Merry

MW00973613

With love,

Megan

2010

thank you for being such a faithful sister & sister in Christ — for that I am truly blessed ♡

Meredith,
"Trust in the Lord
with all your heart!"
Proverbs 3:5-6
Love, Amy
Dec. 2010

When God Intervenes, LET HIM

AMY SIMMONS ALFORD

Amazing Faith
PUBLISHING

Produced with the assistance of Fluency Organization, Inc.

Cover photo by Amy Simmons Alford Photography

www.amyalfordphotos.com

Published by Amazing Faith Publishers
ISBN: 978-0-578-07019-3 (paperback)
ISBN: 978-0-578-07018-6 (hardcover)

Have you ever wondered if God hears your prayers? Or, maybe you believe that He hears them, but you assume that He chooses to ignore some and answer others. This book is real-life testimony that God not only hears your prayers, but He answers every one of them. It is a fast-paced journey through Amy's life, as she vividly recalls the countless times God has intervened and answered her prayers. You will be caught up in the sometimes heart-pounding, sometimes miraculous, but always heart-warming ways in which God has met Amy in her time of need, and provided wisdom and guidance to navigate her through the crisis. In every occasion, Amy has known an inner peace that wasn't shaken by the circumstance or catastrophe. I recommend this book for all who yearn to have that same kind of relationship with God.

Gayle D. Beebe, Ph.D. | President, Westmont College

Through her very personal and fascinating life experiences, Amy beautifully illustrates that *when God intervenes–let Him!* I really enjoyed her book and learned so much about her and her relationship with the Lord. Letting God intervene in her life's journey makes her the SAME KIND OF DIFFERENT AS ME!

Ron Hall | Author of *Same Kind of Different As Me*

This book will keep you on the edge of your seat as Amy describes in detail her incredible life stories. Amy puts her faith into action through the power of prayer, and we as readers are *not* left wondering how to find meaning and fulfillment through a relationship with God.

Joy Weaver | Speaker & author of *Socially Savvy*

When God intervenes in your life, where do you run? This powerful book shows from personal experiences how to really let go and let God. Amy has spoken, and I am listening for this freedom we have in God to let Him have His way.

Thelma Wells, M.Min., D.D. (Hon.) | Speaker & author; President, A Woman of God Ministries

When God Intervenes gives an intimate glimpse inside Amy's daily walk with Christ. Full of heartwarming stories of family and friends, Amy takes you on a journey that testifies to God's faithfulness and love for his children. This will encourage your heart and reaffirm your heart for our loving Creator.

Joe White | President, Kanakuk Kamps; Nationally renowned speaker & author

Amy is amazing. She has such an honest and generous way of sharing her stories and lessons. Sometimes she makes you laugh, and other times she makes you cry…but she always makes you feel better. Her writing style is so natural that you don't realize you are being taught. I think she learned that from Sandy! Her books are a blessing to anyone who reads them, and her passion for God and His Word is contagious.

Kimberly Schlegel Whitman | Founder, RSVPcalendar.com. Author, speaker, and lifestyle expert on DFW's #1 Morning Show

Reading this book made me so teary-eyed. I was riveted by the detailed description and recall of such valuable and powerful events. Anyone who reads this book will be inspired to run to their loved ones...to just appreciate and give thanks for their love. I will share this beautiful collection of stories with everyone I come in contact with! It is such a beautiful reminder how God answers our prayers every day.

Sheree J. Wilson | Film and television actress, featured in *Dallas* and *Walker Texas Ranger*

Also by Amy Simmons Alford

When God Has a Way, No Other Way Works

For my three parents: Mom, Harold, and Dad (who watches from above). All of you raised me in Christian homes and taught me values and morals that shaped my life. Thank you for your encouragement, support, and love throughout my years, especially the rebellious ones. You have been beside me every step of the way, always with encouraging words. Your amazing love and strength has encouraged me. I love you with all my heart.

I want to thank all of you who helped me write and encouraged me to finish this book. The creative team at Fluency spent countless hours skillfully shaping this book to its final form. Joy Weaver, who acted as my "author role model" and soundboard, helped me in many ways—thank you! And for all of you who actually played a part in one or more stories, I'm so glad God protected us and watched over us so we can read this and see how He really did intervene! Most of all, I want to thank my Lord and Savior, Jesus Christ, for being so patient with me when I strayed and for waiting for me when I decided to turn back to Him. May this book glorify You and what You have done in my life.

TABLE OF CONTENTS

DANGER

SCRIPTURE

ABOUT THE AUTHOR

NATIONALLY RENOWNED AUTHOR, SPEAKER, AND photographer Amy Simmons Alford has photographed some of the world's most powerful and respected leaders, including President George W. Bush and his wife Laura, former President George H.W. Bush, Oprah Winfrey, Benjamin Netanyahu, Senator Kay Bailey Hutchinson, and Chuck Norris. However, nothing excites her more than capturing the special moments of children and families in a relaxed, outdoor setting. She graduated from Brooks Institute of Photography, one of the most prestigious colleges for photography in the country.

She loves to travel throughout the world. However, her favorite places include her family farms in Ozark, Arkansas and McKinney, Texas; summers in Aspen, Colorado; and vacationing in Santa Barbara, California. When she is not behind the camera or at her desk writing, she loves adventurous activities like snow skiing, four wheelers, paragliding, and hiking. On the softer side, a beautiful sunset, thunderstorms, and a good fire are at the top of Amy's list of favorites.

Her first book, *When God Has A Way, No Other Way Works,* opened many doors for her to speak and encourage others in their journey. Since her first public speaking engagement at the White House, Amy has spoken at retreats and special events around the country. You may have heard Amy in various radio interviews or even seen her on television shows such as *Daily Talk.*

Showing people there is someone who cares, especially in their time of need, is important to her. Reaching out to people is one of Amy's spiritual gifts, and she supports several charities including Kids Across America and East West Ministries. Amy feels strongly about sponsoring short-term mission trips, following Christ's command to "Go into all nations and spread the Gospel." She also volunteers at her church in the prayer ministry.

Her second book, *When God Intervenes, Let Him,* is a collection of personal experiences when God intervened in her life in special and amazing ways. It shows how God will intervene when you trust Him and are available to Him. She believes everything happens for a reason and is convinced that God has specific plans and purposes for every situation that happens in our lives. She will challenge you to make an investment in a relationship with God so you, too, will agree: When God Intervenes, Let Him!

She resides in Dallas, Texas.

INTRODUCTION

My mentor and adopted grandmother, Sandy, and I used to joke when I told her I wrote my first book about the impact her walk with the Lord and her teachings had on me. She humbly said, "Well, just order a copy for me and one for you and maybe one or two more" (thinking nobody but us would want to read it). We laughed about that until the day *When God Has a Way, No Other Way Works* had sold close to 4000 copies!

We never dreamed the impact our first book would have. The lives it touched, the relationships that were cultivated—God did it all. As you will see in some of the stories in this second book, He had a bigger plan for what He inspired me to write. Every time I put pen to paper to write, I ask the Lord to put His words on the page and to block my way if I try to write something He does not want me to write.

I believe everything happens for a reason. When I endure a trial in my life or I experience a "God thing," I know it's Him working His plan through me. Over the years, I have developed a close and intimate relationship with Christ, and I have experienced things I never knew were possible. Although now I realize that nothing is impossible with God (Luke 1:37)!

At the same time, I also know that I don't have all the answers. But I don't feel I need to know them, because my faith in Christ sustains me in every situation. He has proven His presence, existence, love, mercy, grace, and forgiveness so many times. That's why I don't ask, "Why, Lord?" anymore. Now, when I'm faced with a challenge, I just say, "Help me through this. Guide me, show me what You want me to learn, and thank You, Lord." I don't always understand why God does things. Sometimes I can see why He did something a certain way, but sometimes not. I just know in my heart there is a reason and purpose for everything, so I put my trust and faith in the One who knows, and I go with it!

In this book, I once again use my trials and experiences to relate God's work and His Word to you. I wanted to write these true short stories as evidence for the existence of a loving God so people could relate to what God teaches us through His Word. What has happened in my life proves to me that God exists—and it proves that He loves me and cares for me. He hears our prayers and cries for help. No matter the outcome, He is in control. Therefore, I have total faith that His ways and plans are the best for my life!

For you, the reader, some stories will provide stronger evidence than others that God exists. But for me, all of these stories are evidence that God is real, and He listens to those who love Him. When you develop a love relationship with God (and I hope that you will, or you already have), you will also start seeing how He is working in your life—and you'll have your own stories to share.

"Come and listen, all you who fear God, and I will tell you what he did for me.
For I cried out to him for help, praising him as I spoke...He paid attention to my prayer.
Praise God, who did not ignore my prayer or withdraw his unfailing love from me."

Psalm 66:16-17, 19-20 NKJ

When God Intervenes in FAMILY

A Tale of Two Kidneys

My mom married a man named Harold on June 14, 1980. I am so happy she married someone who loves and adores her and treats her like a queen. They have a very loving and tender marriage. Out of the 30 years they have been married, they have only been apart three nights! Mom is a loving, kind, tender-hearted, and giving woman who loves her family and the Lord. She was a beauty queen at SMU (Southern Methodist University) and still remains as beautiful today (if not more) as she was in college.

Harold was from a small town (population 150) and ended up doing quite well for himself in the business world. To say he is intelligent is an understatement. In my opinion, he is brilliant, and his mind works at a capacity very few people can grasp. He is honest, kind, overly generous, loving, and tender. Both Mom and Harold have taken good care of themselves, and for that I am thankful. Over the years, Harold and I have developed a wonderful, loving relationship. I am so blessed to have parents who love me and care for me the way they do. Some "stepparent" situations are difficult, but I am so blessed to have a stepdad who truly loves and cares for me. Thirty years ago, I had no idea what would be happening in our lives when Mom remarried, but God did. He knew when my mom married Harold what was in store for us as a family, especially in early 2008.

In December of 2007, my mom called me, as she usually does each morning to ask about my day. After I reeled off the day's activities, she casually said, "Honey, Harold has not been feeling well, and we had some tests done. Both of his kidneys are failing, and he needs a kidney transplant."

I was in shock. I remember looking at my dazed reaction in the reflection of my bathroom mirror. I swallowed and said, "Well, where do we get one?"

"We have to find someone to donate."

"Mom, I can do it," I said. "I am the youngest and healthiest, and I can bounce back quicker than anyone."

"Oh, Honey, I couldn't bear to have you and Harold in the hospital at the same time. I'll be talking to the doctors today. I'll get more information and see what we need to do."

I hung up the phone and immediately put together a group of 40 people on an email prayer list. These were people I knew I could count on to pray. I asked them to please pray for the perfect donor for Harold since he needed the surgery fairly quickly. His kidneys were only functioning at about five percent. Soon, over 15 volunteers of close friends, family, and employees were offering their kidney for Harold. My brother, Andy, and I were tested and discovered we were both the same blood type as Harold. However, Mom put us on hold because she didn't want to have her husband and child in surgery at the same time—not for something this serious.

Meanwhile, the other possible donors were being

cut from the list each week. Our concern grew as the surgery date came closer with no firm plans. Harold was deteriorating rapidly. He lost so much weight and looked severely weak and thin. Several times, I had to hide my tears so he wouldn't see. It was killing me and Mom to see him declining so quickly.

I remember one day Harold had been in the hospital for two or three nights having tests done. The phone rang in his room. Mom was there with him and heard him say, "Hello? Hi George...Well, not too good...I have to have a kidney transplant...okay, thank you." And he hung up.

Mom said, "Who was that?"

"George W. Bush," Harold said nonchalantly and picked up his water bottle to take a sip.

"You're kidding! The President? How did he know?" my mom inquired.

"He knows everything," he said with his dry sense of humor.

President Bush had heard from someone that Harold was not doing well. Harold and President Bush had met years ago, and they see each other from time to time. Before the President was governor, he lived three blocks from us when I was growing up. Somehow, he found out where Harold was and called his hospital room. Can you imagine being the hospital receptionist for that call?

I'm not good at handling situations where family members are hurting. I tend to become very emotional and stressed out. About six weeks before Harold's surgery, I began to have a strong pain in my left arm. It was shooting down my shoulder and into my hand, and

I was in constant pain for two weeks. However, I didn't want to burden anyone with my aches and pains in light of everything else going on, so I stayed silent.

One night at dinner, I decided to casually mention the pain. Mom put down her fork and said, "What? Pain in your left arm? You know what that means…heart attack! Honey, please don't have a heart attack! Let's get through the kidney transplant first!"

She said it jokingly and we all giggled, knowing she was kidding. I went home that night, got ready for bed and began flipping pages in my Bible. My friend, Laulie, had emailed a verse for me to read earlier that day, so I looked it up. It read, "Have mercy on me, O God, have mercy on me, for in you my soul takes refuge. I will take refuge in the shadow of your wings until the disaster has passed" Psalm 57:1. Wow. That verse came at the perfect time. I laid the Bible on my chest and thought, "Did God write that for me or what?"

I began to pray aloud, "Lord, I need You to replace my stress and fear with Your peace and comfort. Please remove the pain in my arm. I don't know what is going on with it, but I'm asking You to remove the pain." My next request I had not even thought about saying; it just came out unexpectedly. "…And Lord, if You want me to be the donor, then I want to be in Your will. If I'm the one, then give me a peace about it. All I want is for You to use me for Your purpose." By the time I finished praying, tears were streaming down my face. I also felt as if a ton of weight had been lifted from my shoulders because I had just turned my fears, worries, and stress over to Him. I think I fell asleep with a smile on my face.

The next morning, I spent some time in my "prayer" chair, a comfortable wingback chair in front of the fireplace in my bedroom. That is where I have quiet time in the mornings, my time alone with God. I pray for family, friends, others, myself, our soldiers, our country, and much more. I also read Scripture and a devotional from *Jesus Calling*, by Sarah Young. (Each day applies to my life. I highly recommend reading it!) If I have time, I will read from another daily devotional book called *Experiencing God Day by Day*. I highly recommend everyone getting that book, too. A devotional takes five minutes or less to read, and it is a great way to start your day. After a few minutes of sitting in my prayer chair, I noticed the pain in my left arm was gone. No pain whatsoever. Gone, just like that.

"Lord, I need You to replace my stress and fear with Your peace and comfort."

Almost at the same time, I felt something else—something I've felt before but couldn't identify for a few seconds. Then it hit me: *peace*. I felt it pour over me as if someone had draped a blanket around my shoulders and held me close. It was a feeling I can't explain, but if you have experienced it, you know what I mean.

I sat there and physically felt the Holy Spirit in the room, as if He were holding me. I even looked around the room thinking someone had opened a door. However, the bedroom door was closed. It was a wonderful, peaceful, calming feeling. One thought came to my mind: "I'm going to be the donor." That thought went through my mind over and over, and I had this incredible sense of contentment. It was as if God was letting me know, "You are going to be the donor, and I'm covering you in peace, just as you asked." This feeling lasted about 20 minutes. During that time, I picked up the phone to call my mom. (In our house, if the phone rings before eight in the morning or after ten at night, we know something is wrong.) It was about 7:45 that morning when I called.

"Mom?"

"What?" she said breathlessly. (Her mother's instinct told her something was up.)

"I think I'm going to be the donor," I whispered, as if I might run off the Holy Spirit if I spoke up louder.

"What? Why? What makes you think that?"

"I can feel this great sense of peace. It's in the room with me. I'm supposed to be the donor!"

Mom wasn't convinced. "I don't feel the peace. Give me some of *your* peace," she suggested.

From that day on, I knew in the back of my mind I would be the donor, although we did not act on it right away. We were four weeks away from the surgery, but I went ahead and claimed several scriptures that would help me prepare. I claimed Isaiah 41:10, 13, which says:

"So do not fear, for I am with you; do not be dismayed, for I am your God. I will strengthen you and help you; I will uphold you with my righteous right hand. For I am the LORD, your God, who takes hold of your right hand and says to you, Do not fear; I will help you."

I have all my journals from that time in my life, documenting all my feelings and prayers. I can see where

I wrote one time, "Please give me strength as Mom, Harold, and I approach surgery." I also wrote down Psalm 62:1-2, 5-6 as important verses about calm and peace. That passage reads:

> *"My soul finds rest in God alone;*
> *my salvation comes from him.*
> *He alone is my rock and my salvation;*
> *he is my fortress, I will never be shaken.*
> *Find rest, O my soul, in God alone;*
> *my hope comes from him.*
> *He alone is my rock and my salvation;*
> *he is my fortress, I will not be shaken."*

I read these scriptures repeatedly and prayed over them—even *before* I knew for sure I was the donor. I even emailed several of my friends to pray for the donor to be strong, healthy, and a good match for him. I still have those emails from several friends, and they are so encouraging to read again. We all prayed for the donor long and hard.

Meanwhile, other donors continued to come and go. As time got closer, we were slim on volunteers. Then Ben, my husband at the time, went in for testing. In the meantime, our close family friend, Paul Bass III, offered his kidney as well. Mom has known Paul and his dad all her life. Paul's dad, Paul Bass, Jr., was Mom's best friend throughout her life. They were born six months apart in Tyler, Texas. Paul was an only child, and so was Mom. Their parents were best friends, too. All of Mom's baby pictures were taken with Paul, so they have always thought of themselves as brother and sister. (I even call him Uncle Paul.) One week before the surgery, Paul ended up being a perfect match, and we thought he would be "the" donor. Ben was designated as the "back up" donor. We will always be grateful to both Paul and Ben for their generosity and willingness to donate their kidney to Harold. In this type of surgery, there must always be a back up for the donor, and we would soon find out why.

I went with Ben to see the surgeon before he did his MRI, the last of all the tests. While we waited for the surgeon to arrive, I called Mom to check in. She confirmed that Paul already had a room set up in the hospital and things were going according to plan. Just then, the surgeon came in and began to explain all the details of the surgery. Ben and I sat there listening (or pretending to, since Ben was only the back up). Then the surgeon said, "So, you need to be at the hospital a week from Friday at 5:00am." We perked up our ears.

"Oh wait, Ben's just the back up. We have a donor, Paul Bass."

"He was cut," the surgeon said as he flipped through his chart. "Mr. Bass is no longer the donor; Ben is."

"When was he cut?" I asked, my voice trembling. I'd just talked to my mom and everything was set up for Paul.

"An hour ago. After Mr. Bass's MRI, the doctors decided he was no longer a candidate. Mr. Alford, you are the donor now."

My face went blank as the color drained from my cheeks. Time stopped. I automatically reached down into my purse and grabbed a pen and paper without taking my eyes off the surgeon. Now I was taking notes fast and furiously.

My mind was thinking, "He doesn't know; he must be wrong." Nevertheless, I began asking 50 questions and writing down all the answers. After my barrage of questions, we left the surgeon's office feeling numb. The minute the door closed behind us, I cried out, "He must be wrong, how can this happen?"

Ben was walking ahead of me in silence. He was now the donor, and we were out of volunteers. I fished my cell phone out of my purse and dialed Mom.

My face went blank as the color drained from my cheeks.

"Mom, Paul was cut! Ben is now the donor!" I cried into the phone.

"What are you talking about?" she replied and I explained what the surgeon had said. "Let me call you back," she said. She was calling another doctor to confirm this news.

By now, I was in full panic mode. My emotions were all over the place. Ben and I had only been married three years, and Harold had been my stepdad for over half my life. I didn't feel right about Ben doing this surgery for our family. We were now at the MRI station and Ben was checking in for his test. I was freaking out. He was so calm. As we were sitting in the waiting room, I realized my Bible class was starting in 20 minutes at our house. It was too late to cancel as most of the girls were on their way or already there.

Ben insisted I go home and teach the Bible class. I felt horrible leaving him there all alone to do his MRI, but I went on to the house. As I pulled up, there were two cars in front. Nobody knew about all the chaos that was going on in my life, and I managed to get through my lesson. The minute the girls left, I called Mom for an update.

"So what's the story?" I anxiously hoped that there'd been some mistake and Mom had cleared it up.

"Well, Honey, the surgeon was right...Paul was cut."

I stood there frozen.

She continued, "…and Ben is now the donor. Now, we have to find a back up for Ben. Who should we call?"

Once more, I felt that sense of peace and calmly said, "Mom, it's my turn." She immediately burst into tears.

"I can't let you go! I can't have you and Harold in the hospital at the same time."

"Mom, we've been praying for the perfect donor for two months now. We don't want to mess with God's will, do we?"

"But He doesn't know how I feel!" she said.

"Yes, He does, Mom. I'm totally fine about it, really. I have a sense of peace about it, and I'll be okay. Let me finish my testing, and we can go from there."

We hung up the phone, and in the middle of calamity, another wave of peace washed over me again. I knew I was in God's hands, and I would be okay. He confirmed it through the peace He gave me.

∞

I called the next morning and began a four-day series of tests. One of the tests is an interview with a social worker. Just before she asked me the first question, my cell phone rang. Lately, it seemed as if every time the phone rang it was some kind of bad news.

"Do you need to get that?" she asked politely.

"Yes, it's my mom. I'll be right back," and I dashed out of her office into the hallway.

I talked with Mom briefly and returned to her office. She sat ram rod straight in her chair, her ankles neatly crossed. Her hair was short and perfectly styled like June Cleaver. She had glasses on and was holding a folder with a pen in one hand, ready to capture any sort of stress or anxiety I might indicate regarding the surgery. We sat so close in her tiny office that our knees nearly touched.

"Is everything alright?" she asked, her voice professional and calm.

"Well, our family is in the middle of a tornado right now," I said, referring to the donor situation.

"Oh, the one in Tennessee?" apparently referring to the week's recent weather troubles in the South.

Is she kidding? I thought to myself. "Um, no...I meant what's going on in our family right now."

"Well, let's get started," she decided. "Now Mr. Simmons is your stepdad, is that correct?"

"Yes." She made a note.

"And he is seventy-six years old?"

"Yes." Another note.

Now, she leaned forward and asked in a soft voice, "How would it make you feel if your stepdad did not survive the surgery after you have donated your kidney to him? Do you think that would have an impact on you?"

Without any hesitation I said, "Ma'am, I can tell you this. I wouldn't think twice, even if he only lived for two weeks I would give him my leg, arm, or whatever he needed."

"Uh, okay," she said and skipped over a few pages on her clipboard. "Let's move on to the next session." The rest of the interview was quick and easy.

I knew I was the donor because the Lord had put it on my heart and gave me the peace that surpasses all understanding (Philippians 4:7). And nothing could change my mind.

Even when the doctors told me there was a chance I might not make it and asked if I was sure I wanted to do it, I was certain. All I knew was that I was in the Lord's will, and that's right where I wanted to be. Whether I lived or died, I knew it was His will. I fully trusted Him with my life. If I didn't make it, I knew I was going to heaven, and that was fine with me, too! Therefore, I never had any doubt about doing it. God was in control, and that was a relief.

The following Wednesday, Mom told me the doctor would be calling later that afternoon with all of my test results. I wanted to be there with her and Harold when he called because I knew in my heart I would be the donor. I came in the back door of their house and walked up the stairs. Elna, their house manager, met me in the hallway.

"Where is Mom?" I asked.

"She's in her room, crying."

Right away, I realized the one remaining other potential donor (a lady who had been tested the same week as me) must have been cut. I've only seen Mom cry two or three times in my life—she is such a strong and stable woman. Me? I cry at the drop of a hat. I get that from my dad, Larry; he was like that, too. Slowly, I walked into Mom and Harold's bedroom. Harold was in the middle of his dialysis treatment, lying very still in a hospital bed they had set up at their home. His nurse was beside him, and he was connected to a large machine. Mom was rubbing his feet.

"Hi, Honey," Mom said, mustering up a smile for me. Harold and the nurse joined in a cheery greeting as well.

Whether I lived or died, I knew it was His will.

"How are you feeling, Harold?" I asked, standing beside him.

"Oh, pretty good," he responded, his voice tired.

"Well," Mom began, "the other donor was cut today, so we are waiting for the doctor to call with your results." Ben was already the back up donor—we knew that. Now I was about to find out where I fit into the equation. But I felt I already knew the answer.

About that time, the phone rang. Mom and I went into another room so she could pick it up at her desk. I sat on the other side of her desk listening.

"Hello? Yes, he's doing okay today…" I knew it was the doctor calling about Harold. "So, who is the best donor?"

I looked at Mom as she heard the doctor's response,

and her eyes filled with tears. I knew he had said my name. She leaned her head back on her chair, put her hand on her forehead and said, "How in the world could it come down to the two people I prayed it wouldn't be?" I'm not sure what the doctor's response was to that question; it was probably the first time he had been asked that. She hung up the phone and said, "It's you," her hands on her cheeks.

"Mom, I'm totally fine," I assured her, telling her once more about this strong sense of peace I'd had the entire time. "I'll be alright," I added as I felt another tinge of peace come my way.

"Well, let's go tell Harold," Mom said and stood to her feet. We walked back into the room where Harold was and Mom said, "Well, Ben and Amy are both good matches."

Harold turned to me and said with his characteristic humor, "You gonna flip a coin to see who gets to give their kidney?" Mom smiled softly and went back to rubbing his feet, hesitating only a moment before she spoke.

"Honey, Amy has decided she wants to do it."

Harold extended his arms, and I walked over to hug him, being careful with the tubes and plugs. We hugged, and he had tears streaming down his face; we all did. He said, "I love you so much, thank you."

"I'm happy to do it," I answered. "I love you, too." I truly was happy to be the one. Harold had been so sweet, kind, and generous to me all my life. I could never repay him for all the things he'd given me—trips, college, and so much more. But more than the material things, his love and kindness towards me as his stepdaughter had been the best gift. He went through all my rebellious, selfish, wild, and crazy years…and still loved me. The least I could do was to give him life!

As I sat there looking at him, I realized he'd already saved so many lives through his loving heart and generous donations to people, hospitals, and research. In that moment, I was certain that he could do more for the people in our country in two years than I could do the rest of my lifetime! "Well, I need to go home and talk to Ben," I said, turning to leave.

"Okay, Honey. Call if you need us," Mom said, recalling a phrase I've heard all my life. But now it held special meaning as I realized how blessed I am to have parents who love me, care about me, and want to help me—even when they need help.

In less than two minutes, I was back home. Ben was waiting for me. I said I needed to update him on what was going on, so Ben poured us a glass of wine. I put together some cheese and crackers, and we sat in our den by the fire. I took a deep breath and began to explain what had transpired over the last two hours. We sat on the sofa for at least another two or three hours, discussing what was going to happen in the next few days.

I had never had surgery before, but I was so eager to do this for Harold, no matter the outcome. I was able to convince Ben to let me be the donor, and he remained the back up. After all, I reasoned, he is *my* stepdad. Who knows? Ben might need to give his kidney to one of his family members someday.

By the time we finished talking and praying about it, it was close to 8:00 in the evening on Wednesday, February 20. The surgery was scheduled for 5:00am that Friday. I had one day to cancel photo shoots, meetings, and organize the house to receive guests who might stop by after the surgery.

Next, I sent out an email to the 40 prayer warriors that had been praying for "the perfect donor." I wrote, "I want to thank you all for praying for the perfect donor for Harold. As of today, it's going to be me! So thank you for praying *for me*!" Immediately, I began receiving calls and encouraging emails. My sweet friend, Paige, organized two weeks of meals during my recovery. So many friends joined in and brought some of my favorite dishes like banana pudding, chicken spaghetti, and macaroni and cheese, to name a few!

The night before the surgery, Mom arranged for us to have dinner at the country club with my brother and his family. (They too had offered kidneys but were not a perfect match). It was a joyful time with the family, and we made several toasts to a successful surgery and quick recovery. As we began to leave, we all hugged each other tight and said "I love you" a thousand times. I remember that moment as if it were yesterday.

Four o'clock the next morning came quickly, but I was rested, prayed up, and ready to go! When we arrived at Baylor Hospital, someone was there to greet us and take us to a prep room where I exchanged my clothes for a backless robe. I was sitting on the bed waiting when David, Ben's youngest brother, walked through the door. He just happened to be in Dallas on business that day and found us! He lives a few hours away in Henderson, Texas, with his wife, Fran, and their two daughters. I was glad to see him, and he helped keep my mind off what was about to happen. I have a difficult time with needles and IVs. Before I knew it, there were about nine friends in this tiny space. John Maisel, the president of East West Ministries and a good friend of ours, asked to pray for me. We joined hands in a circle around my bed with Ben, David, Andy, Penny, Paige, Courtney, and "Little A" (my niece, Adrienne). John began to pray an inspiring and encouraging prayer. My emotions took over, and I felt tears filling my eyes. He prayed for the Lord's protection from infection and asked that we would be completely healed. He also prayed for God to guide the doctors and nurses in surgery.

We all hugged each other tight and said "I love you" a thousand times.

To break up the seriousness of the moment afterwards, the nurse came in and gave me a "party hat" that looked like a shower cap! I donned my hat and transferred to a different hospital bed with wheels. I was thankful my young niece was there, or I would have burst into tears right then. But I was holding it together because I didn't want to scare her by seeing Aunt Aim crying or emotional. I wanted to be strong for her. Paige put a coat of my favorite pink lip gloss on as they wheeled me down the hall. Everyone was waving goodbye and saying, "We love you...see you in a couple hours!"

I couldn't tell it, but my friends were crying. Ben walked alongside me holding my hand. "How do I look?" I asked with a smile. It's hard to look cute in a shower cap, but thank goodness I had my pink lip gloss!

"You look great," he said and squeezed my hand. Inside the "pre-op" room, Mom, Harold, my brother, and Uncle Paul were there with the doctors and me. Gary Brandenburg, our pastor, was there to pray over me before they took me back. My family surrounded my hospital bed. Gary was holding my left hand; Mom was holding my right. As Gary began to pray, Mom gasped. I opened my eyes and saw her put her other hand over her mouth. All of this was just about more than she could take. Everyone had tears in their eyes, including me.

After that, the cute anesthesiologist sat beside me and explained what was going to happen next. I jokingly called what he was going to give me the "goo-goo" juice, and within seconds after the injection I was happy and calm. They could have been wheeling me to a furnace, and I would have smiled the whole way. I said goodbye to everyone as they took me down the hall to the operating room.

Once I was in surgery, Harold began his pre-op routine. All along, I'd pictured us going into the operating room together, lying side-by-side and holding hands with our shower caps on like Thelma and Louise. But it wasn't like that at all. I went first, and they removed my left kidney. By then, Harold was prepped and ready, and they literally walked my kidney down the hall to his operating room and put it inside of Harold. Sounds easy, but there was a lot more to it than that! The cuts had to be 100% precise in this very intricate surgery. The surgeons went through the front of my abdomen near the bikini line and through the torso to the back where the kidney is located and pulled it back through the front side.

About 200 of Mom and Harold's friends were anxiously waiting for each doctor's report on me, but mostly about him. Some flew from Santa Barbara to be there for Mom and Harold. Needless to say, they are loved and have many friends who care deeply for them. Mom had secured a hospital room next to Harold's with a sliding partition so she could check on him. While she sat there in the quiet, waiting for the doctor to tell her Harold was out of surgery, a big man with a bright smile came in to clean the room. He saw Mom sitting on the side of the bed, her hands clasped together between her knees.

"Ma'am, how ya doing?" he asked as he emptied the trashcan and went about his duties.

Mom looked up at the unsuspecting man and let out an uncontrollable, ugly cry, "My husband and daughter are both in surgery! My daughter is giving her kidney to my husband!"

"I'm sorry," he offered sheepishly. "I didn't mean to do that to you." He didn't know what to do for a moment, then he said, "My gosh…I need to go get my phone and call my church to pray for them!" And off he went! He came back in a few minutes and said, "Ma'am, the whole church is prayin' for you." They were instant friends. Claude was his name. He came and checked on Mom and Harold every day they were in the hospital. He even came to visit me, but I don't remember meeting him because I slept so much after surgery!

In the recovery room, I remember opening my eyes

and seeing Ben standing over me. “Is Harold okay?” I wanted to know.

“Yes, he is doing well,” Ben assured me.

Madeline, Ben’s youngest daughter, was standing beside him. I felt as if I were in a dream, but at the same time, I knew where I was and what had just happened.

Before I arrived in my hospital room, my longtime friend, Margot, had de-germed the room with Clorox wipes (that’s what friends are for)! The next thing I remember was being in my newly sanitized room with the nurses, dozing in and out of sleep. Before the surgery, I had written out some verses that gave me hope and security. Ben put them on my bulletin board in my hospital room. I was clinging to these verses up until the surgery, including the one my friend had emailed me so long ago from Psalm 57:1 that said:

“Have mercy on me, O God, have mercy on me, for in you my soul takes refuge. I will take refuge in the shadow of your wings until the disaster has passed.”

Mom made sure the nurses who took care of me received a signed copy of my book in hopes that it might encourage them. They were all so nice and helpful to me during my recovery. The entire staff at Baylor Hospital was friendly and anxious to help wherever they could.

The next morning, I woke up and Ben was there on the sofa waiting for me to open my eyes. “How are you feeling?”

“Okay. How’s Harold?” I couldn’t get my stepdad out of my mind.

"He's doing great...he's in his room."

About that time, my brother came in to see me. "Hey, how are you?" he asked and stood at the end of my bed.

"Good...moving slow. Have you seen Harold today?" I had visions of Harold being as out of it as I was.

"He was up walking around the 14th floor earlier," my brother said.

That's nice, I thought. "What? He's walking?" I couldn't get out of bed, much less walk.

"He's lapped the 14th floor a couple of times," my brother said, grinning.

"Call the doctor!" I cried. "Something is wrong with me! I can't even get out of bed!" Our physician came in soon after my panicked request. He explained, "Amy, you're perfectly fine! It's much harder on the donor than it is on the recipient. We will get you up to walk in a couple of hours."

I had written out some verses that gave me hope and security.

A team of people came in after lunch and sat me in a wheelchair so I could go from the 12th floor to the 14th to see Harold for the first time. They wheeled me into the room, and I saw he was in a hospital robe that matched mine. We were both in wheelchairs, so Ben and Mom helped us stand up to hug each other and say, "I love you."

Harold asked me if I wanted to go for a walk. We walked down the hallway, hand-in-hand, Andy pushing the cart behind us with all of Harold's tubes and medicines. Mom was holding me, and Ben was close behind taking photos. It was a sweet and tender moment and one I will always treasure—especially the photographs Ben took of us. He even got a great shot the next day of Harold and I walking and holding hands. Mom was right behind us, faithfully toting a big cup of banana pudding and a spoon. Harold was so thin—she was trying to get him to gain back some weight. So she followed him just in case he would have a hankering for some pudding!

For the four days I was in the hospital, my sweet mom walked up and down the stairs back and forth to visit my room two floors below Harold's. The elevators took too long for Mom, so she took the stairs. Thank goodness she is a spry seventy-three-year-old! When it was time to go home, Mom, a nurse, and a doctor helped me out to the car. When we arrived home, Ben helped me get into my own bed. It was great to be home, but I hated not being close to Harold and Mom. He would be in the hospital for two more days. I now had a special bond with Harold and Mom and didn't want to be away from them.

While Ben was working upstairs in our house, my friends took turns babysitting me. I needed help in and out of bed, walking, and sitting. Everyone was so sweet and gracious to help. I must have had 30 or 40 flower arrangements and more food than I could ever eat. My best friend, Cara, flew in from Arkansas to spend two nights with me. We loved our quiet time together, not blowing and going like we usually do on a visit. Instead, we sat on the sofa or on the bed and talked and watched a movie or two. The doctors said I needed to begin walking every day, so she helped me walk down the street. The first time we walked, we were arm-in-arm taking slow, short steps. I joked, "This will be us in 40 years." We laughed, which kind of hurt my side, so I tried not to laugh anymore. But it is hard not to laugh when you are with your best friends.

The day Cara left, I cried and cried. I wanted her to stay, but she needed to get home to her own kids and husband. I was very grateful, and it meant so much that she came to take care of me. Mom and Harold stopped by to see me on their way home from the hospital. Harold looked 1000 times better. His color had improved, and he didn't seem so weak. It warmed my heart.

A week after the surgery, Mom and Harold had us over to their house for dinner. It was my first outing since I came home, and I decided to dress in a red leather jacket. I never wear red. That jacket is the only red item I have in my closet. Ben helped me through the back door when we got to Mom's, and Harold was standing there in the hall. I couldn't believe my eyes! He was wearing a bright red vest (a color he rarely wears either)! I said, "Oh my gosh, it's the kidney!" We were now thinking alike! What's really funny is we have to go to the bathroom at the same time now!

We celebrated our one-month anniversary, then our one-year anniversary. As of February 22, 2010, it's been two years since our surgery. Both Harold and I are doing great. He was back in the office just a week after the surgery and continues to play golf several times a week. (Thank you, Lord!)

As I look back at the kidney transplant, I realize God knew when Mom married Harold 30 years ago I would be his donor. Over the last 20 years, my relationship with the Lord has grown and strengthened above and beyond what I ever thought it would be. Sandy, my mentor, has had a big part in teaching me over the years to trust God, depend on Him for everything, and be available to Him for His purposes. Had I not learned that from Sandy's teachings, I am not sure I would have been so eager and glad to be Harold's donor. Because I asked God for His will, not mine, He provided a peace, comfort, and assurance that gave me the confidence and encouragement to go through this knowing I was in His hands. He was in control, and that made it easy for me to be the donor. I knew in my heart I was where God wanted me to be—in His will. Throughout the entire ordeal, I was never scared, worried, or afraid, and I never thought twice about doing it. I will never regret it.

I would not trade the past two years spending time with Harold and Mom for anything. God blessed me for obeying Him and desiring to be in His will. My relationship with the Lord has increased tenfold since the kidney transplant. Make that a hundred fold. I know for a fact that nothing is impossible with God. The Bible teaches us that, but I was fortunate enough to learn it from my own experience. Now I know He is real, and He does give us peace in the middle of our trials.

Ephesians 2:8-10 says, "For it is by grace you have been saved, through faith—and this not from yourselves, it is the gift of God—not by works, so that no one can boast. For we are God's workmanship, created in Christ

Jesus to do good works, which God prepared in advance for us to do." This verse clearly says we are saved because of our faith in Christ. It's because we accept Him and believe He alone is our Savior—not Buddha, not a statue—but Jesus Christ Himself. You cannot get to heaven because you are a good person. You cannot get to heaven because you donate to charities and give to the poor. It is by your faith, not what you "do." It is not even by donating a kidney—but by your faith.

The Bible says we were created in Christ Jesus to do "good works." Sure, the good works are great, don't get me wrong, but it's your belief in Jesus Christ that really matters. The last part of that passage in Ephesians says, "…which God prepared in advance for us to do." He knew I was going to donate my kidney before I was born! It was His plan all along, and because I was available to Him to be in His will, He covered me in peace.

He was in control, and that made it easy for me to be the donor.

Philippians 4:6–7 reminds us, "Do not be anxious about anything (even giving up your kidney), but in everything (not just the big things, everything), by prayer and petition, with thanksgiving, present your requests to God. (Ask Him to help you in your time of need, tell Him how you feel and what encouragement or peace you want from Him.) And the peace of God, which transcends all understanding, will guard your hearts and minds in Christ Jesus" (parentheses added). That verse perfectly explains what happened to me! I prayed, made my requests known to God, and His peace guarded my mind.

I cannot explain the amount of peace I felt the morning of my surgery; it was above comprehension. As I've said, He protected me from being anxious, nervous, or afraid. First Peter 5:7 says, "Cast all (not just a few things, but *all*) your anxiety on him (Why?) because he cares for you" (parentheses added). This is another verse telling us to give Him all our stress, troubles, and anxiety because He cares for those who love and believe in Him. Just a few chapters earlier in 1 Peter 1:2, the Bible says, "Grace and peace be yours in abundance through the knowledge of God and of Jesus our Lord." If you don't read the Bible or Scripture, how can you know what the Lord has for you? The more you know about Christ, the more you will begin to trust Him, and He will give you His grace and peace in abundance. My friend, Joy, always says, "How can you know what you don't know?" It's true! You don't have to take my word for it in this story; read the Bible because it is true, and learn all that the Lord has for you as a believer in Jesus Christ.

Dancing at the Sweetheart Ball

The annual fundraiser for the Cardiology Department at UT Southwestern in Dallas is called the Sweetheart Ball. It's by far the most beautiful and elaborate party of the year with a great dinner (and a live band afterwards to dance off the calories!). I don't normally attend this party, but one year a longtime friend was chairing the event and asked me several times to go. When she told me the guests who would be sitting at our table, I decided to go because I'd be with a great group of people. Sure enough, the party was over-the-top incredible—far beyond any party I'd ever attended!

After dinner, Harold came over from across the room and asked me to dance. (He always asks me to dance to the "fast" songs because Mom prefers the slow ones!) This was only a few months after our surgery, but we began to boogie! It didn't bother either one of us that we were the only ones on the dance floor (at least, I don't recall anyone else being there!). We were really cuttin' a rug, as we say in Texas, and having fun. Harold loves dancing. He throws his arms high above his head and occasionally lets out a "woo-hoo." He moves more than most of my friends' husbands, and he is seventy-seven years old! About halfway through the song, I noticed almost everyone was watching us dance. They were smiling, some with tears in their eyes. Couples whispered to one another and exchanged knowing looks. I remember thinking that they either thought we were horrible dancers and looked like fools, or they were talking about what we'd just gone through together.

We danced our way through two or three songs and had a great time. When the music slowed down, we returned to our seats and continued on with the night.

The next day, several people called my mom to tell her what an incredible moment it was to see Harold and me dancing together just two months after our kidney transplant! "There was not a dry eye at our table," one lady said. "Everyone was so touched when they saw them dancing. She gave him his life back." So, they weren't making fun of our dancing after all! They were amazed at his recovery. It made the memories of that fabulous night even more special, if that were possible. It will always be a special moment in my life to think back on how sick Harold was just two months prior, and look at him now!

This story reminds me that God is faithful to his children. Are you a child of God? You are if you have put your trust and faith in Him. If you have done that, you can know God is with you and will fulfill all His promises. If you're not sure you can trust God right now, ask God to reveal His faithfulness to you. Someday, I hope you will do as I did that night at the party and reflect on all God has done and be certain of His absolute faithfulness. Why not start today by thanking the Lord for all He has done for you? Take some time to write down five blessings He has given you, and thank Him for each one.

"For nothing is impossible with God." Luke 1:37

When God Intervenes in PRAYER

God Is Never Late... and Seldom Early

Aspen, Colorado, is one of my favorite places in the world. When I go to Aspen in the summers, I get re-charged in my faith, and my walk with the Lord strengthens. I'll sit on my balcony or porch for hours, praying, reading the Bible, or just looking up at the mountains praising God for the opportunity to be able to come to such a beautiful place. A lot of times when I'm talking to God and thanking Him for everything, the tears start flowing. I feel an overwhelming sense of peace and joy in my soul that causes my eyes to well up in tears. There is something about being in the mountains; maybe it's because I'm closer to God...about 8000 feet closer! I've experienced His provision in so many big and small ways in Aspen, including an episode with a friend who needed to sell her truck.

About six years ago, my good friend, Melissa, was trying to sell her 1989 two-wheel drive Blazer (along with her condo) in Aspen. We both lived in Dallas, and I was planning to go up to Aspen for a month that summer. "Hey Mel," I asked her one day, "I have a proposition for you. If you will let me use your truck in Aspen for the month of July, I'll try to sell it for you while I'm there. That way you won't have to worry about it."

"Sounds great!" she agreed. "But what if you sell it

right away? Then you won't have anything to drive." I was staying in Aspen through the end of July and needed transportation.

"I'll figure something out," I said. "Or I'll just tell the buyer they can't have it until July 31." She wasn't sure that idea would go over so well, since most people would also want to have it for the summer.

"I bet I can work it out," I assured her. That summer, I had been spending a lot of time in prayer. I was growing closer to God and learning to trust Him with everything.

"Alright, girlfriend. Go for it," she said.

I put "For Sale" signs on the truck and placed an ad in the *Aspen Times*. Every day I prayed, "Lord, please bring the perfect person to buy this truck. But You know I need some wheels, so please bring them towards the end of the month." I knew God had a plan, and I was hoping it would accommodate my timing. Three weeks went by, and I only had one looker. Nobody wants a two-wheel drive in Colorado—they're all looking for four-wheel drive to go off-road or use in the snow. When I was halfway through July, Melissa and I started discussing Plan B.

"If we don't sell it, I'll hire someone from Denver to drive it to Dallas," she offered, thinking we'd have a much better chance of selling the truck in Dallas. I couldn't imagine how much that would cost her, and I started feeling guilty that I had used the car all month without anyone making an offer. As the fourth and final week rolled around, I arranged for my "Aspen" friend, Julie, to keep the truck until we could find someone to drive it to Dallas. On July 31, my last day in Aspen, Julie and I drove in the truck to the Aspen airport to drop me off. My mom and Harold (who is a pilot) were flying in to pick me up on their way home. Julie and I sat on the tarmac in the truck, watching my parents' plane approaching.

"Knock, knock, knock," suddenly another pilot was standing outside the truck window, knocking on the glass. I rolled down the window as Mom and Harold taxied down the runway.

"Hi, is your truck for sale?" he asked.

Julie burst out laughing, and we both said, "Yes!"

"My son needs a truck, and he lives in California," the pilot explained, taking a look around the truck. "This would be perfect for him." God brought me the perfect buyer, with only three minutes to spare. We traded phone numbers as I hugged Julie goodbye. She just shook her head and said, "What timing! You sure have a good connection with the guy upstairs!"

This is just one of the many times the Lord intervened and answered my prayers. It was in His timing, and it was by far the best timing! I don't take His answers to my prayers for granted. Every situation like that builds my faith more and more and strengthens my "connection" with God, as my friend said. I have that connection because I have a *relationship* with Him. Christianity is not a set of rules to follow—that's religion. Christianity is a real love relationship with Him. Sandy once told me, "Do not put your trust in religion, but put your trust in Christ." If you put your faith in Jesus, you too will enjoy a good connection with Him and see Him answer your prayers like He has answered mine.

Ring, Ring! It's God Calling!

I had been in Tyler's ICU with Ben's parents, Phyllis and Landon, for three days. His mother had undergone emergency brain surgery as the result of falling the week prior. To make matters worse, Fran, Ben's sister-in-law, had just been diagnosed with stage 3 breast cancer as well. We live two hours away in Dallas, but my friend Jackie is from Tyler and graciously allowed us to stay in her guest home while we helped Ben's family. However, soon after we settled in at her place, Jackie called in despair saying, "My dad was just diagnosed with stage 3 stomach cancer." Her mom had died of cancer 10 years ago, and she was devastated by this sudden news. I myself was feeling overwhelmed with all the crises seeming to pop up all around me.

I started helping Jackie by making phone calls to M.D. Anderson and UT Southwestern to try to get her dad in as soon as possible. He had already hit the road that day to drive from Arkansas to Texas to live with Jackie while he underwent treatment. In the middle of my flurry of phone calls, she called with even worse news. Her dad had flipped his pick-up truck five times on the highway and landed upside down in a creek beside the road! All his clothes and belongings had been strewn all over the ground and the creek. His son, who was driving behind him, witnessed the whole thing. Somehow, Mike wrestled his dad out of the twisted, mangled wreckage, but the helicopter care flight could not land because of fog. Father and son waited for an ambulance instead and finally made it to the same Tyler hospital where I had been all week.

That's when I fell apart. This was the fourth major tragedy that had happened in about eight days. Amid all of this, another friend's child had shot herself and was in ICU, struggling to live (and find the desire to live). Not only that, this same friend's sister-in-law had been rushed to the hospital for immediate surgery to remove a brain tumor they'd just discovered. I began crying and prayed out loud for all these people who were suffering. Then I did what I often do whenever I am stressed out—I called Sandy, who is like an adopted grandmother, friend and mentor to me all rolled into one. She quietly reminded me, "God's in control, and He is faithful." Whenever we talk, I'm usually holding the phone in one hand and a pen in the other so I can write down in my journal the bits of godly wisdom she shares. I took four pages of notes that day. She reminded me that God permitted all of this to happen. And He has a purpose for each disaster—His purpose is that He gets the glory. "We don't know why a problem happens, but He solves it and resolves it," she added. "Leave it in His hands."

This was the fourth major tragedy that had happened in about eight days.

Sandy helped me to see the truth. God didn't say we would understand our problems; He only said,

"Trust Me." I knew that God needed to be the One I was looking to for help. Nothing in my "flesh" could bring me the peace that only He can bring. Philippians 4:6-7 says, "Do not be anxious about anything, but in everything, by prayer and petition, with thanksgiving, present your requests to God. And the peace of God, which transcends all understanding, will guard your hearts and your minds in Christ Jesus." Later in that same chapter, Paul adds, "I can do everything through him who gives me strength" (verse 13). This means I can bear everything with His strength.

Jesus asked in Matthew 6:27, "Who of you by worrying can add a single hour to his life?" We don't understand why God permits these things to happen, but we do know He wants us to come to Him in our time of need. Each trial strengthens our faith more, if we trust and obey Him. "You will see the results, and your faith will increase," Sandy assured me.

While we were talking, someone else called me, but I didn't answer because I didn't recognize the phone number. About an hour and a half later, I remembered to listen to the message. It was a new friend I'd met in a Bible study and had only spoken to her once in the last two months. "Hey Amy, this is Susan McCord," her message began. "I just wanted to call you and let you know I'm praying for you. I know you have a lot on your plate right now, and I felt God's push to call you." I was stunned. How did she know? Then she added, "I'm actually in Bible study right now and stepped out into the hall to call you...just know I'm praying for you."

That may have been Susan on the line, but I knew it

was a call from God! He was letting me know that He had not abandoned me or forgotten me. The next morning, I woke up at four and felt Him impress on me again, "That was Me calling you." He reminded me that He is there for us even when it seems as if everything else is falling apart.

Buster, the Best Dog in the World

Buster was my black-and-white English Springer spaniel and the love of my life. "Bus," one of the nicknames I called him, was the best dog in the world; not to mention the most regal, handsome, perfect dog. His mom was "Spackel," and they looked like twins, but I could always tell them apart. They loved each other so much—always playing, kissing each other, and cuddling together on their bed. I have several thousand photos of Spackel and Buster. (Okay, I am a photographer *and* a dog lover!)

I've always loved dogs, even at two years old. "Mixy," my first dog, was my everything at that age. I loved Spackel, but Buster was my true love. He rode in my car with me everywhere I went. He had "his spot" in the Ford Explorer I drove. His chest would lean on the middle console between the two seats in front—his left paw on my seat, his right paw on the right seat. This position was perfect. It held him in place when Mommy would go around the corners on two wheels. He placed his face perfectly positioned in front of the AC vents to get the maximum amount of cool air (which also gave him full view out the windshield for any possible squirrel sightings). He was so smart to figure that out!

Buster went through so many difficult things with me: my divorce, my dad's death, my engagement to another man (who didn't like Buster or Spackel), my broken engagement (which thrilled everyone, including Buster and Spackel), a very stressful trial my family endured, and Spackel's death. In the summer of 1998, I was living alone in my first home in Dallas. One early Saturday morning, I went out to the front yard to water my impatiens. I was still in my boxers and t-shirt, and Spackel and Buster tumbled out the door together with me. They never left my yard, preferring to stick close to Mommy. While I was watering the flowers, I heard the soundtrack of my worst nightmare: a thump, tires screeching, and a dog yelping. Everything seemed to happen in slow motion as I spun around and saw Buster lying in the street. His screaming and yelping was the worst sound I've ever heard. I ran to him and stood over his mangled, bloody body. We made eye contact, and it was as if he were saying, "Mommy, help me! Help me!"

I immediately scooped him up in my arms. He stopped crying the minute I picked him up. His body, however, was still contorted. Out of the corner of my eye, I saw the car that ran over him turn around and pull up next to me.

"Amy, get in," the driver urged.

"Who is this person?" I thought. "How does she know me?" But Buster needed to go to the vet immediately, so I opened her back door, still holding Buster. I got into the car, called to Spackel to jump in with us, and I shut the door. A blood-curdling yelp came from Spackel. I had shut the door on her tail. I opened the door, got her tail out of the way, and shut it again.

"Amy, where should I go?" the driver asked, terrified. I then realized she was my neighbor who lived a few houses down.

"There's a vet on Mockingbird and Skillman… Hurry!" I yelled at the top of my lungs.

"I'm so sorry. I never saw him. I'm so, so sorry," she kept repeating, visibly upset.

Tears streaming down my face, my cries were uncontrollable. My heart was breaking, and I began to pray out loud, "Lord, please don't take Buster. Please Lord, I'm begging You. Not now. Please don't let him die." I prayed the entire ride there, and my voice grew louder and louder as we approached the vet. We pulled up to the front door, and I jumped out with Buster's lifeless body in my arms. I kicked the double doors open, covered in blood, and yelled, "I need a doctor!" Everyone turned and stared in disbelief.

I heard the soundtrack of my worst nightmare: a thump, tires screeching, and a dog yelping.

The girls behind the counter jumped up quickly to show me where to go. I had never been to this place. I knew my vet very well, but his clinic was too far to drive in Buster's condition. They raced me to the back where they perform surgeries and told me to put Buster on the table. Just as I did, he launched into a full-blown seizure. His front legs went totally stiff, his back rounded upwards. The vet techs were telling me to leave, saying they would take care of him. Distraught and still crying, I refused to leave.

One girl grabbed me by the arm and said, "You have to leave now. We can't start working on him while you're back here." Meanwhile, Buster was having a seizure, I thought he was dying, and I was trying to hold him on the table. I answered her, "Buster has always been there for me. I'm *not* leaving him when he needs me the most! Do what you have to do. I'll stand right here, but I'm not leaving him." At that point, they gave up trying to make me leave.

As promised, I stood back as they held him down and treated the huge spots of open flesh. They used staples to stop the bleeding all over his chest and legs where he had road rash. I could see the black tire marks that started on his stomach between his legs and traveled all the way up his white fur to his neck. I guess his head was to the side, and the tire missed it completely. His hind leg was injured. He held it up in the air and wouldn't walk on it. After they treated his wounds the best they could, they put him in a cage about four feet off the ground—just high enough for me to lean inside and wrap my arms around his body.

I put my head next to his and whispered, "Lord, please, don't take Bus Bus. You know how much I love him. Please, Lord, don't take him now." My tears were rolling past my cheeks, along my throat, and down into chest. I was still covered in blood, but I couldn't have cared less. Buster was all I cared about at that moment. The vet came over to me after about 20 minutes, put her hand on my shoulder and told me, "Let's wait until the end of the day to do X-rays."

I knew what she meant. "Let's see if he lives through the day before we do x-rays." She also mentioned there was probably internal bleeding, based on the tire mark stretching from one end of his body to the other. I still refused to leave Buster's side. I called Mom, who loves animals as much as I do, to tell her about the nightmare I was living and asked her to pray. Then I called my brother to tell him what had happened. We'd made plans that day, and I needed to cancel. He brought me a sandwich to eat—I had been at the vet since nine that morning.

All day long, I leaned in the cage and sang praise and worship songs over Buster. I prayed when I wasn't singing. I loved on him like I'd never see him again, and, quite frankly, I wasn't so sure I would. Now I knew how my parents felt when I was in pain. All day, he whimpered and cried. It broke my heart, but I continued singing songs like "Jesus Loves Me" so he would know I was there.

At 4:00, the vet agreed to do the X-rays. I was thrilled, but scared. *What if his leg, hip, or back was broken? Then what, a doggy cast?* They had to stretch his little weak body out on the cold, hard X-ray table. They allowed me to help them. We waited patiently for the results. Now my prayer was, "Lord, please, no internal bleeding, no broken bones. Let him live." Over and over, I prayed for that. Soon, the vet came in and said with a puzzled look, "Well, no signs of broken bones or dislocated hips. Everything looks good."

I couldn't believe my ears! "Everything looks good?" I asked. I wanted to hear her say it again. "Thank you Lord!" I cried out. "Thank you so much!

"Of course, we better keep him overnight for observation," she added.

I knew that wasn't going to happen. "I'll observe him at home," I said. "What do I need to do?" She had heard I was pretty persistent, I suppose, so she didn't try arguing with me.

"Well, make sure you wake him each hour. He needs pills every four hours, and take him out to the bathroom. Check to see if there is blood in his urine, and come back tomorrow morning."

We made it through the night. Both Spackel and I were great nurses. She was so glad to see him and cleaned his face over and over with lots of "love licks." She knew something had happened and was very gentle and attentive.

The next morning, we went to the vet's office. She came in the exam room and listened to his heart. Whenever one of us pressed on his chest, we could feel and hear all the bones cracking. It was bizarre. However, he checked out fine. She couldn't believe it. I said to her, "Do you believe in God?"

There was a long silence, so I spoke up. "If you don't, this should change your mind. This is a miracle that he lived and has no broken bones, don't you think?"

"Yes. I believe so," was all she could say. There was no other explanation. God heard my cry for help and intervened. He must have. Was Buster just a "lucky dog"? Well, in some ways, yes. I treated him like a king, but as far as surviving a tire rolling over the length of a dog's body, you have to credit God with that one. Still to this day, I give God the glory for saving Buster on that summer Saturday morning.

Buster totally recovered from the incident and lived another six years. I never took one day for granted that he was alive. I know God gave him another lease on life, and that was His answer to my prayer. Buster is buried at my farm, up on a hill overlooking our lake, facing the sunset. Next to his grave is Spackel, Gracie, and Titus (Mom's dogs), and Beau, my niece Adrienne's cocker spaniel. They all have little headstones with their names and the dates they were born and passed away.

Buster has a large rectangle grave bordered in river rock with beautiful flowers inside. A three-foot iron cross is at the top of his grave, and the headstone reads:

Buster

Buster, you brought us so much joy.
You were there for me during the toughest times
and the happiest times of my life. We will always
remember you. Thank You, Lord, for blessing us with
13 wonderful years with Bus Bus.

Almost every time I go to the farm, my new dog "Buddy" and I visit Buster's grave. Buddy runs around, and I enjoy the beauty of the place. Sometimes I sit beside Buster's grave with my morning coffee and say my prayers. As Buddy gets older, he looks more and more like Buster.

I had adopted the little black-and-white Springer when he was four months old as a companion for Buster in his old age. I hoped his youth would help Buster live longer, and I think it did. I even sent out "announcement" cards (as a joke) to let everyone know I had a new child in my home. It took three weeks for

Buster to accept Buddy as his housemate. (Buddy started out being a little brat.) Eventually, they became the best of friends. Buddy loved Buster and took great care of him, especially during the last year of his life when Buster was half-deaf and half-blind. Whenever I called the dogs to come in from the yard, Buddy would go to Buster, bump him and lead him back to me. It was so cute to see Buddy's love for Buster and how he acquired all of Buster's great traits. Buddy has certainly stepped into Buster's paws, but Buster will never be forgotten.

Buddy has now earned the title, "Best Dog in the World," and I thank the Lord each day for him. He, along with all my other dogs, has brought such joy in my life. To me, dogs are just one more bonus God gives to bring us joy while we are here on earth. The entire time I have been writing this story (and this book for the most part) Buddy has been curled up beside me, resting his head on my lap. He is my 60-pound lap dog, and I'm so blessed to have him with me everywhere I go!

Jesus taught us to be persistent in pursuing God—as persistent as I was in the vet's office that day. Sometimes, we give up after a half-hearted effort. Or, if we don't see an answer right away, we quit praying. To know God takes faith. You must believe He exists. Don't give up when you are seeking God. Ask Him for wisdom and knowledge, patience and understanding, and He will give it to you.

Matthew 7:7 reminds us, "Ask, and it will be given to you; seek, and you will find; knock, and the door will be opened to you. For everyone who asks, receives; he who seeks, finds; and to him who knocks, the door will be opened." God tells us to "ask," and when the car hit

Buster, I asked for his life from the bottom of my heart, with everything I had. I knew God could heal Buster if He wanted to do so. God can do anything He wants: heal the sick, calm the winds, and even bring us peace in the middle of our most difficult situations.

Let the following scriptures encourage you to keep praying and asking God for an answer:

Matthew 8:1-3 "When Jesus came down from the mountainside, large crowds followed him. A man with leprosy came and knelt before him and said, 'Lord, if you are willing, you can make me clean.' (Notice the man didn't say, "Heal me right now, I want to be healed!") Jesus reached out His hand and touched the man. 'I am willing,' he said. 'Be clean!' Immediately he was cured of his leprosy." Sometimes God answers our prayers immediately. Sometimes we have to wait, but His timing is always perfect…even if we don't think so.

Jesus taught us to be persistent in pursuing God.

Psalm 91:14-15 "Because he loves me," says the Lord, "I will rescue him; I will protect him, for he acknowledges my name. He will call upon me, and I will answer him: I will be with him in trouble, I will deliver him and honor him." Try substituting your own name in place of "him" and "he" in this verse to make it more personal. For example: "Because **Amy** loves me," says the Lord, "I will rescue **her**; I will protect **Amy**, for **she** acknowledges my name…"

Psalm 100:1-2 "Shout for joy to the Lord, all the earth. Worship the Lord with gladness; come before him with joyful songs…" (Reminds me of singing over Buster.)

Psalm 100:4-5 "…give thanks to him and praise his name. For the Lord is good and his love endures forever; his faithfulness continues through all generations."

Psalm 102:1-2. "Hear my prayer, O Lord; let my cry for help come to you. Do not hide your face from me when I am in distress. Turn your ear to me; when I call, answer me quickly."

Psalm 105:4-5 "Look to the Lord and his strength; seek his face always. Remember the wonders he has done, and his miracles…"

Psalm 119:71 "It was good for me to be afflicted so that I might learn your decrees." Through the trials in my life, I can look back and see that my trust and belief in the Lord was strengthened by my afflictions."

Psalm 145:18-19 "The Lord is near to all that call on him, to all who call on him in truth. He fulfills the desires of those who fear him; he hears their cry and saves them."

Kanakuk Changes Lives

Joe White is the director of Kanakuk, a wonderful Christian camp in Missouri, and has dedicated his life's work to leading kids (along with some of their parents) to Christ. I can't impress enough how important it is to send kids to a Christian camp like Kanakuk! *It will change their lives!*

I prayed for months before one of my stepdaughters went to camp for the first time—for her counselors and cabin mates. I asked that she would be open to hear what God had to say to her through Joe and her counselors. As a camper, I loved getting letters and remembered how much it meant to me to receive mail at camp. I wrote her several times a week and sent several packages.

I went to Kanakuk myself for eight years when I was young. It taught me about the Christian life and what it meant to put your faith in Christ. Even though it took many years for these principles to take effect in my life, camp gave me the foundation I needed. Proverbs 22:6 says, "Train a child in the way he should go, and when he is old he will not turn from it." I was off track for years, but when Dad died, I slowly started my journey back to God.

I warned Ben when we went to Missouri to pick her up. "There's a chance I'm gonna cry when we get to camp."

He looked over at me and said, "That's okay. Why do you think that?"

"Because I have so many great memories here. I remember each year where I was when I saw Mom and Dad for the first time when they came to pick me up." I always dropped whatever I was doing and ran as fast as I could to hug them—often wrapping my arms and legs around Dad in a bear hug. (I would have knocked Mom over had I done that to her!)

At camp, I always pushed the limits on what we were supposed to be doing or not doing. You see, I was a rebellious child too. I loved to get into mischief and see just how far I could bend the rules. I was the one who would organize the "short sheeting" of the beds inside the surrounding cabins. We pulled the top sheet up, tucked it into the top of the mattress, and folded the bottom up so it looked like the top sheet. When someone got into bed at night, their legs only went about two feet into the covers! We would also sneak into other cabins and shake baby powder on each blade of the ceiling fan. When the first person came in and flipped the switch, we would all watch the "white out" from our cabin windows. More often than not, I'd hear a loud scream from the other cabins, "Amy!" They knew I'd done it. When I got in trouble, I had to run laps or memorize Bible verses, but it was always worth it.

Sure enough, as we pulled into camp, I cried. As we drove down the long driveway, I pointed out to Ben the different fields where I played soccer, softball, basketball, tennis, and ran track. You name it; I did it. I won the softball throw every year, hands down. I could throw it further than any girl—and most guys. I don't know where that skill came from, but it came in handy when our "tribe" of campers needed points.

As we walked down into the main area of the camp, the memories flooded my mind. I remembered the time I ran full speed to the trampolines and began jumping from one to the other. That was a huge no-no. The rule was "no jumping without a counselor" (and several "spotters" to push you back on the trampoline if you got off balance). Before anyone could stop me, I'd jumped on all four trampolines and then hit the ground running. The ladies in the office saw me and reported it. Another lap around the field. I was always in great shape after camp.

In the middle of recalling these special memories, I suddenly saw our stepdaughter running up to us and we hugged. She looked happy and introduced us to several friends who were all adorable. We listened to Joe give a talk that night, and the memories surrounded me once again.

As we walked down into the main area of the camp, the memories flooded my mind.

"If only they had camp for forty-year-olds," I sighed, thinking to myself. After he finished, I walked up to the mess hall where all the names of the past camp "princesses" were carved on a wooden plaque. Again, more memories. Sue Moore, Maggie Moore, Judy Griffin, Amy Perry… their faces flashed before me as I thought of so many fun times with these girls. Maggie is the only one I keep up with, and we talk once or twice a year. It's sad to be so close your camp buddies, and then when it's over, life goes on. More than likely, the next time I see most of them will be in heaven. However, I'll never forget them.

On the way home, we kept talking about camp. "So tell me your top three favorite things," I asked her.

She thought for a moment. "Jet skiing, scuba diving, and K-Life."

"Oh, that sounds great! What's K-Life?" I knew what it was, but I wanted to see what she said about it.

"Well, at night the whole camp meets in the gym, and Joe White gives a talk. We sing and they do skits. He did several talks—one on Creation, one on relationships, one on leadership, and one on purity."

I recalled hearing a similar camp talk on Creation many years ago, but I enjoyed hearing about it from her perspective. She explained what she'd learned about how God created the world and universe. "Joe explained that it could *not* be any other way," she said, emphasizing "not." "Darwin's theory had been proven wrong, and the Big Bang Theory doesn't have enough to back itself."

We talked some more, and I could tell that her experience at camp had really impacted her life. When I was a camper, the Holy Spirit moved our hearts in special ways. I know that sounds crazy if you're not a Christian, but when you have experienced that, you will recognize Him immediately. It will bring you to tears, and it's a feeling you can't explain. The closer you come to Christ and begin growing spiritually, you will realize when the Holy Spirit "moves you."

In the car, I had on a Christian radio station I liked. As

we were talking more about camp, she heard the song that was playing on the radio and said, "Oh! That's my new favorite song!" She reached over, turned the volume up, and started singing, "Here I Am to Worship" by Michael W. Smith. And she knew the words! We both started singing the words together. I turned my head to keep her from seeing my tears and pretended as if I were checking the traffic.

We kept singing, and my mind flashbacked to all the months I worried endlessly about her having a good camp experience. God was faithful. He answered my prayers ten-fold. I've never seen a transformation like that in such a short period of time—she was there only two weeks. I felt ashamed for worrying when all along God had heard my prayers. All day, I just kept repeating, "Thank You, Lord."

This story is a huge reminder to me that there is nothing too big for God! He can do anything! He is almighty, all-powerful, and the authority over all.

That night, I recalled how I had felt covered in a peaceful feeling all day. I even wrote Joe an email to thank him. "I know you probably feel this way a lot," I wrote, "but Ben and I are experiencing God's peace and joy in such a way that we can't control our tears. The joy in our hearts is flowing out of us—it is truly amazing! Thank you, Joe, for loving all these kids! Because of your devotion to the Lord, thousands of kids benefit by learning about Jesus Christ and asking Him into their hearts. In such a short time, it transforms their lives!"

Then I thought of all the thousands of parents like me who had prayed for the 15,000 or so children who attend camp over the course of the summer at Kanakuk. God does answer every prayer—all 15,000 of them!

Business Meeting with God

PLAYING TENNIS QUICKLY BECAME A FAVORITE SPORT OF mine. There was a time when I was playing most days of the week, and I ended up joining a TCD (Tennis Competitors of Dallas) team. After years of overhead slams, I began to get tennis elbow. For the most part, I decided to tough it out and just keep swinging. Then the pain became so bad I couldn't squeeze my shampoo bottle, hold a hairbrush, or lift a glass of water to my lips to drink. I fought through that stage, but then the pain increased to the point where it would wake me up in the middle of the night. Something had to be done.

I quit playing and saw a couple of doctors. I tried eight weeks of physical therapy and several other remedies I heard might help. Nothing helped; the only option left was surgery. The kidney transplant was in February, and the trouble with my elbow happened just three months later. My friend, Julie, referred me to a doctor in Vail, Colorado who had fixed a lot of sports celebrity injuries. I told myself that if he was good enough for them, he was good enough for me. His innovative procedure was designed to speed up the recovery. He would take extra blood from my body (ugh) and spin it into a jelly-like substance, then put it back in around the repaired tendon. It sounded promising, so I headed to Vail.

Mom and Harold were supposed to fly to Vail from

Santa Barbara the morning of the surgery (for moral support more than anything). When you're sick or having surgery, we all want our mommies! My surgery was scheduled for 11:00am, and they would arrive just in time. We planned to spend the night in Vail and fly home the next day.

On the morning of the surgery, I woke up about 9:00am. As I sat on the side of the bed, one eye barely open and the other firmly shut, the phone rang. "That's odd," I thought. "Who is calling me now?" I looked at my cell phone and saw it was Mom's number in Santa Barbara where they have a second home. My mind raced..."Wait, shouldn't they be in the air on the way here by now?" I knew something was terribly wrong. I answered, "Mom?"

When you're sick or having surgery, we all want our mommies!

Her voice was weak and tired. "Hi, Honey...well, we are not going to be able to come today. We just got home from the ER, and we are exhausted. Harold started having problems about 1:00 this morning."

I felt the blood drain down to my feet; I fought back tears. "What's wrong? Is he okay?" All I could think about was getting to Santa Barbara to be there with Mom and Harold. But trying to fly from Vail to Santa Barbara would take all day. I felt stranded and helpless. Mom convinced me that he was fine, but she had to stay there with him. My first thought was to cancel my surgery.

Then Mom said, "Honey, Jimmy and Sue are in Vail. They are going to go to the hospital, sit in the waiting room, and wait for you. Then they will help you get back to the hotel room, too."

I should have known Mom already had a Plan B in place. Her friends, Jimmy Westcott and Sue Justice, were in Vail on vacation. They gladly stepped in to comfort me and play "mom." Also Ben would be there to support me, along with my friend, Rachael, whose mom just happened to have back surgery in the same hospital, on the same day. Coincidence? I don't think so—God knew I needed some extra care and support, since "Mommy" was not going to make it.

When I hung up the phone from Mom, I sat in the Vail hotel room with an incredibly heavy heart. I felt as if I were being "pressed down" by Satan. I was completely overwhelmed with the situation that had evolved in the last three minutes. I walked into the living area and looked up toward heaven. With my hands held high, I yelled, "Okay, Lord, I'm falling apart here. I need You! I need to feel Your peace that You talk about, because I am not doing so well right now!" I'm sure some of our hotel neighbors might have heard me having my "business meeting" with God.

I continued praying, "Please comfort me and replace this feeling with Your peace. Please take care of Harold and Mom, and don't let anything happen to them. Lord, here I am at Your mercy. I need You to help me get through this surgery and this day. Amen." Immediately, I felt so much better—as if a great weight had been lifted from my shoulders. He instantly granted me His peace.

I got dressed and we headed to the hospital. I did quite well, although I dreaded the part where they had to take my blood, which took a long time (30 minutes) because of the procedure to spin the platelets. Ben was beside me every second. He talked to me and held my hand during all the questions, needles, and blood work. Then he kissed me goodbye as they wheeled me off to surgery. I came out 45 minutes later, still under the "goo-goo" juice, as I called the anesthesia. I was so happy!

As promised, Jimmy, Sue, Rachael, and Ben were there for me in the recovery room. I felt extra cozy, snuggled under a fancy hospital blanket that pumped warm air inside it. It was the most comfortable I'd ever been, and I apparently kept telling everyone about it! Recovery is normally an hour or so, but mine was four hours because I was still under the influence of the anesthesia and didn't want to get out of that comfy bed!

About four in the afternoon, they devised a plan to get me out because the hospital needed the bed for another patient. First, they convinced me I needed to go to the bathroom. Ben helped me up and into the bathroom. The plan was to get me dressed meanwhile and replace my bed with a recliner! Ben held me tight as we came out of the bathroom and I discovered my bed was gone!

My eyes grew wide and I announced, "We're not in the right room!"

"Yes we are. They just needed your bed, so they took it out."

In my "goo-goo" juiced state, I insisted we were definitely in the wrong room. To keep me quiet, they brought back the heated blanket that I had fallen in love with and coaxed me to sit in the recliner by draping the blanket over me.

Sue, Jimmy, and Rachael had been there all day with me, and when I was finally ready to go back to the hotel it was quite a precession. Ben led the way with my bags, Jimmy pushed me in the wheelchair, Sue followed close behind with huge beautiful flowers, and Rachael parked the car. I'm sure people thought I'd been in the hospital for days! We got up to the hotel room, and the girls helped Ben get me settled. I talked to Mom but don't remember telling her much except that "I was the most comfortable I'd ever been."

This story might seem like no big deal to you. *So my mom couldn't come to be with me during my elbow surgery—big deal, right?* Well, it was a big deal to me. My mom and I are so close—I want her beside me even if it's to pull out a splinter! (Which she has done many times!) Going through the surgery without Mom and Harold there with me was one thing. But knowing Harold was not doing well on the day I was having surgery added a whole other level of stress and anxiety.

The point of my story is that in the midst of my despair, I called out (or yelled, in this case) to God, and He answered my prayers that instant. I knew I could trust Him, based on my previous experiences with Him. And He gave me perfect peace. He relieved all the pain and angst about my situation. God doesn't say He will change our situations, but He does say He will give us peace *in the middle* of our trials. He did that for me during this particular trial. When I gave it to God, He answered my prayers and lifted my burdens immediately.

Harold, and me the day after the kidney ransplant. It was the first time to see each other.

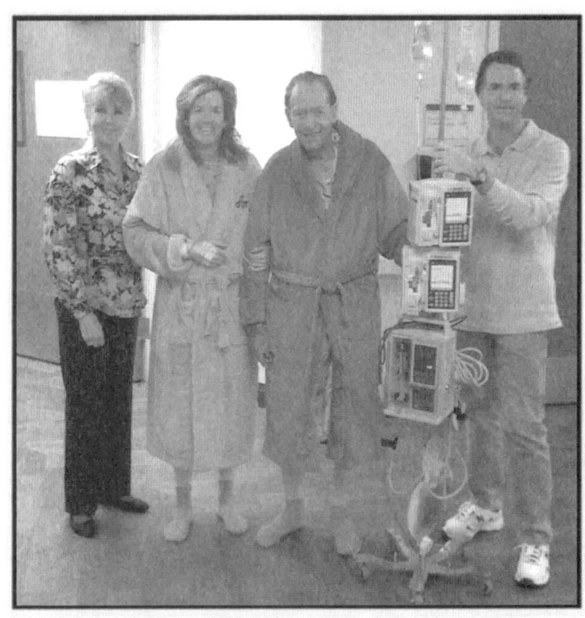

Mom, me, Harold, and my brother Andy, walking the halls at Baylor Hospital.

This is Harold and me on our first walk, unassisted, hand in hand.

Harold and me, one month after the transplant. Mom had a party "celebrating life." Twenty men sang gospel songs while walking through the crowd.

It was a day I'll never forget!

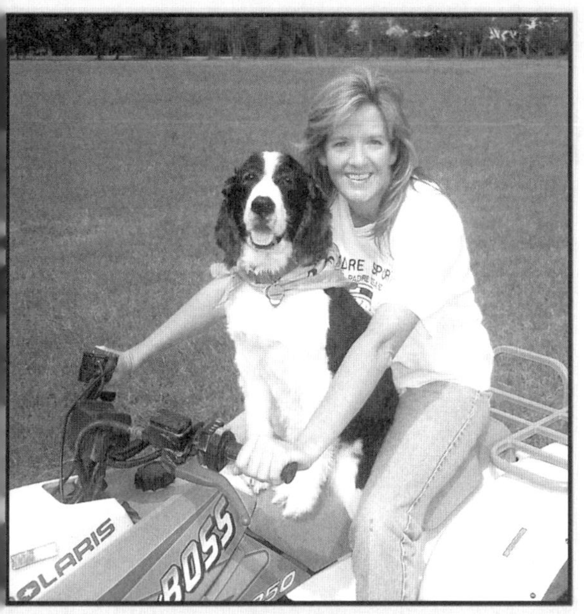

Buster and me on a Saturday afternoon ride at the farm where he was later buried.

He LOVED the farm.

Buster's grave, overlooking our family farm in McKinney, Texas.

Buddy. Funny how much both dogs loved riding 4-wheelers with me!

Buddy and Buster in their monogrammed raincoats so we know whose is whose!

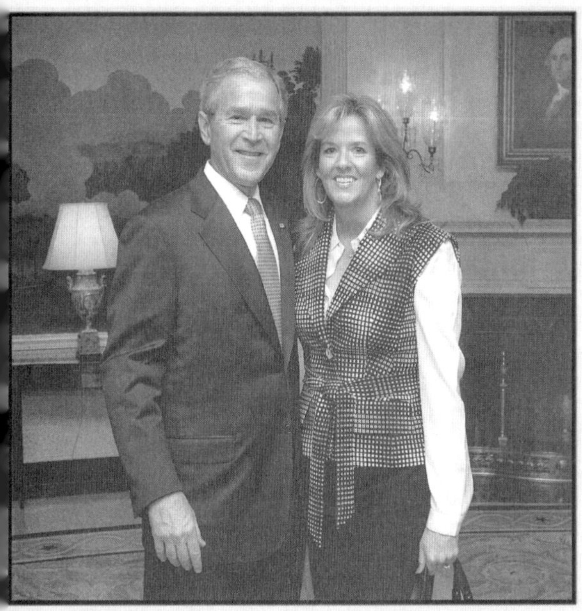

President George Bush and me in the Diplomat Room in the White House.

Exactly five weeks after the kidney transplant.

Standing in front of the Oval Office. Kathy, Susan, Paige, me, and Rachael.

We had a private tour of the West Wing.

Just another day at the farm! 18 years old, and I was just getting started!

It's absolutely beautiful up there.

This was my fourth time up Aspen Mountain. I love being 13,000 feet closer to God!

The morning after the Tea Fire where our next door neighbor lost everything.

I am dousing the flames still burning in the rubble.

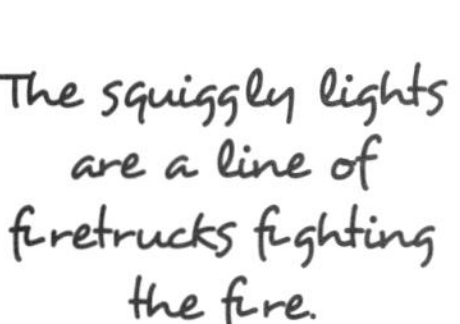

The squiggly lights are a line of firetrucks fighting the fire.

I took this photo of the Tea Fire just 50 feet from the wall in our yard.

Paige, me, Jackie, and Chantell in Paris, France.
Bon Jour!

Trying to navigate our way through Paris.

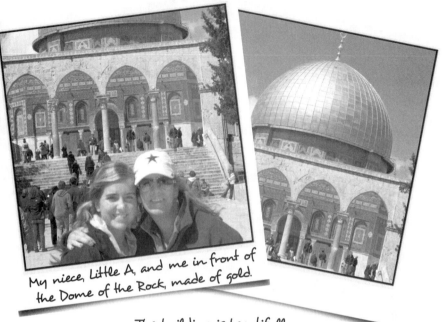

My niece, Little A, and me in front of the Dome of the Rock, made of gold.

The building is beautifully colored with tiny mosaic tiles.

his part of the wall
as there in Jesus' day.

Me praying for my niece, Little A, at the "Wailing Wall."

The Sea of Galilee, so peaceful and pretty.

I think about wha
is was like for the
disciples to see Jesu
walking on the wat
on this very lake!

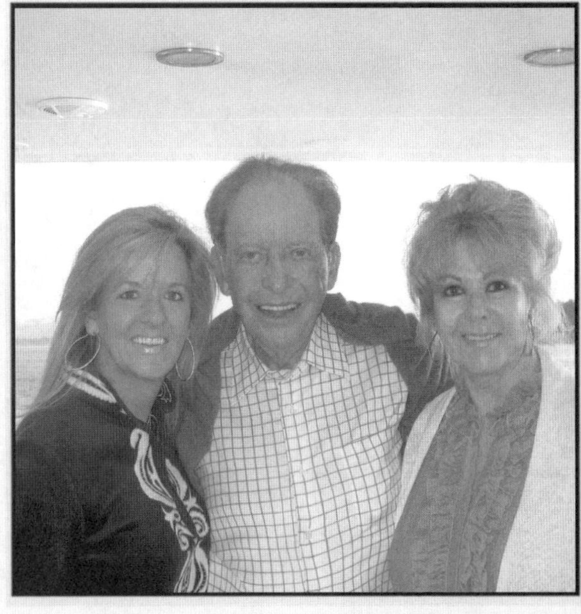

Me, Harold, and Mom in the San Juan islands.

Celebrating my
birthday and the
2 1/2 year anniversary
of the kidney
transplant!

When God Intervenes in MINISTRY

My First Prison Ministry Experience

I HAD ALWAYS WANTED TO VISIT A PRISON. FOR SOME reason, God had put that on my heart. And not just any prison. If I got the chance, I wanted to visit a maximum-security prison where they house the worst of the worst inside.

I wrote about my introduction to prison ministry in my first book, *When God Has a Way No Other Way Works*, and this is the rest of the story! I went to my first prison with a group of 15 people I did not know. However, I got my wish—we were going inside a female prison where the worst of the worst murderers and criminals are spending life sentences.

On December 22, the night before our trip, I got a taste of what it feels like to be "hit on" by the evil one. (I don't even like to acknowledge Satan's name, so I call him "the evil one"). After years of wanting to do prison ministry, I started to have doubts. For one thing, we were supposed to leave at five o'clock Sunday morning (which wipes out any Saturday night plans). The night before, I was beginning to dread how early I would have to get up.

Then I started wondering if it would be worth my while. What if I couldn't talk to the inmates one-on-one? I wanted to share the Gospel with one or two girls and "save" someone in the prison unit. But something made me doubt that I would even get that chance.

So, I began to figure out a way to get out of going—starting with the fact that I didn't want to get up at four o'clock! I decided to call the pastor of Cornerstone Ministries to see if they really needed me.

The phone rang twice before a woman answered.

"Hello?"

"Is Chaplain Gibbons there?" I asked.

"Who's this?" she said in a friendly voice.

"Um, this is Amy Alford…I'm supposed to go with you tomorrow to the Murray Unit but…"

Before I could offer my excuse, she said, "Oh Amy, it's so nice to talk to you, I've heard so much about you, and I'm looking so forward to meeting you tomorrow!"

Oh, great. "Oh, okay." My mind was racing. "Are we going to be able to talk to the girls one-on-one?" I asked. I told myself if I couldn't talk or witness to the girls one-on-one, I might as well stay at home.

"Oh no, Honey. We just pass out 'blessing bags,' have a chapel service, and then we come home. We are so glad you're coming tomorrow!"

I still wanted to back out, but I knew there was no way I could do it now! So I just said, "Great, see you tomorrow" and hung up the phone.

Looking back on that night and that conversation, I realize the "evil one" was working on me. After everything that happened at the prison unit, it's no wonder he put doubtful thoughts in my head to discourage me from going! Now I see his strategy, but at the time I was just making logical excuses not to go.

∞

Despite my doubts, I woke up at four o'clock the next morning and got going. Even after a long van ride down together from Dallas to the Gatesville prison, I still didn't know anyone in my group very well. So, when we entered the prison, I started striking up conversations and trying to get to know some of the female prisoners. It was Christmastime and a chilly 38 degrees outside as we handed out care packages called "blessing bags."

Inside the prison yard, one of the prisoners I'd befriended pointed out another prisoner with shackles who was being escorted by two huge men. This highly visible prisoner had murdered the well-known Hispanic recording artist, Selena. My new friend explained she was under the guards' protection so the other inmates wouldn't harm her!

The security at a maximum-security prison is extraordinarily tight. For example, can you tell the difference between a maximum and minimum-security prison when you drive by? I can now. The maximum-security prison has two rolls of razor wire on top of the fence, while the minimum-security prisons have only one. We gave our drivers licenses at the front office when we arrived, but we had already been thoroughly checked out weeks ahead of time. All visitors are brought into a gated area that has a literal cage. Both the entrance and exit gates lock for a minute or so before the visitors are allowed to pass through to the next section. We went through several secure checkpoints like that before we actually entered the prison yard to pass out our care packages. To say I felt unsafe and afraid in this environment is more than an understatement. I was in a maximum-security prison, virtually on my own.

Luckily, the girls were glad to see us.

After we passed out 1500 bags, our group went into town for lunch, planning to return to the prison later that afternoon. The Texas metropolis of Gatesville has only three fast food restaurants, and Dairy Queen won the popular vote among my group. I followed along like a lost puppy, ordered a basket of greasy steak fingers and sat down with the strangers in my group. My lunch was barely edible, but I found that with enough gravy, I was able to get a few pieces down. I could tell this group had been in prison ministry together for many years, and it was evident they all knew each other well.

They were from the same town, but they had never seen me before in their lives. I looked around and realized how easy it would be for them to accidentally leave me and never miss me until hours later. As they talked and told stories, I intervened at one point and said (only half-jokingly), “No matter what happens today, don’t leave me!” They laughed and went back to their “Belt Buster” hamburgers and fries. Not certain I’d been convincing enough, I made my point again to the van driver and his wife, “Please, please do not leave me.”

You may think I sounded paranoid, but I have this thing—it’s like a hunch or premonition where I often know something’s going to happen long before it does. Whatever you call it, I’m right about 70% of the time. After lunch, we got back in the van and returned to the prison just in time to lead a church service for the prisoners. Again, I had no idea this was part of their routine, but I just followed my group from one activity to the next.

As the 15 people in our group squeezed back into

the "cage" again waiting to be buzzed in, the chaplain said, "Does anyone want to give their testimony during the church service?" No one wanted to make eye contact with him. They either looked down or around, and an awkward silence followed for about 10 seconds. I thought to myself, "I'll say something. What do I have to lose? I'll never see any of these people again." (Or so I thought—remember, God had something else in mind.) I broke the silence and piped up, "I'll say something." Instead of being pleased, the chaplain retorted, "Well, you can't just say *something*…you gotta give your testimony."

I'd never given my testimony in my life. I didn't even know what my "testimony" was. *What would I say?*

I thought to myself, "I'll say something. What do I have to lose?"

Without hesitating, I replied, "Okay, I'll give my testimony." Even as I heard the words come out of my mouth, I thought to myself, *Who just said that? Did I just volunteer to do it?* Any chance I had to change my mind was interrupted by the loud, long "buzzzz" of the gate releasing us into the prison yard. I had a 400-yard walk down the middle of the yard toward the chapel to think of my testimony. We had to walk single file down a marked path, escorted by armed guards. I prayed repeatedly, "Lord, put Your words in my mouth. Let them hear You when I speak, because this is Your deal!" I asked Him to open their hearts to hear Him through me.

The chapel was full with about 400 prisoners. The day before, I'd pictured sharing the Gospel with one or two girls. But God had a different plan, and His plans are so much better than our own!

While we sang worship music, I was frantically looking up scripture verses in my Bible, hoping to find something they could relate to. Before I knew it, I heard the chaplain on the microphone say, "We'd like to call up sister Amy to come speak to you."

I froze. "Let's welcome Amy."

My heart was beating hard enough to make my sweater bounce. I slowly walked up to the stage and stood in front of the microphone to address the women—all dressed in white, all eyes on me. The walls were lined with armed guards. "Okay, Lord," I whispered, "showtime." I hope He "showed" up, because I had never done anything like this before!

Fifteen minutes later, I had finished. I don't remember much except my voice wasn't shaking, and I no longer felt nervous at all. At one point, they were crying, then laughing, then praising God. The last thing I said was, "Remember this: How can you stumble when you're on your knees?" As I walked off the stage and down the aisle next to the armed guards, the prisoners on the edge of the rows were high fivin' me and clapping and cheering. I took my seat on the back row, amazed that my knees did not shake. It was as if my body had been up there on stage, but God had taken control of my words. He used me as His vessel and spoke through me—just exactly as I had prayed.

While the service continued, several young prisoners came over to me. They knelt down on the floor as if not to be seen and said, "We loved what you said…can you go back up and keep talking? We need more people like you to talk to us." That's when I realized they related to younger people and thought of me as closer to their age. (I have to admit, I enjoy a sense of humor and use it every chance I get. They obviously appreciated it in my talk.) I felt honored that so many of the girls felt a connection with me.

I give the glory to God. He's the one who made that happen. It was His doing, not mine. I would never take the credit—especially when I didn't want to go in the first place! I was simply obedient and available for His purpose, and it was obvious He planned to draw them to Christ through the stories He placed on my heart to tell them.

As the worship service came to an end, the girls began filing out in an orderly manner, but some gathered around me. One girl called out, "Hey Amy! I love your hair...I'm going to get mine cut like yours!"

I admit, my first thought was, *Who's going to cut it? Can they have scissors in here?* Several girls told me their story. They asked me to pray for them. I held their hands or put my arm around them (knowing they don't get hugs because it's against prison rules to touch or be affectionate to each other). I was completely caught up in the moment, seeing God at work with these precious girls. Next thing I knew, one of the inmates looked around and said, "Amy, your group left you."

"What?" I tried not to sound startled. "Oh, I'm sure they're just out in the hallway."

"No, they're gone," was the consensus. They were right!

I quickly wrapped up my visit with the girls, grabbed my Bible and coat, and headed into the hallway. No one from my group was there. I dashed out into the 38-degree weather and made my way through the first few gates into the prison yard, all alone. My group was nowhere to be seen. About 400 yards away, I happened to see them entering the last set of gates. I took off running as if I were making a break for it out of this place! I ran down the middle of the prison yard, weaving through all the prisoners. Some of them waved and said, "Bye, Amy! God bless you!" I was calling out *God bless you* here and there, trying to smile and not reveal my sheer panic. It was getting dark by now, and the cold air stung my throat and inside of my chest. I had not run that fast since my eighth grade track meet. I was 100 yards from the last gate when I met eyes with an armed guard. She had this crazy white woman running across the prison yard in her sights.

That's when I began screaming and waving my arms saying, "Wait, wait! I'm with them!" My group had passed through the last secure area and was now headed inside the building. The guard had one hand on her gun and one on the gate. I was completely out of gas but determined not to be locked in with some pretty tough ladies (to put it nicely). I was frantic now, and I knew it showed on my red, cold face as I ran the last 50 yards. As I approached the guard, she said without the slightest hint of humor, "If you were wearing white, you would have been shot." That was the least of my worries!

Finally, I came through the home stretch inside the building and yelled one last time at my group. They nonchalantly turned to see what all the commotion was. I was doubled over trying to catch my breath, and when I did, I managed to heave out, "I…told you…not…to…leave…me." One of the ladies just smiled and said, "Oh, we're sorry. We thought you were with us." I'm now a firm believer in the buddy system.

It's hard to explain the feeling I had on the way home. I forgot all about almost being left in prison! I burst through the back door of my house and yelled out to Ben. My adrenaline was still pounding with joy—a joy that can only come straight from God. It was such an awesome feeling, and Ben was so thrilled for me. He could feel the joy radiating from the inside out. Have you ever had a similar feeling when God seemed to pour His joy over you?

I took off running as if I were making a break for it out of this place!

I had experienced being in God's will, and I saw the results of my obedience to Him. Remember, my original plan was to try and talk to one or two inmates. However, God allowed me to speak to many more. In fact, 22 girls came to Christ that day after hearing my testimony and listening to the chaplain's talk. Twenty-two! It wasn't the experience I had planned (talking to one or two girls), but I'm so glad that God worked His plan in my life instead.

He proved to me once again that He is in control. If we are open and available to Him, He will work His purposes through us. His will *is* far better than ours. Because I was available and compliant with God's will, He used me to lead so many to Him. It's true—when God has a way, no other way works!

Blessed to be a Blessing

After my first experience with prison ministry, I knew it would not be my last. In fact, my friend, Mary Beth Gaylor, and I decided to make a monthly visit to Dawson State Jail in downtown Dallas. On our visits, we usually went from dorm to dorm to distribute Christian books for the inmates to read. I felt led to donate about 60 copies of my first book to the jail, unsure if anyone would read them or not.

One day Mary Beth and I were in the lockdown area waiting to be "buzzed" into the dorms. As we entered, one of the girls seemed to be looking closely at me. Then her eyes grew as big as dinner plates as she exclaimed, "Are you the one on the cover of that book?"

She was obviously referring to one of the books I'd donated, which happens to have a picture of me on the cover walking together in a garden with my mentor, Sandy. Mary Beth giggled under her breath at the stunned look on my face, which she later deemed "priceless." I'd never had that kind of reaction to my book before. Not knowing what else to say to the young woman, I smiled kindly and agreed, "Yes, I am! What's your name?"

"Mary Ann," she said. "My mama is a reverend in Virginia, and I've been writing her and telling her about the things in your book. She sometimes uses what you wrote to preach her sermons on Sundays!"

That made me feel so good to know my book had helped at least two people! I got Mary Ann's and her mom's address that day and sent autographed books to both of them. Soon after, I received a four-page typed letter from her mom thanking me. I then called her mom to thank her for telling me what a difference the principles I'd learned from Sandy had made in Mary Ann's life.

Another friend also told me a great story about someone who was touched by the book. Jackie, my Tyler friend whose dad was undergoing cancer treatment, called one day and said, "I have the neatest story to tell you. While my dad was waiting for his radiation treatment, he was reading your book. A nurse saw the book in his hands, stopped and said, 'Oh my gosh… that's the best book I've ever read!'"

Now, who knows if it was really the best book she's ever read? But still, little stories like that amaze me. Not because of anything I've done—but because of how God can intervene and use anything when we step out in faith for Him.

Another time, two ladies from Sandy's Bible class were at the Dallas Museum of Art. In their conversation with the docent, they discovered the girl was a Christian. After spending some time walking around with them in the museum, the docent revealed that she was going through a bad divorce. She then mentioned a book she'd read that had helped her through tough times. Guess what book it was? You got it.

I recently read a devotional about how we can be a blessing to someone every day. The verse was Romans 1:11, which says, "I long to see you so that I may impart to you some spiritual gift to make you strong..." Paul wanted to be a blessing to other people, so he wrote them a letter of encouragement. You do not need to have written a book to help someone. A few years ago, I'd never written a book before in my life! You don't need to know all the right Bible verses or be a theologian to attract others to the Lord. It's the way we act that gets their attention. (Let me make it clear—I don't always act like Christ. And I know it! But it is something I strive for every day.) You might not realize it, but your life has the potential to bless everyone you meet—even strangers like the ones I mentioned in this story. Your life is the "book" that people around you read every day. When you enter a room, how do others see you? Are you the life of the party? Do you bring others down? Or do people see Jesus in you? Remember, you are blessed in order to be a blessing to those around you every day.

A Private Meeting with the President

When I was at home recovering from my kidney surgery, my friends Rachael and Bob Dedman and Kathy Wills Wright came over to visit and bring me dinner. I met Rachael about 16 years ago in a Bible study and her close friend, Kathy, shortly after that. Kathy and Rachael were fortunate enough to work in the White House, and they still have ties with a lot of people there. As I was telling them about my surgery, Kathy remarked, "Wow, you have an incredible story. Would you consider coming to the White House to speak about your book and tell your kidney story?"

I couldn't believe it, and I immediately agreed to go. I'd only driven by the White House a few times—I'd never actually been inside. And, at the time, I'd only spoken once in public at the prison chapel service. But I just told myself it wouldn't be too much different from the prison. We would be surrounded with guards, only the audience wouldn't be dressed in white this time! Within a couple of weeks, "Robert" contacted me from the White House, and we set the date for April 8.

You might not realize it, but your life has the potential to bless everyone you meet.

Kathy arranged for me to bring Rachael and Paige with me to the White House. My dear friend, Susan Pausky, lives in D.C. and was able to come as well. Robert and I had several phone calls to coordinate the details. During one of our conversations, he said, "I'm going to try to do something special for you. It's a really neat thing to watch the President take off in Marine One from the south lawn. He is scheduled to leave about 10:00 the morning you arrive."

"Oh, do you know where he is going?" I asked him. Silence.

"No…" he said cautiously, not wanting to reveal the President's whereabouts.

"I do," I replied matter-of-factly. About this time, I bet Robert was thinking, "Uh, oh! Security breach!"

"How do you know that?" he asked, curious to see what I'd say.

"He is going to his Crawford ranch to have lunch with my parents." More silence.

"Who are your parents?"

"Annette and Harold."

"Can I call you back?" Robert hung up the phone.

I think he freaked out because I knew where the President was going. My mom had already told me they were going to Crawford to have lunch with George and Laura the day I was to speak in Washington. I didn't think it would be a big deal if I told Robert about the President's lunch plans. Robert called back within the next few days (satisfied that I was no longer a security threat I guess!), and we continued planning the "White House Ministries" speaking engagement.

Paige, Rachael, and I flew out the day before and stayed at a hotel near the White House. We took Kathy to dinner that night and told stories from our college days. That brought back lots of memories. We laughed so hard we might have disturbed the others around us, but we had a great time.

The next morning, I woke up praying and practicing my speech. We were scheduled to arrive at the White House by 9:30am, and I would speak at 11:00. A driver picked us up at the hotel to take us to the White House. On the way there, I said, "Let's say a prayer before we get there." The three of us bowed our heads and held hands in the backseat. "Dear Lord," I began, "thank You for this opportunity to speak to the staff at the White House. Lord, please speak though me so that they can understand what You want to say through me. Open their hearts so they can hear You. Please give me peace and remove any nervousness I feel. This is Your day and Your body that You've given me. Please use me to glorify You. Amen."

Kathy and Susan met us at the West Wing entrance. Security was tight. We received special nametags that gave us certain security clearance. Robert also met us there and Kathy introduced us, although I felt as if I already knew him because of all our phone calls. He was young, slender, and handsome with a great smile. He and Kathy gave us a tour of the West Wing. Kathy knew everybody by name: every policeman, every secret service person, everyone we passed.

We went to the dining room where all the commissioned officers of the White House can eat. The china had a picture of the Presidential seal on it. The photographs that lined the halls were incredible, including a lot of candid shots of the President. One of my favorites was of him and his dog looking at each other at what appeared to be the Crawford ranch. The President was wearing blue jeans and boots, and he was sitting on a wooden bench outside. Another photo of him was at Ground Zero right after 9-11. One of the most moving photographs for me was a picture of Marine One flying over a town that had just been hit by a tornado. You could see the path of destruction winding through the town in the background. Every photograph told a story, and, being a photographer, I loved each one.

Next, we walked past the Oval Office, but we could not go in. The doors were shut, and Robert said there was a meeting going on inside. My mind raced as I thought of all the people who had been there, served there, and lived there. Robert had said there were certain areas where we could not take photos, so I complied (for the most part). My friends and I did take our own photograph in front of the Presidential seal in the West Wing. That was fun! At the end of our tour, we came out into the Rose Garden, the area right outside the Oval Office that I've seen a million times on TV when the President addresses the nation. As we walked along the outside corridor, I held up my pocket-sized camera and just started snapping pictures as we walked along—without even looking through the lens. Now I know where they get the expression "point and shoot."

We walked by the Garden and onto the South Lawn where a few hundred people waited behind a roped-off area. We were standing near the door below all the big white columns, another part of the White House you've likely seen on TV. However, we were not behind the ropes with everyone else. As we stood there waiting, Paige and I could hardly stop smiling. The White House staff did this all the time, and they were used to being at the White House. But we were so excited to be there and see everything in person. As we looked around from our prime spot, Robert suddenly tapped me on the shoulder and said, "Mrs. Alford, you can come with me."

All I could think about was how the surveillance

camera must have caught me shooting photos as we walked along the Rose Garden. I thought I was in big trouble. We walked into the main door into the White House and stood in the Diplomat Room, a large, oval-shaped room. It was blue and yellow and had a fireplace with a portrait of George Washington hanging above the mantel.

"Wow," I thought silently. *Oh wait, am I in trouble?* I still wasn't sure.

We stopped in the middle of the room. Robert had a clipboard in his hand with the President's itinerary on it, containing minute-by-minute details of where he was to be.

"I didn't want to tell you this ahead of time because the President's schedule changes so quickly," Robert explained. "He is upstairs right now in the Blue Room addressing the nation on the war in Iraq. When he finishes, he wants to come down here and meet you."

As we stood there waiting, Paige and I could hardly stop smiling.

Whew. I wasn't in trouble after all! "Meet me? What do I say? How do I address him?" My questions tumbled out all together. "Do I call him George? Mr. Bush? Mr. President? I photographed him when he was Governor, and he said to call him 'George.'"

Robert just smiled patiently and replied, "You need to call him Mr. President. I need to inform you of what will happen when he arrives. About 15-20 Secret Service men will enter the room. They will do a quick check around as the President is walking in. It's rather weird, but they will walk out of the room backwards, almost like a vacuum has sucked them out. Then a photographer will come in and take several photos of you. I'm guessing you'll have about one to two minutes with him before he leaves on Marine One, exiting out the same door that you came in. Any questions?"

"Where will you be?" I asked.

"I will be in the hall with the Secret Service," Robert replied.

"Okay, I think I got it. Can you snap a photo of us before you leave?" I asked.

"I'll try, but I'm not sure if I can." I was still thinking about his answer when a lady came walking through the room carrying a duffle bag in each hand. She was moving pretty quickly. Robert said to her, "Hey Janet. I see you're carrying the football."

"Yes," she replied, not even slowing down.

"That's such a privilege and honor," Robert called after her.

"Oh, I know!' said Janet, but she never missed a step. "I'm loving my job." And she was gone.

"What's the football?" I asked, wondering what was inside those bags.

"Those bags she is carrying," Robert explained, "hold the detonating device and codes in case we are attacked with nuclear bombs. She always travels with the President. I would have tried to get her to slow down and talk to us, but she's not allowed to stop." I was amazed by everything I was seeing, and the President wasn't even here yet!

Next, we walked in the China Room, containing rows and rows of beautiful china plates from all over the world, all neatly displayed on lighted shelves. The room was red with a sitting area in the middle. After I gazed at all the china, I had Robert take a picture in front of the fireplace with the George Washington portrait behind me. He told me he wanted one, too; he'd never been in the Diplomat Room.

Then we walked into the main hallway, and I saw a couple of Secret Service men standing guard. They had on suits, hands folded together in front, and they were wearing earpieces with the telephone cord coming from behind one ear. We ducked back into the Diplomat Room, and just a few moments later I heard the sound of a herd of feet coming quickly down the hall. I thought, "Is that him?" Just then Robert said, "Here comes the President!"

At once, Robert leaped over the ottoman, striding toward the door. I was left standing in the middle of the room. I whispered loudly, "Here, take my picture" and literally threw him my camera. Luckily, he caught it just as the Secret Service rounded the corner.

I flipped my hair, straightened my vest, and stood at attention. I was ready to meet the most powerful man in the world, the President of the United States, George W. Bush. And as he came around the corner, he greeted me with, "Hi Amy! How ya doin'?"

"Good, Mr. President. How are you?" I didn't know what else to say.

"Good, let's get a picture." I looked around. The human vacuum came and started sucking out all the Secret Service, just as Robert had said. We took several pictures. I am not used to being on that side of the camera, so I was trying to give my best "Here I am with the President" smile. By the time the photography session was over, so was the vacuum.

"Let's have a seat," he offered and held out his arms toward the big, yellow, wing-backed chairs in front of the fireplace. He was so relaxed and easy-going. There was a small round table between the chairs, but we were sitting so close I had to be careful not to kick him when I crossed my feet. "What are you doing here?" he asked.

"I am speaking to your staff in the Bible class," I replied.

He nodded. "Which one?"

Oh my gosh, there is more than one Bible class? I said, "All I know is it's called the White House Ministries."

"What are you speaking on?" he wanted to know.

"My book that I wrote." I didn't think to tell him the title!

"What's the name of it?" he leaned back in the chair, so relaxed.

I told him the title and a little bit about the book. "That sounds like a good book," he said. *The President just said my book sounded good!*

"Well, I hope it will encourage and inspire people," I said. "I hear you are having lunch with my parents tomorrow."

"Laura and I are looking forward to it. Say, how's your dad? Last time I talked to him, he was needing a kidney transplant."

I told him Harold had undergone surgery five weeks ago and was doing great.

"Where did he find the kidney?"

I told him I gave him mine.

"What? You're the donor?" He sat up from his initial

relaxed position and looked at me from head to toe as if surprised to see me doing so well. "You're the donor!" He couldn't believe it. "How are you doing?"

"I'm great," I said, smiling. "A tiny bit weak, but other than that, I'm good."

"What a generous, kind act…what a blessing you are to him. I'm so impressed, what a selfless act. And he is good?"

"He's great—working, playing golf. He's so much better."

"What a special person you are to do that," he added. "That's amazing."

I was ready to get the attention off of me, to be honest. So I told him, "I just wanted to tell you that I pray for you and Laura every single day. I pray the Lord will guide you in every decision you make, and I know you have to make some tough ones.

"You know, there are people praying for me that I've never met," he said humbly.

He said that meant a lot to him. "You know, there are people praying for me that I've never met," he said humbly.

"You have no idea!" I said. (I know a lot of people who pray for him.) "It is an honor and a privilege to pray for you, and it makes me feel good to know that you are a Believer and to know our President is being guided by the Lord. It is a comfort to me knowing you have probably prayed about every decision you make." Then I told him about a time I was in a restaurant in the Adirondack Mountains with my parents after 9-11.

I remember the entire place grew quiet when he came on TV to address the nation. I recalled how he quoted Psalm 23: "Even though I walk through the valley of the shadow of death, I will fear no evil, for you are with me, your rod and your staff, they comfort me."

"I don't know how I would do it without Him," he assured me. We talked about a lot of things, including the George Bush Library at SMU in Dallas. He is a genuinely nice, easy-to-be-with, humble president, and he has a great sense of humor as well! Our little get-together lasted almost 20 minutes.

As we said our goodbyes, Marine One was landing outside. He gave me some M&M's that said "The White House" on them, and as he was leaving, he said, "You want to watch me take off?"

"Yes, I'd love to!" and he motioned me outside with him.

As soon as he hit the door, I could hear the crowd cheering and clapping. He began to wave to everyone, and I saw my friends standing there. I'm sure Paige was doing some kind of cheerleading move as he walked by. I heard him say, "Hi girls," as he looked back over his shoulder at me and said, "Are these your friends?"

"Yes!" I replied, hoping Paige had not fainted in the pathway from excitement.

I walked about one step behind the President, waving from side to side as if I were part of the show. I did not follow him all the way out to Marine One, but I was tempted. The departure was indeed quite a sight. I remember the loud humming noise of the engine, the swirling wind around the blades, and the President waving goodbye out the window. They shot off like a cannon out of sight, with the Washington Monument in the background.

My friends were thrilled—our feet were barely touching the ground! Wow, what a day already—and I had not even addressed the White House staff yet. We walked back through the Rose Garden, noting the cherry blossoms blooming. Once again, we stopped and Robert took photos of us with the doors to the Oval Office in the background. I guess that was no longer a security breach after all!

Then we all filed into a large conference room where several of the staff were waiting to hear me speak. It was now almost 11:00, which was perfect because Sandy was teaching Bible class at exactly that time back in Texas. I knew they would all stop and pray for me during the time I was to speak. As I pulled out a chair to sit down, I thought, "Sandy and the class are praying right now for me. That must be why I am not shaking." I felt the same sense of total peace I had when I shared my testimony at the prison. Robert introduced me as a photographer and author and mentioned the famous people I have had the privilege to photograph over the years. It was rather strange listening to someone else speak of my accomplishments and what I've done in my life. I almost felt as if I were at my own funeral.

As Robert finished his introduction, he turned to me and said, "May I introduce Mrs. Amy Alford." *Okay, God, You're up.* I spoke to the group about the things in my life that have strengthened and developed my relationship with the Lord. I told them about how my dad, Larry, had died from cancer at an early age (fifty-seven) and how it was his death that began my walk with the Lord. It took something so devastating like my dad's death to get me on the right track. I said how it felt as if I had a direct connection with heaven, now that my dad was there. Knowing your dad is in the *presence of the Lord* is amazing.

My heart was broken at the time, but I told the people in that conference room how God granted me peace and joy during my crisis. Just knowing Dad was safe in heaven, his body instantly restored, was a relief. I know there is no more pain or suffering, only happiness and joy for him as he stands before the Lord. Even though tears stream down my face whenever I think of him, I also have a smile because I know I will see him again.

His death got me thinking about a question. "What would happen if I died at fifty-seven?" I decided I better shape up and start living the life God intended me to live. *But what does that look like?* I wasn't sure. I started by getting involved in as many Bible studies as I could. I was able to keep up with four a week, and I was excited about each one, each week. I began to learn and grow quickly in my faith, and I desired to learn all I could about Jesus and His will for me.

I told the White House Staff about the Bible classes I did, including *Experiencing God* by Henry Blackaby, several studies by Beth Moore and *The Purpose Driven Life*. I love that book! Reading it inspired me to serve others on mission trips and in prison ministry. Those experiences opened my eyes and heart to a whole new level of compassion, love, and caring. I finished my talk by sharing about how leading people to Christ not only changes their life; it changes yours, too.

God tells us we all have a purpose. We are here for several reasons but mainly to tell others about Christ. Jesus said, "Therefore, go and make disciples of all nations... teaching them to obey everything I have commanded you. And surely I am with you always, to the very end of the age," (Matthew 28:19-20). In other words, we are responsible for telling our kids and grandkids about Jesus Christ and salvation. We are held responsible for each generation that follows us, so that they too will know about Jesus and His sacrificial death on the cross for us.

It took something so devastating like my dad's death to get me on the right track.

Psalm 22:30-31 says, "Posterity will serve him; future generations will be told about the Lord. They will proclaim his righteousness to a people yet unborn—for he has done it." Our faithfulness today matters to tomorrow's generation of men and women. If we fail to do our part and share about Christ with others, especially in our own families, we disrupt the influence God wants us to have on future generations. The Bible says in Proverbs 22:6, "Train a child in the way he should go, and when he is old he will not turn from it." I'm so glad God gave me the opportunity to have some influence, however large or small, on the men and women who were helping shape our country's future.

After I finished my talk, we had a "Q&A" session. My

friend, Susan Pausky, asked, "How has your relationship been with Harold since the kidney transplant?" I told her we'd always had a good relationship, but now we have a special bond. I've always loved him, but this is one way I was able to show him how much, and I would do it all over again if necessary.

Harold has been so sweet to me and done so many things for me that I could never repay. "But I think I'm good for a couple of Christmases!" I joked and everyone laughed. I answered a few more questions, then signed books for the people there. The entire day was something out of a movie; it was a once-in-a-lifetime opportunity, and I'm so blessed and honored. Thank you to everyone for making it possible!

When God Intervenes in CRISIS

Near Tragedy in the Tea Fire

In the fall of 2008, Mom and Harold asked if I wanted to come to Santa Barbara with them for a long weekend at their second home in the foothills of Montecito. I invited my good friend, Beth Montgomery, to go with me on this quick getaway since she'd never been to my parents' house.

Santa Barbara holds a special place in my heart. During my freshman year of college, I took a photography class and watched amazed as my first photo "came to life" in the dark room. I ran outside the room and announced to my professor, "This is what I want to do the rest of my life! What do I need to do now?" He said if I was serious, I needed to go to Brooks Photography Institute in Santa Barbara, the best school for photography.

"Where's that?" I asked, mentally picturing a map of the United States.

"California." Big smile. I was hooked. I called Brooks that day for a brochure and was thrilled to discover the college had three campuses in the area. One was in Montecito (the Beverly Hills of Santa Barbara), and the other two were on the Riviera overlooking Santa Barbara, the harbor, the beach, and the Anacapa Islands. In my opinion, this area is one of the top five most beautiful places in the country.

Next, I called my mother back home and told her I'd figured out what I want to do as a career. She agreed to talk to Harold about flying out there for a visit soon. When we went to Santa Barbara in the summer of 1985 to check out Brooks, Mom and Harold fell in love with Montecito, a small suburb nestled in the mountains above the city! They even ended up buying Piranhurst from Gene Hackman (the actor)—a 1914 estate home and one of the oldest homes in the area. "Perfect!" I thought to myself. "Now I have a place to live while I'm in photography school!"

This area at the top of the Santa Ynez Mountains has an interesting history. In 1895, a man named Henry Bothin bought 325 acres in Montecito and built his dream home at the lower part of the mountain. He named it "Piranhurst" after St. Piran, an Irish saint. "Piranhurst," along with the Bothin name, is chiseled into the stone at the entrance of the property, which is shaped like a vertical rectangle.

The house itself is tucked into the back of the property, with a guesthouse 60 yards from the back gate and fence. A small road runs between the back wall of my parents' property and the rest of the land that is called the Tea House property. My mom loves roses, and one of her most favorite things to do is taking a walk through the rose gardens surrounding the house. She'll cut some beautiful displays of flowers and roses to arrange in vases and place them throughout the house. The roses grow really big in California, some as big as footballs. The property is truly a paradise, and it might even give the Garden of Eden a run for its money!

Mr. Bothin's wife built a "tea house" at the top of the mountain, overlooking their home and providing a beautiful 180-degree view of land and sea. She named the Tea House "Mar Y Cel," the Catalan Spanish translation of "Sea and Sky." She and her friends would spend afternoons at the Tea House enjoying the incredible view of the beach, islands, and ocean. Sometimes when I'm up there with friends, I'll tease and say, "On a really clear day, you can see Maui."

Over the years, the property was split into two pieces. My parents bought the 25-acre piece with Piranhurst and the guesthouse; the rest of the property is mountainous terrain, topped by the Tea House, which is still there today in the middle of 300 underdeveloped acres. I often think of the Bothins and their vision to build this glorious place almost 100 years ago. This beautiful property and home had withstood earthquakes, fires, and floods over the years, but on that fateful visit we made in 2008, it was about to be tested once again.

The roses grow really big in California, some as big as footballs.

The four of us arrived in Santa Barbara later than normal because Sandy and I had just completed our first radio interview about my first book, *When God Has A Way, No Other Way Works*. As soon as the interview was over, I jumped on the plane and headed out. Beth and I unpacked all our things in the guesthouse, and then we went to the main house to watch the sunset. Mom placed her roses in arrangements while Harold, Beth, and I sat on the front porch looking out over the ocean. Harold was telling Beth all about the house and its history when I smelled what I thought was pinion wood burning. The Santa Ana winds had stirred up about 30 minutes after we arrived—very strong winds (up to 70mph) that come from the desert, up over the mountain, and down to the ocean. These bursts of hot air are sometimes very frightening because they are so strong.

I couldn't believe someone was having a fire in those winds. I continued to smell smoke and walked out to the end of the porch. I looked around and didn't see anything, so I sat back down with Beth and Harold. Just then, I saw one fire truck drive past our house toward the Tea House. I remarked, "That can't be good." I got up to go inside and met Mom at the bottom of the stairs. She had a very concerned look on her face. I'd seen that look only a couple of times in my lifetime, but I knew something was terribly wrong.

"We have a huge problem," she announced.

"What?" I felt my stomach grow tight.

"The whole back of the property is on fire. We have to get out now."

I couldn't believe it, so Beth and I jumped in our car and drove out of the courtyard around the back to the guesthouse. I'd never seen anything like it. Flames 200 feet tall were blowing around in 70mph wind. It was massive, barreling down from the Tea House—and we were directly in its path. Beth and I looked up in amazement at the sight, totally still and in shock. "It's going to take the house," was all I could say and think.

A few seconds passed, my mouth wide open, looking up at what used to be my playground in college. "Start praying," I told Beth. And with that, we both began to pray out loud. *Really* loud. We were literally "crying out to God." I whipped the car back into the courtyard, jumped out and ran inside. Mom and Harold stood in the entryway with Andrew and Aldona (our house managers) figuring out a plan.

"Get the van and bring it to the front," Harold told Andrew.

"Mom," I urged. "We have five minutes. What's the most important thing in the house?"

She was still looking at me in disbelief. "Nothing. We need to go."

I took charge and said, "Everybody, grab all the photos and photo albums. Go! Now!" We scattered like mice being chased by an alley cat. Beth was a great help because she had an advantage; she is 5'11" and could reach the photographs on the top shelves in the library. I grabbed an armful of photos off the walls and threw them in the back of my trunk. I came back in for another armful and noticed the portraits of Mom and Harold at the top of the stairs. Mom came by just then with her arms full of things.

"Mom, should I grab the portraits of you and Harold?" She said yes and dashed off outside.

I ran up the staircase skipping two stairs at a time in an effort to save time. A 30x40 portrait of Mom was on one side of the balcony, and another 30x40 portrait of Harold was on the other side. They were hanging rather high, so I stood on my toes and tried to unhook "Harold." I pushed with all my might and it finally came off the wall. I later realized both portraits were actually attached to the wall in case of an earthquake. No wonder I had such a struggle getting them off! I leaned "Harold" up against the wall and went for my mom next. I had recently had elbow surgery, but my adrenaline was running so high that I did not feel any pain until later. I quickly put "Mom" under my left arm and "Harold" under my right. As I took my first step down the stairs from the landing, the heavy portraits caught the first stair, and I was stuck!

I saw Beth running through the entrance hall with both arms full of photo albums and picture frames. She threw her load into the car and came back to help me. Meanwhile, I saw Andrew dart around the corner to the entry hall with an antique silver candelabra in each hand. He saw me on the stairs with Mom and Harold under my arms, obviously stuck.

"Amy, where do you want me to put these?"

I didn't hesitate and said, "In the pool," thinking that would be the safest place of all.

Andrew paused. "How about in the front yard in the grass?"

"They'll melt; throw 'em in the pool," I said as I handed Harold off to Beth and we ran to put both portraits in the van. We came back inside for what would be our last load before evacuating. I ran into one of the guestrooms and stood there trying to think clearly. I couldn't take all the photos—there were too many. So I took the older photos of my brother and me when we were young—the ones I knew we could not replace.

In about six or seven minutes, we all met at the front door after scrambling around and grabbing what we could take with us. Harold was characteristically calm and cool the entire time. Stoic as always, he never panicked and kept his wits about him. We took one last look around and Harold proposed, "Let's follow each other to the Biltmore Hotel (down in Santa Barbara and away from the fire). We'll have dinner there, and then we will figure out what to do."

Mom, Harold and Duke (their Springer spaniel) drove out of the courtyard toward the main entrance of the house. I decided to turn right to see exactly where the fire was at this point. Once again, Beth and I sat in the car mesmerized as we watched the flames and embers soaring across the night sky and over our heads. I had the window rolled down and, as if the flames could hear me, pleaded, "In the name of Jesus, please save the house if it's Your will. It says in the Bible to ask, so I'm asking God now to protect our home and hold back the flames." I think I even remember holding up my hands as if to hold off the flames. While I was praying out loud, so was Beth. I don't know what she was saying, but I know it was from her heart.

"It says in the Bible to ask, so I'm asking God now to protect our home and hold back the flames."

We finished praying, and I took one long last look at the house and yard, then we zoomed around to the side entrance on Cold Springs Road and left through the gate. It was dark as we pulled out, and we saw one lone fireman walking up the street. He was dressed head to toe in yellow protective gear. His fireman's helmet had a light on the front, and he was wearing goggles. He carried a flashlight and seemed to be looking for something. I jumped from the car, ran over to him, and asked what he was looking for. By now, the noise from the roaring fire and blustering winds were extremely loud, so I was yelling.

"I'm looking for people still in their homes," he yelled back. The fire was closer than before, right over us, and I could see it at the end of the street. "In no way do I want to put you in danger, but this is my house," I said and pointed over my shoulder. "What can I do to help you save it?"

"Get your gates open," he commanded me.

"Got it," I said and started back to the car. Then I turned around and put my hand on his shoulder. "I'm praying for you," I said and he thanked me.

I raced back to the car, threw it in reverse and drove backwards up the driveway at about 30mph in the dark. I had to get Andrew to open the back gate.

"Amy, you're going awfully fast," Beth said as she instinctively reached for the door handle.

"Don't worry, I've done this a thousand times," recalling all the years I'd lived there as a college student. I threw the car into park and ran up the back stairs to Andrew and Aldona's room. Andrew came running out to meet me. There was little time to spare.

"How can I get the back gate open and make it stay open for the fire trucks?"

"In the back of the gate, on the motor there is black

lever the size of your pinky finger. Pull that up, and it will release the gate."

While I was talking to Andrew, Beth got out of the car with her video camera, recording the embers raining down on the house and yard. In the video footage, you can hear her saying, "Oh no, this is bad...this is really bad. The embers are landing on the house...go away!" The fire was an orange glow in the sky, and all the embers floated around her.

I flew down the stairs from the back of the house so fast I think I only touched two or three of the steps. I passed my "videographer" friend and urged, "C'mon, Beth, let's go." I was fearless in that moment, determined to save our house. Beth told me later it reminded her of Todd Beamer, the 9/11 passenger whose inspiring last words were, "Let's Roll." I drove the car to the back gate where the fire was racing toward us. Although I knew I was running out of time, I was thinking to myself, "If I can get the back gate open, the fire trucks can come in and save the place." As we pulled up to the gate, it opened automatically. I crouched down and walked behind the gate into the bushes, lit only by the dull orange glow of the fire. The heat was stifling. I felt around in the dark and couldn't see anything like a lever. I looked again, frantically trying to put my hand on that lever. Suddenly my hand grazed something hard.

"I found it!" I yelled to Beth as I pulled and the gate began to open. The yellow-hued shadow of the encroaching fire fell across Beth's face. "We better get outta here, Amy."

I agreed. Embers were landing on the car and falling

on her hair. It was as if we were in a bad movie, with Beth and I in the leading roles. The smoke was thick all around us, and something inside me said, "Beth has a family…get her out of here." Just then, a big SUV pulled up behind us, and a man opened his door. "Amy," the man yelled. "Get down to the bottom gate! Your dad sent me up here to get you."

"I can't get out this way," I explained. The gate was only halfway open. The only way out was to go back down the driveway the way we came. After another ride backwards down the driveway, I turned around in the yard and headed to the winding hairpin-curved driveway at highway speed. We'd only been in California for about two hours, and Beth had had all the fun she could handle. As we hurled down the driveway, Beth said, "Does this normally happen?"

"No, not like this," I assured her and wiped soot off my forehead with the back of my hand.

We reached the front gate and, much to my surprise, Mom and Harold were standing next to the keypad pushing the code over and over. I hadn't thought about the power going out on the electric gate, leaving us stuck inside. I pulled up next to Mom.

"Where have you been?" she cried, thinking we'd be right behind her and Harold when they left.

"I was trying to get the gates open for the firemen," I explained, but it did not seem to erase any worry from her face. Beth got to experience "the look" that I have seen over the years anytime I do something dumb. Behind Mom were six cars in a semi-circle, with their headlights pointing at the gate and us. Little did I know that another actor and Montecito resident, Rob Lowe, had been trying to comfort Mom for the past 20 minutes while his house manager went looking for us. He was the one who found us and told us to get out of there. The six cars were all friends of my parents who live very close and knew the fire had started behind our house. They had risked their own lives to come up and make sure we were okay.

Mom instructed us, "Meet me at the Biltmore." I knew I was in big trouble. "Go straight there!" she added.

The traffic was horrible; there were sightseers and news reporters, fire trucks, police, and people walking around with horses and dogs that they had rescued from residents' property. When I made our way to the fire station (straight down from our house on Cold Springs Road), it was complete chaos. Cars were in a gridlock, people were honking, and policemen were yelling "Move it!" It was crazy. Several firemen were looking at a map, seemingly searching for alternate routes for the fire trucks. I looked at Beth and said, "Call and text all your prayer warrior friends. Ask them to pray for the safety of the firefighters, and ask that the Lord will save our house." We both started calling all the people we knew who would drop what they were doing and start praying for us.

Although we were now stuck in traffic, the prayer chain spread like wildfire, no pun intended.

Although we were now stuck in traffic, the prayer chain spread like wildfire, no pun intended. Within 20-30 minutes after our calls and texts, I am sure about

150 people were praying for the firefighters, the house, and us. My friend, Dana Williams, texted me back Exodus 14:14, “The Lord will fight for you; you need only be still.” Wow. What a great verse!

Since we weren’t going anywhere anytime soon, I got out of the car and walked over to the firemen looking at the map. “Excuse me,” I said and tapped one on the shoulder.

They looked up at me, worry creasing their foreheads. All around was chaos. I just said very calmly, “I want you to know, there is an army of people praying for you.”

“Thank you,” they said and got back to work.

At this point, I was the one now concerned about Mom and Harold’s whereabouts. I had not seen them pass by, and I thought they were right behind us. “Stay here,” I told Beth. “I’m going to see if I can find Mom and Harold.” I walked back up Cold Springs Road and found them in a line of cars about eight-deep. When she saw me, Mom let me know that I needed to be “in my car and headed to the Biltmore.” I didn’t waste anymore time getting out of there!

We pulled up to the Biltmore behind Mom and Harold, and I made one more call to Sandy back in Texas. By now, it was late in the evening in Dallas. I knew it was awfully late to be calling, but I needed her “direct line” to God Himself. She gladly prayed with me over the phone. We said we loved each other, and I went straight back into the chaos that just hours before had been paradise.

The sky was radiant with color now, and smoke billowed all the way down to the ocean. We arrived at the Biltmore, but the fire was getting closer. Harold wisely said, "I don't want to eat here."

"How about the Wharf?" I suggested. 'We can get out on the water and see what's happening with the fire."

"Okay, follow me," he said, but we lost them almost immediately. Our cell phones were not working, so Beth and I made our way down to a beach road called Carrillo. We passed East Beach Grill and could see the Wharf a couple of miles away. At about 7:14, all the power went out in Santa Barbara. It was completely dark except for the glowing fire in the mountains. Even the traffic lights went out.

I thought it was scary up at the house near the fire, but this was ten times worse! With the incredibly strong wind, 15-foot long palm branches were falling in front of us onto the street, and we were all swerving around trying not to hit them. Cars were speeding through intersections without realizing it, then jamming on the brakes in order not to hit the cross-traffic. Between the howling wind and sirens, flying embers, screeching tires, exploding transformers, and maniac drivers, it was like being in the middle of Armageddon.

"Start praying we don't get hit from behind," I said to Beth, knowing all the ambulances and emergency personnel were on the mountain! That was the most defensive driving I'd ever done in my life. Thankfully, since I'd lived in Santa Barbara I knew where all the traffic lights were. I slowed to a stop, while the people behind and beside us would fly right through the middle, barely missing cross-traffic and the cars coming head on. It was intense, to say the least.

"Beth, just so you know, this is but a glimpse of what it

will be like in the End Times," I tried to joke. But I really wasn't kidding. As we made our way down Carrillo, the Wharf was in total darkness. I didn't know if Mom and Harold had already arrived before the power went out. I called Mom a dozen times, but no signals would go through. The Wharf closed just as we were pulling up, so I circled around and parked on Carrillo in front of another parked car. I did that so we would not get rear-ended by a panicked person who might be driving while texting! We sat there in silence—watching house after house, and tree after tree, go up in flames. The fire had now spread to at least five or six different locations because of the embers. The entire mountain before us was ablaze.

In a whisper I said, "I've never seen anything like this."

"Me neither," Beth responded.

Each time a 100-foot eucalyptus tree caught fire, it popped and exploded like a match soaked in gasoline. I knew there was not much hope for our home. Memories from the past 25 years flooded my mind. Some of the best times of my life were spent there. My cell phone suddenly interrupted my thoughts. *Holy cow! It worked!*

"Hello? Mom! Where are you?" I cried into the phone.

"Honey, we couldn't get on the Wharf, so we are headed for the highway. Get on the 101 and head to the airport." We decided to stay on the line to keep our connection going. I put my mom on speakerphone and laid the phone in my lap so I could drive.

"Everyone is panicked and trying to get out of town," I told her, steering around another palm tree as I made my way to the 101 freeway.

"I know, Honey, be careful," my mom cautioned.

Fire trucks continued to squeeze down the middle of the two-lane streets, rushing toward the mountains. We finally got to the freeway, cars zipping in and out of traffic. I looked in my rear view mirror. The sky was raging with flames and smoke. The nightmare was nowhere near over. Mom told us to meet at a restaurant called the Elephant Bar, a place we'd eaten at several years ago in the suburb of Goleta.

We pulled up right behind Mom and Harold, with Duke safely inside. We stood in the parking lot, still only 12 miles away from our home, and watched the flames that were now over the top of the mountain ridge. Only by the grace of God could our house survive. I knew God could do it, but was that His will? I hoped so.

We sat there in silence—watching house after house, and tree after tree, go up in flames.

The people in Goleta were clueless about what was going on just 30 minutes away. I gave the lady our name to wait for a table and walked straight to the bar. Three televisions were showing local and national broadcasts of the fire. Homes were exploding into flames, and every eye in the bar was glued to the television reports.

Mom walked up next to me and swallowed hard, "Have you seen our house?"

"No, not yet," I said, my chest rattling with a deep cough. I had been too close to the fire too long; my eyes were burning and red, and I had a horrible, hurting cough from inhaling smoke.

"I can't watch," Mom said and turned away. "Let me

know if you see our house."

We were completely drained: mentally, physically, and emotionally. They sat us at a booth shortly after we got there, and a cute perky waitress bounced up to our table. "Hi. Welcome to the Elephant Bar," she said, oblivious. "What can I get you to drink?" Without making eye contact, Harold said, "You better bring us four martinis."

Beth whispered to me, "I've never had a martini before."

I whispered back, "Me neither. Tonight's the night."

It was hard to make conversation while silently wondering if our home (and all the memories inside) was burning at that very moment. After dinner, we headed to Bacara resort near Santa Barbara, but a safe distance away. We arrived with all the portraits, photo frames, and albums piled in the backseat and trunk, but no luggage. I just had a small bag with a few items I'd managed to grab. As we stood in the lobby waiting for our rooms, my cell phone rang again. It was 10:30 at night now, and I couldn't imagine who would be calling. I looked down at my phone and noticed it was an 805 area code. That was Santa Barbara.

"Hello?"

"Amy, it's Wayne," said the man who takes care of the property for Mom and Harold. I whispered to Mom, "It's Wayne." We both held our breath.

"I'm at your house—it didn't burn!"

My eyes filled with tears. I let out a loud cry and quickly covered my mouth. Mom and I were looking at each other, and she immediately put her hand over her mouth and began to cry. She thought the house had burned. But I was crying with joy, not grief.

"It's okay!" I said quickly and squeezed her hand. "The house made it!"

"I'm standing in the yard by the guesthouse," Wayne continued. "There is a fire truck in the yard, and they are putting out the flames now."

There was a huge collective sigh from all of us. Then Mom asked me with great anticipation, "Did my roses make it?"

"Wayne, did Mom's roses make it?" I asked, unsure what his answer would be considering all the embers and smoke.

"Yes, the roses are fine!" I nodded to Mom that they were okay. More tears. As I said before, Mom loves her rose garden.

Wayne assured us he would stay until he knew everything was okay, and we agreed to talk in the morning. In all, over 200 homes were destroyed and almost 2000 acres burned. But by His grace, God protected our home, even down to the last rose bush.

Morning could not come fast enough, and I was dying to get back to the house. We didn't know how our neighbors and friends were affected; communication was not easy, and by now it was getting very late. Beth and I collapsed in the beds in our rooms and watched the live news coverage of all the homes burning. It was heartbreaking and devastating to watch, but we couldn't take our eyes off the reports. We eventually turned the TV off, but I never fell asleep.

All night long, the helicopters flew just above us, filling their tanks with water and then heading over to the fire to douse the flames. My first text came at four o'clock in the morning. It was my brother checking to see if we were okay. It was two hours later where he lived, and he was watching the news. We talked briefly before text after text, and call after call, came rolling in from other friends checking on us.

The next morning, I walked next door to Mom and Harold's room and knocked. "Morning!" Harold was all smiles. I asked if they had slept at all, and Harold said he actually slept pretty well!

Mom came around the corner, "Morning, Honey." She was forcing her smile.

I told her Beth and I were headed to the house. "You want to come with us?" I ventured, knowing what her answer might be.

"Honey, no. We don't want to see it. I talked to Andrew, and he said the house is full of smoke and ashes. I don't think it would be a good idea for us to be up in all that. Especially Harold—he doesn't need to fill up his lungs with smoke. But will you get his medications and a couple of things from the house?"

I agreed to call them when I arrived. The TV reports were warning residents of roadblocks everywhere, so I knew it would take us a while to get there.

"Honey, please be careful," she said, a familiar refrain I'd heard a lot in my life. And I assured her I would. We hugged and kissed, I hugged Harold, and off I went.

As Beth and I came up Hot Springs Road, it initially looked okay, although it was eerily quiet. We reached

Sycamore Canyon and East Valley before we met our first roadblock. Policemen were on every corner with wooden roadblocks. Onlookers were creeping around, and the police were waving them off to one side or the other, not allowing them to continue up Sycamore Canyon, which is where we needed to go. I pulled up to the roadblock.

"Amy, what are you going to say?" Beth whispered.

"Just go with it," I said, not sure myself what I would come up with.

"Well, if anyone can get past the cops, you can," she said, smiling.

"Hi Officer," I said as I rolled down my window. "I live on Cold Springs Road, and I need to get some medication for my parents; it will just take a minute." He was not budging.

"Honey, please be careful," she said, a familiar refrain I'd heard a lot in my life.

"Ma'am, we can't let anybody through. There are still fires burning and live electrical lines down."

I explained that Harold had to have his medication, and we needed clothes, too. "I'll be very careful," I added.

He looked at me intently then said, "Okay, but you can get a ticket if the Sergeant catches you. You go up at your own risk."

I thanked him and he moved the roadblock to one side.

"You can talk anyone into anything!" Beth said with a laugh.

We got to the house without being questioned, even though we passed a lot of police and fire trucks. The front gates were wide open as we drove up the driveway. The strong smell of smoke filled the air. As we got close to the house, we could see smoke rising from the scorched ground. Some trees were still smoldering, and some were still burning. There were firefighters all around using shovels to put out whatever was still aflame. We went into Mom and Harold's house first. It was dark, and all the shades were down. It was smoky and smelled like fire. I went to Harold's room to get his medication, and everything I touched was covered in a thick, gritty substance. The desktop, the legal pad, pens—everything had dark grime on it. When we got what we needed, we left and went to the guesthouse.

Helicopters and Coast Guard planes were flying overhead, but aside from the sound of their engines, it was very quiet. We went inside, and it smelled the same as my parents' home. We gathered our clothes and everything we had left behind. We walked around to the back of the guesthouse and noticed the fire had stopped only 30 feet away, although the rest of the back of the property had burned and was still smoldering. In fact, one of the neighbors was on our property putting out a tree with a garden hose. He was blessed, too—his home was still there. I thanked him, and we walked down again toward the main house.

As we walked along the creek bed that runs through the property, I was speechless. The trees, plants, bushes, and ground cover that had been there for so many years were gone. Completely gone. Everything was black. I could now see over to parts of our property I'd never seen before. Everything that remained was spitting out trails of smoke. As we got down toward the garage, I noticed God had spared that building as well. I looked over our wall to another neighbor's house. It was completely gone, except for the chimney, and flames still burned in the rubble.

The wind was blowing, and I was afraid those flames could flare up and come back to our side of the wall. Beth and I carefully walked through the smoldering remains of our yard, climbed the rock wall, grabbed that neighbor's garden house and began spraying the house (or what remained of it). The water pressure was so weak I had to push my fingers hard on the hose to spray it far enough to reach. In the meantime, Beth was taking pictures of everything, including me playing "firefighter." As I finished dousing the flames, a man pulled up beside the house and looked at the rubble. He got out of his car and said, "Oh my gosh…it's totally gone."

I introduced ourselves, fearing we may have pushed our limits since we were only supposed to be there for a few minutes getting Harold's medicine. But here we were, trespassing and playing firefighter. "Did you live here?" I asked sympathetically.

He shook his head. "No, I cleaned the pool here for the last 25 years. Mrs. Johnson lived here for 40 years." Forty years, I thought. Forty years of photographs, memories, everything she owned…gone. Destroyed. "Thank you, Lord" ran through my mind.

"Oh, I'm so sorry. Is she in town?"

"Yes, they barely got out in time," he replied, surveying the damage.

Beth and I walked with him around the remains up

to where the pool used to be. I have never seen such total devastation.

Conscious of our time, Beth and I then hiked back over the wall to our side and continued walking down the yard. We got to a place in the yard I always referred to as "Paradise." A waterfall and creek surrounded by big rocks runs through the lush green grass. There are huge ferns, tall trees, and beautifully colored flowers everywhere. Thankfully, it was still "Paradise"—it had not burned and was still green and lush! I stopped and looked around in awe. Between my feet and the green grass of Paradise stood a four-foot iron cross that Mom found at an antique shop. The fire had suddenly stopped about 30 feet before the cross. I couldn't believe my eyes. We were surrounded by black, burnt trees and burnt ground covering. Everything was black and charred from the fire, and then it just stopped.

Again, it was like a movie, but this was real. God stopped the flames from taking Paradise and the cross that stood in the middle of it. Then He stopped the fire from getting within 50 feet of the main house. People often said afterwards, "Thank goodness the wind changed direction, or it would have burned down your house." But I wanted to say, "Who do you think changed the direction of the wind? Hmmm…Who has that kind of authority?" In Matthew 8:24, the disciples asked after Jesus stilled a storm, "What kind of man is this? Even the winds and the waves obey him."

No one can tell me we are "lucky" that our house did not burn. The fire burned everything in its path on both sides of the house, but it did not get within 50 feet of the main house. Then it went on to the west and burned down 231 homes. We weren't "lucky." We were "blessed." God showed His grace and mercy on us, and this time the magnitude of His mercy was far beyond anything any of us had ever imagined. Let this story remind you today: "with God, all things are possible" (Matthew 19:26).

When God Speaks

When I moved back to Dallas in 1991, my friend, Dottie Poston, invited me to attend Bible Study Fellowship (BSF), a non-denominational Bible study for seekers, baby Christians, and longtime Christians who are familiar with God's Word. It is a great way to study Scripture and learn what the Bible says and also what it means. This study is not anyone's interpretation of the Bible; it's simply what the Bible clearly says. If you are looking to learn God's Word and what He has written to us through His followers, I highly recommend BSF or CBS (Community Bible Study). Both studies will meet you wherever you are in your spiritual walk.

At BSF, I met a girl in my small group named Michelle. During the course of the year, Michelle's forty-nine-year-old husband was diagnosed with multiple myeloma. Cancer. The doctors had prepared Michelle and Gary for the worst: he was going to die. However, I believed God wanted Gary to stay around a little longer.

Our small group prayed diligently for Gary. I would see Michelle from time to time as Gary was fighting the cancer and ask how he was doing. I prayed for them for months and months. After undergoing extensive treatment, and despite bad news from the doctors, he miraculously recovered. His cancer was gone, and we knew it was a total miracle. When he went into remission, we all rejoiced and thanked the Lord for what He had done. The doctors had no other explanation.

One night soon afterwards, I saw Gary and Michelle eating at a restaurant. I was so excited to meet the person for whom I had prayed so long. He looked great, and they were both smiling from ear to ear. I remember the joy I felt in my heart for them at the time.

I lost touch with Michelle after that. About a year went by, and one day I learned Gary was in the hospital again. He was still cancer-free, but his intense course of cancer treatment had taken a toll on his body, leaving his blood unable to coagulate. He contracted a simple urine infection in September and was now in the ICU. My heart broke, and I immediately began to pray—not just once a day, but all through the days and nights ahead. I remember driving home one day in a pouring rainstorm. A Christian song called "Why?" came on the radio by a group named 4Him. The lyrics touched my heart as they sang about the trials we sometimes go through. As the rain pounded on my windshield, I thought about how rain falls on each one of us at some point in life. As I listened to the words of the song, I began to cry. All I could think about was Michelle and Gary's struggle. Their faith in Christ sustained them, even in the worst of times. Their total trust in the Lord was very inspiring to the rest of us who watched and prayed from the sidelines.

I felt compelled to send the song I'd heard to Gary and Michelle, because the Lord impressed on me to do so. There was no doubt in my mind that it was Him, nudging me to go buy the CD and mail it to their home. I felt a bit hesitant, at first, because I didn't know how they would respond. I had not seen or spoken to Michelle in a year. Regardless, I turned the car around and drove to the nearest store to look for the song. I found it, tracked down Michelle's address, wrote a note with the CD, and told them to listen to that particular song.

Their total trust in the Lord was very inspiring to the rest of us who watched and prayed from the sidelines.

I didn't hear back from them.

Weeks went by, and I heard the tragic news that Gary had passed away. I was afraid I had crossed the line by sending the song to them at the wrong time. But I had felt so strongly that I was supposed to do it. I didn't know why I never heard back, but I never stopped praying for them.

Several more months passed after Gary went home (his real home in heaven), and I still had not seen or spoken to Michelle. I noticed she did not come back to BSF, but I continued praying for her anyway. One day while sitting in a BSF lecture, I noticed out of the corner of my eye someone get up and leave the sanctuary. I looked over to see who it was…it was Michelle. I jumped up and went out into the lobby just as she reached the door. I called, "Michelle!" She stopped, and I told her how much I'd been praying for her.

"It's been very difficult," she said quietly. "Thank you for praying."

I wasn't sure if I should mention the CD, but then Michelle said, "Oh, I wanted to thank you for sending Gary that CD with the song. We played it every day in the ICU, and it helped ease our hearts and lift our burden. When he died, we played it again at his funeral."

My heart sank, my lips pursed, and tears began welling up in my eyes. As soon as she turned to leave, I ran outside to my car and cried out loud. I knew I'd felt led to send that gift that day. It was God nudging me to obey Him. That realization wasn't the only reason I was bawling, of course. I just felt so bad for Michelle. She was my age, and Gary was only fifty-two when he died, so young.

Remember the story when God had impressed my friend, Susan, to call me out of the blue during my temporary meltdown? Like me, she had to get out of her comfort zone to respond to God's leading. She'd called me just to say, "I want you to know I'm praying for you." In the same way, God used me to remind Gary and Michelle He was there. There is no way to know how many people were touched by that same song at Gary's funeral, and it showed their strength and faith in the Lord.

I later learned God had worked several miracles in Gary's life before he died. Toward the end of his life, he ended up in a "bubble room" at M.D. Anderson—a germ-free environment that protected him from infections because his immune system was shot.

The doctors injected him with his own stem cells to stimulate his immune system. For the10 days he spent in the "bubble," no one could touch him or enter the airtight room. While he was there, a friend of his named Baron Cass called to wish him well. Gary was allowed a phone inside the room, which was his only way of communicating with others. When he answered, Baron tried cheering him up with a hearty, "How ya doin'?"

However, Gary did not hear what Baron was saying on the other line. Instead, Gary heard a calm voice say to him, "Be still, my son, I am here."

Confused, Gary moved the earpiece of the phone closer to his ear and said, "Hello?"

Baron repeated his hearty greeting, but once again Gary heard another voice speaking. The voice said, "Be still, my son, I am here." Gary was comforted by those words, convinced it was the Lord somehow speaking through Baron and into Gary's heart.

This story reminds me that God orchestrates everything in His timing, and He uses other people to bring us comfort and reassure us when we need it the most. We just have to have open eyes and hearts to see and sense His gentle nudges to get us to do something. And when we do, He works His plan through us. God uses people who are available to Him. If you are not aware of what is going on around you (and how God might be calling you), you will miss out on so many blessings. I can't explain the feeling when you are in God's will and He uses you for His purpose. But I will say there is peace and joy that comes from being blessed by God when you are in His will.

THE POWER OF HOPE

SANDY, MY MENTOR, HAS TAUGHT A POPULAR BIBLE study class in Dallas for years. One of her classes was so good; I had to share it with you. She started her lesson by telling us a tragic story about a friend of hers whose daughter and granddaughter had car trouble while driving on a major highway. They pulled over to the shoulder and waited for help to arrive.

First, a man in an 18-wheeler stopped to lend a hand. He couldn't fix the problem, but he said he would go for help. He never returned. While the mother and nine-year-old daughter were waiting, another man showed up. To make a long story short, he raped both of them, shot them, and left them for dead on the side of the road.

Miraculously, they survived. However, the doctors said the little girl would be blind and unable to talk or walk. The bullet was in an inoperable place in her brain. Sandy went to visit the mom while she was in the hospital. Despite their tragedy, the mother's attitude toward God was inspiring. She said to Sandy, "I have chosen to trust Him with no explanation from Him—and no complaining from me. It's okay if I do not understand why, or if I do not hear from God."

Wow. That is a perfect example of faith and living the Christian life. God doesn't say life will be easy. He says, "Trust Me." That child is now thirty years old. She is married with kids of her own, and she can see, talk, and walk! Most of all, she has a strong, strong faith.

Having told this story, Sandy dove into Romans 8, a chapter about how Christians deal with life's challenges. A great, well-known verse for you to look up on your own is Romans 8:28—keep it in your heart and minds.

But here's another verse you may not know. Romans 8:18 (this is Paul talking) says, "I consider that our present sufferings are not worth comparing with the glory that will be revealed in us." Meaning, when we get to heaven (assuming you believe in Christ) all of the trials and difficult times will not seem so bad when we are filled with His glory, peace, love, comfort...all the things He promises us when we get there. We have *no idea* all the dangers God has kept away from us, but God also allows certain things, at certain times, to cross our path. We simply must desire to be in God's will either way.

God doesn't say life will be easy. He says, "Trust Me."

In fact, God desires for us to *want* to be in His will. Remember Job? If you are not familiar with his story, please read it in the Bible. No matter how difficult your situation may be, when you read about Job, you will feel much better and blessed! Job had everything, and God allowed Satan to take it away. By doing so, God was proving a point to Satan. He knew Job would be faithful and stand with God even during the worst of times. (You've got to read the story!)

Job reminds me of this family's incredible story of

faith. Somehow, their tragedy actually brought them closer to God in the end. When we step aside and let God be in control of our lives, He begins to transform us. Life is not a "do it yourself" project"! If you are going through a difficult trial, don't focus on the things you see or experience. Focus on what is going to last forever: eternity in heaven with God! Look beyond the hardships; God promises us His glory.

When God Intervenes in DANGER

Beating the Odds with 132 Stitches

In 1983, I was a wild and rebellious eighteen-year-old. For graduation at the end of my senior year at Highland Park High School, I got my dream car: a Datsun 280ZX with t-tops and a boombox in the back. I zipped around everywhere I went in that little sports car. I thought I was so cool!

My friend, John McDaniel, held a graduation party one night at a nice private restaurant called The Lancers Club in downtown Dallas. His date was my best friend, Cynthia Love. John had just received the keys to his graduation gift as well—a beautiful Riviera. We decided to follow each other to the party in our brand new cars. It just so happened that my mom was out of town that weekend, visiting friends with Harold. When I was getting ready for the big party, I decided to take advantage of the fact that my mom was gone. Her black-and-white checked fur vest looked so vulnerable, hanging there all alone in her closet. *She will never know I wore it,* I thought to myself as I took it off the hanger. And boy, did it look good over my white lace shirt!

My date was Dan and the four of us headed out for the party about seven that night. I was following John and Cynthia as we zoomed down Turtle Creek Boulevard, a beautiful winding street with huge trees lining the way. As we approached a condo building called the Warrington, I noticed the sprinklers were on, leaving a trail of water streaming across the street. One second later, John and Cynthia hydroplaned and hit a large tree in the median. Both of them simultaneously flew out through the windows onto the median. Their bodies looked like rag dolls, and I couldn't believe my eyes.

Immediately, my car also began swerving from side to side. "Slow down!" Dan yelled. I was turning the wheel as fast as I could, steering back and forth trying to pull us out of a tailspin. My headlights were shining on John's car, which now rested against the tree. Everything was happening in the blink of an eye; I couldn't stop us, even though I tried my best. Spinning out of control, we were now headed straight for John's car at a speed that made NASCAR look slow. Suddenly all went black. Silence.

I landed on Dan's seat—my head on his headrest and my body stretched across the car. Cynthia and John were still sprawled in the median; my car and John's were now one. Fortunately, Cynthia had managed to put her arm in front of her face before she went through the window of John's car, but she was moaning and bleeding, unable to get up. John finally stood to his feet and walked across the street to the Warrington. He dialed the number of The Lancers Club (this was before cell phones) to reach his dad, a doctor, who was waiting there for us along with eight of our closest friends. One of the waiters answered the phone and John asked for his dad. The waiter could tell something was wrong and went to find John's dad.

"Dr. McDaniel, you have a call," the waiter said urgently.

"I'm not taking any calls right now," his dad said,

thinking it may have been work.

"Dr. McDaniel," the waiter said firmly, "it's your son. He says it is an emergency." With that, John's dad jumped to his feet and went to the phone. When he returned to the table, he told our friends to start dinner without him because he and his wife had to leave. Of course, our friends were freaking out because we never showed, and they knew John had called about an emergency.

Back at the accident, Dan got out of the car and checked on us. He was always great at handling tragic situations. Cynthia was moving slowly, but she was alive. He opened my car door to see about me. I was unconscious, but he thought I was dead. He tore off the rearview mirror of my car and held it up to my mouth to see if I was breathing, and luckily I was. He put his hands around my head to try and straighten it out. When he touched my head, both of his hands sank inside the back of my skull.

My head had hit the glass t-top on the roof of the car, splitting my scalp from top to bottom. The split was about seven inches long and ended right at my neck. Thinking quickly, Dan took off his shirt and wrapped it around my head to try and stop the profuse bleeding. My lifeless body now lay in my demolished dream car, my mom's vest covered in blood and laced with tiny shards of glass.

Soon the ambulance arrived, and the EMT began working on me. While all of this was happening, Cynthia's mom and dad "just happened" to drive down the same street on their way to dinner and saw the wreck. Neither of them recognized the cars, which looked like a twisted mess of metal. They drove by, but two blocks later, Karen was unable to get that image out of her mind.

She said, "Honey, which way do you think the kids went to the Lancers Club?"

Her husband, Ross, looked at her and said, "Do you want to go back and check?" Worried, they turned around and headed back to the wreck to see if those were our cars.

They pulled up on the opposite side of the street, and Ross got out of the car. Just as he approached the ambulance, he recognized his daughter, Cynthia. He went back to the car, leaned in and softly said to Karen, "It's our baby."

Karen ran to the ambulance just as they were securing Cynthia's gurney beside mine and began talking to us. I heard a familiar voice talking, but I could not figure it out. It was a voice I knew…soft, sweet, and comforting. My eyes were still closed, but I could hear everything going on around me. I thought I had bitten off my tongue, now a large, soft lump in my mouth. In a daze, I reached my hand to my mouth and handed the lump to the familiar voice behind me. (Fortunately, I later learned it was only my gum!) This gentle voice continued to comfort me with positive words. "Call my mom," I said to her.

Soon I felt someone else squeezing my hand. "Amy, Amy…talk to me," this other voice said. "You're going to be okay. Open your eyes and look at me. Amy, Amy, wake up!" This time the voice was Cynthia's, who was next to me on a gurney, holding my hand. I remember looking up into the EMT's eyes. He was looking into mine with a flashlight.

"What's your name?" he asked, trying to assess how badly I was hurt.

"Is my car okay?" was all I could think to say.

He smiled. "Well, it's pretty banged up," I heard him say before I slipped into an unconscious fog again. Blackness. Silence.

I woke up sometime later and thought, "What is tugging on my head?" More tugging. "Ouch, my head hurts! Who is pulling on my head?" I was no longer in the ambulance, but I couldn't speak.

"I'm glad we got to her when we did," a strange voice said. "She's lost a lot of blood. About two or three pints, I'd say."

My eyes were still closed. I was now stretched out on a cold, hard surface, while the doctors were stitching up my wound and pulling my scalp back together. Then once again, everything went to black.

It was a voice I knew...soft, sweet, and comforting.

I don't know who called my dad, probably the Loves. Cynthia and I had been best friends since first grade, and Karen was like my second mom. My parents were divorced, and for the first time ever, my mom "just happened" to give my dad the phone number where she and Harold were staying that weekend. From the hospital, my dad called Mom at her friends' house to let her know what happened to me.

"Hello?" my parents' friends answered.

"Is Annette there?" my dad asked. "This is Larry Fleck." They put him on hold while they went to find my mom.

"Annette," they said to Mom while she sat at the dinner table with several others, "Larry Fleck is on the phone for you." Her heartbeat tripled, and the blood drained from her face. She knew something was really wrong for my dad to be calling.

"Annette," he began, "it's Amy. She's been in a car wreck." Dad began to cry on the phone, and Mom put her head between her legs so she wouldn't faint. The rest of the dinner party fell silent.

"Is she alive?" Mom asked, hopeful.

"She is in surgery," my dad explained.

"Is she going to make it?"

At that, Dad burst into tears. "They didn't say…she hit her head."

Mom hung up the phone and summoned all her "Mommy strength" to go back to the table and inform her friends what had happened. She and Harold went into the other room where Mom began praying. She asked Harold when they could fly out, thinking he'd be able to take them right away since he had flown his plane there.

"Darling," he said and took her hands, "we can't take off tonight. The airstrip is closed at night. We will have to wait until the morning." Mom was devastated. I was in surgery, she was not sure if I was going to make it, and she couldn't get home until the next day.

Back at the hospital, two nurses approached my dad. "Mr. Fleck, would you like to see your daughter?" They brought Dad into the ER room where they had just taken x-rays of my skull. I heard an unfamiliar voice of a hospital worker say, "Amy, your father's here." It was all I could do to open my eyes. Dad stood over me, tears falling from his eyelashes onto my shoulders.

"Hi Dad," I barely muttered.

"Baby, you're going to be okay. I love you," he said. Just then, I caught a glimpse of my face in the reflection of the x-ray machine above my head. My face was covered in blood, and there was a small puncture under my nose spewing blood everywhere. They whisked Dad out of the room and worked to stop the bleeding, soaking several gauze pads. Blackness. Silence. Unconscious again.

The next thing I knew, people were trying to get me to sit up. "Sit up?" I thought. "I don't know where I am, and my head is killing me for some reason."

It took two or three nurses to get me to sit up and maneuver myself into a wheelchair. They wheeled me to a sink and told me they needed to rinse my hair.

"Where was I, the beauty parlor?"

Before I knew it, they were holding my limp body over an oversized sink. When they bent me over, the pressure inside my skull was so strong and painful I thought my head was going to pop off into the sink! (Actually, I was hoping it *would* pop off—maybe that would relieve the horrible pain I was feeling.) I managed to open my eyes as the warm water washed over my head, but then I saw the sink was full of blood.

While my head was upside down in the sink, I also caught a glimpse of Mom's blood-soaked fur vest. I wasn't sure what had happened, but a wave of nausea came over me, and I began to vomit profusely.

I just *thought* my head hurt before—now it was really hurting! I passed out in the arms of the nurses. Dan was in the waiting room of the hospital. He had his jacket on, no shirt, and was clinging to the one shoe I had on when I arrived at the hospital. Eventually, they released me from the ER, and Dan and Dad brought me home. However, I do not remember anything past when the vomiting started.

I woke up early the next morning, and I was in my room. It was unusually bright; all the shades were open. I was almost sitting up in the bed, with several pillows stacked behind me. Dan and Dad were sitting in chairs on either side of the bed, keeping watch. Dan was still in his suit from the night before, and Dad was smiling at me from his side of the bed. "Hi Baby, how are you feeling?" he asked.

Why are they in my bedroom? I thought. (Boys were not allowed in my room!) I was trying to figure out what was going on. *Why is Dan in a suit with no shirt on? And why is it so bright in my room?* (The boys didn't lower the shades when they brought me home.) *Why does my head hurt? Why is everyone staring at me?*

While I was still trying to solve this mystery, Mom entered the room. I still remember the look on her face, reminiscent of the time she saw the fire coming towards our house. Deeply concerned, her eyes never left mine. She went straight to my side and gently touched my face with her hand. My head was wrapped in a white turban, and I had over 132 stitches. (Thank the Lord they were not in my face.) I suffered memory loss and a concussion. The memory loss was so frustrating. I couldn't remember any of the things I knew that I knew. School was almost out, and all my teachers exempted me from my final exams except for one. If I passed her final, I do not know, but I passed her class and that's all that mattered.

For months, the memory loss and pain in my head lingered. Several times a year, I still have a tingling feeling like mice running over my scar. The doctor told me that several nerve endings were severed in the crash. Whenever I feel that sensation, it's just the cut nerves sending signals searching for their other half. Every time I experience that odd feeling, it reminds me how God protected me and saved me for a reason. He could have easily brought me home that night, but His plans were to let me live and pass these stories onto you. God is real, and He protects His children.

By the way, it turns out Mom could not have cared less about her fur vest. It spent five months at the cleaners, and she gave it to me for Christmas that year. I still have it in my closet, and every time I see it, I say, "Thank You, Lord."

Women in the Wine Country

It was the ultimate girlfriends road trip. My friend, Paige, had invited me on a trip to Paris, San Tropez, and Monte Carlo in the summer of 1998 with two of her friends from college, Jackie and Chantell. I barely knew her college friends, but Paige and I had traveled together quite a bit. Plus, we went to the same church and Bible studies.

Paige is one of my "funnest" friends, if you know what I mean. She is always up for an exciting adventure. If you're having a birthday party, she's the kind of friend you want on your invitation list because she will elevate the "fun factor" ten times. Paige is a beautiful girl, inside and out, and she loves to dress up in designer clothes with matching shoes and purses. In fact, all those girls could have daylong dueling fashion shows with their beautiful boutique designer clothes.

Me? Not so much. I love cute clothes and shoes like any other girl, don't get me wrong. But Paige and I differ greatly in the clothing department. I'm much more comfortable being casual and comfortable. We're also different because I'm quick to respond in a crisis, and she is very laid back and unaffected by urgent matters. I like to be on time; she runs an hour late. That is why she earned the nickname, "Chopper." I'm constantly saying, "Chop, chop! Hurry up," clapping my hands quickly in rounds of two. Actually, we refer to each other as "Chopper" because she says I "chop" her to get going! They say opposites attract, and we couldn't be more different. But we both love to travel and have fun. More importantly, we both love the Lord. When the four of us set out for France, I had no idea what I was in for.

We arrived in Paris and spent three nights there. Then we rented a van for me to drive us out to the wine country. When we went into the rental company office to retrieve our van, we received a surprise. Did you know Paris does not have vans or SUVs? We didn't.

"What, no SUVs? What kind of place is this?" we wondered. We were from Texas—the birthplace of four-wheel drive—and we just assumed every country had them. Instead, we got the keys to a very small, four-door hatchback Volvo. With no bellhop and three fashion queens in tow, we began trying to stuff 18 suitcases into a sardine can. It took all four of us pushing just to shut the hatchback. The girls' feet were slipping in the street because their high heels had no traction. The young man who rented us the car watched from inside, not about to offer to help the four Americans. After we heard the "click" of the now filled-to-capacity hatchback, we squeezed into our seats.

I was familiarizing myself with the car, while Paige manned the CD player and looked over the directions. We headed out from the rental car parking lot straight into a six-street roundabout. We circled very slowly, looking for the right French name on the street signs. We made a complete circle and were back in front of the rental office. Slowly, we made another round, but we could not see which way to go!

With no bellhop and three fashion queens in tow, we began trying to stuff 18 suitcases into a sardine can.

Once again, we were back at the rental office. "Budget boy," as we'd begun calling him, was still watching. We headed out for a third time into the roundabout, this time deciding to chance it and take one of the streets. I'm sure Budget boy was glad to see us go.

We came out onto the main street in Paris, the Avenue des Champs-Élysées, right by the Arc de Triumph. It was a racecar driver's dream: five unmarked lanes of traffic and no speed limit! I'm not so sure my passengers were as excited as I was though. All I heard was, "Watch out…Slow down!...Turn here…Wait…Go!...Do you know where you're going?"

Of course I did not know where I was going; I was in Paris, France, driving a four-door hatchback and couldn't see out of the back window!

We flew through Paris and finally found our way to the right autobahn. Paige was the navigator and our personal GPS. After driving for 30 minutes or so, we came to what seemed to be some kind of tollbooth with a gate. The bar lifted up when we pulled up, but there was no one at the booth, so I drove through. We were rocking out to music, enjoying the beautiful green countryside and trees. About 45 minutes later, we came to another tollbooth, except this time there was a lady inside the booth. We pulled up and she said, "Bonjour."

"Bonjour," I said back with a smile.

"Si vous play…" she began speaking in French.

A blank look came over my face. "What?"

"Si vous play…"

"How…much…do…we…owe?" I interrupted in English, trying to let her know we did not speak French.

Her head turned like a dog that had heard a high-pitched scream. We uselessly exchanged English and French for several minutes before she called the police. Next thing we knew, a bar came down in front of the car and one in the back, trapping us in the tollbooth.

In a moment, five policemen dressed in all-white uniforms with tall white hats and white boots walked over to our hatchback. It must have been a slow day for them. They bent over and inquisitively looked into our car. I quietly said to the girls in the backseat, "Look up 'How much?' in the dictionary." We had an English/French dictionary of short phrases. By now, the policemen had taken off their hats and were scratching their heads as they peered in the open windows. The four of us were scrambling for money and words.

Chantell began to sound out the words in French. She said words that sounded French enough, but I had no clue if they were the right ones.

The policemen looked at each other, then at the French lady in the booth. They seemed confused as they began to chatter back and forth in French. Jackie whispered something to me and I started laughing.

"What are you guys saying?" Chantell asked innocently.

The policemen were not laughing. I braced myself for the worst.

Jackie spoke up between laughs, "Chantell, you just said, 'How bizarre?' not "How much?""

At this point, I'm thinking the fashion queens and I were going to end up in a French prison. After 20 minutes of trying to decipher what we were trying to say, the policemen finally let us go. (That was also after we gave them five dollars.) Later, we discovered that we should have grabbed a ticket in the first tollbooth upon entering. The second tollbooth collects money for the amount of time you spent on the autobahn. I can tell you, at the speed I was going, we probably owed only a few pennies at the most. I love to drive fast, and with not much of a speed limit, "Amy-O-Andretti" was pushing the limits!

Nevertheless, we eventually made it to the wine country in Beaune, France. Beautiful fields with rows of grapes filled the rolling hills, and Mom and Pop stores were scattered along the roads. While we were touring one day, we ended up on a gravel road so narrow I was sure it was a one-way road. The music was still on, and Paige was navigating us to some wineries with cute little outdoor lunch cafés. As I turned left around a blind corner on the one-lane road, to my shock and horror I saw another car coming at me. I swerved to the right to try to avoid a collision but quickly realized the road dropped off there. So, I whipped the wheel back to the left, thinking I'd rather the car hit me than us go over the cliff. As I swerved back to the left, the other car rammed our little hatchback and pushed us to a stop only six inches away from the cliff.

I heard the girls screaming, glass breaking, and that horrible sound of two cars colliding. When we came to a stop, I said, "Is everybody okay?" Everyone was still screaming and discombobulated.

"Is everyone okay?" I repeated, this time a notch louder.

They were all fine.

"Which window broke?" I asked next, remembering the sound of shattered glass.

"It was the wine glasses on the floor from yesterday's winery," Jackie said. Whew. Jackie said that her life had just flashed before her eyes, and I knew what she meant. My heart was beating out of my chest. My entire body was shaking, and I was breathing double time. I got out of the car, my knees knocking, and walked to the edge of the gravel road. Our tires were six inches from going straight over the side of a six-foot drop. Had we gone over the edge in the luggage-packed hatchback, I feel certain it would have caused major injuries or even death. The young French couple that hit us got out of their car, and we greeted each other though we were all still frightened.

His car had a rather large dent in the front left bumper where he'd hit our car. My mind was racing. *Do we have insurance? Yikes! Do we call the police? (I don't speak French. They don't speak English.) No cell phones, and we are in the middle of nowhere—double yikes!* As I looked over the hatchback, I couldn't find a dent anywhere. I know he hit us because I heard it and felt it as his car pushed us to the edge. I examined our vehicle closely at every angle. Nothing. I was confused.

I bent down to see the back left tire and noticed a thumbnail-size gash in the hubcap. "Surely, that's not all that happened," I thought in disbelief. The couple and I exchanged glances and shrugged our shoulders as if to say, "Oh, well." They got back in their car and drove off very slowly. I walked up to the window of our car and said, "If you don't believe in God, come look at this." The girls worked their way out of the car and walked to the front to see where we almost slid off.

"This is a flat out miracle that we didn't go over the edge," I concluded. Everyone agreed. We then packed ourselves back inside the undamaged car, but I was still a nervous wreck. To this day, we realize God had His hand on us. There is no doubt that the Lord intervened for us once again that day and brought us safely back home.

Nothing Good Happens after Midnight

When I was a young girl in high school and college, my mom always said, "Nothing good happens after midnight." I'd usually roll my eyes and say, "Oh, Mom. When the clock strikes 12:00, does the boogie man come out?" A couple of times she responded matter-of-factly that yes, he does. And one evening on that same girls trip overseas, I found out she was right.

I always had a 12:00 curfew, even after college. However, when I was in Paris with my friends Paige, Jackie, and Chantell, we went to dinner and then to a disco for some late night dancing. Paige loves to dance off the calories after dinner, so it's pretty much a given that when you go out to dinner with Paige, you'd better put on your dancing shoes. If you have never been to Europe, let me give you a "heads up." They don't eat dinner until 10:30-11:00 at night. The discos don't really get going until two in the morning! Needless to say, it was already late when we hit the discotheque.

Jackie and Chantell were smart; they went home after about an hour. Paige and I stayed way too long. It was definitely "after midnight" then. We were young and single, and we met some cute Middle Eastern guys while we were there and talked with them for a short while. When we finally decided to go home, Paige and I walked out to get a cab. Thc streets and sidewalks were full of people, and the outdoor cafés were full—even at four in the morning.

Suddenly, a white BMW zoomed up right beside us. One guy was driving, and one was in the backseat. Before I knew what was happening, two more boys flanked Paige and me. They were the boys we met at the disco. My radar went up and I thought to myself, "Something bad is about to happen." Seconds later, the boy next to Paige picked her up from behind and began stuffing her in the back window of his car. The boy inside the car was trying to grab her feet, and she was screaming, "Amy, help! Amy, don't let them take me!"

I was also screaming, "Let her go! Let her go!" and began beating the boy on his chest as hard as I could with my fist. Paige instinctively propped her feet on top of the car, preventing him from shoving her inside. Her back was against the boy's front as he held down her arms and tried to push her in the window. The fourth boy was trying to get me off the boy holding Paige. I was screaming so loudly, but nobody would help us. This struggle went on for what seemed like 20 minutes (but was probably less than 90 seconds).

"Oh, Mom. When the clock strikes 12:00, does the boogie man come out?"

Everything happened so quickly. All I knew to do was to scream and hit. Then, for unknown reasons, the boy suddenly put Paige down. We ran toward a silver Mercedes cab about 40 feet in front of the boys' car. I remember turning around to see if they were chasing us. They were running full speed toward us as we flung open the door to the cab and jumped into the backseat. We screamed to the driver, "Go, go, go!" and looked out the back window—the boys were still running after us!

When they realized they couldn't catch us on foot, they ran back to the car and resumed the chase. Paige and I crouched down in the back of the cab holding each other, completely hysterical. The cab driver drove like a typical cab driver would: fast and crazy—taking the corners on two wheels. Even so, the boys caught up to us in their car and were right on our tail. The cabbie took us down alleyways, around corners, everything he could do to lose these guys. He must have been an angel. Most cabbies would have said, "Get out, I don't need this!" However, he took care of us, knowing he too could have been in danger. I'm just thankful he was not involved with the boys somehow. He could have easily let us out in the alley for the boys to have an easy pick up.

After a hair-raising 20-minute car chase, we lost them. We drove around for quite a while longer to make sure they were gone before going back to our hotel.

If God had not intervened, I shutter to think about what might have happened. *What if they had managed to get Paige in the car? Was I next? Would they have taken her and left me? Would I have ever seen her again? What were they going to do with her?* After I saw the movie, *Taken* (about a girl who finds herself in a similar kidnapping situation) I realized just how awful it could have been. I've run from trouble several times, but I know for a fact that God intervened. He was with us, protected us, and saved us from horrific things that could have happened—things I try not to think about.

There is no doubt in my mind that God had His hand and His angels around us. Psalm 31:14–15 says, "But I trust in you, O Lord; I say, 'You are my God.' My times are in your hands; deliver me from my enemies and from those who pursue me." And Psalm 40:13, 17 says, "O Lord, come quickly to help me. You are my help and my deliverer; O my God, do not delay."

God takes care of us even when we don't realize it until later. As I look back over my life, I see how God intervened so many times. In some of the situations where God rescued me, I realized it immediately and thanked Him right then. At other times, I didn't realize the danger and couldn't see how God rescued me, until years later. Some people claim to have nine lives. I think I have had about 50. God has been so gracious with me over the years and has covered me with His protection. And for that, I am truly grateful.

"For he will command his angels concerning you to guard you in all your ways," Psalm 91:11.

Mark One off the Bucket List

It's crazy. I don't know why, but all my life I have loved mini-bikes, mopeds, and motorcycles when I got older. I rode my first mini-bike (a smaller version of a motorcycle) at the age of eight years old. Mom was a decorator, and she was decorating a lake house one summer in a new development in Tyler called Holly Lake Ranch. We stayed with some friends who happened to have mini-bikes, and I was enamored with them. My sweet dad spent long, hot, dusty days watching me as I rode around and around the driveway. I still have the T-shirt Dad made me for Christmas one year with a picture of me and the mini-bike printed on the shirt! To this day, it's one of my favorite photographs!

My love for mini-bikes soon evolved into mopeds (a motorized bike). When I was a teenager, Harold gave me a bright orange Honda Express in the eighth grade. He and mom were just dating then, but he already had my vote! As I grew older, I continued to feel the need for speed, but this time I wanted something faster—something I could jump some bumps with. As God would have it, Harold enjoyed riding motorcycles, too. He just happened to have a couple of them at his place in Ozark, Arkansas. I'll never forget my first trip with Mom and Harold to Ozark. We pulled up to the "double wide" trailer, and the front yard was full of motorcycles and off-terrain vehicles. As a kid, I wasn't that impressed with the fact Harold could fly his own plane, but he had motorcycles!

My favorite was the Suzuki 125. It didn't take me long to learn how to work the clutch and gearshift. Then I was off riding all over the property for the rest of the day. I remember telling my mom, "Mom, this is so cool! This is the fastest I've ever been on a motorcycle." I went as fast as the 125 could go and hung on, the wind flapping my cheeks. It wasn't too long before Harold showed me my first "jump." We would go really fast up a super steep hill to a point where it leveled off and catch "big air!" Mom would stand at the top and watch so we wouldn't collide as we went up and down. This is when my love for motorcycles really began.

My mom has been awesome through all of my adventuresome endeavors. I can't begin to imagine what

I put her through as the parent of a wild, rebellious, try-anything-once little girl. I know one thing though; she spent many days and hours on her knees, asking God to please protect me. Mom's prayers worked. God has protected me through all my crazy adventures, including: scuba diving to a wrecked sunken ship, motorcycling, skiing on "expert only" slopes, bungee jumping, sky diving, paragliding, and the list goes on. Thank You, Lord, and thank you, Mom!

Since I was thirteen years old, we started going as a family to Aspen, Colorado. I loved watching people race up Aspen Mountain on their colorful dirt bikes, dressed in motorcycle gear from head to toe: helmets, chest protectors (that matched their helmets), elbow pads (that matched their chest protectors and helmets), knee and skin guards (that matched their elbow pads, chest protectors, and helmets). To top it off, they wore cool-looking motorcycle boots (the six-buckle ones that come up to your knees), which matched everything, too. As each summer went by, I watched the riders from my balcony going up and down the mountain and dreamed of the day I would do it, too. It seemed impossible, namely because I didn't have a dirt bike in Aspen. And I didn't know anyone who had one. So, it wasn't until just a few years ago that my childhood dream came true.

I rode my first mini-bike at the age of eight years old.

In July of 2007, I heard about a place called Mountain Adventures that rented four-wheelers and motorcycles. I was staying in Aspen for about a month and immediately called to see what was available.

"Mountain Adventures, this is William," the clerk answered on the first ring.

"Hi!" I said, breathless with excitement. "I was wondering if you rent motorcycles."

"Yes, we do." Big smile. "We have a Honda XR 250 and four-wheelers."

Music to my ears. "Great! I'd like to rent the Honda to go up Aspen Mountain."

I arranged for William to bring the Honda to the home where I was staying. When he arrived, he stepped out of his white pick-up truck wearing jeans and boots. He had sandy blonde hair that resembled John Denver's back in the eighties. I saw he had a pack of Camel cigarettes in his pocket, and he was nearly six feet tall. He smiled sweetly, extended his hand and said, "Hi, I'm William. But you can call me Bill if you want. You must be Amy." He unloaded the red and white Honda 250 and his huge, green four-wheeler. He'd already suggested he go with me, which I was happy for him to do since I wanted to go with someone with experience.

Telling Mom about my adventure was out of the question. *No need to worry her*, I told myself. I didn't have all the matching gear—just a helmet, some gloves I'd bought at the bicycle shop in town, hiking boots, jeans, and a blue jean jacket. I was not quite prepared for the day ahead, but off we went, riding through town up to the base of Aspen Mountain.

My heart was beating extra beats as I looked at the side of the mountain: steep dirt and rocky roads all the way up. I played John Denver's "Rocky Mountain High" on my mobile phone, in honor of my Rocky Mountain adventure! I have to admit I was slightly nervous—given the fear of the unknown. However, once I shot up the first part of the road, my adrenaline was boiling with excitement. I had flashbacks of riding in Ozark on the dirt bike.

I can do this, I thought as I steadily navigated the exceptionally rocky terrain. *Ozark was more dangerous than this,* I assured myself. Every once in a while, I'd looked down the mountain at the town and see the house where our family once owned a home. It was easy to spot because it was a block from "Gazebo" park. Thirty years of great memories from Aspen ran through my mind as John Denver sang in my ears.

We got to the top in just 25 minutes, instead of the hour or two I thought it would take. I pulled over at the skiing gondola, William right behind me. I took off my helmet and shouted, "That was awesome! I loved it!"

"You wanna keep going?" William said. "There's more. We can ride clean to Crested Butte."

"Awesome!" I replied. "Let's go!" I knew Taylor Pass is a beautiful place, and William said it would take us a couple hours to get there.

"Let's go there and see how that goes," he said. I had a sip of water, put my helmet back on, and sped away.

After 30 years of coming to Aspen, I never knew what was beyond the gondola. "Wow," was the first thing that came to my mind. When I lived in Aspen, I'd skied behind the gondola on big snow days on a run we called "Pandora's Box." If you hike beyond the gondola on the left, you can cross under a rope with a sign that reads, "Out of bounds. Ski at your own risk." Naturally, my friends and I would always ski there on powder days. Some days, the snow would come up to our chests—now that was awesome!

On the motorcycle, I went far past Pandora's Box, headed way up the mountain. We soon arrived at a beautiful field covered in wildflowers. I slowed down to look around and take it all in; William pulled up and said, "You want to take a picture?" I'm a professional photographer…of course I wanted a picture!

He took a couple of pictures of me with the field in the background: wildflowers, Christmas trees, and snow-capped mountains. I couldn't think of a word to accurately describe the beauty God had made and allowed me to enjoy. Several times while I was riding I prayed, "Lord, thank You for this incredible place of beauty. Thank You for allowing me the opportunity to be here and experience all You created for me!" I remember speeding along and yelling out in praise, "Woo-hoo!" many times. I couldn't help it! I was experiencing my dream after 30 years!

We made it to the top of onc of the peaks and got off our vehicles to stretch our legs. Within a few minutes, it began to sprinkle, then rain. I had no rain gear. It grew dark, the wind picked up, and it began lightning all around us. William showed no urgency or fear, but I wasn't too sure about being on a mountain peak standing next to two metal objects during a lightning storm. "Should we take cover?" I asked.

"Yeah," he said, looking around for a good place. "Let's ride down to that clump of trees."

It was now pouring rain, and we quickly rode to a nearby thick forest for shelter. The drops felt like toothpicks pricking my face. We rode into the middle of some tall trees and got off the vehicles. The trees helped some to protect us, but the thunder and lightning were getting louder and closer. While we waited for the storm to pass, we talked about our families and our lives. I found out he was a bull rider and a rodeo clown! He also told me he almost lost his family due to a drinking problem. He had been sober 12 years, and I congratulated him on making that decision and sticking to it. He had a genuine, sweet heart and also appreciated living in one of the most beautiful places in the country. When the storm passed, we continued our journey to Taylor Pass.

Thirty years of great memories from Aspen ran through my mind as John Denver sang in my ears.

An hour or so into the ride, we rounded a corner and I noticed the road suddenly went straight up through rocks, with several sharp turns. The rocks were about the size of softballs and footballs and they littered the trail. I never thought twice about the severity of the terrain; I just kept going right on up. About a third of the way, my front tire caught a rock that caused my motorcycle to flip sideways. When I stopped, my front tire was inches from going off the side of the trail. I looked down about 20 feet below and thought, "Holy smokes, that would have hurt if I'd gone over."

I looked down at William, who was behind me. "You

all right?" he called.

"Yeah, I'm good," I said, muscling my handlebars to start backing up.

"You need some help?" he tried again.

"No, I got it." I was backing up the bike as best I could on the rocks.

He offered again to take over, and I declined. So, he just sat and waited. After I backed up pretty far, I turned the wheel and hit the gas. I got about 15 feet higher and the same thing happened. This time, it was so steep my right foot wouldn't touch the ground. I looked down at William again.

"You want me to take it from here?" he asked, a worried expression on his face.

"No, no. I can do it," I said, grimacing and straining to reach my toe on a rock to gain some balance.

"Let me know when you want me to take over…I don't want you to hurt yourself."

"Okay, but I can handle it," I managed to say between grunts, struggling to work the bike back down on my own. I very carefully backed up, this time leaning into the mountain so I wouldn't tumble downhill. With stubborn determination, I continued up the steepest, most difficult terrain I'd ever attempted on a motorcycle. About halfway up, my front tire hit yet another rock just at the right angle and flipped me around again. My heart was pounding; my breath was short and fast. I looked down below at William, his arms crossed over the handlebars and looking very concerned.

"Okay," I said meekly. "I think I'll let you take over."

We switched vehicles and he rode the dirt bike up to

the area where it was smooth again. I followed along on the four-wheeler, but even that was hard to control on this terrain. At the top, we switched again and continued on our journey through the mountains and valleys of Colorado.

I would not have traded that experience for anything, especially after God later revealed to me a greater lesson about my awesome journey up the mountain.

About three months after that experience, I awoke in the middle of the night—which wasn't surprising because I do a lot of praying in the early hours. The moment I opened my eyes, I knew the Lord was relaying something to me, and I did not want to miss the message. I jumped out of bed and walked quickly to my office. Tears began to fill my eyes, and I grabbed a pen and paper. The thoughts were coming too fast, so I grabbed a digital voice recorder instead. The message was clear. God impressed on me something He wanted me to realize and to tell others.

Now, I've never heard God speak audibly (and if I did, I would probably run out of the house). But there was no mistaking what He wanted me to know. As I began speaking into the recorder, I was crying so hard it was hard for me to talk. I don't know why I was so emotional, but then again it's not every day the Lord speaks to me! In Galatians 1:11-12, Paul talks about receiving a revelation from Jesus Christ. I believe that is what I received as well. Paul writes, "I want you to know, brothers, that the gospel I preached is not something that man made up. I did not receive it from any man, nor was I taught it;

rather, I received it by revelation from Jesus Christ."

The message I felt God impressing on my heart was related to my motorcycle ride. He pointed out to me a parallel between that experience and my relationship with Him. You know the story—I rode up that rough, rocky road determined that "I" could do it. William kept asking, "You want me to take it from here? Do you need any help? You want me to take over?" My stubborn answer was always, "No, I got it. I can do it." I refused help from the expert, and he waited and watched patiently while I almost killed myself trying to get through it alone.

My revelation from all of this? We all struggle through rough and rocky roads in our lives. Through it all, God is there: watching to see if we'll call on Him. He is just waiting for us to surrender and say, "Okay, God. I can't do this anymore. I need your help." And that's when He comes in and helps us! For so many years, I've tried to "fix" problems or do things on my own. Often, it's only when I'm at my wits end that I call on God for help. I should be calling on God first, not last!

Psalm 50:15 says, "And call on me in the day of trouble; I will deliver you, and you will honor me." God tells us to call on Him when we are in trouble. That doesn't mean your problem will be solved immediately (although it might be), but it means He will be with you while you are going through your trial. Trust me; you want God with you and on your side when you're going through a rocky time in life. He is the *only one* who can give you peace in the middle of a trial. Don't wait to call on God or use Him as the last resort. He should be first and foremost in your thoughts and priorities because He is there for you.

Take advantage of our God, who loves us and cares for us. Make it a habit to call on Him first, not when all else fails.

Let me ask you something. Have you put your faith in Him? He died for you. If you have not put your faith in Him, I want you to stop right now, be still, and say this prayer:

"Today, I'm putting my faith in You, the One who died for me. I'm trusting You, and I want a relationship with You." First Peter 5:7 says, "Cast all your anxiety on him because he cares for you." It's not during the good times that our faith grows; it's during the trials. We have access to Him, so we can turn over our troubles to Him. When you see how He handles situations, your faith will grow, and you will trust Him more and more. I know Him more intimately in the middle of my trials, because I'm aware that He sustains me during them. He supplies the all-surpassing peace that the Bible says we can't even begin to understand. We reaffirm our faith (to Him and others) whenever we leave it in His hands. Faith is trusting Him.

The message was clear. God impressed on me something He wanted me to realize and to tell others.

Of course, you might have to keep reaffirming your faith because we tend to take it back and "do it ourselves." We all go through difficult times in our lives, and sometimes we think we can "fix things" on our own. I believe God allows things to happen in our lives to bring us closer to Him. You don't develop a closer relationship when everything is going great; it's when you are in the trenches that you call out to God and say, "Okay God, I can't do this on my own! I need Your help, Your guidance, Your peace, Your direction, Your strength, Your encouragement. Help me!" And that's when He takes over.

But you must let Him have it and not keep stepping in and trying to take it back. He is in control; let Him guide and help you in each decision you need to make. This has happened many times in my life, and I'm finally "getting it" after 40 years! Let God be God. I promise, you will be so much better off not trying to "do it yourself!" Like being on a dirt bike trying to get up the side of Aspen Mountain, we can't always see what's ahead; we must put all our faith in the One who knows what's around the corner!

Nay, Nay - Stay Away from Strangers

When I was five years old, my parents decided to move our family to an area of Dallas called Highland Park, a nice area with huge trees and beautiful homes. They chose that area because it has good schools, the neighborhood is safe, and it is full of young families and kids. We lived just four blocks from Bradfield Elementary where I went to school. That's when I met my friend, Cynthia Love, in the first grade. When we reached the second grade, our parents let us walk home from school together since we lived just one block apart.

One day at school, we watched a short film about

staying away from strangers. The reel-to-reel film had a cute little cartoon donkey that warned children, "Nay, nay! Stay away from strangers!" Then he would kick at a cartoon "stranger" to prove his point. As Cynthia and I walked home that very day, two boys (ones I happened to have a crush on) started teasing us and throwing things at us. I walked across the street by myself to get away from them, and Cynthia walked on ahead. She thought I was with the boys, but I was walking alone down a street called Lomo Alto.

Suddenly, I heard a man whisper, "Pssst! Pssst!" I stopped and looked over my right shoulder. I saw a man crouched down in someone's backyard in the bushes. He was wearing a tan corduroy jacket and had sandy, brown hair down to his shoulders. He motioned me closer to him, but there was a chain-link fence between us, covered with thick bushes.

He said, "Hey, do you know what time it is?" I panicked, knowing something was wrong.

"No..." I said quietly, frozen in place.

"Can you help me find my little kitty?" he asked next.

"Um...I can't," I said quickly. "I have a ballet lesson." I was lying; I didn't have ballet, but I was feeling even more anxious at this point.

"It will just take a couple of minutes. I need to find her."

I looked down the street. Cynthia was out of yelling distance, but I could still see her.

"Well, okay," I agreed hesitantly, "but my mom is waiting for me."

I walked into the backyard toward the woodpile.

My arms were full of books, and I was wearing my favorite blue fur.

"Here, kitty kitty kitty," he called. "Hey, let's see if she is in the garage."

The door was rolled up and when I looked inside the garage, there was only a sofa and chair. He said, "Maybe she's on top of the garage door. Why don't you get on my shoulders and see if you can see her?"

"Okay," I agreed, setting my blue fur coat on top of my books near the entrance of the garage. As he helped me up on his shoulders, I suddenly heard a loud, distinct "meow."

"Did you hear that?" he said and walked over closer to the garage door.

"Yes, I did!" I said and peered around, trying to see the cat.

"I can't see anything," I concluded. "I'm not tall enough."

"I have an idea," he suggested. "Why don't you get down, and we will slowly shut the garage door. That way, if she is up there, she can jump down."

I knew as he pulled down the garage door something bad was about to happen. Even as a second-grader, my intuition told me I was not in a good place. I was right—I was not in a good place at all. After he shut the door, it got real dark, real quickly. There was a window in the back of the garage near the sofa and chair, and I could see a neighbor watering his grass two doors down. I was hoping he would somehow see me inside.

Then the man pulled his pants down and said, "Come over here."

I did, but I turned away and continued to watch the neighbor watering his lawn. The stranger was now sitting in the chair beside the sofa. I was so frightened I started praying out loud, "Dear God, please let me go home. God, I want to go home." As my prayers grew louder and louder, he said, "Okay, okay! Shhh! Be quiet. I'll let you go." I ran to my books and gathered up my coat saying, "God! God, help me!"

The man opened the garage door just enough for me to get out. I ran all the way home and through the back alley that I knew so well. Nobody could catch me there.

I popped out of the alley and ran into our driveway. By now, I was crying and very upset. Mom was backing her 1970 yellow and black Pontiac out of our garage. I still remember her expression when she looked at me in total confusion. She threw the car into "park," got out, and wrapped her arms around my blue fur and me. "A man tried to get me," I sobbed.

One day at school, we watched a short film about staying away from strangers.

For the next several weeks, I looked through hundreds of mug shots trying to identify the man. They never caught him. Not many people know this story, only a few close friends. The reason I am telling you this is because I want to stress how important it is to tell children at a very young age about God and Jesus. Maybe God allowed this to happen to me so I could pass this story along to you, 40 years later.

My parents taught me that God was always there for me. Even though I couldn't see Him, He was with me and He loved me no matter what I did. We talked about God and Jesus in our home, at the dinner table, and at night. Each evening, Dad gathered the family together to read family devotionals and pray together before we went to sleep. God was with us everywhere we went. Even at the age of eight, I knew to call on God in the day of trouble. I knew the moment I began calling out to God that He would answer me and protect me from what that man was probably planning to do. God intervened in a huge way for me that day.

When you call out His name, He is there, and He is with you. Not only have I experienced that truth; He confirms it in the Bible. A verse I refer to often is Psalm 50:15: "Call upon me in the day of trouble; I will deliver you, and you will honor me." And Psalm 46:1 says, "God is our refuge (a place of security) and strength, an ever-present help in trouble" (parentheses added). The next verse in that chapter says, "Therefore we will not fear…"

I can't imagine not having God in my life. He is our refuge and strength—He's always there for us and we need not be afraid. If you don't have God in your life, what do you have? You have yourself; you're alone. When you surrender to God and ask Him into your life, you will never be alone. God is always with you.

When God Intervenes in SCRIPTURE

God's Word is for Your Good

It's so important to be firmly planted in God's Word! The Bible says, "All scripture is given by inspiration of God, and is profitable for doctrine, for reproof, for correction, for instruction in righteousness, that the man of God may be complete, thoroughly equipped for every good work" 2 Timothy 3:16-17, NKJ. That means all of Scripture is for our good—His promises *and* His commands. I hope this book encourages you to read more of God's Word. I'll get you started with a list of some of my favorite verses below. Read them for yourself, and commit them to memory.

Exodus 14:14 "The Lord will fight for you, you need only to be still."

2 Chronicles 20:15 "...do not be afraid or discouraged...For the battle is not yours, but God's."

Psalm 31:14 "But I trust in you, O Lord; I say, 'You are my God, my times are in your hands.'"

Psalm 46:1 "God is our refuge and strength, an ever-present help in trouble."

Isaiah 43:2 "When you pass through the waters, I will be with you; and when you pass through the rivers, they will not sweep over you. When you walk through the fire, you will not be burned; the flames will not set you ablaze."

Psalm 57:1 "Have mercy on me, O God, have mercy on me, for in you my soul takes refuge. I will take refuge in the shadow of your wings until the disaster has passed."

Psalm 50:15 "And call upon me in the day of trouble; I will deliver you, and you will honor me."

Psalm 61:1-3 "Hear my cry, O God; listen to my prayer. From the ends of the earth I call to you, I call as my heart grows faint; lead me to the rock that is higher than I. For you have been my refuge, a strong tower against the foe."

Psalm 62:5 "Find rest, O my soul, in God alone; my hope comes from him. He alone is my rock and my salvation; he is my fortress, I will not be shaken."

Isaiah 58:9 "Then you will call, and the Lord will answer; you will cry for help, and he will say: Here am I."

John 6:47 "I tell you the truth, he who believes has everlasting life."

John 8:47 "He who belongs to God hears what God says. The reason you do not hear is that you do not belong to God."

John 11:25-26 "Jesus said to her, 'I am the resurrection and the life. He who believes in me will live, even though he dies; and whoever lives and believes in me will never die. Do you believe this?'"

John 14:6 "Jesus answered, 'I am the way and the truth and the life. No one comes to the Father except through me.'"

Acts 4:12 "Salvation is found in no one else, for there is no other name under heaven given to men by which we must be saved."

Romans 1:4 "…and who through the Spirit of holiness was declared with power to be the Son of God by his resurrection from the dead: Jesus Christ our Lord."

Romans 1:20 "For since the creation of the world God's invisible qualities—his eternal power and divine nature—have been clearly seen, being understood from what has been made, so that men are without excuse."

Romans 5:1-8 "Therefore, since we have been justified through faith, we have peace with God through our Lord Jesus Christ, through whom we have gained access by faith into this grace in which we now stand. And we rejoice in the hope of the glory of God. Not only so, but we also rejoice in our sufferings, because we know that suffering produces perseverance; perseverance, character; and character, hope. And hope does not disappoint us, because God has poured out his love into our hearts by the Holy Spirit, whom he has given us. You see, at just the right time, when we were still powerless, Christ died for the ungodly. Very rarely will anyone die for a righteous man, though for a good man someone might possibly dare to die. But God demonstrates his own love for us in this: While we were still sinners, Christ died for us."

Romans 6:23 "For the wages of sin is death, but the gift of God is eternal life in Christ Jesus our Lord."

Ephesians 2:8-9 "For it is by grace you have been saved, through faith—and this not from yourselves, it is the gift of God—not by works, so that no one can boast."

Ephesians 3:20 "Now to him who is able to do immeasurably more than all we ask or imagine, according to his power that is at work within us, to him be glory in the church and in Christ Jesus throughout all generations, for ever and ever! Amen."

Ephesians 4:5 "...one Lord, one faith, one baptism; one God and Father of all, who is over all and through all and in all."

1 Peter 5:7 "Cast all your anxiety on him, because he cares for you."

1 Peter 5:10-11 "And the God of all grace, who called you to his eternal glory in Christ, after you have suffered a little while, will himself restore you and make you strong, firm and steadfast. To him be the power forever and ever."

Revelation 21:4 "He will wipe every tear from their eyes. There will be no more death or mourning or crying or pain, for the old order of things has passed away."

Walking Where Jesus Walked

I'VE HAD THE OPPORTUNITY TO GO TO ISRAEL AND GREECE twice, and these trips had a tremendous impact on me. In March 2010, I was fortunate to take my niece, Adrienne, on her first trip to Israel. It was one of the most memorable times in my life to spend 10 days with her. I couldn't get enough of the history and the sites where the stories from the Bible actually took place. Even today when I read the Bible, I'm able to picture where those events occurred. For example, I've seen the pool of Bethesda where Jesus healed the lame man. It's a beautiful area in Jerusalem, with tall, stone arches and pathways around pools that used to hold water. The story is told in John 5:1-15:

Some time later, Jesus went up to Jerusalem for a feast

of the Jews. Now there is in Jerusalem near the Sheep Gate a pool, which in Aramaic is called Bethesda and which is surrounded by five covered colonnades. Here a great number of disabled people used to lay—the blind, the lame, the paralyzed. One who was there had been an invalid for thirty-eight years. When Jesus saw him lying there and learned that he had been in this condition for a long time, he asked him, "Do you want to get well?"

"Sir," the invalid replied, "I have no one to help me into the pool when the water is stirred. While I am trying to get in, someone else goes down ahead of me."

Then Jesus said to him, "Get up! Pick up your mat and walk." At once the man was cured; he picked up his mat and walked. The day on which this took place was a Sabbath, and so the Jews said to the man who had been healed, "It is the Sabbath; the law forbids you to carry your mat."

But he replied, "The man who made me well said to me, 'Pick up your mat and walk.' "

So they asked him, "Who is this fellow who told you to pick it up and walk?"

The man who was healed had no idea who it was, for Jesus had slipped away into the crowd that was there.

Later Jesus found him at the temple and said to him, "See, you are well again. Stop sinning or something worse may happen to you." The man went away and told the Jews that it was Jesus who had made him well.

We also visited the Mount of Beatitudes, where Jesus gave the Sermon on the Mount in

Matthew 5, one of His greatest speeches recorded in the Bible. It overlooks the Sea of Galilee, which is actually a big lake (13 miles long, 7 miles wide). It is a beautiful setting up on a hill. As our guide, Dr. Bill Counts, read from the Bible about what took place there, I could look across the fields full of mustard seed flowers and visualize Jesus standing down below. I could picture the hillsides packed with thousands of people anxious to hear what He had to say.

Matthew 5:3-12 says:

Blessed are the poor in spirit,
for theirs is the kingdom of heaven.
Blessed are those who mourn,
for they will be comforted.
Blessed are the meek, for they will inherit the earth.
Blessed are those who hunger and thirst for
righteousness, for they will be filled.
Blessed are the merciful, for they will be shown mercy.
Blessed are the pure in heart, for they will see God.
Blessed are the peacemakers,
for they will be called sons of God.
Blessed are those who are persecuted because of
righteousness, for theirs is the kingdom of heaven.
Blessed are you when people insult you, persecute you,
and falsely say all kinds of evil against you because of
me. Rejoice and be glad, because great is your reward
in heaven, for in the same way they persecuted the
prophets who were before you.

The gardens at the Mount of Beatitudes are beautifully landscaped and have gorgeous two-color roses among many other flowers to enjoy. There are several benches underneath the huge trees that cover the hilltop—a very serene, peaceful, and special place. It was so neat to be there with Little A and see everything through her eyes. I especially enjoyed praying and reading the Bible together in this setting. Praying for her at the Wailing Wall was something we will never forget.

We stayed at a hotel on the Sea of Galilee for two nights. Each morning, I woke up early and full of excitement for the day ahead. I sipped a cup of coffee on my balcony overlooking the lake as the sun came up over the mountains for a beautiful sunrise. Some wooden boats, replicas of the ones back in Jesus' day, quietly sailed through the reflection of the sun off the water. So peaceful. I read from the gospels (Matthew, Mark, Luke, and John) about what Jesus did and where He lived in that particular area.

The second day, we took a boat ride on one of those very boats I'd seen on the water. There were 52 of us from Texas on the boat; it was quite a sight! The ship's crew raised the American flag, and we put our hands on our hearts to sing our national anthem. We also sang several worship songs. Dr. Counts once again read the scriptures that described this beautiful place. He helped us realize we were literally walking in Jesus' footsteps on this trip.

Dr. Counts said, "In Israel, it's possible to know the area (and sometimes very close to the exact spot) where certain biblical events happened or where Jesus walked, spoke, or performed miracles." Then he looked around over the water and added, "We know for certain that the place where we are right now on the Sea of Galilee is the same lake and the same view that Jesus had every day. This is the same lake where He walked on water. These are the very seashores He walked along. And this is the very place where the crowds followed Him, and He spoke to them."

Because the lake is 680 feet below sea level, storms can brew quickly over the mountains without warning. Matthew 8:23-27 tells us about a storm that surprised the disciples on the Sea of Galilee:

Then he got into the boat and his disciples followed him. Without warning, a furious storm came up on the lake, so that the waves swept over the boat. But Jesus was sleeping. The disciples went and woke him, saying, "Lord, save us! We're going to drown!" He replied, "You of little faith, why are you so afraid?" Then he got up and rebuked the winds and the waves, and it was completely calm. The men were amazed and asked, "What kind of man is this? Even the winds and the waves obey him!"

The second day, we took a boat ride on one of those very boats I'd seen on the water.

I know this is a true story because God rebuked the flames that almost engulfed our house in Santa Barbara. He can calm a storm or hold back a 200-foot wall of flames!

Another one of the most memorable stories in the Bible was when Jesus walked on the water. Once again, He was on the Sea of Galilee! Matthew 14:22-32 tells the story:

Immediately Jesus made the disciples get into the boat and go on ahead of him to the other side, while he dismissed the crowd. After he had dismissed them, he went up on a mountainside by himself to pray. When evening came, he was there alone, but the boat was already a considerable distance from land, buffeted by the waves because the wind was against it.

During the fourth watch of the night Jesus went out to them, walking on the lake. When the disciples saw him walking on the lake, they were terrified. "It's a ghost," they said, and cried out in fear.

But Jesus immediately said to them: "Take courage! It is I. Don't be afraid."

"Lord, if it's you," Peter replied, "tell me to come to you on the water."

"Come," he said.

Then Peter got down out of the boat, walked on the water and came toward Jesus. But when he saw the wind, he was afraid and, beginning to sink, cried out, "Lord, save me!"

Immediately Jesus reached out his hand and caught him. "You of little faith," he said, "why did you doubt?"

And when they climbed into the boat, the wind died down. Then those who were in the boat worshiped him, saying, "Truly you are the Son of God."

What an incredible experience to have seen Jesus walking on water, and because of his faith, Peter got out of the boat and went to Jesus. That story is a great reminder to us to "get out of the boat" and go to Jesus in faith, knowing He will be there for us. We must have the faith to step out of the boat, even when we are not sure what is going to happen. We can trust God, no matter the outcome, and have faith that His plans are best—no matter what. The Bible tells us these stories so we can learn by example and take these lessons to heart.

As I look back at my stories in this book, I guess you could say I "got out of the boat" a few times. I left my comfort zone and kept my eyes on Jesus. Did you notice that when Peter took his eyes off Jesus he began to sink? Has that ever happened to you? If you take your focus off Jesus, you begin to sink in despair and things fall apart around you. Keep your eyes on Jesus.

My faith and trust in the Lord allowed me to step out into the unknown and completely depend on the Lord. No matter what my circumstances, the Lord is faithful, and I will forever trust Him with my life. Jesus and I have a pact now. I completely trust and believe in Him for everything, and He takes care of my needs. He gives me the peace that surpasses all understanding, especially in the middle of my trials. It is a relief to know that He is in control, not me!

Remember the story of David and Goliath? We also went to the Valley of Elah where their battle took place. It's a beautiful valley, and it probably looks exactly as it did thousands of years ago, with flowers riddled between the same tall, green grass blowing in the wind. We walked to the riverbed where David gathered his five stones. Our guide, "Shmulik,"

read the story of David and Goliath from 1 Samuel 17 as we stood there. Smulik pointed out where the Israelites assembled their camp and the hill where the Philistines were living. We were standing between the two camps, next to the riverbed that divided the valley. As I listened to the story, I looked around me and visualized David, a "ruddy and handsome" sheepherder going up against Goliath, a nine-foot giant with a shield and sword, covered head to toe in bronze armor. David approached the giant with only his shepherd's staff, five smooth stones, and a slingshot. However, with the first throw, he hit Goliath in the forehead (the one area not covered by his helmet) and that giant dropped like a shot cow. First Samuel 17:46-47 tells us what David said to Goliath right before he killed him:

> "This day the Lord will hand you over to me, and I'll strike you down and cut off your head. Today I will give the carcasses of the Philistine army to the birds of the air and the beasts of the earth, and the whole world will know that there is a God in Israel. All those gathered here will know that it is not by sword or spear that the Lord saves; for the battle is the Lord's, and he will give all of you into our hands."

I don't know about you, but David sounds to me like a man with a strong faith in God! He, too, sends us a great message about trusting in God. Before the battle even started, he boldly declared to his enemy that the Lord would defeat him. Your enemy today is likely not a physical giant like Goliath, but it might be a financial struggle, or a problem in your marriage, or any number of things. The point is that the battle is the Lord's. Trust Him to provide and protect you. And when He gets you through the battles in your life, give him the credit just as David did. Honor God and give Him the glory. It's not what *you* have done or an enemy *you* have defeated; it's what God does *through you*, because you believe.

Of course the Garden of Gethsemane was another incredible sight in Israel. A large garden area filled with old, beautiful olive trees marks the spot where Jesus prayed on the night before He was crucified. It is enclosed by an ancient stone wall and is located just outside the Temple walls and the Old City. Just hours before He was betrayed and arrested, Mark 14:35 tells us Jesus "fell to the ground and prayed that if possible the hour might pass from him." Jesus prayed, "Abba, Father, everything is possible for you. Take this cup from me. Yet not what I will, but what you will."

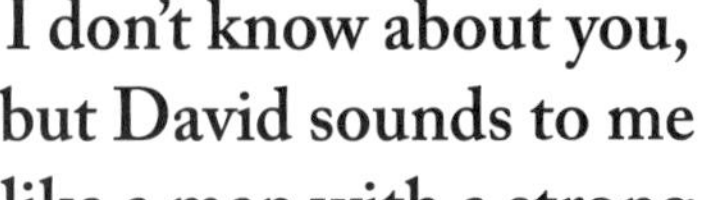

I don't know about you, but David sounds to me like a man with a strong faith in God!

Jesus knew the terrible suffering He was about to endure, yet He prayed for God's will and not His own. He then endured torture far beyond what our minds can comprehend. Why? Because it was His Father's will for Him to die on the cross for our sins. Because Jesus obeyed, we now have the opportunity to receive eternal life. It's a gift. You don't have to earn it. You've been saved through your faith in Jesus; it's not what you do in life that saves you. It is a gift of God—not by your own good deeds, so that no one can brag about it (Ephesians 2:8-9). All you have to do to receive this gift is believe in Jesus. Believe He died for you, He rose three days later, and now He lives in heaven with God the Father.

Many people think they are not "righteous" enough to go to heaven; they fear being "judged" by God. One day, you will stand before the Judge (God) in heaven, and He will ask you one question: "Why didn't you follow Me? You decided to live in sin and shame and do whatever you wanted to do."

You will not have a lawyer with you to defend you when you stand in front of the Judge—it will be only you and Him. However, if you believe in Jesus Christ and have asked Him into your heart and life, things will be very different on that day. You will no longer be standing in front of a Judge—you will be standing before your heavenly Father. Jesus Himself will be standing there with you, and the Father will then say: "I know this one. This one is mine."

What is keeping you from trusting Him right now? Jesus is the one who can set you free from your bondage, guilt, and shame. He died for you so you could be free from all that. What a relief! If you're ready to commit yourself to Christ, ask God silently or aloud (right now!):

"Lord, please come into my life. Open my heart and my eyes to see You and know that You are here for me. I believe You died on the cross for my sins. Because of that fact, I can live my life knowing I am one of Your

children. I know You will always love and care for me. I acknowledge that I am a sinner, and I need Your help. I desire to be in Your will and to follow You. Thank You, Lord, for dying on the cross for me. I praise You and honor You in all that I do. Amen."

That's a pretty detailed prayer, but a simple, "Lord, I ask You to come into my heart," is all you need if you truly believe in Him.

On the other hand, if you are not ready to pray that prayer because you are having a hard time believing in Christ, ask Him to reveal Himself to you. Ask God to open your eyes and your heart to see Him clearly and not be distracted by Satan, the world, or anything or anyone else that would pull you away from the truth. God is real, and He is waiting for you to come and rest in Him.

I've had people ask me, "Why did God send His Son to earth to die for us?" First of all, I don't question why God does things. I trust that He knows best, and He knows the outcome of what He is doing in our lives and in the world.

Still, most people want to know why God does the things He does. Well, I do too! I just believe everything happens for a reason. I might not understand His ways, His purpose, or His reason. I simply trust and have faith in Him. As the title of this book suggests, He has intervened and shown me many times that He is in control. He can handle everything. It's not up to me to try and figure out "why." It's up to me to obey and trust Him. God is so beyond our intelligence; we cannot wrap our minds around Him. Therefore, He sent Jesus, in human form, so we could grasp a little bit of how magnificent He truly is.

I'm not one to insist on seeing "the facts." I simply believe in God because I believe the Bible and what it tells us. Even when Moses asked God to show him His glory, God refused. He said:

"I will cause all my goodness to pass in front of you, and I will proclaim my name, the Lord, in your presence. I will have mercy on whom I will have mercy, and I will have compassion on whom I will have compassion. But," he said, "you cannot see my face, for no one may see me and live." Then the Lord said, "There is a place near me where you may stand on a rock. When my glory passes by, I will put you in a cleft in the rock and cover you with my hand until I have passed by. Then I will remove my hand and you will see my back; but my face must not be seen." Exodus 33:19-23

To see God's "back" means we can only see where God has been. I've seen where God has been and what He has done in my life. I don't have to see His face, because I see *where He has been*.

A Special Note to My Readers: From My Heart to Yours

As the chapters of our lives unfold, so do the opportunities for God to intervene, and I always say…Let Him! The last two years of my life have been a struggle in more ways than one, but never did I sway in my faith. If anything, these trials I endure have brought me closer to the Lord in more ways than I could imagine. I fought the good fight and stuck with what I believe because *When God Has A Way, No Other Way Works.*

Some of you may realize I changed my name—to me, it represents a new beginning in my life. I look forward with great anticipation to see what God has planned for my future. I'm starting fresh and moving on with my life. He once again has brought me peace and comfort through these difficult times.

Just because I have written a book about "God" does not mean I escape hardships and calamity. We will all face trials and tribulations throughout our lives, but if you have God in your heart, and life, He will intervene and give you the peace and strength to sustain you during your trial.

Even today, I thank the Lord for each trial He has set before me. We learn to depend and trust Him during difficulty more so than at any other time. If you find it hard to put your trust in Christ, ask Him to reveal Himself to you. I have chosen to put my trust in Him, and I challenge you to do the same.

Remember, *When God Intervenes, Let Him!*

Beckett COLLECTIBLE

GAMING ALMANAC

A COMPREHENSIVE PRICE GUIDE TO GAMING AND NON-SPORTS CARDS

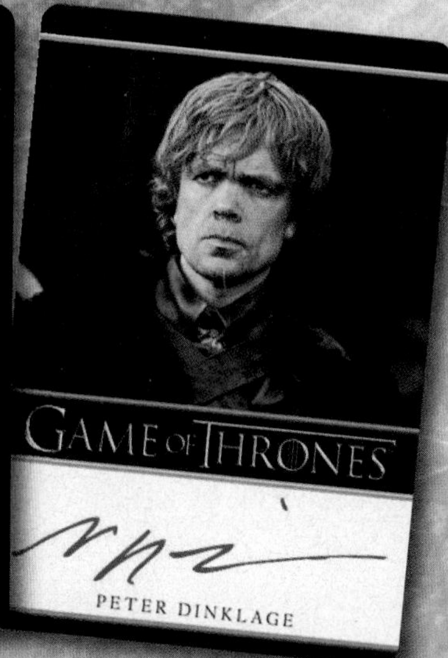

4TH EDITION • 2014

Manufactured in the United States of America
Published by Beckett Media LLC

4635 McEwen Road, Dallas, TX 75244, (972) 991-6657
www.beckett.com

First Printing
ISBN 9781936681785

FEATURES

PRICE GUIDES

Beckett COLLECTIBLE GAMING ALMANAC

4TH EDITION • 2014

A COMPREHENSIVE PRICE GUIDE TO GAMING AND NON-SPORTS CARDS

EDITORIAL

Elliot Ross - **Managing Editor**
Thomas Carroll - **Art Director**

COLLECTIBLES DATA PUBLISHING

Dan Hitt - **Sr. Manager, Sr. Market Analyst**
Brian Fleischer - **Manager, Sr. Market Analyst**
Bryan Hornbeck - **Sr. Market Analyst Staff**
Jeff Camay, Arsenio Tan, Lloyd Almonguera, Kristian Redulla, Rex Pastrana, Justin Grunert, Ryan Altubar, Derek Ficken - **Price Guide Staff**

ADVERTISING

Bill Dumas - **Advertising Director**
972.448.9147, bdumas@beckett.com
Thomas Carroll - **Ad Traffic Coordinator**
tcarroll@beckett.com

BECKETT GRADING SERVICES

Grading Sales - **972.448.9188**
grading@beckett.com

Dallas Office
4635 McEwen, Dallas, TX 75244
Jeromy Murray - **Associate Director**
Mike Simmons - **Southwest Regional Sales Manager**
msimmons@beckett.com
972.448.9144

New York Office
135 W 50th St, 14th Floor
New York, NY 10020
Charles Stabile - **Northeast Regional Sales Manager**
cstabile@beckett.com
212.375.6760

Chicago Office
4839 N. Elston Ave,
Chicago, IL 60630
Dillon Crotty - **Midwest Regional Sales Manager**
DCrotty@Beckett.com
630.303.4755

California Office
22840 Savi Ranch Parkway
Yorba Linda, Ca 92887
Tim E. Kenner - **West Coast Regional Sales Manager**
TKenner@Beckett.com
714-200-1934

OPERATIONS

Gus Alonzo - **Newstand Sales Manager**
Celia Merriday - **Newsstand Analyst**
Amit Sharma - **Newsstand & Production Analyst**
Alberto Chavez - **Sr. Logistics & Facilities Manager**

EDITORIAL, PRODUCTION & SALES OFFICE

4635 McEwen Road, Dallas TX 75244
972.991.6657
www.beckett.com

Letters the Editor:
4635 McEwen Rd., Dallas, TX, 75244

CUSTOMER SERVICE

Beckett Media, LLC
4635 Mc Ewen Road. Dallas, TX 75244

Price Guide Inquiries
customerservice@beckett.com
239.280.2348

Back Issues
www.beckettmedia.com

Dealer Sales
Tim Yoder - **Sr. Manager, Dealer Sales & Production**
239.280.2380 - dealers@beckett.com

Beckett Media, LLC
Sandeep Dua - **Vice President**
Bill Sutherland - **Sr. Director, e-commerce and Hobby Marketing**

Yu-Gi-Oh! HOTLIST

Here's a quick look at the hottest cards from the latest Yu-Gi-Oh! sets

JUDGMENT OF THE LIGHT

COACH SOLDIER WOLFBARK

STAR EATER

TRANSMODIFY

BROTHERHOOD OF THE FIRE FIST - ROOSTER

BUJIN YAMATO

LORD OF THE TACHYON GALAXY

MECHA PHANTOM BEAST DRACOSSACK

SPELLBOOK OF JUDGMENT

BROTHERHOOD OF THE FIRE FIST - CARDINAL

PINPOINT GUARD

EVILSWARM KERYKEION

COZMO BLAZER

DIAMOND DIRE WOLF

NOBLE KNIGHT MEDRAUT

SPELLBOOK OF THE MASTER

BREAKTHROUGH SKILL

BROTHERHOOD OF THE FIRE FIST - BEAR

Yu-gi-oh! World Championship 2013

Shin En Huang is the ultimate Dragon Ruler

Welcome, Duelists—it's been another amazing year of competition! New strategies, new types of monsters, and cards coming back from the Forbidden List that I never thought we'd get to use again. It all came together at the 2013 World Championships, where Shin En Huang of Taiwan piloted a Dragon Rulers deck against David Keener III's prophesy spellbook combo lockdown deck. Let's take a look at what he played and why it worked:

NOTE: This deck was legal during the tournament it was played. The Forbidden and Limited lists have changed since World Championship.

Monsters: 28

3 Blaster, Dragon Ruler of Infernos
2 Burner, Dragon Ruler of Sparks
3 Tempest, Dragon Ruler of Storms
2 Lightning, Dragon Ruler of Drafts
3 Tidal, Dragon Ruler of Waterfalls
2 Stream, Dragon Ruler of Droplets
3 Redox, Dragon Ruler of Boulders
2 Reactan, Dragon Ruler of Pebbles
1 Dragunity Corsesca
1 Light and Darkness Dragon
1 Eclipse Wyvern
3 Maxx "C"
2 Effect Veiler

Spells: 10

2 Sacred Sword of Seven Stars
1 Dragon Ravine
3 Super Rejuvenation
1 Heavy Storm
1 Book of Moon
2 Forbidden Chalice

Traps: 2

2 Vanity's Emptiness

Extra: 15

3 Mecha Phantom Beast Dragossack
3 Number 11: Big Eye
1 Gaia Dragon, the Thunder Charger
1 Mermail Abyssgaios
1 Armory Arm
1 Karakuri Shogun mdl 00 "Burei"
1 Scrap Dragon
1 Thought Ruler Archfiend
1 Colossal Fighter
1 Red Dragon Archfiend
1 Crimson Blader

Side: 15

3 Droll & Lock Bird
2 Tsukuyomi
2 Electric Virus
2 Swift Scarecrow
3 Mystical Space Typhoon
1 Card Destruction
2 DNA Surgery

MONSTERS:

The entire goal of the Dragon Rulers deck is to get out the Dragon Rulers. This is achieved by using the "baby" dragon rulers effect to special summon the big dragons. Once this deck starts to build some momentum you will have some massive threats on the board for your opponent to deal with. Once you have two dragon rulers out you can go for the XYZ summon of Mecha Phantom Beast Dracossack. From there life is really good; you are generating Mecha Dragon Beast tokens once per turn that essentially let you destroy targets one for one while also making the Dracossack invulnerable.

SPELLS:

Super Rejuvenation is what this deck is all about. The whole point of the deck is setting up a staged set of summons using the dragon ruler abilities. This means you want those cards in your graveyard, and Super Rejuvination takes advantage of you putting them there. Drawing a card for discarded dragon is great. Playing a second Super Rejuvination (or a third) can get you two cards from your deck for each discard. This means a possibility of 6 cards drawn if you play it right. The great part is that you may be drawing too many cards and have to discard at end of turn but you want to put those dragon cards there anyway!

TRAPS:

There isn't much to say about traps here. Two copies of Vanity's Emptiness. This is really just a way to control special summons so that they can only happen when you want them to.

WILL NEXT YEAR'S DECKS LOOK ANYTHING LIKE THIS?

The Lord of the Tachyon set was definitely a game changer when it comes to power level. Let's see how it fares on the banned and forbidden list. Will the Dragon Rulers find a way to persevere for 6 more months, or maybe longer? Only time will tell. Until then, play hard, play fair, and enjoy a new season of Yu-Gi-Oh!

Magic: the Gathering HOT LIST

Here's a quick look at the hottest cards from the latest Magic the Gathering sets

THEROS

1. ELSPETH, SUN'S CHAMPION

2. STORMBREATH DRAGON

3. ASHIOK, NIGHTMARE WEAVER

4. THOUGHTSEIZE

5. PURPHOROS, GOD OF THE FORGE

MAGIC 2014

1. ARCHANGEL OF THUNE

2. KALONIAN HYDRA

3. CHANDRA, PYROMASTER

4. GARRUK, CALLER OF BEASTS

5. MUTAVAULT

RETURN TO RAVNICA BLOCK

1. DOMRI RADE

2. BOROS RECKONER

3. JACE, ARCHITECT OF THOUGHT

4. VOICE OF RESURGENCE

5. SACRED FOUNDRY

Magic: The Gathering World Championship

Shahar Shenhar burns his way to the top!

Shahar Shenhar fought his way to the top of this years Magic: The Gathering World Championships, narrowly defeating Reid Duke. Shahar is the second Magic World Champion from Israel, and is one of the youngest Magic champions ever.

Shahar's Red-White-Blue Flash deck was popular, and he faced a nearly identical deck in the semifinals. After proceeding to the finals, Shahar found himself down two games against Reid Duke's Green-White Hexproof deck. Shahar went on to squeak out three wins in a row to become the World Champion.

Looking at the deck he played, it is easy to see that it is meant to be an agressive burn and damage deck. The use of burn spells, Like Lightning Helix and Lightning Bolt and haste creatures such as Vendilion Clique and Snapcaster Mage allowed Shahar to keep pace long enough to overwhelm Reid's defenses. In the fifth game, Shahar utilized a sideboarded Engineered Explosives to gain the win and become your Magic World Champion for 2013.

Red-White-Blue Flash - Modern
Shahar Shenhar, Winner 2013 World Championship

Creatures: 8

- 4 Snapcaster Mage
- 2 Vendilion Clique
- 2 Restoration Angel

Spells: 26

- 2 Sphinx's Revelation
- 4 Lightning Bolt
- 2 Lightning Helix
- 3 Electrolyze
- 3 Path to Exile
- 2 Spell Snare
- 3 Mana Leak
- 3 Cryptic Command
- 2 Shadow of Doubt
- 1 Think Twice
- 1 Ajani Vengeant

Lands: 26

- 4 Celestial Colonnade
- 1 Glacial Fortress
- 2 Hallowed Fountain
- 4 Scalding Tarn
- 2 Steam Vents
- 2 Sulfur Falls
- 3 Arid Mesa
- 1 Sacred Foundry
- 3 Tectonic Edge
- 2 Island
- 1 Mountain
- 1 Plains

Sideboard: 15

- 3 Molten Rain
- 1 Vendilion Clique
- 2 Thundermaw Hellkite
- 2 Pyroclasm
- 2 Supreme Verdict
- 2 Counterflux
- 1 Celestial Purge
- 1 Dispel
- 1 Engineered Explosives

SDCC BLACK PLANES

HASBRO PLEASES AND UPSETS FANS IN ONE FELL SWOOP

2013 saw the release of a very limited and special collectors item. Only available at the Hasbro booth at this years Comic-Con, the SDCC Magic: The Gathering Black Variant Planeswalker set both delighted and upset Magic fans all at once. Fans were awestruck when they saw this beautiful 5 card variant set of the Magic 2014 planeswalker cycle. The only problem with this set was that it was short printed, meaning only a very few people could obtain a copy. These cards have shot up in value on the secondary market due to their scarcity. Fully playable and tournament legal, these cards are a great novelty. These cards are functionally identical to their Magic 2014 core set counterparts, meaning that they don't give high end collectors an unfair advantage in gameplay. Let's hope that these type of creative sets continue to make appearances in the future. Take a look below at the black variation next to the original Magic 2014 card.

SWALKER VARIANTS

Chandra, Pyromaster
Planeswalker — Chandra
+1: Chandra, Pyromaster deals 1 damage to target player and 1 damage to up to one target creature that player controls. That creature can't block this turn.
0: Exile the top card of your library. You may play it this turn.
-7: Exile the top ten cards of your library. Choose an instant or sorcery card exiled this way and copy it three times. You may cast the copies without paying their mana costs.
4
Winona Nelson

Liliana of the Dark Realms
Planeswalker — Liliana
+1: Search your library for a Swamp card, reveal it, and put it into your hand. Then shuffle your library.
-3: Target creature gets +X/+X or -X/-X until end of turn, where X is the number of Swamps you control.
-6: You get an emblem with "Swamps you control have '⊙: Add ●●●● to your mana pool.'"
3
D. Alexander Gregory

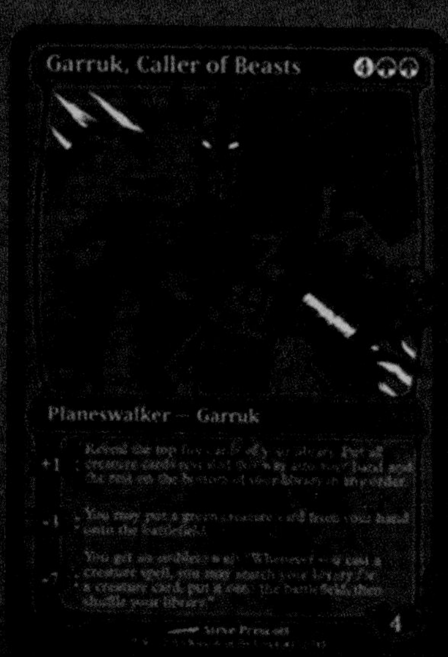

Garruk, Caller of Beasts
Planeswalker — Garruk
+1: Reveal the top five cards of your library. Put all creature cards revealed this way into your hand and the rest on the bottom of your library in any order.
-3: You may put a green creature card from your hand onto the battlefield.
-7: You get an emblem with "Whenever you cast a creature spell, you may search your library for a creature card, put it onto the battlefield, then shuffle your library."
4
Karl Kopinski

HOTLIST

Here's a quick look at the hottest cards from the latest Cardfight Vanguard and World of Warcraft sets

DRAGONIC KAISER VERMILLION THE BLOOD

GHOSTLY CHARGER

DRAGONIC KAISER VERMILLION THE BLOOD

BLUE STORM DRAGON, MAELSTROM

SINESTRA

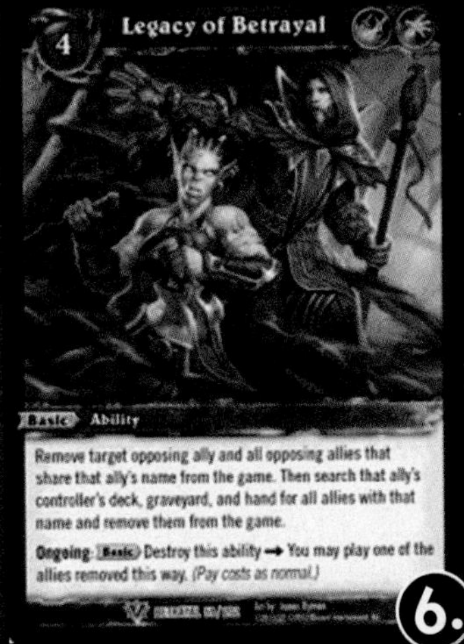

#59 LEGACY OF BETRAYAL

BLAZING LION, PLATINA EZEL

AEGWYNN, GUARDIAN OF TIRISFAL (EXTENDED ART)

CHIEF NURSE, SHAMSIEL

MAZU'KON

Hottest Non-Sport Boxes of

2013 was a bumper crop for Non-Sport cards. From classic movies to the latest new television shows, there was something for almost everybody. Pictured below are 15 of the most popular Non-Sport boxes from the last year.

CASTLE SEASONS ONE AND TWO

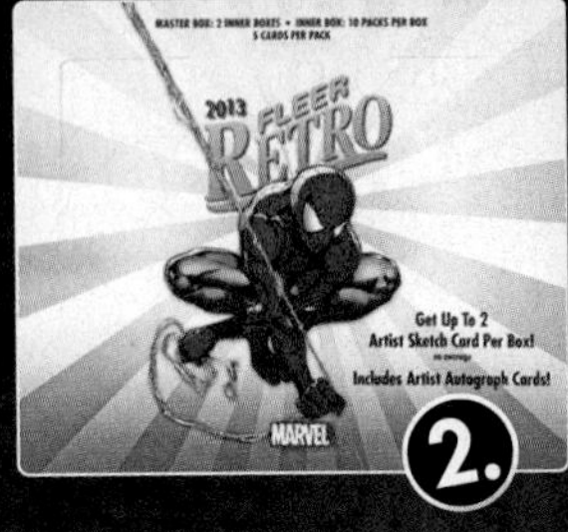

FLEER RETRO MARVEL

FRINGE SEASONS THREE AND FOUR

IRON MAN 3

MARVEL GREATEST BATTLES

PARKS AND RECREATION

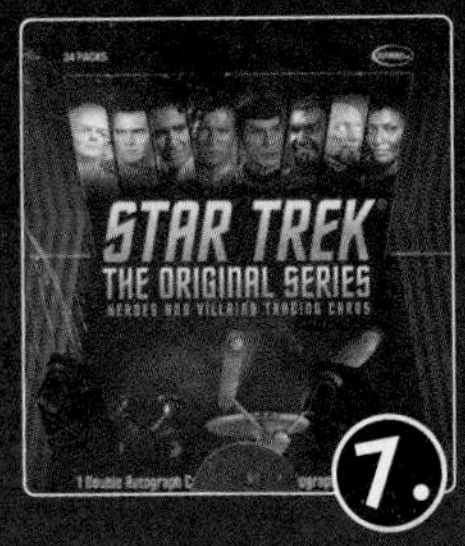

STAR TREK THE ORIGINAL SERIES HEROES AND VILLAINS

STAR WARS GALACTIC FILES 2

STAR WARS JEDI LEGACY

VAMPIRE DIARIES SEASON TWO

DC COMICS THE WOMEN OF LEGEND

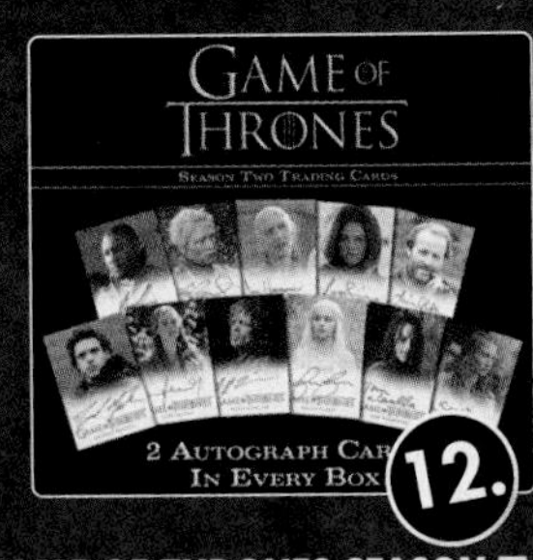

GAME OF THRONES SEASON TWO

GARBAGE PAIL KIDS CHROME

PSYCH SEASONS ONE THROUGH FOUR

TRUE BLOOD ARCHIVES

Beckett Card Gamer HOBBY & ONLINE STORES

ALABAMA

Hobbies & Collectibles
(256) 543-2255
406 Broad St. Gadsden, AL
35901-3718
rmghobbies@comcast.net

ARIZONA

Time Machine Productions
(479) 561-8556
2600 Rogers Ave.,
Fort Smith, AR 72903
hgwelles@hotmail.com

Showtime Cards
(520) 296-5512
5801 E Speedway Blvd.
Tucson, AZ 85712-5037
gmares@aol.com

CALIFORNIA

Russo's Books & Sports Collectibles
(661) 665-4686
9000 Ming Ave, Ste 14
Bakersfield, CA 93311-1321
russosbooks@bak.rr.com

Penninsula Sports Cards
(650) 595-5115
572 El Camino Real
Belmont, CA 94002-2121
PSCSB@aol.com

Comics & Stuff
(619) 316-2425
1020 El Cajon Blvd.
El Cajon, CA 92020
comicsnstuffsd@sbcglobal.net

Sportscards & More
(707) 443-2128
1662 Myrtle Avenue
Eureka, CA 95501

Collector's Paradise
(559) 439-3511
1075 E Bullard Ave.
Fresno, CA 93710

A Baseball Clubhouse
310-675-3333
18308 S Inglewood Ave
Hawthorne, CA 90250
phylbowls@sbcglobal.net

Bill's Bullpen
(831) 636-1180
207 4th St. Hollister, CA
95023-3923
billsbullpen@aol.com

316 Collectible
(408) 504-5557
1012 Newpark Mall
Newark, CA 94560
prostargaming@gmail.com

Affordable Cards
(951) 736-8552
2395 Hamner Ave Unit F
Norco, CA 92860
affordcard@netzero.com

Ardillo's Cards
(760) 433-8591
2001 S Coast Hwy.
Oceanside, CA 92054-6555
pop92056@aol.com

Gold River Distributors
(916) 408-2226
1120 Tara Court, Ste 6
Rocklin, CA 95675
wes@goldriverdist.com

A1 Comics
(916) 783-8005
818 Sunrise Ave.
Roseville, CA 95661
a1roseville@a-1comics.com

HR Sports Cards
(916) 443-1415
2231 10th St Sacramento, CA
95818-1373
vintageparker@yahoo.com

Palmers
(707) 542-1615
932 W College Ave.
Santa Rosa, CA 95401
cardking47@yahoo.com

All Star Cards
(619) 562-7357
8781 Cuyamaca St ., Ste S
Santee, CA 92071-4216
jrmudra@pacbell.net

Comic Collector Shop
(408) 732-8775
574 A East El Camino Real
Sunnyvale, CA 94087

South Bay Sportcards
(408) 530-8250
566 S Murphy Ave.
Sunnyvale, CA 94086-6116
southbaysports@aol.com

COLORADO

All C's
(303) 751-6882
1250 South Abilene St.
Aurora, CO 80012-4629
allcs@comcast.net

Dale's Kardz And Koinz
(719) 528-5959
4341 N Academy Blvd.
Colorado Springs, CO
80918-6623
dalezkardz@earthlink.net

CONNECTICUT

C & S Sports & Hobby
(860) 564-2281
624 Norwich Rd.
Plainfield, CT 6374
steve@cnssportsandhobby.co

A Timeless Journey
(203) 353-1720
2538 Summer St.
Stamford, CT 06905-4302
atimelessjourney@yahoo.com

FLORIDA

7th Inning Stretch
(352) 489-7555
11941 Bostick St , Ste D
Dunnellon, FL 34432-8303
seventhinning2000@yahoo.com

Tbs Comics Inc.
(850) 244-5441
550 Mary Esther Cut Off NW,
Unit 4 Fort Walton Beach, FL
32548-4066

Lakeland Sports Cards
(863) 648-4948
3114 S Florida Ave
Lakeland, FL 33803-4549
lakemiriam@aol.com

Not Just Cardboard
(352) 431-3494
611A S 14th St.
Leesburg, FL 34748
dprler1@yahoo.com

Orlando Sportscards South
(407) 240-0384
9476 S Orange Blossom Trl
Orlando, FL 32837-8321

Eric's Baseball Cards
(321) 383-0947
2400 S Hopkins Ave, Ste B
Titusville, FL 32780-5076
mossland@cfl.rr.com

GEORGIA

Sports Card Alley
(770) 607-9259
28 Copeland Rd NW
Cartersville, GA 30120-4328
bla1124@aol.com

Cornelia Card Shop
(706) 778-2826
711 Leve-Grove Rd.
Cornelia, GA 30531

Book End
(770) 474-1032
6041 North Henry Blvd Ste C
Stockbridge, GA 30281
ps_bookend@hotmail.com

IOWA

Gallagher's
(712) 298-0770
902 Broadway street
Emmetsburg, IA 50536

ILLINOIS

Sportscard Center
(309) 427-1204
705 Suite A S Main St.
Creve Coeur, IL 61610
gd3511@yahoo.com

Kyle's Baseball Cards And More
(618) 876-0221
16 Crossroad Plaza
Granite City , IL 62040
KyleBBcard@yahoo.com

Dean's Dugout
(630) 527-8888
2035 S Washington St.
STE 155-159 Naperville, IL
60565
deans_dugout@hotmail.com

One Stop Comics
(708) 524-2287
111 S Ridgeland Ave.
Oak Park, IL 60302
onestopcomics@sbcglobal.net

KFL Sales
(815) 744-5570
714 Cottage St.
Shorewood, IL 60404-9023
kflsales@aol.com

INDIANA

Reader Copies
(765) 649-5767
315 West 500 North
Anderson, IN 46012
readercopies@aol.com

The Book Broker
(812) 479-5647
2717 Covert Ave.
Evansville, IN 47714-3950

A To Z Coins And Stamps
(260) 483-3743
4201 Coldwater Road,
Ste 102, Fort Wayne IN
46805-1115
azcoins@yahoo.com

LOUISIANA

South East Cards and Comics
(225) 324-4417
6052 Desterhan Dr.
Baton Rouge, LA 70820
southeastcardsand-comics@yahoo.com

Paper Heroes
(337) 478-2143
3941 Ryan St, Ste A
Lake Charles, LA 70605-2835
paperheroeslcla@gmail.com

MASSACHUSETTS

Newsbreak, Inc.
(508) 675-9380
Route 6 Stuarts Plaza
Swansea, MA 2777
newsbreak@cox.net

G2 Sports Cards and Memorabilia
(508) 779-0810
6 South Main Street
Uxbridge, MA 1569
g2sportscards@gmail.com/
g2sportscards.com

MARYLAND

Hall of Fame Cards
(301) 984-3748
11325 Seven Locks Rd.
Potomac, MD 20854-3205
hofcards@aol.com

House Of Cards
(301) 608-0355
900 Silver Spring Ave.
Silver Spring, MD
20910-4618
football@houseofcardsmd.com

MAINE

Republic Coin & Jewelry Co.
(207) 782-9492
212 Center St.
Auburn, ME 04210-6150
chrissy@republicjewelry.com

MICHIGAN

Jim s Cards
(989) 673-5784
201 N State St.
Caro, MI 487231560

The Reading Place
(517) 543-7922
136 S Cochran Ave.
Charlotte, MI 48813-1510

Collectors Inc.
(586) 764-4657
33431 Harper Ave.
Clinton Township, MI 48035
cardsorder@gmail.com

Stadium Cards & Comics
(734) 434-0283
2061 Golfside Dr.
Ypsilanti, MI 48197-1303
fennydude@aol.com

MINNESOTA

Sport Card Central
(218) 825-9610
608 Front St. Brainerd, MN
56401-3602

Twin City Comics
(763) 706-0857
3954 Central Ave. NE
Minneapolis, MN 55421
jeremy@twincitycomics.com

MISSOURI

Coach's Corner Sportscards
(816) 331-6462
110 N Scott Ave, Ste A
Belton, MO 64012-2012

Central Missouri Sportscards
(573) 364-8892
408 S Bishop Ave.
Rolla, MO 65401-4311
lchrisco@fidnet.com

MISSISSIPPI

Gulf Coast Cards & Sports Memo
(228) 388-5178
2600 Beach Blvd.
Biloxi, MS 39531-4606
gulfcoastcards@cableone.net

Gulf Coast Cards & Sports Memo
(601) 599-2273
1000 Turtle Creek Dr, T 56
Hattiesburg, MS 39402-1145
gcc39402@yahoo.com

Van's Comics
(601) 898-9950
398 Highway 51 Suite 202
Ridgeland, MS 39157
vanscomics@gmail.com

MONTANA

KAB Sportscards & Collectibles
(406) 850-1440
710 Grand Ave Suite 13
Billings, MT 59101
kabsportscards@hotmail.com

Action Cards And Collectibles
(406) 453-6629
3909 4th St NE
Great Falls, MT 59404-4244
Scott.Swanke@MALMSTROM.AF.MIL

NORTH DAKOTA

Big Nicks Sports Cards
(701) 277-1989
3902 13th ave S, Suite #100,
West Acres Mall Fargo, ND
58103
bignickscards@cableone.net

NEBRASKA

Joe's Sports Cards and Comics
(402) 462-4838
231 N Lincoln Ave. Hastings,
NE 68901-5149

NEW HAMPSHIRE

The Dugout Collection
(603) 352-4205
800 Park Ave. Keene, NH 3431

NEW JERSEY

Deluca's Baseball Cards
(201) 858-9223
1086 Avenue C Bayonne, NJ
07002-3302
bigbadty@aol.com

Time Warp Comics and Games
(973) 857-9788
555A Pompton Ave.
Cedar Grove, NJ 7009
dave@timewarpcomics.com

New Concept III
(609) 953-0404
676 Stokes Rd. Medford, NJ
08055-2907
newconceptcards@gmail.com

Tem Dee
(856) 228-8645
5051 Rt 42 Turnersville, NJ
08012-1703
sales@temdee.com

The Collectors Den
(201) 819-2100
171 W Prospect St.
Waldwick, NJ 7463
collectorsdennj@gmail.com

Rookies and Stars
(732) 750-3870
530 Amboy Ave.
Woodbridge, NJ 7095
rookies_and_stars@comcast.net

NEW MEXICO

Noble Collectibles
(505) 858-0212
8216 Montgomery Blvd NE
Albuquerque, NM
87109-1602
nobleadamb@aol.com

NEW YORK

Collectibles by Armada
(718) 904-7105
3025b 2nd Floor 3rd Ave Frnt A
Bronx, NY 10455-1208
colbyarmada@optonline.net

The Hot Corner,Inc.
(718) 252-1555
2980 Norstrand Ave.
Brooklyn, NY 11229
clausstadt@aol.com

The Dugout
(607) 758-7435
3933 West Road Plaza
Cortland, NY 13045
pbartolone@stny.rr.com

All Sports
(315) 446-7701
3649 Erie Blvd. E.,
Shoppingtown Mall
Dewitt, NY 13214
rckdsh@aol.com

Who's On First
(718) 358-7047
19907 34th Ave.
Flushing, NY 11358
sarcomano@aol.com

Montasy Comics
(718) 575-8815
7017c Austin St, 2nd Fl
Forest Hills, NY 11375
comic2go@aol.com

Royal Collectibles
(718) 793-0542
9601 Metropolitan Ave.
Forest Hills, NY
11375-6697

Dave & Adam's Card World
716-299-0777
1595 Military Road
Niagra Falls, NY 14304
dacardworld.com

Dave & Adam's Card World
716-677-1840
3217F Southwestern Blvd
Orchard Park, NY 14127
dacardworld.com

Jim s Sports
(802) 363-9219
Champlain Centre Store 60,
Smithfield Blvd
Plattsburgh, NY 12901
jlvitanos@yahoo.com

Greenridge Cards And Gifts
(718) 317-8700
3259 Richmond Ave.
Staten Island, NY
10312-2123
connect123d@yahoo.com

Dave & Adam's Card World
716-837-4920
2217 Sheridan Drive
Tonawanda, NY 14223
dacardworld.com

D'angelo Sports
(516) 679-8331
1890 Wantagh Ave.
Wantagh, NY 11793-3910
dangelosports1890@gmail.com

DCS Sportscards
516-946-6334
3381C Merrick Rd
Wantagh, NY 11793
dcssportscards.com

A&S Sports LLC
(516) 398-7800
825 Carman Ave.
Westbury, NY 11590
www.nysportscards.com

Dave & Adam's Card World
716-689-2273
5575 Transit Rd,
Williamsville, NY 14221
dacardworld.com

OHIO

Queen City Comic & Card Co.
(513) 351-5674
6101 Montgomery Rd.
Cincinnati, OH 45213-1401
qccomics@aol.com

Bases Loaded
(419) 632-0165
35 West Main Shelby, OH
44875

Collector's Palace
(330) 626-2464
9274 State Route 43
Streetsboro, OH 44241
collector33964@sbcglobal.net

OKLAHOMA

Al's Sportscards and Gaming
(405) 348-7583
116 East 15th St.
Edmond, OK 73013-4303
Alscards7599@sbcglobal.net

OREGON

His Junk/Her Treasure
(541) 888-5690
63678 SW 10th Rd.
Coos Bay, OR 97420
deschbil@charter.net

PENNSYLVANIA

Juniata Cards
(814) 944-0810
1019 N 4th Ave.
Altoona, PA 16601-6154
stevejun@verizon.net

Don's Sports Cards
(607) 796-0776
101 Maple St.Athens, PA
18810-1621

Indiana Sportscards
(724) 349-1769
1506 Oakland Ave.
Indiana, PA 15701

VSM Sports Card Outlet
(717) 947-0189
2160 Lincoln Highway East
Suite 3, Lancaster, PA
17602
CWhisman@gesonline.com

Shaffer's Trading Cards
(570) 524-4341
2849 Westbranch Hwy.
Lewisburg, PA 17837

Sports Cards Etc.
(724) 942-8085
110 West McMurray Road
McMurray, PA 15317

RHODE ISLAND

Pitchers Mound
(401) 781-2230
980 Post Rd.
Warwick, RI 02888-3354

SOUTH DAKOTA

Rainbow Sportscards
(605) 338-9519
3310 S Minnesota Ave.
Sioux Falls, SD
57105-6440
jay@rainbowcardsandcomics.com

TENNESSEE

B & M Amusement Company
(423) 490-1162
5036 Highway 58, Ste D
Chattanooga, TN
37416-1843
bandmorders@aol.com

Bob's Collectors Den
(931) 526-2311
206 E 9th St.
Cookeville, TN38501-2617

Cards-R-Fun
(615) 832-3216
15125 Old Hickory Blvd.
Nashville, TN 37211-1318

3 R Baseball Cards
(931) 607-9923
107 Methvin Dr.
Shelbyville, TN
37160-4638

TEXAS

The Old Ballpark
(281) 585-8800
600 E South St.
Alvin, TX 77511-3639
theoldballpark@aol.com

Card Traders Of Austin
(512) 250-0958
8650 Spicewood Springs Rd,
Ste 128, Austin, TX
78759-4323
crdtrade@swbell.net

Card Shack
(713) 455-5357
13018 Woodforest Blvd Suite
M, Houston, TX 77015
cardshackhouston@gmail.com

UTAH

Mr. E's Sports Cards
(801) 224-6677
720 S State St.
Orem, UT 84058-6308
mr.esportscards@gmail.com

VIRGINIA

Blowout Cards - The Fantastic Store
14508 Lee Rd - Unit F
Chantilly, VA 20151
Blowoutcards.com

B & D Cards & Comics
(434) 836-9133
1326 Piney Forest Rd.
Danville, VA 24540-1606

Jerseys Cards And Comics
(757) 890-2842
1818 Todds Ln , Ste G
Hampton, VA 23666-3139

Game Day Sportscards & Collectibles
(434) 221-0861
2143 Holiday Ln.
Lynchburg, VA 24504
randy.scicli@areva.com

Sportscards and Collectibles
(804) 387-1638
7443 Lee Davis Rd, Ste 103
Mechanicsville, VA
23111-4484
djames1503@yahoo.com

Collectors Corner
(703) 450-7280
47024 Harry Byrd Hwy,
Ste 106, Sterling, VA
20164-1829
cardsharkmurph@aol.com

A.J.'s Sport Stop
(703) 938-1688
255 Maple Avenue W
Vienna, VA
22180-5606

Heroes Sports Cards
(757) 313-2694
3936 Virginia Beach Blvd #101
Virginia Beach, VA
23452
sales@heroessportscards.com

VERMONT

Mike's Hobbies
(802) 775-0059
162 N Main St.
Rutland, VT 05701-3024
mhobbies@sober.net

Main Street Sportscards
(802) 655-5751
325 Main St. Suite 7
Winnoski, VT 5404
mainstreetsportscards@comcast.net

WASHINGTON

Jeanne's Trading Cards
(360) 479-5050
2901 Perry Ave Ste#7
Bremerton, WA 98310
mariachal@hotmail.com

Atomic Cards
(866) 440-9224
2008 S 314th St.
Federal Way, WA
98003-5475
westcoastbryan@yahoo.com

Who's On First Sportcards
(360) 653-9014
401 State Ave.
Marysville, WA98270-5029

Shane's Big League Sports Cards
(425) 277-3717
601 S Grady Way, Ste D
Renton, WA 98057-3229
sdschulke@aol.com

Knutsen's Northwest Sportscards
(253) 564-9204
3816 Bridgeport Way West
University Place, WA
98466
northwestsportscards@yahoo.com

Ron's Coin & Book Center
(509) 248-1117
63rd St.
Yakima, WA 98901-2703
ronscoin@hotmail.com

WISCONSIN

Madison Coin And Stamp Shop
(608) 257-9698
1123 South Park St.
Madison, WI 53713
boblee1123@aol.com

Globe News
(715) 392-2090
1430 Tower Ave.
Superior, WI 54880-1526
unterberger@chartermi.net

WEST VIRGINIA

Collectibles Etc.
(304) 776-0020
900 NITRO MARKET PLACE
CROSS LANES, WV
25313
collectiblesetc@msn.com

T&R Sportscards & More
(307) 635-9101
201 W 17th St.
Cheyenne, WY
82001-4518
imelsportscards@aol.com

ONLINE

Blowout Cards
Blowoutcards.com

COMC
www.comc.com

Dave & Adam's Card World
dacardworld.com

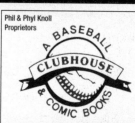

DCS Sportscards
dcssportscards.com

MAGIC The Gathering PRICE GUIDE

THE WORLD'S MOST TRUSTED SOURCE IN COLLECTING™

How To Use And Condition Guide

WHAT'S LISTED
This Beckett Price Guide includes products that are produced by Wizards of the Coast or by licensed manufacturers.

WHAT THE COLUMNS MEAN
The LO and HI columns reflect a range of current retail selling prices and are listed in U.S. dollars. The HI column represents the typical full retail selling price while the LO column represents the lowest price one could expect to find through extensive shopping. Both columns represent the same condition for the card listed. Keep in mind that market conditions can change quickly up or down based on extreme levels of demand. The published HI and LO column prices in this issue are a single snapshot in time and cannot be exact for every card listed.

ONLY A REFERENCE
The data and pricing information contained within this publication is intended for reference only. Beckett's goal is to provide the most accurate and verifiable information in the industry. However, Beckett cannot guarantee the accuracy of all data published and typographical errors occasionally occur. Buyers and sellers of Magic cards should be aware of this and handle their personal transactions at their own risk. If you discover an error or misprint in this issue, please notify us via email at mtg@beckett.com.

MULTIPLIERS
Some parallel Foil sets are listed with multipliers to provide values of unlisted cards. Multiplier ranges (i.e. 1X to 2X HI) apply only to the HI column. Example: If basic-issue card A lists for $2 to $4, and the multiplier is "1X to 2X HI", then the parallel version of card A or the insert card in question is valued at $4 to $8. Please note the term "basic card" used in the Price Guide refers to a standard regular-issue card. A "basic card" cannot be an insert or parallel card.

CARD CONDITION
The value of your card is dependent on the condition or "grade" of your card. Prices in this issue reflect the highest raw condition (i.e. not professionally graded by a third party) of the card most commonly found at shows, shops, on the Internet, and right out of the pack for brand new releases. This generally means Near Mint-Mint condition for all Magic cards. Use the following chart as a guide to estimate the value of your cards in a variety of conditions using the prices found in this issue.

CARD GRADES
Mint (MT) – A card with no wear or flaws. The card has four perfect corners, 60/40 or better centering from top to bottom and from left to right, original gloss, smooth edges and original color borders. A Mint card does not have print spots, color or focus imperfections.

Near Mint-Mint (NRMT-MT) – A card with one minor flaw. Any one of the following would lower a Mint card to Near Mint-Mint: one corner with a slight touch of wear, barely noticeable print spots, color or focus imperfections. This card must have a 60/40 or better centering in both directions, original gloss, smooth edges and original color borders.

Near Mint (NRMT) – A card with one minor flaw. Any one of the following would lower a Mint card to Near Mint: one very slightly scuffed corner or two or four corners with slight touches of wear, 70/30 to 60/40 centering, slightly rough edges, minor print spots, color or focus imperfections. This card must have original gloss and original color borders.

Excellent-Mint (EXMT) – A card with two or three slightly worn corners with centering no worse than 80/20. The card may have no more than two of the following slightly rough edges, very slightly discolored borders, minor print spots, color or focus imperfections. The card must have original gloss.

Excellent (EX) – (a.k.a. SP or Slightly Played.) A card with four slightly worn corners and centering is no worse than 80/20. The card may have a small amount of original gloss lost, rough edges, slightly discolored borders and minor print spots, color or focus imperfections.

Very Good (VG) – A card that has been handled but not abused slightly worn corners with slight layering, slight notching on edges, a significant amount of gloss lost from the surface but no scuffing and moderate discoloration of borders. The card may have a few light creases.

Good (G), Fair (F), Poor (P) – (a.k.a. HP or Heavily Played) A well-worn, mishandled or abused card badly worn corners, lots of scuffing, most or all original gloss missing, seriously discolored borders, moderate or heavy creases, and one or more serious flaws. The grade of Good, Fair or Poor depends on the severity of wear and flaws. Good, Fair and Poor cards generally are used only as fillers.

Special Note: The most widely used grades are defined here. Obviously, many cards will not perfectly match one of the definitions. Therefore, categories between the major grades known as in-between grades are used, such as Good to Very Good (G-VG), Very Good to Excellent (VG-EX), and Excellent-Mint to Near Mint (EXMT-NRMT). Such grades indicate a card with all qualities of the lower category but with at least a few qualities if the higher category.

LEGEND
C – Common Card
C1 – Common Card appeared one time on the press sheet
C2 – Common Card appeared two times on the press sheet
C3 – Common Card appeared three times on the press sheet
C4 – Common Card appeared four times on the press sheet
U – Uncommon Card
U1 – Uncommon Card appeared one time on the press sheet
U2 – Uncommon Card appeared two times on the press sheet
U3 – Uncommon Card appeared three times on the press sheet
R – Rare Card
M – Mythic Rare Card
TR – Timeshifted Rare Card

FOIL – Parallel card. These cards have a special foil-coated film (usually shiny), which separates it from its twin.

PRICE GUIDE PERCENTAGE BY GRADE 1993-PRESENT

MT	100-125%	NRMT	60-75%	EX	20-30%
NRMT-MT	100%	EX-MT	30-50%	VG	5-10%

MAGIC SETS AND SYMBOLS
All set symbols are located on the right side of every card underneath the card's artwork. Some of the early Core sets did not carry a symbol.

CORE SETS
Alpha - 1993
Beta - 1993
Unlimited - 1993
Revised Edition - 1994
Fourth Edition - 1995
Fifth Edition - 1997
Classic (Sixth) Edition - 1999
Seventh Edition - 2001
Eighth Edition - 2003
Ninth Edition - 2005
Tenth Edition - 2007
Magic 2010 - 2009
Magic 2011 - 2010
Magic 2012 - 2011
Magic 2013 - 2012
Magic 2014 - 2013

EXPANSION SETS
Arabian Nights - 1993
Antiquities - 1994
Legends - 1994
The Dark - 1994
Fallen Empires - 1994
Ice Age -1995
Homelands - 1995
Alliances - 1996
Mirage - 1996
Visions - 1997
Weatherlight - 1997
Tempest - 1997
Stronghold - 1998
Exodus - 1998
Urza's Saga - 1998
Urza's Legacy - 1999
Urza's Destiny - 1999
Mercadian Masques - 1999
Nemesis - 2000
Prophecy - 2000
Invasion - 2000
Planeshift - 2001
Apocalypse - 2001
Odyssey - 2001
Torment - 2002
Judgment - 2002
Onslaught - 2002
Legions - 2003
Scourge - 2003
Mirrodin - 2003
Darksteel - 2004
Fifth Dawn - 2004
Champions of Kamigawa - 2004
Betrayers of Kamigawa - 2005
Saviors of Kamigawa - 2005
Ravnica City of Guilds - 2005
Guildpact - 2006
Dissension - 2006
Coldsnap - 2006
Time Spiral - 2006
Planar Chaos - 2007
Future Sight - 2007
Lorwyn - 2007
Morningtide - 2008
Shadowmoor - 2008
Eventide - 2008
Shards of Alara - 2008
Conflux - 2009
Alara Reborn - 2009
Zendikar - 2009
Worldwake - 2010
Rise of the Eldrazi - 2010
Scars of Mirrodin - 2010
Mirrodin Beseiged - 2011
New Phyrexia - 2011
Innistrad - 2011
Dark Ascension - 2012
Avacyn Restored - 2012
Return to Ravnica - 2012
Dragon's Maze - 2013
Gatecrash - 2013
Modern Masters - 2013
Theros - 2013

SPECIAL SETS
Chronicles - 1995
Vanguard - 1997
Unglued - 1998
Unhinged - 2004

STARTER SETS
Portal – 1997
Portal Second Age – 1997
Portal Three Kingdoms – 1999
Starter - 1999

MAGIC: THE GATHERING

Beckett Magic price guide sponsored by GetCashForMagic.com

1993 Magic the Gathering Alpha

Complete Set (295)	12000.00	15000.00
Starter Deck Box (10 Decks)	9000.00	12000.00
Starter Deck (60 Cards)	900.00	1200.00
Booster Box (36 Packs)	12000.00	15000.00
Booster Pack (15 Cards)	375.00	550.00

Released in August 1993
Large rounded corners with black borders.
No Copyright date and name of illustrator at the bottom.

❑ 1 Air Elemental U :B:	5.00	10.00
❑ 2 Ancestral Recall R :B:	550.00	1100.00
❑ 3 Animate Artifact U :B:	2.50	5.00
❑ 4 Animate Dead U :K:	12.00	25.00
❑ 5 Animate Wall R :W:	12.00	25.00
❑ 6 Ankh of Mishra R :A:	30.00	80.00
❑ 7 Armageddon R :W:	40.00	90.00
❑ 8 Aspect of Wolf R :G:	10.00	25.00
❑ 9 Bad Moon R :K:	35.00	70.00
❑ 10 Badlands R :L:	90.00	180.00
❑ 11 Balance R :W:	65.00	125.00
❑ 12 Basalt Monolith U :A:	3.50	7.00
❑ 13 Bayou R :L:	100.00	200.00
❑ 14 Benalish Hero C :W:	1.50	3.00
❑ 15 Berserk U :G:	75.00	150.00
❑ 16 Birds of Paradise R :G:	120.00	230.00
❑ 17 Black Knight U :K:	9.00	18.00
❑ 18 Black Lotus R :A:	2000.00	4000.00
❑ 19 Black Vise U :A:	11.00	22.00
❑ 20 Black Ward U :W:	2.50	5.00
❑ 21 Blaze of Glory R :W:	28.00	55.00
❑ 22 Blessing R :W:	15.00	30.00
❑ 23 Blue Elemental Blast C :B:	4.00	8.00
❑ 24 Blue Ward U :W:	3.50	7.00
❑ 25 Bog Wraith U :K:	2.50	5.00
❑ 26 Braingeyser R :B:	50.00	100.00
❑ 27 Burrowing U :R:	4.00	8.00
❑ 28 Camouflage U :G:	4.00	8.00
❑ 29 Castle U :W:	2.50	5.00
❑ 30 Celestial Prism U :A:	3.00	6.00
❑ 31 Channel U :G:	9.00	18.00
❑ 32 Chaos Orb R :A:	75.00	150.00
❑ 33 Chaoslace R :R:	15.00	30.00
❑ 34 Circle of Protection: Blue C :W:	2.50	5.00
❑ 35 Circle of Protection: Green C :W:	2.50	5.00
❑ 36 Circle of Protection: Red C :W:	2.50	5.00
❑ 37 Circle of Protection: White C :W:	2.50	5.00
❑ 38 Clockwork Beast R :A:	15.00	30.00
❑ 39 Clone U :B:	12.00	25.00
❑ 40 Cockatrice R :G:	15.00	30.00
❑ 41 Consecrate Land U :W:	6.00	12.00
❑ 42 Conservator U :A:	3.00	6.00
❑ 43 Contract from Below R :K:	45.00	90.00
❑ 44 Control Magic U :B:	10.00	20.00
❑ 45 Conversion U :W:	4.00	8.00
❑ 46 Copper Tablet U :A:	6.00	12.00
❑ 47 Copy Artifact R :B:	35.00	70.00
❑ 48 Counterspell U :B:	25.00	50.00
❑ 49 Craw Wurm C :G:	2.00	4.00
❑ 50 Creature Bond C :B:	1.50	3.00
❑ 51 Crusade R :W:	30.00	60.00
❑ 52 Crystal Rod U :A:	2.50	5.00
❑ 53 Cursed Land U :K:	2.50	5.00
❑ 54 Cyclopean Tomb R :A:	75.00	150.00
❑ 55 Dark Ritual C :K:	12.00	25.00
❑ 56 Darkpact R :K:	11.00	22.00
❑ 57 Death Ward C :W:	2.00	4.00
❑ 58 Deathgrip U :K:	4.00	8.00
❑ 59 Deathlace R :K:	12.00	25.00
❑ 60 Demonic Attorney R :K:	11.00	22.00
❑ 61 Demonic Hordes R :K:	28.00	55.00
❑ 62 Demonic Tutor U :K:	50.00	100.00
❑ 63 Dingus Egg R :A:	15.00	30.00
❑ 64 Disenchant C :W:	6.00	12.00
❑ 65 Disintegrate C :R:	2.50	5.00
❑ 66 Disrupting Scepter R :A:	20.00	40.00
❑ 67 Dragon Whelp U :R:	9.00	18.00
❑ 68 Drain Life C :K:	3.50	7.00
❑ 69 Drain Power R :B:	15.00	30.00
❑ 70 Drudge Skeletons C :K:	1.50	3.00
❑ 71 Dwarven Demolition Team U :R:	5.00	10.00
❑ 72 Dwarven Warriors C :R:	1.50	3.00
❑ 73 Earth Elemental U :R:	3.00	6.00
❑ 74 Earthbind C :R:	2.00	4.00
❑ 75 Earthquake R :R:	25.00	50.00
❑ 76 Elvish Archers R :G:	25.00	50.00
❑ 77 Evil Presence U :K:	2.50	5.00
❑ 78 False Orders C :R:	2.50	5.00
❑ 79 Farmstead R :W:	10.00	20.00
❑ 80 Fastbond R :G:	50.00	100.00
❑ 81 Fear C :K:	1.50	3.00
❑ 82 Feedback U :B:	2.50	5.00
❑ 83 Fire Elemental U :R:	3.50	7.00
❑ 84 Fireball C :R:	3.00	6.00
❑ 85 Firebreathing C :R:	1.50	3.00
❑ 86 Flashfires U :R:	5.00	10.00
❑ 87 Flight C :B:	1.50	3.00
❑ 88 Fog C :G:	1.50	3.00
❑ 89 Force of Nature R :G:	55.00	110.00
❑ 90 Forcefield R :A:	70.00	135.00
❑ 91 Forest v1 C :L:	2.00	4.00
❑ 92 Forest v2 C :L:	2.00	4.00
❑ 93 Fork R :R:	70.00	140.00
❑ 94 Frozen Shade C :K:	2.00	4.00
❑ 95 Fungusaur R :G:	12.00	25.00
❑ 96 Gaea's Liege R :G:	12.00	25.00
❑ 97 Gauntlet of Might R :A:	80.00	155.00
❑ 98 Giant Growth C :G:	3.50	7.00
❑ 99 Giant Spider C :G:	2.00	4.00
❑ 100 Glasses of Urza U :A:	3.00	6.00
❑ 101 Gloom U :K:	4.00	8.00
❑ 102 Goblin Balloon Brigade U :R:	5.00	10.00
❑ 103 Goblin King R :R:	25.00	50.00
❑ 104 Granite Gargoyle R :R:	20.00	40.00
❑ 105 Gray Ogre C :R:	1.50	3.00
❑ 106 Green Ward U :W:	3.00	6.00
❑ 107 Grizzly Bears C :G:	1.50	3.00
❑ 108 Guardian Angel C :W:	1.50	3.00
❑ 109 Healing Salve C :W:	1.50	3.00
❑ 110 Helm of Chatzuk R :A:	12.00	25.00
❑ 111 Hill Giant C :R:	1.50	3.00
❑ 112 Hive, The R :A:	11.00	22.00
❑ 113 Holy Armor C :W:	1.50	3.00
❑ 114 Holy Strength C :W:	2.00	4.00
❑ 115 Howl from Beyond C :K:	2.00	4.00
❑ 116 Howling Mine R :A:	50.00	100.00
❑ 117 Hurloon Minotaur C :R:	2.00	4.00
❑ 118 Hurricane U :G:	6.00	12.00
❑ 119 Hypnotic Specter U :K:	45.00	90.00
❑ 120 Ice Storm U :G:	18.00	35.00
❑ 121 Icy Manipulator U :A:	30.00	60.00
❑ 122 Illusionary Mask R :A:	90.00	180.00
❑ 123 Instill Energy U :G:	3.50	7.00
❑ 124 Invisibility C :B:	1.50	3.00
❑ 125 Iron Star U :A:	3.00	6.00
❑ 126 Ironclaw Orcs C :R:	1.50	3.00
❑ 127 Ironroot Treefolk C :G:	1.50	3.00
❑ 128 Island Sanctuary R :W:	12.00	25.00
❑ 129 Island v1 C :L:	1.50	3.00
❑ 130 Island v2 C :L:	1.50	3.00
❑ 131 Ivory Cup U :A:	3.00	6.00
❑ 132 Jade Monolith R :A:	12.00	25.00
❑ 133 Jade Statue U :A:	10.00	20.00
❑ 134 Jayemdae Tome R :A:	25.00	50.00
❑ 135 Juggernaut U :A:	12.00	25.00
❑ 136 Jump C :B:	1.50	3.00
❑ 137 Karma U :W:	4.00	8.00
❑ 138 Keldon Warlord U :R:	5.00	10.00
❑ 139 Kormus Bell R :A:	12.00	25.00
❑ 140 Kudzu R :G:	15.00	30.00
❑ 141 Lance U :W:	3.00	6.00
❑ 142 Ley Druid U :G:	3.00	6.00
❑ 143 Library of Leng U :A:	4.00	8.00
❑ 144 Lich R :K:	40.00	80.00
❑ 145 Lifeforce U :G:	3.50	7.00
❑ 146 Lifelace R :G:	15.00	30.00
❑ 147 Lifetap U :B:	3.00	6.00
❑ 148 Lightning Bolt C :R:	15.00	30.00
❑ 149 Living Artifact R :G:	11.00	22.00
❑ 150 Living Lands R :G:	12.00	25.00
❑ 151 Living Wall U :A:	2.50	5.00
❑ 152 Llanowar Elves C :G:	10.00	20.00
❑ 153 Lord of Atlantis R :B:	28.00	55.00
❑ 154 Lord of the Pit R :K:	40.00	80.00
❑ 155 Lure U :G:	3.00	6.00
❑ 156 Magical Hack R :B:	12.00	25.00
❑ 157 Mahamoti Djinn R :B:	30.00	60.00
❑ 158 Mana Flare R :R:	40.00	75.00
❑ 159 Mana Short R :B:	28.00	55.00
❑ 160 Mana Vault R :A:	60.00	120.00
❑ 161 Manabarbs R :R:	12.00	25.00
❑ 162 Meekstone R :A:	22.00	45.00
❑ 163 Merfolk of the Pearl Trident C :B:	1.50	3.00
❑ 164 Mesa Pegasus C :W:	2.00	4.00
❑ 165 Mind Twist R :K:	70.00	135.00
❑ 166 Mons's Goblin Raiders C :R:	1.50	3.00
❑ 167 Mountain v1 C :L:	1.50	3.00
❑ 168 Mountain v2 C :L:	1.50	3.00
❑ 169 Mox Emerald R :A:	400.00	825.00
❑ 170 Mox Jet R :A:	500.00	1000.00
❑ 171 Mox Pearl R :A:	425.00	850.00
❑ 172 Mox Ruby R :A:	425.00	850.00
❑ 173 Mox Sapphire R :A:	500.00	1000.00
❑ 174 Natural Selection R :G:	25.00	50.00
❑ 175 Nether Shadow R :K:	15.00	30.00
❑ 176 Nettling Imp U :K:	4.00	8.00
❑ 177 Nevinyrral's Disk R :A:	70.00	135.00
❑ 178 Nightmare R :K:	35.00	70.00
❑ 179 Northern Paladin R :W:	20.00	40.00
❑ 180 Obsianus Golem U :A:	3.00	6.00
❑ 181 Orcish Artillery U :R:	12.00	25.00
❑ 182 Orcish Oriflamme U :R:	10.00	20.00
❑ 183 Paralyze C :K:	2.00	4.00
❑ 184 Pearled Unicorn C :W:	2.00	4.00
❑ 185 Personal Incarnation R :W:	12.00	25.00
❑ 186 Pestilence C :K:	2.50	5.00
❑ 187 Phantasmal Forces U :B:	2.50	5.00
❑ 188 Phantasmal Terrain C :B:	1.50	3.00
❑ 189 Phantom Monster U :B:	3.00	6.00
❑ 190 Pirate Ship R :B:	15.00	30.00
❑ 191 Plague Rats C :K:	2.00	4.00
❑ 192 Plains v1 C :L:	1.50	3.00
❑ 193 Plains v2 C :L:	1.50	3.00
❑ 194 Plateau R :L:	100.00	200.00
❑ 195 Power Leak C :B:	1.50	3.00
❑ 196 Power Sink C :B:	2.50	5.00
❑ 197 Power Surge R :R:	12.00	25.00
❑ 198 Prodigal Sorcerer C :B:	2.50	5.00
❑ 199 Psionic Blast U :B:	18.00	35.00
❑ 200 Psychic Venom C :B:	1.50	3.00
❑ 201 Purelace R :W:	12.00	25.00
❑ 202 Raging River R :R:	20.00	40.00
❑ 203 Raise Dead C :K:	1.50	3.00
❑ 204 Red Elemental Blast C :R:	6.00	12.00
❑ 205 Red Ward U :W:	2.50	5.00
❑ 206 Regeneration C :G:	1.50	3.00
❑ 207 Regrowth U :G:	20.00	40.00
❑ 208 Resurrection U :W:	3.00	6.00
❑ 209 Reverse Damage R :W:	12.00	25.00
❑ 210 Righteousness R :W:	12.00	25.00
❑ 211 Roc of Kher Ridges R :R:	12.00	25.00
❑ 212 Rock Hydra R :R:	15.00	30.00
❑ 213 Rod of Ruin U :A:	2.50	5.00
❑ 214 Royal Assassin R :K:	65.00	125.00
❑ 215 Sacrifice U :K:	3.00	6.00
❑ 216 Samite Healer C :W:	1.50	3.00
❑ 217 Savannah Lions R :W:	40.00	75.00
❑ 218 Savannah R :L:	90.00	180.00
❑ 219 Scathe Zombies C :K:	1.50	3.00
❑ 220 Scavenging Ghoul U :K:	3.00	6.00
❑ 221 Scrubland R :L:	100.00	200.00
❑ 222 Scryb Sprites C :G:	2.00	4.00
❑ 223 Sea Serpent C :B:	1.50	3.00
❑ 224 Sedge Troll R :R:	18.00	35.00
❑ 225 Sengir Vampire U :K:	18.00	35.00
❑ 226 Serra Angel U :W:	40.00	80.00
❑ 227 Shanodin Dryads C :G:	1.50	3.00
❑ 228 Shatter C :R:	2.00	4.00
❑ 229 Shivan Dragon R :R:	125.00	250.00
❑ 230 Simulacrum U :K:	3.00	6.00
❑ 231 Sinkhole C :K:	22.00	45.00
❑ 232 Siren's Call U :B:	3.00	6.00
❑ 233 Sleight of Mind R :B:	12.00	25.00
❑ 234 Smoke R :R:	11.00	22.00
❑ 235 Sol Ring U :A:	50.00	100.00
❑ 236 Soul Net U :A:	3.00	6.00
❑ 237 Spell Blast C :B:	2.50	5.00
❑ 238 Stasis R :B:	30.00	60.00
❑ 239 Steal Artifact U :B:	3.50	7.00
❑ 240 Stone Giant U :R:	3.00	6.00
❑ 241 Stone Rain C :R:	3.00	6.00
❑ 242 Stream of Life C :G:	1.50	3.00
❑ 243 Sunglasses of Urza R :A:	11.00	22.00
❑ 244 Swamp v1 C :L:	2.00	4.00
❑ 245 Swamp v2 C :L:	2.00	4.00
❑ 246 Swords to Plowshares U :W:	15.00	30.00
❑ 247 Taiga R :L:	110.00	225.00
❑ 248 Terror C :K:	3.00	6.00
❑ 249 Thicket Basilisk U :G:	3.00	6.00
❑ 250 Thoughtlace R :B:	11.00	22.00
❑ 251 Throne of Bone U :A:	3.00	6.00
❑ 252 Timber Wolves R :G:	11.00	22.00
❑ 253 Time Vault R :A:	80.00	160.00
❑ 254 Time Walk R :B:	450.00	900.00
❑ 255 Timetwister R :B:	300.00	600.00
❑ 256 Tranquility C :G:	2.00	4.00
❑ 257 Tropical Island R :L:	150.00	300.00
❑ 258 Tsunami U :G:	4.00	8.00
❑ 259 Tundra R :L:	125.00	250.00
❑ 260 Tunnel U :R:	3.00	6.00
❑ 261 Twiddle C :B:	2.00	4.00
❑ 262 Two-Headed Giant of Foriys R :R:	28.00	55.00
❑ 263 Underground Sea R :L:	200.00	400.00
❑ 264 Unholy Strength C :K:	3.00	6.00
❑ 265 Unsummon C :B:	3.00	6.00
❑ 266 Uthden Troll U :R:	3.00	6.00
❑ 267 Verduran Enchantress R :G:	22.00	45.00
❑ 268 Vesuvan Doppelganger R :B:	90.00	175.00
❑ 269 Veteran Bodyguard R :W:	12.00	25.00
❑ 270 Volcanic Eruption R :B:	11.00	22.00
❑ 271 Wall of Air U :B:	3.00	6.00
❑ 272 Wall of Bone U :K:	3.00	6.00
❑ 273 Wall of Brambles U :G:	3.00	6.00
❑ 274 Wall of Fire U :R:	3.00	6.00
❑ 275 Wall of Ice U :G:	3.00	6.00
❑ 276 Wall of Stone U :R:	3.50	7.00
❑ 277 Wall of Swords U :W:	3.00	6.00
❑ 278 Wall of Water U :B:	3.00	6.00
❑ 279 Wall of Wood C :G:	1.50	3.00
❑ 280 Wanderlust U :G:	3.00	6.00
❑ 281 War Mammoth C :G:	2.00	4.00
❑ 282 Warp Artifact R :K:	12.00	25.00
❑ 283 Water Elemental U :B:	3.00	6.00
❑ 284 Weakness C :K:	2.00	4.00
❑ 285 Web R :G:	11.00	22.00
❑ 286 Wheel of Fortune R :R:	90.00	175.00
❑ 287 White Knight U :W:	10.00	20.00
❑ 288 White Ward U :W:	3.00	6.00
❑ 289 Wild Growth C :G:	2.00	4.00
❑ 290 Will-O'-The-Wisp R :K:	30.00	60.00
❑ 291 Winter Orb R :A:	45.00	85.00
❑ 292 Wooden Sphere U :A:	2.00	4.00
❑ 293 Word of Command R :K:	45.00	90.00
❑ 294 Wrath of God R :W:	100.00	200.00
❑ 295 Zombie Master R :K:	18.00	35.00

1993 Magic the Gathering Beta

Complete Set (302)	10000.00	15000.00
Starter Deck Box (10 Decks)	12000.00	15000.00
Starter Deck	900.00	1500.00
Booster Box (36 Packs)	15000.00	18000.00
Booster Pack (15 Cards)	375.00	550.00

Released in October 1993
Black borders and no copyright date.
Name of illustrator at the bottom.

❑ 1 Air Elemental U :B:	6.00	12.00
❑ 2 Ancestral Recall R :B:	600.00	1200.00
❑ 3 Animate Artifact U :B:	2.00	4.00
❑ 4 Animate Dead U :K:	10.00	20.00
❑ 5 Animate Wall R :W:	7.50	15.00
❑ 6 Ankh of Mishra R :A:	25.00	50.00
❑ 7 Armageddon R :W:	45.00	90.00
❑ 8 Aspect of Wolf R :G:	9.00	18.00
❑ 9 Bad Moon R :K:	30.00	60.00
❑ 10 Badlands R :L:	300.00	600.00
❑ 11 Balance R :W:	75.00	150.00
❑ 12 Basalt Monolith U :A:	5.00	10.00
❑ 13 Bayou R :L:	350.00	700.00
❑ 14 Benalish Hero C :W:	1.50	3.00
❑ 15 Berserk U :G:	60.00	125.00
❑ 16 Birds of Paradise R :G:	120.00	225.00
❑ 17 Black Knight U :K:	9.00	18.00
❑ 18 Black Lotus R :A:	1200.00	2500.00
❑ 19 Black Vise U :A:	10.00	20.00
❑ 20 Black Ward U :W:	2.00	4.00
❑ 21 Blaze of Glory R :W:	20.00	40.00
❑ 22 Blessing R :W:	9.00	18.00
❑ 23 Blue Elemental Blast C :B:	3.00	6.00
❑ 24 Blue Ward U :W:	3.00	6.00
❑ 25 Bog Wraith U :K:	3.00	6.00
❑ 26 Braingeyser R :B:	45.00	90.00
❑ 27 Burrowing U :R:	3.00	6.00
❑ 28 Camouflage U :G:	4.00	8.00
❑ 29 Castle U :W:	4.00	8.00
❑ 30 Celestial Prism U :A:	2.50	5.00
❑ 31 Channel U :G:	6.00	12.00
❑ 32 Chaos Orb R :A:	65.00	130.00
❑ 33 Chaoslace R :R:	7.50	15.00
❑ 34 Circle of Protection Black C :W:	2.00	4.00
❑ 35 Circle of Protection Blue C :W:	2.00	4.00
❑ 36 Circle of Protection Green C :W:	2.00	4.00
❑ 37 Circle of Protection Red C :W:	2.00	4.00
❑ 38 Circle of Protection White C :W:	2.00	4.00
❑ 39 Clockwork Beast R :A:	9.00	18.00
❑ 40 Clone U :B:	10.00	20.00
❑ 41 Cockatrice R :G:	12.00	25.00
❑ 42 Consecrate Land U :W:	7.50	15.00
❑ 43 Conservator U :A:	3.00	6.00
❑ 44 Contract from Below R :K:	20.00	40.00
❑ 45 Control Magic U :B:	8.00	16.00
❑ 46 Conversion U :W:	3.00	6.00
❑ 47 Copper Tablet U :A:	5.00	10.00
❑ 48 Copy Artifact R :B:	30.00	60.00
❑ 49 Counterspell U :B:	20.00	40.00
❑ 50 Craw Wurm C :G:	1.50	3.00
❑ 51 Creature Bond C :B:	1.50	3.00
❑ 52 Crusade R :W:	28.00	55.00
❑ 53 Crystal Rod U :A:	3.00	6.00
❑ 54 Cursed Land U :K:	3.00	6.00
❑ 55 Cyclopean Tomb R :A:	40.00	75.00
❑ 56 Dark Ritual C :K:	10.00	20.00
❑ 57 Darkpact R :K:	9.00	18.00
❑ 58 Death Ward C :W:	2.50	5.00
❑ 59 Deathgrip U :K:	3.00	6.00
❑ 60 Deathlace R :K:	9.00	18.00
❑ 61 Demonic Attorney R :K:	9.00	18.00
❑ 62 Demonic Hordes R :K:	30.00	60.00
❑ 63 Demonic Tutor U :K:	45.00	90.00
❑ 64 Dingus Egg R :A:	10.00	20.00
❑ 65 Disenchant C :W:	7.50	15.00
❑ 66 Disintegrate C :R:	2.50	5.00
❑ 67 Disrupting Scepter R :A:	20.00	40.00
❑ 68 Dragon Whelp U :R:	9.00	18.00
❑ 69 Drain Life C :K:	3.00	6.00
❑ 70 Drain Power R :B:	11.00	22.00
❑ 71 Drudge Skeletons C :K:	1.50	3.00
❑ 72 Dwarven Demolition Team U :R:	5.00	10.00
❑ 73 Dwarven Warriors C :R:	1.50	3.00
❑ 74 Earth Elemental U :R:	3.00	6.00
❑ 75 Earthbind C :R:	1.50	3.00
❑ 76 Earthquake R :R:	20.00	40.00
❑ 77 Elvish Archers R :G:	22.00	45.00
❑ 78 Evil Presence U :K:	3.00	6.00
❑ 79 False Orders C :R:	2.50	5.00
❑ 80 Farmstead R :W:	9.00	18.00
❑ 81 Fastbond R :G:	45.00	90.00
❑ 82 Fear C :K:	1.50	3.00
❑ 83 Feedback U :B:	3.00	6.00
❑ 84 Fire Elemental U :R:	3.00	6.00
❑ 85 Fireball C :R:	4.00	8.00
❑ 86 Firebreathing C :R:	1.50	3.00
❑ 87 Flashfires U :R:	5.00	10.00
❑ 88 Flight C :B:	1.50	3.00
❑ 89 Fog C :G:	1.50	3.00
❑ 90 Force of Nature R :G:	40.00	75.00
❑ 91 Forcefield R :A:	50.00	100.00
❑ 92 Forest v1 C :L:	1.50	3.00
❑ 93 Forest v2 C :L:	1.50	3.00
❑ 94 Forest v3 C :L:	1.50	3.00
❑ 95 Fork R :R:	75.00	150.00
❑ 96 Frozen Shade C :K:	1.50	3.00
❑ 97 Fungusaur R :G:	9.00	18.00
❑ 98 Gaea's Liege R :G:	10.00	20.00
❑ 99 Gauntlet of Might R :A:	70.00	140.00
❑ 100 Giant Growth C :G:	4.00	8.00
❑ 101 Giant Spider C :G:	1.50	3.00
❑ 102 Glasses of Urza U :A:	3.00	6.00
❑ 103 Gloom U :K:	3.00	6.00
❑ 104 Goblin Balloon Brigade U :R:	4.00	8.00
❑ 105 Goblin King R :R:	25.00	50.00
❑ 106 Granite Gargoyle R :R:	15.00	30.00
❑ 107 Gray Ogre C :R:	1.50	3.00
❑ 108 Green Ward U :W:	3.00	6.00
❑ 109 Grizzly Bears C :G:	2.00	4.00
❑ 110 Guardian Angel C :W:	1.50	3.00
❑ 111 Healing Salve C :W:	1.50	3.00
❑ 112 Helm of Chatzuk R :A:	7.50	15.00
❑ 113 Hill Giant C :R:	1.50	3.00
❑ 114 Hive, The R :A:	9.00	18.00
❑ 115 Holy Armor C :W:	1.50	3.00
❑ 116 Holy Strength C :W:	1.50	3.00
❑ 117 Howl from Beyond C :K:	1.50	3.00
❑ 118 Howling Mine R :A:	45.00	90.00
❑ 119 Hurloon Minotaur C :R:	1.50	3.00
❑ 120 Hurricane U :G:	5.00	10.00
❑ 121 Hypnotic Specter U :K:	40.00	75.00

MAGIC

Card	Low	High
❑ 122 Ice Storm U :G:	20.00	40.00
❑ 123 Icy Manipulator U :A:	28.00	55.00
❑ 124 Illusionary Mask R :A:	80.00	175.00
❑ 125 Instill Energy U :G:	4.00	8.00
❑ 126 Invisibility C :B:	1.50	3.00
❑ 127 Iron Star U :A:	3.00	6.00
❑ 128 Ironclaw Orcs C :R:	1.50	3.00
❑ 129 Ironroot Treefolk C :G:	1.50	3.00
❑ 130 Island Sanctuary R :W:	10.00	20.00
❑ 131 Island v1 C :L:	1.50	3.00
❑ 132 Island v2 C :L:	1.50	3.00
❑ 133 Island v3 C :L:	1.50	3.00
❑ 134 Ivory Cup U :A:	3.00	6.00
❑ 135 Jade Monolith R :A:	9.00	18.00
❑ 136 Jade Statue U :A:	10.00	20.00
❑ 137 Jayemdae Tome R :A:	20.00	40.00
❑ 138 Juggernaut U :A:	12.00	25.00
❑ 139 Jump C :B:	1.50	3.00
❑ 140 Karma U :W:	4.00	8.00
❑ 141 Keldon Warlord U :R:	4.00	8.00
❑ 142 Kormus Bell R :A:	9.00	18.00
❑ 143 Kudzu R :G:	9.00	18.00
❑ 144 Lance U :W:	3.00	6.00
❑ 145 Ley Druid U :G:	3.00	6.00
❑ 146 Library of Leng U :A:	3.00	6.00
❑ 147 Lich R :K:	40.00	75.00
❑ 148 Lifeforce U :G:	3.00	6.00
❑ 149 Lifelace R :G:	7.50	15.00
❑ 150 Lifetap U :B:	3.00	6.00
❑ 151 Lightning Bolt C :R:	10.00	20.00
❑ 152 Living Artifact R :G:	9.00	18.00
❑ 153 Living Lands R :G:	9.00	18.00
❑ 154 Living Wall U :A:	2.50	5.00
❑ 155 Llanowar Elves C :G:	10.00	20.00
❑ 156 Lord of Atlantis R :B:	25.00	50.00
❑ 157 Lord of the Pit R :K:	35.00	70.00
❑ 158 Lure U :G:	3.00	6.00
❑ 159 Magical Hack R :B:	10.00	20.00
❑ 160 Mahamoti Djinn R :B:	30.00	60.00
❑ 161 Mana Flare R :R:	40.00	75.00
❑ 162 Mana Short R :B:	25.00	50.00
❑ 163 Mana Vault R :A:	60.00	120.00
❑ 164 Manabarbs R :R:	9.00	18.00
❑ 165 Meekstone R :A:	20.00	40.00
❑ 166 Merfolk of the Pearl Trident C :B:	1.50	3.00
❑ 167 Mesa Pegasus C :W:	1.50	3.00
❑ 168 Mind Twist R :K:	65.00	130.00
❑ 169 Mons's Goblin Raiders C :R:	1.50	3.00
❑ 170 Mountain v1 C :L:	1.50	3.00
❑ 171 Mountain v2 C :L:	1.50	3.00
❑ 172 Mountain v3 C :L:	1.50	3.00
❑ 173 Mox Emerald R :A:	450.00	900.00
❑ 174 Mox Jet R :A:	600.00	1200.00
❑ 175 Mox Pearl R :A:	450.00	900.00
❑ 176 Mox Ruby R :A:	450.00	900.00
❑ 177 Mox Sapphire R :A:	750.00	1250.00
❑ 178 Natural Selection R :G:	25.00	50.00
❑ 179 Nether Shadow R :K:	18.00	35.00
❑ 180 Nettling Imp U :K:	3.00	6.00
❑ 181 Nevinyrral's Disk R :A:	75.00	150.00
❑ 182 Nightmare R :K:	30.00	60.00
❑ 183 Northern Paladin R :W:	18.00	35.00
❑ 184 Obsianus Golem U :A:	3.00	6.00
❑ 185 Orcish Artillery U :R:	4.00	8.00
❑ 186 Orcish Oriflamme U :R:	4.00	8.00
❑ 187 Paralyze C :K:	1.50	3.00
❑ 188 Pearled Unicorn C :W:	1.50	3.00
❑ 189 Personal Incarnation R :W:	9.00	18.00
❑ 190 Pestilence C :K:	2.50	5.00
❑ 191 Phantasmal Forces U :B:	3.00	6.00
❑ 192 Phantasmal Terrain C :B:	1.50	3.00
❑ 193 Phantom Monster U :B:	3.00	6.00
❑ 194 Pirate Ship R :B:	9.00	18.00
❑ 195 Plague Rats C :K:	2.50	5.00
❑ 196 Plains v1 C :L:	1.50	3.00
❑ 197 Plains v2 C :L:	1.50	3.00
❑ 198 Plains v3 C :L:	1.50	3.00
❑ 199 Plateau R :L:	350.00	700.00
❑ 200 Power Leak C :B:	1.50	3.00
❑ 201 Power Sink C :B:	2.00	4.00
❑ 202 Power Surge R :R:	9.00	18.00
❑ 203 Prodigal Sorcerer C :B:	2.50	5.00
❑ 204 Psionic Blast U :B:	20.00	40.00
❑ 205 Psychic Venom C :B:	1.50	3.00
❑ 206 Purelace R :W:	6.00	12.00
❑ 207 Raging River R :R:	20.00	40.00
❑ 208 Raise Dead C :K:	1.50	3.00
❑ 209 Red Elemental Blast C :R:	5.00	10.00
❑ 210 Red Ward U :W:	3.00	6.00
❑ 211 Regeneration C :G:	1.50	3.00
❑ 212 Regrowth U :G:	20.00	40.00
❑ 213 Resurrection U :W:	3.00	6.00
❑ 214 Reverse Damage R :W:	10.00	20.00
❑ 215 Righteousness R :W:	10.00	20.00
❑ 216 Roc of Kher Ridges R :R:	10.00	20.00
❑ 217 Rock Hydra R :R:	15.00	30.00
❑ 218 Rod of Ruin U :A:	3.00	6.00
❑ 219 Royal Assassin R :K:	50.00	100.00
❑ 220 Sacrifice U :K:	3.00	6.00
❑ 221 Samite Healer C :W:	1.50	3.00
❑ 222 Savannah Lions R :W:	40.00	75.00
❑ 223 Savannah R :L:	350.00	700.00
❑ 224 Scathe Zombies C :K:	1.50	3.00
❑ 225 Scavenging Ghoul U :K:	3.00	6.00
❑ 226 Scrubland R :L:	300.00	600.00
❑ 227 Scryb Sprites C :G:	1.50	3.00
❑ 228 Sea Serpent C :B:	1.50	3.00
❑ 229 Sedge Troll R :R:	18.00	35.00
❑ 230 Sengir Vampire U :K:	15.00	30.00
❑ 231 Serra Angel U :W:	40.00	75.00
❑ 232 Shanodin Dryads C :G:	1.50	3.00
❑ 233 Shatter C :R:	1.50	3.00
❑ 234 Shivan Dragon R :R:	100.00	175.00
❑ 235 Simulacrum U :K:	3.00	6.00
❑ 236 Sinkhole C :K:	15.00	30.00
❑ 237 Siren's Call U :B:	3.00	6.00
❑ 238 Sleight of Mind R :B:	9.00	18.00
❑ 239 Smoke R :R:	9.00	18.00
❑ 240 Sol Ring U :A:	54.00	90.00
❑ 241 Soul Net U :A:	3.00	6.00
❑ 242 Spell Blast C :B:	2.00	4.00
❑ 243 Stasis R :B:	25.00	50.00
❑ 244 Steal Artifact U :B:	3.00	6.00
❑ 245 Stone Giant U :R:	3.00	6.00
❑ 246 Stone Rain C :R:	3.00	6.00
❑ 247 Stream of Life C :G:	1.50	3.00
❑ 248 Sunglasses of Urza R :A:	9.00	18.00
❑ 249 Swamp v1 C :L:	1.50	3.00
❑ 250 Swamp v2 C :L:	1.50	3.00
❑ 251 Swamp v3 C :L:	1.50	3.00
❑ 252 Swords to Plowshares U :W:	12.00	25.00
❑ 253 Taiga R :L:	300.00	600.00
❑ 254 Terror C :K:	2.50	5.00
❑ 255 Thicket Basilisk U :G:	3.00	6.00
❑ 256 Thoughtlace R :B:	9.00	18.00
❑ 257 Throne of Bone U :A:	3.00	6.00
❑ 258 Timber Wolves R :G:	7.50	15.00
❑ 259 Time Vault R :A:	300.00	600.00
❑ 260 Time Walk R :B:	500.00	1000.00
❑ 261 Timetwister R :B:	250.00	500.00
❑ 262 Tranquility C :G:	1.50	3.00
❑ 263 Tropical Island R :L:	700.00	1400.00
❑ 264 Tsunami U :G:	3.00	6.00
❑ 265 Tundra R :L:	700.00	1400.00
❑ 266 Tunnel U :R:	3.00	6.00
❑ 267 Twiddle C :B:	2.00	4.00
❑ 268 Two-Headed Giant of Foriys R :R:	25.00	50.00
❑ 269 Underground Sea R :L:	500.00	1000.00
❑ 270 Unholy Strength C :K:	2.50	5.00
❑ 271 Unsummon C :B:	2.50	5.00
❑ 272 Uthden Troll U :R:	3.00	6.00
❑ 273 Verduran Enchantress R :G:	20.00	40.00
❑ 274 Vesuvan Doppelganger R :B:	75.00	150.00
❑ 275 Veteran Bodyguard R :W:	9.00	18.00
❑ 276 Volcanic Eruption R :B:	7.50	15.00
❑ 277 Volcanic Island R :L:	600.00	1200.00
❑ 278 Wall of Air U :B:	3.00	6.00
❑ 279 Wall of Bone U :K:	3.00	6.00
❑ 280 Wall of Brambles U :G:	3.00	6.00
❑ 281 Wall of Fire U :R:	3.00	6.00
❑ 282 Wall of Ice U :G:	3.00	6.00
❑ 283 Wall of Stone U :R:	3.00	6.00
❑ 284 Wall of Swords U :W:	3.00	6.00
❑ 285 Wall of Water U :B:	3.00	6.00
❑ 286 Wall of Wood C :G:	1.50	3.00
❑ 287 Wanderlust U :G:	3.00	6.00
❑ 288 War Mammoth C :G:	1.50	3.00
❑ 289 Warp Artifact R :K:	7.50	15.00
❑ 290 Water Elemental U :B:	3.00	6.00
❑ 291 Weakness C :K:	1.50	3.00
❑ 292 Web R :G:	7.50	15.00
❑ 293 Wheel of Fortune R :R:	75.00	150.00
❑ 294 White Knight U :W:	9.00	18.00
❑ 295 White Ward U :W:	3.00	6.00
❑ 296 Wild Growth C :G:	2.00	4.00
❑ 297 Will-O'-The-Wisp R :K:	28.00	55.00
❑ 298 Winter Orb R :A:	40.00	75.00
❑ 299 Wooden Sphere U :A:	3.00	6.00
❑ 300 Word of Command R :K:	35.00	70.00
❑ 301 Wrath of God R :W:	80.00	175.00
❑ 302 Zombie Master R :K:	18.00	35.00

1993 Magic the Gathering Unlimited

Item	Low	High
Complete Set (302)	5000.00	7000.00
Starter Deck Box (10 Decks)	4000.00	5500.00
Starter Deck (60 Cards)	500.00	650.00
Booster Box (36 Packs)	5400.00	7500.00
Booster Pack (15 Cards)	150.00	250.00

Released in December 1993
White borders and no copyright date.
Name of illustrator at the bottom.

Card	Low	High
❑ 1 Air Elemental U :B:	1.00	2.00
❑ 2 Ancestral Recall R :B:	350.00	675.00
❑ 3 Animate Artifact U :B:	1.00	2.00
❑ 4 Animate Dead U :K:	4.00	8.00
❑ 5 Animate Wall R :W:	2.50	5.00
❑ 6 Ankh of Mishra R :A:	4.00	8.00
❑ 7 Armageddon R :W:	7.50	15.00
❑ 8 Aspect of Wolf R :G:	3.00	6.00
❑ 9 Bad Moon R :K:	10.00	20.00
❑ 10 Badlands R :L:	35.00	70.00
❑ 11 Balance R :W:	6.00	12.00
❑ 12 Basalt Monolith U :A:	1.00	2.00
❑ 13 Bayou R :L:	50.00	100.00
❑ 14 Benalish Hero C :W:	.25	.50
❑ 15 Berserk U :G:	30.00	60.00
❑ 16 Birds of Paradise R :G:	20.00	40.00
❑ 17 Black Knight U :K:	3.00	6.00
❑ 18 Black Lotus R :A:	750.00	1400.00
❑ 19 Black Vise U :A:	3.00	6.00
❑ 20 Black Ward U :W:	.50	1.00
❑ 21 Blaze of Glory R :W:	10.00	20.00
❑ 22 Blessing R :W:	2.50	5.00
❑ 23 Blue Elemental Blast C :B:	1.00	2.00
❑ 24 Blue Ward U :W:	.50	1.00
❑ 25 Bog Wraith U :K:	.75	1.50
❑ 26 Braingeyser R :B:	7.50	15.00
❑ 27 Burrowing U :R:	.50	1.00
❑ 28 Camouflage U :G:	2.00	4.00
❑ 29 Castle U :W:	1.00	2.00
❑ 30 Celestial Prism U :A:	1.00	2.00
❑ 31 Channel U :G:	2.00	4.00
❑ 32 Chaos Orb R :A:	30.00	60.00
❑ 33 Chaoslace R :R:	2.50	5.00
❑ 34 Circle of Protection: Black C :W:	.25	.50
❑ 35 Circle of Protection: Blue C :W:	.25	.50
❑ 36 Circle of Protection: Green C :W:	.25	.50
❑ 37 Circle of Protection: Red C :W:	.25	.50
❑ 38 Circle of Protection: White C :W:	.25	.50
❑ 39 Clockwork Beast R :A:	2.50	5.00
❑ 40 Clone U :B:	3.50	7.00
❑ 41 Cockatrice R :G:	3.50	7.00
❑ 42 Consecrate Land U :W:	2.00	4.00
❑ 43 Conservator U :A:	.50	1.00
❑ 44 Contract from Below R :K:	4.00	8.00
❑ 45 Control Magic U :B:	3.00	6.00
❑ 46 Conversion U :W:	.50	1.00
❑ 47 Copper Tablet U :A:	2.50	5.00
❑ 48 Copy Artifact R :B:	6.00	12.00
❑ 49 Counterspell U :B:	4.00	8.00
❑ 50 Craw Wurm C :G:	.50	1.00
❑ 51 Creature Bond C :B:	.25	.50
❑ 52 Crusade R :W:	7.50	15.00
❑ 53 Crystal Rod U :A:	.50	1.00
❑ 54 Cursed Land U :K:	.50	1.00
❑ 55 Cyclopean Tomb R :A:	12.00	25.00
❑ 56 Dark Ritual C :K:	2.00	4.00
❑ 57 Darkpact R :K:	1.50	3.00
❑ 58 Death Ward C :W:	.25	.50
❑ 59 Deathgrip U :K:	1.00	2.00
❑ 60 Deathlace R :K:	2.50	5.00
❑ 61 Demonic Attorney R :K:	2.50	5.00
❑ 62 Demonic Hordes R :K:	9.00	18.00
❑ 63 Demonic Tutor U :K:	10.00	20.00
❑ 64 Dingus Egg R :A:	2.50	5.00
❑ 65 Disenchant C :W:	1.00	2.00
❑ 66 Disintegrate C :R:	.50	1.00
❑ 67 Disrupting Scepter R :A:	3.00	6.00
❑ 68 Dragon Whelp U :R:	1.50	3.00
❑ 69 Drain Life C :K:	.50	1.00
❑ 70 Drain Power R :B:	4.00	8.00
❑ 71 Drudge Skeletons C :K:	.25	.50
❑ 72 Dwarven Demolition Team U :R:	1.00	2.00
❑ 73 Dwarven Warriors C :R:	.25	.50
❑ 74 Earth Elemental U :R:	.50	1.00
❑ 75 Earthbind C :R:	.50	1.00
❑ 76 Earthquake R :R:	5.00	10.00
❑ 77 Elvish Archers R :G:	5.00	10.00
❑ 78 Evil Presence U :K:	1.00	2.00
❑ 79 False Orders C :R:	.25	.50
❑ 80 Farmstead R :W:	1.50	3.00
❑ 81 Fastbond R :G:	7.50	15.00
❑ 82 Fear C :K:	.25	.50
❑ 83 Feedback U :B:	.50	1.00
❑ 84 Fire Elemental U :R:	1.00	2.00
❑ 85 Fireball C :R:	1.00	2.00
❑ 86 Firebreathing C :R:	.30	.75
❑ 87 Flashfires U :R:	1.00	2.00
❑ 88 Flight C :B:	.25	.50
❑ 89 Fog C :G:	.25	.50
❑ 90 Force of Nature R :G:	6.00	12.00
❑ 91 Forcefield R :A:	60.00	120.00
❑ 92 Forest v1 C :L:	.25	.50
❑ 93 Forest v2 C :L:	.25	.50
❑ 94 Forest v3 C :L:	.25	.50
❑ 95 Fork R :R:	18.00	35.00
❑ 96 Frozen Shade C :K:	1.00	2.00
❑ 97 Fungusaur R :G:	2.50	5.00
❑ 98 Gaea's Liege R :G:	4.00	8.00
❑ 99 Gauntlet of Might R :A:	60.00	120.00
❑ 100 Giant Growth C :G:	1.00	2.00
❑ 101 Giant Spider C :G:	.25	.50
❑ 102 Glasses of Urza U :A:	1.00	2.00
❑ 103 Gloom U :K:	.50	1.00
❑ 104 Goblin Balloon Brigade U :R:	.50	1.00
❑ 105 Goblin King R :R:	6.00	12.00
❑ 106 Granite Gargoyle R :R:	4.00	8.00
❑ 107 Gray Ogre C :R:	.25	.50
❑ 108 Green Ward U :W:	.50	1.00
❑ 109 Grizzly Bears C :G:	.25	.50
❑ 110 Guardian Angel C :W:	.25	.50
❑ 111 Healing Salve C :W:	.25	.50
❑ 112 Helm of Chatzuk R :A:	2.50	5.00
❑ 113 Hill Giant C :R:	.25	.50
❑ 114 Hive, The R :A:	2.50	5.00
❑ 115 Holy Armor C :W:	.25	.50
❑ 116 Holy Strength C :W:	.25	.50
❑ 117 Howl from Beyond C :K:	.25	.50
❑ 118 Howling Mine R :A:	10.00	20.00
❑ 119 Hurloon Minotaur C :R:	.25	.50
❑ 120 Hurricane U :G:	1.00	2.00
❑ 121 Hypnotic Specter U :K:	10.00	20.00
❑ 122 Ice Storm U :G:	12.00	25.00
❑ 123 Icy Manipulator U :A:	15.00	30.00
❑ 124 Illusionary Mask R :A:	50.00	100.00
❑ 125 Instill Energy U :G:	1.50	3.00
❑ 126 Invisibility C :B:	.50	1.00
❑ 127 Iron Star U :A:	.50	1.00
❑ 128 Ironclaw Orcs C :R:	.25	.50
❑ 129 Ironroot Treefolk C :G:	.25	.50
❑ 130 Island Sanctuary R :W:	3.00	6.00
❑ 131 Island v1 C :L:	.50	1.00
❑ 132 Island v2 C :L:	.50	1.00
❑ 133 Island v3 C :L:	.50	1.00
❑ 134 Ivory Cup U :A:	.50	1.00
❑ 135 Jade Monolith R :A:	2.50	5.00
❑ 136 Jade Statue U :A:	6.00	12.00
❑ 137 Jayemdae Tome R :A:	3.00	6.00
❑ 138 Juggernaut U :A:	3.50	7.00
❑ 139 Jump C :B:	.25	.50
❑ 140 Karma U :W:	2.00	4.00
❑ 141 Keldon Warlord U :R:	1.50	3.00
❑ 142 Kormus Bell R :A:	2.50	5.00
❑ 143 Kudzu R :G:	2.50	5.00
❑ 144 Lance U :W:	.50	1.00
❑ 145 Ley Druid U :G:	.50	1.00
❑ 146 Library of Leng U :A:	1.00	2.00
❑ 147 Lich R :K:	20.00	40.00
❑ 148 Lifeforce U :G:	.50	1.00
❑ 149 Lifelace R :G:	2.00	4.00
❑ 150 Lifetap U :B:	.50	1.00
❑ 151 Lightning Bolt C :R:	4.00	8.00
❑ 152 Living Artifact R :G:	2.50	5.00
❑ 153 Living Lands R :G:	2.50	5.00
❑ 154 Living Wall U :A:	1.50	3.00
❑ 155 Llanowar Elves C :G:	2.00	4.00
❑ 156 Lord of Atlantis R :B:	4.00	8.00
❑ 157 Lord of the Pit R :K:	5.00	10.00
❑ 158 Lure U :G:	2.00	4.00
❑ 159 Magical Hack R :B:	3.00	6.00
❑ 160 Mahamoti Djinn R :B:	7.50	15.00
❑ 161 Mana Flare R :R:	7.50	15.00
❑ 162 Mana Short R :B:	5.00	10.00
❑ 163 Mana Vault R :A:	6.00	12.00
❑ 164 Manabarbs R :R:	2.50	5.00
❑ 165 Meekstone R :A:	6.00	12.00
❑ 166 Merfolk of the Pearl Trident C :B:	.25	.50
❑ 167 Mesa Pegasus C :W:	.25	.50
❑ 168 Mind Twist R :K:	10.00	20.00
❑ 169 Mons's Goblin Raiders C :R:	.25	.50
❑ 170 Mountain v1 C :L:	.25	.50
❑ 171 Mountain v2 C :L:	.25	.50
❑ 172 Mountain v3 C :L:	.25	.50
❑ 173 Mox Emerald R :A:	300.00	600.00
❑ 174 Mox Jet R :A:	350.00	650.00
❑ 175 Mox Pearl R :A:	250.00	500.00
❑ 176 Mox Ruby R :A:	300.00	600.00
❑ 177 Mox Sapphire R :A:	400.00	800.00
❑ 178 Natural Selection R :G:	10.00	20.00
❑ 179 Nether Shadow R :K:	3.50	7.00
❑ 180 Nettling Imp U :K:	1.00	2.00
❑ 181 Nevinyrral's Disk R :A:	10.00	20.00
❑ 182 Nightmare R :K:	9.00	18.00
❑ 183 Northern Paladin R :W:	7.50	15.00
❑ 184 Obsianus Golem U :A:	1.00	2.00
❑ 185 Orcish Artillery U :R:	.50	1.00
❑ 186 Orcish Oriflamme U :R:	1.00	2.00
❑ 187 Paralyze C :K:	.25	.50
❑ 188 Pearled Unicorn C :W:	.25	.50
❑ 189 Personal Incarnation R :W:	2.50	5.00
❑ 190 Pestilence C :K:	.25	.50
❑ 191 Phantasmal Forces U :B:	1.00	2.00
❑ 192 Phantasmal Terrain C :B:	.50	1.00
❑ 193 Phantom Monster U :B:	.50	1.00
❑ 194 Pirate Ship R :B:	2.00	4.00
❑ 195 Plague Rats C :K:	.25	.50
❑ 196 Plains v1 C :L:	.25	.50
❑ 197 Plains v2 C :L:	.25	.50
❑ 198 Plains v3 C :L:	.25	.50
❑ 199 Plateau R :L:	40.00	80.00
❑ 200 Power Leak C :B:	.25	.50
❑ 201 Power Sink C :B:	.25	.50
❑ 202 Power Surge R :R:	2.50	5.00
❑ 203 Prodigal Sorcerer C :B:	.50	1.00
❑ 204 Psionic Blast U :B:	12.00	25.00
❑ 205 Psychic Venom C :B:	.25	.50
❑ 206 Purelace R :W:	2.00	4.00
❑ 207 Raging River R :R:	10.00	20.00
❑ 208 Raise Dead C :K:	.25	.50
❑ 209 Red Elemental Blast C :R:	1.00	2.00
❑ 210 Red Ward U :W:	1.00	2.00
❑ 211 Regeneration C :G:	.25	.50
❑ 212 Regrowth U :G:	3.50	7.00
❑ 213 Resurrection U :W:	1.00	2.00
❑ 214 Reverse Damage R :W:	3.00	6.00
❑ 215 Righteousness R :W:	3.50	7.00
❑ 216 Roc of Kher Ridges R :R:	3.00	6.00
❑ 217 Rock Hydra R :R:	5.00	10.00
❑ 218 Rod of Ruin U :A:	.50	1.00
❑ 219 Royal Assassin R :K:	12.00	25.00
❑ 220 Sacrifice U :K:	.50	1.00
❑ 221 Samite Healer C :W:	.25	.50
❑ 222 Savannah Lions R :L:	10.00	20.00
❑ 223 Savannah R :W:	50.00	100.00
❑ 224 Scathe Zombies C :K:	.25	.50
❑ 225 Scavenging Ghoul U :K:	1.00	2.00
❑ 226 Scrubland R :L:	50.00	100.00
❑ 227 Scryb Sprites C :G:	.25	.50
❑ 228 Sea Serpent C :B:	.25	.50
❑ 229 Sedge Troll R :R:	3.50	7.00
❑ 230 Sengir Vampire U :K:	4.00	8.00
❑ 231 Serra Angel U :W:	7.50	15.00
❑ 232 Shanodin Dryads C :G:	.25	.50
❑ 233 Shatter C :R:	.25	.50
❑ 234 Shivan Dragon R :R:	18.00	35.00
❑ 235 Simulacrum U :K:	.50	1.00
❑ 236 Sinkhole C :K:	15.00	30.00
❑ 237 Siren's Call U :B:	.50	1.00
❑ 238 Sleight of Mind R :B:	4.00	8.00
❑ 239 Smoke R :R:	2.50	5.00
❑ 240 Sol Ring U :A:	12.00	25.00
❑ 241 Soul Net U :A:	1.00	2.00
❑ 242 Spell Blast C :B:	.25	.50
❑ 243 Stasis R :B:	5.00	10.00
❑ 244 Steal Artifact U :B:	.50	1.00
❑ 245 Stone Giant U :R:	.50	1.00
❑ 246 Stone Rain C :R:	1.00	2.00
❑ 247 Stream of Life C :G:	.25	.50
❑ 248 Sunglasses of Urza R :A:	2.00	4.00
❑ 249 Swamp v1 C :L:	.50	1.00
❑ 250 Swamp v2 C :L:	.50	1.00
❑ 251 Swamp v3 C :L:	.50	1.00
❑ 252 Swords to Plowshares U :W:	5.00	10.00
❑ 253 Taiga R :L:	40.00	80.00
❑ 254 Terror C :K:	.50	1.00
❑ 255 Thicket Basilisk U :G:	1.00	2.00
❑ 256 Thoughtlace R :B:	2.50	5.00
❑ 257 Throne of Bone U :A:	1.00	2.00
❑ 258 Timber Wolves R :G:	2.50	5.00
❑ 259 Time Vault R :A:	175.00	350.00
❑ 260 Time Walk R :B:	300.00	600.00
❑ 261 Timetwister R :B:	150.00	300.00
❑ 262 Tranquility C :G:	.25	.50
❑ 263 Tropical Island R :L:	75.00	150.00
❑ 264 Tsunami U :G:	1.00	2.00
❑ 265 Tundra R :L:	75.00	150.00
❑ 266 Tunnel U :R:	.50	1.00
❑ 267 Twiddle C :B:	.25	.50
❑ 268 Two-Headed Giant of Foriys R :R:	15.00	30.00
❑ 269 Underground Sea R :L:	100.00	200.00
❑ 270 Unholy Strength C :K:	.50	1.00
❑ 271 Unsummon C :B:	.50	1.00
❑ 272 Uthden Troll U :R:	.50	1.00
❑ 273 Verduran Enchantress R :G:	3.50	7.00
❑ 274 Vesuvan Doppelganger R :B:	12.00	25.00
❑ 275 Veteran Bodyguard R :W:	3.00	6.00
❑ 276 Volcanic Eruption R :B:	3.00	6.00
❑ 277 Volcanic Island R :L:	75.00	150.00
❑ 278 Wall of Air U :B:	1.50	3.00
❑ 279 Wall of Bone U :K:	1.00	2.00
❑ 280 Wall of Brambles U :G:	.50	1.00
❑ 281 Wall of Fire U :R:	1.00	2.00
❑ 282 Wall of Ice U :G:	1.00	2.00
❑ 283 Wall of Stone U :R:	1.00	2.00
❑ 284 Wall of Swords U :W:	.50	1.00
❑ 285 Wall of Water U :B:	.50	1.00
❑ 286 Wall of Wood C :G:	.50	1.00
❑ 287 Wanderlust U :G:	.50	1.00
❑ 288 War Mammoth C :G:	.25	.50
❑ 289 Warp Artifact R :K:	2.50	5.00
❑ 290 Water Elemental U :B:	1.00	2.00
❑ 291 Weakness C :K:	.25	.50
❑ 292 Web R :G:	2.50	5.00
❑ 293 Wheel of Fortune R :R:	18.00	35.00
❑ 294 White Knight U :W:	3.00	6.00
❑ 295 White Ward U :W:	.50	1.00
❑ 296 Wild Growth C :G:	.25	.50
❑ 297 Will-O'-The-Wisp R :K:	7.50	15.00
❑ 298 Winter Orb R :A:	9.00	18.00
❑ 299 Wooden Sphere U :A:	1.00	2.00
❑ 300 Word of Command R :K:	25.00	50.00
❑ 301 Wrath of God R :W:	10.00	20.00
❑ 302 Zombie Master R :K:	5.00	10.00

1993 Magic the Gathering Arabian Nights

Item	Low	High
Complete Set (92)	900.00	1500.00
Booster Box (60 Packs)	8000.00	10000.00
Booster Pack (8 Cards)	140.00	235.00

With variations there are 92 cards.
Released in December 1993

Card	Low	High
❑ 1 Abu Jafar U3 :W:	4.00	8.00
❑ 2 Aladdin U2 :R:	6.00	12.00
❑ 3 Aladdin's Lamp U2 :A:	5.00	10.00
❑ 4 Aladdin's Ring U2 :A:	5.50	11.00
❑ 5 Ali Baba U3 :R:	3.00	6.00
❑ 6 Ali from Cairo U2 :R:	40.00	80.00
❑ 7 Army of Allah (dark 1) C3 :W:	2.50	5.00
❑ 8 Army of Allah (light 1) C1 :W:	5.00	10.00
❑ 9 Bazaar of Baghdad U3 :L:	175.00	350.00
❑ 10 Bird Maiden (dark 1) C2 :R:	1.00	2.00
❑ 11 Bird Maiden (light 1) C2 :R:	1.00	2.00
❑ 12 Bottle of Suleiman U2 :A:	5.00	10.00
❑ 13 Brass Man U3 :A:	2.50	5.00
❑ 14 Camel C5 :W:	1.00	2.00
❑ 15 City in a Bottle U2 :A:	7.50	15.00
❑ 16 City of Brass U3 :L:	30.00	60.00
❑ 17 Cuombajj Witches C4 :K:	1.00	2.00
❑ 18 Cyclone U3 :G:	2.50	5.00
❑ 19 Dancing Scimitar U2 :A:	4.00	8.00
❑ 20 Dandan C4 :B:	1.00	2.00
❑ 21 Desert C11 :L:	1.00	2.00
❑ 22 Desert Nomads C4 :R:	1.00	2.00
❑ 23 Desert Twister U3 :G:	3.00	6.00
❑ 24 Diamond Valley U2 :L:	75.00	150.00
❑ 25 Drop of Honey U2 :G:	25.00	50.00
❑ 26 Ebony Horse U2 :A:	4.00	8.00
❑ 27 Elephant Graveyard U2 :L:	18.00	35.00
❑ 28 El-Hajjaj U2 :K:	4.00	8.00
❑ 29 Erg Raiders (dark 1) C3 :K:	2.00	4.00
❑ 30 Erg Raiders (light 1) C2 :K:	2.00	4.00
❑ 31 Erhnam Djinn U2 :G:	20.00	40.00
❑ 32 Eye for an Eye U3 :W:	2.50	5.00
❑ 33 Fishliver Oil (dark 1) C3 :B:	1.00	2.00
❑ 34 Fishliver Oil (light 1) C1 :B:	4.00	8.00
❑ 35 Flying Carpet U3 :A:	2.50	5.00
❑ 36 Flying Men C5 :B:	3.50	7.00

MAGIC

Card	Low	High
❑ 37 Ghazban Ogre C4 :G:	1.00	2.00
❑ 38 Giant Tortoise (dark 1) C3 :B:	1.00	2.00
❑ 39 Giant Tortoise (light 1) C1 :B:	4.00	8.00
❑ 40 Guardian Beast U2 :K:	28.00	55.00
❑ 41 Hasran Ogress (dark mana) C3 :K:	1.00	2.00
❑ 42 Hasran Ogress (light mana) C2 :K:	1.00	2.00
❑ 43 Hurr Jackal C4 :R:	1.00	2.00
❑ 44 Ifh-Biff Efreet U2 :G:	15.00	30.00
❑ 45 Island Fish Jasconius U2 :B:	4.00	8.00
❑ 46 Island of Wak-Wak U2 :L:	20.00	40.00
❑ 47 Jandor's Ring U2 :A:	4.00	8.00
❑ 48 Jandor's Saddlebags U2 :A:	4.00	8.00
❑ 49 Jeweled Bird U3 :A:	3.00	6.00
❑ 50 Jihad U2 :W:	25.00	50.00
❑ 51 Junun Efreet U2 :K:	6.00	12.00
❑ 52 Juzam Djinn U2 :K:	110.00	225.00
❑ 53 Khabal Ghoul U3 :K:	15.00	30.00
❑ 54 King Suleiman U2 :W:	12.00	25.00
❑ 55 Kird Ape C5 :R:	2.50	5.00
❑ 56 Library of Alexandria U3 :L:	150.00	300.00
❑ 57 Magnetic Mountain U3 :R:	2.00	4.00
❑ 58 Merchant Ship U3 :B:	3.50	7.00
❑ 59 Metamorphosis C4 :G:	1.00	2.00
❑ 60 Mijae Djinn U2 :R:	4.00	8.00
❑ 61 Moorish Cavalry (dark 2) C4 :W:	1.00	2.00
❑ 62 Moorish Cavalry (light 2) C1 :W:	1.00	2.00
❑ 63 Mountain C1 :L:	9.00	18.00
❑ 64 Nafs Asp (dark 1) C3 :G:	1.00	2.00
❑ 65 Nafs Asp (light 1) C2 :G:	1.00	2.00
❑ 66 Oasis U4 :L:	2.50	5.00
❑ 67 Old Man of the Sea U2 :B:	30.00	60.00
❑ 68 Oubliette (dark 1) C2 :K:	2.50	5.00
❑ 69 Oubliette (light 1) C2 :K:	2.50	5.00
❑ 70 Piety (dark 1) C3 :W:	1.00	2.00
❑ 71 Piety (light 1) C1 :W:	4.00	8.00
❑ 72 Pyramids U2 :A:	10.00	20.00
❑ 73 Repentant Blacksmith U2 :W:	4.00	8.00
❑ 74 Ring of Maruf U2 :A:	20.00	40.00
❑ 75 Rukh Egg (dark 3) C3 :R:	4.00	8.00
❑ 76 Rukh Egg (light 3) C1 :R:	6.00	12.00
❑ 77 Sandals of Abdallah U3 :A:	3.00	6.00
❑ 78 Sandstorm C4 :G:	1.00	2.00
❑ 79 Serendib Djinn U2 :B:	15.00	30.00
❑ 80 Serendib Efreet U2 :B:	28.00	55.00
❑ 81 Shahrazad U2 :W:	35.00	70.00
❑ 82 Sindbad U3 :B:	2.00	4.00
❑ 83 Singing Tree U2 :G:	18.00	35.00
❑ 84 Sorceress Queen U3 :K:	7.50	15.00
❑ 85 Stone-Throwing Devils (dark mana) C3 :K:	3.00	6.00
❑ 86 Stone-Throwing Devils (light mana) C1 :K:	7.50	15.00
❑ 87 Unstable Mutation C5 :B:	1.00	2.00
❑ 88 War Elephant (dark 3) C3 :W:	1.00	2.00
❑ 89 War Elephant (light 3) C1 :W:	4.00	8.00
❑ 90 Wyluli Wolf (dark 1) C4 :G:	1.00	2.00
❑ 91 Wyluli Wolf (light 1) C1 :G:	6.00	12.00
❑ 92 Ydwen Efreet U2 :R:	7.50	15.00

1994 Magic the Gathering Antiquities

	Low	High
Complete Set (100)	450.00	575.00
Booster Box (60 Packs)	1600.00	2000.00
Booster Pack (8 Cards)	35.00	45.00

Released in March 1994

Card	Low	High
❑ 1 Amulet of Kroog C4 :A:	.50	1.00
❑ 2 Argivian Archaeologist U1 :W:	12.00	25.00
❑ 3 Argivian Blacksmith C4 :W:	.50	1.00
❑ 4 Argothian Pixies C4 :G:	.50	1.00
❑ 5 Argothian Treefolk C4 :G:	.50	1.00
❑ 6 Armageddon Clock U2 :A:	2.00	4.00
❑ 7 Artifact Blast C4:R:	.50	1.00
❑ 8 Artifact Possession C4:K:	.50	1.00
❑ 9 Artifact Ward C4:W:	.50	1.00
❑ 10 Ashnod's Altar U2 :A:	1.50	3.00
❑ 11 Ashnod's Battle Gear U2 :A:	.75	1.50
❑ 12 Ashnod's Transmogrant U3 :A:	.75	1.50
❑ 13 Atog C4 :R:	1.50	3.00
❑ 14 Battering Ram C4 :A:	.50	1.00
❑ 15 Bronze Tablet U1 :A:	2.50	5.00
❑ 16 Candelabra of Tawnos U1 :A:	125.00	250.00
❑ 17 Circle of Protection: Artifacts U3 :W:	2.50	5.00
❑ 18 Citanul Druid U3 :G:	2.00	4.00
❑ 19 Clay Statue C4 :A:	.50	1.00
❑ 20 Clockwork Avian U1 :A:	3.50	7.00
❑ 21 Colossus of Sardia U1 :A:	5.00	10.00
❑ 22 Coral Helm U1 :A:	2.50	5.00
❑ 23 Crumble C4 :G:	.50	1.00
❑ 24 Cursed Rack C1 :A:	1.00	2.00
❑ 25 Damping Field U3 :W:	1.00	2.00
❑ 26 Detonate U3 :R:	2.00	4.00
❑ 27 Drafna's Restoration C4 :B:	.50	1.00
❑ 28 Dragon Engine C4 :A:	.50	1.00
❑ 29 Dwarven Weaponsmith U3 :R:	1.00	2.00
❑ 30 Energy Flux U3 :B:	3.00	6.00
❑ 31 Feldon's Cane C1 :A:	3.00	6.00
❑ 32 Gaea's Avenger U1 :G:	5.00	10.00
❑ 33 Gate to Phyrexia U3 :K:	2.50	5.00
❑ 34 Goblin Artisans U3 :R:	1.00	2.00
❑ 35 Golgothian Sylex U1 :A:	3.00	6.00
❑ 36 Grapeshot Catapult C4 :A:	.50	1.00
❑ 37 Haunting Wind U3 :K:	1.00	2.00
❑ 38 Hurkyl's Recall U1 :B:	6.00	12.00
❑ 39 Ivory Tower U3 :A:	5.00	10.00
❑ 40 Jalum Tome U2 :A:	1.50	3.00
❑ 41 Martyrs of Korlis U3 :W:	1.00	2.00
❑ 42 Mightstone U3 :A:	2.00	4.00
❑ 43 Millstone U3 :A:	3.50	7.00
❑ 44 Mishra's Factory, autumn U1 :L:	15.00	30.00
❑ 45 Mishra's Factory, spring C1 :L:	10.00	20.00
❑ 46 Mishra's Factory, summer U1 :L:	20.00	40.00
❑ 47 Mishra's Factory, winter U1 :L:	40.00	80.00
❑ 48 Mishra's War Machine U1 :A:	2.00	4.00
❑ 49 Mishra's Workshop U1 :L:	200.00	400.00
❑ 50 Obelisk of Undoing U1 :A:	2.00	4.00
❑ 51 Onulet U3 :A:	1.00	2.00
❑ 52 Orcish Mechanics C4 :R:	.50	1.00
❑ 53 Ornithopter C4 :A:	1.50	3.00
❑ 54 Phyrexian Gremlins C4 :K:	.50	1.00
❑ 55 Power Artifact U3 :B:	7.50	15.00
❑ 56 Powerleech U3 :G:	1.00	2.00
❑ 57 Priest of Yawgmoth C 4:K:	.50	1.00
❑ 58 Primal Clay U3 :A:	1.00	2.00
❑ 59 Rack, The U3 :A:	3.00	6.00
❑ 60 Rakalite U3 :A:	1.00	2.00
❑ 61 Reconstruction C4 :B:	.50	1.00
❑ 62 Reverse Polarity C4 :W:	.50	1.00
❑ 63 Rocket Launcher U3 :A:	1.50	3.00
❑ 64 Sage of Lat-Nam C4 :B:	.50	1.00
❑ 65 Shapeshifter U1 :A:	2.50	5.00
❑ 66 Shatterstorm U1 :R:	3.50	7.00
❑ 67 Staff of Zegon C4 :A:	.50	1.00
❑ 68 Strip Mine, horizon, even stripe U1 :L:	7.50	15.00
❑ 69 Strip Mine, horizon, uneven stripe U1 :L:	6.00	12.00
❑ 70 Strip Mine, no horizon C1 :L:	6.00	12.00
❑ 71 Strip Mine, small tower in forest U1 :L:	10.00	20.00
❑ 72 Su-Chi U3 :A:	5.00	10.00
❑ 73 Tablet of Epityr C4 :A:	.50	1.00
❑ 74 Tawnos's Coffin U1 :A:	10.00	20.00
❑ 75 Tawnos's Wand U3 :A:	.75	1.50
❑ 76 Tawnos's Weaponry U3 :A:	.50	1.00
❑ 77 Tetravus U1 :A:	3.00	6.00
❑ 78 Titania's Song U3 :G:	1.50	3.00
❑ 79 Transmute Artifact U3 :B:	6.00	12.00
❑ 80 Triskelion U1 :A:	6.00	12.00
❑ 81 Urza's Avenger U1 :A:	3.00	6.00
❑ 82 Urza's Chalice C4 :A:	.50	1.00
❑ 83 Urza's Mine, clawed sphere C2 :L:	1.00	2.00
❑ 84 Urza's Mine, mouth C1 :L:	1.00	2.00
❑ 85 Urza's Mine, pulley C1 :L:	1.50	3.00
❑ 86 Urza's Mine, tower C2 :L:	1.00	2.00
❑ 87 Urza's Miter U1 :A:	3.00	6.00
❑ 88 Urza's Power Plant, bug C2 :L:	1.50	3.00
❑ 89 Urza's Power Plant, columns C1 :L:	1.50	3.00
❑ 90 Urza's Power Plant, rock in pot C1 :L:	1.50	3.00
❑ 91 Urza's Power Plant, sphere C2 :L:	1.50	3.00
❑ 92 Urza's Tower, forest C2 :L:	2.50	5.00
❑ 93 Urza's Tower, mountains C1 :L:	2.50	5.00
❑ 94 Urza's Tower, plains C1 :L:	2.50	5.00
❑ 95 Urza's Tower, shore C1 :L:	2.50	5.00
❑ 96 Wall of Spears U3 :A:	.75	1.50
❑ 97 Weakstone U3 :A:	1.25	2.50
❑ 98 Xenic Poltergeist U3 :K:	1.00	2.00
❑ 99 Yawgmoth Demon U3 :K:	4.00	8.00
❑ 100 Yotian Soldier C4 :A:	.50	1.00

1994 Magic the Gathering Legends

	Low	High
Complete Set (310)	1200.00	1500.00
Booster Box (36 Packs)	1500.00	2000.00
Booster Packs (15 Cards)	42.00	58.00
Italian Booster Box	600.00	700.00

Released in June 1994

Card	Low	High
❑ 1 Abomination U :K:	1.50	3.00
❑ 2 Abyss, The R :K:	60.00	120.00
❑ 3 Acid Rain R :B:	10.00	20.00
❑ 4 Active Volcano C :R:	.30	.75
❑ 5 Adun Oakenshield R :D:	6.00	12.00
❑ 6 Adventurers' Guildhouse U :L:	1.00	2.00
❑ 7 Ærathi Berserker U :R:	1.50	3.00
❑ 8 Aisling Leprechaun C :G:	.25	.50
❑ 9 Akron Legionnaire R :W:	4.00	8.00
❑ 10 Al-abara's Carpet R :A:	5.00	10.00
❑ 11 Alabaster Potion C :W:	.25	.50
❑ 12 Alchor's Tomb R :A:	5.00	10.00
❑ 13 All Hallow's Eve R :K:	20.00	40.00
❑ 14 Amrou Kithkin C :W:	.25	.50
❑ 15 Angelic Voices R :W:	5.00	10.00
❑ 16 Angus Mackenzie R :D:	5.00	10.00
❑ 17 Anti-Magic Aura C :B:	.30	.75
❑ 18 Arboria U :G:	1.50	3.00
❑ 19 Arcades Sabboth R :D:	9.00	18.00
❑ 20 Arena of the Ancients R :A:	3.50	7.00
❑ 21 Avoid Fate C :G:	.50	1.00
❑ 22 Axelrod Gunnarson R :D:	3.50	7.00
❑ 23 Ayesha Tanaka R :D:	3.50	7.00
❑ 24 Azure Drake U :B:	1.00	2.00
❑ 25 Backdraft U :R:	.50	1.00
❑ 26 Backfire U :B:	.75	1.50
❑ 27 Barbary Apes C :G:	.50	1.00
❑ 28 Barktooth Warbeard U :D:	1.00	2.00
❑ 29 Bartel Runeaxe R :D:	5.00	10.00
❑ 30 Beasts of Bogardan U :R:	1.00	2.00
❑ 31 Black Mana Battery U :A:	1.00	2.00
❑ 32 Blazing Effigy C :R:	.25	.50
❑ 33 Blight U :K:	2.00	4.00
❑ 34 Blood Lust U :R:	2.50	5.00
❑ 35 Blue Mana Battery U :A:	.50	1.00
❑ 36 Boomerang C :B:	.30	.75
❑ 37 Boris Devilboon R :D:	5.00	10.00
❑ 38 Brine Hag U :B:	2.00	4.00
❑ 39 Bronze Horse R :A:	3.50	7.00
❑ 40 Brute, The C :R:	.25	.50
❑ 41 Carrion Ants R :K:	4.00	8.00
❑ 42 Cat Warriors C :G:	.25	.50
❑ 43 Cathedral of Serra U :L:	1.50	3.00
❑ 44 Caverns of Despair R :R:	4.00	8.00
❑ 45 Chain Lightning C :R:	6.00	12.00
❑ 46 Chains of Mephistopheles R :K:	40.00	80.00
❑ 47 Chromium R :D:	11.00	22.00
❑ 48 Cleanse R :W:	7.50	15.00
❑ 49 Clergy of the Holy Nimbus C :W:	.50	1.00
❑ 50 Cocoon U :G:	1.00	2.00
❑ 51 Concordant Crossroads R :G:	6.00	12.00
❑ 52 Cosmic Horror R :K:	4.00	8.00
❑ 53 Craw Giant U :G:	1.50	3.00
❑ 54 Crevasse U :R:	1.00	2.00
❑ 55 Crimson Kobolds C :R:	.50	1.00
❑ 56 Crimson Manticore R :R:	3.00	6.00
❑ 57 Crookshank Kobolds C :R:	.50	1.00
❑ 58 Cyclopean Mummy C :K:	.25	.50
❑ 59 Dakkon Blackblade R :D:	11.00	22.00
❑ 60 Darkness C :K:	2.00	4.00
❑ 61 D'Avenant Archer C :W:	.25	.50
❑ 62 Deadfall U :G:	1.00	2.00
❑ 63 Demonic Torment U :K:	1.00	2.00
❑ 64 Devouring Deep C :B:	.50	1.00
❑ 65 Disharmony R :R:	5.00	10.00
❑ 66 Divine Intervention R :W:	7.50	15.00
❑ 67 Divine Offering C :W:	1.00	2.00
❑ 68 Divine Transformation R :W:	4.00	8.00
❑ 69 Dream Coat U :B:	1.00	2.00
❑ 70 Durkwood Boars C :G:	.50	1.00
❑ 71 Dwarven Song U :R:	1.00	2.00
❑ 72 Elder Land Wurm R :W:	4.00	8.00
❑ 73 Elder Spawn R :B:	4.00	8.00
❑ 74 Elven Riders R :G:	4.00	8.00
❑ 75 Emerald Dragonfly C :G:	.25	.50
❑ 76 Enchanted Being C :W:	.50	1.00
❑ 77 Enchantment Alteration C :B:	.50	1.00
❑ 78 Energy Tap C :B:	.50	.75
❑ 79 Equinox C :W:	.50	1.00
❑ 80 Eternal Warrior U :R:	.50	1.00
❑ 81 Eureka R :G:	50.00	100.00
❑ 82 Evil Eye of Orms-By-Gore U :K:	2.50	5.00
❑ 83 Fallen Angel U :K:	3.50	7.00
❑ 84 Falling Star R :R:	6.00	12.00
❑ 85 Feint C :R:	.25	.50
❑ 86 Field of Dreams R :B:	10.00	15.00
❑ 87 Fire Sprites C :G:	.50	1.00
❑ 88 Firestorm Phoenix R :R:	12.00	25.00
❑ 89 Flash Counter C :B:	.25	.50
❑ 90 Flash Flood C :B:	.25	.50
❑ 91 Floral Spuzzem U :G:	1.00	2.00
❑ 92 Force Spike C :B:	2.00	4.00
❑ 93 Forethought Amulet R :A:	4.00	8.00
❑ 94 Fortified Area U :W:	1.00	2.00
❑ 95 Frost Giant U :R:	1.50	3.00
❑ 96 Gabriel Angelfire R :D:	6.00	12.00
❑ 97 Gaseous Form C :B:	.50	1.00
❑ 98 Gauntlets of Chaos R :A:	3.50	7.00
❑ 99 Ghosts of the Damned C :K:	.25	.50
❑ 100 Giant Slug C :K:	.25	.50
❑ 101 Giant Strength C :R:	.25	.50
❑ 102 Giant Turtle C :G:	.25	.50
❑ 103 Glyph of Delusion C :B:	.50	1.00
❑ 104 Glyph of Destruction C :R:	.50	1.00
❑ 105 Glyph of Doom C :K:	.25	.50
❑ 106 Glyph of Life C :W:	.50	1.00
❑ 107 Glyph of Reincarnation C :G:	.50	1.00
❑ 108 Gosta Dirk R :D:	4.00	8.00
❑ 109 Gravity Sphere R :R:	9.00	18.00
❑ 110 Great Defender U :W:	1.00	2.00
❑ 111 Great Wall U :W:	.75	1.50
❑ 112 Greater Realm of Preservation U :W:	1.00	2.00
❑ 113 Greed R :K:	3.50	7.00
❑ 114 Green Mana Battery U :A:	1.00	2.00
❑ 115 Gwendlyn Di Corci R :D:	11.00	22.00
❑ 116 Halfdane R :D:	6.00	12.00
❑ 117 Hammerheim U :L:	1.50	3.00
❑ 118 Hazezon Tamar R :D:	7.50	15.00
❑ 119 Headless Horseman C :K:	.25	.50
❑ 120 Heaven's Gate U :W:	.75	1.50
❑ 121 Hell Swarm C :K:	.25	.50
❑ 122 Hellfire R :K:	11.00	22.00
❑ 123 Hell's Caretaker R :K:	7.50	15.00
❑ 124 Holy Day C :W:	.25	.50
❑ 125 Horn of Deafening R :A:	3.50	7.00
❑ 126 Hornet Cobra C :G:	.25	.50
❑ 127 Horror of Horrors U :K:	1.00	2.00
❑ 128 Hunding Gjornersen U :D:	1.00	2.00
❑ 129 Hyperion Blacksmith U :R:	.50	1.00
❑ 130 Ichneumon Druid U :G:	1.00	2.00
❑ 131 Immolation C :R:	.25	.50
❑ 132 Imprison R :K:	4.00	8.00
❑ 133 In the Eye of Chaos R :B:	15.00	30.00
❑ 134 Indestructible Aura C :W:	.25	.50
❑ 135 Infernal Medusa U :K:	1.00	2.00
❑ 136 Infinite Authority R :W:	5.00	10.00
❑ 137 Invoke Prejudice R :B:	12.00	25.00
❑ 138 Ivory Guardians U :W:	1.00	2.00
❑ 139 Jacques le Vert R :D:	4.00	8.00
❑ 140 Jasmine Boreal U :D:	2.00	4.00
❑ 141 Jedit Ojanen U :D:	2.00	4.00
❑ 142 Jerrard of the Closed Fist U :D:	1.50	3.00
❑ 143 Johan R :D:	4.00	8.00
❑ 144 Jovial Evil R :K:	6.00	12.00
❑ 145 Juxtapose R :B:	3.00	6.00
❑ 146 Karakas U :L:	3.00	6.00
❑ 147 Kasimir the Lone Wolf U :D:	1.00	2.00
❑ 148 Keepers of the Faith C :W:	.25	.50
❑ 149 Kei Takahashi R :D:	3.50	7.00
❑ 150 Killer Bees R :G:	6.00	12.00
❑ 151 Kismet U :W:	2.00	4.00
❑ 152 Knowledge Vault R :A:	4.00	8.00
❑ 153 Kobold Drill Sergeant U :R:	4.00	8.00
❑ 154 Kobold Overlord R :R:	10.00	20.00
❑ 155 Kobold Taskmaster U :R:	4.00	8.00
❑ 156 Kobolds of Kher Keep C :R:	1.00	2.00
❑ 157 Kry Shield U :A:	1.00	2.00
❑ 158 Lady Caleria R :D:	5.00	10.00
❑ 159 Lady Evangela R :D:	5.00	10.00
❑ 160 Lady of the Mountain, The U :D:	1.50	3.00
❑ 161 Lady Orca U :D:	1.00	2.00
❑ 162 Land Equilibrium R :B:	10.00	20.00
❑ 163 Land Tax U :W:	7.50	15.00
❑ 164 Land's Edge R :R:	4.00	8.00
❑ 165 Lesser Werewolf U :K:	1.50	3.00
❑ 166 Life Chisel U :A:	.75	1.50
❑ 167 Life Matrix R :A:	5.00	10.00
❑ 168 Lifeblood R :W:	5.00	10.00
❑ 169 Living Plane R :G:	9.00	18.00
❑ 170 Livonya Silone R :D:	5.00	10.00
❑ 171 Lord Magnus U :D:	1.50	3.00
❑ 172 Lost Soul C :K:	.25	.50
❑ 173 Mana Drain U :B:	75.00	150.00
❑ 174 Mana Matrix R :A:	5.00	10.00
❑ 175 Marble Priest U :A:	.75	1.50
❑ 176 Marhault Elsdragon U :D:	.50	1.00
❑ 177 Master of the Hunt R :G:	10.00	20.00
❑ 178 Mirror Universe R :A:	30.00	60.00
❑ 179 Moat R :W:	175.00	350.00
❑ 180 Mold Demon R :K:	5.00	10.00
❑ 181 Moss Monster C :G:	.25	.50
❑ 182 Mountain Stronghold U :L:	1.00	2.00
❑ 183 Mountain Yeti U :R:	.50	1.00
❑ 184 Nebuchadnezzar R :D:	5.00	10.00
❑ 185 Nether Void R :K:	60.00	120.00
❑ 186 Nicol Bolas R :D:	12.00	25.00
❑ 187 North Star R :A:	5.00	10.00
❑ 188 Nova Pentacle R :A:	6.00	12.00
❑ 189 Osai Vultures C :W:	.25	.50
❑ 190 Palladia-Mors R :D:	10.00	20.00
❑ 191 Part Water U :B:	.50	1.00
❑ 192 Pavel Maliki U :D:	1.00	2.00
❑ 193 Pendelhaven U :L:	3.00	6.00
❑ 194 Petra Sphinx R :W:	3.50	7.00
❑ 195 Pit Scorpion C :K:	.25	.50
❑ 196 Pixie Queen R :G:	7.50	15.00
❑ 197 Planar Gate R :A:	6.00	12.00
❑ 198 Pradesh Gypsies U :G:	.50	1.00
❑ 199 Presence of the Master U :W:	2.00	4.00
❑ 200 Primordial Ooze U :R:	.50	1.00
❑ 201 Princess Lucrezia U :D:	1.00	2.00
❑ 202 Psionic Entity R :B:	3.50	7.00
❑ 203 Psychic Purge C :B:	.25	.50
❑ 204 Puppet Master U :B:	.50	1.00
❑ 205 Pyrotechnics C :R:	.25	.50
❑ 206 Quagmire U :K:	1.00	2.00
❑ 207 Quarum Trench Gnomes R :R:	5.00	10.00
❑ 208 Rabid Wombat U :G:	1.50	3.00
❑ 209 Radjan Spirit U :G:	.50	1.00
❑ 210 Raging Bull C :R:	.25	.50
❑ 211 Ragnar R :D:	5.00	10.00
❑ 212 Ramirez DePietro U :D:	1.50	3.00
❑ 213 Ramses Overdark R :D:	7.50	15.00
❑ 214 Rapid Fire R :W:	4.00	8.00
❑ 215 Rasputin Dreamweaver R :D:	7.50	15.00
❑ 216 Rebirth R :G:	3.00	6.00
❑ 217 Recall R :B:	6.00	12.00
❑ 218 Red Mana Battery U :A:	1.00	2.00
❑ 219 Reincarnation U :G:	1.00	2.00
❑ 220 Relic Barrier U :A:	2.00	4.00
❑ 221 Relic Bind U :B:	.50	1.00
❑ 222 Remove Enchantments C :W:	.25	.50
❑ 223 Remove Soul C :B:	.25	.50
❑ 224 Reset U :B:	12.00	25.00
❑ 225 Revelation R :G:	3.50	7.00
❑ 226 Reverberation R :B:	5.00	10.00
❑ 227 Righteous Avengers U :W:	1.00	2.00
❑ 228 Ring of Immortals R :A:	5.00	10.00
❑ 229 Riven Turnbull U :D:	1.50	3.00
❑ 230 Rohgahh of Kher Keep R :D:	7.50	15.00
❑ 231 Rubinia Soulsinger R :D:	5.00	10.00
❑ 232 Rust C :G:	.25	.50
❑ 233 Sea Kings' Blessing U :B:	1.00	2.00
❑ 234 Seafarer's Quay U :L:	1.00	2.00
❑ 235 Seeker U :W:	1.00	2.00
❑ 236 Segovian Leviathan U :B:	1.00	2.00
❑ 237 Sentinel R :A:	3.50	7.00
❑ 238 Serpent Generator R :A:	5.00	10.00
❑ 239 Shelkin Brownie C :G:	.25	.50
❑ 240 Shield Wall U :W:	1.00	2.00
❑ 241 Shimian Night Stalker U :K:	1.00	2.00
❑ 242 Silhouette U :B:	1.00	2.00
❑ 243 Sir Shandlar of Eberyn U :D:	1.00	2.00
❑ 244 Sivitri Scarzam U :D:	1.00	2.00
❑ 245 Sol'kanar the Swamp King R :D:	10.00	20.00
❑ 246 Spectral Cloak U :B:	2.00	4.00
❑ 247 Spinal Villain R :R:	7.50	15.00
❑ 248 Spirit Link U :W:	2.50	5.00
❑ 249 Spirit Shackle C :K:	.25	.50
❑ 250 Spiritual Sanctuary R :W:	5.00	10.00
❑ 251 Stangg R :D:	5.00	10.00
❑ 252 Storm Seeker U :G:	2.50	5.00
❑ 253 Storm World R :R:	5.00	10.00
❑ 254 Subdue C :G:	.25	.50
❑ 255 Sunastian Falconer U :D:	1.50	3.00
❑ 256 Sword of the Ages R :A:	10.00	20.00
❑ 257 Sylvan Library U :G:	5.00	10.00
❑ 258 Sylvan Paradise U :G:	1.00	2.00
❑ 259 Syphon Soul C :K: :L:	.25	.50
❑ 260 Tabernacle at Pendrell Vale R :L:	175.00	350.00
❑ 261 Takklemaggot U :K:	1.00	2.00
❑ 262 Telekinesis R :B:	4.00	8.00
❑ 263 Teleport R :B:	3.50	7.00
❑ 264 Tempest Efreet R :R:	3.50	7.00
❑ 265 Tetsuo Umezawa R :D:	10.00	20.00
❑ 266 Thunder Spirit R :W:	10.00	20.00
❑ 267 Time Elemental R :B:	7.50	15.00
❑ 268 Tobias Andrion U :D:	1.00	2.00
❑ 269 Tolaria U :L:	1.50	3.00
❑ 270 Tor Wauki U :D:	1.00	2.00
❑ 271 Torsten Von Ursus U :D:	1.00	2.00
❑ 272 Touch of Darkness U :K:	1.00	2.00
❑ 273 Transmutation C :K:	.25	.50
❑ 274 Triassic Egg R :A:	3.00	6.00
❑ 275 Tuknir Deathlock R :D:	5.00	10.00
❑ 276 Tundra Wolves C :W:	.25	.50
❑ 277 Typhoon R :G:	5.00	10.00
❑ 278 Undertow U :B:	1.00	2.00
❑ 279 Underworld Dreams U :K:	10.00	20.00
❑ 280 Unholy Citadel U :L:	1.00	2.00
❑ 281 Untamed Wilds U :G:	1.00	2.00
❑ 282 Urborg U :L:	2.50	5.00
❑ 283 Ur-Drago R :D:	6.00	12.00
❑ 284 Vaevictis Asmadi R :D:	10.00	20.00
❑ 285 Vampire Bats C :K:	.25	.50
❑ 286 Venarian Gold C :B:	.25	.50
❑ 287 Visions U :W:	1.00	2.00
❑ 288 Voodoo Doll R :A:	4.00	8.00
❑ 289 Walking Dead C :K:	.25	.50
❑ 290 Wall of Caltrops C :W:	.25	.50
❑ 291 Wall of Dust U :R:	1.00	2.00
❑ 292 Wall of Earth C :R:	.25	.50
❑ 293 Wall of Heat C :R:	.25	.50
❑ 294 Wall of Light U :W:	1.00	2.00
❑ 295 Wall of Opposition R :R:	3.50	7.00
❑ 296 Wall of Putrid Flesh U :K:	1.00	2.00
❑ 297 Wall of Shadows C :K:	.25	.50
❑ 298 Wall of Tombstones U :K:	1.00	2.00
❑ 299 Wall of Vapor C :B:	.25	.50
❑ 300 Wall of Wonder U :B:	1.00	2.00
❑ 301 Whirling Dervish U :G:	2.00	4.00
❑ 302 White Mana Battery U :A:	1.00	2.00
❑ 303 Willow Satyr R :G:	5.00	10.00
❑ 304 Winds of Change U :R:	1.50	3.00
❑ 305 Winter Blast R :G:	3.00	6.00
❑ 306 Wolverine Pack C :G:	2.50	5.00
❑ 307 Wood Elemental R :G:	5.00	10.00
❑ 308 Wretched, The R :K:	5.00	10.00
❑ 309 Xira Arien R :D:	5.00	10.00
❑ 310 Zephyr Falcon C :B:	.25	.50

1994 Magic the Gathering The Dark

	Low	High
Complete Set (119)	120.00	135.00
Booster Box (60 Packs)	375.00	500.00
Booster Pack (8 Cards)	10.00	15.00

Released in August 1994

Card	Low	High
❑ 1 Amnesia U2 :B:	1.50	3.00
❑ 2 Angry Mob U2 :W:	.50	1.00
❑ 3 Apprentice Wizard U1 :B:	1.00	2.00
❑ 4 Ashes to Ashes C3 :K:	.25	.50
❑ 5 Ball Lightning U1 :R:	10.00	20.00
❑ 6 Banshee U2 :K:	.50	1.00
❑ 7 Barl's Cage U1 :A:	1.00	2.00
❑ 8 Blood Moon U1 :R:	4.00	8.00
❑ 9 Blood of the Martyr U2 :W:	.50	1.00
❑ 10 Bog Imp C3 :K:	.15	.30
❑ 11 Bog Rats C3 :K:	.15	.30
❑ 12 Bone Flute U2 :A:	.50	1.00
❑ 13 Book of Rass U2 :A:	.15	.30
❑ 14 Brainwash C3 :W:	.15	.30
❑ 15 Brothers of Fire U2 :R:	.50	1.00
❑ 16 Carnivorous Plant C3 :G:	.15	.30
❑ 17 Cave People U2 :R:	.50	1.00
❑ 18 City of Shadows U1 :L:	2.00	4.00
❑ 19 Cleansing U1 :W:	1.25	2.50
❑ 20 Coal Golem U2 :A:	1.00	2.00
❑ 21 Curse Artifact U2 :K:	1.00	2.00
❑ 22 Dance of Many U1 :B:	1.00	2.00
❑ 23 Dark Heart of the Wood C3 :D:	.15	.30
❑ 24 Dark Sphere U2 :A:	1.00	2.00
❑ 25 Deep Water C3 :B:	.15	.30
❑ 26 Diabolic Machine U2 :A:	.50	1.00
❑ 27 Drowned C3 :B:	.15	.30
❑ 28 Dust to Dust C3 :W:	.25	.50
❑ 29 Eater of the Dead U2 :K:	1.00	2.00
❑ 30 Electric Eel U2 :B:	.50	1.00
❑ 31 Elves of Deep Shadow U2 :G:	2.00	4.00
❑ 32 Erosion C3 :B:	.15	.30
❑ 33 Eternal Flame U1 :R:	1.00	2.00
❑ 34 Exorcist U1 :W:	2.00	4.00
❑ 35 Fallen, The U2 :K:	.50	1.00
❑ 36 Fasting U2 :W:	.50	1.00
❑ 37 Fellwar Stone U2 :A:	1.50	3.00
❑ 38 Festival C3 :W:	.15	.30
❑ 39 Fire and Brimstone U2 :W:	1.00	2.00
❑ 40 Fire Drake U2 :R:	.50	1.00
❑ 41 Fissure C3 :R:	.15	.30
❑ 42 Flood U2 :B:	.50	1.00
❑ 43 Fountain of Youth U2 :A:	.50	1.00
❑ 44 Frankenstein's Monster U1 :K:	1.50	3.00
❑ 45 Gaea's Touch C3 :G:	.15	.30
❑ 46 Ghost Ship C3 :B:	1.50	3.00
❑ 47 Giant Shark C3 :B:	.15	.30
❑ 48 Goblin Caves C3 :R:	.50	1.00
❑ 49 Goblin Digging Team C3 :R:	.15	.30
❑ 50 Goblin Hero C3 :R:	.15	.30
❑ 51 Goblin Rock Sled C3 :R:	.15	.30
❑ 52 Goblin Shrine C3 :R:	.15	.30
❑ 53 Goblin Wizard U1 :R:	5.00	10.00
❑ 54 Goblins of the Flarg C3 :R:	.15	.30
❑ 55 Grave Robbers U1 :K:	1.00	2.00

MAGIC

Card	Low	High
□ 56 Hidden Path U1 :G:	1.00	2.00
□ 57 Holy Light C3 :W:	.15	.30
□ 58 Inferno U1 :R:	2.00	4.00
□ 59 Inquisition C3 :K:	.15	.30
□ 60 Knights of Thorn U1 :W:	1.50	3.00
□ 61 Land Leeches C3 :G:	.15	.30
□ 62 Leviathan U1 :B:	2.50	5.00
□ 63 Living Armor U2 :A:	.50	1.00
□ 64 Lurker U1 :G:	.50	1.00
□ 65 Mana Clash U1 :R:	1.00	2.00
□ 66 Mana Vortex U1 :B:	1.50	3.00
□ 67 Marsh Gas C3 :K:	.15	.30
□ 68 Marsh Goblins C3 :D:	.15	.30
□ 69 Marsh Viper C3 :G:	.25	.50
□ 70 Martyr's Cry U1 :W:	1.50	3.00
□ 71 Maze of Ith C1 :L:	.15	.30
□ 72 Merfolk Assassin U2 :B:	1.50	3.00
□ 73 Mind Bomb U1 :B:	1.00	2.00
□ 74 Miracle Worker C3 :W:	.15	.30
□ 75 Morale C3 :W:	.15	.30
□ 76 Murk Dwellers C3 :K:	.15	.30
□ 77 Nameless Race U1 :K:	.50	1.00
□ 78 Necropolis U2 :A:	.50	1.00
□ 79 Niall Silvain U1 :G:	.50	1.00
□ 80 Orc General U2 :R:	.50	1.00
□ 81 People of the Woods U2 :G:	.50	1.00
□ 82 Pikemen C3 :W:	.15	.30
□ 83 Preacher U1 :W:	5.00	10.00
□ 84 Psychic Allergy U1 :B:	1.00	2.00
□ 85 Rag Man U1 :K:	1.50	3.00
□ 86 Reflecting Mirror U2 :A:	1.00	2.00
□ 87 Riptide C3 :B:	.15	.30
□ 88 Runesword U2 :A:	.50	1.00
□ 89 Safe Haven U1 :L:	1.50	3.00
□ 90 Savaen Elves C3 :G:	.15	.30
□ 91 Scarecrow U2 :A:	1.00	2.00
□ 92 Scarwood Bandits U1 :G:	1.00	2.00
□ 93 Scarwood Goblins C3 :D:	.15	.30
□ 94 Scarwood Hag U2 :G:	.50	1.00
□ 95 Scavenger Folk C3 :G:	.15	.30
□ 96 Season of the Witch U1 :K:	1.00	2.00
□ 97 Sisters of the Flame U2 :R:	.50	1.00
□ 98 Skull of Orm U2 :A:	2.50	5.00
□ 99 Sorrow's Path U1 :L:	1.00	2.00
□ 100 Spitting Slug U2 :G:	.50	1.00
□ 101 Squire C3 :W:	.15	.30
□ 102 Standing Stones U2 :A:	.50	1.00
□ 103 Stone Calendar U1 :A:	2.00	4.00
□ 104 Sunken City C3 :B:	.15	.30
□ 105 Tangle Kelp U2 :B:	.50	1.00
□ 106 Tivadar's Crusade U2 :W:	1.00	2.00
□ 107 Tormod's Crypt U2 :A:	3.50	7.00
□ 108 Tower of Coireall U2 :A:	.50	1.00
□ 109 Tracker U1 :G:	1.50	3.00
□ 110 Uncle Istvan U2 :K:	1.00	2.00
□ 111 Venom C3 :G:	.15	.30
□ 112 Wand of Ith U2 :A:	1.00	2.00
□ 113 War Barge U2 :A:	1.00	2.00
□ 114 Water Wurm C3 :B:	.15	.30
□ 115 Whippoorwill U2 :G:	.50	1.00
□ 116 Witch Hunter U1 :W:	1.50	3.00
□ 117 Word of Binding C3 :K:	.15	.30
□ 118 Worms of the Earth U1 :K:	1.50	3.00
□ 119 Wormwood Treefolk U1 :G:	1.50	3.00

1994 Magic the Gathering Fallen Empires

Card	Low	High
Complete Set (187)	40.00	65.00
Booster Box (60 Packs)	85.00	125.00
Booster Pack (8 Cards)	125.00	180.00

Released in November 1994

Card	Low	High
□ 1 Aeolipile U :A:	.50	1.00
□ 2 Armor Thrull v1 C :K:	.15	.30
□ 3 Armor Thrull v2 C :K:	.15	.30
□ 4 Armor Thrull v3 C :K:	.15	.30
□ 5 Armor Thrull v4 C :K:	.15	.30
□ 6 Balm of Restoration U :A:	.30	.75
□ 7 Basal Thrull v1 C :K:	.15	.30
□ 8 Basal Thrull v2 C :K:	.15	.30
□ 9 Basal Thrull v3 C :K:	.15	.30
□ 10 Basal Thrull v4 C :K:	.15	.30
□ 11 Bottomless Vault U :L:	1.00	2.00
□ 12 Brassclaw Orcs v1 C :R:	.15	.30
□ 13 Brassclaw Orcs v2 C :R:	.15	.30
□ 14 Brassclaw Orcs v3 C :R:	.15	.30
□ 15 Brassclaw Orcs v4 C :R:	.15	.30
□ 16 Breeding Pit U :K:	1.00	2.00
□ 17 Combat Medic v1 C :W:	.15	.30
□ 18 Combat Medic v2 C :W:	.15	.30
□ 19 Combat Medic v3 C :W:	.15	.30
□ 20 Combat Medic v4 C :W:	.15	.30
□ 21 Conch Horn U :A:	.30	.75
□ 22 Deep Spawn U :B:	.25	.50
□ 23 Delif's Cone C :A:	.15	.30
□ 24 Delif's Cube U :A:	.30	.75
□ 25 Derelor U :K:	.30	.75
□ 26 Draconian Cylix U :A:	.25	.50
□ 27 Dwarven Armorer U :R:	.30	.75
□ 28 Dwarven Catapult U :R:	.25	.50
□ 29 Dwarven Hold U :L:	1.00	2.00
□ 30 Dwarven Lieutenant U :R:	.25	.50
□ 31 Dwarven Ruins U :L:	.50	1.00
□ 32 Dwarven Soldier v1 C :R:	.25	.50
□ 33 Dwarven Soldier v2 C :R:	.15	.30
□ 34 Dwarven Soldier v3 C :R:	.15	.30
□ 35 Ebon Praetor U :K:	1.00	2.00
□ 36 Ebon Stronghold U :L:	.50	1.00
□ 37 Elven Fortress v1 C :G:	.50	1.00
□ 38 Elven Fortress v2 C :G:	.15	.30
□ 39 Elven Fortress v3 C :G:	.15	.30
□ 40 Elven Fortress v4 C :G:	.15	.30
□ 41 Elven Lyre U :A:	.30	.75
□ 42 Elvish Farmer U :G:	2.00	4.00
□ 43 Elvish Hunter v1 C :G:	.25	.50
□ 44 Elvish Hunter v2 C :G:	.15	.30
□ 45 Elvish Hunter v3 C :G:	.15	.30
□ 46 Elvish Scout v1 C :G:	.15	.30
□ 47 Elvish Scout v2 C :G:	.15	.30
□ 48 Elvish Scout v3 C :G:	.15	.30
□ 49 Farrelite Priest U :W:	.25	.50
□ 50 Farrel's Mantle U :W:	.25	.50
□ 51 Farrel's Zealot v1 C :W:	.15	.30
□ 52 Farrel's Zealot v2 C :W:	.15	.30
□ 53 Farrel's Zealot v3 C :W:	.15	.30
□ 54 Feral Thallid U :G:	.25	.50
□ 55 Fungal Bloom U :G:	1.50	3.00
□ 56 Goblin Chirurgeon v1 C :R:	.15	.30
□ 57 Goblin Chirurgeon v2 C :R:	.15	.30
□ 58 Goblin Chirurgeon v3 C :R:	.15	.30
□ 59 Goblin Flotilla U :R:	1.00	2.00
□ 60 Goblin Grenade v1 C :R:	1.00	2.00
□ 61 Goblin Grenade v2 C :R:	1.00	2.00
□ 62 Goblin Grenade v3 C :R:	1.00	2.00
□ 63 Goblin Kites U :R:	.25	.50
□ 64 Goblin War Drums v1 C :R:	.15	.30
□ 65 Goblin War Drums v2 C :R:	.15	.30
□ 66 Goblin War Drums v3 C :R:	.15	.30
□ 67 Goblin War Drums v4 C :R:	.15	.30
□ 68 Goblin Warrens U :R:	1.00	2.00
□ 69 Hand of Justice U :W:	1.00	2.00
□ 70 Havenwood Battleground U :L:	.50	1.00
□ 71 Heroism U :W:	.25	.50
□ 72 High Tide v1 C :B:	.15	.30
□ 73 High Tide v2 C :B:	.15	.30
□ 74 High Tide v3 C :B:	.15	.30
□ 75 Hollow Trees U :L:	1.00	2.00
□ 76 Homarid v1 C :B:	.15	.30
□ 77 Homarid v2 C :B:	.15	.30
□ 78 Homarid v3 C :B:	.15	.30
□ 79 Homarid v4 C :B:	.15	.30
□ 80 Homarid Shaman U :B:	.30	.75
□ 81 Homarid Spawning Bed U :B:	.25	.50
□ 82 Homarid Warrior v1 C :B:	.15	.30
□ 83 Homarid Warrior v2 C :B:	.15	.30
□ 84 Homarid Warrior v3 C :B:	.15	.30
□ 85 Hymn to Tourach v1 C :K:	.50	1.00
□ 86 Hymn to Tourach v2 C :K:	.50	1.00
□ 87 Hymn to Tourach v3 C :K:	.50	1.00
□ 88 Hymn to Tourach v4 C :K:	.50	1.00
□ 89 Icatian Infantry v1 C :W:	.15	.30
□ 90 Icatian Infantry v2 C :W:	.15	.30
□ 91 Icatian Infantry v3 C :W:	.15	.30
□ 92 Icatian Infantry v4 C :W:	.15	.30
□ 93 Icatian Javelineers v1 C :W:	.15	.30
□ 94 Icatian Javelineers v2 C :W:	.15	.30
□ 95 Icatian Javelineers v3 C :W:	.15	.30
□ 96 Icatian Lieutenant U :W:	.30	.75
□ 97 Icatian Moneychanger v1 C :W:	.15	.30
□ 98 Icatian Moneychanger v2 C :W:	.15	.30
□ 99 Icatian Moneychanger v3 C :W:	.15	.30
□ 100 Icatian Phalanx U :W:	.25	.50
□ 101 Icatian Priest U :W:	.25	.50
□ 102 Icatian Scout v1 C :W:	.15	.30
□ 103 Icatian Scout v2 C :W:	.15	.30
□ 104 Icatian Scout v3 C :W:	.15	.30
□ 105 Icatian Scout v4 C :W:	.15	.30
□ 106 Icatian Skirmishers U :W:	.50	1.00
□ 107 Icatian Store U :L:	1.00	2.00
□ 108 Icatian Town U :W:	.50	1.00
□ 109 Implements of Sacrifice U :A:	.25	.50
□ 110 Initiates of the Ebon Hand v1 C :K:	.15	.30
□ 111 Initiates of the Ebon Hand v2 C :K:	.15	.30
□ 112 Initiates of the Ebon Hand v3 C :K:	.15	.30
□ 113 Merseine v1 C :B:	.15	.30
□ 114 Merseine v2 C :B:	.15	.30
□ 115 Merseine v3 C :B:	.15	.30
□ 116 Merseine v4 C :B:	.15	.30
□ 117 Mindstab Thrull v1 C :K:	.15	.30
□ 118 Mindstab Thrull v2 C :K:	.15	.30
□ 119 Mindstab Thrull v3 C :K:	.15	.30
□ 120 Necrite v1 C :K:	.15	.30
□ 121 Necrite v2 C :K:	.15	.30
□ 122 Necrite v3 C :K:	.15	.30
□ 123 Night Soil v1 C :G:	.15	.30
□ 124 Night Soil v2 C :G:	.15	.30
□ 125 Night Soil v3 C :G:	.15	.30
□ 126 Orcish Captain U :R:	.25	.50
□ 127 Orcish Spy v1 C :R:	.15	.30
□ 128 Orcish Spy v2 C :R:	.15	.30
□ 129 Orcish Spy v3 C :R:	.15	.30
□ 130 Orcish Veteran v1 C :R:	.15	.30
□ 131 Orcish Veteran v2 C :R:	.15	.30
□ 132 Orcish Veteran v3 C :R:	.15	.30
□ 133 Orcish Veteran v4 C :R:	.15	.30
□ 134 Order of Leitbur v1 C :W:	.15	.30
□ 135 Order of Leitbur v2 C :W:	.15	.30
□ 136 Order of Leitbur v3 C :W:	.15	.30
□ 137 Order of the Ebon Hand v1 C :K:	.15	.30
□ 138 Order of the Ebon Hand v2 C :K:	.15	.30
□ 139 Order of the Ebon Hand v3 C :K:	.25	.50
□ 140 Orgg U :R:	.50	1.00
□ 141 Raiding Party U :R:	.50	1.00
□ 142 Rainbow Vale U :L:	.75	1.50
□ 143 Ring of Renewal U :A:	.50	1.00
□ 144 River Merfolk U :B:	1.00	2.00
□ 145 Ruins of Trokair U :L:	.50	1.00
□ 146 Sand Silos U :L:	1.00	2.00
□ 147 Seasinger U :B:	.25	.50
□ 148 Soul Exchange U :K:	.50	1.00
□ 149 Spirit Shield U :A:	.30	.75
□ 150 Spore Cloud v1 C :G:	.15	.30
□ 151 Spore Cloud v2 C :G:	.15	.30
□ 152 Spore Cloud v3 C :G:	.15	.30
□ 153 Spore Flower U :G:	.25	.50
□ 154 Svyelunite Priest U :B:	.25	.50
□ 155 Svyelunite Temple U :L:	.25	.50
□ 156 Thallid v1 C :G:	.15	.30
□ 157 Thallid v2 C :G:	.15	.30
□ 158 Thallid v3 C :G:	.15	.30
□ 159 Thallid v4 C :G:	.15	.30
□ 160 Thallid Devourer U :G:	.25	.50
□ 161 Thelonite Druid U :G:	.25	.50
□ 162 Thelonite Monk U :G:	.30	.75
□ 163 Thelon's Chant U :G:	.25	.50
□ 164 Thelon's Curse U :G:	.25	.50
□ 165 Thorn Thallid v1 C :G:	.15	.30
□ 166 Thorn Thallid v2 C :G:	.15	.30
□ 167 Thorn Thallid v3 C :G:	.15	.30
□ 168 Thorn Thallid v4 C :G:	.15	.30
□ 169 Thrull Champion U :K:	1.50	3.00
□ 170 Thrull Retainer U :K:	.25	.50
□ 171 Thrull Wizard U :K:	.25	.50
□ 172 Tidal Flats v1 C :B:	.15	.30
□ 173 Tidal Flats v2 C :B:	.15	.30
□ 174 Tidal Flats v3 C :B:	.15	.30
□ 175 Tidal Influence U :B:	.25	.50
□ 176 Tourach's Chant U :K:	.25	.50
□ 177 Tourach's Gate U :K:	.50	1.00
□ 178 Vodalian Knights U :B:	1.00	2.00
□ 179 Vodalian Mage v1 C :B:	.15	.30
□ 180 Vodalian Mage v2 C :B:	.15	.30
□ 181 Vodalian Mage v3 C :B:	.15	.30
□ 182 Vodalian Soldiers v1 C :B:	.15	.30
□ 183 Vodalian Soldiers v2 C :B:	.15	.30
□ 184 Vodalian Soldiers v3 C :B:	.15	.30
□ 185 Vodalian Soldiers v4 C :B:	.15	.30
□ 186 Vodalian War Machine U :B:	.50	1.00
□ 187 Zelyon Sword U :A:	.50	1.00

1994 Magic the Gathering Revised Edition

Card	Low	High
Complete Set (306)	350.00	500.00
Starter Deck Box	400.00	500.00
Starter Deck	40.00	55.00
Booster Box (36 Packs)	450.00	600.00
Booster Pack (15 Cards)	15.00	20.00

Also Known as 3rd Edition
Released in April 1994
White borders and no copyright date
Pale colors and name of illustrator at the bottom.
No beveled edges inside the colored borders.

Card	Low	High
□ 1 Air Elemental U :B:	.50	1.00
□ 2 Aladdin's Lamp R :A:	1.00	2.50
□ 3 Aladdin's Ring R :A:	1.00	2.50
□ 4 Animate Artifact U :B:	.50	1.00
□ 5 Animate Dead U :K:	.50	1.00
□ 6 Animate Wall R :W:	.50	1.00
□ 7 Ankh of Mishra R :A:	1.50	3.00
□ 8 Armageddon Clock R :A:	.50	1.00
□ 9 Armageddon R :W:	3.50	7.00
□ 10 Aspect of Wolf R :G:	.75	1.50
□ 11 Atog C :R:	.15	.30
□ 12 Bad Moon R :K:	4.00	8.00
□ 13 Badlands R :L:	30.00	60.00
□ 14 Balance R :W:	3.00	6.00
□ 15 Basalt Monolith U :A:	.50	1.00
□ 16 Bayou R :L:	35.00	70.00
□ 17 Benalish Hero C :W:	.15	.30
□ 18 Birds of Paradise R :G:	7.50	15.00
□ 19 Black Knight U :K:	1.00	2.00
□ 20 Black Vise U :A:	1.00	2.00
□ 21 Black Ward U :W:	.50	1.00
□ 22 Blessing R :W:	1.00	2.00
□ 23 Blue Elemental Blast C :B:	.50	1.00
□ 24 Blue Ward U :W:	.50	1.00
□ 25 Bog Wraith U :K:	.50	1.00
□ 26 Bottle of Suleiman R :A:	.50	1.00
□ 27 Braingeyser R :B:	4.00	8.00
□ 28 Brass Man U :A:	.50	1.00
□ 29 Burrowing U :R:	.50	1.00
□ 30 Castle U :W:	.50	1.00
□ 31 Celestial Prism U :A:	.50	1.00
□ 32 Channel U :G:	.75	1.50
□ 33 Chaoslace R :R:	.50	1.00
□ 34 Circle of Protection Black C :W:	.25	.50
□ 35 Circle of Protection Blue C :W:	.25	.50
□ 36 Circle of Protection Green C :W:	.25	.50
□ 37 Circle of Protection Red C :W:	.25	.50
□ 38 Circle of Protection White C :W:	.25	.50
□ 39 Clockwork Beast R :A:	.50	1.00
□ 40 Clone U :B:	1.50	3.00
□ 41 Cockatrice R :G:	.50	1.00
□ 42 Conservator U :A:	.50	1.00
□ 43 Contract from Below R :K:	2.00	4.00
□ 44 Control Magic U :B:	1.00	2.00
□ 45 Conversion U :W:	.50	1.00
□ 46 Copy Artifact R :B:	2.50	5.00
□ 47 Counterspell U :B:	1.50	3.00
□ 48 Craw Wurm C :G:	.25	.50
□ 49 Creature Bond C :B:	.15	.30
□ 50 Crumble U :G:	.50	1.00
□ 51 Crusade R :W:	3.50	7.00
□ 52 Crystal Rod U :A:	.50	1.00
□ 53 Cursed Land U :K:	.50	1.00
□ 54 Dancing Scimitar R :A:	.50	1.00
□ 55 Dark Ritual C :K:	.75	1.50
□ 56 Darkpact R :K:	.50	1.00
□ 57 Death Ward C :W:	.15	.30
□ 58 Deathgrip U :K:	.50	1.00
□ 59 Deathlace R :K:	.50	1.00
□ 60 Demonic Attorney R :K:	.50	1.00
□ 61 Demonic Hordes R :K:	2.00	4.00
□ 62 Demonic Tutor U :K:	6.00	12.00
□ 63 Desert Twister U :G:	.50	1.00
□ 64 Dingus Egg R :A:	1.00	2.00
□ 65 Disenchant C :W:	.15	.30
□ 66 Disintegrate C :R:	.50	1.00
□ 67 Disrupting Scepter R :A:	1.50	3.00
□ 68 Dragon Engine R :A:	1.00	2.00
□ 69 Dragon Whelp U :R:	1.00	2.00
□ 70 Drain Life C :K:	.15	.30
□ 71 Drain Power R :B:	.50	1.00
□ 72 Drudge Skeletons C :K:	.15	.30
□ 73 Dwarven Warriors C :R:	.15	.30
□ 74 Dwarven Weaponsmith U :R:	.50	1.00
□ 75 Earth Elemental U :R:	.50	1.00
□ 76 Earthbind C :R:	.15	.30
□ 77 Earthquake R :R:	2.50	5.00
□ 78 Ebony Horse R :A:	.50	1.00
□ 79 El-Hajjaj R :K: :G:	.50	1.00
□ 80 Elvish Archers R :G:	1.50	3.00
□ 81 Energy Flux U :B:	.50	1.00
□ 82 Erg Raiders C :K:	.15	.30
□ 83 Evil Presence U :K:	.50	1.00
□ 84 Eye for an Eye R :W:	1.00	2.00
□ 85 Farmstead R :W:	.50	1.00
□ 86 Fastbond R :G:	4.00	8.00
□ 87 Fear C :K:	.15	.30
□ 88 Feedback U :B:	.50	1.00
□ 89 Fire Elemental U :R:	.50	1.00
□ 90 Fireball C :R:	.50	1.00
□ 91 Firebreathing C :R:	.15	.30
□ 92 Flashfires U :R:	1.00	2.00
□ 93 Flight C :B:	.15	.30
□ 94 Flying Carpet R :A:	.75	1.50
□ 95 Fog C :G:	.15	.30
□ 96 Force of Nature R :G:	1.50	3.00
□ 97 Forest v1 C :L:	.15	.30
□ 98 Forest v2 C :L:	.15	.30
□ 99 Forest v3 C :L:	.15	.30
□ 100 Fork R :R:	6.00	12.00
□ 101 Frozen Shade C :K:	1.50	3.00
□ 102 Fungusaur R :G:	1.00	2.00
□ 103 Gaea's Liege R :G: :A:	1.50	3.00
□ 104 Giant Growth C :G:	.50	1.00
□ 105 Giant Spider C :G:	.15	.30
□ 106 Glasses of Urza U :A:	.50	1.00
□ 107 Gloom U :K:	.50	1.00
□ 108 Goblin Balloon Brigade U :R:	1.00	2.00
□ 109 Goblin King R :R:	2.00	4.00
□ 110 Granite Gargoyle R :R:	1.50	3.00
□ 111 Gray Ogre C :R:	.15	.30
□ 112 Green Ward U :W:	.50	1.00
□ 113 Grizzly Bears C :G:	.15	.30
□ 114 Guardian Angel C :W:	.15	.30
□ 115 Healing Salve C :W:	.15	.30
□ 116 Helm of Chatzuk R :A:	.75	1.50
□ 117 Hill Giant C :R:	.15	.30
□ 118 Hive, The R :A:	1.00	2.00
□ 119 Holy Armor C :W:	.15	.30
□ 120 Holy Strength C :W:	.15	.30
□ 121 Howl from Beyond C :K:	.15	.30
□ 122 Howling Mine R :A:	4.00	8.00
□ 123 Hurkyl's Recall R :B:	1.00	2.00
□ 124 Hurloon Minotaur C :R:	.15	.30
□ 125 Hurricane U :G:	1.50	3.00
□ 126 Hypnotic Specter U :K:	6.00	12.00
□ 127 Instill Energy U :G:	.50	1.00
□ 128 Iron Star U :A:	1.00	2.00
□ 129 Ironroot Treefolk C :G:	.15	.30
□ 130 Island Fish Jasconius R :B:	1.00	2.00
□ 131 Island Sanctuary R :W:	1.00	2.00
□ 132 Island v1 C :L:	.15	.30
□ 133 Island v2 C :L:	.15	.30
□ 134 Island v3 C :L: :A:	.15	.30
□ 135 Ivory Cup U :A:	.50	1.00
□ 136 Ivory Tower R :A:	3.50	7.00
□ 137 Jade Monolith R :A:	1.00	2.00
□ 138 Jandor's Ring R :A:	1.00	2.00
□ 139 Jandor's Saddlebags R :A:	1.00	2.00
□ 140 Jayemdae Tome R :A:	1.00	2.00
□ 141 Juggernaut U :A:	1.50	3.00
□ 142 Jump C :B:	.15	.30
□ 143 Karma U :W:	.50	1.00
□ 144 Keldon Warlord U :R:	1.00	2.00
□ 145 Kird Ape C :R:	.50	1.00
□ 146 Kormus Bell R :A:	1.00	2.00
□ 147 Kudzu R :G:	1.00	2.00
□ 148 Lance U :W:	.50	1.00
□ 149 Ley Druid U :G:	.50	1.00
□ 150 Library of Leng U :A:	.50	1.00
□ 151 Lifeforce U :G:	.50	1.00
□ 152 Lifelace R :G:	1.00	2.00
□ 153 Lifetap U :B:	.50	1.00
□ 154 Lightning Bolt C :R:	2.50	5.00
□ 155 Living Artifact R :G:	1.00	2.00
□ 156 Living Lands R :G:	1.00	2.00
□ 157 Living Wall U :A:	.50	1.00
□ 158 Llanowar Elves C :G:	.50	1.00
□ 159 Lord of Atlantis R :B:	2.00	4.00
□ 160 Lord of the Pit R :K:	1.50	3.00
□ 161 Lure U :G:	1.00	2.00
□ 162 Magical Hack R :B:	1.00	2.00
□ 163 Magnetic Mountain R :R:	1.00	2.00
□ 164 Mahamoti Djinn R :B:	2.50	5.00
□ 165 Mana Flare R :R:	3.00	6.00
□ 166 Mana Short R :B:	2.00	4.00
□ 167 Mana Vault R :A:	3.00	6.00
□ 168 Manabarbs R :R:	1.00	2.00
□ 169 Meekstone R :A:	1.50	3.00
□ 170 Merfolk of the Pearl Trident C :B:	.15	.30
□ 171 Mesa Pegasus C :W:	.15	.30
□ 172 Mijae Djinn R :R:	1.00	2.00
□ 173 Millstone R :A: :K:	2.50	5.00
□ 174 Mind Twist R :K:	3.50	7.00
□ 175 Mishra's War Machine R :A:	1.00	2.00
□ 176 Mons's Goblin Raiders C :R:	.15	.30
□ 177 Mountain v1 C :L:	.15	.30
□ 178 Mountain v2 C :L:	.15	.30
□ 179 Mountain v3 C :L:	.15	.30
□ 180 Nether Shadow R :K:	1.00	2.00
□ 181 Nettling Imp U :K:	.50	1.00
□ 182 Nevinyrral's Disk R :A:	4.00	8.00
□ 183 Nightmare R :K:	3.50	7.00
□ 184 Northern Paladin R :W:	2.50	5.00
□ 185 Obsianus Golem U :A:	.50	1.00
□ 186 Onulet R :A:	1.00	2.00
□ 187 Orcish Artillery U :R:	.50	1.00
□ 188 Orcish Oriflamme U :R:	.50	1.00
□ 189 Ornithopter U :A:	1.00	2.00
□ 190 Paralyze C :K:	.15	.30
□ 191 Pearled Unicorn C :W:	.15	.30
□ 192 Personal Incarnation R :W:	1.00	2.00
□ 193 Pestilence C :K:	.15	.30
□ 194 Phantasmal Forces U :B:	.50	1.00
□ 195 Phantasmal Terrain C :B:	.15	.30
□ 196 Phantom Monster U :B:	.50	1.00
□ 197 Pirate Ship R :B:	.50	1.00
□ 198 Plague Rats C :K:	.15	.30
□ 199 Plains v1 C :L:	.15	.30
□ 200 Plains v2 C :L:	.15	.30
□ 201 Plains v3 C :L:	.15	.30
□ 202 Plateau R :L:	25.00	50.00
□ 203 Power Leak C :B:	.15	.30
□ 204 Power Sink C :B:	.15	.30
□ 205 Power Surge R :R:	1.00	2.00
□ 206 Primal Clay R :A:	1.00	2.00
□ 207 Prodigal Sorcerer C :B:	.15	.30
□ 208 Psychic Venom C :B:	.15	.30
□ 209 Purelace R :W:	1.00	2.00
□ 210 Rack, The U :A:	1.50	3.00
□ 211 Raise Dead C :K:	.15	.30
□ 212 Reconstruction C :B:	.15	.30
□ 213 Red Elemental Blast C :R:	.15	.30
□ 214 Red Ward U :W:	.50	1.00
□ 215 Regeneration C :G:	.15	.30
□ 216 Regrowth U :G:	1.00	2.00
□ 217 Resurrection U :W:	.50	1.00
□ 218 Reverse Damage R :W:	1.00	2.00
□ 219 Reverse Polarity U :W:	.50	1.00
□ 220 Righteousness R :W:	.50	1.00
□ 221 Roc of Kher Ridges R :R:	2.00	4.00
□ 222 Rock Hydra R :R:	2.00	4.00
□ 223 Rocket Launcher R :A:	1.50	3.00
□ 224 Rod of Ruin U :A:	.50	1.00
□ 225 Royal Assassin R :K:	5.00	10.00
□ 226 Sacrifice U :K:	.50	1.00
□ 227 Samite Healer C :W:	.15	.30
□ 228 Savannah Lions R :W:	4.00	8.00
□ 229 Savannah R :L:	40.00	80.00
□ 230 Scathe Zombies C :K:	.15	.30
□ 231 Scavenging Ghoul U :K:	.50	1.00
□ 232 Scrubland R :L:	30.00	60.00
□ 233 Scryb Sprites C :G:	.15	.30
□ 234 Sea Serpent C :B:	.15	.30
□ 235 Sedge Troll R :R:	2.00	4.00
□ 236 Sengir Vampire U :K:	2.00	4.00
□ 237 Serendib Efreet R :B:	3.00	6.00
□ 238 Serra Angel U :W:	3.00	6.00
□ 239 Shanodin Dryads C :G:	.15	.30
□ 240 Shatter C :R:	.15	.30
□ 241 Shatterstorm U :R:	1.00	2.00
□ 242 Shivan Dragon R :R:	6.00	12.00
□ 243 Simulacrum U :K:	.50	1.00
□ 244 Siren's Call U :B:	.50	1.00
□ 245 Sleight of Mind R :B:	1.00	2.00
□ 246 Smoke R :R:	1.00	2.00
□ 247 Sol Ring U :A:	7.50	15.00
□ 248 Sorceress Queen R :K:	2.00	4.00
□ 249 Soul Net U :A:	.50	1.00
□ 250 Spell Blast C :B:	.15	.30
□ 251 Stasis R :B:	2.50	5.00
□ 252 Steal Artifact U :B:	.50	1.00
□ 253 Stone Giant U :R:	.50	1.00
□ 254 Stone Rain C :R:	.15	.30
□ 255 Stream of Life C :G:	.15	.30
□ 256 Sunglasses of Urza R :A:	1.00	2.00
□ 257 Swamp v1 C :L:	.15	.30
□ 258 Swamp v2 C :L:	.15	.30
□ 259 Swamp v3 C :L:	.15	.30
□ 260 Swords to Plowshares U :W:	1.50	3.00
□ 261 Taiga R :L:	30.00	60.00
□ 262 Terror C :K:	.15	.30
□ 263 Thicket Basilisk U :G:	.50	1.00
□ 264 Thoughtlace R :B:	1.00	2.00
□ 265 Throne of Bone U :A:	.50	1.00
□ 266 Timber Wolves R :G:	1.00	2.00
□ 267 Titania's Song R :G:	1.00	2.00

❑ 268 Tranquility C :G: .15 .30
❑ 269 Tropical Island R :L: 50.00 100.00
❑ 270 Tsunami U :G: 1.00 2.00
❑ 271 Tundra R :L: 60.00 120.00
❑ 272 Tunnel U :R: :B: :R: .50 1.00
❑ 273 Underground Sea R :L: 60.00 120.00
❑ 274 Unholy Strength C :K: .15 .30
❑ 275 Unstable Mutation C :B: .15 .30
❑ 276 Unsummon C :B: .15 .30
❑ 277 Uthden Troll U :R: .50 1.00
❑ 278 Verduran Enchantress R :G: 1.50 3.00
❑ 279 Vesuvan Doppelganger R :B: 5.00 10.00
❑ 280 Veteran Bodyguard R :W: 2.50 5.00
❑ 281 Volcanic Eruption R :B: 1.00 2.00
❑ 282 Volcanic Island R :L: 50.00 100.00
❑ 283 Wall of Air U :B: .50 1.00
❑ 284 Wall of Bone U :K: .50 1.00
❑ 285 Wall of Brambles U :G: .50 1.00
❑ 286 Wall of Fire U :R: .50 1.00
❑ 287 Wall of Ice U :G: .50 1.00
❑ 288 Wall of Stone U :R: .50 1.00
❑ 289 Wall of Swords U :W: .50 1.00
❑ 290 Wall of Water U :B: .50 1.00
❑ 291 Wall of Wood C :G: .15 .30
❑ 292 Wanderlust U :G: .50 1.00
❑ 293 War Mammoth C :G: .15 .30
❑ 294 Warp Artifact R :K: .50 1.00
❑ 295 Water Elemental U :B: .50 1.00
❑ 296 Weakness C :K: .15 .30
❑ 297 Web R :G: .50 1.00
❑ 298 Wheel of Fortune R :R: 6.00 12.00
❑ 299 White Knight U :W: 1.00 2.00
❑ 300 White Ward U :W: .50 1.00
❑ 301 Wild Growth C :G: .15 .30
❑ 302 Will-O'-The-Wisp R :K: 4.00 8.00
❑ 303 Winter Orb R :A: 3.50 7.00
❑ 304 Wooden Sphere U :A: .50 1.00
❑ 305 Wrath of God R :W: 7.50 15.00
❑ 306 Zombie Master R :K: 1.50 3.00

1995 Magic the Gathering 4th Edition

Complete Set (378) 170.00 275.00
Starter Deck Box (10 Decks) 100.00 150.00
Starter Deck 13.00 17.00
Booster Box (36 Packs) 175.00 225.00
Booster Pack (15 Cards) 5.00 7.00
Released in April 1995
White borders and a 1995 copyright date

❑ 1 Abomination U :K: .50 1.00
❑ 2 Air Elemental U :B: 1.00 2.00
❑ 3 Alabaster Potion C :W: .15 .30
❑ 4 Aladdin's Lamp R :A: 1.00 2.00
❑ 5 Aladdin's Ring R :A: 1.00 2.00
❑ 6 Ali Baba U :R: .50 1.00
❑ 7 Amrou Kithkin C :W: .15 .30
❑ 8 Amulet of Kroog C :A: .25 .50
❑ 9 Angry Mob U :W: .50 1.00
❑ 10 Animate Artifact U :B: .50 1.00
❑ 11 Animate Dead U :K: 1.00 2.00
❑ 12 Animate Wall R :W: 1.00 2.00
❑ 13 Ankh of Mishra R :A: 1.50 3.00
❑ 14 Apprentice Wizard C :B: .15 .30
❑ 15 Armageddon R :W: 3.00 6.00
❑ 16 Armageddon Clock R :A: 1.00 2.00
❑ 17 Ashes to Ashes U :K: .50 1.00
❑ 18 Ashnod's Battle Gear U :A: .50 1.00
❑ 19 Aspect of Wolf R :G: 1.00 2.00
❑ 20 Backfire U :B: .50 1.00
❑ 21 Bad Moon R :K: 3.50 7.00
❑ 22 Balance R :W: 2.50 5.00
❑ 23 Ball Lightning R :R: 7.50 15.00
❑ 24 Battering Ram C :A: .15 .30
❑ 25 Benalish Hero C :W: .15 .30
❑ 26 Bird Maiden C :R: .15 .30
❑ 27 Birds of Paradise R :G: 7.50 15.00
❑ 28 Black Knight U :K: 1.00 2.00
❑ 29 Black Mana Battery R :A: 1.00 2.00
❑ 30 Black Vise U :A: 1.00 2.00
❑ 31 Black Ward U :W: .50 1.00
❑ 32 Blessing R :W: 1.50 3.00
❑ 33 Blight U :K: .50 1.00
❑ 34 Blood Lust C :R: .50 1.00
❑ 35 Blue Elemental Blast C :B: .50 1.00
❑ 36 Blue Mana Battery R :A: 1.00 2.00
❑ 37 Blue Ward U :W: .50 1.00
❑ 38 Bog Imp C :K: .15 .30
❑ 39 Bog Wraith U :K: .50 1.00
❑ 40 Bottle of Suleiman R :A: 1.50 3.00
❑ 41 Brainwash C :W: .15 .30
❑ 42 Brass Man U :A: .50 1.00
❑ 43 Bronze Tablet R :A: 1.00 2.00
❑ 44 Brothers of Fire C :R: .15 .30
❑ 45 Brute, The C :R: .15 .30
❑ 46 Burrowing U :R: .50 1.00
❑ 47 Carnivorous Plant C :G: .15 .30
❑ 48 Carrion Ants U :K: .50 1.00
❑ 49 Castle U :W: .50 1.00
❑ 50 Cave People U :R: .50 1.00
❑ 51 Celestial Prism U :A: .50 1.00
❑ 52 Channel U :G: 1.00 2.00
❑ 53 Chaoslace R :R: 1.00 2.00
❑ 54 Circle of Protection Artifacts U :W: .50 1.00
❑ 55 Circle of Protection Black C :W: .15 .30
❑ 56 Circle of Protection Blue C :W: .15 .30
❑ 57 Circle of Protection Green C :W: .15 .30
❑ 58 Circle of Protection Red C :W: .15 .30
❑ 59 Circle of Protection: White C :W: .15 .30
❑ 60 Clay Statue C :A: .15 .30
❑ 61 Clockwork Avian R :A: 1.50 3.00
❑ 62 Clockwork Beast R :A: 1.00 2.00
❑ 63 Cockatrice R :G: 1.00 2.00
❑ 64 Colossus of Sardia R :A: 1.50 3.00
❑ 65 Conservator U :A: .50 1.00
❑ 66 Control Magic U :B: 1.00 2.00
❑ 67 Conversion U :W: .50 1.00
❑ 68 Coral Helm R :A: 1.00 2.00
❑ 69 Cosmic Horror R :K: 1.00 2.00
❑ 70 Counterspell U :B: 1.50 3.00
❑ 71 Craw Wurm C :G: .15 .30
❑ 72 Creature Bond C :B: .15 .30
❑ 73 Crimson Manticore R :R: 1.50 3.00
❑ 74 Crumble U :G: .50 1.00
❑ 75 Crusade R :W: 3.00 6.00
❑ 76 Crystal Rod U :A: .50 1.00
❑ 77 Cursed Land U :K: .50 1.00
❑ 78 Cursed Rack U :A: .50 1.00
❑ 79 Cyclopean Mummy C :K: .15 .30
❑ 80 Dancing Scimitar R :A: 1.00 2.00
❑ 81 Dark Ritual C :K: .15 .30
❑ 82 Death Ward C :W: .15 .30
❑ 83 Deathgrip U :K: .50 1.00
❑ 84 Deathlace R :K: .15 .30
❑ 85 Desert Twister U :G: .30 .75
❑ 86 Detonate U :R: .50 1.00
❑ 87 Diabolic Machine U :A: .50 1.00
❑ 88 Dingus Egg R :A: 1.50 3.00
❑ 89 Disenchant C :W: .15 .30
❑ 90 Disintegrate C :R: .15 .30
❑ 91 Disrupting Scepter R :A: 1.50 3.00
❑ 92 Divine Transformation U :W: .50 1.00
❑ 93 Dragon Engine R :A: 1.00 2.00
❑ 94 Dragon Whelp U :R: .50 1.00
❑ 95 Drain Life C :K: .15 .30
❑ 96 Drain Power R :B: 1.00 2.00
❑ 97 Drudge Skeletons C :K: .15 .30
❑ 98 Durkwood Boars C :G: .15 .30
❑ 99 Dwarven Warriors C :R: .15 .30
❑ 100 Earth Elemental U :R: .25 .50
❑ 101 Earthquake R :R: .75 1.50
❑ 102 Ebony Horse R :A: 1.00 2.00
❑ 103 Elder Land Wurm R :W: 1.00 2.00
❑ 104 El-Hajjaj R :K: 1.00 2.00
❑ 105 Elven Riders U :G: .25 .50
❑ 106 Elvish Archers R :G: 1.00 2.00
❑ 107 Energy Flux U :B: 1.00 2.00
❑ 108 Energy Tap C :B: .15 .30
❑ 109 Erg Raiders C :K: .15 .30
❑ 110 Erosion C :B: .15 .30
❑ 111 Eternal Warrior C :R: .15 .30
❑ 112 Evil Presence U :K: .25 .50
❑ 113 Eye for an Eye R :W: 1.50 3.00
❑ 114 Fear C :K: .15 .30
❑ 115 Feedback U :B: .25 .50
❑ 116 Fellwar Stone U :A: .25 .50
❑ 117 Fire Elemental U :R: .25 .50
❑ 118 Fireball C :R: .15 .30
❑ 119 Firebreathing C :R: .15 .30
❑ 120 Fissure C :R: .15 .30
❑ 121 Flashfires U :R: .25 .50
❑ 122 Flight C :B: .15 .30
❑ 123 Flood C :B: .15 .30
❑ 124 Flying Carpet R :A: 1.00 2.00
❑ 125 Fog C :G: .15 .30
❑ 126 Force of Nature R :G: 2.00 4.00
❑ 127 Forest v1 C :L: .15 .30
❑ 128 Forest v2 C :L: .15 .30
❑ 129 Forest v3 C :L: .15 .30
❑ 130 Fortified Area C :W: .15 .30
❑ 131 Frozen Shade C :K: .15 .30
❑ 132 Fungusaur R :G: 1.00 2.00
❑ 133 Gaea's Liege R :G: 1.00 2.00
❑ 134 Gaseous Form C :B: .15 .30
❑ 135 Ghost Ship U :B: .25 .50
❑ 136 Giant Growth C :G: .15 .30
❑ 137 Giant Spider C :G: .15 .30
❑ 138 Giant Strength C :R: .15 .30
❑ 139 Giant Tortoise C :B: .15 .30
❑ 140 Glasses of Urza U :A: .25 .50
❑ 141 Gloom U :K: .25 .50
❑ 142 Goblin Balloon Brigade U :R: .50 1.00
❑ 143 Goblin King R :R: 2.00 4.00
❑ 144 Goblin Rock Sled C :R: .15 .30
❑ 145 Grapeshot Catapult C :A: .15 .30
❑ 146 Gray Ogre C :R: .15 .30
❑ 147 Greed R :K: 1.00 2.00
❑ 148 Green Mana Battery R :A: 1.50 3.00
❑ 149 Green Ward U :W: .50 1.00
❑ 150 Grizzly Bears C :G: .15 .30
❑ 151 Healing Salve C :W: .15 .30
❑ 152 Helm of Chatzuk R :A: 1.00 2.00
❑ 153 Hill Giant C :R: .15 .30
❑ 154 Hive, The R :A: 1.00 2.00
❑ 155 Holy Armor C :W: .15 .30
❑ 156 Holy Strength C :W: .15 .30
❑ 157 Howl from Beyond C :K: .15 .30
❑ 158 Howling Mine R :A: 3.50 7.00
❑ 159 Hurkyl's Recall R :B: 2.00 4.00
❑ 160 Hurloon Minotaur C :R: .15 .30
❑ 161 Hurr Jackal R :R: 1.00 2.00
❑ 162 Hurricane U :G: .50 1.00
❑ 163 Hypnotic Specter U :K: 5.00 10.00
❑ 164 Immolation C :R: .15 .30
❑ 165 Inferno R :R: 1.50 3.00
❑ 166 Instill Energy U :G: .50 1.00
❑ 167 Iron Star U :A: .25 .50
❑ 168 Ironclaw Orcs C :R: .15 .30
❑ 169 Ironroot Treefolk C :G: .15 .30
❑ 170 Island v1 C :L: .15 .30
❑ 171 Island v2 C :L: .15 .30
❑ 172 Island v3 C :L: .15 .30
❑ 173 Island Fish Jasconius R :B: 1.00 2.00
❑ 174 Island Sanctuary R :W: 1.00 2.00
❑ 175 Ivory Cup U :A: .25 .50
❑ 176 Ivory Tower R :A: 3.00 6.00
❑ 177 Jade Monolith R :A: 1.00 2.00
❑ 178 Jandor's Saddlebags R :A: 1.00 2.00
❑ 179 Jayemdae Tome R :A: 1.00 2.00
❑ 180 Jump C :B: .15 .30
❑ 181 Junún Efreet U :K: .25 .50
❑ 182 Karma U :W: .25 .50
❑ 183 Keldon Warlord U :R: .50 1.00
❑ 184 Killer Bees U :G: 1.50 3.00
❑ 185 Kismet U :W: .50 1.00
❑ 186 Kormus Bell R :A: 1.00 2.00
❑ 187 Land Leeches C :G: .15 .30
❑ 188 Land Tax R :W: 4.00 8.00
❑ 189 Leviathan R :B: 1.50 3.00
❑ 190 Ley Druid U :G: .25 .50
❑ 191 Library of Leng U :A: .50 1.00
❑ 192 Lifeforce U :G: .25 .50
❑ 193 Lifelace R :G: 1.00 2.00
❑ 194 Lifetap U :B: .25 .50
❑ 195 Lightning Bolt C :R: 2.00 4.00
❑ 196 Living Artifact R :G: 1.00 2.00
❑ 197 Living Lands R :G: 1.00 2.00
❑ 198 Llanowar Elves C :G: .25 .50
❑ 199 Lord of Atlantis R :B: 2.00 4.00
❑ 200 Lord of the Pit R :K: 2.50 5.00
❑ 201 Lost Soul C :K: .15 .30
❑ 202 Lure U :G: .25 .50
❑ 203 Magical Hack R :B: 1.00 2.00
❑ 204 Magnetic Mountain R :R: 1.00 2.00
❑ 205 Mahamoti Djinn R :B: 1.50 3.00
❑ 206 Mana Clash R :R: 1.00 2.00
❑ 207 Mana Flare R :R: 2.50 5.00
❑ 208 Mana Short R :B: 2.00 4.00
❑ 209 Mana Vault R :A: 2.00 4.00
❑ 210 Manabarbs R :R: 1.00 2.00
❑ 211 Marsh Gas C :K: .15 .30
❑ 212 Marsh Viper C :G: .15 .30
❑ 213 Meekstone R :A: 1.00 2.00
❑ 214 Merfolk of the Pearl Trident C :B: .15 .30
❑ 215 Mesa Pegasus C :W: .15 .30
❑ 216 Millstone R :A: 2.00 4.00
❑ 217 Mind Bomb U :B: .25 .50
❑ 218 Mind Twist R :K: 3.00 6.00
❑ 219 Mishra's Factory U :L: 3.00 6.00
❑ 220 Mishra's War Machine R :A: 1.00 2.00
❑ 221 Mons's Goblin Raiders C :R: .15 .30
❑ 222 Morale C :W: .15 .30
❑ 223 Mountain v1 C :L: .15 .30
❑ 224 Mountain v2 C :L: .15 .30
❑ 225 Mountain v3 C :L: .15 .30
❑ 226 Murk Dwellers C :K: .15 .30
❑ 227 Nafs Asp C :G: .15 .30
❑ 228 Nether Shadow R :K: 1.00 2.00
❑ 229 Nevinyrral's Disk R :A: 3.50 7.00
❑ 230 Nightmare R :K: 3.00 6.00
❑ 231 Northern Paladin R :W: 1.00 2.00
❑ 232 Oasis U :L: .25 .50
❑ 233 Obsianus Golem U :A: .25 .50
❑ 234 Onulet R :A: 1.00 2.00
❑ 235 Orcish Artillery U :R: .25 .50
❑ 236 Orcish Oriflamme U :R: .25 .50
❑ 237 Ornithopter U :A: 1.00 2.00
❑ 238 Osai Vultures U :W: .25 .50
❑ 239 Paralyze C :K: .15 .30
❑ 240 Pearled Unicorn C :W: .15 .30
❑ 241 Personal Incarnation R :W: 1.00 2.00
❑ 242 Pestilence C :K: .15 .30
❑ 243 Phantasmal Forces U :B: .25 .50
❑ 244 Phantasmal Terrain C :B: .15 .30
❑ 245 Phantom Monster U :B: .25 .50
❑ 246 Piety C :W: .15 .30
❑ 247 Pikemen C :W: .15 .30
❑ 248 Pirate Ship R :B: 1.00 2.00
❑ 249 Pit Scorpion C :K: .25 .50
❑ 250 Plague Rats C :K: .15 .30
❑ 251 Plains (ver. 1) C :L: .15 .30
❑ 252 Plains (ver. 2) C :L: .15 .30
❑ 253 Plains (ver. 3) C :L: .15 .30
❑ 254 Power Leak C :B: .15 .30
❑ 255 Power Sink C :B: .15 .30
❑ 256 Power Surge R :R: 1.00 2.00
❑ 257 Pradesh Gypsies C :G: .15 .30
❑ 258 Primal Clay R :A: 1.00 2.00
❑ 259 Prodigal Sorcerer C :B: .15 .30
❑ 260 Psionic Entity R :B: 1.00 2.00
❑ 261 Psychic Venom C :B: .15 .30
❑ 262 Purelace R :W: 1.00 2.00
❑ 263 Pyrotechnics U :R: .25 .50
❑ 264 Rack, The U :A: 1.00 2.00
❑ 265 Radjan Spirit U :G: .25 .50
❑ 266 Rag Man R :K: 1.00 2.00
❑ 267 Raise Dead C :K: .15 .30
❑ 268 Rebirth R :G: 1.00 2.00
❑ 269 Red Elemental Blast C :R: .15 .30
❑ 270 Red Mana Battery R :A: 1.00 2.00
❑ 271 Red Ward U :W: .25 .50
❑ 272 Regeneration C :G: .15 .30
❑ 273 Relic Bind R :B: .50 1.00
❑ 274 Reverse Damage R :W: .50 1.00
❑ 275 Righteousness R :W: 1.50 3.00
❑ 276 Rod of Ruin U :A: .25 .50
❑ 277 Royal Assassin R :K: 4.00 8.00
❑ 278 Samite Healer C :W: .15 .30
❑ 279 Sandstorm C :G: .15 .30
❑ 280 Savannah Lions R :W: 4.00 8.00
❑ 281 Scathe Zombies C :K: .15 .30
❑ 282 Scavenging Ghoul U :K: .25 .50
❑ 283 Scryb Sprites C :G: .15 .30
❑ 284 Sea Serpent C :B: .15 .30
❑ 285 Seeker C :W: .15 .30
❑ 286 Segovian Leviathan U :B: .25 .50
❑ 287 Sengir Vampire U :K: 2.00 4.00
❑ 288 Serra Angel U :W: 2.50 5.00
❑ 289 Shanodin Dryads C :G: .15 .30
❑ 290 Shapeshifter U :A: .25 .50
❑ 291 Shatter C :R: .15 .30
❑ 292 Shivan Dragon R :R: 3.50 7.00
❑ 293 Simulacrum U :K: .25 .50
❑ 294 Sindbad U :B: .25 .50
❑ 295 Siren's Call U :B: .25 .50
❑ 296 Sisters of the Flame C :R: .15 .30
❑ 297 Sleight of Mind R :B: 1.50 3.00
❑ 298 Smoke R :R: 1.50 3.00
❑ 299 Sorceress Queen R :K: 2.00 4.00
❑ 300 Soul Net U :A: .25 .50
❑ 301 Spell Blast C :B: .15 .30
❑ 302 Spirit Link U :W: 1.00 2.00
❑ 303 Spirit Shackle U :K: .25 .50
❑ 304 Stasis R :B: 2.00 4.00
❑ 305 Steal Artifact U :B: .25 .50
❑ 306 Stone Giant U :R: .25 .50
❑ 307 Stone Rain C :R: .15 .30
❑ 308 Stream of Life C :G: .15 .30
❑ 309 Strip Mine U :L: 2.00 4.00
❑ 310 Sunglasses of Urza R :A: 1.50 3.00
❑ 311 Sunken City C :B: .15 .30
❑ 312 Swamp v1 C :L: .15 .30
❑ 313 Swamp v2 C :L: .15 .30
❑ 314 Swamp v3 C :L: .15 .30
❑ 315 Swords to Plowshares U :W: 2.00 4.00
❑ 316 Sylvan Library R :G: 2.00 4.00
❑ 317 Tawnos's Wand U :A: .25 .50
❑ 318 Tawnos's Weaponry U :A: .25 .50
❑ 319 Tempest Efreet R :R: 1.50 3.00
❑ 320 Terror C :K: .15 .30
❑ 321 Tetravus R :A: 1.00 2.00
❑ 322 Thicket Basilisk U :G: .25 .50
❑ 323 Thoughtlace R :B: 1.00 2.00
❑ 324 Throne of Bone U :A: .25 .50
❑ 325 Timber Wolves R :G: .15 .30
❑ 326 Time Elemental R :B: 2.00 4.00
❑ 327 Titania's Song R :G: 1.50 3.00
❑ 328 Tranquility C :G: .15 .30
❑ 329 Triskelion R :A: 2.00 4.00
❑ 330 Tsunami U :G: .25 .50
❑ 331 Tundra Wolves C :W: .15 .30
❑ 332 Tunnel U :R: .25 .50
❑ 333 Twiddle C :B: .15 .30
❑ 334 Uncle Istvan U :K: .50 1.00
❑ 335 Unholy Strength C :K: .15 .30
❑ 336 Unstable Mutation C :B: .15 .30
❑ 337 Unsummon C :B: .15 .30
❑ 338 Untamed Wilds U :G: .25 .50
❑ 339 Urza's Avenger R :A: 1.00 2.00
❑ 340 Uthden Troll U :R: .25 .50
❑ 341 Vampire Bats C :K: .15 .30
❑ 342 Venom C :G: .25 .50
❑ 343 Verduran Enchantress R :G: 1.50 3.00
❑ 344 Visions U :W: .25 .50
❑ 345 Volcanic Eruption R :B: 1.50 3.00
❑ 346 Wall of Air U :B: .25 .50
❑ 347 Wall of Bone U :K: .25 .50
❑ 348 Wall of Brambles U :G: .25 .50
❑ 349 Wall of Dust U :R: .25 .50
❑ 350 Wall of Fire U :R: .25 .50
❑ 351 Wall of Ice U :G: .25 .50
❑ 352 Wall of Spears C :A: .15 .30
❑ 353 Wall of Stone U :R: .25 .50
❑ 354 Wall of Swords U :W: .25 .50
❑ 355 Wall of Water U :B: .25 .50
❑ 356 Wall of Wood C :G: .15 .30
❑ 357 Wanderlust U :G: .25 .50
❑ 358 War Mammoth C :G: .15 .30
❑ 359 Warp Artifact R :K: 1.50 3.00
❑ 360 Water Elemental U :B: .25 .50
❑ 361 Weakness C :K: .15 .30
❑ 362 Web R :G: 1.50 3.00
❑ 363 Whirling Dervish U :G: .25 .50
❑ 364 White Knight U :W: .50 1.00
❑ 365 White Mana Battery R :A: 1.00 2.00
❑ 366 White Ward U :W: .25 .50
❑ 367 Wild Growth C :G: .15 .30
❑ 368 Will-O'-The-Wisp R :K: 3.00 6.00
❑ 369 Winds of Change R :R: 1.00 2.00
❑ 370 Winter Blast U :G: .25 .50
❑ 371 Winter Orb R :A: 2.50 5.00
❑ 372 Wooden Sphere U :A: .25 .50
❑ 373 Word of Binding C :K: .15 .30
❑ 374 Wrath of God R :W: 7.50 15.00
❑ 375 Xenic Poltergeist R :K: 1.00 2.00
❑ 376 Yotian Soldier C :A: .15 .30
❑ 377 Zephyr Falcon C :B: .25 .50
❑ 378 Zombie Master R :K: 2.00 4.00

1995 Magic the Gathering Ice Age

Complete Set (383) 175.00 200.00
Starter Deck Box (10 Decks) 150.00 165.00
Starter Deck 15.00 20.00
Booster Box (36 Packs) 175.00 190.00
Booster Pack (15 Cards) 6.00 8.00
Released in June 1995

❑ 1 Abyssal Specter U :K: .50 1.00
❑ 2 Adarkar Sentinel U :A: .50 1.00
❑ 3 Adarkar Unicorn C :W: .15 .30
❑ 4 Adarkar Wastes R :L: 4.00 8.00
❑ 5 Aegis of the Meek R :A: 1.00 2.00
❑ 6 Aggression U :R: .50 1.00
❑ 7 Altar of Bone R :D: 1.25 2.50
❑ 8 Amulet of Quoz R :A: 1.25 2.50
❑ 9 Anarchy U :R: 1.00 2.00
❑ 10 Arctic Foxes C :W: .15 .30
❑ 11 Arcum's Sleigh U :A: .25 .50
❑ 12 Arcum's Weathervane U :A: .25 .50
❑ 13 Arcum's Whistle U :A: .25 .50
❑ 14 Arenson's Aura C :W: .15 .30
❑ 15 Armor of Faith C :W: .15 .30
❑ 16 Arnjlot's Ascent C :B: .15 .30
❑ 17 Ashen Ghoul U :K: .50 1.00
❑ 18 Aurochs C :G: .15 .30
❑ 19 Avalanche U :R: .25 .50
❑ 20 Balduvian Barbarians C :R: .15 .30
❑ 21 Balduvian Bears C :G: .15 .30
❑ 22 Balduvian Conjurer U :B: .50 1.00
❑ 23 Balduvian Hydra R :R: 1.50 3.00
❑ 24 Balduvian Shaman C :B: .15 .30
❑ 25 Barbarian Guides C :R: .15 .30
❑ 26 Barbed Sextant C :A: .15 .30
❑ 27 Baton of Morale U :A: .50 1.00
❑ 28 Battle Cry U :W: .50 1.00
❑ 29 Battle Frenzy C :R: .15 .30
❑ 30 Binding Grasp U :B: .50 1.00
❑ 31 Black Scarab U :W: .50 1.00
❑ 32 Blessed Wine C :W: .15 .30
❑ 33 Blinking Spirit R :W: 2.00 4.00
❑ 34 Blizzard R :G: 1.50 3.00
❑ 35 Blue Scarab U :W: .50 1.00
❑ 36 Bone Shaman C :R: .15 .30
❑ 37 Brainstorm C :B: 1.00 2.00
❑ 38 Brand of Ill Omen R :R: 1.00 2.00
❑ 39 Breath of Dreams U :B: .50 1.00
❑ 40 Brine Shaman C :K: .15 .30
❑ 41 Brown Ouphe C :G: .15 .30
❑ 42 Brushland R :L: 3.50 7.00
❑ 43 Burnt Offering C :K: .15 .30
❑ 44 Call to Arms R :W: 1.00 2.00
❑ 45 Caribou Range R :W: 1.00 2.00
❑ 46 Celestial Sword R :A: 1.00 2.00
❑ 47 Centaur Archer U :D: .50 1.00
❑ 48 Chaos Lord R :R: 1.00 2.00
❑ 49 Chaos Moon R :R: 1.00 2.00
❑ 50 Chromatic Armor R :D: 1.00 2.00
❑ 51 Chub Toad C :G: :W: :W: :W: :W: :W: .15 .30
❑ 52 Circle of Protection Black C :W: .15 .30
❑ 53 Circle of Protection Blue C :W: .15 .30
❑ 54 Circle of Protection Green C :W: .15 .30
❑ 55 Circle of Protection Red C :W: .15 .30
❑ 56 Circle of Protection White C :W: .15 .30
❑ 57 Clairvoyance C :B: .15 .30
❑ 58 Cloak of Confusion C :K: .15 .30
❑ 59 Cold Snap U :W: .50 1.00
❑ 60 Conquer U :R: .50 1.00
❑ 61 Cooperation C :W: .15 .30
❑ 62 Counterspell C :B: 1.00 2.00
❑ 63 Crown of the Ages R :A: 1.00 2.00
❑ 64 Curse of Marit Lage R :R: 1.00 2.00
❑ 65 Dance of the Dead U :K: 1.50 3.00
❑ 66 Dark Banishing C :K: .15 .30
❑ 67 Dark Ritual C :K: .50 1.00
❑ 68 Death Ward C :W: .15 .30
❑ 69 Deflection R :B: 1.50 3.00
❑ 70 Demonic Consultation U :K: 1.00 2.00
❑ 71 Despotic Scepter R :A: 1.50 3.00
❑ 72 Diabolic Vision U :D: .50 1.00
❑ 73 Dire Wolves C :G: .15 .30
❑ 74 Disenchant C :W: .15 .30
❑ 75 Dread Wight R :K: 1.00 2.00
❑ 76 Dreams of the Dead U :B: .50 1.00
❑ 77 Drift of the Dead U :K: .50 1.00
❑ 78 Drought U :W: .50 1.00
❑ 79 Dwarven Armory R :R: 1.00 2.00
❑ 80 Earthlink R :D: 1.00 2.00
❑ 81 Earthlore C :G: .15 .30
❑ 82 Elder Druid R :G: 1.00 2.00
❑ 83 Elemental Augury R :D: 1.50 3.00
❑ 84 Elkin Bottle R :A: 1.00 2.00
❑ 85 Elvish Healer C :W: .15 .30
❑ 86 Enduring Renewal R :W: 3.50 7.00
❑ 87 Energy Storm R :W: 1.50 3.00
❑ 88 Enervate C :B: .15 .30
❑ 89 Errant Minion C :B: .15 .30
❑ 90 Errantry C :R: .15 .30
❑ 91 Essence Filter C :G: .15 .30
❑ 92 Essence Flare C :B: .15 .30
❑ 93 Essence Vortex U :D: .25 .50
❑ 94 Fanatical Fever U :G: .25 .50
❑ 95 Fear C :K: .15 .30
❑ 96 Fiery Justice R :D: 1.00 2.00
❑ 97 Fire Covenant U :D: .25 .50
❑ 98 Flame Spirit U :R: .25 .50
❑ 99 Flare C :R: .15 .30
❑ 100 Flooded Woodlands R :D: 1.00 2.00
❑ 101 Flow of Maggots R :K: 1.00 2.00
❑ 102 Folk of the Pines C :G: .15 .30
❑ 103 Forbidden Lore R :G: 1.50 3.00
❑ 104 Force Void U :B: .50 1.00
❑ 105 Forest v1 L :L: .25 .50
❑ 106 Forest v2 L :L: .25 .50

MAGIC

Card	Low	High
☐ 107 Forest v3 L :L:	.25	.50
☐ 108 Forgotten Lore U :G:	.50	1.00
☐ 109 Formation R :W:	1.50	3.00
☐ 110 Foul Familiar C :K:	.15	.30
☐ 111 Foxfire C :G:	.15	.30
☐ 112 Freyalise Supplicant U :G:	.50	1.00
☐ 113 Freyalise's Charm U :G:	.50	1.00
☐ 114 Freyalise's Winds R :G:	1.00	2.00
☐ 115 Fumarole U :D:	.50	1.00
☐ 116 Fylgja C :W:	.15	.30
☐ 117 Fyndhorn Bow U :A:	.50	1.00
☐ 118 Fyndhorn Brownie C :G:	.15	.30
☐ 119 Fyndhorn Elder U :G:	.50	1.00
☐ 120 Fyndhorn Elves C :G:	1.00	2.00
☐ 121 Fyndhorn Pollen R :G:	1.50	3.00
☐ 122 Game of Chaos R :R:	1.50	3.00
☐ 123 Gangrenous Zombies C :K:	.15	.30
☐ 124 Gaze of Pain C :K:	.15	.30
☐ 125 General Jarkeld R :W:	1.00	2.00
☐ 126 Ghostly Flame R :D:	1.50	3.00
☐ 127 Giant Growth C :G:	.15	.30
☐ 128 Giant Trap Door Spider U :D:	.50	1.00
☐ 129 Glacial Chasm U :L:	.50	1.00
☐ 130 Glacial Crevasses R :R:	1.50	3.00
☐ 131 Glacial Wall U :B:	.50	1.00
☐ 132 Glaciers R :D:	1.50	3.00
☐ 133 Goblin Lyre R :A:	1.50	3.00
☐ 134 Goblin Mutant U :R:	.50	1.00
☐ 135 Goblin Sappers C :R:	.15	.30
☐ 136 Goblin Ski Patrol C :R:	.15	.30
☐ 137 Goblin Snowman U :R:	.50	1.00
☐ 138 Gorilla Pack C :G:	.15	.30
☐ 139 Gravebind R :K:	1.50	3.00
☐ 140 Green Scarab U :W:	.50	1.00
☐ 141 Grizzled Wolverine C :R:	.15	.30
☐ 142 Hallowed Ground U :W:	.50	1.00
☐ 143 Halls of Mist R :L:	1.00	2.00
☐ 144 Heal C :W:	.15	.30
☐ 145 Hecatomb R :K:	2.00	4.00
☐ 146 Hematite Talisman U :A:	.50	1.00
☐ 147 Hipparion U :W:	.50	1.00
☐ 148 Hoar Shade C :K:	.15	.30
☐ 149 Hot Springs R :G:	1.50	3.00
☐ 150 Howl from Beyond C :K:	.15	.30
☐ 151 Hurricane U :G:	.50	1.00
☐ 152 Hyalopterous Lemure U :K:	.50	1.00
☐ 153 Hydroblast C :B:	.15	.30
☐ 154 Hymn of Rebirth U :D:	.50	1.00
☐ 155 Ice Cauldron R :A:	1.50	3.00
☐ 156 Ice Floe U :L:	.50	1.00
☐ 157 Iceberg U :B:	.50	1.00
☐ 158 Icequake U :K:	.50	1.00
☐ 159 Icy Manipulator U :A:	2.00	4.00
☐ 160 Icy Prison R :B:	1.50	3.00
☐ 161 Illusionary Forces C :B:	1.00	2.00
☐ 162 Illusionary Presence R :B:	.50	1.00
☐ 163 Illusionary Terrain U :B:	.15	.30
☐ 164 Illusionary Wall C :B:	.15	.30
☐ 165 Illusions of Grandeur R :B:	3.50	7.00
☐ 166 Imposing Visage C :R:	.15	.30
☐ 167 Incinerate C :R:	.50	1.00
☐ 168 Infernal Darkness R :K:	1.00	2.00
☐ 169 Infernal Denizen R :K:	1.00	2.00
☐ 170 Infinite Hourglass R :A:	1.00	2.00
☐ 171 Infuse C :B:	.15	.30
☐ 172 Island v1 L :L:	.25	.50
☐ 173 Island v2 L :L:	.25	.50
☐ 174 Island v3 L :L:	.25	.50
☐ 175 Jester's Cap R :A:	3.00	6.00
☐ 176 Jester's Mask R :A:	2.00	4.00
☐ 177 Jeweled Amulet U :A:	.50	1.00
☐ 178 Johtull Wurm U :G:	.50	1.00
☐ 179 Jokulhaups R :R:	2.00	4.00
☐ 180 Juniper Order Druid C :G:	.15	.30
☐ 181 Justice U :W:	.50	1.00
☐ 182 Karplusan Forest R :L:	2.50	5.00
☐ 183 Karplusan Giant U :R:	.50	1.00
☐ 184 Karplusan Yeti R :R:	1.50	3.00
☐ 185 Kelsinko Ranger C :W:	.15	.30
☐ 186 Kjeldoran Dead C :K:	.15	.30
☐ 187 Kjeldoran Elite Guard U :W:	.50	1.00
☐ 188 Kjeldoran Frostbeast U :D:	.50	1.00
☐ 189 Kjeldoran Guard C :W:	.15	.30
☐ 190 Kjeldoran Knight R :W:	1.00	2.00
☐ 191 Kjeldoran Phalanx R :W:	1.00	2.00
☐ 192 Kjeldoran Royal Guard R :W:	1.00	2.00
☐ 193 Kjeldoran Skycaptain U :W:	.50	1.00
☐ 194 Kjeldoran Skyknight C :W:	.15	.30
☐ 195 Kjeldoran Warrior C :W:	.15	.30
☐ 196 Knight of Stromgald U :K:	.50	1.00
☐ 197 Krovikan Elementalist U :K:	.50	1.00
☐ 198 Krovikan Fetish C :K:	.15	.30
☐ 199 Krovikan Sorcerer C :B:	.15	.30
☐ 200 Krovikan Vampire U :K:	1.00	2.00
☐ 201 Land Cap R :L:	1.00	2.00
☐ 202 Lapis Lazuli Talisman U :A:	.50	1.00
☐ 203 Lava Burst C :R:	.25	.50
☐ 204 Lava Tubes R :L:	1.00	2.00
☐ 205 Legions of Lim-Dûl C :K:	.15	.30
☐ 206 Leshrac's Rite U :K:	.50	1.00
☐ 207 Leshrac's Sigil U :K:	.50	1.00
☐ 208 Lhurgoyf R :G:	2.00	4.00
☐ 209 Lightning Blow R :W:	1.50	3.00
☐ 210 Lim-Dûl's Cohort C :K:	.15	.30
☐ 211 Lim-Dûl's Hex U :K:	.50	1.00
☐ 212 Lost Order of Jarkeld R :W:	1.50	3.00
☐ 213 Lure U :G:	.50	1.00
☐ 214 Maddening Wind U :G:	.50	1.00
☐ 215 Magus of the Unseen R :B:	1.00	2.00
☐ 216 Malachite Talisman U :A:	.50	1.00
☐ 217 Márton Stromgald R :R:	2.00	4.00
☐ 218 Melee U :R:	.50	1.00
☐ 219 Melting U :R:	.50	1.00
☐ 220 Mercenaries R :W:	1.00	2.00
☐ 221 Merieke Ri Berit R :D:	1.00	2.00
☐ 222 Mesmeric Trance R :B:	1.00	2.00
☐ 223 Meteor Shower C :R:	.15	.30
☐ 224 Mind Ravel C :K:	.15	.30
☐ 225 Mind Warp U :K:	.50	1.00
☐ 226 Mind Whip R :K:	1.00	2.00
☐ 227 Minion of Leshrac R :K:	1.50	3.00
☐ 228 Minion of Tevesh Szat R :K:	1.00	2.00
☐ 229 Mistfolk C :B:	.15	.30
☐ 230 Mole Worms U :K:	.50	1.00
☐ 231 Monsoon R :D:	1.50	3.00
☐ 232 Moor Fiend C :K:	.15	.30
☐ 233 Mountain v1 L :L:	.25	.50
☐ 234 Mountain v2 L :L:	.25	.50
☐ 235 Mountain v3 L :L:	.25	.50
☐ 236 Mountain Goat C :R:	.15	.30
☐ 237 Mountain Titan R :D:	1.50	3.00
☐ 238 Mudslide R :R:	1.50	3.00
☐ 239 Musician R :B:	1.50	3.00
☐ 240 Mystic Might R :B:	1.50	3.00
☐ 241 Mystic Remora C :B:	.15	.30
☐ 242 Nacre Talisman U :A:	.50	1.00
☐ 243 Naked Singularity R :A:	1.50	3.00
☐ 244 Nature's Lore U :G:	.50	1.00
☐ 245 Necropotence R :K:	3.00	6.00
☐ 246 Norritt C :K:	.15	.30
☐ 247 Oath of Lim-Dûl R :K:	1.50	3.00
☐ 248 Onyx Talisman U :A:	.50	1.00
☐ 249 Orcish Cannoneers U :R:	.50	1.00
☐ 250 Orcish Conscripts C :R:	.15	.30
☐ 251 Orcish Farmer C :R:	.15	.30
☐ 252 Orcish Healer U :R:	.50	1.00
☐ 253 Orcish Librarian R :R:	1.50	3.00
☐ 254 Orcish Lumberjack C :R:	.15	.30
☐ 255 Orcish Squatters R :R:	1.50	3.00
☐ 256 Order of the Sacred Torch R :W:	1.00	2.00
☐ 257 Order of the White Shield U :W:	.50	1.00
☐ 258 Pale Bears R :G:	1.00	2.00
☐ 259 Panic C :R:	.15	.30
☐ 260 Pentagram of the Ages R :A:	1.00	2.00
☐ 261 Pestilence Rats C :K:	.15	.30
☐ 262 Phantasmal Mount U :B:	.50	1.00
☐ 263 Pit Trap U :A:	.50	1.00
☐ 264 Plains v1 L :L:	.25	.50
☐ 265 Plains v2 L :L:	.25	.50
☐ 266 Plains v3 L7 :L:	.25	.50
☐ 267 Polar Kraken R :B:	2.00	4.00
☐ 268 Portent C :B:	.15	.30
☐ 269 Power Sink C :B:	.15	.30
☐ 270 Pox R :K:	2.00	4.00
☐ 271 Prismatic Ward C :W:	.15	.30
☐ 272 Pygmy Allosaurus R :G:	2.00	4.00
☐ 273 Pyknite C :G:	.15	.30
☐ 274 Pyroblast C :R:	.15	.30
☐ 275 Pyroclasm U :R:	1.50	3.00
☐ 276 Rally C :W:	.15	.30
☐ 277 Ray of Command C :B:	.15	.30
☐ 278 Ray of Erasure C :B:	.15	.30
☐ 279 Reality Twist R :B:	1.00	2.00
☐ 280 Reclamation R :D:	1.00	2.00
☐ 281 Red Scarab U :W:	.50	1.00
☐ 282 Regeneration C :G:	.15	.30
☐ 283 Rime Dryad C :G:	.15	.30
☐ 284 Ritual of Subdual R :G:	1.00	2.00
☐ 285 River Delta R :L:	1.00	2.00
☐ 286 Runed Arch R :A:	1.00	2.00
☐ 287 Sabretooth Tiger C :R:	.15	.30
☐ 288 Sacred Boon U :W:	.25	.50
☐ 289 Scaled Wurm C :G:	.15	.30
☐ 290 Sea Spirit U :B:	.50	1.00
☐ 291 Seizures C :K:	.15	.30
☐ 292 Seraph R :W:	2.00	4.00
☐ 293 Shambling Strider C :G:	.15	.30
☐ 294 Shatter C :R:	.15	.30
☐ 295 Shield Bearer C :W:	.15	.30
☐ 296 Shield of the Ages U :A:	.50	1.00
☐ 297 Shyft R :B:	1.00	2.00
☐ 298 Sibilant Spirit R :B:	2.00	4.00
☐ 299 Silver Erne U :B:	.50	1.00
☐ 300 Skeleton Ship R :D:	1.50	3.00
☐ 301 Skull Catapult U :A:	.50	1.00
☐ 302 Sleight of Mind U :B:	.50	1.00
☐ 303 Snow Devil C :B:	.15	.30
☐ 304 Snow Fortress R :A:	1.50	3.00
☐ 305 Snow Hound U :W:	.50	1.00
☐ 306 Snowblind R :G:	1.00	2.00
☐ 307 Snow-Covered Forest L :L:	.25	.50
☐ 308 Snow-Covered Island L :L:	.25	.50
☐ 309 Snow-Covered Mountain L :L:	.25	.50
☐ 310 Snow-Covered Plains L :L:	.25	.50
☐ 311 Snow-Covered Swamp L :L:	.50	1.00
☐ 312 Snowfall C :B:	.25	.50
☐ 313 Soldevi Golem R :A:	1.00	2.00
☐ 314 Soldevi Machinist U :B:	.50	1.00
☐ 315 Soldevi Simulacrum U :A:	.50	1.00
☐ 316 Songs of the Damned C :K:	.15	.30
☐ 317 Soul Barrier U :B:	.50	1.00
☐ 318 Soul Burn C :K:	.15	.30
☐ 319 Soul Kiss C :K:	.15	.30
☐ 320 Spectral Shield U :D:	.50	1.00
☐ 321 Spoils of Evil R :K:	1.00	2.00
☐ 322 Spoils of War R :K:	1.00	2.00
☐ 323 Staff of the Ages R :A:	1.00	2.00
☐ 324 Stampede R :G:	1.00	2.00
☐ 325 Stench of Evil U :K:	.50	1.00
☐ 326 Stone Rain C :R:	.15	.30
☐ 327 Stone Spirit U :R:	.50	1.00
☐ 328 Stonehands C :R:	.15	.30
☐ 329 Storm Spirit R :D:	1.00	2.00
☐ 330 Stormbind R :D:	2.00	4.00
☐ 331 Stromgald Cabal R :K:	1.00	2.00
☐ 332 Stunted Growth R :G:	2.00	4.00
☐ 333 Sulfurous Springs R :L:	3.50	7.00
☐ 334 Sunstone U :A:	.50	1.00
☐ 335 Swamp v1 L :L:	.25	.50
☐ 336 Swamp v2 L :L:	.25	.50
☐ 337 Swamp v3 L :L:	.25	.50
☐ 338 Swords to Plowshares U :W:	2.50	5.00
☐ 339 Tarpan C :G:	.15	.30
☐ 340 Thermokarst U :G:	1.00	2.00
☐ 341 Thoughtleech U :G:	.50	1.00
☐ 342 Thunder Wall U :B:	.50	1.00
☐ 343 Timberline Ridge R :L:	1.00	2.00
☐ 344 Time Bomb R :A:	1.50	3.00
☐ 345 Tinder Wall C :G:	.50	1.00
☐ 346 Tor Giant C :R:	.15	.30
☐ 347 Total War R :R:	1.50	3.00
☐ 348 Touch of Death C :K:	.15	.30
☐ 349 Touch of Vitae U :G:	.50	1.00
☐ 350 Trailblazer R :G:	1.00	2.00
☐ 351 Underground River R :L:	2.50	5.00
☐ 352 Updraft U :B:	.50	1.00
☐ 353 Urza's Bauble U :A:	.50	1.00
☐ 354 Veldt R :L:	1.00	2.00
☐ 355 Venomous Breath U :G:	.50	1.00
☐ 356 Vertigo U :R:	.50	1.00
☐ 357 Vexing Arcanix R :A:	1.50	3.00
☐ 358 Vibrating Sphere R :A:	1.00	2.00
☐ 359 Walking Wall U :A:	.50	1.00
☐ 360 Wall of Lava U :R:	.50	1.00
☐ 361 Wall of Pine Needles U :G:	.50	1.00
☐ 362 Wall of Shields U :A:	.50	1.00
☐ 363 War Chariot U :A:	.50	1.00
☐ 364 Warning C :W:	.15	.30
☐ 365 Whalebone Glider U :A:	.50	1.00
☐ 366 White Scarab U :W:	.50	1.00
☐ 367 Whiteout U :G:	.50	1.00
☐ 368 Wiitigo R :G:	1.00	2.00
☐ 369 Wild Growth C :G:	.15	.30
☐ 370 Wind Spirit U :B:	1.00	2.00
☐ 371 Wings of Aesthir U :D:	.50	1.00
☐ 372 Winter's Chill R :B:	1.50	3.00
☐ 373 Withering Wisps U :K:	.50	1.00
☐ 374 Woolly Mammoths C :G:	.15	.30
☐ 375 Woolly Spider C :G:	.15	.30
☐ 376 Word of Blasting U :R:	.50	1.00
☐ 377 Word of Undoing C :B:	.15	.30
☐ 378 Wrath of Marit Lage R :B:	1.00	2.00
☐ 379 Yavimaya Gnats U :G:	.50	1.00
☐ 380 Zuran Enchanter C :B:	.15	.30
☐ 381 Zuran Orb U :A:	2.00	4.00
☐ 382 Zuran Spellcaster C :B:	.15	.30
☐ 383 Zur's Weirding R :B:	1.50	3.00

1995 Magic the Gathering Homelands

	Low	High
Complete Set (140)	30.00	60.00
Booster Box (60 Packs)	70.00	100.00
Booster Pack (8 Cards)	2.50	3.25
Released in October 1995		
☐ 1 Abbey Gargoyles U :W:	.50	1.00
☐ 2 Abbey Matron v1 C :W:	.15	.30
☐ 3 Abbey Matron v2 C :W:	.15	.30
☐ 4 AEther Storm U :B:	.25	.50
☐ 5 Aliban's Tower v1 C :R:	.15	.30
☐ 6 Aliban's Tower v2 C :R:	.15	.30
☐ 7 Ambush C :R:	.15	.30
☐ 8 Ambush Party v1 C :R:	.15	.30
☐ 9 Ambush Party v2 C :R:	.15	.30
☐ 10 Anaba Ancestor U :R:	1.00	2.00
☐ 11 Anaba Bodyguard v1 C :R:	.15	.30
☐ 12 Anaba Bodyguard v2 C :R:	.15	.30
☐ 13 Anaba Shaman v1 C :R:	.15	.30
☐ 14 Anaba Shaman v2 C :R:	.15	.30
☐ 15 Anaba Spirit Crafter U :R:	.50	1.00
☐ 16 An-Havva Constable U :G:	.50	1.00
☐ 17 An-Havva Inn U :G:	.50	1.00
☐ 18 An-Havva Township U :L:	.50	1.00
☐ 19 An-Zerrin Ruins U :R:	.50	1.00
☐ 20 Apocalypse Chime U :A:	.50	1.00
☐ 21 Autumn Willow U :G:	1.00	2.00
☐ 22 Aysen Abbey U :L:	.25	.50
☐ 23 Aysen Bureaucrats v1 C :W:	.15	.30
☐ 24 Aysen Bureaucrats v2 C :W:	.15	.30
☐ 25 Aysen Crusader U :W:	.50	1.00
☐ 26 Aysen Highway U :W:	.50	1.00
☐ 27 Baki's Curse U :B:	.50	1.00
☐ 28 Baron Sengir U :K:	5.00	10.00
☐ 29 Beast Walkers U :W:	.50	1.00
☐ 30 Black Carriage U :K:	.50	1.00
☐ 31 Broken Visage U :K:	.50	1.00
☐ 32 Carapace v1 C :G:	.15	.30
☐ 33 Carapace v2 C :G:	.15	.30
☐ 34 Castle Sengir U :L:	.50	1.00
☐ 35 Cemetery Gate v1 C :K:	.15	.30
☐ 36 Cemetery Gate v2 C :K:	.15	.30
☐ 37 Chain Stasis U :B:	.50	1.00
☐ 38 Chandler U :R:	.25	.50
☐ 39 Clockwork Gnomes C :A:	.15	.30
☐ 40 Clockwork Steed C :A:	.15	.30
☐ 41 Clockwork Swarm C :A:	.15	.30
☐ 42 Coral Reef C :B:	.15	.30
☐ 43 Dark Maze v1 C :B:	.15	.30
☐ 44 Dark Maze v2 C :B:	.15	.30
☐ 45 Daughter of Autumn U :G:	.50	1.00
☐ 46 Death Speakers U :W:	.25	.50
☐ 47 Didgeridoo U :A:	1.50	3.00
☐ 48 Drudge Spell U :K:	.50	1.00
☐ 49 Dry Spell v1 C :K:	.15	.30
☐ 50 Dry Spell v2 C :K:	.15	.30
☐ 51 Dwarven Pony U :R:	.50	1.00
☐ 52 Dwarven Sea Clan U :R:	.50	1.00
☐ 53 Dwarven Trader v1 C :R:	.15	.30
☐ 54 Dwarven Trader v2 C :R:	.15	.30
☐ 55 Ebony Rhino C :A:	.15	.30
☐ 56 Eron the Relentless U :R:	.50	1.00
☐ 57 Evaporate U :R:	.50	1.00
☐ 58 Faerie Noble U :G:	1.50	3.00
☐ 59 Feast of the Unicorn v1 C :K:	.15	.30
☐ 60 Feast of the Unicorn v2 C :K:	.15	.30
☐ 61 Feroz's Ban U :A:	.50	1.00
☐ 62 Folk of An-Havva v1 C :G:	.15	.30
☐ 63 Folk of An-Havva v2 C :G:	.15	.30
☐ 64 Forget U :B:	.50	1.00
☐ 65 Funeral March C :K:	.15	.30
☐ 66 Ghost Hounds U :K:	.25	.50
☐ 67 Giant Albatross v1 C :B:	.15	.30
☐ 68 Giant Albatross v2 C :B:	.15	.30
☐ 69 Giant Oyster U :B:	.25	.50
☐ 70 Grandmother Sengir U :K:	1.50	3.00
☐ 71 Greater Werewolf U :K:	.25	.50
☐ 72 Hazduhr the Abbot U :W:	.50	1.00
☐ 73 Headstone C :K:	.15	.30
☐ 74 Heart Wolf U :R:	.50	1.00
☐ 75 Hungry Mist v1 C :G:	.15	.30
☐ 76 Hungry Mist v2 C :G:	.15	.30
☐ 77 Ihsan's Shade U :K:	1.00	2.00
☐ 78 Irini Sengir U :K:	.50	1.00
☐ 79 Ironclaw Curse U :R:	.50	1.00
☐ 80 Jinx C :B:	.15	.30
☐ 81 Joven U :R:	.25	.50
☐ 82 Joven's Ferrets C :G:	.25	.50
☐ 83 Joven's Tools U :A:	.25	.50
☐ 84 Koskun Falls U :K:	.50	1.00
☐ 85 Koskun Keep U :L:	.25	.50
☐ 86 Labyrinth Minotaur v1 C :B:	.15	.30
☐ 87 Labyrinth Minotaur v2 C :B:	.15	.30
☐ 88 Leaping Lizard C :G:	.15	.30
☐ 89 Leeches U :W:	.50	1.00
☐ 90 Mammoth Harness U :G:	.50	1.00
☐ 91 Marjhan U :B:	.50	1.00
☐ 92 Memory Lapse v1 C :B:	.15	.30
☐ 93 Memory Lapse v2 C :B:	.15	.30
☐ 94 Merchant Scroll C :B:	1.50	3.00
☐ 95 Mesa Falcon v1 C :W:	.15	.30
☐ 96 Mesa Falcon v2 C :W:	.15	.30
☐ 97 Mystic Decree U :B:	1.00	2.00
☐ 98 Narwhal U :B:	.50	1.00
☐ 99 Orcish Mine U :R:	.25	.50
☐ 100 Primal Order U :G:	1.00	2.00
☐ 101 Prophecy U :W:	.25	.50
☐ 102 Rashka the Slayer U :W:	.25	.50
☐ 103 Reef Pirates v1 C :B:	.15	.30
☐ 104 Reef Pirates v2 C :B:	.15	.30
☐ 105 Renewal C :G:	.15	.30
☐ 106 Retribution U :R:	.25	.50
☐ 107 Reveka, Wizard Savant U :B:	1.00	2.00
☐ 108 Root Spider U :G:	.25	.50
☐ 109 Roots U :G:	.25	.50
☐ 110 Roterothopter C :A:	.15	.30
☐ 111 Rysorian Badger U :G:	.50	1.00
☐ 112 Samite Alchemist v1 C :W:	.15	.30
☐ 113 Samite Alchemist v2 C :W:	.15	.30
☐ 114 Sea Sprite U :B:	.50	1.00
☐ 115 Sea Troll U :B:	.50	1.00
☐ 116 Sengir Autocrat U :K:	1.50	3.00
☐ 117 Sengir Bats v1 C :K:	.15	.30
☐ 118 Sengir Bats v2 C :K:	.15	.30
☐ 119 Serra Aviary U :W:	1.00	2.00
☐ 120 Serra Bestiary U :W:	.25	.50
☐ 121 Serra Inquisitors U :W:	.25	.50
☐ 122 Serra Paladin C :W:	.15	.30
☐ 123 Serrated Arrows C :A:	.15	.30
☐ 124 Shrink v1 C :G:	.15	.30
☐ 125 Shrink v2 C :G:	.15	.30
☐ 126 Soraya the Falconer U :W:	1.00	2.00
☐ 127 Spectral Bears U :G:	.50	1.00
☐ 128 Timmerian Fiends U :K:	.50	1.00
☐ 129 Torture v1 C :K:	.15	.30
☐ 130 Torture v2 C :K:	.15	.30
☐ 131 Trade Caravan v1 C :W:	.15	.30
☐ 132 Trade Caravan v2 C :W:	.15	.30
☐ 133 Truce U :W:	1.00	2.00
☐ 134 Veldrane of Sengir U :K:	1.00	2.00
☐ 135 Wall of Kelp U :B:	1.50	3.00
☐ 136 Willow Faerie v1 C :G:	.15	.30
☐ 137 Willow Faerie v2 C :G:	.15	.30
☐ 138 Willow Priestess U :G:	1.50	3.00
☐ 139 Winter Sky U :R:	.50	1.00
☐ 140 Wizards' School U :L:	.50	1.00

1996 Magic the Gathering Alliances

	Low	High
Complete Set (199)	120.00	130.00
Booster Box (45 Packs)	190.00	250.00
Booster Pack (12 Cards)	5.00	8.00
Released in June 1996		
☐ 1 Aesthir Glider v1 C :A:	.15	.30
☐ 2 Aesthir Glider v2 C :A:	.15	.30
☐ 3 Agent of Stromgald v1 C :R:	.15	.30
☐ 4 Agent of Stromgald v2 C :R:	.15	.30
☐ 5 Arcane Denial v1 C :B:	1.00	2.00
☐ 6 Arcane Denial v2 C :B:	1.00	2.00
☐ 7 Ashnod's Cylix R :A:	1.00	2.00
☐ 8 Astrolabe v1 C :A:	.15	.30
☐ 9 Astrolabe v2 C :A:	.15	.30
☐ 10 Awesome Presence v1 C :B:	.15	.30
☐ 11 Awesome Presence v2 C :B:	.15	.30
☐ 12 Balduvian Dead U :K:	.25	.50
☐ 13 Balduvian Horde R :R:	2.50	5.00
☐ 14 Balduvian Trading Post R :L:	1.50	3.00
☐ 15 Balduvian War-Makers v1 C :R:	.15	.30
☐ 16 Balduvian War-Makers v2 C :R:	.15	.30
☐ 17 Benthic Explorers v1 C :B:	.15	.30
☐ 18 Benthic Explorers v2 C :B:	.15	.30
☐ 19 Bestial Fury v1 C :R:	.15	.30
☐ 20 Bestial Fury v2 C :R:	.15	.30
☐ 21 Bounty of the Hunt U :G:	.50	1.00
☐ 22 Browse U :B:	.50	1.00
☐ 23 Burnout U :R:	.50	1.00
☐ 24 Carrier Pigeons v1 C :W:	.15	.30
☐ 25 Carrier Pigeons v2 C :W:	.15	.30
☐ 26 Casting of Bones v1 C :K:	.15	.30
☐ 27 Casting of Bones v2 C :K:	.15	.30
☐ 28 Chaos Harlequin R :R:	1.00	2.00
☐ 29 Contagion U :K: :G: :G:	1.00	2.00
☐ 30 Deadly Insect v1 U :G:	.25	.50
☐ 31 Deadly Insect v2 U :G:	.25	.50
☐ 32 Death Spark U :R:	.25	.50
☐ 33 Diminishing Returns R :B:	1.50	3.00
☐ 34 Diseased Vermin U :K:	.50	1.00
☐ 35 Dystopia R :K:	1.00	2.00
☐ 36 Elvish Bard U :G:	.25	.50
☐ 37 Elvish Ranger v1 C :G:	.15	.30
☐ 38 Elvish Ranger v2 C :G:	.15	.30
☐ 39 Elvish Spirit Guide U :G:	3.00	6.00
☐ 40 Energy Arc U :D:	.25	.50
☐ 41 Enslaved Scout v1 C :R:	.15	.30
☐ 42 Enslaved Scout v2 C :R:	.15	.30
☐ 43 Errand of Duty v1 C :W:	.15	.30
☐ 44 Errand of Duty v2 C :W:	.15	.30
☐ 45 Exile R :W: :B: :B:	1.50	3.00
☐ 46 False Demise v1 U :B:	.50	1.00
☐ 47 False Demise v2 U :B:	.50	1.00
☐ 48 Fatal Lore R :K: :K: :K:	1.00	2.00
☐ 49 Feast or Famine v1 U :K:	.50	1.00
☐ 50 Feast or Famine v2 U :K:	.50	1.00
☐ 51 Fevered Strength v1 C :K:	.15	.30
☐ 52 Fevered Strength v2 C :K:	.15	.30
☐ 53 Floodwater Dam R :A:	1.00	2.00
☐ 54 Force of Will U :B:	50.00	100.00
☐ 55 Foresight v1 C :B:	.15	.30
☐ 56 Foresight v2 C :B:	.15	.30
☐ 57 Fyndhorn Druid v1 C :G:	.15	.30
☐ 58 Fyndhorn Druid v2 C :G:	.15	.30
☐ 59 Gargantuan Gorilla R :G:	1.00	2.00
☐ 60 Gift of the Woods v1 C :G:	.15	.30
☐ 61 Gift of the Woods v2 C :G:	.15	.30
☐ 62 Gorilla Berserkers v1 C :G:	.15	.30
☐ 63 Gorilla Berserkers v2 C :G:	.15	.30
☐ 64 Gorilla Chieftain v1 C :G:	.15	.30
☐ 65 Gorilla Chieftain v2 C :G: :R:	.15	.30
☐ 66 Gorilla Shaman v1 U :R:	.50	1.00
☐ 67 Gorilla Shaman v2 U :R:	.50	1.00
☐ 68 Gorilla War Cry v1 C :R:	.15	.30
☐ 69 Gorilla War Cry v2 C :R:	.15	.30
☐ 70 Guerrilla Tactics v1 C :R:	.15	.30
☐ 71 Guerrilla Tactics v2 C :R:	.15	.30
☐ 72 Gustha's Scepter R :A:	1.50	3.00
☐ 73 Hail Storm U :G:	.25	.50
☐ 74 Heart of Yavimaya R :L:	1.00	2.00
☐ 75 Helm of Obedience R :A:	1.50	3.00
☐ 76 Inheritance U :W:	.25	.50
☐ 77 Insidious Bookworms v1 C :K:	.15	.30
☐ 78 Insidious Bookworms v2 C :K:	.15	.30
☐ 79 Ivory Gargoyle R :W:	1.50	3.00
☐ 80 Juniper Order Advocate U :W:	.25	.50
☐ 81 Kaysa R :G:	1.50	3.00
☐ 82 Keeper of Tresserhorn R :K:	1.00	2.00
☐ 83 Kjeldoran Escort v1 C :W:	.15	.30
☐ 84 Kjeldoran Escort v2 C :W:	.15	.30
☐ 85 Kjeldoran Home Guard U :W:	.50	1.00
☐ 86 Kjeldoran Outpost R :L:	3.00	6.00
☐ 87 Kjeldoran Pride v1 C :W:	.15	.30
☐ 88 Kjeldoran Pride v2 C :W:	.15	.30
☐ 89 Krovikan Horror R :K:	1.50	3.00
☐ 90 Krovikan Plague U :K:	.25	.50
☐ 91 Lake of the Dead R :L:	4.00	8.00
☐ 92 Lat-Nam's Legacy v1 C :B:	.15	.30
☐ 93 Lat-Nam's Legacy v2 C :B:	.15	.30
☐ 94 Library of Lat-Nam R :B:	1.00	2.00
☐ 95 Lim-Dûl's High Guard v1 C :K:	.15	.30
☐ 96 Lim-Dûl's High Guard v2 C :K:	.15	.30
☐ 97 Lim-Dûl's Paladin U :D:	1.00	2.00
☐ 98 Lim-Dûl's Vault U :D:	1.00	2.00
☐ 99 Lodestone Bauble R :A:	1.00	2.00
☐ 100 Lord of Tresserhorn R :D:	1.50	3.00
☐ 101 Martyrdom v1 C :W:	.15	.30
☐ 102 Martyrdom v2 C :W:	.15	.30
☐ 103 Misfortune R :D:	1.00	2.00
☐ 104 Mishra's Groundbreaker U :A:	.25	.50
☐ 105 Misinformation U :K:	.25	.50
☐ 106 Mystic Compass U :A:	.25	.50
☐ 107 Nature's Blessing U :D:	.30	.75

MAGIC

❑ 108 Nature's Chosen U :G: .50 1.00
❑ 109 Nature's Wrath R :G: 1.50 3.00
❑ 110 Noble Steeds v1 C :W: .15 .30
❑ 111 Noble Steeds v2 C :W: .15 .30
❑ 112 Omen of Fire R :R: 1.00 2.00
❑ 113 Phantasmal Fiend v1 C :K: .15 .30
❑ 114 Phantasmal Fiend v2 C :K: .15 .30
❑ 115 Phantasmal Sphere R :B: 1.00 2.00
❑ 116 Phelddagrif R :D: 1.00 2.00
❑ 117 Phyrexian Boon v1 C :K: .15 .30
❑ 118 Phyrexian Boon v2 C :K: .15 .30
❑ 119 Phyrexian Devourer R :A: 1.00 2.00
❑ 120 Phyrexian Portal R :A: 1.00 2.00
❑ 121 Phyrexian War Beast v1 C :A: .15 .30
❑ 122 Phyrexian War Beast v2 C :A: .15 .30
❑ 123 Pillage U :R: 1.00 2.00
❑ 124 Primitive Justice U :R: .50 1.00
❑ 125 Pyrokinesis U :R: 1.00 2.00
❑ 126 Reinforcements v1 C :W: .15 .30
❑ 127 Reinforcements v2 C :W: .15 .30
❑ 128 Reprisal v1 U :W: .25 .50
❑ 129 Reprisal v2 U :W: .25 .50
❑ 130 Ritual of the Machine R :K: 1.00 2.00
❑ 131 Rogue Skycaptain R :R: 1.00 2.00
❑ 132 Royal Decree R :W: 1.00 2.00
❑ 133 Royal Herbalist v1 C :W: .15 .30
❑ 134 Royal Herbalist v2 C :W: .15 .30
❑ 135 Scarab of the Unseen U :A: .25 .50
❑ 136 Scars of the Veteran U :W: .30 .75
❑ 137 School of the Unseen U :L: .25 .50
❑ 138 Seasoned Tactician U :W: .25 .50
❑ 139 Sheltered Valley R :L: 1.00 2.00
❑ 140 Shield Sphere U :A: 1.50 3.00
❑ 141 Sol Grail R :A: 1.00 2.00
❑ 142 Soldevi Adnate v1 C :K: .15 .30
❑ 143 Soldevi Adnate v2 C :K: .15 .30
❑ 144 Soldevi Digger R :A: 1.50 3.00
❑ 145 Soldevi Excavations R :L: 1.00 2.00
❑ 146 Soldevi Heretic v1 C :B: .15 .30
❑ 147 Soldevi Heretic v2 C :B: .15 .30
❑ 148 Soldevi Sage v1 C :B: .15 .30
❑ 149 Soldevi Sage v2 C :B: .15 .30
❑ 150 Soldevi Sentry v1 C :A: .15 .30
❑ 151 Soldevi Sentry v2 C :A: .15 .30
❑ 152 Soldevi Steam Beast v1 C :A: .15 .30
❑ 153 Soldevi Steam Beast v2 C :A: .15 .30
❑ 154 Soldier of Fortune U :R: .50 1.00
❑ 155 Spiny Starfish U :B: .25 .50
❑ 156 Splintering Wind R :G: 1.00 2.00
❑ 157 Stench of Decay v1 C :K: .15 .30
❑ 158 Stench of Decay v2 C :K: .15 .30
❑ 159 Storm Cauldron R :A: 1.00 2.00
❑ 160 Storm Crow v1 C :B: .15 .30
❑ 161 Storm Crow v2 C :B: .15 .30
❑ 162 Storm Elemental U :B: .25 .50
❑ 163 Storm Shaman v1 C :R: .15 .30
❑ 164 Storm Shaman v2 C :R: .15 .30
❑ 165 Stromgald Spy U :K: .25 .50
❑ 166 Suffocation U :B: .25 .50
❑ 167 Surge of Strength U :D: .25 .50
❑ 168 Sustaining Spirit R :W: 1.00 2.00
❑ 169 Swamp Mosquito v1 C :K: .15 .30
❑ 170 Swamp Mosquito v2 C :K: .15 .30
❑ 171 Sworn Defender R :W: 1.00 2.00
❑ 172 Taste of Paradise v1 C :G: .15 .30
❑ 173 Taste of Paradise v2 C :G: .15 .30
❑ 174 Thawing Glaciers R :L: 3.50 7.00
❑ 175 Thought Lash R :B: 1.50 3.00
❑ 176 Tidal Control R :B: 1.50 3.00
❑ 177 Tornado R :G: 1.00 2.00
❑ 178 Undergrowth v1 C :G: .15 .30
❑ 179 Undergrowth v2 C :G: .15 .30
❑ 180 Unlikely Alliance U :W: .50 1.00
❑ 181 Urza's Engine R :A: 1.00 2.00
❑ 182 Varchild's Crusader v1 C :R: .15 .30
❑ 183 Varchild's Crusader v2 C :R: .15 .30
❑ 184 Varchild's War-Riders R :R: 1.50 3.00
❑ 185 Veteran's Voice v1 C :R: .15 .30
❑ 186 Veteran's Voice v2 C :R: .15 .30
❑ 187 Viscerid Armor v1 C :B: .15 .30
❑ 188 Viscerid Armor v2 C :B: .15 .30
❑ 189 Viscerid Drone U :B: .25 .50
❑ 190 Wandering Mage R :D: 1.00 2.00
❑ 191 Whip Vine v1 C :G: .15 .30
❑ 192 Whip Vine v2 C :G: .15 .30
❑ 193 Whirling Catapult R :A: 1.00 2.00
❑ 194 Wild Aesthir v1 C :W: .15 .30
❑ 195 Wild Aesthir v2 C :W: .15 .30
❑ 196 Winter's Night R :D: 1.00 2.00
❑ 197 Yavimaya Ancients v1 C :G: .15 .30
❑ 198 Yavimaya Ancients v2 C :G: .15 .30
❑ 199 Yavimaya Ants U :G: .50 1.00

1996 Magic the Gathering Mirage

Complete Set (350) 110.00 150.00
Starter Deck Box 100.00 140.00
Starter Deck 12.00 18.00
Booster Box (36 Packs) 175.00 200.00
Booster Pack (15 Cards) 7.00 9.00
Released in October 1996

❑ 1 Abyssal Hunter R :K: 1.00 2.00
❑ 2 Acidic Dagger R :A: 1.00 2.00
❑ 3 Afiya Grove R :G: 1.00 2.00
❑ 4 Afterlife U :W: .25 .50
❑ 5 Agility C :R: .15 .30
❑ 6 Alarum C :W: .15 .30
❑ 7 Aleatory U :R: .25 .50
❑ 8 Amber Prison R :A: 1.00 2.00
❑ 9 Amulet of Unmaking R :A: 1.00 2.00
❑ 10 Ancestral Memories R :B: 1.00 2.00
❑ 11 Armor of Thorns C :G: .15 .30
❑ 12 Armorer Guildmage C :R: .15 .30
❑ 13 Ashen Powder R :K: 1.00 2.00
❑ 14 Asmira, Holy Avenger R :D: 1.00 2.00
❑ 15 Auspicious Ancestor R :W: 1.00 2.00
❑ 16 Azimaet Drake C :B: .15 .30
❑ 17 Bad River U :L: .50 1.00
❑ 18 Barbed Foliage U :G: .25 .50
❑ 19 Barbed-Back Wurm U :K: .25 .50
❑ 20 Barreling Attack R :R: 1.00 2.00
❑ 21 Basalt Golem U :A: .25 .50
❑ 22 Bay Falcon C :B: .15 .30
❑ 23 Bazaar of Wonders R :B: 1.00 2.00
❑ 24 Benevolent Unicorn C :W: .15 .30
❑ 25 Benthic Djinn R :D: 1.00 2.00
❑ 26 Binding Agony C :K: .15 .30
❑ 27 Blighted Shaman U :K: .25 .50
❑ 28 Blind Fury U :R: .25 .50
❑ 29 Blinding Light U :W: .25 .50
❑ 30 Blistering Barrier C :R: .15 .30
❑ 31 Bone Harvest C :K: .15 .30
❑ 32 Bone Mask R :A: 1.00 2.00
❑ 33 Boomerang C :B: .15 .30
❑ 34 Breathstealer C :K: .15 .30
❑ 35 Brushwagg R :G: 1.50 3.00
❑ 36 Builder's Bane C :R: .15 .30
❑ 37 Burning Palm Efreet U :R: .25 .50
❑ 38 Burning Shield Askari C :R: .15 .30
❑ 39 Cadaverous Bloom R :D: 2.00 4.00
❑ 40 Cadaverous Knight C :K: .50 1.00
❑ 41 Canopy Dragon R :G: 2.00 4.00
❑ 42 Carrion R :K: 1.00 2.00
❑ 43 Catacomb Dragon R :K: 3.50 7.00
❑ 44 Celestial Dawn R :W: 1.25 2.50
❑ 45 Cerulean Wyvern U :B: .25 .50
❑ 46 Chaos Charm C :R: .15 .30
❑ 47 Chaosphere R :R: 1.00 2.00
❑ 48 Charcoal Diamond U :A: .50 1.00
❑ 49 Chariot of the Sun U :A: .50 1.00
❑ 50 Choking Sands C :K: .15 .30
❑ 51 Cinder Cloud U :R: .25 .50
❑ 52 Circle of Despair R :D: 1.00 2.00
❑ 53 Civic Guildmage C :W: .15 .30
❑ 54 Cloak of Invisibility C :B: .15 .30
❑ 55 Consuming Ferocity U :R: .25 .50
❑ 56 Coral Fighters U :B: .25 .50
❑ 57 Crash of Rhinos C :G: .15 .30
❑ 58 Crimson Hellkite R :R: 2.50 5.00
❑ 59 Crimson Roc U :R: .25 .50
❑ 60 Crypt Cobra U :K: 1.50 3.00
❑ 61 Crystal Golem U :A: .25 .50
❑ 62 Crystal Vein U :L: .50 1.00
❑ 63 Cursed Totem R :A: 1.00 2.00
❑ 64 Cycle of Life R :G: .50 1.00
❑ 65 Daring Apprentice R :B: 1.00 2.00
❑ 66 Dark Banishing C :K: .15 .30
❑ 67 Dark Ritual C :K: 1.00 2.00
❑ 68 Dazzling Beauty C :W: .25 .50
❑ 69 Decomposition U :G: .25 .50
❑ 70 Delirium U :D: .50 1.00
❑ 71 Dirtwater Wraith C :K: .15 .30
❑ 72 Discordant Spirit R :D: 1.00 2.00
❑ 73 Disempower C :W: .15 .30
❑ 74 Disenchant C :W: .15 .30
❑ 75 Dissipate U :B: 2.00 4.00
❑ 76 Divine Offering C :W: .15 .30
❑ 77 Divine Retribution R :W: 1.00 2.00
❑ 78 Drain Life C :K: .50 1.00
❑ 79 Dread Specter U :K: .25 .50
❑ 80 Dream Cache C :B: .15 .30
❑ 81 Dream Fighter C :B: .15 .30
❑ 82 Dwarven Miner U :R: .25 .50
❑ 83 Dwarven Nomad C :R: .15 .30
❑ 84 Early Harvest R :G: 3.50 7.00
❑ 85 Ebony Charm C :K: .15 .30
❑ 86 Ekundu Cyclops C :R: .15 .30
❑ 87 Ekundu Griffin C :W: .15 .30
❑ 88 Elixir of Vitality U :A: .25 .50
❑ 89 Emberwilde Caliph R :D: 1.00 2.00
❑ 90 Emberwilde Djinn R :R: 1.50 3.00
❑ 91 Energy Bolt R :D: 1.00 2.00
❑ 92 Energy Vortex R :B: 1.00 2.00
❑ 93 Enfeeblement C :K: .15 .30
❑ 94 Enlightened Tutor U :W: 4.00 8.00
❑ 95 Ersatz Gnomes U :A: .50 1.00
❑ 96 Ether Well U :B: .25 .50
❑ 97 Ethereal Champion R :W: 1.50 3.00
❑ 98 Fallow Earth U :G: .50 1.00
❑ 99 Favorable Destiny U :W: .50 1.00
❑ 100 Femeref Archers U :G: .50 1.00
❑ 101 Femeref Healer C :W: .15 .30
❑ 102 Femeref Knight C :W: .15 .30
❑ 103 Femeref Scouts C :W: .15 .30
❑ 104 Feral Shadow C :K: .15 .30
❑ 105 Fetid Horror C :K: .15 .30
❑ 106 Final Fortune R :R: 1.00 2.00
❑ 107 Fire Diamond U :A: .25 .50
❑ 108 Firebreathing C :R: .15 .30
❑ 109 Flame Elemental U :R: .25 .50
❑ 110 Flare C :R: .15 .30
❑ 111 Flash R :B: 1.00 2.00
❑ 112 Flood Plain U :L: .50 1.00
❑ 113 Floodgate U :B: .50 1.00
❑ 114 Fog C :G: .15 .30
❑ 115 Foratog U :G: .50 1.00
❑ 116 Forbidden Crypt R :K: 1.00 2.00
❑ 117 Forest A L :L: .25 .50
❑ 118 Forest B L :L: .25 .50
❑ 119 Forest C L :L: .25 .50
❑ 120 Forest D L :L: .25 .50
❑ 121 Forsaken Wastes R :K: 1.50 3.00
❑ 122 Frenetic Efreet R :D: 1.00 2.00
❑ 123 Giant Mantis C :G: .15 .30
❑ 124 Gibbering Hyenas C :G: .15 .30
❑ 125 Goblin Elite Infantry C :R: .50 1.00
❑ 126 Goblin Scouts U :R: .50 1.00
❑ 127 Goblin Soothsayer U :R: .50 1.00
❑ 128 Goblin Tinkerer C :R: .15 .30
❑ 129 Granger Guildmage C :G: .15 .30
❑ 130 GrassLands U :L: .25 .50
❑ 131 Grave Servitude C :K: .15 .30
❑ 132 Gravebane Zombie C :K: .15 .30
❑ 133 Grim Feast R :D: 1.00 2.00
❑ 134 Grinning Totem R :A: 1.00 2.00
❑ 135 Hakim, Loreweaver R :B: 1.00 2.00
❑ 136 Hall of Gemstone R :G: 1.00 2.00
❑ 137 Hammer of Bogardan R :R: 3.00 6.00
❑ 138 Harbinger of Night R :K: 1.50 3.00
❑ 139 Harbor Guardian U :D: .25 .50
❑ 140 Harmattan Efreet U :B: .25 .50
❑ 141 Haunting Apparition U :D: .25 .50
❑ 142 Hazerider Drake U :D: .25 .50
❑ 143 Healing Salve C :W: .15 .30
❑ 144 Hivis of the Scale R :R: 1.50 3.00
❑ 145 Horrible Hordes U :A: .25 .50
❑ 146 Igneous Golem U :A: .25 .50
❑ 147 Illicit Auction R :R: 1.00 2.00
❑ 148 Illumination U :W: .25 .50
❑ 149 Incinerate C :R: 1.50 3.00
❑ 150 Infernal Contract R :K: 1.00 2.00
❑ 151 Iron Tusk Elephant U :W: .25 .50
❑ 152 Island A L :L: .25 .50
❑ 153 Island B L :L: .25 .50
❑ 154 Island C L :L: .25 .50
❑ 155 Island D L :L: .25 .50
❑ 156 Ivory Charm C :W: .15 .30
❑ 157 Jabari's Influence R :W: 1.00 2.00
❑ 158 Jolrael's Centaur C :G: .15 .30
❑ 159 Jolt C :B: .15 .30
❑ 160 Jungle Patrol R :G: 1.00 2.00
❑ 161 Jungle Troll U :D: .25 .50
❑ 162 Jungle Wurm C :G: .15 .30
❑ 163 Kaervek's Hex U :K: .25 .50
❑ 164 Kaervek's Purge U :D: .25 .50
❑ 165 Kaervek's Torch C :R: .15 .30
❑ 166 Karoo Meerkat U :G: .25 .50
❑ 167 Kukemssa Pirates R :B: 1.00 2.00
❑ 168 Kukemssa Serpent C :B: .15 .30
❑ 169 Lead Golem U :A: .50 1.00
❑ 170 Leering Gargoyle R :D: 1.00 2.00
❑ 171 Lightning Reflexes C :R: .15 .30
❑ 172 Lion's Eye Diamond R :A: 5.00 10.00
❑ 173 Locust Swarm U :G: .50 1.00
❑ 174 Lure of Prey R :G: 1.00 2.00
❑ 175 Malignant Growth R :D: 1.00 2.00
❑ 176 Mana Prism U :A: .50 1.00
❑ 177 Mangara's Blessing U :W: .50 1.00
❑ 178 Mangara's Equity U :W: .50 1.00
❑ 179 Mangara's Tome R :A: 1.50 3.00
❑ 180 Marble Diamond U :A: .50 1.00
❑ 181 Maro R :G: 1.50 3.00
❑ 182 Meddle U :B: .50 1.00
❑ 183 Melesse Spirit U :W: 1.50 3.00
❑ 184 Memory Lapse C :B: .15 .30
❑ 185 Merfolk Raiders C :B: .15 .30
❑ 186 Merfolk Seer C :B: .15 .30
❑ 187 Mind Bend U :B: 1.00 2.00
❑ 188 Mind Harness U :B: .50 1.00
❑ 189 Mindbender Spores R :G: 1.00 2.00
❑ 190 Mire Shade U :K: .50 1.00
❑ 191 Misers' Cage R :A: 1.50 3.00
❑ 192 Mist Dragon R :B: 2.00 4.00
❑ 193 Moss Diamond U :A: .50 1.00
❑ 194 Mountain A L :L: .25 .50
❑ 195 Mountain B L :L: .25 .50
❑ 196 Mountain C L :L: .25 .50
❑ 197 Mountain D L :L: .25 .50
❑ 198 Mountain Valley U :L: .50 1.00
❑ 199 Mtenda Griffin U :W: .50 1.00
❑ 200 Mtenda Herder C :W: .15 .30
❑ 201 Mtenda Lion C :G: .15 .30
❑ 202 Mystical Tutor U :B: 2.50 5.00
❑ 203 Natural Balance R :G: 1.00 2.00
❑ 204 Nettletooth Djinn U :G: .50 1.00
❑ 205 Noble Elephant C :W: .15 .30
❑ 206 Nocturnal Raid U :K: .25 .50
❑ 207 Null Chamber R :W: 1.00 2.00
❑ 208 Pacifism C :W: .15 .30
❑ 209 Painful Memories U :K: .25 .50
❑ 210 Patagia Golem U :A: .50 1.00
❑ 211 Paupers' Cage R :A: 1.00 2.00
❑ 212 Pearl Dragon R :W: 1.50 3.00
❑ 213 Phyrexian Dreadnought R :A: 5.00 10.00
❑ 214 Phyrexian Purge R :D: 1.50 3.00
❑ 215 Phyrexian Tribute R :K: 1.50 3.00
❑ 216 Phyrexian Vault U :A: .50 1.00
❑ 217 Plains A L :L: .25 .50
❑ 218 Plains B L :L: .25 .50
❑ 219 Plains C L :L: .25 .50
❑ 220 Plains D L :L: .25 .50
❑ 221 Political Trickery R :B: 1.00 2.00
❑ 222 Polymorph R :B: 1.00 2.00
❑ 223 Power Sink C :B: .15 .30
❑ 224 Preferred Selection R :G: 1.00 2.00
❑ 225 Prismatic Boon U :D: .50 1.00
❑ 226 Prismatic Circle C :W: .15 .30
❑ 227 Prismatic Lace R :B: 1.50 3.00
❑ 228 Psychic Transfer R :B: 1.00 2.00
❑ 229 Purgatory R :D: 1.50 3.00
❑ 230 Purraj of Urborg R :K: 1.50 3.00
❑ 231 Pyric Salamander C :R: .15 .30
❑ 232 Quirion Elves C :G: .15 .30
❑ 233 Radiant Essence U :D: .25 .50
❑ 234 Raging Spirit C :R: .15 .30
❑ 235 Rampant Growth C :G: .15 .30
❑ 236 Rashida Scalebane R :W: 1.50 3.00
❑ 237 Ravenous Vampire U :K: .50 1.00
❑ 238 Ray of Command C :B: .15 .30
❑ 239 Razor Pendulum R :A: 1.00 2.00
❑ 240 Reality Ripple C :B: .15 .30
❑ 241 Reckless Embermage R :R: 1.00 2.00
❑ 242 Reflect Damage R :D: 1.50 3.00
❑ 243 Regeneration C :G: .15 .30
❑ 244 Reign of Chaos U :R: .50 1.00
❑ 245 Reign of Terror U :K: .50 1.00
❑ 246 Reparations R :D: 1.50 3.00
❑ 247 Restless Dead C :K: .15 .30
❑ 248 Ritual of Steel C :W: .15 .30
❑ 249 Rock Basilisk R :D: 1.00 2.00
❑ 250 Rocky Tar Pit U :L: .50 1.00
❑ 251 Roots of Life U :G: .50 1.00
❑ 252 Sabertooth Cobra C :G: .15 .30
❑ 253 Sacred Mesa R :W: 1.50 3.00
❑ 254 Sand Golem U :A: .25 .50
❑ 255 Sandbar Crocodile C :B: .15 .30
❑ 256 Sandstorm C :G: .15 .30
❑ 257 Sapphire Charm C :B: .15 .30
❑ 258 Savage Twister U :D: .50 1.00
❑ 259 Sawback Manticore R :D: 1.00 2.00
❑ 260 Sea Scryer C :B: .15 .30
❑ 261 Sealed Fate U :D: .25 .50
❑ 262 Searing Spear Askari C :R: .15 .30
❑ 263 Seedling Charm C :G: .15 .30
❑ 264 Seeds of Innocence R :G: 1.50 3.00
❑ 265 Serene Heart C :G: .15 .30
❑ 266 Sewer Rats C :K: .15 .30
❑ 267 Shadow Guildmage C :K: .15 .30
❑ 268 Shadowbane U :W: .25 .50
❑ 269 Shallow Grave R :K: 1.00 2.00
❑ 270 Shaper Guildmage C :B: .15 .30
❑ 271 Shauku, Endbringer R :K: 1.50 3.00
❑ 272 Shauku's Minion U :D: .50 1.00
❑ 273 Shimmer R :B: 1.50 3.00
❑ 274 Sidar Jabari R :W: 1.50 3.00
❑ 275 Sirocco U :R: .50 1.00
❑ 276 Skulking Ghost C :K: .15 .30
❑ 277 Sky Diamond U :A: .50 1.00
❑ 278 Soar C :B: .15 .30
❑ 279 Soul Echo R :W: 1.50 3.00
❑ 280 Soul Rend U :K: .25 .50
❑ 281 Soulshriek C :K: .25 .50
❑ 282 Spatial Binding U :D: .25 .50
❑ 283 Spectral Guardian R :W: 1.50 3.00
❑ 284 Spirit of the Night R :K: 6.00 12.00
❑ 285 Spitting Earth C :R: .15 .30
❑ 286 Stalking Tiger C :G: .15 .30
❑ 287 Stone Rain C :R: .15 .30
❑ 288 Stupor U :K: .25 .50
❑ 289 Subterranean Spirit R :R: 1.50 3.00
❑ 290 Sunweb R :W: 1.50 3.00
❑ 291 Superior Numbers U :G: .25 .50
❑ 292 Suq'Ata Firewalker U :B: 1.50 3.00
❑ 293 Swamp A L :L: .25 .50
❑ 294 Swamp B L :L: .25 .50
❑ 295 Swamp C L :L: .25 .50
❑ 296 Swamp D L :L: .25 .50
❑ 297 Tainted Specter R :K: 1.00 2.00
❑ 298 Talruum Minotaur C :R: .15 .30
❑ 299 Taniwha R :B: 1.00 2.00
❑ 300 Teeka's Dragon R :A: 4.00 8.00
❑ 301 Teferi's Curse C :B: .15 .30
❑ 302 Teferi's Drake C :B: .15 .30
❑ 303 Teferi's Imp R :B: 1.50 3.00
❑ 304 Teferi's Isle R :L: 1.50 3.00
❑ 305 Telim'Tor R :R: 1.50 3.00
❑ 306 Telim'Tor's Darts U :A: .25 .50
❑ 307 Telim'Tor's Edict R :R: 1.00 2.00
❑ 308 Teremko Griffin C :W: .15 .30
❑ 309 Thirst C :B: .15 .30
❑ 310 Tidal Wave U :B: .25 .50
❑ 311 Tombstone Stairwell R :K: 1.00 2.00
❑ 312 Torrent of Lava R :R: 1.00 2.00
❑ 313 Tranquil Domain C :G: .15 .30
❑ 314 Tropical Storm U :G: .25 .50
❑ 315 Uktabi Faerie C :G: .15 .30
❑ 316 Uktabi Wildcats R :G: 1.50 3.00
❑ 317 Unerring Sling U :A: .50 1.00
❑ 318 Unfulfilled Desires R :D: 1.00 2.00
❑ 319 Unseen Walker U :G: .50 1.00
❑ 320 Unyaro Bee Sting U :G: .50 1.00
❑ 321 Unyaro Griffin U :W: .50 1.00
❑ 322 Urborg Panther C :K: .15 .30
❑ 323 Vaporous Djinn U :B: .25 .50
❑ 324 Ventifact Bottle R :A: 1.50 3.00
❑ 325 Viashino Warrior C :R: .15 .30
❑ 326 Vigilant Martyr U :W: .50 1.00
❑ 327 Village Elder C :G: .15 .30
❑ 328 Vitalizing Cascade U :D: .50 1.00
❑ 329 Volcanic Dragon R :R: 3.00 6.00
❑ 330 Volcanic Geyser U :R: .50 1.00
❑ 331 Waiting in the Weeds R :G: 1.50 3.00
❑ 332 Wall of Corpses C :K: .15 .30
❑ 333 Wall of Resistance C :W: .15 .30
❑ 334 Wall of Roots C :G: .15 .30
❑ 335 Ward of Lights C :W: .15 .30
❑ 336 Warping Wurm R :D: 1.50 3.00
❑ 337 Wave Elemental U :B: .25 .50
❑ 338 Wellspring R :D: .25 .50
❑ 339 Wild Elephant C :G: .15 .30
❑ 340 Wildfire Emissary U :R: .25 .50
❑ 341 Windreaper Falcon U :D: .25 .50
❑ 342 Withering Boon U :K: .25 .50
❑ 343 Worldly Tutor U :G: 4.00 8.00
❑ 344 Yare R :W: 1.50 3.00
❑ 345 Zebra Unicorn U :D: .25 .50
❑ 346 Zhalfirin Commander U :W: .50 1.00
❑ 347 Zhalfirin Knight C :W: .15 .30
❑ 348 Zirilan of the Claw R :R: 2.00 4.00
❑ 349 Zombie Mob U :K: .50 1.00
❑ 350 Zuberi, Golden Feather R :W: 1.00 2.00

1997 Magic the Gathering 5th Edition

Complete Set (434) 190.00 250.00
Starter Deck Box (10 Decks) 120.00 150.00
Booster Box (36 Packs) 140.00 185.00
Starter Deck 12.00 15.00
Booster Pack (15 Cards) 4.50 6.00
Released in March 1997
White borders and a 1997 copyright date

❑ 1 Abbey Gargoyles U :W: .50 1.00
❑ 2 Abyssal Specter U :K: .50 1.00
❑ 3 Adarkar Wastes R :L: 3.50 7.00
❑ 4 Aether Storm U :B: .50 1.00
❑ 5 Air Elemental U :B: .50 1.00
❑ 6 Akron Legionnaire R :W: 1.00 2.00
❑ 7 Alabaster Potion C :W: .15 .30
❑ 8 Aladdin's Ring R :A: 1.50 3.00
❑ 9 Ambush Party C :R: .15 .30
❑ 10 Amulet of Kroog C :A: .15 .30
❑ 11 Angry Mob U :W: .25 .50
❑ 12 An-Havva Constable R :G: 1.50 3.00
❑ 13 Animate Dead U :K: 2.00 4.00
❑ 14 Animate Wall R :W: 1.50 3.00
❑ 15 Ankh of Mishra R :A: 1.50 3.00
❑ 16 Anti-Magic Aura U :B: .50 1.00
❑ 17 Arenson's Aura U :W: .50 1.00
❑ 18 Armageddon R :W: 3.00 6.00
❑ 19 Armor of Faith C :W: .15 .30
❑ 20 Ashes to Ashes U :K: .25 .50
❑ 21 Ashnod's Altar U :A: .50 1.00
❑ 22 Ashnod's Transmogrant C :A: .15 .30
❑ 23 Aspect of Wolf R :G: 2.00 4.00
❑ 24 Atog U :R: 1.00 2.00
❑ 25 Aurochs C :G: .15 .30
❑ 26 Aysen Bureaucrats C :W: .15 .30
❑ 27 Azure Drake U :B: .25 .50
❑ 28 Bad Moon R :K: 4.00 8.00
❑ 29 Ball Lightning R :R: 3.00 6.00
❑ 30 Barbed Sextant C :A: .15 .30
❑ 31 Barl's Cage R :A: 1.50 3.00
❑ 32 Battering Ram C :A: .15 .30
❑ 33 Benalish Hero C :W: .15 .30
❑ 34 Binding Grasp U :B: .50 1.00
❑ 35 Bird Maiden C :R: .15 .30
❑ 36 Birds of Paradise R :G: 5.00 10.00
❑ 37 Black Knight U :K: 1.00 2.00
❑ 38 Blessed Wine C :W: .15 .30
❑ 39 Blight U :K: .50 1.00
❑ 40 Blinking Spirit R :W: 1.50 3.00
❑ 41 Blood Lust C :R: .15 .30
❑ 42 Bog Imp C :K: .15 .30
❑ 43 Bog Rats C :K: .15 .30
❑ 44 Bog Wraith U :K: .25 .50
❑ 45 Boomerang C :B: .15 .30
❑ 46 Bottle of Suleiman R :A: 1.50 3.00
❑ 47 Bottomless Vault R :L: 1.50 3.00
❑ 48 Brainstorm C :B: .50 1.00
❑ 49 Brainwash C :W: .15 .30
❑ 50 Brassclaw Orcs C :R: .15 .30
❑ 51 Breeding Pit U :K: 1.00 2.00
❑ 52 Broken Visage R :K: 1.00 2.00
❑ 53 Brothers of Fire C :R: .15 .30
❑ 54 Brushland R :L: 3.50 7.00
❑ 55 Brute, The C :R: .15 .30
❑ 56 Carapace C :G: .15 .30
❑ 57 Caribou Range R :W: 1.00 2.00
❑ 58 Carrion Ants U :K: .50 1.00
❑ 59 Castle U :W: .25 .50
❑ 60 Cat Warriors C :G: .15 .30
❑ 61 Cave People U :R: .50 1.00
❑ 62 Chub Toad C :G: .15 .30
❑ 63 City of Brass R :L: 3.50 7.00
❑ 64 Clay Statue C :A: .15 .30
❑ 65 Cloak of Confusion C :K: .15 .30
❑ 66 Clockwork Beast R :A: 2.00 4.00
❑ 67 Clockwork Steed U :A: .25 .50
❑ 68 Cockatrice R :G: 2.00 4.00
❑ 69 Colossus of Sardia R :A: 2.00 4.00
❑ 70 Conquer U :R: .50 1.00
❑ 71 CoP: Artifacts U :W: .50 1.00
❑ 72 CoP: Black C :W: .15 .30
❑ 73 CoP: Blue C :W: .15 .30
❑ 74 CoP: Green C :W: .15 .30
❑ 75 CoP: Red C :W: .15 .30
❑ 76 CoP: White C :W: .15 .30
❑ 77 Coral Helm R :A: 1.50 3.00
❑ 78 Counterspell C :B: 1.00 2.00
❑ 79 Craw Giant U :G: .50 1.00
❑ 80 Craw Wurm C :G: .15 .30
❑ 81 Crimson Manticore R :R: 2.00 4.00

MAGIC

Card	Low	High
❑ 82 Crown of the Ages R :A:	1.50	3.00
❑ 83 Crumble U :G:	.50	1.00
❑ 84 Crusade R :W:	3.00	6.00
❑ 85 Crystal Rod U :A:	.25	.50
❑ 86 Cursed Land U :K:	.50	1.00
❑ 87 D'Avenant Archer C :W:	.15	.30
❑ 88 Dance of Many R :B:	1.50	3.00
❑ 89 Dancing Scimitar R :A:	1.00	2.00
❑ 90 Dandân C :B:	.15	.30
❑ 91 Dark Maze C :B:	.15	.30
❑ 92 Dark Ritual C :K:	.75	1.50
❑ 93 Death Speakers C :W:	.15	.30
❑ 94 Death Ward C :W:	.15	.30
❑ 95 Deathgrip U :K:	.50	1.00
❑ 96 Deflection R :B:	2.00	4.00
❑ 97 Derelor R :K:	1.00	2.00
❑ 98 Desert Twister U :G:	.50	1.00
❑ 99 Detonate U :R:	.50	1.00
❑ 100 Diabolic Machine U :A:	.50	1.00
❑ 101 Dingus Egg R :A:	1.50	3.00
❑ 102 Disenchant C :W:	.25	.50
❑ 103 Disintegrate C :R:	.25	.50
❑ 104 Disrupting Scepter R :A:	1.50	3.00
❑ 105 Divine Offering C :W:	.15	.30
❑ 106 Divine Transformation U :W:	.50	1.00
❑ 107 Dragon Engine R :A:	1.50	3.00
❑ 108 Drain Life C :K:	.50	1.00
❑ 109 Drain Power R :B:	1.50	3.00
❑ 110 Drudge Skeletons C :K:	.15	.30
❑ 111 Durkwood Boars C :G:	.15	.30
❑ 112 Dust to Dust U :W:	1.00	2.00
❑ 113 Dwarven Catapult U :R:	.25	.50
❑ 114 Dwarven Hold R :L:	1.50	3.00
❑ 115 Dwarven Ruins U :L:	.50	1.00
❑ 116 Dwarven Soldier C :R:	.15	.30
❑ 117 Dwarven Warriors C :R:	.15	.30
❑ 118 Earthquake R :R:	2.00	4.00
❑ 119 Ebon Stronghold U :L:	.50	1.00
❑ 120 Elder Druid R :G:	1.00	2.00
❑ 121 Elkin Bottle R :A:	1.50	3.00
❑ 122 Elven Riders U :G:	.25	.50
❑ 123 Elvish Archers R :G:	2.00	4.00
❑ 124 Energy Flux U :B:	1.00	2.00
❑ 125 Enervate C :B:	.15	.30
❑ 126 Erg Raiders C :K:	.15	.30
❑ 127 Errantry C :R:	.15	.30
❑ 128 Eternal Warrior C :R:	.15	.30
❑ 129 Evil Eye of Orms-by-Gore U :K:	.30	.75
❑ 130 Evil Presence U :K:	1.00	2.00
❑ 131 Eye for an Eye R :W:	2.00	4.00
❑ 132 Fallen Angel U :K:	.50	1.00
❑ 133 Fear C :K:	.15	.30
❑ 134 Feedback U :B:	.25	.50
❑ 135 Feldon's Cane U :A:	2.00	4.00
❑ 136 Fellwar Stone U :A:	1.00	2.00
❑ 137 Feroz's Ban R :A:	2.00	4.00
❑ 138 Fire Drake U :R:	.25	.50
❑ 139 Fireball C :R:	.25	.50
❑ 140 Firebreathing C :R:	.15	.30
❑ 141 Flame Spirit U :R:	.25	.50
❑ 142 Flare C :R:	.15	.30
❑ 143 Flashfires U :R:	.50	1.00
❑ 144 Flight C :B:	.15	.30
❑ 145 Flood C :B:	.15	.30
❑ 146 Flying Carpet R :A:	1.00	2.00
❑ 147 Fog C :G:	.15	.30
❑ 148 Force of Nature R :G:	2.50	5.00
❑ 149 Force Spike C :B:	.25	.50
❑ 150 Forest L :L:	.50	1.00
❑ 151 Forget R :B:	1.00	2.00
❑ 152 Fountain of Youth U :A:	.50	1.00
❑ 153 Foxfire C :G:	.15	.30
❑ 154 Frozen Shade C :K:	.25	.50
❑ 155 Funeral March C :K:	.15	.30
❑ 156 Fungusaur R :G:	1.50	3.00
❑ 157 Fyndhorn Elder U :G:	.50	1.00
❑ 158 Game of Chaos R :R:	1.50	3.00
❑ 159 Gaseous Form C :B:	.15	.30
❑ 160 Gauntlets of Chaos R :A:	1.00	2.00
❑ 161 Ghazbán Ogre C :G:	.50	1.00
❑ 162 Giant Growth C :G:	.50	1.00
❑ 163 Giant Spider C :G:	.15	.30
❑ 164 Giant Strength C :R:	.15	.30
❑ 165 Glacial Wall U :B:	.25	.50
❑ 166 Glasses of Urza U :A:	.50	1.00
❑ 167 Gloom U :K:	.50	1.00
❑ 168 Goblin Digging Team C :R:	.15	.30
❑ 169 Goblin Hero C :R:	.15	.30
❑ 170 Goblin King R :R:	2.50	5.00
❑ 171 Goblin War Drums C :R:	.15	.30
❑ 172 Goblin Warrens R :R:	1.50	3.00
❑ 173 Grapeshot Catapult C :A:	.15	.30
❑ 174 Greater Realm of Preservation U :W:	.25	.50
❑ 175 Greater Werewolf U :K:	.25	.50
❑ 176 Grizzly Bears C :G:	.15	.30
❑ 177 Havenwood Battleground U :L:	.50	1.00
❑ 178 Heal C :W:	.15	.30
❑ 179 Healing Salve C :W:	.15	.30
❑ 180 Hecatomb R :K:	2.00	4.00
❑ 181 Helm of Chatzuk R :A:	1.00	2.00
❑ 182 Hill Giant C :R:	.15	.30
❑ 183 Hipparion C :W:	.15	.30
❑ 184 Hive, The R :A:	1.50	3.00
❑ 185 Hollow Trees R :L:	1.50	3.00
❑ 186 Holy Strength C :W:	.15	.30
❑ 187 Homarid Warrior C :B:	.15	.30
❑ 188 Howl from Beyond C :K:	.15	.30
❑ 189 Howling Mine R :A:	3.50	7.00
❑ 190 Hungry Mist C :G:	.15	.30
❑ 191 Hurkyl's Recall R :B:	1.50	3.00
❑ 192 Hurloon Minotaur C :R:	.15	.30
❑ 193 Hurricane U :G:	.50	1.00
❑ 194 Hydroblast U :B:	.50	1.00
❑ 195 Icatian Phalanx U :W:	.50	1.00
❑ 196 Icatian Scout C :W:	.15	.30
❑ 197 Icatian Store R :L:	1.50	3.00
❑ 198 Icatian Town R :W:	1.50	3.00
❑ 199 Ice Floe U :L:	.50	1.00
❑ 200 Imposing Visage C :R:	.15	.30
❑ 201 Incinerate C :R:	.50	1.00
❑ 202 Inferno R :R:	1.50	3.00
❑ 203 Infinite Hourglass R :A:	1.50	3.00
❑ 204 Initiates of the Ebon Hand C :K:	.15	.30
❑ 205 Instill Energy U :G:	.50	1.00
❑ 206 Iron Star U :A:	.50	1.00
❑ 207 Ironclaw Curse R :R:	1.50	3.00
❑ 208 Ironclaw Orcs C :R:	.15	.30
❑ 209 Ironroot Treefolk C :G:	.15	.30
❑ 210 Island L :L:	.25	.50
❑ 211 Island Sanctuary R :W:	1.50	3.00
❑ 212 Ivory Cup U :A:	.50	1.00
❑ 213 Ivory Guardians U :W:	.25	.50
❑ 214 Jade Monolith R :A:	1.50	3.00
❑ 215 Jalum Tome R :A:	1.00	2.00
❑ 216 Jandor's Saddlebags R :A:	1.50	3.00
❑ 217 Jayemdae Tome R :A:	1.00	2.00
❑ 218 Jester's Cap R :A:	3.00	6.00
❑ 219 Johtull Wurm U :G:	.25	.50
❑ 220 Jokulhaups R :R:	2.00	4.00
❑ 221 Joven's Tools U :A:	.25	.50
❑ 222 Justice U :W:	.25	.50
❑ 223 Juxtapose R :B:	1.50	3.00
❑ 224 Karma U :W:	.50	1.00
❑ 225 Karplusan Forest R :L:	3.50	7.00
❑ 226 Keldon Warlord U :R:	.50	1.00
❑ 227 Killer Bees U :G:	.75	1.50
❑ 228 Kismet U :W:	.50	1.00
❑ 229 Kjeldoran Dead C :K:	.15	.30
❑ 230 Kjeldoran Royal Guard R :W:	1.50	3.00
❑ 231 Kjeldoran Skycaptain U :W:	.50	1.00
❑ 232 Knight of Stromgald U :K:	.50	1.00
❑ 233 Krovikan Fetish C :K:	.15	.30
❑ 234 Krovikan Sorcerer C :B:	.15	.30
❑ 235 Labyrinth Minotaur C :B:	.15	.30
❑ 236 Leshrac's Rite U :K:	.50	1.00
❑ 237 Leviathan R :B:	1.50	3.00
❑ 238 Ley Druid C :G:	.15	.30
❑ 239 Lhurgoyf R :G:	2.00	4.00
❑ 240 Library of Leng U :A:	1.00	2.00
❑ 241 Lifeforce U :G:	.50	1.00
❑ 242 Lifetap U :B:	.25	.50
❑ 243 Living Artifact R :G:	1.50	3.00
❑ 244 Living Lands R :G:	1.50	3.00
❑ 245 Llanowar Elves C :G:	.50	1.00
❑ 246 Lord of Atlantis R :B:	2.00	4.00
❑ 247 Lord of the Pit R :K:	2.50	5.00
❑ 248 Lost Soul C :K:	.15	.30
❑ 249 Lure U :G:	.50	1.00
❑ 250 Magical Hack R :B:	2.00	4.00
❑ 251 Magus of the Unseen R :B:	1.00	2.00
❑ 252 Mana Clash R :R:	1.00	2.00
❑ 253 Mana Flare R :R:	3.00	6.00
❑ 254 Mana Vault R :A:	2.50	5.00
❑ 255 Manabarbs R :R:	1.50	3.00
❑ 256 Marsh Viper C :G:	.15	.30
❑ 257 Meekstone R :A:	2.00	4.00
❑ 258 Memory Lapse C :B:	.15	.30
❑ 259 Merfolk of the Pearl Trident C :B:	.15	.30
❑ 260 Mesa Falcon C :W:	.15	.30
❑ 261 Mesa Pegasus C :W:	.15	.30
❑ 262 Millstone R :A:	3.00	6.00
❑ 263 Mind Bomb U :B:	.50	1.00
❑ 264 Mind Ravel C :K:	.15	.30
❑ 265 Mind Warp U :K:	.50	1.00
❑ 266 Mindstab Thrull C :K:	.15	.30
❑ 267 Mole Worms U :K:	.25	.50
❑ 268 Mons's Goblin Raiders C :R:	.15	.30
❑ 269 Mountain Goat C :R:	.15	.30
❑ 270 Mountain L :L:	.50	1.00
❑ 271 Murk Dwellers C :K:	.15	.30
❑ 272 Nature's Lore C :G:	.15	.30
❑ 273 Necrite C :K:	.15	.30
❑ 274 Necropotence R :K:	3.00	6.00
❑ 275 Nether Shadow R :K:	1.50	3.00
❑ 276 Nevinyrral's Disk R :A:	4.00	8.00
❑ 277 Nightmare R :K:	2.50	5.00
❑ 278 Obelisk of Undoing R :A:	1.00	2.00
❑ 279 Orcish Artillery U :R:	.25	.50
❑ 280 Orcish Captain U :R:	.25	.50
❑ 281 Orcish Conscripts C :R:	.15	.30
❑ 282 Orcish Farmer C :R:	.15	.30
❑ 283 Orcish Oriflamme U :R:	.50	1.00
❑ 284 Orcish Squatters R :R:	1.50	3.00
❑ 285 Order of the Sacred Torch R :W:	1.50	3.00
❑ 286 Order of the White Shield U :W:	.50	1.00
❑ 287 Orgg R :R:	1.50	3.00
❑ 288 Ornithopter U :A:	1.00	2.00
❑ 289 Panic C :R:	.15	.30
❑ 290 Paralyze C :K:	.15	.30
❑ 291 Pearled Unicorn C :W:	.15	.30
❑ 292 Pentagram of the Ages R :A:	1.50	3.00
❑ 293 Personal Incarnation R :W:	1.50	3.00
❑ 294 Pestilence C :K:	.15	.30
❑ 295 Phantasmal Forces U :B:	.15	.30
❑ 296 Phantasmal Terrain C :B:	.15	.30
❑ 297 Phantom Monster U :B:	.50	1.00
❑ 298 Pikemen C :W:	.15	.30
❑ 299 Pirate Ship R :B:	1.50	3.00
❑ 300 Pit Scorpion C :K:	.25	.50
❑ 301 Plague Rats C :K:	.25	.50
❑ 302 Plains L :L:	.25	.50
❑ 303 Portent C :B:	.15	.30
❑ 304 Power Sink U :B:	.50	1.00
❑ 305 Pox R :K:	1.50	3.00
❑ 306 Pradesh Gypsies C :G:	.15	.30
❑ 307 Primal Clay R :A:	1.50	3.00
❑ 308 Primal Order R :G:	1.50	3.00
❑ 309 Primordial Ooze U :R:	.25	.50
❑ 310 Prismatic Ward C :W:	.15	.30
❑ 311 Prodigal Sorcerer C :B:	.15	.30
❑ 312 Psychic Venom C :B:	.15	.30
❑ 313 Pyroblast U :R:	.50	1.00
❑ 314 Pyrotechnics U :R:	1.00	2.00
❑ 315 Rabid Wombat U :G:	.50	1.00
❑ 316 Radjan Spirit U :G:	.50	1.00
❑ 317 Rag Man R :K:	1.50	3.00
❑ 318 Raise Dead C :K:	.15	.30
❑ 319 Ray of Command C :B:	.15	.30
❑ 320 Recall R :B:	1.50	3.00
❑ 321 Reef Pirates C :B:	.15	.30
❑ 322 Regeneration C :G:	.15	.30
❑ 323 Remove Soul C :B:	.15	.30
❑ 324 Repentant Blacksmith C :W:	.15	.30
❑ 325 Reverse Damage R :W:	1.50	3.00
❑ 326 Righteousness R :W:	1.50	3.00
❑ 327 Rod of Ruin U :A:	.50	1.00
❑ 328 Ruins of Trokair U :L:	.50	1.00
❑ 329 Sabretooth Tiger C :R:	.15	.30
❑ 330 Sacred Boon U :W:	.50	1.00
❑ 331 Samite Healer C :W:	.15	.30
❑ 332 Sand Silos R :L:	1.50	3.00
❑ 333 Scaled Wurm C :G:	.15	.30
❑ 334 Scathe Zombies C :K:	.15	.30
❑ 335 Scavenger Folk C :G:	.15	.30
❑ 336 Scryb Sprites C :G:	.15	.30
❑ 337 Sea Serpent C :B:	.15	.30
❑ 338 Sea Spirit U :B:	.50	1.00
❑ 339 Sea Sprite U :B:	.50	1.00
❑ 340 Seasinger U :B:	.50	1.00
❑ 341 Segovian Leviathan U :B:	.50	1.00
❑ 342 Sengir Autocrat R :K:	2.00	4.00
❑ 343 Seraph R :W:	3.00	6.00
❑ 344 Serpent Generator R :A:	2.00	4.00
❑ 345 Serra Bestiary U :W:	.25	.50
❑ 346 Serra Paladin U :W:	.50	1.00
❑ 347 Shanodin Dryads C :G:	.15	.30
❑ 348 Shapeshifter U :A:	.50	1.00
❑ 349 Shatter C :R:	.50	1.00
❑ 350 Shatterstorm U :R:	1.00	2.00
❑ 351 Shield Bearer C :W:	.15	.30
❑ 352 Shield Wall C :W:	.15	.30
❑ 353 Shivan Dragon R :R:	3.00	6.00
❑ 354 Shrink C :G:	.15	.30
❑ 355 Sibilant Spirit R :B:	1.50	3.00
❑ 356 Skull Catapult U :A:	1.00	2.00
❑ 357 Sleight of Mind R :B:	1.50	3.00
❑ 358 Smoke R :R:	1.50	3.00
❑ 359 Sorceress Queen R :K:	2.00	4.00
❑ 360 Soul Barrier C :B:	.15	.30
❑ 361 Soul Net U :A:	.25	.50
❑ 362 Spell Blast C :B:	.15	.30
❑ 363 Spirit Link U :W:	.50	1.00
❑ 364 Stampede R :G:	1.50	3.00
❑ 365 Stasis R :B:	2.50	5.00
❑ 366 Steal Artifact U :B:	.25	.50
❑ 367 Stone Giant U :R:	.50	1.00
❑ 368 Stone Rain C :R:	.50	1.00
❑ 369 Stone Spirit U :R:	.25	.50
❑ 370 Stream of Life C :G:	.25	.50
❑ 371 Stromgald Cabal R :K:	1.50	3.00
❑ 372 Sulfurous Springs R :L:	3.00	6.00
❑ 373 Svyelunite Temple U :L:	.50	1.00
❑ 374 Swamp L :L:	.50	1.00
❑ 375 Sylvan Library R :G:	3.50	7.00
❑ 376 Tarpan C :G:	.15	.30
❑ 377 Tawnos's Weaponry U :A:	.50	1.00
❑ 378 Terror C :K:	.15	.30
❑ 379 Thicket Basilisk U :G:	.25	.50
❑ 380 Throne of Bone U :A:	1.00	2.00
❑ 381 Thrull Retainer U :K:	.50	1.00
❑ 382 Time Bomb R :A:	1.50	3.00
❑ 383 Time Elemental R :B:	2.00	4.00
❑ 384 Titania's Song R :G:	1.50	3.00
❑ 385 Torture C :K:	.15	.30
❑ 386 Touch of Death C :K:	.15	.30
❑ 387 Tranquility C :G:	.15	.30
❑ 388 Truce R :W:	1.50	3.00
❑ 389 Tsunami U :G:	.50	1.00
❑ 390 Tundra Wolves C :W:	.15	.30
❑ 391 Twiddle C :B:	.15	.30
❑ 392 Underground River R :L:	4.00	8.00
❑ 393 Unholy Strength C :K:	.15	.30
❑ 394 Unstable Mutation C :B:	.25	.50
❑ 395 Unsummon C :B:	.25	.50
❑ 396 Untamed Wilds U :G:	.25	.50
❑ 397 Updraft C :B:	.15	.30
❑ 398 Urza's Avenger R :A:	1.50	3.00
❑ 399 Urza's Bauble U :A:	.50	1.00
❑ 400 Urza's Mine C :L:	.50	1.00
❑ 401 Urza's Power Plant C :L:	.50	1.00
❑ 402 Urza's Tower C :L:	.50	1.00
❑ 403 Vampire Bats C :K:	.15	.30
❑ 404 Venom C :G:	.25	.50
❑ 405 Verduran Enchantress R :G:	1.50	3.00
❑ 406 Vodalian Soldiers C :B:	.15	.30
❑ 407 Wall of Air U :B:	.50	1.00
❑ 408 Wall of Bone U :K:	.50	1.00
❑ 409 Wall of Brambles U :G:	.50	1.00
❑ 410 Wall of Fire U :R:	.50	1.00
❑ 411 Wall of Spears C :A:	.15	.30
❑ 412 Wall of Stone U :R:	.30	.75
❑ 413 Wall of Swords U :W:	.50	1.00
❑ 414 Wanderlust U :G:	.50	1.00
❑ 415 War Mammoth C :G:	.15	.30
❑ 416 Warp Artifact R :K:	1.50	3.00
❑ 417 Weakness C :K:	.15	.30
❑ 418 Whirling Dervish U :G:	.50	1.00
❑ 419 White Knight U :W:	1.00	2.00
❑ 420 Wild Growth C :G:	.15	.30
❑ 421 Wind Spirit U :B:	.50	1.00
❑ 422 Winds of Change R :R:	1.50	3.00
❑ 423 Winter Blast U :G:	.50	1.00
❑ 424 Winter Orb R :A:	2.50	5.00
❑ 425 Wolverine Pack U :G:	.50	1.00
❑ 426 Wooden Sphere U :A:	.50	1.00
❑ 427 Word of Blasting U :R:	.50	1.00
❑ 428 Wrath of God R :W:	4.00	10.00
❑ 429 Wretched, The R :K:	1.50	3.00
❑ 430 Wyluli Wolf R :G:	1.00	2.00
❑ 431 Xenic Poltergeist R :K:	1.50	3.00
❑ 432 Zephyr Falcon C :B:	.15	.30
❑ 433 Zombie Master R :K:	2.00	4.00
❑ 434 Zur's Weirding R :B:	1.00	2.00

1997 Magic the Gathering Visions

Card	Low	High
Complete Set (167)	85.00	110.00
Booster Box (36 Packs)	175.00	200.00
Booster Pack (15 Cards)	5.00	7.00
Released in February 1997		
❑ 1 Aku Djinn R :K:	1.00	3.00
❑ 2 Anvil of Bogardan R :A:	2.00	5.00
❑ 3 Archangel R :W:	4.00	6.00
❑ 4 Army Ants U :D:	.50	1.00
❑ 5 Betrayal C :B:	.15	.30
❑ 6 Blanket of Night U :K:	.75	1.50
❑ 7 Bogardan Phoenix R :R:	2.00	4.00
❑ 8 Brass-Talon Chimera U :A:	.50	1.00
❑ 9 Breathstealer's Crypt R :D:	1.50	3.00
❑ 10 Breezekeeper C :B:	.15	.30
❑ 11 Brood of Cockroaches U :K:	.50	1.00
❑ 12 Bull Elephant C :G:	.15	.30
❑ 13 Chronatog R :B:	2.00	4.00
❑ 14 City of Solitude R :G:	2.00	4.00
❑ 15 Cloud Elemental C :B:	.15	.30
❑ 16 Coercion C :K:	.15	.30
❑ 17 Coral Atoll U :L:	.50	1.00
❑ 18 Corrosion R :D:	1.00	2.00
❑ 19 Creeping Mold U :G:	.50	1.00
❑ 20 Crypt Rats C :K:	.15	.30
❑ 21 Daraja Griffin U :W:	.50	1.00
❑ 22 Dark Privilege C :K:	.15	.30
❑ 23 Death Watch C :K:	.15	.30
❑ 24 Desertion R :B:	2.00	4.00
❑ 25 Desolation U :K:	.50	1.00
❑ 26 Diamond Kaleidoscope R :A:	1.00	3.00
❑ 27 Dormant Volcano U :L:	.50	1.00
❑ 28 Dragon Mask U :A:	.50	1.00
❑ 29 Dream Tides U :B:	.50	1.00
❑ 30 Dwarven Vigilantes C :R:	.15	.30
❑ 31 Elephant Grass U :G:	.50	1.00
❑ 32 Elkin Lair R :R:	1.00	2.00
❑ 33 Elven Cache C :G:	.15	.30
❑ 34 Emerald Charm C :G:	.50	1.00
❑ 35 Equipoise R :W:	1.00	2.00
❑ 36 Everglades U :L:	.50	1.00
❑ 37 Eye of Singularity R :W:	1.00	2.00
❑ 38 Fallen Askari C :K:	.15	.30
❑ 39 Femeref Enchantress R :D:	1.50	3.00
❑ 40 Feral Instinct C :G:	.15	.30
❑ 41 Fireblast C :R:	.30	.75
❑ 42 Firestorm Hellkite R :D:	2.00	4.00
❑ 43 Flooded Shoreline R :B:	1.00	3.00
❑ 44 Forbidden Ritual R :K:	1.00	3.00
❑ 45 Foreshadow U :B:	.50	1.00
❑ 46 Freewind Falcon C :W:	.15	.30
❑ 47 Funeral Charm C :K:	.15	.30
❑ 48 Giant Caterpillar C :G:	.15	.30
❑ 49 Goblin Recruiter U :R:	2.00	4.00
❑ 50 Goblin Swine-Rider C :R:	.15	.30
❑ 51 Gossamer Chains C :W:	.15	.30
❑ 52 Griffin Canyon R :L:	1.00	2.00
❑ 53 Guiding Spirit R :D:	1.00	2.00
❑ 54 Hearth Charm C :R:	.15	.30
❑ 55 Heat Wave U :R:	1.00	2.00
❑ 56 Helm of Awakening U :A:	2.00	3.50
❑ 57 Honorable Passage U :W:	1.00	2.00
❑ 58 Hope Charm C :W:	.15	.30
❑ 59 Hulking Cyclops U :R:	.50	1.00
❑ 60 Impulse C :B:	.25	.50
❑ 61 Infantry Veteran C :W:	.15	.30
❑ 62 Infernal Harvest C :K:	.15	.30
❑ 63 Inspiration C :B:	.15	.30
❑ 64 Iron-Heart Chimera U :A:	.50	1.00
❑ 65 Jamuraan Lion C :W:	.15	.30
❑ 66 Juju Bubble U :A:	.50	1.00
❑ 67 Jungle Basin U :L:	.50	1.00
❑ 68 Kaervek's Spite R :K:	2.00	3.00
❑ 69 Karoo U :L:	.50	1.00
❑ 70 Katabatic Winds R :G:	1.50	3.00
❑ 71 Keeper of Kookus C :R:	.15	.30
❑ 72 King Cheetah C :G:	.15	.30
❑ 73 Knight of the Mists C :B:	.15	.30
❑ 74 Knight of Valor C :W:	.15	.30
❑ 75 Kookus R :R:	1.50	3.00
❑ 76 Kyscu Drake U :G:	1.00	2.00
❑ 77 Lead-Belly Chimera U :A:	.50	1.00
❑ 78 Lichenthrope R :G:	1.50	3.00
❑ 79 Lightning Cloud R :R:	1.00	2.00
❑ 80 Longbow Archer U :W:	2.50	4.00
❑ 81 Magma Mine U :A:	1.00	2.00
❑ 82 Man-o'-War C :B:	.50	1.00
❑ 83 Matopi Golem U :A:	.50	1.00
❑ 84 Miraculous Recovery U :W:	.50	1.00
❑ 85 Mob Mentality U :R:	.50	1.00
❑ 86 Mortal Wound C :G:	.15	.30
❑ 87 Mundungu U :D:	.50	1.00
❑ 88 Mystic Veil C :B:	.15	.30
❑ 89 Natural Order R :G:	4.00	6.00
❑ 90 Necromancy U :K:	1.50	3.00
❑ 91 Necrosavant R :K:	3.00	6.00
❑ 92 Nekrataal U :K:	1.00	2.00
❑ 93 Ogre Enforcer R :R:	1.00	2.00
❑ 94 Ovinomancer U :B:	.50	1.00
❑ 95 Panther Warriors C :G:	.15	.30
❑ 96 Parapet C :W:	.15	.30
❑ 97 Peace Talks U :W:	.50	1.00
❑ 98 Phyrexian Marauder R :A:	1.00	2.50
❑ 99 Phyrexian Walker C :A:	.15	.30
❑ 100 Pillar Tombs of Aku R :K:	1.00	2.00
❑ 101 Prosperity U :B:	1.00	3.00
❑ 102 Pygmy Hippo R :D:	2.00	3.00
❑ 103 Python C :K:	.15	.30
❑ 104 Quicksand U :L:	1.00	2.00
❑ 105 Quirion Druid R :G:	2.00	4.00
❑ 106 Quirion Ranger C :G:	.15	.30
❑ 107 Raging Gorilla C :R:	.15	.30
❑ 108 Rainbow Efreet R :B:	2.00	4.00
❑ 109 Relentless Assault R :R:	3.00	6.00
❑ 110 Relic Ward U :W:	.50	1.00
❑ 111 Remedy C :W:	.15	.30
❑ 112 Resistance Fighter C :W:	.15	.30
❑ 113 Retribution of the Meek R :W:	1.00	2.00
❑ 114 Righteous Aura C :W:	.15	.30
❑ 115 Righteous War R :D:	1.00	2.00
❑ 116 River Boa C :G:	.75	1.50
❑ 117 Rock Slide C :R:	.15	.30
❑ 118 Rowen R :G:	2.00	4.00
❑ 119 Sands of Time R :A:	1.00	2.00
❑ 120 Scalebane's Elite U :D:	.50	1.00
❑ 121 Shimmering Efreet U :B:	.50	1.00
❑ 122 Shrieking Drake C :B:	.15	.30
❑ 123 Simoon U :D:	.50	1.00
❑ 124 Sisay's Ring C :A:	.15	.30
❑ 125 Snake Basket R :A:	2.00	3.00
❑ 126 Solfatara C :R:	.15	.30
❑ 127 Song of Blood C :R:	.15	.30
❑ 128 Spider Climb C :G:	.15	.30
❑ 129 Spitting Drake U :R:	.50	1.00
❑ 130 Squandered Resources R :D:	3.00	5.00
❑ 131 Stampeding Wildebeests U :G:	.50	1.00
❑ 132 Suleiman's Legacy R :D:	1.00	2.00
❑ 133 Summer Bloom U :G:	.50	1.00
❑ 134 Sun Clasp C :W:	.15	.30
❑ 135 Suq'Ata Assassin U :K:	.50	1.00
❑ 136 Suq'Ata Lancer C :R:	.15	.30
❑ 137 Talruum Champion C :R:	.15	.30
❑ 138 Talruum Piper U :R:	.50	1.00
❑ 139 Tar Pit Warrior C :K:	.15	.30
❑ 140 Teferi's Honor Guard U :W:	.50	1.00
❑ 141 Teferi's Puzzle Box R :A:	2.00	4.00
❑ 142 Teferi's Realm R :B:	2.00	4.00
❑ 143 Tempest Drake U :D:	.50	1.00
❑ 144 Three Wishes R :B:	1.50	3.00
❑ 145 Time and Tide U :B:	.50	1.00
❑ 146 Tin-Wing Chimera U :A:	.50	1.00
❑ 147 Tithe R :W:	3.00	6.00
❑ 148 Tremor C :R:	.15	.30
❑ 149 Triangle of War R :A:	1.00	3.00
❑ 150 Uktabi Orangutan U :G:	1.00	2.00
❑ 151 Undiscovered Paradise R :L:	3.00	7.00
❑ 152 Undo C :B:	.15	.30
❑ 153 Urborg Mindsucker C :K:	.15	.30
❑ 154 Vampiric Tutor R :K:	20.00	25.00
❑ 155 Vampirism U :K:	1.00	2.00
❑ 156 Vanishing C :B:	.15	.30
❑ 157 Viashino Sandstalker U :R:	1.00	2.00
❑ 158 Viashivan Dragon R :D:	2.00	5.00
❑ 159 Vision Charm C :B:	.15	.30
❑ 160 Wake of Vultures C :K:	.15	.30
❑ 161 Wand of Denial R :A:	2.00	4.00
❑ 162 Warrior's Honor C :W:	.15	.30
❑ 163 Warthog C :G:	.15	.30
❑ 164 Waterspout Djinn U :B:	1.00	2.00
❑ 165 Wicked Reward C :K:	.15	.30
❑ 166 Wind Shear U :G:	.50	1.00
❑ 167 Zhalfirin Crusader R :W:	1.50	3.00

1997 Magic the Gathering Weatherlight

Card	Low	High
Complete Set (167)	75.00	110.00
Booster Box (36 Packs)	165.00	185.00
Booster Pack (15 Cards)	5.00	6.50
Released in June 1997		
❑ 1 Abduction U :B:	.50	1.00
❑ 2 Abeyance R :W:	3.00	6.00
❑ 3 Abjure C :B:	.15	.30
❑ 4 Aboroth R :G:	1.50	3.00

Card	Low	High
❑ 5 Abyssal Gatekeeper C :K:	.15	.30
❑ 6 AEther Flash U :R:	.50	1.00
❑ 7 Agonizing Memories U :K:	.50	1.00
❑ 8 Alabaster Dragon R :W:	2.00	4.00
❑ 9 Alms C :W:	.15	.30
❑ 10 Ancestral Knowledge R :B:	1.00	2.00
❑ 11 Angelic Renewal C :W:	.15	.30
❑ 12 Apathy C :B:	.15	.30
❑ 13 Arctic Wolves U :G:	.50	1.00
❑ 14 Ardent Militia C :W:	.15	.30
❑ 15 Argivian Find U :W:	.50	1.00
❑ 16 Argivian Restoration U :B:	.50	1.00
❑ 17 Aura of Silence U :W:	.75	1.50
❑ 18 Avizoa R :B:	1.00	2.00
❑ 19 Barishi U :G:	.50	1.00
❑ 20 Barrow Ghoul C :K:	.15	.30
❑ 21 Benalish Infantry C :W:	.15	.30
❑ 22 Benalish Knight C :W:	.15	.30
❑ 23 Benalish Missionary C :W:	.15	.30
❑ 24 Betrothed of Fire C :R:	.15	.30
❑ 25 Bloodrock Cyclops C :R:	.15	.30
❑ 26 Blossoming Wreath C :G:	.15	.30
❑ 27 Bogardan Firefiend C :R:	.15	.30
❑ 28 Boiling Blood C :R:	.15	.30
❑ 29 Bone Dancer R :K:	2.00	4.00
❑ 30 Bosium Strip R :A:	2.00	4.00
❑ 31 Briar Shield C :G:	.50	1.00
❑ 32 Bubble Matrix R :A:	2.00	4.00
❑ 33 Buried Alive U :K:	2.00	4.00
❑ 34 Call of the Wild R :G:	1.50	3.00
❑ 35 Chimeric Sphere U :A:	.50	1.00
❑ 36 Choking Vines C :G:	.15	.30
❑ 37 Cinder Giant U :R:	.50	1.00
❑ 38 Cinder Wall C :R:	.15	.30
❑ 39 Circling Vultures U :K:	.50	1.00
❑ 40 Cloud Djinn U :B:	.50	1.00
❑ 41 Coils of the Medusa C :K:	.15	.30
❑ 42 Cone of Flame U :R:	.50	1.00
❑ 43 Debt of Loyalty R :W:	1.50	3.00
❑ 44 Dense Foliage R :G:	1.00	2.00
❑ 45 Desperate Gambit U :R:	1.00	2.00
❑ 46 Dingus Staff U :A:	.50	1.00
❑ 47 Disrupt C :B:	.15	.30
❑ 48 Doomsday R :K:	1.50	3.00
❑ 49 Downdraft U :G:	.50	1.00
❑ 50 Duskrider Falcon C :W:	.15	.30
❑ 51 Dwarven Berserker C :R:	.15	.30
❑ 52 Dwarven Thaumaturgist R :R:	1.50	3.00
❑ 53 Empyrial Armor C :W:	.15	.30
❑ 54 Ertai's Familiar R :B:	1.50	3.00
❑ 55 Fallow Wurm U :G:	.50	1.00
❑ 56 Familiar Ground U :G:	1.00	2.00
❑ 57 Fatal Blow C :K:	.15	.30
❑ 58 Fervor R :R:	1.50	3.00
❑ 59 Festering Evil U :K:	.50	1.00
❑ 60 Fire Whip C :R:	.15	.30
❑ 61 Firestorm R :R:	2.50	5.00
❑ 62 Fit of Rage C :R:	.15	.30
❑ 63 Fledgling Djinn C :K:	.15	.30
❑ 64 Flux C :B:	.15	.30
❑ 65 Fog Elemental C :B:	.15	.30
❑ 66 Foriysian Brigade U :W:	.50	1.00
❑ 67 Fungus Elemental R :G:	1.50	3.00
❑ 68 Gaea's Blessing U :G:	2.00	4.00
❑ 69 Gallowbraid R :K:	1.50	3.00
❑ 70 Gemstone Mine U :L:	2.50	5.00
❑ 71 Gerrard's Wisdom U :W:	1.00	2.00
❑ 72 Goblin Bomb R :R:	2.00	4.00
❑ 73 Goblin Grenadiers U :R:	.50	1.00
❑ 74 Goblin Vandal C :R:	.15	.30
❑ 75 Guided Strike C :W:	.15	.30
❑ 76 Harvest Wurm C :G:	.15	.30
❑ 77 Haunting Misery C :K:	.15	.30
❑ 78 Heart of Bogardan R :R:	1.50	3.00
❑ 79 Heat Stroke R :R:	1.00	2.00
❑ 80 Heavy Ballista C :W:	.15	.30
❑ 81 Hidden Horror U :K:	.75	1.50
❑ 82 Hurloon Shaman U :R:	.50	1.00
❑ 83 Infernal Tribute R :K:	1.00	2.00
❑ 84 Inner Sanctum R :W:	1.00	2.00
❑ 85 Jabari's Banner U :A:	.50	1.00
❑ 86 Jangling Automaton C :A:	.15	.30
❑ 87 Kithkin Armor C :W:	.15	.30
❑ 88 Lava Hounds U :R:	.75	1.50
❑ 89 Lava Storm C :R:	.15	.30
❑ 90 Liege of the Hollows R :G:	1.50	3.00
❑ 91 Llanowar Behemoth U :G:	.50	1.00
❑ 92 Llanowar Druid C :G:	.15	.30
❑ 93 Llanowar Sentinel C :G:	.15	.30
❑ 94 Lotus Vale R :L:	4.00	8.00
❑ 95 Mana Chains C :B:	.15	.30
❑ 96 Mana Web R :A:	2.00	4.00
❑ 97 Manta Ray C :B:	.15	.30
❑ 98 Maraxus of Keld R :R:	1.50	3.00
❑ 99 Master of Arms U :W:	.50	1.00
❑ 100 Merfolk Traders C :B:	.15	.30
❑ 101 Mind Stone C :A:	.15	.30
❑ 102 Mischievous Poltergeist U :K:	.50	1.00
❑ 103 Mistmoon Griffin U :W:	.50	1.00
❑ 104 Morinfen R :K:	1.00	2.00
❑ 105 Mwonvuli Ooze R :G:	1.00	2.00
❑ 106 Nature's Kiss C :G:	.15	.30
❑ 107 Nature's Resurgence R :G:	2.00	4.00
❑ 108 Necratog U :K:	.50	1.00
❑ 109 Noble Benefactor U :B:	.50	1.00
❑ 110 Null Rod R :A:	6.00	12.00
❑ 111 Odylic Wraith U :K:	1.00	2.00
❑ 112 Ophidian C :B:	.15	.30
❑ 113 Orcish Settlers U :R:	.50	1.00
❑ 114 Paradigm Shift R :B:	1.00	2.00
❑ 115 Peacekeeper R :W:	2.00	4.00
❑ 116 Pendrell Mists R :B:	1.50	3.00
❑ 117 Phantom Warrior U :B:	.50	1.00
❑ 118 Phantom Wings C :B:	.15	.30
❑ 119 Phyrexian Furnace U :A:	2.00	4.00
❑ 120 Psychic Vortex R :B:	2.00	4.00
❑ 121 Razortooth Rats C :K:	.15	.30
❑ 122 Redwood Treefolk C :G:	.15	.30
❑ 123 Relearn U :B:	.50	1.00
❑ 124 Revered Unicorn U :W:	.50	1.00
❑ 125 Roc Hatchling U :R:	.50	1.00
❑ 126 Rogue Elephant C :G:	.50	1.00
❑ 127 Sage Owl C :B:	.15	.30
❑ 128 Sawtooth Ogre C :R:	.15	.30
❑ 129 Scorched Ruins R :L:	1.50	3.00
❑ 130 Serenity R :W:	1.50	3.00
❑ 131 Serra's Blessing U :W:	1.00	2.00
❑ 132 Serrated Biskelion U :A:	.50	1.00
❑ 133 Shadow Rider C :K:	.15	.30
❑ 134 Shattered Crypt C :K:	.15	.30
❑ 135 Soul Shepherd C :W:	.15	.30
❑ 136 Southern Paladin R :W:	2.00	4.00
❑ 137 Spinning Darkness C :K:	1.00	2.00
❑ 138 Steel Golem U :A:	.50	1.00
❑ 139 Strands of Night U :K:	.50	1.00
❑ 140 Straw Golem U :A:	.50	1.00
❑ 141 Striped Bears C :G:	.15	.30
❑ 142 Sylvan Hierophant U :G:	.50	1.00
❑ 143 Tariff R :W:	2.00	4.00
❑ 144 Teferi's Veil U :B:	.50	1.00
❑ 145 Tendrils of Despair C :K:	.15	.30
❑ 146 Thran Forge U :A:	.50	1.00
❑ 147 Thran Tome R :A:	2.00	4.00
❑ 148 Thunderbolt C :R:	.15	.30
❑ 149 Thundermare R :R:	2.00	4.00
❑ 150 Timid Drake U :B:	.50	1.00
❑ 151 Tolarian Drake C :B:	.15	.30
❑ 152 Tolarian Entrancer R :B:	1.50	3.00
❑ 153 Tolarian Serpent R :B:	2.00	4.00
❑ 154 Touchstone U :A:	.50	1.00
❑ 155 Tranquil Grove R :G:	2.00	4.00
❑ 156 Uktabi Efreet C :G:	.15	.30
❑ 157 Urborg Justice R :K:	2.00	4.00
❑ 158 Urborg Stalker R :K:	1.50	3.00
❑ 159 Veteran Explorer U :G:	.50	1.00
❑ 160 Vitalize C :G:	.15	.30
❑ 161 Vodalian Illusionist U :B:	.50	1.00
❑ 162 Volunteer Reserves U :W:	.50	1.00
❑ 163 Wave of Terror R :K:	2.00	4.00
❑ 164 Well of Knowledge R :A:	1.50	3.00
❑ 165 Winding Canyons R :L:	2.00	4.00
❑ 166 Xanthic Statue R :A:	1.50	3.00
❑ 167 Zombie Scavengers C :K:	.15	.30

1997 Magic the Gathering Tempest

Complete Set (335)	200.00	300.00
Starter Deck Box (12 Decks)	175.00	250.00
Starter Deck	20.00	25.00
Booster Box (36 Packs)	275.00	380.00
Booster Pack (15 Cards)	10.00	15.00

Released in October 1997

Card	Low	High
❑ 1 Abandon Hope U :K:	.25	.50
❑ 2 Advance Scout C :W:	.15	.30
❑ 3 Aftershock C :R:	.15	.30
❑ 4 Altar of Dementia R :A:	3.00	6.00
❑ 5 Aluren R :G:	5.00	10.00
❑ 6 Ancient Runes U :R:	.50	1.00
❑ 7 Ancient Tomb U :L:	1.50	3.00
❑ 8 Angelic Protector U :W:	.50	1.00
❑ 9 Anoint C :W:	.15	.30
❑ 10 Apes of Rath U :G:	.25	.50
❑ 11 Apocalypse R :R:	1.50	3.00
❑ 12 Armor Sliver U :W:	1.00	2.00
❑ 13 Armored Pegasus C :W:	.15	.30
❑ 14 Auratog R :W:	2.00	4.00
❑ 15 Avenging Angel R :W:	2.00	4.00
❑ 16 Barbed Sliver U :R:	1.00	2.00
❑ 17 Bayou Dragonfly C :G:	.15	.30
❑ 18 Bellowing Fiend R :K:	1.00	2.00
❑ 19 Benthic Behemoth R :B:	1.50	3.00
❑ 20 Blood Frenzy C :R:	.15	.30
❑ 21 Blood Pet C :K:	.15	.30
❑ 22 Boil U :R:	1.00	2.00
❑ 23 Booby Trap R :A:	2.00	4.00
❑ 24 Bottle Gnomes U :A:	.75	1.50
❑ 25 Bounty Hunter R :K:	2.50	5.00
❑ 26 Broken Fall C :G:	.15	.30
❑ 27 Caldera Lake R :L:	1.50	3.00
❑ 28 Canopy Spider C :G:	.15	.30
❑ 29 Canyon Drake R :R:	.50	1.00
❑ 30 Canyon Wildcat C :R:	.15	.30
❑ 31 Capsize C :B:	.50	1.00
❑ 32 Carrionette R :K:	1.50	3.00
❑ 33 Chaotic Goo R :R:	1.00	2.00
❑ 34 Charging Rhino U :G:	.50	1.00
❑ 35 Chill U :B:	2.00	4.00
❑ 36 Choke U :G:	.50	1.00
❑ 37 Cinder Marsh U :L:	.50	1.00
❑ 38 Circle of Protection Black C :W:	.15	.30
❑ 39 Circle of Protection Blue C :W:	.15	.30
❑ 40 Circle of Protection Green C :W:	.15	.30
❑ 41 Circle of Protection Red C :W:	.15	.30
❑ 42 Circle of Protection Shadow C :W:	.15	.30
❑ 43 Circle of Protection White C :W:	.15	.30
❑ 44 Clergy en-Vec C :W:	.15	.30
❑ 45 Clot Sliver C :K:	.50	1.00
❑ 46 Cloudchaser Eagle C :W:	.15	.30
❑ 47 Coercion C :K:	.15	.30
❑ 48 Coffin Queen R :K:	2.50	5.00
❑ 49 Coiled Tinviper C :A:	.15	.30
❑ 50 Cold Storage R :A:	1.50	3.00
❑ 51 Commander Greven il-Vec R :K:	2.50	5.00
❑ 52 Corpse Dance R :K:	3.00	6.00
❑ 53 Counterspell C :B:	1.00	2.00
❑ 54 Crazed Armodon R :G:	1.00	2.00
❑ 55 Crown of Flames C :R:	.15	.30
❑ 56 Cursed Scroll R :A:	8.00	16.00
❑ 57 Dark Banishing C :K:	.15	.30
❑ 58 Dark Ritual C :K:	.50	1.00
❑ 59 Darkling Stalker C :K:	.15	.30
❑ 60 Dauthi Embrace U :K:	.50	1.00
❑ 61 Dauthi Ghoul U :K:	.50	1.00
❑ 62 Dauthi Horror C :K:	.15	.30
❑ 63 Dauthi Marauder C :K:	.15	.30
❑ 64 Dauthi Mercenary U :K:	.50	1.00
❑ 65 Dauthi Mindripper U :K:	.50	1.00
❑ 66 Dauthi Slayer C :K:	.50	1.00
❑ 67 Deadshot R :R:	1.00	2.00
❑ 68 Death Pits of Rath R :K:	2.00	4.00
❑ 69 Diabolic Edict C :K:	1.50	3.00
❑ 70 Dirtcowl Wurm R :G:	.75	1.50
❑ 71 Disenchant C :W:	.15	.30
❑ 72 Dismiss U :B:	.75	1.50
❑ 73 Disturbed Burial C :K:	.15	.30
❑ 74 Dracoplasm R :D:	1.00	2.00
❑ 75 Dread of Night U :K:	.50	1.00
❑ 76 Dream Cache C :B:	.15	.30
❑ 77 Dregs of Sorrow R :K:	1.00	2.00
❑ 78 Duplicity R :B:	1.00	2.00
❑ 79 Earthcraft R :G:	5.00	10.00
❑ 80 Echo Chamber R :A:	1.00	2.00
❑ 81 Eladamri, Lord of Leaves R :G:	3.50	7.00
❑ 82 Eladamri's Vineyard R :G:	2.00	4.00
❑ 83 Elite Javelineer C :W:	.15	.30
❑ 84 Elven Warhounds R :G:	1.00	2.00
❑ 85 Elvish Fury C :G:	.15	.30
❑ 86 Emerald Medallion R :A:	3.00	6.00
❑ 87 Emmessi Tome R :A:	1.00	2.00
❑ 88 Endless Scream C :K:	.15	.30
❑ 89 Energizer R :A:	1.00	2.00
❑ 90 Enfeeblement C :K:	.15	.30
❑ 91 Enraging Licid U :R:	.25	.50
❑ 92 Ertai's Meddling R :B:	1.00	2.00
❑ 93 Escaped Shapeshifter R :B:	1.00	2.00
❑ 94 Essence Bottle U :A:	.50	1.00
❑ 95 Evincar's Justice C :K:	.15	.30
❑ 96 Excavator U :A:	.25	.50
❑ 97 Extinction R :K:	2.00	4.00
❑ 98 Fevered Convulsions R :K:	1.50	3.00
❑ 99 Field of Souls R :W:	1.00	2.00
❑ 100 Fighting Drake U :B:	.25	.50
❑ 101 Firefly U :R:	.25	.50
❑ 102 Fireslinger C :R:	.15	.30
❑ 103 Flailing Drake U :G:	.25	.50
❑ 104 Flickering Ward U :W:	1.00	2.00
❑ 105 Flowstone Giant C :R:	.15	.30
❑ 106 Flowstone Salamander U :R:	.50	1.00
❑ 107 Flowstone Sculpture R :A:	1.50	3.00
❑ 108 Flowstone Wyvern R :R:	1.00	2.00
❑ 109 Fool's Tome R :A:	1.00	2.00
❑ 110 Forest (4 versions) L :L:	.15	.30
❑ 111 Frog Tongue C :G:	.15	.30
❑ 112 Fugitive Druid R :G:	1.50	3.00
❑ 113 Furnace of Rath R :R:	2.50	5.00
❑ 114 Fylamarid U :B:	.50	1.00
❑ 115 Gallantry U :W:	.50	1.00
❑ 116 Gaseous Form C :B:	.15	.30
❑ 117 Gerrard's Battle Cry R :W:	1.00	2.00
❑ 118 Ghost Town U :L:	.50	1.00
❑ 119 Giant Crab C :B:	.15	.30
❑ 120 Giant Strength C :R:	.15	.30
❑ 121 Goblin Bombardment U :R:	1.00	2.00
❑ 122 Gravedigger C :K:	.15	.30
❑ 123 Grindstone R :A:	4.00	8.00
❑ 124 Hand to Hand R :R:	1.50	3.00
❑ 125 Hanna's Custody R :W:	1.50	3.00
❑ 126 Harrow U :G:	.50	1.00
❑ 127 Havoc U :R:	.50	1.00
❑ 128 Heart Sliver C :R:	.50	1.00
❑ 129 Heartwood Dryad C :G:	.15	.30
❑ 130 Heartwood Giant R :G:	1.00	2.00
❑ 131 Heartwood Treefolk U :G:	.50	1.00
❑ 132 Helm of Possession R :A:	1.50	3.00
❑ 133 Hero's Resolve C :W:	.15	.30
❑ 134 Horned Sliver U :G:	2.00	4.00
❑ 135 Horned Turtle C :B:	.15	.30
❑ 136 Humility R :W:	3.50	7.00
❑ 137 Imps' Taunt U :K:	.50	1.00
❑ 138 Insight U :B:	.50	1.00
❑ 139 Interdict U :B:	.50	1.00
❑ 140 Intuition R :B:	15.00	30.00
❑ 141 Invulnerability U :W:	.50	1.00
❑ 142 Island (4 versions) L :L:	.15	.30
❑ 143 Jackal Pup U :R:	2.00	4.00
❑ 144 Jet Medallion R :A:	3.50	7.00
❑ 145 Jinxed Idol R :A:	1.50	3.00
❑ 146 Kezzerdrix R :K:	1.50	3.00
❑ 147 Kindle C :R:	.25	.50
❑ 148 Knight of Dawn U :W:	.50	1.00
❑ 149 Knight of Dusk U :K:	.50	1.00
❑ 150 Krakilin U :G:	.50	1.00
❑ 151 Leeching Licid U :K:	.50	1.00
❑ 152 Legacy's Allure U :B:	.50	1.00
❑ 153 Legerdemain U :B:	.50	1.00
❑ 154 Light of Day U :W:	1.00	2.00
❑ 155 Lightning Blast C :R:	.25	.50
❑ 156 Lightning Elemental C :R:	.15	.30
❑ 157 Living Death R :K:	6.00	12.00
❑ 158 Lobotomy U :D:	.50	1.00
❑ 159 Lotus Petal C :A:	1.50	3.00
❑ 160 Lowland Giant C :R:	.15	.30
❑ 161 Maddening Imp R :K:	1.00	2.00
❑ 162 Magmasaur R :R:	1.00	2.00
❑ 163 Magnetic Web R :A:	1.00	2.00
❑ 164 Mana Severance R :B:	2.50	5.00
❑ 165 Manakin C :A:	.15	.30
❑ 166 Manta Riders C :B:	.15	.30
❑ 167 Marble Titan R :W:	1.00	2.00
❑ 168 Marsh Lurker C :K:	.15	.30
❑ 169 Master Decoy C :W:	.15	.30
❑ 170 Mawcor R :B:	1.00	2.00
❑ 171 Maze of Shadows U :L:	.50	1.00
❑ 172 Meditate R :B:	3.00	6.00
❑ 173 Metallic Sliver C :A:	.50	1.00
❑ 174 Mindwhip Sliver U :K:	1.00	2.00
❑ 175 Minion of the Wastes R :K:	1.50	3.00
❑ 176 Mirri's Guile R :G:	2.50	5.00
❑ 177 Mnemonic Sliver U :B:	1.00	2.00
❑ 178 Mogg Cannon U :A:	.25	.50
❑ 179 Mogg Conscripts C :R:	.15	.30
❑ 180 Mogg Fanatic C :R:	1.00	2.00
❑ 181 Mogg Hollows U :L:	.50	1.00
❑ 182 Mogg Raider C :R:	.15	.30
❑ 183 Mogg Squad U :R:	.50	1.00
❑ 184 Mongrel Pack R :G:	1.50	3.00
❑ 185 Mountain (4 versions) L :L:	.15	.30
❑ 186 Mounted Archers C :W:	.15	.30
❑ 187 Muscle Sliver C :G:	1.00	2.00
❑ 188 Natural Spring C :G:	.15	.30
❑ 189 Nature's Revolt R :G:	1.50	3.00
❑ 190 Needle Storm U :G:	.50	1.00
❑ 191 No Quarter R :R:	1.00	2.00
❑ 192 Nurturing Licid U :G:	.50	1.00
❑ 193 Opportunist U :R:	.50	1.00
❑ 194 Oracle en-Vec R :W:	1.50	3.00
❑ 195 Orim, Samite Healer R :W:	1.50	3.00
❑ 196 Orim's Prayer U :W:	1.00	2.00
❑ 197 Overrun U :G:	1.50	3.00
❑ 198 Pacifism C :W:	.15	.30
❑ 199 Pallimud R :R:	1.00	2.00
❑ 200 Patchwork Gnomes U :A:	.50	1.00
❑ 201 Pearl Medallion R :A:	3.50	7.00
❑ 202 Pegasus Refuge R :W:	1.50	3.00
❑ 203 Perish U :K:	1.00	2.00
❑ 204 Phyrexian Grimoire R :A:	1.00	2.00
❑ 205 Phyrexian Hulk U :A:	.50	1.00
❑ 206 Phyrexian Splicer U :A:	.50	1.00
❑ 207 Pincher Beetles C :G:	.15	.30
❑ 208 Pine Barrens R :L:	1.00	2.00
❑ 209 Pit Imp C :K: :L:	.15	.30
❑ 210 Plains L :L:	.15	.30
❑ 211 Power Sink C :B:	.15	.30
❑ 212 Precognition R :B:	1.00	2.00
❑ 213 Propaganda U :B:	1.50	3.00
❑ 214 Puppet Strings U :A:	.50	1.00
❑ 215 Quickening Licid U :W:	.50	1.00
❑ 216 Rain of Tears U :K:	.50	1.00
❑ 217 Rampant Growth C :G:	.15	.30
❑ 218 Ranger en-Vec U :D:	.50	1.00
❑ 219 Rathi Dragon R :R:	3.50	7.00
❑ 220 Rats of Rath C :K:	.15	.30
❑ 221 Reality Anchor C :G:	.15	.30
❑ 222 Reanimate U :K:	3.00	6.00
❑ 223 Reap U :G:	.25	.50
❑ 224 Reckless Spite U :K:	.50	1.00
❑ 225 Recycle R :G:	2.00	4.00
❑ 226 Reflecting Pool R :L:	5.00	10.00
❑ 227 Renegade Warlord U :R:	.50	1.00
❑ 228 Repentance U :W:	.50	1.00
❑ 229 Respite C :G:	.15	.30
❑ 230 Rolling Thunder C :R:	.15	.30
❑ 231 Root Maze R :G:	1.50	3.00
❑ 232 Rootbreaker Wurm C :G:	.15	.30
❑ 233 Rootwalla C :G:	.15	.30
❑ 234 Rootwater Depths U :L:	.50	1.00
❑ 235 Rootwater Diver U :B:	.50	1.00
❑ 236 Rootwater Hunter C :B:	.15	.30
❑ 237 Rootwater Matriarch R :B:	1.00	2.00
❑ 238 Rootwater Shaman R :B:	1.00	2.00
❑ 239 Ruby Medallion R :A:	3.00	6.00
❑ 240 Sacred Guide R :W:	1.50	3.00
❑ 241 Sadistic Glee C :K:	.15	.30
❑ 242 Safeguard R :W:	1.00	2.00
❑ 243 Salt Flats R :L:	1.00	2.00
❑ 244 Sandstone Warrior C :R:	.15	.30
❑ 245 Sapphire Medallion R :A:	5.00	10.00
❑ 246 Sarcomancy R :K:	3.00	6.00
❑ 247 Scabland R :L:	1.00	2.00
❑ 248 Scalding Tongs R :A:	2.00	4.00
❑ 249 Scorched Earth R :R:	1.50	3.00
❑ 250 Scragnoth U :G:	.50	1.00
❑ 251 Screeching Harpy U :K:	.50	1.00
❑ 252 Scroll Rack R :A:	4.00	8.00
❑ 253 Sea Monster C :B:	.15	.30
❑ 254 Searing Touch U :R:	.50	1.00
❑ 255 Seeker of Skybreak C :G:	.15	.30
❑ 256 Segmented Wurm U :D:	.50	1.00
❑ 257 Selenia, Dark Angel R :D:	2.50	5.00
❑ 258 Serene Offering U :W:	.50	1.00
❑ 259 Servant of Volrath C :K:	.15	.30
❑ 260 Shadow Rift C :B:	.15	.30
❑ 261 Shadowstorm U :R:	.50	1.00
❑ 262 Shatter C :R:	.15	.30
❑ 263 Shimmering Wings C :B:	.15	.30
❑ 264 Shocker R :R:	1.50	3.00
❑ 265 Sky Spirit U :D:	.50	1.00
❑ 266 Skyshroud Condor U :B:	.50	1.00
❑ 267 Skyshroud Elf C :G:	.15	.30
❑ 268 Skyshroud Forest R :L:	1.50	3.00
❑ 269 Skyshroud Ranger C :G:	.15	.30
❑ 270 Skyshroud Troll C :G:	.15	.30
❑ 271 Skyshroud Vampire U :K:	.50	1.00
❑ 272 Soltari Crusader U :W:	.50	1.00
❑ 273 Soltari Emissary R :W:	1.50	3.00
❑ 274 Soltari Foot Soldier C :W:	.15	.30
❑ 275 Soltari Guerrillas R :D:	1.50	3.00
❑ 276 Soltari Lancer C :W:	.15	.30
❑ 277 Soltari Monk U :W:	1.50	3.00
❑ 278 Soltari Priest U :W:	1.50	3.00
❑ 279 Soltari Trooper C :W:	.15	.30
❑ 280 Souldrinker U :K:	.50	1.00
❑ 281 Spell Blast C :B:	.15	.30
❑ 282 Spike Drone C :G:	.15	.30
❑ 283 Spinal Graft C :K:	.15	.30
❑ 284 Spirit Mirror R :W:	1.00	2.00
❑ 285 Spontaneous Combustion U :D:	.50	1.00
❑ 286 Squee's Toy C :A:	.15	.30
❑ 287 Stalking Stones U :L:	.50	1.00
❑ 288 Starke of Rath R :R:	1.00	2.00
❑ 289 Static Orb R :A:	2.50	5.00
❑ 290 Staunch Defenders U :W:	.50	1.00
❑ 291 Steal Enchantment U :B:	.50	1.00
❑ 292 Stinging Licid U :B:	.50	1.00
❑ 293 Stone Rain C :R:	.15	.30
❑ 294 Storm Front U :G:	.50	1.00
❑ 295 Stun C :R:	.15	.30
❑ 296 Sudden Impact U :R:	.50	1.00
❑ 297 Swamp (4 versions) L :L:	.15	.30
❑ 298 Tahngarth's Rage U :R:	.50	1.00
❑ 299 Talon Sliver C :W:	.50	1.00
❑ 300 Telethopter U :A:	.50	1.00
❑ 301 Thalakos Dreamsower U :B:	.50	1.00
❑ 302 Thalakos Lowlands U :L:	.50	1.00
❑ 303 Thalakos Mistfolk C :B:	.15	.30
❑ 304 Thalakos Seer C :B:	.15	.30
❑ 305 Thalakos Sentry C :B:	.15	.30
❑ 306 Thumbscrews R :A:	1.00	2.00
❑ 307 Time Ebb C :B:	.15	.30
❑ 308 Time Warp R :B:	4.00	8.00
❑ 309 Tooth and Claw R :R:	1.50	3.00
❑ 310 Torture Chamber R :A:	1.00	2.00
❑ 311 Tradewind Rider R :B:	4.00	8.00
❑ 312 Trained Armodon C :G:	.15	.30
❑ 313 Tranquility C :G:	.15	.30
❑ 314 Trumpeting Armodon U :G:	.25	.50
❑ 315 Twitch C :B:	.15	.30
❑ 316 Unstable Shapeshifter R :B:	1.00	2.00
❑ 317 Vec Townships U :L:	.50	1.00
❑ 318 Verdant Force R :G:	6.00	12.00
❑ 319 Verdigris U :G:	.25	.50
❑ 320 Vhati il-Dal R :D:	1.50	3.00
❑ 321 Volrath's Curse C :B:	.15	.30
❑ 322 Wall of Diffusion C :R:	.15	.30
❑ 323 Warmth U :W:	.25	.50
❑ 324 Wasteland U :L:	30.00	60.00
❑ 325 Watchdog U :A:	.25	.50
❑ 326 Whim of Volrath R :B:	1.50	3.00
❑ 327 Whispers of the Muse U :B:	.50	1.00
❑ 328 Wild Wurm U :R:	.50	1.00
❑ 329 Wind Dancer U :B:	.25	.50
❑ 330 Wind Drake C :B:	.15	.30
❑ 331 Winds of Rath R :W:	2.00	4.00
❑ 332 Winged Sliver C :B:	1.00	2.00
❑ 333 Winter's Grasp U :G:	1.00	2.00
❑ 334 Wood Sage R :D:	1.00	2.00
❑ 335 Worthy Cause U :W:	1.50	3.00

1998 Magic the Gathering Stronghold

Complete Set (143)	100.00	175.00
Starter Deck Box (12 Decks)	125.00	175.00
Starter Deck	15.00	20.00
Booster Box (36 Packs)	128.00	155.00
Booster Pack (15 Cards)	5.00	6.50

Released in February 1998

Card	Low	High
❑ 1 Acidic Sliver U :D:	1.50	3.00
❑ 2 Amok R :R:	1.00	2.00
❑ 3 Awakening R :G:	1.00	2.00
❑ 4 Bandage C :W:	.15	.30
❑ 5 Bottomless Pit U :K:	.25	.50
❑ 6 Brush With Death C :K:	.15	.30
❑ 7 Bullwhip U :A:	.25	.50
❑ 8 Burgeoning R :G:	1.50	3.00
❑ 9 Calming Licid U :W:	.25	.50
❑ 10 Cannibalize C :K:	.15	.30
❑ 11 Cardassid R :G:	1.00	2.00
❑ 12 Change of Heart C :W:	.15	.30
❑ 13 Cloud Spirit C :B:	.15	.30
❑ 14 Constant Mists U :G:	1.00	2.00
❑ 15 Contemplation U :W:	.50	1.00
❑ 16 Contempt C :B:	.15	.30
❑ 17 Conviction C :W:	.15	.30
❑ 18 Convulsing Licid U :R:	.25	.50
❑ 19 Corrupting Licid U :K:	.25	.50
❑ 20 Craven Giant C :R:	.15	.30
❑ 21 Crossbow Ambush C :G:	.15	.30
❑ 22 Crovax, The Cursed R :K:	1.50	3.00
❑ 23 Crystalline Sliver U :D:	4.00	8.00
❑ 24 Dauthi Trapper U :K:	.50	1.00
❑ 25 Death Stroke C :K:	.15	.30
❑ 26 Dream Halls R :B:	1.50	3.00

MAGIC

❑ 27 Dream Prowler C :B:	.15	.30
❑ 28 Duct Crawler C :R:	.15	.30
❑ 29 Dungeon Shade C :K:	.15	.30
❑ 30 Elven Rite U :G:	.25	.50
❑ 31 Endangered Armodon C :G:	.15	.30
❑ 32 Ensnaring Bridge R :A:	3.00	6.00
❑ 33 Evacuation R :B:	2.00	4.00
❑ 34 Fanning the Flames U :R:	.75	1.50
❑ 35 Flame Wave U :R:	.75	1.50
❑ 36 Fling C :R:	1.00	2.00
❑ 37 Flowstone Blade C :R:	.15	.30
❑ 38 Flowstone Hellion U :R:	.50	1.00
❑ 39 Flowstone Mauler R :R:	1.00	2.00
❑ 40 Flowstone Shambler C :R:	.15	.30
❑ 41 Foul Imp C :K:	.15	.30
❑ 42 Furnace Spirit C :R:	.15	.30
❑ 43 Gliding Licid U :B:	.50	1.00
❑ 44 Grave Pact R :K:	4.00	8.00
❑ 45 Hammerhead Shark C :B:	.15	.30
❑ 46 Heartstone U :A:	1.00	2.00
❑ 47 Heat of Battle U :R:	.50	1.00
❑ 48 Hermit Druid R :G:	1.00	2.00
❑ 49 Hesitation U :B:	.50	1.00
❑ 50 Hibernation Sliver U :D:	1.00	2.00
❑ 51 Hidden Retreat R :W:	1.00	2.00
❑ 52 Honor Guard C :W:	.15	.30
❑ 53 Horn of Greed R :A:	2.50	5.00
❑ 54 Hornet Cannon U :A:	.25	.50
❑ 55 Intruder Alarm R :B:	4.00	8.00
❑ 56 Invasion Plans R :R:	1.00	2.00
❑ 57 Jinxed Ring R :A:	1.50	3.00
❑ 58 Lab Rats C :K:	.15	.30
❑ 59 Lancers en-Kor U :W:	.25	.50
❑ 60 Leap C :B:	.15	.30
❑ 61 Lowland Basilisk C :G:	.15	.30
❑ 62 Mana Leak C :B:	1.50	3.00
❑ 63 Mask of the Mimic U :B:	1.00	2.00
❑ 64 Megrim U :K:	1.50	3.00
❑ 65 Mind Games C :B:	.15	.30
❑ 66 Mind Peel U :K:	.50	1.00
❑ 67 Mindwarper R :K:	1.00	2.00
❑ 68 Mob Justice C :R:	.15	.30
❑ 69 Mogg Bombers C :R:	.15	.30
❑ 70 Mogg Flunkies C :R:	.15	.30
❑ 71 Mogg Infestation R :R:	1.50	3.00
❑ 72 Mogg Maniac U :R:	1.00	2.00
❑ 73 Morgue Thrull C :K:	.15	.30
❑ 74 Mortuary R :K:	1.50	3.00
❑ 75 Mox Diamond R :A:	25.00	50.00
❑ 76 Mulch C :G:	.15	.30
❑ 77 Nomads en-Kor C :W:	.50	1.00
❑ 78 Overgrowth C :G:	.15	.30
❑ 79 Portcullis R :A:	1.50	3.00
❑ 80 Primal Rage U :G:	1.00	2.00
❑ 81 Provoke C :G:	.15	.30
❑ 82 Pursuit of Knowledge R :W:	1.50	3.00
❑ 83 Rabid Rats C :K:	.15	.30
❑ 84 Ransack U :B:	.50	1.00
❑ 85 Rebound U :B:	1.00	2.00
❑ 86 Reins of Power R :B:	1.00	2.00
❑ 87 Revenant R :K:	1.00	2.00
❑ 88 Rolling Stones R :W:	1.00	2.00
❑ 89 Ruination R :R:	1.00	2.00
❑ 90 Sacred Ground R :W:	2.00	4.00
❑ 91 Samite Blessing C :W:	.15	.30
❑ 92 Scapegoat U :W:	.50	1.00
❑ 93 Seething Anger C :R:	.15	.30
❑ 94 Serpent Warrior C :K:	.15	.30
❑ 95 Shaman en-Kor R :W:	3.00	6.00
❑ 96 Shard Phoenix R :R:	2.00	4.00
❑ 97 Shifting Wall U :A:	1.00	2.00
❑ 98 Shock C :R:	.15	.30
❑ 99 Sift C :B:	.15	.30
❑ 100 Silver Wyvern R :B:	1.00	2.00
❑ 101 Skeleton Scavengers R :K:	1.50	3.00
❑ 102 Skyshroud Archer C :G:	.15	.30
❑ 103 Skyshroud Falcon C :W:	.15	.30
❑ 104 Skyshroud Troopers C :G:	.15	.30
❑ 105 Sliver Queen R :D:	15.00	30.00
❑ 106 Smite C :W:	.15	.30
❑ 107 Soltari Champion R :W:	2.50	5.00
❑ 108 Spike Breeder R :G:	1.50	3.00
❑ 109 Spike Colony C :G:	.15	.30
❑ 110 Spike Feeder U :G:	1.00	2.00
❑ 111 Spike Soldier U :G:	.50	1.00
❑ 112 Spike Worker C :G:	.15	.30
❑ 113 Spindrift Drake C :B:	.15	.30
❑ 114 Spined Sliver U :D:	1.00	2.00
❑ 115 Spined Wurm C :G:	.15	.30
❑ 116 Spirit en-Kor C :W:	.15	.30
❑ 117 Spitting Hydra R :R:	.50	1.00
❑ 118 Stronghold Assassin R :K:	1.00	2.00
❑ 119 Stronghold Taskmaster U :K:	.50	1.00
❑ 120 Sword of the Chosen R :A:	1.50	3.00
❑ 121 Temper U :W:	.50	1.00
❑ 122 Tempting Licid U :G:	.25	.50
❑ 123 Thalakos Deceiver R :B:	2.00	4.00
❑ 124 Tidal Surge C :B:	.15	.30
❑ 125 Tidal Warrior C :B:	.15	.30
❑ 126 Torment C :K:	.15	.30
❑ 127 Tortured Existence C :K:	.50	1.00
❑ 128 Venerable Monk C :W:	.15	.30
❑ 129 Verdant Touch R :G:	1.50	3.00
❑ 130 Victual Sliver U :D:	1.50	3.00
❑ 131 Volrath's Gardens R :G:	1.00	2.00
❑ 132 Volrath's Laboratory R :A:	1.00	2.00
❑ 133 Volrath's Shapeshifter R :B:	2.00	4.00
❑ 134 Volrath's Stronghold R :L:	4.00	8.00
❑ 135 Walking Dream U :B:	.50	1.00
❑ 136 Wall of Blossoms U :G:	2.50	5.00
❑ 137 Wall of Essence U :W:	.50	1.00
❑ 138 Wall of Razors U :R:	.50	1.00
❑ 139 Wall of Souls U :K:	1.50	3.00
❑ 140 Wall of Tears U :B:	.50	1.00
❑ 141 Warrior Angel R :W:	2.00	4.00
❑ 142 Warrior en-Kor U :W:	.50	1.00
❑ 143 Youthful Knight C :W:	.15	.30

1998 Magic the Gathering Exodus

Complete Set (143)	100.00	135.00
Theme Deck	20.00	30.00
Booster Box	200.00	275.00
Booster Pack	7.00	9.00
Released in June 1998		
❑ 1 AEther Tide C :B:	.15	.30
❑ 2 Allay C :W:	.25	.50
❑ 3 Anarchist C :R:	.15	.30
❑ 4 Angelic Blessing C :W:	.15	.30
❑ 5 Avenging Druid C :G:	.15	.30
❑ 6 Bequeathal C :G:	.25	.50
❑ 7 Carnophage C :K:	.50	1.00
❑ 8 Cartographer U :G:	.50	1.00
❑ 9 Cat Burglar C :K:	.15	.30
❑ 10 Cataclysm R :W:	2.50	5.00
❑ 11 Charging Paladin C :W:	.15	.30
❑ 12 Cinder Crawler C :R:	.15	.30
❑ 13 City of Traitors R :L:	4.00	8.00
❑ 14 Coat of Arms R :A:	7.50	15.00
❑ 15 Convalescence R :W:	2.00	4.00
❑ 16 Crashing Boars U :G:	.50	1.00
❑ 17 Culling the Weak C :K:	.50	1.00
❑ 18 Cunning C :B:	.15	.30
❑ 19 Curiosity U :B:	.75	1.50
❑ 20 Cursed Flesh C :K:	.15	.30
❑ 21 Dauthi Cutthroat U :K:	1.00	2.00
❑ 22 Dauthi Jackal C :K:	.15	.30
❑ 23 Dauthi Warlord U :K:	1.00	2.00
❑ 24 Death's Duet C :K:	.15	.30
❑ 25 Dizzying Gaze C :R:	.15	.30
❑ 26 Dominating Licid R :B:	2.00	4.00
❑ 27 Elven Palisade U :G:	.25	.50
❑ 28 Elvish Berserker C :G:	.25	.50
❑ 29 Entropic Specter R :K:	1.00	2.00
❑ 30 Ephemeron R :B:	1.00	2.00
❑ 31 Equilibrium R :B:	1.50	3.00
❑ 32 Erratic Portal R :A:	1.50	3.00
❑ 33 Ertai, Wizard Adept R :B:	4.00	8.00
❑ 34 Exalted Dragon R :W:	2.00	4.00
❑ 35 Fade Away C :B:	.15	.30
❑ 36 Fighting Chance R :R:	1.50	3.00
❑ 37 Flowstone Flood U :R:	.25	.50
❑ 38 Forbid U :B:	1.00	2.00
❑ 39 Fugue U :K:	.50	1.00
❑ 40 Furnace Brood C :R:	.15	.30
❑ 41 Grollub C :K:	.15	.30
❑ 42 Hatred R :K:	4.00	8.00
❑ 43 High Ground U :W:	.50	1.00
❑ 44 Jackalope Herd C :G:	.15	.30
❑ 45 Keeper of the Beasts U :G:	.50	1.00
❑ 46 Keeper of the Dead U :K:	.50	1.00
❑ 47 Keeper of the Flame U :R:	.50	1.00
❑ 48 Keeper of the Light U :W:	.50	1.00
❑ 49 Keeper of the Mind U :B:	.50	1.00
❑ 50 Killer Whale U :B:	.50	1.00
❑ 51 Kor Chant C :W:	.15	.30
❑ 52 Limited Resources R :W:	2.00	4.00
❑ 53 Mage il-Vec C :R:	.15	.30
❑ 54 Mana Breach U :B:	.50	1.00
❑ 55 Manabond R :G:	1.50	3.00
❑ 56 Maniacal Rage C :R:	.15	.30
❑ 57 Medicine Bag U :A:	.50	1.00
❑ 58 Memory Crystal R :A:	1.50	3.00
❑ 59 Merfolk Looter C :B:	.25	.50
❑ 60 Mind Maggots U :K:	.50	1.00
❑ 61 Mind Over Matter R :B:	2.50	5.00
❑ 62 Mindless Automaton R :A:	2.00	4.00
❑ 63 Mirozel U :B:	.50	1.00
❑ 64 Mirri, Cat Warrior R :G:	2.50	5.00
❑ 65 Mogg Assassin U :R:	1.00	2.00
❑ 66 Monstrous Hound R :R:	1.00	2.00
❑ 67 Nausea C :K:	.25	.50
❑ 68 Necrologia U :K:	.50	1.00
❑ 69 Null Brooch R :A:	2.00	4.00
❑ 70 Oath of Druids R :G:	7.50	15.00
❑ 71 Oath of Ghouls R :K:	1.50	3.00
❑ 72 Oath of Lieges R :W:	1.50	3.00
❑ 73 Oath of Mages R :R:	1.50	3.00
❑ 74 Oath of Scholars R :B:	1.50	3.00
❑ 75 Ogre Shaman R :R:	1.00	2.00
❑ 76 Onslaught C :R:	.15	.30
❑ 77 Paladin en-Vec R :W:	1.50	3.00
❑ 78 Pandemonium R :R:	4.00	8.00
❑ 79 Paroxysm U :R:	.50	1.00
❑ 80 Peace of Mind U :W:	.50	1.00
❑ 81 Pegasus Stampede U :W:	.50	1.00
❑ 82 Penance U :W:	.50	1.00
❑ 83 Pit Spawn R :K:	1.50	3.00
❑ 84 Plaguebearer R :K:	1.50	3.00
❑ 85 Plated Rootwalla C :G:	.15	.30
❑ 86 Predatory Hunger C :G:	.15	.30
❑ 87 Price of Progress U :R:	1.00	2.00
❑ 88 Pygmy Troll C :G:	.15	.30
❑ 89 Rabid Wolverines C :G:	.15	.30
❑ 90 Raging Goblin C :R:	.15	.30
❑ 91 Ravenous Baboons R :R:	1.00	2.00
❑ 92 Reaping the Rewards C :W:	.15	.30
❑ 93 Reckless Ogre C :R:	.15	.30
❑ 94 Reclaim C :G:	.15	.30
❑ 95 Reconnaissance U :W:	.50	1.00
❑ 96 Recurring Nightmare R :K:	6.00	12.00
❑ 97 Resuscitate U :G:	.25	.50
❑ 98 Robe of Mirrors C :B:	.15	.30
❑ 99 Rootwater Alligator C :G:	.15	.30
❑ 100 Rootwater Mystic C :B:	.15	.30
❑ 101 Sabertooth Wyvern U :R:	.50	1.00
❑ 102 Scalding Salamander U :R:	.50	1.00
❑ 103 Scare Tactics C :K:	.15	.30
❑ 104 School of Piranha C :B:	.15	.30
❑ 105 Scrivener U :B:	.50	1.00
❑ 106 Seismic Assault R :R:	2.00	4.00
❑ 107 Shackles C :W:	.15	.30
❑ 108 Shattering Pulse C :R:	.25	.50
❑ 109 Shield Mate C :W:	.15	.30
❑ 110 Skyshaper U :A:	.50	1.00
❑ 111 Skyshroud Elite U :G:	1.00	2.00
❑ 112 Skyshroud War Beast R :G:	1.50	3.00
❑ 113 Slaughter U :K:	.50	1.00
❑ 114 Soltari Visionary C :W:	.15	.30
❑ 115 Song of Serenity U :G:	.50	1.00
❑ 116 Sonic Burst C :R:	.15	.30
❑ 117 Soul Warden C :W:	.15	.30
❑ 118 Spellbook U :A:	1.00	2.00
❑ 119 Spellshock U :R:	.50	1.00
❑ 120 Sphere of Resistance R :A:	2.50	5.00
❑ 121 Spike Cannibal U :K:	.50	1.00
❑ 122 Spike Hatcher R :G:	1.50	3.00
❑ 123 Spike Rogue U :G:	.25	.50
❑ 124 Spike Weaver R :G:	2.50	5.00
❑ 125 Standing Troops C :W:	.15	.30
❑ 126 Survival of the Fittest R :G:	15.00	30.00
❑ 127 Thalakos Drifters R :B:	1.50	3.00
❑ 128 Thalakos Scout C :B:	.15	.30
❑ 129 Theft of Dreams C :B:	.15	.30
❑ 130 Thopter Squadron R :A:	1.00	2.00
❑ 131 Thrull Surgeon C :K:	.15	.30
❑ 132 Transmogrifying Licid U :A:	.50	1.00
❑ 133 Treasure Hunter U :W:	.50	1.00
❑ 134 Treasure Trove U :B:	.50	1.00
❑ 135 Vampire Hounds C :K:	.15	.30
❑ 136 Volrath's Dungeon R :K:	1.00	2.00
❑ 137 Wall of Nets R :W:	2.00	4.00
❑ 138 Wayward Soul C :B:	.15	.30
❑ 139 Welkin Hawk C :W:	.15	.30
❑ 140 Whiptongue Frog C :B:	.15	.30
❑ 141 Wood Elves C :G:	.15	.30
❑ 142 Workhorse R :A:	1.50	3.00
❑ 143 Zealots en-Dal U :W:	.50	1.00

1998 Magic the Gathering Urza's Saga

Complete Set (350)	325.00	425.00
Starter Deck Box (12 Decks)	190.00	250.00
Starter Deck	20.00	30.00
Booster Box (36 Packs)	330.00	450.00
Booster Pack (15 Cards)	15.00	20.00
Released in September 1998		
❑ 1 Absolute Grace U :W:	1.00	2.00
❑ 2 Absolute Law U :W:	1.00	2.00
❑ 3 Abundance R :G:	1.50	3.00
❑ 4 Abyssal Horror R :K:	1.00	2.00
❑ 5 Academy Researchers U :B:	.25	.50
❑ 6 Acidic Soil U :R:	.25	.50
❑ 7 Acridian C :G:	.15	.30
❑ 8 Albino Troll U :G:	1.00	2.00
❑ 9 Anaconda U :G:	.25	.50
❑ 10 Angelic Chorus R :W:	5.00	10.00
❑ 11 Angelic Page C :W:	.15	.30
❑ 12 Annul C :B:	.50	1.00
❑ 13 Antagonism R :R:	1.00	2.00
❑ 14 Arc Lightning C :R:	.15	.30
❑ 15 Arcane Laboratory U :B:	1.00	2.00
❑ 16 Argothian Elder U :G:	1.00	2.00
❑ 17 Argothian Enchantress R :G:	6.00	12.00
❑ 18 Argothian Swine C :G:	.15	.30
❑ 19 Argothian Wurm R :G:	3.00	6.00
❑ 20 Attunement R :B:	1.00	2.00
❑ 21 Back to Basics R :B:	2.50	5.00
❑ 22 Barrin, Master Wizard R :B:	1.00	2.00
❑ 23 Barrin's Codex R :A:	1.00	2.00
❑ 24 Bedlam R :R:	2.00	4.00
❑ 25 Befoul C :K:	.15	.30
❑ 26 Bereavement U :K:	.25	.50
❑ 27 Blanchwood Armor U :G:	1.00	2.00
❑ 28 Blanchwood Treefolk C :G:	.15	.30
❑ 29 Blasted Landscape U :L:	.50	1.00
❑ 30 Blood Vassal C :K:	.15	.30
❑ 31 Bog Raiders C :K:	.15	.30
❑ 32 Brand R :R:	1.50	3.00
❑ 33 Bravado C :R:	.15	.30
❑ 34 Breach C :K:	.15	.30
❑ 35 Brilliant Halo C :W:	.15	.30
❑ 36 Bull Hippo U :G:	.25	.50
❑ 37 Bulwark R :R:	1.50	3.00
❑ 38 Cackling Fiend C :K:	.15	.30
❑ 39 Carpet of Flowers U :G:	.50	1.00
❑ 40 Carrion Beetles C :K:	.15	.30
❑ 41 Catalog C :B:	.15	.30
❑ 42 Catastrophe R :W:	2.00	4.00
❑ 43 Cathodion U :A:	.50	1.00
❑ 44 Cave Tiger C :G:	.15	.30
❑ 45 Child of Gaea R :G:	2.50	5.00
❑ 46 Chimeric Staff R :A:	2.00	4.00
❑ 47 Citanul Centaurs R :G:	1.50	3.00
❑ 48 Citanul Flute R :A:	1.50	3.00
❑ 49 Citanul Hierophants R :G:	1.50	3.00
❑ 50 Claws of Gix U :A:	.50	1.00
❑ 51 Clear U :W:	.50	1.00
❑ 52 Cloak of Mists C :B:	.15	.30
❑ 53 Confiscate U :B:	.50	1.00
❑ 54 Congregate C :W:	.50	1.00
❑ 55 Contamination R :K:	2.50	5.00
❑ 56 Copper Gnomes R :A:	1.50	3.00
❑ 57 Coral Merfolk C :B:	.15	.30
❑ 58 Corrupt C :K:	.15	.30
❑ 59 Cradle Guard U :G:	.50	1.00
❑ 60 Crater Hellion R :R:	2.50	5.00
❑ 61 Crazed Skirge U :K:	.50	1.00
❑ 62 Crosswinds U :G:	.50	1.00
❑ 63 Crystal Chimes U :A:	.50	1.00
❑ 64 Curfew C :B:	.15	.30
❑ 65 Dark Hatchling R :K:	2.00	4.00
❑ 66 Dark Ritual C :K:	.50	1.00
❑ 67 Darkest Hour R :K:	2.00	4.00
❑ 68 Defensive Formation U :W:	.50	1.00
❑ 69 Despondency C :K:	.15	.30
❑ 70 Destructive Urge U :R:	.75	1.50
❑ 71 Diabolic Servitude U :K:	.75	1.50
❑ 72 Disciple of Grace C :W:	.15	.30
❑ 73 Disciple of Law C :W:	.15	.30
❑ 74 Discordant Dirge R :K:	1.00	2.00
❑ 75 Disenchant C :W:	.50	1.00
❑ 76 Disorder U :R:	.50	1.00
❑ 77 Disruptive Student C :B:	.15	.30
❑ 78 Douse U :B:	.50	1.00
❑ 79 Dragon Blood U :A:	.50	1.00
❑ 80 Drifting Djinn R :B:	2.00	4.00
❑ 81 Drifting Meadow C :L:	.15	.30
❑ 82 Dromosaur C :R:	.15	.30
❑ 83 Duress C :K:	2.50	5.00
❑ 84 Eastern Paladin R :K:	2.00	4.00
❑ 85 Electryte R :R:	1.50	3.00
❑ 86 Elite Archers R :W:	1.00	2.00
❑ 87 Elvish Herder C :G:	1.00	2.00
❑ 88 Elvish Lyrist C :G:	.15	.30
❑ 89 Enchantment Alteration U :B:	.50	1.00
❑ 90 Endless Wurm R :G:	3.00	6.00
❑ 91 Endoskeleton U :A:	.25	.50
❑ 92 Energy Field R :B:	2.00	4.00
❑ 93 Exhaustion U :B:	.50	1.00
❑ 94 Exhume C :K:	.15	.30
❑ 95 Exploration R :G:	7.50	15.00
❑ 96 Expunge C :K:	.15	.30
❑ 97 Faith Healer R :W:	1.00	2.00
❑ 98 Falter C :R:	.15	.30
❑ 99 Fault Line R :R:	1.50	3.00
❑ 100 Fecundity U :G:	1.50	3.00
❑ 101 Fertile Ground C :G:	.15	.30
❑ 102 Fiery Mantle C :R:	.15	.30
❑ 103 Fire Ants U :R:	.50	1.00
❑ 104 Flesh Reaver U :K:	.50	1.00
❑ 105 Fluctuator R :A:	3.50	7.00
❑ 106 Fog Bank U :B:	1.00	2.00
❑ 107 Forest L :L:	.25	.50
❑ 108 Forest L :L:	.25	.50
❑ 109 Forest L :L:	.25	.50
❑ 110 Forest L :L:	.25	.50
❑ 111 Fortitude C :G:	.15	.30
❑ 112 Gaea's Bounty C :G:	.15	.30
❑ 113 Gaea's Cradle R :L:	40.00	80.00
❑ 114 Gaea's Embrace U :G:	1.00	2.00
❑ 115 Gamble R :R:	2.50	5.00
❑ 116 Gilded Drake R :B:	5.00	10.00
❑ 117 Glorious Anthem R :W:	4.00	8.00
❑ 118 Goblin Cadets U :R:	1.00	2.00
❑ 119 Goblin Lackey U :R:	5.00	10.00
❑ 120 Goblin Matron C :R:	1.50	3.00
❑ 121 Goblin Offensive U :R:	1.00	2.00
❑ 122 Goblin Patrol C :R:	.50	1.00
❑ 123 Goblin Raider C :R:	.15	.30
❑ 124 Goblin Spelunkers C :R:	.15	.30
❑ 125 Goblin War Buggy C :R:	.25	.50
❑ 126 Gorilla Warrior C :G:	.15	.30
❑ 127 Grafted Skullcap R :A:	2.00	4.00
❑ 128 Great Whale R :B:	2.00	4.00
❑ 129 Greater Good R :G:	7.50	15.00
❑ 130 Greener Pastures R :G:	1.50	3.00
❑ 131 Guma U :R:	.50	1.00
❑ 132 Hawkeater Moth U :G:	.50	1.00
❑ 133 Headlong Rush C :R:	.15	.30
❑ 134 Healing Salve C :W:	.15	.30
❑ 135 Heat Ray C :R:	.15	.30
❑ 136 Herald of Serra R :W:	2.00	4.00
❑ 137 Hermetic Study C :B:	.15	.30
❑ 138 Hibernation U :B:	.75	1.50
❑ 139 Hidden Ancients U :G:	.50	1.00
❑ 140 Hidden Guerrillas U :G:	.50	1.00
❑ 141 Hidden Herd R :G:	1.50	3.00
❑ 142 Hidden Predators R :G:	2.00	4.00
❑ 143 Hidden Spider C :G:	.15	.30
❑ 144 Hidden Stag R :G:	1.50	3.00
❑ 145 Hollow Dogs C :K:	.15	.30
❑ 146 Hopping Automaton U :A:	.50	1.00
❑ 147 Horseshoe Crab C :B:	.15	.30
❑ 148 Humble U :W:	.50	1.00
❑ 149 Hush C :G:	.15	.30
❑ 150 Ill-Gotten Gains R :K:	1.50	3.00
❑ 151 Imaginary Pet R :B:	1.50	3.00
❑ 152 Intrepid Hero R :W:	2.50	5.00
❑ 153 Island L :L:	.25	.50
❑ 154 Island L :L:	.25	.50
❑ 155 Island L :L:	.25	.50
❑ 156 Island L :L:	.25	.50
❑ 157 Jagged Lightning U :R:	.50	1.00
❑ 158 Karn, Silver Golem R :A:	3.50	7.00
❑ 159 Launch C :B:	.15	.30
❑ 160 Lay Waste C :R:	.15	.30
❑ 161 Lifeline R :A:	5.00	10.00
❑ 162 Lightning Dragon R :R:	5.00	10.00
❑ 163 Lilting Refrain U :B:	.50	1.00
❑ 164 Lingering Mirage U :B:	.50	1.00
❑ 165 Looming Shade C :K:	.15	.30
❑ 166 Lotus Blossom R :A:	2.00	4.00
❑ 167 Lull C :G:	.15	.30
❑ 168 Lurking Evil R :K:	1.50	3.00
❑ 169 Mana Leech U :K:	.50	1.00
❑ 170 Meltdown U :R:	1.00	2.00
❑ 171 Metrognome R :A:	1.50	3.00
❑ 172 Midsummer Revel R :G:	1.50	3.00
❑ 173 Mishra's Helix R :A:	2.50	5.00
❑ 174 Mobile Fort U :A:	.25	.50
❑ 175 Monk Idealist U :W:	.50	1.00
❑ 176 Monk Realist C :W:	.15	.30
❑ 177 Morphling R :B:	7.50	15.00
❑ 178 Mountain L :L:	.25	.50
❑ 179 Mountain L :L:	.25	.50
❑ 180 Mountain L :L:	.25	.50
❑ 181 Mountain L :L:	.25	.50
❑ 182 No Rest for the Wicked U :K:	.50	1.00
❑ 183 Noetic Scales R :A:	1.50	3.00
❑ 184 Okk R :R:	1.50	3.00
❑ 185 Opal Acrolith U :W:	.25	.50
❑ 186 Opal Archangel R :W:	2.50	5.00
❑ 187 Opal Caryatid C :W:	.15	.30
❑ 188 Opal Gargoyle C :W:	.15	.30
❑ 189 Opal Titan R :W:	1.50	3.00
❑ 190 Oppression R :K:	1.50	3.00
❑ 191 Order of Yawgmoth U :K:	.50	1.00
❑ 192 Outmaneuver U :R:	.50	1.00
❑ 193 Pacifism C :W:	.15	.30
❑ 194 Parasitic Bond U :K:	.50	1.00
❑ 195 Pariah R :W:	2.00	4.00
❑ 196 Path of Peace C :W:	.15	.30
❑ 197 Pegasus Charger C :W:	.15	.30
❑ 198 Pendrell Drake C :B:	.15	.30
❑ 199 Pendrell Flux C :B:	.15	.30
❑ 200 Peregrine Drake U :B:	.50	1.00
❑ 201 Persecute R :K:	4.00	8.00
❑ 202 Pestilence C :K:	.15	.30
❑ 203 Phyrexian Colossus R :A:	1.50	3.00
❑ 204 Phyrexian Ghoul C :K:	.15	.30
❑ 205 Phyrexian Processor R :A:	4.00	8.00
❑ 206 Phyrexian Tower R :L:	2.00	4.00
❑ 207 Pit Trap U :A:	.30	.75
❑ 208 Plains L :L:	.25	.50
❑ 209 Plains L :L:	.25	.50
❑ 210 Plains L :L:	.25	.50
❑ 211 Plains L :L:	.25	.50
❑ 212 Planar Birth R :W:	1.50	3.00
❑ 213 Planar Void U :K:	1.50	3.00
❑ 214 Polluted Mire C :L:	.15	.30
❑ 215 Pouncing Jaguar C :G:	.50	1.00
❑ 216 Power Sink C :B:	.15	.30
❑ 217 Power Taint C :B:	.15	.30
❑ 218 Presence of the Master U :W:	.50	1.00
❑ 219 Priest of Gix U :K:	1.00	2.00
❑ 220 Priest of Titania C :G:	2.50	5.00
❑ 221 Purging Scythe R :A:	1.00	2.00
❑ 222 Rain of Filth U :K:	.50	1.00
❑ 223 Rain of Salt U :R:	.50	1.00
❑ 224 Ravenous Skirge C :K:	.15	.30
❑ 225 Raze C :R:	.15	.30
❑ 226 Recantation R :B:	1.50	3.00
❑ 227 Reclusive Wight U :K:	.50	1.00
❑ 228 Redeem U :W:	.50	1.00
❑ 229 Reflexes C :R:	.15	.30
❑ 230 Rejuvenate C :G:	.15	.30
❑ 231 Remembrance R :W:	1.50	3.00
❑ 232 Remote Isle C :L:	.15	.30
❑ 233 Reprocess R :K:	1.50	3.00
❑ 234 Rescind C :B:	.15	.30
❑ 235 Retaliation U :G:	.50	1.00
❑ 236 Retromancer C :R:	.15	.30
❑ 237 Rewind C :B:	.15	.30
❑ 238 Rumbling Crescendo R :R:	1.50	3.00
❑ 239 Rune of Protection Artifacts U :W:	.25	.50
❑ 240 Rune of Protection Black C :W:	.15	.30
❑ 241 Rune of Protection Blue C :W:	.15	.30
❑ 242 Rune of Protection Green C :W:	.15	.30
❑ 243 Rune of Protection Lands R :W:	.15	.30
❑ 244 Rune of Protection Red C :W:	.15	.30
❑ 245 Rune of Protection White C :W:	.15	.30
❑ 246 Sanctum Custodian C :W:	.15	.30
❑ 247 Sanctum Guardian U :W:	.30	.75
❑ 248 Sandbar Merfolk C :B:	.15	.30
❑ 249 Sandbar Serpent U :B:	.25	.50
❑ 250 Sanguine Guard U :K:	.25	.50
❑ 251 Scald U :R:	.50	1.00
❑ 252 Scoria Wurm R :R:	2.00	4.00
❑ 253 Scrap C :R:	.15	.30
❑ 254 Seasoned Marshal U :W:	.50	1.00
❑ 255 Serra Avatar R :W:	12.00	25.00
❑ 256 Serra Zealot C :W:	.15	.30
❑ 257 Serra's Embrace U :W:	1.00	2.00
❑ 258 Serra's Hymn U :W:	.50	1.00
❑ 259 Serra's Liturgy R :W:	1.50	3.00

Card	Low	High
❑ 260 Serra's Sanctum R :L:	4.00	8.00
❑ 261 Shimmering Barrier U :W:	.50	1.00
❑ 262 Shivan Gorge R :L:	2.00	4.00
❑ 263 Shivan Hellkite R :R:	4.00	8.00
❑ 264 Shivan Raptor U :R:	.50	1.00
❑ 265 Shiv's Embrace U :R:	.50	1.00
❑ 266 Show and Tell R :B:	3.00	6.00
❑ 267 Shower of Sparks C :R:	.15	.30
❑ 268 Sicken C :K:	.15	.30
❑ 269 Silent Attendant C :W:	.15	.30
❑ 270 Skirge Familiar U :K:	.50	1.00
❑ 271 Skittering Skirge C :K:	.15	.30
❑ 272 Sleeper Agent R :K:	2.00	4.00
❑ 273 Slippery Karst C :L:	.15	.30
❑ 274 Smokestack R :A:	3.00	6.00
❑ 275 Smoldering Crater C :L:	.15	.30
❑ 276 Sneak Attack R :R:	15.00	30.00
❑ 277 Somnophore R :B:	1.50	3.00
❑ 278 Songstitcher U :W:	.50	1.00
❑ 279 Soul Sculptor R :W:	2.00	4.00
❑ 280 Spined Fluke U :K:	.50	1.00
❑ 281 Spire Owl C :B:	.15	.30
❑ 282 Sporogenesis R :G:	1.50	3.00
❑ 283 Spreading Algae U :G:	.50	1.00
❑ 284 Steam Blast U :R:	.50	1.00
❑ 285 Stern Proctor U :B:	.50	1.00
❑ 286 Stroke of Genius R :B:	5.00	10.00
❑ 287 Sulfuric Vapors R :R:	2.00	4.00
❑ 288 Sunder R :B:	1.00	2.00
❑ 289 Swamp L :L:	.25	.50
❑ 290 Swamp L :L:	.25	.50
❑ 291 Swamp L :L:	.25	.50
❑ 292 Swamp L :L:	.25	.50
❑ 293 Symbiosis C :G:	.15	.30
❑ 294 Tainted 'ther R :K:	2.00	4.00
❑ 295 Telepathy U :B:	.50	1.00
❑ 296 Temporal Aperture R :A:	1.50	3.00
❑ 297 Thran Quarry R :L:	3.50	7.00
❑ 298 Thran Turbine U :A:	.50	1.00
❑ 299 Thundering Giant U :R:	.50	1.00
❑ 300 Time Spiral R :B:	4.00	8.00
❑ 301 Titania's Boon U :G:	.50	1.00
❑ 302 Titania's Chosen U :G:	2.00	4.00
❑ 303 Tolarian Academy R :L:	20.00	40.00
❑ 304 Tolarian Winds C :B:	.50	1.00
❑ 305 Torch Song U :R:	.50	1.00
❑ 306 Treefolk Seedlings U :G:	.50	1.00
❑ 307 Treetop Rangers C :G:	.15	.30
❑ 308 Turnabout U :B:	1.50	3.00
❑ 309 Umbilicus R :A:	2.00	4.00
❑ 310 Unnerve C :K:	.15	.30
❑ 311 Unworthy Dead C :K:	.15	.30
❑ 312 Urza's Armor U :A:	.75	1.50
❑ 313 Vampiric Embrace U :K:	1.00	2.00
❑ 314 Vebulid R :K:	1.50	3.00
❑ 315 Veil of Birds C :B:	.15	.30
❑ 316 Veiled Apparition U :B:	.50	1.00
❑ 317 Veiled Crocodile R :B:	1.50	3.00
❑ 318 Veiled Sentry U :B:	.50	1.00
❑ 319 Veiled Serpent C :B:	.15	.30
❑ 320 Venomous Fangs C :G:	.50	1.00
❑ 321 Vernal Bloom R :G:	3.00	6.00
❑ 322 Viashino Outrider C :R:	.15	.30
❑ 323 Viashino Runner C :R:	.15	.30
❑ 324 Viashino Sandswimmer R :R:	2.00	4.00
❑ 325 Viashino Weaponsmith C :R:	.15	.30
❑ 326 Victimize U :K:	1.00	2.00
❑ 327 Vile Requiem U :K:	.50	1.00
❑ 328 Voice of Grace U :W:	1.00	2.00
❑ 329 Voice of Law U :W:	1.00	2.00
❑ 330 Voltaic Key U :A:	1.50	3.00
❑ 331 Vug Lizard U :R:	.50	1.00
❑ 332 Wall of Junk U :A:	.50	1.00
❑ 333 War Dance U :G:	.50	1.00
❑ 334 Waylay U :W:	.50	1.00
❑ 335 Western Paladin R :K:	2.00	4.00
❑ 336 Whetstone R :A:	2.00	4.00
❑ 337 Whirlwind R :G:	1.50	3.00
❑ 338 Wild Dogs C :G:	.15	.30
❑ 339 Wildfire R :R:	1.00	2.00
❑ 340 Windfall U :B:	.50	1.00
❑ 341 Winding Wurm C :G:	.15	.30
❑ 342 Wirecat U :A:	.50	1.00
❑ 343 Witch Engine R :K:	1.00	2.00
❑ 344 Wizard Mentor C :B:	.15	.30
❑ 345 Worn Powerstone U :A:	1.00	2.00
❑ 346 Worship R :W:	4.00	8.00
❑ 347 Yawgmoth's Edict U :K:	.50	1.00
❑ 348 Yawgmoth's Will R :K:	8.00	16.00
❑ 349 Zephid R :B:	1.50	3.00
❑ 350 Zephid's Embrace U :B:	.50	1.00

1999 Magic the Gathering Urza's Legacy

Card	Low	High
Complete Set (143)	115.00	130.00
❑ 1 About Face C :R:	.15	.30
❑ 2 Angelic Curator C :W:	.15	.30
❑ 3 Angel's Trumpet U :A:	.50	1.00
❑ 4 Anthroplasm R :B:	1.50	3.00
❑ 5 Archivist R :B:	2.00	4.00
❑ 6 Aura Flux C :B:	.15	.30
❑ 7 Avalanche Riders U :R:	1.00	2.00
❑ 8 Beast of Burden R :A:	2.00	4.00
❑ 9 Blessed Reversal R :W:	2.00	4.00
❑ 10 Bloated Toad U :G:	.15	.30
❑ 11 Bone Shredder U :K:	.50	1.00
❑ 12 Bouncing Beebles C :B:	.15	.30
❑ 13 Brink of Madness R :K:	1.50	3.00
❑ 14 Burst of Energy C :W:	.15	.30
❑ 15 Cessation C :W:	.15	.30
❑ 16 Cloud of Faeries C :B:	.15	.30
❑ 17 Crawlspace R :A:	2.00	4.00
❑ 18 Crop Rotation C :G:	.15	.30
❑ 19 Damping Engine R :A:	1.50	3.00
❑ 20 Darkwatch Elves U :G:	.25	.50
❑ 21 Defender of Chaos C :R:	.15	.30
❑ 22 Defender of Law C :W:	.15	.30
❑ 23 Defense Grid R :A:	2.50	5.00
❑ 24 Defense of the Heart R :G:	4.00	8.00
❑ 25 Delusions of Mediocrity R :B:	2.00	4.00
❑ 26 Deranged Hermit R :G:	6.00	12.00
❑ 27 Devout Harpist C :W:	.15	.30
❑ 28 Engineered Plague U :K:	1.00	2.00
❑ 29 Erase C :W:	.15	.30
❑ 30 Eviscerator R :K:	1.50	3.00
❑ 31 Expendable Troops C :W:	.15	.30
❑ 32 Faerie Conclave U :L:	1.00	2.00
❑ 33 Fleeting Image R :B:	1.00	2.00
❑ 34 Fog of Gnats C :K:	.15	.30
❑ 35 Forbidding Watchtower U :L:	.50	1.00
❑ 36 Frantic Search C :B:	.15	.30
❑ 37 Gang of Elk U :G:	.25	.50
❑ 38 Ghitu Encampment U :L:	1.00	2.00
❑ 39 Ghitu Fire-Eater U :R:	.50	1.00
❑ 40 Ghitu Slinger C :R:	.15	.30
❑ 41 Ghitu War Cry U :R:	.25	.50
❑ 42 Giant Cockroach C :K:	.15	.30
❑ 43 Goblin Medics C :R:	.15	.30
❑ 44 Goblin Welder R :R:	7.50	15.00
❑ 45 Granite Grip C :R:	.15	.30
❑ 46 Grim Monolith R :A:	15.00	30.00
❑ 47 Harmonic Convergence U :G:	.25	.50
❑ 48 Hidden Gibbons R :G:	2.00	4.00
❑ 49 Hope and Glory U :W:	.30	.75
❑ 50 Impending Disaster R :R:	1.50	3.00
❑ 51 Intervene C :B:	.15	.30
❑ 52 Iron Maiden R :A:	1.50	3.00
❑ 53 Iron Will C :W:	.15	.30
❑ 54 Jhoira's Toolbox U :A:	.30	.75
❑ 55 Karmic Guide R :W:	1.50	3.00
❑ 56 King Crab U :B:	.25	.50
❑ 57 Knighthood U :W:	.25	.50
❑ 58 Last-Ditch Effort U :R:	.25	.50
❑ 59 Lava Axe C :R:	.15	.30
❑ 60 Levitation U :B:	.25	.50
❑ 61 Lone Wolf U :G:	.25	.50
❑ 62 Lurking Skirge R :K:	1.50	3.00
❑ 63 Martyr's Cause U :W:	.25	.50
❑ 64 Memory Jar R :A:	2.00	4.00
❑ 65 Might of Oaks R :G:	3.00	6.00
❑ 66 Miscalculation C :B:	.15	.30
❑ 67 Molten Hydra R :R:	2.00	4.00
❑ 68 Mother of Runes U :W:	1.50	3.00
❑ 69 Multani, Maro-Sorcerer R :G:	3.00	6.00
❑ 70 Multani's Acolyte C :G:	.15	.30
❑ 71 Multani's Presence U :G:	.25	.50
❑ 72 No Mercy R :K:	3.00	6.00
❑ 73 Opal Avenger R :W:	2.00	4.00
❑ 74 Opal Champion C :W:	.15	.30
❑ 75 Opportunity U :B:	.50	1.00
❑ 76 Ostracize C :K:	.15	.30
❑ 77 Palinchron R :B:	2.50	5.00
❑ 78 Parch C :R:	.15	.30
❑ 79 Peace and Quiet U :W:	.25	.50
❑ 80 Phyrexian Broodlings C :K:	.15	.30
❑ 81 Phyrexian Debaser C :K:	.15	.30
❑ 82 Phyrexian Defiler U :K:	.25	.50
❑ 83 Phyrexian Denouncer C :K:	.15	.30
❑ 84 Phyrexian Plaguelord R :K:	2.00	4.00
❑ 85 Phyrexian Reclamation U :K:	.50	1.00
❑ 86 Plague Beetle C :K:	.15	.30
❑ 87 Planar Collapse R :W:	1.50	3.00
❑ 88 Purify R :W:	1.50	3.00
❑ 89 Pygmy Pyrosaur C :R:	.15	.30
❑ 90 Pyromancy R :R:	1.00	2.00
❑ 91 Quicksilver Amulet R :A:	4.00	8.00
❑ 92 Rack and Ruin U :R:	1.00	2.00
❑ 93 Radiant, Archangel R :W:	.50	1.00
❑ 94 Radiant's Dragoons U :W:	.50	1.00
❑ 95 Radiant's Judgment C :W:	.15	.30
❑ 96 Rancor C :G:	1.50	3.00
❑ 97 Rank and File U :K:	.25	.50
❑ 98 Raven Familiar U :B:	.50	1.00
❑ 99 Rebuild U :B:	1.00	2.00
❑ 100 Repopulate C :G:	.15	.30
❑ 101 Ring of Gix R :A:	1.00	2.00
❑ 102 Rivalry R :R:	1.00	2.00
❑ 103 Scrapheap R :A:	1.00	2.00
❑ 104 Second Chance R :B:	2.00	4.00
❑ 105 Shivan Phoenix R :R:	2.00	4.00
❑ 106 Sick and Tired C :K:	.15	.30
❑ 107 Silk Net C :G:	.15	.30
❑ 108 Simian Grunts C :G:	.15	.30
❑ 109 Sleeper's Guile C :K:	.15	.30
❑ 110 Slow Motion C :B:	.15	.30
❑ 111 Sluggishness C :R:	.15	.30
❑ 112 Snap C :B:	.15	.30
❑ 113 Spawning Pool U :L:	.15	.30
❑ 114 Subversion R :K:	1.50	3.00
❑ 115 Sustainer of the Realm U :W:	.25	.50
❑ 116 Swat C :K:	.15	.30
❑ 117 Tethered Skirge U :K:	.25	.50
❑ 118 Thornwind Faeries C :B:	.15	.30
❑ 119 Thran Lens R :A:	1.50	3.00
❑ 120 Thran War Machine R :A:	.25	.50
❑ 121 Thran Weaponry R :A:	2.00	4.00
❑ 122 Ticking Gnomes U :A:	.25	.50
❑ 123 Tinker U :B:	2.00	4.00
❑ 124 Tragic Poet C :W:	.15	.30
❑ 125 Treacherous Link U :K:	.25	.50
❑ 126 Treefolk Mystic C :G:	.15	.30
❑ 127 Treetop Village U :L:	1.50	3.00
❑ 128 Unearth C :K:	.15	.30
❑ 129 Urza's Blueprints R :A:	2.00	4.00
❑ 130 Viashino Bey C :R:	.15	.30
❑ 131 Viashino Cutthroat U :R:	.25	.50
❑ 132 Viashino Heretic U :R:	.50	1.00
❑ 133 Viashino Sandscout C :R:	.15	.30
❑ 134 Vigilant Drake C :B:	.15	.30
❑ 135 Walking Sponge U :B:	.25	.50
❑ 136 Weatherseed Elf C :G:	.15	.30
❑ 137 Weatherseed Faeries C :B:	.15	.30
❑ 138 Weatherseed Treefolk R :G:	2.00	4.00
❑ 139 Wheel of Torture R :A:	2.00	4.00
❑ 140 Wing Snare U :G:	.25	.50
❑ 141 Yavimaya Granger C :G:	.15	.30
❑ 142 Yavimaya Scion C :G:	.15	.30
❑ 143 Yavimaya Wurm C :G:	.15	.30

1999 Magic the Gathering Urza's Legacy Foil

Card	Low	High
COMPLETE SET (143)	375.00	500.00

*Foil: 1X to 2X Basic Cards

1999 Magic the Gathering Urza's Destiny

Card	Low	High
Complete Set (143)	100.00	150.00
Booster Box (36 Packs)	225.00	300.00
Booster Pack (15 Cards)	8.00	11.00
❑ 1 Academy Rector R :W:	4.00	8.00
❑ 2 Aether Sting U :R:	.50	1.00
❑ 3 Ancient Silverback R :G:	2.00	4.00
❑ 4 Apprentice Necromancer R :K:	1.50	3.00
❑ 5 Archery Training U :W:	.50	1.00
❑ 6 Attrition R :K:	2.00	4.00
❑ 7 Aura Thief R :B:	2.00	4.00
❑ 8 Blizzard Elemental R :B:	1.50	3.00
❑ 9 Bloodshot Cyclops R :R:	2.00	4.00
❑ 10 Body Snatcher R :K:	1.50	3.00
❑ 11 Braidwood Cup U :A:	.50	1.00
❑ 12 Braidwood Sextant U :A:	.50	1.00
❑ 13 Brass Secretary U :A:	.50	1.00
❑ 14 Brine Seer U :B:	.50	1.00
❑ 15 Bubbling Beebles C :B:	.15	.30
❑ 16 Bubbling Muck C :K:	.15	.30
❑ 17 Caltrops U :A:	.50	1.00
❑ 18 Capashen Knight C :W:	.15	.30
❑ 19 Capashen Standard C :W:	.15	.30
❑ 20 Capashen Templar C :W:	.15	.30
❑ 21 Carnival of Souls R :K:	1.00	2.00
❑ 22 Chime of Night C :K:	.15	.30
❑ 23 Cinder Seer U :R:	.50	1.00
❑ 24 Colos Yearling C :R:	.15	.30
❑ 25 Compost U :G:	1.00	2.00
❑ 26 Covetous Dragon R :R:	3.00	6.00
❑ 27 Disappear U :B:	.50	1.00
❑ 28 Disease Carriers C :K:	.15	.30
❑ 29 Donate R :B:	2.50	5.00
❑ 30 Dying Wail C :K:	.15	.30
❑ 31 Elvish Lookout C :G:	.15	.30
❑ 32 Elvish Piper R :G:	5.00	10.00
❑ 33 Emperor Crocodile R :G:	2.00	4.00
❑ 34 Encroach U :K:	.25	.50
❑ 35 Eradicate U :K:	1.25	2.50
❑ 36 Extruder U :A:	.25	.50
❑ 37 False Prophet R :W:	2.00	4.00
❑ 38 Fatigue C :B:	.15	.30
❑ 39 Fend Off C :W:	.15	.30
❑ 40 Festering Wound U :K:	.25	.50
❑ 41 Field Surgeon C :W:	.15	.30
❑ 42 Flame Jet C :R:	.15	.30
❑ 43 Fledgling Osprey C :B:	.15	.30
❑ 44 Flicker R :W:	1.50	3.00
❑ 45 Fodder Cannon U :A:	.50	1:00
❑ 46 Gamekeeper U :G:	.50	1.00
❑ 47 Goblin Berserker U :R:	.50	1.00
❑ 48 Goblin Festival R :R:	2.00	4.00
❑ 49 Goblin Gardener C :R:	.15	.30
❑ 50 Goblin Marshal R :R:	2.00	4.00
❑ 51 Goblin Masons C :R:	.15	.30
❑ 52 Goliath Beetle C :G:	.15	.30
❑ 53 Heart Warden C :G:	.15	.30
❑ 54 Hulking Ogre C :R:	.15	.30
❑ 55 Hunting Moa U :G:	.50	1.00
❑ 56 Illuminated Wings C :B:	.15	.30
❑ 57 Impatience R :R:	1.00	2.00
❑ 58 Incendiary U :R:	.50	1.00
❑ 59 Iridescent Drake U :B:	.50	1.00
❑ 60 Ivy Seer U :G:	.50	1.00
❑ 61 Jasmine Seer U :W:	.50	1.00
❑ 62 Junk Diver R :A:	1.50	3.00
❑ 63 Keldon Champion U :R:	.50	1.00
❑ 64 Keldon Vandals C :R:	.15	.30
❑ 65 Kingfisher C :B:	.15	.30
❑ 66 Landslide U :R:	.50	1.00
❑ 67 Lurking Jackals U :K:	.50	1.00
❑ 68 Magnify C :G:	.15	.30
❑ 69 Mantis Engine U :A:	.50	1.00
❑ 70 Mark of Fury C :R:	.15	.30
❑ 71 Marker Beetles C :G:	.15	.30
❑ 72 Mask of Law and Grace C :W:	.15	.30
❑ 73 Master Healer R :W:	2.00	4.00
❑ 74 Masticore R :A:	10.00	20.00
❑ 75 Mental Discipline C :B:	.15	.30
❑ 76 Metalworker R :A:	4.00	8.00
❑ 77 Metathran Elite U :B:	.50	1.00
❑ 78 Metathran Soldier C :B:	.15	.30
❑ 79 Momentum U :G:	.50	1.00
❑ 80 Multani's Decree C :G:	.15	.30
❑ 81 Nightshade Seer U :K:	.50	1.00
❑ 82 Opalescence R :W:	2.00	4.00
❑ 83 Opposition R :B:	3.00	6.00
❑ 84 Pattern of Rebirth R :G:	2.50	5.00
❑ 85 Phyrexian Monitor C :K:	.15	.30
❑ 86 Phyrexian Negator R :K:	5.00	10.00
❑ 87 Plague Dogs U :K:	.50	1.00
❑ 88 Plated Spider C :G:	.15	.30
❑ 89 Plow Under R :G:	5.00	10.00
❑ 90 Powder Keg R :A:	4.00	8.00
❑ 91 Private Research U :B:	.50	1.00
❑ 92 Quash U :B:	1.25	2.50
❑ 93 Rapid Decay R :K:	2.00	4.00
❑ 94 Ravenous Rats C :K:	.15	.30
❑ 95 Rayne, Academy Chancellor R :B:	1.00	2.00
❑ 96 Reckless Abandon C :R:	.15	.30
❑ 97 Reliquary Monk C :W:	.15	.30
❑ 98 Repercussion R :R:	2.00	4.00
❑ 99 Replenish R :W:	4.00	8.00
❑ 100 Rescue C :B:	.15	.30
❑ 101 Rofellos, Llanowar Emissary R :G:	5.00	10.00
❑ 102 Rofellos's Gift C :G:	.15	.30
❑ 103 Sanctimony U :W:	1.00	2.00
❑ 104 Scent of Brine C :B:	.15	.30
❑ 105 Scent of Cinder C :R:	.15	.30
❑ 106 Scent of Ivy C :G:	.15	.30
❑ 107 Scent of Jasmine C :W:	.15	.30
❑ 108 Scent of Nightshade C :K:	.15	.30
❑ 109 Scour U :W:	.50	1.00
❑ 110 Scrying Glass R :A:	2.00	4.00
❑ 111 Serra Advocate U :W:	.50	1.00
❑ 112 Sigil of Sleep C :B:	.15	.30
❑ 113 Skittering Horror C :K:	.15	.30
❑ 114 Slinking Skirge C :K:	.15	.30
❑ 115 Solidarity C :W:	.15	.30
❑ 116 Soul Feast U :K:	.50	1.00
❑ 117 Sowing Salt U :R:	.50	1.00
❑ 118 Splinter U :G:	1.00	2.00
❑ 119 Squirming Mass C :K:	.15	.30
❑ 120 Storage Matrix R :A:	1.50	3.00
❑ 121 Taunting Elf C :G:	.15	.30
❑ 122 Telepathic Spies C :B:	.15	.30
❑ 123 Temporal Adept R :B:	2.00	4.00
❑ 124 Tethered Griffin R :W:	1.50	3.00
❑ 125 Thieving Magpie U :B:	1.00	2.00
❑ 126 Thorn Elemental R :G:	3.00	6.00
❑ 127 Thran Dynamo U :A:	1.50	3.00
❑ 128 Thran Foundry U :A:	.50	1.00
❑ 129 Thran Golem R :A:	2.00	4.00
❑ 130 Tormented Angel C :W:	.15	.30
❑ 131 Treachery R :B:	3.00	6.00
❑ 132 Trumpet Blast C :R:	.15	.30
❑ 133 Twisted Experiment C :K:	.15	.30
❑ 134 Urza's Incubator R :A:	3.00	6.00
❑ 135 Voice of Duty U :W:	.50	1.00
❑ 136 Voice of Reason U :W:	.50	1.00
❑ 137 Wake of Destruction R :R:	2.00	4.00
❑ 138 Wall of Glare C :W:	.15	.30
❑ 139 Wild Colos C :R:	.15	.30
❑ 140 Yavimaya Elder C :G:	.15	.30
❑ 141 Yavimaya Enchantress U :G:	1.00	2.00
❑ 142 Yavimaya Hollow R :L:	2.00	4.00
❑ 143 Yawgmoth's Bargain R :K: :R:	4.00	8.00

1999 Magic the Gathering Urza's Destiny Foil

Card	Low	High
COMPLETE SET (143)	450.00	650.00

*Foil: 1X to 2X Basic Cards

1999 Magic the Gathering Classic Sixth Edition

Card	Low	High
Complete Set (350)	200.00	300.00
Starter Deck Box (12 Decks)	100.00	150.00
Starter Deck	10.00	16.00
Booster Box (36 Packs)	120.00	170.00
Booster Pack (15 Cards)	4.50	5.50

Released in July 1999

Card	Low	High
❑ 1 Abduction U :B:	.50	1.00
❑ 2 Abyssal Hunter R :K:	1.00	2.00
❑ 3 Abyssal Specter U :K:	.25	.50
❑ 4 Adarkar Wastes R :L:	3.00	6.00
❑ 5 Aether Flash U :R:	.25	.50
❑ 6 Agonizing Memories U :K:	.25	.50
❑ 7 Air Elemental U :B:	.50	1.00
❑ 8 Aladdin's Ring R :A:	1.00	2.50
❑ 9 Amber Prison R :A:	1.00	2.00
❑ 10 Anaba Bodyguard C :R:	.15	.30
❑ 11 Anaba Shaman C :R:	.15	.30
❑ 12 Ancestral Memories R :B:	.50	1.00
❑ 13 Animate Wall R :W:	1.00	2.00
❑ 14 Ankh of Mishra R :A:	1.50	3.00
❑ 15 Archangel R :W:	4.00	8.00
❑ 16 Ardent Militia U :W:	.25	.50
❑ 17 Armageddon R :W:	4.00	8.00
❑ 18 Armored Pegasus C :W:	.15	.30
❑ 19 Ashen Powder R :K:	1.00	2.00
❑ 20 Ashnod's Altar U :A:	.50	1.00
❑ 21 Balduvian Barbarians C :R:	.15	.30
❑ 22 Balduvian Horde R :R:	2.00	4.00
❑ 23 Birds of Paradise R :G:	9.00	18.00
❑ 24 Blaze U :R:	.50	1.00
❑ 25 Blight U :K:	.25	.50
❑ 26 Blighted Shaman U :K:	.25	.50
❑ 27 Blood Pet C :K:	.25	.50
❑ 28 Bog Imp C :K:	.15	.30
❑ 29 Bog Rats C :K:	.15	.30
❑ 30 Bog Wraith U :K:	.25	.50
❑ 31 Boil U :R:	.50	1.00
❑ 32 Boomerang C :B:	.25	.50
❑ 33 Bottle of Suleiman R :A:	1.50	3.00
❑ 34 Browse U :B:	.50	1.00
❑ 35 Brushland R :L:	3.00	6.00
❑ 36 Burrowing U :R:	.25	.50
❑ 37 Call of the Wild R :G:	1.50	3.00
❑ 38 Castle U :W:	.25	.50
❑ 39 Cat Warriors C :G:	.15	.30
❑ 40 Celestial Dawn R :W:	1.50	3.00
❑ 41 Charcoal Diamond U :A:	.25	.50
❑ 42 Chill U :B:	2.50	5.00
❑ 43 Circle of Protection Black C :W:	.15	.30
❑ 44 Circle of Protection Blue C :W:	.15	.30
❑ 45 Circle of Protection Green C :W:	.15	.30
❑ 46 Circle of Protection Red C :W:	.15	.30
❑ 47 Circle of Protection White C :W:	.15	.30
❑ 48 City of Brass R :L:	4.00	8.00
❑ 49 Coercion C :K:	.15	.30
❑ 50 Conquer U :R:	.50	1.00
❑ 51 Counterspell C :B:	1.00	2.00
❑ 52 Creeping Mold U :G:	.25	.50
❑ 53 Crimson Hellkite R :R:	3.00	6.00
❑ 54 Crusade R :W:	3.00	6.00
❑ 55 Crystal Rod U :A:	.25	.50
❑ 56 Crystal Vein U :L:	.50	1.00
❑ 57 Cursed Totem R :A:	1.50	3.00
❑ 58 Dancing Scimitar R :A:	1.50	3.00
❑ 59 Daraja Griffin U :W:	.25	.50
❑ 60 Daring Apprentice R :B:	1.50	3.00
❑ 61 D'Avenant Archer C :W:	.15	.30
❑ 62 Deflection R :B:	1.50	3.00
❑ 63 Dense Foliage R :G:	1.00	2.00
❑ 64 Derelor R :K:	1.50	3.00
❑ 65 Desertion R :B:	2.00	4.00
❑ 66 Diminishing Returns R :B:	1.50	3.00
❑ 67 Dingus Egg R :A:	1.50	3.00
❑ 68 Disenchant C :W:	.15	.30
❑ 69 Disrupting Scepter R :A:	.50	1.00
❑ 70 Divine Transformation U :W:	.50	1.00
❑ 71 Doomsday R :K:	2.00	4.00
❑ 72 Dragon Engine R :A:	1.50	3.00
❑ 73 Dragon Mask U :A:	.50	1.00
❑ 74 Dread of Night U :K:	.50	1.00
❑ 75 Dream Cache C :B:	.15	.30
❑ 76 Drudge Skeletons C :K:	.15	.30
❑ 77 Dry Spell C :K:	.15	.30
❑ 78 Dwarven Ruins U :L:	.50	1.00
❑ 79 Early Harvest R :G:	2.00	4.00
❑ 80 Earthquake R :R:	1.00	2.00
❑ 81 Ebon Stronghold U :L:	.50	1.00
❑ 82 Ekundu Griffin C :W:	.25	.50
❑ 83 Elder Druid R :G:	1.00	2.00
❑ 84 Elven Cache C :G:	.25	.50
❑ 85 Elven Riders U :G:	.50	1.00
❑ 86 Elvish Archers R :G:	1.50	3.00
❑ 87 Enfeeblement C :K:	.15	.30
❑ 88 Enlightened Tutor U :W:	4.00	8.00
❑ 89 Ethereal Champion R :W:	1.00	2.00
❑ 90 Evil Eye of Orms-by-Gore U :K:	.50	1.00
❑ 91 Exile R :W:	2.50	5.00
❑ 92 Fallen Angel R :K:	2.00	4.00
❑ 93 Fallow Earth U :G:	.25	.50
❑ 94 Familiar Ground U :G:	.25	.50
❑ 95 Fatal Blow C :K:	.25	.50
❑ 96 Fear C :K:	.15	.30
❑ 97 Feast of the Unicorn C :K:	.15	.30
❑ 98 Femeref Archers U :G:	.25	.50
❑ 99 Feral Shadow C :K:	.15	.30
❑ 100 Fervor R :R:	2.00	4.00
❑ 101 Final Fortune R :R:	1.50	3.00
❑ 102 Fire Diamond U :A:	.50	1.00
❑ 103 Fire Elemental U :R:	.50	1.00
❑ 104 Firebreathing C :R:	.15	.30
❑ 105 Fit of Rage C :R:	.15	.30
❑ 106 Flame Spirit C :R:	.15	.30
❑ 107 Flash R :B:	1.00	2.00
❑ 108 Flashfires U :R:	.25	.50
❑ 109 Flight C :B:	.15	.30
❑ 110 Flying Carpet R :A:	1.50	3.00
❑ 111 Fog C :G:	.15	.30
❑ 112 Fog Elemental C :B:	.15	.30
❑ 113 Forbidden Crypt R :K:	1.50	3.00
❑ 114 Forest L :L:	.25	.50
❑ 115 Forest L :L:	.25	.50
❑ 116 Forest L :L:	.25	.50
❑ 117 Forest L :L:	.25	.50
❑ 118 Forget R :B:	1.00	2.00
❑ 119 Fountain of Youth U :A:	.50	1.00
❑ 120 Fyndhorn Brownie C :G:	.15	.30
❑ 121 Fyndhorn Elder U :G:	.50	1.00
❑ 122 Gaseous Form C :B:	.15	.30
❑ 123 Giant Growth C :G:	.15	.30
❑ 124 Giant Spider C :G:	.15	.30
❑ 125 Giant Strength C :R:	.15	.30
❑ 126 Glacial Wall U :B:	.25	.50
❑ 127 Glasses of Urza U :A:	.25	.50
❑ 128 Goblin Digging Team C :R:	.15	.30
❑ 129 Goblin Elite Infantry C :R:	.15	.30
❑ 130 Goblin Hero C :R:	.15	.30
❑ 131 Goblin King R :R:	2.00	4.00
❑ 132 Goblin Recruiter U :R:	1.50	3.00
❑ 133 Goblin Warrens R :R:	.15	.30
❑ 134 Gorilla Chieftain C :G:	.15	.30
❑ 135 Gravebane Zombie U :K:	.50	1.00
❑ 136 Gravedigger C :K:	.15	.30
❑ 137 Greed R :K:	1.50	3.00
❑ 138 Grinning Totem R :A:	1.50	3.00

MAGIC

☐ 139 Grizzly Bears C :G: .15 .30
☐ 140 Hammer of Bogardan R :R: 3.00 6.00
☐ 141 Harmattan Efreet U :B: .25 .50
☐ 142 Havenwood Battleground U :L: .50 1.00
☐ 143 Healing Salve C :W: .15 .30
☐ 144 Heavy Ballista U :W: .25 .50
☐ 145 Hecatomb R :K: 1.50 3.00
☐ 146 Hero's Resolve C :W: .25 .50
☐ 147 Hidden Horror U :K: .25 .50
☐ 148 Horned Turtle C :B: .15 .30
☐ 149 Howl from Beyond C :K: .15 .30
☐ 150 Howling Mine R :A: 3.00 6.00
☐ 151 Hulking Cyclops U :R: .25 .50
☐ 152 Hurricane R :G: .25 .50
☐ 153 Icatian Town R :W: 1.50 3.00
☐ 154 Illicit Auction R :R: 1.00 2.00
☐ 155 Infantry Veteran C :W: .15 .30
☐ 156 Infernal Contract R :K: 1.00 2.00
☐ 157 Inferno R :R: 1.50 3.00
☐ 158 Insight U :B: .50 1.00
☐ 159 Inspiration C :B: .15 .30
☐ 160 Iron Star U :A: .25 .50
☐ 161 Island L :L: .25 .50
☐ 162 Island L :L: .25 .50
☐ 163 Island L :L: .25 .50
☐ 164 Island L :L: .25 .50
☐ 165 Ivory Cup U :A: .25 .50
☐ 166 Jade Monolith R :A: 1.50 3.00
☐ 167 Jalum Tome R :A: 1.00 2.00
☐ 168 Jayemdae Tome R :A: 1.00 2.00
☐ 169 Jokulhaups R :R: 2.00 4.00
☐ 170 Juxtapose R :B: 1.50 3.00
☐ 171 Karplusan Forest R :L: 4.00 8.00
☐ 172 Kismet U :W: .50 1.00
☐ 173 Kjeldoran Dead C :K: .15 .30
☐ 174 Kjeldoran Royal Guard R :W: 1.50 3.00
☐ 175 Lead Golem U :A: .25 .50
☐ 176 Leshrac's Rite U :K: .25 .50
☐ 177 Library of Lat-Nam R :B: 1.00 2.00
☐ 178 Light of Day U :W: 1.00 2.00
☐ 179 Lightning Blast C :R: .50 1.00
☐ 180 Living Lands R :G: 1.50 3.00
☐ 181 Llanowar Elves C :G: .50 1.00
☐ 182 Longbow Archer U :W: .50 1.00
☐ 183 Lord of Atlantis R :B: 2.00 4.00
☐ 184 Lost Soul C :K: .15 .30
☐ 185 Lure U :G: .50 1.00
☐ 186 Mana Prism U :A: .50 1.00
☐ 187 Mana Short R :B: 2.00 4.00
☐ 188 Manabarbs R :R: 1.00 2.00
☐ 189 Marble Diamond U :A: .15 .30
☐ 190 Maro R :G: 2.00 4.00
☐ 191 Meekstone R :A: 1.50 3.00
☐ 192 Memory Lapse C :B: .25 .50
☐ 193 Merfolk of the Pearl Trident C :B: .15 .30
☐ 194 Mesa Falcon C :W: .15 .30
☐ 195 Millstone R :A: 2.00 4.00
☐ 196 Mind Warp U :K: .25 .50
☐ 197 Mischievous Poltergeist U :K: .25 .50
☐ 198 Moss Diamond U :A: .25 .50
☐ 199 Mountain Goat C :R: .15 .30
☐ 200 Mountain L :L: .25 .50
☐ 201 Mountain L :L: .25 .50
☐ 202 Mountain L :L: .25 .50
☐ 203 Mountain L :L: .25 .50
☐ 204 Mystic Compass U :A: .25 .50
☐ 205 Mystical Tutor U :B: 2.00 4.00
☐ 206 Nature's Resurgence R :G: 1.50 3.00
☐ 207 Necrosavant R :K: 1.00 2.00
☐ 208 Nightmare R :K: 2.00 4.00
☐ 209 Obsianus Golem U :A: .25 .50
☐ 210 Orcish Artillery U :R: .25 .50
☐ 211 Orcish Oriflamme U :R: .25 .50
☐ 212 Order of the Sacred Torch R :W: 1.50 3.00
☐ 213 Ornithopter U :A: 1.00 2.00
☐ 214 Pacifism C :W: .25 .50
☐ 215 Painful Memories C :K: .15 .30
☐ 216 Panther Warriors C :G: .15 .30
☐ 217 Patagia Golem U :A: .25 .50
☐ 218 Pearl Dragon R :W: 2.00 4.00
☐ 219 Pentagram of the Ages R :A: 1.00 2.00
☐ 220 Perish U :K: 1.00 2.00
☐ 221 Pestilence U :K: .25 .50
☐ 222 Phantasmal Terrain C :B: .15 .30
☐ 223 Phantom Warrior U :B: .50 1.00
☐ 224 Phyrexian Vault U :A: .50 1.00
☐ 225 Pillage U :R: .50 1.00
☐ 226 Plains L :L: .25 .50
☐ 227 Plains L :L: .25 .50
☐ 228 Plains L :L: .25 .50
☐ 229 Plains L :L: .25 .50
☐ 230 Polymorph R :B: 1.50 3.00
☐ 231 Power Sink U :B: .50 1.00
☐ 232 Pradesh Gypsies C :G: .15 .30
☐ 233 Primal Clay R :A: 1.00 2.00
☐ 234 Prodigal Sorcerer C :B: .15 .30
☐ 235 Prosperity U :B: 1.00 2.00
☐ 236 Psychic Transfer R :B: 1.00 2.00
☐ 237 Psychic Venom C :B: .15 .30
☐ 238 Pyrotechnics C :R: .15 .30
☐ 239 Python C :K: .15 .30
☐ 240 Radjan Spirit U :G: .25 .50
☐ 241 Rag Man R :K: 1.50 3.00
☐ 242 Raging Goblin C :R: .15 .30
☐ 243 Raise Dead C :K: .15 .30
☐ 244 Rampant Growth C :G: .25 .50
☐ 245 Razortooth Rats C :K: .25 .50
☐ 246 Recall R :B: 2.00 4.00
☐ 247 Reckless Embermage R :R: 1.50 3.00
☐ 248 Redwood Treefolk C :G: .15 .30
☐ 249 Regal Unicorn C :W: .15 .30
☐ 250 Regeneration C :G: .15 .30
☐ 251 Relearn U :B: .50 1.00
☐ 252 Relentless Assault R :R: 2.00 4.00
☐ 253 Remedy C :W: .15 .30
☐ 254 Remove Soul C :B: .25 .50
☐ 255 Reprisal U :W: .50 1.00
☐ 256 Resistance Fighter C :W: .15 .30
☐ 257 Reverse Damage R :W: 1.50 3.00
☐ 258 River Boa U :G: 1.00 2.00
☐ 259 Rod of Ruin U :A: .25 .50
☐ 260 Rowen R :G: 1.50 3.00
☐ 261 Ruins of Trokair U :L: .50 1.00
☐ 262 Sabretooth Tiger C :R: .15 .30
☐ 263 Sage Owl C :B: .25 .50
☐ 264 Samite Healer C :W: .15 .30
☐ 265 Scaled Wurm C :G: .15 .30
☐ 266 Scathe Zombies C :K: .15 .30
☐ 267 Sea Monster C :B: .15 .30
☐ 268 Segovian Leviathan U :B: .25 .50
☐ 269 Sengir Autocrat R :K: 1.50 3.00
☐ 270 Serenity R :W: 1.50 3.00
☐ 271 Serra's Blessing U :W: 2.50 5.00
☐ 272 Shanodin Dryads C :G: .15 .30
☐ 273 Shatter C :R: .15 .30
☐ 274 Shatterstorm R :R: 1.50 3.00
☐ 275 Shock C :R: .15 .30
☐ 276 Sibilant Spirit R :B: 1.00 2.00
☐ 277 Skull Catapult U :A: .25 .50
☐ 278 Sky Diamond U :A: .25 .50
☐ 279 Snake Basket R :A: 2.50 5.00
☐ 280 Soldevi Sage U :B: .25 .50
☐ 281 Soul Net U :A: .25 .50
☐ 282 Spell Blast C :B: .15 .30
☐ 283 Spirit Link U :W: .25 .50
☐ 284 Spitting Drake U :R: .25 .50
☐ 285 Spitting Earth C :R: .15 .30
☐ 286 Stalking Tiger C :G: .15 .30
☐ 287 Standing Troops C :W: .15 .30
☐ 288 Staunch Defenders U :W: .50 1.00
☐ 289 Stone Rain C :R: .15 .30
☐ 290 Storm Cauldron R :A: 1.00 2.00
☐ 291 Storm Crow C :B: .15 .30
☐ 292 Strands of Night U :K: .50 1.00
☐ 293 Stream of Life C :G: .25 .50
☐ 294 Stromgald Cabal R :K: 1.00 2.00
☐ 295 Stupor U :K: .50 1.00
☐ 296 Sulfurous Springs R :L: 3.00 6.00
☐ 297 Summer Bloom U :G: .50 1.00
☐ 298 Sunweb R :W: 1.50 3.00
☐ 299 Svyelunite Temple U :L: .50 1.00
☐ 300 Swamp L :L: .25 .50
☐ 301 Swamp L :L: .25 .50
☐ 302 Swamp L :L: .25 .50
☐ 303 Swamp L :L: .25 .50
☐ 304 Syphon Soul C :K: .50 1.00
☐ 305 Talruum Minotaur C :R: .15 .30
☐ 306 Tariff R :W: 1.00 2.00
☐ 307 Teferi's Puzzle Box R :A: 1.50 3.00
☐ 308 Terror C :K: .25 .50
☐ 309 The Hive R :A: 1.00 2.00
☐ 310 Thicket Basilisk U :G: .50 1.00
☐ 311 Throne of Bone U :A: .25 .50
☐ 312 Tidal Surge C :B: .15 .30
☐ 313 Trained Armodon C :G: .15 .30
☐ 314 Tranquil Grove R :G: 1.50 3.00
☐ 315 Tranquility C :G: .15 .30
☐ 316 Tremor C :R: .15 .30
☐ 317 Tundra Wolves C :W: .15 .30
☐ 318 Uktabi Orangutan U :G: 1.00 2.00
☐ 319 Uktabi Wildcats R :G: 1.00 2.00
☐ 320 Underground River R :L: 4.00 8.00
☐ 321 Unseen Walker U :G: .25 .50
☐ 322 Unsummon C :B: .15 .30
☐ 323 Untamed Wilds U :G: .15 .30
☐ 324 Unyaro Griffin U :W: .25 .50
☐ 325 Vampiric Tutor R :K: 12.00 25.00
☐ 326 Venerable Monk C :W: .15 .30
☐ 327 Verduran Enchantress R :G: 1.00 2.00
☐ 328 Vertigo U :R: .25 .50
☐ 329 Vieshino Warrior C :R: .15 .30
☐ 330 Vitalize C :G: .15 .30
☐ 331 Vodalian Soldiers C :B: .15 .30
☐ 332 Volcanic Dragon R :R: 3.00 6.00
☐ 333 Volcanic Geyser U :R: .50 1.00
☐ 334 Waiting in the Weeds R :G: 1.00 2.00
☐ 335 Wall of Air U :B: .50 1.00
☐ 336 Wall of Fire U :R: .50 1.00
☐ 337 Wall of Swords U :W: .25 .50
☐ 338 Wand of Denial R :A: 1.00 2.00
☐ 339 Warmth U :W: .25 .50
☐ 340 Warrior's Honor C :W: .15 .30
☐ 341 Warthog U :G: .25 .50
☐ 342 Wild Growth C :G: .15 .30
☐ 343 Wind Drake C :B: .15 .30
☐ 344 Wind Spirit U :B: .15 .30
☐ 345 Wooden Sphere U :A: .25 .50
☐ 346 Worldly Tutor U :G: 2.50 5.00
☐ 347 Wrath of God R :W: 7.50 15.00
☐ 348 Wyluli Wolf R :G: 1.00 2.00
☐ 349 Zombie Master R :K: 3.00 6.00
☐ 350 Zur's Weirding R :B: 1.00 2.00

1999 Magic the Gathering Mercadian Masques

Complete Set (350) 150.00 200.00
☐ 1 Aerial Caravan R :B: 1.00 2.00
☐ 2 Afterlife U :W: .25 .50
☐ 3 Alabaster Wall C :W: .15 .30
☐ 4 Alley Grifters C :K: .15 .30
☐ 5 Ancestral Mask C :G: .50 1.00
☐ 6 Armistice R :W: 1.00 2.00
☐ 7 Arms Dealer U :R: .50 1.00
☐ 8 Arrest U :W: .50 1.00
☐ 9 Assembly Hall R :A: 1.00 2.00
☐ 10 Ballista Squad U :W: .50 1.00
☐ 11 Balloon Peddler C :B: .15 .30
☐ 12 Barbed Wire U :A: .50 1.00
☐ 13 Bargaining Table R :A: 1.50 3.00
☐ 14 Battle Rampart C :R: .15 .30
☐ 15 Battle Squadron R :R: 1.00 2.00
☐ 16 Bifurcate R :G: 1.50 3.00
☐ 17 Black Market R :K: 1.00 2.00
☐ 18 Blaster Mage C :R: .15 .30
☐ 19 Blockade Runner C :B: .15 .30
☐ 20 Blood Hound R :R: 1.00 2.00
☐ 21 Blood Oath R :R: 1.50 3.00
☐ 22 Boa Constrictor U :G: .50 1.00
☐ 23 Bog Smugglers C :K: .15 .30
☐ 24 Bog Witch C :K: .15 .30
☐ 25 Brainstorm C :B: 2.00 4.00
☐ 26 Brawl R :R: 1.00 2.00
☐ 27 Briar Patch U :G: .50 1.00
☐ 28 Bribery R :B: 5.00 10.00
☐ 29 Buoyancy C :B: .15 .30
☐ 30 Cackling Witch U :K: .50 1.00
☐ 31 Caller of the Hunt R :G: 1.50 3.00
☐ 32 Cateran Brute C :K: .15 .30
☐ 33 Cateran Enforcer U :K: .50 1.00
☐ 34 Cateran Kidnappers U :K: .50 1.00
☐ 35 Cateran Overlord R :K: 2.00 4.00
☐ 36 Cateran Persuader C :K: .15 .30
☐ 37 Cateran Slaver R :K: 1.00 2.00
☐ 38 Cateran Summons U :K: .50 1.00
☐ 39 Caustic Wasps U :G: .50 1.00
☐ 40 Cave Sense C :R: .15 .30
☐ 41 Cave-In R :R: 2.00 4.00
☐ 42 Cavern Crawler C :R: .15 .30
☐ 43 Ceremonial Guard C :R: .15 .30
☐ 44 Chambered Nautilus U :B: .50 1.00
☐ 45 Chameleon Spirit U :B: .50 1.00
☐ 46 Charisma R :B: 3.00 6.00
☐ 47 Charm Peddler C :W: .15 .30
☐ 48 Charmed Griffin U :W: .50 1.00
☐ 49 Cho-Arrim Alchemist R :W: 1.50 3.00
☐ 50 Cho-Arrim Bruiser R :W: 1.00 2.00
☐ 51 Cho-Arrim Legate U :W: .50 1.00
☐ 52 Cho-Manno, Revolutionary R :W: 1.50 3.00
☐ 53 Cho-Manno's Blessing C :W: .15 .30
☐ 54 Cinder Elemental U :R: .50 1.00
☐ 55 Clear the Land R :G: 1.50 3.00
☐ 56 Close Quarters U :R: .50 1.00
☐ 57 Cloud Sprite C :B: .15 .30
☐ 58 Coastal Piracy U :B: 1.00 2.00
☐ 59 Collective Unconscious R :G: 1.50 3.00
☐ 60 Common Cause R :W: 1.00 2.00
☐ 61 Conspiracy R :K: 1.50 3.00
☐ 62 Cornered Market R :W: 1.00 2.00
☐ 63 Corrupt Official R :K: 1.00 2.00
☐ 64 Counterspell C :B: 1.00 2.00
☐ 65 Cowardice R :B: 1.50 3.00
☐ 66 Crackdown R :W: 1.50 3.00
☐ 67 Crag Saurian R :R: 1.00 2.00
☐ 68 Crash C :R: .15 .30
☐ 69 Credit Voucher U :A: .50 1.00
☐ 70 Crenellated Wall U :A: .50 1.00
☐ 71 Crooked Scales R :A: 1.00 2.00
☐ 72 Crossbow Infantry C :W: .15 .30
☐ 73 Crumbling Sanctuary R :A: 1.50 3.00
☐ 74 Customs Depot U :B: .50 1.00
☐ 75 Dark Ritual C :K: .50 1.00
☐ 76 Darting Merfolk C :B: .15 .30
☐ 77 Dawnstrider R :G: 1.00 2.00
☐ 78 Deadly Insect C :G: .15 .30
☐ 79 Deathgazer U :K: .50 1.00
☐ 80 Deepwood Drummer C :G: .15 .30
☐ 81 Deepwood Elder R :G: 1.00 2.00
☐ 82 Deepwood Ghoul C :K: .15 .30
☐ 83 Deepwood Legate U :K: .50 1.00
☐ 84 Deepwood Tantiv U :G: .50 1.00
☐ 85 Deepwood Wolverine C :G: .15 .30
☐ 86 Dehydration C :B: .15 .30
☐ 87 Delraich R :K: 2.00 4.00
☐ 88 Desert Twister U :G: .50 1.00
☐ 89 Devout Witness C :W: .15 .30
☐ 90 Diplomatic Escort U :B: .50 1.00
☐ 91 Diplomatic Immunity C :B: .50 1.00
☐ 92 Disenchant C :W: .15 .30
☐ 93 Distorting Lens R :A: 1.50 3.00
☐ 94 Drake Hatchling C :B: .15 .30
☐ 95 Dust Bowl R :L: 3.00 6.00
☐ 96 Embargo R :B: 1.00 2.00
☐ 97 Energy Flux U :B: 2.00 4.00
☐ 98 Enslaved Horror U :K: .50 1.00
☐ 99 Erithizon R :G: 1.50 3.00
☐ 100 Extortion R :K: 1.50 3.00
☐ 101 Extravagant Spirit R :B: 1.00 2.00
☐ 102 Eye of Ramos R :A: 1.00 2.00
☐ 103 False Demise U :B: .50 1.00
☐ 104 Ferocity C :G: .15 .30
☐ 105 Flailing Manticore R :R: 1.00 2.00
☐ 106 Flailing Ogre U :R: .25 .50
☐ 107 Flailing Soldier C :R: .15 .30
☐ 108 Flaming Sword C :R: .15 .30
☐ 109 Food Chain R :G: 4.00 8.00
☐ 110 Forced March R :K: 1.00 2.00
☐ 111 Forest C :L: .25 .50
☐ 112 Forest C :L: .25 .50
☐ 113 Forest C :L: .25 .50
☐ 114 Forest C :L: .25 .50
☐ 115 Foster R :G: 1.00 2.00
☐ 116 Fountain of Cho U :L: .25 .50
☐ 117 Fountain Watch R :W: 4.00 8.00
☐ 118 Fresh Volunteers C :W: .15 .30
☐ 119 Furious Assault C :R: .15 .30
☐ 120 Game Preserve R :G: 1.00 2.00
☐ 121 General's Regalia R :A: 1.00 2.00
☐ 122 Gerrard's Irregulars C :R: .15 .30
☐ 123 Ghoul's Feast U :K: .25 .50
☐ 124 Giant Caterpillar C :G: .15 .30
☐ 125 Glowing Anemone U :B: .25 .50
☐ 126 Groundskeeper U :G: .50 1.00
☐ 127 Gush C :B: .15 .30
☐ 128 Hammer Mage U :R: .25 .50
☐ 129 Haunted Crossroads U :K: 1.00 2.00
☐ 130 Heart of Ramos R :A: 1.00 2.00
☐ 131 Henge Guardian U :A: .50 1.00
☐ 132 Henge of Ramos U :L: .50 1.00
☐ 133 Hickory Woodlot C :L: .15 .30
☐ 134 High Market R :L: 1.50 3.00
☐ 135 High Seas U :B: .50 1.00
☐ 136 Highway Robber C :K: .15 .30
☐ 137 Hired Giant U :R: .50 1.00
☐ 138 Honor the Fallen R :W: 1.50 3.00
☐ 139 Hoodwink C :B: .15 .30
☐ 140 Horn of Plenty R :A: 1.00 2.00
☐ 141 Horn of Ramos R :A: 1.50 3.00
☐ 142 Horned Troll C :G: .15 .30
☐ 143 Howling Wolf C :G: .15 .30
☐ 144 Hunted Wumpus U :G: .50 1.00
☐ 145 Ignoble Soldier U :W: .50 1.00
☐ 146 Indentured Djinn U :B: .50 1.00
☐ 147 Instigator R :K: 1.00 2.00
☐ 148 Insubordination C :K: .15 .30
☐ 149 Intimidation U :K: .75 1.50
☐ 150 Invigorate C :G: .15 .30
☐ 151 Inviolability C :W: .15 .30
☐ 152 Iron Lance U :A: .50 1.00
☐ 153 Island C :L: .15 .30
☐ 154 Island C :L: .15 .30
☐ 155 Island C :L: .15 .30
☐ 156 Island C :L: .15 .30
☐ 157 Ivory Mask R :W: 2.50 5.00
☐ 158 Jeweled Torque U :A: .50 1.00
☐ 159 Jhovall Queen R :W: 1.50 3.00
☐ 160 Jhovall Rider U :W: .25 .50
☐ 161 Kam's Touch R :B: .50 1.00
☐ 162 Kris Mage C :R: .15 .30
☐ 163 Kyren Archive R :A: 1.00 2.00
☐ 164 Kyren Glider C :R: .15 .30
☐ 165 Kyren Legate U :R: .50 1.00
☐ 166 Kyren Negotiations U :R: .50 1.00
☐ 167 Kyren Sniper C :R: .15 .30
☐ 168 Kyren Toy R :A: 1.00 2.00
☐ 169 Land Grant C :G: .15 .30
☐ 170 Larceny U :K: 1.00 2.00
☐ 171 Last Breath U :W: .50 1.00
☐ 172 Lava Runner R :R: 1.50 3.00
☐ 173 Ley Line U :G: .50 1.00
☐ 174 Liability R :K: 1.00 2.00
☐ 175 Lightning Hounds C :R: .15 .30
☐ 176 Lithophage R :R: 1.50 3.00
☐ 177 Lumbering Satyr U :G: .25 .50
☐ 178 Lunge C :R: .15 .30
☐ 179 Lure U :G: .25 .50
☐ 180 Maggot Therapy C :K: .15 .30
☐ 181 Magistrate's Scepter R :A: 2.50 5.00
☐ 182 Magistrate's Veto U :R: .50 1.00
☐ 183 Megatherium R :G: 1.00 2.00
☐ 184 Mercadian Atlas R :A: 1.00 2.00
☐ 185 Mercadian Bazaar U :L: .50 1.00
☐ 186 Mercadian Lift R :A: 1.50 3.00
☐ 187 Mercadia's Downfall U :R: .50 1.00
☐ 188 Midnight Ritual R :K: 1.50 3.00
☐ 189 Misdirection R :B: 7.50 15.00
☐ 190 Misshapen Fiend C :K: .15 .30
☐ 191 Misstep C :B: .15 .30
☐ 192 Molting Harpy U :K: .50 1.00
☐ 193 Moment of Silence C :W: .15 .30
☐ 194 Monkey Cage R :A: 1.50 3.00
☐ 195 Moonlit Wake U :W: .50 1.00
☐ 196 Mountain C :L: .15 .30
☐ 197 Mountain C :L: .15 .30
☐ 198 Mountain C :L: .15 .30
☐ 199 Mountain C :L: .15 .30
☐ 200 Muzzle C :W: .15 .30
☐ 201 Natural Affinity R :G: 1.50 3.00
☐ 202 Nether Spirit R :K: 2.50 5.00
☐ 203 Nightwind Glider C :W: .15 .30
☐ 204 Noble Purpose U :W: 1.00 2.00
☐ 205 Notorious Assassin R :K: 1.00 2.00
☐ 206 Ogre Taskmaster U :R: .25 .50
☐ 207 Orim's Cure C :W: .15 .30
☐ 208 Overtaker R :B: 1.00 2.00
☐ 209 Panacea U :A: .25 .50
☐ 210 Pangosaur R :G: 1.00 2.00
☐ 211 Peat Bog C :L: .15 .30
☐ 212 Pious Warrior C :W: .15 .30
☐ 213 Plains C :L: .15 .30
☐ 214 Plains C :L: .15 .30
☐ 215 Plains C :L: .15 .30
☐ 216 Plains C :L: .15 .30
☐ 217 Port Inspector C :B: .15 .30
☐ 218 Power Matrix R :A: 2.00 4.00
☐ 219 Pretender's Claim U :K: .50 1.00
☐ 220 Primeval Shambler U :K: .50 1.00
☐ 221 Puffer Extract U :A: .50 1.00
☐ 222 Pulverize R :R: 1.50 3.00
☐ 223 Puppet's Verdict R :R: 1.00 2.00
☐ 224 Putrefaction U :K: .50 1.00
☐ 225 Quagmire Lamprey U :K: .50 1.00
☐ 226 Rain of Tears U :K: .50 1.00
☐ 227 Ramosian Captain U :W: .50 1.00
☐ 228 Ramosian Commander U :W: .50 1.00
☐ 229 Ramosian Lieutenant C :W: .15 .30
☐ 230 Ramosian Rally C :W: .15 .30
☐ 231 Ramosian Sergeant C :W: .15 .30
☐ 232 Ramosian Sky Marshal R :W: 1.00 2.00
☐ 233 Rampart Crawler C :K: .15 .30
☐ 234 Rappelling Scouts R :W: 1.00 2.00
☐ 235 Remote Farm C :L: .15 .30
☐ 236 Renounce U :W: .50 1.00
☐ 237 Revered Elder C :W: .15 .30
☐ 238 Reverent Mantra R :W: .50 1.00
☐ 239 Revive U :G: .50 1.00
☐ 240 Righteous Aura U :W: .25 .50
☐ 241 Righteous Indignation U :W: .25 .50
☐ 242 Rishadan Airship C :B: .15 .30
☐ 243 Rishadan Brigand R :B: 1.00 2.00
☐ 244 Rishadan Cutpurse C :B: .15 .30
☐ 245 Rishadan Footpad U :B: .50 1.00
☐ 246 Rishadan Pawnshop R :A: 1.00 2.00
☐ 247 Rishadan Port R :L: 7.50 15.00
☐ 248 Robber Fly U :R: .50 1.00
☐ 249 Rock Badger U :R: .50 1.00
☐ 250 Rouse C :K: .15 .30
☐ 251 Rushwood Dryad C :G: .15 .30
☐ 252 Rushwood Elemental R :G: 2.50 5.00
☐ 253 Rushwood Grove U :L: .50 1.00
☐ 254 Rushwood Herbalist C :G: .15 .30
☐ 255 Rushwood Legate U :G: .25 .50
☐ 256 Saber Ants U :G: .50 1.00
☐ 257 Sacred Prey C :G: .15 .30
☐ 258 Sailmonger U :B: .25 .50
☐ 259 Sand Squid R :B: 1.00 2.00
☐ 260 Sandstone Needle C :L: .15 .30
☐ 261 Saprazzan Bailiff R :B: 1.00 2.00
☐ 262 Saprazzan Breaker U :B: .25 .50
☐ 263 Saprazzan Cove U :L: .50 1.00
☐ 264 Saprazzan Heir R :B: 1.50 3.00
☐ 265 Saprazzan Legate U :B: .25 .50
☐ 266 Saprazzan Outrigger C :B: .15 .30
☐ 267 Saprazzan Raider C :B: .15 .30
☐ 268 Saprazzan Skerry C :L: .15 .30
☐ 269 Scandalmonger U :K: .25 .50
☐ 270 Security Detail R :W: 1.00 2.00
☐ 271 Seismic Mage R :R: 1.00 2.00
☐ 272 Sever Soul C :K: .15 .30
☐ 273 Shock Troops C :R: .15 .30
☐ 274 Shoving Match U :B: .25 .50
☐ 275 Silent Assassin R :K: .50 1.00
☐ 276 Silverglade Elemental C :G: .15 .30
☐ 277 Silverglade Pathfinder U :G: .25 .50
☐ 278 Sizzle C :R: .15 .30
☐ 279 Skulking Fugitive C :K: .15 .30
☐ 280 Skull of Ramos R :A: 1.00 2.00
☐ 281 Snake Pit U :G: .50 1.00
☐ 282 Snorting Gahr C :G: .15 .30
☐ 283 Snuff Out C :K: .15 .30
☐ 284 Soothing Balm C :W: .15 .30
☐ 285 Soothsaying U :B: .75 1.50
☐ 286 Soul Channeling C :K: .15 .30
☐ 287 Specter's Wail C :K: .15 .30
☐ 288 Spidersilk Armor C :G: .15 .30
☐ 289 Spiritual Focus R :W: 1.00 2.00
☐ 290 Spontaneous Generation R :G: 1.50 3.00
☐ 291 Squall C :G: .15 .30
☐ 292 Squallmonger U :G: .25 .50
☐ 293 Squee, Goblin Nabob R :R: 6.00 12.00
☐ 294 Squeeze R :B: 1.00 2.00
☐ 295 Stamina U :G: 1.00 2.00
☐ 296 Statecraft R :B: 1.00 2.00
☐ 297 Steadfast Guard C :W: .15 .30
☐ 298 Stinging Barrier C :B: .15 .30
☐ 299 Stone Rain C :R: .15 .30
☐ 300 Story Circle U :W: 1.50 3.00
☐ 301 Strongarm Thug U :K: .25 .50
☐ 302 Subterranean Hangar U :L: .25 .50
☐ 303 Sustenance U :G: .25 .50
☐ 304 Swamp C :L: .15 .30
☐ 305 Swamp C :L: .15 .30
☐ 306 Swamp C :L: .15 .30
☐ 307 Swamp C :L: .15 .30
☐ 308 Task Force C :W: .15 .30
☐ 309 Tectonic Break R :R: 1.00 2.00
☐ 310 Territorial Dispute R :R: 1.00 2.00
☐ 311 Thermal Glider C :W: .15 .30
☐ 312 Thieves' Auction R :R: 1.00 2.00
☐ 313 Thrashing Wumpus R :K: 1.50 3.00
☐ 314 Thunderclap C :R: .15 .30
☐ 315 Thwart U :B: 1.00 2.00
☐ 316 Tidal Bore C :B: .15 .30
☐ 317 Tidal Kraken R :B: 2.00 4.00
☐ 318 Tiger Claws C :G: .15 .30
☐ 319 Timid Drake U :B: .25 .50
☐ 320 Tonic Peddler U :W: .25 .50

MAGIC

Card	Low	High
❑ 321 Tooth of Ramos R :A:	1.00	2.00
❑ 322 Tower of the Magistrate R :L:	1.50	3.00
❑ 323 Toymaker U :A:	.25	.50
❑ 324 Trade Routes R :B:	2.00	4.00
❑ 325 Tranquility C :G:	.15	.30
❑ 326 Trap Runner U :W:	.25	.50
❑ 327 Tremor C :R:	.15	.30
❑ 328 Two-Headed Dragon R :R:	4.00	8.00
❑ 329 Undertaker C :K:	.15	.30
❑ 330 Unmask R :K:	2.50	5.00
❑ 331 Unnatural Hunger R :K:	1.00	2.00
❑ 332 Uphill Battle U :R:	.25	.50
❑ 333 Vendetta C :K:	.15	.30
❑ 334 Venomous Breath U :G:	.25	.50
❑ 335 Venomous Dragonfly C :G:	.15	.30
❑ 336 Vernal Equinox R :G:	1.00	2.00
❑ 337 Vine Dryad R :G:	2.00	4.00
❑ 338 Vine Trellis C :G:	.15	.30
❑ 339 Volcanic Wind U :R:	.50	1.00
❑ 340 Wall of Distortion C :K:	.15	.30
❑ 341 War Cadence U :R:	.50	1.00
❑ 342 War Tax U :B:	.50	1.00
❑ 343 Warmonger U :R:	.50	1.00
❑ 344 Warpath U :R:	.50	1.00
❑ 345 Waterfront Bouncer C :B:	.15	.30
❑ 346 Wave of Reckoning R :W:	1.00	2.00
❑ 347 Wild Jhovall C :R:	.15	.30
❑ 348 Wishmonger U :W:	.50	1.00
❑ 349 Word of Blasting U :R:	.50	1.00
❑ 350 Worry Beads R :A:	1.00	2.00

1999 Magic the Gathering Mercadian Masques Foil

COMPLETE SET (350)	500.00	750.00

*Foil: 1X to 2X Basic Cards

2000 Magic the Gathering Nemesis

Item	Low	High
Complete Set (143)	75.00	90.00
Starter Deck Box (12 Decks)	90.00	125.00
Starter Deck	10.00	12.50
Booster Box (36 Packs)	90.00	125.00
Booster Pack (15 Cards)	3.75	4.50
Fat Pack	40.00	50.00
❑ 1 Ather Barrier R :B:	1.00	2.00
❑ 2 Accumulated Knowledge C :B: :B:	.50	1.00
❑ 3 Air Bladder C :B:	.12	.30
❑ 4 Ancient Hydra U :R:	.20	.50
❑ 5 Angelic Favor U :W:	.20	.50
❑ 6 Animate Land U :G:	.50	1.00
❑ 7 Arc Mage U :R:	.20	.50
❑ 8 Ascendant Evincar R :K:	2.50	5.00
❑ 9 Avenger en-Dal R :W:	1.00	2.00
❑ 10 Battlefield Percher U :K:	.20	.50
❑ 11 Belbe's Armor U :A:	.20	.50
❑ 12 Belbe's Percher C :K:	.12	.30
❑ 13 Belbe's Portal R :A:	2.00	4.00
❑ 14 Blastoderm C :G:	.12	.30
❑ 15 Blinding Angel R :W:	4.00	8.00
❑ 16 Bola Warrior C :R:	.12	.30
❑ 17 Carrion Wall U :K:	.20	.50
❑ 18 Chieftain en-Dal U :W:	.20	.50
❑ 19 Cloudskate C :B:	.12	.30
❑ 20 Coiling Woodworm U :G:	.20	.50
❑ 21 Complex Automaton R :A:	1.00	2.00
❑ 22 Dark Triumph U :K:	.20	.50
❑ 23 Daze C :B:	.12	.30
❑ 24 Death Pit Offering R :K:	2.00	4.00
❑ 25 Defender en-Vec C :W:	.12	.30
❑ 26 Defiant Falcon C :W:	.12	.30
❑ 27 Defiant Vanguard U :W:	.50	1.00
❑ 28 Divining Witch R :K:	1.00	2.00
❑ 29 Dominate U :B:	.50	1.00
❑ 30 Downhill Charge C :R:	.12	.30
❑ 31 Ensnare U :B:	.50	1.00
❑ 32 Eye of Yawgmoth R :A:	1.00	2.00
❑ 33 Fanatical Devotion C :W:	.12	.30
❑ 34 Flame Rift C :R:	.12	.30
❑ 35 Flint Golem U :A:	.20	.50
❑ 36 Flowstone Armor U :A:	.20	.50
❑ 37 Flowstone Crusher C :R:	.12	.30
❑ 38 Flowstone Overseer R :R:	1.00	2.00
❑ 39 Flowstone Slide R :R:	1.00	2.00
❑ 40 Flowstone Strike C :R:	.12	.30
❑ 41 Flowstone Surge U :R:	.20	.50
❑ 42 Flowstone Thopter U :A:	.20	.50
❑ 43 Flowstone Wall C :R:	.12	.30
❑ 44 Fog Patch C :G:	.12	.30
❑ 45 Harvest Mage C :G:	.12	.30
❑ 46 Infiltrate C :B:	.12	.30
❑ 47 Jolting Merfolk U :B:	.20	.50
❑ 48 Kill Switch R :A:	1.00	2.00
❑ 49 Kor Haven R :L:	1.50	3.00
❑ 50 Laccolith Grunt C :R:	.12	.30
❑ 51 Laccolith Rig C :R:	.12	.30
❑ 52 Laccolith Titan R :R:	1.00	2.00
❑ 53 Laccolith Warrior U :R:	.20	.50
❑ 54 Laccolith Whelp C :R:	.12	.30
❑ 55 Lashknife C :W:	.12	.30
❑ 56 Lawbringer C :W:	.12	.30
❑ 57 Lightbringer C :W:	.12	.30
❑ 58 Lin Sivvi, Defiant Hero R :W:	3.00	6.00
❑ 59 Mana Cache R :R:	1.00	2.00
❑ 60 Massacre U :K:	.20	.50
❑ 61 Mind Slash U :K:	.20	.50
❑ 62 Mind Swords C :K:	.12	.30
❑ 63 Mogg Alarm U :R:	.20	.50
❑ 64 Mogg Salvage U :R:	.20	.50
❑ 65 Mogg Toady C :R:	.12	.30
❑ 66 Moggcatcher R :R:	1.00	2.00
❑ 67 Mossdog C :G:	.12	.30
❑ 68 Murderous Betrayal R :K:	1.00	2.00
❑ 69 Nesting Wurm U :G:	.50	1.00
❑ 70 Netter en-Dal C :W:	.12	.30
❑ 71 Noble Stand U :W:	.20	.50
❑ 72 Off Balance C :W:	.12	.30
❑ 73 Oracle's Attendants R :W:	1.00	2.00
❑ 74 Oraxid C :B:	.12	.30
❑ 75 Overlaid Terrain R :G:	1.00	2.00
❑ 76 Pack Hunt R :G:	1.00	2.00
❑ 77 Pale Moon R :B:	1.00	2.00
❑ 78 Parallax Dementia C :K:	.12	.30
❑ 79 Parallax Inhibitor R :A:	1.00	2.00
❑ 80 Parallax Nexus R :K:	1.00	2.00
❑ 81 Parallax Tide R :B:	2.00	4.00
❑ 82 Parallax Wave R :W:	2.00	4.00
❑ 83 Phyrexian Driver C :K:	.12	.30
❑ 84 Phyrexian Prowler U :K:	.50	1.00
❑ 85 Plague Witch C :K:	.12	.30
❑ 86 Predator, Flagship R :A:	2.00	4.00
❑ 87 Rackling U :A:	.50	1.00
❑ 88 Rathi Assassin R :K:	2.00	4.00
❑ 89 Rathi Fiend U :K:	.50	1.00
❑ 90 Rathi Intimidator C :K:	.12	.30
❑ 91 Rath's Edge R :L:	1.00	2.00
❑ 92 Refreshing Rain U :G:	.50	1.00
❑ 93 Rejuvenation Chamber U :A:	.50	1.00
❑ 94 Reverent Silence C :G:	.12	.30
❑ 95 Rhox R :G:	2.00	4.00
❑ 96 Rising Waters R :B:	1.50	3.00
❑ 97 Rootwater Commando C :B:	.12	.30
❑ 98 Rootwater Thief R :B:	4.00	8.00
❑ 99 Rupture U :R:	.20	.50
❑ 100 Rusting Golem U :A:	.20	.50
❑ 101 Saproling Burst R :G:	2.00	4.00
❑ 102 Saproling Cluster R :G:	1.50	3.00
❑ 103 Seahunter R :B:	1.00	2.00
❑ 104 Seal of Cleansing C :W:	.12	.30
❑ 105 Seal of Doom C :K:	.12	.30
❑ 106 Seal of Fire C :R:	.12	.30
❑ 107 Seal of Removal C :B:	.12	.30
❑ 108 Seal of Strength C :G:	.12	.30
❑ 109 Shrieking Mogg R :R:	1.00	2.00
❑ 110 Silkenfist Fighter C :W:	.12	.30
❑ 111 Silkenfist Order U :W:	.20	.50
❑ 112 Sivvi's Ruse U :W:	.20	.50
❑ 113 Sivvi's Valor R :W:	1.00	2.00
❑ 114 Skyshroud Behemoth R :G:	1.50	3.00
❑ 115 Skyshroud Claim C :G:	.12	.30
❑ 116 Skyshroud Cutter C :G:	.12	.30
❑ 117 Skyshroud Poacher R :G:	2.50	5.00
❑ 118 Skyshroud Ridgeback C :G:	.12	.30
❑ 119 Skyshroud Sentinel C :G:	.12	.30
❑ 120 Sliptide Serpent R :B:	1.00	2.00
❑ 121 Sneaky Homunculus C :B:	.12	.30
❑ 122 Spineless Thug C :K:	.12	.30
❑ 123 Spiritual Asylum R :W:	1.00	2.00
❑ 124 Spiteful Bully C :K:	.12	.30
❑ 125 Stampede Driver U :G:	.20	.50
❑ 126 Stronghold Biologist U :B:	.50	1.00
❑ 127 Stronghold Discipline C :K:	.12	.30
❑ 128 Stronghold Gambit R :R:	1.00	2.00
❑ 129 Stronghold Machinist U :B:	.50	1.00
❑ 130 Stronghold Zeppelin U :B:	.20	.50
❑ 131 Submerge U :B:	.20	.50
❑ 132 Tangle Wire R :A:	5.00	10.00
❑ 133 Terrain Generator U :L:	.50	1.00
❑ 134 Topple C :W:	.12	.30
❑ 135 Treetop Bracers C :G:	.12	.30
❑ 136 Trickster Mage C :B:	.12	.30
❑ 137 Vicious Hunger C :K:	.12	.30
❑ 138 Viseling U :A:	.50	1.00
❑ 139 Voice of Truth U :W:	.50	1.00
❑ 140 Volrath the Fallen R :K:	2.50	5.00
❑ 141 Wandering Eye C :B:	.12	.30
❑ 142 Wild Mammoth U :G:	.20	.50
❑ 143 Woodripper U :G:	.20	.50

2000 Magic the Gathering Nemesis Foil

COMPLETE SET (143)	275.00	350.00

*Foil: 1X to 2X Basic Cards

2000 Magic the Gathering Prophecy

Item	Low	High
Complete Set (143)	50.00	100.00
Starter Deck Box (12 Decks)	120.00	175.00
Starter Deck	15.00	20.00
Booster Box (36 Packs)	100.00	150.00
Booster Pack (15 Cards)	4.00	5.00
Fat Pack	30.00	60.00
❑ 1 Abolish U :W:	.50	1.00
❑ 2 Agent of Shauku C :K:	.12	.30
❑ 3 Alexi, Zephyr Mage R :B:	1.50	3.00
❑ 4 Alexi's Cloak C :B:	.12	.30
❑ 5 Aura Fracture C :W:	.12	.30
❑ 6 Avatar of Fury R :R:	4.00	8.00
❑ 7 Avatar of Hope R :W:	4.00	8.00
❑ 8 Avatar of Might R :G:	4.00	8.00
❑ 9 Avatar of Will R :B:	3.00	6.00
❑ 10 Avatar of Woe R :K:	10.00	20.00
❑ 11 Barbed Field U :R:	.20	.50
❑ 12 Blessed Wind R :W:	1.50	3.00
❑ 13 Bog Elemental R :K:	1.00	2.00
❑ 14 Bog Glider C :K:	.12	.30
❑ 15 Branded Brawlers C :R:	.12	.30
❑ 16 Brutal Suppression U :R:	.20	.50
❑ 17 Calming Verse C :G:	.12	.30
❑ 18 Celestial Convergence R :W:	1.00	2.00
❑ 19 Chilling Apparition U :K:	.50	1.00
❑ 20 Chimeric Idol U :A:	1.00	2.00
❑ 21 Citadel of Pain U :R:	.50	1.00
❑ 22 Coastal Hornclaw C :B:	.12	.30
❑ 23 Coffin Puppets R :K:	1.00	2.00
❑ 24 Copper-Leaf Angel R :A:	2.00	4.00
❑ 25 Darba U :G:	.20	.50
❑ 26 Death Charmer C :K:	.12	.30
❑ 27 Denying Wind R :B:	1.50	3.00
❑ 28 Despoil C :K:	.12	.30
❑ 29 Devastate C :R:	.12	.30
❑ 30 Diving Griffin C :W:	.12	.30
❑ 31 Dual Nature R :G:	1.00	2.00
❑ 32 Elephant Resurgence R :G:	1.00	2.00
❑ 33 Endbringer's Revel U :K:	.20	.50
❑ 34 Entangler U :W:	1.00	2.00
❑ 35 Excavation U :B:	.20	.50
❑ 36 Excise C :W:	.12	.30
❑ 37 Fault Riders C :R:	.12	.30
❑ 38 Fen Stalker C :K:	.12	.30
❑ 39 Fickle Efreet R :R:	1.00	2.00
❑ 40 Flameshot U :R:	.20	.50
❑ 41 Flay C :K:	.12	.30
❑ 42 Flowering Field U :W:	.20	.50
❑ 43 Foil U :B:	1.00	2.00
❑ 44 Forgotten Harvest R :G:	1.00	2.00
❑ 45 Glittering Lion U :W:	.30	.75
❑ 46 Glittering Lynx C :W:	.12	.30
❑ 47 Greel, Mind Raker R :K:	1.50	3.00
❑ 48 Greel's Caress C :K:	.12	.30
❑ 49 Gulf Squid C :B:	.12	.30
❑ 50 Hazy Homunculus C :B:	.12	.30
❑ 51 Heightened Awareness R :B:	1.00	2.00
❑ 52 Hollow Warrior U :A:	.20	.50
❑ 53 Infernal Genesis R :K:	1.00	2.00
❑ 54 Inflame C :R:	.12	.30
❑ 55 Jeweled Spirit R :W:	1.00	2.00
❑ 56 Jolrael, Empress of Beasts R :G:	2.00	4.00
❑ 57 Jolrael's Favor C :G:	.12	.30
❑ 58 Keldon Arsonist U :R:	.20	.50
❑ 59 Keldon Battlewagon R :A:	1.00	2.00
❑ 60 Keldon Berserker C :R:	.12	.30
❑ 61 Keldon Firebombers R :R:	1.00	2.00
❑ 62 Latulla, Keldon Overseer R :R:	2.00	4.00
❑ 63 Latulla's Orders C :R:	.12	.30
❑ 64 Lesser Gargadon U :R:	.20	.50
❑ 65 Living Terrain U :G:	.20	.50
❑ 66 Mageta the Lion R :W:	2.00	4.00
❑ 67 Mageta's Boon C :W:	.12	.30
❑ 68 Mana Vapors U :B:	.50	1.00
❑ 69 Marsh Boa C :G:	.12	.30
❑ 70 Mercenary Informer R :W:	1.00	2.00
❑ 71 Mine Bearer C :W:	.12	.30
❑ 72 Mirror Strike U :W:	.50	1.00
❑ 73 Mungha Wurm R :G:	1.00	2.00
❑ 74 Nakaya Shade U :K:	.20	.50
❑ 75 Noxious Field U :K:	.20	.50
❑ 76 Outbreak U :K:	.20	.50
❑ 77 Overburden R :B:	1.50	3.00
❑ 78 Panic Attack C :R:	.12	.30
❑ 79 Pit Raptor U :K:	.20	.50
❑ 80 Plague Fiend C :K:	.12	.30
❑ 81 Plague Wind R :K:	2.00	4.00
❑ 82 Psychic Theft R :B:	1.00	2.00
❑ 83 Pygmy Razorback C :G:	.12	.30
❑ 84 Quicksilver Wall U :B:	.20	.50
❑ 85 Rebel Informer R :K:	1.00	2.00
❑ 86 Rethink C :B:	.12	.30
❑ 87 Reveille Squad U :W:	.50	1.00
❑ 88 Rhystic Cave U :L:	.50	1.00
❑ 89 Rhystic Circle C :W:	.12	.30
❑ 90 Rhystic Deluge C :B:	.12	.30
❑ 91 Rhystic Lightning C :R:	.12	.30
❑ 92 Rhystic Scrying U :B:	.50	1.00
❑ 93 Rhystic Shield C :W:	.12	.30
❑ 94 Rhystic Study C :B:	.12	.30
❑ 95 Rhystic Syphon U :K:	.20	.50
❑ 96 Rhystic Tutor R :K:	2.00	4.00
❑ 97 Rib Cage Spider C :G:	.12	.30
❑ 98 Ribbon Snake C :B:	.12	.30
❑ 99 Ridgeline Rager C :R:	.12	.30
❑ 100 Root Cage U :G:	.20	.50
❑ 101 Samite Sanctuary R :W:	1.00	2.00
❑ 102 Scoria Cat U :R:	.20	.50
❑ 103 Search for Survivors R :R:	1.00	2.00
❑ 104 Searing Wind R :R:	1.00	2.00
❑ 105 Sheltering Prayers R :W:	1.00	2.00
❑ 106 Shield Dancer U :W:	.20	.50
❑ 107 Shrouded Serpent R :B:	1.00	2.00
❑ 108 Silt Crawler C :G:	.12	.30
❑ 109 Snag U :G:	.20	.50
❑ 110 Soul Charmer C :W:	.12	.30
❑ 111 Soul Strings C :K:	.12	.30
❑ 112 Spiketail Drake U :B:	.50	1.00
❑ 113 Spiketail Hatchling C :B:	.12	.30
❑ 114 Spitting Spider U :G:	.20	.50
❑ 115 Spore Frog C :G:	.12	.30
❑ 116 Spur Grappler C :R:	.12	.30
❑ 117 Squirrel Wrangler R :G:	2.00	4.00
❑ 118 Steal Strength C :K:	.12	.30
❑ 119 Stormwatch Eagle C :B:	.12	.30
❑ 120 Sunken Field U :B:	.20	.50
❑ 121 Sword Dancer U :W:	.20	.50
❑ 122 Task Mage Assembly R :R:	1.00	2.00
❑ 123 Thresher Beast C :G:	.12	.30
❑ 124 Thrive C :G:	.12	.30
❑ 125 Trenching Steed C :W:	.12	.30
❑ 126 Troubled Healer C :W:	.12	.30
❑ 127 Troublesome Spirit R :B:	1.00	2.00
❑ 128 Verdant Field U :G:	.20	.50
❑ 129 Veteran Brawlers R :R:	1.50	3.00
❑ 130 Vintara Elephant C :G:	.12	.30
❑ 131 Vintara Snapper U :G:	.20	.50
❑ 132 Vitalizing Wind R :G:	2.00	4.00
❑ 133 Wall of Vipers U :K:	.20	.50
❑ 134 Well of Discovery R :A:	1.00	2.00
❑ 135 Well of Life U :A:	.50	1.00
❑ 136 Whip Sergeant U :R:	.50	1.00
❑ 137 Whipstitched Zombie C :K:	.12	.30
❑ 138 Wild Might C :G:	.12	.30
❑ 139 Windscouter U :B:	.20	.50
❑ 140 Wing Storm U :G:	.20	.50
❑ 141 Wintermoon Mesa R :L:	1.00	2.00
❑ 142 Withdraw C :B:	.12	.30
❑ 143 Zerapa Minotaur C :R:	.12	.30

2000 Magic the Gathering Prophecy Foil

COMPLETE SET (143)	250.00	350.00

*Foil: 1X to 2X Basic Cards

2000 Magic the Gathering Invasion

Item	Low	High
Complete Set (340)	175.00	225.00
Starter Deck Box (12 Decks)	110.00	160.00
Starter Deck	15.00	20.00
Booster Box (36 Packs)	125.00	165.00
Booster Pack (15 Cards)	4.00	6.00
Fat Pack	35.00	40.00
❑ 1 Absorb R :D:	4.00	8.00
❑ 2 Addle U :K:	.20	.50
❑ 3 AEther Rift R :D:	1.50	3.00
❑ 4 Aggressive Urge C :G:	.12	.30
❑ 5 Agonizing Demise C :K:	.12	.30
❑ 6 Alabaster Leech R :W:	1.50	3.00
❑ 7 Alloy Golem U :A:	.12	.30
❑ 8 Ancient Kavu C :R:	.12	.30
❑ 9 Ancient Spring C :L:	.12	.30
❑ 10 Andradite Leech R :K:	1.00	2.00
❑ 11 Angel of Mercy U :W:	.50	1.00
❑ 12 Angelic Shield U :D:	.50	1.00
❑ 13 Annihilate U :K:	.50	1.00
❑ 14 Archaeological Dig U :L:	.50	1.00
❑ 15 Ardent Soldier C :W:	.12	.30
❑ 16 Armadillo Cloak C :D:	.12	.30
❑ 17 Armored Guardian R :D:	1.00	2.00
❑ 18 Artifact Mutation R :D:	2.00	4.00
❑ 19 Assault/Battery (Assault) U :R:	.50	1.00
❑ 20 Assault/Battery (Battery) U :G:	.50	1.00
❑ 21 Atalya, Samite Master R :W:	1.50	3.00
❑ 22 Aura Mutation R :D:	1.50	3.00
❑ 23 Aura Shards U :D:	.50	1.00
❑ 24 Backlash U :D:	.50	1.00
❑ 25 Barrin's Spite R :D:	1.00	2.00
❑ 26 Barrin's Unmaking C :B:	.12	.30
❑ 27 Benalish Emissary U :W:	.50	1.00
❑ 28 Benalish Heralds U :W:	.50	1.00
❑ 29 Benalish Lancer C :W:	.12	.30
❑ 30 Benalish Trapper C :W:	.12	.30
❑ 31 Bend or Break R :R:	1.50	3.00
❑ 32 Bind R :G:	1.50	3.00
❑ 33 Blazing Specter R :D:	2.50	5.00
❑ 34 Blind Seer R :B:	1.50	3.00
❑ 35 Blinding Light U :W:	.50	1.00
❑ 36 Bloodstone Cameo U :A:	.20	.50
❑ 37 Blurred Mongoose R :G:	2.00	4.00
❑ 38 Bog Initiate C :K:	.12	.30
❑ 39 Breaking Wave R :B:	1.00	2.00
❑ 40 Breath of Darigaaz U :R:	.20	.50
❑ 41 Callous Giant R :R:	1.50	3.00
❑ 42 Canopy Surge U :G:	.20	.50
❑ 43 Capashen Unicorn C :W:	.12	.30
❑ 44 Captain Sisay R :D:	2.00	4.00
❑ 45 Cauldron Dance U :D:	.50	1.00
❑ 46 Chaotic Strike U :R:	.20	.50
❑ 47 Charging Troll U :D:	.50	1.00
❑ 48 Chromatic Sphere U :A:	.50	1.00
❑ 49 Cinder Shade U :D:	.50	1.00
❑ 50 Coalition Victory R :D:	2.00	4.00
❑ 51 Coastal Tower U :L:	1.00	2.00
❑ 52 Collapsing Borders R :R:	1.00	2.00
❑ 53 Collective Restraint R :B:	1.50	3.00
❑ 54 Cremate U :K:	.20	.50
❑ 55 Crimson Acolyte C :W:	.12	.30
❑ 56 Crosis, the Purger R :D:	4.00	8.00
❑ 57 Crosis's Attendant U :A:	.50	1.00
❑ 58 Crown of Flames C :R:	.12	.30
❑ 59 Crusading Knight R :W:	2.00	4.00
❑ 60 Crypt Angel R :K:	1.50	3.00
❑ 61 Crystal Spray R :B:	1.50	3.00
❑ 62 Cursed Flesh C :K:	.12	.30
❑ 63 Darigaaz, the Igniter R :D:	4.00	8.00
❑ 64 Darigaaz's Attendant U :A:	.50	1.00
❑ 65 Death or Glory R :W:	1.50	3.00
❑ 66 Defiling Tears U :K:	.50	1.00
❑ 67 Desperate Research R :K:	1.50	3.00
❑ 68 Devouring Strossus R :K:	2.00	4.00
❑ 69 Dismantling Blow C :W:	.12	.30
❑ 70 Disrupt U :B:	.50	1.00
❑ 71 Distorting Wake R :B:	1.50	3.00
❑ 72 Divine Presence R :W:	1.50	3.00
❑ 73 Do or Die R :K:	1.50	3.00
❑ 74 Drake-Skull Cameo U :A:	.50	1.00
❑ 75 Dream Thrush C :B:	.12	.30
❑ 76 Dredge U :K:	.50	1.00
❑ 77 Dromar, the Banisher R :D:	4.00	8.00
❑ 78 Dromar's Attendant U :A:	.50	1.00
❑ 79 Dueling Grounds R :D:	2.00	4.00
❑ 80 Duskwalker C :K:	.12	.30
❑ 81 Elfhame Palace U :L:	1.00	2.00
❑ 82 Elfhame Sanctuary U :G:	.50	1.00
❑ 83 Elvish Champion R :G:	4.00	8.00
❑ 84 Empress Galina R :B:	1.00	2.00
❑ 85 Essence Leak U :B:	.50	1.00
❑ 86 Exclude C :B:	.12	.30
❑ 87 Exotic Curse C :K:	.12	.30
❑ 88 Explosive Growth C :G:	.12	.30
❑ 89 Fact or Fiction U :B:	3.00	6.00
❑ 90 Faerie Squadron C :B:	.12	.30
❑ 91 Fertile Ground C :G:	.12	.30
❑ 92 Fight or Flight R :W:	1.50	3.00
❑ 93 Firebrand Ranger U :R:	.50	1.00
❑ 94 Fires of Yavimaya U :D:	.50	1.00
❑ 95 Firescreamer C :K:	.12	.30
❑ 96 Forest C :L:	.12	.30
❑ 97 Frenzied Tilling C :D:	.12	.30
❑ 98 Galina's Knight C :D:	.12	.30
❑ 99 Geothermal Crevice C :L:	.12	.30
❑ 100 Ghitu Fire R :R:	1.50	3.00
❑ 101 Glimmering Angel C :W:	.12	.30
❑ 102 Global Ruin R :W:	1.50	3.00
❑ 103 Goblin Spy U :R:	.50	1.00
❑ 104 Goham Djinn U :K:	.50	1.00
❑ 105 Halam Djinn U :R:	.50	1.00
❑ 106 Hanna, Ship's Navigator R :D:	2.00	4.00
❑ 107 Harrow C :G:	.12	.30
❑ 108 Harsh Judgment R :W:	1.50	3.00
❑ 109 Hate Weaver U :K:	.50	1.00
❑ 110 Heroes' Reunion U :D:	.50	1.00
❑ 111 Holy Day C :W:	.12	.30
❑ 112 Hooded Kavu C :R:	.12	.30
❑ 113 Horned Cheetah U :D:	.50	1.00
❑ 114 Hunting Kavu U :D:	.50	1.00
❑ 115 Hypnotic Cloud C :K:	.12	.30
❑ 116 Irrigation Ditch C :L:	.12	.30
❑ 117 Island C :L:	.12	.30
❑ 118 Jade Leech R :G:	2.00	4.00
❑ 119 Juntu Stakes R :A:	1.50	3.00
❑ 120 Kangee, Aerie Keeper R :D:	1.50	3.00
❑ 121 Kavu Aggressor C :R:	.12	.30
❑ 122 Kavu Chameleon U :G:	.50	1.00
❑ 123 Kavu Climber C :G:	.12	.30
❑ 124 Kavu Lair R :G:	1.50	3.00
❑ 125 Kavu Monarch R :R:	2.00	4.00
❑ 126 Kavu Runner U :R:	.50	1.00
❑ 127 Kavu Scout C :R:	.12	.30
❑ 128 Kavu Titan R :G:	2.00	4.00
❑ 129 Keldon Necropolis R :L:	1.50	3.00
❑ 130 Liberate U :W:	.50	1.00
❑ 131 Lightning Dart U :R:	.50	1.00
❑ 132 Llanowar Cavalry C :G:	.12	.30
❑ 133 Llanowar Elite C :G:	.12	.30
❑ 134 Llanowar Knight C :D:	.12	.30
❑ 135 Llanowar Vanguard C :G:	.12	.30
❑ 136 Loafing Giant R :R:	1.50	3.00
❑ 137 Lobotomy U :D:	.50	1.00
❑ 138 Lotus Guardian R :A:	1.00	2.00
❑ 139 Mages' Contest R :R:	1.50	3.00
❑ 140 Mana Maze R :B:	1.50	3.00
❑ 141 Maniacal Rage C :R:	.12	.30
❑ 142 Manipulate Fate U :B:	.50	1.00
❑ 143 Marauding Knight R :K:	1.50	3.00
❑ 144 Metathran Aerostat R :B:	1.00	2.00
❑ 145 Metathran Transport U :B:	.50	1.00
❑ 146 Metathran Zombie C :B:	.12	.30
❑ 147 Meteor Storm R :D:	1.50	3.00
❑ 148 Might Weaver U :G:	1.50	3.00
❑ 149 Molimo, Maro-Sorcerer R :G:	2.00	4.00
❑ 150 Mountain C :L:	.12	.30
❑ 151 Mourning C :K:	.12	.30
❑ 152 Nightscape Apprentice C :K:	.12	.30
❑ 153 Nightscape Master R :K:	2.00	4.00
❑ 154 Noble Panther R :D:	2.00	4.00
❑ 155 Nomadic Elf C :G:	.12	.30
❑ 156 Obliterate R :R:	3.00	6.00
❑ 157 Obsidian Acolyte C :W:	.12	.30
❑ 158 Opt C :B:	.12	.30
❑ 159 Ordered Migration U :D:	.50	1.00
❑ 160 Orim's Touch C :W:	.12	.30
❑ 161 Overabundance R :D:	1.50	3.00
❑ 162 Overload C :R:	.12	.30
❑ 163 Pain/Suffering (Pain) U :K:	.50	1.00
❑ 164 Pain/Suffering (Suffering) U :R:	.50	1.00
❑ 165 Phantasmal Terrain C :B:	.12	.30
❑ 166 Phyrexian Altar R :A:	1.00	2.00
❑ 167 Phyrexian Battleflies C :K:	.12	.30
❑ 168 Phyrexian Delver R :K:	1.00	2.00
❑ 169 Phyrexian Infiltrator R :K:	1.00	2.00
❑ 170 Phyrexian Lens R :A:	1.00	2.00
❑ 171 Phyrexian Reaper C :K:	.12	.30
❑ 172 Phyrexian Slayer C :K:	.12	.30
❑ 173 Pincer Spider C :G:	.12	.30
❑ 174 Plague Spitter U :K:	.50	1.00
❑ 175 Plague Spores C :D:	.12	.30
❑ 176 Plains C :L:	.12	.30
❑ 177 Planar Portal R :A:	2.00	4.00
❑ 178 Pledge of Loyalty U :W:	.50	1.00
❑ 179 Pouncing Kavu C :R:	.12	.30
❑ 180 Power Armor U :A:	.50	1.00
❑ 181 Prison Barricade C :W:	.12	.30
❑ 182 Probe C :B:	.12	.30
❑ 183 Prohibit C :B:	.12	.30
❑ 184 Protective Sphere C :W:	.12	.30
❑ 185 Psychic Battle R :B:	1.00	2.00
❑ 186 Pulse of Llanowar U :G:	.50	1.00
❑ 187 Pure Reflection R :W:	1.50	3.00
❑ 188 Pyre Zombie R :D:	2.00	4.00

❑	Card	Low	High
❑ 189	Quirion Elves C :G:	.12	.30
❑ 190	Quirion Sentinel C :G:	.12	.30
❑ 191	Quirion Trailblazer C :G:	.12	.30
❑ 192	Rage Weaver U :R:	.50	1.00
❑ 193	Raging Kavu R :D:	1.50	3.00
❑ 194	Rainbow Crow U :B:	.50	1.00
❑ 195	Rampant Elephant C :W:	.12	.30
❑ 196	Ravenous Rats C :K:	.12	.30
❑ 197	Razorfoot Griffin C :W:	.12	.30
❑ 198	Reckless Assault R :D:	1.50	3.00
❑ 199	Reckless Spite U :K:	.50	1.00
❑ 200	Recoil C :D:	.12	.30
❑ 201	Recover C :K:	.12	.30
❑ 202	Repulse C :B:	.12	.30
❑ 203	Restock R :G:	1.50	3.00
❑ 204	Restrain C :W:	.12	.30
❑ 205	Reviving Dose C :W:	.12	.30
❑ 206	Reviving Vapors U :D:	.50	1.00
❑ 207	Rewards of Diversity U :W:	.50	1.00
❑ 208	Reya Dawnbringer R :W:	10.00	20.00
❑ 209	Riptide Crab U :D:	.50	1.00
❑ 210	Rith, the Awakener R :D:	5.00	10.00
❑ 211	Rith's Attendant U :A:	.50	1.00
❑ 212	Rogue Kavu C :R:	.12	.30
❑ 213	Rooting Kavu U :G:	.50	1.00
❑ 214	Rout R :W:	2.50	5.00
❑ 215	Ruby Leech R :R:	1.50	3.00
❑ 216	Ruham Djinn U :W:	.50	1.00
❑ 217	Sabertooth Nishoba R :D:	2.00	4.00
❑ 218	Salt Marsh U :L:	1.00	2.00
❑ 219	Samite Archer U :D:	.50	1.00
❑ 220	Samite Ministration U :W:	.50	1.00
❑ 221	Sapphire Leech R :B:	1.50	3.00
❑ 222	Saproling Infestation R :G:	2.00	4.00
❑ 223	Saproling Symbiosis R :G:	2.00	4.00
❑ 224	Savage Offensive C :R:	.12	.30
❑ 225	Scarred Puma C :R:	.12	.30
❑ 226	Scavenged Weaponry C :K:	.12	.30
❑ 227	Scorching Lava C :R:	.12	.30
❑ 228	Scouting Trek U :G:	.50	1.00
❑ 229	Searing Rays U :R:	.50	1.00
❑ 230	Seashell Cameo U :A:	.50	1.00
❑ 231	Seer's Vision U :D:	.50	1.00
❑ 232	Serpentine Kavu C :G:	.12	.30
❑ 233	Shackles C :W:	.12	.30
❑ 234	Shimmering Wings C :B:	.12	.30
❑ 235	Shivan Emissary U :R:	.50	1.00
❑ 236	Shivan Harvest U :R:	.50	1.00
❑ 237	Shivan Oasis U :L:	1.00	2.00
❑ 238	Shivan Zombie C :D:	.12	.30
❑ 239	Shoreline Raider C :B:	.12	.30
❑ 240	Simoon U :D:	.50	1.00
❑ 241	Skittish Kavu U :R:	.50	1.00
❑ 242	Skizzik R :R:	3.00	6.00
❑ 243	Sky Weaver U :B:	.50	1.00
❑ 244	Sleeper's Robe U :D:	.50	1.00
❑ 245	Slimy Kavu C :R:	.12	.30
❑ 246	Slinking Serpent U :D:	.50	1.00
❑ 247	Smoldering Tar U :D:	.50	1.00
❑ 248	Soul Burn C :K:	.12	.30
❑ 249	Sparring Golem U :A:	.50	1.00
❑ 250	Spinal Embrace R :D:	1.50	3.00
❑ 251	Spirit of Resistance R :W:	1.50	3.00
❑ 252	Spirit Weaver U :W:	.50	1.00
❑ 253	Spite/Malice (Malice) U :K:	.50	1.00
❑ 254	Spite/Malice (Spite) U :B:	.50	1.00
❑ 255	Spreading Plague R :K:	1.00	2.00
❑ 256	Stalking Assassin R :D:	1.50	3.00
❑ 257	Stand or Fall R :R:	1.50	3.00
❑ 258	Stand/Deliver (Deliver) U :B:	.50	1.00
❑ 259	Stand/Deliver (Stand) U :W:	.50	1.00
❑ 260	Sterling Grove U :D:	1.00	2.00
❑ 261	Stormscape Apprentice C :B:	.12	.30
❑ 262	Stormscape Master R :B:	1.50	3.00
❑ 263	Strength of Unity C :W:	.12	.30
❑ 264	Stun C :R:	.12	.30
❑ 265	Sulam Djinn U :G:	.50	1.00
❑ 266	Sulfur Vent C :L:	.12	.30
❑ 267	Sunscape Apprentice C :W:	.12	.30
❑ 268	Sunscape Master R :W:	2.00	4.00
❑ 269	Swamp C :L:	.12	.30
❑ 270	Sway of Illusion U :B:	.50	1.00
❑ 271	Tainted Well C :K:	.12	.30
❑ 272	Tangle U :G:	1.00	2.00
❑ 273	Tectonic Instability R :R:	1.50	3.00
❑ 274	Teferi's Care U :W:	.50	1.00
❑ 275	Teferi's Moat R :D:	2.00	4.00
❑ 276	Teferi's Response R :B:	1.50	3.00
❑ 277	Tek R :A:	2.00	4.00
❑ 278	Temporal Distortion R :B:	1.50	3.00
❑ 279	Thicket Elemental R :G:	2.00	4.00
❑ 280	Thornscape Apprentice C :G:	.12	.30
❑ 281	Thornscape Master R :G:	2.00	4.00
❑ 282	Thunderscape Apprentice C :R:	.12	.30
❑ 283	Thunderscape Master R :R:	1.50	3.00
❑ 284	Tidal Visionary C :B:	.12	.30
❑ 285	Tigereye Cameo U :A:	.50	1.00
❑ 286	Tinder Farm C :L:	.12	.30
❑ 287	Tolarian Emissary U :B:	.50	1.00
❑ 288	Tower Drake C :B:	.12	.30
❑ 289	Tranquility C :G:	.12	.30
❑ 290	Traveler's Cloak C :B:	.12	.30
❑ 291	Treefolk Healer U :G:	.50	1.00
❑ 292	Trench Wurm U :K:	.50	1.00
❑ 293	Treva, the Renewer R :D:	4.00	8.00
❑ 294	Treva's Attendant U :A:	.50	1.00
❑ 295	Tribal Flames C :R:	.12	.30
❑ 296	Troll-Horn Cameo U :A:	.50	1.00
❑ 297	Tsabo Tavoc R :D:	2.00	4.00
❑ 298	Tsabo's Assassin R :K:	1.50	3.00
❑ 299	Tsabo's Decree R :K:	2.00	4.00
❑ 300	Tsabo's Web R :A:	2.00	4.00
❑ 301	Turf Wound C :R:	.12	.30
❑ 302	Twilight's Call R :K:	1.50	3.00
❑ 303	Undermine R :D:	5.00	10.00
❑ 304	Urborg Drake U :D:	.50	1.00
❑ 305	Urborg Emissary U :K:	.50	1.00
❑ 306	Urborg Phantom C :K:	.12	.30
❑ 307	Urborg Shambler U :K:	.50	1.00
❑ 308	Urborg Skeleton C :K:	.12	.30
❑ 309	Urborg Volcano U :L:	1.00	2.00
❑ 310	Urza's Filter R :A:	1.00	2.00
❑ 311	Urza's Rage R :R:	5.00	10.00
❑ 312	Utopia Tree R :G:	2.50	5.00
❑ 313	Verdeloth the Ancient R :G:	2.00	4.00
❑ 314	Verduran Emissary U :G:	.50	1.00
❑ 315	Viashino Grappler C :R:	.12	.30
❑ 316	Vicious Kavu U :D:	.50	1.00
❑ 317	Vigorous Charge C :G:	.12	.30
❑ 318	Vile Consumption R :D:	1.50	3.00
❑ 319	Vodalian Hypnotist U :B:	.50	1.00
❑ 320	Vodalian Merchant C :B:	.12	.30
❑ 321	Vodalian Serpent C :B:	.12	.30
❑ 322	Vodalian Zombie C :D:	.12	.30
❑ 323	Void R :D:	1.00	2.00
❑ 324	Voracious Cobra U :D:	.50	1.00
❑ 325	Wallop U :G:	.50	1.00
❑ 326	Wandering Stream C :G:	.12	.30
❑ 327	Wash Out U :B:	.50	1.00
❑ 328	Wax/Wane (Wane) U :W:	.50	1.00
❑ 329	Wax/Wane (Wax) U :G:	.50	1.00
❑ 330	Wayfaring Giant U :W:	.50	1.00
❑ 331	Well-Laid Plans R :B:	.50	1.00
❑ 332	Whip Silk C :G:	.12	.30
❑ 333	Wings of Hope C :D:	.12	.30
❑ 334	Winnow R :W:	1.00	2.00
❑ 335	Worldly Counsel C :B:	.12	.30
❑ 336	Yavimaya Barbarian C :D:	.12	.30
❑ 337	Yavimaya Kavu U :D:	.50	1.00
❑ 338	Yawgmoth's Agenda R :K:	1.50	3.00
❑ 339	Zanam Djinn U :B:	.50	1.00
❑ 340	Zap C :R:	.12	.30

2000 Magic the Gathering Invasion Foil

Item	Low	High
COMPLETE SET (340)	600.00	800.00

*Foil: 1X to 2X Basic Cards

2001 Magic the Gathering 7th Edition

Item	Low	High
Complete Set (350)	140.00	200.00
Starter Deck	6.00	10.00
Theme Deck Box (15 Decks)	70.00	90.00
Booster Box (36 Packs)	120.00	140.00
Booster Pack (15 Cards)	4.00	6.00

❑	Card	Low	High
❑ 1	Abyssal Horror R :K:	1.00	2.00
❑ 2	Abyssal Specter U :K:	.20	.50
❑ 3	Adarkar Wastes R :L:	3.00	6.00
❑ 4	AEther Flash U :R:	.20	.50
❑ 5	Agonizing Memories U :K:	.20	.50
❑ 6	Air Elemental U :B:	.20	.50
❑ 7	Aladdin's Ring R :A:	1.50	3.00
❑ 8	Anaconda U :G:	.20	.50
❑ 9	Ancestral Memories R :B:	1.00	2.00
❑ 10	Ancient Silverback R :G:	1.00	2.00
❑ 11	Angelic Page C :W:	.12	.30
❑ 12	Arcane Laboratory U :B:	.50	1.00
❑ 13	Archivist R :B:	.50	1.00
❑ 14	Ardent Militia U :W:	.20	.50
❑ 15	Balduvian Barbarians C :R:	.12	.30
❑ 16	Baleful Stare U :B:	.20	.50
❑ 17	Beast of Burden R :A:	1.50	3.00
❑ 18	Bedlam R :R:	1.50	3.00
❑ 19	Befoul U :K:	.20	.50
❑ 20	Bellowing Fiend R :K:	1.00	2.00
❑ 21	Benthic Behemoth R :B:	1.00	2.00
❑ 22	Bereavement U :K:	.20	.50
❑ 23	Birds of Paradise R :G:	9.00	18.00
❑ 24	Blanchwood Armor U :G:	1.00	2.00
❑ 25	Blaze U :R:	.50	1.00
❑ 26	Blessed Reversal R :W:	1.00	2.00
❑ 27	Blood Pet C :K:	.12	.30
❑ 28	Bloodshot Cyclops R :R:	1.00	2.00
❑ 29	Bog Imp C :K:	.12	.30
❑ 30	Bog Wraith U :K:	.20	.50
❑ 31	Boil U :R:	.50	1.00
❑ 32	Boomerang C :B:	.12	.30
❑ 33	Breath of Life U :W:	.50	1.00
❑ 34	Brushland R :L:	3.00	6.00
❑ 35	Bull Hippo U :G:	.20	.50
❑ 36	Caltrops U :A:	.20	.50
❑ 37	Canopy Spider C :G:	.12	.30
❑ 38	Castle U :W:	.20	.50
❑ 39	Charcoal Diamond U :A:	.20	.50
❑ 40	Circle of Protection Black C :W:	.12	.30
❑ 41	Circle of Protection Blue C :W:	.12	.30
❑ 42	Circle of Protection Green C :W:	.12	.30
❑ 43	Circle of Protection Red C :W:	.12	.30
❑ 44	Circle of Protection White C :W:	.12	.30
❑ 45	City of Brass R :L:	4.00	8.00
❑ 46	Cloudchaser Eagle C :W:	.12	.30
❑ 47	Coat of Arms R :A:	7.50	15.00
❑ 48	Compost U :G:	.50	1.00
❑ 49	Confiscate U :B:	.20	.50
❑ 50	Coral Merfolk C :B:	.12	.30
❑ 51	Corrupt C :K:	.12	.30
❑ 52	Counterspell C :B:	1.00	2.00
❑ 53	Creeping Mold U :G:	.50	1.00
❑ 54	Crimson Hellkite R :R:	2.00	4.00
❑ 55	Crossbow Infantry C :W:	.12	.30
❑ 56	Crypt Rats U :K:	.50	1.00
❑ 57	Crystal Rod U :A:	.20	.50
❑ 58	Dakmor Lancer U :K:	.20	.50
❑ 59	Daring Apprentice R :B:	1.00	2.00
❑ 60	Dark Banishing C :K:	.12	.30
❑ 61	Darkest Hour R :K:	1.50	3.00
❑ 62	Deflection R :B:	1.00	2.00
❑ 63	Delusions of Mediocrity R :B:	1.00	2.00
❑ 64	Dingus Egg R :A:	1.00	2.00
❑ 65	Disenchant C :W:	.12	.30
❑ 66	Disorder U :R:	.20	.50
❑ 67	Disrupting Scepter R :A:	1.00	2.00
❑ 68	Dregs of Sorrow R :K:	1.00	2.00
❑ 69	Drudge Skeletons C :K:	.12	.30
❑ 70	Duress C :K:	1.25	2.50
❑ 71	Eager Cadet C :W:	.12	.30
❑ 72	Early Harvest R :G:	3.00	6.00
❑ 73	Earthquake R :R:	1.00	2.00
❑ 74	Eastern Paladin R :K:	1.00	2.00
❑ 75	Elder Druid R :G:	1.00	2.00
❑ 76	Elite Archers R :W:	1.00	2.00
❑ 77	Elvish Archers R :G:	1.50	3.00
❑ 78	Elvish Champion R :G:	3.00	6.00
❑ 79	Elvish Lyrist U :G:	.20	.50
❑ 80	Elvish Piper R :G:	5.00	10.00
❑ 81	Engineered Plague U :K:	1.25	2.50
❑ 82	Ensnaring Bridge R :A:	2.00	4.00
❑ 83	Equilibrium R :B:	1.00	2.00
❑ 84	Evacuation R :B:	1.00	2.00
❑ 85	Fallen Angel R :K:	2.00	4.00
❑ 86	Familiar Ground U :G:	.20	.50
❑ 87	Fear C :K:	.12	.30
❑ 88	Femeref Archers U :G:	.12	.30
❑ 89	Feroz's Ban R :A:	.50	1.00
❑ 90	Fervor R :R:	1.00	2.00
❑ 91	Fighting Drake U :B:	.20	.50
❑ 92	Final Fortune R :R:	1.50	3.00
❑ 93	Fire Diamond U :A:	.50	1.00
❑ 94	Fire Elemental U :R:	.20	.50
❑ 95	Fleeting Image R :B:	1.00	2.00
❑ 96	Flight C :B:	.20	.50
❑ 97	Flying Carpet R :A:	1.00	2.00
❑ 98	Fog C :G:	.12	.30
❑ 99	Force Spike C :B:	.50	1.00
❑ 100	Forest L :L:	.20	.50
❑ 101	Forest L :L:	.20	.50
❑ 102	Forest L :L:	.50	1.00
❑ 103	Forest L :L:	.50	1.00
❑ 104	Foul Imp U :K:	.20	.50
❑ 105	Fugue U :K:	.12	.30
❑ 106	Fyndhorn Elder U :G:	.50	1.00
❑ 107	Gang of Elk U :G:	.50	1.00
❑ 108	Gerrard's Wisdom U :W:	.20	.50
❑ 109	Ghitu Fire-Eater U :R:	.20	.50
❑ 110	Giant Cockroach C :K:	.12	.30
❑ 111	Giant Growth C :G:	.12	.30
❑ 112	Giant Octopus C :B:	.12	.30
❑ 113	Giant Spider C :G:	.12	.30
❑ 114	Glacial Wall U :B:	.20	.50
❑ 115	Glorious Anthem R :W:	3.00	6.00
❑ 116	Goblin Chariot C :R:	.12	.30
❑ 117	Goblin Digging Team C :R:	.12	.30
❑ 118	Goblin Elite Infantry C :R:	.12	.30
❑ 119	Goblin Gardener C :R:	.12	.30
❑ 120	Goblin Glider U :R:	.20	.50
❑ 121	Goblin King R :R:	2.00	4.00
❑ 122	Goblin Matron U :R:	.50	1.00
❑ 123	Goblin Raider C :R:	.12	.30
❑ 124	Goblin Spelunkers C :R:	.12	.30
❑ 125	Goblin War Drums U :R:	.20	.50
❑ 126	Gorilla Chieftain C :G:	.12	.30
❑ 127	Grafted Skullcap R :A:	1.00	2.00
❑ 128	Granite Grip C :R:	.12	.30
❑ 129	Grapeshot Catapult U :A:	.20	.50
❑ 130	Gravedigger C :K:	.12	.30
❑ 131	Greed R :K:	1.00	2.00
❑ 132	Grizzly Bears C :G:	.12	.30
❑ 133	Healing Salve C :W:	.12	.30
❑ 134	Heavy Ballista U :W:	.20	.50
❑ 135	Hibernation U :B:	.20	.50
❑ 136	Hill Giant C :R:	.12	.30
❑ 137	Hollow Dogs C :K:	.12	.30
❑ 138	Holy Strength C :W:	.12	.30
❑ 139	Honor Guard C :W:	.12	.30
❑ 140	Horned Turtle C :B:	.12	.30
❑ 141	Howl from Beyond C :K:	.12	.30
❑ 142	Howling Mine R :A:	2.50	5.00
❑ 143	Hurricane R :G:	1.00	2.00
❑ 144	Impatience R :R:	1.00	2.00
❑ 145	Infernal Contract R :K:	1.00	2.00
❑ 146	Inferno R :R:	1.00	2.00
❑ 147	Inspiration C :B:	1.00	2.00
❑ 148	Intrepid Hero R :W:	2.00	4.00
❑ 149	Iron Star U :A:	.20	.50
❑ 150	Island L :L:	.20	.50
❑ 151	Island L :L:	.20	.50
❑ 152	Island L :L:	.20	.50
❑ 153	Island L :L:	.20	.50
❑ 154	Ivory Cup U :A:	.20	.50
❑ 155	Jalum Tome R :A:	1.00	2.00
❑ 156	Jandor's Saddlebags R :A:	1.00	2.00
❑ 157	Jayemdae Tome R :A:	1.00	2.00
❑ 158	Karplusan Forest R :L:	4.00	8.00
❑ 159	Kjeldoran Royal Guard R :W:	1.00	2.00
❑ 160	Knight Errant C :W:	.12	.30
❑ 161	Knighthood U :W:	.50	1.00
❑ 162	Lava Axe C :R:	.12	.30
❑ 163	Leshrac's Rite U :K:	.20	.50
❑ 164	Levitation U :B:	.20	.50
❑ 165	Lightning Blast C :R:	.12	.30
❑ 166	Lightning Elemental C :R:	.12	.30
❑ 167	Llanowar Elves C :G:	.50	1.00
❑ 168	Lone Wolf C :G:	.12	.30
❑ 169	Longbow Archer U :W:	.50	1.00
❑ 170	Looming Shade C :K:	.12	.30
❑ 171	Lord of Atlantis R :B:	2.00	4.00
❑ 172	Lure U :G:	.20	.50
❑ 173	Mahamoti Djinn R :B:	2.00	4.00
❑ 174	Mana Breach U :B:	.20	.50
❑ 175	Mana Clash R :R:	1.00	2.00
❑ 176	Mana Short R :B:	1.50	3.00
❑ 177	Marble Diamond U :A:	.20	.50
❑ 178	Maro R :G:	1.00	2.00
❑ 179	Master Healer R :W:	1.00	2.00
❑ 180	Mawcor R :B:	1.00	2.00
❑ 181	Meekstone R :A:	1.50	3.00
❑ 182	Megrim U :K:	1.00	2.00
❑ 183	Memory Lapse C :B:	.12	.30
❑ 184	Merfolk Looter U :B:	.50	1.00
❑ 185	Merfolk of the Pearl Trident C :B:	.12	.30
❑ 186	Might of Oaks R :G:	2.50	5.00
❑ 187	Millstone R :A:	1.50	3.00
❑ 188	Mind Rot C :K:	.12	.30
❑ 189	Monstrous Growth C :G:	.12	.30
❑ 190	Moss Diamond U :A:	.20	.50
❑ 191	Mountain L :L:	.20	.50
❑ 192	Mountain L :L:	.20	.50
❑ 193	Mountain L :L:	.20	.50
❑ 194	Mountain L :L:	.20	.50
❑ 195	Nature's Resurgence R :G:	1.00	2.00
❑ 196	Nature's Revolt R :G:	1.00	2.00
❑ 197	Nausea C :K:	.12	.30
❑ 198	Necrologia U :K:	.20	.50
❑ 199	Nightmare R :K:	2.50	5.00
❑ 200	Nocturnal Raid U :K:	.20	.50
❑ 201	Northern Paladin R :W:	1.00	2.00
❑ 202	Ogre Taskmaster U :R:	.20	.50
❑ 203	Okk R :R:	1.00	2.00
❑ 204	Opportunity U :B:	.20	.50
❑ 205	Opposition R :B:	2.50	5.00
❑ 206	Oppression R :K:	1.00	2.00
❑ 207	Orcish Artillery U :R:	.20	.50
❑ 208	Orcish Oriflamme U :R:	.20	.50
❑ 209	Ostracize C :K:	.12	.30
❑ 210	Pacifism C :W:	.12	.30
❑ 211	Pariah R :W:	2.50	5.00
❑ 212	Patagia Golem U :A:	.20	.50
❑ 213	Persecute R :K:	3.00	6.00
❑ 214	Phantom Warrior U :B:	.20	.50
❑ 215	Phyrexian Colossus R :A:	2.00	4.00
❑ 216	Phyrexian Hulk U :A:	.20	.50
❑ 217	Pillage U :R:	1.50	3.00
❑ 218	Pit Trap U :A:	.20	.50
❑ 219	Plague Beetle C :K:	.12	.30
❑ 220	Plains L :L:	.20	.50
❑ 221	Plains L :L:	.20	.50
❑ 222	Plains L :L:	.20	.50
❑ 223	Plains L :L:	.20	.50
❑ 224	Pride of Lions U :G:	.50	1.00
❑ 225	Prodigal Sorcerer C :B:	.12	.30
❑ 226	Purify R :W:	1.00	2.00
❑ 227	Pygmy Pyrosaur C :R:	.12	.30
❑ 228	Pyroclasm U :R:	1.50	3.00
❑ 229	Pyrotechnics U :R:	.20	.50
❑ 230	Rag Man R :K:	1.00	2.00
❑ 231	Raging Goblin C :R:	.12	.30
❑ 232	Raise Dead C :K:	.12	.30
❑ 233	Rampant Growth C :G:	.12	.30
❑ 234	Razorfoot Griffin C :W:	.12	.30
❑ 235	Razortooth Rats C :K:	.12	.30
❑ 236	Reckless Embermage R :R:	1.00	2.00
❑ 237	Reclaim C :G:	.50	1.00
❑ 238	Redwood Treefolk C :G:	.12	.30
❑ 239	Reflexes C :R:	.12	.30
❑ 240	Regeneration C :G:	.12	.30
❑ 241	Relentless Assault R :R:	.50	1.00
❑ 242	Remove Soul C :B:	.12	.30
❑ 243	Reprisal U :W:	.50	1.00
❑ 244	Reprocess R :K:	1.00	2.00
❑ 245	Revenant R :K:	1.00	2.00
❑ 246	Reverse Damage R :W:	1.00	2.00
❑ 247	Rod of Ruin U :A:	.20	.50
❑ 248	Rolling Stones R :W:	1.00	2.00
❑ 249	Rowen R :G:	1.00	2.00
❑ 250	Sabretooth Tiger C :R:	.12	.30
❑ 251	Sacred Ground R :W:	2.00	4.00
❑ 252	Sacred Nectar C :W:	.12	.30
❑ 253	Sage Owl C :B:	.12	.30
❑ 254	Samite Healer C :W:	.12	.30
❑ 255	Sanctimony U :W:	.20	.50
❑ 256	Scathe Zombies C :K:	.20	.50
❑ 257	Scavenger Folk U :G:	.20	.50
❑ 258	Sea Monster C :B:	.12	.30
❑ 259	Seasoned Marshal U :W:	.20	.50
❑ 260	Seeker of Skybreak C :G:	.20	.50
❑ 261	Seismic Assault R :R:	1.00	2.00
❑ 262	Serpent Warrior C :K:	.12	.30
❑ 263	Serra Advocate U :W:	.20	.50
❑ 264	Serra Angel R :W:	3.00	6.00
❑ 265	Serra's Embrace U :W:	.50	1.00
❑ 266	Shanodin Dryads C :G:	.12	.30
❑ 267	Shatter C :R:	.12	.30
❑ 268	Shield Wall C :W:	.12	.30
❑ 269	Shivan Dragon R :R:	3.00	6.00
❑ 270	Shock C :R:	.12	.30
❑ 271	Sisay's Ring U :A:	.20	.50
❑ 272	Sky Diamond U :A:	.20	.50
❑ 273	Skyshroud Falcon C :W:	.12	.30
❑ 274	Sleight of Hand C :B:	.12	.30
❑ 275	Soul Feast U :K:	.50	1.00
❑ 276	Soul Net U :A:	.50	1.00
❑ 277	Southern Paladin R :W:	1.25	2.50
❑ 278	Spellbook U :A:	.50	1.00
❑ 279	Spined Wurm C :G:	.12	.30
❑ 280	Spineless Thug C :K:	.12	.30
❑ 281	Spirit Link U :W:	.50	1.00
❑ 282	Spitting Earth C :R:	.12	.30
❑ 283	Squall C :G:	.12	.30
❑ 284	Standing Troops C :W:	.12	.30
❑ 285	Starlight U :W:	.20	.50
❑ 286	Static Orb R :A:	1.50	3.00
❑ 287	Staunch Defenders U :W:	.50	1.00
❑ 288	Steal Artifact U :B:	.20	.50
❑ 289	Stone Rain C :R:	.20	.50
❑ 290	Storm Cauldron R :A:	1.00	2.00
❑ 291	Storm Crow C :B:	.20	.50
❑ 292	Storm Shaman U :R:	.20	.50
❑ 293	Strands of Night U :K:	.20	.50
❑ 294	Stream of Life C :G:	.20	.50
❑ 295	Stronghold Assassin R :K:	1.00	2.00
❑ 296	Sudden Impact U :R:	.20	.50
❑ 297	Sulfurous Springs R :L:	3.00	6.00
❑ 298	Sunweb R :W:	1.50	3.00
❑ 299	Sustainer of the Realm U :W:	.20	.50
❑ 300	Swamp L :L:	.20	.50
❑ 301	Swamp L :L:	.20	.50
❑ 302	Swamp L :L:	.20	.50
❑ 303	Swamp L :L:	.20	.50
❑ 304	Tainted Æther R :K:	1.50	3.00
❑ 305	Teferi's Puzzle Box R :A:	1.50	3.00
❑ 306	Telepathic Spies C :B:	.12	.30
❑ 307	Telepathy U :B:	.50	1.00
❑ 308	Temporal Adept R :B:	2.00	4.00
❑ 309	Thieving Magpie U :B:	.20	.50
❑ 310	Thorn Elemental R :G:	2.00	4.00
❑ 311	Thoughtleech U :G:	.50	1.00
❑ 312	Throne of Bone U :A:	.20	.50
❑ 313	Tolarian Winds C :B:	.12	.30
❑ 314	Trained Armodon C :G:	.12	.30
❑ 315	Trained Orgg R :R:	1.00	2.00
❑ 316	Tranquility C :G:	.12	.30
❑ 317	Treasure Trove U :B:	.20	.50
❑ 318	Treefolk Seedlings U :G:	.20	.50
❑ 319	Tremor C :R:	.12	.30
❑ 320	Twiddle C :B:	.12	.30
❑ 321	Uktabi Wildcats R :G:	1.00	2.00
❑ 322	Underground River R :L:	5.00	10.00
❑ 323	Unholy Strength C :K:	.12	.30
❑ 324	Unsummon C :B:	.12	.30
❑ 325	Untamed Wilds U :G:	.20	.50
❑ 326	Venerable Monk C :W:	.12	.30
❑ 327	Vengeance U :W:	.20	.50
❑ 328	Verduran Enchantress R :G:	1.50	3.00
❑ 329	Vernal Bloom R :G:	2.50	5.00
❑ 330	Vigilant Drake C :B:	.12	.30
❑ 331	Vizzerdrix R :B:	1.00	2.00
❑ 332	Volcanic Hammer C :R:	.12	.30
❑ 333	Wall of Air U :B:	.50	1.00
❑ 334	Wall of Bone U :K:	.50	1.00
❑ 335	Wall of Fire U :R:	.50	1.00
❑ 336	Wall of Spears U :A:	.20	.50
❑ 337	Wall of Swords U :W:	.50	1.00
❑ 338	Wall of Wonder R :B:	1.00	2.00
❑ 339	Western Paladin R :K:	1.00	2.00
❑ 340	Wild Growth C :G:	.12	.30
❑ 341	Wildfire R :R:	2.00	4.00
❑ 342	Wind Dancer U :B:	.20	.50
❑ 343	Wind Drake C :B:	.12	.30
❑ 344	Wing Snare U :G:	.20	.50
❑ 345	Wood Elves C :G:	.12	.30
❑ 346	Wooden Sphere U :A:	.20	.50
❑ 347	Worship R :W:	4.00	8.00
❑ 348	Wrath of God R :W:	10.00	20.00
❑ 349	Yavimaya Enchantress U :G:	.20	.50
❑ 350	Yawgmoth's Edict U :K:	.20	.50

2001 Magic the Gathering 7th Edition Foil

Item	Low	High
COMPLETE SET (350)	600.00	900.00

*Foil: 1X to 2X Basic Cards

2001 Magic the Gathering Planeshift

Item	Low	High
Complete Set (143)	75.00	110.00
Theme Deck Box	100.00	125.00
Theme Deck	10.00	13.50
Booster Box (36 Packs)	100.00	160.00
Booster Pack (15 Cards)	4.50	5.50
Fat Pack	40.00	50.00

❑	Card	Low	High
❑ 1	Allied Strategies U :B:	.50	1.00
❑ 2	Alpha Kavu U :G:	.50	1.00
❑ 3	Amphibious Kavu C :G:	.12	.30
❑ 4	Ancient Spider R :D:	1.00	2.00
❑ 5	Arctic Merfolk C :B:	.12	.30
❑ 6	Aura Blast C :W:	.12	.30
❑ 7	Aurora Griffin C :W:	.12	.30
❑ 8	Bog Down C :K:	.12	.30
❑ 9	Caldera Kavu C :R:	.12	.30
❑ 10	Cavern Harpy C :D:	.12	.30
❑ 11	Cloud Cover R :D:	2.00	3.00
❑ 12	Confound C :B:	.12	.30

Card	Low	High
❑ 13 Crosis's Catacombs U :L:	1.00	2.00
❑ 14 Crosis's Charm U :D:	.20	.50
❑ 15 Darigaaz's Caldera U :L:	1.00	2.00
❑ 16 Darigaaz's Charm U :D:	.20	.50
❑ 17 Daring Leap C :D:	.12	.30
❑ 18 Dark Suspicions R :K:	2.00	4.00
❑ 19 Deadapult R :R:	1.00	2.00
❑ 20 Death Bomb C :K:	.12	.30
❑ 21 Destructive Flow R :D:	1.00	2.00
❑ 22 Diabolic Intent R :K:	2.00	3.00
❑ 23 Disciple of Kangee C :W:	.12	.30
❑ 24 Dominaria's Judgment R :W:	2.00	3.00
❑ 25 Doomsday Specter R :D:	2.00	4.00
❑ 26 Draco R :A:	4.00	8.00
❑ 27 Dralnu's Crusade R :D:	1.00	2.00
❑ 28 Dralnu's Pet R :B:	1.50	3.00
❑ 29 Dromar's Cavern U :L:	1.00	2.00
❑ 30 Dromar's Charm U :D:	.50	1.00
❑ 31 Eladamri's Call R :D:	3.00	5.00
❑ 32 Ertai, the Corrupted R :D:	1.50	3.00
❑ 33 Ertai's Trickery U :B:	.50	1.00
❑ 34 Escape Routes C :B:	.12	.30
❑ 35 Exotic Disease U :K:	.20	.50
❑ 36 Falling Timber C :G:	.12	.30
❑ 37 Flametongue Kavu U :R:	3.00	5.00
❑ 38 Fleetfoot Panther U :D:	.50	1.00
❑ 39 Forsaken City R :L:	2.00	3.00
❑ 40 Gaea's Herald R :G:	2.00	3.00
❑ 41 Gaea's Might C :G:	.12	.30
❑ 42 Gainsay U :B:	.50	1.00
❑ 43 Gerrard's Command C :D:	.12	.30
❑ 44 Goblin Game R :R:	2.00	4.00
❑ 45 Guard Dogs U :W:	.50	1.00
❑ 46 Heroic Defiance C :W:	.12	.30
❑ 47 Hobble C :W:	.12	.30
❑ 48 Honorable Scout C :W:	.12	.30
❑ 49 Horned Kavu C :D:	.12	.30
❑ 50 Hull Breach C :D:	.12	.30
❑ 51 Hunting Drake C :B:	.12	.30
❑ 52 Implode U :R:	.20	.50
❑ 53 Insolence C :R:	.12	.30
❑ 54 Kavu Recluse C :R:	.12	.30
❑ 55 Keldon Mantle C :R:	.12	.30
❑ 56 Keldon Twilight R :D:	1.00	2.00
❑ 57 Lashknife Barrier U :W:	.50	1.00
❑ 58 Lava Zombie C :D:	.12	.30
❑ 59 Lord of the Undead R :K:	3.50	6.00
❑ 60 Maggot Carrier C :K:	.12	.30
❑ 61 Magma Burst C :R:	.12	.30
❑ 62 Magnigoth Treefolk R :G:	2.00	3.00
❑ 63 Malicious Advice C :D:	.12	.30
❑ 64 Mana Cylix U :A:	.50	1.00
❑ 65 March of Souls R :W:	1.00	2.00
❑ 66 Marsh Crocodile U :D:	.50	1.00
❑ 67 Meddling Mage R :D:	18.00	20.00
❑ 68 Meteor Crater R :L:	1.50	3.00
❑ 69 Mire Kavu C :R:	.12	.30
❑ 70 Mirrorwood Treefolk U :G:	.50	1.00
❑ 71 Mogg Jailer U :R:	.50	1.00
❑ 72 Mogg Sentry R :R:	2.00	4.00
❑ 73 Morgue Toad C :K:	.12	.30
❑ 74 Multani's Harmony U :G:	.50	1.00
❑ 75 Natural Emergence R :D:	1.50	3.00
❑ 76 Nemata, Grove Guardian R :G:	2.00	4.00
❑ 77 Nightscape Battlemage U :K:	.20	.50
❑ 78 Nightscape Familiar C :K:	.12	.30
❑ 79 Noxious Vapors U :K:	.50	1.00
❑ 80 Orim's Chant R :W:	18.00	22.00
❑ 81 Phyrexian Bloodstock C :K:	.12	.30
❑ 82 Phyrexian Scuta R :K:	3.50	6.00
❑ 83 Phyrexian Tyranny R :D:	1.50	3.00
❑ 84 Planar Overlay R :B:	1.50	3.00
❑ 85 Planeswalker's Favor R :G:	1.50	3.00
❑ 86 Planeswalker's Fury R :R:	2.00	4.00
❑ 87 Planeswalker's Mirth R :W:	1.50	3.00
❑ 88 Planeswalker's Mischief R :B:	1.50	3.00
❑ 89 Planeswalker's Scorn R :K:	1.50	3.00
❑ 90 Pollen Remedy C :W:	.12	.30
❑ 91 Primal Growth C :G:	.12	.30
❑ 92 Pygmy Kavu C :G:	.12	.30
❑ 93 Questing Phelddagrif R :D:	1.00	2.00
❑ 94 Quirion Dryad R :G:	2.00	4.00
❑ 95 Quirion Explorer C :G:	.12	.30
❑ 96 Radiant Kavu R :D:	1.00	2.00
❑ 97 Razing Snidd U :D:	.20	.50
❑ 98 Rith's Charm U :D:	.50	1.00
❑ 99 Rith's Grove U :L:	.75	1.50
❑ 100 Root Greevil C :G:	.12	.30
❑ 101 Rushing River C :B:	.12	.30
❑ 102 Samite Elder R :W:	2.00	3.00
❑ 103 Samite Pilgrim C :W:	.12	.30
❑ 104 Sawtooth Loon U :D:	.20	.50
❑ 105 Sea Snidd C :B:	.12	.30
❑ 106 Shifting Sky U :B:	.50	1.00
❑ 107 Shivan Wurm R :D:	4.00	7.00
❑ 108 Shriek of Dread C :K:	.12	.30
❑ 109 Silver Drake C :D:	.12	.30
❑ 110 Singe C :R:	.12	.30
❑ 111 Sinister Strength C :K:	.12	.30
❑ 112 Sisay's Ingenuity C :B:	.12	.30
❑ 113 Skyship Weatherlight R :A:	1.50	3.00
❑ 114 Skyshroud Blessing U :G:	.50	1.00
❑ 115 Slay U :K:	.50	1.00
❑ 116 Sleeping Potion C :B:	.12	.30
❑ 117 Slingshot Goblin C :R:	.12	.30
❑ 118 Sparkcaster U :D:	.20	.50
❑ 119 Star Compass U :A:	.20	.50
❑ 120 Steel Leaf Paladin C :D:	.12	.30
❑ 121 Stone Kavu C :G:	.12	.30
❑ 122 Stormscape Battlemage U :B:	.20	.50
❑ 123 Stormscape Familiar C :B:	.12	.30
❑ 124 Strafe U :R:	.20	.50
❑ 125 Stratadon U :A:	.50	1.00
❑ 126 Sunken Hope R :B:	2.00	3.00
❑ 127 Sunscape Battlemage U :W:	.20	.50
❑ 128 Sunscape Familiar C :W:	.12	.30
❑ 129 Surprise Deployment U :W:	.20	.50
❑ 130 Tahngarth, Talruum Hero R :R:	1.00	2.00
❑ 131 Terminal Moraine U :L:	.20	.50
❑ 132 Terminate C :D:	.30	.75
❑ 133 Thornscape Battlemage U :G:	.20	.50
❑ 134 Thornscape Familiar C :G:	.12	.30
❑ 135 Thunderscape Battlemage U :R:	.20	.50
❑ 136 Thunderscape Familiar C :R:	.12	.30
❑ 137 Treva's Charm U :D:	.50	1.00
❑ 138 Treva's Ruins U :L:	1.00	2.00
❑ 139 Urza's Guilt R :D:	1.50	3.00
❑ 140 Voice of All U :W:	1.00	2.00
❑ 141 Volcano Imp C :K:	.12	.30
❑ 142 Warped Devotion U :K:	.50	1.00
❑ 143 Waterspout Elemental R :B:	1.50	3.00

2001 Magic the Gathering Planeshift Foil

COMPLETE SET (143)	300.00	500.00

*Foil: 1X to 2X Basic Cards

2001 Magic the Gathering Apocalypse

Card	Low	High
Complete Set (143)	75.00	110.00
Theme Deck Box	110.00	150.00
Theme Deck	12.00	15.00
Booster Box (36 Packs)	175.00	225.00
Booster Pack (15 Cards)	5.00	7.00
Fat Pack	30.00	60.00
❑ 1 AEther Mutation U :D:	.20	.50
❑ 2 Ana Disciple C :G:	.12	.30
❑ 3 Ana Sanctuary U :G:	.50	1.00
❑ 4 Anavolver R :G:	1.50	3.00
❑ 5 Angelfire Crusader C :W:	.12	.30
❑ 6 Battlefield Forge R :L:	5.00	10.00
❑ 7 Bloodfire Colossus R :R:	2.00	4.00
❑ 8 Bloodfire Dwarf C :R:	.12	.30
❑ 9 Bloodfire Infusion C :R:	.12	.30
❑ 10 Bloodfire Kavu U :R:	.50	1.00
❑ 11 Bog Gnarr C :G:	.12	.30
❑ 12 Brass Herald U :A:	.50	1.00
❑ 13 Captain's Maneuver U :D:	.50	1.00
❑ 14 Caves of Koilos R :L:	5.00	10.00
❑ 15 Ceta Disciple C :B:	.12	.30
❑ 16 Ceta Sanctuary U :B:	.50	1.00
❑ 17 Cetavolver R :B:	1.50	3.00
❑ 18 Chaos/Order U :R:/:W:	.50	1.00
❑ 19 Coalition Flag U :W:	.50	1.00
❑ 20 Coalition Honor Guard C :W:	.12	.30
❑ 21 Coastal Drake C :B:	.12	.30
❑ 22 Consume Strength C :D:	.12	.30
❑ 23 Cromat R :D:	1.50	3.00
❑ 24 Day/Night U :W:/:K:	.50	1.00
❑ 25 Dead Ringers C :K:	.12	.30
❑ 26 Death Grasp R :D:	2.00	4.00
❑ 27 Death Mutation U :D:	.50	1.00
❑ 28 Death/Life U :G:/:K:	.50	1.00
❑ 29 Dega Disciple C :W:	.12	.30
❑ 30 Dega Sanctuary U :W:	.50	1.00
❑ 31 Degavolver R :W:	1.50	3.00
❑ 32 Desolation Angel R :K:	2.50	5.00
❑ 33 Desolation Giant R :R:	1.00	2.00
❑ 34 Diversionary Tactics U :W:	.50	1.00
❑ 35 Divine Light C :W:	.12	.30
❑ 36 Dodecapod U :A:	.50	1.00
❑ 37 Dragon Arch U :A:	1.00	2.00
❑ 38 Dwarven Landslide C :R:	.12	.30
❑ 39 Dwarven Patrol U :R:	.50	1.00
❑ 40 Ebony Treefolk U :D:	.50	1.00
❑ 41 Emblazoned Golem U :A:	.50	1.00
❑ 42 Enlistment Officer U :W:	.20	.50
❑ 43 Evasive Action U :B:	.50	1.00
❑ 44 False Dawn R :W:	1.00	2.50
❑ 45 Fervent Charge R :D:	1.50	3.00
❑ 46 Fire/Ice U :R:/:B:	1.50	3.00
❑ 47 Flowstone Charger U :D:	.20	.50
❑ 48 Foul Presence U :K:	.20	.50
❑ 49 Fungal Shambler R :D:	1.50	3.00
❑ 50 Gaea's Balance U :G:	.50	1.00
❑ 51 Gaea's Skyfolk C :D:	.12	.30
❑ 52 Gerrard Capashen R :W:	1.50	3.00
❑ 53 Gerrard's Verdict U :D:	.50	1.00
❑ 54 Glade Gnarr C :G:	.12	.30
❑ 55 Goblin Legionnaire C :D:	.12	.30
❑ 56 Goblin Ringleader U :R:	1.50	3.00
❑ 57 Goblin Trenches R :D:	2.00	4.00
❑ 58 Grave Defiler U :K:	.50	1.00
❑ 59 Guided Passage R :D:	1.00	2.00
❑ 60 Haunted Angel U :W:	.50	1.00
❑ 61 Helionaut C :W:	.12	.30
❑ 62 Ice Cave R :B:	1.00	2.00
❑ 64 Illuminate U :R:	.50	1.00
❑ 65 Illusion/Reality U :B:/:G:	.50	1.00
❑ 66 Index C :B:	.12	.30
❑ 67 Jaded Response C :B:	.12	.30
❑ 68 Jilt C :B:	.12	.30
❑ 69 Jungle Barrier U :D:	.50	1.00
❑ 70 Kavu Glider C :R:	.12	.30
❑ 71 Kavu Howler U :G:	.50	1.00
❑ 72 Kavu Mauler R :G:	1.50	3.00
❑ 73 Last Caress C :K:	.12	.30
❑ 74 Last Stand R :D:	1.00	2.50
❑ 75 Lay of the Land C :G:	.12	.30
❑ 76 Legacy Weapon R :A:	1.50	3.00
❑ 78 Lightning Angel R :D:	2.50	5.00
❑ 79 Living Airship C :B:	.12	.30
❑ 80 Llanowar Dead C :D:	.12	.30
❑ 81 Llanowar Wastes R :L:	5.00	10.00
❑ 82 Manacles of Decay C :W:	.12	.30
❑ 83 Martyrs' Tomb U :D:	.50	1.00
❑ 84 Mask of Intolerance R :A:	1.00	2.00
❑ 85 Mind Extraction C :K:	.12	.30
❑ 86 Minotaur Illusionist U :D:	.50	1.00
❑ 87 Minotaur Tactician C :R:	.12	.30
❑ 88 Mournful Zombie C :K:	.12	.30
❑ 89 Mystic Snake R :D:	2.50	5.00
❑ 90 Necra Disciple C :K:	.12	.30
❑ 91 Necra Sanctuary U :K:	.50	1.00
❑ 92 Necravolver R :K:	1.00	2.00
❑ 95 Orim's Thunder C :W:	.12	.30
❑ 96 Overgrown Estate R :D:	1.00	2.00
❑ 97 Penumbra Bobcat C :G:	.12	.30
❑ 98 Penumbra Kavu U :G:	.30	.75
❑ 99 Penumbra Wurm R :G:	2.00	4.00
❑ 100 Pernicious Deed R :D:	7.50	15.00
❑ 101 Phyrexian Arena R :K:	3.00	6.00
❑ 102 Phyrexian Gargantua U :K:	.30	.75
❑ 103 Phyrexian Rager C :K:	.12	.30
❑ 104 Planar Despair R :K:	1.00	2.00
❑ 105 Powerstone Minefield R :D:	2.00	4.00
❑ 106 Prophetic Bolt R :D:	1.00	2.00
❑ 107 Putrid Warrior C :D:	.12	.30
❑ 108 Quagmire Druid C :K:	.12	.30
❑ 109 Quicksilver Dagger C :D:	.12	.30
❑ 110 Raka Disciple C :R:	.12	.30
❑ 111 Raka Sanctuary U :R:	.30	.75
❑ 112 Rakavolver R :R:	1.00	2.00
❑ 113 Razorfin Hunter C :D:	.12	.30
❑ 115 Reef Shaman C :B:	.12	.30
❑ 116 Savage Gorilla C :G:	.12	.30
❑ 117 Shield of Duty and Reason C :W:	.12	.30
❑ 118 Shimmering Mirage C :B:	.12	.30
❑ 119 Shivan Reef R :L:	6.00	12.00
❑ 120 Smash C :R:	.12	.30
❑ 121 Soul Link C :D:	.12	.30
❑ 122 Spectral Lynx R :W:	2.00	4.00
❑ 123 Spiritmonger R :D:	6.00	12.00
❑ 124 Squee's Embrace C :D:	.12	.30
❑ 125 Squee's Revenge U :D:	.20	.50
❑ 126 Standard Bearer C :W:	.12	.30
❑ 127 Strength of Night C :G:	.12	.30
❑ 128 Suffocating Blast R :D:	1.50	3.00
❑ 129 Suppress U :K:	.30	.75
❑ 130 Sylvan Messenger U :G:	.50	1.00
❑ 131 Symbiotic Deployment R :G:	1.00	2.00
❑ 132 Tahngarth's Glare C :R:	.12	.30
❑ 133 Temporal Spring C :D:	.12	.30
❑ 134 Tidal Courier U :B:	.30	.75
❑ 135 Tranquil Path C :G:	.12	.30
❑ 136 Tundra Kavu C :R:	.12	.30
❑ 137 Unnatural Selection R :B:	2.00	4.00
❑ 138 Urborg Elf C :G:	.12	.30
❑ 139 Urborg Uprising C :K:	.12	.30
❑ 140 Vindicate R :D:	6.00	12.00
❑ 141 Vodalian Mystic U :B:	.50	1.00
❑ 142 Whirlpool Drake U :B:	.50	1.00
❑ 143 Whirlpool Rider C :B:	.12	.30
❑ 144 Whirlpool Warrior R :B:	1.50	3.00
❑ 145 Wild Research R :R:	1.50	3.00
❑ 146 Yavimaya Coast R :L:	5.00	10.00
❑ 147 Yavimaya's Embrace R :D:	1.00	2.50
❑ 148 Zombie Boa C :K:	.12	.30

2001 Magic the Gathering Apocalypse Foil

*Foil: 1X to 2X Basic Cards

2001 Magic the Gathering Odyssey

Card	Low	High
Complete Set (350)	125.00	200.00
Theme Deck Box	75.00	100.00
Theme Deck	9.00	12.00
Booster Box (36 Packs)	100.00	120.00
Booster Pack (15 Cards)	4.00	5.00
Fat Pack	30.00	40.00
❑ 1 Abandoned Outpost C :L:	.12	.30
❑ 2 Aboshan, Cephalid Emperor R :B:	2.00	4.00
❑ 3 Aboshan's Desire C :B:	.12	.30
❑ 4 Acceptable Losses C :R:	.12	.30
❑ 5 Aegis of Honor R :W:	2.00	4.00
❑ 6 AEther Burst C :B:	.12	.30
❑ 7 Afflict C :K:	.12	.30
❑ 8 Amugaba R :B:	1.50	3.00
❑ 9 Anarchist C :R:	.12	.30
❑ 10 Ancestral Tribute R :W:	1.00	2.00
❑ 11 Angelic Wall C :W:	.12	.30
❑ 12 Animal Boneyard U :W:	.50	1.00
❑ 13 Ashen Firebeast R :R:	1.50	3.00
❑ 14 Atogatog R :D:	1.50	3.00
❑ 15 Aura Graft U :B:	.20	.50
❑ 16 Auramancer C :W:	.12	.30
❑ 17 Aven Archer U :W:	.50	1.00
❑ 18 Aven Cloudchaser C :W:	.12	.30
❑ 19 Aven Fisher C :B:	.12	.30
❑ 20 Aven Flock C :W:	.12	.30
❑ 21 Aven Shrine R :W:	1.00	2.00
❑ 22 Aven Smokeweaver U :B:	.50	1.00
❑ 23 Aven Windreader C :B:	.12	.30
❑ 24 Balancing Act R :W:	1.50	3.00
❑ 25 Balshan Beguiler U :B:	.50	1.00
❑ 26 Balshan Griffin U :B:	.50	1.00
❑ 27 Bamboozle U :B:	.50	1.00
❑ 28 Barbarian Lunatic C :R:	.12	.30
❑ 29 Barbarian Ring U :L:	.50	1.00
❑ 30 Bash to Bits U :R:	.50	1.00
❑ 31 Battle of Wits R :B:	1.50	3.00
❑ 32 Battle Strain U :R:	.20	.50
❑ 33 Bearscape R :G:	2.00	4.00
❑ 34 Beast Attack U :G:	.50	1.00
❑ 35 Beloved Chaplain U :W:	.50	1.00
❑ 36 Blazing Salvo C :R:	.12	.30
❑ 37 Blessed Orator U :W:	.50	1.00
❑ 38 Bloodcurdler R :K:	1.00	2.00
❑ 39 Bog Wreckage C :L:	.12	.30
❑ 40 Bomb Squad R :R:	.50	1.00
❑ 41 Braids, Cabal Minion R :K:	2.50	5.00
❑ 42 Buried Alive U :K:	1.50	3.00
❑ 43 Burning Sands R :R:	1.50	3.00
❑ 44 Cabal Inquisitor C :K:	.12	.30
❑ 45 Cabal Patriarch R :K:	1.50	3.00
❑ 46 Cabal Pit U :L:	.50	1.00
❑ 47 Cabal Shrine R :K:	1.00	2.00
❑ 48 Call of the Herd R :G:	5.00	10.00
❑ 49 Cantivore R :W:	1.00	2.00
❑ 50 Careful Study C :B:	.12	.30
❑ 51 Cartographer C :G:	.12	.30
❑ 52 Catalyst Stone R :A:	1.50	3.00
❑ 53 Caustic Tar U :K:	.50	1.00
❑ 54 Cease-Fire C :W:	.12	.30
❑ 55 Centaur Garden U :L:	.20	.50
❑ 56 Cephalid Broker U :B:	.50	1.00
❑ 57 Cephalid Coliseum U :L:	.50	1.00
❑ 58 Cephalid Looter C :B:	.12	.30
❑ 59 Cephalid Retainer R :B:	1.50	3.00
❑ 60 Cephalid Scout C :B:	.12	.30
❑ 61 Cephalid Shrine R :B:	1.00	2.00
❑ 62 Chainflinger C :R:	.12	.30
❑ 63 Chamber of Manipulation U :B:	.50	1.00
❑ 64 Chance Encounter R :R:	1.00	2.00
❑ 65 Charmed Pendant R :A:	1.00	2.50
❑ 66 Chatter of the Squirrel C :G:	.12	.30
❑ 67 Childhood Horror U :K:	.50	1.00
❑ 68 Chlorophant R :G:	1.50	3.00
❑ 69 Coffin Purge C :K:	.12	.30
❑ 70 Cognivore R :B:	1.50	3.00
❑ 71 Concentrate U :B:	.50	1.00
❑ 72 Confessor C :W:	.12	.30
❑ 73 Crashing Centaur U :G:	.20	.50
❑ 74 Crypt Creeper C :K:	.12	.30
❑ 75 Crystal Quarry R :L:	2.50	5.00
❑ 76 Cultural Exchange R :B:	1.00	2.00
❑ 77 Cursed Monstrosity R :K:	1.50	3.00
❑ 78 Darkwater Catacombs R :L:	2.00	4.00
❑ 79 Darkwater Egg U :A:	.50	1.00
❑ 80 Decaying Soil R :K:	1.00	2.00
❑ 81 Decimate R :D:	1.50	3.00
❑ 82 Decompose U :K:	.50	1.00
❑ 83 Dedicated Martyr C :W:	.12	.30
❑ 84 Deep Reconnaissance U :G:	.50	1.00
❑ 85 Delaying Shield R :W:	1.00	2.00
❑ 86 Deluge U :B:	.20	.50
❑ 87 Dematerialize C :B:	.12	.30
❑ 88 Demolish U :R:	.50	1.00
❑ 89 Demoralize C :R:	.12	.30
❑ 90 Deserted Temple R :L:	1.50	3.00
❑ 91 Devoted Caretaker R :W:	2.00	4.00
❑ 92 Diabolic Tutor U :K:	1.50	3.00
❑ 93 Diligent Farmhand C :G:	.12	.30
❑ 94 Dirty Wererat C :K:	.12	.30
❑ 95 Divert R :B:	1.00	2.00
❑ 96 Divine Sacrament R :W:	2.00	4.00
❑ 97 Dogged Hunter R :W:	1.00	2.50
❑ 98 Dreamwinder C :B:	.12	.30
❑ 99 Druid Lyrist C :G:	.12	.30
❑ 100 Druid's Call U :G:	.50	1.00
❑ 101 Dusk Imp C :K:	.12	.30
❑ 102 Dwarven Grunt C :R:	.12	.30
❑ 103 Dwarven Recruiter U :R:	.50	1.00
❑ 104 Dwarven Shrine R :R:	1.00	2.00
❑ 105 Dwarven Strike Force U :R:	.50	1.00
❑ 106 Earnest Fellowship R :W:	1.50	3.00
❑ 107 Earth Rift C :R:	.12	.30
❑ 108 Elephant Ambush C :G:	.12	.30
❑ 109 Ember Beast C :R:	.12	.30
❑ 110 Embolden C :W:	.12	.30
❑ 111 Engulfing Flames U :R:	.50	1.00
❑ 112 Entomb R :K:	4.00	8.00
❑ 113 Epicenter R :R:	1.00	2.00
❑ 114 Escape Artist C :B:	.12	.30
❑ 115 Execute U :K:	.50	1.00
❑ 116 Extract R :B:	2.00	4.00
❑ 117 Face of Fear U :K:	.50	1.00
❑ 118 Famished Ghoul U :K:	.50	1.00
❑ 119 Fervent Denial U :B:	.20	.50
❑ 120 Filthy Cur C :K:	.12	.30
❑ 121 Firebolt C :R:	.12	.30
❑ 122 Flame Burst C :R:	.12	.30
❑ 123 Fledgling Imp C :K:	.12	.30
❑ 124 Forest v1 C :L:	.12	.30
❑ 125 Forest v2 C :L:	.12	.30
❑ 126 Forest v3 C :L:	.12	.30
❑ 127 Forest v4 C :L:	.12	.30
❑ 128 Frenetic Ogre U :R:	.50	1.00
❑ 129 Frightcrawler C :K:	.12	.30
❑ 130 Gallantry U :W:	.50	1.00
❑ 131 Ghastly Demise C :K:	.12	.30
❑ 132 Gorilla Titan U :G:	.50	1.00
❑ 133 Graceful Antelope R :W:	1.00	2.00
❑ 134 Gravedigger C :K:	.12	.30
❑ 135 Gravestorm R :K:	2.00	4.00
❑ 136 Ground Seal R :G:	2.00	4.00
❑ 137 Halberdier C :R:	.12	.30
❑ 138 Hallowed Healer C :W:	.12	.30
❑ 139 Haunting Echoes R :K:	6.00	12.00
❑ 140 Hint of Insanity R :K:	1.00	2.00
❑ 141 Holistic Wisdom R :G:	2.00	4.00
❑ 142 Howling Gale U :G:	.50	1.00
❑ 143 Immobilizing Ink C :B:	.12	.30
❑ 144 Impulsive Maneuvers R :R:	1.00	2.00
❑ 145 Infected Vermin U :K:	.50	1.00
❑ 146 Innocent Blood C :K:	.12	.30
❑ 147 Iridescent Angel R :D:	5.00	10.00
❑ 148 Island v1 C :L:	.12	.30
❑ 149 Island v2 C :L:	.12	.30
❑ 150 Island v3 C :L:	.12	.30
❑ 151 Island v4 C :L:	.12	.30
❑ 152 Ivy Elemental R :G:	2.00	4.00
❑ 153 Junk Golem R :A:	1.00	2.00
❑ 154 Kamahl, Pit Fighter R :R:	3.00	6.00
❑ 155 Kamahl's Desire C :R:	.12	.30
❑ 156 Karmic Justice R :W:	1.50	3.00
❑ 157 Kirtar's Desire C :W:	.12	.30
❑ 158 Kirtar's Wrath R :W:	2.00	4.00
❑ 159 Krosan Archer C :G:	.12	.30
❑ 160 Krosan Avenger C :G:	.12	.30
❑ 161 Krosan Beast R :G:	2.00	4.00
❑ 162 Laquatus's Creativity U :B:	.50	1.00
❑ 163 Last Rites C :K:	.12	.30
❑ 164 Lava Blister U :R:	.50	1.00
❑ 165 Leaf Dancer C :G:	.12	.30
❑ 166 Lieutenant Kirtar R :W:	2.00	4.00
❑ 167 Life Burst C :W:	.12	.30
❑ 168 Limestone Golem U :A:	.50	1.00
❑ 169 Liquid Fire U :R:	.50	1.00
❑ 170 Lithatog U :D:	.50	1.00
❑ 171 Luminous Guardian U :W:	.50	1.00
❑ 172 Mad Dog C :R:	.12	.30
❑ 173 Magma Vein U :R:	.20	.50
❑ 174 Magnivore R :R:	1.00	2.00
❑ 175 Malevolent Awakening U :K:	.20	.50
❑ 176 Master Apothecary R :W:	1.50	3.00
❑ 177 Metamorphic Wurm U :G:	.50	1.00
❑ 178 Millikin U :A:	.50	1.00
❑ 179 Mind Burst C :K:	.12	.30
❑ 180 Mindslicer R :K:	2.00	4.00
❑ 181 Mine Layer R :R:	1.50	3.00
❑ 182 Minotaur Explorer U :R:	.50	1.00
❑ 183 Mirari R :A:	6.00	12.00
❑ 184 Molten Influence R :R:	2.00	4.00
❑ 185 Moment's Peace C :G:	.12	.30
❑ 186 Morbid Hunger C :K:	.12	.30
❑ 187 Morgue Theft C :K:	.12	.30
❑ 188 Mortivore R :K:	2.50	5.00
❑ 189 Mossfire Egg U :A:	.50	1.00
❑ 190 Mossfire Valley R :L:	2.00	4.00
❑ 191 Mountain v1 C :L:	.12	.30
❑ 192 Mountain v2 C :L:	.12	.30
❑ 193 Mountain v3 C :L:	.12	.30
❑ 194 Mountain v4 C :L:	.12	.30
❑ 195 Mudhole R :R:	1.50	3.00
❑ 196 Muscle Burst C :G:	.12	.30
❑ 197 Mystic Crusader R :W:	2.00	4.00
❑ 198 Mystic Enforcer R :D:	3.00	6.00
❑ 199 Mystic Penitent U :W:	.50	1.00
❑ 200 Mystic Visionary C :W:	.12	.30
❑ 201 Mystic Zealot C :W:	.12	.30
❑ 202 Nantuko Disciple C :G:	.12	.30
❑ 203 Nantuko Elder U :G:	.50	1.00
❑ 204 Nantuko Mentor R :G:	1.50	3.00
❑ 205 Nantuko Shrine R :G:	1.50	3.00
❑ 206 Need for Speed R :R:	1.50	3.00
❑ 207 Nefarious Lich R :K:	1.50	3.00
❑ 208 New Frontiers R :G:	2.00	4.00
❑ 209 Nimble Mongoose U :G:	.50	1.00
❑ 210 Nomad Decoy U :W:	.50	1.00
❑ 211 Nomad Stadium U :L:	.50	1.00
❑ 212 Nut Collector R :G:	2.50	5.00
❑ 213 Obstinate Familiar R :R:	1.50	3.00
❑ 214 Otarian Juggernaut R :A:	1.50	3.00
❑ 215 Overeager Apprentice C :K:	.12	.30
❑ 216 Overrun U :G:	1.00	2.00
❑ 217 Painbringer U :K:	.50	1.00
❑ 218 Pardic Firecat C :R:	.12	.30
❑ 219 Pardic Miner R :R:	1.50	3.00
❑ 220 Pardic Swordsmith C :R:	.12	.30
❑ 221 Patchwork Gnomes U :A:	.50	1.00
❑ 222 Patriarch's Desire C :K:	.12	.30
❑ 223 Patrol Hound C :W:	.12	.30
❑ 224 Patron Wizard R :B:	2.00	4.00
❑ 225 Pedantic Learning R :B:	1.50	3.00
❑ 226 Peek C :B:	.12	.30
❑ 227 Persuasion R :B:	1.50	3.00
❑ 228 Petrified Field R :L:	1.50	3.00
❑ 229 Phantatog U :D:	.50	1.00
❑ 230 Phantom Whelp C :B:	.12	.30
❑ 231 Pianna, Nomad Captain R :W:	2.00	4.00
❑ 232 Pilgrim of Justice C :W:	.12	.30
❑ 233 Pilgrim of Virtue C :W:	.12	.30
❑ 234 Piper's Melody U :G:	.20	.50
❑ 235 Plains v1 C :L:	.12	.30
❑ 236 Plains v2 C :L:	.12	.30
❑ 237 Plains v3 C :L:	.12	.30
❑ 238 Plains v4 C :L:	.12	.30
❑ 239 Predict U :B:	.20	.50
❑ 240 Price of Glory U :R:	.20	.50
❑ 241 Primal Frenzy C :G:	.12	.30
❑ 242 Psionic Gift C :B:	.12	.30
❑ 243 Psychatog U :D:	2.00	4.00

MAGIC

Card	Low	High
❑ 244 Pulsating Illusion U :B:	.50	1.00
❑ 245 Puppeteer U :B:	.50	1.00
❑ 246 Rabid Elephant C :G:	.12	.30
❑ 247 Ravaged Highlands C :L:	.12	.30
❑ 248 Ray of Distortion C :W:	.12	.30
❑ 249 Reckless Charge C :R:	.12	.30
❑ 250 Recoup U :R:	.50	1.00
❑ 251 Refresh C :G:	.12	.30
❑ 252 Repel C :B:	.12	.30
❑ 253 Repentant Vampire R :K:	2.00	4.00
❑ 254 Resilient Wanderer U :W:	.20	.50
❑ 255 Rites of Initiation C :R:	.12	.30
❑ 256 Rites of Refusal C :B:	.12	.30
❑ 257 Rites of Spring C :G:	.12	.30
❑ 258 Roar of the Wurm U :G:	1.50	3.00
❑ 259 Rotting Giant U :K:	.20	.50
❑ 260 Sacred Rites C :W:	.12	.30
❑ 261 Sadistic Hypnotist U :K:	.20	.50
❑ 262 Sandstone Deadfall U :A:	.20	.50
❑ 263 Sarcatog U :D:	.50	1.00
❑ 264 Savage Firecat R :R:	1.50	3.00
❑ 265 Scorching Missile C :R:	.12	.30
❑ 266 Screams of the Damned U :K:	.20	.50
❑ 267 Scrivener C :B:	.12	.30
❑ 268 Seafloor Debris C :L:	.12	.30
❑ 269 Second Thoughts C :W:	.12	.30
❑ 270 Seize the Day R :R:	1.50	3.00
❑ 271 Seton, Krosan Protector R :G:	1.50	3.00
❑ 272 Seton's Desire C :G:	.12	.30
❑ 273 Shadowblood Egg U :A:	.50	1.00
❑ 274 Shadowblood Ridge R :L:	2.00	4.00
❑ 275 Shadowmage Infiltrator R :D:	5.00	10.00
❑ 276 Shelter C :W:	.12	.30
❑ 277 Shifty Doppelganger R :B:	1.00	2.00
❑ 278 Shower of Coals U :R:	.50	1.00
❑ 279 Simplify C :G:	.12	.30
❑ 280 Skeletal Scrying U :K:	.50	1.00
❑ 281 Skull Fracture U :K:	.50	1.00
❑ 282 Skycloud Egg U :A:	.50	1.00
❑ 283 Skycloud Expanse R :L:	2.00	4.00
❑ 284 Skyshooter U :G:	.20	.50
❑ 285 Soulcatcher U :W:	.50	1.00
❑ 286 Spark Mage U :R:	.20	.50
❑ 287 Spellbane Centaur R :G:	2.00	4.00
❑ 288 Sphere of Duty U :W:	.20	.50
❑ 289 Sphere of Grace U :W:	.50	1.00
❑ 290 Sphere of Law U :W:	.20	.50
❑ 291 Sphere of Reason U :W:	.20	.50
❑ 292 Sphere of Truth U :W:	.50	1.00
❑ 293 Spiritualize U :W:	.20	.50
❑ 294 Springing Tiger C :G:	.12	.30
❑ 295 Squirrel Mob R :G:	2.50	5.00
❑ 296 Squirrel Nest U :G:	2.50	5.00
❑ 297 Stalking Bloodsucker R :K:	1.50	3.00
❑ 298 Standstill U :B:	2.50	5.00
❑ 299 Steam Vines U :R:	.50	1.00
❑ 300 Steamclaw U :A:	.20	.50
❑ 301 Still Life U :G:	.50	1.00
❑ 302 Stone-Tongue Basilisk R :G:	2.00	4.00
❑ 303 Sungrass Egg U :A:	.50	1.00
❑ 304 Sungrass Prairie R :L:	2.00	4.00
❑ 305 Swamp v1 C :L:	.12	.30
❑ 306 Swamp v2 C :L:	.12	.30
❑ 307 Swamp v3 C :L:	.12	.30
❑ 308 Swamp v4 C :L:	.12	.30
❑ 309 Sylvan Might U :G:	.50	1.00
❑ 310 Syncopate C :B:	.12	.30
❑ 311 Tainted Pact R :K:	2.00	4.00
❑ 312 Tarnished Citadel R :L:	1.00	2.00
❑ 313 Tattoo Ward U :W:	.20	.50
❑ 314 Terravore R :G:	2.00	4.00
❑ 315 Testament of Faith U :W:	.20	.50
❑ 316 Thaumatog U :D:	.20	.50
❑ 317 Thermal Blast C :R:	.12	.30
❑ 318 Think Tank U :B:	.20	.50
❑ 319 Thought Devourer R :B:	1.00	2.00
❑ 320 Thought Eater U :B:	.20	.50
❑ 321 Thought Nibbler C :B:	.12	.30
❑ 322 Timberland Ruins C :L:	.12	.30
❑ 323 Time Stretch R :B:	2.50	5.00
❑ 324 Tireless Tribe C :W:	.12	.30
❑ 325 Tombfire R :K:	1.50	3.00
❑ 326 Touch of Invisibility C :B:	.12	.30
❑ 327 Traumatize R :B:	7.50	15.00
❑ 328 Traveling Plague R :K:	1.50	3.00
❑ 329 Treetop Sentinel U :B:	.20	.50
❑ 330 Tremble C :R:	.12	.30
❑ 331 Twigwalker U :G:	.20	.50
❑ 332 Unifying Theory R :B:	1.00	2.00
❑ 333 Upheaval R :B:	4.00	8.00
❑ 334 Vampiric Dragon R :D:	5.00	10.00
❑ 335 Verdant Succession R :G:	2.00	4.00
❑ 336 Vivify U :G:	.50	1.00
❑ 337 Volcanic Spray U :R:	.50	1.00
❑ 338 Volley of Boulders R :R:	1.00	2.00
❑ 339 Wayward Angel R :W:	2.00	4.00
❑ 340 Werebear C :G:	.12	.30
❑ 341 Whipkeeper U :R:	.20	.50
❑ 342 Whispering Shade C :K:	.12	.30
❑ 343 Wild Mongrel C :G:	.12	.30
❑ 344 Woodland Druid C :G:	.12	.30
❑ 345 Words of Wisdom C :B:	.12	.30
❑ 346 Zombie Assassin C :K:	.12	.30
❑ 347 Zombie Cannibal C :K:	.12	.30
❑ 348 Zombie Infestation U :K:	1.00	2.00
❑ 349 Zombify U :K:	1.00	2.00
❑ 350 Zoologist R :G:	1.00	2.00

2001 Magic the Gathering Odyssey Foil

COMPLETE SET (350)	500.00	800.00

*Foil: 1X to 2X Basic Cards

2002 Magic the Gathering Torment

Complete Set (143)	80.00	125.00
Theme Deck Box	120.00	170.00
Theme Deck	12.00	17.00
Booster Box (36 Packs)	120.00	185.00
Booster Pack (15 Cards)	4.50	6.50

Card	Low	High
❑ 1 Accelerate C :R:	.10	.30
❑ 2 Acorn Harvest C :G:	.10	.30
❑ 3 Alter Reality R :B:	1.50	3.00
❑ 4 Ambassador Laquatus R :B:	2.50	5.00
❑ 5 Angel of Retribution R :W:	2.00	4.00
❑ 6 Anurid Scavenger U :G:	.20	.50
❑ 7 Aquamoeba C :B:	.10	.30
❑ 8 Arrogant Wurm U :G:	1.50	3.00
❑ 9 Aven Trooper C :W:	.10	.30
❑ 10 Balshan Collaborator U :B:	.20	.50
❑ 11 Balthor the Stout R :R:	1.50	3.00
❑ 12 Barbarian Outcast C :R:	.10	.30
❑ 13 Basking Rootwalla C :G:	.10	.30
❑ 14 Boneshard Slasher U :K:	.20	.50
❑ 15 Breakthrough U :B:	.20	.50
❑ 16 Cabal Coffers U :L:	4.00	8.00
❑ 17 Cabal Ritual C :K:	.10	.30
❑ 18 Cabal Surgeon C :K:	.10	.30
❑ 19 Cabal Torturer C :K:	.10	.30
❑ 20 Carrion Rats C :K:	.10	.30
❑ 21 Carrion Wurm U :K:	.20	.50
❑ 22 Centaur Chieftain U :G:	.20	.50
❑ 23 Centaur Veteran C :G:	.10	.30
❑ 24 Cephalid Aristocrat C :B:	.10	.30
❑ 25 Cephalid Illusionist U :B:	.20	.50
❑ 26 Cephalid Sage U :B:	.20	.50
❑ 27 Cephalid Snitch C :B:	.10	.30
❑ 28 Cephalid Vandal R :B:	1.00	2.00
❑ 29 Chainer, Dementia Master R :K:	2.50	5.00
❑ 30 Chainer's Edict U :K:	2.00	4.00
❑ 31 Churning Eddy C :B:	.10	.30
❑ 32 Circular Logic U :B:	2.50	5.00
❑ 33 Cleansing Meditation U :W:	.20	.50
❑ 34 Compulsion U :B:	.75	1.50
❑ 35 Coral Net C :B:	.10	.30
❑ 36 Crackling Club C :R:	.10	.30
❑ 37 Crazed Firecat U :R:	.20	.50
❑ 38 Crippling Fatigue C :K:	.10	.30
❑ 39 Dawn of the Dead R :K:	1.50	3.00
❑ 40 Deep Analysis C :B:	.10	.30
❑ 41 Devastating Dreams R :R:	1.50	3.00
❑ 42 Dwell on the Past U :G:	.50	1.00
❑ 43 Enslaved Dwarf C :R:	.10	.30
❑ 44 Equal Treatment U :W:	.20	.50
❑ 45 Faceless Butcher C :K:	.10	.30
❑ 46 False Memories R :B:	1.50	3.00
❑ 47 Far Wanderings C :G:	.10	.30
❑ 48 Fiery Temper C :R:	.10	.30
❑ 49 Flaming Gambit U :R:	.50	1.00
❑ 50 Flash of Defiance C :R:	.10	.30
❑ 51 Floating Shield C :W:	.10	.30
❑ 52 Frantic Purification C :W:	.10	.30
❑ 53 Ghostly Wings C :B:	.10	.30
❑ 54 Gloomdrifter U :K:	.20	.50
❑ 55 Gravegouger C :K:	.10	.30
❑ 56 Grim Lavamancer R :R:	6.00	12.00
❑ 57 Grotesque Hybrid U :K:	.20	.50
❑ 58 Gurzigost R :G:	2.00	4.00
❑ 59 Hell-Bent Raider R :R:	2.00	4.00
❑ 60 Hydromorph Guardian C :B:	.10	.30
❑ 61 Hydromorph Gull U :B:	.20	.50
❑ 62 Hypnox R :K:	2.50	5.00
❑ 63 Hypochondria U :W:	.20	.50
❑ 64 Ichorid R :K:	3.00	6.00
❑ 65 Insidious Dreams R :K:	2.00	4.00
❑ 66 Insist R :G:	1.50	3.00
❑ 67 Invigorating Falls C :G:	.10	.30
❑ 68 Kamahl's Sledge C :R:	.10	.30
❑ 69 Krosan Constrictor C :G:	.10	.30
❑ 70 Krosan Restorer C :G:	.10	.30
❑ 71 Laquatus's Champion R :K:	3.00	6.00
❑ 72 Last Laugh R :K:	1.00	2.00
❑ 73 Liquify C :B:	.10	.30
❑ 74 Llawan, Cephalid Empress R :B:	1.50	3.00
❑ 75 Longhorn Firebeast C :R:	.10	.30
❑ 76 Major Teroh R :W:	2.00	4.00
❑ 77 Mesmeric Fiend C :K:	.10	.30
❑ 78 Militant Monk C :W:	.10	.30
❑ 79 Mind Sludge U :K:	.50	1.00
❑ 80 Morningtide R :W:	1.50	3.00
❑ 81 Mortal Combat R :K:	1.50	3.00
❑ 82 Mortiphobia U :K:	.20	.50
❑ 83 Mutilate R :K:	4.00	8.00
❑ 84 Mystic Familiar C :W:	.10	.30
❑ 85 Nantuko Blightcutter R :G:	1.50	3.00
❑ 86 Nantuko Calmer C :G:	.10	.30
❑ 87 Nantuko Cultivator R :G:	1.50	3.00
❑ 88 Nantuko Shade R :K:	7.00	14.00
❑ 89 Narcissism U :G:	.20	.50
❑ 90 Nostalgic Dreams R :G:	2.00	4.00
❑ 91 Obsessive Search C :B:	.10	.30
❑ 92 Organ Grinder C :K:	.10	.30
❑ 93 Overmaster R :R:	1.00	2.00
❑ 94 Parallel Evolution R :G:	2.50	5.00
❑ 95 Pardic Arsonist U :R:	.20	.50
❑ 96 Pardic Collaborator U :R:	.20	.50
❑ 97 Pardic Lancer C :R:	.10	.30
❑ 98 Pay No Heed C :W:	.10	.30
❑ 99 Petradon R :R:	1.50	3.00
❑ 100 Petravark C :R:	.10	.30
❑ 101 Pitchstone Wall U :R:	.20	.50
❑ 102 Plagiarize R :B:	2.00	4.00
❑ 103 Possessed Aven R :B:	1.50	3.00
❑ 104 Possessed Barbarian R :R:	1.50	3.00
❑ 105 Possessed Centaur R :G:	1.50	3.00
❑ 106 Possessed Nomad R :W:	1.50	3.00
❑ 107 Psychotic Haze C :K:	.10	.30
❑ 108 Putrid Imp C :K:	.10	.30
❑ 109 Pyromania U :R:	.20	.50
❑ 110 Radiate R :R:	2.50	5.00
❑ 111 Rancid Earth C :K:	.10	.30
❑ 112 Reborn Hero R :W:	2.00	4.00
❑ 113 Restless Dreams C :K:	.10	.30
❑ 114 Retraced Image R :B:	1.50	3.00
❑ 115 Sengir Vampire R :K:	2.50	5.00
❑ 116 Seton's Scout U :G:	.20	.50
❑ 117 Shade's Form C :K:	.10	.30
❑ 118 Shambling Swarm R :K:	2.00	4.00
❑ 119 Sickening Dreams U :K:	.50	-1.00
❑ 120 Skullscorch R :R:	3.00	5.00
❑ 121 Skywing Aven C :B:	.10	.30
❑ 122 Slithery Stalker U :K:	.20	.50
❑ 123 Sonic Seizure C :R:	.10	.30
❑ 124 Soul Scourge C :K:	.10	.30
❑ 125 Spirit Flare C :W:	.10	.30
❑ 126 Stern Judge U :W:	.30	.75
❑ 127 Strength of Isolation U :W:	.20	.50
❑ 128 Strength of Lunacy U :K:	.20	.50
❑ 129 Stupefying Touch U :B:	.20	.50
❑ 130 Tainted Field U :L:	1.00	2.00
❑ 131 Tainted Isle U :L:	1.00	2.00
❑ 132 Tainted Peak U :L:	1.00	2.00
❑ 133 Tainted Wood U :L:	1.00	2.00
❑ 134 Temporary Insanity U :R:	.20	.50
❑ 135 Teroh's Faithful C :W:	.10	.30
❑ 136 Teroh's Vanguard U :W:	.20	.50
❑ 137 Transcendence R :W:	1.00	2.00
❑ 138 Turbulent Dreams R :B:	1.00	2.00
❑ 139 Unhinge C :K:	.10	.30
❑ 140 Vengeful Dreams R :W:	1.50	3.00
❑ 141 Violent Eruption U :R:	.75	1.50
❑ 142 Waste Away C :K:	.10	.30
❑ 143 Zombie Trailblazer U :K:	.50	1.00

2002 Magic the Gathering Torment Foil

COMPLETE SET (143)	275.00	350.00

*Foil: 1X to 2X Basic Cards

2002 Magic the Gathering Judgment

Complete Set (143)	75.00	125.00
Theme Deck Box	140.00	200.00
Theme Deck	15.00	20.00
Booster Box (36 Packs)	100.00	120.00
Booster Pack (15 Cards)	3.50	4.00
Fat Pack	40.00	50.00

Card	Low	High
❑ 1 Ancestor's Chosen U :W:	.50	1.00
❑ 2 Anger U :R:	1.00	2.00
❑ 3 Anurid Barkripper C :G:	.10	.30
❑ 4 Anurid Brushhopper R :D:	2.50	5.00
❑ 5 Anurid Swarmsnapper U :G:	.20	.50
❑ 6 Arcane Teachings C :R:	.10	.30
❑ 7 Aven Fogbringer C :B:	.10	.30
❑ 8 Aven Warcraft U :W:	.20	.50
❑ 9 Balthor the Defiled R :K:	2.00	4.00
❑ 10 Barbarian Bully C :R:	.10	.30
❑ 11 Battle Screech U :W:	.50	1.00
❑ 12 Battlefield Scrounger C :G:	.10	.30
❑ 13 Battlewise Aven C :W:	.10	.30
❑ 14 Benevolent Bodyguard C :W:	.10	.30
❑ 15 Book Burning C :R:	.10	.30
❑ 16 Border Patrol C :W:	.10	.30
❑ 17 Brawn U :G:	.50	1.00
❑ 18 Breaking Point R :R:	2.50	5.00
❑ 19 Browbeat U :R:	2.00	4.00
❑ 20 Burning Wish R :R:	4.00	8.00
❑ 21 Cabal Therapy U :K:	3.50	7.00
❑ 22 Cabal Trainee C :K:	.10	.30
❑ 23 Cagemail C :W:	.10	.30
❑ 24 Canopy Claws C :G:	.10	.30
❑ 25 Centaur Rootcaster C :G:	.10	.30
❑ 26 Cephalid Constable R :B:	1.50	3.00
❑ 27 Cephalid Inkshrouder U :B:	.50	1.00
❑ 28 Chastise U :W:	.50	1.00
❑ 29 Commander Eesha R :W:	2.00	4.00
❑ 30 Crush of Wurms R :G:	2.00	4.00
❑ 31 Cunning Wish R :B:	8.00	15.00
❑ 32 Death Wish R :K:	1.00	2.00
❑ 33 Defy Gravity C :B:	.10	.30
❑ 34 Dwarven Bloodboiler R :R:	1.00	2.00
❑ 35 Dwarven Driller U :R:	.50	1.00
❑ 36 Dwarven Scorcher C :R:	.10	.30
❑ 37 Earsplitting Rats C :K:	.10	.30
❑ 38 Elephant Guide U :G:	.75	1.50
❑ 39 Ember Shot C :R:	.10	.30
❑ 40 Envelop C :B:	.10	.30
❑ 41 Epic Struggle R :G:	1.50	3.00
❑ 42 Erhnam Djinn R :G:	2.00	4.00
❑ 43 Exoskeletal Armor U :G:	.50	1.00
❑ 44 Filth U :K:	.20	.50
❑ 45 Firecat Blitz U :R:	.20	.50
❑ 46 Flaring Pain C :R:	.10	.30
❑ 47 Flash of Insight U :B:	.20	.50
❑ 48 Fledgling Dragon R :R:	3.00	6.00
❑ 49 Folk Medicine C :G:	.10	.30
❑ 50 Forcemage Advocate U :G:	.20	.50
❑ 51 Funeral Pyre C :W:	.10	.30
❑ 52 Genesis R :G:	3.50	7.00
❑ 53 Giant Warthog C :G:	.10	.30
❑ 54 Glory R :W:	2.00	4.00
❑ 55 Golden Wish R :W:	1.50	3.00
❑ 56 Goretusk Firebeast C :R:	.10	.30
❑ 57 Grave Consequences U :K:	.50	1.00
❑ 58 Grip of Amnesia C :B:	.10	.30
❑ 59 Grizzly Fate U :G:	.50	1.00
❑ 60 Guided Strike C :W:	.10	.30
❑ 61 Guiltfeeder R :K:	2.00	4.00
❑ 62 Hapless Researcher C :B:	.10	.30
❑ 63 Harvester Druid C :G:	.10	.30
❑ 64 Hunting Grounds R :D:	1.50	3.00
❑ 65 Infectious Rage U :R:	.20	.50
❑ 66 Ironshell Beetle C :G:	.10	.30
❑ 67 Jeska, Warrior Adept R :R:	1.50	3.00
❑ 68 Keep Watch C :B:	.10	.30
❑ 69 Krosan Reclamation U :G:	.50	1.00
❑ 70 Krosan Verge U :L:	.50	1.00
❑ 71 Krosan Wayfarer C :G:	.10	.30
❑ 72 Laquatus's Disdain U :B:	.20	.50
❑ 73 Lava Dart C :R:	.10	.30
❑ 74 Lead Astray C :W:	.10	.30
❑ 75 Liberated Dwarf C :R:	.10	.30
❑ 76 Lightning Surge R :R:	1.50	3.00
❑ 77 Living Wish R :G:	6.00	12.00
❑ 78 Lost in Thought C :B:	.10	.30
❑ 79 Masked Gorgon R :K:	1.50	3.00
❑ 80 Mental Note C :B:	.10	.30
❑ 81 Mirari's Wake R :D:	4.00	8.00
❑ 82 Mirror Wall C :B:	.10	.30
❑ 83 Mist of Stagnation R :B:	1.00	2.00
❑ 84 Morality Shift R :K:	1.00	2.00
❑ 85 Nantuko Monastery U :L:	.50	1.00
❑ 86 Nantuko Tracer C :G:	.10	.30
❑ 87 Nomad Mythmaker R :W:	1.50	3.00
❑ 88 Nullmage Advocate C :G:	.10	.30
❑ 89 Phantom Centaur U :G:	1.00	2.00
❑ 90 Phantom Flock U :W:	.50	1.00
❑ 91 Phantom Nantuko R :G:	1.50	3.00
❑ 92 Phantom Nishoba R :D:	3.00	6.00
❑ 93 Phantom Nomad C :W:	.10	.30
❑ 94 Phantom Tiger C :G:	.10	.30
❑ 95 Planar Chaos U :R:	.20	.50
❑ 96 Prismatic Strands C :W:	.10	.30
❑ 97 Pulsemage Advocate R :W:	1.50	3.00
❑ 98 Quiet Speculation U :B:	.50	1.00
❑ 99 Rats' Feast C :K:	.10	.30
❑ 100 Ray of Revelation C :W:	.10	.30
❑ 101 Riftstone Portal U :L:	.50	1.00
❑ 102 Scalpelexis R :B:	2.00	4.00
❑ 103 Seedtime R :G:	2.00	4.00
❑ 104 Selfless Exorcist R :W:	1.50	3.00
❑ 105 Serene Sunset U :G:	.20	.50
❑ 106 Shaman's Trance R :R:	1.00	2.00
❑ 107 Shieldmage Advocate C :W:	.10	.30
❑ 108 Silver Seraph R :W:	2.50	5.00
❑ 109 Solitary Confinement R :W:	2.00	4.00
❑ 110 Soulcatchers' Aerie U :W:	.50	1.00
❑ 111 Soulgorger Orgg U :R:	.20	.50
❑ 112 Spellgorger Barbarian C :R:	.10	.30
❑ 113 Spelljack R :B:	2.00	4.00
❑ 114 Spirit Cairn U :W:	.75	1.50
❑ 115 Spurnmage Advocate U :W:	.20	.50
❑ 116 Stitch Together U :K:	.75	1.50
❑ 117 Sudden Strength C :G:	.10	.30
❑ 118 Suntail Hawk C :W:	.10	.30
❑ 119 Sutured Ghoul R :K:	1.50	3.00
❑ 120 Swelter U :R:	.20	.50
❑ 121 Swirling Sandstorm C :R:	.10	.30
❑ 122 Sylvan Safekeeper R :G:	1.50	3.00
❑ 123 Telekinetic Bonds R :B:	1.50	3.00
❑ 124 Test of Endurance R :W:	3.00	6.00
❑ 125 Thriss, Nantuko Primus R :G:	1.50	3.00
❑ 126 Toxic Stench C :K:	.10	.30
❑ 127 Trained Pronghorn C :W:	.10	.30
❑ 128 Treacherous Vampire U :K:	.50	1.00
❑ 129 Treacherous Werewolf C :K:	.10	.30
❑ 130 Tunneler Wurm U :G:	.20	.50
❑ 131 Unquestioned Authority U :W:	.50	1.00
❑ 132 Valor U :W:	.50	1.00
❑ 133 Venomous Vines C :G:	.10	.30
❑ 134 Vigilant Sentry C :W:	.10	.30
❑ 135 Web of Inertia U :B:	.50	1.00
❑ 136 Wonder U :B:	1.25	2.50
❑ 137 Worldgorger Dragon R :R:	3.00	6.00
❑ 138 Wormfang Behemoth R :B:	1.25	2.50
❑ 139 Wormfang Crab U :B:	.20	.50
❑ 140 Wormfang Drake C :B:	.10	.30
❑ 141 Wormfang Manta R :B:	1.00	2.00
❑ 142 Wormfang Newt C :B:	.10	.30
❑ 143 Wormfang Turtle U :B:	.50	1.00

2002 Magic the Gathering Judgment Foil

COMPLETE SET (143)	300.00	400.00

*Foil: 1X to 2X Basic Cards

2002 Magic the Gathering Onslaught

Complete Set (350)	150.00	250.00
Theme Deck Box	90.00	110.00
Theme Deck	10.00	14.00
Booster Box	85.00	100.00
Booster Pack	3.50	4.00
Fat Pack	40.00	50.00

Card	Low	High
❑ 1 Accursed Centaur C :K:	.10	.30
❑ 2 AEther Charge U :R:	.50	1.00
❑ 3 Aggravated Assault R :R:	1.25	2.50
❑ 4 Airborne Aid C :B:	.10	.30
❑ 5 Airdrop Condor U :R:	.20	.50
❑ 6 Akroma's Blessing U :W:	.50	1.00
❑ 7 Akroma's Vengeance R :W:	3.00	6.00
❑ 8 Ancestor's Prophet R :W:	1.50	3.00
❑ 9 Animal Magnetism R :G:	1.25	2.50
❑ 10 Annex U :B:	.50	1.00
❑ 11 Anurid Murkdiver C :K:	.10	.30
❑ 12 Aphetto Alchemist U :B:	1.00	2.00
❑ 13 Aphetto Dredging C :K:	.10	.30
❑ 14 Aphetto Grifter U :B:	.20	.50
❑ 15 Aphetto Vulture U :K:	.20	.50
❑ 16 Arcanis the Omnipotent R :B:	3.00	6.00
❑ 17 Artificial Evolution R :B:	1.50	3.00
❑ 18 Ascending Aven C :B:	.10	.30
❑ 19 Astral Slide U :W:	1.00	2.00
❑ 20 Aura Extraction U :W:	.20	.50
❑ 21 Aurification R :W:	1.00	2.00
❑ 22 Avarax U :R:	.50	1.00
❑ 23 Aven Brigadier R :W:	2.00	4.00
❑ 24 Aven Fateshaper U :B:	.20	.50
❑ 25 Aven Soulgazer U :W:	.20	.50
❑ 26 Backslide C :B:	.10	.30
❑ 27 Barkhide Mauler C :G:	.10	.30
❑ 28 Barren Moor C :L:	.10	.30
❑ 29 Battering Craghorn C :R:	.10	.30
❑ 30 Battlefield Medic C :W:	.10	.30
❑ 31 Biorhythm R :G:	2.00	4.00
❑ 32 Birchlore Rangers C :G:	.10	.30
❑ 33 Blackmail U :K:	.75	1.50
❑ 34 Blatant Thievery R :B:	1.50	3.00
❑ 35 Blistering Firecat R :R:	4.00	8.00
❑ 36 Bloodline Shaman U :G:	.20	.50
❑ 37 Bloodstained Mire R :L:	10.00	20.00
❑ 38 Boneknitter U :K:	.50	1.00
❑ 39 Break Open C :R:	.10	.30
❑ 40 Brightstone Ritual C :R:	.10	.30
❑ 41 Broodhatch Nantuko U :G:	.20	.50
❑ 42 Butcher Orgg R :R:	1.50	3.00
❑ 43 Cabal Archon U :K:	.50	1.00
❑ 44 Cabal Executioner U :K:	.20	.50
❑ 45 Cabal Slaver U :K:	.20	.50
❑ 46 Callous Oppressor R :B:	1.50	3.00
❑ 47 Catapult Master R :W:	1.00	2.00
❑ 48 Catapult Squad U :W:	.20	.50
❑ 49 Centaur Glade U :G:	.50	1.00
❑ 50 Chain of Acid U :G:	.20	.50
❑ 51 Chain of Plasma U :R:	.20	.50
❑ 52 Chain of Silence U :W:	.20	.50
❑ 53 Chain of Smog U :K:	.20	.50
❑ 54 Chain of Vapor U :B:	.50	1.00
❑ 55 Charging Slateback C :R:	.10	.30
❑ 56 Choking Tethers C :B:	.10	.30
❑ 57 Circle of Solace R :W:	1.50	3.00
❑ 58 Clone R :B:	2.00	4.00
❑ 59 Commando Raid U :R:	.20	.50
❑ 60 Complicate U :B:	.50	1.00
❑ 61 Contested Cliffs R :L:	2.00	4.00
❑ 62 Convalescent Care R :W:	1.50	3.00
❑ 63 Cover of Darkness R :K:	2.00	4.00
❑ 64 Crafty Pathmage C :B:	.10	.30
❑ 65 Crowd Favorites U :W:	.20	.50
❑ 66 Crown of Ascension C :B:	.10	.30
❑ 67 Crown of Awe C :W:	.10	.30
❑ 68 Crown of Fury C :R:	.10	.30
❑ 69 Crown of Suspicion C :K:	.10	.30
❑ 70 Crown of Vigor C :G:	.10	.30
❑ 71 Crude Rampart U :W:	.20	.50
❑ 72 Cruel Revival C :K:	.10	.30
❑ 73 Cryptic Gateway R :A:	2.00	4.00
❑ 74 Custody Battle U :R:	.20	.50
❑ 75 Daru Cavalier C :W:	.10	.30
❑ 76 Daru Encampment U :L:	.50	1.00
❑ 77 Daru Healer C :W:	.10	.30
❑ 78 Daru Lancer C :W:	.10	.30
❑ 79 Daunting Defender C :W:	.10	.30
❑ 80 Dawning Purist U :W:	.20	.50
❑ 81 Death Match R :K:	1.50	3.00
❑ 82 Death Pulse U :K:	.20	.50
❑ 83 Defensive Maneuvers C :W:	.10	.30
❑ 84 Demystify C :W:	.10	.30
❑ 85 Dirge of Dread C :K:	.10	.30
❑ 86 Disciple of Grace C :W:	.10	.30
❑ 87 Disciple of Malice C :K:	.10	.30
❑ 88 Discombobulate U :B:	.50	1.00
❑ 89 Dispersing Orb U :B:	.20	.50
❑ 90 Disruptive Pitmage C :B:	.10	.30
❑ 91 Dive Bomber C :W:	.10	.30
❑ 92 Doom Cannon R :A:	1.00	2.00
❑ 93 Doomed Necromancer R :K:	2.00	4.00
❑ 94 Doubtless One U :W:	1.00	2.00
❑ 95 Dragon Roost R :R:	2.50	5.00
❑ 96 Dream Chisel R :A:	1.50	3.00
❑ 97 Dwarven Blastminer U :R:	.50	1.00
❑ 98 Ebonblade Reaper R :K:	2.00	4.00
❑ 99 Elven Riders U :G:	.50	1.00
❑ 100 Elvish Guidance C :G:	.10	.30
❑ 101 Elvish Pathcutter C :G:	.10	.30
❑ 102 Elvish Pioneer C :G:	.10	.30
❑ 103 Elvish Scrapper U :G:	.50	1.00
❑ 104 Elvish Vanguard R :G:	2.00	4.00
❑ 105 Elvish Warrior C :G:	.10	.30
❑ 106 Embermage Goblin U :R:	.50	1.00
❑ 107 Enchantress's Presence R :G:	2.00	4.00

Card	Low	High
☐ 108 Endemic Plague R :K:	1.50	3.00
☐ 109 Entrails Feaster R :K:	1.50	3.00
☐ 110 Erratic Explosion C :R:	.10	.30
☐ 111 Essence Fracture U :B:	.20	.50
☐ 112 Everglove Courier U :G:	.20	.50
☐ 113 Exalted Angel R :W:	10.00	20.00
☐ 114 Explosive Vegetation U :G:	.50	1.00
☐ 115 Fade from Memory U :K:	.50	1.00
☐ 116 Fallen Cleric C :K:	.10	.30
☐ 117 False Cure R :K:	2.00	4.00
☐ 118 Feeding Frenzy U :K:	.20	.50
☐ 119 Festering Goblin C :K:	.10	.30
☐ 120 Fever Charm C :R:	.10	.30
☐ 121 Flamestick Courier U :R:	.20	.50
☐ 122 Fleeting Aven U :B:	.20	.50
☐ 123 Flooded Strand R :L:	10.00	20.00
☐ 124 Foothill Guide C :W:	.10	.30
☐ 125 Forest C :L:	.10	.30
☐ 126 Forest C :L:	.10	.30
☐ 127 Forest C :L:	.10	.30
☐ 128 Forest C :L:	.10	.30
☐ 129 Forgotten Cave C :L:	.10	.30
☐ 130 Frightshroud Courier U :K:	.20	.50
☐ 131 Future Sight R :B:	2.50	5.00
☐ 132 Gangrenous Goliath R :K:	1.50	3.00
☐ 133 Ghosthelm Courier U :B:	.20	.50
☐ 134 Gigapede R :G:	1.50	3.00
☐ 135 Glarecaster R :W:	1.50	3.00
☐ 136 Glory Seeker C :W:	.10	.30
☐ 137 Gluttonous Zombie U :K:	.20	.50
☐ 138 Goblin Burrows U :L:	.50	1.00
☐ 139 Goblin Machinist U :R:	.20	.50
☐ 140 Goblin Piledriver R :R:	8.00	15.00
☐ 141 Goblin Pyromancer R :R:	1.50	3.00
☐ 142 Goblin Sharpshooter R :R:	5.00	10.00
☐ 143 Goblin Sky Raider C :R:	.10	.30
☐ 144 Goblin Sledder C :R:	.10	.30
☐ 145 Goblin Taskmaster C :R:	.10	.30
☐ 146 Grand Coliseum R :L:	3.00	6.00
☐ 147 Grand Melee R :R:	1.00	2.00
☐ 148 Grassland Crusader C :W:	.10	.30
☐ 149 Gratuitous Violence R :R:	2.00	4.00
☐ 150 Gravel Slinger C :W:	.10	.30
☐ 151 Gravespawn Sovereign R :K:	2.00	4.00
☐ 152 Graxiplon U :B:	.20	.50
☐ 153 Grinning Demon R :K:	3.00	6.00
☐ 154 Gustcloak Harrier C :W:	.10	.30
☐ 155 Gustcloak Runner C :W:	.10	.30
☐ 156 Gustcloak Savior R :W:	1.50	3.00
☐ 157 Gustcloak Sentinel U :W:	.20	.50
☐ 158 Gustcloak Skirmisher U :W:	.20	.50
☐ 159 Harsh Mercy R :W:	2.00	4.00
☐ 160 Haunted Cadaver C :K:	.10	.30
☐ 161 Head Games R :K:	1.00	2.00
☐ 162 Headhunter U :K:	.20	.50
☐ 163 Heedless One U :G:	2.00	4.00
☐ 164 Hystrodon R :G:	1.00	2.00
☐ 165 Imagecrafter C :B:	.10	.30
☐ 166 Improvised Armor U :W:	.20	.50
☐ 167 Infest U :K:	1.00	2.00
☐ 168 Information Dealer C :B:	.10	.30
☐ 169 Inspirit U :W:	.20	.50
☐ 170 Insurrection R :R:	1.50	3.00
☐ 171 Invigorating Boon U :G:	.20	.50
☐ 172 Ironfist Crusher U :W:	.20	.50
☐ 173 Island C :L:	.10	.30
☐ 174 Island C :L:	.10	.30
☐ 175 Island C :L:	.10	.30
☐ 176 Island C :L:	.10	.30
☐ 177 Ixidor, Reality Sculptor R :B:	2.00	4.00
☐ 178 Ixidor's Will C :B:	.10	.30
☐ 179 Jareth, Leonine Titan R :W:	4.00	8.00
☐ 180 Kaboom! R :R:	1.50	3.00
☐ 181 Kamahl, Fist of Krosa R :G:	4.00	8.00
☐ 182 Kamahl's Summons U :G:	.50	1.00
☐ 183 Krosan Colossus R :G:	2.00	4.00
☐ 184 Krosan Groundshaker U :G:	.20	.50
☐ 185 Krosan Tusker C :G:	.10	.30
☐ 186 Lavamancer's Skill C :R:	.10	.30
☐ 187 Lay Waste C :R:	.10	.30
☐ 188 Leery Fogbeast C :G:	.10	.30
☐ 189 Lightning Rift U :R:	.50	1.00
☐ 190 Lonely Sandbar C :L:	.10	.30
☐ 191 Mage's Guile C :B:	.10	.30
☐ 192 Mana Echoes R :R:	1.50	3.00
☐ 193 Meddle U :B:	.20	.50
☐ 194 Menacing Ogre R :R:	1.50	3.00
☐ 195 Misery Charm C :K:	.10	.30
☐ 196 Mistform Dreamer C :B:	.10	.30
☐ 197 Mistform Mask C :B:	.10	.30
☐ 198 Mistform Mutant U :B:	.20	.50
☐ 199 Mistform Shrieker U :B:	.20	.50
☐ 200 Mistform Skyreaver R :B:	1.50	3.00
☐ 201 Mistform Stalker U :B:	.20	.50
☐ 202 Mistform Wall C :B:	.10	.30
☐ 203 Mobilization R :W:	3.00	6.00
☐ 204 Mountain C :L:	.10	.30
☐ 205 Mountain C :L:	.10	.30
☐ 206 Mountain C :L:	.10	.30
☐ 207 Mountain C :L:	.10	.30
☐ 208 Mythic Proportions R :G:	1.50	3.00
☐ 209 Nameless One U :B:	.50	1.00
☐ 210 Nantuko Husk C :K:	.10	.30
☐ 211 Naturalize C :G:	.10	.30
☐ 212 Nosy Goblin C :R:	.10	.30
☐ 213 Nova Cleric U :W:	.20	.50
☐ 214 Oblation R :W:	1.50	3.00
☐ 215 Oversold Cemetery R :K:	3.00	6.00
☐ 216 Overwhelming Instinct U :G:	.20	.50
☐ 217 Pacifism C :W:	.10	.30
☐ 218 Patriarch's Bidding R :K:	4.00	8.00
☐ 219 Pearlspear Courier U :W:	.20	.50
☐ 220 Peer Pressure R :B:	1.50	3.00
☐ 221 Piety Charm C :W:	.10	.30
☐ 222 Pinpoint Avalanche C :R:	.10	.30
☐ 223 Plains C :L:	.10	.30
☐ 224 Plains C :L:	.10	.30
☐ 225 Plains C :L:	.10	.30
☐ 226 Plains C :L:	.10	.30
☐ 227 Polluted Delta R :L:	10.00	20.00
☐ 228 Primal Boost U :G:	.20	.50
☐ 229 Profane Prayers C :K:	.10	.30
☐ 230 Prowling Pangolin U :K:	.20	.50
☐ 231 Psychic Trance R :B:	1.50	3.00
☐ 232 Quicksilver Dragon R :B:	3.00	6.00
☐ 233 Ravenous Baloth R :G:	5.00	10.00
☐ 234 Read the Runes R :B:	1.50	3.00
☐ 235 Reckless One U :R:	.75	1.50
☐ 236 Reminisce U :B:	.50	1.00
☐ 237 Renewed Faith C :W:	.10	.30
☐ 238 Righteous Cause U :W:	.50	1.00
☐ 239 Riptide Biologist C :B:	.10	.30
☐ 240 Riptide Chronologist U :B:	.50	1.00
☐ 241 Riptide Entrancer R :B:	1.25	2.50
☐ 242 Riptide Laboratory R :L:	1.50	3.00
☐ 243 Riptide Replicator R :A:	2.50	5.00
☐ 244 Riptide Shapeshifter U :B:	.20	.50
☐ 245 Risky Move R :R:	1.50	3.00
☐ 246 Rorix Bladewing R :R:	4.00	8.00
☐ 247 Rotlung Reanimator R :K:	4.00	8.00
☐ 248 Rummaging Wizard U :B:	.50	1.00
☐ 249 Run Wild U :G:	.50	1.00
☐ 250 Sage Aven C :B:	.10	.30
☐ 251 Sandskin C :W:	.10	.30
☐ 252 Screaming Seahawk C :B:	.10	.30
☐ 253 Screeching Buzzard C :K:	.10	.30
☐ 254 Sea's Claim C :B:	.10	.30
☐ 255 Searing Flesh U :R:	.50	1.00
☐ 256 Seaside Haven U :L:	.20	.50
☐ 257 Secluded Steppe C :L:	.10	.30
☐ 258 Serpentine Basilisk U :G:	.20	.50
☐ 259 Severed Legion C :K:	.10	.30
☐ 260 Shade's Breath U :K:	.20	.50
☐ 261 Shaleskin Bruiser U :R:	.20	.50
☐ 262 Shared Triumph R :W:	2.50	5.00
☐ 263 Shepherd of Rot C :K:	.10	.30
☐ 264 Shieldmage Elder U :W:	.50	1.00
☐ 265 Shock C :R:	.10	.30
☐ 266 Sigil of the New Dawn R :W:	2.00	4.00
☐ 267 Silent Specter R :K:	1.50	3.00
☐ 268 Silklash Spider R :G:	2.00	4.00
☐ 269 Silvos, Rogue Elemental R :G:	4.00	8.00
☐ 270 Skirk Commando C :R:	.10	.30
☐ 271 Skirk Fire Marshal R :R:	2.00	4.00
☐ 272 Skirk Prospector C :R:	.10	.30
☐ 273 Skittish Valesk U :R:	.20	.50
☐ 274 Slate of Ancestry R :A:	2.00	4.00
☐ 275 Slice and Dice U :R:	1.00	2.00
☐ 276 Slipstream Eel C :B:	.10	.30
☐ 277 Smother U :K:	1.00	2.00
☐ 278 Snapping Thragg U :R:	.50	1.00
☐ 279 Snarling Undorak C :G:	.10	.30
☐ 280 Solar Blast C :R:	.10	.30
☐ 281 Soulless One U :K:	1.00	2.00
☐ 282 Sparksmith C :R:	.10	.30
☐ 283 Spined Basher C :K:	.10	.30
☐ 284 Spitfire Handler U :R:	.20	.50
☐ 285 Spitting Gourna C :G:	.10	.30
☐ 286 Spurred Wolverine C :R:	.10	.30
☐ 287 Spy Network C :B:	.10	.30
☐ 288 Slag Beetle R :G:	1.50	3.00
☐ 289 Standardize R :B:	1.50	3.00
☐ 290 Starlit Sanctum U :L:	1.00	2.00
☐ 291 Starstorm R :R:	3.00	6.00
☐ 292 Steely Resolve R :G:	2.50	5.00
☐ 293 Strongarm Tactics R :K:	1.50	3.00
☐ 294 Sunfire Balm U :W:	.20	.50
☐ 295 Supreme Inquisitor R :B:	2.00	4.00
☐ 296 Swamp C :L:	.10	.30
☐ 297 Swamp C :L:	.10	.30
☐ 298 Swamp C :L:	.10	.30
☐ 299 Swamp C :L:	.10	.30
☐ 300 Swat C :K:	.10	.30
☐ 301 Symbiotic Beast U :G:	.20	.50
☐ 302 Symbiotic Elf C :G:	.10	.30
☐ 303 Symbiotic Wurm R :G:	2.00	4.00
☐ 304 Syphon Mind C :K:	.10	.30
☐ 305 Syphon Soul C :K:	.10	.30
☐ 306 Taunting Elf C :G:	.10	.30
☐ 307 Tempting Wurm R :G:	1.50	3.00
☐ 308 Tephraderm R :R:	1.50	3.00
☐ 309 Thoughtbound Primoc U :R:	.20	.50
☐ 310 Thrashing Mudspawn U :K:	.20	.50
☐ 311 Threaten U :R:	.50	1.00
☐ 312 Thunder of Hooves U :R:	.20	.50
☐ 313 Towering Baloth U :G:	.20	.50
☐ 314 Trade Secrets R :B:	1.50	3.00
☐ 315 Tranquil Thicket C :L:	.10	.30
☐ 316 Treespring Lorian C :G:	.10	.30
☐ 317 Tribal Golem R :A:	1.50	3.00
☐ 318 Tribal Unity U :G:	.50	1.00
☐ 319 Trickery Charm C :B:	.10	.30
☐ 320 True Believer R :W:	2.50	5.00
☐ 321 Undead Gladiator R :K:	2.00	4.00
☐ 322 Unholy Grotto R :L:	2.00	4.00
☐ 323 Unified Strike C :W:	.10	.30
☐ 324 Venomspout Brackus U :G:	.20	.50
☐ 325 Visara the Dreadful R :K:	6.00	12.00
☐ 326 Vitality Charm C :G:	.10	.30
☐ 327 Voice of the Woods R :G:	2.50	5.00
☐ 328 Voidmage Prodigy R :B:	3.00	6.00
☐ 329 Walking Desecration U :K:	.20	.50
☐ 330 Wall of Mulch U :G:	.20	.50
☐ 331 Wave of Indifference C :R:	.10	.30
☐ 332 Weathered Wayfarer R :W:	2.00	4.00
☐ 333 Weird Harvest R :G:	1.50	3.00
☐ 334 Wellwisher C :G:	.10	.30
☐ 335 Wheel and Deal R :B:	2.00	4.00
☐ 336 Whipcorder U :W:	.50	1.00
☐ 337 Windswept Heath R :L:	7.00	14.00
☐ 338 Wirewood Elf C :G:	.10	.30
☐ 339 Wirewood Herald C :G:	.10	.30
☐ 340 Wirewood Lodge U :L:	1.25	2.50
☐ 341 Wirewood Pride C :G:	.10	.30
☐ 342 Wirewood Savage C :G:	.10	.30
☐ 343 Withering Hex U :K:	.20	.50
☐ 344 Wooded Foothills R :L:	8.00	15.00
☐ 345 Words of War R :R:	1.50	3.00
☐ 346 Words of Waste R :K:	1.50	3.00
☐ 347 Words of Wilding R :G:	1.50	3.00
☐ 348 Words of Wind R :B:	1.50	3.00
☐ 349 Words of Worship R :W:	1.50	3.00
☐ 350 Wretched Anurid C :K:	.10	.30

2002 Magic the Gathering Onslaught Foil

COMPLETE SET (350)	500.00	700.00

*Foil: 1X to 2X Basic Cards

2003 Magic the Gathering 8th Edition

Item	Low	High
Complete Set	150.00	250.00
Theme Deck Box	125.00	140.00
Theme Deck	8.00	10.00
Booster Box (36 Packs)	80.00	125.00
Booster Pack (15 Cards)	3.50	4.00
☐ 1 Abyssal Specter U :K:	.20	.50
☐ 2 Air Elemental U :B:	.20	.50
☐ 3 Aladdin's Ring R :A:	1.00	2.00
☐ 4 Ambition's Cost U :K:	.20	.50
☐ 5 Anaba Shaman C :R:	.10	.30
☐ 6 Angel of Mercy U :W:	.50	1.00
☐ 7 Angelic Page C :W:	.10	.30
☐ 8 Archivist R :B:	1.00	2.00
☐ 9 Ardent Militia U :W:	.50	1.00
☐ 10 Avatar of Hope R :W:	1.50	3.00
☐ 11 Aven Cloudchaser C :W:	.10	.30
☐ 12 Aven Fisher C :B:	.10	.30
☐ 13 Aven Flock C :W:	.10	.30
☐ 14 Balance of Power R :B:	2.00	4.00
☐ 15 Balduvian Barbarians C :R:	.10	.30
☐ 16 Beast of Burden R :A:	1.00	2.00
☐ 17 Birds of Paradise R :G:	8.00	15.00
☐ 18 Blanchwood Armor U :G:	.50	1.00
☐ 19 Blaze U :R:	.50	1.00
☐ 20 Blessed Reversal R :W:	1.50	3.00
☐ 21 Blinding Angel R :W:	4.00	8.00
☐ 22 Blood Moon R :R:	2.00	4.00
☐ 23 Bloodshot Cyclops R :R:	2.00	4.00
☐ 24 Bog Imp C :K:	.10	.30
☐ 25 Bog Wraith U :K:	.50	1.00
☐ 26 Boil U :R:	.50	1.00
☐ 27 Boomerang C :B:	.10	.30
☐ 28 Brass Herald R :A:	1.00	2.00
☐ 29 Bribery R :B:	5.00	10.00
☐ 30 Call of the Wild R :G:	1.50	3.00
☐ 31 Canopy Spider C :G:	.10	.30
☐ 32 Canyon Wildcat C :R:	.10	.30
☐ 33 Carrion Wall U :K:	.20	.50
☐ 34 Catalog C :B:	.10	.30
☐ 35 Chastise U :W:	.20	.50
☐ 36 Choke U :G:	.20	.50
☐ 37 Cinder Wall C :R:	.10	.30
☐ 38 Circle of Protection: Black U :W:	.20	.50
☐ 39 Circle of Protection: Blue U :W:	.20	.50
☐ 40 Circle of Protection: Green U :W:	.20	.50
☐ 41 Circle of Protection: Red U :W:	.20	.50
☐ 42 Circle of Protection: White U :W:	.20	.50
☐ 43 City of Brass R :L:	4.00	8.00
☐ 44 Coastal Hornclaw C :B:	.10	.30
☐ 45 Coastal Piracy R :B:	1.00	2.00
☐ 46 Coastal Tower U :L:	.50	1.00
☐ 47 Coat of Arms R :A:	6.00	12.00
☐ 48 Coercion C :K:	.10	.30
☐ 49 Collective Unconscious R :G:	1.00	2.00
☐ 50 Concentrate U :B:	.20	.50
☐ 51 Confiscate U :B:	.20	.50
☐ 52 Coral Eel C :B:	.10	.30
☐ 53 Cowardice R :B:	1.50	3.00
☐ 54 Craw Wurm C :G:	.10	.30
☐ 55 Creeping Mold U :G:	.20	.50
☐ 56 Crossbow Infantry C :W:	.10	.30
☐ 57 Crystal Rod U :A:	.20	.50
☐ 58 Curiosity U :B:	.20	.50
☐ 59 Daring Apprentice R :B:	1.50	3.00
☐ 60 Dark Banishing C :K:	.10	.30
☐ 61 Death Pit Offering R :K:	1.50	3.00
☐ 62 Death Pits of Rath R :K:	1.50	3.00
☐ 63 Deathgazer U :K:	.20	.50
☐ 64 Deepwood Ghoul C :K:	.10	.30
☐ 65 Defense Grid R :A:	2.00	4.00
☐ 66 Deflection R :B:	2.00	4.00
☐ 67 Dehydration C :B:	.10	.30
☐ 68 Demolish U :R:	.20	.50
☐ 69 Demystify C :W:	.10	.30
☐ 70 Diabolic Tutor U :K:	1.00	2.00
☐ 71 Dingus Egg R :A:	1.00	2.00
☐ 72 Disrupting Scepter R :A:	1.00	2.00
☐ 73 Distorting Lens R :A:	2.00	4.00
☐ 74 Diving Griffin C :W:	.10	.30
☐ 75 Drudge Skeletons C :K:	.10	.30
☐ 76 Dusk Imp C :K:	.10	.30
☐ 77 Dwarven Demolition Team U :R:	.20	.50
☐ 78 Eastern Paladin R :K:	1.00	2.00
☐ 78A Eager Cadet C :W:	.75	1.50
☐ 79 Elfhame Palace U :L:	.50	1.00
☐ 80 Elite Archers R :W:	1.50	3.00
☐ 81 Elite Javelineer U :W:	.20	.50
☐ 82 Elvish Champion R :G:	3.00	6.00
☐ 83 Elvish Lyrist U :G:	.50	1.00
☐ 84 Elvish Pioneer C :G:	.10	.30
☐ 85 Elvish Piper R :G:	5.00	10.00
☐ 86 Elvish Scrapper U :G:	.20	.50
☐ 87 Emperor Crocodile R :G:	2.00	4.00
☐ 87A Enormous Baloth U :G:	.20	.50
☐ 88 Enrage U :R:	.20	.50
☐ 89 Ensnaring Bridge R :A:	4.00	8.00
☐ 90 Evacuation R :B:	1.50	3.00
☐ 91 Execute U :K:	.20	.50
☐ 92 Fallen Angel R :K:	2.00	4.00
☐ 93 Fear C :K:	.10	.30
☐ 94 Fecundity U :G:	.50	1.00
☐ 95 Fertile Ground C :G:	.10	.30
☐ 96 Fighting Drake U :B:	.20	.50
☐ 97 Flash Counter C :B:	.10	.30
☐ 98 Flashfires U :R:	.20	.50
☐ 99 Fleeting Image R :B:	1.50	3.00
☐ 100 Flight C :B:	.10	.30
☐ 101 Flying Carpet R :A:	1.00	2.00
☐ 102 Fodder Cannon U :A:	.20	.50
☐ 103 Foratog U :G:	.20	.50
☐ 104 Forest L :L:	.10	.30
☐ 105 Forest L :L:	.10	.30
☐ 106 Forest L :L:	.10	.30
☐ 107 Forest L :L:	.10	.30
☐ 108 Fugitive Wizard C :B:	.10	.30
☐ 109 Fungusaur R :G:	1.00	2.00
☐ 110 Furnace of Rath R :R:	2.00	4.00
☐ 111 Fyndhorn Elder U :G:	.20	.50
☐ 112 Gaea's Herald R :G:	1.50	3.00
☐ 113 Giant Badger C :G:	.10	.30
☐ 114 Giant Cockroach C :K:	.10	.30
☐ 115 Giant Growth C :G:	.10	.30
☐ 115A Giant Octopus C :B:	.50	1.00
☐ 116 Giant Spider C :G:	.10	.30
☐ 117 Glorious Anthem R :W:	3.00	6.00
☐ 118 Glory Seeker C :W:	.10	.30
☐ 119 Gluttonous Zombie U :K:	.20	.50
☐ 120 Goblin Chariot C :R:	.10	.30
☐ 121 Goblin Glider U :R:	.20	.50
☐ 122 Goblin King R :R:	2.00	4.00
☐ 123 Goblin Raider C :R:	.10	.30
☐ 124 Grave Pact R :K:	5.00	10.00
☐ 125 Gravedigger C :K:	.10	.30
☐ 126 Grizzly Bears C :G:	.10	.30
☐ 127 Guerrilla Tactics U :R:	.20	.50
☐ 128 Hammer of Bogardan R :R:	4.00	8.00
☐ 129 Healing Salve C :W:	.10	.30
☐ 130 Hibernation U :B:	.20	.50
☐ 131 Hill Giant C :R:	.10	.30
☐ 132 Holy Day C :W:	.10	.30
☐ 133 Holy Strength C :W:	.10	.30
☐ 134 Honor Guard C :W:	.10	.30
☐ 135 Horned Troll C :G:	.10	.30
☐ 136 Horned Turtle C :B:	.10	.30
☐ 137 Howling Mine R :A:	3.00	6.00
☐ 138 Hulking Cyclops U :R:	.20	.50
☐ 139 Hunted Wumpus U :G:	.20	.50
☐ 140 Index C :B:	.10	.30
☐ 141 Inferno R :R:	1.50	3.00
☐ 142 Inspiration C :B:	.10	.30
☐ 143 Intrepid Hero R :W:	2.00	4.00
☐ 144 Intruder Alarm R :B:	2.00	4.00
☐ 145 Invisibility U :B:	.20	.50
☐ 146 Iron Star U :A:	.20	.50
☐ 147 Island L :L:	.10	.30
☐ 148 Island L :L:	.10	.30
☐ 149 Island L :L:	.10	.30
☐ 150 Island L :L:	.10	.30
☐ 151 Ivory Cup U :A:	.20	.50
☐ 152 Ivory Mask R :W:	3.00	6.00
☐ 153 Jayemdae Tome R :A:	1.00	2.00
☐ 154 Karma U :W:	.20	.50
☐ 155 Larceny R :K:	1.00	2.00
☐ 156 Lava Axe C :R:	.10	.30
☐ 157 Lava Hounds R :R:	1.50	3.00
☐ 158 Lesser Gargadon U :R:	.20	.50
☐ 159 Lhurgoyf R :G:	1.50	3.00
☐ 160 Lightning Blast U :R:	.20	.50
☐ 161 Lightning Elemental C :R:	.10	.30
☐ 162 Living Terrain U :G:	.20	.50
☐ 163 Llanowar Behemoth U :G:	.20	.50
☐ 164 Lone Wolf C :G:	.10	.30
☐ 165 Looming Shade C :K:	.10	.30
☐ 166 Lord of the Undead R :K:	3.00	6.00
☐ 167 Lure U :G:	.20	.50
☐ 168 Maggot Carrier C :K:	.10	.30
☐ 169 Mahamoti Djinn R :B:	2.00	4.00
☐ 170 Mana Clash R :R:	1.50	3.00
☐ 171 Mana Leak C :B:	.10	.30
☐ 172 Maro R :G:	1.00	2.00
☐ 173 Master Decoy C :W:	.10	.30
☐ 174 Master Healer R :W:	1.00	2.00
☐ 175 Megrim U :K:	.20	.50
☐ 176 Merchant of Secrets C :B:	.10	.30
☐ 177 Merchant Scroll U :B:	.20	.50
☐ 178 Might of Oaks R :G:	2.00	4.00
☐ 179 Millstone R :A:	1.50	3.00
☐ 180 Mind Bend R :B:	1.50	3.00
☐ 181 Mind Rot C :K:	.10	.30
☐ 182 Mind Slash U :K:	.20	.50
☐ 183 Mind Sludge U :K:	.20	.50
☐ 184 Mogg Sentry R :R:	1.50	3.00
☐ 185 Monstrous Growth C :G:	.10	.30
☐ 186 Moss Monster C :G:	.10	.30
☐ 187 Mountain L :L:	.10	.30
☐ 188 Mountain L :L:	.10	.30
☐ 189 Mountain L :L:	.10	.30
☐ 190 Mountain L :L:	.10	.30
☐ 191 Murderous Betrayal R :K:	1.00	2.00
☐ 192 Nantuko Disciple C :G:	.10	.30
☐ 193 Natural Affinity R :G:	1.50	3.00
☐ 194 Naturalize C :G:	.10	.30
☐ 195 Nausea C :K:	.10	.30
☐ 196 Nekrataal U :K:	.20	.50
☐ 197 Nightmare R :K:	2.00	4.00
☐ 198 Noble Purpose R :W:	1.50	3.00
☐ 199 Norwood Ranger C :G:	.10	.30
☐ 200 Obliterate R :R:	2.50	5.00
☐ 201 Ogre Taskmaster U :R:	.20	.50
☐ 202 Okk R :R:	1.00	2.00
☐ 203 Oracle's Attendants R :W:	1.00	2.00
☐ 204 Orcish Artillery U :R:	.20	.50
☐ 205 Orcish Spy C :R:	.10	.30
☐ 206 Pacifism C :W:	.10	.30
☐ 207 Panic Attack C :R:	.10	.30
☐ 208 Patagia Golem U :A:	.20	.50
☐ 209 Peach Garden Oath U :W:	.20	.50
☐ 210 Persecute R :K:	3.00	6.00
☐ 211 Phantom Warrior U :B:	.20	.50
☐ 212 Phyrexian Arena R :K:	3.00	6.00
☐ 213 Phyrexian Colossus R :A:	2.00	4.00
☐ 214 Phyrexian Hulk U :A:	.20	.50
☐ 215 Phyrexian Plaguelord R :K:	2.00	4.00
☐ 216 Plague Beetle C :K:	.10	.30
☐ 217 Plague Wind R :K:	2.00	4.00
☐ 218 Plains L :L:	.10	.30
☐ 219 Plains L :L:	.10	.30
☐ 220 Plains L :L:	.10	.30
☐ 221 Plains L :L:	.10	.30
☐ 222 Planar Portal R :A:	2.00	4.00
☐ 223 Plow Under R :G:	5.00	10.00
☐ 224 Primeval Force R :G:	1.00	2.00
☐ 225 Primeval Shambler U :K:	.20	.50
☐ 226 Puppeteer U :B:	.20	.50
☐ 227 Pyroclasm U :R:	1.00	2.00
☐ 228 Pyrotechnics U :R:	.20	.50
☐ 229 Raging Goblin C :R:	.10	.30
☐ 230 Rain of Blades U :W:	.20	.50
☐ 231 Raise Dead C :K:	.10	.30
☐ 232 Rampant Growth C :G:	.10	.30
☐ 233 Ravenous Rats C :K:	.10	.30
☐ 234 Razorfoot Griffin C :W:	.10	.30
☐ 235 Redeem C :W:	.10	.30
☐ 236 Reflexes C :R:	.10	.30
☐ 237 Regeneration C :G:	.10	.30
☐ 238 Relentless Assault R :R:	1.00	2.00
☐ 239 Remove Soul C :B:	.10	.30
☐ 240 Revive U :G:	.20	.50
☐ 241 Rewind U :B:	.50	1.00
☐ 242 Rhox R :G:	1.50	3.00
☐ 243 Ridgeline Rager C :R:	.10	.30
☐ 244 Rod of Ruin U :A:	.20	.50
☐ 245 Rolling Stones R :W:	1.50	3.00
☐ 246 Royal Assassin R :K:	5.00	10.00
☐ 247 Rukh Egg R :R:	2.00	4.00
☐ 248 Rushwood Dryad C :G:	.10	.30
☐ 249 Sabretooth Tiger C :R:	.10	.30
☐ 250 Sacred Ground R :W:	2.00	4.00
☐ 251 Sacred Nectar C :W:	.10	.30
☐ 252 Sage of Lat-Nam R :B:	1.50	3.00
☐ 253 Sage Owl C :B:	.10	.30
☐ 254 Salt Marsh U :L:	.20	.50
☐ 255 Samite Healer C :W:	.10	.30
☐ 256 Sanctimony U :W:	.20	.50
☐ 257 Savannah Lions R :W:	3.00	6.00
☐ 258 Scathe Zombies C :K:	.10	.30
☐ 259 Sea Monster C :B:	.10	.30
☐ 260 Searing Wind R :R:	2.00	4.00
☐ 261 Seasoned Marshal U :W:	.10	.30
☐ 262 Seismic Assault R :R:	1.00	2.00
☐ 263 Serpent Warrior C :K:	.10	.30
☐ 264 Serra Angel R :W:	4.00	8.00
☐ 265 Sever Soul U :K:	.20	.50
☐ 266 Severed Legion C :K:	.10	.30
☐ 267 Shatter C :R:	.10	.30
☐ 268 Shifting Sky R :B:	1.50	3.00
☐ 269 Shivan Dragon R :R:	4.00	8.00
☐ 270 Shivan Oasis U :L:	.20	.50
☐ 271 Shock C :R:	.10	.30
☐ 272 Shock Troops C :R:	.10	.30
☐ 272A Silverback Ape U :G:	.75	1.50
☐ 273 Sizzle C :R:	.10	.30
☐ 274 Skull of Orm R :A:	1.50	3.00

MAGIC

❑ 275 Slay U :K: .20 .50
❑ 276 Sneaky Homunculus C :B: .10 .30
❑ 277 Solidarity C :W: .10 .30
❑ 278 Soul Feast U :K: .20 .50
❑ 279 Spellbook U :A: .20 .50
❑ 280 Spiketail Hatchling U :B: .20 .50
❑ 281 Spined Wurm C :G: .10 .30
❑ 282 Spineless Thug C :K: .10 .30
❑ 283 Spirit Link U :W: .20 .50
❑ 284 Spitting Spider U :G: .20 .50
❑ 285 Spreading Algae U :G: .20 .50
❑ 286 Standing Troops C :W: .10 .30
❑ 287 Star Compass U :A: .20 .50
❑ 288 Staunch Defenders U :W: .20 .50
❑ 289 Steal Artifact U :B: .20 .50
❑ 290 Stone Rain C :R: .10 .30
❑ 291 Storm Crow C :B: .10 .30
❑ 292 Story Circle R :W: 2.00 4.00
❑ 293 Stream of Life U :G: .20 .50
❑ 294 Sudden Impact U :R: .20 .50
❑ 295 Suntail Hawk C :W: .10 .30
❑ 296 Sunweb R :W: 1.00 2.00
❑ 297 Swamp L :L: .10 .30
❑ 298 Swamp L :L: .10 .30
❑ 299 Swamp L :L: .10 .30
❑ 300 Swamp L :L: .10 .30
❑ 301 Swarm of Rats U :K: .20 .50
❑ 302 Sword Dancer U :W: .20 .50
❑ 303 Teferi's Puzzle Box R :A: 1.50 3.00
❑ 304 Telepathy U :B: .20 .50
❑ 305 Temporal Adept R :B: 2.00 4.00
❑ 306 Thieves' Auction R :R: 1.00 2.00
❑ 307 Thieving Magpie U :B: .20 .50
❑ 308 Thorn Elemental R :G: 2.00 4.00
❑ 309 Throne of Bone U :A: .20 .50
❑ 310 Tidal Kraken R :B: 2.00 4.00
❑ 311 Trade Routes R :B: 1.00 2.00
❑ 312 Trained Armodon C :G: .10 .30
❑ 313 Treasure Trove U :B: .20 .50
❑ 314 Tremor C :R: .10 .30
❑ 315 Tundra Wolves C :W: .10 .30
❑ 316 Twiddle C :B: .10 .30
❑ 317 Two-Headed Dragon R :R: 5.00 10.00
❑ 318 Underworld Dreams R :K: 6.00 12.00
❑ 319 Unholy Strength C :K: .10 .30
❑ 320 Unsummon C :B: .10 .30
❑ 321 Urborg Volcano U :L: .20 .50
❑ 322 Urza's Armor R :A: 1.50 3.00
❑ 323 Urza's Mine U :L: .20 .50
❑ 324 Urza's Power Plant U :L: .20 .50
❑ 325 Urza's Tower U :L: .20 .50
❑ 326 Vampiric Spirit R :K: 1.50 3.00
❑ 327 Venerable Monk C :W: .10 .30
❑ 327A Vengence U :W: 4.00 8.00
❑ 328 Verduran Enchantress R :G: 1.50 3.00
❑ 329 Vernal Bloom R :G: 2.50 5.00
❑ 330 Vexing Arcanix R :A: 1.00 2.00
❑ 331 Viashino Sandstalker U :R: .20 .50
❑ 332 Vicious Hunger C :K: .10 .30
❑ 333 Vine Trellis C :G: .10 .30
❑ 333A Vizzerdrix R :B: .50 1.00
❑ 334 Volcanic Hammer C :R: .10 .30
❑ 335 Wall of Air U :B: .20 .50
❑ 336 Wall of Spears U :A: .20 .50
❑ 337 Wall of Stone U :R: .20 .50
❑ 338 Wall of Swords U :W: .20 .50
❑ 339 Warped Devotion R :K: 1.00 2.00
❑ 340 Western Paladin R :K: 1.00 2.00
❑ 341 Wind Drake C :B: .10 .30
❑ 342 Wing Snare U :G: .20 .50
❑ 343 Wood Elves C :G: .10 .30
❑ 344 Wooden Sphere U :A: .20 .50
❑ 345 Worship R :W: 3.00 6.00
❑ 346 Wrath of God R :W: 8.00 15.00
❑ 347 Wrath of Marit Lage U :B: .20 .50
❑ 348 Yavimaya Enchantress U :G: .20 .50
❑ 349 Zombify U :K: .20 .50
❑ 350 Zur's Weirding R :B: 1.50 3.00

2003 Magic the Gathering 8th Edition Foil

COMPLETE SET (350) 900.00 1300.00
*Foil: 1X to 2X Basic Cards

2003 Magic the Gathering Legions

Complete Set (145) 75.00 125.00
Theme Deck Box 125.00 150.00
Them Deck 7.00 14.00
Booster Box (36 Packs) 120.00 140.00
Booster Pack (12 Cards) 4.00 5.00
Fat pack 38.00 45.00

❑ 1 Akroma, Angel of Wrath R :W: 15.00 30.00
❑ 2 Akroma's Devoted U :W: .50 1.00
❑ 3 Aphetto Exterminator U :K: .20 .50
❑ 4 Aven Envoy C :B: .10 .30
❑ 5 Aven Redeemer C :W: .10 .30
❑ 6 Aven Warhawk U :W: .20 .50
❑ 7 Bane of the Living R :K: 1.50 3.00
❑ 8 Beacon of Destiny R :W: 1.50 3.00
❑ 9 Berserk Murlodont C :G: .10 .30
❑ 10 Blade Sliver U :R: 1.00 2.00
❑ 11 Blood Celebrant C :K: .10 .30
❑ 12 Bloodstoke Howler C :R: .10 .30
❑ 13 Branchsnap Lorian U :G: .20 .50
❑ 14 Brontotherium U :G: .20 .50
❑ 15 Brood Sliver R :G: 3.00 6.00
❑ 16 Caller of the Claw R :G: 2.00 4.00
❑ 17 Canopy Crawler U :G: .20 .50
❑ 18 Celestial Gatekeeper R :W: 1.50 3.00
❑ 19 Cephalid Pathmage C :B: .10 .30
❑ 20 Chromeshell Crab R :B: 2.00 4.00
❑ 21 Clickslither R :R: 1.00 2.00
❑ 22 Cloudreach Cavalry U :W: .20 .50
❑ 23 Corpse Harvester U :K: .20 .50
❑ 24 Covert Operative C :B: .10 .30
❑ 25 Crested Craghorn C :R: .10 .30
❑ 26 Crookclaw Elder U :B: .20 .50
❑ 27 Crypt Sliver C :K: .10 .30
❑ 28 Dark Supplicant U :K: .50 1.00
❑ 29 Daru Mender U :W: .20 .50
❑ 30 Daru Sanctifier C :W: .10 .30
❑ 31 Daru Stinger C :W: .10 .30
❑ 32 Deathmark Prelate U :K: .20 .50
❑ 33 Defender of the Order R :W: 1.00 2.00
❑ 34 Defiant Elf C :G: .10 .30
❑ 35 Deftblade Elite C :W: .10 .30
❑ 36 Dermoplasm R :B: 1.00 2.00
❑ 37 Dreamborn Muse R :B: 1.50 3.00
❑ 38 Drinker of Sorrow R :K: 1.00 2.00
❑ 39 Dripping Dead C :K: .10 .30
❑ 40 Earthblighter U :K: .20 .50
❑ 41 Echo Tracer C :B: .10 .30
❑ 42 Elvish Soultiller R :G: 1.50 3.00
❑ 43 Embalmed Brawler C :K: .10 .30
❑ 44 Enormous Baloth U :G: .20 .50
❑ 45 Essence Sliver R :W: 3.00 6.00
❑ 46 Feral Throwback R :G: 1.00 2.00
❑ 47 Flamewave Invoker C :R: .10 .30
❑ 48 Frenetic Raptor U :R: .20 .50
❑ 49 Fugitive Wizard C :B: .10 .30
❑ 50 Gempalm Avenger C :W: .10 .30
❑ 51 Gempalm Incinerator U :R: .75 1.50
❑ 52 Gempalm Polluter C :K: .10 .30
❑ 53 Gempalm Sorcerer U :B: .20 .50
❑ 54 Gempalm Strider U :G: .20 .50
❑ 55 Ghastly Remains R :K: 1.50 3.00
❑ 56 Glintwing Invoker C :B: .10 .30
❑ 57 Glowering Rogon C :G: .10 .30
❑ 58 Glowrider R :W: 1.50 3.00
❑ 59 Goblin Assassin U :R: .20 .50
❑ 60 Goblin Clearcutter U :R: .20 .50
❑ 61 Goblin Dynamo U :R: .20 .50
❑ 62 Goblin Firebug C :R: .10 .30
❑ 63 Goblin Goon R :R: 2.00 4.00
❑ 64 Goblin Grappler C :R: .10 .30
❑ 65 Goblin Lookout C :R: .10 .30
❑ 66 Goblin Turncoat C :K: .10 .30
❑ 67 Graveborn Muse R :K: 1.00 2.00
❑ 68 Havoc Demon R :K: 1.50 3.00
❑ 69 Hollow Specter R :K: 1.50 3.00
❑ 70 Hundroog C :G: .10 .30
❑ 71 Hunter Sliver C :R: .10 .30
❑ 72 Imperial Hellkite R :R: 2.00 4.00
❑ 73 Infernal Caretaker C :K: .10 .30
❑ 74 Keeneye Aven C :B: .10 .30
❑ 75 Keeper of the Nine Gales R :B: 1.00 2.00
❑ 76 Kilnmouth Dragon R :R: 4.00 8.00
❑ 77 Krosan Cloudscraper R :G: 4.00 8.00
❑ 78 Krosan Vorine C :G: .10 .30
❑ 79 Lavaborn Muse R :R: 1.50 3.00
❑ 80 Liege of the Axe U :W: .20 .50
❑ 81 Lowland Tracker C :W: .10 .30
❑ 82 Macetail Hystrodon C :R: .10 .30
❑ 83 Magma Sliver R :R: 2.50 5.00
❑ 84 Master of the Veil U :B: .20 .50
❑ 85 Merchant of Secrets C :B: .10 .30
❑ 86 Mistform Seaswift C :B: .10 .30
❑ 87 Mistform Sliver C :B: .10 .30
❑ 88 Mistform Ultimus R :B: 1.00 2.00
❑ 89 Mistform Wakecaster U :B: .20 .50
❑ 90 Nantuko Vigilante C :G: .10 .30
❑ 91 Needleshot Gourna C :G: .10 .30
❑ 92 Noxious Ghoul U :K: 1.00 2.00
❑ 93 Patron of the Wild C :G: .10 .30
❑ 94 Phage the Untouchable R :K: 5.00 10.00
❑ 95 Planar Guide R :W: 1.50 3.00
❑ 96 Plated Sliver C :W: .10 .30
❑ 97 Primal Whisperer R :G: 1.00 2.00
❑ 98 Primoc Escapee U :B: .20 .50
❑ 99 Quick Sliver C :G: .10 .30
❑ 100 Ridgetop Raptor U :R: .20 .50
❑ 101 Riptide Director R :B: 1.50 3.00
❑ 102 Riptide Mangler R :B: 1.50 3.00
❑ 103 Rockshard Elemental R :R: 1.50 3.00
❑ 104 Root Sliver U :G: .50 1.00
❑ 105 Scion of Darkness R :K: 4.00 8.00
❑ 106 Seedborn Muse R :G: 4.00 8.00
❑ 107 Shaleskin Plower C :R: .10 .30
❑ 108 Shifting Sliver U :B: .50 1.00
❑ 109 Skinthinner C :K: .10 .30
❑ 110 Skirk Alarmist R :R: 1.00 2.00
❑ 111 Skirk Drill Sergeant U :R: .50 1.00
❑ 112 Skirk Marauder C :R: .10 .30
❑ 113 Skirk Outrider C :R: .10 .30
❑ 114 Smokespew Invoker C :K: .10 .30
❑ 115 Sootfeather Flock C :K: .10 .30
❑ 116 Spectral Sliver U :K: .50 1.00
❑ 117 Starlight Invoker C :W: .10 .30
❑ 118 Stoic Champion U :W: .20 .50
❑ 119 Stonewood Invoker C :G: .10 .30
❑ 120 Sunstrike Legionnaire R :W: 1.50 3.00
❑ 121 Swooping Talon U :W: .20 .50
❑ 122 Synapse Sliver R :B: 2.00 4.00
❑ 123 Timberwatch Elf C :G: .10 .30
❑ 124 Totem Speaker U :G: .20 .50
❑ 125 Toxin Sliver R :K: 4.00 8.00
❑ 126 Tribal Forcemage R :G: 1.50 3.00
❑ 127 Unstable Hulk R :R: 1.00 2.00
❑ 128 Vexing Beetle R :G: 1.00 2.00
❑ 129 Vile Deacon C :K: .10 .30
❑ 130 Voidmage Apprentice C :B: .10 .30
❑ 131 Wall of Deceit U :B: .20 .50
❑ 132 Wall of Hope C :W: .10 .30
❑ 133 Warbreak Trumpeter U :R: .20 .50
❑ 134 Ward Sliver U :W: 1.50 3.00
❑ 135 Warped Researcher U :B: .20 .50
❑ 136 Weaver of Lies R :B: 1.00 2.00
❑ 137 Whipgrass Entangler C :W: .10 .30
❑ 138 White Knight U :W: .75 1.50
❑ 139 Willbender U :B: .50 1.00
❑ 140 Windborn Muse R :W: 2.00 4.00
❑ 141 Wingbeat Warrior C :W: .10 .30
❑ 142 Wirewood Channeler U :G: 1.50 3.00
❑ 143 Wirewood Hivemaster U :G: 1.50 3.00
❑ 144 Withered Wretch U :K: 1.00 2.00
❑ 145 Zombie Brute U :K: .20 .50

2003 Magic the Gathering Legions Foil

COMPLETE SET (145) 250.00 375.00
*Foil: 1X to 2X Basic Cards

2003 Magic the Gathering Scourge

Complete Set (143) 90.00 140.00
Theme Deck Box 90.00 110.00
Theme Deck 10.00 12.00
Booster Box (36 Packs) 80.00 120.00
Booster Pack (15 Cards) 3.50 4.00
Fat Pack 25.00 30.00

❑ 1 Accelerated Mutation C :G: .10 .30
❑ 2 Ageless Sentinels R :W: 1.50 3.00
❑ 3 Alpha Status U :G: 1.00 2.00
❑ 4 Ambush Commander R :G: 2.50 5.00
❑ 5 Ancient Ooze R :G: 2.00 4.00
❑ 6 Aphetto Runecaster U :B: .50 1.00
❑ 7 Ark of Blight U :A: .50 1.00
❑ 8 Astral Steel C :W: .10 .30
❑ 9 Aven Farseer C :W: .10 .30
❑ 10 Aven Liberator C :W: .10 .30
❑ 11 Bladewing the Risen R :D: 2.00 4.00
❑ 12 Bladewing's Thrall U :K: .20 .50
❑ 13 Bonethorn Valesk C :R: .10 .30
❑ 14 Brain Freeze U :B: 2.00 4.00
❑ 15 Break Asunder C :G: .10 .30
❑ 16 Cabal Conditioning R :K: 1.00 2.00
❑ 17 Cabal Interrogator U :K: .50 1.00
❑ 18 Call to the Grave R :K: 3.00 6.00
❑ 19 Carbonize U :R: .20 .50
❑ 20 Carrion Feeder C :K: .10 .30
❑ 21 Chartooth Cougar C :R: .10 .30
❑ 22 Chill Haunting U :K: .30 .75
❑ 23 Claws of Wirewood U :G: .30 .75
❑ 24 Clutch of Undeath C :K: .10 .30
❑ 25 Coast Watcher C :B: .10 .30
❑ 26 Consumptive Goo R :K: 1.50 3.00
❑ 27 Daru Spiritualist C :W: .10 .30
❑ 28 Daru Warchief U :W: 1.00 2.00
❑ 29 Dawn Elemental R :W: 2.00 4.00
❑ 30 Day of the Dragons R :B: 2.50 5.00
❑ 31 Death's-Head Buzzard C :K: .10 .30
❑ 32 Decree of Annihilation R :R: 3.00 6.00
❑ 33 Decree of Justice R :W: 4.00 8.00
❑ 34 Decree of Pain R :K: 2.00 4.00
❑ 35 Decree of Savagery R :G: 1.50 3.00
❑ 36 Decree of Silence R :B: 2.00 4.00
❑ 37 Dimensional Breach R :W: 1.50 3.00
❑ 38 Dispersal Shield C :B: .10 .30
❑ 39 Divergent Growth C :G: .10 .30
❑ 40 Dragon Breath C :R: .10 .30
❑ 41 Dragon Fangs C :G: .10 .30
❑ 42 Dragon Mage R :R: 2.50 4.00
❑ 43 Dragon Scales C :W: .10 .30
❑ 44 Dragon Shadow C :K: .10 .30
❑ 45 Dragon Tyrant R :R: 3.00 6.00
❑ 46 Dragon Wings C :B: .10 .30
❑ 47 Dragonspeaker Shaman U :R: 1.00 2.00
❑ 48 Dragonstalker U :W: .30 .75
❑ 49 Dragonstorm R :R: 2.50 5.00
❑ 50 Edgewalker U :D: .75 1.50
❑ 51 Elvish Aberration U :G: .50 1.00
❑ 52 Enrage U :R: .20 .50
❑ 53 Eternal Dragon R :W: 6.00 12.00
❑ 54 Exiled Doomsayer R :W: 1.50 3.00
❑ 55 Extra Arms U :R: .20 .50
❑ 56 Faces of the Past R :B: 1.50 3.00
❑ 57 Fatal Mutation U :K: .20 .50
❑ 58 Fierce Empath C :G: .10 .30
❑ 59 Final Punishment R :K: 1.50 3.00
❑ 60 Force Bubble R :W: 1.50 3.00
❑ 61 Forgotten Ancient R :G: 4.00 8.00
❑ 62 Form of the Dragon R :R: 2.50 5.00
❑ 63 Frontline Strategist C :W: .10 .30
❑ 64 Frozen Solid C :B: .10 .30
❑ 65 Gilded Light U :W: .50 1.00
❑ 66 Goblin Brigand C :R: .10 .30
❑ 67 Goblin Psychopath U :R: .30 .75
❑ 68 Goblin War Strike C :R: .10 .30
❑ 69 Goblin Warchief U :R: 2.00 4.00
❑ 70 Grip of Chaos R :R: 1.00 2.00
❑ 71 Guilty Conscience C :W: .10 .30
❑ 72 Hindering Touch C :B: .10 .30
❑ 73 Hunting Pack U :G: .20 .50
❑ 74 Karona, False God R :D: 2.00 4.00
❑ 75 Karona's Zealot U :W: .20 .50
❑ 76 Krosan Drover C :G: .10 .30
❑ 77 Krosan Warchief U :G: .75 1.50
❑ 78 Kurgadon U :G: .20 .50
❑ 79 Lethal Vapors R :K: 2.00 4.00
❑ 80 Lingering Death C :K: .10 .30
❑ 81 Long-Term Plans U :B: .20 .50
❑ 82 Mercurial Kite C :B: .10 .30
❑ 83 Metamorphose U :B: .20 .50
❑ 84 Mind's Desire R :B: 2.00 4.00
❑ 85 Mischievous Quanar R :B: 1.00 2.00
❑ 86 Misguided Rage C :R: .10 .30
❑ 87 Mistform Warchief U :B: .20 .50
❑ 88 Nefashu R :K: 1.50 3.00
❑ 89 Noble Templar C :W: .10 .30
❑ 90 One with Nature U :G: .50 1.00
❑ 91 Parallel Thoughts R :B: 1.00 2.00
❑ 92 Pemmin's Aura U :B: 1.00 2.00
❑ 93 Primitive Etchings R :G: 1.50 3.00
❑ 94 Proteus Machine U :A: .30 .75
❑ 95 Putrid Raptor U :K: .20 .50
❑ 96 Pyrostatic Pillar U :R: .20 .50
❑ 97 Rain of Blades U :W: .20 .50
❑ 98 Raven Guild Initiate C :B: .10 .30
❑ 99 Raven Guild Master R :B: 4.00 8.00
❑ 100 Reaping the Graves C :K: .10 .30
❑ 101 Recuperate C :W: .10 .30
❑ 102 Reward the Faithful U :W: .20 .50
❑ 103 Riptide Survivor U :B: .20 .50
❑ 104 Rock Jockey C :R: .10 .30
❑ 105 Root Elemental R :G: 1.50 3.00
❑ 106 Rush of Knowledge C :B: .10 .30
❑ 107 Scattershot C :R: .10 .30
❑ 108 Scornful Egotist C :B: .10 .30
❑ 109 Shoreline Ranger C :B: .10 .30
❑ 110 Siege-Gang Commander R :R: 3.00 6.00
❑ 111 Silver Knight U :W: 1.00 2.00
❑ 112 Skirk Volcanist U :R: .20 .50
❑ 113 Skulltap C :K: .10 .30
❑ 114 Sliver Overlord R :D: 4.00 8.00
❑ 115 Soul Collector R :K: 2.00 4.00
❑ 116 Spark Spray C :R: .10 .30
❑ 117 Sprouting Vines C :G: .10 .30
❑ 118 Stabilizer R :A: 1.00 2.00
❑ 119 Stifle R :B: 4.00 8.00
❑ 120 Sulfuric Vortex R :R: 2.00 4.00
❑ 121 Temple of the False God U :L: .50 1.00
❑ 122 Temporal Fissure C :B: .10 .30
❑ 123 Tendrils of Agony U :K: .75 1.50
❑ 124 Thundercloud Elemental U :B: .30 .75
❑ 125 Titanic Bulvox C :G: .10 .30
❑ 126 Torrent of Fire C :R: .10 .30
❑ 127 Trap Digger R :W: 1.50 3.00
❑ 128 Treetop Scout C :G: .10 .30
❑ 129 Twisted Abomination C :K: .10 .30
❑ 130 Unburden C :K: .10 .30
❑ 131 Uncontrolled Infestation C :R: .10 .30
❑ 132 Undead Warchief U :K: 1.00 2.50
❑ 133 Unspeakable Symbol U :K: .20 .50
❑ 134 Upwelling R :G: 2.00 4.00
❑ 135 Vengeful Dead C :K: .10 .30
❑ 136 Wing Shards U :W: 1.00 2.00
❑ 137 Wipe Clean C :W: .10 .30
❑ 138 Wirewood Guardian C :G: .10 .30
❑ 139 Wirewood Symbiote U :G: .50 1.00
❑ 140 Woodcloaker C :G: .10 .30
❑ 141 Xantid Swarm R :G: 2.00 4.00
❑ 142 Zealous Inquisitor C :W: .10 .30
❑ 143 Zombie Cutthroat C :K: .10 .30

2003 Magic the Gathering Scourge Foil

*Foil: 1X to 2X Basic Cards

2003 Magic the Gathering Mirrodin

Complete Set (306) 125.00 200.00
Starter Box (12 Decks) 80.00 125.00
Starter Deck 10.00 13.00
Booster Box (36 Packs) 80.00 110.00
Booster Pack (15 Cards) 3.50 4.00
Fat Pack 30.00 38.00

❑ 1 AEther Spellbomb C :A: .10 .30
❑ 2 Alpha Myr C :A: .10 .30
❑ 3 Altar of Shadows R :A: 1.50 3.00
❑ 4 Altar's Light U :W: .50 1.00
❑ 5 Ancient Den C :L: .10 .30
❑ 6 Annul C :B: .10 .30
❑ 7 Arc-Slogger R :R: 2.50 5.00
❑ 8 Arrest C :W: .10 .30
❑ 9 Assert Authority U :B: .50 1.00
❑ 10 Alog U :R: .50 1.00
❑ 11 Auriok Bladewarden U :W: .50 1.00
❑ 12 Auriok Steelshaper R :W: 2.00 4.00
❑ 13 Auriok Transfixer C :W: .10 .30
❑ 14 Awe Strike C :W: .10 .30
❑ 15 Banshee's Blade U :A: .50 1.00
❑ 16 Barter in Blood U :K: .50 1.00
❑ 17 Battlegrowth C :G: .10 .30
❑ 18 Betrayal of Flesh U :K: .30 .75
❑ 19 Blinding Beam C :W: .10 .30
❑ 20 Blinkmoth Urn R :A: 1.00 2.00
❑ 21 Blinkmoth Well U :L: .50 1.00
❑ 22 Bloodscent U :G: .50 1.00
❑ 23 Bonesplitter C :A: .10 .30
❑ 24 Bosh, Iron Golem R :A: 2.00 4.00
❑ 25 Bottle Gnomes U :A: .50 1.00
❑ 26 Broodstar R :B: 2.50 5.00
❑ 27 Brown Ouphe U :G: .50 1.00
❑ 28 Cathodion U :A: .50 1.00
❑ 29 Chalice of the Void R :A: 2.50 5.00
❑ 30 Chimney Imp C :K: .10 .30
❑ 31 Chromatic Sphere C :A: .10 .30
❑ 32 Chrome Mox R :A: 10.00 20.00
❑ 33 Clockwork Beetle C :A: .10 .30
❑ 34 Clockwork Condor C :A: .10 .30
❑ 35 Clockwork Dragon R :A: 2.00 4.00
❑ 36 Clockwork Vorrac U :A: .20 .50
❑ 37 Cloudpost C :L: .10 .30
❑ 38 Cobalt Golem C :A: .10 .30
❑ 39 Confusion in the Ranks R :R: 1.50 3.00
❑ 40 Consume Spirit C :K: .10 .30
❑ 41 Contaminated Bond C :K: .10 .30
❑ 42 Copper Myr C :A: .10 .30
❑ 43 Copperhoof Vorrac R :G: 1.00 2.00
❑ 44 Creeping Mold U :G: .20 .50
❑ 45 Crystal Shard U :A: .20 .50
❑ 46 Culling Scales R :A: 1.00 2.00
❑ 47 Damping Matrix R :A: 2.00 4.00
❑ 48 Dead-Iron Sledge U :A: .20 .50
❑ 49 Deconstruct C :G: .10 .30
❑ 50 Detonate U :R: .50 1.00
❑ 51 Disarm C :B: .10 .30
❑ 52 Disciple of the Vault C :K: .10 .30
❑ 53 Domineer U :B: .20 .50
❑ 54 Dragon Blood U :A: .50 1.00
❑ 55 Dream's Grip C :B: .10 .30
❑ 56 Dross Harvester R :K: 1.50 3.00
❑ 57 Dross Prowler C :K: .10 .30
❑ 58 Dross Scorpion C :A: .10 .30
❑ 59 Duplicant R :A: 2.50 5.00
❑ 60 Duskworker U :A: .20 .50
❑ 61 Electrostatic Bolt C :R: .20 .30
❑ 62 Elf Replica C :A: .10 .30
❑ 63 Empyrial Plate R :A: 2.00 4.00
❑ 64 Extraplanar Lens R :A: 2.50 5.00
❑ 65 Fabricate U :B: 1.00 2.00
❑ 66 Fangren Hunter C :G: .10 .30
❑ 67 Farsight Mask U :A: .20 .50
❑ 68 Fatespinner R :B: 1.50 3.00
❑ 69 Fiery Gambit R :R: 1.00 2.00
❑ 70 Fireshrieker U :A: 1.00 2.00
❑ 71 Fists of the Anvil C :R: .10 .30
❑ 72 Flayed Nim U :K: .20 .50
❑ 73 Forest L :L: .10 .30
❑ 74 Forest L :L: .10 .30
❑ 75 Forest L :L: .10 .30
❑ 76 Forest L :L: .10 .30
❑ 77 Forge Armor U :R: .20 .50
❑ 78 Fractured Loyalty U :R: .20 .50
❑ 79 Frogmite C :A: .10 .30
❑ 80 Galvanic Key C :A: .10 .30
❑ 81 Gate to the Æther R :A: 1.50 3.00
❑ 82 Gilded Lotus R :A: 3.00 6.00
❑ 83 Glimmervoid R :L: 5.00 10.00
❑ 84 Glissa Sunseeker R :G: 2.00 4.00
❑ 85 Goblin Charbelcher R :A: 2.50 5.00
❑ 86 Goblin Dirigible U :A: .20 .50
❑ 87 Goblin Replica C :A: .10 .30
❑ 88 Goblin Striker C :R: .10 .30
❑ 89 Goblin War Wagon C :A: .10 .30
❑ 90 Gold Myr C :A: .10 .30
❑ 91 Golem-Skin Gauntlets U :A: .50 1.00
❑ 92 Grab the Reins U :R: .50 1.00
❑ 93 Granite Shard U :A: .20 .50
❑ 94 Great Furnace C :L: .20 .50
❑ 95 Grid Monitor R :A: 2.00 4.00
❑ 96 Grim Reminder R :K: 1.00 2.00
❑ 97 Groffskithur C :G: .10 .30
❑ 98 Heartwood Shard U :A: .20 .50
❑ 99 Hematite Golem C :A: .10 .30
❑ 100 Hum of the Radix R :G: 1.50 3.00
❑ 101 Icy Manipulator U :A: 1.00 2.00
❑ 102 Incite War C :R: .10 .30
❑ 103 Inertia Bubble C :B: .10 .30
❑ 104 Iron Myr C :A: .10 .30
❑ 105 Irradiate C :K: .10 .30
❑ 106 Island L :L: .10 .30
❑ 107 Island L :L: .10 .30
❑ 108 Island L :L: .10 .30
❑ 109 Island L :L: .10 .30
❑ 110 Isochron Scepter U :A: 4.00 8.00
❑ 111 Jinxed Choker R :A: 1.00 2.00
❑ 112 Journey of Discovery C :G: .10 .30
❑ 113 Krark-Clan Grunt C :R: .10 .30
❑ 114 Krark-Clan Shaman C :R: .10 .30
❑ 115 Krark's Thumb R :A: 1.00 2.00
❑ 116 Leaden Myr C :A: .10 .30
❑ 117 Leonin Abunas R :W: 2.50 5.00
❑ 118 Leonin Bladetrap U :A: .20 .50
❑ 119 Leonin Den-Guard C :W: .10 .30
❑ 120 Leonin Elder C :W: .10 .30
❑ 121 Leonin Scimitar C :A: .10 .30
❑ 122 Leonin Skyhunter U :W: 1.00 2.00
❑ 123 Leonin Sun Standard R :A: 1.50 3.00
❑ 124 Leveler R :A: 1.50 3.00
❑ 125 Liar's Pendulum R :A: 1.00 2.00
❑ 126 Lifespark Spellbomb C :A: .10 .30
❑ 127 Lightning Coils R :A: 2.00 4.00
❑ 128 Lightning Greaves U :A: 1.00 2.00
❑ 129 Living Hive R :G: 1.50 3.00
❑ 130 Lodestone Myr R :A: 1.50 3.00
❑ 131 Looming Hoverguard U :B: .20 .50
❑ 132 Loxodon Mender C :W: .10 .30
❑ 133 Loxodon Peacekeeper R :W: 1.50 3.00
❑ 134 Loxodon Punisher R :W: 1.00 2.00
❑ 135 Loxodon Warhammer U :A: 1.00 2.00
❑ 136 Lumengrid Augur R :B: 1.00 2.00
❑ 137 Lumengrid Sentinel U :B: .20 .50
❑ 138 Lumengrid Warden C :B: .10 .30

❑ 139 Luminous Angel R :W: 2.00 4.00
❑ 140 Malachite Golem C :A: .10 .30
❑ 141 March of the Machines R :B: 3.00 6.00
❑ 142 Mask of Memory U :A: .20 .50
❑ 143 Mass Hysteria R :R: 1.50 3.00
❑ 144 Megatog R :R: 2.00 4.00
❑ 145 Mesmeric Orb R :A: 1.50 3.00
❑ 146 Mind's Eye R :A: 1.50 3.00
❑ 147 Mindslaver R :A: 4.00 8.00
❑ 148 Mindstorm Crown U :A: .20 .50
❑ 149 Mirror Golem U :A: .20 .50
❑ 150 Molder Slug R :G: 2.00 4.00
❑ 151 Molten Rain C :R: .10 .30
❑ 152 Moriok Scavenger C :K: .10 .30
❑ 153 Mountain L :L: .10 .30
❑ 154 Mountain L :L: .10 .30
❑ 155 Mountain L :L: .10 .30
❑ 156 Mountain L :L: .10 .30
❑ 157 Mourner's Shield U :A: .20 .50
❑ 158 Myr Adapter C :A: .10 .30
❑ 159 Myr Enforcer C :A: .10 .30
❑ 160 Myr Incubator R :A: 2.00 4.00
❑ 161 Myr Mindservant U :A: .20 .50
❑ 162 Myr Prototype U :A: .20 .50
❑ 163 Myr Retriever U :A: 1.00 2.00
❑ 164 Necrogen Mists R :K: 1.50 3.00
❑ 165 Necrogen Spellbomb C :A: .10 .30
❑ 166 Needlebug U :A: .20 .50
❑ 167 Neurok Familiar C :B: .10 .30
❑ 168 Neurok Hoversail C :A: .10 .30
❑ 169 Neurok Spy C :B: .10 .30
❑ 170 Nightmare Lash R :A: 1.00 2.00
❑ 171 Nim Devourer R :K: 1.00 2.00
❑ 172 Nim Lasher C :K: .10 .30
❑ 173 Nim Replica C :A: .10 .30
❑ 174 Nim Shambler U :K: .20 .50
❑ 175 Nim Shrieker C :K: .10 .30
❑ 176 Nuisance Engine U :A: .20 .50
❑ 177 Oblivion Stone R :A: 4.00 8.00
❑ 178 Ogre Leadfoot C :R: .10 .30
❑ 179 Omega Myr C :A: .10 .30
❑ 180 One Dozen Eyes U :G: .20 .50
❑ 181 Ornithopter U :A: 1.00 2.00
❑ 182 Override C :B: .10 .30
❑ 183 Pearl Shard U :A: .20 .50
❑ 184 Pentavus R :A: 1.50 3.00
❑ 185 Pewter Golem C :A: .10 .30
❑ 186 Plains L :L: .10 .30
❑ 187 Plains L :L: .10 .30
❑ 188 Plains L :L: .10 .30
❑ 189 Plains L :L: .10 .30
❑ 190 Plated Slagwurm R :G: 1.50 3.00
❑ 191 Platinum Angel R :A: 8.00 15.00
❑ 192 Power Conduit U :A: .50 1.00
❑ 193 Predator's Strike C :G: .10 .30
❑ 194 Promise of Power R :K: 1.50 3.00
❑ 195 Proteus Staff R :A: 1.50 3.00
❑ 196 Psychic Membrane U :B: .20 .50
❑ 197 Psychogenic Probe R :A: 1.00 2.00
❑ 198 Pyrite Spellbomb C :A: .10 .30
❑ 199 Quicksilver Elemental R :B: 1.00 2.00
❑ 200 Quicksilver Fountain R :A: 1.00 2.00
❑ 201 Raise the Alarm C :W: .10 .30
❑ 202 Razor Barrier C :W: .10 .30
❑ 203 Regress C :B: .10 .30
❑ 204 Reiver Demon R :K: 2.50 5.00
❑ 205 Relic Bane U :K: .20 .50
❑ 206 Roar of the Kha U :W: .20 .50
❑ 207 Rule of Law R :W: 1.50 3.00
❑ 208 Rust Elemental U :A: .20 .50
❑ 209 Rustmouth Ogre U :R: .30 .75
❑ 210 Rustspore Ram U :A: .20 .50
❑ 211 Scale of Chiss-Goria C :A: .10 .30
❑ 212 Scrabbling Claws U :A: .20 .50
❑ 213 Sculpting Steel R :A: 2.00 4.00
❑ 214 Scythe of the Wretched R :A: 1.50 3.00
❑ 215 Seat of the Synod C :L: .20 .50
❑ 216 Second Sunrise R :W: 2.00 4.00
❑ 217 Seething Song C :R: .10 .30
❑ 218 Serum Tank U :A: .20 .50
❑ 219 Shared Fate R :B: 1.50 3.00
❑ 220 Shatter C :R: .10 .30
❑ 221 Shrapnel Blast U :R: 1.00 2.00
❑ 222 Silver Myr C :A: .10 .30
❑ 223 Skeleton Shard U :A: .20 .50
❑ 224 Skyhunter Cub C :W: .10 .30
❑ 225 Skyhunter Patrol C :W: .10 .30
❑ 226 Slagwurm Armor C :A: .10 .30
❑ 227 Slith Ascendant U :W: .20 .50
❑ 228 Slith Bloodletter U :K: .20 .50
❑ 229 Slith Firewalker U :R: 1.00 2.00
❑ 230 Slith Predator U :G: .20 .50
❑ 231 Slith Strider U :B: .20 .50
❑ 232 Solar Tide R :W: 1.50 3.00
❑ 233 Soldier Replica C :A: .10 .30
❑ 234 Solemn Simulacrum R :A: 4.00 8.00
❑ 235 Somber Hoverguard C :B: .10 .30
❑ 236 Soul Foundry R :A: 2.00 4.00
❑ 237 Soul Nova U :W: .20 .50
❑ 238 Spellweaver Helix R :A: 1.50 3.00
❑ 239 Sphere of Purity C :W: .10 .30
❑ 240 Spikeshot Goblin C :R: .10 .30
❑ 241 Spoils of the Vault R :K: 1.50 3.00
❑ 242 Stalking Stones U :L: .20 .50
❑ 243 Steel Wall C :A: .10 .30
❑ 244 Sun Droplet U :A: .50 1.00
❑ 245 Sunbeam Spellbomb C :A: .10 .30
❑ 246 Swamp L :L: .10 .30
❑ 247 Swamp L :L: .10 .30
❑ 248 Swamp L :L: .10 .30
❑ 249 Swamp L :L: .10 .30
❑ 250 Sword of Kaldra R :A: 3.00 6.00
❑ 251 Sylvan Scrying U :G: .50 1.00
❑ 252 Synod Sanctum U :A: .20 .50
❑ 253 Taj-Nar Swordsmith U :W: .20 .50
❑ 254 Talisman of Dominance U :A: .50 1.00
❑ 255 Talisman of Impulse U :A: .20 .50
❑ 256 Talisman of Indulgence U :A: .20 .50
❑ 257 Talisman of Progress U :A: .50 1.00
❑ 258 Talisman of Unity U :A: .20 .50
❑ 259 Tanglebloom C :A: .10 .30
❑ 260 Tangleroot R :A: 1.00 2.00
❑ 261 Tel-Jilad Archers C :G: .10 .30
❑ 262 Tel-Jilad Chosen C :G: .10 .30
❑ 263 Tel-Jilad Exile C :G: .10 .30
❑ 264 Tel-Jilad Stylus U :A: .20 .50
❑ 265 Tempest of Light U :W: .20 .50
❑ 266 Temporal Cascade R :B: 1.50 3.00
❑ 267 Terror C :K: .10 .30
❑ 268 Thirst for Knowledge U :B: 1.00 2.00
❑ 269 Thought Prison U :A: .20 .50
❑ 270 Thoughtcast C :B: .20 .50
❑ 271 Timesifter R :A: 1.50 3.00
❑ 272 Titanium Golem C :A: .10 .30
❑ 273 Tooth and Nail R :G: 4.00 8.00
❑ 274 Tooth of Chiss-Goria C :A: .10 .30
❑ 275 Tower of Champions R :A: 1.00 2.00
❑ 276 Tower of Eons R :A: 1.50 3.00
❑ 277 Tower of Fortunes R :A: 1.50 3.00
❑ 278 Tower of Murmurs R :A: 1.50 3.00
❑ 279 Trash for Treasure R :R: 1.50 3.00
❑ 280 Tree of Tales C :L: .10 .30
❑ 281 Triskelion R :A: 2.00 4.00
❑ 282 Troll Ascetic R :G: 5.00 10.00
❑ 283 Trolls of Tel-Jilad U :G: .20 .50
❑ 284 Turn to Dust C :G: .10 .30
❑ 285 Vault of Whispers C :L: .10 .30
❑ 286 Vedalken Archmage R :B: 1.50 3.00
❑ 287 Vermiculos R :K: 1.00 2.00
❑ 288 Viridian Joiner C :G: .10 .30
❑ 289 Viridian Longbow C :A: .10 .30
❑ 290 Viridian Shaman U :G: .50 1.00
❑ 291 Vorrac Battlehorns C :A: .10 .30
❑ 292 Vulshok Battlegear U :A: .20 .50
❑ 293 Vulshok Battlemaster R :R: 1.00 2.00
❑ 294 Vulshok Berserker C :R: .10 .30
❑ 295 Vulshok Gauntlets C :A: .10 .30
❑ 296 Wail of the Nim C :K: .10 .30
❑ 297 Wall of Blood U :K: .20 .50
❑ 298 Wanderguard Sentry C :B: .10 .30
❑ 299 War Elemental R :R: 1.50 3.00
❑ 300 Welding Jar C :A: .10 .30
❑ 301 Wizard Replica C :A: .10 .30
❑ 302 Woebearer U :K: .20 .50
❑ 303 Worldslayer R :A: 1.50 3.00
❑ 304 Wrench Mind C :K: .10 .30
❑ 305 Wurmskin Forger C :G: .10 .30
❑ 306 Yotian Soldier C :A: .10 .30

2003 Magic the Gathering Mirrodin Foil

*Foil: 1X to 2X Basic Cards

2004 Magic the Gathering Darksteel

Complete Set (165) 125.00 200.00
Booster Box (36 Packs) 150.00 250.00
Booster Pack (15 Cards) 4.50 8.00
Fat Pack 30.00 60.00

❑ 1 AEther Snap R :K: .30 .75
❑ 2 AEther Vial U :A: 6.00 15.00
❑ 3 Ageless Entity R :G: .50 1.25
❑ 4 Angel's Feather U :A: .20 .50
❑ 5 Arcane Spyglass C :A: .10 .25
❑ 6 Arcbound Bruiser C :A: .10 .25
❑ 7 Arcbound Crusher U :A: .40 1.00
❑ 8 Arcbound Fiend U :A: .20 .50
❑ 9 Arcbound Hybrid C :A: .10 .25
❑ 10 Arcbound Lancer U :A: .20 .50
❑ 11 Arcbound Overseer R :A: 1.00 2.50
❑ 12 Arcbound Ravager R :A: 10.00 25.00
❑ 13 Arcbound Reclaimer R :A: .50 1.25
❑ 14 Arcbound Slith U :A: .30 .75
❑ 15 Arcbound Stinger C :A: .10 .25
❑ 16 Arcbound Worker C :A: .20 .50
❑ 17 Auriok Glaivemaster C :W: .10 .25
❑ 18 Auriok Siege Sled U :A: .20 .50
❑ 19 Barbed Lightning C :R: .10 .25
❑ 20 Blinkmoth Nexus R :L: 6.00 15.00
❑ 21 Burden of Greed C :K: .10 .25
❑ 22 Carry Away U :B: .20 .50
❑ 23 Chimeric Egg U :A: .20 .50
❑ 24 Chittering Rats C :K: .10 .25
❑ 25 Chromescale Drake R :B: .30 .75
❑ 26 Coretapper U :A: .40 1.00
❑ 27 Crazed Goblin C :R: .10 .25
❑ 28 Darksteel Brute U :A: .20 .50
❑ 29 Darksteel Citadel C :L: .60 1.50
❑ 30 Darksteel Colossus R :A: 2.50 6.00
❑ 31 Darksteel Forge R :A: 5.00 12.00
❑ 32 Darksteel Gargoyle U :A: .20 .50
❑ 33 Darksteel Ingot C :A: .30 .75
❑ 34 Darksteel Pendant C :A: .10 .25
❑ 35 Darksteel Reactor R :A: 1.25 3.00
❑ 36 Death Cloud R :K: 1.00 2.50
❑ 37 Death-Mask Duplicant U :A: .20 .50
❑ 38 Demon's Horn U :A: .20 .50
❑ 39 Dismantle U :R: .20 .50
❑ 40 Dragon's Claw U :A: .20 .50
❑ 41 Drill-Skimmer C :A: .10 .25
❑ 42 Drooling Ogre C :R: .10 .25
❑ 43 Dross Golem C :A: .10 .25
❑ 44 Eater of Days R :A: .40 1.00
❑ 45 Echoing Calm C :W: .10 .25
❑ 46 Echoing Courage C :G: .10 .25
❑ 47 Echoing Decay C :K: .10 .25
❑ 48 Echoing Ruin C :R: .10 .25
❑ 49 Echoing Truth C :B: .30 .75
❑ 50 Emissary of Despair U :K: .20 .50
❑ 51 Emissary of Hope U :W: .20 .50
❑ 52 Essence Drain C :K: .10 .25
❑ 53 Fangren Firstborn R :G: .40 1.00
❑ 54 Fireball U :R: .20 .50
❑ 55 Flamebreak R :R: .75 2.00
❑ 56 Furnace Dragon R :R: .30 .75
❑ 57 Gemini Engine R :A: .30 .75
❑ 58 Genesis Chamber U :A: .40 1.00
❑ 59 Geth's Grimoire U :A: .20 .50
❑ 60 Goblin Archaeologist U :R: .20 .50
❑ 61 Greater Harvester R :K: .30 .75
❑ 62 Grimclaw Bats C :K: .10 .25
❑ 63 Hallow C :W: .10 .25
❑ 64 Heartseeker R :A: .40 1.00
❑ 65 Hoverguard Observer U :B: .20 .50
❑ 66 Hunger of the Nim C :K: .10 .25
❑ 67 Infested Roothold U :G: .20 .50
❑ 68 Inflame C :R: .10 .25
❑ 69 Juggernaut U :A: .20 .50
❑ 70 Karstoderm U :G: .20 .50
❑ 71 Kraken's Eye U :A: .20 .50
❑ 72 Krark-Clan Stoker C :R: .10 .25
❑ 73 Last Word R :B: .40 1.00
❑ 74 Leonin Battlemage U :W: .20 .50
❑ 75 Leonin Bola C :A: .10 .25
❑ 76 Leonin Shikari R :W: 1.50 4.00
❑ 77 Lich's Tomb R :A: .30 .75
❑ 78 Loxodon Mystic C :W: .10 .25
❑ 79 Machinate C :B: .10 .25
❑ 80 Magnetic Flux C :B: .10 .25
❑ 81 Memnarch R :A: 2.50 6.00
❑ 82 Mephitic Ooze R :K: .30 .75
❑ 83 Metal Fatigue C :W: .10 .25
❑ 84 Mirrodin's Core U :L: .40 1.00
❑ 85 Murderous Spoils U :K: .20 .50
❑ 86 Mycosynth Lattice R :A: 3.00 8.00
❑ 87 Myr Landshaper C :A: .10 .25
❑ 88 Myr Matrix R :A: 1.50 4.00
❑ 89 Myr Moonvessel C :A: .10 .25
❑ 90 Nemesis Mask U :A: .20 .50
❑ 91 Neurok Prodigy C :B: .10 .25
❑ 92 Neurok Transmuter U :B: .20 .50
❑ 93 Nim Abomination U :K: .20 .50
❑ 94 Nourish C :G: .10 .25
❑ 95 Oxidda Golem C :A: .10 .25
❑ 96 Oxidize U :G: .20 .50
❑ 97 Panoptic Mirror R :A: 1.50 4.00
❑ 98 Pristine Angel R :W: 1.50 4.00
❑ 99 Psychic Overload U :B: .20 .50
❑ 100 Pteron Ghost C :W: .10 .25
❑ 101 Pulse of the Dross R :K: .30 .75
❑ 102 Pulse of the Fields R :W: .40 1.00
❑ 103 Pulse of the Forge R :R: .40 1.00
❑ 104 Pulse of the Grid R :B: .30 .75
❑ 105 Pulse of the Tangle R :G: .30 .75
❑ 106 Purge U :W: .20 .50
❑ 107 Quicksilver Behemoth C :B: .10 .25
❑ 108 Razor Golem C :A: .10 .25
❑ 109 Reap and Sow C :G: .10 .25
❑ 110 Rebuking Ceremony R :G: .30 .75
❑ 111 Reshape R :B: .60 1.50
❑ 112 Retract R :B: .30 .75
❑ 113 Ritual of Restoration C :W: .10 .25
❑ 114 Roaring Slagwurm R :G: .30 .75
❑ 115 Savage Beating R :R: .40 1.00
❑ 116 Scavenging Scarab C :K: .10 .25
❑ 117 Screams from Within U :K: .20 .50
❑ 118 Scrounge U :K: .20 .50
❑ 119 Second Sight U :B: .20 .50
❑ 120 Serum Powder R :A: .50 1.25
❑ 121 Shield of Kaldra R :A: 2.00 5.00
❑ 122 Shriveling Rot R :K: .30 .75
❑ 123 Shunt R :R: .30 .75
❑ 124 Skullclamp U :A: 1.25 3.00
❑ 125 Slobad, Goblin Tinkerer R :R: .30 .75
❑ 126 Soulscour R :W: .30 .75
❑ 127 Spawning Pit U :A: .20 .50
❑ 128 Specter's Shroud U :A: .20 .50
❑ 129 Spellbinder R :A: .30 .75
❑ 130 Spincrusher U :A: .20 .50
❑ 131 Spire Golem C :A: .10 .25
❑ 132 Stand Together U :G: .20 .50
❑ 133 Steelshaper Apprentice R :W: .30 .75
❑ 134 Stir the Pride U :W: .20 .50
❑ 135 Sundering Titan R :A: 1.25 3.00
❑ 136 Surestrike Trident U :A: .20 .50
❑ 137 Sword of Fire and Ice R :A: 20.00 40.00
❑ 138 Sword of Light and Shadow R :A: 15.00 30.00
❑ 139 Synod Artificer R :B: .30 .75
❑ 140 Talon of Pain U :A: .20 .50
❑ 141 Tangle Golem C :A: .10 .25
❑ 142 Tangle Spider C :G: .10 .25
❑ 143 Tanglewalker U :G: .20 .50
❑ 144 Tears of Rage U :R: .20 .50
❑ 145 Tel-Jilad Outrider C :G: .10 .25
❑ 146 Tel-Jilad Wolf C :G: .10 .25
❑ 147 Test of Faith U :W: .20 .50
❑ 148 Thought Dissector R :A: .30 .75
❑ 149 Thunderstaff U :A: .30 .75
❑ 150 Trinisphere R :A: 1.25 3.00
❑ 151 Turn the Tables R :W: .30 .75
❑ 152 Unforge C :R: .10 .25
❑ 153 Ur-Golem's Eye C :A: .10 .25
❑ 154 Vedalken Engineer C :B: .10 .25
❑ 155 Vex C :B: .10 .25
❑ 156 Viridian Acolyte C :G: .10 .25
❑ 157 Viridian Zealot R :G: .75 2.00
❑ 158 Voltaic Construct U :A: .20 .50
❑ 159 Vulshok Morningstar C :A: .10 .25
❑ 160 Vulshok War Boar U :R: .20 .50
❑ 161 Wand of the Elements R :A: .30 .75
❑ 162 Well of Lost Dreams R :A: 1.00 2.50
❑ 163 Whispersilk Cloak C :A: .30 .75
❑ 164 Wirefly Hive U :A: .20 .50
❑ 165 Wurm's Tooth U :A: .20 .50

2004 Magic the Gathering Darksteel Foil

Complete Set (165) 250.00 400.00
*Foil: .8X to 2X Basic Cards

2004 Magic the Gathering Fifth Dawn

Complete Set (165) 100.00 175.00
Booster Box (36 Packs) 125.00 200.00
Booster Pack (15 Cards) 3.50 6.00
Fat Pack 30.00 50.00
Theme Deck 10.00 15.00

❑ 1 Abuna's Chant C :W: .10 .25
❑ 2 Acquire R :B: 1.00 2.50
❑ 3 Advanced Hoverguard C :B: .10 .25
❑ 4 All Suns' Dawn R :G: .40 1.00
❑ 5 Anodet Lurker C :A: .10 .25
❑ 6 Arachnoid U :A: .20 .50
❑ 7 Arcbound Wanderer U :A: .20 .50
❑ 8 Armed Response C :W: .10 .25
❑ 9 Artificer's Intuition R :B: .30 .75
❑ 10 Auriok Champion R :W: 2.00 5.00
❑ 11 Auriok Salvagers U :W: .25 .60
❑ 12 Auriok Windwalker R :W: .30 .75
❑ 13 Avarice Totem U :A: .20 .50
❑ 14 Baton of Courage C :A: .10 .25
❑ 15 Battered Golem C :A: .10 .25
❑ 16 Beacon of Creation R :G: 1.25 3.00
❑ 17 Beacon of Destruction R :R: .40 1.00
❑ 18 Beacon of Immortality R :W: 1.50 4.00
❑ 19 Beacon of Tomorrows R :B: 1.00 2.50
❑ 20 Beacon of Unrest R :K: 1.50 4.00
❑ 21 Blasting Station U :A: .60 1.50
❑ 22 Blind Creeper C :K: .10 .25
❑ 23 Blinkmoth Infusion R :B: .30 .75
❑ 24 Bringer of the Black Dawn R :K: .75 2.00
❑ 25 Bringer of the Blue Dawn R :B: 1.25 3.00
❑ 26 Bringer of the Green Dawn R :G: .60 1.50
❑ 27 Bringer of the Red Dawn R :R: .60 1.50
❑ 28 Bringer of the White Dawn R :W: .75 2.00
❑ 29 Cackling Imp C :K: .10 .25
❑ 30 Channel the Suns U :G: .30 .75
❑ 31 Chimeric Coils U :A: .20 .50
❑ 32 Circle of Protection: Artifacts U :W: .20 .50
❑ 33 Clearwater Goblet R :A: .40 1.00
❑ 34 Clock of Omens U :A: .25 .60
❑ 35 Composite Golem U :A: .25 .60
❑ 36 Condescend C :B: .25 .60
❑ 37 Conjurer's Bauble C :A: .10 .25
❑ 38 Cosmic Larva R :R: .30 .75
❑ 39 Cranial Plating C :A: .75 2.00
❑ 40 Crucible of Worlds R :A: 10.00 25.00
❑ 41 Dawn's Reflection C :G: .10 .25
❑ 42 Desecration Elemental R :K: .30 .75
❑ 43 Devour in Shadow U :K: .20 .50
❑ 44 Disruption Aura U :B: .20 .50
❑ 45 Door to Nothingness R :A: .75 2.00
❑ 46 Doubling Cube R :A: 1.50 4.00
❑ 47 Dross Crocodile C :K: .10 .25
❑ 48 Early Frost C :B: .10 .25
❑ 49 Ebon Drake U :K: .20 .50
❑ 50 Endless Whispers R :K: .30 .75
❑ 51 Energy Chamber U :A: .75 2.00
❑ 52 Engineered Explosives R :A: 6.00 15.00
❑ 53 Ensouled Scimitar U :A: .20 .50
❑ 54 Eon Hub R :A: .50 1.25
❑ 55 Etched Oracle U :A: .25 .60
❑ 56 Eternal Witness U :G: 2.00 5.00
❑ 57 Eyes of the Watcher U :B: .20 .50
❑ 58 Fangren Pathcutter U :G: .20 .50
❑ 59 Feedback Bolt U :R: .20 .50
❑ 60 Ferocious Charge C :G: .10 .25
❑ 61 Ferropede U :A: .20 .50
❑ 62 Fill with Fright C :K: .10 .25
❑ 63 Fist of Suns R :A: .75 2.00
❑ 64 Fleshgrafter C :K: .10 .25
❑ 65 Fold into Æther U :B: .20 .50
❑ 66 Furnace Whelp U :R: .25 .60
❑ 67 Gemstone Array U :A: .25 .60
❑ 68 Goblin Brawler C :R: .10 .25
❑ 69 Goblin Cannon U :A: .20 .50
❑ 70 Grafted Wargear U :A: .50 1.25
❑ 71 Granulate R :R: .30 .75
❑ 72 Grinding Station U :A: .25 .60
❑ 73 Guardian Idol U :A: .25 .60
❑ 74 Healer's Headdress C :A: .10 .25
❑ 75 Heliophial C :A: .10 .25
❑ 76 Helm of Kaldra R :A: 2.00 5.00
❑ 77 Horned Helm C :A: .10 .25
❑ 78 Hoverguard Sweepers R :B: .25 .60
❑ 79 Infused Arrows U :A: .20 .50
❑ 80 Into Thin Air C :B: .10 .25
❑ 81 Ion Storm R :R: .30 .75
❑ 82 Iron-Barb Hellion U :R: .20 .50
❑ 83 Joiner Adept R :G: .75 2.00
❑ 84 Krark-Clan Engineers U :R: .20 .50
❑ 85 Krark-Clan Ironworks U :A: .40 1.00
❑ 86 Krark-Clan Ogre C :R: .10 .25
❑ 87 Lantern of Insight U :A: .20 .50
❑ 88 Leonin Squire C :W: .10 .25
❑ 89 Lose Hope C :K: .10 .25
❑ 90 Loxodon Anchorite C :W: .10 .25
❑ 91 Loxodon Stalwart U :W: .20 .50
❑ 92 Lunar Avenger U :A: .20 .50
❑ 93 Magma Giant R :R: .25 .60
❑ 94 Magma Jet U :R: 1.50 4.00
❑ 95 Magnetic Theft U :R: .20 .50
❑ 96 Mana Geyser C :R: .10 .25
❑ 97 Mephidross Vampire R :K: 3.00 8.00
❑ 98 Moriok Rigger R :K: .30 .75
❑ 99 Mycosynth Golem R :A: 5.00 12.00
❑ 100 Myr Quadropod C :A: .10 .25
❑ 101 Myr Servitor C :A: .30 .75
❑ 102 Neurok Stealthsuit C :A: .10 .25
❑ 103 Night's Whisper U :K: .60 1.50
❑ 104 Nim Grotesque U :K: .20 .50
❑ 105 Opaline Bracers C :A: .10 .25
❑ 106 Ouphe Vandals U :G: .20 .50
❑ 107 Paradise Mantle U :A: 1.25 3.00
❑ 108 Pentad Prism C :A: .10 .25
❑ 109 Plasma Elemental U :B: .20 .50
❑ 110 Plunge into Darkness R :K: .50 1.25
❑ 111 Possessed Portal R :A: .25 .60
❑ 112 Qumulox U :B: .20 .50
❑ 113 Rain of Rust C :R: .10 .25
❑ 114 Raksha Golden Cub R :W: .75 2.00
❑ 115 Razorgrass Screen C :A: .10 .25
❑ 116 Razormane Masticore R :A: .30 .75
❑ 117 Relentless Rats U :K: .60 1.50
❑ 118 Relic Barrier U :A: .25 .60
❑ 119 Retaliate R :W: .30 .75
❑ 120 Reversal of Fortune R :R: .25 .60
❑ 121 Rite of Passage R :G: .30 .75
❑ 122 Roar of Reclamation R :W: .30 .75
❑ 123 Rude Awakening R :G: .40 1.00
❑ 124 Salvaging Station R :A: .30 .75
❑ 125 Sawtooth Thresher C :A: .10 .25
❑ 126 Screaming Fury C :R: .10 .25
❑ 127 Serum Visions C :B: .60 1.50
❑ 128 Shattered Dreams U :K: .20 .50
❑ 129 Silent Arbiter R :A: 1.25 3.00
❑ 130 Skullcage U :A: .20 .50
❑ 131 Skyhunter Prowler C :W: .10 .25
❑ 132 Skyhunter Skirmisher U :W: .25 .60
❑ 133 Skyreach Manta C :A: .10 .25
❑ 134 Solarion R :A: .40 1.00
❑ 135 Spark Elemental C :R: .25 .60
❑ 136 Sparring Collar C :A: .10 .25
❑ 137 Spectral Shift R :B: .25 .60
❑ 138 Spinal Parasite U :A: .20 .50
❑ 139 Staff of Domination R :A: 2.50 6.00
❑ 140 Stand Firm C :W: .10 .25
❑ 141 Stasis Cocoon C :W: .10 .25
❑ 142 Steelshaper's Gift U :W: 2.00 5.00
❑ 143 Summoner's Egg R :A: .40 1.00
❑ 144 Summoning Station R :A: .40 1.00
❑ 145 Suncrusher R :A: .25 .60
❑ 146 Suntouched Myr C :A: .10 .25
❑ 147 Sylvok Explorer C :G: .10 .25
❑ 148 Synod Centurion U :A: .20 .50
❑ 149 Tangle Asp C :G: .10 .25
❑ 150 Tel-Jilad Justice U :G: .20 .50
❑ 151 Tel-Jilad Lifebreather C :G: .10 .25
❑ 152 Thermal Navigator C :A: .10 .25
❑ 153 Thought Courier C :B: .10 .25
❑ 154 Tornado Elemental R :G: .50 1.25
❑ 155 Trinket Mage C :B: .25 .60
❑ 156 Tyrranax C :G: .10 .25
❑ 157 Vanquish U :W: .20 .50
❑ 158 Vedalken Mastermind U :B: .25 .60
❑ 159 Vedalken Orrery R :A: 2.00 5.00
❑ 160 Vedalken Shackles R :A: 8.00 20.00
❑ 161 Vicious Betrayal C :K: .10 .25
❑ 162 Viridian Lorebearers U :G: .20 .50
❑ 163 Viridian Scout C :G: .10 .25
❑ 164 Vulshok Sorcerer C :R: .10 .25
❑ 165 Wayfarer's Bauble C :A: .10 .25

2004 Magic the Gathering Fifth Dawn Foil

Complete Set (165) 200.00 350.00
*Foil: .8X to 2X Basic Cards

2004 Magic the Gathering Champions of Kamigawa

Complete Set (307) 125.00 200.00
Theme Deck 9.00 12.00
Booster Box (36 Packs) 175.00 250.00
Booster Pack (15 Cards) 5.00 8.00

❑ 1 Akki Avalanchers C :R: .10 .25
❑ 2 Akki Coalflinger U :R: .20 .50
❑ 3 Akki Lavarunner R :R: .30 .75
❑ 4 Akki Rockspeaker C :R: .10 .25
❑ 5 Akki Underminer U :R: .25 .60
❑ 6 Ashen-Skin Zubera C :K: .10 .25
❑ 7 Aura of Dominion U :B: .20 .50
❑ 8 Azami, Lady of Scrolls R :B: .75 2.00
❑ 9 Azusa, Lost but Seeking R :G: 2.00 5.00
❑ 10 Battle-Mad Ronin C :R: .10 .25
❑ 11 Befoul C :K: .10 .25

MAGIC

No.	Card	Low	High
☐ 12	Ben-Ben, Akki Hermit R :R:	.30	.75
☐ 13	Blessed Breath C :W:	.10	.25
☐ 14	Blind with Anger U :R:	.25	.60
☐ 15	Blood Rites U :R:	.20	.50
☐ 16	Blood Speaker U :K:	.25	.60
☐ 17	Bloodthirsty Ogre U :K:	.25	.60
☐ 18	Boseiju, Who Shelters All R :L:	2.00	5.00
☐ 19	Brothers Yamazaki U :R:	.30	.75
☐ 20	Brothers Yamazaki U :R:	.30	.75
☐ 21	Brutal Deceiver C :R:	.10	.25
☐ 22	Budoka Gardener R :G:	.40	1.00
☐ 23	Burr Grafter C :G:	.10	.25
☐ 24	Bushi Tenderfoot U :W:	.25	.60
☐ 25	Cage of Hands C :W:	.10	.25
☐ 26	Call to Glory C :W:	.10	.25
☐ 27	Callous Deceiver C :B:	.10	.25
☐ 28	Candles' Glow U :W:	.20	.50
☐ 29	Cleanfall U :W:	.25	.60
☐ 30	Cloudcrest Lake U :L:	.25	.60
☐ 31	Commune with Nature C :G:	.10	.25
☐ 32	Consuming Vortex C :B:	.10	.25
☐ 33	Counsel of the Soratami C :B:	.10	.25
☐ 34	Cranial Extraction R :K:	.75	2.00
☐ 35	Cruel Deceiver C :K:	.10	.25
☐ 36	Crushing Pain C :R:	.10	.25
☐ 37	Cursed Ronin C :K:	.10	.25
☐ 38	Cut the Tethers U :B:	.20	.50
☐ 39	Dampen Thought U :B:	.25	.60
☐ 40	Dance of Shadows U :K:	.25	.60
☐ 41	Deathcurse Ogre C :K:	.10	.25
☐ 42	Desperate Ritual C :R:	.40	1.00
☐ 43	Devoted Retainer C :W:	.10	.25
☐ 44	Devouring Greed C :K:	.10	.25
☐ 45	Devouring Rage C :R:	.10	.25
☐ 46	Distress C :K:	.10	.25
☐ 47	Dosan the Falling Leaf R :G:	.30	.75
☐ 48	Dripping-Tongue Zubera C :G:	.10	.25
☐ 49	Earthshaker U :R:	.20	.50
☐ 50	Eerie Procession U :B:	.25	.60
☐ 51	Eiganjo Castle R :L:	.75	2.00
☐ 52	Eight-and-a-Half-Tails R :W:	1.50	4.00
☐ 53	Ember-Fist Zubera C :R:	.10	.25
☐ 54	Ethereal Haze C :W:	.10	.25
☐ 55	Eye of Nowhere C :B:	.10	.25
☐ 56	Feast of Worms U :G:	.20	.50
☐ 57	Feral Deceiver C :G:	.10	.25
☐ 58	Field of Reality C :B:	.10	.25
☐ 59	Floating-Dream Zubera C :B:	.10	.25
☐ 60	Forbidden Orchard R :L:	2.50	6.00
☐ 61	Forest L :L:	.10	.25
☐ 62	Forest L :L:	.10	.25
☐ 63	Forest L :L:	.10	.25
☐ 64	Forest L :L:	.10	.25
☐ 65	Frostwielder C :R:	.10	.25
☐ 66	Gale Force U :G:	.20	.50
☐ 67	General's Kabuto R :A:	.75	2.00
☐ 68	Ghostly Prison U :W:	1.50	4.00
☐ 69	Gibbering Kami C :K:	.10	.25
☐ 70	Gifts Ungiven R :B:	5.00	12.00
☐ 71	Glacial Ray C :R:	.10	.25
☐ 72	Glimpse of Nature R :G:	8.00	20.00
☐ 73	Godo, Bandit Warlord R :R:	.75	2.00
☐ 74	Graceful Adept U :B:	.25	.60
☐ 75	Guardian of Solitude U :B:	.20	.50
☐ 76	Gutwrencher Oni U :K:	.25	.60
☐ 77	Hair-Strung Koto R :A:	.30	.75
☐ 78	Hall of the Bandit Lord R :L:	.50	1.25
☐ 79	Hana Kami U :G:	.25	.60
☐ 80	Hanabi Blast U :R:	.20	.50
☐ 81	Hankyu U :A:	.20	.50
☐ 82	Harsh Deceiver C :W:	.10	.25
☐ 83	He Who Hungers R :K:	.30	.75
☐ 84	Heartbeat of Spring R :G:	.60	1.50
☐ 85	Hearth Kami C :R:	.10	.25
☐ 86	Hideous Laughter U :K:	.25	.60
☐ 87	Hikari, Twilight Guardian R :W:	.30	.75
☐ 88	Hinder U :B:	.40	1.00
☐ 89	Hisoka, Minamo Sensei R :B:	.10	.25
☐ 90	Hisoka's Defiance C :B:	.10	.25
☐ 91	Hisoka's Guard C :B:	.30	.75
☐ 92	Hold the Line R :W:	.30	.75
☐ 93	Honden of Cleansing Fire U :W:	.30	.75
☐ 94	Honden of Infinite Rage U :R:	.25	.60
☐ 95	Honden of Life's Web U :G:	.25	.60
☐ 96	Honden of Night's Reach U :K:	.25	.60
☐ 97	Honden of Seeing Winds U :B:	.30	.75
☐ 98	Honor-Worn Shaku U :A:	.20	.50
☐ 99	Horizon Seed U :W:	.20	.50
☐ 100	Horobi, Death's Wail R :K:	.30	.75
☐ 101	Humble Budoka C :G:	.10	.25
☐ 102	Hundred-Talon Kami C :W:	.10	.25
☐ 103	Imi Statue R :A:	.30	.75
☐ 104	Iname, Death Aspect R :K:	.30	.75
☐ 105	Iname, Life Aspect R :G:	.30	.75
☐ 106	Indomitable Will C :W:	.10	.25
☐ 107	Initiate of Blood U :R:	.20	.50
☐ 108	Innocence Kami U :W:	.20	.50
☐ 109	Isamaru, Hound of Konda R :W:	1.25	3.00
☐ 110	Island L :L:	.10	.25
☐ 111	Island L :L:	.10	.25
☐ 112	Island L :L:	.10	.25
☐ 113	Island L :L:	.10	.25
☐ 114	Jade Idol U :A:	.20	.50
☐ 115	Journeyer's Kite R :A:	1.25	3.00
☐ 116	Joyous Respite C :G:	.10	.25
☐ 117	Jugan, the Rising Star R :G:	1.25	3.00
☐ 118	Jukai Messenger C :G:	.10	.25
☐ 119	Junkyo Bell R :A:	.30	.75
☐ 120	Jushi Apprentice R :B:	.30	.75
☐ 121	Kabuto Moth C :W:	.10	.25
☐ 122	Kami of Ancient Law C :W:	.10	.25
☐ 123	Kami of Fire's Roar C :R:	.10	.25
☐ 124	Kami of Lunacy U :K:	.20	.50
☐ 125	Kami of Old Stone U :W:	.20	.50
☐ 126	Kami of the Hunt C :G:	.10	.25
☐ 127	Kami of the Painted Road C :W:	.10	.25
☐ 128	Kami of the Palace Fields U :W:	.20	.50
☐ 129	Kami of the Waning Moon C :K:	.10	.25
☐ 130	Kami of Twisted Reflection C :B:	.10	.25
☐ 131	Kashi-Tribe Reaver U :G:	.25	.60
☐ 132	Kashi-Tribe Warriors C :G:	.10	.25
☐ 133	Keiga, the Tide Star R :B:	2.50	6.00
☐ 134	Kiki-Jiki, Mirror Breaker R :R:	6.00	15.00
☐ 135	Kiku, Night's Flower R :K:	.40	1.00
☐ 136	Kitsune Blademaster C :W:	.10	.25
☐ 137	Kitsune Diviner C :W:	.10	.25
☐ 138	Kitsune Healer C :W:	.10	.25
☐ 139	Kitsune Mystic R :W:	.30	.75
☐ 140	Kitsune Riftwalker C :W:	.10	.25
☐ 141	Kodama of the North Tree R :G:	.40	1.00
☐ 142	Kodama of the South Tree R :G:	.30	.75
☐ 143	Kodama's Might C :G:	.10	.25
☐ 144	Kodama's Reach C :G:	.30	.75
☐ 145	Kokusho, the Evening Star R :K:	4.00	10.00
☐ 146	Konda, Lord of Eiganjo R :W:	1.25	3.00
☐ 147	Konda's Banner R :A:	.25	.60
☐ 148	Konda's Hatamoto U :W:	1.25	3.00
☐ 149	Kumano, Master Yamabushi R :R:	.30	.75
☐ 150	Kumano's Pupils U :R:	.20	.50
☐ 151	Kuro, Pitlord R :K:	.30	.75
☐ 152	Kusari-Gama R :A:	.30	.75
☐ 153	Lantern Kami C :W:	.10	.25
☐ 154	Lantern-Lit Graveyard U :L:	.25	.60
☐ 155	Lava Spike C :R:	1.25	3.00
☐ 156	Lifted by Clouds C :B:	.10	.25
☐ 157	Long-Forgotten Gohei R :A:	.30	.75
☐ 158	Lure U :G:	.25	.60
☐ 159	Mana Seism U :R:	.20	.50
☐ 160	Marrow-Gnawer R :K:	1.50	4.00
☐ 161	Masako the Humorless R :W:	.30	.75
☐ 162	Matsu-Tribe Decoy C :G:	.10	.25
☐ 163	Meloku the Clouded Mirror R :B:	.75	2.00
☐ 164	Midnight Covenant C :K:	.10	.25
☐ 165	Minamo, School at Water's Edge R :L:	2.00	5.00
☐ 166	Mindblaze R :R:	.30	.75
☐ 167	Moonring Mirror R :A:	.30	.75
☐ 168	Moss Kami C :G:	.10	.25
☐ 169	Mothrider Samurai C :W:	.10	.25
☐ 170	Mountain L :L:	.10	.25
☐ 171	Mountain L :L:	.10	.25
☐ 172	Mountain L :L:	.10	.25
☐ 173	Mountain L :L:	.10	.25
☐ 174	Myojin of Cleansing Fire R :W:	.60	1.50
☐ 175	Myojin of Infinite Rage R :R:	.40	1.00
☐ 176	Myojin of Life's Web R :G:	1.25	3.00
☐ 177	Myojin of Night's Reach R :K:	.75	2.00
☐ 178	Myojin of Seeing Winds R :B:	.30	.75
☐ 179	Mystic Restraints C :B:	.10	.25
☐ 180	Nagao, Bound by Honor U :W:	.25	.60
☐ 181	Nature's Will R :G:	.30	.75
☐ 182	Nezumi Bone-Reader U :K:	.25	.60
☐ 183	Nezumi Cutthroat C :K:	.10	.25
☐ 184	Nezumi Graverobber U :K:	.30	.75
☐ 185	Nezumi Ronin C :K:	.10	.25
☐ 186	Nezumi Shortfang R :K:	1.25	3.00
☐ 187	Night Dealings R :K:	.30	.75
☐ 188	Night of Souls' Betrayal R :K:	.30	.75
☐ 189	Nine-Ringed Bo U :A:	.20	.50
☐ 190	No-Dachi U :A:	.25	.60
☐ 191	Numai Outcast U :K:	.20	.50
☐ 192	Oathkeeper, Takeno's Daisho R :A:	.30	.75
☐ 193	Okina, Temple to the Grandfathers R :L:	.40	1.00
☐ 194	Oni Possession U :K:	.20	.50
☐ 195	Orbweaver Kumo U :G:	.20	.50
☐ 196	Order of the Sacred Bell C :G:	.10	.25
☐ 197	Ore Gorger U :R:	.20	.50
☐ 198	Orochi Eggwatcher U :G:	.25	.60
☐ 199	Orochi Hatchery R :A:	.30	.75
☐ 200	Orochi Leafcaller C :G:	.10	.25
☐ 201	Orochi Ranger C :G:	.10	.25
☐ 202	Orochi Sustainer C :G:	.10	.25
☐ 203	Otherworldly Journey U :W:	.25	.60
☐ 204	Pain Kami U :R:	.20	.50
☐ 205	Painwracker Oni U :K:	.20	.50
☐ 206	Part the Veil R :B:	.30	.75
☐ 207	Peer Through Depths C :B:	.30	.75
☐ 208	Petals of Insight U :B:	.25	.60
☐ 209	Pinecrest Ridge U :L:	.25	.60
☐ 210	Pious Kitsune C :W:	.10	.25
☐ 211	Plains L :L:	.10	.25
☐ 212	Plains L :L:	.10	.25
☐ 213	Plains L :L:	.10	.25
☐ 214	Plains L :L:	.10	.25
☐ 215	Psychic Puppetry C :B:	.10	.25
☐ 216	Pull Under C :K:	.10	.25
☐ 217	Quiet Purity C :W:	.10	.25
☐ 218	Rag Dealer C :K:	.10	.25
☐ 219	Ragged Veins C :K:	.10	.25
☐ 220	Reach Through Mists C :B:	.10	.25
☐ 221	Reciprocate U :W:	.25	.60
☐ 222	Reito Lantern U :A:	.25	.60
☐ 223	Rend Flesh C :K:	.25	.60
☐ 224	Rend Spirit C :K:	.10	.25
☐ 225	Reverse the Sands R :W:	.30	.75
☐ 226	Reweave R :B:	.30	.75
☐ 227	River Kaijin C :B:	.10	.25
☐ 228	Ronin Houndmaster C :R:	.10	.25
☐ 229	Rootrunner U :G:	.20	.50
☐ 230	Ryusei, the Falling Star R :R:	.75	2.00
☐ 231	Sachi, Daughter of Seshiro U :G:	.25	.60
☐ 232	Sakura-Tribe Elder C :G:	.40	1.00
☐ 233	Samurai Enforcers U :W:	.25	.60
☐ 234	Samurai of the Pale Curtain U :W:	.30	.75
☐ 235	Scuttling Death C :K:	.10	.25
☐ 236	Seizan, Perverter of Truth R :K:	.30	.75
☐ 237	Sensei Golden-Tail R :W:	.40	1.00
☐ 238	Sensei's Divining Top U :A:	6.00	15.00
☐ 239	Serpent Skin C :G:	.10	.25
☐ 240	Seshiro the Anointed R :G:	.60	1.50
☐ 241	Shell of the Last Kappa R :A:	.30	.75
☐ 242	Shimatsu the Bloodcloaked R :R:	.30	.75
☐ 243	Shinka, the Bloodsoaked Keep R :L:	.40	1.00
☐ 244	Shisato, Whispering Hunter R :G:	.30	.75
☐ 245	Shizo, Death's Storehouse R :L:	1.50	4.00
☐ 246	Sideswipe U :R:	.20	.50
☐ 247	Sift Through Sands C :B:	.10	.25
☐ 248	Silent-Chant Zubera C :W:	.10	.25
☐ 249	Sire of the Storm U :B:	.25	.60
☐ 250	Soilshaper U :G:	.20	.50
☐ 251	Sokenzan Bruiser C :R:	.10	.25
☐ 252	Soratami Cloudskater C :B:	.10	.25
☐ 253	Soratami Mirror-Guard C :B:	.10	.25
☐ 254	Soratami Mirror-Mage U :B:	.20	.50
☐ 255	Soratami Rainshaper C :B:	.10	.25
☐ 256	Soratami Savant U :B:	.25	.60
☐ 257	Soratami Seer U :B:	.20	.50
☐ 258	Sosuke, Son of Seshiro U :G:	.25	.60
☐ 259	Soul of Magma C :R:	.10	.25
☐ 260	Soulblast R :R:	.30	.75
☐ 261	Soulless Revival C :K:	.10	.25
☐ 262	Squelch U :B:	.25	.60
☐ 263	Stone Rain C :R:	.10	.25
☐ 264	Strange Inversion U :R:	.20	.50
☐ 265	Strength of Cedars U :G:	.20	.50
☐ 266	Struggle for Sanity U :K:	.20	.50
☐ 267	Student of Elements U :B:	.20	.50
☐ 268	Swallowing Plague U :K:	.20	.50
☐ 269	Swamp L :L:	.10	.25
☐ 270	Swamp L :L:	.10	.25
☐ 271	Swamp L :L:	.10	.25
☐ 272	Swamp L :L:	.10	.25
☐ 273	Swirl the Mists R :B:	.30	.75
☐ 274	Takeno, Samurai General R :W:	.30	.75
☐ 275	Tatsumasa, the Dragon's Fang R :A:	1.00	2.50
☐ 276	Teller of Tales C :B:	.10	.25
☐ 277	Tenza, Godo's Maul U :A:	.25	.60
☐ 278	Terashi's Cry C :W:	.10	.25
☐ 279	The Unspeakable R :B:	.30	.75
☐ 280	Thief of Hope U :K:	.25	.60
☐ 281	Thoughtbind C :B:	.10	.25
☐ 282	Thousand-legged Kami U :G:	.20	.50
☐ 283	Through the Breach R :R:	2.50	6.00
☐ 284	Tide of War R :R:	.30	.75
☐ 285	Time of Need U :G:	.30	.75
☐ 286	Time Stop R :B:	.50	1.25
☐ 287	Tranquil Garden U :L:	.25	.60
☐ 288	Uba Mask R :A:	.30	.75
☐ 289	Uncontrollable Anger C :R:	.10	.25
☐ 290	Unearthly Blizzard C :R:	.10	.25
☐ 291	Unnatural Speed C :R:	.10	.25
☐ 292	Untaidake, the Cloud Keeper R :L:	.30	.75
☐ 293	Uyo, Silent Prophet R :B:	.30	.75
☐ 294	Vassal's Duty R :W:	.30	.75
☐ 295	Venerable Kumo C :G:	.10	.25
☐ 296	Vigilance C :W:	.10	.25
☐ 297	Villainous Ogre C :K:	.10	.25
☐ 298	Vine Kami C :G:	.10	.25
☐ 299	Waking Nightmare C :K:	.10	.25
☐ 300	Wandering Ones C :B:	.10	.25
☐ 301	Waterveil Cavern U :L:	.25	.60
☐ 302	Wear Away C :G:	.10	.25
☐ 303	Wicked Akuba C :K:	.10	.25
☐ 304	Yamabushi's Flame C :R:	.10	.25
☐ 305	Yamabushi's Storm C :R:	.10	.25
☐ 306	Yosei, the Morning Star R :W:	3.00	8.00
☐ 307	Zo-Zu the Punisher R :R:	.30	.75

2004 Magic the Gathering Champions of Kamigawa Foil

Complete Set (307)	250.00	400.00

*Foil: .8X to 2X Basic Cards

2005 Magic the Gathering 9th Edition

Complete Set (350)	125.00	200.00

No.	Card	Low	High
☐ 1	Adarkar Wastes R :L:	1.00	2.50
☐ 2	Air Elemental U :B:	.10	.25
☐ 3	Aladdin's Ring R :A:	.25	.60
☐ 4	Anaba Shaman C :R:	.08	.20
☐ 5	Anaconda U :G:	.10	.25
☐ 6	Anarchist U :R:	.10	.25
☐ 7	Ancient Silverback R :G:	.30	.75
☐ 8	Angel of Mercy U :W:	.15	.40
☐ 9	Angel's Feather U :A:	.10	.25
☐ 10	Angelic Blessing C :W:	.08	.20
☐ 11	Annex U :B:	.15	.40
☐ 12	Archivist R :B:	.40	1.00
☐ 13	Aven Cloudchaser C :W:	.08	.20
☐ 14	Aven Fisher C :B:	.08	.20
☐ 15	Aven Flock C :W:	.08	.20
☐ 16	Aven Windreader C :B:	.08	.20
☐ 17	Azure Drake U :B:	.10	.25
☐ 18	Balduvian Barbarians C :R:	.08	.20
☐ 19	Baleful Stare U :B:	.10	.25
☐ 20	Ballista Squad U :W:	.10	.25
☐ 21	Battle of Wits R :B:	.40	1.00
☐ 22	Battlefield Forge R :L:	1.00	2.50
☐ 23	Beast of Burden R :A:	.40	1.00
☐ 24	Biorhythm R :G:	.50	1.25
☐ 25	Blackmail U :K:	.40	1.00
☐ 26	Blanchwood Armor U :G:	.50	1.25
☐ 27	Blaze U :R:	.20	.50
☐ 28	Blessed Orator U :W:	.10	.25
☐ 29	Blinding Angel R :W:	1.25	3.00
☐ 30	Blinking Spirit R :W:	.30	.75
☐ 31	Blood Moon R :R:	2.50	6.00
☐ 32	Bloodfire Colossus R :R:	.25	.60
☐ 33	Bog Imp C :K:	.08	.20
☐ 34	Bog Wraith U :K:	.10	.25
☐ 35	Boiling Seas U :R:	.15	.40
☐ 36	Booby Trap R :A:	.50	1.25
☐ 37	Boomerang C :B:	.08	.20
☐ 38	Bottle Gnomes U :A:	.15	.40
☐ 39	Brushland R :L:	.75	2.00
☐ 40	Caves of Koilos R :L:	1.00	2.50
☐ 41	Chastise U :W:	.15	.40
☐ 42	Circle of Protection: Black U :W:	.10	.25
☐ 43	Circle of Protection: Red U :W:	.20	.50
☐ 44	Clone R :B:	.40	1.00
☐ 45	Coat of Arms R :A:	2.00	5.00
☐ 46	Coercion C :K:	.08	.20
☐ 47	Confiscate U :B:	.15	.40
☐ 48	Consume Spirit U :K:	.10	.25
☐ 49	Contaminated Bond C :K:	.08	.20
☐ 50	Coral Eel C :B:	.08	.20
☐ 51	Counsel of the Soratami C :B:	.08	.20
☐ 52	Cowardice R :B:	.25	.60
☐ 53	Crafty Pathmage C :B:	.08	.20
☐ 54	Craw Wurm C :G:	.08	.20
☐ 55	Creeping Mold U :G:	.10	.25
☐ 56	Crossbow Infantry C :W:	.08	.20
☐ 57	Cruel Edict U :K:	.50	1.25
☐ 58	Dancing Scimitar U :A:	.10	.25
☐ 59	Daring Apprentice R :B:	.30	.75
☐ 60	Dark Banishing C :K:	.08	.20
☐ 61	Death Pits of Rath R :K:	.40	1.00
☐ 62	Deathgazer U :K:	.10	.25
☐ 63	Defense Grid R :A:	.75	2.00
☐ 64	Dehydration C :B:	.08	.20
☐ 65	Demolish U :R:	.10	.25
☐ 66	Demon's Horn U :A:	.15	.40
☐ 67	Demystify C :W:	.08	.20
☐ 68	Diabolic Tutor U :K:	.50	1.25
☐ 69	Disrupting Scepter R :A:	.25	.60
☐ 70	Dragon's Claw U :A:	.20	.50
☐ 71	Dream Prowler U :B:	.10	.25
☐ 72	Drudge Skeletons U :K:	.10	.25
☐ 73	Eager Cadet C :W:	.08	.20
☐ 74	Early Harvest R :G:	.60	1.50
☐ 75	Elvish Bard U :G:	.10	.25
☐ 76	Elvish Berserker C :G:	.08	.20
☐ 77	Elvish Champion R :G:	2.00	5.00
☐ 78	Elvish Piper R :G:	2.50	6.00
☐ 79	Elvish Warrior C :G:	.08	.20
☐ 80	Emperor Crocodile R :G:	.25	.60
☐ 81	Enfeeblement C :K:	.08	.20
☐ 82	Enormous Baloth U :G:	.15	.40
☐ 83	Enrage U :R:	.10	.25
☐ 84	Evacuation R :B:	.75	2.00
☐ 85	Execute U :K:	.10	.25
☐ 86	Exhaustion U :B:	.20	.50
☐ 87	Fear C :K:	.08	.20
☐ 88	Fellwar Stone U :A:	.20	.50
☐ 89	Festering Goblin C :K:	.08	.20
☐ 90	Final Punishment R :K:	.30	.75
☐ 91	Firebreathing C :R:	.08	.20
☐ 92	Fishliver Oil C :B:	.08	.20
☐ 93	Flame Wave U :R:	.15	.40
☐ 94	Flashfires U :R:	.10	.25
☐ 95	Fleeting Image R :B:	.25	.60
☐ 96	Flight C :B:	.08	.20
☐ 97	Flowstone Crusher U :R:	.10	.25
☐ 98	Flowstone Shambler C :R:	.08	.20
☐ 99	Flowstone Slide R :R:	.25	.60
☐ 100	Foot Soldiers C :W:	.08	.20
☐ 101	Force of Nature R :G:	.30	.75
☐ 102	Forest L :L:	.08	.20
☐ 103	Forest L :L:	.08	.20
☐ 104	Forest L :L:	.08	.20
☐ 105	Forest L :L:	.08	.20
☐ 106	Form of the Dragon R :R:	.50	1.25
☐ 107	Foul Imp C :K:	.08	.20
☐ 108	Fugitive Wizard C :B:	.08	.20
☐ 109	Furnace of Rath R :R:	.60	1.50
☐ 110	Giant Cockroach C :K:	.08	.20
☐ 111	Giant Growth C :G:	.08	.20
☐ 112	Giant Octopus C :B:	.10	.25
☐ 113	Giant Spider C :G:	.08	.20
☐ 114	Gift of Estates U :W:	.75	2.00
☐ 115	Glorious Anthem R :W:	1.00	2.50
☐ 116	Glory Seeker C :W:	.08	.20
☐ 117	Gluttonous Zombie U :K:	.10	.25
☐ 118	Goblin Balloon Brigade U :R:	.10	.25
☐ 119	Goblin Brigand C :R:	.08	.20
☐ 120	Goblin Chariot C :R:	.08	.20
☐ 121	Goblin King R :R:	.75	2.00
☐ 122	Goblin Mountaineer C :R:	.08	.20
☐ 123	Goblin Piker C :R:	.08	.20
☐ 124	Goblin Raider C :R:	.08	.20
☐ 125	Goblin Sky Raider C :R:	.08	.20
☐ 126	Grave Pact R :K:	2.50	6.00
☐ 127	Gravedigger C :K:	.08	.20
☐ 128	Greater Good R :G:	1.50	4.00
☐ 129	Grizzly Bears C :G:	.08	.20
☐ 130	Groundskeeper U :G:	.10	.25
☐ 131	Guerrilla Tactics U :R:	.10	.25
☐ 132	Hell's Caretaker R :K:	1.25	3.00
☐ 133	Highway Robber C :K:	.08	.20
☐ 134	Hill Giant C :R:	.08	.20
☐ 135	Hollow Dogs C :K:	.08	.20
☐ 136	Holy Day C :W:	.10	.25
☐ 137	Holy Strength C :W:	.08	.20
☐ 138	Honor Guard C :W:	.08	.20
☐ 139	Horned Turtle C :B:	.08	.20
☐ 140	Horror of Horrors U :K:	.10	.25
☐ 141	Howling Mine R :A:	1.25	3.00
☐ 142	Hunted Wumpus U :G:	.10	.25
☐ 143	Hypnotic Specter R :K:	1.00	2.50
☐ 144	Icy Manipulator U :A:	.30	.75
☐ 145	Imaginary Pet R :B:	.30	.75
☐ 146	Index C :B:	.20	.50
☐ 147	Infantry Veteran C :W:	.08	.20
☐ 148	Inspirit U :W:	.10	.25
☐ 149	Island L :L:	.08	.20
☐ 150	Island L :L:	.08	.20
☐ 151	Island L :L:	.08	.20
☐ 152	Island L :L:	.08	.20
☐ 153	Ivory Mask R :W:	.75	2.00
☐ 154	Jade Statue R :A:	.25	.60
☐ 155	Jester's Cap R :A:	1.00	2.50
☐ 156	Kami of Old Stone U :W:	.10	.25
☐ 157	Karplusan Forest R :L:	1.00	2.50
☐ 158	Karplusan Yeti R :R:	.25	.60
☐ 159	Kavu Climber C :G:	.08	.20
☐ 160	King Cheetah U :G:	.10	.25
☐ 161	Kird Ape U :R:	.60	1.50
☐ 162	Kraken's Eye U :A:	.10	.25
☐ 163	Lava Axe C :R:	.08	.20
☐ 164	Leonin Skyhunter U :W:	.20	.50
☐ 165	Levitation U :B:	.10	.25
☐ 166	Ley Druid U :G:	.10	.25
☐ 167	Lightning Elemental C :R:	.08	.20
☐ 168	Llanowar Behemoth U :G:	.10	.25
☐ 169	Llanowar Elves C :G:	.20	.50
☐ 170	Llanowar Wastes R :L:	1.25	3.00
☐ 171	Looming Shade C :K:	.08	.20
☐ 172	Lord of the Undead R :K:	4.00	10.00
☐ 173	Loxodon Warhammer R :A:	1.00	2.50
☐ 174	Lumengrid Warden C :B:	.08	.20
☐ 175	Magnivore R :R:	.40	1.00
☐ 176	Mahamoti Djinn R :B:	.25	.60
☐ 177	Mana Clash R :R:	.30	.75
☐ 178	Mana Leak C :B:	.40	1.00
☐ 179	Marble Titan R :W:	.30	.75
☐ 180	Maro R :G:	.40	1.00
☐ 181	Master Decoy C :W:	.08	.20
☐ 182	Master Healer R :W:	.25	.60
☐ 183	Megrim U :K:	.50	1.25
☐ 184	Mending Hands C :W:	.08	.20
☐ 185	Might of Oaks R :G:	.50	1.25
☐ 186	Millstone R :A:	.50	1.25
☐ 187	Mind Bend R :B:	.25	.60
☐ 188	Mind Rot C :K:	.08	.20
☐ 189	Mindslicer R :K:	.50	1.25
☐ 190	Mogg Sentry R :R:	.30	.75
☐ 191	Mortivore R :K:	.75	2.00
☐ 192	Mountain L :L:	.08	.20
☐ 193	Mountain L :L:	.08	.20
☐ 194	Mountain L :L:	.08	.20
☐ 195	Mountain L :L:	.08	.20
☐ 196	Nantuko Husk U :K:	.10	.25
☐ 197	Natural Affinity R :G:	.40	1.00
☐ 198	Natural Spring C :G:	.08	.20
☐ 199	Naturalize C :G:	.08	.20
☐ 200	Needle Storm U :G:	.10	.25
☐ 201	Nekrataal U :K:	.20	.50
☐ 202	Nightmare R :K:	.40	1.00
☐ 203	Norwood Ranger C :G:	.08	.20
☐ 204	Ogre Taskmaster U :R:	.10	.25
☐ 205	Oracle's Attendants R :W:	.25	.60
☐ 206	Orcish Artillery U :R:	.10	.25
☐ 207	Order of the Sacred Bell C :G:	.08	.20
☐ 208	Ornithopter U :A:	.50	1.25
☐ 209	Overgrowth C :G:	.08	.20
☐ 210	Pacifism C :W:	.08	.20
☐ 211	Paladin en-Vec R :W:	.75	2.00
☐ 212	Panic Attack C :R:	.08	.20
☐ 213	Peace of Mind U :W:	.10	.25
☐ 214	Pegasus Charger C :W:	.08	.20
☐ 215	Persecute R :K:	.75	2.00
☐ 216	Phantom Warrior U :B:	.10	.25
☐ 217	Phyrexian Arena R :K:	1.50	4.00
☐ 218	Phyrexian Gargantua U :K:	.10	.25
☐ 219	Phyrexian Hulk U :A:	.10	.25
☐ 220	Plagiarize R :B:	.30	.75
☐ 221	Plague Beetle C :K:	.08	.20
☐ 222	Plague Wind R :K:	.75	2.00
☐ 223	Plains L :L:	.08	.20
☐ 224	Plains L :L:	.08	.20
☐ 225	Plains L :L:	.08	.20
☐ 226	Plains L :L:	.08	.20
☐ 227	Polymorph R :B:	.60	1.50
☐ 228	Puppeteer U :B:	.10	.25
☐ 229	Pyroclasm U :R:	.40	1.00
☐ 230	Quicksand U :L:	.15	.40
☐ 231	Raging Goblin C :R:	.08	.20
☐ 232	Raise Dead C :K:	.08	.20
☐ 233	Rampant Growth C :G:	.08	.20

Card	Low	High
❑ 234 Rathi Dragon R :R:	.50	1.25
❑ 235 Ravenous Rats C :K:	.08	.20
❑ 236 Razortooth Rats C :K:	.08	.20
❑ 237 Reclaim C :G:	.08	.20
❑ 238 Reflexes C :R:	.08	.20
❑ 239 Regeneration U :G:	.10	.25
❑ 240 Relentless Assault R :R:	.30	.75
❑ 241 Reminisce U :B:	.15	.40
❑ 242 Remove Soul C :B:	.08	.20
❑ 243 Reverse Damage R :W:	.40	1.00
❑ 244 Rewind U :B:	.50	1.25
❑ 245 Righteousness R :W:	.25	.60
❑ 246 River Bear U :G:	.10	.25
❑ 247 Rod of Ruin U :A:	.10	.25
❑ 248 Rogue Kavu C :R:	.08	.20
❑ 249 Rootbreaker Wurm U :G:	.10	.25
❑ 250 Rootwalla C :G:	.08	.20
❑ 251 Royal Assassin R :K:	.60	1.50
❑ 252 Rukh Egg R :R:	.40	1.00
❑ 253 Sacred Ground R :W:	.40	1.00
❑ 254 Sacred Nectar C :W:	.08	.20
❑ 255 Sage Aven C :B:	.08	.20
❑ 256 Samite Healer C :W:	.08	.20
❑ 257 Sanctum Guardian U :W:	.10	.25
❑ 258 Sandstone Warrior C :R:	.08	.20
❑ 259 Savannah Lions R :W:	.75	2.00
❑ 260 Scaled Wurm C :G:	.08	.20
❑ 261 Scathe Zombies C :K:	.08	.20
❑ 262 Sea Monster C :B:	.08	.20
❑ 263 Sea's Claim C :B:	.08	.20
❑ 264 Seasoned Marshal U :W:	.10	.25
❑ 265 Seedborn Muse R :G:	2.00	5.00
❑ 266 Seething Song C :R:	.75	2.00
❑ 267 Sengir Vampire R :K:	.50	1.25
❑ 268 Serpent Warrior C :K:	.08	.20
❑ 269 Serra Angel R :W:	.60	1.50
❑ 270 Serra's Blessing U :W:	.60	1.50
❑ 271 Shard Phoenix R :R:	.40	1.00
❑ 272 Shatter C :R:	.08	.20
❑ 273 Shivan Dragon R :R:	.50	1.25
❑ 274 Shivan Reef R :L:	2.00	5.00
❑ 275 Shock C :R:	.10	.25
❑ 276 Sift C :B:	.08	.20
❑ 277 Silklash Spider R :G:	.60	1.50
❑ 278 Skyhunter Prowler C :W:	.08	.20
❑ 279 Slate of Ancestry R :A:	.60	1.50
❑ 280 Slay U :K:	.10	.25
❑ 281 Sleight of Hand C :B:	.60	1.50
❑ 282 Soul Feast U :K:	.10	.25
❑ 283 Soul Warden U :W:	.40	1.00
❑ 284 Spellbook U :A:	.20	.50
❑ 285 Spined Wurm C :G:	.08	.20
❑ 286 Spineless Thug C :K:	.08	.20
❑ 287 Spirit Link U :W:	.20	.50
❑ 288 Stone Rain C :R:	.08	.20
❑ 289 Storage Matrix R :A:	.40	1.00
❑ 290 Storm Crow C :B:	.08	.20
❑ 291 Story Circle R :W:	.75	2.00
❑ 292 Stream of Life U :G:	.10	.25
❑ 293 Sudden Impact U :R:	.10	.25
❑ 294 Sulfurous Springs R :L:	.75	2.00
❑ 295 Summer Bloom U :G:	.40	1.00
❑ 296 Suntail Hawk C :W:	.08	.20
❑ 297 Swamp L :L:	.08	.20
❑ 298 Swamp L :L:	.08	.20
❑ 299 Swamp L :L:	.08	.20
❑ 300 Swamp L :L:	.08	.20
❑ 301 Swarm of Rats U :K:	.20	.50
❑ 302 Tanglebloom U :A:	.10	.25
❑ 303 Teferi's Puzzle Box R :A:	.60	1.50
❑ 304 Telepathy U :B:	.10	.25
❑ 305 Tempest of Light U :W:	.10	.25
❑ 306 Temporal Adept R :B:	.60	1.50
❑ 307 Thieving Magpie U :B:	.10	.25
❑ 308 Thought Courier U :B:	.10	.25
❑ 309 Thran Golem R :A:	.30	.75
❑ 310 Threaten U :R:	.15	.40
❑ 311 Thundermare R :R:	.50	1.25
❑ 312 Tidal Kraken R :B:	.50	1.25
❑ 313 Tidings U :B:	.30	.75
❑ 314 Time Ebb C :B:	.08	.20
❑ 315 Trade Routes R :B:	.30	.75
❑ 316 Trained Armodon C :G:	.08	.20
❑ 317 Traumatize R :B:	1.00	2.50
❑ 318 Treasure Trove U :B:	.10	.25
❑ 319 Tree Monkey C :G:	.08	.20
❑ 320 Treetop Bracers C :G:	.08	.20
❑ 321 Underground River R :L:	1.25	3.00
❑ 322 Underworld Dreams R :K:	.75	2.00
❑ 323 Unholy Strength C :K:	.08	.20
❑ 324 Ur-Golem's Eye U :A:	.10	.25
❑ 325 Urza's Mine U :L:	.60	1.50
❑ 326 Urza's Power Plant U :L:	.60	1.50
❑ 327 Urza's Tower U :L:	.60	1.50
❑ 328 Utopia Tree R :G:	.75	2.00
❑ 329 Venerable Monk C :W:	.08	.20
❑ 330 Vengeance U :W:	.10	.25
❑ 331 Verdant Force R :G:	.75	2.00
❑ 332 Verduran Enchantress R :G:	.40	1.00
❑ 333 Veteran Cavalier C :W:	.08	.20
❑ 334 Viashino Sandstalker U :R:	.10	.25
❑ 335 Viridian Shaman U :G:	.10	.25
❑ 336 Vizzerdrix R :B:	.25	.60
❑ 337 Volcanic Hammer C :R:	.08	.20
❑ 338 Vulshok Morningstar U :A:	.10	.25
❑ 339 Wanderguard Sentry C :B:	.08	.20
❑ 340 Warrior's Honor C :W:	.08	.20
❑ 341 Weathered Wayfarer R :W:	2.00	5.00
❑ 342 Web U :G:	.10	.25
❑ 343 Weird Harvest R :G:	.60	1.50
❑ 344 Whip Sergeant U :R:	.10	.25
❑ 345 Wildfire R :R:	.50	1.25
❑ 346 Will-o'-the-Wisp R :K:	1.25	3.00
❑ 347 Wind Drake C :B:	.08	.20
❑ 348 Withering Gaze U :B:	.10	.25
❑ 349 Wood Elves C :G:	.10	.25
❑ 350 Worship R :W:	1.25	3.00
❑ 351 Wrath of God R :W:	4.00	10.00
❑ 352 Wurm's Tooth U :A:	.10	.25
❑ 353 Yavimaya Coast R :L:	1.25	3.00
❑ 354 Yavimaya Enchantress U :G:	.15	.40
❑ 355 Yawgmoth Demon R :K:	.30	.75
❑ 356 Zealous Inquisitor U :W:	.10	.25
❑ 357 Zodiac Monkey C :G:	.08	.20
❑ 358 Zombify U :K:	.60	1.50
❑ 359 Zur's Weirding R :B:	.30	.75

2005 Magic the Gathering 9th Edition Foil

*Foil: .8X to 2X Basic Cards

2005 Magic the Gathering Betrayers of Kamigawa

Item	Low	High
Complete Set (165)	75.00	150.00
Booster Box (36 Packs)	150.00	200.00
Booster Pack (15 Cards)	4.00	6.00
Theme Deck	10.00	25.00
Fat Pack	40.00	80.00
❑ 1 Akki Blizzard-Herder C :R:	.08	.20
❑ 2 Akki Raider U :R:	.10	.25
❑ 3 Ashen Monstrosity U :R:	.10	.25
❑ 4 Aura Barbs U :R:	.10	.25
❑ 5 Baku Altar R :A:	.25	.60
❑ 6 Bile Urchin C :K:	.08	.20
❑ 7 Blademane Baku C :R:	.08	.20
❑ 8 Blazing Shoal R :R:	1.50	4.00
❑ 9 Blessing of Leeches C :K:	.08	.20
❑ 10 Blinding Powder U :A:	.20	.50
❑ 11 Body of Jukai U :G:	.10	.25
❑ 12 Budoka Pupil U :G:	.10	.25
❑ 13 Call for Blood C :K:	.08	.20
❑ 14 Callow Jushi U :B:	.10	.25
❑ 15 Child of Thorns C :G:	.08	.20
❑ 16 Chisei, Heart of Oceans R :B:	.25	.60
❑ 17 Clash of Realities R :R:	.25	.60
❑ 18 Crack the Earth C :R:	.08	.20
❑ 19 Crawling Filth C :K:	.08	.20
❑ 20 Cunning Bandit U :R:	.10	.25
❑ 21 Day of Destiny R :W:	.30	.75
❑ 22 Disrupting Shoal R :B:	2.00	5.00
❑ 23 Empty-Shrine Kannushi U :W:	.12	.30
❑ 24 Enshrined Memories R :G:	.30	.75
❑ 25 Eradicate U :K:	.30	.75
❑ 26 Faithful Squire U :W:	.10	.25
❑ 27 Final Judgment R :W:	1.25	3.00
❑ 28 First Volley C :R:	.08	.20
❑ 29 Flames of the Blood Hand U :R:	.60	1.50
❑ 30 Floodbringer C :B:	.08	.20
❑ 31 Forked-Branch Garami U :G:	.10	.25
❑ 32 Frost Ogre C :R:	.08	.20
❑ 33 Frostling C :R:	.08	.20
❑ 34 Fumiko the Lowblood R :R:	.50	1.25
❑ 35 Genju of the Cedars U :G:	.15	.40
❑ 36 Genju of the Falls U :B:	.15	.40
❑ 37 Genju of the Fens U :K:	.12	.30
❑ 38 Genju of the Fields U :W:	.20	.50
❑ 39 Genju of the Realm R :D:	.60	1.50
❑ 40 Genju of the Spires U :R:	.30	.75
❑ 41 Gnarled Mass C :G:	.08	.20
❑ 42 Goblin Cohort C :R:	.08	.20
❑ 43 Gods' Eye, Gate to the Reikai U :L:	.20	.50
❑ 44 Goryo's Vengeance R :K:	2.00	5.00
❑ 45 Harbinger of Spring C :G:	.08	.20
❑ 46 Heart of Light C :W:	.08	.20
❑ 47 Heartless Hidetsugu R :R:	.30	.75
❑ 48 Heed the Mists U :B:	.10	.25
❑ 49 Hero's Demise R :K:	.30	.75
❑ 50 Higure, the Still Wind R :B:	.75	2.00
❑ 51 Hired Muscle U :K:	.10	.25
❑ 52 Hokori, Dust Drinker R :W:	.40	1.00
❑ 53 Horobi's Whisper C :K:	.08	.20
❑ 54 Hundred-Talon Strike C :W:	.08	.20
❑ 55 In the Web of War R :R:	.30	.75
❑ 56 Indebted Samurai U :W:	.20	.50
❑ 57 Ink-Eyes, Servant of Oni R :K:	5.00	12.00
❑ 58 Ire of Kaminari C :R:	.08	.20
❑ 59 Isao, Enlightened Bushi R :G:	.30	.75
❑ 60 Ishi-Ishi, Akki Crackshot R :R:	.25	.60
❑ 61 Iwamori of the Open Fist R :G:	.30	.75
❑ 62 Jetting Glasskite U :B:	.10	.25
❑ 63 Kaijin of the Vanishing Touch U :B:	.12	.30
❑ 64 Kami of False Hope C :W:	.08	.20
❑ 65 Kami of Tattered Shoji C :W:	.08	.20
❑ 66 Kami of the Honored Dead U :W:	.10	.25
❑ 67 Kentaro, the Smiling Cat R :W:	.30	.75
❑ 68 Kira, Great Glass-Spinner R :B:	8.00	20.00
❑ 69 Kitsune Palliator U :W:	.10	.25
❑ 70 Kodama of the Center Tree R :G:	.25	.60
❑ 71 Kumano's Blessing C :R:	.08	.20
❑ 72 Kyoki, Sanity's Eclipse R :K:	.25	.60
❑ 73 Lifegift R :G:	.50	1.25
❑ 74 Lifespinner U :G:	.12	.30
❑ 75 Loam Dweller U :G:	.10	.25
❑ 76 Mannichi, the Fevered Dream R :R:	.25	.60
❑ 77 Mark of Sakiko U :G:	.12	.30
❑ 78 Mark of the Oni U :K:	.10	.25
❑ 79 Matsu-Tribe Sniper C :G:	.08	.20
❑ 80 Mending Hands C :W:	.08	.20
❑ 81 Minamo Sightbender U :B:	.10	.25
❑ 82 Minamo's Meddling C :B:	.08	.20
❑ 83 Mirror Gallery R :A:	1.50	4.00
❑ 84 Mistblade Shinobi C :B:	.10	.25
❑ 85 Moonlit Strider C :W:	.08	.20
❑ 86 Neko-Te R :A:	.50	1.25
❑ 87 Nezumi Shadow-Watcher U :K:	.10	.25
❑ 88 Ninja of the Deep Hours C :B:	.20	.50
❑ 89 Nourishing Shoal R :G:	.25	.60
❑ 90 Ogre Marauder U :K:	.15	.40
❑ 91 Ogre Recluse U :R:	.10	.25
❑ 92 Okiba-Gang Shinobi C :K:	.10	.25
❑ 93 Opal-Eye, Konda's Yojimbo R :W:	.40	1.00
❑ 94 Orb of Dreams R :A:	.30	.75
❑ 95 Ornate Kanzashi R :A:	.25	.60
❑ 96 Overblaze U :R:	.10	.25
❑ 97 Oyobi, Who Split the Heavens R :W:	.25	.60
❑ 98 Patron of the Akki R :R:	.25	.60
❑ 99 Patron of the Kitsune R :W:	.25	.60
❑ 100 Patron of the Moon R :B:	.30	.75
❑ 101 Patron of the Nezumi R :K:	.25	.60
❑ 102 Patron of the Orochi R :G:	1.00	2.50
❑ 103 Petalmane Baku C :G:	.08	.20
❑ 104 Phantom Wings C :B:	.08	.20
❑ 105 Psychic Spear C :K:	.08	.20
❑ 106 Pus Kami U :K:	.10	.25
❑ 107 Quash U :B:	.20	.50
❑ 108 Quillmane Baku C :B:	.08	.20
❑ 109 Reduce to Dreams R :B:	.25	.60
❑ 110 Ribbons of the Reikai C :B:	.08	.20
❑ 111 Roar of Jukai C :G:	.08	.20
❑ 112 Ronin Cliffrider U :R:	.10	.25
❑ 113 Ronin Warclub U :A:	.15	.40
❑ 114 Sakiko, Mother of Summer R :G:	.30	.75
❑ 115 Sakura-Tribe Springcaller C :G:	.08	.20
❑ 116 Scaled Hulk C :G:	.08	.20
❑ 117 Scour U :W:	.12	.30
❑ 118 Scourge of Numai U :K:	.10	.25
❑ 119 Shimmering Glasskite C :B:	.08	.20
❑ 120 Shining Shoal R :W:	.40	1.00
❑ 121 Shinka Gatekeeper C :R:	.08	.20
❑ 122 Shirei, Shizo's Caretaker R :K:	.60	1.50
❑ 123 Shizuko, Caller of Autumn R :G:	.25	.60
❑ 124 Shuko U :A:	.20	.50
❑ 125 Shuriken U :A:	.20	.50
❑ 126 Sickening Shoal R :K:	.40	1.00
❑ 127 Silverstorm Samurai C :W:	.08	.20
❑ 128 Skullmane Baku C :K:	.08	.20
❑ 129 Skullsnatcher C :K:	.08	.20
❑ 130 Slumbering Tora R :A:	.25	.60
❑ 131 Soratami Mindsweeper U :B:	.10	.25
❑ 132 Sosuke's Summons U :G:	.30	.75
❑ 133 Sowing Salt U :R:	.12	.30
❑ 134 Splinter U :G:	.15	.40
❑ 135 Split-Tail Miko C :W:	.08	.20
❑ 136 Stir the Grave C :K:	.08	.20
❑ 137 Stream of Consciousness U :B:	.10	.25
❑ 138 Sway of the Stars R :B:	.25	.60
❑ 139 Takeno's Cavalry C :W:	.08	.20
❑ 140 Takenuma Bleeder C :K:	.08	.20
❑ 141 Tallowisp U :W:	.15	.40
❑ 142 Teardrop Kami C :B:	.08	.20
❑ 143 Tendo Ice Bridge R :L:	1.25	3.00
❑ 144 Terashi's Grasp C :W:	.08	.20
❑ 145 Terashi's Verdict U :W:	.10	.25
❑ 146 That Which Was Taken R :A:	1.50	4.00
❑ 147 Threads of Disloyalty R :B:	2.00	5.00
❑ 148 Three Tragedies U :K:	.10	.25
❑ 149 Throat Slitter U :K:	.50	1.25
❑ 150 Toils of Night and Day C :B:	.08	.20
❑ 151 Tomorrow, Azami's Familiar R :B:	.25	.60
❑ 152 Torrent of Stone C :R:	.08	.20
❑ 153 Toshiro Umezawa R :K:	.30	.75
❑ 154 Traproot Kami C :G:	.08	.20
❑ 155 Twist Allegiance R :R:	.25	.60
❑ 156 Umezawa's Jitte R :A:	8.00	20.00
❑ 157 Unchecked Growth U :G:	.10	.25
❑ 158 Uproot C :G:	.08	.20
❑ 159 Veil of Secrecy C :B:	.08	.20
❑ 160 Vital Surge C :G:	.08	.20
❑ 161 Walker of Secret Ways U :B:	.25	.60
❑ 162 Ward of Piety U :W:	.10	.25
❑ 163 Waxmane Baku C :W:	.08	.20
❑ 164 Yomiji, Who Bars the Way R :W:	.25	.60
❑ 165 Yukora, the Prisoner R :K:	.25	.60

2005 Magic the Gathering Betrayers of Kamigawa Foil

Item	Low	High
Complete Set (165)	2.00	3.00
*Foil: .8X to 2X Basic Cards		
❑ 1 Akki Blizzard-Herder C :R:	.15	.40
❑ 2 Akki Raider U :R:	.20	.50
❑ 3 Ashen Monstrosity U :R:	.20	.50
❑ 4 Aura Barbs U :R:	.20	.50
❑ 5 Baku Altar R :A:	.50	1.25
❑ 6 Bile Urchin C :K:	.15	.40
❑ 7 Blademane Baku C :R:	.15	.40
❑ 8 Blazing Shoal R :R:	3.00	8.00
❑ 9 Blessing of Leeches C :K:	.15	.40
❑ 10 Blinding Powder U :A:	.40	1.00
❑ 11 Body of Jukai U :G:	.20	.50
❑ 12 Budoka Pupil U :G:	.20	.50
❑ 13 Call for Blood C :K:	.15	.40
❑ 14 Callow Jushi U :B:	.20	.50
❑ 15 Child of Thorns C :G:	.15	.40
❑ 16 Chisei, Heart of Oceans R :B:	.50	1.25
❑ 17 Clash of Realities R :R:	.50	1.25
❑ 18 Crack the Earth C :R:	.15	.40
❑ 19 Crawling Filth C :K:	.15	.40
❑ 20 Cunning Bandit U :R:	.20	.50
❑ 21 Day of Destiny R :W:	.60	1.50
❑ 22 Disrupting Shoal R :B:	4.00	10.00
❑ 23 Empty-Shrine Kannushi U :W:	.25	.60
❑ 24 Enshrined Memories R :G:	.60	1.50
❑ 25 Eradicate U :K:	.60	1.50
❑ 26 Faithful Squire U :W:	.20	.50
❑ 27 Final Judgment R :W:	2.50	6.00
❑ 28 First Volley C :R:	.15	.40
❑ 29 Flames of the Blood Hand U :R:	1.25	3.00
❑ 30 Floodbringer C :B:	.15	.40
❑ 31 Forked-Branch Garami U :G:	.20	.50
❑ 32 Frost Ogre C :R:	.15	.40
❑ 33 Frostling C :R:	.15	.40
❑ 34 Fumiko the Lowblood R :R:	1.00	2.50
❑ 35 Genju of the Cedars U :G:	.30	.75
❑ 36 Genju of the Falls U :B:	.30	.75
❑ 37 Genju of the Fens U :K:	.25	.60
❑ 38 Genju of the Fields U :W:	.40	1.00
❑ 39 Genju of the Realm R :Z:	1.25	3.00
❑ 40 Genju of the Spires U :R:	.60	1.50
❑ 41 Gnarled Mass C :G:	.15	.40
❑ 42 Goblin Cohort C :R:	.15	.40
❑ 43 Gods' Eye, Gate to the Reikai U :L:	.40	1.00
❑ 44 Goryo's Vengeance R :K:	4.00	10.00
❑ 45 Harbinger of Spring C :G:	.15	.40
❑ 46 Heart of Light C :W:	.15	.40
❑ 47 Heartless Hidetsugu R :R:	.60	1.50
❑ 48 Heed the Mists U :B:	.20	.50
❑ 49 Hero's Demise R :K:	.60	1.50
❑ 50 Higure, the Still Wind R :B:	1.50	4.00
❑ 51 Hired Muscle U :K:	.20	.50
❑ 52 Hokori, Dust Drinker R :W:	.75	2.00
❑ 53 Horobi's Whisper C :K:	.15	.40
❑ 54 Hundred-Talon Strike C :W:	.15	.40
❑ 55 In the Web of War R :R:	.60	1.50
❑ 56 Indebted Samurai U :W:	.40	1.00
❑ 57 Ink-Eyes, Servant of Oni R :K:	10.00	25.00
❑ 58 Ire of Kaminari C :R:	.15	.40
❑ 59 Isao, Enlightened Bushi R :G:	.60	1.50
❑ 60 Ishi-Ishi, Akki Crackshot R :R:	.50	1.25
❑ 61 Iwamori of the Open Fist R :G:	.60	1.50
❑ 62 Jetting Glasskite U :B:	.20	.50
❑ 63 Kaijin of the Vanishing Touch U :B:	.25	.60
❑ 64 Kami of False Hope C :W:	.15	.40
❑ 65 Kami of Tattered Shoji C :W:	.15	.40
❑ 66 Kami of the Honored Dead U :W:	.20	.50
❑ 67 Kentaro, the Smiling Cat R :W:	.60	1.50
❑ 68 Kira, Great Glass-Spinner R :B:	15.00	40.00
❑ 69 Kitsune Palliator U :W:	.20	.50
❑ 70 Kodama of the Center Tree R :G:	.50	1.25
❑ 71 Kumano's Blessing C :R:	.15	.40
❑ 72 Kyoki, Sanity's Eclipse R :K:	.50	1.25
❑ 73 Lifegift R :G:	1.00	2.50
❑ 74 Lifespinner U :G:	.25	.60
❑ 75 Loam Dweller U :G:	.20	.50
❑ 76 Mannichi, the Fevered Dream R :R:	.50	1.25
❑ 77 Mark of Sakiko U :G:	.25	.60
❑ 78 Mark of the Oni U :K:	.20	.50
❑ 79 Matsu-Tribe Sniper C :G:	.15	.40
❑ 80 Mending Hands C :W:	.15	.40
❑ 81 Minamo Sightbender U :B:	.20	.50
❑ 82 Minamo's Meddling C :B:	.15	.40
❑ 83 Mirror Gallery R :A:	3.00	8.00
❑ 84 Mistblade Shinobi C :B:	.20	.50
❑ 85 Moonlit Strider C :W:	.15	.40
❑ 86 Neko-Te R :A:	1.00	2.50
❑ 87 Nezumi Shadow-Watcher U :K:	.20	.50
❑ 88 Ninja of the Deep Hours C :B:	.40	1.00
❑ 89 Nourishing Shoal R :G:	.50	1.25
❑ 90 Ogre Marauder U :K:	.30	.75
❑ 91 Ogre Recluse U :R:	.20	.50
❑ 92 Okiba-Gang Shinobi C :K:	.20	.50
❑ 93 Opal-Eye, Konda's Yojimbo R :W:	.75	2.00
❑ 94 Orb of Dreams R :A:	.60	1.50
❑ 95 Ornate Kanzashi R :A:	.50	1.25
❑ 96 Overblaze U :R:	.20	.50
❑ 97 Oyobi, Who Split the Heavens R :W:	.50	1.25
❑ 98 Patron of the Akki R :R:	.50	1.25
❑ 99 Patron of the Kitsune R :W:	.50	1.25
❑ 100 Patron of the Moon R :B:	.60	1.50
❑ 101 Patron of the Nezumi R :K:	.50	1.25
❑ 102 Patron of the Orochi R :G:	2.00	5.00
❑ 103 Petalmane Baku C :G:	.15	.40
❑ 104 Phantom Wings C :B:	.15	.40
❑ 105 Psychic Spear C :K:	.15	.40
❑ 106 Pus Kami U :K:	.20	.50
❑ 107 Quash U :B:	.40	1.00
❑ 108 Quillmane Baku C :B:	.15	.40
❑ 109 Reduce to Dreams R :B:	.50	1.25
❑ 110 Ribbons of the Reikai C :B:	.15	.40
❑ 111 Roar of Jukai C :G:	.15	.40
❑ 112 Ronin Cliffrider U :R:	.20	.50
❑ 113 Ronin Warclub U :A:	.30	.75
❑ 114 Sakiko, Mother of Summer R :G:	.60	1.50
❑ 115 Sakura-Tribe Springcaller C :G:	.15	.40
❑ 116 Scaled Hulk C :G:	.15	.40
❑ 117 Scour U :W:	.25	.60
❑ 118 Scourge of Numai U :K:	.20	.50
❑ 119 Shimmering Glasskite C :B:	.15	.40
❑ 120 Shining Shoal R :W:	.75	2.00
❑ 121 Shinka Gatekeeper C :R:	.15	.40
❑ 122 Shirei, Shizo's Caretaker R :K:	1.25	3.00
❑ 123 Shizuko, Caller of Autumn R :G:	.50	1.25
❑ 124 Shuko U :A:	.40	1.00
❑ 125 Shuriken U :A:	.40	1.00
❑ 126 Sickening Shoal R :K:	.75	2.00
❑ 127 Silverstorm Samurai C :W:	.15	.40
❑ 128 Skullmane Baku C :K:	.15	.40
❑ 129 Skullsnatcher C :K:	.15	.40
❑ 130 Slumbering Tora R :A:	.50	1.25
❑ 131 Soratami Mindsweeper U :B:	.20	.50
❑ 132 Sosuke's Summons U :G:	.60	1.50
❑ 133 Sowing Salt U :R:	.25	.60
❑ 134 Splinter U :G:	.30	.75
❑ 135 Split-Tail Miko C :W:	.15	.40
❑ 136 Stir the Grave C :K:	.15	.40
❑ 137 Stream of Consciousness U :B:	.20	.50
❑ 138 Sway of the Stars R :B:	.50	1.25
❑ 139 Takeno's Cavalry C :W:	.15	.40
❑ 140 Takenuma Bleeder C :K:	.15	.40
❑ 141 Tallowisp U :W:	.30	.75
❑ 142 Teardrop Kami C :B:	.15	.40
❑ 143 Tendo Ice Bridge R :L:	2.50	6.00
❑ 144 Terashi's Grasp C :W:	.15	.40
❑ 145 Terashi's Verdict U :W:	.20	.50
❑ 146 That Which Was Taken R :A:	3.00	8.00
❑ 147 Threads of Disloyalty R :B:	4.00	10.00
❑ 148 Three Tragedies U :K:	.20	.50
❑ 149 Throat Slitter U :K:	1.00	2.50
❑ 150 Toils of Night and Day C :B:	.15	.40
❑ 151 Tomorrow, Azami's Familiar R :B:	.50	1.25
❑ 152 Torrent of Stone C :R:	.15	.40
❑ 153 Toshiro Umezawa R :K:	.60	1.50
❑ 154 Traproot Kami C :G:	.15	.40
❑ 155 Twist Allegiance R :R:	.50	1.25
❑ 156 Umezawa's Jitte R :A:	15.00	40.00
❑ 157 Unchecked Growth U :G:	.20	.50
❑ 158 Uproot C :G:	.15	.40
❑ 159 Veil of Secrecy C :B:	.15	.40
❑ 160 Vital Surge C :G:	.15	.40
❑ 161 Walker of Secret Ways U :B:	.50	1.25
❑ 162 Ward of Piety U :W:	.20	.50
❑ 163 Waxmane Baku C :W:	.15	.40
❑ 164 Yomiji, Who Bars the Way R :W:	.50	1.25
❑ 165 Yukora, the Prisoner R :K:	.50	1.25

2005 Magic the Gathering Saviors of Kamigawa

Item	Low	High
Complete Set (165)	75.00	150.00
Booster Box (36 Packs)	100.00	150.00
Booster Pack (15 Cards)	3.00	5.00
Theme Deck	5.00	10.00
Fat Pack	25.00	50.00
❑ 1 Adamaro, First to Desire R :R:	.25	.60
❑ 2 AEther Shockwave U :W:	.10	.25
❑ 3 Akki Drillmaster C :R:	.08	.20
❑ 4 Akki Underling C :R:	.08	.20
❑ 5 Akuta, Born of Ash R :K:	.25	.60
❑ 6 Araba Mothrider C :W:	.08	.20
❑ 7 Arashi, the Sky Asunder R :G:	.50	1.25
❑ 8 Ashes of the Fallen R :A:	.25	.60
❑ 9 Ayumi, the Last Visitor R :G:	.30	.75
❑ 10 Barrel Down Sokenzan C :R:	.08	.20
❑ 11 Blood Clock R :A:	.30	.75
❑ 12 Bounteous Kirin R :G:	.25	.60
❑ 13 Briarknit Kami U :G:	.20	.50
❑ 14 Burning-Eye Zubera U :R:	.10	.25
❑ 15 Captive Flame U :R:	.10	.25
❑ 16 Celestial Kirin R :W:	.30	.75
❑ 17 Charge Across the Araba U :W:	.10	.25
❑ 18 Choice of Damnations R :K:	1.00	2.50
❑ 19 Cloudhoof Kirin R :B:	.25	.60
❑ 20 Cowed by Wisdom C :W:	.08	.20
❑ 21 Curtain of Light C :W:	.08	.20
❑ 22 Cut the Earthly Bond C :B:	.08	.20
❑ 23 Death Denied C :K:	.08	.20
❑ 24 Death of a Thousand Stings C :K:	.08	.20
❑ 25 Deathknell Kami C :K:	.08	.20
❑ 26 Deathmask Nezumi C :K:	.08	.20
❑ 27 Dense Canopy U :G:	.10	.25
❑ 28 Descendant of Kiyomaro U :W:	.10	.25
❑ 29 Descendant of Masumaro U :G:	.10	.25
❑ 30 Descendant of Soramaro C :B:	.08	.20
❑ 31 Dosan's Oldest Chant C :G:	.08	.20
❑ 32 Dreamcatcher C :B:	.08	.20
❑ 33 Ebony Owl Netsuke U :A:	.20	.50
❑ 34 Eiganjo Free-Riders U :W:	.10	.25
❑ 35 Elder Pine of Jukai C :G:	.08	.20
❑ 36 Endless Swarm R :G:	.30	.75
❑ 37 Enduring Ideal R :W:	.75	2.00
❑ 38 Erayo, Soratami Ascendant R :B:	3.00	8.00
❑ 39 Eternal Dominion R :B:	1.00	2.50
❑ 40 Evermind U :B:	.10	.25
❑ 41 Exile into Darkness U :K:	.10	.25
❑ 42 Feral Lightning U :R:	.10	.25
❑ 43 Fiddlehead Kami C :G:	.08	.20
❑ 44 Footsteps of the Goryo U :K:	.20	.50
❑ 45 Freed from the Real C :B:	.20	.50
❑ 46 Gaze of Adamaro U :R:	.10	.25
❑ 47 Ghost-Lit Nourisher U :G:	.10	.25
❑ 48 Ghost-Lit Raider U :R:	.10	.25
❑ 49 Ghost-Lit Redeemer U :W:	.20	.50
❑ 50 Ghost-Lit Stalker U :K:	.10	.25
❑ 51 Ghost-Lit Warder U :B:	.10	.25
❑ 52 Glitterfang C :R:	.08	.20
❑ 53 Gnat Miser C :K:	.08	.20
❑ 54 Godo's Irregulars U :R:	.10	.25
❑ 55 Hail of Arrows U :W:	.10	.25
❑ 56 Hand of Cruelty U :K:	.30	.75
❑ 57 Hand of Honor U :W:	.50	1.25
❑ 58 Haru-Onna U :G:	.10	.25
❑ 59 Hidetsugu's Second Rite R :R:	.50	1.25

MAGIC

Card	Low	High
❑ 60 Homura, Human Ascendant R :R:	.50	1.25
❑ 61 Ideas Unbound C :B:	.20	.50
❑ 62 Iizuka the Ruthless R :R:	.30	.75
❑ 63 Iname as One R :D:	.30	.75
❑ 64 Infernal Kirin R :K:	.30	.75
❑ 65 Inner Calm, Outer Strength C :G:	.08	.20
❑ 66 Inner Fire C :R:	.08	.20
❑ 67 Inner-Chamber Guard U :W:	.20	.50
❑ 68 Into the Fray C :R:	.08	.20
❑ 69 Ivory Crane Netsuke U :A:	.10	.25
❑ 70 Jiwari, the Earth Aflame R :R:	.25	.60
❑ 71 Kagemaro, First to Suffer R :K:	.60	1.50
❑ 72 Kagemaro's Clutch C :K:	.08	.20
❑ 73 Kaho, Minamo Historian R :B:	.40	1.00
❑ 74 Kami of Empty Graves C :K:	.08	.20
❑ 75 Kami of the Crescent Moon R :B:	.60	1.50
❑ 76 Kami of the Tended Garden U :G:	.10	.25
❑ 77 Kashi-Tribe Elite U :G:	.25	.60
❑ 78 Kataki, War's Wage R :W:	2.50	6.00
❑ 79 Kemuri-Onna U :K:	.10	.25
❑ 80 Kiku's Shadow U :K:	.20	.50
❑ 81 Kiri-Onna U :B:	.10	.25
❑ 82 Kitsune Bonesetter C :W:	.08	.20
❑ 83 Kitsune Dawnblade C :W:	.08	.20
❑ 84 Kitsune Loreweaver C :W:	.08	.20
❑ 85 Kiyomaro, First to Stand R :W:	.25	.60
❑ 86 Kuon, Ogre Ascendant R :K:	.25	.60
❑ 87 Kuro's Taken C :K:	.08	.20
❑ 88 Locust Miser U :K:	.20	.50
❑ 89 Maga, Traitor to Mortals R :K:	.50	1.25
❑ 90 Manriki-Gusari U :A:	.60	1.50
❑ 91 Masumaro, First to Live R :G:	.30	.75
❑ 92 Matsu-Tribe Birdstalker C :G:	.08	.20
❑ 93 Measure of Wickedness U :K:	.10	.25
❑ 94 Meishin, the Mind Cage R :B:	.30	.75
❑ 95 Michiko Konda, Truth Seeker R :W:	1.25	3.00
❑ 96 Mikokoro, Center of the Sea R :L:	2.00	5.00
❑ 97 Minamo Scrollkeeper C :B:	.08	.20
❑ 98 Miren, the Moaning Well R :L:	2.50	6.00
❑ 99 Molting Skin U :G:	.10	.25
❑ 100 Moonbow Illusionist C :B:	.08	.20
❑ 101 Moonwing Moth C :W:	.08	.20
❑ 102 Murmurs from Beyond C :B:	.08	.20
❑ 103 Neverending Torment R :K:	.30	.75
❑ 104 Nightsoil Kami C :G:	.08	.20
❑ 105 Nikko-Onna U :W:	.10	.25
❑ 106 Oboro Breezecaller C :B:	.08	.20
❑ 107 Oboro Envoy U :B:	.10	.25
❑ 108 Oboro, Palace in the Clouds R :L:	1.00	2.50
❑ 109 Okina Nightwatch C :G:	.08	.20
❑ 110 O-Naginata U :A:	.25	.60
❑ 111 One with Nothing R :K:	.30	.75
❑ 112 Oni of Wild Places U :R:	.10	.25
❑ 113 Oppressive Will C :B:	.08	.20
❑ 114 Overwhelming Intellect U :B:	.20	.50
❑ 115 Pain's Reward R :K:	.30	.75
❑ 116 Path of Anger's Flame C :R:	.08	.20
❑ 117 Pithing Needle R :A:	1.50	4.00
❑ 118 Plow Through Reito C :W:	.08	.20
❑ 119 Presence of the Wise U :W:	.10	.25
❑ 120 Promise of Bunrei R :W:	.75	2.00
❑ 121 Promised Kannushi C :G:	.08	.20
❑ 122 Pure Intentions R :W:	.25	.60
❑ 123 Rally the Horde R :R:	.25	.60
❑ 124 Raving Oni-Slave C :K:	.08	.20
❑ 125 Razorjaw Oni U :K:	.10	.25
❑ 126 Reki, the History of Kamigawa R :G:	.30	.75
❑ 127 Rending Vines C :G:	.08	.20
❑ 128 Reverence R :W:	.30	.75
❑ 129 Ronin Cavekeeper C :R:	.08	.20
❑ 130 Rune-Tail, Kitsune Ascendant R :W:	1.25	3.00
❑ 131 Rushing-Tide Zubera U :B:	.10	.25
❑ 132 Sakashima the Impostor R :B:	2.00	5.00
❑ 133 Sakura-Tribe Scout C :G:	.10	.25
❑ 134 Sasaya, Orochi Ascendant R :G:	.30	.75
❑ 135 Scroll of Origins R :A:	.25	.60
❑ 136 Secretkeeper U :B:	.10	.25
❑ 137 Seed the Land R :G:	.30	.75
❑ 138 Seek the Horizon U :G:	.20	.50
❑ 139 Sekki, Seasons' Guide R :G:	.40	1.00
❑ 140 Shape Stealer U :B:	.20	.50
❑ 141 Shifting Borders U :B:	.10	.25
❑ 142 Shinen of Fear's Chill C :K:	.08	.20
❑ 143 Shinen of Flight's Wings C :B:	.08	.20
❑ 144 Shinen of Fury's Fire C :R:	.08	.20
❑ 145 Shinen of Life's Roar C :G:	.08	.20
❑ 146 Shinen of Stars' Light C :W:	.08	.20
❑ 147 Sink into Takenuma C :K:	.08	.20
❑ 148 Skull Collector U :K:	.10	.25
❑ 149 Skyfire Kirin R :R:	.25	.60
❑ 150 Sokenzan Renegade U :R:	.08	.20
❑ 151 Sokenzan Spellblade C :R:	.08	.20
❑ 152 Soramaro, First to Dream R :B:	.25	.60
❑ 153 Soratami Cloud Chariot U :A:	.10	.25
❑ 154 Spiraling Embers C :R:	.08	.20
❑ 155 Spiritual Visit C :W:	.08	.20
❑ 156 Stampeding Serow U :G:	.10	.25
❑ 157 Sunder from Within U :R:	.10	.25
❑ 158 Thoughts of Ruin R :R:	.30	.75
❑ 159 Tomb of Urami R :L:	.30	.75
❑ 160 Torii Watchward C :W:	.08	.20
❑ 161 Trusted Advisor U :B:	.10	.25
❑ 162 Twincast R :B:	1.25	3.00
❑ 163 Undying Flames R :R:	.25	.60
❑ 164 Wine of Blood and Iron R :A:	.25	.60
❑ 165 Yuki-Onna U :R:	.10	.25

2005 Magic the Gathering Saviors of Kamigawa Foil

Complete Set (165)	150.00	300.00

*Foil: .8X to 2X Basic Cards

2005 Magic the Gathering Ravnica: City of Guilds

Card	Low	High
Complete Set (306)	125.00	200.00
Booster Box (36 Packs)	300.00	400.00
Booster Pack (15 Cards)	9.00	12.00
Fat Pack	175.00	250.00
Theme Deck	20.00	30.00
❑ 1 Agrus Kos, WojekVeteran R :D:	.25	.60
❑ 2 Auratouched Mage U :W:	.12	.30
❑ 3 Autochthon Wurm R :D:	.40	1.00
❑ 4 Barbarian Riftcutter C :R:	.08	.20
❑ 5 Bathe in Light U :W:	.12	.30
❑ 6 Belltower Sphinx U :B:	.12	.30
❑ 7 Benevolent Ancestor C :W:	.08	.20
❑ 8 Birds of Paradise R :G:	2.50	6.00
❑ 9 Blazing Archon R :W:	1.25	3.00
❑ 10 Blockbuster U :R:	.12	.30
❑ 11 Blood Funnel R :K:	.25	.60
❑ 12 Bloodbond March R :D:	.25	.60
❑ 13 Bloodletter Quill R :A:	.25	.60
❑ 14 Boros Fury-Shield C :W:	.08	.20
❑ 15 Boros Garrison C :L:	.20	.50
❑ 16 Boros Guildmage U :R:W:	.12	.30
❑ 17 Boros Recruit C :R:W:	.08	.20
❑ 18 Boros Signet C :A:	.12	.30
❑ 19 Boros Swiftblade U :D:	.20	.50
❑ 20 Bottled Cloister R :A:	.25	.60
❑ 21 Brainspoil C :K:	.08	.20
❑ 22 Bramble Elemental C :G:	.08	.20
❑ 23 Breath of Fury R :R:	.25	.60
❑ 24 Brightflame R :D:	.30	.75
❑ 25 Caregiver C :W:	.08	.20
❑ 26 Carrion Howler U :K:	.12	.30
❑ 27 Carven Caryatid U :G:	.20	.50
❑ 28 Centaur Safeguard C :G:W:	.08	.20
❑ 29 Cerulean Sphinx R :B:	.25	.60
❑ 30 Chant of Vitu-Ghazi U :W:	.12	.30
❑ 31 Char R :R:	.40	1.00
❑ 32 Chord of Calling R :G:	5.00	12.00
❑ 33 Chorus of the Conclave R :D:	.25	.60
❑ 34 Circu, Dimir Lobotomist R :D:	2.00	5.00
❑ 35 Civic Wayfinder C :G:	.08	.20
❑ 36 Cleansing Beam U :R:	.12	.30
❑ 37 Clinging Darkness C :K:	.08	.20
❑ 38 Cloudstone Curio R :A:	1.25	3.00
❑ 39 Clutch of the Undercity U :D:	.20	.50
❑ 40 Coalhauler Swine C :R:	.08	.20
❑ 41 Compulsive Research C :B:	.12	.30
❑ 42 Concerted Effort R :W:	1.00	2.50
❑ 43 Conclave Equenaut C :W:	.08	.20
❑ 44 Conclave Phalanx U :W:	.12	.30
❑ 45 Conclave's Blessing C :W:	.08	.20
❑ 46 Congregation at Dawn U :D:	.30	.75
❑ 47 Consult the Necrosages C :D:	.08	.20
❑ 48 Convolute C :B:	.08	.20
❑ 49 Copy Enchantment R :B:	1.25	3.00
❑ 50 Courier Hawk C :W:	.08	.20
❑ 51 Crown of Convergence R :A:	.25	.60
❑ 52 Cyclopean Snare U :A:	.12	.30
❑ 53 Dark Confidant R :K:	25.00	50.00
❑ 54 Dark Heart of the Wood U :D:	.12	.30
❑ 55 Darkblast U :K:	.25	.60
❑ 56 Devouring Light U :W:	.20	.50
❑ 57 Dimir Aqueduct C :L:	.30	.75
❑ 58 Dimir Cutpurse R :D:	.50	1.25
❑ 59 Dimir Doppelganger R :D:	1.00	2.50
❑ 60 Dimir Guildmage U :B:K:	.20	.50
❑ 61 Dimir House Guard C :K:	.08	.20
❑ 62 Dimir Infiltrator C :D:	.08	.20
❑ 63 Dimir Machinations U :K:	.20	.50
❑ 64 Dimir Signet C :A:	.12	.30
❑ 65 Disembowel C :K:	.08	.20
❑ 66 Divebomber Griffin U :W:	.12	.30
❑ 67 Dizzy Spell C :B:	.08	.20
❑ 68 Dogpile C :R:	.08	.20
❑ 69 Doubling Season R :G:	15.00	30.00
❑ 70 Dowsing Shaman U :G:	.12	.30
❑ 71 Drake Familiar C :B:	.08	.20
❑ 72 Dream Leash R :B:	.25	.60
❑ 73 Drift of Phantasms C :B:	.12	.30
❑ 74 Dromad Purebred C :W:	.08	.20
❑ 75 Drooling Groodion U :D:	.12	.30
❑ 76 Dryad's Caress C :G:	.08	.20
❑ 77 Duskmantle,HouseofShadow U :L:	.12	.30
❑ 78 Elves of Deep Shadow C :G:	.08	.20
❑ 79 Elvish Skysweeper C :G:	.08	.20
❑ 80 Empty the Catacombs R :K:	.25	.60
❑ 81 Ethereal Usher U :B:	.12	.30
❑ 82 Excruciator R :R:	.25	.60
❑ 83 Eye of the Storm R :B:	.25	.60
❑ 84 Faith's Fetters C :W:	.12	.30
❑ 85 Farseek C :G:	.08	.20
❑ 86 Festival of the Guildpact U :W:	.12	.30
❑ 87 Fiery Conclusion C :R:	.08	.20
❑ 88 Firemane Angel R :D:	.60	1.50
❑ 89 Fists of Ironwood C :G:	.08	.20
❑ 90 Flame Fusillade R :R:	.25	.60
❑ 91 Flame-Kin Zealot U :D:	.20	.50
❑ 92 Flash Conscription U :R:	.12	.30
❑ 93 Flickerform R :W:	.25	.60
❑ 94 Flight of Fancy C :B:	.08	.20
❑ 95 Flow of Ideas U :B:	.12	.30
❑ 96 Followed Footsteps R :B:	1.50	4.00
❑ 97 Forest C :L:	.08	.20
❑ 98 Frenzied Goblin U :R:	.12	.30
❑ 99 Galvanic Arc C :R:	.08	.20
❑ 100 Gate Hound C :W:	.08	.20
❑ 101 Gather Courage C :G:	.08	.20
❑ 102 Gaze of the Gorgon C :K:G:	.08	.20
❑ 103 Ghosts of the Innocent R :W:	.25	.60
❑ 104 Glare of Subdual R :D:	.50	1.25
❑ 105 Glass Golem U :A:	.12	.30
❑ 106 Gleancrawler R :K:G:	.50	1.25
❑ 107 Glimpse the Unthinkable R :D:	6.00	15.00
❑ 108 Goblin Fire Fiend C :R:	.08	.20
❑ 109 Goblin Spelunkers C :R:	.08	.20
❑ 110 Golgari Brownscale C :G:	.08	.20
❑ 111 Golgari Germination U :D:	.20	.50
❑ 112 Golgari Grave-Troll R :G:	1.50	4.00
❑ 113 Golgari Guildmage U :K:G:	.12	.30
❑ 114 Golgari Rot Farm C :L:	.25	.60
❑ 115 Golgari Rotwurm C :D:	.08	.20
❑ 116 Golgari Signet C :A:	.12	.30
❑ 117 Golgari Thug U :K:	.75	2.00
❑ 118 Goliath Spider U :G:	.12	.30
❑ 119 Grave-Shell Scarab R :D:	.30	.75
❑ 120 Grayscaled Gharial C :B:	.08	.20
❑ 121 Greater Forgeling U :R:	.12	.30
❑ 122 Greater Mossdog C :G:	.08	.20
❑ 123 Grifter's Blade U :A:	.12	.30
❑ 124 Grozoth R :B:	.30	.75
❑ 125 Guardian of Vitu-Ghazi C :D:	.08	.20
❑ 126 Halcyon Glaze U :B:	.12	.30
❑ 127 Hammerfist Giant R :R:	.25	.60
❑ 128 Helldozer R :K:	.50	1.25
❑ 129 Hex R :K:	.30	.75
❑ 130 Hour of Reckoning R :W:	.30	.75
❑ 131 Hunted Dragon R :R:	.50	1.25
❑ 132 Hunted Horror R :K:	.75	2.00
❑ 133 Hunted Lammasu R :W:	.25	.60
❑ 134 Hunted Phantasm R :B:	.40	1.00
❑ 135 Hunted Troll R :G:	.30	.75
❑ 136 Incite Hysteria C :R:	.08	.20
❑ 137 Indentured Oaf U :R:	.12	.30
❑ 138 Induce Paranoia C :B:	.12	.30
❑ 139 Infectious Host C :K:	.08	.20
❑ 140 Instill Furor U :R:	.12	.30
❑ 141 Island C :L:	.08	.20
❑ 142 Ivy Dancer U :G:	.12	.30
❑ 143 Junktroller U :A:	.12	.30
❑ 144 Keening Banshee U :K:	.12	.30
❑ 145 Last Gasp C :K:	.08	.20
❑ 146 Leashling U :A:	.12	.30
❑ 147 Leave No Trace C :W:	.08	.20
❑ 148 Life from the Loam R :G:	6.00	15.00
❑ 149 Light of Sanction R :W:	.25	.60
❑ 150 Lightning Helix U :D:	1.25	3.00
❑ 151 Lore Broker U :B:	.12	.30
❑ 152 Loxodon Gatekeeper R :W:	.30	.75
❑ 153 Loxodon Hierarch R :D:	.60	1.50
❑ 154 Lurking Informant C :B:K:	.08	.20
❑ 155 Mark of Eviction U :B:	.12	.30
❑ 156 Master Warcraft R :R:W:	.40	1.00
❑ 157 Mausoleum Turnkey U :K:	.12	.30
❑ 158 Mindleech Mass R :D:	.40	1.00
❑ 159 Mindmoil R :R:	.25	.60
❑ 160 Mnemonic Nexus U :B:	.12	.30
❑ 161 Moldervine Cloak U :G:	.20	.50
❑ 162 Molten Sentry R :R:	.25	.60
❑ 163 Moonlight Bargain R :K:	.25	.60
❑ 164 Moroii U :D:	.20	.50
❑ 165 Mortipede C :K:	.08	.20
❑ 166 Mountain C :L:	.08	.20
❑ 167 Muddle the Mixture C :B:	.30	.75
❑ 168 Necromantic Thirst C :K:	.08	.20
❑ 169 Necroplasm R :K:	.30	.75
❑ 170 Netherborn Phalanx U :K:	.12	.30
❑ 171 Nightguard Patrol C :W:	.08	.20
❑ 172 Nightmare Void U :K:	.12	.30
❑ 173 Nullmage Shepherd U :G:	.20	.50
❑ 174 Nullstone Gargoyle R :A:	.25	.60
❑ 175 Oathsworn Giant U :W:	.20	.50
❑ 176 Ordruun Commando C :R:	.08	.20
❑ 177 Overgrown Tomb R :L:	8.00	20.00
❑ 178 Overwhelm U :G:	.12	.30
❑ 179 Pariah's Shield R :A:	.75	2.00
❑ 180 Peel from Reality C :B:	.08	.20
❑ 181 Peregrine Mask U :A:	.12	.30
❑ 182 Perilous Forays U :G:	.12	.30
❑ 183 Perplex C :D:	.12	.30
❑ 184 Phytohydra R :D:	.60	1.50
❑ 185 Plague Boiler R :A:	.25	.60
❑ 186 Plains C :L:	.08	.20
❑ 187 Pollenbright Wings U :D:	.12	.30
❑ 188 Primordial Sage R :G:	.30	.75
❑ 189 Privileged Position R :G:W:	4.00	10.00
❑ 190 Psychic Drain U :D:	.25	.60
❑ 191 Putrefy U :D:	.60	1.50
❑ 192 Quickchange C :B:	.08	.20
❑ 193 Rain of Embers C :R:	.08	.20
❑ 194 Rally the Righteous C :D:	.08	.20
❑ 195 Razia, Boros Archangel R :D:	.60	1.50
❑ 196 Razia's Purification R :D:	.30	.75
❑ 197 Recollect U :G:	.12	.30
❑ 198 Remand U :B:	3.00	8.00
❑ 199 Reroute U :R:	.12	.30
❑ 200 Ribbons of Night U :K:	.12	.30
❑ 201 Rolling Spoil U :R:	.12	.30
❑ 202 Roofstalker Wight C :K:	.08	.20
❑ 203 Root-Kin Ally U :G:	.12	.30
❑ 204 Sabertooth Alley Cat C :R:	.08	.20
❑ 205 Sacred Foundry R :L:	6.00	15.00
❑ 206 Sadistic Augermage C :K:	.08	.20
❑ 207 Sandsower U :W:	.12	.30
❑ 208 Savra,Queen of the Golgari R :D:	.40	1.00
❑ 209 Scatter the Seeds C :G:	.08	.20
❑ 210 Scion of the Wild R :G:	.25	.60
❑ 211 Screeching Griffin C :W:	.08	.20
❑ 212 Searing Meditation R :D:	.30	.75
❑ 213 Seed Spark U :W:	.12	.30
❑ 214 Seeds of Strength C :D:	.08	.20
❑ 215 Seismic Spike C :R:	.08	.20
❑ 216 Selesnya Evangel C :D:	.08	.20
❑ 217 Selesnya Guildmage U :G:W:	.12	.30
❑ 218 Selesnya Sagittars U :D:	.12	.30
❑ 219 Selesnya Sanctuary C :L:	.20	.50
❑ 220 Selesnya Signet C :A:	.12	.30
❑ 221 Sell-Sword Brute C :R:	.08	.20
❑ 222 Sewerdreg C :K:	.08	.20
❑ 223 Shadow of Doubt R :B:K:	.30	.75
❑ 224 Shambling Shell C :D:	.08	.20
❑ 225 Shred Memory C :K:	.08	.20
❑ 226 Siege Wurm C :G:	.08	.20
❑ 227 Sins of the Past R :K:	.25	.60
❑ 228 Sisters of Stone Death R :D:	.50	1.25
❑ 229 Skyknight Legionnaire C :D:	.08	.20
❑ 230 Smash C :R:	.08	.20
❑ 231 Snapping Drake C :B:	.08	.20
❑ 232 Sparkmage Apprentice C :R:	.08	.20
❑ 233 Spawnbroker R :B:	.25	.60
❑ 234 Spectral Searchlight U :A:	.20	.50
❑ 235 Stasis Cell C :B:	.08	.20
❑ 236 Stinkweed Imp C :K:	.20	.50
❑ 237 Stone-Seeder Hierophant C :G:	.08	.20
❑ 238 Stoneshaker Shaman U :R:	.12	.30
❑ 239 Strands of Undeath C :K:	.08	.20
❑ 240 Sundering Vitae C :G:	.08	.20
❑ 241 Sunforger R :A:	.50	1.25
❑ 242 Sunhome Enforcer U :D:	.12	.30
❑ 243 Sunhome,Fortress U :L:	.20	.50
❑ 244 Suppression Field U :W:	.20	.50
❑ 245 Surge of Zeal C :R:	.08	.20
❑ 246 Surveilling Sprite C :B:	.08	.20
❑ 247 Svogthos,Restless Tomb U :L:	.12	.30
❑ 248 Swamp C :L:	.08	.20
❑ 249 Szadek, Lord of Secrets R :D:	.40	1.00
❑ 250 Tattered Drake C :B:	.08	.20
❑ 251 Telling Time U :B:	.20	.50
❑ 252 Temple Garden R :L:	8.00	20.00
❑ 253 Terraformer C :B:	.08	.20
❑ 254 Terrarion C :A:	.08	.20
❑ 255 Thoughtpicker Witch C :K:	.08	.20
❑ 256 Three Dreams R :W:	.30	.75
❑ 257 Thundersong Trumpeter C :D:	.08	.20
❑ 258 Tidewater Minion C :B:	.08	.20
❑ 259 Tolsimir Wolfblood R :D:	.60	1.50
❑ 260 Torpid Moloch C :R:	.08	.20
❑ 261 Transluminant C :G:	.08	.20
❑ 262 Trophy Hunter U :G:	.12	.30
❑ 263 Tunnel Vision R :B:	.40	1.00
❑ 264 Twilight Drover R :W:	.75	2.00
❑ 265 Twisted Justice U :D:	.12	.30
❑ 266 Undercity Shade U :K:	.12	.30
❑ 267 Ursapine R :G:	.25	.60
❑ 268 Vedalken Dismisser C :B:	.08	.20
❑ 269 Vedalken Entrancer C :B:	.08	.20
❑ 270 Veteran Armorer C :W:	.08	.20
❑ 271 Viashino Fangtail C :R:	.08	.20
❑ 272 Viashino Slasher C :R:	.08	.20
❑ 273 Vigor Mortis U :K:	.12	.30
❑ 274 Vindictive Mob U :K:	.12	.30
❑ 275 Vinelasher Kudzu R :G:	.50	1.25
❑ 276 Vitu-Ghazi, City-Tree U :L:	.20	.50
❑ 277 Votary of the Conclave C :W:	.08	.20
❑ 278 Voyager Staff U :A:	.12	.30
❑ 279 Vulturous Zombie R :D:	.60	1.50
❑ 280 Warp World R :R:	.08	.20
❑ 281 War-Torch Goblin C :R:	.25	.60
❑ 282 Watchwolf U :D:	.40	1.00
❑ 283 Watery Grave R :L:	8.00	20.00
❑ 284 Wizened Snitches U :B:	.12	.30
❑ 285 Woebringer Demon R :K:	.25	.60
❑ 286 Wojek Apothecary U :W:	.12	.30
❑ 287 Wojek Embermage U :R:	.12	.30
❑ 288 Wojek Siren C :W:	.08	.20
❑ 289 Woodwraith Corrupter R :D:	.25	.60
❑ 290 Woodwraith Strangler C :D:	.08	.20
❑ 291 Zephyr Spirit C :B:	.08	.20

2005 Magic the Gathering Ravnica: City of Guilds Foil

*Foil: .8X to 2X Basic Cards

2006 Magic the Gathering Guildpact

Card	Low	High
Complete Set (165)	100.00	175.00
Booster Box (36 Packs)	175.00	300.00
Booster Pack (15 Cards)	5.00	10.00
Theme Deck	10.00	20.00
Fat Pack	40.00	80.00
❑ 1 Absolver Thrull C :W:	.10	.20
❑ 2 Abyssal Nocturnus R :K:	.40	1.00
❑ 3 AEtherplasm U :B:	.15	.40
❑ 4 Agent of Masks U :D:	.15	.40
❑ 5 Angel of Despair R :D:	2.50	6.00
❑ 6 Battering Wurm U :G:	.12	.30
❑ 7 Beastmaster's Magemark C :G:	.10	.20
❑ 8 Belfry Spirit U :W:	.12	.30
❑ 9 Benediction of Moons C :W:	.10	.20
❑ 10 Bioplasm R :G:	.25	.60
❑ 11 Blind Hunter C :D:	.10	.20
❑ 12 Bloodscale Prowler C :R:	.10	.20
❑ 13 Borborygmos R :D:	.30	.75
❑ 14 Burning-Tree Bloodscale C :D:	.10	.20
❑ 15 Burning-Tree Shaman R :D:	6.00	1.50
❑ 16 Castigate C :D:	.10	.20
❑ 17 Caustic Rain U :K:	.12	.30
❑ 18 Cerebral Vortex R :D:	.30	.75
❑ 19 Conjurer's Ban U :D:	.15	.40
❑ 20 Crash Landing U :G:	.12	.30
❑ 21 Cremate C :K:	.10	.20
❑ 22 Cry of Contrition C :K:	.10	.20
❑ 23 Cryptwailing U :K:	.12	.30
❑ 24 Crystal Seer C :B:	.10	.20
❑ 25 Culling Sun R :D:	.30	.75
❑ 26 Daggerclaw Imp U :K:	.12	.30
❑ 27 Debtors' Knell R :D:	4.00	10.00
❑ 28 Djinn Illuminatus R :D:	6.00	1.50
❑ 29 Douse in Gloom C :K:	.10	.20
❑ 30 Droning Bureaucrats U :W:	.12	.30
❑ 31 Drowned Rusalka U :B:	.12	.30
❑ 32 Dryad Sophisticate U :G:	.15	.40
❑ 33 Dune-Brood Nephilim R :D:	.30	.75
❑ 34 Earth Surge R :G:	.25	.60
❑ 35 Electrolyze U :D:	.40	1.00
❑ 36 Exhumer Thrull U :K:	.12	.30
❑ 37 Fencer's Magemark C :R:	.10	.20
❑ 38 Feral Animist U :D:	.12	.30
❑ 39 Frazzle U :B:	.12	.30
❑ 40 Gatherer of Graces U :G:	.12	.30
❑ 41 Gelectrode U :D:	6.00	1.50
❑ 42 Ghor-Clan Bloodscale U :R:	.12	.30
❑ 43 Ghor-Clan Savage C :G:	.10	.20
❑ 44 Ghost Council of Orzhova R :D:	6.00	1.50
❑ 45 Ghost Warden C :W:	.10	.20
❑ 46 Ghostway R :W:	1.00	2.50
❑ 47 Giant Solifuge R :D:	6.00	1.50
❑ 48 Gigadrowse C :B:	.10	.20
❑ 49 Glint-Eye Nephilim R :D:	.30	.75
❑ 50 Goblin Flectomancer U :D:	.12	.30
❑ 51 Godless Shrine R :L:	8.00	20.00
❑ 52 Graven Dominator R :W:	.25	.60
❑ 53 Gristleback U :G:	.12	.30
❑ 54 Gruul Guildmage U :D:	.15	.40
❑ 55 Gruul Nodorog C :G:	.10	.20
❑ 56 Gruul Scrapper C :G:	.10	.20
❑ 57 Gruul Signet C :A:	.10	.20
❑ 58 Gruul Turf C :L:	.15	.40
❑ 59 Gruul War Plow R :A:	.30	.75
❑ 60 Guardian's Magemark C :W:	.10	.20
❑ 61 Harrier Griffin U :W:	.12	.30
❑ 62 Hatching Plans R :B:	.30	.75
❑ 63 Hissing Miasma U :K:	.15	.40
❑ 64 Hypervolt Grasp U :R:	.12	.30
❑ 65 Infiltrator's Magemark C :B:	.10	.20
❑ 66 Ink-Treader Nephilim R :D:	.30	.75
❑ 67 Invoke the Firemind R :D:	.30	.75
❑ 68 Izzet Boilerworks C :L:	.30	.75
❑ 69 Izzet Chronarch C :D:	.10	.20
❑ 70 Izzet Guildmage U :D:	.30	.75
❑ 71 Izzet Signet C :A:	.10	.20
❑ 72 Killer Instinct R :D:	.25	.60
❑ 73 Leap of Flame C :D:	.10	.20
❑ 74 Leyline of Lifeforce R :G:	.40	1.00
❑ 75 Leyline of Lightning R :R:	.30	.75
❑ 76 Leyline of Singularity R :B:	.40	1.00
❑ 77 Leyline of the Meek R :W:	1.00	2.50
❑ 78 Leyline of the Void R :K:	1.00	2.50
❑ 79 Lionheart Maverick C :W:	.10	.20
❑ 80 Living Inferno R :R:	.25	.60
❑ 81 Martyred Rusalka U :W:	.12	.30
❑ 82 Mimeofacture R :B:	.25	.60
❑ 83 Mizzium Transreliquat R :A:	.30	.75
❑ 84 Moratorium Stone R :A:	.30	.75
❑ 85 Mortify U :D:	6.00	1.50
❑ 86 Mourning Thrull C :D:	.10	.20
❑ 87 Necromancer's Magemark C :K:	.10	.20
❑ 88 Nivix, Aerie of the Firemind U :L:	.12	.30
❑ 89 Niv-Mizzet, the Firemind R :D:	6.00	15.00
❑ 90 Ogre Savant C :R:	.12	.30
❑ 91 Order of the Stars U :W:	.15	.40
❑ 92 Orzhov Basilica C :L:	.15	.40
❑ 93 Orzhov Euthanist C :K:	.10	.20
❑ 94 Orzhov Guildmage U :D:	.15	.40
❑ 95 Orzhov Pontiff R :D:	.40	1.00
❑ 96 Orzhov Signet C :A:	.10	.20
❑ 97 Orzhova, the Church of Deals U :L:	.12	.30
❑ 98 Ostiary Thrull C :K:	.10	.20
❑ 99 Parallectric Feedback R :R:	.30	.75
❑ 100 Petrahydrox C :D:	.10	.20
❑ 101 Petrified Wood-Kin R :G:	.25	.60
❑ 102 Pillory of the Sleepless C :D:	.12	.30
❑ 103 Plagued Rusalka U :K:	.15	.40
❑ 104 Poisonbelly Ogre C :K:	.10	.20
❑ 105 Predatory Focus U :G:	.12	.30
❑ 106 Primeval Light U :G:	.15	.40
❑ 107 Pyromatics C :R:	.10	.20
❑ 108 Quicken R :B:	.30	.75
❑ 109 Rabble-Rouser U :R:	.12	.30
❑ 110 Repeal C :B:	.15	.40
❑ 111 Restless Bones C :K:	.10	.20

MAGIC

Card	Low	High
❑ 112 Revenant Patriarch U :K:	.12	.30
❑ 113 Rumbling Slum R :D:	.40	1.00
❑ 114 Runeboggle C :B:	.10	.20
❑ 115 Sanguine Praetor R :K:	.25	.60
❑ 116 Savage Twister U :D:	.25	.60
❑ 117 Scab-Clan Mauler C :D:	.10	.20
❑ 118 Schismotivate U :D:	.12	.30
❑ 119 Scorched Rusalka U :R:	.15	.40
❑ 120 Seize the Soul R :K:	.25	.60
❑ 121 Shadow Lance U :W:	.12	.30
❑ 122 Shattering Spree U :R:	1.50	4.00
❑ 123 Shrieking Grotesque C :W:	.10	.20
❑ 124 Siege of Towers R :R:	.25	.60
❑ 125 Silhana Ledgewalker C :G:	.15	.40
❑ 126 Silhana Starfletcher C :G:	.10	.20
❑ 127 Sinstriker's Will U :W:	.12	.30
❑ 128 Skarrg, the Rage Pits U :L:	.15	.40
❑ 129 Skarrgan Firebird R :R:	.25	.60
❑ 130 Skarrgan Pit-Skulk C :G:	.10	.20
❑ 131 Skarrgan Skybreaker U :D:	.12	.30
❑ 132 Skeletal Vampire R :K:	6.00	1.50
❑ 133 Sky Swallower R :B:	.30	.75
❑ 134 Skyrider Trainee C :W:	.10	.20
❑ 135 Smogsteed Rider U :K:	.12	.30
❑ 136 Souls of the Faultless U :D:	.40	1.00
❑ 137 Spelltithe Enforcer R :W:	.25	.60
❑ 138 Starved Rusalka U :G:	.12	.30
❑ 139 Steam Vents R :L:	10.00	25.00
❑ 140 Steamcore Weird C :B:	.10	.20
❑ 141 Stitch in Time R :D:	6.00	1.50
❑ 142 Stomping Ground R :L:	8.00	20.00
❑ 143 Storm Herd R :W:	.40	1.00
❑ 144 Stratozeppelid U :B:	.12	.30
❑ 145 Streetbreaker Wurm C :D:	.10	.20
❑ 146 Sword of the Paruns R :A:	.30	.75
❑ 147 Teysa, Orzhov Scion R :D:	.40	1.00
❑ 148 Thunderheads U :B:	.12	.30
❑ 149 Tibor and Lumia R :D:	.40	1.00
❑ 150 Tin Street Hooligan C :R:	.10	.20
❑ 151 To Arms! U :W:	.15	.40
❑ 152 Torch Drake C :B:	.10	.20
❑ 153 Train of Thought C :B:	.12	.30
❑ 154 Ulasht, the Hate Seed R :D:	.30	.75
❑ 155 Vacuumelt U :B:	.12	.30
❑ 156 Vedalken Plotter U :B:	.12	.30
❑ 157 Vertigo Spawn U :B:	.12	.30
❑ 158 Wee Dragonauts C :D:	.12	.30
❑ 159 Wild Cantor C :D:	.10	.20
❑ 160 Wildsize C :G:	.10	.20
❑ 161 Witch-Maw Nephilim R :D:	.30	.75
❑ 162 Withstand C :W:	.10	.20
❑ 163 Wreak Havoc U :D:	.30	.75
❑ 164 Wurmweaver Coil R :G:	.25	.60
❑ 165 Yore-Tiller Nephilim R :D:	.30	.75

2006 Magic the Gathering Guildpact Foil

Card	Low	High
Complete Set (165)	200.00	350.00
*Foil: .8X to 2X Basic Cards		
❑ 1 Absolver Thrull C :W:	.15	.40
❑ 2 Abyssal Nocturnus R :K:	.75	2.00
❑ 3 AEtherplasm U :B:	.30	.75
❑ 4 Agent of Masks U :D:	.30	.75
❑ 5 Angel of Despair R :D:	5.00	12.00
❑ 6 Battering Wurm U :G:	.25	.60
❑ 7 Beastmaster's Magemark C :G:	.15	.40
❑ 8 Belfry Spirit U :W:	.25	.60
❑ 9 Benediction of Moons C :W:	.15	.40
❑ 10 Bioplasm R :G:	.50	1.25
❑ 11 Blind Hunter C :D:	.15	.40
❑ 12 Bloodscale Prowler C :R:	.15	.40
❑ 13 Borborygmos R :D:	.60	1.50
❑ 14 Burning-Tree Bloodscale C :D:	.15	.40
❑ 15 Burning-Tree Shaman R :D:	1.25	3.00
❑ 16 Castigate C :D:	.15	.40
❑ 17 Caustic Rain U :K:	.25	.60
❑ 18 Cerebral Vortex R :D:	.60	1.50
❑ 19 Conjurer's Ban U :D:	.30	.75
❑ 20 Crash Landing U :G:	.25	.60
❑ 21 Cremate C :K:	.15	.40
❑ 22 Cry of Contrition C :K:	.15	.40
❑ 23 Cryptwailing U :K:	.25	.60
❑ 24 Crystal Seer C :B:	.15	.40
❑ 25 Culling Sun R :D:	.60	1.50
❑ 26 Daggerclaw Imp U :K:	.25	.60
❑ 27 Debtors' Knell R :D:	8.00	20.00
❑ 28 Djinn Illuminatus R :D:	1.25	3.00
❑ 29 Douse in Gloom C :K:	.15	.40
❑ 30 Droning Bureaucrats U :W:	.25	.60
❑ 31 Drowned Rusalka U :B:	.25	.60
❑ 32 Dryad Sophisticate U :G:	.30	.75
❑ 33 Dune-Brood Nephilim R :D:	.60	1.50
❑ 34 Earth Surge R :G:	.50	1.25
❑ 35 Electrolyze U :D:	.75	2.00
❑ 36 Exhumer Thrull U :K:	.25	.60
❑ 37 Fencer's Magemark C :R:	.15	.40
❑ 38 Feral Animist U :D:	.25	.60
❑ 39 Frazzle U :B:	.25	.60
❑ 40 Gatherer of Graces U :G:	.25	.60
❑ 41 Gelectrode U :D:	1.25	3.00
❑ 42 Ghor-Clan Bloodscale U :R:	.25	.60
❑ 43 Ghor-Clan Savage C :G:	.15	.40
❑ 44 Ghost Council of Orzhova R :D:	1.25	3.00
❑ 45 Ghost Warden C :W:	.15	.40
❑ 46 Ghostway R :W:	2.00	5.00
❑ 47 Giant Solifuge R :D:	1.25	3.00
❑ 48 Gigadrowse C :B:	.15	.40
❑ 49 Glint-Eye Nephilim R :D:	.60	1.50
❑ 50 Goblin Flectomancer U :D:	.25	.60
❑ 51 Godless Shrine R :L:	15.00	40.00
❑ 52 Graven Dominator R :W:	.50	1.25
❑ 53 Gristleback U :G:	.25	.60
❑ 54 Gruul Guildmage U :D:	.30	.75
❑ 55 Gruul Nodorog C :G:	.15	.40
❑ 56 Gruul Scrapper C :G:	.15	.40
❑ 57 Gruul Signet C :A:	.15	.40
❑ 58 Gruul Turf C :L:	.30	.75
❑ 59 Gruul War Plow R :A:	.60	1.50
❑ 60 Guardian's Magemark C :W:	.15	.40
❑ 61 Harrier Griffin U :W:	.25	.60
❑ 62 Hatching Plans R :B:	.60	1.50
❑ 63 Hissing Miasma U :K:	.30	.75
❑ 64 Hypervolt Grasp U :R:	.25	.60
❑ 65 Infiltrator's Magemark C :B:	.15	.40
❑ 66 Ink-Treader Nephilim R :D:	.60	1.50
❑ 67 Invoke the Firemind R :D:	.60	1.50
❑ 68 Izzet Boilerworks C :L:	.60	1.50
❑ 69 Izzet Chronarch C :D:	.15	.40
❑ 70 Izzet Guildmage U :D:	.60	1.50
❑ 71 Izzet Signet C :A:	.15	.40
❑ 72 Killer Instinct R :D:	.50	1.25
❑ 73 Leap of Flame C :D:	.15	.40
❑ 74 Leyline of Lifeforce R :G:	.75	2.00
❑ 75 Leyline of Lightning R :R:	.60	1.50
❑ 76 Leyline of Singularity R :B:	.75	2.00
❑ 77 Leyline of the Meek R :W:	2.00	5.00
❑ 78 Leyline of the Void R :K:	2.00	5.00
❑ 79 Lionheart Maverick C :W:	.15	.40
❑ 80 Living Inferno R :R:	.50	1.25
❑ 81 Martyred Rusalka U :W:	.25	.60
❑ 82 Mimeofacture R :B:	.50	1.25
❑ 83 Mizzium Transreliquat R :A:	.60	1.50
❑ 84 Moratorium Stone R :A:	.60	1.50
❑ 85 Mortify U :D:	1.25	3.00
❑ 86 Mourning Thrull C :D:	.15	.40
❑ 87 Necromancer's Magemark C :K:	.15	.40
❑ 88 Nivix, Aerie of the Firemind U :L:	.25	.60
❑ 89 Niv-Mizzet, the Firemind R :D:	12.00	30.00
❑ 90 Ogre Savant C :R:	.25	.60
❑ 91 Order of the Stars U :W:	.30	.75
❑ 92 Orzhov Basilica C :L:	.30	.75
❑ 93 Orzhov Euthanist C :K:	.15	.40
❑ 94 Orzhov Guildmage U :D:	.30	.75
❑ 95 Orzhov Pontiff R :D:	.75	2.00
❑ 96 Orzhov Signet C :A:	.15	.40
❑ 97 Orzhova, the Church of Deals U :L:	.25	.60
❑ 98 Ostiary Thrull C :K:	.15	.40
❑ 99 Parallectric Feedback R :R:	.60	1.50
❑ 100 Petrahydrox C :D:	.15	.40
❑ 101 Petrified Wood-Kin R :G:	.50	1.25
❑ 102 Pillory of the Sleepless C :D:	.15	.40
❑ 103 Plagued Rusalka U :K:	.30	.75
❑ 104 Poisonbelly Ogre C :K:	.30	.75
❑ 105 Predatory Focus U :G:	.25	.60
❑ 106 Primeval Light U :G:	.30	.75
❑ 107 Pyromatics C :R:	.15	.40
❑ 108 Quicken R :B:	.60	1.50
❑ 109 Rabble-Rouser U :R:	.25	.60
❑ 110 Repeal C :B:	.30	.75
❑ 111 Restless Bones C :K:	.15	.40
❑ 112 Revenant Patriarch U :K:	.25	.60
❑ 113 Rumbling Slum R :D:	.75	2.00
❑ 114 Runeboggle C :B:	.15	.40
❑ 115 Sanguine Praetor R :K:	.50	1.25
❑ 116 Savage Twister U :D:	.50	1.25
❑ 117 Scab-Clan Mauler C :D:	.15	.40
❑ 118 Schismotivate U :D:	.25	.60
❑ 119 Scorched Rusalka U :R:	.30	.75
❑ 120 Seize the Soul R :K:	.50	1.25
❑ 121 Shadow Lance U :W:	.25	.60
❑ 122 Shattering Spree U :R:	3.00	8.00
❑ 123 Shrieking Grotesque C :W:	.15	.40
❑ 124 Siege of Towers R :R:	.50	1.25
❑ 125 Silhana Ledgewalker C :G:	.30	.75
❑ 126 Silhana Starfletcher C :G:	.15	.40
❑ 127 Sinstriker's Will U :W:	.25	.60
❑ 128 Skarrg, the Rage Pits U :L:	.30	.75
❑ 129 Skarrgan Firebird R :R:	.50	1.25
❑ 130 Skarrgan Pit-Skulk C :G:	.15	.40
❑ 131 Skarrgan Skybreaker U :D:	.25	.60
❑ 132 Skeletal Vampire R :K:	1.25	3.00
❑ 133 Sky Swallower R :B:	.60	1.50
❑ 134 Skyrider Trainee C :W:	.15	.40
❑ 135 Smogsteed Rider U :K:	.25	.60
❑ 136 Souls of the Faultless U :D:	.75	2.00
❑ 137 Spelltithe Enforcer R :W:	.50	1.25
❑ 138 Starved Rusalka U :G:	.25	.60
❑ 139 Steam Vents R :L:	20.00	50.00
❑ 140 Steamcore Weird C :B:	.15	.40
❑ 141 Stitch in Time R :D:	1.25	3.00
❑ 142 Stomping Ground R :L:	15.00	40.00
❑ 143 Storm Herd R :W:	.75	2.00
❑ 144 Stratozeppelid U :B:	.25	.60
❑ 145 Streetbreaker Wurm C :D:	.15	.40
❑ 146 Sword of the Paruns R :A:	.60	1.50
❑ 147 Teysa, Orzhov Scion R :D:	.75	2.00
❑ 148 Thunderheads U :B:	.25	.60
❑ 149 Tibor and Lumia R :D:	.75	2.00
❑ 150 Tin Street Hooligan C :R:	.15	.40
❑ 151 To Arms! U :W:	.30	.75
❑ 152 Torch Drake C :B:	.15	.40
❑ 153 Train of Thought C :B:	.25	.60
❑ 154 Ulasht, the Hate Seed R :D:	.60	1.50
❑ 155 Vacuumelt U :B:	.25	.60
❑ 156 Vedalken Plotter U :B:	.25	.60
❑ 157 Vertigo Spawn U :B:	.25	.60
❑ 158 Wee Dragonauts C :D:	.25	.60
❑ 159 Wild Cantor C :D:	.15	.40
❑ 160 Wildsize C :G:	.15	.40
❑ 161 Witch-Maw Nephilim R :D:	.60	1.50
❑ 162 Withstand C :W:	.15	.40
❑ 163 Wreak Havoc U :D:	.60	1.50
❑ 164 Wurmweaver Coil R :G:	.50	1.25
❑ 165 Yore-Tiller Nephilim R :D:	.60	1.50

2006 Magic the Gathering Dissension

Card	Low	High
Complete Set (180)	100.00	200.00
Booster Box (36 Packs)	175.00	250.00
Booster Pack (15 Cards)	5.00	8.00
❑ 1 AEthermage's Touch R :W: :B:	.40	1.00
❑ 2 Anthem of Rakdos R :K: :R:	.40	1.00
❑ 3 Aquastrand Spider C :G:	.08	.20
❑ 4 Assault Zeppelid C :G: :B:	.08	.20
❑ 5 Aurora Eidolon C :W:	.08	.20
❑ 6 Avatar of Discord R :K:/:R:	1.00	2.50
❑ 7 Azorius AEthermage U :W: :B:	.10	.25
❑ 8 Azorius Chancery C :L:	.40	1.00
❑ 9 Azorius First-Wing C :W:/:B:	.08	.20
❑ 10 Azorius Guildmage U :W:/:B:	.30	.75
❑ 11 Azorius Herald U :W:	.20	.50
❑ 12 Azorius Ploy U :W: :B:	.10	.25
❑ 13 Azorius Signet C :A:	.20	.50
❑ 14 Beacon Hawk C :W:	.08	.20
❑ 15 Biomantic Mastery R :G:/:B:	.40	1.00
❑ 16 Blessing of the Nephilim U :W:	.20	.50
❑ 17 Blood Crypt R :L:	8.00	20.00
❑ 18 Bond of Agony U :K:	.40	1.00
❑ 19 Bound // Determined R :K: :G:	.40	1.00
❑ 20 Brace for Impact U :W:	.10	.25
❑ 21 Brain Pry U :K:	.10	.25
❑ 22 Breeding Pool R :L:	12.00	30.00
❑ 23 Bronze Bombshell R :A:	.50	1.25
❑ 24 Cackling Flames C :R:	.08	.20
❑ 25 Carom C :W:	.08	.20
❑ 26 Celestial Ancient R :W:	.50	1.25
❑ 27 Coiling Oracle C :G: :B:	.30	.75
❑ 28 Condemn U :W:	.50	1.25
❑ 29 Court Hussar U :B:	.20	.50
❑ 30 Crime // Punishment R :W: :K:	.75	2.00
❑ 31 Crypt Champion U :K:	.20	.50
❑ 32 Cytoplast Manipulator R :B:	1.00	2.50
❑ 33 Cytoplast Root-Kin R :G:	.75	2.00
❑ 34 Cytoshape R :G: :B:	.50	1.25
❑ 35 Cytospawn Shambler C :G:	.08	.20
❑ 36 Delirium Skeins C :K:	.08	.20
❑ 37 Demon's Jester C :K:	.08	.20
❑ 38 Demonfire R :R:	.75	2.00
❑ 39 Dovescape R :K:/:B:	.60	1.50
❑ 40 Dread Slag R :K: :R:	.25	.60
❑ 41 Drekavac U :K:	.10	.25
❑ 42 Elemental Resonance R :G:	.40	1.00
❑ 43 Enemy of the Guildpact C :K:	.08	.20
❑ 44 Enigma Eidolon C :B:	.08	.20
❑ 45 Entropic Eidolon C :K:	.08	.20
❑ 46 Evolution Vat R :A:	.40	1.00
❑ 47 Experiment Kraj R :G: :B:	.60	1.50
❑ 48 Fertile Imagination U :G:	.10	.25
❑ 49 Flame-Kin War Scout U :R:	.10	.25
❑ 50 Flaring Flame-Kin U :R:	.20	.50
❑ 51 Flash Foliage U :G:	.10	.25
❑ 52 Freewind Equenaut C :W:	.08	.20
❑ 53 Ghost Quarter U :L:	1.00	2.50
❑ 54 Gnat Alley Creeper U :R:	.10	.25
❑ 55 Gobhobbler Rats C :K: :R:	.08	.20
❑ 56 Govern the Guildless R :B:	.25	.60
❑ 57 Grand Arbiter Augustin IV R :W: :B:	4.00	10.00
❑ 58 Guardian of the Guildpact C :W:	.08	.20
❑ 59 Haazda Exonerator C :W:	.08	.20
❑ 60 Haazda Shield Mate R :W:	.25	.60
❑ 61 Hallowed Fountain R :L:	12.00	30.00
❑ 62 Helium Squirter C :B:	.08	.20
❑ 63 Hellhole Rats U :K: :R:	.20	.50
❑ 64 Hide // Seek R :R: :W:	.75	2.00
❑ 65 Hit // Run U :K:/:R:	.20	.50
❑ 66 Ignorant Bliss U :R:	.20	.50
❑ 67 Indrik Stomphowler U :G:	.20	.50
❑ 68 Infernal Tutor R :K:	4.00	10.00
❑ 69 Isperia the Inscrutable R :W: :B:	.25	.60
❑ 70 Jagged Poppet U :K: :R:	.10	.25
❑ 71 Kill-Suit Cultist C :R:	.08	.20
❑ 72 Kindle the Carnage U :R:	.10	.25
❑ 73 Leafdrake Roost U :G: :B:	.10	.25
❑ 74 Loaming Shaman R :G:	.60	1.50
❑ 75 Lyzolda, the Blood Witch R :K: :R:	.40	1.00
❑ 76 Macabre Waltz C :K:	.08	.20
❑ 77 Magewright's Stone U :A:	.20	.50
❑ 78 Might of the Nephilim U :G:	.20	.50
❑ 79 Minister of Impediments C :W:/:B:	.08	.20
❑ 80 Mistral Charger U :W:	.10	.25
❑ 81 Momir Vig, Simic Visionary R :G:/:B:	1.50	4.00
❑ 82 Muse Vessel R :A:	.40	1.00
❑ 83 Nettling Curse C :K:	.08	.20
❑ 84 Nightcreep U :K:	.10	.25
❑ 85 Nihilistic Glee R :K:	.25	.60
❑ 86 Novijen Sages R :B:	.40	1.00
❑ 87 Novijen, Heart of Progress U :L:	.20	.50
❑ 88 Ocular Halo C :B:	.08	.20
❑ 89 Odds // Ends R :B: :R:	.50	1.25
❑ 90 Ogre Gatecrasher C :R:	.08	.20
❑ 91 Omnibian R :G: :B:	.40	1.00
❑ 92 Overrule C :W: :B:	.08	.20
❑ 93 Pain Magnification U :K: :R:	.20	.50
❑ 94 Paladin of Prahv U :W:	.10	.25
❑ 95 Palliation Accord U :W: :B:	.10	.25
❑ 96 Patagia Viper U :G:	.10	.25
❑ 97 Pillar of the Paruns R :L:	1.50	4.00
❑ 98 Plaxcaster Frogling U :G: :B:	.50	1.25
❑ 99 Plaxmanta U :B:	.20	.50
❑ 100 Plumes of Peace C :W: :B:	.08	.20
❑ 101 Prahv, Spires of Order U :L:	.20	.50
❑ 102 Pride of the Clouds R :W:/:B:	1.00	2.50
❑ 103 Proclamation of Rebirth R :W:	3.00	8.00
❑ 104 Proper Burial R :W:	.50	1.25
❑ 105 Protean Hulk R :G:	1.25	3.00
❑ 106 Psychic Possession R :B:	.40	1.00
❑ 107 Psychotic Fury C :R:	.08	.20
❑ 108 Pure // Simple U :R: :G:	.20	.50
❑ 109 Ragamuffyn U :K:	.10	.25
❑ 110 Rain of Gore R :K: :R:	.60	1.50
❑ 111 Rakdos Augermage R :K: :R:	.40	1.00
❑ 112 Rakdos Carnarium C :L:	.30	.75
❑ 113 Rakdos Guildmage U :K:/:R:	.20	.50
❑ 114 Rakdos Ickspitter C :K: :R:	.08	.20
❑ 115 Rakdos Pit Dragon R :R:	1.00	2.50
❑ 116 Rakdos Riteknife R :A:	.25	.60
❑ 117 Rakdos Signet C :A:	.08	.20
❑ 118 Rakdos the Defiler R :K: :R:	.75	2.00
❑ 119 Ratcatcher R :K:	.50	1.25
❑ 120 Research // Development R :G: :B:	.50	1.25
❑ 121 Riot Spikes C :K:/:R:	.08	.20
❑ 122 Rise // Fall U :B:/:K:	.20	.50
❑ 123 Rix Maadi, Dungeon Palace U :L:	.10	.25
❑ 124 Sandstorm Eidolon C :R:	.08	.20
❑ 125 Seal of Doom C :K:	.08	.20
❑ 126 Seal of Fire C :R:	.10	.25
❑ 127 Shielding Plax C :G:/:B:	.08	.20
❑ 128 Silkwing Scout C :B:	.08	.20
❑ 129 Simic Basilisk U :G:	.10	.25
❑ 130 Simic Growth Chamber C :L:	.30	.75
❑ 131 Simic Guildmage U :G:/:B:	.30	.75
❑ 132 Simic Initiate C :G:	.08	.20
❑ 133 Simic Ragworm C :G:	.08	.20
❑ 134 Simic Signet C :A:	.08	.20
❑ 135 Simic Sky Swallower R :G: :B:	1.25	3.00
❑ 136 Skullmead Cauldron U :A:	.10	.25
❑ 137 Sky Hussar U :W: :B:	.30	.75
❑ 138 Skyscribing U :B:	.10	.25
❑ 139 Slaughterhouse Bouncer C :K:	.08	.20
❑ 140 Slithering Shade U :K:	.10	.25
❑ 141 Soulsworn Jury C :W:	.08	.20
❑ 142 Spell Snare U :B:	5.00	12.00
❑ 143 Sporeback Troll C :G:	.08	.20
❑ 144 Sprouting Phytohydra R :G:	.50	1.25
❑ 145 Squealing Devil U :R:	.10	.25
❑ 146 Stalking Vengeance R :R:	.50	1.25
❑ 147 Steeling Stance C :W:	.08	.20
❑ 148 Stoic Ephemera U :W:	.10	.25
❑ 149 Stomp and Howl U :G:	.10	.25
❑ 150 Stormscale Anarch R :R:	.25	.60
❑ 151 Street Savvy C :G:	.08	.20
❑ 152 Supply // Demand U :G:/:W:	.30	.75
❑ 153 Swift Silence R :W: :B:	.25	.60
❑ 154 Taste for Mayhem C :R:	.08	.20
❑ 155 Thrive C :G:	.08	.20
❑ 156 Tidespout Tyrant R :B:	1.00	2.50
❑ 157 Transguild Courier U :A:	.20	.50
❑ 158 Trial // Error U :W: :B:	.10	.25
❑ 159 Trygon Predator U :G: :B:	1.50	4.00
❑ 160 Twinstrike U :K: :R:	.10	.25
❑ 161 Unliving Psychopath R :K:	.40	1.00
❑ 162 Utopia Sprawl C :G:	.20	.50
❑ 163 Utvara Scalper C :R:	.08	.20
❑ 164 Valor Made Real C :W:	.08	.20
❑ 165 Verdant Eidolon C :G:	.08	.20
❑ 166 Vesper Ghoul C :K:	.08	.20
❑ 167 Vigean Graftmage U :B:	.20	.50
❑ 168 Vigean Hydropon C :G:/:B:	.08	.20
❑ 169 Vigean Intuition U :G: :B:	.10	.25
❑ 170 Vision Skeins C :B:	.08	.20
❑ 171 Voidslime R :G: :B:	2.00	5.00
❑ 172 Wakestone Gargoyle R :W:	.25	.60
❑ 173 Walking Archive R :A:	.40	1.00
❑ 174 War's Toll R :R:	.40	1.00
❑ 175 Weight of Spires U :R:	.10	.25
❑ 176 Whiptail Moloch C :R:	.08	.20
❑ 177 Windreaver R :W: :B:	.40	1.00
❑ 178 Wit's End R :K:	.25	.60
❑ 179 Wrecking Ball C :K:/:R:	.08	.20
❑ 180 Writ of Passage C :B:	.08	.20

2006 Magic the Gathering Dissension Foil

Card	Low	High
Complete Set (180)	250.00	400.00
*Foil: .8X to 2X Basic Cards		

2006 Magic the Gathering Coldsnap

Card	Low	High
Complete Set (155)	75.00	125.00
Booster Box (36 Packs)	125.00	175.00
Booster Pack (15 Cards)	4.00	6.00
Fat Pack	40.00	80.00
❑ 1 Adarkar Valkyrie R :W:	4.00	10.00
❑ 2 Adarkar Windform U :B:	.10	.25
❑ 3 Allosaurus Rider R :G:	.40	1.00
❑ 4 Arctic Flats U :L:	.50	1.25
❑ 5 Arctic Nishoba U :G:	.10	.25
❑ 6 Arcum Dagsson R :B:	.75	2.00
❑ 7 Aurochs Herd C :G:	.08	.20
❑ 8 Balduvian Fallen U :K:	.10	.25
❑ 9 Balduvian Frostwaker U :B:	.10	.25
❑ 10 Balduvian Rage U :R:	.10	.25
❑ 11 Balduvian Warlord U :R:	.10	.25
❑ 12 Blizzard Specter U :D:	.60	1.50
❑ 13 Boreal Centaur C :G:	.08	.20
❑ 14 Boreal Druid C :G:	.10	.25
❑ 15 Boreal Griffin C :W:	.08	.20
❑ 16 Boreal Shelf U :L:	.50	1.25
❑ 17 Braid of Fire R :R:	3.00	8.00
❑ 18 Brooding Saurian R :G:	.25	.60
❑ 19 Bull Aurochs C :G:	.08	.20
❑ 20 Chill to the Bone C :K:	.08	.20
❑ 21 Chilling Shade C :K:	.08	.20
❑ 22 Coldsteel Heart U :A:	.50	1.25
❑ 23 Commandeer R :B:	1.25	3.00
❑ 24 Controvert U :B:	.10	.25
❑ 25 Counterbalance U :B:	3.00	8.00
❑ 26 Cover of Winter R :W:	.25	.60
❑ 27 Cryoclasm U :R:	.20	.50
❑ 28 Darien, King of Kjeldor R :W:	1.50	4.00
❑ 29 Dark Depths R :L:	8.00	20.00
❑ 30 Deathmark U :K:	.20	.50
❑ 31 Deepfire Elemental U :D:	.10	.25
❑ 32 Diamond Faerie R :D:	.20	.50
❑ 33 Disciple of Tevesh Szat C :K:	.08	.20
❑ 34 Drelnoch C :B:	.08	.20
❑ 35 Earthen Goo U :R:	.10	.25
❑ 36 Feast of Flesh C :K:	.08	.20
❑ 37 Field Marshal R :W:	2.50	6.00
❑ 38 Flashfreeze U :B:	.20	.50
❑ 39 Freyalise's Radiance U :G:	.10	.25
❑ 40 Frost Marsh U :L:	.60	1.50
❑ 41 Frost Raptor C :B:	.08	.20
❑ 42 Frostweb Spider C :G:	.08	.20
❑ 43 Frozen Solid C :B:	.08	.20
❑ 44 Fury of the Horde R :R:	.25	.60
❑ 45 Garza Zol, Plague Queen R :D:	.50	1.25
❑ 46 Garza's Assassin R :K:	.20	.50
❑ 47 Gelid Shackles C :W:	.08	.20
❑ 48 Glacial Plating U :W:	.10	.25
❑ 49 Goblin Furrier C :R:	.08	.20
❑ 50 Goblin Rimerunner C :R:	.08	.20
❑ 51 Greater Stone Spirit U :R:	.10	.25
❑ 52 Grim Harvest C :K:	.08	.20
❑ 53 Gristle Grinner U :K:	.10	.25
❑ 54 Gutless Ghoul C :K:	.08	.20
❑ 55 Haakon, Stromgald Scourge R :K:	3.00	8.00
❑ 56 Heidar, Rimewind Master R :B:	.20	.50
❑ 57 Herald of Leshrac R :K:	.60	1.50
❑ 58 Hibernation's End R :G:	.30	.75
❑ 59 Highland Weald U :L:	.40	1.00
❑ 60 Icefall C :R:	.08	.20
❑ 61 Into the North C :G:	.08	.20
❑ 62 Jester's Scepter R :A:	.50	1.25
❑ 63 Jokulmorder R :B:	.20	.50
❑ 64 Jotun Grunt U :W:	1.00	2.50
❑ 65 Jotun Owl Keeper U :W:	.10	.25
❑ 66 Juniper Order Ranger U :D:	.75	2.00
❑ 67 Karplusan Minotaur R :R:	.25	.60
❑ 68 Karplusan Strider U :G:	.10	.25
❑ 69 Karplusan Wolverine C :R:	.08	.20
❑ 70 Kjeldoran Gargoyle U :W:	.10	.25
❑ 71 Kjeldoran Javelineer C :W:	.08	.20
❑ 72 Kjeldoran Outrider C :W:	.08	.20
❑ 73 Kjeldoran War Cry C :W:	.08	.20
❑ 74 Krovikan Mist C :B:	.30	.75
❑ 75 Krovikan Rot U :K:	.10	.25
❑ 76 Krovikan Scoundrel C :K:	.08	.20
❑ 77 Krovikan Whispers U :B:	.10	.25
❑ 78 Lightning Serpent R :R:	.75	2.00
❑ 79 Lightning Storm U :R:	.10	.25
❑ 80 Lovisa Coldeyes R :R:	.30	.75
❑ 81 Luminesce U :W:	.10	.25
❑ 82 Magmatic Core U :R:	.10	.25
❑ 83 Martyr of Ashes C :R:	.08	.20
❑ 84 Martyr of Bones C :K:	.08	.20
❑ 85 Martyr of Frost C :B:	.08	.20
❑ 86 Martyr of Sands C :W:	.30	.75
❑ 87 Martyr of Spores C :G:	.08	.20
❑ 88 Mishra's Bauble U :A:	.50	1.25
❑ 89 Mouth of Ronom U :L:	.30	.75
❑ 90 Mystic Melting U :G:	.10	.25
❑ 91 Ohran Viper R :G:	2.00	5.00
❑ 92 Ohran Yeti C :R:	.08	.20
❑ 93 Orcish Bloodpainter C :R:	.08	.20
❑ 94 Panglacial Wurm R :G:	1.25	3.00
❑ 95 Perilous Research U :B:	.20	.50
❑ 96 Phobian Phantasm U :K:	.10	.25
❑ 97 Phyrexian Etchings R :K:	.20	.50
❑ 98 Phyrexian Ironfoot U :A:	.20	.50
❑ 99 Phyrexian Snowcrusher U :A:	.20	.50
❑ 100 Phyrexian Soulgorger R :A:	.25	.60
❑ 101 Resize U :G:	.10	.25
❑ 102 Rime Transfusion U :K:	.10	.25
❑ 103 Rimebound Dead C :K:	.08	.20
❑ 104 Rimefeather Owl R :B:	.20	.50
❑ 105 Rimehorn Aurochs U :G:	.10	.25
❑ 106 Rimescale Dragon R :R:	.60	1.50
❑ 107 Rimewind Cryomancer U :B:	.10	.25
❑ 108 Rimewind Taskmage C :B:	.08	.20
❑ 109 Rite of Flame C :R:	1.50	4.00
❑ 110 Ronom Hulk C :G:	.08	.20
❑ 111 Ronom Serpent C :B:	.08	.20
❑ 112 Ronom Unicorn C :W:	.08	.20
❑ 113 Rune Snag C :B:	.50	1.25
❑ 114 Scrying Sheets R :L:	1.25	3.00
❑ 115 Sek'Kuar, Deathkeeper R :D:	.30	.75
❑ 116 Shape of the Wiitigo R :G:	.20	.50
❑ 117 Sheltering Ancient U :G:	.20	.50
❑ 118 Simian Brawler C :G:	.08	.20
❑ 119 Skred C :R:	.10	.25
❑ 120 Snow-Covered Forest C :L:	.30	.75

No.	Card	Low	High
121	Snow-Covered Island C :L:	.40	1.00
122	Snow-Covered Mountain C :L:	.40	1.00
123	Snow-Covered Plains C :L:	.30	.75
124	Snow-Covered Swamp C :L:	.30	.75
125	Soul Spike R :K:	.30	.75
126	Sound the Call C :G:	.08	.20
127	Squall Drifter C :W:	.08	.20
128	Stalking Yeti U :R:	.10	.25
129	Steam Spitter U :G:	.10	.25
130	Stromgald Crusader U :K:	1.25	3.00
131	Sun's Bounty C :W:	.08	.20
132	Sunscour R :W:	.40	1.00
133	Surging AEther C :B:	.08	.20
134	Surging Dementia C :K:	.08	.20
135	Surging Flame C :R:	.08	.20
136	Surging Might C :G:	.08	.20
137	Surging Sentinels C :W:	.08	.20
138	Survivor of the Unseen C :B:	.08	.20
139	Swift Maneuver C :W:	.08	.20
140	Tamanoa R :D:	.30	.75
141	Thermal Flux C :B:	.08	.20
142	Thermopod C :R:	.08	.20
143	Thrumming Stone R :A:	3.00	8.00
144	Tresserhorn Sinks U :L:	.40	1.00
145	Tresserhorn Skyknight U :K:	.10	.25
146	Ursine Fylgja U :W:	.10	.25
147	Vanish into Memory U :D:	.10	.25
148	Vexing Sphinx R :B:	.30	.75
149	Void Maw R :K:	.20	.50
150	Wall of Shards U :W:	.20	.50
151	White Shield Crusader U :W:	.20	.50
152	Wilderness Elemental U :D:	.10	.25
153	Woolly Razorback R :W:	.25	.60
154	Zombie Musher C :K:	.08	.20
155	Zur the Enchanter R :D:	1.50	4.00

2006 Magic the Gathering Coldsnap Foil

	Low	High
Complete Set (155)	125.00	250.00

*Foil: .8X to 2X Basic Cards

2006 Magic the Gathering Time Spiral

	Low	High
Complete Set (301)	100.00	175.00
Booster Box (36 Packs)	150.00	200.00
Booster Pack (15 Cards)	4.00	6.00
Theme Deck	8.00	15.00
Fat Pack	40.00	60.00

No.	Card	Low	High
1	Academy Ruins R :L:	4.00	10.00
2	AEther Web C :G:	.10	.20
3	AEtherflame Wall C :R:	.10	.20
4	Amrou Scout C :W:	.10	.20
5	Amrou Seekers C :W:	.10	.20
6	Ancestral Vision R :B:	2.00	5.00
7	Ancient Grudge C :R:	.15	.40
8	Angel's Grace R :W:	2.50	6.00
9	Ashcoat Bear C :G:	.10	.20
10	Aspect of Mongoose U :G:	.20	.50
11	Assassinate C :K:	.10	.20
12	Assembly-Worker U :A:	.12	.30
13	Barbed Shocker U :R:	.15	.40
14	Basal Sliver C :K:	.10	.20
15	Basalt Gargoyle U :R:	.12	.30
16	Benalish Cavalry C :W:	.10	.20
17	Bewilder C :B:	.10	.20
18	Blazing Blade Askari C :R:	.10	.20
19	Bogardan Hellkite R :R:	1.50	4.00
20	Bogardan Rager C :R:	.10	.20
21	Bonesplitter Sliver C :R:	.10	.20
22	Brass Gnat C :A:	.10	.20
23	Brine Elemental U :B:	.12	.30
24	Calciform Pools U :L:	.20	.50
25	Call to the Netherworld C :K:	.10	.20
26	Cancel C :B:	.10	.20
27	Candles of Leng R :A:	.25	.60
28	Careful Consideration U :B:	.12	.30
29	Castle Raptors C :W:	.10	.20
30	Cavalry Master U :W:	.12	.30
31	Celestial Crusader U :W:	.20	.50
32	Chameleon Blur C :G:	.10	.20
33	Children of Korlis C :W:	.10	.20
34	Chromatic Star C :A:	.15	.40
35	Chronatog Totem U :A:	.12	.30
36	Chronosavant R :W:	.25	.60
37	Clockspinning C :B:	.15	.40
38	Clockwork Hydra U :A:	.12	.30
39	Cloudchaser Kestrel C :W:	.10	.20
40	Coal Stoker C :R:	.10	.20
41	Conflagrate U :R:	.12	.30
42	Coral Trickster C :B:	.10	.20
43	Corpulent Corpse C :K:	.10	.20
44	Crookclaw Transmuter C :B:	.10	.20
45	Curse of the Cabal R :K:	.30	.75
46	Cyclopean Giant C :K:	.10	.20
47	Dark Withering C :K:	.10	.20
48	D'Avenant Healer C :W:	.10	.20
49	Deathspore Thallid C :K:	.10	.20
50	Deep-Sea Kraken R :B:	1.25	3.00
51	Dementia Sliver U :D:	.15	.40
52	Demonic Collusion R :K:	.30	.75
53	Detainment Spell C :W:	.10	.20
54	Divine Congregation C :W:	.10	.20
55	Draining Whelk R :B:	1.00	2.50
56	Dralnu, Lich Lord R :D:	.75	2.00
57	Dread Return U :K:	.75	2.00
58	Dreadship Reef U :L:	.25	.60
59	Dream Stalker C :B:	.10	.20
60	Drifter il-Dal C :B:	.10	.20
61	Drudge Reavers C :K:	.10	.20
62	Durkwood Baloth C :G:	.10	.20
63	Durkwood Tracker U :G:	.12	.30
64	Duskrider Peregrine U :W:	.12	.30
65	Empty the Warrens C :R:	.30	.75
66	Endrek Sahr, Master Breeder R :K:	.30	.75
67	Errant Doomsayers C :W:	.10	.20
68	Errant Ephemeron C :B:	.10	.20
69	Eternity Snare C :B:	.10	.20
70	Evangelize R :W:	.25	.60
71	Evil Eye of Urborg U :K:	.12	.30
72	Faceless Devourer U :K:	.12	.30
73	Fallen Ideal U :K:	.12	.30
74	Fathom Seer C :B:	.12	.30
75	Feebleness C :K:	.10	.20
76	Firemaw Kavu U :R:	.12	.30
77	Firewake Sliver U :D:	.15	.40
78	Flagstones of Trokair R :L:	3.00	8.00
79	Flamecore Elemental C :R:	.10	.20
80	Fledgling Mawcor U :B:	.12	.30
81	Flickering Spirit C :W:	.10	.20
82	Flowstone Channeler C :R:	.10	.20
83	Fool's Demise U :B:	.15	.40
84	Forest L :L:	.10	.20
85	Forest L :L:	.10	.20
86	Forest L :L:	.10	.20
87	Forest L :L:	.10	.20
88	Foriysian Interceptor C :W:	.10	.20
89	Foriysian Totem U :A:	.12	.30
90	Fortify C :W:	.10	.20
91	Fortune Thief R :R:	.25	.60
92	Fungal Reaches U :L:	.20	.50
93	Fungus Sliver R :G:	.30	.75
94	Fury Sliver U :R:	.20	.50
95	Gauntlet of Power R :A:	4.00	10.00
96	Gaze of Justice C :W:	.10	.20
97	Gemhide Sliver C :G:	.40	1.00
98	Gemstone Caverns R :L:	.75	2.00
99	Ghitu Firebreathing C :R:	.10	.20
100	Ghostflame Sliver U :D:	.15	.40
101	Glass Asp C :G:	.10	.20
102	Goblin Skycutter C :R:	.10	.20
103	Gorgon Recluse C :K:	.10	.20
104	Grapeshot C :R:	.30	.75
105	Greater Gargadon R :R:	1.50	4.00
106	Greenseeker C :G:	.10	.20
107	Griffin Guide U :W:	.15	.40
108	Ground Rift C :R:	.10	.20
109	Gustcloak Cavalier U :W:	.12	.30
110	Harmonic Sliver U :D:	.75	2.00
111	Haunting Hymn U :K:	.12	.30
112	Havenwood Wurm C :G:	.10	.20
113	Herd Gnarr C :G:	.10	.20
114	Hivestone R :A:	.40	1.00
115	Hypergenesis R :G:	2.00	5.00
116	Ib Halfheart, Goblin Tactician R :R:	.25	.60
117	Icatian Crier C :W:	.10	.20
118	Ignite Memories U :R:	.15	.40
119	Ironclaw Buzzardiers C :R:	.10	.20
120	Island L :L:	.10	.20
121	Island L :L:	.10	.20
122	Island L :L:	.10	.20
123	Island L :L:	.10	.20
124	Ith, High Arcanist R :D:	.40	1.00
125	Ivory Giant C :W:	.10	.20
126	Ixidron R :B:	.30	.75
127	Jaya Ballard, Task Mage R :R:	.30	.75
128	Jedit's Dragoons C :W:	.10	.20
129	Jhoira's Timebug C :A:	.10	.20
130	Kaervek the Merciless R :D:	.30	.75
131	Keldon Halberdier C :R:	.10	.20
132	Kher Keep R :L:	.60	1.50
133	Knight of the Holy Nimbus U :W:	.20	.50
134	Krosan Grip U :G:	1.50	4.00
135	Liege of the Pit R :K:	.25	.60
136	Lightning Axe C :R:	.10	.20
137	Lim-Dûl the Necromancer R :K:	1.25	3.00
138	Living End R :K:	1.50	4.00
139	Locket of Yesterdays U :A:	.12	.30
140	Looter il-Kor C :B:	.10	.20
141	Lotus Bloom R :A:	4.00	10.00
142	Magus of the Candelabra R :G:	.60	1.50
143	Magus of the Disk R :W:	.60	1.50
144	Magus of the Jar R :B:	.25	.60
145	Magus of the Mirror R :K:	.25	.60
146	Magus of the Scroll R :R:	.25	.60
147	Mana Skimmer C :K:	.10	.20
148	Mangara of Corondor R :W:	1.25	3.00
149	Might of Old Krosa U :G:	.20	.50
150	Might Sliver U :G:	.30	.75
151	Mindlash Sliver C :K:	.10	.20
152	Mindstab C :K:	.10	.20
153	Mishra, Artificer Prodigy R :D:	.30	.75
154	Mogg War Marshal C :R:	.40	1.00
155	Molder C :G:	.10	.20
156	Molten Slagheap U :L:	.15	.40
157	Momentary Blink C :W:	.20	.50
158	Moonlace R :B:	.25	.60
159	Mountain L :L:	.10	.20
160	Mountain L :L:	.10	.20
161	Mountain L :L:	.10	.20
162	Mountain L :L:	.10	.20
163	Mwonvuli Acid-Moss C :G:	.15	.40
164	Mystical Teachings C :B:	.20	.50
165	Nantuko Shaman C :G:	.10	.20
166	Nether Traitor R :K:	2.00	5.00
167	Nightshade Assassin U :K:	.12	.30
168	Norin the Wary R :R:	.25	.60
169	Opal Guardian R :W:	.25	.60
170	Opaline Sliver U :D:	.20	.50
171	Ophidian Eye C :B:	.10	.20
172	Orcish Cannonade C :R:	.10	.20
173	Outrider en-Kor U :W:	.12	.30
174	Paradise Plume U :A:	.12	.30
175	Paradox Haze U :B:	1.25	3.00
176	Pardic Dragon R :R:	.25	.60
177	Pendelhaven Elder U :G:	.12	.30
178	Pentarch Paladin R :W:	1.00	2.50
179	Pentarch Ward C :W:	.15	.40
180	Penumbra Spider C :G:	.10	.20
181	Phantom Wurm U :G:	.12	.30
182	Phthisis U :K:	.12	.30
183	Phyrexian Totem U :A:	.15	.40
184	Pit Keeper C :K:	.10	.20
185	Plague Sliver R :K:	.30	.75
186	Plains L :L:	.10	.20
187	Plains L :L:	.10	.20
188	Plains L :L:	.10	.20
189	Plains L :L:	.10	.20
190	Plated Pegasus U :W:	.12	.30
191	Plunder C :R:	.10	.20
192	Premature Burial U :K:	.12	.30
193	Primal Forcemage U :G:	.15	.40
194	Prismatic Lens C :A:	.10	.20
195	Psionic Sliver R :B:	.30	.75
196	Psychotic Episode C :K:	.10	.20
197	Pull from Eternity U :W:	.12	.30
198	Pulmonic Sliver R :W:	1.25	3.00
199	Quilled Sliver U :W:	.15	.40
200	Reiterate R :R:	1.25	3.00
201	Restore Balance R :W:	.75	2.00
202	Return to Dust U :W:	.25	.60
203	Rift Bolt C :R:	1.25	3.00
204	Riftwing Cloudskate U :B:	.12	.30
205	Saffi Eriksdotter R :D:	.75	2.00
206	Sage of Epityr C :B:	.10	.20
207	Saltcrusted Steppe U :L:	.20	.50
208	Sangrophage C :K:	.10	.20
209	Sarpadian Empires, Vol. VII R :A:	.25	.60
210	Savage Thallid C :G:	.10	.20
211	Scarwood Treefolk C :G:	.10	.20
212	Scion of the Ur-Dragon R :D:	1.25	3.00
213	Screeching Sliver C :B:	.10	.20
214	Scryb Ranger U :G:	.25	.60
215	Search for Tomorrow C :G:	.10	.20
216	Sedge Sliver R :R:	1.00	2.50
217	Sengir Nosferatu R :K:	.25	.60
218	Serra Avenger R :W:	3.00	8.00
219	Shadow Sliver C :B:	.10	.20
220	Sidewinder Sliver C :W:	.10	.20
221	Skittering Monstrosity U :K:	.12	.30
222	Skulking Knight C :K:	.10	.20
223	Slipstream Serpent C :B:	.10	.20
224	Smallpox U :K:	.30	.75
225	Snapback C :B:	.10	.20
226	Spectral Force R :G:	.25	.60
227	Spell Burst U :B:	.15	.40
228	Spike Tiller R :G:	.25	.60
229	Spiketail Drakeling C :B:	.10	.20
230	Spinneret Sliver C :G:	.10	.20
231	Spirit Loop U :W:	.40	1.00
232	Sporesower Thallid U :G:	.25	.60
233	Sprite Noble R :B:	.30	.75
234	Sprout C :G:	.10	.20
235	Squall Line R :G:	.25	.60
236	Stonebrow, Krosan Hero R :D:	.25	.60
237	Stonewood Invocation R :G:	.25	.60
238	Stormcloud Djinn U :B:	.12	.30
239	Strangling Soot C :K:	.10	.20
240	Strength in Numbers C :G:	.10	.20
241	Stronghold Overseer R :K:	.30	.75
242	Stuffy Doll R :A:	3.00	8.00
243	Subterranean Shambler C :R:	.10	.20
244	Sudden Death U :K:	.20	.50
245	Sudden Shock U :R:	.20	.50
246	Sudden Spoiling R :K:	1.50	4.00
247	Sulfurous Blast U :R:	.15	.40
248	Swamp L :L:	.10	.20
249	Swamp L :L:	.10	.20
250	Swamp L :L:	.10	.20
251	Swamp L :L:	.10	.20
252	Swarmyard R :L:	1.50	4.00
253	Tectonic Fiend U :R:	.12	.30
254	Teferi, Mage of Zhalfir R :B:	2.50	6.00
255	Telekinetic Sliver U :B:	.20	.50
256	Temporal Eddy C :B:	.10	.20
257	Temporal Isolation C :W:	.10	.20
258	Tendrils of Corruption C :K:	.10	.20
259	Terramorphic Expanse C :L:	.20	.50
260	Thallid Germinator C :G:	.10	.20
261	Thallid Shell-Dweller C :G:	.10	.20
262	Thelon of Havenwood R :G:	.30	.75
263	Thelonite Hermit R :G:	.30	.75
264	Thick-Skinned Goblin U :R:	.12	.30
265	Think Twice C :B:	.15	.40
266	Thrill of the Hunt C :G:	.10	.20
267	Thunder Totem U :A:	.12	.30
268	Tivadar of Thorn R :W:	.25	.60
269	Tolarian Sentinel C :B:	.10	.20
270	Traitor's Clutch C :K:	.10	.20
271	Trespasser il-Vec C :K:	.10	.20
272	Trickbind R :B:	2.00	5.00
273	Triskelavus R :A:	.25	.60
274	Tromp the Domains U :G:	.12	.30
275	Truth or Tale U :B:	.15	.40
276	Two-Headed Sliver C :R:	.10	.20
277	Undying Rage U :R:	.15	.40
278	Unyaro Bees R :G:	.25	.60
279	Urborg Syphon-Mage C :K:	.10	.20
280	Urza's Factory U :L:	.25	.60
281	Vampiric Sliver U :K:	.20	.50
282	Venser's Sliver C :A:	.10	.20
283	Verdant Embrace R :G:	.30	.75
284	Vesuva R :L:	6.00	15.00
285	Vesuvan Shapeshifter R :B:	1.25	3.00
286	Viashino Bladescout C :R:	.10	.20
287	Viscerid Deepwalker C :B:	.10	.20
288	Viscid Lemures C :K:	.10	.20
289	Voidmage Husher U :B:	.15	.40
290	Volcanic Awakening U :R:	.12	.30
291	Walk the Aeons R :B:	.60	1.50
292	Watcher Sliver C :W:	.10	.20
293	Weathered Bodyguards R :W:	.25	.60
294	Weatherseed Totem U :A:	.12	.30
295	Wheel of Fate R :R:	1.25	3.00
296	Wipe Away U :B:	.20	.50
297	Word of Seizing R :R:	.25	.60
298	Wormwood Dryad C :G:	.10	.20
299	Wurmcalling R :G:	.25	.60
300	Yavimaya Dryad U :G:	.15	.40
301	Zealot il-Vec C :W:	.10	.20

2006 Magic the Gathering Time Spiral Foil

*Foil: .8X to 2X Basic Cards

No.	Card	Low	High
1	Academy Ruins R :L:	8.00	20.00
2	AEther Web C :G:	.15	.40
3	AEtherflame Wall C :R:	.15	.40
4	Amrou Scout C :W:	.15	.40
5	Amrou Seekers C :W:	.15	.40
6	Ancestral Vision R :B:	4.00	10.00
7	Ancient Grudge C :R:	.30	.75
8	Angel's Grace R :W:	5.00	12.00
9	Ashcoat Bear C :G:	.15	.40
10	Aspect of Mongoose U :G:	.40	1.00
11	Assassinate C :K:	.15	.40
12	Assembly-Worker U :A:	.25	.60
13	Barbed Shocker U :R:	.30	.75
14	Basal Sliver C :K:	.15	.40
15	Basalt Gargoyle U :R:	.25	.60
16	Benalish Cavalry C :W:	.15	.40
17	Bewilder C :B:	.15	.40
18	Blazing Blade Askari C :R:	.15	.40
19	Bogardan Hellkite R :R:	3.00	8.00
20	Bogardan Rager C :R:	.15	.40
21	Bonesplitter Sliver C :R:	.15	.40
22	Brass Gnat C :A:	.15	.40
23	Brine Elemental U :B:	.25	.60
24	Calciform Pools U :L:	.40	1.00
25	Call to the Netherworld C :K:	.15	.40
26	Cancel C :B:	.15	.40
27	Candles of Leng R :A:	.50	1.25
28	Careful Consideration U :B:	.25	.60
29	Castle Raptors C :W:	.15	.40
30	Cavalry Master U :W:	.25	.60
31	Celestial Crusader U :W:	.40	1.00
32	Chameleon Blur C :G:	.15	.40
33	Children of Korlis C :W:	.15	.40
34	Chromatic Star C :A:	.30	.75
35	Chronatog Totem U :A:	.25	.60
36	Chronosavant R :W:	.50	1.25
37	Clockspinning C :B:	.30	.75
38	Clockwork Hydra U :A:	.25	.60
39	Cloudchaser Kestrel C :W:	.15	.40
40	Coal Stoker C :R:	.15	.40
41	Conflagrate U :R:	.25	.60
42	Coral Trickster C :B:	.15	.40
43	Corpulent Corpse C :K:	.15	.40
44	Crookclaw Transmuter C :B:	.15	.40
45	Curse of the Cabal R :K:	.60	1.50
46	Cyclopean Giant C :K:	.15	.40
47	Dark Withering C :K:	.15	.40
48	D'Avenant Healer C :W:	.15	.40
49	Deathspore Thallid C :K:	.15	.40
50	Deep-Sea Kraken R :B:	2.50	6.00
51	Dementia Sliver U :D:	.30	.75
52	Demonic Collusion R :K:	.60	1.50
53	Detainment Spell C :W:	.15	.40
54	Divine Congregation C :W:	.15	.40
55	Draining Whelk R :B:	2.00	5.00
56	Dralnu, Lich Lord R :D:	1.50	4.00
57	Dread Return U :K:	1.50	4.00
58	Dreadship Reef U :L:	.50	1.25
59	Dream Stalker C :B:	.15	.40
60	Drifter il-Dal C :B:	.15	.40
61	Drudge Reavers C :K:	.15	.40
62	Durkwood Baloth C :G:	.15	.40
63	Durkwood Tracker U :G:	.25	.60
64	Duskrider Peregrine U :W:	.25	.60
65	Empty the Warrens C :R:	.60	1.50
66	Endrek Sahr, Master Breeder R :K:	.60	1.50
67	Errant Doomsayers C :W:	.15	.40
68	Errant Ephemeron C :B:	.15	.40
69	Eternity Snare C :B:	.15	.40
70	Evangelize R :W:	.50	1.25
71	Evil Eye of Urborg U :K:	.25	.60
72	Faceless Devourer U :K:	.25	.60
73	Fallen Ideal U :K:	.25	.60
74	Fathom Seer C :B:	.25	.60
75	Feebleness C :K:	.15	.40
76	Firemaw Kavu U :R:	.25	.60
77	Firewake Sliver U :D:	.30	.75
78	Flagstones of Trokair R :L:	6.00	15.00
79	Flamecore Elemental C :R:	.15	.40
80	Fledgling Mawcor U :B:	.25	.60
81	Flickering Spirit C :W:	.15	.40
82	Flowstone Channeler C :R:	.15	.40
83	Fool's Demise U :B:	.30	.75
84	Forest L :L:	.15	.40
85	Forest L :L:	.15	.40
86	Forest L :L:	.15	.40
87	Forest L :L:	.15	.40
88	Foriysian Interceptor C :W:	.15	.40
89	Foriysian Totem U :A:	.25	.60
90	Fortify C :W:	.15	.40
91	Fortune Thief R :R:	.50	1.25
92	Fungal Reaches U :L:	.40	1.00
93	Fungus Sliver R :G:	.60	1.50
94	Fury Sliver U :R:	.40	1.00
95	Gauntlet of Power R :A:	8.00	20.00
96	Gaze of Justice C :W:	.15	.40
97	Gemhide Sliver C :G:	.75	2.00
98	Gemstone Caverns R :L:	1.50	4.00
99	Ghitu Firebreathing C :R:	.15	.40
100	Ghostflame Sliver U :D:	.30	.75
101	Glass Asp C :G:	.15	.40
102	Goblin Skycutter C :R:	.15	.40
103	Gorgon Recluse C :K:	.15	.40
104	Grapeshot C :R:	.60	1.50
105	Greater Gargadon R :R:	3.00	8.00
106	Greenseeker C :G:	.15	.40
107	Griffin Guide U :W:	.30	.75
108	Ground Rift C :R:	.15	.40
109	Gustcloak Cavalier U :W:	.25	.60
110	Harmonic Sliver U :D:	1.50	4.00
111	Haunting Hymn U :K:	.25	.60
112	Havenwood Wurm C :G:	.15	.40
113	Herd Gnarr C :G:	.15	.40
114	Hivestone R :A:	.75	2.00
115	Hypergenesis R :G:	4.00	10.00
116	Ib Halfheart, Goblin Tactician R :R:	.50	1.25
117	Icatian Crier C :W:	.15	.40
118	Ignite Memories U :R:	.30	.75
119	Ironclaw Buzzardiers C :R:	.15	.40
120	Island L :L:	.15	.40
121	Island L :L:	.15	.40
122	Island L :L:	.15	.40
123	Island L :L:	.15	.40
124	Ith, High Arcanist R :D:	.75	2.00
125	Ivory Giant C :W:	.15	.40
126	Ixidron R :B:	.60	1.50
127	Jaya Ballard, Task Mage R :R:	.60	1.50
128	Jedit's Dragoons C :W:	.15	.40
129	Jhoira's Timebug C :A:	.15	.40
130	Kaervek the Merciless R :D:	.60	1.50
131	Keldon Halberdier C :R:	.15	.40
132	Kher Keep R :L:	1.25	3.00
133	Knight of the Holy Nimbus U :W:	.40	1.00
134	Krosan Grip U :G:	3.00	8.00
135	Liege of the Pit R :K:	.50	1.25
136	Lightning Axe C :R:	.15	.40
137	Lim-Dûl the Necromancer R :K:	2.50	6.00
138	Living End R :K:	3.00	8.00
139	Locket of Yesterdays U :A:	.25	.60
140	Looter il-Kor C :B:	.15	.40
141	Lotus Bloom R :A:	8.00	20.00
142	Magus of the Candelabra R :G:	1.25	3.00
143	Magus of the Disk R :W:	1.25	3.00
144	Magus of the Jar R :B:	.50	1.25
145	Magus of the Mirror R :K:	.50	1.25
146	Magus of the Scroll R :R:	.50	1.25
147	Mana Skimmer C :K:	.15	.40
148	Mangara of Corondor R :W:	2.50	6.00
149	Might of Old Krosa U :G:	.40	1.00
150	Might Sliver U :G:	.60	1.50
151	Mindlash Sliver C :K:	.15	.40
152	Mindstab C :K:	.15	.40
153	Mishra, Artificer Prodigy R :D:	.60	1.50
154	Mogg War Marshal C :R:	.75	2.00
155	Molder C :G:	.15	.40
156	Molten Slagheap U :L:	.30	.75
157	Momentary Blink C :W:	.40	1.00
158	Moonlace R :B:	.50	1.25
159	Mountain L :L:	.15	.40
160	Mountain L :L:	.15	.40
161	Mountain L :L:	.15	.40
162	Mountain L :L:	.15	.40
163	Mwonvuli Acid-Moss C :G:	.30	.75
164	Mystical Teachings C :B:	.40	1.00
165	Nantuko Shaman C :G:	.15	.40
166	Nether Traitor R :K:	4.00	10.00
167	Nightshade Assassin U :K:	.25	.60
168	Norin the Wary R :R:	.50	1.25
169	Opal Guardian R :W:	.50	1.25
170	Opaline Sliver U :D:	.40	1.00
171	Ophidian Eye C :B:	.15	.40
172	Orcish Cannonade C :R:	.15	.40
173	Outrider en-Kor U :W:	.25	.60
174	Paradise Plume U :A:	.25	.60
175	Paradox Haze U :B:	2.50	6.00
176	Pardic Dragon R :R:	.50	1.25
177	Pendelhaven Elder U :G:	.25	.60
178	Pentarch Paladin R :W:	2.00	5.00
179	Pentarch Ward C :W:	.30	.75
180	Penumbra Spider C :G:	.15	.40
181	Phantom Wurm U :G:	.25	.60
182	Phthisis U :K:	.25	.60
183	Phyrexian Totem U :A:	.30	.75
184	Pit Keeper C :K:	.15	.40
185	Plague Sliver R :K:	.60	1.50
186	Plains L :L:	.15	.40
187	Plains L :L:	.15	.40
188	Plains L :L:	.15	.40

MAGIC

Card	Low	High
❑ 189 Plains L :L:	.15	.40
❑ 190 Plated Pegasus U :W:	.25	.60
❑ 191 Plunder C :R:	.15	.40
❑ 192 Premature Burial U :K:	.25	.60
❑ 193 Primal Forcemage U :G:	.30	.75
❑ 194 Prismatic Lens C :A:	.15	.40
❑ 195 Psionic Sliver R :B:	.60	1.50
❑ 196 Psychotic Episode C :K:	.15	.40
❑ 197 Pull from Eternity U :W:	.25	.60
❑ 198 Pulmonic Sliver R :W:	2.50	6.00
❑ 199 Quilled Sliver U :W:	.30	.75
❑ 200 Reiterate R :R:	2.50	6.00
❑ 201 Restore Balance R :W:	1.50	4.00
❑ 202 Return to Dust U :W:	.50	1.25
❑ 203 Rift Bolt C :R:	2.50	6.00
❑ 204 Riftwing Cloudskate U :B:	.25	.60
❑ 205 Saffi Eriksdotter R :D:	1.50	4.00
❑ 206 Sage of Epityr C :B:	.25	.60
❑ 207 Saltcrusted Steppe U :L:	.40	1.00
❑ 208 Sangrophage C :K:	.15	.40
❑ 209 Sarpadian Empires, Vol. VII R :A:	.50	1.25
❑ 210 Savage Thallid C :G:	.15	.40
❑ 211 Scarwood Treefolk C :G:	.15	.40
❑ 212 Scion of the Ur-Dragon R :D:	2.50	6.00
❑ 213 Screeching Sliver C :B:	.15	.40
❑ 214 Scryb Ranger U :G:	.50	1.25
❑ 215 Search for Tomorrow C :G:	.15	.40
❑ 216 Sedge Sliver R :R:	2.00	5.00
❑ 217 Sengir Nosferatu R :K:	.50	1.25
❑ 218 Serra Avenger R :W:	6.00	15.00
❑ 219 Shadow Sliver C :B:	.15	.40
❑ 220 Sidewinder Sliver C :W:	.15	.40
❑ 221 Skittering Monstrosity U :K:	.25	.60
❑ 222 Skulking Knight C :K:	.15	.40
❑ 223 Slipstream Serpent C :B:	.15	.40
❑ 224 Smallpox U :K:	.60	1.50
❑ 225 Snapback C :B:	.15	.40
❑ 226 Spectral Force R :G:	.50	1.25
❑ 227 Spell Burst U :B:	.30	.75
❑ 228 Spike Tiller R :G:	.50	1.25
❑ 229 Spiketail Drakeling C :B:	.15	.40
❑ 230 Spinneret Sliver C :G:	.15	.40
❑ 231 Spirit Loop U :W:	.75	2.00
❑ 232 Sporesower Thallid U :G:	.50	1.25
❑ 233 Sprite Noble R :B:	.60	1.50
❑ 234 Sprout C :G:	.15	.40
❑ 235 Squall Line R :G:	.50	1.25
❑ 236 Stonebrow, Krosan Hero R :D:	.50	1.25
❑ 237 Stonewood Invocation R :G:	.50	1.25
❑ 238 Stormcloud Djinn U :B:	.25	.60
❑ 239 Strangling Soot C :K:	.15	.40
❑ 240 Strength in Numbers C :G:	.15	.40
❑ 241 Stronghold Overseer R :K:	.60	1.50
❑ 242 Stuffy Doll R :A:	6.00	15.00
❑ 243 Subterranean Shambler C :R:	.15	.40
❑ 244 Sudden Death U :K:	.40	1.00
❑ 245 Sudden Shock U :R:	.40	1.00
❑ 246 Sudden Spoiling R :K:	3.00	8.00
❑ 247 Sulfurous Blast U :R:	.30	.75
❑ 248 Swamp L :L:	.15	.40
❑ 249 Swamp L :L:	.15	.40
❑ 250 Swamp L :L:	.15	.40
❑ 251 Swamp L :L:	.15	.40
❑ 252 Swarmyard R :L:	3.00	8.00
❑ 253 Tectonic Fiend U :R:	.25	.60
❑ 254 Teferi, Mage of Zhalfir R :B:	5.00	12.00
❑ 255 Telekinetic Sliver U :B:	.40	1.00
❑ 256 Temporal Eddy C :B:	.15	.40
❑ 257 Temporal Isolation C :W:	.15	.40
❑ 258 Tendrils of Corruption C :K:	.15	.40
❑ 259 Terramorphic Expanse C :L:	.40	1.00
❑ 260 Thallid Germinator C :G:	.15	.40
❑ 261 Thallid Shell-Dweller C :G:	.15	.40
❑ 262 Thelon of Havenwood R :G:	.60	1.50
❑ 263 Thelonite Hermit R :G:	.60	1.50
❑ 264 Thick-Skinned Goblin U :R:	.25	.60
❑ 265 Think Twice C :B:	.30	.75
❑ 266 Thrill of the Hunt C :G:	.15	.40
❑ 267 Thunder Totem U :A:	.25	.60
❑ 268 Tivadar of Thorn R :W:	.50	1.25
❑ 269 Tolarian Sentinel C :B:	.15	.40
❑ 270 Traitor's Clutch C :K:	.15	.40
❑ 271 Trespasser Il-Vec C :K:	.15	.40
❑ 272 Trickbind R :B:	4.00	10.00
❑ 273 Triskelavus R :A:	.50	1.25
❑ 274 Tromp the Domains U :G:	.25	.60
❑ 275 Truth or Tale U :B:	.30	.75
❑ 276 Two-Headed Sliver C :R:	.15	.40
❑ 277 Undying Rage U :R:	.30	.75
❑ 278 Unyaro Bees R :G:	.50	1.25
❑ 279 Urborg Syphon-Mage C :K:	.15	.40
❑ 280 Urza's Factory U :L:	.50	1.25
❑ 281 Vampiric Sliver U :K:	.40	1.00
❑ 282 Venser's Sliver C :A:	.15	.40
❑ 283 Verdant Embrace R :G:	.60	1.50
❑ 284 Vesuva R :L:	12.00	30.00
❑ 285 Vesuvan Shapeshifter R :B:	2.50	6.00
❑ 286 Viashino Bladescout C :R:	.15	.40
❑ 287 Viscerid Deepwalker C :B:	.15	.40
❑ 288 Viscid Lemures C :K:	.15	.40
❑ 289 Voidmage Husher U :B:	.30	.75
❑ 290 Volcanic Awakening U :R:	.25	.60
❑ 291 Walk the Aeons R :B:	1.25	3.00
❑ 292 Watcher Sliver C :W:	.15	.40
❑ 293 Weathered Bodyguards R :W:	.50	1.25
❑ 294 Weatherseed Totem U :A:	.25	.60
❑ 295 Wheel of Fate R :R:	2.50	6.00
❑ 296 Wipe Away U :B:	.40	1.00
❑ 297 Word of Seizing R :R:	.50	1.25
❑ 298 Wormwood Dryad C :G:	.15	.40
❑ 299 Wurmcalling R :G:	.50	1.25
❑ 300 Yavimaya Dryad U :G:	.30	.75
❑ 301 Zealot Il-Vec C :W:	.15	.40

2007 Magic the Gathering 10th Edition

Card	Low	High
Complete Set (383)	125.00	200.00
❑ 1 Abundance R :G:	.40	1.00
❑ 2 Academy Researchers U :B:	.20	.50
❑ 3 Adarkar Wastes R :L:	1.25	3.00
❑ 4 Afflict C :K:	.10	.25
❑ 5 Aggressive Urge C :G:	.10	.25
❑ 6 Agonizing Memories U :K:	.20	.50
❑ 7 Air Elemental U :B:	.20	.50
❑ 8 Ambassador Laquatus R :B:	.60	1.50
❑ 9 Anaba Bodyguard C :R:	.10	.25
❑ 10 Ancestor's Chosen U :W:	.20	.50
❑ 11 Angel of Mercy U :W:	.20	.50
❑ 12 Angelic Blessing C :W:	.20	.50
❑ 13 Angelic Chorus R :W:	.10	.25
❑ 14 Angelic Wall C :W:	1.50	4.00
❑ 15 Angel's Feather U :A:	.20	.50
❑ 16 Arcane Teachings U :R:	.20	.50
❑ 17 Arcanis the Omnipotent R :B:	2.00	5.00
❑ 18 Ascendant Evincar R :K:	.75	2.00
❑ 19 Assassinate C :K:	.10	.25
❑ 20 Aura Graft U :B:	.20	.50
❑ 21 Aura of Silence U :W:	.60	1.50
❑ 22 Avatar of Might R :G:	.40	1.00
❑ 23 Aven Cloudchaser C :W:	.10	.25
❑ 24 Aven Fisher C :B:	.10	.25
❑ 25 Aven Windreader C :B:	.10	.25
❑ 26 Ballista Squad U :W:	.20	.50
❑ 27 Bandage C :W:	.10	.25
❑ 28 Battlefield Forge R :L:	1.25	2.50
❑ 29 Beacon of Destruction R :R:	.50	1.25
❑ 30 Beacon of Immortality R :W:	2.00	5.00
❑ 31 Beacon of Unrest R :K:	1.50	4.00
❑ 32 Benalish Knight C :W:	.10	.25
❑ 33 Birds of Paradise R :G:	2.50	6.00
❑ 34 Blanchwood Armor U :G:	.50	1.25
❑ 35 Blaze U :R:	.25	.60
❑ 36 Bloodfire Colossus R :R:	.30	.75
❑ 37 Bloodrock Cyclops C :R:	.10	.25
❑ 38 Bog Wraith U :K:	.20	.50
❑ 39 Bogardan Firefiend C :R:	.10	.25
❑ 40 Boomerang C :B:	.20	.50
❑ 41 Bottle Gnomes U :A:	.20	.50
❑ 42 Brushland R :L:	.75	2.00
❑ 43 Cancel C :B:	.20	.50
❑ 44 Canopy Spider C :G:	.10	.25
❑ 45 Caves of Koilos R :L:	1.25	3.00
❑ 46 Cephalid Constable R :B:	.30	.75
❑ 47 Chimeric Staff R :A:	.30	.75
❑ 48 Cho-Manno, Revolutionary R :W:	.40	1.00
❑ 49 Chromatic Star U :A:	.25	.60
❑ 50 Citanul Flute R :A:	.40	1.00
❑ 51 Civic Wayfinder C :G:	.10	.25
❑ 52 Clone R :B:	.40	1.00
❑ 53 Cloud Elemental C :B:	.10	.25
❑ 54 Cloud Sprite C :B:	.10	.25
❑ 55 Coat of Arms R :A:	2.50	6.00
❑ 56 Colossus of Sardia R :A:	.30	.75
❑ 57 Commune with Nature C :G:	.10	.25
❑ 58 Composite Golem U :A:	.20	.50
❑ 59 Condemn U :W:	.40	1.00
❑ 60 Cone of Flame U :R:	.20	.50
❑ 61 Consume Spirit U :K:	.20	.50
❑ 62 Contaminated Bond C :K:	.10	.25
❑ 63 Counsel of the Soratami C :B:	.10	.25
❑ 64 Crafty Pathmage C :B:	.10	.25
❑ 65 Craw Wurm C :G:	.10	.25
❑ 66 Creeping Mold U :G:	.20	.50
❑ 67 Crucible of Worlds R :A:	15.00	30.00
❑ 68 Cruel Edict U :K:	.60	1.50
❑ 69 Cryoclasm U :R:	.40	1.00
❑ 70 Deathmark U :K:	.25	.60
❑ 71 Dehydration C :B:	.10	.25
❑ 72 Deluge U :B:	.20	.50
❑ 73 Demolish C :R:	.10	.25
❑ 74 Demon's Horn U :A:	.20	.50
❑ 75 Demystify C :W:	.10	.25
❑ 76 Denizen of the Deep R :B:	.30	.75
❑ 77 Diabolic Tutor U :K:	.50	1.25
❑ 78 Discombobulate U :B:	.20	.50
❑ 79 Distress C :K:	.10	.25
❑ 80 Doomed Necromancer R :K:	1.25	2.50
❑ 81 Doubling Cube R :A:	2.00	5.00
❑ 82 Dragon Roost R :R:	.60	1.50
❑ 83 Dragon's Claw U :A:	.25	.60
❑ 84 Dreamborn Muse R :B:	.30	.75
❑ 85 Dross Crocodile C :K:	.10	.25
❑ 86 Drudge Skeletons U :K:	.20	.50
❑ 87 Duct Crawler C :R:	.10	.25
❑ 88 Dusk Imp C :K:	.10	.25
❑ 89 Earth Elemental U :R:	.20	.50
❑ 90 Elven Riders U :G:	.20	.50
❑ 91 Elvish Berserker C :G:	.10	.25
❑ 92 Elvish Champion R :G:	2.50	6.00
❑ 93 Elvish Piper R :G:	3.00	8.00
❑ 94 Enormous Baloth U :G:	.20	.50
❑ 95 Essence Drain C :K:	.10	.25
❑ 96 Evacuation R :B:	1.25	3.00
❑ 97 Faerie Conclave U :L:	.75	2.00
❑ 98 Fear C :K:	.10	.25
❑ 99 Femeref Archers U :G:	.20	.50
❑ 100 Festering Goblin C :K:	.10	.25
❑ 101 Field Marshal R :W:	2.50	6.00
❑ 102 Firebreathing C :R:	.10	.25
❑ 103 Fists of the Anvil C :R:	.10	.25
❑ 104 Flamewave Invoker U :R:	.20	.50
❑ 105 Flashfreeze U :B:	.30	.75
❑ 106 Flowstone Slide R :R:	.30	.75
❑ 107 Fog Elemental U :B:	.20	.50
❑ 108 Forbidding Watchtower U :L:	.30	.75
❑ 109 Forest :L:	.20	.50
❑ 110 Forest :L:	.20	.50
❑ 111 Forest :L:	.20	.50
❑ 112 Forest :L:	.20	.50
❑ 113 Fountain of Youth U :A:	.20	.50
❑ 114 Fugitive Wizard C :B:	.10	.25
❑ 115 Furnace of Rath R :R:	.60	1.50
❑ 116 Furnace Whelp U :R:	.20	.50
❑ 117 Gaea's Herald R :G:	.40	1.00
❑ 118 Ghitu Encampment U :L:	.30	.75
❑ 119 Ghost Warden C :W:	.10	.25
❑ 120 Giant Growth C :G:	.10	.25
❑ 121 Giant Spider C :G:	.10	.25
❑ 122 Glorious Anthem R :W:	1.25	3.00
❑ 123 Goblin Elite Infantry C :R:	.10	.25
❑ 124 Goblin King R :R:	1.25	3.00
❑ 125 Goblin Lore U :R:	.40	1.00
❑ 126 Goblin Piker C :R:	.10	.25
❑ 127 Goblin Sky Raider C :R:	.10	.25
❑ 128 Grave Pact R :K:	2.50	6.00
❑ 129 Graveborn Muse R :K:	.50	1.25
❑ 130 Gravedigger C :K:	.10	.25
❑ 131 Grizzly Bears C :G:	.10	.25
❑ 132 Guerrilla Tactics U :R:	.20	.50
❑ 133 Hail of Arrows U :W:	.20	.50
❑ 134 Hate Weaver U :K:	.20	.50
❑ 135 Head Games R :K:	.30	.75
❑ 136 Heart of Light C :W:	.10	.25
❑ 137 Hidden Horror U :K:	.20	.50
❑ 138 High Ground U :W:	.20	.50
❑ 139 Highway Robber C :K:	.10	.25
❑ 140 Hill Giant C :R:	.10	.25
❑ 141 Holy Day C :W:	.25	.60
❑ 142 Holy Strength C :W:	.10	.25
❑ 143 Honor Guard C :W:	.10	.25
❑ 144 Horseshoe Crab C :B:	.10	.25
❑ 145 Howling Mine R :A:	1.50	4.00
❑ 146 Hunted Wumpus U :G:	.20	.50
❑ 147 Hurkyl's Recall R :B:	1.25	3.00
❑ 148 Hurricane R :G:	.30	.75
❑ 149 Hypnotic Specter R :K:	1.25	3.00
❑ 150 Icatian Priest U :W:	.20	.50
❑ 151 Icy Manipulator U :A:	.30	.75
❑ 152 Incinerate C :R:	.30	.75
❑ 153 Island :L:	.20	.50
❑ 154 Island :L:	.20	.50
❑ 155 Island :L:	.20	.50
❑ 156 Island :L:	.20	.50
❑ 157 Jayemdae Tome R :A:	.30	.75
❑ 158 Joiner Adept R :G:	1.25	3.00
❑ 159 Juggernaut U :A:	.20	.50
❑ 160 Kamahl, Pit Fighter R :R:	.30	.75
❑ 161 Karplusan Forest R :L:	1.25	3.00
❑ 162 Karplusan Strider U :G:	.20	.50
❑ 163 Kavu Climber C :G:	.10	.25
❑ 164 Kjeldoran Royal Guard R :W:	.30	.75
❑ 165 Knight of Dusk U :K:	.25	.60
❑ 166 Kraken's Eye U :A:	.20	.50
❑ 167 Lava Axe C :R:	.10	.25
❑ 168 Lavaborn Muse R :R:	.30	.75
❑ 169 Legacy Weapon R :A:	.40	1.00
❑ 170 Leonin Scimitar U :A:	.20	.50
❑ 171 Lightning Elemental C :R:	.10	.25
❑ 172 Llanowar Elves C :G:	.30	.75
❑ 173 Llanowar Sentinel C :G:	.10	.25
❑ 174 Llanowar Wastes R :L:	1.25	3.00
❑ 175 Looming Shade C :K:	.10	.25
❑ 176 Lord of the Pit R :K:	.30	.75
❑ 177 Lord of the Undead R :K:	6.00	15.00
❑ 178 Loxodon Mystic C :W:	.10	.25
❑ 179 Loxodon Warhammer R :A:	1.25	3.00
❑ 180 Loyal Sentry R :W:	.40	1.00
❑ 181 Lumengrid Warden C :B:	.10	.25
❑ 182 Luminesce U :W:	.20	.50
❑ 183 Lure U :G:	.20	.50
❑ 184 Mahamoti Djinn R :B:	.30	.75
❑ 185 Manabarbs R :R:	.30	.75
❑ 186 Mantis Engine U :A:	.20	.50
❑ 187 March of the Machines R :B:	.30	.75
❑ 188 Mass of Ghouls C :K:	.10	.25
❑ 189 Megrim U :K:	.40	1.00
❑ 190 Merfolk Looter C :B:	.20	.50
❑ 191 Midnight Ritual R :K:	.30	.75
❑ 192 Might of Oaks R :G:	.30	.75
❑ 193 Might Weaver U :G:	.20	.50
❑ 194 Millstone R :A:	.40	1.00
❑ 195 Mind Bend R :B:	.30	.75
❑ 196 Mind Rot C :K:	.10	.25
❑ 197 Mind Stone U :A:	.40	1.00
❑ 198 Mirri, Cat Warrior R :G:	.50	1.25
❑ 199 Mobilization R :W:	1.25	3.00
❑ 200 Mogg Fanatic U :R:	.60	1.50
❑ 201 Molimo, Maro-Sorcerer R :G:	.30	.75
❑ 202 Mortal Combat R :K:	.30	.75
❑ 203 Mortivore R :K:	.75	2.00
❑ 204 Mountain :L:	.20	.50
❑ 205 Mountain :L:	.20	.50
❑ 206 Mountain :L:	.20	.50
❑ 207 Mountain :L:	.20	.50
❑ 208 Nantuko Husk U :K:	.20	.50
❑ 209 Natural Spring C :G:	.10	.25
❑ 210 Naturalize C :G:	.10	.25
❑ 211 Nekrataal U :K:	.25	.60
❑ 212 Nightmare R :K:	.30	.75
❑ 213 No Rest for the Wicked U :K:	.20	.50
❑ 214 Nomad Mythmaker R :W:	.60	1.50
❑ 215 Orcish Artillery U :R:	.20	.50
❑ 216 Ornithopter U :A:	.40	1.00
❑ 217 Overgrowth C :G:	.20	.50
❑ 218 Overrun U :G:	.30	.75
❑ 219 Pacifism C :W:	.10	.25
❑ 220 Paladin en-Vec R :W:	.75	2.00
❑ 221 Pariah R :W:	1.50	4.00
❑ 222 Peek C :B:	.10	.25
❑ 223 Persuasion U :B:	.25	.60
❑ 224 Phage the Untouchable R :K:	2.50	6.00
❑ 225 Phantom Warrior U :B:	.25	.60
❑ 226 Phyrexian Rager C :K:	.10	.25
❑ 227 Phyrexian Vault U :A:	.20	.50
❑ 228 Pincher Beetles C :G:	.10	.25
❑ 229 Pithing Needle R :A:	1.50	4.00
❑ 230 Plagiarize R :B:	.30	.75
❑ 231 Plague Beetle C :K:	.10	.25
❑ 232 Plague Wind R :K:	1.25	3.00
❑ 233 Plains :L:	.20	.50
❑ 234 Plains :L:	.20	.50
❑ 235 Plains :L:	.20	.50
❑ 236 Plains :L:	.20	.50
❑ 237 Platinum Angel R :A:	2.00	5.00
❑ 238 Primal Rage U :G:	.60	1.50
❑ 239 Prodigal Pyromancer C :R:	.10	.25
❑ 240 Puppeteer U :B:	.20	.50
❑ 241 Pyroclasm U :R:	.40	1.00
❑ 242 Quicksand U :L:	.20	.50
❑ 243 Quirion Dryad R :G:	.60	1.50
❑ 244 Rage Weaver U :R:	.20	.50
❑ 245 Raging Goblin C :R:	.10	.25
❑ 246 Rain of Tears U :K:	.25	.60
❑ 247 Rampant Growth C :G:	.20	.50
❑ 248 Ravenous Rats C :K:	.20	.50
❑ 249 Razormane Masticore R :A:	.40	1.00
❑ 250 Recollect U :G:	.20	.50
❑ 251 Recover C :K:	.10	.25
❑ 252 Regeneration U :G:	.20	.50
❑ 253 Relentless Assault R :R:	.30	.75
❑ 254 Relentless Rats U :K:	.75	2.00
❑ 255 Reminisce U :B:	.20	.50
❑ 256 Remove Soul C :B:	.10	.25
❑ 257 Reviving Dose C :W:	.10	.25
❑ 258 Reya Dawnbringer R :W:	2.50	6.00
❑ 259 Rhox R :G:	.30	.75
❑ 260 Righteousness R :W:	.30	.75
❑ 261 Robe of Mirrors C :B:	.10	.25
❑ 262 Rock Badger C :R:	.10	.25
❑ 263 Rod of Ruin U :A:	.20	.50
❑ 264 Root Maze R :G:	.30	.75
❑ 265 Rootwalla C :G:	.10	.25
❑ 266 Rootwater Commando C :B:	.10	.25
❑ 267 Rootwater Matriarch R :B:	.60	1.50
❑ 268 Royal Assassin R :K:	.75	2.00
❑ 269 Rule of Law U :W:	.40	1.00
❑ 270 Rushwood Dryad C :G:	.10	.25
❑ 271 Sage Owl C :B:	.10	.25
❑ 272 Samite Healer C :W:	.10	.25
❑ 273 Scalpelexis R :B:	.30	.75
❑ 274 Scathe Zombies C :K:	.10	.25
❑ 275 Scion of the Wild R :G:	.30	.75
❑ 276 Scoria Wurm R :R:	.30	.75
❑ 277 Sculpting Steel R :A:	2.00	5.00
❑ 278 Sea Monster C :B:	.10	.25
❑ 279 Seedborn Muse R :G:	2.50	6.00
❑ 280 Seismic Assault R :R:	1.25	2.50
❑ 281 Sengir Vampire R :K:	.50	1.25
❑ 282 Serra Angel R :W:	.40	1.00
❑ 283 Serra's Embrace U :W:	.25	.60
❑ 284 Severed Legion C :K:	.10	.25
❑ 285 Shatterstorm U :R:	.30	.75
❑ 286 Shimmering Wings C :B:	.10	.25
❑ 287 Shivan Dragon R :R:	.30	.75
❑ 288 Shivan Hellkite R :R:	.40	1.00
❑ 289 Shivan Reef R :L:	2.50	6.00
❑ 290 Shock C :R:	.20	.50
❑ 291 Shunt R :R:	.30	.75
❑ 292 Siege-Gang Commander R :R:	1.25	2.50
❑ 293 Sift C :B:	.10	.25
❑ 294 Sky Weaver U :B:	.20	.50
❑ 295 Skyhunter Patrol C :W:	.10	.25
❑ 296 Skyhunter Prowler C :W:	.10	.25
❑ 297 Skyhunter Skirmisher U :W:	.20	.50
❑ 298 Skyshroud Ranger C :G:	.20	.50
❑ 299 Sleeper Agent R :K:	.30	.75
❑ 300 Smash C :R:	.10	.25
❑ 301 Snapping Drake C :B:	.10	.25
❑ 302 Soul Feast U :K:	.20	.50
❑ 303 Soul Warden U :W:	.30	.75
❑ 304 Soulblast R :R:	.30	.75
❑ 305 Spark Elemental U :R:	.40	1.00
❑ 306 Spawning Pool U :L:	.25	.60
❑ 307 Spellbook U :A:	.25	.60
❑ 308 Spiketail Hatchling U :B:	.20	.50
❑ 309 Spined Wurm C :G:	.10	.25
❑ 310 Spineless Thug C :K:	.10	.25
❑ 311 Spirit Link U :W:	.25	.60
❑ 312 Spirit Weaver U :W:	.20	.50
❑ 313 Spitting Earth C :R:	.10	.25
❑ 314 Squee, Goblin Nabob R :R:	2.00	5.00
❑ 315 Stalking Tiger C :G:	.10	.25
❑ 316 Stampeding Wildebeests U :G:	.20	.50
❑ 317 Starlight Invoker U :W:	.20	.50
❑ 318 Steadfast Guard C :W:	.10	.25
❑ 319 Steel Golem U :A:	.20	.50
❑ 320 Story Circle R :W:	.75	2.00
❑ 321 Stronghold Discipline U :K:	.20	.50
❑ 322 Stun C :R:	.10	.25
❑ 323 Sudden Impact U :R:	.20	.50
❑ 324 Sulfurous Springs R :L:	1.25	3.00
❑ 325 Sunken Hope R :B:	.30	.75
❑ 326 Suntail Hawk C :W:	.10	.25
❑ 327 Swamp :L:	.20	.50
❑ 328 Swamp :L:	.20	.50
❑ 329 Swamp :L:	.20	.50
❑ 330 Swamp :L:	.20	.50
❑ 331 Sylvan Basilisk U :G:	.25	.60
❑ 332 Sylvan Scrying U :G:	.40	1.00
❑ 333 Tangle Spider U :G:	.20	.50
❑ 334 Telepathy U :B:	.20	.50
❑ 335 Telling Time U :B:	.30	.75
❑ 336 Tempest of Light U :W:	.20	.50
❑ 337 Terramorphic Expanse C :L:	.25	.60
❑ 338 Terror C :K:	.25	.60
❑ 339 The Hive R :A:	.30	.75
❑ 340 Thieving Magpie U :B:	.20	.50
❑ 341 Threaten U :R:	.20	.50
❑ 342 Thrull Surgeon U :K:	.20	.50
❑ 343 Thundering Giant U :R:	.20	.50
❑ 344 Tidings U :B:	.40	1.00
❑ 345 Time Stop R :B:	.75	2.00
❑ 346 Time Stretch R :B:	2.00	5.00
❑ 347 Traumatize R :B:	1.25	2.50
❑ 348 Treasure Hunter U :W:	.20	.50
❑ 349 Treetop Bracers C :G:	.10	.25
❑ 350 Treetop Village U :L:	1.25	2.50
❑ 351 Troll Ascetic R :G:	1.25	2.50
❑ 352 True Believer R :W:	1.25	2.50
❑ 353 Tundra Wolves C :W:	.10	.25
❑ 354 Twincast R :B:	1.25	3.00
❑ 355 Twitch C :B:	.10	.25
❑ 356 Uncontrollable Anger C :R:	.10	.25
❑ 357 Underground River R :L:	1.50	4.00
❑ 358 Underworld Dreams R :K:	1.25	2.50
❑ 359 Unholy Strength C :K:	.10	.25
❑ 360 Unsummon C :B:	.10	.25
❑ 361 Upwelling R :G:	.30	.75
❑ 362 Vampire Bats C :K:	.10	.25
❑ 363 Vedalken Mastermind U :B:	.20	.50
❑ 364 Venerable Monk C :W:	.10	.25
❑ 365 Verdant Force R :G:	.75	2.00
❑ 366 Viashino Runner C :R:	.10	.25
❑ 367 Viashino Sandscout C :R:	.10	.25
❑ 368 Viridian Shaman U :G:	.25	.60
❑ 369 Voice of All R :W:	.60	1.50
❑ 370 Wall of Air U :B:	.20	.50
❑ 371 Wall of Fire U :R:	.20	.50
❑ 372 Wall of Swords U :W:	.20	.50
❑ 373 Wall of Wood C :G:	.10	.25
❑ 374 Warp World R :R:	.30	.75
❑ 375 Warrior's Honor C :W:	.10	.25
❑ 376 Whispersilk Cloak U :A:	.40	1.00
❑ 377 Wild Griffin C :W:	.10	.25
❑ 378 Windborn Muse R :W:	.75	2.00
❑ 379 Wrath of God R :W:	6.00	15.00
❑ 380 Wurm's Tooth U :A:	.20	.50
❑ 381 Yavimaya Coast R :L:	1.50	4.00
❑ 382 Yavimaya Enchantress U :G:	.25	.60
❑ 383 Youthful Knight C :W:	.10	.25

2007 Magic the Gathering 10th Edition Foil

*Foil: .8X to 2X Basic Cards

2007 Magic the Gathering Elves vs Goblins

Card	Low	High
Duel Deck	100.00	200.00
❑ 1 Ambush Commander R :G:	1.50	4.00
❑ 2 Allosaurus Rider R :G:	.40	1.00
❑ 3 Elvish Eulogist C :G:	.10	.25
❑ 4 Elvish Harbinger U :G:	1.25	3.00
❑ 5 Elvish Warrior C :G:	.10	.25
❑ 6 Gempalm Strider U :G:	.20	.50
❑ 7 Heedless One U :G:	1.50	4.00
❑ 8 Imperious Perfect U :G:	2.50	6.00
❑ 9 Llanowar Elves C :G:	.20	.50
❑ 10 Lys Alana Huntmaster C :G:	.30	.75
❑ 11 Stonewood Invoker C :G:	.10	.25
❑ 12 Sylvan Messenger U :G:	.75	2.00
❑ 13 Timberwatch Elf C :G:	.60	1.50
❑ 14 Voice of the Woods R :G:	.60	1.50
❑ 15 Wellwisher C :G:	.75	2.00
❑ 16 Wirewood Herald C :G:	.20	.75
❑ 17 Wirewood Symbiote U :G:	1.25	3.00
❑ 18 Wood Elves C :G:	.10	.25
❑ 19 Wren's Run Vanquisher U :G:	.75	2.00
❑ 20 Elvish Promenade U :G:	1.50	4.00
❑ 21 Giant Growth C :G:	.10	.25
❑ 22 Harmonize U :G:	.75	2.00
❑ 23 Wildsize C :G:	.10	.25
❑ 24 Moonglove Extract C	.10	.25
❑ 25 Slate of Ancestry R	.50	1.00
❑ 26 Wirewood Lodge U	1.25	3.00
❑ 27 Tranquil Thicket C	.10	.25
❑ 28 Forest L	.10	.40
❑ 29 Forest L	.10	.40
❑ 30 Forest L	.10	.40
❑ 31 Forest L	.10	.40
❑ 32 Siege-Gang Commander R :R:	1.25	3.00
❑ 33 Akki Coalflinger U :R:	.20	.50
❑ 34 Clickslither R :R:	.40	.75
❑ 35 Emberwilde Augur C :R:	.10	.25

Card	Low	High
❑ 36 Flamewave Invoker U :R:	.20	.50
❑ 37 Gempalm Incinerator U :R:	.60	1.50
❑ 38 Goblin Cohort C :R:	.10	.25
❑ 39 Goblin Matron U :R:	.75	2.00
❑ 40 Goblin Ringleader U :R:	1.25	3.00
❑ 41 Goblin Sledder C :R:	.10	.25
❑ 42 Goblin Warchief U :R:	1.50	4.00
❑ 43 Ib Halfheart, Goblin Tactician R :R:	.30	.75
❑ 44 Mogg Fanatic U :R:	.60	1.50
❑ 45 Mogg War Marshal C :R:	.40	1.00
❑ 46 Mudbutton Torchrunner C :R:	.10	.25
❑ 47 Raging Goblin C :R:	.10	.25
❑ 48 Reckless One U :R:	.30	.75
❑ 49 Skirk Drill Sergeant U :R:	.20	.50
❑ 50 Skirk Fire Marshal R :R:	.40	1.00
❑ 51 Skirk Prospector C :R:	.20	.50
❑ 52 Skirk Shaman C :R:	.10	.25
❑ 53 Tar Pitcher U :R:	.20	.50
❑ 54 Boggart Shenanigans U :R:	.30	.50
❑ 55 Spitting Earth C :R:	.10	.25
❑ 56 Tarfire C :R:	.10	.25
❑ 57 Forgotten Cave C	.10	.25
❑ 58 Goblin Burrows U	.20	.50
❑ 59 Mountain L	.10	.40
❑ 60 Mountain L	.10	.40
❑ 61 Mountain L	.10	.40
❑ 62 Mountain L	.10	.40
❑ T1 Token: Elemental C	.40	.75
❑ T2 Token: Elf Warrior C	.40	1.00
❑ T3 Token: Goblin C	.40	1.00

2007 Magic the Gathering Planar Chaos

Card	Low	High
Complete Set (165)	75.00	125.00
Booster Box (36 Packs)	150.00	250.00
Booster Pack (15 Cards)	5.00	8.00
Theme Deck	8.00	15.00
Fat Pack	30.00	60.00
❑ 1 Aeon Chronicler R :B:	.40	1.00
❑ 2 AEther Membrane U :R:	.20	.50
❑ 3 Akroma, Angel of Fury R :R:	1.25	3.00
❑ 4 Ana Battlemage U :G:	.15	.40
❑ 5 Aquamorph Entity C :B:	.10	.25
❑ 6 Auramancer's Guise U :B:	.15	.40
❑ 7 Aven Riftwatcher C :W:	.10	.25
❑ 8 Battering Sliver C :R:	.10	.25
❑ 9 Benalish Commander R :W:	.60	1.50
❑ 10 Big Game Hunter U :K:	.20	.50
❑ 11 Blightspeaker C :K:	.10	.25
❑ 12 Blood Knight U :R:	.30	.75
❑ 13 Body Double R :B:	.75	2.00
❑ 14 Bog Serpent C :K:	.10	.25
❑ 15 Boom // Bust R :R:	.60	1.50
❑ 16 Braids, Conjurer Adept R :B:	.25	.60
❑ 17 Brain Gorgers C :K:	.10	.25
❑ 18 Brute Force C :R:	.15	.40
❑ 19 Calciderm U :W:	.20	.50
❑ 20 Cautery Sliver U :D:	.20	.50
❑ 21 Chronozoa R :B:	.60	1.50
❑ 22 Circle of Affliction U :K:	.15	.40
❑ 23 Citanul Woodreaders C :G:	.10	.25
❑ 24 Cradle to Grave C :K:	.10	.25
❑ 25 Crovax, Ascendant Hero R :W:	.40	1.00
❑ 26 Damnation R :K:	10.00	25.00
❑ 27 Darkheart Sliver U :D:	.20	.50
❑ 28 Dash Hopes C :K:	.20	.50
❑ 29 Dawn Charm C :W:	.20	.50
❑ 30 Dead // Gone C :R:	.10	.25
❑ 31 Deadly Grub C :K:	.10	.25
❑ 32 Deadwood Treefolk U :G:	.15	.40
❑ 33 Detritivore R :R:	.25	.60
❑ 34 Dichotomancy R :B:	.25	.60
❑ 35 Dismal Failure U :B:	.15	.40
❑ 36 Dormant Sliver U :D:	.20	.50
❑ 37 Dreamscape Artist C :B:	.10	.25
❑ 38 Dunerider Outlaw U :K:	.15	.40
❑ 39 Dust Corona C :R:	.10	.25
❑ 40 Dust Elemental R :W:	.25	.60
❑ 41 Enslave U :K:	.20	.50
❑ 42 Erratic Mutation C :B:	.10	.25
❑ 43 Essence Warden C :G:	.25	.60
❑ 44 Evolution Charm C :G:	.10	.25
❑ 45 Extirpate R :K:	3.00	8.00
❑ 46 Fa'adiyah Seer C :G:	.10	.25
❑ 47 Fatal Frenzy R :R:	.25	.60
❑ 48 Firefright Mage C :R:	.10	.25
❑ 49 Frenetic Sliver U :D:	.15	.40
❑ 50 Frozen AEther U :B:	.25	.60
❑ 51 Fungal Behemoth R :G:	.25	.60
❑ 52 Fury Charm C :R:	.10	.25
❑ 53 Gaea's Anthem R :G:	1.00	2.50
❑ 54 Ghost Tactician C :W:	.10	.25
❑ 55 Giant Dustwasp C :G:	.10	.25
❑ 56 Gossamer Phantasm C :B:	.10	.25
❑ 57 Groundbreaker R :G:	.75	2.00
❑ 58 Hammerheim Deadeye U :R:	.15	.40
❑ 59 Harmonize U :G:	.75	2.00
❑ 60 Healing Leaves C :G:	.10	.25
❑ 61 Hedge Troll U :G:	.15	.40
❑ 62 Heroes Remembered R :W:	.25	.60
❑ 63 Hunting Wilds U :G:	.15	.40
❑ 64 Imp's Mischief R :K:	.25	.60
❑ 65 Intet, the Dreamer R :D:	.40	1.00
❑ 66 Jedit Ojanen of Efrava R :G:	.25	.60
❑ 67 Jodah's Avenger U :B:	.15	.40
❑ 68 Kavu Predator U :G:	.75	2.00
❑ 69 Keen Sense U :G:	.20	.50
❑ 70 Keldon Marauders C :R:	.20	.50
❑ 71 Kor Dirge U :K:	.15	.40
❑ 72 Lavacore Elemental U :R:	.15	.40
❑ 73 Life and Limb R :G:	.25	.60
❑ 74 Magus of the Arena R :R:	.25	.60
❑ 75 Magus of the Bazaar R :B:	.25	.60
❑ 76 Magus of the Coffers R :K:	.40	1.00
❑ 77 Magus of the Library R :G:	.25	.60
❑ 78 Magus of the Tabernacle R :W:	.25	.60
❑ 79 Malach of the Dawn U :W:	.15	.40
❑ 80 Mana Tithe C :W:	.20	.50
❑ 81 Mantle of Leadership U :W:	.15	.40
❑ 82 Melancholy C :K:	.10	.25
❑ 83 Merfolk Thaumaturgist C :B:	.10	.25
❑ 84 Mesa Enchantress R :W:	.25	.60
❑ 85 Midnight Charm C :K:	.10	.25
❑ 86 Mire Boa C :G:	.15	.40
❑ 87 Mirri the Cursed R :K:	1.00	2.50
❑ 88 Molten Firebird R :R:	.25	.60
❑ 89 Muck Drubb U :K:	.15	.40
❑ 90 Mycologist U :W:	.15	.40
❑ 91 Necrotic Sliver U :D:	.40	1.00
❑ 92 Needlepeak Spider C :R:	.10	.25
❑ 93 Null Profusion R :K:	.25	.60
❑ 94 Numot, the Devastator R :D:	.60	1.50
❑ 95 Oros, the Avenger R :D:	.25	.60
❑ 96 Ovinize U :B:	.15	.40
❑ 97 Pallid Mycoderm C :W:	.10	.25
❑ 98 Phantasmagorian U :K:	.20	.50
❑ 99 Piracy Charm C :B:	.10	.25
❑ 100 Pongify U :B:	.20	.50
❑ 101 Porphyry Nodes R :W:	.25	.60
❑ 102 Poultice Sliver C :W:	.10	.25
❑ 103 Pouncing Wurm U :G:	.15	.40
❑ 104 Primal Plasma C :B:	.10	.25
❑ 105 Prodigal Pyromancer C :R:	.10	.25
❑ 106 Psychotrope Thallid U :G:	.30	.75
❑ 107 Pyrohemia U :R:	.20	.50
❑ 108 Radha, Heir to Keld R :D:	.30	.75
❑ 109 Rathi Trapper C :K:	.10	.25
❑ 110 Reality Acid C :B:	.10	.25
❑ 111 Rebuff the Wicked U :W:	.50	1.25
❑ 112 Reckless Wurm U :R:	.20	.50
❑ 113 Reflex Sliver C :G:	.10	.25
❑ 114 Retether R :W:	.25	.60
❑ 115 Revered Dead C :W:	.10	.25
❑ 116 Ridged Kusite C :K:	.10	.25
❑ 117 Riftmarked Knight U :W:	.15	.40
❑ 118 Riptide Pilferer U :B:	.15	.40
❑ 119 Roiling Horror R :K:	.25	.60
❑ 120 Rough // Tumble U :R:	.20	.50
❑ 121 Saltblast U :W:	.15	.40
❑ 122 Saltfield Recluse C :W:	.10	.25
❑ 123 Seal of Primordium C :G:	.10	.25
❑ 124 Serendib Sorcerer R :B:	.25	.60
❑ 125 Serra Sphinx R :B:	.40	1.00
❑ 126 Serra's Boon U :W:	.15	.40
❑ 127 Shade of Trokair C :W:	.10	.25
❑ 128 Shaper Parasite C :B:	.10	.25
❑ 129 Shivan Meteor U :R:	.20	.50
❑ 130 Shivan Wumpus R :R:	.40	1.00
❑ 131 Shrouded Lore U :K:	.15	.40
❑ 132 Simian Spirit Guide C :R:	.25	.60
❑ 133 Sinew Sliver C :W:	.20	.50
❑ 134 Skirk Shaman C :R:	.10	.25
❑ 135 Sophic Centaur U :G:	.15	.40
❑ 136 Spellshift R :B:	.25	.60
❑ 137 Spitting Sliver C :K:	.10	.25
❑ 138 Stingscourger C :R:	.10	.25
❑ 139 Stonecloaker U :W:	.20	.50
❑ 140 Stormfront Riders U :W:	.15	.40
❑ 141 Sulfur Elemental U :R:	.40	1.00
❑ 142 Sunlance C :W:	.10	.25
❑ 143 Synchronous Sliver C :B:	.10	.25
❑ 144 Temporal Extortion R :K:	1.00	2.50
❑ 145 Teneb, the Harvester R :D:	.60	1.50
❑ 146 Tidewalker U :B:	.15	.40
❑ 147 Timbermare R :G:	.25	.60
❑ 148 Timebender U :B:	.15	.40
❑ 149 Timecrafting U :R:	.15	.40
❑ 150 Torchling R :R:	.25	.60
❑ 151 Treacherous Urge U :K:	.15	.40
❑ 152 Uktabi Drake C :G:	.10	.25
❑ 153 Urborg, Tomb of Yawgmoth R :L:	8.00	20.00
❑ 154 Utopia Vow C :G:	.10	.25
❑ 155 Vampiric Link C :K:	.20	.50
❑ 156 Veiling Oddity C :B:	.10	.25
❑ 157 Venarian Glimmer U :B:	.15	.40
❑ 158 Vitaspore Thallid C :G:	.10	.25
❑ 159 Voidstone Gargoyle R :W:	.25	.60
❑ 160 Volcano Hellion R :R:	.25	.60
❑ 161 Vorosh, the Hunter R :D:	.40	1.00
❑ 162 Waning Wurm U :K:	.15	.40
❑ 163 Whitemane Lion C :W:	.10	.25
❑ 164 Wild Pair R :G:	.50	1.25
❑ 165 Wistful Thinking C :B:	.10	.25

2007 Magic the Gathering Planar Chaos Foil

Complete Set (165)
*Foil: .8X to 2X Basic Cards

Card	Low	High
❑ 1 Aeon Chronicler R :B:	.75	2.00
❑ 2 AEther Membrane U :R:	.40	1.00
❑ 3 Akroma, Angel of Fury R :R:	2.50	6.00
❑ 4 Ana Battlemage U :G:	.30	.75
❑ 5 Aquamorph Entity C :B:	.20	.50
❑ 6 Auramancer's Guise U :B:	.30	.75
❑ 7 Aven Riftwatcher C :W:	.20	.50
❑ 8 Battering Sliver C :R:	.20	.50
❑ 9 Benalish Commander R :W:	1.25	3.00
❑ 10 Big Game Hunter U :K:	.40	1.00
❑ 11 Blightspeaker C :K:	.20	.50
❑ 12 Blood Knight U :R:	.60	1.50
❑ 13 Body Double R :B:	1.50	4.00
❑ 14 Bog Serpent C :K:	.20	.50
❑ 15 Boom // Bust R :R:	1.25	3.00
❑ 16 Braids, Conjurer Adept R :B:	.50	1.25
❑ 17 Brain Gorgers C :K:	.20	.50
❑ 18 Brute Force C :R:	.30	.75
❑ 19 Calciderm U :W:	.40	1.00
❑ 20 Cautery Sliver U :D:	.40	1.00
❑ 21 Chronozoa R :B:	1.25	3.00
❑ 22 Circle of Affliction U :K:	.30	.75
❑ 23 Citanul Woodreaders C :G:	.20	.50
❑ 24 Cradle to Grave C :K:	.20	.50
❑ 25 Crovax, Ascendant Hero R :W:	.75	2.00
❑ 26 Damnation R :K:	20.00	50.00
❑ 27 Darkheart Sliver U :D:	.40	1.00
❑ 28 Dash Hopes C :K:	.40	1.00
❑ 29 Dawn Charm C :W:	.40	1.00
❑ 30 Dead // Gone C :R:	.20	.50
❑ 31 Deadly Grub C :K:	.20	.50
❑ 32 Deadwood Treefolk U :G:	.30	.75
❑ 33 Detritivore R :R:	.50	1.25
❑ 34 Dichotomancy R :B:	.50	1.25
❑ 35 Dismal Failure U :B:	.30	.75
❑ 36 Dormant Sliver U :D:	.40	1.00
❑ 37 Dreamscape Artist C :B:	.20	.50
❑ 38 Dunerider Outlaw U :K:	.30	.75
❑ 39 Dust Corona C :R:	.20	.50
❑ 40 Dust Elemental R :W:	.50	1.25
❑ 41 Enslave U :K:	.40	1.00
❑ 42 Erratic Mutation C :B:	.20	.50
❑ 43 Essence Warden C :G:	.50	1.25
❑ 44 Evolution Charm C :G:	.20	.50
❑ 45 Extirpate R :K:	6.00	15.00
❑ 46 Fa'adiyah Seer C :G:	.20	.50
❑ 47 Fatal Frenzy R :R:	.50	1.25
❑ 48 Firefright Mage C :R:	.20	.50
❑ 49 Frenetic Sliver U :D:	.30	.75
❑ 50 Frozen Æther U :B:	.50	1.25
❑ 51 Fungal Behemoth R :G:	.50	1.25
❑ 52 Fury Charm C :R:	.20	.50
❑ 53 Gaea's Anthem R :G:	2.00	5.00
❑ 54 Ghost Tactician C :W:	.20	.50
❑ 55 Giant Dustwasp C :G:	.20	.50
❑ 56 Gossamer Phantasm C :B:	.20	.50
❑ 57 Groundbreaker R :G:	1.50	4.00
❑ 58 Hammerheim Deadeye U :R:	.30	.75
❑ 59 Harmonize U :G:	1.50	4.00
❑ 60 Healing Leaves C :G:	.20	.50
❑ 61 Hedge Troll U :G:	.30	.75
❑ 62 Heroes Remembered R :W:	.50	1.25
❑ 63 Hunting Wilds U :G:	.30	.75
❑ 64 Imp's Mischief R :K:	.50	1.25
❑ 65 Intet, the Dreamer R :D:	.75	2.00
❑ 66 Jedit Ojanen of Efrava R :G:	.50	1.25
❑ 67 Jodah's Avenger U :B:	.30	.75
❑ 68 Kavu Predator U :G:	1.50	4.00
❑ 69 Keen Sense U :G:	.40	1.00
❑ 70 Keldon Marauders C :R:	.40	1.00
❑ 71 Kor Dirge U :K:	.30	.75
❑ 72 Lavacore Elemental U :R:	.30	.75
❑ 73 Life and Limb R :G:	.50	1.25
❑ 74 Magus of the Arena R :R:	.50	1.25
❑ 75 Magus of the Bazaar R :B:	.50	1.25
❑ 76 Magus of the Coffers R :K:	.75	2.00
❑ 77 Magus of the Library R :G:	.50	1.25
❑ 78 Magus of the Tabernacle R :W:	.50	1.25
❑ 79 Malach of the Dawn U :W:	.30	.75
❑ 80 Mana Tithe C :W:	.40	1.00
❑ 81 Mantle of Leadership U :W:	.30	.75
❑ 82 Melancholy C :K:	.20	.50
❑ 83 Merfolk Thaumaturgist C :B:	.20	.50
❑ 84 Mesa Enchantress R :W:	.50	1.25
❑ 85 Midnight Charm C :K:	.20	.50
❑ 86 Mire Boa C :G:	.30	.75
❑ 87 Mirri the Cursed R :K:	2.00	5.00
❑ 88 Molten Firebird R :R:	.50	1.25
❑ 89 Muck Drubb U :K:	.30	.75
❑ 90 Mycologist U :W:	.30	.75
❑ 91 Necrotic Sliver U :D:	.75	2.00
❑ 92 Needlepeak Spider C :R:	.20	.50
❑ 93 Null Profusion R :K:	.50	1.25
❑ 94 Numot, the Devastator R :D:	1.25	3.00
❑ 95 Oros, the Avenger R :D:	.50	1.25
❑ 96 Ovinize U :B:	.30	.75
❑ 97 Pallid Mycoderm C :W:	.20	.50
❑ 98 Phantasmagorian U :K:	.40	1.00
❑ 99 Piracy Charm C :B:	.20	.50
❑ 100 Pongify U :B:	.40	1.00
❑ 101 Porphyry Nodes R :W:	.50	1.25
❑ 102 Poultice Sliver C :W:	.20	.50
❑ 103 Pouncing Wurm U :G:	.30	.75
❑ 104 Primal Plasma C :B:	.20	.50
❑ 105 Prodigal Pyromancer C :R:	.20	.50
❑ 106 Psychotrope Thallid U :G:	.60	1.50
❑ 107 Pyrohemia U :R:	.40	1.00
❑ 108 Radha, Heir to Keld R :D:	.60	1.50
❑ 109 Rathi Trapper C :K:	.20	.50
❑ 110 Reality Acid C :B:	.20	.50
❑ 111 Rebuff the Wicked U :W:	1.00	2.50
❑ 112 Reckless Wurm U :R:	.40	1.00
❑ 113 Reflex Sliver C :G:	.20	.50
❑ 114 Retether R :W:	.50	1.25
❑ 115 Revered Dead C :W:	.20	.50
❑ 116 Ridged Kusite C :K:	.20	.50
❑ 117 Riftmarked Knight U :W:	.30	.75
❑ 118 Riptide Pilferer U :B:	.30	.75
❑ 119 Roiling Horror R :K:	.50	1.25
❑ 120 Rough // Tumble U :R:	.40	1.00
❑ 121 Saltblast U :W:	.30	.75
❑ 122 Saltfield Recluse C :W:	.20	.50
❑ 123 Seal of Primordium C :G:	.20	.50
❑ 124 Serendib Sorcerer R :B:	.50	1.25
❑ 125 Serra Sphinx R :B:	.75	2.00
❑ 126 Serra's Boon U :W:	.30	.75
❑ 127 Shade of Trokair C :W:	.20	.50
❑ 128 Shaper Parasite C :B:	.20	.50
❑ 129 Shivan Meteor U :R:	.40	1.00
❑ 130 Shivan Wumpus R :R:	.75	2.00
❑ 131 Shrouded Lore U :K:	.30	.75
❑ 132 Simian Spirit Guide C :R:	.50	1.25
❑ 133 Sinew Sliver C :W:	.40	1.00
❑ 134 Skirk Shaman C :R:	.20	.50
❑ 135 Sophic Centaur U :G:	.30	.75
❑ 136 Spellshift R :B:	.50	1.25
❑ 137 Spitting Sliver C :K:	.20	.50
❑ 138 Stingscourger C :R:	.20	.50
❑ 139 Stonecloaker U :W:	.40	1.00
❑ 140 Stormfront Riders U :W:	.30	.75
❑ 141 Sulfur Elemental U :R:	.75	2.00
❑ 142 Sunlance C :W:	.20	.50
❑ 143 Synchronous Sliver C :B:	.20	.50
❑ 144 Temporal Extortion R :K:	2.00	5.00
❑ 145 Teneb, the Harvester R :D:	1.25	3.00
❑ 146 Tidewalker U :B:	.30	.75
❑ 147 Timbermare R :G:	.50	1.25
❑ 148 Timebender U :B:	.30	.75
❑ 149 Timecrafting U :R:	.30	.75
❑ 150 Torchling R :R:	.50	1.25
❑ 151 Treacherous Urge U :K:	.30	.75
❑ 152 Uktabi Drake C :G:	.20	.50
❑ 153 Urborg, Tomb of Yawgmoth R :L:	15.00	40.00
❑ 154 Utopia Vow C :G:	.20	.50
❑ 155 Vampiric Link C :K:	.40	1.00
❑ 156 Veiling Oddity C :B:	.20	.50
❑ 157 Venarian Glimmer U :B:	.30	.75
❑ 158 Vitaspore Thallid C :G:	.20	.50
❑ 159 Voidstone Gargoyle R :W:	.50	1.25
❑ 160 Volcano Hellion R :R:	.50	1.25
❑ 161 Vorosh, the Hunter R :D:	.75	2.00
❑ 162 Waning Wurm U :K:	.30	.75
❑ 163 Whitemane Lion C :W:	.20	.50
❑ 164 Wild Pair R :G:	1.00	2.50
❑ 165 Wistful Thinking C :B:	.20	.50

2007 Magic the Gathering Future Sight

Card	Low	High
Complete Set (180)	200.00	275.00
Booster Box (36 Packs)	200.00	350.00
Booster Pack (15 Cards)	6.00	10.00
Theme Deck	8.00	15.00
Fat Pack	40.00	80.00
❑ 1 Akroma's Memorial R :A:	6.00	15.00
❑ 2 Angel of Salvation R :W:	.25	.60
❑ 3 Arc Blade U :R:	.15	.40
❑ 4 Arcanum Wings U :B:	.15	.40
❑ 5 Augur il-Vec C :W:	.10	.25
❑ 6 Augur of Skulls C :K:	.10	.25
❑ 7 Aven Augur C :B:	.10	.25
❑ 8 Aven Mindcensor U :W:	1.25	3.00
❑ 9 Barren Glory R :W:	.25	.60
❑ 10 Baru, Fist of Krosa R :G:	.25	.60
❑ 11 Bitter Ordeal R :K:	.60	1.50
❑ 12 Blade of the Sixth Pride C :W:	.10	.25
❑ 13 Blind Phantasm C :B:	.10	.25
❑ 14 Bloodshot Trainee U :R:	.15	.40
❑ 15 Bogardan Lancer C :R:	.10	.25
❑ 16 Boldwyr Intimidator U :R:	.15	.40
❑ 17 Bonded Fetch U :B:	.15	.40
❑ 18 Bound in Silence U :W:	.15	.40
❑ 19 Bridge from Below R :K:	8.00	20.00
❑ 20 Centaur Omenreader U :G:	.15	.40
❑ 21 Char-Rumbler U :R:	.15	.40
❑ 22 Chronomantic Escape U :W:	.15	.40
❑ 23 Cloud Key R :A:	1.25	3.00
❑ 24 Cloudseeder U :B:	.15	.40
❑ 25 Coalition Relic R :A:	1.50	4.00
❑ 26 Cryptic Annelid U :B:	.15	.40
❑ 27 Cutthroat il-Dal C :K:	.10	.25
❑ 28 Cyclical Evolution U :G:	.15	.40
❑ 29 Dakmor Salvage U :L:	.30	.75
❑ 30 Darksteel Garrison R :A:	.25	.60
❑ 31 Daybreak Coronet R :W:	1.25	3.00
❑ 32 Death Rattle C :K:	.10	.25
❑ 33 Deepcavern Imp C :K:	.10	.25
❑ 34 Delay U :B:	.25	.60
❑ 35 Dryad Arbor U :L:	1.50	4.00
❑ 36 Dust of Moments U :W:	.15	.40
❑ 37 Edge of Autumn C :G:	.10	.25
❑ 38 Emberwilde Augur C :R:	.10	.25
❑ 39 Emblem of the Warmind U :R:	.15	.40
❑ 40 Epochrasite R :A:	.60	1.50
❑ 41 Even the Odds U :W:	.15	.40
❑ 42 Fatal Attraction C :R:	.10	.25
❑ 43 Festering March U :K:	.15	.40
❑ 44 Fleshwrither U :K:	.15	.40
❑ 45 Flowstone Embrace C :R:	.10	.25
❑ 46 Fomori Nomad C :R:	.10	.25
❑ 47 Force of Savagery R :G:	.25	.60
❑ 48 Foresee C :B:	.10	.25
❑ 49 Frenzy Sliver C :K:	.10	.25
❑ 50 Gathan Raiders C :R:	.10	.25
❑ 51 Ghostfire C :R:	.10	.25
❑ 52 Gibbering Descent R :K:	.25	.60
❑ 53 Gift of Granite C :W:	.10	.25
❑ 54 Glittering Wish R :D:	.60	1.50
❑ 55 Goldmeadow Lookout U :W:	.15	.40
❑ 56 Grave Peril C :R:	.10	.25
❑ 57 Grave Scrabbler C :K:	.10	.25
❑ 58 Graven Cairns R :L:	1.25	3.00
❑ 59 Grinning Ignus C :R:	.10	.25
❑ 60 Grove of the Burnwillows R :L:	5.00	12.00
❑ 61 Haze of Rage U :R:	.15	.40
❑ 62 Heartwood Storyteller R :G:	.30	.75
❑ 63 Henchfiend of Ukor C :R:	.10	.25
❑ 64 Homing Sliver C :R:	.10	.25
❑ 65 Horizon Canopy R :L:	3.00	8.00
❑ 66 Ichor Slick C :K:	.10	.25
❑ 67 Imperial Mask R :W:	.25	.60
❑ 68 Imperiosaur U :G:	.15	.40
❑ 69 Infiltrator il-Kor C :B:	.10	.25
❑ 70 Intervention Pact R :W:	.40	1.00
❑ 71 Jhoira of the Ghitu R :D:	1.50	4.00
❑ 72 Judge Unworthy C :W:	.10	.25
❑ 73 Kavu Primarch C :G:	.10	.25
❑ 74 Keldon Megaliths U :L:	.15	.40
❑ 75 Knight of Sursi C :W:	.10	.25
❑ 76 Korlash, Heir to Blackblade R :K:	2.50	6.00
❑ 77 Leaden Fists C :B:	.10	.25
❑ 78 Linessa, Zephyr Mage R :B:	.25	.60
❑ 79 Llanowar Augur C :G:	.10	.25
❑ 80 Llanowar Empath C :G:	.10	.25
❑ 81 Llanowar Mentor U :G:	.25	.60
❑ 82 Llanowar Reborn U :L:	.25	.60
❑ 83 Logic Knot C :B:	.10	.25
❑ 84 Lost Auramancers U :W:	.15	.40
❑ 85 Lost Hours C :K:	.10	.25
❑ 86 Lucent Liminid C :W:	.10	.25
❑ 87 Lumithread Field C :W:	.10	.25
❑ 88 Lymph Sliver C :W:	.10	.25
❑ 89 Maelstrom Djinn R :B:	.25	.60
❑ 90 Magus of the Abyss R :K:	.25	.60
❑ 91 Magus of the Future R :B:	.50	1.25
❑ 92 Magus of the Moat R :W:	1.00	2.50
❑ 93 Magus of the Moon R :R:	2.50	6.00
❑ 94 Magus of the Vineyard R :G:	.25	.60
❑ 95 Marshaling Cry C :W:	.10	.25
❑ 96 Mass of Ghouls C :K:	.10	.25
❑ 97 Mesmeric Sliver C :B:	.10	.25
❑ 98 Minions' Murmurs U :K:	.15	.40
❑ 99 Mistmeadow Skulk U :W:	.15	.40
❑ 100 Molten Disaster R :R:	.25	.60
❑ 101 Muraganda Petroglyphs R :G:	.25	.60
❑ 102 Mystic Speculation U :B:	.25	.60
❑ 103 Nacatl War-Pride U :G:	.15	.40
❑ 104 Narcomoeba U :B:	1.00	2.50
❑ 105 Nessian Courser C :G:	.10	.25
❑ 106 New Benalia U :L:	.15	.40
❑ 107 Nihilith R :K:	.25	.60
❑ 108 Nimbus Maze R :L:	1.00	2.50
❑ 109 Nix R :B:	.25	.60
❑ 110 Oblivion Crown C :K:	.10	.25
❑ 111 Oriss, Samite Guardian R :W:	.30	.75
❑ 112 Pact of Negation R :B:	8.00	20.00
❑ 113 Pact of the Titan R :R:	.75	2.00
❑ 114 Patrician's Scorn C :W:	.10	.25
❑ 115 Petrified Plating C :G:	.10	.25
❑ 116 Phosphorescent Feast U :G:	.15	.40
❑ 117 Pooling Venom U :K:	.15	.40
❑ 118 Putrid Cyclops C :K:	.10	.25
❑ 119 Pyromancer's Swath R :R:	.75	2.00
❑ 120 Quagnoth R :G:	.25	.60
❑ 121 Quiet Disrepair C :G:	.10	.25
❑ 122 Ramosian Revivalist U :W:	.15	.40
❑ 123 Ravaging Riftwurm U :G:	.15	.40
❑ 124 Reality Strobe U :B:	.15	.40
❑ 125 Riddle of Lightning C :R:	.10	.25
❑ 126 Rift Elemental C :R:	.10	.25
❑ 127 Riftsweeper U :G:	.15	.40
❑ 128 Rites of Flourishing R :G:	.40	1.00
❑ 129 River of Tears R :L:	1.00	2.50
❑ 130 Saltskitter C :W:	.10	.25
❑ 131 Samite Censer-Bearer C :W:	.10	.25
❑ 132 Sarcomite Myr C :B:	.10	.25
❑ 133 Scourge of Kher Ridges R :R:	.75	2.00
❑ 134 Scout's Warning R :W:	.25	.60
❑ 135 Second Wind U :B:	.15	.40
❑ 136 Seht's Tiger R :W:	.25	.60
❑ 137 Shah of Naar Isle R :R:	.25	.60
❑ 138 Shapeshifter's Marrow R :B:	.25	.60
❑ 139 Shimian Specter R :K:	.75	2.00
❑ 140 Shivan Sand-Mage U :R:	.15	.40
❑ 141 Skirk Ridge Exhumer U :K:	.15	.40
❑ 142 Skizzik Surger U :R:	.15	.40
❑ 143 Slaughter Pact R :K:	1.25	3.00
❑ 144 Sliver Legion R :D:	4.00	10.00
❑ 145 Sliversmith U :A:	.15	.40
❑ 146 Snake Cult Initiation U :K:	.15	.40
❑ 147 Soultether Golem U :A:	.15	.40
❑ 148 Sparkspitter U :R:	.15	.40
❑ 149 Spellweaver Volute R :B:	.25	.60
❑ 150 Spellwild Ouphe U :G:	.15	.40
❑ 151 Spin into Myth U :B:	.15	.40
❑ 152 Spirit en-Dal U :W:	.15	.40
❑ 153 Sporoloth Ancient C :G:	.10	.25
❑ 154 Sprout Swarm C :G:	.10	.25
❑ 155 Steamflogger Boss R :R:	.30	.75
❑ 156 Storm Entity U :R:	.15	.40
❑ 157 Street Wraith U :K:	.75	2.00
❑ 158 Stronghold Rats U :K:	.15	.40
❑ 159 Summoner's Pact R :G:	4.00	10.00

Card	Low	High
☐ 160 Sword of the Meek U :A:	.75	2.00
☐ 161 Take Possession R :B:	.30	.75
☐ 162 Tarmogoyf R :G:	75.00	125.00
☐ 163 Tarox Bladewing R :R:	.25	.60
☐ 164 Thornweald Archer C :G:	.15	.40
☐ 165 Thunderblade Charge R :R:	.25	.60
☐ 166 Tolaria West U :L:	.75	2.00
☐ 167 Tombstalker R :K:	4.00	10.00
☐ 168 Unblinking Bleb C :B:	.10	.25
☐ 169 Utopia Mycon U :G:	.50	1.25
☐ 170 Vedalken AEthermage C :B:	.10	.25
☐ 171 Veilstone Amulet R :A:	.25	.60
☐ 172 Venser, Shaper Savant R :B:	.25	.60
☐ 173 Venser's Diffusion C :B:	2.00	5.00
☐ 174 Virulent Sliver C :G:	.15	.40
☐ 175 Whetwheel R :A:	.25	.60
☐ 176 Whip-Spine Drake C :B:	.10	.25
☐ 177 Witch's Mist U :K:	.15	.40
☐ 178 Wrap in Vigor C :G:	.10	.25
☐ 179 Yixlid Jailer U :K:	.15	.40
☐ 180 Zoetic Cavern U :L:	.15	.40

2007 Magic the Gathering Future Sight Foil

Card	Low	High
Complete Set (180)	300.00	450.00
*Foil: .8X to 2X Basic Cards		
☐ 1 Akroma's Memorial R :A:	12.00	30.00
☐ 2 Angel of Salvation R :W:	.50	1.25
☐ 3 Arc Blade U :R:	.30	.75
☐ 4 Arcanum Wings U :B:	.30	.75
☐ 5 Augur il-Vec C :W:	.20	.50
☐ 6 Augur of Skulls C :K:	.20	.50
☐ 7 Aven Augur C :B:	.20	.50
☐ 8 Aven Mindcensor U :W:	2.50	6.00
☐ 9 Barren Glory R :W:	.50	1.25
☐ 10 Baru, Fist of Krosa R :G:	.50	1.25
☐ 11 Bitter Ordeal R :K:	1.25	3.00
☐ 12 Blade of the Sixth Pride C :W:	.20	.50
☐ 13 Blind Phantasm C :B:	.20	.50
☐ 14 Bloodshot Trainee U :R:	.30	.75
☐ 15 Bogardan Lancer C :R:	.20	.50
☐ 16 Boldwyr Intimidator U :R:	.30	.75
☐ 17 Bonded Fetch U :B:	.30	.75
☐ 18 Bound in Silence U :W:	.30	.75
☐ 19 Bridge from Below R :K:	15.00	40.00
☐ 20 Centaur Omenreader U :G:	.30	.75
☐ 21 Char-Rumbler U :R:	.30	.75
☐ 22 Chronomantic Escape U :W:	.30	.75
☐ 23 Cloud Key R :A:	2.50	6.00
☐ 24 Cloudseeder U :B:	.30	.75
☐ 25 Coalition Relic R :A:	3.00	8.00
☐ 26 Cryptic Annelid U :B:	.30	.75
☐ 27 Cutthroat il-Dal C :K:	.20	.50
☐ 28 Cyclical Evolution U :G:	.30	.75
☐ 29 Dakmor Salvage U :L:	.60	1.50
☐ 30 Darksteel Garrison R :A:	.50	1.25
☐ 31 Daybreak Coronet R :W:	2.50	6.00
☐ 32 Death Rattle C :K:	.20	.50
☐ 33 Deepcavern Imp C :K:	.20	.50
☐ 34 Delay U :B:	.50	1.25
☐ 35 Dryad Arbor U :L:	3.00	8.00
☐ 36 Dust of Moments U :W:	.30	.75
☐ 37 Edge of Autumn C :G:	.20	.50
☐ 38 Emberwilde Augur C :R:	.20	.50
☐ 39 Emblem of the Warmind U :R:	.30	.75
☐ 40 Epochrasite R :A:	1.25	3.00
☐ 41 Even the Odds U :W:	.30	.75
☐ 42 Fatal Attraction C :R:	.20	.50
☐ 43 Festering March U :K:	.30	.75
☐ 44 Fleshwrither U :K:	.30	.75
☐ 45 Flowstone Embrace C :R:	.20	.50
☐ 46 Fomori Nomad C :R:	.20	.50
☐ 47 Force of Savagery R :G:	.50	1.25
☐ 48 Foresee C :B:	.20	.50
☐ 49 Frenzy Sliver C :K:	.20	.50
☐ 50 Gathan Raiders C :R:	.20	.50
☐ 51 Ghostfire C :R:	.20	.50
☐ 52 Gibbering Descent R :K:	.50	1.25
☐ 53 Gift of Granite C :W:	.20	.50
☐ 54 Glittering Wish R :D:	1.25	3.00
☐ 55 Goldmeadow Lookout U :W:	.30	.75
☐ 56 Grave Peril C :K:	.20	.50
☐ 57 Grave Scrabbler C :K:	.20	.50
☐ 58 Graven Cairns R :L:	2.50	6.00
☐ 59 Grinning Ignus C :R:	.20	.50
☐ 60 Grove of the Burnwillows R :L:	10.00	25.00
☐ 61 Haze of Rage U :R:	.30	.75
☐ 62 Heartwood Storyteller R :G:	.60	1.50
☐ 63 Henchfiend of Ukor C :R:	.20	.50
☐ 64 Homing Sliver C :R:	.20	.50
☐ 65 Horizon Canopy R :L:	6.00	15.00
☐ 66 Ichor Slick C :K:	.20	.50
☐ 67 Imperial Mask R :W:	.50	1.25
☐ 68 Imperiosaur U :G:	.30	.75
☐ 69 Infiltrator il-Kor C :B:	.20	.50
☐ 70 Intervention Pact R :W:	.75	2.00
☐ 71 Jhoira of the Ghitu R :D:	3.00	8.00
☐ 72 Judge Unworthy C :W:	.20	.50
☐ 73 Kavu Primarch C :G:	.20	.50
☐ 74 Keldon Megaliths U :L:	.30	.75
☐ 75 Knight of Sursi C :W:	.20	.50
☐ 76 Korlash, Heir to Blackblade R :K:	5.00	12.00
☐ 77 Leaden Fists C :B:	.20	.50
☐ 78 Linessa, Zephyr Mage R :B:	.50	1.25
☐ 79 Llanowar Augur C :G:	.20	.50
☐ 80 Llanowar Empath C :G:	.20	.50
☐ 81 Llanowar Mentor U :G:	.50	1.25
☐ 82 Llanowar Reborn U :L:	.50	1.25
☐ 83 Logic Knot C :B:	.20	.50
☐ 84 Lost Auramancers U :W:	.30	.75
☐ 85 Lost Hours C :K:	.20	.50
☐ 86 Lucent Liminid C :W:	.20	.50
☐ 87 Lumithread Field C :W:	.20	.50
☐ 88 Lymph Sliver C :W:	.20	.50
☐ 89 Maelstrom Djinn R :B:	.50	1.25
☐ 90 Magus of the Abyss R :K:	.50	1.25
☐ 91 Magus of the Future R :B:	1.00	2.50
☐ 92 Magus of the Moat R :W:	2.00	5.00
☐ 93 Magus of the Moon R :R:	5.00	12.00
☐ 94 Magus of the Vineyard R :G:	.50	1.25
☐ 95 Marshaling Cry C :W:	.20	.50
☐ 96 Mass of Ghouls C :K:	.20	.50
☐ 97 Mesmeric Sliver C :B:	.20	.50
☐ 98 Minions' Murmurs U :K:	.30	.75
☐ 99 Mistmeadow Skulk U :W:	.30	.75
☐ 100 Molten Disaster R :R:	.50	1.25
☐ 101 Muraganda Petroglyphs R :G:	.50	1.25
☐ 102 Mystic Speculation U :B:	.50	1.25
☐ 103 Nacatl War-Pride U :G:	.30	.75
☐ 104 Narcomoeba U :B:	2.00	5.00
☐ 105 Nessian Courser C :G:	.20	.50
☐ 106 New Benalia U :L:	.30	.75
☐ 107 Nihilith R :K:	.50	1.25
☐ 108 Nimbus Maze R :L:	2.00	5.00
☐ 109 Nix R :B:	.50	1.25
☐ 110 Oblivion Crown C :K:	.20	.50
☐ 111 Oriss, Samite Guardian R :W:	.60	1.50
☐ 112 Pact of Negation R :B:	15.00	40.00
☐ 113 Pact of the Titan R :R:	1.50	4.00
☐ 114 Patrician's Scorn C :W:	.20	.50
☐ 115 Petrified Plating C :G:	.20	.50
☐ 116 Phosphorescent Feast U :G:	.30	.75
☐ 117 Pooling Venom U :K:	.30	.75
☐ 118 Putrid Cyclops C :K:	.20	.50
☐ 119 Pyromancer's Swath R :R:	1.50	4.00
☐ 120 Quagnoth R :G:	.50	1.25
☐ 121 Quiet Disrepair C :G:	.20	.50
☐ 122 Ramosian Revivalist U :W:	.30	.75
☐ 123 Ravaging Riftwurm U :G:	.30	.75
☐ 124 Reality Strobe U :B:	.30	.75
☐ 125 Riddle of Lightning C :R:	.20	.50
☐ 126 Rift Elemental C :R:	.20	.50
☐ 127 Riftsweeper U :G:	.30	.75
☐ 128 Rites of Flourishing R :G:	.75	2.00
☐ 129 River of Tears R :L:	2.00	5.00
☐ 130 Saltskitter C :W:	.20	.50
☐ 131 Samite Censer-Bearer C :W:	.20	.50
☐ 132 Sarcomite Myr C :B:	.20	.50
☐ 133 Scourge of Kher Ridges R :R:	1.50	4.00
☐ 134 Scout's Warning R :W:	.50	1.25
☐ 135 Second Wind U :B:	.30	.75
☐ 136 Seht's Tiger R :W:	.50	1.25
☐ 137 Shah of Naar Isle R :R:	.50	1.25
☐ 138 Shapeshifter's Marrow R :B:	.50	1.25
☐ 139 Shimian Specter R :K:	1.50	4.00
☐ 140 Shivan Sand-Mage U :R:	.30	.75
☐ 141 Skirk Ridge Exhumer U :K:	.30	.75
☐ 142 Skizzik Surger U :R:	.30	.75
☐ 143 Slaughter Pact R :K:	2.50	6.00
☐ 144 Sliver Legion R :D:	8.00	20.00
☐ 145 Sliversmith U :A:	.30	.75
☐ 146 Snake Cult Initiation U :K:	.30	.75
☐ 147 Soultether Golem U :A:	.30	.75
☐ 148 Sparkspitter U :R:	.30	.75
☐ 149 Spellweaver Volute R :B:	.50	1.25
☐ 150 Spellwild Ouphe U :G:	.30	.75
☐ 151 Spin into Myth U :B:	.30	.75
☐ 152 Spirit en-Dal U :W:	.30	.75
☐ 153 Sporoloth Ancient C :G:	.20	.50
☐ 154 Sprout Swarm C :G:	.20	.50
☐ 155 Steamflogger Boss R :R:	.60	1.50
☐ 156 Storm Entity U :R:	.30	.75
☐ 157 Street Wraith U :K:	1.50	4.00
☐ 158 Stronghold Rats U :K:	.30	.75
☐ 159 Summoner's Pact R :G:	8.00	20.00
☐ 160 Sword of the Meek U :A:	1.50	4.00
☐ 161 Take Possession R :B:	.60	1.50
☐ 162 Tarmogoyf R :G:	200.00	300.00
☐ 163 Tarox Bladewing R :R:	.50	1.25
☐ 164 Thornweald Archer C :G:	.30	.75
☐ 165 Thunderblade Charge R :R:	.50	1.25
☐ 166 Tolaria West U :L:	1.50	4.00
☐ 167 Tombstalker R :K:	8.00	20.00
☐ 168 Unblinking Bleb C :B:	.20	.50
☐ 169 Utopia Mycon U :G:	1.00	2.50
☐ 170 Vedalken AEthermage C :B:	.20	.50
☐ 171 Veilstone Amulet R :A:	.50	1.25
☐ 172 Venser, Shaper Savant R :B:	.20	.50
☐ 173 Venser's Diffusion C :B:	4.00	10.00
☐ 174 Virulent Sliver C :G:	.30	.75
☐ 175 Whetwheel R :A:	.50	1.25
☐ 176 Whip-Spine Drake C :B:	.20	.50
☐ 177 Witch's Mist U :K:	.30	.75
☐ 178 Wrap in Vigor C :G:	.20	.50
☐ 179 Yixlid Jailer U :K:	.30	.75
☐ 180 Zoetic Cavern U :L:	.30	.75

2007 Magic the Gathering Lorwyn

Card	Low	High
Complete Set (301)	250.00	350.00
☐ 1 Ajani Goldmane R :W:	4.00	10.00
☐ 2 Arbiter of Knollridge R :W:	.25	.60
☐ 3 Austere Command R :W:	1.50	4.00
☐ 4 Avian Changeling C :W:	.10	.25
☐ 5 Battle Mastery U :W:	.40	1.00
☐ 6 Brigid, Hero of Kinsbaile R :W:	.40	1.00
☐ 7 Burrenton Forge-Tender U :W:	.20	.50
☐ 8 Cenn's Heir C :W:	.10	.25
☐ 9 Changeling Hero U :W:	.20	.50
☐ 10 Cloudgoat Ranger U :W:	.20	.50
☐ 11 Crib Swap U :W:	.30	.75
☐ 12 Dawnfluke C :W:	.10	.25
☐ 13 Entangling Trap U :W:	.15	.40
☐ 14 Favor of the Mighty R :W:	.25	.60
☐ 15 Galepowder Mage R :W:	.40	1.00
☐ 16 Goldmeadow Dodger C :W:	.10	.25
☐ 17 Goldmeadow Harrier C :W:	.10	.25
☐ 18 Goldmeadow Stalwart U :W:	.20	.50
☐ 19 Harpoon Sniper U :W:	.12	.30
☐ 20 Hillcomber Giant C :W:	.10	.25
☐ 21 Hoofprints of the Stag R :W:	.40	1.00
☐ 22 Judge of Currents C :W:	.12	.30
☐ 23 Kinsbaile Balloonist C :W:	.10	.25
☐ 24 Kinsbaile Skirmisher C :W:	.10	.25
☐ 25 Kithkin Greatheart C :W:	.10	.25
☐ 26 Kithkin Harbinger U :W:	.20	.50
☐ 27 Kithkin Healer C :W:	.10	.25
☐ 28 Knight of Meadowgrain U :W:	1.25	3.00
☐ 29 Lairwatch Giant C :W:	.10	.25
☐ 30 Militia's Pride R :W:	.50	1.25
☐ 31 Mirror Entity R :W:	4.00	10.00
☐ 32 Neck Snap C :W:	.10	.25
☐ 33 Oaken Brawler C :W:	.10	.25
☐ 34 Oblivion Ring C :W:	.25	.60
☐ 35 Plover Knights C :W:	.10	.25
☐ 36 Pollen Lullaby U :W:	.20	.50
☐ 37 Purity R :W:	.50	1.25
☐ 38 Sentry Oak U :W:	.12	.30
☐ 39 Shields of Velis Vel C :W:	.10	.25
☐ 40 Soaring Hope C :W:	.10	.25
☐ 41 Springjack Knight C :W:	.10	.25
☐ 42 Summon the School U :W:	.20	.50
☐ 43 Surge of Thoughtweft C :W:	.12	.30
☐ 44 Thoughtweft Trio R :W:	.40	1.00
☐ 45 Triclopean Sight C :W:	.10	.25
☐ 46 Veteran of the Depths U :W:	.12	.30
☐ 47 Wellgabber Apothecary C :W:	.10	.25
☐ 48 Wispmare C :W:	.12	.30
☐ 49 Wizened Cenn U :W:	.20	.50
☐ 50 Aethersnipe C :B:	.10	.25
☐ 51 Amoeboid Changeling C :B:	.10	.25
☐ 52 Aquitect's Will C :B:	.10	.25
☐ 53 Benthicore U :B:	.12	.30
☐ 54 Broken Ambitions C :B:	.12	.30
☐ 55 Captivating Glance U :B:	.12	.30
☐ 56 Cryptic Command R :B:	20.00	40.00
☐ 57 Deeptread Merrow C :B:	.10	.25
☐ 58 Drowner of Secrets U :B:	.20	.50
☐ 59 Ego Erasure U :B:	.12	.30
☐ 60 Ethereal Whiskergill U :B:	.12	.30
☐ 61 Faerie Harbinger U :B:	.12	.30
☐ 62 Faerie Trickery C :B:	.12	.30
☐ 63 Fallowsage U :B:	.15	.40
☐ 64 Familiar's Ruse U :B:	.12	.30
☐ 65 Fathom Trawl R :B:	.25	.60
☐ 66 Forced Fruition R :B:	.75	2.00
☐ 67 Glen Elendra Pranksters U :B:	.12	.30
☐ 68 Glimmerdust Nap C :B:	.10	.25
☐ 69 Guile R :B:	.40	1.00
☐ 70 Inkfathom Divers C :B:	.10	.25
☐ 71 Jace Beleren R :B:	4.00	10.00
☐ 72 Merrow Commerce U :B:	.40	1.00
☐ 73 Merrow Harbinger U :B:	.20	.50
☐ 74 Merrow Reejerey U :B:	1.25	3.00
☐ 75 Mistbind Clique R :B:	1.25	3.00
☐ 76 Mulldrifter C :B:	.15	.40
☐ 77 Paperfin Rascal C :B:	.10	.25
☐ 78 Pestermite C :B:	.40	1.00
☐ 79 Ponder C :B:	.40	1.00
☐ 80 Protective Bubble C :B:	.10	.25
☐ 81 Ringskipper C :B:	.10	.25
☐ 82 Scattering Stroke U :B:	.12	.30
☐ 83 Scion of Oona R :B:	3.00	8.00
☐ 84 Sentinels of Glen Elendra C :B:	.10	.25
☐ 85 Shapesharer R :B:	.75	2.00
☐ 86 Silvergill Adept U :B:	.40	1.00
☐ 87 Silvergill Douser C :B:	.10	.25
☐ 88 Sower of Temptation R :B:	4.00	10.00
☐ 89 Spellstutter Sprite C :B:	.40	1.00
☐ 90 Stonybrook Angler C :B:	.10	.25
☐ 91 Streambed Aquitects C :B:	.10	.25
☐ 92 Surgespanner R :B:	.25	.60
☐ 93 Tideshaper Mystic C :B:	.10	.25
☐ 94 Turtleshell Changeling U :B:	.12	.30
☐ 95 Wanderwine Prophets R :B:	.25	.60
☐ 96 Whirlpool Whelm C :B:	.10	.25
☐ 97 Wings of Velis Vel C :B:	.10	.25
☐ 98 Zephyr Net C :B:	.10	.25
☐ 99 Black Poplar Shaman C :K:	.10	.25
☐ 100 Bog Hoodlums C :K:	.10	.25
☐ 101 Boggart Birth Rite C :K:	.10	.25
☐ 102 Boggart Harbinger U :K:	.20	.50
☐ 103 Boggart Loggers C :K:	.10	.25
☐ 104 Boggart Mob R :K:	.40	1.00
☐ 105 Cairn Wanderer R :K:	.60	1.50
☐ 106 Colfenor's Plans R :K:	.25	.60
☐ 107 Dread R :K:	1.25	3.00
☐ 108 Dreamspoiler Witches R :K:	.25	.60
☐ 109 Exiled Boggart C :K:	.10	.25
☐ 110 Eyeblight's Ending C :K:	.12	.30
☐ 111 Facevaulter C :K:	.10	.25
☐ 112 Faerie Tauntings C :K:	.20	.50
☐ 113 Final Revels U :K:	.12	.30
☐ 114 Fodder Launch U :K:	.25	.60
☐ 115 Footbottom Feast U :K:	.12	.30
☐ 116 Ghostly Changeling C :K:	.12	.30
☐ 117 Hoarder's Greed U :K:	.12	.30
☐ 118 Hornet Harasser R :K:	.25	.60
☐ 119 Hunter of Eyeblights C :K:	.12	.30
☐ 120 Knucklebone Witch U :K:	.50	1.25
☐ 121 Liliana Vess R :K:	4.00	10.00
☐ 122 Lys Alana Scarblade R :K:	.25	.60
☐ 123 Mad Auntie R :K:	.60	1.50
☐ 124 Makeshift Mannequin U :K:	.25	.60
☐ 125 Marsh Flitter R :K:	.25	.60
☐ 126 Moonglove Winnower U :K:	.12	.30
☐ 127 Mournwhelk U :K:	.12	.30
☐ 128 Nameless Inversion C :K:	.12	.30
☐ 129 Nath's Buffoon C :K:	.10	.25
☐ 130 Nectar Faerie R :K:	.25	.60
☐ 131 Nettlevine Blight C :K:	.25	.60
☐ 132 Nightshade Stinger U :K:	.12	.30
☐ 133 Oona's Prowler R :K:	1.00	2.50
☐ 134 Peppersmoke C :K:	.12	.30
☐ 135 Profane Command R :K:	1.50	4.00
☐ 136 Prowess of the Fair C :K:	.20	.50
☐ 137 Quill-Slinger Boggart R :K:	.10	.25
☐ 138 Scarred Vinebreeder U :K:	.12	.30
☐ 139 Shriekmaw C :K:	.40	1.00
☐ 140 Skeletal Changeling C :K:	.10	.25
☐ 141 Spiderwig Boggart U :K:	.12	.30
☐ 142 Squeaking Pie Sneak C :K:	.15	.40
☐ 143 Thieving Sprite C :K:	.10	.25
☐ 144 Thorntooth Witch U :K:	.12	.30
☐ 145 Thoughtseize R :K:	35.00	70.00
☐ 146 Warren Pilferers C :K:	.10	.25
☐ 147 Weed Strangle C :K:	.10	.25
☐ 148 Adder-Staff Boggart C :R:	.10	.25
☐ 149 Ashling the Pilgrim R :R:	.40	1.00
☐ 150 Ashling's Prerogative R :R:	.25	.60
☐ 151 Axegrinder Giant C :R:	.10	.25
☐ 152 Blades of Velis Vel C :R:	.10	.25
☐ 153 Blind-Spot Giant C :R:	.10	.25
☐ 154 Boggart Forager C :R:	.10	.25
☐ 155 Boggart Shenanigans U :R:	.25	.60
☐ 156 Boggart Sprite-Chaser C :R:	.10	.25
☐ 157 Caterwauling Boggart C :R:	.10	.25
☐ 158 Ceaseless Searblades U :R:	.12	.30
☐ 159 Chandra Nalaar R :R:	1.50	4.00
☐ 160 Changeling Berserker U :R:	.12	.30
☐ 161 Consuming Bonfire C :R:	.10	.25
☐ 162 Crush Underfoot U :R:	.12	.30
☐ 163 Faultgrinder C :R:	.10	.25
☐ 164 Fire-Belly Changeling C :R:	.10	.25
☐ 165 Flamekin Bladewhirl U :R:	.25	.60
☐ 166 Flamekin Brawler C :R:	.10	.25
☐ 167 Flamekin Harbinger U :R:	.75	2.00
☐ 168 Flamekin Spitfire U :R:	.12	.30
☐ 169 Giant Harbinger U :R:	.20	.50
☐ 170 Giant's Ire C :R:	.10	.25
☐ 171 Glarewielder U :R:	.12	.30
☐ 172 Goatnapper U :R:	.12	.30
☐ 173 Hamletback Goliath R :R:	.25	.60
☐ 174 Hearthcage Giant U :R:	.12	.30
☐ 175 Heat Shimmer R :R:	.25	.60
☐ 176 Hostility R :R:	.40	1.00
☐ 177 Hurly-Burly C :R:	.10	.25
☐ 178 Incandescent Soulstoke R :R:	1.25	3.00
☐ 179 Incendiary Command R :R:	.60	1.50
☐ 180 Ingot Chewer C :R:	.12	.30
☐ 181 Inner-Flame Acolyte C :R:	.10	.25
☐ 182 Inner-Flame Igniter U :R:	.12	.30
☐ 183 Lash Out C :R:	.12	.30
☐ 184 Lowland Oaf C :R:	.10	.25
☐ 185 Mudbutton Torchrunner C :R:	.10	.25
☐ 186 Needle Drop C :R:	.10	.25
☐ 187 Nova Chaser R :R:	1.25	3.00
☐ 188 Rebellion of the Flamekin U :R:	.12	.30
☐ 189 Smokebraider C :R:	.12	.30
☐ 190 Soulbright Flamekin C :R:	.10	.25
☐ 191 Stinkdrinker Daredevil C :R:	.10	.25
☐ 192 Sunrise Sovereign R :R:	.25	.60
☐ 193 Tar Pitcher U :R:	.12	.30
☐ 194 Tarfire C :R:	.12	.30
☐ 195 Thundercloud Shaman U :R:	.12	.30
☐ 196 Wild Ricochet R :R:	.40	1.00
☐ 197 Battlewand Oak C :G:	.10	.25
☐ 198 Bog-Strider Ash C :G:	.10	.25
☐ 199 Briarhorn U :G:	.20	.50
☐ 200 Changeling Titan U :G:	.20	.50
☐ 201 Cloudcrown Oak C :G:	.10	.25
☐ 202 Cloudthresher R :G:	.40	1.00
☐ 203 Dauntless Dourbark R :G:	1.50	4.00
☐ 204 Elvish Branchbender C :G:	.10	.25
☐ 205 Elvish Eulogist C :G:	.10	.25
☐ 206 Elvish Handservant C :G:	.10	.25
☐ 207 Elvish Harbinger U :G:	.75	2.00
☐ 208 Elvish Promenade U :G:	1.50	4.00
☐ 209 Epic Proportions R :G:	.25	.60
☐ 210 Eyes of the Wisent R :G:	.40	1.00
☐ 211 Fertile Ground C :G:	.12	.30
☐ 212 Fistful of Force C :G:	.10	.25
☐ 213 Garruk Wildspeaker R :G:	4.00	10.00
☐ 214 Gilt-Leaf Ambush C :G:	.10	.25
☐ 215 Gilt-Leaf Seer C :G:	.10	.25
☐ 216 Guardian of Cloverdell U :G:	.12	.30
☐ 217 Heal the Scars C :G:	.10	.25
☐ 218 Hunt Down C :G:	.10	.25
☐ 219 Immaculate Magistrate R :G:	4.00	10.00
☐ 220 Imperious Perfect U :G:	3.00	8.00
☐ 221 Incremental Growth U :G:	.12	.30
☐ 222 Jagged-Scar Archers U :G:	1.00	2.50
☐ 223 Kithkin Daggerdare C :G:	.10	.25
☐ 224 Kithkin Mourncaller U :G:	.12	.30
☐ 225 Lace with Moonglove C :G:	.10	.25
☐ 226 Lammastide Weave U :G:	.12	.30
☐ 227 Leaf Gilder C :G:	.12	.30
☐ 228 Lignify C :G:	.10	.25
☐ 229 Lys Alana Huntmaster C :G:	.10	.25
☐ 230 Masked Admirers R :G:	.40	1.00
☐ 231 Nath's Elite C :G:	.10	.25
☐ 232 Oakgnarl Warrior C :G:	.10	.25
☐ 233 Primal Command R :G:	2.00	5.00
☐ 234 Rootgrapple C :G:	.10	.25
☐ 235 Seedguide Ash U :G:	.12	.30
☐ 236 Spring Cleaning C :G:	.10	.25
☐ 237 Sylvan Echoes U :G:	.12	.30
☐ 238 Timber Protector R :G:	3.00	8.00
☐ 239 Treefolk Harbinger U :G:	.60	1.50
☐ 240 Vigor R :G:	6.00	15.00
☐ 241 Warren-Scourge Elf C :G:	.10	.25
☐ 242 Woodland Changeling C :G:	.10	.25
☐ 243 Woodland Guidance U :G:	.10	.25
☐ 244 Wren's Run Packmaster R :G:	1.00	2.50
☐ 245 Wren's Run Vanquisher U :G:	.40	1.00
☐ 246 Brion Stoutarm R :W/R:	.40	1.00
☐ 247 Doran, the Siege Tower R :W/K/G:	2.50	6.00
☐ 248 Gaddock Teeg R :W/G:	3.00	8.00
☐ 249 Horde of Notions R :W/B/K/R/G:	.40	1.00
☐ 250 Nath of the Gilt-Leaf R :K/G:	.60	1.50
☐ 251 Sygg, River Guide R :W/B:	.40	1.00
☐ 252 Wort, Boggart Auntie R :K/R:	.75	2.00
☐ 253 Wydwen, the Biting Gale R :B/K:	.40	1.00
☐ 254 Colfenor's Urn R :A:	.25	.60
☐ 255 Deathrender R :A:	3.00	8.00
☐ 256 Dolmen Gate R :A:	1.50	4.00
☐ 257 Herbal Poultice C :A:	.10	.25
☐ 258 Moonglove Extract C :A:	.10	.25
☐ 259 Rings of Brighthearth R :A:	2.00	5.00
☐ 260 Runed Stalactite C :A:	.10	.25
☐ 261 Springleaf Drum C :A:	.40	1.00
☐ 262 Thorn of Amethyst R :A:	1.25	3.00
☐ 263 Thousand-Year Elixir R :A:	2.50	6.00
☐ 264 Twinning Glass R :A:	.25	.60
☐ 265 Wanderer's Twig C :A:	.10	.25
☐ 266 Ancient Amphitheater R :L:	.30	.75
☐ 267 Auntie's Hovel R :L:	1.00	2.50
☐ 268 Gilt-Leaf Palace R :L:	1.25	3.00
☐ 269 Howltooth Hollow R :L:	.30	.75
☐ 270 Mosswort Bridge R :L:	1.25	3.00
☐ 271 Secluded Glen R :L:	1.00	2.50
☐ 272 Shelldock Isle R :L:	.40	1.00
☐ 273 Shimmering Grotto C :L:	.12	.30
☐ 274 Spinerock Knoll R :L:	.60	1.50
☐ 275 Vivid Crag U :L:	.30	.75
☐ 276 Vivid Creek U :L:	.40	1.00
☐ 277 Vivid Grove U :L:	.30	.75
☐ 278 Vivid Marsh U :L:	.30	.75
☐ 279 Vivid Meadow U :L:	.30	.75
☐ 280 Wanderwine Hub R :L:	1.25	3.00
☐ 281 Windbrisk Heights R :L:	2.00	5.00
☐ 282 Plains C :L:	.20	.50
☐ 283 Plains C :L:	.20	.50
☐ 284 Plains C :L:	.20	.50
☐ 285 Plains C :L:	.20	.50
☐ 286 Island C :L:	.20	.50
☐ 287 Island C :L:	.20	.50
☐ 288 Island C :L:	.20	.50
☐ 289 Island C :L:	.20	.50
☐ 290 Swamp C :L:	.20	.50
☐ 291 Swamp C :L:	.20	.50
☐ 292 Swamp C :L:	.20	.50
☐ 293 Swamp C :L:	.20	.50
☐ 294 Mountain C :L:	.20	.50
☐ 295 Mountain C :L:	.20	.50
☐ 296 Mountain C :L:	.20	.50
☐ 297 Mountain C :L:	.20	.50
☐ 298 Forest C :L:	.20	.50
☐ 299 Forest C :L:	.20	.50
☐ 300 Forest C :L:	.20	.50
☐ 301 Forest C :L:	.20	.50

2007 Magic the Gathering Lorwyn Foil

Card	Low	High
*Foil: .8X to 2X Basic Cards		
☐ 1 Ajani Goldmane R :W:	8.00	20.00
☐ 2 Arbiter of Knollridge R :W:	.50	1.25
☐ 3 Austere Command R :W:	3.00	8.00
☐ 4 Avian Changeling C :W:	.20	.50
☐ 5 Battle Mastery U :W:	.75	2.00
☐ 6 Brigid, Hero of Kinsbaile R :W:	.75	2.00
☐ 7 Burrenton Forge-Tender U :W:	.40	1.00
☐ 8 Cenn's Heir C :W:	.20	.50
☐ 9 Changeling Hero U :W:	.40	1.00
☐ 10 Cloudgoat Ranger U :W:	.40	1.00
☐ 11 Crib Swap U :W:	.60	1.50
☐ 12 Dawnfluke C :W:	.20	.50
☐ 13 Entangling Trap U :W:	.30	.75
☐ 14 Favor of the Mighty R :W:	.50	1.25
☐ 15 Galepowder Mage R :W:	.75	2.00
☐ 16 Goldmeadow Dodger C :W:	.20	.50
☐ 17 Goldmeadow Harrier C :W:	.20	.50
☐ 18 Goldmeadow Stalwart U :W:	.40	1.00
☐ 19 Harpoon Sniper U :W:	.25	.60
☐ 20 Hillcomber Giant C :W:	.20	.50
☐ 21 Hoofprints of the Stag R :W:	.75	2.00
☐ 22 Judge of Currents C :W:	.25	.60
☐ 23 Kinsbaile Balloonist C :W:	.20	.50
☐ 24 Kinsbaile Skirmisher C :W:	.20	.50
☐ 25 Kithkin Greatheart C :W:	.20	.50
☐ 26 Kithkin Harbinger U :W:	.40	1.00
☐ 27 Kithkin Healer C :W:	.20	.50
☐ 28 Knight of Meadowgrain U :W:	2.50	6.00

MAGIC

Card	Low	High
❑ 29 Lairwatch Giant C :W:	.20	.50
❑ 30 Militia's Pride R :W:	1.00	2.50
❑ 31 Mirror Entity R :W:	8.00	20.00
❑ 32 Neck Snap C :W:	.20	.50
❑ 33 Oaken Brawler C :W:	.20	.50
❑ 34 Oblivion Ring C :W:	.50	1.25
❑ 35 Plover Knights C :W:	.20	.50
❑ 36 Pollen Lullaby U :W:	.40	1.00
❑ 37 Purity R :W:	1.00	2.50
❑ 38 Sentry Oak U :W:	.25	.60
❑ 39 Shields of Velis Vel C :W:	.20	.50
❑ 40 Soaring Hope C :W:	.20	.50
❑ 41 Springjack Knight C :W:	.20	.50
❑ 42 Summon the School U :W:	.40	1.00
❑ 43 Surge of Thoughtweft C :W:	.25	.60
❑ 44 Thoughtweft Trio R :W:	.75	2.00
❑ 45 Triclopean Sight C :W:	.20	.50
❑ 46 Veteran of the Depths U :W:	.25	.60
❑ 47 Wellgabber Apothecary C :W:	.20	.50
❑ 48 Wispmare C :W:	.25	.60
❑ 49 Wizened Cenn U :W:	.40	1.00
❑ 50 Aethersnipe C :B:	.20	.50
❑ 51 Amoeboid Changeling C :B:	.20	.50
❑ 52 Aquitect's Will C :B:	.20	.50
❑ 53 Benthicore U :B:	.25	.60
❑ 54 Broken Ambitions C :B:	.25	.60
❑ 55 Captivating Glance U :B:	.25	.60
❑ 56 Cryptic Command R :B:	40.00	80.00
❑ 57 Deeptread Merrow C :B:	.20	.50
❑ 58 Drowner of Secrets U :B:	.40	1.00
❑ 59 Ego Erasure U :B:	.25	.60
❑ 60 Ethereal Whiskergill U :B:	.25	.60
❑ 61 Faerie Harbinger U :B:	.25	.60
❑ 62 Faerie Trickery C :B:	.25	.60
❑ 63 Fallowsage U :B:	.30	.75
❑ 64 Familiar's Ruse U :B:	.25	.60
❑ 65 Fathom Trawl R :B:	.50	1.25
❑ 66 Forced Fruition R :B:	1.50	4.00
❑ 67 Glen Elendra Pranksters U :B:	.25	.60
❑ 68 Glimmerdust Nap C :B:	.20	.50
❑ 69 Guile R :B:	.75	2.00
❑ 70 Inkfathom Divers C :B:	.20	.50
❑ 71 Jace Beleren R :B:	8.00	20.00
❑ 72 Merrow Commerce U :B:	.75	2.00
❑ 73 Merrow Harbinger U :B:	.40	1.00
❑ 74 Merrow Reejerey U :B:	2.50	6.00
❑ 75 Mistbind Clique R :B:	2.50	6.00
❑ 76 Mulldrifter C :B:	.30	.75
❑ 77 Paperfin Rascal C :B:	.20	.50
❑ 78 Pestermite C :B:	.75	2.00
❑ 79 Ponder C :B:	.75	2.00
❑ 80 Protective Bubble C :B:	.20	.50
❑ 81 Ringskipper C :B:	.20	.50
❑ 82 Scattering Stroke U :B:	.25	.60
❑ 83 Scion of Oona R :B:	6.00	15.00
❑ 84 Sentinels of Glen Elendra C :B:	.20	.50
❑ 85 Shapesharer R :B:	1.50	4.00
❑ 86 Silvergill Adept U :B:	.75	2.00
❑ 87 Silvergill Douser C :B:	.20	.50
❑ 88 Sower of Temptation R :B:	8.00	20.00
❑ 89 Spellstutter Sprite C :B:	.75	2.00
❑ 90 Stonybrook Angler C :B:	.20	.50
❑ 91 Streambed Aquitects C :B:	.20	.50
❑ 92 Surgespanner R :B:	.50	1.25
❑ 93 Tideshaper Mystic C :B:	.20	.50
❑ 94 Turtleshell Changeling U :B:	.25	.60
❑ 95 Wanderwine Prophets R :B:	.50	1.25
❑ 96 Whirlpool Whelm C :B:	.20	.50
❑ 97 Wings of Velis Vel C :B:	.20	.50
❑ 98 Zephyr Net C :B:	.20	.50
❑ 99 Black Poplar Shaman C :K:	.20	.50
❑ 100 Bog Hoodlums C :K:	.20	.50
❑ 101 Boggart Birth Rite C :K:	.20	.50
❑ 102 Boggart Harbinger U :K:	.40	1.00
❑ 103 Boggart Loggers C :K:	.20	.50
❑ 104 Boggart Mob R :K:	.75	2.00
❑ 105 Cairn Wanderer R :K:	1.25	3.00
❑ 106 Colfenor's Plans R :K:	.50	1.25
❑ 107 Dread R :K:	2.50	6.00
❑ 108 Dreamspoiler Witches R :K:	.50	1.25
❑ 109 Exiled Boggart C :K:	.20	.50
❑ 110 Eyeblight's Ending C :K:	.25	.60
❑ 111 Facevaulter C :K:	.20	.50
❑ 112 Faerie Tauntings C :K:	.40	1.00
❑ 113 Final Revels U :K:	.25	.60
❑ 114 Fodder Launch U :K:	.50	1.25
❑ 115 Footbottom Feast U :K:	.25	.60
❑ 116 Ghostly Changeling C :K:	.25	.60
❑ 117 Hoarder's Greed U :K:	.25	.60
❑ 118 Hornet Harasser R :K:	.50	1.25
❑ 119 Hunter of Eyeblights C :K:	.25	.60
❑ 120 Knucklebone Witch U :K:	1.00	2.50
❑ 121 Liliana Vess R :K:	8.00	20.00
❑ 122 Lys Alana Scarblade R :K:	.50	1.25
❑ 123 Mad Auntie R :K:	1.25	3.00
❑ 124 Makeshift Mannequin U :K:	.50	1.25
❑ 125 Marsh Flitter R :K:	.50	1.25
❑ 126 Moonglove Winnower U :K:	.25	.60
❑ 127 Mournwhelk U :K:	.25	.60
❑ 128 Nameless Inversion C :K:	.25	.60
❑ 129 Nath's Buffoon C :K:	.20	.50
❑ 130 Nectar Faerie R :K:	.50	1.25
❑ 131 Nettlevine Blight C :K:	.50	1.25
❑ 132 Nightshade Stinger U :K:	.25	.60
❑ 133 Oona's Prowler R :K:	2.00	5.00
❑ 134 Peppersmoke C :K:	.25	.60
❑ 135 Profane Command R :K:	3.00	8.00
❑ 136 Prowess of the Fair C :K:	.40	1.00
❑ 137 Quill-Slinger Boggart R :K:	.20	.50
❑ 138 Scarred Vinebreeder U :K:	.25	.60
❑ 139 Shriekmaw C :K:	.75	2.00
❑ 140 Skeletal Changeling C :K:	.20	.50
❑ 141 Spiderwig Boggart U :K:	.25	.60
❑ 142 Squeaking Pie Sneak C :K:	.30	.75
❑ 143 Thieving Sprite C :K:	.20	.50
❑ 144 Thorntooth Witch U :K:	.25	.60
❑ 145 Thoughtseize R :K:	70.00	140.00
❑ 146 Warren Pilferers C :K:	.20	.50
❑ 147 Weed Strangle C :K:	.20	.50
❑ 148 Adder-Staff Boggart C :R:	.20	.50
❑ 149 Ashling the Pilgrim R :R:	.75	2.00
❑ 150 Ashling's Prerogative R :R:	.50	1.25
❑ 151 Axegrinder Giant C :R:	.20	.50
❑ 152 Blades of Velis Vel C :R:	.20	.50
❑ 153 Blind-Spot Giant C :R:	.20	.50
❑ 154 Boggart Forager C :R:	.20	.50
❑ 155 Boggart Shenanigans U :R:	.50	1.25
❑ 156 Boggart Sprite-Chaser C :R:	.20	.50
❑ 157 Caterwauling Boggart C :R:	.20	.50
❑ 158 Ceaseless Searblades U :R:	.25	.60
❑ 159 Chandra Nalaar R :R:	3.00	8.00
❑ 160 Changeling Berserker U :R:	.25	.60
❑ 161 Consuming Bonfire C :R:	.20	.50
❑ 162 Crush Underfoot U :R:	.25	.60
❑ 163 Faultgrinder C :R:	.20	.50
❑ 164 Fire-Belly Changeling C :R:	.20	.50
❑ 165 Flamekin Bladewhirl U :R:	.50	1.25
❑ 166 Flamekin Brawler C :R:	.20	.50
❑ 167 Flamekin Harbinger U :R:	1.50	4.00
❑ 168 Flamekin Spitfire U :R:	.25	.60
❑ 169 Giant Harbinger U :R:	.40	1.00
❑ 170 Giant's Ire C :R:	.20	.50
❑ 171 Glarewielder U :R:	.25	.60
❑ 172 Goatnapper U :R:	.25	.60
❑ 173 Hamletback Goliath R :R:	.50	1.25
❑ 174 Hearthcage Giant U :R:	.25	.60
❑ 175 Heat Shimmer R :R:	.50	1.25
❑ 176 Hostility R :R:	.75	2.00
❑ 177 Hurly-Burly C :R:	.20	.50
❑ 178 Incandescent Soulstoke R :R:	2.50	6.00
❑ 179 Incendiary Command R :R:	1.25	3.00
❑ 180 Ingot Chewer C :R:	.25	.60
❑ 181 Inner-Flame Acolyte C :R:	.20	.50
❑ 182 Inner-Flame Igniter U :R:	.25	.60
❑ 183 Lash Out C :R:	.25	.60
❑ 184 Lowland Oaf C :R:	.20	.50
❑ 185 Mudbutton Torchrunner C :R:	.20	.50
❑ 186 Needle Drop C :R:	.20	.50
❑ 187 Nova Chaser R :R:	2.50	6.00
❑ 188 Rebellion of the Flamekin U :R:	.25	.60
❑ 189 Smokebraider C :R:	.25	.60
❑ 190 Soulbright Flamekin C :R:	.20	.50
❑ 191 Stinkdrinker Daredevil C :R:	.20	.50
❑ 192 Sunrise Sovereign R :R:	.50	1.25
❑ 193 Tar Pitcher U :R:	.25	.60
❑ 194 Tarfire C :R:	.25	.60
❑ 195 Thundercloud Shaman U :R:	.25	.60
❑ 196 Wild Ricochet R :R:	.75	2.00
❑ 197 Battlewand Oak C :G:	.20	.50
❑ 198 Bog-Strider Ash C :G:	.20	.50
❑ 199 Briarhorn U :G:	.40	1.00
❑ 200 Changeling Titan U :G:	.40	1.00
❑ 201 Cloudcrown Oak C :G:	.20	.50
❑ 202 Cloudthresher R :G:	.75	2.00
❑ 203 Dauntless Dourbark R :G:	3.00	8.00
❑ 204 Elvish Branchbender C :G:	.20	.50
❑ 205 Elvish Eulogist C :G:	.20	.50
❑ 206 Elvish Handservant C :G:	.20	.50
❑ 207 Elvish Harbinger U :G:	1.50	4.00
❑ 208 Elvish Promenade U :G:	3.00	8.00
❑ 209 Epic Proportions R :G:	.50	1.25
❑ 210 Eyes of the Wisent R :G:	.75	2.00
❑ 211 Fertile Ground C :G:	.25	.60
❑ 212 Fistful of Force C :G:	.20	.50
❑ 213 Garruk Wildspeaker R :G:	8.00	20.00
❑ 214 Gilt-Leaf Ambush C :G:	.20	.50
❑ 215 Gilt-Leaf Seer C :G:	.20	.50
❑ 216 Guardian of Cloverdell U :G:	.25	.60
❑ 217 Heal the Scars C :G:	.20	.50
❑ 218 Hunt Down C :G:	.20	.50
❑ 219 Immaculate Magistrate R :G:	8.00	20.00
❑ 220 Imperious Perfect U :G:	6.00	15.00
❑ 221 Incremental Growth U :G:	.25	.60
❑ 222 Jagged-Scar Archers U :G:	2.00	5.00
❑ 223 Kithkin Daggerdare C :G:	.20	.50
❑ 224 Kithkin Mourncaller U :G:	.25	.60
❑ 225 Lace with Moonglove C :G:	.20	.50
❑ 226 Lammastide Weave U :G:	.25	.60
❑ 227 Leaf Gilder C :G:	.25	.60
❑ 228 Lignify C :G:	.20	.50
❑ 229 Lys Alana Huntmaster C :G:	.20	.50
❑ 230 Masked Admirers R :G:	.75	2.00
❑ 231 Nath's Elite C :G:	.20	.50
❑ 232 Oakgnarl Warrior C :G:	.20	.50
❑ 233 Primal Command R :G:	4.00	10.00
❑ 234 Rootgrapple C :G:	.20	.50
❑ 235 Seedguide Ash U :G:	.25	.60
❑ 236 Spring Cleaning C :G:	.20	.50
❑ 237 Sylvan Echoes U :G:	.25	.60
❑ 238 Timber Protector R :G:	6.00	15.00
❑ 239 Treefolk Harbinger U :G:	1.25	3.00
❑ 240 Vigor R :G:	12.00	30.00
❑ 241 Warren-Scourge Elf C :G:	.20	.50
❑ 242 Woodland Changeling C :G:	.20	.50
❑ 243 Woodland Guidance U :G:	.20	.50
❑ 244 Wren's Run Packmaster R :G:	2.00	5.00
❑ 245 Wren's Run Vanquisher U :G:	.75	2.00
❑ 246 Brion Stoutarm R :W/R:	.75	2.00
❑ 247 Doran, the Siege Tower R :W/K/G:	5.00	12.00
❑ 248 Gaddock Teeg R :W/G:	6.00	15.00
❑ 249 Horde of Notions R :W/B/K/R/G:	.75	2.00
❑ 250 Nath of the Gilt-Leaf R :K/G:	1.25	3.00
❑ 251 Sygg, River Guide R :W/B:	.75	2.00
❑ 252 Wort, Boggart Auntie R :K/R:	1.50	4.00
❑ 253 Wydwen, the Biting Gale R :B/K:	.75	2.00
❑ 254 Colfenor's Urn R :A:	.50	1.25
❑ 255 Deathrender R :A:	6.00	15.00
❑ 256 Dolmen Gate R :A:	3.00	8.00
❑ 257 Herbal Poultice C :A:	.20	.50
❑ 258 Moonglove Extract C :A:	.20	.50
❑ 259 Rings of Brighthearth R :A:	4.00	10.00
❑ 260 Runed Stalactite C :A:	.20	.50
❑ 261 Springleaf Drum C :A:	.75	2.00
❑ 262 Thorn of Amethyst R :A:	2.50	6.00
❑ 263 Thousand-Year Elixir R :A:	5.00	12.00
❑ 264 Twinning Glass R :A:	.50	1.25
❑ 265 Wanderer's Twig C :A:	.20	.50
❑ 266 Ancient Amphitheater R :L:	.60	1.50
❑ 267 Auntie's Hovel R :L:	2.00	5.00
❑ 268 Gilt-Leaf Palace R :L:	2.50	6.00
❑ 269 Howltooth Hollow R :L:	.60	1.50
❑ 270 Mosswort Bridge R :L:	2.50	6.00
❑ 271 Secluded Glen R :L:	2.00	5.00
❑ 272 Shelldock Isle R :L:	.75	2.00
❑ 273 Shimmering Grotto C :L:	.25	.60
❑ 274 Spinerock Knoll R :L:	1.25	3.00
❑ 275 Vivid Crag U :L:	.60	1.50
❑ 276 Vivid Creek U :L:	.75	2.00
❑ 277 Vivid Grove U :L:	.60	1.50
❑ 278 Vivid Marsh U :L:	.60	1.50
❑ 279 Vivid Meadow U :L:	.60	1.50
❑ 280 Wanderwine Hub R :L:	2.50	6.00
❑ 281 Windbrisk Heights R :L:	4.00	10.00
❑ 282 Plains C :L:	.40	1.00
❑ 283 Plains C :L:	.40	1.00
❑ 284 Plains C :L:	.40	1.00
❑ 285 Plains C :L:	.40	1.00
❑ 286 Island C :L:	.40	1.00
❑ 287 Island C :L:	.40	1.00
❑ 288 Island C :L:	.40	1.00
❑ 289 Island C :L:	.40	1.00
❑ 290 Swamp C :L:	.40	1.00
❑ 291 Swamp C :L:	.40	1.00
❑ 292 Swamp C :L:	.40	1.00
❑ 293 Swamp C :L:	.40	1.00
❑ 294 Mountain C :L:	.40	1.00
❑ 295 Mountain C :L:	.40	1.00
❑ 296 Mountain C :L:	.40	1.00
❑ 297 Mountain C :L:	.40	1.00
❑ 298 Forest C :L:	.40	1.00
❑ 299 Forest C :L:	.40	1.00
❑ 300 Forest C :L:	.40	1.00
❑ 301 Forest C :L:	.40	1.00

2008 Magic the Gathering Jace vs Chandra

Card	Low	High
Duel Deck	50.00	100.00
❑ 1 Jace Beleren M :B:	6.00	15.00
❑ 1 Elemental Shaman C	.20	.50
❑ 2 Martyr of Frost C :B:	.10	.25
❑ 3 Fathom Seer C :B:	.10	.25
❑ 4 Voidmage Apprentice C :B:	.10	.25
❑ 5 Wall of Deceit U :B:	.20	.50
❑ 6 Willbender U :B:	.25	.60
❑ 7 Bottle Gnomes U	.20	.50
❑ 8 Man-o'-War C :B:	.30	.75
❑ 9 Ophidian C :B:	.10	.25
❑ 10 Fledgling Mawcor U :B:	.20	.50
❑ 11 Waterspout Djinn U :B:	.20	.50
❑ 12 Mulldrifter C :B:	.40	1.00
❑ 13 Air Elemental U :B:	.20	.50
❑ 14 Guile R :B:	.50	1.25
❑ 15 Riftwing Cloudskate U :B:	.20	.50
❑ 16 Spire Golem C	.10	.25
❑ 17 AEthersnipe C :B:	.10	.25
❑ 18 Brine Elemental U :B:	.20	.50
❑ 19 Quicksilver Dragon R :B:	.50	1.25
❑ 20 Errant Ephemeron C :B:	.20	.50
❑ 21 Ancestral Vision R :B:	2.00	5.00
❑ 22 Mind Stone U	.50	1.25
❑ 23 Daze C :B:	1.50	4.00
❑ 24 Counterspell C :B:	4.00	10.00
❑ 25 Repulse C :B:	.10	.25
❑ 26 Fact or Fiction U :B:	1.50	4.00
❑ 27 Gush C :B:	.40	1.00
❑ 28 Condescend C :B:	.20	.50
❑ 29 Terrain Generator U	.60	1.50
❑ 30 Island L	.10	.25
❑ 31 Island L	.10	.25
❑ 32 Island L	.10	.25
❑ 33 Island L	.10	.25
❑ 34 Chandra Nalaar M :R:	3.00	8.00
❑ 35 Flamekin Brawler C :R:	.10	.25
❑ 36 Fireslinger C :R:	.10	.25
❑ 37 Soulbright Flamekin C :R:	.20	.50
❑ 38 Pyre Charger U :R:	.20	.50
❑ 39 Slith Firewalker U :R:	.20	.50
❑ 40 Flamewave Invoker U :R:	.20	.50
❑ 41 Inner-Flame Acolyte C :R:	.10	.25
❑ 42 Flametongue Kavu U :R:	.60	1.50
❑ 43 Furnace Whelp U :R:	.20	.50
❑ 44 Rakdos Pit Dragon R :R:	.75	2.00
❑ 45 Ingot Chewer C :R:	.20	.50
❑ 46 Oxidda Golem C	.10	.25
❑ 47 Chartooth Cougar C :R:	.10	.25
❑ 48 Hostility R :R:	.40	1.00
❑ 49 Firebolt C :R:	.10	.25
❑ 50 Seal of Fire C :R:	.20	.50
❑ 51 Incinerate C :R:	.60	1.50
❑ 52 Magma Jet U :R:	2.00	5.00
❑ 53 Flame Javelin U :R:	.60	1.50
❑ 54 Cone of Flame U :R:	.20	.50
❑ 55 Fireblast C :R:	.75	2.00
❑ 56 Fireball U :R:	.20	.50
❑ 57 Demonfire R :R:	.50	1.25
❑ 58 Keldon Megaliths U	.25	.60
❑ 59 Mountain L	.10	.25
❑ 60 Mountain L	.10	.25
❑ 61 Mountain L	.10	.25
❑ 62 Mountain L	.10	.25

2008 Magic the Gathering Morningtide

Card	Low	High
Complete Set (150)	120.00	200.00
Booster Box (36 Packs)	175.00	275.00
Booster Pack (15 Cards)	5.00	8.00
Theme Deck	10.00	20.00
Fat Pack	40.00	80.00
❑ 1 Ambassador Oak C :G:	.10	.25
❑ 2 Auntie's Snitch R :K:	.25	.60
❑ 3 Ballyrush Banneret C :W:	.15	.40
❑ 4 Battletide Alchemist R :W:	.25	.60
❑ 5 Bitterblossom R :K:	6.00	15.00
❑ 6 Blightsoil Druid C :K:	.10	.25
❑ 7 Boldwyr Heavyweights R :R:	.25	.60
❑ 8 Boldwyr Intimidator U :R:	.15	.40
❑ 9 Borderland Behemoth R :R:	.25	.60
❑ 10 Bosk Banneret C :G:	.15	.40
❑ 11 Bramblewood Paragon U :G:	.60	1.50
❑ 12 Brighthearth Banneret C :R:	.10	.25
❑ 13 Burrenton Bombardier C :W:	.10	.25
❑ 14 Burrenton Shield-Bearers C :W:	.10	.25
❑ 15 Cenn's Tactician U :W:	.20	.50
❑ 16 Chameleon Colossus R :G:	1.50	4.00
❑ 17 Changeling Sentinel C :W:	.10	.25
❑ 18 Cloak and Dagger U :A:	.20	.50
❑ 19 Coordinated Barrage C :W:	.10	.25
❑ 20 Countryside Crusher R :R:	1.00	2.50
❑ 21 Cream of the Crop R :G:	.25	.60
❑ 22 Daily Regimen U :W:	.15	.40
❑ 23 Declaration of Naught R :B:	.25	.60
❑ 24 Deglamer C :G:	.10	.25
❑ 25 Dewdrop Spy C :B:	.10	.25
❑ 26 Disperse C :B:	.10	.25
❑ 27 Distant Melody C :B:	.10	.25
❑ 28 Diviner's Wand U :A:	.15	.40
❑ 29 Door of Destinies R :A:	4.00	10.00
❑ 30 Earthbrawn C :G:	.10	.25
❑ 31 Earwig Squad R :K:	.60	1.50
❑ 32 Elvish Warrior C :G:	.10	.25
❑ 33 Everbark Shaman C :G:	.10	.25
❑ 34 Fencer Clique C :B:	.10	.25
❑ 35 Fendeep Summoner R :K:	.25	.60
❑ 36 Fertilid C :G:	.10	.25
❑ 37 Festercreep C :K:	.10	.25
❑ 38 Feudkiller's Verdict R :W:	.25	.60
❑ 39 Final-Sting Faerie C :K:	.10	.25
❑ 40 Fire Juggler C :R:	.10	.25
❑ 41 Floodchaser C :B:	.10	.25
❑ 42 Forfend C :W:	.10	.25
❑ 43 Frogtosser Banneret C :K:	.10	.25
❑ 44 Game-Trail Changeling C :G:	.10	.25
❑ 45 Gilt-Leaf Archdruid R :G:	.40	1.00
❑ 46 Graceful Reprieve U :W:	.15	.40
❑ 47 Greatbow Doyen R :G:	.25	.60
❑ 48 Grimoire Thief R :B:	1.25	3.00
❑ 49 Heritage Druid U :G:	1.00	2.50
❑ 50 Hostile Realm C :R:	.10	.25
❑ 51 Hunting Triad U :G:	.15	.40
❑ 52 Idyllic Tutor R :W:	2.50	6.00
❑ 53 Indomitable Ancients R :W:	.60	1.50
❑ 54 Ink Dissolver C :B:	.10	.25
❑ 55 Inspired Sprite U :B:	.15	.40
❑ 56 Kindled Fury C :R:	.10	.25
❑ 57 Kinsbaile Borderguard R :W:	.60	1.50
❑ 58 Kinsbaile Cavalier R :W:	1.50	4.00
❑ 59 Kithkin Zephyrnaut C :W:	.10	.25
❑ 60 Knowledge Exploitation R :B:	.25	.60
❑ 61 Latchkey Faerie C :B:	.10	.25
❑ 62 Leaf-Crowned Elder R :G:	1.50	4.00
❑ 63 Lightning Crafter R :R:	.75	2.00
❑ 64 Luminescent Rain C :G:	.10	.25
❑ 65 Lunk Errant C :R:	.10	.25
❑ 66 Lys Alana Bowmaster C :G:	.10	.25
❑ 67 Maralen of the Mornsong R :K:	.30	.75
❑ 68 Meadowboon U :W:	.15	.40
❑ 69 Merrow Witsniper C :B:	.10	.25
❑ 70 Mind Shatter R :K:	.25	.60
❑ 71 Mind Spring R :B:	.25	.60
❑ 72 Moonglove Changeling C :K:	.10	.25
❑ 73 Morsel Theft C :K:	.10	.25
❑ 74 Mosquito Guard C :W:	.10	.25
❑ 75 Mothdust Changeling C :B:	.10	.25
❑ 76 Mudbutton Clanger C :R:	.10	.25
❑ 77 Murmuring Bosk R :L:	2.00	5.00
❑ 78 Mutavault R :L:	12.00	30.00
❑ 79 Negate C :B:	.15	.40
❑ 80 Nevermaker U :B:	.15	.40
❑ 81 Nightshade Schemers U :K:	.15	.40
❑ 82 Noggin Whack U :K:	.20	.50
❑ 83 Notorious Throng R :B:	.25	.60
❑ 84 Obsidian Battle-Axe U :A:	.20	.50
❑ 85 Offalsnout U :K:	.15	.40
❑ 86 Oona's Blackguard U :K:	.20	.50
❑ 87 Orchard Warden U :G:	.15	.40
❑ 88 Order of the Golden Cricket C :W:	.10	.25
❑ 89 Pack's Disdain C :K:	.10	.25
❑ 90 Preeminent Captain R :W:	2.50	6.00
❑ 91 Prickly Boggart C :K:	.10	.25
❑ 92 Primal Beyond R :L:	.60	1.50
❑ 93 Pulling Teeth C :K:	.10	.25
❑ 94 Pyroclast Consul U :R:	.15	.40
❑ 95 Rage Forger U :R:	.15	.40
❑ 96 Reach of Branches R :G:	.25	.60
❑ 97 Recross the Paths U :G:	.15	.40
❑ 98 Redeem the Lost U :W:	.15	.40
❑ 99 Reins of the Vinesteed C :G:	.10	.25
❑ 100 Release the Ants U :R:	.15	.40
❑ 101 Research the Deep U :B:	.15	.40
❑ 102 Reveillark R :W:	2.00	5.00
❑ 103 Revive the Fallen U :K:	.15	.40
❑ 104 Rhys the Exiled R :G:	.60	1.50
❑ 105 Rivals' Duel U :R:	.15	.40
❑ 106 Roar of the Crowd C :R:	.10	.25
❑ 107 Rustic Clachan R :L:	.30	.75
❑ 108 Sage of Fables U :B:	.20	.50
❑ 109 Sage's Dousing U :B:	.20	.50
❑ 110 Scapeshift R :G:	1.50	4.00
❑ 111 Scarblade Elite R :K:	.25	.60
❑ 112 Seething Pathblazer C :R:	.10	.25
❑ 113 Sensation Gorger R :R:	.25	.60
❑ 114 Shard Volley C :R:	.15	.40
❑ 115 Shared Animosity R :R:	.25	.60
❑ 116 Shinewend C :W:	.10	.25
❑ 117 Sigil Tracer R :B:	.40	1.00
❑ 118 Slithermuse R :B:	.25	.60
❑ 119 Spitebellows U :R:	.15	.40
❑ 120 Squeaking Pie Grubfellows C :K:	.10	.25
❑ 121 Stenchskipper R :K:	.25	.60
❑ 122 Stingmoggie C :R:	.10	.25
❑ 123 Stinkdrinker Bandit U :K:	.15	.40
❑ 124 Stomping Slabs U :R:	.15	.40
❑ 125 Stonehewer Giant R :W:	2.50	6.00
❑ 126 Stonybrook Banneret C :B:	.20	.50
❑ 127 Stonybrook Schoolmaster C :W:	.10	.25
❑ 128 Stream of Unconsciousness C :B:	.10	.25
❑ 129 Sunflare Shaman C :R:	.10	.25
❑ 130 Supreme Exemplar R :B:	.25	.60
❑ 131 Swell of Courage U :W:	.15	.40
❑ 132 Taurean Mauler R :R:	.75	2.00
❑ 133 Thieves' Fortune U :B:	.15	.40
❑ 134 Thornbite Staff U :A:	.15	.40
❑ 135 Titan's Revenge R :R:	.25	.60
❑ 136 Unstoppable Ash R :G:	.30	.75
❑ 137 Vendilion Clique R :B:	12.00	30.00
❑ 138 Vengeful Firebrand R :R:	.25	.60
❑ 139 Veteran's Armaments U :A:	.20	.50
❑ 140 Violet Pall C :K:	.10	.25
❑ 141 Walker of the Grove U :G:	.15	.40
❑ 142 Wandering Graybeard U :W:	.15	.40
❑ 143 Warren Weirding U :K:	.10	.25
❑ 144 War-Spike Changeling C :R:	.20	.50
❑ 145 Waterspout Weavers U :B:	.15	.40
❑ 146 Weed-Pruner Poplar C :K:	.10	.25
❑ 147 Weight of Conscience C :W:	.10	.25
❑ 148 Weirding Shaman R :K:	.25	.60
❑ 149 Winnower Patrol C :G:	.10	.25
❑ 150 Wolf-Skull Shaman U :G:	.25	.60

2008 Magic the Gathering Morningtide Foil

Card	Low	High
Complete Set (150)	200.00	300.00
*Foil: .8X to 2X Basic Cards		
❑ 1 Ambassador Oak C :G:	.20	.50
❑ 2 Auntie's Snitch R :K:	.50	1.25
❑ 3 Ballyrush Banneret C :W:	.30	.75
❑ 4 Battletide Alchemist R :W:	.50	1.25
❑ 5 Bitterblossom R :K:	12.00	30.00
❑ 6 Blightsoil Druid C :K:	.20	.50
❑ 7 Boldwyr Heavyweights R :R:	.50	1.25
❑ 8 Boldwyr Intimidator U :R:	.30	.75
❑ 9 Borderland Behemoth R :R:	.50	1.25
❑ 10 Bosk Banneret C :G:	.30	.75
❑ 11 Bramblewood Paragon U :G:	1.25	3.00
❑ 12 Brighthearth Banneret C :R:	.20	.50
❑ 13 Burrenton Bombardier C :W:	.20	.50
❑ 14 Burrenton Shield-Bearers C :W:	.20	.50
❑ 15 Cenn's Tactician U :W:	.40	1.00
❑ 16 Chameleon Colossus R :G:	3.00	8.00
❑ 17 Changeling Sentinel C :W:	.20	.50
❑ 18 Cloak and Dagger U :A:	.40	1.00
❑ 19 Coordinated Barrage C :W:	.20	.50
❑ 20 Countryside Crusher R :R:	2.00	5.00
❑ 21 Cream of the Crop R :G:	.50	1.25
❑ 22 Daily Regimen U :W:	.30	.75
❑ 23 Declaration of Naught R :B:	.50	1.25
❑ 24 Deglamer C :G:	.20	.50
❑ 25 Dewdrop Spy C :B:	.20	.50
❑ 26 Disperse C :B:	.20	.50
❑ 27 Distant Melody C :B:	.20	.50
❑ 28 Diviner's Wand U :A:	.30	.75
❑ 29 Door of Destinies R :A:	8.00	20.00
❑ 30 Earthbrawn C :G:	.20	.50
❑ 31 Earwig Squad R :K:	1.25	3.00
❑ 32 Elvish Warrior C :G:	.20	.50
❑ 33 Everbark Shaman C :G:	.20	.50
❑ 34 Fencer Clique C :B:	.20	.50
❑ 35 Fendeep Summoner R :K:	.50	1.25
❑ 36 Fertilid C :G:	.20	.50
❑ 37 Festercreep C :K:	.20	.50
❑ 38 Feudkiller's Verdict R :W:	.50	1.25

Card	Low	High
❑ 39 Final-Sting Faerie C :K:	.20	.50
❑ 40 Fire Juggler C :R:	.20	.50
❑ 41 Floodchaser C :B:	.20	.50
❑ 42 Forfend C :W:	.20	.50
❑ 43 Frogtosser Banneret C :K:	.20	.50
❑ 44 Game-Trail Changeling C :G:	.20	.50
❑ 45 Gilt-Leaf Archdruid R :G:	.75	2.00
❑ 46 Graceful Reprieve U :W:	.30	.75
❑ 47 Greatbow Doyen R :G:	.50	1.25
❑ 48 Grimoire Thief R :B:	2.50	6.00
❑ 49 Heritage Druid U :G:	2.00	5.00
❑ 50 Hostile Realm C :R:	.20	.50
❑ 51 Hunting Triad U :G:	.30	.75
❑ 52 Idyllic Tutor R :W:	5.00	12.00
❑ 53 Indomitable Ancients R :W:	1.25	3.00
❑ 54 Ink Dissolver C :B:	.20	.50
❑ 55 Inspired Sprite U :B:	.30	.75
❑ 56 Kindled Fury C :R:	.20	.50
❑ 57 Kinsbaile Borderguard R :W:	1.25	3.00
❑ 58 Kinsbaile Cavalier R :W:	3.00	8.00
❑ 59 Kithkin Zephyrnaut C :W:	.20	.50
❑ 60 Knowledge Exploitation R :B:	.50	1.25
❑ 61 Latchkey Faerie C :B:	.20	.50
❑ 62 Leaf-Crowned Elder R :G:	3.00	8.00
❑ 63 Lightning Crafter R :R:	1.50	4.00
❑ 64 Luminescent Rain C :G:	.20	.50
❑ 65 Lunk Errant C :R:	.20	.50
❑ 66 Lys Alana Bowmaster C :G:	.20	.50
❑ 67 Maralen of the Mornsong R :K:	.60	1.50
❑ 68 Meadowboon U :W:	.30	.75
❑ 69 Merrow Witsniper C :B:	.20	.50
❑ 70 Mind Shatter R :K:	.50	1.25
❑ 71 Mind Spring R :B:	.50	1.25
❑ 72 Moonglove Changeling C :K:	.20	.50
❑ 73 Morsel Theft C :K:	.20	.50
❑ 74 Mosquito Guard C :W:	.20	.50
❑ 75 Mothdust Changeling C :B:	.20	.50
❑ 76 Mudbutton Clanger C :R:	.20	.50
❑ 77 Murmuring Bosk R :L:	4.00	10.00
❑ 78 Mutavault R :L:	25.00	60.00
❑ 79 Negate C :B:	.30	.75
❑ 80 Nevermaker U :B:	.30	.75
❑ 81 Nightshade Schemers U :K:	.30	.75
❑ 82 Noggin Whack U :K:	.40	1.00
❑ 83 Notorious Throng R :B:	.50	1.25
❑ 84 Obsidian Battle-Axe U :A:	.40	1.00
❑ 85 Offalsnout U :K:	.30	.75
❑ 86 Oona's Blackguard U :K:	.40	1.00
❑ 87 Orchard Warden U :G:	.30	.75
❑ 88 Order of the Golden Cricket C :W:	.20	.50
❑ 89 Pack's Disdain C :K:	.20	.50
❑ 90 Preeminent Captain R :W:	5.00	12.00
❑ 91 Prickly Boggart C :K:	.20	.50
❑ 92 Primal Beyond R :L:	1.25	3.00
❑ 93 Pulling Teeth C :K:	.20	.50
❑ 94 Pyroclast Consul U :R:	.30	.75
❑ 95 Rage Forger U :R:	.30	.75
❑ 96 Reach of Branches R :G:	.50	1.25
❑ 97 Recross the Paths U :G:	.30	.75
❑ 98 Redeem the Lost U :W:	.30	.75
❑ 99 Reins of the Vinesteed C :G:	.20	.50
❑ 100 Release the Ants U :R:	.30	.75
❑ 101 Research the Deep U :B:	.30	.75
❑ 102 Reveillark R :W:	4.00	10.00
❑ 103 Revive the Fallen U :K:	.30	.75
❑ 104 Rhys the Exiled R :G:	1.25	3.00
❑ 105 Rivals' Duel U :R:	.30	.75
❑ 106 Roar of the Crowd C :R:	.20	.50
❑ 107 Rustic Clachan R :L:	.60	1.50
❑ 108 Sage of Fables U :B:	.40	1.00
❑ 109 Sage's Dousing U :B:	.40	1.00
❑ 110 Scapeshift R :G:	3.00	8.00
❑ 111 Scarblade Elite R :K:	.50	1.25
❑ 112 Seething Pathblazer C :R:	.20	.50
❑ 113 Sensation Gorger R :R:	.50	1.25
❑ 114 Shard Volley C :R:	.30	.75
❑ 115 Shared Animosity R :R:	.50	1.25
❑ 116 Shinewend C :W:	.20	.50
❑ 117 Sigil Tracer R :B:	.75	2.00
❑ 118 Slithermuse R :B:	.50	1.25
❑ 119 Spitebellows U :R:	.30	.75
❑ 120 Squeaking Pie Grubfellows C :K:	.20	.50
❑ 121 Stenchskipper R :K:	.50	1.25
❑ 122 Stingmoggie C :R:	.20	.50
❑ 123 Stinkdrinker Bandit U :K:	.30	.75
❑ 124 Stomping Slabs U :R:	.30	.75
❑ 125 Stonehewer Giant R :W:	5.00	12.00
❑ 126 Stonybrook Banneret C :B:	.40	1.00
❑ 127 Stonybrook Schoolmaster C :W:	.20	.50
❑ 128 Stream of Unconsciousness C :B:	.20	.50
❑ 129 Sunflare Shaman C :R:	.20	.50
❑ 130 Supreme Exemplar R :B:	.50	1.25
❑ 131 Swell of Courage U :W:	.30	.75
❑ 132 Taurean Mauler R :R:	1.50	4.00
❑ 133 Thieves' Fortune U :B:	.30	.75
❑ 134 Thornbite Staff U :A:	.30	.75
❑ 135 Titan's Revenge R :R:	.50	1.25
❑ 136 Unstoppable Ash R :G:	.60	1.50
❑ 137 Vendilion Clique R :B:	25.00	60.00
❑ 138 Vengeful Firebrand R :R:	.50	1.25
❑ 139 Veteran's Armaments U :A:	.40	1.00
❑ 140 Violet Pall C :K:	.20	.50
❑ 141 Walker of the Grove U :G:	.30	.75
❑ 142 Wandering Graybeard U :W:	.30	.75
❑ 143 Warren Weirding U :K:	.20	.50
❑ 144 War-Spike Changeling C :R:	.40	1.00
❑ 145 Waterspout Weavers U :B:	.30	.75
❑ 146 Weed-Pruner Poplar C :K:	.20	.50
❑ 147 Weight of Conscience C :W:	.20	.50
❑ 148 Weirding Shaman R :K:	.50	1.25
❑ 149 Winnower Patrol C :G:	.20	.50
❑ 150 Wolf-Skull Shaman U :G:	.50	1.25

2008 Magic the Gathering Shadowmoor

Card	Low	High
Complete Set (301)	150.00	225.00
Booster Box (36 Packs)	150.00	225.00
Booster Pack (15 Cards)	5.00	8.00
Theme Deck	20.00	40.00
Fat Pack	50.00	100.00
❑ 1 Advice from the Fae U :B:	.15	.40
❑ 2 AEthertow C :W: :B:	.10	.25
❑ 3 Aphotic Wisps C :K:	.10	.25
❑ 4 Apothecary Initiate C :W:	.10	.25
❑ 5 Armored Ascension U :W:	.15	.40
❑ 6 Ashenmoor Cohort C :K:	.10	.25
❑ 7 Ashenmoor Gouger U :K: :R:	.15	.40
❑ 8 Ashenmoor Liege R :K: :R:	1.50	4.00
❑ 9 Augury Adept R :W: :B:	.60	1.50
❑ 10 Ballynock Cohort C :W:	.10	.25
❑ 11 Barkshell Blessing C :G: :W:	.10	.25
❑ 12 Barrenton Cragtreads C :W: :B:	.10	.25
❑ 13 Barrenton Medic C :W:	.10	.25
❑ 14 Beseech the Queen U :K:	.60	1.50
❑ 15 Biting Tether U :B:	.15	.40
❑ 16 Blazethorn Scarecrow C :A:	.10	.25
❑ 17 Blight Sickle C :A:	.10	.25
❑ 18 Blistering Dieflyn C :R:	.10	.25
❑ 19 Bloodmark Mentor U :R:	.15	.40
❑ 20 Bloodshed Fever C :R:	.10	.25
❑ 21 Blowfly Infestation U :K:	.15	.40
❑ 22 Boartusk Liege R :R: :G:	1.50	4.00
❑ 23 Boggart Arsonists C :R:	.10	.25
❑ 24 Boggart Ram-Gang U :R: :G:	.60	1.50
❑ 25 Boon Reflection R :W:	1.25	3.00
❑ 26 Briarberry Cohort C :B:	.10	.25
❑ 27 Burn Trail C :R:	.10	.25
❑ 28 Cauldron of Souls R :A:	.75	2.00
❑ 29 Cemetery Puca R :B: :K:	.30	.75
❑ 30 Cerulean Wisps C :B:	.10	.25
❑ 31 Chainbreaker C :A:	.10	.25
❑ 32 Cinderbones C :K:	.10	.25
❑ 33 Cinderhaze Wretch C :K:	.10	.25
❑ 34 Consign to Dream C :B:	.10	.25
❑ 35 Corrosive Mentor U :K:	.15	.40
❑ 36 Corrupt U :K:	.15	.40
❑ 37 Counterbore R :B:	.40	1.00
❑ 38 Crabapple Cohort C :G:	.10	.25
❑ 39 Cragganwick Cremator R :R:	.25	.60
❑ 40 Crimson Wisps C :R:	.10	.25
❑ 41 Crowd of Cinders U :K:	.15	.40
❑ 42 Cultbrand Cinder C :K: :R:	.10	.25
❑ 43 Curse of Chains C :W: :B:	.10	.25
❑ 44 Cursecatcher U :B:	1.50	4.00
❑ 45 Dawnglow Infusion U :G: :W:	.15	.40
❑ 46 Deepchannel Mentor U :B:	.20	.50
❑ 47 Deep-Slumber Titan R :R:	.25	.60
❑ 48 Demigod of Revenge R :K: :R:	2.50	6.00
❑ 49 Deus of Calamity R :R: :G:	1.50	4.00
❑ 50 Devoted Druid C :G:	.20	.50
❑ 51 Din of the Fireherd R :K: :R:	.25	.60
❑ 52 Dire Undercurrents R :B: :K:	.30	.75
❑ 53 Disturbing Plot C :K:	.10	.25
❑ 54 Dramatic Entrance R :G:	.30	.75
❑ 55 Dream Salvage U :B: :K:	.15	.40
❑ 56 Drove of Elves U :G:	.75	2.00
❑ 57 Drowner Initiate C :B:	.10	.25
❑ 58 Dusk Urchins R :K:	.40	1.00
❑ 59 Elemental Mastery R :R:	.30	.75
❑ 60 Elsewhere Flask C :A:	.10	.25
❑ 61 Elvish Hexhunter C :G: :W:	.10	.25
❑ 62 Ember Gale C :R:	.10	.25
❑ 63 Emberstrike Duo C :K: :R:	.10	.25
❑ 64 Enchanted Evening R :W: :B:	.60	1.50
❑ 65 Everlasting Torment R :K: :R:	.75	2.00
❑ 66 Faerie Macabre C :K:	.15	.40
❑ 67 Faerie Swarm U :B:	.15	.40
❑ 68 Farhaven Elf C :G:	.15	.40
❑ 69 Fate Transfer C :B: :K:	.10	.25
❑ 70 Fire-Lit Thicket R :L:	1.50	4.00
❑ 71 Firespout U :R: :G:	.75	2.00
❑ 72 Fists of the Demigod C :K: :R:	.10	.25
❑ 73 Flame Javelin U :R:	.40	1.00
❑ 74 Flourishing Defenses U :G:	.15	.40
❑ 75 Flow of Ideas U :B:	.15	.40
❑ 76 Forest L :L:	.10	.25
❑ 77 Forest L :L:	.10	.25
❑ 78 Forest L :L:	.10	.25
❑ 79 Forest L :L:	.10	.25
❑ 80 Fossil Find U :R: :G:	.15	.40
❑ 81 Foxfire Oak C :G:	.10	.25
❑ 82 Fracturing Gust R :G: :W:	.50	1.25
❑ 83 Fulminator Mage R :K: :R:	1.50	4.00
❑ 84 Furystoke Giant R :R:	.25	.60
❑ 85 Ghastlord of Fugue R :B: :K:	1.25	3.00
❑ 86 Ghastly Discovery C :B:	.10	.25
❑ 87 Giantbaiting C :R: :G:	.10	.25
❑ 88 Glamer Spinners U :W: :B:	.15	.40
❑ 89 Gleeful Sabotage C :G:	.10	.25
❑ 90 Glen Elendra Liege R :B: :K:	1.50	4.00
❑ 91 Gloomlance C :K:	.10	.25
❑ 92 Gloomwidow U :G:	.15	.40
❑ 93 Gloomwidow's Feast C :G:	.10	.25
❑ 94 Gnarled Effigy U :A:	.15	.40
❑ 95 Godhead of Awe R :W: :B:	.75	2.00
❑ 96 Goldenglow Moth C :W:	.10	.25
❑ 97 Gravelgill Axeshark C :B: :K:	.10	.25
❑ 98 Gravelgill Duo C :B: :K:	.10	.25
❑ 99 Graven Cairns R :L:	1.50	4.00
❑ 100 Greater Auramancy R :W:	2.50	6.00
❑ 101 Grief Tyrant U :K: :R:	.15	.40
❑ 102 Grim Poppet R :A:	.30	.75
❑ 103 Guttural Response U :R: :G:	.40	1.00
❑ 104 Heap Doll U :A:	.15	.40
❑ 105 Heartmender R :G: :W:	.50	1.25
❑ 106 Helm of the Ghastlord C :B: :K:	.10	.25
❑ 107 Hollowborn Barghest R :K:	.25	.60
❑ 108 Hollowsage U :K:	.15	.40
❑ 109 Horde of Boggarts U :R:	.15	.40
❑ 110 Howl of the Night Pack U :G:	.15	.40
❑ 111 Hungry Spriggan C :G:	.10	.25
❑ 112 Illuminated Folio U :A:	.15	.40
❑ 113 Impromptu Raid R :R: :G:	.25	.60
❑ 114 Incremental Blight U :K:	.15	.40
❑ 115 Inescapable Brute C :R:	.10	.25
❑ 116 Inkfathom Infiltrator U :B: :K:	.30	.75
❑ 117 Inkfathom Witch U :B: :K:	.15	.40
❑ 118 Inquisitor's Snare C :W:	.10	.25
❑ 119 Intimidator Initiate C :R:	.10	.25
❑ 120 Island L :L:	.10	.25
❑ 121 Island L :L:	.10	.25
❑ 122 Island L :L:	.10	.25
❑ 123 Island L :L:	.10	.25
❑ 124 Isleback Spawn R :B:	.25	.60
❑ 125 Jaws of Stone U :R:	.15	.40
❑ 126 Juvenile Gloomwidow C :G:	.10	.25
❑ 127 Kinscaer Harpoonist C :B:	.10	.25
❑ 128 Kitchen Finks U :G: :W:	4.00	10.00
❑ 129 Kithkin Rabble U :W:	.15	.40
❑ 130 Kithkin Shielddare C :W:	.10	.25
❑ 131 Knacksaw Clique R :B:	.25	.60
❑ 132 Knollspine Dragon R :R:	.40	1.00
❑ 133 Knollspine Invocation R :R:	.25	.60
❑ 134 Kulrath Knight U :K: :R:	.40	1.00
❑ 135 Last Breath C :W:	.15	.40
❑ 136 Leech Bonder U :B:	.15	.40
❑ 137 Leechridden Swamp U :L:	.20	.50
❑ 138 Loamdragger Giant C :R: :G:	.10	.25
❑ 139 Loch Korrigan C :K:	.10	.25
❑ 140 Lockjaw Snapper U :A:	.15	.40
❑ 141 Lurebound Scarecrow U :A:	.15	.40
❑ 142 Madblind Mountain U :L:	.15	.40
❑ 143 Mana Reflection R :G:	2.50	6.00
❑ 144 Manaforge Cinder C :K: :R:	.10	.25
❑ 145 Manamorphose C :R: :G:	1.00	2.50
❑ 146 Mass Calcify R :W:	.40	1.00
❑ 147 Medicine Runner C :G: :W:	.10	.25
❑ 148 Memory Plunder R :B: :K:	.60	1.50
❑ 149 Memory Sluice C :B: :K:	.30	.75
❑ 150 Mercy Killing U :G: :W:	.20	.50
❑ 151 Merrow Grimeblotter U :B: :K:	.15	.40
❑ 152 Merrow Wavebreakers C :B:	.10	.25
❑ 153 Midnight Banshee R :K:	.60	1.50
❑ 154 Mine Excavation C :W:	.10	.25
❑ 155 Mirrorweave R :W: :B:	.40	1.00
❑ 156 Mistmeadow Skulk U :W:	.15	.40
❑ 157 Mistmeadow Witch U :W: :B:	.15	.40
❑ 158 Mistveil Plains U :L:	.30	.75
❑ 159 Moonring Island U :L:	.15	.40
❑ 160 Morselhoarder C :R: :G:	.10	.25
❑ 161 Mossbridge Troll R :G:	.30	.75
❑ 162 Mountain L :L:	.10	.25
❑ 163 Mountain L :L:	.10	.25
❑ 164 Mountain L :L:	.10	.25
❑ 165 Mountain L :L:	.10	.25
❑ 166 Mudbrawler Cohort C :R:	.10	.25
❑ 167 Mudbrawler Raiders C :R: :G:	.10	.25
❑ 168 Murderous Redcap U :K: :R:	.50	1.25
❑ 169 Mystic Gate R :L:	2.50	6.00
❑ 170 Niveous Wisps C :W:	.10	.25
❑ 171 Nurturer Initiate C :G:	.10	.25
❑ 172 Old Ghastbark C :G: :W:	.10	.25
❑ 173 Oona, Queen of the Fae R :B: :K:	2.00	5.00
❑ 174 Oona's Gatewarden C :B: :K:	.10	.25
❑ 175 Oracle of Nectars R :G: :W:	.75	2.00
❑ 176 Order of Whiteclay R :W:	.30	.75
❑ 177 Oversoul of Dusk R :G: :W:	1.25	3.00
❑ 178 Painter's Servant R :A:	2.50	6.00
❑ 179 Pale Wayfarer U :W:	.15	.40
❑ 180 Parapet Watchers C :B:	.10	.25
❑ 181 Pili-Pala C :A:	.15	.40
❑ 182 Plague of Vermin R :K:	.25	.60
❑ 183 Plains L :L:	.10	.25
❑ 184 Plains L :L:	.10	.25
❑ 185 Plains L :L:	.10	.25
❑ 186 Plains L :L:	.10	.25
❑ 187 Plumeveil U :W: :B:	.30	.75
❑ 188 Poison the Well C :K: :R:	.10	.25
❑ 189 Polluted Bonds R :K:	.40	1.00
❑ 190 Power of Fire C :R:	.10	.25
❑ 191 Presence of Gond C :G:	.10	.25
❑ 192 Prismatic Omen R :G:	1.50	4.00
❑ 193 Prismwake Merrow C :B:	.10	.25
❑ 194 Prison Term U :W:	.25	.60
❑ 195 Puca's Mischief R :B:	.25	.60
❑ 196 Puncture Bolt C :R:	.10	.25
❑ 197 Puppeteer Clique R :K:	.60	1.50
❑ 198 Puresight Merrow U :W: :B:	.15	.40
❑ 199 Put Away C :B:	.10	.25
❑ 200 Pyre Charger U :R:	.15	.40
❑ 201 Rage Reflection R :R:	.30	.75
❑ 202 Raking Canopy U :G:	.15	.40
❑ 203 Rattleblaze Scarecrow C :A:	.10	.25
❑ 204 Raven's Run Dragoon C :G: :W:	.10	.25
❑ 205 Reaper King R :A:	1.50	4.00
❑ 206 Reflecting Pool R :L:	4.00	10.00
❑ 207 Reknit U :G: :W:	.15	.40
❑ 208 Repel Intruders U :W: :B:	.15	.40
❑ 209 Resplendent Mentor U :W:	.15	.40
❑ 210 Revelsong Horn U :A:	.15	.40
❑ 211 Rhys the Redeemed R :G: :W:	3.00	8.00
❑ 212 Rite of Consumption C :K:	.10	.25
❑ 213 River Kelpie R :B:	.25	.60
❑ 214 River's Grasp U :B: :K:	.15	.40
❑ 215 Rosheen Meanderer R :R: :G:	.25	.60
❑ 216 Roughshod Mentor U :G:	.15	.40
❑ 217 Rune-Cervin Rider C :W:	.10	.25
❑ 218 Runed Halo R :W:	1.25	3.00
❑ 219 Runes of the Deus C :R: :G:	.10	.25
❑ 220 Rustrazor Butcher C :R:	.10	.25
❑ 221 Safehold Duo C :G: :W:	.10	.25
❑ 222 Safehold Elite C :G: :W:	.10	.25
❑ 223 Safehold Sentry C :W:	.10	.25
❑ 224 Safewright Quest C :G: :W:	.10	.25
❑ 225 Sapseep Forest U :L:	.15	.40
❑ 226 Savor the Moment R :B:	.50	1.25
❑ 227 Scar C :K: :R:	.10	.25
❑ 228 Scarscale Ritual C :B: :K:	.10	.25
❑ 229 Scrapbasket C :A:	.10	.25
❑ 230 Scuttlemutt C :A:	.15	.40
❑ 231 Scuzzback Marauders C :R: :G:	.10	.25
❑ 232 Scuzzback Scrapper C :R: :G:	.10	.25
❑ 233 Seedcradle Witch U :G: :W:	.15	.40
❑ 234 Shield of the Oversoul C :G: :W:	.30	.75
❑ 235 Sickle Ripper C :K:	.10	.25
❑ 236 Silkbind Faerie C :W: :B:	.10	.25
❑ 237 Sinking Feeling C :B:	.10	.25
❑ 238 Slinking Giant U :R:	.15	.40
❑ 239 Smash to Smithereens C :R:	.30	.75
❑ 240 Smolder Initiate C :K:	.10	.25
❑ 241 Somnomancer C :W: :B:	.10	.25
❑ 242 Sootstoke Kindler C :K: :R:	.10	.25
❑ 243 Sootwalkers C :K: :R:	.10	.25
❑ 244 Spawnwrithe R :G:	.25	.60
❑ 245 Spectral Procession U :W:	1.25	3.00
❑ 246 Spell Syphon C :B:	.10	.25
❑ 247 Spiteflame Witch U :K: :R:	.15	.40
❑ 248 Spiteful Visions R :K: :R:	.30	.75
❑ 249 Splitting Headache C :K:	.10	.25
❑ 250 Steel of the Godhead C :W: :B:	.20	.50
❑ 251 Strip Bare C :W:	.10	.25
❑ 252 Sunken Ruins R :L:	2.50	6.00
❑ 253 Swamp L :L:	.10	.25
❑ 254 Swamp L :L:	.10	.25
❑ 255 Swamp L :L:	.10	.25
❑ 256 Swamp L :L:	.10	.25
❑ 257 Swans of Bryn Argoll R :W: :B:	1.00	2.50
❑ 258 Sygg, River Cutthroat R :B: :K:	.75	2.00
❑ 259 Tatterkite U :A:	.15	.40
❑ 260 Tattermunge Duo C :R: :G:	.10	.25
❑ 261 Tattermunge Maniac U :R: :G:	.20	.50
❑ 262 Tattermunge Witch U :R: :G:	.15	.40
❑ 263 Thistledown Duo C :W: :B:	.10	.25
❑ 264 Thistledown Liege R :W: :B:	.60	1.50
❑ 265 Thornwatch Scarecrow C :A:	.10	.25
❑ 266 Thought Reflection R :B:	.30	.75
❑ 267 Thoughtweft Gambit U :W: :B:	.15	.40
❑ 268 Toil to Renown C :G:	.10	.25
❑ 269 Torpor Dust C :B: :K:	.10	.25
❑ 270 Torrent of Souls U :K: :R:	.15	.40
❑ 271 Torture C :K:	.10	.25
❑ 272 Tower Above U :G:	.15	.40
❑ 273 Traitor's Roar C :K: :R:	.10	.25
❑ 274 Trip Noose U :A:	.15	.40
❑ 275 Turn to Mist C :W: :B:	.10	.25
❑ 276 Twilight Shepherd R :W:	1.00	2.50
❑ 277 Tyrannize R :K: :R:	.25	.60
❑ 278 Umbral Mantle U :A:	.15	.40
❑ 279 Valleymaker R :R: :G:	.25	.60
❑ 280 Vexing Shusher R :R: :G:	1.25	3.00
❑ 281 Viridescent Wisps C :G:	.10	.25
❑ 282 Wanderbrine Rootcutters C :B: :K:	.10	.25
❑ 283 Wasp Lancer U :B: :K:	.15	.40
❑ 284 Watchwing Scarecrow C :A:	.10	.25
❑ 285 Wheel of Sun and Moon R :G: :W:	1.50	4.00
❑ 286 Whimwader C :B:	.10	.25
❑ 287 Wicker Warcrawler U :A:	.15	.40
❑ 288 Wild Swing U :R:	.15	.40
❑ 289 Wildslayer Elves C :G:	.10	.25
❑ 290 Wilt-Leaf Cavaliers U :G: :W:	.40	1.00
❑ 291 Wilt-Leaf Liege R :G: :W:	2.00	5.00
❑ 292 Windbrisk Raptor R :W:	.25	.60
❑ 293 Wingrattle Scarecrow C :A:	.10	.25
❑ 294 Witherscale Wurm R :G:	.25	.60
❑ 295 Woeleecher C :W:	.10	.25
❑ 296 Wooded Bastion R :L:	1.50	4.00
❑ 297 Woodfall Primus R :G:	3.00	8.00
❑ 298 Worldpurge R :W: :B:	.25	.60
❑ 299 Wort, the Raidmother R :R: :G:	.40	1.00
❑ 300 Wound Reflection R :K:	.30	.75
❑ 301 Zealous Guardian C :W: :B:	.10	.25

2008 Magic the Gathering Shadowmoor Foil

Card	Low	High
Complete Set (301)	250.00	350.00
*Foil: .8X to 2X Basic Cards		
❑ 1 Advice from the Fae U :B:	.50	1.25
❑ 2 AEthertow C :W: :B:	.30	.75
❑ 3 Aphotic Wisps C :K:	.30	.75
❑ 4 Apothecary Initiate C :W:	.30	.75
❑ 5 Armored Ascension U :W:	.40	1.00
❑ 6 Ashenmoor Cohort C :K:	.30	.75
❑ 7 Ashenmoor Gouger U :K: :R:	.60	1.50
❑ 8 Ashenmoor Liege R :K: :R:	2.50	6.00
❑ 9 Augury Adept R :W: :B:	2.50	6.00
❑ 10 Ballynock Cohort C :W:	.30	.75
❑ 11 Barkshell Blessing C :G: :W:	.30	.75
❑ 12 Barrenton Cragtreads C :W: :B:	.30	.75
❑ 13 Barrenton Medic C :W:	.30	.75
❑ 14 Beseech the Queen U :K:	1.50	4.00
❑ 15 Biting Tether U :B:	.30	.75
❑ 16 Blazethorn Scarecrow C :A:	.30	.75
❑ 17 Blight Sickle C :A:	.30	.75
❑ 18 Blistering Dieflyn C :R:	.30	.75
❑ 19 Bloodmark Mentor U :R:	.30	.75
❑ 20 Bloodshed Fever C :R:	.30	.75
❑ 21 Blowfly Infestation U :K:	.40	1.00
❑ 22 Boartusk Liege R :R: :G:	2.50	6.00
❑ 23 Boggart Arsonists C :R:	.30	.75
❑ 24 Boggart Ram-Gang U :R: :G:	1.50	4.00
❑ 25 Boon Reflection R :W:	1.50	4.00
❑ 26 Briarberry Cohort C :B:	.30	.75
❑ 27 Burn Trail C :R:	.30	.75
❑ 28 Cauldron of Souls R :A:	.40	1.00
❑ 29 Cemetery Puca R :B: :K:	1.25	3.00
❑ 30 Cerulean Wisps C :B:	.30	.75
❑ 31 Chainbreaker C :A:	.30	.75
❑ 32 Cinderbones C :K:	.30	.75
❑ 33 Cinderhaze Wretch C :K:	.30	.75
❑ 34 Consign to Dream C :B:	.30	.75
❑ 35 Corrosive Mentor U :K:	.30	.75
❑ 36 Corrupt U :K:	1.00	2.50
❑ 37 Counterbore R :B:	2.50	6.00
❑ 38 Crabapple Cohort C :G:	.30	.75
❑ 39 Cragganwick Cremator R :R:	.60	1.50
❑ 40 Crimson Wisps C :R:	.30	.75
❑ 41 Crowd of Cinders U :K:	.30	.75
❑ 42 Cultbrand Cinder C :K: :R:	.30	.75
❑ 43 Curse of Chains C :W: :B:	.30	.75
❑ 44 Cursecatcher U :B:	1.25	3.00
❑ 45 Dawnglow Infusion U :G: :W:	.60	1.50
❑ 46 Deepchannel Mentor U :B:	.30	.75
❑ 47 Deep-Slumber Titan R :R:	1.00	2.50
❑ 48 Demigod of Revenge R :K: :R:	8.00	20.00
❑ 49 Deus of Calamity R :R: :G:	3.00	8.00
❑ 50 Devoted Druid C :G:	.40	1.00
❑ 51 Din of the Fireherd R :K: :R:	1.25	3.00
❑ 52 Dire Undercurrents R :B: :K:	1.25	3.00
❑ 53 Disturbing Plot C :K:	.30	.75
❑ 54 Dramatic Entrance R :G:	1.50	4.00
❑ 55 Dream Salvage U :B: :K:	.50	1.25
❑ 56 Drove of Elves U :G:	1.00	2.50
❑ 57 Drowner Initiate C :B:	.30	.75
❑ 58 Dusk Urchins R :K:	4.00	10.00
❑ 59 Elemental Mastery R :R:	1.00	2.50
❑ 60 Elsewhere Flask C :A:	.30	.75
❑ 61 Elvish Hexhunter C :G: :W:	.30	.75
❑ 62 Ember Gale C :R:	.30	.75
❑ 63 Emberstrike Duo C :K: :R:	.30	.75
❑ 64 Enchanted Evening R :W: :B:	2.50	6.00
❑ 65 Everlasting Torment R :K: :R:	3.00	8.00
❑ 66 Faerie Macabre C :K:	1.00	2.50
❑ 67 Faerie Swarm U :B:	.30	.75
❑ 68 Farhaven Elf C :G:	.40	1.00
❑ 69 Fate Transfer C :B: :K:	.30	.75
❑ 70 Fire-Lit Thicket R :L:	4.00	10.00
❑ 71 Firespout U :R: :G:	2.00	5.00
❑ 72 Fists of the Demigod C :K: :R:	.30	.75
❑ 73 Flame Javelin U :R:	1.50	4.00
❑ 74 Flourishing Defenses U :G:	.30	.75
❑ 75 Flow of Ideas U :B:	.30	.75
❑ 76 Forest L :L:	.30	.75
❑ 77 Forest L :L:	.30	.75
❑ 78 Forest L :L:	.30	.75
❑ 79 Forest L :L:	.30	.75
❑ 80 Fossil Find U :R: :G:	.40	1.00
❑ 81 Foxfire Oak C :G:	.30	.75
❑ 82 Fracturing Gust R :G: :W:	1.50	4.00
❑ 83 Fulminator Mage R :K: :R:	4.00	10.00
❑ 84 Furystoke Giant R :R:	1.25	3.00
❑ 85 Ghastlord of Fugue R :B: :K:	1.50	4.00
❑ 86 Ghastly Discovery C :B:	.30	.75
❑ 87 Giantbaiting C :R: :G:	.30	.75
❑ 88 Glamer Spinners U :W: :B:	.30	.75
❑ 89 Gleeful Sabotage C :G:	.40	1.00
❑ 90 Glen Elendra Liege R :B: :K:	2.00	5.00
❑ 91 Gloomlance C :K:	.30	.75
❑ 92 Gloomwidow U :G:	.30	.75
❑ 93 Gloomwidow's Feast C :G:	.30	.75
❑ 94 Gnarled Effigy U :A:	.30	.75
❑ 95 Godhead of Awe R :W: :B:	2.50	6.00
❑ 96 Goldenglow Moth C :W:	.30	.75
❑ 97 Gravelgill Axeshark C :B: :K:	.30	.75
❑ 98 Gravelgill Duo C :B: :K:	.30	.75
❑ 99 Graven Cairns R :L:	3.00	8.00
❑ 100 Greater Auramancy R :W:	1.25	3.00
❑ 101 Grief Tyrant U :K: :R:	.30	.75
❑ 102 Grim Poppet R :A:	1.50	4.00
❑ 103 Guttural Response U :R: :G:	1.25	3.00
❑ 104 Heap Doll U :A:	.30	.75
❑ 105 Heartmender R :G: :W:	2.50	6.00
❑ 106 Helm of the Ghastlord C :B: :K:	.30	.75
❑ 107 Hollowborn Barghest R :K:	1.00	2.50
❑ 108 Hollowsage U :K:	.30	.75
❑ 109 Horde of Boggarts U :R:	.30	.75
❑ 110 Howl of the Night Pack U :G:	.40	1.00
❑ 111 Hungry Spriggan C :G:	.30	.75
❑ 112 Illuminated Folio U :A:	.30	.75
❑ 113 Impromptu Raid R :R: :G:	.60	1.50
❑ 114 Incremental Blight U :K:	.50	1.25
❑ 115 Inescapable Brute C :R:	.30	.75
❑ 116 Inkfathom Infiltrator U :B: :K:	.50	1.25

MAGIC

❑ 117 Inkfathom Witch U :B: :K: .30 .75
❑ 118 Inquisitor's Snare C :W: .30 .75
❑ 119 Intimidator Initiate C :R: .30 .75
❑ 120 Island L :L: .30 .75
❑ 121 Island L :L: .30 .75
❑ 122 Island L :L: .30 .75
❑ 123 Island L :L: .30 .75
❑ 124 Isleback Spawn R :B: .60 1.50
❑ 125 Jaws of Stone U :R: .30 .75
❑ 126 Juvenile Gloomwidow C :G: .30 .75
❑ 127 Kinscaer Harpoonist C :B: .30 .75
❑ 128 Kitchen Finks U :G: :W: 3.00 8.00
❑ 129 Kithkin Rabble U :W: .30 .75
❑ 130 Kithkin Shielddare C :W: .30 .75
❑ 131 Knacksaw Clique R :B: .75 2.00
❑ 132 Knollspine Dragon R :R: 1.50 4.00
❑ 133 Knollspine Invocation R :R: .40 1.00
❑ 134 Kulrath Knight U :K: :R: .40 1.00
❑ 135 Last Breath C :W: .30 .75
❑ 136 Leech Bonder U :B: .30 .75
❑ 137 Leechridden Swamp U :L: .50 1.25
❑ 138 Loamdragger Giant C :R: :G: .30 .75
❑ 139 Loch Korrigan C :K: .30 .75
❑ 140 Lockjaw Snapper U :A: .30 .75
❑ 141 Lurebound Scarecrow U :A: .30 .75
❑ 142 Madblind Mountain U :L: .30 .75
❑ 143 Mana Reflection R :G: 1.50 4.00
❑ 144 Manaforge Cinder C :K: :R: .30 .75
❑ 145 Manamorphose C :R: :G: 1.00 2.50
❑ 146 Mass Calcify R :W: .75 2.00
❑ 147 Medicine Runner C :G: :W: .30 .75
❑ 148 Memory Plunder R :B: :K: 2.00 5.00
❑ 149 Memory Sluice C :B: :K: .40 1.00
❑ 150 Mercy Killing U :G: :W: .40 1.00
❑ 151 Merrow Grimeblotter U :B: :K: .30 .75
❑ 152 Merrow Wavebreakers C :B: .30 .75
❑ 153 Midnight Banshee R :K: 1.50 4.00
❑ 154 Mine Excavation C :W: .30 .75
❑ 155 Mirrorweave R :W: :B: 2.50 6.00
❑ 156 Mistmeadow Skulk U :W: .40 1.00
❑ 157 Mistmeadow Witch U :W: :B: .50 1.25
❑ 158 Mistveil Plains U :L: .50 1.25
❑ 159 Moonring Island U :L: .40 1.00
❑ 160 Morselhoarder C :R: :G: .30 .75
❑ 161 Mossbridge Troll R :G: 1.00 2.50
❑ 162 Mountain L :L: .30 .75
❑ 163 Mountain L :L: .30 .75
❑ 164 Mountain L :L: .30 .75
❑ 165 Mountain L :L: .30 .75
❑ 166 Mudbrawler Cohort C :R: .30 .75
❑ 167 Mudbrawler Raiders C :R: :G: .30 .75
❑ 168 Murderous Redcap U :K: :R: 1.25 3.00
❑ 169 Mystic Gate R :L: 8.00 20.00
❑ 170 Niveous Wisps C :W: .30 .75
❑ 171 Nurturer Initiate C :G: .30 .75
❑ 172 Old Ghastbark C :G: :W: .30 .75
❑ 173 Oona, Queen of the Fae R :B: :K: 4.00 10.00
❑ 174 Oona's Gatewarden C :B: :K: .30 .75
❑ 175 Oracle of Nectars R :G: :W: 1.25 3.00
❑ 176 Order of Whiteclay R :W: 1.25 3.00
❑ 177 Oversoul of Dusk R :G: :W: 4.00 10.00
❑ 178 Painter's Servant R :A: 6.00 15.00
❑ 179 Pale Wayfarer U :W: .30 .75
❑ 180 Parapet Watchers C :B: .30 .75
❑ 181 Pili-Pala C :A: .30 .75
❑ 182 Plague of Vermin R :K: .60 1.50
❑ 183 Plains L :L: .30 .75
❑ 184 Plains L :L: .30 .75
❑ 185 Plains L :L: .30 .75
❑ 186 Plains L :L: .30 .75
❑ 187 Plumeveil U :W: :B: .60 1.50
❑ 188 Poison the Well C :K: :R: .30 .75
❑ 189 Polluted Bonds R :K: 1.00 2.50
❑ 190 Power of Fire C :R: .30 .75
❑ 191 Presence of Gond C :G: .30 .75
❑ 192 Prismatic Omen R :G: 3.00 8.00
❑ 193 Prismwake Merrow C :B: .30 .75
❑ 194 Prison Term U :W: .60 1.50
❑ 195 Puca's Mischief R :B: 1.25 3.00
❑ 196 Puncture Bolt C :R: .30 .75
❑ 197 Puppeteer Clique R :K: 3.00 8.00
❑ 198 Puresight Merrow U :W: :B: .30 .75
❑ 199 Put Away C :B: .30 .75
❑ 200 Pyre Charger U :R: .30 .75
❑ 201 Rage Reflection R :R: 1.00 2.50
❑ 202 Raking Canopy U :G: .50 1.25
❑ 203 Rattleblaze Scarecrow C :A: .30 .75
❑ 204 Raven's Run Dragoon C :G: :W: .30 .75
❑ 205 Reaper King R :A: 3.00 8.00
❑ 206 Reflecting Pool R :L: 15.00 30.00
❑ 207 Reknit U :G: :W: .30 .75
❑ 208 Repel Intruders U :W: :B: .30 .75
❑ 209 Resplendent Mentor U :W: .30 .75
❑ 210 Revelsong Horn U :A: .30 .75
❑ 211 Rhys the Redeemed R :G: :W: 2.00 5.00
❑ 212 Rite of Consumption C :K: .40 1.00
❑ 213 River Kelpie R :B: 1.50 4.00
❑ 214 River's Grasp U :B: :K: .30 .75
❑ 215 Rosheen Meanderer R :R: :G: 1.25 3.00
❑ 216 Roughshod Mentor U :G: .30 .75
❑ 217 Rune-Cervin Rider C :W: .30 .75
❑ 218 Runed Halo R :W: 3.00 8.00
❑ 219 Runes of the Deus C :R: :G: .30 .75
❑ 220 Rustrazor Butcher C :R: .30 .75
❑ 221 Safehold Duo C :G: :W: .30 .75
❑ 222 Safehold Elite C :G: :W: .30 .75
❑ 223 Safehold Sentry C :W: .30 .75
❑ 224 Safewright Quest C :G: :W: .30 .75
❑ 225 Sapseep Forest U :L: .40 1.00
❑ 226 Savor the Moment R :B: 1.00 2.50
❑ 227 Scar C :K: :R: .30 .75
❑ 228 Scarscale Ritual C :B: :K: .30 .75
❑ 229 Scrapbasket C :A: .30 .75
❑ 230 Scuttlemutt C :A: .30 .75
❑ 231 Scuzzback Marauders C :R: :G: .30 .75
❑ 232 Scuzzback Scrapper C :R: :G: .30 .75
❑ 233 Seedcradle Witch U :G: :W: .30 .75
❑ 234 Shield of the Oversoul C :G: :W: .50 1.25
❑ 235 Sickle Ripper C :K: .30 .75
❑ 236 Silkbind Faerie C :W: :B: .30 .75
❑ 237 Sinking Feeling C :B: .30 .75
❑ 238 Slinking Giant U :R: .30 .75
❑ 239 Smash to Smithereens C :R: .50 1.25
❑ 240 Smolder Initiate C :K: .30 .75
❑ 241 Somnomancer C :W: :B: .30 .75
❑ 242 Sootstoke Kindler C :K: :R: .30 .75
❑ 243 Sootwalkers C :K: :R: .30 .75
❑ 244 Spawnwrithe R :G: 1.50 4.00
❑ 245 Spectral Procession U :W: 1.25 3.00
❑ 246 Spell Syphon C :B: .30 .75
❑ 247 Spiteflame Witch U :K: :R: .30 .75
❑ 248 Spiteful Visions R :K: :R: .60 1.50
❑ 249 Splitting Headache C :K: .30 .75
❑ 250 Steel of the Godhead C :W: :B: .40 1.00
❑ 251 Strip Bare C :W: .30 .75
❑ 252 Sunken Ruins R :L: 6.00 15.00
❑ 253 Swamp L :L: .30 .75
❑ 254 Swamp L :L: .30 .75
❑ 255 Swamp L :L: .30 .75
❑ 256 Swamp L :L: .30 .75
❑ 257 Swans of Bryn Argoll R :W: :B: 4.00 10.00
❑ 258 Sygg, River Cutthroat R :B: :K: 1.25 3.00
❑ 259 Tatterkite U :A: .30 .75
❑ 260 Tattermunge Duo C :R: :G: .30 .75
❑ 261 Tattermunge Maniac U :R: :G: 2.00 5.00
❑ 262 Tattermunge Witch U :R: :G: .30 .75
❑ 263 Thistledown Duo C :W: :B: .30 .75
❑ 264 Thistledown Liege R :W: :B: 2.00 5.00
❑ 265 Thornwatch Scarecrow C :A: .30 .75
❑ 266 Thought Reflection R :B: .40 1.00
❑ 267 Thoughtweft Gambit U :W: :B: .30 .75
❑ 268 Toil to Renown C :G: .30 .75
❑ 269 Torpor Dust C :B: :K: .30 .75
❑ 270 Torrent of Souls U :K: :R: .50 1.25
❑ 271 Torture C :K: .30 .75
❑ 272 Tower Above U :G: .50 1.25
❑ 273 Traitor's Roar C :K: :R: .30 .75
❑ 274 Trip Noose U :A: .30 .75
❑ 275 Turn to Mist C :W: :B: .30 .75
❑ 276 Twilight Shepherd R :W: 4.00 10.00
❑ 277 Tyrannize R :K: :R: 1.00 2.50
❑ 278 Umbral Mantle U :A: .30 .75
❑ 279 Valleymaker R :R: :G: 1.00 2.50
❑ 280 Vexing Shusher R :R: :G: 4.00 10.00
❑ 281 Viridescent Wisps C :G: .30 .75
❑ 282 Wanderbrine Rootcutters C :B: :K: .30 .75
❑ 283 Wasp Lancer U :B: :K: .40 1.00
❑ 284 Watchwing Scarecrow C :A: .30 .75
❑ 285 Wheel of Sun and Moon R :G: :W: 2.50 6.00
❑ 286 Whimwader C :B: .30 .75
❑ 287 Wicker Warcrawler U :A: .30 .75
❑ 288 Wild Swing U :R: .30 .75
❑ 289 Wildslayer Elves C :G: .30 .75
❑ 290 Wilt-Leaf Cavaliers U :G: :W: .75 2.00
❑ 291 Wilt-Leaf Liege R :G: :W: 6.00 15.00
❑ 292 Windbrisk Raptor R :W: 1.00 2.50
❑ 293 Wingrattle Scarecrow C :A: .30 .75
❑ 294 Witherscale Wurm R :G: .60 1.50
❑ 295 Woeleecher C :W: .30 .75
❑ 296 Wooded Bastion R :L: 6.00 15.00
❑ 297 Woodfall Primus R :G: 1.25 3.00
❑ 298 Worldpurge R :W: :B: 1.00 2.50
❑ 299 Wort, the Raidmother R :R: :G: 1.50 4.00
❑ 300 Wound Reflection R :K: 1.25 3.00
❑ 301 Zealous Guardian C :W: :B: .30 .75

2008 Magic the Gathering Eventide

Complete Set (180) 150.00 250.00
Booster Box (36 Packs) 100.00 175.00
Booster Pack (15 Cards) 3.50 5.00
Theme Deck 10.00 20.00
Fat Pack 40.00 80.00

❑ 1 Aerie Ouphes C :G: .10 .25
❑ 2 Altar Golem R :A: .30 .75
❑ 3 Antler Skulkin C :A: .10 .25
❑ 4 Archon of Justice R :W: .40 1.00
❑ 5 Ashling, the Extinguisher R :K: .75 2.00
❑ 6 Balefire Liege R :R: :W: 2.00 5.00
❑ 7 Ballynock Trapper C :W: .10 .25
❑ 8 Banishing Knack C :B: .10 .25
❑ 9 Battlegate Mimic C :R: :W: .10 .25
❑ 10 Batwing Brume U :W: :K: .30 .75
❑ 11 Beckon Apparition C :W: :K: .15 .40
❑ 12 Belligerent Hatchling U :R: :W: .20 .50
❑ 13 Bloodied Ghost U :W: :K: .15 .40
❑ 14 Bloom Tender R :G: 1.50 4.00
❑ 15 Cache Raiders U :B: .15 .40
❑ 16 Call the Skybreaker R :B: :R: .30 .75
❑ 17 Canker Abomination U :K: :G: .15 .40
❑ 18 Cankerous Thirst U :K: :G: .15 .40
❑ 19 Cascade Bluffs R :L: 4.00 10.00
❑ 20 Cauldron Haze U :W: :K: .20 .50
❑ 21 Cenn's Enlistment C :W: .10 .25
❑ 22 Chaotic Backlash U :R: .15 .40
❑ 23 Cinder Pyromancer C :R: .10 .25
❑ 24 Clout of the Dominus C :B: :R: .10 .25
❑ 25 Cold-Eyed Selkie R :G: :B: 2.00 5.00
❑ 26 Crackleburr R :B: :R: .60 1.50
❑ 27 Crag Puca U :B: :R: .15 .40
❑ 28 Creakwood Ghoul U :K: .15 .40
❑ 29 Creakwood Liege R :K: :G: 3.00 8.00
❑ 30 Crumbling Ashes U :K: .25 .60
❑ 31 Deathbringer Liege R :W: :K: 5.00 12.00
❑ 32 Deity of Scars R :K: :G: .75 2.00
❑ 33 Desecrator Hag C :K: :G: .10 .25
❑ 34 Divinity of Pride R :W: :K: 4.00 10.00
❑ 35 Dominus of Fealty R :B: :R: 1.25 3.00
❑ 36 Doomgape R :K: :G: .75 2.00
❑ 37 Double Cleave C :R: :W: .10 .25
❑ 38 Drain the Well C :K: :G: .10 .25
❑ 39 Dream Fracture U :B: .25 .60
❑ 40 Dream Thief C :B: .10 .25
❑ 41 Duergar Assailant C :R: :W: .10 .25
❑ 42 Duergar Cave-Guard U :R: .15 .40
❑ 43 Duergar Hedge-Mage U :R: :W: .20 .50
❑ 44 Duergar Mine-Captain U :R: :W: .15 .40
❑ 45 Duskdale Wurm U :G: .15 .40
❑ 46 Edge of the Divinity C :W: :K: .15 .40
❑ 47 Endless Horizons R :W: .60 1.50
❑ 48 Endure U :W: .15 .40
❑ 49 Evershrike R :W: :K: .50 1.25
❑ 50 Fable of Wolf and Owl R :G: :B: .60 1.50
❑ 51 Fang Skulkin C :A: .10 .25
❑ 52 Favor of the Overbeing C :G: :B: .10 .25
❑ 53 Fetid Heath R :L: 5.00 12.00
❑ 54 Fiery Bombardment R :R: .25 .60
❑ 55 Figure of Destiny R :R: :W: 3.00 8.00
❑ 56 Fire at Will C :R: :W: .10 .25
❑ 57 Flame Jab C :R: .10 .25
❑ 58 Flickerwisp U :W: .40 1.00
❑ 59 Flooded Grove R :L: 3.00 8.00
❑ 60 Gift of the Deity C :K: :G: .10 .25
❑ 61 Gilder Bairn U :G: :B: .60 1.50
❑ 62 Glamerdye R :B: .25 .60
❑ 63 Glen Elendra Archmage R :B: 3.00 8.00
❑ 64 Grazing Kelpie C :G: :B: .10 .25
❑ 65 Groundling Pouncer U :G: :B: .15 .40
❑ 66 Gwyllion Hedge-Mage U :W: :K: .15 .40
❑ 67 Hag Hedge-Mage U :K: :G: .15 .40
❑ 68 Hallowed Burial R :W: 1.25 3.00
❑ 69 Harvest Gwyllion C :W: :K: .10 .25
❑ 70 Hatchet Bully U :R: .15 .40
❑ 71 Hateflayer R :R: .30 .75
❑ 72 Hearthfire Hobgoblin U :R: :W: .30 .75
❑ 73 Heartlash Cinder C :R: .10 .25
❑ 74 Helix Pinnacle R :G: .75 2.00
❑ 75 Hobgoblin Dragoon C :R: :W: .10 .25
❑ 76 Hoof Skulkin C :A: .10 .25
❑ 77 Hotheaded Giant C :R: .10 .25
❑ 78 Idle Thoughts U :B: .15 .40
❑ 79 Impelled Giant U :R: .15 .40
❑ 80 Indigo Faerie U :B: .15 .40
❑ 81 Inside Out C :B: :R: .10 .25
❑ 82 Inundate R :B: .25 .60
❑ 83 Invert the Skies U :G: :B: .15 .40
❑ 84 Jawbone Skulkin C :A: .10 .25
❑ 85 Kithkin Spellduster C :W: .10 .25
❑ 86 Kithkin Zealot C :W: .10 .25
❑ 87 Leering Emblem R :A: .25 .60
❑ 88 Light from Within R :W: .75 2.00
❑ 89 Lingering Tormentor U :K: .15 .40
❑ 90 Loyal Gyrfalcon U :W: .15 .40
❑ 91 Marshdrinker Giant U :G: .15 .40
❑ 92 Merrow Bonegnawer C :K: .10 .25
❑ 93 Merrow Levitator C :B: .10 .25
❑ 94 Mindwrack Liege R :B: :R: .75 2.00
❑ 95 Mirror Sheen R :B: :R: .30 .75
❑ 96 Monstrify C :G: .10 .25
❑ 97 Moonhold U :R: :W: .15 .40
❑ 98 Murkfiend Liege R :G: :B: 2.00 5.00
❑ 99 Necroskitter R :K: 2.00 5.00
❑ 100 Needle Specter R :K: .40 1.00
❑ 101 Nettle Sentinel C :G: .25 .60
❑ 102 Nightmare Incursion R :K: .25 .60
❑ 103 Nightsky Mimic C :W: :K: .10 .25
❑ 104 Nip Gwyllion C :W: :K: .10 .25
❑ 105 Nobilis of War R :R: :W: .60 1.50
❑ 106 Noggle Bandit C :B: :R: .10 .25
❑ 107 Noggle Bridgebreaker C :B: :R: .10 .25
❑ 108 Noggle Hedge-Mage U :B: :R: .15 .40
❑ 109 Noggle Ransacker U :B: :R: .15 .40
❑ 110 Noxious Hatchling U :K: :G: .25 .60
❑ 111 Nucklavee U :B: :R: .15 .40
❑ 112 Odious Trow C :K: :G: .10 .25
❑ 113 Oona's Grace C :B: .10 .25
❑ 114 Outrage Shaman U :R: .15 .40
❑ 115 Overbeing of Myth R :G: :B: 1.00 2.50
❑ 116 Patrol Signaler U :W: .15 .40
❑ 117 Phosphorescent Feast U :G: .15 .40
❑ 118 Primalcrux R :G: 2.00 5.00
❑ 119 Puncture Blast C :R: .10 .25
❑ 120 Pyrrhic Revival R :W: :K: .30 .75
❑ 121 Quillspike U :K: :G: .30 .75
❑ 122 Raven's Crime C :K: .10 .25
❑ 123 Razorfin Abolisher U :B: .15 .40
❑ 124 Recumbent Bliss C :W: .10 .25
❑ 125 Regal Force R :G: 2.50 6.00
❑ 126 Rekindled Flame R :R: .25 .60
❑ 127 Rendclaw Trow C :K: :G: .10 .25
❑ 128 Restless Apparition U :W: :K: .15 .40
❑ 129 Rise of the Hobgoblins R :R: :W: 1.00 2.50
❑ 130 Riverfall Mimic C :B: :R: .10 .25
❑ 131 Rugged Prairie R :L: 3.00 8.00
❑ 132 Sanity Grinding R :B: 1.25 3.00
❑ 133 Sapling of Colfenor R :K: :G: .60 1.50
❑ 134 Savage Conception U :G: .15 .40
❑ 135 Scarecrone R :A: 1.25 3.00
❑ 136 Scourge of the Nobilis C :R: :W: .10 .25
❑ 137 Selkie Hedge-Mage U :G: :B: .15 .40
❑ 138 Shell Skulkin C :A: .10 .25
❑ 139 Shorecrasher Mimic C :G: :B: .10 .25
❑ 140 Shrewd Hatchling U :B: :R: .20 .50
❑ 141 Slippery Bogle C :G: :B: .10 .25
❑ 142 Smoldering Butcher C :K: .10 .25
❑ 143 Snakeform C :G: :B: .10 .25
❑ 144 Soot Imp U :K: .15 .40
❑ 145 Soul Reap C :K: .10 .25
❑ 146 Soul Snuffers U :K: .25 .60
❑ 147 Spirit of the Hearth R :W: .40 1.00
❑ 148 Spitemare U :R: :W: .25 .60
❑ 149 Spitting Image R :G: :B: .60 1.50
❑ 150 Springjack Pasture R :L: .60 1.50
❑ 151 Springjack Shepherd U :W: .20 .50
❑ 152 Stalker Hag U :K: :G: .15 .40
❑ 153 Stigma Lasher R :R: 1.25 3.00
❑ 154 Stillmoon Cavalier R :W: :K: 2.50 6.00
❑ 155 Stream Hopper C :B: :R: .10 .25
❑ 156 Sturdy Hatchling U :G: :B: .15 .40
❑ 157 Suture Spirit U :W: .15 .40
❑ 158 Swirling Spriggan U :G: .15 .40
❑ 159 Syphon Life U :K: .15 .40
❑ 160 Talara's Bane C :K: .10 .25
❑ 161 Talara's Battalion R :G: 1.50 4.00
❑ 162 Talonrend U :B: .15 .40
❑ 163 Thunderblust R :R: .40 1.00
❑ 164 Tilling Treefolk C :G: .10 .25
❑ 165 Trapjaw Kelpie C :G: :B: .10 .25
❑ 166 Twilight Mire R :L: 3.00 8.00
❑ 167 Twinblade Slasher U :G: .25 .60
❑ 168 Umbra Stalker R :K: .25 .60
❑ 169 Unmake C :W: :K: .40 1.00
❑ 170 Unnerving Assault U :B: :R: .15 .40
❑ 171 Unwilling Recruit U :R: .20 .50
❑ 172 Voracious Hatchling U :W: :K: .30 .75
❑ 173 Wake Thrasher R :B: 1.50 4.00
❑ 174 Ward of Bones R :A: .30 .75
❑ 175 Waves of Aggression R :R: :W: .30 .75
❑ 176 Wickerbough Elder C :G: .10 .25
❑ 177 Wilderness Hypnotist C :B: .10 .25
❑ 178 Wistful Selkie U :G: :B: .15 .40
❑ 179 Woodlurker Mimic C :K: :G: .10 .25
❑ 180 Worm Harvest R :K: :G: .40 1.00

2008 Magic the Gathering Eventide Foil

Complete Set (180) 250.00 400.00
*Foil: .8X to 2X Basic Cards

❑ 1 Aerie Ouphes C :G: .20 .50
❑ 2 Altar Golem R :A: .60 1.50
❑ 3 Antler Skulkin C :A: .20 .50
❑ 4 Archon of Justice R :W: .75 2.00
❑ 5 Ashling, the Extinguisher R :K: 1.50 4.00
❑ 6 Balefire Liege R :R: :W: 4.00 10.00
❑ 7 Ballynock Trapper C :W: .20 .50
❑ 8 Banishing Knack C :B: .20 .50
❑ 9 Battlegate Mimic C :R: :W: .20 .50
❑ 10 Batwing Brume U :W: :K: .60 1.50
❑ 11 Beckon Apparition C :W: :K: .30 .75
❑ 12 Belligerent Hatchling U :R: :W: .40 1.00
❑ 13 Bloodied Ghost U :W: :K: .30 .75
❑ 14 Bloom Tender R :G: 3.00 8.00
❑ 15 Cache Raiders U :B: .30 .75
❑ 16 Call the Skybreaker R :B: :R: .60 1.50
❑ 17 Canker Abomination U :K: :G: .30 .75
❑ 18 Cankerous Thirst U :K: :G: .30 .75
❑ 19 Cascade Bluffs R :L: 8.00 20.00
❑ 20 Cauldron Haze U :W: :K: .40 1.00
❑ 21 Cenn's Enlistment C :W: .20 .50
❑ 22 Chaotic Backlash U :R: .30 .75
❑ 23 Cinder Pyromancer C :R: .20 .50
❑ 24 Clout of the Dominus C :B: :R: .20 .50
❑ 25 Cold-Eyed Selkie R :G: :B: 4.00 10.00
❑ 26 Crackleburr R :B: :R: 1.25 3.00
❑ 27 Crag Puca U :B: :R: .30 .75
❑ 28 Creakwood Ghoul U :K: .30 .75
❑ 29 Creakwood Liege R :K: :G: 6.00 15.00
❑ 30 Crumbling Ashes U :K: .50 1.25
❑ 31 Deathbringer Liege R :W: :K: 10.00 25.00
❑ 32 Deity of Scars R :K: :G: 1.50 4.00
❑ 33 Desecrator Hag C :K: :G: .20 .50
❑ 34 Divinity of Pride R :W: :K: 8.00 20.00
❑ 35 Dominus of Fealty R :B: :R: 2.50 6.00
❑ 36 Doomgape R :K: :G: 1.50 4.00
❑ 37 Double Cleave C :R: :W: .20 .50
❑ 38 Drain the Well C :K: :G: .20 .50
❑ 39 Dream Fracture U :B: .50 1.25
❑ 40 Dream Thief C :B: .20 .50
❑ 41 Duergar Assailant C :R: :W: .20 .50
❑ 42 Duergar Cave-Guard U :R: .30 .75
❑ 43 Duergar Hedge-Mage U :R: :W: .40 1.00
❑ 44 Duergar Mine-Captain U :R: :W: .30 .75
❑ 45 Duskdale Wurm U :G: .30 .75
❑ 46 Edge of the Divinity C :W: :K: .30 .75
❑ 47 Endless Horizons R :W: 1.25 3.00
❑ 48 Endure U :W: .30 .75
❑ 49 Evershrike R :W: :K: 1.00 2.50
❑ 50 Fable of Wolf and Owl R :G: :B: 1.25 3.00
❑ 51 Fang Skulkin C :A: .20 .50
❑ 52 Favor of the Overbeing C :G: :B: .20 .50
❑ 53 Fetid Heath R :L: 10.00 25.00
❑ 54 Fiery Bombardment R :R: .50 1.25
❑ 55 Figure of Destiny R :R: :W: 6.00 15.00
❑ 56 Fire at Will C :R: :W: .20 .50
❑ 57 Flame Jab C :R: .20 .50
❑ 58 Flickerwisp U :W: .75 2.00
❑ 59 Flooded Grove R :L: 6.00 15.00
❑ 60 Gift of the Deity C :K: :G: .20 .50
❑ 61 Gilder Bairn U :G: :B: 1.25 3.00
❑ 62 Glamerdye R :B: .50 1.25
❑ 63 Glen Elendra Archmage R :B: 6.00 15.00
❑ 64 Grazing Kelpie C :G: :B: .20 .50
❑ 65 Groundling Pouncer U :G: :B: .30 .75
❑ 66 Gwyllion Hedge-Mage U :W: :K: .30 .75
❑ 67 Hag Hedge-Mage U :K: :G: .30 .75
❑ 68 Hallowed Burial R :W: 2.50 6.00
❑ 69 Harvest Gwyllion C :W: :K: .20 .50
❑ 70 Hatchet Bully U :R: .30 .75
❑ 71 Hateflayer R :R: .60 1.50
❑ 72 Hearthfire Hobgoblin U :R: :W: .60 1.50
❑ 73 Heartlash Cinder C :R: .20 .50
❑ 74 Helix Pinnacle R :G: 1.50 4.00
❑ 75 Hobgoblin Dragoon C :R: :W: .20 .50
❑ 76 Hoof Skulkin C :A: .20 .50
❑ 77 Hotheaded Giant C :R: .20 .50
❑ 78 Idle Thoughts U :B: .30 .75
❑ 79 Impelled Giant U :R: .30 .75
❑ 80 Indigo Faerie U :B: .30 .75
❑ 81 Inside Out C :B: :R: .20 .50
❑ 82 Inundate R :B: .50 1.25
❑ 83 Invert the Skies U :G: :B: .30 .75
❑ 84 Jawbone Skulkin C :A: .20 .50
❑ 85 Kithkin Spellduster C :W: .20 .50
❑ 86 Kithkin Zealot C :W: .20 .50
❑ 87 Leering Emblem R :A: .50 1.25
❑ 88 Light from Within R :W: 1.50 4.00
❑ 89 Lingering Tormentor U :K: .30 .75
❑ 90 Loyal Gyrfalcon U :W: .30 .75
❑ 91 Marshdrinker Giant U :G: .30 .75
❑ 92 Merrow Bonegnawer C :K: .20 .50
❑ 93 Merrow Levitator C :B: .20 .50
❑ 94 Mindwrack Liege R :B: :R: 1.50 4.00
❑ 95 Mirror Sheen R :B: :R: .60 1.50
❑ 96 Monstrify C :G: .20 .50
❑ 97 Moonhold U :R: :W: .30 .75
❑ 98 Murkfiend Liege R :G: :B: 4.00 10.00
❑ 99 Necroskitter R :K: 4.00 10.00
❑ 100 Needle Specter R :K: .75 2.00
❑ 101 Nettle Sentinel C :G: .50 1.25
❑ 102 Nightmare Incursion R :K: .50 1.25
❑ 103 Nightsky Mimic C :W: :K: .20 .50
❑ 104 Nip Gwyllion C :W: :K: .20 .50
❑ 105 Nobilis of War R :R: :W: 1.25 3.00
❑ 106 Noggle Bandit C :B: :R: .20 .50
❑ 107 Noggle Bridgebreaker C :B: :R: .20 .50
❑ 108 Noggle Hedge-Mage U :B: :R: .30 .75
❑ 109 Noggle Ransacker U :B: :R: .30 .75
❑ 110 Noxious Hatchling U :K: :G: .50 1.25
❑ 111 Nucklavee U :B: :R: .30 .75
❑ 112 Odious Trow C :K: :G: .20 .50
❑ 113 Oona's Grace C :B: .20 .50
❑ 114 Outrage Shaman U :R: .30 .75
❑ 115 Overbeing of Myth R :G: :B: 2.00 5.00
❑ 116 Patrol Signaler U :W: .30 .75
❑ 117 Phosphorescent Feast U :G: .30 .75
❑ 118 Primalcrux R :G: 4.00 10.00
❑ 119 Puncture Blast C :R: .20 .50
❑ 120 Pyrrhic Revival R :W: :K: .60 1.50
❑ 121 Quillspike U :K: :G: .60 1.50
❑ 122 Raven's Crime C :K: .20 .50
❑ 123 Razorfin Abolisher U :B: .30 .75
❑ 124 Recumbent Bliss C :W: .20 .50
❑ 125 Regal Force R :G: 5.00 12.00
❑ 126 Rekindled Flame R :R: .50 1.25
❑ 127 Rendclaw Trow C :K: :G: .20 .50
❑ 128 Restless Apparition U :W: :K: .30 .75
❑ 129 Rise of the Hobgoblins R :R: :W: 2.00 5.00
❑ 130 Riverfall Mimic C :B: :R: .20 .50
❑ 131 Rugged Prairie R :L: 6.00 15.00
❑ 132 Sanity Grinding R :B: 2.50 6.00
❑ 133 Sapling of Colfenor R :K: :G: 1.25 3.00
❑ 134 Savage Conception U :G: .30 .75
❑ 135 Scarecrone R :A: 2.50 6.00
❑ 136 Scourge of the Nobilis C :R: :W: .20 .50
❑ 137 Selkie Hedge-Mage U :G: :B: .30 .75
❑ 138 Shell Skulkin C :A: .20 .50
❑ 139 Shorecrasher Mimic C :G: :B: .20 .50
❑ 140 Shrewd Hatchling U :B: :R: .40 1.00
❑ 141 Slippery Bogle C :G: :B: .20 .50
❑ 142 Smoldering Butcher C :K: .20 .50
❑ 143 Snakeform C :G: :B: .20 .50
❑ 144 Soot Imp U :K: .30 .75
❑ 145 Soul Reap C :K: .20 .50
❑ 146 Soul Snuffers U :K: .50 1.25
❑ 147 Spirit of the Hearth R :W: .75 2.00
❑ 148 Spitemare U :R: :W: .50 1.25
❑ 149 Spitting Image R :G: :B: 1.25 3.00
❑ 150 Springjack Pasture R :L: 1.25 3.00
❑ 151 Springjack Shepherd U :W: .40 1.00
❑ 152 Stalker Hag U :K: :G: .30 .75
❑ 153 Stigma Lasher R :R: 2.50 6.00
❑ 154 Stillmoon Cavalier R :W: :K: 5.00 12.00
❑ 155 Stream Hopper C :B: :R: .20 .50
❑ 156 Sturdy Hatchling U :G: :B: .30 .75
❑ 157 Suture Spirit U :W: .30 .75
❑ 158 Swirling Spriggan U :G: .30 .75
❑ 159 Syphon Life U :K: .30 .75
❑ 160 Talara's Bane C :K: .20 .50
❑ 161 Talara's Battalion R :G: 3.00 8.00

❑ 162 Talonrend U :B: .30 .75
❑ 163 Thunderblust R :R: .75 2.00
❑ 164 Tilling Treefolk C :G: .20 .50
❑ 165 Trapjaw Kelpie C :G: :B: .20 .50
❑ 166 Twilight Mire R :L: 6.00 15.00
❑ 167 Twinblade Slasher U :G: .50 1.25
❑ 168 Umbra Stalker R :K: .50 1.25
❑ 169 Unmake C :W: :K: .75 2.00
❑ 170 Unnerving Assault U :B: :R: .30 .75
❑ 171 Unwilling Recruit U :R: .40 1.00
❑ 172 Voracious Hatchling U :W: :K: .60 1.50
❑ 173 Wake Thrasher R :B: 3.00 8.00
❑ 174 Ward of Bones R :A: .60 1.50
❑ 175 Waves of Aggression R :R: :W: .60 1.50
❑ 176 Wickerbough Elder C :G: .20 .50
❑ 177 Wilderness Hypnotist C :B: .20 .50
❑ 178 Wistful Selkie U :G: :B: .30 .75
❑ 179 Woodlurker Mimic C :K: :G: .20 .50
❑ 180 Worm Harvest R :K: :G: .75 2.00

2008 Magic the Gathering Shards of Alara

Complete Set (249) 125.00 200.00
Booster Box (36 Packs) 100.00 150.00
Booster Pack (15 Cards) 3.50 5.00
Theme Decks 10.00 15.00
Fat Pack 30.00 60.00

❑ 1 Ad Nauseam R :K: .60 1.50
❑ 2 Agony Warp C :D: .10 .25
❑ 3 Ajani Vengeant M :D: 2.50 6.00
❑ 4 Akrasan Squire C :W: .20 .50
❑ 5 Algae Gharial U :G: .20 .50
❑ 6 Angel's Herald U :W: .20 .50
❑ 7 Angelic Benediction U :W: .20 .50
❑ 8 Angelsong C :W: .10 .25
❑ 9 Arcane Sanctum U :L: 1.00 2.50
❑ 10 Archdemon of Unx R :K: .30 .75
❑ 11 Banewasp Affliction C :K: .10 .25
❑ 12 Bant Battlemage U :W: .20 .50
❑ 13 Bant Charm U :D: .50 1.25
❑ 14 Bant Panorama C :L: .10 .25
❑ 15 Battlegrace Angel R :W: 1.25 3.00
❑ 16 Behemoth's Herald U :G: .20 .50
❑ 17 Blightning C :D: .60 1.50
❑ 18 Blister Beetle C :K: .10 .25
❑ 19 Blood Cultist U :D: .20 .50
❑ 20 Bloodpyre Elemental C :R: .10 .25
❑ 21 Bloodthorn Taunter C :R: .20 .50
❑ 22 Bone Splinters C :K: .10 .25
❑ 23 Branching Bolt C :D: .10 .25
❑ 24 Brilliant Ultimatum R :D: .30 .75
❑ 25 Broodmate Dragon R :D: 1.50 4.00
❑ 26 Bull Cerodon U :D: .20 .50
❑ 27 Caldera Hellion R :R: .30 .75
❑ 28 Call to Heel C :B: .10 .25
❑ 29 Cancel C :B: .10 .25
❑ 30 Carrion Thrash C :D: .10 .25
❑ 31 Cathartic Adept C :B: .10 .25
❑ 32 Cavern Thoctar C :G: .10 .25
❑ 33 Clarion Ultimatum R :D: .30 .75
❑ 34 Cloudheath Drake C :B: .10 .25
❑ 35 Coma Veil C :B: .10 .25
❑ 36 Corpse Connoisseur U :K: .20 .50
❑ 37 Courier's Capsule C :B: .10 .25
❑ 38 Court Archers C :G: .10 .25
❑ 39 Covenant of Minds R :B: .25 .60
❑ 40 Cradle of Vitality R :W: .60 1.50
❑ 41 Crucible of Fire R :R: 1.50 4.00
❑ 42 Cruel Ultimatum R :D: .60 1.50
❑ 43 Crumbling Necropolis U :L: .75 2.00
❑ 44 Cunning Lethemancer R :K: .30 .75
❑ 45 Cylian Elf C :G: .10 .25
❑ 46 Dawnray Archer U :B: .20 .50
❑ 47 Death Baron R :K: 6.00 15.00
❑ 48 Deathgreeter C :K: .10 .25
❑ 49 Deft Duelist C :D: .10 .25
❑ 50 Demon's Herald U :K: .20 .50
❑ 51 Dispeller's Capsule C :W: .10 .25
❑ 52 Dragon Fodder C :R: .20 .50
❑ 53 Dragon's Herald U :R: .20 .50
❑ 54 Dreg Reaver C :K: .10 .25
❑ 55 Dregscape Zombie C :K: .10 .25
❑ 56 Druid of the Anima C :G: .10 .25
❑ 57 Drumhunter U :G: .20 .50
❑ 58 Elspeth, Knight-Errant M :W: 12.00 30.00
❑ 59 Elvish Visionary C :G: .12 .30
❑ 60 Empyrial Archangel M :D: 2.50 6.00
❑ 61 Esper Battlemage U :B: .20 .50
❑ 62 Esper Charm U :D: .50 1.25
❑ 63 Esper Panorama C :L: .10 .25
❑ 64 Etherium Astrolabe U :B: .10 .25
❑ 65 Etherium Sculptor C :B: .75 2.00
❑ 66 Ethersworn Canonist R :W: 6.00 15.00
❑ 67 Excommunicate C :W: .08 .20
❑ 68 Executioner's Capsule C :K: .10 .25
❑ 69 Exuberant Firestoker U :R: .20 .50
❑ 70 Fatestitcher U :B: .20 .50
❑ 71 Feral Hydra R :G: .30 .75
❑ 72 Filigree Sages U :B: .20 .50
❑ 73 Fire-Field Ogre U :D: .20 .50
❑ 74 Flameblast Dragon R :R: .50 1.25
❑ 75 Fleshbag Marauder U :K: .20 .50
❑ 76 Forest L :L: .10 .25
❑ 77 Forest L :L: .10 .25
❑ 78 Forest L :L: .10 .25
❑ 79 Forest L :L: .10 .25
❑ 80 Gather Specimens R :B: .30 .75
❑ 81 Gift of the Gargantuan C :G: .10 .25
❑ 82 Glaze Fiend C :K: .10 .25
❑ 83 Goblin Assault R :R: .60 1.50
❑ 84 Goblin Deathraiders C :D: .10 .25
❑ 85 Goblin Mountaineer C :R: .10 .25
❑ 86 Godsire M :D: 1.50 4.00
❑ 87 Godtoucher C :G: .10 .25
❑ 88 Grixis Battlemage U :K: .20 .50
❑ 89 Grixis Charm U :D: .20 .50
❑ 90 Grixis Panorama C :L: .12 .30
❑ 91 Guardians of Akrasa C :W: .10 .25
❑ 92 Gustrider Exuberant C :W: .10 .25
❑ 93 Hell's Thunder R :R: 2.00 5.00
❑ 94 Hellkite Overlord M :D: 2.50 6.00
❑ 95 Hindering Light C :D: .20 .50
❑ 96 Hissing Iguanar C :R: .10 .25
❑ 97 Immortal Coil R :K: .30 .75
❑ 98 Incurable Ogre C :R: .10 .25
❑ 99 Infest U :K: .25 .60
❑ 100 Invincible Hymn R :W: .25 .60
❑ 101 Island L :L: .10 .25
❑ 102 Island L :L: .10 .25
❑ 103 Island L :L: .10 .25
❑ 104 Island L :L: .10 .25
❑ 105 Jhessian Infiltrator U :D: .25 .60
❑ 106 Jhessian Lookout C :B: .10 .25
❑ 107 Jund Battlemage U :R: .20 .50
❑ 108 Jund Charm U :D: .20 .50
❑ 109 Jund Panorama C :L: .10 .25
❑ 110 Jungle Shrine U :L: .60 1.50
❑ 111 Jungle Weaver C :G: .10 .25
❑ 112 Kathari Screecher C :B: .10 .25
❑ 113 Kederekt Creeper C :D: .10 .25
❑ 114 Kederekt Leviathan R :B: .25 .60
❑ 115 Keeper of Progenitus R :G: .30 .75
❑ 116 Kiss of the Amesha U :D: .20 .50
❑ 117 Knight of the Skyward Eye C :W: .10 .25
❑ 118 Knight of the White Orchid R :W: 1.50 4.00
❑ 119 Knight-Captain of Eos R :W: .30 .75
❑ 120 Kresh the Bloodbraided M :D: .75 2.00
❑ 121 Lich's Mirror M :A: 1.00 2.50
❑ 122 Lightning Talons C :R: .10 .25
❑ 123 Lush Growth C :G: .10 .25
❑ 124 Magma Spray C :R: .10 .25
❑ 125 Manaplasm R :G: .25 .60
❑ 126 Marble Chalice C :W: .10 .25
❑ 127 Master of Etherium R :B: 2.50 6.00
❑ 128 Mayael the Anima M :D: 1.00 2.50
❑ 129 Memory Erosion R :B: 1.50 4.00
❑ 130 Metallurgeon U :W: .20 .50
❑ 131 Mighty Emergence U :G: .20 .50
❑ 132 Mindlock Orb R :B: .30 .75
❑ 133 Minion Reflector R :A: .30 .75
❑ 134 Mosstodon C :G: .10 .25
❑ 135 Mountain L :L: .10 .25
❑ 136 Mountain L :L: .10 .25
❑ 137 Mountain L :L: .10 .25
❑ 138 Mountain L :L: .10 .25
❑ 139 Mycoloth R :G: 2.00 5.00
❑ 140 Naturalize C :G: .10 .25
❑ 141 Naya Battlemage U :G: .20 .50
❑ 142 Naya Charm U :D: .20 .50
❑ 143 Naya Panorama C :L: .10 .25
❑ 144 Necrogenesis U :D: .20 .50
❑ 145 Obelisk of Bant C :A: .10 .25
❑ 146 Obelisk of Esper C :A: .10 .25
❑ 147 Obelisk of Grixis C :A: .10 .25
❑ 148 Obelisk of Jund C :A: .10 .25
❑ 149 Obelisk of Naya C :A: .10 .25
❑ 150 Oblivion Ring C :W: .60 1.50
❑ 151 Onyx Goblet C :K: .10 .25
❑ 152 Ooze Garden R :G: .30 .75
❑ 153 Outrider of Jhess C :B: .10 .25
❑ 154 Plains L :L: .10 .25
❑ 155 Plains L :L: .10 .25
❑ 156 Plains L :L: .10 .25
❑ 157 Plains L :L: .10 .25
❑ 158 Predator Dragon R :R: .40 1.00
❑ 159 Prince of Thralls M :D: 1.25 3.00
❑ 160 Protomatter Powder U :B: .20 .50
❑ 161 Punish Ignorance R :D: .30 .75
❑ 162 Puppet Conjurer U :K: .20 .50
❑ 163 Qasali Ambusher U :D: .20 .50
❑ 164 Quietus Spike R :A: 1.50 4.00
❑ 165 Rafiq of the Many M :D: 2.50 6.00
❑ 166 Rakeclaw Gargantuan C :D: .10 .25
❑ 167 Ranger of Eos R :W: 2.00 5.00
❑ 168 Realm Razer R :D: .30 .75
❑ 169 Relic of Progenitus C :A: .60 1.50
❑ 170 Resounding Roar C :G: .10 .25
❑ 171 Resounding Scream C :K: .10 .25
❑ 172 Resounding Silence C :W: .10 .25
❑ 173 Resounding Thunder C :R: .10 .25
❑ 174 Resounding Wave C :B: .10 .25
❑ 175 Rhox Charger U :G: .20 .50
❑ 176 Rhox War Monk U :D: .25 .60
❑ 177 Ridge Rannet C :R: .10 .25
❑ 178 Rip-Clan Crasher C :D: .10 .25
❑ 179 Rockcaster Platoon U :W: .20 .50
❑ 180 Rockslide Elemental U :R: .20 .50
❑ 181 Sacellum Godspeaker R :G: .25 .60
❑ 182 Salvage Titan R :K: .30 .75
❑ 183 Sanctum Gargoyle C :W: .10 .25
❑ 184 Sangrite Surge U :D: .20 .50
❑ 185 Sarkhan Vol M :D: 6.00 15.00
❑ 186 Savage Hunger C :G: .10 .25
❑ 187 Savage Lands U :L: .75 2.00
❑ 188 Scavenger Drake U :K: .20 .50
❑ 189 Scourge Devil U :R: .20 .50
❑ 190 Scourglass R :W: .60 1.50
❑ 191 Seaside Citadel U :L: .75 2.00
❑ 192 Sedraxis Specter R :D: .40 1.00
❑ 193 Sedris, the Traitor King M :D: 1.00 2.50
❑ 194 Shadowfeed C :K: .10 .25
❑ 195 Sharding Sphinx R :B: .30 .75
❑ 196 Sharuum the Hegemon M :D: 1.50 4.00
❑ 197 Shore Snapper C :K: .10 .25
❑ 198 Sighted-Caste Sorcerer C :W: .10 .25
❑ 199 Sigil Blessing C :D: .10 .25
❑ 200 Sigil of Distinction R :A: .30 .75
❑ 201 Sigiled Paladin U :W: .40 1.00
❑ 202 Skeletal Kathari C :K: .10 .25
❑ 203 Skeletonize U :R: .20 .50
❑ 204 Skill Borrower R :B: .30 .75
❑ 205 Skullmulcher R :G: .25 .60
❑ 206 Soul's Fire C :R: .10 .25
❑ 207 Soul's Grace C :W: .10 .25
❑ 208 Soul's Might C :G: .10 .25
❑ 209 Spearbreaker Behemoth R :G: .30 .75
❑ 210 Spell Snip C :B: .10 .25
❑ 211 Sphinx Sovereign M :D: .60 1.50
❑ 212 Sphinx's Herald U :B: .20 .50
❑ 213 Sprouting Thrinax U :D: .25 .60
❑ 214 Steelclad Serpent C :B: .10 .25
❑ 215 Steward of Valeron C :D: .20 .50
❑ 216 Stoic Angel R :D: .75 2.00
❑ 217 Sunseed Nurturer U :W: .20 .50
❑ 218 Swamp L :L: .10 .25
❑ 219 Swamp L :L: .10 .25
❑ 220 Swamp L :L: .10 .25
❑ 221 Swamp L :L: .10 .25
❑ 222 Swerve U :D: .25 .60
❑ 223 Tar Fiend R :K: .25 .60
❑ 224 Tezzeret the Seeker M :B: 3.00 8.00
❑ 225 Thorn-Thrash Viashino C :R: .20 .50
❑ 226 Thoughtcutter Agent U :D: .20 .50
❑ 227 Thunder-Thrash Elder U :R: .20 .50
❑ 228 Tidehollow Sculler U :D: .40 1.00
❑ 229 Tidehollow Strix C :D: .20 .50
❑ 230 Titanic Ultimatum R :D: .25 .60
❑ 231 Topan Ascetic U :G: .20 .50
❑ 232 Tortoise Formation C :B: .10 .25
❑ 233 Tower Gargoyle U :D: .20 .50
❑ 234 Undead Leotau C :K: .10 .25
❑ 235 Vectis Silencers C :B: .10 .25
❑ 236 Vein Drinker R :K: .30 .75
❑ 237 Viashino Skeleton C :R: .10 .25
❑ 238 Vicious Shadows R :R: .25 .60
❑ 239 Violent Ultimatum R :D: .30 .75
❑ 240 Viscera Dragger C :K: .10 .25
❑ 241 Vithian Stinger C :R: .10 .25
❑ 242 Volcanic Submersion C :R: .10 .25
❑ 243 Waveskimmer Aven C :D: .10 .25
❑ 244 Welkin Guide C :W: .10 .25
❑ 245 Where Ancients Tread R :R: .25 .60
❑ 246 Wild Nacatl C :G: .20 .50
❑ 247 Windwright Mage C :D: .10 .25
❑ 248 Woolly Thoctar U :D: .50 1.25
❑ 249 Yoked Plowbeast C :W: .10 .25

2008 Magic the Gathering Shards of Alara Foil

Complete Set (249) 250.00 350.00
*Foil: .8X to 2X Basic Cards

❑ 1 Ad Nauseam R :K: 1.25 3.00
❑ 2 Agony Warp C :D: .20 .50
❑ 3 Ajani Vengeant M :D: 5.00 12.00
❑ 4 Akrasan Squire C :W: .40 1.00
❑ 5 Algae Gharial U :G: .40 1.00
❑ 6 Angel's Herald U :W: .40 1.00
❑ 7 Angelic Benediction U :W: .40 1.00
❑ 8 Angelsong C :W: .20 .50
❑ 9 Arcane Sanctum U :L: 2.00 5.00
❑ 10 Archdemon of Unx R :K: .60 1.50
❑ 11 Banewasp Affliction C :K: .20 .50
❑ 12 Bant Battlemage U :W: .40 1.00
❑ 13 Bant Charm U :D: 1.00 2.50
❑ 14 Bant Panorama C :L: .20 .50
❑ 15 Battlegrace Angel R :W: 2.50 6.00
❑ 16 Behemoth's Herald U :G: .40 1.00
❑ 17 Blightning C :D: 1.25 3.00
❑ 18 Blister Beetle C :K: .20 .50
❑ 19 Blood Cultist U :D: .40 1.00
❑ 20 Bloodpyre Elemental C :R: .20 .50
❑ 21 Bloodthorn Taunter C :R: .40 1.00
❑ 22 Bone Splinters C :K: .20 .50
❑ 23 Branching Bolt C :D: .20 .50
❑ 24 Brilliant Ultimatum R :D: .60 1.50
❑ 25 Broodmate Dragon R :D: 3.00 8.00
❑ 26 Bull Cerodon U :D: .40 1.00
❑ 27 Caldera Hellion R :R: .60 1.50
❑ 28 Call to Heel C :B: .20 .50
❑ 29 Cancel C :B: .20 .50
❑ 30 Carrion Thrash C :D: .20 .50
❑ 31 Cathartic Adept C :B: .20 .50
❑ 32 Cavern Thoctar C :G: .20 .50
❑ 33 Clarion Ultimatum R :D: .60 1.50
❑ 34 Cloudheath Drake C :B: .20 .50
❑ 35 Coma Veil C :B: .20 .50
❑ 36 Corpse Connoisseur U :K: .40 1.00
❑ 37 Courier's Capsule C :B: .20 .50
❑ 38 Court Archers C :G: .20 .50
❑ 39 Covenant of Minds R :B: .40 1.00
❑ 40 Cradle of Vitality R :W: 1.25 3.00
❑ 41 Crucible of Fire R :R: 3.00 8.00
❑ 42 Cruel Ultimatum R :D: 1.25 3.00
❑ 43 Crumbling Necropolis U :L: 1.50 4.00
❑ 44 Cunning Lethemancer R :K: .60 1.50
❑ 45 Cylian Elf C :G: .20 .50
❑ 46 Dawnray Archer U :B: .40 1.00
❑ 47 Death Baron R :K: 12.00 30.00
❑ 48 Deathgreeter C :K: .20 .50
❑ 49 Deft Duelist C :D: .20 .50
❑ 50 Demon's Herald U :K: .40 1.00
❑ 51 Dispeller's Capsule C :W: .20 .50
❑ 52 Dragon Fodder C :R: .40 1.00
❑ 53 Dragon's Herald U :R: .40 1.00
❑ 54 Dreg Reaver C :K: .20 .50
❑ 55 Dregscape Zombie C :K: .20 .50
❑ 56 Druid of the Anima C :G: .20 .50
❑ 57 Drumhunter U :G: .40 1.00
❑ 58 Elspeth, Knight-Errant M :W: 25.00 60.00
❑ 59 Elvish Visionary C :G: .20 .50
❑ 60 Empyrial Archangel M :D: 5.00 12.00
❑ 61 Esper Battlemage U :B: .40 1.00
❑ 62 Esper Charm U :D: 1.00 2.50
❑ 63 Esper Panorama C :L: .20 .50
❑ 64 Etherium Astrolabe U :B: .40 1.00
❑ 65 Etherium Sculptor C :B: 1.50 4.00
❑ 66 Ethersworn Canonist R :W: 12.00 30.00
❑ 67 Excommunicate C :W: .20 .50
❑ 68 Executioner's Capsule C :K: .20 .50
❑ 69 Exuberant Firestoker U :R: .40 1.00
❑ 70 Fatestitcher U :B: .40 1.00
❑ 71 Feral Hydra R :G: .60 1.50
❑ 72 Filigree Sages U :B: .40 1.00
❑ 73 Fire-Field Ogre U :D: .40 1.00
❑ 74 Flameblast Dragon R :R: 1.00 2.50
❑ 75 Fleshbag Marauder U :K: .40 1.00
❑ 76 Forest L :L: .20 .50
❑ 77 Forest L :L: .20 .50
❑ 78 Forest L :L: .20 .50
❑ 79 Forest L :L: .20 .50
❑ 80 Gather Specimens R :B: .60 1.50
❑ 81 Gift of the Gargantuan C :G: .20 .50
❑ 82 Glaze Fiend C :K: .20 .50
❑ 83 Goblin Assault R :R: 1.25 3.00
❑ 84 Goblin Deathraiders C :D: .20 .50
❑ 85 Goblin Mountaineer C :R: .20 .50
❑ 86 Godsire M :D: 5.00 12.00
❑ 87 Godtoucher C :G: .20 .50
❑ 88 Grixis Battlemage U :K: .40 1.00
❑ 89 Grixis Charm U :D: .40 1.00
❑ 90 Grixis Panorama C :L: .20 .50
❑ 91 Guardians of Akrasa C :W: .20 .50
❑ 92 Gustrider Exuberant C :W: .20 .50
❑ 93 Hell's Thunder R :R: 2.50 6.00
❑ 94 Hellkite Overlord M :D: 5.00 12.00
❑ 95 Hindering Light C :D: .40 1.00
❑ 96 Hissing Iguanar C :R: .20 .50
❑ 97 Immortal Coil R :K: .60 1.50
❑ 98 Incurable Ogre C :R: .20 .50
❑ 99 Infest U :K: .40 1.00
❑ 100 Invincible Hymn R :W: .50 1.25
❑ 101 Island L :L: .20 .50
❑ 102 Island L :L: .20 .50
❑ 103 Island L :L: .20 .50
❑ 104 Island L :L: .20 .50
❑ 105 Jhessian Infiltrator U :D: .40 1.00
❑ 106 Jhessian Lookout C :B: .20 .50
❑ 107 Jund Battlemage U :R: .40 1.00
❑ 108 Jund Charm U :D: .40 1.00
❑ 109 Jund Panorama C :L: .20 .50
❑ 110 Jungle Shrine U :L: 1.25 3.00
❑ 111 Jungle Weaver C :G: .20 .50
❑ 112 Kathari Screecher C :B: .20 .50
❑ 113 Kederekt Creeper C :D: .20 .50
❑ 114 Kederekt Leviathan R :B: .50 1.25
❑ 115 Keeper of Progenitus R :G: .50 1.25
❑ 116 Kiss of the Amesha U :D: .40 1.00
❑ 117 Knight of the Skyward Eye C :W: .20 .50
❑ 118 Knight of the White Orchid R :W: 3.00 8.00
❑ 119 Knight-Captain of Eos R :W: .60 1.50
❑ 120 Kresh the Bloodbraided M :D: 1.50 4.00
❑ 121 Lich's Mirror M :A: 2.00 5.00
❑ 122 Lightning Talons C :R: .20 .50
❑ 123 Lush Growth C :G: .20 .50
❑ 124 Magma Spray C :R: .20 .50
❑ 125 Manaplasm R :G: .40 1.00
❑ 126 Marble Chalice C :W: .20 .50
❑ 127 Master of Etherium R :B: 5.00 12.00
❑ 128 Mayael the Anima M :D: 2.00 5.00
❑ 129 Memory Erosion R :B: 3.00 8.00
❑ 130 Metallurgeon U :W: .40 1.00
❑ 131 Mighty Emergence U :G: .40 1.00
❑ 132 Mindlock Orb R :B: .60 1.50
❑ 133 Minion Reflector R :A: .60 1.50
❑ 134 Mosstodon C :G: .20 .50
❑ 135 Mountain L :L: .20 .50
❑ 136 Mountain L :L: .20 .50
❑ 137 Mountain L :L: .20 .50
❑ 138 Mountain L :L: .20 .50
❑ 139 Mycoloth R :G: 4.00 10.00
❑ 140 Naturalize C :G: .20 .50
❑ 141 Naya Battlemage U :G: .40 1.00
❑ 142 Naya Charm U :D: .40 1.00
❑ 143 Naya Panorama C :L: .20 .50
❑ 144 Necrogenesis U :D: .40 1.00
❑ 145 Obelisk of Bant C :A: .20 .50
❑ 146 Obelisk of Esper C :A: .20 .50
❑ 147 Obelisk of Grixis C :A: .20 .50
❑ 148 Obelisk of Jund C :A: .20 .50
❑ 149 Obelisk of Naya C :A: .20 .50
❑ 150 Oblivion Ring C :W: 1.25 3.00
❑ 151 Onyx Goblet C :K: .20 .50
❑ 152 Ooze Garden R :G: .60 1.50
❑ 153 Outrider of Jhess C :B: .20 .50
❑ 154 Plains L :L: .20 .50
❑ 155 Plains L :L: .20 .50
❑ 156 Plains L :L: .20 .50
❑ 157 Plains L :L: .20 .50
❑ 158 Predator Dragon R :R: .75 2.00
❑ 159 Prince of Thralls M :D: 2.50 6.00
❑ 160 Protomatter Powder U :B: .40 1.00
❑ 161 Punish Ignorance R :D: .60 1.50
❑ 162 Puppet Conjurer U :K: .40 1.00
❑ 163 Qasali Ambusher U :D: .40 1.00
❑ 164 Quietus Spike R :A: 3.00 8.00
❑ 165 Rafiq of the Many M :D: 5.00 12.00
❑ 166 Rakeclaw Gargantuan C :D: .20 .50
❑ 167 Ranger of Eos R :W: 4.00 10.00
❑ 168 Realm Razer R :D: .60 1.50
❑ 169 Relic of Progenitus C :A: 1.25 3.00
❑ 170 Resounding Roar C :G: .20 .50
❑ 171 Resounding Scream C :K: .20 .50
❑ 172 Resounding Silence C :W: .20 .50
❑ 173 Resounding Thunder C :R: .20 .50
❑ 174 Resounding Wave C :B: .20 .50
❑ 175 Rhox Charger U :G: .40 1.00
❑ 176 Rhox War Monk U :D: .50 1.25
❑ 177 Ridge Rannet C :R: .20 .50
❑ 178 Rip-Clan Crasher C :D: .20 .50
❑ 179 Rockcaster Platoon U :W: .40 1.00
❑ 180 Rockslide Elemental U :R: .40 1.00
❑ 181 Sacellum Godspeaker R :G: .40 1.00
❑ 182 Salvage Titan R :K: .60 1.50
❑ 183 Sanctum Gargoyle C :W: .20 .50
❑ 184 Sangrite Surge U :D: .40 1.00
❑ 185 Sarkhan Vol M :D: 12.00 30.00
❑ 186 Savage Hunger C :G: .20 .50
❑ 187 Savage Lands U :L: 1.50 4.00
❑ 188 Scavenger Drake U :K: .40 1.00
❑ 189 Scourge Devil U :R: .40 1.00
❑ 190 Scourglass R :W: 1.25 3.00
❑ 191 Seaside Citadel U :L: 1.50 4.00
❑ 192 Sedraxis Specter R :D: .75 2.00
❑ 193 Sedris, the Traitor King M :D: 2.00 5.00
❑ 194 Shadowfeed C :K: .20 .50
❑ 195 Sharding Sphinx R :B: .60 1.50
❑ 196 Sharuum the Hegemon M :D: 3.00 8.00
❑ 197 Shore Snapper C :K: .20 .50
❑ 198 Sighted-Caste Sorcerer C :W: .20 .50
❑ 199 Sigil Blessing C :D: .20 .50
❑ 200 Sigil of Distinction R :A: .60 1.50
❑ 201 Sigiled Paladin U :W: .75 2.00
❑ 202 Skeletal Kathari C :K: .20 .50
❑ 203 Skeletonize U :R: .40 1.00
❑ 204 Skill Borrower R :B: .60 1.50
❑ 205 Skullmulcher R :G: .50 1.25
❑ 206 Soul's Fire C :R: .20 .50
❑ 207 Soul's Grace C :W: .20 .50
❑ 208 Soul's Might C :G: .20 .50
❑ 209 Spearbreaker Behemoth R :G: .60 1.50
❑ 210 Spell Snip C :B: .20 .50
❑ 211 Sphinx Sovereign M :D: 1.25 3.00
❑ 212 Sphinx's Herald U :B: .40 1.00
❑ 213 Sprouting Thrinax U :D: .50 1.25
❑ 214 Steelclad Serpent C :B: .20 .50
❑ 215 Steward of Valeron C :D: .40 1.00
❑ 216 Stoic Angel R :D: 1.50 4.00
❑ 217 Sunseed Nurturer U :W: .40 1.00
❑ 218 Swamp L :L: .20 .50
❑ 219 Swamp L :L: .20 .50
❑ 220 Swamp L :L: .20 .50
❑ 221 Swamp L :L: .20 .50
❑ 222 Swerve U :D: .50 1.25
❑ 223 Tar Fiend R :K: .40 1.00
❑ 224 Tezzeret the Seeker M :B: 6.00 15.00
❑ 225 Thorn-Thrash Viashino C :R: .40 1.00
❑ 226 Thoughtcutter Agent U :D: .40 1.00
❑ 227 Thunder-Thrash Elder U :R: .40 1.00
❑ 228 Tidehollow Sculler U :D: .75 2.00
❑ 229 Tidehollow Strix C :D: .40 1.00
❑ 230 Titanic Ultimatum R :D: .50 1.25
❑ 231 Topan Ascetic U :G: .40 1.00
❑ 232 Tortoise Formation C :B: .20 .50
❑ 233 Tower Gargoyle U :D: .40 1.00
❑ 234 Undead Leotau C :K: .20 .50
❑ 235 Vectis Silencers C :B: .20 .50
❑ 236 Vein Drinker R :K: .60 1.50
❑ 237 Viashino Skeleton C :R: .20 .50
❑ 238 Vicious Shadows R :R: .40 1.00
❑ 239 Violent Ultimatum R :D: .60 1.50
❑ 240 Viscera Dragger C :K: .20 .50
❑ 241 Vithian Stinger C :R: .20 .50
❑ 242 Volcanic Submersion C :R: .20 .50
❑ 243 Waveskimmer Aven C :D: .20 .50
❑ 244 Welkin Guide C :W: .20 .50
❑ 245 Where Ancients Tread R :R: .40 1.00
❑ 246 Wild Nacatl C :G: .40 1.00
❑ 247 Windwright Mage C :D: .20 .50
❑ 248 Woolly Thoctar U :D: 1.00 2.50
❑ 249 Yoked Plowbeast C :W: .20 .50

2009 Magic the Gathering Magic 2010

Complete Set (234) 100.00 175.00

❑ 1 Acidic Slime U :G: .20 .50
❑ 2 Acolyte of Xathrid C :K: .10 .25
❑ 3 Act of Treason U :R: .20 .50
❑ 4 Air Elemental U :B: .20 .50
❑ 5 Ajani Goldmane M :W: 2.50 6.00
❑ 6 Alluring Siren U :B: .20 .50
❑ 7 Angel's Feather U :A: .20 .50
❑ 8 Angel's Mercy C :W: .10 .25
❑ 9 Ant Queen R :G: .30 .75

MAGIC

Card	Low	High
❑ 10 Armored Ascension U :W:	.20	.50
❑ 11 Assassinate C :K:	.10	.25
❑ 12 Awakener Druid U :G:	.20	.50
❑ 13 Ball Lightning R :R:	1.25	3.00
❑ 14 Baneslayer Angel M :W:	5.00	12.00
❑ 15 Berserkers of Blood Ridge C :R:	.10	.25
❑ 16 Birds of Paradise R :G:	2.00	5.00
❑ 17 Black Knight U :K:	.30	.75
❑ 18 Blinding Mage C :W:	.10	.25
❑ 19 Bog Wraith U :K:	.20	.50
❑ 20 Bogardan Hellkite M :R:	.75	2.00
❑ 21 Borderland Ranger C :G:	.10	.25
❑ 22 Bountiful Harvest C :G:	.10	.25
❑ 23 Bramble Creeper C :G:	.10	.25
❑ 24 Burning Inquiry C :R:	.10	.25
❑ 25 Burst of Speed C :R:	.10	.25
❑ 26 Cancel C :B:	.10	.25
❑ 27 Canyon Minotaur C :R:	.10	.25
❑ 28 Capricious Efreet R :R:	.30	.75
❑ 29 Captain of the Watch R :W:	2.00	5.00
❑ 30 Celestial Purge U :W:	.20	.50
❑ 31 Cemetery Reaper R :K:	1.50	4.00
❑ 32 Centaur Courser C :G:	.10	.25
❑ 33 Chandra Nalaar M :R:	1.50	4.00
❑ 34 Child of Night C :K:	.10	.25
❑ 35 Clone R :B:	.30	.75
❑ 36 Coat of Arms R :A:	2.00	5.00
❑ 37 Consume Spirit U :K:	.20	.50
❑ 38 Convincing Mirage C :B:	.10	.25
❑ 39 Coral Merfolk C :B:	.10	.25
❑ 40 Craw Wurm C :G:	.10	.25
❑ 41 Cudgel Troll U :G:	.20	.50
❑ 42 Darksteel Colossus M :A:	2.00	5.00
❑ 43 Deadly Recluse C :G:	.20	.50
❑ 44 Deathmark U :K:	.30	.75
❑ 45 Demon's Horn U :A:	.20	.50
❑ 46 Diabolic Tutor U :K:	.30	.75
❑ 47 Disentomb C :K:	.10	.25
❑ 48 Disorient C :B:	.10	.25
❑ 49 Divination C :B:	.10	.25
❑ 50 Divine Verdict C :W:	.10	.25
❑ 51 Djinn of Wishes R :B:	.30	.75
❑ 52 Doom Blade C :K:	.20	.50
❑ 53 Dragon Whelp U :R:	.20	.50
❑ 54 Dragon's Claw U :A:	.20	.50
❑ 55 Dragonskull Summit R :L:	1.50	4.00
❑ 56 Dread Warlock C :K:	.10	.25
❑ 57 Drowned Catacomb R :L:	3.00	8.00
❑ 58 Drudge Skeletons C :K:	.10	.25
❑ 59 Duress C :K:	.20	.50
❑ 60 Earthquake R :R:	.40	1.00
❑ 61 Elite Vanguard U :W:	.30	.75
❑ 62 Elvish Archdruid R :G:	.75	2.00
❑ 63 Elvish Piper R :G:	2.00	5.00
❑ 64 Elvish Visionary C :G:	.20	.50
❑ 65 Emerald Oryx C :G:	.10	.25
❑ 66 Enormous Baloth U :G:	.20	.50
❑ 67 Entangling Vines C :G:	.10	.25
❑ 68 Essence Scatter C :B:	.10	.25
❑ 69 Excommunicate C :W:	.10	.25
❑ 70 Fabricate U :B:	.40	1.00
❑ 71 Fiery Hellhound C :R:	.10	.25
❑ 72 Fireball U :R:	.20	.50
❑ 73 Firebreathing C :R:	.10	.25
❑ 74 Flashfreeze U :B:	.20	.50
❑ 75 Fog C :G:	.10	.25
❑ 76 Forest C :L:	.10	.25
❑ 77 Gargoyle Castle R :L:	.40	1.00
❑ 78 Garruk Wildspeaker M :G:	2.50	6.00
❑ 79 Giant Growth C :G:	.10	.25
❑ 80 Giant Spider C :G:	.10	.25
❑ 81 Glacial Fortress R :L:	2.00	5.00
❑ 82 Glorious Charge C :W:	.10	.25
❑ 83 Goblin Artillery U :R:	.20	.50
❑ 84 Goblin Chieftain R :R:	.60	1.50
❑ 85 Goblin Piker C :R:	.10	.25
❑ 86 Gorgon Flail U :A:	.30	.75
❑ 87 Gravedigger C :K:	.10	.25
❑ 88 Great Sable Stag R :G:	.60	1.50
❑ 89 Griffin Sentinel C :W:	.10	.25
❑ 90 Guardian Seraph R :W:	.30	.75
❑ 91 Harm's Way U :W:	.30	.75
❑ 92 Haunting Echoes R :K:	.40	1.00
❑ 93 Hive Mind R :B:	.40	1.00
❑ 94 Holy Strength C :W:	.10	.25
❑ 95 Honor of the Pure R :W:	1.50	4.00
❑ 96 Horned Turtle C :B:	.10	.25
❑ 97 Howl of the Night Pack U :G:	.20	.50
❑ 98 Howling Banshee U :K:	.20	.50
❑ 99 Howling Mine R :A:	1.25	3.00
❑ 100 Hypnotic Specter R :K:	.75	2.00
❑ 101 Ice Cage C :B:	.10	.25
❑ 102 Ignite Disorder U :R:	.20	.50
❑ 103 Illusionary Servant C :B:	.10	.25
❑ 104 Indestructibility R :W:	.40	1.00
❑ 105 Inferno Elemental U :R:	.20	.50
❑ 106 Island C :L:	.10	.25
❑ 107 Jace Beleren M :B:	2.00	5.00
❑ 108 Jackal Familiar C :R:	.10	.25
❑ 109 Jump C :B:	.10	.25
❑ 110 Kalonian Behemoth R :G:	.40	1.00
❑ 111 Kelinore Bat C :K:	.10	.25
❑ 112 Kindled Fury C :R:	.10	.25
❑ 113 Kraken's Eye U :A:	.20	.50
❑ 114 Lava Axe C :R:	.10	.25
❑ 115 Levitation U :B:	.20	.50
❑ 116 Lifelink C :W:	.10	.25
❑ 117 Lightning Bolt C :R:	.40	1.00
❑ 118 Lightning Elemental C :R:	.10	.25
❑ 119 Lightwielder Paladin R :W:	.30	.75
❑ 120 Liliana Vess M :K:	3.00	8.00
❑ 121 Llanowar Elves C :G:	.20	.50
❑ 122 Looming Shade C :K:	.10	.25
❑ 123 Lurking Predators R :G:	.40	1.00
❑ 124 Magebane Armor R :A:	.30	.75
❑ 125 Magma Phoenix R :R:	.30	.75
❑ 126 Manabarbs R :R:	.30	.75
❑ 127 Master of the Wild Hunt M :G:	2.50	6.00
❑ 128 Megrim U :K:	.30	.75
❑ 129 Merfolk Looter C :B:	.10	.25
❑ 130 Merfolk Sovereign R :B:	.30	.75
❑ 131 Mesa Enchantress R :W:	.30	.75
❑ 132 Might of Oaks R :G:	.30	.75
❑ 133 Mind Control U :B:	.30	.75
❑ 134 Mind Rot C :K:	.10	.25
❑ 135 Mind Shatter R :K:	.30	.75
❑ 136 Mind Spring R :B:	.30	.75
❑ 137 Mirror of Fate R :A:	.30	.75
❑ 138 Mist Leopard C :G:	.10	.25
❑ 139 Mold Adder U :G:	.20	.50
❑ 140 Mountain C :L:	.10	.25
❑ 141 Naturalize C :G:	.10	.25
❑ 142 Nature's Spiral U :G:	.20	.50
❑ 143 Negate C :B:	.10	.25
❑ 144 Nightmare R :K:	.30	.75
❑ 145 Oakenform C :G:	.10	.25
❑ 146 Open the Vaults R :W:	.30	.75
❑ 147 Ornithopter U :A:	.30	.75
❑ 148 Overrun U :G:	.30	.75
❑ 149 Pacifism C :W:	.10	.25
❑ 150 Palace Guard C :W:	.10	.25
❑ 151 Panic Attack C :R:	.10	.25
❑ 152 Phantom Warrior U :B:	.20	.50
❑ 153 Pithing Needle R :A:	1.50	4.00
❑ 154 Plains C :L:	.10	.25
❑ 155 Planar Cleansing R :W:	.30	.75
❑ 156 Platinum Angel M :A:	2.00	5.00
❑ 157 Polymorph R :B:	.40	1.00
❑ 158 Ponder C :B:	.40	1.00
❑ 159 Prized Unicorn U :G:	.20	.50
❑ 160 Prodigal Pyromancer U :R:	.20	.50
❑ 161 Protean Hydra M :G:	.60	1.50
❑ 162 Pyroclasm U :R:	.30	.75
❑ 163 Raging Goblin C :R:	.10	.25
❑ 164 Rampant Growth C :G:	.10	.25
❑ 165 Razorfoot Griffin C :W:	.10	.25
❑ 166 Regenerate C :G:	.10	.25
❑ 167 Relentless Rats U :K:	.60	1.50
❑ 168 Rhox Pikemaster U :W:	.20	.50
❑ 169 Righteousness U :W:	.20	.50
❑ 170 Rise from the Grave U :K:	.20	.50
❑ 171 Rod of Ruin U :A:	.20	.50
❑ 172 Rootbound Crag R :L:	2.00	5.00
❑ 173 Royal Assassin R :K:	.30	.75
❑ 174 Runeclaw Bear C :G:	.10	.25
❑ 175 Safe Passage C :W:	.10	.25
❑ 176 Sage Owl C :B:	.10	.25
❑ 177 Sanguine Bond R :K:	3.00	8.00
❑ 178 Seismic Strike C :R:	.10	.25
❑ 179 Serpent of the Endless Sea C :B:	.10	.25
❑ 180 Serra Angel U :W:	.30	.75
❑ 181 Shatter C :R:	.10	.25
❑ 182 Shivan Dragon R :R:	.30	.75
❑ 183 Siege Mastodon C :W:	.10	.25
❑ 184 Siege-Gang Commander R :R:	.75	2.00
❑ 185 Sign in Blood C :K:	.20	.50
❑ 186 Silence R :W:	.60	1.50
❑ 187 Silvercoat Lion C :W:	.10	.25
❑ 188 Sleep U :B:	.30	.75
❑ 189 Snapping Drake C :B:	.10	.25
❑ 190 Solemn Offering C :W:	.10	.25
❑ 191 Soul Bleed C :K:	.10	.25
❑ 192 Soul Warden C :W:	.20	.50
❑ 193 Sparkmage Apprentice C :R:	.10	.25
❑ 194 Spellbook U :A:	.20	.50
❑ 195 Sphinx Ambassador M :B:	.60	1.50
❑ 196 Stampeding Rhino C :G:	.10	.25
❑ 197 Stone Giant U :R:	.20	.50
❑ 198 Stormfront Pegasus C :W:	.10	.25
❑ 199 Sunpetal Grove R :L:	1.50	4.00
❑ 200 Swamp C :L:	.10	.25
❑ 201 Telepathy U :B:	.20	.50
❑ 202 Tempest of Light U :W:	.20	.50
❑ 203 Tendrils of Corruption C :K:	.10	.25
❑ 204 Terramorphic Expanse C :L:	.10	.25
❑ 205 Time Warp M :B:	2.50	6.00
❑ 206 Tome Scour C :B:	.10	.25
❑ 207 Traumatize R :B:	.60	1.50
❑ 208 Trumpet Blast C :R:	.10	.25
❑ 209 Twincast R :B:	1.00	2.50
❑ 210 Undead Slayer U :W:	.20	.50
❑ 211 Underworld Dreams R :K:	.60	1.50
❑ 212 Unholy Strength C :K:	.10	.25
❑ 213 Unsummon C :B:	.10	.25
❑ 214 Vampire Aristocrat C :K:	.10	.25
❑ 215 Vampire Nocturnus M :K:	8.00	20.00
❑ 216 Veteran Armorsmith C :W:	.10	.25
❑ 217 Veteran Swordsmith C :W:	.10	.25
❑ 218 Viashino Spearhunter C :R:	.10	.25
❑ 219 Wall of Bone U :K:	.20	.50
❑ 220 Wall of Faith C :W:	.10	.25
❑ 221 Wall of Fire U :R:	.20	.50
❑ 222 Wall of Frost U :B:	.20	.50
❑ 223 Warp World R :R:	.30	.75
❑ 224 Warpath Ghoul C :K:	.10	.25
❑ 225 Weakness C :K:	.10	.25
❑ 226 Whispersilk Cloak U :A:	.30	.75
❑ 227 White Knight U :W:	.20	.50
❑ 228 Wind Drake C :B:	.10	.25
❑ 229 Windstorm U :G:	.20	.50
❑ 230 Wurm's Tooth U :A:	.20	.50
❑ 231 Xathrid Demon M :K:	.40	1.00
❑ 232 Yawning Fissure C :R:	.10	.25
❑ 233 Zephyr Sprite C :B:	.10	.25
❑ 234 Zombie Goliath C :K:	.10	.25

2009 Magic the Gathering Magic 2010 Foil

*Foil: .8X to 2X Basic Cards

2009 Magic the Gathering Alara Reborn

Card	Low	High
Complete Set (145)	100.00	175.00
Booster Box (36 Packs)	100.00	175.00
Booster Pack (15 Cards)	4.00	5.00
Theme Decks	8.00	10.00
Fat Pack	50.00	100.00
❑ 1 Anathemancer U :D:	.30	.75
❑ 2 Architects of Will C :D:	.10	.25
❑ 3 Ardent Plea U :D:	.25	.60
❑ 4 Arsenal Thresher C :W: :K: :B:	.10	.25
❑ 5 Aven Mimeomancer R :D:	.30	.75
❑ 6 Bant Sojourners C :D:	.10	.25
❑ 7 Bant Sureblade C :G: :B: :W:	.10	.25
❑ 8 Behemoth Sledge U :D:	.60	1.50
❑ 9 Bituminous Blast U :D:	.30	.75
❑ 10 Blitz Hellion R :D:	.30	.75
❑ 11 Bloodbraid Elf U :D:	1.25	3.00
❑ 12 Brainbite C :D:	.10	.25
❑ 13 Breath of Malfegor C :D:	.10	.25
❑ 14 Captured Sunlight C :D:	.10	.25
❑ 15 Cerodon Yearling C :D:	.10	.25
❑ 16 Cloven Casting R :D:	.30	.75
❑ 17 Colossal Might C :D:	.10	.25
❑ 18 Crystallization C :G: :B: :W:	.10	.25
❑ 19 Dauntless Escort R :D:	.75	2.00
❑ 20 Deadshot Minotaur C :D:	.10	.25
❑ 21 Deathbringer Thoctar R :D:	.30	.75
❑ 22 Defiler of Souls M :D:	.75	2.00
❑ 23 Demonic Dread C :D:	.10	.25
❑ 24 Demonspine Whip U :D:	.20	.50
❑ 25 Deny Reality C :D:	.10	.25
❑ 26 Double Negative U :D:	.20	.50
❑ 27 Dragon Appeasement U :D:	.20	.50
❑ 28 Dragon Broodmother M :D:	3.00	8.00
❑ 29 Drastic Revelation U :D:	.20	.50
❑ 30 Enigma Sphinx R :D:	.30	.75
❑ 31 Enlisted Wurm U :D:	.20	.50
❑ 32 Esper Sojourners C :D:	.10	.25
❑ 33 Esper Stormblade C :W: :K: :B:	.10	.25
❑ 34 Ethercaste Knight C :D:	.10	.25
❑ 35 Etherium Abomination C :D:	.10	.25
❑ 36 Ethersworn Shieldmage C :D:	.10	.25
❑ 37 Etherwrought Page U :D:	.20	.50
❑ 38 Fieldmist Borderpost C :D:	.20	.50
❑ 39 Fight to the Death R :D:	.30	.75
❑ 40 Filigree Angel R :D:	.40	1.00
❑ 41 Finest Hour R :D:	.60	1.50
❑ 42 Firewild Borderpost C :D:	.10	.25
❑ 43 Flurry of Wings U :D:	.20	.50
❑ 44 Giant Ambush Beetle U :K: :G: :R:	.20	.50
❑ 45 Glassdust Hulk C :D:	.10	.25
❑ 46 Glory of Warfare R :D:	.40	1.00
❑ 47 Gloryscale Viashino U :D:	.20	.50
❑ 48 Godtracker of Jund C :D:	.10	.25
❑ 49 Gorger Wurm C :D:	.10	.25
❑ 50 Grixis Grimblade C :B: :R: :K:	.20	.50
❑ 51 Grixis Sojourners C :D:	.10	.25
❑ 52 Grizzled Leotau C :D:	.10	.25
❑ 53 Identity Crisis R :D:	.30	.75
❑ 54 Igneous Pouncer C :D:	.10	.25
❑ 55 Illusory Demon U :D:	.20	.50
❑ 56 Intimidation Bolt U :D:	.20	.50
❑ 57 Jenara, Asura of War M :D:	2.50	6.00
❑ 58 Jhessian Zombies C :D:	.10	.25
❑ 59 Jund Hackblade C :K: :G: :R:	.10	.25
❑ 60 Jund Sojourners C :D:	.10	.25
❑ 61 Karrthus, Tyrant of Jund M :D:	3.00	8.00
❑ 62 Kathari Bomber C :D:	.10	.25
❑ 63 Kathari Remnant U :D:	.20	.50
❑ 64 Knight of New Alara R :D:	.60	1.50
❑ 65 Knotvine Paladin R :D:	.40	1.00
❑ 66 Lavalanche R :D:	.30	.75
❑ 67 Leonin Armorguard C :D:	.10	.25
❑ 68 Lich Lord of Unx R :D:	2.50	6.00
❑ 69 Lightning Reaver R :D:	.40	1.00
❑ 70 Lord of Extinction M :D:	3.00	8.00
❑ 71 Lorescale Coatl U :D:	.40	1.00
❑ 72 Madrush Cyclops R :D:	.30	.75
❑ 73 Maelstrom Nexus M :D:	1.00	2.50
❑ 74 Maelstrom Pulse R :D:	6.00	15.00
❑ 75 Mage Slayer U :D:	.25	.60
❑ 76 Magefire Wings C :D:	.10	.25
❑ 77 Marisi's Twinclaws U :R: :W: :G:	.20	.50
❑ 78 Marrow Chomper U :D:	.20	.50
❑ 79 Mask of Riddles U :D:	.20	.50
❑ 80 Mayael's Aria R :D:	.75	2.00
❑ 81 Meddling Mage R :D:	1.25	3.00
❑ 82 Messenger Falcons U :G: :B: :W:	.20	.50
❑ 83 Mind Funeral U :D:	2.00	5.00
❑ 84 Mistvein Borderpost C :D:	.20	.50
❑ 85 Monstrous Carabid C :D:	.10	.25
❑ 86 Morbid Bloom U :D:	.20	.50
❑ 87 Mycoid Shepherd R :D:	.30	.75
❑ 88 Naya Hushblade C :R: :W: :G:	.10	.25
❑ 89 Naya Sojourners C :D:	.10	.25
❑ 90 Necromancer's Covenant R :D:	.30	.75
❑ 91 Nemesis of Reason R :D:	2.00	5.00
❑ 92 Nulltread Gargantuan U :D:	.25	.60
❑ 93 Offering to Asha C :D:	.10	.25
❑ 94 Pale Recluse C :D:	.10	.25
❑ 95 Predatory Advantage R :D:	.30	.75
❑ 96 Putrid Leech C :D:	.20	.50
❑ 97 Qasali Pridemage C :D:	.60	1.50
❑ 98 Reborn Hope U :D:	.20	.50
❑ 99 Retaliator Griffin R :D:	.30	.75
❑ 100 Rhox Brute C :D:	.10	.25
❑ 101 Sages of the Anima R :D:	.30	.75
❑ 102 Sanctum Plowbeast C :D:	.10	.25
❑ 103 Sangrite Backlash C :K: :G: :R:	.10	.25
❑ 104 Sanity Gnawers U :D:	.20	.50
❑ 105 Sen Triplets M :D:	3.00	8.00
❑ 106 Sewn-Eye Drake C :B: :R: :K:	.10	.25
❑ 107 Shield of the Righteous U :D:	.20	.50
❑ 108 Sigil Captain U :D:	.20	.50
❑ 109 Sigil of the Nayan Gods C :D:	.10	.25
❑ 110 Sigiled Behemoth C :D:	.10	.25
❑ 111 Singe-Mind Ogre C :D:	.10	.25
❑ 112 Skyclaw Thrash U :D:	.20	.50
❑ 113 Slave of Bolas U :B: :R: :K:	.20	.50
❑ 114 Soul Manipulation C :D:	.10	.25
❑ 115 Soulquake R :D:	.30	.75
❑ 116 Sovereigns of Lost Alara R :D:	.75	2.00
❑ 117 Spellbound Dragon R :D:	.30	.75
❑ 118 Spellbreaker Behemoth R :D:	.75	2.00
❑ 119 Sphinx of the Steel Wind M :D:	4.00	10.00
❑ 120 Stormcaller's Boon C :D:	.10	.25
❑ 121 Stun Sniper U :D:	.20	.50
❑ 122 Tainted Sigil U :D:	.20	.50
❑ 123 Talon Trooper C :D:	.10	.25
❑ 124 Terminate C :D:	.60	1.50
❑ 125 Thopter Foundry U :W: :K: :B:	.40	1.00
❑ 126 Thought Hemorrhage R :D:	.60	1.50
❑ 127 Thraximundar M :D:	5.00	12.00
❑ 128 Time Sieve R :D:	1.00	2.50
❑ 129 Trace of Abundance C :R: :W: :G:	.20	.50
❑ 130 Unbender Tine U :D:	.20	.50
❑ 131 Unscythe, Killer of Kings R :D:	.40	1.00
❑ 132 Uril, the Miststalker M :D:	1.25	3.00
❑ 133 Valley Rannet C :D:	.10	.25
❑ 134 Vectis Dominator C :D:	.10	.25
❑ 135 Vedalken Ghoul C :D:	.10	.25
❑ 136 Vedalken Heretic R :D:	.30	.75
❑ 137 Veinfire Borderpost C :D:	.20	.50
❑ 138 Vengeful Rebirth U :D:	.20	.50
❑ 139 Violent Outburst C :D:	.10	.25
❑ 140 Vithian Renegades U :D:	.20	.50
❑ 141 Wall of Denial U :D:	.75	2.00
❑ 142 Wargate R :D:	.60	1.50
❑ 143 Wildfield Borderpost C :D:	.20	.50
❑ 144 Winged Coatl C :D:	.10	.25
❑ 145 Zealous Persecution U :D:	.30	.75

2009 Magic the Gathering Alara Reborn Foil

*Foil: .8X to 2X Basic Cards

2009 Magic the Gathering Conflux

Card	Low	High
Complete Set (145)	75.00	125.00
Booster Box (36 Packs)	150.00	200.00
Booster Pack (15 Cards)	5.00	6.00
Theme Decks	8.00	10.00
Fat Pack	30.00	40.00
❑ 1 Absorb Vis C :K:	.20	.50
❑ 2 Aerie Mystics U :W:	.20	.50
❑ 3 Ancient Ziggurat U :L:	.75	2.00
❑ 4 Apocalypse Hydra M :D:	2.00	5.00
❑ 5 Armillary Sphere C :A:	.10	.25
❑ 6 Asha's Favor C :W:	.10	.25
❑ 7 Aven Squire C :W:	.10	.25
❑ 8 Aven Trailblazer C :W:	.10	.25
❑ 9 Banefire R :R:	1.25	3.00
❑ 10 Beacon Behemoth C :G:	.10	.25
❑ 11 Blood Tyrant R :D:	.40	1.00
❑ 12 Bloodhall Ooze R :R:	.30	.75
❑ 13 Bone Saw C :A:	.10	.25
❑ 14 Brackwater Elemental C :B:	.10	.25
❑ 15 Canyon Minotaur C :R:	.10	.25
❑ 16 Celestial Purge U :W:	.25	.60
❑ 17 Charnelhoard Wurm R :D:	.40	1.00
❑ 18 Child of Alara M :D:	.75	2.00
❑ 19 Cliffrunner Behemoth R :G:	.40	1.00
❑ 20 Conflux M :D:	.75	2.00
❑ 21 Constricting Tendrils C :B:	.10	.25
❑ 22 Controlled Instincts U :B:	.20	.50
❑ 23 Corrupted Roots U :K:	.20	.50
❑ 24 Countersquall U :D:	.50	1.25
❑ 25 Court Homunculus C :W:	.10	.25
❑ 26 Cumber Stone U :B:	.20	.50
❑ 27 Cylian Sunsinger R :G:	.40	1.00
❑ 28 Dark Temper C :R:	.10	.25
❑ 29 Darklit Gargoyle C :W:	.10	.25
❑ 30 Drag Down C :K:	.10	.25
❑ 31 Dragonsoul Knight U :R:	.20	.50
❑ 32 Dreadwing U :K:	.20	.50
❑ 33 Elder Mastery U :D:	.20	.50
❑ 34 Ember Weaver C :G:	.10	.25
❑ 35 Esper Cormorants C :D:	.10	.25
❑ 36 Esperzoa U :B:	.25	.60
❑ 37 Ethersworn Adjudicator M :B:	1.25	3.00
❑ 38 Exotic Orchard R :L:	.75	2.00
❑ 39 Exploding Borders C :D:	.10	.25
❑ 40 Extractor Demon R :K:	.40	1.00
❑ 41 Faerie Mechanist C :B:	.10	.25
❑ 42 Fiery Fall C :R:	.10	.25
❑ 43 Filigree Fracture U :G:	.20	.50
❑ 44 Fleshformer U :K:	.20	.50
❑ 45 Font of Mythos R :A:	1.50	4.00
❑ 46 Frontline Sage C :B:	.10	.25
❑ 47 Fusion Elemental U :D:	.25	.60
❑ 48 Giltspire Avenger R :D:	.40	1.00
❑ 49 Gleam of Resistance C :W:	.10	.25
❑ 50 Gluttonous Slime U :G:	.20	.50
❑ 51 Goblin Outlander C :D:	.10	.25
❑ 52 Goblin Razerunners R :R:	.40	1.00
❑ 53 Grixis Illusionist C :B:	.10	.25
❑ 54 Grixis Slavedriver U :K:	.20	.50
❑ 55 Gwafa Hazid, Profiteer R :D:	.30	.75
❑ 56 Hellkite Hatchling U :D:	.25	.60
❑ 57 Hellspark Elemental U :R:	.75	2.00
❑ 58 Ignite Disorder U :R:	.20	.50
❑ 59 Infectious Horror C :K:	.10	.25
❑ 60 Inkwell Leviathan R :B:	1.25	3.00
❑ 61 Jhessian Balmgiver U :D:	.20	.50
❑ 62 Kaleidostone C :A:	.10	.25
❑ 63 Kederekt Parasite R :K:	.40	1.00
❑ 64 Knight of the Reliquary R :D:	6.00	15.00
❑ 65 Knotvine Mystic U :D:	.30	.75
❑ 66 Kranioceros C :R:	.10	.25
❑ 67 Lapse of Certainty C :W:	.10	.25
❑ 68 Maelstrom Archangel M :D:	3.00	8.00
❑ 69 Magister Sphinx R :D:	.40	1.00
❑ 70 Malfegor M :D:	.75	2.00
❑ 71 Mana Cylix C :A:	.10	.25
❑ 72 Manaforce Mace U :A:	.20	.50
❑ 73 Maniacal Rage C :R:	.10	.25
❑ 74 Mark of Asylum R :W:	.40	1.00
❑ 75 Martial Coup R :W:	1.50	4.00
❑ 76 Master Transmuter R :B:	3.00	8.00
❑ 77 Matca Rioters C :G:	.10	.25
❑ 78 Meglonoth R :D:	.40	1.00
❑ 79 Might of Alara C :G:	.10	.25
❑ 80 Mirror-Sigil Sergeant M :W:	.75	2.00
❑ 81 Molten Frame C :R:	.10	.25
❑ 82 Nacatl Hunt-Pride U :W:	.20	.50
❑ 83 Nacatl Outlander C :D:	.10	.25
❑ 84 Nacatl Savage C :G:	.10	.25
❑ 85 Nicol Bolas, Planeswalker M :D:	6.00	15.00
❑ 86 Noble Hierarch R :G:	12.00	30.00
❑ 87 Nyxathid R :K:	.75	2.00
❑ 88 Obelisk of Alara R :A:	.40	1.00
❑ 89 Paleoloth R :G:	.40	1.00
❑ 90 Paragon of the Amesha U :W:	.20	.50
❑ 91 Parasitic Strix C :B:	.10	.25
❑ 92 Path to Exile U :W:	2.00	5.00
❑ 93 Pestilent Kathari C :K:	.10	.25
❑ 94 Progenitus M :D:	8.00	20.00
❑ 95 Quenchable Fire C :R:	.10	.25
❑ 96 Rakka Mar R :R:	.40	1.00
❑ 97 Reliquary Tower U :L:	2.00	5.00
❑ 98 Rhox Bodyguard C :D:	.10	.25
❑ 99 Rhox Meditant C :W:	.10	.25
❑ 100 Rotting Rats C :K:	.10	.25
❑ 101 Rupture Spire C :L:	.25	.60
❑ 102 Sacellum Archers U :G:	.20	.50
❑ 103 Salvage Slasher C :K:	.10	.25
❑ 104 Scarland Thrinax U :D:	.20	.50
❑ 105 Scattershot Archer C :G:	.10	.25
❑ 106 Scepter of Dominance R :W:	.30	.75
❑ 107 Scepter of Fugue R :K:	.40	1.00
❑ 108 Scepter of Insight R :B:	.30	.75
❑ 109 Scornful AEther-Lich U :B:	.20	.50
❑ 110 Sedraxis Alchemist C :K:	.20	.50
❑ 111 Shambling Remains U :D:	.30	.75
❑ 112 Shard Convergence U :G:	.20	.50
❑ 113 Sigil of the Empty Throne R :W:	.75	2.00
❑ 114 Skyward Eye Prophets U :D:	.20	.50
❑ 115 Sludge Strider U :D:	.20	.50
❑ 116 Soul's Majesty R :G:	.30	.75
❑ 117 Sphinx Summoner R :D:	.60	1.50
❑ 118 Spore Burst U :G:	.20	.50
❑ 119 Suicidal Charge C :D:	.10	.25
❑ 120 Sylvan Bounty C :G:	.10	.25
❑ 121 Telemin Performance R :B:	.60	1.50
❑ 122 Thornling M :G:	1.00	2.50
❑ 123 Toxic Iguanar C :R:	.10	.25
❑ 124 Traumatic Visions C :B:	.10	.25
❑ 125 Tukatongue Thallid C :G:	.10	.25
❑ 126 Unstable Frontier U :L:	.20	.50
❑ 127 Unsummon C :B:	.10	.25
❑ 128 Vagrant Plowbeasts U :D:	.20	.50
❑ 129 Valeron Outlander C :D:	.10	.25
❑ 130 Valiant Guard C :W:	.10	.25
❑ 131 Vectis Agents C :D:	.10	.25
❑ 132 Vedalken Outlander C :D:	.10	.25
❑ 133 Viashino Slaughtermaster U :R:	.20	.50
❑ 134 View from Above U :B:	.20	.50
❑ 135 Voices from the Void U :K:	.20	.50
❑ 136 Volcanic Fallout U :R:	.75	2.00
❑ 137 Voracious Dragon R :R:	.40	1.00
❑ 138 Wall of Reverence R :W:	1.25	3.00
❑ 139 Wandering Goblins C :R:	.10	.25
❑ 140 Wild Leotau C :G:	.10	.25
❑ 141 Worldheart Phoenix R :R:	.30	.75
❑ 142 Worldly Counsel C :B:	.10	.25
❑ 143 Wretched Banquet C :K:	.10	.25
❑ 144 Yoke of the Damned C :K:	.10	.25
❑ 145 Zombie Outlander C :D:	.10	.25

2009 Magic the Gathering Conflux Foil

Card	Low	High
Complete Set (145)	150.00	200.00

*Foil: .8X to 2X Basic Cards

Card	Low	High
❑ 1 Absorb Vis C :K:	.30	.75
❑ 2 Aerie Mystics U :W:	.30	.75
❑ 3 Ancient Ziggurat U :L:	1.50	4.00
❑ 4 Apocalypse Hydra M :D:	3.00	8.00
❑ 5 Armillary Sphere C :A:	.40	1.00
❑ 6 Asha's Favor C :W:	.30	.75
❑ 7 Aven Squire C :W:	.30	.75
❑ 8 Aven Trailblazer C :W:	.30	.75
❑ 9 Banefire R :R:	6.00	15.00
❑ 10 Beacon Behemoth C :G:	.30	.75
❑ 11 Blood Tyrant R :D:	1.00	2.50
❑ 12 Bloodhall Ooze R :R:	1.50	4.00
❑ 13 Bone Saw C :A:	.30	.75
❑ 14 Brackwater Elemental C :B:	.30	.75
❑ 15 Canyon Minotaur C :R:	.30	.75
❑ 16 Celestial Purge U :W:	1.25	3.00
❑ 17 Charnelhoard Wurm R :D:	1.00	2.50
❑ 18 Child of Alara M :D:	1.00	2.50
❑ 19 Cliffrunner Behemoth R :G:	1.50	4.00
❑ 20 Conflux M :D:	3.00	8.00
❑ 21 Constricting Tendrils C :B:	.30	.75
❑ 22 Controlled Instincts U :B:	.30	.75
❑ 23 Corrupted Roots U :K:	.30	.75
❑ 24 Countersquall U :D:	1.25	3.00
❑ 25 Court Homunculus C :W:	.30	.75
❑ 26 Cumber Stone U :B:	.50	1.25
❑ 27 Cylian Sunsinger R :G:	.75	2.00
❑ 28 Dark Temper C :R:	.30	.75
❑ 29 Darklit Gargoyle C :W:	.30	.75
❑ 30 Drag Down C :K:	.30	.75
❑ 31 Dragonsoul Knight U :R:	.30	.75
❑ 32 Dreadwing U :K:	.30	.75
❑ 33 Elder Mastery U :D:	.30	.75
❑ 34 Ember Weaver C :G:	.30	.75
❑ 35 Esper Cormorants C :D:	.30	.75
❑ 36 Esperzoa U :B:	1.25	3.00
❑ 37 Ethersworn Adjudicator M :B:	3.00	8.00
❑ 38 Exotic Orchard R :L:	3.00	8.00
❑ 39 Exploding Borders C :D:	.30	.75
❑ 40 Extractor Demon R :K:	1.00	2.50
❑ 41 Faerie Mechanist C :B:	.30	.75
❑ 42 Fiery Fall C :R:	.30	.75
❑ 43 Filigree Fracture U :G:	.50	1.25
❑ 44 Fleshformer U :K:	.30	.75
❑ 45 Font of Mythos R :A:	4.00	10.00
❑ 46 Frontline Sage C :B:	.30	.75
❑ 47 Fusion Elemental U :D:	.50	1.25
❑ 48 Giltspire Avenger R :D:	1.25	3.00
❑ 49 Gleam of Resistance C :W:	.30	.75
❑ 50 Gluttonous Slime U :G:	.30	.75
❑ 51 Goblin Outlander C :D:	.30	.75
❑ 52 Goblin Razerunners R :R:	1.25	3.00
❑ 53 Grixis Illusionist C :B:	.30	.75
❑ 54 Grixis Slavedriver U :K:	.30	.75
❑ 55 Gwafa Hazid, Profiteer R :D:	1.25	3.00
❑ 56 Hellkite Hatchling U :D:	.40	1.00
❑ 57 Hellspark Elemental U :R:	1.25	3.00
❑ 58 Ignite Disorder U :R:	.40	1.00
❑ 59 Infectious Horror C :K:	.30	.75
❑ 60 Inkwell Leviathan R :B:	4.00	10.00
❑ 61 Jhessian Balmgiver U :D:	.30	.75
❑ 62 Kaleidostone C :A:	.40	1.00
❑ 63 Kederekt Parasite R :K:	1.50	4.00
❑ 64 Knight of the Reliquary R :D:	10.00	25.00
❑ 65 Knotvine Mystic U :D:	.40	1.00
❑ 66 Kranioceros C :R:	.30	.75
❑ 67 Lapse of Certainty C :W:	.50	1.25
❑ 68 Maelstrom Archangel M :D:	2.00	5.00
❑ 69 Magister Sphinx R :D:	1.25	3.00
❑ 70 Malfegor M :D:	2.50	6.00
❑ 71 Mana Cylix C :A:	.30	.75
❑ 72 Manaforce Mace U :A:	.30	.75
❑ 73 Maniacal Rage C :R:	.30	.75
❑ 74 Mark of Asylum R :W:	1.25	3.00
❑ 75 Martial Coup R :W:	4.00	10.00
❑ 76 Master Transmuter R :B:	4.00	10.00
❑ 77 Matca Rioters C :G:	.30	.75
❑ 78 Meglonoth R :D:	1.25	3.00
❑ 79 Might of Alara C :G:	.60	1.50
❑ 80 Mirror-Sigil Sergeant M :W:	2.50	6.00
❑ 81 Molten Frame C :R:	.30	.75
❑ 82 Nacatl Hunt-Pride U :W:	.30	.75
❑ 83 Nacatl Outlander C :D:	.30	.75
❑ 84 Nacatl Savage C :G:	.30	.75
❑ 85 Nicol Bolas, Planeswalker M :D:	15.00	30.00
❑ 86 Noble Hierarch R :G:	18.00	35.00
❑ 87 Nyxathid R :K:	3.00	8.00
❑ 88 Obelisk of Alara R :A:	1.00	2.50
❑ 89 Paleoloth R :G:	.60	1.50
❑ 90 Paragon of the Amesha U :W:	.30	.75
❑ 91 Parasitic Strix C :B:	.30	.75
❑ 92 Path to Exile U :W:	5.00	12.00
❑ 93 Pestilent Kathari C :K:	.30	.75
❑ 94 Progenitus M :D:	8.00	20.00
❑ 95 Quenchable Fire C :R:	.30	.75
❑ 96 Rakka Mar R :R:	1.25	3.00
❑ 97 Reliquary Tower U :L:	.50	1.25
❑ 98 Rhox Bodyguard C :D:	.30	.75
❑ 99 Rhox Meditant C :W:	.30	.75
❑ 100 Rotting Rats C :K:	.30	.75
❑ 101 Rupture Spire C :L:	.60	1.50
❑ 102 Sacellum Archers U :G:	.30	.75
❑ 103 Salvage Slasher C :K:	.30	.75
❑ 104 Scarland Thrinax U :D:	.40	1.00
❑ 105 Scattershot Archer C :G:	.40	1.00
❑ 106 Scepter of Dominance R :W:	2.50	6.00
❑ 107 Scepter of Fugue R :K:	2.50	6.00
❑ 108 Scepter of Insight R :B:	1.00	2.50
❑ 109 Scornful Æther-Lich U :B:	.30	.75
❑ 110 Sedraxis Alchemist C :K:	.30	.75
❑ 111 Shambling Remains U :D:	1.25	3.00
❑ 112 Shard Convergence U :G:	.40	1.00
❑ 113 Sigil of the Empty Throne R :W:	1.50	4.00
❑ 114 Skyward Eye Prophets U :D:	.30	.75
❑ 115 Sludge Strider U :D:	.30	.75
❑ 116 Soul's Majesty R :G:	1.00	2.50
❑ 117 Sphinx Summoner R :D:	2.00	5.00
❑ 118 Spore Burst U :G:	.30	.75
❑ 119 Suicidal Charge C :D:	.30	.75
❑ 120 Sylvan Bounty C :G:	.30	.75
❑ 121 Telemin Performance R :B:	1.50	4.00
❑ 122 Thornling M :G:	5.00	12.00
❑ 123 Toxic Iguanar C :R:	.30	.75
❑ 124 Traumatic Visions C :B:	.30	.75
❑ 125 Tukatongue Thallid C :G:	.30	.75
❑ 126 Unstable Frontier U :L:	.30	.75
❑ 127 Unsummon C :B:	.30	.75
❑ 128 Vagrant Plowbeasts U :D:	.30	.75
❑ 129 Valeron Outlander C :D:	.30	.75
❑ 130 Valiant Guard C :W:	.30	.75
❑ 131 Vectis Agents C :D:	.30	.75
❑ 132 Vedalken Outlander C :D:	.30	.75
❑ 133 Viashino Slaughtermaster U :R:	.60	1.50
❑ 134 View from Above U :B:	.30	.75
❑ 135 Voices from the Void U :K:	.30	.75
❑ 136 Volcanic Fallout U :R:	2.00	5.00
❑ 137 Voracious Dragon R :R:	1.50	4.00
❑ 138 Wall of Reverence R :W:	2.50	6.00
❑ 139 Wandering Goblins C :R:	.30	.75
❑ 140 Wild Leotau C :G:	.30	.75
❑ 141 Worldheart Phoenix R :R:	.75	2.00
❑ 142 Worldly Counsel C :B:	.30	.75
❑ 143 Wretched Banquet C :K:	.30	.75
❑ 144 Yoke of the Damned C :K:	.30	.75
❑ 145 Zombie Outlander C :D:	.30	.75

2009 Magic the Gathering Divine vs Demonic

Card	Low	High
❑ 1 Akroma, Angel of Wrath M :W:	12.00	30.00
❑ 2 Icatian Priest U :W:	.20	.50
❑ 3 Angelic Page C :W:	.20	.50
❑ 4 Charging Paladin C :W:	.10	.25
❑ 5 Venerable Monk C :W:	.10	.25
❑ 6 Angelic Protector U :W:	.20	.50
❑ 7 Serra Advocate U :W:	.20	.50
❑ 8 Sustainer of the Realm U :W:	.20	.50
❑ 9 Angel of Mercy U :W:	.20	.50
❑ 10 Serra Angel R :W:	.30	.75
❑ 11 Twilight Shepherd R :W:	1.25	3.00
❑ 12 Luminous Angel R :W:	3.00	8.00
❑ 13 Reya Dawnbringer R :W:	3.00	8.00
❑ 14 Healing Salve C :W:	.10	.25
❑ 15 Angelsong C :W:	.10	.25
❑ 16 Otherworldly Journey U :W:	.20	.50
❑ 17 Pacifism C :W:	.10	.25
❑ 18 Serra's Boon U :W:	.20	.50
❑ 19 Angelic Benediction U :W:	.20	.50
❑ 20 Faith's Fetters C :W:	.30	.75
❑ 21 Serra's Embrace U :W:	.30	.75
❑ 22 Righteous Cause U :W:	.20	.50
❑ 23 Angel's Feather U	.20	.50
❑ 24 Marble Diamond U	.20	.50
❑ 25 Secluded Steppe C	.10	.25
❑ 26 Plains L	.20	.50
❑ 27 Plains L	.20	.50
❑ 28 Plains L	.20	.50
❑ 29 Plains L	.20	.50
❑ 30 Lord of the Pit M :K:	1.50	4.00
❑ 31 Abyssal Gatekeeper C :K:	.10	.25
❑ 32 Foul Imp C :K:	.10	.25
❑ 33 Daggerclaw Imp U :K:	.20	.50
❑ 34 Dusk Imp C :K:	.10	.25
❑ 35 Overeager Apprentice C :K:	.10	.25
❑ 36 Stinkweed Imp C :K:	2.00	5.00
❑ 37 Soot Imp U :K:	.20	.50
❑ 38 Demon's Jester C :K:	.10	.25
❑ 39 Souldrinker U :K:	.20	.50
❑ 40 Abyssal Specter U :K:	.20	.50
❑ 41 Cackling Imp C :K:	.10	.25
❑ 42 Fallen Angel R :K:	.30	.75
❑ 43 Reiver Demon R :K:	.75	2.00
❑ 44 Kuro, Pitlord R :K:	.30	.75
❑ 45 Dark Ritual C :K:	1.25	3.00
❑ 46 Duress C :K:	.40	1.00
❑ 47 Unholy Strength C :K:	.10	.25
❑ 48 Cruel Edict U :K:	.40	1.00
❑ 49 Demonic Tutor U :K:	12.00	30.00
❑ 50 Dark Banishing C :K:	.10	.25
❑ 51 Oni Possession U :K:	.20	.50
❑ 52 Barter in Blood U :K:	.40	1.00
❑ 53 Breeding Pit U :K:	.30	.75
❑ 54 Promise of Power R :K:	.40	1.00
❑ 55 Corrupt U :K:	.20	.50
❑ 56 Consume Spirit U :K:	.20	.50
❑ 57 Demon's Horn U	.20	.50
❑ 58 Barren Moor C	.20	.50
❑ 59 Swamp L	.20	.50
❑ 60 Swamp L	.20	.50
❑ 61 Swamp L	.20	.50
❑ 62 Swamp L	.20	.50
❑ T1 Spirit - Token C	.40	1.00
❑ T2 Demon - Token C	.40	1.00
❑ T3 Thrull - Token C	.60	1.50

2009 Magic the Gathering Garruk vs Liliana

Card	Low	High
Duel Deck	30.00	50.00
❑ 1 Garruk Wildspeaker M :G:	6.00	15.00
❑ 2 Basking Rootwalla C :G:	.30	.75
❑ 3 Albino Troll U :G:	.30	.75
❑ 4 Vine Trellis C :G:	.10	.25
❑ 5 Wild Mongrel C :G:	.10	.25
❑ 6 Wirewood Savage C :G:	.10	.25
❑ 7 Blastoderm C :G:	.10	.25
❑ 8 Ravenous Baloth R :G:	1.50	4.00
❑ 9 Stampeding Wildebeests U :G:	.20	.50
❑ 10 Indrik Stomphowler U :G:	.20	.50
❑ 11 Krosan Tusker C :G:	.10	.25
❑ 12 Plated Slagwurm R :G:	1.25	3.00
❑ 13 Genju of the Cedars U :G:	.20	.50
❑ 14 Giant Growth C :G:	.20	.50
❑ 15 Rancor C :G:	.10	.25
❑ 16 Lignify C :G:	.10	.25
❑ 17 Nature's Lore C :G:	.10	.25
❑ 18 Elephant Guide U :G:	.20	.50
❑ 19 Invigorate C :G:	.20	.50
❑ 20 Serrated Arrows C	.10	.25
❑ 21 Harmonize U :G:	.20	.50
❑ 22 Rude Awakening R :G:	.60	1.50
❑ 23 Beast Attack U :G:	.20	.50
❑ 24 Overrun U :G:	.20	.50
❑ 25 Windstorm U :G:	.20	.50
❑ 26 Slippery Karst C	.10	.25
❑ 27 Treetop Village U	.20	.50
❑ 28 Forest L	.10	.25
❑ 29 Forest L	.10	.25
❑ 30 Forest L	.10	.25
❑ 31 Forest L	.10	.25
❑ 32 Liliana Vess M :K:	6.00	15.00
❑ 33 Deathgreeter C :K:	.10	.25
❑ 34 Ghost-Lit Stalker U :K:	.20	.50
❑ 35 Vampire Bats C :K:	.10	.25
❑ 36 Drudge Skeletons C :K:	.10	.25
❑ 37 Ravenous Rats C :K:	.10	.25
❑ 38 Fleshbag Marauder U :K:	.20	.50
❑ 39 Phyrexian Rager C :K:	.10	.25
❑ 40 Urborg Syphon-Mage C :K:	.10	.25
❑ 41 Wall of Bone U :K:	.20	.50
❑ 42 Faerie Macabre C :K:	.10	.25
❑ 43 Howling Banshee U :K:	.20	.50
❑ 44 Keening Banshee U :K:	.20	.50
❑ 45 Twisted Abomination C :K:	.10	.25
❑ 46 Skeletal Vampire R :K:	1.25	3.00
❑ 47 Genju of the Fens U :K:	.20	.50
❑ 48 Bad Moon R :K:	2.50	6.00
❑ 49 Sign in Blood C :K:	.10	.25
❑ 50 Vicious Hunger C :K:	.10	.25
❑ 51 Ichor Slick C :K:	.10	.25
❑ 52 Hideous End C :K:	.10	.25
❑ 53 Snuff Out C :K:	.10	.25
❑ 54 Tendrils of Corruption C :K:	.10	.25
❑ 55 Mutilate R :K:	2.50	6.00
❑ 56 Rise from the Grave U :K:	.20	.50
❑ 57 Corrupt U :K:	.20	.50
❑ 58 Enslave U :K:	.20	.50
❑ 59 Polluted Mire C	.10	.25
❑ 60 Swamp L	.10	.25
❑ 61 Swamp L	.10	.25
❑ 62 Swamp L	.10	.25
❑ 63 Swamp L	.10	.25
❑ T1 Beast - Token C	.20	.50
❑ T2 Beast - Token C	.20	.50
❑ T3 Elephant - Token C	.40	1.00

2009 Magic the Gathering Zendikar

Card	Low	High
Complete Set (234)	100.00	175.00
Booster Box (36 Packs)	100.00	200.00
Booster Pack (15 Cards)	4.00	6.00
Theme Decks	7.50	15.00
Fat Pack	60.00	120.00
❑ 1 Adventuring Gear C :A:	.10	.25
❑ 2 Aether Figment U :B:	.20	.50
❑ 3 Akoum Refuge U :L:	.30	.75
❑ 4 Archive Trap R :B:	1.25	3.00
❑ 5 Archmage Ascension R :B:	.30	.75
❑ 6 Arid Mesa R :L:	6.00	15.00
❑ 7 Armament Master R :W:	.30	.75
❑ 8 Arrow Volley Trap U :W:	.12	.30
❑ 9 Bala Ged Thief R :K:	.30	.75
❑ 10 Baloth Cage Trap U :G:	.15	.40
❑ 11 Baloth Woodcrasher U :G:	.20	.50
❑ 12 Beast Hunt C :G:	.10	.25
❑ 13 Beastmaster Ascension R :G:	.75	2.00
❑ 14 Blade of the Bloodchief R :A:	1.25	3.00
❑ 15 Bladetusk Boar C :R:	.10	.25
❑ 16 Blazing Torch U :A:	.20	.50
❑ 17 Blood Seeker C :K:	.10	.25
❑ 18 Blood Tribute R :K:	.40	1.00
❑ 19 Bloodchief Ascension R :K:	1.25	3.00
❑ 20 Bloodghast R :K:	2.50	6.00
❑ 21 Bog Tatters C :K:	.10	.25
❑ 22 Bold Defense C :W:	.10	.25
❑ 23 Brave the Elements U :W:	.40	1.00
❑ 24 Burst Lightning C :R:	.30	.75
❑ 25 Caller of Gales C :B:	.10	.25
❑ 26 Cancel C :B:	.10	.25
❑ 27 Caravan Hurda C :W:	.10	.25
❑ 28 Carnage Altar U :A:	.20	.50
❑ 29 Celestial Mantle R :W:	1.25	3.00
❑ 30 Chandra Ablaze M :R:	2.50	6.00
❑ 31 Cliff Threader C :W:	.08	.20
❑ 32 Cobra Trap U :G:	.20	.50
❑ 33 Conqueror's Pledge R :W:	.75	2.00
❑ 34 Cosi's Trickster R :B:	.30	.75
❑ 35 Crypt of Agadeem R :L:	.40	1.00
❑ 36 Crypt Ripper C :K:	.10	.25
❑ 37 Day of Judgment R :W:	1.00	2.50
❑ 38 Demolish C :R:	.10	.25
❑ 39 Desecrated Earth C :K:	.08	.20
❑ 40 Devout Lightcaster R :W:	.30	.75
❑ 41 Disfigure C :K:	.12	.30
❑ 42 Eldrazi Monument M :A:	2.50	6.00
❑ 43 Electropotence R :R:	.25	.60
❑ 44 Elemental Appeal R :R:	.30	.75
❑ 45 Emeria Angel R :W:	.75	2.00
❑ 46 Emeria, the Sky Ruin R :L:	1.50	4.00
❑ 47 Eternity Vessel M :A:	.75	2.00
❑ 48 Expedition Map C :A:	.30	.75
❑ 49 Explorer's Scope C :A:	.10	.25
❑ 50 Feast of Blood U :K:	.30	.75
❑ 51 Felidar Sovereign M :W:	2.00	5.00
❑ 52 Forest C :L:	.60	1.50
❑ 53 Frontier Guide U :G:	.20	.50
❑ 54 Gatekeeper of Malakir U :K:	.60	1.50
❑ 55 Geyser Glider U :R:	.20	.50
❑ 56 Giant Scorpion C :K:	.10	.25
❑ 57 Gigantiform R :G:	.30	.75
❑ 58 Goblin Bushwhacker C :R:	.20	.50
❑ 59 Goblin Guide R :R:	3.00	8.00
❑ 60 Goblin Ruinblaster U :R:	.20	.50
❑ 61 Goblin Shortcutter C :R:	.08	.20
❑ 62 Goblin War Paint C :R:	.10	.25
❑ 63 Gomazoa U :B:	.20	.50
❑ 64 Grappling Hook R :A:	.30	.75
❑ 65 Graypelt Refuge U :L:	.30	.75
❑ 66 Grazing Gladehart C :G:	.10	.25
❑ 67 Greenweaver Druid U :G:	.20	.50
❑ 68 Grim Discovery C :K:	.10	.25
❑ 69 Guul Draz Specter R :K:	.30	.75
❑ 70 Guul Draz Vampire C :K:	.10	.25
❑ 71 Hagra Crocodile C :K:	.10	.25
❑ 72 Hagra Diabolist U :K:	.20	.50
❑ 73 Halo Hunter R :K:	.30	.75
❑ 74 Harrow C :G:	.20	.50
❑ 75 Heartstabber Mosquito C :K:	.08	.20
❑ 76 Hedron Crab U :B:	.75	2.00
❑ 77 Hedron Scrabbler C :A:	.10	.25
❑ 78 Hellfire Mongrel U :R:	.20	.50
❑ 79 Hellkite Charger R :R:	.40	1.00
❑ 80 Hideous End C :K:	.12	.30
❑ 81 Highland Berserker C :R:	.10	.25
❑ 82 Inferno Trap U :R:	.12	.30
❑ 83 Into the Roil C :B:	.30	.75
❑ 84 Iona, Shield of Emeria M :W:	3.00	8.00
❑ 85 Ior Ruin Expedition C :B:	.10	.25
❑ 86 Island C :L:	.12	.30
❑ 87 Joraga Bard C :G:	.10	.25
❑ 88 Journey to Nowhere C :W:	.12	.30
❑ 89 Jwar Isle Refuge U :L:	.30	.75
❑ 90 Kabira Crossroads C :L:	.10	.25
❑ 91 Kabira Evangel R :W:	.40	1.00
❑ 92 Kalitas, Bloodchief of Ghet M :K:	1.50	4.00
❑ 93 Kazandu Blademaster U :W:	.30	.75
❑ 94 Kazandu Refuge U :L:	.20	.50
❑ 95 Kazuul Warlord R :R:	.30	.75
❑ 96 Khalni Gem U :A:	.20	.50
❑ 97 Khalni Heart Expedition C :G:	.12	.30
❑ 98 Kor Aeronaut U :W:	.20	.50
❑ 99 Kor Cartographer C :W:	.08	.20
❑ 100 Kor Duelist U :W:	.20	.50
❑ 101 Kor Hookmaster C :W:	.08	.20
❑ 102 Kor Outfitter C :W:	.10	.25
❑ 103 Kor Sanctifiers C :W:	.12	.30
❑ 104 Kor Skyfisher C :W:	.20	.50
❑ 105 Kraken Hatchling C :B:	.10	.25
❑ 106 Landbind Ritual U :W:	.20	.50
❑ 107 Lavaball Trap R :R:	.30	.75
❑ 108 Lethargy Trap C :B:	.10	.25
❑ 109 Living Tsunami U :B:	.20	.50
❑ 110 Lorthos, the Tidemaker M :B:	.75	2.00
❑ 111 Lotus Cobra M :G:	3.00	8.00
❑ 112 Lullmage Mentor R :B:	.30	.75
❑ 113 Luminarch Ascension R :W:	1.25	3.00
❑ 114 Magma Rift C :R:	.10	.25
❑ 115 Magosi, the Waterveil R :L:	.30	.75
❑ 116 Makindi Shieldmate C :W:	.10	.25
❑ 117 Malakir Bloodwitch R :K:	.75	2.00
❑ 118 Mark of Mutiny U :R:	.20	.50
❑ 119 Marsh Casualties U :K:	.20	.50
❑ 120 Marsh Flats R :L:	6.00	15.00
❑ 121 Merfolk Seastalkers U :B:	.20	.50
❑ 122 Merfolk Wayfinder U :B:	.20	.50
❑ 123 Mind Sludge U :K:	.20	.50
❑ 124 Mindbreak Trap M :B:	2.00	5.00
❑ 125 Mindless Null C :K:	.08	.20
❑ 126 Mire Blight C :K:	.10	.25
❑ 127 Misty Rainforest R :L:	6.00	15.00
❑ 128 Mold Shambler C :G:	.10	.25
❑ 129 Molten Ravager C :R:	.08	.20
❑ 130 Mountain C :L:	.60	1.50
❑ 131 Murasa Pyromancer U :R:	.20	.50
❑ 132 Narrow Escape C :W:	.10	.25
❑ 133 Needlebite Trap U :K:	.20	.50
❑ 134 Nimana Sell-Sword C :K:	.10	.25
❑ 135 Nimbus Wings C :W:	.10	.25
❑ 136 Nissa Revane M :G:	3.00	8.00
❑ 137 Nissa's Chosen C :G:	.20	.50
❑ 138 Noble Vestige C :W:	.08	.20
❑ 139 Ob Nixilis, the Fallen M :K:	1.25	3.00
❑ 140 Obsidian Fireheart M :R:	1.00	2.50
❑ 141 Ondu Cleric C :W:	.10	.25
❑ 142 Oracle of Mul Daya R :G:	1.25	4.00
❑ 143 Oran-Rief Recluse C :G:	.10	.25
❑ 144 Oran-Rief Survivalist C :G:	.12	.30
❑ 145 Oran-Rief, the Vastwood R :L:	1.00	2.50
❑ 146 Paralyzing Grasp C :B:	.08	.20
❑ 147 Pillarfield Ox C :W:	.10	.25
❑ 148 Piranha Marsh C :L:	.08	.20
❑ 149 Pitfall Trap U :W:	.20	.50
❑ 150 Plains C :L:	.12	.30
❑ 151 Plated Geopede C :R:	.20	.50
❑ 152 Predatory Urge R :G:	.30	.75
❑ 153 Primal Bellow U :G:	.20	.50
❑ 154 Punishing Fire U :R:	.20	.50
❑ 155 Pyromancer Ascension R :R:	.75	2.00
❑ 156 Quest for Ancient Secrets U :B:	.20	.50
❑ 157 Quest for Pure Flame U :R:	.20	.50
❑ 158 Quest for the Gemblades U :G:	.20	.50
❑ 159 Quest for the Gravelord U :K:	.20	.50
❑ 160 Quest for the Holy Relic U :W:	.40	1.00
❑ 161 Rampaging Baloths M :G:	1.50	4.00
❑ 162 Ravenous Trap U :K:	.20	.50
❑ 163 Reckless Scholar C :B:	.10	.25
❑ 164 Relic Crush C :G:	.10	.25
❑ 165 Rite of Replication R :B:	1.25	3.00
❑ 166 River Boa U :G:	.20	.50
❑ 167 Roil Elemental R :B:	.40	1.00
❑ 168 Ruinous Minotaur C :R:	.10	.25
❑ 169 Runeflare Trap U :R:	.20	.50
❑ 170 Sadistic Sacrament R :K:	.60	1.50
❑ 171 Savage Silhouette C :G:	.10	.25
❑ 172 Scalding Tarn R :L:	8.00	20.00
❑ 173 Scute Mob R :G:	.75	2.00
❑ 174 Scythe Tiger C :G:	.10	.25
❑ 175 Sea Gate Loremaster R :B:	.30	.75
❑ 176 Seascape Aerialist U :B:	.20	.50
❑ 177 Seismic Shudder C :R:	.10	.25
❑ 178 Sejiri Refuge U :L:	.30	.75
❑ 179 Shatterskull Giant C :R:	.10	.25
❑ 180 Shepherd of the Lost U :W:	.20	.50
❑ 181 Shieldmate's Blessing C :W:	.10	.25
❑ 182 Shoal Serpent C :B:	.10	.25
❑ 183 Sky Ruin Drake C :B:	.10	.25
❑ 184 Slaughter Cry C :R:	.10	.25
❑ 185 Soaring Seacliff C :L:	.10	.25
❑ 186 Sorin Markov M :K:	2.50	6.00
❑ 187 Soul Stair Expedition C :K:	.10	.25
❑ 188 Spell Pierce C :B:	.50	1.25
❑ 189 Sphinx of Jwar Isle R :B:	.40	1.00
❑ 190 Sphinx of Lost Truths R :B:	.30	.75
❑ 191 Spidersilk Net C :A:	.10	.25
❑ 192 Spire Barrage C :R:	.10	.25
❑ 193 Spreading Seas C :B:	.30	.75
❑ 194 Steppe Lynx C :W:	.20	.50
❑ 195 Stonework Puma C :A:	.10	.25
❑ 196 Summoner's Bane U :B:	.20	.50
❑ 197 Summoning Trap R :G:	.75	2.00
❑ 198 Sunspring Expedition C :W:	.10	.25
❑ 199 Surrakar Marauder C :K:	.10	.25
❑ 200 Swamp C :L:	.60	1.50
❑ 201 Tajuru Archer U :G:	.20	.50
❑ 202 Tanglesap C :G:	.10	.25
❑ 203 Teetering Peaks C :L:	.20	.50
❑ 204 Tempest Owl C :B:	.10	.25
❑ 205 Terra Stomper R :G:	.40	1.00
❑ 206 Territorial Baloth C :G:	.10	.25
❑ 207 Timbermaw Larva C :G:	.10	.25
❑ 208 Torch Slinger C :R:	.10	.25
❑ 209 Trailblazer's Boots U :A:	.20	.50
❑ 210 Trapfinder's Trick C :B:	.10	.25
❑ 211 Trapmaker's Snare U :B:	.20	.50
❑ 212 Trusty Machete U :A:	.20	.50
❑ 213 Tuktuk Grunts C :R:	.10	.25
❑ 214 Turntimber Basilisk U :G:	.20	.50
❑ 215 Turntimber Grove C :L:	.10	.25
❑ 216 Turntimber Ranger R :G:	.30	.75
❑ 217 Umara Raptor C :B:	.10	.25
❑ 218 Unstable Footing U :R:	.20	.50
❑ 219 Valakut, the Molten Pinnacle R :L:	.75	2.00
❑ 220 Vampire Hexmage U :K:	.40	1.00
❑ 221 Vampire Lacerator C :K:	.10	.25
❑ 222 Vampire Nighthawk U :K:	.75	2.00
❑ 223 Vampire's Bite C :K:	.10	.25
❑ 224 Vastwood Gorger C :G:	.10	.25
❑ 225 Verdant Catacombs R :L:	6.00	15.00
❑ 226 Vines of Vastwood C :G:	.30	.75
❑ 227 Warren Instigator M :R:	2.00	5.00
❑ 228 Welkin Tern C :B:	.10	.25
❑ 229 Whiplash Trap C :B:	.10	.25
❑ 230 Windborne Charge U :W:	.20	.50
❑ 231 Windrider Eel C :B:	.10	.25
❑ 232 World Queller R :W:	.30	.75
❑ 233 Zektar Shrine Expedition C :R:	.10	.25
❑ 234 Zendikar Farguide C :G:	.10	.25

2009 Magic the Gathering Zendikar Foil

*Foil: .8X to 2X Basic Cards

2010 Magic the Gathering Magic 2011

Card	Low	High
Complete Set (249)	75.00	150.00
❑ 1 Acidic Slime U :G:	.20	.50
❑ 2 Act of Treason U :R:	.20	.50
❑ 3 Aether Adept C :B:	.10	.25
❑ 4 Air Servant U :B:	.20	.50
❑ 5 Ajani Goldmane M :W:	3.00	8.00
❑ 6 Ajani's Mantra C :W:	.10	.25
❑ 7 Ajani's Pridemate U :W:	.40	1.00

❑ 8 Alluring Siren U :B: .20 .50
❑ 9 Ancient Hellkite R :R: .30 .75
❑ 10 Angel's Feather U .20 .50
❑ 11 Angelic Arbiter R :W: .30 .75
❑ 12 Arc Runner C :R: .10 .25
❑ 13 Armored Ascension U :W: .20 .50
❑ 14 Armored Cancrix C :B: .10 .25
❑ 15 Assassinate C :K: .10 .25
❑ 16 Assault Griffin C :W: .10 .25
❑ 17 Augury Owl C :B: .10 .25
❑ 18 Autumn's Veil U :G: .20 .50
❑ 19 Awakener Druid U :G: .20 .50
❑ 20 Azure Drake U :B: .20 .50
❑ 21 Back to Nature U :G: .20 .50
❑ 22 Baneslayer Angel M :W: 5.00 12.00
❑ 23 Barony Vampire C :K: .10 .25
❑ 24 Berserkers of Blood Ridge C :R: .10 .25
❑ 25 Birds of Paradise R :G: 2.50 6.00
❑ 26 Black Knight U :K: .20 .50
❑ 27 Blinding Mage C :W: .10 .25
❑ 28 Blood Tithe C :K: .10 .25
❑ 29 Bloodcrazed Goblin C :R: .10 .25
❑ 30 Bloodthrone Vampire C :K: .10 .25
❑ 31 Bog Raiders C :K: .10 .25
❑ 32 Brindle Boar C :G: .10 .25
❑ 33 Brittle Effigy R .40 1.00
❑ 34 Call to Mind U :B: .20 .50
❑ 35 Cancel C :B: .10 .25
❑ 36 Canyon Minotaur C :R: .10 .25
❑ 37 Captivating Vampire R :K: 3.00 8.00
❑ 38 Celestial Purge U :W: .20 .50
❑ 39 Chandra Nalaar M :R: 1.50 4.00
❑ 40 Chandra's Outrage C :R: .10 .25
❑ 41 Chandra's Spitfire U :R: .20 .50
❑ 42 Child of Night C :K: .10 .25
❑ 43 Clone R :B: .40 1.00
❑ 44 Cloud Crusader C :W: .10 .25
❑ 45 Cloud Elemental C :B: .10 .25
❑ 46 Combust U :R: .20 .50
❑ 47 Condemn U :W: .30 .75
❑ 48 Conundrum Sphinx R :B: .40 1.00
❑ 49 Corrupt U :K: .20 .50
❑ 50 Crystal Ball U .30 .75
❑ 51 Cudgel Troll U :G: .20 .50
❑ 52 Cultivate C :G: .30 .75
❑ 53 Cyclops Gladiator R :R: .30 .75
❑ 54 Dark Tutelage R :K: .40 1.00
❑ 55 Day of Judgment R :W: 1.25 3.00
❑ 56 Deathmark U :K: .20 .50
❑ 57 Demolish C :R: .10 .25
❑ 58 Demon of Death's Gate M :K: 1.25 3.00
❑ 59 Demon's Horn U .20 .50
❑ 60 Destructive Force R :R: .40 1.00
❑ 61 Diabolic Tutor U :K: .30 .75
❑ 62 Diminish C :B: .10 .25
❑ 63 Disentomb C :K: .10 .25
❑ 64 Doom Blade C :K: .20 .50
❑ 65 Dragon's Claw U .20 .50
❑ 66 Dragonskull Summit R :L: 2.00 5.00
❑ 67 Drowned Catacomb R :L: 3.00 8.00
❑ 68 Dryad's Favor C :G: .10 .25
❑ 69 Duress C :K: .20 .50
❑ 70 Duskdale Wurm U :G: .20 .50
❑ 71 Earth Servant U :R: .20 .50
❑ 72 Elite Vanguard U :W: .20 .50
❑ 73 Elixir of Immortality U .40 1.00
❑ 74 Elvish Archdruid R :G: .60 1.50
❑ 75 Ember Hauler U :R: .30 .75
❑ 76 Excommunicate C :W: .10 .25
❑ 77 Fauna Shaman R :G: 2.50 6.00
❑ 78 Fiery Hellhound C :R: .10 .25
❑ 79 Fire Servant U :R: .30 .75
❑ 80 Fireball U :R: .20 .50
❑ 81 Flashfreeze U :B: .20 .50
❑ 82 Fling C :R: .10 .25
❑ 83 Fog C :G: .10 .25
❑ 84 Foresee C :B: .10 .25
❑ 85 Forest - A L :L: .10 .25
❑ 86 Forest - B L :L: .10 .25
❑ 87 Forest - C L :L: .10 .25
❑ 88 Forest - D L :L: .10 .25
❑ 89 Frost Titan M :B: 1.50 4.00
❑ 90 Gaea's Revenge M :G: .75 2.00
❑ 91 Gargoyle Sentinel U .20 .50
❑ 92 Garruk Wildspeaker M :G: 2.50 6.00
❑ 93 Garruk's Companion C :G: .10 .25
❑ 94 Garruk's Packleader U :G: .20 .50
❑ 95 Giant Growth C :G: .10 .25
❑ 96 Giant Spider C :G: .10 .25
❑ 97 Glacial Fortress R :L: 2.50 6.00
❑ 98 Goblin Balloon Brigade C :R: .10 .25
❑ 99 Goblin Chieftain R :R: .60 1.50
❑ 100 Goblin Piker C :R: .10 .25
❑ 101 Goblin Tunneler C :R: .10 .25
❑ 102 Goldenglow Moth C :W: .10 .25
❑ 103 Grave Titan M :K: 4.00 10.00
❑ 104 Gravedigger C :K: .10 .25
❑ 105 Greater Basilisk C :G: .10 .25
❑ 106 Harbor Serpent C :B: .10 .25
❑ 107 Haunting Echoes R :K: .40 1.00
❑ 108 Hoarding Dragon R :R: .30 .75
❑ 109 Holy Strength C :W: .10 .25
❑ 110 Honor of the Pure R :W: 1.50 4.00
❑ 111 Hornet Sting C :G: .10 .25
❑ 112 Howling Banshee U :K: .20 .50
❑ 113 Hunters' Feast C :G: .10 .25
❑ 114 Ice Cage C :B: .10 .25
❑ 115 Incite C :R: .10 .25
❑ 116 Infantry Veteran C :W: .10 .25
❑ 117 Inferno Titan M :R: 2.00 5.00
❑ 118 Inspired Charge C :W: .10 .25
❑ 119 Island L :L: .10 .25
❑ 120 Island - B L :L: .10 .25
❑ 121 Island - C L :L: .10 .25
❑ 122 Island - D L :L: .10 .25
❑ 123 Jace Beleren M :B: 3.00 8.00
❑ 124 Jace's Erasure C :B: .10 .25
❑ 125 Jace's Ingenuity U :B: .20 .50
❑ 126 Jinxed Idol R .30 .75
❑ 127 Juggernaut U .20 .50
❑ 128 Knight Exemplar R :W: 1.50 4.00
❑ 129 Kraken's Eye U .20 .50
❑ 130 Lava Axe R :R: .10 .25
❑ 131 Leyline of Anticipation R :B: .60 1.50
❑ 132 Leyline of Punishment R :R: .40 1.00
❑ 133 Leyline of Sanctity R :W: 2.50 6.00
❑ 134 Leyline of the Void R :K: .75 2.00
❑ 135 Leyline of Vitality R :G: .40 1.00
❑ 136 Lightning Bolt C :R: .60 1.50
❑ 137 Liliana Vess M :K: 3.00 8.00
❑ 138 Liliana's Caress U :K: .75 2.00
❑ 139 Liliana's Specter C :K: .10 .25
❑ 140 Llanowar Elves C :G: .20 .50
❑ 141 Magma Phoenix R :R: .30 .75
❑ 142 Mana Leak C :B: .40 1.00
❑ 143 Manic Vandal C :R: .10 .25
❑ 144 Maritime Guard C :B: .10 .25
❑ 145 Mass Polymorph R :B: .30 .75
❑ 146 Merfolk Sovereign R :B: .40 1.00
❑ 147 Merfolk Spy C :B: .10 .25
❑ 148 Mighty Leap C :W: .10 .25
❑ 149 Mind Control U :B: .20 .50
❑ 150 Mind Rot C :K: .10 .25
❑ 151 Mitotic Slime R :G: .40 1.00
❑ 152 Mountain L :L: .10 .25
❑ 153 Mountain - B L :L: .10 .25
❑ 154 Mountain - C L :L: .10 .25
❑ 155 Mountain - D L :L: .10 .25
❑ 156 Mystifying Maze R :L: .40 1.00
❑ 157 Nantuko Shade R :K: .60 1.50
❑ 158 Naturalize C :G: .10 .25
❑ 159 Nature's Spiral U :G: .20 .50
❑ 160 Necrotic Plague C :K: .30 .75
❑ 161 Negate C :B: .10 .25
❑ 162 Nether Horror C :K: .20 .50
❑ 163 Nightwing Shade C :K: .10 .25
❑ 164 Obstinate Baloth U :G: .60 1.50
❑ 165 Ornithopter U .40 1.00
❑ 166 Overwhelming Stampede R :G: .60 1.50
❑ 167 Pacifism C :W: .10 .25
❑ 168 Palace Guard C :W: .10 .25
❑ 169 Phantom Beast C :B: .10 .25
❑ 170 Phylactery Lich R :K: .60 1.50
❑ 171 Plains L :L: .10 .25
❑ 172 Plains - B L :L: .10 .25
❑ 173 Plains - C L :L: .10 .25
❑ 174 Plains - D L :L: .10 .25
❑ 175 Platinum Angel M 2.00 5.00
❑ 176 Plummet C :G: .10 .25
❑ 177 Preordain C :B: .40 1.00
❑ 178 Primal Cocoon C :G: .10 .25
❑ 179 Primeval Titan M :G: 8.00 20.00
❑ 180 Prized Unicorn U :G: .20 .50
❑ 181 Prodigal Pyromancer U :R: .20 .50
❑ 182 Protean Hydra R :G: .40 1.00
❑ 183 Pyretic Ritual C :R: .10 .25
❑ 184 Pyroclasm U :R: .30 .75
❑ 185 Quag Sickness C :K: .10 .25
❑ 186 Reassembling Skeleton U :K: .20 .50
❑ 187 Redirect R :B: .40 1.00
❑ 188 Relentless Rats U :K: .60 1.50
❑ 189 Reverberate R :R: .40 1.00
❑ 190 Rise from the Grave U :K: .20 .50
❑ 191 Roc Egg U :W: .20 .50
❑ 192 Rootbound Crag R :L: 2.00 5.00
❑ 193 Rotting Legion C :K: .10 .25
❑ 194 Royal Assassin R :K: .40 1.00
❑ 195 Runeclaw Bear C :G: .10 .25
❑ 196 Sacred Wolf C :G: .10 .25
❑ 197 Safe Passage C :W: .10 .25
❑ 198 Scroll Thief C :B: .10 .25
❑ 199 Serra Angel U :W: .20 .50
❑ 200 Serra Ascendant R :W: 2.50 6.00
❑ 201 Shiv's Embrace U :R: .20 .50
❑ 202 Siege Mastodon C :W: .10 .25
❑ 203 Sign in Blood C :K: .20 .50
❑ 204 Silence R :W: .40 1.00
❑ 205 Silvercoat Lion C :W: .10 .25
❑ 206 Sleep U :B: .20 .50
❑ 207 Solemn Offering C :W: .10 .25
❑ 208 Sorcerer's Strongbox U .20 .50
❑ 209 Spined Wurm C :G: .10 .25
❑ 210 Squadron Hawk C :W: .40 1.00
❑ 211 Stabbing Pain C :K: .10 .25
❑ 212 Steel Overseer R 2.50 6.00
❑ 213 Stone Golem U .20 .50
❑ 214 Stormfront Pegasus C :W: .10 .25
❑ 215 Stormtide Leviathan R :B: .40 1.00
❑ 216 Sun Titan M :W: 2.50 6.00
❑ 217 Sunpetal Grove R :L: 1.50 4.00
❑ 218 Swamp L :L: .10 .25
❑ 219 Swamp - B L :L: .10 .25
❑ 220 Swamp - C L :L: .10 .25
❑ 221 Swamp - D L :L: .10 .25
❑ 222 Sword of Vengeance R .60 1.50
❑ 223 Sylvan Ranger C :G: .10 .25
❑ 224 Temple Bell R .40 1.00
❑ 225 Terramorphic Expanse C :L: .20 .50
❑ 226 Thunder Strike C :R: .10 .25
❑ 227 Time Reversal M :B: .60 1.50
❑ 228 Tireless Missionaries C :W: .10 .25
❑ 229 Tome Scour C :B: .10 .25
❑ 230 Traumatize R :B: 1.25 3.00
❑ 231 Triskelion R .30 .75
❑ 232 Unholy Strength C :K: .10 .25
❑ 233 Unsummon C :B: .10 .25
❑ 234 Vengeful Archon R :W: .30 .75
❑ 235 Viscera Seer C :K: .10 .25
❑ 236 Volcanic Strength C :R: .10 .25
❑ 237 Voltaic Key U .40 1.00
❑ 238 Vulshok Berserker C :R: .10 .25
❑ 239 Wall of Frost U :B: .20 .50
❑ 240 Wall of Vines C :G: .10 .25
❑ 242 Warlord's Axe U .20 .50
❑ 241 War Priest of Thune U :W: .20 .50
❑ 243 Water Servant U :B: .20 .50
❑ 244 Whispersilk Cloak U .30 .75
❑ 245 White Knight U :W: .20 .50
❑ 246 Wild Evocation R :R: .30 .75
❑ 247 Wild Griffin C :W: .10 .25
❑ 248 Wurm's Tooth U .20 .50
❑ 249 Yavimaya Wurm C :G: .10 .25
❑ R1 Rules Tip: Planeswalker Cards .10 .25
❑ R2 Rules Tip: Parts of the Turn .10 .25
❑ R3 Rules Tip: Deathtouch .10 .25
❑ R4 Rules Tip: Tokens and Counters .10 .25
❑ R5 Rules Tip: Building a Deck .10 .25
❑ R6 Rules Tip: Limited Play .10 .25
❑ R7 Rules Tip: The Stack .10 .25
❑ R8 Rules Tip: Gatherer Card Database .10 .25
❑ R9 Rules Tip: Leylines .10 .25
❑ T1 Token: Avatar .10 .25
❑ T2 Token: Bird .10 .25
❑ T3 Token: Zombie .10 .25
❑ T4 Token: Beast .10 .25
❑ T5 Token: Ooze (2/2) .10 .25
❑ T6 Token: Ooze (1/1) .10 .25

2010 Magic the Gathering Magic 2011 Foil

Complete Set (249) 150.00 300.00
*Foil: .8X to 2X Basic Cards

❑ 1 Acidic Slime U :G: .40 1.00
❑ 2 Act of Treason U :R: .40 1.00
❑ 3 Aether Adept C :B: .20 .50
❑ 4 Air Servant U :B: .40 1.00
❑ 5 Ajani Goldmane M :W: 6.00 15.00
❑ 6 Ajani's Mantra C :W: .20 .50
❑ 7 Ajani's Pridemate U :W: .75 2.00
❑ 8 Alluring Siren U :B: .40 1.00
❑ 9 Ancient Hellkite R :R: .60 1.50
❑ 10 Angel's Feather U .40 1.00
❑ 11 Angelic Arbiter R :W: .60 1.50
❑ 12 Arc Runner C :R: .20 .50
❑ 13 Armored Ascension U :W: .40 1.00
❑ 14 Armored Cancrix C :B: .20 .50
❑ 15 Assassinate C :K: .20 .50
❑ 16 Assault Griffin C :W: .20 .50
❑ 17 Augury Owl C :B: .20 .50
❑ 18 Autumn's Veil U :G: .40 1.00
❑ 19 Awakener Druid U :B: .40 1.00
❑ 20 Azure Drake U :B: .40 1.00
❑ 21 Back to Nature U :G: .40 1.00
❑ 22 Baneslayer Angel M :W: 10.00 25.00
❑ 23 Barony Vampire C :K: .20 .50
❑ 24 Berserkers of Blood Ridge C :R: .20 .50
❑ 25 Birds of Paradise R :G: 5.00 12.00
❑ 26 Black Knight U :K: .40 1.00
❑ 27 Blinding Mage C :W: .20 .50
❑ 28 Blood Tithe C :K: .20 .50
❑ 29 Bloodcrazed Goblin C :R: .20 .50
❑ 30 Bloodthrone Vampire C :K: .20 .50
❑ 31 Bog Raiders C :K: .20 .50
❑ 32 Brindle Boar C :G: .20 .50
❑ 33 Brittle Effigy R .75 2.00
❑ 34 Call to Mind U :B: .40 1.00
❑ 35 Cancel C :B: .20 .50
❑ 36 Canyon Minotaur C :R: .20 .50
❑ 37 Captivating Vampire R :K: 6.00 15.00
❑ 38 Celestial Purge U :W: .40 1.00
❑ 39 Chandra Nalaar M :R: 3.00 8.00
❑ 40 Chandra's Outrage C :R: .20 .50
❑ 41 Chandra's Spitfire U :R: .40 1.00
❑ 42 Child of Night C :K: .20 .50
❑ 43 Clone R :B: .75 2.00
❑ 44 Cloud Crusader C :W: .20 .50
❑ 45 Cloud Elemental C :B: .20 .50
❑ 46 Combust U :R: .40 1.00
❑ 47 Condemn U :W: .60 1.50
❑ 48 Conundrum Sphinx R :B: .75 2.00
❑ 49 Corrupt U :K: .40 1.00
❑ 50 Crystal Ball U .60 1.50
❑ 51 Cudgel Troll U :G: .40 1.00
❑ 52 Cultivate C :G: .60 1.50
❑ 53 Cyclops Gladiator R :R: .60 1.50
❑ 54 Dark Tutelage R :K: .75 2.00
❑ 55 Day of Judgment R :W: 2.50 6.00
❑ 56 Deathmark U :K: .40 1.00
❑ 57 Demolish C :R: .20 .50
❑ 58 Demon of Death's Gate M :K: 2.50 6.00
❑ 59 Demon's Horn U .40 1.00
❑ 60 Destructive Force R :R: .75 2.00
❑ 61 Diabolic Tutor U :K: .60 1.50
❑ 62 Diminish C :B: .20 .50
❑ 63 Disentomb C :K: .20 .50
❑ 64 Doom Blade C :K: .40 1.00
❑ 65 Dragon's Claw U .40 1.00
❑ 66 Dragonskull Summit R :L: 4.00 10.00
❑ 67 Drowned Catacomb R :L: 6.00 15.00
❑ 68 Dryad's Favor C :G: .20 .50
❑ 69 Duress C :K: .40 1.00
❑ 70 Duskdale Wurm U :G: .40 1.00
❑ 71 Earth Servant U :R: .40 1.00
❑ 72 Elite Vanguard U :W: .40 1.00
❑ 73 Elixir of Immortality U .75 2.00
❑ 74 Elvish Archdruid R :G: 1.25 3.00
❑ 75 Ember Hauler U :R: .60 1.50
❑ 76 Excommunicate C :W: .20 .50
❑ 77 Fauna Shaman R :G: 5.00 12.00
❑ 78 Fiery Hellhound C :R: .20 .50
❑ 79 Fire Servant U :R: .60 1.50
❑ 80 Fireball U :R: .40 1.00
❑ 81 Flashfreeze U :B: .40 1.00
❑ 82 Fling C :R: .20 .50
❑ 83 Fog C :G: .20 .50
❑ 84 Foresee C :B: .20 .50
❑ 85 Forest L :L: .20 .50
❑ 86 Forest - B L :L: .20 .50
❑ 87 Forest - C L :L: .20 .50
❑ 88 Forest - D L :L: .20 .50
❑ 89 Frost Titan M :B: 3.00 8.00
❑ 90 Gaea's Revenge M :G: 1.50 4.00
❑ 91 Gargoyle Sentinel U .40 1.00
❑ 92 Garruk Wildspeaker M :G: 5.00 12.00
❑ 93 Garruk's Companion C :G: .20 .50
❑ 94 Garruk's Packleader U :G: .40 1.00
❑ 95 Giant Growth C :G: .20 .50
❑ 96 Giant Spider C :G: .20 .50
❑ 97 Glacial Fortress R :L: 5.00 12.00
❑ 98 Goblin Balloon Brigade C :R: .20 .50
❑ 99 Goblin Chieftain R :R: 1.25 3.00
❑ 100 Goblin Piker C :R: .20 .50
❑ 101 Goblin Tunneler C :R: .20 .50
❑ 102 Goldenglow Moth C :W: .20 .50
❑ 103 Grave Titan M :K: 8.00 20.00
❑ 104 Gravedigger C :K: .20 .50
❑ 105 Greater Basilisk C :G: .20 .50
❑ 106 Harbor Serpent C :B: .20 .50
❑ 107 Haunting Echoes R :K: .75 2.00
❑ 108 Hoarding Dragon R :R: .60 1.50
❑ 109 Holy Strength C :W: .20 .50
❑ 110 Honor of the Pure R :W: 3.00 8.00
❑ 111 Hornet Sting C :G: .20 .50
❑ 112 Howling Banshee U :K: .40 1.00
❑ 113 Hunters' Feast C :G: .20 .50
❑ 114 Ice Cage C :B: .20 .50
❑ 115 Incite C :R: .20 .50
❑ 116 Infantry Veteran C :W: .20 .50
❑ 117 Inferno Titan M :R: 4.00 10.00
❑ 118 Inspired Charge C :W: .20 .50
❑ 119 Island L :L: .20 .50
❑ 120 Island - B L :L: .20 .50
❑ 121 Island - C L :L: .20 .50
❑ 122 Island - D L :L: .20 .50
❑ 123 Jace Beleren M :B: 6.00 15.00
❑ 124 Jace's Erasure C :B: .20 .50
❑ 125 Jace's Ingenuity U :B: .40 1.00
❑ 126 Jinxed Idol R .60 1.50
❑ 127 Juggernaut U .40 1.00
❑ 128 Knight Exemplar R :W: 3.00 8.00
❑ 129 Kraken's Eye U .40 1.00
❑ 130 Lava Axe R :R: .20 .50
❑ 131 Leyline of Anticipation R :B: 1.25 3.00
❑ 132 Leyline of Punishment R :R: .75 2.00
❑ 133 Leyline of Sanctity R :W: 5.00 12.00
❑ 134 Leyline of the Void R :K: 1.50 4.00
❑ 135 Leyline of Vitality R :G: .75 2.00
❑ 136 Lightning Bolt C :R: 1.25 3.00
❑ 137 Liliana Vess M :K: 6.00 15.00
❑ 138 Liliana's Caress U :K: 1.50 4.00
❑ 139 Liliana's Specter C :K: .20 .50
❑ 140 Llanowar Elves C :G: .40 1.00
❑ 141 Magma Phoenix R :R: .60 1.50
❑ 142 Mana Leak C :B: .75 2.00
❑ 143 Manic Vandal C :R: .20 .50
❑ 144 Maritime Guard C :B: .20 .50
❑ 145 Mass Polymorph R :B: .60 1.50
❑ 146 Merfolk Sovereign R :B: .75 2.00
❑ 147 Merfolk Spy C :B: .20 .50
❑ 148 Mighty Leap C :W: .20 .50
❑ 149 Mind Control U :B: .40 1.00
❑ 150 Mind Rot C :K: .20 .50
❑ 151 Mitotic Slime R :G: .75 2.00
❑ 152 Mountain L :L: .20 .50
❑ 153 Mountain - B L :L: .20 .50
❑ 154 Mountain - C L :L: .20 .50
❑ 155 Mountain - D L :L: .20 .50
❑ 156 Mystifying Maze R :L: .75 2.00
❑ 157 Nantuko Shade R :K: 1.25 3.00
❑ 158 Naturalize C :G: .20 .50
❑ 159 Nature's Spiral U :G: .40 1.00
❑ 160 Necrotic Plague C :K: .60 1.50
❑ 161 Negate C :B: .20 .50
❑ 162 Nether Horror C :K: .40 1.00
❑ 163 Nightwing Shade C :K: .20 .50
❑ 164 Obstinate Baloth U :G: 1.25 3.00
❑ 165 Ornithopter U .75 2.00
❑ 166 Overwhelming Stampede R :G: 1.25 3.00
❑ 167 Pacifism C :W: .20 .50
❑ 168 Palace Guard C :W: .20 .50
❑ 169 Phantom Beast C :B: .20 .50
❑ 170 Phylactery Lich R :K: 1.25 3.00
❑ 171 Plains L :L: .20 .50
❑ 172 Plains - B L :L: .20 .50
❑ 173 Plains - C L :L: .20 .50
❑ 174 Plains - D L :L: .20 .50
❑ 175 Platinum Angel M 4.00 10.00
❑ 176 Plummet C :G: .20 .50
❑ 177 Preordain C :B: .75 2.00
❑ 178 Primal Cocoon C :G: .20 .50
❑ 179 Primeval Titan M :G: 15.00 40.00
❑ 180 Prized Unicorn U :G: .40 1.00
❑ 181 Prodigal Pyromancer U :R: .40 1.00
❑ 182 Protean Hydra R :G: .75 2.00
❑ 183 Pyretic Ritual C :R: .20 .50
❑ 184 Pyroclasm U :R: .60 1.50
❑ 185 Quag Sickness C :K: .20 .50
❑ 186 Reassembling Skeleton U :K: .40 1.00
❑ 187 Redirect R :B: .75 2.00
❑ 188 Relentless Rats U :K: 1.25 3.00
❑ 189 Reverberate R :R: .75 2.00
❑ 190 Rise from the Grave U :K: .40 1.00
❑ 191 Roc Egg U :W: .40 1.00
❑ 192 Rootbound Crag R :L: 4.00 10.00
❑ 193 Rotting Legion C :K: .20 .50
❑ 194 Royal Assassin R :K: .75 2.00
❑ 195 Runeclaw Bear C :G: .20 .50
❑ 196 Sacred Wolf C :G: .20 .50
❑ 197 Safe Passage C :W: .20 .50
❑ 198 Scroll Thief C :B: .20 .50
❑ 199 Serra Angel U :W: .40 1.00
❑ 200 Serra Ascendant R :W: 5.00 12.00
❑ 201 Shiv's Embrace U :R: .40 1.00
❑ 202 Siege Mastodon C :W: .20 .50
❑ 203 Sign in Blood C :K: .40 1.00
❑ 204 Silence R :W: .75 2.00
❑ 205 Silvercoat Lion C :W: .20 .50
❑ 206 Sleep U :B: .40 1.00
❑ 207 Solemn Offering C :W: .20 .50
❑ 208 Sorcerer's Strongbox U .40 1.00
❑ 209 Spined Wurm C :G: .20 .50
❑ 210 Squadron Hawk C :W: .75 2.00
❑ 211 Stabbing Pain C :K: .20 .50
❑ 212 Steel Overseer R 5.00 12.00
❑ 213 Stone Golem U .40 1.00
❑ 214 Stormfront Pegasus C :W: .20 .50
❑ 215 Stormtide Leviathan R :B: .75 2.00
❑ 216 Sun Titan M :W: 5.00 12.00
❑ 217 Sunpetal Grove R :L: 3.00 8.00
❑ 218 Swamp L :L: .20 .50
❑ 219 Swamp - B L :L: .20 .50
❑ 220 Swamp - C L :L: .20 .50
❑ 221 Swamp - D L :L: .20 .50
❑ 222 Sword of Vengeance R 1.25 3.00
❑ 223 Sylvan Ranger C :G: .20 .50
❑ 224 Temple Bell R .75 2.00
❑ 225 Terramorphic Expanse C :L: .40 1.00
❑ 226 Thunder Strike C :R: .20 .50
❑ 227 Time Reversal M :B: 1.25 3.00
❑ 228 Tireless Missionaries C :W: .20 .50
❑ 229 Tome Scour C :B: .20 .50
❑ 230 Traumatize R :B: 2.50 6.00
❑ 231 Triskelion R .60 1.50
❑ 232 Unholy Strength C :K: .20 .50
❑ 233 Unsummon C :B: .20 .50
❑ 234 Vengeful Archon R :W: .60 1.50
❑ 235 Viscera Seer C :K: .20 .50
❑ 236 Volcanic Strength C :R: .20 .50
❑ 237 Voltaic Key U .75 2.00
❑ 238 Vulshok Berserker C :R: .20 .50
❑ 239 Wall of Frost U :B: .40 1.00
❑ 240 Wall of Vines C :G: .20 .50
❑ 242 Warlord's Axe U .40 1.00
❑ 241 War Priest of Thune U :W: .40 1.00
❑ 243 Water Servant U :B: .40 1.00
❑ 244 Whispersilk Cloak U .60 1.50
❑ 245 White Knight U :W: .40 1.00
❑ 246 Wild Evocation R :R: .60 1.50
❑ 247 Wild Griffin C :W: .20 .50
❑ 248 Wurm's Tooth U .40 1.00
❑ 249 Yavimaya Wurm C :G: .20 .50

2010 Magic the Gathering Elspeth vs Tezzeret

Duel Deck 30.00 50.00

❑ 1 Elspeth, Knight-Errant M :W: 8.00 20.00
❑ 2 Elite Vanguard U :W: .20 .50
❑ 3 Goldmeadow Harrier C :W: .10 .25
❑ 4 Infantry Veteran C :W: .10 .25
❑ 5 Loyal Sentry R :W: .30 .75
❑ 6 Mosquito Guard C :W: .10 .25
❑ 7 Glory Seeker C :W: .10 .25
❑ 8 Kor Skyfisher C :W: .10 .25
❑ 9 Temple Acolyte C :W: .10 .25
❑ 10 Kor Aeronaut U :W: .20 .50
❑ 11 Burrenton Bombardier C :W: .10 .25
❑ 12 Kor Hookmaster C :W: .10 .25
❑ 13 Kemba's Skyguard C :W: .10 .25
❑ 14 Celestial Crusader U :W: .20 .50
❑ 15 Seasoned Marshal U :W: .20 .50
❑ 16 Conclave Phalanx U :W: .20 .50
❑ 17 Stormfront Riders U :W: .20 .50
❑ 18 Catapult Master R :W: .30 .75
❑ 19 Conclave Equenaut C :W: .10 .25
❑ 20 Angel of Salvation R :W: .30 .75

❑ 21 Sunlance C :W: .10 .25
❑ 22 Swords to Plowshares U :W: 2.00 5.00
❑ 23 Journey to Nowhere C :W: .30 .75
❑ 24 Mighty Leap C :W: .10 .25
❑ 25 Raise the Alarm C :W: .10 .25
❑ 26 Razor Barrier C :W: .10 .25
❑ 27 Crusade R :W: .60 1.50
❑ 28 Blinding Beam C :W: .10 .25
❑ 29 Abolish U :W: .20 .50
❑ 30 Saltblast U :W: .20 .50
❑ 31 Swell of Courage U :W: .20 .50
❑ 32 Daru Encampment U .20 .50
❑ 33 Kabira Crossroads C .10 .25
❑ 34 Rustic Clachan R .30 .75
❑ 35 Plains L .10 .25
❑ 36 Plains L .10 .25
❑ 37 Plains L .10 .25
❑ 38 Plains L .10 .25
❑ 39 Tezzeret the Seeker M :B: 2.50 6.00
❑ 40 Arcbound Worker C .20 .50
❑ 41 Steel Wall C .10 .25
❑ 42 Runed Servitor U .20 .50
❑ 43 Silver Myr C .10 .25
❑ 44 Steel Overseer R 2.00 5.00
❑ 45 Assembly-Worker U .20 .50
❑ 46 Serrated Biskelion U .20 .50
❑ 47 Esperzoa U :B: .20 .50
❑ 48 Master of Etherium R :B: 2.00 5.00
❑ 49 Trinket Mage C :B: .20 .50
❑ 50 Clockwork Condor C .10 .25
❑ 51 Frogmite C .30 .75
❑ 52 Juggernaut U .20 .50
❑ 53 Synod Centurion U .20 .50
❑ 54 Faerie Mechanist C :B: .10 .25
❑ 55 Clockwork Hydra U .20 .50
❑ 56 Razormane Masticore R .30 .75
❑ 57 Triskelion R .30 .75
❑ 58 Pentavus R .20 .50
❑ 59 Qumulox U :B: .20 .50
❑ 60 Everflowing Chalice U .75 2.00
❑ 61 AEther Spellbomb C .10 .25
❑ 62 Elixir of Immortality U .40 1.00
❑ 63 Contagion Clasp U .40 1.00
❑ 64 Energy Chamber U .75 2.00
❑ 65 Trip Noose U .20 .50
❑ 66 Echoing Truth C :B: .40 1.00
❑ 67 Moonglove Extract C .10 .25
❑ 68 Thirst for Knowledge U :B: .40 1.00
❑ 69 Argivian Restoration U :B: .20 .50
❑ 70 Foil U :B: .30 .75
❑ 71 Thoughtcast C :B: .30 .75
❑ 72 Darksteel Citadel C .75 2.00
❑ 73 Mishra's Factory U 2.00 5.00
❑ 74 Seat of the Synod C .75 2.00
❑ 75 Stalking Stones U .20 .50
❑ 76 Island L .10 .25
❑ 77 Island L .10 .25
❑ 78 Island L .10 .25
❑ 79 Island L .10 .25
❑ T1 Token: Soldier .10 .25

2010 Magic the Gathering Phyrexia vs The Coalition

Duel Deck 20.00 40.00
❑ 1 Phyrexian Negator M :K: .75 2.00
❑ 1 Hornet - Token C .10 .25
❑ 2 Minion - Token C .10 .25
❑ 2 Carrion Feeder C :K: .20 .50
❑ 3 Phyrexian Battleflies C :K: .10 .25
❑ 3 Saproling - Token C .10 .25
❑ 4 Phyrexian Denouncer C :K: .10 .25
❑ 5 Bone Shredder U :K: .20 .50
❑ 6 Phyrexian Ghoul C :K: .10 .25
❑ 7 Priest of Gix U :K: .20 .50
❑ 8 Phyrexian Broodlings C :K: .10 .25
❑ 9 Sanguine Guard U :K: .20 .50
❑ 10 Phyrexian Debaser C :K: .10 .25
❑ 11 Order of Yawgmoth U :K: .20 .50
❑ 12 Phyrexian Defiler U :K: .20 .50
❑ 13 Phyrexian Plaguelord R :K: .30 .75
❑ 14 Phyrexian Hulk U .20 .50
❑ 15 Phyrexian Gargantua U :K: .20 .50
❑ 16 Phyrexian Colossus R .30 .75
❑ 17 Voltaic Key U .40 1.00
❑ 18 Dark Ritual C :K: .75 2.00
❑ 19 Lightning Greaves U 1.00 2.50
❑ 20 Phyrexian Totem U .20 .50
❑ 21 Phyrexian Vault U .20 .50
❑ 22 Puppet Strings U .20 .50
❑ 23 Whispersilk Cloak U .30 .75
❑ 24 Worn Powerstone U .40 1.00
❑ 25 Slay U :K: .20 .50
❑ 26 Hideous End C :K: .10 .25
❑ 27 Phyrexian Arena R :K: 1.25 3.00
❑ 28 Hornet Cannon U .20 .50
❑ 29 Phyrexian Processor R .75 2.00
❑ 30 Tendrils of Corruption C :K: .10 .25
❑ 31 Living Death R :K: 1.00 2.50
❑ 32 Swamp L .10 .25
❑ 33 Swamp L .10 .25
❑ 34 Swamp L .10 .25
❑ 35 Swamp L .10 .25
❑ 36 Urza's Rage M :R: .60 1.50
❑ 37 Thornscape Apprentice C :G: .10 .25
❑ 38 Nomadic Elf C :G: .10 .25
❑ 39 Quirion Elves C :G: .10 .25
❑ 40 Sunscape Battlemage U :W: .20 .50
❑ 41 Thunderscape Battlemage U :R: .20 .50
❑ 42 Thornscape Battlemage U :G: .20 .50
❑ 43 Verduran Emissary U :G: .20 .50
❑ 44 Yavimaya Elder C :G: .40 1.00
❑ 45 Charging Troll U :W/G: .20 .50
❑ 46 Gerrard Capashen R :W: .30 .75
❑ 47 Darigaaz, the Igniter R :K/R/G: .60 1.50
❑ 48 Rith, the Awakener R :W/R/G: .75 2.00
❑ 49 Treva, the Renewer R :W/L/G: .75 2.00
❑ 50 Evasive Action U :B: .20 .50
❑ 51 Tribal Flames C :R: .20 .50
❑ 52 Fertile Ground C :G: .10 .25
❑ 53 Gerrard's Command C :W/G: .10 .25
❑ 54 Coalition Relic R 1.50 4.00
❑ 55 Narrow Escape C :W: .10 .25
❑ 56 Exotic Curse C :K: .10 .25
❑ 57 Harrow C :G: .20 .50
❑ 58 Armadillo Cloak C :W/G: .40 1.00
❑ 59 Darigaaz's Charm U :K/R/G: .20 .50
❑ 60 Rith's Charm U :W/R/G: .20 .50
❑ 61 Treva's Charm U :W/L/G: .20 .50
❑ 62 Power Armor U .20 .50
❑ 63 Allied Strategies U :B: .20 .50
❑ 64 Elfhame Palace U .20 .50
❑ 65 Shivan Oasis U .20 .50
❑ 66 Terramorphic Expanse C .20 .50
❑ 67 Plains L .10 .25
❑ 68 Island L .10 .25
❑ 69 Mountain L .10 .25
❑ 70 Forest L .10 .25
❑ 71 Forest L .10 .25
❑ T1 Token: Hornet .10 .25
❑ T2 Token: Minion .10 .25
❑ T3 Token: Saproling .10 .25

2010 Magic the Gathering Rise of the Eldrazi

Complete Set (248) 100.00 200.00
Booster Box (36 Packs) 125.00 200.00
Booster Pack (15 Cards) 4.00 6.00
Theme Decks 8.00 12.00
Fat Pack 30.00 50.00
❑ 1 Affa Guard Hound U :W: .20 .50
❑ 2 Akoum Boulderfoot U :R: .20 .50
❑ 3 All Is Dust M 5.00 12.00
❑ 4 Ancient Stirrings C :G: .10 .25
❑ 5 Angelheart Vial R .30 .75
❑ 6 Arrogant Bloodlord U :K: .20 .50
❑ 7 Artisan of Kozilek U .20 .50
❑ 8 Aura Finesse C :B: .10 .25
❑ 9 Aura Gnarlid C :G: .10 .25
❑ 10 Awakening Zone R :G: 1.00 2.50
❑ 11 Bala Ged Scorpion C :G: .10 .25
❑ 12 Baneful Omen R :K: .30 .75
❑ 13 Battle Rampart C :R: .10 .25
❑ 14 Battle-Rattle Shaman C :R: .10 .25
❑ 15 Bear Umbra R :G: .60 1.50
❑ 16 Beastbreaker of Bala Ged U :G: .20 .50
❑ 17 Bloodrite Invoker C :K: .10 .25
❑ 18 Bloodthrone Vampire C :K: .10 .25
❑ 19 Boar Umbra U :G: .20 .50
❑ 20 Bramblesnap U :G: .20 .50
❑ 21 Brimstone Mage U :R: .20 .50
❑ 22 Brood Birthing C :R: .10 .25
❑ 23 Broodwarden U :G: .20 .50
❑ 24 Cadaver Imp C :K: .10 .25
❑ 25 Caravan Escort C :W: .10 .25
❑ 26 Cast Through Time M :B: .40 1.00
❑ 27 Champion's Drake C :B: .10 .25
❑ 28 Conquering Manticore R :R: .30 .75
❑ 29 Consume the Meek R :K: .40 1.00
❑ 30 Consuming Vapors R :K: .40 1.00
❑ 31 Contaminated Ground C :K: .10 .25
❑ 32 Coralhelm Commander R :B: 2.00 5.00
❑ 33 Corpsehatch U :K: .20 .50
❑ 34 Crab Umbra U :B: .20 .50
❑ 35 Curse of Wizardry U :K: .20 .50
❑ 36 Daggerback Basilisk C :G: .10 .25
❑ 37 Dawnglare Invoker C :W: .10 .25
❑ 38 Death Cultist C :K: .10 .25
❑ 39 Deathless Angel R :W: .60 1.50
❑ 40 Demonic Appetite C :K: .10 .25
❑ 41 Demystify C :W: .10 .25
❑ 42 Deprive C :B: .20 .50
❑ 43 Devastating Summons R :R: .30 .75
❑ 44 Disaster Radius R :R: .30 .75
❑ 45 Distortion Strike C :B: .20 .50
❑ 46 Domestication U :B: .20 .50
❑ 47 Dormant Gomazoa R :B: .30 .75
❑ 48 Drake Umbra U :B: .20 .50
❑ 49 Drana, Kalastria Bloodchief R :K: 1.00 2.50
❑ 50 Dread Drone C :K: .10 .25
❑ 51 Dreamstone Hedron U .20 .50
❑ 52 Echo Mage R :B: .60 1.50
❑ 53 Eel Umbra C :B: .10 .25
❑ 54 Eland Umbra C :W: .10 .25
❑ 55 Eldrazi Conscription R 2.00 5.00
❑ 56 Eldrazi Temple R :L: 1.00 2.50
❑ 57 Emerge Unscathed U :W: .20 .50
❑ 58 Emrakul's Hatcher C :R: .10 .25
❑ 59 Emrakul, the Aeons Torn M 8.00 20.00
❑ 60 Enatu Golem U .20 .50
❑ 61 Enclave Cryptologist U :B: .20 .50
❑ 62 Escaped Null U :K: .20 .50
❑ 63 Essence Feed C :K: .10 .25
❑ 64 Evolving Wilds C .10 .25
❑ 65 Explosive Revelation U :R: .20 .50
❑ 66 Fissure Vent C :R: .10 .25
❑ 67 Flame Slash C :R: .20 .50
❑ 68 Fleeting Distraction C :B: .10 .25
❑ 69 Forest (a) L .20 .50
❑ 70 Forest (b) L .10 .25
❑ 71 Forest (c) L .10 .25
❑ 72 Forest (d) L .10 .25
❑ 73 Forked Bolt U :R: .20 .50
❑ 74 Frostwind Invoker C :B: .10 .25
❑ 75 Gelatinous Genesis R :G: .30 .75
❑ 76 Gideon Jura M :W: 5.00 12.00
❑ 77 Gigantomancer R :G: .30 .75
❑ 78 Gloomhunter C :B: .10 .25
❑ 79 Glory Seeker C :W: .10 .25
❑ 80 Goblin Arsonist C :R: .10 .25
❑ 81 Goblin Tunneler C :R: .10 .25
❑ 82 Gravitational Shift R :B: .30 .75
❑ 83 Gravity Well U :G: .20 .50
❑ 84 Grotag Siege-Runner C :R: .10 .25
❑ 85 Growth Spasm C :G: .10 .25
❑ 86 Guard Duty C :W: .10 .25
❑ 87 Guard Gomazoa U :B: .20 .50
❑ 88 Guul Draz Assassin R :K: 2.00 5.00
❑ 89 Hada Spy Patrol U :B: .20 .50
❑ 90 Halimar Wavewatch C :B: .10 .25
❑ 91 Hand of Emrakul C .20 .50
❑ 92 Harmless Assault C :W: .10 .25
❑ 93 Haze Frog C :G: .10 .25
❑ 94 Heat Ray C :R: .10 .25
❑ 95 Hedron Matrix R .30 .75
❑ 96 Hedron-Field Purists R :W: .30 .75
❑ 97 Hellcarver Demon M :K: .40 1.00
❑ 98 Hellion Eruption R :R: .30 .75
❑ 99 Hyena Umbra C :W: .20 .50
❑ 100 Ikiral Outrider C :W: .10 .25
❑ 101 Induce Despair C :B: .10 .25
❑ 102 Inquisition of Kozilek U :B: 2.00 5.00
❑ 103 Irresistible Prey U :G: .20 .50
❑ 104 Island (a) L .20 .50
❑ 105 Island (b) L .10 .25
❑ 106 Island (c) L .10 .25
❑ 107 Island (d) L .10 .25
❑ 108 It That Betrays R 3.00 8.00
❑ 109 Jaddi Lifestrider U :G: .20 .50
❑ 110 Joraga Treespeaker U :G: 1.00 2.50
❑ 111 Jwari Scuttler C :B: .10 .25
❑ 112 Kabira Vindicator U :W: .20 .50
❑ 113 Kargan Dragonlord M :R: 2.50 6.00
❑ 114 Kazandu Tuskcaller R :G: .30 .75
❑ 115 Keening Stone R .60 1.50
❑ 116 Khalni Hydra M :G: 2.50 6.00
❑ 117 Kiln Fiend C :R: .20 .50
❑ 118 Knight of Cliffhaven C :W: .10 .25
❑ 119 Kor Line-Slinger C :W: .10 .25
❑ 120 Kor Spiritdancer R :W: .75 2.00
❑ 121 Kozilek's Predator C :G: .20 .50
❑ 122 Kozilek, Butcher of Truth M 8.00 20.00
❑ 123 Lagac Lizard C :R: .10 .25
❑ 124 Last Kiss C :K: .10 .25
❑ 125 Lavafume Invoker C :R: .10 .25
❑ 126 Lay Bare C :B: .10 .25
❑ 127 Leaf Arrow C :G: .10 .25
❑ 128 Lighthouse Chronologist M :B: 2.50 6.00
❑ 129 Lightmine Field R :W: .30 .75
❑ 130 Linvala, Keeper of Silence M :W: 4.00 10.00
❑ 131 Living Destiny C :G: .10 .25
❑ 132 Lone Missionary C :W: .10 .25
❑ 133 Lord of Shatterskull Pass R :R: .30 .75
❑ 134 Luminous Wake U :W: .20 .50
❑ 135 Lust for War U :R: .20 .50
❑ 136 Magmaw R :R: .30 .75
❑ 137 Makindi Griffin C :W: .10 .25
❑ 138 Mammoth Umbra U :W: .20 .50
❑ 139 Merfolk Observer C :B: .10 .25
❑ 140 Merfolk Skyscout U :B: .20 .50
❑ 141 Might of the Masses C :G: .10 .25
❑ 142 Mnemonic Wall C :B: .10 .25
❑ 143 Momentous Fall R :G: .60 1.50
❑ 144 Mortician Beetle R :K: .30 .75
❑ 145 Mountain (a) L .10 .25
❑ 146 Mountain (b) L .10 .25
❑ 147 Mountain (c) L .10 .25
❑ 148 Mountain (d) L .10 .25
❑ 149 Mul Daya Channelers R :G: .40 1.00
❑ 150 Narcolepsy C :B: .10 .25
❑ 151 Naturalize C :G: .10 .25
❑ 152 Near-Death Experience R :W: .30 .75
❑ 153 Nema Siltlurker C :G: .10 .25
❑ 154 Nest Invader C :G: .20 .50
❑ 155 Nighthaze C :K: .10 .25
❑ 156 Nirkana Cutthroat U :K: .20 .50
❑ 157 Nirkana Revenant M :K: 4.00 10.00
❑ 158 Nomads' Assembly R :W: .30 .75
❑ 159 Not Of This World U .20 .50
❑ 160 Null Champion C :B: .10 .25
❑ 161 Ogre Sentry C :R: .10 .25
❑ 162 Ogre's Cleaver U .20 .50
❑ 163 Ondu Giant C :G: .10 .25
❑ 164 Oust U :W: .20 .50
❑ 165 Overgrown Battlement C :G: .20 .50
❑ 166 Pathrazer of Ulamog U .20 .50
❑ 167 Pawn of Ulamog U :K: .20 .50
❑ 168 Pelakka Wurm U :G: .20 .50
❑ 169 Pennon Blade U .20 .50
❑ 170 Perish the Thought C :K: .10 .25
❑ 171 Pestilence Demon R :K: .30 .75
❑ 172 Phantasmal Abomination U :B: .20 .50
❑ 173 Plains (a) L .10 .25
❑ 174 Plains (b) L .10 .25
❑ 175 Plains (c) L .10 .25
❑ 176 Plains (d) L .10 .25
❑ 177 Prey's Vengeance U :G: .20 .50
❑ 178 Prophetic Prism C .10 .25
❑ 179 Puncturing Light C :W: .10 .25
❑ 180 Rage Nimbus R :R: .30 .75
❑ 181 Raid Bombardment C :R: .10 .25
❑ 182 Rapacious One U :R: .20 .50
❑ 183 Reality Spasm U :B: .20 .50
❑ 184 Realms Uncharted R :G: .40 1.00
❑ 185 Recurring Insight R :B: .30 .75
❑ 186 Regress C :B: .10 .25
❑ 187 Reinforced Bulwark C .10 .25
❑ 188 Renegade Doppelganger R :B: .30 .75
❑ 189 Repay In Kind R :K: .30 .75
❑ 190 Repel the Darkness C :W: .10 .25
❑ 191 Runed Servitor U .20 .50
❑ 192 Sarkhan the Mad M :K/R: 2.50 6.00
❑ 193 Sea Gate Oracle C :B: .20 .50
❑ 194 See Beyond C :B: .20 .50
❑ 195 Shared Discovery C :B: .10 .25
❑ 196 Shrivel C :K: .10 .25
❑ 197 Skeletal Wurm U :K: .20 .50
❑ 198 Skittering Invasion U .20 .50
❑ 199 Skywatcher Adept C :B: .10 .25
❑ 200 Smite C :W: .10 .25
❑ 201 Snake Umbra C :G: .10 .25
❑ 202 Soul's Attendant C :W: .10 .25
❑ 203 Soulbound Guardians U :W: .20 .50
❑ 204 Soulsurge Elemental U :R: .20 .50
❑ 205 Spawning Breath C :R: .10 .25
❑ 206 Spawnsire of Ulamog R .60 1.50
❑ 207 Sphinx of Magosi R :B: .30 .75
❑ 208 Sphinx-Bone Wand R .30 .75
❑ 209 Spider Umbra C :G: .10 .25
❑ 210 Splinter Twin R :R: 2.00 5.00
❑ 211 Sporecap Spider C :G: .10 .25
❑ 212 Staggershock C :R: .20 .50
❑ 213 Stalwart Shield-Bearers C :W: .10 .25
❑ 214 Stomper Cub C :G: .10 .25
❑ 215 Student of Warfare R :W: 2.00 5.00
❑ 216 Suffer the Past U :K: .20 .50
❑ 217 Surrakar Spellblade R :B: .30 .75
❑ 218 Surreal Memoir U :R: .20 .50
❑ 219 Survival Cache U :W: .20 .50
❑ 220 Swamp (a) L .10 .25
❑ 221 Swamp (b) L .10 .25
❑ 222 Swamp (c) L .10 .25
❑ 223 Swamp (d) L .10 .25
❑ 224 Tajuru Preserver R :G: .30 .75
❑ 225 Thought Gorger R :K: .30 .75
❑ 226 Time of Heroes U :W: .20 .50
❑ 227 Totem-Guide Hartebeest C :W: .10 .25
❑ 228 Training Grounds R :B: .75 2.00
❑ 229 Traitorous Instinct U :R: .20 .50
❑ 230 Transcendent Master M :W: 2.00 5.00
❑ 231 Tuktuk the Explorer R :R: .40 1.00
❑ 232 Ulamog's Crusher C .20 .50
❑ 233 Ulamog, the Infinite Gyre M 6.00 15.00
❑ 234 Umbra Mystic R :W: .30 .75
❑ 235 Unified Will U :B: .20 .50
❑ 236 Valakut Fireboar U :R: .20 .50
❑ 237 Vendetta C :K: .10 .25
❑ 238 Venerated Teacher C :B: .10 .25
❑ 239 Vengevine M :G: 6.00 15.00
❑ 240 Vent Sentinel C :R: .10 .25
❑ 241 Virulent Swipe U :K: .20 .50
❑ 242 Wall of Omens U :W: .60 1.50
❑ 243 Warmonger's Chariot U .20 .50
❑ 244 Wildheart Invoker C :G: .10 .25
❑ 245 World at War R :R: .30 .75
❑ 246 Wrap in Flames C :R: .10 .25
❑ 247 Zof Shade C :K: .10 .25
❑ 248 Zulaport Enforcer C :K: .10 .25
❑ R1 Rules Tip: Levelers .10 .25
❑ R2 Rules Tip: Eldrazi .10 .25
❑ R3 Rules Tip: Eldrazi Abilities .10 .25
❑ R4 Rules Tip: Rebound .10 .25
❑ R5 Rules Tip: Totem Armor .10 .25
❑ T1a Token: Eldrazi Spawn (Aleksi Briclot) .10 .25
❑ T1b Token: Eldrazi Spawn (Mark Tedin) .10 .25
❑ T1c Token: Eldrazi Spawn (Veronique Meignaud) .10 .25
❑ T2 Token: Elemental .10 .25
❑ T3 Token: Hellion .10 .25
❑ T4 Token: Ooze .10 .25
❑ T5 Token: Tuktuk the Returned .10 .25

2010 Magic the Gathering Rise of the Eldrazi Foil

*Foil: .8X to 2X Basic Cards

2010 Magic the Gathering Scars of Mirrodin

Complete Set (249) 100.00 200.00
Booster Box (36 Packs) 75.00 150.00
Booster Pack (15 Cards) 3.50 5.00
Fat Pack 30.00 40.00
Released October 2010
❑ 1 Abuna Acolyte U :W: .20 .50
❑ 2 Arrest C :W: .10 .25
❑ 3 Auriok Edgewright U :W: .20 .50
❑ 4 Auriok Sunchaser C :W: .10 .25
❑ 5 Dispense Justice U :W: .20 .50
❑ 6 Elspeth Tirel M :W: 6.00 15.00
❑ 7 Fulgent Distraction C :W: .10 .25
❑ 8 Ghalma's Warden C :W: .10 .25
❑ 9 Glimmerpoint Stag U :W: .20 .50
❑ 10 Glint Hawk C :W: .10 .25
❑ 11 Indomitable Archangel M :W: 1.25 3.00
❑ 12 Kemba, Kha Regent R :W: .30 .75
❑ 13 Kemba's Skyguard C :W: .10 .25
❑ 14 Leonin Arbiter R :W: .40 1.00
❑ 15 Loxodon Wayfarer C :W: .10 .25
❑ 16 Myrsmith U :W: .10 .25
❑ 17 Razor Hippogriff U :W: .20 .50
❑ 18 Revoke Existence C :W: .10 .25
❑ 19 Salvage Scout C :W: .10 .25
❑ 20 Seize the Initiative C :W: .10 .25
❑ 21 Soul Parry C :W: .10 .25
❑ 22 Sunblast Angel R :W: .40 1.00
❑ 23 Sunspear Shikari C :W: .10 .25
❑ 24 Tempered Steel R :W: 2.00 5.00
❑ 25 True Conviction R :W: .40 1.00
❑ 26 Vigil for the Lost U :W: .20 .50
❑ 27 Whitesun's Passage C :W: .10 .25
❑ 28 Argent Sphinx R :B: .30 .75
❑ 29 Bonds of Quicksilver C :B: .10 .25
❑ 30 Darkslick Drake U :B: .20 .50
❑ 31 Disperse C :B: .10 .25
❑ 32 Dissipation Field R :B: .60 1.50
❑ 33 Grand Architect R :B: 1.25 3.00
❑ 34 Halt Order U :B: .20 .50
❑ 35 Inexorable Tide R :B: .30 .75
❑ 36 Lumengrid Drake C :B: .10 .25
❑ 37 Neurok Invisimancer C :B: .10 .25
❑ 38 Plated Seastrider C :B: .10 .25
❑ 39 Quicksilver Gargantuan M :B: .60 1.50
❑ 40 Riddlesmith U :B: .20 .50
❑ 41 Scrapdiver Serpent C :B: .10 .25
❑ 42 Screeching Silcaw C :B: .10 .25
❑ 43 Shape Anew R :B: .30 .75
❑ 44 Sky-Eel School C :B: .10 .25
❑ 45 Steady Progress C :B: .10 .25
❑ 46 Stoic Rebuttal C :B: .20 .50
❑ 47 Thrummingbird U :B: .30 .75
❑ 48 Trinket Mage U :B: .20 .50
❑ 49 Turn Aside C :B: .10 .25
❑ 50 Twisted Image U :B: .20 .50
❑ 51 Vault Skyward C :B: .10 .25
❑ 52 Vedalken Certarch C :B: .10 .25
❑ 53 Volition Reins U :B: .30 .75
❑ 54 Blackcleave Goblin C :K: .10 .25
❑ 55 Bleak Coven Vampires C :K: .10 .25
❑ 56 Blistergrub C :K: .10 .25
❑ 57 Carnifex Demon R :K: .30 .75
❑ 58 Contagious Nim C :K: .10 .25
❑ 59 Corrupted Harvester U :K: .20 .50
❑ 60 Dross Hopper C :K: .10 .25
❑ 61 Exsanguinate U :K: .40 1.00
❑ 62 Flesh Allergy U :K: .20 .50
❑ 63 Fume Spitter C :K: .10 .25
❑ 64 Geth, Lord of the Vault M :K: 1.50 4.00
❑ 65 Grasp of Darkness C :K: .10 .25
❑ 66 Hand of the Praetors R :K: 1.25 3.00
❑ 67 Ichor Rats U :K: .20 .50
❑ 68 Instill Infection C :K: .10 .25
❑ 69 Memoricide R :K: .75 2.00
❑ 70 Moriok Reaver C :K: .10 .25
❑ 71 Necrogen Scudder U :K: .20 .50
❑ 72 Necrotic Ooze R :K: 1.00 2.50
❑ 73 Painful Quandary R :K: .30 .75
❑ 74 Painsmith U :K: .20 .50
❑ 75 Plague Stinger C :K: .10 .25
❑ 76 Psychic Miasma C :K: .10 .25
❑ 77 Relic Putrescence C :K: .10 .25
❑ 78 Skinrender U :K: .30 .75
❑ 79 Skithiryx, the Blight Dragon M :K: 3.00 8.00
❑ 80 Tainted Strike C :K: .10 .25
❑ 81 Arc Trail U :R: .60 1.50
❑ 82 Assault Strobe C :R: .10 .25
❑ 83 Barrage Ogre U :R: .20 .50
❑ 84 Blade-Tribe Berserkers C :R: .10 .25
❑ 85 Bloodshot Trainee U :R: .20 .50
❑ 86 Cerebral Eruption R :R: .30 .75
❑ 87 Embersmith U :R: .20 .50
❑ 88 Ferrovore C :R: .10 .25
❑ 89 Flameborn Hellion C :R: .10 .25
❑ 90 Furnace Celebration U :R: .20 .50
❑ 91 Galvanic Blast C :R: .30 .75
❑ 92 Goblin Gaveleer C :R: .10 .25
❑ 93 Hoard-Smelter Dragon R :R: .30 .75
❑ 94 Koth of the Hammer M :R: 5.00 12.00
❑ 95 Kuldotha Phoenix R :R: .30 .75
❑ 96 Kuldotha Rebirth C :R: .10 .25
❑ 97 Melt Terrain C :R: .10 .25
❑ 98 Molten Psyche R :R: .30 .75
❑ 99 Ogre Geargrabber U :R: .20 .50
❑ 100 Oxidda Daredevil C :R: .10 .25
❑ 101 Oxidda Scrapmelter U :R: .20 .50
❑ 102 Scoria Elemental C :R: .10 .25
❑ 103 Shatter C :R: .10 .25
❑ 104 Spikeshot Elder R :R: .75 2.00
❑ 105 Tunnel Ignus R :R: .40 1.00
❑ 106 Turn to Slag C :R: .10 .25
❑ 107 Vulshok Heartstoker C :R: .10 .25
❑ 108 Acid Web Spider U :G: .20 .50
❑ 109 Alpha Tyrranax C :G: .10 .25
❑ 110 Asceticism R :G: 2.00 5.00
❑ 111 Bellowing Tanglewurm U :G: .20 .50
❑ 112 Blight Mamba C :G: .10 .25
❑ 113 Blunt the Assault C :G: .10 .25
❑ 114 Carapace Forger C :G: .10 .25
❑ 115 Carrion Call U :G: .20 .50
❑ 116 Copperhorn Scout C :G: .10 .25
❑ 117 Cystbearer C :G: .10 .25
❑ 118 Engulfing Slagwurm R :G: .30 .75
❑ 119 Ezuri, Renegade Leader R :G: 1.00 2.50
❑ 120 Ezuri's Archers C :G: .10 .25
❑ 121 Ezuri's Brigade R :G: .60 1.50

MAGIC

MAGIC

❑ 122 Genesis Wave R :G:	.75	2.00
❑ 123 Liege of the Tangle M :G:	1.25	3.00
❑ 124 Lifesmith U :G:	.20	.50
❑ 125 Molder Beast C :G:	.10	.25
❑ 126 Putrefax R :G:	.40	1.00
❑ 127 Slice in Twain U :G:	.20	.50
❑ 128 Tangle Angler U :G:	.20	.50
❑ 129 Tel-Jilad Defiance C :G:	.10	.25
❑ 130 Tel-Jilad Fallen C :G:	.10	.25
❑ 131 Untamed Might C :G:	.10	.25
❑ 132 Viridian Revel U :G:	.20	.50
❑ 133 Wing Puncture C :G:	.20	.50
❑ 134 Withstand Death C :G:	.10	.25
❑ 135 Venser, the Sojourner M :G:	4.00	10.00
❑ 136 Accorder's Shield C	.10	.25
❑ 137 Argentum Armor R	1.00	2.50
❑ 138 Auriok Replica C	.10	.25
❑ 139 Barbed Battlegear U	.20	.50
❑ 140 Bladed Pinions C	.10	.25
❑ 141 Chimeric Mass R	.40	1.00
❑ 142 Chrome Steed C	.10	.25
❑ 143 Clone Shell U	.20	.50
❑ 144 Contagion Clasp U	.40	1.00
❑ 145 Contagion Engine R	.75	2.00
❑ 146 Copper Myr C	.10	.25
❑ 147 Corpse Cur C	.10	.25
❑ 148 Culling Dais U	.20	.50
❑ 149 Darksteel Axe U	.20	.50
❑ 150 Darksteel Juggernaut R	.30	.75
❑ 151 Darksteel Myr U	.30	.75
❑ 152 Darksteel Sentinel U	.20	.50
❑ 153 Echo Circlet C	.10	.25
❑ 154 Etched Champion R	2.50	6.00
❑ 155 Flight Spellbomb C	.10	.25
❑ 156 Glint Hawk Idol C	.10	.25
❑ 157 Gold Myr C	.10	.25
❑ 158 Golden Urn C	.10	.25
❑ 159 Golem Artisan U	.20	.50
❑ 160 Golem Foundry C	.10	.25
❑ 161 Golem's Heart U	.20	.50
❑ 162 Grafted Exoskeleton U	.20	.50
❑ 163 Grindclock R	.30	.75
❑ 164 Heavy Arbalest U	.20	.50
❑ 165 Horizon Spellbomb C	.10	.25
❑ 166 Ichorclaw Myr C	.30	.75
❑ 167 Infiltration Lens U	.40	1.00
❑ 168 Iron Myr C	.10	.25
❑ 169 Kuldotha Forgemaster R	.40	1.00
❑ 170 Leaden Myr C	.10	.25
❑ 171 Liquimetal Coating U	.20	.50
❑ 172 Livewire Lash R	.40	1.00
❑ 173 Lux Cannon M	1.25	3.00
❑ 174 Memnite U	.60	1.50
❑ 175 Mimic Vat R	1.25	3.00
❑ 176 Mindslaver M	.75	2.00
❑ 177 Molten-Tail Masticore M	.75	2.00
❑ 178 Moriok Replica C	.10	.25
❑ 179 Mox Opal M	8.00	20.00
❑ 180 Myr Battlesphere R	.75	2.00
❑ 181 Myr Galvanizer U	.40	1.00
❑ 182 Myr Propagator R	.30	.75
❑ 183 Myr Reservoir R	.30	.75
❑ 184 Necrogen Censer C	.10	.25
❑ 185 Necropede U	.30	.75
❑ 186 Neurok Replica C	.10	.25
❑ 187 Nihil Spellbomb C	.30	.75
❑ 188 Nim Deathmantle R	.30	.75
❑ 189 Origin Spellbomb C	.10	.25
❑ 190 Palladium Myr U	.40	1.00
❑ 191 Panic Spellbomb C	.10	.25
❑ 192 Perilous Myr C	.20	.50
❑ 193 Platinum Emperion M	1.50	4.00
❑ 194 Precursor Golem R	.40	1.00
❑ 195 Prototype Portal R	.40	1.00
❑ 196 Ratchet Bomb R	3.00	8.00
❑ 197 Razorfield Thresher C	.10	.25
❑ 198 Rust Tick U	.20	.50
❑ 199 Rusted Relic U	.20	.50
❑ 200 Saberclaw Golem C	.10	.25
❑ 201 Semblance Anvil R	.60	1.50
❑ 202 Silver Myr C	.10	.25
❑ 203 Snapsail Glider C	.10	.25
❑ 204 Soliton C	.10	.25
❑ 205 Steel Hellkite R	.75	2.00
❑ 206 Strata Scythe R	.30	.75
❑ 207 Strider Harness C	.10	.25
❑ 208 Sword of Body and Mind M	5.00	12.00
❑ 209 Sylvok Lifestaff C	.10	.25
❑ 210 Sylvok Replica C	.10	.25
❑ 211 Throne of Geth U	.20	.50
❑ 212 Tower of Calamities R	.30	.75
❑ 213 Trigon of Corruption U	.20	.50
❑ 214 Trigon of Infestation U	.20	.50
❑ 215 Trigon of Mending U	.20	.50
❑ 216 Trigon of Rage U	.20	.50
❑ 217 Trigon of Thought U	.20	.50
❑ 218 Tumble Magnet C	.20	.50
❑ 219 Vector Asp C	.10	.25
❑ 220 Venser's Journal R	.75	2.00
❑ 221 Vulshok Replica C	.10	.25
❑ 222 Wall of Tanglecord C	.10	.25
❑ 223 Wurmcoil Engine M	8.00	20.00
❑ 224 Blackcleave Cliffs R	3.00	8.00
❑ 225 Copperline Gorge R	5.00	12.00
❑ 226 Darkslick Shores R	8.00	20.00
❑ 227 Glimmerpost C	.10	.25
❑ 228 Razorverge Thicket R	4.00	10.00
❑ 229 Seachrome Coast R	8.00	20.00
❑ 230 Plains L	.10	.25
❑ 231 Plains L	.10	.25
❑ 232 Plains L	.10	.25
❑ 233 Plains L	.10	.25
❑ 234 Island L	.10	.25
❑ 235 Island L	.10	.25
❑ 236 Island L	.10	.25
❑ 237 Island L	.10	.25
❑ 238 Swamp L	.10	.25
❑ 239 Swamp L	.10	.25
❑ 240 Swamp L	.10	.25
❑ 241 Swamp L	.10	.25
❑ 242 Mountain L	.10	.25
❑ 243 Mountain L	.10	.25
❑ 244 Mountain L	.10	.25
❑ 245 Mountain L	.10	.25
❑ 246 Forest L	.10	.25
❑ 247 Forest L	.10	.25
❑ 248 Forest L	.10	.25
❑ 249 Forest L	.10	.25
❑ PC Poison Counter	.10	.25
❑ R1 Rules Tip: Infect	.10	.25
❑ R2 Rules Tip: Metalcraft	.10	.25
❑ R3 Rules Tip: Proliferate	.10	.25
❑ R4 Rules Tip: Imprint	.10	.25
❑ R5 Rules Tip: Poison and Emblems	.10	.25
❑ T1 Token: Cat	.10	.25
❑ T2 Token: Soldier	.10	.25
❑ T3 Token: Goblin	.10	.25
❑ T4 Token: Insect	.10	.25
❑ T5 Token: Wolf	.10	.25
❑ T6 Token: Golem	.10	.25
❑ T7 Token: Myr	.10	.25
❑ T8 Token: Wurm (Deathtouch)	.10	.25
❑ T9 Token: Wurm (Lifelink)	.10	.25

2010 Magic the Gathering Scars of Mirrodin Foil

*Foil: .8X to 2X Basic Cards

2010 Magic the Gathering Worldwake

Card		
Complete Set (145)	125.00	200.00
Booster Box (36 Packs)	200.00	300.00
Booster Pack (15 Cards)	6.00	10.00
Theme Decks	10.00	20.00
Fat Pack	75.00	125.00
❑ 1 Abyssal Persecutor M :K:	3.00	8.00
❑ 2 Admonition Angel M :W:	2.00	5.00
❑ 3 Aether Tradewinds C :L:	.10	.25
❑ 4 Agadeem Occultist R :K:	.60	1.50
❑ 5 Akoum Battlesinger C :R:	.10	.25
❑ 6 Amulet of Vigor R	.75	2.00
❑ 7 Anowon, the Ruin Sage R :K:	1.50	4.00
❑ 8 Apex Hawks C :W:	.20	.50
❑ 9 Arbor Elf C :G:	.30	.75
❑ 10 Archon of Redemption R :W:	.60	1.50
❑ 11 Avenger of Zendikar M :G:	2.50	6.00
❑ 12 Basilisk Collar R	2.50	6.00
❑ 13 Battle Hurda C :W:	.10	.25
❑ 14 Bazaar Trader R :R:	.60	1.50
❑ 15 Bestial Menace U :G:	.30	.75
❑ 16 Bloodhusk Ritualist U :K:	.30	.75
❑ 17 Bojuka Bog C	.20	.50
❑ 18 Bojuka Brigand C :K:	.10	.25
❑ 19 Brink of Disaster C :K:	.10	.25
❑ 20 Bull Rush C :R:	.10	.25
❑ 21 Butcher of Malakir R :K:	.60	1.50
❑ 22 Calcite Snapper C :B:	.10	.25
❑ 23 Canopy Cover U :G:	.30	.75
❑ 24 Caustic Crawler U :K:	.30	.75
❑ 25 Celestial Colonnade R	2.00	5.00
❑ 26 Chain Reaction R :R:	.60	1.50
❑ 27 Claws of Valakut C :R:	.10	.25
❑ 28 Comet Storm M :R:	1.00	2.50
❑ 29 Corrupted Zendikon C :K:	.10	.25
❑ 30 Cosi's Ravager C :R:	.10	.25
❑ 31 Creeping Tar Pit R	2.50	6.00
❑ 32 Crusher Zendikon C :R:	.10	.25
❑ 33 Cunning Sparkmage U :R:	.30	.75
❑ 34 Dead Reckoning C :K:	.10	.25
❑ 35 Death's Shadow R :K:	.60	1.50
❑ 36 Deathforge Shaman U :R:	.20	.50
❑ 37 Dispel C :B:	.30	.75
❑ 38 Dragonmaster Outcast M :R:	4.00	10.00
❑ 39 Dread Statuary U	.20	.50
❑ 40 Enclave Elite C :B:	.10	.25
❑ 41 Everflowing Chalice U	1.00	2.50
❑ 42 Explore C :G:	.40	1.00
❑ 43 Eye of Ugin M	2.00	5.00
❑ 44 Feral Contest C :G:	.10	.25
❑ 45 Fledgling Griffin C :W:	.10	.25
❑ 46 Gnarlid Pack C :G:	.10	.25
❑ 47 Goblin Roughrider C :R:	.10	.25
❑ 48 Goliath Sphinx R :B:	.60	1.50
❑ 49 Grappler Spider C :G:	.10	.25
❑ 50 Graypelt Hunter C :G:	.10	.25
❑ 51 Grotag Thrasher C :R:	.10	.25
❑ 52 Groundswell C :G:	.20	.50
❑ 53 Guardian Zendikon C :W:	.10	.25
❑ 54 Hada Freeblade U :W:	.30	.75
❑ 55 Halimar Depths C	.30	.75
❑ 56 Halimar Excavator C :B:	.10	.25
❑ 57 Hammer of Ruin U	.30	.75
❑ 58 Harabaz Druid R :G:	.75	2.00
❑ 59 Hedron Rover C	.20	.50
❑ 60 Horizon Drake U :B:	.20	.50
❑ 61 Iona's Judgment C :W:	.10	.25
❑ 62 Jace, the Mind Sculptor M :B:	35.00	70.00
❑ 63 Jagwasp Swarm C :K:	.10	.25
❑ 64 Join the Ranks C :W:	.20	.50
❑ 65 Joraga Warcaller R :G:	2.00	5.00
❑ 66 Jwari Shapeshifter R :B:	.75	2.00
❑ 67 Kalastria Highborn R :K:	2.50	6.00
❑ 68 Kazuul, Tyrant of the Cliffs R :R:	.60	1.50
❑ 69 Khalni Garden C	.30	.75
❑ 70 Kitesail C	.10	.25
❑ 71 Kitesail Apprentice C :W:	.10	.25
❑ 72 Kor Firewalker U :W:	.75	2.00
❑ 73 Lavaclaw Reaches R	1.50	4.00
❑ 74 Leatherback Baloth U :G:	.30	.75
❑ 75 Lightkeeper of Emeria U :W:	.20	.50
❑ 76 Loam Lion U :W:	.40	1.00
❑ 77 Lodestone Golem R	.75	2.00
❑ 78 Marsh Threader C :W:	.10	.25
❑ 79 Marshal's Anthem R :W:	.60	1.50
❑ 80 Mire's Toll C :K:	.10	.25
❑ 81 Mordant Dragon R :R:	.60	1.50
❑ 82 Mysteries of the Deep C :B:	.10	.25
❑ 83 Nature's Claim C :G:	.30	.75
❑ 84 Nemesis Trap U :K:	.30	.75
❑ 85 Novablast Wurm M :W/G:	1.50	4.00
❑ 86 Omnath, Locus of Mana M :G:	2.00	5.00
❑ 87 Perimeter Captain U :W:	.40	1.00
❑ 88 Permafrost Trap U :B:	.20	.50
❑ 89 Pilgrim's Eye C	.10	.25
❑ 90 Pulse Tracker C :K:	.30	.75
❑ 91 Quag Vampires C :K:	.10	.25
❑ 92 Quest for Renewal U :G:	.40	1.00
❑ 93 Quest for the Goblin Lord U :R:	.40	1.00
❑ 94 Quest for the Nihil Stone R :K:	.60	1.50
❑ 95 Quest for Ula's Temple R :B:	.60	1.50
❑ 96 Quicksand C	.20	.50
❑ 97 Raging Ravine R	2.00	5.00
❑ 98 Razor Boomerang U	.40	1.00
❑ 99 Refraction Trap U :W:	.40	1.00
❑ 100 Rest for the Weary C :W:	.20	.50
❑ 101 Ricochet Trap U :R:	.40	1.00
❑ 102 Roiling Terrain C :R:	.20	.50
❑ 103 Ruin Ghost U :W:	.40	1.00
❑ 104 Rumbling Aftershocks U :R:	.20	.50
❑ 105 Ruthless Cullblade C :K:	.10	.25
❑ 106 Scrib Nibblers U :K:	.20	.50
❑ 107 Searing Blaze C :R:	.30	.75
❑ 108 Seer's Sundial R	.60	1.50
❑ 109 Sejiri Merfolk U :B:	.40	1.00
❑ 110 Sejiri Steppe C	.20	.50
❑ 411 Selective Memory R :B:	.60	1.50
❑ 112 Shoreline Salvager U :K:	.20	.50
❑ 113 Skitter of Lizards C :R:	.10	.25
❑ 114 Slavering Nulls U :R:	.40	1.00
❑ 115 Slingbow Trap U :G:	.40	1.00
❑ 116 Smoldering Spires C	.20	.50
❑ 117 Smother U :K:	.40	1.00
❑ 118 Snapping Creeper C :G:	.10	.25
❑ 119 Spell Contortion U :B:	.40	1.00
❑ 120 Stirring Wildwood R	1.00	2.50
❑ 121 Stone Idol Trap R :R:	.60	1.50
❑ 122 Stoneforge Mystic R :W:	5.00	12.00
❑ 123 Strength of the Tajuru R :G:	.60	1.50
❑ 124 Summit Apes U :G:	.40	1.00
❑ 125 Surrakar Banisher C :B:	.10	.25
❑ 126 Talus Paladin R :W:	.75	2.00
❑ 127 Tectonic Edge U	1.50	4.00
❑ 128 Terastodon R :G:	.75	2.00
❑ 129 Terra Eternal R :W:	.60	1.50
❑ 130 Thada Adel, Acquisitor R :B:	.60	1.50
❑ 131 Tideforce Elemental U :B:	.20	.50
❑ 132 Tomb Hex C :K:	.10	.25
❑ 133 Treasure Hunt C :B:	.20	.50
❑ 134 Tuktuk Scrapper U :R:	.40	1.00
❑ 135 Twitch C :B:	.10	.25
❑ 136 Urge to Feed U :K:	.40	1.00
❑ 137 Vapor Snare U :B:	.40	1.00
❑ 138 Vastwood Animist U :G:	.40	1.00
❑ 139 Vastwood Zendikon C :G:	.10	.25
❑ 140 Veteran's Reflexes C :W:	.10	.25
❑ 141 Voyager Drake U :B:	.20	.50
❑ 142 Walking Atlas C	.10	.25
❑ 143 Wind Zendikon C :B:	.10	.25
❑ 144 Wolfbriar Elemental R :G:	.75	2.00
❑ 145 Wrexial, the Risen Deep M :B/K:	.75	2.00
❑ R1 Rules Tip: Landfall	.10	.25
❑ R2 Rules Tip: Multikicker	.10	.25
❑ R3 Rules Tip: Lands Alive	.10	.25
❑ R4 Rules Tip: Allies and Quests	.10	.25
❑ R5 Rules Tip: Traps	.10	.25
❑ T1 Token: Soldier Ally	.10	.25
❑ T2 Token: Dragon	.10	.25
❑ T3 Token: Ogre	.10	.25
❑ T4 Token: Elephant	.10	.25
❑ T5 Token: Plant	.10	.25
❑ T6 Token: Construct	.10	.25

2010 Magic the Gathering Worldwake Foil

*Foil: .8X to 2X Basic Cards

2011 Magic the Gathering Magic 2012

Card		
Complete Set (249)	125.00	250.00
❑ 1 Aegis Angel R :W:	.40	1.00
❑ 2 Alabaster Mage U :W:	.20	.50
❑ 3 Angelic Destiny M :W:	6.00	15.00
❑ 4 Angel's Mercy C :W:	.10	.25
❑ 5 Arbalest Elite U :W:	.20	.50
❑ 6 Archon of Justice R :W:	.40	1.00
❑ 7 Armored Warhorse C :W:	.10	.25
❑ 8 Assault Griffin C :W:	.10	.25
❑ 9 Auramancer C :W:	.10	.25
❑ 10 Benalish Veteran C :W:	.10	.25
❑ 11 Celestial Purge U :W:	.20	.50
❑ 12 Day of Judgment R :W:	1.25	3.00
❑ 13 Demystify C :W:	.10	.25
❑ 14 Divine Favor C :W:	.10	.25
❑ 15 Elite Vanguard U :W:	.20	.50
❑ 16 Gideon Jura M :W:	5.00	12.00
❑ 17 Gideon's Avenger R :W:	.60	1.50
❑ 18 Gideon's Lawkeeper C :W:	.10	.25
❑ 19 Grand Abolisher R :W:	3.00	8.00
❑ 20 Griffin Rider C :W:	.10	.25
❑ 21 Griffin Sentinel C :W:	.10	.25
❑ 22 Guardians' Pledge C :W:	.10	.25
❑ 23 Honor of the Pure R :W:	1.25	3.00
❑ 24 Lifelink C :W:	.10	.25
❑ 25 Mesa Enchantress R :W:	.40	1.00
❑ 26 Mighty Leap C :W:	.10	.25
❑ 27 Oblivion Ring U :W:	.60	1.50
❑ 28 Pacifism C :W:	.10	.25
❑ 29 Peregrine Griffin C :W:	.10	.25
❑ 30 Personal Sanctuary R :W:	.40	1.00
❑ 31 Pride Guardian C :W:	.10	.25
❑ 32 Roc Egg U :W:	.20	.50
❑ 33 Serra Angel U :W:	.20	.50
❑ 34 Siege Mastodon C :W:	.10	.25
❑ 35 Spirit Mantle U :W:	.40	1.00
❑ 36 Stave Off C :W:	.10	.25
❑ 37 Stonehorn Dignitary C :W:	.10	.25
❑ 38 Stormfront Pegasus C :W:	.10	.25
❑ 39 Sun Titan M :W:	2.50	6.00
❑ 40 Timely Reinforcements U :W:	1.00	2.50
❑ 41 AEther Adept C :B:	.10	.25
❑ 42 Alluring Siren U :B:	.20	.50
❑ 43 Amphin Cutthroat C :B:	.10	.25
❑ 44 Aven Fleetwing C :B:	.10	.25
❑ 45 Azure Mage U :B:	.20	.50
❑ 46 Belltower Sphinx U :B:	.20	.50
❑ 47 Cancel C :B:	.10	.25
❑ 48 Chasm Drake C :B:	.10	.25
❑ 49 Coral Merfolk C :B:	.10	.25
❑ 50 Divination C :B:	.10	.25
❑ 51 Djinn of Wishes R :B:	.40	1.00
❑ 52 Flashfreeze U :B:	.20	.50
❑ 53 Flight C :B:	.10	.25
❑ 54 Frost Breath C :B:	.10	.25
❑ 55 Frost Titan M :B:	1.50	4.00
❑ 56 Harbor Serpent C :B:	.10	.25
❑ 57 Ice Cage C :B:	.10	.25
❑ 58 Jace, Memory Adept M :B:	6.00	15.00
❑ 59 Jace's Archivist R :B:	.75	2.00
❑ 60 Jace's Erasure C :B:	.10	.25
❑ 61 Levitation U :B:	.20	.50
❑ 62 Lord of the Unreal R :B:	.75	2.00
❑ 63 Mana Leak C :B:	.40	1.00
❑ 64 Master Thief U :B:	.20	.50
❑ 65 Merfolk Looter C :B:	.10	.25
❑ 66 Merfolk Mesmerist C :B:	.10	.25
❑ 67 Mind Control U :B:	.20	.50
❑ 68 Mind Unbound R :B:	.40	1.00
❑ 69 Negate C :B:	.10	.25
❑ 70 Phantasmal Bear C :B:	.10	.25
❑ 71 Phantasmal Dragon U :B:	.20	.50
❑ 72 Phantasmal Image R :B:	6.00	15.00
❑ 73 Ponder C :B:	.60	1.50
❑ 74 Redirect R :B:	.60	1.50
❑ 75 Skywinder Drake C :B:	.10	.25
❑ 76 Sphinx of Uthuun R :B:	.40	1.00
❑ 77 Time Reversal M :B:	.60	1.50
❑ 78 Turn to Frog U :B:	.20	.50
❑ 79 Unsummon C :B:	.10	.25
❑ 80 Visions of Beyond R :B:	1.00	2.50
❑ 81 Blood Seeker C :K:	.10	.25
❑ 82 Bloodlord of Vaasgoth M :K:	1.25	3.00
❑ 83 Bloodrage Vampire C :K:	.10	.25
❑ 84 Brink of Disaster C :K:	.10	.25
❑ 85 Call to the Grave R :K:	.60	1.50
❑ 86 Cemetery Reaper R :K:	1.50	4.00
❑ 87 Child of Night C :K:	.10	.25
❑ 88 Consume Spirit U :K:	.20	.50
❑ 89 Dark Favor C :K:	.10	.25
❑ 90 Deathmark U :K:	.20	.50
❑ 91 Devouring Swarm C :K:	.10	.25
❑ 92 Diabolic Tutor U :K:	.40	1.00
❑ 93 Disentomb C :K:	.10	.25
❑ 94 Distress C :K:	.10	.25
❑ 95 Doom Blade C :K:	.20	.50
❑ 96 Drifting Shade C :K:	.10	.25
❑ 97 Duskhunter Bat C :K:	.10	.25
❑ 98 Grave Titan M :K:	4.00	10.00
❑ 99 Gravedigger C :K:	.10	.25
❑ 100 Hideous Visage C :K:	.10	.25
❑ 101 Mind Rot C :K:	.10	.25
❑ 102 Monomania R :K:	.40	1.00
❑ 103 Onyx Mage U :K:	.20	.50
❑ 104 Reassembling Skeleton U :K:	.20	.50
❑ 105 Royal Assassin R :K:	.40	1.00
❑ 106 Rune-Scarred Demon R :K:	1.00	2.50
❑ 107 Sengir Vampire U :K:	.20	.50
❑ 108 Smallpox U :K:	.40	1.00
❑ 109 Sorin Markov M :K:	2.50	6.00
❑ 110 Sorin's Thirst C :K:	.10	.25
❑ 111 Sorin's Vengeance R :K:	.60	1.50
❑ 112 Sutured Ghoul R :K:	.40	1.00
❑ 113 Taste of Blood C :K:	.10	.25
❑ 114 Tormented Soul C :K:	.10	.25
❑ 115 Vampire Outcasts U :K:	.20	.50
❑ 116 Vengeful Pharaoh R :K:	.75	2.00
❑ 117 Warpath Ghoul C :K:	.10	.25
❑ 118 Wring Flesh C :K:	.10	.25
❑ 119 Zombie Goliath C :K:	.10	.25
❑ 120 Zombie Infestation U :K:	.40	1.00
❑ 121 Act of Treason C :R:	.10	.25
❑ 122 Blood Ogre C :R:	.10	.25
❑ 123 Bonebreaker Giant C :R:	.10	.25
❑ 124 Chandra, the Firebrand M :R:	5.00	12.00
❑ 125 Chandra's Outrage C :R:	.10	.25
❑ 126 Chandra's Phoenix R :R:	2.50	6.00
❑ 127 Circle of Flame U :R:	.20	.50
❑ 128 Combust U :R:	.20	.50
❑ 129 Crimson Mage U :R:	.20	.50
❑ 130 Fiery Hellhound C :R:	.10	.25
❑ 131 Fireball U :R:	.20	.50
❑ 132 Firebreathing C :R:	.10	.25
❑ 133 Flameblast Dragon R :R:	.40	1.00
❑ 134 Fling C :R:	.10	.25
❑ 135 Furyborn Hellkite M :R:	1.25	3.00
❑ 136 Goblin Arsonist C :R:	.10	.25
❑ 137 Goblin Bangchuckers U :R:	.20	.50
❑ 138 Goblin Chieftain R :R:	.60	1.50
❑ 139 Goblin Fireslinger C :R:	.10	.25
❑ 140 Goblin Grenade U :R:	.40	1.00
❑ 141 Goblin Piker C :R:	.10	.25
❑ 142 Goblin Tunneler C :R:	.10	.25
❑ 143 Goblin War Paint C :R:	.10	.25
❑ 144 Gorehorn Minotaurs C :R:	.10	.25
❑ 145 Grim Lavamancer R :R:	2.00	5.00
❑ 146 Incinerate C :R:	.40	1.00
❑ 147 Inferno Titan M :R:	2.50	6.00
❑ 148 Lava Axe C :R:	.10	.25
❑ 149 Lightning Elemental C :R:	.10	.25
❑ 150 Manabarbs R :R:	.40	1.00
❑ 151 Manic Vandal C :R:	.10	.25
❑ 152 Reverberate R :R:	.40	1.00
❑ 153 Scrambleverse R :R:	.40	1.00
❑ 154 Shock C :R:	.10	.25
❑ 155 Slaughter Cry C :R:	.10	.25
❑ 156 Stormblood Berserker U :R:	.60	1.50
❑ 157 Tectonic Rift U :R:	.20	.50
❑ 158 Volcanic Dragon U :R:	.20	.50
❑ 159 Wall of Torches C :R:	.10	.25
❑ 160 Warstorm Surge R :R:	.40	1.00
❑ 161 Acidic Slime U :G:	.20	.50
❑ 162 Arachnus Spinner R :G:	.40	1.00
❑ 163 Arachnus Web C :G:	.10	.25
❑ 164 Autumn's Veil U :G:	.20	.50
❑ 165 Birds of Paradise R :G:	2.00	5.00
❑ 166 Bountiful Harvest C :G:	.10	.25
❑ 167 Brindle Boar C :G:	.10	.25
❑ 168 Carnage Wurm U :G:	.20	.50
❑ 169 Cudgel Troll U :G:	.20	.50
❑ 170 Doubling Chant R :G:	.40	1.00
❑ 171 Dungrove Elder R :G:	2.00	5.00
❑ 172 Elvish Archdruid R :G:	.75	2.00
❑ 173 Fog C :G:	.10	.25
❑ 174 Garruk, Primal Hunter M :G:	6.00	15.00
❑ 175 Garruk's Companion C :G:	.10	.25
❑ 176 Garruk's Horde R :G:	.40	1.00
❑ 177 Giant Spider C :G:	.10	.25
❑ 178 Gladecover Scout C :G:	.10	.25
❑ 179 Greater Basilisk C :G:	.10	.25
❑ 180 Hunter's Insight U :G:	.20	.50
❑ 181 Jade Mage U :G:	.20	.50
❑ 182 Llanowar Elves C :G:	.10	.25
❑ 183 Lure U :G:	.20	.50
❑ 184 Lurking Crocodile C :G:	.10	.25
❑ 185 Naturalize C :G:	.10	.25
❑ 186 Overrun U :G:	.20	.50
❑ 187 Plummet C :G:	.10	.25
❑ 188 Primeval Titan M :G:	8.00	20.00
❑ 189 Primordial Hydra M :G:	2.50	6.00
❑ 190 Rampant Growth C :G:	.10	.25
❑ 191 Reclaim C :G:	.10	.25
❑ 192 Rites of Flourishing R :G:	.40	1.00
❑ 193 Runeclaw Bear C :G:	.10	.25
❑ 194 Sacred Wolf C :G:	.10	.25
❑ 195 Skinshifter R :G:	.75	2.00
❑ 196 Stampeding Rhino C :G:	.10	.25
❑ 197 Stingerfling Spider U :G:	.20	.50
❑ 198 Titanic Growth C :G:	.10	.25
❑ 199 Trollhide C :G:	.10	.25
❑ 200 Vastwood Gorger C :G:	.10	.25
❑ 201 Adaptive Automaton R	1.50	4.00
❑ 202 Angel's Feather U	.20	.50
❑ 203 Crown of Empires U	.20	.50
❑ 204 Crumbling Colossus U	.20	.50
❑ 205 Demon's Horn U	.20	.50
❑ 206 Dragon's Claw U	.20	.50
❑ 207 Druidic Satchel R	.60	1.50
❑ 208 Elixir of Immortality U	.40	1.00
❑ 209 Greatsword U	.20	.50
❑ 210 Kite Shield U	.20	.50
❑ 211 Kraken's Eye U	.20	.50
❑ 212 Manalith C	.20	.50
❑ 213 Pentavus R	.40	1.00
❑ 214 Quicksilver Amulet R	1.50	4.00
❑ 215 Rusted Sentinel U	.20	.50
❑ 216 Scepter of Empires U	.20	.50
❑ 217 Solemn Simulacrum R	4.00	10.00
❑ 218 Sundial of the Infinite R	.60	1.50
❑ 219 Swiftfoot Boots U	.75	2.00
❑ 220 Thran Golem U	.20	.50
❑ 221 Throne of Empires R	.40	1.00
❑ 222 Worldslayer R	.40	1.00
❑ 223 Wurm's Tooth U	.20	.50

□ 224 Buried Ruin U .40 1.00
□ 225 Dragonskull Summit R 2.00 5.00
□ 226 Drowned Catacomb R 3.00 8.00
□ 227 Glacial Fortress R 2.50 6.00
□ 228 Rootbound Crag R 2.00 5.00
□ 229 Sunpetal Grove R 2.50 6.00
□ 230 Plains L .10 .25
□ 231 Plains L .10 .25
□ 232 Plains L .10 .25
□ 233 Plains L .10 .25
□ 234 Island L .10 .25
□ 235 Island L .10 .25
□ 236 Island L .10 .25
□ 237 Island L .10 .25
□ 238 Swamp L .10 .25
□ 239 Swamp L .10 .25
□ 240 Swamp L .10 .25
□ 241 Swamp L .10 .25
□ 242 Mountain L .10 .25
□ 243 Mountain L .10 .25
□ 244 Mountain L .10 .25
□ 245 Mountain L .10 .25
□ 246 Forest L .10 .25
□ 247 Forest L .10 .25
□ 248 Forest L .10 .25
□ 249 Forest L .10 .25
□ T1 Token: Bird .10 .25
□ T2 Token: Soldier .10 .25
□ T3 Token: Zombie .10 .25
□ T4 Token: Beast .10 .25
□ T5 Token: Saproling .10 .25
□ T6 Token: Wurm .10 .25
□ T7 Token: Pentavite .10 .25

2011 Magic the Gathering Magic 2012 Foil

*Foil: .8X to 2X Basic Cards

2011 Magic the Gathering Ajani vs Nicol Bolas

Duel Deck 15.00 30.00

□ 1 Ajani Vengeant M :W/R: 2.50 6.00
□ 2 Kird Ape U :R: .50 1.25
□ 3 Essence Warden C :G: .20 .50
□ 4 Wild Nacatl C :G: .20 .50
□ 5 Loam Lion U :W: .20 .50
□ 6 Canyon Wildcat C :R: .10 .25
□ 7 Jade Mage U :G: .20 .50
□ 8 Sylvan Ranger C :G: .10 .25
□ 9 Ajani's Pridemate U :W: .40 1.00
□ 10 Qasali Pridemage C :W/G: .40 1.00
□ 11 Grazing Gladehart C :G: .10 .25
□ 12 Fleetfoot Panther U :W/G: .20 .50
□ 13 Woolly Thoctar U :W/R/G: .30 .75
□ 14 Briarhorn U :G: .20 .50
□ 15 Loxodon Hierarch R :W/G: .60 1.50
□ 16 Spitemare U :W/R: .20 .50
□ 17 Marisi's Twinclaws U :W/R/G: .20 .50
□ 18 Ageless Entity R :G: .50 1.25
□ 19 Pride of Lions U :G: .20 .50
□ 20 Nacatl Hunt-Pride U :W: .20 .50
□ 21 Firemane Angel R :W/R: .75 2.00
□ 22 Ajani's Mantra C :W: .10 .25
□ 23 Lightning Helix U :W/R: 2.00 4.00
□ 24 Lead the Stampede U :G: .20 .50
□ 25 Griffin Guide U :W: .20 .50
□ 26 Recumbent Bliss C :W: .10 .25
□ 27 Searing Meditation R :W/R: .40 1.00
□ 28 Behemoth Sledge U :W/G: .60 1.50
□ 29 Naya Charm U :W/R/G: .20 .50
□ 30 Sylvan Bounty C :G: .10 .25
□ 31 Titanic Ultimatum R :W/R/G: .40 1.00
□ 32 Evolving Wilds C .30 .75
□ 33 Graypelt Refuge U .30 .75
□ 34 Jungle Shrine U .75 2.00
□ 35 Kazandu Refuge U .30 .75
□ 36 Sapseep Forest U .20 .50
□ 37 Vitu-Ghazi, the City-Tree U .20 .50
□ 38 Forest L .10 .25
□ 39 Forest L .10 .25
□ 40 Plains L .10 .25
□ 41 Mountain L .10 .25
□ 42 Nicol Bolas, Planeswalker M :B/K/R: 5.00 12.00
□ 43 Surveilling Sprite C :B: .10 .25
□ 44 Nightscape Familiar C :K: .20 .50
□ 45 Slavering Nulls U :R: .20 .50
□ 46 Brackwater Elemental C :B: .10 .25
□ 47 Morgue Toad C :K: .10 .25
□ 48 Hellfire Mongrel U :R: .20 .50
□ 49 Dimir Cutpurse R :B/K: .60 1.50
□ 50 Steamcore Weird C :B: .10 .25
□ 51 Moroii U :B/K: .20 .50
□ 52 Blazing Specter R :K/R: .60 1.50
□ 53 Fire-Field Ogre U :B/K/R: .20 .50
□ 54 Shriekmaw U :K: .60 1.50
□ 55 Ogre Savant C :R: .10 .25
□ 56 Jhessian Zombies C :B/K: .10 .25
□ 57 Igneous Pouncer C :K/R: .10 .25
□ 58 Vapor Snag C :B: .50 1.25
□ 59 Countersquall U :B/K: .60 1.50
□ 60 Obelisk of Grixis C .10 .25
□ 61 Recoil C :B/K: .20 .50
□ 62 Undermine R :B/K: 1.25 3.00
□ 63 Grixis Charm U :B/K/R: .20 .50
□ 64 Icy Manipulator U .20 .50
□ 65 Deep Analysis U :B: .50 1.25
□ 66 Agonizing Demise C :K: .10 .25
□ 67 Slave of Bolas U :B/K/R: .20 .50
□ 68 Elder Mastery U :B/K/R: .20 .50
□ 69 Cruel Ultimatum R :B/K/R: .75 2.00
□ 70 Profane Command R :K: .75 2.00
□ 71 Spite/Malice U :B/K: .20 .50
□ 72 Pain/Suffering U :K/R: .20 .50
□ 73 Rise/Fall U :B/K/R: .20 .50
□ 74 Crumbling Necropolis U .75 2.00
□ 75 Rupture Spire C .20 .50
□ 76 Terramorphic Expanse C .20 .50
□ 77 Swamp L .10 .25
□ 78 Swamp L .10 .25
□ 79 Island L .10 .25
□ 80 Mountain L .10 .25
□ T1 Token: Griffin .10 .25
□ T2 Token: Saproling .10 .25

2011 Magic the Gathering Ajani vs Nicol Bolas Foil

*Foil: .8X to 2X Basic Cards

2011 Magic the Gathering Innistrad

Complete Set 125.00 200.00
Booster Box (36 packs) 75.00 125.00
Booster Pack (15 cards) 3.00 4.00

□ 1 Abbey Griffin C :W: .10 .25
□ 2 Angel of Flight Alabaster R :W: .40 1.00
□ 3 Angelic Overseer M :W: 1.50 4.00
□ 4 Avacynian Priest C :W: .10 .25
□ 5 Bonds of Faith C :W: .10 .25
□ 6 Champion of the Parish R :W: 3.00 8.00
□ 7 Chapel Geist C :W: .10 .25
□ 8 Cloistered Youth/Unholy Fiend U :W/K: .20 .50
□ 9 Dearly Departed R :W: .40 1.00
□ 10 Divine Reckoning R :W: .60 1.50
□ 11 Doomed Traveler C :W: .30 .75
□ 12 Elder Cathar C :W: .10 .25
□ 13 Elite Inquisitor R :W: .75 2.00
□ 14 Feeling of Dread C :W: .10 .25
□ 15 Fiend Hunter U :W: .50 1.25
□ 16 Gallows Warden U :W: .20 .50
□ 17 Geist-Honored Monk R :W: .75 2.00
□ 18 Ghostly Possession C :W: .10 .25
□ 19 Intangible Virtue U :W: .75 2.00
□ 20 Mausoleum Guard U :W: .20 .50
□ 21 Mentor of the Meek R :W: 1.00 2.50
□ 22 Midnight Haunting U :W: .50 1.25
□ 23 Mikaeus, the Lunarch M :W: 2.00 5.00
□ 24 Moment of Heroism C :W: .10 .25
□ 25 Nevermore R :W: .75 2.00
□ 26 Paraselene U :W: .20 .50
□ 27 Purify the Grave U :W: .20 .50
□ 28 Rally the Peasants U :W: .20 .50
□ 29 Rebuke C :W: .10 .25
□ 30 Selfless Cathar C :W: .10 .25
□ 31 Silverchase Fox C :W: .30 .75
□ 32 Slayer of the Wicked U :W: .20 .50
□ 33 Smite the Monstrous C :W: .10 .25
□ 34 Spare from Evil C :W: .10 .25
□ 35 Spectral Rider U :W: .20 .50
□ 36 Stony Silence R :W: .60 1.50
□ 37 Thraben Purebloods C :W: .10 .25
□ 38 Thraben Sentry/Thraben Militia C :W: .10 .25
□ 39 Unruly Mob C :W: .10 .25
□ 40 Urgent Exorcism C :W: .10 .25
□ 41 Village Bell-Ringer C :W: .10 .25
□ 42 Voiceless Spirit C :W: .10 .25
□ 43 Armored Skaab C :B: .10 .25
□ 44 Back from the Brink R :B: .40 1.00
□ 45 Battleground Geist U :B: .20 .50
□ 46 Cackling Counterpart R :B: .60 1.50
□ 47 Civilized Scholar/Homicidal Brute U :B/R: .20 .50
□ 48 Claustrophobia C :B: .10 .25
□ 49 Curiosity U :B: .30 .75
□ 50 Curse of the Bloody Tome C :B: .10 .25
□ 51 Delver of Secrets/Insectile Aberration C :B: .50 1.25
□ 52 Deranged Assistant C :B: .10 .25
□ 53 Dissipate U :B: .60 1.50
□ 54 Dream Twist C :B: .10 .25
□ 55 Forbidden Alchemy C :B: .40 1.00
□ 56 Fortress Crab C :B: .10 .25
□ 57 Frightful Delusion C :B: .10 .25
□ 58 Grasp of Phantoms U :B: .20 .50
□ 59 Hysterical Blindness C :B: .10 .25
□ 60 Invisible Stalker U :B: .60 1.50
□ 61 Laboratory Maniac R :B: .60 1.50
□ 62 Lantern Spirit U :B: .20 .50
□ 63 Lost in the Mist C :B: .10 .25
□ 64 Ludevic's Test Subject
Ludevic's Abomination R :B: .75 2.00
□ 65 Makeshift Mauler C :B: .10 .25
□ 66 Memory's Journey U :B: .20 .50
□ 67 Mindshrieker R :B: 1.00 2.50
□ 68 Mirror-Mad Phantasm M :B: 1.00 2.50
□ 69 Moon Heron C :B: .10 .25
□ 70 Murder of Crows U :B: .30 .75
□ 71 Rooftop Storm R :B: .50 1.25
□ 72 Runic Repetition U :B: .20 .50
□ 73 Selhoff Occultist C :B: .10 .25
□ 74 Sensory Deprivation C :B: .10 .25
□ 75 Silent Departure C :B: .10 .25
□ 76 Skaab Goliath U :B: .20 .50
□ 77 Skaab Ruinator M :B: 1.50 4.00
□ 78 Snapcaster Mage R :B: 12.00 30.00
□ 79 Spectral Flight C :B: .10 .25
□ 80 Stitched Drake C :B: .10 .25
□ 81 Stitcher's Apprentice C :B: .10 .25
□ 82 Sturmgeist R :B: .40 1.00
□ 83 Think Twice C :B: .20 .50
□ 84 Undead Alchemist R :B: .60 1.50
□ 85 Abattoir Ghoul U :K: .20 .50
□ 86 Altar's Reap C :K: .10 .25
□ 87 Army of the Damned M :K: 1.50 4.00
□ 88 Bitterheart Witch U :K: .20 .50
□ 89 Bloodgift Demon R :K: 1.00 2.50
□ 90 Bloodline Keeper/Lord of Lineage R :K: 2.50 6.00
□ 91 Brain Weevil C :K: .10 .25
□ 92 Bump in the Night C :K: .10 .25
□ 93 Corpse Lunge C :K: .10 .25
□ 94 Curse of Death's Hold R :K: .60 1.50
□ 95 Curse of Oblivion C :K: .10 .25
□ 96 Dead Weight C :K: .10 .25
□ 97 Diregraf Ghoul U :K: .50 1.25
□ 98 Disciple of Griselbrand U :K: .20 .50
□ 99 Endless Ranks of the Dead R :K: 1.00 2.50
□ 100 Falkenrath Noble U :K: .20 .50
□ 101 Ghoulcaller's Chant C :K: .10 .25
□ 102 Ghoulraiser C :K: .10 .25
□ 103 Gruesome Deformity C :K: .10 .25
□ 104 Heartless Summoning R :K: 1.25 3.00
□ 105 Liliana of the Veil M :K: 12.00 30.00
□ 106 Manor Skeleton C :K: .10 .25
□ 107 Markov Patrician C :K: .10 .25
□ 108 Maw of the Mire C :K: .10 .25
□ 109 Moan of the Unhallowed U :K: .20 .50
□ 110 Morkrut Banshee U :K: .20 .50
□ 111 Night Terrors C :K: .20 .50
□ 112 Reaper from the Abyss M :K: .75 2.00
□ 113 Rotting Fensnake C :K: .10 .25
□ 114 Screeching Bat/Stalking Vampire U :K: .20 .50
□ 115 Sever the Bloodline R :K: .60 1.50
□ 116 Skeletal Grimace C :K: .10 .25
□ 117 Skirsdag High Priest R :K: .75 2.00
□ 118 Stromkirk Patrol C :K: .10 .25
□ 119 Tribute to Hunger U :K: .40 1.00
□ 120 Typhoid Rats C :K: .10 .25
□ 121 Unbreathing Horde R :K: 1.00 2.50
□ 122 Unburial Rites U :K: .50 1.25
□ 123 Vampire Interloper C :K: .10 .25
□ 124 Victim of Night C :K: .10 .25
□ 125 Village Cannibals U :K: .20 .50
□ 126 Walking Corpse C :K: .10 .25
□ 127 Ancient Grudge C :R: .10 .25
□ 128 Ashmouth Hound C :R: .10 .25
□ 129 Balefire Dragon M :R: 1.00 2.50
□ 130 Blasphemous Act R :R: .60 1.50
□ 131 Bloodcrazed Neonate C :R: .10 .25
□ 132 Brimstone Volley C :R: .40 1.00
□ 133 Burning Vengeance U :R: .30 .75
□ 134 Charmbreaker Devils R :R: .40 1.00
□ 135 Crossway Vampire C :R: .10 .25
□ 136 Curse of Stalked Prey R :R: .60 1.50
□ 137 Curse of the Nightly Hunt U :R: .20 .50
□ 138 Curse of the Pierced Heart C :R: .10 .25
□ 139 Desperate Ravings U :R: .20 .50
□ 140 Devil's Play R :R: .60 1.50
□ 141 Falkenrath Marauders R :R: .60 1.50
□ 142 Feral Ridgewolf C :R: .10 .25
□ 143 Furor of the Bitten C :R: .10 .25
□ 144 Geistflame C :R: .20 .50
□ 145 Hanweir Watchkeep/Bane of Hanweir U :R: .20 .50
□ 146 Harvest Pyre C :R: .10 .25
□ 147 Heretic's Punishment R :R: .40 1.00
□ 148 Infernal Plunge C :R: .10 .25
□ 149 Instigator Gang/Wildblood Pack R :R: .60 1.50
□ 150 Into the Maw of Hell U :R: .20 .50
□ 151 Kessig Wolf C :R: .10 .25
□ 152 Kruin Outlaw/Terror of Kruin Pass R :R: .75 2.00
□ 153 Night Revelers C :R: .10 .25
□ 154 Nightbird's Clutches C :R: .10 .25
□ 155 Past in Flames M :R: 1.50 4.00
□ 156 Pitchburn Devils C :R: .10 .25
□ 157 Rage Thrower U :R: .20 .50
□ 158 Rakish Heir U :R: .40 1.00
□ 159 Reckless Waif/Merciless Predator U :R: .50 1.25
□ 160 Riot Devils C :R: .10 .25
□ 161 Rolling Temblor U :R: .20 .50
□ 162 Scourge of Geier Reach U :R: .20 .50
□ 163 Skirsdag Cultist U :R: .30 .75
□ 164 Stromkirk Noble R :R: 2.50 6.00
□ 165 Tormented Pariah/Rampaging Werewolf C :R: .10 .25
□ 166 Traitorous Blood C :R: .30 .75
□ 167 Vampiric Fury C :R: .10 .25
□ 168 Village Ironsmith/Ironfang C :R: .10 .25
□ 169 Ambush Viper C :G: .10 .25
□ 170 Avacyn's Pilgrim C :G: .10 .25
□ 171 Boneyard Wurm U :G: .30 .75
□ 172 Bramblecrush U :G: .20 .50
□ 173 Caravan Vigil C :G: .10 .25
□ 174 Creeping Renaissance R :G: .40 1.00
□ 175 Darkthicket Wolf C :G: .10 .25
□ 176 Daybreak Ranger/Nightfall Predator R :G: 1.25 3.00
□ 177 Elder of Laurels R :G: .40 1.00
□ 178 Essence of the Wild M :G: .60 1.50
□ 179 Festerhide Boar C :G: .10 .25
□ 180 Full Moon's Rise U :G: .30 .75
□ 181 Garruk Relentless/Garruk 6.00 15.00
the Veil-Cursed M :K/G:
□ 182 Gatstaf Shepherd/Gatstaf Howler U :G: .20 .50
□ 183 Gnaw to the Bone C :G: .10 .25
□ 184 Grave Bramble C :G: .10 .25
□ 185 Grizzled Outcasts/Krallenhorde Wantons C :G: .10 .25
□ 186 Gutter Grime R :G: .40 1.00
□ 187 Hamlet Captain U :G: .20 .50
□ 188 Hollowhenge Scavenger U :G: .30 .75
□ 189 Kessig Cagebreakers R :G: .60 1.50
□ 190 Kindercatch C :G: .10 .25
□ 191 Lumberknot U :G: .20 .50
□ 192 Make a Wish U :G: .20 .50
□ 193 Mayor of Avabruck/Howlpack Alpha R :G: 2.00 5.00
□ 194 Moldgraf Monstrosity R :G: .40 1.00
□ 195 Moonmist C :G: .20 .50
□ 196 Mulch C :G: .10 .25
□ 197 Naturalize C :G: .10 .25
□ 198 Orchard Spirit C :G: .10 .25
□ 199 Parallel Lives R :G: 1.50 4.00
□ 200 Prey Upon C :G: .10 .25
□ 201 Ranger's Guile C :G: .10 .25
□ 202 Somberwald Spider C :G: .10 .25
□ 203 Spider Spawning U :G: .20 .50
□ 204 Spidery Grasp C :G: .30 .75
□ 205 Splinterfright R :G: .60 1.50
□ 206 Travel Preparations C :G: .10 .25
□ 207 Tree of Redemption M :G: 1.25 3.00
□ 208 Ulvenwald Mystics/Ulvenwald Primordials U :G: .20 .50
□ 209 Villagers of Estwald/Howlpack of Estwald C :G: .10 .25
□ 210 Woodland Sleuth C :G: .10 .25
□ 211 Wreath of Geists U :G: .20 .50
□ 212 Evil Twin R :B/K: .60 1.50
□ 213 Geist of Saint Traft M :W/B: 10.00 25.00
□ 214 Grimgrin, Corpse-Born M :B/K: 1.50 4.00
□ 215 Olivia Voldaren M :K/R: 2.50 6.00
□ 216 Blazing Torch C .10 .25
□ 217 Butcher's Cleaver U .20 .50
□ 218 Cellar Door U .20 .50
□ 219 Cobbled Wings C .10 .25
□ 220 Creepy Doll R .40 1.00
□ 221 Demonmail Hauberk U .20 .50
□ 222 Galvanic Juggernaut U .20 .50
□ 223 Geistcatcher's Rig U .60 1.50
□ 224 Ghoulcaller's Bell C .10 .25
□ 225 Graveyard Shovel U .20 .50
□ 226 Grimoire of the Dead M 1.50 4.00
□ 227 Inquisitor's Flail U .20 .50
□ 228 Manor Gargoyle R .40 1.00
□ 229 Mask of Avacyn U .30 .75
□ 230 One-Eyed Scarecrow C .10 .25
□ 231 Runechanter's Pike R 1.00 2.50
□ 232 Sharpened Pitchfork U .20 .50
□ 233 Silver-Inlaid Dagger U .20 .50
□ 234 Traveler's Amulet C .10 .25
□ 235 Trepanation Blade U .30 .75
□ 236 Witchbane Orb R .60 1.50
□ 237 Wooden Stake C .30 .75
□ 238 Clifftop Retreat R 3.00 8.00
□ 239 Gavony Township R 1.25 3.00
□ 240 Ghost Quarter U .60 1.50
□ 241 Hinterland Harbor R 3.00 8.00
□ 242 Isolated Chapel R 5.00 12.00
□ 243 Kessig Wolf Run R 1.50 4.00
□ 244 Moorland Haunt R 1.50 4.00
□ 245 Nephalia Drownyard R .60 1.50
□ 246 Shimmering Grotto C .10 .25
□ 247 Stensia Bloodhall R .40 1.00
□ 248 Sulfur Falls R 3.00 8.00
□ 249 Woodland Cemetery R 3.00 8.00
□ 250 Plains L .10 .25
□ 251 Plains L .10 .25
□ 252 Plains L .10 .25
□ 253 Island L .10 .25
□ 254 Island L .10 .25
□ 255 Island L .10 .25
□ 256 Swamp L .10 .25
□ 257 Swamp L .10 .25
□ 258 Swamp L .10 .25
□ 259 Mountain L .10 .25
□ 260 Mountain L .10 .25
□ 261 Mountain L .10 .25
□ 262 Forest L .10 .25
□ 263 Forest L .10 .25
□ 264 Forest L .10 .25
□ CL Checklist .10 .25
□ T1 Token: Angel .10 .25
□ T2 Token: Spirit .10 .25
□ T3 Token: Homunculus .10 .25
□ T4 Token: Demon .10 .25
□ T5 Token: Vampire .10 .25
□ T6 Token: Wolf BLACK .10 .25
□ T7 Zombie (Lucas Graciano) .10 .25
□ T8 Zombie (Christopher Moeller) .10 .25
□ T9 Zombie (Cynthia Sheppard) .10 .25
□ T10 Token: Ooze .10 .25
□ T11 Token: Spider .10 .25
□ T12 Token: Wolf GREEN .10 .25

2011 Magic the Gathering Innistrad Foil

*Foil: .8X to 2X Basic Cards

2011 Magic the Gathering Knights vs Dragons

Duel Deck 20.00 40.00

□ 1 Knight of the Reliquary M :W/G: 4.00 10.00
□ 2 Caravan Escort C :W: .10 .25
□ 3 Lionheart Maverick C :W: .10 .25
□ 4 Knight of Cliffhaven C :W: .10 .25
□ 5 Knight of Meadowgrain U :W: 1.25 3.00
□ 6 Knight of the White Orchid R :W: 1.25 3.00
□ 7 Leonin Skyhunter U :W: .20 .50
□ 8 Silver Knight U :W: .75 2.00
□ 9 White Knight U :W: .30 .75
□ 10 Knotvine Paladin R :W/G: .40 1.00
□ 11 Steward of Valeron C :W/G: .10 .25
□ 12 Benalish Lancer C :W: .10 .25
□ 13 Zhalfirin Commander U :W: .20 .50
□ 14 Knight Exemplar R :W: 1.50 4.00
□ 15 Wilt-Leaf Cavaliers U :W/G: .75 2.00
□ 16 Kabira Vindicator U :W: .20 .50
□ 17 Kinsbaile Cavalier R :W: 1.50 4.00
□ 18 Alaborn Cavalier U :W: .20 .50
□ 19 Skyhunter Patrol C :W: .10 .25
□ 20 Plover Knights C :W: .20 .50
□ 21 Juniper Order Ranger U :W/G: .75 2.00
□ 22 Paladin of Prahv U :W: .20 .50
□ 23 Harm's Way U :W: .20 .50
□ 24 Reciprocate U :W: .30 .75
□ 25 Edge of Autumn C :G: .10 .25
□ 26 Mighty Leap C :W: .10 .25
□ 27 Reprisal U :W: .20 .50
□ 28 Test of Faith U :W: .20 .50
□ 29 Heroes' Reunion U :W/G: .30 .75
□ 30 Sigil Blessing C :W/G: .10 .25
□ 31 Loxodon Warhammer R 1.00 2.50
□ 32 Spidersilk Armor C :G: .20 .50
□ 33 Griffin Guide U :W: .20 .50
□ 34 Oblivion Ring C :W: 1.25 3.00
□ 35 Grasslands U .20 .50
□ 36 Sejiri Steppe C .10 .25
□ 37 Selesnya Sanctuary C .20 .50
□ 38 Treetop Village U 1.25 3.00
□ 39 Plains L .10 .25
□ 40 Plains L .10 .25
□ 41 Plains L .10 .25
□ 42 Plains L .10 .25
□ 43 Forest L .10 .25
□ 44 Forest L .10 .25
□ 45 Forest L .10 .25
□ 46 Forest L .10 .25
□ 47 Bogardan Hellkite M :R: 2.00 5.00
□ 48 Cinder Wall C :R: .10 .25
□ 49 Skirk Prospector C :R: .20 .50
□ 50 Bloodmark Mentor U :R: .40 1.00
□ 51 Fire-Belly Changeling C :R: .10 .25
□ 52 Mudbutton Torchrunner C :R: .20 .50
□ 53 Dragonspeaker Shaman U :R: 1.25 3.00
□ 54 Dragon Whelp U :R: .20 .50
□ 55 Henge Guardian U .20 .50
□ 56 Voracious Dragon R :R: .40 1.00
□ 57 Bogardan Rager C :R: .10 .25
□ 58 Mordant Dragon R :R: .40 1.00
□ 59 Kilnmouth Dragon R :R: 1.25 3.00
□ 60 Shivan Hellkite R :R: .40 1.00
□ 61 Thunder Dragon R :R: .75 2.00
□ 62 Armillary Sphere C .10 .25
□ 63 Dragon's Claw U .20 .50
□ 64 Breath of Darigaaz U :R: .20 .50
□ 65 Dragon Fodder C :R: .20 .50
□ 66 Punishing Fire U :R: .40 1.00
□ 67 Spitting Earth C :R: .10 .25
□ 68 Captive Flame U :R: .20 .50
□ 69 Ghostfire C .10 .25
□ 70 Seething Song C :R: 1.25 3.00
□ 71 Seismic Strike C :R: .20 .50
□ 72 Claws of Valakut C :R: .10 .25
□ 73 Temporary Insanity U :R: .20 .50
□ 74 Shiv's Embrace U :R: .40 1.00
□ 75 Cone of Flame U :R: .20 .50
□ 76 Fiery Fall C :R: .10 .25
□ 77 Jaws of Stone U :R: .20 .50
□ 78 Mountain L .10 .25
□ 79 Mountain L .10 .25
□ 80 Mountain L .10 .25
□ 81 Mountain L .10 .25
□ T1 Token: Goblin .10 .25

2011 Magic the Gathering Knights vs Dragons Foil

*Foil: .8X to 2X Basic Cards

2011 Magic the Gathering Mirrodin Besieged

Complete Set (155) 60.00 120.00
Booster Box (36 Packs) 100.00 150.00
Booster Pack (16 Cards) 3.00 4.00

□ 1 Accorder Paladin U :W: .30 .75
□ 2 Ardent Recruit C :W: .10 .25
□ 3 Banishment Decree C :W: .10 .25
□ 4 Choking Fumes U :W: .20 .50
□ 5 Divine Offering C :W: .20 .50
□ 6 Frantic Salvage C :W: .10 .25
□ 7 Gore Vassal U :W: .20 .50
□ 8 Hero of Bladehold M :W: 6.00 15.00
□ 9 Kemba's Legion U :W: .20 .50
□ 10 Leonin Relic-Warder U :W: .20 .50
□ 11 Leonin Skyhunter C :W: .30 .75
□ 12 Loxodon Partisan C :W: .10 .25
□ 13 Master's Call C :W: .40 1.00
□ 14 Mirran Crusader R :W: 3.00 8.00
□ 15 Phyrexian Rebirth R :W: .40 1.00
□ 16 Priests of Norn C :W: .10 .25
□ 17 Tine Shrike C :W: .10 .25
□ 18 Victory's Herald R :W: .40 1.00
□ 19 White Sun's Zenith R :W: .75 2.00
□ 20 Blue Sun's Zenith R :B: 1.25 3.00
□ 21 Consecrated Sphinx M :B: 4.00 10.00
□ 22 Corrupted Conscience U :B: .20 .50
□ 23 Cryptoplasm R :B: .40 1.00
□ 24 Distant Memories R :B: .40 1.00
□ 25 Fuel for the Cause C :B: .10 .25
□ 26 Mirran Spy C :B: .10 .25
□ 27 Mitotic Manipulation R :B: .40 1.00
□ 28 Neurok Commando U :B: .20 .50
□ 29 Oculus C :B: .10 .25
□ 30 Quicksilver Geyser C :B: .10 .25
□ 31 Serum Raker C :B: .10 .25
□ 32 Spire Serpent C :B: .10 .25
□ 33 Steel Sabotage C :B: .10 .25
□ 34 Treasure Mage U :B: .30 .75
□ 35 Turn the Tide C :B: .10 .25

MAGIC

❑ 36 Vedalken Anatomist U :B:	.20	.50
❑ 37 Vedalken Infuser U :B:	.20	.50
❑ 38 Vivisection C :B:	.10	.25
❑ 39 Black Sun's Zenith R :K:	3.00	8.00
❑ 40 Caustic Hound C :K:	.10	.25
❑ 41 Flensermite C :K:	.10	.25
❑ 42 Flesh-Eater Imp U :K:	.20	.50
❑ 43 Go for the Throat U :K:	1.25	3.00
❑ 44 Gruesome Encore U :K:	.20	.50
❑ 45 Horrifying Revelation C :K:	.10	.25
❑ 46 Massacre Wurm M :K:	2.50	6.00
❑ 47 Morbid Plunder C :K:	.10	.25
❑ 48 Nested Ghoul U :K:	.20	.50
❑ 49 Phyresis C :K:	.10	.25
❑ 50 Phyrexian Crusader R :K:	2.50	6.00
❑ 51 Phyrexian Rager C :K:	.10	.25
❑ 52 Phyrexian Vatmother R :K:	.75	2.00
❑ 53 Sangromancer R :K:	.75	2.00
❑ 54 Scourge Servant C :K:	.10	.25
❑ 55 Septic Rats U :K:	.20	.50
❑ 56 Spread the Sickness C :K:	.20	.50
❑ 57 Virulent Wound C :K:	.10	.25
❑ 58 Blisterstick Shaman C :R:	.10	.25
❑ 59 Burn the Impure C :R:	.10	.25
❑ 60 Concussive Bolt C :R:	.10	.25
❑ 61 Crush C :R:	.10	.25
❑ 62 Galvanoth R :R:	.40	1.00
❑ 63 Gnathosaur C :R:	.10	.25
❑ 64 Goblin Wardriver U :R:	.40	1.00
❑ 65 Hellkite Igniter R :R:	.40	1.00
❑ 66 Hero of Oxid Ridge M :R:	1.50	4.00
❑ 67 Into the Core U :R:	.20	.50
❑ 68 Koth's Courier C :R:	.10	.25
❑ 69 Kuldotha Flamefiend U :R:	.20	.50
❑ 70 Kuldotha Ringleader C :R:	.10	.25
❑ 71 Metallic Mastery U :R:	.20	.50
❑ 72 Ogre Resister C :R:	.10	.25
❑ 73 Rally the Forces C :R:	.10	.25
❑ 74 Red Sun's Zenith R :R:	.75	2.00
❑ 75 Slagstorm R :R:	2.50	6.00
❑ 76 Spiraling Duelist U :R:	.20	.50
❑ 77 Blightwidow C :G:	.10	.25
❑ 78 Creeping Corrosion R :G:	.40	1.00
❑ 79 Fangren Marauder C :G:	.10	.25
❑ 80 Glissa's Courier C :G:	.10	.25
❑ 81 Green Sun's Zenith R :G:	5.00	12.00
❑ 82 Lead the Stampede U :G:	.30	.75
❑ 83 Melira's Keepers U :G:	.20	.50
❑ 84 Mirran Mettle C :G:	.10	.25
❑ 85 Phyrexian Hydra R :G:	.40	1.00
❑ 86 Pistus Strike C :G:	.10	.25
❑ 87 Plaguemaw Beast U :G:	.20	.50
❑ 88 Praetor's Counsel M :G:	.75	2.00
❑ 89 Quilled Slagwurm U :G:	.20	.50
❑ 90 Rot Wolf C :G:	.10	.25
❑ 91 Tangle Mantis C :G:	.10	.25
❑ 92 Thrun, the Last Troll M :G:	6.00	15.00
❑ 93 Unnatural Predation C :G:	.10	.25
❑ 94 Viridian Corrupter U :G:	.20	.50
❑ 95 Viridian Emissary C :G:	.40	1.00
❑ 96 Glissa, the Traitor M :K/G:	1.50	4.00
❑ 97 Tezzeret, Agent of Bolas M :B/K:	6.00	15.00
❑ 98 Bladed Sentinel C	.10	.25
❑ 99 Blightsteel Colossus M	3.00	8.00
❑ 100 Bonehoard R	.60	1.50
❑ 101 Brass Squire U	.30	.75
❑ 102 Copper Carapace C	.10	.25
❑ 103 Core Prowler U	.20	.50
❑ 104 Darksteel Plate R	1.50	4.00
❑ 105 Decimator Web R	.40	1.00
❑ 106 Dross Ripper C	.10	.25
❑ 107 Flayer Husk C	.10	.25
❑ 108 Gust-Skimmer C	.10	.25
❑ 109 Hexplate Golem C	.10	.25
❑ 110 Ichor Wellspring C	.10	.25
❑ 111 Knowledge Pool R	.40	1.00
❑ 112 Lumengrid Gargoyle U	.20	.50
❑ 113 Magnetic Mine R	.40	1.00
❑ 114 Mirrorworks R	.40	1.00
❑ 115 Mortarpod U	.40	1.00
❑ 116 Myr Sire C	.10	.25
❑ 117 Myr Turbine R	1.00	2.50
❑ 118 Myr Welder R	.40	1.00
❑ 119 Peace Strider U	.20	.50
❑ 120 Phyrexian Digester C	.10	.25
❑ 121 Phyrexian Juggernaut U	.20	.50
❑ 122 Phyrexian Revoker R	1.00	2.50
❑ 123 Pierce Strider U	.20	.50
❑ 124 Piston Sledge U	.20	.50
❑ 125 Plague Myr U	.60	1.50
❑ 126 Psychosis Crawler R	.40	1.00
❑ 127 Razorfield Rhino C	.10	.25
❑ 128 Rusted Slasher C	.10	.25
❑ 129 Shimmer Myr R	.40	1.00
❑ 130 Shriekhorn C	.10	.25
❑ 131 Signal Pest U	.60	1.50
❑ 132 Silverskin Armor U	.20	.50
❑ 133 Skinwing U	.20	.50
❑ 134 Sphere of the Suns U	.75	2.00
❑ 135 Spin Engine C	.10	.25
❑ 136 Spine of Ish Sah R	.40	1.00
❑ 137 Strandwalker U	.20	.50
❑ 138 Sword of Feast and Famine M	12.00	30.00
❑ 139 Tangle Hulk C	.10	.25
❑ 140 Thopter Assembly R	.40	1.00
❑ 141 Titan Forge R	.40	1.00
❑ 142 Training Drone C	.10	.25
❑ 143 Viridian Claw U	.20	.50
❑ 144 Contested War Zone R	1.25	3.00
❑ 145 Inkmoth Nexus R	5.00	12.00
❑ 146 Plains L	.10	.25
❑ 147 Plains L	.10	.25
❑ 148 Island L	.10	.25
❑ 149 Island L	.10	.25
❑ 150 Swamp L	.10	.25
❑ 151 Swamp L	.10	.25
❑ 152 Mountain L	.10	.25
❑ 153 Mountain L	.10	.25
❑ 154 Forest L	.10	.25
❑ 155 Forest L	.10	.25
❑ PC Poison Counter	.10	.25
❑ R1 Rules Tip: Battle Cry	.10	.25
❑ R2 Rules Tip: Metalcraft Imprint	.10	.25
❑ R3 Rules Tip: Living Weapon	.10	.25
❑ R4 Rules Tip: Infect	.10	.25
❑ R5 Rules Tip: Proliferate	.10	.25
❑ T1 Token: Germ	.10	.25
❑ T2 Token: Zombie	.10	.25
❑ T3 Token: Golem	.10	.25
❑ T4 Token: Horror	.10	.25
❑ T5 Token: Thopter	.10	.25

2011 Magic the Gathering Mirrodin Besieged Foil

*Foil: .8X to 2X Basic Cards

2011 Magic the Gathering New Phyrexia

Complete Set (175)	60.00	120.00
Booster Box (36 packs)	100.00	175.00
Booster Pack (15 cards)	3.00	5.00
❑ 1 Karn Liberated M	8.00	20.00
❑ 2 Apostle's Blessing C :W:	.10	.25
❑ 3 Auriok Survivors U :W:	.20	.50
❑ 4 Blade Splicer R :W:	2.00	5.00
❑ 5 Cathedral Membrane U :W:	.20	.50
❑ 6 Chancellor of the Annex R :W:	.60	1.50
❑ 7 Dispatch U :W:	1.00	2.50
❑ 8 Due Respect U :W:	.20	.50
❑ 9 Elesh Norn, Grand Cenobite M :W:	12.00	30.00
❑ 10 Exclusion Ritual U :W:	.20	.50
❑ 11 Forced Worship C :W:	.10	.25
❑ 12 Inquisitor Exarch U :W:	.20	.50
❑ 13 Lost Leonin C :W:	.10	.25
❑ 14 Loxodon Convert C :W:	.10	.25
❑ 15 Marrow Shards U :W:	.40	1.00
❑ 16 Master Splicer U :W:	.20	.50
❑ 17 Norn's Annex R :W:	.75	2.00
❑ 18 Phyrexian Unlife R :W:	.60	1.50
❑ 19 Porcelain Legionnaire C :W:	.10	.25
❑ 20 Puresteel Paladin R :W:	1.50	4.00
❑ 21 Remember the Fallen C :W:	.10	.25
❑ 22 Sensor Splicer C :W:	.10	.25
❑ 23 Shattered Angel U :W:	.20	.50
❑ 24 Shriek Raptor C :W:	.10	.25
❑ 25 Suture Priest C :W:	.10	.25
❑ 26 War Report C :W:	.10	.25
❑ 27 Argent Mutation U :B:	.20	.50
❑ 28 Arm with AEther U :B:	.40	1.00
❑ 29 Blighted Agent C :B:	.10	.25
❑ 30 Chained Throatseeker C :B:	.10	.25
❑ 31 Chancellor of the Spires R :B:	.60	1.50
❑ 32 Corrupted Resolve U :B:	.40	1.00
❑ 33 Deceiver Exarch U :B:	.40	1.00
❑ 34 Defensive Stance C :B:	.10	.25
❑ 35 Gitaxian Probe C :B:	.60	1.50
❑ 36 Impaler Shrike C :B:	.10	.25
❑ 37 Jin-Gitaxias, Core Augur M :B:	3.00	8.00
❑ 38 Mental Misstep U :B:	1.50	4.00
❑ 39 Mindculling U :B:	.60	1.50
❑ 40 Numbing Dose C :B:	.10	.25
❑ 41 Phyrexian Ingester R :B:	.60	1.50
❑ 42 Phyrexian Metamorph R :B:	4.00	10.00
❑ 43 Psychic Barrier C :B:	.10	.25
❑ 44 Psychic Surgery R :B:	.60	1.50
❑ 45 Spined Thopter C :B:	.10	.25
❑ 46 Spire Monitor C :B:	.10	.25
❑ 47 Tezzeret's Gambit U :B:	1.25	3.00
❑ 48 Vapor Snag C :B:	.75	2.00
❑ 49 Viral Drake U :B:	.20	.50
❑ 50 Wing Splicer U :B:	.20	.50
❑ 51 Xenograft R :B:	.60	1.50
❑ 52 Blind Zealot C :K:	.10	.25
❑ 53 Caress of Phyrexia U :K:	.40	1.00
❑ 54 Chancellor of the Dross R :K:	1.00	2.50
❑ 55 Dementia Bat C :K:	.10	.25
❑ 56 Despise U :K:	1.00	2.50
❑ 57 Dismember U :K:	1.50	4.00
❑ 58 Enslave U :K:	.20	.50
❑ 59 Entomber Exarch U :K:	.20	.50
❑ 60 Evil Presence C :K:	.10	.25
❑ 61 Geth's Verdict C :K:	.40	1.00
❑ 62 Glistening Oil R :K:	.60	1.50
❑ 63 Grim Affliction C :K:	.10	.25
❑ 64 Ichor Explosion U :K:	.20	.50
❑ 65 Life's Finale R :K:	1.00	2.50
❑ 66 Mortis Dogs C :K:	.10	.25
❑ 67 Parasitic Implant C :K:	.10	.25
❑ 68 Phyrexian Obliterator M :K:	10.00	25.00
❑ 69 Pith Driller C :K:	.10	.25
❑ 70 Postmortem Lunge U :K:	.20	.50
❑ 71 Praetor's Grasp R :K:	.75	2.00
❑ 72 Reaper of Sheoldred U :K:	.20	.50
❑ 73 Sheoldred, Whispering One M :K:	2.50	6.00
❑ 74 Surgical Extraction R :K:	4.00	10.00
❑ 75 Toxic Nim C :K:	.10	.25
❑ 76 Vault Skirge C :K:	.20	.50
❑ 77 Whispering Specter U :K:	.75	2.00
❑ 78 Act of Aggression U :R:	.40	1.00
❑ 79 Artillerize C :R:	.10	.25
❑ 80 Bludgeon Brawl R :R:	.60	1.50
❑ 81 Chancellor of the Forge R :R:	.60	1.50
❑ 82 Fallen Ferromancer U :R:	.20	.50
❑ 83 Flameborn Viron C :R:	.10	.25
❑ 84 Furnace Scamp C :R:	.10	.25
❑ 85 Geosurge U :R:	.20	.50
❑ 86 Gut Shot U :R:	1.50	4.00
❑ 87 Invader Parasite R :R:	.60	1.50
❑ 88 Moltensteel Dragon R :R:	.75	2.00
❑ 89 Ogre Menial C :R:	.10	.25
❑ 90 Priest of Urabrask U :R:	.60	1.50
❑ 91 Rage Extractor U :R:	.20	.50
❑ 92 Razor Swine C :R:	.10	.25
❑ 93 Ruthless Invasion C :R:	.10	.25
❑ 94 Scrapyard Salvo C :R:	.10	.25
❑ 95 Slag Fiend R :R:	1.50	4.00
❑ 96 Slash Panther C :R:	.10	.25
❑ 97 Tormentor Exarch U :R:	.20	.50
❑ 98 Urabrask the Hidden M :R:	2.00	5.00
❑ 99 Victorious Destruction C :R:	.10	.25
❑ 100 Volt Charge C :R:	.10	.25
❑ 101 Vulshok Refugee U :R:	.40	1.00
❑ 102 Whipflare U :R:	1.00	2.50
❑ 103 Beast Within U :G:	1.50	4.00
❑ 104 Birthing Pod R :G:	2.00	5.00
❑ 105 Brutalizer Exarch U :G:	.20	.50
❑ 106 Chancellor of the Tangle R :G:	.60	1.50
❑ 107 Corrosive Gale U :G:	.60	1.50
❑ 108 Death-Hood Cobra C :G:	.10	.25
❑ 109 Fresh Meat R :G:	.60	1.50
❑ 110 Glissa's Scorn C :G:	.10	.25
❑ 111 Glistener Elf C :G:	.10	.25
❑ 112 Greenhilt Trainee U :G:	.20	.50
❑ 113 Leeching Bite C :G:	.10	.25
❑ 114 Maul Splicer C :G:	.10	.25
❑ 115 Melira, Sylvok Outcast R :G:	1.25	3.00
❑ 116 Mutagenic Growth C :G:	.10	.25
❑ 117 Mycosynth Fiend U :G:	.20	.50
❑ 118 Noxious Revival U :G:	1.00	2.50
❑ 119 Phyrexian Swarmlord R :G:	.60	1.50
❑ 120 Rotted Hystrix C :G:	.10	.25
❑ 121 Spinebiter U :G:	.20	.50
❑ 122 Thundering Tanadon C :G:	.10	.25
❑ 123 Triumph of the Hordes U :G:	.40	1.00
❑ 124 Viridian Betrayers C :G:	.10	.25
❑ 125 Viridian Harvest C :G:	.10	.25
❑ 126 Vital Splicer U :G:	.20	.50
❑ 127 Vorinclex, Voice of Hunger M :G:	2.00	5.00
❑ 128 Jor Kadeen, the Prevailer R :W/R:	.75	2.00
❑ 129 Alloy Myr U	.60	1.50
❑ 130 Batterskull M	8.00	20.00
❑ 131 Blinding Souleater C	.10	.25
❑ 132 Caged Sun R	1.25	3.00
❑ 133 Conversion Chamber U	.20	.50
❑ 134 Darksteel Relic U	.20	.50
❑ 135 Etched Monstrosity M	1.00	2.50
❑ 136 Gremlin Mine C	.10	.25
❑ 137 Hex Parasite R	1.50	4.00
❑ 138 Hovermyr C	.10	.25
❑ 139 Immolating Souleater C	.10	.25
❑ 140 Insatiable Souleater C	.10	.25
❑ 141 Isolation Cell U	.20	.50
❑ 142 Kiln Walker U	.20	.50
❑ 143 Lashwrithe R	1.50	4.00
❑ 144 Mindcrank U	.60	1.50
❑ 145 Mycosynth Wellspring C	.10	.25
❑ 146 Myr Superion R	1.25	3.00
❑ 147 Necropouncer U	.20	.50
❑ 148 Omen Machine R	.60	1.50
❑ 149 Pestilent Souleater C	.10	.25
❑ 150 Phyrexian Hulk C	.10	.25
❑ 151 Pristine Talisman C	.10	.25
❑ 152 Shrine of Boundless Growth U	.20	.50
❑ 153 Shrine of Burning Rage U	1.50	4.00
❑ 154 Shrine of Limitless Power U	.20	.50
❑ 155 Shrine of Loyal Legions U	.75	2.00
❑ 156 Shrine of Piercing Vision U	.20	.50
❑ 157 Sickleslicer U	.40	1.00
❑ 158 Soul Conduit R	.60	1.50
❑ 159 Spellskite R	2.50	6.00
❑ 160 Surge Node U	.40	1.00
❑ 161 Sword of War and Peace M	15.00	40.00
❑ 162 Torpor Orb R	1.25	3.00
❑ 163 Trespassing Souleater C	.10	.25
❑ 164 Unwinding Clock R	1.00	2.50
❑ 165 Phyrexia's Core U	.40	1.00
❑ 166 Plains L	.10	.25
❑ 167 Plains L	.10	.25
❑ 168 Island L	.10	.25
❑ 169 Island L	.10	.25
❑ 170 Swamp L	.10	.25
❑ 171 Swamp L	.10	.25
❑ 172 Mountain L	.10	.25
❑ 173 Mountain L	.10	.25
❑ 174 Forest L	.10	.25
❑ 175 Forest L	.10	.25
❑ PC Poison Counter	.10	.25
❑ R1 Rules Tip: Phyrexian Mana	.10	.25
❑ R2 Rules Tip: Living Weapon	.10	.25
❑ R3 Rules Tip: Infect	.10	.25
❑ R4 Rules Tip: Proliferate	.10	.25
❑ T1 Token: Beast	.10	.25
❑ T2 Token: Goblin	.10	.25
❑ T3 Token: Golem	.10	.25
❑ T4 Token: Myr	.10	.25

2011 Magic the Gathering New Phyrexia Foil

*Foil: .8X to 2X Basic Cards

2012 Magic the Gathering Magic 2013

Complete Set	200.00	350.00
❑ 1 Ajani, Caller of the Pride M :W:	6.00	15.00
❑ 2 Ajani's Sunstriker C :W:	.10	.25
❑ 3 Angel's Mercy C :W:	.10	.25
❑ 4 Angelic Benediction U :W:	.20	.50
❑ 5 Attended Knight C :W:	.10	.25
❑ 6 Aven Squire C :W:	.10	.25
❑ 7 Battleflight Eagle C :W:	.10	.25
❑ 8 Captain of the Watch R :W:	.75	2.00
❑ 9 Captain's Call C :W:	.10	.25
❑ 10 Crusader of Odric U :W:	.40	1.00
❑ 11 Divine Favor C :W:	.10	.25
❑ 12 Divine Verdict C :W:	.10	.25
❑ 13 Erase C :W:	.10	.25
❑ 14 Faith's Reward R :W:	.60	1.50
❑ 15 Glorious Charge C :W:	.10	.25
❑ 16 Griffin Protector C :W:	.10	.25
❑ 17 Guardian Lions C :W:	.10	.25
❑ 18 Guardians of Akrasa C :W:	.10	.25
❑ 19 Healer of the Pride U :W:	.20	.50
❑ 20 Intrepid Hero R :W:	.60	1.50
❑ 21 Knight of Glory U :W:	.30	.75
❑ 22 Oblivion Ring U :W:	.50	1.25
❑ 23 Odric, Master Tactician R :W:	1.50	4.00
❑ 24 Pacifism C :W:	.10	.25
❑ 25 Pillarfield Ox C :W:	.10	.25
❑ 26 Planar Cleansing R :W:	.60	1.50
❑ 27 Prized Elephant U :W:	.20	.50
❑ 28 Rain of Blades U :W:	.20	.50
❑ 29 Rhox Faithmender R :W:	.75	2.00
❑ 30 Safe Passage C :W:	.10	.25
❑ 31 Serra Angel U :W:	.20	.50
❑ 32 Serra Avatar M :W:	2.00	5.00
❑ 33 Serra Avenger R :W:	1.50	4.00
❑ 34 Show of Valor C :W:	.10	.25
❑ 35 Silvercoat Lion C :W:	.10	.25
❑ 36 Sublime Archangel M :W:	6.00	15.00
❑ 37 Touch of the Eternal R :W:	.60	1.50
❑ 38 War Falcon C :W:	.10	.25
❑ 39 War Priest of Thune U :W:	.20	.50
❑ 40 Warclamp Mastiff C :W:	.10	.25
❑ 41 Archaeomancer C :B:	.10	.25
❑ 42 Arctic Aven U :B:	.20	.50
❑ 43 Augur of Bolas U :B:	.50	1.25
❑ 44 Battle of Wits R :B:	.60	1.50
❑ 45 Clone R :B:	.60	1.50
❑ 46 Courtly Provocateur U :B:	.20	.50
❑ 47 Divination C :B:	.10	.25
❑ 48 Downpour C :B:	.10	.25
❑ 49 Encrust C :B:	.10	.25
❑ 50 Essence Scatter C :B:	.10	.25
❑ 51 Faerie Invaders C :B:	.10	.25
❑ 52 Fog Bank U :B:	.40	1.00
❑ 53 Harbor Serpent C :B:	.10	.25
❑ 54 Hydrosurge C :B:	.10	.25
❑ 55 Index C :B:	.10	.25
❑ 56 Jace, Memory Adept M :B:	6.00	15.00
❑ 57 Jace's Phantasm U :B:	.75	2.00
❑ 58 Kraken Hatchling C :B:	.10	.25
❑ 59 Master of the Pearl Trident R :B:	2.50	6.00
❑ 60 Merfolk of the Pearl Trident C :B:	.10	.25
❑ 61 Mind Sculpt C :B:	.10	.25
❑ 62 Negate C :B:	.10	.25
❑ 63 Omniscience M :B:	4.00	10.00
❑ 64 Redirect R :B:	.60	1.50
❑ 65 Rewind U :B:	.30	.75
❑ 66 Scroll Thief C :B:	.10	.25
❑ 67 Sleep U :B:	.20	.50
❑ 68 Spelltwine R :B:	.60	1.50
❑ 69 Sphinx of Uthuun R :B:	.60	1.50
❑ 70 Stormtide Leviathan R :B:	.60	1.50
❑ 71 Switcheroo U :B:	.20	.50
❑ 72 Talrand, Sky Summoner R :B:	1.50	4.00
❑ 73 Talrand's Invocation U :B:	.20	.50
❑ 74 Tricks of the Trade C :B:	.10	.25
❑ 75 Unsummon C :B:	.10	.25
❑ 76 Vedalken Entrancer C :B:	.10	.25
❑ 77 Void Stalker R :B:	.75	2.00
❑ 78 Watercourser C :B:	.10	.25
❑ 79 Welkin Tern C :B:	.10	.25
❑ 80 Wind Drake C :B:	.10	.25
❑ 81 Blood Reckoning U :K:	.20	.50
❑ 82 Bloodhunter Bat C :K:	.10	.25
❑ 83 Bloodthrone Vampire C :K:	.10	.25
❑ 84 Cower in Fear U :K:	.20	.50
❑ 85 Crippling Blight C :K:	.10	.25
❑ 86 Dark Favor C :K:	.10	.25
❑ 87 Diabolic Revelation R :K:	.60	1.50
❑ 88 Disciple of Bolas R :K:	1.50	4.00
❑ 89 Disentomb C :K:	.10	.25
❑ 90 Duress C :K:	.10	.25
❑ 91 Duskmantle Prowler U :K:	.20	.50
❑ 92 Duty-Bound Dead C :K:	.10	.25
❑ 93 Essence Drain C :K:	.10	.25
❑ 94 Giant Scorpion C :K:	.10	.25
❑ 95 Harbor Bandit U :K:	.20	.50
❑ 96 Knight of Infamy U :K:	.30	.75
❑ 97 Liliana of the Dark Realms M :K:	6.00	15.00
❑ 98 Liliana's Shade C :K:	.10	.25
❑ 99 Mark of the Vampire C :K:	.10	.25
❑ 100 Mind Rot C :K:	.10	.25
❑ 101 Murder C :K:	.10	.25
❑ 102 Mutilate R :K:	2.50	6.00
❑ 103 Nefarox, Overlord of Grixis R :K:	1.00	2.50
❑ 104 Phylactery Lich R :K:	.60	1.50
❑ 105 Public Execution U :K:	.20	.50
❑ 106 Ravenous Rats C :K:	.10	.25
❑ 107 Rise from the Grave U :K:	.20	.50
❑ 108 Servant of Nefarox C :K:	.10	.25
❑ 109 Shimian Specter R :K:	.60	1.50
❑ 110 Sign in Blood C :K:	.10	.25
❑ 111 Tormented Soul C :K:	.10	.25
❑ 112 Vampire Nighthawk U :K:	.60	1.50
❑ 113 Vampire Nocturnus M :K:	3.00	8.00
❑ 114 Veilborn Ghoul U :K:	.20	.50
❑ 115 Vile Rebirth C :K:	.10	.25
❑ 116 Walking Corpse C :K:	.10	.25
❑ 117 Wit's End R :K:	.60	1.50
❑ 118 Xathrid Gorgon R :K:	.60	1.50
❑ 119 Zombie Goliath C :K:	.10	.25
❑ 120 Arms Dealer U :R:	.20	.50
❑ 121 Bladetusk Boar C :R:	.10	.25
❑ 122 Canyon Minotaur C :R:	.10	.25
❑ 123 Chandra, the Firebrand M :R:	2.50	6.00
❑ 124 Chandra's Fury C :R:	.10	.25
❑ 125 Cleaver Riot U :R:	.20	.50
❑ 126 Craterize C :R:	.10	.25
❑ 127 Crimson Muckwader U :R:	.20	.50
❑ 128 Dragon Hatchling C :R:	.10	.25
❑ 129 Fervor R :R:	.60	1.50
❑ 130 Fire Elemental C :R:	.10	.25
❑ 131 Firewing Phoenix R :R:	.60	1.50
❑ 132 Flames of the Firebrand U :R:	.40	1.00
❑ 133 Furnace Whelp U :R:	.20	.50
❑ 134 Goblin Arsonist C :R:	.10	.25
❑ 135 Goblin Battle Jester C :R:	.10	.25
❑ 136 Hamletback Goliath R :R:	.60	1.50
❑ 137 Kindled Fury C :R:	.10	.25
❑ 138 Krenko, Mob Boss R :R:	2.00	5.00
❑ 139 Krenko's Command C :R:	.10	.25
❑ 140 Magmaquake R :R:	.75	2.00
❑ 141 Mark of Mutiny U :R:	.20	.50
❑ 142 Mindclaw Shaman U :R:	.20	.50
❑ 143 Mogg Flunkies C :R:	.10	.25
❑ 144 Reckless Brute C :R:	.10	.25
❑ 145 Reverberate R :R:	.60	1.50
❑ 146 Rummaging Goblin C :R:	.10	.25
❑ 147 Searing Spear C :R:	.10	.25
❑ 148 Slumbering Dragon R :R:	1.25	3.00
❑ 149 Smelt C :R:	.10	.25
❑ 150 Thundermaw Hellkite M :R:	12.00	30.00
❑ 151 Torch Fiend U :R:	.20	.50
❑ 152 Trumpet Blast C :R:	.10	.25
❑ 153 Turn to Slag C :R:	.10	.25
❑ 154 Volcanic Geyser U :R:	.20	.50
❑ 155 Volcanic Strength C :R:	.10	.25
❑ 156 Wall of Fire C :R:	.10	.25
❑ 157 Wild Guess C :R:	.10	.25
❑ 158 Worldfire M :R:	.75	2.00
❑ 159 Acidic Slime U :G:	.20	.50
❑ 160 Arbor Elf C :G:	.10	.25
❑ 161 Bond Beetle C :G:	.10	.25
❑ 162 Boundless Realms R :G:	.60	1.50
❑ 163 Bountiful Harvest C :G:	.10	.25
❑ 164 Centaur Courser C :G:	.10	.25
❑ 165 Deadly Recluse C :G:	.10	.25
❑ 166 Duskdale Wurm U :G:	.20	.50
❑ 167 Elderscale Wurm M :G:	2.00	5.00
❑ 168 Elvish Archdruid R :G:	.60	1.50
❑ 169 Elvish Visionary C :G:	.10	.25
❑ 170 Farseek C :G:	.10	.25
❑ 171 Flinthoof Boar U :G:	.30	.75
❑ 172 Fog C :G:	.10	.25
❑ 173 Fungal Sprouting U :G:	.20	.50
❑ 174 Garruk, Primal Hunter M :G:	6.00	15.00
❑ 175 Garruk's Packleader U :G:	.20	.50
❑ 176 Ground Seal R :G:	.60	1.50
❑ 177 Mwonvuli Beast Tracker U :G:	.30	.75
❑ 178 Naturalize C :G:	.10	.25
❑ 179 Plummet C :G:	.10	.25
❑ 180 Predatory Rampage R :G:	.60	1.50
❑ 181 Prey Upon C :G:	.10	.25
❑ 182 Primal Huntbeast C :G:	.10	.25
❑ 183 Primordial Hydra M :G:	4.00	10.00
❑ 184 Quirion Dryad R :G:	.60	1.50
❑ 185 Rancor U :G:	1.00	2.50
❑ 186 Ranger's Path C :G:	.10	.25
❑ 187 Revive U :G:	.20	.50
❑ 188 Roaring Primadox U :G:	.20	.50
❑ 189 Sentinel Spider C :G:	.10	.25
❑ 190 Serpent's Gift C :G:	.10	.25
❑ 191 Silklash Spider R :G:	.60	1.50
❑ 192 Spiked Baloth C :G:	.10	.25
❑ 193 Thragtusk R :G:	4.00	10.00
❑ 194 Timberpack Wolf C :G:	.10	.25
❑ 195 Titanic Growth C :G:	.10	.25
❑ 196 Vastwood Gorger C :G:	.10	.25
❑ 197 Yeva, Nature's Herald R :G:	.60	1.50
❑ 198 Yeva's Forcemage C :G:	.10	.25
❑ 199 Nicol Bolas, Planeswalker M :B/K/R:	3.00	8.00
❑ 200 Akroma's Memorial M	4.00	10.00
❑ 201 Chronomatom U	.20	.50
❑ 202 Clock of Omens U	.20	.50
❑ 203 Door to Nothingness R	.60	1.50
❑ 204 Elixir of Immortality U	.25	.60
❑ 205 Gem of Becoming U	.20	.50
❑ 206 Gilded Lotus R	2.00	5.00
❑ 207 Jayemdae Tome U	.20	.50
❑ 208 Kitesail U	.20	.50
❑ 209 Phyrexian Hulk U	.20	.50

MAGIC

❑ 210 Primal Clay U .20 .50
❑ 211 Ring of Evos Isle U .25 .60
❑ 212 Ring of Kalonia U .25 .60
❑ 213 Ring of Thune U .25 .60
❑ 214 Ring of Valkas U .25 .60
❑ 215 Ring of Xathrid U .25 .60
❑ 216 Sands of Delirium R .75 2.00
❑ 217 Staff of Nin R .60 1.50
❑ 218 Stuffy Doll R 1.25 3.00
❑ 219 Tormod's Crypt U .75 2.00
❑ 220 Trading Post R .75 2.00
❑ 221 Cathedral of War R 1.50 4.00
❑ 222 Dragonskull Summit R 2.00 5.00
❑ 223 Drowned Catacomb R 2.00 5.00
❑ 224 Evolving Wilds C .10 .25
❑ 225 Glacial Fortress R 2.00 5.00
❑ 226 Hellion Crucible R .75 2.00
❑ 227 Reliquary Tower U .75 2.00
❑ 228 Rootbound Crag R 1.25 3.00
❑ 229 Sunpetal Grove R 2.00 5.00
❑ 230 Plains L .10 .25
❑ 231 Plains L .10 .25
❑ 232 Plains L .10 .25
❑ 233 Plains L .10 .25
❑ 234 Island L .10 .25
❑ 235 Island L .10 .25
❑ 236 Island L .10 .25
❑ 237 Island L .10 .25
❑ 238 Swamp L .10 .25
❑ 239 Swamp L .10 .25
❑ 240 Swamp L .10 .25
❑ 241 Swamp L .10 .25
❑ 242 Mountain L .10 .25
❑ 243 Mountain L .10 .25
❑ 244 Mountain L .10 .25
❑ 245 Mountain L .10 .25
❑ 246 Forest L .10 .25
❑ 247 Forest L .10 .25
❑ 248 Forest L .10 .25
❑ 249 Forest L .10 .25
❑ T1 Token: Cat .10 .25
❑ T2 Token: Goat .10 .25
❑ T3 Token: Soldier .10 .25
❑ T4 Token: Drake .10 .25
❑ T5 Token: Zombie .10 .25
❑ T6 Token: Goblin .10 .25
❑ T7 Token: Hellion .10 .25
❑ T8 Token: Beast .10 .25
❑ T9 Token: Saproling .10 .25
❑ T10 Token: Wurm .10 .25
❑ T11 Emblem: Liliana of the Dark Realms .10 .25

2012 Magic the Gathering Magic 2013 Foil

*Foil: .8X to 2X Basic Cards

2012 Magic the Gathering Avacyn Restored

Complete Set (244) 150.00 250.00
Booster Box 75.00 125.00
Booster Pack 3.00 4.00

❑ 1 Angel of Glory's Rise R :W: .75 2.00
❑ 2 Angel of Jubilation R :W: 2.00 5.00
❑ 3 Angel's Mercy C :W: .10 .25
❑ 4 Angelic Wall C :W: .10 .25
❑ 5 Archangel U :W: .20 .50
❑ 6 Avacyn, Angel of Hope M :W: 6.00 15.00
❑ 7 Banishing Stroke U :W: .20 .50
❑ 8 Builder's Blessing U :W: .20 .50
❑ 9 Call to Serve C :W: .10 .25
❑ 10 Cathars' Crusade R :W: 1.00 2.50
❑ 11 Cathedral Sanctifier C :W: .10 .25
❑ 12 Cloudshift C :W: .10 .25
❑ 13 Commander's Authority U :W: .20 .50
❑ 14 Cursebreak C :W: .10 .25
❑ 15 Defang C :W: .10 .25
❑ 16 Defy Death U :W: .20 .50
❑ 17 Devout Chaplain U :W: .20 .50
❑ 18 Divine Deflection R :W: 1.50 4.00
❑ 19 Emancipation Angel U :W: .20 .50
❑ 20 Entreat the Angels M :W: 6.00 15.00
❑ 21 Farbog Explorer C :W: .10 .25
❑ 22 Goldnight Commander U :W: .20 .50
❑ 23 Goldnight Redeemer U :W: .20 .50
❑ 24 Herald of War R :W: 1.50 4.00
❑ 25 Holy Justiciar U :W: .20 .50
❑ 26 Leap of Faith C :W: .10 .25
❑ 27 Midnight Duelist C :W: .10 .25
❑ 28 Midvast Protector C :W: .10 .25
❑ 29 Moonlight Geist C :W: .10 .25
❑ 30 Moorland Inquisitor C :W: .10 .25
❑ 31 Nearheath Pilgrim U :W: .20 .50
❑ 32 Restoration Angel R :W: 3.00 8.00
❑ 33 Riders of Gavony R :W: .75 2.00
❑ 34 Righteous Blow C :W: .10 .25
❑ 35 Seraph of Dawn C :W: .10 .25
❑ 36 Silverblade Paladin R :W: 2.50 6.00
❑ 37 Spectral Gateguards C :W: .10 .25
❑ 38 Terminus R :W: 2.50 6.00
❑ 39 Thraben Valiant C :W: .10 .25
❑ 40 Voice of the Provinces C :W: .10 .25
❑ 41 Zealous Strike C :W: .10 .25
❑ 42 Alchemist's Apprentice C :B: .10 .25
❑ 43 Amass the Components C :B: .10 .25
❑ 44 Arcane Melee R :B: .60 1.50
❑ 45 Captain of the Mists R :B: .60 1.50
❑ 46 Crippling Chill C :B: .10 .25
❑ 47 Deadeye Navigator R :B: .60 1.50
❑ 48 Devastation Tide R :B: 1.50 4.00
❑ 49 Dreadwaters C :B: .10 .25
❑ 50 Elgaud Shieldmate C :B: .10 .25
❑ 51 Favorable Winds U :B: .20 .50
❑ 52 Fettergeist U :B: .20 .50
❑ 53 Fleeting Distraction C :B: .10 .25
❑ 54 Galvanic Alchemist C :B: .10 .25
❑ 55 Geist Snatch C :B: .10 .25
❑ 56 Ghostform C :B: .10 .25
❑ 57 Ghostly Flicker C :B: .10 .25
❑ 58 Ghostly Touch U :B: .20 .50
❑ 59 Gryff Vanguard C :B: .10 .25
❑ 60 Havengul Skaab C :B: .10 .25
❑ 61 Infinite Reflection R :B: .60 1.50
❑ 62 Into the Void U :B: .20 .50
❑ 63A Latch Seeker U :B: .20 .50
❑ 63B Latch Seeker U :B: 2.00 5.00
(Full Art Promo)
❑ 64 Lone Revenant R :B: .60 1.50
❑ 65 Lunar Mystic R :B: .60 1.50
❑ 66 Mass Appeal U :B: .20 .50
❑ 67 Mist Raven C :B: .10 .25
❑ 68 Misthollow Griffin M :B: 2.00 5.00
❑ 69 Nephalia Smuggler U :B: .20 .50
❑ 70 Outwit C :B: .10 .25
❑ 71 Peel from Reality C :B: .10 .25
❑ 72 Rotcrown Ghoul C :B: .10 .25
❑ 73 Scrapskin Drake C :B: .10 .25
❑ 74 Second Guess U :B: .20 .50
❑ 75 Spectral Prison C :B: .10 .25
❑ 76 Spirit Away R :B: .60 1.50
❑ 77 Stern Mentor U :B: .20 .50
❑ 78 Stolen Goods R :B: .75 2.00
❑ 79 Tamiyo, the Moon Sage M :B: 8.00 20.00
❑ 80 Tandem Lookout U :B: .20 .50
❑ 81 Temporal Mastery M :B: 6.00 15.00
❑ 82 Vanishment U :B: .20 .50
❑ 83 Wingcrafter C :B: .10 .25
❑ 84 Appetite for Brains U :K: .20 .50
❑ 85 Barter in Blood U :K: .20 .50
❑ 86 Blood Artist U :K: .20 .50
❑ 87 Bloodflow Connoisseur C :K: .10 .25
❑ 88 Bone Splinters C :K: .10 .25
❑ 89 Butcher Ghoul C :K: .10 .25
❑ 90 Corpse Traders U :K: .20 .50
❑ 91 Crypt Creeper C :K: .10 .25
❑ 92 Dark Impostor R :K: .75 2.00
❑ 93 Death Wind C :K: .10 .25
❑ 94 Demonic Rising R :K: .60 1.50
❑ 95 Demonic Taskmaster U :K: .20 .50
❑ 96 Demonlord of Ashmouth R :K: 1.00 2.50
❑ 97 Descent into Madness M :K: 1.25 3.00
❑ 98 Dread Slaver R :K: .60 1.50
❑ 99 Driver of the Dead C :K: .10 .25
❑ 100 Essence Harvest C :K: .10 .25
❑ 101 Evernight Shade U :K: .20 .50
❑ 102 Exquisite Blood R :K: .75 2.00
❑ 103 Ghoulflesh C :K: .10 .25
❑ 104 Gloom Surgeon R :K: .60 1.50
❑ 105 Grave Exchange C :K: .10 .25
❑ 106 Griselbrand M :K: 6.00 15.00
❑ 107 Harvester of Souls R :K: 1.00 2.50
❑ 108 Homicidal Seclusion U :K: .20 .50
❑ 109 Human Frailty U :K: .20 .50
❑ 110 Hunted Ghoul C :K: .10 .25
❑ 111A Killing Wave R :K: 1.25 3.00
❑ 111B Killing Wave R :K: 6.00 15.00
(Full Art Promo)
❑ 112 Maalfeld Twins U :K: .20 .50
❑ 113 Marrow Bats U :K: .20 .50
❑ 114 Mental Agony C :K: .10 .25
❑ 115 Necrobite C :K: .10 .25
❑ 116 Polluted Dead C :K: .10 .25
❑ 117 Predator's Gambit C :K: .10 .25
❑ 118 Renegade Demon C :K: .10 .25
❑ 119 Searchlight Geist C :K: .10 .25
❑ 120 Soulcage Fiend C :K: .10 .25
❑ 121 Treacherous Pit-Dweller R :K: .75 2.00
❑ 122 Triumph of Cruelty U :K: .20 .50
❑ 123 Undead Executioner C :K: .10 .25
❑ 124 Unhallowed Pact C :K: .10 .25
❑ 125 Aggravate U :R: .20 .50
❑ 126 Archwing Dragon R :R: 1.25 3.00
❑ 127 Banners Raised C :R: .10 .25
❑ 128 Battle Hymn C :R: .10 .25
❑ 129 Bonfire of the Damned M :R: 8.00 20.00
❑ 130 Burn at the Stake R :R: .75 2.00
❑ 131 Dangerous Wager C :R: .10 .25
❑ 132 Demolish C :R: .10 .25
❑ 133 Dual Casting R :R: 1.00 2.50
❑ 134 Falkenrath Exterminator U :R: .20 .50
❑ 135 Fervent Cathar C :R: .10 .25
❑ 136 Gang of Devils U :R: .20 .50
❑ 137 Guise of Fire C :R: .10 .25
❑ 138 Hanweir Lancer C :R: .10 .25
❑ 139 Havengul Vampire U :R: .20 .50
❑ 140 Heirs of Stromkirk C :R: .10 .25
❑ 141 Hound of Griselbrand R :R: 1.25 3.00
❑ 142 Kessig Malcontents U :R: .20 .50
❑ 143 Kruin Striker C :R: .10 .25
❑ 144 Lightning Mauler U :R: .20 .50
❑ 145 Lightning Prowess U :R: .20 .50
❑ 146 Mad Prophet C :R: .10 .25
❑ 147 Malicious Intent C :R: .10 .25
❑ 148 Malignus M :R: 1.25 3.00
❑ 149 Pillar of Flame C :R: .10 .25
❑ 150 Raging Poltergeist C :R: .10 .25
❑ 151 Reforge the Soul R :R: 1.50 4.00
❑ 152 Riot Ringleader C :R: .10 .25
❑ 153 Rite of Ruin R :R: .60 1.50
❑ 154 Rush of Blood U :R: .20 .50
❑ 155 Scalding Devil C :R: .10 .25
❑ 156 Somberwald Vigilante C :R: .10 .25
❑ 157 Stonewright U :R: .20 .50
❑ 158 Thatcher Revolt C :R: .10 .25
❑ 159 Thunderbolt C :R: .10 .25
❑ 160 Thunderous Wrath U :R: .20 .50
❑ 161 Tibalt, the Fiend-Blooded M :R: 6.00 15.00
❑ 162 Tyrant of Discord R :R: .60 1.50
❑ 163 Uncanny Speed C :R: .10 .25
❑ 164 Vexing Devil R :R: 6.00 15.00
❑ 165 Vigilante Justice U :R: .20 .50
❑ 166 Zealous Conscripts R :R: 1.50 4.00
❑ 167 Abundant Growth C :G: .10 .25
❑ 168 Blessings of Nature U :G: .20 .50
❑ 169 Borderland Ranger C :G: .10 .25
❑ 170 Bower Passage U :G: .20 .50
❑ 171 Champion of Lambholt R :G: 1.50 4.00
❑ 172 Craterhoof Behemoth M :G: 1.25 3.00
❑ 173 Descendants' Path R :G: 1.50 4.00
❑ 174 Diregraf Escort C :G: .10 .25
❑ 175 Druid's Familiar U :G: .20 .50
❑ 176 Druids' Repository R :G: .75 2.00
❑ 177 Eaten by Spiders U :G: .20 .50
❑ 178 Flowering Lumberknot C :G: .10 .25
❑ 179 Geist Trappers C :G: .10 .25
❑ 180 Gloomwidow U :G: .20 .50
❑ 181 Grounded C :G: .10 .25
❑ 182 Howlgeist U :G: .20 .50
❑ 183 Joint Assault C :G: .10 .25
❑ 184 Lair Delve C :G: .10 .25
❑ 185 Natural End C :G: .10 .25
❑ 186 Nettle Swine C :G: .10 .25
❑ 187 Nightshade Peddler C :G: .10 .25
❑ 188 Pathbreaker Wurm C :G: .10 .25
❑ 189 Primal Surge M :G: 1.25 3.00
❑ 190 Rain of Thorns U :G: .20 .50
❑ 191 Revenge of the Hunted R :G: 1.25 3.00
❑ 192 Sheltering Word C :G: .10 .25
❑ 193 Snare the Skies C :G: .10 .25
❑ 194 Somberwald Sage R :G: 1.50 4.00
❑ 195 Soul of the Harvest R :G: .60 1.50
❑ 196 Terrifying Presence C :G: .10 .25
❑ 197 Timberland Guide C :G: .10 .25
❑ 198 Triumph of Ferocity U :G: .20 .50
❑ 199 Trusted Forcemage C :G: .10 .25
❑ 200 Ulvenwald Tracker R :G: 1.25 3.00
❑ 201 Vorstclaw U :G: .20 .50
❑ 202 Wandering Wolf C :G: .10 .25
❑ 203 Wild Defiance R :G: .75 2.00
❑ 204 Wildwood Geist C :G: .10 .25
❑ 205 Wolfir Avenger U :G: .20 .50
❑ 206 Wolfir Silverheart R :G: 3.00 8.00
❑ 207 Yew Spirit U :G: .20 .50
❑ 208 Bruna, Light of Alabaster M :W/B: 3.00 8.00
❑ 209 Gisela, Blade of Goldnight M :W/R: 5.00 12.00
❑ 210 Sigarda, Host of Herons M :W/G: 6.00 15.00
❑ 211 Angel's Tomb U .20 .50
❑ 212 Angelic Armaments U .20 .50
❑ 213 Bladed Bracers C .10 .25
❑ 214 Conjurer's Closet R .60 1.50
❑ 215 Gallows at Willow Hill R .60 1.50
❑ 216 Haunted Guardian U .20 .50
❑ 217 Moonsilver Spear R 1.25 3.00
❑ 218 Narstad Scrapper C .10 .25
❑ 219 Otherworld Atlas R .60 1.50
❑ 220 Scroll of Avacyn C .10 .25
❑ 221 Scroll of Griselbrand C .10 .25
❑ 222 Tormentor's Trident U .20 .50
❑ 223 Vanguard's Shield C .10 .25
❑ 224 Vessel of Endless Rest U .20 .50
❑ 225 Alchemist's Refuge R 1.50 4.00
❑ 226 Cavern of Souls R 15.00 30.00
❑ 227 Desolate Lighthouse R 1.50 4.00
❑ 228 Seraph Sanctuary C .10 .25
❑ 229 Slayers' Stronghold R 1.50 4.00
❑ 230 Plains L .10 .25
❑ 231 Plains L .10 .25
❑ 232 Plains L .10 .25
❑ 233 Island L .10 .25
❑ 234 Island L .10 .25
❑ 235 Island L .10 .25
❑ 236 Swamp L .10 .25
❑ 237 Swamp L .10 .25
❑ 238 Swamp L .10 .25
❑ 239 Mountain L .10 .25
❑ 240 Mountain L .10 .25
❑ 241 Mountain L .10 .25
❑ 242 Forest L .10 .25
❑ 243 Forest L .10 .25
❑ 244 Forest L .10 .25
❑ T1 Token: Angel .10 .25
❑ T2 Token: Human .10 .25
❑ T3 Token: Spirit WHITE .10 .25
❑ T4 Token: Spirit BLUE .10 .25
❑ T5 Token: Demon .10 .25
❑ T6 Token: Zombie .10 .25
❑ T7 Token: Human .10 .25
❑ T8 Emblem: Tamiyo, The Moon Sage .10 .25

2012 Magic the Gathering Avacyn Restored Foil

*Foil: .8X to 2X Basic Cards

2012 Magic the Gathering Dark Ascension

Complete Set (158) 150.00 300.00
Booster Box 75.00 150.00
Booster Pack 3.00 5.00

❑ 1 Archangel's Light M :W: 1.00 2.50
❑ 2 Bar the Door C :W: .10 .25
❑ 3 Break of Day C :W: .10 .25
❑ 4 Burden of Guilt C :W: .10 .25
❑ 5 Curse of Exhaustion U :W: .20 .50
❑ 6 Elgaud Inquisitor C :W: .10 .25
❑ 7 Faith's Shield U :W: .20 .50
❑ 8 Gather the Townsfolk C :W: .10 .25
❑ 9 Gavony Ironwright U :W: .20 .50
❑ 10 Hollowhenge Spirit U :W: .20 .50
❑ 11 Increasing Devotion R :W: 2.00 5.00
❑ 12 Lingering Souls U :W: .20 .50
❑ 13 Loyal Cathar/Unhallowed Cathar C :W/K: .10 .25
❑ 14 Midnight Guard C :W: .10 .25
❑ 15 Niblis of the Mist C :W: .10 .25
❑ 16 Niblis of the Urn U :W: .20 .50
❑ 17 Ray of Revelation C :W: .10 .25
❑ 18 Requiem Angel R :W: 1.00 2.50
❑ 19 Sanctuary Cat C :W: .10 .25
❑ 20 Seance R :W: 1.00 2.50
❑ 21 Silverclaw Griffin C :W: .10 .25
❑ 22 Skillful Lunge C :W: .10 .25
❑ 23 Sudden Disappearance R :W: 1.00 2.50
❑ 24 Thalia, Guardian of Thraben R :W: 3.00 8.00
❑ 25 Thraben Doomsayer R :W: 2.00 5.00
❑ 26 Thraben Heretic U :W: .20 .50
❑ 27 Artful Dodge C :B: .10 .25
❑ 28 Beguiler of Wills M :B: 1.50 4.00
❑ 29 Bone to Ash C :B: .10 .25
❑ 30 Call to the Kindred R :B: 1.00 2.50
❑ 31 Chant of the Skifsang C :B: .10 .25
❑ 32 Chill of Foreboding U :B: .20 .50
❑ 33 Counterlash R :B: 1.25 3.00
❑ 34 Curse of Echoes R :B: .60 1.50
❑ 35 Divination C :B: .10 .25
❑ 36 Dungeon Geists R :B: 2.00 5.00
❑ 37 Geralf's Mindcrusher R :B: .60 1.50
❑ 38 Griptide C :B: .10 .25
❑ 39 Havengul Runebinder R :B: .60 1.50
❑ 40 Headless Skaab C :B: .10 .25
❑ 41 Increasing Confusion R :B: 2.00 5.00
❑ 42 Mystic Retrieval U :B: .20 .50
❑ 43 Nephalia Seakite C :B: .10 .25
❑ 44 Niblis of the Breath U :B: .20 .50
❑ 45 Relentless Skaabs U :B: .20 .50
❑ 46 Saving Grasp C :B: .10 .25
❑ 47 Screeching Skaab C :B: .10 .25
❑ 48 Secrets of the Dead U :B: .20 .50
❑ 49 Shriekgeist C :B: .10 .25
❑ 50 Soul Seizer/Ghastly Haunting U :B: .20 .50
❑ 51 Stormbound Geist C :B: .10 .25
❑ 52 Thought Scour C :B: .10 .25
❑ 53 Tower Geist U :B: .20 .50
❑ 54 Black Cat C :K: .10 .25
❑ 55 Chosen of Markov/Markov's Servant C :K: .10 .25
❑ 56 Curse of Misfortunes R :K: .60 1.50
❑ 57 Curse of Thirst U :K: .20 .50
❑ 58 Deadly Allure U :K: .20 .50
❑ 59 Death's Caress C :K: .10 .25
❑ 60 Falkenrath Torturer C :K: .10 .25
❑ 61 Farbog Boneflinger U :K: .20 .50
❑ 62 Fiend of the Shadows R :K: 1.25 3.00
❑ 63 Geralf's Messenger R :K: 5.00 12.00
❑ 64 Gravecrawler R :K: 4.00 10.00
❑ 65 Gravepurge C :K: .10 .25
❑ 66 Gruesome Discovery C :K: .10 .25
❑ 67 Harrowing Journey U :K: .20 .50
❑ 68 Highborn Ghoul C :K: .10 .25
❑ 69 Increasing Ambition R :K: .60 1.50
❑ 70 Mikaeus, the Unhallowed M :K: 3.00 8.00
❑ 71 Ravenous Demon/Archdemon of Greed R :K: 2.00 5.00
❑ 72 Reap the Seagraf C :K: .10 .25
❑ 73 Sightless Ghoul C :K: .10 .25
❑ 74 Skirsdag Flayer U :K: .20 .50
❑ 75 Spiteful Shadows C :K: .10 .25
❑ 76 Tragic Slip C :K: .10 .25
❑ 77 Undying Evil C :K: .10 .25
❑ 78 Vengeful Vampire U :K: .20 .50
❑ 79 Wakedancer U :K: .20 .50
❑ 80 Zombie Apocalypse R :K: 2.50 6.00
❑ 81 Afflicted Deserter/Werewolf Ransacker U :R: .20 .50
❑ 82 Alpha Brawl R :R: .60 1.50
❑ 83 Blood Feud U :R: .20 .50
❑ 84 Burning Oil U :R: .20 .50
❑ 85 Curse of Bloodletting R :R: 1.00 2.50
❑ 86 Erdwal Ripper C :R: .10 .25
❑ 87 Faithless Looting C :R: .10 .25
❑ 88 Fires of Undeath C :R: .10 .25
❑ 89 Flayer of the Hatebound R :R: 1.00 2.50
❑ 90 Fling C :R: .10 .25
❑ 91 Forge Devil C :R: .10 .25
❑ 92 Heckling Fiends U :R: .20 .50
❑ 93 Hellrider R :R: 1.50 4.00
❑ 94 Hinterland Hermit/Hinterland Scourge C :R: .10 .25
❑ 95 Increasing Vengeance R :R: 1.50 4.00
❑ 96 Markov Blademaster R :R: 1.50 4.00
❑ 97 Markov Warlord U :R: .20 .50
❑ 98 Mondronen Shaman/Tovolar's Magehunter R :R: 1.00 2.50
❑ 99 Moonveil Dragon M :R: 1.50 4.00
❑ 100 Nearheath Stalker C :R: .10 .25
❑ 101 Pyreheart Wolf U :R: .20 .50
❑ 102 Russet Wolves C :R: .10 .25
❑ 103 Scorch the Fields C :R: .10 .25
❑ 104 Shattered Perception U :R: .20 .50
❑ 105 Talons of Falkenrath C :R: .10 .25
❑ 106 Torch Fiend C :R: .10 .25
❑ 107 Wrack with Madness C :R: .10 .25
❑ 108 Briarpack Alpha U :G: .20 .50
❑ 109 Clinging Mists C :G: .10 .25
❑ 110 Crushing Vines C :G: .10 .25
❑ 111 Dawntreader Elk C :G: .10 .25
❑ 112 Deranged Outcast R :G: .60 1.50
❑ 113 Favor of the Woods C :G: .10 .25
❑ 114 Feed the Pack R :G: .60 1.50
❑ 115 Ghoultree R :G: 1.50 4.00
❑ 116 Gravetiller Wurm U :G: .20 .50
❑ 117 Grim Flowering U :G: .20 .50
❑ 118 Hollowhenge Beast C :G: .10 .25
❑ 119 Hunger of the Howlpack C :G: .10 .25
❑ 120 Increasing Savagery R :G: 1.00 2.50
❑ 121 Kessig Recluse C :G: .10 .25
❑ 122 Lambholt Elder/Silverpelt Werewolf U :G: .20 .50
❑ 123 Lost in the Woods R :G: .60 1.50
❑ 124 Predator Ooze R :G: 2.50 6.00
❑ 125 Scorned Villager/Moonscarred Werewolf C :G: .10 .25
❑ 126 Somberwald Dryad C :G: .10 .25
❑ 127 Strangleroot Geist U :G: .20 .50
❑ 128 Tracker's Instincts U :G: .20 .50
❑ 129 Ulvenwald Bear C :G: .10 .25
❑ 130 Village Survivors U :G: .20 .50
❑ 131 Vorapede M :G: 3.00 8.00
❑ 132 Wild Hunger C :G: .10 .25
❑ 133 Wolfbitten Captive/Krallenhorde Killer R :G: 2.00 5.00
❑ 134 Young Wolf C :G: .10 .25
❑ 135 Diregraf Captain U :B/K: .20 .50
❑ 136 Drogskol Captain U :W/B: .20 .50
❑ 137 Drogskol Reaver M :W/B: 5.00 12.00
❑ 138 Falkenrath Aristocrat M :K/R: 5.00 12.00
❑ 139 Havengul Lich M :B/K: 5.00 12.00
❑ 140 Huntmaster of the Fells 12.00 30.00
Ravager of the Fells M :R/G:
❑ 141 Immerwolf U :R/G: .20 .50
❑ 142 Sorin, Lord of Innistrad M :W/K: 20.00 40.00
❑ 143 Stromkirk Captain U :K/R: .20 .50
❑ 144 Altar of the Lost U .20 .50
❑ 145 Avacyn's Collar U .20 .50
❑ 146 Chalice of Life/Chalice of Death U .20 .50
❑ 147 Elbrus, the Binding Blade 3.00 8.00
Withengar Unbound M :K:
❑ 148 Executioner's Hood C .10 .25
❑ 149 Grafdigger's Cage R 2.50 6.00
❑ 150 Heavy Mattock C .10 .25
❑ 151 Helvault M 2.00 5.00
❑ 152 Jar of Eyeballs R .60 1.50
❑ 153 Warden of the Wall U .20 .50
❑ 154 Wolfhunter's Quiver U .20 .50
❑ 155 Evolving Wilds C .10 .25
❑ 156 Grim Backwoods R 1.00 2.50
❑ 157 Haunted Fengraf C .10 .25
❑ 158 Vault of the Archangel R 3.00 8.00
❑ CL Checklist .10 .25
❑ T1 Token: Human .10 .25
❑ T2 Token: Vampire .10 .25
❑ T3 Emblem: Sorin, Lord of Innistrad .10 .25

2012 Magic the Gathering Dark Ascension Foil

*Foil: .8X to 2X Basic Cards

2012 Magic the Gathering Planechase

Chaos Reigns deck 25.00 50.00
Night of the Ninja deck 30.00 60.00
Primordial Hunger deck 20.00 40.00
Savage Auras deck 20.00 40.00

❑ 1 Armored Griffin U :W: .15 .40
❑ 2 Auramancer C :W: .10 .25
❑ 3 Auratouched Mage U :W: .15 .40
❑ 4 Cage of Hands C :W: .10 .25
❑ 5 Celestial Ancient R :W: .30 .75
❑ 6 Felidar Umbra U :W: 1.50 4.00
❑ 7 Ghostly Prison U :W: 2.00 5.00
❑ 8 Hyena Umbra C :W: .30 .75
❑ 9 Kor Spiritdancer R :W: 4.00 10.00
❑ 10 Mammoth Umbra U :W: .15 .40
❑ 11 Sigil of the Empty Throne R :W: .75 2.00
❑ 12 Spirit Mantle U :W: 1.00 2.50
❑ 13 Three Dreams R :W: .30 .75
❑ 14 Augury Owl C :B: .10 .25
❑ 15 Cancel C :B: .10 .25
❑ 16 Concentrate U :B: .15 .40
❑ 17 Guard Gomazoa U :B: .40 1.00
❑ 18 Higure, the Still Wind R :B: .40 1.00
❑ 19 Illusory Angel U :B: 1.25 3.00
❑ 20 Mistblade Shinobi C :B: .15 .40
❑ 21 Ninja of the Deep Hours C :B: .30 .75
❑ 22 Peregrine Drake U :B: .15 .40
❑ 23 Primal Plasma C :B: .10 .25
❑ 24 Sakashima's Student R :B: 3.00 8.00
❑ 25 See Beyond C :B: .10 .25
❑ 26 Sunken Hope R :B: .30 .75
❑ 27 Walker of Secret Ways U :B: .15 .40
❑ 28 Wall of Frost U :B: .15 .40
❑ 29 Whirlpool Warrior R :B: .30 .75
❑ 30 Assassinate C :K: .10 .25
❑ 31 Cadaver Imp C :K: .10 .25
❑ 32 Dark Hatchling R :K: .30 .75
❑ 33 Ink-Eyes, Servant of Oni R :K: 1.50 4.00
❑ 34 Liliana's Specter C :K: .10 .25
❑ 35 Okiba-Gang Shinobi C :K: .30 .75
❑ 36 Skullsnatcher C :K: .10 .25
❑ 37 Throat Slitter U :K: .40 1.00
❑ 38 Tormented Soul C :K: .10 .25
❑ 39 Arc Trail U :R: .15 .40
❑ 40 Beetleback Chief U :R: .75 2.00
❑ 41 Erratic Explosion C :R: .10 .25
❑ 42 Fiery Conclusion C :R: .10 .25
❑ 43 Fiery Fall C :R: .10 .25
❑ 44 Fling C :R: .10 .25
❑ 45 Hellion Eruption R :R: .30 .75

❑ 46 Hissing Iguanar C :R: .10 .25
❑ 47 Mark of Mutiny U :R: .15 .40
❑ 48 Mass Mutiny R :R: .40 1.00
❑ 49 Mudbutton Torchrunner C :R: .10 .25
❑ 50 Preyseizer Dragon R :R: 2.00 5.00
❑ 51 Rivals' Duel U :R: .15 .40
❑ 52 Thorn-Thrash Viashino C :R: .10 .25
❑ 53 Thunder-Thrash Elder U :R: .15 .40
❑ 54 Warstorm Surge R :R: .30 .75
❑ 55 Aura Gnarlid C :G: .10 .25
❑ 56 Awakening Zone R :G: .75 2.00
❑ 57 Beast Within U :G: .75 2.00
❑ 58 Boar Umbra U :G: .15 .40
❑ 59 Bramble Elemental C :G: .10 .25
❑ 60 Brindle Shoat U :G: .15 .40
❑ 61 Brutalizer Exarch U :G: .15 .40
❑ 62 Cultivate C :G: .75 2.00
❑ 63 Dowsing Shaman U :G: .15 .40
❑ 64 Dreampod Druid U :G: .15 .40
❑ 65 Gluttonous Slime U :G: .15 .40
❑ 66 Lumberknot U :G: .15 .40
❑ 67 Mitotic Slime R :G: .30 .75
❑ 68 Mycoloth R :G: 2.00 5.00
❑ 69 Nest Invader C :G: .10 .25
❑ 70 Nullmage Advocate C :G: .10 .25
❑ 71 Ondu Giant C :G: .10 .25
❑ 72 Overrun U :G: .15 .40
❑ 73 Penumbra Spider C :G: .10 .25
❑ 74 Predatory Urge R :G: .30 .75
❑ 75 Quiet Disrepair C :G: .10 .25
❑ 76 Rancor C :G: .75 2.00
❑ 77 Silhana Ledgewalker C :G: .75 2.00
❑ 78 Snake Umbra C :G: .10 .25
❑ 79 Tukatongue Thallid C :G: .10 .25
❑ 80 Viridian Emissary C :G: .10 .25
❑ 81 Wall of Blossoms U :G: 1.00 2.50
❑ 82 Baleful Strix U :B/K: 10.00 25.00
❑ 83 Bituminous Blast U :K/R: .15 .40
❑ 84 Bloodbraid Elf U :R/G: .75 2.00
❑ 85 Deny Reality C :B/K: .10 .25
❑ 86 Dimir Infiltrator C :B/K: .10 .25
❑ 87 Dragonlair Spider R :R/G: 1.50 4.00
❑ 88 Elderwood Scion R :W/G: .75 2.00
❑ 89 Enigma Sphinx R :W/B/K: .30 .75
❑ 90 Enlisted Wurm U :W/G: .15 .40
❑ 91 Etherium-Horn Sorcerer R :B/R: .75 2.00
❑ 92 Fires of Yavimaya U :R/G: .40 1.00
❑ 93 Fusion Elemental U :W/B/K/R/G: .15 .40
❑ 94 Glen Elendra Liege R :B/K: .75 2.00
❑ 95 Hellkite Hatchling U :R/G: .15 .40
❑ 96 Indrik Umbra R :W/G: .75 2.00
❑ 97 Inkfathom Witch U :B/K: .15 .40
❑ 98 Kathari Remnant U :B/K: .15 .40
❑ 99 Krond the Dawn-Clad M :W/G: 1.25 3.00
❑ 100 Last Stand R :W/B/K/R/G: .30 .75
❑ 101 Maelstrom Wanderer M :B/R/G: 3.00 8.00
❑ 102 Noggle Ransacker U :B/R: .15 .40
❑ 103 Pollenbright Wings U :W/G: .15 .40
❑ 104 Shardless Agent U :B/G: 8.00 20.00
❑ 105 Silent-Blade Oni R :B/K: 3.00 8.00
❑ 106 Thromok the Insatiable M :R/G: 2.00 5.00
❑ 107 Vela the Night-Clad M :B/K: 1.50 4.00
❑ 108 Armillary Sphere C .10 .25
❑ 109 Farsight Mask U .15 .40
❑ 110 Flayer Husk C .10 .25
❑ 111 Fractured Powerstone C .10 .25
❑ 112 Quietus Spike R .75 2.00
❑ 113 Sai of the Shinobi U .15 .40
❑ 114 Thran Golem U .15 .40
❑ 115 Whispersilk Cloak U .40 1.00
❑ 116 Dimir Aqueduct C .60 1.50
❑ 117 Exotic Orchard R .60 1.50
❑ 118 Graypelt Refuge U .15 .40
❑ 119 Gruul Turf C .10 .25
❑ 120 Jwar Isle Refuge U .30 .75
❑ 121 Kazandu Refuge U .15 .40
❑ 122 Khalni Garden C .10 .25
❑ 123 Krosan Verge U .15 .40
❑ 124 Rupture Spire C .10 .25
❑ 125 Selesnya Sanctuary C .30 .75
❑ 126 Shimmering Grotto C .10 .25
❑ 127 Skarrg, the Rage Pits U .15 .40
❑ 128 Tainted Isle U .75 2.00
❑ 129 Terramorphic Expanse C .10 .25
❑ 130 Vitu-Ghazi, the City-Tree U .15 .40
❑ 131 Vivid Creek U .30 .75
❑ 132 Plains L .10 .25
❑ 133 Plains L .10 .25
❑ 134 Plains L .10 .25
❑ 135 Plains L .10 .25
❑ 136 Plains L .10 .25
❑ 137 Island L .10 .25
❑ 138 Island L .10 .25
❑ 139 Island L .10 .25
❑ 140 Island L .10 .25
❑ 141 Island L .10 .25
❑ 142 Swamp L .10 .25
❑ 143 Swamp L .10 .25
❑ 144 Swamp L .10 .25
❑ 145 Swamp L .10 .25
❑ 146 Swamp L .10 .25
❑ 147 Mountain L .10 .25
❑ 148 Mountain L .10 .25
❑ 149 Mountain L .10 .25
❑ 150 Mountain L .10 .25
❑ 151 Forest L .10 .25
❑ 152 Forest L .10 .25
❑ 153 Forest L .10 .25
❑ 154 Forest L .10 .25
❑ 155 Forest L .10 .25
❑ 156 Forest L .10 .25

2012 Magic the Gathering Return to Ravnica

Complete Set 175.00 300.00
Booster Box (36 Packs) 80.00 120.00
Booster Pack (15 Cards) 3.00 4.00

❑ 1 Angel of Serenity M :W: 5.00 12.00
❑ 2 Armory Guard C :W: .10 .25
❑ 3 Arrest U :W: .20 .50
❑ 4 Avenging Arrow C :W: .10 .25
❑ 5 Azorius Arrester C :W: .10 .25
❑ 6 Azorius Justiciar U :W: .20 .50
❑ 7 Bazaar Krovod U :W: .20 .50
❑ 8 Concordia Pegasus C :W: .10 .25
❑ 9 Ethereal Armor C :W: .10 .25
❑ 10 Eyes in the Skies C :W: .10 .25
❑ 11 Fencing Ace U :W: .20 .50
❑ 12 Keening Apparition C :W: .10 .25
❑ 13 Knightly Valor C :W: .10 .25
❑ 14 Martial Law R :W: .40 1.00
❑ 15 Palisade Giant R :W: .40 1.00
❑ 16 Phantom General U :W: .20 .50
❑ 17 Precinct Captain R :W: .75 2.00
❑ 18 Rest in Peace R :W: 1.00 2.50
❑ 19 Rootborn Defenses C :W: .10 .25
❑ 20 Security Blockade U :W: .20 .50
❑ 21 Selesnya Sentry C :W: .10 .25
❑ 22 Seller of Songbirds C :W: .10 .25
❑ 23 Soul Tithe U :W: .20 .50
❑ 24 Sphere of Safety U :W: .20 .50
❑ 25 Sunspire Griffin C :W: .10 .25
❑ 26 Swift Justice C :W: .10 .25
❑ 27 Trained Caracal C :W: .10 .25
❑ 28 Trostani's Judgment C :W: .10 .25
❑ 29 Aquus Steed U :B: .20 .50
❑ 30 Blustersquall U :B: .20 .50
❑ 31 Cancel C :B: .10 .25
❑ 32 Chronic Flooding C :B: .10 .25
❑ 33 Conjured Currency R :B: .40 1.00
❑ 34 Crosstown Courier C :B: .10 .25
❑ 35 Cyclonic Rift R :B: 1.50 4.00
❑ 36 Dispel C :B: .10 .25
❑ 37 Doorkeeper C :B: .10 .25
❑ 38 Downsize C :B: .10 .25
❑ 39 Faerie Impostor U :B: .20 .50
❑ 40 Hover Barrier U :B: .20 .50
❑ 41 Inaction Injunction C :B: .10 .25
❑ 42 Inspiration C :B: .10 .25
❑ 43 Isperia's Skywatch C :B: .10 .25
❑ 44 Jace, Architect of Thought M :B: 6.00 15.00
❑ 45 Mizzium Skin C :B: .10 .25
❑ 46 Paralyzing Grasp C :B: .10 .25
❑ 47 Psychic Spiral U :B: .20 .50
❑ 48 Runewing C :B: .10 .25
❑ 49 Search the City R :B: .40 1.00
❑ 50 Skyline Predator U :B: .20 .50
❑ 51 Soulsworn Spirit U :B: .20 .50
❑ 52 Sphinx of the Chimes R :B: .40 1.00
❑ 53 Stealer of Secrets C :B: .10 .25
❑ 54 Syncopate U :B: .20 .50
❑ 55 Tower Drake C :B: .10 .25
❑ 56 Voidwielder C :B: .10 .25
❑ 57 Assassin's Strike U :K: .20 .50
❑ 58 Catacomb Slug C :K: .10 .25
❑ 59 Cremate C :K: .10 .25
❑ 60 Daggerdrome Imp C :K: .10 .25
❑ 61 Dark Revenant U :K: .20 .50
❑ 62 Dead Reveler C :K: .10 .25
❑ 63 Desecration Demon R :K: 1.25 3.00
❑ 64 Destroy the Evidence C :K: .10 .25
❑ 65 Deviant Glee C :K: .10 .25
❑ 66 Drainpipe Vermin C :K: .10 .25
❑ 67 Grave Betrayal R :K: .40 1.00
❑ 68 Grim Roustabout C :K: .10 .25
❑ 69 Launch Party C :K: .10 .25
❑ 70 Mind Rot C :K: .10 .25
❑ 71 Necropolis Regent M :K: .75 2.00
❑ 72 Ogre Jailbreaker C :K: .10 .25
❑ 73 Pack Rat R :K: .40 1.00
❑ 74 Perilous Shadow C :K: .10 .25
❑ 75 Sewer Shambler C :K: .10 .25
❑ 76 Shrieking Affliction U :K: .20 .50
❑ 77 Slum Reaper U :K: .20 .50
❑ 78 Stab Wound C :K: .10 .25
❑ 79 Tavern Swindler U :K: .20 .50
❑ 80 Terrus Wurm C :K: .10 .25
❑ 81 Thrill-Kill Assassin U :K: .20 .50
❑ 82 Ultimate Price U :K: .40 1.00
❑ 83 Underworld Connections R :K: .60 1.50
❑ 84 Zanikev Locust U :K: .20 .50
❑ 85 Annihilating Fire C :R: .10 .25
❑ 86 Ash Zealot R :R: 2.50 6.00
❑ 87 Batterhorn C :R: .10 .25
❑ 88 Bellows Lizard C :R: .10 .25
❑ 89 Bloodfray Giant U :R: .20 .50
❑ 90 Chaos Imps R :R: .40 1.00
❑ 91 Cobblebrute C :R: .10 .25
❑ 92 Dynacharge C :R: .10 .25
❑ 93 Electrickery C :R: .10 .25
❑ 94 Explosive Impact C :R: .10 .25
❑ 95 Goblin Rally U :R: .20 .50
❑ 96 Gore-House Chainwalker C :R: .10 .25
❑ 97 Guild Feud R :R: .40 1.00
❑ 98 Guttersnipe U :R: .50 1.25
❑ 99 Lobber Crew C :R: .10 .25
❑ 100 Minotaur Aggressor U :R: .20 .50
❑ 101 Mizzium Mortars R :R: 1.50 4.00
❑ 102 Pursuit of Flight C :R: .10 .25
❑ 103 Pyroconvergence U :R: .20 .50
❑ 104 Racecourse Fury U :R: .20 .50
❑ 105 Splatter Thug C :R: .10 .25
❑ 106 Street Spasm U :R: .20 .50
❑ 107 Survey the Wreckage C :R: .10 .25
❑ 108 Tenement Crasher C :R: .10 .25
❑ 109 Traitorous Instinct C :R: .10 .25
❑ 110 Utvara Hellkite M :R: 1.00 2.50
❑ 111 Vandalblast U :R: .20 .50
❑ 112 Viashino Racketeer C :R: .10 .25
❑ 113 Aerial Predation C :G: .10 .25
❑ 114 Archweaver U :G: .20 .50
❑ 115 Axebane Guardian C :G: .10 .25
❑ 116 Axebane Stag C :G: .10 .25
❑ 117 Brushstrider U :G: .20 .50
❑ 118 Centaur's Herald C :G: .10 .25
❑ 119 Chorus of Might C :G: .10 .25
❑ 120 Deadbridge Goliath R :G: .40 1.00
❑ 121 Death's Presence R :G: .40 1.00
❑ 122 Drudge Beetle C :G: .10 .25
❑ 123 Druid's Deliverance C :G: .10 .25
❑ 124 Gatecreeper Vine C :G: .10 .25
❑ 125 Giant Growth C :G: .10 .25
❑ 126 Gobbling Ooze U :G: .20 .50
❑ 127 Golgari Decoy U :G: .20 .50
❑ 128 Horncaller's Chant C :G: .10 .25
❑ 129 Korozda Monitor C :G: .10 .25
❑ 130 Mana Bloom R :G: .40 1.00
❑ 131 Oak Street Innkeeper U :G: .20 .50
❑ 132 Rubbleback Rhino C :G: .10 .25
❑ 133 Savage Surge U :G: .20 .50
❑ 134 Seek the Horizon U :G: .20 .50
❑ 135 Slime Molding U :G: .20 .50
❑ 136 Stonefare Crocodile C :G: .10 .25
❑ 137 Towering Indrik C :G: .10 .25
❑ 138 Urban Burgeoning C :G: .10 .25
❑ 139 Wild Beastmaster R :G: .40 1.00
❑ 140 Worldspine Wurm M :G: 1.00 2.50
❑ 141 Abrupt Decay R :K/G: 3.00 8.00
❑ 142 Archon of the Triumvirate R :W/B: .40 1.00
❑ 143 Armada Wurm M :W/G: 2.00 5.00
❑ 144 Auger Spree C :K/R: .10 .25
❑ 145 Azorius Charm U :W/B: .50 1.25
❑ 146 Call of the Conclave U :W/G: .40 1.00
❑ 147 Carnival Hellsteed R :K/R: .40 1.00
❑ 148 Centaur Healer C :W/G: .10 .25
❑ 149 Chemister's Trick C :B/R: .10 .25
❑ 150 Collective Blessing R :W/G: .40 1.00
❑ 151 Common Bond C :W/G: .10 .25
❑ 152 Corpsejack Menace R :K/G: .75 2.00
❑ 153 Counterflux R :B/R: .75 2.00
❑ 154 Coursers' Accord C :W/G: .10 .25
❑ 155 Detention Sphere R :W/B: 1.50 4.00
❑ 156 Dramatic Rescue C :W/B: .10 .25
❑ 157 Dreadbore R :K/R: 2.00 5.00
❑ 158 Dreg Mangler U :K/G: .40 1.00
❑ 159 Epic Experiment M :B/R: 1.25 3.00
❑ 160 Essence Backlash C :B/R: .10 .25
❑ 161 Fall of the Gavel U :W/B: .20 .50
❑ 162 Firemind's Foresight R :B/R: .40 1.00
❑ 163 Goblin Electromancer C :B/R: .10 .25
❑ 164 Golgari Charm U :K/G: .20 .50
❑ 165 Grisly Salvage C :K/G: .10 .25
❑ 166 Havoc Festival R :K/R: .40 1.00
❑ 167 Hellhole Flailer U :K/R: .20 .50
❑ 168 Heroes' Reunion U :W/G: .20 .50
❑ 169 Hussar Patrol C :W/B: .10 .25
❑ 170 Hypersonic Dragon R :B/R: .40 1.00
❑ 171 Isperia, Supreme Judge M :W/B: 1.25 3.00
❑ 172 Izzet Charm U :B/R: .40 1.00
❑ 173 Izzet Staticaster U :B/R: .20 .50
❑ 174 Jarad, Golgari Lich Lord M :K/G: .75 2.00
❑ 175 Jarad's Orders R :K/G: .40 1.00
❑ 176 Korozda Guildmage U :K/G: .20 .50
❑ 177 Lotleth Troll R :K/G: 1.50 4.00
❑ 178 Loxodon Smiter R :W/G: 2.00 5.00
❑ 179 Lyev Skyknight U :W/B: .20 .50
❑ 180 Mercurial Chemister R :B/R: .40 1.00
❑ 181 New Prahv Guildmage U :W/B: .20 .50
❑ 182 Nivix Guildmage U :B/R: .20 .50
❑ 183 Niv-Mizzet, Dracogenius M :B/R: 2.00 5.00
❑ 184 Rakdos Charm U :K/R: .20 .50
❑ 185 Rakdos Ragemutt U :K/R: .20 .50
❑ 186 Rakdos Ringleader U :K/R: .20 .50
❑ 187 Rakdos, Lord of Riots M :K/R: 2.00 5.00
❑ 188 Rakdos's Return M :K/R: 2.50 6.00
❑ 189 Righteous Authority R :W/B: .40 1.00
❑ 190 Risen Sanctuary U :W/G: .20 .50
❑ 191 Rites of Reaping U :K/G: .20 .50
❑ 192 Rix Maadi Guildmage U :K/R: .20 .50
❑ 193 Search Warrant C :W/B: .10 .25
❑ 194 Selesnya Charm U :W/G: .50 1.25
❑ 195 Skull Rend C :K/R: .10 .25
❑ 196 Skymark Roc U :W/B: .20 .50
❑ 197 Slaughter Games R :K/R: .75 2.00
❑ 198 Sluiceway Scorpion C :K/G: .10 .25
❑ 199 Spawn of Rix Maadi C :K/R: .10 .25
❑ 200 Sphinx's Revelation M :W/B: 10.00 25.00
❑ 201 Supreme Verdict R :W/B: 2.50 6.00
❑ 202 Teleportal U :B/R: .20 .50
❑ 203 Thoughtflare U :B/R: .20 .50
❑ 204 Treasured Find U :K/G: .20 .50
❑ 205 Trestle Troll C :K/G: .10 .25
❑ 206 Trostani, Selesnya's Voice M :W/G: 3.00 8.00
❑ 207 Vitu-Ghazi Guildmage U :W/G: .20 .50
❑ 208 Vraska the Unseen M :K/G: 4.00 10.00
❑ 209 Wayfaring Temple R :W/G: .60 1.50
❑ 210 Azor's Elocutors R :W/B: .40 1.00
❑ 211 Blistercoil Weird U :B/R: .20 .50
❑ 212 Cryptborn Horror R :K/R: .40 1.00
❑ 213 Deathrite Shaman R :K/G: 6.00 15.00
❑ 214 Dryad Militant U :W/G: .40 1.00
❑ 215 Frostburn Weird C :B/R: .10 .25
❑ 216 Golgari Longlegs C :K/G: .10 .25
❑ 217 Growing Ranks R :W/G: .75 2.00
❑ 218 Judge's Familiar U :W/B: .40 1.00
❑ 219 Nivmagus Elemental R :B/R: .60 1.50
❑ 220 Rakdos Cackler U :K/R: .40 1.00
❑ 221 Rakdos Shred-Freak C :K/R: .10 .25
❑ 222 Slitherhead U :K/G: .20 .50
❑ 223 Sundering Growth C :W/G: .10 .25
❑ 224 Vassal Soul C :W/B: .10 .25
❑ 225 Azorius Keyrune U .20 .50
❑ 226 Chromatic Lantern R 2.00 5.00
❑ 227 Civic Saber U .20 .50
❑ 228 Codex Shredder U .20 .50
❑ 229 Golgari Keyrune U .20 .50
❑ 230 Izzet Keyrune U .20 .50
❑ 231 Pithing Needle R .60 1.50
❑ 232 Rakdos Keyrune U .20 .50
❑ 233 Selesnya Keyrune U .20 .50
❑ 234 Street Sweeper U .20 .50
❑ 235 Tablet of the Guilds U .20 .50
❑ 236 Volatile Rig R .40 1.00
❑ 237 Azorius Guildgate C .10 .25
❑ 238 Blood Crypt R 6.00 15.00
❑ 239 Golgari Guildgate C .10 .25
❑ 240 Grove of the Guardian R .40 1.00
❑ 241 Hallowed Fountain R 5.00 12.00
❑ 242 Izzet Guildgate C .10 .25
❑ 243 Overgrown Tomb R 6.00 15.00
❑ 244 Rakdos Guildgate C .10 .25
❑ 245 Rogue's Passage U .20 .50
❑ 246 Selesnya Guildgate C .10 .25
❑ 247 Steam Vents R 4.00 10.00
❑ 248 Temple Garden R 6.00 15.00
❑ 249 Transguild Promenade C .10 .25
❑ 250 Plains L .10 .25
❑ 251 Plains L .10 .25
❑ 252 Plains L .10 .25
❑ 253 Plains L .10 .25
❑ 254 Plains L .10 .25
❑ 255 Island L .10 .25
❑ 256 Island L .10 .25
❑ 257 Island L .10 .25
❑ 258 Island L .10 .25
❑ 259 Island L .10 .25
❑ 260 Swamp L .10 .25
❑ 261 Swamp L .10 .25
❑ 262 Swamp L .10 .25
❑ 263 Swamp L .10 .25
❑ 264 Swamp L .10 .25
❑ 265 Mountain L .10 .25
❑ 266 Mountain L .10 .25
❑ 267 Mountain L .10 .25
❑ 268 Mountain L .10 .25
❑ 269 Mountain L .10 .25
❑ 270 Forest L .10 .25
❑ 271 Forest L .10 .25
❑ 272 Forest L .10 .25
❑ 273 Forest L .10 .25
❑ 274 Forest L .10 .25
❑ T1 Bird .20 .50
❑ T2 Knight .20 .50
❑ T3 Soldier .20 .50
❑ T4 Assassin .60 1.50
❑ T5 Dragon .60 1.50
❑ T6 Goblin .20 .50
❑ T7 Centaur .20 .50
❑ T8 Ooze .20 .50
❑ T9 Rhino .20 .50
❑ T10 Saproling .20 .50
❑ T11 Wurm .60 1.50
❑ T12 Elemental .40 1.00

2012 Magic the Gathering Return to Ravnica Foil

*Foil: .8X to 2X Basic Cards

2012 Magic the Gathering Venser vs Koth

Duel Deck 20.00 40.00

❑ 1 Venser, the Sojourner M :W/B: 4.00 10.00
❑ 2 Whitemane Lion C :W: .20 .50
❑ 3 Augury Owl C :B: .10 .25
❑ 4 Coral Fighters U :B: .20 .50
❑ 5 Minamo Sightbender U :B: .20 .50
❑ 6 Mistmeadow Witch U :W/B: .20 .50
❑ 7 Scroll Thief C :B: .10 .25
❑ 8 Neurok Invisimancer C :B: .10 .25
❑ 9 Slith Strider U :B: .20 .50
❑ 10 Sky Spirit U :W/B: .20 .50
❑ 11 Wall of Denial U :W/B: .60 1.50
❑ 12 Galepowder Mage R :W: .40 1.00
❑ 13 Kor Cartographer C :W: .10 .25
❑ 14 Clone R :B: .40 1.00
❑ 15 Cryptic Annelid U :B: .20 .50
❑ 16 Primal Plasma C :B: .10 .25
❑ 17 Sawtooth Loon U :W/B: .20 .50
❑ 18 Cache Raiders U :B: .20 .50
❑ 19 Windreaver R :W/B: .40 1.00
❑ 20 Jedit's Dragoons C :W: .10 .25
❑ 21 Sunblast Angel R :W: .40 1.00
❑ 22 Sphinx of Uthuun R :B: .40 1.00
❑ 23 Path to Exile U :W: 3.00 8.00
❑ 24 Preordain C :B: .60 1.50
❑ 25 Sigil of Sleep C :B: .20 .50
❑ 26 Revoke Existence C :W: .10 .25
❑ 27 Angelic Shield U :W/B: .20 .50
❑ 28 Oblivion Ring U :W: .60 1.50
❑ 29 Safe Passage C :W: .10 .25
❑ 30 Steel of the Godhead C :W/B: .30 .75
❑ 31 Vanish into Memory U :W/B: .20 .50
❑ 32 Overrule C :W/B: .20 .50
❑ 33 Azorius Chancery C .20 .50
❑ 34 Flood Plain U .30 .75
❑ 35 New Benalia U .20 .50
❑ 36 Sejiri Refuge U .30 .75
❑ 37 Soaring Seacliff C .10 .25
❑ 38 Plains L .10 .25
❑ 39 Plains L .10 .25
❑ 40 Plains L .10 .25
❑ 41 Island L .10 .25
❑ 42 Island L .10 .25
❑ 43 Island L .10 .25
❑ 44 Koth of the Hammer M :R: 4.00 10.00
❑ 45 Plated Geopede C :R: .30 .75
❑ 46 Pygmy Pyrosaur C :R: .10 .25
❑ 47 Pilgrim's Eye C .20 .50
❑ 48 AEther Membrane U :R: .20 .50
❑ 49 Fiery Hellhound C :R: .10 .25
❑ 50 Vulshok Sorcerer C :R: .10 .25
❑ 51 Anger U :R: .60 1.50
❑ 52 Cosi's Ravager C :R: .10 .25
❑ 53 Vulshok Berserker C :R: .10 .25
❑ 54 Bloodfire Kavu U :R: .20 .50
❑ 55 Stone Giant U :R: .20 .50
❑ 56 Geyser Glider U :R: .20 .50
❑ 57 Lithophage R :R: .40 1.00
❑ 58 Torchling R :R: .40 1.00
❑ 59 Chartooth Cougar C :R: .30 .75
❑ 60 Earth Servant U :R: .20 .50
❑ 61 Greater Stone Spirit U :R: .20 .50
❑ 62 Bloodfire Colossus R :R: .40 1.00
❑ 63 Wayfarer's Bauble C .20 .50
❑ 64 Armillary Sphere C .10 .25
❑ 65 Journeyer's Kite R .75 2.00
❑ 66 Vulshok Morningstar U .20 .50
❑ 67 Searing Blaze C :R: .10 .25
❑ 68 Vulshok Battlegear U .20 .50
❑ 69 Downhill Charge C :R: .10 .25
❑ 70 Seismic Strike C :R: .10 .25
❑ 71 Spire Barrage C :R: .10 .25
❑ 72 Jaws of Stone U :R: .20 .50
❑ 73 Volley of Boulders R :R: .40 1.00
❑ 74 Mountain L .10 .25
❑ 75 Mountain L .10 .25
❑ 76 Mountain L .10 .25
❑ 77 Mountain L .10 .25

2012 Magic the Gathering Venser vs Koth Foil

*Foil: .8X to 2X Basic Cards

2013 Magic the Gathering Magic 2014

Complete Set 200.00 300.00

❑ 1 Ajani, Caller of the Pride M :W: 3.00 8.00
❑ 2 Ajani's Chosen R :W: .30 .75
❑ 3 Angelic Accord U :W: .20 .50
❑ 5 Archangel of Thune M :W: 12.00 30.00
❑ 7 Banisher Priest U :W: .30 .75
❑ 8 Blessing U :W: .15 .40
❑ 9 Bonescythe Sliver R :W: 1.25 3.00
❑ 10 Brave the Elements U :W: .20 .50
❑ 14 Congregate U :W: .15 .40
❑ 16 Devout Invocation M :W: 1.00 2.50
❑ 18 Fiendslayer Paladin R :W: 3.00 8.00
❑ 21 Hive Stirrings C :W: .20 .50
❑ 22 Imposing Sovereign R :W: 1.50 4.00
❑ 23 Indestructibility R :W: .30 .75
❑ 26 Path of Bravery R :W: .60 1.50
❑ 29 Planar Cleansing R :W: .30 .75
❑ 31 Seraph of the Sword R :W: .60 1.50
❑ 32 Serra Angel U :W: .15 .40
❑ 35 Silence R :W: .40 1.00
❑ 38 Steelform Sliver U :W: .20 .50
❑ 39 Stonehorn Chanter U :W: .15 .40
❑ 41 Wall of Swords U :W: .15 .40
❑ 42 Air Servant U :B: .15 .40
❑ 47 Clone R :B: .30 .75
❑ 48 Colossal Whale R :B: .30 .75
❑ 50 Dismiss into Dream R :B: .30 .75
❑ 53 Domestication R :B: .30 .75
❑ 54 Elite Arcanist R :B: .40 1.00
❑ 57 Galerider Sliver R :B: 1.50 4.00
❑ 58 Glimpse the Future U :B: .15 .40
❑ 59 Illusionary Armor U :B: .15 .40
❑ 60 Jace, Memory Adept M :B: 3.00 8.00
❑ 61 Jace's Mindseeker R :B: .30 .75
❑ 66 Opportunity U :B: .15 .40
❑ 67 Phantom Warrior U :B: .15 .40
❑ 68 Quicken R :B: .40 1.00
❑ 72 Spell Blast U :B: .15 .40
❑ 73 Tidebinder Mage R :B: .60 1.50
❑ 77 Traumatize R :B: .40 1.00
❑ 78 Wall of Frost U :B: .15 .40
❑ 79 Warden of Evos Isle U :B: .15 .40
❑ 80 Water Servant U :B: .15 .40
❑ 81 Windreader Sphinx M :B: .75 2.00
❑ 85 Artificer's Hex U :K: .15 .40
❑ 86 Blightcaster U :K: .15 .40
❑ 88 Bogbrew Witch R :K: .30 .75
❑ 91 Corrupt U :K: .15 .40

❑ 93 Dark Prophecy R :K: .40 1.00
❑ 95 Diabolic Tutor U :K: .15 .40
❑ 96 Doom Blade U :K: .15 .40
❑ 99 Gnawing Zombie U :K: .15 .40
❑ 100 Grim Return R :K: .60 1.50
❑ 101 Lifebane Zombie R :K: 3.00 8.00
❑ 102 Liliana of the Dark Realms M :K: 2.50 6.00
❑ 103 Liliana's Reaver R :K: .60 1.50
❑ 108 Nightmare R :K: .30 .75
❑ 111 Rise of the Dark Realms M :K: 1.25 3.00
❑ 112 Sanguine Bond R :K: .75 2.00
❑ 113 Sengir Vampire U :K: .15 .40
❑ 114 Shadowborn Apostle C :K: .40 1.00
❑ 115 Shadowborn Demon M :K: 3.00 8.00
❑ 117 Syphon Sliver R :K: .60 1.50
❑ 118 Tenacious Dead U :K: .15 .40
❑ 120 Vampire Warlord U :K: .15 .40
❑ 123 Xathrid Necromancer R :K: 3.00 8.00
❑ 126 Awaken the Ancient R :R: .30 .75
❑ 127 Barrage of Expendables U :R: .15 .40
❑ 128 Battle Sliver U :R: .20 .50
❑ 130 Burning Earth R :R: 1.25 3.00
❑ 132 Chandra, Pyromaster M :R: 6.00 15.00
❑ 134 Chandra's Phoenix R :R: .60 1.50
❑ 137 Dragon Egg U :R: .15 .40
❑ 139 Flames of the Firebrand U :R: .15 .40
❑ 140 Fleshpulper Giant U :R: .15 .40
❑ 141 Goblin Diplomats R :R: .40 1.00
❑ 146 Mindsparker R :R: .75 2.00
❑ 147 Molten Birth U :R: .15 .40
❑ 148 Ogre Battledriver R :R: 1.25 3.00
❑ 151 Scourge of Valkas M :R: 2.50 6.00
❑ 153 Shiv's Embrace U :R: .15 .40
❑ 154 Shivan Dragon R :R: .30 .75
❑ 158 Thorncaster Sliver R :R: .60 1.50
❑ 160 Volcanic Geyser U :R: .15 .40
❑ 162 Wild Ricochet R :R: .30 .75
❑ 163 Young Pyromancer U :R: .75 2.00
❑ 165 Bramblecrush U :G: .15 .40
❑ 166 Briarpatch Alpha U :G: .15 .40
❑ 169 Elvish Mystic C :G: .20 .50
❑ 170 Enlarge U :G: .15 .40
❑ 172 Garruk, Caller of Beasts M :G: 8.00 20.00
❑ 173 Garruk's Horde R :G: .30 .75
❑ 178 Howl of the Night Pack U :G: .15 .40
❑ 180 Into the Wilds R :G: .40 1.00
❑ 181 Kalonian Hydra M :G: 12.00 30.00
❑ 182 Kalonian Tusker U :G: .20 .50
❑ 184 Manaweft Sliver U :G: .60 1.50
❑ 185 Megantic Sliver R :G: .60 1.50
❑ 187 Oath of the Ancient Wood R :G: .30 .75
❑ 189 Predatory Sliver C :G: .40 1.00
❑ 190 Primeval Bounty M :G: 3.00 8.00
❑ 194 Savage Summoning R :G: 1.00 2.50
❑ 195 Scavenging Ooze R :G: 6.00 15.00
❑ 198 Vastwood Hydra R :G: .40 1.00
❑ 200 Voracious Wurm U :G: .20 .50
❑ 201 Windstorm U :G: .15 .40
❑ 202 Witchstalker R :G: 2.00 5.00
❑ 203 Woodborn Behemoth U :G: .15 .40
❑ 204 Accorder's Shield U .15 .40
❑ 205 Bubbling Cauldron U .15 .40
❑ 206 Darksteel Forge M 1.50 4.00
❑ 207 Darksteel Ingot U .15 .40
❑ 208 Door of Destinies R 1.25 3.00
❑ 209 Elixir of Immortality U .15 .40
❑ 210 Fireshrieker U .15 .40
❑ 211 Guardian of the Ages R .30 .75
❑ 212 Haunted Plate Mail R .40 1.00
❑ 213 Millstone U .15 .40
❑ 214 Pyromancer's Gauntlet R .30 .75
❑ 215 Ratchet Bomb R .60 1.50
❑ 216 Ring of Three Wishes M 1.00 2.50
❑ 217 Rod of Ruin U .15 .40
❑ 219 Staff of the Death Magus U .15 .40
❑ 220 Staff of the Flame Magus U .15 .40
❑ 221 Staff of the Mind Magus U .15 .40
❑ 222 Staff of the Sun Magus U .15 .40
❑ 223 Staff of the Wild Magus U .15 .40
❑ 224 Strionic Resonator R .75 2.00
❑ 225 Trading Post R .30 .75
❑ 226 Vial of Poison U .15 .40
❑ 227 Encroaching Wastes U .20 .50
❑ 228 Mutavault R 8.00 20.00
❑ 229 Shimmering Grotto U .15 .40
❑ T4 Goat .20 .50
❑ T12 Emblem: Liliana of the Dark Realms .40 1.00
❑ T13 Emblem: Garruk, Caller of Beasts .75 2.00

2013 Magic the Gathering Magic 2014 Foil

*Foil: .8X to 2X Basic Cards

2013 Magic the Gathering Dragon's Maze

Complete Set 175.00 250.00

❑ 1 Boros Mastiff C :W: .10 .25
❑ 2 Haazda Snare Squad C :W: .10 .25
❑ 3 Lyev Decree C :W: .10 .25
❑ 4 Maze Sentinel C :W: .10 .25
❑ 5 Renounce the Guilds R :W: .50 1.25
❑ 6 Riot Control C :W: .10 .25
❑ 7 Scion of Vitu-Ghazi R :W: .40 1.00
❑ 8 Steeple Roc C :W: .10 .25
❑ 9 Sunspire Gatekeepers C :W: .10 .25
❑ 10 Wake the Reflections C :W: .10 .25
❑ 11 AEtherling R :B: 1.50 4.00
❑ 12 Hidden Strings C :B: .10 .25
❑ 13 Maze Glider C :B: .10 .25
❑ 14 Mindstatic C :B: .10 .25
❑ 15 Murmuring Phantasm C :B: .10 .25
❑ 16 Opal Lake Gatekeepers C :B: .10 .25
❑ 17 Runner's Bane C :B: .10 .25
❑ 18 Trait Doctoring R :B: .30 .75
❑ 19 Uncovered Clues C :B: .10 .25
❑ 20 Wind Drake C :B: .10 .25
❑ 21 Bane Alley Blackguard C :K: .10 .25
❑ 22 Blood Scrivener R :K: 1.50 4.00
❑ 23 Crypt Incursion C :K: .10 .25
❑ 24 Fatal Fumes C :K: .10 .25
❑ 25 Hired Torturer C :K: .10 .25
❑ 26 Maze Abomination C :K: .10 .25
❑ 27 Pontiff of Blight R :K: .30 .75
❑ 28 Rakdos Drake C :K: .10 .25
❑ 29 Sinister Possession C :K: .10 .25
❑ 30 Ubul Sar Gatekeepers C :K: .10 .25
❑ 31 Awe for the Guilds C :R: .10 .25
❑ 32 Clear a Path C :R: .10 .25
❑ 33 Maze Rusher C :R: .10 .25
❑ 34 Possibility Storm R :R: .30 .75
❑ 35 Punish the Enemy C :R: .10 .25
❑ 36 Pyrewild Shaman R :R: .50 1.25
❑ 37 Riot Piker C :R: .10 .25
❑ 38 Rubblebelt Maaka C :R: .10 .25
❑ 39 Smelt-Ward Gatekeepers C :R: .10 .25
❑ 40 Weapon Surge C :R: .10 .25
❑ 41 Battering Krasis C :G: .10 .25
❑ 42 Kraul Warrior C :G: .10 .25
❑ 43 Maze Behemoth C :G: .10 .25
❑ 44 Mending Touch C :G: .10 .25
❑ 45 Mutant's Prey C :G: .10 .25
❑ 46 Phytoburst C :G: .10 .25
❑ 47 Renegade Krasis R :G: .30 .75
❑ 48 Saruli Gatekeepers C :G: .10 .25
❑ 49 Skylasher R :G: .75 2.00
❑ 50 Thrashing Mossdog C :G: .10 .25
❑ 51 Advent of the Wurm R :W/G: 3.00 8.00
❑ 52 Armored Wolf-Rider C :W/G: .10 .25
❑ 53 Ascended Lawmage U :W/B: .15 .40
❑ 54 Beetleform Mage C :B/G: .10 .25
❑ 55 Blast of Genius U :B/R: .15 .40
❑ 56 Blaze Commando U :W/R: .15 .40
❑ 57 Blood Baron of Vizkopa M :W/K: 4.00 10.00
❑ 58 Boros Battleshaper R :W/R: .30 .75
❑ 59 Bred for the Hunt U :B/G: .15 .40
❑ 60 Bronzebeak Moa U :W/G: .15 .40
❑ 61 Carnage Gladiator U :K/R: .15 .40
❑ 62 Council of the Absolute M :W/B: 1.50 4.00
❑ 63 Deadbridge Chant M :K/G: 3.00 8.00
❑ 64 Debt to the Deathless U :W/K: .15 .40
❑ 65 Deputy of Acquittals C :W/B: .10 .25
❑ 66 Dragonshift R :B/R: .30 .75
❑ 67 Drown in Filth C :K/G: .10 .25
❑ 68 Emmara Tandris R :W/G: .30 .75
❑ 69 Exava, Rakdos Blood Witch R :K/R: .60 1.50
❑ 70 Feral Animist U :R/G: .15 .40
❑ 71 Fluxcharger U :B/R: .15 .40
❑ 72 Gaze of Granite R :K/G: .75 2.00
❑ 73 Gleam of Battle U :W/R: .15 .40
❑ 74 Goblin Test Pilot U :B/R: .15 .40
❑ 75 Gruul War Chant U :R/G: .15 .40
❑ 76 Haunter of Nightveil U :B/K: .15 .40
❑ 77 Jelenn Sphinx U :W/B: .15 .40
❑ 78 Korozda Gorgon U :K/G: .15 .40
❑ 79 Krasis Incubation U :B/G: .15 .40
❑ 80 Lavinia of the Tenth R :W/B: .40 1.00
❑ 81 Legion's Initiative M :W/R: 3.00 8.00
❑ 82 Master of Cruelties M :K/R: 3.00 8.00
❑ 83 Maw of the Obzedat U :W/K: .15 .40
❑ 84 Melek, Izzet Paragon R :B/R: .30 .75
❑ 85 Mirko Vosk, Mind Drinker R :B/K: .50 1.25
❑ 86 Morgue Burst C :K/R: .10 .25
❑ 87 Nivix Cyclops C :B/R: .10 .25
❑ 88 Notion Thief R :B/K: 1.00 2.50
❑ 89 Obzedat's Aid R :W/K: .60 1.50
❑ 90 Pilfered Plans C :B/K: .10 .25
❑ 91 Plasm Capture R :B/G: 1.25 3.00
❑ 92 Progenitor Mimic M :B/G: 2.00 5.00
❑ 93 Putrefy U :K/G: .30 .75
❑ 94 Ral Zarek M :B/R: 8.00 20.00
❑ 95 Reap Intellect M :B/K: .60 1.50
❑ 96 Render Silent R :W/B: 1.00 2.50
❑ 97 Restore the Peace U :W/B: .15 .40
❑ 98 Rot Farm Skeleton U :K/G: .15 .40
❑ 99 Ruric Thar, the Unbowed R :R/G: .60 1.50
❑ 100 Savageborn Hydra M :R/G: 2.00 5.00
❑ 101 Scab-Clan Giant U :R/G: .15 .40
❑ 102 Showstopper U :K/R: .15 .40
❑ 103 Sin Collector U :W/K: .30 .75
❑ 104 Sire of Insanity R :K/R: 1.50 4.00
❑ 105 Species Gorger U :B/G: .15 .40
❑ 106 Spike Jester U :K/R: .15 .40
❑ 107 Tajic, Blade of the Legion R :W/R: 1.00 2.50
❑ 108 Teysa, Envoy of Ghosts R :W/K: .50 1.25
❑ 109 Tithe Drinker C :W/K: .10 .25
❑ 110 Trostani's Summoner U :W/G: .15 .40
❑ 111 Unflinching Courage U :W/G: .30 .75
❑ 112 Varolz, the Scar-Striped R :K/G: 1.50 4.00
❑ 113 Viashino Firstblade C :W/R: .10 .25
❑ 114 Voice of Resurgence M :W/G: 20.00 40.00
❑ 115 Vorel of the Hull Clade R :B/G: .60 1.50
❑ 116 Warleader's Helix U :W/R: .30 .75
❑ 117 Warped Physique U :B/K: .15 .40
❑ 118 Woodlot Crawler U :B/K: .15 .40
❑ 119 Zhur-Taa Ancient R :R/G: .30 .75
❑ 120 Zhur-Taa Druid C :R/G: .10 .25
❑ 121 Alive/Well U :G/W: .15 .40
❑ 122 Armed/Dangerous U :R/G: .15 .40
❑ 123 Beck/Call R :B/G/W: 1.00 2.50
❑ 124 Breaking/Entering R :B/K: .50 1.25
❑ 125 Catch/Release R :B/R/W: .30 .75
❑ 126 Down/Dirty U :K/G: .15 .40
❑ 127 Far/Away U :B/K: .30 .75
❑ 128 Flesh/Blood R :K/G/R: .30 .75
❑ 129 Give/Take U :G/B: .15 .40
❑ 130 Profit/Loss U :W/K: .15 .40
❑ 131 Protect/Serve U :W/B: .15 .40
❑ 132 Ready/Willing R :W/G/K: .60 1.50
❑ 133 Toil/Trouble U :K/R: .15 .40
❑ 134 Turn/Burn U :B/R: .30 .75
❑ 135 Wear/Tear U :R/W: .15 .40
❑ 136 Azorius Cluestone C .10 .25
❑ 137 Boros Cluestone C .10 .25
❑ 138 Dimir Cluestone C .10 .25
❑ 139 Golgari Cluestone C .10 .25
❑ 140 Gruul Cluestone C .10 .25
❑ 141 Izzet Cluestone C .10 .25
❑ 142 Orzhov Cluestone C .10 .25
❑ 143 Rakdos Cluestone C .10 .25
❑ 144 Selesnya Cluestone C .10 .25
❑ 145 Simic Cluestone C .10 .25
❑ 146 Azorius Guildgate C .10 .25
❑ 147 Boros Guildgate C .10 .25
❑ 148 Dimir Guildgate C .10 .25
❑ 149 Golgari Guildgate C .10 .25
❑ 150 Gruul Guildgate C .10 .25
❑ 151 Izzet Guildgate C .10 .25
❑ 152 Maze's End M 1.25 3.00
❑ 153 Orzhov Guildgate C .10 .25
❑ 154 Rakdos Guildgate C .10 .25
❑ 155 Selesnya Guildgate C .10 .25
❑ 156 Simic Guildgate C .10 .25
❑ T1 Bird .10 .25
❑ T2 Elemental .10 .25

2013 Magic the Gathering Dragon's Maze Foil

*Foil: .8X to 2X Basic Cards

2013 Magic the Gathering Gatecrash

Complete Set 175.00 300.00

❑ 1 Aerial Maneuver C :W: .10 .25
❑ 2 Angelic Edict C :W: .20 .50
❑ 3 Angelic Skirmisher R :W: .60 1.50
❑ 4 Assault Griffin C :W: .10 .25
❑ 5 Basilica Guards C :W: .10 .25
❑ 6 Blind Obedience R :W: 2.50 6.00
❑ 7 Boros Elite U :W: .20 .50
❑ 8 Court Street Denizen C :W: .10 .25
❑ 9 Daring Skyjek C :W: .10 .25
❑ 10 Debtor's Pulpit U :W: .20 .50
❑ 11 Dutiful Thrull C :W: .10 .25
❑ 12 Frontline Medic R :W: 3.00 8.00
❑ 13 Gideon, Champion of Justice M :W: 4.00 10.00
❑ 14 Guardian of the Gateless U :W: .20 .50
❑ 15 Guildscorn Ward C :W: .10 .25
❑ 16 Hold the Gates U :W: .20 .50
❑ 17 Holy Mantle U :W: .20 .50
❑ 18 Knight of Obligation U :W: .20 .50
❑ 19 Knight Watch C :W: .10 .25
❑ 20 Luminate Primordial R :W: .40 1.00
❑ 21 Murder Investigation U :W: .20 .50
❑ 22 Nav Squad Commandos C :W: .10 .25
❑ 23 Righteous Charge U :W: .20 .50
❑ 24 Shielded Passage C :W: .10 .25
❑ 25 Smite C :W: .10 .25
❑ 26 Syndic of Tithes C :W: .10 .25
❑ 27 Urbis Protector U :W: .20 .50
❑ 28 Zarichi Tiger C :W: .10 .25
❑ 29 AEtherize U :B: .20 .50
❑ 30 Agoraphobia U :B: .20 .50
❑ 31 Clinging Anemones C :B: .10 .25
❑ 32 Cloudfin Raptor C :B: .10 .25
❑ 33 Diluvian Primordial R :B: .40 1.00
❑ 34 Enter the Infinite M :B: 1.25 3.00
❑ 35 Frilled Oculus C :B: .20 .50
❑ 36 Gridlock U :B: .20 .50
❑ 37 Hands of Binding C :B: .10 .25
❑ 38 Incursion Specialist U :B: .20 .50
❑ 39 Keymaster Rogue C :B: .10 .25
❑ 40 Last Thoughts C :B: .10 .25
❑ 41 Leyline Phantom C :B: .10 .25
❑ 42 Metropolis Sprite C :B: .10 .25
❑ 43 Mindeye Drake U :B: .20 .50
❑ 44 Rapid Hybridization U :B: .20 .50
❑ 45 Realmwright R :B: .75 2.00
❑ 46 Sage's Row Denizen C :B: .10 .25
❑ 47 Sapphire Drake U :B: .20 .50
❑ 48 Scatter Arc C :B: .10 .25
❑ 49 Simic Fluxmage U :B: .20 .50
❑ 50 Simic Manipulator R :B: .60 1.50
❑ 51 Skygames C :B: .10 .25
❑ 52 Spell Rupture C :B: .10 .25
❑ 53 Stolen Identity R :B: .40 1.00
❑ 54 Totally Lost C :B: .10 .25
❑ 55 Voidwalk U :B: .20 .50
❑ 56 Way of the Thief C :B: .10 .25
❑ 57 Balustrade Spy C :K: .10 .25
❑ 58 Basilica Screecher C :K: .10 .25
❑ 59 Contaminated Ground C :K: .10 .25
❑ 60 Corpse Blockade C :K: .10 .25
❑ 61 Crypt Ghast R :K: 1.25 3.00
❑ 62 Death's Approach C :K: .10 .25
❑ 63 Devour Flesh C :K: .10 .25
❑ 64 Dying Wish U :K: .20 .50
❑ 65 Gateway Shade U :K: .20 .50
❑ 66 Grisly Spectacle C :K: .10 .25
❑ 67 Gutter Skulk C :K: .10 .25
❑ 68 Horror of the Dim C :K: .10 .25
❑ 69 Illness in the Ranks U :K: .20 .50
❑ 70 Killing Glare U :K: .20 .50
❑ 71 Lord of the Void M :K: 1.25 3.00
❑ 72 Mental Vapors U :K: .20 .50
❑ 73 Midnight Recovery C :K: .20 .50
❑ 74 Ogre Slumlord R :K: .40 1.00
❑ 75 Sepulchral Primordial R :K: .40 1.00
❑ 76 Shadow Alley Denizen C :K: .10 .25
❑ 77 Shadow Slice C :K: .10 .25
❑ 78 Slate Street Ruffian C :K: .10 .25
❑ 79 Smog Elemental U :K: .20 .50
❑ 80 Syndicate Enforcer C :K: .10 .25
❑ 81 Thrull Parasite U :K: .20 .50
❑ 82 Undercity Informer U :K: .20 .50
❑ 83 Undercity Plague R :K: .40 1.00
❑ 84 Wight of Precinct Six U :K: .20 .50
❑ 85 Act of Treason C :R: .10 .25
❑ 86 Bomber Corps C :R: .10 .25
❑ 87 Cinder Elemental U :R: .20 .50
❑ 88 Crackling Perimeter U :R: .20 .50
❑ 89 Ember Beast C :R: .10 .25
❑ 90 Firefist Striker U :R: .20 .50
❑ 91 Five-Alarm Fire R :R: .40 1.00
❑ 92 Foundry Street Denizen C :R: .10 .25
❑ 93 Furious Resistance C :R: .10 .25
❑ 94 Hellkite Tyrant M :R: 1.00 2.50
❑ 95 Hellraiser Goblin U :R: .20 .50
❑ 96 Homing Lightning U :R: .20 .50
❑ 97 Legion Loyalist R :R: 2.50 6.00
❑ 98 Madcap Skills C :R: .10 .25
❑ 99 Mark for Death U :R: .20 .50
❑ 100 Massive Raid C :R: .10 .25
❑ 101 Molten Primordial R :R: .40 1.00
❑ 102 Mugging C :R: .10 .25
❑ 103 Ripscale Predator U :R: .20 .50
❑ 104 Scorchwalker C :R: .10 .25
❑ 105 Skinbrand Goblin C :R: .10 .25
❑ 106 Skullcrack U :R: .75 2.00
❑ 107 Structural Collapse C :R: .10 .25
❑ 108 Tin Street Market C :R: .10 .25
❑ 109 Towering Thunderfist C :R: .10 .25
❑ 110 Viashino Shanktail U :R: .20 .50
❑ 111 Warmind Infantry C :R: .10 .25
❑ 112 Wrecking Ogre R :R: .40 1.00
❑ 113 Adaptive Snapjaw C :G: .10 .25
❑ 114 Alpha Authority U :G: .20 .50
❑ 115 Burst of Strength C :G: .10 .25
❑ 116 Crocanura C :G: .10 .25
❑ 117 Crowned Ceratok U :G: .20 .50
❑ 118 Disciple of the Old Ways C :G: .10 .25
❑ 119 Experiment One U :G: .30 .75
❑ 120 Forced Adaptation C :G: .10 .25
❑ 121 Giant Adephage M :G: 1.25 3.00
❑ 122 Greenside Watcher C :G: .10 .25
❑ 123 Gyre Sage R :G: 1.00 2.50
❑ 124 Hindervines U :G: .20 .50
❑ 125 Ivy Lane Denizen C :G: .10 .25
❑ 126 Miming Slime U :G: .20 .50
❑ 127 Naturalize C :G: .10 .25
❑ 128 Ooze Flux R :G: .40 1.00
❑ 129 Predator's Rapport C :G: .10 .25
❑ 130 Rust Scarab U :G: .20 .50
❑ 131 Scab-Clan Charger C :G: .10 .25
❑ 132 Serene Remembrance U :G: .20 .50
❑ 133 Skarrg Goliath R :G: .40 1.00
❑ 134 Slaughterhorn C :G: .10 .25
❑ 135 Spire Tracer C :G: .10 .25
❑ 136 Sylvan Primordial R :G: .75 2.00
❑ 137 Tower Defense U :G: .20 .50
❑ 138 Verdant Haven C :G: .10 .25
❑ 139 Wasteland Viper U :G: .20 .50
❑ 140 Wildwood Rebirth C :G: .10 .25
❑ 141 Alms Beast R :W/K: .40 1.00
❑ 142 Assemble the Legion R :W/R: .75 2.00
❑ 143 Aurelia, the Warleader M :W/R: 4.00 10.00
❑ 144 Aurelia's Fury M :W/R: 2.50 6.00
❑ 145 Bane Alley Broker U :B/K: .20 .50
❑ 146 Biovisionary R :B/G: .40 1.00
❑ 147 Borborygmos Enraged M :R/G: 1.50 4.00
❑ 148 Boros Charm U :W/R: 1.50 4.00
❑ 149 Call of the Nightwing U :B/K: .20 .50
❑ 150 Cartel Aristocrat U :W/K: .20 .50
❑ 151 Clan Defiance R :R/G: 1.25 3.00
❑ 152 Consuming Aberration R :B/K: .75 2.00
❑ 153 Deathpact Angel M :W/K: 2.00 5.00
❑ 154 Dimir Charm U :B/K: .30 .75
❑ 155 Dinrova Horror U :B/K: .20 .50
❑ 156 Domri Rade M :R/G: 8.00 20.00
❑ 157 Drakewing Krasis C :B/G: .10 .25
❑ 158 Duskmantle Guildmage U :B/K: .20 .50
❑ 159 Duskmantle Seer M :B/K: 3.00 8.00
❑ 160 Elusive Krasis U :B/G: .20 .50
❑ 161 Executioner's Swing C :W/K: .10 .25
❑ 162 Fathom Mage R :B/G: .60 1.50
❑ 163 Firemane Avenger R :W/R: 1.25 3.00
❑ 164 Fortress Cyclops U :W/R: .20 .50
❑ 165 Foundry Champion R :W/R: .40 1.00
❑ 166 Frenzied Tilling U :R/G: .20 .50
❑ 167 Ghor-Clan Rampager U :R/G: .30 .75
❑ 168 Ground Assault U :R/G: .20 .50
❑ 169 Gruul Charm U :R/G: .20 .50
❑ 170 Gruul Ragebeast R :R/G: .40 1.00
❑ 171 High Priest of Penance R :W/K: 1.25 3.00
❑ 172 Hydroform C :B/G: .10 .25
❑ 173 Kingpin's Pet C :W/K: .10 .25
❑ 174 Lazav, Dimir Mastermind M :B/K: 3.00 8.00
❑ 175 Martial Glory C :W/R: .10 .25
❑ 176 Master Biomancer M :B/G: 4.00 10.00
❑ 177 Merciless Eviction R :W/K: .75 2.00
❑ 178 Mind Grind R :B/K: 1.25 3.00
❑ 179 Mortus Strider C :B/K: .10 .25
❑ 180 Mystic Genesis R :B/G: .40 1.00
❑ 181 Nimbus Swimmer U :B/G: .20 .50
❑ 182 Obzedat, Ghost Council M :W/K: 5.00 12.00
❑ 183 One Thousand Lashes U :W/K: .20 .50
❑ 184 Ordruun Veteran U :W/R: .20 .50
❑ 185 Orzhov Charm U :W/K: .40 1.00
❑ 186 Paranoid Delusions C :B/K: .10 .25
❑ 187 Primal Visitation C :R/G: .10 .25
❑ 188 Prime Speaker Zegana M :B/G: 5.00 12.00
❑ 189 Psychic Strike C :B/K: .10 .25
❑ 190 Purge the Profane C :W/K: .10 .25
❑ 191 Rubblehulk R :R/G: .40 1.00
❑ 192 Ruination Wurm C :R/G: .10 .25
❑ 193 Shambleshark C :B/G: .10 .25
❑ 194 Signal the Clans R :R/G: .60 1.50
❑ 195 Simic Charm U :B/G: .40 1.00
❑ 196 Skarrg Guildmage U :R/G: .20 .50
❑ 197 Skyknight Legionnaire C :W/R: .10 .25
❑ 198 Soul Ransom R :B/K: .60 1.50
❑ 199 Spark Trooper R :W/R: 1.25 3.00
❑ 200 Sunhome Guildmage U :W/R: .20 .50
❑ 201 Treasury Thrull R :W/K: .40 1.00
❑ 202 Truefire Paladin U :W/R: .20 .50
❑ 203 Unexpected Results R :B/G: .75 2.00
❑ 204 Urban Evolution U :B/G: .20 .50
❑ 205 Vizkopa Confessor U :W/K: .20 .50
❑ 206 Vizkopa Guildmage U :W/K: .20 .50
❑ 207 Whispering Madness R :B/K: .60 1.50
❑ 208 Wojek Halberdiers C :W/R: .10 .25
❑ 209 Zameck Guildmage U :B/G: .20 .50
❑ 210 Zhur-Taa Swine C :R/G: .10 .25
❑ 211 Arrows of Justice U :W/R: .20 .50
❑ 212 Beckon Apparition C :W/K: .10 .25
❑ 213 Biomass Mutation R :B/G: .40 1.00
❑ 214 Bioshift C :B/G: .10 .25
❑ 215 Boros Reckoner R :W/R: 8.00 20.00
❑ 216 Burning-Tree Emissary U :R/G: .60 1.50
❑ 217 Coerced Confession U :B/K: .20 .50
❑ 218 Deathcult Rogue C :B/K: .10 .25
❑ 219 Gift of Orzhova U :W/K: .20 .50
❑ 220 Immortal Servitude R :W/K: .75 2.00
❑ 221 Merfolk of the Depths U :B/G: .20 .50
❑ 222 Nightveil Specter R :B/K: .75 2.00
❑ 223 Pit Fight C :R/G: .10 .25
❑ 224 Rubblebelt Raiders R :R/G: .75 2.00
❑ 225 Shattering Blow C :W/R: .10 .25
❑ 226 Armored Transport C .10 .25
❑ 227 Boros Keyrune U .20 .50
❑ 228 Dimir Keyrune U .20 .50
❑ 229 Glaring Spotlight R .75 2.00
❑ 230 Gruul Keyrune U .20 .50
❑ 231 Illusionist's Bracers R .75 2.00
❑ 232 Millennial Gargoyle C .10 .25
❑ 233 Orzhov Keyrune U .20 .50
❑ 234 Prophetic Prism C .10 .25
❑ 235 Razortip Whip C .10 .25
❑ 236 Riot Gear C .10 .25
❑ 237 Simic Keyrune U .20 .50
❑ 238 Skyblinder Staff C .10 .25
❑ 239 Boros Guildgate C .20 .50
❑ 240 Breeding Pool R 6.00 15.00
❑ 241 Dimir Guildgate C .10 .25
❑ 242 Godless Shrine R 6.00 15.00
❑ 243 Gruul Guildgate C .10 .25
❑ 244 Orzhov Guildgate C .10 .25
❑ 245 Sacred Foundry R 8.00 20.00
❑ 246 Simic Guildgate C .10 .25
❑ 247 Stomping Ground R 6.00 15.00
❑ 248 Thespian's Stage R 2.00 5.00
❑ 249 Watery Grave R 6.00 15.00
❑ T1 Angel .10 .25
❑ T2 Rat .10 .25
❑ T3 Frog Lizard .10 .25
❑ T4 Cleric .60 1.50
❑ T5 Horror .10 .25
❑ T6 Soldier .10 .25
❑ T7 Spirit .10 .25
❑ T8 Emblem: Domri Rade .40 1.00

2013 Magic the Gathering Gatecrash Foil

*Foil: .8X to 2X Basic Cards

2013 Magic the Gathering Modern Masters

❑ 1 Adarkar Valkyrie R :W: 1.25 3.00
❑ 2 Amrou Scout C :W: .12 .30
❑ 3 Amrou Seekers C :W: .12 .30
❑ 4 Angel's Grace R :W: .50 1.25
❑ 5 Auriok Salvagers R :W: .40 1.00
❑ 6 Avian Changeling C :W: .12 .30
❑ 7 Blinding Beam C :W: .12 .30
❑ 8 Bound in Silence C :W: .12 .30
❑ 9 Cenn's Enlistment C :W: .12 .30
❑ 10 Cloudgoat Ranger U :W: .25 .60
❑ 11 Court Homunculus C :W: .12 .30
❑ 12 Dispeller's Capsule C :W: .12 .30
❑ 13 Elspeth, Knight-Errant M :W: 10.00 25.00
❑ 14 Ethersworn Canonist R :W: 2.00 5.00
❑ 15 Feudkiller's Verdict U :W: .25 .60
❑ 16 Flickerwisp U :W: .30 .75
❑ 17 Gleam of Resistance C :W: .12 .30
❑ 18 Hillcomber Giant C :W: .12 .30

MAGIC

❑ 19 Ivory Giant C :W: .12 .30
❑ 20 Kataki, War's Wage R :W: 1.25 3.00
❑ 21 Kithkin Greatheart C :W: .12 .30
❑ 22 Meadowboon U :W: .25 .60
❑ 23 Otherworldly Journey C :W: .12 .30
❑ 24 Pallid Mycoderm C :W: .12 .30
❑ 25 Path to Exile U :W: 2.50 6.00
❑ 26 Reveillark R :W: 1.50 4.00
❑ 27 Saltfield Recluse C :W: .12 .30
❑ 28 Sanctum Gargoyle C :W: .12 .30
❑ 29 Sandsower U :W: .25 .60
❑ 30 Stir the Pride U :W: .25 .60
❑ 31 Stonehewer Giant R :W: 1.25 3.00
❑ 32 Terashi's Grasp U :W: .25 .60
❑ 33 Test of Faith C :W: .12 .30
❑ 34 Veteran Armorer C :W: .12 .30
❑ 35 Yosei, the Morning Star M :W: 2.00 5.00
❑ 36 AEthersnipe C :B: .12 .30
❑ 37 Careful Consideration U :B: .25 .60
❑ 38 Cryptic Command R :B: 10.00 25.00
❑ 39 Dampen Thought C :B: .12 .30
❑ 40 Echoing Truth C :B: .20 .50
❑ 41 Errant Ephemeron C :B: .12 .30
❑ 42 Erratic Mutation C :B: .12 .30
❑ 43 Esperzoa U :B: .25 .60
❑ 44 Etherium Sculptor C :B: .20 .50
❑ 45 Faerie Mechanist C :B: .12 .30
❑ 46 Gifts Ungiven R :B: 2.00 5.00
❑ 47 Glen Elendra Archmage R :B: 2.00 5.00
❑ 48 Keiga, the Tide Star M :B: 1.50 4.00
❑ 49 Kira, Great Glass-Spinner R :B: 2.50 6.00
❑ 50 Latchkey Faerie C :B: .12 .30
❑ 51 Logic Knot C :B: .12 .30
❑ 52 Meloku the Clouded Mirror R :B: .50 1.25
❑ 53 Mothdust Changeling C :B: .12 .30
❑ 54 Mulldrifter U :B: .25 .60
❑ 55 Narcomoeba U :B: .40 1.00
❑ 56 Pact of Negation R :B: 2.50 6.00
❑ 57 Peer Through Depths C :B: .20 .50
❑ 58 Perilous Research C :B: .12 .30
❑ 59 Pestermite C :B: .20 .50
❑ 60 Petals of Insight C :B: .12 .30
❑ 61 Reach Through Mists C :B: .12 .30
❑ 62 Riftwing Cloudskate U :B: .25 .60
❑ 63 Scion of Oona R :B: 1.00 2.50
❑ 64 Spell Snare U :B: 1.50 4.00
❑ 65 Spellstutter Sprite C :B: .20 .50
❑ 66 Take Possession U :B: .25 .60
❑ 67 Thirst for Knowledge U :B: .25 .60
❑ 68 Traumatic Visions C :B: .12 .30
❑ 69 Vedalken Dismisser C :B: .12 .30
❑ 70 Vendilion Clique M :B: 25.00 50.00
❑ 71 Absorb Vis C :K: .12 .30
❑ 72 Auntie's Snitch U :K: .25 .60
❑ 73 Blightspeaker C :K: .12 .30
❑ 74 Bridge from Below R :K: 2.50 6.00
❑ 75 Dark Confidant M :K: 35.00 70.00
❑ 76 Death Cloud R :K: .50 1.25
❑ 77 Death Denied C :K: .20 .50
❑ 78 Death Rattle U :K: .25 .60
❑ 79 Deepcavern Imp C :K: .12 .30
❑ 80 Drag Down C :K: .12 .30
❑ 81 Dreamspoiler Witches C :K: .12 .30
❑ 82 Earwig Squad R :K: .40 1.00
❑ 83 Executioner's Capsule U :K: .25 .60
❑ 84 Extirpate R :K: 1.50 4.00
❑ 85 Facevaulter C :K: .12 .30
❑ 86 Faerie Macabre C :K: .20 .50
❑ 87 Festering Goblin C :K: .12 .30
❑ 88 Horobi's Whisper U :K: .25 .60
❑ 89 Kokusho, the Evening Star M :K: 4.00 10.00
❑ 90 Mad Auntie U :K: .25 .60
❑ 91 Marsh Flitter U :K: .25 .60
❑ 92 Peppersmoke C :K: .12 .30
❑ 93 Phthisis U :K: .25 .60
❑ 94 Rathi Trapper C :K: .12 .30
❑ 95 Raven's Crime C :K: .12 .30
❑ 96 Skeletal Vampire R :K: .40 1.00
❑ 97 Slaughter Pact R :K: .75 2.00
❑ 98 Stinkweed Imp C :K: .12 .30
❑ 99 Street Wraith C :K: .40 1.00
❑ 100 Syphon Life C :K: .12 .30
❑ 101 Thieving Sprite C :K: .12 .30
❑ 102 Tombstalker R :K: 1.00 2.50
❑ 103 Warren Pilferers C :K: .12 .30
❑ 104 Warren Weirding C :K: .20 .50
❑ 105 Blind-Spot Giant C :R: .12 .30
❑ 106 Blood Moon R :R: 3.00 8.00
❑ 107 Brute Force C :R: .12 .30
❑ 108 Countryside Crusher R :R: .50 1.25
❑ 109 Crush Underfoot C :R: .12 .30
❑ 110 Desperate Ritual U :R: .25 .60
❑ 111 Dragonstorm R :R: .50 1.25
❑ 112 Empty the Warrens C :R: .20 .50
❑ 113 Fiery Fall C :R: .12 .30
❑ 114 Fury Charm C :R: .12 .30
❑ 115 Glacial Ray C :R: .12 .30
❑ 116 Grapeshot C :R: .20 .50
❑ 117 Greater Gargadon R :R: .50 1.25
❑ 118 Grinning Ignus U :R: .25 .60
❑ 119 Hammerheim Deadeye C :R: .12 .30
❑ 120 Kiki-Jiki, Mirror Breaker M :R: 8.00 20.00
❑ 121 Lava Spike C :R: .60 1.50
❑ 122 Mogg War Marshal C :R: .20 .50
❑ 123 Molten Disaster R :R: .40 1.00
❑ 124 Pardic Dragon U :R: .25 .60
❑ 125 Pyromancer's Swath R :R: .40 1.00
❑ 126 Rift Bolt C :R: .50 1.25
❑ 127 Rift Elemental C :R: .12 .30
❑ 128 Ryusei, the Falling Star M :R: 1.00 2.50
❑ 129 Shrapnel Blast U :R: .30 .75
❑ 130 Squee, Goblin Nabob R :R: .50 1.25
❑ 131 Stingscourger C :R: .12 .30
❑ 132 Stinkdrinker Daredevil C :R: .12 .30
❑ 133 Sudden Shock U :R: .25 .60
❑ 134 Tar Pitcher U :R: .25 .60
❑ 135 Thundercloud Shaman U :R: .25 .60
❑ 136 Thundering Giant C :R: .12 .30
❑ 137 Torrent of Stone C :R: .12 .30
❑ 138 Tribal Flames U :R: .25 .60
❑ 139 War-Spike Changeling C :R: .12 .30
❑ 140 Citanul Woodreaders C :G: .12 .30
❑ 141 Doubling Season R :G: 6.00 15.00
❑ 142 Durkwood Baloth C :G: .12 .30
❑ 143 Echoing Courage C :G: .12 .30
❑ 144 Eternal Witness U :G: .60 1.50
❑ 145 Giant Dustwasp C :G: .12 .30
❑ 146 Greater Mossdog C :G: .12 .30
❑ 147 Hana Kami C :G: .12 .30
❑ 148 Imperiosaur C :G: .12 .30
❑ 149 Incremental Growth U :G: .25 .60
❑ 150 Jugan, the Rising Star M :G: 1.00 2.50
❑ 151 Kodama's Reach C :G: .20 .50
❑ 152 Krosan Grip U :G: .40 1.00
❑ 153 Life from the Loam R :G: 1.25 3.00
❑ 154 Masked Admirers U :G: .25 .60
❑ 155 Moldervine Cloak C :G: .12 .30
❑ 156 Nantuko Shaman C :G: .12 .30
❑ 157 Penumbra Spider C :G: .12 .30
❑ 158 Reach of Branches U :G: .25 .60
❑ 159 Riftsweeper U :G: .25 .60
❑ 160 Rude Awakening R :G: .40 1.00
❑ 161 Search for Tomorrow C :G: .12 .30
❑ 162 Sporesower Thallid U :G: .25 .60
❑ 163 Sporoloth Ancient C :G: .12 .30
❑ 164 Summoner's Pact R :G: 2.00 5.00
❑ 165 Sylvan Bounty C :G: .12 .30
❑ 166 Tarmogoyf M :G: 75.00 150.00
❑ 167 Thallid C :G: .12 .30
❑ 168 Thallid Germinator C :G: .12 .30
❑ 169 Thallid Shell-Dweller C :G: .12 .30
❑ 170 Tooth and Nail R :G: 2.50 6.00
❑ 171 Tromp the Domains U :G: .25 .60
❑ 172 Verdeloth the Ancient R :G: .40 1.00
❑ 173 Walker of the Grove C :G: .12 .30
❑ 174 Woodfall Primus R :G: 2.00 5.00
❑ 175 Electrolyze U :B/R: .50 1.25
❑ 176 Grand Arbiter Augustin IV R :W/B: 1.50 4.00
❑ 177 Jhoira of the Ghitu R :B/R: 1.00 2.50
❑ 178 Knight of the Reliquary R :W/G: 2.50 6.00
❑ 179 Lightning Helix U :W/R: 1.50 4.00
❑ 180 Maelstrom Pulse R :K/G: 3.00 8.00
❑ 181 Mind Funeral U :B/K: 1.00 2.50
❑ 182 Progenitus M :W/B/K/R/G: 4.00 10.00
❑ 183 Sarkhan Vol M :R/G: 6.00 15.00
❑ 184 Tidehollow Sculler U :W/K: .25 .60
❑ 185 Trygon Predator U :B/G: .50 1.25
❑ 186 Cold-Eyed Selkie R :B/G: .75 2.00
❑ 187 Demigod of Revenge R :K/R: 1.50 4.00
❑ 188 Divinity of Pride R :W/K: 2.00 5.00
❑ 189 Figure of Destiny R :W/R: 1.50 4.00
❑ 190 Kitchen Finks U :W/G: 2.00 5.00
❑ 191 Manamorphose U :R/G: .75 2.00
❑ 192 Murderous Redcap U :K/R: .30 .75
❑ 193 Oona, Queen of the Fae R :B/K: 1.00 2.50
❑ 194 Plumeveil U :W/B: .25 .60
❑ 195 Worm Harvest U :K/G: .25 .60
❑ 196 AEther Spellbomb C .12 .30
❑ 197 AEther Vial R 6.00 15.00
❑ 198 Arcbound Ravager R 8.00 20.00
❑ 199 Arcbound Stinger C .12 .30
❑ 200 Arcbound Wanderer C .12 .30
❑ 201 Arcbound Worker C .12 .30
❑ 202 Bonesplitter C .20 .50
❑ 203 Chalice of the Void R 2.50 6.00
❑ 204 Engineered Explosives R 3.00 8.00
❑ 205 Epochrasite U .25 .60
❑ 206 Etched Oracle U .25 .60
❑ 207 Frogmite C .20 .50
❑ 208 Lotus Bloom R 2.50 6.00
❑ 209 Myr Enforcer C .20 .50
❑ 210 Myr Retriever U .25 .60
❑ 211 Paradise Mantle U .60 1.50
❑ 212 Pyrite Spellbomb C .12 .30
❑ 213 Relic of Progenitus U .50 1.25
❑ 214 Runed Stalactite C .12 .30
❑ 215 Skyreach Manta C .12 .30
❑ 216 Sword of Fire and Ice M 12.00 30.00
❑ 217 Sword of Light and Shadow M 10.00 25.00
❑ 218 Vedalken Shackles M 6.00 15.00
❑ 219 Academy Ruins R 2.00 5.00
❑ 220 Blinkmoth Nexus R 4.00 10.00
❑ 221 City of Brass R 2.00 5.00
❑ 222 Dakmor Salvage U .25 .60
❑ 223 Glimmervoid R 4.00 10.00
❑ 224 Terramorphic Expanse C .12 .30
❑ 225 Vivid Crag U .25 .60
❑ 226 Vivid Creek U .25 .60
❑ 227 Vivid Grove U .25 .60
❑ 228 Vivid Marsh U .25 .60
❑ 229 Vivid Meadow U .25 .60
❑ T1 Giant Warrior .12 .30
❑ T2 Kithkin Soldier .12 .30
❑ T3 Soldier .60 1.50
❑ T4 Illusion .40 1.00
❑ T5 Bat .25 .60
❑ T6 Goblin Rogue .12 .30
❑ T7 Spider .12 .30
❑ T8 Zombie .12 .30
❑ T9 Dragon .40 1.00
❑ T10 Goblin .12 .30
❑ T11 Elemental .12 .30
❑ T12 Saproling .12 .30
❑ T13 Treefolk Shaman .12 .30
❑ T14 Faerie Rogue .12 .30
❑ T15 Worm .12 .30
❑ T16 Emblem: Elspeth, Knight-Errant 3.00 8.00

2013 Magic the Gathering Modern Masters Foil

*Foil: .8X to 2X Basic Cards

2013 Magic the Gathering Theros

Complete Set 200.00 300.00
❑ 1 Battlewise Valor C :W: .10 .25
❑ 2 Cavalry Pegasus C :W: .10 .25
❑ 3 Celestial Archon R :W: .30 .75
❑ 4 Chained to the Rocks R :W: 1.25 3.00
❑ 5 Chosen by Heliod C :W: .10 .25
❑ 6 Dauntless Onslaught U :W: .20 .50
❑ 7 Decorated Griffin U :W: .15 .40
❑ 8 Divine Verdict C :W: .10 .25
❑ 9 Elspeth, Sun's Champion M :W: 20.00 40.00
❑ 10 Ephara's Warden C :W: .10 .25
❑ 11 Evangel of Heliod U :W: .15 .40
❑ 12 Fabled Hero R :W: .60 1.50
❑ 13 Favored Hoplite U :W: .15 .40
❑ 14 Gift of Immortality R :W: .40 1.00
❑ 15 Glare of Heresy U :W: .20 .50
❑ 16 Gods Willing C :W: .10 .25
❑ 17 Heliod, God of the Sun M :W: 4.00 10.00
❑ 18 Heliod's Emissary U :W: .15 .40
❑ 19 Hopeful Eidolon C :W: .10 .25
❑ 20 Hundred-Handed One R :W: .30 .75
❑ 21 Lagonna-Band Elder C :W: .10 .25
❑ 22 Last Breath C :W: .10 .25
❑ 23 Leonin Snarecaster C :W: .10 .25
❑ 24 Observant Alseid C :W: .10 .25
❑ 25 Ordeal of Heliod U :W: .20 .50
❑ 26 Phalanx Leader U :W: .30 .75
❑ 27 Ray of Dissolution C :W: .10 .25
❑ 28 Scholar of Athreos C :W: .10 .25
❑ 29 Setessan Battle Priest C :W: .10 .25
❑ 30 Setessan Griffin C :W: .10 .25
❑ 31 Silent Artisan C :W: .10 .25
❑ 32 Soldier of the Pantheon R :W: 1.25 3.00
❑ 33 Spear of Heliod R :W: 1.00 2.50
❑ 34 Traveling Philosopher C :W: .10 .25
❑ 35 Vanquish the Foul U :W: .15 .40
❑ 36 Wingsteed Rider C :W: .10 .25
❑ 37 Yoked Ox C :W: .10 .25
❑ 38 Annul C :B: .10 .25
❑ 39 Aqueous Form C :B: .10 .25
❑ 40 Artisan of Forms R :B: .40 1.00
❑ 41 Benthic Giant C :B: .10 .25
❑ 42 Bident of Thassa R :B: .30 .75
❑ 43 Breaching Hippocamp C :B: .10 .25
❑ 44 Coastline Chimera C :B: .10 .25
❑ 45 Crackling Triton C :B: .10 .25
❑ 46 Curse of the Swine R :B: .40 1.00
❑ 47 Dissolve U :B: .40 1.00
❑ 48 Fate Foretold C :B: .10 .25
❑ 49 Gainsay U :B: .15 .40
❑ 50 Griptide C :B: .10 .25
❑ 51 Horizon Scholar U :B: .15 .40
❑ 52 Lost in a Labyrinth C :B: .10 .25
❑ 53 Master of Waves M :B: 2.50 6.00
❑ 54 Meletis Charlatan R :B: .30 .75
❑ 55 Mnemonic Wall C :B: .10 .25
❑ 56 Nimbus Naiad C :B: .10 .25
❑ 57 Omenspeaker C :B: .10 .25
❑ 58 Ordeal of Thassa U :B: .15 .40
❑ 59 Prescient Chimera C :B: .10 .25
❑ 60 Prognostic Sphinx R :B: .40 1.00
❑ 61 Sea God's Revenge U :B: .15 .40
❑ 62 Sealock Monster U :B: .15 .40
❑ 63 Shipbreaker Kraken R :B: .30 .75
❑ 64 Stymied Hopes C :B: .10 .25
❑ 65 Swan Song R :B: 1.00 2.50
❑ 66 Thassa, God of the Sea M :B: 6.00 15.00
❑ 67 Thassa's Bounty C :B: .10 .25
❑ 68 Thassa's Emissary U :B: .15 .40
❑ 69 Triton Fortune Hunter U :B: .15 .40
❑ 70 Triton Shorethief C :B: .10 .25
❑ 71 Triton Tactics U :B: .20 .50
❑ 72 Vaporkin C :B: .10 .25
❑ 73 Voyage's End C :B: .10 .25
❑ 74 Wavecrash Triton C :B: .10 .25
❑ 75 Abhorrent Overlord R :K: .30 .75
❑ 76 Agent of the Fates R :K: .60 1.50
❑ 77 Asphodel Wanderer C :K: .10 .25
❑ 78 Baleful Eidolon C :K: .10 .25
❑ 79 Blood-Toll Harpy C :K: .10 .25
❑ 80 Boon of Erebos C :K: .10 .25
❑ 81 Cavern Lampad C :K: .10 .25
❑ 82 Cutthroat Maneuver U :K: .15 .40
❑ 83 Dark Betrayal U :K: .15 .40
❑ 84 Disciple of Phenax C :K: .10 .25
❑ 85 Erebos, God of the Dead M :K: 3.00 8.00
❑ 86 Erebos's Emissary U :K: .15 .40
❑ 87 Felhide Minotaur C :K: .10 .25
❑ 88 Fleshmad Steed C :K: .10 .25
❑ 89 Gray Merchant of Asphodel C :K: .10 .25
❑ 90 Hero's Downfall R :K: 2.50 6.00
❑ 91 Hythonia the Cruel M :K: .60 1.50
❑ 92 Insatiable Harpy U :K: .15 .40
❑ 93 Keepsake Gorgon U :K: .15 .40
❑ 94 Lash of the Whip C :K: .10 .25
❑ 95 Loathsome Catoblepas C :K: .10 .25
❑ 96 March of the Returned C :K: .10 .25
❑ 97 Mogis's Marauder U :K: .15 .40
❑ 98 Nighthowler R :K: .40 1.00
❑ 99 Ordeal of Erebos U :K: .15 .40
❑ 100 Pharika's Cure C :K: .10 .25
❑ 101 Read the Bones C :K: .10 .25
❑ 102 Rescue from the Underworld U :K: .20 .50
❑ 103 Returned Centaur C :K: .10 .25
❑ 104 Returned Phalanx C :K: .10 .25
❑ 105 Scourgemark C :K: .10 .25
❑ 106 Sip of Hemlock C :K: .10 .25
❑ 107 Thoughtseize R :K: 8.00 20.00
❑ 108 Tormented Hero U :K: .20 .50
❑ 109 Viper's Kiss C :K: .10 .25
❑ 110 Whip of Erebos R :K: .75 2.00
❑ 111 Akroan Crusader C :R: .10 .25
❑ 112 Anger of the Gods R :R: 2.50 6.00
❑ 113 Arena Athlete U :R: .15 .40
❑ 114 Borderland Minotaur C :R: .10 .25
❑ 115 Boulderfall C :R: .10 .25
❑ 116 Coordinated Assault U :R: .15 .40
❑ 117 Deathbellow Raider C :R: .10 .25
❑ 118 Demolish C :R: .10 .25
❑ 119 Dragon Mantle C :R: .10 .25
❑ 120 Ember Swallower R :R: .30 .75
❑ 121 Fanatic of Mogis U :R: .15 .40
❑ 122 Firedrinker Satyr R :R: .50 1.25
❑ 123 Flamespeaker Adept U :R: .15 .40
❑ 124 Hammer of Purphoros R :R: .75 2.00
❑ 125 Ill-Tempered Cyclops C :R: .10 .25
❑ 126 Labyrinth Champion R :R: .30 .75
❑ 127 Lightning Strike C :R: .20 .50
❑ 128 Magma Jet U :R: .75 2.00
❑ 129 Messenger's Speed C :R: .10 .25
❑ 130 Minotaur Skullcleaver C :R: .10 .25
❑ 131 Ordeal of Purphoros U :R: .15 .40
❑ 132 Peak Eruption U :R: .15 .40
❑ 133 Portent of Betrayal C :R: .10 .25
❑ 134 Priest of Iroas C :R: .10 .25
❑ 135 Purphoros, God of the Forge M :R: 8.00 20.00
❑ 136 Purphoros's Emissary U :R: .15 .40
❑ 137 Rage of Purphoros C :R: .10 .25
❑ 138 Rageblood Shaman R :R: .40 1.00
❑ 139 Satyr Rambler C :R: .10 .25
❑ 140 Spark Jolt C :R: .10 .25
❑ 141 Spearpoint Oread C :R: .10 .25
❑ 142 Stoneshock Giant U :R: .15 .40
❑ 143 Stormbreath Dragon M :R: 12.00 30.00
❑ 144 Titan of Eternal Fire R :R: .30 .75
❑ 145 Titan's Strength C :R: .10 .25
❑ 146 Two-Headed Cerberus C :R: .10 .25
❑ 147 Wild Celebrants C :R: .10 .25
❑ 148 Agent of Horizons C :G: .10 .25
❑ 149 Anthousa, Setessan Hero R :G: .30 .75
❑ 150 Arbor Colossus R :G: .30 .75
❑ 151 Artisan's Sorrow U :G: .15 .40
❑ 152 Boon Satyr R :G: 1.00 2.50
❑ 153 Bow of Nylea R :G: 1.00 2.50
❑ 154 Centaur Battlemaster U :G: .20 .50
❑ 155 Commune with the Gods C :G: .10 .25
❑ 156 Defend the Hearth C :G: .10 .25
❑ 157 Fade into Antiquity C :G: .30 .75
❑ 158 Feral Invocation C :G: .15 .40
❑ 159 Hunt the Hunter U :G: .15 .40
❑ 160 Karametra's Acolyte U :G: .15 .40
❑ 161 Leafcrown Dryad C :G: .10 .25
❑ 162 Mistcutter Hydra R :G: 1.00 2.50
❑ 163 Nemesis of Mortals U :G: .20 .50
❑ 164 Nessian Asp C :G: .10 .25
❑ 165 Nessian Courser C :G: .10 .25
❑ 166 Nylea, God of the Hunt M :G: 3.00 8.00
❑ 167 Nylea's Disciple C :G: .10 .25
❑ 168 Nylea's Emissary U :G: .15 .40
❑ 169 Nylea's Presence C :G: .10 .25
❑ 170 Ordeal of Nylea U :G: .15 .40
❑ 171 Pheres-Band Centaurs C :G: .10 .25
❑ 172 Polukranos, World Eater M :G: 2.50 6.00
❑ 173 Reverent Hunter R :G: .40 1.00
❑ 174 Satyr Hedonist C :G: .10 .25
❑ 175 Satyr Piper U :G: .15 .40
❑ 176 Savage Surge C :G: .10 .25
❑ 177 Sedge Scorpion C :G: .10 .25
❑ 178 Shredding Winds C :G: .10 .25
❑ 179 Staunch-Hearted Warrior C :G: .10 .25
❑ 180 Sylvan Caryatid R :G: 2.00 5.00
❑ 181 Time to Feed C :G: .10 .25
❑ 182 Voyaging Satyr C :G: .10 .25
❑ 183 Vulpine Goliath C :G: .10 .25
❑ 184 Warriors' Lesson U :G: .15 .40
❑ 185 Akroan Hoplite U :W/R: .15 .40
❑ 186 Anax and Cymede R :W/R: .40 1.00
❑ 187 Ashen Rider M :W/K: 1.50 4.00
❑ 188 Ashiok, Nightmare Weaver M :B/K: 10.00 25.00
❑ 189 Battlewise Hoplite U :W/B: .15 .40
❑ 190 Chronicler of Heroes U :W/G: .15 .40
❑ 191 Daxos of Meletis R :W/B: .60 1.50
❑ 192 Destructive Revelry U :R/G: .30 .75
❑ 193 Fleecemane Lion R :W/G: 4.00 10.00
❑ 194 Horizon Chimera U :B/G: .15 .40
❑ 195 Kragma Warcaller U :K/R: .15 .40
❑ 196 Medomai the Ageless M :W/B: 1.25 3.00
❑ 197 Pharika's Mender U :K/G: .15 .40
❑ 198 Polis Crusher R :R/G: .40 1.00
❑ 199 Prophet of Kruphix R :B/G: .75 2.00
❑ 200 Psychic Intrusion R :B/K: .40 1.00
❑ 201 Reaper of the Wilds R :K/G: .75 2.00
❑ 202 Sentry of the Underworld U :W/K: .15 .40
❑ 203 Shipwreck Singer U :B/K: .15 .40
❑ 204 Spellheart Chimera U :B/R: .30 .75
❑ 205 Steam Augury R :B/R: .75 2.00
❑ 206 Triad of Fates R :W/K: .40 1.00
❑ 207 Tymaret, the Murder King R :K/R: .40 1.00
❑ 208 Underworld Cerberus M :K/R: 1.50 4.00
❑ 209 Xenagos, the Reveler M :R/G: 8.00 20.00
❑ 210 Akroan Horse R .30 .75
❑ 211 Anvilwrought Raptor U .15 .40
❑ 212 Bronze Sable C .10 .25
❑ 213 Burnished Hart U .15 .40
❑ 214 Colossus of Akros R .30 .75
❑ 215 Flamecast Wheel U .15 .40
❑ 216 Fleetfeather Sandals C .10 .25
❑ 217 Guardians of Meletis C .10 .25
❑ 218 Opaline Unicorn C .10 .25
❑ 219 Prowler's Helm U .15 .40
❑ 220 Pyxis of Pandemonium R .30 .75
❑ 221 Traveler's Amulet C .10 .25
❑ 222 Witches' Eye U .15 .40
❑ 223 Nykthos, Shrine to Nyx R 2.50 6.00
❑ 224 Temple of Abandon R 1.50 4.00
❑ 225 Temple of Deceit R 2.00 5.00
❑ 226 Temple of Mystery R 1.50 4.00
❑ 227 Temple of Silence R 2.00 5.00
❑ 228 Temple of Triumph R 2.00 5.00
❑ 229 Unknown Shores C .10 .25
❑ 230 Plains L .10 .25
❑ 231 Plains L .10 .25
❑ 232 Plains L .10 .25
❑ 233 Plains L .10 .25
❑ 234 Island L .10 .25
❑ 235 Island L .10 .25
❑ 236 Island L .10 .25
❑ 237 Island L .10 .25
❑ 238 Swamp L .10 .25
❑ 239 Swamp L .10 .25
❑ 240 Swamp L .10 .25
❑ 241 Swamp L .10 .25
❑ 242 Mountain L .10 .25
❑ 243 Mountain L .10 .25
❑ 244 Mountain L .10 .25
❑ 245 Mountain L .10 .25
❑ 246 Forest L .10 .25
❑ 247 Forest L .10 .25
❑ 248 Forest L .10 .25
❑ 249 Forest L .10 .25
❑ T1 Cleric .20 .50
❑ T2 Soldier (white) .10 .25
❑ T3 Soldier (white) .10 .25
❑ T4 Bird .20 .50
❑ T5 Elemental .20 .50
❑ T6 Harpy .10 .25
❑ T7 Soldier (red) .10 .25
❑ T8 Boar .10 .25
❑ T9 Satyr .30 .75
❑ T10 Golem .20 .50
❑ T11 Emblem: Elspeth, Sun's Champion 1.25 3.00

2013 Magic the Gathering Theros Foil

*Foil: .8X to 2X Basic Cards

1997 Magic the Gathering Portal

Complete Set (222) 200.00 300.00
Booster Box (36 Packs) 120.00 160.00
Booster Pack (15 Cards) 5.00 7.00
❑ 1 Alabaster Dragon R :W: 4.00 8.00
❑ 2 Alluring Scent R :G: 1.50 3.00
❑ 3 Anaconda v1 C :G: .50 1.00
❑ 4 Anaconda v2 U :G: .25 .50
❑ 5 Ancestral Memories R :B: 2.00 4.00
❑ 6 Angelic Blessing C :W: .15 .30
❑ 7 Archangel R :W: 5.00 10.00
❑ 8 Ardent Militia U :W: .25 .50
❑ 9 Armageddon R :W: 5.00 10.00
❑ 10 Armored Pegasus C :W: .15 .30
❑ 11 Arrogant Vampire U :K: .50 1.00
❑ 12 Assassin's Blade U :K: .50 1.00
❑ 13 Balance of Power R :B: 2.00 4.00
❑ 14 Baleful Stare U :B: .50 1.00
❑ 15 Bee Sting U :G: .25 .50
❑ 16 Blaze v1 C :R: .50 1.00
❑ 17 Blaze v2 U :R: .50 1.00
❑ 18 Blessed Reversal R :W: 2.00 4.00
❑ 19 Blinding Light R :W: 2.00 4.00
❑ 20 Bog Imp C :K: .15 .30
❑ 21 Bog Raiders C :K: .15 .30
❑ 22 Bog Wraith U :K: .25 .50
❑ 23 Boiling Seas U :K: .50 1.00
❑ 24 Border Guard C :W: .15 .30
❑ 25 Breath of Life C :W: .15 .30
❑ 26 Bull Hippo U :G: .25 .50
❑ 27 Burning Cloak C :R: .15 .30
❑ 28 Capricious Sorcerer R :B: 2.00 4.00
❑ 29 Charging Bandits U :K: .25 .50
❑ 30 Charging Paladin U :W: .25 .50
❑ 31 Charging Rhino R :G: 2.00 4.00
❑ 32 Cloak of Feathers C :B: .15 .30
❑ 33 Cloud Dragon R :B: 7.50 15.00
❑ 34 Cloud Pirates C :B: .15 .30
❑ 35 Cloud Spirit U :B: .50 1.00

☐ 36 Command of Unsummoning U :B: .25 .50
☐ 37 Coral Eel C :B: .15 .30
☐ 38 Craven Giant C :R: .15 .30
☐ 39 Craven Knight C :K: .15 .30
☐ 40 Cruel Bargain R :K: 10.00 20.00
☐ 41 Cruel Fate R :B: 2.00 4.00
☐ 42 Cruel Tutor R :K: 9.00 18.00
☐ 43 Deep Wood U :G: .25 .50
☐ 44 Deep-Sea Serpent U :B: .25 .50
☐ 45 Defiant Stand U :W: .25 .50
☐ 46 Deja Vu C :B: .15 .30
☐ 47 Desert Drake U :R: .25 .50
☐ 48 Devastation R :R: 4.00 8.00
☐ 49 Devoted Hero C :W: .15 .30
☐ 50 Djinn of the Lamp R :B: 2.50 5.00
☐ 51 Dread Charge R :K: 2.00 4.00
☐ 52 Dread Reaper R :K: 2.00 4.00
☐ 53 Dry Spell U :K: .25 .50
☐ 54 Earthquake R :R: 4.00 8.00
☐ 55 Ebon Dragon R :K: 7.50 15.00
☐ 56 Elite Cat Warrior v1 C :G: .15 .30
☐ 57 Elite Cat Warrior v2 C :G: .15 .30
☐ 58 Elven Cache C :G: .15 .30
☐ 59 Elvish Ranger C :G: .15 .30
☐ 60 Endless Cockroaches R :K: 5.00 10.00
☐ 61 Exhaustion R :B: 2.50 5.00
☐ 62 False Peace C :W: .15 .30
☐ 63 Feral Shadow C :K: .15 .30
☐ 64 Final Strike R :K: 2.00 4.00
☐ 65 Fire Dragon R :R: 10.00 20.00
☐ 66 Fire Imp U :R: .25 .50
☐ 67 Fire Snake C :R: .15 .30
☐ 68 Fire Tempest R :R: 2.00 4.00
☐ 69 Flashfires U :R: .50 1.00
☐ 70 Fleet-Footed Monk C :W: .15 .30
☐ 71 Flux U :B: .50 1.00
☐ 72 Foot Soldiers C :W: .15 .30
☐ 73 Forest A C :L: .15 .30
☐ 74 Forest B C :L: .15 .30
☐ 75 Forest C C :L: .15 .30
☐ 76 Forest D C :L: .15 .30
☐ 77 Forked Lightning R :R: 2.50 5.00
☐ 78 Fruition C :G: .15 .30
☐ 79 Giant Octopus C :B: .15 .30
☐ 80 Giant Spider C :G: .15 .30
☐ 81 Gift of Estates R :W: 5.00 10.00
☐ 82 Goblin Bully C :R: .15 .30
☐ 83 Gorilla Warrior C :G: .15 .30
☐ 84 Gravedigger U :K: .25 .50
☐ 85 Grizzly Bears C :G: .15 .30
☐ 86 Hand of Death v1 C :K: .15 .30
☐ 87 Hand of Death v2 C :K: .15 .30
☐ 88 Harsh Justice R :W: 3.00 6.00
☐ 89 Highland Giant C :R: .15 .30
☐ 90 Hill Giant C :R: .15 .30
☐ 91 Horned Turtle C :B: .15 .30
☐ 92 Howling Fury C :K: .15 .30
☐ 93 Hulking Cyclops U :R: .50 1.00
☐ 94 Hulking Goblin C :R: .15 .30
☐ 95 Hurricane R :G: 2.00 4.00
☐ 96 Ingenious Thief U :B: .25 .50
☐ 97 Island A C :L: .15 .30
☐ 98 Island B C :L: .15 .30
☐ 99 Island C C :L: .15 .30
☐ 100 Island D C :L: .15 .30
☐ 101 Jungle Lion C :G: .15 .30
☐ 102 Keen-Eyed Archers C :W: .15 .30
☐ 103 King's Assassin R :K: 5.00 10.00
☐ 104 Knight Errant C :W: .15 .30
☐ 105 Last Chance R :R: 3.00 6.00
☐ 106 Lava Axe C :R: .15 .30
☐ 107 Lava Flow U :R: .25 .50
☐ 108 Lizard Warrior C :R: .15 .30
☐ 109 Man-o'-War U :B: .25 .50
☐ 110 Mercenary Knight R :K: 7.50 15.00
☐ 111 Merfolk of the Pearl Trident C :B: .15 .30
☐ 112 Mind Knives C :K: .15 .30
☐ 113 Mind Rot C :K: .15 .30
☐ 114 Minotaur Warrior C :R: .15 .30
☐ 115 Mobilize C :G: .15 .30
☐ 116 Monstrous Growth v1 C :G: .15 .30
☐ 117 Monstrous Growth v2 C :G: .15 .30
☐ 118 Moon Sprite U :G: .75 1.50
☐ 119 Mountain A C :L: .15 .30
☐ 120 Mountain B C :L: .15 .30
☐ 121 Mountain C C :L: .15 .30
☐ 122 Mountain D C :L: .15 .30
☐ 123 Mountain Goat U :R: .25 .50
☐ 124 Muck Rats C :K: .15 .30
☐ 125 Mystic Denial U :B: .50 1.00
☐ 126 Natural Order R :G: 3.00 6.00
☐ 127 Natural Spring U :G: .25 .50
☐ 128 Nature's Cloak R :G: 2.00 4.00
☐ 129 Nature's Lore C :G: .15 .30
☐ 130 Nature's Ruin U :K: .25 .50
☐ 131 Needle Storm U :G: .25 .50
☐ 132 Noxious Toad U :K: .25 .50
☐ 133 Omen C :B: .15 .30
☐ 134 Owl Familiar C :B: .15 .30
☐ 135 Panther Warriors C :G: .15 .30
☐ 136 Path of Peace C :W: .15 .30
☐ 137 Personal Tutor U :B: 5.00 10.00
☐ 138 Phantom Warrior R :B: 2.00 4.00
☐ 139 Pillaging Horde R :R: 3.00 6.00
☐ 140 Plains A C :L: .15 .30
☐ 141 Plains B C :L: .15 .30
☐ 142 Plains C C :L: .15 .30
☐ 143 Plains D C :L: .15 .30
☐ 144 Plant Elemental U :G: 1.50 3.00
☐ 145 Primeval Force R :G: 2.50 5.00
☐ 146 Prosperity R :B: 2.50 5.00
☐ 147 Pyroclasm R :R: 3.50 7.00
☐ 148 Python C :K: .15 .30
☐ 149 Raging Cougar C :R: .15 .30
☐ 150 Raging Goblin v1 C :R: .15 .30
☐ 151 Raging Goblin v2 C :R: .15 .30
☐ 152 Raging Minotaur C :R: .15 .30
☐ 153 Rain of Salt U :R: .50 1.00
☐ 154 Rain of Tears U :K: 1.00 2.00
☐ 155 Raise Dead C :K: .15 .30
☐ 156 Redwood Treefolk C :G: .15 .30
☐ 157 Regal Unicorn C :W: .15 .30
☐ 158 Renewing Dawn U :W: .25 .50
☐ 159 Rowan Treefolk C :G: .15 .30
☐ 160 Sacred Knight C :W: .15 .30
☐ 161 Sacred Nectar C :W: .15 .30
☐ 162 Scorching Spear C :R: .15 .30
☐ 163 Scorching Winds U :R: .25 .50
☐ 164 Seasoned Marshal U :W: .25 .50
☐ 165 Serpent Assassin R :K: 2.50 5.00
☐ 166 Serpent Warrior C :K: .15 .30
☐ 167 Skeletal Crocodile C :K: .15 .30
☐ 168 Skeletal Snake C :K: .15 .30
☐ 169 Snapping Drake C :B: .15 .30
☐ 170 Sorcerous Sight C :B: .15 .30
☐ 171 Soul Shred C :K: .15 .30
☐ 172 Spined Wurm C :G: .15 .30
☐ 173 Spiritual Guardian R :W: 2.00 4.00
☐ 174 Spitting Earth C :R: .15 .30
☐ 175 Spotted Griffin C :W: .15 .30
☐ 176 Stalking Tiger C :G: .15 .30
☐ 177 Starlight U :W: .25 .50
☐ 178 Starlit Angel U :W: 3.00 6.00
☐ 179 Steadfastness C :W: .15 .30
☐ 180 Stern Marshal R :W: 2.00 4.00
☐ 181 Stone Rain C :R: .15 .30
☐ 182 Storm Crow C :B: .15 .30
☐ 183 Summer Bloom R :G: 2.00 4.00
☐ 184 Swamp A C :L: .15 .30
☐ 185 Swamp B C :L: .15 .30
☐ 186 Swamp C C :L: .15 .30
☐ 187 Swamp D C :L: .75 1.50
☐ 188 Sylvan Tutor R :G: 4.00 8.00
☐ 189 Symbol of Unsummoning C :B: .15 .30
☐ 190 Taunt R :B: 2.00 4.00
☐ 191 Temporary Truce R :W: 2.00 4.00
☐ 192 Theft of Dreams U :B: .25 .50
☐ 193 Thing from the Deep R :B: 3.50 7.00
☐ 194 Thundering Wurm R :G: 2.00 4.00
☐ 195 Thundermare R :R: 3.00 6.00
☐ 196 Tidal Surge C :B: .15 .30
☐ 197 Time Ebb C :B: .15 .30
☐ 198 Touch of Brilliance C :G: .15 .30
☐ 199 Treetop Defense R :K: 1.00 2.00
☐ 200 Undying Beast C :G: .15 .30
☐ 201 Untamed Wilds U :G: .25 .50
☐ 202 Valorous Charge U :W: .25 .50
☐ 203 Vampiric Feast U :K: .50 1.00
☐ 204 Vampiric Touch C :K: .15 .30
☐ 205 Venerable Monk U :W: .25 .50
☐ 206 Vengeance U :W: .25 .50
☐ 207 Virtue's Ruin U :K: .50 1.00
☐ 208 Volcanic Dragon R :R: 4.00 8.00
☐ 209 Volcanic Hammer C :R: .15 .30
☐ 210 Wall of Granite U :R: .25 .50
☐ 211 Wall of Swords U :W: .50 1.00
☐ 212 Warrior's Charge v1 C :W: .15 .30
☐ 213 Warrior's Charge v2 C :W: .15 .30
☐ 214 Whiptail Wurm U :G: .25 .50
☐ 215 Wicked Pact R :K: 2.00 4.00
☐ 216 Willow Dryad C :G: .15 .30
☐ 217 Wind Drake C :B: .15 .30
☐ 218 Winds of Change R :R: 2.50 5.00
☐ 219 Winter's Grasp U :G: .50 1.00
☐ 220 Withering Gaze U :B: .50 1.00
☐ 221 Wood Elves R :G: 2.50 5.00
☐ 222 Wrath of God R :W: 12.00 25.00

1997 Magic the Gathering Portal Second Age

Complete Set (165) 150.00 225.00
Starter Deck Box 70.00 110.00
Starter Deck 8.00 11.00
Booster Box 125.00 175.00
Booster Pack 5.00 7.00
Released in June 1998

☐ 1 Abyssal Nightstalker U :K: .50 1.00
☐ 2 Air Elemental U :B: .50 1.00
☐ 3 Alaborn Cavalier U :W: .50 1.00
☐ 4 Alaborn Grenadier C :W: .15 .30
☐ 5 Alaborn Musketeer C :W: .15 .30
☐ 6 Alaborn Trooper C :W: .15 .30
☐ 7 Alaborn Veteran R :W: 2.00 4.00
☐ 8 Alaborn Zealot U :W: .25 .50
☐ 9 Alluring Scent R :G: 2.00 4.00
☐ 10 Ancient Craving R :K: 3.00 6.00
☐ 11 Angel of Fury R :W: 6.00 12.00
☐ 12 Angel of Mercy U :W: 1.00 2.00
☐ 13 Angelic Blessing C :W: .15 .30
☐ 14 Angelic Wall C :W: .15 .30
☐ 15 Apprentice Sorcerer U :B: .50 1.00
☐ 16 Archangel R :W: 9.00 18.00
☐ 17 Armageddon R :W: 5.00 10.00
☐ 18 Armored Galleon U :B: 1.00 2.00
☐ 19 Armored Griffin U :W: .50 1.00
☐ 20 Barbtooth Wurm C :G: .15 .30
☐ 21 Bargain U :W: .75 1.50
☐ 22 Bear Cub C :G: .15 .30
☐ 23 Bee Sting U :G: .25 .50
☐ 24 Blaze U :R: 1.00 2.00
☐ 25 Bloodcurdling Scream U :K: .50 1.00
☐ 26 Breath of Life C :K: .15 .30
☐ 27 Brimstone Dragon R :R: 10.00 20.00
☐ 28 Brutal Nightstalker U :K: .50 1.00
☐ 29 Chorus of Woe C :K: .15 .30
☐ 30 Coastal Wizard R :B: 2.50 5.00
☐ 31 Coercion U :K: .50 1.00
☐ 32 Cruel Edict C :K: .15 .30
☐ 33 Cunning Giant R :R: 3.00 6.00
☐ 34 Dakmor Bat C :K: .15 .30
☐ 35 Dakmor Plague U :K: .50 1.00
☐ 36 Dakmor Scorpion C :K: .15 .30
☐ 37 Dakmor Sorceress R :K: 6.00 12.00
☐ 38 Dark Offering U :K: .50 1.00
☐ 39 Deathcoil Wurm R :G: 5.00 10.00
☐ 40 Deep Wood U :G: .25 .50
☐ 41 Deja Vu C :B: .15 .30
☐ 42 Denizen of the Deep R :B: 5.00 10.00
☐ 43 Earthquake R :R: 3.00 6.00
☐ 44 Exhaustion R :B: 2.00 4.00
☐ 45 Extinguish C :B: .15 .30
☐ 46 Eye Spy U :B: .50 1.00
☐ 47 False Summoning C :B: .15 .30
☐ 48 Festival of Trokin C :W: .15 .30
☐ 49 Forest C :L: .15 .30
☐ 50 Forest B C :L: .15 .30
☐ 51 Forest C C :L: .15 .30
☐ 52 Foul Spirit U :K: .50 1.00
☐ 53 Goblin Cavaliers C :R: .15 .30
☐ 54 Goblin Firestarter U :R: 1.00 2.00
☐ 55 Goblin General R :R: 5.00 10.00
☐ 56 Goblin Glider C :R: .15 .30
☐ 57 Goblin Lore U :R: 2.50 5.00
☐ 58 Goblin Matron U :R: 1.25 2.50
☐ 59 Goblin Mountaineer C :R: .15 .30
☐ 60 Goblin Piker C :R: .15 .30
☐ 61 Goblin Raider C :R: .15 .30
☐ 62 Goblin War Cry U :R: .50 1.00
☐ 63 Goblin War Strike C :R: .15 .30
☐ 64 Golden Bear C :G: .15 .30
☐ 65 Hand of Death C :K: .15 .30
☐ 66 Harmony of Nature U :G: 1.00 2.00
☐ 67 Hidden Horror R :K: 2.50 5.00
☐ 68 Hurricane R :G: 2.00 4.00
☐ 69 Ironhoof Ox U :G: .50 1.00
☐ 70 Island C :L: .15 .30
☐ 71 Island B C :L: .15 .30
☐ 72 Island C C :L: .15 .30
☐ 73 Jagged Lightning U :R: .25 .50
☐ 74 Just Fate R :W: 2.50 5.00
☐ 75 Kiss of Death U :K: .50 1.00
☐ 76 Lava Axe C :R: .15 .30
☐ 77 Lone Wolf U :G: .25 .50
☐ 78 Lurking Nightstalker C :K: .15 .30
☐ 79 Lynx C :G: .15 .30
☐ 80 Magma Giant R :R: 2.00 4.00
☐ 81 Mind Rot C :K: .15 .30
☐ 82 Moaning Spirit C :K: .15 .30
☐ 83 Monstrous Growth C :G: .15 .30
☐ 84 Mountain C :L: .15 .30
☐ 85 Mountain B C :L: .15 .30
☐ 86 Mountain C C :L: .15 .30
☐ 87 Muck Rats C :K: .15 .30
☐ 88 Mystic Denial U :B: .50 1.00
☐ 89 Natural Spring C :G: .15 .30
☐ 90 Nature's Lore C :G: .15 .30
☐ 91 Nightstalker Engine R :K: 2.50 5.00
☐ 92 Norwood Archers C :G: .15 .30
☐ 93 Norwood Priestess R :G: 12.00 25.00
☐ 94 Norwood Ranger C :G: .15 .30
☐ 95 Norwood Riders C :G: .15 .30
☐ 96 Norwood Warrior C :G: .15 .30
☐ 97 Obsidian Giant U :R: .50 1.00
☐ 98 Ogre Arsonist U :R: .50 1.00
☐ 99 Ogre Berserker C :R: .15 .30
☐ 100 Ogre Taskmaster U :R: .25 .50
☐ 101 Ogre Warrior C :R: .15 .30
☐ 102 Path of Peace C :W: .15 .30
☐ 103 Piracy R :B: 7.50 15.00
☐ 104 Plains C :L: .15 .30
☐ 105 Plains B C :L: .15 .30
☐ 106 Plains C C :L: .15 .30
☐ 107 Plated Wurm C :G: .15 .30
☐ 108 Predatory Nightstalker U :K: .50 1.00
☐ 109 Prowling Nightstalker C :K: .15 .30
☐ 110 Raging Goblin C :R: .15 .30
☐ 111 Raiding Nightstalker C :K: .15 .30
☐ 112 Rain of Daggers R :K: 5.00 10.00
☐ 113 Raise Dead C :K: .15 .30
☐ 114 Rally the Troops U :W: .50 1.00
☐ 115 Ravenous Rats C :K: .15 .30
☐ 116 Razorclaw Bear R :G: 4.00 8.00
☐ 117 Relentless Assault R :R: 2.00 4.00
☐ 118 Remove U :B: .25 .50
☐ 119 Renewing Touch U :G: .25 .50
☐ 120 Return of the Nightstalkers R :K: 4.00 8.00
☐ 121 Righteous Charge C :W: .15 .30
☐ 122 Righteous Fury R :W: 4.00 8.00
☐ 123 River Bear U :G: .50 1.00
☐ 124 Salvage C :G: .15 .30
☐ 125 Screeching Drake C :B: .15 .30
☐ 126 Sea Drake U :B: 15.00 30.00
☐ 127 Sleight of Hand C :B: .15 .30
☐ 128 Spitting Earth C :R: .15 .30
☐ 129 Steam Catapult R :W: 4.00 8.00
☐ 130 Steam Frigate C :B: .15 .30
☐ 131 Stone Rain C :R: .15 .30
☐ 132 Swamp C :L: .15 .30
☐ 133 Swamp B C :K: .15 .30
☐ 134 Swamp C C :G: .15 .30
☐ 135 Swarm of Rats C :G: .15 .30
☐ 136 Sylvan Basilisk R :B: 5.00 10.00
☐ 137 Sylvan Yeti R :B: 2.50 5.00
☐ 138 Talas Air Ship C :B: .15 .30
☐ 139 Talas Explorer C :B: .15 .30
☐ 140 Talas Merchant C :B: .15 .30
☐ 141 Talas Researcher R :B: 4.00 8.00
☐ 142 Talas Scout C :B: .15 .30
☐ 143 Talas Warrior R :B: 2.50 5.00
☐ 144 Temple Acolyte C :W: .15 .30
☐ 145 Temple Elder U :W: .50 1.00
☐ 146 Temporal Manipulation R :B: 30.00 60.00
☐ 147 Theft of Dreams U :B: .50 1.00
☐ 148 Tidal Surge C :B: .15 .30
☐ 149 Time Ebb C :B: .15 .30
☐ 150 Touch of Brilliance C :B: .15 .30
☐ 151 Town Sentry C :W: .15 .30
☐ 152 Tree Monkey C :G: .15 .30
☐ 153 Tremor C :R: .15 .30
☐ 154 Trokin High Guard C :W: .15 .30
☐ 155 Undo U :B: .25 .50
☐ 156 Untamed Wilds U :G: .50 1.00
☐ 157 Vampiric Spirit R :K: 4.00 8.00
☐ 158 Vengeance U :W: .25 .50
☐ 159 Volcanic Hammer C :R: .15 .30
☐ 160 Volunteer Militia C :W: .15 .30
☐ 161 Warrior's Stand U :W: .25 .50
☐ 162 Wild Griffin C :W: .15 .30
☐ 163 Wild Ox U :G: .25 .50
☐ 164 Wildfire R :R: 4.00 8.00
☐ 165 Wind Sail C :B: .15 .30

1999 Magic the Gathering Portal Three Kingdoms

Complete Set (180) 600.00 850.00
Starter Deck 10.00 30.00
Booster Box 1100.00 1250.00
Booster Pack 15.00 25.00
Released in July 1999

☐ 1 Alert Shu Infantry U :W: 2.00 4.00
☐ 2 Ambition's Cost R :K: 3.00 6.00
☐ 3 Balance of Power R :B: 5.00 10.00
☐ 4 Barbarian General U :R: 1.50 3.00
☐ 5 Barbarian Horde C :R: .50 1.00
☐ 6 Blaze U :R: 2.00 4.00
☐ 7 Borrowing 100,000 Arrows U :B: 2.50 5.00
☐ 8 Borrowing the East Wind R :G: 6.00 12.00
☐ 9 Brilliant Plan U :B: 2.00 4.00
☐ 10 Broken Dam C :B: .50 1.00
☐ 11 Burning Fields C :R: .50 1.00
☐ 12 Burning of Xinye R :R: 7.50 15.00
☐ 13 Cao Cao, Lord of Wei R :K: 7.50 15.00
☐ 14 Cao Ren, Wei Commander R :K: 4.00 8.00
☐ 15 Capture of Jingzhou R :B: 150.00 300.00
☐ 16 Champion's Victory U :B: 2.00 4.00
☐ 17 Coercion U :K: 2.00 4.00
☐ 18 Control of the Court U :R: 1.00 2.00
☐ 19 Corrupt Court Official U :K: 2.00 4.00
☐ 20 Corrupt Eunuchs U :R: 2.00 4.00
☐ 21 Council of Advisors U :B: 2.00 4.00
☐ 22 Counterintelligence U :B: 2.00 4.00
☐ 23 Cunning Advisor U :K: 2.00 4.00
☐ 24 Deception C :K: .50 1.00
☐ 25 Desert Sandstorm C :R: .50 1.00
☐ 26 Desperate Charge U :K: 1.00 2.00
☐ 27 Diaochan, Artful Beauty R :R: 6.00 12.00
☐ 28 Dong Zhou, the Tyrant R :R: 6.00 12.00
☐ 29 Eightfold Maze R :W: 6.00 12.00
☐ 30 Empty City Ruse U :W: 2.00 4.00
☐ 31 Eunuchs' Intrigues U :R: 2.00 4.00
☐ 32 Exhaustion R :B: 6.00 12.00
☐ 33 Extinguish C :B: .50 1.00
☐ 34 False Defeat C :W: .50 1.00
☐ 35 False Mourning U :G: 3.00 6.00
☐ 36 Famine U :K: 2.00 4.00
☐ 37 Fire Ambush C :R: .50 1.00
☐ 38 Fire Bowman U :R: 2.00 4.00
☐ 39 Flanking Troops U :W: 1.00 2.00
☐ 40 Forced Retreat C :B: .50 1.00
☐ 41 Forest Bear C :G: .50 1.00
☐ 42 Forest C :L: .50 1.00
☐ 43 Forest C :L: .50 1.00
☐ 44 Forest C :L: .50 1.00
☐ 45 Ghostly Visit C :K: .50 1.00
☐ 46 Guan Yu, Sainted Warrior R :W: 7.50 15.00
☐ 47 Guan Yu's 1,000-Li March R :W: 10.00 20.00
☐ 48 Heavy Fog U :G: 1.50 3.00
☐ 49 Hua Tuo, Honored Physician R :G: 5.00 10.00
☐ 50 Huang Zhong, Shu General R :W: 4.00 8.00
☐ 51 Hunting Cheetah U :G: 2.00 4.00
☐ 52 Imperial Edict C :K: .50 1.00
☐ 53 Imperial Recruiter U :R: 4.00 8.00
☐ 54 Imperial Seal R :K: 350.00 700.00
☐ 55 Independent Troops C :R: .50 1.00
☐ 56 Island C :L: .50 1.00
☐ 57 Island C :L: .50 1.00
☐ 58 Island C :L: .50 1.00
☐ 59 Kongming, Sleeping Dragon R :W: 10.00 20.00
☐ 60 Kongming's Contraptions R :W: 4.00 8.00
☐ 61 Lady Sun R :B: 6.00 12.00
☐ 62 Lady Zhurong, Warrior Queen R :G: 6.00 12.00
☐ 63 Liu Bei, Lord of Shu R :W: 6.00 12.00
☐ 64 Lone Wolf U :G: 1.50 3.00
☐ 65 Loyal Retainers U :W: 2.00 4.00
☐ 66 Lu Bu, Master-at-Arms R :R: 7.50 15.00
☐ 67 Lu Meng, Wu General R :B: 4.00 8.00
☐ 68 Lu Su, Wu Advisor R :B: 4.00 8.00
☐ 69 Lu Xun, Scholar General R :B: 3.00 6.00
☐ 70 Ma Chao, Western Warrior R :R: 4.00 8.00
☐ 71 Marshaling the Troops R :G: 5.00 10.00
☐ 72 Meng Huo, Barbarian King R :G: 15.00 30.00
☐ 73 Meng Huo's Horde C :G: .50 1.00
☐ 74 Misfortune's Gain C :W: .50 1.00
☐ 75 Mountain Bandit C :R: .50 1.00
☐ 76 Mountain C :L: .50 1.00
☐ 77 Mountain C :L: .50 1.00
☐ 78 Mountain C :L: .50 1.00
☐ 79 Mystic Denial U :B: 2.00 4.00
☐ 80 Overwhelming Forces R :K: 60.00 120.00
☐ 81 Pang Tong, Young Phoenix R :W: 4.00 8.00
☐ 82 Peach Garden Oath U :W: 2.00 4.00
☐ 83 Plains C :L: .50 1.00
☐ 84 Plains C :L: .50 1.00
☐ 85 Plains C :L: .50 1.00
☐ 86 Poison Arrow U :K: 2.00 4.00
☐ 87 Preemptive Strike C :B: .50 1.00
☐ 88 Rally the Troops U :W: 2.00 4.00
☐ 89 Ravages of War R :W: 100.00 200.00
☐ 90 Ravaging Horde U :R: 2.00 4.00
☐ 91 Red Cliffs Armada U :B: 2.00 4.00
☐ 92 Relentless Assault R :R: 4.00 8.00
☐ 93 Renegade Troops U :R: 2.00 4.00
☐ 94 Return to Battle C :K: .50 1.00
☐ 95 Riding Red Hare C :W: .50 1.00
☐ 96 Riding the Dilu Horse R :G: 4.00 8.00
☐ 97 Rockslide Ambush U :R: 2.00 4.00
☐ 98 Rolling Earthquake R :R: 60.00 120.00
☐ 99 Sage's Knowledge C :B: .50 1.00
☐ 100 Shu Cavalry C :W: .50 1.00
☐ 101 Shu Defender C :W: .50 1.00
☐ 102 Shu Elite Companions U :W: 2.00 4.00
☐ 103 Shu Elite Infantry C :W: .50 1.00
☐ 104 Shu Farmer C :W: .50 1.00
☐ 105 Shu Foot Soldiers C :W: .50 1.00
☐ 106 Shu General U :W: 2.00 4.00
☐ 107 Shu Grain Caravan C :W: .50 1.00
☐ 108 Shu Soldier-Farmers U :W: 2.00 4.00
☐ 109 Sima Yi, Wei Field Marshal R :K: 4.00 8.00
☐ 110 Slashing Tiger R :G: 4.00 8.00
☐ 111 Southern Elephant C :G: .50 1.00
☐ 112 Spoils of Victory U :G: 2.00 4.00
☐ 113 Spring of Eternal Peace C :G: .50 1.00
☐ 114 Stalking Tiger C :G: .50 1.00
☐ 115 Stolen Grain U :K: 2.00 4.00
☐ 116 Stone Catapult R :K: 5.00 10.00
☐ 117 Stone Rain C :R: .50 1.00
☐ 118 Strategic Planning U :B: 2.00 4.00
☐ 119 Straw Soldiers C :B: .50 1.00
☐ 120 Sun Ce, Young Conquerer R :B: 6.00 12.00
☐ 121 Sun Quan, Lord of Wu R :B: 6.00 12.00
☐ 122 Swamp C :L: .50 1.00
☐ 123 Swamp C :L: .50 1.00
☐ 124 Swamp C :L: .50 1.00
☐ 125 Taoist Hermit U :G: 2.00 4.00
☐ 126 Taoist Mystic R :G: 3.00 6.00
☐ 127 Taunting Challenge R :G: 4.00 8.00
☐ 128 Three Visits C :G: .50 1.00
☐ 129 Trained Cheetah U :G: 2.00 4.00
☐ 130 Trained Jackal C :G: .50 1.00
☐ 131 Trip Wire U :G: 2.00 4.00
☐ 132 Vengeance U :W: 2.00 4.00
☐ 133 Virtuous Charge C :W: .50 1.00
☐ 134 Volunteer Militia C :W: .50 1.00
☐ 135 Warrior's Oath R :R: 4.00 8.00
☐ 136 Warrior's Stand U :W: 2.00 4.00
☐ 137 Wei Ambush Force C :K: .50 1.00
☐ 138 Wei Assassins U :K: 2.00 4.00
☐ 139 Wei Elite Companions U :K: 2.00 4.00
☐ 140 Wei Infantry C :K: .50 1.00
☐ 141 Wei Night Raiders U :K: 2.00 4.00
☐ 142 Wei Scout C :K: .50 1.00
☐ 143 Wei Strike Force C :K: .50 1.00
☐ 144 Wielding the Green Dragon C :G: .50 1.00
☐ 145 Wolf Pack R :G: 15.00 30.00
☐ 146 Wu Admiral U :B: 2.00 4.00
☐ 147 Wu Elite Cavalry C :B: .50 1.00
☐ 148 Wu Infantry C :B: .50 1.00
☐ 149 Wu Light Cavalry C :B: .50 1.00
☐ 150 Wu Longbowman U :B: 2.00 4.00
☐ 151 Wu Scout C :B: .50 1.00
☐ 152 Wu Spy U :B: 2.00 4.00
☐ 153 Wu Warship C :B: .50 1.00
☐ 154 Xiahou Dun, the One-Eyed R :K: 75.00 150.00
☐ 155 Xun Yu, Wei Advisor R :K: 4.00 8.00
☐ 156 Yellow Scarves Cavalry C :R: .50 1.00
☐ 157 Yellow Scarves General R :R: 4.00 8.00
☐ 158 Yellow Scarves Troops C :R: .50 1.00
☐ 159 Young Wei Recruit C :K: .50 1.00
☐ 160 Yuan Shao, the Indecisive R :R: 4.00 8.00
☐ 161 Yuan Shao's Infantry U :R: 2.00 4.00
☐ 162 Zhang Fei, Fierce Warrior R :W: 6.00 12.00
☐ 163 Zhang He, Wei General R :K: 5.00 10.00
☐ 164 Zhang Liao, Hero of Hefei R :K: 4.00 8.00
☐ 165 Zhao Zilong, Tiger General R :W: 5.00 10.00
☐ 166 Zhou Yu, Chief Commander R :B: 5.00 10.00
☐ 167 Zhuge Jin, Wu Strategist R :B: 5.00 10.00
☐ 168 Zodiac Dog C :R: .50 1.00
☐ 169 Zodiac Dragon R :R: 100.00 200.00
☐ 170 Zodiac Goat C :R: .50 1.00
☐ 171 Zodiac Horse U :G: 2.00 4.00

❑ 172 Zodiac Monkey C :G:	.50	1.00
❑ 173 Zodiac Ox U :G:	2.00	4.00
❑ 174 Zodiac Pig U :K:	2.00	4.00
❑ 175 Zodiac Rabbit C :G:	.50	1.00
❑ 176 Zodiac Rat C :K:	.50	1.00
❑ 177 Zodiac Rooster C :G:	.50	1.00
❑ 178 Zodiac Snake C :K:	.50	1.00
❑ 179 Zodiac Tiger U :G:	2.00	4.00
❑ 180 Zuo Ci, the Mocking Sage R :G:	4.00	8.00

1999 Magic the Gathering Starter

Complete Set (173)	250.00	300.00
Starter Deck Box (12 Decks)	150.00	250.00
Starter Deck	18.00	30.00
Booster Box (36 Packs)	175.00	250.00
Booster Pack (15 Cards)	5.00	8.00
Released in July 1999		
❑ 1 Abyssal Horror R :K:	1.00	2.00
❑ 2 Air Elemental U :B:	.25	.50
❑ 3 Alluring Scent R :G:	1.00	2.00
❑ 4 Ancient Craving R :K:	1.50	3.00
❑ 5 Angel of Light U :W:	.25	.50
❑ 6 Angel of Mercy U :W:	.25	.50
❑ 7 Angelic Blessing C :W:	.15	.30
❑ 8 Archangel R :W:	4.00	8.00
❑ 9 Ardent Militia U :W:	.25	.50
❑ 10 Armageddon R :W:	2.50	5.00
❑ 11 Barbtooth Wurm C :G:	.15	.30
❑ 12 Bargain U :W:	.25	.50
❑ 13 Blinding Light R :W:	1.50	3.00
❑ 14 Bog Imp C :K:	.15	.30
❑ 15 Bog Raiders C :K:	.15	.30
❑ 16 Bog Wraith U :K:	.50	1.00
❑ 17 Border Guard C :W:	.15	.30
❑ 18 Breath of Life U :W:	.25	.50
❑ 19 Bull Hippo U :G:	.30	.75
❑ 20 Champion Lancer R :W:	2.00	4.00
❑ 21 Charging Paladin U :W:	.25	.50
❑ 22 Chorus of Woe C :K:	.15	.30
❑ 23 Cinder Storm U :R:	.25	.50
❑ 24 Coercion U :K:	.25	.50
❑ 25 Coral Eel C :B:	.15	.30
❑ 26 Counterspell U :B:	.25	.50
❑ 27 Dakmor Ghoul U :K:	.25	.50
❑ 28 Dakmor Lancer R :K:	1.50	3.00
❑ 29 Dakmor Plague U :K:	.25	.50
❑ 30 Dakmor Scorpion C :K:	.15	.30
❑ 31 Dakmor Sorceress R :K:	5.00	10.00
❑ 32 Dark Offering U :K:	.25	.50
❑ 33 Denizen of the Deep R :B:	2.50	5.00
❑ 34 Devastation R :R:	1.50	3.00
❑ 35 Devoted Hero C :W:	.15	.30
❑ 36 Devout Monk C :W:	.15	.30
❑ 37 Dread Reaper R :K:	1.50	3.00
❑ 38 Durkwood Boars C :G:	.15	.30
❑ 39 Eager Cadet C* :W:	.15	.30
❑ 40 Earth Elemental U :R:	.25	.50
❑ 41 Exhaustion U :B:	.25	.50
❑ 42 Extinguish C :B:	.15	.30
❑ 43 Eye Spy U :B:	.25	.50
❑ 44 False Peace U :W:	.25	.50
❑ 45 Feral Shadow C :K:	.15	.30
❑ 46 Fire Elemental U :R:	.25	.50
❑ 47 Fire Tempest R :R:	1.00	2.00
❑ 48 Foot Soldiers C :W:	.15	.30
❑ 49 Forest L :L:	.15	.30
❑ 50 Forest L :L:	.15	.30
❑ 51 Forest L :L:	.15	.30
❑ 52 Forest L :L:	.15	.30
❑ 53 Gerrard's Wisdom R :W:	1.50	3.00
❑ 54 Giant Octopus C :B:	.15	.30
❑ 55 Goblin Cavaliers C :R:	.15	.30
❑ 56 Goblin Chariot C :R:	.15	.30
❑ 57 Goblin Commando U :R:	.25	.50
❑ 58 Goblin General U :R:	.25	.50
❑ 59 Goblin Glider U :R:	.25	.50
❑ 60 Goblin Hero R* :R:	2.00	4.00
❑ 61 Goblin Lore U :R:	.25	.50
❑ 62 Goblin Mountaineer C :R:	.15	.30
❑ 63 Goblin Settler U :R:	.25	.50
❑ 64 Gorilla Warrior C :G:	.15	.30
❑ 65 Gravedigger U :K:	.25	.50
❑ 66 Grim Tutor R :K:	125.00	200.00
❑ 67 Grizzly Bears C :G:	.15	.30
❑ 68 Hand of Death C :K:	.15	.30
❑ 69 Hollow Dogs C :K:	.15	.30
❑ 70 Howling Fury U :K:	.25	.50
❑ 71 Hulking Goblin C :R:	.15	.30
❑ 72 Hulking Ogre U :R:	.25	.50
❑ 73 Ingenious Thief C :B:	.15	.30
❑ 74 Island L :L:	.15	.30
❑ 75 Island L :L:	.15	.30
❑ 76 Island L :L:	.15	.30
❑ 77 Island L :L:	.15	.30
❑ 78 Jagged Lightning U :R:	.50	1.00
❑ 79 Knight Errant C :W:	.15	.30
❑ 80 Last Chance R :R:	1.50	3.00
❑ 81 Lava Axe C :R:	.15	.30
❑ 82 Lone Wolf C :G:	.15	.30
❑ 83 Loyal Sentry R :W:	1.00	2.00
❑ 84 Lynx U :G:	.25	.50
❑ 85 Man-o-War U :B:	.25	.50
❑ 86 Merfolk of the Pearl Trident C* :B:	.15	.30
❑ 87 Mind Rot C :K:	.15	.30
❑ 88 Mons's Goblin Raiders R* :R:	1.00	2.00
❑ 89 Monstrous Growth C :G:	.15	.30
❑ 90 Moon Sprite U :G:	.25	.50
❑ 91 Mountain L :L:	.15	.30
❑ 92 Mountain L :L:	.15	.30
❑ 93 Mountain L :L:	.15	.30
❑ 94 Mountain L :L:	.15	.30
❑ 95 Muck Rats C :K:	.15	.30
❑ 96 Natural Spring U :G:	.25	.50
❑ 97 Nature's Cloak R :G:	1.00	2.00
❑ 98 Nature's Lore C :G:	.15	.30
❑ 99 Norwood Archers C :G:	.15	.30
❑ 100 Norwood Ranger C :G:	.15	.30
❑ 101 Ogre Warrior C :R:	.15	.30
❑ 102 Owl Familiar U :B:	.25	.50
❑ 103 Path of Peace C :W:	.15	.30
❑ 104 Phantom Warrior R :B:	1.00	2.00
❑ 105 Piracy R :B:	5.00	10.00
❑ 106 Plains L :L:	.15	.30
❑ 107 Plains L :L:	.15	.30
❑ 108 Plains L :L:	.15	.30
❑ 109 Plains L :L:	.15	.30
❑ 110 Pride of Lions U :G:	.25	.50
❑ 111 Psychic Transfer R :B:	1.50	3.00
❑ 112 Raging Goblin C :R:	.15	.30
❑ 113 Raise Dead C :K:	.15	.30
❑ 114 Ransack R :B:	1.00	2.00
❑ 115 Ravenous Rats U :K:	.50	1.00
❑ 116 Relearn U :B:	.25	.50
❑ 117 Relentless Assault R :R:	2.00	4.00
❑ 118 Remove Soul C :B:	.15	.30
❑ 119 Renewing Touch U :G:	.25	.50
❑ 120 Righteous Charge U :W:	2.50	5.00
❑ 121 Righteous Fury R :W:	1.00	2.00
❑ 122 Royal Falcon C* :W:	.15	.30
❑ 123 Royal Trooper U :W:	.25	.50
❑ 124 Sacred Nectar C :W:	.15	.30
❑ 125 Scathe Zombies C* :K:	.15	.30
❑ 126 Scorching Spear C :R:	.15	.30
❑ 127 Sea Eagle C* :B:	.15	.30
❑ 128 Serpent Warrior C :K:	.15	.30
❑ 129 Shrieking Specter U :K:	.25	.50
❑ 130 Silverback Ape U :G:	.25	.50
❑ 131 Sleight of Hand C :B:	.15	.30
❑ 132 Snapping Drake C :B:	.15	.30
❑ 133 Soul Feast U :K:	.25	.50
❑ 134 Southern Elephant C :G:	.15	.30
❑ 135 Spitting Earth U :R:	.25	.50
❑ 136 Squall C :G:	.15	.30
❑ 137 Steadfastness C :W:	.15	.30
❑ 138 Stone Rain C :R:	.15	.30
❑ 139 Storm Crow C :B:	.15	.30
❑ 140 Stream of Acid U :K:	.25	.50
❑ 141 Summer Bloom R :G:	1.00	2.00
❑ 142 Swamp L :L:	.15	.30
❑ 143 Swamp L :L:	.15	.30
❑ 144 Swamp L :L:	.15	.30
❑ 145 Swamp L :L:	.15	.30
❑ 146 Sylvan Basilisk R :G:	1.50	3.00
❑ 147 Sylvan Yeti R :G:	1.00	2.00
❑ 148 Thorn Elemental R :G:	1.00	2.00
❑ 149 Thunder Dragon R :R:	20.00	35.00
❑ 150 Tidings U :B:	.25	.50
❑ 151 Time Ebb C :B:	.15	.30
❑ 152 Time Warp R :B:	3.00	6.00
❑ 153 Touch of Brilliance C :B:	.15	.30
❑ 154 Trained Orgg R :R:	1.00	2.00
❑ 155 Tremor C :R:	.15	.30
❑ 156 Undo U :B:	.25	.50
❑ 157 Untamed Wilds U :G:	.25	.50
❑ 158 Venerable Monk C :W:	.15	.30
❑ 159 Vengeance U :W:	.25	.50
❑ 160 Veteran Cavalier U :W:	.25	.50
❑ 161 Vizzerdrix R :B:	1.00	2.00
❑ 162 Volcanic Dragon R :R:	2.00	4.00
❑ 163 Volcanic Hammer C :R:	.15	.30
❑ 164 Water Elemental U :B:	.25	.50
❑ 165 Whiptail Wurm U :G:	.25	.50
❑ 167 Wicked Pact R :K:	1.50	3.00
❑ 168 Wild Griffin C :W:	.15	.30
❑ 169 Wild Ox U :G:	.25	.50
❑ 170 Willow Elf C* :G:	.15	.30
❑ 171 Wind Drake C :B:	.15	.30
❑ 172 Wind Sail U :B:	.25	.50
❑ 173 Wood Elves U :G:	.25	.50

1995 Magic the Gathering Chronicles

Complete Set (125)	50.00	100.00
Booster Box (45 Packs)	100.00	200.00
Booster Pack (12 Cards)	5.00	7.00
Released in September 1995		
❑ 1 Abu Ja'far U	.25	.50
❑ 2 Active Volcano C	.15	.30
❑ 3 Akron Legionnaire U	.25	.50
❑ 4 Aladdin U	.25	.50
❑ 5 Angelic Voices U	.25	.50
❑ 6 Arcades Sabboth U	2.00	4.00
❑ 7 Arena of the Ancients U	.50	1.00
❑ 8 Argothian Pixies C	.15	.30
❑ 9 Ashnod's Altar C	.15	.30
❑ 10 Ashnod's Transmogrant C	.15	.30
❑ 11 Axelrod Gunnarson U	.50	1.00
❑ 12 Ayesha Tanaka U	.50	1.00
❑ 13 Azure Drake U	.50	1.00
❑ 14 Banshee U	.50	1.00
❑ 15 Barl's Cage U	.50	1.00
❑ 16 Beasts of Bogardan U	.50	1.00
❑ 17 Blood Moon U	2.00	4.00
❑ 18 Blood of the Martyr U	.50	1.00
❑ 19 Bog Rats C	.15	.30
❑ 20 Book of Rass U	.50	1.00
❑ 21 Boomerang C	.15	.30
❑ 22 Bronze Horse U	.50	1.00
❑ 23 Cat Warriors C	.15	.30
❑ 24 Chromium U	2.00	4.00
❑ 25 City of Brass U	4.00	8.00
❑ 26 Cocoon U	.50	1.00
❑ 27 Concordant Crossroads U	2.50	5.00
❑ 28 Craw Giant U	.50	1.00
❑ 29 Cuombajj Witches C	.15	.30
❑ 30 Cyclone U	.50	1.00
❑ 31 Dakkon Blackblade U	1.50	3.00
❑ 32 Dance of Many U	.50	1.00
❑ 33 Dandân C	.15	.30
❑ 34 D'Avenant Archer C	.15	.30
❑ 35 Divine Offering C	.15	.30
❑ 36 Emerald Dragonfly C	.15	.30
❑ 37 Enchantment Alteration U	.50	1.00
❑ 38 Erhnam Djinn U	.50	1.00
❑ 39 Fallen Angel U	.50	1.00
❑ 40 Fallen, The U	.50	1.00
❑ 41 Feldon's Cane C	.15	.30
❑ 42 Fire Drake U	.50	1.00
❑ 43 Fishliver Oil C	.15	.30
❑ 44 Flash Flood C	.15	.30
❑ 45 Fountain of Youth C	.15	.30
❑ 46 Gabriel Angelfire U	1.00	2.00
❑ 47 Gauntlets of Chaos U	.50	1.00
❑ 48 Ghazbán Ogre C	.15	.30
❑ 49 Giant Slug C	.15	.30
❑ 50 Goblin Artisans U	.50	1.00
❑ 51 Goblin Digging Team C	.15	.30
❑ 52 Goblin Shrine C	.15	.30
❑ 53 Goblins of the Flarg C	.15	.30
❑ 54 Hasran Ogress C	.15	.30
❑ 55 Hell's Caretaker U	2.50	5.00
❑ 56 Horn of Deatening U	.50	1.00
❑ 57 Indestructible Aura C	.15	.30
❑ 58 Ivory Guardians U	.50	1.00
❑ 59 Jalum Tome U	.50	1.00
❑ 60 Jeweled Bird U	1.00	2.00
❑ 61 Johan U	.50	1.00
❑ 62 Juxtapose U	.50	1.00
❑ 63 Keepers of the Faith C	.15	.30
❑ 64 Kei Takahashi C	.15	.30
❑ 65 Land's Edge U	.50	1.00
❑ 66 Living Armor C	.15	.30
❑ 67 Marhault Elsdragon C	.15	.30
❑ 68 Metamorphosis C	.15	.30
❑ 69 Mountain Yeti C	.15	.30
❑ 70 Nebuchadnezzar U	1.00	2.00
❑ 71 Nicol Bolas U	2.00	4.00
❑ 72 Obelisk of Undoing U	.50	1.00
❑ 73 Palladia-Mors U	2.00	4.00
❑ 74 Petra Sphinx U	.50	1.00
❑ 75 Primordial Ooze U	.15	.30
❑ 76 Puppet Master U	.50	1.00
❑ 77 Rabid Wombat U	.50	1.00
❑ 78 Rakalite U	.50	1.00
❑ 79 Recall U	.50	1.00
❑ 80 Remove Soul C	.15	.30
❑ 81 Repentant Blacksmith C	.15	.30
❑ 82 Revelation U	.50	1.00
❑ 83 Rubinia Soulsinger U	1.00	2.00
❑ 84 Runesword C	.15	.30
❑ 85 Safe Haven U	1.00	2.00
❑ 86 Scavenger Folk C	.15	.30
❑ 87 Sentinel U	.50	1.00
❑ 88 Serpent Generator U	1.00	2.00
❑ 89 Shield Wall U	.50	1.00
❑ 90 Shimian Night Stalker U	.50	1.00
❑ 91 Sivitri Scarzam C	.15	.30
❑ 92 Sol'kanar the Swamp King U	1.50	3.00
❑ 93 Stangg U	.50	1.00
❑ 94 Storm Seeker U	.50	1.00
❑ 95 Takklemaggot U	.50	1.00
❑ 96 Teleport U	.50	1.00
❑ 97 Tobias Andrion C	.15	.30
❑ 98 Tor Wauki C	.15	.30
❑ 99 Tormod's Crypt C	.30	.75
❑ 100 Transmutation C	.15	.30
❑ 101 Triassic Egg U	.50	1.00
❑ 102 Urza's Mine C	.15	.30
❑ 103 Urza's Mine C	.15	.30
❑ 104 Urza's Mine C	.15	.30
❑ 105 Urza's Mine C	.15	.30
❑ 106 Urza's Power Plant C	.15	.30
❑ 107 Urza's Power Plant C	.15	.30
❑ 108 Urza's Power Plant C	.15	.30
❑ 109 Urza's Power Plant C	.15	.30
❑ 110 Urza's Tower C	.15	.30
❑ 111 Urza's Tower C	.15	.30
❑ 112 Urza's Tower C	.15	.30
❑ 113 Urza's Tower C	.15	.30
❑ 114 Vaevictis Asmadi U	2.00	4.00
❑ 115 Voodoo Doll U	.50	1.00
❑ 116 Wall of Heat C	.15	.30
❑ 117 Wall of Opposition U	.50	1.00
❑ 118 Wall of Shadows C	.15	.30
❑ 119 Wall of Vapor C	.15	.30
❑ 120 Wall of Wonder U	.50	1.00
❑ 121 War Elephant C	.15	.30
❑ 122 Witch Hunter U	.50	1.00
❑ 123 Wretched, The U	1.50	3.00
❑ 124 Xira Arien U	.50	1.00
❑ 125 Yawgmoth Demon U	.50	1.00

1997 Magic the Gathering Vanguard

Complete Set (32)	150.00	200.00
Booster Pack	40.00	60.00
❑ 1 Ashnod R	3.00	5.00
❑ 2 Barrin R	3.00	5.00
❑ 3 Crovax R	3.00	5.00
❑ 4 Eladamri R	3.00	5.00
❑ 5 Ertai R	3.00	5.00
❑ 6 Gerrard R	3.00	5.00
❑ 7 Gix R	3.00	5.00
❑ 8 Greven il-Vec R	3.00	5.00
❑ 9 Hanna R	3.00	6.00
❑ 10 Karn R	3.00	5.00
❑ 11 Lyna R-	3.00	5.00
❑ 12 Maraxus R	3.00	5.00
❑ 13 Mirri R	4.00	7.00
❑ 14 Mishra R	3.00	5.00
❑ 15 Multani R	4.00	7.00
❑ 16 Oracle R	3.00	5.00
❑ 17 Orim R	3.00	5.00
❑ 18 Rofellos R	3.00	5.00
❑ 19 Selenia R	3.00	5.00
❑ 20 Serra R	3.00	5.00
❑ 21 Sidar Kondo R	3.00	5.00
❑ 22 Sisay R	3.00	6.00
❑ 23 Sliver Queen, Brood Mother R	7.00	12.00
❑ 24 Squee R	3.00	5.00
❑ 25 Starke R	3.00	5.00
❑ 26 Tahngarth R	3.00	5.00
❑ 27 Takara R	3.00	6.00
❑ 28 Tawnos R	4.00	6.00
❑ 29 Titania R	3.00	6.00
❑ 30 Urza R	3.00	6.00
❑ 31 Volrath R	3.00	5.00
❑ 32 Xantcha R	3.00	5.00

1998 Magic the Gathering Unglued

Complete Set (93)	50.00	90.00
Booster Box (48 Packs)	225.00	300.00
Booster Pack (15 Cards)	7.00	10.00
Released in August 1998		
❑ 1 Ashnod's Coupon R :A: :K:	4.00	8.00
❑ 2 Big Furry Monster-L R :K:	6.00	12.00
❑ 2A Big Furry Monster-R R :K:	6.00	12.00
❑ 3 Blacker Lotus R :A:	3.50	7.00
❑ 4 Bronze Calendar U :A:	.50	1.00
❑ 5 Bureaucracy R :B:	1.00	2.00
❑ 6 Burning Cinder Fury of Crimson/ Chaos Fire R :R:	1.50	3.00
❑ 7 Cardboard Carapace R :G:	1.50	3.00
❑ 8 Censorship U :B:	1.00	2.00
❑ 9 Chaos Confetti C :A:	.15	.30
❑ 10 Charm School U :W:	.50	1.00
❑ 11 Checks and Balances U :B:	.50	1.00
❑ 12 Chicken a la King R :B:	1.50	3.00
❑ 13 Chicken Egg C :R:	.15	.30
❑ 14 Clam Session C :B:	.15	.30
❑ 15 Clambassadors C :B:	.15	.30
❑ 16 Clam-I-Am C :B:	.15	.30
❑ 17 Clay Pigeon U :A:	.50	1.00
❑ 18 Common Courtesy U :B:	1.00	2.00
❑ 19 Deadhead C :K:	.15	.30
❑ 20 Denied! C :B:	.15	.30
❑ 21 Double Cross C :K:	.15	.30
❑ 22 Double Deal C :R:	.15	.30
❑ 23 Double Dip C :W:	.15	.30
❑ 24 Double Play C :G:	.15	.30
❑ 25 Double Take C :B:	.15	.30
❑ 26 Elvish Impersonators C :G:	.15	.30
❑ 27 Flock of Rabid Sheep U :G:	1.00	2.00
❑ 28 Forest C :G:	1.50	3.00
❑ 29 Fowl Play C :B:	.15	.30
❑ 30 Free-for-All R :B:	1.00	2.00
❑ 31 Free-Range Chicken C :G:	.15	.30
❑ 32 Gerrymandering U :G:	.50	1.00
❑ 33 Get a Life U :W:	.50	1.00
❑ 34 Ghazban Ogress C :G:	.15	.30
❑ 35 Giant Fan R :A:	1.00	2.00
❑ 36 Goblin Bookie C :R:	.15	.30
❑ 37 Goblin Bowling Team C :R:	.15	.30
❑ 38 Goblin Tutor U :R:	1.00	2.00
❑ 39 Goblin U :R:	.50	1.00
❑ 40 Growth Spurt C :G:	.15	.30
❑ 41 Gus C :G:	.15	.30
❑ 42 Handcuffs U :K:	.50	1.00
❑ 43 Hungry Hungry Heifer U :G:	.50	1.00
❑ 44 Hurloon Wrangler C :R:	.15	.30
❑ 45 I'm Rubber, You're Glue R :W:	2.00	4.00
❑ 46 Incoming! R :G:	2.00	4.00
❑ 47 Infernal Spawn of Evil R :K:	4.00	8.00
❑ 48 Island C :B:	1.50	3.00
❑ 49 Jack-in-the-Mox R :A:	1.50	3.00
❑ 50 Jalum Grifter R :R:	1.50	3.00
❑ 51 Jester's Sombrero R :A:	1.50	3.00
❑ 52 Jumbo Imp U :K:	.50	1.00
❑ 53 Knight of the Hokey Pokey C :W:	.15	.30
❑ 54 Krazy Kow C :R:	.15	.30
❑ 55 Landfill R :R:	1.00	2.00
❑ 56 Lexivore U :W:	.50	1.00
❑ 57 Look at Me, I'm the DCI R :W:	1.50	3.00
❑ 58 Mesa Chicken C :W:	.15	.30
❑ 59 Mine, Mine, Mine! R :G:	2.50	5.00
❑ 60 Mirror Mirror R :A:	1.50	3.00
❑ 61 Miss Demeanor U :W:	1.00	2.00
❑ 62 Mountain C :R:	1.00	2.00
❑ 63 Once More with Feeling R :W:	1.50	3.00
❑ 64 Organ Harvest C :K:	.15	.30
❑ 65 Ow R :K:	1.50	3.00
❑ 66 Paper Tiger C :A:	.15	.30
❑ 67 Pegasus U :W:	.50	1.00
❑ 68 Plains C :W:	1.00	2.00
❑ 69 Poultrygeist C :K:	.15	.30
❑ 70 Prismatic Wardrobe C :W:	.15	.30
❑ 71 Psychic Network R :B:	1.00	2.00
❑ 72 Ricochet U :R:	.50	1.00
❑ 73 Rock Lobster C :A:	.15	.30
❑ 74 Scissors Lizard C :A:	.15	.30
❑ 75 Sex Appeal C :W:	.15	.30
❑ 76 Sheep U :G:	1.00	2.00
❑ 77 Soldier U :W:	.50	1.00
❑ 78 Sorry U :B:	.50	1.00
❑ 79 Spark Fiend R :R:	1.50	3.00
❑ 80 Spatula of the Ages U :A:	.50	1.00
❑ 81 Squirrel Farm R :G:	2.00	4.00
❑ 82 Squirrel U :G:	1.50	3.00
❑ 83 Strategy, Schmategy R :R:	2.00	4.00
❑ 84 Swamp C :K:	1.00	2.00
❑ 85 Team Spirit C :G:	.15	.30
❑ 86 Temp of the Damned C :K:	.15	.30
❑ 87 The Cheese Stands Alone R :W:	3.00	6.00
❑ 88 The Ultimate Nightmare U :B:	1.00	2.00
❑ 89 Timmy, Power Gamer R :G:	2.50	5.00
❑ 90 Urza's Contact Lenses U :A:	.50	1.00
❑ 91 Urza's Science Fair Project U :A:	.50	1.00
❑ 92 Volrath's Motion Sensor U :K:	.50	1.00
❑ 93 Zombie U :K:	.75	1.50

2004 Magic the Gathering Unhinged

Complete Set	60.00	120.00
Booster Box (36 Packs)	200.00	250.00
Booster Pack (15 Cards)	6.00	8.00
❑ 1 ___ U :B:	.20	.50
❑ 2 Ach! Hans, Run! R :D:	.30	.75
❑ 3 Aesthetic Consultation R :K:	.30	.75
❑ 4 Ambiguity R :B:	.30	.75
❑ 5 Artful Looter C :B:	.10	.25
❑ 6 Ass Whuppin' R :D:	.50	1.25
❑ 7 Assquatch R :R:	.40	1.00
❑ 8 Atinlay Igpay U :W:	.20	.50
❑ 9 Avatar of Me R :B:	.60	1.50
❑ 10 AWOL C :W:	.20	.50
❑ 11 Bad Ass C :K:	.10	.25
❑ 12 B-I-N-G-O R :G:	.40	1.00
❑ 13 Blast from the Past R :R:	.50	1.25
❑ 14 Bloodletter C :K:	.10	.25
❑ 15 Booster Tutor U :K:	.20	.50
❑ 16 Bosom Buddy U :W:	.20	.50
❑ 17 Brushstroke Paintermage C :B:	.10	.25
❑ 18 Bursting Beebles C :B:	.10	.25
❑ 19 Cardpecker C :W:	.10	.25
❑ 20 Carnivorous Death-Parrot C :B:	.10	.25
❑ 21 Cheap Ass C :W:	.10	.25
❑ 22 Cheatyface U :B:	.75	2.00
❑ 23 Circle of Protection: Art C :W:	.10	.25
❑ 24 City of Ass R :L:	1.50	4.00
❑ 25 Collector Protector R :W:	.30	.75
❑ 26 Creature Guy U :G:	.20	.50
❑ 27 Curse of the Fire Penguin R :R:	.30	.75
❑ 28 Deal Damage U :R:	.20	.50
❑ 29 Double Header C :B:	.10	.25
❑ 30 Drawn Together R :W:	.30	.75
❑ 31 Duh C :K:	.10	.25
❑ 32 Dumb Ass C :R:	.10	.25
❑ 33 Elvish House Party U :G:	.20	.50
❑ 34 Emcee U :W:	.20	.50
❑ 35 Enter the Dungeon R :K:	.40	1.00
❑ 36 Erase C :W:	.10	.25
❑ 37 Eye to Eye U :K:	.20	.50
❑ 38 Face to Face U :R:	.20	.50
❑ 39 Farewell to Arms C :K:	.10	.25
❑ 40 Fascist Art Director C :W:	.10	.25
❑ 41 Fat Ass C :G:	.10	.25
❑ 42 First Come, First Served U :W:	.20	.50
❑ 43 Flaccify C :B:	.10	.25
❑ 44 Forest L :L:	2.00	5.00
❑ 45 Form of the Squirrel R :G:	.30	.75
❑ 46 Fraction Jackson R :G:	.30	.75
❑ 47 Framed! C :B:	.10	.25
❑ 48 Frankie Peanuts R :W:	.30	.75
❑ 49 Frazzled Editor C :R:	.10	.25
❑ 50 Gleemax R :A:	.75	2.00
❑ 51 Gluetius Maximus U :G:	.20	.50
❑ 52 Goblin Mime C :R:	.10	.25
❑ 53 Goblin S.W.A.T. Team C :R:	.10	.25
❑ 54 Goblin Secret Agent C :R:	.10	.25
❑ 55 Granny's Payback U :G:	.20	.50
❑ 56 Graphic Violence C :G:	.10	.25
❑ 57 Greater Morphling R :B:	.50	1.25
❑ 58 Head to Head U :W:	.20	.50
❑ 59 Infernal Spawn of Infernal Spawn of Evil R :K:	.75	2.00
❑ 60 Island L :L:	2.50	6.00
❑ 61 Johnny, Combo Player R :B:	.75	2.00
❑ 62 Keeper of the Sacred Word C :G:	.10	.25
❑ 63 Kill! Destroy! U :K:	.20	.50
❑ 64 Ladies' Knight U :W:	.20	.50
❑ 65 Land Aid '04 C :G:	.10	.25
❑ 66 Laughing Hyena C :G:	.10	.25
❑ 67 Letter Bomb R :A:	.50	1.25
❑ 68 Little Girl C :W:	.20	.50
❑ 69 Look at Me, I'm R&D R :W:	.30	.75
❑ 70 Loose Lips C :B:	.10	.25
❑ 71 Magical Hacker U :B:	.20	.50
❑ 72 Man of Measure C :W:	.10	.25
❑ 73 Mana Flair C :R:	.10	.25
❑ 74 Mana Screw U :A:	.20	.50
❑ 75 Market Research Long Card Name C :G:	.10	.25
❑ 76 Meddling Kids R :D:	.40	1.00

❑ 77 Mise U :B: .20 .50
❑ 78 Moniker Mage C :B: .10 .25
❑ 79 Monkey Monkey Monkey C :G: .10 .25
❑ 80 Mons's Goblin Waiters C :R: .10 .25
❑ 81 Mother of Goons C :K: .10 .25
❑ 82 Mountain L :L: 2.00 5.00
❑ 83 Mouth to Mouth U :B: .20 .50
❑ 84 Mox Lotus R :A: 4.00 10.00
❑ 85 My First Tome U :A: .20 .50
❑ 86 Name Dropping U :G: .20 .50
❑ 87 Necro-Impotence R :K: .30 .75
❑ 88 Now I Know My ABC's R :B: .30 .75
❑ 89 Number Crunch C :B: .10 .25
❑ 90 Old Fogey R :G: .30 .75
❑ 91 Orcish Paratroopers C :R: .10 .25
❑ 92 Persecute Artist U :K: .20 .50
❑ 93 Phyrexian Librarian U :K: .20 .50
❑ 94 Plains L :L: 2.00 5.00
❑ 95 Pointy Finger of Doom R :A: .40 1.00
❑ 96 Punctuate C :R: .10 .25
❑ 97 Pygmy Giant U :R: .20 .50
❑ 98 Question Elemental? U :B: .20 .50
❑ 99 R&D's Secret Lair R :L: .40 1.00
❑ 100 Rare-B-Gone R :D: .40 1.00
❑ 101 Red-Hot Hottie C :R: .10 .25
❑ 102 Remodel C :G: .10 .25
❑ 103 Richard Garfield, Ph.D. R :B: 1.00 2.50
❑ 104 Rocket-Powered Turbo Slug U :R: .40 1.00
❑ 105 Rod of Spanking U :A: .20 .50
❑ 106 S.N.O.T. C :G: .20 .50
❑ 107 Sauté C :R: .10 .25
❑ 108 Save Life U :W: .20 .50
❑ 109 Shoe Tree C :G: .10 .25
❑ 110 Side to Side U :G: .20 .50
❑ 111 Six-y Beast U :R: .20 .50
❑ 112 Smart Ass C :B: .10 .25
❑ 113 Spell Counter U :B: .20 .50
❑ 114 Standing Army C :W: .10 .25
❑ 115 Staying Power R :W: .30 .75
❑ 116 Stone-Cold Basilisk U :G: .20 .50
❑ 117 Stop That C :K: .10 .25
❑ 118 Supersize C :G: .10 .25
❑ 119 Swamp L :L: 2.50 6.00
❑ 120 Symbol Status U :G: .20 .50
❑ 121 Tainted Monkey C :K: .10 .25
❑ 122 The Fallen Apart C :K: .10 .25
❑ 123 Time Machine R :A: .30 .75
❑ 124 Togglodyte U :A: .20 .50
❑ 125 Topsy Turvy R :B: .30 .75
❑ 126 Touch and Go C :R: .10 .25
❑ 127 Toy Boat U :A: .20 .50
❑ 128 Uktabi Kong R :G: .40 1.00
❑ 129 Urza's Hot Tub U :A: .20 .50
❑ 130 Vile Bile C :K: .10 .25
❑ 131 Water Gun Balloon Game R :A: .30 .75
❑ 132 Wet Willie of the Damned C :K: .10 .25
❑ 133 When Fluffy Bunnies Attack C :K: .10 .25
❑ 134 Who/What/When/Where/Why R :D: .60 1.50
❑ 135 Wordmail C :W: .10 .25
❑ 136 Working Stiff U :K: .20 .50
❑ 137 World-Bottling Kit R :A: .30 .75
❑ 138 Yet Another Æther Vortex R :R: .30 .75
❑ 139 Zombie Fanboy U :K: .20 .50
❑ 140 Zzzyxas's Abyss R :K: .30 .75
❑ 141 Super Secret Tech R :A: 4.00 10.00

2004 Magic the Gathering Unhinged Foil

Complete Set (141) 150.00 250.00
*Foil: .8X to 2X Basic Cards

2005 Magic the Gathering Ravnica Pro Tour Player Set

Complete Set 6.00 12.00
❑ 1 Kai Budde 1.00 2.00
❑ 2 Dave Humphrey .50 1.00
❑ 3 Osyp Lebedowicz .75 1.50
❑ 4 Julien Nuijten .50 1.00
❑ 5 Masashi Oiso .50 1.00
❑ 6 Olivier Ruel .50 1.00

2008 Magic the Gathering From the Vault Dragons

Complete Set (15) 75.00 150.00
❑ 1 Bladewing the Risen R :D: 3.00 8.00
❑ 2 Bogarden Hellkite R :R: 2.50 6.00
❑ 3 Draco R :A: 2.00 5.00
❑ 4 Dragon Whelp R :R: .75 2.00
❑ 5 Dragonstorm R :R: 5.00 12.00
❑ 6 Ebon Dragon R :K: 3.00 8.00
❑ 7 Form of the Dragon R :R: 3.00 8.00
❑ 8 Hellkite Overlord R :D: 3.00 8.00
❑ 9 Kokusho, the Evening Star R :K: 8.00 20.00
❑ 10 Nicol Bolas R :D: 25.00 50.00
❑ 11 Niv-Mizzet, the Firemind R :D: 8.00 20.00
❑ 12 Rith, the Awakener R :D: 3.00 8.00
❑ 13 Shivan Dragon R :R: 1.50 4.00
❑ 14 Thunder Dragon R :R: 4.00 10.00
❑ 15 Two-Headed Dragon R :R: 2.00 5.00

2009 Magic the Gathering From the Vault Exiled

Complete Set (15) 75.00 125.00
❑ 1 Balance R :W: 2.50 6.00
❑ 2 Berserk R :G: 20.00 50.00
❑ 3 Channel R :G: 2.00 5.00
❑ 4 Gifts Ungiven R :B: 3.00 8.00
❑ 5 Goblin Lackey R :R: 6.00 15.00
❑ 6 Kird Ape R :R: 1.50 4.00
❑ 7 Lotus Petal R :A: 4.00 10.00
❑ 8 Mystical Tutor R :B: 4.00 10.00
❑ 9 Necropotence R :K: 3.00 8.00
❑ 10 Sensei's Divining Top R :A: 12.00 30.00
❑ 11 Serendib Efreet R :B: 2.50 6.00
❑ 12 Skullclamp R :A: 2.50 6.00
❑ 13 Strip Mine R :L: 6.00 15.00
❑ 14 Tinker R :B: 4.00 10.00
❑ 15 Trinisphere R :A: 1.50 4.00

2010 Magic the Gathering From the Vault Relics

Complete Set (15) 75.00 125.00
❑ 1 Aether Vial M 10.00 25.00
❑ 2 Black Vise M 1.25 3.00
❑ 3 Isochron Scepter M 4.00 10.00
❑ 4 Ivory Tower M 1.50 4.00
❑ 5 Jester's Cap M 1.25 3.00
❑ 6 Karn, Silver Golem M 2.50 6.00
❑ 7 Masticore M 1.25 3.00
❑ 8 Memory Jar M 2.00 5.00
❑ 9 Mirari M 1.50 4.00
❑ 10 Mox Diamond M 12.00 30.00
❑ 11 Nevinyrral's Disk M 6.00 15.00
❑ 12 Sol Ring M 12.00 30.00
❑ 13 Sundering Titan M 1.50 4.00
❑ 14 Sword of Body and Mind M 5.00 12.00
❑ 15 Zuran Orb M 1.25 3.00

2011 Magic the Gathering From the Vault Legends

Complete Set (15) 60.00 100.00
❑ 1 Cao Cao, Lord of Wei M :K: 1.25 3.00
❑ 2 Captain Sisay M :W/G: 1.50 4.00
❑ 3 Doran, the Siege Tower M :W/B/G: 2.50 6.00
❑ 4 Kiki-Jiki, Mirror Breaker M :R: 10.00 25.00
❑ 5 Kresh the Bloodbraided M :K/R/G: 1.50 4.00
❑ 6 Mikaeus, the Lunarch M :W: 1.25 3.00
❑ 7 Omnath, Locus of Mana M :G: 3.00 8.00
❑ 8 Oona, Queen of the Fae M :B/K: 2.00 5.00
❑ 9 Progenitus M :W/B/K/R/G: 6.00 15.00
❑ 10 Rafiq of the Many M :W/B/G: 4.00 10.00
❑ 11 Sharuum the Hegemon M :W/B/K: 2.00 5.00
❑ 12 Sun Quan, Lord of Wu M :B: 1.50 4.00
❑ 13 Teferi, Mage of Zhalfir M :B: 4.00 10.00
❑ 14 Ulamog, the Infinite Gyre M 20.00 40.00
❑ 15 Visara the Dreadful M :K: 3.00 8.00

2012 Magic the Gathering From the Vault Realms

Complete Set 75.00 150.00
❑ 1 Ancient Tomb M 10.00 25.00
❑ 2 Boseiju, Who Shelters All M 3.00 8.00
❑ 3 Cephalid Coliseum M 4.00 10.00
❑ 4 Desert M 1.50 4.00
❑ 5 Dryad Arbor M :G: 6.00 15.00
❑ 6 Forbidden Orchard M 3.00 8.00
❑ 7 Glacial Chasm M 2.50 6.00
❑ 8 Grove of the Burnwillows M 6.00 15.00
❑ 9 High Market M 2.50 6.00
❑ 10 Maze of Ith M 25.00 50.00
❑ 11 Murmuring Bosk M 2.50 6.00
❑ 12 Shivan Gorge M 2.00 5.00
❑ 13 Urborg, Tomb of Yawgmoth M 8.00 20.00
❑ 14 Vesuva M 6.00 15.00
❑ 15 Windbrisk Heights M 3.00 8.00

2009 Magic the Gathering Premium Deck Series Slivers

❑ 1 Acidic Sliver U :D: .40 1.00
❑ 2 Amoeboid Changeline C :B: .20 .50
❑ 3 Ancient Ziggurat U :L: 1.25 3.00
❑ 4 Aphetto Dredging C :K: .20 .50
❑ 5 Armor Sliver U :W: .30 .75
❑ 6 Barbed Sliver U :R: .30 .75
❑ 7 Brood Sliver R :G: 1.50 4.00
❑ 8 Clot Sliver C :K: .20 .50
❑ 9 Coat of Arms R :A: 2.00 5.00
❑ 10 Crystalline Sliver U :D: 2.00 5.00
❑ 11 Distant Melody C :B: .20 .50
❑ 12 Forest C :L: .20 .50
❑ 13 Frenzy Sliver C :K: .20 .50
❑ 14 Fungus Sliver R :G: .75 2.00
❑ 15 Fury Sliver U :R: .40 1.00
❑ 16 Gemhide Sliver C :G: .75 2.00
❑ 17 Heart Sliver C :R: .75 2.00
❑ 18 Heartstone U :A: .60 1.50
❑ 19 Hibernation Sliver U :D: .30 .75
❑ 20 Homing Sliver C :R: .30 .75
❑ 21 Island C :L: .30 .75
❑ 22 Metallic Sliver C :A: .30 .75
❑ 23 Might Sliver U :G: .60 1.50
❑ 24 Mountain C :L: .30 .75
❑ 25 Muscle Sliver C :G: .75 2.00
❑ 26 Necrotic Sliver U :D: 1.25 3.00
❑ 27 Plains C :L: .30 .75
❑ 28 Quick Sliver C :G: .20 .50
❑ 29 Rootbound Crag R :L: 2.00 5.00
❑ 30 Rupture Spire C :L: .30 .75
❑ 31 Sliver Overlord M :D: 2.00 5.00
❑ 32 Spectral Sliver U :K: .30 .75
❑ 33 Spined Sliver U :D: .30 .75
❑ 34 Swamp C :L: .30 .75
❑ 35 Terramorphic Expanse C :L: .30 .75
❑ 36 Victual Sliver U :D: .30 .75
❑ 37 Virulent Sliver C :G: .30 .75
❑ 38 Vivid Creek U :L: .60 1.50
❑ 39 Vivid Grove U :L: .60 1.50
❑ 40 Wild Pair R :G: 1.00 2.50
❑ 41 Winged Sliver C :B: 1.25 3.00

1993-2010 Magic the Gathering Special Sets

All sets are complete.
❑ 1 Anthologies Set 40.00 60.00
❑ 3 Battle Royale Set 50.00 85.00
❑ 4 Beatdown Set 90.00 150.00
❑ 5 Beta Collector's Edition Set 800.00 1000.00
❑ 6 Deckmasters 35.00 45.00
❑ 78 Garfield/Finkel Deckmaster set 30.00 50.00
❑ 100 1997 World Champ Deck 25.00 35.00
❑ 110 1998 World Champ Deck 15.00 20.00
❑ 111 1998 World Champ Buehler Deck 20.00 30.00
❑ 120 1999 World Champ Deck 12.00 15.00
❑ 130 2000 World Champ Deck 15.00 25.00
❑ 140 2001 World Champ Deck 10.00 15.00
❑ 150 2002 World Champ Deck 12.00 18.00
❑ 151 2002 World Champ Kibler Deck 20.00 30.00
❑ 160 2003 World Champ Deck 10.00 12.00
❑ 170 2004 World Champ Deck 8.00 12.00

1993-2010 Magic the Gathering Promos

❑ 11 Accumulated Knowledge (FNM) FOIL 10.00 15.00
❑ 22 Albino Troll (FNM) FOIL 4.00 8.00
❑ 33 APAC Land Set - a 12.00 18.00
❑ 44 APAC Land Set - b 12.00 18.00
❑ 55 APAC Land Set - c 12.00 18.00
❑ 66 Arc Lightning - FOIL 5.00 12.00
❑ 77 Archangel - Glossy Japanese 25.00 50.00
❑ 88 Arena 6.00 8.00
❑ 99 ARENA 2004 Land Set 8.00 11.00
❑ 111 Argothian Enchantress - FOIL 15.00 30.00
❑ 122 Armageddon - FOIL 35.00 50.00
❑ 133 Ashnod's Coupon - FOIL 5.00 10.00
❑ 144 Ass Whuppin' - FOIL 3.50 6.00
❑ 155 Aura of Silence (FNM) FOIL 3.00 6.00
❑ 166 Avalanche Riders (FNM) FOIL 6.00 10.00
❑ 177 Avatar of Hope - FOIL 5.00 12.00
❑ 188 Balance (Judge Rew) FOIL 45.00 80.00
❑ 199 Balance - Oversized 6X9 10.00 18.00
❑ 211 Balduvian Horde (Judge Rew) FOIL 7.00 15.00
❑ 222 Balduvian Horde - Oversized 6X9 7.00 10.00
❑ 233 Ball Lightning (Judge Rew) FOIL 18.00 30.00
❑ 244 Baron Sengir - Oversized 6X9 6.00 12.00
❑ 255 Beast of Burden - FOIL 3.00 6.00
❑ 266 Beast of Burden - FOIL Misprint 10.00 16.00
❑ 277 Black Knight - FOIL 8.00 11.00
❑ 288 Black Knight - Oversized 6X9 9.00 12.00
❑ 299 Black Lotus - Oversized 6X9 13.00 18.00
❑ 311 Blacker Lotus - Oversized 6X9 6.00 12.00
❑ 322 Blastoderm - FOIL 2.00 5.00
❑ 333 Blinking Spirit - Oversized 6X9 6.00 10.00
❑ 344 Bonesplitter - FOIL 3.00 7.00
❑ 355 Booster Tutor 4.00 7.00
❑ 366 Bottle Gnomes - FOIL 3.00 7.00
❑ 377 Brainstorm (FNM) FOIL 12.00 18.00
❑ 388 Brushland - Oversized 6X9 2.00 5.00
❑ 399 Budoka Pupil - FOIL 4.00 8.00
❑ 411 Cabal Therapy (FNM) 10.00 16.00
❑ 422 Cadaverous Bloom - Oversized 6X9 9.00 17.00
❑ 433 Call From the Grave - Oversized 6X9 6.00 12.00
❑ 444 Capsize (FNM) FOIL 4.00 8.00
❑ 455 Carnophage - FOIL 6.00 8.00
❑ 466 Carrion Feeder (FNM) FOIL 4.00 8.00
❑ 477 Chaos Orb - Oversized 6X9 6.00 8.00
❑ 488 Chill - FOIL 6.00 8.00
❑ 499 Circle of Protection: Art 5.00 8.00
❑ 511 City of Brass (JSS) FOIL 15.00 30.00
❑ 522 City Of Brass - Oversized 6X9 12.00 22.00
❑ 525 Counterspell 10.00 15.00
❑ 544 Counterspell (Judge Rew) FOIL 10.00 20.00
❑ 555 Creeping Mold - FOIL 5.00 10.00
❑ 566 Crimson Hellkite - Oversized 6X9 6.00 12.00
❑ 577 Crusade (JSS) FOIL 9.00 15.00
❑ 588 Crystalline Sliver - FOIL 40.00 100.00
❑ 599 Cursed Scroll - Oversized 6X9 12.00 23.00
❑ 611 Dark Banishing - Oversized 6X9 10.00 16.00
❑ 622 Darksteel Ingot - FOIL 7.00 12.00
❑ 633 Dauthi Slayer - FOIL 6.00 10.00
❑ 644 Deranged Hermit (JUDGE) FOIL 8.00 15.00
❑ 655 Deflection - Oversized 6X9 6.00 8.00
❑ 666 Diabolic Edict - FOIL 12.00 18.00
❑ 677 Dirtcowl Wurm 7.00 10.00
❑ 688 Disenchant 7.00 10.00
❑ 699 Disenchant (FNM) FOIL 8.00 15.00
❑ 711 Disenchant - Oversized 6X9 8.00 12.00
❑ 722 Dismiss - FOIL 2.00 5.00
❑ 733 Dissipate (FNM) FOIL 4.00 7.00
❑ 744 Dissipate - Oversized 6X9 5.00 8.00
❑ 745 Drain Life (FNM) FOIL 5.00 8.00
❑ 755 Drain Life - Oversized 6X9 10.00 15.00
❑ 766 Duress - FOIL 8.00 15.00
❑ 777 Earthquake - Oversized 6X9 4.00 7.00
❑ 788 Elvish Aberration - FOIL 2.00 4.00
❑ 799 Elvish Lyrist (JSS) FOIL 2.00 4.00
❑ 812 Empyrial Armor - FOIL 3.00 6.00
❑ 822 Enduring Renewal - Oversized 6X9 10.00 15.00
❑ 833 Enlightened Tutor - FOIL 7.00 12.00
❑ 844 Erhnam Djinn - Oversized 6X9 8.00 12.00
❑ 855 Eternal Dragon (DCI) FOIL 25.00 50.00
❑ 866 Exalted Angel - FOIL 80.00 125.00
❑ 877 Faerie Dragon - Oversized 6X9 3.00 6.00
❑ 888 Fallen Angel - Oversized 6X9 10.00 17.00
❑ 899 False Prophet - FOIL 3.00 6.00
❑ 900 Feral Throwback - FOIL 2.00 4.00
❑ 911 Fireball 6.00 8.00
❑ 922 Fireball - Oversized 6X9 5.00 8.00
❑ 933 Fireball - Textless 4.00 7.00
❑ 944 Fireblast (FNM) FOIL 6.00 10.00
❑ 955 Fireslinger (FNM) FOIL 2.00 4.00
❑ 966 Flametongue Kavu (FNM) FOIL 7.00 10.00
❑ 977 Fling - FOIL 5.00 8.00
❑ 988 Forbid (FNM) FOIL 5.00 10.00
❑ 999 Force Of Nature - Oversized 6X9 6.00 12.00
❑ 1111 Forest - 1996 Arena 5.00 8.00
❑ 1122 Forest - 2003 Arena 2.00 4.00
❑ 1133 Forest - 2004 Arena 2.00 4.00
❑ 1144 Forest - APAC (Blue) 1.50 3.00
❑ 1155 Forest - APAC (Clear) 2.00 4.00
❑ 1166 Forest - APAC (Red) 2.00 4.00
❑ 1177 Forest - EURO (Blue) 4.00 7.00
❑ 1188 Forest - EURO (Purple) 4.00 7.00
❑ 1199 Forest - EURO (Red) 4.00 7.00
❑ 1222 Forest - FOIL Beta 3.00 6.00
❑ 1233 Forest - FOIL Ice Age 2.00 4.00
❑ 1244 Forest - FOIL Urza's Saga 3.00 5.00
❑ 1255 Forest - GURU 15.00 30.00
❑ 1266 Forest - Oversized 6X9 2.00 4.00
❑ 1278 Fruitcake Elemental FOIL 25.00 50.00
❑ 1288 Fungal Shambler - FOIL 2.00 4.00
❑ 1299 Gaea's Blessing - FOIL 6.00 12.00
❑ 1344 Gemstone Mine (JUDGE) 50.00 85.00
❑ 1355 Gaea's Cradle - FOIL 35.00 60.00
❑ 1366 Gemstone Mine (DCI) FOIL 50.00 70.00
❑ 1377 Genju of Spires 8.00 12.00
❑ 1388 Giant Badger 4.00 7.00
❑ 1499 Giant Growth (FNM) FOIL 3.00 6.00
❑ 1599 Giant Growth - FOIL Beta 3.00 5.00
❑ 1611 Gleancrawler FOIL 1.00 2.00
❑ 1622 Glory - FOIL 4.00 6.00
❑ 1623 Goblin Bombardment (FNM) FOIL 3.00 6.00
❑ 1624 Goblin Mime 5.00 8.00
❑ 1625 Granny's Payback 3.00 6.00
❑ 1627 Grim Lavamancer (DCI) FOIL 45.00 80.00
❑ 1699 Hammer of Bogardan - FOIL 10.00 15.00
❑ 1711 Helm of Kaldra - FOIL 2.00 5.00
❑ 1722 Hermit Druid (Judge Rew) FOIL 15.00 25.00
❑ 1733 Hypnotic Specter (Play.Rev) 15.00 20.00
❑ 1744 Impulse - FOIL 6.00 10.00
❑ 1755 Incinerate 4.00 7.00
❑ 1766 Ink-Eyes, Sérvant of Oni - FOIL 6.00 8.00
❑ 1777 Intuition (Judge Rew) FOIL 35.00 50.00
❑ 1788 Island - 1996 Arena 3.00 6.00
❑ 1799 Island - 2003 Arena FOIL 2.00 4.00
❑ 1811 Island - 2004 Arena FOIL 2.00 3.00
❑ 1822 Island - APAC (Blue) 3.00 6.00
❑ 1825 Island - APAC (Clear) 3.00 6.00
❑ 1833 Island - APAC (Red) 3.00 6.00
❑ 1844 Island - EURO (Blue) 4.00 7.00
❑ 1855 Island - EURO (Purple) 4.00 7.00
❑ 1866 Island - EURO (Red) 4.00 7.00
❑ 1877 Island 2002- FOIL Beta 2.00 3.00
❑ 1888 Island 2001 - FOIL Ice Age 2.00 4.00
❑ 1899 Island 1999 - FOIL Urza's Saga 3.00 6.00
❑ 1900 Island 1999 - FOIL Urza's Saga/ No Symbol10.00 18.00
❑ 1911 Island - GURU 25.00 40.00
❑ 1922 Juggernaut (FNM) FOIL 8.00 10.00
❑ 1933 Jackal Pup (FNM) FOIL 4.00 8.00
❑ 1944 Karn Silver Golem - FOIL 8.00 15.00
❑ 1955 Krosan Tusker (FNM) FOIL 2.00 5.00
❑ 1966 Krosan Warchief (FNM) FOIL 2.00 4.00
❑ 1977 Laquatus's Champion - FOIL 3.00 5.00
❑ 1988 Lightning Bolt (Judge Rew) FOIL 20.00 35.00
❑ 1999 Lightning Dragon - FOIL 8.00 15.00
❑ 2000 Lightning Helix FOIL 25.00 35.00
❑ 2011 Lightning Hounds - FOIL 1.00 2.00
❑ 2022 Lightning Rift (FNM) FOIL 2.00 3.00
❑ 2033 Living Death (Judge Rew) FOIL 20.00 30.00
❑ 2044 Llanowar Elves (FNM) FOIL 10.00 18.00
❑ 2055 Longbow Archer (FNM) FOIL 3.00 5.00
❑ 2066 Lord of Atlantis (JSS) FOIL 4.00 7.00
❑ 2077 Lotus Bloom (DCI) FOIL 10.00 20.00
❑ 2088 Lu Bu- Master-at-Arms (Singapore) 6.00 11.00
❑ 2099 Man-o'-War - FOIL 3.00 6.00
❑ 2100 Mana Crypt 30.00 50.00
❑ 2111 Mana Leak - FOIL 7.00 11.00
❑ 2122 Meddling Mage (DCI) FOIL 60.00 100.00
❑ 2127 Memory Lapse (Judge Rew) FOIL 6.00 10.00
❑ 2133 Mind Warp (FNM) FOIL 3.00 5.00
❑ 2144 Mise 4.00 7.00
❑ 2155 Mishra's Factory (DCI) FOIL 50.00 80.00
❑ 2166 Mogg Fanatic (FNM) FOIL 6.00 10.00
❑ 2177 Monstrouse Hound 1.00 3.00
❑ 2188 Mother of Runes (FNM) FOIL 5.00 10.00
❑ 2199 Mountain - 1996 Arena 3.00 6.00
❑ 2200 Mountain - 2003 Arena 2.00 3.00
❑ 2222 Mountain - 2004 Arena 2.00 3.00
❑ 2233 Mountain - APAC (Blue) 2.00 3.00
❑ 2244 Mountain - APAC (Clear) 3.00 5.00
❑ 2255 Mountain - APAC (Red) 3.00 5.00
❑ 2266 Mountain - EURO (Blue) 4.00 7.00
❑ 2277 Mountain - EURO (Purple) 4.00 7.00
❑ 2299 Mountain - EURO (Red) 4.00 7.00
❑ 2322 Mountain - FOIL Ice Age 2.00 3.00
❑ 2344 Mountain - FOIL Urza's Saga 3.00 5.00
❑ 2355 Mountain - GURU 20.00 35.00
❑ 2366 Muscle Sliver (FNM) FOIL 5.00 10.00
❑ 2377 Nalathni Dragon (Dragon Con 94) 2.00 4.00
❑ 2388 Niv-Mizzet (DCI) FOIL 30.00 50.00
❑ 2399 Oath of Druids (Judge Rew) FOIL 15.00 25.00
❑ 2411 Ophidian (FNM) FOIL 4.00 7.00
❑ 2455 Overtaker - FOIL 1.00 2.00
❑ 2466 Oxidize - Textless 4.00 7.00
❑ 2477 Pernicous Deed (DCI) FOIL 40.00 80.00
❑ 2488 Phyrexian Negator - FOIL 20.00 40.00
❑ 2499 Pillage - FOIL 3.00 6.00
❑ 2522 Plains - 1996 Arena 2.00 3.00
❑ 2533 Plains - 2003 Arena 2.00 3.00
❑ 2544 Plains - 2004 Arena 2.00 3.00
❑ 2555 Plains - APAC (Blue) 3.00 5.00
❑ 2557 Plains - APAC (Clear) 3.00 5.00
❑ 2666 Plains - APAC (Red) 2.00 4.00
❑ 2777 Plains - EURO (Blue) 4.00 7.00
❑ 2888 Plains - EURO (Purple) 4.00 7.00
❑ 2999 Plains - EURO (Red) 4.00 7.00
❑ 3111 Plains 2001 - FOIL Ice Age 2.00 4.00
❑ 3222 Plains 1999 - FOIL Urza's Saga 2.00 4.00
❑ 3333 Plains - GURU 28.00 40.00
❑ 3399 Pouncing Jaguar - FOIL 3.00 6.00
❑ 3444 Powder Keg - FOIL 5.00 8.00
❑ 3455 Priest of Titania (FNM) FOIL 5.00 11.00
❑ 3466 Prodigal Sorcerer (FNM) FOIL 4.00 7.00
❑ 3488 Psychatog - FOIL 7.00 12.00
❑ 3499 Questing Phelddagrif - FOIL 1.00 2.00
❑ 3511 Quirion Ranger (FNM) FOIL 3.00 6.00
❑ 3522 Raging Kavu - FOIL 2.00 4.00
❑ 3533 Rakdos Guildmage (DCI) FOIL 20.00 25.00
❑ 3544 Rancor (FNM) FOIL 6.00 10.00
❑ 3555 Rathi Assassin - FOIL 2.00 4.00
❑ 3566 Reanimate (FNM) FOIL 6.00 10.00
❑ 3577 Regrowth (DCI) FOIL 40.00 50.00
❑ 3588 Revenant 5.00 8.00
❑ 3599 Rewind - FOIL 6.00 11.00
❑ 3622 Rhox - FOIL 2.00 4.00
❑ 3633 River Boa (FNM) FOIL 6.00 10.00
❑ 3644 Royal Assassin (JSS) FOIL 15.00 25.00
❑ 3655 Rukh Egg - FOIL 2.00 4.00
❑ 3666 Ryusei, the Falling Star - FOIL 4.00 7.00
❑ 3677 Scent of Cinder 5.00 8.00
❑ 3688 Scragnoth (FNM) FOIL 1.00 2.00
❑ 3699 Seal of Cleansing - FOIL 5.00 8.00
❑ 3711 Serra Angel - FOIL 40.00 70.00
❑ 3722 Serra Avatar (JSS) FOIL 25.00 40.00
❑ 3733 Serum Visions - FOIL 1.00 2.00
❑ 3744 Sewers of Estark 1.00 3.00
❑ 3755 Shard Phoenix (JSS) FOIL 10.00 18.00
❑ 3766 Shield of Kaldra - FOIL 2.00 5.00
❑ 3777 Shivan Dragon (Japanese Coro Coro) 5.00 10.00
❑ 3788 Shock (FNM) FOIL 4.00 8.00
❑ 3799 Silent Specter - FOIL 3.00 5.00
❑ 3811 Silver Knight (FNM) FOIL 3.00 5.00
❑ 3822 Skirk Marauder - FOIL 1.00 2.00
❑ 3833 Skittering Skirge - FOIL 2.00 4.00
❑ 3833 Slice and Dice (FNM) FOIL 2.00 4.00
❑ 3844 Slith Firewalker (JSS) FOIL 6.00 10.00
❑ 3855 Smother (FNM) FOIL 3.00 6.00
❑ 3866 Sol Ring (DCI) FOIL 30.00 60.00
❑ 3877 Soltari Priest (FNM) FOIL 5.00 8.00
❑ 3888 Soul Collector - FOIL 3.00 6.00
❑ 3899 Sparksmith (FNM) FOIL 3.00 6.00
❑ 3911 Spined Wurm (Top Deck) 5.00 10.00
❑ 4111 Spike Feeder (FNM) FOIL 3.00 6.00
❑ 4122 Splendid Genesis 1000.00 2000.00
❑ 4123 Staunch Defender (FNM) FOIL 1.00 3.00
❑ 4233 Stone Rain (FNM) FOIL 5.00 8.00
❑ 4234 Stone-Tongue Basilisk - FOIL 1.00 2.00
❑ 4255 Stroke of Genius (Judge Rew) FOIL 18.00 30.00
❑ 4266 Stupor - FOIL 2.00 4.00
❑ 4288 Swamp - 1996 Arena 2.00 4.00
❑ 4299 Swamp - 2003 Arena 2.00 3.00
❑ 4311 Swamp - 2004 Arena 2.00 3.00
❑ 4322 Swamp - APAC (Blue) 2.00 4.00
❑ 4333 Swamp - APAC (Clear) 2.00 5.00
❑ 4344 Swamp - APAC (Red) 2.00 4.00
❑ 4355 Swamp - EURO (Blue) 4.00 8.00
❑ 4366 Swamp - EURO (Purple) 4.00 8.00
❑ 4377 Swamp - EURO (Red) 4.00 8.00
❑ 4388 Swamp 2001 - FOIL Ice Age 2.00 3.00
❑ 4399 Swamp 1999 - FOIL Urza's Saga 3.00 5.00
❑ 4411 Swamp - GURU 25.00 40.00
❑ 4422 Sword of Kaldra - FOIL 3.00 5.00
❑ 4433 Swords To Plowshares (FNM) FOIL 20.00 30.00
❑ 4444 Terror (FNM) FOIL 6.00 12.00
❑ 4455 Terror - Textless 5.00 8.00
❑ 4466 Thorn Elemental (Japanese) 5.00 10.00
❑ 4477 Thran Quarry (JSS) FOIL 6.00 11.00
❑ 4488 Time Warp (Judge Rew) FOIL 25.00 40.00
❑ 4499 Tradewind Rider (Judge Rew) FOIL 12.00 20.00
❑ 4511 Treetop Village (FNM) FOIL 4.00 7.00
❑ 4522 Underworld Dreams (2HG) FOIL 5.00 7.00
❑ 4523 Two-Headed Dragon (JSS) FOIL 15.00 25.00
❑ 4533 Uktabi Orangutan - FOIL 2.00 4.00
❑ 4544 Underworld (DCI) FOIL 6.00 8.00
❑ 4555 Vampiric Tutor - FOIL 20.00 40.00
❑ 4566 Voidmage Prodigy - Alt Art 3.00 5.00
❑ 4577 Voidslime (DCI) FOIL 40.00 60.00
❑ 4588 Volcanic Geyser (FNM) FOIL 2.00 4.00
❑ 4599 Volcanic Hammer (JSS) FOIL 2.00 4.00
❑ 4611 Wall of Blossoms (FNM) FOIL 6.00 10.00
❑ 4622 Warmonger - FOIL 1.00 2.00
❑ 4633 Wasteland (DCI) FOIL 15.00 25.00
❑ 4644 Whipcorder (FNM) FOIL 2.00 3.00
❑ 4655 White Knight (FNM) FOIL 4.00 7.00
❑ 4666 Willbender (FNM) FOIL 1.00 2.00
❑ 4677 Windseeker Centaur 2.00 4.00
❑ 4688 Withered Wretch (FNM) FOIL 2.00 5.00
❑ 4699 Wrath of God (DCI) FOIL 20.00 40.00
❑ 4711 Yawgmoth's Will (JUDGE) FOIL 25.00 50.00

YU-GI-OH!

HOW TO USE

What's Listed
Products listed in the Price Guide typically: 1) are produced by licensed manufacturers, 2) are widely available and 3) have market activity on single items.

What the Columns Mean
The LO and HI columns reflect current retail selling ranges. The HI column on the right generally represents the full retail selling price. The LO column on the left generally represents the lowest price one would expect to find with extensive shopping.

Grading
All cards in the Price Guide are based on NrMint to Mint condition. Damaged cards are generally sold for 25 to 75 percent of Mint value. Toy prices are based on mint condition. Toys that are loose (out of package), are generally sold for 50 percent of the listed price.

Currency
This Price Guide is intended to reflect the entire North American market. All listed prices are in U.S. dollars.

Legend
(R) - Rare card. The name of the card is printed in silver foil.

(SCR) - Secret Rare card. The name of the card is printed in silver foil. These cards are glossy and feature a sparkling holographic illustration.

(SP) - Short Printed card.

(SSP) - Super Short Printed card.

(SR) - Super Rare card. The illustrations on these cards are printed with a foil background.

(UR) - Ultra Rare card. The name of the card is printed in gold foil. The illustration and sometimes the frame contain a foil background.

(UTR) - Ultimate Rare card. Gold foil lettering & holographic picture with a raised image (embossed).

(GR) - Ghost Rare card. White background, gold foil holographic lettering, and holographic picture.

Please Note: Beckett does not sell single Yu-Gi-Oh cards.

2000 Yu-Gi-Oh Curse of Anubis

Complete Set (52)	60.00	110.00
Booster Box (30 packs)	45.00	60.00
Booster Pack (5 cards)	2.00	3.50
❑ CA1 Iron Arm Golem	.10	.30
❑ CA2 Three-Head Gidou	.10	.30
❑ CA3 Parasite (PR)	10.00	20.00
❑ CA3 Parasite (UR)	5.00	12.00
❑ CA4 7 Card	.25	.50
❑ CA5 Hand-Sealing Light Sword (SR)	4.00	8.00
❑ CA6 Chain Destruction (PR)	15.00	25.00
❑ CA6 Chain Destruction (UR)	5.00	10.00
❑ CA7 Seal of Time	.10	.30
❑ CA8 Tomb Raider	.50	1.00
❑ CA9 Holy Elf's Blessing	.10	.30
❑ CA10 Eye of Truth	1.00	2.00
❑ CA11 Desert Cyclone	.10	.30
❑ CA12 Cry of the Living Dead (SP)	2.00	4.00
❑ CA13 Book of Solomon (R)	1.00	2.00
❑ CA14 Land Reformation	.10	.30
❑ CA15 Holy Javelin	.10	.30
❑ CA16 Silver Screen Mirror Wall (SR)	3.00	7.00
❑ CA17 Gale	.10	.30
❑ CA18 Blizzard	.10	.30
❑ CA19 Glass Armour	.10	.30
❑ CA20 World Peace	.10	.30
❑ CA21 Magic Stone Tablet	.10	.30
❑ CA22 Metal Detector	.10	.30
❑ CA23 White-Robed Angel	.50	1.00
❑ CA24 Take Advantage	1.00	2.00
❑ CA25 Forced Takeover	.10	.30
❑ CA26 DNA Modify Operation		
❑ CA27 Racial Trial	.10	.30
❑ CA28 Back-Up Members	.10	.30
❑ CA29 Big Commotion	.10	.30
❑ CA30 Peace Treaty	.10	.30
❑ CA31 Holy Shine	.10	.30
❑ CA32 Righteousness	.10	.30
❑ CA33 Imperial Rebellion (SR)	5.00	10.00
❑ CA34 Magical Silk Hat (SR)	6.00	10.00
❑ CA35 Messiah of Genocide (R)	2.00	5.00
❑ CA36 Messiah of Annihilation (R)	3.00	6.00
❑ CA37 Shallow Grave (R)	3.00	6.00
❑ CA38 Early Burial (R)	5.00	10.00
❑ CA39 Examine	.10	.30
❑ CA40 Restriction Order (R)	2.00	4.00
❑ CA41 Chaos Pot	.10	.30
❑ CA42 Flame Killer	.10	.30
❑ CA43 Big Burn Dragon	.50	1.00
❑ CA44 Burning Soldier	.10	.30
❑ CA45 Mr. Volcano	.10	.30
❑ CA46 Flame Samurai	.25	.50
❑ CA47 Mental Parasitic Host	.10	.30
❑ CA48 Mecha Falcon	.25	.50
❑ CA49 Flying Mantis	.10	.30
❑ CA50 Bird Man	.10	.30
❑ CA51 Buster Blader (PR)	12.00	25.00
❑ CA51 Buster Blader (UR)	7.00	15.00
❑ CA00 Jinzo (SCR)	10.00	22.00

2000 Yu-Gi-Oh EX Starter

Complete Set (87) 20.00 40.00
Released November 2000 (Reprints from Starter EX plus 2 Cards)

❑ EX1 Holy Elf	.10	.30
❑ EX2 Gremlin	.10	.30
❑ EX3 Fortress- Guard Winged Dragon (SR)	.50	1.00
❑ EX4 Demon's Summon	.10	.30
❑ EX5 Luis	.10	.30
❑ EX6 Black Magician (UR)	6.00	12.00
❑ EX7 Dark Knight Gaia	.50	1.00
❑ EX8 Curse of Dragon	.10	.30
❑ EX9 Elven Swordsman	.10	.30
❑ EX10 Mammoth's Grave	.10	.30
❑ EX11 Great White	.10	.30
❑ EX12 Silver Fang	.10	.30
❑ EX13 Giant Stone Soldier	.10	.30
❑ EX14 Dragon Zombie	.10	.30
❑ EX15 Death Mute Angel- Doma	.10	.30
❑ EX16 Assasin	.10	.30
❑ EX17 Demon Death- Satan	.10	.30
❑ EX18 Killer the Claw	.10	.30
❑ EX19 Berserker	.10	.30
❑ EX20 Dark Destruction Sword	.10	.30
❑ EX21 Secret Tecnique Manual	.10	.30
❑ EX22 Black Hole	.10	.30
❑ EX23 Healing Goddess	.10	.30
❑ EX24 Ancient Elf	.10	.30
❑ EX25 Magical Ghost	.10	.30
❑ EX26 Earth Crack	.10	.30
❑ EX27 Pitfall	.10	.30
❑ EX28 Pinsir Attack	.10	.30
❑ EX29 Magic Cancel	.10	.30
❑ EX30 Resurrect	.10	.30
❑ EX31 Reinforcements	.10	.30
❑ EX32 Change of Heart	.50	1.00
❑ EX33 Strict Old Magician	.10	.30
❑ EX34 Illusion Wall	.10	.30
❑ EX35 Magic Swordsman- Neo	.10	.30
❑ EX36 Evil Sword- Baron	.10	.30
❑ EX37 Man- Eating Treasure Box	.10	.30
❑ EX38 Death Sorceror	.10	.30
❑ EX39 Will	.10	.30
❑ EX40 Missionary of Harmony	.10	.30
❑ EX41 Trap Master	.10	.30
❑ EX42 Dragon- Sealing Pot	.10	.30
❑ EX43 Darkness	.10	.30
❑ EX44 Man- Eating Bug	.10	.30
❑ EX45 Curse of Amanojyaku	.10	.30
❑ EX46 Trap Destroy	.10	.30
❑ EX47 Castle Wall	.10	.30
❑ EX48 Blood Compensation	.10	.30
❑ EX49 Blue Eyes White Dragon (UR)	8.00	15.00
❑ EX50 Cyclops	.10	.30
❑ EX51 Gargoyle	.10	.30
❑ EX52 Evil Worm- Beast	.10	.30
❑ EX53 Minotaurus	.10	.30
❑ EX54 Devil Dragon	.25	.50
❑ EX55 Judge Man (SR)	2.00	4.00
❑ EX56 Holy Doll	.10	.30
❑ EX57 Demon Tamer	.10	.30
❑ EX58 Wild Raptor	.10	.30
❑ EX59 Goddess of Opposites	.10	.30
❑ EX60 Kentauros	.10	.30
❑ EX61 Demon Terra	.10	.30
❑ EX62 Dark Demon- Nightmare	.10	.30
❑ EX63 Dark Assasin	.10	.30
❑ EX64 Master & Expert	.10	.30
❑ EX65 Evil Nameless Warrior	.10	.30
❑ EX66 Dark Shadow Ghost King	.10	.30
❑ EX67 Dark Energy	.10	.30
❑ EX68 Awakening	.10	.30
❑ EX69 Midnight Fire Outbreak	.10	.30
❑ EX70 Gargoyle Powered	.10	.30
❑ EX71 Vengeful Sword- Stalker	.10	.30
❑ EX72 Lamp Genie	.10	.30
❑ EX73 Lude Kaiser	.10	.30
❑ EX74 Destructive Golem	.10	.30
❑ EX75 Sky Hunter	.10	.30
❑ EX76 Drago-Human	.10	.30
❑ EX77 Pale Beast	.10	.30
❑ EX78 Inexperienced Detective	.10	.30
❑ EX79 Ancient Telescope	.10	.30
❑ EX80 Retribution	1.00	2.00
❑ EX81 Mysterious Puppet Master	.10	.30
❑ EX82 Grassy Plains	.10	.30
❑ EX83 Hane-Hane	.10	.30
❑ EX84 Lord of Dragon (UR)	5.00	10.00
❑ EX85 Dragon- Calling Horn (UR)	5.00	10.00
❑ EX86 Cross Soul (SR)	2.00	5.00
❑ EX87 Hand Obliteration (SR)	2.00	4.00

2000 Yu-Gi-Oh Legend of Blue Eyes White Dragon

Complete Set (61)	65.00	125.00
Booster Box (30 packs)	60.00	80.00
Booster Pack (5 cards)	3.00	4.50
❑ LB1 Blue Eyes White Dragon (UR)	15.00	25.00
❑ LB2 Cyclops	.10	.30
❑ LB3 Flame Swordsman (UR)	8.00	15.00
❑ LB4 Wyde	.10	.30
❑ LB5 Black Magician (UR)	8.00	16.00
❑ LB6 Black Knight Gaia (UR)	8.00	15.00
❑ LB7 Basic Insect	.10	.30
❑ LB8 Mammoth's Graveyard	.10	.30
❑ LB9 Silver Fang	.10	.30
❑ LB10 Dark Grey	.10	.30
❑ LB11 Hell's Judgement (R)	1.00	2.00
❑ LB12 Sleeping Child	.10	.30
❑ LB13 The 13th Grave Digger (R)	1.00	2.00
❑ LB14 Fire Knight	.20	.50
❑ LB15 Fire-User	.20	.50
❑ LB16 Monster Egg	.20	.50
❑ LB17 Flame Grass	.20	.50
❑ LB18 Dark Flame Dragon	.50	1.00
❑ LB19 Ruler of the Underworld (R)	1.00	2.00
❑ LB20 Mirage	.10	.30
❑ LB21 Fusionist	.10	.30
❑ LB22 Turtle Tiger (R)	1.00	2.00
❑ LB23 Puchi-Ryu	.10	.30
❑ LB24 Puchi-Tenshin	.10	.30
❑ LB25 Sting	.10	.30
❑ LB26 Aqua Madoll (R)	1.00	2.00
❑ LB27 Purple Flame Kage-Musha	.10	.30
❑ LB28 Flame Ghost	.10	.30
❑ LB29 Two-Mouthed Dark Ruler	.10	.30
❑ LB30 Mug-Man	.10	.30
❑ LB31 Root Water	.10	.30
❑ LB32 Furious Sea King	.10	.30
❑ LB33 Tree Spirit King	.10	.30
❑ LB34 Northern Wind & Sun	.10	.30
❑ LB35 King Smog	.10	.30
❑ LB36 Sleepy	.10	.30
❑ LB37 Legendary Swordsman Masaki	.10	.30
❑ LB38 Drake	.10	.30
❑ LB39 Legendary Sword	.10	.30
❑ LB40 Wild Beast's Teeth	.10	.30
❑ LB41 Purple Crystal	.10	.30
❑ LB42 Secret Magic Manual	.10	.30
❑ LB43 Poseidon's Power	.10	.30
❑ LB44 Dragon-Sealing Pot	.10	.30
❑ LB45 Forest (R)	1.00	2.00
❑ LB46 Dry Plains (R)	1.00	2.00
❑ LB47 Moutain (R)	1.00	2.00
❑ LB48 Grassy Plains (R)	1.00	2.00
❑ LB49 Sea (R)	1.00	2.00
❑ LB50 Darkness (R)	1.00	2.00
❑ LB51 Black Hole (SR)	5.00	12.00
❑ LB52 Raigeki (SR)	5.00	10.00
❑ LB53 Red Potion	.10	.30
❑ LB54 Fire Powder	.10	.30
❑ LB55 Fire Ball	.10	.30
❑ LB56 Earth Shatter (SR)	3.00	6.00
❑ LB57 Pitfall (SR)	3.00	6.00
❑ LB58 Polymerization (SR)	9.00	15.00
❑ LB59 Trap Destroy	.10	.30
❑ LB60 Pinsir Attack	.10	.30
❑ LB00 Elven Swordsman (SCR)	15.00	25.00

2000 Yu-Gi-Oh Magic Ruler

Complete Set (50)	60.00	100.00
Booster Box (30 packs)	45.00	70.00
Booster Pack (5 cards)	2.00	3.50
❑ MR1 Penguin Knight	.50	1.00
❑ MR2 Demon's Axe (SR)	8.00	15.00
❑ MR3 Black Pendant (R)	1.00	2.00
❑ MR4 Horn of Light	.10	.30
❑ MR5 Demon's Kiss	.10	.30
❑ MR6 Hexagram Curse (UR)	5.00	10.00
❑ MR6 Hexagram Curse (PR)	8.00	20.00
❑ MR7 Metal Fish	.10	.30
❑ MR8 Electric Snake	.10	.30
❑ MR9 Queen Bird	.50	1.00
❑ MR10 Amoeba	.20	.50
❑ MR11 Kujacku	.10	.30
❑ MR12 Maha Vailo	1.00	2.00
❑ MR13 Royal Hall Guardian	.10	.30
❑ MR14 Fire Kraken	.10	.30
❑ MR15 Eevy	.10	.30
❑ MR16 Guriguru	.10	.30
❑ MR17 Red Dragon	.50	1.00
❑ MR18 Elder of the Deep Forest	.10	.30
❑ MR19 Valkyrie	.10	.30
❑ MR20 Weather Report	.10	.30
❑ MR21 Mechanical Snail	.10	.30
❑ MR22 Fire-Eating Turtle	.50	1.00
❑ MR23 Liquid Beast	.10	.30
❑ MR24 Demonic Investigator (SR)	3.00	6.00
❑ MR25 Lake Merman	.10	.30
❑ MR26 Royal Throne Infiltrator (SR)	5.00	10.00
❑ MR27 Whiptail Gargoyle	.10	.30
❑ MR28 Slot Machine AM-7 (UR)	5.00	10.00
❑ MR28 Slot Machine Am-7 (PR)	15.00	25.00
❑ MR29 Sacrifice (UR)	4.00	8.00
❑ MR30 Bow-Pulling Mermaid	.10	.30
❑ MR31 Graveyard Familiar	.10	.30
❑ MR32 Demonic Ritual	.10	.30
❑ MR33 Wealthy Goblin	.10	.30
❑ MR34 Toll (R)	1.00	2.00
❑ MR35 Final Battle	.10	.30
❑ MR36 Theft	.10	.30
❑ MR37 Holy Song	.50	1.00
❑ MR38 Confiscate (R)	1.00	2.00
❑ MR39 Mischievous Twin Demons	.25	.50
❑ MR40 Dark Visitor (R)	1.00	2.00
❑ MR41 Angel's Mirror	.10	.30
❑ MR42 Change of Hands	.25	.50
❑ MR43 Charge	.10	.30
❑ MR44 Reliable Defender	.10	.30
❑ MR45 Aggressive Guard (SR)	3.00	6.00
❑ MR46 Magical Chain	.25	.50
❑ MR47 Cyclone	.10	.30
❑ MR48 Hurricane	.10	.30
❑ MR49 Tough Choice	.50	1.00
❑ MR50 Venomous Snake Fang	.50	1.00

2000 Yu-Gi-Oh Phantom God

Complete Set (65)	60.00	100.00
Booster Box (30 packs)	60.00	100.00
Booster Pack (5 cards)	2.00	4.00
❑ PG1 Holy Elf (SR)	5.00	10.00
❑ PG2 Typhoon	.10	.30
❑ PG3 Lewis	.10	.30
❑ PG4 Dragon Knight Gaia (PR)	15.00	30.00
❑ PG4 Dragon Knight Gaia (UR)	8.00	15.00
❑ PG5 Curse of Dragon (SR)	3.00	6.00
❑ PG6 Karponara Soldier	.10	.30
❑ PG7 Giant Stone Soldier	.10	.30
❑ PG8 Wild Raptor	.10	.30
❑ PG9 Red Eyes Black Dragon (UR)	12.00	25.00
❑ PG9 Red Eyes B Dragon (PR)	20.00	40.00
❑ PG10 Card Reaper (SR)	3.00	6.00
❑ PG11 Demon Death Satan	.10	.30
❑ PG12 Rabuss	.10	.30
❑ PG13 Hard Armor	.10	.30
❑ PG14 Man-Eater	.10	.30
❑ PG15 Magnuts No.1	.10	.30
❑ PG16 Magnuts No.2	.10	.30
❑ PG17 Harp Elf	.10	.30
❑ PG18 Air Mail	.10	.30
❑ PG19 Demon Terra	.10	.30
❑ PG20 Killer Panda	.50	1.00
❑ PG21 Spider Man	.50	1.00
❑ PG22 Dark Napoleon	.10	.30
❑ PG23 Wandering Mermaid	.50	1.00
❑ PG24 Fire Majin	.10	.30
❑ PG25 Magic Knight Dragoness	.10	.30
❑ PG26 One-Eyed Shield Dragon	.50	1.00
❑ PG27 Dark Energy (R)	1.00	2.00
❑ PG28 Laser Cannon Armor (R)	1.00	2.00
❑ PG29 Demon Germs (R)	1.00	2.00
❑ PG30 Silver Bow (R)	1.00	2.00
❑ PG31 Dragon's Secret Pearl (R)	2.00	4.00
❑ PG32 Electric Whip (R)	1.00	2.00
❑ PG33 Magical moon (R)	1.00	2.00
❑ PG34 Disable Defense (R)	2.00	4.00
❑ PG35 Machinery Upgrade Factory (R)	2.00	4.00
❑ PG36 Body Temprature Rise (R)	1.00	2.00
❑ PG37 Follow Wind	.10	.30
❑ PG38 Goblin's Secret Medicine	.10	.30
❑ PG39 Fire Execution	.10	.30

- PG40 Sealing Swords of Light (UR) 9.00 18.00
- PG41 Metal Dragon .50 1.00
- PG42 Spike Seadra .10 .30
- PG43 Land Mine Beast .10 .30
- PG44 Sky Hunter .10 .30
- PG45 Blue Ninja .10 .30
- PG46 Flower Wolf .10 .30
- PG47 Man-Eating Bug (SR) 3.00 6.00
- PG48 Sand Stone .10 .30
- PG49 Hane-Hane (SR) 3.00 6.00
- PG50 Nail .10 .30
- PG51 Huge Iron Statue .10 .30
- PG52 Leather Dragon .10 .30
- PG53 Demon Plant .10 .30
- PG54 Blood-Thirsty Reptile .10 .30
- PG55 Armored Starfish .10 .30
- PG56 Succubus Knight .25 .50
- PG57 Magic Cancel (R) 1.00 2.00
- PG58 Resurrect (UR) 5.00 10.00
- PG59 Pot of Strong Desire (NR) 2.00 4.00
- PG60 Grave-Digging Ghoul .10 .30
- PG61 Sealed Exodia's Right Leg (SCR) 15.00 25.00
- PG62 Sealed Exodia's Left Leg (SCR) 15.00 25.00
- PG63 Sealed Exodia's Right Arm (SCR) 15.00 25.00
- PG64 Sealed Exodia's Left Arm (SCR) 15.00 25.00
- PG65 Sealed Exodia (SCR) 25.00 40.00

2000 Yu-Gi-Oh Pharoah's Servant

Complete Set (51) 70.00 120.00
Booster Box (30 packs) 45.00 65.00
Booster Pack (5 cards) 2.00 3.75

- PS1 Octo-Baza .10 .30
- PS2 Psyco Kappa .10 .30
- PS3 Unicorn's Horn (SR) 2.00 4.00
- PS4 Labyrinth Wall (SP) 2.00 4.00
- PS5 Wall Shadow .10 .30
- PS6 Twin Tail .10 .30
- PS7 Stone Giant .10 .30
- PS8 Labyrinth Change .10 .30
- PS9 Baptism .10 .30
- PS10 Giant Growth (R) 4.00 8.00
- PS11 Dancer's Ritual .10 .30
- PS12 Hamburger Reciepe .10 .30
- PS13 House of Sticky Tape .10 .30
- PS14 Mouse Trap .10 .30
- PS15 Turtle's Oath .10 .30
- PS16 Dancing Soldier .50 1.00
- PS17 Hungry Burger .50 1.00
- PS18 Crab Turtle .50 1.00
- PS19 Dragon Egger 1.00 2.00
- PS20 Toon Dragon Egger 2.00 4.00
- PS21 Toon Mermaid (SR) 5.00 10.00
- PS22 Toon Demon (PR) 12.00 22.00
- PS22 Toon Demon (UR) 6.00 12.00
- PS23 Time Bomber (R) 1.00 2.00
- PS24 Diamond Dragon (UR) 10.00 20.00
- PS25 Toon World (UR) 6.00 12.00
- PS25 Toon World (PR) 10.00 20.00
- PS26 Cyber Pod .10 .30
- PS27 Light Pursuer (R) 1.00 3.00
- PS28 Big Nezumi .10 .30
- PS29 Senju God (SR) 4.00 8.00
- PS30 UFO Turtle .50 1.00
- PS31 Stealthy Assasin .50 1.00
- PS32 Karate Man .50 1.00
- PS33 Dark Zebra .10 .30
- PS34 Giant Virus (R) 2.00 4.00
- PS35 Flying Squirrel (R) 1.00 2.00
- PS36 Dark Familiar .10 .30
- PS37 Shine Angel .10 .30
- PS38 Boar Soldier 1.00 2.00
- PS39 Grizzly Mother .10 .30
- PS40 Dragon Fly .25 .50
- PS41 Ceremony Bell .10 .30
- PS42 Sonic Bird .10 .30
- PS43 Killer Tomato .50 1.00
- PS44 Kotodama .10 .30
- PS45 Gaia Power .10 .30
- PS46 Water World .10 .30
- PS47 Burning Cloud .10 .30
- PS48 Desert Storm .10 .30
- PS49 Shine Spark .10 .30
- PS50 Dark Zone .10 .30
- PS51 Messenger of Peace (SR) 4.00 8.00
- PS00 Blue Eyes Toon Dragon (UR) 15.00 25.00
- PS00 Blue Eyes Toon Dragon (SCR) 10.00 20.00

2000 Yu-Gi-Oh Premium Pack 3

Complete Set (10) 100.00 150.00
Booster Pack 15.00 30.00

- P3-1 Blue Eyes Ultimate Dragon (UR) 25.00 50.00
- P3-2 Meteor Black Dragon (UR) 10.00 20.00
- P3-3 Fire Wing Pegasus (PR) .10 .30
- P3-3 Fire Wing Pegasus (UR) 6.00 12.00
- P3-4 Tri-Horned Dragon (PR) 20.00 30.00
- P3-4 Tri-Horned Dragon (UR) 4.00 8.00
- P3-5 Millennium Prehistoric Man(UR) .20 .50
- P3-6 Evil Night Dragon (UR) 4.00 6.00
- P3-6 Evil Night Dragon (PR) 8.00 15.00
- P3-7 Magician of Black Chaos (PR) 12.00 20.00
- P3-7 Magician of Black Chaos (UR) 5.00 12.00
- P3-8 Gate Guardian (UR) 10.00 20.00
- P3-9 Meteor Dragon (PR) 15.00 30.00
- P3-9 Meteor Dragon (UR) 10.00 20.00
- P3-10 Chaos Magic Ritual (PR) 6.00 12.00
- P3-10 Chaos Magic Ritual (UR) 4.00 8.00

2000 Yu-Gi-Oh Revival of Black Demons Dragon

Complete Set (60) 85.00 100.00
Booster Box (30 packs) 30.00 40.00
Booster Pack (5 cards) 2.00 3.00

- RB1 Gremlin .10 .30
- RB2 Fortress-Guard Dragon .10 .30
- RB3 Summoned Skull (UR) 12.00 20.00
- RB4 Stone Demon-Ogre Rock .10 .30
- RB5 Armored Lizard .10 .30
- RB6 Killer Bee .10 .30
- RB7 Larva Moth (R) 1.00 2.00
- RB8 Harpy Lady .50 1.00
- RB9 Harpy Lady Triplets (PR) 15.00 25.00
- RB9 Harpy Lady Triplets (UR) 8.00 18.00
- RB10 Demon Hunter .10 .30
- RB11 Evolution Cocoon (R) 1.00 2.00
- RB12 Earth Dragon .50 1.00
- RB13 Armored Samurai Zombie .10 .30
- RB14 Dark Mask (R) 2.00 5.00
- RB15 Mute Death Angel- Doma .10 .30
- RB16 White Thief (R) 2.00 4.00
- RB17 King of Eyeballs (R) 1.00 2.00
- RB18 Black Demons Dragon (UR) 10.00 18.00
- RB19 Masked Magician (R) 2.00 5.00
- RB20 Sea Serpent .10 .30
- RB21 Water Dancer .10 .30
- RB22 Land-Battle Type Bacross .10 .30
- RB23 Puchi (Baby) Moth .10 .30
- RB24 Thousand Prism Mirrors (R) 1.00 2.00
- RB25 Thunder Guardian- Saanga (SR) 6.00 12.00
- RB26 Wind Guardian- Hyuuga (SR) 6.00 12.00
- RB27 Water Guardian- Suuga (SR) 6.00 12.00
- RB28 Magical Lamp .10 .30
- RB29 Iron Scorpion .50 1.00
- RB30 Enzell Ears .10 .30
- RB31 Leguil 45.00 70.00
- RB32 Large Mouse .10 .30
- RB33 Leogon .10 .30
- RB34 Mr. Bomber (R) 1.00 2.00
- RB35 Android No. 7 .10 .30
- RB36 Saint Magician (SR) 4.00 8.00
- RB37 Ancient Elf .50 1.00
- RB38 Deep-Sea Shark .10 .30
- RB39 God Fish .10 .30
- RB40 Destructive Golem .10 .30
- RB41 Thunder God's Anger .10 .30
- RB42 Rainbow Flower .10 .30
- RB43 Mgrinfen .10 .30
- RB44 Mega Thunderball .10 .30
- RB45 Tongue Fish .10 .30
- RB46 Judgemerit Queen .10 .30
- RB47 Pale Beast .10 .30
- RB48 Electric Lizard .10 .30
- RB49 Hunter Spider .10 .30
- RB50 Golden Lizard Warrior .25 .50
- RB51 Kage-Musha Queen .10 .30
- RB52 Tront .10 .30
- RB53 Disc Magician .50 1.00
- RB54 Hiyousube .10 .30
- RB55 Siren .10 .30
- RB56 Fake Trap (R) 3.00 6.00
- RB57 To Welcome the Dead (SR) 4.00 8.00
- RB58 Spiritual Release (R) 2.00 4.00
- RB59 Funeral Release (R) 2.00 4.00
- RB60 Change of Heart (PR) 15.00 25.00
- RB60 Change of Heart (UR) 8.00 15.00

2000 Yu-Gi-Oh Thousand Eyes Bible

Complete Set (52) 50.00 100.00
Booster Box (30 packs) 30.00 50.00
Booster Pack (5 cards) 2.00 3.50

- TB1 Take You With Me (R) 2.00 4.00
- TB2 Goblin Grunt .10 .30
- TB3 Gamble .10 .30
- TB4 Melee (R) 1.00 2.00
- TB5 God's Blessing .10 .30
- TB6 Evil Spirit's Temptation .10 .30
- TB7 Death Hamster .10 .30
- TB8 Dark Bat .10 .30
- TB9 Ghost Tank T-34 .10 .30
- TB10 Galling Buggy .20 .50
- TB11 Burning Earth .10 .30
- TB12 Deep Freeze .10 .30
- TB13 Meteor Strike .10 .30
- TB14 Limit Break .10 .30
- TB15 Blessed Rain .10 .30
- TB16 Monster Recall (SR) 3.00 6.00
- TB17 Shift Change (UR) 5.00 10.00
- TB18 Egg .10 .30
- TB19 Worm Hole (R) 1.00 3.00
- TB20 Sinking Territory .10 .30
- TB21 Magic Drain (SR) 4.00 8.00
- TB22 Ant Hell .10 .30
- TB23 Gravity Bind .10 .30
- TB24 Type Zero: Magic Cruncher .10 .30
- TB25 Seductive Shadow (R) 3.00 6.00
- TB26 Legendary Fisherman (SR) 4.00 10.00
- TB27 Sword Hunter .10 .30
- TB28 Tunnel Worm .10 .30
- TB29 Deep Sea Warrior .10 .30
- TB30 Jade Shoe .10 .30
- TB31 Spike Head .10 .30
- TB32 Dark Hypnotist Lucifer (R) 1.00 2.00
- TB33 Thousand Eyes Evil Cult God (NR) 6.00 12.00
- TB34 Thousand Eyes Sacrifice (PR) 15.00 27.00
- TB34 Thousand Eyes Sacrifice (UTR) 20.00 35.00
- TB34 Thousand Eyes Sacrifice (UR) 7.00 15.00
- TB35 Guillotine Kuwagada .10 .30
- TB36 Pidgeon Knight .10 .30
- TB37 Bomber Bug .10 .30
- TB38 4-Star Death Bug .10 .30
- TB39 Vic Viper .10 .30
- TB40 Vampire Baby .20 .50
- TB41 Sword-Tusked Beast .10 .30
- TB42 Pirate Ship Skull-Blood .10 .30
- TB43 White Tiger .10 .30
- TB44 Goblin Assault Team .50 1.00
- TB45 Island Turtle .10 .30
- TB46 Winged Messenger 2.00 4.00
- TB47 Science Bio-Soldier .10 .30
- TB48 Unrest Souls .10 .30
- TB49 Death Boomerang .10 .30
- TB50 Magic Giga-Cyber (UR) 9.00 18.00
- TB51 Iron Knight Gear-Freed (SR) 4.00 8.00
- TB52 Anti-Insect Barrier (R) 1.00 2.00

2001 Yu-Gi-Oh Booster Chronicle

Complete Set (80) 70.00 110.00
Booster Box (30 packs) 40.00 60.00
Booster Pack (5 cards) 2.00 3.50

- BC1 Thunder Guy .10 .30
- BC2 Vampire Guy .10 .30
- BC3 Light of Elf .10 .30
- BC4 Metal Shell .10 .30
- BC5 Life Blood of Angel .10 .30
- BC6 Brighten Light (R) 1.00 2.00
- BC7 Bean Soldier .10 .30
- BC8 Statue of Easter Island .10 .30
- BC9 Skull Shark .10 .30
- BC10 Fish Fin Warrior .10 .30
- BC11 Guardian of Fortress #2 .10 .30
- BC12 Dimensional Warrior .10 .30
- BC13 Spirit of Light .10 .30
- BC14 Blue Potion .10 .30
- BC15 Roll of Thunder .10 .30
- BC16 Burning Spear .10 .30
- BC17 Fan with Sudden Gust .10 .30
- BC18 Wicked Worm Beast .10 .30
- BC19 Giant Beetle .10 .30
- BC20 Tiger Axe .10 .30
- BC21 Axe Raider (PR) 10.00 20.00
- BC21 Axe Raider (UR) 5.00 10.00
- BC22 Elder Winged Beast Spirit .10 .30
- BC23 Winged Beast of Holy Light .10 .30
- BC24 God's Left Hand Final Judge .10 .30
- BC25 Pretty Samurai .10 .30
- BC26 Man in the Forest .10 .30
- BC27 Metabolic Soldier of Hell .10 .30
- BC28 Miss Sonic .10 .30
- BC29 Metabolic Pod (SR) 6.00 12.00
- BC30 Red Dragon .50 1.00
- BC31 Bug Warrior .10 .30
- BC32 Fierce Beetle .10 .30
- BC33 Winged Turtle .10 .30
- BC34 Gemini (UTR) 22.00 40.00
- BC34 Gemini (UR) 12.00 25.00
- BC34 Gemini (PR) 15.00 30.00
- BC35 Giant Beetle King .10 .30
- BC36 Machinery Investigator .10 .30
- BC37 Unfortunate Bird .10 .30
- BC38 Sandglass of Courage .10 .30
- BC39 Death Suit of Battlefield .10 .30
- BC40 Elf of Fountain .10 .30
- BC41 Goddess of the Moon .10 .30
- BC42 Queen of Red Leaves .10 .30
- BC43 White Hole .10 .30
- BC44 Alms by Angel (SR) 4.00 8.00
- BC45 Scream from Cemetery .10 .30
- BC46 Two Heads King Rex (PR) 7.00 15.00
- BC46 Two Heads King-Rex (UR) 5.00 10.00
- BC47 Garzas .10 .30
- BC48 Sea Serpent God .10 .30
- BC49 Dinosaur Zombie .10 .30
- BC50 Dragon Zombie .10 .30
- BC51 Goddess of Mind's Eye (R) 3.00 6.00
- BC52 Ra Shin of the Lamp .10 .30
- BC53 Devil Beast King (R) 1.00 2.00
- BC54 Destruction God (R) 1.00 2.00
- BC55 Cuckoo Dragon .10 .30
- BC56 Bull Soul of the Lamp .10 .30
- BC57 Hundred Eyes .10 .30
- BC58 Machine King (R) 3.00 6.00
- BC59 Devil Franken (SR) 5.00 10.00
- BC60 Sky Dragon .10 .30
- BC61 Slimness Dragon .10 .30
- BC62 Water Wizard .10 .30
- BC63 Snipe Eagle .10 .30
- BC64 Red Sun Chicken .10 .30
- BC65 Joker Riding Dragon .10 .30
- BC66 Fiend of Sea Urchin .10 .30
- BC67 Dragon Killer .10 .30
- BC68 Giant Dinosaur .10 .30
- BC69 Needle Worm .10 .30
- BC70 Doppleganger (R) 3.00 6.00
- BC71 Mecca Hunter (SR) 3.00 6.00
- BC72 Penguin Soldier (SR) 5.00 10.00
- BC73 Amphibian Tank .10 .30
- BC74 Illusion Sheep (R) 1.00 2.00
- BC75 Rule of Royal Palace (SR) 5.00 10.00
- BC76 Witch Hunt .10 .30
- BC77 Devil Purification (R) 1.00 2.00
- BC78 Thorn of Magic (R) 2.00 4.00
- BC79 Revolution .10 .30
- BC80 Sage of Fusion 1.00 2.00
- BC00 Absolute Def.General (SCR) 5.00 10.00

2001 Yu-Gi-Oh Labyrinth of Nightmare

Complete Set (53) 75.00 120.00
Booster Box (30 packs) 45.00 60.00
Booster Pack (5 cards) 2.00 3.50

- LN1 Possessed Painting .10 .30
- LN2 Demon Dream Ghost .10 .30
- LN3 Headless Knight .10 .30
- LN4 Earthbound Spirit (SR) 3.00 6.00
- LN5 Ghost Duke .10 .30
- LN6 Bone Seahorse .10 .30
- LN7 Flame Dancer .10 .30
- LN8 Spherus Lady .10 .30
- LN9 Electric Eel .10 .30
- LN10 Controller of the Dead .10 .30
- LN11 Turner of the Dead .10 .30
- LN12 Illusionary Fusionist .10 .30
- LN13 Eater of Souls .10 .30
- LN14 Dark Necrophia (UR) 15.00 25.00
- LN15 Holy Shine Soul .10 .30
- LN16 Spirit of Fire .10 .30
- LN17 Spirit of Water .10 .30
- LN18 Spirit of Rock .10 .30
- LN19 Spirit of Wind .10 .30
- LN20 Fleet Footed Gilazaurus .10 .30
- LN21 Tornado Bird .10 .30
- LN22 Illusionary Spirit .10 .30
- LN23 Dark Hero Zombie (SP) 2.00 5.00
- LN24 Material Supplier .10 .30
- LN25 Magic Absorber .10 .30
- LN26 Final Soldier of a Planet (PR) 5.00 10.00
- LN26 Final Soldier of Planet (UR) 8.00 15.00
- LN27 Intensify Power .10 .30
- LN28 Dark Spirit of Silence (R) 3.00 6.00
- LN29 Imperial Comand (SR) 6.00 12.00
- LN30 Force Field (SR) 4.00 8.00
- LN31 Nest of Ghosts .10 .30
- LN32 Wrath from Beyond Grave .10 .30
- LN33 Charm of Spirit Protection .10 .30
- LN34 Counter Punch .10 .30
- LN35 Indiscriminate Destruction .10 .30
- LN36 The Naked King .10 .30
- LN37 Ouija Board (PR) 15.00 25.00
- LN37 Ouija Board (UR) 8.00 15.00
- LN38 Death Message E (R) 2.00 4.00
- LN39 Death Message A (R) 2.00 4.00
- LN40 Death Message T (R) 2.00 4.00
- LN41 Death Message H (R) 2.00 4.00
- LN42 Dark Corridor .10 .30
- LN43 Poltergeist (R) 4.00 8.00
- LN44 Cyclone Laser .10 .30
- LN45 Decoy Doll .10 .30
- LN46 Fusion Cancel (SR) 4.00 8.00
- LN47 Fusion Gate 1.00 2.00
- LN48 Infectious Virus .10 .30
- LN49 Mysterious Findings .10 .30
- LN50 Dragon Power .10 .30
- LN51 Soul Remover .10 .30
- LN52 Field of Bitter Souls .10 .30
- LN53 Dark Magician (UTR) 30.00 55.00

2001 Yu-Gi-Oh Metal Raiders

Complete Set (84) 80.00 125.00
Booster Box (30 packs) 50.00 60.00
Booster Pack (5 cards) 2.50 4.00

- ME1 Baby Dragon .50 1.00
- ME2 Dark Dragon .50 1.00
- ME3 Barbarian No.2 .10 .30
- ME4 Cow Demon .10 .30
- ME5 Dark Clown Zagi .10 .40
- ME6 Pot Demon .10 .30
- ME7 Illusionist No-Face .10 .30
- ME8 Critter (R) 4.00 8.00
- ME9 Great Moth (SR) 2.00 4.00
- ME10 Kuribo (R) 4.00 8.00
- ME11 Thousand Dragon (UR) 8.00 15.00
- ME12 Jelly Fish .10 .30
- ME13 Dark Castle 1.00 2.00
- ME14 King of the Demon World .10 .30
- ME15 Catapult Turtle (R) 2.00 4.00
- ME16 Kentauros .10 .30
- ME17 Mino-Centaur .10 .30
- ME18 Murder Circus .10 .30
- ME19 Ghost King- Pump King .10 .30
- ME20 Dream Pierro .10 .30
- ME21 Demon's Intelligence .10 .30
- ME22 Demonic Old Man .10 .30
- ME23 Nether World Soldier .10 .30
- ME24 Prevent Rat .10 .30
- ME25 Little Swordsman of Airu 1.00 2.00
- ME26 Sword Queen (R) 4.00 8.00
- ME27 Royal Throne Protector .10 .30
- ME28 Flame Hell (R) 1.00 2.00
- ME29 Land Mine Spider .10 .30
- ME30 Shadow Ghoul (R) 1.00 2.00
- ME31 Dungeon's Demon Tank 1.00 2.00
- ME32 Gargoyle Powered .10 .30
- ME33 Devil Box .10 .30
- ME34 Magic Knight- Giltia .10 .30
- ME35 TM-1 Launcher Spider 1.00 2.00
- ME36 Gigatec Wolf .10 .30
- ME37 Thunder Dragon .10 .30
- ME38 Rainbow Fish .10 .30
- ME39 Thunder Saint .10 .30
- ME40 Judgement Eagle .10 .30
- ME41 Air Insect Soldier .10 .30
- ME42 Super Star .10 .30
- ME43 Musician King .10 .30
- ME44 Yado-Karyu .10 .30
- ME45 Mega Saurus .10 .30
- ME46 Cannon Soldier (R) 2.00 4.00
- ME47 Muka-Muka (R) 1.00 2.00
- ME48 Devil Cook .10 .30
- ME49 Star Boy .10 .30
- ME50 Millis Rediant .10 .30
- ME51 Flame Cereberus .10 .30
- ME52 Ko-Ke .10 .30
- ME53 Dark Elf 1.00 2.00
- ME54 Matango .10 .30
- ME55 Barbarian No.1 .10 .30
- ME56 Black Forest Witch (R) 2.00 4.00
- ME57 Little Chimera .10 .30
- ME58 Blade Fly .10 .30
- ME59 High Priestess .10 .30
- ME60 Two-Headed Thunder Dragon (SR) 3.00 6.00
- ME61 Apprentice Witch .10 .30
- ME62 Crown-Wearing Blue Wings .10 .30
- ME63 Skull Bishop .10 .30
- ME64 Garnesha Elephants (UR) 3.00 6.00
- ME65 Revolver Dragon (UR) 5.00 10.00
- ME66 God's Declaration (SR) 3.00 6.00
- ME67 Magic Jammer (SR) 8.00 15.00
- ME68 Thief's Pocket Knife (SR) 5.00 10.00
- ME69 Rising Horn (SR) 2.00 4.00
- ME70 Attack-Defense Change (SR) 2.00 4.00
- ME71 Vengeful Sword .10 .30
- ME72 Disable Attack .10 .30
- ME73 Unfortunate Pretty Girl (R) 3.00 6.00
- ME74 Thieving Goblin (R) 4.00 8.00
- ME75 Viral Infection .10 .30
- ME76 Paralysis Potion .10 .30
- ME77 Holy Barrier Mirror Force (UR) 8.00 15.00
- ME78 Magnetic Ring .10 .30
- ME79 Share the Pain .10 .30
- ME80 Doping .10 .30
- ME81 Big Storm .10 .30
- ME82 Griffon's Wing .50 1.00
- ME83 Illusion Beast Gazelle (SR) 8.00 15.00
- ME00 Time Magician (SCR) 12.00 20.00

2001 Yu-Gi-Oh Spell of Mask

Complete Set (52) 80.00 125.00
Booster Box (30 packs) 45.00 60.00
Booster Pack (5 cards) 2.00 3.50

- SM1 Landstar Swordsman .10 .30
- SM2 Humanoid Slime .10 .30
- SM3 Worm Drake .10 .30
- SM4 Humanoid Drake .10 .30
- SM5 Revival Slime (SR) 3.00 6.00
- SM6 Flying Fish .10 .30
- SM7 Fisher Beast .10 .30
- SM8 Shine Abyss .10 .30
- SM9 Gadget Soldier .25 .50
- SM10 Cursed Gyura 1.00 2.00
- SM11 Maekid: Four Faced Beast .10 .30
- SM12 Temptress Nuvia (UR) 5.00 12.00
- SM13 The Chosen One (R) 1.00 2.00
- SM14 Mask of Weakening .10 .30
- SM15 Masked Beast Ritual .10 .30
- SM16 Mask of Magic Loss (SPR) 3.00 6.00
- SM17 Sacrifice-Prohibit Mask (UR) 6.00 15.00
- SM17 Sacrifice-Prohib Mask (PR) 20.00 40.00
- SM18 Mask of Cursed Souls (SR) 4.00 10.00
- SM19 Mask of Atrocity .10 .30
- SM20 Restore Life (R) 2.00 4.00
- SM21 Lightning Sword .10 .30
- SM22 Tornado Wall .10 .30
- SM23 Monster Box .25 .50
- SM24 Tidal Wave (R) 5.00 12.00
- SM25 Slime Multiplication Furnace (R) 2.00 4.00
- SM26 Unlimited Hand Size .10 .30
- SM27 Defense Slime .10 .30
- SM28 Valuable Card of Revival (PR) 12.00 25.00
- SM28 Valuable Card of Revival (UR) 6.00 15.00
- SM29 Lady Panther .10 .30
- SM30 Ally-Killing Female Knight .10 .30
- SM31 Amazon Archer .10 .30
- SM32 Red Guardian .10 .30
- SM33 Big Bang Girl (SR) 8.00 20.00
- SM34 Flame Assasin .10 .30
- SM35 Fire Sorceror .10 .30
- SM36 Wind Sprite .10 .30
- SM37 Dancing Fairy .10 .30
- SM38 Pixie Guardian .10 .30
- SM39 Queen Kamagiri .10 .30
- SM40 Mermaid Princess .10 .30
- SM41 Hysteric Angel .10 .30
- SM42 Bio Cleric .10 .30
- SM43 Remorseful Nun .10 .30
- SM44 Saint Jeanne .10 .30
- SM45 Fallen Angel Mary (R) 3.00 6.00
- SM46 Vase of Strong Desire .10 .30
- SM47 Mystifying Scroll .10 .30
- SM48 Power of Unity 1.00 2.00
- SM49 Magician's Power .10 .30
- SM50 Offerings to the Dead (R) 2.00 4.00
- SM51 Blue Eyes White Dragon (UTR) 30.00 55.00
- SM00 Masked Hell-Raiser (UTR) 20.00 40.00
- SM00 Masked Hell-Raiser (SCR) 12.00 25.00

2001 Yu-Gi-Oh Struggle of Chaos

Complete Set (50) 85.00 130.00
Booster Box (30 packs) 40.00 70.00
Booster Pack (5 cards) 2.00 3.50

- SC1 Lord of Netherworld (UR) 8.00 15.00
- SC1 Lord of Netherworld (PR) 20.00 30.00
- SC2 Demon Dark Baltar (SR) 3.00 6.00
- SC3 Lesser Demon (R) 5.00 10.00
- SC4 Haunting Blood Soul .10 .30
- SC5 Ha-Des Familiar .10 .30
- SC6 Skull Knight .10 .30
- SC7 Gargoyle Deceiver .10 1.00
- SC8 Twin-Head Kerberos .10 .30
- SC9 Red Cyclops (SP) 1.00 3.00
- SC10 Grasp of the Underworld .10 .30
- SC11 Death Calculator (R) 3.00 6.00
- SC12 Life Absorber .10 .30
- SC13 Revival from the Underworld .10 .30
- SC14 Soul Smash .10 .30
- SC15 Double Trap .10 .30
- SC16 Undefeated General (PR) 15.00 25.00
- SC16 Undefeated General (UR) 6.00 12.00
- SC17 Sling Troops .10 .30
- SC18 Standing Troops .10 .30
- SC19 Dragon Warrior (SR) 3.00 8.00
- SC20 Warrior Dai Greyfar .10 .30
- SC21 Holy Defender .10 .30
- SC22 Birder Wiseman .10 .30
- SC23 Initiate Troops .10 .30
- SC24 Hunter with 7 Weapons .10 .30
- SC25 Demon Tamer (R) 3.00 6.00
- SC26 Dragon Rider C .10 .30
- SC27 United Army .10 .30
- SC28 Calling Reinforcements .10 .30
- SC29 Sealing Light Formation (R) 3.00 6.00
- SC30 Warrior Reborn .10 .30
- SC31 Assault Preparations .10 .30
- SC32 Military Movements .10 .30
- SC33 Emergency Rations .10 .30
- SC34 Tyrant Dragon (UR) 15.00 25.00
- SC34 Tyrant Dragon (PR) 18.00 30.00
- SC35 Spear Dragon (R) 2.00 4.00
- SC36 Spirit Dragon .50 1.00
- SC37 Cave Dragon .50 1.00
- SC38 Lizard Soldier .10 .30
- SC39 Death Demon Dragon (SR) 4.00 10.00
- SC40 Grand Dragon .10 .30
- SC41 Grey Wing .10 .30
- SC42 Dragon Troops .50 1.00
- SC43 Dragon's Jewel (R) 3.00 6.00
- SC44 Dragon Feather Burst .10 .30
- SC45 Fire Blast of Flame Dragon .10 .30
- SC46 Stomping Crash .10 .30
- SC47 Super Regeneration .10 .30
- SC48 Dragon Scales .10 .30
- SC49 Burst Breath .10 .30
- SC50 Emerald Dragon (SR) 5.00 10.00
- SC51 Summon Skull (UTR) 20.00 40.00

2002 Yu-Gi-Oh Advent of Union

Complete Set (55) 90.00 150.00
Booster Box (30 packs) 40.00 60.00
Booster Pack (5 Cards) 2.00 4.00

- 302-001 Escape People .10 .30
- 302-002 Oppressed People .10 .30
- 302-003 Resistance Unit .10 .30
- 302-004 X Head Cannon (SR) 3.00 6.00
- 302-005 Y Dragon Head (UR) 5.00 10.00
- 302-006 Z Metal Caterpillar (SR) 3.00 6.00
- 302-007 Fighter of Dark World (SR) 3.00 6.00
- 302-008 Dragon of Darkness 1.00 2.00
- 302-009 Horseman Dragon .10 .30
- 302-010 Decaying General .10 .30
- 302-011 Zombie Tiger .10 .30
- 302-012 Gaint Goblin .10 .30
- 302-013 Second Goblin .10 .30
- 302-014 Demon Tree .10 .30
- 302-015 Demon Grass .10 .30
- 302-016 Flint Stone Beast .10 .30
- 302-017 Freeze Crystal Beast .10 .30
- 302-018 Union Rider .10 .30
- 302-019 Dimensional Beast .10 .30
- 302-020 Magic Canceller (UR) 6.00 12.00
- 302-021 Cat of Richie (SP) 1.00 2.00
- 302-022 Combat Auto-Bot (R) 1.00 2.00
- 302-023 Dimensional Pot .10 .30

❑ 302-024 The Great Thief (R)	1.00	2.00
❑ 302-025 Roulette Bomber	.10	.30
❑ 302-026 White Dragon Rider (UR)	10.00	20.00
❑ 302-027 Advent of White Dragon	.10	.30
❑ 302-028 Advance Base	.10	.30
❑ 302-029 Demotion Disposal	.10	.30
❑ 302-030 Combination Attack (R)	1.00	2.00
❑ 302-031 Kaiser Coliseum	.10	.30
❑ 302-032 Automatic Unit	.10	.30
❑ 302-033 Poison and Potion	.10	.30
❑ 302-034 Anti Game (R)	1.00	2.00
❑ 302-035 Black Cores (R)	2.00	4.00
❑ 302-036 Gold Armor	.10	.30
❑ 302-037 Silver Armor	.10	.30
❑ 302-038 Soul of Bushido	.10	.30
❑ 302-039 Tribute Doll (R)	2.00	4.00
❑ 302-040 Super Charge Cannon	.10	.30
❑ 302-041 Great Revolution	.10	.30
❑ 302-042 Road of Champion	.10	.30
❑ 302-043 Multiplex Wear (SR)	3.00	6.00
❑ 302-044 Meteor Rain	.10	.30
❑ 302-045 Pineapple Bomb	.10	.30
❑ 302-046 Machine Gun	.10	.30
❑ 302-047 Physical Offshoot	.10	.30
❑ 302-048 Rivalry of Barons	.10	.30
❑ 302-049 Two Side Attack	.10	.30
❑ 302-050 Adhesion Trap	.10	.30
❑ 302-051 XY Dragon Cannon (SCR)	5.00	10.00
❑ 302-051 XY Dragon Cannon (UTR)	7.00	15.00
❑ 302-052 XYZ Dragon Cannon (UTR)	7.00	15.00
❑ 302-052 XYZ Dragon Cannon (SCR)	5.00	10.00
❑ 302-053 XZ Dragon Cannon (SCR)	5.00	10.00
❑ 302-053 XZ Dragon Cannon (UTR)	7.00	15.00
❑ 302-054 YZ Dragon Cannon (UTR)	5.00	10.00
❑ 302-054 YZ Dragon Cannon (SCR)	5.00	10.00
❑ 302-055 Barrel Dragon (UTR)	20.00	40.00

2002 Yu-Gi-Oh Duelist Legacy 1

Complete Set (136)	120.00	200.00
Booster Box (30 packs)	30.00	50.00
Booster Pack (5 cards)	2.00	3.50
❑ DL1000 Dark Sage (UTR)	12.00	25.00
❑ DL1001 Penguin Knight	.10	.30
❑ DL1002 Demon's Axe (SR)	3.00	6.00
❑ DL1003 Black Pendant (R)	1.00	2.00
❑ DL1004 Horn of Light	.10	.30
❑ DL1005 Kiss of Demon	.10	.30
❑ DL1006 Hexagram Curse	.10	.30
❑ DL1007 Thunder Snake	.10	.30
❑ DL1008 Amoeba	.10	.30
❑ DL1009 Magic Warrior (R)	1.00	2.00
❑ DL1010 Royal Throne Guardian	.10	.30
❑ DL1011 Envy	.10	.30
❑ DL1012 Green Buddy	.10	.30
❑ DL1013 Weather Report	.10	.30
❑ DL1014 Demonic Investigator	.10	.30
❑ DL1015 Lake Merman	.10	.30
❑ DL1016 Throne Infiltrator	.10	.30
❑ DL1017 Slot Machine	.10	.32
❑ DL1018 Relinquished (PR)	10.00	20.00
❑ DL1018 Relinquished (UR)	5.00	10.00
❑ DL1019 Mermaid	.10	.30
❑ DL1020 Grave Familiar	.10	.30
❑ DL1021 Demonic Ritual	.10	.30
❑ DL1022 Wealthy Goblin	.10	.30
❑ DL1023 Toll	.10	.30
❑ DL1024 Final Battle	.10	.30
❑ DL1025 Theft (SR)	3.00	6.00
❑ DL1026 Holy Song	.10	.30
❑ DL1027 Confiscation (R)	1.00	2.00
❑ DL1028 Twin Demons (SR)	3.00	6.00
❑ DL1029 Dark Visitor	.10	.30
❑ DL1030 Angelic Mirror	.10	.30
❑ DL1031 Change of Cloth	.10	.30
❑ DL1032 Charge	.10	.30
❑ DL1033 Reliable Guardian	.10	.30
❑ DL1034 Forcible Guard	.10	.30
❑ DL1035 Magical Bond	.10	.30
❑ DL1036 Cyclone (R)	1.00	2.00
❑ DL1037 Hurricane (R)	1.00	2.00
❑ DL1038 Tough Decision	.10	.30
❑ DL1039 Snake Fang	.10	.30
❑ DL1040 Unicorn's Horn	.10	.30
❑ DL1041 Labyrinth Wall	.10	.20
❑ DL1042 Wall Shadow	.10	.30
❑ DL1043 Labyrinth Change	.10	.30
❑ DL1044 Baptism	.10	.30
❑ DL1045 Giant Growth (SR)	3.00	6.00
❑ DL1046 Dance Ritual	.10	.30
❑ DL1047 Burger Recipe	.10	.30
❑ DL1048 Sticky House	.10	.30
❑ DL1049 Mouse Trap	.10	.30
❑ DL1050 Turtle's Oath	.10	.30
❑ DL1051 Dancing Queen	.10	.30
❑ DL1052 Burger Senior	.10	.30
❑ DL1053 Crab Turtle	.10	.30
❑ DL1054 Dragon Egger	.10	.30
❑ DL1055 Toon Egger	.50	1.00
❑ DL1056 Toon Mermaid	2.00	5.00
❑ DL1057 Toon Summoned Skull (SR)	5.00	12.00
❑ DL1058 Time Bomber	.10	.30
❑ DL1059 Diamond Dragon	.10	.30
❑ DL1060 Toon World (R)	3.00	6.00
❑ DL1061 Cyber Pot (R)	1.00	2.00
❑ DL1062 Light Purser (R)	1.00	2.00
❑ DL1063 Giant Mouse (R)	1.00	2.00
❑ DL1064 Senju God	1.00	2.00
❑ DL1065 UFO Turtle	.10	.30
❑ DL1066 Assassin	.10	.30
❑ DL1067 Mr.Karate (R)	1.00	2.00
❑ DL1068 Dark Zebra	.10	.30
❑ DL1069 Big Virus (R)	1.00	2.00
❑ DL1070 Speedy Squirrel	.10	.30
❑ DL1071 Dark Familiar	.10	.30
❑ DL1072 Shine Angel	.10	.30
❑ DL1073 Boar Warrior	.10	.30
❑ DL1074 Grizzle	.10	.30
❑ DL1075 Dragon Fly	.10	.30
❑ DL1076 Ceremony Bell	.10	.30
❑ DL1077 Sonic Bird	.10	.30
❑ DL1078 Killer Tomato (R)	1.00	2.00
❑ DL1079 Kotoro	.10	.30
❑ DL1080 Gaia Power	.10	.30
❑ DL1081 Water World	.10	.30
❑ DL1082 Burning Volcano	.10	.30
❑ DL1083 Desert Storm	.10	.30
❑ DL1084 Shine Spark	.10	.30
❑ DL1085 Dark Force	.10	.30
❑ DL1086 Messenger of Peace	.10	.30
❑ DL1087 Blue Eyes Toon Dragon (PR)	20.00	30.00
❑ DL1087 Blue Eyes Toon Dragon (UR)	12.00	20.00
❑ DL1088 Silver Armstrong	.10	.30
❑ DL1089 Three Head Demon	.10	.30
❑ DL1090 Android Psycho Shocker (UR)	6.00	12.00
❑ DL1090 Android Psycho Shocker (PR)	10.00	20.00
❑ DL1091 Parasite (R)	1.00	2.00
❑ DL1092 7 Card	.10	.30
❑ DL1093 Hand-Sealing Sword (R)	1.00	2.00
❑ DL1094 Chain Destruction	.10	.30
❑ DL1095 Seal of Time	.10	.30
❑ DL1096 Tomb Raider	.10	.30
❑ DL1097 Holy Elf's Blessing	.10	.30
❑ DL1098 Eye of Truth	.10	.30
❑ DL1099 Desert Cyclone (R)	1.00	2.00
❑ DL1100 Cry of Living Dead (SR)	3.00	6.00
❑ DL1101 Book of Solomon	.10	.30
❑ DL1102 Land Reformation	.10	.30
❑ DL1103 Holy Javelin	.10	.30
❑ DL1104 Silver Screen Mirror Wall (R)	1.00	2.00
❑ DL1105 Gale	.10	.30
❑ DL1106 Blizzard	.10	.30
❑ DL1107 Glass Armor	.10	.30
❑ DL1108 World Peace	.10	.30
❑ DL1109 Magic Stone Tablet	.10	.30
❑ DL1110 Metal Detector	.10	.30
❑ DL1111 White-Robed Angel	.10	.30
❑ DL1112 Take Advantage (R)	1.00	2.00
❑ DL1113 Forceful Takeover	.10	.30
❑ DL1114 DNA Modify Operation	.10	.30
❑ DL1115 Racial Trial	.10	.30
❑ DL1116 Back-up Members	.10	.30
❑ DL1117 Big Commotion	.10	.30
❑ DL1118 Peace Treaty (R)	1.00	2.00
❑ DL1119 Holy Shrine	.10	.30
❑ DL1120 Righteousness	.10	.30
❑ DL1121 Imperial Rebellion (SR)	4.00	8.00
❑ DL1122 Magical Silk Hat (R)	1.00	2.00
❑ DL1123 Messiah of Genocide (R)	.50	1.00
❑ DL1124 Messiah of Annihilation (R)	1.00	2.00
❑ DL1125 Shallow Grave	.10	.30
❑ DL1126 Early Burial (SR)	4.00	8.00
❑ DL1127 Examine	.10	.30
❑ DL1128 Restriction Order	.10	.30
❑ DL1129 Chaos Pot (R)	1.00	2.00
❑ DL1130 Flame Samurai	.10	.30
❑ DL1131 Mental Parasitic Host	.10	.30
❑ DL1132 Mecha Falcon	.10	.30
❑ DL1133 Flying Mantis	.10	.30
❑ DL1134 Bird Man	.10	.30
❑ DL1135 Buster Blader (PR)	12.00	25.00
❑ DL1135 Buster Blader (UR)	7.00	12.00
❑ DL1136 Big Shield Guardian (UTR)	12.00	25.00

2002 Yu-Gi-Oh Duelist Legacy 2

Complete Set	100.00	175.00
Booster Box (30 packs)	45.00	65.00
Booster Pack (5 cards)	2.00	4.00
❑ DL2000 Dark Executer Makura (UTR)	8.00	16.00
❑ DL2001 Blue-Eyes White Dragon (UR)	6.00	12.00
❑ DL2002 Hitotsu-Me Giant	.10	.30
❑ DL2003 Flame Swordsman (R)	2.00	5.00
❑ DL2004 Skull Servant	.10	.30
❑ DL2005 Dark Magician (UR)	5.00	10.00
❑ DL2006 Gaia the Fierce Knight (R)	1.00	2.00
❑ DL2007 Celtic Guardian	.10	.30
❑ DL2008 Basic Insect	.10	.30
❑ DL2009 Mammoth Graveyard	.10	.30
❑ DL2010 Silver Fang	.10	.30
❑ DL2011 Trial of Hell	.10	.30
❑ DL2012 The 13th Grave	.10	.30
❑ DL2013 Flame Manipulater	.10	.30
❑ DL2014 Dark King of Abyss	.10	.30
❑ DL2015 Fiend Reflection #2	.10	.30
❑ DL2016 Aqua Madoor (R)	1.00	2.00
❑ DL2017 Two-Mouth Darkruler	.10	.30
❑ DL2018 Ray & Temperature	.10	.30
❑ DL2019 King Fog	.10	.30
❑ DL2020 Masaki the Legendary Swordsman	.10	.30
❑ DL2021 Legendary Sword	.10	.30
❑ DL2022 Beast Fangs	.10	.30
❑ DL2023 Violet Crystal	.10	.30
❑ DL2024 Book of Secret Arts	.10	.30
❑ DL2025 Power of Kaishin	.10	.30
❑ DL2026 Dragon Capture Jar	.10	.30
❑ DL2027 Forest	.10	.30
❑ DL2028 Wasteland	.10	.30
❑ DL2029 Moutain	.10	.30
❑ DL2030 Sogen	.10	.30
❑ DL2031 Umi	.10	.30
❑ DL2032 Yami	.10	.30
❑ DL2033 Dark Hole (SR)	2.00	5.00
❑ DL2034 Raigeki (SR)	5.00	10.00
❑ DL2035 Red Medicine	.10	.30
❑ DL2036 Sparks	.10	.30
❑ DL2037 Hinotama	.10	.30
❑ DL2038 Fissure (R)	1.00	2.00
❑ DL2039 Trap Hole (R)	1.00	2.00
❑ DL2040 Polymerization (R)	6.00	12.00
❑ DL2041 Remove Trap	.10	.30
❑ DL2042 Two-Pronged Attack	.10	.30
❑ DL2043 Mystical Elf (R)	1.00	2.00
❑ DL2044 Tyhone	.10	.30
❑ DL2045 Beaver Warrior	.10	.30
❑ DL2046 Gaia the Dragon Champion (SR)	3.00	6.00
❑ DL2047 Curse of Dragon (R)	1.00	2.00
❑ DL2048 Giant Soldier of Stone	.10	.30
❑ DL2049 Uraby	.10	.30
❑ DL2050 Red Eyes B Dragon (UR)	8.00	15.00
❑ DL2051 Reaper of the Cards (R)	1.00	2.00
❑ DL2052 Witty of Phantom	.10	.30
❑ DL2053 Spirit of the Harp	.10	.30
❑ DL2054 Terra the Terrible	.10	.30
❑ DL2055 Enchanting Mermaid	.10	.30
❑ DL2056 Fireyarou	.10	.30
❑ DL2057 Dark Energy	.10	.30
❑ DL2058 Laser Cannon Armor	.10	.30
❑ DL2059 Vile Germs	.10	.30
❑ DL2060 Silver Bow and Arrow	.10	.30
❑ DL2061 Dragon Treasure	.10	.30
❑ DL2062 Electro-Whip	.10	.30
❑ DL2063 Mystical Moon	.10	.30
❑ DL2064 Stop Defense	.10	.30
❑ DL2065 Machine Conversion Factory	.10	.30
❑ DL2066 Raise Body Heat	.10	.30
❑ DL2067 Follow Wind	.10	.30
❑ DL2068 Goblin's Secret Remedy	.10	.30
❑ DL2069 Final Flame	.10	.30
❑ DL2070 Swords of Revealing Light (SR)	3.00	6.00
❑ DL2071 Metal Dragon	.10	.30
❑ DL2072 Spike Seadra	.10	.30
❑ DL2073 Skull Red Bird	.10	.30
❑ DL2074 Armed Ninja (R)	1.00	2.00
❑ DL2075 Man-Eater Bug (R)	1.00	2.00
❑ DL2076 Sand Stone	.10	.30
❑ DL2077 Hane-Hane (R)	1.00	2.00
❑ DL2078 Steel Ogre Grotto #1	.10	.30
❑ DL2079 Lesser Dragon	.10	.30
❑ DL2080 Succubus Knight	.10	.30
❑ DL2081 De-Spell	.10	.30
❑ DL2082 Monster Reborn (SR)	3.00	6.00
❑ DL2083 Pot of Greed (R)	2.00	4.00
❑ DL2084 Gravedigger Ghoul (R)	1.00	2.00
❑ DL2085 Right Leg of the Forbidden One (R)	8.00	15.00
❑ DL2086 Left Leg of the Forbidden One (R)	8.00	15.00
❑ DL2087 Right Arm of the Forbidden One (R)	8.00	15.00
❑ DL2088 Left Arm of the Forbidden One (R)	8.00	15.00
❑ DL2089 Exodia the Forbidden One (UR)	15.00	25.00
❑ DL2090 Feral Imp	.10	.30
❑ DL2091 Winged Dragon	.10	.30
❑ DL2092 Summoned Skull (SR)	3.00	6.00
❑ DL2093 Rock Ogre Grotto #1	.10	.30
❑ DL2094 Armored Lizard	.10	.30
❑ DL2095 Killer Needle	.10	.30
❑ DL2096 Larvae Moth	.10	.30
❑ DL2097 Harpie Lady	.50	1.00
❑ DL2098 Harpie Lady Sisters (R)	1.00	2.00
❑ DL2099 Kojikocky	.10	.30
❑ DL2100 Cocoon of Evolution	.10	.30
❑ DL2101 Crawling Dragon	.10	.30
❑ DL2102 Armored Zombie	.10	.30
❑ DL2103 Mask of Darkness (R)	1.00	2.00
❑ DL2104 White Magical Hat (R)	1.00	2.00
❑ DL2105 Big Eye	.10	.30
❑ DL2106 B Skull Dragon (SR)	4.00	8.00
❑ DL2107 Masked Sorcerer (R)	1.00	2.00
❑ DL2108 Roaring Ocean Snake	.10	.30
❑ DL2109 Water Omotics	.10	.30
❑ DL2110 Ground Attacker Bugroth	.10	.30
❑ DL2111 Petit Moth	.10	.30
❑ DL2112 Elegant Egotist	.10	.30
❑ DL2113 Sanga of Thunder (R)	3.00	6.00
❑ DL2114 Kazejin (R)	3.00	6.00
❑ DL2115 Suijin (R)	2.00	4.00
❑ DL2116 Mystic Lamp	.10	.30
❑ DL2117 Steel Scorpion	.10	.30
❑ DL2118 Leghul	.10	.30
❑ DL2119 Ooguchi	.10	.30
❑ DL2120 Leogun	.10	.30
❑ DL2121 Blast Juggler	.10	.30
❑ DL2122 Jinzo #7	.10	.30
❑ DL2123 Magician of Faith (R)	3.00	6.00
❑ DL2124 Rainbow Flower	.10	.30
❑ DL2125 Pale Beast	.10	.30
❑ DL2126 Electric Lizard	.10	.30
❑ DL2127 Hunter Spider	.10	.30
❑ DL2128 Ancient Lizard Warrior	.10	.30
❑ DL2129 Queen's Double	.10	.30
❑ DL2130 Trent	.10	.30
❑ DL2131 Fake Trap	.10	.30
❑ DL2132 Tribute to Doomed (R)	1.00	2.00
❑ DL2133 Soul Release (R)	2.00	4.00
❑ DL2134 Cheerful Coffin (R)	1.00	3.00
❑ DL2135 Change of Heart (SR)	4.00	8.00
❑ DL2136 Card Exchange (UTR)	10.00	20.00

2002 Yu-Gi-Oh Legend of Blue Eyes White Dragon 1st Edition

Card		
Complete Set (126)	400.00	550.00
Booster Box (24 packs)	250.00	350.00
Booster Pack (9 cards)	12.00	15.00
❑ LOB-0 Tri-Horned Dragon (SCR)	10.00	25.00
❑ LOB-1 Blue-Eyes White Dragon (UR)	20.00	40.00
❑ LOB-2 Hitotsu-Me Giant	.30	.75
❑ LOB-3 Flame Swordsman (SR)	4.00	10.00
❑ LOB-4 Skull Servant	.40	1.00
❑ LOB-5 Dark Magician (UR)	15.00	30.00
❑ LOB-6 Gaia The Fierce Knight (UR)	5.00	12.00
❑ LOB-7 Celtic Guardian (SR)	2.50	6.00
❑ LOB-8 Basic Insect	.30	.75
❑ LOB-9 Mammoth Graveyard	.30	.75
❑ LOB-10 Silver Fang	.30	.75
❑ LOB-11 Dark Gray	.30	.75
❑ LOB-12 Trial of Hell	.40	1.00
❑ LOB-13 Nemuriko	.30	.75
❑ LOB-14 The 13th Grave	.30	.75
❑ LOB-15 Charubin Fire Knight (R)	1.50	4.00
❑ LOB-16 Flame Manipulator	.30	.75
❑ LOB-17 Monster Egg	.30	.75
❑ LOB-18 Firegrass	.40	1.00
❑ LOB-19 Darkfire Dragon (R)	2.00	5.00
❑ LOB-20 Dark King of Abyss	.30	.75
❑ LOB-21 Fiend Reflection #2	.30	.75
❑ LOB-22 Fusionist (R)	1.50	4.00
❑ LOB-23 Turtle Tiger	.30	.75
❑ LOB-24 Petit Dragon	.30	.75
❑ LOB-25 Petit Angel	.30	.75
❑ LOB-26 Hinotama Soul	.40	1.00
❑ LOB-27 Aqua Madoor (R)	.75	2.00
❑ LOB-28 Kagemusha of Blue Flame	.30	.75
❑ LOB-29 Flame Ghost (R)	1.25	3.00
❑ LOB-30 Two-Mouth Darkruler	.30	.75
❑ LOB-31 Dissolverock	.30	.75
❑ LOB-32 Root Water	.40	1.00
❑ LOB-33 The Furious Sea King	.40	1.00
❑ LOB-34 Green Phantom King	.30	.75
❑ LOB-35 Ray & Temperature	.30	.75
❑ LOB-36 King Fog	.30	.75
❑ LOB-37 Mystical Sheep #2	.30	.75
❑ LOB-38 Masaki Legendary Swordsman	.30	.75
❑ LOB-39 Kurama	.30	.75
❑ LOB-40 Legendary Sword (SP)	.75	2.00
❑ LOB-41 Beast Fangs (SP)	.40	1.00
❑ LOB-42 Violet Crystal (SP)	.75	2.00
❑ LOB-43 Book of Secret Arts (SP)	.75	2.00
❑ LOB-44 Power of Kaishin (SP)	.75	2.00
❑ LOB-45 Dragon Capture Jar (R)	1.50	4.00
❑ LOB-46 Forest	.30	.75
❑ LOB-47 Wasteland	.30	.75
❑ LOB-48 Mountain	.30	.75
❑ LOB-49 Sogen	.30	.75
❑ LOB-50 Umi	.40	1.00
❑ LOB-51 Yami	.40	1.00
❑ LOB-52 Dark Hole (SR)	10.00	25.00
❑ LOB-53 Raigeki (SR)	6.00	15.00
❑ LOB-54 Red Medicine	.30	.75
❑ LOB-55 Sparks	.30	.75
❑ LOB-56 Hinotama	.30	.75
❑ LOB-57 Fissure (R)	1.00	2.50
❑ LOB-58 Trap Hole (SR)	3.00	8.00
❑ LOB-59 Polymerization (SR)	8.00	20.00
❑ LOB-60 Remove Trap	.75	2.00
❑ LOB-61 Two-Pronged Attack (R)	.75	2.00
❑ LOB-62 Mystical Elf (SR)	3.00	8.00
❑ LOB-63 Tyhone	.30	.75
❑ LOB-64 Beaver Warrior	.30	.75
❑ LOB-65 Gravedigger Ghoul (R)	.75	2.00
❑ LOB-66 Curse of Dragon (SR)	5.00	12.00
❑ LOB-67 Karbonala Warrior (R)	1.50	4.00
❑ LOB-68 Giant Soldier of Stone (R)	1.50	4.00
❑ LOB-69 Uraby	.40	1.00
❑ LOB-70 Red Eyes B Dragon (UR)	15.00	30.00
❑ LOB-71 Reaper of the Cards (R)	1.00	2.50
❑ LOB-72 Witty Phantom	.30	.75
❑ LOB-73 Larvas	.30	.75
❑ LOB-74 Hard Armor	.30	.75
❑ LOB-75 Man Eater	.40	1.00
❑ LOB-76 M-Warrior #1	.30	.75
❑ LOB-77 M-Warrior #2	.30	.75
❑ LOB-78 Spirit of the Harp (R)	.75	2.00
❑ LOB-79 Armaill	.40	1.00
❑ LOB-80 Terra the Terrible	.30	.75
❑ LOB-81 Frenzied Panda	.30	.75
❑ LOB-82 Kumootoko	.30	.75
❑ LOB-83 Meda Bat	.40	1.00
❑ LOB-84 Enchanting Mermaid	.30	.75
❑ LOB-85 Fireyarou	.30	.75
❑ LOB-86 Dragoness The Wicked K(R)	1.25	3.00
❑ LOB-87 One-Eyed Shield Dragon	.30	.75
❑ LOB-88 Dark Energy (SP)	.75	2.00
❑ LOB-89 Laser Cannon Armor (SP)	.75	2.00
❑ LOB-90 Vile Germs (SP)	.75	2.00
❑ LOB-91 Silver Bow and Arrow (SP)	.75	2.00
❑ LOB-92 Dragon Treasure (SP)	.75	2.00
❑ LOB-93 Electro-Whip	.30	.75
❑ LOB-94 Mystical Moon (SP)	.75	2.00
❑ LOB-95 Stop Defense (R)	.75	2.00
❑ LOB-96 Machine Convers. Factory (SP)	1.50	4.00
❑ LOB-97 Raise Body Heat (SSP)	.75	2.00
❑ LOB-98 Follow Wind (SSP)	.75	2.00
❑ LOB-99 Goblin's Secret Remedy (R)	.75	2.00
❑ LOB-100 Final Flame (R)	1.25	3.00
❑ LOB-101 Swords of Rev. Light (SR)	4.00	10.00
❑ LOB-102 Metal Dragon (R)	1.25	3.00
❑ LOB-103 Spike Seadra	.30	.75
❑ LOB-104 Tripwire Beast	.30	.75
❑ LOB-105 Skull Red Bird	.30	.75
❑ LOB-106 Armed Ninja (R)	.75	2.00
❑ LOB-107 Flower Wolf (R)	.75	2.00
❑ LOB-108 Man-Eater Bug (SR)	3.00	8.00
❑ LOB-109 Sand Stone	.30	.75
❑ LOB-110 Hane-Hane (R)	.75	2.00
❑ LOB-111 Misairuzame	.30	.75
❑ LOB-112 Steel Ogre Grotto #1	.30	.75
❑ LOB-113 Lesser Dragon	.30	.75
❑ LOB-114 Darkworld Thorns	.30	.75
❑ LOB-115 Drooling Lizard	.30	.75
❑ LOB-116 Armored Starfish	.30	.75
❑ LOB-117 Succubus Knight	.30	.75
❑ LOB-118 Monster Reborn (UR)	75.00	125.00
❑ LOB-119 Pot of Greed (R)	3.00	8.00
❑ LOB-120 Right Leg of Forbid.One (UR)	20.00	40.00
❑ LOB-121 Left Leg of Forbid.One (UR)	15.00	30.00
❑ LOB-122 Right Arm of Forbid.One (UR)	25.00	50.00
❑ LOB-123 Left Arm of Forbid.One (UR)	15.00	30.00
❑ LOB-124 Exodia the Forbidden One (UR)	25.00	50.00
❑ LOB-125 Gaia the Dragon Champion (SCR)	8.00	20.00

2002 Yu-Gi-Oh Lord of Dark Magician

Complete Set (54)	60.00	100.00
Booster Box (30 packs)	45.00	65.00
Booster Pack (5 cards)	2.00	4.00
❑ 303-001 Great Beast	.10	.30
❑ 303-002 Aitshi the Red Guy	.10	.30
❑ 303-003 Sonic Duck	.50	1.00
❑ 303-004 Sapphire Dragon (SR)	4.00	8.00
❑ 303-005 Amazon Holy Warrior	.20	.50
❑ 303-006 Amazon Martial Warrior	.20	.50
❑ 303-007 Amazon Swordsman (UR)	6.00	12.00
❑ 303-007 Amazon Swordsman (PR)	10.00	20.00
❑ 303-008 Amazon Blow Gunner	.10	.30
❑ 303-009 Amazon Pet Tiger	.10	.30
❑ 303-010 Skillful White Magician (SR)	5.00	10.00
❑ 303-011 Skillful Black Magician (SR)	4.00	8.00
❑ 303-012 Trainee Magician (R)	1.00	2.00
❑ 303-013 Deep-Seated Old Magician	.50	1.00
❑ 303-014 Chaos Magician (UR)	7.00	15.00
❑ 303-015 Chaos Magician (PR)	10.00	20.00
❑ 303-016 Pixie Knight	.10	.30
❑ 303-017 Magic Marionette	.10	.30
❑ 303-018 Mandragora	.10	.30
❑ 303-019 Magical Scientist	.10	.30
❑ 303-020 Royal Magic Library	.10	.30
❑ 303-021 Magical Armor Axe (R)	1.00	2.00
❑ 303-022 Race Infection Virus	.10	.30
❑ 303-023 Death Koala	.10	.30
❑ 303-024 Trap Remover - Clinton	.10	.30
❑ 303-025 Magical Goods Merchant	.10	.30
❑ 303-026 Koitsu The Blue Guy	.10	.30
❑ 303-027 Cat Baby Triplet	.10	.30
❑ 303-028 Obedience Demon	5.00	10.00
❑ 303-029 White Tailed Black Cat	.50	1.00
❑ 303-030 Amazon Wizard	.50	1.00
❑ 303-031 Counter Machine Gun Punch	.20	.50
❑ 303-032 Big Bang Shoot (R)	1.00	2.00
❑ 303-033 Moral Clarity	.10	.30
❑ 303-034 Mass Driver	.10	.30
❑ 303-035 Eye of Thousand Miles	.10	.30
❑ 303-036 Proof of Dragon Destruction	.10	.30
❑ 303-037 Pot Stealing	.10	.30
❑ 303-038 Body Shield	.10	.30
❑ 303-039 Spell Book Arrangement	.10	.30
❑ 303-040 Megaton Magical Cannon (R)	1.00	2.00
❑ 303-041 Power Stone of Darkness	.10	.30
❑ 303-042 Amazon Crossbow Team (SR)	3.00	6.00
❑ 303-043 Quick Save Drama (R)	1.00	2.00
❑ 303-044 Magical Drought	.10	.30
❑ 303-045 Hidden Spell Book	.10	.30
❑ 303-046 Miraculous Revival	.10	.30
❑ 303-047 Control Release	.10	.30
❑ 303-048 Disarmament	.10	.30
❑ 303-049 Confrontation Spell	.10	.30
❑ 303-050 Life Absorption Spell	.10	.30
❑ 303-051 Super Hero Paladin (UTR)	12.00	25.00
❑ 303-051 Super Hero Paladin (SCR)	10.00	20.00
❑ 303-052 Double Magic (SCR)	8.00	15.00
❑ 303-053 Diffusion Wave (SCR)	8.00	15.00
❑ 303-054 Buster Blader (UTR)	15.00	30.00

2002 Yu-Gi-Oh Magic Ruler 1st Edition

Complete Set (104)	100.00	175.00
Hobby Booster Box (24 packs)	75.00	100.00
Retail Booster Box (36 packs)	90.00	120.00
Booster Pack (9 cards)	4.00	6.00
❑ MRL-0 Blue Eyes Toon Dragon (SCR)	6.00	15.00
❑ MRL-1 Penguin Knight	.30	.75
❑ MRL-2 Axe of Despair (UR)	4.00	10.00
❑ MRL-3 Black Pendant (SR)	.75	2.00
❑ MRL-4 Horn of Light	.30	.75
❑ MRL-5 Malevolent Nuzzler	.30	.75
❑ MRL-6 Spellbinding Circle (UR)	3.00	8.00
❑ MRL-7 Metal Fish	.30	.75
❑ MRL-8 Electric Snake	.30	.75
❑ MRL-9 Queen Bird	.30	.75
❑ MRL-10 Ameba (R)	.40	1.00
❑ MRL-11 Peacock	.30	.75
❑ MRL-12 Maha Vailo (SR)	.75	2.00
❑ MRL-13 Guardian of Throne Room	.30	.75
❑ MRL-14 Fire Kraken	.30	.75
❑ MRL-15 Minar	.30	.75
❑ MRL-16 Griggle	.30	.75
❑ MRL-17 Tyhone #2	.60	1.50
❑ MRL-18 Ancient One of Deep Forest	.30	.75
❑ MRL-19 Dark Witch	.30	.75
❑ MRL-20 Weather Report	.30	.75
❑ MRL-21 Mechanical Snail	.30	.75
❑ MRL-22 Giant Turtle Feeds on Flames	.30	.75
❑ MRL-23 Liquid Beast	.30	.75
❑ MRL-24 Hiro's Shadow Scout (R)	.40	1.00
❑ MRL-25 High Tide Gyojin	.30	.75
❑ MRL-26 Invader of the Throne (SR)	.75	2.00
❑ MRL-27 Whiptail Crow	.30	.75
❑ MRL-28 Slot Machine	.30	.75
❑ MRL-29 Relinquished (UR)	3.00	8.00
❑ MRL-30 Red Archery Girl	.30	.75
❑ MRL-31 Gravekeeper's Servant	1.50	4.00
❑ MRL-32 Curse of Fiend	.40	1.00
❑ MRL-33 Upstart Goblin	1.50	4.00
❑ MRL-34 Toll	.30	.75
❑ MRL-35 Final Destiny	.30	.75
❑ MRL-36 Snatch Steal (UR)	3.00	8.00
❑ MRL-37 Chorus of Sanctuary	.30	.75
❑ MRL-38 Confiscation (SR)	1.00	2.50
❑ MRL-39 Delinquent Duo (UR)	4.00	10.00
❑ MRL-40 Darkness Approaches	.30	.75
❑ MRL-41 Fairy's Hand Mirror	.40	1.00
❑ MRL-42 Tailor of the Fickle	.30	.75
❑ MRL-43 Rush Recklessly (R)	.40	1.00
❑ MRL-44 The Reliable Guardian	.30	.75
❑ MRL-45 The Forceful Sentry (UR)	1.50	4.00
❑ MRL-46 Chain Energy	.40	1.00
❑ MRL-47 Mystical Space Typhoon (UR)	25.00	50.00
❑ MRL-48 Giant Trunade (SR)	2.00	5.00
❑ MRL-49 Painful Choice (SR)	1.00	2.50
❑ MRL-50 Snake Fang	.30	.75
❑ MRL-51 Black Illusion Ritual (SR)	2.50	6.00
❑ MRL-52 Octoberser	.30	.75
❑ MRL-53 Psychic Kappa	.30	.75
❑ MRL-54 Horn of the Unicorn (R)	.40	1.00
❑ MRL-55 Labyrinth Wall	.30	.75
❑ MRL-56 Wall Shadow	.30	.75
❑ MRL-57 Twin Long Rods #2	.30	.75
❑ MRL-58 Stone Ogre Grotto	.30	.75
❑ MRL-59 Magical Labyrinth	.30	.75
❑ MRL-60 Eternal Rest	.30	.75
❑ MRL-61 Megamorph (UR)	3.00	8.00
❑ MRL-62 Commencement Dance	.30	.75
❑ MRL-63 Hamburger Recipe	.40	1.00
❑ MRL-64 House of Adhesive Tape	.30	.75
❑ MRL-65 Eatgaboon	.30	.75
❑ MRL-66 Turtle Oath	.30	.75
❑ MRL-67 Performance of Sword	.30	.75
❑ MRL-68 Hungry Burger	.30	.75
❑ MRL-69 Crab Turtle	.30	.75
❑ MRL-70 Ryu-Ran	.30	.75
❑ MRL-71 Manga Ryu-Ran (R)	.40	1.00
❑ MRL-72 Toon Mermaid (UR)	2.00	5.00
❑ MRL-73 Toon Summoned Skull (UR)	2.00	5.00
❑ MRL-74 Jigen Bakudan	.30	.75
❑ MRL-75 Hyozanryu (R)	.40	1.00
❑ MRL-76 Toon World (SR)	1.50	4.00
❑ MRL-77 Cyber Jar (R)	.75	2.00
❑ MRL-78 Banisher of the Light (SR)	.75	2.00
❑ MRL-79 Giant Rat (R)	.40	1.00
❑ MRL-80 Senju of Thousand Hands (R)	.40	1.00
❑ MRL-81 UFO Turtle (R)	.40	1.00
❑ MRL-82 Flash Assailant	.30	.75
❑ MRL-83 Karate Man (R)	.30	.75
❑ MRL-84 Dark Zebra	.30	.75
❑ MRL-85 Giant Germ (R)	.75	2.00
❑ MRL-86 Nimble Momonga (R)	.75	2.00
❑ MRL-87 Spear Cretin	.30	.75
❑ MRL-88 Shining Angel (R)	.60	1.50
❑ MRL-89 Boar Soldier	.30	.75
❑ MRL-90 Mother Grizzly (R)	.40	1.00
❑ MRL-91 Flying Kamakiri #1 (R)	.40	1.00
❑ MRL-92 Ceremonial Bell	.30	.75
❑ MRL-93 Sonic Bird	.30	.75
❑ MRL-94 Mystic Tomato (R)	.40	1.00

❑ MRL-95 Kotodama .30 .75
❑ MRL-96 Gaia Power .30 .75
❑ MRL-97 Umiiruka .40 1.00
❑ MRL-98 Molten Destruction .40 1.00
❑ MRL-99 Rising Air Current .40 1.00
❑ MRL-100 Luminous Spark .60 1.50
❑ MRL-101 Mystic Plasma Zone .60 1.50
❑ MRL-102 Messenger of Peace (SR) 4.00 10.00
❑ MRL-103 Serpent Night Dragon (SCR) 2.50 6.00

2002 Yu-Gi-Oh Metal Raiders 1st Edition

Complete Set (144) 150.00 300.00
Booster Box (24 packs) 100.00 175.00
Booster Pack (9 cards) 5.00 8.00

❑ MRD-0 Gate Guardian (SCR) 15.00 30.00
❑ MRD-1 Feral Imp (SP) .75 2.00
❑ MRD-2 Winged Dragon .40 1.00
❑ MRD-3 Summoned Skull (UR) 6.00 15.00
❑ MRD-4 Rock Ogre Grotto 1 .30 .75
❑ MRD-5 Armored Lizard .30 .75
❑ MRD-6 Killer Needle .30 .75
❑ MRD-7 Larvae Moth .40 1.00
❑ MRD-8 Harpie Lady 1.25 3.00
❑ MRD-9 Harpie Lady Sisters (SR) 6.00 15.00
❑ MRD-10 Kojikocy .30 .75
❑ MRD-11 Cocoon of Evolution (SSP) .60 1.50
❑ MRD-12 Crawling Dragon .30 .75
❑ MRD-13 Armored Zombie .30 .75
❑ MRD-14 Mask of Darkness (R) 1.00 2.50
❑ MRD-15 Doma the Angel of Silence .30 .75
❑ MRD-16 White Magical Hat (R) .40 1.00
❑ MRD-17 Big Eye .30 .75
❑ MRD-18 B Skull Dragon (UR) 15.00 30.00
❑ MRD-19 Masked Sorcerer (R) .40 1.00
❑ MRD-20 Roaring Ocean Snake .30 .75
❑ MRD-21 Water Omotics .30 .75
❑ MRD-22 Ground Attacker Bugroth .40 1.00
❑ MRD-23 Petit Moth .30 .75
❑ MRD-24 Elegant Egotist (R) 4.00 10.00
❑ MRD-25 Sanga of Thunder (SR) 2.50 6.00
❑ MRD-26 Kazejin (SR) 4.00 10.00
❑ MRD-27 Suijin (SR) 4.00 10.00
❑ MRD-28 Mystic Lamp (SP) .30 .75
❑ MRD-29 Steel Scorpion .30 .75
❑ MRD-30 Ocubeam .30 .75
❑ MRD-31 Leghul (SP) .30 .75
❑ MRD-32 Ooguchi (SP) .30 .75
❑ MRD-33 Leogun .30 .75
❑ MRD-34 Blast Juggler .30 .75
❑ MRD-35 Jinzo #7 (SP) .60 1.50
❑ MRD-36 Magician of Faith (R) 2.00 5.00
❑ MRD-37 Ancient Elf .30 .75
❑ MRD-38 Deepsea Shark .30 .75
❑ MRD-39 Bottom Dweller .30 .75
❑ MRD-40 Destroyer Golem .40 1.00
❑ MRD-41 Kaminari Attack .40 1.00
❑ MRD-42 Rainbow Flower (SP) .40 1.00
❑ MRD-43 Morinphen .30 .75
❑ MRD-44 Mega Thunderball .30 .75
❑ MRD-45 Tongyo .30 .75
❑ MRD-46 Empress Judge .30 .75
❑ MRD-47 Pale Beast .30 .75
❑ MRD-48 Electric Lizard .30 .75
❑ MRD-49 Hunter Spider .30 .75
❑ MRD-50 Ancient Lizard Warrior .30 .75
❑ MRD-51 Queen's Double (SP) 1.25 3.00
❑ MRD-52 Trent .30 .75
❑ MRD-53 Disk Magician .30 .75
❑ MRD-54 Hyosube .30 .75
❑ MRD-55 Hibikime .40 1.00
❑ MRD-56 Fake Trap (R) .60 1.50
❑ MRD-57 Tribute to the Doomed (SR) 1.50 4.00
❑ MRD-58 Soul Release .75 2.00
❑ MRD-59 Cheerful Coffin .40 1.00
❑ MRD-60 Change of Heart (UR) 6.00 15.00
❑ MRD-61 Baby Dragon (SP) .40 1.00
❑ MRD-62 Blackland Fire Dragon .30 .75
❑ MRD-63 Swamp Battleguard .40 1.00
❑ MRD-64 Battle Steer .30 .75
❑ MRD-65 Time Wizard (UR) 4.00 10.00
❑ MRD-66 Saggi the Dark Clown .30 .75
❑ MRD-67 Dragon Piper .40 1.00
❑ MRD-68 Illusionist Faceless Mage .30 .75
❑ MRD-69 Sangan (R) 2.50 6.00
❑ MRD-70 Great Moth (R) 1.25 3.00
❑ MRD-71 Kuriboh (SR) 4.00 10.00
❑ MRD-72 Jellyfish .30 .75
❑ MRD-73 Castle of Dark Illusions 1.25 3.00
❑ MRD-74 King of Yamimakai .30 .75
❑ MRD-75 Catapult Turtle (SR) 2.00 5.00
❑ MRD-76 Mystic Horseman .30 .75
❑ MRD-77 Rabid Horseman .40 1.00
❑ MRD-78 Crass Clown (SP) .75 2.00
❑ MRD-79 Pumpking King of Ghosts .30 .75
❑ MRD-80 Dream Clown (SP) .75 2.00
❑ MRD-81 Tainted Wisdom .30 .75
❑ MRD-82 Ancient Brain .40 1.00
❑ MRD-83 Guardian of Labyrinth .30 .75
❑ MRD-84 Prevent Rat .30 .75
❑ MRD-85 Little Swordsman of Aile .30 .75
❑ MRD-86 Princess of Tsurugi (R) .50 1.25
❑ MRD-87 Protector of the Throne .30 .75
❑ MRD-88 Tremendous Fire .40 1.00
❑ MRD-89 Jirai Gumo .30 .75
❑ MRD-90 Shadow Ghoul (R) .75 2.00
❑ MRD-91 Labyrinth Tank .30 .75
❑ MRD-92 Ryu-Kishin Powered .30 .75
❑ MRD-93 Bickuribox .30 .75
❑ MRD-94 Gillia the D Knight .60 1.50
❑ MRD-95 Launcher Spider .30 .75
❑ MRD-96 Giga-Tech Wolf .30 .75
❑ MRD-97 Thunder Dragon (SP) 2.00 5.00
❑ MRD-98 7 Colored Fish .30 .75
❑ MRD-99 Immortal of Thunder .30 .75
❑ MRD-100 Punished Eagle .30 .75
❑ MRD-101 Insect Soldiers of the Sky .30 .75
❑ MRD-102 Hoshiningen (R) .40 1.00
❑ MRD-103 Musician King .40 1.00
❑ MRD-104 Yado Karu .30 .75
❑ MRD-105 Cyber Saurus 1.50 4.00
❑ MRD-106 Cannon Soldier (R) .40 1.00
❑ MRD-107 Muka Muka (R) .40 1.00
❑ MRD-108 The Bistro Butcher .30 .75
❑ MRD-109 Star Boy (R) .60 1.50
❑ MRD-110 Milus Radiant (R) .40 1.00
❑ MRD-111 Flame Cerebus .30 .75
❑ MRD-112 Niwatori .30 .75
❑ MRD-113 Dark Elf (R) .40 1.00
❑ MRD-114 Mushroom Man #2 .30 .75
❑ MRD-115 Lava Battleguard .30 .75
❑ MRD-116 Witch of Black Forest (R) .75 2.00
❑ MRD-117 Little Chimera (R) .40 1.00
❑ MRD-118 Bladefly (R) .40 1.00
❑ MRD-119 Lady of Faith .30 .75
❑ MRD-120 Twin-Headed Thunder Dragon (SR)1.00 2.50
❑ MRD-121 Witch's Apprentice (R) .40 1.00
❑ MRD-122 Blue-Winged Crown .30 .75
❑ MRD-123 Skull Knight .30 .75
❑ MRD-124 Gazelle King of Myth Beasts (SSP) .40 1.00
❑ MRD-125 Garnecia Elefantis (SR) .75 2.00
❑ MRD-126 Barrel Dragon (UR) 4.00 10.00
❑ MRD-127 Solemn Judgment (UR) 20.00 40.00
❑ MRD-128 Magic Jammer (UR) 3.00 8.00
❑ MRD-129 7 Tools of the Bandit (UR) 8.00 20.00
❑ MRD-130 Horn of Heaven (UR) 4.00 10.00
❑ MRD-131 Shield and Sword (R) .40 1.00
❑ MRD-132 Sword of Deep-Seated .30 .75
❑ MRD-133 Block Attack .30 .75
❑ MRD-134 The Unhappy Maiden (SP) .40 1.00
❑ MRD-135 Robbin Goblin (R) .40 1.00
❑ MRD-136 Germ Infection .30 .75
❑ MRD-137 Paralyzing Potion .30 .75
❑ MRD-138 Mirror Force (UR) 40.00 80.00
❑ MRD-139 Ring of Magnetism .40 1.00
❑ MRD-140 Share the Pain .30 .75
❑ MRD-141 Stim-pack (SP) .30 .75
❑ MRD-142 Heavy Storm (SR) 8.00 20.00
❑ MRD-143 Thousand Dragon (SCR) 3.00 8.00

2001 Yu-Gi-Oh Pegasus Structure Deck

❑ PE-1 Red Archery Girl 5.00 10.00
❑ PE-2 Thousand Eyes Idol 3.00 6.00
❑ PE-3 Illusionist .40 1.00
❑ PE-4 Parrot Dragon .40 1.00
❑ PE-5 Dark Toon Rabbit 5.00 10.00
❑ PE-6 Mystical Doll .40 1.00
❑ PE-7 Toon Alligator .40 1.00
❑ PE-8 Toon Goblin Attack Force .40 1.00
❑ PE-9 Toon Cannon Soldier (SR) 5.00 10.00
❑ PE-10 Toon Gemini Elf (SR) 5.00 10.00
❑ PE-11 Toon Masked Sorcerer .40 1.00
❑ PE-12 Toon Summoned Skull 3.00 6.00
❑ PE-13 Toon Mermaid 2.00 4.00
❑ PE-14 Blue-Eyes Toon Dragon 5.00 10.00
❑ PE-15 Sangan .40 1.00
❑ PE-16 Witch of Black Forest .40 1.00
❑ PE-17 Magician of Faith .40 1.00
❑ PE-18 Senju the Thousand Hand .40 1.00
❑ PE-19 Mystic Tomato .40 1.00
❑ PE-20 Jigen Bakudan .40 1.00
❑ PE-21 Sonic Bird .40 1.00
❑ PE-22 Relinquished 1.00 2.00
❑ PE-23 Snatch Steal .40 1.00
❑ PE-24 Toon World 2.00 4.00
❑ PE-25 Raigeki 2.00 5.00
❑ PE-26 Heavy Storm .40 1.00
❑ PE-27 Soul Exchange .40 1.00
❑ PE-28 Change of Heart .40 1.00
❑ PE-29 Fissure .40 1.00
❑ PE-30 Monster Reborn .40 1.00
❑ PE-31 Polymerization 5.00 10.00
❑ PE-32 Magician of Fusion .40 1.00
❑ PE-33 Giant Trunade .40 1.00
❑ PE-34 Iron Cage of Nightmares .40 1.00
❑ PE-35 Black Illusion Ritual .40 1.00
❑ PE-36 Swamp of Soul .40 1.00
❑ PE-37 Toon Index (SR) 4.00 8.00
❑ PE-38 Toon Defense .40 1.00
❑ PE-39 Jar of Greed .40 1.00
❑ PE-40 Thousand Eyes Restrict 1.00 2.00
❑ PE-41 Ryu-Ran .40 1.00
❑ PE-42 Manga Ryu-Ran .40 1.00
❑ PE-43 Illusionary Summoner .40 1.00
❑ PE-44 Dark Eyes Illusionist .40 1.00
❑ PE-45 Dream Clown .40 1.00
❑ PE-46 Dragon Piper .40 1.00
❑ PE-47 Fusion Cancelation .40 1.00
❑ PE-48 Dimension Hole .40 1.00
❑ PE-49 Shine Castle .40 1.00
❑ PE-50 The Eye of Truth .40 1.00
❑ PE-51 Dragon Capture Jar .40 1.00
❑ PE-52 Illness Prediction .40 1.00
❑ PE-53 Life Absorber .40 1.00
❑ PE-54 Forcefield .40 1.00
❑ PE-55 Respect Player .40 1.00

2001 Yu-Gi-Oh Premium Pack 4

Complete Set (6) 18.00 35.00
Booster Pack 7.00 15.00

❑ P4-1 Dark Magician Girl (UR) 8.00 15.00
❑ P4-2 Dark Magician (UR) 5.00 12.00
❑ P4-3 Thousand Knives (UR) 2.00 4.00
❑ P4-4 Black Magic Curtain (UR) 2.00 5.00
❑ P4-5 Magic Box of Death (UR) 2.00 4.00
❑ P4-6 Magic Cylinder (UR) 2.00 4.00

2002 Yu-Gi-Oh Mythological Age

Complete Set (52) 60.00 100.00
Booster Box (30 packs) 30.00 50.00
Booster Pack (9 cards) 2.00 3.50

❑ MA1 Machine Corp .20 .50
❑ MA2 Beowulf .10 .30
❑ MA3 Magic Gentleman .10 .30
❑ MA4 Metal Lady .10 .30
❑ MA5 Metal Man .10 .30
❑ MA6 Fiber Pod .10 .30
❑ MA7 Naga .10 .30
❑ MA8 Noble Du Noir .10 .30
❑ MA9 Voltage Girl (R) 10.00 20.00
❑ MA10 Option .10 .30
❑ MA11 Injection Angel Lily (SP) 4.00 8.00
❑ MA12 Leaf Fairie .10 .30
❑ MA13 Sky Knight (SR) 6.00 15.00
❑ MA14 Doll Dra .10 .30
❑ MA15 Illumination Spirit .10 .30
❑ MA16 Pathfinder Spirit .10 .30
❑ MA17 Giant Crows .10 .30
❑ MA18 Divine Emperor Thunder (PR) 22.00 40.00
❑ MA18 Divine Emperor Thunder (UR) 12.00 20.00
❑ MA19 Eight-Headed Serpent (UR) 5.00 10.00
❑ MA19 Eight-Headed Serpent (PR) 30.00 50.00
❑ MA20 Great Sky Dog .10 .30
❑ MA21 Dragon Princess .10 .30
❑ MA22 Fire Starter (PR) 20.00 30.00
❑ MA22 Fire Starter (UR) 10.00 20.00
❑ MA23 Asura (SR) 7.00 15.00
❑ MA24 Undefeatable Firebird .10 .30
❑ MA25 Rare Metal Valkyrie .10 .30
❑ MA26 Rare Metal Knight .10 .30
❑ MA27 Spirit-Sealing Mirror .10 .30
❑ MA28 Elemental Spring .10 .30
❑ MA29 Mind that Reflects as Water .10 .30
❑ MA30 Legendary City Atlantis .10 .30
❑ MA31 Fusion Weapon (R) 2.00 4.00
❑ MA32 Thieving Smoke Bomb .50 1.00
❑ MA33 Forced Transfer .10 .30
❑ MA34 Spirit Syphon Equipment .10 .30
❑ MA35 Second Chance (R) 1.00 2.00
❑ MA36 Disturb. between Heav & Earth .10 .30
❑ MA37 Quiet Theft .10 .30
❑ MA38 Genocide War (R) 3.00 6.00
❑ MA39 Magic Gardner (SR) 3.00 6.00
❑ MA40 Chained Dynamite (R) 3.00 8.00
❑ MA41 Lost .10 .30
❑ MA42 Bubble Crush .10 .30
❑ MA43 Imperial Oppression (R) 4.00 9.00
❑ MA44 Bottomless Pit Fall .10 .30
❑ MA45 Drug Reaction .10 .30
❑ MA46 Fortuneless Prediction .10 .30
❑ MA47 Invitation from Spirits .10 .30
❑ MA48 Body Strength Supplement .10 .30
❑ MA49 Vanishing Pit .10 .30
❑ MA50 Devil Comedian .10 .30
❑ MA51 Last Battle (SR) 6.00 12.00
❑ MA52 Black Demon Dragon (UTR) 25.00 45.00

2002 Yu-Gi-Oh New Ruler

Complete Set (50) 75.00 110.00
Booster Box (30 packs) 45.00 65.00
Booster Pack (5 cards) 2.00 4.00

❑ 301-01 Master Kyonshi .10 .30
❑ 301-02 Giant Kabazaurus .10 .30
❑ 301-03 Tree-man 18 .10 .30
❑ 301-04 Dark Jiroido (SR) 5.00 10.00
❑ 301-05 Nyudoryua .10 .30
❑ 301-06 Hell Poet (UR) 6.00 12.00
❑ 301-06 Hell Poet (PR) 10.00 20.00
❑ 301-07 Gravekeeper Detective .10 .30
❑ 301-08 Gravekeeper Chanter .10 .30
❑ 301-09 Gravekeeper Guard .10 .30
❑ 301-10 Gravekeeper Commander .10 .30
❑ 301-11 Gravekeeper Follower .10 .30
❑ 301-12 Gravekeeper Observer (R) 1.00 2.00
❑ 301-13 Gravekeeper Leader (SR) 3.00 6.00
❑ 301-14 Gravekeeper Gunner .10 .30
❑ 301-15 Gravekeeper Assassin .10 .30
❑ 301-16 The Man With Eye of Ujat .10 .30
❑ 301-17 Jackal Paladin (UR) 6.00 12.00
❑ 301-17 Jackal Paladin (PR) 12.00 22.00
❑ 301-18 Black Cat Brings Unhappiness .10 .30
❑ 301-19 Ship to the Sunset .10 .30
❑ 301-20 Winged Sage Falcos (R) 1.00 2.00
❑ 301-21 Owl Brings Unhappiness .10 .30
❑ 301-22 Shabti's Protector .10 .30
❑ 301-23 Snake Pod (R) 1.00 2.00
❑ 301-24 Soul-hunting Spirit .10 .30
❑ 301-25 Nightmare Horse .10 .30
❑ 301-26 Nightmare-shaving Spirit .10 .30
❑ 301-27 Dark Tudor (R) 1.00 2.00
❑ 301-28 Shotgun Shuffle .10 .30
❑ 301-29 Reputation .10 .30
❑ 301-30 Torture Room of Nightmares(R) .10 .30
❑ 301-31 Time Capsule .10 .30
❑ 301-32 Necro Val. Royal Fam Sleep(UR) 3.00 6.00
❑ 301-33 Buster Launcher .10 .30
❑ 301-34 Heliograph Tablet .10 .30
❑ 301-35 Black Snake Sickness .10 .30
❑ 301-36 Terra Forming .10 .30
❑ 301-37 Symbol of Courage .10 .30
❑ 301-38 Metamorphosis .10 .30
❑ 301-39 Imperial Sacrifice .10 .30
❑ 301-40 The Reverse Quiz .10 .30
❑ 301-41 Coffin Sale .10 .30
❑ 301-42 Curse of Aging .10 .30
❑ 301-43 The Key Opens Hell's Door .10 .30
❑ 301-44 Thunder Break .10 .30
❑ 301-45 Narrow Passage .10 .30
❑ 301-46 Confusing Battle .10 .30
❑ 301-47 Trap of Blackboard Cleaner(R) 1.00 2.00
❑ 301-48 Ritual of the Spirits .10 .30
❑ 301-49 Invasion of Territory .10 .30
❑ 301-50 Blood of Dragons .10 .30
❑ 301-51 Lava Evil Spirit (UTR) 12.00 25.00
❑ 301-51 Lava Evil Spirit (SCR) 6.00 12.00
❑ 301-52 Baisa Shook (SCR) 6.00 12.00
❑ 301-52 Baisa Shook (UTR) 15.00 30.00
❑ 301-53 Quiz (SCR) 15.00 25.00
❑ 301-54 Rope of Life (SCR) 10.00 20.00
❑ 301-55 Torture Wheel (SCR) 6.00 12.00
❑ 301-56 Red Eyes Black Dragon (UTR) 20.00 40.00

2002 Yu-Gi-Oh Pharaoh's Servant 1st Edition

Complete Set (105) 100.00 150.00
Hobby Booster Box (24 packs) 75.00 125.00
Retail Booster Box (36 packs) 100.00 175.00
Booster Pack (9 cards) 4.00 6.00

❑ PSV-0 Jinzo (SCR) 10.00 25.00
❑ PSV-1 Steel Ogre Grotto #2 .30 .75
❑ PSV-2 Three-Headed Geedo .30 .75
❑ PSV-3 Parasite Paracide (SR) .75 2.00
❑ PSV-4 7 Completed .30 .75
❑ PSV-5 Lightforce Sword (R) .30 .75
❑ PSV-6 Chain Destruction (UR) 1.50 4.00
❑ PSV-7 Time Seal (SP) .30 .75
❑ PSV-8 Graverobber (SR) .75 2.00
❑ PSV-9 Gift of the Mystical Elf (SP) .30 .75
❑ PSV-10 The Eye of Truth (SP) .30 .75
❑ PSV-11 Dust Tornado (SR) 2.00 5.00
❑ PSV-12 Call of the Haunted (UR) 6.00 15.00
❑ PSV-13 Solomon's Lawbook .30 .75
❑ PSV-14 Earthshaker .30 .75
❑ PSV-15 Enchanted Javelin .30 .75
❑ PSV-16 Mirror Wall (SR) .75 2.00
❑ PSV-17 Gust .30 .75
❑ PSV-18 Driving Snow .30 .75
❑ PSV-19 Armored Glass .30 .75
❑ PSV-20 World Suppression .30 .75
❑ PSV-21 Mystic Probe .30 .75
❑ PSV-22 Metal Detector .30 .75
❑ PSV-23 Numinous Healer (SSP) .30 .75
❑ PSV-24 Appropriate (R) .75 2.00
❑ PSV-25 Forced Requisition (R) .75 2.00
❑ PSV-26 DNA Surgery (SP) 3.00 6.00
❑ PSV-27 The Regulation of Tribe .30 .75
❑ PSV-28 Backup Soldier (SR) .75 2.00
❑ PSV-29 Major Riot (SSP) .30 .75
❑ PSV-30 Ceasefire (UR) 1.50 4.00
❑ PSV-31 Light of Intervention .30 .75
❑ PSV-32 Respect Play .30 .75
❑ PSV-33 Magical Hats (SR) 1.50 4.00
❑ PSV-34 Nobleman of Crossout (SR) 1.00 2.50
❑ PSV-35 Nobleman of Extermination (R) .75 2.00
❑ PSV-36 The Shallow Grave (R) .75 2.00
❑ PSV-37 Premature Burial (UR) 3.00 8.00
❑ PSV-38 Inspection (SP) .40 1.00
❑ PSV-39 Prohibition (R) 1.00 2.50
❑ PSV-40 Morphing Jar #2 (R) 1.25 3.00
❑ PSV-41 Flame Champion .30 .75
❑ PSV-42 Twin-Headed Fire Dragon .30 .75
❑ PSV-43 Darkfire Soldier .30 .75
❑ PSV-44 Mr.Volcano .30 .75
❑ PSV-45 Darkfire Soldier #2 .30 .75
❑ PSV-46 Kiseitai (SP) .30 .75
❑ PSV-47 Cyber Falcon .30 .75
❑ PSV-48 Flying Kamakiri #2 .30 .75
❑ PSV-49 Harpie's Brother .30 .75
❑ PSV-50 Buster Blader (UR) 4.00 10.00
❑ PSV-51 Michizure (R) .40 1.00
❑ PSV-52 Minor Goblin Official (SP) .30 .75
❑ PSV-53 Gamble .30 .75
❑ PSV-54 Attack and Receive .30 .75
❑ PSV-55 Solemn Wishes (SSP) 1.50 4.00
❑ PSV-56 Skull Invitation (R) .40 1.00
❑ PSV-57 Bubonic Vermin .30 .75
❑ PSV-58 Dark Bat .30 .75
❑ PSV-59 Oni Tank T-34 .30 .75
❑ PSV-60 Overdrive .30 .75
❑ PSV-61 Burning Land .30 .75
❑ PSV-62 Cold Wave .30 .75
❑ PSV-63 Fairy Meteor Crush (SR) .75 2.00
❑ PSV-64 Limiter Removal (SR) .75 2.00
❑ PSV-65 Rain of Mercy .30 .75
❑ PSV-66 Monster Recovery (R) .40 1.00
❑ PSV-67 Shift (R) .40 1.00
❑ PSV-68 Insect Imitation .60 1.50
❑ PSV-69 Dimensionhole (R) .30 .75
❑ PSV-70 Ground Collapse .30 .75
❑ PSV-71 Magic Drain (R) .60 1.50
❑ PSV-72 Infinite Dismissal .30 .75
❑ PSV-73 Gravity Bind (R) 1.25 3.00
❑ PSV-74 Type Zero Magic Crusher .30 .75
❑ PSV-75 Shadow of Eyes .30 .75
❑ PSV-76 The Legendary Fisherman (UR) 4.00 10.00
❑ PSV-77 Sword Hunter (SP) .30 .75
❑ PSV-78 Drill Bug .30 .75
❑ PSV-79 Deepsea Warrior .30 .75
❑ PSV-80 Bite Shoes .30 .75
❑ PSV-81 Spikebot .30 .75
❑ PSV-82 Invitation to a Dark Sleep .30 .75
❑ PSV-83 Thousand-Eyes Idol (SSP) .40 1.00
❑ PSV-84 Thousand-Eyes Restrict (UR) 3.00 8.00
❑ PSV-85 Girochin Kuwagata .30 .75
❑ PSV-86 Hayabusa Knight (R) .40 1.00
❑ PSV-87 Bombardment Beetle (SP) .30 .75
❑ PSV-88 4-Starred Ladybug of Doom (SP) .30 .75
❑ PSV-89 Gradius (SP) .30 .75
❑ PSV-90 Red-Moon Baby (R) .40 1.00
❑ PSV-91 Mad Sword Beast (R) .30 .75
❑ PSV-92 Skull Mariner .30 .75
❑ PSV-93 The All-Seeing White Tiger .30 .75
❑ PSV-94 Goblin Attack Force (UR) 2.50 6.00
❑ PSV-95 Island Turtle (SP) .30 .75
❑ PSV-96 Wingweaver .30 .75
❑ PSV-97 Science Soldier .30 .75
❑ PSV-98 Souls of the Forbidden .30 .75
❑ PSV-99 Dokuroyaiba .30 .75
❑ PSV-100 The Fiend Megacyber (UR) 2.00 5.00
❑ PSV-101 Gearfried the Iron Knight (SR) .75 2.00
❑ PSV-102 Insect Barrier .30 .75
❑ PSV-103 Beast Talwar (UR) 2.00 5.00
❑ PSV-104 Imperial Order (SCR) 1.25 3.00

2002 Yu-Gi-Oh Pharaonic Guardian

Complete Set (51) 80.00 140.00
Booster Box (30 packs) 45.00 65.00
Booster Pack (5 cards) 2.50 4.00

❑ PH1 Magma Giant .10 .30
❑ PH2 Shapesnatch .10 .30
❑ PH3 Soul-eater .10 .30
❑ PH4 Wan-fu Tiger King (R) 2.00 5.00
❑ PH5 Birdface .10 .30
❑ PH6 Cruel .10 .30
❑ PH7 Armored Fly .10 .30
❑ PH8 Mermaid Princess (SP) 3.00 6.00
❑ PH9 Xeno .10 .30
❑ PH10 Time Eater .10 .30
❑ PH11 Gurrage .10 .30
❑ PH12 Mysterious Sevant .10 .30
❑ PH13 Moist Alien (SR) 4.00 8.00
❑ PH14 Gora-Turtle .10 .30
❑ PH15 Super Slash Samurai (SR) 5.00 10.00
❑ PH16 Poison Mummy .10 .30
❑ PH17 Sandstorm Poltergeist .10 .30
❑ PH18 Pharaoh's Guardian .10 .30
❑ PH19 Wandering Mummy (R) 2.00 4.00
❑ PH20 De-zard the Great Priest (UR) 10.00 22.00
❑ PH20 De-Zard the Great Priest (PR) 15.00 30.00
❑ PH21 Scarab Swarm .10 .30
❑ PH22 Locust Swarm .10 .30
❑ PH23 Fat Mummy .10 .30
❑ PH24 Octo-Pion .10 .30
❑ PH25 Guardian Sphynx (PR) 20.00 35.00
❑ PH25 Guardian Sphynx (UR) 10.00 22.00
❑ PH26 Pyramurtle .10 .30
❑ PH27 Dice Pot .10 .30
❑ PH28 Black Scorpion Gang .10 .30
❑ PH29 Don Zaruug (UR) 10.00 20.00
❑ PH29 Don Zaruug (PR) 20.00 35.00
❑ PH30 Camel Mummy .10 .30
❑ PH31 Suksy Serpent Man (R) 1.00 2.00
❑ PH32 Book of Life (SR) 9.00 18.00
❑ PH33 Book of Sun .20 .50
❑ PH34 Book of Moon .20 .50
❑ PH35 Nightmare Shimmer .10 .30
❑ PH36 Secret Door .10 .30
❑ PH37 Call of the Mummy .10 .30
❑ PH38 Scaredy Cat .10 .30
❑ PH39 Pyramid Power .10 .30
❑ PH40 Pharoah's Mask .10 .30
❑ PH41 Traveller's Ordeal (R) 2.00 4.00
❑ PH42 Bottomless Quicksand .10 .30
❑ PH43 Curse of Pharoah (R) 2.00 4.00
❑ PH44 Spiked Ceiling Trap .10 .30
❑ PH45 Golden Statue of Evil (SR) 4.00 8.00
❑ PH46 Cursed Sarcophagus .10 .30
❑ PH47 Spiked Wall Trap .10 .30
❑ PH48 Dust Chute .10 .30
❑ PH49 Sundial of Destiny .10 .30
❑ PH50 Greedy Fool .10 .30
❑ PH51 Treasure Chest (R) 2.00 5.00
❑ PH00 Lich Undead King (SCR) 10.00 20.00

2002 Yu-Gi-Oh Power of Guardian

Complete Set (54) 60.00 100.00
Booster Box (30 packs) 45.00 65.00
Booster Pack (5 cards) 2.00 4.00

❑ 304-001 Football Warrior .10 .30
❑ 304-002 Ninja Dog .10 .30
❑ 304-003 Metal Monkey .10 .30
❑ 304-004 Weapon Summoner .10 .30
❑ 304-005 Guardian Alma .10 .30
❑ 304-006 Guardian Seal (UR) 5.00 10.00
❑ 304-007 Guardian Powell (UR) 5.00 10.00
❑ 304-008 Guardian Barol (R) 2.00 4.00
❑ 304-009 Guardian Christine .10 .30
❑ 304-010 Guardian Double (R) 1.00 2.00
❑ 304-011 Cybernetics Radar Warrior .10 .30
❑ 304-012 Magician of Magical Mirror (SR) 4.00 8.00
❑ 304-013 Tiny Winged Warrior .10 .30
❑ 304-014 Death Feral Imp (UR) 5.00 10.00
❑ 304-015 Twilight Zone (R) 1.00 2.00
❑ 304-016 King of Sky Shinato (R) 1.00 2.00
❑ 304-017 Dark Flare Knight (R) 1.00 2.00
❑ 304-018 Miracle Knight (R) 1.00 2.00
❑ 304-019 Berserk Death Dragon (R) 1.00 2.00
❑ 304-020 Exodia Necros (R) 6.00 12.00
❑ 304-021 Panda Attack (R) 1.00 2.00
❑ 304-022 Mindless Obedience Goblin .10 .30
❑ 304-023 Darkness of Despair .10 .30
❑ 304-024 Composition Beast .10 .30
❑ 304-025 Darkness of Fear (R) 1.00 2.00
❑ 304-026 Black Scorpion .10 .30
❑ 304-027 Twilight Zone Female Warrior (SR) 8.00 16.00
❑ 304-028 The Thousand Needles .10 .30
❑ 304-029 Miracle Ark .10 .30
❑ 304-030 Bargain with Demon .10 .30
❑ 304-031 Pact of Exodia 4.00 8.00
❑ 304-032 Dagger of Butterfly (SR) 4.00 8.00
❑ 304-033 Bow of Meteor .10 .30
❑ 304-034 Axe of Gravity .10 .30
❑ 304-035 Sword of Evil Breaker (SR) 4.00 8.00
❑ 304-036 Rod of Silence .10 .30
❑ 304-037 Twin Swords of Flash Light .10 .30
❑ 304-038 Treasure of Hell .10 .30
❑ 304-039 Blade of Third Eye .10 .30
❑ 304-040 Spirit of the Spring .10 .30
❑ 304-041 Harvest of Token Festival .10 .30
❑ 304-042 Morale Evevation .10 .30
❑ 304-043 Absolute Magic Probation Zone .10 .30
❑ 304-044 Twilight Zone Isolation Machine (R) 1.00 2.00
❑ 304-045 Final Attack Order .10 .30
❑ 304-046 Powerful Enemy Temptation .10 .30
❑ 304-047 Obstacle Trio .10 .30
❑ 304-048 Armory Robbery .10 .30
❑ 304-049 Effect Absorbption (R) 2.00 4.00
❑ 304-050 Big Eternal Rest .10 .30
❑ 304-051 Kaiser Glider (SR)(UTR) 5.00 12.00
❑ 304-052 Sub-space Material Transfer Device (SR)4.00 8.00
❑ 304-053 Cost Reduction (SR) 4.00 8.00
❑ 304-054 Black Luster Soldier (UR) 10.00 18.00

2003 Yu-Gi-Oh Dark Crisis 1st Edition

Complete Set (106) 125.00 179.00
Hobby Booster Box (24 packs) 100.00 175.00
Retail Booster Box (36 packs) 125.00 200.00
Booster Pack (9 cards) 4.50 8.00

❑ DCR-0 Vampire Lord (SCR) 5.00 12.00
❑ DCR-1 Battle Footballer .30 .75
❑ DCR-2 Nin-Ken Dog 1.00 2.50
❑ DCR-3 Acrobat Monkey .30 .75
❑ DCR-4 Arsenal Summoner .30 .75
❑ DCR-5 Guardian Elma .30 .75
❑ DCR-6 Guardian Ceal (UR) .60 1.50
❑ DCR-7 Guardian Grarl (UR) 1.25 3.00
❑ DCR-8 Guardian Baou (R) .40 1.00
❑ DCR-9 Guardian Kay'est .30 .75
❑ DCR-10 Guardian Tryce (R) .40 1.00
❑ DCR-11 Cyber Raider (SP) .30 .75
❑ DCR-12 Reflect Bounder (UR) 3.00 8.00
❑ DCR-13 Little-Winguard (SP) .30 .75
❑ DCR-14 Des Feral Imp (R) .40 1.00
❑ DCR-15 Different Dimension Dragon (SR) .60 1.50
❑ DCR-16 Shinato, King of a Higher Plane(UR) 4.00 10.00
❑ DCR-17 Dark Flare Knight (SR) 1.25 3.00
❑ DCR-18 Mirage Knight (SR) 1.25 3.00
❑ DCR-19 Berserk Dragon (SR) 1.50 4.00
❑ DCR-20 Exodia Necross (UR) 6.00 15.00
❑ DCR-21 Gyaku-Gire Panda (SP) .30 .75
❑ DCR-22 Blindly Loyal Goblin .30 .75
❑ DCR-23 Despair from the Dark (SP) .30 .75
❑ DCR-24 Maju Garzett (SP) .30 .75
❑ DCR-25 Fear from the Dark (R) .40 1.00
❑ DCR-26 Dark Scorpion - Chick the Yellow .30 .75
❑ DCR-27 D. D. Warrior Lady (SR) 1.00 2.50
❑ DCR-28 Thousand Needles .30 .75
❑ DCR-29 Shinato's Ark (SP) .40 1.00

- DCR-30 A Deal with Dark Ruler (SP) .50 1.25
- DCR-31 Contract with Exodia (SP) .75 2.00
- DCR-32 Butterfly Dagger - Elma (SR) .60 1.50
- DCR-33 Shooting Star Bow - Ceal .20 .75
- DCR-34 Gravity Axe - Grarl .20 .75
- DCR-35 Wicked-Breaking Flamberge (R) .40 1.00
- DCR-36 Rod of Silence - Kay'est .30 .75
- DCR-37 Twin Swords of Flashing Light .30 .75
- DCR-38 Precious Cards from Beyond .30 .75
- DCR-39 Rod of the Mind's Eye .30 .75
- DCR-40 Fairy of the Spring .30 .75
- DCR-41 Token Thanksgiving .30 .75
- DCR-42 Morale Boost .30 .75
- DCR-43 Non-Spellcasting Area .30 .75
- DCR-44 Different Dimension Gate (R) .40 1.00
- DCR-45 Final Attack Orders .30 .75
- DCR-46 Staunch Defender .30 .75
- DCR-47 Ojama Trio (SP) 1.00 2.00
- DCR-48 Arsenal Robber .30 .75
- DCR-49 Skill Drain (R) 2.00 5.00
- DCR-50 Really Eternal Rest .30 .75
- DCR-51 Kaiser Glider (UR) 1.25 3.00
- DCR-52 Interdimensional Matter Trans.(UR) 1.25 3.00
- DCR-53 Cost Down (UR) 1.50 4.00
- DCR-54 Gagagigo .30 .75
- DCR-55 D. D. Trainer .30 .75
- DCR-56 Ojama Green .30 .75
- DCR-57 Archfiend Soldier (R) 1.25 3.00
- DCR-58 Pandemonium Watchbear .30 .75
- DCR-59 Sasuke Samurai #2 .30 .75
- DCR-60 Dark Scorpion - Gorg .30 .75
- DCR-61 Dark Scorpion - Meanae .30 .75
- DCR-62 Outstanding Dog Marron (SP) .30 .75
- DCR-63 Great Maju Garzett (R) 1.50 4.00
- DCR-64 Iron Blacksmith Kotetsu .30 .75
- DCR-65 Goblin of Greed .30 .75
- DCR-66 Mefist the Infernal General (R) .40 1.00
- DCR-67 Vilepawn Archfiend .30 .75
- DCR-68 Shadowknight Archfiend .30 .75
- DCR-69 Darkbishop Archfiend (R) .40 1.00
- DCR-70 Desrook Archfiend .30 .75
- DCR-71 Infernalqueen Archfiend (R) .40 1.00
- DCR-72 Terrorking Archfiend (SR) 1.50 4.00
- DCR-73 Skull Archfiend of Lightning (UR) 1.50 4.00
- DCR-74 Metallizing Parasite - Lunatite(R) .40 1.00
- DCR-75 Tsukuyomi (R) 1.50 4.00
- DCR-76 Mudora (SR) .40 1.00
- DCR-77 Keldo .30 .75
- DCR-78 Kelbek .30 .75
- DCR-79 Zolga .30 .75
- DCR-80 Agido .30 .75
- DCR-81 Legendary Flame Lord (R) .40 1.00
- DCR-82 Dark Master - Zorc (SR) .60 1.50
- DCR-83 Spell Reproduction .30 .75
- DCR-84 Dragged Down into Grave 2.00 5.00
- DCR-85 Incandescent Ordeal (SP) .30 .75
- DCR-86 Contract with the Abyss (R) .40 1.00
- DCR-87 Contract with the Dark Master (SP) .30 .75
- DCR-88 Falling Down (SP) 3.00 8.00
- DCR-89 Checkmate .30 .75
- DCR-90 Cestus of Dagla .30 .75
- DCR-91 Final Countdown (SP) 2.00 5.00
- DCR-92 Archfiend's Oath .30 .75
- DCR-93 Mustering of Dark Scorpions .30 .75
- DCR-94 Pandemonium (SP) .60 1.50
- DCR-95 Altar for Tribute .30 .75
- DCR-96 Frozen soul .30 .75
- DCR-97 Battle-Scarred .30 .75
- DCR-98 Dark Scorpion Combination(R) .40 1.00
- DCR-99 Archfiend's Roar .75 2.00
- DCR-100 Dice Re-Roll (SP) .40 1.00
- DCR-101 Spell Vanishing (SR) .30 .75
- DCR-102 Sakuretsu Armor .50 1.25
- DCR-103 Ray of Hope .30 .75
- DCR-104 Blast Held by a Tribute (UR) 2.00 5.00
- DCR-105 Judgment of Anubis (SCR) 1.50 4.00

2003 Yu-Gi-Oh Labyrinth of Nightmare 1st Edition

Complete Set (105)	100.00	150.00
Hobby Booster Box (24 packs)	70.00	100.00
Retail Booster Box (36 packs)	80.00	125.00
Booster Pack (9 cards)	3.50	5.00

- LON-0 Gemini Elf (SCR) 3.00 8.00
- LON-1 The Masked Beast (UR) 4.00 10.00
- LON-2 Swordsman of Landstar .30 .75
- LON-3 Humanoid Slime (SP) .40 1.00
- LON-4 Worm Drake .30 .75
- LON-5 Humanoid Worm Drake .30 .75
- LON-6 Revival Jam (SR) 2.00 5.00
- LON-7 Flying Fish .30 .75
- LON-8 Amphibian Beast (R) .40 1.00
- LON-9 Shining Abyss .30 .75
- LON-10 Gadget Soldier .30 .75
- LON-11 Grand Tiki Elder .30 .75
- LON-12 Melchid the Four-Face Beast .30 .75
- LON-13 Nuvia the Wicked (R) .40 1.00
- LON-14 Chosen One .30 .75
- LON-15 Mask of Weakness .30 .75
- LON-16 Curse of the Masked Beast .40 1.00
- LON-17 Mask of Dispel (SR) .75 2.00
- LON-18 Mask of Restrict (UR) 2.00 5.00
- LON-19 Mask of the Accursed (SR) 1.00 2.50
- LON-20 Mask of Brutality (R) .40 1.00
- LON-21 Return of the Doomed (R) .30 .75
- LON-22 Lightning Blade .30 .75
- LON-23 Tornado Wall .40 1.00
- LON-24 Fairy Box 1.25 3.00
- LON-25 Torrential Tribute (UR) 15.00 30.00
- LON-26 Jam Breeding Machine (R) .40 1.00
- LON-27 Infinite Cards (R) 2.50 6.00
- LON-28 Jam Defender (SP) .30 .75
- LON-29 Card of Safe Return (UR) 2.50 6.00
- LON-30 Lady Panther .30 .75
- LON-31 The Unfriendly Amazon .30 .75
- LON-32 Amazon Archer .30 .75
- LON-33 Crimson Sentry .30 .75
- LON-34 Fire Princess (SR) .75 2.00
- LON-35 Lady Assailant of Flames .30 .75
- LON-36 Fire Sorcerer .30 .75
- LON-37 Spirit of the Breeze (R) .40 1.00
- LON-38 Dancing Fairy .30 .75
- LON-39 Fairy Guardian .30 .75
- LON-40 Empress Mantis .30 .75
- LON-41 Cure Mermaid .30 .75
- LON-42 Hysteric Fairy .30 .75
- LON-43 Bio-Mage .30 .75
- LON-44 The Forgiving Maiden .30 .75
- LON-45 St. Joan .30 .75
- LON-46 Marie the Fallen One (R) .40 1.00
- LON-47 Jar of Greed (SR) 2.00 5.00
- LON-48 Scroll of Bewitchment .30 .75
- LON-49 United We Stand (UR) 5.00 12.00
- LON-50 Mage Power (UR) 4.00 10.00
- LON-51 Offerings to the Doomed .30 .75
- LON-52 The Portrait's Secret .30 .75
- LON-53 The Gross Ghost of Fled Dreams .30 .75
- LON-54 Headless Knight .30 .75
- LON-55 Earthbound Spirit .30 .75
- LON-56 The Earl of Demise .30 .75
- LON-57 Boneheimer .30 .75
- LON-58 Flame Dancer .30 .75
- LON-59 Soherous Lady .30 .75
- LON-60 Lightning Conger .30 .75
- LON-61 Jowgen the Spiritualist (R) 4.00 10.00
- LON-62 Kycoo the Ghost Destroyer (SR) 3.00 8.00
- LON-63 Summoner of Illusions .30 .75
- LON-64 Bazoo the Soul-Eater (SR) .75 2.00
- LON-65 Dark Necrofear (UR) 2.00 5.00
- LON-66 Soul of Purity and Light .30 .75
- LON-67 Spirit of Flames .30 .75
- LON-68 Aqua Spirit .30 .75
- LON-69 The Rock Spirit .30 .75
- LON-70 Garuda the Wind Spirit .30 .75
- LON-71 Gilasaurus (R) .40 1.00
- LON-72 Tornado Bird (R) .40 1.00
- LON-73 Dreamsprite .30 .75
- LON-74 Zombyra the Dark .40 1.00
- LON-75 Supply .30 .75
- LON-76 Maryokutai .30 .75
- LON-77 Last Warrior from Another Planet (UR)1.50 4.00
- LON-78 Collected Power .30 .75
- LON-79 Dark Spirit of the Silent (SR) .60 1.50
- LON-80 Royal Command (UR) .75 2.00
- LON-81 Riryoku Field (SR) .75 2.00
- LON-82 Skull Lair .60 1.50
- LON-83 Graverobber's Retribution .30 .75
- LON-84 Deal of Phantom .40 1.00
- LON-85 Destruction Punch (R) .40 1.00
- LON-86 Blind Destruction .30 .75
- LON-87 The Emperor's Holiday .30 .75
- LON-88 Destiny Board (UR) 2.50 6.00
- LON-89 Spirit Message I (R) .40 1.00
- LON-90 Spirit Message N (R) .40 1.00
- LON-91 Spirit Message A (R) .40 1.00
- LON-92 Spirit Message L (R) .40 1.00
- LON-93 The Dark Door .30 .75
- LON-94 Spiritualism (R) .40 1.00
- LON-95 Cyclon Laser .30 .75
- LON-96 Bait Doll .30 .75
- LON-97 De-Fusion (SR) .75 2.00
- LON-98 Fusion Gate 3.00 8.00
- LON-99 Ekibyo Drakmord .30 .75
- LON-100 Miracle Dig .30 .75
- LON-101 Dragonic Attack .30 .75
- LON-102 Spirit Elimination .30 .75
- LON-103 Vengeful Bog Spirit (SP) .40 1.00
- LON-104 Magic Cylinder (SCR) 5.00 12.00

2003 Yu-Gi-Oh Legacy of Darkness 1st Edition

Complete Set (101)	100.00	150.00
Hobby Booster Box (24 packs)	60.00	90.00
Retail Booster Box (36 packs)	75.00	110.00
Booster Pack (9 cards)	3.00	5.00

- LOD-0 Yata-Garasu (SCR) 5.00 12.00
- LOD-1 Dark Ruler Ha Des (UR) 1.00 2.50
- LOD-2 Dark Balter the Terrible (SR) .75 2.00
- LOD-3 Lesser Fiend (R) .40 1.00
- LOD-4 Possessed Dark Soul .30 .75
- LOD-5 Winged Minion .30 .75
- LOD-6 Skull Knight #2 .30 .75
- LOD-7 Ryu-Kishin Clown .30 .75
- LOD-8 Twin-Headed Wolf .30 .75
- LOD-9 Opticlops (R) .40 1.00
- LOD-10 Bark of Dark Ruler .30 .75
- LOD-11 Fatal Abacus (R) .40 1.00
- LOD-12 Life Absorbing Machine .30 .75
- LOD-13 The Puppet Magic of Dark Ruler .30 .75
- LOD-14 Soul Demolition .30 .75
- LOD-15 Double Snare .30 .75
- LOD-16 Freed the Matchless General(UR) .75 2.00
- LOD-17 Throwstone Unit .30 .75
- LOD-18 Marauding Captain (UR) 2.50 6.00
- LOD-19 Ryu Senshi (SR) .60 1.50
- LOD-20 Warrior Dai Grepher .30 .75
- LOD-21 Mysterious Guard .30 .75
- LOD-22 Frontier Wiseman .30 .75
- LOD-23 Exiled Force (SR) .60 1.50
- LOD-24 The Hunter with 7 Weapons .30 .75
- LOD-25 Shadow Tamer (R) .40 1.00
- LOD-26 Dragon Manipulator .30 .75
- LOD-27 The A Forces (R) .75 2.00
- LOD-28 Reinforcements of the Army(SR) 2.50 6.00
- LOD-29 Array of Revealing Light (R) .40 1.00
- LOD-30 The Warrior Returning Alive (R) .60 1.50
- LOD-31 Ready for Intercepting .30 .75
- LOD-32 A Feint Plan .30 .75
- LOD-33 Emergency Provisions .40 1.00
- LOD-34 Tyrant Dragon (UR) 4.00 10.00
- LOD-35 Spear Dragon (SR) .75 2.00
- LOD-36 Spirit Ryu .30 .75
- LOD-37 The Dragon Dwelling in the Cave .30 .75
- LOD-38 Lizard Soldier .30 .75
- LOD-39 Fiend Skull Dragon (SR) .60 1.50
- LOD-40 Cave Dragon (SSP) .60 1.50
- LOD-41 Gray Wing .30 .75
- LOD-42 Troop Dragon .30 .75
- LOD-43 The Dragon's Bead (R) .40 1.00
- LOD-44 A Wingbeat of Giant Dragon .40 1.00
- LOD-45 Dragon's Gunfire .30 .75
- LOD-46 Stamping Destruction .30 .75
- LOD-47 Super Rejuvenation 5.00 12.00
- LOD-48 Dragon's Rage .50 1.00
- LOD-49 Burst Breath .30 .75
- LOD-50 Luster Dragon (SR) 2.00 5.00
- LOD-51 Robotic Knight .30 .75
- LOD-52 Wolf Axwielder .30 .75
- LOD-53 The Illusory Gentleman .30 .75
- LOD-54 Robolady .30 .75
- LOD-55 Roboyarou .30 .75
- LOD-56 Fiber Jar (UR) 4.00 10.00
- LOD-57 Serpentine Princess .30 .75
- LOD-58 Patrician of Darkness .30 .75
- LOD-59 Thunder Nyan Nyan (R) .40 1.00
- LOD-60 Gradius Option .30 .75
- LOD-61 Woodland Sprite .30 .75
- LOD-62 Airknight Parshath (UR) 2.00 5.00
- LOD-63 Twin-Headed Behemoth (SR) .60 1.50
- LOD-64 Maharaghi (SSP) .30 .75
- LOD-65 Inaba White Rabbit (SSP) .60 1.50
- LOD-66 Susa Soldier (R) .40 1.00
- LOD-67 Yamata Dragon (UR) 2.00 5.00
- LOD-68 Great Long Nose (SP) .30 .75
- LOD-69 Otohime (SSP) .40 1.00
- LOD-70 Hino-Kagu-Tsuchi (UR) 3.00 8.00
- LOD-71 Asura Priest (SR) .75 2.00
- LOD-72 Fushi No Tori .30 .75
- LOD-73 Super Robolady .30 .75
- LOD-74 Super Roboyarou .30 .75
- LOD-75 Fengsheng Mirror .30 .75
- LOD-76 Spring of Rebirth .30 .75
- LOD-77 Heart of Clear Water .50 1.25
- LOD-78 A Legendary Ocean .30 .75
- LOD-79 Fusion Sword Murasame Blade(R) .40 1.00
- LOD-80 Smoke Grenade of the Thief (SP) .60 1.50
- LOD-81 Creature Swap (UR) 3.00 8.00
- LOD-82 Spiritual Energy Settle Machine .30 .75
- LOD-83 Second Coin Toss (R) .60 1.50
- LOD-84 Convulsion of Nature .30 .75
- LOD-85 The Secret of the Bandit .30 .75
- LOD-86 After Genocide (R) .40 1.00
- LOD-87 Magic Reflector (R) .40 1.00
- LOD-88 Blast with Chain (R) .40 1.00
- LOD-89 Disppear (SP) .30 .75
- LOD-90 Bubble Crash .30 .75
- LOD-91 Royal Oppression (R) .75 2.00
- LOD-92 Bottomless Trap Hole (R) 4.00 8.00
- LOD-93 Bad Reaction to Simochi .60 1.50
- LOD-94 Ominous Fortunetelling .30 .75
- LOD-95 Spirit's Invitation .30 .75
- LOD-96 Nutrient Z .40 1.00
- LOD-97 Drop Off (SR) .75 2.00
- LOD-98 Fiend Comedian .30 .75
- LOD-99 Last Turn (UR) 2.50 6.00
- LOD-100 Injection Fairy Lily (SCR) 6.00 15.00

2003 Yu-Gi-Oh Magician's Force 1st Edition

Complete Set (108)	175.00	250.00
Booster Box (36 packs)	250.00	350.00
Booster Pack	7.00	10.00

- MFC-0 Dark Magician Girl (SCR) 25.00 50.00
- MFC-1 People Running About .30 .75
- MFC-2 Oppressed People .50 1.00
- MFC-3 United Resistance .30 .75
- MFC-4 X-Head Cannon (SR) 2.00 5.00
- MFC-5 Y-Dragon Head (SR) 1.25 3.00
- MFC-6 Z-Metal Tank (SR) .75 2.00
- MFC-7 Dark Blade (R) .60 1.50
- MFC-8 Pitch-Dark Dragon .30 .75
- MFC-9 Kiryu .30 .75
- MFC-10 Decayed Commander .30 .75
- MFC-11 Zombie Tiger .30 .75
- MFC-12 Giant Orc .30 .75
- MFC-13 Second Goblin .30 .75
- MFC-14 Vampire Orchis .30 .75
- MFC-15 Des Dendle .30 .75
- MFC-16 Burning Beast .30 .75
- MFC-17 Freezing Beast .30 .75
- MFC-18 Union Rider .30 .75
- MFC-19 D.D. Crazy Beast (R) .40 1.00
- MFC-20 Spell Canceller (UR) 6.00 15.00
- MFC-21 Neko Mane King .50 1.00
- MFC-22 Helping Robo For Combat (R) .40 1.00
- MFC-23 Dimension Jar (SSP) .30 .75
- MFC-24 Great Phantom Thief (R) .40 1.00
- MFC-25 Roulette Barrel .30 .75
- MFC-26 Paladin of White Dragon (UR) 2.00 5.00
- MFC-27 White Dragon Ritual .30 .75
- MFC-28 Frontline Base .30 .75
- MFC-29 Demotion (SP) .30 .75
- MFC-30 Combination Attack (R) .40 1.00
- MFC-31 Kaiser Colosseum .40 1.00
- MFC-32 Autonomous Action Unit .30 .75
- MFC-33 Poison of the Old Man .30 .75
- MFC-34 Ante (R) .40 1.00
- MFC-35 Dark Core (R) 1.00 2.00
- MFC-36 Raregold Armor .40 1.00
- MFC-37 Metalsilver Armor .30 .75
- MFC-38 Kishido Spirit .30 .75
- MFC-39 Tribute Doll (R) .40 1.00
- MFC-40 Wave-Motion Cannon (SP) 4.00 8.00
- MFC-41 Huge Revolution .30 .75
- MFC-42 Thunder of Ruler .50 1.00
- MFC-43 Spell Shield Type-8 (SR) .75 2.00
- MFC-44 Meteorain .30 .75
- MFC-45 Pineapple Blast .30 .75
- MFC-46 Secret Barrel (SP) 2.00 4.00
- MFC-47 Physical Double .30 .75
- MFC-48 Rivalry of Warlords .40 1.00
- MFC-49 Formation Union .30 .75
- MFC-50 Adhesion Trap Hole .50 1.00
- MFC-51 XY-Dragon Cannon (UR) 5.00 12.00
- MFC-52 XYZ-Dragon Cannon (UR) 1.50 4.00
- MFC-53 XZ-Tank Cannon (SR) 1.50 4.00
- MFC-54 YZ-Tank Dragon (SR) 2.00 5.00
- MFC-55 Great Angus .30 .75
- MFC-56 Aitsu .30 .75
- MFC-57 Sonic Duck .30 .75
- MFC-58 Luster Dragon (UR) 2.00 5.00
- MFC-59 Amazoness Paladin .30 .75
- MFC-60 Amazoness Fighter (SP) .40 1.00
- MFC-61 Amazoness Swords Woman (UR) 1.50 4.00
- MFC-62 Amazoness Blowpiper .30 .75
- MFC-63 Amazoness Tiger (R) .40 1.00
- MFC-64 Skilled White Magician (SR) 1.25 3.00
- MFC-65 Skilled Dark Magician (SR) 2.50 6.00
- MFC-66 Apprentice Magician (R) .50 1.25
- MFC-67 Old Vindictive Magician .30 .75
- MFC-68 Chaos Command Magician (UR) 3.00 8.00
- MFC-69 Magical Marionette .30 .75
- MFC-70 Pixie Knight .30 .75
- MFC-71 Breaker the Magical Warrior (UR) 3.00 8.00
- MFC-72 Magical Plant Mandragola .30 .75
- MFC-73 Magical Scientist .30 .75
- MFC-74 Royal Magical Library .30 .75
- MFC-75 Armor Exe (R) .40 1.00
- MFC-76 Tribe-Infecting Virus (SR) 1.50 4.00
- MFC-77 Des Koala (R) .60 1.50
- MFC-78 Cliff the Trap Remover (SP) .40 1.00
- MFC-79 Magical Merchant .60 1.50
- MFC-80 Koitsu .30 .75
- MFC-81 Cat's Ear Tribe (R) .40 1.00
- MFC-82 Ultimate Obedient Fiend (SP) .75 2.00
- MFC-83 Dark Cat with White Tail .30 .75
- MFC-84 Amazoness Spellcaster .30 .75
- MFC-85 Continuous Destruction Punch (R) .40 1.00
- MFC-86 Big Bang Shot (R) .40 1.00
- MFC-87 Gather Your Mind .30 .75
- MFC-88 Mass Driver .30 .75
- MFC-89 Senri Eye (SP) .30 .75
- MFC-90 Emblem of Dragon Destroyer .50 1.00
- MFC-91 Jar Robber .30 .75
- MFC-92 My Body as a Shield .30 .75
- MFC-93 Pigeonholing Books of Spell (SP) .30 .75
- MFC-94 Mega Ton Magical Cannon (R) .40 1.00
- MFC-95 Pitch-Black Power Stone (SP) .40 1.00
- MFC-96 Amazoness Archers (SR) .75 2.00
- MFC-97 Dramatic Rescue (R) .40 1.00
- MFC-98 Exhausting Spell .30 .75
- MFC-99 Hidden Book of Spell .30 .75
- MFC-100 Miracle Restoring .30 .75
- MFC-101 Remove Brainwashing .50 1.00
- MFC-102 Disarmament .30 .75
- MFC-103 Anti-Spell .30 .75
- MFC-104 The Spell Absorbing Life .30 .75
- MFC-105 Dark Paladin w/ring in back (UR) 10.00 25.00
- MFC-105 Dark Paladin (mail-in redemp) (UR)30.00 60.00
- MFC-106 Double Spell (UR) 2.00 5.00
- MFC-107 Diffussion Wave-Motion (SCR) .60 1.50

2003 Yu-Gi-Oh Pharaonic Guardian 1st Edition

Complete Set (108)	50.00	100.00
Hobby Booster Box (24 packs)	60.00	90.00
Retail Booster Box (36 packs)	75.00	120.00
Booster Pack (9 cards)	3.50	5.00

- PGD-0 Ring of Destruction (SCR) 3.00 8.00
- PGD-1 Molten Behemoth .30 .75
- PGD-2 Snapesnatch .30 .75
- PGD-3 Souleater .30 .75
- PGD-4 King Tiger Wanghu .60 1.50
- PGD-5 Birdface .30 .75
- PGD-6 Kryuel .30 .75
- PGD-7 Arsenal Bug .30 .75
- PGD-8 Madien of the Aqua .40 1.00
- PGD-9 Jowl of Dark Demise (R) .40 1.00
- PGD-10 Timeater .30 .75
- PGD-11 Mucus Yolk .30 .75
- PGD-12 Servant of Catabolism .30 .75
- PGD-13 Moisture Creature (R) .40 1.00
- PGD-14 Gora Turtle (R) .40 1.00
- PGD-15 Sasuke Samurai (SR) .60 1.50
- PGD-16 Poison Mummy .30 .75
- PGD-17 Dark Dust Spirit .30 .75
- PGD-18 Royal Keeper .30 .75
- PGD-19 Wandering Mummy (R) .30 .75
- PGD-20 Great Dezard (UR) .60 1.50
- PGD-21 Swarm of Scarabs .30 .75
- PGD-22 Swarm of Locusts .30 .75
- PGD-23 Giant Axe Mummy .30 .75
- PGD-24 8-Claws Scorpion .30 .75
- PGD-25 Guardian Sphinx (UR) .60 1.50
- PGD-26 Pyramid Turtle (R) .40 1.00
- PGD-27 Dice Jar .75 2.00
- PGD-28 Dark Scorpion Burglars .30 .75
- PGD-29 Don Zaloog (UR) 1.00 2.50
- PGD-30 Des Lacooda .30 .75
- PGD-31 Fushioh Richie (UR) .60 1.50
- PGD-32 Cobraman Sakuzy .30 .75
- PGD-33 Book of Life (SR) 1.25 3.00
- PGD-34 Book of Taiyou .75 2.00
- PGD-35 Book of Moon (R) 1.25 3.00
- PGD-36 Mirage of Nightmare (SR) .60 1.50
- PGD-37 Secret Pass to the Treasure .30 .75
- PGD-38 Call of the Mummy .30 .75
- PGD-39 Timidity .30 .75
- PGD-40 Pyramid Energy .30 .75
- PGD-41 Tutan Mask .30 .75
- PGD-42 Ordeal of a Traveler (SP) .60 1.50
- PGD-43 Bottomless Shifting Sand .30 .75
- PGD-44 Curse of Royal (R) .40 1.00
- PGD-45 Needle Ceiling .30 .75
- PGD-46 Statue of the Wicked (SR) .60 1.50
- PGD-47 Dark Coffin .30 .75
- PGD-48 Needle Wall .30 .75
- PGD-49 Trap Dustshoot .40 1.00
- PGD-50 Pyro Clock of Destiny .30 .75
- PGD-51 Reckless Greed (R) .60 1.50
- PGD-52 Pharaoh's Treasure (R) .40 1.00
- PGD-53 Master Kyonshee .30 .75
- PGD-54 Kabazauls 1.00 2.50
- PGD-55 Inpachi .30 .75
- PGD-56 Dark Jeroid (R) .40 1.00
- PGD-57 Newdoria (R) .40 1.00
- PGD-58 Helpoemer (UR) 3.00 8.00
- PGD-59 Gravekeeper's Spy .30 .75
- PGD-60 Gravekeeper's Curse .30 .75
- PGD-61 Gravekeeper's Guard .30 .75
- PGD-62 Gravekeeper's Spear Soldier .30 .75
- PGD-63 Gravekeeper's Vassal .60 1.50
- PGD-64 Gravekeeper's Watcher (R) .40 1.00
- PGD-65 Gravekeeper's Chief (SR) .60 1.50
- PGD-66 Gravekeeper's Cannonholder .30 .75
- PGD-67 Gravekeeper's Assailant .30 .75
- PGD-68 A Man with Wdjat .30 .75
- PGD-69 Mystical Knight of Jackal (UR) .75 2.00
- PGD-70 A Cat of Ill Omen 2.50 6.00
- PGD-71 Yomi Ship .40 1.00
- PGD-72 Winged Sage Falcos (R) .30 .75
- PGD-73 An Owl of Luck .30 .75
- PGD-74 Charm of Shabti .30 .75
- PGD-75 Cobra Jar (SP) .30 .75
- PGD-76 Spirit Reaper (R) 1.25 3.00
- PGD-77 Nightmare Horse (SSP) .40 1.00
- PGD-78 Reaper on the Nightmare (SR) 1.25 3.00
- PGD-79 Dark Designator (R) .40 1.00
- PGD-80 Card Shuffle .30 .75
- PGD-81 Reasoning .30 .75
- PGD-82 Dark Room of Nightmare (SR) .60 1.50
- PGD-83 Different Dimension Capsule .30 .75
- PGD-84 Necrovalley (SR) .75 2.00
- PGD-85 Buster Rancher .30 .75
- PGD-86 Hieroglyph Lithograph .30 .75
- PGD-87 Dark Snake Syndrome .30 .75
- PGD-88 Terraforming .40 1.00
- PGD-89 Banner of Courage .30 .75
- PGD-90 Metamorphosis .30 .75
- PGD-91 Royal Tribute .60 1.50
- PGD-92 Reversal Quiz (SP) .60 1.50
- PGD-93 Coffin Seller (R) .40 1.00
- PGD-94 Curse of Aging .30 .75
- PGD-95 Barrel Behind the Door (SR) .60 1.50
- PGD-96 Raigeki Break .40 1.00
- PGD-97 Narrow Pass .30 .75
- PGD-98 Disturbance Strategy .30 .75
- PGD-99 Trap of Board Eraser (SR) .60 1.50
- PGD-100 Rite of Spirit .30 .75
- PGD-101 Non Aggression Area .30 .75
- PGD-102 D. Tribe .30 .75
- PGD-103 Byser Shock (UR) .60 1.50
- PGD-104 Question (UR) 1.25 3.00
- PGD-105 Rope of Life (UR) .60 1.50
- PGD-106 Nightmare Wheel (UR) 2.00 5.00
- PGD-107 Lava Golem (SCR) 2.50 6.00

2004 Yu-Gi-Oh Ancient Sanctuary 1st Edition

Complete Set (112)	75.00	125.00
Booster Box (24 packs)	60.00	90.00
Booster Pack (9 cards)	3.00	5.00

- AST-0 The End of Anubis (SCR) 5.00 12.00
- AST-1 Gogiga Gagagigo .20 .50
- AST-2 Warrior of Zera .30 .75
- AST-3 Sealmaster Meisei (R) .30 .75
- AST-4 Mystical Shine Ball .50 1.25
- AST-5 Metal Armored Bug .20 .50
- AST-6 The Agent of Judgment Saturn (UR) .75 2.00
- AST-7 The Agent of Wisdom Mercury (R) .30 .75
- AST-8 The Agent of Creation Venus (R) .75 2.00
- AST-9 The Agent of Force Mars (SR) .40 1.00
- AST-10 The Unhappy Girl .20 .50
- AST-11 Soul-Absorbing Bone Tower (R) 1.00 2.50
- AST-12 The Kick Man .20 .50
- AST-13 Vampire Lady .20 .50
- AST-14 Stone Statue of the Aztecs (SR) .40 1.00
- AST-15 Rocket Jumper .20 .50
- AST-16 Avatar of the Pot (R) .30 .75
- AST-17 Legendary Jujitsu Master .30 .75
- AST-18 Gear Golem the Moving Fortress (UR) .75 2.00
- AST-19 KA-2 Des Scissors .20 .50
- AST-20 Needle Burrower (SR) .30 .75
- AST-21 Sonic Jammer .20 .50
- AST-22 Blowback Dragon (UR) 1.00 2.50
- AST-23 Zaborg the Thunder Monarch (SR) .75 2.00
- AST-24 Atomic Firefly .20 .50
- AST-25 Mermaid Knight .20 .50
- AST-26 Piranha Army .20 .50
- AST-27 Two Thousand Needles .20 .50
- AST-28 Disc Fighter .20 .50
- AST-29 Arcane Archer of the Forest .20 .50
- AST-30 Lady Ninja Yae .60 1.50
- AST-31 Goblin King .20 .50
- AST-32 Solar Flare Dragon .20 .50
- AST-33 White Magician Pikeru .20 .50
- AST-34 Archlord Zerato (UR) 2.00 5.00
- AST-35 Opti-Camouflage Armor 1.00 2.50
- AST-36 Mystik Wok .20 .50
- AST-37 Enemy Controller (UR) 3.00 8.00
- AST-38 Burst Stream of Destruction (UR) 4.00 10.00
- AST-39 Monster Gate .20 .50
- AST-40 Amplifier (SR) 1.25 3.00
- AST-41 Weapon Change .20 .50
- AST-42 The Sanctuary in the Sky (SR) 1.50 4.00
- AST-43 Earthquake .20 .50
- AST-44 Talisman of Trap Sealing (R) .30 .75
- AST-45 Goblin Thief .20 .50
- AST-46 Backfire .20 .50
- AST-47 Micro Ray .20 .50
- AST-48 Light of Judgment .20 .50
- AST-49 Talisman of Spell Sealing (R) .30 .75
- AST-50 Wall of Revealing Light .40 1.00
- AST-51 Solar Ray .20 .50
- AST-52 Ninjitsu Art of Transformation .50 1.25
- AST-53 Beckoning Light .20 .50
- AST-54 Draining Shield (R) .75 2.00
- AST-55 Armor Break .20 .50
- AST-56 Gigobyte .20 .50
- AST-57 Mokey Mokey 1.00 2.50
- AST-58 Kozaky .20 .50
- AST-59 Fiend Scorpion .20 .50
- AST-60 Pharaoh's Servant .20 .50
- AST-61 Pharaonic Protector .20 .50
- AST-62 Spirit of the Pharaoh (UR) .75 2.00
- AST-63 Theban Nightmare (R) .30 .75
- AST-64 Aswan Apparition .20 .50
- AST-65 Protector of the Sanctuary .20 .50
- AST-66 Nubian Guard .20 .50
- AST-67 Legacy Hunter (SR) .40 1.00
- AST-68 Desertapir .20 .50
- AST-69 Sand Gambler .20 .50
- AST-70 3-Hump Lacooda .20 .50
- AST-71 Ghost Knight of Jackal (UR) .50 1.25
- AST-72 Absorbing Kid from the Sky .20 .50
- AST-73 Elephant Statue of Blessing .20 .50
- AST-74 Elephant Statue of Disaster .20 .50
- AST-75 Spirit Caller .20 .50
- AST-76 Emissary of the Afterlife (SR) 1.00 2.50
- AST-77 Grave Protector (R) .30 .75
- AST-78 Double Coston (R) .30 .75
- AST-79 Regenerating Mummy .20 .50
- AST-80 Night Assailant .40 1.00
- AST-81 Man-Thro' Tro' .20 .50
- AST-82 King of the Swamp (R) 2.00 5.00
- AST-83 Emissary of the Oasis .20 .50

Card	Low	High
AST-84 Special Hurricane (R)	.30	.75
AST-85 Order to Charge	.20	.50
AST-86 Sword of the Soul-Eater	.20	.50
AST-87 Dust Barrier	.20	.50
AST-88 Soul Reversal	.20	.50
AST-89 Spell Economics (R)	.30	.75
AST-90 Blessings of the Nile	.20	.50
AST-91 7	.20	.50
AST-92 Level Limit - Area B (SP)	2.00	5.00
AST-93 Enchanting Fitting Room	.20	.50
AST-94 The Law of the Normal	.20	.50
AST-95 Dark Magic Attack (UR)	1.50	4.00
AST-96 Delta Attacker	.20	.50
AST-97 Thousand Energy (R)	.30	.75
AST-98 Triangle Power (R)	.30	.75
AST-99 The Third Sarcophagus	.20	.50
AST-100 The Second Sarcophagus	.20	.50
AST-101 The First Sarcophagus (SR)	.40	1.00
AST-102 Dora of Fate	.20	.50
AST-103 Judgment of the Desert	.20	.50
AST-104 Human-Wave Tactics	.20	.50
AST-105 Curse of Anubis (UR)	.75	2.00
AST-106 Desert Sunlight	.20	.50
AST-107 Des Counterblow (SR)	.30	.75
AST-108 Labyrinth of Nightmare	.20	.50
AST-109 Soul Resurrection (R)	.30	.75
AST-110 Order to Smash	.20	.50
AST-111 Mazera DeVille (SCR)	.75	2.00

2004 Yu-Gi-Oh Dark Beginnings 1

Card	Low	High
Complete Set (250)	175.00	250.00
Booster Box (24 packs)	100.00	150.00
Booster Pack (12 Cards)	4.00	7.00
DB1EN001 Penguin Knight	.10	.25
DB1EN002 Axe of Despair (R)	.60	1.50
DB1EN003 Black Pendant (R)	.25	.60
DB1EN004 Horn of Light	.10	.25
DB1EN005 Malevolent Nuzzler	.10	.25
DB1EN006 Spellbinding Circle (R)	.25	.60
DB1EN007 Electric Snake	.10	.25
DB1EN008 Ameba	.10	.25
DB1EN009 Maha Vailo	.10	.25
DB1EN010 Minar	.10	.25
DB1EN011 Griggle	.10	.25
DB1EN012 Hiro's Shadow Scout	.10	.25
DB1EN013 Invader of the Throne	.10	.25
DB1EN014 Slot Machine	.10	.25
DB1EN015 Relinquished (SR)	.40	1.00
DB1EN016 Red Archery Girl	.10	.25
DB1EN017 Gravekeeper's Servant	.60	1.50
DB1EN018 Upstart Goblin	1.25	3.00
DB1EN019 Toll	.10	.25
DB1EN020 Final Destiny	.10	.25
DB1EN021 Snatch Steal (UR)	1.50	4.00
DB1EN022 Chorus of Sanctuary	.10	.25
DB1EN023 Confiscation	.10	.25
DB1EN024 Delinquent Duo (SR)	1.25	3.00
DB1EN025 Fairy's Hand Mirror	.10	.25
DB1EN026 Tailor of the Fickle	.10	.25
DB1EN027 Rush Recklessly	.10	.25
DB1EN028 The Reliable Guardian	.10	.25
DB1EN029 The Forceful Sentry (R)	.25	.60
DB1EN030 Chain Energy	.10	.25
DB1EN031 Mystical Space Typhoon (SR)	10.00	25.00
DB1EN032 Giant Trunade (R)	.25	.60
DB1EN033 Painful Choice	.10	.25
DB1EN034 Horn of the Unicorn	.10	.25
DB1EN035 Labyrinth Wall	.10	.25
DB1EN036 Eternal Rest	.10	.25
DB1EN037 Megamorph (SR)	.75	2.00
DB1EN038 Manga Ryu-Ran	.10	.25
DB1EN039 Toon Mermaid	.10	.25
DB1EN040 Toon Summoned Skull (R)	.50	1.00
DB1EN041 Hyozanryu	.10	.25
DB1EN042 Toon World	.10	.25
DB1EN043 Cyber Jar (R)	.40	1.00
DB1EN044 Banisher of the Light	.25	.60
DB1EN045 Giant Rat (R)	.25	.60
DB1EN046 Senju of the Thousand Hands	.25	.60
DB1EN047 UFO Turtle	.10	.25
DB1EN048 Flash Assailant	.10	.25
DB1EN049 Karate Man	.10	.25
DB1EN050 Giant Germ	.40	1.00
DB1EN051 Nimble Momonga (R)	.40	1.00
DB1EN052 Shining Angel	.10	.25
DB1EN053 Mother Grizzly	.10	.25
DB1EN054 Flying Kamakiri #1	.10	.25
DB1EN055 Ceremonial Bell	.10	.25
DB1EN056 Sonic Bird	.10	.25
DB1EN057 Mystic Tomato (R)	.40	1.00
DB1EN058 Kotodama	.10	.25
DB1EN059 Gaia Power	.10	.25
DB1EN060 Umiiruka	.10	.25
DB1EN061 Molten Destruction	.10	.25
DB1EN062 Rising Air Current	.20	.50
DB1EN063 Luminous Spark	.25	.60
DB1EN064 Mystic Plasma Zone	.10	.25
DB1EN065 Messenger of Peace	1.25	3.00
DB1EN066 Blue-Eyes Toon Dragon (SR)	1.25	3.00
DB1EN067 Jinzo (UR)	3.00	8.00
DB1EN068 Parasite Paracide	.10	.25
DB1EN069 Lightforce Sword	.10	.25
DB1EN070 Chain Destruction	.40	1.00
DB1EN071 Time Seal	.10	.25
DB1EN072 Graverobber	.10	.25
DB1EN073 Gift of the Mystical Elf	.10	.25
DB1EN074 The Eye of Truth	.10	.25
DB1EN075 Dust Tornado (R)	.25	.60
DB1EN076 Call Of The Haunted (SR)	1.50	4.00
DB1EN077 Enchanted Javelin	.10	.25
DB1EN078 Mirror Wall	.10	.25
DB1EN079 Numinous Healer	.10	.25
DB1EN080 Forced Requisition	.25	.60
DB1EN081 DNA Surgery	.10	.25
DB1EN082 Backup Soldier	.10	.25
DB1EN083 Ceasefire (SR)	.25	.60
DB1EN084 Light of Intervention	.10	.25
DB1EN085 Respect Play	.10	.25
DB1EN086 Imperial Order (UR)	.60	1.50
DB1EN087 Magical Hats (R)	.50	1.25
DB1EN088 Nobleman of Crossout (SR)	.40	1.00
DB1EN089 Nobleman of Extermination	.10	.25
DB1EN090 The Shallow Grave	.40	1.00
DB1EN091 Premature Burial (SR)	.40	1.00
DB1EN092 Morphing Jar #2 (R)	1.00	2.00

Card	Low	High
DB1EN093 Kiseitai	.10	.25
DB1EN094 Harpie's Brother	.10	.25
DB1EN095 Buster Blader (SR)	1.25	3.00
DB1EN096 Dark Sage (UR)	4.00	10.00
DB1EN097 Big Shield Guardna (UR)	1.00	2.50
DB1EN098 Blue-Eyes White Dragon (UR)	2.50	6.00
DB1EN099 Hitotsu-Me Giant	.10	.25
DB1EN100 Flame Swordsman (R)	.25	.60
DB1EN101 Skull Servant	.40	1.00
DB1EN102 Dark Magician (UR)	1.00	2.50
DB1EN103 Gaia The Fierce Knight (R)	.25	.60
DB1EN104 Celtic Guardian	.10	.25
DB1EN105 Mammoth Graveyard	.10	.25
DB1EN106 Silver Fang	.10	.25
DB1EN107 Flame Manipulator	.10	.25
DB1EN108 Dark King of the Abyss	.10	.25
DB1EN109 Aqua Madoor	.10	.25
DB1EN110 Masaki the Legendary Swordsman	.10	.25
DB1EN111 Dragon Capture Jar	.10	.25
DB1EN112 Umi	.10	.25
DB1EN113 Dark Hole (SR)	3.00	8.00
DB1EN114 Raigeki (UR)	5.00	12.00
DB1EN115 Red Medicine	.10	.25
DB1EN116 Hinotama	.10	.25
DB1EN117 Fissure (R)	.25	.60
DB1EN118 Trap Hole (R)	.25	.60
DB1EN119 Polymerization	2.50	6.00
DB1EN120 Mystical Elf	.10	.25
DB1EN121 Beaver Warrior	.10	.25
DB1EN122 Gaia the Dragon Champion (R)	.40	1.00
DB1EN123 Curse of Dragon	.10	.25
DB1EN124 Giant Soldier of Stone	.10	.25
DB1EN125 Uraby	.10	.25
DB1EN126 Red-Eyes B. Dragon (SR)	.75	2.00
DB1EN127 Reaper of the Cards	.10	.25
DB1EN128 Stop Defense	.10	.25
DB1EN129 Swords of Revealing Light (SR)	1.50	4.00
DB1EN130 Armed Ninja	.10	.25
DB1EN131 Man-Eater Bug (R)	.40	1.00
DB1EN132 Hane-Hane	.10	.25
DB1EN133 Monster Reborn (UR)	8.00	20.00
DB1EN134 Pot of Greed (SR)	3.00	8.00
DB1EN135 Right Leg of the Forbidden One	2.50	6.00
DB1EN136 Left Leg of the Forbidden One	2.00	5.00
DB1EN137 Right Arm of the Forbidden One	2.00	5.00
DB1EN138 Left Arm of the Forbidden One	2.00	5.00
DB1EN139 Exodia the Forbidden One (UR)	8.00	20.00
DB1EN140 Feral Imp	.10	.25
DB1EN141 Winged Dragon Guardian of the Fortress #1	.10	.25
DB1EN142 Summoned Skull (SR)	.60	1.50
DB1EN143 Armored Lizard	.10	.25
DB1EN144 Larvae Moth	.10	.25
DB1EN145 Harpie Lady	.10	.25
DB1EN146 Harpie Lady Sisters	.10	.25
DB1EN147 Kojikocy	.10	.25
DB1EN148 Cocoon of Evolution	.25	.60
DB1EN149 Armored Zombie	.10	.25
DB1EN150 Mask of Darkness	.10	.25
DB1EN151 White Magical Hat	.10	.25
DB1EN152 Big Eye	.10	.25
DB1EN153 B. Skull Dragon (SR)	5.00	12.00
DB1EN154 Masked Sorcerer	.10	.25
DB1EN155 Petit Moth	.10	.25
DB1EN156 Elegant Egotist	.40	1.00
DB1EN157 Sanga of the Thunder	.75	2.00
DB1EN158 Kazejin	.10	.25
DB1EN159 Suijin	.25	.60
DB1EN160 Mystic Lamp	.10	.25
DB1EN161 Blast Juggler	.10	.25
DB1EN162 Jinzo #7	.10	.25
DB1EN163 Magician of Faith (R)	.40	1.00
DB1EN164 Fake Trap	.10	.25
DB1EN165 Tribute to The Doomed (R)	.25	.60
DB1EN166 Soul Release	.25	.60
DB1EN167 The Cheerful Coffin	.40	1.00
DB1EN168 Change of Heart (UR)	1.50	4.00
DB1EN169 Makyura the Destructor (SR)	2.00	5.00
DB1EN170 Exchange (SR)	.75	2.00
DB1EN171 Minor Goblin Official	.10	.25
DB1EN172 Gamble	.10	.25
DB1EN173 Attack and Receive	.10	.25
DB1EN174 Solemn Wishes	.60	1.50
DB1EN175 Skull Invitation	.10	.25
DB1EN176 Bubonic Vermin	.10	.25
DB1EN177 Burning Land	.10	.25
DB1EN178 Fairy Meteor Crush (R)	.25	.60
DB1EN179 Limiter Removal (R)	.25	.60
DB1EN180 Rain of Mercy	.10	.25
DB1EN181 Monster Recovery	.10	.25
DB1EN182 Shift	.10	.25
DB1EN183 Dimensionhole	.10	.25
DB1EN184 Ground Collapse	.10	.25
DB1EN185 Magic Drain (R)	.25	.60
DB1EN186 Infinite Dismissal	.10	.25
DB1EN187 Gravity Bind	.10	.25
DB1EN188 Type Zero Magic Crusher	.10	.25
DB1EN189 Shadow of Eyes (R)	.25	.60
DB1EN190 The Legendary Fisherman (R)	1.50	4.00
DB1EN191 Sword Hunter	.10	.25
DB1EN192 Drill Bug	.10	.25
DB1EN193 Deepsea Warrior	.10	.25
DB1EN194 Thousand-Eyes Idol	.10	.25
DB1EN195 Thousand-Eyes Restrict (UR)	1.50	4.00
DB1EN196 Hayabusa Knight (R)	.25	.60
DB1EN197 Bombardment Beetle	.10	.25
DB1EN198 4-Starred Ladybug of Doom	.10	.25
DB1EN199 Gradius	.10	.25
DB1EN200 Red-Moon Baby	.10	.25
DB1EN201 Mad Sword Beast (R)	.25	.60
DB1EN202 Goblin Attack Force (SR)	.40	1.00
DB1EN203 The Fiend Megacyber (R)	.75	2.00
DB1EN204 Gearfried the Iron Knight (R)	.25	.60
DB1EN205 Insect Barrier	.10	.25
DB1EN206 Swordsman of Landstar	.10	.25
DB1EN207 Humanoid Slime	.10	.25
DB1EN208 Worm Drake	.10	.25
DB1EN209 Humanoid Worm Drake	.10	.25
DB1EN210 Revival Jam	.75	2.00
DB1EN211 Amphibian Beast	.10	.25
DB1EN212 Shining Abyss	.10	.25
DB1EN213 Grand Tiki Elder	.10	.25
DB1EN214 The Masked Beast (SR)	.40	1.00
DB1EN215 Melchid the Four-Face Beast	.10	.25
DB1EN216 Nuvia the Wicked	.10	.25
DB1EN217 Chosen One	.10	.25
DB1EN218 Mask of Weakness	.10	.25
DB1EN219 Curse of the Masked Beast	.10	.25
DB1EN220 Mask of Dispel	.10	.25
DB1EN221 Mask of Restrict	.50	1.25
DB1EN222 Mask of the Accursed	.10	.25
DB1EN223 Mask of Brutality	.10	.25
DB1EN224 Return of the Doomed	.10	.25
DB1EN225 Lightning Blade	.10	.25
DB1EN226 Tornado Wall	.10	.25
DB1EN227 Fairy Box	.10	.25
DB1EN228 Torrential Tribute (UR)	4.00	10.00
DB1EN229 Jam Breeding Machine	.10	.25
DB1EN230 Infinite Cards	.10	.25
DB1EN231 Jam Defender	.10	.25
DB1EN232 Card of Safe Return	.25	.60
DB1EN233 Amazoness Archer	.10	.25
DB1EN234 Fire Princess	.10	.25
DB1EN235 Spirit of the Breeze	.10	.25
DB1EN236 Dancing Fairy	.10	.25
DB1EN237 Cure Mermaid	.10	.25
DB1EN238 Hysteric Fairy	.10	.25
DB1EN239 The Forgiving Maiden	.10	.25
DB1EN240 St. Joan	.10	.25
DB1EN241 Marie the Fallen One	.10	.25
DB1EN242 Jar of Greed (R)	.60	1.50
DB1EN243 Scroll of Bewitchment	.25	.60
DB1EN244 United We Stand (UR)	2.50	6.00
DB1EN245 Mage Power (UR)	2.00	5.00
DB1EN246 The Portrait's Secret	.10	.25
DB1EN247 The Gross Ghost of Fled Dreams	.10	.25
DB1EN248 Headless Knight	.10	.25
DB1EN249 Earthbound Spirit	.10	.25
DB1EN250 The Earl of Demise	.10	.25

2004 Yu-Gi-Oh Invasion of Chaos 1st Edition

Card	Low	High
Complete Set (112)	150.00	225.00
Hobby Booster Box (24 packs)	80.00	120.00
Retail Booster Box (24 packs)	75.00	110.00
Booster Pack (9 cards)	4.00	6.00
Special Edition Box (3 packs 1 Var. card)	15.00	20.00
IOC-0 Chaos Emperor Dragon (SCR)	20.00	40.00
IOC-1 Ojama Yellow	.20	.50
IOC-2 Ojama Black	.20	.50
IOC-3 Soul Tiger	.20	.50
IOC-4 Big Koala	.20	.50
IOC-5 DesKangaroo	.20	.50
IOC-6 Crimson Ninja	.20	.50
IOC-7 Strike Ninja (UR)	2.50	6.00
IOC-8 Gale Lizard	.20	.50
IOC-9 Spirit of the Pot of Greed (SP)	.20	.50
IOC-10 Chopman the Desperate Outlaw	.20	.50
IOC-11 Sasuke Samurai #3 (R)	.30	.75
IOC-12 D.D. Scout Plane (SR)	.60	1.50
IOC-13 Beserk Gorilla (R)	.40	1.00
IOC-14 Freed the Brave Wanderer (SR)	.40	1.00
IOC-15 Coach Goblin	.20	.50
IOC-16 Witch Doctor of Chaos (SP)	.20	.50
IOC-17 Chaos Necromancer (SP)	.30	.75
IOC-18 Chaosrider Gustaph (SR)	.60	1.50
IOC-19 Inferno	.20	.50
IOC-20 Fenrir	.20	.50
IOC-21 Gigantes	.20	.50
IOC-22 Silpheed	.20	.50
IOC-23 Chaos Sorcerer	.30	.75
IOC-24 Gren Maju Da Eiza	.40	1.00
IOC-25 Black Luster Soldier (UR)	25.00	50.00
IOC-26 Drillago (R)	.30	.75
IOC-27 Lekunga (R)	.30	.75
IOC-28 Lord Poison (SP)	.40	1.00
IOC-29 Bowganian (SP)	.20	.50
IOC-30 Granadora (SP)	.20	.50
IOC-31 Fuhma Shuriken (R)	.30	.75
IOC-32 Heart of the Underdog (SP)	.60	1.50
IOC-33 Wild Nature's Release (SR)	.30	.75
IOC-34 Ojama Delta Hurricane (SP)	.20	.50
IOC-35 Stumbling (SP)	.60	1.50
IOC-36 Chaos End	.20	.50
IOC-37 Yellow Luster Shield	.20	.50
IOC-38 Chaos Greed	.20	.50
IOC-39 D.D. Designator (SR)	.60	1.50
IOC-40 D.D. Borderline	.20	.50
IOC-41 Recycle	.20	.50
IOC-42 Primal Seed	.20	.50
IOC-43 Thunder Crash (SP)	.20	.50
IOC-44 Dimension Distortion (SP)	.20	.50
IOC-45 Reload (SR)	.50	1.25
IOC-46 Soul Absorption	.60	1.50
IOC-47 Big Burn (SR)	.40	1.00
IOC-48 Blasting the Ruins	.40	1.00
IOC-49 Cursed Seal of Forbidden Spell	.75	2.00
IOC-50 Tower of Babel	.20	.50
IOC-51 Spatial Collapse	.20	.50
IOC-52 Chain Disappearance (R)	.75	2.00
IOC-53 Zero Gravity	.20	.50
IOC-54 Dark Mirror Force (UR)	2.00	5.00
IOC-55 Energy Drain	.20	.50
IOC-56 Giga Gagagigo (SP)	.60	1.50
IOC-57 Mad Dog of Darkness (R)	.30	.75
IOC-58 Neo Bug	.20	.50
IOC-59 Sea Serpent Warrior of Darkness	.20	.50
IOC-60 Terrorking Salmon	.20	.50
IOC-61 Blazing Inpachi	.20	.50
IOC-62 Burning Algae	.20	.50
IOC-63 The Thing in the Crater	.20	.50
IOC-64 Molten Zombie	.20	.50
IOC-65 Dark Magician of Chaos (UR)	12.00	30.00
IOC-66 Gora Turtle of Illusion	.20	.50
IOC-67 Manticore of Darkness (UR)	1.25	3.00
IOC-68 Stealth Bird (SP)	.30	.75
IOC-69 Sacred Crane	.40	1.00
IOC-70 Enraged Battle Ox (R)	.30	.75
IOC-71 Don Turtle (SP)	.30	.75
IOC-72 Balloon Lizard	.20	.50
IOC-73 Dark Driceratops (R)	.30	.75
IOC-74 Hyper Hammerhead (SP)	.20	.50
IOC-75 Black Tyranno (UR)	1.00	2.50
IOC-76 Anti-Aircraft Flower (SP)	.20	.50
IOC-77 Prickle Fairy	.20	.50
IOC-78 Pinch Hopper (SP)	.75	2.00
IOC-79 Skull-Mark Ladybug (SP)	.20	.50
IOC-80 Insect Princess (UR)	.60	1.50
IOC-81 Amphibious Bugroth MK-3	.20	.50
IOC-82 Torpedo Fish (SP)	.20	.50
IOC-83 Levia-Dragon Daedalus (UR)	2.00	5.00
IOC-84 Orca Mega-Fortress of Darkness (SR)	.40	1.00
IOC-85 Cannonball Spear Shellfish (SP)	.30	.75
IOC-86 Mataza the Zapper (R)	.30	.75
IOC-87 Guardian Angel Joan (UR)	1.50	4.00
IOC-88 Manju of Ten Thousand Hands (SP)	1.50	4.00
IOC-89 Getsu Fuhma (R)	.30	.75
IOC-90 Ryu Kokki	.20	.50
IOC-91 Gryphon's Feather Duster	.20	.50
IOC-92 Stray Lambs (R)	.20	.50
IOC-93 Smashing Ground (SP)	.60	1.50
IOC-94 Dimension Fusion (UR)	3.00	8.00
IOC-95 Dedication through Light & Darkness(SR)	.50	1.25
IOC-96 Salvage	.50	1.25
IOC-97 Ultra Evolution Pill (R)	.30	.75
IOC-98 Multiplication of Ants	.20	.50
IOC-99 Earth Chant (SP)	.20	.50
IOC-100 Jade Insect Whistle	.20	.50
IOC-101 Destruction Ring (R)	.30	.75
IOC-102 Fiend's Hand Mirror	.20	.50
IOC-103 Compulsory Evacuation Device (R)	2.00	5.00
IOC-104 A Hero Emerges	.20	.50
IOC-105 Self-Destruct Button (SP)	1.50	4.00
IOC-106 Curse of Darkness (R)	2.00	5.00
IOC-107 Begone, Knave!	.20	.50
IOC-108 DNA Transplant	.20	.50
IOC-109 Robbin' Zombie (R)	.30	.75
IOC-110 Trap Jammer (SR)	.75	2.00
IOC-111 Invader of Darkness (SCR)	.60	1.50

2004 Yu-Gi-Oh Rise of Destiny 1st Edition

Card	Low	High
Complete Set (60)	30.00	60.00
Complete Master Set (85)	50.00	100.00
Booster Box (24 packs)	40.00	75.00
Booster Pack (9 cards)	2.50	4.00
SE Box (3 packs, 1 variant)	6.00	12.00
RDSEN01 Woodborg Inpachi	.20	.50
RDSEN02 Mighty Guard	.20	.50
RDSEN03 Bokoichi the Freightening Car	.20	.50
RDSEN04 Harpie Girl	.20	.50
RDSEN05 The Creator (UR)	.40	1.00
RDSEN05 The Creator (UTR)	1.25	3.00
RDSEN06 The Creator Incarnate	.20	.50
RDSEN07 Ultimate Insect LV3 (R)	.30	.75
RDSEN07 Ultimate Insect LV3 (UTR)	.60	1.50
RDSEN08 Mystic Swordsman LV6 (UR)	2.00	5.00
RDSEN08 Mystic Swordsman LV6 (UTR)	3.00	8.00
RDSEN09 Silent Swordsman LV3 (UR)	2.00	5.00
RDSEN09 Silent Swordsman LV3 (UTR)	1.50	4.00
RDSEN10 Nightmare Penguin	.20	.50
RDSEN11 Heavy Mech Support Platform	.20	.50
RDSEN12 Perfect Machine King (UR)	1.50	4.00
RDSEN12 Perfect Machine King (UTR)	2.50	6.00
RDSEN13 Element Magician	.20	.50
RDSEN14 Element Saurus	.20	.50
RDSEN15 Roc from the Valley of Haze	.20	.50
RDSEN16 Sasuke Samurai #4 (R)	.30	.75
RDSEN16 Sasuke Samurai #4 (UTR)	.60	1.50
RDSEN17 Harpie Lady 1	.40	1.00
RDSEN18 Harpie Lady 2	.20	.50
RDSEN19 Harpie Lady 3	.20	.50
RDSEN20 Raging Flame Sprite	.20	.50
RDSEN21 Thestalos the Firestorm/Monarch (UTR)	2.00	5.00
RDSEN21 Thestalos the Firestorm/Monarch (SR)	.40	1.00
RDSEN22 Eagle Eye	.20	.50
RDSEN23 Tactical Espionage Expert	.20	.50
RDSEN24 Invasion of Flames	.20	.50
RDSEN25 Creeping Doom Manta	.20	.50
RDSEN26 Pitch-Black Warwolf	.20	.50
RDSEN27 Mirage Dragon	.30	.75
RDSEN28 Gaia Soul the Combust Collective (R)	.30	.75
RDSEN28 Gaia Soul the Combust Collective (UTR)	.60	1.50
RDSEN29 Fox Fire	.20	.50
RDSEN30 Big Core (UTR)	.60	1.50
RDSEN30 Big Core (SR)	.30	.75
RDSEN31 Fusilier Dragon, Duel Mode Beast (R)	1.50	4.00
RDSEN31 Fusilier Dragon, Duel Mode Beast (UTR)	6.00	15.00
RDSEN32 Dekoichi the Battle. Locomotive (R)	.30	.75
RDSEN32 Dekoichi the Battle./ Locomotive (UTR)	2.00	5.00
RDSEN33 A-Team: Trap Disposal Unit (UTR)	.60	1.50
RDSEN33 A-Team: Trap Disposal Unit (R)	.30	.75
RDSEN34 Homunculus the Alchemic Being	.20	.50
RDSEN35 Dark Blade the Dragon Knight (R)	.30	.75
RDSEN35 Dark Blade the Dragon Knight (UTR)	1.00	2.50
RDSEN36 Mokey Mokey King	.20	.50
RDSEN37 Serial Spell (R)	.30	.75
RDSEN37 Serial Spell (UTR)	.60	1.50
RDSEN38 Harpies' Hunting Ground	.20	.50
RDSEN39 Triangle Ecstasy Spark (UR)	.40	1.00
RDSEN39 Triangle Ecstasy Spark (UTR)	2.00	5.00
RDSEN40 Necklace of Command (UTR)	.60	1.50
RDSEN40 Necklace of Command (R)	.30	.75
RDSEN41 Machine Duplication (R)	.30	.75
RDSEN41 Machine Duplication (UTR)	1.25	3.00
RDSEN42 Flint (R)	.30	.75
RDSEN42 Flint (UTR)	.60	1.50
RDSEN43 Mokey Mokey Smackdown	.20	.50
RDSEN44 Back to Square One	.20	.50
RDSEN45 Monster Reincarnation (UTR)	5.00	12.00
RDSEN45 Monster Reincarnation (SR)	.75	2.00
RDSEN46 Ballista of Rampart Smashing	.20	.50
RDSEN47 Lighten the Load	.20	.50
RDSEN48 Malice Dispersion	.20	.50
RDSEN49 Tragedy (UTR)	.60	1.50
RDSEN49 Tragedy (SR)	.30	.75
RDSEN50 Divine Wrath (UTR)	3.00	8.00
RDSEN50 Divine Wrath (SR)	.60	1.50
RDSEN51 Xing Zhen Hu	.20	.50
RDSEN52 Rare Metalmorph (R)	.30	.75
RDSEN52 Rare Metalmorph (UTR)	.60	1.50
RDSEN53 Fruits of Kozaky's Studies	.20	.50
RDSEN54 Mind Haxorz	.20	.50
RDSEN55 Fuh-Rin-Ka-Zan	.20	.50
RDSEN56 Chain Burst (R)	.30	.75
RDSEN56 Chain Burst (UTR)	.60	1.50
RDSEN57 Pikeru's Circle of Enchantment (UTR)	.75	2.00
RDSEN57 Pikeru's Circle of Enchantment (SR)	.30	.75
RDSEN58 Spell Purification	.20	.50
RDSEN59 Astral Barrier	.20	.50
RDSEN60 Covering Fire (R)	.30	.75
RDSEN60 Covering Fire (UTR)	.60	1.50

2004 Yu-Gi-Oh Soul of the Duelist 1st Edition

Card	Low	High
Complete Set (60)	50.00	100.00
Complete Master Set (85)	125.00	200.00
Booster Box (24 packs)	60.00	100.00
Booster Pack (9 cards)	3.50	5.00
SODEN01 Charcoal Inpachi (R)	.30	.75
SODEN01 Charcoal Inpachi (UTR)	2.00	5.00
SODEN02 Neo Aqua Madoor	.20	.50
SODEN03 Skull Dog Marron	.20	.50
SODEN04 Goblin Calligrapher	.20	.50
SODEN05 Ultimate Insect LV1 (R)	.30	.75
SODEN05 Ultimate Insect LV1 (UTR)	.75	2.00
SODEN06 Horus the Black Flame Dragon LV4 (R)	1.50	4.00
SODEN06 Horus the Blk Flame Dragon LV4 (UTR)	5.00	12.00
SODEN07 Horus the Blk Flame Dragon LV6 (UTR)	5.00	12.00
SODEN07 Horus the Black Flame Dragon LV6 (SR)	2.50	6.00
SODEN08 Horus the Blk Flame Dragon LV8 (UTR)	25.00	50.00
SODEN08 Horus the Blk Flame Dragon LV8 (UR)	4.00	10.00
SODEN09 Dark Mimic LV1	.20	.50
SODEN10 Dark Mimic LV3 (R)	.30	.75
SODEN10 Dark Mimic LV3 (UTR)	4.00	10.00
SODEN11 Mystic Swordsman LV2 (UTR)	1.50	4.00
SODEN11 Mystic Swordsman LV2 (R)	.30	.75
SODEN12 Mystic Swordsman LV4 (UR)	.75	2.00
SODEN12 Mystic Swordsman LV4 (UTR)	2.50	6.00
SODEN13 Armed Dragon LV3	.20	.50
SODEN14 Armed Dragon LV5 (R)	.30	.75
SODEN14 Armed Dragon LV5 (UTR)	3.00	8.00
SODEN15 Armed Dragon LV7 (UR)	4.00	10.00
SODEN15 Armed Dragon LV7 (UTR)	8.00	20.00
SODEN16 Horus' Servant	.20	.50
SODEN17 Red-Eyes B. Chick	.30	.75
SODEN18 Malice Doll of Demise	.20	.50
SODEN19 Ninja Grandmaster Sasuke (UTR)	4.00	10.00
SODEN19 Ninja Grandmaster Sasuke (R)	.40	1.00
SODEN20 Rafflesia Seduction (R)	.30	.75
SODEN20 Rafflesia Seduction (UTR)	.75	2.00
SODEN21 Ultimate Baseball Kid	.20	.50
SODEN22 Mobius the Frost Monarch	.75	2.00
SODEN22 Mobius the Frost Monarch (UTR)	5.00	12.00
SODEN23 Element Dragon	.20	.50
SODEN24 Element Soldier	.20	.50
SODEN25 Howling Insect	.20	.50
SODEN26 Masked Dragon	.30	.75
SODEN27 Mind on Air (R)	.30	.75
SODEN27 Mind on Air (UTR)	1.00	2.50
SODEN28 Unshaven Angler	.20	.50
SODEN29 The Trojan Horse	.20	.50
SODEN30 Nobleman-Eater Bug	.20	.50
SODEN31 Enraged Muka Muka	.20	.50
SODEN32 Hade-Hane	.20	.50
SODEN33 Penumbral Soldier Lady (SR)	.40	1.00
SODEN33 Penumbral Soldier Lady (UTR)	.75	2.00
SODEN34 Ojama King (UTR)	2.00	5.00
SODEN34 Ojama King (R)	.40	1.00
SODEN35 Master of Oz (UTR)	3.00	8.00
SODEN35 Master of Oz (R)	.30	.75
SODEN36 Sanwitch	.20	.50
SODEN37 Dark Factory of Mass Production	.60	1.50
SODEN38 Hammer Shot (UTR)	2.50	6.00
SODEN38 Hammer Shot (R)	.30	.75
SODEN39 Mind Wipe	.20	.50
SODEN40 Abyssal Designator	.20	.50
SODEN41 Level Up!	.30	.75
SODEN42 Inferno Fire Blast (UR)	1.50	4.00
SODEN42 Inferno Fire Blast (UTR)	3.00	8.00
SODEN43 Ectoplasmer (SR)	.40	1.00
SODEN43 Ectoplasmer (UTR)	.60	1.50
SODEN44 The Graveyard in the Fourth Dimension	.20	.50
SODEN45 Two-Man Cell Battle	.20	.50
SODEN46 Big Wave Small Wave	.20	.50
SODEN47 Fusion Weapon	.20	.50
SODEN48 Ritual Weapon	.20	.50
SODEN49 Taunt	.20	.50
SODEN50 Absolute End	.20	.50
SODEN51 Spirit Barrier (UTR)	4.00	10.00
SODEN51 Spirit Barrier (R)	1.50	4.00
SODEN52 Ninjitsu Art of Decoy	.20	.50
SODEN53 Enervating Mist (R)	.30	.75
SODEN53 Enervating Mist (UTR)	4.00	10.00
SODEN54 Heavy Slump	.30	.75
SODEN55 Greed (UTR)	.60	1.50
SODEN55 Greed (SR)	.40	1.00
SODEN56 Mind Crush	.60	1.50
SODEN57 Null and Void (UTR)	.60	1.50
SODEN57 Null and Void (SR)	.40	1.00
SODEN58 Gorgon's Eye	.20	.50
SODEN59 Cemetary Bomb	.20	.50
SODEN60 Hallowed Life Barrier (UTR)	.75	2.00
SODEN60 Hallowed Life Barrier (SR)	.40	1.00

2005 Yu-Gi-Oh Cybernetic Revolution 1st Edition

Card	Low	High
Complete Set (60)	140.00	200.00
Booster Box (24 packs)	72.00	90.00
Booster Pack (9 cards)	3.50	4.50
CRV-1 Cycloid	.10	.20
CRV-2 Soitsu	.10	.20
CRV-3 Mad Lobster	.10	.20
CRV-4 Jelly Beans Man	.10	.20
CRV-5 Winged Kuriboh LV 10 (UR)	18.00	30.00
CRV-5 Winged Kuriboh LV 10 (UTR)	30.00	45.00
CRV-6 Patroid	.10	.20
CRV-7 Gyroid	.10	.20
CRV-8 Steamroid	.10	.20
CRV-9 Drillroid	.10	.20
CRV-10 UFOroid (SR)	4.00	8.00
CRV-10 UFOroid (UTR)	6.00	12.00
CRV-11 Jetroid	.10	.30
CRV-12 Wroughtweiler (UTR)	5.00	11.00
CRV-12 Wroughtweiler (R)	1.00	2.00
CRV-13 Dark Catapulter (R)	1.00	2.00
CRV-13 Dark Catapulter (UTR)	4.00	10.00
CRV-14 Elemental Hero Bubbleman (R)	2.00	5.00
CRV-14 Elemental Hero Bubbleman (UTR)	10.00	20.00
CRV-15 Cyber Dragon (SR)	12.00	30.00
CRV-15 Cyber Dragon (UTR)	30.00	40.00
CRV-16 Cybernetic Magician (SR)	8.00	12.00

❑ CRV-16 Cybernetic Magician (UTR) 15.00 22.00
❑ CRV-17 Cybernetic Cyclops .10 .20
❑ CRV-18 Mechanical Hound .10 .20
❑ CRV-19 Cyber Archfiend .10 .20
❑ CRV-20 Goblin Elite Attack Force (SR) 4.00 8.00
❑ CRV-20 Goblin Elite Attack Force (UTR) 8.00 12.00
❑ CRV-21 B.E.S. Crystal Core (SR) 4.00 6.00
❑ CRV-21 B.E.S. Crystal Core (UTR) 6.00 10.00
❑ CRV-22 Giant Kozaky .10 .20
❑ CRV-23 Indomitable Fighter Lei Lei .10 .20
❑ CRV-24 Protective Soul Ailin .10 .20
❑ CRV-25 Doitsu .10 .20
❑ CRV-26 Des Frog .10 .20
❑ CRV-27 T.A.D.P.O.L.E. .10 .20
❑ CRV-28 Poison Draw Frog .10 .20
❑ CRV-29 Tyranno Infinity .10 .20
❑ CRV-30 Batteryman .10 .20
❑ CRV-31 Ebon Magician Curran .10 .20
❑ CRV-32 D.D.M. Different Dimension Master (R) 1.00 2.00
❑ CRV-32 D.D.M. Different Dimension Master (UTR) 4.00 8.00
❑ CRV-33 Steam Gyroid .10 .20
❑ CRV-34 UFOroid Fighter (UR) 8.00 15.00
❑ CRV-34 UFOroid Fighter (UTR) 15.00 22.00
❑ CRV-35 Cyber Twin Dragon (SR) 10.00 18.00
❑ CRV-35 Cyber Twin Dragon (UTR) 20.00 30.00
❑ CRV-36 Cyber End Dragon (UR) 6.00 12.00
❑ CRV-36 Cyber End Dragon (UTR) 10.00 20.00
❑ CRV-37 Power Bond (UR) 8.00 15.00
❑ CRV-37 Power Bond (UTR) 20.00 28.00
❑ CRV-38 Fusion Recovery .10 .20
❑ CRV-39 Miracle Fusion (R) 2.00 4.00
❑ CRV-39 Miracle Fusion (UTR) 7.00 14.00
❑ CRV-40 Dragon's Mirror .10 .20
❑ CRV-41 System Down (R) 1.00 2.00
❑ CRV-41 System Down (UTR) 7.00 12.00
❑ CRV-42 Des Croaking .10 .20
❑ CRV-43 Pot of Generosity .10 .20
❑ CRV-44 Shien's Spy .10 .20
❑ CRV-45 Transcendant Wings (R) 1.00 2.00
❑ CRV-45 Transcendant Wings (UTR) 8.00 17.00
❑ CRV-46 Bubble Shuffle (R) 1.00 2.00
❑ CRV-46 Bubble Shuffle (UTR) 5.00 10.00
❑ CRV-47 Spark Blaster (R) 1.00 2.00
❑ CRV-47 Spark Blaster (UTR) 4.00 10.00
❑ CRV-48 Skyscraper (SR) 3.00 6.00
❑ CRV-48 Skyscraper (UTR) 7.00 15.00
❑ CRV-49 Fire Darts (UTR) 3.00 6.00
❑ CRV-49 Fire Darts (R) 1.00 2.00
❑ CRV-50 Spiritual Earth Art - Kurogane .10 .20
❑ CRV-51 Spiritual Water Art - Aoi .10 .20
❑ CRV-52 Spiritual Fire Art - Kurenai .10 .20
❑ CRV-53 Spiritual Wind Art - Miyabi .10 .20
❑ CRV-54 A Rival Appears! .10 .20
❑ CRV-55 Magical Explosion (R) 1.00 2.00
❑ CRV-55 Magical Explosion (UTR) 5.00 10.00
❑ CRV-56 Rising Energy (R) 1.00 2.00
❑ CRV-56 Rising Energy (UTR) 5.00 12.00
❑ CRV-57 D.D. Trap Hole (R) 1.00 2.00
❑ CRV-57 D.D. Trap Hole (UTR) 5.00 10.00
❑ CRV-58 Conscription .10 .20
❑ CRV-59 Dimension Wall (R) 1.00 2.00
❑ CRV-59 Dimension Wall (UTR) 7.00 12.00
❑ CRV-60 Prepare to Strike Back .10 .20

2005 Yu-Gi-Oh Dark Beginnings 2

Complete Set (250) 140.00 225.00
Booster Box (24 Packs) 65.00 85.00
Booster Pack (13 cards) 3.00 3.75

❑ DB2001 Jowgen the Spiritualist (R) 1.00 2.00
❑ DB2002 Kycoo the Ghost Destroyer (R) 1.00 2.00
❑ DB2003 Bazoo the Soul-Eater (R) 2.00 4.00
❑ DB2004 Dark Necrofear (UR) 4.00 7.00
❑ DB2005 Soul of Purity and Light .10 .20
❑ DB2006 Aqua Spirit .10 .20
❑ DB2007 The Rock Spirit .10 .20
❑ DB2008 Gilasaurus .10 .20
❑ DB2009 Tornado Bird .10 .20
❑ DB2010 Zombyra the Dark .10 .20
❑ DB2011 Maryokutai .10 .20
❑ DB2012 The Last Warrior from Another Planet (SR) 3.00 6.00
❑ DB2013 Dark Spirit of the Silent .10 .20
❑ DB2014 Royal Command (R) 1.00 2.00
❑ DB2015 Riryoku Field (R) 1.00 2.00
❑ DB2016 Skull Lair .10 .20
❑ DB2017 Graverobber's Retribution .10 .20
❑ DB2018 Destruction Punch .10 .20
❑ DB2019 Blind Destruction .10 .20
❑ DB2020 The Emperor's Holiday .10 .20
❑ DB2021 Destiny Board .10 .20
❑ DB2022 Spirit Message 'I' .10 .20
❑ DB2023 Spirit Message 'N' .10 .20
❑ DB2024 Spirit Message 'A' .10 .20
❑ DB2025 Spirit Message 'L' .10 .20
❑ DB2026 The Dark Door .10 .20
❑ DB2027 Spiritualism (R) 1.00 2.00
❑ DB2028 Cyclon Laser .10 .20
❑ DB2029 De-Fusion .10 .20
❑ DB2030 Fusion Gate (R) 3.00 6.00
❑ DB2031 Ekibyo Drakmord .10 .20
❑ DB2032 Miracle Dig .10 .20
❑ DB2033 Vengeful Bog Spirit .10 .20
❑ DB2034 Blade Knight (UR) 4.00 8.00
❑ DB2035 Baby Dragon .50 1.00
❑ DB2036 Blackland Fire Dragon .20 .50
❑ DB2037 Battle Steer .10 .20
❑ DB2038 Time Wizard (SR) 3.00 6.00
❑ DB2039 Saggi the Dark Clown .10 .20
❑ DB2040 Dragon Piper .10 .20
❑ DB2041 Illusionist Faceless Mage .10 .20
❑ DB2042 Sangan (R) 1.00 2.00
❑ DB2043 Great Moth .20 .50
❑ DB2044 Kuriboh (R) 1.00 2.00
❑ DB2045 Thousand Dragon .20 .50
❑ DB2046 King of Yamimakai .10 .20
❑ DB2047 Catapult Turtle (SR) 3.00 7.00
❑ DB2048 Mystic Horseman .10 .20
❑ DB2049 Rabid Horseman .10 .20
❑ DB2050 Crass Clown .10 .20
❑ DB2051 Dream Clown .10 .20
❑ DB2052 Princess of Tsurugi .10 .20
❑ DB2053 Tremendous Fire .10 .20
❑ DB2054 Jirai Gumo .10 .20
❑ DB2055 Shadow Ghoul .10 .20
❑ DB2056 Ryu-Kishin Powered .10 .20
❑ DB2057 Launcher Spider .20 .50

❑ DB2058 Thunder Dragon .50 1.00
❑ DB2059 The Immortal of Thunder .10 .20
❑ DB2060 Hoshiningen .10 .20
❑ DB2061 Cannon Soldier (SR) 5.00 10.00
❑ DB2062 Muka Muka .10 .20
❑ DB2063 The Bistro Butcher .10 .20
❑ DB2064 Star Boy .10 .20
❑ DB2065 Milus Radiant .10 .20
❑ DB2066 Witch of the Black Forest (R) 2.00 4.00
❑ DB2067 Little Chimera .10 .20
❑ DB2068 Bladefly .10 .20
❑ DB2069 Twin-Headed Thunder Dragon .20 .50
❑ DB2070 Witch's Apprentice .10 .20
❑ DB2071 Gazelle the King of Mythical Beasts .10 .20
❑ DB2072 Barrel Dragon (UR) 5.00 10.00
❑ DB2073 Solemn Judgment (SR) 10.00 20.00
❑ DB2074 Magic Jammer (SR) 3.00 6.00
❑ DB2075 Seven Tools of the Bandit (SR) 3.00 6.00
❑ DB2076 Horn of Heaven (R) 1.00 2.00
❑ DB2077 Shield & Sword .10 .20
❑ DB2078 Block Attack .10 .20
❑ DB2079 The Unhappy Maiden .10 .20
❑ DB2080 Robbin' Goblin .10 .20
❑ DB2081 Mirror Force (SR) 20.00 30.00
❑ DB2082 Ring of Magnetism (R) 1.00 2.00
❑ DB2083 Share the Pain .10 .20
❑ DB2084 Heavy Storm (SR) 5.00 10.00
❑ DB2085 Oscillo Hero #2 .10 .20
❑ DB2086 Soul of the Pure .10 .20
❑ DB2087 Dark-Piercing Light .10 .20
❑ DB2088 The Statue of Easter Island .10 .20
❑ DB2089 Shining Friendship .10 .20
❑ DB2090 The Wicked Worm Beast .10 .20
❑ DB2091 Tiger Axe .10 .20
❑ DB2092 Axe Raider .10 .20
❑ DB2093 Mechanicalchaser 1.00 2.00
❑ DB2094 Gemini Elf .50 1.00
❑ DB2095 Graceful Charity (R) 2.00 4.00
❑ DB2096 Two-Headed King Rex .10 .20
❑ DB2097 Goddess with the Third Eye .10 .20
❑ DB2098 Lord of the Lamp .10 .20
❑ DB2099 Machine King .10 .20
❑ DB2100 Cyber-Stein (R) 7.00 15.00
❑ DB2101 Dragon Seeker .10 .20
❑ DB2102 Needle Worm 2.00 6.00
❑ DB2103 Greenkappa .10 .20
❑ DB2104 Morphing Jar (R) 8.00 16.00
❑ DB2105 Penguin Soldier .10 .20
❑ DB2106 Royal Decree (SR) 7.00 15.00
❑ DB2107 Magical Thorn .50 1.00
❑ DB2108 Restructer Revolution .10 .20
❑ DB2109 Fusion Sage .10 .20
❑ DB2110 Total Defense Shogun (SR) 3.00 6.00
❑ DB2111 Swift Gaia the Fierce Knight (UR) 4.00 8.00
❑ DB2112 Obnoxious Celtic Guard (UR) 5.00 12.00
❑ DB2113 Luminous Soldier 1.00 2.00
❑ DB2114 Command Knight (SR) 3.00 6.00
❑ DB2115 Kaiser Sea Horse .10 .20
❑ DB2116 Vampire Lord (UR) 8.00 12.00
❑ DB2117 Toon Goblin Attack Force .10 .20
❑ DB2118 Toon Cannon Soldier 1.00 2.00
❑ DB2119 Toon Gemini Elf .50 1.00
❑ DB2120 Toon Masked Sorcerer .10 .20
❑ DB2121 Toon Table of Contents .10 .20
❑ DB2122 Toon Defense .10 .20
❑ DB2123 Insect Queen (UR) 8.00 12.00
❑ DB2124 Dark Ruler Ha Des (UR) 5.00 10.00
❑ DB2125 Dark Balter the Terrible (R) 2.00 4.00
❑ DB2126 Lesser Fiend .10 .20
❑ DB2127 Possessed Dark Soul .10 .20
❑ DB2128 Winged Minion .10 .20
❑ DB2129 Skull Knight #2 .10 .20
❑ DB2130 Twin-Headed Wolf .10 .20
❑ DB2131 Opticlops .10 .20
❑ DB2132 Bark of Dark Ruler .10 .20
❑ DB2133 Fatal Abacus .10 .20
❑ DB2134 The Puppet Magic of Dark Ruler .20 .50
❑ DB2135 Soul Demolition .10 .20
❑ DB2136 Double Snare .10 .20
❑ DB2137 Freed the Matchless General (UR) 7.00 12.00
❑ DB2138 Marauding Captain (R) 2.00 4.00
❑ DB2139 Ryu Senshi (R) 1.00 2.00
❑ DB2140 Warrior Dai Grepher .10 .20
❑ DB2141 Mysterious Guard .10 .20
❑ DB2142 Frontier Wiseman .10 .20
❑ DB2143 Exiled Force .10 .20
❑ DB2144 Shadow Tamer .10 .20
❑ DB2145 Dragon Manipulator .10 .20
❑ DB2146 The A. Forces .10 .20
❑ DB2147 Reinforcement of the Army (R) 1.00 2.00
❑ DB2148 Array of Revealing Light .10 .20
❑ DB2149 The Warrior Returning Alive .10 .20
❑ DB2150 Emergency Provisions (R) 2.00 4.00
❑ DB2151 Tyrant Dragon (UR) 6.00 14.00
❑ DB2152 Spear Dragon (SR) 5.00 8.00
❑ DB2153 Spirit Ryu .10 .20
❑ DB2154 Fiend Skull Dragon (R) 1.00 2.00
❑ DB2155 Cave Dragon .10 .20
❑ DB2156 Gray Wing .10 .20
❑ DB2157 Troop Dragon .20 .50
❑ DB2158 The Dragon's Bead .10 .20
❑ DB2159 A Wingbeat of Giant Dragon .10 .20
❑ DB2160 Dragon's Gunfire .10 .20
❑ DB2161 Stamping Destruction .10 .20
❑ DB2162 Super Rejuvenation .10 .20
❑ DB2163 Dragon's Rage .10 .20
❑ DB2164 Burst Breath .10 .20
❑ DB2165 Luster Dragon #2 .10 .20
❑ DB2166 Fiber Jar (R) 3.00 6.00
❑ DB2167 Serpentine Princess .10 .20
❑ DB2168 Patrician of Darkness .10 .20
❑ DB2169 Thunder Nyan Nyan (R) 1.00 2.00
❑ DB2170 Gradius' Option .10 .20
❑ DB2171 Injection Fairy Lily (UR) 12.00 20.00
❑ DB2172 Woodland Sprite .10 .20
❑ DB2173 Airknight Parshath (SR) 8.00 14.00
❑ DB2174 Twin-Headed Behemoth .20 .50
❑ DB2175 Maharaghi .10 .20
❑ DB2176 Inaba White Rabbit .10 .20
❑ DB2177 Yata-Garasu .10 .20
❑ DB2178 Susa Soldier (SR) 2.00 4.00
❑ DB2179 Yamata Dragon (SR) 3.00 6.00
❑ DB2180 Great Long Nose .10 .20
❑ DB2181 Otohime .10 .20
❑ DB2182 Hino-Kagu-Tsuchi (UR) 5.00 9.00
❑ DB2183 Asura Priest .10 .20
❑ DB2184 Fushi No Tori .10 .20
❑ DB2185 Spring of Rebirth .10 .20
❑ DB2186 Heart of Clear Water .10 .20
❑ DB2187 A Legendary Ocean .10 .20
❑ DB2188 Fusion Sword Murasame Blade .10 .20
❑ DB2189 Smoke Grenade of the Thief .10 .20
❑ DB2190 Creature Swap (SR) 4.00 9.00
❑ DB2191 Spiritual Energy Settle Machine .10 .20
❑ DB2192 Second Coin Toss .10 .20
❑ DB2193 Convulsion of Nature .10 .20
❑ DB2194 The Secret of the Bandit .10 .20
❑ DB2195 After the Struggle .10 .20
❑ DB2196 Magic Reflector .10 .20
❑ DB2197 Blast with Chain (R) 1.00 2.00
❑ DB2198 Disappear .10 .20
❑ DB2199 Bubble Crash .10 .20
❑ DB2200 Royal Oppression (R) 1.00 2.00
❑ DB2201 Bottomless Trap Hole .10 .20
❑ DB2202 Bad Reaction to Simochi .10 .20
❑ DB2203 Ominous Fortunetelling .10 .20
❑ DB2204 Spirit's Invitation .10 .20
❑ DB2205 Drop Off .10 .20
❑ DB2206 Last Turn (R) 1.00 2.00
❑ DB2207 King Tiger Wanghu .10 .20
❑ DB2208 Birdface .10 .20
❑ DB2209 Kryuel .10 .20
❑ DB2210 Arsenal Bug .10 .20
❑ DB2211 Maiden of the Aqua .10 .20
❑ DB2212 Jowls of Dark Demise .10 .20
❑ DB2213 Mucus Yolk .10 .20
❑ DB2214 Moisture Creature .10 .20
❑ DB2215 Gora Turtle .10 .20
❑ DB2216 Sasuke Samurai (R) 1.00 2.00
❑ DB2217 Dark Dust Spirit .10 .20
❑ DB2218 Royal Keeper .10 .20
❑ DB2219 Wandering Mummy .10 .20
❑ DB2220 Great Dezard (SR) 3.00 6.00
❑ DB2221 Swarm of Scarabs .10 .20
❑ DB2222 Swarm of Locusts .10 .20
❑ DB2223 Giant Axe Mummy .10 .20
❑ DB2224 Guardian Sphinx (UR) 5.00 10.00
❑ DB2225 Pyramid Turtle (R) 1.00 2.00
❑ DB2226 Dice Jar .10 .20
❑ DB2227 Dark Scorpion Burglars .10 .20
❑ DB2228 Don Zaloog (SR) 7.00 15.00
❑ DB2229 Fushioh Richie (UR) 7.00 12.00
❑ DB2230 Book of Life (SR) 4.00 8.00
❑ DB2231 Book of Taiyou .10 .20
❑ DB2232 Book of Moon .10 .20
❑ DB2233 Mirage of Nightmare .10 .20
❑ DB2234 Secret Pass to the Treasures .10 .20
❑ DB2235 Call of the Mummy .10 .20
❑ DB2236 Timidity .10 .20
❑ DB2237 Pyramid Energy .10 .20
❑ DB2238 Tutan Mask .10 .20
❑ DB2239 Ordeal of a Traveler .10 .20
❑ DB2240 Bottomless Shifting Sand .10 .20
❑ DB2241 Curse of Royal .10 .20
❑ DB2242 Needle Ceiling .10 .20
❑ DB2243 Statue of the Wicked (R) 1.00 2.00
❑ DB2244 Dark Coffin .10 .20
❑ DB2245 Needle Wall .10 .20
❑ DB2246 Trap Dustshoot .10 .20
❑ DB2247 Reckless Greed .10 .20
❑ DB2248 Pharaoh's Treasure .10 .20
❑ DB2249 Perfectly Ultimate Great Moth (UR) 5.00 10.00
❑ DB2250 Black Illusion Ritual .10 .20

2005 Yu-Gi-Oh Dark Revelation 1

Complete Set (267) 175.00 300.00
Booster Box (24 packs) 60.00 80.00
Booster Pack (13 cards) 3.50 4.00

❑ DR1001 Master Kyonshee .10 .20
❑ DR1002 Kabazauls .10 .20
❑ DR1003 Inpachi .10 .20
❑ DR1004 Dark Jeroid (R) 1.00 2.00
❑ DR1005 Newdoria (R) 1.00 2.00
❑ DR1006 Helpoemer (SR) 5.00 10.00
❑ DR1007 Gravekeeper's Spy 4.00 8.00
❑ DR1008 Gravekeeper's Curse .10 .20
❑ DR1009 Gravekeeper's Guard .10 .20
❑ DR1010 Gravekeeper's Spear Soldier .10 .20
❑ DR1011 Gravekeeper's Vassal .10 .20
❑ DR1012 Gravekeeper's Watcher .10 .20
❑ DR1013 Gravekeeper's Chief (R) 2.00 4.00
❑ DR1014 Gravekeeper's Cannonholder .10 .20
❑ DR1015 Gravekeeper's Assailant .10 .20
❑ DR1016 A Man with Wdjat .10 .20
❑ DR1017 Mystical Knight of Jackal (SR) 7.00 10.00
❑ DR1018 A Cat of Ill Omen .10 .20
❑ DR1019 Yomi Ship .10 .20
❑ DR1020 Winged Sage Falcos .10 .20
❑ DR1021 An Owl of Luck .10 .20
❑ DR1022 Charm of Shabti .10 .20
❑ DR1023 Cobra Jar .10 .20
❑ DR1024 Spirit Reaper (R) 2.00 5.00
❑ DR1025 Nightmare Horse .10 .20
❑ DR1026 Reaper on the Nightmare (R) 1.00 2.00
❑ DR1027 Dark Designator .10 .20
❑ DR1028 Card Shuffle .10 .20
❑ DR1029 Reasoning .10 .20
❑ DR1030 Dark Room of Nightmare .10 .20
❑ DR1031 Different Dimension Capsule .10 .20
❑ DR1032 Necrovalley (SR) 3.00 5.00
❑ DR1033 Buster Rancher .10 .20
❑ DR1034 Hieroglyph Lithograph .10 .20
❑ DR1035 Dark Snake Syndrome .10 .20
❑ DR1036 Terraforming .10 .20
❑ DR1037 Banner of Courage .10 .20
❑ DR1038 Metamorphosis .10 .20
❑ DR1039 Roayl Tribute .10 .20
❑ DR1040 Reversal Quiz .10 .20
❑ DR1041 Coffin Seller (SR) 3.00 5.00
❑ DR1042 Curse of Aging .10 .20
❑ DR1043 Barrel Behind the Door (R) 1.00 2.00
❑ DR1044 Raigeki Break .10 .20
❑ DR1045 Narrow Pass .10 .20
❑ DR1046 Disturbance Strategy .10 .20
❑ DR1047 Trap of Board .10 .20
❑ DR1048 Rite of Spirit .10 .20
❑ DR1049 Non Aggression Area .10 .20
❑ DR1050 D. Tribe .10 .20
❑ DR1051 Lava Golem (UR) 6.00 14.00
❑ DR1052 Byser Shock (UR) 6.00 10.00
❑ DR1053 Question (SR) 3.00 5.00
❑ DR1054 Rope of Life (R) 1.00 2.00
❑ DR1055 Nightmare Wheel (UR) 6.00 10.00
❑ DR1056 People Running About .10 .20
❑ DR1057 Oppressed People .10 .20
❑ DR1058 United Resistance .10 .20
❑ DR1059 Z-head Cannon (R) 2.00 5.00
❑ DR1060 Y-Dragon Head (R) 3.00 7.00
❑ DR1061 Z-Metal Tank (R) 2.00 5.00
❑ DR1062 Dark Blade .10 .20
❑ DR1063 Pitch-Dark Dragon .20 .50
❑ DR1064 Kiryu .10 .20
❑ DR1065 Decayed Commander .10 .20
❑ DR1066 Zombie Tiger .10 .20
❑ DR1067 Giant Orc .10 .20
❑ DR1068 Second Goblin .10 .20
❑ DR1069 Vampire Orchis .10 .20
❑ DR1070 Des Dendle .10 .20
❑ DR1071 Burning Beast .10 .20
❑ DR1072 Freezing Beast .10 .20
❑ DR1073 Union Rider .10 .20
❑ DR1074 D.D. Crazy Beast .10 .20
❑ DR1075 Spell Canceller (UR) 6.00 12.00
❑ DR1076 Neko Mane King .10 .20
❑ DR1077 Helping Robo For Combat .10 .20
❑ DR1078 Dimension Jar .10 .20
❑ DR1079 Great Phantom Thief .10 .20
❑ DR1080 Roulette Barrel .10 .20
❑ DR1081 Paladin of White Dragon (SR) 6.00 10.00
❑ DR1082 White Dragon Ritual .10 .20
❑ DR1083 Frontline Base .10 .20
❑ DR1084 Demotion .10 .20
❑ DR1085 Combination Attack .10 .20
❑ DR1086 Kaiser Colosseum .10 .20
❑ DR1087 Autonomous Action Unit .10 .20
❑ DR1088 Poison of the Old Man .10 .20
❑ DR1089 Ante .10 .20
❑ DR1090 Dark Core .10 .20
❑ DR1091 Raregold Armor .10 .20
❑ DR1092 Metalsilver .10 .20
❑ DR1093 Kishido Spirit .10 .20
❑ DR1094 Tribute Doll .10 .20
❑ DR1095 Wave-Motion Cannon 3.00 6.00
❑ DR1096 Huge Revolution .10 .20
❑ DR1097 Thunder of Ruler .10 .20
❑ DR1098 Spell Shield Type-8 (SR) 3.00 6.00
❑ DR1099 Meteorain .10 .20
❑ DR1100 Pineapple Blast .10 .20
❑ DR1101 Secret Barrel .10 .20
❑ DR1102 Physical Double .10 .20
❑ DR1103 Rivalry of Warlords .10 .20
❑ DR1104 Formation Union .10 .20
❑ DR1105 Adhesion Trap Hole .10 .20
❑ DR1106 XY-Dragon Cannon (R) 3.00 7.00
❑ DR1107 XYZ-Dragon Cannon (UR) 7.00 15.00
❑ DR1108 XZ-Tank Cannon (R) 2.00 5.00
❑ DR1109 YZ-Tank Cannon (R) 2.00 4.00
❑ DR1110 Great Angus .10 .20
❑ DR1111 Aitsu .10 .20
❑ DR1112 Sonic Duck .10 .20
❑ DR1113 Luster Dragon 1.00 2.00
❑ DR1114 Amazoness Paladin .10 .20
❑ DR1115 Amazoness Fighter .10 .20
❑ DR1116 Amazoness Swords Woman (SR) 10.00 19.00
❑ DR1117 Amazoness Blowpiper .10 .20
❑ DR1118 Amazoness Tiger .10 .20
❑ DR1119 Skilled White Magician (R) 2.00 4.00
❑ DR1120 Skilled Dark Magician (R) 2.00 5.00
❑ DR1121 Apprentice Magician .10 .20
❑ DR1122 Old Vindictive Magician .10 .20
❑ DR1123 Chaos Command Magician (SR) 8.00 12.00
❑ DR1124 Magical Marionette .10 .20
❑ DR1125 Pixie Knight .10 .20
❑ DR1126 Breaker the Magical Warrior (UR) 8.00 16.00
❑ DR1127 Magical Plant Mandragola .10 .20
❑ DR1128 Magical Scientist (R) 1.00 2.00
❑ DR1129 Royal Magical Library .10 .20
❑ DR1130 Armor Exe .10 .20
❑ DR1131 Tribe-Infecting Virus (R) 3.00 5.00
❑ DR1132 Des Koala (R) 1.00 2.00
❑ DR1133 Cliff the Trap Remover .10 .20
❑ DR1134 Magical Merchant .10 .20
❑ DR1135 Koitsu .10 .20
❑ DR1136 Cat's Ear Tribe .10 .20
❑ DR1137 Ultimate Obedient Fiend .10 .20
❑ DR1138 Dark Cat with White Tail .10 .20
❑ DR1139 Amazoness Spellcaster .10 .20
❑ DR1140 Continuous Destruction Punch .10 .20
❑ DR1141 Big Bang Shot (R) 1.00 2.00
❑ DR1142 Gather Your Mind .10 .20
❑ DR1143 Mass Driver .10 .20
❑ DR1144 Senri Eye .10 .20
❑ DR1145 Emblem of Dragon Destroyer .10 .20
❑ DR1146 Jar Robber .10 .20
❑ DR1147 My Body as a Shield .10 .20
❑ DR1148 Pigeonholing Books of Spell .10 .20
❑ DR1149 Mega Ton Magical Cannon .10 .20
❑ DR1150 Pitch-Black Power Stone .10 .20
❑ DR1151 Amazoness Archers (SR) 3.00 6.00
❑ DR1152 Dramatic Rescue (R) 1.00 2.00
❑ DR1153 Exhausting Spell .10 .20
❑ DR1154 Hidden Book of Spell .10 .20
❑ DR1155 Miracle Restoring .10 .20
❑ DR1156 Remove Brainwashing .10 .20
❑ DR1157 Disarmament .10 .20
❑ DR1158 Anti-Spell .10 .20
❑ DR1159 The Spell Absorbing Life .10 .20
❑ DR1160 Dark Paladin (UR) 10.00 18.00
❑ DR1161 Double Spell (UR) 7.00 15.00
❑ DR1162 Diffusion Wave-Motion 6.00 10.00
❑ DR1163 Battle Footballer .10 .20
❑ DR1164 Nin-Ken Dog .10 .20
❑ DR1165 Acrobat Monkey .10 .20
❑ DR1166 Arsenal Summoner .10 .20
❑ DR1167 Guardian Elma .10 .20
❑ DR1168 Guardian Ceal (R) 2.00 5.00
❑ DR1169 Guardian Grarl (R) 1.00 2.00
❑ DR1170 Guardian Baou .10 .20
❑ DR1171 Guardian Kay'est .10 .20
❑ DR1172 Guardian Tryce .10 .20
❑ DR1173 Cyber Raider .10 .20
❑ DR1174 Reflect Bounder (SR) 15.00 22.00
❑ DR1175 Little-Winguard .10 .20
❑ DR1176 Des Feral Imp .10 .20
❑ DR1177 Different Dimension Dragon (SR) 5.00 10.00
❑ DR1178 Sinato, King of a Higher Plane (SR) 7.00 15.00
❑ DR1179 Dark Flare Knight (SR) 6.00 12.00
❑ DR1180 Mirage Knight (SR) 5.00 10.00
❑ DR1181 Berserk Dragon (SR) 6.00 12.00
❑ DR1182 Exodia Necross (SR) 7.00 15.00
❑ DR1183 Gyaku-Gire Panda .10 .20
❑ DR1184 Blindly Loyal Goblin .10 .20
❑ DR1185 Despair from the Dark .10 .20
❑ DR1186 Maju Garzett .10 .20
❑ DR1187 Fear from the Dark (R) 1.00 2.00
❑ DR1188 Dark Scorpion Chick the Yellow .10 .20
❑ DR1189 D.D. Warrior Lady (SR) 12.00 18.00
❑ DR1190 Thousand Needles .10 .20
❑ DR1191 Shinato's Ark .10 .20
❑ DR1192 A Deal with Dark Ruler .10 .20
❑ DR1193 Contract with Exodia 1.00 2.00
❑ DR1194 Butterfly Dagger - Elma (R) 2.00 4.00
❑ DR1195 Shooting Star Bow - Ceal .10 .20
❑ DR1196 Gravity Axe - Grarl .10 .20
❑ DR1197 Wicked-Breaking Flamberge Baou .10 .20
❑ DR1198 Rod of Silence - Kay'est .10 .20
❑ DR1199 Twin Swords of Flashing Light - Tryce .10 .20
❑ DR1200 Precious Cards from Beyond .10 .20
❑ DR1201 Rod of the Mind's Eye .10 .20
❑ DR1202 Fairy of the Spring .10 .20
❑ DR1203 Token Thanksgiving .10 .20
❑ DR1204 Morale Boost .10 .20
❑ DR1205 Non-Spellcasting Area .10 .20
❑ DR1206 Different Dimension Gate (R) 2.00 4.00
❑ DR1207 Final Attack Orders .10 .20
❑ DR1208 Staunch Defender .10 .20
❑ DR1209 Ojama Trio .10 .20
❑ DR1210 Arsenal Robber .10 .20
❑ DR1211 Skill Drain (R) 1.00 2.00
❑ DR1212 Really Eternal Rest .10 .20
❑ DR1213 Kaiser Glider (UR) 9.00 15.00
❑ DR1214 Interdimensional Matter Trans (UR) 5.00 12.00
❑ DR1215 Cost Down (UR) 8.00 15.00
❑ DR1216 Gagagigo .10 .20
❑ DR1217 D.D. Trainer .10 .20
❑ DR1218 Ojama Green .10 .20
❑ DR1219 Archfiend Soldier .10 .20
❑ DR1220 Pandemonium Watchbear .10 .20
❑ DR1221 Sasuke Samurai #2 .10 .20
❑ DR1222 Dark Scorpion Gorg the Strong .10 .20
❑ DR1223 Dark Scorpion Meanae the Thorn .10 .20
❑ DR1224 Outstanding Dog Marron .10 .20
❑ DR1225 Great Maju Garzett .10 .20
❑ DR1226 Iron Blacksmith Kotetsu .10 .20
❑ DR1227 Goblin of Greed .10 .20
❑ DR1228 Mefist the Infernal General .10 .20
❑ DR1229 Vilepawn Archfiend .10 .20
❑ DR1230 Shadowknight Archfiend .10 .20
❑ DR1231 Darkbishop Archfiend .10 .20
❑ DR1232 Desrook Archfiend .10 .20
❑ DR1233 Infernalqueen Archfiend .10 .20
❑ DR1234 Terrorking Archfiend (SR) 4.00 8.00
❑ DR1235 Skull Archfiend of Lightning (UR) 7.00 14.00
❑ DR1236 Metallizing Parasite Lunatite .10 .20
❑ DR1237 Tsukuyomi .10 .20
❑ DR1238 Mudora (R) 1.00 2.00
❑ DR1239 Keldo .10 .20
❑ DR1240 Kelbek .10 .20
❑ DR1241 Zolga .10 .20
❑ DR1242 Agido .10 .20
❑ DR1243 Legendary Flame Lord (R) 2.00 4.00
❑ DR1244 Dark Master Zorc (SR) 5.00 9.00
❑ DR1245 Spell Reproduction .10 .20
❑ DR1246 Dragged Down into the Grave .10 .20
❑ DR1247 Incandescent Ordeal .10 .20
❑ DR1248 Contract with the Abyss .10 .20
❑ DR1249 Contract with the Dark Master .10 .20
❑ DR1250 Falling Down .10 .20
❑ DR1251 Checkmate .10 .20
❑ DR1252 Cestus of Dagla .10 .20
❑ DR1253 Final Countdown .10 .20
❑ DR1254 Archfiend's Oath .10 .20
❑ DR1255 Mustering of the Dark Scorpions .10 .20
❑ DR1256 Pandemonium (R) 1.00 2.00
❑ DR1257 Altar for Tribute .10 .20
❑ DR1258 Frozen Soul .10 .20
❑ DR1259 Battle-Scarred .10 .20
❑ DR1260 Dark Scorpion Combination .10 .20
❑ DR1261 Archfiend's Roar .10 .20
❑ DR1262 Dice Re-Roll .10 .20
❑ DR1263 Spell Vanishing (R) 2.00 4.00
❑ DR1264 Sakuretsu 2.00 4.00
❑ DR1265 Ray of Hope .10 .20
❑ DR1266 Blast Held by a Tribute (UR) 5.00 10.00
❑ DR1267 Judgment of Anubis (UR) 5.00 10.00

2005 Yu-Gi-Oh Dark Revelation 2

Complete Set (224) 110.00 185.00
Booster Box (24 packs) 70.00 90.00
Booster Pack (13 cards) 3.75 4.00

❑ DR2001 Ojama Yellow .10 .20
❑ DR2002 Ojama Black .10 .20
❑ DR2003 Soul Tiger .10 .20
❑ DR2004 Big Koala .10 .20
❑ DR2005 Des Kangaroo .10 .20
❑ DR2006 Crimson Ninja .10 .20
❑ DR2007 Strike Ninja (UR) 6.00 12.00
❑ DR2008 Gale Lizard .10 .20
❑ DR2009 Spirit of the Pot of Greed .10 .20
❑ DR2010 Chopman the Desperate Outlaw .10 .20
❑ DR2011 Sasuke Samurai #3 .10 .20
❑ DR2012 D.D. Scout Plane (R) 2.00 4.00
❑ DR2013 Berserk Gorilla (R) 1.00 2.00
❑ DR2014 Freed the Brave Wanderer (SR) 3.00 6.00
❑ DR2015 Coach Goblin .10 .20
❑ DR2016 Witch Doctor of Chaos .10 .20
❑ DR2017 Chaos Necromancer .10 .20
❑ DR2018 Chaosrider Gustaph (SR) 3.00 6.00
❑ DR2019 Inferno .10 .20
❑ DR2020 Fenrir (R) 1.00 2.00
❑ DR2021 Gigantes .10 .20
❑ DR2022 Silpheed .10 .20

YU-GI-OH

❑ DR2023 Chaos Sorcerer .10 .20
❑ DR2024 Gren Maju Da Eiza .10 .20
❑ DR2025 Black Luster Soldier - EOB (UR) 7.00 15.00
❑ DR2026 Drillago (R) 1.00 2.00
❑ DR2027 Lekunga (R) 1.00 2.00
❑ DR2028 Lord Poison .10 .20
❑ DR2029 Bowganian .10 .20
❑ DR2030 Granadora .10 .20
❑ DR2031 Fuhma Shuriken .10 .20
❑ DR2032 Heart of the Underdog .10 .20
❑ DR2033 Wild Nature's Release (R) 1.00 2.00
❑ DR2034 Ojama Delta Hurricane!! .10 .20
❑ DR2035 Stumbling .10 .20
❑ DR2036 Chaos End .10 .20
❑ DR2037 Yellow Luster Shield .10 .20
❑ DR2038 Chaos Greed .10 .20
❑ DR2039 D.D. Designator (SR) 3.00 6.00
❑ DR2040 D.D. Borderline .10 .20
❑ DR2041 Recycle .10 .20
❑ DR2042 Primal Seed .10 .20
❑ DR2043 Thunder Crash .10 .20
❑ DR2044 Dimension Distortion .10 .20
❑ DR2045 Reload (SR) 3.00 6.00
❑ DR2046 Soul Absorption .10 .20
❑ DR2047 Big Burn (SR) 3.00 6.00
❑ DR2048 Blasting the Ruins .10 .20
❑ DR2049 Cursed Seal of the Forbidden Spell .10 .20
❑ DR2050 Tower of Babel .10 .20
❑ DR2051 Spatial Collapse .10 .20
❑ DR2052 Chain Disappearance (R) 1.00 2.00
❑ DR2053 Zero Gravity .10 .20
❑ DR2054 Dark Mirror Force (SR) 5.00 8.00
❑ DR2055 Energy Drain .10 .20
❑ DR2056 Chaos Emperor Dragon - EOE (UR) 14.00 22.00
❑ DR2057 Giga Gagagigo .10 .20
❑ DR2058 Mad Dog of Darkness .10 .20
❑ DR2059 Neo Bug .10 .20
❑ DR2060 Sea Serpent Warrior of Darkness .20 .40
❑ DR2061 Terrorking Salmon .10 .20
❑ DR2062 Blazing Inpachi .10 .20
❑ DR2063 Burning Algae .10 .20
❑ DR2064 The Thing in the Crater .10 .20
❑ DR2065 Molten Zombie .10 .20
❑ DR2066 Dark Magician of Chaos (UR) 25.00 38.00
❑ DR2067 Gora Turtle of Illusion .10 .20
❑ DR2068 Manticore of Darkness (SR) 3.00 7.00
❑ DR2069 Stealth Bird (R) 1.00 2.00
❑ DR2070 Sacred Crane .10 .20
❑ DR2071 Enraged Battle Ox .10 .20
❑ DR2072 Don Turtle .10 .20
❑ DR2073 Balloon Lizard .10 .20
❑ DR2074 Dark Driceratops .10 .20
❑ DR2075 Hyper Hammerhead .10 .20
❑ DR2076 Black Tyranno (UR) 5.00 10.00
❑ DR2077 Anti-Aircraft Flower .10 .20
❑ DR2078 Prickle Fairy .10 .20
❑ DR2079 Pinch Hopper .10 .20
❑ DR2080 Skull-Mark Ladybug .10 .20
❑ DR2081 Insect Princess (UR) 5.00 10.00
❑ DR2082 Amphibious Bugroth MK-3 (R) 1.00 2.00
❑ DR2083 Torpedo Fish .10 .20
❑ DR2084 Levia-Dragon - Daedalus (UR) 5.00 12.00
❑ DR2085 Orca Mega-Fortress of Drknss (R) 1.00 2.00
❑ DR2086 Cannonball Spear Shellfish .10 .20
❑ DR2087 Mataza the Zapper (R) 1.00 2.00
❑ DR2088 Guardian Angel Joan (SR) 4.00 8.00
❑ DR2089 Manju of the Ten Thousand Hands .10 .20
❑ DR2090 Getsu Fuhma .10 .20
❑ DR2091 Ryu Kokki (SR) 9.00 17.00
❑ DR2092 Gryphon's Feather Duster .10 .20
❑ DR2093 Stray Lambs (R) 1.00 2.00
❑ DR2094 Smashing Ground 5.00 9.00
❑ DR2095 Dimension Fusion (SR) 5.00 10.00
❑ DR2096 Dedication Light and Darkness (SR) 3.00 6.00
❑ DR2097 Salvage .10 .20
❑ DR2098 Ultra Evolution Pill .10 .20
❑ DR2099 Multiplication of Ants .10 .20
❑ DR2100 Earth Chant .10 .20
❑ DR2101 Jade Insect Whistle .10 .20
❑ DR2102 Destruction Ring .10 .20
❑ DR2103 Fiend's Hand Mirror .10 .20
❑ DR2104 Compulsory Evacuation Device (R) 1.00 2.00
❑ DR2105 A Hero Emerges .10 .20
❑ DR2106 Self-Destruct Button .10 .20
❑ DR2107 Curse of Darkness (R) 1.00 2.00
❑ DR2108 Begone, Knave! .10 .20
❑ DR2109 DNA Transplant .10 .20
❑ DR2110 Robbin' Zombie (R) 1.00 2.00
❑ DR2111 Trap Jammer (R) 1.00 2.00
❑ DR2112 Invader of Darkness (UR) 5.00 11.00
❑ DR2113 Gogiga Gagagigo .10 .20
❑ DR2114 Warrior of Zera .10 .20
❑ DR2115 Sealmaster Meisei .10 .20
❑ DR2116 Mystic Shine Ball .10 .20
❑ DR2117 Metal Armored Bug .10 .20
❑ DR2118 The Agent of Judgment - Saturn (SR) 3.00 6.00
❑ DR2119 The Agent of Wisdom - Mercury .10 .20
❑ DR2120 The Agent of Creation - Venus .10 .20
❑ DR2121 The Agent of Force - Mars .10 .20
❑ DR2122 The Unhappy Girl .10 .20
❑ DR2123 Soul-Absorbing Bone Tower .10 .20
❑ DR2124 The Kick Man .10 .20
❑ DR2125 Vampire Lady .10 .20
❑ DR2126 Stone Statue of the Aztecs (R) 1.00 2.00
❑ DR2127 Rocket Jumper .10 .20
❑ DR2128 Avatar of the Pot .10 .20
❑ DR2129 Legendary Jujitsu Master .10 .20
❑ DR2130 Gear Golem the Moving Fortress (SR) 3.00 6.00
❑ DR2131 KA-2 Des Scissors .10 .20
❑ DR2132 Needle Burrower (R) 1.00 2.00
❑ DR2133 Sonic Jammer .10 .20
❑ DR2134 Blowback Dragon (UR) 5.00 10.00
❑ DR2135 Zaborg the Thunder Monarch (SR) 8.00 15.00
❑ DR2136 Atomic Firefly .10 .20
❑ DR2137 Mermaid Knight (R) 1.00 2.00
❑ DR2138 Piranha Army .10 .20
❑ DR2139 Two Thousand Needles .10 .20
❑ DR2140 Disc Fighter .10 .20
❑ DR2141 Arcane Archer of the Forest .10 .20
❑ DR2142 Lady Ninja Yae .20 .50
❑ DR2143 Goblin King .10 .20
❑ DR2144 Solar Flare Dragon .10 .20
❑ DR2145 White Magician Pikeru .10 .20
❑ DR2146 Archlord Zerato (UR) 5.00 10.00
❑ DR2147 Opti-Camouflage Armor .10 .20
❑ DR2148 Mystik Wok .10 .20
❑ DR2149 Enemy Controller (SR) 9.00 18.00
❑ DR2150 Burst Stream of Destruction (SR) 4.00 10.00
❑ DR2151 Monster Gate .10 .20
❑ DR2152 Amplifier (R) 1.00 2.00
❑ DR2153 Weapon Change .10 .20
❑ DR2154 The Sanctuary in the Sky .10 .20
❑ DR2155 Earthquake .10 .20
❑ DR2156 Talisman of Trap Sealing .10 .20
❑ DR2157 Goblin Thief .10 .20
❑ DR2158 Backfire .10 .20
❑ DR2159 Micro Ray .10 .20
❑ DR2160 Light of Judgment .10 .20
❑ DR2161 Talisman of Spell Sealing .10 .20
❑ DR2162 Wall of Revealing Light .10 .20
❑ DR2163 Solar Ray .10 .20
❑ DR2164 Ninjitsu Art of Transformation .10 .20
❑ DR2165 Beckoning Light .10 .20
❑ DR2166 Draining Shield (R) 1.00 2.00
❑ DR2167 Armor Break .10 .20
❑ DR2168 Mazera DeVille (UR) 5.00 10.00
❑ DR2169 Gigobyte .10 .20
❑ DR2170 Mokey Mokey .10 .20
❑ DR2171 Kozaky .10 .20
❑ DR2172 Fiend Scorpion .10 .20
❑ DR2173 Pharaoh's Servant .10 .20
❑ DR2174 Pharaonic Protector .10 .20
❑ DR2175 Spirit of the Pharaoh (UR) 6.00 11.00
❑ DR2176 Theban Nightmare (R) 1.00 2.00
❑ DR2177 Aswan Apparition .10 .20
❑ DR2178 Protector of the Sanctuary (R) 1.00 2.00
❑ DR2179 Nubian Guard .10 .20
❑ DR2180 Legacy Hunter (SR) 3.00 6.00
❑ DR2181 Desertapir .10 .20
❑ DR2182 Sand Gambler .10 .20
❑ DR2183 3-Hump Lacooda .10 .20
❑ DR2184 Ghost Knight of Jackal (UR) 5.00 10.00
❑ DR2185 Absorbing Kid from the Sky .10 .20
❑ DR2186 Elephant Statue of Blessing .10 .20
❑ DR2187 Elephant Statue of Disaster .10 .20
❑ DR2188 Spirit Caller .10 .20
❑ DR2189 Emissary of the Afterlife (SR) 3.00 6.00
❑ DR2190 Grave Protector .10 .20
❑ DR2191 Double Coston (R) 1.00 2.00
❑ DR2192 Regenerating Mummy .10 .20
❑ DR2193 Night Assailant (R) 1.00 2.00
❑ DR2194 Man-Thro' Tro' .10 .20
❑ DR2195 King of the Swamp .10 .20
❑ DR2196 Emissary of the Oasis .10 .20
❑ DR2197 Special Hurricane (R) 1.00 2.00
❑ DR2198 Order to Charge .10 .20
❑ DR2199 Sword of the Soul-Eater .10 .20
❑ DR2200 Dust Barrier .10 .20
❑ DR2201 Soul Reversal .10 .20
❑ DR2202 Spell Economics (R) 1.00 2.00
❑ DR2203 Blessings of the Nile .10 .20
❑ DR2204 7 .10 .20
❑ DR2205 Level Limit - Area B (R) 1.00 2.00
❑ DR2206 Enchanting Fitting Room .10 .20
❑ DR2207 The Law of the Normal .10 .20
❑ DR2208 Dark Magic Attack (UR) 5.00 10.00
❑ DR2209 Delta Attacker .10 .20
❑ DR2210 Thousand Energy .10 .20
❑ DR2211 Triangle Power .10 .20
❑ DR2212 The Third Sarcophagus .10 .20
❑ DR2213 The Second Sarcophagus .10 .20
❑ DR2214 The First Sarcophagus (SR) 3.00 6.00
❑ DR2215 Dora of Fate .10 .20
❑ DR2216 Judgment of the Desert .10 .20
❑ DR2217 Human-Wave Tactics .10 .20
❑ DR2218 Curse of Anubis (SR) 3.00 6.00
❑ DR2219 Desert Sunlight .10 .20
❑ DR2220 Des Counterblow (R) 1.00 2.00
❑ DR2221 Labyrinth of Nightmare .10 .20
❑ DR2222 Soul Resurrection (R) 1.00 2.00
❑ DR2223 Order to Smash .10 .20
❑ DR2224 The End of Anubis (UR) 5.00 10.00

2005 Yu-Gi-Oh Elemental Energy 1st Edition

Complete Set (60) 130.00 180.00
Booster Box (24 packs) 62.00 85.00
Booster Pack (9 cards) 3.75 4.00

❑ EEN-1 Zure, Knight of Dark World .10 .20
❑ EEN-2 V-Tiger Jet .10 .20
❑ EEN-3 Blade Skater .10 .20
❑ EEN-4 Queen's Knight (UTR) 8.00 20.00
❑ EEN-4 Queen's Knight (R) 1.00 3.00
❑ EEN-5 Jack's Knight (UTR) 6.00 12.00
❑ EEN-5 Jack's Knight (R) 1.00 2.00
❑ EEN-6 King's Knight (UTR) 6.00 12.00
❑ EEN-6 King's Knight (R) 1.00 2.00
❑ EEN-7 Elemental Hero Bladedge (SR) 6.00 12.00
❑ EEN-7 Elemental Hero Bladedge (UTR) 10.00 20.00
❑ EEN-8 Elemental Hero Wildheart .20 .50
❑ EEN-9 Reborn Zombie .10 .20
❑ EEN-10 Chthonian Soldier (UTR) 4.00 8.00
❑ EEN-10 Chthonian Soldier (R) 1.00 2.00
❑ EEN-11 W-Wing Catapult .10 .20
❑ EEN-12 Infernal Incinerator .10 .20
❑ EEN-13 Hydrogeddon .10 .20
❑ EEN-14 Oxygeddon .10 .20
❑ EEN-15 Water Dragon (SR) 6.00 10.00
❑ EEN-15 Water Dragon (UTR) 10.00 20.00
❑ EEN-16 Etoile Cyber .10 .20
❑ EEN-17 B.E.S. Tetran (UTR) 2.00 4.00
❑ EEN-17 B.E.S. Tetran (SR) 1.00 2.00
❑ EEN-18 Nanobreaker .10 .20
❑ EEN-19 Rapid-Fire Magician (R) 1.00 2.00
❑ EEN-19 Rapid-Fire Magician (UTR) 2.00 4.00
❑ EEN-20 Beiige, Vanguard of Dark World .10 .20
❑ EEN-21 Broww, Huntsman of Dark World (UTR) 4.00 9.00
❑ EEN-21 Broww, Huntsman of Dark World (R) 1.00 2.00
❑ EEN-22 Brron, Mad King of Dark World (R) 1.00 2.00
❑ EEN-22 Brron, Mad King of Dark World (UTR) 5.00 10.00
❑ EEN-23 Sillva, Warlord of Dark World (R) 1.00 2.00
❑ EEN-23 Sillva, Warlord of Dark World (UTR) 5.00 10.00
❑ EEN-24 Goldd, Wu-Lord of Dark World (UTR) 10.00 20.00
❑ EEN-24 Goldd, Wu-Lord of Dark World (SR) 6.00 10.00
❑ EEN-25 Scarr, Scout of Dark World .10 .20
❑ EEN-26 Familiar-Possessed - Aussa .10 .20
❑ EEN-27 Familiar-Possessed - Eria .10 .20
❑ EEN-28 Familiar-Possessed - Hiita .10 .20
❑ EEN-29 Familiar-Possessed - Wynn .10 .20
❑ EEN-30 VW-Tiger Catapult .10 .20
❑ EEN-31 VWXYZ-Dragon Catapult Cannon (SR) 3.00 6.00
❑ EEN-31 VWXYZ-Dragon Catapult Cannon (UTR) 6.00 12.00
❑ EEN-32 Cyber Blader (SR) 3.00 7.00
❑ EEN-32 Cyber Blader (UTR) 8.00 15.00
❑ EEN-33 Elemental Hero Rampart Blaster (UR) 7.00 15.00
❑ EEN-33 Elemental Hero Rampart (UTR) 15.00 25.00
❑ EEN-34 Elemental Hero Tempest (UR) 9.00 18.00
❑ EEN-34 Elemental Hero Tempest (UTR) 12.00 25.00
❑ EEN-35 Elemental Hero Wildedge (UTR) 15.00 30.00
❑ EEN-35 Elemental Hero Wildedge (UR) 10.00 20.00
❑ EEN-36 Elemental Hero Shining Flare Wingman (UTR) 15.00 30.00
❑ EEN-36 Elemental Hero Shining Flare Wingman (UR) 10.00 20.00
❑ EEN-37 Pot of Avarice (UTR) 15.00 25.00
❑ EEN-37 Pot of Avarice (SR) 5.00 10.00
❑ EEN-38 Dark World Lightning .10 .20
❑ EEN-39 Level Modulation .10 .20
❑ EEN-40 Ojamagic .10 .20
❑ EEN-41 Ojamuscle .10 .20
❑ EEN-42 Feather Shot (UTR) 2.00 4.00
❑ EEN-42 Feather Shot (R) 1.00 2.00
❑ EEN-43 Bonding - H2O .10 .20
❑ EEN-44 Chthonian Alliance (R) 1.00 2.00
❑ EEN-44 Chthonian Alliance (UTR) 2.00 5.00
❑ EEN-45 Armed Changer (R) 1.00 2.00
❑ EEN-45 Armed Changer (UTR) 2.00 5.00
❑ EEN-46 Branch! .10 .20
❑ EEN-47 Boss Rush .10 .20
❑ EEN-48 Gateway to Dark World .20 .50
❑ EEN-49 Hero Barrier (UTR) 2.00 5.00
❑ EEN-49 Hero Barrier (R) 1.00 2.00
❑ EEN-50 Chthonian Blast (R) 1.00 2.00
❑ EEN-50 Chthonian Blast (UTR) 2.00 5.00
❑ EEN-51 The Forces of Darkness .10 .20
❑ EEN-52 Dark Deal .10 .20
❑ EEN-53 Simultaneous Loss .10 .20
❑ EEN-54 Weed Out .10 .20
❑ EEN-55 The League of Uniform Nomenclature .10 .20
❑ EEN-56 Roll Out! .10 .20
❑ EEN-57 Chthonian Polymer .10 .20
❑ EEN-58 Feather Wind .10 .20
❑ EEN-59 Non-Fusion Area .10 .20
❑ EEN-60 Level Limit - Area A (R) 1.00 2.00
❑ EEN-60 Level Limit - Area A (UTR) 2.00 5.00

2005 Yu-Gi-Oh Flaming Eternity 1st Edition

Comp.Set w/o UTR(60) 150.00 200.00
Complete Set (85) 200.00 300.00
Booster Box (24) 70.00 80.00
Booster Pack (9 cards) 4.00 5.00

❑ FETEN1 Space Mambo .10 .30
❑ FETEN2 Divine Dragon Ragnarok .10 .30
❑ FETEN3 Chu-Ske The Mouse Fighter .10 .30
❑ FETEN4 Insect Knight .10 .30
❑ FETEN5 Sacred Phoenix of Nephthys (UTR) 15.00 30.00
❑ FETEN5 Sacred Phoenix of Nephthys (UR) 10.00 20.00
❑ FETEN6 Hand of Nephthys .10 .30
❑ FETEN7 Ultimate Insect LV5 (R) 1.00 2.00
❑ FETEN7 Ultimate Insect LV5 (UTR) 6.00 12.00
❑ FETEN8 Silent Swordsman LV5 (UR) 12.00 25.00
❑ FETEN8 Silent Swordsman LV5 (UTR) 15.00 30.00
❑ FETEN9 Granmarg the Rock Monarch (SR) 3.00 6.00
❑ FETEN9 Granmarg the Rock Monarch (UTR) 7.00 15.00
❑ FETEN10 Element Valkyrie .10 .30
❑ FETEN11 Element Doom .10 .30
❑ FETEN12 Maji-Gire Panda .10 .30
❑ FETEN13 Catnipped Kitty .10 .30
❑ FETEN14 Behemoth the King of all Animals (SR) 2.00 5.00
❑ FETEN14 Behemoth the King of all Animals (UTR) 8.00 18.00
❑ FETEN15 Big-Tusked Mammoth (UTR) 5.00 10.00
❑ FETEN15 Big-Tusked Mammoth (R) 1.00 2.00
❑ FETEN16 Kangaroo Champ .10 .30
❑ FETEN17 Hyena .10 .30
❑ FETEN18 Blade Rabbit .10 .30
❑ FETEN19 Mecha-Dog Marron .10 .30
❑ FETEN20 Blast Magician (SR) 6.00 12.00
❑ FETEN20 Blast Magician (UTR) 10.00 20.00
❑ FETEN21 Chiron the Mage (UTR) 7.00 14.00
❑ FETEN21 Chiron the Mage (R) 1.00 2.00
❑ FETEN22 Gearfried the Swordsmaster (UR) 10.00 20.00
❑ FETEN22 Gearfried the Swordsman (UTR) 15.00 30.00
❑ FETEN23 Armed Samurai - Ben Kei .10 .30
❑ FETEN24 Shadowslayer (R) 1.00 2.00
❑ FETEN24 Shadowslayer (UTR) 5.00 10.00
❑ FETEN25 Golem Sentry .10 .30
❑ FETEN26 Abare Ushioni .10 .30
❑ FETEN27 The Light - Hex-Sealed Fusion .10 .30
❑ FETEN28 The Dark - Hex-Sealed Fusion .10 .30
❑ FETEN29 The Earth - Hex-Sealed Fusion .10 .30
❑ FETEN30 Whirlwind Prodigy .10 .30
❑ FETEN31 Flame Ruler .10 .30
❑ FETEN32 Firebird .10 .30
❑ FETEN33 Rescue Cat .10 .30
❑ FETEN34 Brain Jacker (UTR) 6.00 12.00
❑ FETEN34 Brain Jacker (R) 1.00 2.00
❑ FETEN35 Gatling Dragon (UTR) 10.00 20.00
❑ FETEN35 Gatling Dragon (UR) 6.00 12.00
❑ FETEN36 King Dragun (SR) 7.00 15.00
❑ FETEN36 King Dragun (UTR) 10.00 20.00
❑ FETEN37 A Feather of the Phoenix (UTR) 10.00 18.00
❑ FETEN37 A Feather of the Phoenix (SR) 3.00 6.00
❑ FETEN38 Poison Fangs .10 .30
❑ FETEN39 Spell Absorption (R) 1.00 2.00
❑ FETEN39 Spell Absorption (UTR) 7.00 15.00
❑ FETEN40 Lightning Vortex (SR) 7.00 15.00
❑ FETEN40 Lightning Vortex (UTR) 15.00 30.00
❑ FETEN41 Meteor of Destruction (UTR) 6.00 12.00
❑ FETEN41 Meteor of Destruction (R) 1.00 2.00
❑ FETEN42 Swords of Concealing Light (R) 1.00 2.00
❑ FETEN42 Swords of Concealing Light (UTR) 5.00 10.00
❑ FETEN43 Spiral Spear Strike (UTR) 4.00 8.00
❑ FETEN43 Spiral Spear Strike (R) 1.00 2.00
❑ FETEN44 Release Restraint .10 .30
❑ FETEN45 Centrifugal Field .10 .30
❑ FETEN46 Fulfillment of the Contract .10 .30
❑ FETEN47 Re-Fusion .10 .30
❑ FETEN48 The Big March of Animals .10 .30
❑ FETEN49 Cross Counter (UTR) 5.00 10.00
❑ FETEN49 Cross Counter (R) 1.00 2.00
❑ FETEN50 Pole Position .10 .30
❑ FETEN51 Penalty Game! (UTR) 7.00 15.00
❑ FETEN51 Penalty Game! (R) 1.00 2.00
❑ FETEN52 Threatening Roar .10 .30
❑ FETEN53 Phoenix Wing Wind (UTR) 10.00 20.00
❑ FETEN53 Phoenix Wing Wind Blast (R) 4.00 8.00
❑ FETEN54 Good Goblin Housekeeping .10 .30
❑ FETEN55 Beast Soul Swap .10 .30
❑ FETEN56 Assault on GHQ (R) 1.00 2.00
❑ FETEN56 Assault on GHQ (UTR) 4.00 8.00
❑ FETEN57 D.D. Dynamite .10 .30
❑ FETEN58 Deck Devastation Virus (SR) 7.00 14.00
❑ FETEN58 Deck Devastation (UTR) 10.00 20.00
❑ FETEN59 Elemental Burst .20 .50
❑ FETEN60 Forced Ceasefire (UTR) 7.00 15.00
❑ FETEN60 Forced Ceasefire (R) 1.00 2.00

2005 Yu-Gi-Oh The Lost Millennium 1st Edition

Complete Set (85) 200.00 275.00
Booster Box (24 packs) 70.00 90.00
Booster Pack (9 cards) 3.75 4.50
SE Pack 10.00 14.00

❑ SE-1 Invader of Darkness 1.00 2.00
❑ SE-2 Chaos Emperor Dragon 6.00 12.00
❑ SE-3 Mazera Deville 1.00 2.00
❑ SE-4 End of Anubis 2.00 4.00
❑ TLM-1 Elemental Hero Avian .20 .50
❑ TLM-2 Elemental Hero Burstinatrix .20 .50
❑ TLM-3 Elemental Hero Clayman .20 .50
❑ TLM-4 Elemental Hero Sparkman .20 .50
❑ TLM-5 Winged Kuriboh (UTR) 20.00 35.00
❑ TLM-5 Winged Kuriboh (SR) 7.00 15.00
❑ TLM-6 Ancient Gear Golem (UTR) 10.00 20.00
❑ TLM-6 Ancient Gear Golem (UR) 9.00 18.00
❑ TLM-7 Ancient Gear Beast (R) 1.00 2.00
❑ TLM-7 Ancient Gear Beast (UTR) 6.00 10.00
❑ TLM-8 Ancient Gear Soldier .10 .30
❑ TLM-9 Millennium Scorpion (UTR) 6.00 12.00
❑ TLM-9 Millennium Scorpion (R) 3.00 7.00
❑ TLM-10 Ultimate Insect LV7 (SR) 5.00 10.00
❑ TLM-10 Ultimate Insect LV7 (UTR) 10.00 20.00
❑ TLM-11 Lost Guardian .10 .30
❑ TLM-12 Hieracosphinx (SR) 5.00 10.00
❑ TLM-12 Hieracosphinx (UTR) 10.00 20.00
❑ TLM-13 Criosphinx (UTR) 6.00 12.00
❑ TLM-13 Criosphinx (R) 1.00 2.00
❑ TLM-14 Moai Interceptor Cannons .10 .30
❑ TLM-15 Megarock Dragon (UTR) 10.00 20.00
❑ TLM-15 Megarock Dragon (SR) 5.00 10.00
❑ TLM-16 Dummy Golem .30 .75
❑ TLM-17 Grave Ohja (R) 1.00 2.00
❑ TLM-17 Grave Ohja (UTR) 6.00 12.00
❑ TLM-18 Mine Golem .10 .30
❑ TLM-19 Monk Fighter .10 .30
❑ TLM-20 Master Monk (SR) 3.00 6.00
❑ TLM-20 Master Monk (UTR) 8.00 15.00
❑ TLM-21 Guardian Statue .30 .75
❑ TLM-22 Medusa Worm .30 1.00
❑ TLM-23 D.D. Survivor (R) 3.00 7.00
❑ TLM-23 D.D. Survivor (UTR) 9.00 18.00
❑ TLM-24 Mid Shield Gardna (UTR) 15.00 25.00
❑ TLM-24 Mid Shield Gardna (R) 1.00 2.00
❑ TLM-25 White Ninja .30 .75
❑ TLM-26 Aussa the Earth Charmer .10 .30
❑ TLM-27 Eria the Water Charmer .10 .30
❑ TLM-28 Hiita the Fire Charmer .10 .30
❑ TLM-29 Wynn the Wind Charmer .10 .30
❑ TLM-30 Batteryman AA .10 .30
❑ TLM-31 Des Wombat .30 .75
❑ TLM-32 King of the Skull Servants .10 .30
❑ TLM-33 Reshef the Dark Being (UR) 15.00 25.00
❑ TLM-33 Reshef the Dark Being (UTR) 20.00 30.00
❑ TLM-34 Elemental Mistress Doriado (UTR) 9.00 18.00
❑ TLM-34 Elemental Mistress Doriado (R) 2.00 5.00
❑ TLM-35 Elemental Hero Flame Wingman (UR) 5.00 10.00
❑ TLM-35 Elemental Hero Flame Wingman (UTR) 10.00 20.00
❑ TLM-36 Elemental Hero Thunder Giant (UTR) 8.00 15.00
❑ TLM-36 Elemental Hero Thunder Giant (UR) 5.00 10.00
❑ TLM-37 Card of Sanctity (UTR) 8.00 15.00
❑ TLM-37 Card of Sanctity (SR) 3.00 6.00
❑ TLM-38 Brain Control (UTR) 10.00 20.00
❑ TLM-38 Brain Control (SR) 9.00 18.00
❑ TLM-39 Gift of the Martyr .10 .30
❑ TLM-40 Double Attack .10 .30
❑ TLM-41 Battery Charger .10 .30
❑ TLM-42 Kaminote Blow .10 .30
❑ TLM-43 Doriado's Blessing .10 .30
❑ TLM-44 Final Ritual of the Ancients .10 .30
❑ TLM-45 Legendary Black Belt (UTR) 6.00 12.00
❑ TLM-45 Legendary Black Belt (R) 1.00 2.00
❑ TLM-46 Nitro Unit (R) 2.00 5.00
❑ TLM-46 Nitro Unit (UTR) 7.00 15.00
❑ TLM-47 Shifting Shadows .10 .30
❑ TLM-48 Impenetrable Formation .10 .30
❑ TLM-49 Hero Signal (R) 1.00 2.00
❑ TLM-49 Hero Signal (UTR) 7.00 15.00
❑ TLM-50 Pikeru's Second Sight .10 .30
❑ TLM-51 Minefield Eruption .10 .30
❑ TLM-52 Kozaky's Self-Destruct Button (R) 1.00 2.00
❑ TLM-52 Kozaky's Self-Destruct Button (UTR) 6.00 12.00
❑ TLM-53 Mispolymerization .30 .75
❑ TLM-54 Level Conversion Lab .30 .75
❑ TLM-55 Rock Bombardment .10 .30
❑ TLM-56 Grave Lure .10 .30
❑ TLM-57 Token Feastevil (UTR) 6.00 12.00
❑ TLM-57 Token Feastevil (R) 2.00 5.00
❑ TLM-58 Spell-Stopping Statute (R) 2.00 4.00
❑ TLM-58 Spell-Stopping Statute (UTR) 6.00 12.00
❑ TLM-59 Royal Surrender (UTR) 10.00 20.00
❑ TLM-59 Royal Surrender (R) 1.00 2.00
❑ TLM-60 Lone Wolf .10 .30

2006 Yu-Gi-Oh Cyberdark Impact 1st Edition

Complete Set (60) 100.00 160.00
Booster Box (24 packs) 75.00 90.00
Booster Pack (9 cards) 3.50 4.50

❑ CDIP1 Cyberdark Horn (SR) 2.00 5.00
❑ CDIP1 Cyberdark Horn (ULT) 8.00 15.00
❑ CDIP2 Cyberdark Edge (SR) 4.00 8.00
❑ CDIP2 Cyberdark Edge (ULT) 7.00 15.00
❑ CDIP3 Cyberdark Keel (SR) 3.00 6.00
❑ CDIP3 Cyberdark Keel (ULT) 7.00 15.00
❑ CDIP4 Cyber Ogre .10 .20
❑ CDIP5 Cyber Esper (ULT) 3.00 6.00
❑ CDIP5 Cyber Esper (SR) 10.00 20.00
❑ CDIP6 Allure Queen LV3 .10 .20
❑ CDIP7 Allure Queen LV5 (R) .75 2.00
❑ CDIP7 Allure Queen LV5 (ULT) 4.00 8.00
❑ CDIP8 Allure Queen LV7 (ULT) 10.00 20.00
❑ CDIP8 Allure Queen LV7 (UR) 7.00 15.00
❑ CDIP9 Dark Lucius LV4 .10 .20
❑ CDIP10 Dark Lucius LV6 (ULT) 3.00 7.00
❑ CDIP10 Dark Lucius LV6 (R) .75 2.00
❑ CDIP11 Dark Lucius LV8 (UR) 4.00 7.00
❑ CDIP11 Dark Lucius LV8 (ULT) 7.00 15.00
❑ CDIP12 Stray Asmodian .10 .20
❑ CDIP13 Abaki .10 .20
❑ CDIP14 Flame Ogre .10 .20
❑ CDIP15 Snipe Hunter 2.00 3.00
❑ CDIP16 Blast Asmodian .10 .20
❑ CDIP17 Vanity's Fiend (R) .75 2.00
❑ CDIP17 Vanity's Fiend (ULT) 3.00 5.00
❑ CDIP18 Barrier Statue of the Abyss .10 .20
❑ CDIP19 Barrier Statue of the Torrent .10 .20
❑ CDIP20 Barrier Statue of the Inferno .10 .20
❑ CDIP21 Barrier Statue of the Stormwinds .10 .20
❑ CDIP22 Barrier Statue of the Drought .10 .20
❑ CDIP23 Barrier Statue of the Heavens .10 .20
❑ CDIP24 Vanity's Ruler (ULT) 4.00 10.00
❑ CDIP24 Vanity's Ruler (R) .75 2.00
❑ CDIP25 Iris, the Earth Mother (ULT) 3.00 7.00
❑ CDIP25 Iris, the Earth Mother (R) .75 2.00
❑ CDIP26 Lightning Punisher (R) .75 2.00
❑ CDIP26 Lightning Punisher (ULT) 3.00 7.00
❑ CDIP27 Queen's Bodyguard .10 .20
❑ CDIP28 Combo Fighter .10 .20
❑ CDIP29 Combo Master (ULT) 3.00 7.00
❑ CDIP29 Combo Master (R) .75 2.00
❑ CDIP30 Man Beast of Ares .10 .20
❑ CDIP31 Rampaging Rhynos (ULT) 3.00 7.00
❑ CDIP31 Rampaging Rhynos (R) .75 2.00
❑ CDIP32 Storm Shooter (ULT) 7.00 15.00
❑ CDIP32 Storm Shooter (SR) 3.00 6.00
❑ CDIP33 Alien Infiltrator .10 .20
❑ CDIP34 Alien Mars .10 .20
❑ CDIP35 Cyberdark Dragon (UR) 6.00 12.00
❑ CDIP35 Cyberdark Dragon (ULT) 10.00 20.00
❑ CDIP36 Cyber Ogre 2 (UR) 12.00 20.00
❑ CDIP36 Cyber Ogre 2 (ULT) 15.00 28.00
❑ CDIP37 Corruption Cell A .10 .20
❑ CDIP38 Flash of the Forbidden Spell (R) .75 2.00
❑ CDIP38 Flash of the Forbidden Spell(ULT) 3.00 7.00
❑ CDIP39 Ritual Foregone .10 .20
❑ CDIP40 Instant Fusion .10 .20
❑ CDIP41 Counter Cleaner .10 .20
❑ CDIP42 Linear Accelerator Cannon .10 .20
❑ CDIP43 Chain Strike .10 .20
❑ CDIP44 Miraculous Rebirth (ULT) 4.00 8.00
❑ CDIP44 Miraculous Rebirth (R) .75 2.00
❑ CDIP45 Mystical Wind Typhoon .10 .20
❑ CDIP46 Level Down!? .10 .20
❑ CDIP47 Degenerate Circuit (R) .75 2.00
❑ CDIP47 Degenerate Circuit (ULT) 4.00 8.00
❑ CDIP48 Senet Switch .10 .20
❑ CDIP49 Blasting Fuse (R) .75 2.00
❑ CDIP49 Blasting Fuse (ULT) 4.00 8.00
❑ CDIP50 Straight Flush .10 .20
❑ CDIP51 Justi-Break .10 .20
❑ CDIP52 Dimensional Inversion (ULT) 4.00 8.00
❑ CDIP52 Dimensional Inversion (R) .75 2.00
❑ CDIP53 Chain Healing .10 .20
❑ CDIP54 Chain Detonation .10 .20
❑ CDIP55 Byroad Sacrifice .10 .20
❑ CDIP56 Trojan Blast (ULT) 5.00 10.00
❑ CDIP56 Trojan Blast (SR) 2.00 4.00
❑ CDIP57 Accumulated Fortune .10 .20
❑ CDIP58 Cyber Shadow Gardna (SR) 4.00 8.00
❑ CDIP58 Cyber Shadow Gardna (ULT) 10.00 20.00
❑ CDIP59 Vanity's Call .10 .20
❑ CDIP60 Black Horn of Heaven (R) .75 2.00
❑ CDIP60 Black Horn of Heaven (ULT) 5.00 10.00

2006 Yu-Gi-Oh Dark Revelation 3

Complete Set (240) 250.00 300.00
Booster Box (24 packs) 45.00 65.00
Booster Pack (12 cards) 2.00 3.00

❑ DR3001 Charcoal Inpachi (R) 1.00 2.00
❑ DR3002 Neo Aqua Madoor .10 .20
❑ DR3003 Skull Dog Marron .10 .20
❑ DR3004 Goblin Calligrapher .10 .20
❑ DR3005 Ultimate Insect LV1 (R) 1.00 2.00
❑ DR3006 Horus, Black Flame Dragon LV4 (R) 1.00 2.00
❑ DR3007 Horus, Black Flame Dragon LV6 (SR) 4.00 8.00
❑ DR3008 Horus, Black Flame Dragon LV8 (UR) 6.00 12.00
❑ DR3009 Dark Mimic LV1 .10 .20
❑ DR3010 Dark Mimic LV3 (R) .40 1.00
❑ DR3011 Mystic Swordsman LV2 (R) 1.00 2.00
❑ DR3012 Mystic Swordsman LV4 (UR) 4.00 8.00
❑ DR3013 Armed Dragon LV3 .10 .20
❑ DR3014 Armed Dragon LV5 (R) 1.00 2.00
❑ DR3015 Armed Dragon LV7 (UR) 4.00 8.00
❑ DR3016 Horus' Servant .10 .20
❑ DR3017 Red-Eyes B. Chick .10 .20
❑ DR3018 Malice Doll of Demise .10 .20
❑ DR3019 Ninja Grandmaster Sasuke (R) .40 1.00
❑ DR3020 Rafflesia Seduction (R) .40 1.00
❑ DR3021 Ultimate Baseball Kid .10 .20
❑ DR3022 Mobius the Frost Monarch (SR) 4.00 8.00
❑ DR3023 Element Dragon .10 .20
❑ DR3024 Element Soldier .10 .20
❑ DR3025 Howling Insect .10 .20
❑ DR3026 Masked Dragon .10 .20
❑ DR3027 Mind on Air (R) .40 1.00
❑ DR3028 Unshaven Angler .10 .20
❑ DR3029 The Trojan Horse .10 .20
❑ DR3030 Nobleman-Eater Bug .10 .20
❑ DR3031 Enraged Muka Muka .10 .20
❑ DR3032 Hade-Hane .10 .20
❑ DR3033 Penumbral Soldier Lady (SR) 2.00 5.00
❑ DR3034 Ojama King (R) 1.00 2.00
❑ DR3035 Master of OZ (R) 1.00 3.00
❑ DR3036 Sanwitch .10 .20
❑ DR3037 Dark Factory of Mass Production .10 .20
❑ DR3038 Hammer Shot (R) .40 1.00
❑ DR3039 Mind Wipe .10 .20

- DR3040 Abyssal Designator .10 .20
- DR3041 Level Up! .10 .20
- DR3042 Inferno Fire Blast (UR) 3.00 7.00
- DR3043 Ectoplasmer (SR) 2.00 4.00
- DR3044 The Graveyard in the 4th Dimension .10 .20
- DR3045 Two-Man Cell Battle .10 .20
- DR3046 Big Wave Small Wave .10 .20
- DR3047 Fusion Weapon .10 .20
- DR3048 Ritual Weapon .10 .20
- DR3049 Taunt .10 .20
- DR3050 Absolute End .10 .20
- DR3051 Spirit Barrier (R) 1.00 2.00
- DR3052 Ninjitsu Art of Decoy .10 .20
- DR3053 Enervating Mist (R) .40 1.00
- DR3054 Heavy Slump .10 .20
- DR3055 Greed (SR) 1.00 2.00
- DR3056 Mind Crush .10 .20
- DR3057 Null and Void (SR) 2.00 4.00
- DR3058 Gorgon's Eye .10 .20
- DR3059 Cemetery Bomb .10 .20
- DR3060 Hallowed Life Barrier (SR) 2.00 4.00
- DR3061 Woodborg Inpachi .10 .20
- DR3062 Mighty Guard .10 .20
- DR3063 Bokoichi the Freightening Car .10 .20
- DR3064 Harpie Girl .10 .20
- DR3065 The Creator (UR) 3.00 5.00
- DR3066 The Creator Incarnate .10 .20
- DR3067 Ultimate Insect LV3 (R) 1.00 2.00
- DR3068 Mystic Swordsman LV6 (UR) 6.00 13.00
- DR3069 Silent Swordsman LV3 (UR) 6.00 12.00
- DR3070 Nightmare Penguin .10 .20
- DR3071 Heavy Mech Support Platform .10 .20
- DR3072 Perfect Machine King (UR) 4.00 10.00
- DR3073 Element Magician .10 .20
- DR3074 Element Saurus .10 .20
- DR3075 Roc from the Valley of Haze .10 .20
- DR3076 Sasuke Samurai #4 (R) 1.00 2.00
- DR3077 Harpie Lady 1 .10 .20
- DR3078 Harpie Lady 2 .10 .20
- DR3079 Harpie Lady 3 .10 .20
- DR3080 Raging Flame Sprite .10 .20
- DR3081 Thestalos the Firestorm Monarch (SR)1.00 2.00
- DR3082 Eagle Eye .10 .20
- DR3083 Tactical Espionage Expert .10 .20
- DR3084 Invasion of Flames .10 .20
- DR3085 Creeping Doom Manta .10 .20
- DR3086 Pitch-Black Warwolf .10 .20
- DR3087 Mirage Dragon .10 .20
- DR3088 Gaia Soul the Combustible Collective (R).40 1.00
- DR3089 Fox Fire .10 .20
- DR3090 Big Core (SR) 2.00 4.00
- DR3091 Fusilier Dragon, the Dual-Mode Beast (R)1.00 3.00
- DR3092 Dekoichi the Battlechanted Locomotive (R) 1.00 2.00
- DR3093 A-Team: Trap Disposal Unit (R) .40 1.00
- DR3094 Homunculus the Alchemic Being .10 .20
- DR3095 Dark Blade the Dragon Knight (R) 1.00 2.00
- DR3096 Mokey Mokey King .10 .20
- DR3097 Serial Spell (R) .10 .20
- DR3098 Harpies' Hunting Ground .10 .20
- DR3099 Triangle Ecstasy Spark (SR) 1.00 2.00
- DR3100 Necklace of Command (R) .40 1.00
- DR3101 Machine Duplication (R) .40 1.00
- DR3102 Flint (R) .10 .20
- DR3103 Mokey Mokey Smackdown .10 .20
- DR3104 Back to Square One .10 .20
- DR3105 Monster Reincarnation (SR) 2.00 4.00
- DR3106 Ballista of Rampart Smashing .10 .20
- DR3107 Lighten the Load .10 .20
- DR3108 Malice Dispersion .10 .20
- DR3109 Tragedy (SR) 2.00 4.00
- DR3110 Divine Wrath (SR) 2.00 4.00
- DR3111 Xing Zhen Hu .10 .20
- DR3112 Rare Metalmorph (R) .40 1.00
- DR3113 Fruits of Kozaky's Studies .10 .20
- DR3114 Mind Haxorz .10 .20
- DR3115 Fuh-Rin-Ka-Zan .10 .20
- DR3116 Chain Burst (R) 1.00 3.00
- DR3117 Pikeru's Circle of Enchantment (SR) 3.00 6.00
- DR3118 Spell Purification .10 .20
- DR3119 Astral Barrier .10 .20
- DR3120 Covering Fire (R) .40 1.00
- DR3121 Space Mambo .10 .20
- DR3122 Divine Dragon Ragnarok .10 .20
- DR3123 Chu-Ske the Mouse Fighter .10 .20
- DR3124 Insect Knight .10 .20
- DR3125 Sacred Phoenix of Nephthys (UR) 10.00 18.00
- DR3126 Hand of Nephthys .10 .20
- DR3127 Ultimate Insect LV5 (R) 1.00 2.00
- DR3128 Silent Swordsman LV5 (UR) 6.00 12.00
- DR3129 Granmarg the Rock Monarch (SR) 1.00 2.00
- DR3130 Element Valkyrie .10 .20
- DR3131 Element Doom .10 .20
- DR3132 Maji-Gire Panda .10 .20
- DR3133 Catnipped Kitty .10 .20
- DR3134 Behemoth the King of All Animals (SR)7.00 15.00
- DR3135 Big-Tusked Mammoth (R) 1.00 2.00
- DR3136 Kangaroo Champ .10 .20
- DR3137 Hyena .10 .20
- DR3138 Blade Rabbit .10 .20
- DR3139 Mecha-Dog Marron .10 .20
- DR3140 Blast Magician (SR) 4.00 8.00
- DR3141 Chiron the Mage (R) 1.00 2.00
- DR3142 Gearfried the Swordmaster (UR) 1.00 3.00
- DR3143 Armed Samurai - Ben Kei .10 .20
- DR3144 Shadowslayer (R) .40 1.00
- DR3145 Golem Sentry .10 .20
- DR3146 Abare Ushioni .10 .20
- DR3147 The Light - Hex-Sealed Fusion .10 .20
- DR3148 The Dark - Hex-Sealed Fusion .10 .20
- DR3149 The Earth - Hex-Sealed Fusion .10 .20
- DR3150 Whirlwind Prodigy .10 .20
- DR3151 Flame Ruler .10 .20
- DR3152 Firebird .10 .20
- DR3153 Rescue Cat .10 .20
- DR3154 Brain Jacker (R) 1.00 2.00
- DR3155 Gatling Dragon (UR) 3.00 6.00
- DR3156 King Dragun (SR) 3.00 6.00
- DR3157 A Feather of the Phoenix (SR) 1.00 3.00
- DR3158 Poison Fangs .10 .20
- DR3159 Spell Absorption (R) 1.00 2.00
- DR3160 Lightning Vortex (SR) 3.00 6.00
- DR3161 Meteor of Destruction (R) .40 1.00
- DR3162 Swords of Concealing Light (R) .40 1.00
- DR3163 Spiral Spear Strike (R) .40 1.00
- DR3164 Release Restraint .10 .20
- DR3165 Centrifugal Field .10 .20
- DR3166 Fulfillment of the Contract .10 .20
- DR3167 Re-Fusion .10 .20
- DR3168 The Big March of Animals .10 .20
- DR3169 Cross Counter (R) .40 1.00
- DR3170 Pole Position .10 .20
- DR3171 Penalty Game! (R) .40 1.00
- DR3172 Threatening Roar .10 .20
- DR3173 Phoenix Wing Wind Blast (R) 3.00 6.00
- DR3174 Good Goblin Housekeeping .10 .20
- DR3175 Beast Soul Swap .10 .20
- DR3176 Assault on GHQ (R) .40 1.00
- DR3177 D.D. Dynamite .10 .20
- DR3178 Deck Devastation Virus (SR) 3.00 6.00
- DR3179 Elemental Burst .10 .20
- DR3180 Forced Ceasefire (R) .40 1.00
- DR3181 Elemental Hero Avian .10 .20
- DR3182 Elemental Hero Burstinatrix .10 .20
- DR3183 Elemental Hero Clayman .10 .20
- DR3184 Elemental Hero Sparkman .10 .20
- DR3185 Winged Kuriboh (SR) 2.00 4.00
- DR3186 Ancient Gear Golem (UR) 7.00 15.00
- DR3187 Ancient Gear Beast (R) 1.00 2.00
- DR3188 Ancient Gear Soldier .10 .20
- DR3189 Millennium Scorpion (R) .40 1.00
- DR3190 Ultimate Insect LV7 (SR) 2.00 4.00
- DR3191 Lost Guardian .10 .20
- DR3192 Hieracosphinx (SR) 2.00 4.00
- DR3193 Criosphinx (R) .40 1.00
- DR3194 Moai Interceptor Cannons .10 .20
- DR3195 Megarock Dragon (SR) 2.00 4.00
- DR3196 Dummy Golem .10 .20
- DR3197 Grave Ohja (R) .40 1.00
- DR3198 Mine Golem .10 .20
- DR3199 Monk Fighter .10 .20
- DR3200 Master Monk (SR) 1.00 3.00
- DR3201 Guardian Statue .10 .20
- DR3202 Medusa Worm .10 .20
- DR3203 D.D. Survivor (R) .40 1.00
- DR3204 Mid Shield Gardna (R) .40 1.00
- DR3205 White Ninja .10 .20
- DR3206 Aussa the Earth Charmer .10 .20
- DR3207 Eria the Water Charmer .10 .20
- DR3208 Hiita the Fire Charmer .10 .20
- DR3209 Wynn the Wind Charmer .10 .20
- DR3210 Batteryman AA .10 .20
- DR3211 Des Wombat .10 .20
- DR3212 King of the Skull Servants .10 .20
- DR3213 Reshef the Dark Being (UR) 3.00 6.00
- DR3214 Elemental Mistress Doriado (R) 1.00 2.00
- DR3215 Elemental Hero Flame Wingman (UR)5.00 10.00
- DR3216 Elemental Hero Thunder Giant (UR) 3.00 6.00
- DR3217 Card of Sanctity (SR) 3.00 6.00
- DR3218 Brain Control (SR) 3.00 6.00
- DR3219 Gift of the Martyr .10 .20
- DR3220 Double Attack .10 .20
- DR3221 Battery Charger .10 .20
- DR3222 Kaminote Blow .10 .20
- DR3223 Doriado's Blessing .10 .20
- DR3224 Final Ritual of the Ancients .10 .20
- DR3225 Legendary Black Bel (R) .40 1.00
- DR3226 Nitro Unit (R) .40 1.00
- DR3227 Shifting Shadows .10 .20
- DR3228 Impenetrable Formation .10 .20
- DR3229 Hero Signal (R) .40 1.00
- DR3230 Pikeru's Second Sight .10 .20
- DR3231 Minefield Eruption .10 .20
- DR3232 Kozaky's Self-Destruct Button (R) .40 1.00
- DR3233 Mispolymerization .10 .20
- DR3234 Level Conversion Lab .10 .20
- DR3235 Rock Bombardment .10 .20
- DR3236 Grave Lure .10 .20
- DR3237 Token Feastevil (R) .60 1.50
- DR3238 Spell-Stopping StatuteRare (R) .40 1.00
- DR3239 Royal Surrender (R) .40 1.00
- DR3240 Lone Wolf .10 .20

2006 Yu-Gi-Oh Enemy of Justice 1st Edition

- Complete Set (60) 90.00 150.00
- Booster Box (24 packs) 50.00 75.00
- Booster Pack (9 cards) 3.50 4.00

- EOJ-1 Destiny Hero - Doom Lord .10 .20
- EOJ-2 Destiny Hero - Captain Tenacious .10 .20
- EOJ-3 Destiny Hero - Diamond Dude (R) 3.00 6.00
- EOJ-3 Destiny Hero - Diamond Dude (UTR) 7.00 15.00
- EOJ-4 Destiny Hero - Dreadmaster (UR) 10.00 20.00
- EOJ-4 Destiny Hero - Dreadmaster (UTR) 15.00 30.00
- EOJ-5 Cyber Tutu .10 .20
- EOJ-6 Cyber Gymnast .10 .20
- EOJ-7 Cyber Prima (SR) 3.00 5.00
- EOJ-7 Cyber Prima (UTR) 5.00 10.00
- EOJ-8 Cyber Kirin .10 .20
- EOJ-9 Cyber Phoenix (UTR) 8.00 18.00
- EOJ-9 Cyber Phoenix (SR) 6.00 12.00
- EOJ-10 Searchlightman .10 .20
- EOJ-11 Victory Viper XX03 (SR) 11.00 18.00
- EOJ-11 Victory Viper XX03 (UTR) 4.00 8.00
- EOJ-12 Swift Birdman Joe .10 .20
- EOJ-13 Harpie's Pet Baby Dragon (R) 1.00 2.00
- EOJ-13 Harpie's Pet Baby Dragon (UTR) 10.00 20.00
- EOJ-14 Majestic Mech - Senku .10 .20
- EOJ-15 Majestic Mech - Ohka (R) 2.00 4.00
- EOJ-15 Majestic Mech - Ohka (UTR) 10.00 18.00
- EOJ-16 Majestic Mech - Goryu (SR) 2.00 4.00
- EOJ-16 Majestic Mech - Goryu (UTR) 6.00 12.00
- EOJ-17 Royal Knight .10 .20
- EOJ-18 Herald of Green Light (UTR) 1.00 2.00
- EOJ-18 Herald of Green Light (R) .40 1.00
- EOJ-19 Herald of Purple Light (UTR) 2.00 4.00
- EOJ-19 Herald of Purple Light (R) 1.00 2.00
- EOJ-20 Bountiful Artemis .10 .20
- EOJ-21 Layard the Liberator .10 .20
- EOJ-22 Banisher of Radiance (UTR) 7.00 14.00
- EOJ-22 Banisher of the Radiance (R) 1.00 3.00
- EOJ-23 Voltanis the Adjudicator (UTR) 10.00 20.00
- EOJ-23 Voltanis the Adjudicator (UR) 7.00 12.00
- EOJ-24 Guard Dog .10 .20
- EOJ-25 Whirlwind Weasel .10 .20
- EOJ-26 Avalanching Aussa .10 .20
- EOJ-27 Raging Eria .10 .20
- EOJ-28 Blazing Hiita .10 .20
- EOJ-29 Storming Wynn .10 .20
- EOJ-30 Batteryman D .10 .20
- EOJ-31 Super-Electro. Voltech Dragon (SR) 2.00 4.00
- EOJ-31 Super-Electro. Voltech Dragon (UTR) 3.00 6.00
- EOJ-32 Elemental Hero Phoenix Enforcer (UR)10.00 20.00
- EOJ-32 Elemental Hero Phoenix Enforcer (UTR)15.00 30.00
- EOJ-33 Elemental Hero Shining Phoenix Enf. (UTR) 15.00 30.00
- EOJ-33 Elemental Hero Shining Phoenix Enf. (UR) 10.00 20.00
- EOJ-34 Elemental Hero Mariner .10 .20
- EOJ-35 Elemental Hero Wild Wingman (UTR)7.00 15.00
- EOJ-35 Elemental Hero Wild Wingman (SR) 5.00 10.00
- EOJ-36 Elemental Hero Necroid Shaman .20 .40
- EOJ-37 Misfortune .10 .20
- EOJ-38 H - Heated Heart .10 .20
- EOJ-39 E - Emergency Call .10 .20
- EOJ-40 R - Righteous Justice .10 .20
- EOJ-41 O - Oversoul .10 .20
- EOJ-42 HERO Flash!! (UTR) 3.00 6.00
- EOJ-42 HERO Flash!! (R) 1.00 2.00
- EOJ-43 Power Capsule .10 .20
- EOJ-44 Celestial Transformation .10 .20
- EOJ-45 Guard Penalty (UTR) 3.00 5.00
- EOJ-45 Guard Penalty (R) 1.00 2.00
- EOJ-46 Grand Convergence .10 .20
- EOJ-47 Dimensional Fissure .10 .20
- EOJ-48 Clock Tower Prison (SR) 2.00 4.00
- EOJ-48 Clock Tower Prison (UTR) 3.00 6.00
- EOJ-49 Life Equilizer (UTR) 3.00 6.00
- EOJ-49 Life Equalizer (R) 1.00 2.00
- EOJ-50 Elemental Recharge .10 .20
- EOJ-51 Destruction of Destiny (R) .40 1.00
- EOJ-51 Destruction of Destiny (UTR) 1.00 3.00
- EOJ-52 Destiny Signal .10 .20
- EOJ-53 D - Time (R) 1.00 2.00
- EOJ-53 D - Time (UTR) 2.00 4.00
- EOJ-54 D - Shield .10 .20
- EOJ-55 Icarus Attack .10 .20
- EOJ-56 Elemental Absorber (R) .40 1.00
- EOJ-56 Elemental Absorber (UTR) 1.00 2.00
- EOJ-57 Macro Cosmos .10 .20
- EOJ-58 Miraculous Descent (UTR) 1.00 2.00
- EOJ-58 Miraculous Descent (R) .40 1.00
- EOJ-59 Shattered Axe .10 .20
- EOJ-60 Forced Back (R) 2.00 4.00
- EOJ-60 Forced Back (UTR) 7.00 15.00

2006 Yu-Gi-Oh Power of the Duelist 1st Edition

- Complete Set (60) 95.00 125.00
- Booster Box (24 packs) 50.00 75.00
- Booster Pack (9 cards) 3.00 4.00

- POTD1 Elemental Hero Neos .10 .20
- POTD2 Sabersaurus .10 .20
- POTD3 Neo-Spacian Aqua Dolphin (SR) 2.00 4.00
- POTD3 Neo-Spacian Aqua Dolphin (UTR) 7.00 15.00
- POTD4 Neo Spacian Flare Scarab (SR) 2.00 4.00
- POTD4 Neo Spacian Flare Scarab (UTR) 3.00 6.00
- POTD5 Neo-Spacian Dark Panther (UTR) 8.00 15.00
- POTD5 Neo-Spacian Dark Panther (SR) 3.00 6.00
- POTD6 Chryalis Dolphin .10 .20
- POTD7 Rallis The Star Bird .10 .20
- POTD8 Submarineroid (R) 1.00 2.00
- POTD8 Submarineroid (UTR) 3.00 6.00
- POTD9 Ambulanceroid .10 .20
- POTD10 Decoyroid .10 .20
- POTD11 Rescueroid .10 .20
- POTD12 Destiny Hero-Double Dude (SR) 3.00 6.00
- POTD12 Destiny Hero-Double Dude (UTR) 4.00 8.00
- POTD13 Destiny Hero-Defender .10 .20
- POTD14 Destiny Hero-Dogma (SR) 3.00 6.00
- POTD14 Destiny Hero-Dogma (UTR) 5.00 10.00
- POTD15 Destiny Hero-Blade Master .10 .20
- POTD16 Destiny Hero-Fear Monger .10 .20
- POTD17 Destiny Hero-Dasher (UTR) 15.00 30.00
- POTD17 Destiny Hero-Dasher (R) 1.00 2.00
- POTD18 Black Ptera .10 .20
- POTD19 Black Stego .10 .20
- POTD20 Ultimate Tyranno (SR) 3.00 6.00
- POTD20 Ultimate Tyranno (UTR) 4.00 8.00
- POTD21 Miracle Jurassic Egg .10 .20
- POTD22 Babycerasaurus .10 .20
- POTD23 Bitelon .10 .20
- POTD24 Alien Grey .10 .20
- POTD25 Alien Skull .10 .20
- POTD26 Alien Hunter .10 .20
- POTD27 Alien Warrior (UTR) 4.00 8.00
- POTD27 Alien Warrior (R) 1.00 2.00
- POTD28 Alien Mother (R) .40 1.00
- POTD28 Alien Mother (UTR) 4.00 8.00
- POTD29 Cosmic Horror Gangi'el (UTR) 4.00 8.00
- POTD29 Cosmic Horror Gangi'el (R) 1.00 2.00
- POTD30 Flying Saucer Muusik'I .10 .20
- POTD31 Elemental Hero Aqua Neos (UR) 6.00 12.00
- POTD31 Elemental Hero Aqua Neos (UTR) 15.00 26.00
- POTD32 Elemental Hero Flare Neos (UR) 6.00 12.00
- POTD32 Elemental Hero Flare Neos (UTR) 10.00 20.00
- POTD33 Elemental Hero Dark Neos (UTR) 15.00 28.00
- POTD33 Elemental Hero Dark Neos (UR) 15.00 25.00
- POTD34 Chimeratech Overdragon (UTR) 15.00 30.00
- POTD34 Chimeratech Overdragon (UR) 6.00 12.00
- POTD35 Ambulance Rescueroid .10 .20
- POTD36 Super Vehicroid Jumbo Drill (SR) 2.00 4.00
- POTD36 Super Vehicroid Jumbo Drill (UTR) 3.00 6.00
- POTD37 Contact .10 .20
- POTD38 Fake Hero .10 .20
- POTD39 Spell Casting (UTR) 2.00 4.00
- POTD39 Spell Calling (R) .40 1.00
- POTD40 Vehicroid Connection Zone .10 .20
- POTD41 D-Spirit .10 .20
- POTD42 Overload Fusion (UTR) 3.00 6.00
- POTD42 Overload Fusion (R) 1.00 2.00
- POTD43 Cyclone Blade (UTR) 3.00 6.00
- POTD43 Cyclone Blade (R) .40 1.00
- POTD44 Future Fusion (R) 1.00 2.00
- POTD44 Future Fusion (UTR) 7.00 15.00
- POTD45 Common Soul .10 .20
- POTD46 Neo Space (R) .40 1.00
- POTD46 Neo Space (UTR) 3.00 6.00
- POTD47 Mausoleum of the Emperor .10 .20
- POTD48 Dark City (R) .40 1.00
- POTD48 Dark City (UTR) 3.00 6.00
- POTD49 Destiny Mirage .10 .20
- POTD50 D-Chain (UTR) 3.00 6.00
- POTD50 D-Chain (R) .40 1.00
- POTD51 Crop Circles .10 .20
- POTD52 The Paths of Destiny .10 .20
- POTD53 Orbital Bombardment .10 .20
- POTD54 Royal Writ of Taxation .10 .20
- POTD55 Wonder Garage .10 .20
- POTD56 Supercharge (R) .40 1.00
- POTD56 Supercharge (UTR) 3.00 6.00
- POTD57 Cyber Summon Blaster (R) .40 1.00
- POTD57 Cyber Summon Blaster (UTR) 3.00 6.00
- POTD58 Fossil Excavation .10 .20
- POTD59 Synthetic Seraphim .10 .20
- POTD60 Brainwashing Beam .10 .20

2006 Yu-Gi-Oh Shadow of Infinity 1st Edition

- Complete Set (60) 100.00 150.00
- Booster Box (24 packs) 65.00 85.00
- Booster Pack (9 cards) 3.50 4.00

- SOI-1 Uria, Lord of Searing Flames (UTR) 12.00 25.00
- SOI-1 Uria, Lord of Searing Flames (UR) 8.00 16.00
- SOI-2 Hamon, Lord of Striking Thunder (UTR)15.00 30.00
- SOI-2 Hamon, Lord of Striking Thunder (UR) 8.00 15.00
- SOI-3 Raviel, Lord of Phantasms (UTR) 15.00 30.00
- SOI-3 Raviel, Lord of Phantasms (UR) 10.00 20.00
- SOI-4 Elemental Hero Neo Bubbleman .50 1.00
- SOI-5 Hero Kid .10 .20
- SOI-6 Cyber Barrier Dragon (UTR) 10.00 20.00
- SOI-6 Cyber Barrier Dragon (SR) 7.00 12.00
- SOI-7 Cyber Laser Dragon (UTR) 15.00 30.00
- SOI-7 Cyber Laser Dragon (UR) 10.00 20.00
- SOI-8 Ancient Gear .10 .20
- SOI-9 Ancient Gear Cannon .10 .20
- SOI-10 Proto-Cyber Dragon (UTR) 10.00 20.00
- SOI-10 Proto-Cyber Dragon (R) 4.00 7.00
- SOI-11 Adhesive Explosive (UTR) 5.00 10.00
- SOI-11 Adhesive Explosive (R) 3.00 6.00
- SOI-12 Machine King Prototype .10 .20
- SOI-13 B.E.S. Covered Core (UTR) 8.00 15.00
- SOI-13 B.E.S. Covered Core (SR) 3.00 6.00
- SOI-14 D.D. Guide .10 .20
- SOI-15 Chain Thrasher .10 .20
- SOI-16 Disciple of the Forbidden Spell .10 .20
- SOI-17 Tenkabito Shien .10 .20
- SOI-18 Parasitic Ticky .10 .20
- SOI-19 Gokipon .10 .20
- SOI-20 Silent Insect .10 .20
- SOI-21 Chainsaw Insect (UTR) 6.00 12.00
- SOI-21 Chainsaw Insect (R) 3.00 6.00
- SOI-22 Anteatereatingant .10 .20
- SOI-23 Saber Beetle .10 .20
- SOI-24 Doom Dozer (UTR) 8.00 18.00
- SOI-24 Doom Dozer (R) 5.00 10.00
- SOI-25 Treeborn Frog (UTR) 8.00 18.00
- SOI-25 Treeborn Frog (R) 2.00 4.00
- SOI-26 Beelze Frog .20 .50
- SOI-27 Princess Pikeru (UTR) 5.00 10.00
- SOI-27 Princess Pikeru (R) .75 2.00
- SOI-28 Princess Curran (UTR) 5.00 10.00
- SOI-28 Princess Curran (R) .75 2.00
- SOI-29 Memory Crusher (UTR) 4.00 8.00
- SOI-29 Memory Crusher (R) .75 2.00
- SOI-30 Malice Ascendant .10 .20
- SOI-31 Grass Phantom .10 .20
- SOI-32 Sand Moth .10 .20
- SOI-33 Divine Dragon-Excelion (UTR) 8.00 18.00
- SOI-33 Divine Dragon - Excelion (SR) 4.00 8.00
- SOI-34 Ruin, Queen of Oblivion (UTR) 10.00 20.00
- SOI-34 Ruin, Queen of Oblivion (SR) 1.00 2.00
- SOI-35 Demise, King of Armageddon (UTR) 9.00 18.00
- SOI-35 Demise, King of Armageddon (SR) 6.00 12.00
- SOI-36 D.3.S. Frog .10 .20
- SOI-37 Hero Heart .10 .20
- SOI-38 Magnet Circle LV2 .10 .20
- SOI-39 Ancient Gear Factory .10 .20
- SOI-40 Ancient Gear Drill .10 .20
- SOI-41 Phantasmal Martyrs (R) .75 2.00
- SOI-41 Phantasmal Martyrs (UTR) 3.00 6.00
- SOI-42 Cyclone Boomerang (R) .75 2.00
- SOI-42 Cyclone Bommerang (UTR) 3.00 6.00
- SOI-43 Symbol of Heritage .10 .20
- SOI-44 Trial of the Princesses .10 .20
- SOI-45 Photon Generator Unit .10 .20
- SOI-46 End of the World .10 .20
- SOI-47 Ancient Gear Castle (SR) 3.00 6.00
- SOI-47 Ancient Gear Castle (UTR) 5.00 10.00
- SOI-48 Samsara .10 .20
- SOI-49 Super Junior Confrontation .10 .20
- SOI-50 Miracle Kids .10 .20
- SOI-51 Attack Reflector Unit .10 .20
- SOI-52 Damage Condenser (UTR) 6.00 12.00
- SOI-52 Damage Condenser (SR) 3.00 6.00
- SOI-53 Karma Cut (UTR) 3.00 6.00
- SOI-53 Karma Cut (R) .75 2.00
- SOI-54 Next to be Lost .10 .20
- SOI-55 Generation Shift .10 .20
- SOI-56 Full Salvo .10 .20
- SOI-57 Success Probability 0% .10 .20
- SOI-58 Option Hunter (UTR) 3.00 6.00
- SOI-58 Option Hunter (R) .75 2.00
- SOI-59 Goblin Out of the Frying Pan (R) .75 2.00
- SOI-59 Goblin Out of the Frying Pan (UTR) 3.00 6.00
- SOI-60 Malfunction (UTR) 4.00 8.00
- SOI-60 Malfunction (R) .75 2.00

2007 Yu-Gi-Oh Dark Revelation 4

- Complete Set (240) 300.00 400.00
- Booster Box (24 packs) 100.00 150.00
- Booster Pack (12 cards) 4.00 6.00

- DR041 Cycroid .10 .20
- DR042 Soitsu .10 .20
- DR043 Mad Lobster .10 .20
- DR044 Jerry Beans Man .10 .20
- DR045 Winged Kuriboh LV10 (UR) 2.50 5.00
- DR046 Patroid .10 .20
- DR047 Gyroid (R) .75 2.00
- DR048 Steamroid (R) .75 2.00
- DR049 Drillroid (SR) 1.50 4.00
- DR0410 UFOroid .10 .20
- DR0411 Jetroid .10 .20
- DR0412 Wroughtweiler .10 .20
- DR0413 Dark Catapulter .10 .20
- DR0414 Elemental Hero Bubbleman .10 .20
- DR0415 Cyber Dragon (UR) 15.00 30.00
- DR0416 Cybernetic Magician (R) 1.50 4.00
- DR0417 Cybernetic Cyclopean .10 .20
- DR0418 Mechanical Hound .10 .20
- DR0419 Cyber Archfiend .10 .20
- DR0420 Goblin Elite Attack Force (SR) 1.00 2.50
- DR0421 B.E.S. Crystal Core (SR) 1.50 4.00
- DR0422 Giant Kozaky .10 .20
- DR0423 Indomitable Fighter Lei Lei .10 .20
- DR0424 Protective Soul Ailin .10 .20
- DR0425 Doitsu .10 .20
- DR0426 Des Frog .10 .20
- DR0427 T.A.D.P.O.L.E. .10 .20
- DR0428 Poison Draw Frog .10 .20
- DR0429 Tyranno Infinity (R) .75 2.00
- DR0430 Batteryman C .10 .20
- DR0431 Ebon Magician Curran .10 .20
- DR0432 D.D.M. - Different Dimension Master (R)1.50 4.00
- DR0433 Steam Gyroid .10 .20
- DR0434 UFOroid Fighter (R) .75 2.00
- DR0435 Cyber Twin Dragon (UR) 3.00 8.00
- DR0436 Cyber End Dragon (UR) 2.50 6.00
- DR0437 Power Bond (SR) 3.00 8.00
- DR0438 Fusion Recovery .10 .20
- DR0439 Miracle Fusion (SR) 15.00 30.00
- DR0440 Dragon's Mirror (SR) 8.00 15.00
- DR0441 System Down (R) .75 2.00
- DR0442 Des Croaking .10 .20
- DR0443 Pot of Generosity .10 .20
- DR0444 Shien's Spy .10 .20
- DR0445 Transcendent Wings .10 .20
- DR0446 Bubble Shuffle .10 .20
- DR0447 Spark Blaster .10 .20
- DR0448 Skyscraper (R) 1.00 2.50
- DR0449 Fire Darts .10 .20
- DR0450 Spiritual Earth Art - Kurogane .10 .20
- DR0451 Spiritual Water Art - Aoi .10 .20
- DR0452 Spiritual Fire Art - Kurenai .10 .20
- DR0453 Spiritual Wind Art - Miyabi .10 .20
- DR0454 A Rival Appears! .10 .20
- DR0455 Magical Explosion .10 .20
- DR0456 Rising Energy (R) .60 4.00
- DR0457 D.D. Trap Hole .10 .20
- DR0458 Conscription .10 .20
- DR0459 Dimension Wall (R) 1.00 2.50
- DR0460 Prepare to Strike Back .10 .20
- DR0461 Zure, Knight of Dark World .10 .20
- DR0462 V-Tiger Jet .10 .20
- DR0463 Blade Skater .10 .20
- DR0464 Queen's Knight (R) 1.50 4.00
- DR0465 Jack's Knight (R) .75 2.00
- DR0466 King's Knight (R) .75 2.00
- DR0467 Elemental Hero Bladedge (SR) 1.00 2.50
- DR0468 Elemental Hero Wildheart (SR) 3.00 8.00
- DR0469 Reborn Zombie .10 .20
- DR0470 Chthonian Soldier .10 .20
- DR0471 W-Wing Catapult .10 .20
- DR0472 Infernal Incinerator .10 .20
- DR0473 Hydrogeddon (SR) 6.00 15.00
- DR0474 Oxygeddon .10 .20
- DR0475 Water Dragon (R) .75 2.00
- DR0476 Etoile Cyber .10 .20
- DR0477 B.E.S. Tetran (SR) 2.00 5.00
- DR0478 Nanobreaker .10 .20
- DR0479 Rapid-Fire Magician (R) 1.00 2.50
- DR0480 Beiige, Vanguard of Dark World .10 .20
- DR0481 Broww, Huntsman of Dark World (R) 2.00 5.00
- DR0482 Brron, Mad King of Dark World (R) 2.50 6.00
- DR0483 Sillva, Warlord of Dark World (UR) 8.00 20.00
- DR0484 Goldd, Wu-Lord of Dark World (UR) 8.00 15.00
- DR0485 Scarr, Scout of Dark World .10 .20
- DR0486 Familiar-Possessed - Aussa .10 .20
- DR0487 Familiar-Possessed - Eria .10 .20
- DR0488 Familiar-Possessed - Hiita .10 .20
- DR0489 Familiar-Possessed - Wynn .10 .20
- DR0490 VW-Tiger Catapult .10 .20
- DR0491 VWXYZ-Dragon Catapult Cannon (R)1.50 8.00
- DR0492 Cyber Blader (R) 1.50 4.00
- DR0493 Elemental Hero Rampart Blaster (R) 2.00 5.00
- DR0494 Elemental Hero Tempest (SR) 6.00 15.00
- DR0495 Elemental Hero Wildedge (R) 2.50 6.00
- DR0496 Elemental Hero Shining Flare Wingman (UR) 8.00 20.00
- DR0497 Pot of Avarice (UR) 15.00 30.00
- DR0498 Dark World Lightning (R) 1.50 4.00
- DR0499 Level Modulation .10 .20
- DR04100 Ojamagic (R) 1.00 4.00
- DR04101 Ojamuscle .10 .20
- DR04102 Feather Shot .10 .20
- DR04103 Bonding - H2O .10 .20
- DR04104 Chthonian Alliance .10 .20
- DR04105 Armed Changer .10 .20
- DR04106 Branch! .10 .20
- DR04107 Boss Rush .10 .20
- DR04108 Gateway to Dark World .10 .20
- DR04109 Hero Barrier .10 .20
- DR04110 Chthonian Blast .10 .20
- DR04111 The Forces of Darkness .10 .20
- DR04112 Dark Deal (R) 1.00 2.50
- DR04113 Simultaneous Loss .10 .20
- DR04114 Weed Out .10 .20
- DR04115 The League of Uniform Nomenclature.10 .20
- DR04116 Roll Out! .10 .20
- DR04117 Chthonian Polymer .10 .20
- DR04118 Feather Wind .10 .20
- DR04119 Non-Fusion Area .10 .20
- DR04120 Level Limit - Area A (R) 1.00 2.50
- DR04121 Uria, Lord of Searing Flames (UR) 15.00 30.00
- DR04122 Hamon, Lord of Striking Thunder (UR)8.00 20.00
- DR04123 Raviel, Lord of Phantasms (UR) 5.00 12.00
- DR04124 Elemental Hero Neo Bubbleman .10 .20
- DR04125 Hero Kid (R) .75 2.00
- DR04126 Cyber Barrier Dragon (R) 1.00 2.50
- DR04127 Cyber Laser Dragon (R) 2.50 6.00
- DR04128 Ancient Gear .10 .20
- DR04129 Ancient Gear Cannon .10 .20
- DR04130 Proto-Cyber Dragon (SR) 2.50 6.00
- DR04131 Adhesive Explosive .10 .20
- DR04132 Machine King Prototype .10 .20
- DR04133 B.E.S. Covered Core (SR) 1.50 4.00
- DR04134 D.D. Guide .10 .20

Card	Name	Low	High
❑ DR04135	Chain Thrasher	.10	.20
❑ DR04136	Disciple of the Forbidden Spell	.10	.20
❑ DR04137	Tenkabito Shien (R)	3.00	8.00
❑ DR04138	Parasitic Ticky	.10	.20
❑ DR04139	Gokipon	.10	.20
❑ DR04140	Silent Insect	.10	.20
❑ DR04141	Chainsaw Insect (R)	2.00	5.00
❑ DR04142	Anteatereatingant (R)	1.50	8.00
❑ DR04143	Saber Beetle (R)	.75	2.00
❑ DR04144	Doom Dozer (R)	1.00	2.50
❑ DR04145	Treeborn Frog (UR)	15.00	30.00
❑ DR04146	Beelze Frog	.10	.20
❑ DR04147	Princess Pikeru (R)	.75	2.00
❑ DR04148	Princess Curran (R)	.75	2.00
❑ DR04149	Memory Crusher	.10	.20
❑ DR04150	Malice Ascendant	.10	.20
❑ DR04151	Grass Phantom	.10	.20
❑ DR04152	Sand Moth (R)	.75	2.00
❑ DR04153	Divine Dragon - Excelion (SR)	2.00	5.00
❑ DR04154	Ruin, Queen of Oblivion (SR)	3.00	8.00
❑ DR04155	Demise, King of Armageddon (SR)	4.00	10.00
❑ DR04156	D.3.S. Frog	.10	.20
❑ DR04157	Hero Heart	.10	.20
❑ DR04158	Magnet Circle LV2	.10	.20
❑ DR04159	Ancient Gear Factory	.10	.20
❑ DR04160	Ancient Gear Drill (R)	1.50	4.00
❑ DR04161	Phantasmal Martyrs	.10	.20
❑ DR04162	Cyclone Boomerang	.10	.20
❑ DR04163	Symbol of Heritage	.10	.20
❑ DR04164	Trial of the Princesses	.10	.20
❑ DR04165	Photon Generator Unit	.10	.20
❑ DR04166	End of the World	.10	.20
❑ DR04167	Ancient Gear Castle (SR)	2.00	5.00
❑ DR04168	Samsara	.10	.20
❑ DR04169	Super Junior Confrontation	.10	.20
❑ DR04170	Miracle Kids	.10	.20
❑ DR04171	Attack Reflector Unit	.10	.20
❑ DR04172	Damage Condenser (SR)	2.00	5.00
❑ DR04173	Karma Cut (SR)	3.00	8.00
❑ DR04174	Next to be Lost	.10	.20
❑ DR04175	Generation Shift	.10	.20
❑ DR04176	Full Salvo	.10	.20
❑ DR04177	Success Probability 0	.10	.20
❑ DR04178	Option Hunter	.10	.20
❑ DR04179	Goblin Out of the Frying Pan (R)	1.00	2.50
❑ DR04180	Malfunction (R)	1.00	2.50
❑ DR04181	Destiny Hero - Doom Lord (R)	6.00	15.00
❑ DR04182	Destiny Hero - Captain Tenacious	.10	.20
❑ DR04183	Destiny Hero - Diamond Dude (SR)	15.00	30.00
❑ DR04184	Destiny Hero - Dreadmaster (R)	2.00	5.00
❑ DR04185	Cyber Tutu	.10	.20
❑ DR04186	Cyber Gymnast (R)	1.50	4.00
❑ DR04187	Cyber Prima (R)	1.50	4.00
❑ DR04188	Cyber Kirin	.10	.20
❑ DR04189	Cyber Phoenix (UR)	2.50	6.00
❑ DR04190	Searchlightman	.10	.20
❑ DR04191	Victory Viper XX03 (SR)	2.00	5.00
❑ DR04192	Swift Birdman Joe	.10	.20
❑ DR04193	Harpie's Pet Baby Dragon (R)	.75	2.00
❑ DR04194	Majestic Mech - Senku	.10	.20
❑ DR04195	Majestic Mech - Ohka (SR)	2.00	5.00
❑ DR04196	Majestic Mech - Goryu (SR)	1.00	2.50
❑ DR04197	Royal Knight	.10	.20
❑ DR04198	Herald of Green Light (R)	.75	2.00
❑ DR04199	Herald of Purple Light (R)	1.50	4.00
❑ DR04200	Bountiful Artemis (SR)	25.00	50.00
❑ DR04201	Layard the Liberator	.10	.20
❑ DR04202	Banisher of the Radiance (SR)	8.00	20.00
❑ DR04203	Voltanis the Adjudicator (UR)	2.50	6.00
❑ DR04204	Guard Dog	.10	.20
❑ DR04205	Whirlwind Weasel	.10	.20
❑ DR04206	Avalanching Aussa	.10	.20
❑ DR04207	Raging Eria	.10	.20
❑ DR04208	Blazing Hiita	.10	.20
❑ DR04209	Storming Wynn	.10	.20
❑ DR04210	Batteryman D	.10	.20
❑ DR04211	Super-Electromagnetic Voltech Dragon (UR)	2.00	5.00
❑ DR04212	Elemental Hero Phoenix Enforcer (R)	3.00	8.00
❑ DR04213	Elemental Hero Shining Phoenix Enforcer (UR)	2.00	5.00
❑ DR04214	Elemental Hero Mariner	.10	.20
❑ DR04215	Elemental Hero Wild Wingman (R)	2.50	5.00
❑ DR04216	Elemental Hero Necroid Shaman	.10	.20
❑ DR04217	Misfortune	.10	.20
❑ DR04218	H - Heated Heart	.10	.20
❑ DR04219	E - Emergency Call	.10	.20
❑ DR04220	R - Righteous Justice	.10	.20
❑ DR04221	O - Oversoul	.10	.20
❑ DR04222	HERO Flash!!	.10	.20
❑ DR04223	Power Capsule	.10	.20
❑ DR04224	Celestial Transformation (R)	1.00	2.50
❑ DR04225	Guard Penalty (R)	1.00	2.50
❑ DR04226	Grand Convergence (R)	1.00	2.50
❑ DR04227	Dimensional Fissure (R)	2.50	6.00
❑ DR04228	Clock Tower Prison (R)	1.00	2.50
❑ DR04229	Life Equalizer (R)	1.00	5.00
❑ DR04230	Elemental Recharge	.10	.20
❑ DR04231	Destruction of Destiny	.10	.20
❑ DR04232	Destiny Signal (R)	1.00	2.50
❑ DR04233	D - Time	.10	.20
❑ DR04234	D - Shield	.10	.20
❑ DR04235	Icarus Attack (SR)	30.00	60.00
❑ DR04236	Elemental Absorber	.10	.20
❑ DR04237	Macro Cosmos (SR)	15.00	30.00
❑ DR04238	Miraculous Descent (SR)	2.00	5.00
❑ DR04239	Shattered Axe	.10	.20
❑ DR04240	Forced Back (R)	2.00	5.00
❑ DR04241	Satellite Cannon (SCR)	10.00	25.00
❑ DR04242	Gilford the Lightning (SCR)	8.00	15.00
❑ DR04243	Exarion Universe (SCR)	8.00	15.00
❑ DR04244	D.D. Assailant (SCR)	20.00	40.00
❑ DR04245	Kaibaman (SCR)	5.00	12.00

2007 Yu-Gi-Oh Force of the Breaker 1st Edition

Card	Name	Low	High
	Complete Regular Set (60)	80.00	130.00
	Booster Box (24 packs)	50.00	80.00
	Booster Pack (9 cards)	3.00	4.00
❑ FOTB0	Volcanic Rocket (SCR)	15.00	30.00
❑ FOTB1	Crystal Beast Ruby Carbuncle	.10	.20
❑ FOTB2	Crystal Beast Amethyst Cat	.25	.75
❑ FOTB3	Crystal Beast Emerald Tortoise	.10	.20
❑ FOTB4	Crystal Beast Topaz Tiger (R)	2.00	4.00
❑ FOTB4	Crystal Beast Topaz Tiger(UTR)	6.00	12.00
❑ FOTB5	Crystal Beast Amber Mammoth	.10	.50
❑ FOTB6	Crystal Beast Cobalt Eagle	.10	.20
❑ FOTB7	Crystal Beast Sapphire Pegasus(UTR)	10.00	20.00
❑ FOTB7	Crystal Beast Sapphire Pegasus (UR)	7.00	15.00
❑ FOTB8	Volcanic Doomfire (UTR)	10.00	20.00
❑ FOTB8	Volcanic Doomfire (UR)	8.00	15.00
❑ FOTB9	Volcanic Shell (UTR)	.10	.30
❑ FOTB9	Volcanic Shell (R)	1.00	2.00
❑ FOTB10	Volcanic Scattershot	.10	.20
❑ FOTB11	Volcanic Blaster	.10	.20
❑ FOTB12	Volcanic Slicer (R)	1.00	2.00
❑ FOTB12	Volcanic Slicer (UTR)	3.00	7.00
❑ FOTB13	Volcanic Hammerer	.10	.20
❑ FOTB14	Elemental Hero Captain Gold(UTR)	7.00	15.00
❑ FOTB14	Elemental Hero Captain Gold (UR)	5.00	12.00
❑ FOTB15	Gravekeeper's Commandant (UTR)	3.00	6.00
❑ FOTB15	Gravekeeper's Commandant (R)	1.00	2.00
❑ FOTB16	Warrior of Atlantis (R)	.40	1.00
❑ FOTB16	Warrior of Atlantis (UTR)	2.00	4.00
❑ FOTB17	Destroyersaurus (R)	2.00	4.00
❑ FOTB17	Destroyersaurus (UTR)	2.00	4.00
❑ FOTB18	Zeradias, Herald of Heaven(UTR)	4.00	8.00
❑ FOTB18	Zeradias, Herald of Heaven (R)	1.00	2.00
❑ FOTB19	Archfiend General (UTR)	3.00	6.00
❑ FOTB19	Archfiend General (R)	1.00	2.00
❑ FOTB20	Harpie Queen (UTR)	3.00	6.00
❑ FOTB20	Harpie Queen (R)	1.00	2.00
❑ FOTB21	Sky Scourge Enrise (SR)	3.00	6.00
❑ FOTB21	Sky Scourge Enrise (UTR)	5.00	10.00
❑ FOTB22	Sky Scourge Norleras (UTR)	7.00	15.00
❑ FOTB22	Sky Scourge Norleras (SR)	3.00	6.00
❑ FOTB23	Sky Scourge Invicil (UTR)	5.00	10.00
❑ FOTB23	Sky Scourge Invicil (SR)	3.00	6.00
❑ FOTB24	Goe Goe the Gallant Ninja (R)	.40	1.00
❑ FOTB24	Goe Goe the Gallant Ninja (UTR)	2.00	4.00
❑ FOTB25	Mei-Kou, Master of Barriers	.10	.20
❑ FOTB26	Raiza the Storm Monarch (SR)	15.00	25.00
❑ FOTB26	Raiza the Storm Monarch (UTR)	20.00	35.00
❑ FOTB27	Seismic Crasher	.10	.20
❑ FOTB28	Dweller in the Depths	.10	.20
❑ FOTB29	Magna-Slash Dragon	.10	.20
❑ FOTB30	Gravi-Crush Dragon	.10	.20
❑ FOTB31	Soul of Fire (UTR)	3.00	5.00
❑ FOTB31	Soul of Fire (SR)	1.00	3.00
❑ FOTB32	Crystal Beacon	.10	.20
❑ FOTB33	Rare Value (R)	6.00	12.00
❑ FOTB33	Rare Value (UTR)	12.00	20.00
❑ FOTB34	Crystal Blessing	.10	.20
❑ FOTB35	Crystal Abundance	.10	.20
❑ FOTB36	Crystal Promise	.10	.20
❑ FOTB37	Lucky Iron Axe (UTR)	2.00	4.00
❑ FOTB37	Lucky Iron Axe (R)	.40	1.00
❑ FOTB38	Tornado	.10	.20
❑ FOTB39	Wild Fire	.10	.20
❑ FOTB40	Blaze Accelerator	.10	.20
❑ FOTB41	Tri-Blaze Accelerator (SR)	2.00	4.00
❑ FOTB41	Tri-Blaze Accelerator (UTR)	3.00	6.00
❑ FOTB42	Field Barrier	.10	.20
❑ FOTB43	A Cell Breeding Device	.10	.20
❑ FOTB44	Otherworld - The A Zone	.10	.20
❑ FOTB45	Ancient City - Rainbow Ruins(UTR)	2.00	5.00
❑ FOTB45	Ancient City - Rainbow Ruins (R)	1.00	2.00
❑ FOTB46	Triggered Summon (UTR)	2.00	4.00
❑ FOTB46	Triggered Summon (R)	.40	1.00
❑ FOTB47	Last Resort	.10	.20
❑ FOTB48	Crystal Raigeki	.10	.20
❑ FOTB49	Volcanic Recharge	.10	.20
❑ FOTB50	Terrible Deal	.10	.20
❑ FOTB51	Breakthrough!	.10	.20
❑ FOTB52	Backs to the Wall	.10	.20
❑ FOTB53	Introduction to Gallantry	.10	.20
❑ FOTB54	Secrets of the Gallant	.10	.20
❑ FOTB55	Radiant Mirror Force (UTR)	4.00	8.00
❑ FOTB55	Radiant Mirror Force (SR)	2.00	4.00
❑ FOTB56	Hard-sellin' Goblin	.10	.20
❑ FOTB57	Hard-sellin' Zombie	.10	.20
❑ FOTB58	Mass Hypnosis	.10	.20
❑ FOTB59	Gem Flash Energy	.10	.20
❑ FOTB60	Firewall (R)	.40	1.00
❑ FOTB60	Firewall (UTR)	2.00	4.00
❑ FOTB61	Diabolos, King of the Abyss (SCR)	12.00	20.00
❑ FOTB62	Lich Lord, King of the Underworld (SCR)	12.00	20.00
❑ FOTB63	Prometheus (SCR)	25.00	40.00
❑ FOTB64	Mist Archfield (SCR)	12.00	20.00
❑ FOTB65	Plague Wolf (SCR)	12.00	20.00
❑ FOTB66	Recurring Nightmare (SCR)	15.00	25.00
❑ FOTB67	Sword of Dark Rites (SCR)	12.00	18.00
❑ FOTB68	Eradicator Epidemic (SCR)	20.00	40.00

2007 Yu-Gi-Oh Gladiators Assault 1st Edition

Card	Name	Low	High
	Complete Set	150.00	200.00
	Booster Box (24 packs)	60.00	80.00
	Booster Pack (9 cards)	3.50	4.00
❑ GLAS0	Gladiator Beast Octavius (SCR)	10.00	20.00
❑ GLAS1	Chamberlain of Six Samurai	.10	.20
❑ GLAS2	Cloudian Smoke Ball	.10	.20
❑ GLAS3	Evil Hero Malicious Edge (UTR)	7.00	15.00
❑ GLAS3	Evil Hero Malicious Edge (SR)	4.00	8.00
❑ GLAS4	Evil Hero Infernal Gainer (R)	.40	1.00
❑ GLAS5	Cloudian Eye of Typhoon (UTR)	3.00	6.00
❑ GLAS5	Cloudian Eye of Typhoon (SR)	2.00	4.00
❑ GLAS6	Cloudian Ghost Fog	.10	.20
❑ GLAS7	Cloudian Nimbusman	.10	.20
❑ GLAS8	Cloudian Sheep Cloud (UTR)	3.00	6.00
❑ GLAS8	Cloudian Sheep Cloud (SR)	2.00	4.00
❑ GLAS9	Cloudian Poison Cloud	.10	.20
❑ GLAS10	Cloudian Acid Cloud (R)	.40	1.00
❑ GLAS11	Cloudian Cirrostratus (R)	.40	1.00
❑ GLAS12	Cloudian Altus (R)	.40	1.00
❑ GLAS13	Cloudian Turbulence	.10	.20
❑ GLAS14	Truckroid	.10	.20
❑ GLAS15	Stealthroid	.10	.20
❑ GLAS16	Expressroid (R)	.40	1.00
❑ GLAS17	Gladiator Beast Alexander (UTR)	5.00	10.00
❑ GLAS17	Gladiator Beast Alexander (SR)	2.00	4.00
❑ GLAS18	Gladiator Beast Spartacus (R)	.40	1.00
❑ GLAS19	Gladiator Beast Murmillo (R)	.40	1.00
❑ GLAS20	Gladiator Beast Bestiari	.10	.20
❑ GLAS21	Gladiator Beast Laquari (R)	5.00	10.00
❑ GLAS22	Gladiator Beast Hoplomus	.10	.20
❑ GLAS23	Gladiator Beast Dimacari	.10	.20
❑ GLAS24	Gladiator Beast Secutor	.10	.20
❑ GLAS25	Test Ape	.10	.20
❑ GLAS26	Witch Doctor of Sparta	.10	.20
❑ GLAS27	Infinity Dark	.10	.20
❑ GLAS28	Magical Reflect Slime	.10	.20
❑ GLAS29	Ancient Gear Knight	.10	.20
❑ GLAS30	Goblin Black Ops (R)	.40	1.00
❑ GLAS31	Gambler of Legend	.10	.20
❑ GLAS32	Enishi, Shiens Chancellor (UTR)	15.00	25.00
❑ GLAS32	Enishi, Shiens Chancellor (UR)	9.00	18.00
❑ GLAS33	Spirit of the Six Samurai	.10	.20
❑ GLAS34	Alien Telepath (R)	.40	1.00
❑ GLAS35	Alien Hypno	.10	.20
❑ GLAS36	Elemental Hero Chaos Neos (GR)	6.00	15.00
❑ GLAS36	Elemental Hero Chaos Neos (SCR)	12.00	20.00
❑ GLAS37	Elemental Hero Plasma Vice (SCR)	8.00	16.00
❑ GLAS38	Evil Hero Inferno Wing (UTR)	5.00	10.00
❑ GLAS38	Evil Hero Inferno Wing (UR)	4.00	8.00
❑ GLAS39	Evil Hero Lightning Golem (UR)	4.00	8.00
❑ GLAS39	Evil Hero Lightning Golem (UTR)	5.00	10.00
❑ GLAS40	Evil Hero Dark Gaia (R)	.75	2.00
❑ GLAS41	Super Vehicroid Stealth Un (SCR)	12.00	22.00
❑ GLAS42	Superalloy Beast Raptinus	.10	.20
❑ GLAS43	Gladiator Beast Gaiodiaz (R)	.40	1.00
❑ GLAS44	Gladiator Beast Heraklinos (SCR)	50.00	100.00
❑ GLAS45	Contact Out	.10	.20
❑ GLAS46	Swing of Memories	.10	.20
❑ GLAS47	Dark Fusion (R)	.75	2.00
❑ GLAS48	Diamond-Dust Cyclone (R)	.40	1.00
❑ GLAS49	Summon Cloud	.10	.20
❑ GLAS50	Lucky Cloud	.10	.20
❑ GLAS51	Fog Control	.10	.20
❑ GLAS52	Cloudian Squall	.10	.20
❑ GLAS53	Super Double Summon	.10	.20
❑ GLAS54	Colosseum Cage Gladiatr Bsts (R)	.40	1.00
❑ GLAS55	Glad.Beasts Bttle Halberd	.10	.20
❑ GLAS56	Glad. Beasts Battle Gladius	.10	.20
❑ GLAS57	Glad.Beasts Battle Manica (R)	.40	1.00
❑ GLAS58	Gladiator Beasts Respite (R)	.40	1.00
❑ GLAS59	Gladiators Return	.10	.20
❑ GLAS60	Soul Devouring Bamboo Sword	.10	.20
❑ GLAS61	Cunning of the Six Samurai (UTR)	5.00	10.00
❑ GLAS61	Cunning of the Six Samurai (SR)	7.00	15.00
❑ GLAS62	A Cell Incubator	.10	.20
❑ GLAS63	Over Limit	.10	.20
❑ GLAS64	No Entry!!	.10	.20
❑ GLAS65	Natural Disaster	.10	.20
❑ GLAS66	Rain Storm	.10	.20
❑ GLAS67	Updraft (UTR)	3.00	6.00
❑ GLAS67	Updraft (SR)	.75	2.00
❑ GLAS68	Release from Stone	.10	.20
❑ GLAS69	Light-Imprisoning Mirror	.10	.20
❑ GLAS70	Shadow-Imprisoning Mirror	.10	.20
❑ GLAS71	Disarm	.10	.20
❑ GLAS72	Parry	.10	.20
❑ GLAS73	Swiftstrike Armor	.10	.20
❑ GLAS74	DoubleEdged Sword Tech	.10	.20
❑ GLAS75	Energy-Absorbing Monolith (UTR)	3.00	6.00
❑ GLAS75	Energy-Absorbing Monolith (SR)	2.00	4.00
❑ GLAS76	Cell Explosion Virus (R)	.40	1.00
❑ GLAS77	Detonator Circle A	.10	.20
❑ GLAS78	Interdimensional Warp	.10	.20
❑ GLAS79	Foolish Revival	.10	.20
❑ GLAS80	An Unfortunate Report	.10	.20
❑ GLAS81	Gladiator Beast Torax (UTR)	3.00	6.00
❑ GLAS81	Gladiator Beast Torax (SR)	2.00	4.00
❑ GLAS82	Test Tiger (UR)	9.00	18.00
❑ GLAS82	Test Tiger (UTR)	12.00	22.00
❑ GLAS83	Defensive Tactics (UTR)	3.00	6.00
❑ GLAS83	Defensive Tactics (SR)	2.00	4.00
❑ GLAS84	Dragon Ice (SCR)	20.00	40.00
❑ GLAS85	Tongue Twister (SCR)	10.00	20.00
❑ GLAS86	Skreech (SCR)	12.00	22.00
❑ GLAS87	Royal Firestorm Guards (SCR)	20.00	40.00
❑ GLAS88	Veil of Darkness (SCR)	20.00	40.00
❑ GLAS89	Security Orb (UTR)	3.00	6.00
❑ GLAS89	Security Orb (UR)	2.00	4.00
❑ GLAS90	Necroface (SCR)	25.00	50.00
❑ GLAS91	Gilgarth (SCR)	15.00	30.00
❑ GLAS92	Soul Taker (SCR)	25.00	50.00
❑ GLAS93	Magic Formula (SCR)	40.00	80.00
❑ GLAS94	Silent Doom (SCR)	25.00	50.00

2007 Yu-Gi-Oh Strike of Neos 1st Edition

Card	Name	Low	High
	Complete Regular Set (60)	100.00	150.00
	Booster Box (24)	70.00	90.00
	Booster Pack (9 cards)	3.50	4.00
❑ STON0	Grandmaster of Six Samurai (SCR)	25.00	50.00
❑ STON1	Gene-Warped Warwolf (UTR)	6.00	10.00
❑ STON1	Gene-Warped Warwolf (SR)	3.00	6.00
❑ STON2	Frostosaurus (UTR)	4.00	10.00
❑ STON2	Frostosaurus (R)	.75	2.00
❑ STON3	Spiral Serpent (R)	.75	2.00
❑ STON3	Spiral Serpent (UTR)	2.00	4.00
❑ STON4	Neo-Spacian Air Hummingbird (UTR)	7.00	15.00
❑ STON4	Neo-Spacian Air Hummingbird (SR)	4.00	10.00
❑ STON5	Neo-Spacian Grand Mole (UTR)	15.00	25.00
❑ STON5	Neo-Spacian Grand Mole (R)	3.00	6.00
❑ STON6	Neo-Spacian Glow Moss	.10	.20
❑ STON7	The Six Samurai - Yaichi	.10	.20
❑ STON8	The Six Samurai - Kamon	.10	.20
❑ STON9	The Six Samurai - Yariza	.10	.20
❑ STON10	The Six Samurai - Nisashi	.10	.20
❑ STON11	The Six Samurai - Zanji	.10	.20
❑ STON12	The Six Samurai - Irou	.10	.20
❑ STON13	Great Shogun Shien (UTR)	7.00	15.00
❑ STON13	Great Shogun Shien (SR)	5.00	11.00
❑ STON14	Shien's Footsoldier	.10	.20
❑ STON15	Sage of Silence (UTR)	2.00	5.00
❑ STON15	Sage of Silence (R)	.75	2.00
❑ STON16	Sage of Stillness	.10	.20
❑ STON17	Reign-Beaux, Overlord of Dark World (UTR)	20.00	40.00
❑ STON17	Reign-Beaux, Overlord of Dark World (UR)	12.00	25.00
❑ STON18	Kahkki, Guerilla of Dark World	.20	.50
❑ STON19	Gren, Tactician of Dark World	.20	.50
❑ STON20	Fusion Devourer (UTR)	2.00	5.00
❑ STON20	Fusion Devourer (R)	.75	2.00
❑ STON21	Electric Virus	.10	.20
❑ STON22	Puppet Plant	.10	.20
❑ STON23	Marionette Mite	.10	.20
❑ STON24	D.D. Crow (R)	.75	2.00
❑ STON24	D.D. Crow (UTR)	10.00	25.00
❑ STON25	Silent Abyss	.10	.20
❑ STON26	Firestorm Prominence	.10	.20
❑ STON27	Raging Earth	.10	.20
❑ STON28	Destruction Cyclone	.10	.20
❑ STON29	Radiant Spirit	.10	.20
❑ STON30	Umbral Soul	.10	.20
❑ STON31	Alien Psychic	.10	.20
❑ STON32	Lycanthrope	.10	.20
❑ STON33	CA° Chulainn the Awakened	.10	.20
❑ STON34	Elemental Hero Air Neos (UR)	10.00	20.00
❑ STON34	Elemental Hero Air Neos (UTR)	20.00	30.00
❑ STON35	Elemental Hero Grand Neos (UTR)	20.00	35.00
❑ STON35	Elemental Hero Grand Neos (UR)	10.00	20.00
❑ STON36	Elemental Hero Glow Neos (UR)	10.00	20.00
❑ STON36	Elemental Hero Glow Neos (UTR)	20.00	35.00
❑ STON37	Ancient Rules (UTR)	4.00	10.00
❑ STON37	Ancient Rules (R)	.75	2.00
❑ STON38	Dark World Dealings (SR)	3.00	6.00
❑ STON38	Dark World Dealings (UTR)	5.00	10.00
❑ STON39	Neos Force (UTR)	2.00	5.00
❑ STON39	Neos Force (R)	.75	2.00
❑ STON40	Legendary Ebon Steed	.10	.20
❑ STON41	A Cell Scatter Burst	.10	.20
❑ STON42	Twister (R)	.75	2.00
❑ STON42	Twister (UTR)	6.00	12.00
❑ STON43	Synthesis Spell	.10	.20
❑ STON44	Emblem of the Awakening	.10	.20
❑ STON45	Advanced Ritual Art	.10	.20
❑ STON46	Card Trader (UTR)	4.00	8.00
❑ STON46	Card Trader (SR)	2.00	4.00
❑ STON47	Shienâ€™s Castle of Mist	.10	.20
❑ STON48	Skyscraper 2 - Hero City (UTR)	4.00	8.00
❑ STON48	Skyscraper 2 - Hero City (SR)	2.00	4.00
❑ STON49	Change of Hero - Reflector Ray	.20	.50
❑ STON50	Hero Medal (R)	.75	2.00
❑ STON50	Hero Medal (UTR)	2.00	4.00
❑ STON51	Return of the Six Samurai	.10	.20
❑ STON52	Eliminating the League (UTR)	2.00	5.00
❑ STON52	Eliminating the League (R)	.75	2.00
❑ STON53	Flashbang	.10	.20
❑ STON54	The Transmigration Prophecy (R)	.75	2.00
❑ STON54	The Transmigration Prophecy (UTR)	2.00	5.00
❑ STON55	Anti-Fusion Device	.10	.20
❑ STON56	Ritual Sealing	.10	.20
❑ STON57	Birthright (UTR)	4.00	8.00
❑ STON57	Birthright (SR)	2.00	4.00
❑ STON58	Swift Samurai Storm!	.10	.20
❑ STON59	Cloak and Dagger (UTR)	2.00	5.00
❑ STON59	Cloak and Dagger (R)	.75	2.00
❑ STON60	Pulling the Rug (R)	3.00	6.00
❑ STON60	Pulling the Rug (UTR)	7.00	15.00
❑ STON61	Neo-Parshath, Sky Paladin (SCR)	15.00	25.00
❑ STON62	Metiel, Sage of the Sky (SCR)	30.00	50.00
❑ STON63	Harvest Angel of Wisdom (SCR)	20.00	40.00
❑ STON64	Freya, Spirit of Victory (SCR)	15.00	25.00
❑ STON65	Nova Summoner (SCR)	20.00	35.00
❑ STON66	Radiant Jeral (SCR)	10.00	20.00
❑ STON67	Gellenduo (SCR)	32.00	50.00
❑ STON68	Aegis of Gaia (SCR)	10.00	20.00

2007 Yu-Gi-Oh Tactical Evolution 1st Edition

Card	Name	Low	High
	Regular Set (89)	180.00	300.00
	Booster Box (24 Packs)	60.00	85.00
	Booster Pack (9 cards)	3.50	4.00
❑ TAEV000	Gemini Summoner (SCR)	4.00	10.00
❑ TAEV1	Alien Shocktrooper	.10	.20
❑ TAEV2	Volcanic Rat	.10	.20
❑ TAEV3	Renge Gatekeeper Dark World	.10	.20
❑ TAEV4	Hunter Dragon (R)	1.00	2.00
❑ TAEV5	Venom Cobra	.10	.20
❑ TAEV6	Rainbow Dragon (SCR)	15.00	30.00
❑ TAEV7	Chrysalis Pantail	.10	.20
❑ TAEV8	Chrysalis Chicky	.10	.20
❑ TAEV9	Chrysalis Pinny	.10	.20
❑ TAEV10	Chrysalis Larva	.10	.20
❑ TAEV11	Chrysalis Mole	.10	.20
❑ TAEV12	Necro Gardna (SR)	4.00	8.00
❑ TAEV12	Necro Gardna (UTR)	10.00	20.00
❑ TAEV13	Vennominaga, the Deity of Poisonous Snakes (SCR)	35.00	50.00
❑ TAEV14	Vennominon, the King of Poisonous Snakes (UTR)	3.00	8.00
❑ TAEV14	Vennominon, the King of Poisonous Snakes (UR)	4.00	10.00
❑ TAEV15	Venom Snake	.10	.20
❑ TAEV16	Venom Boa	.10	.20
❑ TAEV17	Venom Serpent	.10	.20
❑ TAEV18	Elemental Hero Neos Alius (UTR)	5.00	10.00
❑ TAEV18	Elemental Hero Neos Alius (SR)	12.00	25.00
❑ TAEV19	Chthonian Emperor Dragon (UTR)	7.50	15.00
❑ TAEV19	Chthonian Emperor Dragon (UR)	4.00	10.00
❑ TAEV20	Aquarian Alessa (SR)	2.00	4.00
❑ TAEV20	Aquarian Alessa (UTR)	4.00	7.00
❑ TAEV21	Lucky Pied Piper (UTR)	4.00	8.00
❑ TAEV21	Lucky Pied Piper (SR)	1.00	2.00
❑ TAEV22	Grasschopper (R)	.50	1.00
❑ TAEV23	Goggle Golem	.10	.20
❑ TAEV24	Dawnbreak Gardna	.10	.20
❑ TAEV25	Doom Shaman (UTR)	5.00	10.00
❑ TAEV25	Doom Shaman (SR)	3.00	6.00
❑ TAEV26	King Pyron	.10	.20
❑ TAEV27	Shadow Delver	.10	.20
❑ TAEV28	Flint Lock	.10	.20
❑ TAEV29	Gravitic Orb	.10	.20
❑ TAEV30	Phantom Cricket	.10	.20
❑ TAEV31	Crystal Seer (UTR)	10.00	20.00
❑ TAEV31	Crystal Seer (UR)	7.50	15.00
❑ TAEV32	Neo Space Pathfinder (R)	1.00	2.00
❑ TAEV33	Frost and Flame Dragon (SCR)	10.00	20.00
❑ TAEV34	Desert Twister (UR)	4.00	10.00
❑ TAEV34	Desert Twister (UTR)	5.00	10.00
❑ TAEV35	Ritual Raven	.10	.20
❑ TAEV36	Razor Lizard	.10	.20
❑ TAEV37	Light Effigy	.10	.20
❑ TAEV38	Dark Effigy	.10	.20
❑ TAEV39	Zombie Master (UTR)	10.00	20.00
❑ TAEV39	Zombie Master (SR)	5.00	10.00
❑ TAEV40	Neo-Spacian Marine Dolphin	.10	.20
❑ TAEV41	Elemental Hero Marine Neos (R)	1.00	2.00
❑ TAEV42	Elemental Hero Darkbright (UTR)	4.00	10.00
❑ TAEV42	Elemental Hero Darkbright (UR)	5.00	10.00
❑ TAEV43	Elemental Hero Magma Neos (SCR)	20.00	40.00
❑ TAEV44	Ojama Knight	.10	.20
❑ TAEV45	Fifth Hope (UTR)	2.00	5.00
❑ TAEV45	Fifth Hope (SR)	2.00	4.00
❑ TAEV46	Reverse of Neos	.10	.20
❑ TAEV47	Convert Contract	.10	.20
❑ TAEV48	Cocoon Party	.10	.20
❑ TAEV49	NEX	.10	.20
❑ TAEV50	Cocoon Rebirth	.10	.20
❑ TAEV52	Snake Rain (R)	.50	1.00
❑ TAEV53	Venom Shot	.10	.20
❑ TAEV54	Cyberdark Impact! (SCR)	15.00	30.00
❑ TAEV55	Flint Missile	.10	.20
❑ TAEV56	Double Summon (R)	1.00	2.00
❑ TAEV57	Summoner's Art (R)	.50	1.00
❑ TAEV58	Creature Seizure	.10	.20
❑ TAEV59	Phalanx Pike (R)	.50	1.00
❑ TAEV60	Symbols of Duty (R)	.50	1.00
❑ TAEV61	Amulet of Ambition	.10	.20
❑ TAEV62	Broken Bamboo Sword	.10	.20
❑ TAEV63	Mirror Gate (UTR)	4.00	8.00
❑ TAEV63	Mirror Gate (SR)	2.00	4.00
❑ TAEV64	Hero Counterattack	.10	.20
❑ TAEV65	Cocoon Veil	.10	.20
❑ TAEV66	Snake Whistle	.10	.20
❑ TAEV67	Damage = Reptile (R)	.50	1.00
❑ TAEV68	Snake Deity's Command (R)	.50	1.00
❑ TAEV69	Rise of the Snake Deity	.10	.20
❑ TAEV70	Ambush Fangs	.10	.20
❑ TAEV71	Venom Burn	.10	.20
❑ TAEV72	Common Charity (R)	.50	1.00
❑ TAEV73	Destructive Draw	.10	.20
❑ TAEV74	Shield Spear	.10	.20
❑ TAEV75	Strike Slash	.10	.20
❑ TAEV76	Spell Reclamation (R)	.50	1.00
❑ TAEV77	Trap Reclamation (R)	.50	1.00
❑ TAEV78	Gift Card	.10	.20
❑ TAEV79	The Gift of Greed	.10	.20
❑ TAEV80	Counter Counter	.10	.20
❑ TAEV81	Ocean's Keeper (R)	.50	1.00
❑ TAEV82	Thousand-Eyes Jellyfish (R)	.50	1.00
❑ TAEV83	Cranium Fish (SCR)	7.50	15.00
❑ TAEV84	Abyssal Kingshark (SCR)	7.50	15.00
❑ TAEV85	Mormolith (SCR)	4.00	10.00
❑ TAEV86	Fossil Tusker (R)	.50	1.00
❑ TAEV87	Phantom Dragonray Bronto (R)	.50	1.00
❑ TAEV88	Il Blud (SCR)	10.00	20.00
❑ TAEV89	Blazewing Butterfly (UTR)	3.00	8.00
❑ TAEV89	Blazewing Butterfly (SR)	2.00	4.00

2008 Yu-Gi-Oh Phantom Darkness 1st Edition

Card	Name	Low	High
	Complete Set (100)	225.00	400.00
	Booster Box (36 packs)	70.00	90.00
	Booster Pack (9 cards)	3.50	4.00
❑ PTDN0	Dark Grepher (SCR)	15.00	25.00
❑ PTDN1	Atlantean Pikeman	.10	.25
❑ PTDN3	Rainbow Dark Dragon (SCR)	25.00	40.00
❑ PTDN4	Samsara Lotus	.10	.25
❑ PTDN5	Regenerating Rose	.10	.25
❑ PTDN6	Yubel (SR)	5.00	10.00
❑ PTDN7	Yubel - Terror Incarnate (UR)	7.00	15.00
❑ PTDN7	Yubel - Terror Incarnate (UTR)	10.00	20.00
❑ PTDN8	Yubel - The Ultimate Nightmare (SCR)	25.00	45.00
❑ PTDN9	Armored Cybern	.10	.25
❑ PTDN10	Cyber Valley (SR)	10.00	18.00
❑ PTDN11	Cyber Ouroboros	.10	.25
❑ PTDN12	Volcanic Counter (SR)	5.00	10.00
❑ PTDN13	Fire Trooper	.10	.25
❑ PTDN14	Destiny Hero - Dunker	.10	.25
❑ PTDN15	Destiny Hero - Departed	.10	.25
❑ PTDN16	Dark Horus (UR)	5.00	10.00
❑ PTDN17	The Dark Creator (SCR)	30.00	50.00
❑ PTDN18	Dark Nephthys (UTR)	10.00	20.00
❑ PTDN18	Dark Nephthys (UR)	8.00	15.00
❑ PTDN19	Dark Armed Dragon (SCR)	50.00	100.00
❑ PTDN20	Dark Crusader	.10	.25
❑ PTDN21	Armageddon Knight (SR)	5.00	10.00
❑ PTDN22	Doomsday Horror (SR)	2.00	3.00
❑ PTDN23	Obsidian Dragon	.10	.25
❑ PTDN24	Shadowpriestess of Ohm (R)	.50	1.00
❑ PTDN25	Gemini Lancer	.10	.25
❑ PTDN26	Gigaplant (R)	.50	1.00
❑ PTDN27	Future Samurai (R)	.50	1.00
❑ PTDN28	Vengeful Shinobi	.10	.25
❑ PTDN29	The Immortal Bushi	.10	.25
❑ PTDN30	Field-Commander Rahz (SR)	2.00	4.00
❑ PTDN31	Gladiator Beast Darius	.10	.25
❑ PTDN32	Imprisoned Queen Archfiend	.10	.25
❑ PTDN33	Black Veloci	.10	.25
❑ PTDN34	Superancient Deepsea King Coelacanth (SR)	3.00	6.00
❑ PTDN34	Superancient Deepsea King Coelacanth (UTR)	4.00	8.00
❑ PTDN35	Cannon Soldier MK-2	.10	.25
❑ PTDN36	The Calculator	.10	.25
❑ PTDN37	Sea Koala	.10	.25
❑ PTDN38	Blue Thunder T-45	.10	.25
❑ PTDN39	Magnetic Mosquito	.10	.25
❑ PTDN40	Earth Effigy	.10	.25
❑ PTDN41	Wind Effigy	.10	.25
❑ PTDN42	Neo-Spacian Twinkle Moss	.10	.25
❑ PTDN43	Elemental Hero Storm Neos (SR)	2.00	4.00
❑ PTDN44	Rainbow Neos (SCR)	15.00	25.00
❑ PTDN44	Rainbow Neos (GR)	20.00	30.00
❑ PTDN45	Rainbow Veil	.10	.25
❑ PTDN46	Super Polymerization (R)	.50	1.00
❑ PTDN47	Vicious Claw	.10	.25
❑ PTDN48	Instant Neo Space	.10	.25
❑ PTDN49	Mirage Tube	.10	.25
❑ PTDN50	Spell Chronicle	.10	.25
❑ PTDN51	Dimension Explosion	.10	.25
❑ PTDN52	Cybernetic Zone	.10	.25
❑ PTDN53	The Beginning of the End (UR)	4.00	8.00
❑ PTDN53	The Beginning of the End (UTR)	6.00	12.00
❑ PTDN54	Dark Eruption (SR)	2.00	4.00
❑ PTDN55	Fires of Doomsday (R)	.50	1.00
❑ PTDN56	Unleash Your Power!	.10	.25
❑ PTDN57	Chain Summoning	.10	.25
❑ PTDN58	Acidic Downpour	.10	.25
❑ PTDN59	Six Samurai United (R)	.50	1.00
❑ PTDN60	Gladiator Beast's Battle Archf.Shield	.10	.25
❑ PTDN61	Gladiator Proving Ground	.10	.25
❑ PTDN62	Dark World Grimoire	.10	.25

❑ PTDN63 Rainbow Path	.10	.25
❑ PTDN64 Rainbow Life (R)	.50	1.00
❑ PTDN65 Sinister Seeds	.10	.25
❑ PTDN66 Hate Buster (R)	.50	1.00
❑ PTDN67 Chain Material	.10	.25
❑ PTDN68 Alchemy Cycle	.10	.25
❑ PTDN69 Cybernetic Hidden Technology	.10	.25
❑ PTDN70 Dark Spirit Art - Greed (R)	.50	1.00
❑ PTDN71 Dark Illusion (R)	.50	1.00
❑ PTDN72 Escape from Dark Dimension (SR)	2.00	4.00
❑ PTDN73 Gemini Trap Hole	.10	.25
❑ PTDN74 Drastic Drop Off (UTR)	5.00	10.00
❑ PTDN74 Drastic Drop Off (UR)	3.00	7.00
❑ PTDN75 All-Out Attacks	.10	.25
❑ PTDN76 Double Tag Team	.10	.25
❑ PTDN77 Offering to the Snake Deity (R)	.50	1.00
❑ PTDN78 Cry Havoc! (R)	.50	1.00
❑ PTDN79 Transmigration Break	.10	.25
❑ PTDN80 Fine	.10	.25
❑ PTDN81 Darklord Zerato (SCR)	30.00	50.00
❑ PTDN82 Darknight Parshath (UTR)	7.00	14.00
❑ PTDN82 Darknight Parshath (UR)	4.00	8.00
❑ PTDN83 Deepsea Macrotrema (R)	.50	1.00
❑ PTDN84 Allure of Darkness (UTR)	30.00	50.00
❑ PTDN84 Allure of Darkness (UR)	20.00	40.00
❑ PTDN85 Metabo Globster (R)	.50	1.00
❑ PTDN86 Golden Flying Fish (SR)	1.00	2.00
❑ PTDN87 Prime Material Dragon (SR)	4.00	9.00
❑ PTDN88 Lonefire Blossom (R)	.50	1.00
❑ PTDN89 Aztekipede, the Worm Warrior (R)	.50	1.00
❑ PTDN90 Vampire's Curse (UTR)	9.00	18.00
❑ PTDN90 Vampire's Curse (UR)	4.00	8.00
❑ PTDN91 Castle Gate (R)	.50	1.00
❑ PTDN92 Dark-Eyes Illusionist (R)	.50	1.00
❑ PTDN93 Legendary Fiend (R)	.50	1.00
❑ PTDN94 Metal Reflect Slime (UTR)	9.00	18.00
❑ PTDN94 Metal Reflect Slime (UR)	6.00	12.00
❑ PTDN95 Zoma the Spirit (SR)	3.00	6.00
❑ PTDN96 Call of the Earthbound (R)	.50	1.00
❑ PTDN97 Dark Red Enchanter (SCR)	20.00	38.00
❑ PTDN98 Goblin Zombie (SCR)	25.00	45.00
❑ PTDN99 Belial Marquis of Darkness (SCR)	18.00	28.00

2008 Yu-Gi-Oh Gold

Complete Set (45)	100.00	150.00
Booster Box	250.00	350.00
Booster Pack (25 cards)	50.00	75.00
❑ GLD1-1 7 Colored Fish	.10	.25
❑ GLD1-2 Sonic Bird	.10	.25
❑ GLD1-3 Jinzo (GUR)	12.00	18.00
❑ GLD1-4 Summoner Of Illusions	.10	.25
❑ GLD1-5 Fire Princess	.10	.25
❑ GLD1-6 Needle Worm	.25	.50
❑ GLD1-7 8-Claws Scorpion	.10	.25
❑ GLD1-8 Swarm Of Scarabs	.10	.25
❑ GLD1-9 Swarm Of Locusts	.10	.25
❑ GLD110 Des Lacooda	.10	.25
❑ GLD111 Newdoria	.10	.25
❑ GLD112 Don Zaloog (GUR)	2.00	5.00
❑ GLD113 Old Vindictive Magician	.10	.25
❑ GLD114 Breaker the Magical Warrior (GUR)	1.50	3.00
❑ GLD115 D.D. Warrior Lady (GUR)	1.00	2.00
❑ GLD116 Dark Magician of Chaos (GUR)	10.00	20.00
❑ GLD117 Stealth Bird	.10	.25
❑ GLD118 Regenerating Mummy	.10	.25
❑ GLD119 Solar Flare Dragon	.10	.25
❑ GLD120 Rare Metal Dragon	.10	.25
❑ GLD121 Nightmare Penguin	.10	.25
❑ GLD122 Cyber Dragon (GUR)	6.00	12.00
❑ GLD123 Sillva, Warlord Of Dark World	.25	.50
❑ GLD124 Goldd, Wu-Lord Of Dark World (GUR)	1.00	2.00
❑ GLD125 Doom Dozer	.10	.25
❑ GLD126 Grandmaster of the Six Samurai (GUR)	10.00	20.00
❑ GLD127 Prometheus, King Of Shadows (GUR)	3.00	6.00
❑ GLD128 Blue-Eyes Ultimate Dragon (GUR)	3.00	6.00
❑ GLD129 Chimeratech Overdragon (GUR)	1.00	2.00
❑ GLD130 Swords of Revealing Light (GUR)	1.00	2.00
❑ GLD131 Heavy Storm (GUR)	1.00	2.00
❑ GLD132 Reinforcement of the Army (GUR)	1.00	2.00
❑ GLD133 Brain Control (GUR)	1.00	2.00
❑ GLD134 Offerings To The Doomed	.10	.25
❑ GLD135 Non-Spellcasting Area	.10	.25
❑ GLD136 Mist Body	.10	.25
❑ GLD137 Pandemonium	.10	.25
❑ GLD138 Crush Card Virus (GUR)	40.00	80.00
❑ GLD139 Mirror Force (GUR)	25.00	36.00
❑ GLD140 Torrential Tribute (GUR)	1.00	2.00
❑ GLD141 Needle Ceiling	.10	.25
❑ GLD142 Royal Command	.10	.25
❑ GLD143 Rivalry Of Warlords	.10	.25
❑ GLD144 Skill Drain	.10	.25
❑ GLD145 Spell Shield Type-8	.10	.25

2008 Yu-Gi-Oh Light of Destruction 1st Edition

Complete Set (100)	200.00	300.00
Booster Box (24 packs)	70.00	90.00
Booster Pack (9 cards)	3.50	4.00
❑ LODT0 Guardian of Order (SCR)	10.00	20.00
❑ LODT1 Honest (SCR)	30.00	50.00
❑ LODT2 Cross Porter	.10	.25
❑ LODT3 Miracle Flipper	.10	.25
❑ LODT4 Destiny Hero - Dread Servant	.10	.25
❑ LODT5 Volcanic Queen	.10	.25
❑ LODT6 Jinzo - Returner (R)	.50	1.00
❑ LODT7 Jinzo - Lord (SR)	2.00	4.00
❑ LODT8 Arcana Force 0 - The Fool	.10	.25
❑ LODT9 Arcana Force I - The Magician	.10	.25
❑ LODT10 Arcana Force III - The Empress	.10	.25
❑ LODT11 Arcana Force IV - The Emperor	.10	.25
❑ LODT12 Arcana Force VI - The Lovers	.10	.25
❑ LODT13 Arcana Force VII - The Chariot	.10	.25
❑ LODT14 Arcana Force XIV - Temperance (R)	.50	1.00
❑ LODT15 Arcana Force XVIII - The Moon	.10	.25
❑ LODT16 Arcana Force XXI - The World (UTR)	10.00	20.00
❑ LODT16 Arcana Force XXI - The World (UR)	5.00	10.00
❑ LODT17 Arcana Force EX/ The Dark Ruler (SCR)	15.00	25.00
❑ LODT19 Lyla, Lightsworn Sorceress (UR)	10.00	20.00
❑ LODT19 Lyla, Lightsworn Sorceress (UTR)	12.00	25.00
❑ LODT20 Garoth, Lightsworn Warrior	.10	.25
❑ LODT21 Lumina, Lightsworn Summoner (R)	.50	1.00
❑ LODT22 Ryko, Lightsworn Hunter (SR)	3.00	6.00
❑ LODT23 Wulf, Lightsworn Beast (SR)	3.00	6.00
❑ LODT24 Celestia, Lightsworn Angel (UR)	6.00	12.00
❑ LODT24 Celestia, Lightsworn Angel (UTR)	8.00	16.00
❑ LODT25 Gragonith, Lightsworn Dragon	.10	.25
❑ LODT26 Judgment Dragon (SCR)	50.00	80.00
❑ LODT27 Dark Valkyria (R)	.50	1.00
❑ LODT28 Substitoad (R)	.20	.50
❑ LODT29 Unifrog	.10	.25
❑ LODT30 Batteryman Charger	.10	.25
❑ LODT31 Batteryman Industrial Strength (R)	.50	1.00
❑ LODT32 Batteryman Micro-Cell	.10	.25
❑ LODT33 Goblin Recon Squad	.10	.25
❑ LODT34 Interplanetary Invader A	.10	.25
❑ LODT35 Diskblade Rider (R)	.60	1.00
❑ LODT36 Golden Ladybug (R)	.50	1.00
❑ LODT37 DUCKER Mobile Cannon (SR)	1.00	2.00
❑ LODT38 The Lady in Wight	.10	.25
❑ LODT39 Simorgh, Bird of Ancestry (R)	.50	1.00
❑ LODT40 Cloudian - Storm Dragon	.10	.25
❑ LODT41 Phantom Dragon (UR)	2.00	4.00
❑ LODT41 Phantom Dragon (UTR)	3.00	6.00
❑ LODT42 Destiny End Dragoon (UTR)	4.00	8.00
❑ LODT42 Destiny End Dragoon (UR)	3.00	6.00
❑ LODT43 Ultimate Ancient Gear Golem (UR)	3.00	6.00
❑ LODT43 Ultimate Ancient Gear Golem (UTR)	4.00	8.00
❑ LODT44 Gladiator Beast Gyzarus (SR)	6.00	12.00
❑ LODT45 Hero Mask	.10	.25
❑ LODT46 Space Gift	.10	.25
❑ LODT47 Demise of the Land	.10	.25
❑ LODT48 D - Formation	.10	.25
❑ LODT49 Spell Gear	.10	.25
❑ LODT50 Cup of Ace	.10	.25
❑ LODT51 Light Barrier (R)	.20	.50
❑ LODT52 Solar Recharge (UR)	10.00	20.00
❑ LODT52 Solar Recharge (UTR)	15.00	25.00
❑ LODT53 Realm of Light	.10	.25
❑ LODT54 Wetlands	.10	.25
❑ LODT55 Quick Charger	.10	.25
❑ LODT56 Short Circuit	.10	.25
❑ LODT57 Light of Redemption (SR)	1.00	2.00
❑ LODT58 Mystical Cards of Light (SP)	.20	.50
❑ LODT59 Level Tuning (SP)	.20	.50
❑ LODT60 Deck Lockdown (R)	.20	.50
❑ LODT61 Ribbon of Rebirth (R)	.20	.50
❑ LODT62 Golden Bamboo Sword (SP)	.20	.50
❑ LODT63 Limit Reverse	.10	.25
❑ LODT64 Hero Blast (R)	.20	.50
❑ LODT65 Rainbow Gravity	.10	.25
❑ LODT66 D - Fortune	.10	.25
❑ LODT67 Reversal of Fate	.10	.25
❑ LODT68 Tour of Doom (SP)	.20	.50
❑ LODT69 Arcana Call	.10	.25
❑ LODT70 Light Spiral	.10	.25
❑ LODT71 Glorious Illusion (R)	.20	.50
❑ LODT72 Destruction Jammer (R)	.20	.50
❑ LODT73 Froggy Forcefield (R)	.20	.50
❑ LODT74 Portable Battery Pack	.10	.25
❑ LODT75 Gladiator Lash	.10	.25
❑ LODT76 Raging Cloudian	.10	.25
❑ LODT77 Sanguine Swamp	.10	.25
❑ LODT78 Lucky Chance	.10	.25
❑ LODT79 Summon Limit	.10	.25
❑ LODT80 Dice Try!	.10	.25
❑ LODT81 Aurkus, Lightsworn Druid (SR)	2.00	5.00
❑ LODT82 Ehren, Lightsworn Monk (SCR)	30.00	50.00
❑ LODT83 Dark General Freed (SCR)	10.00	20.00
❑ LODT84 Magical Exemplar (SR)	2.00	4.00
❑ LODT85 Maniacal Servant (R)	.20	.50
❑ LODT86 Nimble Musasabi (R)	.20	.50
❑ LODT87 Flame Spirit Ignis (R)	.20	.50
❑ LODT88 Super-Ancient Dinobeast (UR)	2.00	4.00
❑ LODT88 Super-Ancient Dinobeast (UTR)	3.00	6.00
❑ LODT89 Vanquishing Light (SR)	2.00	4.00
❑ LODT90 Tualatin (SCR)	10.00	20.00
❑ LODT91 Divine Knight Ishzark (SR)	2.00	5.00
❑ LODT92 Angel O7 (SCR)	10.00	20.00
❑ LODT93 Union Attack (SR)	2.00	4.00
❑ LODT94 Owner's Seal (R)	.50	1.00
❑ LODT95 Helios Trice Megistus (SR)	2.00	4.00
❑ LODT96 Dangerous Machine Type-6 (UR)	2.00	4.00
❑ LODT96 Dangerous Machine Type-6 (UTR)	3.00	6.00
❑ LODT97 Maximum Six (UR)	2.00	4.00
❑ LODT97 Maximum Six (UTR)	3.00	6.00
❑ LODT98 Fog King (SCR)	10.00	18.00
❑ LODT99 Fossil Dyna Pachycephalo (SCR)	25.00	40.00

2008 Yu-Gi-Oh The Duelist Genesis 1st Edition

Complete Set (100)	200.00	300.00
Booster Box (24 packs)	70.00	90.00
Booster Pack (9 cards)	3.50	4.00
❑ 1 Turbo Booster	.10	.25
❑ 2 Nitro Synchron (SR)	1.00	2.00
❑ 3 Quillbolt Hedgehog	.10	.25
❑ 4 Ghost Gardna	.10	.25
❑ 6 Small Piece Golem	.10	.25
❑ 7 Medium Piece Golem	.10	.25
❑ 8 Big Piece Golem (R)	.50	1.00
❑ 9 Sinister Sprocket (SR)	1.00	2.00
❑ 10 Dark Resonator (R)	.50	1.00
❑ 11 Twin-Shield Defender	.10	.25
❑ 12 Jutte Fighter	.10	.25
❑ 13 Handcuffs Dragon (R)	1.00	2.00
❑ 14 Montage Dragon (UR)	6.00	12.00
❑ 14 Montage Dragon (UTR)	7.00	15.00
❑ 15 Gonogo	.10	.25
❑ 16 Mind Master (R)	.50	1.00
❑ 17 Doctor Cranium	.10	.25
❑ 18 Krebons	.10	.25
❑ 19 Mind Protector	.10	.25
❑ 20 Psychic Commander	.10	.25
❑ 21 Psychic Snail	.10	.25
❑ 22 Telekinetic Shocker	.10	.25
❑ 23 Destructotron	.10	.25
❑ 24 Gladiator Beast Equeste	.10	.25
❑ 25 Jenis, Lightsworn Mender	.10	.25
❑ 26 Dharc the Dark Charmer	.10	.25
❑ 27 Mecha Bunny	.10	.25
❑ 28 Oyster Meister	.10	.25
❑ 29 Twin-Barrel Dragon (SR)	1.00	2.00
❑ 30 Izanagi (SR)	1.00	2.00
❑ 31 Kunoichi	.10	.25
❑ 32 Beast of the Pharaoh	.10	.25
❑ 33 Dark Hunter (UR)	4.00	8.00
❑ 34 Kinka-byo (SR)	2.00	4.00
❑ 35 Yamato-no-Kami (R)	.50	1.00
❑ 36 Silent Strider	.10	.25
❑ 37 Noisy Gnat	.10	.25
❑ 38 Multiple Piece Golem (UR)	4.00	8.00
❑ 39 Nitro Warrior (UR)	4.00	8.00
❑ 40 Stardust Dragon (UR)	10.00	15.00
❑ 41 Red Dragon Archfiend (UR)	7.00	15.00
❑ 42 Goyo Guardian (UR)	25.00	45.00
❑ 43 Magical Android (SR)	5.00	10.00
❑ 44 Thought Ruler Archfiend (UR)	5.00	10.00
❑ 45 Fighting Spirit (R)	.50	1.00
❑ 46 Domino Effect	.10	.25
❑ 47 Junk Barrage	.10	.25
❑ 48 Battle Tuned	.10	.25
❑ 49 De-Synchro (R)	.50	1.00
❑ 50 Lightwave Tuning	.10	.25
❑ 51 Psi-Station	.10	.25
❑ 52 Psi-Impulse	.10	.25
❑ 53 Emergency Teleport (UR)	20.00	40.00
❑ 53 Emergency Teleport (UTR)	30.00	50.00
❑ 54 Sword of Kusanagi	.10	.25
❑ 55 Orb of Yasaka	.10	.25
❑ 56 Mirror of Yata	.10	.25
❑ 57 Geartown	.10	.25
❑ 58 Power Filter (SR)	1.00	3.00
❑ 59 Lightsworn Sabre (SR)	1.00	3.00
❑ 60 Unstable Evolution (SR)	1.00	3.00
❑ 61 Recycling Batteries	.10	.25
❑ 62 Book of Eclipse (SP)	.20	.50
❑ 63 Equip Shot (SP)	.20	.50
❑ 64 Graceful Revival (R)	.50	1.00
❑ 65 Defense Draw (R)	.50	1.00
❑ 66 Remote Revenge	.10	.25
❑ 67 Spacegate	.10	.25
❑ 68 Synchro Deflector	.10	.25
❑ 69 Broken Blocker (SR)	1.00	3.00
❑ 70 Psychic Overload (UR)	4.00	8.00
❑ 70 Psychic Overload (UTR)	5.00	10.00
❑ 71 Psychic Rejuvenation	.10	.25
❑ 72 Telepathic Power	.10	.25
❑ 73 Mind Over Matter (R)	.50	1.00
❑ 74 Gladiator Beast War Chariot (SR)	4.00	8.00
❑ 75 Lightsworn Barrier	.10	.25
❑ 76 Intercept (SR)	1.00	2.00
❑ 77 Judgment of Thunder	.10	.25
❑ 78 Fish Depth Charge	.10	.25
❑ 79 Needlebug Nest (SP)	.20	.50
❑ 80 Overworked (SP)	.20	.50
❑ 81 Counselor Lily (SR)	1.00	3.00
❑ 82 Herald of Orange Light (R)	.50	1.00
❑ 83 Izanami (R)	.50	1.00
❑ 84 Maiden of Macabre (R)	.50	1.00
❑ 85 Hand of the Six Samurai (SCR)	25.00	45.00
❑ 86 Cyber Shark (SCR)	10.00	20.00
❑ 87 Grapple Blocker (R)	.50	1.00
❑ 88 Telekinetic Charging Cell (R)	.50	1.00
❑ 89 Charge of the Light Brigade (SCR)	50.00	100.00
❑ 90 The Tricky (R)	.50	1.00
❑ 91 Tricky Spell 4	.10	.25
❑ 92 Trap of Darkness (R)	.50	1.00
❑ 93 The Selection (R)	.50	1.00
❑ 94 Splendid Venus (SCR)	15.00	30.00
❑ 95 Fiendish Engine W (SCR)	7.00	15.00
❑ 96 Cold Enchanter (R)	.50	1.00
❑ 97 Ice Master (SCR)	15.00	25.00
❑ 98 Kunai with Chain (SR)	2.00	4.00
❑ 99 Toy Magician (SCR)	20.00	40.00
❑ 0 Avenging Knight Parshath (SCR)	12.00	22.00

2008 Yu-Gi-Oh Crossroads of Chaos 1st Edition

Complete Set (100)	175.00	250.00
Booster Box (24 packs)	75.00	100.00
Booster Pack (9 cards)	3.00	4.00
❑ CSOC0 Rose, Warrior of Revenge (UTR)	6.00	15.00
❑ CSOC0 Rose, Warrior of Revenge (UR)	5.00	12.00
❑ CSOC1 Healing Wave Generator	.10	.25
❑ CSOC2 Turbo Synchron (R)	1.00	2.50
❑ CSOC3 Mad Archfiend (R)	.75	2.00
❑ CSOC4 Wall of Ivy	.10	.25
❑ CSOC5 Copy Plant	.10	.25
❑ CSOC6 Morphtronic Celfon	.10	.25
❑ CSOC7 Morphtronic Magnen	.10	.25
❑ CSOC8 Morphtronic Datatron	.10	.25
❑ CSOC9 Morphtronic Boomboxen (R)	.60	1.50
❑ CSOC10 Morphtronic Cameran	.10	.25
❑ CSOC11 Morphtronic Radion (R)	.75	2.00
❑ CSOC12 Morphtronic Clocken	.10	.25
❑ CSOC13 Gadget Hauler	.10	.25
❑ CSOC14 Gadget Driver	.10	.25
❑ CSOC15 Search Striker (R)	.75	2.00
❑ CSOC16 Pursuit Chaser	.10	.25
❑ CSOC17 Iron Chain Repairman (R)	.60	1.50
❑ CSOC18 Iron Chain Snake	.10	.25
❑ CSOC19 Iron Chain Blaster	.10	.25
❑ CSOC20 Iron Chain Coil	.10	.25
❑ CSOC21 Power Injector	.10	.25
❑ CSOC22 Storm Caller (R)	.75	2.00
❑ CSOC23 Psychic Jumper	.10	.25
❑ CSOC24 Nettles	.10	.25
❑ CSOC25 Gigantic Cephalotus	.10	.25
❑ CSOC26 Horseytail	.10	.25
❑ CSOC27 Botanical Girl	.10	.25
❑ CSOC28 Cursed Fig (SP)	.10	.25
❑ CSOC29 Tytannial, Princess of Camellias (UR)	6.00	15.00
❑ CSOC29 Tytannial, Princess of Camellias (UTR)	10.00	25.00
❑ CSOC30 Zombie Mammoth	.10	.25
❑ CSOC31 Plaguespreader Zombie (UTR)	30.00	60.00
❑ CSOC31 Plaguespreader Zombie (UR)	25.00	50.00
❑ CSOC32 Goblin Decoy Squad	.10	.25
❑ CSOC33 Comrade Swordsman of Landstar	.10	.25
❑ CSOC34 Hanewata (SR)	1.25	3.00
❑ CSOC35 The White Stone of Legend (SP)	.10	.25
❑ CSOC36 Tiger Dragon (R)	1.25	3.00
❑ CSOC37 Jade Knight (SP)	.10	.25
❑ CSOC38 Turbo Warrior (UTR)	4.00	10.00
❑ CSOC38 Turbo Warrior (UR)	3.00	8.00
❑ CSOC39 Black Rose Dragon (GR)	15.00	30.00
❑ CSOC39 Black Rose Dragon (UR)	8.00	20.00
❑ CSOC39 Black Rose Dragon (UTR)	10.00	25.00
❑ CSOC40 Iron Chain Dragon (R)	1.50	4.00
❑ CSOC41 Psychic Lifetrancer (R)	1.50	4.00
❑ CSOC42 Queen of Thorns (SR)	1.50	4.00
❑ CSOC43 Doomkaiser Dragon (UR)	4.00	10.00
❑ CSOC43 Doomkaiser Dragon (UTR)	5.00	12.00
❑ CSOC44 Revived King Ha Des (UR)	4.00	10.00
❑ CSOC44 Revived King Ha Des (UTR)	5.00	12.00
❑ CSOC45 Card Rotator	.10	.25
❑ CSOC46 Seed of Deception	.10	.25
❑ CSOC47 Mark of the Rose (UR)	4.00	10.00
❑ CSOC47 Mark of the Rose (UTR)	5.00	12.00
❑ CSOC48 Black Garden (SR)	4.00	10.00
❑ CSOC49 Factory of 100 Machines	.10	.25
❑ CSOC50 Morphtronic Accelerator (R)	.60	1.50
❑ CSOC51 Morphtronic Cord	.10	.25
❑ CSOC52 Morphtronic Engine	.10	.25
❑ CSOC53 Poison Chain	.10	.25
❑ CSOC54 Paralyzing Chain (R)	.60	1.50
❑ CSOC55 Teleport	.10	.25
❑ CSOC56 Psychokinesis (UR)	2.00	5.00
❑ CSOC56 Psychokinesis (UTR)	3.00	8.00
❑ CSOC57 Miracle Fertilizer (R)	.75	2.00
❑ CSOC58 Fragrance Storm	.10	.25
❑ CSOC59 The World Tree (R)	.75	2.00
❑ CSOC60 Everliving Underworld Cannon	.10	.25
❑ CSOC61 Secret Village of the Spellcasters (SR)	10.00	25.00
❑ CSOC62 Omega Goggles (SP)	.10	.25
❑ CSOC63 Battle Mania (SR)	.75	2.00
❑ CSOC64 Confusion Chaff	.10	.25
❑ CSOC65 Urgent Tuning (SR)	1.25	3.00
❑ CSOC66 Synchro Strike	.10	.25
❑ CSOC67 Prideful Roar (R)	.75	2.00
❑ CSOC68 Revival Gift	.10	.25
❑ CSOC69 Lineage of Destruction	.10	.25
❑ CSOC70 Doppelganger	.10	.25
❑ CSOC71 Morphtransition	.10	.25
❑ CSOC72 Morphtronic Monitron	.10	.25
❑ CSOC73 Psychic Trigger (SR)	1.00	2.50
❑ CSOC74 Pollinosis (R)	.40	1.00
❑ CSOC75 Bamboo Scrap	.10	.25
❑ CSOC76 Plant Food Chain	.10	.25
❑ CSOC77 Trap of the Imperial Tomb (R)	.40	1.00
❑ CSOC78 DNA Checkup	.10	.25
❑ CSOC79 Gozen Match	.10	.25
❑ CSOC80 Giant Trap Hole	.10	.25
❑ CSOC81 Seed of Flame (UR)	2.00	5.00
❑ CSOC81 Seed of Flame (UTR)	3.00	8.00
❑ CSOC82 Cactus Fighter (R)	.60	1.50
❑ CSOC83 Overdrive Teleporter (SCR)	10.00	25.00
❑ CSOC84 Rai-Jin (SR)	.75	2.00
❑ CSOC85 Rai-Mei (SR)	2.00	5.00
❑ CSOC86 Gladiator Beast Retiari (SCR)	20.00	40.00
❑ CSOC87 Night's End Sorcerer (SR)	4.00	10.00
❑ CSOC88 Tempest Magician (SCR)	25.00	50.00
❑ CSOC89 Treacherous Trap Hole (SCR)	20.00	40.00
❑ CSOC90 Puppet Master (SR)	.75	2.00
❑ CSOC91 Time Machine (SCR)	10.00	25.00
❑ CSOC92 Virus Cannon (R)	.60	1.50
❑ CSOC93 Machine Lord Ür (SCR)	6.00	15.00
❑ CSOC94 Mosaic Manticore (R)	.40	1.00
❑ CSOC95 Goka, the Pyre of Malice (SR)	.75	2.00
❑ CSOC96 Red Ogre (SR)	.75	2.00
❑ CSOC97 Neos Wiseman (SCR)	10.00	25.00
❑ CSOC98 Elemental Hero Divine Neos (SCR)	10.00	25.00
❑ CSOC99 Botanical Lion (SR)	3.00	8.00

2008 Yu-Gi-Oh Retro Pack 1

Complete Set (100)	400.00	500.00
Booster Pack (9 cards)	8.00	10.00
Set (3 packs)	25.00	30.00
Box (8 sets)	80.00	100.00
❑ RP01-0 Blue-Eyes Ultimate Dragon (SCR)	3.00	8.00
❑ RP01-1 Blue-Eyes White Dragon (UR)	8.00	20.00
❑ RP01-3 Dark Magician (UR)	3.00	8.00
❑ RP01-5 Raigeki (UR)	10.00	25.00
❑ RP01-6 Fissure (R)	1.50	4.00
❑ RP01-11 Red-Eyes B. Dragon (UR)	4.00	10.00
❑ RP01-12 Swords of Revealing Light (SR)	2.50	6.00
❑ RP01-16 Monster Reborn (SR)	5.00	12.00
❑ RP01-17 Right Leg of the Forbidden One (R)	5.00	12.00
❑ RP01-18 Left Leg of the Forbidden One (R)	5.00	12.00
❑ RP01-19 Right Arm of the Forbidden One (R)	5.00	12.00
❑ RP01-20 Left Arm of the Forbidden One (R)	5.00	12.00
❑ RP01-21 Exodia the Forbidden One (UR)	20.00	40.00
❑ RP01-22 Gaia the Dragon Champion (SR)	2.00	5.00
❑ RP01-23 Gate Guardian (UR)	10.00	25.00
❑ RP01-24 Summoned Skull (SR)	2.50	6.00
❑ RP01-26 Harpie Lady Sisters (R)	1.00	2.50
❑ RP01-28 B. Skull Dragon (R)	1.50	4.00
❑ RP01-30 Sanga of the Thunder (R)	2.00	5.00
❑ RP01-31 Kazejin (R)	1.50	4.00
❑ RP01-32 Suijin (R)	1.50	4.00
❑ RP01-33 Magician of Faith (R)	1.50	4.00
❑ RP01-35 Time Wizard (SR)	2.50	6.00
❑ RP01-36 Sangan (SR)	6.00	15.00
❑ RP01-37 Kuriboh (SR)	1.00	2.50
❑ RP01-38 Catapult Turtle (SR)	2.00	5.00
❑ RP01-44 Barrel Dragon (R)	2.50	6.00
❑ RP01-45 Solemn Judgment (SR)	20.00	40.00
❑ RP01-48 Heavy Storm (R)	1.25	3.00
❑ RP01-50 Blue-Eyes Toon Dragon (R)	1.25	3.00
❑ RP01-51 Axe of Despair (R)	1.25	3.00
❑ RP01-54 Relinquished (UR)	3.00	8.00
❑ RP01-59 Painful Choice (R)	1.50	4.00
❑ RP01-61 Megamorph (R)	1.00	2.50
❑ RP01-82 Messenger of Peace (R)	1.50	4.00
❑ RP01-84 Card Destruction (R)	2.50	6.00
❑ RP01-85 La Jinn the Mystical Genie of the Lamp (SR)	2.50	6.00
❑ RP01-86 Lord of D. (R)	1.00	2.50
❑ RP01-87 The Flute of Summoning Dragon (R)	1.50	4.00
❑ RP01-88 Graceful Charity (R)	1.50	4.00
❑ RP01-90 Scapegoat (UR)	10.00	25.00
❑ RP01-91 Blast Sphere (SCR)	20.00	40.00
❑ RP01-92 Copycat (SCR)	25.00	50.00
❑ RP01-93 Relieve Monster (SCR)	10.00	25.00
❑ RP01-94 Cloning (SCR)	20.00	40.00
❑ RP01-95 Kaibaman (SCR)	20.00	40.00
❑ RP01-96 Cyber Harpie Lady (SCR)	20.00	40.00
❑ RP01-97 Amazoness Chain Master (SCR)	20.00	40.00
❑ RP01-98 Embodiment of Apophis (SCR)	15.00	30.00
❑ RP01-99 Exchange of the Spirit (SCR)	15.00	30.00
❑ RP01-100 Ancient Lamp (SCR)	20.00	40.00

2009 Yu-Gi-Oh Ancient Prophecy 1st Edition

Complete Set (100)	200.00	300.00
Booster Box (24 packs)	70.00	90.00
Booster Pack (9 cards)	3.00	4.00
❑ ANPR0 XX-Saber Gardestrike (SCR)	8.00	20.00
❑ ANPR1 Kuribon (R)	.60	1.50
❑ ANPR2 Sunny Pixie	.10	.25
❑ ANPR3 Sunlight Unicorn	.10	.25
❑ ANPR4 Blackwing - Mistral the Silver Shield	.10	.25
❑ ANPR5 Blackwing Vayu the Emblem of Honor (UR)	30.00	60.00
❑ ANPR5 Blackwing Vayu the Emblem of Honor (UTR)	25.00	50.00
❑ ANPR6 Blackwing - Fane the Steel Chain	.10	.25
❑ ANPR7 Morphtronic Magnen Bar	.10	.25
❑ ANPR8 Jester Lord (R)	.40	1.00
❑ ANPR9 Jester Confit (SR)	1.25	3.00
❑ ANPR10 Fortune Lady Light (R)	1.00	2.50
❑ ANPR11 Fortune Lady Fire (R)	.75	2.00
❑ ANPR12 Infernity Beast	.10	.25
❑ ANPR13 Darksea Rescue (R)	.40	1.00
❑ ANPR14 Darksea Float	.10	.25
❑ ANPR15 Turbo Rocket (R)	.75	2.00
❑ ANPR16 Earthbound Immortal Cusillu (UTR)	6.00	15.00
❑ ANPR16 Earthbound Immortal Cusillu (UR)	4.00	10.00
❑ ANPR17 Earthbound Immortal Chacu Challhua (UTR)	6.00	15.00
❑ ANPR17 Earthbound Immortal Chacu Challhua (UR)	4.00	10.00
❑ ANPR18 Koa'ki Meiru Boulder	.10	.25
❑ ANPR19 Koa'ki Meiru Crusader (SR)	2.00	5.00
❑ ANPR20 Koa'ki Meiru Speeder (R)	.60	1.50
❑ ANPR21 Koa'ki Meiru Tornado (R)	.60	1.50
❑ ANPR22 Koa'ki Meiru Hydro Barrier	.10	.25
❑ ANPR23 Scary Moth	.10	.25
❑ ANPR24 Shiny Black C	.10	.25
❑ ANPR25 Armed Sea Hunter	.10	.25
❑ ANPR26 Divine Dragon Aquabizarre	.10	.25
❑ ANPR27 Fishborg Blaster	.10	.25
❑ ANPR28 Shark Cruiser	.10	.25
❑ ANPR29 Armored Axon Kicker	.10	.25
❑ ANPR30 Genetic Woman	.10	.25
❑ ANPR31 Magicat (R)	.40	1.00
❑ ANPR32 Cyborg Doctor	.10	.25
❑ ANPR33 White Potan	.10	.25
❑ ANPR34 Minefieldriller (SR)	.60	1.50
❑ ANPR35 XX-Saber Faultroll (SR)	6.00	15.00
❑ ANPR36 XX-Saber Ragigura	.10	.25
❑ ANPR37 Flamvell Firedog (R)	1.50	4.00
❑ ANPR38 Ancient Crimson Ape	.10	.25
❑ ANPR39 Falchion (R)	.40	1.00
❑ ANPR40 Ancient Fairy Dragon (UTR)	7.00	18.00
❑ ANPR40 Ancient Fairy Dragon (UR)	6.00	15.00
❑ ANPR40 Ancient Fairy Dragon (GR)	8.00	20.00
❑ ANPR41 Turbo Cannon (SR)	2.00	5.00
❑ ANPR42 Archfiend Zombie-Skull (SR)	1.50	4.00
❑ ANPR43 Ancient Sacred Wyvern (UR)	3.00	8.00
❑ ANPR43 Ancient Sacred Wyvern (UTR)	4.00	10.00
❑ ANPR44 XX-Saber Gottoms (UR)	5.00	12.00
❑ ANPR44 XX-Saber Gottoms (UTR)	6.00	15.00
❑ ANPR45 Release Restraint Wave	.10	.25
❑ ANPR46 Silver Wing	.10	.25
❑ ANPR47 Advance Draw	.10	.25
❑ ANPR48 Ancient Forest (SR)	3.00	8.00
❑ ANPR49 Emergency Assistance	.10	.25
❑ ANPR50 Spirit Burner	.10	.25
❑ ANPR51 Future Visions (SR)	6.00	15.00
❑ ANPR52 Core Compression (SR)	1.00	2.50
❑ ANPR53 Core Blaster	.10	.25
❑ ANPR54 Solidarity (R)	1.00	2.50
❑ ANPR55 Hydro Pressure Cannon	.10	.25
❑ ANPR56 Water Hazard	.10	.25
❑ ANPR57 Brain Research Lab	.10	.25
❑ ANPR58 Saber Slash (SR)	5.00	12.00
❑ ANPR59 Sword of Sparkles	.10	.25
❑ ANPR60 Rekindling	.10	.25
❑ ANPR61 Ancient Leaf	.10	.25
❑ ANPR62 Fossil Dig	.10	.25
❑ ANPR63 Skill Successor (SR)	.75	2.00
❑ ANPR64 Reinforce Truth (R)	.60	1.50
❑ ANPR65 Pixie Ring	.10	.25
❑ ANPR66 Fairy Wind	.10	.25
❑ ANPR67 Imperial Custom	.10	.25
❑ ANPR68 Discord (SR)	.40	1.00
❑ ANPR69 Slip of Fortune	.10	.25
❑ ANPR70 Depth Amulet	.10	.25
❑ ANPR71 Damage Translation	.10	.25
❑ ANPR72 Battle Teleportation	.10	.25
❑ ANPR73 Core Reinforcement (R)	.40	1.00
❑ ANPR74 Iron Core Luster	.10	.25
❑ ANPR75 Battle of the Elements	.10	.25
❑ ANPR76 Aegis of the Ocean Dragon Lord	.10	.25
❑ ANPR77 Psychic Soul	.10	.25
❑ ANPR78 Flamvell Counter	.10	.25
❑ ANPR79 At One With the Sword	.10	.25
❑ ANPR80 A Major Upset	.10	.25
❑ ANPR81 XX-Saber Fulhelmknight (R)	1.50	4.00
❑ ANPR82 Koa'ki Meiru Ghoulungulate (UTR)	4.00	10.00
❑ ANPR82 Koa'ki Meiru Ghoulungulate (UR)	3.00	8.00
❑ ANPR83 Koa'ki Meiru Gravirose (UTR)	4.00	10.00
❑ ANPR83 Koa'ki Meiru Gravirose (UR)	3.00	8.00
❑ ANPR84 Psychic Emperor (R)	.40	1.00
❑ ANPR85 Card Guard (SCR)	8.00	20.00
❑ ANPR86 Flamvell Commando (UTR)	3.00	8.00
❑ ANPR86 Flamvell Commando (UR)	2.50	6.00
❑ ANPR87 Pseudo Space (R)	.60	1.50
❑ ANPR88 Greed Grado (SCR)	6.00	15.00
❑ ANPR89 Revival of the Immortals (SR)	1.25	3.00
❑ ANPR90 Arcana Knight Joker (R)	.60	1.50
❑ ANPR91 Armityle the Chaos Phantom (SCR)	5.00	12.00
❑ ANPR92 White Night Dragon (SCR)	20.00	40.00
❑ ANPR93 Card Blocker (SCR)	4.00	10.00
❑ ANPR94 Gaia Plate the Earth Giant (UTR)	2.50	6.00
❑ ANPR94 Gaia Plate the Earth Giant (UR)	2.00	5.00
❑ ANPR95 Sauropod Brachion (R)	.40	1.00
❑ ANPR96 Gaap the Divine Soldier (R)	.40	1.00
❑ ANPR97 Beast Machine King Barbaros Ur (SR)	2.50	6.00
❑ ANPR98 Kasha (SCR)	8.00	20.00
❑ ANPR99 Elemental Hero Gaia (SCR)	25.00	50.00

2009 Yu-Gi-Oh Crimson Crisis 1st Edition

Complete Set (100)	175.00	250.00
Booster Box (24 packs)	75.00	100.00
Booster Pack (9 cards)	3.00	4.00

YU-GI-OH!

❑ CRMS0 Colossal Fighter/Assault Mode (SCR) 5.00 12.00
❑ CRMS1 Turret Warrior (SR) 1.25 3.00
❑ CRMS2 Debris Dragon (R) .75 2.00
❑ CRMS3 Hyper Synchron (R) .75 2.00
❑ CRMS4 Red Dragon Archfiend/Assault Mode (UR) 5.00 12.00
❑ CRMS4 Red Dragon Archfiend/Assault Mode (GR) 8.00 20.00
❑ CRMS4 Red Dragon Archfiend/Assault Mode (UTR) 6.00 15.00
❑ CRMS5 Trap Eater .10 .25
❑ CRMS6 Twin-Sword Marauder .10 .25
❑ CRMS7 Dark Tinker .10 .25
❑ CRMS8 Blackwing - Gale the Whirlwind (R) 3.00 8.00
❑ CRMS9 Blackwing - Bora the Spear .10 .25
❑ CRMS10 Blackwing - Sirocco the Dawn .10 .25
❑ CRMS11 Twilight Rose Knight (SR) 3.00 8.00
❑ CRMS12 Summon Reactor・SK .10 .25
❑ CRMS13 Trap Reactor・Y FI .10 .25
❑ CRMS14 Spell Reactor・RE .10 .25
❑ CRMS15 Black Salvo (SR) 3.00 8.00
❑ CRMS16 Flying Fortress SKY FIRE (R) .40 1.00
❑ CRMS17 Morphtronic Boarden .10 .25
❑ CRMS18 Morphtronic Slingen .10 .25
❑ CRMS19 Doomkaiser Dragon Assault Mode (UTR) 2.50 6.00
❑ CRMS19 Doomkaiser Dragon Assault Mode (UR) 2.00 5.00
❑ CRMS20 Hyper Psychic Blaster Assault Mode (UTR) 2.50 6.00
❑ CRMS20 Hyper Psychic Blaster Assault Mode (UR) 2.00 5.00
❑ CRMS21 Arcanite Magician/Assault Mode (UTR) 2.50 6.00
❑ CRMS21 Arcanite Magician/Assault Mode (UR) 2.00 5.00
❑ CRMS22 Arcane Apprentice (R) .60 1.50
❑ CRMS23 Assault Mercenary .10 .25
❑ CRMS24 Assault Beast (R) .60 1.50
❑ CRMS25 Night Wing Sorceress .10 .25
❑ CRMS26 Lifeforce Harmonizer (UTR) 2.50 6.00
❑ CRMS26 Lifeforce Harmonizer (UR) 2.00 5.00
❑ CRMS27 Gladiator Beast Samnite (R) 2.50 6.00
❑ CRMS28 Dupe Frog .10 .25
❑ CRMS29 Flip Flop Frog .10 .25
❑ CRMS30 B.E.S. Big Core MK-2 (R) .60 1.50
❑ CRMS31 Inmato (R) .60 1.50
❑ CRMS32 Scanner (SR) 1.00 2.50
❑ CRMS33 Dimension Fortress Weapon (SR) 1.25 3.00
❑ CRMS34 Desert Protector .10 .25
❑ CRMS35 Cross-Sword Beetle .10 .25
❑ CRMS36 Bee List Soldier .10 .25
❑ CRMS37 Hydra Viper (SP) .10 .25
❑ CRMS38 Alien Overlord (R) .40 1.00
❑ CRMS39 Alien Ammonite (R) .40 1.00
❑ CRMS40 Dark Strike Fighter (SR) 15.00 30.00
❑ CRMS41 Blackwing Armor Master (UTR) 25.00 50.00
❑ CRMS41 Blackwing Armor Master (UR) 20.00 40.00
❑ CRMS42 Hyper Psychic Blaster (UTR) 3.00 8.00
❑ CRMS42 Hyper Psychic Blaster (UR) 2.50 6.00
❑ CRMS43 Arcanite Magician (SR) 8.00 20.00
❑ CRMS44 Cosmic Fortress Gol'gar (UR) 3.00 8.00
❑ CRMS44 Cosmic Fortress Gol'gar (UTR) 4.00 10.00
❑ CRMS45 Prevention Star .10 .25
❑ CRMS46 Vengeful Servant .10 .25
❑ CRMS47 Star Blast (R) .40 1.00
❑ CRMS48 Raptor Wing Strike .10 .25
❑ CRMS49 Morphtronic Rusty Engine .10 .25
❑ CRMS50 Morphtronic Map .10 .25
❑ CRMS51 Assault Overload .10 .25
❑ CRMS52 Assault Teleport .10 .25
❑ CRMS53 Assault Revival (SP) .10 .25
❑ CRMS54 Psychic Sword .10 .25
❑ CRMS55 Telekinetic Power Well .10 .25
❑ CRMS56 Indomitable Gladiator Beast (SP) .10 .25
❑ CRMS57 Seed Cannon .10 .25
❑ CRMS58 Super Solar Nutrient .10 .25
❑ CRMS59 Six Scrolls of the Samurai .10 .25
❑ CRMS60 Verdant Sanctuary .10 .25
❑ CRMS61 Arcane Barrier (R) .40 1.00
❑ CRMS62 Mysterious Triangle .10 .25
❑ CRMS63 Assault Mode Activate .10 .25
❑ CRMS64 Spirit Force (SR) 1.50 4.00
❑ CRMS65 Descending Lost Star .10 .25
❑ CRMS66 Shining Silver Force (R) .40 1.00
❑ CRMS67 Half or Nothing .10 .25
❑ CRMS68 Nightmare Archfiends (SP) .10 .25
❑ CRMS69 Ebon Arrow .10 .25
❑ CRMS70 Ivy Shackles .10 .25
❑ CRMS71 Fake Explosion .10 .25
❑ CRMS72 Morphtronic Forcefield .10 .25
❑ CRMS73 Morphtronic Mix-up .10 .25
❑ CRMS74 Assault Slash .10 .25
❑ CRMS75 Assault Counter .10 .25
❑ CRMS76 Psychic Tuning (R) .60 1.50
❑ CRMS77 Metaphysical Regeneration .10 .25
❑ CRMS78 Trojan Gladiator Beast .10 .25
❑ CRMS79 Wall of Thorns (R) .60 1.50
❑ CRMS80 Planet Pollutant Virus (R) .60 1.50
❑ CRMS81 Dark Voltanis (SCR) 8.00 20.00
❑ CRMS82 Prime Material Falcon (SCR) 5.00 12.00
❑ CRMS83 Bone Crusher (UR) 2.50 6.00
❑ CRMS83 Bone Crusher (UTR) 3.00 8.00
❑ CRMS84 Alien Kid (SR) 1.50 4.00
❑ CRMS85 Totem Dragon (SR) 2.50 6.00
❑ CRMS86 Royal Swamp Eel (SR) 2.50 6.00
❑ CRMS87 Submarine Frog .10 .25
❑ CRMS88 Code A Ancient Ruins (SR) 1.50 4.00
❑ CRMS89 Synchro Change (R) .60 1.50
❑ CRMS90 Multiply (SR) 1.00 2.50
❑ CRMS91 Makiu, the Magical Mist (R) .40 1.00
❑ CRMS92 Assault Armor (R) .60 1.50
❑ CRMS93 Puppet King (SCR) 5.00 12.00
❑ CRMS94 Zeta Reticulant (SCR) 6.00 15.00
❑ CRMS95 Tethys, Goddess of Light (SCR) 15.00 30.00
❑ CRMS96 Ido the Supreme Magical Force (SCR) 6.00 15.00
❑ CRMS97 Violet Witch (UTR) 3.00 8.00
❑ CRMS97 Violet Witch (UR) 2.50 6.00
❑ CRMS98 Greed Quasar (SCR) 8.00 20.00
❑ CRMS99 Armoroid (SR) 1.25 3.00

2009 Yu-Gi-Oh Gold Series 2

Complete Set (100) 125.00 200.00
Booster Box (5 packs) 100.00 150.00
Booster Pack (25 cards) 25.00 30.00

❑ GLD2-1 Sangan (GUR) 4.00 10.00
❑ GLD2-2 Des Volstgalph (GUR) 6.00 15.00
❑ GLD2-3 Lekunga .20 .50
❑ GLD2-4 Lord Poison .20 .50
❑ GLD2-5 Rigorous Reaver .20 .50
❑ GLD2-6 Zaborg the Thunder Monarch .20 .50
❑ GLD2-7 Mobius the Frost Monarch .20 .50
❑ GLD2-8 Thestalos the Firestorm Monarch .20 .50
❑ GLD2-9 Granmarg the Rock Monarch .20 .50
❑ GLD2-10 Treeborn Frog .20 .50
❑ GLD2-11 Phantom Beast Cross-Wing .20 .50
❑ GLD2-12 Phantom Beast Wild-Horn .20 .50
❑ GLD2-13 Phantom Beast Thunder-Pegasus .20 .50
❑ GLD2-14 Phantom Beast Rock-Lizard .20 .50
❑ GLD2-15 Winged Rhynos .20 .50
❑ GLD2-16 Snipe Hunter .20 .50
❑ GLD2-17 The Six Samurai - Yaichi .20 .50
❑ GLD2-18 The Six Samurai - Kamon .20 .50
❑ GLD2-19 The Six Samurai - Yariza .20 .50
❑ GLD2-20 The Six Samurai - Nisashi .20 .50
❑ GLD2-21 The Six Samurai - Zanji .20 .50
❑ GLD2-22 The Six Samurai - Irou .20 .50
❑ GLD2-23 Volcanic Rocket (GUR) 6.00 15.00
❑ GLD2-24 Volcanic Shell .20 .50
❑ GLD2-25 Elemental Hero Captain Gold (GUR) 1.50 4.00
❑ GLD2-26 Raiza the Storm Monarch (GUR) 5.00 12.00
❑ GLD2-27 Necro Gardna (GUR) 4.00 10.00
❑ GLD2-28 Elemental Hero Neos Alius .20 .50
❑ GLD2-29 Test Tiger (GUR) 6.00 15.00
❑ GLD2-30 Royal Firestorm Guards (GUR) 3.00 8.00
❑ GLD2-31 Dark Armed Dragon (GUR) 25.00 50.00
❑ GLD2-32 Prime Material Dragon (GUR) 5.00 12.00
❑ GLD2-33 Caius the Shadow Monarch (GUR) 5.00 12.00
❑ GLD2-34 Exile of the Wicked .20 .50
❑ GLD2-35 Warrior Elimination .20 .50
❑ GLD2-36 Giant Trunade .20 .50
❑ GLD2-37 Mind Control (GUR) 6.00 15.00
❑ GLD2-38 Skyscraper .20 .50
❑ GLD2-39 Future Fusion (GUR) 4.00 10.00
❑ GLD2-40 Gold Sarcophagus (GUR) 30.00 60.00
❑ GLD2-41 Shien's Castle of Mist .20 .50
❑ GLD2-42 Six Samurai United .20 .50
❑ GLD2-43 Veil of Darkness (GUR) 5.00 12.00
❑ GLD2-44 Solemn Judgment (GUR) 10.00 25.00
❑ GLD2-45 Bottomless Trap Hole (GUR) 5.00 12.00
❑ GLD2-46 Compulsory Evacuation Device .20 .50
❑ GLD2-47 Begone, Knave! .20 .50
❑ GLD2-48 Phoenix Wing Wind Blast (GUR) 5.00 12.00
❑ GLD2-49 Return of the Six Samurai .20 .50
❑ GLD2-50 Double-Edged Sword Technique .20 .50

2009 Yu-Gi-Oh Hidden Arsenal

Complete Set (30) 80.00 120.00
Booster Box (30 packs) 100.00 140.00
Booster Pack (5 cards) 3.00 4.00

❑ HA01-1 Blizzed, Defender of the Ice Barrier (SCR) .75 2.00
❑ HA01-2 Blizzard Warrior (SR) .40 1.00
❑ HA01-3 Cryomancer of the Ice Barrier (SCR) .60 1.50
❑ HA01-4 Mist Valley Thunderbird (SCR) .60 1.50
❑ HA01-5 Mist Valley Shaman (SCR) .60 1.50
❑ HA01-6 Mist Valley Soldier (SCR) 1.50 4.00
❑ HA01-7 Flamvell Dragnov (SR) .60 1.50
❑ HA01-8 Flamvell Magician (SR) .60 1.50
❑ HA01-9 Flamvell Guard (SR) .40 1.00
❑ HA01-10 X-Saber Axel (SR) .40 1.00
❑ HA01-11 X-Saber Airbellum (SCR) 2.50 6.00
❑ HA01-12 X-Saber Uruz (SR) .40 1.00
❑ HA01-13 Commander Gottoms Swordmaster (SCR) .75 2.00
❑ HA01-14 Ally of Justice Clausolas (SR) .40 1.00
❑ HA01-15 Ally of Justice Garadholg (SR) .40 1.00
❑ HA01-16 Ally of Justice Rudra (SR) .40 1.00
❑ HA01-17 Worm Apocalypse (SR) .40 1.00
❑ HA01-18 Worm Barses (SR) .40 1.00
❑ HA01-19 Worm Cartaros (SR) .40 1.00
❑ HA01-20 Worm Dimikles (SR) .40 1.00
❑ HA01-21 Worm Erokin (SCR) .40 1.00
❑ HA01-22 Brionac Dragon of the Ice Barrier (SCR) 15.00 30.00
❑ HA01-23 Mist Wurm (SCR) 8.00 20.00
❑ HA01-24 Flamvell Uruquizas (SCR) .60 1.50
❑ HA01-25 X-Saber Urbellum (SCR) .60 1.50
❑ HA01-26 Ally of Justice Catastor (SCR) 10.00 25.00
❑ HA01-27 Wrath of Neos (SCR) .75 2.00
❑ HA01-28 Detonate (SR) .40 1.00
❑ HA01-29 Berserker Crush (SR) .40 1.00
❑ HA01-30 Evolution Burst (SCR) .60 1.50

2009 Yu-Gi-Oh Raging Battle 1st Edition

Complete Set (100) 150.00 250.00
Booster Box (24 packs) 70.00 90.00
Booster Pack (9 cards) 3.00 4.00

❑ RGBT0 Battlestorm (SCR) 2.50 6.00
❑ RGBT1 Rockstone Warrior (SCR) 1.50 4.00
❑ RGBT2 Level Warrior (SCR) 8.00 20.00
❑ RGBT3 Strong Wind Dragon (UTR) 3.00 8.00
❑ RGBT3 Strong Wind Dragon (UR) 2.50 6.00
❑ RGBT4 Dark Verger (R) .60 1.50
❑ RGBT5 Phoenixian Seed .10 .25
❑ RGBT6 Phoenixian Cluster Amaryllis (SCR) 1.00 2.50
❑ RGBT7 Rose Tentacles .10 .25
❑ RGBT8 Hedge Guard .10 .25
❑ RGBT9 Evil Thorn .10 .25
❑ RGBT10 Blackwing - Blizzard the Far North (R) 2.00 5.00
❑ RGBT11 Blackwing - Shura the Blue Flame .10 .25
❑ RGBT12 Blackwing - Kalut the Moon Shadow .10 .25
❑ RGBT13 Blackwing - Elphin the Raven (UR) 4.00 10.00
❑ RGBT13 Blackwing - Elphin the Raven (UTR) 5.00 12.00
❑ RGBT14 Morphtronic Remoten (R) .40 1.00
❑ RGBT15 Morphtronic Videon .10 .25
❑ RGBT16 Morphtronic Scopen .10 .25
❑ RGBT17 Gadget Arms .10 .25
❑ RGBT18 Torapart (R) .60 1.50
❑ RGBT19 Earthbound Immortal Aslla piscu (UTR) 5.00 12.00
❑ RGBT19 Earthbound Immortal Aslla piscu (UR) 3.00 8.00
❑ RGBT20 Earthbound Immortal Ccapac Apu (UTR) 5.00 12.00
❑ RGBT20 Earthbound Immortal Ccapac Apu (UR) 3.00 8.00
❑ RGBT21 Koa'ki Meiru Valafar (SCR) 1.50 4.00
❑ RGBT22 Koa'ki Meiru Powerhand (SCR) 1.50 4.00
❑ RGBT23 Koa'ki Meiru Guardian .10 .25
❑ RGBT24 Koa'ki Meiru Drago (UR) 2.50 6.00
❑ RGBT24 Koa'ki Meiru Drago (UTR) 4.00 10.00
❑ RGBT25 Koa'ki Meiru Ice (R) .60 1.50
❑ RGBT26 Koa'ki Meiru Doom .10 .25
❑ RGBT27 Brain Golem (R) .40 1.00
❑ RGBT28 Minoan Centaur .10 .25
❑ RGBT29 Reinforced Human Psychic Borg (SCR) 1.25 3.00
❑ RGBT30 Master Gig .10 .25
❑ RGBT31 Emissary from Pandemonium .10 .25
❑ RGBT32 Gigastone Omega .10 .25
❑ RGBT33 Alien Dog .10 .25
❑ RGBT34 Spined Gillman .10 .25
❑ RGBT35 Deep Sea Diva (R) 3.00 8.00
❑ RGBT36 Mermaid Archer .10 .25
❑ RGBT37 Lava Dragon .10 .25
❑ RGBT38 Vanguard of the Dragon .10 .25
❑ RGBT39 G.B. Hunter .10 .25
❑ RGBT40 Exploder Dragonwing (UTR) 3.00 8.00
❑ RGBT40 Exploder Dragonwing (UR) 2.50 6.00
❑ RGBT41 Blackwing Armed Wing (SCR) 15.00 30.00
❑ RGBT42 Power Tool Dragon (UR) 3.00 8.00
❑ RGBT42 Power Tool Dragon (UTR) 5.00 12.00
❑ RGBT42 Power Tool DragonGhost 6.00 15.00
❑ RGBT43 Trident Dragion (UTR) 3.00 8.00
❑ RGBT43 Trident Dragion (UR) 2.00 5.00
❑ RGBT44 Sea Dragon Lord Gishilnodon (SCR) 3.00 8.00
❑ RGBT45 One for One (R) .75 2.00
❑ RGBT46 Mind Trust .10 .25
❑ RGBT47 Thorn of Malice .10 .25
❑ RGBT48 Magic Planter (SCR) 1.00 2.50
❑ RGBT49 Wonder Clover .10 .25
❑ RGBT50 Against the Wind (R) .60 1.50
❑ RGBT51 Black Whirlwind .10 .25
❑ RGBT52 Junk Box .10 .25
❑ RGBT53 Double Tool C&D .10 .25
❑ RGBT54 Morphtronic Repair Unit .10 .25
❑ RGBT55 Iron Core of Koa'ki Meiru (R) .40 1.00
❑ RGBT56 Iron Core Immediate Disposal .10 .25
❑ RGBT57 Urgent Synthesis .10 .25
❑ RGBT58 Psychic Path .10 .25
❑ RGBT59 Natural Tune .10 .25
❑ RGBT60 Supremacy Berry .10 .25
❑ RGBT61 Forbidden Chalice (UR) 4.00 10.00
❑ RGBT61 Forbidden Chalice (UTR) 5.00 12.00
❑ RGBT62 Calming Magic (R) .40 1.00
❑ RGBT63 Miracle Locus .10 .25
❑ RGBT64 Crimson Fire .10 .25
❑ RGBT65 Tuner Capture .10 .25
❑ RGBT66 Overdoom Line .10 .25
❑ RGBT67 Wicked Rebirth .10 .25
❑ RGBT68 Delta Crow - Anti Reverse (SCR) 3.00 8.00
❑ RGBT69 Level Retuner .10 .25
❑ RGBT70 Fake Feather .10 .25
❑ RGBT71 Trap Stun .10 .25
❑ RGBT72 Morphtronic Bind .10 .25
❑ RGBT73 Reckoned Power .10 .25
❑ RGBT74 Automatic Laser .10 .25
❑ RGBT75 Attack of the Cornered Rat .10 .25
❑ RGBT76 Proof of Powerlessness .10 .25
❑ RGBT77 Bone Temple Block .10 .25
❑ RGBT78 Grave of the Super Ancient Organism (UR) 1.50 4.00
❑ RGBT78 Grave of the Super Ancient Organism (UTR) 2.00 5.00
❑ RGBT79 Swallow Flip (SCR) .60 1.50
❑ RGBT80 Mirror of Oaths .10 .25
❑ RGBT81 Koa'ki Meiru War Arms (SCR) 1.50 4.00
❑ RGBT82 Immortal Ruler (SCR) 2.50 6.00
❑ RGBT83 Hardened Armed Dragon (SCR) 10.00 25.00
❑ RGBT84 Moja (R) .60 1.50
❑ RGBT85 Beast Striker (SCR) 2.00 5.00
❑ RGBT86 King of the Beasts (SCR) 3.00 8.00
❑ RGBT87 Swallow's Nest (SCR) 4.00 10.00
❑ RGBT88 Overwhelm (SCR) 4.00 10.00
❑ RGBT89 Berserking (R) .60 1.50
❑ RGBT90 Spell of Pain (R) .60 1.50
❑ RGBT91 Light End Dragon (SCR) 1.50 4.00
❑ RGBT92 Chaos-End Master (SCR) 6.00 15.00
❑ RGBT93 Sphere of Chaos (SCR) 4.00 10.00
❑ RGBT94 Snowman Eater (R) .60 1.50
❑ RGBT95 Tree Otter (R) .60 1.50
❑ RGBT96 Ojama Red (R) .40 1.00
❑ RGBT97 Ojama Blue (R) .60 1.50
❑ RGBT98 Ojama Country (R) .60 1.50
❑ RGBT99 Emperor Sem (R) .60 1.50

2009 Yu-Gi-Oh Retro Pack 2

Complete Set (100) 180.00 250.00
Booster Pack (9 cards) 8.00 10.00
Set (3 packs) 24.00 30.00
Box (8 sets) 125.00 175.00

❑ RP02-0 Gorz the Emissary of Darkness (SCR) 1.25 3.00
❑ RP02-1 Jinzo (UR) 5.00 12.00
❑ RP02-4 Chain Destruction (R) .75 2.00
❑ RP02-7 Mirror Wall (UR) 2.50 6.00
❑ RP02-9 Ceasefire (R) .75 2.00
❑ RP02-10 Magical Hats (R) .60 1.50
❑ RP02-13 Buster Blader (SR) .60 1.50
❑ RP02-15 Limiter Removal (SR) 1.50 4.00
❑ RP02-19 The Legendary Fisherman (R) .60 1.50
❑ RP02-21 Thousand-Eyes Restrict (UR) 1.50 4.00
❑ RP02-25 Gearfried the Iron Knight (R) .60 1.50
❑ RP02-27 The Masked Beast (SR) .40 1.00
❑ RP02-28 Revival Jam (R) 1.00 2.50
❑ RP02-35 Infinite Cards (R) .40 1.00
❑ RP02-36 Jam Defender (SR) .60 1.50
❑ RP02-38 United We Stand (UR) 6.00 15.00
❑ RP02-39 Mage Power (R) .75 2.00
❑ RP02-42 Dark Necrofear (SR) .40 1.00
❑ RP02-45 Destiny Board (SR) .60 1.50
❑ RP02-50 Magic Cylinder (R) .60 1.50
❑ RP02-52 Dark Ruler Ha Des (UR) .75 2.00
❑ RP02-54 Freed the Matchless General (R) .60 1.50
❑ RP02-56 Tyrant Dragon (SR) 1.50 4.00
❑ RP02-58 Airknight Parshath (R) 1.25 3.00
❑ RP02-59 Yamata Dragon (R) .40 1.00
❑ RP02-60 Hino-Kagu-Tsuchi (SR) 2.50 6.00
❑ RP02-65 Injection Fairy Lily (UR) 4.00 10.00
❑ RP02-66 Ring of Destruction (SCR) 3.00 8.00
❑ RP02-68 Don Zaloog (R) 1.25 3.00
❑ RP02-72 Dark Jeroid (R) .40 1.00
❑ RP02-73 Newdoria (R) .60 1.50
❑ RP02-74 Helpoemer (UR) .75 2.00
❑ RP02-79 Necrovalley (R) 1.50 4.00
❑ RP02-81 Nightmare Wheel (R) 1.50 4.00
❑ RP02-82 Lava Golem (SR) 3.00 8.00
❑ RP02-83 Morphing Jar (R) 2.50 6.00
❑ RP02-84 Royal Decree (R) 3.00 8.00
❑ RP02-85 Swift Gaia the Fierce Knight (UR) 1.00 2.50
❑ RP02-86 Obnoxious Celtic Guardian (R) .40 1.00
❑ RP02-87 Kaiser Sea Horse (R) .40 1.00
❑ RP02-88 Insect Queen (SR) .60 1.50
❑ RP02-89 Alpha The Magnet Warrior (R) .60 1.50
❑ RP02-90 Beta The Magnet Warrior (R) .60 1.50
❑ RP02-91 Gamma The Magnet Warrior (R) .60 1.50
❑ RP02-92 Valkyrion the Magna Warrior (SCR) 6.00 15.00
❑ RP02-93 Harpie's Pet Dragon (SCR) 20.00 40.00
❑ RP02-94 Archfiend of Gilfer (SCR) 6.00 15.00
❑ RP02-95 Light and Darkness Dragon (SCR) 8.00 20.00
❑ RP02-96 Blue-Eyes Shining Dragon (SCR) 15.00 30.00
❑ RP02-97 Dragon Master Knight (SCR) 8.00 20.00
❑ RP02-98 Victory Dragon (SCR) 5.00 12.00
❑ RP02-99 Green Baboon, Defender of the Forest (SCR) 4.00 10.00
❑ RP02-100 Dreadscythe Harvester (SCR) 4.00 10.00

2009 Yu-Gi-Oh Stardust Overdrive 1st Edition

Complete Set (100) 200.00 250.00
Booster Box (24 packs) 70.00 90.00
Booster Pack (9 cards) 3.00 3.50

❑ SOVR0 Koa'ki Meiru Beetle (SR) .75 2.00
❑ SOVR1 Majestic Dragon (SR) 3.00 8.00
❑ SOVR2 Stardust Xiaolong (R) .60 1.50
❑ SOVR3 Max Warrior (SR) 1.00 2.50
❑ SOVR4 Quickdraw Synchron .10 .25
❑ SOVR5 Level Eater .10 .25
❑ SOVR6 Zero Gardna (R) .60 1.50
❑ SOVR7 Regulus .10 .25
❑ SOVR8 Infernity Necromancer .10 .25
❑ SOVR9 Fortune Lady Wind (R) .75 2.00
❑ SOVR10 Fortune Lady Water (R) .75 2.00
❑ SOVR11 Fortune Lady Dark (R) .75 2.00
❑ SOVR12 Fortune Lady Earth (R) .75 2.00
❑ SOVR13 Solitaire Magician .10 .25
❑ SOVR14 Catoblepas and the Witch of Fate (R) .40 1.00
❑ SOVR15 Dark Spider .10 .25
❑ SOVR16 Ground Spider .10 .25
❑ SOVR17 Relinquished Spider .10 .25
❑ SOVR18 Spyder Spider .10 .25
❑ SOVR19 Mother Spider (R) .40 1.00
❑ SOVR20 Reptilianne Gorgon .10 .25
❑ SOVR21 Reptilianne Medusa .10 .25
❑ SOVR22 Reptilianne Scylla .10 .25
❑ SOVR23 Reptilianne Viper .10 .25
❑ SOVR24 Earthbound Immortal Ccarayhua (UTR) 3.00 8.00
❑ SOVR24 Earthbound Immortal Ccarayhua (UR) 2.50 6.00
❑ SOVR25 Earthbound Immortal Uru (UTR) 5.00 12.00
❑ SOVR25 Earthbound Immortal Uru (UR) 4.00 10.00
❑ SOVR26 Earthbound Immortal Wiraqocha Rasca (UR) 2.50 6.00
❑ SOVR26 Earthbound Immortal Wiraqocha Rasca (UTR) 3.00 8.00
❑ SOVR27 Koa'ki Meiru Sea Panther .10 .25
❑ SOVR28 Koa'ki Meiru Rooklord (SR) 1.00 2.50
❑ SOVR29 Tuned Magician .10 .25
❑ SOVR30 Crusader of Endymion (UR) 6.00 15.00
❑ SOVR30 Crusader of Endymion (UTR) 8.00 20.00
❑ SOVR31 Woodland Archer .10 .25
❑ SOVR32 Knight of the Red Lotus (SR) 1.00 2.50
❑ SOVR33 Energy Bravery .10 .25
❑ SOVR34 Swap Frog .10 .25
❑ SOVR35 Lord British Space Fighter (R) .60 1.50
❑ SOVR36 Oshaleon .10 .25
❑ SOVR37 Djinn Releaser of Rituals (R) .60 1.50
❑ SOVR38 Djinn Presider of Rituals (R) .40 1.00
❑ SOVR39 Divine Grace - Northwemko (UTR) 4.00 10.00
❑ SOVR39 Divine Grace - Northwemko (UR) 3.00 8.00
❑ SOVR40 Majestic Star Dragon (GR) 6.00 15.00
❑ SOVR40 Majestic Star Dragon (UR) 3.00 8.00
❑ SOVR40 Majestic Star Dragon (UTR) 4.00 10.00
❑ SOVR41 Blackwing Silverwind the Ascendant (UTR) 15.00 30.00
❑ SOVR41 Blackwing Silverwind the Ascendant (UR) 8.00 20.00
❑ SOVR42 Reptilianne Hydra (SR) .75 2.00
❑ SOVR43 Black Brutdrago (SR) 2.00 5.00
❑ SOVR44 Explosive Magician (UR) 2.50 6.00
❑ SOVR44 Explosive Magician (UTR) 3.00 8.00
❑ SOVR45 Spider Web .10 .25
❑ SOVR46 Earthbound Whirlwind (SR) .60 1.50
❑ SOVR47 Savage Colosseum .10 .25
❑ SOVR48 Attack Pheromones .10 .25
❑ SOVR49 Molting Escape .10 .25
❑ SOVR50 Reptilianne Spawn .10 .25
❑ SOVR51 Fortune's Future (SR) 4.00 10.00
❑ SOVR52 Time Passage .10 .25
❑ SOVR53 Iron Core Armor .10 .25
❑ SOVR54 Herculean Power .10 .25
❑ SOVR55 Gemini Spark .10 .25
❑ SOVR56 Ritual of Grace .10 .25
❑ SOVR57 Preparation of Rites (SR) 1.50 4.00
❑ SOVR58 Moray of Greed .10 .25
❑ SOVR59 Spiritual Forest .10 .25
❑ SOVR60 Raging Mad Plants (R) .40 1.00
❑ SOVR61 Insect Neglect .10 .25
❑ SOVR62 Faustian Bargain .10 .25
❑ SOVR63 Slip Summon .10 .25
❑ SOVR64 Synchro Barrier .10 .25
❑ SOVR65 Enlightenment .10 .25
❑ SOVR66 Bending Destiny .10 .25
❑ SOVR67 Inherited Fortune (R) .40 1.00
❑ SOVR68 Spider Egg .10 .25
❑ SOVR69 Wolf in Sheep's Clothing .10 .25
❑ SOVR70 Earthbound Wave .10 .25
❑ SOVR71 Roar of the Earthbound .10 .25
❑ SOVR72 Limit Impulse .10 .25
❑ SOVR73 Infernity Force .10 .25
❑ SOVR74 Nega-Ton Corepanel (R) .40 1.00
❑ SOVR75 Gemini Counter .10 .25
❑ SOVR76 Gemini Booster .10 .25
❑ SOVR77 Ritual Buster .10 .25
❑ SOVR78 Stygian Dirge .10 .25
❑ SOVR79 Seal of Wickedness (SR) .75 2.00
❑ SOVR80 Appointer of the Red Lotus .10 .25
❑ SOVR81 Koa'ki Meiru Maximus (UTR) 3.00 8.00
❑ SOVR81 Koa'ki Meiru Maximus (UR) 2.00 5.00
❑ SOVR82 Shire, Lightsworn Spirit (SR) 2.00 5.00
❑ SOVR83 Rinyan, Lightsworn Rogue (R) 3.00 8.00
❑ SOVR84 Yellow Baboon, Archer of the Forest (UR) 2.00 5.00
❑ SOVR84 Yellow Baboon, Archer of the Forest (UTR) 2.50 6.00
❑ SOVR85 Gemini Scorpion (R) .40 1.00
❑ SOVR86 Metabo-Shark (SR) 1.00 2.50
❑ SOVR87 Earthbound Revival (R) .40 1.00
❑ SOVR88 Reptilianne Poison (R) .40 1.00
❑ SOVR89 Gateway of the Six (SR) 6.00 15.00
❑ SOVR90 Dark Rabbit (R) .40 1.00
❑ SOVR91 Shine Palace (R) .60 1.50
❑ SOVR92 Dark Simorgh (SCR) 40.00 60.00
❑ SOVR93 Victoria (SCR) 15.00 30.00
❑ SOVR94 Ice Queen (SCR) 6.00 15.00
❑ SOVR95 Shutendoji (SCR) 25.00 50.00
❑ SOVR96 Archlord Kristya (SCR) 60.00 90.00
❑ SOVR97 Guardian Eatos (SCR) 30.00 60.00
❑ SOVR98 Clear Vice Dragon (SCR) 10.00 25.00
❑ SOVR99 Clear World (SCR) 6.00 15.00

2010 Yu-Gi-Oh Absolute Powerforce 1st Edition

Complete Set (100) 200.00 250.00
Booster Box (24 packs) 70.00 90.00
Booster Pack (9 cards) 3.00 3.50

❑ ABPF0 Gravekeeper's Priestess (SR) 1.50 4.00
❑ ABPF1 Unicycular .10 .25
❑ ABPF2 Bicular .10 .25
❑ ABPF3 Tricular .75 2.00
❑ ABPF4 Drill Synchron (R) 1.00 2.50
❑ ABPF5 Ogre of the Scarlet Sorrow (SR) 20.00 40.00
❑ ABPF6 Battle Fader (UTR) 2.00 5.00
❑ ABPF6 Battle Fader (UR) 25.00 50.00
❑ ABPF7 Power Supplier .10 .25
❑ ABPF8 Magic Hole Golem .10 .25
❑ ABPF9 Power Invader .75 2.00
❑ ABPF10 Dark Bug (R) .40 1.00
❑ ABPF11 Sword Master 3.00 8.00
❑ ABPF12 Witch of the Black Rose (UTR) 2.00 5.00
❑ ABPF12 Witch of the Black Rose (UR) 4.00 10.00
❑ ABPF13 Rose Fairy 1.50 4.00
❑ ABPF14 Dragon Queen of Tragic Endings (SR) 1.00 2.50
❑ ABPF15 Reptilianne Servant .10 .25
❑ ABPF16 Reptilianne Gardna .10 .25
❑ ABPF17 Reptilianne Naga .10 .25
❑ ABPF18 Reptilianne Vaskii (R) .75 2.00
❑ ABPF19 Oracle of the Sun (SR) 5.00 12.00
❑ ABPF20 Fire Ant Ascator .10 .25
❑ ABPF21 Weeping Idol .10 .25
❑ ABPF22 Apocatequil .10 .25
❑ ABPF23 Supay .10 .25
❑ ABPF24 Informer Spider .10 .25
❑ ABPF25 Koa'ki Meiru Urnight (UR) 5.00 12.00
❑ ABPF25 Koa'ki Meiru Urnight (UTR) 6.00 15.00
❑ ABPF26 XX-Saber Garsem (R) 1.25 3.00
❑ ABPF27 Gravekeeper's Visionary (SR) 4.00 10.00
❑ ABPF28 Gravekeeper's Descendant (R) 1.00 2.50
❑ ABPF29 Black Potan .10 .25
❑ ABPF30 Shreddder .10 .25
❑ ABPF31 Pandaborg .10 .25
❑ ABPF32 Codarus .10 .25
❑ ABPF33 Consecrated Light .10 .25
❑ ABPF34 Gundari .10 .25
❑ ABPF35 Cyber Dragon Zwei (R) 1.50 4.00
❑ ABPF36 Oilman .10 .25
❑ ABPF37 Djinn Cursenchanter of Rituals (R) .40 1.00
❑ ABPF38 Djinn Prognosticator of Rituals (R) .40 1.00
❑ ABPF39 Garlandolf, King of Destruction (UTR) 5.00 12.00
❑ ABPF39 Garlandolf, King of Destruction (UR) 4.00 10.00
❑ ABPF40 Majestic Red Dragon (GR) 8.00 20.00
❑ ABPF40 Majestic Red Dragon (UTR) 6.00 15.00
❑ ABPF40 Majestic Red Dragon (UR) 5.00 12.00
❑ ABPF41 Drill Warrior (UR) 5.00 12.00
❑ ABPF41 Drill Warrior (UTR) 6.00 15.00
❑ ABPF42 Sun Dragon Inti (UR) 4.00 10.00
❑ ABPF42 Sun Dragon Inti (UTR) 5.00 12.00
❑ ABPF43 Moon Dragon Quilla (UR) 4.00 10.00
❑ ABPF43 Moon Dragon Quilla (UTR) 5.00 12.00
❑ ABPF44 XX-Saber Hyunlei (UTR) 6.00 15.00
❑ ABPF44 XX-Saber Hyunlei (UR) 4.00 10.00
❑ ABPF45 Cards of Consonance (SR) 3.00 8.00
❑ ABPF46 Variety Comes Out .10 .25
❑ ABPF47 Reptilianne Rage .10 .25
❑ ABPF48 Advance Force .10 .25
❑ ABPF49 Viper's Rebirth .10 .25
❑ ABPF50 Temple of the Sun .10 .25
❑ ABPF51 Rocket Pilder .10 .25
❑ ABPF52 Break! Draw! .10 .25
❑ ABPF53 Power Pickaxe (R) .60 1.50
❑ ABPF54 Spider's Lair .10 .25
❑ ABPF55 Iron Core Specimen Lab (SR) 1.50 4.00
❑ ABPF56 Gravekeeper's Stele .10 .25
❑ ABPF57 Machine Assembly Line .10 .25
❑ ABPF58 Ritual of Destruction .10 .25
❑ ABPF59 Ascending Soul (R) .60 1.50
❑ ABPF60 Ritual Cage (R) .60 1.50
❑ ABPF61 Pot of Benevolence .10 .25
❑ ABPF62 Synchro Control (SR) 1.00 2.50
❑ ABPF63 Changing Destiny .10 .25
❑ ABPF64 Fiendish Chain (SR) 1.25 3.00
❑ ABPF65 Nature's Reflection .10 .25
❑ ABPF66 Serpent Suppression .10 .25
❑ ABPF67 Meteor Flare .10 .25
❑ ABPF68 Offering to the Immortals (R) .40 1.00
❑ ABPF69 Destruct Potion .10 .25
❑ ABPF70 Call of the Reaper .10 .25
❑ ABPF71 Lair Wire .10 .25
❑ ABPF72 Core Blast (R) .40 1.00
❑ ABPF73 Saber Hole (SR) 3.00 8.00
❑ ABPF74 Machine King - 3000 B.C. .10 .25
❑ ABPF75 Alien Brain .10 .25
❑ ABPF76 Forgotten Temple of the Deep .10 .25
❑ ABPF77 Tuner's Scheme (SR) 1.50 4.00
❑ ABPF78 Psi-Curse .10 .25
❑ ABPF79 Widespread Dud .10 .25
❑ ABPF80 Inverse Universe .10 .25
❑ ABPF81 XX-Saber Emmersblade (SCR) 60.00 90.00
❑ ABPF82 Alchemist of Black Spells (UTR) 3.00 8.00
❑ ABPF82 Alchemist of Black Spells (UR) 2.50 6.00
❑ ABPF83 Super-Nimble Mega Hamster (SR) 15.00 30.00
❑ ABPF84 Cactus Bouncer (SCR) 5.00 12.00
❑ ABPF85 Dragonic Guard (SR) .75 2.00
❑ ABPF86 The Dragon Dwelling in the Deep (SR) 1.00 2.50
❑ ABPF87 Djinn Disserere of Rituals (SCR) 8.00 20.00
❑ ABPF88 Earthbound Linewalker .10 .25
❑ ABPF89 Core Transport Unit (SCR) 6.00 15.00

ABPF90 Gale Dogra (R)	.60	1.50
ABPF91 Berfomet (R)	.60	1.50
ABPF92 Chimera the Flying Mythical Beast (R)	.60	1.50
ABPF93 Viser Des (R)	.60	1.50
ABPF94 Evil Blast (R)	.60	1.50
ABPF95 Shield Wing (SCR)	15.00	30.00
ABPF96 Underground Arachnid (SCR)	6.00	15.00
ABPF97 Zeman the Ape King (SCR)	6.00	15.00
ABPF98 Skull Conductor (R)	.60	1.50
ABPF99 Shield Worm (R)	.60	1.50

2010 Yu-Gi-Oh Duelist Revolution

Booster Box (24 packs)	75.00	100.00
Booster Pack (9 cards)	3.00	4.00
DREV0 Scrap Archfiend (SR)	2.00	5.00
DREV1 Earthquake Giant	.10	.25
DREV2 Effect Veiler (UR)	20.00	40.00
DREV2 Effect Veiler (UTR)	20.00	40.00
DREV3 Dash Warrior	.10	.25
DREV4 Damage Eater	.10	.25
DREV5 A/D Changer	.10	.25
DREV6 Stronghold Guardian	.10	.25
DREV7 Playful Possum (R)	.20	.50
DREV8 Egotistical Ape (R)	.20	.50
DREV9 Uni-Horned Familiar	.10	.25
DREV10 Monoceros	.10	.25
DREV11 D.D. Unicorn Knight (R)	.20	.50
DREV12 Unibird (SR)	.60	1.50
DREV13 Bicorn Re'em	.10	.25
DREV14 Mine Mole	.10	.25
DREV15 Trident Warrior (SR)	.60	1.50
DREV16 Delta Flyer (R)	.40	1.00
DREV17 Rhinotaurus	.10	.25
DREV18 Hypnocorn (R)	.20	.50
DREV19 Scrap Chimera (SR)	6.00	15.00
DREV20 Scrap Goblin	.20	.50
DREV21 Scrap Beast (R)	.40	1.00
DREV22 Scrap Hunter (R)	.20	.50
DREV23 Scrap Golem (R)	.40	1.00
DREV24 Wattbetta	.10	.25
DREV25 Wattlemur	.10	.25
DREV26 Wattpheasant	.10	.25
DREV27 Naturia Mosquito	.10	.25
DREV28 Naturia Beans	.10	.25
DREV29 Naturia Bamboo Shoot (UR)	5.00	12.00
DREV29 Naturia Bamboo Shoot (UTR)	10.00	25.00
DREV30 Amazoness Sage	.20	.50
DREV31 Amazoness Trainee	.20	.50
DREV32 Amazoness Queen (SR)	1.50	4.00
DREV33 Lock Cat	.10	.25
DREV34 Elephun	.10	.25
DREV35 Synchro Fusionist (R)	.20	.50
DREV36 Ambitious Gofer (R)	.20	.50
DREV37 Final Psychic Ogre	.20	.50
DREV38 Dragon Knight Draco-Equiste (UTR)	2.00	5.00
DREV38 Dragon Knight Draco-Equiste (UR)	1.50	4.00
DREV39 Ultimate Axon Kicker (SR)	.75	2.00
DREV40 Thunder Unicorn (UTR)	2.50	6.00
DREV40 Thunder Unicorn (UR)	1.50	4.00
DREV41 Voltic Bicorn (UTR)	2.50	6.00
DREV41 Voltic Bicorn (UR)	2.00	5.00
DREV42 Lightning Tricorn (UTR)	2.50	6.00
DREV42 Lightning Tricorn (UR)	1.50	4.00
DREV43 Scrap Dragon (UR)	20.00	40.00
DREV43 Scrap Dragon (UTR)	30.00	60.00
DREV44 Wattchimera (UTR)	2.50	6.00
DREV44 Wattchimera (UR)	2.00	5.00
DREV45 Blind Spot Strike	.10	.25
DREV46 Double Cyclone	.20	.50
DREV47 Scrapyard (SR)	3.00	8.00
DREV48 Scrapstorm (SR)	3.00	8.00
DREV49 Scrap Sheen	.10	.25
DREV50 Wattcine	.10	.25
DREV51 Naturia Forest	.10	.25
DREV52 Landoise's Luminous Moss (R)	.20	.50
DREV53 Amazoness Village (R)	.40	1.00
DREV54 Amazoness Fighting Spirit	.20	.50
DREV55 Unicorn Beacon (SR)	.40	1.00
DREV56 Beast Rage	.10	.25
DREV57 Miracle Synchro Fusion	.20	.50
DREV58 Pestilence	.10	.25
DREV59 Cursed Armaments	.20	.50
DREV60 Wiseman's Chalice (SR)	.40	1.00
DREV61 Summoning Curse	.20	.50
DREV62 Pot of Duality (SCR)	150.00	200.00
DREV63 Desperate Tag	.10	.25
DREV64 Battle Instinct	.10	.25
DREV65 Howl of the Wild	.10	.25
DREV66 Parallel Selection (R)	.20	.50
DREV67 Reanimation Wave (R)	.20	.50
DREV68 Barrier Wave	.10	.25
DREV69 Chain Whirlwind	.20	.50
DREV70 Scrap Rage	.10	.25
DREV71 Wattcannon	.10	.25
DREV72 Amazoness Willpower (R)	.40	1.00
DREV73 Queen's Pawn	.20	.50
DREV74 Beast Rising	.10	.25
DREV75 Horn of the Phantom Beast (R)	.20	.50
DREV76 Paradox Fusion (SR)	1.50	4.00
DREV77 Solemn Warning (UTR)	75.00	100.00
DREV77 Solemn Warning (UR)	75.00	100.00
DREV78 Anti-Magic Prism	.10	.25
DREV79 Chivalry (UTR)	3.00	8.00
DREV79 Chivalry (UR)	2.50	6.00
DREV80 Light of Destruction	.20	.50
DREV81 Amazoness Scouts (R)	.20	.50
DREV82 Naturia Pineapple (SCR)	15.00	30.00
DREV83 D.D. Destroyer (R)	.20	.50
DREV84 Dark Desertapir (R)	.20	.50
DREV85 Psychic Nightmare (SCR)	6.00	15.00
DREV86 Guts of Steel (R)	.20	.50
DREV87 Amazoness Heirloom (SR)	1.25	3.00
DREV88 Amazoness Shamanism (SR)	.60	1.50
DREV89 Super Rush Recklessly (SR)	.60	1.50
DREV90 Mystical Refpanel (SCR)	4.00	10.00
DREV91 Fabled Raven (SCR)	20.00	40.00
DREV92 Ally of Justice Cyclone Creator (SCR)	4.00	10.00
DREV93 Miracle's Wake (SCR)	3.00	8.00
DREV94 Flamvell Poun	.10	.25
DREV95 Flamvell Archer	.10	.25
DREV96 Flamvell Fiend	.10	.25
DREV97 Genex Worker	.10	.25
DREV98 Genex Power Planner	.10	.25
DREV99 Stygian Street Patrol (SCR)	10.00	20.00

2010 Yu-Gi-Oh Gold Series 3

GLD3-1 Mist Valley Watcher	.10	.25
GLD3-2 Vice Dragon (GUR)	3.00	8.00
GLD3-3 Amazoness Archer	.10	.25
GLD3-4 Amazoness Paladin	.10	.25
GLD3-5 Amazoness Fighter	.10	.25
GLD3-6 Amazoness Swords Woman	.20	.50
GLD3-7 Amazoness Blowpiper	.10	.25
GLD3-8 Amazoness Tiger	.10	.25
GLD3-9 Destiny Hero - Malicious	.60	1.50
GLD3-10 Freya, Spirit of Victory	.20	.50
GLD3-11 Nova Summoner	.20	.50
GLD3-12 Exploder Dragon (GUR)	1.25	3.00
GLD3-13 Goblin Zombie	.20	.50
GLD3-14 Elemental Hero Prisma (GUR)	4.00	10.00
GLD3-15 Dimensional Alchemist (GUR)	1.25	3.00
GLD3-16 Judgment Dragon (GUR)	5.00	12.00
GLD3-17 Amazoness Chain Master	.10	.25
GLD3-18 Mezuki (GUR)	2.00	5.00
GLD3-19 Plaguespreader Zombie (GUR)	5.00	12.00
GLD3-20 Thunder King Rai-Oh (GUR)	10.00	20.00
GLD3-21 Blackwing - Gale the Whirlwind (GUR)	2.00	5.00
GLD3-22 Blackwing - Bora the Spear	.10	.25
GLD3-23 Blackwing - Sirocco the Dawn	.40	1.00
GLD3-24 Blackwing - Blizzard the Far North	.40	1.00
GLD3-25 Blackwing - Shura the Blue Flame	.20	.50
GLD3-26 Blackwing - Kalut the Moon Shadow	.20	.50
GLD3-27 Infernity Archfiend (GUR)	3.00	8.00
GLD3-28 Infernity Dwarf	.10	.25
GLD3-29 Infernity Guardian	.10	.25
GLD3-30 Reese the Ice Mistress	.20	.50
GLD3-31 Numbing Grub in the Ice Barrier	.10	.25
GLD3-32 Mist Condor	.10	.25
GLD3-33 Mist Valley Windmaster	.10	.25
GLD3-34 Worm Falco	.10	.25
GLD3-35 Worm Gulse	.10	.25
GLD3-36 Worm Hope	.10	.25
GLD3-37 Stardust Dragon (GUR)	6.00	15.00
GLD3-38 Blackwing Armor Master (GUR)	5.00	12.00
GLD3-39 Blackwing Armed Wing (GUR)	2.50	6.00
GLD3-40 Mystical Space Typhoon (GUR)	1.25	3.00
GLD3-41 My Body as a Shield (GUR)	2.50	6.00
GLD3-42 Smashing Ground (GUR)	1.50	4.00
GLD3-43 Enemy Controller (GUR)	.75	2.00
GLD3-44 Destiny Draw	.30	.75
GLD3-45 Black Whirlwind	.20	.50
GLD3-46 Amazoness Archers	.10	.25
GLD3-47 Dramatic Rescue	.10	.25
GLD3-48 Magical Arm Shield	.10	.25
GLD3-49 Icarus Attack (GUR)	2.50	6.00
GLD3-50 Aegis of Gaia	.10	.25

2010 Yu-Gi-Oh Hidden Arsenal 2

Booster Box (24 packs)	50.00	75.00
Booster Pack (5 cards)	2.00	3.00
HA02-1 Naturia Beetle (SR)	.40	1.00
HA02-2 Naturia Rock (SR)	.40	1.00
HA02-3 Naturia Guardian (SCR)	.60	1.50
HA02-4 Naturia Vein (SR)	.40	1.00
HA02-5 Genex Furnace (SR)	.40	1.00
HA02-6 Genex Gaia (SR)	.40	1.00
HA02-7 Genex Spare (SR)	.40	1.00
HA02-8 Genex Turbine (SR)	.40	1.00
HA02-9 Genex Doctor (SR)	.40	1.00
HA02-10 Genex Solar (SCR)	.60	1.50
HA02-11 Dai-sojo of the Ice Barrier (SCR)	.60	1.50
HA02-12 Medium of the Ice Barrier (SR)	.60	1.50
HA02-13 Mist Valley Baby Roc (SR)	.40	1.00
HA02-14 Mist Valley Executor (SR)	.40	1.00
HA02-15 Flamvell Grunika (SR)	.40	1.00
HA02-16 Flamvell Baby (SR)	.40	1.00
HA02-17 Ally Mind (SR)	.40	1.00
HA02-18 Ally of Justice Nullfier (SR)	.40	1.00
HA02-19 Ally of Justice Searcher (SR)	.40	1.00
HA02-20 Ally of Justice Enemy Catcher (SR)	.40	1.00
HA02-21 Ally of Justice Thunder Armor (SR)	.40	1.00
HA02-22 Ally of Justice Cosmic Gateway (SCR)	.60	1.50
HA02-23 Worm Linx (SR)	.40	1.00
HA02-24 Worm Millidith (SR)	.40	1.00
HA02-25 Worm Noble (SR)	.40	1.00
HA02-26 Naturia Beast (SCR)	12.00	25.00
HA02-27 Dewloren Tiger King of the Ice Barrier (SCR)	8.00	15.00
HA02-28 Thermal Genex (SCR)	.60	1.50
HA02-29 Geo Genex (SCR)	.60	1.50
HA02-30 Ally of Justice Field Marshal (SCR)	1.00	2.50
HA02-31 Fabled Lurrie (SR)	.40	1.00
HA02-32 Fabled Grimro (SCR)	8.00	15.00
HA02-33 Fabled Gallabas (SCR)	.60	1.50
HA02-34 Fabled Kushano (SR)	.75	2.00
HA02-35 Jurrac Protops (SR)	.40	1.00
HA02-36 Jurrac Velo (SR)	.60	1.50
HA02-37 Jurrac Monoloph (SR)	.40	1.00
HA02-38 Jurrac Tyrannus (SCR)	.60	1.50
HA02-39 Naturia Antjaw (SR)	.40	1.00
HA02-40 Naturia Spiderfang (SR)	.40	1.00
HA02-41 Naturia Rosewhip (SR)	.60	1.50
HA02-42 Naturia Cosmobeet (SR)	.40	1.00
HA02-43 Genex Blastfan (SR)	.40	1.00
HA02-44 Genex Recycled (SR)	.40	1.00
HA02-45 Genex Army (SCR)	.60	1.50
HA02-46 Pilgrim of the Ice Barrier (SR)	.40	1.00
HA02-47 Geomancer of the Ice Barrier (SR)	.40	1.00
HA02-48 Mist Valley Falcon (SR)	.60	1.50
HA02-49 Mist Valley Apex Avian (SCR)	.60	1.50
HA02-50 Ally of Justice Reverse Break (SR)	.40	1.00
HA02-51 Ally of Justice Unlimiter (SR)	.40	1.00
HA02-52 Worm Opera (SR)	.40	1.00
HA02-53 Worm Prince (SR)	.40	1.00
HA02-54 Worm Queen (SCR)	.60	1.50
HA02-55 Worm Rakuyeh (SR)	.40	1.00
HA02-56 Fabled Valkyrus (SCR)	4.00	10.00
HA02-57 Jurrac Giganoto (SCR)	2.00	5.00
HA02-58 Naturia Leodrake (SCR)	.60	1.50
HA02-59 Windmill Genex (SCR)	.60	1.50
HA02-60 Mist Valley Thunder Lord (SCR)	.60	1.50

2010 Yu-Gi-Oh Hidden Arsenal 3

Booster Box (24 packs)	50.00	75.00
Booster Pack (5 cards)	2.00	3.00
HA03EN001 Fabled Urustos SR	.25	.60
HA03EN002 Fabled Krus SCR	6.00	15.00
HA03EN003 Fabled Topi SR	.25	.60
HA03EN004 Fabled Soulkius SCR	1.50	4.00
HA03EN005 Fabled Miztoji SR	.25	.60
HA03EN006 Jurrac Ptera SR	.25	.60
HA03EN007 Jurrac Iguanon SR	.25	.60
HA03EN008 Jurrac Brachis SR	.25	.60
HA03EN009 Jurrac Spinos SR	.25	.60
HA03EN010 Naturia Dragonfly SR	.25	.60
HA03EN011 Naturia Sunflower SR	.25	.60
HA03EN012 Naturia Cliff SCR	3.00	8.00
HA03EN013 Naturia Tulip SR	.25	.60
HA03EN014 R-Genex Turbo SR	.25	.60
HA03EN015 R-Genex Overseer SR	.25	.60
HA03EN016 R-Genex Crusher SR	.25	.60
HA03EN017 R-Genex Magma SR	.25	.60
HA03EN018 Shock Troops of the Ice Barrier SR	.30	.75
HA03EN019 Samurai of the Ice Barrier SR	.25	.60
HA03EN020 Dewdark of the Ice Barrier SR	.50	1.25
HA03EN021 Caravan of the Ice Barrier SR	.25	.60
HA03EN022 Worm Solid SR	.25	.60
HA03EN023 Worm Tentacles SR	.25	.60
HA03EN024 Worm Ugly SR	.25	.60
HA03EN025 Worm Victory SCR	.50	1.25
HA03EN026 Fabled Leviathan SCR	2.50	6.00
HA03EN027 Jurrac Velphito SCR	1.50	4.00
HA03EN028 Naturia Barkion SCR	20.00	40.00
HA03EN029 Locomotion R-Genex SCR	4.00	10.00
HA03EN030 Gungnir, Dragon of the Ice Barrier SCR	20.00	40.00
HA03EN031 Dragunity Dux SCR	2.50	6.00
HA03EN032 Dragunity Legionnaire SR	.25	.60
HA03EN033 Dragunity Tribus SR	.25	.60
HA03EN034 Dragunity Darkspear SR	.30	.75
HA03EN035 Dragunity Phalanx SCR	15.00	30.00
HA03EN036 Fabled Dyf SR	.25	.60
HA03EN037 Fabled Ashenveil SCR	.60	1.50
HA03EN038 Fabled Oltro SR	.25	.60
HA03EN039 Jurrac Titano SCR	1.25	3.00
HA03EN040 Jurrac Guaiba SR	.25	.60
HA03EN041 Jurrac Stauriko SR	.25	.60
HA03EN042 Naturia Horneedle SR	.25	.60
HA03EN043 Naturia Fruitfly SR	.25	.60
HA03EN044 Naturia Hydrangea SR	.25	.60
HA03EN045 R-Genex Accelerator SR	.25	.60
HA03EN046 R-Genex Oracle SR	.25	.60
HA03EN047 R-Genex Ultimum SR	.25	.60
HA03EN048 Spellbreaker of the Ice Barrier SR	.25	.60
HA03EN049 General Grunard of the Ice Barrier SCR	1.25	3.00
HA03EN050 Ally of Justice Omni-Weapon SCR	.50	1.25
HA03EN051 Ally of Justice Quarantine SR	.25	.60
HA03EN052 Ally of Justice Cycle Reader SR	.25	.60
HA03EN053 Worm Warlord SR	.25	.60
HA03EN054 Worm Xex SR	.25	.60
HA03EN055 Worm Yagan SR	.25	.60
HA03EN056 Worm Zero SCR	.60	1.50
HA03EN057 Dragunity Knight - Gae Bulg SCR	2.00	5.00
HA03EN058 Fabled Ragin SCR	3.00	8.00
HA03EN059 Vindikite R-Genex SCR	.50	1.25
HA03EN060 Ally of Justice Decisive Armor SCR	6.00	15.00

2010 Yu-Gi-Oh The Shining Darkness

Booster Box (24 packs)	50.00	75.00
Booster Pack (9)	2.00	3.00
TSHD0 XX-Saber Boggart Knight (SR)	2.00	5.00
TSHD1 Blackwing - Ghibli the Searing Wind	.10	.25
TSHD2 Blackwing - Gust the Backblast (R)	1.00	2.50
TSHD3 Blackwing - Breeze the Zephyr (UR)	8.00	20.00
TSHD3 Blackwing - Breeze the Zephyr (UTR)	10.00	25.00
TSHD4 Changer Synchron	.10	.25
TSHD5 Card Breaker	.10	.25
TSHD6 Second Booster	.10	.25
TSHD7 Archfiend Interceptor	.10	.25
TSHD8 Dread Dragon (R)	.40	1.00
TSHD9 Trust Guardian (SR)	1.25	3.00
TSHD10 Flare Resonator	.10	.25
TSHD11 Synchro Magnet	.10	.25
TSHD12 Infernity Mirage (SR)	5.00	12.00
TSHD13 Infernity Randomizer	.10	.25
TSHD14 Infernity Beetle (R)	1.50	4.00
TSHD15 Infernity Avenger (R)	.75	2.00
TSHD16 Revival Rose (R)	.40	1.00
TSHD17 Morphtronic Vacuumen	.10	.25
TSHD18 Bird of Roses (SR)	.75	2.00
TSHD19 Spore	.10	.25
TSHD20 Fairy Archer	.10	.25
TSHD21 Biofalcon	.10	.25
TSHD22 Cherry Inmato (R)	.40	1.00
TSHD23 Magidog (R)	.40	1.00
TSHD24 Lyna the Light Charmer	.10	.25
TSHD25 Wattgiraffe (SR)	1.25	3.00
TSHD26 Wattfox	.10	.25
TSHD27 Wattwoodpecker	.10	.25
TSHD28 Koa'ki Meiru Sandman	.10	.25
TSHD29 Memory Crush King	.10	.25
TSHD30 Delta Tri (R)	.40	1.00
TSHD31 Trigon	.10	.25
TSHD32 Testudo Erat Numen (SP)	.20	.50
TSHD33 Ronintoadin	.10	.25
TSHD34 Batteryman AAA	.10	.25
TSHD35 Batteryman Fuel Cell (R)	.40	1.00
TSHD36 Key Mouse	.10	.25
TSHD37 Ally of Justice Core Destroyer (R)	.40	1.00
TSHD38 Hunter of Black Feathers (SP)	.20	.50
TSHD39 Herald of Perfection (UR)	4.00	10.00
TSHD39 Herald of Perfection (UTR)	5.00	12.00
TSHD40 Black-Winged Dragon (GR)	6.00	15.00
TSHD40 Black-Winged Dragon (UTR)	4.00	10.00
TSHD40 Black-Winged Dragon (UR)	3.00	8.00
TSHD41 Chaos King Archfiend (UTR)	2.50	6.00
TSHD41 Chaos King Archfiend (UR)	1.50	4.00
TSHD42 Infernity Doom Dragon (UR)	4.00	10.00
TSHD42 Infernity Doom Dragon (UTR)	5.00	12.00
TSHD43 Splendid Rose (UTR)	2.00	5.00
TSHD43 Splendid Rose (UR)	1.25	3.00
TSHD44 Chaos Goddess (SCR)	4.00	10.00
TSHD45 Black-Winged Strafe	.10	.25
TSHD46 Cards for Black Feathers (UTR)	6.00	15.00
TSHD46 Cards for Black Feathers (UR)	4.00	10.00
TSHD47 ZERO-MAX (SR)	1.00	2.50
TSHD48 Infernity Launcher (SR)	6.00	15.00
TSHD49 Into The Void (UTR)	2.50	6.00
TSHD49 Into The Void (UR)	2.00	5.00
TSHD50 Intercept Wave (UTR)	2.50	6.00
TSHD50 Intercept Wave (UR)	1.50	4.00
TSHD51 Pyramid of Wonders (R)	.40	1.00
TSHD52 The Fountain in the Sky (R)	.60	1.50
TSHD53 Dragon Laser	.10	.25
TSHD54 Wattcube	.10	.25
TSHD55 Electromagnetic Shield (R)	.40	1.00
TSHD56 Worm Call	.10	.25
TSHD57 Magic Triangle of the Ice Barrier	.10	.25
TSHD58 Koa'ki Meiru Initialize	.10	.25
TSHD59 Dawn of the Herald	.10	.25
TSHD60 Forbidden Graveyard	.10	.25
TSHD61 Leeching the Light	.10	.25
TSHD62 Corridor of Agony (SP)	.20	.50
TSHD63 Power Frame (SR)	1.25	3.00
TSHD64 Blackwing - Backlash (R)	.60	1.50
TSHD65 Blackwing - Bombardment	.10	.25
TSHD66 Black Thunder	.10	.25
TSHD67 Guard Mines (R)	.40	1.00
TSHD68 Infernity Reflector	.10	.25
TSHD69 Infernity Break	.10	.25
TSHD70 Damage Gate (SR)	1.00	2.50
TSHD71 Infernity Inferno (R)	.40	1.00
TSHD72 Phantom Hand	.10	.25
TSHD73 Assault Spirits	.10	.25
TSHD74 Blossom Bombardment	.10	.25
TSHD75 Morphtronics, Scramble!	.10	.25
TSHD76 Power Break	.10	.25
TSHD77 Koa'ki Meiru Shield (R)	.40	1.00
TSHD78 Crevice into the Different Dimension	.10	.25
TSHD79 Synchro Ejection (SR)	.60	1.50
TSHD80 Chaos Trap Hole (SP)	.20	.50
TSHD81 XX-Saber Darksoul (UTR)	20.00	40.00
TSHD81 XX-Saber Darksoul (UR)	12.00	30.00
TSHD82 Koa'ki Meiru Prototype (R)	.40	1.00
TSHD83 Snyffus (SCR)	6.00	15.00
TSHD84 Nimble Sunfish (SR)	.60	1.50
TSHD85 Akz, the Pumer (R)	.40	1.00
TSHD86 Saber Vault (SCR)	3.00	8.00
TSHD87 Core Overclock (SR)	1.50	4.00
TSHD88 Wave-Motion Inferno (SCR)	1.50	4.00
TSHD89 Infernity Barrier (SCR)	25.00	50.00
TSHD90 Genex Controller	.10	.25
TSHD91 Genex Undine	.10	.25
TSHD92 Genex Searcher (R)	.60	1.50
TSHD93 X-Saber Palomuro	.10	.25
TSHD94 X-Saber Pashuul	.10	.25
TSHD95 Hydro Genex (SR)	1.50	4.00
TSHD96 Ally of Justice Light Gazer (SR)	2.00	5.00
TSHD97 Genex Neutron (SCR)	3.00	8.00
TSHD98 Infernity Destroyer (SCR)	4.00	10.00
TSHD99 Koa'ki Meiru Bergzak (SCR)	4.00	10.00

2010 Yu-Gi-Oh Starstrike Blast

Booster Box	50.00	75.00
Booster Pack	2.00	3.00
STBLEN000 Archfiend Empress (SR)	1.50	4.00
STBLEN001 Swift Scarecrow	.20	.50
STBLEN002 Mirror Ladybug	.15	.40
STBLEN003 Reed Butterfly	.15	.40
STBLEN004 Needle Soldier	.15	.40
STBLEN005 Necro Linker	.15	.40
STBLEN006 Rescue Warrior	.15	.40
STBLEN007 Power Giant (UTR)	4.00	10.00
STBLEN008 Vice Berserker	.15	.40
STBLEN009 Lancer Archfiend (R)	.60	1.50
STBLEN010 Power Breaker (SR)	1.50	4.00
STBLEN011 Extra Veiler	.15	.40
STBLEN012 Synchro Soldier	.15	.40
STBLEN013 Creation Resonator (R)	.60	1.50
STBLEN014 Attack Gainer	.15	.40
STBLEN015 Blackwing Elesian of Two Swords	.20	.50
STBLEN016 Blackwing Aurora the Northern Lights (R)	.75	2.00
STBLEN017 Blackwing Abrolhos the Megaquake (R)	.75	2.00
STBLEN018 Glow-Up Bulb (UTR)	30.00	60.00
STBLEN019 Karakuri Soldier mdl 236 Nisamu	.15	.40
STBLEN020 Karakuri Merchant mdl 177 Inashichi (R)	.60	1.50
STBLEN021 Karakuri Strategist mdl 248 Nishipachi	.15	.40
STBLEN022 Karakuri Ninja mdl 339 Sazank (SR)	3.00	8.00
STBLEN023 Karakuri Bushi mdl 6318 Muzanichiha (R)	.60	1.50
STBLEN024 Scrap Soldier (R)	.75	2.00
STBLEN025 Scrap Searcher	.15	.40
STBLEN026 Wattkiwi	.15	.40
STBLEN027 Watthopper	.15	.40
STBLEN028 Wattdragonfly	.15	.40
STBLEN029 Wattsquirrel (R)	.60	1.50
STBLEN030 Naturia Cherries (SR)	4.00	10.00
STBLEN031 Naturia Pumpkin	.15	.40
STBLEN032 Naturia Stag Beetle	.20	.50
STBLEN033 Dance Princess of the Ice Barrier (SR)	3.00	8.00
STBLEN034 Chain Dog (R)	1.25	3.00
STBLEN035 Wightmare	.20	.50
STBLEN036 Anarchist Monk Ranshin (SR)	1.50	4.00
STBLEN037 Delg the Dark Monarch (SR)	3.00	8.00
STBLEN038 Supreme Arcanite Magician (UTR)	5.00	12.00
STBLEN039 Gaia Drake, the Universal Force (UTR)	4.00	10.00
STBLEN040 Shooting Star Dragon (GR)	15.00	30.00
STBLEN041 Formula Synchron (R)	4.00	10.00
STBLEN042 Red Nova Dragon (UTR)	6.00	15.00
STBLEN043 Karakuri Shogun mdl/ 00 Burei (UTR)	15.00	30.00
STBLEN044 Scrap Twin Dragon (UTR)	15.00	30.00
STBLEN045 Tuning (UTR)	20.00	40.00
STBLEN046 Karakuri Showdown Castle (R)	.75	2.00
STBLEN047 Golden Gearbox	.15	.40
STBLEN048 Karakuri Anatomy	.15	.40
STBLEN049 Scrap Lube	.15	.40
STBLEN050 Wattcastle (R)	.75	2.00
STBLEN051 Wattjustment	.15	.40
STBLEN052 Barkion's Bark	.15	.40
STBLEN053 Leodrake's Mane	.15	.40
STBLEN054 Medallion of the Ice Barrier	.15	.40
STBLEN055 Mirror of the Ice Barrier	.15	.40
STBLEN056 Koa'ki Ring	.15	.40
STBLEN057 Darkworld Shackles	.15	.40
STBLEN058 Axe of Fools	.15	.40
STBLEN059 Cursed Bill	.15	.40
STBLEN060 Tokkosho of Ghost Destroying (R)	.60	1.50
STBLEN061 Heat Wave (R)	.60	1.50
STBLEN062 White Elephant's Gift	.40	1.00
STBLEN063 D2 Shield (SR)	1.50	4.00
STBLEN064 Red Screen	.15	.40
STBLEN065 Blackback (SR)	2.00	5.00
STBLEN066 Defenders Intersect	.15	.40
STBLEN067 Gravity Collapse (R)	.60	1.50
STBLEN068 Blackwing - Boobytrap	.15	.40
STBLEN069 Star Siphon	.15	.40
STBLEN070 Half Counter	.15	.40
STBLEN071 Karakuri Trick House	.15	.40
STBLEN072 Karakuri Klock (SR)	1.50	4.00
STBLEN073 Scrap Crash	.40	1.00
STBLEN074 Wattkeeper	.15	.40
STBLEN075 Exterio's Fang	.15	.40
STBLEN076 Vanity's Emptiness	.30	.75
STBLEN077 Different Dimension Ground (SR)	1.50	4.00
STBLEN078 Powersink Stone	.15	.40
STBLEN079 Tyrant's Temper (SR)	2.50	6.00
STBLEN080 Dark Trap Hole	.50	1.25
STBLEN081 Skull Meister (SCR)	6.00	15.00
STBLEN082 Droll & Lock Bird (R)	.60	1.50
STBLEN083 Spellstone Sorcerer Karood (SCR)	6.00	15.00
STBLEN084 Scrap Mind Reader (SCR)	8.00	20.00
STBLEN085 Gravekeeper's Recruiter (R)	1.25	3.00
STBLEN086 Psi-Blocker (SCR)	8.00	20.00
STBLEN087 Koa'ki Meiru Wall (R)	.75	2.00
STBLEN088 Karakuri Barrel mdl 96 Shinkuro (R)	.60	1.50
STBLEN089 Mischief of the Yokai (UTR)	4.00	10.00
STBLEN090 Karakuri Spider	.15	.40
STBLEN091 Royal Knight of the Ice Barrier (SR)	1.25	3.00
STBLEN092 Ally Salvo (R)	.60	1.50
STBLEN093 Ally of Justice Thousand Arms	.15	.40
STBLEN094 Ally of Justice Unknown Crusher	.15	.40
STBLEN095 Genex Ally Duradark (SCR)	6.00	15.00
STBLEN096 The Fabled Rubyruda (SCR)	10.00	25.00
STBLEN097 Dragunity Knight - Vajrayana (SR)	4.00	10.00
STBLEN098 Dragunity Knight - Gae Dearg (SCR)	20.00	40.00
STBLEN099 Genex Ally Axel (SCR)	4.00	10.00

2011 Yu-Gi-Oh Extreme Victory

Booster Box (24 packs)	50.00	75.00
Booster Pack (9 cards)	2.50	4.00
EXVC000 Reborn Tengu (SR)	10.00	25.00
EXVC001 Junk Servant (R)	.50	1.25
EXVC002 Unknown Synchron	.30	.75
EXVC003 Salvage Warrior (R)	.30	.75
EXVC004 Necro Defender (R)	.30	.75
EXVC005 Mystic Piper (SCR)	10.00	25.00
EXVC006 Force Resonator	.15	.40
EXVC007 Clock Resonator	.15	.40
EXVC008 Blackwing - Hillen the Tengu-wind (SR)	1.25	3.00
EXVC009 Blackwing Kogarashi the Wanderer (UTR)	5.00	12.00
EXVC009 Blackwing Kogarashi the Wanderer (UR)	3.00	8.00
EXVC010 Morphtronic Lantron	.15	.40
EXVC011 Morphtronic Staplen	.15	.40
EXVC012 Meklord Army of Wisel	.30	.75
EXVC013 Meklord Army of Skiel	.30	.75
EXVC014 Meklord Army of Granel (R)	.60	1.50
EXVC015 Meklord Astro Dragon Asterisk (SR)	1.50	4.00
EXVC016 T.G. Cyber Magician (SR)	8.00	20.00
EXVC017 T.G. Striker (R)	1.25	3.00
EXVC018 T.G. Jet Falcon	.15	.40
EXVC019 T.G. Catapult Dragon	.25	.60
EXVC020 T.G. Warwolf	.15	.40
EXVC021 T.G. Rush Rhino (R)	.40	1.00
EXVC022 Buster Blaster (R)	.50	1.25
EXVC023 Esper Girl	.40	1.00
EXVC024 Mental Seeker	.25	.60
EXVC025 Silent Psychic Wizard (SR)	5.00	12.00
EXVC026 Serene Psychic Witch	.25	.60
EXVC027 Hushed Psychic Cleric (R)	.75	2.00
EXVC028 Elder of the Six Samurai	.25	.60
EXVC029 Shien's Advisor (SR)	1.00	2.50
EXVC030 Karakuri Komachi mdl 224 Ninishi	.25	.60
EXVC031 Karakuri Ninja mdl 7749 Nanashick	.15	.40
EXVC032 Scrap Kong	.15	.40
EXVC033 Tradetoad (R)	.30	.75
EXVC034 Gladiator Beast Tygerius	.15	.40
EXVC035 Jar Turtle	.25	.60
EXVC036 Aurora Paragon	.25	.60
EXVC037 Junk Berserker (GR)	6.00	15.00
EXVC037 Junk Berserker (UTR)	6.00	15.00
EXVC038 Life Stream Dragon (UR)	5.00	12.00
EXVC038 Life Stream Dragon (UTR)	6.00	15.00
EXVC039 T.G. Recipro Dragonfly (R)	.75	2.00
EXVC040 T.G. Wonder Magician (UTR)	10.00	25.00
EXVC040 T.G. Wonder Magician (UR)	10.00	25.00
EXVC041 T.G. Power Gladiator (SR)	2.50	6.00
EXVC042 T.G. Blade Blaster (UTR)	6.00	15.00
EXVC042 T.G. Blade Blaster (UR)	5.00	12.00
EXVC043 T.G. Halberd Cannon (UR)	4.00	10.00
EXVC043 T.G. Halberd Cannon (UTR)	6.00	15.00
EXVC044 Overmind Archfiend (UTR)	5.00	12.00
EXVC044 Overmind Archfiend (UR)	3.00	8.00
EXVC045 Scarlet Security	.30	.75
EXVC046 Red Dragon Vase	.15	.40
EXVC047 Resonator Call (R)	.60	1.50
EXVC048 Resonant Destruction	.15	.40
EXVC049 Fortissimo the Mobile Fortress	.15	.40
EXVC050 Boon of the Meklord Emperor	.15	.40
EXVC051 The Resolute Meklord Army	.15	.40
EXVC052 Reboot	.15	.40
EXVC053 TGX1-HL	.15	.40
EXVC054 TGX300	.30	.75
EXVC055 ESP Amplifier	.15	.40
EXVC056 Psychic Feel Zone (R)	.30	.75
EXVC057 Shien's Dojo (SR)	6.00	15.00
EXVC058 Runaway Karakuri	.15	.40
EXVC059 Contact with the Aquamirror	.15	.40
EXVC060 Soundproofed (R)	.30	.75
EXVC061 Out of the Blue	.15	.40
EXVC062 Self-Mummification	.15	.40
EXVC063 Red Carpet	.25	.60
EXVC064 Power-Up Adapter	.15	.40
EXVC065 Chaos Infinity (R)	.50	1.25
EXVC066 Mektimed Blast	.15	.40
EXVC067 Meklord Factory	.30	.75
EXVC068 TGX3-DX2 (R)	.50	1.25
EXVC069 TG-SX1	.15	.40
EXVC070 TG1-EM1	.15	.40
EXVC071 Psychic Reactor	.15	.40
EXVC072 Brain Hazard (R)	.50	1.25

- ☐ EXVC073 Six Style - Dual Wield .25 .60
- ☐ EXVC074 Karakuri Cash Shed (SR) 2.00 5.00
- ☐ EXVC075 Tyrant's Tantrum .15 .40
- ☐ EXVC076 Debunk (SR) 4.00 10.00
- ☐ EXVC077 Sealing Ceremony of Mokuten .15 .40
- ☐ EXVC078 Safe Zone (SR) 6.00 15.00
- ☐ EXVC079 Localized Tornado .30 .75
- ☐ EXVC080 W Nebula Meteorite .60 1.50
- ☐ EXVC081 Vampire Dragon (SCR) 3.00 8.00
- ☐ EXVC082 Dodger Dragon (SR) 5.00 12.00
- ☐ EXVC083 Mara of the Nordic Alfar (UR) 3.00 8.00
- ☐ EXVC083 Mara of the Nordic Alfar (UTR) 5.00 12.00
- ☐ EXVC084 Tour Guide From the Underworld (SCR)30.00 60.00
- ☐ EXVC085 Psi-Beast (R) .60 1.50
- ☐ EXVC086 Gladiator Beast Essedarii (UR) 6.00 15.00
- ☐ EXVC086 Gladiator Beast Essedarii (UTR) 8.00 20.00
- ☐ EXVC087 Gladiator Taming (SCR) 5.00 12.00
- ☐ EXVC088 Full House (R) .50 1.25
- ☐ EXVC089 Psychic Shockwave (SCR) 6.00 15.00
- ☐ EXVC090 Axe Dragonute 4.00 10.00
- ☐ EXVC091 Lancer Dragonute (SR) 1.00 2.50
- ☐ EXVC092 Lancer Lindwurm .25 .60
- ☐ EXVC093 Elemental Hero Neos Knight (UR) 3.00 8.00
- ☐ EXVC093 Elemental Hero Neos Knight (UTR) 5.00 12.00
- ☐ EXVC094 Meklord Emperor Skiel (SCR) 2.00 5.00
- ☐ EXVC095 Meklord Fortress (R) .75 2.00
- ☐ EXVC096 Blackwing - Jin the Rain Shadow (R) .60 1.50
- ☐ EXVC097 Scrap Orthros (SCR) 8.00 20.00
- ☐ EXVC098 Naturia Eggplant (SR) 1.50 4.00
- ☐ EXVC099 Blue Rose Dragon (SCR) 8.00 20.00

2011 Yu-Gi-Oh Gold Series 4

Complete Set 100.00 175.00
Booster Box (5 Packs) 60.00 120.00
Booster Pack (25 cards) 15.00 30.00

- ☐ GLD4001 Millennium Shield .50 1.25
- ☐ GLD4002 Pendulum Machine .25 .60
- ☐ GLD4003 The Wicked Worm Beast .75 2.00
- ☐ GLD4004 Goddess with the Third Eye .25 .60
- ☐ GLD4005 Beastking of the Swamps .30 .75
- ☐ GLD4006 Versago the Destroyer .25 .60
- ☐ GLD4007 Morphing Jar (GUR) 4.00 10.00
- ☐ GLD4008 Goddess of Whim .25 .60
- ☐ GLD4009 Injection Fairy Lily 1.00 2.50
- ☐ GLD4010 Gravekeeper's Spy (GUR) 3.00 8.00
- ☐ GLD4011 Spirit Reaper (GUR) 5.00 12.00
- ☐ GLD4012 Chaos Sorcerer (GUR) 8.00 20.00
- ☐ GLD4013 Black Luster Soldier 30.00 60.00 Envoy of the Beginning (GUR)
- ☐ GLD4014 White-Horned Dragon .50 1.25
- ☐ GLD4015 Toon Dark Magician Girl 1.00 2.50
- ☐ GLD4016 Meltiel, Sage of the Sky 1.00 2.50
- ☐ GLD4017 Radiant Jeral .30 .75
- ☐ GLD4018 Diabolos, King of the Abyss .50 1.25
- ☐ GLD4019 Lich Lord, King of the Underworld .50 1.25
- ☐ GLD4020 Prometheus, King of the Shadows .50 1.25
- ☐ GLD4021 Mormolith .50 1.25
- ☐ GLD4022 Darklord Zerato (GUR) 3.00 8.00
- ☐ GLD4023 Doomcaliber Knight (GUR) 10.00 25.00
- ☐ GLD4024 Ryko, Lightsworn Hunter (GUR) 6.00 15.00
- ☐ GLD4025 Celestia, Lightsworn Angel (GUR) 3.00 8.00
- ☐ GLD4026 Tytannial, Princess of Camellias (GUR)3.00 8.00
- ☐ GLD4027 Summoner Monk (GUR) 4.00 10.00
- ☐ GLD4028 Genesis Dragon .60 1.50
- ☐ GLD4029 Orichalcos Shunoros .30 .75
- ☐ GLD4030 Obelisk the Tormentor (GUR) 6.00 15.00
- ☐ GLD4031 Five-Headed Dragon (GUR) 6.00 15.00
- ☐ GLD4032 Gladiator Beast Gyzarus (GUR) 2.50 6.00
- ☐ GLD4033 Eternal Drought .25 .60
- ☐ GLD4034 Eradicating Aerosol .25 .60
- ☐ GLD4035 Soul Exchange .30 .75
- ☐ GLD4036 Toon World .30 .75
- ☐ GLD4037 Graceful Dice .30 .75
- ☐ GLD4038 Sage's Stone .40 1.00
- ☐ GLD4039 Toon Table of Contents (GUR) 3.00 8.00
- ☐ GLD4040 Pot of Avarice (GUR) 5.00 12.00
- ☐ GLD4041 Recurring Nightmare .75 2.00
- ☐ GLD4042 Sword of Dark Rites .50 1.25
- ☐ GLD4043 Trade-In 1.25 3.00
- ☐ GLD4044 Magic Formula .30 .75
- ☐ GLD4045 Robbin' Goblin .25 .60
- ☐ GLD4046 Skull Dice .30 .75
- ☐ GLD4047 Royal Oppression (GUR) 5.00 12.00
- ☐ GLD4048 Xing Zhen Hu .30 .75
- ☐ GLD4049 Deck Devastation Virus 1.00 2.50
- ☐ GLD4050 Trap Stun (GUR) 5.00 12.00

2011 Yu-Gi-Oh Generation Force

Booster Box (24 packs) 60.00 80.00
Booster Pack (9 cards) 2.50 4.00

- ☐ GENFEN000 Xyz Veil (SR) 1.50 4.00
- ☐ GENFEN001 Gagaga Magician (SR) 4.00 10.00
- ☐ GENFEN002 Gogogo Golem .25 .60
- ☐ GENFEN003 Achacha Archer .25 .60
- ☐ GENFEN004 Goblindbergh .25 .60
- ☐ GENFEN005 Big Jaws (R) .60 1.50
- ☐ GENFEN006 Skull Kraken .25 .60
- ☐ GENFEN007 Drill Barnacle .25 .60
- ☐ GENFEN008 Jawsman (R) .30 .75
- ☐ GENFEN009 Crashbug X .25 .60
- ☐ GENFEN010 Crashbug Y .25 .60
- ☐ GENFEN011 Crashbug Z .25 .60
- ☐ GENFEN012 Super Crashbug (SR) .60 1.50
- ☐ GENFEN013 Wind-Up Soldier .25 .60
- ☐ GENFEN014 Wind-Up Magician (R) .30 .75
- ☐ GENFEN015 Wind-Up Juggler (SR) 1.50 4.00
- ☐ GENFEN016 Wind-Up Dog .25 .60
- ☐ GENFEN017 Wind-Up Snail (R) .30 .75
- ☐ GENFEN018 Spearfish Soldier .30 .75
- ☐ GENFEN019 Flyfang .25 .60
- ☐ GENFEN020 Skystarray (R) .30 .75
- ☐ GENFEN021 Airorca (R) .60 1.50
- ☐ GENFEN022 Wingtortoise (R) .60 1.50
- ☐ GENFEN023 Space-Time Police (UR) 1.25 3.00
- ☐ GENFEN023 Space-Time Police (UTR) 2.00 5.00
- ☐ GENFEN024 Time Escaper (SR) .60 1.50
- ☐ GENFEN025 Gem-Elephant .25 .60
- ☐ GENFEN026 Laval Magma Cannoneer .25 .60
- ☐ GENFEN027 Gishki Diviner (R) .30 .75
- ☐ GENFEN028 Gusto Codor .30 .75
- ☐ GENFEN029 Saambell the Summoner .25 .60
- ☐ GENFEN030 Geargiano .25 .60
- ☐ GENFEN031 Poki Draco .25 .60
- ☐ GENFEN032 Master of the Flaming Dragonswords.25 .60
- ☐ GENFEN033 Perditious Puppeteer .30 .75
- ☐ GENFEN034 Blue-Blooded Oni (SR) 1.50 4.00
- ☐ GENFEN035 Ghost Ship (R) .40 1.00
- ☐ GENFEN036 Absolute Crusader (SR) 1.25 3.00
- ☐ GENFEN037 Big Emperor Penguin .30 .75
- ☐ GENFEN038 Mitla the Temporal Magician .60 1.50
- ☐ GENFEN039 Number 17: Leviathan Dragon (UR)6.00 15.00
- ☐ GENFEN039 Number 17: Leviathan Dragon (GR)8.00 20.00
- ☐ GENFEN039 Number 17: Leviathan Dragon (UTR)6.00 15.00
- ☐ GENFEN040 Submersible Carrier Aero Shark (SR)1.50 4.00
- ☐ GENFEN041 Number 34: Terror-Byte (UR) 3.00 8.00
- ☐ GENFEN041 Number 34: Terror-Byte (UTR) 4.00 10.00
- ☐ GENFEN042 Wind-Up Zenmaister (UR) 3.00 8.00
- ☐ GENFEN042 Wind-Up Zenmaister (UTR) 3.00 8.00
- ☐ GENFEN043 Leviair the Sea Dragon (UR) 20.00 40.00
- ☐ GENFEN043 Leviair the Sea Dragon (UTR) 20.00 40.00
- ☐ GENFEN044 Tiras, Keeper of Genesis (SCR) 15.00 30.00
- ☐ GENFEN045 Wonder Wand (UTR) 4.00 10.00
- ☐ GENFEN045 Wonder Wand (UR) 6.00 15.00
- ☐ GENFEN046 Double Up Chance .30 .75
- ☐ GENFEN047 Thunder Short .25 .60
- ☐ GENFEN048 Aqua Jet .25 .60
- ☐ GENFEN049 Surface (SR) 4.00 10.00
- ☐ GENFEN050 Crashbug Road .25 .60
- ☐ GENFEN051 Infected Mail (SR) .75 2.00
- ☐ GENFEN052 Cracking .25 .60
- ☐ GENFEN053 Legendary Wind-Up .25 .60
- ☐ GENFEN054 Wind-Up Factory (SR) 3.00 8.00
- ☐ GENFEN055 Fish and Kicks .25 .60
- ☐ GENFEN056 Future Glow .30 .75
- ☐ GENFEN057 Vylon Filament .25 .60
- ☐ GENFEN058 Quill Pen of Gulldos (SR) 1.50 4.00
- ☐ GENFEN059 Star Changer (R) .40 1.00
- ☐ GENFEN060 Oni-Gami Combo .25 .60
- ☐ GENFEN061 Resonance Device (R) .30 .75
- ☐ GENFEN062 Peeking Goblin .25 .60
- ☐ GENFEN063 Asleep at the Switch .25 .60
- ☐ GENFEN064 Poseidon Waves .30 .75
- ☐ GENFEN065 Explosive Urchin .25 .60
- ☐ GENFEN066 Damage Vaccine MAX .25 .60
- ☐ GENFEN067 Overwind .25 .60
- ☐ GENFEN068 Underworld Egg Clutch .25 .60
- ☐ GENFEN069 Oh F!sh! (R) .75 2.00
- ☐ GENFEN070 Bright Future (R) .30 .75
- ☐ GENFEN071 Past Image .30 .75
- ☐ GENFEN072 Burgeoning Whirlflame .25 .60
- ☐ GENFEN073 Treaty on Uniform Nomenclature .30 .75
- ☐ GENFEN074 Utopian Aura .25 .60
- ☐ GENFEN075 United Front (R) .60 1.50
- ☐ GENFEN076 Curse of the Circle (R) .60 1.50
- ☐ GENFEN077 Tyrant's Tummyache .25 .60
- ☐ GENFEN078 Attention! (R) .30 .75
- ☐ GENFEN079 Raigeki Bottle (UR) .75 2.00
- ☐ GENFEN079 Raigeki Bottle (UTR) .75 2.00
- ☐ GENFEN080 Gravelstorm .25 .60
- ☐ GENFEN081 Sea Lancer (R) .60 1.50
- ☐ GENFEN082 Piercing Moray (UR) 1.25 3.00
- ☐ GENFEN082 Piercing Moray (UTR) 2.00 5.00
- ☐ GENFEN083 Lost Blue Breaker (SCR) 8.00 20.00
- ☐ GENFEN084 Pain Painter (SCR) 8.00 20.00
- ☐ GENFEN085 Orient Dragon (SCR) 20.00 40.00
- ☐ GENFEN086 Adreus 15.00 30.00 Keeper of Armageddon (SCR)
- ☐ GENFEN087 Fish and Swaps (R) .60 1.50
- ☐ GENFEN088 Painful Return (R) .60 1.50
- ☐ GENFEN089 Smashing Horn (SCR) 5.00 12.00
- ☐ GENFEN090 Elemental HERO Flash .25 .60
- ☐ GENFEN091 Vision HERO Trinity (SR) 1.25 3.00
- ☐ GENFEN092 Phantom Magician .25 .60
- ☐ GENFEN093 Elemental HERO Nova Master (UTR)5.00 12.00
- ☐ GENFEN093 Elemental HERO Nova Master (UR)5.00 12.00
- ☐ GENFEN094 Masked HERO Goka (R) .60 1.50
- ☐ GENFEN095 Masked HERO Vapor (SR) 2.50 6.00
- ☐ GENFEN096 Vision HERO Adoration (SCR) 10.00 25.00
- ☐ GENFEN097 Mask Change .25 .60
- ☐ GENFEN098 A Hero Lives (UR) 8.00 20.00
- ☐ GENFEN098 A Hero Lives (UTR) 3.00 8.00
- ☐ GENFEN099 Steelswarm Roach (SCR) 30.00 60.00

2011 Yu-Gi-Oh Hidden Arsenal 4

Booster Box (24 packs) 60.00 90.00
Booster Pack (5 cards) 2.50 4.00

- ☐ HA04EN001 Genex Ally Remote SR .25 .60
- ☐ HA04EN002 Genex Ally Powercell SCR .25 .60
- ☐ HA04EN003 Genex Ally Changer SR .15 .40
- ☐ HA04EN004 Genex Ally Volcannon SR .15 .40
- ☐ HA04EN005 Genex Ally Solid SR .15 .40
- ☐ HA04EN006 The Fabled Chawa SR .15 .40
- ☐ HA04EN007 The Fabled Catsith SR .75 2.00
- ☐ HA04EN008 The Fabled Cerburrel SCR 8.00 20.00
- ☐ HA04EN009 The Fabled Ganashia SR .75 2.00
- ☐ HA04EN010 The Fabled Nozoochee SR .25 .60
- ☐ HA04EN011 Dragunity Militum SR .25 .60
- ☐ HA04EN012 Dragunity Primus Pilus SCR .25 .60
- ☐ HA04EN013 Dragunity Brandistock SR .15 .40
- ☐ HA04EN014 Dragunity Javelin SR .15 .40
- ☐ HA04EN015 Jurrac Dino SR .40 1.00
- ☐ HA04EN016 Jurrac Gallim SR .25 .60
- ☐ HA04EN017 Jurrac Aeolo SR .30 .75
- ☐ HA04EN018 Jurrac Herra SR .30 .75
- ☐ HA04EN019 Naturia Butterfly SR .25 .60
- ☐ HA04EN020 Naturia Ladybug SR .25 .60
- ☐ HA04EN021 Naturia Strawberry SR .15 .40
- ☐ HA04EN022 Defender of the Ice Barrier SR .25 .60
- ☐ HA04EN023 Warlock of the Ice Barrier SR .25 .60
- ☐ HA04EN024 Sacred Spirit of the Ice Barrier SR.25 .60
- ☐ HA04EN025 General Raiho of the Ice Barrier SCR.75 2.00
- ☐ HA04EN026 Genex Ally Triarm SCR .30 .75
- ☐ HA04EN027 The Fabled Unicore SCR 1.25 3.00
- ☐ HA04EN028 Dragunity Knight - Trident SCR 2.50 6.00
- ☐ HA04EN029 Jurrac Meteor SCR .75 2.00
- ☐ HA04EN030 Naturia Landoise SCR 2.50 6.00
- ☐ HA04EN031 Neo Flamvell Origin SR .25 .60
- ☐ HA04EN032 Neo Flamvell Hedgehog SR .25 .60
- ☐ HA04EN033 Neo Flamvell Shaman SR .25 .60
- ☐ HA04EN034 Neo Flamvell Garuda SR .15 .40
- ☐ HA04EN035 Neo Flamvell Sabre SCR .30 .75
- ☐ HA04EN036 Genex Ally Chemistrer SR .15 .40
- ☐ HA04EN037 Genex Ally Birdman SR 3.00 8.00
- ☐ HA04EN038 Genex Ally Bellflame SR .15 .40
- ☐ HA04EN039 Genex Ally Crusher SR .40 1.00
- ☐ HA04EN040 Genex Ally Reliever SCR .25 .60
- ☐ HA04EN041 The Fabled Peggulsus SR .25 .60
- ☐ HA04EN042 The Fabled Kokkator SR .25 .60
- ☐ HA04EN043 Fabled Dianaira SCR .25 .60
- ☐ HA04EN044 Dragunity Corsesca SR .30 .75
- ☐ HA04EN045 Dragunity Partisan SR .25 .60
- ☐ HA04EN046 Dragunity Pilum SR .25 .60
- ☐ HA04EN047 Dragunity Angusticlavii SR .25 .60
- ☐ HA04EN048 Naturia Stinkbug SR .25 .60
- ☐ HA04EN049 Naturia Mantis SR .25 .60
- ☐ HA04EN050 Naturia Ragweed SR .25 .60
- ☐ HA04EN051 Naturia White Oak SCR .40 1.00
- ☐ HA04EN052 Strategist of the Ice Barrier SR .25 .60
- ☐ HA04EN053 Secret Guards of the Ice Barrier SR.25 .60
- ☐ HA04EN054 General Gantala of the .75 2.00 Ice Barrier SCR
- ☐ HA04EN055 Naturia Exterio SCR .75 2.00
- ☐ HA04EN056 Ancient Flamvell Deity SCR .75 2.00
- ☐ HA04EN057 Genex Ally Triforce SCR .75 2.00
- ☐ HA04EN058 The Fabled Kudabbi SCR .75 2.00
- ☐ HA04EN059 Dragunity Knight - Barcha SCR 2.50 6.00
- ☐ HA04EN060 Trishula, Dragon of the 30.00 60.00 Ice Barrier SCR

2011 Yu-Gi-Oh Hidden Arsenal 5

Complete Set 30.00 60.00
Booster Box 30.00 60.00
Booster Pack

- ☐ HA05001 Gem-Knight Garnet (SR) .15 .40
- ☐ HA05002 Gem-Knight Sapphire (SR) .25 .60
- ☐ HA05003 Gem-Knight Tourmaline (SR) .60 1.50
- ☐ HA05004 Gem-Knight Alexandrite (SCR) 1.00 2.50
- ☐ HA05005 Gem-Armadillo (SCR) 1.00 2.50
- ☐ HA05006 Gem-Merchant (SR) .15 .40
- ☐ HA05007 Laval Miller (SR) .30 .75
- ☐ HA05008 Soaring Eagle Above the .15 .40 Searing Land (SR)
- ☐ HA05009 Laval Warrior (SR) .15 .40
- ☐ HA05010 Prominence, Molten Swordsman (SR).25 .60
- ☐ HA05011 Laval Forest Sprite (SR) .30 .75
- ☐ HA05012 Kayenn .40 1.00 the Master Magma Blacksmith (SR)
- ☐ HA05013 Laval Burner (SR) .15 .40
- ☐ HA05014 Laval Judgment Lord (SCR) 1.00 2.50
- ☐ HA05015 Vylon Cube (SR) .15 .40
- ☐ HA05016 Vylon Vanguard (SR) .15 .40
- ☐ HA05017 Vylon Charger (SR) .15 .40
- ☐ HA05018 Vylon Soldier (SR) .15 .40
- ☐ HA05019 Gem-Knight Ruby (SCR) 1.50 4.00
- ☐ HA05020 Gem-Knight Aquamarine (SCR) 1.25 3.00
- ☐ HA05021 Gem-Knight Topaz (SCR) 1.25 3.00
- ☐ HA05022 Lavalval Dragon (SCR) 2.00 5.00
- ☐ HA05023 Laval the Greater (SCR) 1.50 4.00
- ☐ HA05024 Vylon Sigma (SCR) 1.25 3.00
- ☐ HA05025 Vylon Epsilon (SCR) 4.00 10.00
- ☐ HA05026 Gem-Knight Fusion (SR) .60 1.50
- ☐ HA05027 Searing Fire Wall (SR) .15 .40
- ☐ HA05028 Vylon Material (SR) .15 .40
- ☐ HA05029 Gem-Enhancement (SR) .60 1.50
- ☐ HA05030 Molten Whirlwind Wall (SR) .15 .40
- ☐ HA05031 Gishki Abyss (SR) .60 1.50
- ☐ HA05032 Gishki Vanity (SR) .15 .40
- ☐ HA05033 Gishki Marker (SR) .15 .40
- ☐ HA05034 Gishki Chain (SCR) 2.00 5.00
- ☐ HA05035 Gishki Ariel (SR) .40 1.00
- ☐ HA05036 Gishki Shadow (SR) .60 1.50
- ☐ HA05037 Gusto Gulldo (SR) .25 .60
- ☐ HA05038 Gusto Egul (SR) .25 .60
- ☐ HA05039 Gusto Thunbolt (SR) .15 .40
- ☐ HA05040 Winda, Priestess of Gusto (SR) .60 1.50
- ☐ HA05041 Caam, Serenity of Gusto (SCR) 6.00 15.00
- ☐ HA05042 Windaar, Sage of Gusto (SR) .15 .40
- ☐ HA05043 Steelswarm Cell (SR) .15 .40
- ☐ HA05044 Steelswarm Scout (SR) .15 .40
- ☐ HA05045 Steelswarm Gatekeeper (SR) .15 .40
- ☐ HA05046 Steelswarm Caller (SR) .15 .40
- ☐ HA05047 Steelswarm Mantis (SCR) 1.25 3.00
- ☐ HA05048 Steelswarm Moth (SR) .15 .40
- ☐ HA05049 Steelswarm Girastag (SCR) 3.00 8.00
- ☐ HA05050 Steelswarm Caucastag (SCR) 4.00 10.00
- ☐ HA05051 Evigishki Mind Augus (SCR) 1.50 4.00
- ☐ HA05052 Evigishki Soul Ogre (SCR) 2.00 5.00
- ☐ HA05053 Daigusto Gulldos (SCR) 1.50 4.00
- ☐ HA05054 Daigusto Eguls (SCR) 1.50 4.00
- ☐ HA05055 Gishki Aquamirror (SR) 1.00 2.50
- ☐ HA05056 Contact with Gusto (SCR) 1.00 2.50
- ☐ HA05057 First Step Towards Infestation (SR) .25 .60
- ☐ HA05058 Aquamirror Meditation (SR) .15 .40
- ☐ HA05059 Blessings for Gusto (SR) .15 .40
- ☐ HA05060 Infestation Wave (SR) .15 .40

2011 Yu-Gi-Oh Legendary Collection 2

- ☐ LC02001 Uria, Lord of Searing Flames (UR) .75 2.00
- ☐ LC02002 Hamon, Lord of Striking Thunder (UR).75 2.00
- ☐ LC02003 Raviel, Lord of Phantasms (UR) .75 2.00
- ☐ LC02004 Darklord Asmodeus (UR) .75 2.00
- ☐ LC02005 Darklord Superbia (UR) 4.00 10.00
- ☐ LC02006 Darklord Edeh Arae (UR) .75 2.00
- ☐ LC02007 Cyber Larva (UR) .25 .60
- ☐ LC02008 Lion Alligator (UR) .25 .60
- ☐ LC02009 Spawn Alligator (UR) .25 .60
- ☐ LC02010 Elemental HERO Great Tornado (UR)2.50 6.00
- ☐ LC02011 Parallel World Fusion (UR) 2.50 6.00
- ☐ LC02012 Dragonic Tactics (UR) .25 .60
- ☐ LC02013 Court of Justice (UR) .25 .60
- ☐ LCGX001 Elemental HERO Avian .25 .60
- ☐ LCGX002 Elemental HERO Avian (alt) (SCR) 3.00 8.00
- ☐ LCGX003 Elemental HERO Burstinatrix .20 .50
- ☐ LCGX004 Elemental HERO Burstinatrix (alt) (SCR)4.00 10.00
- ☐ LCGX005 Elemental HERO Clayman .20 .50
- ☐ LCGX006 Elemental HERO Sparkman .20 .50
- ☐ LCGX007 Elemental HERO Sparkman (alt) (SCR)3.00 8.00
- ☐ LCGX008 Elemental HERO Neos .20 .50
- ☐ LCGX009 Winged Kuriboh .20 .50
- ☐ LCGX010 Winged Kuriboh LV10 .20 .50
- ☐ LCGX011 Wroughtweiler .20 .50
- ☐ LCGX012 Elemental HERO Bubbleman .20 .50
- ☐ LCGX013 Elemental HERO Bladedge .20 .50
- ☐ LCGX014 Elemental HERO Wildheart .20 .50
- ☐ LCGX015 Elemental HERO Necroshade (R) .75 2.00
- ☐ LCGX016 Hero Kid .20 .50
- ☐ LCGX017 Neo-Spacian Aqua Dolphin .20 .50
- ☐ LCGX018 Neo-Spacian Flare Scarab .20 .50
- ☐ LCGX019 Neo-Spacian Dark Panther .20 .50
- ☐ LCGX020 Card Trooper 1.50 4.00
- ☐ LCGX021 Neo-Spacian Air Hummingbird .20 .50
- ☐ LCGX022 Neo-Spacian Grand Mole .75 2.00
- ☐ LCGX023 Neo-Spacian Glow Moss .20 .50
- ☐ LCGX024 Elemental HERO Stratos .75 2.00
- ☐ LCGX025 Elemental HERO Ocean (R) 1.50 4.00
- ☐ LCGX026 Elemental HERO Captain Gold .20 .50
- ☐ LCGX027 Necro Gardna (SCR) 8.00 20.00
- ☐ LCGX028 Elemental HERO Neos Alius (SCR) 6.00 15.00
- ☐ LCGX029 Evil HERO Malicious Edge (SCR) 2.50 6.00
- ☐ LCGX030 Evil HERO Infernal Gainer .20 .50
- ☐ LCGX031 Evil HERO Infernal Prodigy (R) .40 1.00
- ☐ LCGX032 Card Ejector (SR) .75 2.00
- ☐ LCGX033 Elemental Hero Prisma 4.00 10.00
- ☐ LCGX034 Elemental HERO Woodsman (SR) 1.50 4.00
- ☐ LCGX035 Elemental HERO Knospe (R) .25 .60
- ☐ LCGX036 Elemental HERO Poison Rose (R) .25 .60
- ☐ LCGX037 Elemental HERO Heat .40 1.00
- ☐ LCGX038 Elemental HERO Lady Heat .40 1.00
- ☐ LCGX039 Elemental HERO Voltic .75 2.00
- ☐ LCGX040 Neos Wiseman (UR) 1.50 4.00
- ☐ LCGX041 Gallis the Star Beast (SCR) 8.00 20.00
- ☐ LCGX042 Dandylion (SCR) 8.00 20.00
- ☐ LCGX043 Winged Kuriboh LV9 (SCR) 3.00 8.00
- ☐ LCGX044 Card Blocker (UR) .75 2.00
- ☐ LCGX045 Elemental HERO Flame Wingman (SCR)3.00 8.00
- ☐ LCGX046 Elemental HERO Thunder Giant .40 1.00
- ☐ LCGX047 Elemental HERO Rampart Blaster (SR).75 2.00
- ☐ LCGX048 Elemental HERO Tempest (SR) 3.00 8.00
- ☐ LCGX049 Elemental HERO Wildedge .40 1.00
- ☐ LCGX050 Elemental HERO 2.50 6.00 Shining Flare Wingman (SCR)
- ☐ LCGX051 Elemental HERO Steam Healer (R) 1.50 4.00
- ☐ LCGX052 Elemental HERO Electrum (UR) 3.00 8.00
- ☐ LCGX053 Elemental HERO Mudballman (SR) 3.00 8.00
- ☐ LCGX054 Elemental HERO Mariner .25 .60
- ☐ LCGX055 Elemental HERO Wild Wingman .25 .60
- ☐ LCGX056 Elemental HERO Necroid Shaman .25 .60
- ☐ LCGX057 Elemental HERO Aqua Neos (SR) .40 1.00
- ☐ LCGX058 Elemental HERO Flare Neos .25 .60
- ☐ LCGX059 Elemental HERO Dark Neos (SCR) 1.50 4.00
- ☐ LCGX060 Elemental HERO Grand Neos (SR) .75 2.00
- ☐ LCGX061 Elemental HERO Glow Neos (R) 1.50 4.00
- ☐ LCGX062 Elemental HERO Marine Neos .25 .60
- ☐ LCGX063 Elemental HERO Darkbright (SR) .75 2.00
- ☐ LCGX064 Elemental HERO Magma Neos (SR) 3.00 8.00
- ☐ LCGX065 Elemental HERO Chaos Neos (UR) 2.00 5.00
- ☐ LCGX066 Elemental HERO Plasma Vice .40 1.00
- ☐ LCGX067 Evil HERO Inferno Wing (SR) 1.50 4.00
- ☐ LCGX068 Evil HERO Lightning Golem (SR) .75 2.00
- ☐ LCGX069 Evil HERO Dark Gaia (SR) 1.50 4.00
- ☐ LCGX070 Evil HERO Wild Cyclone (SR) 1.25 3.00
- ☐ LCGX071 Evil HERO Infernal Sniper (UR) .75 2.00
- ☐ LCGX072 Evil HERO Malicious Fiend (SR) 2.50 6.00
- ☐ LCGX073 Elemental HERO Storm Neos .25 .60
- ☐ LCGX074 Rainbow Neos (SR) 2.50 6.00
- ☐ LCGX075 Elemental HERO Terra Firma (SR) .75 2.00
- ☐ LCGX076 Elemental HERO Inferno (SR) .75 2.00
- ☐ LCGX077 Elemental HERO Divine Neos (UR) 2.50 6.00
- ☐ LCGX078 Miracle Fusion (UR) 10.00 25.00
- ☐ LCGX079 Transcendent Wings .20 .50
- ☐ LCGX080 Bubble Shuffle (R) .25 .60
- ☐ LCGX081 Spark Blaster .20 .50
- ☐ LCGX082 Skyscraper .25 .60
- ☐ LCGX083 Feather Shot (R) .25 .60
- ☐ LCGX084 Burst Return (R) .25 .60
- ☐ LCGX085 Hero Heart .20 .50
- ☐ LCGX086 Cyclone Boomerang .20 .50
- ☐ LCGX087 The Flute of Summoning Kuriboh (UR)2.50 6.00
- ☐ LCGX088 H - Heated Heart .20 .50
- ☐ LCGX089 E - Emergency Call .30 .75
- ☐ LCGX090 R - Righteous Justice .20 .50
- ☐ LCGX091 O - Oversoul .20 .50
- ☐ LCGX092 Hero Flash!! (R) .25 .60
- ☐ LCGX093 Fake Hero (R) .25 .60
- ☐ LCGX094 Neo Space (R) .25 .60
- ☐ LCGX095 Instant Fusion (UR) 6.00 15.00
- ☐ LCGX096 Neos Force .20 .50
- ☐ LCGX097 Skyscraper 2 - Hero City (SCR) 1.50 4.00
- ☐ LCGX098 Fifth Hope (SCR) 1.50 4.00
- ☐ LCGX099 Dark Fusion (UR) 1.50 4.00
- ☐ LCGX100 Dark Calling (R) .75 2.00
- ☐ LCGX101 Super Polymerization (SCR) 20.00 40.00
- ☐ LCGX102 Instant Neo Space .20 .50
- ☐ LCGX103 Hero Mask .20 .50
- ☐ LCGX104 Space Gift .20 .50
- ☐ LCGX105 Rose Bud (R) .25 .60
- ☐ LCGX106 HERO's Bond .20 .50
- ☐ LCGX107 Hero Signal .20 .50
- ☐ LCGX108 Hero Barrier .20 .50
- ☐ LCGX109 Feather Wind .20 .50
- ☐ LCGX110 Hero Ring (SR) .75 2.00
- ☐ LCGX111 Clay Charge .20 .50
- ☐ LCGX112 Miracle Kids .20 .50
- ☐ LCGX113 Edge Hammer .20 .50
- ☐ LCGX114 Kid Guard (UR) .75 2.00
- ☐ LCGX115 Elemental Recharge .20 .50
- ☐ LCGX116 Change of Hero - Reflector Ray .20 .50
- ☐ LCGX117 Hero Spirit .20 .50
- ☐ LCGX118 Hero Counterattack .20 .50
- ☐ LCGX119 Mirror Gate (UR) .40 1.00
- ☐ LCGX120 Hero Blast .75 2.00
- ☐ LCGX121 Terra Firma Gravity (R) .25 .60
- ☐ LCGX122 Destiny HERO - Doom Lord .25 .60
- ☐ LCGX123 Destiny HERO - Captain Tenacious .25 .60
- ☐ LCGX124 Destiny HERO - Diamond Dude (SR)5.00 12.00
- ☐ LCGX125 Destiny HERO - Dreadmaster (SR) .75 2.00
- ☐ LCGX126 Destiny HERO - Double Dude .25 .60
- ☐ LCGX127 Destiny HERO - Defender (R) .25 .60
- ☐ LCGX128 Destiny HERO - Dogma (SR) .75 2.00
- ☐ LCGX129 Destiny HERO - Blade Master .25 .60
- ☐ LCGX130 Destiny HERO - Fear Monger .25 .60
- ☐ LCGX131 Destiny HERO - Dasher .25 .60
- ☐ LCGX132 Destiny HERO - Malicious 1.50 4.00
- ☐ LCGX133 Destiny HERO 4.00 10.00 Disk Commander (SCR)
- ☐ LCGX134 Destiny HERO - Plasma (SR) 3.00 8.00
- ☐ LCGX135 Destiny HERO - Dunker .25 .60
- ☐ LCGX136 Destiny HERO - Departed .25 .60
- ☐ LCGX137 Destiny HERO - Dread Servant .25 .60
- ☐ LCGX138 Elemental HERO Phoenix Enforcer (SR).75 2.00
- ☐ LCGX139 Elemental HERO 1.50 4.00 Shining Phoenix Enforcer (SCR)
- ☐ LCGX140 Destiny End Dragoon (SR) 1.50 4.00
- ☐ LCGX141 Clock Tower Prison .25 .60
- ☐ LCGX142 D - Spirit .20 .50
- ☐ LCGX143 Cyclone Blade .20 .50
- ☐ LCGX144 Dark City .25 .60
- ☐ LCGX145 Destiny Draw (SCR) 6.00 15.00
- ☐ LCGX146 Over Destiny (R) .25 .60
- ☐ LCGX147 D - Formation .20 .50
- ☐ LCGX148 Destiny Signal .20 .50
- ☐ LCGX149 D-Time (R) .25 .60
- ☐ LCGX150 D - Shield .20 .50
- ☐ LCGX151 Destiny Mirage (R) .25 .60
- ☐ LCGX152 D - Chain .20 .50
- ☐ LCGX153 D - Counter .20 .50
- ☐ LCGX154 D - Fortune .20 .50
- ☐ LCGX155 Crystal Beast Ruby Carbuncle .20 .50
- ☐ LCGX156 Crystal Beast Amethyst Cat .20 .50
- ☐ LCGX157 Crystal Beast Emerald Tortoise .20 .50
- ☐ LCGX158 Crystal Beast Topaz Tiger .25 .60
- ☐ LCGX159 Crystal Beast Amber Mammoth .20 .50
- ☐ LCGX160 Crystal Beast Cobalt Eagle .25 .60
- ☐ LCGX161 Crystal Beast Sapphire Pegasus (SR)3.00 8.00
- ☐ LCGX162 Rainbow Dragon (UR) 3.00 8.00
- ☐ LCGX163 Crystal Beacon (R) .25 .60
- ☐ LCGX164 Rare Value (UR) 3.00 8.00
- ☐ LCGX165 Crystal Blessing (R) .25 .60
- ☐ LCGX166 Crystal Abundance (R) .30 .75
- ☐ LCGX167 Crystal Promise (R) .25 .60
- ☐ LCGX168 Ancient City - Rainbow Ruins .25 .60
- ☐ LCGX169 Crystal Release (UR) 1.50 4.00
- ☐ LCGX170 Crystal Tree (UR) 1.25 3.00
- ☐ LCGX171 Crystal Raigeki .20 .50
- ☐ LCGX172 Crystal Pair .25 .60
- ☐ LCGX173 Rainbow Path .20 .50
- ☐ LCGX174 Rainbow Gravity .20 .50
- ☐ LCGX175 Cyber Dragon (UR) 6.00 15.00
- ☐ LCGX176 Cyber Dragon (alt) (SCR) 10.00 25.00
- ☐ LCGX177 Proto-Cyber Dragon (UR) 3.00 8.00
- ☐ LCGX178 Cyber Phoenix (UR) 1.50 4.00
- ☐ LCGX179 Cyber Valley (UR) 3.00 8.00
- ☐ LCGX180 Cyber Twin Dragon (SCR) 2.50 6.00
- ☐ LCGX181 Cyber End Dragon (SCR) 4.00 10.00
- ☐ LCGX182 Cyber End Dragon (alt) (SCR) 4.00 10.00
- ☐ LCGX183 Chimeratech Overdragon (SCR) 4.00 10.00
- ☐ LCGX184 Power Bond (SCR) 2.50 6.00
- ☐ LCGX185 Overload Fusion (R) .25 .60
- ☐ LCGX186 Future Fusion (UR) 6.00 15.00
- ☐ LCGX187 Magical Mallet (UR) .75 2.00
- ☐ LCGX188 Dark End Dragon (SCR) 6.00 15.00
- ☐ LCGX189 Light End Dragon (UR) 4.00 10.00
- ☐ LCGX190 Hydrogeddon (UR) 4.00 10.00
- ☐ LCGX191 Vennominaga the Deity 8.00 20.00 of Poisonous Snakes (UR)
- ☐ LCGX192 Vennominon the King 1.25 3.00 of Poisonous Snakes (SR)
- ☐ LCGX193 Phantom of Chaos (SCR) 5.00 12.00
- ☐ LCGX194 Phantom Skyblaster (SCR) 4.00 10.00
- ☐ LCGX195 Grave Squirmer .25 .60
- ☐ LCGX196 Grinder Golem .40 1.00
- ☐ LCGX197 Yubel (SCR) 3.00 8.00
- ☐ LCGX198 Yubel - Terror Incarnate (SCR) 2.50 6.00
- ☐ LCGX199 Yubel - The Ultimate Nightmare (SCR)6.00 15.00
- ☐ LCGX200 Mezuki .40 1.00
- ☐ LCGX201 Cold Enchanter .25 .60
- ☐ LCGX202 Ice Master .40 1.00
- ☐ LCGX203 Thunder King Rai-Oh 6.00 15.00
- ☐ LCGX204 Darkness Destroyer (SCR) 2.50 6.00
- ☐ LCGX205 White Night Dragon (UR) 4.00 10.00
- ☐ LCGX206 Kasha (UR) 2.50 6.00
- ☐ LCGX207 Ice Queen (UR) .75 2.00
- ☐ LCGX208 Shutendoji (UR) 2.50 6.00
- ☐ LCGX209 Clear Vice Dragon (SR) .75 2.00
- ☐ LCGX210 Darklord Desire (SR) 2.50 6.00
- ☐ LCGX211 Armityle the Chaos Phantom (UR) 2.50 6.00
- ☐ LCGX212 Fusion Recovery .25 .60
- ☐ LCGX213 System Down .75 2.00
- ☐ LCGX214 Grand Convergence (R) .25 .60
- ☐ LCGX215 Dimensional Fissure (SCR) 8.00 20.00
- ☐ LCGX216 Venom Swamp .25 .60
- ☐ LCGX217 Clear World (SR) .75 2.00
- ☐ LCGX218 Macro Cosmos (UR) 6.00 15.00
- ☐ LCGX219 Rise of the Snake Deity .25 .60
- ☐ LCGX220 Dimensional Prison (UR) 15.00 30.00
- ☐ LCGX221 Offering to the Snake Deity .75 2.00
- ☐ LCGX222 Chamberlain of the Six Samurai .20 .50
- ☐ LCGX223 Gladiator Beast Andal .25 .60
- ☐ LCGX224 D.D. Survivor .40 1.00
- ☐ LCGX225 Banisher of the Radiance (SCR) 6.00 15.00
- ☐ LCGX226 Grandmaster of the Six Samurai 1.50 4.00
- ☐ LCGX227 The Six Samurai - Yaichi .25 .60
- ☐ LCGX228 The Six Samurai - Kamon .25 .60
- ☐ LCGX229 The Six Samurai - Yariza .25 .60
- ☐ LCGX230 The Six Samurai - Nisashi .25 .60
- ☐ LCGX231 The Six Samurai - Zanji .25 .60
- ☐ LCGX232 The Six Samurai - Irou .25 .60
- ☐ LCGX233 Great Shogun Shien (SCR) 5.00 12.00
- ☐ LCGX234 D.D. Crow (SR) 10.00 25.00
- ☐ LCGX235 Gladiator Beast Octavius (UR) 1.50 4.00
- ☐ LCGX236 Gladiator Beast Murmillo (SCR) 4.00 10.00
- ☐ LCGX237 Gladiator Beast Bestiari (SCR) 6.00 15.00
- ☐ LCGX238 Gladiator Beast Laquari (SCR) 10.00 25.00
- ☐ LCGX239 Gladiator Beast Hoplomus (SCR) 3.00 8.00
- ☐ LCGX240 Gladiator Beast Secutor (SCR) 4.00 10.00
- ☐ LCGX241 Enishi, Shien's Chancellor (SR) 1.25 3.00
- ☐ LCGX242 Test Tiger (SCR) 6.00 15.00
- ☐ LCGX243 Rainbow Dark Dragon (UR) 5.00 12.00
- ☐ LCGX244 Gladiator Beast Darius (SCR) 5.00 12.00
- ☐ LCGX245 Jain, Lightsworn Paladin (UR) 6.00 15.00
- ☐ LCGX246 Garoth, Lightsworn Warrior (UR) 3.00 8.00
- ☐ LCGX247 Lumina, Lightsworn Summoner (UR)10.00 25.00
- ☐ LCGX248 Wulf, Lightsworn Beast (UR) 6.00 15.00
- ☐ LCGX249 Judgment Dragon 3.00 8.00
- ☐ LCGX250 Aurkus, Lightsworn Druid (UR) 3.00 8.00
- ☐ LCGX251 Gladiator Beast Equeste (SCR) 5.00 12.00
- ☐ LCGX252 Gladiator Beast Lanista (UR) 8.00 20.00
- ☐ LCGX253 Gladiator Beast Heraklinos (SR) .75 2.00
- ☐ LCGX254 Gladiator Beast's Respite (R) 1.50 4.00
- ☐ LCGX255 Gladiator's Return (R) .25 .60
- ☐ LCGX256 Cunning of the Six Samurai .40 1.00
- ☐ LCGX257 Gladiator Proving Ground (R) .40 1.00
- ☐ LCGX258 Light of Redemption .40 1.00
- ☐ LCGX259 Gateway of the Six 1.50 4.00
- ☐ LCGX260 Non-Fusion Area .20 .50
- ☐ LCGX261 Success Probability 0 .20 .50
- ☐ LCGX262 Return of the Six Samurai .25 .60
- ☐ LCGX263 Swiftstrike Armor (R) .25 .60
- ☐ LCGX264 Double-Edged Sword Technique .40 1.00

Card	Low	High
❑ LCGX265 Defensive Tactics (UR)	.75	2.00
❑ LCGX266 Gladiator Beast War Chariot (SCR)	6.00	15.00

2011 Yu-Gi-Oh Photon Shockwave

Card	Low	High
Booster Box	50.00	75.00
Booster Pack	2.50	4.00
❑ PHSW000 Alexandrite Dragon (SR)	4.00	10.00
❑ PHSW001 Bunilla	.25	.60
❑ PHSW002 Rabidragon	.25	.60
❑ PHSW003 Rai Rider	.15	.40
❑ PHSW004 Stinging Swordsman	.15	.40
❑ PHSW005 Kagetokage (R)	.25	.60
❑ PHSW006 Acorno	.15	.40
❑ PHSW007 Pinecono	.15	.40
❑ PHSW008 Friller Rabca (SR)	.75	2.00
❑ PHSW009 Shark Stickers	.15	.40
❑ PHSW010 Needle Sunfish	.15	.40
❑ PHSW011 Galaxy-Eyes Photon Dragon (GR)	10.00	25.00
❑ PHSW011 Galaxy-Eyes Photon Dragon (UR)	1.25	3.00
❑ PHSW011 Galaxy-Eyes Photon Dragon (UTR)	2.00	5.00
❑ PHSW012 Daybreaker (R)	.25	.60
❑ PHSW013 Lightserpent (SR)	.30	.75
❑ PHSW014 Plasma Ball	.15	.40
❑ PHSW015 Photon Cerberus (R)	.25	.60
❑ PHSW016 Evoltile Gephyro	.25	.60
❑ PHSW017 Evoltile Westlo (SR)	1.25	3.00
❑ PHSW018 Evoltile Odonto	.25	.60
❑ PHSW019 Evolsaur Vulcano (R)	.25	.60
❑ PHSW020 Evolsaur Cerato (UTR)	4.00	10.00
❑ PHSW020 Evolsaur Cerato (UR)	3.00	8.00
❑ PHSW021 Evolsaur Diplo (R)	.25	.60
❑ PHSW022 Wind-Up Warrior	.25	.60
❑ PHSW023 Wind-Up Knight (R)	.25	.60
❑ PHSW024 Wind-Up Hunter (SR)	1.50	4.00
❑ PHSW025 Wind-Up Bat	.25	.60
❑ PHSW026 Wind-Up Kitten (UR)	2.50	6.00
❑ PHSW026 Wind-Up Kitten (UTR)	3.00	8.00
❑ PHSW027 D.D. Telepon (R)	.25	.60
❑ PHSW028 Wattcobra	.25	.60
❑ PHSW029 Naturia Marron	.15	.40
❑ PHSW030 Prior of the Ice Barrier	.30	.75
❑ PHSW031 Senior Silver Ninja	.15	.40
❑ PHSW032 Rodenut	.15	.40
❑ PHSW033 Fenghuang (SR)	.40	1.00
❑ PHSW034 Tribe-Shocking Virus (R)	.25	.60
❑ PHSW035 Goblin Pothole Squad	.25	.60
❑ PHSW036 Creepy Coney	.15	.40
❑ PHSW037 Rescue Rabbit (SCR)	75.00	150.00
❑ PHSW038 Baby Tiragon (R)	.40	1.00
❑ PHSW039 Number 83: Galaxy Queen (SR)	1.50	4.00
❑ PHSW040 Black Ray Lancer (SR)	.75	2.00
❑ PHSW041 Number 10: Illumiknight (UR)	1.25	3.00
❑ PHSW041 Number 10: Illumiknight (UTR)	1.50	4.00
❑ PHSW042 Number 20: Giga-Brilliant (SR)	1.50	4.00
❑ PHSW043 Evolzar Laggia (UTR)	30.00	60.00
❑ PHSW043 Evolzar Laggia (UR)	20.00	40.00
❑ PHSW044 Thunder End Dragon (UTR)	4.00	10.00
❑ PHSW044 Thunder End Dragon (UR)	3.00	8.00
❑ PHSW045 Attraffic Control	.15	.40
❑ PHSW046 Ego Boost	.25	.60
❑ PHSW047 Monster Slots	.25	.60
❑ PHSW048 Cross Attack	.15	.40
❑ PHSW049 Xyz Gift (UTR)	.75	2.00
❑ PHSW049 Xyz Gift (UR)	.40	1.00
❑ PHSW050 Photon Veil (UTR)	1.50	4.00
❑ PHSW050 Photon Veil (UR)	1.25	3.00
❑ PHSW051 Photon Lead	.25	.60
❑ PHSW052 Photon Booster (R)	.25	.60
❑ PHSW053 Evo-Karma	.15	.40
❑ PHSW054 Evo-Miracle	.15	.40
❑ PHSW055 Zenmaifunction	.25	.60
❑ PHSW056 Extra Gate (SR)	.40	1.00
❑ PHSW057 Shard of Greed (SCR)	15.00	30.00
❑ PHSW058 Murmur of the Forest (R)	.25	.60
❑ PHSW059 Tri-Wight	.25	.60
❑ PHSW060 One Day of Peace	.75	2.00
❑ PHSW061 Space Cyclone	.15	.40
❑ PHSW062 Poisonous Winds	.15	.40
❑ PHSW063 Heartfelt Appeal	.15	.40
❑ PHSW064 Fiery Fervor	.15	.40
❑ PHSW065 Damage Diet	.25	.60
❑ PHSW066 Copy Knight (R)	.25	.60
❑ PHSW067 Mirror Mail	.25	.60
❑ PHSW068 Fish Rain	.15	.40
❑ PHSW069 Icy Crevasse	.15	.40
❑ PHSW070 Lumenize	.25	.60
❑ PHSW071 Evolutionary Bridge	.15	.40
❑ PHSW072 Zenmairch	.15	.40
❑ PHSW073 Wattcancel	.25	.60
❑ PHSW074 Champion's Vigilance	.15	.40
❑ PHSW075 Darklight (SR)	.30	.75
❑ PHSW076 Tyrant's Throes (R)	.25	.60
❑ PHSW077 Sound the Retreat!	.15	.40
❑ PHSW078 Deep Dark Trap Hole (R)	.25	.60
❑ PHSW079 Eisbahn (R)	.40	1.00
❑ PHSW080 Sealing Ceremony of Suiton	.15	.40
❑ PHSW081 Photon Sabre Tiger (SR)	3.00	8.00
❑ PHSW082 Evolsaur Pelta (R)	.25	.60
❑ PHSW083 Wind-Up Rabbit (SCR)	15.00	30.00
❑ PHSW084 D-Boyz (SCR)	5.00	12.00
❑ PHSW085 Latinum, Exarch of Dark World (UR)	1.25	3.00
❑ PHSW085 Latinum, Exarch of Dark World (UTR)	2.00	5.00
❑ PHSW086 Evolzar Dolkka (SCR)	20.00	40.00
❑ PHSW087 Wind-Up Zenmaines (SCR)	30.00	60.00
❑ PHSW088 Xyz Territory (R)	.25	.60
❑ PHSW089 Dark Smog (SCR)	20.00	40.00
❑ PHSW090 Sergeant Electro (UR)	.40	1.00
❑ PHSW090 Sergeant Electro (UTR)	.75	2.00
❑ PHSW091 Vylon Ohm	.25	.60
❑ PHSW092 Laval Dual Slasher	.25	.60
❑ PHSW093 Gem-Turtle (SR)	.30	.75
❑ PHSW094 Laval Lancelord	.25	.60
❑ PHSW095 Gishki Beast (R)	.75	2.00
❑ PHSW096 Gem-Knight Emerald (R)	.25	.60
❑ PHSW097 Junk Defender (R)	.25	.60
❑ PHSW098 Metaion, the Timelord (SCR)	8.00	20.00
❑ PHSW099 Infernity Knight (SR)	1.25	3.00

2011 Yu-Gi-Oh Storm of Ragnarok

Card	Low	High
Booster Box (24 packs)	50.00	75.00
Booster Pack (9 cards)	2.50	4.00
❑ STOR000 Vortex the Whirlwind (SR)	2.00	5.00
❑ STOR001 Cosmic Compass	.25	.60
❑ STOR002 Doppelwarrior (R)	.40	1.00
❑ STOR003 Stardust Phantom (R)	.40	1.00
❑ STOR004 D.D. Sprite (SR)	2.00	5.00
❑ STOR005 Top Runner	.25	.60
❑ STOR006 Barrier Resonator	.25	.60
❑ STOR007 Blackwing - Boreas the Sharp (R)	.40	1.00
❑ STOR008 Blackwing - Brisote the Tailwind	.25	.60
❑ STOR009 Blackwing - Calima the Haze	.25	.60
❑ STOR010 Tanngrisnir of the Nordic Beasts (SR)	1.50	4.00
❑ STOR011 Guldfaxe of the Nordic Beasts (R)	.75	2.00
❑ STOR012 Garmr of the Nordic Beasts	.30	.75
❑ STOR013 Tanngnjostr of the Nordic Beasts (R)	.75	2.00
❑ STOR014 Ljosalf of the Nordic Alfar	.30	.75
❑ STOR015 Svartalf of the Nordic Alfar (SR)	2.50	6.00
❑ STOR016 Dverg of the Nordic Alfar (R)	.75	2.00
❑ STOR017 Valkyrie of the Nordic Ascendant (SR)	2.50	6.00
❑ STOR018 Mimir of the Nordic Ascendant	.25	.60
❑ STOR019 Tyr of the Nordic Champions (R)	.75	2.00
❑ STOR020 Legendary Six Samurai - Kizan (SR)	20.00	40.00
❑ STOR021 Legendary Six Samurai - Enishi (UR)	1.50	4.00
❑ STOR021 Legendary Six Samurai - Enishi (UTR)	2.00	5.00
❑ STOR022 Legendary Six Samurai - Kageki (R)	3.00	8.00
❑ STOR023 Legendary Six Samurai - Shinai	.40	1.00
❑ STOR024 Legendary Six Samurai - Mizuho	.40	1.00
❑ STOR025 Kagemusha of the Six Samurai	.75	2.00
❑ STOR026 Shien's Squire	.25	.60
❑ STOR027 Karakuri Watchdog mdl 313 Saizan	.25	.60
❑ STOR028 Karakuri Ninja mdl 919 Kuick	.25	.60
❑ STOR029 Scrap Worm (R)	.40	1.00
❑ STOR030 Scrap Shark	.25	.60
❑ STOR031 Wattberyx (R)	.40	1.00
❑ STOR032 Wattmole	.25	.60
❑ STOR033 Symphonic Warrior Basses (SR)	.40	1.00
❑ STOR034 Symphonic Warrior Drumss (SR)	.40	1.00
❑ STOR035 Symphonic Warrior Piano (R)	.30	.75
❑ STOR036 Majioshaleon	.15	.40
❑ STOR037 Yaksha	.15	.40
❑ STOR038 Thor, Lord of the Aesir (UTR)	5.00	12.00
❑ STOR038 Thor, Lord of the Aesir (UR)	4.00	10.00
❑ STOR039 Loki, Lord of the Aesir (UR)	2.00	5.00
❑ STOR039 Loki, Lord of the Aesir (UTR)	3.00	8.00
❑ STOR040 Odin, Father of the Aesir (GR)	6.00	15.00
❑ STOR040 Odin, Father of the Aesir (UTR)	4.00	10.00
❑ STOR040 Odin, Father of the Aesir (UR)	4.00	10.00
❑ STOR041 Legendary Six Samurai - Shi En (UR)	30.00	60.00
❑ STOR041 Legendary Six Samurai - Shi En (UTR)	30.00	60.00
❑ STOR042 Karakuri Steel Shogun mdl 00X Bureido (UR)	6.00	15.00
❑ STOR042 Karakuri Steel Shogun mdl 00X Bureido (UTR)	8.00	20.00
❑ STOR043 Atomic Scrap Dragon (UR)	2.00	5.00
❑ STOR043 Atomic Scrap Dragon (UTR)	4.00	10.00
❑ STOR044 Wattkydra (SR)	1.50	4.00
❑ STOR045 Nordic Relic Draupnir	.25	.60
❑ STOR046 Gotterdammerung	.30	.75
❑ STOR047 March Towards Ragnarok (R)	.50	1.25
❑ STOR048 Shien's Smoke Signal (R)	3.00	8.00
❑ STOR049 Six Strike - Triple Impact	.40	1.00
❑ STOR050 Asceticism of the Six Samurai (R)	.50	1.25
❑ STOR051 Temple of the Six (SR)	2.50	6.00
❑ STOR052 Karakuri Cash Cache	.25	.60
❑ STOR053 Karakuri Gold Dust	.15	.40
❑ STOR054 Wattkey	.25	.60
❑ STOR055 Stardust Shimmer (SR)	2.50	6.00
❑ STOR056 Resonator Engine	.15	.40
❑ STOR057 Token Sundae	.15	.40
❑ STOR058 Foolish Return (R)	.30	.75
❑ STOR059 Divine Wind of Mist Valley	.25	.60
❑ STOR060 Vylon Matter	.25	.60
❑ STOR061 Forbidden Lance (SR)	15.00	30.00
❑ STOR062 Terminal World	.15	.40
❑ STOR063 Hope for Escape (R)	.40	1.00
❑ STOR064 Zero Force	.25	.60
❑ STOR065 Blackboost	.25	.60
❑ STOR066 Divine Relic Mjollnir	.25	.60
❑ STOR067 Solemn Authority	.25	.60
❑ STOR068 Nordic Relic Brisingamen	.25	.60
❑ STOR069 Nordic Relic Laevateinn	.25	.60
❑ STOR070 Nordic Relic Gungnir (R)	.50	1.25
❑ STOR071 The Golden Apples (SCR)	10.00	25.00
❑ STOR072 Odin's Eye	.25	.60
❑ STOR073 Gleipnir, the Fetters of Fenrir (UR)	6.00	15.00
❑ STOR073 Gleipnir, the Fetters of Fenrir (UTR)	8.00	20.00
❑ STOR074 Musakani Magatama (R)	1.50	4.00
❑ STOR075 Shien's Scheme	.30	.75
❑ STOR076 Token Stampede	.15	.40
❑ STOR077 Xing Zhen Hu Replica	.25	.60
❑ STOR078 Tyrant's Tirade	.25	.60
❑ STOR079 Tiki Curse	.25	.60
❑ STOR080 Tiki Soul	.25	.60
❑ STOR081 Vanadis of the Nordic Ascendant (SCR)	30.00	60.00
❑ STOR082 Shien's Daredevil (R)	.40	1.00
❑ STOR083 Karakuri Muso mdl 818 Haipa (UTR)	2.50	6.00
❑ STOR083 Karakuri Muso mdl 818 Haipa (UR)	2.00	5.00
❑ STOR084 Scrap Breaker (SCR)	2.50	6.00
❑ STOR085 Chaos Hunter (SCR)	6.00	15.00
❑ STOR086 Maxx C (SCR)	6.00	15.00
❑ STOR087 The Nordic Lights (UR)	2.50	6.00
❑ STOR087 The Nordic Lights (UTR)	4.00	10.00
❑ STOR088 Nordic Relic Megingjord (SCR)	2.50	6.00
❑ STOR089 Six Strike - Thunder Blast (SCR)	1.50	4.00
❑ STOR090 Cyber Shield	.25	.60
❑ STOR091 Hourglass of Courage	.15	.40
❑ STOR092 Needle Ball	.15	.40
❑ STOR093 Blood Sucker	.15	.40
❑ STOR094 Overpowering Eye (R)	.40	1.00
❑ STOR095 Worm Illidan	.25	.60
❑ STOR096 Worm Jetelikpse	.25	.60
❑ STOR097 Worm King (SR)	.40	1.00
❑ STOR098 Elemental Hero Ice Edge (SR)	1.50	4.00
❑ STOR099 Vylon Delta (SCR)	2.00	5.00

2012 Yu-Gi-Oh Abyss Rising

Card	Low	High
Complete Set	300.00	500.00
Booster Box (24 Packs)	50.00	80.00
Booster Pack (9 Cards)	3.00	4.50
❑ ABYR000 Ignoble Knight of Black Laundsallyn (SR)	1.00	2.50
❑ ABYR001 Gagaga Caesar (R)	.25	.60
❑ ABYR002 Bull Blader	.15	.40
❑ ABYR003 Achacha Chanbara	.15	.40
❑ ABYR004 Mogmole	.15	.40
❑ ABYR005 Grandram	.15	.40
❑ ABYR006 Tripod Fish	.15	.40
❑ ABYR007 Deep Sweeper	.15	.40
❑ ABYR008 Heroic Challenger - Extra Sword	.15	.40
❑ ABYR009 Heroic Challenger - Night Watchman	.15	.40
❑ ABYR010 Planet Pathfinder	.15	.40
❑ ABYR011 Solar Wind Jammer	.15	.40
❑ ABYR012 Heraldic Beast Aberconway	.15	.40
❑ ABYR013 Heraldic Beast Berners Falcon	.15	.40
❑ ABYR014 Mermail Abysslinde (UTR)	8.00	20.00
❑ ABYR014 Mermail Abysslinde (UR)	6.00	15.00
❑ ABYR015 Mermail Abyssgunde (R)	.25	.60
❑ ABYR016 Mermail Abysshilde	.15	.40
❑ ABYR017 Mermail Abyssturge (R)	.25	.60
❑ ABYR018 Mermail Abysspike (R)	.40	1.00
❑ ABYR019 Mermail Abysslung	.15	.40
❑ ABYR020 Mermail Abyssmegalo (SCR)	15.00	40.00
❑ ABYR021 Stoic of Prophecy	.15	.40
❑ ABYR022 Hermit of Prophecy	.15	.40
❑ ABYR023 Justice of Prophecy (R)	.60	1.50
❑ ABYR024 Emperor of Prophecy (R)	.25	.60
❑ ABYR025 Madolche Croiwanssant	.15	.40
❑ ABYR026 Madolche Marmalmaid	.15	.40
❑ ABYR027 Madolche Messengelato (R)	.40	1.00
❑ ABYR028 Abyss Warrior	.15	.40
❑ ABYR029 Snowman Creator	.15	.40
❑ ABYR030 Fishborg Planter	.15	.40
❑ ABYR031 Nimble Angler	.15	.40
❑ ABYR032 Shore Knight (R)	.25	.60
❑ ABYR033 Mecha Sea Dragon Plesion	.15	.40
❑ ABYR034 Metallizing Parasite - Soltite	.15	.40
❑ ABYR035 Moulinglacia the Elemental Lord (SCR)	10.00	25.00
❑ ABYR036 House Duston	.15	.40
❑ ABYR037 Puny Penguin (SP)	.15	.40
❑ ABYR038 Missing Force (SP)	.15	.40
❑ ABYR039 Number C32: Shark Drake Veiss (UR)	2.50	6.00
❑ ABYR039 Number C32: Shark Drake Veiss (GR)	3.00	8.00
❑ ABYR039 Number C32: Shark Drake Veiss (UTR)	2.00	5.00
❑ ABYR040 One-Eyed Skill Gainer (SR)	.75	2.00
❑ ABYR041 Gagaga Cowboy (SR)	6.00	15.00
❑ ABYR042 Heroic Champion - Gandiva (UTR)	2.50	6.00
❑ ABYR042 Heroic Champion - Gandiva (UR)	2.50	6.00
❑ ABYR043 Heroic Champion - Kusanagi (SR)	1.50	4.00
❑ ABYR044 Number 9: Dyson Sphere (UR)	1.50	4.00
❑ ABYR044 Number 9: Dyson Sphere (UTR)	2.00	5.00
❑ ABYR045 Number 8: Heraldic King Genom-Heritage (SR)	1.25	3.00
❑ ABYR046 Mermail Abyssgaios (UR)	2.00	5.00
❑ ABYR046 Mermail Abyssgaios (UTR)	2.00	5.00
❑ ABYR047 Empress of Prophecy (UTR)	1.25	3.00
❑ ABYR047 Empress of Prophecy (UR)	1.00	2.50
❑ ABYR048 Madolche Queen Tiaramisu (UR)	5.00	12.00
❑ ABYR048 Madolche Queen Tiaramisu (UTR)	6.00	15.00
❑ ABYR049 Snowdust Giant (R)	.25	.60
❑ ABYR050 Gagagigo the Risen (R)	.25	.60
❑ ABYR051 One-Shot Wand	.15	.40
❑ ABYR052 Different Dimension Deepsea Trench	.15	.40
❑ ABYR053 Tannhauser Gate (SR)	.40	1.00
❑ ABYR054 Gravity Blaster	.15	.40
❑ ABYR055 Advanced Heraldry Art (R)	.25	.60
❑ ABYR056 Abyss-scale of the Kraken	.15	.40
❑ ABYR057 Lemuria, the Forgotten City	.15	.40
❑ ABYR058 Spellbook of Eternity (R)	.25	.60
❑ ABYR059 Spellbook of Fate (UTR)	2.50	6.00
❑ ABYR059 Spellbook of Fate (UR)	2.00	5.00
❑ ABYR060 The Grand Spellbook Tower (SCR)	12.00	30.00
❑ ABYR061 Madolche Ticket	.15	.40
❑ ABYR062 Forbidden Dress (SR)	2.50	6.00
❑ ABYR063 Final Gesture	.15	.40
❑ ABYR064 Mind Pollutant (R)	.25	.60
❑ ABYR065 The Humble Sentry (SP)	.15	.40
❑ ABYR066 Battle Break	.15	.40
❑ ABYR067 Bubble Bringer (SR)	.40	1.00
❑ ABYR068 Heroic Gift	.15	.40
❑ ABYR069 Heroic Advance	.15	.40
❑ ABYR070 Xyz Xtreme !!	.15	.40
❑ ABYR071 Abyss-squall (SR)	1.50	4.00
❑ ABYR072 Abyss-sphere (UTR)	8.00	20.00
❑ ABYR072 Abyss-sphere (UR)	5.00	12.00
❑ ABYR073 Abyss-strom (R)	.25	.60
❑ ABYR074 Madolchepalooza (SR)	1.50	4.00
❑ ABYR075 Memory of an Adversary (SR)	.75	2.00
❑ ABYR076 Magic Deflector	.15	.40
❑ ABYR077 That Wacky Alchemy! (UTR)	.40	1.00
❑ ABYR077 That Wacky Alchemy! (UR)	.40	1.00
❑ ABYR078 Cash Back (SP)	.15	.40
❑ ABYR079 Unification	.15	.40
❑ ABYR080 Retort (SCR)	2.00	5.00
❑ ABYR081 Mermail Abyssmander (R)	.25	.60
❑ ABYR082 Red Dragon Ninja (SR)	.75	2.00
❑ ABYR083 Slushy (R)	.25	.60
❑ ABYR084 Abyss Dweller (SR)	4.00	10.00
❑ ABYR085 Giant Soldier of Steel (SCR)	1.50	4.00
❑ ABYR086 Noble Arms - Arfeudutyr (R)	.25	.60
❑ ABYR087 Spellbook Library of the Heliosphere (SCR)	2.00	5.00
❑ ABYR088 Spellbook Star Hall (R)	.25	.60
❑ ABYR089 Attack the Moon! (SR)	.40	1.00
❑ ABYR090 Electromagnetic Bagworm	.15	.40
❑ ABYR091 Rage of the Deep Sea	.15	.40
❑ ABYR092 Ape Magician	.15	.40
❑ ABYR093 Snowdust Dragon	.15	.40
❑ ABYR094 Snow Dragon	.15	.40
❑ ABYR095 Uminotaurus (R)	.25	.60
❑ ABYR096 Fishborg Launcher	.15	.40
❑ ABYR097 Papa-Corn (R)	.25	.60
❑ ABYR098 Thunder Sea Horse (SCR)	10.00	25.00
❑ ABYR099 Bahamut Shark (SCR)	10.00	25.00

2012 Yu-Gi-Oh Abyss Rising Special Edition

One Card Per Special Edition Box

Card	Low	High
❑ ABYRSE1 Gagaga Girl (SR)	1.00	2.50
❑ ABYRSE2 Dark Smog (SR)	1.00	2.50

2012 Yu-Gi-Oh Battle Pack Epic Dawn

Card	Low	High
Complete Set	75.00	150.00
Booster Box (36 Packs)	50.00	80.00
Booster Pack (5 Cards)	3.00	4.00
❑ BP01001 Witch of the Black Forest (R)	.30	.75
❑ BP01002 Cyber Jar (R)	.40	1.00
❑ BP01003 Jinzo (R)	.50	1.25
❑ BP01004 Injection Fairy Lily (R)	.30	.75
❑ BP01005 Dark Dust Spirit (R)	.30	.75
❑ BP01006 Skull Archfiend of Lightning (R)	.30	.75
❑ BP01007 Dark Magician of Chaos (R)	.75	2.00
❑ BP01008 Blowback Dragon (R)	.30	.75
❑ BP01009 Mobius the Frost Monarch (R)	.30	.75
❑ BP01010 Fox Fire (R)	.30	.75
❑ BP01011 Ancient Gear Golem (R)	.40	1.00
❑ BP01012 Treeborn Frog (R)	.60	1.50
❑ BP01013 Super Conductor Tyranno (R)	.30	.75
❑ BP01014 Gorz the Emissary of Darkness (R)	1.00	2.50
❑ BP01015 Raiza the Storm Monarch (R)	.30	.75
❑ BP01016 White Night Dragon (R)	.30	.75
❑ BP01017 Deep Diver (R)	.30	.75
❑ BP01018 Caius the Shadow Monarch (R)	.50	1.25
❑ BP01019 Krebons (R)	.30	.75
❑ BP01020 Tragoedia (R)	.40	1.00
❑ BP01021 Obelisk the Tormentor (R)	1.00	2.50
❑ BP01022 Machina Fortress (R)	.40	1.00
❑ BP01023 Tour Guide From the Underworld (R)	8.00	20.00
❑ BP01024 Number 39: Utopia (R)	.50	1.25
❑ BP01025 Gachi Gachi Gantetsu (R)	.30	.75
❑ BP01026 Grenosaurus (R)	.30	.75
❑ BP01027 Number 17: Leviathan Dragon (R)	.50	1.25
❑ BP01028 Wind-Up Zenmaister (R)	.30	.75
❑ BP01029 Tiras, Keeper of Genesis (R)	1.50	4.00
❑ BP01030 Adreus, Keeper of Armageddon (R)	2.00	5.00
❑ BP01031 Gem-Knight Pearl (R)	.50	1.25
❑ BP01032 Raigeki (R)	.60	1.50
❑ BP01033 Swords of Revealing Light (R)	.40	1.00
❑ BP01034 Pot of Greed (R)	.50	1.25
❑ BP01035 Harpie's Feather Duster (R)	.30	.75
❑ BP01036 Graceful Charity (R)	.30	.75
❑ BP01037 Change of Heart (R)	.30	.75
❑ BP01038 Heavy Storm (R)	.40	1.00
❑ BP01039 Snatch Steal (R)	.30	.75
❑ BP01040 Premature Burial (R)	.30	.75
❑ BP01041 Soul Exchange (R)	.30	.75
❑ BP01042 Scapegoat (R)	.30	.75
❑ BP01043 United We Stand (R)	.30	.75
❑ BP01044 Creature Swap (R)	.30	.75
❑ BP01045 Burden of the Mighty (R)	.30	.75
❑ BP01046 Pot of Duality (R)	5.00	12.00
❑ BP01047 Solemn Judgment (R)	.60	1.50
❑ BP01048 Mirror Force (R)	.60	1.50
❑ BP01049 Call of the Haunted (R)	.40	1.00
❑ BP01050 Ring of Destruction (R)	.40	1.00
❑ BP01051 Torrential Tribute (R)	.75	2.00
❑ BP01052 Metal Reflect Slime (R)	.30	.75
❑ BP01053 Skill Drain (R)	1.50	4.00
❑ BP01054 Divine Wrath (R)	.30	.75
❑ BP01055 Dark Bribe (R)	.30	.75
❑ BP01056 Greenkappa	.10	.25
❑ BP01057 Penguin Soldier	.10	.25
❑ BP01058 Mysterious Guard	.10	.25
❑ BP01059 Exiled Force	.10	.25
❑ BP01060 Old Vindictive Magician	.10	.25
❑ BP01061 Breaker the Magical Warrior	.30	.75
❑ BP01062 Grave Squirmer	.10	.25
❑ BP01063 Ryko, Lightsworn Hunter	.20	.50
❑ BP01064 Snowman Eater	.50	1.25
❑ BP01065 Fissure	.10	.25
❑ BP01066 Tribute to the Doomed	.10	.25
❑ BP01067 Axe of Despair	.20	.50
❑ BP01068 Mystical Space Typhoon	.30	.75
❑ BP01069 Horn of the Unicorn	.10	.25
❑ BP01070 Offerings to the Doomed	.10	.25
❑ BP01071 Bait Doll	.10	.25
❑ BP01072 Book of Moon	.30	.75
❑ BP01073 Autonomous Action Unit	.10	.25
❑ BP01074 Ante	.10	.25
❑ BP01075 Big Bang Shot	.10	.25
❑ BP01076 Fiend's Sanctuary	.10	.25
❑ BP01077 Different Dimension Gate	.20	.50
❑ BP01078 Enemy Controller	.20	.50
❑ BP01079 Monster Gate	.10	.25
❑ BP01080 Shield Crush	.10	.25
❑ BP01081 Fighting Spirit	.10	.25
❑ BP01082 Forbidden Chalice	1.00	2.50
❑ BP01083 Darkworld Shackles	.20	.50
❑ BP01084 Forbidden Lance	1.50	4.00
❑ BP01085 Infected Mail	.10	.25
❑ BP01086 Ego Boost	.10	.25
❑ BP01087 Kunai with Chain	.10	.25
❑ BP01088 Dust Tornado	.10	.25
❑ BP01089 Windstorm of Etaqua	.20	.50
❑ BP01090 Magic Drain	.10	.25
❑ BP01091 Magic Cylinder	.20	.50
❑ BP01092 Shadow Spell	.10	.25
❑ BP01093 Blast with Chain	.10	.25
❑ BP01094 Needle Ceiling	.10	.25
❑ BP01095 Reckless Greed	.20	.50
❑ BP01096 Nightmare Wheel	.10	.25
❑ BP01097 Spell Shield Type-8	.10	.25
❑ BP01098 Interdimensional Matter Transporter	.10	.25
❑ BP01099 Compulsory Evacuation Device	.40	1.00
❑ BP01100 Prideful Roar	.10	.25
❑ BP01101 Half or Nothing	.10	.25
❑ BP01102 Skill Successor	.10	.25
❑ BP01103 Pixie Ring	.10	.25
❑ BP01104 Changing Destiny	.10	.25
❑ BP01105 Fiendish Chain	1.50	4.00
❑ BP01106 Inverse Universe	.10	.25
❑ BP01107 Miracle's Wake	.10	.25
❑ BP01108 Power Frame	.10	.25
❑ BP01109 Damage Gate	.10	.25
❑ BP01110 Liberty at Last!	.20	.50
❑ BP01111 Luster Dragon	.10	.25
❑ BP01112 Archfiend Soldier	.20	.50
❑ BP01113 Mad Dog of Darkness	.10	.25
❑ BP01114 Charcoal Inpachi	.10	.25
❑ BP01115 Insect Knight	.10	.25
❑ BP01116 Gene-Warped Warwolf	.10	.25
❑ BP01117 Buster Blader	.20	.50
❑ BP01118 Goblin Attack Force	.10	.25
❑ BP01119 Bazoo the Soul-Eater	.10	.25
❑ BP01120 Zombyra the Dark	.20	.50
❑ BP01121 Slate Warrior	.10	.25
❑ BP01122 Dark Ruler Ha Des	.10	.25
❑ BP01123 Freed the Matchless General	.10	.25
❑ BP01124 Airknight Parshath	.10	.25
❑ BP01125 Asura Priest	.10	.25
❑ BP01126 Exarion Universe	.10	.25
❑ BP01127 Vampire Lord	.10	.25
❑ BP01128 Toon Gemini Elf	.10	.25
❑ BP01129 King Tiger Wanghu	.30	.75
❑ BP01130 Guardian Sphinx	.10	.25
❑ BP01131 Skilled White Magician	.10	.25
❑ BP01132 Zaborg the Thunder Monarch	.10	.25
❑ BP01133 D.D. Assailant	.20	.50
❑ BP01134 Theban Nightmare	.10	.25
❑ BP01135 The Tricky	.75	2.00
❑ BP01136 Raging Flame Sprite	.10	.25
❑ BP01137 Chiron the Mage	.10	.25
❑ BP01138 Cyber Dragon	.30	.75
❑ BP01139 Cybernetic Magician	.10	.25
❑ BP01140 Goblin Elite Attack Force	.10	.25
❑ BP01141 Doomcaliber Knight	.50	1.25
❑ BP01142 Chainsaw Insect	.10	.25
❑ BP01143 Card Trooper	.20	.50
❑ BP01144 Voltic Kong	.20	.50
❑ BP01145 Botanical Lion	.10	.25
❑ BP01146 Ancient Gear Knight	.20	.50
❑ BP01147 Blizzard Dragon	.20	.50
❑ BP01148 Beast King Barbaros	.30	.75
❑ BP01149 The Calculator	.10	.25
❑ BP01150 Gaap the Divine Soldier	.10	.25
❑ BP01151 Arcana Force XIV - Temperance	.10	.25
❑ BP01152 Dark Valkyria	.20	.50
❑ BP01153 Alector, Sovereign of Birds	.10	.25
❑ BP01154 Twin-Barrel Dragon	.10	.25
❑ BP01155 Abyssal Kingshark	.10	.25
❑ BP01156 Jurrac Protops	.10	.25
❑ BP01157 Hedge Guard	.10	.25
❑ BP01158 Fabled Ashenveil	.10	.25
❑ BP01159 Backup Warrior	.40	1.00
❑ BP01160 Ambitious Gofer	.10	.25
❑ BP01161 Power Giant	.10	.25
❑ BP01162 Card Guard	.10	.25
❑ BP01163 Yaksha	.10	.25
❑ BP01164 Gogogo Golem	.10	.25
❑ BP01165 Big Jaws	.10	.25
❑ BP01166 Wind-Up Soldier	.10	.25
❑ BP01167 Wind-Up Dog	.10	.25
❑ BP01168 Milla the Temporal Magician	.10	.25
❑ BP01169 Ape Fighter	.10	.25
❑ BP01170 Wind-Up Warrior	.20	.50
❑ BP01171 Giant Soldier of Stone	.10	.25
❑ BP01172 Mask of Darkness	.10	.25
❑ BP01173 Morphing Jar	.50	1.25
❑ BP01174 Muka Muka	.10	.25
❑ BP01175 Blast Sphere	.10	.25
❑ BP01176 Big Shield Gardna	.10	.25
❑ BP01177 Gilasaurus	.10	.25
❑ BP01178 Possessed Dark Soul	.10	.25
❑ BP01179 Twin-Headed Behemoth	.10	.25
❑ BP01180 Makyura the Destructor	.20	.50
❑ BP01181 Helping Robo for Combat	.10	.25
❑ BP01182 Zolga	.10	.25
❑ BP01183 Chaos Necromancer	.10	.25
❑ BP01184 Stealth Bird	.10	.25
❑ BP01185 Hyper Hammerhead	.10	.25
❑ BP01186 Grave Protector	.10	.25
❑ BP01187 Night Assailant	.20	.50
❑ BP01188 Pitch-Black Warwolf	.10	.25
❑ BP01189 Dekoichi the Battlechanted Locomotive	.20	.50
❑ BP01190 Gyroid	.10	.25
❑ BP01191 Drillroid	.10	.25
❑ BP01192 Gravitic Orb	.20	.50
❑ BP01193 Cloudian - Poison Cloud	.10	.25
❑ BP01194 Des Mosquito	.20	.50
❑ BP01195 Mad Reloader	.10	.25
❑ BP01196 Phantom of Chaos	.30	.75
❑ BP01197 Cyber Valley	.30	.75
❑ BP01198 Blue Thunder T-45	.10	.25
❑ BP01199 Vortex Trooper	.20	.50
❑ BP01200 DUCKER Mobile Cannon	.10	.25
❑ BP01201 Worm Barses	.10	.25
❑ BP01202 Shield Warrior	.10	.25
❑ BP01203 Dark Resonator	.10	.25
❑ BP01204 Noisy Gnat	.10	.25
❑ BP01205 Fabled Raven	1.00	2.50
❑ BP01206 Fortress Warrior	.10	.25
❑ BP01207 Twin-Sword Marauder	.10	.25
❑ BP01208 Level Warrior	.10	.25
❑ BP01209 Level Eater	.10	.25
❑ BP01210 Naturia Strawberry	.10	.25
❑ BP01211 Battle Fader	.30	.75
❑ BP01212 Amazoness Sage	.10	.25
❑ BP01213 Amazoness Trainee	.10	.25
❑ BP01214 Hardened Armed Dragon	.20	.50
❑ BP01215 Blackwing - Zephyros the Elite	.75	2.00
❑ BP01216 Tanngrisnir of the Nordic Beasts	.10	.25
❑ BP01217 Shine Knight	.10	.25
❑ BP01218 Gagaga Magician	.20	.50
❑ BP01219 Goblindbergh	.10	.25
❑ BP01220 Psi-Blocker	.10	.25

2012 Yu-Gi-Oh Battle Pack Epic Dawn Starfoil

*Starfoil: .6X to 1.5X Basic Cards
Stated Odds One Per Pack

2012 Yu-Gi-Oh Galactic Overlord

Card	Low	High
Complete Set	250.00	350.00
Booster Box	60.00	90.00
Booster Pack	3.00	4.00
❑ GAOV000 Noble Knight Artorigus (SR)	.75	2.00
❑ GAOV001 Wattaildragon	.15	.40
❑ GAOV002 Hieratic Seal of the Sun Dragon Overlord	.15	.40
❑ GAOV003 Overlay Owl	.15	.40
❑ GAOV004 Tasuke Knight (SR)	.75	2.00
❑ GAOV005 Gagaga Gardna (R)	.25	.60
❑ GAOV006 Cardcar D (SCR)	60.00	120.00
❑ GAOV007 Overlay Eater	.15	.40
❑ GAOV008 Hammer Shark (R)	.25	.60
❑ GAOV009 Hammer Bounzer (SR)	1.25	3.00
❑ GAOV010 Blade Bounzer	.15	.40
❑ GAOV011 Phantom Bounzer	.15	.40
❑ GAOV012 Morpho Butterspy	.15	.40
❑ GAOV013 Swallowtail Butterspy	.15	.40
❑ GAOV014 Moonlit Papillon	.15	.40
❑ GAOV015 Jumbo Drill (SR)	1.00	2.50
❑ GAOV016 Rocket Arrow Express (R)	.25	.60
❑ GAOV017 Cameraclops	.15	.40
❑ GAOV018 Hieratic Dragon of Nuit	.15	.40
❑ GAOV019 Hieratic Dragon of Gebeb (SR)	5.00	12.00
❑ GAOV020 Hieratic Dragon of Eset	.15	.40
❑ GAOV021 Hieratic Dragon of Nebthet	.15	.40
❑ GAOV022 Hieratic Dragon of Tefnuit (R)	.25	.60
❑ GAOV023 Hieratic Dragon of Su	.15	.40

❑ GAOV024 Hieratic Dragon of Asar (R) .25 .60
❑ GAOV025 Hieratic Dragon of Sutekh (UR) 4.00 10.00
❑ GAOV025 Hieratic Dragon of Sutekh (UTR) 3.00 8.00
❑ GAOV026 Evoltile Lagosucho .15 .40
❑ GAOV027 Evolsaur Darwino .15 .40
❑ GAOV028 Inzektor Firefly .15 .40
❑ GAOV029 Inzektor Ladybug .15 .40
❑ GAOV030 Inzektor Earwig .15 .40
❑ GAOV031 Inzektor Giga-Cricket (R) .25 .60
❑ GAOV032 Lightray Sorcerer (R) .25 .60
❑ GAOV033 Lightray Daedalus .15 .40
❑ GAOV034 Lightray Gearfried (R) .25 .60
❑ GAOV035 Lightray Diabolos (R) .25 .60
❑ GAOV036 Lady of D. .15 .40
❑ GAOV037 Absorbing Jar (R) .25 .60
❑ GAOV038 Red-Headed Oni .15 .40
❑ GAOV039 Flame Tiger .15 .40
❑ GAOV040 Nomadic Force .15 .40
❑ GAOV041 Neo Galaxy-Eyes Photon Dragon (GR)10.00 25.00
❑ GAOV041 Neo Galaxy-Eyes Photon Dragon (UR)6.00 15.00
❑ GAOV041 Neo Galaxy-Eyes Photon Dragon (UTR)6.00 15.00
❑ GAOV042 Number 32: Shark Drake (UTR) 6.00 15.00
❑ GAOV042 Number 32: Shark Drake (UR) 5.00 12.00
❑ GAOV043 Photon Strike Bounzer (SCR) 25.00 50.00
❑ GAOV044 Photon Papilloperative (R) 1.00 2.50
❑ GAOV045 Number 25: Force Focus (UR) 4.00 10.00
❑ GAOV045 Number 25: Force Focus (UTR) 4.00 10.00
❑ GAOV046 Gaia Dragon, the Thunder Charger (SR)10.00 25.00
❑ GAOV047 Hieratic Dragon King of Atum (SR)15.00 40.00
❑ GAOV048 Hieratic Sun Dragon 25.00 50.00
Overlord of Heliopolis (SCR)
❑ GAOV049 Queen Dragun Djinn (SR) 6.00 15.00
❑ GAOV050 Inzektor Exa-Stag (UTR) 5.00 12.00
❑ GAOV050 Inzektor Exa-Stag (UR) 4.00 10.00
❑ GAOV051 Bound Wand (SR) 2.50 6.00
❑ GAOV052 Mini-Guts .15 .40
❑ GAOV053 Falling Current .15 .40
❑ GAOV054 Berserk Scales .15 .40
❑ GAOV055 Night Beam (UR) 10.00 25.00
❑ GAOV055 Night Beam (UTR) 12.00 30.00
❑ GAOV056 Hieratic Seal of Convocation (R) .25 .60
❑ GAOV057 Hieratic Seal of Supremacy .15 .40
❑ GAOV058 Evo-Diversity (R) .25 .60
❑ GAOV059 Evo-Price (R) .25 .60
❑ GAOV060 Final Inzektion (R) .25 .60
❑ GAOV061 Inzektor Crossbow - Zektarrow (R) .25 .60
❑ GAOV062 Xyz Unit (UR) 2.50 6.00
❑ GAOV062 Xyz Unit (UTR) 2.00 5.00
❑ GAOV063 That Wacky Magic .15 .40
❑ GAOV064 Constellar Belt .15 .40
❑ GAOV065 Storm .15 .40
❑ GAOV066 Nitwit Outwit .15 .40
❑ GAOV067 Gamushara .15 .40
❑ GAOV068 Commander of Swords .15 .40
❑ GAOV069 Bounzer Guard .15 .40
❑ GAOV070 Butterflyoke .15 .40
❑ GAOV071 Hieratic Seal of Banishment .15 .40
❑ GAOV072 Hieratic Seal of Reflection (SR) 2.50 6.00
❑ GAOV073 Zekt Conversion (UTR) 3.00 8.00
❑ GAOV073 Zekt Conversion (UR) 2.00 5.00
❑ GAOV074 Inzektor Gauntlet .15 .40
❑ GAOV075 Return .15 .40
❑ GAOV076 Dimension Slice (R) .25 .60
❑ GAOV077 Spiritual Light Art - Hijiri (SR) 2.00 5.00
❑ GAOV078 Sealing Ceremony of Raiton .15 .40
❑ GAOV079 Aquamirror Cycle .15 .40
❑ GAOV080 Double Payback .15 .40
❑ GAOV081 Ancient Dragon (R) .25 .60
❑ GAOV082 Hieratic Seal of the Dragon King .15 .40
❑ GAOV083 Evoltile Elginero (SR) 3.00 8.00
❑ GAOV084 Lightray Grepher (R) .25 .60
❑ GAOV085 Tardy Orc (SCR) 4.00 10.00
❑ GAOV086 Draconnection (UTR) 3.00 8.00
❑ GAOV086 Draconnection (UR) 3.00 8.00
❑ GAOV087 Trial and Tribulation (SCR) 8.00 20.00
❑ GAOV088 Hieratic Seal From the Ashes (SCR)10.00 25.00
❑ GAOV089 Xyz Wrath .15 .40
❑ GAOV090 Number 11: Big Eye (SCR) 12.00 30.00
❑ GAOV091 Number 7: Lucky Straight (SCR) 8.00 20.00
❑ GAOV092 Beetron (UR) 5.00 12.00
❑ GAOV092 Beetron (UTR) 4.00 10.00
❑ GAOV093 Influence Dragon .15 .40
❑ GAOV094 Bright Star Dragon .15 .40
❑ GAOV095 Buten .15 .40
❑ GAOV096 Doom Donuts .15 .40
❑ GAOV097 Nimble Manta .15 .40
❑ GAOV098 Shining Elf (SR) 2.00 5.00
❑ GAOV099 Flelf (SR) .75 2.00

2012 Yu-Gi-Oh Gold Series Haunted Mine

Complete Set 50.00 100.00
Booster Box 40.00 80.00
Booster Pack 10.00 20.00

❑ GLD5001 Blue-Eyes White Dragon (GGR) 3.00 8.00
❑ GLD5002 Patrician of Darkness .10 .25
❑ GLD5003 Pyramid Turtle .10 .25
❑ GLD5004 Dark Scorpion Burglars .10 .25
❑ GLD5005 Don Zaloog .20 .50
❑ GLD5006 Helpoemer .10 .25
❑ GLD5007 Dark Scorpion - Cliff the Trap Remover.10 .25
❑ GLD5008 Despair from the Dark .10 .25
❑ GLD5009 Fear from the Dark .10 .25
❑ GLD5010 Dark Scorpion - Chick the Yellow .10 .25
❑ GLD5011 Dark Scorpion - Gorg the Strong .10 .25
❑ GLD5012 Dark Scorpion - Meanae the Thorn .10 .25
❑ GLD5013 Ryu Kokki .10 .25
❑ GLD5014 Vampire Lady .10 .25
❑ GLD5015 Double Coston .10 .25
❑ GLD5016 Regenerating Mummy .10 .25
❑ GLD5017 Dark Mimic LV1 .10 .25
❑ GLD5018 Dark Mimic LV3 .10 .25
❑ GLD5019 Zombie Master .10 .25
❑ GLD5020 Gernia .10 .25
❑ GLD5021 Goblin Zombie .10 .25
❑ GLD5022 The Lady in Wight .10 .25
❑ GLD5023 Red Ogre .10 .25
❑ GLD5024 Gorz the Emissary of Darkness (GGR)2.50 6.00
❑ GLD5025 Bone Crusher .10 .25
❑ GLD5026 Fabled Grimro (GR) .75 2.00
❑ GLD5027 Master Hyperion (GR) .40 1.00
❑ GLD5028 Grapha 1.00 2.50
Dragon Lord of Dark World (GR)
❑ GLD5029 Sephylon, the Ultimate Timelord (GR)1.25 3.00
❑ GLD5030 Herald of Perfection (GGR) 1.25 3.00
❑ GLD5031 Brionac, Dragon of the Ice Barrier (GR)5.00 12.00
❑ GLD5032 Naturia Beast (GR) 6.00 15.00
❑ GLD5033 Naturia Barkion (GGR) 6.00 15.00
❑ GLD5034 Formula Synchron (GR) 2.00 5.00
❑ GLD5035 Karakuri Steel Shogun .75 2.00
mdl 00X Bureido (GR)
❑ GLD5036 Number 39: Utopia (GR) 1.00 2.50
❑ GLD5037 Dark Hole (GR) 2.50 6.00
❑ GLD5038 Mystical Space Typhoon (GGR) 8.00 20.00
❑ GLD5039 Book of Life .10 .25
❑ GLD5040 Call of the Mummy .10 .25
❑ GLD5041 Spellbook Organization .10 .25
❑ GLD5042 Mustering of the Dark Scorpions .10 .25
❑ GLD5043 Pyramid of Wonders .10 .25
❑ GLD5044 Dawn of the Herald .10 .25
❑ GLD5045 Solemn Judgment (GGR) 3.00 8.00
❑ GLD5046 Call of the Haunted (GR) 1.50 4.00
❑ GLD5047 Physical Double .10 .25
❑ GLD5048 Hidden Spellbook .10 .25
❑ GLD5049 Zoma the Spirit .10 .25
❑ GLD5050 Embodiment of Apophis .10 .25
❑ GLD5051 Machine King - 3000 B.C. .10 .25
❑ GLD5052 Starlight Road (GR) 1.25 3.00
❑ GLD5053 Tiki Curse .10 .25
❑ GLD5054 Tiki Soul .10 .25
❑ GLD5055 Copy Knight .10 .25

2012 Yu-Gi-Oh Hidden Arsenal 6

Complete Set (60) 50.00 100.00
Booster Box (24 Packs) 50.00 75.00
Booster Pack (5 Cards) 2.50 4.00

❑ HA06001 Gem-Knight Crystal .10 .25
❑ HA06002 Laval Volcano Handmaiden 1.00 2.50
❑ HA06003 Laval Cannon (SCR) 2.50 6.00
❑ HA06004 Vylon Sphere .10 .25
❑ HA06005 Vylon Tetra .10 .25
❑ HA06006 Vylon Stella .10 .25
❑ HA06007 Vylon Prism .20 .50
❑ HA06008 Vylon Hept .10 .25
❑ HA06009 Gishki Reliever .10 .25
❑ HA06010 Gishki Noellia (SR) .10 .25
❑ HA06011 Gusto Squirro .10 .25
❑ HA06012 Reeze, Whirlwind of Gusto .10 .25
❑ HA06013 Steelswarm Genome .10 .25
❑ HA06014 Steelswarm Sentinel .10 .25
❑ HA06015 Steelswarm Sting .10 .25
❑ HA06016 Steelswarm Longhorn (SCR) .30 .75
❑ HA06017 Steelswarm Hercules (SCR) .40 1.00
❑ HA06018 Evigishki Tetrogre (SCR) .75 2.00
❑ HA06019 Gem-Knight Citrine (SCR) 1.25 3.00
❑ HA06020 Gem-Knight Prismaura (SCR) 1.25 3.00
❑ HA06021 Laval Stennon (SCR) .75 2.00
❑ HA06022 Vylon Alpha (SCR) .60 1.50
❑ HA06023 Vylon Omega (SCR) .75 2.00
❑ HA06024 Daigusto Sphreez (SCR) 1.25 3.00
❑ HA06025 Vylon Component .10 .25
❑ HA06026 Vylon Element .10 .25
❑ HA06027 Forbidden Arts of the Gishki .10 .25
❑ HA06028 Pyroxene Fusion .10 .25
❑ HA06029 Infestation Ripples .10 .25
❑ HA06030 Infestation Tool .10 .25
❑ HA06031 Gem-Knight Obsidian .50 1.25
❑ HA06032 Gem-Knight Iolite .20 .50
❑ HA06033 Gem-Knight Amber .10 .25
❑ HA06034 Laval Lakeside Lady (SCR) 2.00 5.00
❑ HA06035 Laval Coatl .10 .25
❑ HA06036 Laval Blaster .10 .25
❑ HA06037 Vylon Pentachloro .10 .25
❑ HA06038 Vylon Tesseract .10 .25
❑ HA06039 Vylon Stigma .10 .25
❑ HA06040 Gishki Vision .60 1.50
❑ HA06041 Gishki Emilia (SR) .10 .25
❑ HA06042 Gishki Mollusk .10 .25
❑ HA06043 Gusto Falco .10 .25
❑ HA06044 Kamui, Hope of Gusto .10 .25
❑ HA06045 Musto, Oracle of Gusto .10 .25
❑ HA06046 Evigishki Gustkraken (SCR) 2.50 6.00
❑ HA06047 Gem-Knight Amethyst (SCR) .40 1.00
❑ HA06048 Lavalval Dragun (SCR) .60 1.50
❑ HA06049 Daigusto Falcos (SCR) .50 1.25
❑ HA06050 Gem-Knight Pearl (SCR) 1.50 4.00
❑ HA06051 Lavalval Ignis (SCR) .60 1.50
❑ HA06052 Vylon Disigma (SCR) 6.00 15.00
❑ HA06053 Evigishki Merrowgeist (SCR) 4.00 10.00
❑ HA06054 Daigusto Phoenix (SCR) 15.00 40.00
❑ HA06055 Particle Fusion .10 .25
❑ HA06056 Vylon Polytope .10 .25
❑ HA06057 Vylon Segment .10 .25
❑ HA06058 Dustflame Blast .10 .25
❑ HA06059 Aquamirror Illusion .10 .25
❑ HA06060 Whirlwind of Gusto .10 .25

2012 Yu-Gi-Oh Legendary Collection 3 Yugi's World

Booster Box 20.00 30.00

❑ LCYW001 Dark Magician (SCR) .60 1.50
❑ LCYW002 Gaia The Fierce Knight (SR) .30 .75
❑ LCYW003 Celtic Guardian (SR) .30 .75
❑ LCYW004 Silver Fang (UR) .40 1.00
❑ LCYW005 Mystical Elf .15 .40
❑ LCYW006 Curse of Dragon (R) .25 .60
❑ LCYW007 Giant Soldier of Stone .15 .40
❑ LCYW008 Feral Imp .15 .40
❑ LCYW009 Winged Dragon .40 1.00
Guardian of the Fortress #1 (UR)
❑ LCYW010 Summoned Skull (SR) .30 .75
❑ LCYW011 Gazelle the King of .40 1.00
Mythical Beasts (UR)
❑ LCYW012 Alpha the Magnet Warrior .15 .40
❑ LCYW013 Beta the Magnet Warrior .15 .40
❑ LCYW014 Gamma the Magnet Warrior .15 .40
❑ LCYW015 Queen's Knight (UR) .60 1.50
❑ LCYW016 Jack's Knight (UR) .50 1.25
❑ LCYW017 King's Knight (UR) .60 1.50
❑ LCYW018 Kuriboh (SR) .40 1.00
❑ LCYW019 Catapult Turtle (R) .25 .60
❑ LCYW020 Buster Blader (SCR) .60 1.50
❑ LCYW021 Valkyrion the Magna Warrior (SR) .75 2.00
❑ LCYW022 Dark Magician Girl (SCR) 8.00 20.00
❑ LCYW023 Breaker the Magical Warrior (UR) .60 1.50
❑ LCYW024 Mirage Knight .15 .40
❑ LCYW025 Black Luster Soldier 12.00 30.00
Envoy of the Beginning (SCR)
❑ LCYW026 Dark Magician of Chaos (SCR) 4.00 10.00
❑ LCYW027 Dark Sage .25 .60
❑ LCYW028 Dark Magician Knight .25 .60
❑ LCYW029 Sorcerer of Dark Magic .15 .40
❑ LCYW030 Watapon .15 .40
❑ LCYW031 Swift Gaia the Fierce Knight .15 .40
❑ LCYW032 Big Shield Gardna (SCR) .60 1.50
❑ LCYW033 Silent Swordsman LV3 .15 .40
❑ LCYW034 Silent Swordsman LV5 .15 .40
❑ LCYW035 Silent Swordsman LV7 .15 .40
❑ LCYW036 Obnoxious Celtic Guard .15 .40
❑ LCYW037 Silent Magician LV4 .40 1.00
❑ LCYW038 Silent Magician LV8 .40 1.00
❑ LCYW039 Green Gadget (UR) 1.25 3.00
❑ LCYW040 Red Gadget (UR) 1.25 3.00
❑ LCYW041 Yellow Gadget (UR) 1.25 3.00
❑ LCYW042 Archfiend of Gilfer (R) .25 .60
❑ LCYW043 The Tricky .25 .60
❑ LCYW044 Gorz the Emissary of Darkness (UR)1.25 3.00
❑ LCYW045 Berfomet (SR) .30 .75
❑ LCYW046 Black Luster Soldier .50 1.25
❑ LCYW047 Magician of Black Chaos .25 .60
❑ LCYW048 Dark Paladin (SCR) 6.00 15.00
❑ LCYW049 Dark Flare Knight .15 .40
❑ LCYW050 Dragon Master Knight (SR) .50 1.25
❑ LCYW051 Arcana Knight Joker (SCR) .75 2.00
❑ LCYW052 Chimera the Flying Mythical Beast (SR).30 .75
❑ LCYW053 Dark Hole (SCR) 4.00 10.00
❑ LCYW054 Raigeki (SCR) 1.00 2.50
❑ LCYW055 Fissure (SR) .30 .75
❑ LCYW056 Polymerization (SR) .75 2.00
❑ LCYW057 Swords of Revealing Light (UR) .40 1.00
❑ LCYW058 Monster Reborn (UR) 6.00 15.00
❑ LCYW059 Pot of Greed (SCR) 1.00 2.50
❑ LCYW060 Card Destruction (SCR) .50 1.25
❑ LCYW061 Heavy Storm (UR) 1.50 4.00
❑ LCYW062 Mystical Space Typhoon (SCR) 6.00 15.00
❑ LCYW063 De-Fusion .15 .40
❑ LCYW064 Graceful Charity (SCR) .50 1.25
❑ LCYW065 Double Spell (SR) .30 .75
❑ LCYW066 Diffusion Wave-Motion (SR) .30 .75
❑ LCYW067 Thousand Knives .15 .40
❑ LCYW068 Heart of the Underdog .15 .40
❑ LCYW069 Dedication through .50 1.25
Light and Darkness (SCR)
❑ LCYW070 Black Luster Ritual .15 .40
❑ LCYW071 Dark Magic Attack .15 .40
❑ LCYW072 Knight's Title .15 .40
❑ LCYW073 Sage's Stone (R) .25 .60
❑ LCYW074 Brain Control (SCR) .50 1.25
❑ LCYW075 Magical Dimension .15 .40
❑ LCYW076 Mystic Box .15 .40
❑ LCYW077 Magicians Unite .15 .40
❑ LCYW078 Black Magic Ritual .15 .40
❑ LCYW079 Dark Magic Curtain (R) .25 .60
❑ LCYW080 Gold Sarcophagus 1.25 3.00
❑ LCYW081 Soul Taker .50 1.25
❑ LCYW082 Magic Formula .15 .40
❑ LCYW083 Union Attack .15 .40
❑ LCYW084 Tricky Spell 4 .15 .40
❑ LCYW085 Spell Shattering Arrow .15 .40
❑ LCYW086 Multiply (R) .25 .60
❑ LCYW087 Makiu, the Magical Mist .15 .40
❑ LCYW088 Detonate .15 .40
❑ LCYW089 Seven Tools of the Bandit (SCR) .50 1.25
❑ LCYW090 Horn of Heaven (SCR) .50 1.25
❑ LCYW091 Mirror Force (SCR) 4.00 10.00
❑ LCYW092 Spellbinding Circle .15 .40
❑ LCYW093 Lightforce Sword (SR) .30 .75
❑ LCYW094 Chain Destruction .15 .40
❑ LCYW095 Dust Tornado (UR) .50 1.25
❑ LCYW096 Magical Hats .15 .40
❑ LCYW097 Shift (SR) .30 .75
❑ LCYW098 Collected Power .15 .40
❑ LCYW099 Magic Cylinder (SR) .50 1.25
❑ LCYW100 Magician's Circle (SR) .30 .75
❑ LCYW101 Stronghold the Moving Fortress (UR).40 1.00
❑ LCYW102 Soul Rope .15 .40
❑ LCYW103 Blue-Eyes Toon Dragon (R) .25 .60
❑ LCYW104 Manga Ryu-Ran (R) .25 .60
❑ LCYW105 Toon Mermaid (R) .25 .60
❑ LCYW106 Toon Summoned Skull (R) .25 .60
❑ LCYW107 Toon Gemini Elf (R) .25 .60
❑ LCYW108 Toon Goblin Attack Force (R) .25 .60
❑ LCYW109 Toon Cannon Soldier (R) .25 .60
❑ LCYW110 Toon Masked Sorcerer (R) .25 .60
❑ LCYW111 Toon Dark Magician Girl (R) .25 .60
❑ LCYW112 Dark-Eyes Illusionist (R) .25 .60
❑ LCYW113 Relinquished (R) .25 .60
❑ LCYW114 Black Illusion Ritual (R) .25 .60
❑ LCYW115 Toon World (R) .25 .60
❑ LCYW116 Toon Table of Contents (R) .75 2.00
❑ LCYW117 Dragon Capture Jar (R) .25 .60
❑ LCYW118 Toon Defense (R) .25 .60
❑ LCYW119 Man-Eater Bug .15 .40
❑ LCYW120 Sangan (SCR) 2.00 5.00
❑ LCYW121 Morphing Jar (UR) 1.00 2.50
❑ LCYW122 Puppet Master .15 .40
❑ LCYW123 Dark Master - Zorc .15 .40
❑ LCYW124 Change of Heart (SCR) .50 1.25
❑ LCYW125 Exchange (SCR) .50 1.25
❑ LCYW126 The Dark Door (R) .25 .60
❑ LCYW127 Spiritualism .15 .40
❑ LCYW128 Contract with the Dark Master .15 .40
❑ LCYW129 Guardian Elma .15 .40
❑ LCYW130 Guardian Ceal .15 .40
❑ LCYW131 Guardian Grarl .15 .40
❑ LCYW132 Guardian Baou .15 .40
❑ LCYW133 Guardian Kay'est .15 .40
❑ LCYW134 Guardian Tryce .15 .40
❑ LCYW135 My Body as a Shield .25 .60
❑ LCYW136 Butterfly Dagger - Elma .15 .40
❑ LCYW137 Shooting Star Bow - Ceal .15 .40
❑ LCYW138 Gravity Axe - Grarl .15 .40
❑ LCYW139 Wicked-Breaking Flamberge - Baou .15 .40
❑ LCYW140 Rod of Silence - Kay'est .15 .40
❑ LCYW141 Twin Swords of Flashing Light - Tryce.15 .40
❑ LCYW142 Monster Reincarnation (R) .25 .60
❑ LCYW143 Gil Garth (UR) .40 1.00
❑ LCYW144 Bowganian (SR) .30 .75
❑ LCYW145 Machine Duplication (SR) .30 .75
❑ LCYW146 Hidden Soldiers (R) .25 .60
❑ LCYW147 Rope of Life (SCR) .50 1.25
❑ LCYW148 Malevolent Catastrophe (SR) .30 .75
❑ LCYW149 Harpie's Feather Duster (SCR) 1.00 2.50
❑ LCYW150 Gravity Bind (SR) .40 1.00
❑ LCYW151 Mechanicalchaser (UR) .60 1.50
❑ LCYW152 Solemn Judgment (SCR) 2.00 5.00
❑ LCYW153 Magic Jammer (SCR) .50 1.25
❑ LCYW154 Sinister Serpent (SCR) .60 1.50
❑ LCYW155 Mirage of Nightmare (SCR) .50 1.25
❑ LCYW156 Ordeal of a Traveler .15 .40
❑ LCYW157 Tri-Horned Dragon (SR) .30 .75
❑ LCYW158 Two-Headed King Rex (SCR) .75 2.00
❑ LCYW159 Millennium Shield (SR) .30 .75
❑ LCYW160 Cosmo Queen (UR) .60 1.50
❑ LCYW161 Fire Princess (UR) .40 1.00
❑ LCYW162 Command Knight .15 .40
❑ LCYW163 Malice Doll of Demise (R) .25 .60
❑ LCYW164 White-Horned Dragon (SR) .30 .75
❑ LCYW165 Green Baboon, Defender of the Forest.15 .40
❑ LCYW166 Summoner Monk (UR) .75 2.00
❑ LCYW167 Commander Covington (SCR) .50 1.25
❑ LCYW168 Machina Soldier (SCR) .50 1.25
❑ LCYW169 Machina Sniper (SCR) .50 1.25
❑ LCYW170 Machina Defender (SCR) .50 1.25
❑ LCYW171 Machina Force (SCR) .75 2.00
❑ LCYW172 Limiter Removal (UR) .40 1.00
❑ LCYW173 Reinforcement of the Army (SR) .60 1.50
❑ LCYW174 Dragged Down into the Grave (SR) 3.00 8.00
❑ LCYW175 Ectoplasmer (R) .25 .60
❑ LCYW176 Mind Control (UR) 1.50 4.00
❑ LCYW177 Trap Hole (UR) .40 1.00
❑ LCYW178 Imperial Order (SCR) .60 1.50
❑ LCYW179 Mask of Restrict .15 .40
❑ LCYW180 Torrential Tribute (SCR) 3.00 8.00
❑ LCYW181 Bottomless Trap Hole (UR) 4.00 10.00
❑ LCYW182 Royal Decree (UR) 4.00 10.00
❑ LCYW183 Gravekeeper's Spy (UR) .75 2.00
❑ LCYW184 Gravekeeper's Guard (UR) .60 1.50
❑ LCYW185 Gravekeeper's Spear Soldier (UR) .40 1.00
❑ LCYW186 Gravekeeper's Watcher .15 .40
❑ LCYW187 Gravekeeper's Chief (UR) .40 1.00
❑ LCYW188 Gravekeeper's Cannonholder (UR) .40 1.00
❑ LCYW189 Gravekeeper's Assailant (UR) .40 1.00
❑ LCYW190 Charm of Shabti .15 .40
❑ LCYW191 Gravekeeper's Commandant (UR) 1.25 3.00
❑ LCYW192 Gravekeeper's Descendant (UR) 1.25 3.00
❑ LCYW193 Gravekeeper's Recruiter (UR) 3.00 8.00
❑ LCYW194 Necrovalley (UR) .60 1.50
❑ LCYW195 Royal Tribute (UR) 2.00 5.00
❑ LCYW196 Rite of Spirit .15 .40
❑ LCYW197 Horus the Black Flame Dragon LV4 .25 .60
❑ LCYW198 Horus the Black Flame Dragon LV6 .25 .60
❑ LCYW199 Horus the Black Flame Dragon LV8 .50 1.25
❑ LCYW200 Mystic Swordsman LV2 .15 .40
❑ LCYW201 Mystic Swordsman LV4 .15 .40
❑ LCYW202 Mystic Swordsman LV6 .15 .40
❑ LCYW203 Armed Dragon LV3 .15 .40
❑ LCYW204 Armed Dragon LV5 .15 .40
❑ LCYW205 Armed Dragon LV7 .25 .60
❑ LCYW206 Horus' Servant .15 .40
❑ LCYW207 Level Up! .15 .40
❑ LCYW208 Dark Grepher .60 1.50
❑ LCYW209 Dark Horus .15 .40
❑ LCYW210 The Dark Creator .15 .40
❑ LCYW211 Dark Nephthys .15 .40
❑ LCYW212 Darklord Zerato .25 .60
❑ LCYW213 Darknight Parshath .15 .40
❑ LCYW214 Dark General Freed .15 .40
❑ LCYW215 D.D. Warrior Lady (R) .25 .60
❑ LCYW216 D.D. Scout Plane (R) .25 .60
❑ LCYW217 D.D. Assailant (R) .25 .60
❑ LCYW218 D.D. Warrior (R) .25 .60
❑ LCYW219 Skull Servant (UR) .60 1.50
❑ LCYW220 Dark King of the Abyss (SCR) .50 1.25
❑ LCYW221 Aqua Madoor (SCR) .50 1.25
❑ LCYW222 Yaranzo (SR) .30 .75
❑ LCYW223 Takriminos (SR) .30 .75
❑ LCYW224 Megasonic Eye (SR) .30 .75
❑ LCYW225 Yamadron (SR) .30 .75
❑ LCYW226 Three-Legged Zombie (SR) .30 .75
❑ LCYW227 Fairy's Gift (SR) .30 .75
❑ LCYW228 Kanan the Swordmistress (UR) .75 2.00
❑ LCYW229 Mystical Shine Ball (SR) 1.50 4.00
❑ LCYW230 Big Eye (R) .25 .60
❑ LCYW231 Banisher of the Light .15 .40
❑ LCYW232 Giant Rat (SCR) .50 1.25
❑ LCYW233 UFO Turtle (SCR) .50 1.25
❑ LCYW234 Giant Germ .15 .40
❑ LCYW235 Nimble Momonga .15 .40
❑ LCYW236 Shining Angel (SCR) .50 1.25
❑ LCYW237 Mother Grizzly (SCR) .50 1.25
❑ LCYW238 Flying Kamakiri #1 (SCR) .50 1.25
❑ LCYW239 Mystic Tomato (SCR) .60 1.50
❑ LCYW240 Morphing Jar #2 (SR) .30 .75
❑ LCYW241 Goddess of Whim .15 .40
❑ LCYW242 Kycoo the Ghost Destroyer (SCR) .60 1.50
❑ LCYW243 Summoner of Illusions .15 .40
❑ LCYW244 Needle Worm (UR) .60 1.50
❑ LCYW245 Pyramid Turtle (SCR) .50 1.25
❑ LCYW246 Spirit Reaper (UR) 1.00 2.50
❑ LCYW247 Arsenal Summoner .15 .40
❑ LCYW248 Chaos Sorcerer (SR) .75 2.00
❑ LCYW249 Levia-Dragon - Daedalus (SCR) .60 1.50
❑ LCYW250 Manju of the Ten Thousand Hands .25 .60
❑ LCYW251 Invader of Darkness .15 .40
❑ LCYW252 The Agent of Wisdom - Mercury (SR).30 .75
❑ LCYW253 The Agent of Creation - Venus (SR)1.50 4.00
❑ LCYW254 Solar Flare Dragon (SR) .30 .75
❑ LCYW255 Emissary of the Afterlife .15 .40
❑ LCYW256 King of the Swamp .50 1.25
❑ LCYW257 The Creator .15 .40
❑ LCYW258 The Creator Incarnate .15 .40
❑ LCYW259 Sacred Phoenix of Nephthys (SR) .30 .75
❑ LCYW260 Hand of Nephthys (R) .25 .60
❑ LCYW261 Armed Samurai - Ben Kei .15 .40
❑ LCYW262 The Light - Hex-Sealed Fusion .15 .40
❑ LCYW263 The Dark - Hex-Sealed Fusion .15 .40
❑ LCYW264 The Earth - Hex-Sealed Fusion .15 .40
❑ LCYW265 Upstart Goblin (UR) 1.50 4.00
❑ LCYW266 Messenger of Peace .40 1.00
❑ LCYW267 Prohibition (SCR) .75 2.00
❑ LCYW268 Fusion Gate (SR) .75 2.00
❑ LCYW269 Creature Swap (UR) .40 1.00
❑ LCYW270 Book of Moon (SCR) 3.00 8.00
❑ LCYW271 Dark Snake Syndrome (R) .25 .60
❑ LCYW272 Non-Spellcasting Area .15 .40
❑ LCYW273 Contract with the Abyss .15 .40
❑ LCYW274 Stray Lambs .15 .40
❑ LCYW275 Smashing Ground (UR) .50 1.25
❑ LCYW276 Salvage (SR) 1.50 4.00
❑ LCYW277 Earth Chant .15 .40
❑ LCYW278 Spell Economics .15 .40
❑ LCYW279 Level Limit - Area B .75 2.00
❑ LCYW280 A Feather of the Phoenix (SCR) .50 1.25
❑ LCYW281 Swords of Concealing Light (UR) .40 1.00
❑ LCYW282 Centrifugal Field .25 .60
❑ LCYW283 Acid Trap Hole (R) .25 .60
❑ LCYW284 DNA Surgery .25 .60
❑ LCYW285 Reckless Greed (SR) 1.25 3.00
❑ LCYW286 Raigeki Break (SR) .60 1.50
❑ LCYW287 Goblin Fan .15 .40
❑ LCYW288 Sakuretsu Armor (SR) .30 .75
❑ LCYW289 Chain Disappearance .75 2.00
❑ LCYW290 Dark Mirror Force (R) .25 .60
❑ LCYW291 Compulsory Evacuation Device (SCR)8.00 20.00
❑ LCYW292 DNA Transplant .15 .40
❑ LCYW293 Beckoning Light (UR) .40 1.00
❑ LCYW294 Draining Shield .15 .40
❑ LCYW295 Mind Crush (UR) 1.25 3.00
❑ LCYW296 Penalty Game! .15 .40
❑ LCYW297 Threatening Roar (SCR) .60 1.50
❑ LCYW298 Phoenix Wing Wind Blast (SCR) .60 1.50
❑ LCYW299 Level Limit - Area A .15 .40
❑ LCYW300 Black Horn of Heaven (SCR) .75 2.00
❑ LCYW301 Solemn Warning 2.00 5.00
❑ LCYW302 Right Leg of the Forbidden One (SCR)3.00 8.00
❑ LCYW303 Left Leg of the Forbidden One (SCR)3.00 8.00
❑ LCYW304 Right Arm of the Forbidden One (SCR)3.00 8.00
❑ LCYW305 Left Arm of the Forbidden One (SCR)3.00 8.00
❑ LCYW306 Exodia the Forbidden One (SCR) 8.00 20.00

2012 Yu-Gi-Oh Legendary Collection 3 Yugi's World Box Bonus

Complete Set (7) 4.00 8.00
One Set Per Legendary Collection Box

❑ LC03001 The Seal of Orichalcos (UR) .60 1.50
❑ LC03002 Dark Necrofear (UR) .40 1.00
❑ LC03003 Guardian Eatos (UR) .40 1.00
❑ LC03004 Five-Headed Dragon (UR) .40 1.00
❑ LC03005 Emissary of Darkness Token (UR) .40 1.00
❑ LC03006 Pink Kuriboh Token (UR) .40 1.00
❑ LC03007 Orange Kuriboh Token (UR) .40 1.00

2012 Yu-Gi-Oh Order of Chaos

Complete Set 250.00 350.00
Booster Box 60.00 90.00
Booster Pack 3.00 4.00

❑ ORCS000 Inzektor Axe - Zektahawk (UR) 2.00 5.00
❑ ORCS000 Inzektor Axe - Zektahawk (SR) 1.50 4.00
❑ ORCS001 Kurivolt .15 .40
❑ ORCS002 Darklon .15 .40
❑ ORCS003 Gagaga Girl (SCR) 20.00 40.00
❑ ORCS004 Gogogo Giant (R) .60 1.50
❑ ORCS005 ZW - Unicorn Spear (R) .25 .60
❑ ORCS006 Shocktopus .15 .40
❑ ORCS007 Photon Lizard (R) .25 .60
❑ ORCS008 Photon Thrasher (R) .75 2.00
❑ ORCS009 Photon Crusher .15 .40
❑ ORCS010 Photon Leo .15 .40
❑ ORCS011 Photon Circle .15 .40
❑ ORCS012 Reverse Buster (R) .25 .60
❑ ORCS013 Flame Armor Ninja .15 .40
❑ ORCS014 Air Armor Ninja .15 .40
❑ ORCS015 Aqua Armor Ninja .15 .40
❑ ORCS016 Earth Armor Ninja .15 .40
❑ ORCS017 Inzektor Hornet (SR) 25.00 50.00
❑ ORCS018 Inzektor Ant .15 .40
❑ ORCS019 Inzektor Centipede .15 .40
❑ ORCS020 Inzektor Dragonfly (R) 1.50 4.00
❑ ORCS021 Inzektor Giga-Mantis (UTR) 8.00 20.00
❑ ORCS021 Inzektor Giga-Mantis (UR) 8.00 20.00
❑ ORCS022 Inzektor Giga-Weevil .15 .40
❑ ORCS023 Wind-Up Rat (SR) 12.00 25.00
❑ ORCS024 Wind-Up Honeybee .15 .40
❑ ORCS025 Evoltile Pleuro .15 .40
❑ ORCS026 Evoltile Casinerio (R) .25 .60
❑ ORCS027 Evolsaur Elias .15 .40
❑ ORCS028 Evolsaur Terias .15 .40
❑ ORCS029 Ninja Grandmaster Hanzo (UTR) 15.00 30.00
❑ ORCS029 Ninja Grandmaster Hanzo (UR) 15.00 30.00
❑ ORCS030 Masked Ninja Ebisu .15 .40
❑ ORCS031 Upstart Golden Ninja .15 .40
❑ ORCS032 Chow Len the Prophet .15 .40
❑ ORCS033 Familiar-Possessed - Dharc .15 .40
❑ ORCS034 Dark Blade .60 1.50
the Captain of the Evil World (R)
❑ ORCS035 Trance Archfiend (SP) .75 2.00
❑ ORCS036 Divine Dragon Apocralyph .15 .40
❑ ORCS037 Darkstorm Dragon (SR) 1.00 2.50
❑ ORCS038 Numen erat Testudo .15 .40
❑ ORCS039 Twin Photon Lizard (UTR) 2.00 5.00
❑ ORCS039 Twin Photon Lizard (UR) 1.50 4.00
❑ ORCS040 Number C39: Utopia Ray (GR) 10.00 25.00
❑ ORCS040 Number C39: Utopia Ray (UR) 5.00 12.00
❑ ORCS040 Number C39: Utopia Ray (UTR) 6.00 15.00
❑ ORCS041 Blade Armor Ninja (SR) 5.00 12.00
❑ ORCS042 Number 12 5.00 12.00
Crimson Shadow Armor Ninja (UR)
❑ ORCS042 Number 12 6.00 15.00
Crimson Shadow Armor Ninja (UTR)
❑ ORCS043 Number 96: Dark Mist (UR) 4.00 10.00
❑ ORCS043 Number 96: Dark Mist (UTR) 6.00 15.00
❑ ORCS044 Wind-Up Carrier Zenmaity (UR) 20.00 40.00
❑ ORCS044 Wind-Up Carrier Zenmaity (UTR) 25.00 50.00
❑ ORCS045 Evolzar Solda (UTR) 6.00 15.00
❑ ORCS045 Evolzar Solda (UR) 5.00 12.00
❑ ORCS046 Inzektor Exa-Beetle (SCR) 12.00 30.00
❑ ORCS047 Full-Force Strike .15 .40
❑ ORCS048 Gagagabolt (R) .25 .60
❑ ORCS049 Double Defender .15 .40
❑ ORCS050 Galaxy Storm .15 .40
❑ ORCS051 Armor Ninjitsu Art of Alchemy (SR) 1.00 2.50
❑ ORCS052 Star Light, Star Bright .15 .40
❑ ORCS053 Armor Blast (SR) 1.00 2.50
❑ ORCS054 Inzektor Sword - Zektkaliber (UR) 1.25 3.00
❑ ORCS054 Inzektor Sword - Zektkaliber (UTR) 2.50 6.00
❑ ORCS055 Weights & Zenmaisures (R) .25 .60
❑ ORCS056 Primordial Soup .15 .40
❑ ORCS057 Evo-Force (SR) 2.50 6.00

❑ ORCS058 Dark Mambele .15 .40
❑ ORCS059 Creeping Darkness (SR) 2.00 5.00
❑ ORCS060 Shrine of Mist Valley (R) .25 .60
❑ ORCS061 Xyz Burst .15 .40
❑ ORCS062 Galaxy Wave .15 .40
❑ ORCS063 Dicephoon .15 .40
❑ ORCS064 Counterforce .15 .40
❑ ORCS065 Gagagaguard (R) .60 1.50
❑ ORCS066 Xyz Reflect (UTR) 2.50 6.00
❑ ORCS066 Xyz Reflect (UR) 1.50 4.00
❑ ORCS067 Splash Capture .15 .40
❑ ORCS068 Armor Ninjitsu Art of Freezing .15 .40
❑ ORCS069 Armor Ninjitsu Art of Rust Mist (SR)1.50 4.00
❑ ORCS070 Inzektor Orb (R) .25 .60
❑ ORCS071 Variable Form .15 .40
❑ ORCS072 Zenmailstrom .15 .40
❑ ORCS073 Degen-Force .15 .40
❑ ORCS074 Evo-Branch .15 .40
❑ ORCS075 Ninjitsu Art of Super-Transformation (SR) 3.00 8.00
❑ ORCS076 Xyz Reborn (SCR) 12.00 30.00
❑ ORCS077 Over Capacity (R) .25 .60
❑ ORCS078 The Huge Revolution is Over .15 .40
❑ ORCS079 Royal Prison (R) .75 2.00
❑ ORCS080 Sealing Ceremony of Katon .15 .40
❑ ORCS081 Inzektor Hopper (R) .25 .60
❑ ORCS082 Wind-Up Shark (SR) 12.00 30.00
❑ ORCS083 Evoltile Najasho (SR) 2.50 6.00
❑ ORCS084 White Dragon Ninja (SCR) 20.00 40.00
❑ ORCS085 Interplanetarypurplythorny Dragon .60 1.50
❑ ORCS086 Tour Bus From the Underworld (SCR)50.00 100.00
❑ ORCS087 Photon Trident .15 .40
❑ ORCS088 Evo-Instant (R) .25 .60
❑ ORCS089 Ninjitsu Art of Duplication (R) .60 1.50
❑ ORCS090 White Night Queen (R) .25 .60
❑ ORCS091 Danipon .15 .40
❑ ORCS092 Sweet Corn .15 .40
❑ ORCS093 Vampire Koala .15 .40
❑ ORCS094 Koalo-Koala .15 .40
❑ ORCS095 Dark Diviner (SR) 1.50 4.00
❑ ORCS096 Dark Flattop (R) .25 .60
❑ ORCS097 Driven Daredevil (SCR) 8.00 20.00
❑ ORCS098 Wind-Up Arsenal Zenmaioh (SCR)12.00 30.00
❑ ORCS099 M-X-Saber Invoker (SCR) 10.00 25.00
❑ ORCSSP1 Inzektor Axe - Zektahawk PROMO 2.00 5.00

2012 Yu-Gi-Oh Order of Chaos Special Edition

Complete Set (2) 5.00 10.00
One Card Per Special Edition Box
❑ ORCSSE1 Effect Veiler (SR) 4.00 10.00
❑ ORCSSE2 The Winged Dragon of Ra (SR) 1.50 4.00

2012 Yu-Gi-Oh Ra Yellow Mega Pack

Complete Set (113) 60.00 120.00
Booster Box (24 Packs) 60.00 90.00
Booster Pack (11 Cards) 3.00 4.00
❑ RYMP001 Elemental HERO Avian ALT .15 .40
❑ RYMP002 Elemental HERO Burstinatrix ALT .15 .40
❑ RYMP003 Elemental HERO Sparkman ALT .15 .40
❑ RYMP004 Elemental HERO Neos .15 .40
❑ RYMP005 Elemental HERO Necroshade .15 .40
❑ RYMP006 Card Trooper .15 .40
❑ RYMP007 Neo-Spacian Grand Mole (SR) 1.50 4.00
❑ RYMP008 Elemental HERO Stratos .15 .40
❑ RYMP009 Necro Gardna (SCR) 1.50 4.00
❑ RYMP010 Elemental HERO Neos Alius (SCR) 2.00 5.00
❑ RYMP011 Card Ejector .15 .40
❑ RYMP012 Elemental HERO Prisma .15 .40
❑ RYMP013 Gallis the Star Beast .15 .40
❑ RYMP014 Winged Kuriboh LV9 (R) .25 .60
❑ RYMP015 Card Blocker .15 .40
❑ RYMP016 Elemental HERO Flame Wingman (R).25 .60
❑ RYMP017 Elemental HERO Electrum .15 .40
❑ RYMP018 Elemental HERO Mudballman .15 .40
❑ RYMP019 Rainbow Neos .15 .40
❑ RYMP020 Elemental HERO Divine Neos .15 .40
❑ RYMP021 Miracle Fusion (UR) 3.00 8.00
❑ RYMP022 The Flute of Summoning Kuriboh .15 .40
❑ RYMP023 H - Heated Heart (SCR) 1.00 2.50
❑ RYMP024 E - Emergency Call (SCR) 3.00 8.00
❑ RYMP025 R - Righteous Justice (SCR) 1.25 3.00
❑ RYMP026 O - Oversoul (SCR) 1.25 3.00
❑ RYMP027 Hero Flash!! (SCR) 1.00 2.50
❑ RYMP028 Instant Fusion (UR) 1.25 3.00
❑ RYMP029 Super Polymerization (SCR) 4.00 10.00
❑ RYMP030 Hero Mask .15 .40
❑ RYMP031 Hero Signal (SR) .40 1.00
❑ RYMP032 Hero Blast (SR) 1.50 4.00
❑ RYMP033 Destiny HERO - Diamond Dude .15 .40
❑ RYMP034 Destiny HERO - Malicious (SCR) 2.00 5.00
❑ RYMP035 Destiny HERO - Disk Commander (R).25 .60
❑ RYMP036 Destiny HERO - Plasma .15 .40
❑ RYMP037 Destiny Draw (SCR) 1.00 2.50
❑ RYMP038 Destiny Signal (SR) .40 1.00
❑ RYMP039 Destiny Mirage .15 .40
❑ RYMP040 Crystal Beast Ruby Carbuncle (SR) 1.25 3.00
❑ RYMP041 Crystal Beast Amethyst Cat (SR) .75 2.00
❑ RYMP042 Crystal Beast Emerald Tortoise (SR)1.00 2.50
❑ RYMP043 Crystal Beast Topaz Tiger (SR) 1.25 3.00
❑ RYMP044 Crystal Beast Amber Mammoth (SR)1.00 2.50
❑ RYMP045 Crystal Beast Cobalt Eagle (SR) .75 2.00
❑ RYMP046 Crystal Beast Sapphire Pegasus .15 .40
❑ RYMP047 Rainbow Dragon .15 .40
❑ RYMP048 Crystal Beacon (SCR) 1.00 2.50
❑ RYMP049 Rare Value .15 .40
❑ RYMP050 Crystal Blessing (SCR) .75 2.00
❑ RYMP051 Crystal Abundance (SCR) 1.00 2.50
❑ RYMP052 Crystal Promise (SCR) 1.00 2.50
❑ RYMP053 Ancient City - Rainbow Ruins .15 .40
❑ RYMP054 Crystal Release .15 .40
❑ RYMP055 Crystal Raigeki (SR) .75 2.00
❑ RYMP056 Rainbow Path .15 .40
❑ RYMP057 Rainbow Gravity .15 .40
❑ RYMP058 Cyber Dragon 1.25 3.00
❑ RYMP059 Cyber Dragon ALT (SCR) 3.00 8.00
❑ RYMP060 Cyber End Dragon ALT (R) .75 2.00
❑ RYMP061 Chimeratech Overdragon (R) .60 1.50
❑ RYMP062 Power Bond .15 .40
❑ RYMP063 Overload Fusion .15 .40
❑ RYMP064 Future Fusion (UR) 2.00 5.00
❑ RYMP065 Magical Mallet .15 .40
❑ RYMP066 Dark End Dragon (SR) 1.00 2.50
❑ RYMP067 Light End Dragon (SR) .75 2.00
❑ RYMP068 Vennominaga the Deity of Poisonous Snakes (R) .25 .60
❑ RYMP069 Vennominon the King of Poisonous Snakes .15 .40
❑ RYMP070 Yubel (R) .50 1.25
❑ RYMP071 Yubel - Terror Incarnate (R) .40 1.00
❑ RYMP072 Yubel - The Ultimate Nightmare (R) .40 1.00
❑ RYMP073 Mezuki .15 .40
❑ RYMP074 Thunder King Rai-Oh .15 .40
❑ RYMP075 Kasha .15 .40
❑ RYMP076 Shutendoji .15 .40
❑ RYMP077 Darklord Desire .15 .40
❑ RYMP078 Fusion Recovery .15 .40
❑ RYMP079 System Down .15 .40
❑ RYMP080 Grand Convergence .15 .40
❑ RYMP081 Dimensional Fissure (SCR) 1.50 4.00
❑ RYMP082 Macro Cosmos (UR) 1.25 3.00
❑ RYMP083 Rise of the Snake Deity .15 .40
❑ RYMP084 Dimensional Prison (UR) 6.00 15.00
❑ RYMP085 Offering to the Snake Deity .15 .40
❑ RYMP086 D.D. Survivor .15 .40
❑ RYMP087 Grandmaster of the Six Samurai .15 .40
❑ RYMP088 The Six Samurai - Yaichi (UR) .75 2.00
❑ RYMP089 The Six Samurai - Kamon (UR) 1.50 4.00
❑ RYMP090 The Six Samurai - Yariza (UR) 1.00 2.50
❑ RYMP091 The Six Samurai - Nisashi (UR) 1.00 2.50
❑ RYMP092 The Six Samurai - Zanji (UR) 1.00 2.50
❑ RYMP093 The Six Samurai - Irou (UR) 1.25 3.00
❑ RYMP094 Great Shogun Shien .15 .40
❑ RYMP095 D.D. Crow (SR) 1.50 4.00
❑ RYMP096 Gladiator Beast Laquari (SCR) 1.25 3.00
❑ RYMP097 Enishi, Shien's Chancellor .15 .40
❑ RYMP098 Test Tiger .15 .40
❑ RYMP099 Rainbow Dark Dragon .15 .40
❑ RYMP100 Jain, Lightsworn Paladin (UR) 1.00 2.50
❑ RYMP101 Garoth, Lightsworn Warrior (R) .25 .60
❑ RYMP102 Lumina, Lightsworn Summoner (UR)3.00 8.00
❑ RYMP103 Wulf, Lightsworn Beast (UR) 1.25 3.00
❑ RYMP104 Judgement Dragon .15 .40
❑ RYMP105 Aurkus, Lightsworn Druid .15 .40
❑ RYMP106 Gladiator Beast Lanista .15 .40
❑ RYMP107 Gladiator Beast's Respite .15 .40
❑ RYMP108 Gladiator's Return .15 .40
❑ RYMP109 Cunning of the Six Samurai .15 .40
❑ RYMP110 Gladiator Proving Ground (UR) 1.00 2.50
❑ RYMP111 Gateway of the Six .15 .40
❑ RYMP112 Double-Edged Sword Technique (UR)1.50 4.00
❑ RYMP113 Gladiator Beast War Chariot (R) .40 1.00

2012 Yu-Gi-Oh Return of the Duelist

Complete Set 250.00 350.00
Booster Box (24 Packs) 50.00 80.00
Booster Pack (9 Cards) 3.00 4.00
❑ REDU000 Noble Knight Gawayn (SR) .75 2.00
❑ REDU001 Trance the Magic Swordsman .15 .40
❑ REDU002 Damage Mage .15 .40
❑ REDU003 ZW - Phoenix Bow (R) .25 .60
❑ REDU004 Photon Caesar .15 .40
❑ REDU005 Heroic Challenger - Spartan .15 .40
❑ REDU006 Heroic Challenger - War Hammer .15 .40
❑ REDU007 Heroic Challenger - Swordshield .15 .40
❑ REDU008 Heroic Challenger - Double Lance (R).40 1.00
❑ REDU009 Chronomaly Mayan Machine .15 .40
❑ REDU010 Chronomaly Colossal Head (R) .25 .60
❑ REDU011 Chronomaly Golden Jet .15 .40
❑ REDU012 Chronomaly Crystal Bones (R) .25 .60
❑ REDU013 Chronomaly Crystal Skull (R) .25 .60
❑ REDU014 Chronomaly Moai .15 .40
❑ REDU015 Spellbook Magician of Prophecy (UTR)5.00 12.00
❑ REDU015 Spellbook Magician of Prophecy (UR)6.00 15.00
❑ REDU016 Amores of Prophecy .15 .40
❑ REDU017 Temperance of Prophecy (SR) 2.50 6.00
❑ REDU018 Strength of Prophecy .15 .40
❑ REDU019 Charioteer of Prophecy .15 .40
❑ REDU020 High Priestess of Prophecy (SCR) 50.00 100.00
❑ REDU021 Madolche Mewfeuille .15 .40
❑ REDU022 Madolche Baaple .15 .40
❑ REDU023 Madolche Chouxvalier (R) .50 1.25
❑ REDU024 Madolche Magileine (SR) 5.00 12.00
❑ REDU025 Madolche Butlerusk .15 .40
❑ REDU026 Madolche Puddingcess (UTR) 5.00 12.00
❑ REDU026 Madolche Puddingcess (UR) 6.00 15.00
❑ REDU027 Geargiano Mk-II (R) .40 1.00
❑ REDU028 Geargiaccelerator .15 .40
❑ REDU029 Geargiarsenal (R) .60 1.50
❑ REDU030 Geargiarmor (SR) 3.00 8.00
❑ REDU031 Unifiora, Mystical Beast of the Forest .15 .40
❑ REDU032 Little Trooper .15 .40
❑ REDU033 Silver Sentinel (UTR) 4.00 10.00
❑ REDU033 Silver Sentinel (UR) 4.00 10.00
❑ REDU034 Dust Knight (R) .25 .60
❑ REDU035 Block Golem .15 .40
❑ REDU036 Atlantean Attack Squad .15 .40
❑ REDU037 Illusory Snatcher (SR) 1.50 4.00
❑ REDU038 Grandsoil the Elemental Lord (SCR)8.00 20.00
❑ REDU039 Three Thousand Needles (SP) .15 .40
❑ REDU040 Goblin Marauding Squad (SP) .15 .40
❑ REDU041 Heroic Champion - Excalibur (UR) 6.00 15.00
❑ REDU041 Heroic Champion - Excalibur (GR) 2.50 6.00
❑ REDU041 Heroic Champion - Excalibur (UTR)3.00 8.00
❑ REDU042 Chronomaly Crystal Chrononaut (SR)2.00 5.00
❑ REDU043 Number 33 Chronomaly Machu Mech (UR) 3.00 8.00
❑ REDU043 Number 33 Chronomaly Machu Mech (UTR) 2.50 6.00
❑ REDU044 Superdimensional Robot Galaxy Destroyer (UTR) 1.50 4.00
❑ REDU044 Superdimensional Robot Galaxy Destroyer (UR) 2.00 5.00
❑ REDU045 Hierophant of Prophecy (UR) 3.00 8.00
❑ REDU045 Hierophant of Prophecy (UTR) 2.50 6.00
❑ REDU046 Gear Gigant X (SCR) 20.00 40.00
❑ REDU047 Alchemic Magician (SR) 2.00 5.00
❑ REDU048 Soul of Silvermountain (SR) 1.50 4.00
❑ REDU049 Fairy King Albverdich (R) .60 1.50
❑ REDU050 Sword Breaker (SR) 2.00 5.00
❑ REDU051 Gagagarevenge (SR) 1.25 3.00
❑ REDU052 Overlay Regen .15 .40
❑ REDU053 Heroic Chance .15 .40
❑ REDU054 Chronomaly Technology .15 .40
❑ REDU055 Chronomaly Pyramid Eye Tablet .15 .40
❑ REDU056 Galaxy Queen's Light .15 .40
❑ REDU057 Spellbook of Secrets (UR) 6.00 15.00
❑ REDU057 Spellbook of Secrets (UTR) 5.00 12.00
❑ REDU058 Spellbook of Power .15 .40
❑ REDU059 Spellbook of Life (SR) 2.50 6.00
❑ REDU060 Spellbook of Wisdom (R) .40 1.00
❑ REDU061 Madolche Chateau .15 .40
❑ REDU062 Where Arf Thou? .15 .40
❑ REDU063 Generation Force .15 .40
❑ REDU064 Catapult Zone .15 .40
❑ REDU065 Cold Feet (SP) .15 .40
❑ REDU066 Impenetrable Attack .15 .40
❑ REDU067 Gagagarush .15 .40
❑ REDU068 Heroic Retribution Sword .15 .40
❑ REDU069 Stonehenge Methods .15 .40
❑ REDU070 Madolche Lesson .15 .40
❑ REDU071 Madolche Waltz .15 .40
❑ REDU072 Madolche Tea Break (R) .40 1.00
❑ REDU073 Xyz Soul .15 .40
❑ REDU074 Compulsory Escape Device .15 .40
❑ REDU075 Turnabout .15 .40
❑ REDU076 Void Trap Hole (SR) 1.00 2.50
❑ REDU077 Three of a Kind .15 .40
❑ REDU078 Soul Drain (R) .50 1.25
❑ REDU079 Rebound (SR) .30 .75
❑ REDU080 Lucky Punch (SP) .15 .40
❑ REDU081 Prophecy Destroyer (UTR) 2.00 5.00
❑ REDU081 Prophecy Destroyer (UR) 2.50 6.00
❑ REDU082 Lightray Madoor .15 .40
❑ REDU083 Blue Dragon Ninja (SR) .60 1.50
❑ REDU084 Imairuka (R) .25 .60
❑ REDU085 Revival Golem (R) .30 .75
❑ REDU086 Noble Arms - Gallatin .15 .40
❑ REDU087 Spellbook Library of the Crescent (R).30 .75
❑ REDU088 Advance Zone (SCR) 3.00 8.00
❑ REDU089 Ninjitsu Art of Shadow Sealing .15 .40
❑ REDU090 Chewbone .15 .40
❑ REDU091 Eco, Mystical Spirit of the Forest (R) .25 .60
❑ REDU092 Number 6: Chronomaly Atlandis (SCR)6.00 15.00
❑ REDU093 Miracle Contact (SCR) 5.00 12.00
❑ REDU094 Advanced Dark (SCR) 3.00 8.00
❑ REDU095 Pahunder (R) .25 .60
❑ REDU096 Mahunder (R) .30 .75
❑ REDU097 Sishunder (R) .25 .60
❑ REDU098 Number 91 Thunder Spark Dragon (UR) 4.00 10.00
❑ REDU098 Number 91 Thunder Spark Dragon (UTR) 3.00 8.00
❑ REDU099 Spirit Converter (SCR) 2.50 6.00

2012 Yu-Gi-Oh Return of the Duelist Special Edition

Complete Set 2.00 5.00
One Card Per Special Edition Box
❑ REDUSE1 T.G. Hyper Librarian (SR) 1.50 4.00
❑ REDUSE2 Number 30 Acid Golem of Destruction (SR) 1.00 2.50

2013 Yu-Gi-Oh Battle Pack 2 War of the Giants

Complete Set
Booster Box (36 packs)
Booster Pack (5 cards)
❑ BP02001 Luster Dragon .10 .25
❑ BP02002 Gene-Warped Warwolf .10 .25
❑ BP02003 Frostosaurus (R) .25 .60
❑ BP02004 Alexandrite Dragon .30 .75
❑ BP02005 Magician of Faith (R) .25 .60
❑ BP02006 Maha Vailo .10 .25
❑ BP02007 Cyber Jar (R) .25 .60
❑ BP02008 Goblin Attack Force .10 .25
❑ BP02009 The Fiend Megacyber (R) .25 .60
❑ BP02010 Revival Jam .10 .25
❑ BP02011 Kycoo the Ghost Destroyer .20 .50
❑ BP02012 Bazoo the Soul-Eater .10 .25
❑ BP02013 Gilasaurus .10 .25
❑ BP02014 Zombyra the Dark .10 .25
❑ BP02015 Sinister Serpent .10 .25
❑ BP02016 Airknight Parshath (R) .25 .60
❑ BP02017 Twin-Headed Behemoth .10 .25
❑ BP02018 Injection Fairy Lily (R) .25 .60
❑ BP02019 Helping Robo for Combat .10 .25
❑ BP02020 Little-Winguard .10 .25
❑ BP02021 D.D. Warrior Lady (R) .25 .60
❑ BP02022 Zolga .10 .25
❑ BP02023 Dark Magician of Chaos (R) .60 1.50
❑ BP02024 Hyper Hammerhead .10 .25
❑ BP02025 Mataza the Zapper .10 .25
❑ BP02026 Guardian Angel Joan (R) .25 .60
❑ BP02027 Slate Warrior (R) .25 .60
❑ BP02028 D.D. Assailant (R) .25 .60
❑ BP02029 Ninja Grandmaster Sasuke .10 .25
❑ BP02030 Pitch-Black Warwolf .10 .25
❑ BP02031 Mirage Dragon .10 .25
❑ BP02032 Big Shield Gardna .10 .25
❑ BP02033 Toon Gemini Elf .10 .25
❑ BP02034 Chiron the Mage .10 .25
❑ BP02035 Ancient Gear Golem (R) .25 .60
❑ BP02036 Gyroid .10 .25
❑ BP02037 Steamroid .10 .25
❑ BP02038 Drillroid .10 .25
❑ BP02039 Cyber Dragon .40 1.00
❑ BP02040 Goblin Elite Attack Force .10 .25
❑ BP02041 Exarion Universe .10 .25
❑ BP02042 Mythical Beast Cerberus .10 .25
❑ BP02043 Treeborn Frog .20 .50
❑ BP02044 Submarineroid .10 .25
❑ BP02045 Ultimate Tyranno (R) .25 .60
❑ BP02046 Super Conductor Tyranno (R) .25 .60
❑ BP02047 Brain Crusher (R) .25 .60
❑ BP02048 Card Trooper .10 .25
❑ BP02049 Blockman .10 .25
❑ BP02050 Spell Striker .10 .25
❑ BP02051 Winged Rhynos .10 .25
❑ BP02052 Necro Gardna .10 .25
❑ BP02053 Herald of Creation .10 .25
❑ BP02054 Evil HERO Malicious Edge (R) .25 .60
❑ BP02055 Truckroid (R) .25 .60
❑ BP02056 Ancient Gear Knight .10 .25
❑ BP02057 Dragon Ice .10 .25
❑ BP02058 Copycat .10 .25
❑ BP02059 Cyber Valley (R) .25 .60
❑ BP02060 Darklord Zerato (R) .25 .60
❑ BP02061 Belial - Marquis of Darkness (R) .25 .60
❑ BP02062 Doomcaliber Knight .20 .50
❑ BP02063 Exodius the Ultimate Forbidden Lord .20 .50
❑ BP02064 Dark Valkyria (R) .25 .60
❑ BP02065 Phantom Dragon (R) .25 .60
❑ BP02066 Shield Warrior .10 .25
❑ BP02067 Dark Resonator .10 .25
❑ BP02068 Krebons (R) .25 .60
❑ BP02069 The Tricky .10 .25
❑ BP02070 Splendid Venus (R) .25 .60
❑ BP02071 Plaguespreader Zombie 1.00 2.50
❑ BP02072 Machine Lord Ür .10 .25
❑ BP02073 Mosaic Manticore (R) .25 .60
❑ BP02074 Botanical Lion .10 .25
❑ BP02075 Blizzard Dragon .20 .50
❑ BP02076 Des Mosquito .10 .25
❑ BP02077 Dandylion .20 .50
❑ BP02078 Fortress Warrior .10 .25
❑ BP02079 Twin-Sword Marauder .10 .25
❑ BP02080 Beast King Barbaros (R) .25 .60
❑ BP02081 Hedge Guard .10 .25
❑ BP02082 Card Guard .10 .25
❑ BP02083 White Night Dragon (R) .25 .60
❑ BP02084 Beast Machine King Barbaros Ür (R).25 .60
❑ BP02085 Evocator Chevalier .10 .25
❑ BP02086 Battle Fader .30 .75
❑ BP02087 Oracle of the Sun .10 .25
❑ BP02088 Samurai of the Ice Barrier .10 .25
❑ BP02089 Jurrac Titano (R) .25 .60
❑ BP02090 Darklord Desire (R) .25 .60
❑ BP02091 Power Giant .10 .25
❑ BP02092 Anarchist Monk Ranshin .10 .25
❑ BP02093 Ape Fighter .10 .25
❑ BP02094 Tanngrisnir of the Nordic Beasts .10 .25
❑ BP02095 Chaos Hunter (R) .60 1.50
❑ BP02096 Axe Dragonute .10 .25
❑ BP02097 Vylon Soldier .10 .25
❑ BP02098 Blackwing - Zephyros the Elite .75 2.00
❑ BP02099 Zubaba Knight .10 .25
❑ BP02100 Gogogo Golem .10 .25
❑ BP02101 Needle Sunfish .10 .25
❑ BP02102 Shocktopus .10 .25
❑ BP02103 Photon Thrasher .60 1.50
❑ BP02104 Interplanetarypurplythorny Dragon .10 .25
❑ BP02105 Tour Bus From the Underworld .50 1.25
❑ BP02106 Vylon Tetra .10 .25
❑ BP02107 Vylon Stella .10 .25
❑ BP02108 Vylon Prism .10 .25
❑ BP02109 Photon Wyvern (R) .25 .60
❑ BP02110 Tasuke Knight .10 .25
❑ BP02111 Gagaga Gardna .10 .25
❑ BP02112 Cardcar D (R) 2.00 5.00
❑ BP02113 Flame Tiger .10 .25
❑ BP02114 Tardy Orc .10 .25
❑ BP02115 Bull Blader (R) .25 .60
❑ BP02116 Solar Wind Jammer .10 .25
❑ BP02117 Mermail Abyssmegalo (R) 5.00 12.00
❑ BP02118 Dododo Bot .10 .25
❑ BP02119 Bacon Saver .10 .25
❑ BP02120 Amarylease .10 .25
❑ BP02121 Hyper-Ancient Shark Megalodon (R) .25 .60
❑ BP02122 Pyrotech Mech - Shiryu (R) .25 .60
❑ BP02123 Aye-Iron .10 .25
❑ BP02124 Mecha Phantom Beast Hamstrat .10 .25
❑ BP02128 Monster Reborn (R) 1.00 2.50
❑ BP02129 Pot of Greed (R) .25 .60
❑ BP02130 Shield & Sword .10 .25
❑ BP02131 Axe of Despair .10 .25
❑ BP02132 Malevolent Nuzzler .10 .25
❑ BP02133 Rush Recklessly .10 .25
❑ BP02134 Horn of the Unicorn .10 .25
❑ BP02135 Premature Burial (R) .25 .60
❑ BP02136 Scapegoat .10 .25
❑ BP02137 Graceful Charity (R) .25 .60
❑ BP02138 Book of Moon .10 .25
❑ BP02139 Reasoning .10 .25
❑ BP02140 Autonomous Action Unit .10 .25
❑ BP02141 Big Bang Shot .10 .25
❑ BP02142 Riryoku .10 .25
❑ BP02143 Gravity Axe - Grarl .10 .25
❑ BP02144 Enemy Controller .10 .25
❑ BP02145 Earthquake .10 .25
❑ BP02146 Shrink .10 .25
❑ BP02147 Swords of Concealing Light .30 .75
❑ BP02148 Nightmare's Steelcage .10 .25
❑ BP02149 Mausoleum of the Emperor .10 .25
❑ BP02150 Card Trader (R) .25 .60
❑ BP02151 Fiend's Sanctuary .10 .25
❑ BP02152 Union Attack .10 .25
❑ BP02153 Fighting Spirit .10 .25
❑ BP02154 Star Blast .10 .25
❑ BP02155 Forbidden Chalice .40 1.00
❑ BP02156 Reptilianne Rage .10 .25
❑ BP02157 Rocket Pilder .10 .25
❑ BP02158 Half Shut .10 .25
❑ BP02159 Cursed Armaments .10 .25
❑ BP02160 Pot of Duality (R) 1.50 4.00
❑ BP02161 Axe of Fools .10 .25
❑ BP02162 Forbidden Lance 2.50 6.00
❑ BP02163 Blustering Winds .10 .25
❑ BP02164 Ego Boost .10 .25
❑ BP02165 Shard of Greed (R) .25 .60
❑ BP02166 Full-Force Strike (R) .25 .60
❑ BP02167 Photon Sanctuary .40 1.00
❑ BP02168 Forbidden Dress 1.25 3.00
❑ BP02169 Reverse Trap .10 .25
❑ BP02170 Waboku .20 .50
❑ BP02171 Call of the Haunted (R) .25 .60
❑ BP02172 Mirror Wall .10 .25
❑ BP02173 Metalmorph .10 .25
❑ BP02174 Mask of Weakness .10 .25
❑ BP02175 Reckless Greed (R) .25 .60
❑ BP02176 Rope of Life .10 .25
❑ BP02177 Windstorm of Etaqua .10 .25
❑ BP02178 Zero Gravity .10 .25
❑ BP02179 A Hero Emerges .10 .25
❑ BP02180 Embodiment of Apophis .10 .25
❑ BP02181 Draining Shield .10 .25
❑ BP02182 Curse of Anubis .10 .25
❑ BP02183 Labyrinth of Nightmare .10 .25
❑ BP02184 Threatening Roar .40 1.00
❑ BP02185 Rising Energy .10 .25
❑ BP02186 Magical Arm Shield .10 .25
❑ BP02187 Shattered Axe .10 .25
❑ BP02188 Stronghold the Moving Fortress .10 .25
❑ BP02189 Strike Slash .10 .25
❑ BP02190 No Entry!! .10 .25
❑ BP02191 Cloning .10 .25
❑ BP02192 Sinister Seeds .10 .25
❑ BP02193 Metal Reflect Slime .20 .50
❑ BP02194 Zoma the Spirit .10 .25
❑ BP02195 Miniaturize .10 .25
❑ BP02196 Spacegate .10 .25
❑ BP02197 Overworked .20 .50
❑ BP02198 Kunai with Chain .10 .25
❑ BP02199 Prideful Roar .10 .25
❑ BP02200 Time Machine .10 .25
❑ BP02201 Half or Nothing .10 .25
❑ BP02202 Miracle Locus .10 .25
❑ BP02203 Skill Successor .10 .25
❑ BP02204 Power Frame .10 .25
❑ BP02205 Damage Gate .10 .25
❑ BP02206 Miracle's Wake .10 .25
❑ BP02207 Half Counter .10 .25
❑ BP02208 The Golden Apples (R) .40 1.00
❑ BP02209 Tiki Curse .10 .25
❑ BP02210 Tiki Soul .10 .25
❑ BP02211 Impenetrable Attack .10 .25
❑ BP02212 Memory of an Adversary (R) .25 .60
❑ BP02213 Dimension Gate .10 .25
❑ BP02214 Spikeshield with Chain (R) .25 .60
❑ BP02215 Breakthrough Skill 4.00 10.00

2013 Yu-Gi-Oh Battle Pack 2 War of the Giants Mosaic Rare

*Mosaic Rare: .6X to 1.5X Basic Cards
One Mosaic Rare Per Pack
❑ BP02125 Obelisk the Tormentor
❑ BP02126 The Winged Dragon of Ra
❑ BP02127 Slifer the Sky Dragon

2013 Yu-Gi-Oh Cosmo Blazer

Complete Set 350.00 500.00
Booster Box (24 Packs) 50.00 80.00
Booster Pack (9 Cards) 3.00 4.50
❑ CBLZ000 Noble Arms - Caliburn (SR) .75 2.00
❑ CBLZ001 Dododo Bot .15 .40
❑ CBLZ002 Gogogo Ghost .15 .40
❑ CBLZ003 Bacon Saver .15 .40
❑ CBLZ004 Amarylease .15 .40
❑ CBLZ005 ZW - Lightning Blade (R) .25 .60
❑ CBLZ006 ZW - Tornado Bringer (R) .25 .60
❑ CBLZ007 ZW - Ultimate Shield .15 .40
❑ CBLZ008 Gagaga Clerk (SR) 1.50 4.00
❑ CBLZ009 Spear Shark .15 .40
❑ CBLZ010 Double Shark .15 .40
❑ CBLZ011 Xyz Remora .15 .40
❑ CBLZ012 Hyper-Ancient Shark Megalodon (R) .25 .60
❑ CBLZ013 Heraldic Beast Basilisk .15 .40
❑ CBLZ014 Heraldic Beast Eale .15 .40
❑ CBLZ015 Heraldic Beast Twin-Headed Eagle (R).25 .60
❑ CBLZ016 Heraldic Beast Unicorn .15 .40
❑ CBLZ017 Heraldic Beast Leo (R) .25 .60
❑ CBLZ018 Garbage Ogre .15 .40
❑ CBLZ019 Garbage Lord .15 .40
❑ CBLZ020 Orbital 7 (SR) .75 2.00
❑ CBLZ021 Brotherhood of the Fire Fist - Hawk .15 .40
❑ CBLZ022 Brotherhood of the Fire Fist - Raven .15 .40
❑ CBLZ023 Brotherhood of the Fire Fist - Gorilla (R).25 .60
❑ CBLZ024 Brotherhood of the Fire Fist Bear (UTR) 30.00 60.00
❑ CBLZ024 Brotherhood of the Fire Fist - Bear (UR)30.00 60.00
❑ CBLZ025 Brotherhood of the Fire Fist Dragon (SR) 5.00 12.00
❑ CBLZ026 Brotherhood of the Fire Fist Snake (SR) 2.00 5.00
❑ CBLZ027 Brotherhood of the Fire Fist Swallow (SR) 1.00 2.50
❑ CBLZ028 Hazy Flame Cerbereus .15 .40
❑ CBLZ029 Hazy Flame Griffin .15 .40
❑ CBLZ030 Hazy Flame Sphynx .15 .40
❑ CBLZ031 Hazy Flame Peryton (R) .25 .60
❑ CBLZ032 Mermail Abyssdine (SR) 2.00 5.00
❑ CBLZ033 Mermail Abyssnose .15 .40
❑ CBLZ034 Mermail Abyssleed (SCR) 10.00 25.00
❑ CBLZ035 Fool of Prophecy (SR) 1.50 4.00
❑ CBLZ036 Reaper of Prophecy (SR) 2.50 6.00
❑ CBLZ037 Brushfire Knight (R) .25 .60
❑ CBLZ038 Inari Fire .15 .40
❑ CBLZ039 Valkyrian Knight (SR) .75 2.00
❑ CBLZ040 Pyrorex the Elemental Lord (SCR) 8.00 20.00
❑ CBLZ041 Pyrotech Mech - Shiryu .15 .40
❑ CBLZ042 Leotaur .15 .40
❑ CBLZ043 Star Drawing (SP) .40 1.00
❑ CBLZ044 Red Duston (SP) .15 .40
❑ CBLZ045 Number 92: Heart-eartH Dragon (UR)4.00 10.00
❑ CBLZ045 Number 92: Heart-eartH Dragon (GR)5.00 12.00
❑ CBLZ045 Number 92: Heart-eartH Dragon (UTR)6.00 15.00
❑ CBLZ046 Number 53: Heart-eartH (UTR) 6.00 15.00
❑ CBLZ046 Number 53: Heart-eartH (UR) 3.00 8.00
❑ CBLZ047 ZW - Leo Arms (UTR) 2.00 5.00
❑ CBLZ047 ZW - Leo Arms (UR) 2.00 5.00
❑ CBLZ048 Brotherhood of the Fire Fist Tiger King (UTR) 15.00 30.00
❑ CBLZ048 Brotherhood of the Fire Fist Tiger King (UR) 10.00 25.00
❑ CBLZ049 Hazy Flame Basiltrice (R) .25 .60
❑ CBLZ050 Mermail Abysstrite (SR) 1.50 4.00
❑ CBLZ051 Diamond Dire Wolf (SCR) 25.00 50.00
❑ CBLZ052 Lightning Chidori (UTR) 8.00 20.00
❑ CBLZ052 Lightning Chidori (UR) 10.00 25.00
❑ CBLZ053 Slacker Magician (R) .25 .60
❑ CBLZ054 Zerozerock .15 .40
❑ CBLZ055 Gagagadraw (SR) .75 2.00
❑ CBLZ056 Xyz Double Back .15 .40
❑ CBLZ057 Heraldry Reborn (R) .25 .60
❑ CBLZ058 Fire Formation - Tensu .15 .40
❑ CBLZ059 Fire Formation - Tenki .75 2.00
❑ CBLZ060 Hazy Pillar .15 .40
❑ CBLZ061 Abyss-scale of Cetus .15 .40
❑ CBLZ062 Spellbook of the Master (SCR) 25.00 50.00
❑ CBLZ063 The Big Cattle Drive .15 .40
❑ CBLZ064 March of the Monarchs .15 .40
❑ CBLZ065 Quick Booster (UTR) 1.50 4.00
❑ CBLZ065 Quick Booster (UR) 1.00 2.50
❑ CBLZ066 After the Storm .15 .40
❑ CBLZ067 Goblin Circus (SP) .15 .40
❑ CBLZ068 Dimension Gate .15 .40
❑ CBLZ069 Xyz Dimension Splash .15 .40

YU-GI-OH!

❑ CBLZ070 Heraldry Change .15 .40
❑ CBLZ071 Fire Formation - Tensen .15 .40
❑ CBLZ072 Fire Formation - Tenken .15 .40
❑ CBLZ073 Ultimate Fire Formation - Seito (R) .25 .60
❑ CBLZ074 Hazy Glory .15 .40
❑ CBLZ075 Abyss-scorn .15 .40
❑ CBLZ076 Spikeshield with Chain .15 .40
❑ CBLZ077 Xyz Tribalrivals .15 .40
❑ CBLZ078 Breakthrough Skill (UR) 8.00 20.00
❑ CBLZ078 Breakthrough Skill (UTR) 10.00 25.00
❑ CBLZ079 Jurrac Impact .15 .40
❑ CBLZ080 Dice-nied (SP) .15 .40
❑ CBLZ081 Noble Knight Medraut (SCR) 12.00 30.00
❑ CBLZ082 Hazy Flame Mantikor (R) .25 .60
❑ CBLZ083 Mermail Abyssteus (UTR) 10.00 25.00
❑ CBLZ083 Mermail Abyssteus (UR) 8.00 20.00
❑ CBLZ084 Bonfire Colossus (SCR) 4.00 10.00
❑ CBLZ085 Mystical Fairy Elfuria (SCR) 6.00 15.00
❑ CBLZ086 Artorigus King of the Noble Knights (UR) 4.00 10.00
❑ CBLZ086 Artorigus King of the Noble Knights (UTR) 5.00 12.00
❑ CBLZ087 Infernal Flame Vixen (R) .25 .60
❑ CBLZ088 Spell Wall .15 .40
❑ CBLZ089 Kickfire (SCR) 2.00 5.00
❑ CBLZ090 Crimson Sunbird .15 .40
❑ CBLZ091 Ignition Beast Volcannon .15 .40
❑ CBLZ092 Noble Knight Joan (R) .25 .60
❑ CBLZ093 Crimson Blader (R) .25 .60
❑ CBLZ094 Infernity Archer (R) .25 .60
❑ CBLZ095 Blackwing Gladius the Midnight Sun (R) .25 .60
❑ CBLZ096 Blackwing Damascus the Polar Night (R) .25 .60
❑ CBLZ097 Brotherhood of the Fire Fist Horse Prince (SR) 2.50 6.00
❑ CBLZ098 Brotherhood of the Fire Fist - Spirit (R) .25 .60
❑ CBLZ099 Brotherhood of the Fire Fist Lion Emperor (SR) 3.00 8.00

2013 Yu-Gi-Oh Cosmo Blazer Special Edition

One Card Per Special Edition Box

❑ CBLZSE1 Wind-Up Shark (SR) .75 2.00
❑ CBLZSE2 Blade Armor Ninja (SR) 1.50 4.00

2013 Yu-Gi-Oh Hidden Arsenal 7

Complete Set 60.00 120.00
Booster Box (24 Packs) 60.00 90.00
Booster Pack (5 Cards) 3.00 4.50

❑ HA07001 Gem-Knight Sardonyx (SR) .40 1.00
❑ HA07002 Laval Phlogis (SR) .15 .40
❑ HA07003 Gishki Avance (SR) .15 .40
❑ HA07004 Gusto Griffin (SR) .15 .40
❑ HA07005 Constellar Sheratan (SR) .30 .75
❑ HA07006 Constellar Aldebaran (SR) .15 .40
❑ HA07007 Constellar Algiedi (SR) .40 1.00
❑ HA07008 Constellar Pollux (SR) 1.25 3.00
❑ HA07009 Constellar Zubeneschamali (SR) .40 1.00
❑ HA07010 Constellar Virgo (SR) .15 .40
❑ HA07011 Evilswarm Heliotrope (SR) 1.50 4.00
❑ HA07012 Evilswarm Zahak (SR) .15 .40
❑ HA07013 Evilswarm Ketos (SR) .15 .40
❑ HA07014 Evilswarm O'lantern (SR) .15 .40
❑ HA07015 Evilswarm Mandragora (SR) 1.25 3.00
❑ HA07016 Evilswarm Hraesvelg (SR) .15 .40
❑ HA07017 Evigishki Levianima (SCR) .30 .75
❑ HA07018 Gem-Knight Zirconia (SR) .40 1.00
❑ HA07019 Lavalval Chain (SCR) 12.00 25.00
❑ HA07020 Daigusto Emeral (SCR) 12.00 25.00
❑ HA07021 Constellar Hyades (SCR) .40 1.00
❑ HA07022 Constellar Pleiades (SCR) 2.50 6.00
❑ HA07023 Evilswarm Nightmare (SCR) .40 1.00
❑ HA07024 Evilswarm Bahamut (SCR) 3.00 8.00
❑ HA07025 Molten Conduction Field (SCR) .75 2.00
❑ HA07026 Gishki Photomirror (SR) .15 .40
❑ HA07027 Constellar Star Chart (SCR) .40 1.00
❑ HA07028 Fragment Fusion (SR) .15 .40
❑ HA07029 Dust Storm of Gusto (SR) .15 .40
❑ HA07030 Infestation Infection (SCR) .40 1.00
❑ HA07031 D.D. Esper Star Sparrow (SCR) .30 .75
❑ HA07032 Beast-Warrior Puma (SR) .15 .40
❑ HA07033 Phoenix Beast Gairuda (SR) .15 .40
❑ HA07034 Ironhammer the Giant (SR) .15 .40
❑ HA07035 D.D. Jet Iron (SR) .15 .40
❑ HA07036 Aye-Iron (SR) .15 .40
❑ HA07037 Tin Goldfish (SR) 2.00 5.00
❑ HA07038 Gearspring Spirit (SR) .15 .40
❑ HA07039 Gem-Knight Lazuli (SR) .40 1.00
❑ HA07040 Gishki Natalia (SR) .15 .40
❑ HA07041 Constellar Siat (SR) .30 .75
❑ HA07042 Constellar Rasalhague (SR) .15 .40
❑ HA07043 Constellar Leonis (SR) .30 .75
❑ HA07044 Constellar Acubens (SR) .15 .40
❑ HA07045 Constellar Kaus (SCR) 1.50 4.00
❑ HA07046 Constellar Alrescha (SR) .15 .40
❑ HA07047 Constellar Antares (SR) .15 .40
❑ HA07048 Evilswarm Castor (SR) 1.25 3.00
❑ HA07049 Evilswarm Obliviwisp (SR) .15 .40
❑ HA07050 Evilswarm Azzathoth (SR) .15 .40
❑ HA07051 Evilswarm Thunderbird (SCR) 3.00 8.00
❑ HA07052 Evilswarm Salamandra (SR) .15 .40
❑ HA07053 Evilswarm Golem (SR) .15 .40
❑ HA07054 Evilswarm Coppelia (SR) .15 .40
❑ HA07055 Sophia, Goddess of Rebirth (SCR) .30 .75
❑ HA07056 Gishki Psychelone (SR) .15 .40
❑ HA07057 Gishki Zielgigas (SCR) .30 .75
❑ HA07058 Gem-Knight Seraphinite (SR) .30 .75
❑ HA07059 Gem-Knight Master Diamond (SCR) .40 1.00
❑ HA07060 Tin Archduke (SCR) .30 .75
❑ HA07061 Constellar Praesepe (SCR) .60 1.50
❑ HA07062 Constellar Ptolemy M7 (SCR) 10.00 20.00
❑ HA07063 Evilswarm Thanatos (SCR) .40 1.00
❑ HA07064 Evilswarm Ophion (SCR) 12.00 25.00
❑ HA07065 Evilswarm Ouroboros (SCR) 10.00 20.00
❑ HA07066 Iron Call (SCR) .60 1.50
❑ HA07067 Constellar Star Cradle (SR) .15 .40
❑ HA07068 Infestation Pandemic (SCR) 2.00 5.00
❑ HA07069 Constellar Meteor (SR) .15 .40
❑ HA07070 Infestation Terminus (SR) .15 .40

2013 Yu-Gi-Oh Judgement of the Light

Booster Box (24 Packs) 50.00 70.00
Booster Pack (9 Cards) 2.50 4.00

❑ JOTL000 Galaxy Serpent (SR) .60 1.50

❑ JOTL001 DZW - Chimera Clad (R) .25 .60
❑ JOTL002 V Salamander (R) .25 .60
❑ JOTL003 Interceptomato .15 .40
❑ JOTL004 Spell Recycler .15 .40
❑ JOTL005 Xyz Agent .15 .40
❑ JOTL006 Super Defense Robot Lio .15 .40
❑ JOTL007 Super Defense Robot Elephan .15 .40
❑ JOTL008 Super Defense Robot Monki .15 .40
❑ JOTL009 Star Seraph Scout .15 .40
❑ JOTL010 Star Seraph Sage .15 .40
❑ JOTL011 Star Seraph Sword .15 .40
❑ JOTL012 Umbral Horror Ghoul .15 .40
❑ JOTL013 Umbral Horror Unform .15 .40
❑ JOTL014 Umbral Horror Will o' the Wisp .15 .40
❑ JOTL015 Schwarzschild Limit Dragon .15 .40
❑ JOTL016 Bujin Yamato (UR) 15.00 40.00
❑ JOTL017 Bujingi Quilin (SR) 2.00 5.00
❑ JOTL018 Bujingi Turtle .15 .40
❑ JOTL019 Bujingi Wolf .15 .40
❑ JOTL020 Bujingi Crane (R) .25 .60
❑ JOTL021 Bujingi Ophidian .15 .40
❑ JOTL022 Mecha Phantom Beast Warbluran (R) .25 .60
❑ JOTL023 Mecha Phantom Beast Blue Impala (UR) 2.00 5.00
❑ JOTL024 Mecha Phantom Beast Coltwing .15 .40
❑ JOTL025 Mecha Phantom Beast Harrliard .15 .40
❑ JOTL026 Brotherhood of the Fire Fist - Boar (R) .25 .60
❑ JOTL027 Brotherhood of the Fire Fist - Caribou .15 .40
❑ JOTL028 World of Prophecy (SCR) 10.00 25.00
❑ JOTL029 Archfiend Heiress (R) .25 .60
❑ JOTL030 Archfiend Cavalry (R) .25 .60
❑ JOTL031 Archfiend Emperor the First Lord of Horror (R) .25 .60
❑ JOTL032 Traptrix Atrax (R) .25 .60
❑ JOTL033 Traptrix Myrmeleo (R) .25 .60
❑ JOTL034 Traptrix Nepenthes .15 .40
❑ JOTL035 The Calibrator .15 .40
❑ JOTL036 Talaya Princess of Cherry Blossoms (SR) .40 1.00
❑ JOTL037 Cheepcheepcheep .15 .40
❑ JOTL038 Masked Chameleon (UR) 4.00 10.00
❑ JOTL039 Flying C (SP) .60 1.50
❑ JOTL040 Yellow Duston (SP) .15 .40
❑ JOTL041 Mecha Phantom Beast Concoruda (SR) .75 2.00
❑ JOTL042 Brotherhood of the Fire Fist - Kirin (R) .25 .60
❑ JOTL043 Mist Bird Clausolas (SR) .60 1.50
❑ JOTL044 Underworld Fighter Balmung (R) .40 1.00
❑ JOTL045 Armades, Keeper of Boundaries (SCR) 10.00 25.00
❑ JOTL046 HTS Psyhemuth (SR) .75 2.00
❑ JOTL047 Star Eater (SCR) 8.00 20.00
❑ JOTL047 Star Eater (GR) 12.00 30.00
❑ JOTL047 Star Eater (UTR) 10.00 25.00
❑ JOTL048 Number C39: Utopia Ray Victory (UTR) 2.50 6.00
❑ JOTL048 Number C39: Utopia Ray Victory (SR) 1.50 4.00
❑ JOTL049 Shark Caesar .15 .40
❑ JOTL050 Starliege Lord Galaxion (SR) .75 2.00
❑ JOTL051 Googly-Eyes Drum Dragon .15 .40
❑ JOTL052 Ice Princess Zereort .15 .40
❑ JOTL053 Number 102: Star Seraph Sentry (R) .25 .60
❑ JOTL054 Number 66: Master Key Beetle (SR) 6.00 15.00
❑ JOTL055 Number 104: Masquerade (R) .25 .60
❑ JOTL056 Number C104 Umbral Horror Masquerade (UTR) .75 2.00
❑ JOTL056 Number C104 Umbral Horror Masquerade (SR) 1.00 2.50
❑ JOTL057 Bujintei Susanowo (UTR) 4.00 10.00
❑ JOTL057 Bujintei Susanowo (UR) 3.00 8.00
❑ JOTL058 Herald of Pure Light (SR) .75 2.00
❑ JOTL059 Rank-Up-Magic Numeron Force (UR) 1.25 3.00
❑ JOTL059 Rank-Up-Magic Numeron Force (UTR) 1.50 4.00
❑ JOTL060 Xyz Reception .15 .40
❑ JOTL061 Sargasso the D.D. Battlefield .15 .40
❑ JOTL062 Sargasso Lighthouse .15 .40
❑ JOTL063 Bujincarnation (R) .25 .60
❑ JOTL064 Vertical Landing .15 .40
❑ JOTL065 Fire Formation - Yoko (SR) .60 1.50
❑ JOTL066 Archfiend Palabyrinth (R) .25 .60
❑ JOTL067 Transmodify (SCR) 15.00 40.00
❑ JOTL068 Black and White Wave .15 .40
❑ JOTL069 Single Purchase (SP) .15 .40
❑ JOTL070 Reverse Glasses .15 .40
❑ JOTL071 Xyz Revenge Shuffle .15 .40
❑ JOTL072 Corrupted Keys (R) .25 .60
❑ JOTL073 Vain Betrayer .15 .40
❑ JOTL074 Bujin Regalia - The Sword .15 .40
❑ JOTL075 Bujinfidel .15 .40
❑ JOTL076 Sonic Boom .15 .40
❑ JOTL077 Traptrix Trap Hole Nightmare (SR) .75 2.00
❑ JOTL078 Xyz Reversal .15 .40
❑ JOTL079 Shapesister (UR) .75 2.00
❑ JOTL080 Armageddon Designator (SP) .15 .40
❑ JOTL081 Bujingi Warg .15 .40
❑ JOTL082 Mecha Phantom Beast Aerosguin (UR) 1.00 2.50
❑ JOTL083 Cockadoodledoo (UR) 1.50 4.00
❑ JOTL084 Noble Knight Drystan (SCR) 10.00 25.00
❑ JOTL085 Tour Bus To Forbidden Realms (R) .25 .60
❑ JOTL086 Confronting the C (R) .25 .60
❑ JOTL087 Angel of Zera (SCR) 6.00 15.00
❑ JOTL088 Xyz Encore (UR) 3.00 8.00
❑ JOTL089 Moon Dance Ritual (R) .25 .60
❑ JOTL090 The Atmosphere .15 .40
❑ JOTL091 Junk Blader .15 .40
❑ JOTL092 Coach Captain Bearman (UR) .40 1.00
❑ JOTL093 Coach Soldier Wolfbark (SCR) 25.00 50.00
❑ JOTL094 Brotherhood of the Fire Fist Rooster (SCR) 30.00 60.00
❑ JOTL095 Fire King Avatar Yaksha (SR) 2.50 6.00
❑ JOTL096 Fishborg Archer .15 .40
❑ JOTL097 Fencing Fire Ferret .15 .40
❑ JOTL098 Kujakujaku .15 .40
❑ JOTL099 Madolche Chickolates .15 .40

2013 Yu-Gi-Oh Lord of the Tachyon Galaxy

Booster Box (24 Packs) 75.00 100.00
Booster Pack (9 Cards) 4.00 5.00

❑ LTGY000 Mecha Phantom Beast Turtletracer (SR) .30 .75
❑ LTGY001 Bachibachibachi .15 .40
❑ LTGY002 Gogogo Gigas (R) .25 .60
❑ LTGY003 Mimimic .15 .40
❑ LTGY004 Doledotengu .15 .40
❑ LTGY005 Tatakawa Knight .15 .40
❑ LTGY006 Little Fairy .15 .40
❑ LTGY007 Sharkraken .15 .40
❑ LTGY008 Big Whale (R) .25 .60
❑ LTGY009 Starfish .15 .40
❑ LTGY010 Panther Shark .15 .40
❑ LTGY011 Eagle Shark .15 .40
❑ LTGY012 Blizzard Falcon .15 .40
❑ LTGY013 Aurora Wing .15 .40
❑ LTGY014 Radius, the Half-Moon Dragon .15 .40
❑ LTGY015 Parsec, the Interstellar Dragon .15 .40
❑ LTGY016 Battlin' Boxer Headgeared .15 .40
❑ LTGY017 Battlin' Boxer Glassjaw .15 .40
❑ LTGY018 Battlin' Boxer Sparrer .15 .40
❑ LTGY019 Battlin' Boxer Switchitter .15 .40
❑ LTGY020 Battlin' Boxer Counterpunch .15 .40
❑ LTGY021 Mecha Phantom Beast Megaraptor (SR) 1.25 3.00
❑ LTGY022 Mecha Phantom Beast Tetherwolf (R) .25 .60
❑ LTGY023 Mecha Phantom Beast Blackfalcon .15 .40
❑ LTGY024 Mecha Phantom Beast Stealthray .15 .40
❑ LTGY025 Mecha Phantom Beast Hamstrat (UR) .75 2.00
❑ LTGY025 Mecha Phantom Beast Hamstrat (UTR) 1.25 3.00
❑ LTGY026 Brotherhood of the Fire Fist - Wolf .15 .40
❑ LTGY027 Brotherhood of the Fire Fist - Leopard .15 .40
❑ LTGY028 Brotherhood of the Fire Fist - Rhino (R) .25 .60
❑ LTGY029 Brotherhood of the Fire Fist - Buffalo (R) .25 .60
❑ LTGY030 Mermail Abyssocea .15 .40
❑ LTGY031 Wheel of Prophecy (R) .25 .60
❑ LTGY032 Madolche Hootcake (SR) 2.00 5.00
❑ LTGY033 Legendary Atlantean Tridon .15 .40
❑ LTGY034 Fire King Avatar Garunix .15 .40
❑ LTGY035 Harpie Channeler (UR) 2.00 5.00
❑ LTGY035 Harpie Channeler (UTR) 2.50 6.00
❑ LTGY036 Altitude Knight (R) .25 .60
❑ LTGY037 Windrose the Elemental Lord (SCR) 2.00 5.00
❑ LTGY038 Redox, Dragon Ruler of Boulders (R) 3.00 8.00
❑ LTGY039 Tidal, Dragon Ruler of Waterfalls (R) 3.00 8.00
❑ LTGY040 Blaster, Dragon Ruler of Infernos (R) 4.00 10.00
❑ LTGY041 Tempest, Dragon Ruler of Storms (R) 3.00 8.00
❑ LTGY042 Risebell the Star Adjuster (SP) .15 .40
❑ LTGY043 Green Duston (SP) .15 .40
❑ LTGY044 Number 107 Galaxy-Eyes Tachyon Dragon (GR) 4.00 10.00
❑ LTGY044 Number 107 Galaxy-Eyes Tachyon Dragon (UTR) 5.00 12.00
❑ LTGY044 Number 107 Galaxy-Eyes Tachyon Dragon (UR) 5.00 12.00
❑ LTGY045 Gauntlet Launcher (UTR) 1.50 4.00
❑ LTGY045 Gauntlet Launcher (UR) 1.00 2.50
❑ LTGY046 Fairy Cheer Girl (R) .25 .60
❑ LTGY047 CXyz Dark Fairy Cheer Girl (R) .25 .60
❑ LTGY048 Shark Fortress .15 .40
❑ LTGY049 Ice Beast Zerofyne (R) .25 .60
❑ LTGY050 Battlin' Boxer Lead Yoke (R) .25 .60
❑ LTGY051 Number 105 Battlin' Boxer Star Cestus (SR) 1.50 4.00
❑ LTGY052 Number C105 Battlin' Boxer Comet Cestus (UR) 2.50 6.00
❑ LTGY052 Number C105 Battlin' Boxer Comet Cestus (UTR) 3.00 8.00
❑ LTGY053 Mecha Phantom Beast Dracossack (SCR) 75.00 150.00
❑ LTGY054 Brotherhood of the Fire Fist Cardinal (SCR) 4.00 10.00
❑ LTGY055 Harpie's Pet Phantasmal Dragon (R) .25 .60
❑ LTGY056 King of the Feral Imps .15 .40
❑ LTGY057 Gagagawind .15 .40
❑ LTGY058 Magnum Shield .15 .40
❑ LTGY059 Xyz Revenge (R) .25 .60
❑ LTGY060 Rank-Up-Magic Barian's Force (UTR) 2.50 6.00
❑ LTGY060 Rank-Up-Magic Barian's Force (UR) 2.50 6.00
❑ LTGY061 Scramble!! Scramble!! (UTR) .75 2.00
❑ LTGY061 Scramble!! Scramble!! (UR) .60 1.50
❑ LTGY062 Fire Formation - Gyokkou (SR) .75 2.00
❑ LTGY063 Spellbook of Judgment (SCR) 40.00 80.00
❑ LTGY064 Abyss-scale of the Mizuchi .15 .40
❑ LTGY065 Hysteric Sign (SR) 1.00 2.50
❑ LTGY066 Sacred Sword of Seven Stars (SR) 2.00 5.00
❑ LTGY067 Jewels of the Valiant .15 .40
❑ LTGY068 Summon Breaker (SP) .15 .40
❑ LTGY069 Pinpoint Guard (SCR) 5.00 12.00
❑ LTGY070 Memory Loss .15 .40
❑ LTGY071 Torrential Reborn (SCR) 1.25 3.00
❑ LTGY072 Xyz Block .15 .40
❑ LTGY073 Aerial Recharge .15 .40
❑ LTGY074 Do a Barrel Roll (R) .25 .60
❑ LTGY075 Fire Formation - Kaiyo .15 .40
❑ LTGY076 Madolche Nights (SR) .40 1.00
❑ LTGY077 Geargiagear (SR) .30 .75
❑ LTGY078 High Tide on Fire Island .15 .40
❑ LTGY079 Mind Drain .15 .40
❑ LTGY080 Dragoncarnation (SP) .15 .40
❑ LTGY081 Noble Knight Gwalchavad (UR) 1.00 2.50
❑ LTGY081 Noble Knight Gwalchavad (UTR) 1.25 3.00
❑ LTGY082 Brotherhood of the Fire Fist Coyote (SCR) 1.25 3.00
❑ LTGY083 Mermail Abyssbalaen (UTR) .60 1.50
❑ LTGY083 Mermail Abyssbalaen (UR) .40 1.00
❑ LTGY084 Trifortressops (R) .25 .60
❑ LTGY085 Ghost Fairy Elfobia (SR) .40 1.00
❑ LTGY086 Totem Bird (SCR) 1.25 3.00
❑ LTGY087 Noble Arms of Destiny (SR) .60 1.50
❑ LTGY088 Spellbook of Miracles .15 .40
❑ LTGY089 Five Brothers Explosion .15 .40
❑ LTGY090 Sonic Warrior .15 .40
❑ LTGY091 Constellar Omega (UR) 2.50 6.00
❑ LTGY091 Constellar Omega (UTR) 3.00 8.00
❑ LTGY092 Number 69: Heraldry Crest (R) .30 .75
❑ LTGY093 Constellar Sombre (SR) 4.00 10.00
❑ LTGY094 Evilswarm Kerykeion (SR) 10.00 25.00
❑ LTGY095 Reactan, Dragon Ruler of Pebbles .15 .40
❑ LTGY096 Stream, Dragon Ruler of Droplets .15 .40
❑ LTGY097 Burner, Dragon Ruler of Sparks .15 .40
❑ LTGY098 Lightning, Dragon Ruler of Drafts .15 .40
❑ LTGY099 Duck Fighter (SR) .30 .75

2013 Yu-Gi-Oh Number Hunters

Complete Set (60) 40.00 80.00
Booster Box (24 packs) 25.00 50.00
Booster Pack (5 cards) 2.00 3.00

❑ NUMH001 Chronomaly Aztec Mask Golem (SR) .20 .50
❑ NUMH002 Chronomaly Cabrera Trebuchet (SR) .20 .50
❑ NUMH003 Chronomaly Mud Golem (SR) .20 .50
❑ NUMH004 Chronomaly Sol Monolith (SR) .20 .50
❑ NUMH005 Gimmick Puppet Egg Head (SR) .20 .50
❑ NUMH006 Gimmick Puppet Gear Changer (SR) .20 .50
❑ NUMH007 Gimmick Puppet Twilight Joker (SR) .20 .50
❑ NUMH008 Gimmick Puppet Scissor Arms (SR) .20 .50
❑ NUMH009 Gimmick Puppet Nightmare (SR) .20 .50
❑ NUMH010 Heroic Challenger Ambush Soldier (SCR) .30 .75
❑ NUMH011 Heroic Challenger - Clasp Sword (SR) .20 .50
❑ NUMH012 Blue Mountain Butterspy (SR) .40 1.00
❑ NUMH013 Box of Friends (SCR) 2.00 5.00
❑ NUMH014 Zombowwow (SR) .20 .50
❑ NUMH015 Gash the Dust Lord (SR) .20 .50
❑ NUMH016 Zubaba Knight (SR) .20 .50
❑ NUMH017 Gogogo Golem (SR) .20 .50
❑ NUMH018 Kagetokage (SR) .50 1.25
❑ NUMH019 Kurivolt (SR) .20 .50
❑ NUMH020 Gogogo Giant (SR) .20 .50
❑ NUMH021 Gagaga Gardna (SR) .20 .50
❑ NUMH022 Photon Cerberus (SR) .20 .50
❑ NUMH023 Photon Lizard (SR) .20 .50
❑ NUMH024 Rocket Arrow Express (SR) .20 .50
❑ NUMH025 Battle Warrior (SR) .20 .50
❑ NUMH026 Number 54: Lion Heart (SCR) .75 2.00
❑ NUMH027 Number 15 Gimmick Puppet Giant Grinder (SCR) 1.25 3.00
❑ NUMH028 Number 44: Sky Pegasus (SCR) .75 2.00
❑ NUMH029 Number 49: Fortune Tune (SCR) 2.00 5.00
❑ NUMH030 Number 57 Tri-Head Dust Dragon (SCR) .50 1.25
❑ NUMH031 Number 63: Shamoji Soldier (SR) .40 1.00
❑ NUMH032 Number 74: Master of Blades (SCR) 6.00 15.00
❑ NUMH033 Number 85: Crazy Box (SR) 2.50 6.00
❑ NUMH034 Number 87: Queen of the Night (SR) .40 1.00
❑ NUMH035 Mechquipped Angineer (SR) .20 .50
❑ NUMH036 CXyz Mechquipped Djinn Angeneral (SR) .20 .50
❑ NUMH037 Coach King Giantrainer (SCR) .75 2.00
❑ NUMH038 CXyz Coach Lord Ultimatrainer (SCR) .40 1.00
❑ NUMH039 Norito the Moral Leader (SCR) 1.25 3.00
❑ NUMH040 CXyz Simon the Great Moral Leader (SCR) .30 .75
❑ NUMH041 Comics Hero King Arthur (SCR) .75 2.00
❑ NUMH042 CXyz Comics Hero Legend Arthur (SCR) .40 1.00
❑ NUMH043 Battlecruiser Dianthus (SR) .40 1.00
❑ NUMH044 CXyz Battleship Cherry Blossom (SCR) .30 .75
❑ NUMH045 Skypalace Gangaridai (SCR) .40 1.00
❑ NUMH046 CXyz Skypalace Babylon (SCR) .30 .75
❑ NUMH047 Photon Alexandra Queen (SCR) .30 .75
❑ NUMH048 Night Papilloperative (SR) .20 .50
❑ NUMH049 Unformed Void (SR) .20 .50
❑ NUMH050 Princess Cologne (SCR) .75 2.00
❑ NUMH051 Baby Tiragon (SR) .20 .50
❑ NUMH052 Chakra (SR) .20 .50
❑ NUMH053 Resurrection of Chakra (SR) .20 .50
❑ NUMH054 Gimmick Puppet Ritual (SR) .20 .50
❑ NUMH055 Stoic Challenge (SR) .20 .50
❑ NUMH056 Overlay Capture (SR) .20 .50
❑ NUMH057 Insect Armor with Laser Cannon (SR) .20 .50
❑ NUMH058 Number Wall (SCR) .40 1.00
❑ NUMH059 Heraldry Record (SR) .20 .50
❑ NUMH060 Butterspy Protection (SR) .20 .50

2013 Yu-Gi-Oh Star Pack 2013

Booster Box (50 Packs) 40.00 70.00
Booster Pack (3 Cards) 1.25 2.00

❑ SP13001 Zubaba Knight .25 .60
❑ SP13002 Gagaga Magician .40 1.00
❑ SP13003 Gogogo Golem .25 .60
❑ SP13004 Achacha Archer .40 1.00
❑ SP13005 Goblindbergh .25 .60
❑ SP13006 Big Jaws .15 .40
❑ SP13007 Skull Kraken .25 .60
❑ SP13008 Galaxy-Eyes Photon Dragon .75 2.00
❑ SP13009 Kagetokage .25 .60
❑ SP13010 Friller Rabca .15 .40
❑ SP13011 Needle Sunfish .15 .40
❑ SP13012 Photon Cerberus .25 .60
❑ SP13013 Kurivolt .25 .60
❑ SP13014 Darklon .15 .40
❑ SP13015 Flame Armor Ninja .15 .40
❑ SP13016 Air Armor Ninja .15 .40
❑ SP13017 Aqua Armor Ninja .15 .40
❑ SP13018 Earth Armor Ninja .15 .40
❑ SP13019 Flelf .15 .40
❑ SP13020 Chewbone .25 .60
❑ SP13021 Number 39: Utopia .25 .60
❑ SP13022 Grenosaurus .25 .60
❑ SP13023 Number 17: Leviathan Dragon .60 1.50
❑ SP13024 Submersible Carrier Aero Shark .40 1.00
❑ SP13025 Number 34: Terror-Byte .15 .40
❑ SP13026 Number 10: Illumiknight .40 1.00
❑ SP13027 Baby Tiragon .15 .40
❑ SP13028 Number 83: Galaxy Queen .25 .60
❑ SP13029 Black Ray Lancer .40 1.00
❑ SP13030 Number 12 Crimson Shadow Armor Ninja .75 2.00
❑ SP13031 Number 96: Dark Mist 1.50 4.00
❑ SP13032 Wonder Wand 2.00 5.00
❑ SP13033 Infected Mail .15 .40
❑ SP13034 Ego Boost .40 1.00
❑ SP13035 Monster Slots .25 .60
❑ SP13036 Heartfelt Appeal .25 .60
❑ SP13037 Icy Crevasse .15 .40
❑ SP13038 Nitwit Outwit .25 .60
❑ SP13039 Faith Bird .25 .60
❑ SP13040 Gilford the Lightning .25 .60
❑ SP13041 Gandora the Dragon of Destruction .60 1.50
❑ SP13042 Metalmorph .25 .60
❑ SP13043 Arcana Force EX - The Dark Ruler 1.25 3.00
❑ SP13044 Arcana Force EX - The Light Ruler .40 1.00
❑ SP13045 Barbaroid, the Ultimate Battle Machine .40 1.00
❑ SP13046 Elemental HERO Escuridao 2.50 6.00
❑ SP13047 Meklord Emperor Wisel .40 1.00
❑ SP13048 Seven Swords Warrior .60 1.50
❑ SP13049 Catapult Warrior .40 1.00
❑ SP13050 One for One .40 1.00

2013 Yu-Gi-Oh Star Pack 2013 Starfoil

*Starfoil: .6X to 1.5X Basic Card
Stated Odds One Per Pack

2004 Yu-Gi-Oh Exclusive Pack

Booster Box (20 packs) 40.00 80.00
Booster Pack (8 cards) 4.00 6.00

❑ EP1EN1 Theinen The Great Sphinx (UR) 2.00 4.00
❑ EP1EN2 Andro Sphinx (UR) 1.00 3.00
❑ EP1EN3 Sphinx Teleia (UR) 1.00 3.00
❑ EP1EN4 Rare Metal Dragon .25 .50
❑ EP1EN5 Peten The Dark Clown .50 1.00
❑ EP1EN6 Familiar Knight .50 1.00
❑ EP1EN7 Inferno Tempest .25 .50
❑ EP1EN8 Return From The Different Dimension 1.00 3.00

2004 Yu-Gi-Oh The Movie

Complete Set (4) 8.00 15.00
Booster Pack (1 card) 1.00 3.00

❑ MOV-EN1 Blue-Eyes Shining Dragon (SR) 4.00 10.00
❑ MOV-EN2 Sorcerer of Dark Magic 2.00 4.00
❑ MOV-EN3 Watapon .50 1.50
❑ MOV-EN4 Pyramid of Light 2.00 4.00

2011 Yu-Gi-Oh 3D Bonds Beyond Time Movie

Booster Box (20 packs) 40.00 75.00
Booster Pack (5 cards) 2.50 4.00

❑ YMP1EN001 Malefic Red-Eyes B. Dragon SCR .75 2.00
❑ YMP1EN002 Malefic Blue Eyes White Dragon SCR .75 2.00
❑ YMP1EN003 Malefic Parallel Gear SCR .75 2.00
❑ YMP1EN004 Malefic Cyber End Dragon SCR 6.00 15.00
❑ YMP1EN005 Malefic Rainbow Dragon SCR 1.25 3.00
❑ YMP1EN006 Junk Gardna SCR .75 2.00
❑ YMP1EN007 Malefic Paradox Dragon SCR 2.00 5.00
❑ YMP1EN008 Malefic World SCR .75 2.00
❑ YMP1EN009 Malefic Claw Stream SCR .40 1.00

2002 Yu-Gi-Oh Kaiba Starter Deck 1st Edition

Complete Set (50) 35.00 50.00

❑ SDK-1 Blue Eyes White Dragon (UR) 8.00 20.00
❑ SDK-2 Hitotsu-Me Giant .20 .50
❑ SDK-3 Ryu-Kishin .20 .50
❑ SDK-4 Wicked Worm Beast .20 .50
❑ SDK-5 Battle Ox .20 .50
❑ SDK-6 Koumori Dragon .20 .50
❑ SDK-7 Judge Man .20 .50
❑ SDK-8 Rogue Doll .20 .50
❑ SDK-9 Kojikocy .20 .50
❑ SDK-10 Uraby .20 .50
❑ SDK-11 Gyakutenno Megami .20 .50
❑ SDK-12 Mystic Horseman .20 .50
❑ SDK-13 Terra the Terrible .20 .50
❑ SDK-14 Dark Titan of Terror .20 .50
❑ SDK-15 Dark Assassin .50 1.00
❑ SDK-16 Master and Expert .20 .50
❑ SDK-17 Unknown Warrior of Fiend .20 .50
❑ SDK-18 Mystic Clown .20 .50
❑ SDK-19 Ogre of Black Shadow .20 .50
❑ SDK-20 Dark Energy .20 .50
❑ SDK-21 Invigoration .20 .50
❑ SDK-22 Dark Hole .50 1.00
❑ SDK-23 Ookazi .20 .50
❑ SDK-24 Ryu-Kishin Powered .20 .50
❑ SDK-25 Swordstalker .20 .50
❑ SDK-26 La Jinn the Mystical Genie 1.00 2.00
❑ SDK-27 Rude Kaiser .50 1.00
❑ SDK-28 Destroyer Golem .20 .50
❑ SDK-29 Skull Red Bird .20 .50
❑ SDK-30 D. Human .20 .50
❑ SDK-31 Pale Beast .20 .50
❑ SDK-32 Fissure .50 1.00
❑ SDK-33 Trap Hole .20 .50
❑ SDK-34 Two-Pronged Attack .20 .50
❑ SDK-35 De-Spell .20 .50
❑ SDK-36 Monster Reborn 2.00 4.00
❑ SDK-37 Inexperienced Spy .20 .50
❑ SDK-38 Reinforcements .20 .50
❑ SDK-39 Ancient Telescope .20 .50
❑ SDK-40 Just Desserts .20 .50
❑ SDK-41 Lord of D. (SR) 3.00 6.00
❑ SDK-42 Flute of Summoning Dragon (SR) 2.00 4.00
❑ SDK-43 Mysterious Puppeteer .20 .50
❑ SDK-44 Trap Master .10 .30
❑ SDK-45 Sogen .20 .50
❑ SDK-46 Hane-Hane .20 .50
❑ SDK-47 Reverse Trap .20 .50
❑ SDK-48 Reverse Trap .20 .50
❑ SDK-49 Castle Walls .20 .50
❑ SDK-50 Ultimate Offering .20 .50

2002 Yu-Gi-Oh Kaiba Starter Deck Unlimited

Complete Set (50) 12.00 20.00

❑ SDK-1 Blue Eyes White Dragon (UR) 4.00 10.00
❑ SDK-2 Hitotsu-Me Giant .20 .40
❑ SDK-3 Ryu-Kishin .20 .40
❑ SDK-4 Wicked Worm Beast .20 .40
❑ SDK-5 Battle Ox .20 .40
❑ SDK-6 Koumori Dragon .20 .40
❑ SDK-7 Judge Man .20 .40
❑ SDK-8 Rogue Doll .20 .40
❑ SDK-9 Kojikocy .20 .40
❑ SDK-10 Uraby .20 .40
❑ SDK-11 Gyakutenno Megami .20 .40
❑ SDK-12 Mystic Horseman .20 .40
❑ SDK-13 Terra the Terrible .20 .40
❑ SDK-14 Dark Titan of Terror .20 .40
❑ SDK-15 Dark Assassin .50 1.00
❑ SDK-16 Master and Expert .20 .40
❑ SDK-17 Unknown Warrior of Fiend .20 .40
❑ SDK-18 Mystic Clown .20 .40
❑ SDK-19 Ogre of Black Shadow .20 .40
❑ SDK-20 Dark Energy .20 .40
❑ SDK-21 Invigoration .20 .40
❑ SDK-22 Dark Hole .50 1.00
❑ SDK-23 Ookazi .20 .40
❑ SDK-24 Ryu-Kishin Powered .20 .40
❑ SDK-25 Swordstalker .20 .40
❑ SDK-26 La Jinn the Mystical Genie 1.25 2.50
❑ SDK-27 Rude Kaiser .50 1.00
❑ SDK-28 Destroyer Golem .20 .40
❑ SDK-29 Skull Red Bird .20 .40
❑ SDK-30 D. Human .20 .40
❑ SDK-31 Pale Beast .20 .40
❑ SDK-32 Fissure .50 1.00
❑ SDK-33 Trap Hole .20 .40
❑ SDK-34 Two-Pronged Attack .20 .40
❑ SDK-35 De-Spell .20 .40
❑ SDK-36 Monster Reborn 1.00 2.50
❑ SDK-37 Inexperienced Spy .20 .40

YU-GI-OH!

❑ SDK-38 Reinforcements	.20	.40
❑ SDK-39 Ancient Telescope	.20	.40
❑ SDK-40 Just Desserts	.20	.40
❑ SDK-41 Lord of D. (SR)	2.00	4.00
❑ SDK-42 Flute of Summoning Dragon (SR)	1.00	3.00
❑ SDK-43 Mysterious Puppeteer	.20	.40
❑ SDK-44 Trap Master	.20	.40
❑ SDK-45 Sogen	.20	.40
❑ SDK-46 Hane-Hane	.30	.75
❑ SDK-47 Reverse Trap	.20	.40
❑ SDK-48 Reverse Trap	.20	.40
❑ SDK-49 Castle Walls	.20	.40
❑ SDK-50 Ultimate Offering	.20	.40

2002 Yu-Gi-Oh Yugi Starter Deck 1st Edition

Complete Set (50)	30.00	50.00
❑ SDY-1 Mystical Elf	.20	.50
❑ SDY-2 Feral Imp	.20	.50
❑ SDY-3 Winged Dragon Guardian	.20	.50
❑ SDY-4 Summoned Skull	2.00	6.00
❑ SDY-5 Beaver Warrior	.20	.50
❑ SDY-6 Dark Magician (UR)	7.00	15.00
❑ SDY-7 Gaia The Fierce Knight	2.00	4.00
❑ SDY-8 Curse of Dragon	.20	.50
❑ SDY-9 Celtic Guardian	1.00	2.00
❑ SDY-10 Mammoth Graveyard	.20	.50
❑ SDY-11 Great White	.20	.50
❑ SDY-12 Silver Fang	.20	.50
❑ SDY-13 Giant Soldier of Stone	.20	.50
❑ SDY-14 Dragon Zombie	.20	.50
❑ SDY-15 Doma Angel of Silence	.20	.50
❑ SDY-16 Ansatsu	.20	.50
❑ SDY-17 Witty Phantom	.20	.50
❑ SDY-18 Claw Reacher	.20	.50
❑ SDY-19 Mystic Clown	.20	.50
❑ SDY-20 Sword of Dark Destruction	.20	.50
❑ SDY-21 Book of Secret Arts	.20	.50
❑ SDY-22 Dark Hole	.20	.50
❑ SDY-23 Dian Keto the Cure Master	.20	.50
❑ SDY-24 Ancient Elf	.20	.50
❑ SDY-25 Magical Ghost	.20	.50
❑ SDY-26 Fissure	.50	1.00
❑ SDY-27 Trap Hole	.20	.50
❑ SDY-28 Two-Pronged Attack	.20	.50
❑ SDY-29 De-Spell	.20	.50
❑ SDY-30 Monster Reborn	1.00	3.00
❑ SDY-31 Reinforcements	.20	.50
❑ SDY-32 Change of Heart	1.00	2.00
❑ SDY-33 The Stern Mystic	.20	.50
❑ SDY-34 Wall of Illusion	.20	.50
❑ SDY-35 Neo the Magic Swordsman	.20	.50
❑ SDY-36 Baron of Fiend Sword	.20	.50
❑ SDY-37 Man-Eating Treasure Chest	.20	.50
❑ SDY-38 Sorcerer of the Doomed	.20	.50
❑ SDY-39 Last Will	.20	.50
❑ SDY-40 Waboku	1.00	2.00
❑ SDY-41 Soul Exchange (SR)	2.00	5.00
❑ SDY-42 Card Destruction (SR)	2.00	5.00
❑ SDY-43 Trap Master	.20	.50
❑ SDY-44 Dragon Capture Jar	.20	.50
❑ SDY-45 Yami	.20	.50
❑ SDY-46 Man-Eater Bug	.20	.50
❑ SDY-47 Reverse Trap	.20	.50
❑ SDY-48 Remove Trap	.20	.50
❑ SDY-49 Castle Walls	.20	.50
❑ SDY-50 Ultimate Offering	.20	.50

2002 Yu-Gi-Oh Yugi Starter Deck Unlimited

Complete Set (50)	12.00	20.00
❑ SDY-1 Mystical Elf	.20	.40
❑ SDY-2 Feral Imp	.20	.40
❑ SDY-3 Winged Dragon Guardian	.20	.40
❑ SDY-4 Summoned Skull	2.00	5.00
❑ SDY-5 Beaver Warrior	.20	.40
❑ SDY-6 Dark Magician (UR)	4.00	8.00
❑ SDY-7 Gaia The Fierce Knight	1.00	2.50
❑ SDY-8 Curse of Dragon	.20	.40
❑ SDY-9 Celtic Guardian	.50	1.50
❑ SDY-10 Mammoth Graveyard	.20	.40
❑ SDY-11 Great White	.20	.40
❑ SDY-12 Silver Fang	.20	.40
❑ SDY-13 Giant Soldier of Stone	.20	.40
❑ SDY-14 Dragon Zombie	.20	.40
❑ SDY-15 Doma Angel of Silence	.20	.40
❑ SDY-16 Ansatsu	.20	.40
❑ SDY-17 Witty Phantom	.20	.40
❑ SDY-18 Claw Reacher	.20	.40
❑ SDY-19 Mystic Clown	.20	.40
❑ SDY-20 Sword of Dark Destruction	.20	.40
❑ SDY-21 Book of Secret Arts	.20	.40
❑ SDY-22 Dark Hole	.50	1.00
❑ SDY-23 Dian Keto the Cure Master	.20	.40
❑ SDY-24 Ancient Elf	.20	.40
❑ SDY-25 Magical Ghost	.20	.40
❑ SDY-26 Fissure	.50	1.00
❑ SDY-27 Trap Hole	.20	.40
❑ SDY-28 Two-Pronged Attack	.20	.40
❑ SDY-29 De-Spell	.20	.40
❑ SDY-30 Monster Reborn	1.00	2.00
❑ SDY-31 Reinforcements	.20	.40
❑ SDY-32 Change of Heart	.75	1.50
❑ SDY-33 The Stern Mystic	.20	.40
❑ SDY-34 Wall of Illusion	.20	.40
❑ SDY-35 Neo the Magic Swordsman	.20	.40
❑ SDY-36 Baron of Fiend Sword	.20	.40
❑ SDY-37 Man-Eating Treasure Chest	.20	.40
❑ SDY-38 Sorcerer of the Doomed	.20	.40
❑ SDY-39 Last Will	.20	.40
❑ SDY-40 Waboku	.75	1.50
❑ SDY-41 Soul Exchange (SR)	1.00	3.00
❑ SDY-42 Card Destruction (SR)	1.00	3.00
❑ SDY-43 Trap Master	.20	.40
❑ SDY-44 Dragon Capture Jar	.20	.40
❑ SDY-45 Yami	.20	.40
❑ SDY-46 Man-Eater Bug	.20	.40
❑ SDY-47 Reverse Trap	.20	.40
❑ SDY-48 Remove Trap	.20	.40
❑ SDY-49 Castle Walls	.20	.40
❑ SDY-50 Ultimate Offering	.20	.40

2003 Yu-Gi-Oh Joey Starter Deck 1st Edition

Complete Set (50)	12.00	24.00
❑ SDJ-1 Red-Eyes B. Dragon (UR)	6.00	12.00
❑ SDJ-2 Swordsman of Landstar	.20	.50
❑ SDJ-3 Baby Dragon	1.00	2.00
❑ SDJ-4 Spirit of the Harp	.20	.50
❑ SDJ-5 Island Turtle	.20	.50
❑ SDJ-6 Flame Manipulator	.20	.50
❑ SDJ-7 Masaki The Legendary Swordsman	.20	.50
❑ SDJ-8 7 Colored Fish	.50	1.00
❑ SDJ-9 Armored Lizard	.20	.50
❑ SDJ-10 Darkfire Soldier #1	.20	.50
❑ SDJ-11 Harpie's Brother	.20	.50
❑ SDJ-12 Gearfried the Iron Knight	.20	.50
❑ SDJ-13 Karate Man	.20	.50
❑ SDJ-14 Milus Radiant	.20	.50
❑ SDJ-15 Time Wizard	5.00	10.00
❑ SDJ-16 Maha Vailo	.50	1.00
❑ SDJ-17 Magician of Faith	.20	.50
❑ SDJ-18 Big Eye	.20	.50
❑ SDJ-19 Sangan	.50	1.00
❑ SDJ-20 Princess of Tsurugi	.20	.50
❑ SDJ-21 White Magical Hat	.20	.50
❑ SDJ-22 Penguin Soldier (SR)	2.00	4.00
❑ SDJ-23 Thousand Dragon	.50	1.00
❑ SDJ-24 Flame Swordsman	2.00	4.00
❑ SDJ-25 Malevolent Nuzzler	.20	.50
❑ SDJ-26 Dark Hole	.20	.50
❑ SDJ-27 Dian Keto	.20	.50
❑ SDJ-28 Fissure	.20	.50
❑ SDJ-29 De-Spell	.20	.50
❑ SDJ-30 Change of Heart	.20	.50
❑ SDJ-31 Block Attack	.20	.50
❑ SDJ-32 Giant Trunade	.20	.50
❑ SDJ-33 The Reliable Guardian	.20	.50
❑ SDJ-34 Remove Trap	.20	.50
❑ SDJ-35 Monster Reborn	1.00	2.00
❑ SDJ-36 Polymerization	5.00	10.00
❑ SDJ-37 Mountain	.20	.50
❑ SDJ-38 Dragon Treasure	.20	.50
❑ SDJ-39 Eternal Rest	.20	.50
❑ SDJ-40 Shield & Sword	.20	.50
❑ SDJ-41 Scapegoat (SR)	3.00	6.00
❑ SDJ-42 Just Desserts	.20	.50
❑ SDJ-43 Trap Hole	.20	.50
❑ SDJ-44 Reinforcements	.20	.50
❑ SDJ-45 Castle Walls	.20	.50
❑ SDJ-46 Waboku	.20	.50
❑ SDJ-47 Ultimate Offering	.20	.50
❑ SDJ-48 Seven Tools of the Bandit	.20	.50
❑ SDJ-49 Fake Trap	.20	.50
❑ SDJ-50 Reverse Trap	.20	.50

2003 Yu-Gi-Oh Joey Starter Deck Unlimited

Complete Set (50)	9.00	14.00
❑ SDJ-1 Red-Eyes B. Dragon (UR)	4.00	7.00
❑ SDJ-2 Swordsman of Landstar	.20	.40
❑ SDJ-3 Baby Dragon	1.00	2.00
❑ SDJ-4 Spirit of the Harp	.20	.40
❑ SDJ-5 Island Turtle	.20	.40
❑ SDJ-6 Flame Manipulator	.20	.40
❑ SDJ-7 Masaki The Legendary Swordsman	.20	.40
❑ SDJ-8 7 Colored Fish	.50	1.00
❑ SDJ-9 Armored Lizard	.20	.40
❑ SDJ-10 Darkfire Soldier #1	.20	.40
❑ SDJ-11 Harpie's Brother	.20	.40
❑ SDJ-12 Gearfried the Iron Knight	.20	.40
❑ SDJ-13 Karate Man	.20	.40
❑ SDJ-14 Milus Radiant	.20	.40
❑ SDJ-15 Time Wizard	3.00	5.00
❑ SDJ-16 Maha Vailo	.30	.75
❑ SDJ-17 Magician of Faith	.20	.40
❑ SDJ-18 Big Eye	.20	.40
❑ SDJ-19 Sangan	.20	.40
❑ SDJ-20 Princess of Tsurugi	.20	.40
❑ SDJ-21 White Magical Hat	.20	.40
❑ SDJ-22 Penguin Soldier (SR)	1.50	3.00
❑ SDJ-23 Thousand Dragon	.75	1.50
❑ SDJ-24 Flame Swordsman	1.50	3.00
❑ SDJ-25 Malevolent Nuzzler	.20	.40
❑ SDJ-26 Dark Hole	.20	.40
❑ SDJ-27 Dian Keto	.20	.40
❑ SDJ-28 Fissure	.20	.40
❑ SDJ-29 De-Spell	.20	.40
❑ SDJ-30 Change of Heart	.20	.40
❑ SDJ-31 Block Attack	.20	.40
❑ SDJ-32 Giant Trunade	.20	.40
❑ SDJ-33 The Reliable Guardian	.20	.40
❑ SDJ-34 Remove Trap	.20	.40
❑ SDJ-35 Monster Reborn	.75	1.50
❑ SDJ-36 Polymerization	4.00	7.00
❑ SDJ-37 Mountain	.20	.40
❑ SDJ-38 Dragon Treasure	.20	.40
❑ SDJ-39 Eternal Rest	.20	.40
❑ SDJ-40 Shield & Sword	.20	.40
❑ SDJ-41 Scapegoat (SR)	2.00	4.00
❑ SDJ-42 Just Desserts	.20	.40
❑ SDJ-43 Trap Hole	.20	.40
❑ SDJ-44 Reinforcements	.20	.40
❑ SDJ-45 Castle Walls	.20	.40
❑ SDJ-46 Waboku	.20	.40
❑ SDJ-47 Ultimate Offering	.20	.40
❑ SDJ-48 Seven Tools of the Bandit	.20	.40
❑ SDJ-49 Fake Trap	.20	.40
❑ SDJ-50 Reverse Trap	.20	.40

2003 Yu-Gi-Oh Pegasus Starter Deck 1st Edition

Complete Set (50)	15.00	25.00
❑ SDP-1 Relinquished (UR)	5.00	10.00
❑ SDP-2 Red Archery Girl	.20	.50
❑ SDP-3 Ryu-Ran	.20	.50
❑ SDP-4 Illusionist Faceless Mage	.20	.50
❑ SDP-5 Rogue Doll	.20	.50
❑ SDP-6 Uraby	.20	.50
❑ SDP-7 Giant Soldier of Stone	.20	.50
❑ SDP-8 Aqua Madoor	.20	.50
❑ SDP-9 Toon Alligator	.50	1.00
❑ SDP-10 Hane-Hane	.20	.50
❑ SDP-11 Sonic Bird	.20	.50
❑ SDP-12 Jigen Bakudan	.20	.50
❑ SDP-13 Mask of Darkness	.20	.50
❑ SDP-14 Witch of the Black Forest	.20	.50
❑ SDP-15 Man-Eater Bug	.20	.50
❑ SDP-16 Muka Muka	.20	.50
❑ SDP-17 Dream Clown	.20	.50
❑ SDP-18 Armed Ninja	.20	.50
❑ SDP-19 Hiro's Shadow	.20	.50
❑ SDP-20 Blue-Eyes Toon Dragon	.50	1.00
❑ SDP-21 Toon Summoned Skull	.20	.50
❑ SDP-22 Manga Ryu-Ran	.20	.50
❑ SDP-23 Toon Mermaid	.20	1.00
❑ SDP-24 Toon World	1.00	2.00
❑ SDP-25 Black Pendant	.20	.50
❑ SDP-26 Dark Hole	.20	1.00
❑ SDP-27 Dian Keto The Cure Master	.20	.50
❑ SDP-28 Fissure	.20	.50
❑ SDP-29 De-Spell	.20	.50
❑ SDP-30 Change of Heart	.20	.50
❑ SDP-31 Stop Defense	.20	.50
❑ SDP-32 Mystical Space Typhoon	.20	.50
❑ SDP-33 Rush Recklessly	.20	.50
❑ SDP-34 Remove Trap	.20	.50
❑ SDP-35 Monster Reborn	.50	1.00
❑ SDP-36 Soul Release	.20	.50
❑ SDP-37 Yami	.20	.50
❑ SDP-38 Black Illusion Ritual	.20	.50
❑ SDP-39 Ring of Magnetism	.20	.50
❑ SDP-40 Graceful Charity (SR)	2.00	5.00
❑ SDP-41 Trap Hole	.20	.50
❑ SDP-42 Reinforcements	.20	.50
❑ SDP-43 Castle Walls	.20	.50
❑ SDP-44 Waboku	.20	.50
❑ SDP-45 Seven Tools of the Bandit	.20	.50
❑ SDP-46 Ultimate Offering	.20	.50
❑ SDP-47 Robbin Gobblin	.20	.50
❑ SDP-48 Magic Jammer	.20	.50
❑ SDP-49 Enchanted Javelin	.20	.50
❑ SDP-50 Gryphon Wing (SR)	1.00	3.00

2003 Yu-Gi-Oh Pegasus Starter Deck Unlimited

Complete Set (50)	9.00	14.00
❑ SDP-1 Relinquished (UR)	4.00	8.00
❑ SDP-2 Red Archery Girl	.20	.40
❑ SDP-3 Ryu-Ran	.20	.40
❑ SDP-4 Illusionist Faceless Mage	.20	.40
❑ SDP-5 Rogue Doll	.20	.40
❑ SDP-6 Uraby	.20	.40
❑ SDP-7 Giant Soldier of Stone	.20	.40
❑ SDP-8 Aqua Madoor	.20	.40
❑ SDP-9 Toon Alligator	.50	1.00
❑ SDP-10 Hane-Hane	.20	.40
❑ SDP-11 Sonic Bird	.20	.40
❑ SDP-12 Jigen Bakudan	.20	.40
❑ SDP-13 Mask of Darkness	.20	.40
❑ SDP-14 Witch of the Black Forest	.20	.40
❑ SDP-15 Man-Eater Bug	.20	.40
❑ SDP-16 Muka Muka	.20	.40
❑ SDP-17 Dream Clown	.20	.40
❑ SDP-18 Armed Ninja	.20	.40
❑ SDP-19 Hiro's Shadow	.20	.40
❑ SDP-20 Blue-Eyes Toon Dragon	.75	1.50
❑ SDP-21 Toon Summoned Skull	.20	.40
❑ SDP-22 Manga Ryu-Ran	.20	.40
❑ SDP-23 Toon Mermaid	.50	1.00
❑ SDP-24 Toon World	.75	1.50
❑ SDP-25 Black Pendant	.20	.40
❑ SDP-26 Dark Hole	.20	.40
❑ SDP-27 Dian Keto The Cure Master	.20	.40
❑ SDP-28 Fissure	.20	.40
❑ SDP-29 De-Spell	.20	.40
❑ SDP-30 Change of Heart	.20	.40
❑ SDP-31 Stop Defense	.20	.40
❑ SDP-32 Mystical Space Typhoon	.20	.40
❑ SDP-33 Rush Recklessly	.20	.40
❑ SDP-34 Remove Trap	.20	.40
❑ SDP-35 Monster Reborn	.50	1.00
❑ SDP-36 Soul Release	.20	.40
❑ SDP-37 Yami	.20	.40
❑ SDP-38 Black Illusion Ritual	.20	.40
❑ SDP-39 Ring of Magnetism	.20	.40
❑ SDP-40 Graceful Charity (SR)	1.00	3.00
❑ SDP-41 Trap Hole	.20	.40
❑ SDP-42 Reinforcements	.20	.40
❑ SDP-43 Castle Walls	.20	.40
❑ SDP-44 Waboku	.20	.40
❑ SDP-45 Seven Tools of the Bandit	.20	.40
❑ SDP-46 Ultimate Offering	.20	.40
❑ SDP-47 Robbin Gobblin	.20	.40
❑ SDP-48 Magic Jammer	1.00	2.00
❑ SDP-49 Enchanted Javelin	.20	.40
❑ SDP-50 Gryphon Wing (SR)	2.00	4.00

2004 Yu-Gi-Oh Kaiba Evolution Starter Deck 1st Edition

Complete Set (50)	3.00	6.00
❑ SKE-1 Blue-Eyes White Dragon (UR)	5.00	10.00

2004 Yu-Gi-Oh Kaiba Evolution Starter Deck Unlimited

Complete Set (50)	9.00	12.00
*Unlimited Cards: .4X to .8X 1st Edition		
❑ SKE-1 Blue-Eyes White Dragon (UR)	3.00	6.00

2004 Yu-Gi-Oh Yugi Evolution Starter Deck 1st Edition

Complete Set (50)	12.00	20.00
❑ SYE-1 Dark Magician (UR)	3.00	6.00
❑ SYE-24 Black Luster Soldier	2.00	5.00

2004 Yu-Gi-Oh Yugi Evolution Starter Deck Unlimited

Complete Set (50)	9.00	12.00
*Unlimited Cards: .4X to .8X 1st Edition		
❑ SYE-1 Dark Magician (UR)	2.00	4.00
❑ SYE-24 Black Luster Soldier	1.00	3.00

2005 Yu-Gi-Oh Dragon's Roar Structure Deck 1st Edition

Complete Set (28)	10.00	17.00
❑ SD1E1 Red-Eyes Darkness Dragon (UR)	5.00	10.00
❑ SD1E2 Red-Eyes B. Dragon	1.00	2.00
❑ SD1E3 Luster Dragon	1.00	2.00
❑ SD1E4 Twin-Headed Behemoth	.20	.50
❑ SD1E5 Armed Dragon LV3	.20	.50
❑ SD1E6 Armed Dragon LV5	.20	.50
❑ SD1E7 Red-Eyes B. Chick	.20	.50
❑ SD1E8 Element Dragon	.20	.50
❑ SD1E9 Masked Dragon	.20	.50
❑ SD1E10 Snatch Steal	.20	.50
❑ SD1E11 Mystical Space Typhoon	.20	.50
❑ SD1E12 Nobleman of Crossout	.20	.50
❑ SD1E13 Premature Burial	.20	.50
❑ SD1E14 Swords of Revealing Light	.20	.50
❑ SD1E15 Pot of Greed	.20	.50
❑ SD1E16 Heavy Storm	.20	.50
❑ SD1E17 Stamping Destruction	.20	.50
❑ SD1E18 Creature Swap	.20	.50
❑ SD1E19 Reload	.20	.50
❑ SD1E20 The Graveyard in the Fourth Dimension	.20	.50
❑ SD1E21 Call of the Haunted	.20	.50
❑ SD1E22 Ceasefire	.20	.50
❑ SD1E23 The Dragon's Bead	.20	.50
❑ SD1E24 Dragon's Rage	.20	.50
❑ SD1E25 Reckless Greed	.20	.50
❑ SD1E26 Interdimensional Matter	.20	.50
❑ SD1E27 Trap Jammer	.20	.50
❑ SD1E28 Curse of Anubis	1.00	2.00

2005 Yu-Gi-Oh Zombie Madness Structure Deck 1st Edition

Complete Set (28)	10.00	15.00
❑ SD2E1 Vampire Genesis (UR)	3.00	6.00
❑ SD2E2 Master Kyonshee	.20	.50
❑ SD2E3 Vampire Lord	1.00	2.00
❑ SD2E4 Dark Dust Spirit	.20	.50
❑ SD2E5 Pyramid Turtle	.20	.50
❑ SD2E6 Spirit Reaper	.20	.50
❑ SD2E7 Despair From The Dark	.20	.50
❑ SD2E8 Ryu Kokki	.20	.50
❑ SD2E9 Soul-Absorbing Bone Tower	.20	.50
❑ SD2E10 Vampire Lady	.20	.50
❑ SD2E11 Double Coston	.20	.50
❑ SD2E12 Regenerating Mummy	.20	.50
❑ SD2E13 Snatch Steal	1.00	2.00
❑ SD2E14 Mystical Space Typhoon	.20	.50
❑ SD2E15 Giant Trunade	.20	.50
❑ SD2E16 Nobleman of Crossout	.20	.50
❑ SD2E17 Pot of Greed	.20	.50
❑ SD2E18 Card of Safe Return	.20	.50
❑ SD2E19 Heavy Storm	.20	.50
❑ SD2E20 Creature Swap	.20	.50
❑ SD2E21 Book of Life	.20	.50
❑ SD2E22 Call of the Mummy	.20	.50
❑ SD2E23 Reload	.20	.50
❑ SD2E24 Dust Tornado	.20	.50
❑ SD2E25 Torrential Tribute	.20	.50
❑ SD2E26 Magic Jammer	.20	.50
❑ SD2E27 Reckless Greed	.20	.50
❑ SD2E28 Compulsory Evacuation Device	.20	.50

2005 Yu-Gi-Oh Blaze of Destruction Structure Deck

Complete Set (31)	6.00	15.00
Structure Deck	8.00	20.00
❑ SD3001 Infernal Flame Emperor (UR)	.30	.75
❑ SD3002 Great Angus	.10	.25
❑ SD3003 Blazing Inpachi	.10	.25
❑ SD3004 UFO Turtle	.10	.25
❑ SD3005 Little Chimera	.10	.25
❑ SD3006 Inferno	.10	.25
❑ SD3007 Molten Zombie	.10	.25
❑ SD3008 Solar Flare Dragon	.20	.50
❑ SD3009 Ultimate Baseball Kid	.10	.25
❑ SD3010 Raging Flame Sprite	.20	.50
❑ SD3011 Thestalos the Firestorm Monarch	.50	1.25
❑ SD3012 Gaia Soul the Combustible Collective	.10	.25
❑ SD3013 Fox Fire	.10	.25
❑ SD3014 Snatch Steal	.30	.75
❑ SD3015 Mystical Space Typhoon	.60	1.50
❑ SD3016 Molten Destruction	.10	.25
❑ SD3017 Nobleman of Crossout	.20	.50
❑ SD3018 Premature Burial	.20	.50
❑ SD3019 Pot of Greed	.75	2.00
❑ SD3020 Tribute to the Doomed	.10	.25
❑ SD3021 Heavy Storm	.60	1.50
❑ SD3022 Dark Room of Nightmare	.20	.50
❑ SD3023 Reload	.10	.25
❑ SD3024 Level Limit - Area B	1.25	3.00
❑ SD3025 Necklace of Command	.10	.25
❑ SD3026 Meteor of Destruction	.40	1.00
❑ SD3027 Dust Tornado	.10	.25
❑ SD3028 Call of the Haunted	.60	1.50
❑ SD3029 Jar of Greed	.40	1.00
❑ SD3030 Spell Shield Type-8	.10	.25
❑ SD3031 Backfire	.20	.50

2005 Yu-Gi-Oh Fury From The Deep Structure Deck

Complete Set (32)	10.00	25.00
Structure Deck	12.00	30.00
❑ SD4001 Ocean Dragon Lord (UR)	.40	1.00
❑ SD4002 7 Colored Fish	.10	.25
❑ SD4003 Sea Serpent Warrior of Darkness	.10	.25
❑ SD4004 Space Mambo	.10	.25
❑ SD4005 Mother Grizzly	.10	.25
❑ SD4006 Star Boy	.10	.25
❑ SD4007 Tribe-Infecting Virus	.75	2.00
❑ SD4008 Fenrir	.10	.25
❑ SD4009 Amphibious Bugroth MK-3	.20	.50
❑ SD4010 Levia-Dragon - Daedalus	1.25	3.00
❑ SD4011 Mermaid Knight	.10	.25
❑ SD4012 Mobius the Frost Monarch	.60	1.50
❑ SD4013 Unshaven Angler	.20	.50
❑ SD4014 Creeping Doom Manta	.10	.25
❑ SD4015 Snatch Steal	.30	.75
❑ SD4016 Mystical Space Typhoon	.50	1.25
❑ SD4017 Premature Burial	.30	.75
❑ SD4018 Pot of Greed	.75	2.00
❑ SD4019 Heavy Storm	.60	1.50
❑ SD4020 A Legendary Ocean	.20	.50
❑ SD4021 Creature Swap	.20	.50
❑ SD4022 Reload	.10	.25
❑ SD4023 Salvage	1.00	2.50
❑ SD4024 Hammer Shot	.30	.75
❑ SD4025 Big Wave Small Wave	.30	.75
❑ SD4026 Dust Tornado	.10	.25
❑ SD4027 Call of the Haunted	.50	1.25
❑ SD4028 Gravity Bind	.75	2.00
❑ SD4029 Tornado Wall	.30	.75
❑ SD4030 Torrential Tribute	1.50	4.00
❑ SD4031 Spell Shield Type-8	.20	.50
❑ SD4032 Xing Zhen Hu	.20	.50

2006 Yu-Gi-Oh Dinosaur's Rage Structure Deck

Complete Set	6.00	12.00
Structure Deck	6.00	12.00
Special Edition Deck w/5-Headed Dragon	10.00	20.00
Five-Headed Dragon is a Wal-Mart Exclusive		
❑ SD9001 Super Conductor Tyranno (UR)	.40	1.00
❑ SD9002 Kabazauls	.40	1.00
❑ SD9003 Sabersaurus	.60	1.50
❑ SD9004 Mad Sword Beast	.10	.25
❑ SD9005 Gilasaurus	.10	.25
❑ SD9006 Dark Driceratops	.10	.25
❑ SD9007 Hyper Hammerhead	.10	.25
❑ SD9008 Black Tyranno	.30	.75
❑ SD9009 Tyranno Infinity	.10	.25
❑ SD9010 Hydrogeddon	.20	.50
❑ SD9011 Oxygeddon	.10	.25
❑ SD9012 Black Ptera	.10	.25
❑ SD9013 Black Stego	.10	.25
❑ SD9014 Ultimate Tyranno	.20	.50
❑ SD9015 Miracle Jurassic Egg	.10	.25
❑ SD9016 Babycerasaurus	.10	.25
❑ SD9017 Big Evolution Pill	.30	.75
❑ SD9018 Tail Swipe	.20	.50
❑ SD9019 Jurassic World	.50	1.25
❑ SD9020 Sebek's Blessing	.20	.50
❑ SD9021 Riryoku	.20	.50
❑ SD9022 Mesmeric Control	.10	.25
❑ SD9023 Mystical Space Typhoon	.60	1.50
❑ SD9024 Megamorph	.30	.75
❑ SD9025 Heavy Storm	.75	2.00
❑ SD9026 Lightning Vortex	.40	1.00
❑ SD9027 Magical Mallet	.20	.50
❑ SD9028 Hunting Instinct	.20	.50
❑ SD9029 Survival Instinct	.20	.50
❑ SD9030 Volcanic Eruption	.20	.50
❑ SD9031 Seismic Shockwave	.20	.50
❑ SD9032 Magical Arm Shield	.20	.50
❑ SD9033 Negate Attack	.40	1.00
❑ SD9034 Goblin Out of the Frying Pan	.10	.25
❑ SD9035 Malfunction	.10	.25
❑ SD9036 Fossil Excavation	.10	.25
❑ SD9SS1 Five-Headed Dragon	5.00	12.00

2006 Yu-Gi-Oh Invincible Fortress Structure Deck 1st Edition

Complete Set (32)	6.00	15.00
Structure Deck	8.00	20.00
❑ SD7001 Exxod, Master of the Guard (UR)	.60	1.50
❑ SD7002 Great Spirit	.20	.50
❑ SD7003 Giant Rat	.10	.25
❑ SD7004 Maharaghi	.10	.25
❑ SD7005 Guardian Sphinx	.30	.75
❑ SD7006 Gigantes	.10	.25
❑ SD7007 Stone Statue of the Aztecs	.10	.25
❑ SD7008 Golem Sentry	.30	.75
❑ SD7009 Hieracosphinx	.20	.50
❑ SD7010 Criosphinx	.10	.25
❑ SD7011 Moai Interceptor Cannons	.10	.25
❑ SD7012 Megarock Dragon	.10	.25
❑ SD7013 Guardian Statue	.10	.25
❑ SD7014 Medusa Worm	.10	.25
❑ SD7015 Sand Moth	.10	.25
❑ SD7016 Canyon	.40	1.00
❑ SD7017 Mystical Space Typhoon	.60	1.50
❑ SD7018 Premature Burial	.30	.75
❑ SD7019 Swords of Revealing Light	.30	.75
❑ SD7020 Shield & Sword	.10	.25
❑ SD7021 Magical Mallet	.50	1.25
❑ SD7022 Hammer Shot	.10	.25
❑ SD7023 Ectoplasmer	.20	.50
❑ SD7024 Brain Control	.40	1.00
❑ SD7025 Shifting Shadows	.10	.25
❑ SD7026 Waboku	.40	1.00
❑ SD7027 Ultimate Offering	.50	1.25
❑ SD7028 Magic Drain	.20	.50
❑ SD7029 Robbin' Goblin	.10	.25
❑ SD7030 Ordeal of a Traveler	.30	.75
❑ SD7031 Reckless Greed	.60	1.50
❑ SD7032 Compulsory Evacuation Device	.75	2.00

2006 Yu-Gi-Oh Lord of the Storm Structure Deck

Complete Set (36)	6.00	15.00
Structure Deck	8.00	20.00
❑ SD8001 Simorgh, Bird of Divinity (UR)	.30	.75
❑ SD8002 Sonic Shooter	.10	.25
❑ SD8003 Sonic Duck	.10	.25
❑ SD8004 Harpie Girl	.10	.25
❑ SD8005 Slate Warrior	1.25	3.00
❑ SD8006 Flying Kamakiri #1	.10	.25
❑ SD8007 Harpie Lady Sisters	.10	.25
❑ SD8008 Bladefly	.10	.25
❑ SD8009 Birdface	.10	.25
❑ SD8010 Silpheed	.10	.25
❑ SD8011 Lady Ninja Yae	.40	1.00
❑ SD8012 Roc from the Valley of Haze	.10	.25
❑ SD8013 Harpie Lady 1	.20	.50
❑ SD8014 Harpie Lady 2	.25	.50
❑ SD8015 Harpie Lady 3	.25	.50
❑ SD8016 Swift Birdman Joe	.10	.25
❑ SD8017 Harpie's Pet Baby Dragon	.10	.25
❑ SD8018 Card Destruction	.10	.25
❑ SD8019 Mystical Space Typhoon	.50	1.25
❑ SD8020 Nobleman of Crossout	.10	.25
❑ SD8021 Elegant Egotist	.10	.25
❑ SD8022 Heavy Storm	.60	1.50
❑ SD8023 Reload	.10	.25
❑ SD8024 Harpies' Hunting Ground	.30	.75
❑ SD8025 Triangle Ecstasy Spark	.30	.75
❑ SD8026 Lightning Vortex	.40	1.00
❑ SD8027 Hysteric Party	2.00	5.00
❑ SD8028 Aqua Chorus	.10	.25
❑ SD8029 Dust Tornado	.10	.25
❑ SD8030 Call of the Haunted	.50	1.25
❑ SD8031 Magic Jammer	.10	.25
❑ SD8032 Dark Coffin	.25	.50
❑ SD8033 Reckless Greed	.50	1.25

- ❑ SD8034 Sakuretsu Armor .30 .75
- ❑ SD8035 Ninjitsu Art of Transformation .30 .75
- ❑ SD8036 Icarus Attack .40 1.00

2006 Yu-Gi-Oh Spellcaster's Judgement Structure Deck

- Complete Set (36) 15.00 30.00
- Structure Deck 20.00 40.00
- ❑ SD6001 Dark Eradicator Warlock (UR) 1.50 4.00
- ❑ SD6002 Mythical Beast Cerberus .10 .25
- ❑ SD6003 Dark Magician .50 1.25
- ❑ SD6004 Gemini Elf .40 1.00
- ❑ SD6005 Magician of Faith .20 .50
- ❑ SD6006 Skilled Dark Magician .40 1.00
- ❑ SD6007 Apprentice Magician .10 .25
- ❑ SD6008 Chaos Command Magician .75 2.00
- ❑ SD6009 Breaker the Magical Warrior .75 2.00
- ❑ SD6010 Royal Magical Library .15 .40
- ❑ SD6011 Tsukuyomi .60 1.50
- ❑ SD6012 Chaos Sorcerer .75 2.00
- ❑ SD6013 White Magician Pikeru .20 .50
- ❑ SD6014 Blast Magician .10 .25
- ❑ SD6015 Ebon Magician Curran .15 .40
- ❑ SD6016 Rapid-Fire Magician .10 .25
- ❑ SD6017 Magical Blast .15 .40
- ❑ SD6018 Mystical Space Typhoon .60 1.50
- ❑ SD6019 Nobleman of Crossout .10 .25
- ❑ SD6020 Premature Burial .30 .75
- ❑ SD6021 Swords of Revealing Light .40 1.00
- ❑ SD6022 Mage Power .50 1.25
- ❑ SD6023 Heavy Storm .60 1.50
- ❑ SD6024 Diffusion Wave-Motion .10 .25
- ❑ SD6025 Reload .10 .25
- ❑ SD6026 Dark Magic Attack 1.25 3.00
- ❑ SD6027 Spell Absorption .20 .50
- ❑ SD6028 Lightning Vortex .30 .75
- ❑ SD6029 Magical Dimension .75 2.00
- ❑ SD6030 Mystic Box 1.25 3.00
- ❑ SD6031 Nightmare's Steelcage .20 .50
- ❑ SD6032 Call of the Haunted .60 1.50
- ❑ SD6033 Spell Shield Type-8 .10 .25
- ❑ SD6034 Pitch-Black Power Stone .10 .25
- ❑ SD6035 Divine Wrath .60 1.50
- ❑ SD6036 Magic Cylinder 1.25 3.00

2006 Yu-Gi-Oh Warrior's Triumph Structure Deck

- Complete Set (36) 10.00 25.00
- Structure Deck 12.00 30.00
- ❑ SD5001 Gilford the Legend (UR) .40 1.00
- ❑ SD5002 Warrior Lady of the Wasteland .60 1.50
- ❑ SD5003 Dark Blade .10 .25
- ❑ SD5004 Goblin Attack Force .15 .40
- ❑ SD5005 Gearfried the Iron Knight .10 .25
- ❑ SD5006 Swift Gaia the Fierce Knight .10 .25
- ❑ SD5007 Obnoxious Celtic Guard .20 .50
- ❑ SD5008 Command Knight .60 1.50
- ❑ SD5009 Marauding Captain .15 .40
- ❑ SD5010 Exiled Force .10 .25
- ❑ SD5011 D.D. Warrior Lady .50 1.25
- ❑ SD5012 Mataza the Zapper .10 .25
- ❑ SD5013 Mystic Swordsman LV2 .20 .50
- ❑ SD5014 Mystic Swordsman LV4 .40 1.00
- ❑ SD5015 Ninja Grandmaster Sasuke .20 .50
- ❑ SD5016 Gearfried the Swordmaster .60 1.50
- ❑ SD5017 Armed Samurai - Ben Kei .10 .25
- ❑ SD5018 Divine Sword - Phoenix Blade .10 .25
- ❑ SD5019 Snatch Steal .15 .40
- ❑ SD5020 Mystical Space Typhoon .60 1.50
- ❑ SD5021 Giant Trunade .10 .25
- ❑ SD5022 Lightning Blade .10 .25
- ❑ SD5023 Heavy Storm .75 2.00
- ❑ SD5024 Reinforcement of the Army .15 .40
- ❑ SD5025 The Warrior Returning Alive .10 .25
- ❑ SD5026 Fusion Sword Murasame Blade .10 .25
- ❑ SD5027 Wicked-Breaking Flamberge - Baou .10 .25
- ❑ SD5028 Fairy of the Spring .10 .25
- ❑ SD5029 Reload .10 .25
- ❑ SD5030 Lightning Vortex .30 .75
- ❑ SD5031 Swords of Concealing Light .60 1.50
- ❑ SD5032 Release Restraint .10 .25
- ❑ SD5033 Call of the Haunted .60 1.50
- ❑ SD5034 Magic Jammer .15 .40
- ❑ SD5035 Royal Decree 4.00 10.00
- ❑ SD5036 Blast with Chain .10 .25

2007 Yu-Gi-Oh Machine Re-Volt Structure Deck

- Complete Set (37) 8.00 20.00
- Structure Deck 10.00 25.00
- ❑ SD10001 Ancient Gear Dragon Gadjiltron (UR) 2.00 5.00
- ❑ SD10002 Ancient Gear Gadjiltron Chimera .40 1.00
- ❑ SD10003 Ancient Gear Engineer .50 1.25
- ❑ SD10004 Boot-Up Soldier - Dread Dynamo .10 .25
- ❑ SD10005 Mechanicalchaser .10 .25
- ❑ SD10006 Green Gadget .10 .25
- ❑ SD10007 Red Gadget .20 .50
- ❑ SD10008 Yellow Gadget .20 .50
- ❑ SD10009 Cannon Soldier .20 .50
- ❑ SD10010 Gear Golem the Moving Fortress .50 1.25
- ❑ SD10011 Heavy Mech Support Platform .10 .25
- ❑ SD10012 Ancient Gear Golem 1.25 3.00
- ❑ SD10013 Ancient Gear Beast .10 .25
- ❑ SD10014 Ancient Gear Soldier .10 .25
- ❑ SD10015 Ancient Gear .10 .25
- ❑ SD10016 Ancient Gear Cannon .10 .25
- ❑ SD10017 Ancient Gear Workshop .20 .50
- ❑ SD10018 Ancient Gear Tank .10 .25
- ❑ SD10019 Ancient Gear Explosive .10 .25
- ❑ SD10020 Ancient Gear Fist .10 .25
- ❑ SD10021 Ancient Gear Factory .10 .25
- ❑ SD10022 Ancient Gear Drill .10 .25
- ❑ SD10023 Ancient Gear Castle .20 .50
- ❑ SD10024 Mystical Space Typhoon .60 1.50
- ❑ SD10025 Limiter Removal .10 .25
- ❑ SD10026 Heavy Storm .75 2.00
- ❑ SD10027 Enemy Controller .50 1.25
- ❑ SD10028 Weapon Change .10 .25
- ❑ SD10029 Machine Duplication .20 .50
- ❑ SD10030 Pot of Avarice 2.00 5.00
- ❑ SD10031 Stronghold the Moving Fortress .20 .50
- ❑ SD10032 Ultimate Offering .75 2.00
- ❑ SD10033 Sakuretsu Armor .40 1.00
- ❑ SD10034 Micro Ray .10 .25
- ❑ SD10035 Rare Metalmorph .10 .25
- ❑ SD10036 Covering Fire .10 .25
- ❑ SD10037 Roll Out! .10 .25

2008 Yu-Gi-Oh Zombie World Structure Deck

- Structure Deck Zombie World 8.00 10.00
- ❑ SDZW1 Red-Eyes Zombie Dragon (UR) 2.00 5.00
- ❑ SDZW2 Malevolent Mech - Goku En .10 .25
- ❑ SDZW3 Paladin of the Cursed Dragon .75 2.00
- ❑ SDZW4 Gernia .10 .25
- ❑ SDZW5 Patrician of Darkness .10 .25
- ❑ SDZW6 Royal Keeper .10 .25
- ❑ SDZW7 Pyramid Turtle .10 .25
- ❑ SDZW8 Master Kyonshee .10 .25
- ❑ SDZW9 Spirit Reaper .75 2.00
- ❑ SDZW10 Getsu Fuhma .10 .25
- ❑ SDZW11 Ryu Kokki .10 .25
- ❑ SDZW12 Regenerating Mummy .10 .25
- ❑ SDZW13 Des Lacooda .10 .25
- ❑ SDZW14 Marionette Mite .10 .25
- ❑ SDZW15 Plague Wolf .10 .25
- ❑ SDZW16 Zombie Master .40 1.00
- ❑ SDZW17 Zombie World 1.50 4.00
- ❑ SDZW18 Spell Shattering Arrow .10 .25
- ❑ SDZW19 Cold Wave .10 .25
- ❑ SDZW20 Magical Stone Excavation 1.00 2.50
- ❑ SDZW21 Card of Safe Return .10 .25
- ❑ SDZW22 Creature Swap .10 .25
- ❑ SDZW23 Book of Life .10 .25
- ❑ SDZW24 Call of the Mummy .10 .25
- ❑ SDZW25 Terraforming .20 .50
- ❑ SDZW26 Pot of Avarice 1.50 4.00
- ❑ SDZW27 Shrink 1.25 3.00
- ❑ SDZW28 Field Barrier .10 .25
- ❑ SDZW29 Soul Taker .75 2.00
- ❑ SDZW30 Ribbon of Rebirth .10 .25
- ❑ SDZW31 Card Destruction .10 .25
- ❑ SDZW32 Imperial Iron Wall .75 2.00
- ❑ SDZW33 Dust Tornado .20 .50
- ❑ SDZW34 Bottomless Trap Hole 2.00 5.00
- ❑ SDZW35 Tutan Mask .10 .25
- ❑ SDZW36 Waboku .75 2.00
- ❑ SDZW37 Magical Arm Shield .10 .25

2009 Yu-Gi-Oh Spellcaster's Command Structure Deck

- Structure Deck Spellcaster's Command 10.00 12.00
- ❑ SDSC1 Endymion, the Master Magician (UR) 1.25 3.00
- ❑ SDSC2 Disenchanter .10 .25
- ❑ SDSC3 Defender, the Magical Knight .75 2.00
- ❑ SDSC4 Hannibal Necromancer .10 .25
- ❑ SDSC5 Summoner Monk 1.50 4.00
- ❑ SDSC6 Dark Red Enchanter .10 .25
- ❑ SDSC7 Skilled Dark Magician .75 2.00
- ❑ SDSC8 Apprentice Magician .10 .25
- ❑ SDSC9 Old Vindictive Magician .10 .25
- ❑ SDSC10 Magical Marionette .10 .25
- ❑ SDSC11 Breaker the Magical Warrior 1.50 4.00
- ❑ SDSC12 Magical Plant Mandragola .10 .25
- ❑ SDSC13 Royal Magical Library .10 .25
- ❑ SDSC14 Blast Magician 1.25 3.00
- ❑ SDSC15 Mythical Beast Cerberus .10 .25
- ❑ SDSC16 Mei-Kou, Master of Barriers .10 .25
- ❑ SDSC17 Crystal Seer .10 .25
- ❑ SDSC18 Magical Exemplar .10 .25
- ❑ SDSC19 Magical Citadel of Endymion 1.50 4.00
- ❑ SDSC20 Spell Power Grasp .60 1.50
- ❑ SDSC21 Magicians Unite .10 .25
- ❑ SDSC22 Mist Body .10 .25
- ❑ SDSC23 Malevolent Nuzzler .10 .25
- ❑ SDSC24 Giant Trunade .10 .25
- ❑ SDSC25 Fissure .10 .25
- ❑ SDSC26 Swords of Revealing Light .75 2.00
- ❑ SDSC27 Mage Power 2.00 5.00
- ❑ SDSC28 Terraforming .40 1.00
- ❑ SDSC29 Enemy Controller .75 2.00
- ❑ SDSC30 Book of Moon 1.50 4.00
- ❑ SDSC31 Magical Blast .10 .25
- ❑ SDSC32 Magical Dimension .10 .25
- ❑ SDSC33 Twister .10 .25
- ❑ SDSC34 Field Barrier .10 .25
- ❑ SDSC35 Magician's Circle .75 2.00
- ❑ SDSC36 Pitch-Black Power Stone .10 .25
- ❑ SDSC37 Tower of Babel .10 .25
- ❑ SDSC38 Magic Cylinder 1.50 4.00

2009 Yu-Gi-Oh Warrior's Strike Structure Deck

- Structure Deck Warrior's Strike 8.00 12.00
- ❑ SDWS1 Phoenix Gearfried (UR) .40 1.00
- ❑ SDWS2 Evocator Chevalier (SR) .10 .25
- ❑ SDWS3 Featherizer (SR) .10 .25
- ❑ SDWS4 Gemini Soldier .10 .25
- ❑ SDWS5 Spell Striker .10 .25
- ❑ SDWS6 Freed the Matchless General .10 .25
- ❑ SDWS7 Marauding Captain .10 .25
- ❑ SDWS8 Exiled Force .10 .25
- ❑ SDWS9 D.D. Warrior Lady .60 1.50
- ❑ SDWS10 Card Trooper .10 .25
- ❑ SDWS11 Gemini Summoner .10 .25
- ❑ SDWS12 Blazewing Butterfly .10 .25
- ❑ SDWS13 D.D. Warrior .10 .25
- ❑ SDWS14 Future Samurai .10 .25
- ❑ SDWS15 Field-Commander Rahz .10 .25
- ❑ SDWS16 Dark Valkyria .10 .25
- ❑ SDWS17 Supervise .10 .25
- ❑ SDWS18 Mind Control .10 .25
- ❑ SDWS19 Burden of the Mighty .75 2.00
- ❑ SDWS20 Silent Doom .10 .25
- ❑ SDWS21 Hidden Armory .60 1.50
- ❑ SDWS22 Nightmare's Steelcage .10 .25
- ❑ SDWS23 Mystical Space Typhoon .10 .25
- ❑ SDWS24 Ekibyo Drakmord .10 .25
- ❑ SDWS25 Reinforcement of the Army .10 .25
- ❑ SDWS26 Big Bang Shot .10 .25
- ❑ SDWS27 Divine Sword - Phoenix Blade .10 .25
- ❑ SDWS28 Double Summon .10 .25
- ❑ SDWS29 Symbols of Duty .10 .25
- ❑ SDWS30 Swing of Memories .10 .25
- ❑ SDWS31 Unleash Your Power! .10 .25
- ❑ SDWS32 Dark Bribe .10 .25
- ❑ SDWS33 Kunai with Chain .10 .25
- ❑ SDWS34 Sakuretsu Armor .60 1.50
- ❑ SDWS35 Soul Resurrection .10 .25
- ❑ SDWS36 Justi-Break .10 .25
- ❑ SDWS37 Birthright .10 .25
- ❑ SDWS38 Gemini Trap Hole .10 .25

2010 Yu-Gi-Oh Machina Mayhem Structure Deck

- Structure Deck Machina Mayhem 8.00 20.00
- ❑ SDMM1 Machina Fortress (UR) .75 2.00
- ❑ SDMM2 Machina Gearframe (SR) .60 1.50
- ❑ SDMM3 Machina Peacekeeper (SR) .60 1.50
- ❑ SDMM4 Scrap Recycler .10 .25
- ❑ SDMM5 Commander Covington .10 .25
- ❑ SDMM6 Machina Soldier .40 1.00
- ❑ SDMM7 Machina Sniper .10 .25
- ❑ SDMM8 Machina Defender .10 .25
- ❑ SDMM9 Machina Force .10 .25
- ❑ SDMM10 Kinetic Soldier .10 .25
- ❑ SDMM11 Blast Sphere .10 .25
- ❑ SDMM12 Heavy Mech Support Platform .10 .25
- ❑ SDMM13 Cyber Dragon .10 .25
- ❑ SDMM14 Proto-Cyber Dragon .10 .25
- ❑ SDMM15 Green Gadget .10 .25
- ❑ SDMM16 Red Gadget .10 .25
- ❑ SDMM17 Yellow Gadget .10 .25
- ❑ SDMM18 Armored Cybern .10 .25
- ❑ SDMM19 Cyber Valley 1.25 3.00
- ❑ SDMM20 The Big Saturn .10 .25
- ❑ SDMM21 Machina Armored Unit .10 .25
- ❑ SDMM22 Prohibition .10 .25
- ❑ SDMM23 Swords of Revealing Light .10 .25
- ❑ SDMM24 Shrink .10 .25
- ❑ SDMM25 Frontline Base .10 .25
- ❑ SDMM26 Machine Duplication .10 .25
- ❑ SDMM27 Inferno Reckless Summon .10 .25
- ❑ SDMM28 Hand Destruction .75 2.00
- ❑ SDMM29 Card Trader .10 .25
- ❑ SDMM30 Solidarity .40 1.00
- ❑ SDMM31 Time Machine .10 .25
- ❑ SDMM32 Dimensional Prison 2.50 6.00
- ❑ SDMM33 Metalmorph .10 .25
- ❑ SDMM34 Rare Metalmorph .10 .25
- ❑ SDMM35 Ceasefire .10 .25
- ❑ SDMM36 Compulsory Evacuation Device .10 .25
- ❑ SDMM37 Roll Out! .10 .25

2010 Yu-Gi-Oh Marik Structure Deck

- Complete Set (38) 8.00 20.00
- ❑ SDMA01 Gil Garth .15 .40
- ❑ SDMA02 Mystic Tomato .15 .40
- ❑ SDMA03 Viser Des .15 .40
- ❑ SDMA04 Legendary Fiend .15 .40
- ❑ SDMA05 Dark Jeroid .15 .40
- ❑ SDMA06 Newdoria .15 .40
- ❑ SDMA07 Gravekeeper's Spy .75 2.00
- ❑ SDMA08 Gravekeeper's Curse .15 .40
- ❑ SDMA09 Gravekeeper's Guard .75 2.00
- ❑ SDMA10 Gravekeeper's Spear Soldier .25 .60
- ❑ SDMA11 Gravekeeper's Chief .25 .60
- ❑ SDMA12 Gravekeeper's Cannonholder .25 .60
- ❑ SDMA13 Gravekeeper's Assailant .25 .60
- ❑ SDMA14 Lava Golem (UR) .75 2.00
- ❑ SDMA15 Drillago .15 .40
- ❑ SDMA16 Bowganian .15 .40
- ❑ SDMA17 Gravekeeper's Commandant .25 .60
- ❑ SDMA18 Gravekeeper's Visionary .25 .60
- ❑ SDMA19 Gravekeeper's Descendant .25 .60
- ❑ SDMA20 Mystical Space Typhoon .75 2.00
- ❑ SDMA21 Nightmare's Steelcage .25 .60
- ❑ SDMA22 Creature Swap .25 .60
- ❑ SDMA23 Book of Moon 2.00 5.00
- ❑ SDMA24 Dark Room of Nightmare .15 .40
- ❑ SDMA25 Necrovalley .40 1.00
- ❑ SDMA26 Foolish Burial .40 1.00
- ❑ SDMA27 Magical Stone Excavation .25 .60
- ❑ SDMA28 Allure of Darkness 1.50 4.00
- ❑ SDMA29 Acid Trap Hole .15 .40
- ❑ SDMA30 Mirror Force 2.50 6.00
- ❑ SDMA31 Skull Invitation .15 .40
- ❑ SDMA32 Coffin Seller .15 .40
- ❑ SDMA33 Nightmare Wheel .30 .75
- ❑ SDMA34 Metal Reflect Slime .30 .75
- ❑ SDMA35 Malevolent Catastrophe .25 .60
- ❑ SDMA36 Dark Illusion .25 .60
- ❑ SDMA37 Mystical Beast of Serket (UR) .40 1.00
- ❑ SDMA38 Temple of the Kings (UR) .40 1.00

2011 Yu-Gi-Oh Dragunity Legion Structure Deck

- Complete Set (39) 8.00 20.00
- ❑ SDDL01 Dragunity Arma Leyvaten (UTR) .75 2.00
- ❑ SDDL02 Dragunity Arma Mystletainn (SR) .75 2.00
- ❑ SDDL03 Dragunity Aklys (SR) .75 2.00
- ❑ SDDL04 Dragunity Dux .25 .60
- ❑ SDDL05 Dragunity Legionnaire .15 .40
- ❑ SDDL06 Dragunity Tribus .15 .40
- ❑ SDDL07 Dragunity Darkspear .15 .40
- ❑ SDDL08 Dragunity Militum .15 .40
- ❑ SDDL09 Dragunity Primus Pilus .15 .40
- ❑ SDDL10 Dragunity Brandistock .15 .40
- ❑ SDDL11 Dragunity Javelin .15 .40
- ❑ SDDL12 Mist Valley Falcon .15 .40
- ❑ SDDL13 Hunter Owl .15 .40
- ❑ SDDL14 Garuda the Wind Spirit .15 .40
- ❑ SDDL15 Flying Kamakiri #1 .15 .40
- ❑ SDDL16 Spear Dragon .15 .40
- ❑ SDDL17 Twin-Headed Behemoth .15 .40
- ❑ SDDL18 Armed Dragon LV3 .15 .40
- ❑ SDDL19 Armed Dragon LV5 .15 .40
- ❑ SDDL20 Masked Dragon .25 .60
- ❑ SDDL21 Dragon Ravine 1.50 4.00
- ❑ SDDL22 Dragon Mastery 50.00 75.00
- ❑ SDDL23 United We Stand 1.25 3.00
- ❑ SDDL24 Mage Power .40 1.00
- ❑ SDDL25 Dragon's Gunfire .15 .40
- ❑ SDDL26 Stamping Destruction .15 .40
- ❑ SDDL27 Creature Swap .25 .60
- ❑ SDDL28 Monster Reincarnation .25 .60
- ❑ SDDL29 Foolish Burial .40 1.00
- ❑ SDDL30 Card Destruction .15 .40
- ❑ SDDL31 Windstorm of Etaqua .15 .40
- ❑ SDDL32 Relieve Monster .25 .60
- ❑ SDDL33 Legacy of Yata-Garasu .15 .40
- ❑ SDDL34 Final Attack Orders .15 .40
- ❑ SDDL35 Mirror Force 2.50 6.00
- ❑ SDDL36 Dragon's Rage .15 .40
- ❑ SDDL37 Bottomless Trap Hole 2.00 5.00
- ❑ SDDL38 Spiritual Wind Art - Miyabi .15 .40
- ❑ SDDL39 Icarus Attack .75 2.00

2011 Yu-Gi-Oh Lost Sanctuary Structure Deck

- Complete Set (38) 8.00 20.00
- ❑ SDLS01 Master Hyperion (UR) 2.00 5.00
- ❑ SDLS02 The Agent of Mystery - Earth (SR) 1.00 2.50
- ❑ SDLS03 The Agent of Miracles - Jupiter (SR) .75 2.00
- ❑ SDLS04 The Agent of Judgement - Saturn .30 .75
- ❑ SDLS05 The Agent of Wisdom - Mercury .30 .75
- ❑ SDLS06 The Agent of Creation - Venus .30 .75
- ❑ SDLS07 The Agent of Force - Mars .30 .75
- ❑ SDLS08 Mystical Shine Ball .30 .75
- ❑ SDLS09 Splendid Venus .50 1.25
- ❑ SDLS10 Tethys, Goddess of Light .75 2.00
- ❑ SDLS11 Victoria .60 1.50
- ❑ SDLS12 Athena .40 1.00
- ❑ SDLS13 Marshmallon 1.00 2.50
- ❑ SDLS14 Hecatrice .40 1.00
- ❑ SDLS15 Shining Angel .60 1.50
- ❑ SDLS16 Soul of Purity and Light .60 1.50
- ❑ SDLS17 Airknight Parshath .30 .75
- ❑ SDLS18 Nova Summoner .60 1.50
- ❑ SDLS19 Zeradias, Herald of Heaven .30 .75
- ❑ SDLS20 Honest .75 2.00
- ❑ SDLS21 Hanewata .30 .75
- ❑ SDLS22 Consecrated Light .60 1.50
- ❑ SDLS23 Cards from the Sky 1.00 2.50
- ❑ SDLS24 Valhalla, Hall of the Fallen .50 1.25
- ❑ SDLS25 Terraforming .60 1.50
- ❑ SDLS26 Smashing Ground 1.00 2.50
- ❑ SDLS27 The Sanctuary in the Sky .75 2.00
- ❑ SDLS28 Celestial Transformation .30 .75
- ❑ SDLS29 Burial from a Different Dimension 1.50 4.00
- ❑ SDLS30 Mausoleum of the Emperor .60 1.50
- ❑ SDLS31 Solidarity 1.50 4.00
- ❑ SDLS32 The Fountain in the Sky .30 .75
- ❑ SDLS33 Divine Punishment .60 1.50
- ❑ SDLS34 Return from the Different Dimension .60 1.50
- ❑ SDLS35 Torrential Tribute 1.50 4.00
- ❑ SDLS36 Beckoning Light .40 1.00
- ❑ SDLS37 Miraculous Descent .30 .75
- ❑ SDLS38 Solemn Judgment 4.00 10.00

2012 Yu-Gi-Oh Realm of the Sea Emperor Structure Deck

- Structure Deck 5.00 10.00
- ❑ SDRE001 Poseidra, the Atlantean Dragon (UR) .75 2.00
- ❑ SDRE002 Atlantean Dragoons (SR) 1.00 2.50
- ❑ SDRE003 Atlantean Marksman .20 .50
- ❑ SDRE004 Atlantean Heavy Infantry .10 .25
- ❑ SDRE005 Atlantean Pikeman .10 .25
- ❑ SDRE006 Atlantean Attack Squad .10 .25
- ❑ SDRE007 Lost Blue Breaker .10 .25
- ❑ SDRE008 Armed Sea Hunter .10 .25
- ❑ SDRE009 Spined Gillman .10 .25
- ❑ SDRE010 Deep Sea Diva .40 1.00
- ❑ SDRE011 Mermaid Archer .10 .25
- ❑ SDRE012 Codarus .10 .25
- ❑ SDRE013 Warrior of Atlantis .10 .25
- ❑ SDRE014 Abyss Soldier .10 .25
- ❑ SDRE015 Skreech .10 .25
- ❑ SDRE016 Snowman Eater .20 .50
- ❑ SDRE017 Nightmare Penguin .10 .25
- ❑ SDRE018 Penguin Soldier .10 .25
- ❑ SDRE019 Deep Diver .10 .25
- ❑ SDRE020 Reese the Ice Mistress .10 .25
- ❑ SDRE021 Mother Grizzly .10 .25
- ❑ SDRE022 Friller Rabca .10 .25
- ❑ SDRE023 Call of the Atlanteans (SR) .40 1.00
- ❑ SDRE024 A Legendary Ocean .10 .25
- ❑ SDRE025 Terraforming .10 .25
- ❑ SDRE026 Water Hazard .10 .25
- ❑ SDRE027 Aqua Jet .10 .25
- ❑ SDRE028 Surface .10 .25
- ❑ SDRE029 Moray of Greed .10 .25
- ❑ SDRE030 Salvage .10 .25
- ❑ SDRE031 Dark Hole .20 .50
- ❑ SDRE032 Big Wave Small Wave .10 .25
- ❑ SDRE033 Aegis of the Ocean Dragon Lord .10 .25
- ❑ SDRE034 Forgotten Temple of the Deep .10 .25
- ❑ SDRE035 Tornado Wall .10 .25
- ❑ SDRE036 Torrential Tribute .40 1.00
- ❑ SDRE037 Spiritual Water Art - Aoi .10 .25
- ❑ SDRE038 Gravity Bind .10 .25
- ❑ SDRE039 Poseidon Wave .10 .25

2012 Yu-Gi-Oh Samurai Warlords Structure Deck

- Complete Set (41) 6.00 12.00
- Structure Deck 7.50 15.00
- ❑ SDWA001 Chamberlain of the Six Samurai .10 .25
- ❑ SDWA002 Grandmaster of the Six Samurai .15 .40
- ❑ SDWA003 The Six Samurai - Yaiza .10 .25
- ❑ SDWA004 The Six Samurai - Zanji .10 .25
- ❑ SDWA005 The Six Samurai - Nisashi .10 .25
- ❑ SDWA006 The Six Samurai - Yaichi .10 .25
- ❑ SDWA007 The Six Samurai - Kamon .10 .25
- ❑ SDWA008 The Six Samurai - Irou .10 .25
- ❑ SDWA009 Great Shogun Shien .15 .40
- ❑ SDWA010 Shien's Footsoldier .10 .25
- ❑ SDWA011 Enishi, Shien's Chancellor .10 .25
- ❑ SDWA012 Spirit of the Six Samurai .10 .25
- ❑ SDWA013 Future Samurai .10 .25
- ❑ SDWA014 The Immortal Bushi .10 .25
- ❑ SDWA015 Hand of the Six Samurai .10 .25
- ❑ SDWA016 Legendary Six Samurai - Kizan 1.00 2.50
- ❑ SDWA017 Legendary Six Samurai - Enishi .20 .50
- ❑ SDWA018 Legendary Six Samurai - Kageki (SR) .40 1.00
- ❑ SDWA019 Shien's Squire .10 .25
- ❑ SDWA020 Shien's Daredevil .10 .25
- ❑ SDWA021 Elder of the Six Samurai .10 .25
- ❑ SDWA022 Shien's Advisor .10 .25
- ❑ SDWA023 Dark Hole .60 1.50
- ❑ SDWA024 The A. Forces .10 .25
- ❑ SDWA025 Reinforcement of the Army .10 .25
- ❑ SDWA026 The Warrior Returning Alive .10 .25
- ❑ SDWA027 Cunning of the Six Samurai .10 .25
- ❑ SDWA028 Six Samurai United .40 1.00
- ❑ SDWA029 Gateway of the Six .15 .40
- ❑ SDWA030 Shien's Smoke Signal (SR) .40 1.00
- ❑ SDWA031 Temple of the Six .10 .25
- ❑ SDWA032 Shien's Dojo .30 .75
- ❑ SDWA033 Rivalry of Warlords .15 .40
- ❑ SDWA034 Return of the Six Samurai .10 .25
- ❑ SDWA035 Double-Edged Sword Technique .15 .40
- ❑ SDWA036 Fiendish Chain 1.00 2.50
- ❑ SDWA037 Musakani Magatama .10 .25
- ❑ SDWA038 Shien's Scheme .10 .25
- ❑ SDWA039 Six Strike - Thunder Blast .10 .25
- ❑ SDWA040 Six Style - Dual Wield .10 .25
- ❑ SDWA041 Shadow of the Six Samurai Shien (UR) 1.25 3.00

2012 Yu-Gi-Oh Xyz Symphony Starter Deck

- Complete Set (43) 4.00 8.00
- Starter Deck 6.00 12.00
- ❑ YS12001 Alexandrite Dragon .40 1.00
- ❑ YS12002 Spirit of the Harp .10 .25
- ❑ YS12003 Frostosaurus .10 .25
- ❑ YS12004 Zubaba Knight .10 .25
- ❑ YS12005 Ganbara Knight .10 .25
- ❑ YS12006 Gogogo Golem .10 .25
- ❑ YS12007 Gogogo Giant .10 .25
- ❑ YS12008 Goblindbergh .10 .25
- ❑ YS12009 Feedback Warrior .10 .25
- ❑ YS12010 Shine Knight .10 .25
- ❑ YS12011 Cyber Dragon .40 1.00
- ❑ YS12012 Trident Warrior .10 .25
- ❑ YS12013 Chiron the Mage .10 .25
- ❑ YS12014 Marauding Captain .10 .25
- ❑ YS12015 Penguin Soldier .10 .25
- ❑ YS12016 Sangan .10 .25
- ❑ YS12017 Giant Rat .10 .25
- ❑ YS12018 Shining Angel .10 .25
- ❑ YS12019 Blustering Winds .10 .25
- ❑ YS12020 Ego Boost .10 .25
- ❑ YS12021 Xyz Energy .10 .25
- ❑ YS12022 Star Changer .10 .25
- ❑ YS12023 Swords of Revealing Light .10 .25
- ❑ YS12024 Mystical Space Typhoon .60 1.50
- ❑ YS12025 Fissure .10 .25
- ❑ YS12026 Gravity Axe - Grarl .10 .25
- ❑ YS12027 Reinforcement of the Army .10 .25
- ❑ YS12028 Burden of the Mighty .20 .50
- ❑ YS12029 Heartfelt Appeal .10 .25
- ❑ YS12030 Xyz Effect .10 .25
- ❑ YS12031 Raigeki Break .10 .25
- ❑ YS12032 Trap Hole .10 .25
- ❑ YS12033 Dust Tornado .10 .25
- ❑ YS12034 Magic Cylinder .20 .50
- ❑ YS12035 Draining Shield .10 .25
- ❑ YS12036 Call of the Haunted .10 .25
- ❑ YS12037 Limit Reverse .10 .25
- ❑ YS12038 Seven Tools of the Bandit .10 .25
- ❑ YS12039 Number 39: Utopia (UR) 1.00 2.50
- ❑ YS12040 Muzurhythm the String Djinn (SR) .20 .50
- ❑ YS12041 Temtempo the Percussion Djinn (SR) .40 1.00
- ❑ YS12042 Melomelody the Brass Djinn (SR) .40 1.00
- ❑ YS12043 Maestroke the Symphony Djinn (SR) 1.50 4.00

2013 Yu-Gi-Oh Onslaught of the Fire Kings Structure Deck

- Complete Set 6.00 12.00
- Structure Deck 7.50 15.00
- ❑ SDOK001 Fire King High Avatar Garunix (UR) 1.00 2.50
- ❑ SDOK002 Fire King Avatar Barong .75 2.00
- ❑ SDOK003 Fire King Avatar Kirin .15 .40
- ❑ SDOK004 Sacred Phoenix of Nephthys .15 .40
- ❑ SDOK005 Manticore of Darkness .15 .40
- ❑ SDOK006 Goka, the Pyre of Malice .15 .40
- ❑ SDOK007 Hazy Flame Hyppogrif .15 .40
- ❑ SDOK008 Laval Lancelord .15 .40
- ❑ SDOK009 Flamvell Firedog .30 .75
- ❑ SDOK010 Flamvell Poun .15 .40
- ❑ SDOK011 Neo Flamvell Sabre .15 .40
- ❑ SDOK012 Royal Firestorm Guards .25 .60
- ❑ SDOK013 Volcanic Rocket .15 .40
- ❑ SDOK014 Volcanic Counter .15 .40
- ❑ SDOK015 Molten Zombie .15 .40
- ❑ SDOK016 Spirit of Flames .15 .40
- ❑ SDOK017 Raging Flame Sprite .15 .40
- ❑ SDOK018 Fox Fire .15 .40
- ❑ SDOK019 Flame Tiger .15 .40
- ❑ SDOK020 Little Chimera .15 .40
- ❑ SDOK021 UFO Turtle .15 .40
- ❑ SDOK022 Onslaught of the Fire Kings (SR) 1.00 2.50
- ❑ SDOK023 Circle of the Fire Kings (SR) 1.00 2.50
- ❑ SDOK024 Rekindling .40 1.00
- ❑ SDOK025 Blaze Accelerator .15 .40
- ❑ SDOK026 Wild Nature's Release .15 .40
- ❑ SDOK027 Pot of Duality 2.50 6.00
- ❑ SDOK028 Hand Destruction .60 1.50
- ❑ SDOK029 Creature Swap .15 .40
- ❑ SDOK030 Burden of the Mighty .15 .40
- ❑ SDOK031 Backfire .15 .40
- ❑ SDOK032 Flamvell Counter .15 .40
- ❑ SDOK033 Phoenix Wing Wind Blast .15 .40
- ❑ SDOK034 Horn of the Phantom Beast .30 .75
- ❑ SDOK035 Blast with Chain .15 .40
- ❑ SDOK036 Spiritual Fire Art - Kurenai .15 .40
- ❑ SDOK037 Regretful Rebirth .15 .40
- ❑ SDOK038 Nightmare Wheel .15 .40
- ❑ SDOK039 Call of the Haunted .15 .40

2013 Yu-Gi-Oh Super Starter V For Victory Starter Deck

- Structure Deck 6.00 12.00
- ❑ YS13001 Cosmo Queen .15 .40
- ❑ YS13002 Trance the Magic Swordsman .15 .40
- ❑ YS13003 Neo the Magic Swordsman .15 .40
- ❑ YS13004 Mystical Elf .15 .40
- ❑ YS13005 Chamberlain of the Six Samurai .15 .40
- ❑ YS13006 Gagaga Child .40 1.00
- ❑ YS13007 Magical Undertaker .15 .40
- ❑ YS13008 Caligo Claw Crow .15 .40
- ❑ YS13009 Gagaga Magician .15 .40
- ❑ YS13010 Gagaga Girl .15 .40
- ❑ YS13011 Gagaga Gardna .15 .40
- ❑ YS13012 Zubaba Knight .15 .40
- ❑ YS13013 Ganbara Knight .15 .40

- ❑ YS13014 Achacha Archer .15 .40
- ❑ YS13015 Goblindbergh .15 .40
- ❑ YS13016 Kagetokage .60 1.50
- ❑ YS13017 Tasuke Knight .15 .40
- ❑ YS13018 ZW - Unicorn Spear .15 .40
- ❑ YS13019 Marauding Captain .15 .40
- ❑ YS13020 Old Vindictive Magician .15 .40
- ❑ YS13021 Swords of Burning Light .15 .40
- ❑ YS13022 Blustering Winds .15 .40
- ❑ YS13023 Wonder Wand .15 .40
- ❑ YS13024 Double or Nothing .15 .40
- ❑ YS13025 Ego Boost .15 .40
- ❑ YS13026 Gagagarevenge .15 .40
- ❑ YS13027 Xyz Unit .15 .40
- ❑ YS13028 The A. Forces .15 .40
- ❑ YS13029 Reinforcement of the Army .15 .40
- ❑ YS13030 The Warrior Returning Alive .15 .40
- ❑ YS13031 Puzzle Reborn .15 .40
- ❑ YS13032 Gagagashield .15 .40
- ❑ YS13033 Copy Knight .15 .40
- ❑ YS13034 Impenetrable Attack .15 .40
- ❑ YS13035 Utopian Aura .15 .40
- ❑ YS13036 Xyz Effect .15 .40
- ❑ YS13037 Shadow Spell .15 .40
- ❑ YS13038 Dust Tornado .15 .40
- ❑ YS13039 Call of the Haunted .15 .40
- ❑ YS13040 Dark Bribe .40 1.00
- ❑ YS13041 Number 39: Utopia (SR) .40 1.00
- ❑ YS13042 Number C39: Utopia Ray (UR) 1.25 3.00

2013 Yu-Gi-Oh Super Starter V For Victory Starter Deck Power Up Pack

Two Packs per Starter Deck

- ❑ YS13V01 Number C39: Utopia Ray V (UR) .60 1.50
- ❑ YS13V02 Rank-Up Magic Limited Barian's Force (UR) .75 2.00
- ❑ YS13V03 ZW - Eagle Claw .15 .40
- ❑ YS13V04 Ganbara Lancer .15 .40
- ❑ YS13V05 Bite Bug .15 .40
- ❑ YS13V06 Crane Crane .75 2.00
- ❑ YS13V07 Gentlemander .15 .40
- ❑ YS13V08 Grenosaurus .15 .40
- ❑ YS13V09 Number 30: Acid Golem of Destruction .15 .40
- ❑ YS13V10 Shining Elf .15 .40
- ❑ YS13V11 Number 6: Chronomaly Atlandis .40 1.00
- ❑ YS13V12 Mystical Space Typhoon (SR) 1.00 2.50
- ❑ YS13V13 Swords of Revealing Light (SR) .40 1.00
- ❑ YS13V14 Mirror Force (SR) 1.50 4.00
- ❑ YS13V15 Magic Cylinder (SR) .60 1.50

2002 Yu-Gi-Oh Collector Tins

- Complete Set Sealed (6) 150.00 175.00
- Black Skull Dragon Sealed Box 30.00 45.00
- Black Skull Dragon Tin Only 8.00 15.00
- Blue Eyes White Dragon Sealed Box 25.00 35.00
- Blue Eyes White Dragon Tin Only 8.00 12.00
- Dark Magician Sealed Box 25.00 30.00
- Dark Magician Tin Only 5.00 8.00
- Lord of D Sealed Box 20.00 28.00
- Lord of D Tin Only 4.00 7.00
- Red Eyes B Dragon Sealed Box 30.00 35.00
- Red Eyes B Dragon Tin Only 6.00 10.00
- Summoned Skull Sealed Box 22.00 30.00
- Summoned Skull Tin Only 4.00 8.00
- ❑ BPT001 Dark Magician (SCR) 3.00 8.00
- ❑ BPT002 Summoned Skull (SCR) 2.50 6.00
- ❑ BPT003 Blue Eyes White Dragon (SCR) 2.00 5.00
- ❑ BPT004 Lord of D (SCR) 1.00 2.50
- ❑ BPT005 Red Eyes B Dragon (SCR) 1.50 4.00
- ❑ BPT006 B. Skull Dragon (SCR) 2.50 6.00

2003 Yu-Gi-Oh Collector Tins

- Complete Tin Set sealed (6) 140.00 200.00
- Blue-Eyes White Dragon Sealed Box 25.00 35.00
- Blue-Eyes White Dragon Tin Only 5.00 10.00
- Buster Blader Sealed Box 20.00 30.00
- Buster Blader Tin Only 4.00 7.00
- Dark Magician Sealed Box 22.00 30.00
- Dark Magician Tin Only 5.00 8.00
- Gearfried the Iron Knight Sealed Box 15.00 20.00
- Gearfried the Iron Knight Tin Only 3.00 5.00
- Jinzo Sealed Box 30.00 45.00
- Jinzo Tin Only 7.00 15.00
- XYZ-Dragon Cannon Sealed Box 20.00 28.00
- XYZ-Dragon Cannon Tin Only 5.00 10.00
- ❑ BPT007 Dark Magician 2.00 5.00
- ❑ BPT008 Buster Blader 1.25 3.00
- ❑ BPT009 Blue-Eyes White Dragon 3.00 8.00
- ❑ BPT010 XYZ-Dragon Cannon 1.00 2.50
- ❑ BPT011 Jinzo 2.50 6.00
- ❑ BPT012 Gearfried the Iron Knight .75 2.00

2004 Yu-Gi-Oh Collector Tins

- Complete Tin Set sealed (6) 90.00 130.00
- Blade Knight Sealed Tin 20.00 27.00
- Command Knight Sealed Tin 20.00 27.00
- Insect Queen Sealed Tin 20.00 27.00
- Obnoxious Celtic Guardian Sealed Tin 20.00 25.00
- Swift Knight Gaia Sealed Tin 18.00 22.00
- Total Defense Shogun Sealed Tin 18.00 22.00
- ❑ CT1001 Total Defense Shogun .75 2.00
- ❑ CT1002 Blade Knight .75 2.00
- ❑ CT1003 Command Knight 1.00 2.50
- ❑ CT1004 Swift Gaia The Fierce Knight .75 2.00
- ❑ CT1005 Insect Queen 1.25 3.00
- ❑ CT1006 Obnoxious Celtic Guardian 1.00 2.50

2005 Yu-Gi-Oh Collector Tins

- Collector Tins (empty) 3.00 5.00
- Gilford the Lightning Sealed Tin 15.00 25.00
- Exarion Sealed Tin 15.00 22.00
- Vorse Raider Sealed Tin 15.00 19.00
- Dark Magician Girl Sealed Tin 20.00 30.00
- Rocket Warrior Sealed Tin 15.00 22.00
- Panther Warrior Sealed Tin 15.00 22.00
- ❑ CT2001 Gilford the Lightning 1.00 2.50
- ❑ CT2002 Exarion Universe .75 2.00
- ❑ CT2003 Vorse Raider 6.00 15.00
- ❑ CT2004 Dark Magician Girl 6.00 15.00
- ❑ CT2005 Rockety Warrior 2.00 5.00
- ❑ CT2006 Panther Warrior 1.00 2.50

2006 Yu-Gi-Oh Collector Tins

- ❑ CT03001 Elemental HERO Neos (SCR) 2.00 5.00
- ❑ CT03002 Cyber Dragon (SCR) 1.50 4.00

- ❑ CT03003 Raviel, Lord of Phantasms (SCR) 1.50 4.00
- ❑ CT03004 Elemental HERO Shining Flare Wingman (SCR) 2.00 5.00
- ❑ CT03005 Uria, Lord of Searing Flames (SCR) 2.50 6.00
- ❑ CT03006 Hamon, Lord of Striking Thunder (SCR) 2.00 5.00

2007 Yu-Gi-Oh Collector Tins

- ❑ CT04001 Elemental HERO Grand Neos (SCR) .75 2.00
- ❑ CT04002 Crystal Beast Sapphire Pegasus (SCR) 2.00 5.00
- ❑ CT04003 Destiny HERO - Plasma (SCR) 1.25 3.00
- ❑ CT04004 Volcanic Doomfire (SCR) 1.50 4.00
- ❑ CT04005 Rainbow Dragon (SCR) 2.50 6.00
- ❑ CT04006 Elemental HERO Plasma Vice (SCR) 1.00 2.50

2008 Yu-Gi-Oh Collector Tins

- Stardust Dragon Tin 30.00 40.00
- Red Dragon Archfiend Tin 30.00 40.00
- Black Rose Dragon Tin 30.00 40.00
- Turbo Warrior Tin 25.00 35.00
- Yusei Fudo Tin 30.00 40.00
- ❑ CT05001 Stardust Dragon (SCR) 8.00 20.00
- ❑ CT05002 Red Dragon Archfiend (SCR) 3.00 8.00
- ❑ CT05003 Black Rose Dragon (SCR) 8.00 20.00
- ❑ CT05004 Turbo Warrior (SCR) .75 2.00
- ❑ CT05S01 Montage Dragon (SR) 2.00 5.00
- ❑ CT05S02 Nitro Warrior (SR) .75 2.00
- ❑ CT05S03 Goyo Guardian (SR) 3.00 8.00

2009 Yu-Gi-Oh Collector Tins

- Ancient Fairy Dragon Tin 15.00 25.00
- Power Tool Dragon Tin 15.00 25.00
- Majestic Star Dragon Tin 15.00 25.00
- Earthbound Immortal Wiraquocha Rasca Tin 15.00 25.00
- ❑ CT06001 Power Tool Dragon (SCR) 2.00 5.00
- ❑ CT06002 Ancient Fairy Dragon (SCR) 3.00 8.00
- ❑ CT06003 Majestic Star Dragon (SCR) 1.50 4.00
- ❑ CT06004 Earthbound Immortal Wiragocha 1.00 2.50
- ❑ CT06S01 Blackwing - Elphin the Raven (SCR) 1.00 2.50
- ❑ CT06S02 Earthbound Immortal Aslla piscu (SCR) 2.00 5.00
- ❑ CT06S03 Earthbound Immortal Chacu 2.50 6.00
- ❑ CT06S04 XX-Saber Gottoms (SCR) .75 2.00
- ❑ DP09001 Stardust Dragon/Assault Mode (UR) 1.00 2.50
- ❑ RGBTPP1 Iron Core of Koa'ki Meiru (UR) .60 1.50
- ❑ RGBTPP2 Blackwing - Shura the Blue Flame (SR) .60 1.50
- ❑ RGBTPP3 Koa'ki Meiru Guardian (SR) .60 1.50
- ❑ RGBTPP4 Moja (UR) .60 1.50
- ❑ RGBTPP5 Master Gig (SR) .60 1.50
- ❑ RGBTPP6 Level Retuner (SR) .60 1.50

2010 Yu-Gi-Oh Collector Tins

- ❑ CT07001 Majestic Red Dragon (SCR) .75 2.00
- ❑ CT07002 Black-Winged Dragon (SCR) 1.25 3.00
- ❑ CT07003 Dragon Knight Draco-Equiste (SCR) .75 2.00
- ❑ CT07004 Shooting Star Dragon (SCR) 2.50 6.00
- ❑ CT07005 Red Nova Dragon (SCR) 2.00 5.00
- ❑ CT07006 Elemental HERO Stratos (SR) 1.50 4.00
- ❑ CT07007 Van'Dalgyon the Dark Dragon Lord (SR) .75 2.00
- ❑ CT07008 Cyber Dinosaur (SR) .75 2.00
- ❑ CT07009 Battle Fader (SR) 1.25 3.00
- ❑ CT07010 Green Baboon Defender of the Forest (SR) .75 2.00
- ❑ CT07011 The Wicked Eraser (SR) .75 2.00
- ❑ CT07012 Blackwing Vayu the Emblem of Honor (SR) 1.50 4.00
- ❑ CT07013 Chimeratech Fortress Dragon (SR) 2.50 6.00
- ❑ CT07014 Archfiend of Gilfer (SR) .75 2.00
- ❑ CT07015 The Wicked Dreadroot (SR) 1.50 4.00
- ❑ CT07016 Dark Armed Dragon (SR) 2.50 6.00
- ❑ CT07017 Dragonic Knight (SR) .75 2.00
- ❑ CT07018 Elemental HERO Ocean (SR) 1.25 3.00
- ❑ CT07019 Dreadscythe Harvester (SR) .75 2.00
- ❑ CT07020 Gandora the Dragon of Destruction (SR) .75 2.00
- ❑ CT07021 Stardust Dragon (SR) 8.00 20.00
- ❑ CT07022 Magician's Valkyria (SR) 3.00 8.00
- ❑ CT07023 The Wicked Avatar (SR) .75 2.00
- ❑ CT07024 Exodius the Ultimate Forbidden Lord (SR) 1.25 3.00
- ❑ CT07025 Red Dragon Archfiend (SR) 2.50 6.00

2011 Yu-Gi-Oh Collector Tins

- ❑ CT08001 Number 17: Leviathan Dragon (SCR) 1.50 4.00
- ❑ CT08002 Wind-Up Zenmaister (SCR) .75 2.00
- ❑ CT08003 Galaxy-Eyes Photon Dragon (SCR) 2.00 5.00
- ❑ CT08004 Number 10: Illumiknight (SCR) .75 2.00
- ❑ CT08005 Beast King Barbaros (SR) 1.00 2.50
- ❑ CT08006 Dark Simorgh (SR) .75 2.00
- ❑ CT08007 Stygian Street Patrol (SR) 1.00 2.50
- ❑ CT08008 Pot of Duality (SR) 3.00 8.00
- ❑ CT08009 Neo-Parshath, the Sky Paladin (SR) .75 2.00
- ❑ CT08010 Archlord Kristya (SR) 1.50 4.00
- ❑ CT08011 Elemental HERO Gaia (SR) .75 2.00
- ❑ CT08012 Fossil Dyna Pachycephalo (SR) 1.50 4.00
- ❑ CT08013 Guardian Eatos (SR) .75 2.00
- ❑ CT08014 Malefic Stardust Dragon (SR) .75 2.00
- ❑ CT08015 Solemn Warning (SR) 3.00 8.00
- ❑ CT08016 Ehren, Lightsworn Monk (SR) .75 2.00
- ❑ CT08017 XX-Saber Darksoul (SR) .75 2.00
- ❑ CT08018 The Tyrant Neptune (SR) .75 2.00

2012 Yu-Gi-Oh Collector Tins

- ❑ CT09001 Evolzar Dolkka (SCR) 1.00 2.50
- ❑ CT09002 Heroic Champion - Excalibur (SCR) 1.50 4.00
- ❑ CT09003 Ninja Grandmaster Hanzo (SCR) .75 2.00
- ❑ CT09004 Hieratic Sun Dragon Overlord of Heliopolis (SCR) .75 2.00
- ❑ CT09005 Genex Neutron (SR) .75 2.00
- ❑ CT09006 Scrap Dragon (SR) 1.00 2.50
- ❑ CT09007 Dark Highlander (SR) .75 2.00
- ❑ CT09008 Wind-Up Zenmaines (SR) 1.00 2.50
- ❑ CT09009 Blizzard Princess (SR) .75 2.00
- ❑ CT09010 Wind-Up Rabbit (SR) .75 2.00
- ❑ CT09011 Evolzar Laggia (SR) 1.00 2.50
- ❑ CT09012 Maxx C (SR) 3.00 8.00
- ❑ CT09013 Tour Guide From the Underworld (SR) 4.00 10.00
- ❑ CT09014 Number 16: Shock Master (SR) 1.50 4.00
- ❑ CT09015 Rescue Rabbit (SR) .75 2.00
- ❑ CT09016 Malefic Truth Dragon (SR) .75 2.00
- ❑ CT09017 X-Saber Souza (SR) .75 2.00
- ❑ CT09018 Leviair the Sea Dragon (SR) 2.50 6.00
- ❑ CT09019 Prophecy Destroyer (SR) 1.25 3.00
- ❑ CT09020 Endless Decay (SR) 1.50 4.00
- ❑ CT09021 Steelswarm Roach (SR) 3.00 8.00
- ❑ CT09022 Photon Strike Bounzer (SR) 2.50 6.00
- ❑ CT09023 Infernity Barrier (SR) 2.00 5.00

2013 Yu-Gi-Oh Zexal Collection Tin

- Complete Set 8.00 20.00
- ❑ ZTIN001 Dododo Warrior (SR) .20 .50
- ❑ ZTIN002 Number 61: Volcasaurus (UR) 4.00 10.00
- ❑ ZTIN003 Number 19: Freezadon (UR) 1.00 2.50
- ❑ ZTIN004 Gagagaback (SR) .20 .50
- ❑ ZTIN005 Gagagashield (UR) .60 1.50
- ❑ ZTIN006 Photon Pirate (SR) .20 .50
- ❑ ZTIN007 Photon Satellite (SR) .40 1.00
- ❑ ZTIN008 Photon Slasher (SR) .40 1.00
- ❑ ZTIN009 Kuriphoton (UR) .40 1.00
- ❑ ZTIN010 Dimension Wanderer (SR) .20 .50
- ❑ ZTIN011 Galaxy Wizard (UR) 1.25 3.00
- ❑ ZTIN012 Galaxy Knight (UR) 2.00 5.00
- ❑ ZTIN013 Number 56: Gold Rat (SR) .75 2.00
- ❑ ZTIN014 Starliege Paladynamo (UR) 3.00 8.00
- ❑ ZTIN015 Message in a Bottle (SR) .60 1.50
- ❑ ZTIN016 Accellight (UR) .60 1.50
- ❑ ZTIN017 Galaxy Expedition (UR) 1.25 3.00
- ❑ ZTIN018 Galaxy Zero (SR) .60 1.50
- ❑ ZTIN019 Triple Star Trion (SR) .20 .50
- ❑ ZTIN020 Zubaba Buster (SR) .20 .50
- ❑ ZTIN021 Chachaka Archer (SR) .20 .50
- ❑ ZTINV01 Gagaga Magician (UTR) .75 2.00
- ❑ ZTINV02 Number 20: Giga-Brilliant (UTR) 1.25 3.00
- ❑ ZTINV03 Gagagabolt (UTR) .75 2.00

2006 Yu-Gi-Oh Duelist Pack Jaden Yuki

- Complete Set (30) 35.00 60.00
- Booster Box (30 packs) 30.00 50.00
- Booster Pack (6 cards) 2.00 3.00
- ❑ DP1-5 Winged Kuriboh .75 1.50
- ❑ DP1-10 Elemental Hero Flame Wingman (UR) 5.00 10.00
- ❑ DP1-13 Elemental Hero Steam Healer (UR) 15.00 26.00

2006 Yu-Gi-Oh Duelist Pack Chazz Princeton

- Complete Set (30) 40.00 60.00
- Booster Box (30 packs) 30.00 50.00
- Booster Pack (6 cards) 2.00 3.00
- ❑ DP2-12 Armed Dragon LV7 (SR) 7.00 14.00
- ❑ DP2-13 Armed Dragon LV10 (UR) 15.00 25.00

2006 Yu-Gi-Oh Duelist Pack Special Edition

English cards have EN Prefix

- ❑ DPK-SE1 Blockman (LE) (SR) 1.00 3.00
- ❑ DPK-SE2 Treasure Map (LE) (SR) 1.00 2.00
- ❑ DPK-SE3 Hero Spirit (LE) (SR) 1.00 2.00

2007 Yu-Gi-Oh Duelist Pack Aster Phoenix

- Complete Set (30) 75.00 125.00
- Booster Box (30 packs) 50.00 75.00
- Booster Pack (6 cards) 3.00 4.00
- ❑ DP5-4 Destiny Hero Dreadmaster (R) .50 1.00
- ❑ DP5-6 Destiny Hero Defender (R) .50 1.00
- ❑ DP5-7 Destiny Hero Dogma (R) .50 1.00
- ❑ DP5-9 Destiny Hero Fear Monger (R) .50 1.00
- ❑ DP5-11 Destiny Hero Malicious (UR) 20.00 32.00
- ❑ DP5-12 Elemental Hero Phoenix Enforcer (R) 1.00 2.00
- ❑ DP5-13 Elemental Hero Shining Phoenix Enforcer (SR) 1.00 2.00
- ❑ DP5-16 Clock Tower Prison (R) .50 1.00
- ❑ DP5-20 Destiny Draw (UR) 20.00 40.00
- ❑ DP5-21 Over Destiny (SR) 1.00 3.00
- ❑ DP5-29 D - Counter (SR) 1.00 3.00
- ❑ DP5-30 Eternal Dread (SR) 1.00 3.00

2007 Yu-Gi-Oh Duelist Pack Jaden Yuki 2

- Complete Set (30) 30.00 50.00
- Booster Box (30 packs) 35.00 50.00
- Booster Pack (6 cards) 2.00 3.00
- ❑ DP3-2 Elemental Hero Bladedge (R) .50 1.00
- ❑ DP3-5 Neo-Spacian Aqua Dolphin (R) .50 1.00
- ❑ DP3-6 Neo-Spacian Flare Scarab (R) .50 1.00
- ❑ DP3-7 Neo-Spacian Dark Panther (R) .50 1.00
- ❑ DP3-9 Card Trooper (UR) 20.00 30.00
- ❑ DP3-10 Elemental Hero Wildedge (R) .50 1.00
- ❑ DP3-12 Elemental Hero Aqua Neos (R) .50 1.00
- ❑ DP3-13 Elemental Hero Flare Neos (R) 1.00 3.00
- ❑ DP3-14 Elemental Hero Dark Neos (SR) 2.00 4.00
- ❑ DP3-25 Light Laser (SR) 1.00 3.00
- ❑ DP3-26 Burial From Different Dimen (UR) 5.00 10.00
- ❑ DP3-29 Edge Hammer (SR) 1.00 3.00
- ❑ DP3-30 Kids Guard (SR) 1.00 3.00

2007 Yu-Gi-Oh Duelist Pack Zane Truesdale

- Complete Set (30) 80.00 120.00
- Booster Box (30 packs) 90.00 120.00
- Booster Pack (6 cards) 3.00 4.00
- ❑ DP4-1 Cyber Dragon (R) 15.00 30.00
- ❑ DP4-2 Cyber Barrier Dragon (R) .60 1.50
- ❑ DP4-3 Cyber Laser Dragon (R) .60 1.50
- ❑ DP4-10 Internal Dragon (UR) 10.00 25.00
- ❑ DP4-11 Cyber Twin Dragon (R) 1.50 4.00
- ❑ DP4-12 Cyber End Dragon (R) .60 1.50
- ❑ DP4-13 Chimeratech Overdragon (R) 1.50 4.00
- ❑ DP4-14 Cyberdark Dragon (SR) 3.00 8.00
- ❑ DP4-20 Power Bond (R) 1.50 4.00
- ❑ DP4-24 Ruthless Denial (SR) 1.50 4.00
- ❑ DP4-28 Return Soul (SR) 1.25 3.00
- ❑ DP4-29 Damage Polarizer (UR) 3.00 8.00
- ❑ DP4-30 Fusion Guard (SR) .75 2.00

2008 Yu-Gi-Oh Duelist Pack Jaden Yuki 3

- Complete Set (30) 80.00 120.00
- Booster Box (30 packs) 90.00 120.00
- Booster Pack (6 cards) 3.00 4.00
- ❑ DP6-2 Neo-Spacian Grand Mole (R) 1.25 3.00
- ❑ DP6-4 Elemental Hero Captain Gold (R) .60 1.50
- ❑ DP6-6 Evil Hero Malicious Edge (SR) 1.50 4.00
- ❑ DP6-8 Evil Hero Infernal Prodigy (SR) 2.00 5.00
- ❑ DP6-9 Armor Breaker (R) .40 1.00
- ❑ DP6-11 Evil Hero Wild Cyclone (UR) 4.00 10.00
- ❑ DP6-12 Evil Hero Infernal Sniper (SR) 1.50 4.00
- ❑ DP6-13 Evil Hero Malicious Fiend (UR) 8.00 20.00
- ❑ DP6-14 Skyscraper 2 - Hero City (SR) 1.50 4.00
- ❑ DP6-19 Dark Calling (R) 1.50 4.00
- ❑ DP6-20 Revoke Fusion (R) .60 1.50
- ❑ DP6-25 Hero's Rule 2 (R) .60 1.50

2008 Yu-Gi-Oh Duelist Pack Jesse Anderson

- Complete Set (30) 80.00 120.00
- Booster Box (30 packs) 90.00 120.00
- Booster Pack (6 cards) 3.00 4.00
- ❑ DP7-2 Crystal Beast Amethyst Cat (R) .40 1.00
- ❑ DP7-4 Crystal Beast Topaz Tiger (R) .60 1.50
- ❑ DP7-7 Phantom Skyblaster (UR) 8.00 20.00
- ❑ DP7-8 Grave Squirmer (SR) .60 1.50
- ❑ DP7-9 Grinder Golem (SR) 1.50 4.00
- ❑ DP7-15 Crystal Abundance (R) .60 1.50
- ❑ DP7-17 Ancient City - Rainbow Ruins (R) .75 2.00
- ❑ DP7-18 Hand Destruction (R) 3.00 8.00
- ❑ DP7-19 Crystal Release (SR) 3.00 8.00
- ❑ DP7-20 Crystal Tree (SR) 3.00 8.00
- ❑ DP7-24 Crystal Counter (UR) 3.00 8.00
- ❑ DP7-25 Crystal Pair (R) .75 2.00

2009 Yu-Gi-Oh Duelist Pack Yugi

- Complete Set (30) 140.00 180.00
- Booster Box (30 packs) 90.00 120.00
- Booster Pack (6 cards) 3.00 4.00
- ❑ DPYG-1 Dark Magician (R) .60 1.50
- ❑ DPYG-2 Summoned Skull (R) .60 1.50
- ❑ DPYG-8 Dark Magician Girl (SR) 4.00 10.00
- ❑ DPYG-10 Sorcerer of Dark Magic (SR) 2.00 5.00
- ❑ DPYG-15 Marshmallon (R) 1.50 4.00
- ❑ DPYG-16 Dark Paladin (UR) 5.00 12.00
- ❑ DPYG-17 Black Luster Soldier (R) .40 1.00
- ❑ DPYG-19 Monster Reborn (R) .60 1.50
- ❑ DPYG-20 Polymerization (SR) 4.00 10.00
- ❑ DPYG-21 Exchange (R) .60 1.50
- ❑ DPYG-25 Card of Sanctity (R) .60 1.50
- ❑ DPYG-27 Mirror Force (UR) 30.00 60.00
- ❑ DPYG-28 Magical Hats (R) .40 1.00

2009 Yu-Gi-Oh Duelist Pack Yusei Fudo 1

- Complete Set (30) 80.00 120.00
- Booster Box (30 packs) 90.00 120.00
- Booster Pack (6 cards) 3.00 4.00
- ❑ DP8-4 Nitro Synchron (R) .60 1.50
- ❑ DP8-9 Turbo Synchron (R) .60 1.50
- ❑ DP8-10 Fortress Warrior (SR) .60 1.50
- ❑ DP8-11 Tuningware (UR) 4.00 10.00
- ❑ DP8-12 Junk Warrior (R) .75 2.00
- ❑ DP8-13 Nitro Warrior (R) .60 1.50
- ❑ DP8-14 Stardust Dragon (SR) 10.00 25.00
- ❑ DP8-15 Turbo Warrior (R) .40 1.00
- ❑ DP8-16 Armory Arm (UR) 6.00 15.00
- ❑ DP8-25 Battle Mania (R) .60 1.50
- ❑ DP8-27 Urgent Tuning (R) .60 1.50
- ❑ DP8-29 Give and Take (SR) .75 2.00
- ❑ DP8-30 Limiter Overload (SR) .75 2.00

2010 Yu-Gi-Oh Duelist Pack Collection Tins

- Red Tin 15.00 25.00
- Yellow Tin 15.00 25.00
- Purple Tin 15.00 25.00

Three Cards per tin
One Starlight Road per tin

- ❑ DPCTY01 Junk Synchron (UR) 3.00 8.00
- ❑ DPCTY02 Quillbolt Hedgehog (SR) 1.50 4.00
- ❑ DPCTY03 Synchro Blast Wave (SR) 1.50 4.00
- ❑ DPCTY04 Drill Synchron (UR) 2.50 6.00
- ❑ DPCTY05 Speed Warrior (SR) 1.25 3.00
- ❑ DPCTY06 Advance Draw (SR) 1.25 3.00
- ❑ DPCTY07 Scrap-Iron Scarecrow (UR) 2.50 6.00
- ❑ DPCTY08 Level Eater (SR) 1.25 3.00
- ❑ DPCTY09 One for One (SR) 1.25 3.00
- ❑ DPCT004 Starlight Road (SCR) 4.00 10.00

2010 Yu-Gi-Oh Duelist Pack Kaiba

- Booster Box (36 packs) 75.00 125.00
- Booster Pack (5 cards) 3.50 5.00
- ❑ DPKB-01 Blue-Eyes White Dragon (SR) 6.00 15.00
- ❑ DPKB-02 Hitotsu-Me Giant .30 .75
- ❑ DPKB-03 Judge Man .30 .75
- ❑ DPKB-04 Swordstalker .30 .75
- ❑ DPKB-05 La Jinn the Mystical Genie of the Lamp .50 1.25
- ❑ DPKB-06 Saggi the Dark Clown .30 .75
- ❑ DPKB-07 X-Head Cannon .40 1.00
- ❑ DPKB-08 Vorse Raider .50 1.25
- ❑ DPKB-09 Lord of D. .40 1.00
- ❑ DPKB-10 Cyber Jar (UTR) 10.00 25.00
- ❑ DPKB-11 Y-Dragon Head .40 1.00
- ❑ DPKB-12 Z-Metal Tank .40 1.00
- ❑ DPKB-13 Vampire Lord (R) .60 1.50
- ❑ DPKB-14 Different Dimension Dragon (R) .60 1.50
- ❑ DPKB-15 Kaiser Glider (R) .50 1.25
- ❑ DPKB-16 Chaos Emperor Dragon Envoy of the End (UTR) 15.00 30.00
- ❑ DPKB-17 Kaiser Sea Horse (R) .40 1.00
- ❑ DPKB-18 Enraged Battle Ox .30 .75
- ❑ DPKB-19 Peten the Dark Clown (R) .50 1.25
- ❑ DPKB-20 Familiar Knight .30 .75
- ❑ DPKB-21 Ancient Lamp .30 .75
- ❑ DPKB-22 The White Stone of Legend (SR) 10.00 25.00
- ❑ DPKB-23 Malefic Blue-Eyes White Dragon (UR) 15.00 30.00
- ❑ DPKB-24 Paladin of White Dragon (R) .50 1.25
- ❑ DPKB-25 XYZ-Dragon Cannon (SR) 3.00 8.00
- ❑ DPKB-26 Blue-Eyes Ultimate Dragon (UR) 5.00 12.00
- ❑ DPKB-27 Dragon Master Knight (UR) 4.00 10.00
- ❑ DPKB-28 Polymerization 1.50 4.00
- ❑ DPKB-29 Pot of Greed (UTR) 15.00 30.00
- ❑ DPKB-30 The Flute of Summoning Dragon .30 .75
- ❑ DPKB-31 Magic Reflector .30 .75
- ❑ DPKB-32 White Dragon Ritual .40 1.00
- ❑ DPKB-33 Cost Down (R) 1.50 4.00
- ❑ DPKB-34 Ring of Defense .40 1.00
- ❑ DPKB-35 Fiend's Sanctuary (SR) 6.00 15.00
- ❑ DPKB-36 Ring of Destruction (UTR) 8.00 20.00
- ❑ DPKB-37 Interdimensional Matter Transporter .40 1.00
- ❑ DPKB-38 Return from the Different Dimension (SR) 4.00 10.00
- ❑ DPKB-39 Crush Card Virus (UTR) 20.00 40.00
- ❑ DPKB-40 Cloning .30 .75

2010 Yu-Gi-Oh Duelist Pack Yusei Fudo 2

- Complete Set (30) 80.00 120.00
- Booster Box (30 packs) 90.00 120.00
- Booster Pack (6 cards) 3.00 4.00
- ❑ DP09001 Stardust Dragon/Assault Mode (SR) 2.00 5.00
- ❑ DP09002 Road Synchron (R) .60 1.50
- ❑ DP09003 Turret Warrior (R) .40 1.00
- ❑ DP09004 Debris Dragon .12 .30
- ❑ DP09005 Hyper Synchron .12 .30
- ❑ DP09006 Rockstone Warrior (R) .40 1.00
- ❑ DP09007 Level Warrior .12 .30
- ❑ DP09008 Majestic Dragon .12 .30
- ❑ DP09009 Max Warrior (R) .40 1.00
- ❑ DP09010 Quickdraw Synchron .12 .30
- ❑ DP09011 Level Eater .12 .30
- ❑ DP09012 Zero Gardna .12 .30
- ❑ DP09013 Gauntlet Warrior (UR) 3.00 8.00
- ❑ DP09014 Eccentric Boy (SR) 3.00 8.00
- ❑ DP09015 Road Warrior (R) .40 1.00
- ❑ DP09016 Junk Archer (UR) 8.00 20.00
- ❑ DP09017 Prevention Star .12 .30
- ❑ DP09018 One for One (R) .60 1.50
- ❑ DP09019 Release Restraint Wave .12 .30
- ❑ DP09020 Silver Wing .12 .30
- ❑ DP09021 Advance Draw .12 .30
- ❑ DP09022 Assault Mode Activate .12 .30
- ❑ DP09023 Spirit Force .12 .30
- ❑ DP09024 Descending Lost Star .12 .30
- ❑ DP09025 Miracle Locus .12 .30
- ❑ DP09026 Skill Successor (R) .40 1.00
- ❑ DP09027 Reinforce Truth .12 .30
- ❑ DP09028 Slip Summon .12 .30
- ❑ DP09029 Scrubbed Raid (SR) 2.00 5.00
- ❑ DP09030 Tuner's Barrier (SR) 2.00 5.00
- ❑ DP0901 Power Up the Warriors STRAT .08 .20
- ❑ DP0902 Super Synchro Summon STRAT .08 .20
- ❑ DP0903 Substitute Synchron STRAT .08 .20
- ❑ DP0904 Combo Chain STRAT .08 .20
- ❑ DP0905 Protect Your Tuner and Gain the Edge STRAT .08 .20
- ❑ DP0906 Bring Assault Mode Activate to Your Hand STRAT .08 .20
- ❑ DP0907 Match the Level and Draw STRAT .08 .20
- ❑ DP0908 Deploy Monsters from the Deck STRAT .08 .20
- ❑ DP0909 Emissary Eater STRAT .08 .20
- ❑ DP0910 Checklist STRAT .08 .20

2011 Yu-Gi-Oh Duelist Pack Crow

- Unlisted Commons .15 .40
- Booster Box (36 packs) 40.00 60.00
- Booster Pack (5 cards) 2.00 3.00
- ❑ DP11EN001 Blackwing - Gale the Whirlwind (R) .40 1.00
- ❑ DP11EN002 Blackwing - Bora the Spear (R) .30 .75
- ❑ DP11EN003 Blackwing - Blizzard the Far North .15 .40
- ❑ DP11EN004 Blackwing - Shura the Blue Flame (R) .25 .60
- ❑ DP11EN005 Blackwing - Elphin the Raven (R) .30 .75
- ❑ DP11EN006 Blackwing - Mistral the Silver Shield .15 .40
- ❑ DP11EN007 Blackwing - Fane the Steel Chain .15 .40
- ❑ DP11EN008 Blackwing - Ghibli the Searing Wind .15 .40
- ❑ DP11EN009 Blackwing - Gust the Backblast .15 .40
- ❑ DP11EN010 Blackwing - Kochi the Daybreak (R) .75 2.00
- ❑ DP11EN011 Blackwing - Jetstream the Blue Sky (UR) 3.00 8.00
- ❑ DP11EN012 Blackwing - Zephyros the Elite (UR) 15.00 30.00
- ❑ DP11EN013 Blackwing Armor Master (SR) 3.00 8.00
- ❑ DP11EN014 Blackwing Armed Wing (R) 1.50 4.00
- ❑ DP11EN015 Blackwing Silverwind the Ascendant (R) .75 2.00
- ❑ DP11EN016 Black-Winged Dragon (SR) .40 1.00
- ❑ DP11EN017 Raptor Wing Strike .15 .40
- ❑ DP11EN018 Against the Wind .15 .40
- ❑ DP11EN019 Black-Winged Strafe .15 .40
- ❑ DP11EN020 Cards for Black Feathers .30 .75
- ❑ DP11EN021 Ebon Arrow .15 .40
- ❑ DP11EN022 Delta Crow - Anti Reverse .40 1.00
- ❑ DP11EN023 Level Retuner .15 .40
- ❑ DP11EN024 Fake Feather .15 .40
- ❑ DP11EN025 Blackwing - Backlash .15 .40
- ❑ DP11EN026 Blackwing - Bombardment .15 .40
- ❑ DP11EN027 Black Thunder .15 .40
- ❑ DP11EN028 Guard Mines .15 .40
- ❑ DP11EN029 Black Feather Beacon (SR) .75 2.00
- ❑ DP11EN030 Black Return (SR) 1.50 4.00

2011 Yu-Gi-Oh Duelist Pack Yusei Fudo 3

- Booster Box (36 packs) 30.00 50.00
- Booster Pack (6 cards) 1.25 2.00
- ❑ DP10EN001 Sonic Chick .50 1.25
- ❑ DP10EN002 Shield Wing 2.00 5.00
- ❑ DP10EN003 Stardust Xiaolong .50 1.25
- ❑ DP10EN004 Drill Synchron .50 1.25
- ❑ DP10EN005 Card Breaker .50 1.25
- ❑ DP10EN006 Second Booster .75 2.00
- ❑ DP10EN007 Effect Veiler (R) 10.00 25.00
- ❑ DP10EN008 Dash Warrior .50 1.25
- ❑ DP10EN009 Damage Eater .50 1.25
- ❑ DP10EN010 A/D Changer .50 1.25
- ❑ DP10EN011 Stronghold Guardian .50 1.25
- ❑ DP10EN012 Boost Warrior (SR) 6.00 15.00
- ❑ DP10EN013 Justice Bringer (UR) 15.00 30.00
- ❑ DP10EN014 Bri Synchron (UR) 15.00 30.00
- ❑ DP10EN015 Big One Warrior (SR) 5.00 12.00
- ❑ DP10EN016 Dragon Knight Draco-Equiste (SR) 4.00 10.00
- ❑ DP10EN017 Majestic Star Dragon (R) 3.00 8.00
- ❑ DP10EN018 Drill Warrior (R) 3.00 8.00
- ❑ DP10EN019 Cards of Consonance 2.00 5.00
- ❑ DP10EN020 Variety Comes Out .50 1.25
- ❑ DP10EN021 Blind Spot Strike .50 1.25
- ❑ DP10EN022 Double Cyclone .50 1.25
- ❑ DP10EN023 Battle Waltz (R) 3.00 8.00
- ❑ DP10EN024 Synchro Gift (R) 3.00 8.00
- ❑ DP10EN025 Starlight Road (R) 5.00 12.00
- ❑ DP10EN026 Synchro Barrier .50 1.25
- ❑ DP10EN027 Power Frame .75 2.00
- ❑ DP10EN028 Desperate Tag .75 2.00
- ❑ DP10EN029 Cards of Sacrifice (R) 3.00 8.00
- ❑ DP10EN030 Synchro Material (SR) 8.00 20.00

2002 Yu-Gi-Oh Tournament Series 1

- Complete Set (30) 85.00 150.00
- Booster Pack (3 cards) 7.00 12.00

❑ TP1001 Mechanical Chaser (UR) 20.00 40.00
❑ TP1002 Axe Raider (SR) 10.00 20.00
❑ TP1003 Kwagar Hercules (SR) 8.00 15.00
❑ TP1004 Patrol Robo (SR) 6.00 12.00
❑ TP1005 White Hole (SR) 12.00 30.00
❑ TP1006 Elf's Light (R) 5.00 10.00
❑ TP1007 Steel Shell (R) 10.00 20.00
❑ TP1008 Blue Medicine (R) 3.00 6.00
❑ TP1009 Raimei (R) 7.00 14.00
❑ TP1010 Burning Spear (R) 7.00 14.00
❑ TP1011 Gust Fan (R) 3.00 6.00
❑ TP1012 Tiger Axe (R) 3.00 6.00
❑ TP1013 Goddess with Third Eye (R) 4.00 8.00
❑ TP1014 Beastking of Swamps (R) 3.00 6.00
❑ TP1015 Versago the Destroyer (R) 3.00 6.00
❑ TP1016 Oscillo Hero #2 1.00 2.00
❑ TP1017 Giant Flea 1.00 2.00
❑ TP1018 Bean Soldier 2.00 4.00
❑ TP1019 The Statue of Easter Island 1.50 3.00
❑ TP1020 Corroding Shark 1.00 2.00
❑ TP1021 WOW Warrior 1.00 2.00
❑ TP1022 Winged Dragon 2.00 4.00
❑ TP1023 Oscillo Hero 1.00 2.00
❑ TP1024 Shining Friendship 1.50 3.00
❑ TP1025 Hercules Beetle 1.50 3.00
❑ TP1026 Judgement Hand 1.00 2.00
❑ TP1027 Wodan The Resident 1.00 2.00
❑ TP1028 Cyber Soldier 1.00 2.00
❑ TP1029 Cockroach Knight 3.00 6.00
❑ TP1030 Kuwagata Alpha 1.00 2.00

2002 Yu-Gi-Oh Tournament Series 2

Complete Set (30) 150.00 200.00
Booster Pack (3 cards) 4.00 7.00

❑ TP2030 Water Magician .50 1.00
❑ TP2001 Morphing Jar (UR) 75.00 125.00
❑ TP2002 Dragon Seeker (SR) 12.00 25.00
❑ TP2003 Giant Red Seasnake (SR) 10.00 20.00
❑ TP2004 Exile of the Wicked (SR) 10.00 20.00
❑ TP2005 Call of the Grave (SR) 8.00 15.00
❑ TP2006 Mikazukinoyaiba (R) 8.00 15.00
❑ TP2007 Skull Guardian (R) 7.00 15.00
❑ TP2008 Novox's Prayer (R) 8.00 18.00
❑ TP2009 Dokurorider (R) 10.00 20.00
❑ TP2010 Revival of Dokurorider (R) 4.00 8.00
❑ TP2011 Beautiful Headhuntress (R) 5.00 12.00
❑ TP2012 Sonic Maid (R) 10.00 20.00
❑ TP2013 Mystical Sheep #1 (R) 5.00 12.00
❑ TP2014 Warrior of Tradition (R) 5.00 12.00
❑ TP2015 Soul of the Pure (R) 6.00 12.00
❑ TP2016 Dancing Elf 1.00 2.00
❑ TP2017 Turu-Purun .50 1.00
❑ TP2018 Dharma Cannon .50 1.00
❑ TP2019 Stuffed Animal .50 1.00
❑ TP2020 Spirit of the Books .50 1.00
❑ TP2021 Faith Bird 1.00 2.00
❑ TP2022 Takuhee .50 1.00
❑ TP2023 Maiden of the Moonlight .50 1.00
❑ TP2024 Queen of Autumn Leaves 1.00 2.00
❑ TP2025 Two-Headed King Rex 4.00 10.00
❑ TP2026 Garoozis 5.00 10.00
❑ TP2027 Crawling Dragon 1.00 2.00
❑ TP2028 Parrot Dragon 2.00 6.00
❑ TP2029 Sky Dragon 2.00 5.00

2003 Yu-Gi-Oh Tournament Series 3

Complete Set (20) 150.00 200.00
Booster Pack (3 cards) 7.00 12.00

❑ TP3001 Needle Worm (UR) 30.00 50.00
❑ TP3002 Anti Raigeki (SR) 9.00 20.00
❑ TP3003 Mechanicalchaser (SR) 10.00 20.00
❑ TP3004 B.Skull Dragon (SR) 15.00 30.00
❑ TP3005 Horn of Heaven (SR) 8.00 16.00
❑ TP3006 Axe Raider (R) 4.00 10.00
❑ TP3007 Kwagar Hercules (R) 2.00 4.00
❑ TP3008 Patrol Robo (R) 3.00 6.00
❑ TP3009 White Hole (R) 3.00 6.00
❑ TP3010 Dragon Capture Jar 1.00 3.00
❑ TP3011 Goblin's Secret Remedy 1.00 2.00
❑ TP3012 Final Flame 1.00 2.00
❑ TP3013 Spirit of the Harp 1.00 3.00
❑ TP3014 Pot of Greed 1.00 4.00
❑ TP3015 Karbonala Warrior 1.00 3.00
❑ TP3016 Darkfire Dragon 2.00 4.00
❑ TP3017 Elegant Egotist 2.00 4.00
❑ TP3018 Dark Elf 1.00 3.00
❑ TP3019 Little Chimera 1.00 2.00
❑ TP3020 Bladefly 1.00 3.00

2003 Yu-Gi-Oh Tournament Series 4

Complete Set (20) 65.00 100.00
Booster Pack (3 cards) 5.00 10.00
Booster Box (20 packs) 120.00 150.00

❑ TP4001 Royal Decree (UR) 20.00 30.00
❑ TP4002 Morphing Jar (SR) 25.00 48.00
❑ TP4003 Megamorph (SR) 7.00 14.00
❑ TP4004 Chain Destruction (SR) 8.00 16.00
❑ TP4005 The Fiend Megacyber (SR) 4.00 10.00
❑ TP4006 Dragon Seeker (R) 5.00 10.00
❑ TP4007 Giant Red Seasnake (R) 2.00 4.00
❑ TP4008 Exile of the Wicked (R) 2.00 4.00
❑ TP4009 Call of the Grave (R) 2.00 4.00
❑ TP4010 Rush Recklessly 1.00 2.00
❑ TP4011 Giant Rat 1.00 2.00
❑ TP4012 Senju of Thousand Hands 1.00 2.00
❑ TP4013 Karate Man 1.00 2.00
❑ TP4014 Nimble Momonga 1.00 2.00
❑ TP4015 Mystic Tomato 1.00 2.00
❑ TP4016 Nobleman of Extermination 1.00 2.00
❑ TP4017 Magic Drain 1.00 2.00
❑ TP4018 Gravity Bind 1.00 2.00
❑ TP4019 Hayabusa Knight 1.00 2.00
❑ TP4020 Mad Sword Beast 1.00 2.00

2004 Yu-Gi-Oh Tournament Series 5

Complete Set (20) 50.00 100.00
Booster Box (20 Packs) 60.00 100.00
Booster Pack (3 Cards) 4.00 7.00

❑ TP5001 Luminous Soldier (UR) 9.00 20.00
❑ TP5002 Big Shield Gardna (SR) 20.00 30.00
❑ TP5003 Magical Thorn (SR) 5.00 10.00
❑ TP5004 Luster Dragon (SR) 7.00 15.00
❑ TP5005 Needle Worm (SR) 15.00 30.00
❑ TP5006 Kycoo the Ghost Destroyer (R) 3.00 5.00

Beckett Yu-Gi-Oh! price guide sponsored by YugiohMint.com

❑ TP5007 Bazoo the Soul-Eater (R) 3.00 5.00
❑ TP5008 Book of Life (R) 3.00 5.00
❑ TP5009 Trap Board Eraser (R) 1.00 3.00
❑ TP5010 Goddess with the Third Eye .50 1.00
❑ TP5011 Jowgen the Spiritualist .50 1.00
❑ TP5012 Tornado Bird .50 1.00
❑ TP5013 Destruction Punch .50 1.00
❑ TP5014 Beastking of the Swamps .50 1.00
❑ TP5015 Versago the Destroyer 5.00 12.00
❑ TP5016 Mysticak Sheep #1 .50 1.00
❑ TP5017 Pyramid Turtle .50 1.00
❑ TP5018 Curse of Royal .50 1.00
❑ TP5019 Winged Sage Falcos .50 1.00
❑ TP5020 Dark Designator .50 1.00

2005 Yu-Gi-Oh Tournament Series 6

Complete Set (20) 60.00 120.00
Booster Box (20 packs) 45.00 70.00
Booster Pack (3 cards) 3.00 6.00

❑ TP6001 Toon Cannon Soldier (UR) 10.00 20.00
❑ TP6002 Toon Table of Contents (SR) 9.00 20.00
❑ TP6003 Fusion Sage (SR) 8.00 15.00
❑ TP6004 Royal Decree (SR) 10.00 20.00
❑ TP6005 Restructer Revolution (SR) 5.00 10.00
❑ TP6006 Spear Dragon (R) 3.00 6.00
❑ TP6007 Airknight Parshath (R) 3.00 7.00
❑ TP6008 Susa Soldier (R) 3.00 6.00
❑ TP6009 Yamata Dragon (R) 3.00 6.00
❑ TP6010 Dark Balter the Terrible .40 1.00
❑ TP6011 Ryu Senshi .40 1.00
❑ TP6012 Emergency Provisions .40 1.00
❑ TP6013 Fiend Skull Dragon .40 1.00
❑ TP6014 Thunder Nyan Nyan .40 1.00
❑ TP6015 Last Turn .40 1.00
❑ TP6016 Archfiend Marmot of Nefariousness .40 1.00
❑ TP6017 Sleeping Lion .40 1.00
❑ TP6018 Nekogal #1 .40 1.00
❑ TP6019 Burglar .40 1.00
❑ TP6020 Clown Zombie .40 1.00

2006 Yu-Gi-Oh Tournament Series 7

Complete Set (20) 75.00 125.00
Booster Pack (3 cards) 4.00 7.00

❑ TP7-1 D.D. Warrior (UR) 30.00 60.00
❑ TP7-2 Warrior Eliminator (SR) 10.00 20.00
❑ TP7-3 Fortress Whale (SR) 10.00 20.00
❑ TP7-4 Luminous Soldier (SR) 5.00 10.00
❑ TP7-5 Breaker the Magical Warrior (SR) 10.00 20.00
❑ TP7-6 Goblin Attack Force (R) 1.00 3.00
❑ TP7-7 Amazoness Swords Woman (R) 2.00 4.00
❑ TP7-8 Chaos Command Magician (R) 1.00 3.00
❑ TP7-9 Scapegoat (R) 1.00 3.00

2006 Yu-Gi-Oh Tournament Series 8

Complete Set 80.00 125.00
Booster Box 30.00 50.00
Booster Pack 2.00 3.00

❑ TP8-1 Magical Arm Shield (UR) 15.00 30.00
❑ TP8-2 Harpies Feather Duster (SR) 10.00 20.00
❑ TP8-3 Slate Warrior (SR) 10.00 18.00
❑ TP8-4 Dunames Dark Witch (SR) 15.00 32.00
❑ TP8-5 Garma Sword (SR) 10.00 20.00
❑ TP8-6 Zaborg the Thunder Monarch (SR) 15.00 25.00
❑ TP8-8 Mobius Frost Monarch 3.00 7.00

2006 Yu-Gi-Oh Champion Pack Game One

Complete Set (20) 80.00 150.00
Booster Pack 3.00 5.00

❑ CP1-1 Satellite Cannon (UR) 30.00 55.00
❑ CP1-2 Book of Moon (SR) 15.00 25.00
❑ CP1-3 Metamorphosis (SR) 8.00 14.00
❑ CP1-4 Sakuretsu Armor (SR) 20.00 30.00
❑ CP1-5 Night Assailant (SR) 10.00 20.00
❑ CP1-6 Big Shield Gardna (R) 2.00 4.00
❑ CP1-7 Limiter Removal (R) .50 1.00
❑ CP1-8 Solemn Judgment (R) 2.00 4.00
❑ CP1-9 Reflect Bounder (R) 3.00 6.00
❑ CP1-10 Enemy Controller (R) 1.00 3.00
❑ CP1-11 Pot of Avarice (R) 1.00 2.00
❑ CP1-12 Thunder Kid .10 .25
❑ CP1-13 Mysterious Guard .10 .25
❑ CP1-14 King Tiger Wanghu .10 .25
❑ CP1-15 My Body as a Shield .10 .25
❑ CP1-16 Final Countdown .10 .25
❑ CP1-17 Mudora .10 .25
❑ CP1-18 Stealth Bird .10 .25
❑ CP1-19 Emissary of the Afterlife .10 .25
❑ CP1-20 Threatening Roar .10 .25

2006 Yu-Gi-Oh Champion Pack Game Two

Complete Set (20) 80.00 150.00
Booster Pack (3 cards) 2.00 4.00

❑ CP2-1 Magical Stone Excavation (UR) 20.00 40.00
❑ CP2-2 Nimble Momonga (SR) 5.00 10.00
❑ CP2-3 Magician of Faith (SR) 6.00 12.00
❑ CP2-4 Pyramid Turtle (SR) 5.00 10.00
❑ CP2-5 Smashing Ground (SR) 20.00 30.00
❑ CP2-6 Kuriboh (R) 2.00 4.00
❑ CP2-7 Abyss Solider (R) 1.00 2.00
❑ CP2-8 Ring of Destruction (R) 3.00 6.00
❑ CP2-9 Morphing Jar (R) 4.00 7.00
❑ CP2-10 Dark Master - Zorc (R) 1.00 2.00
❑ CP2-11 Magical Dimension (R) 1.00 2.00
❑ CP2-12 Happy Lover .10 .25
❑ CP2-13 Rush Recklessly .10 .25
❑ CP2-14 Ceasefire .10 .25
❑ CP2-15 Thunder Dragon .10 .25
❑ CP2-16 Twin-Headed Behemoth .10 .25
❑ CP2-17 Book of Taiyou .10 .25
❑ CP2-18 Terraforming .10 .25
❑ CP2-19 Big Bang Shot .10 .25
❑ CP2-20 Stray Lambs .10 .25

2007 Yu-Gi-Oh Champion Pack Game Three

❑ CP3-1 Magicians Unite 10.00 20.00
❑ CP3-2 Spirit Reaper 15.00 25.00
❑ CP3-3 Gravekeeper Spy 20.00 35.00
❑ CP3-4 Sniper Hunter 15.00 30.00
❑ CP3-5 Dark World Lightning 4.00 8.00
❑ CP3-6 D.D. Assailant 3.00 6.00
❑ CP3-7 Goldd Wu-Lord 1.00 2.00

2007 Yu-Gi-Oh Champion Pack Game Four

❑ CP4-1 Germa 15.00 25.00
❑ CP4-2 Ultimate Offering 5.00 10.00
❑ CP4-3 Bottomless Trap Hole 15.00 25.00
❑ CP4-4 Apprentice Magician 15.00 25.00
❑ CP4-5 Hydrogeddon 5.00 10.00

2008 Yu-Gi-Oh Champion Pack Game Five

Booster Pack

❑ CP5-1 Fiend's Sanctuary (UR) 25.00 45.00
❑ CP5-2 Giant Germ (SR) 7.00 14.00
❑ CP5-3 Magical Merchant (SR) 3.00 6.00
❑ CP5-4 Wave Motion Cannon (SR) 10.00 18.00
❑ CP5-5 Trap Dustshoot (SR) 7.00 14.00

2008 Yu-Gi-Oh Champion Pack Game Six

Complete Set (20) 90.00 120.00
Booster Pack 2.50 4.00

❑ CP6-1 Rigorous Reaver (UR) 8.00 20.00
❑ CP6-2 Destiny Hero - Fear Monger (SR) 8.00 20.00
❑ CP6-3 Old Vindictive Magician (SR) 6.00 15.00
❑ CP6-4 Phoenix Wing Wind Blast (SR) 20.00 40.00
❑ CP6-5 Blaze Accelerator (SR) 4.00 10.00
❑ CP6-6 Call of Darkness (SR) .75 2.00
❑ CP6-7 Blade Knight (SR) .75 2.00
❑ CP6-8 Super-Electromagnetic Voltech Dragon (SR) .75 2.00
❑ CP6-9 Elemental Hero Stratos (R) 6.00 15.00
❑ CP6-10 Helios Duo Megistus (R) .75 2.00
❑ CP6-11 Mage Power (R) 2.00 5.00
❑ CP6-12 Sentinel of the Seas .75 2.00
❑ CP6-13 Batteryman AA .75 2.00
❑ CP6-14 Theban Nightmare .75 2.00
❑ CP6-15 Majestic Mech - Ohka .75 2.00
❑ CP6-16 Soul of Purity and Light .75 2.00
❑ CP6-17 Amplifier .75 2.00
❑ CP6-18 Cold Wave .75 2.00
❑ CP6-19 Magical Hats .75 2.00
❑ CP6-20 Dimension Wall .75 2.00

2008 Yu-Gi-Oh Champion Pack Game Seven

Complete Set (20) 150.00 200.00
Booster Pack 2.50 4.00

❑ CP7-1 Voltic Kong (UR) 8.00 20.00
❑ CP7-2 Legendary Jujitsu Master (SR) 15.00 30.00
❑ CP7-3 Threatening Roar (SR) 20.00 40.00
❑ CP7-4 Gladiator Beast Bestiari (SR) 15.00 30.00
❑ CP7-5 Lonefire Blossom (SR) 8.00 20.00
❑ CP7-6 Elemental Hero Ocean (R) 4.00 10.00
❑ CP7-7 Fairy King Truesdale (R) 1.50 4.00
❑ CP7-8 Spell Striker (R) 1.25 3.00
❑ CP7-9 Vanity's Fiend (R) 1.25 3.00
❑ CP7-10 Dark World Dealings (R) 2.50 6.00
❑ CP7-11 Doom Shaman (R) 1.25 3.00
❑ CP7-12 Shovel Crusher .75 2.00
❑ CP7-13 Life Absorbing Machine .75 2.00
❑ CP7-14 Fusilier Dragon, the Dual-Mode Beast .75 2.00
❑ CP7-15 Homunculus the Alchemic Being .75 2.00
❑ CP7-16 Memory Crusher .75 2.00
❑ CP7-17 Instant Fusion .75 2.00
❑ CP7-18 Dimensional Inversion .75 2.00
❑ CP7-19 Ancient Rules 2.00 5.00
❑ CP7-20 Counter Counter .75 2.00

2009 Yu-Gi-Oh Champion Pack Game Eight

Complete Set (20) 150.00 200.00
Booster Pack 2.50 4.00

❑ CP8-1 Gravity Behemoth (UR) 5.00 12.00
❑ CP8-2 Prohibition (SR) 6.00 15.00
❑ CP8-3 Mind Crush (SR) 15.00 30.00
❑ CP8-4 Dimensional Fissure (SR) 8.00 20.00
❑ CP8-5 Lumina, Lightsworn Summoner (SR) 50.00 80.00
❑ CP8-6 Magician's Valkyria (R) 5.00 12.00
❑ CP8-7 Silent Magician LV4 (R) 2.50 6.00
❑ CP8-8 Great Shogun Shien (R) 2.50 6.00
❑ CP8-9 Herald of Creation (R) 1.50 4.00
❑ CP8-10 Burial from a Different Dimension (R) 10.00 25.00
❑ CP8-11 Necro Gardna (R) 3.00 8.00
❑ CP8-12 Mushroom Man .75 2.00
❑ CP8-13 Royal Oppression 3.00 8.00
❑ CP8-14 Beckoning Light .75 2.00
❑ CP8-15 Neo-Spacian Dark Panther .75 2.00
❑ CP8-16 Alien Warrior .75 2.00
❑ CP8-17 Alien Mother .75 2.00
❑ CP8-18 Vanity's Ruler .75 2.00
❑ CP8-19 Miraculous Rebirth .75 2.00
❑ CP8-20 Cell Explosion.Virus .75 2.00

2009 Yu-Gi-Oh Turbo Pack 1

Complete Set (21) 200.00 300.00
Booster Box (3 packs) 4.00 6.00

❑ TU1-0 Judgment Dragon (UR) 60.00 100.00
❑ TU1-1 Doomcaliber Knight (UR) 25.00 50.00
❑ TU1-2 Garoth, Lightsworn Warrior (SR) 10.00 25.00
❑ TU1-3 Krebons (SR) 10.00 25.00
❑ TU1-4 Gladiator Beast Samnite (SR) 8.00 20.00
❑ TU1-5 Black Whirlwind (SR) 15.00 30.00
❑ TU1-6 Crush Card Virus (R) 6.00 15.00
❑ TU1-7 Satellite Cannon (R) .60 1.50
❑ TU1-8 Rescue Cat (R) .60 1.50
❑ TU1-9 Grandmaster of the Six Samurai (R) .60 1.50
❑ TU1-10 Trade-In (R) 1.50 4.00
❑ TU1-11 Armageddon Knight (R) .75 2.00
❑ TU1-12 Book of Moon .40 1.00
❑ TU1-13 Terraforming .40 1.00
❑ TU1-14 Hand Destruction .40 1.00
❑ TU1-15 Gladiator Beast Murmillo .40 1.00
❑ TU1-16 Gladiator Beast Bestiari .40 1.00
❑ TU1-17 Gladiator Beast Laquari .40 1.00
❑ TU1-18 Golden Flying Fish .40 1.00
❑ TU1-19 Ryko, Lightsworn Hunter .40 1.00
❑ TU1-20 D.D.R. - Different Dimension Reincarnation .40 1.00

2010 Yu-Gi-Oh Turbo Pack 2

Complete Set (21) 100.00 140.00
Booster Box (3 packs) 3.00 5.00

❑ TU2-0 Gladiator Beast Heraklinos (UR) 8.00 20.00
❑ TU2-1 Chaos Sorcerer (UR) 20.00 40.00
❑ TU2-2 Gravekeeper's Assailant (SR) 5.00 12.00
❑ TU2-3 Magical Dimension (SR) 5.00 12.00
❑ TU2-4 Foolish Burial (SR) 15.00 30.00
❑ TU2-5 Beckoning Light (SR) 15.00 30.00
❑ TU2-6 Gravekeeper's Spear Soldier (R) .75 2.00
❑ TU2-7 My Body as a Shield (R) 3.00 8.00
❑ TU2-8 Magical Stone Excavation (R) .60 1.50
❑ TU2-9 Mist Archfiend (R) .60 1.50
❑ TU2-10 Light-Imprisoning Mirror (R) .75 2.00
❑ TU2-11 Shadow-Imprisoning Mirror (R) .60 1.50
❑ TU2-12 Anti-Spell Fragrance .40 1.00
❑ TU2-13 Gravekeeper's Cannonholder .40 1.00
❑ TU2-14 Necrovalley .40 1.00
❑ TU2-15 Autonomous Action Unit .40 1.00
❑ TU2-16 Anti-Spell .40 1.00
❑ TU2-17 Reflect Bounder .40 1.00
❑ TU2-18 Mausoleum of the Emperor .40 1.00
❑ TU2-19 Gravekeeper's Commandant .40 1.00
❑ TU2-20 Iron Core of Koa'ki Meiru .40 1.00

2002-2011 Yu-Gi-Oh Promos

❑ YR01 Van'Dalgyon the Dark Dragon Lord 5.00 12.00
❑ YR03 Gorz the Emissary of Darkness 6.00 15.00
❑ YR04 Angel O7 6.00 15.00
❑ YR05 Alector, Sovereign of Birds 10.00 25.00
❑ CMC-1 Abyss Soldier 6.00 15.00
❑ CMC-2 Inferno Hammer 3.00 8.00
❑ CMC-3 Teva 3.00 8.00
❑ DBT-1 Emes the Infinity 3.00 8.00
❑ DBT-2 D.D. Assailant 10.00 25.00
❑ DBT-3 Twinheaded Beast 3.00 8.00
❑ DDS-1 Blue-Eyes White Dragon 25.00 50.00
❑ DDS-2 Dark Magician 10.00 25.00
❑ DDS-3 Exodia 8.00 20.00
❑ DDS-4 Seiyaryu 6.00 15.00
❑ DDS-5 Acid Trap Hole 3.00 8.00
❑ DDS-6 Salamandra 3.00 8.00
❑ DL1-1 Thousand-Eyes Restrict 3.00 8.00
❑ DL1-2 Buster Blader 3.00 8.00
❑ DL2-1 Masked Beast 3.00 8.00
❑ DL2-2 Dark Necrofear 3.00 8.00
❑ DL3-1 Necrovalley 1.50 4.00
❑ DL4-1 Machine King 2.00 5.00
❑ DL5-1 Restructer Revolution 1.25 3.00
❑ DL6-1 Toon Gemini Elf 3.00 8.00
❑ DMG-1 Dark Paladin 6.00 15.00
❑ DOD-1 The Winged Dragon of Ra 15.00 30.00
❑ DOD-2 Dark Sage 10.00 25.00
❑ DOD-3 Widespread Ruin 8.00 20.00
❑ DOR-1 Alpha the Magnetic Warrior 3.00 8.00
❑ DOR-2 Beta the Magnetic Warrior 6.00 15.00
❑ DOR-3 Gamma the Magnetic Warrior 3.00 8.00
❑ EDS-1 Exchange 3.00 8.00
❑ EDS-2 Graceful Dice 3.00 8.00
❑ EDS-3 Skull Dice 3.00 8.00
❑ FMR-1 Red-Eyes Black Metal Dragon 25.00 50.00
❑ FMR-2 Harpie's Pet Dragon 20.00 40.00
❑ FMR-3 Metalmorph 20.00 40.00
❑ FTK-1 Zoa 4.00 10.00
❑ FTK-2 MetalZoa 6.00 15.00
❑ FTK-3 Goblin Fan 6.00 15.00
❑ HL1-1 Lord of the Lamp 1.25 3.00
❑ HL1-2 Green Kappa 1.25 3.00
❑ HL1-3 A Legendary Ocean .60 1.50
❑ HL1-4 Levia-Dragon - Daedalus 1.50 4.00
❑ HL1-5 Fusion Gate 1.25 3.00
❑ HL1-6 King of the Swamp 10.00 25.00
❑ HL2-1 Cyber Jar 1.25 3.00
❑ HL2-2 Mystical Space Typhoon 3.00 8.00
❑ HL2-3 Sangan 2.00 5.00
❑ HL2-4 Heavy Storm 2.00 5.00
❑ HL2-5 Mauruading Captain .75 2.00
❑ HL2-6 Fissure 1.25 3.00
❑ HL3-1 Giant Rat .75 2.00
❑ HL3-2 Creature Swap 1.50 4.00
❑ HL3-3 Trap Hole 1.25 3.00
❑ HL3-4 Spear Dragon .75 2.00
❑ HL3-5 Mystic Tomato 3.00 8.00
❑ HL3-6 Royal Decree 3.00 8.00
❑ HL3-7 Dark Balter the Terrible .60 1.50
❑ HL4-1 Exiled Force 1.25 3.00
❑ HL4-2 Swords of Revealing Light 1.50 4.00
❑ HL4-3 Asura Priest .75 2.00
❑ HL4-4 Graceful Charity 2.00 5.00
❑ HL4-5 Kycoo the Ghost Destroyer 2.00 5.00
❑ HL4-6 Torrential Tribute 2.50 6.00
❑ HL5-1 Crystal Beast Ruby Carbuncle .60 1.50
❑ HL5-2 Green Gadget 3.00 8.00
❑ HL5-3 Crystal Beacon .75 2.00
❑ HL5-4 Dekoichi the Battlechanted Locomotive 1.25 3.00
❑ HL5-5 The Six Samurai - Zanji 2.50 6.00
❑ HL5-6 Scapegoat 1.25 3.00
❑ HL6-1 Nobleman of Crossout .60 1.50
❑ HL6-2 Limiter Removal 1.25 3.00
❑ HL6-3 D.D. Warrior Lady .75 2.00
❑ HL6-4 Reinforcement of the Army 1.00 2.50
❑ HL6-5 Call of the Haunted 1.25 3.00
❑ HL6-6 Shining Angel 1.25 3.00
❑ HL7-1 Monster Reborn 2.00 5.00
❑ HL7-2 Neo-Spacian Grand Mole 1.50 4.00
❑ HL7-3 Dark Dust Spirit .75 2.00
❑ HL7-4 Red Gadget 2.00 5.00
❑ HL7-5 Card of Safe Return 1.25 3.00
❑ HL7-6 Yellow Gadget 1.25 3.00
❑ JMP-1 Blue-Eyes White Dragon 6.00 15.00
❑ JMP-2 Red-Eyes B.Dragon 2.50 6.00
❑ JMP-3 Archfiend of Gilfer 4.00 10.00
❑ JMP-4 Obelisk the Tormentor 20.00 40.00
❑ JMP-5 Blue-Eyes Ultimate Dragon 3.00 8.00
❑ JUMP6 Unity 2.50 6.00
❑ JUMP7 Yu-Jo Friendship 3.00 8.00
❑ JUMP8 Judgment of the Pharoah 3.00 8.00
❑ JUMP9 Magician's Valkyria 5.00 12.00
❑ MC1-1 Exodia 10.00 25.00
❑ MC1-2 Barrel Dragon 2.00 5.00
❑ MC1-3 Relinquished 1.25 3.00
❑ MC1-4 Thousand-Eyes Restrict 2.50 6.00
❑ MC1-5 Dark Necrofear 2.50 6.00
❑ MC1-6 Dark Ruler Ha Des 2.50 6.00
❑ MC2-1 Guardian Sphinx 2.00 5.00
❑ MC2-2 Breaker the Magical Warrior 5.00 12.00
❑ MC2-3 Exodia Necross 2.50 6.00
❑ MC2-4 Black Luster Soldier 6.00 15.00
❑ MC2-5 Blowback Dragon 2.50 6.00
❑ MC2-6 Theinen the Great Sphinx .75 2.00
❑ MF2-3 Cyber End Dragon 10.00 25.00
❑ PCJ-1 Red-Eyes B. Dragon 8.00 20.00
❑ PCJ-2 Sebek's Blessing 8.00 20.00
❑ PCJ-3 Sword of Dragon's Soul 3.00 8.00
❑ PCK-1 Blue-Eyes White Dragon 8.00 20.00
❑ PCK-2 Aqua Chorus 2.50 6.00
❑ PCK-3 Seal of the Ancients 6.00 15.00
❑ PCY-1 Windstorm of Etaqua 8.00 20.00
❑ PCY-2 Anti-spell Fragrance 6.00 15.00
❑ PCY-3 Thousand Knives 8.00 20.00
❑ ROD-1 Dark Magician Knight 6.00 15.00
❑ ROD-2 Knight's Tale 3.00 8.00
❑ ROD-3 Sage's Stone 3.00 8.00
❑ SDD-1 Valkyrion The Magna Warrior 8.00 20.00
❑ SDD-2 Sinister Serpent 5.00 12.00
❑ SDD-3 Harpie's Feather Duster 8.00 20.00
❑ SDY-4 Summoned Skull 2.50 6.00
❑ SJC-1 Cyber-Stein 400.00 500.00
❑ SP1-1 Cyber Harpie Lady 4.00 10.00
❑ SP2-1 Ancient Lamp 1.50 4.00
❑ TSC-1 Perfectly Ultimate Great Moth 5.00 12.00
❑ TSC-2 Riryoku 4.00 10.00
❑ TSC-3 Negate Attack 5.00 12.00
❑ WC4-1 Fairy King Truesdale 5.00 12.00
❑ WC4-2 Kinetic Soldier 3.00 8.00
❑ WC4-3 Slate Warrior 6.00 15.00
❑ WC5-1 Silent Swordsman 10.00 25.00
❑ WC5-2 Kaibaman 6.00 15.00
❑ WCS-403 Sengenjin 10.00 25.00
❑ WC5-3 Mind Control 4.00 10.00
❑ WC7-1 Spell Striker 2.50 6.00
❑ WCS-1 Kanan the Swordmistress 100.00 150.00
❑ JUMP10 Toon Dark Magician Girl 2.50 6.00
❑ JUMP11 Victory Dragon 3.00 8.00
❑ JUMP12 Elemental Hero Stratos 6.00 15.00
❑ JUMP13 Elemental Hero Ocean 4.00 10.00
❑ JUMP14 Green Baboon, Defender of the Forest 6.00 15.00
❑ JUMP15 Dreadscythe Harvester 2.00 5.00
❑ JUMP16 The Wicked Eraser 2.50 6.00
❑ JUMP17 The Wicked Avatar 3.00 8.00
❑ JUMP18 The Wicked Dreadroot 4.00 10.00
❑ JUMP19 Blast Sphere 2.00 5.00
❑ JUMP20 Copycat 2.50 6.00
❑ JUMP21 Relieve Monster .75 2.00
❑ JUMP22 Cloning 1.50 4.00
❑ JUMP23 Van'Dalgyon the Dark Dragon Lord 3.00 8.00
❑ JUMP24 Cyber Dinosaur 1.25 3.00
❑ JUMP25 Exodius the Ultimate Forbidden Lord 6.00 15.00
❑ JUMP26 Dragonic Knight 1.25 3.00
❑ JUMP27 Arcana Force Ex - the Light Ruler 1.50 4.00
❑ JUMP28 Gandora the Dragon of Destruction 3.00 8.00
❑ JUMP29 Dandylion 3.00 8.00
❑ JUMP30 Red-Eyes Darkness Metal Dragon 8.00 20.00
❑ JUMP31 Chimeratech Fortress Dragon 6.00 15.00
❑ JUMP32 Beast King Barbaros 8.00 20.00
❑ JUMP33 Tragoedia 6.00 15.00
❑ JUMP34 Genesis Dragon 10.00 25.00
❑ JUMP35 Orichalcos Shunoros 4.00 10.00
❑ JUMP36 Darkness Neosphere 2.00 5.00
❑ JUMP37 Obelisk the Tormentor 8.00 20.00
❑ JUMP38 Cyber Eltanin 1.25 3.00
❑ JUMP39 Hundred-Eyes Dragon 2.50 6.00
❑ JUMP40 Golem Dragon 2.00 5.00
❑ PCY-4 Dark Magician 25.00 50.00
❑ PCY-E005 Kuriboh 30.00 60.00
❑ SJCS-4 Crush Card Virus 350.00 400.00
❑ TWED-1 Honest 1.25 3.00
❑ DPK-SE1 Blockman .75 2.00
❑ DPK-SE2 Treasure Map .40 1.00
❑ DPK-SE3 Hero Spirit .40 1.00
❑ EEN-SE1 Horus the Black Flame Dragon LV8 3.00 8.00
❑ EEN-SE2 The Creator 1.50 4.00
❑ EEN-SE3 Sacred Phoenix of Nephthys 1.50 4.00
❑ EEN-SE4 Silent Swordsman LV5 1.25 3.00
❑ IOC-SE1 Gemini Elf .60 1.50
❑ IOC-SE2 Magic Cylinder 1.50 4.00
❑ IOC-SE3 Ring of Destruction 2.50 6.00
❑ IOC-SE4 Lava Golem 1.25 3.00
❑ RDS-SE1 Diffusion Wave-Motion .40 1.00
❑ RDS-SE2 Dark Magician Girl 4.00 10.00
❑ RDS-SE3 Judgment of Anubis 1.25 3.00
❑ RDS-SE4 Vampire Lord 1.00 2.50
❑ SOI-SE1 Acid Trap Hole .40 1.00
❑ SOI-SE2 Riryoku .60 1.50
❑ SOI-SE3 Windstorm of Etaqua .40 1.00
❑ SOI-SE4 Mesmeric Control .40 1.00
❑ TLM-SE1 Invader of Darkness .60 1.50
❑ TLM-SE2 Chaos Emperor Dragon Envoy of the End 3.00 8.00
❑ TLM-SE3 Mazera DeVille .60 1.50
❑ TLM-SE4 The End of Anubis 1.00 2.50
❑ WCS-503 Firewing Pegasus 150.00 200.00
❑ ABPF-SE1 Dandylion 1.25 3.00
❑ ABPF-SE2 Red-Eyes Darkness Metal Dragon 2.00 5.00
❑ ANPR-SE1 Solar Recharge 2.00 5.00
❑ ANPR-SE2 Red-Eyes Wyvern 2.00 5.00
❑ CSOC-SE1 Harvest Angel of Wisdom .40 1.00
❑ CSOC-SE2 Il Blud .75 2.00
❑ FOTB-SE1 Phantom Beast Rock-Lizard .40 1.00
❑ FOTB-SE2 Winged Rhynos .40 1.00
❑ GLAS-SE1 Phantom of Chaos 2.00 5.00
❑ GLAS-SE2 Vortex Trooper .40 1.00
❑ LODT-SE1 Kuraz the Light Monarch 1.25 3.00
❑ LODT-SE2 Soul Rope .60 1.50
❑ PTDN-SE1 Mutant Mindmaster .60 1.50
❑ PTDN-SE2 Hannibal Necromancer .40 1.00
❑ RGBT-SE1 The Dark Creator 1.50 4.00
❑ RGBT-SE2 Allure of Darkness 4.00 10.00
❑ SOVR-SE1 Tempest Magician 1.25 3.00
❑ SOVR-SE2 Charge of the Light Brigade 1.25 3.00
❑ STON-SE1 Cyber End Dragon 1.50 4.00
❑ STON-SE2 Shrink 1.25 3.00
❑ TAEV-SE1 Masked Beast Des Gardius .60 1.50
❑ TAEV-SE2 The Mask of Remnants .60 1.50
❑ TDGS-SE1 Eradicator Epidemic Virus .40 1.00
❑ TDGS-SE2 Gladiator Beast Heraklinos 1.00 2.50

YU-GI-OH!

TRADING CARD GAMES

HOW TO USE

What's Listed
Products listed in the Price Guide typically: 1) are produced by licensed manufacturers, 2) are widely available and 3) have market activity on single items.

What the Columns Mean
The LO and HI columns reflect current retail selling ranges. The HI column on the right generally represents the full retail selling price. The LO column on the left generally represents the lowest price one would expect to find with extensive shopping.

Grading
All cards in the Price Guide are based on NrMint to Mint condition. Damaged cards are generally sold for 25 to 75 percent of Mint value.

Currency
This Price Guide is intended to reflect the entire North American market. All listed prices are in U.S. dollars.

Legend
Rarity structure can vary greatly across different games; a full description of the rarity structure in every game is beyond the scope of this book. Below are some of the most commonly used rarity abbreviations, which we've tried to incorporate in our listings.

F - Fixed card, typically found in starter decks.

C - Common card.

U - Uncommon card.

R - Rare card.

SR/UR - Super/Ultra Rare card. Rarity may vary, but is typically found in one of every X (3, 6, 12, 24, etc.) packs.

CH, X - Chase card. As with SR/UR designation, typcially found in one of every X packs; often alternate-art or other variation on "normal" card.

PR - Promo card.

Note: Beckett does not sell individual cards, for any game.

2009 Battle Spirits Call of the Core

Item	LO	HI
BOOSTER BOX (32 PACKS)	30.00	60.00
BOOSTER PACK (8 CARDS)	1.25	2.50
❑ 1 Gora C	.10	.20
❑ 2 Rokceratops C	.10	.20
❑ 3 Teranosaber C	.10	.20
❑ 4 The Scout Dragno C	.10	.20
❑ 5 Eyeburn C	.10	.20
❑ 6 Merat C	.10	.20
❑ 7 Hummerdrake C	.10	.20
❑ 8 Metalburn C	.10	.20
❑ 9 Volc-Baboon C	.10	.20
❑ 10 Chakrambat C	.10	.20
❑ 11 Dragsaurus U	.20	.50
❑ 12 Tryswordon C	.10	.20
❑ 13 Taurusknight C	.10	.20
❑ 14 The Shaman Dragno R	.40	1.00
❑ 15 Spinoaxe C	.10	.20
❑ 16 Skelton-Jaw U	.20	.50
❑ 17 Lanceraptor C	.10	.20
❑ 18 Lizardman C	.10	.20
❑ 19 Jurassickle C	.10	.20
❑ 20 The BladeDragon Steelanodon U	.20	.50
❑ 21 The FlameDragon Ma-Gwo MR	1.25	3.00
❑ 22 The Sickle Fool-Joker R	.75	2.00
❑ 23 The Fire LithoGraphica Phoenixious MR	1.25	3.00
❑ 24 The Dragon Diamat R	.75	2.00
❑ 25 The DragonicFortress Giga MR	2.00	5.00
❑ 26 Foger C	.10	.20
❑ 27 Will-Orb C	.10	.20
❑ 28 Skulldevil C	.10	.20
❑ 29 Rib-Reaper C	.10	.20
❑ 30 Grip-Hands C	.10	.20
❑ 31 Death-Haides C	.10	.20
❑ 32 Gawrm C	.10	.20
❑ 33 Disaster C	.10	.20
❑ 34 Bi-Python U	.20	.50
❑ 35 Bone-Gladiator C	.10	.20
❑ 36 Sha-Zoo C	.10	.20
❑ 37 Illusiona C	.10	.20
❑ 38 Skel-Viper C	.10	.20
❑ 39 The Mysteryman Dionaeman C	.10	.20
❑ 40 Darkwitch R	.40	1.00
❑ 41 Cobraiga C	.10	.20
❑ 42 Mistweasel C	.10	.20
❑ 43 Draculious R	.40	1.00
❑ 44 The PhantomBull Smowg U	.20	.50
❑ 45 The Ripper Headiless C	.10	.20
❑ 46 The PhantomDragon Sheyron MR	1.25	3.00
❑ 47 The Witch Naja R	.40	1.00
❑ 48 The PrincessVampire Vampiles U	.20	.50
❑ 49 The Phantom Horseman MR	1.25	3.00
❑ 50 Beatbeetle C	.10	.20
❑ 51 Flyingmirage C	.10	.20
❑ 52 Pelileaf C	.10	.20
❑ 53 Leavwolf C	.10	.20
❑ 54 Shockeater C	.10	.20
❑ 55 Emeant C	.10	.20
❑ 56 Matchra C	.10	.20
❑ 57 Gularva C	.10	.20
❑ 58 Hercules-Geo C	.10	.20
❑ 59 Shidafukurou C	.10	.20
❑ 60 Eagrass C	.10	.20
❑ 61 Apewhip R	.40	1.00
❑ 62 Hungrytree R	.40	1.00
❑ 63 Emeraldscissor C	.10	.20
❑ 64 Ziga-Wasp C	.10	.20
❑ 65 Killikabut C	.10	.20
❑ 66 Stagrove U	.20	.50
❑ 67 Swallowivy U	.20	.50
❑ 68 The BlastTiger Tigald U	.20	.50
❑ 69 The AirMaster Aquilers C	.10	.20
❑ 70 The MeteoriteArmor Monoqueiroz C	.10	.20
❑ 71 The Charger Blanboar R	.40	1.00
❑ 72 Gowsilvia MR	1.25	3.00
❑ 73 The GaudyFeather Vulpelture MR	1.25	3.00
❑ 74 Warrior-Gun C	.10	.20
❑ 75 IceDroid C	.10	.20
❑ 76 Ray-Bullet C	.10	.20
❑ 77 Baby-Loki C	.10	.20
❑ 78 The AutoLady Mani C	.10	.20
❑ 79 Rainbowpapillon C	.10	.20
❑ 80 Fenrircannon C	.10	.20
❑ 81 The SilverScale Nithhoggr C	.10	.20
❑ 82 Ur-Dine C	.10	.20
❑ 83 Rabicrysta C	.10	.20
❑ 84 Gatlingstand C	.10	.20
❑ 85 Elephantite U	.20	.50
❑ 86 Queen-Valkyrie C	.10	.20
❑ 87 Metaldy-Bug U	.20	.50
❑ 88 Towermittcrab C	.10	.20
❑ 89 Dualcannon-Bell C	.10	.20
❑ 90 Kell-Blindi U	.20	.50
❑ 91 The Artifact Laguna U	.20	.50
❑ 92 The CarrierWhale Mobileflow C	.10	.20
❑ 93 The ShieldSpirit Dis MR	1.25	3.00
❑ 94 Gran-Dolbalkan R	.40	1.00
❑ 95 The ArmoredBeast Bear-Gelmir MR	1.25	3.00
❑ 96 The AutoEmpress Sol R	.40	1.00
❑ 97 The SteelWyvern R	.40	1.00
❑ 98 The Burning Battlefield U	.20	.50
❑ 99 The Canyon Where Sage lives U	.20	.50
❑ 100 The Ruby Sun C	.10	.20
❑ 101 The Ancient Dragon Territory C	.10	.20
❑ 102 The Lost of Old Castle C	.10	.20
❑ 103 The Swamp of Drain Life U	.20	.50
❑ 104 The Historic Battlefield of the Cursed R	.40	1.00
❑ 105 The Shackles of Doom U	.20	.50
❑ 106 The Hermit Wise Tree R	.40	1.00
❑ 107 The Fruit of Life U	.20	.50
❑ 108 The Anthill U	.20	.50
❑ 109 The Hill of Violent Wind C	.10	.20
❑ 110 The Timeless Ice Field U	.20	.50
❑ 111 The Diamond Moon C	.10	.20
❑ 112 The Castle of Eternal Snow U	.20	.50
❑ 113 The Invaded Silver Snow C	.10	.20
❑ 114 Buster Spear R	.40	1.00
❑ 115 Awaken C	.10	.20
❑ 116 Offensive Aura C	.10	.20
❑ 117 Double Draw C	.10	.20
❑ 118 Call of Lost C	.10	.20
❑ 119 Burst Fire C	.10	.20
❑ 120 Buster Phalanx U	.20	.50
❑ 121 Flame Dance C	.10	.20
❑ 122 Flame Tempest R	.40	1.00
❑ 123 Return Draw C	.10	.20
❑ 124 Cemetery Aura U	.20	.50
❑ 125 Deadly Balance C	.10	.20
❑ 126 Shadow Elixir U	.20	.50
❑ 127 Killer Telescope C	.10	.20
❑ 128 Chaos Draw R	.40	1.00
❑ 129 Poison Shoot C	.10	.20
❑ 130 Changing Cores C	.10	.20
❑ 131 Dark Coffin C	.10	.20
❑ 132 Storm Draw C	.10	.20
❑ 133 Wild Power C	.10	.20
❑ 134 Binding Thorn C	.10	.20
❑ 135 Power Aura C	.10	.20
❑ 136 Gather Forces U	.20	.50
❑ 137 Relation Soul C	.10	.20
❑ 138 Hand Reverse U	.20	.50
❑ 139 Feather Barrier C	.10	.20
❑ 140 Binding Woods R	.40	1.00
❑ 141 Invisible Cloak R	.40	1.00
❑ 142 Pure Elixir C	.10	.20
❑ 143 Divine Chain R	.40	1.00
❑ 144 Silent Wall U	.20	.50
❑ 145 Defensive Aura C	.10	.20
❑ 146 Dream Ribbon C	.10	.20
❑ 147 Dream Chest C	.10	.20
❑ 148 Leak Drive C	.10	.20
❑ 149 Attack Shift C	.10	.20
❑ X1 The DragonEmperor Siegfried XR	6.00	15.00
❑ X2 The SevenShogun Desperado XR	6.00	15.00
❑ X3 The Duke Kingtaurus XR	6.00	15.00
❑ X4 The ImpregnableFortress Odin XR	6.00	15.00

2009 Battle Spirits Rise of the Angels

Item	LO	HI
BOOSTER BOX (32 PACKS)	30.00	60.00
BOOSTER PACK (8 CARDS)	1.25	2.50
❑ 1 Lizardedge C	.10	.20
❑ 2 The Acrobat Juggline U	.20	.50
❑ 3 Dinohound C	.10	.20
❑ 4 Orcaria C	.10	.20
❑ 5 The Charger Dragno C	.10	.20
❑ 6 Pteratomahawk C	.10	.20
❑ 7 The RiseDragon Balmung C	.10	.20
❑ 8 Fisdragoon C	.10	.20
❑ 9 The DragonBuster Archeorni C	.10	.20
❑ 10 The LavaDragon Plesios R	.40	1.00
❑ 11 Zwei-Howle C	.10	.20
❑ 12 The Conqueror Cendragos MR	1.00	2.50
❑ 13 Bat-Bat C	.10	.20
❑ 14 Phantasma C	.10	.20
❑ 15 Humpdump C	.10	.20
❑ 16 Slimy C	.10	.20
❑ 17 Mummella C	.10	.20
❑ 18 Top Supra C	.10	.20
❑ 19 Bottom Desuper C	.10	.20
❑ 20 Lady-Frankelly U	.20	.50
❑ 21 The SkullKnight Zo-Goin C	.10	.20
❑ 22 The Marquis Cocytus R	.40	1.00
❑ 23 The TwinSnake Hydram C	.10	.20
❑ 24 The General Bloody-Caesar MR	1.00	2.50
❑ 25 Sheep man C	.10	.20
❑ 26 MachG C	.10	.20
❑ 27 Caprihorn C	.10	.20
❑ 28 Xscissors C	.10	.20
❑ 29 Bathopper C	.10	.20
❑ 30 The Soldier Ant U	.20	.50
❑ 31 Scorpede C	.10	.20
❑ 32 Dachono C	.10	.20
❑ 33 The CavalryBeast Sleiphorse C	.10	.20
❑ 34 The OldSage Trenton C	.10	.20
❑ 35 The DarkFeather Yatagross R	.40	1.00
❑ 36 The Great Kaiseleon MR	1.00	2.50
❑ 37 Sphereroid C	.10	.20
❑ 38 The Buckler Langlies C	.10	.20
❑ 39 The Sacred Mjolnir C	.10	.20
❑ 40 Lobsterk C	.10	.20
❑ 41 Liorider C	.10	.20
❑ 42 Skuldia C	.10	.20
❑ 43 Arma-Dillo C	.10	.20
❑ 44 The CannonArtifact Megarock C	.10	.20
❑ 45 The ShieldDragon Fevnir MR	1.00	2.50
❑ 46 Wingur C	.10	.20
❑ 47 The AutoPriest Freyr U	.20	.50
❑ 48 The DragonTank Earthguard R	.40	1.00
❑ 49 Piyon C	.10	.20
❑ 50 Koristal C	.10	.20
❑ 51 Chunpopo C	.10	.20
❑ 52 Chagamaru U	.20	.50
❑ 53 The Fairy Tanya C	.10	.20
❑ 54 Pom C	.10	.20
❑ 55 Chauw C	.10	.20
❑ 56 Arcanabeast-Ken C	.10	.20
❑ 57 The FairyQueen Ti-Tanya U	.20	.50
❑ 58 Pentan C	.10	.20
❑ 59 Lom C	.10	.20
❑ 60 The Clown Clan C	.10	.20
❑ 61 The Angelia Angu C	.10	.20
❑ 62 Porkne C	.10	.20
❑ 63 The HellDog Cerru-Berus R	.40	1.00
❑ 64 The Melodybird Crewc C	.10	.20
❑ 65 The BlossomChild Lip R	.40	1.00
❑ 66 Arcanadoll-Pan C	.10	.20
❑ 67 The Angelia Virchu MR	1.00	2.50
❑ 68 The whiteTiger Huck C	.10	.20
❑ 69 The BlackTiger Kuron C	.10	.20
❑ 70 Arcanaprince-Obero U	.20	.50
❑ 71 The PreciousBeast Carbulc R	.40	1.00
❑ 72 Trickster MR	1.00	2.50
❑ 73 The Kaiser Empereur U	.20	.50
❑ 74 The BalloonMan Barball C	.10	.20
❑ 75 The GreatAngelia Principearl MR	1.00	2.50
❑ 76 The Ancient Fault C	.10	.20
❑ 77 The Plateau of Duel U	.20	.50
❑ 78 The Evil Coffin U	.20	.50
❑ 79 The Forest of Amethyst C	.10	.20
❑ 80 The Limestone Cave of Emerald C	.10	.20
❑ 81 The Budding Plain U	.20	.50
❑ 82 The Artifact Plant C	.10	.20
❑ 83 The Corridor of Mirrors U	.20	.50
❑ 84 The Blessed Sanctuary C	.10	.20
❑ 85 The Topaz Meteor R	.40	1.00
❑ 86 The Spiral Tower C	.10	.20
❑ 87 The Sealed Spellbook R	.40	1.00
❑ 88 Cross Fire C	.10	.20
❑ 89 Spirit Link C	.10	.20
❑ 90 Mind Flare U	.20	.50
❑ 91 Seventh Crimson R	.40	1.00
❑ 92 Energy Drain C	.10	.20
❑ 93 Mind Control R	.40	1.00
❑ 94 Bloody Rain U	.20	.50
❑ 95 Sacrifice C	.10	.20
❑ 96 Divine Wind U	.20	.50
❑ 97 Nature Forces C	.10	.20
❑ 98 Cast Off C	.10	.20
❑ 99 Life Chain R	.40	1.00
❑ 100 Invincible Shield C	.10	.20
❑ 101 Reflection Armor C	.10	.20
❑ 102 White Potion U	.20	.50
❑ 103 Reload Cores R	.40	1.00
❑ 104 Additional Color C	.10	.20
❑ 105 Great Wall C	.10	.20
❑ 106 Royal Potion C	.10	.20
❑ 107 Time Reap C	.10	.20
❑ 108 Magic Book R	.40	1.00
❑ 109 Angel Voice C	.10	.20
❑ 110 Heavy Gate C	.10	.20
❑ 111 Spirit Illusion U	.20	.50
❑ X5 The TwinRowdy Diranos XR	6.00	15.00

Card	Low	High
❑ X6 The SevenShogun Destlord XR	6.00	15.00
❑ X7 The Gigantic Thor XR	6.00	15.00
❑ X8 The ArcAngelia Mikafar XR	6.00	15.00

2010 Battle Spirits Ascension of Dragons

Card	Low	High
BOOSTER BOX (32 PACKS)	30.00	60.00
BOOSTER PACK (8 CARDS)	1.25	2.50
❑ 1 Kunanomi C	.10	.20
❑ 2 Chamelewhip C	.10	.20
❑ 3 DarkGoradon C	.10	.20
❑ 4 DarkDinohound C	.10	.20
❑ 5 Chain-Dragon C	.10	.20
❑ 6 The ZombieDragon Zom-Sauru U	.20	.50
❑ 7 The Guardsman Dragno U	.20	.50
❑ 8 The AncientDragon Ba-Gaw MR	1.50	4.00
❑ 9 The FlameEmperor Kujaraku C	.10	.20
❑ 10 The ThunderDragon El-Clair R	.40	1.00
❑ 11 The Tyrant Fuhjaus MR	1.25	3.00
❑ 12 Banshee C	.10	.20
❑ 13 Skulldemon C	.10	.20
❑ 14 Shadowjuggler C	.10	.20
❑ 15 Cyclo-Winder C	.10	.20
❑ 16 The FallenAngelia Azel U	.20	.50
❑ 17 Hellwitch C	.10	.20
❑ 18 The WaterSnake Seaserpenta U	.20	.50
❑ 19 Headless Carriage C	.10	.20
❑ 20 The DarkDragon Ops-Curite R	.40	1.00
❑ 21 The Vampire Dampeel R	.40	1.00
❑ 22 The KingSnake Quetzalcoatl MR	1.25	3.00
❑ 23 Giraffen C	.10	.20
❑ 24 Duckle C	.10	.20
❑ 25 Fal-Condor C	.10	.20
❑ 26 BlackMachG C	.10	.20
❑ 27 Alligade U	.20	.50
❑ 28 Sevenspot U	.20	.50
❑ 29 BlackMonoqueiroz C	.10	.20
❑ 30 The AppetiteFlower Bug-Lesia C	.10	.20
❑ 31 The GroundDragon Fon-Daxion R	.40	1.00
❑ 32 The SpearBeetle Lucanidos R	.40	1.00
❑ 33 The CrustaceanFighter Longhorn MR	1.25	3.00
❑ 34 Vidohunir C	.10	.20
❑ 35 Berserker-Magnum C	.10	.20
❑ 36 Oddsay C	.10	.20
❑ 37 The ArmoredBeast Heith-Rune U	.20	.50
❑ 38 The Reconnaissance Magni C	.10	.20
❑ 39 The JewelBug Scaraveil U	.20	.50
❑ 40 The ArmoredBeast Gullin-Bullsty C	.10	.20
❑ 41 Fenrircannon Mk-II C	.10	.20
❑ 42 The BeastMaster Dvergr C	.10	.20
❑ 43 The Valkyrie-Hildr MR	1.25	3.00
❑ 44 The SkyDragon Le-Ciel R	.40	1.00
❑ 45 The IceGoddess Frigg MR	1.25	3.00
❑ 46 The Fairy Dorothy C	.10	.20
❑ 47 Wiseless-Scarecrow U	.20	.50
❑ 48 DarkPiyon C	.10	.20
❑ 49 The BlackFairy Ti-Tanya C	.10	.20
❑ 50 Heartless-Tin U	.20	.50
❑ 51 Arcanabeast-Hart C	.10	.20
❑ 52 The Postman Pentan C	.10	.20
❑ 53 The Angelia Throne R	.40	1.00
❑ 54 Arcanasoldier-Cinq C	.10	.20
❑ 55 The LightDragon Lumiere R	.40	1.00
❑ 56 Braveless-Leo C	.10	.20
❑ 57 The GreatAngelia Seraphy MR	1.25	3.00
❑ 58 The RatMan Zurich C	.10	.20
❑ 59 The Pharmacist Girmamarl C	.10	.20
❑ 60 The Soldier Gustav C	.10	.20
❑ 61 The BattleBeast Jacker C	.10	.20
❑ 62 The ApeMan Mongoku U	.20	.50
❑ 63 The Two-Sword Ambrose C	.10	.20
❑ 64 Ugarurum C	.10	.20
❑ 65 The Spinner Har?elicite C	.10	.20
❑ 66 The CatLady Abyssinia C	.10	.20
❑ 67 Dra-Golem U	.20	.50
❑ 68 Iron-Golem C	.10	.20
❑ 69 The Illusionist Mirage C	.10	.20
❑ 70 The BattleBeast Diatryma C	.10	.20
❑ 71 Steam-Golem C	.10	.20
❑ 72 Rabirabi C	.10	.20
❑ 73 The SeaDragon Courant-Marin R	.40	1.00
❑ 74 The ChimeraDragon Hydrus R	.40	1.00
❑ 75 The LegendaryGiant Jude MR	1.25	3.00
❑ 76 The BombSoldier Dragno C	.10	.20
❑ 77 The MysteriousFox Cubic U	.20	.50
❑ 78 The ScarletDragonRider Rosso R	.40	1.00
❑ 79 The UnicornDragon Volsung U	.20	.50
❑ 80 The Dictator Volcanos MR	1.25	3.00
❑ 81 Sandman C	.10	.20
❑ 82 Fallenpaladin C	.10	.20
❑ 83 The PurpleDragonRider Violet R	.40	1.00
❑ 84 The EvilAdmiral Negapluto U	.20	.50
❑ 85 Pineappopotamus C	.10	.20
❑ 86 The SeaHorse Kelpie C	.10	.20
❑ 87 The Yojinbo Antman U	.20	.50
❑ 88 The ViridianDragonRider Grun R	.40	1.00
❑ 89 Armetcrab C	.10	.20
❑ 90 Pantomeister C	.10	.20
❑ 91 The WhiteDragonRider Albus R	.40	1.00
❑ 92 The EvilDeity Big-Loki U	.20	.50
❑ 93 The IceWitch Hel MR	1.25	3.00
❑ 94 The Angelia Kleio C	.10	.20
❑ 95 The Princess- Snowwhite U	.20	.50
❑ 96 Arcanafighter-Quatre C	.10	.20
❑ 97 The YellowDragonRider Flavum R	.40	1.00
❑ 98 Dwarf-Seven C	.10	.20
❑ 99 The BattleBeast Babeaver C	.10	.20
❑ 100 Bronze-Golem C	.10	.20
❑ 101 The GiantKnight Aldous MR	1.25	3.00
❑ 102 Mithril-Golem C	.10	.20
❑ 103 The BlueDragonRider Azure R	.40	1.00
❑ 104 The IronHammer Oswald U	.20	.50
❑ 105 The Airspace of Pterosaurs C	.10	.20
❑ 106 The Seven Dragons' Throne C	.10	.20
❑ 107 The Shadow Street C	.10	.20
❑ 108 The King Snake Nest C	.10	.20
❑ 109 The Whirlwind Ravine U	.20	.50
❑ 110 The Strong-Dominated Earth C	.10	.20
❑ 111 The Inviolable Sanctuary C	.10	.20
❑ 112 The Steel Forest U	.20	.50
❑ 113 The Miraculous Hill C	.10	.20
❑ 114 The Spring of Full Magical Powers C	.10	.20
❑ 115 The Ancient Arena U	.20	.50
❑ 116 The Heart-Buster Huge Slope C	.10	.20
❑ 117 The Victory Stand of the Glory C	.10	.20
❑ 118 The Ruby Empty Sky C	.10	.20
❑ 119 The Amethyst Empty Sky C	.10	.20
❑ 120 The Emerald Empty Sky C	.10	.20
❑ 121 The Diamond Empty Sky C	.10	.20
❑ 122 The Topaz Empty Sky C	.10	.20
❑ 123 The Sapphire Empty Sky C	.10	.20
❑ 124 Great Link C	.10	.20
❑ 125 The Ring of Nibelungen C	.10	.20
❑ 126 Lightning Ballista R	.40	1.00
❑ 127 Dragons' Rush C	.10	.20
❑ 128 Merciful Release C	.10	.20
❑ 129 Danse Macabre C	.10	.20
❑ 130 Venom Shot U	.20	.50
❑ 131 Inferno Eyes R	.40	1.00
❑ 132 Forest Aura C	.10	.20
❑ 133 Full Charge C	.10	.20
❑ 134 Ground Howling R	.40	1.00
❑ 135 Jungle Law C	.10	.20
❑ 136 Mist Curtain C	.10	.20
❑ 137 Dream Hand C	.10	.20
❑ 138 High Ether C	.10	.20
❑ 139 Glacial Breath R	.40	1.00
❑ 140 Trick Prank C	.10	.20
❑ 141 Gleam Hope C	.10	.20
❑ 142 Judgment Lights R	.40	1.00
❑ 143 Straight Flush U	.20	.50
❑ 144 Switch Hitter C	.10	.20
❑ 145 Lead Wall U	.20	.50
❑ 146 Magic Drill C	.10	.20
❑ 147 Massive Up C	.10	.20
❑ 148 Nexus Repair C	.10	.20
❑ 149 Tidal Tide R	.40	1.00
❑ 150 Warning Attack C	.10	.20
❑ 151 Absorb Symbol C	.10	.20
❑ 152 Branch Lock C	.10	.20
❑ 153 Eternal Shield C	.10	.20
❑ 154 Chorus Birds C	.10	.20
❑ 155 Magic Spanner C	.10	.20
❑ 156 Potential Power U	.20	.50
❑ X13 The DarkDragonEmperor Siegfried XR	6.00	15.00
❑ X14 The SevenShogun Pandemium XR	6.00	15.00
❑ X15 The Emperor Kaiseratlas XR	6.00	15.00
❑ X16 The MobileFortress Castle-Golem XR	6.00	15.00
❑ X17 The PhantomLord Rean XR	6.00	15.00
❑ X18 The HugeBeastLord Behedoth XR	6.00	15.00

2010 Battle Spirits Dawn of the Ancients

Card	Low	High
BOOSTER BOX (32 PACKS)	30.00	60.00
BOOSTER PACK (8 CARDS)	1.25	2.50
❑ 1 The FanDragon Sordes C	.10	.20
❑ 2 Dimetrodoron C	.10	.20
❑ 3 Wyarm C	.10	.20
❑ 4 The DragonicFortress Megaron C	.10	.20
❑ 5 Redcap C	.10	.20
❑ 6 Blindsnake C	.10	.20
❑ 7 Gastoras U	.20	.50
❑ 8 The MischievousFairy Imp C	.10	.20
❑ 9 The QueenVampire Carmilla MR	1.50	4.00
❑ 10 Pollu?&Castar C	.10	.20
❑ 11 Gengoron C	.10	.20
❑ 12 Mothleaf C	.10	.20
❑ 13 The GodTree Dionaeus MR	1.25	3.00
❑ 14 The SaberTiger Xen-Fu U	.20	.50
❑ 15 The Artifact Embla C	.10	.20
❑ 16 The GunKnight Heavybarrel C	.10	.20
❑ 17 The CoralCrab Siomanekid U	.20	.50
❑ 18 The GiantMobile Ymir C	.10	.20
❑ 19 Shesas U	.20	.50
❑ 20 The MorningFairy Napalco C	.10	.20
❑ 21 The GreatAngelia Sophia MR	1.50	4.00
❑ 22 LittleKnight-Lancelot C	.10	.20
❑ 23 The ChimeraDinosaur Dinozaur C	.10	.20
❑ 24 The WolfMan Wolfy C	.10	.20
❑ 25 MCPanther U	.20	.50
❑ 26 Erimakilizard C	.10	.20
❑ 27 Katanakasago C	.10	.20
❑ 28 Ankillersaurus C	.10	.20
❑ 29 The Infantry Dragron C	.10	.20
❑ 30 Tartargar C	.10	.20
❑ 31 The FineDragon Windrake U	.20	.50
❑ 32 Styrahorn C	.10	.20
❑ 33 The ThunderEmperorDragon Siegwurm MR	1.25	3.00
❑ 34 Bone-Dog C	.10	.20
❑ 35 Komoribrella C	.10	.20
❑ 36 The HellFighter Balam C	.10	.20
❑ 37 The DoubleHead Snake U	.20	.50
❑ 38 The HellFencer Berith R	.40	1.00
❑ 39 Skunks C	.10	.20
❑ 40 Hacchidori C	.10	.20
❑ 41 Amenborg C	.10	.20
❑ 42 The HeavyArmoredBug Caterbarga U	.20	.50
❑ 43 The Hunter Kinggheppardo R	.40	1.00
❑ 44 Momongul C	.10	.20
❑ 45 Hitodem C	.10	.20
❑ 46 The Sacred Gungnir C	.10	.20
❑ 47 Glasscargot C	.10	.20
❑ 48 The Artifact Droiden C	.10	.20
❑ 49 The CentaurusSoldier Atrithr U	.20	.50
❑ 50 The ArmoredBeast Skoll C	.10	.20
❑ 51 The IronKnight Yggdrasill MR	1.25	3.00
❑ 52 Oviraptt C	.10	.20
❑ 53 Iguaknife C	.10	.20
❑ 54 The FierceHeadBeast Horngrizzly C	.10	.20
❑ 55 The Decurion Dragron C	.10	.20
❑ 56 The DinosaurPrincess Jura C	.10	.20
❑ 57 Sabecaulus C	.10	.20
❑ 58 The ShamshirDinosaur Parasaur U	.20	.50
❑ 59 The Scabbardfish Espada C	.10	.20
❑ 60 The CloudBladeDragon Swordlagoon C	.10	.20
❑ 61 The BattleAxe Apollodinos R	.40	1.00
❑ 62 The IronScorpionDragon Scord-Goran R	.40	1.00
❑ 63 The HugeDinosaur Giganoton MR	1.25	3.00
❑ 64 Pigeonheadless C	.10	.20
❑ 65 Smoggoat C	.10	.20
❑ 66 Straysoul C	.10	.20
❑ 67 Bronzemaiden C	.10	.20
❑ 68 The HellAirMan Buney C	.10	.20
❑ 69 The Werewolf Loup-Gawrou C	.10	.20
❑ 70 The HellMusician Mur C	.10	.20
❑ 71 Skullgoyle C	.10	.20
❑ 72 The SnakeEmpress Medousa U	.20	.50
❑ 73 The ChopSword Shadowslicer R	.40	1.00
❑ 74 The DarkBishop Daculus R	.40	1.00
❑ 75 The HellKnight Andra MR	1.25	3.00
❑ 76 Mepon C	.10	.20
❑ 77 Caracalossom C	.10	.20
❑ 78 Gazellecaid C	.10	.20
❑ 79 Gabunohashi C	.10	.20
❑ 80 Mamrot U	.20	.50
❑ 81 The Worker Antman C	.10	.20
❑ 82 Mitsujarashi C	.10	.20
❑ 83 Woodykong C	.10	.20
❑ 84 The Baron Jacobino C	.10	.20
❑ 85 The IronFist Cactusgaroo R	.40	1.00
❑ 86 Tsukushinmoa R	.40	1.00
❑ 87 The FangTree Rafflesio MR	1.25	3.00
❑ 88 TwinFairies Hugin?Munin C	.10	.20
❑ 89 Senzangou C	.10	.20
❑ 90 The FloatingFish Molamola C	.10	.20
❑ 91 The ChiefMaid Fulla C	.10	.20
❑ 92 The ArmoredBeast Audhumla C	.10	.20
❑ 93 The AutoMarine Seerauber U	.20	.50
❑ 94 The ShieldSoldier Balder C	.10	.20
❑ 95 Reindeer C	.10	.20
❑ 96 Tonbeaul C	.10	.20
❑ 97 The KeyMaul Valgrind R	.40	1.00
❑ 98 The ShineDragonPalace Breidhablic R	.40	1.00
❑ 99 The SilverWolfEmperor Gagnrathr MR	1.25	3.00
❑ 100 Pyorit C	.10	.20
❑ 101 The SnowKiddie Yeti C	.10	.20
❑ 102 Gremly C	.10	.20
❑ 103 The Chick Pentan C	.10	.20
❑ 104 The FortuneTeller Pentan C	.10	.20
❑ 105 Laserpanda C	.10	.20
❑ 106 Cotton-Candele C	.10	.20
❑ 107 The CatKnight Cait-Sith R	.40	1.00
❑ 108 ArcanaKing-Charle MR	1.25	3.00
❑ 109 ArcanaKnight-Hex C	.10	.20
❑ 110 The CleverBeast Iberix U	.20	.50
❑ 111 The GreatAngelia Fanim MR	1.25	3.00
❑ 112 Dolphino C	.10	.20
❑ 113 The BattlingBeast Zouuchi C	.10	.20
❑ 114 The GolemCraftEngineer Gatan C	.10	.20
❑ 115 Mantigore U	.20	.50
❑ 116 Block-Golem C	.10	.20
❑ 117 The MuscleBraggart Humphrey C	.10	.20
❑ 118 The WeaponDealer Goron-Garan C	.10	.20
❑ 119 The Tactician Shoujouji C	.10	.20
❑ 120 Tsathoggua C	.10	.20
❑ 121 The BlastingGiant Douglas MR	1.25	3.00
❑ 122 The HeavyJavelin Morgan R	.40	1.00
❑ 123 The HugeGiant Eurytos MR	1.25	3.00
❑ 124 The Great Ancient Dragon's Jaw U	.20	.50
❑ 125 The Remain of Scaffold U	.20	.50
❑ 126 The Thorny Colosseum U	.20	.50
❑ 127 The Eternal Glacier Palace U	.20	.50
❑ 128 The Empire of Pentan U	.20	.50
❑ 129 The Sacred Torch scorched the Sky R	.40	1.00
❑ 130 The Big Lavafalls C	.10	.20
❑ 131 The Cursed Shrine R	.40	1.00
❑ 132 The Wriggle Catacomb C	.10	.20
❑ 133 The Earth of Fertility R	.40	1.00
❑ 134 The Cape in the Red Sky C	.10	.20
❑ 135 The Protection of Sacred Artifacts C	.10	.20
❑ 136 The Burning Canyon C	.10	.20
❑ 137 The Ruby Volcanic Bombs C	.10	.20
❑ 138 The Deity in the Sacred Mountains U	.20	.50
❑ 139 The Digged Tombstone C	.10	.20
❑ 140 The Depths of the Darkness U	.20	.50
❑ 141 The Doom Coffin C	.10	.20
❑ 142 The Forest of the Sacred Conifer C	.10	.20
❑ 143 The Storm Highland U	.20	.50
❑ 144 The Fruit of Wise Tree C	.10	.20
❑ 145 The Infinite Mother Ship U	.20	.50
❑ 146 The Lighthouse of Hope C	.10	.20
❑ 147 The Invaded Castle C	.10	.20
❑ 148 The Chaotic Magic Laboratory C	.10	.20
❑ 149 The Opened Spellbook C	.10	.20
❑ 150 The Phantom Paradise U	.20	.50
❑ 151 The Intentional Scuffle C	.10	.20
❑ 152 The Battle?ield enclosed by the Chains C	.10	.20
❑ 153 The Honorable Fight U	.20	.50
❑ 154 Synchronicity C	.10	.20
❑ 155 Transmigration R	.40	1.00
❑ 156 Soul Crash R	.40	1.00
❑ 157 Reanimate C	.10	.20
❑ 158 God Speed R	.40	1.00
❑ 159 Brave Charge C	.10	.20
❑ 160 Crystal Aura R	.40	1.00
❑ 161 Icicle Assault C	.10	.20
❑ 162 Three Cards C	.10	.20
❑ 163 Nexus Blockade R	.40	1.00
❑ 164 CircularSaw Arm C	.10	.20
❑ 165 Victory Fire R	.40	1.00
❑ 166 Extra Draw U	.20	.50
❑ 167 Sudden Death Draw C	.10	.20
❑ 168 Curse Enchant U	.20	.50
❑ 169 Carry Cores C	.10	.20
❑ 170 Emerald Boost U	.20	.50
❑ 171 Blizzard Wall R	.40	1.00
❑ 172 Armor Purge U	.20	.50
❑ 173 Buster Javelin C	.10	.20
❑ 174 Excavation U	.20	.50
❑ 175 Lightning Aura C	.10	.20
❑ 176 Trident Flare R	.40	1.00
❑ 177 Burial Draw C	.10	.20
❑ 178 Level Drain C	.10	.20
❑ 179 Bloody Coffin U	.20	.50
❑ 180 Counter Curse R	.40	1.00
❑ 181 Savage Power C	.10	.20
❑ 182 Thorn Prison R	.40	1.00
❑ 183 Mistral Core C	.10	.20
❑ 184 Speed Star U	.20	.50
❑ 185 Chivalry U	.20	.50
❑ 186 Avalanche Aura C	.10	.20
❑ 187 Holy Elixir C	.10	.20
❑ 188 White Hole R	.40	1.00
❑ 189 Second Sight C	.10	.20
❑ 190 Discontinue U	.20	.50
❑ 191 Archaic Smile R	.40	1.00
❑ 192 Imagine Field C	.10	.20
❑ 193 Reclamation C	.10	.20
❑ 194 Muscle Charge C	.10	.20
❑ 195 Maximum Break U	.20	.50
❑ 196 Demolish R	.40	1.00
❑ X19 The SacredEmperor Siegfrieden XR	6.00	15.00
❑ X20 The GreatArmoredLord Deathtaurus XR	6.00	15.00
❑ X21 The Deity Catastrophedragon XR	6.00	15.00
❑ X22 The SevenShogun Beelzebeat XR	6.00	15.00
❑ X23 The Providence Hououga XR	6.00	15.00
❑ X24 The ArmoredSacred Walhalance XR	6.00	15.00

2010 Battle Spirits Scars of Battle

Card	Low	High
BOOSTER BOX (32 PACKS)	30.00	60.00
BOOSTER PACK (8 CARDS)	1.25	2.50
❑ 1 The FireSpirit Salamandert C	.10	.20
❑ 2 Edgehog C	.10	.20
❑ 3 The Assassin Dragno C	.10	.20
❑ 4 Brontrident C	.10	.20
❑ 5 Enchu C	.10	.20
❑ 6 Runkaphorhynchus C	.10	.20
❑ 7 Flame-Elk U	.20	.50
❑ 8 The BladeDragon Stegorasaurus C	.10	.20
❑ 9 The FireBlower Melt C	.10	.20
❑ 10 The BlackDragon Vritra R	.40	1.00
❑ 11 The DinoCavalry Diridalus MR	1.25	3.00
❑ 12 The GrandBishop Levia R	.40	1.00
❑ 13 Hellscorpio C	.10	.20
❑ 14 Fish-Skull C	.10	.20
❑ 15 The EvilGrass Mindragora C	.10	.20
❑ 16 The InvisibleMan Eclear C	.10	.20
❑ 17 The GhostCaptain Silvershark C	.10	.20
❑ 18 Blackwraith C	.10	.20
❑ 19 The EvilTactician Hellmia U	.20	.50
❑ 20 Mega-HumDum C	.10	.20
❑ 21 The Count Wyhl C	.10	.20
❑ 22 The DarkReefDiva Seiren R	.40	1.00
❑ 23 The ArtificialCreature No.44 U	.20	.50
❑ 24 The VampireKnight Nosferat MR	1.50	4.00
❑ 25 Stagscissor C	.10	.20
❑ 26 The WoodenSpirit Dryadena C	.10	.20
❑ 27 Fullmingo U	.20	.50
❑ 28 Mogrunner C	.10	.20
❑ 29 Machfly C	.10	.20
❑ 30 The Master Rainer Bros. C	.10	.20
❑ 31 The BlackWind Panther C	.10	.20
❑ 32 The Spider Arachnet U	.20	.50
❑ 33 The Beatpriest C	.10	.20
❑ 34 The FightingBird Bishamon C	.10	.20
❑ 35 The GoldenFlower Zonne-Bloem R	.40	1.00
❑ 36 The GodBird Peagod MR	1.25	3.00
❑ 37 Ratatoscr C	.10	.20
❑ 38 Angelafish C	.10	.20
❑ 39 The Piper Heimdall C	.10	.20
❑ 40 Ver-Thandia C	.10	.20
❑ 41 The Artifact Asc C	.10	.20
❑ 42 The SeaCreature Dugong C	.10	.20
❑ 43 Hotaruri C	.10	.20
❑ 44 The Metal Surtr R	.40	1.00
❑ 45 The SilverFox Hati R	.40	1.00
❑ 46 The Unicorn Einhorn C	.10	.20
❑ 47 The CrystalGoddess Freyr U	.20	.50
❑ 48 The ArmoredSnake Mithgarth MR	1.25	3.00
❑ 49 Mycanaen C	.10	.20
❑ 50 Kinokonoko C	.10	.20
❑ 51 Dongurin C	.10	.20
❑ 52 Frog Fisher C	.10	.20
❑ 53 The HundredFaces Flatface U	.20	.50
❑ 54 Arcanadoll-Tria C	.10	.20
❑ 55 Gomazarashi C	.10	.20
❑ 56 Ochogo C	.10	.20
❑ 57 Jellfy C	.10	.20
❑ 58 The Fairy Tinguly C	.10	.20
❑ 59 Arcanabeast-Paira U	.20	.50
❑ 60 Rumpkin C	.10	.20
❑ 61 The StrawberryGirl Strawberi C	.10	.20
❑ 62 Chihuahl C	.10	.20
❑ 63 Ponysus C	.10	.20
❑ 64 The RoseLady Barossa R	.40	1.00
❑ 65 The Angelia Curio R	.40	1.00
❑ 66 The Angelia Archre MR	1.25	3.00
❑ 67 Arcanaprincess-Un U	.20	.50
❑ 68 Forthros C	.10	.20
❑ 69 The Rockhopper Pentan U	.20	.50
❑ 70 The GreatAngelia Exsia MR	1.25	3.00
❑ 71 The BattlingBeast Bulltop C	.10	.20
❑ 72 The Pikeman Jeffrey C	.10	.20
❑ 73 Stone-Statue C	.10	.20
❑ 74 The BattlingBeast Doben C	.10	.20
❑ 75 The DogMan Murdoch C	.10	.20
❑ 76 The ClawSword Lazarus C	.10	.20
❑ 77 The AssaultSoldier Norman C	.10	.20
❑ 78 The Berserk Troll C	.10	.20
❑ 79 The StaffOfficer Foxin C	.10	.20
❑ 80 Rock-Golem C	.10	.20
❑ 81 The GiganticCentaurusSoldier Danston C	.10	.20
❑ 82 Sharkhammer C	.10	.20
❑ 83 The BearMan Beard C	.10	.20
❑ 84 The GiganticCat Blynx U	.20	.50
❑ 85 Wood-Golem C	.10	.20
❑ 86 The Repairer Baran-Baran U	.20	.50
❑ 87 The BattlingBeast Rhino-Ceros C	.10	.20
❑ 88 The FortressCrasher Dennis C	.10	.20
❑ 89 Deep-Arnold C	.10	.20
❑ 90 The DragonSlayBlade Guy U	.20	.50
❑ 91 The BattlingBeast Bun-Ffalo C	.10	.20
❑ 92 The GroundSupporter Francis U	.20	.50
❑ 93 The BuffaloMan Bulltania C	.10	.20
❑ 94 The Weaponsmith Bagin U	.20	.50
❑ 95 The Conjurer Oliver R	.40	1.00
❑ 96 The GiantKing Randolph MR	1.25	3.00
❑ 97 The BirdMan R	.40	1.00
❑ 98 The BattleDragon Wyvern MR	1.25	3.00
❑ 99 The IronFist Tiga C	.10	.20
❑ 100 The WeaponCollector MR	1.25	3.00
❑ 101 Volcano-Golem R	.40	1.00
❑ 102 The Outlaw Wasteland U	.20	.50
❑ 103 The Middle of Hard Battle C	.10	.20
❑ 104 The Crossroads of Destiny U	.20	.50
❑ 105 The Dark Reef Sea Area C	.10	.20
❑ 106 The Sea of Trees in Dark Green U	.20	.50
❑ 107 The Endless Horizon C	.10	.20
❑ 108 The High Sky Covered by Metal U	.20	.50
❑ 109 The Earth of Aurora C	.10	.20
❑ 110 The Sacred Place in Falling Stars C	.10	.20
❑ 111 The Child's Room in Midnight U	.20	.50
❑ 112 The Kingdom of Cards C	.10	.20
❑ 113 The Absorption Triumphal Arch R	.40	1.00
❑ 114 The Rampart of Sapphire U	.20	.50
❑ 115 The Collapse of Battle Line C	.10	.20
❑ 116 The Loss of Heroes R	.40	1.00
❑ 117 The H.Q. filled with Fighting Spirits C	.10	.20
❑ 118 Fourth Draw R	.40	1.00
❑ 119 Buster Lance C	.10	.20
❑ 120 Flame Cyclone C	.10	.20
❑ 121 Double Hearts R	.40	1.00
❑ 122 Fall Down C	.10	.20
❑ 123 Necromancy C	.10	.20
❑ 124 Poison Mist C	.10	.20
❑ 125 Weakness U	.20	.50
❑ 126 Potion Berry U	.20	.50
❑ 127 Ivy Cage C	.10	.20
❑ 128 Multiple Cores C	.10	.20
❑ 129 Flock Recovery C	.10	.20
❑ 130 Möbius Loop R	.40	1.00
❑ 131 United Power C	.10	.20
❑ 132 Perfect Guard C	.10	.20
❑ 133 High Elixir R	.40	1.00
❑ 134 Puppet String C	.10	.20
❑ 135 Escape Route C	.10	.20
❑ 136 Focus Light C	.10	.20
❑ 137 Four Cards U	.20	.50
❑ 138 Teleport Change R	.40	1.00
❑ 139 Same Tired R	.40	1.00
❑ 140 Shining Magic U	.20	.50
❑ 141 Build Up C	.10	.20
❑ 142 Salvage C	.10	.20
❑ 143 Blitz C	.10	.20
❑ 144 Magic Hammer C	.10	.20
❑ 145 Scramble C	.10	.20

TCG/C

Card	Low	High
☐ 146 Nexus Register C	.10	.20
☐ 147 Golem Craft R	.40	1.00
☐ 148 Construction U	.20	.50
☐ 149 Delta Crash U	.20	.50
☐ X9 The SavageKnight Hercules XR	6.00	15.00
☐ X10 The IceBeast Mam-Morl XR	6.00	15.00
☐ X11 The ArcAngelia Valiero XR	6.00	15.00
☐ X12 The GiantHero Titus XR	6.00	15.00

2001 Buffy the Vampire Slayer Pergamum Prophecy

Card	Low	High
BOOSTER BOX (36 PACKS)	30.00	60.00
BOOSTER PACK (12 CARDS)	1.50	3.00
☐ 1 Feeding Time C	.10	.20
☐ 2 From the Ashes of Five Dead C	.10	.20
☐ 3 Young Frankenstein C	.10	.20
☐ 4 Facing Your Fear C	.10	.20
☐ 5 Welcome to the Harvest C	.10	.20
☐ 6 Abduction C	.10	.20
☐ 7 Body Switch C	.10	.20
☐ 8 On Patrol C	.10	.20
☐ 9 A Quick Jaunt to the Funeral Home C	.10	.20
☐ 10 Cheerleader Tryouts C	.10	.20
☐ 11 Oh, May Queen C	.10	.20
☐ 12 Mayhem at the Bronze C	.10	.20
☐ 13 A Dead Cheerleader Is a Good Cheerleader C	.10	.20
☐ 14 You Can Trust the Technopagan C	.10	.20
☐ 15 The Bronze C	.10	.20
☐ 16 Weatherly Park Bike Trail C	.10	.20
☐ 17 Natalie French's Cellar C	.10	.20
☐ 18 The Nest C	.10	.20
☐ 19 Pool of Blood C	.10	.20
☐ 20 Streets of Sunnydale C	.10	.20
☐ 21 Mausoleum C	.10	.20
☐ 22 Power Station C	.10	.20
☐ 23 Public Restroom C	.10	.20
☐ 24 Sunnydale School Hallways C	.10	.20
☐ 25 Animal Intensity C	.10	.20
☐ 26 Varsity Training C	.10	.20
☐ 27 Electrical Tunnels Schematic C	.10	.20
☐ 28 Empty Puppet Case C	.10	.20
☐ 29 Number 1 Alternate C	.10	.20
☐ 30 Testosterone C	.10	.20
☐ 31 Priority Check C	.10	.20
☐ 32 Two Gun Woo C	.10	.20
☐ 33 New Kid On The Block C	.10	.20
☐ 34 Demon Theory C	.10	.20
☐ 35 Feast on Virgins C	.10	.20
☐ 36 Overhand Toss C	.10	.20
☐ 37 Wooly-Headed Liberal Thinking C	.10	.20
☐ 38 My Spider-Sense Is Tingling C	.10	.20
☐ 39 Aaack! Spiders! C	.10	.20
☐ 40 The CPR Thing C	.10	.20
☐ 41 Watch Zebras Mating C	.10	.20
☐ 42 Not Prepared for Farrah Hair C	.10	.20
☐ 43 Bow Before the Idiot Box C	.10	.20
☐ 44 Thrown to the Hyenas C	.10	.20
☐ 45 Hit the Streets C	.10	.20
☐ 46 The Old Madison Body Switch U	.20	.50
☐ 47 Primal Urges U	.20	.50
☐ 48 Reviving the Master U	.20	.50
☐ 49 Festival of Saint Vigeous U	.20	.50
☐ 50 Turn Them On Each Other U	.20	.50
☐ 51 Hyenas in the Principal's Office U	.20	.50
☐ 52 Never Kill a Boy on the First Date U	.20	.50
☐ 53 When Good Mothers Go Bad U	.20	.50
☐ 54 Why Yes, I am a Praying Mantis U	.20	.50
☐ 55 Parent Teacher Night U	.20	.50
☐ 56 Billy Palmer U	.20	.50
☐ 57 Cordelia U	.20	.50
☐ 58 Jenny Calendar U	.20	.50
☐ 59 Owen Thurman U	.20	.50
☐ 60 Sid U	.20	.50
☐ 61 Xander U	.20	.50
☐ 62 Jesse U	.20	.50
☐ 63 Andrew Borba U	.20	.50
☐ 64 Catherine Madison U	.20	.50
☐ 65 Chris Epps U	.20	.50
☐ 66 Claw U	.20	.50
☐ 67 Fritz U	.20	.50
☐ 68 Luke U	.20	.50
☐ 69 Moloch, the Corruptor U	.20	.50
☐ 70 Natalie French U	.20	.50
☐ 71 The Ugly Man U	.20	.50
☐ 72 The Pack U	.20	.50
☐ 73 The Three U	.20	.50
☐ 74 Marc, The Organ Stealer U	.20	.50
☐ 75 Absalom U	.20	.50
☐ 76 Dr. Gregory U	.20	.50
☐ 77 Joyce Summers U	.20	.50
☐ 78 Coach Herrold U	.20	.50
☐ 79 Mitch U	.20	.50
☐ 80 Harmony U	.20	.50
☐ 81 Hank Summers U	.20	.50
☐ 82 Blayne Mall U	.20	.50
☐ 83 Amber Grove U	.20	.50
☐ 84 Sunnydale High School Library U	.20	.50
☐ 85 1630 Revello Drive (Summer's House) U	.20	.50
☐ 86 Tunnels U	.20	.50
☐ 87 Madison House U	.20	.50
☐ 88 Sunnydale Funeral Home U	.20	.50
☐ 89 Cemetary U	.20	.50
☐ 90 Hyena Exhibit U	.20	.50
☐ 91 Sunnydale High School Computer Lab U	.20	.50
☐ 92 CRD U	.20	.50
☐ 93 Sunnydale School Lawn U	.20	.50
☐ 94 Warehouse U	.20	.50
☐ 95 Watcher Training U	.20	.50
☐ 96 Off-the-charts Smart U	.20	.50
☐ 97 Expert on the Weird U	.20	.50
☐ 98 Babe-li-tude U	.20	.50
☐ 99 Power of the Black Mass U	.20	.50
☐ 100 Technopaganism U	.20	.50
☐ 101 Scully Me U	.20	.50
☐ 102 Demonology 101 U	.20	.50
☐ 103 Gone Binary U	.20	.50
☐ 104 Morning Person U	.20	.50
☐ 105 Pack Rat U	.20	.50
☐ 106 Fast Pace U	.20	.50
☐ 107 Stake & Crossbow U	.20	.50
☐ 108 Lucky 19 Baseball Jersey U	.20	.50
☐ 109 May Queen Dress U	.20	.50
☐ 110 Tome of Moloch U	.20	.50
☐ 111 Fire Axe U	.20	.50
☐ 112 Ring of Prophecy U	.20	.50
☐ 113 Bat Sonar U	.20	.50
☐ 114 Metal Robot Body U	.20	.50
☐ 115 Sledgehammer U	.20	.50
☐ 116 Sentient Cheerleading Trophy U	.20	.50
☐ 117 Giles-mobile U	.20	.50
☐ 118 An Innocent Guillotine U	.20	.50
☐ 119 Hair Flip U	.20	.50
☐ 120 Book Learning U	.20	.50
☐ 121 Creep Factor U	.20	.50
☐ 122 Vampire Embrace U	.20	.50
☐ 123 Cafeteria Soylent Green U	.20	.50
☐ 124 Dig Up The Corpses U	.20	.50
☐ 125 Stake 'em High U	.20	.50
☐ 126 I Quit U	.20	.50
☐ 127 Computer Invasion U	.20	.50
☐ 128 Clumsy Fingers U	.20	.50
☐ 129 Lounging About With Imbeciles U	.20	.50
☐ 130 A Friend In Need U	.20	.50
☐ 131 Trading Clothing U	.20	.50
☐ 132 Talent Show U	.20	.50
☐ 133 Oh, the 'Other' Cemetery U	.20	.50
☐ 134 Offer of Ugly Death U	.20	.50
☐ 135 Shaky on the Dismount U	.20	.50
☐ 136 Trans-possession R	1.00	2.50
☐ 137 Hot Dog Surprise R	1.00	2.50
☐ 138 Cricket Snack R	1.00	2.50
☐ 139 A Boy and His Guillotine R	1.00	2.50
☐ 140 I Robot, You Jane R	1.00	2.50
☐ 141 The Master Returns R	1.00	2.50
☐ 142 Pergamum Prophecy R	1.00	2.50
☐ 143 The Talent Show Must Go On R	1.00	2.50
☐ 144 Nightmares of Mine R	1.00	2.50
☐ 145 Demonic Smackdown R	1.00	2.50
☐ 146 Angel R	1.00	2.50
☐ 147 Angel R	1.00	2.50
☐ 148 Buffy Summers R	1.00	2.50
☐ 149 Rupert Giles R	1.00	2.50
☐ 150 Rupert Giles R	1.00	2.50
☐ 151 Willow Rosenberg R	1.00	2.50
☐ 152 Willow Rosenberg R	1.00	2.50
☐ 153 Collin, the Annointed One R	1.00	2.50
☐ 154 Collin, the Annointed One R	1.00	2.50
☐ 155 Darla R	1.00	2.50
☐ 156 Drusilla R	1.00	2.50
☐ 157 Drusilla R	1.00	2.50
☐ 158 Spike R	1.00	2.50
☐ 159 Spike R	1.00	2.50
☐ 160 The Master R	1.00	2.50
☐ 161 Sunnydale High School Auditorium R	1.00	2.50
☐ 162 Lair of the Master R	1.00	2.50
☐ 163 Hospital R	1.00	2.50
☐ 164 Football Field R	1.00	2.50
☐ 165 Real Literary-like R	1.00	2.50
☐ 166 Spellcasting Dolls R	1.00	2.50
☐ 167 Pergamum Codex R	1.00	2.50
☐ 168 Ashes of Five Dead R	1.00	2.50
☐ 169 Supernatural Boost R	1.00	2.50
☐ 170 Self-Referential Humor R	1.00	2.50
☐ 171 Go Home and Listen to Country Music R	1.00	2.50
☐ 172 Circle of Kayless R	1.00	2.50
☐ 173 Alone R	1.00	2.50
☐ 174 Inside Joke R	1.00	2.50
☐ 175 Superior Fighting R	1.00	2.50
☐ 176 Master Bones R	1.00	2.50
☐ 177 Run, Fast R	1.00	2.50
☐ 178 Join the Pep Squad R	1.00	2.50
☐ 179 Decisions, Decisions R	1.00	2.50
☐ 180 Sunset R	1.00	2.50
☐ 181 The Master UR	4.00	10.00
☐ 182 Buffy Summers UR	6.00	15.00
☐ 183 The Dead Have Risen UR	5.00	12.00
☐ 184 Primal Connection UR	6.00	15.00
☐ 185 Angel F	1.50	4.00
☐ 186 Buffy Summers F	1.50	4.00
☐ 187 Rupert Giles F	1.50	4.00
☐ 188 Willow Rosenberg F	1.50	4.00
☐ 189 Collin, the Annointed One F	1.50	4.00
☐ 190 Drusilla F	1.50	4.00
☐ 191 Spike F	1.50	4.00
☐ 192 The Master F	1.50	4.00
☐ 193 Buffy F	1.50	4.00
☐ 194 Giles F	1.50	4.00
☐ 195 Willow F	1.50	4.00
☐ 196 Angel F	1.50	4.00
☐ 197 The Master F	1.50	4.00
☐ 198 Collin F	1.50	4.00
☐ 199 Spike F	1.50	4.00
☐ 200 Drusilla F	1.50	4.00

2001 Buffy the Vampire Slayer Pergamum Prophecy First Patrol

Card	Low	High
☐ 1 Buffy Summers FP R	2.00	5.00
☐ 2 Buffy Summers FP F	1.50	4.00
☐ 3 Spike FP F	1.25	3.00
☐ 4 Buffy FP F	1.50	4.00
☐ 5 Spike FP F	1.25	3.00

2001 Buffy the Vampire Slayer Pergamum Prophecy Preview

Card	Low	High
☐ 1 Alley C	.10	.25
☐ 2 Sunnydale High School Lobby C	.10	.25
☐ 3 Breaking the Bones U	.30	.75
☐ 4 Principal Snyder U	.30	.75
☐ 5 Manacles R	.60	1.50
☐ 6 Hide Until It Goes Away R	.60	1.50

2002 Buffy the Vampire Slayer Angel's Curse

Card	Low	High
BOOSTER BOX (36)	15.00	30.00
BOOSTER PACK	.75	1.50
☐ 1 Bad Eggs C	.10	.20
☐ 2 Die Young and Stay Pretty C	.10	.20
☐ 3 Love Sucks C	.10	.20
☐ 4 Death Stalks the Dream C	.10	.20
☐ 5 Coach Marin C	.10	.20
☐ 6 Dalton C	.10	.20
☐ 7 50's Time Capsule C	.10	.20
☐ 8 Dragon's Cove Magic Shop C	.10	.20
☐ 9 Ethan's Costume Shop C	.10	.20
☐ 10 Sunset Club C	.10	.20
☐ 11 Body of a Dead Cheerleader C	.10	.20
☐ 12 Gypsy Curse C	.10	.20
☐ 13 Machiavellian Ingenuity C	.10	.20
☐ 14 Ritual of Restoration C	.10	.20
☐ 15 Spike's Car C	.10	.20
☐ 16 The Look C	.10	.20
☐ 17 Tweed Mail C	.10	.20
☐ 18 Wisdom C	.10	.20
☐ 19 PDA C	.10	.20
☐ 20 Something Weird C	.10	.20
☐ 21 The Plan C	.10	.20
☐ 22 A Lover's Gift C	.10	.20
☐ 23 Angry Mob C	.10	.20
☐ 24 Anywhere But Here C	.10	.20
☐ 25 Confrontation C	.10	.20
☐ 26 Cut From the Same Cloth C	.10	.20
☐ 27 Going Goth C	.10	.20
☐ 28 Hot Sheets C	.10	.20
☐ 29 Soda Machine Raid C	.10	.20
☐ 30 Total Lecture Overload C	.10	.20
☐ 31 Tremors C	.10	.20
☐ 32 Unwelcome Surprise C	.10	.20
☐ 33 A Soul's Revenge U	.20	.50
☐ 34 An American Werewolf in Sunnydale U	.20	.50
☐ 35 New Dad in Town U	.20	.50
☐ 36 Something Fishy This Way Comes U	.20	.50
☐ 37 The Dark Age U	.20	.50
☐ 38 Amy Madison U	.20	.50
☐ 39 Billy Fordham U	.20	.50
☐ 40 Cameron Walker U	.20	.50
☐ 41 Der Kindestod U	.20	.50
☐ 42 Doug Perren U	.20	.50
☐ 43 Ethan Rayne U	.20	.50
☐ 44 Gill Monster U	.20	.50
☐ 45 Kendra U	.20	.50
☐ 46 Oz U	.20	.50
☐ 47 Oz U	.20	.50
☐ 48 Ted Buchanan U	.20	.50
☐ 49 Willy U	.20	.50
☐ 50 Xander U	.20	.50
☐ 51 Army Base U	.20	.50
☐ 52 Sunnydale City Morgue U	.20	.50
☐ 53 Willy's Bar U	.20	.50
☐ 54 Black Lagoon Aromatherapy U	.20	.50
☐ 55 Diana's Touch U	.20	.50
☐ 56 Mummy's Seal U	.20	.50
☐ 57 Tattoo Remover (Acid) U	.20	.50
☐ 58 Video Camera U	.20	.50
☐ 59 Wavering Power U	.20	.50
☐ 60 Weapon's Expert U	.20	.50
☐ 61 A Fervant Wish U	.20	.50
☐ 62 Immolation-O-Gram U	.20	.50
☐ 63 B.O. U	.20	.50
☐ 64 Bad Alcohol U	.20	.50
☐ 65 Blind Panic U	.20	.50
☐ 66 Box of Goodies U	.20	.50
☐ 67 Choke Hold U	.20	.50
☐ 68 Competition Appraisal U	.20	.50
☐ 69 Desperate Maneuvers U	.20	.50
☐ 70 Fatal Recovery U	.20	.50
☐ 71 Gathering of Scoobies U	.20	.50
☐ 72 Grounded U	.20	.50
☐ 73 Henchmen-R-Us U	.20	.50
☐ 74 Homeric Insensitivity U	.20	.50
☐ 75 Hypnotic Grasp U	.20	.50
☐ 76 Master of Ceremonies U	.20	.50
☐ 77 No More Soul U	.20	.50
☐ 78 Slay Industries U	.20	.50
☐ 79 Surprise U	.20	.50
☐ 80 Here's How You Eat It U	.20	.50
☐ 81 Visions U	.20	.50
☐ 82 What Comes Around ... U	.20	.50
☐ 83 It's The End of the World As We Know It R	1.00	2.50
☐ 84 Jigsaw Judge R	1.00	2.50
☐ 85 Ritual of Eligor R	1.00	2.50
☐ 86 Angel R	1.00	2.50
☐ 87 Angelus R	1.00	2.50
☐ 88 Angelus R	1.00	2.50
☐ 89 Buffy Summers R	1.00	2.50
☐ 90 Collin, The Annointed One R	1.00	2.50
☐ 91 Cordelia R	1.00	2.50
☐ 92 Drusilla R	1.00	2.50
☐ 93 Jenny Calendar R	1.00	2.50
☐ 94 Kendra R	1.00	2.50
☐ 95 Principal Snyder R	1.00	2.50
☐ 96 Rupert Giles R	1.00	2.50
☐ 97 Spike R	1.00	2.50
☐ 98 The Judge R	1.00	2.50
☐ 99 The Master R	1.00	2.50
☐ 100 Uncle Enyos R	1.00	2.50
☐ 101 Willow Rosenberg R	1.00	2.50
☐ 102 Natural History Museum R	1.00	2.50
☐ 103 Vampire Mansion R	1.00	2.50
☐ 104 Claddagh Ring R	1.00	2.50
☐ 105 Disembodied Arm R	1.00	2.50
☐ 106 Mr. Pointy R	1.00	2.50
☐ 107 Orb of Thesulah R	1.00	2.50
☐ 108 Rocket Launcher R	1.00	2.50
☐ 109 Silver Locket R	1.00	2.50
☐ 110 What Doesn't Kill You ... R	1.00	2.50
☐ 111 Death R	1.00	2.50
☐ 112 Slayer's Burden R	1.00	2.50
☐ 113 Breaking Free R	1.00	2.50
☐ 114 Concealed Weapon R	1.00	2.50
☐ 115 Finding Your Destiny R	1.00	2.50
☐ 116 Flashy Swordfight R	1.00	2.50
☐ 117 Hypnotism R	1.00	2.50
☐ 118 Vampiric Expertise R	1.00	2.50
☐ 119 Ritual of Acathla R	1.00	2.50
☐ 120 St. Du Lac Mausoleum UR	15.00	30.00
☐ 121 Wrath of Angelus UR	15.00	30.00
☐ 122 Xander F	.75	2.00
☐ 123 Kendra F	.75	2.00
☐ 124 Cordelia F	.75	2.00
☐ 125 Angelus F	.75	2.00

2002 Buffy the Vampire Slayer Angel's Curse Preview

Card	Low	High
☐ Pre1 Forceful Persuasion C	.10	.25
☐ Pre2 Home Again U	.30	.75
☐ Pre3 Lily R	.60	1.50

2002 Buffy the Vampire Slayer Class of '99

Card	Low	High
BOOSTER BOX (36 PACKS)	20.00	40.00
BOOSTER PACK (12 CARDS)	1.00	2.00
☐ 1 Dead Man's Party C	.10	.20
☐ 2 Homecoming C	.10	.20
☐ 3 Eliminati Vamps C	.10	.20
☐ 4 Hellhound C	.10	.20
☐ 5 Percy West C	.10	.20
☐ 6 Scott Hope C	.10	.20
☐ 7 The Harbingers C	.10	.20
☐ 8 April Fools Dress Ship C	.10	.20
☐ 9 Boiler Room C	.10	.20
☐ 10 Faith's Motel C	.10	.20
☐ 11 Garden Shed C	.10	.20
☐ 12 Eliminati Swords C	.10	.20
☐ 13 Formal Wear C	.10	.20
☐ 14 Holy Hand Grenade C	.10	.20
☐ 15 Living Flame C	.10	.20
☐ 16 Maps and Stuff C	.10	.20
☐ 17 Slayer Kryptonite C	.10	.20
☐ 18 Witch Pez Dispenser C	.10	.20
☐ 19 Cross-Referencing C	.10	.20
☐ 20 Demonology, Ph.D C	.10	.20
☐ 21 Knife Practice C	.10	.20
☐ 22 Necronomenclature C	.10	.20
☐ 23 Slayer's Fortitude C	.10	.20
☐ 24 Slayer's Training C	.10	.20
☐ 25 Spells, Cursies and Whammies C	.10	.20
☐ 26 Telekinesis C	.10	.20
☐ 27 Telepathic Block C	.10	.20
☐ 28 Tutoring C	.10	.20
☐ 29 Birthday Tradition C	.10	.20
☐ 30 Caught in the Crossfire C	.10	.20
☐ 31 Come to the Dark Side C	.10	.20
☐ 32 Disciplinary Council C	.10	.20
☐ 33 Locker Search C	.10	.20
☐ 34 All's Well That Ends Well C	.10	.20
☐ 35 Big Bang C	.10	.20
☐ 36 Book Cramming C	.10	.20
☐ 37 Book Learning C	.10	.20
☐ 38 Cluck-Cluck C	.10	.20
☐ 39 Creep Factor C	.10	.20
☐ 40 Discovery C	.10	.20
☐ 41 Don't Get Killed C	.10	.20
☐ 42 Dramatic Irony C	.10	.20
☐ 43 Drive Like Crazy C	.10	.20
☐ 44 Group Support C	.10	.20
☐ 45 Hair Flip C	.10	.20
☐ 46 If at First You Don't Succeed C	.10	.20
☐ 47 Knowledge is Power C	.10	.20
☐ 48 Manic-Depressive Chick C	.10	.20
☐ 49 Neat Freak C	.10	.20
☐ 50 Off My Game C	.10	.20
☐ 51 Full-On Monster Fighting C	.10	.20
☐ 52 Prom C	.10	.20
☐ 53 Testosterone C	.10	.20
☐ 54 The Help of the Merry Men C	.10	.20
☐ 55 Tranquilized C	.10	.20
☐ 56 Untrustworthy C	.10	.20
☐ 57 Vampire Embrace C	.10	.20
☐ 58 Want, Take, Have C	.10	.20
☐ 59 And Hell Follows Him U	.20	.50
☐ 60 Fairy Tales are Real U	.20	.50
☐ 61 Gingerbread U	.20	.50
☐ 62 Hell's Angel U	.20	.50
☐ 63 Price of True Evil U	.20	.50
☐ 64 Tento di Cruciamentum U	.20	.50
☐ 65 Through the Demon Portal U	.20	.50
☐ 66 Amy Madison U	.20	.50
☐ 67 Angel U	.20	.50
☐ 68 Anyanka U	.20	.50
☐ 69 Buffy Summers U	.20	.50
☐ 70 Faith U	.20	.50
☐ 71 Faith U	.20	.50
☐ 72 Hansel and Gretal U	.20	.50
☐ 73 Jack O'Toole U	.20	.50
☐ 74 Pat U	.20	.50
☐ 75 Jonathan Levenson U	.20	.50
☐ 76 Ken U	.20	.50
☐ 77 Lunch Lady U	.20	.50
☐ 78 Mr. Trick U	.20	.50
☐ 79 Oz U	.20	.50
☐ 80 Pete U	.20	.50
☐ 81 Rupert Giles U	.20	.50
☐ 82 Tucker Wells U	.20	.50
☐ 83 Wesley Wyndam-Pryce U	.20	.50
☐ 84 Willow Rosenberg U	.20	.50
☐ 85 Xander Harris U	.20	.50
☐ 86 Hell U	.20	.50
☐ 87 Sporting Goods Store U	.20	.50
☐ 88 Sunnydale Arms U	.20	.50
☐ 89 Balthazar's Amulet U	.20	.50
☐ 90 Disturbing Features U	.20	.50
☐ 91 Faith's Knife U	.20	.50
☐ 92 Haphazard Bomb U	.20	.50
☐ 93 Killer of the Dead U	.20	.50
☐ 94 Love Tattoo U	.20	.50
☐ 95 Tranquilizer Gun U	.20	.50
☐ 96 Channeled Aggresion U	.20	.50
☐ 97 Charming U	.20	.50
☐ 98 Gourmet Cuisine U	.20	.50
☐ 99 Homecoming Queen U	.20	.50
☐ 100 Invulnerability U	.20	.50
☐ 101 Scoring Well U	.20	.50
☐ 102 Warding U	.20	.50
☐ 103 In the Past U	.20	.50
☐ 104 Young at Heart U	.20	.50
☐ 105 Bad Girls Part 1 U	.20	.50
☐ 106 Band Candy Part 1 U	.20	.50
☐ 107 Graduation Day Part 1 U	.20	.50
☐ 108 Lover's Walk Part 1 U	.20	.50
☐ 109 The Zeppo Part 1 U	.20	.50
☐ 110 Done! U	.20	.50
☐ 111 I Quit U	.20	.50
☐ 112 Lust For Her Death U	.20	.50
☐ 113 Modern Day Vampire U	.20	.50
☐ 114 Preparing for Ascension U	.20	.50
☐ 115 Slayer's Lust U	.20	.50
☐ 116 Unknown Outcome U	.20	.50
☐ 117 Ascension of Olivikan R	1.00	2.50
☐ 118 Commencement Ceremonies R	1.00	2.50
☐ 119 Flamma Vitae R	1.00	2.50
☐ 120 Angel R	1.00	2.50
☐ 121 Angel R	1.00	2.50
☐ 122 Anyanka R	1.00	2.50
☐ 123 Balthazar R	1.00	2.50
☐ 124 Buffy Summers R	1.00	2.50
☐ 125 Buffy Summers R	1.00	2.50
☐ 126 Cordelia R	1.00	2.50
☐ 127 Faith R	1.00	2.50
☐ 128 Faith R	1.00	2.50
☐ 129 Faith R	1.00	2.50
☐ 130 Faith R	1.00	2.50
☐ 131 Gwendolyn Post R	1.00	2.50
☐ 132 Mayor Richard Wilkins III R	1.00	2.50
☐ 133 Mayor Richard Wilkins III R	1.00	2.50
☐ 134 Mr. Trick R	1.00	2.50
☐ 135 Oz R	1.00	2.50
☐ 136 Rupert Giles R	1.00	2.50
☐ 137 Spike R	1.00	2.50
☐ 138 The First R	1.00	2.50
☐ 139 The Master R	1.00	2.50
☐ 140 Vamp Willow R	1.00	2.50
☐ 141 Willow R	1.00	2.50
☐ 142 Xander R	1.00	2.50
☐ 143 Band Candy Warehouse R	1.00	2.50
☐ 144 Fountain Quad R	1.00	2.50
☐ 145 Box of Gavrok R	1.00	2.50
☐ 146 Candy Bars R	1.00	2.50
☐ 147 Glove of Myhnegon R	1.00	2.50
☐ 148 Compound Bow R	1.00	2.50
☐ 149 Mask of Ovu Mobani R	1.00	2.50
☐ 150 Symbol of Anyanka R	1.00	2.50
☐ 151 Tome of Mediocrity R	1.00	2.50
☐ 152 Verbal Non-Verbal R	1.00	2.50
☐ 153 Eventful Combat R	1.00	2.50
☐ 154 Initiation R	1.00	2.50
☐ 155 Bad Girls Part 2 R	1.00	2.50

❑ 156 Band Candy Part 2 R 1.00 2.50
❑ 157 Graduation Day Part 2 R 1.00 2.50
❑ 158 Lover's Walk Part 2 R 1.00 2.50
❑ 159 The Zeppo Part 2 R 1.00 2.50
❑ 160 A Crazy Plan R 1.00 2.50
❑ 161 Ambushed R 1.00 2.50
❑ 162 Been There, Killed That R 1.00 2.50
❑ 163 Bored Now R 1.00 2.50
❑ 164 Crushing Blow R 1.00 2.50
❑ 165 Demon in Sheep's Clothing R 1.00 2.50
❑ 166 Kicking Demon A$$ R 1.00 2.50
❑ 167 Make It A Double R 1.00 2.50
❑ 168 Raising the Stakes R 1.00 2.50
❑ 169 Rivalry R 1.00 2.50
❑ 170 Three-some R 1.00 2.50
❑ 171 A Thing F .60 1.50
❑ 172 Class Protector F .60 1.50
❑ 173 Demon Hunting F .60 1.50
❑ 174 Morality Lecture F .60 1.50
❑ 175 Slayer's Handiwork F .60 1.50
❑ 176 Mobile Tracking System F .60 1.50
❑ 177 Quality Rage F .60 1.50
❑ 178 Black Hat F .60 1.50
❑ 179 Caught Off Guard F .60 1.50
❑ 180 Hidden Allies F .60 1.50
❑ 181 Lover's Return F .60 1.50
❑ 182 Spring Madness F .60 1.50
❑ 183 The Big Night F .60 1.50
❑ 184 Young, Fast and Hot-Blooded F .60 1.50
❑ 185 Beauty and the Beast F .60 1.50
❑ 186 Bring Me My Amulet F .60 1.50
❑ 187 One Man Army F .60 1.50
❑ 188 Return of The First F .60 1.50
❑ 189 Slayerfest F .60 1.50
❑ 190 Lunch Special F .60 1.50
❑ 191 Doppelgangland F .60 1.50
❑ 192 Power of the Wish F .60 1.50
❑ 193 Start the Juicer F .60 1.50
❑ 194 Wish Granted F .60 1.50
❑ 195 Larry Blaisdell F .60 1.50
❑ 196 Zachary Kralik F .60 1.50
❑ 197 Bizarro Blood Bottling Plant F .60 1.50
❑ 198 Bizarro Bronze F .60 1.50
❑ 199 Bizarro Streets of Sunnydale F .60 1.50
❑ 200 Bizarro Sun Cinema F .60 1.50
❑ 201 Bizarro Sunnydale High School F .60 1.50
❑ 202 Bizarro Sunnydale School Library F .60 1.50
❑ 203 Deserted Cabin F .60 1.50
❑ 204 Eye of Rat F .60 1.50
❑ 205 Hallway Scene-making F .60 1.50
❑ 206 Major Wiggins F .60 1.50
❑ 207 Trade Talks F .60 1.50
❑ 208 Fast Food F .60 1.50
❑ 209 Out of Options F .60 1.50
❑ 210 The Wish Part 1 F .60 1.50
❑ 211 The Wish Part 2 F .60 1.50
❑ 212 Blood and Crumpets F .60 1.50
❑ 213 Broken Wishes F .60 1.50
❑ 214 Clarion Call F .60 1.50
❑ 215 I Love This Part F .60 1.50
❑ 216 I'm A Blood Sucking Fiend F .60 1.50
❑ 217 Oh Fff.... F .60 1.50
❑ 218 Oz Watch F .60 1.50
❑ 219 Tiny Victory F .60 1.50
❑ 220 Watching Playtime F .60 1.50
❑ 221 Who Do You Work For F .60 1.50
❑ 222 Wish: The Weirding F .60 1.50
❑ 223 Angel F .60 1.50
❑ 224 Anyanka F .60 1.50
❑ 225 Buffy Summers F .60 1.50
❑ 226 Bizarro Buffy F .60 1.50
❑ 227 Cordelia F .60 1.50
❑ 228 Faith F .60 1.50
❑ 229 Kakistos F .60 1.50
❑ 230 Mayor Richard Wilkins III F .60 1.50
❑ 231 Mr. Trick F .60 1.50
❑ 232 Oz F .60 1.50
❑ 233 Rupert Giles F .60 1.50
❑ 234 The Master F .60 1.50
❑ 235 Vamp Willow F .60 1.50
❑ 236 Vamp Xander F .60 1.50
❑ 237 Willow F .60 1.50
❑ 238 Xander F .60 1.50
❑ 239 Buffy/Riley F .60 1.50
❑ 240 Xander/Anya F .60 1.50
❑ 241 Angel/Spike F .60 1.50
❑ 242 Willow/Tara F .60 1.50
❑ 243 The Mayor/Kathy F .60 1.50
❑ 244 Mr. Trick/Harmony F .60 1.50
❑ 245 Kakistos/Maggie Walsh F .60 1.50
❑ 246 Faith/Adam F .60 1.50
❑ 247 Vamp Willow/Vamp Xander F .60 1.50
❑ 249 The Master/Anyanka F .60 1.50
❑ 251 Oz/Buffy Bizarro Land F .60 1.50
❑ 253 Giles/Cordelia F .60 1.50
❑ 255 City Hall UR 20.00 40.00
❑ 256 Books of Ascension UR 20.00 40.00
❑ 257 Day of Ascension UR 20.00 40.00
❑ 258 Calling in the Heavy Artillery UR 20.00 40.00

2002 Buffy the Vampire Slayer Class of '99 First Patrol

❑ 124 Buffy Summers FP R 2.00 5.00
❑ 225 Buffy Summers FP F 1.50 4.00
❑ 228 Faith FP F 1.25 3.00
❑ 239 Buffy FP F 1.50 4.00
❑ 246 Faith FP F 1.25 3.00

2002 Buffy the Vampire Slayer Class of '99 Preview

❑ 1 Initiative Commandos C .10 .25
❑ 2 UC Sunnydale Commons C .10 .25
❑ 3 Espresso Pump U .30 .75
❑ 4 Freshman Year U .30 .75
❑ 5 Maggie Walsh R .60 1.50
❑ 6 Riley Finn R .60 1.50

2011 Cardfight Vanguard Descent of the King of Knights

Unlisted Common .10 .25
Booster Box (30 Packs) 50.00 80.00
Booster Pack (5 Cards) 2.50 4.00

❑ BT01001 King of Knights, Alfred RRR 12.00 30.00
❑ BT01002 Blaster Blade RRR 6.00 15.00
❑ BT01003 Barcgal RRR 4.00 10.00
❑ BT01004 Dragonic Overlord RRR 4.00 10.00
❑ BT01005 Embodiment of Victory, Aleph RRR 2.50 6.00
❑ BT01006 CEO Amaterasu RRR 8.00 20.00
❑ BT01007 Battle Sister, Cocoa RRR 8.00 20.00
❑ BT01008 Asura Kaiser RRR 4.00 10.00
❑ BT01009 Demon Slaying Knight, Lohengrin RR 1.50 4.00
❑ BT01010 Solitary Knight, Gancelot RR 1.50 4.00
❑ BT01011 Flash Shield, Iseult RR 8.00 20.00
❑ BT01012 Future Knight, Llew RR 6.00 15.00
❑ BT01013 Vortex Dragon RR 3.00 8.00
❑ BT01014 Dragon Knight, Aleph RR 4.00 10.00
❑ BT01015 Wyvern Guard, Barri RR 8.00 20.00
❑ BT01016 Lizard Soldier, Conroe RR 2.50 6.00
❑ BT01017 Maiden of Libra RR 2.00 5.00
❑ BT01018 Battle Sister, Mocha RR 3.00 8.00
❑ BT01019 Battle Sister, Chocolat RR 6.00 15.00
❑ BT01020 Juggernaut Maximum RR 1.50 4.00
❑ BT01021 Knight of Silence, Gallatin R .20 .50
❑ BT01022 Dragon Knight, Nehalem R .20 .50
❑ BT01023 Wyvern Strike, Tejas R .20 .50
❑ BT01024 Embodiment of Spear, Tahr R 2.00 5.00
❑ BT01025 Oracle Guardian, Apollon R .75 2.00
❑ BT01026 Oracle Guardian, Wiseman R .75 2.00
❑ BT01027 Lozenge Magus R 2.00 5.00
❑ BT01028 Mr. Invincible R .40 1.00
❑ BT01029 Brutal Jack R .75 2.00
❑ BT01030 King of Sword R .40 1.00
❑ BT01031 Queen of Heart R .40 1.00
❑ BT01032 Battleraizer R .60 1.50
❑ BT01033 Tyrant, Deathrex R .20 .50
❑ BT01034 Assault Dragon, Blightops R .20 .50
❑ BT01035 Stealth Dragon, Voidmaster R .20 .50
❑ BT01036 Demon Eater R .20 .50
❑ BT01037 Monster Frank R .20 .50
❑ BT01038 Commodore Blueblood R .60 1.50
❑ BT01039 Hell Spider R .20 .50
❑ BT01040 Bloody Hercules R .20 .50

2011 Cardfight Vanguard Descent of the King of Knights SP

❑ BT01S01 King of Knights, Alfred 25.00 60.00
❑ BT01S02 Blaster Blade 15.00 40.00
❑ BT01S03 Barcgal 10.00 25.00
❑ BT01S04 Dragonic Overlord 12.00 30.00
❑ BT01S05 CEO Amaterasu 25.00 60.00
❑ BT01S06 Battle Sister, Cocoa 12.00 30.00
❑ BT01S07 Asura Kaiser 12.00 30.00
❑ BT01S08 Solitary Knight, Gancelot 10.00 25.00
❑ BT01S09 Vortex Dragon 8.00 20.00
❑ BT01S10 Maiden of Libra 8.00 20.00
❑ BT01S11 Lozenge Magus 20.00 50.00
❑ BT01S12 Battleraizer 12.00 30.00

2012 Cardfight Vanguard Breaker of Limits

Unlisted Common .10 .25
Booster Box (30 Packs) 60.00 90.00
Booster Pack (5 Cards) 2.50 4.00

❑ BT06001 Circular Saw, Kiriel RRR 5.00 12.00
❑ BT06002 Battle Cupid, Nociel RRR 4.00 10.00
❑ BT06003 Ice Prison Necromancer, Cocytus RRR 5.00 12.00
❑ BT06004 Incandescent Lion, Blond Ezel RRR 12.00 30.00
❑ BT06005 Player of the Holy Bow, Viviane RRR 6.00 15.00
❑ BT06006 Dragonic Kaiser, Vermillion RRR 15.00 40.00
❑ BT06007 Desert Gunner, Shiden RRR 3.00 8.00
❑ BT06008 Beast Deity, Azure Dragon RRR 5.00 12.00
❑ BT06009 Cosmo Healer, Ergodiel RR 2.00 5.00
❑ BT06010 Core Memory, Armaros RR 2.50 6.00
❑ BT06011 Love Machine Gun, Nociel RR 2.50 6.00
❑ BT06012 Pure Keeper, Requiel RR 5.00 12.00
❑ BT06013 Deadly Swordmaster RR 2.00 5.00
❑ BT06014 Death Seeker, Thanatos RR 2.00 5.00
❑ BT06015 Knight of Fury, Agravain RR 2.00 5.00
❑ BT06016 Sleygal Dagger RR 2.00 5.00
❑ BT06017 Halo Shield, Mark RR 12.00 30.00
❑ BT06018 Vajra Emperor, Indra RR 2.00 5.00
❑ BT06019 Dragonic Deathscythe RR 3.00 8.00
❑ BT06020 Wyvern Guard, Guld RR 6.00 15.00
❑ BT06021 Mobile Hospital, Feather Palace R .60 1.50
❑ BT06022 Drill Bullet, Geniel R .60 1.50
❑ BT06023 The Phoenix, Calamity Flame R .60 1.50
❑ BT06024 Gattling Shot, Barbiel R .75 2.00
❑ BT06025 Fate Healer, Ergodiel R .60 1.50
❑ BT06026 Miracle Feather Nurse R .60 1.50
❑ BT06027 Master Swordsman, Nightstorm R .40 1.00
❑ BT06028 Skeleton Demon World Knight R .40 1.00
❑ BT06029 Deadly Spirit R .60 1.50
❑ BT06030 Three Star Chef, Pietro R .60 1.50
❑ BT06031 Deadly Nightmare R .60 1.50
❑ BT06032 Knight of Superior Skills, Beaumains R .60 1.50
❑ BT06033 Mage of Calamity, Tripp R .60 1.50
❑ BT06034 Player of the Holy Axe, Nimue R .75 2.00
❑ BT06035 Crimson Lion Cub, Kyrph R .60 1.50
❑ BT06036 Riot General, Gyras R .60 1.50
❑ BT06037 Thunderstorm Dragoon R .40 1.00
❑ BT06038 Demonic Dragon Berserker, Garuda R .60 1.50
❑ BT06039 Desert Gunner, Raien R .60 1.50
❑ BT06040 Photon Bomber Wyvern R .60 1.50
❑ BT06041 Lizard Soldier, Saishin R .60 1.50
❑ BT06042 Beast Deity, White Tiger R .60 1.50

2012 Cardfight Vanguard Breaker of Limits SP

❑ BT06S01 Circular Saw, Kiriel 10.00 25.00
❑ BT06S02 Battle Cupid, Nociel 6.00 15.00
❑ BT06S03 Ice Prison Necromancer, Cocytus 8.00 20.00
❑ BT06S04 Incandescent Lion, Blond Ezel 30.00 60.00
❑ BT06S05 Player of the Holy Bow, Viviane 12.00 30.00
❑ BT06S06 Dragonic Kaiser, Vermillion 30.00 60.00
❑ BT06S07 Desert Gunner, Shiden 6.00 15.00
❑ BT06S08 Beast Deity, Azure Dragon 8.00 20.00
❑ BT06S09 Cosmo Healer, Ergodiel 6.00 15.00
❑ BT06S10 Death Seeker, Thanatos 6.00 15.00
❑ BT06S11 Knight of Fury, Agravain 6.00 15.00
❑ BT06S12 Vajra Emperor, Indra 6.00 15.00

2012 Cardfight Vanguard Cavalry of Black Steel

Complete Set (47)
Unlisted Common .10 .25
Booster Box (15 Packs) 30.00 50.00
Booster Pack (5 Cards) 2.50 4.00

❑ EB03001 Demonic Lord, Dudley Emperor RRR 5.00 12.00
❑ EB03002 Spectral Duke Dragon RRR 10.00 25.00
❑ EB03003 Reckless Express RR 2.50 6.00
❑ EB03004 Martial Arts Mutant, Master Beetle RR 2.50 6.00
❑ EB03005 White Dragon Knight, Pendragon RR 2.50 6.00
❑ EB03006 Origin Mage, Ildona RR 2.50 6.00
❑ EB03007 Dragonic Lawkeeper RR 4.00 10.00
❑ EB03008 Jelly Beans R .60 1.50
❑ EB03009 Dudley Daisy R .60 1.50
❑ EB03010 Bewitching Officer, Lady Butterfly R .75 2.00
❑ EB03011 Toxic Trooper R .60 1.50
❑ EB03012 Toxic Soldier R .75 2.00
❑ EB03013 Gigantech Destroyer R 1.00 2.50
❑ EB03014 Black Dragon Knight, Vortimer R 1.25 3.00
❑ EB03015 Black Dragon Whelp, Vortimer R .75 2.00
❑ EB03016 Twin Shine Swordsman, Marhaus R 1.00 2.50
❑ EB03017 Dragonic Executioner R 1.00 2.50
❑ EB03033 Scout of Darkness, Vortimer C .30 .75
❑ EB03035 War-horse, Raging Storm C .20 .50
❑ EB03036 Falcon Knight of the Azure C .20 .50
❑ EB03037 Knight of Determination, Lamorak C .20 .50

2012 Cardfight Vanguard Cavalry of Black Steel SP

❑ EB03S01 Demonic Lord, Dudley Emperor 25.00 50.00
❑ EB03S02 Spectral Duke Dragon 40.00 80.00
❑ EB03S03 Martial Arts Mutant, Master Beetle 20.00 40.00
❑ EB03S04 White Dragon Knight, Pendragon 12.00 25.00
❑ EB03S05 Origin Mage, Ildona 12.00 25.00
❑ EB03S06 Dragonic Lawkeeper 20.00 40.00

2012 Cardfight Vanguard Demonic Lord Invasion

Unlisted Common .10 .25
Booster Box (30 Packs) 50.00 80.00
Booster Pack (5 Cards) 2.50 4.00

❑ BT03001 Stil Vampir RRR 2.00 5.00
❑ BT03002 Demon World Marquis, Amon RRR 8.00 20.00
❑ BT03003 Nightmare Doll, Alice RRR 8.00 20.00
❑ BT03004 Ravenous Dragon, Gigarex RRR 2.00 5.00
❑ BT03005 Swordsman of the Explosive Flames 12.00 30.00
Palamedes RRR
❑ BT03006 Goddess of the Full Moon 10.00 25.00
Tsukuyomi RRR
❑ BT03007 Goddess of the Half Moon, Tsukuyomi RRR12.00 30.00
❑ BT03008 Ultimate Lifeform, Cosmo Lord RRR 1.00 2.50
❑ BT03009 Edel Rose RR 1.50 4.00
❑ BT03010 Gwynn the Ripper RR 1.25 3.00
❑ BT03011 March Rabbit of Nightmareland RR 6.00 15.00
❑ BT03012 Doreen the Thruster RR 2.50 6.00
❑ BT03013 Dusk Illusionist, Robert RR 1.25 3.00
❑ BT03014 Crimson Beast Tamer RR 6.00 15.00
❑ BT03015 Mirror Demon RR 1.25 3.00
❑ BT03016 Hades Hypnotist RR 8.00 20.00
❑ BT03017 Archbird RR 5.00 12.00
❑ BT03018 Knight of Godly Speed, Galahad RR 3.00 8.00
❑ BT03019 Dual Axe Archdragon RR 2.50 6.00
❑ BT03020 Super Dimensional Robo, Daiyusha RR 4.00 10.00
❑ BT03021 Imprisoned Fallen Angel, Saraqael R .40 1.00
❑ BT03022 Werwolf Sieger R .50 1.25
❑ BT03023 Demon of Aspiration, Amon R .40 1.00
❑ BT03024 Alluring Succubus R 1.25 3.00
❑ BT03025 Vermillion Gatekeeper R .40 1.00
❑ BT03026 Bloody Calf R .40 1.00
❑ BT03027 Barking Manticore R .50 1.25
❑ BT03028 Barking Cerberus R .40 1.00
❑ BT03029 Skull Juggler R .40 1.00
❑ BT03030 Midnight Bunny R 1.00 2.50
❑ BT03031 Turquoise Beast Tamer R .50 1.25
❑ BT03032 Hades Ringmaster R .40 1.00
❑ BT03033 Raging Dragon, Blastsaurus R .60 1.50
❑ BT03034 Ravenous Dragon, Megarex R 1.00 2.50
❑ BT03035 Savage Warrior R .40 1.00
❑ BT03036 Toypugal R .75 2.00
❑ BT03037 Drangal R .50 1.25
❑ BT03038 Oracle Guardian, Blue Eye R .40 1.00
❑ BT03039 Godhawk, Ichibyoshi R .40 1.00
❑ BT03040 Circle Magus R .50 1.25
❑ BT03041 Death Army Lady R .75 2.00
❑ BT03042 Death Army Guy R 1.00 2.50

2012 Cardfight Vanguard Demonic Lord Invasion SP

❑ BT03S02 Demon World Marquis, Amon 12.00 30.00
❑ BT03S03 Nightmare Doll, Alice 12.00 30.00
❑ BT03S04 Ravenous Dragon, Gigarex 6.00 15.00
❑ BT03S05 Swordsman of the Explosive Flames 25.00 50.00
Palamedes
❑ BT03S06 Goddess of the Full Moon, Tsukuyomi30.00 60.00
❑ BT03S08 Ultimate Lifeform, Cosmo Lord 6.00 15.00
❑ BT03S10 Gwynn the Ripper 8.00 20.00
❑ BT03S14 Crimson Beast Tamer 15.00 40.00
❑ BT03S18 Knight of Godly Speed, Galahad 6.00 15.00
❑ BT03S19 Dual Axe Archdragon 8.00 20.00
❑ BT03S20 Super Dimensional Robo, Daiyusha 20.00 40.00
❑ BT03S30 Turquoise Beast Tamer 25.00 50.00

2012 Cardfight Vanguard Eclipse of Illusionary Shadows

Complete Set (82)
Unlisted Common .10 .25
Booster Box (30 packs)
Booster Pack (5 cards)

❑ BT04001 Phantom Blaster Dragon RRR 15.00 40.00
❑ BT04002 Darkness Maiden, Macha RRR 6.00 15.00
❑ BT04003 Skull Witch, Nemain RRR 8.00 20.00
❑ BT04004 Enigman Storm RRR 3.00 8.00
❑ BT04005 Evil Armor General, Giraffa RRR 5.00 12.00
❑ BT04006 Amber Dragon, Eclipse RRR 5.00 12.00
❑ BT04007 Heatnail Salamander RRR 4.00 10.00
❑ BT04008 Stern Blaukluger RRR 6.00 15.00
❑ BT04009 Dark Metal Dragon RR 3.00 8.00
❑ BT04010 Gururubau RR 3.00 8.00
❑ BT04011 Dark Shield, Mac Lir RR 10.00 25.00
❑ BT04012 Enigman Wave RR 2.50 6.00
❑ BT04013 Cosmo Break RR 3.00 8.00
❑ BT04014 Diamond Ace RR 5.00 12.00
❑ BT04015 Commander Laurel RR 2.50 6.00
❑ BT04016 Elite Mutant, Giraffa RR 3.00 8.00
❑ BT04017 Paralize Madonna RR 4.00 10.00
❑ BT04018 Amber Dragon, Dusk RR 3.00 8.00
❑ BT04019 Blaukluger RR 5.00 12.00
❑ BT04020 Fang of Light, Garmore RR 4.00 10.00
❑ BT04021 Silver Spear Demon, Gusion R .40 1.00
❑ BT04022 Dark Mage, Badhabh Caar R .75 2.00
❑ BT04023 Knight of Darkness, Rugos R .75 2.00
❑ BT04024 Blaster Dark R 5.00 12.00
❑ BT04025 Cursed Lancer R .75 2.00
❑ BT04026 Fullbau R .40 1.00
❑ BT04027 Enigman Rain R .40 1.00
❑ BT04028 Twin Order R .40 1.00
❑ BT04029 Platinum Ace R .40 1.00
❑ BT04030 Cosmo Roar R .75 2.00
❑ BT04031 Enigman Flow R .40 1.00
❑ BT04032 Death Warden Ant Lion R .75 2.00
❑ BT04033 Violent Vesper R .40 1.00
❑ BT04034 Water Gang R .40 1.00
❑ BT04035 Gloom Flyman R .40 1.00
❑ BT04036 Megacolony Battler B R .75 2.00
❑ BT04037 Larva Mutant, Giraffa R .40 1.00
❑ BT04038 Lizard Soldier, Raopia R .40 1.00
❑ BT04039 Amber Dragon, Dawn R .75 2.00
❑ BT04040 Armored Fairy, Shubiela R .40 1.00
❑ BT04041 Blaujunger R .40 1.00
❑ BT04042 Beast Knight, Garmore R .40 1.00

2012 Cardfight Vanguard Eclipse of Illusionary Shadows SP

❑ BT04S01 Phantom Blaster Dragon 50.00 100.00
❑ BT04S02 Darkness Maiden, Macha 25.00 50.00
❑ BT04S03 Skull Witch, Nemain 20.00 40.00
❑ BT04S04 Enigman Storm 10.00 25.00
❑ BT04S05 Evil Armor General, Giraffa 10.00 25.00
❑ BT04S06 Amber Dragon, Eclipse 12.00 30.00
❑ BT04S07 Stern Blaukluger 20.00 40.00
❑ BT04S08 Dark Metal Dragon 10.00 25.00
❑ BT04S09 Amber Dragon, Dusk 12.00 30.00
❑ BT04S10 Blaukluger 10.00 25.00
❑ BT04S11 Fang of Light, Garmore 10.00 25.00
❑ BT04S12 Blaster Dark 60.00 120.00

2012 Cardfight Vanguard Onslaught of Dragon Souls

Complete Set (80)
Unlisted Common .10 .25
Booster Box (30 Packs) 50.00 80.00
Booster Pack (5 Cards) 2.50 4.00

❑ BT02001 Sky Diver RRR 6.00 15.00
❑ BT02002 Spirit Exceed RRR 2.50 6.00
❑ BT02003 Ruin Shade RRR 8.00 20.00
❑ BT02004 Soul Savior Dragon RRR 15.00 30.00
❑ BT02005 Blazing Flare Dragon RRR 6.00 15.00
❑ BT02006 Seal Dragon, Blockade RRR 4.00 10.00
❑ BT02007 Scarlet Witch, Coco RRR 2.00 5.00
❑ BT02008 Lion Heat RRR 3.00 8.00
❑ BT02009 General Seifried RR 2.00 5.00
❑ BT02010 Cheer Girl, Marilyn RR 6.00 15.00
❑ BT02011 King of Demonic Seas, Basskirk RR 3.00 8.00
❑ BT02012 Witch Doctor of the Abyss, Negromarl RR1.25 3.00
❑ BT02013 Captain Nightmist RR 3.00 8.00
❑ BT02014 Gust Jinn RR 6.00 15.00
❑ BT02015 Young Pegasus Knight RR 2.50 6.00
❑ BT02016 Chain-attack Sutherland RR 1.00 2.50
❑ BT02017 Silent Tom RR 8.00 20.00
❑ BT02018 Magician Girl Kirara RR 1.50 4.00
❑ BT02019 Twin Blader RR 8.00 20.00
❑ BT02020 Top Idol, Flores RR 1.00 2.50
❑ BT02021 Unite Attacker R .20 .50
❑ BT02022 Treasured, Black Panther R .20 .50
❑ BT02023 Dudley Dan R .30 .75
❑ BT02024 Mecha Trainer R .20 .50
❑ BT02025 Dancing Cutlass R .20 .50
❑ BT02026 Chappie the Ghostie R .30 .75
❑ BT02027 Gigantech Charger R .30 .75
❑ BT02028 Great Sage, Barron R .20 .50
❑ BT02029 High Dog Breeder, Akane R .40 1.00
❑ BT02030 Pongal R 1.00 2.50
❑ BT02031 Blazing Core Dragon R 1.25 3.00
❑ BT02032 Demonic Dragon Mage, Kimnara R 1.25 3.00
❑ BT02033 Luck Bird R .20 .50
❑ BT02034 Winged Dragon, Skyptero R .20 .50
❑ BT02035 Dragon Egg R .20 .50
❑ BT02036 Top Idol, Aqua R .20 .50
❑ BT02037 Bermuda Triangle Cadet, Caravel R .20 .50
❑ BT02038 Master Fraude R .20 .50
❑ BT02039 Scientist Monkey Rue R .20 .50
❑ BT02040 Geograph Giant R .20 .50
❑ BT02056 Knight of Truth, Gordon C .40 1.00
❑ BT02064 Gattling Claw Dragon C .30 .75

2012 Cardfight Vanguard Onslaught of Dragon Souls SP

❑ BT02S01 Sky Diver 10.00 25.00
❑ BT02S02 Spirit Exceed 8.00 20.00
❑ BT02S03 Ruin Shade 15.00 30.00
❑ BT02S04 Soul Savior Dragon 30.00 60.00
❑ BT02S05 Blazing Flare Dragon 15.00 30.00
❑ BT02S06 Seal Dragon, Blockade 8.00 20.00
❑ BT02S07 Scarlet Witch, Coco 10.00 25.00
❑ BT02S08 Lion Heat 15.00 30.00
❑ BT02S09 General Seifried 8.00 20.00
❑ BT02S10 Witch Doctor of the Abyss, Negromarl 4.00 10.00
❑ BT02S11 Top Idol, Flores 20.00 40.00
❑ BT02S12 Top Idol, Aqua 15.00 30.00

2013 Cardfight Vanguard Awakening of Twin Blades

Unlisted Common .10 .25
Booster Box (30 Packs)
Booster Pack (5 Cards)

❑ BT05001 Covert Demonic Dragon 5.00 12.00
Mandala Lord RRR
❑ BT05002 Majesty Lord Blaster RRR 12.00 30.00
❑ BT05003 Star Call Trumpeter RRR 6.00 15.00
❑ BT05004 Phantom Blaster Overlord RRR 12.00 30.00
❑ BT05005 Dragonic Overlord The End RRR 25.00 50.00
❑ BT05006 Miracle Beauty RRR 4.00 10.00
❑ BT05007 King of Diptera, Beelzebub RRR 2.00 5.00
❑ BT05008 Mistress Hurricane RRR 1.50 4.00
❑ BT05009 Maiden of Trailing Rose RR 4.00 10.00
❑ BT05010 Glass Beads Dragon RR 2.00 5.00
❑ BT05011 Maiden of Blossom Rain RR 5.00 12.00
❑ BT05012 Stealth Fiend, Midnight Crow RR 1.25 3.00
❑ BT05013 Stealth Beast, Leaves Mirage RR 5.00 12.00
❑ BT05014 Knight of Loyalty, Bedivere RR 4.00 10.00
❑ BT05015 Knight of Friendship, Kay RR 3.00 8.00
❑ BT05016 Wingal Brave RR 3.00 8.00
❑ BT05017 Moonlight Witch, Vaha RR 1.50 4.00
❑ BT05018 Knight of Nullity, Masquerade RR 5.00 12.00
❑ BT05019 Evil-eye Princess, Euryale RR 1.50 4.00
❑ BT05020 Street Bouncer RR 1.25 3.00
❑ BT05021 Frontline Valkyrie, Laurel R 1.00 2.50
❑ BT05022 Knight of Harvest, Gene R .60 1.50
❑ BT05023 Avatar of the Plains, Behemoth R .60 1.50
❑ BT05024 Iris Knight R .60 1.50
❑ BT05025 Hey Yo Pineapple R .60 1.50
❑ BT05026 Shield Seed Squire R .60 1.50
❑ BT05027 Stealth Fiend, Kurama Lord R .60 1.50
❑ BT05028 Stealth Dragon, Voidgelga R .75 2.00
❑ BT05029 Stealth Beast, Bloody Mist R .60 1.50
❑ BT05030 Caped Stealth Rogue, Shanaou R .40 1.00
❑ BT05031 Stealth Dragon, Cursed Breath R .75 2.00
❑ BT05032 Stealth Dragon, Turbulent Edge R .75 2.00
❑ BT05033 Stealth Beast, Million Rat R .75 2.00
❑ BT05034 Stealth Beast, Evil Ferret R .60 1.50
❑ BT05035 Conjurer of Mithril R .75 2.00
❑ BT05036 Knight of Purgatory, Skull Face R .75 2.00
❑ BT05037 Apocalypse Bat R .75 2.00
❑ BT05038 Burning Horn Dragon R 1.25 3.00
❑ BT05039 Flame of Promise, Aermo R .75 2.00
❑ BT05040 Demonic Dragon Mage, Mahoraga R .60 1.50
❑ BT05041 Magical Police Quilt R .75 2.00
❑ BT05042 Devil Child R .75 2.00

2013 Cardfight Vanguard Awakening of Twin Blades SP

❑ BT05S01 Covert Demonic Dragon, Mandala Lord 15.00 40.00
❑ BT05S02 Majesty Lord Blaster 30.00 60.00
❑ BT05S03 Star Call Trumpeter 8.00 20.00
❑ BT05S04 Phantom Blaster Overlord 25.00 50.00
❑ BT05S05 Dragonic Overlord the End 30.00 60.00
❑ BT05S06 Miracle Beauty 8.00 20.00
❑ BT05S07 King of Diptera, Beelzebub 8.00 20.00
❑ BT05S08 Mistress Hurricane 6.00 15.00

❑ BT05S09 Maiden of Trailing Rose 8.00 20.00
❑ BT05S10 Stealth Fiend, Midnight Crow 6.00 15.00

2013 Cardfight Vanguard Blue Storm Armada

Unlisted Common .10 .25
❑ BT08001 Ultimate Dimensional Robo 6.00 15.00
Great Daiyusha RRR
❑ BT08002 Galactic Beast, Zeal RRR 3.00 8.00
❑ BT08003 Arboros Dragon, Sephirot RRR 4.00 10.00
❑ BT08004 White Lily Musketeer, Cecilia RRR 5.00 12.00
❑ BT08005 Blue Storm Dragon, Maelstrom RRR 10.00 25.00
❑ BT08006 Hydro Hurricane Dragon RRR 2.00 5.00
❑ BT08007 Storm Rider, Basil RRR 8.00 20.00
❑ BT08008 Sealed Demon Dragon, Dungaree RRR 2.00 5.00
❑ BT08009 Operator Girl, Mika RR .60 1.50
❑ BT08010 Dimensional Robo, Daidragon RR 2.50 6.00
❑ BT08011 Cherry Blossom Musketeer, Augusto RR 1.50 4.00
❑ BT08012 Lily of the Valley Musketeer, Kaivant RR .75 2.00
❑ BT08013 Maiden of Rainbow Wood RR .75 2.00
❑ BT08014 Water Lily Musketeer, Ruth RR 1.25 3.00
❑ BT08015 Lily of the Valley Musketeer, Rebecca RR 1.50 4.00
❑ BT08016 Military Dragon, Raptor Colonel RR 5.00 12.00
❑ BT08017 Destruction Dragon, Dark Rex RR 2.00 5.00
❑ BT08018 Tear Knight, Valeria RR 2.00 5.00
❑ BT08019 Emerald Shield, Paschal RR 10.00 25.00
❑ BT08020 Armed Instructor, Bison RR .60 1.50
❑ BT08021 Enigman Cyclone R .25 .60
❑ BT08022 Lady Justice R .25 .60
❑ BT08023 Subterranean Beast, Magma Lord R .25 .60
❑ BT08024 Devourer of Planets, Zeal R .25 .60
❑ BT08025 Dimensional Robo, Dailander R .40 1.00
❑ BT08026 Dimensional Robo, Goyusha R .25 .60
❑ BT08027 Larva Beast, Zeal R .25 .60
❑ BT08028 Arboros Dragon, Timber R .40 1.00
❑ BT08029 Arboros Dragon, Ratoon R .25 .60
❑ BT08030 Military Dragon, Raptor Captain R .40 1.00
❑ BT08031 Winged Dragon, Slashptero R .25 .60
❑ BT08032 Assault Dragon, Pachyphalos R .25 .60
❑ BT08033 Winged Dragon, Beamptero R .25 .60
❑ BT08034 Military Dragon, Raptor Soldier R .25 .60
❑ BT08035 Storm Rider, Diamantes R .40 1.00
❑ BT08036 Tear Knight, Lazarus R .25 .60
❑ BT08037 Storm Rider, Eugen R .25 .60
❑ BT08038 Torpedo Rush Dragon R .25 .60
❑ BT08039 Aqua Breath Dracokid R .25 .60
❑ BT08040 Thunder Spear Wielding .25 .60
Exorcist Knight R
❑ BT08041 Compass Lion R .25 .60
❑ BT08042 Coiling Duckbill R .25 .60

2013 Cardfight Vanguard Blue Storm Armada SP

❑ BT08S01 Ultimate Dimensional Robo 10.00 25.00
Great Daiyusha
❑ BT08S02 Galactic Beast, Zeal 8.00 20.00
❑ BT08S03 Arboros Dragon, Sephirot 8.00 20.00
❑ BT08S04 White Lily Musketeer, Cecilia 10.00 25.00
❑ BT08S05 Blue Storm Dragon, Maelstrom 30.00 60.00
❑ BT08S06 Hydro Hurricane Dragon 5.00 12.00
❑ BT08S07 Storm Rider, Basil 15.00 40.00
❑ BT08S08 Sealed Demon Dragon, Dungaree 8.00 20.00
❑ BT08S09 Operator Girl, Mika 12.00 30.00
❑ BT08S10 Maiden of Rainbow Wood 12.00 30.00
❑ BT08S11 Military Dragon, Raptor Colonel 6.00 15.00
❑ BT08S12 Destruction Dragon, Dark Rex 8.00 20.00

2013 Cardfight Vanguard Clash of the Knights and Dragons

Unlisted Common .10 .25
❑ BT09001 Covert Demonic Dragon 3.00 8.00
Magatsu Storm RRR
❑ BT09002 Blue Storm Supreme Dragon 8.00 20.00
Glory Maelstrom RRR
❑ BT09003 Goddess of the Sun, Amaterasu RRR 4.00 10.00
❑ BT09004 Ultra Beast Deity, Illuminal Dragon RRR 4.00 10.00
❑ BT09005 Crimson Impact, Metatron RRR 5.00 12.00
❑ BT09006 Blazing Lion, Platina Ezel RRR 12.00 30.00
❑ BT09007 Conviction Dragon 6.00 15.00
Chromejailer Dragon RRR
❑ BT09008 Dragonic Kaiser Vermillion 15.00 40.00
THE BLOOD RRR
❑ BT09009 Fantasy Petal Storm, Shirayuki RR 2.50 6.00
❑ BT09010 Platinum Blond Fox Spirit, Tamamo RR 2.00 5.00
❑ BT09011 Tri-Stinger DragonRR .40 1.00
❑ BT09012 Battle Sister, Cookie RR 2.00 5.00
❑ BT09013 Battler of the Twin Brush, Polaris RR 1.25 3.00
❑ BT09014 Halo Shield, Mark RR 5.00 12.00
❑ BT09015 Lord of the Demonic Winds, Vayu RR .40 1.00
❑ BT09016 Wyvern Guard, Guld RR 3.00 8.00
❑ BT09017 Starlight Melody Tamer, Farah RR 1.25 3.00
❑ BT09018 Nightmare Summoner, Raqiel RR 1.00 2.50
❑ BT09019 Blaster Blade Spirit RR 2.50 6.00
❑ BT09020 Blaster Dark Spirit RR 1.50 4.00
❑ BT09021 Stealth Dragon, Magatsu Gale R .40 1.00
❑ BT09022 Stealth Fiend, Oboro Cart R .25 .60
❑ BT09023 Stealth Dragon, Magatsu Wind R .25 .60
❑ BT09024 Storm Rider, Lysander R .25 .60
❑ BT09025 Storm Rider, Damon R .25 .60
❑ BT09026 Battle Siren, Theresa R .25 .60
❑ BT09027 Storm Rider, Nicolas R .25 .60
❑ BT09028 Tri-holl DracokidR .25 .60
❑ BT09029 Battle Deity, Susanoo R .25 .60
❑ BT09030 Battle Maiden, Sayorihime R .25 .60
❑ BT09031 Beast Deity, Yamatano Drake R .25 .60
❑ BT09032 Hollow Nomad R .25 .60
❑ BT09033 Beast Deity, Golden Anglet R .40 1.00
❑ BT09034 Beast Deity, Blank Marsh R .30 .75
❑ BT09035 Mobile Hospital, Elysium R .25 .60
❑ BT09036 Knight of Passion, Bagdemagus R .40 1.00
❑ BT09037 Advance of the Black Chains, Kahedin R .25 .60
❑ BT09038 Dreaming Sage, Corron R .25 .60
❑ BT09039 Dusty Plasma Dragon R 1.00 2.50
❑ BT09040 Exorcist Demonic Dragon, Indigo R .25 .60
❑ BT09041 Barking Wyvern R .25 .60
❑ BT09042 Fire Juggler R .25 .60
❑ BT09052 Fox Tamer, Izuna C .20 .50
❑ BT09076 Crimson Drive, Aphrodite C .20 .50
❑ BT09078 Crimson Mind, Baruch C .20 .50
❑ BT09083 Fever Therapy Nurse C .20 .50
❑ BT09099 Spark Edge Dracokid C .20 .50

2013 Cardfight Vanguard Clash of the Knights and Dragons SP

❑ BT09S01 Covert Demonic Dragon, Magatsu Storm 8.00 20.00
❑ BT09S02 Blue Storm Supreme Dragon 15.00 40.00
Glory Maelstrom
❑ BT09S03 Goddess of the Sun, Amaterasu 15.00 40.00
❑ BT09S04 Ultra Beast Deity, Illuminal Dragon 10.00 25.00
❑ BT09S05 Crimson Impact, Metatron 12.00 30.00
❑ BT09S06 Blazing Lion, Platina Ezel 25.00 60.00
❑ BT09S07 Conviction Dragon, Chromejailer Dragon 12.00 30.00
❑ BT09S08 Dragonic Kaiser Vermillion THE BLOOD35.00 70.00
❑ BT09S09 Battle Sister, Cookie 12.00 30.00
❑ BT09S10 Starlight Melody Tamer, Farah 8.00 20.00
❑ BT09S11 Blaster Blade Spirit 10.00 25.00
❑ BT09S12 Blaster Dark Spirit 12.00 30.00

2013 Cardfight Vanguard Rampage of the Beast

Unlisted Common .10 .25
❑ BT07001 School Hunter, Leo-paid RRR 5.00 12.00
❑ BT07002 Guardian of Truth, Lox RRR 2.00 5.00
❑ BT07003 Binoculus Tiger RRR 6.00 15.00
❑ BT07004 Silver Thorn Dragon Tamer, Luquier RRR10.00 25.00
❑ BT07005 Dark Lord of Abyss RRR 2.50 6.00
❑ BT07006 Emerald Witch, LaLa RRR 2.00 5.00
❑ BT07007 White Hare in the Moon's Shadow 5.00 12.00
Pellinore RRR
❑ BT07008 Chief Nurse, Shamsiel RRR 8.00 20.00
❑ BT07009 School Dominator, Apt RR 1.00 2.50
❑ BT07010 Lamp Camel RR 1.00 2.50
❑ BT07011 Monoculus Tiger RR 1.25 3.00
❑ BT07012 Cable Sheep RR 5.00 12.00
❑ BT07013 Sword Magician, Sarah RR 2.50 6.00
❑ BT07014 Fire Breeze, Carrie RR 1.00 2.50
❑ BT07015 Peek-a-boo RR 1.00 2.50
❑ BT07016 Magician of Quantum Mechanics RR 1.00 2.50
❑ BT07017 Blade Wing Reijy RR 5.00 12.00
❑ BT07018 Emblem Master RR 3.00 8.00
❑ BT07019 Yellow Bolt RR 3.00 8.00
❑ BT07020 Listener of Truth, Dindrane RR 5.00 12.00
❑ BT07021 Pencil Hero, Hammsuke R .25 .60
❑ BT07022 Dumbbell Kangaroo R .25 .60
❑ BT07023 Magnet Crocodile R .40 1.00
❑ BT07024 Law Official, Lox R .25 .60
❑ BT07025 Pencil Squire, Hammsuke R .75 2.00
❑ BT07026 Thermometer Giraffe R .25 .60
❑ BT07027 Tank Mouse R .25 .60
❑ BT07028 Flask Marmoset R .25 .60
❑ BT07029 Midnight Invader R .40 1.00
❑ BT07030 Dancing Princess of the Night Sky R .40 1.00
❑ BT07031 Bull's Eye, Mia R .25 .60
❑ BT07032 Purple Trapezist R 1.50 4.00
❑ BT07033 Evil Eye Basilisk R .25 .60
❑ BT07034 Hades Carriage of the Witching Hour R .25 .60
❑ BT07035 Free Traveler R .25 .60
❑ BT07036 Courting Succubus R 1.25 3.00
❑ BT07037 Sky Witch, NaNa R .25 .60
❑ BT07038 Battle Sister, Glace R .75 2.00
❑ BT07039 Little Witch, LuLu R .25 .60
❑ BT07040 Photon Archer, Griflet R .40 1.00
❑ BT07041 Lop Ear Shooter R 2.00 5.00
❑ BT07042 Spring Breeze Messenger R .25 .60
❑ BT07060 Triangle Cobra C .20 .50
❑ BT07061 Fortune-bringing Cat C .20 .50
❑ BT07064 Dictionary Goat C .40 1.00
❑ BT07065 Ruler Chameleon C .20 .50
❑ BT07078 Popcorn Boy C .20 .50
❑ BT07079 Poison Juggler C .40 1.00
❑ BT07083 Demon Bike of the Witching Hour C .20 .50
❑ BT07091 Cheshire Cat of Nightmareland C .20 .50
❑ BT07092 Dark Knight of Nightmareland C .40 1.00
❑ BT07098 Disciple of Pain C .20 .50
❑ BT07099 Speeder Hound C .20 .50

2013 Cardfight Vanguard Rampage of the Beast SP

❑ BT07S01 School Hunter, Leo-paid 8.00 20.00
❑ BT07S02 Guardian of Truth, Lox 4.00 10.00
❑ BT07S03 Binoculus Tiger 6.00 15.00
❑ BT07S04 Silver Thorn Dragon Tamer, Luquier 15.00 40.00
❑ BT07S05 Dark Lord of Abyss 6.00 15.00
❑ BT07S06 Emerald Witch, LaLa 5.00 12.00
❑ BT07S07 White Hare in the Moon's Shadow 10.00 25.00
Pellinore
❑ BT07S08 Chief Nurse, Shamsiel 15.00 40.00
❑ BT07S09 School Dominator, Apt 4.00 10.00
❑ BT07S10 Monoculus Tiger 4.00 10.00
❑ BT07S11 Sword Magician, Sarah 10.00 25.00
❑ BT07S12 Blade Wing Reijy 12.00 30.00

1995 Dragon Ball Z Ani-Mayhem

Complete Set (232) 125.00 175.00
Booster Box (60 packs) 120.00 200.00
Booster Packs (9 cards) 5.00 9.00
Starter Deck 15.00 30.00
❑ 1 Adult Gohan R 4.00 8.00
❑ 2 Atlia U .50 1.00
❑ 3 Baba R 2.00 4.00
❑ 4 Baby Gohan C 1.00 2.00
❑ 5 Bubbles R 3.00 6.00
❑ 6 Bulma C 2.00 4.00
❑ 7 Chi-Chi C 1.00 2.00
❑ 8 Chiao-Tzu R 1.00 3.00
❑ 9 Farmer with shotgun C .10 .25
❑ 10 Future Trunks UR 8.00 16.00
❑ 11 Gohan the Barbarian U .50 1.00
❑ 12 Goku C 2.00 4.00
❑ 13 Goku (different)R 6.00 12.00
❑ 14 Goten R 4.00 8.00
❑ 15 Gregory R 1.00 3.00
❑ 16 Kami R 3.00 6.00
❑ 17 Krillin C 1.00 2.00
❑ 18 Lunch U 1.00 2.00
❑ 19 Master Roshi U 1.00 2.00
❑ 20 Nail U 2.00 4.00
❑ 21 Oolong U 1.00 2.00
❑ 22 Ox-King U 1.00 2.00
❑ 23 Piccolo R 4.00 8.00
❑ 24 Super Saiyan Goku UR 10.00 20.00
❑ 25 Super Saiyan Goten UR 8.00 16.00
❑ 26 Super Saiyan Trunks UR 8.00 16.00
❑ 27 Tien (Tenshinhan)C 1.00 2.00
❑ 28 Trunks C 1.00 3.00
❑ 29 Yajirobe C 1.00 2.00
❑ 30 Yamcha C .10 .25
❑ 31 Young Gohan U 2.00 4.00
❑ 32 Bump on the Head R 1.50 3.00
❑ 33 Good Deed U .25 .50
❑ 34 Heavy Gravity Training R 2.00 4.00
❑ 35 Leap of Faith U .25 .50
❑ 36 M.V.P. C .10 .25
❑ 37 Speed II C .10 .25
❑ 38 Spirit C .10 .25
❑ 39 Spirit Fighting C .10 .25
❑ 40 Survey R 1.00 3.00
❑ 41 Survival Training U .25 .50
❑ 42 Weighted Clothing U .25 .50
❑ 43 Algebra R 1.00 3.00
❑ 44 Airbus U .25 .50
❑ 45 Blasters C .10 .25
❑ 46 Dragon Radar R 1.00 3.00
❑ 47 Dream Mirror R 1.00 3.00
❑ 48 Floating Car C .10 .25
❑ 49 Giant's Toy Biplane U .25 .50
❑ 50 Goz' Flying Machine R 1.00 3.00
❑ 51 Gravity Ship R 1.00 3.00
❑ 52 Hand Gun U .25 .50
❑ 53 Kai's Dimensional Sedan R 1.00 3.00
❑ 54 Light R 1.00 3.00
❑ 55 Namek Ship R 1.00 3.00
❑ 56 Razor Balls C .10 .25
❑ 57 Rocket Launcher U .25 .50
❑ 58 Saiyan Space Pod C .10 .25
❑ 59 Scouter C .50 1.00
❑ 60 Change Direction C .10 .25
❑ 61 Destructo Disc R 1.00 3.00
❑ 62 Divert Attack R 3.00 6.00
❑ 63 Dodonpa C .10 .25
❑ 64 Fake Item R 1.00 3.00
❑ 65 False Moon R 2.00 4.00
❑ 66 Genki-Dama (Spirit Ball)R 3.00 6.00
❑ 67 Gohan is Angry C .25 .50
❑ 68 Haste U .25 .50
❑ 69 Hey, You're not Dead C .10 .25
❑ 70 High Ground C .10 .25
❑ 71 Jan-ken-Po C .10 .25
❑ 72 Just a Scratch R 1.00 3.00
❑ 73 Kamehameha U 1.00 3.00
❑ 74 Keen Observation R 1.00 3.00
❑ 75 Know When to Run U .25 .50
❑ 76 Laser Eyes C .10 .25
❑ 77 Makkankoupousou R 2.00 4.00
❑ 78 Meltdown R 1.00 3.00
❑ 79 Mindtrap R 2.00 4.00
❑ 80 Moon Destruction C .10 .25
❑ 81 Mother Instinct U .25 .50
❑ 82 Out of the Frying Pan U .25 .50
❑ 83 Regeneration U .25 .50
❑ 84 Rescue R 1.00 3.00
❑ 85 Shen Lon UR 6.00 12.00
❑ 86 Shield R 1.00 3.00
❑ 87 Spilt Form C .10 .25
❑ 88 Sunshine Daydream U .25 .50
❑ 89 Telekinese R 2.00 4.00
❑ 90 Time Out! C .10 .25
❑ 91 Ultimate Sacrifice R 1.00 3.00
❑ 92 Who Sows the Wind C .10 .25
❑ 93 Equipment Retrieval U 1.50 3.00
❑ 94 Frothy Mugs of Water C .10 .25
❑ 95 Great King Yemma R 1.00 3.00
❑ 96 Guardian of the Earth R 1.00 3.00
❑ 97 Guru R 1.00 3.00
❑ 98 Hiding Out U .25 .50
❑ 99 King Kai C .25 .50
❑ 100 Medical Regenerator U .25 .50
❑ 101 Power Sense U .25 .50
❑ 102 Power Up U 1.00 3.00
❑ 103 Refuge R 1.00 3.00
❑ 104 Slow Moving Traffic C .10 .25
❑ 105 Training with Kami U .25 .50
❑ 106 Gohan's Cave C .10 .25
❑ 107 King Kai's Bungalow U 1.00 2.00
❑ 108 Lunch's House C .10 .25
❑ 109 Roshi's Veranda C 1.00 3.00
❑ 110 Otherworld Lounge U .25 .50
❑ 111 West Side City Hospital U .25 .50
❑ 112 Dragon Ball C .10 .25
❑ 113 2 Dragon Balls U 3.00 6.00
❑ 114 3 Dragon Balls R 4.00 8.00
❑ 115 Baby Dragon U .25 .50
❑ 116 Capsule Army Knife C .10 .25
❑ 117 Firewood C .10 .25
❑ 118 Flying Nimbus R 2.00 4.00
❑ 119 Gohan's Supplies C .10 .25
❑ 120 King Yemma's Fruit U .25 .50
❑ 121 Lemila C .10 .25
❑ 122 Mighty Fridge C .10 .25
❑ 123 Presents U .25 .50
❑ 124 Samurai Gohan R 2.00 4.00
❑ 125 Senzu Beans R 2.00 4.00
❑ 126 Ships Auto-Toilet R 1.00 3.00
❑ 127 Sleepy Grass C .10 .25
❑ 128 Tail Steak C .10 .25
❑ 129 Technological Artifact C .10 .25
❑ 130 Tortoise R 1.00 3.00
❑ 131 Alien Jungle C .10 .25
❑ 132 Alien Landing Site C .10 .25
❑ 133 Arena C .10 .25
❑ 134 Baseball Stadium C .25 .50
❑ 135 Beware: Bathroom! C .50 1.00
❑ 136 Café C .10 .25
❑ 137 Campground U .25 .50
❑ 138 Capsule Corporation U .25 .50
❑ 139 Desert Battleground C .10 .25
❑ 140 Dr. Weelo's Fortress R 1.00 3.00
❑ 141 Forest Glade U .25 .50
❑ 142 Freeza's Ship R 2.00 4.00
❑ 143 Frozen Wastes C .10 .25
❑ 144 Garlic Jr.'s Palace U .25 .50
❑ 145 Goku and Chi-Chi's House U .50 1.00
❑ 146 Hong Kong U .25 .50
❑ 147 Illusionary Castle C .10 .25
❑ 148 Kami's Floating Palace U .25 .50
❑ 149 King Kai's Planetoid R 1.00 3.00
❑ 150 King Yemma's Palace C .50 1.00
❑ 151 Pendulum Training Room R 1.00 3.00
❑ 152 Planet Arlia C .10 .25
❑ 153 Planet Freeza C 1.00 2.00
❑ 154 Planet Namek R 1.00 3.00
❑ 155 Planet Vegeta R 2.00 4.00
❑ 156 Princess Snake's Palace R 1.00 3.00
❑ 157 Snake Way U .25 .50
❑ 158 Dodria C .75 1.50
❑ 159 Freeza (1st form)R 4.00 8.00
❑ 160 Garlic Jr. U 1.00 3.00
❑ 161 Ginger C .10 .25
❑ 162 Ginyu U .75 1.50
❑ 163 Kidnapped C .10 .25
❑ 164 Nappa C 1.00 2.00
❑ 165 Princess Snake U .25 .50
❑ 166 Raditz C .25 .50
❑ 167 Raiichi and Zaakro C .10 .25
❑ 168 Recoom C .75 1.50
❑ 169 Sabre-Toothed Tiger C .10 .25
❑ 170 Tares R 2.00 4.00
❑ 171 The Dead Zone U .25 .50
❑ 172 Vegeta U 4.00 8.00
❑ 173 Acid Head U .25 .50
❑ 174 Asteroid Field U .25 .50
❑ 175 Baby Saiyan R 3.00 6.00
❑ 176 Catch Bubbles R 1.00 3.00
❑ 177 Demon Hordes U .25 .50
❑ 178 Don't Be A Dummy C .10 .25
❑ 179 Dr. Weelo R 1.00 3.00
❑ 180 Dr. Weelo's Bio Men U 1.00 2.00
❑ 181 Ebi-Furiya U .25 .50
❑ 182 Excessive Gravity U .25 .50
❑ 183 Full Moon U 1.00 2.00
❑ 184 Goz C .10 .25
❑ 185 Guldo C .10 .25
❑ 186 Homework C .10 .25
❑ 187 Hungry Dinasaur C .10 .25
❑ 188 Ibuprofen and Quickly! U .25 .50
❑ 189 Impending Doom U .25 .50
❑ 190 Kishiime C .10 .25
❑ 191 Loner U .25 .50
❑ 192 Mez C .10 .25
❑ 193 Miso-Cutsun U .25 .50
❑ 194 Mystery Foe R 2.00 4.00
❑ 195 No Help! U .25 .50
❑ 196 Overload C .10 .25
❑ 197 Property Damage U .25 .50
❑ 198 Pterodactyl C .10 .25
❑ 199 Saibamen U .25 .50
❑ 200 Shinseiju Tree R 2.00 4.00
❑ 201 Squeeeeeeeeeze! U .25 .50
❑ 202 The Pit C .10 .25
❑ 203 Watch That 1st Step U .25 .50
❑ 204 Willpower U .25 .50
❑ 205 Zarbon R 1.00 3.00
❑ 206 Back Kick U .25 .50
❑ 207 Be with you C .10 .25
❑ 208 Bench Brawl U .25 .50
❑ 209 Berserk U .25 .50
❑ 210 Crushing Left U .25 .50
❑ 211 Devestating Attack C .10 .25
❑ 212 Double Blow C .25 .50
❑ 213 Drop Kick C .10 .25
❑ 214 Films About Gladiators U .25 .50
❑ 215 Flying Kick C .10 .25
❑ 216 Fried C .10 .25
❑ 217 Grace C .10 .25
❑ 218 Gut Punch C .10 .25
❑ 219 Head Butt C .10 .25
❑ 220 In My Sights C .10 .25
❑ 221 Incoming C .10 .25
❑ 222 Just a Trim C .10 .25
❑ 223 Leg Sweep C .10 .25
❑ 224 Lunch Break U .25 .50
❑ 225 Oooh! It Got Me! U .25 .50
❑ 226 Pinned C .10 .25
❑ 227 Pummel C .10 .25
❑ 228 Screwed U .25 .50
❑ 229 Shock C .10 .25
❑ 230 To Much Sun C .10 .25
❑ 231 Wild Swing C .10 .25
❑ 232 Yipes C .10 .25

2000 Dragon Ball Z Saiyan Saga

Complete Set (250) 75.00 150.00
Unopened Box (36 packs) 40.00 50.00
Unopened Pack (9 cards) 2.00 3.00
Limited Edition cards add 10% to value.
❑ 1 Orange Standing Fist Punch C .25 .50
❑ 2 Orange One Knuckle Punch C .25 .50
❑ 3 Orange Two Knuckle Punch C .25 .50
❑ 4 Orange Leg Sweep C .25 .50
❑ 5 Orange Arm Bar C .25 .50
❑ 6 Red Lunge Punch C .25 .50
❑ 7 Red Reverse Punch C .25 .50
❑ 8 Red Knife Hand C .25 .50
❑ 9 Red Palm Heel Strike C .50 .75
❑ 10 Red Elbow StrikeC .25 .50
❑ 11 Blue Forward Foot Sweep C .25 .50
❑ 12 Blue Hip Spring Throw C .25 .50
❑ 13 Blue Round Throw C .25 .50
❑ 14 Blue Shoulder Wheel C .25 .50
❑ 15 Earth Dragon Ball 1 C .50 1.00
❑ 16 Earth Dragon Ball 2 C .50 1.00
❑ 17 Hidden Power Level C .25 .50
❑ 18 Saiyan Arm Throw C .25 .50
❑ 19 Saiyan Full Spin Kick C .25 .50
❑ 20 Saiyan Pressure Punch C .25 .50
❑ 21 Saiyan Neck Hold C .25 .50
❑ 22 Power Up C .50 1.00
❑ 23 Burning Rage C .25 .50
❑ 24 Goku's Surprise Attack C .50 1.00
❑ 25 Goku's Physical Attack C .50 1.00
❑ 26 Gohan's Physical Attack C .25 .50
❑ 27 Tien's Physical Attack C .25 .50
❑ 28 Vegeta's Physical Stance C .25 .50
❑ 29 Yajirobe's Physical Attack C .10 .25
❑ 30 Fall 7 times, get up 8 times C .10 .25
❑ 31 Fortify Your Spirit C .10 .25
❑ 32 The Untroubled Mind is Focused C .10 .25
❑ 33 It's the Little Things That Matter C .10 .25
❑ 34 Straining Off-Balancing Move C .10 .25
❑ 35 Straining, Penetrating Attack Move C .10 .25
❑ 36 Straining Fake Left Move C .10 .25
❑ 37 Straining Tripping Move C .10 .25
❑ 38 Straining Arm Drag Move C .10 .25
❑ 39 Straining Ankle Smash Move C .10 .25
❑ 40 Straining Energy Defense Move C .10 .25
❑ 41 Straining Head Lock Move C .10 .25
❑ 42 Straining Rolling Escape Move C .10 .25
❑ 43 Senzu Bean C .50 1.00
❑ 44 Goku Body Throw C .25 .50
❑ 45 Saiyan City Destruction C .10 .25
❑ 46 Goku Anger Attack C .25 .50
❑ 47 Raditz Total Defense C .25 .50
❑ 48 Goku's Touch C .25 .50
❑ 49 Orange Wrist Flex Takedown C .10 .25
❑ 50 Orange Shoulder Throw C .10 .25
❑ 51 Orange Hip Throw C .10 .25
❑ 52 Orange Neck Restraints C .10 .25
❑ 53 Orange Holding After Takedown C .10 .25
❑ 54 Red Knee Strike C .10 .25
❑ 55 Red Front Kick C .10 .25
❑ 56 Red Side Kick C .10 .25
❑ 57 Red Round Kick C .10 .25
❑ 58 Red Back Kick C .10 .25
❑ 59 Blue Big Outside Drop C .10 .25
❑ 60 Blue One Arm Shoulder Throw C .10 .25
❑ 61 Blue Body Drop Throw U .50 1.00
❑ 62 Blue Inner Leg Throw U .50 1.00
❑ 63 Blue Big Whirl Throw U .50 1.00
❑ 64 Blue Ground Holding U .50 1.00
❑ 65 Black Fore Fist Punch U .50 1.00
❑ 66 Black Knife Hand Strike U .50 1.00
❑ 67 Black Elbow Strike U .50 1.00
❑ 68 Black Front Kick U 1.00 2.00
❑ 69 Black Side Kick U 1.00 2.00
❑ 70 Black Turning Kick U .50 1.00

❑ 71 Black Back Kick U 1.00 2.00
❑ 72 Black Axe Heel Kick U .50 1.00
❑ 73 Black Rear Spin Kick U .50 1.00
❑ 74 Black Jump Turn Kick U .50 1.00
❑ 75 Earth Dragon Ball 3 U 1.00 2.00
❑ 76 Earth Dragon Ball 4 U .50 1.00
❑ 77 Earth Dragon Ball 5 U .50 1.00
❑ 78 Roshi Training U .75 1.50
❑ 79 King Kai Training U .50 1.00
❑ 80 Saiyan Training U .50 1.00
❑ 81 Saiyan Armor U .50 1.00
❑ 82 Tien U .50 1.00
❑ 83 Tien U .50 1.00
❑ 84 Yamcha U .50 1.00
❑ 85 Yamcha U .50 1.00
❑ 86 Chi-Chi U .50 1.00
❑ 87 Bulma U 1.00 2.00
❑ 88 King Kai Uniform U .50 1.00
❑ 89 Dream Chamber Training U .50 1.00
❑ 90 Mother's Touch U .50 1.00
❑ 91 Saiyan Energy Throw U 1.00 2.00
❑ 92 Saiyan Energy Defense U 1.00 2.00
❑ 93 Saiyan Mental Energy Attack U 1.00 2.00
❑ 94 Saiyan Energy Blast U 1.00 2.00
❑ 95 Saiyan Energy Aura U .50 1.00
❑ 96 Saiyan Sweeping Defense U 1.00 2.00
❑ 97 Power Up More U .50 1.00
❑ 98 Power Up the Most U .50 1.00
❑ 99 Blazing Anger U .50 1.00
❑ 100 Vegeta's Surprise Defense U .75 1.50
❑ 101 Goku Honor Duel U 1.00 2.00
❑ 102 Raditz Honor Duel U .50 1.00
❑ 103 Piccolo Honor Duel U 1.00 2.00
❑ 104 Chiaotzu U .75 1.50
❑ 105 Chiaotzu U .50 1.00
❑ 106 Yajirobe U .50 1.00
❑ 107 Yajirobe U .50 1.00
❑ 108 Goku's Energy Defense U 1.00 2.00
❑ 109 Piccolo's Energy Attack U .50 1.00
❑ 110 Piccolo's Physical Defense U .50 1.00
❑ 111 Gohan's Energy Defense U 1.00 2.00
❑ 112 Krillin's Physical Defense U .50 1.00
❑ 113 Krillin's Energy Attack U .50 1.00
❑ 114 Tien's Energy Defense U .50 1.00
❑ 115 Yamcha's Energy Attack U .50 1.00
❑ 116 Yamcha's Physical Defense U .50 1.00
❑ 117 Raditz Energy Wall U .50 1.00
❑ 118 Raditz Physical Defense U .50 1.00
❑ 119 Vegeta's Energy Blast U .50 1.00
❑ 120 Nappa's Energy Aura U 1.00 2.00
❑ 121 Nappa's Physical Resistance U .50 1.00
❑ 122 Yajirobe's Energy Attack U .50 1.00
❑ 123 Chiaotzu's Energy Manipulation U .50 1.00
❑ 124 Red Penetrating Defense Drill U .50 1.00
❑ 125 Blue Off-Balancing Opponent Drill U 1.00 2.00
❑ 126 Orange Lifting Drill U .50 1.00
❑ 127 Black Takedown Drill U .50 1.00
❑ 128 Red Knee Pick Drill U .50 1.00
❑ 129 Blue Deceiving Drill U 1.00 2.00
❑ 130 Orange Tripping Drill U .50 1.00
❑ 131 Black Bear Hug Drill U .50 1.00
❑ 132 Red Rolling Drill U .50 1.00
❑ 133 Blue Reversal Drill U .50 1.00
❑ 134 Orange Off-Balancing Drill U .50 1.00
❑ 135 Black Arm Bar Drill U .50 1.00
❑ 136 Black Free-Style Drill U .50 1.00
❑ 137 Orange Spontaneous Drill U .50 1.00
❑ 138 Blue Cradle Drill U .50 1.00
❑ 139 Red Wrist Control Drill U .50 1.00
❑ 140 Red Reading Drill U .50 1.00
❑ 141 Blue Enemies Drill U .50 1.00
❑ 142 Orange Energy Drill U .75 1.50
❑ 143 Black Physical Drill U .50 1.00
❑ 144 Red Coordination Drill U .50 1.00
❑ 145 Blue Breakfall Drill U .50 1.00
❑ 146 Orange Body Shifting Drill U 1.00 2.00
❑ 147 Black Striking Drill U .50 1.00
❑ 148 Red Pressure- Point Drill U .50 1.00
❑ 149 Meditation Drill U 1.00 2.00
❑ 150 Blue Neck Restraint Drill U .50 1.00
❑ 151 Orange Joint Restraint Drill U .50 1.00
❑ 152 Black Defender Drill U 1.00 2.00
❑ 153 Goku Energy Blast U .50 1.00
❑ 154 Piccolo Sidestep U .50 1.00
❑ 155 Piccolo Defense Drill U .50 1.00
❑ 156 Ally's Sacrifice U .50 1.00
❑ 157 Eyes of the Dragon U .50 1.00
❑ 158 Goku (Level 1) P 2.00 4.00
❑ 159 Goku (Level 2) P 2.00 4.00
❑ 160 Goku (Level 3) P 2.00 4.00
❑ 161 Piccolo (Level 1) P 1.00 2.00
❑ 162 Piccolo (Level 2) P 1.00 2.00
❑ 163 Piccolo (Level 3) P 2.00 4.00
❑ 164 Gohan (Level 1) P 1.50 3.00
❑ 165 Gohan (Level 2) P 1.00 2.00
❑ 166 Gohan (Level 3) P 1.00 2.00
❑ 167 Krillin (Level 1) P .50 1.00
❑ 168 Krillin (Level 2) P .50 1.00
❑ 169 Krillin (Level 3) P .50 1.00
❑ 170 Raditz (Level 1) P 1.00 3.00
❑ 171 Raditz (Level 2) P 1.00 3.00
❑ 172 Raditz (Level 3) P 1.00 3.00
❑ 173 Vegeta (Level 1) P 4.00 8.00
❑ 174 Vegeta (Level 2) P 3.00 6.00
❑ 175 Vegeta (Level 3) P 3.00 6.00
❑ 176 Nappa (Level 1) P .50 1.00
❑ 177 Nappa (Level 2) P .50 1.00
❑ 178 Nappa (Level 3) P .50 1.00
❑ 179 Goku (Level 1) P 3.00 5.00
❑ 180 Piccolo (Level 1) P 3.00 5.00
❑ 181 Gohan (Level 1) P 3.00 5.00
❑ 182 Krillin (Level 1) P 4.00 6.00
❑ 183 Raditz (Level 1) P 4.00 8.00
❑ 184 Vegeta (Level 1) P 4.00 8.00
❑ 185 Nappa (Level 1) P 2.00 4.00
❑ 186 Earth Dragon Ball 6 R 2.00 5.00
❑ 187 Earth Dragon Ball 7 R 2.00 5.00
❑ 188 Earth Dragon Ball Capture R 2.00 5.00
❑ 189 Earth Dragon Ball Combat R 2.00 4.00
❑ 190 Enraged R 3.00 6.00
❑ 191 A Beginner's Heart is Dedicated R 2.00 4.00
❑ 192 Teaching the Unteachable Observation R 2.00 4.00
❑ 193 Respect the Spirit R 2.00 4.00
❑ 194 Unselfish Behavior is the Best R 2.50 5.00
❑ 195 Hero Advantage R 2.00 4.00
❑ 196 Saiyan Honor Quest R 2.00 4.00
❑ 197 Saiyan Battle Terms R 2.00 4.00
❑ 198 Saiyan Appraisal Maneuver R 2.00 4.00
❑ 199 Dream Fighting R 2.00 4.00
❑ 200 Cutting the Tail R 2.00 4.00
❑ 201 The Tail Grows Back R 2.50 5.00
❑ 202 Goku's Lucky Break R 2.00 4.00
❑ 203 Saiyan Truce Card R 3.00 6.00
❑ 204 Battle Pausing R 3.00 6.00
❑ 205 Grabbing the Tail R 2.00 4.00
❑ 206 Nappa's Blinding Stare R 2.00 4.00
❑ 207 Power Gifting R 2.00 4.00
❑ 208 Terrible Wounds R 2.00 4.00
❑ 209 Broken Scouter R 2.00 4.00
❑ 210 Raditz Flying Kick R 3.00 6.00
❑ 211 Tien Mind Reading Trick R 2.00 4.00
❑ 212 Piccolo's Flight R 3.00 5.00
❑ 213 Plant Two Saibaimen R 2.00 4.00
❑ 214 Gohan's Father Save R 3.00 6.00
❑ 215 Krillin's Drill R 3.00 6.00
❑ 216 Krillins's Energy Disk R 2.00 4.00
❑ 217 Ribs Broken R 1.00 3.00
❑ 218 Unexpected Allies R 2.00 4.00
❑ 219 Raditz Energy Burst R 2.00 4.00
❑ 220 Vegeta's Stance R 3.00 6.00
❑ 221 Vegeta's Quickness Drill R 4.00 8.00
❑ 222 Bulma Finds a Dragon Ball R 2.00 4.00
❑ 223 Bulma Finds a Drill R 2.00 4.00
❑ 224 Baba Witch Viewing Drill R 3.00 6.00
❑ 225 Baba Energy Blast R 2.00 4.00
❑ 226 T-Rex Defense R 2.00 4.00
❑ 227 T-Rex Offense R 2.00 4.00
❑ 228 Vegeta's Plans R 4.00 8.00
❑ 229 Ally Wins R 2.00 4.00
❑ 230 Chiaotzu's Drill R 3.00 6.00
❑ 231 Goku's Mixing Drill R 4.00 6.00
❑ 232 Red Life Attack Drill R 3.00 6.00
❑ 233 Blue Life Defense Drill R 2.00 4.00
❑ 234 Orange Focusing Drill R 2.00 4.00
❑ 235 Black Shadow Drill R 2.00 4.00
❑ 236 Saiyan Power Drill R 2.00 4.00
❑ 237 Goku's Capturing Drill R 4.00 6.00
❑ 238 Kings Kai's Calming R 3.00 6.00
❑ 239 Roshi's Calming R 3.00 5.00
❑ 240 Vegeta's Trick R 2.00 4.00
❑ 241 Vegeta's Dragon Ball Capture R 2.00 4.00
❑ 242 Dream Machine Battle R 2.00 4.00
❑ 243 Saibaimen R 1.00 3.00
❑ 244 Saibaimen R 1.00 3.00
❑ 245 Saibaimen R 1.00 3.00
❑ 246 Saibaimen R 2.00 4.00
❑ 247 Goku's Truce UR 15.00 20.00
❑ 248 Goku's Plan UR 15.00 25.00
❑ 249 Medic Kit UR 20.00 30.00
❑ 250 Chiaotzu's Physical Defense UR 15.00 25.00

2000 Dragon Ball Z Frieza Preview

Complete Set (6) 6.00 12.00
Inserts in Frieza Saga Booster Packs

❑ PV1 The Talking Ends Here! C 1.00 2.00
❑ PV2 Just Kidding C 1.00 2.00
❑ PV3 No, Really Drill? U 1.00 3.00
❑ PV4 Good Advice U 2.00 4.00
❑ PV5 The Luck of Trunks R 2.00 4.00
❑ PV6 Trunks Makes Himself Clear R 3.00 6.00

2000 Dragon Ball Z Frieza Saga

Complete Set (125) 100.00 150.00
Booster Box (36 Packs) 50.00 100.00
Booster Pack (11 Cards) 3.00 4.00
*Foil: 1X to 2X Basic Cards

❑ 1 Orange Planet Destruction C .25 .50
❑ 2 Orange Kamehameha Attack C .10 .25
❑ 3 Orange Taunting Attack C .10 .25
❑ 4 Red Energy Suspension C .10 .25
❑ 5 Red Energy Disk C .10 .25
❑ 6 Red Energy Disk Blasting C .10 .25
❑ 7 Blue Energy Flight C .10 .25
❑ 8 Recoome Boom C .10 .25
❑ 9 Saiyan Rapture C .25 .50
❑ 10 Saiyan Concussion Punch C .25 .50
❑ 11 Saiyan Rapid Deflection C .25 .50
❑ 12 Saiyan Energy Focus C .25 .50
❑ 13 Empowerment C .10 .25
❑ 14 Goku's Righteous Force C .25 .75
❑ 15 Gohan's Temper C .25 .50
❑ 16 Tien's Jolting Aura C .25 .50
❑ 17 Vegeta's Jolting Slash C .25 .75
❑ 18 Saiyan Concentration C .10 .25
❑ 19 Powerful Followers C .10 .25
❑ 20 Straining, Floating Attack Move C .10 .25
❑ 21 Straining Blasting Move C .10 .25
❑ 22 Straining Energy Move C .10 .25
❑ 23 Straining Defense Move C .10 .25
❑ 24 Straining Blocking Move C .10 .25
❑ 25 Straining Focusing Move C .10 .25
❑ 26 A Hospital Stay C .10 .25
❑ 27 Orange Thumbs Up C .10 .25
❑ 28 Orange Fist Detonation C .10 .25
❑ 29 Goku's Sudden Outburst C .25 .50
❑ 30 Time's a Warrior Tool C .50 .75
❑ 31 Dodoria Energy Attack C .10 .25
❑ 32 Dodoria Flames of Fury C .10 .25
❑ 33 Jeice Flash Attack C .10 .25
❑ 34 Saiyan Planet Explosion C .10 .25
❑ 35 Saiyan Focusing Power C .10 .25
❑ 36 Alien Anger C .10 .25
❑ 37 Jeice (level 1) U .50 1.00
❑ 38 Dodoria (level 1) U .50 1.00
❑ 39 Tien (level 3) U 1.00 2.00
❑ 40 Yamcha (level 3) U .75 1.50
❑ 41 Chi-Chi (level 2) U 1.00 2.00
❑ 42 Bulma (level 2) U .50 1.00
❑ 43 Chiaotzu (level 3) U .50 1.00
❑ 44 Yajirobe the Hero (level 3) U 1.00 2.00
❑ 45 Guldo (level 1) U 1.00 2.00
❑ 46 Guldo (level 2) U .50 1.00
❑ 47 Guldo (level 3) U .50 1.00
❑ 48 Dende the unlikely Hero (level 1) U 1.00 3.00
❑ 49 Frieza Smiles U 1.00 2.00
❑ 50 Captain Ginyu Realization U 1.00 2.00
❑ 51 Jeice Shouts U .50 1.00
❑ 52 Jeice Comet Attack U .25 .50
❑ 53 Dodoria Boom U .25 .50
❑ 54 Goku's Energy Absorbtion U .50 1.00
❑ 55 Guldo's Time Feeze Drill U .25 .50
❑ 56 Gohan's Anger Blast U 1.00 2.00
❑ 57 Krillin's Anger Blast U .50 1.00
❑ 58 Tien's Power Burst U .25 .50
❑ 59 Yamcha's Skillful Defense U .25 .50
❑ 60 Vegeta's Gallic Gun U .50 1.00
❑ 61 Vegeta's Powering Up U 1.00 2.00
❑ 62 Captain Ginyu's Visionary Attack U .50 1.00
❑ 63 Yajirobe's Gifting Drill U .50 1.00
❑ 64 Chiaotzu's Glaring Power U .50 1.00
❑ 65 Red Energy Defense Drill U .50 1.00
❑ 66 Blue Mental Drill U .50 1.00
❑ 67 Orange Destruction Drill U .50 1.00
❑ 68 Black Zarbon Transformation Drill U .50 1.00
❑ 69 Red Phasing Drill U .50 1.00
❑ 70 Blue Allies Drill U 1.00 2.00
❑ 71 Orange Leg Drill U .50 1.00
❑ 72 Black Energy Stamina Drill U .50 1.00
❑ 73 Red Implosion Drill U 1.00 2.00
❑ 74 Captain Ginyu Reversal Drill U 1.00 2.00
❑ 75 Jeice's Style Drill U .50 1.00
❑ 76 Vegeta Getting Bashed Drill U .50 1.00
❑ 77 Dende Healing Drill U 1.00 2.00
❑ 78 Gohan Anger Drill U 1.00 2.00
❑ 79 Frieza's Influencing Drill U .50 1.00
❑ 80 Black Erasing Drill U .25 .50
❑ 81 Krillin's Power Block U 1.00 2.00
❑ 82 Black Standing Position U .25 .50
❑ 83 Black Right Cross U .50 1.00
❑ 84 Black Driving Leg Throw U .25 .50
❑ 85 Straining Outburst Move U .25 .50
❑ 86 Straining Neck Move U .25 .50
❑ 87 Krillin's Concentration U .25 1.00
❑ 88 Hero Enraged U .25 .50
❑ 89 Vegeta On Namek (level 4) R 3.00 6.00
❑ 90 Krillin On Namek (level 4) R 2.00 4.00
❑ 91 Nappa Restored (level 4) R 2.00 4.00
❑ 92 Raditz Restored (level 4) R 2.00 4.00
❑ 93 Goku On Namek (level 4) R 3.00 6.00
❑ 94 Piccolo (level 4) R 3.00 6.00
❑ 95 Gohan (level 4) R 4.00 8.00
❑ 96 Nail The Namekian (level 1) R 2.00 4.00
❑ 97 Straining Force Positioning Move R 2.00 4.00
❑ 98 Blue Stance R 2.00 4.00
❑ 99 Blue Energy Outburst R 2.00 4.00
❑ 100 Kami as Your Ally R 2.50 5.00
❑ 101 Hero Teamwork Drill R 3.00 6.00
❑ 102 Villain's TeamworkDrill R 3.00 6.00
❑ 103 Human Technology R 2.00 4.00
❑ 104 Power R 2.00 4.00
❑ 105 Dende's Help R 2.00 4.00
❑ 106 Goku's Super Saiyan Blast R 4.00 8.00
❑ 107 Piccolo's Wisdom R 1.00 3.00
❑ 108 Yamcha's Good Wishes R 3.00 6.00
❑ 109 Captain Ginyu's Sacrifice R 1.00 3.00
❑ 110 Nail the Namekian Hero (level 3) R 4.00 8.00
❑ 111 Krillin's Power Tap R 2.00 4.00
❑ 112 Black Swift Elbow Strike R 3.00 6.00
❑ 113 Kami Fades R 3.00 6.00
❑ 114 Gohan's Stomp R 1.00 3.00
❑ 115 Piccolo's Stomp R 2.00 4.00
❑ 116 Goku's Quickness R 3.00 6.00
❑ 117 Nail Inspired (level 2) R 3.00 6.00
❑ 118 The Plan R 2.00 4.00
❑ 119 Mommy's Coming Dear R 3.00 6.00
❑ 120 Bulma's Scouter R 2.00 4.00
❑ 121 This Too Shall Past R 2.00 4.00
❑ 122 Focusing Is Everything R 2.00 4.00
❑ 123 Red Foot Jolt R 3.00 6.00
❑ 124 Frieza the Master UR 20.00 40.00
❑ 125 Super Saiyan Goku (level 4) UR 30.00 50.00

2001 Dragon Ball Z Trunks Preview

Complete Set (6 Cards) 5.00 10.00
Inserts in Trunks Saga Booster Packs

❑ PV1 Android 20 Absorbing Drill C .50 1.00
❑ PV2 Android 20 Powers Up C .50 1.00
❑ PV3 Android Effect U 1.00 2.00
❑ PV4 Super Saiyan Effect U 1.00 2.00
❑ PV5 Too Late R 2.00 4.00
❑ PV6 Trunks Finds the Answer R 2.00 4.00

2001 Dragon Ball Z Trunks Saga

Complete Set (200) 175.00 250.00
Unopened Box (36 Packs) 125.00 200.00
Unopened Pack (11 Cards) 4.00 6.00
Starter Deck 12.00 20.00
*Foil: .75X to 1.5X Basic Cards

❑ 1 Orange Energy Blast C .25 .50
❑ 2 Red Kienzan Discs C .25 .50
❑ 3 Namek Dragon Ball 2 C .25 .50
❑ 4 Captain Ginyu Frog C .25 .50
❑ 5 Krillin's Kamehameha Outburst C .25 .50
❑ 6 Straining Outburst Move C .25 .50
❑ 7 Namekian Glare Attack C .25 .50
❑ 8 Namekian Braced Attack C .25 .50
❑ 9 Namekian Thrust C .25 .50
❑ 10 Namekian Blocking Defense C .25 .50
❑ 11 Red Implosion Lunge C .25 .50
❑ 12 Blue Stomach Eruption C .25 .50
❑ 13 Orange Power Shifting Drill C .25 .50
❑ 14 Orange Surprise Blast C .25 .50
❑ 15 Orange Dashing Gut Punch C .25 .50
❑ 16 Orange Straight Jab C .25 .50
❑ 17 Black Defensive Aura C .25 .50
❑ 18 Black Flying Kick C .25 .50
❑ 19 Black Finger Block C .25 .50
❑ 20 Black Defensive Burst C .25 .50
❑ 21 Black Overpowering Attack C .50 1.00
❑ 22 Red Blazing Aura C .25 .50
❑ 23 Red Gravity Drill C .25 .50
❑ 24 Red Energy Shield C .25 .50
❑ 25 Namek Dragon Ball 1 C .50 .75
❑ 26 Spice and his friends C .25 .50
❑ 27 Spice Prepares an Energy Blast C .25 .50
❑ 28 Vinegar has Plans C .25 .50
❑ 29 Vinegar's Revenge C .25 .50
❑ 30 Black Water Confusion Drill C .25 .50
❑ 31 Garlic Jr's Kyokaika Technique C .25 .50
❑ 32 Garlic Jr's Energy Blast C .25 .50
❑ 33 Garlic Jr's Black Water Mist C .25 .50
❑ 34 Krillin Lashes Out C .25 .50
❑ 35 Krillin takes a Shot C .25 .50
❑ 36 Frieza's Finger Tip Energy Blast C .75 1.50
❑ 37 King Cold Smiles C .25 .50
❑ 38 King Cold's End C .25 .50
❑ 39 Goku's Ready C .50 1.00
❑ 40 Tien's Ready C .25 .50
❑ 41 Blue Driving Face Off U .50 1.00
❑ 42 Breakthrough Drill U .50 1.00
❑ 43 Blue Thrusting Fist Strike U .50 1.00
❑ 44 Chiaotzu's Psychic Halt U .50 1.00
❑ 45 Black Head Strike U .50 1.00
❑ 46 Black Hug Maneuver U .50 1.00
❑ 47 Black Driving Palm Strike U .50 1.00
❑ 48 Dodoria's Waiting Game U .50 1.00
❑ 49 Frieza's Aura Shot U .50 1.00
❑ 50 Saiyan Knee Strike U .50 1.00
❑ 51 Frieza's Powering Rage U .50 1.00
❑ 52 Namekian Fighting U .50 1.00
❑ 53 Captain Ginyu Moves to Attack U .50 1.00
❑ 54 Captain Ginyu's Energy Attack U .50 1.00
❑ 55 Namekian Attack Drill U .50 1.00
❑ 56 Frieza's Tail Hold U .50 1.00
❑ 57 Frieza's Irritation Grows U .50 1.00
❑ 58 Scoring Aura Shot U .50 1.00
❑ 59 Frieza is Ready U .50 1.00
❑ 60 Namekian Physical Drill U .50 1.00
❑ 61 Namekian Energy Drill U .50 1.00
❑ 62 Burter's Power Stance U .50 1.00
❑ 63 Red Shattering Leap U .50 1.00
❑ 64 Gohan's Quest U .50 1.00
❑ 65 Krillin's Quest U .50 1.00
❑ 66 Namekian's Head Strike U .50 1.00
❑ 67 Red Knee Eruption U .50 1.00
❑ 68 Red Face Upheaval U .50 1.00
❑ 69 Orange Special Beam Cannon U .50 1.00
❑ 70 Orange Resistance U .50 1.00
❑ 71 Orange Special Beam Cannon Drill U .50 1.00
❑ 72 Black Energy Web U .50 1.00
❑ 73 Black Energy Blast U 1.00 2.00
❑ 74 Black Energy Deflection Drill U 1.00 2.00
❑ 75 Red Power Rush U .50 1.00
❑ 76 Red Lightning Slash U .50 1.00
❑ 77 Red Energy Blast U 1.00 2.00
❑ 78 Red Eye Laser Assault U .50 1.00
❑ 79 Namek Dragon Ball 3 U 1.00 2.00
❑ 80 Namek Dragon Ball 4 U 1.00 2.00
❑ 81 Trunks Slash U 1.00 3.00
❑ 82 Trunks High Strike U 1.00 3.00
❑ 83 Trunks Cuts Down U 1.00 3.00
❑ 84 Trunks Energy Sphere U 5.00 10.00
❑ 85 Trunks Effortless Drill U 1.00 3.00
❑ 86 Trunks Planning Drill U 1.00 3.00
❑ 87 Trunks Sword Position 1 U 2.00 4.00
❑ 88 Trunks Sword Position 2 U 2.00 4.00
❑ 89 Trunks Sword Position 3 U 2.00 4.00
❑ 90 Trunks Sword Position 4 U 2.00 4.00
❑ 91 Expectant Trunks U 1.00 3.00
❑ 92 Trunks Draws Steel U 1.00 3.00
❑ 93 Trunks Stands Ready U 1.00 3.00
❑ 94 Double Saiyans U 1.00 3.00
❑ 95 Blue Softening Stance U .50 1.00
❑ 96 Blue Awakening U .50 1.00
❑ 97 Blue Leaving U .50 1.00
❑ 98 Trunks Strikes U 1.00 3.00
❑ 99 Trunks Swiftly Moving U 1.00 3.00
❑ 100 Frieza, the Revived (level 4) U 3.00 6.00
❑ 101 Garlic Jr. the Void Master (level 4) U 1.00 3.00
❑ 102 Spice, the Punisher (level 4) U 1.00 2.00
❑ 103 Vinegar, the Attacker (level 4) U 2.00 4.00
❑ 104 Jeice, With Style (level 2) U 1.00 3.00
❑ 105 Jeice Attacks (level 3) U .50 1.00
❑ 106 Captain Ginyu (level 1) U .50 1.00
❑ 107 Captain Ginyu the Leader (level 2) U .50 1.00
❑ 108 Captain Ginyu Changes (level 3) U .50 1.00
❑ 109 Dodoria (level 1) U 1.00 3.00
❑ 110 Dodoria, in Flight (level 2) U 1.00 2.00
❑ 111 Dodoria the Mocking (level 3) U 1.00 2.00
❑ 112 Guru as your ally R 1.00 3.00
❑ 113 Namek Dragon Ball 6 R 2.00 4.00
❑ 114 Namek Dragon Ball 7 R 2.00 4.00
❑ 115 Namekian Dragon Ball Combat R 1.00 3.00
❑ 116 Guru Fades R 1.00 3.00
❑ 117 Frieza's Featherlight Touch R 1.00 3.00
❑ 118 What Was I Thinking R 1.00 3.00
❑ 119 Hero's Lucky Break R 1.00 3.00
❑ 120 Thought Comes Before Action R 1.00 3.00
❑ 121 A Hero's Heart Is Strong R 1.00 3.00
❑ 122 An Amusing Trick R 1.00 3.00
❑ 123 Drills Are For The Weak R 1.00 3.00
❑ 124 Hero's Way R 1.00 3.00
❑ 125 Don't You Just Hate That R 1.00 3.00
❑ 126 Vegeta Scans the City R 2.00 4.00
❑ 127 Goku's Battle Ready R 2.00 4.00
❑ 128 Gohan Spots the Imposter Drill R 2.00 4.00
❑ 129 Piccolo and Heroes Gather R 1.00 3.00
❑ 130 Krillin's Heat Seaking Blast R 3.00 6.00
❑ 131 Chi-Chi Searches R .75 2.50
❑ 132 Nail Takes Extra Effort R 1.00 3.00
❑ 133 Roshi's Thoughts R 1.00 3.00
❑ 134 King Kai's Thoughts R 1.00 3.00
❑ 135 Namek Dragon Ball Wish R 2.00 4.00
❑ 136 Namek Dragon Ball 5 R 3.00 6.00
❑ 137 Nail Combat Drill R 1.00 3.00
❑ 138 Orange Energy Dan Drill R 2.00 3.00
❑ 139 Orange Junction Energy Blast R 1.00 3.00
❑ 140 Black Smoothness Drill R 4.00 8.00
❑ 141 Black Physical Focus R 2.00 4.00
❑ 142 Red Evasion Drill R 1.00 3.00
❑ 143 Red King Cold Observation R 3.00 6.00
❑ 144 Red Style Mastery R 6.00 10.00
❑ 145 Black Style Mastery R 8.00 12.00
❑ 146 Orange Style Mastery R 5.00 10.00
❑ 147 Namekian Style Mastery R 5.00 8.00
❑ 148 Saiyan Style Mastery R 8.00 12.00
❑ 149 Blue Style Mastery R 8.00 12.00
❑ 150 Trunks the Hero (level 4) R 6.00 10.00
❑ 151 Vegeta, Saiyan Prince (level 4) R 4.00 8.00
❑ 152 Gohan Empowered (level 4) R 5.00 10.00
❑ 153 Piccolo Enraged (level 4) R 4.00 8.00
❑ 154 Krillin (level 1) R 4.00 8.00
❑ 155 Krillin Enraged (level 2) R 6.00 10.00
❑ 156 Krillin, the Warrior (level 3) R 4.00 8.00
❑ 157 Where There's Life There's Hope UR 40.00 80.00
❑ 158 Villain's True Power UR 20.00 40.00
❑ 159 Goku, the Unbeatable UR 30.00 50.00
❑ 160 King Cold, the All Powerful UR 20.00 40.00
❑ 161 Frieza the Monster (level 1) P 3.00 6.00
❑ 162 Frieza the Conqueror (level 2) P 3.00 6.00
❑ 163 Frieza the Cyborg (level 3) P 3.00 6.00
❑ 164 Goku, the Leader (level 1) P 2.00 4.00
❑ 165 Goku, the Defender (level 2) P 2.00 4.00
❑ 166 Goku, the Protector (level 3) P 2.00 4.00
❑ 167 Piccolo, the Avenger (level 1) P 2.00 4.00
❑ 168 Piccolo, Revived (level 2) P 2.00 4.00
❑ 169 Piccolo, the Hero (level 3) P 3.00 7.00
❑ 170 Gohan, the Furious (level 1) P 2.00 4.00
❑ 171 Gohan, the Fighter (level 2) P 2.00 4.00
❑ 172 Gohan, the Warrior (level 3) P 2.00 4.00
❑ 173 Vegeta, the Determined (level 1) P 2.00 4.00
❑ 174 Vegeta, the Powerful (level 2) P 3.00 6.00
❑ 175 Vegeta, in Training (level 3) P 3.00 6.00
❑ 176 Garlic Jr. (level 1) P 2.00 4.00
❑ 177 Garlic Jr. the Master (level 2) P 2.00 4.00
❑ 178 Garlic Jr. the Monster (level 3) P 2.00 4.00
❑ 179 Spice (level 1) P 2.00 4.00
❑ 180 Spice, the Leader (level 2) P 2.00 4.00
❑ 181 Spice, the Warrior (level 3) P 2.00 4.00
❑ 182 Vinegar (level 1) P 2.00 4.00
❑ 183 Vinegar, the Fighter (level 2) P 1.00 3.00
❑ 184 Vinegar, the Henchman (level 3) P 1.00 3.00
❑ 185 Trunks (level 1) P 3.00 6.00
❑ 186 Trunks, the Swordsman (level 2) P 3.00 6.00

☐ 187 Super Saiyan Trunks (level 3) P 3.00 6.00
☐ 188 King Cold (level 1) P 3.00 6.00
☐ 189 King Cold, the Destroyer (level 2) P 2.00 4.00
☐ 190 King Cold, the Ruler (level 3) P 2.00 4.00
☐ 191 Frieza the Master (level 2) HT 3.00 6.00
☐ 192 Goku (level 2) HT 4.00 8.00
☐ 193 Piccolo (level 2) HT 4.00 8.00
☐ 194 Gohan (level 2) HT 3.00 6.00
☐ 195 Vegeta (level 2) HT 4.00 8.00
☐ 196 Garlic Jr., the Merciless (level 2) HT 2.00 4.00
☐ 197 Spice, the Enchanter (level 2) HT 3.00 6.00
☐ 198 Vinegar, the Battler (level 2) HT 3.00 6.00
☐ 199 Trunks, the Saiyan (level 2) HT 6.00 12.00
☐ 200 King Cold, Galactic Ruler (level 2) HT 4.00 8.00

2001 Dragon Ball Z Android Saga

Complete Set (125) 100.00 150.00
Unopened Box (36 Packs) 45.00 60.00
Unopened Pack (12 Cards) 3.00 4.00
*Foil: .75X to 1.5X Basic Cards

☐ 1 Android 17's Neck Hold C .25 .50
☐ 2 Android 18's Low Blow C .25 .50
☐ 3 Android 19's Body Slam C .50 1.00
☐ 4 Android 19's Energy Burst C .50 1.00
☐ 5 Android 20 Is Caught Off Guard C .50 1.00
☐ 6 Android 20's Energy Burst C .50 1.00
☐ 7 Blasted Land C .50 1.00
☐ 8 Gravity Chamber C .50 1.00
☐ 9 Black Confusion Drill C .50 1.00
☐ 10 Black Draining Aura C .25 .50
☐ 11 Black Jump Kick C .25 .50
☐ 12 Black Taunting Attack C .50 1.00
☐ 13 Blue Defensive Flight C .50 1.00
☐ 14 Blue Foot Smash C .25 .50
☐ 15 Blue Glare Attack C .25 .50
☐ 16 Blue Idea C .25 .50
☐ 17 Blue Sidestep C .25 .50
☐ 18 Gohan's Ready C .25 .50
☐ 19 Goku's Conquering Stance C .50 1.00
☐ 20 Goku's Right Knee Smash C .50 1.00
☐ 21 Namekian Blocking Stance C .25 .50
☐ 22 Namekian Defensive Stance C .25 .50
☐ 23 Namekian Determination C .25 .50
☐ 24 Namekian Dodging Technique C .25 .50
☐ 25 Namekian Energy Absorption C .25 .50
☐ 26 Namekian Wrist Grab C .25 .50
☐ 27 Orange Fist Catch C .25 .50
☐ 28 Orange Palm Blast C .25 .50
☐ 29 Piccolo's Stance C .50 1.00
☐ 30 Red Burning Stance C .50 1.00
☐ 31 Red Energy Charge (C0 .25 .50
☐ 32 Red Power Drain C .25 .50
☐ 33 Red Power Lift C .50 1.00
☐ 34 Blue Battle Readiness C .25 .50
☐ 35 Saiyan Glare C .50 1.00
☐ 36 Saiyan Inspection C .50 1.00
☐ 37 Android 17's Back Bash U .50 1.00
☐ 38 Android 17's Haymaker U .50 1.00
☐ 39 Android 20's Energy Drive U .25 .50
☐ 40 Android 20's Enraged U .25 .50
☐ 41 Android 20's Search Pattern U .50 1.00
☐ 42 Android Attack Drill U .50 1.00
☐ 43 Hyperbolic Time Chamber U .25 .50
☐ 44 Master Roshi's Island U 1.00 2.00
☐ 45 Black Anger Stance U 1.00 2.00
☐ 46 Black Energy Assault U .50 1.00
☐ 47 Black Gut Wrench U .50 1.00
☐ 48 Black Off-Balancing Punch U .50 1.00
☐ 49 Gohan's Peaceful Stance U 1.00 3.00
☐ 50 Black Power Up U .50 1.00
☐ 51 Black Searching Technique U .50 1.00
☐ 52 Black Side Thrust U .50 1.00
☐ 53 Black Studying Drill U .50 1.00
☐ 54 Blue Betrayal U .50 1.00
☐ 55 Blue Holding Drill U .50 1.00
☐ 56 Blue Right Cross U .50 1.00
☐ 57 Blue Rush U 1.00 2.00
☐ 58 Blue Smirk U 1.00 2.00
☐ 59 Bulma's Looking Good U 1.00 2.00
☐ 60 Goku's Training U 1.00 2.00
☐ 61 Namekian Elbow Smash U 1.00 2.00
☐ 62 Namekian Finishing Effort U 1.00 2.00
☐ 63 Namekian Focusing Effort U 1.00 2.00
☐ 64 Namekian Forearm Smash U 1.00 3.00
☐ 65 Orange Aura Drill U 1.00 2.00
☐ 66 Orange Energy Glare U .50 1.00
☐ 67 Orange Energy Phasing Drill U 1.00 3.00
☐ 68 Orange Power Ball U .50 1.00
☐ 69 Orange Power Beam U .50 1.00
☐ 70 Orange Stare Down U .50 1.00
☐ 71 Orange Sword Slash U .50 1.00
☐ 72 Orange Uppercut U 1.00 2.00
☐ 73 Red Dueling Drill U 1.00 2.00
☐ 74 Red Hunting Drill U 1.00 2.00
☐ 75 Red Knee Bash U 1.00 2.00
☐ 76 Saiyan Flying Tackle U .50 1.00
☐ 77 Saiyan Focus U 2.00 4.00
☐ 78 Saiyan Heads Up U .50 1.00
☐ 79 Saiyan Left Kick U 1.00 3.00
☐ 80 Saiyan Wrist Block U .50 1.00
☐ 81 Saiyan Destiny U 1.50 3.00
☐ 82 Senzu Effect U 1.00 2.00
☐ 83 Straining Energy Blast Move U 1.00 2.00
☐ 84 Straining Jump Kick Move U 1.00 2.00
☐ 85 Red Lifting KickU 2.00 4.00
☐ 86 Tien's Mental Conditioning U 1.00 2.00
☐ 87 Tien's Solar Flare U 1.00 2.00
☐ 88 Unexpected Company U 1.00 2.00
☐ 89 Android 17 Smirks R 2.00 4.00
☐ 90 Android 18's Stare Down R 5.00 10.00
☐ 91 Android 19's Distress R 2.00 4.00
☐ 92 City in Turmoil R 2.00 4.00
☐ 93 Winter Countryside R 2.00 4.00
☐ 94 Kami's Floating Island R 1.00 3.00
☐ 95 Defenseless Beach R 2.00 4.00
☐ 96 Dying Planet R 2.00 4.00
☐ 97 Black Mischievous Drill R 4.00 8.00
☐ 98 Black Scout Maneuver R 3.00 6.00
☐ 99 Blue Terror R 2.00 4.00
☐ 100 Goku's Heart Disease R 2.00 4.00
☐ 101 Knockout Drill R 1.00 3.00
☐ 102 Namekian Friendship R 2.00 4.00
☐ 103 Namekian Teamwork R 4.00 8.00
☐ 104 Orange Eye Beam R 2.00 4.00
☐ 105 Orange Rage R 1.50 3.00
☐ 106 Orange Searching Maneuver R 2.00 4.00
☐ 107 Rebellion R 2.00 4.00
☐ 108 Red Counterstrike R 1.00 3.00
☐ 109 Red Tactical Drill R 2.00 4.00
☐ 110 Saiyan Face Stomp R 3.00 5.00

Beckett Dragonball price guide sponsored by wholesalegaming.com

☐ 111 Saiyan Lightning Dodge R 3.00 6.00
☐ 112 Severe Bruises R 2.00 4.00
☐ 113 Tien's Flight R 2.00 4.00
☐ 114 Android 16 (level 1) R 4.00 8.00
☐ 115 Android 17 (level 1) R 4.00 8.00
☐ 116 Android 18 Standing (level 1) R 4.00 8.00
☐ 116 Android 18 Running (level 1) R 3.00 6.00
☐ 117 Android 19 (level 1) R 4.00 8.00
☐ 118 Android 20 (level 1) R 4.00 8.00
☐ 119 Piccolo, The Trained (level 1) R 4.00 8.00
☐ 120 Tien, The Watcher (level 4) R 3.00 6.00
☐ 121 Vegeta, The Ready (level 1) R 4.00 8.00
☐ 122 Yajirobe, The Unstoppable (level 4) R 2.00 4.00
☐ 123 Yamcha Is There (level 4) R 8.00 12.00
☐ 124 The Hero Is Down UR 20.00 40.00
☐ 125 Trunks Guardian Drill UR 30.00 60.00

2001 Dragon Ball Z Cell Preview

Complete Set 6.00 12.00
Inserts in Android Saga Booster Packs

☐ C1 Cell Smiles 1.00 3.00
☐ C2 Cell's Dark Attack 2.00 4.00
☐ C3 Cell's Energy Blast 1.00 3.00
☐ C4 Cell's Defense 2.00 4.00
☐ C5 Awful Abrasions 2.00 4.00
☐ C6 Cell's Threatening Position 2.00 4.00

2001 Dragon Ball Z Cell Saga

Complete Set (200) 175.00 200.00
Booster Box (36 Packs) 45.00 80.00
Booster Pack (12 Cards) 3.00 4.00
Starter Deck 15.00 20.00
Limited Edition cards add 10% to value.

☐ 1 Blue Sliding Dodge C .25 .50
☐ 2 Red Side Step C .25 .50
☐ 3 Blue Fist Strike C .25 .50
☐ 4 Orange Focused Blast C .25 .50
☐ 5 Orange Blast C .25 .50
☐ 6 Saiyan Right Cross C .25 .50
☐ 7 Namekian Energy Ray C .25 .50
☐ 8 Black Fatality C .25 .50
☐ 9 Blue Fight C .25 .50
☐ 10 Saiyan Defensive Stance C .25 .50
☐ 11 Namekian Backflip C .25 .50
☐ 12 Namekian Physical Stance C .25 .50
☐ 13 Namekian Destruction Blast C .25 .50
☐ 14 Saiyan Energy Orb C .50 .75
☐ 15 Saiyan Counterstrike C .25 .50
☐ 16 Saiyan Energy Attack C .25 .50
☐ 17 Blue Backflip C .25 .50
☐ 18 Saiyan Left Hook C .25 .50
☐ 19 Black Power Punch C .25 .50
☐ 20 Black Quick Blast C .25 .50
☐ 21 Orange Sidestep C .25 .50
☐ 22 Namekian Headbutt C .25 .50
☐ 23 Black Twin Blast C .25 .50
☐ 24 Saiyan Palm Blast C .50 1.00
☐ 25 Blue Swift Dodge C .25 .50
☐ 26 Black Forearm Block C .25 .50
☐ 27 Red Flight C .25 .50
☐ 28 Red Defensive Jump C .25 .50
☐ 29 Orange Strike C .25 .50
☐ 30 Black Strike C .25 .50
☐ 31 Orange Energy Deflection C .25 .50
☐ 32 Red Power Strike C .25 .50
☐ 33 Red Face Strike C .25 .50
☐ 34 Namekian Power Kick C .25 .50
☐ 35 Orange Left Kick C .25 .50
☐ 36 Red Driving Jab C .25 .50
☐ 37 Red Crush C .25 .50
☐ 38 Black Neck Break C .25 .50
☐ 39 Dende Dragon Ball 1 C .50 1.00
☐ 40 Dende Dragon Ball 2 C .50 1.00
☐ 41 Saiyan Tripple Kick U .50 1.00
☐ 42 Namekian Fist Block U .50 1.00
☐ 43 Namekian Special Beam Cannon U .50 1.00
☐ 44 Namekian Bash U .50 1.00
☐ 45 Namekian Energy Catch U .50 1.00
☐ 46 Red Offensive Stance U .50 1.00
☐ 47 Blue Evasion U .50 1.00
☐ 48 Orange Energy Focus U 1.00 2.00
☐ 49 Namekian Upward Dash U .50 1.00
☐ 50 Saiyan Left Punch U 1.00 2.00
☐ 51 Black Dodge U .50 1.00
☐ 52 Orange Energy Discharge U .50 1.00
☐ 53 Saiyan Power Kick U .50 1.00
☐ 54 Saiyan Strike U 1.00 2.00
☐ 55 Orange Power Blast U .50 1.00
☐ 56 Blue Palm Shot U .50 1.00
☐ 57 Red Jump U .50 1.00
☐ 58 Namekian Rock Crush U 1.00 2.00
☐ 59 Saiyan High Jump Kick U .50 1.00
☐ 60 Saiyan Flying Kick U .50 1.00
☐ 61 Orange Solar Flare U 1.00 2.00
☐ 62 Red Dodge U .50 1.00
☐ 63 Orange Sideshot U 1.00 2.00
☐ 64 Black Side Block U .50 1.00
☐ 65 Blue Blackflip U .50 1.00
☐ 66 Blue Wrist Block U .50 1.00
☐ 67 Orange Ally Drill U .50 1.00
☐ 68 Heroes Discovery U .50 1.00
☐ 69 Piccolo's Determination U .50 1.00
☐ 70 The Car U .50 1.00
☐ 71 Krillin's Thoughts U .50 1.00
☐ 72 Capsule Corp. Ship U .50 1.00
☐ 73 Dende Dragon Ball 3 U 2.00 4.00
☐ 74 Dende Dragon Ball 4 U 2.00 4.00
☐ 75 Dende Dragon Ball 5 U 2.00 4.00
☐ 76 Exuastion U .50 1.00
☐ 77 Trunks Prepares U .50 1.00
☐ 78 Smokescreen U .50 1.00
☐ 79 Time Chamber Training U .50 1.00
☐ 80 Gohan's Stance U 1.00 2.00
☐ 81 Grappling Stance U .50 1.00
☐ 82 Cell's Android Absorbtion U 1.00 2.00
☐ 83 Ally Rescue U .50 1.00
☐ 84 Yamcha, the Friend (Level 1) U .50 1.00
☐ 85 Yamcha, the Battler (Level 2) U .50 1.00
☐ 86 Tien, the Swift (Level 1) U .50 1.00
☐ 87 Tien, the Leader (Level 3) U 1.00 2.00
☐ 88 Yamcha, the Powerful (Level 3) U .50 1.00
☐ 89 Krillin, the Friend (Level 1) U .50 1.00
☐ 90 Android 19 (Level 1) U 2.00 4.00
☐ 91 Tien's Tri-Beam U .50 1.00
☐ 92 Orange Deflection U .50 1.00
☐ 93 Krillin's Solar Flare U 1.00 2.00
☐ 94 Namekian Side Kick U .50 1.00
☐ 95 Android 19, Recalled (Level 2) U 2.00 4.00
☐ 96 Namekian Energy Deflection U 1.00 2.00
☐ 97 Krillin, the Champion (Level 3) U 1.00 2.00
☐ 98 Android 19, Recharged (Level 3) U 1.00 2.00
☐ 99 Krillin, the Hero (Level 2) U 1.00 2.00
☐ 100 Speaking With The King Drill U 1.00 2.00
☐ 101 Orange Goku's Kamehameha U 1.00 2.00
☐ 102 Straining Hand Blast Move U 1.00 2.00
☐ 103 Tien, the Quick (Level 2) U .50 1.00
☐ 104 Blue Straight Jab U .50 1.00
☐ 105 Namekian Power Up U 1.00 2.00
☐ 106 Android 16 Detects U .50 1.00
☐ 107 Orange Gaze U 1.00 2.00
☐ 108 Namekian Energy Beam U .50 1.00
☐ 109 Bulma, the Expert (Level 3) U 1.00 3.00
☐ 110 Krillin Asks For Help U .50 1.00
☐ 111 Namekian Regeneration U 1.00 2.00
☐ 112 Namekian Dash Attack R 2.00 4.00
☐ 113 Madness R 2.00 4.00
☐ 114 Chi-Chi, the Wife (Level 3) R 2.00 4.00
☐ 115 Focusing R 2.00 4.00
☐ 116 Stunned R 2.00 4.00
☐ 117 Blue Assistance Drill R 2.00 4.00
☐ 118 Mr. Popo's Calming R 2.00 4.00
☐ 119 Namekian Preparation Drill R 2.00 4.00
☐ 120 Krillin Unleashed R 2.00 4.00
☐ 121 Dende Dragon Ball 6 R 3.00 6.00
☐ 122 Dende Dragon Ball 7 R 3.00 6.00
☐ 123 Cell's Power Drain R 2.00 4.00
☐ 124 Saiyan Power Blast R 3.00 6.00
☐ 125 Run Away R 2.00 4.00
☐ 126 Blue Style Mastery R 2.00 4.00
☐ 127 Trunks, the Powerful (Level 4) R 3.00 6.00
☐ 128 Blueprints R 2.00 4.00
☐ 129 Black Style Mastery R 4.00 8.00
☐ 130 Saiyan Style Mastery R 4.00 8.00
☐ 131 Red Style Mastery R 4.00 8.00
☐ 132 Piccolo, the Namek (Level 4) R 3.00 6.00
☐ 133 Android 18 (Level 4) 4.00 8.00
☐ 134 Gohan, the Winner (Level 5) R 5.00 8.00
☐ 135 Goku (Level 4) R 5.00 10.00
☐ 136 Cell, the Master (Level 5) R 4.00 8.00
☐ 137 Cell, the Destroyer (Level 4) R 4.00 8.00
☐ 138 Gohan, Ascendant (Level 4) R 5.00 8.00
☐ 139 Krillin, the Mighty (Level 4) R 3.00 6.00
☐ 140 Orange Style Mastery R 4.00 8.00
☐ 141 Namekian Style Mastery R 3.00 6.00
☐ 142 Red Feint R 2.00 4.00
☐ 143 Blue Elbow Drop R 1.00 3.00
☐ 144 Blue Driving Punch Drill R 2.00 4.00
☐ 145 Blue Left Cross Punch R 1.00 3.00
☐ 146 Orange City Destruction R 2.00 4.00
☐ 147 Orange Halting Drill R 3.00 6.00
☐ 148 Saiyan Offensive Rush R 3.00 6.00
☐ 149 Namekian Fusion R 2.00 4.00
☐ 150 Android 16's Battle Charge R 2.00 4.00
☐ 151 Namekian Fist Smash R 2.00 4.00
☐ 152 Android 16's Rage R 2.00 4.00
☐ 153 Namekian Energy Focus R 2.00 4.00
☐ 154 Vegeta, Ascendant (Level 4) R 6.00 12.00
☐ 155 Saiyan Rapid Fire R 3.00 6.00
☐ 156 Blue Head Charge R 2.00 4.00
☐ 157 Z Warriors Gather UR 25.00 50.00
☐ 158 Cell's Presence UR 25.00 50.00
☐ 159 Vegeta, the Revitalized (lvl 5) UR 40.00 75.00
☐ 160 Goku, the All Powerful (lvl 5) UR 40.00 75.00
☐ 161 Goku, the Hero (Level 1) P 3.00 6.00
☐ 162 Goku, the Saiyan (Level 2 P 3.00 6.00
☐ 163 Goku, the Perfect Warrior (Level 3) P 4.00 8.00
☐ 164 Gohan, the Champion (Level 1) P 3.00 6.00
☐ 165 Gohan, the Swift (Level 2) P 3.00 6.00
☐ 166 Gohan, the Mighty (Level 3) P 3.00 6.00
☐ 167 Vegeta, the Powerful (Level 1) P 3.00 6.00
☐ 168 Vegeta, the All Powerful (Level 2) P 3.00 6.00
☐ 169 Vegeta, the Prince (Level 3) P 4.00 8.00
☐ 170 Piccolo, the Warrior (Level 1) P 3.00 6.00
☐ 171 Piccolo, the Champion (Level 2) P 3.00 6.00
☐ 172 Piccolo, the Destroyer (Level 3) P 4.00 8.00
☐ 173 Trunks, the Swift (Level 1) P 3.00 6.00
☐ 174 Trunks, the Quick (Level 2) P 3.00 6.00
☐ 175 Trunks, the Mighty (Level 3) P 4.00 8.00
☐ 176 Android 16 (Level 1) P 2.00 4.00
☐ 177 Android 16, the Machine (Level 2) P 3.00 6.00
☐ 178 Android 16, the Battler (Level 3) P 2.00 4.00
☐ 179 Android 17 (Level 1) P 3.00 6.00
☐ 180 Android 17, the Leader (Level 2) P 4.00 8.00
☐ 181 Android 17, the Fighter (Level 3) P 3.00 6.00
☐ 182 Android 18 (Level 1) P 3.00 6.00
☐ 183 Android 18, the Model (Level 2) P 4.00 6.00
☐ 184 Android 18, the Machine (Level 3) P 3.00 6.00
☐ 185 Android 20 (Level 1) P 3.00 6.00
☐ 186 Android 20, the Doctor (Level 2) P 3.00 6.00
☐ 187 Android 20, Schemer (Level 3) P 3.00 6.00
☐ 188 Cell, Stage One (Level 1) P 3.00 6.00
☐ 189 Cell, Stage Two (Level 2) P 3.00 6.00
☐ 190 Cell, Perfect (Level 3) P 4.00 8.00
☐ 191 Goku, Earth's Hero (Level 3) HT 4.00 8.00
☐ 192 Gohan, Super Saiyan (Level 3) HT 4.00 8.00
☐ 193 Vegeta, the Last Prince (Level 3) HT 4.00 8.00
☐ 194 Piccolo, Earth's Protector (lvl 3) HT 3.00 6.00
☐ 195 Trunks, Time's Hero (Level 3) HT 4.00 8.00
☐ 196 Android 16, the Fighter (Level 3) HT 5.00 8.00
☐ 197 Android 17, the Destroyer (lvl 3) HT 3.00 6.00
☐ 198 Android 18, the Smart One (lvl 3) HT 5.00 8.00
☐ 199 Android 20, the Destructor (lvl 3) HT 4.00 8.00
☐ 200 Cell, the Perfect Warrior (Level 3) HT 7.00 14.00

2002 Dragon Ball Z Cell Games Saga Preview

Complete Set (6) 5.00 10.00
Inserts in Android Saga Booster Packs.

☐ 1 Cell's Draining .50 1.00
☐ 2 Cell's Arena 1.00 2.00
☐ 3 Cell's Last Strike 1.00 2.00
☐ 4 They're All There 1.00 2.00
☐ 5 Heroes Battleground 2.00 4.00
☐ 6 Cell's Style 2.00 4.00

2002 Dragon Ball Z Cell Games Saga

Complete Set (125) 150.00 200.00
Unopened Box (36 Packs) 50.00 70.00
Unopened Pack (12 cards) 3.00 4.00
*Foil: .75X to 1.5X Basic Cards

☐ 1 Black Explosion C .25 .50
☐ 2 Black Fist Lock C .25 .50
☐ 3 Black Preparation C .25 .50
☐ 4 Blue Forced Punch C .25 .50
☐ 5 Blue Thrusted Blast C .25 .50
☐ 6 Deadly Attack C .25 .50
☐ 7 Flashback C .25 .50
☐ 8 Gohan's Kick C .50 1.00
☐ 9 Gohan's Strike C .50 1.00
☐ 10 Namekian Crushing Hold C .25 .50
☐ 11 Namekian Fist Dodge C .25 .50
☐ 12 Namekian Flying Kick C .25 .50
☐ 13 Namekian Foot Lunge C .25 .50
☐ 14 Orange Dragon Aid C .25 .50
☐ 15 Orange Uniting Strike C .25 .50
☐ 16 Power Boost C .25 .50
☐ 17 Red Anger Rising C .50 1.00
☐ 18 Red Drop Kick C 1.00 2.00
☐ 19 Red Duck C .25 .50
☐ 20 Red Fist Lunge C .25 .50
☐ 21 Red Flying Attack C .50 1.00
☐ 22 Red Shifty Maneuver C .25 .50
☐ 23 Saiyan Ally Strike C 1.00 2.00
☐ 24 Saiyan Blocking Technique C .25 .50
☐ 25 Saiyan Energy Surprise C .25 .50
☐ 26 Saiyan Fist Attack C .50 1.00
☐ 27 Saiyan Knee Block C .25 .50
☐ 28 Saiyan Power Rush C .25 .50
☐ 29 Saiyan Triple Blast C .25 .50
☐ 30 Strength Training C .25 .50
☐ 31 Time to Party C .50 1.00
☐ 32 Black Anticipation Drill U .50 1.00
☐ 33 Black Blasting Beam U .50 1.00
☐ 34 Double Black Attack Drill U .50 1.00
☐ 35 Black Hand Energy Blast U 1.00 2.00
☐ 36 Black Face Slap U .50 1.00
☐ 37 Black Recovery U .50 1.00
☐ 38 Black Saving Drill U .50 1.00
☐ 39 Black Shifting Drill U 1.00 2.00
☐ 40 Black Wrist Block U .50 1.00
☐ 41 Blue Arm Blast U .50 1.00
☐ 42 Blue Defensive Effect U .50 1.00
☐ 43 Blue Energy Arrow U .50 1.00
☐ 44 Blue Energy Blast U .50 1.00
☐ 45 Blue Prepared Drill U .50 1.00
☐ 46 Blue Recovery Drill U .50 1.00
☐ 47 Blue Pivot Kick U .50 1.00
☐ 48 Blue Stamina Drill U .50 1.00
☐ 49 Blue Total Resistance U .50 1.00
☐ 50 Bracing for Impact U .50 1.00
☐ 51 Caught in the Act U .50 1.00
☐ 52 Cell's Power Burst U 2.00 4.00
☐ 53 Cell's Instant Transmission U 1.00 2.00
☐ 54 Cell's Swift Strike U 1.00 2.00
☐ 55 Energy Rush U .50 1.00
☐ 56 Everyone is Attacked! U .50 1.00
☐ 57 Fighting in Cover U .50 1.00
☐ 58 Cell's Backslap U 1.00 2.00
☐ 59 Namekian Restoration U .50 1.00
☐ 60 Namekian Dragon Blast U .50 1.00
☐ 61 Namekian Energy Spike U .50 1.00
☐ 62 Namekian Face Smack U .50 1.00
☐ 63 Namekian Piercing Beam U .50 1.00
☐ 64 Namekian Power Stance Drill U 1.00 2.00
☐ 65 Namekian Quick Blast U .50 1.00
☐ 66 Namekian Ready Drill U .50 1.00
☐ 67 Namekian Right Cross U .50 1.00
☐ 68 Namekian Scouting U .50 1.00
☐ 69 Orange Beatdown U 1.00 2.00
☐ 70 Orange Burning Aura Drill U 1.00 2.00
☐ 71 Orange Energy Concentration U 2.00 4.00
☐ 72 Orange Energy Setup U .50 1.00
☐ 73 Orange Energy Shot U .50 1.00
☐ 74 Orange Fateful Attack U .50 1.00
☐ 75 Orange Aggressive Technique U 1.00 2.00
☐ 76 Orange Steady Drill U 1.00 2.00
☐ 77 Piccolo's Fury U .50 1.00
☐ 78 Prepared Dodge U .50 1.00
☐ 79 Protective Shelter U .50 1.00
☐ 80 Quick Combat Drill U 1.00 2.00
☐ 81 Red Energy Drill U 1.00 2.00
☐ 82 Red Energy Surprise U 1.00 2.00
☐ 83 Red Forward Stance Drill U 1.00 2.00
☐ 84 Red Overhand Slash U 1.00 2.00
☐ 85 Red Power Punch U 2.00 4.00
☐ 86 Red Shielded Strike U 1.00 2.00
☐ 87 Saiyan Energy Drill U .50 1.00
☐ 88 Saiyan Protectant Drill U .50 1.00
☐ 89 Saiyan Pride U .50 1.00
☐ 90 Senzu Drill U 1.00 2.00
☐ 91 Something Dangerous is Coming! U .50 1.00
☐ 92 Tien's Block U .50 1.00
☐ 93 Blue Windup Blast R 2.00 4.00
☐ 94 Cell Jr. 1 (Level 1) R 3.00 6.00
☐ 95 Injured R 1.00 3.00
☐ 96 Saiyan Face Smash R 1.00 3.00
☐ 97 Surprise Hit R 1.00 3.00
☐ 98 Cell Jr. 2 (Level 1) R 3.00 6.00
☐ 99 Goku's Farewell R 4.00 8.00
☐ 100 Korin's Tower R 1.00 3.00
☐ 101 The Power of the Dragon R 3.00 5.00
☐ 102 Megaton Bull Crusher R 2.00 4.00
☐ 103 Orange Energy Smash R 2.00 4.00
☐ 104 Blue Fist Smash R 1.00 3.00
☐ 105 Double Teaming R 1.00 3.00
☐ 106 Straining Rebirth Move R 1.00 3.00
☐ 107 Android 18's Effect R 2.00 4.00
☐ 108 Aura Clash R 3.00 6.00
☐ 109 Group Attack R 3.00 6.00
☐ 110 Orange Focused Attack R 1.00 3.00
☐ 111 Caught Off Guard Drill R 3.00 6.00
☐ 112 Vegeta's Anger Drill R 2.00 4.00
☐ 113 Who's da Man! R 3.00 6.00
☐ 114 Dende (Level 2) R 2.00 4.00
☐ 115 Cell Jr. 1 (Level 2) R 3.00 6.00
☐ 116 Goku's Dragon Ball Quest R 2.00 4.00
☐ 117 Chazke Village R 1.00 3.00
☐ 118 Vegeta's Surprised R 2.00 4.00
☐ 119 Gohan's Elbow Block R 2.00 4.00
☐ 120 Straining Destruction Move R 2.00 4.00
☐ 121 Cosmic Backlash R 3.00 6.00
☐ 122 Chiaotzu (Level 2) R 3.00 6.00
☐ 123 Dragon's Victory R 2.00 4.00
☐ 124 Trunks, the Battler UR 50.00 80.00
☐ 125 Piccolo, the Defender (Level 5) UR 40.00 75.00

2002 Dragon Ball Z Cell Games Saga - Tuff Enuff

Complete Set (22) 20.00 40.00
Inserts in Cell Games Saga Boosters

☐ TF1 Black Smackdown 2.00 4.00
☐ TF2 Blue Smackdown 2.00 4.00
☐ TF3 Namekian Smackdown 1.00 2.00
☐ TF4 Orange Smackdown 2.00 4.00
☐ TF5 Red Smackdown 2.00 4.00
☐ TF6 Saiyan Smackdown 2.00 4.00

TCG/CCG

- ❑ TF7 Garlic Jr.'s Palm Blast 1.00 3.00
- ❑ TF8 Loser With Style Drill 2.00 4.00
- ❑ TF9 Krillin's Coolness Drill 2.00 4.00
- ❑ TF10 Are You Tuff Enough??? 2.00 4.00
- ❑ TF11 Bubbles Drill 1.50 3.00
- ❑ TF12 Namekain Side Swipe 1.00 3.00
- ❑ TF13 Orange Energy Stance 2.00 4.00
- ❑ TF14 Namekian Charging Stance 1.00 3.00
- ❑ TF15 Blue Show Off 1.00 3.00
- ❑ TF16 Straining Double Strike Move 2.00 4.00
- ❑ TF17 Saiyan Anger Strike 2.00 4.00
- ❑ TF18 Black Energy Stance 2.00 4.00
- ❑ TF19 Blue Goku's Power Kick 2.00 4.00
- ❑ TF20 Blue Frustration Drill 2.00 4.00
- ❑ TF21 Black Transformation (CC Pwr Pk) 3.00 5.00
- ❑ TF22 Tien and Yamcha Strike (CC Pwr Pk) 3.00 5.00

2002 Dragon Ball Z World Games Saga Preview

Complete Set (7) 10.00 20.00
Inserts in Cell Games Saga Booster Packs

- ❑ 1 Celestial Games Begin C 1.00 3.00
- ❑ 2 Goku Helping Drill C 1.00 3.00
- ❑ 3 Gohan Meditates U 2.00 4.00
- ❑ 4 Gathering of Warriors U 1.50 2.50
- ❑ 5 Brothers in Training R 2.00 4.00
- ❑ 6 Chi-Chi on Attack! R 2.00 4.00
- ❑ 7 Learning the Moves (CC Pwr Pk) 3.00 6.00

2002 Dragon Ball Z World Games Saga

Complete Set (201) 200.00 300.00
Booster Box (36 Packs) 45.00 70.00
Booster Pack (12 Cards) 3.00 3.75
Celestial Fighter Starter Deck 10.00 15.00
*Foil: .75X to 1.5X Basic Cards

- ❑ 1 Black Back Power Hit C .25 .50
- ❑ 2 Black Defensive Stance C .25 .50
- ❑ 3 Black Elbow Counter C .25 .50
- ❑ 4 Black Light Jab C .25 .50
- ❑ 5 Black Quick Strike C .25 .50
- ❑ 6 Black Reversal Strike C .25 .50
- ❑ 7 Blue Defensive Stance C .25 .50
- ❑ 8 Blue Fire Kick C .25 .50
- ❑ 9 Blue Flying Kick C .25 .50
- ❑ 10 Blue Forearm Block C .25 .50
- ❑ 11 Blue Right Power Strike C .25 .50
- ❑ 12 Blue Sneak Attack C .25 .50
- ❑ 13 Blue Thunder Flash C .25 .50
- ❑ 14 Goten's Focused Blast C .25 .50
- ❑ 15 Earth Dragon Ball 3 C .50 1.00
- ❑ 16 Namekian Battle Stance C .25 .50
- ❑ 17 Namekian Elbow Strike C .25 .50
- ❑ 18 Namekian Halting Stance C .25 .50
- ❑ 19 Namekian Light Jab C .25 .50
- ❑ 20 Namekian Surprise Attack C .25 .50
- ❑ 21 Namekian Throw C .25 .50
- ❑ 22 Orange Flying Drop Kick C .25 .50
- ❑ 23 Orange Gut Wrench C .25 .50
- ❑ 24 Orange Knockout C .25 .50
- ❑ 25 Orange Palm Block C .25 .50
- ❑ 26 Red Creative Block C .25 .50
- ❑ 27 Red Energy Defensive Stance C .25 .50
- ❑ 28 Red Flying Kick C .25 .50
- ❑ 29 Red Goku's Energy Blast C .25 .50
- ❑ 30 Red Kid Trunks' Blast C .25 .50
- ❑ 31 Saiyan Abduction C .25 .50
- ❑ 32 Saiyan Defensive Sphere C .25 .50
- ❑ 33 Saiyan Energy Ball C .25 .50
- ❑ 34 Saiyan Readied Attack C .25 .50
- ❑ 35 Straining Cry Baby Move C .25 .50
- ❑ 36 Straining Diving Punch Move C .25 .50
- ❑ 37 Straining Reversal Move C .25 .50
- ❑ 38 The Middle of Nowhere C .25 .50
- ❑ 39 Kid Trunks' Palm Blast C .25 .50
- ❑ 40 Black Back Breaker U .50 1.00
- ❑ 41 Black Driving Elbow Strike U .50 1.00
- ❑ 42 Black Duck U .50 1.00
- ❑ 43 Black Fist Catch U .50 1.00
- ❑ 44 Black Majin Blast U .50 1.00
- ❑ 45 Black Point Blank Kamehameha U 1.00 2.00
- ❑ 46 Black Super Kick U .50 1.00
- ❑ 47 Black Triple Team U .50 1.00
- ❑ 48 Black Videl's Power Kick U .50 1.00
- ❑ 49 Blue Back Kick U .50 1.00
- ❑ 50 Blue Energy Transformation U .50 1.00
- ❑ 51 Blue Heat Seeking Blast U .50 1.00
- ❑ 52 Blue Lightning Block U .50 1.00
- ❑ 53 Blue Quick Blast U .50 1.00
- ❑ 54 Blue Rebound U .50 1.00
- ❑ 55 Blue Videl's Knee Bash U .75 1.50
- ❑ 56 Chapuchai's Multiform U .50 1.00
- ❑ 57 Goku"s Quickness Drill U 1.00 2.00
- ❑ 58 Hercule's Drop Kick U .50 1.00
- ❑ 59 Hero's Drill U .50 1.00
- ❑ 60 Jackie Chun's Energy Attack U 1.00 2.00
- ❑ 61 Like Father, Like Son U .50 1.00
- ❑ 62 Majin Fist Block U .50 1.00
- ❑ 63 Majin Display of Power U 1.00 2.00
- ❑ 64 Majin Knee Strike U .50 1.00
- ❑ 65 Majin Overwhelming Attack U .50 1.00
- ❑ 66 Namekian Combo U .50 1.00
- ❑ 67 Namekian Double Blast U .50 1.00
- ❑ 68 Namekian Ducking Technique U .50 1.00
- ❑ 69 Namekian Eye Beam U .50 1.00
- ❑ 70 Namekian Final Flash U .50 1.00
- ❑ 71 Namekian Flight U .50 1.00
- ❑ 72 Namekian Focused Blast U .50 1.00
- ❑ 73 Namekian Focused Jab U 1.00 2.00
- ❑ 74 Namekian Focused Kick U 1.00 2.00
- ❑ 75 Namekian Heat Seeking Blast U .50 1.00
- ❑ 76 Namekian Knee Strike U .50 1.00
- ❑ 77 Namekian Offense U .50 1.00
- ❑ 78 Namekian Pikkon's Defense U .50 1.00
- ❑ 79 Namekian Swift Strike U .50 1.00
- ❑ 80 Namekian Tornado Attack U .50 1.00
- ❑ 81 Orange Close Call U 1.00 2.00
- ❑ 82 Orange Direct Strike U .50 1.00
- ❑ 83 Orange Diving Attack U 1.00 2.00
- ❑ 84 Orange Friendship U .50 1.00
- ❑ 85 Orange Light Jab U .50 1.00
- ❑ 86 Orange Overpowering Attack U 1.00 2.00
- ❑ 87 Orange Power Grip U .50 1.00
- ❑ 88 Orange Power Kick U 1.00 2.00
- ❑ 89 Orange Power Stance U .50 1.00
- ❑ 90 Orange Right Cross U .50 1.00
- ❑ 91 Arqua's Arena U .50 1.00
- ❑ 92 Orange Videl's Jump Kick U .75 1.50
- ❑ 93 Pikkon's Truce U .50 1.00
- ❑ 94 Red Aggression U .50 1.00
- ❑ 95 Red Double Strike U .50 1.00
- ❑ 96 Red Energy Drill U .50 1.00
- ❑ 97 Red Energy Focus U 1.00 2.00
- ❑ 98 Red Heat Seeking Blast U .50 1.00
- ❑ 99 Krillin, the Father U 1.00 2.00
- ❑ 100 Red Light Jab U .50 1.00
- ❑ 101 Red Lightning Strike U .50 1.00
- ❑ 102 Red Solar Flare U .50 1.00
- ❑ 103 Red Trap U .50 1.00
- ❑ 104 Red Videl's Elbow Smash U .50 1.00
- ❑ 105 Saiyan Discharge U .50 1.00
- ❑ 106 Saiyan Finger Block U .50 1.00
- ❑ 107 Saiyan Flight U 1.00 2.00
- ❑ 108 Saiyan Focused Block U .50 1.00
- ❑ 109 Saiyan Heritage Drill U .50 1.00
- ❑ 110 Saiyan Jump Shot U .50 1.00
- ❑ 111 Saiyan Kamehameha U .50 1.00
- ❑ 112 Saiyan Light Jab U .50 1.00
- ❑ 113 Saiyan Side Step U .50 1.00
- ❑ 114 Saiyan Swift Kick U .50 1.00
- ❑ 115 Saiyan Uppercut U .50 1.00
- ❑ 116 Straining Counterstrike Move U .50 1.00
- ❑ 117 Straining Focused Move U .50 1.00
- ❑ 118 The Truck U 1.00 2.00
- ❑ 119 Black Style Mastery R 5.00 10.00
- ❑ 120 Blue Style Mastery R 5.00 10.00
- ❑ 121 Capsule Corp. R 1.00 3.00
- ❑ 122 Chapuchai R 2.00 4.00
- ❑ 123 Chapuchai, the Tiny R 2.00 4.00
- ❑ 124 Chapuchai, the Tenacious R 2.00 4.00
- ❑ 125 East Kai Sensei R 5.00 8.00
- ❑ 126 Freestyle Mastery R 6.00 10.00
- ❑ 127 Froug R 2.00 4.00
- ❑ 128 Froug, the Underdog R 2.00 4.00
- ❑ 129 Froug, the Huge R 2.00 4.00
- ❑ 130 Gohan, the Energized R 4.00 8.00
- ❑ 131 Goku, the King's Pupil R 4.00 8.00
- ❑ 132 Grand Kai R 5.00 8.00
- ❑ 133 Red Jump Kick R 4.00 8.00
- ❑ 134 Krillin, the Husband R 2.00 4.00
- ❑ 135 Krillin, the Great R 2.00 4.00
- ❑ 136 Majin Spopovich R 3.00 6.00
- ❑ 137 Majin Spopovich, the Empowered R 3.00 6.00
- ❑ 138 Majin Spopovich, the Revitalized R 3.00 6.00
- ❑ 139 Namekian Style Mastery R 3.00 6.00
- ❑ 140 North Kai Sensei R 4.00 8.00
- ❑ 141 Olibu, the Honorable R 3.00 6.00
- ❑ 142 Orange Style Mastery R 3.00 6.00
- ❑ 143 Torbie, the Silent R 2.00 4.00
- ❑ 144 Torbie, the Prepared R 2.00 4.00
- ❑ 145 Torbie, Unleashed R 2.00 4.00
- ❑ 146 Pikkon, the Hero R 4.00 6.00
- ❑ 147 Red Style Mastery R 3.00 6.00
- ❑ 148 Saiyan Style Mastery R 4.00 8.00
- ❑ 149 South Kai Sensei R 4.00 8.00
- ❑ 150 Tapkar R 3.00 6.00
- ❑ 151 Tapkar, the Speedy R 3.00 6.00
- ❑ 152 Tapkar, the Fastest R 3.00 6.00
- ❑ 153 Arqua, the Water Champion R 2.00 4.00
- ❑ 154 Arqua, the Agile R 2.00 4.00
- ❑ 155 Arqua, Unleashed R 2.00 4.00
- ❑ 156 West Kai Sensei R 4.00 8.00
- ❑ 157 World Tournament R 4.00 8.00
- ❑ 158 Evil Presence Drill UR 15.00 30.00
- ❑ 159 Goku, the Galaxy's Hero UR 30.00 60.00
- ❑ 160 Goku's Blinding Strike UR 25.00 50.00
- ❑ 161 Pikkon, the Prized Fighter UR 25.00 50.00
- ❑ 162 Vegeta, the Proud (Level 1) P 3.00 6.00
- ❑ 163 Vegeta, the Mighty (Level 2) P 3.00 6.00
- ❑ 164 Vegeta, the Dark Hero (Level 3) P 3.00 6.00
- ❑ 165 Vegeta (Level 1) HT 4.00 8.00
- ❑ 166 Gohan, the Great Saiyaman (Level 1) P 1.00 3.00
- ❑ 167 Gohan, the Protector (Level 2) P 1.00 3.00
- ❑ 168 Gohan, the Righteous (Level 3) P 1.00 3.00
- ❑ 169 Gohan (Level 1) HT 3.00 6.00
- ❑ 170 Goku, the Warrior (Level 1) P 3.00 6.00
- ❑ 171 Goku, the Competitor (Level 2) P 3.00 6.00
- ❑ 172 Goku, the Proud (Level 3) P 3.00 6.00
- ❑ 173 Goku (Level 1) HT 6.00 12.00
- ❑ 174 Goten, the Playful (Level 1) P 3.00 6.00
- ❑ 175 Goten, the Brother (Level 2) P 3.00 6.00
- ❑ 176 Goten, the Young Saiyan (Level 3) P 3.00 6.00
- ❑ 177 Goten (Level 1) HT 4.00 8.00
- ❑ 178 Kid Trunks, the Junior Champion (Level 1) P2.00 4.00
- ❑ 179 Kid Trunks, the Boastful (Level 2) P 2.00 4.00
- ❑ 180 Kid Trunks, the Young Saiyan (Level 3) P 2.00 4.00
- ❑ 181 Kid Trunks (Level 1) HT 3.00 6.00
- ❑ 182 Maraikoh, the Vicious (Level 1) P 2.00 4.00
- ❑ 183 Maraikoh, the Strong (Level 2) P 2.00 4.00
- ❑ 184 Maraikoh, the Mighty (Level 3) P 2.00 4.00
- ❑ 185 Maraikoh (Level 1) HT 2.00 4.00
- ❑ 186 Olibu, the Magical Hero (Level 1) P 2.00 4.00
- ❑ 187 Olibu, the Courageous (Level 2) P 2.00 4.00
- ❑ 188 Olibu, the Powerful (Level 3) P 2.00 4.00
- ❑ 189 Olibu (Level 1) HT 2.00 4.00
- ❑ 190 Pikkon, the Silent (Level 1) P 1.00 3.00
- ❑ 191 Pikkon, the Serious (Level 2) P 1.00 3.00
- ❑ 192 Pikkon, the Powerful (Level 3) P 1.00 3.00
- ❑ 193 Pikkon (Level 1) HT 2.00 4.00
- ❑ 194 Piccolo, the Majunior (Level 1) P 3.00 5.00
- ❑ 195 Piccolo, the Mentor (Level 2) P 3.00 5.00
- ❑ 196 Piccolo, the Former Guardian (Level 3) P 3.00 5.00
- ❑ 197 Piccolo (Level 1) HT 5.00 8.00
- ❑ 198 Videl, the Student (Level 1) P 3.00 4.00
- ❑ 199 Videl, the Protector (Level 2) P 3.00 4.00
- ❑ 200 Videl, the Determined (Level 3) P 3.00 4.00
- ❑ 201 Videl (Level 1) HT 4.00 6.00

2002 Babidi Saga Preview Cards

Inserts in World Games Saga Booster Packs

- ❑ 1 Face Off (C) 1.00 3.00
- ❑ 2 Righteous Strike (C) 1.00 3.00
- ❑ 3 Evil's True Face (U) 2.00 4.00
- ❑ 4 Energy Drain (U) 2.00 4.00
- ❑ 5 Supreme Kai's Power Hold (R) 5.00 10.00
- ❑ 6 Supreme Kai (R) 7.00 14.00
- ❑ 7 Majin Vegeta, the Dark Prince (R) 8.00 15.00

2003 Dragon Ball Z Babidi Saga

Complete Set (123) 150.00 225.00
Booster Box (36 Packs) 45.00 80.00
Booster Pack (12 Cards) 3.00 4.00
*Foil: .75X to 1.5X Basic Cards

- ❑ 1 Android 18's Iron Defense C .25 .50
- ❑ 2 Black Chained Strike C .75 1.50
- ❑ 3 Black Palm Reversal C .25 .50
- ❑ 4 Black Personal Smack C .50 1.00
- ❑ 5 Black Power Catch C .25 .50
- ❑ 6 Black Quick Kick C .25 .50
- ❑ 7 Blue Cape Swing C .25 .50
- ❑ 8 Blue Reflexes C .25 .50
- ❑ 9 Blue Shifting Maneuver C .25 .50
- ❑ 10 Blue Speediness C .25 .50
- ❑ 11 Combo C .50 1.00
- ❑ 12 Entering the Arena C .25 .50
- ❑ 13 Hercule's Power Stance C .25 .50
- ❑ 14 Heroic Shoulder Slam C .25 .50
- ❑ 15 Majin Death Focus C .25 .50
- ❑ 16 Orange Crushing Kick C .25 .50
- ❑ 17 Orange Dodge C .25 .50
- ❑ 18 Orange Elbow Smash C .25 .50
- ❑ 19 Orange Firebreath C .25 .50
- ❑ 20 Orange Right Punch C .25 .50
- ❑ 21 Red Forearm Block C .25 .50
- ❑ 22 Red Resistance C .25 .50
- ❑ 23 Red Slide C .25 .50
- ❑ 24 Red Thrusting Beam C .25 .50
- ❑ 25 Red Uppercut C .25 .50
- ❑ 26 Saiyan Duck C .25 .50
- ❑ 27 Saiyan Energy Rapture C .25 .50
- ❑ 28 Saiyan Might C .25 .50
- ❑ 29 Saiyan Power Block C .25 .50
- ❑ 30 Saiyan Prepared Smash C .25 .50
- ❑ 31 Straining Counter Punch U .25 .50
- ❑ 32 Android 18's Kneeing Drill U .25 .50
- ❑ 33 Android 18's Pressure Routine U .25 .50
- ❑ 34 Android 18's Throwing Drill U .25 .50
- ❑ 35 Majin Babidi's Ship U .25 .50
- ❑ 36 Black Backstab U .25 .50
- ❑ 37 Black Conservation Drill U .25 .50
- ❑ 38 Black Face Crush U .25 .50
- ❑ 39 Black Pummeling Strike U .25 .50
- ❑ 40 Black Reverse Kick U .25 .50
- ❑ 41 Black Surprise Maneuver U .25 .50
- ❑ 42 Blue Destruction Beam U .25 .50
- ❑ 43 Blue Leverage U .25 .50
- ❑ 44 Blue Palm Sphere U .25 .50
- ❑ 45 Blue Prevention Drill U .25 .50
- ❑ 46 Blue Torso Strike U .25 .50
- ❑ 47 Majin Vegeta U 3.00 6.00
- ❑ 48 Chi-Chi's Cheering Drill U .50 1.00
- ❑ 49 Majin Dabura's Offensive Leverage U .50 1.00
- ❑ 50 Majin Dabura's Petrifying Spit U .50 1.00
- ❑ 51 Energy Empowerment Drill U .50 1.00
- ❑ 52 Energy Storage Drill U .50 1.00
- ❑ 53 Goku's Berserk U .50 1.00
- ❑ 54 Goku's Shifted Balance Drill U .50 1.00
- ❑ 55 Goten's Flying Drill U .50 1.00
- ❑ 56 Hercule, the World Champion U .50 1.00
- ❑ 57 Majin Vegeta, the Evil U 2.00 4.00
- ❑ 58 In the Grove U .50 1.00
- ❑ 59 Majin Buu's Egg Drill U .50 1.00
- ❑ 60 Majin Defense Drill U .50 1.00
- ❑ 61 Majin Lightning Hit U .50 1.00
- ❑ 62 Majin Power Deflection U .50 1.00
- ❑ 63 Majin Power Drill U .50 1.00
- ❑ 64 Majin Power Shift U .50 1.00
- ❑ 65 Majin Pui Pui U .50 1.00
- ❑ 66 Majin Pui Pui, the Henchman U .50 1.00
- ❑ 67 Majin Babidi U 3.00 6.00
- ❑ 68 Majin Vegeta's Frantic Attack U .50 1.00
- ❑ 69 Majin Vegeta's Powerful Drill U .50 1.00
- ❑ 70 Majin Yakon U 1.00 3.00
- ❑ 71 Majin Yakon, the Monster U 1.00 3.00
- ❑ 72 Majin Babidi, the Wizard U 1.00 3.00
- ❑ 73 Majin Dabura U .50 1.00
- ❑ 74 Orange Critical Hit U .50 1.00
- ❑ 75 Orange High Block U .50 1.00
- ❑ 76 Orange Body Kick U .50 1.00
- ❑ 77 Orange Surprise Reaction U 1.00 2.00
- ❑ 78 Orange Temple Strike U .50 1.00
- ❑ 79 Paper, Rock, Sissors U .50 1.00
- ❑ 80 Red Energy Outburst U .50 1.00
- ❑ 81 Majin Dabura, King of Fighting U .50 1.00
- ❑ 82 Red Air Kick U .50 1.00
- ❑ 83 Red Physical Drill U .50 1.00
- ❑ 84 Splash Damage Drill U .50 1.00
- ❑ 85 Surprising Strength Drill U .50 1.00
- ❑ 86 Red Tilted Punch U .50 1.00
- ❑ 87 Saiyan Chin Kick U .50 1.00
- ❑ 88 Saiyan Movement U .50 1.00
- ❑ 89 Saiyan Aura Blast U .50 1.00
- ❑ 90 Saiyan Suspended Blast U .50 1.00
- ❑ 91 Majin Vegeta's Rage U 3.00 6.00
- ❑ 92 Videl, Tournament Ready U 1.00 3.00
- ❑ 93 Android 18, the Mom R 2.00 4.00
- ❑ 94 Majin Babidi's Power Extension R 2.00 4.00
- ❑ 95 Black Pivot Kick R 1.00 3.00
- ❑ 96 Blue Energy Dive R 2.00 4.00
- ❑ 97 Daughter's Joy R 2.00 4.00
- ❑ 98 Gohan, Energized R 3.00 6.00
- ❑ 99 Goku, the Legendary R 5.00 10.00
- ❑ 100 Hercule's Close Save U 2.00 4.00
- ❑ 101 Heroic Force R 2.00 4.00
- ❑ 102 Initiative R 2.00 4.00
- ❑ 103 M R 1.00 3.00
- ❑ 104 Majin Pui Pui, the Flashy R 2.00 4.00
- ❑ 105 Majin Yakon, the Absorber R 1.00 3.00
- ❑ 106 Majin Babidi, the Evil Genius R 3.00 5.00
- ❑ 107 Orange Backstab R 1.00 3.00
- ❑ 108 Red Face Slap R 1.00 3.00
- ❑ 109 Majin Dabura, Meditated R 3.00 6.00
- ❑ 110 Majin Quickness R 4.00 8.00
- ❑ 111 Blue Trapped Strike R 2.00 4.00
- ❑ 112 Heroic Sword Catch R 2.00 4.00
- ❑ 113 Majin Vegeta, Uncontrollable R 4.00 8.00
- ❑ 114 Majin Vegeta, the Malicious R 4.00 8.00
- ❑ 115 Orange Rapid Attack R 3.00 6.00
- ❑ 116 Red Energy Rings R 1.00 3.00
- ❑ 117 Red Meditation Drill R 2.00 4.00
- ❑ 118 Red Sniping Shot R 3.00 6.00
- ❑ 119 Risky Maneuver R 3.00 6.00
- ❑ 120 Saiyan Headshot R 3.00 5.00
- ❑ 121 Surpreme Kai, the Mentor (R) 2.00 4.00
- ❑ 122 Majin Vegeta UR 30.00 60.00
- ❑ 123 Majin Vegeta, the Malevolent UR 50.00 80.00

2003 Dragon Ball Z Babidi Saga Android Movie

Inserted in the Babidi Saga card packs.

- ❑ M1 Android 13 5.00 10.00
- ❑ M2 Android 13 5.00 10.00
- ❑ M3 Super Android 13 6.00 12.00
- ❑ M4 Android 15 4.00 8.00
- ❑ M5 Android 15 4.00 8.00
- ❑ M6 Android 15 5.00 8.00
- ❑ M7 Android 14 8.00 12.00
- ❑ M8 Super Android 13's Destruction Bomb 5.00 10.00
- ❑ M9 Super Android 13's Ridge Hand 2.00 4.00
- ❑ M10 Android 13's Prepared Stance 6.00 12.00
- ❑ M11 Goku's Defense Drill 3.00 6.00
- ❑ M12 Blue Android 15's Energy Ball 2.00 4.00
- ❑ M13 Gohan's Braced Energy Beam 3.00 6.00
- ❑ M14 Android 14's Power Kick 4.00 8.00
- ❑ M15 Gohan 5.00 10.00
- ❑ M16 Super Saiyan Goku 5.00 10.00
- ❑ M17 Saiyan Power Stance 2.00 4.00
- ❑ M18 Goku's Quick Save 2.00 4.00
- ❑ M19 Straining Spirit Bomb 2.00 4.00
- ❑ M20 Super Android 13's Physical Resistance 2.00 4.00
- ❑ M21 Red Android 13's Rapid Blast 3.00 6.00
- ❑ M22 Heroic Final Strike 2.00 4.00
- ❑ M23 Super Saiyan Trunks 6.00 10.00
- ❑ M24 Trunks Swordplay Drill 10.00 15.00
- ❑ M25 Android 18's Drop Kick 3.00 6.00
- ❑ M26 Android 16's Grapple 2.00 4.00
- ❑ M27 Breakfall 2.00 4.00
- ❑ M28 Android 17's Left Blast 2.00 4.00
- ❑ M29 Android Tag Team 3.00 6.00
- ❑ M30 Android 18's Palm Blast 3.00 6.00
- ❑ M31 Android 19's Dodge 2.00 4.00
- ❑ M32 Android 18's Left Hook 2.00 4.00
- ❑ M33 Betrayal 2.00 4.00
- ❑ M34 Injured Circuits 3.00 6.00

2003 Dragon Ball Z Buu Saga

Complete Set (200) 225.00 275.00
Booster Box (36 Packs) 50.00 75.00
Booster Pack (12 Cards) 3.00 4.00
*Foil: .75X to 1.5X Basic Cards

- ❑ 1 Alt. Dende Dragon Ball 1 C .50 1.00
- ❑ 2 Alt. Dende Dragon Ball 2 C .50 1.00
- ❑ 3 Black Arm Stretch C .25 .50
- ❑ 4 Black Head Crush C .25 .50
- ❑ 5 Black Floating Popo Defense C .25 .50
- ❑ 6 Black Diving Energy Drop C .25 .50
- ❑ 7 Blue Healing Ray C .25 .50
- ❑ 8 Blue High Block C .25 .50
- ❑ 9 Blue Slam C .25 .50
- ❑ 10 Carpet Attack Technique C .25 .50
- ❑ 11 Energy Gathering C .25 .50
- ❑ 12 Focused Sword Strike C .25 .50
- ❑ 13 Gohan's Sword Slash C .50 1.00
- ❑ 14 Gohan's Sword Sweep C .50 1.00
- ❑ 15 Gohan's Sword Thrust C .50 1.00
- ❑ 16 Goku's Power Attack C .25 .50
- ❑ 17 Heroic Quick Kick C .25 .50
- ❑ 18 Horrified C .25 .50
- ❑ 19 Krillin's Flight C .25 .50
- ❑ 20 Majin Demise C .25 .50
- ❑ 21 Majin Hand Clap C .25 .50
- ❑ 22 Orange Chin Break C .25 .50
- ❑ 23 Orange Energy Catch C .25 .50
- ❑ 24 Orange Energy Guard C .25 .50
- ❑ 25 Orange Spy Drill C .25 .50
- ❑ 26 Red Ball Throw C .25 .50
- ❑ 27 Red Fast Ball C .25 .50
- ❑ 28 Red Fist Catch C .25 .50
- ❑ 29 Red Passive Block C .25 .50
- ❑ 30 Red Power Block C .25 .50
- ❑ 31 Red Vigor Orb C .25 .50
- ❑ 32 Saiyan Energy Deflection C .25 .50
- ❑ 33 Saiyan Hand Swipe C .25 .50
- ❑ 34 Saiyan Snap Kick C .25 .50
- ❑ 35 Saiyan Direct Strike C .25 .50
- ❑ 36 Underwater Kick C .25 .50
- ❑ 37 West City U .50 1.00
- ❑ 38 Alt. Dende Dragon Ball 3 U .75 1.50
- ❑ 39 Alt. Dende Dragon Ball 4 U .75 1.50
- ❑ 40 Alt. Dende Dragon Ball 5 U .75 1.50
- ❑ 41 Bee U .75 1.50
- ❑ 42 Black Face Smash U .50 1.00
- ❑ 43 Black Gambit U .50 1.00
- ❑ 44 Black Gravity Drop U .50 1.00
- ❑ 45 Black Heoric Side Kick (U) .50 1.00
- ❑ 46 Black Overhead Smack U .50 1.00
- ❑ 47 Black Secret U .50 1.00
- ❑ 48 Black Snap Kick U .50 1.00
- ❑ 49 Black Weakness Drill U .50 1.00
- ❑ 50 Blue Devastation U .50 1.00
- ❑ 51 Blue Belly Kick U .50 1.00
- ❑ 52 Blue Draining Blast U .50 1.00
- ❑ 53 Blue Energy Cannon U .50 1.00
- ❑ 54 Blue Eye Gouge U .50 1.00
- ❑ 55 Blue Friendship U .50 1.00
- ❑ 56 Blue Gambit U .50 1.00
- ❑ 57 Blue Head Kick U .50 1.00
- ❑ 58 Blue Protective Bubble U 1.00 2.00
- ❑ 59 Blue Stomach Smash U .50 1.00
- ❑ 60 Blue Upward Block U .50 1.00
- ❑ 61 City Ablaze U .50 1.00
- ❑ 62 Cookie! U .75 1.50
- ❑ 63 Energy Ricochet U .50 1.00
- ❑ 64 Flight Training (U) 1.00 2.00
- ❑ 65 Gohan's Swordplay Drill U .50 1.00
- ❑ 66 Goku Swiftly Moving U .50 1.00
- ❑ 67 Gouku's Escape (U) .50 1.00
- ❑ 68 Healing Magic U .50 1.00
- ❑ 69 Herecule's Underground Training Area (U) .50 1.00
- ❑ 70 Heroic Head Kick U .50 1.00
- ❑ 71 Heroic Kamehameha U .50 1.00
- ❑ 72 Krillin, Z Warrior U .50 1.00
- ❑ 73 Majin Buu's House U 1.00 2.00
- ❑ 74 Majin Buu's Invincibility U 1.00 2.00
- ❑ 75 Majin Buu's Magical Ray U .50 1.00
- ❑ 76 Majin Buu's Stomach Throw U .50 1.00
- ❑ 77 Majin Head Blow U 1.00 2.00
- ❑ 78 Namekian Gambit U .50 1.00
- ❑ 79 Namekian Shield Destruction U .75 1.50
- ❑ 80 Namekian Shuto U .50 1.00
- ❑ 81 Orange Car Push U .50 1.00
- ❑ 82 Orange Face Breaker U .50 1.00
- ❑ 83 Orange Face Crunch U .50 1.00
- ❑ 84 Orange Flight U .50 1.00
- ❑ 85 Orange Gambit U .50 1.00
- ❑ 86 Orange Hiding Drill U .50 1.00
- ❑ 87 Orange Mouth Shot U .50 1.00
- ❑ 88 Orange Right Hook U .50 1.00
- ❑ 89 Orange Sneak Attack U .50 1.00
- ❑ 90 Orange Trick Shot U .50 1.00
- ❑ 91 Physical Defense Drill U .50 1.00
- ❑ 92 Red Arm Swioe U .50 1.00
- ❑ 93 Red Force Punch U .50 1.00
- ❑ 94 Red Front Jab U .50 1.00
- ❑ 95 Red Gambit U .50 1.00
- ❑ 96 Red Joker Drill U .50 1.00
- ❑ 97 Red Overhead Crush U .50 1.00
- ❑ 98 Red Pressure Technique U .50 1.00
- ❑ 99 Red Spiked Blast U .50 1.00
- ❑ 100 Saiyan Assault U .50 1.00
- ❑ 101 Saiyan Energy Bomb U .50 1.00
- ❑ 102 Saiyan Concentrated Blast U .50 1.00
- ❑ 103 Saiyan Gambit U .50 1.00

TCG/CCG

#	Card	Low	High
☐ 104	Saiyan Hurricane Kick U	.50	1.00
☐ 105	Saiyan Ki Ball U	1.00	2.00
☐ 106	Saiyan Onslaught U	.50	1.00
☐ 107	Saiyan Overwhelming Drill U	.50	1.00
☐ 108	Saiyan Power Beam U	.50	1.00
☐ 109	Saiyan Strength Blast U	.50	1.00
☐ 110	The Other World U	.50	1.00
☐ 111	Vegeta's Sacrifice U	1.00	2.00
☐ 112	Whiplash U	.50	1.50
☐ 113	Z Sword Plateau U	.50	1.00
☐ 114	Majin Buu U	1.00	2.00
☐ 115	Korin R	1.00	3.00
☐ 116	Goku, Super Saiyan Ascended R	2.00	4.00
☐ 117	Kid Trunks R	1.00	2.00
☐ 118	Goten R	2.00	4.00
☐ 119	Majin Dabura D.O.A. R	2.00	4.00
☐ 120	Majin Babidi R	1.00	2.00
☐ 121	Alt. Dende Dragon Ball 6 R	1.00	2.00
☐ 122	Alt. Dende Dragon Ball 7 R	1.00	2.00
☐ 123	Black Front Punch R	1.00	3.00
☐ 124	Black Right Kick R	1.00	3.00
☐ 125	Black Royal Flush Drill R	1.00	3.00
☐ 126	Black Style Mastery R	3.00	5.00
☐ 127	Blue Electrical Gunk R	1.00	3.00
☐ 128	Blue Style Mastery R	3.00	5.00
☐ 129	Deal! R	1.00	3.00
☐ 130	Dende R	1.00	3.00
☐ 131	Freestyle Mastery R	2.00	4.00
☐ 132	Gotenks' Flight R	1.00	3.00
☐ 133	Herecule (R)	1.00	3.00
☐ 134	Losing Battle R	1.00	2.00
☐ 135	Majin Buu's Body Slam R	1.00	2.00
☐ 136	Majin Buu's Charged Attack R	1.00	2.00
☐ 137	Majin Buu's Flight R	3.00	5.00
☐ 138	Elder Kai Sensei R	4.00	6.00
☐ 139	Namekian Style Mastery R	2.00	4.00
☐ 140	Oolong R	1.00	3.00
☐ 141	Orange Destruction Ball R	1.00	2.00
☐ 142	Orange Style Mastery R	2.00	4.00
☐ 143	Red Cross Punch R	1.00	3.00
☐ 144	Red Style Mastery R	2.00	4.00
☐ 145	Saiyan Pressure Technique R	1.00	3.00
☐ 146	Saiyan Style Mastery R	5.00	10.00
☐ 147	Supreme Kai's Help R	2.00	4.00
☐ 148	Supreme Kai's Ki Push (R)	2.00	4.00
☐ 149	The Fusion Dance R	3.00	6.00
☐ 150	The Eternal Dragon Quest UR	25.00	50.00
☐ 151	Majin Buu UR	30.00	60.00
☐ 152	Goku, Super Saiyan 3 UR	50.00	80.00
☐ 153	Master Roshi Sensei UR	30.00	60.00
☐ 154	Gotenks (PC) HT	15.00	20.00
☐ 155	Gotenks, Super Saiyan (PC) HT	20.00	35.00
☐ 156	Goku	3.00	5.00
☐ 157	Goku, Super Saiyan	3.00	5.00
☐ 158	Goku, Super Saiyan 2	3.00	5.00
☐ 159	Goku HT	4.00	8.00
☐ 160	Goku GF	4.00	8.00
☐ 161	Gohan	3.00	5.00
☐ 162	Gohan	3.00	5.00
☐ 163	Gohan, Mystic Training	4.00	8.00
☐ 164	Gohan HT	4.00	8.00
☐ 165	Gohan GF	4.00	8.00
☐ 166	Kid Trunks	2.00	4.00
☐ 167	Kid Trunks	2.00	4.00
☐ 168	Kid Trunks	2.00	4.00
☐ 169	Kid Trunks HT	3.00	6.00
☐ 170	Kid Trunks GF	2.00	4.00
☐ 171	Goten	2.00	4.00
☐ 172	Goten	2.00	4.00
☐ 173	Goten	2.00	4.00
☐ 174	Goten HT	3.00	5.00
☐ 175	Goten GF	3.00	5.00
☐ 176	Piccolo	2.00	4.00
☐ 177	Piccolo	2.00	4.00
☐ 178	Piccolo	2.00	4.00
☐ 179	Piccolo HT	3.00	5.00
☐ 180	Majin Dabura	1.00	3.00
☐ 181	Majin Dabura	1.00	3.00
☐ 182	Majin Dabura	1.00	3.00
☐ 183	Majin Dabura HT	2.00	4.00
☐ 184	Majin Babidi	1.00	3.00
☐ 185	Majin Babidi	1.00	3.00
☐ 186	Majin Babidi	1.00	3.00
☐ 187	Majin Babidi HT	2.00	4.00
☐ 188	Majin Babidi GF	2.00	4.00
☐ 189	Majin Vegeta	3.00	5.00
☐ 190	Majin Vegeta	3.00	5.00
☐ 191	Majin Vegeta	3.00	5.00
☐ 192	Majin Vegeta HT	4.00	8.00
☐ 193	Majin Vegeta GF	4.00	8.00
☐ 194	Majin Buu	2.00	4.00
☐ 195	Majin Buu, the Rotund	2.00	4.00
☐ 196	Majin Buu, Pink People Eater	2.00	4.00
☐ 197	Majin Buu HT	4.00	8.00
☐ 198	Majin Buu GF	4.00	8.00
☐ 199	Majin Buu HT	4.00	8.00
☐ 200	Majin Buu GF	4.00	8.00

2003 Dragon Ball Z Buu Saga Broly Movie

Inserted in the Buu Saga card packs

#	Card	Low	High
☐ 1	Broly	12.00	20.00
☐ 2	Broly, the Enraged Saiyan	12.00	20.00
☐ 3	Broly, Super Saiyan	12.00	20.00
☐ 4	Broly, the Legendary Saiyan	20.00	30.00
☐ 5	Broly, the Unstoppable	8.00	15.00
☐ 6	Broly's Energy Burst	6.00	12.00
☐ 7	Broly's Evil Drill	4.00	8.00
☐ 8	Broly's Might	4.00	8.00
☐ 9	Broly's Overwhelming Attacks	4.00	8.00
☐ 10	Broly's Supreme Power	4.00	8.00
☐ 11	Saiyan Broly Smash	5.00	8.00
☐ 12	Saiyan Charge	3.00	6.00
☐ 13	Saiyan Cliff Slam	3.00	5.00
☐ 14	Saiyan Clothesline	2.00	4.00
☐ 15	Saiyan Enraged	3.00	6.00
☐ 16	Saiyan Setup	3.00	6.00
☐ 17	Saiyan Surprise	4.00	8.00
☐ 18	Battle of the Saiyans	2.00	4.00
☐ 19	Common Techniques	1.00	3.00
☐ 20	Goku's Instant Teleportation	2.00	4.00
☐ 21	Goku's Running Defense	3.00	6.00
☐ 22	Heroic Drill	3.00	6.00
☐ 23	Power Smack	1.00	3.00
☐ 24	Pure Defense	2.00	4.00
☐ 25	Krillin's Quick Kicks	2.00	4.00
☐ 26	Efficient Medicine	.50	1.00
☐ 27	Master Roshi	2.00	4.00
☐ 28	Comet Kumolre	1.00	2.00
☐ 29	Mind Control Device	2.00	4.00
☐ 30	New Vegeta	3.00	6.00
☐ 31	Paragus	1.00	2.00
☐ 32	Heroic Double Team	2.00	4.00
☐ 33	Namekian Precise Aim Drill	2.00	4.00
☐ 34	Power Transfer	.50	1.00
☐ 35	Saiyan Energy Toss	1.00	2.00
☐ 36	Vegeta's Energy Blast	3.00	6.00

2003 Dragon Ball Z Fusion Saga Preview

		Low	High
	Complete Set	8.00	15.00

Inserts in Babidi Saga booster packs

#	Card	Low	High
☐ 1	Red Pulverize	.50	1.00
☐ 2	Surrounded!	1.00	2.00
☐ 3	Orange 5-Finger Focus	1.00	2.00
☐ 4	Watching From Afar	1.00	2.00
☐ 5	Vegeta's Pride Drill	3.00	6.00
☐ 6	Gohan, Mystic	5.00	10.00

2003 Dragon Ball Z Fusion Saga

		Low	High
	Complete Set (125)	150.00	200.00
	Booster Box (36 Packs)	55.00	75.00
	Booster Pack (12 Cards)	3.00	4.00

*Foil: .75X to 1.5x Basic Cards

#	Card	Low	High
☐ 1	Black High Kick C	.25	.50
☐ 2	Black Jaw Hammer C	.25	.50
☐ 3	Black Shift Kick C	.25	.50
☐ 4	Blue Knockdown C	.25	.50
☐ 5	Determination Drill C	.25	.50
☐ 6	Dimension Scream C	.25	.50
☐ 7	Hercule's Assault Drill C	.25	.50
☐ 8	Hercule's Immunity C	.25	.50
☐ 9	Heroic Effort C	.25	.50
☐ 10	Majin Buu, Evil Buu (Level 1) C	.50	1.00
☐ 11	Majin Buu's Heel Kick C	.50	1.00
☐ 12	Majin Buu's Taunt C	.25	.50
☐ 13	Noooooooooooooo! C	.25	.50
☐ 14	Orange Splitting Headache C	.25	.50
☐ 15	Orange Strength C	.25	.50
☐ 16	Paused Pose C	.25	.50
☐ 17	Red Holding Drill C	.25	.50
☐ 18	Red Striking Drill C	.25	.50
☐ 19	Release C	.25	.50
☐ 20	Saiyan Neutralization C	.25	.50
☐ 21	Saiyan Power C	.25	.50
☐ 22	Saiyan Spindletop Punch C	.25	.50
☐ 23	Taking Cover C	.25	.50
☐ 24	Tien's Surprise Technique C	.25	.50
☐ 25	Underdog Drill C	.25	.50
☐ 26	Underdog Drop Kick C	.25	.50
☐ 27	Up Close and Personal C	.25	.50
☐ 28	Vegito's Charged Blast C	.25	.50
☐ 29	Vegito's Drop Kick C	.25	.50
☐ 30	Vegito's Leg Catch C	.25	.50
☐ 31	Vegito's Uppercut C	.25	.50
☐ 32	Advanced Basics C	.25	.50
☐ 33	Apocalyptic Battle U	.30	.75
☐ 34	Black Big Bang U	.30	.75
☐ 35	Black Dark Energy U	.30	.75
☐ 36	Black Jawbreaker U	.30	.75
☐ 37	Black Karmic Strike U	.30	.75
☐ 38	Black Protection Orb U	.30	.75
☐ 39	Black Restraint U	.30	.75
☐ 40	Black Spin Kick U	.30	.75
☐ 41	Blue Beatdown U	.30	.75
☐ 42	Blue Energy Guard U	.30	.75
☐ 43	Blue Forceful Explosion U	.30	.75
☐ 44	Blue Gut Implosion U	.30	.75
☐ 45	Blue Longshot U	.30	.75
☐ 46	Blue Multi-Jab U	.30	.75
☐ 47	Blue Stopping Technique U	.30	.75
☐ 48	Blue Weaving U	.30	.75
☐ 49	Boomstick U	.30	.75
☐ 50	Devious Moves U	.30	.75
☐ 51	Elder Kai's Sacrifice U	.30	.75
☐ 52	Gohan's Forearm Block U	.30	.75
☐ 53	Gohan's Left Energy Release U	.30	.75
☐ 54	Heroic Charge U	.30	.75
☐ 55	Intensity Drill U	.30	.75
☐ 56	Krillin's Sacrifice U	.50	1.00
☐ 57	Majin Buu, Piccolo Absorbed (Level 3) U	1.00	2.00
☐ 58	Majin Buu, Super Buu (Level 2) U	1.00	2.00
☐ 59	Majin Buu's Bicycle Kick U	.30	.75
☐ 60	Majin Buu's Goo U	.30	.75
☐ 61	Majin Buu's Stomach U	.30	.75
☐ 62	Majin Static Orb U	.30	.75
☐ 63	Namekian Finger Blast U	.30	.75
☐ 64	Narrow Escape U	.30	.75
☐ 65	Orange Energy Break U	.30	.75
☐ 66	Orange Headshot U	.30	.75
☐ 67	Orange Laser Drill U	.30	.75
☐ 68	Orange Protection Drill U	.30	.75
☐ 69	Orange Rush U	.30	.75
☐ 70	Overcharge U	.30	.75
☐ 71	Ready for Action U	.30	.75
☐ 72	Red Cross Slash U	.30	.75
☐ 73	Red Energy Slap U	.30	.75
☐ 74	Red Physical Fortification U	.30	.75
☐ 75	Red Rapid Deflection U	.30	.75
☐ 76	Red Rapid Energy U	.30	.75
☐ 77	Red Repeated Flares U	.30	.75
☐ 78	Red Static Shot U	.30	.75
☐ 79	Redeemed U	.30	.75
☐ 80	Saiyan Blitz U	.30	.75
☐ 81	Saiyan Elusion U	.30	.75
☐ 82	Saiyan Explosion U	.30	.75
☐ 83	Saiyan Gut Kick U	.30	.75
☐ 84	Saiyan Neckbreaker U	.30	.75
☐ 85	Saiyan Perfect Defense U	.30	.75
☐ 86	Saiyan Push U	.30	.75
☐ 87	Saiyan Two Gun Woo U	.30	.75
☐ 88	Sneaky Tricks U	.30	.75
☐ 89	Unlocked Potential U	.30	.75
☐ 90	Vegeta, the Celestial (Level 1) U	.75	1.50
☐ 91	Vegeta's Blurred Kick U	.30	.75
☐ 92	Yamcha, the Amazing (Level 1) U	.30	.75
☐ 93	Black Energy Swirl R	1.00	2.00
☐ 94	Black Uppercut R	2.00	4.00
☐ 95	Blue Backhand R	1.00	3.00
☐ 96	Blue Leapfrog Drill R	1.00	3.00
☐ 97	Blue Lunge R	2.00	4.00
☐ 98	Dazed R	1.00	3.00
☐ 99	Den-Goku (Level 1) R	3.00	5.00
☐ 100	Gohan, Earth's Protector (Level 5) R	3.00	6.00
☐ 101	Gohan, Mystic Empowered (Level 4) R	2.00	4.00
☐ 102	Gotenks' Kamikaze Ghost R	3.00	6.00
☐ 103	Hercule-Goku (Level 1) R	3.00	6.00
☐ 104	Last Ditch Effort R	1.00	3.00
☐ 105	Majin Buu, Gohan Absorbed (Level 5) R	3.00	6.00
☐ 106	Majin Buu, Gotenks Absorbed (Level 4) R	3.00	6.00
☐ 107	Majin Buu's Energy Spray R	1.00	3.00
☐ 108	Majin Buu's Kamikaze Ghost (Level 1) R	2.00	4.00
☐ 109	Majin Buu's New House R	1.00	3.00
☐ 110	Majin Planet Destruction Blast R	1.00	3.00
☐ 111	Majin Thrust R	2.00	4.00
☐ 112	Namekian Door Explosion R	1.00	3.00
☐ 113	Orange Reflex R	1.00	3.00
☐ 114	Potara Earrings R	4.00	8.00
☐ 115	Red Drop R	1.00	3.00
☐ 116	Red Leverage Blast R	1.00	3.00
☐ 117	Red Mouth Cannon R	1.00	3.00
☐ 118	Red Whiplash R	2.00	4.00
☐ 119	Saiyan Overcharged Blast R	1.00	3.00
☐ 120	Straining Power Move R	1.00	3.00
☐ 121	Transformation R	2.00	4.00
☐ 122	Vegeta's Fury R	1.00	3.00
☐ 123	Vegito (Level 1) R	6.00	12.00
☐ 124	Gotenks, Super Saiyan 3 (Level 3) UR	50.00	75.00
☐ 125	Vegito, Super Saiyan (Level 2) UR	50.00	75.00

2003 Dragon Ball Z Fusion Saga Cosmic Anthology

Inserted in the Fusion Saga card packs

#	Card	Low	High
☐ CA1	Supreme West Kai (Level 1)	8.00	16.00
☐ CA2	Supreme West Kai (Level 2)	6.00	10.00
☐ CA3	Supreme West Kai (Level 3)	5.00	10.00
☐ CA4	Dr. Willow (Level 1)	3.00	6.00
☐ CA5	Dr. Willow (Level 2)	3.00	6.00
☐ CA6	Dr. Willow (Level 3)	3.00	6.00
☐ CA7	Zarbon (Level 1)	2.00	4.00
☐ CA8	Zarbon, Transformed (Level 2)	2.00	4.00
☐ CA9	Zarbon, Fanatical (Level 3)	2.00	4.00
☐ CA10	Turles, the Mysterious (Level 1)	4.00	8.00
☐ CA11	Turles, the Proud (level 2)	2.00	4.00
☐ CA12	Turles, the Saiyan Warrior (level 3)	2.00	4.00
☐ CA13	Caterpy (Level 1)	3.00	6.00
☐ CA14	Caterpy, the Grappler (Level 2)	2.00	4.00
☐ CA15	Caterpy, the Tenacious (Level 3)	.10	.25
☐ CA16	Gohan's Immense Power	2.00	4.00
☐ CA17	Goku's Power Pole	4.00	8.00
☐ CA18	Energetic Fruit	2.00	4.00
☐ CA19	Icarus	3.00	6.00
☐ CA20	Tree of Might	3.00	6.00
☐ CA21	Goku's Super Saiyan Catch	4.00	8.00
☐ CA22	Knowledge Transfer	3.00	6.00
☐ CA23	Piccolo's Power Blast	5.00	10.00
☐ CA24	Cooler's Surprise Attack	3.00	6.00
☐ CA25	Returning the Favor	1.00	3.00
☐ CA26	Ingrain in the Membrane	1.00	3.00
☐ CA27	Alt. Earth Dragon Ball 3	3.00	6.00
☐ CA28	Goku's Quick Dodge	5.00	10.00
☐ CA29	Energy Pouch	4.00	6.00
☐ CA30	Master Roshi's Back Kick	3.00	6.00
☐ CA31	Gohan's Energy Deflection	2.00	4.00
☐ CA32	Makyo Star	3.00	6.00
☐ CA33	Piccolo's Destruction Attack	2.00	4.00
☐ CA34	Blue Style Mastery	3.00	6.00
☐ CA35	A Hero's Heart is Strong	2.00	4.00
☐ CA36	Black Scout Maneuver	3.00	6.00

2003 Dragon Ball Z Kid Buu Saga Preview

Inserts in the Fusion Saga packs

#	Card	Low	High
☐ 1	Goku's Flight C	.25	.50
☐ 2	Majin Buu's Choke Hold C	.25	.50
☐ 3	Majin Babidi, the Mastermind U	.30	.75
☐ 4	Peaceful times U	.30	.75
☐ 5	The Power of Porunga R	1.00	3.00

2003 Dragon Ball Z Kid Buu Saga

		Low	High
	Complete Set (125)	120.00	200.00
	Booster Box (36 packs)	45.00	65.00
	Booster Pack (12 cards)	2.50	3.50

*Foil: 1X to 2X Basic Cards

#	Card	Low	High
☐ 1	Alt. Namek Dragon Ball 1 C	.25	.50
☐ 2	Alt. Namek Dragon Ball 2 C	.25	.50
☐ 3	Alt. Namek Dragon Ball 3 C	.25	.50
☐ 4	Black Exertion C	.25	.50
☐ 5	Black Groveling Drill C	.25	.50
☐ 6	Black Magic C	.25	.50
☐ 7	Black Parry C	.25	.50
☐ 8	Blue Biting Drill C	.25	.50
☐ 9	Blue Double Blast C	.25	.50
☐ 10	Blue Ki Build Up C	.25	.50
☐ 11	Blue Sledgehammer C	.25	.50
☐ 12	Blue Stretch Kick C	.25	.50
☐ 13	Fierce Left Kick C	.25	.50
☐ 14	Hercule's Realization C	.25	.50
☐ 15	Heroic Power Detonation C	.25	.50
☐ 16	Ki Catalyst C	.25	.50
☐ 17	Majin Hair Pull C	.25	.50
☐ 18	Namekian Remedy Drill C	.25	.50
☐ 19	Orange Arm Break C	.25	.50
☐ 20	Orange Discharge Drill C	.25	.50
☐ 21	Orange Hand-clasp Drill C	.25	.50
☐ 22	Overwhelmed C	.25	.50
☐ 23	Pan's High Slap C	.25	.50
☐ 24	Red Bullrush Drill C	.25	.50
☐ 25	Red Kaio-Ken Drill C	.25	.50
☐ 26	Red Puppy Slap C	.25	.50
☐ 27	Saiyan Aggression Drill C	.25	.50
☐ 28	Saiyan Dashing Kick C	.25	.50
☐ 29	Saiyan Stop C	.25	.50
☐ 30	Stupendous Strike C	.25	.50
☐ 31	The Help of Earth C	.25	.50
☐ 32	Alt. Namek Dragon Ball 4 U	1.00	3.00
☐ 33	Alt. Namek Dragon Ball 5 U	1.00	3.00
☐ 34	Android 18, the Mom (Level 1) U	1.00	3.00
☐ 35	Black Bicycle Kick U	.30	.75
☐ 36	Black Buffer Block U	.30	.75
☐ 37	Black Impressive Slap U	.30	.75
☐ 38	Black Swivel Attack U	.30	.75
☐ 39	Blue Alliance U	.30	.75
☐ 40	Blue Deviation Drill U	.30	.75
☐ 41	Blue Dikaio Blast U	.30	.75
☐ 42	Blue Face Crunch U	.30	.75
☐ 43	Blue Impulse U	.30	.75
☐ 44	Blue Villains Drill U	.30	.75
☐ 45	Bulma, the Wife (Level 1) U	1.00	3.00
☐ 46	CHARGE! U	.30	.75
☐ 47	Chi-chi, the Grandmother (Level 1) U	1.00	3.00
☐ 48	Earth's Demise U	.30	.75
☐ 49	Energy Lob U	.30	.75
☐ 50	Goku's Setup Strike U	1.00	3.00
☐ 51	Goku's Supreme Kamehameha U	1.00	3.00
☐ 52	Hercule, the Everlasting World Champ (Level 1) U	2.00	4.00
☐ 53	Kid Trunks, Teenager (Level 1) U	3.00	6.00
☐ 54	Krillin's Destructo Disk U	1.00	3.00
☐ 55	Majin Buu, Kid Buu (Level 2) U	2.00	5.00
☐ 56	Majin Buu, Kid Buu (Level 3) U	2.00	5.00
☐ 57	Majin Buu's Backstabbing Kick U	1.00	3.00
☐ 58	Majin Dabura, the Redeemed (Level 1) U	.30	.75
☐ 59	Billions of Mini Majin Buus U	2.00	5.00
☐ 60	Masterful Moves U	.30	.75
☐ 61	Orange Carnage U	2.00	5.00
☐ 62	Orange Gutter Swipe U	.30	.75
☐ 63	Orange Might U	.30	.75
☐ 64	Orange Obliteration U	.30	.75
☐ 65	Orange Vegeta's Assault U	1.00	3.00
☐ 66	Pan, Granddaughter of Goku (Level 1) U	1.00	3.00
☐ 67	Poof! U	.30	.75
☐ 68	Power Headbutt U	.30	.75
☐ 69	Provoke Drill U	.30	.75
☐ 70	Quick Teleportation Drill U	2.00	5.00
☐ 71	Recoome's Vogue Drill U	.30	.75
☐ 72	Red Aerial Force U	.30	.75
☐ 73	Red Annihilation U	.30	.75
☐ 74	Red Clap U	.30	.75
☐ 75	Red Elbow Drop U	.30	.75
☐ 76	Red Power Slam U	.30	.75
☐ 77	Red Sword Cleave U	.30	.75
☐ 78	Red Thunder Clap U	.30	.75
☐ 79	Saiyan Brace U	.30	.75
☐ 80	Saiyan Desperation U	.30	.75
☐ 81	Saiyan Energy Bullet U	.30	.75
☐ 82	Saiyan Jeering Drill U	.30	.75
☐ 83	Saiyan Youth Bruise U	.30	.75
☐ 84	Ultimate Defense U	.30	.75
☐ 85	Ultra Uppercut U	2.00	5.00
☐ 86	Uub (Level 1) U	1.00	3.00
☐ 87	Uub, the Quick Learner (Level 2) U	1.00	3.00
☐ 88	Vegeta's Ill Temper U	.30	.75
☐ 89	Videl, the Heroic (Level 1) U	1.00	3.00
☐ 90	Welcome Home Drill U	.30	.75
☐ 91	Yajirobe, Retired (Level 1) U	1.00	3.00
☐ 92	Yamcha, the Single (Level 2) U	1.00	3.00
☐ 93	Alt. Namek Dragon Ball 6 R	3.00	5.00
☐ 94	Alt. Namek Dragon Ball 7 R	3.00	5.00
☐ 95	Black Chaos Detonation R	1.00	3.00
☐ 96	Black Disarray Drill R	1.00	3.00
☐ 97	Black Drop Kick R	1.00	3.00
☐ 98	Black Swerve R	1.00	3.00
☐ 99	Blue Reverse R	1.00	3.00
☐ 100	Fond Memories R	1.00	3.00
☐ 101	Gohan, the Bookworm (Level 1) R	3.00	6.00
☐ 102	Goku Sensei R	4.00	8.00
☐ 103	Hercule's "Dream Sequence" R	1.00	3.00
☐ 104	King Kai, Earth's Mentor (Level 1) R	1.00	3.00
☐ 105	Majin Buu, Kid Buu (Level 4) R	3.00	6.00
☐ 106	Majin Buu, Kid Buu (Level 5) R	4.00	8.00
☐ 107	Majin Buu's Prepped Crash R	1.00	3.00
☐ 108	Orange Head Mash R	1.00	3.00
☐ 109	Orange Intense Power R	1.00	3.00
☐ 110	Orange Ki Assailment R	1.00	3.00
☐ 111	Orange Massacre R	1.00	3.00
☐ 112	Red Axe Heel Kick R	1.00	3.00
☐ 113	Red Hunger Drill R	1.00	3.00
☐ 114	Red Left Bolt R	1.00	3.00
☐ 115	Red Voltage Missle R	1.00	3.00
☐ 116	Saiyan Acute Rapid Slam R	1.00	3.00
☐ 117	Saiyan Beef R	2.00	4.00
☐ 118	Saiyan Handstand R	1.00	3.00
☐ 119	Saiyan Lurch R	1.00	3.00
☐ 120	Intense Observation Drill R	2.00	4.00
☐ 121	Uub, Enraged (Level 3) R	2.00	4.00
☐ 122	Vegeta, Settled Down (Level 2) R	2.00	4.00
☐ 123	Vile Energy R	1.00	3.00
☐ 124	Earth's Spirit Bomb UR	25.00	40.00
☐ 125	Piccolo Sensei UR	25.00	40.00

2003 Dragon Ball Z Kid Buu Saga Bojack Unbound

Inserted in the Kid Buu Saga packs

#	Card	Low	High
☐ 1	Ohhhhhhhhhhhh YEAH!	3.00	6.00
☐ 2	Krillin's Smoothness Drill	2.00	4.00
☐ 3	Trunks, the Weaponmaster (Level 1)	8.00	12.00
☐ 4	Kogu (Level 1)	3.00	6.00
☐ 5	Zangya (Level 1)	5.00	10.00
☐ 6	Bujin (Level 1)	4.00	8.00
☐ 7	Bido (Level 1)	5.00	10.00
☐ 8	Bojack (Level 1)	8.00	16.00
☐ 9	Bojack, the Villianous (Level 2)	4.00	10.00
☐ 10	Bojack, the Notorious (Level 3)	8.00	16.00
☐ 11	The Sword of Trunks	6.00	10.00
☐ 12	Snake Way	1.00	3.00
☐ 13	Saiyan Outburst	1.00	3.00
☐ 14	Vegeta's Elbow Slam	5.00	10.00
☐ 15	Orange Brick Breaker	1.00	3.00
☐ 16	Red Plasma Catapult	2.00	4.00
☐ 17	Black Eradication	1.00	3.00
☐ 18	Master Roshi's Gawking Drill	2.00	4.00
☐ 19	Bulma and Chi-chi's Stare Off	1.00	3.00
☐ 20	Tien's Focused Beam	2.00	4.00
☐ 21	Trunks' Back Bash	2.00	4.00
☐ 22	Zangya's Leaping Rush Down	1.00	3.00
☐ 23	Kogu's Dual Strike	2.00	4.00
☐ 24	Trunks' Deadly Impact	2.00	4.00
☐ 25	Heroic Power Shot	1.00	3.00
☐ 26	Triple Torpedo	6.00	10.00
☐ 27	Bojack's Overhead Toss	3.00	6.00
☐ 28	Bojack's Left Palm Charge	3.00	6.00
☐ 29	Bojack's Defensive Shield	3.00	6.00
☐ 30	Zangya's Entrapping Strings	1.00	3.00
☐ 31	Gohan's Obliteration	2.00	4.00
☐ 32	Power Overwhelming	1.00	3.00
☐ 33	Bojack's Extreme Assailment	3.00	6.00
☐ 34	Bido's Charge	3.00	6.00
☐ 35	Bojack's Double-Palmed Blitz	.50	1.00
☐ 36	Empowered Kamehameha	2.00	4.00

2003 Dragon Ball GT Saga Preview

		Low	High
	Complete Set (6)	10.00	20.00

Inserted in Kidd Buu Saga packs

#	Card	Low	High
☐ 1	Trunks Aerial Kick C	1.00	3.00
☐ 2	Pan's Right Blast C	1.00	2.00
☐ 3	Uub's Energy Drill U	2.00	4.00
☐ 4	Super Saiyan Stepup U	2.00	4.00
☐ 5	Goku, Young Again (Level 1) R	4.00	6.00
☐ 6	The Might of Shenron R	5.00	10.00

2004 Dragon Ball GT Baby Saga

		Low	High
	Complete Set (301)	175.00	225.00
	Booster Box (24 packs)	45.00	70.00
	Booster Pack (12 cards)	3.00	3.75

*Foil: 1X to 2X Basic Cards

#	Card	Low	High
☐ 1	Metal Mending ST	.20	.50
☐ 2	Goku's Finger Throw ST	.50	1.00
☐ 3	Saiyan Lift ST	.20	.50
☐ 4	Orange Double Shot ST	.20	.50
☐ 5	Saiyan Soaring Swerve ST	.20	.50
☐ 6	Red Close Call ST	.10	.25
☐ 7	Red Ducking Coverage ST	.10	.25
☐ 8	Blue Concentrated Blast ST	.20	.50
☐ 9	Orange Close Guard ST	.10	.25

Card	Low	High
❑ 10 Baby Vegeta's Immobile Defense C	.10	.25
❑ 11 Baby Vegeta's Viciousness C	.10	.25
❑ 12 Baby's Surprise Grapple C	.10	.25
❑ 13 Black Agile Reaction C	.10	.25
❑ 14 Black Buffer C	.10	.25
❑ 15 Black Combat Defense C	.10	.25
❑ 16 Black Energy Dodge C	.10	.25
❑ 17 Black Firebreath C	.10	.25
❑ 18 Black Flight C	.10	.25
❑ 19 Black Full Force Impact C	.10	.25
❑ 20 Black Laser Beams C	.10	.25
❑ 21 Black Laser Dodge C	.10	.25
❑ 22 Black Precise Aim C	.10	.25
❑ 23 Black Robot Wallop C	.10	.25
❑ 24 Black Star Dragon Ball 1 C	.10	.25
❑ 25 Black Star Dragon Ball 2 C	.10	.25
❑ 26 Black Thwack C	.10	.25
❑ 27 Black Torso Shift C	.10	.25
❑ 28 Blue Aversion C	.10	.25
❑ 29 Blue Distorted Knee C	.10	.25
❑ 30 Blue Double Barrel C	.10	.25
❑ 31 Blue Fallback C	.10	.25
❑ 32 Blue Forced Impact C	.10	.25
❑ 33 Blue Full Defense C	.10	.25
❑ 34 Blue Gliding Shirk C	.10	.25
❑ 35 Blue Hand Clasp C	.10	.25
❑ 36 Blue Ki Burst C	.10	.25
❑ 37 Blue Lofty Finesse C	.10	.25
❑ 38 Blue Power Absorption C	.10	.25
❑ 39 Blue Resistance C	.10	.25
❑ 40 Elevation C	.10	.25
❑ 41 Energy Overload Drill C	.10	.25
❑ 42 Fiesta Pan C	.10	.25
❑ 43 Flying Blades C	.10	.25
❑ 44 General Rilldo's Rocket Punch C	.10	.25
❑ 45 Goku to the Rescue C	.10	.25
❑ 46 Goku's Chin Break C	.10	.25
❑ 47 Goku's Energy Spray C	.10	.25
❑ 48 Hidden Power Level C	.10	.25
❑ 49 Inner Strength Drill C	.10	.25
❑ 50 Lookin' Pimp-like C	.10	.25
❑ 51 Orange Blurred Movement C	.10	.25
❑ 52 Orange Distortion C	.10	.25
❑ 53 Orange Dogfight C	.10	.25
❑ 54 Orange Drill C	.10	.25
❑ 55 Orange Ducking Resistance C	.10	.25
❑ 56 Orange Hand Lock C	.10	.25
❑ 57 Orange Revealing Attack C	.10	.25
❑ 58 Orange Revenge Death Ball C	.10	.25
❑ 59 Orange Scolding C	.10	.25
❑ 60 Orange Soaring Evasion C	.10	.25
❑ 61 Orange Stomach Slam C	.10	.25
❑ 62 Orange Warm-up Drill C	.10	.25
❑ 63 Orange Wrist Interception C	.10	.25
❑ 64 Pan's Anger Strike C	.10	.25
❑ 65 Pan's Spirit Attack C	.10	.25
❑ 66 Red Aerial Glide C	.10	.25
❑ 67 Red Blindside C	.10	.25
❑ 68 Red Crash C	.10	.25
❑ 69 Red Crippler C	.10	.25
❑ 70 Red Earth Shatter C	.10	.25
❑ 71 Red Erratic Flutter C	.10	.25
❑ 72 Red Headbutt C	.10	.25
❑ 73 Red Hypersonic Knockout C	.10	.25
❑ 74 Red Mix Up C	.10	.25
❑ 75 Red Perfection C	.10	.25
❑ 76 Red Stout Restraint C	.10	.25
❑ 77 Red Strength Squeeze C	.10	.25
❑ 78 Red Surprise Launch C	.10	.25
❑ 79 Saiyan Anchored Clamp C	.10	.25
❑ 80 Saiyan Arrogant Snare C	.10	.25
❑ 81 Saiyan Braced Resistance C	.10	.25
❑ 82 Saiyan Choke Hold C	.10	.25
❑ 83 Saiyan Cross Punch C	.10	.25
❑ 84 Saiyan Elbow Slam C	.10	.25
❑ 85 Saiyan Flawless Snatch C	.10	.25
❑ 86 Saiyan Fly Swat C	.10	.25
❑ 87 Saiyan Headbutt C	.10	.25
❑ 88 Saiyan Love C	.10	.25
❑ 89 Saiyan Sole Stop C	.10	.25
❑ 90 Saiyan Space Nova C	.10	.25
❑ 91 Saiyan Stomp C	.10	.25
❑ 92 Saiyan Weighted Lunge C	.10	.25
❑ 93 Strengthened Ki Drill C	.10	.25
❑ 94 Super Saiyans Unite C	.10	.25
❑ 95 Trunks' Flying Uppercut C	.10	.25
❑ 96 Trunks' Horizontal Encounter C	.10	.25
❑ 97 Uub's Blitz C	.10	.25
❑ 98 Uub's Finger Blast C	.10	.25
❑ 99 Uub's Majin Focus C	.10	.25
❑ 100 Wink Wink, Nudge Nudge C	.10	.25
❑ 101 Baby Gohan (Level 1) U	.30	.75
❑ 102 Baby Goten (Level 1) U	.30	.75
❑ 103 Baby Vegeta's Flaming Death Ball U	.50	1.00
❑ 104 Baby's Breakout U	.50	1.00
❑ 105 Baby's Liquidity U	.50	1.00
❑ 106 Black Butterfingers U	.30	.75
❑ 107 Black Covert Operations Drill U	.30	.75
❑ 108 Black Elbow Block U	.30	.75
❑ 109 Black Opposition U	.30	.75
❑ 110 Black Power Strike U	.30	.75
❑ 111 Black Rising Knee U	.30	.75
❑ 112 Black Star Dragon Ball 3 U	.50	1.00
❑ 113 Black Star Dragon Ball 4 U	.50	1.00
❑ 114 Black Uber Blast U	.30	.75
❑ 115 Blue Announcer Drill U	.30	.75
❑ 116 Blue Body Manipulation U	.30	.75
❑ 117 Blue Data Download U	.30	.75
❑ 118 Blue Draining Kamehameha U	.50	1.00
❑ 119 Blue Imminent Destruction U	.30	.75
❑ 120 Blue Plea U	.30	.75
❑ 121 Blue Power Boost U	.30	.75
❑ 122 Blue Prepped Attack U	.30	.75
❑ 123 Blue Seizure U	.30	.75
❑ 124 Bulla (Level 1) U	.30	.75
❑ 125 Bulma, the Mom (Level 1) U	.30	.75
❑ 126 Dr. Myuu's Destiny U	.30	.75
❑ 127 Dr. Myuu's Horror U	.30	.75
❑ 128 Elder Kai (Level 1) U	.30	.75
❑ 129 Emperor Pilaf (Level 1) U	.30	.75
❑ 130 General Rilldo's Metalization U	.30	.75
❑ 131 Giru (Level 1) U	.30	.75
❑ 132 Giru, the Helper (Level 2) U	.30	.75
❑ 133 Gohan (Level 1) U	.50	1.00
❑ 134 Goten (Level 1) U	.50	1.00
❑ 135 Hercule (Level 1) U	.30	.75
❑ 136 Hercule, the Great (Level 2) U	.30	.75
❑ 137 Kabito Kai (Level 1) U	.30	.75
❑ 138 Mai (Level 1) U	.30	.75
❑ 139 Majin Buu (Level 1) U	.50	1.00
❑ 140 Majin Buu, the Cherub (Level 2) U	.50	1.00
❑ 141 Mutant Robot (Level 1) U	.30	.75
❑ 142 Orange Effective Illusion U	.30	.75
❑ 143 Orange Fierce Discharge U	.30	.75
❑ 144 Orange Ki Assault U	.30	.75
❑ 145 Orange Menacing Attack U	.30	.75
❑ 146 Orange Proximity Blasts U	.30	.75
❑ 147 Orange Reverse Elbow U	.30	.75
❑ 148 Orange Safety Drill U	.30	.75
❑ 149 Orange Slide U	.30	.75
❑ 150 Power Up the Most U	.30	.75
❑ 151 Red Anticipation U	.30	.75
❑ 152 Red Dice Chucker U	.30	.75
❑ 153 Red Double Guard U	.30	.75
❑ 154 Red Hasty Release U	.30	.75
❑ 155 Red Scissors U	.30	.75
❑ 156 Red Snappy Reflexes U	.30	.75
❑ 157 Red Torso Pound U	.30	.75
❑ 158 Red Traverse Punch U	.30	.75
❑ 159 Road Rage U	.30	.75
❑ 160 Saiyan Agile Swerve U	.30	.75
❑ 161 Saiyan Charged Kamehameha U	.30	.75
❑ 162 Saiyan Destiny U	.30	.75
❑ 163 Saiyan Exertive Attack U	.30	.75
❑ 164 Saiyan Planet Explosion U	.30	.75
❑ 165 Saiyan Power Deflection U	.30	.75
❑ 166 Saiyan Spirit Shock U	.30	.75
❑ 167 Saiyan Strength Drill U	.50	1.00
❑ 168 Shu (Level 1) U	.30	.75
❑ 169 Shusugoro (Level 1) U	.30	.75
❑ 170 Sigma Force (Level 1) U	.30	.75
❑ 171 Sugoro (Level 1) U	.30	.75
❑ 172 Sugoro, Shapeshifter (Level 2) U	.30	.75
❑ 173 Trunks Searching U	.50	1.00
❑ 174 Vegeta (Level 1) U	1.00	2.00
❑ 175 Videl (Level 1) U	.30	.75
❑ 176 Baby (Level 4) R	1.00	2.00
❑ 177 Baby Vegeta (Level 4) R	3.00	6.00
❑ 178 Black Concealed Weaponry Drill R	1.00	2.00
❑ 179 Black Coolness Drill R	1.00	2.00
❑ 180 Black Geezer Patrol R	1.00	2.00
❑ 181 Black Interruption R	1.00	2.00
❑ 182 Black Leadership Drill R	1.00	2.00
❑ 183 Black Parental Guidance R	1.00	2.00
❑ 184 Black Star Dragon Ball 5 R	2.00	4.00
❑ 185 Black Star Dragon Ball 6 R	3.00	6.00
❑ 186 Black Star Dragon Ball 7 R	2.00	4.00
❑ 187 Black Style Mastery R	3.00	8.00
❑ 188 Black Style Mastery R	3.00	8.00
❑ 189 Black Throwdown R	1.00	2.00
❑ 190 Blue Ball Control Drill R	1.00	2.00
❑ 191 Blue Ball Gathering R	1.00	2.00
❑ 192 Blue Clobber R	1.00	2.00
❑ 193 Blue Kamehameha R	1.00	3.00
❑ 194 Blue Might Drill R	1.00	2.00
❑ 195 Blue Slipup R	1.00	2.00
❑ 196 Blue Style Mastery R	3.00	6.00
❑ 197 Blue Style Mastery R	3.00	6.00
❑ 198 Blue Trap Drill R	1.00	2.00
❑ 199 Champions of Earth R	1.00	2.00
❑ 200 Chi-chi, the Grandmother (Level 1) R	1.00	2.00
❑ 201 Dr. Myuu (Level 4) R	1.00	2.00
❑ 202 Epic Battle of Saiyans R	2.00	4.00
❑ 203 Fistful of Pain R	1.00	2.00
❑ 204 General Rilldo's Force Field R	2.00	4.00
❑ 205 General Rilldo's Invulnerability R	1.00	2.00
❑ 206 Goku, Golden Oozaru (Level 4) R	4.00	8.00
❑ 207 Goku's Brawling R	1.00	3.00
❑ 208 Goku's Mixing Drill R	1.00	3.00
❑ 209 Hercule, the Colossal (Level 3) R	1.00	2.00
❑ 210 Majin Buu, the Benevolent (Level 3) R	2.00	4.00
❑ 211 Masterful Defense R	1.00	2.00
❑ 212 Meanacing Evil R	1.00	2.00
❑ 213 Orange Absorbing Drill R	1.00	2.00
❑ 214 Orange Augmenting Drill R	1.00	2.00
❑ 215 Orange Escaping Drill R	1.00	2.00
❑ 216 Orange Family R	1.00	2.00
❑ 217 Orange Focusing Drill R	1.00	2.00
❑ 218 Orange Gameshow Drill R	1.00	2.00
❑ 219 Orange Removal System R	1.00	2.00
❑ 220 Orange Style Mastery R	3.00	6.00
❑ 221 Orange Style Mastery R	3.00	6.00
❑ 222 Pan, the Spirited (Level 4) R	1.00	2.00
❑ 223 Red Blowback R	1.00	2.00
❑ 224 Red Bolstered Defense R	1.00	2.00
❑ 225 Red Fingertip Blast R	1.00	2.00
❑ 226 Red Jumping Smash R	1.00	2.00
❑ 227 Red Personal Vendetta R	1.00	2.00
❑ 228 Red Shaving Drill R	1.00	2.00
❑ 229 Red Style Mastery R	5.00	8.00
❑ 230 Red Style Mastery R	5.00	8.00
❑ 231 Red Tail Pull R	1.00	2.00
❑ 232 Saiyan Firm Stance R	1.00	2.00
❑ 233 Saiyan Jump Kick R	1.00	2.00
❑ 234 Saiyan Outrage R	1.00	2.00
❑ 235 Saiyan Power Punch R	1.00	2.00
❑ 236 Saiyan Quest R	1.00	2.00
❑ 237 Saiyan Rage Drill R	1.00	2.00
❑ 238 Saiyan Style Mastery R	1.00	2.00
❑ 239 Saiyan Supreme Mastery R	5.00	9.00
❑ 240 Saiyan Trickery Drill R	1.00	2.00
❑ 241 Super Gallic Gun R	1.00	2.00
❑ 242 The Dragon Awaits R	1.00	3.00
❑ 243 Trunks, the Brilliant (Level 4) R	1.00	3.00
❑ 244 Majuub (Level 4) R	1.00	3.00
❑ 245 Vegeta's Quickness Drill R	1.00	2.00
❑ 246 Baby Vegeta, Golden Oozaru (Level 5) UR	20.00	30.00
❑ 247 Black Crosscheck UR	10.00	18.00
❑ 248 Blue Narrow Escape UR	10.00	18.00
❑ 249 Goku, Super Saiyan 4 (Level 5) UR	35.00	50.00
❑ 250 It's the Inside That Counts UR	8.00	18.00
❑ 251 Orange Fishing Drill UR	8.00	18.00
❑ 252 Red Toe Pierce UR	15.00	25.00
❑ 253 Saiyan Ground Slide UR	8.00	18.00
❑ 254 Baby (Level 2) ST	2.00	5.00
❑ 255 Baby (Level 3) ST	2.00	5.00
❑ 256 Baby (Level 1) ST	2.00	5.00
❑ 257 Baby Vegeta (Level 3) ST	2.00	5.00
❑ 258 Baby Vegeta (Level 1) ST	2.00	5.00
❑ 259 Baby Vegeta (Level 2) ST	2.00	5.00
❑ 260 Dr. Myuu (Level 1) ST	1.00	3.00
❑ 261 Dr. Myuu (Level 2) ST	1.00	3.00
❑ 262 Dr. Myuu (Level 3) ST	1.00	3.00
❑ 263 General Rilldo (Level 3) ST	1.00	3.00
❑ 264 General Rilldo (Level 1) ST	1.00	3.00
❑ 265 General Rilldo (Level 2) ST	1.00	3.00
❑ 266 Goku (Level 1) ST	2.00	4.00
❑ 267 Goku, Super Saiyan (Level 2) ST	2.00	4.00
❑ 268 Goku, Super Saiyan 3 (Level 3) ST	2.00	4.00
❑ 269 Pan (Level 1) ST	1.00	3.00
❑ 270 Pan, the Young Saiyan (Level 3) ST	1.00	3.00
❑ 271 Pan, the Youthful (Level 2) ST	1.00	3.00
❑ 272 Trunks (Level 1) ST	1.00	3.00
❑ 273 Trunks, Super Saiyan (Level 3) ST	1.00	3.00
❑ 274 Trunks, the Scientific (Level 2) ST	1.00	3.00
❑ 275 Uub (Level 1) ST	1.00	2.00
❑ 276 Majuub (Level 3) ST	1.00	2.00
❑ 277 Majuub (Level 2) ST	1.00	2.00
❑ 278 Baby (Level 1) (HT) ST	1.00	3.00
❑ 279 Baby (Level 2) (HT) ST	1.00	3.00
❑ 280 Baby (Level 3) (HT) ST	1.00	3.00
❑ 281 Baby Vegeta (Level 2) (HT) ST	2.00	4.00
❑ 282 Baby Vegeta (Level 3) (HT) ST	2.00	4.00
❑ 283 Baby Vegeta (Level 1) (HT) ST	2.00	4.00
❑ 284 Dr. Myuu (Level 3) (HT) ST	1.00	2.00
❑ 285 Dr. Myuu (Level 3) (HT) ST	1.00	2.00
❑ 286 Dr. Myuu (Level 2) (HT) ST	1.00	2.00
❑ 287 General Rilldo (Level 3) (HT) ST	1.00	2.00
❑ 288 General Rilldo (Level 1) (HT) ST	1.00	2.00
❑ 289 General Rilldo (Level 2) (HT) ST	1.00	2.00
❑ 290 Goku (Level 1) (HT) ST	2.00	4.00
❑ 291 Goku, Earth's Protector (Level 3) (HT) ST	2.00	4.00
❑ 292 Goku, Energized (Level 2) (HT) ST	2.00	4.00
❑ 293 Pan (Level 1) (HT) ST	1.00	2.50
❑ 294 Pan, the Agile (Level 2) (HT) ST	1.00	2.50
❑ 295 Pan, the Vivacious (Level 3) (HT) ST	1.00	2.50
❑ 296 Trunks (Level 1) (HT) ST	1.00	2.00
❑ 297 Trunks (Level 3) (HT) ST	1.00	2.00
❑ 298 Trunks, Teen Saiyan (Level 2) (HT) ST	1.00	2.00
❑ 299 Majuub (Level 3) (HT) ST	1.50	3.50
❑ 300 Uub (Level 1) (HT) ST	1.50	3.50
❑ 301 Majuub (Level 2) (HT) ST	1.50	3.50

2004 Dragon Ball GT Super 17 Saga

Card	Low	High
Complete Set (154)	150.00	275.00
Booster Box (24 packs)	50.00	75.00
Booster Pack (10 cards)	3.00	4.00
*Foil: 1.5X to 3X Baxic Cards		
❑ 105 Android Rocket Crush R	1.00	2.00
❑ 106 Black Fallback R	1.00	2.00
❑ 107 Black Good-bye R	1.00	2.00
❑ 108 Black Gripe R	1.00	2.00
❑ 109 Black Hidden Drill R	1.00	2.00
❑ 110 Black Morbid Cuisine Drill R	1.00	2.00
❑ 111 Black Tickle Drill R	1.00	2.00
❑ 112 Blue Android 18's Grieving R	1.00	2.00
❑ 113 Blue Defensive Posture R	1.00	2.00
❑ 114 Blue Restriction R	2.00	4.00
❑ 115 Blue Safeguard R	1.00	2.00
❑ 116 Blue Scattershot Drill R	1.00	3.00
❑ 117 Blue Searching R	1.00	2.00
❑ 118 Blue Soul Alignment R	1.00	2.00
❑ 119 Chi Chi's Broom Bustle R	1.00	2.00
❑ 120 City Rampage R	1.00	2.00
❑ 121 Final Breath R	5.00	9.00
❑ 122 Flight Drill R	1.00	2.00
❑ 123 Goku's Sacrifical Restraint R	1.00	2.00
❑ 124 Massive Destruction R	1.00	2.00
❑ 125 Ornage Amazing Rescue R	1.00	2.00
❑ 126 Orange Android 17's Electric Shot R	2.00	4.00
❑ 127 Orange Android 17's Personal Touch R	2.00	4.00
❑ 128 Orange Conference Drill R	2.00	4.00
❑ 129 Orange Dual Aura Drill R	2.00	4.00
❑ 130 Orange Juke R	1.00	2.00
❑ 131 Orange Power Transmission Drill R	1.00	2.00
❑ 132 Piccolo's Destruction Drill R	2.00	5.00
❑ 133 Red Cell's tail Trap R	2.00	4.00
❑ 134 Red Disc Toss R	1.00	2.00
❑ 135 Red Gatling Gun R	1.00	2.00
❑ 136 Red Illusion R	2.00	4.00
❑ 137 Red Old Friends R	1.00	2.00
❑ 138 Red Ring-Out R	2.00	4.00
❑ 139 Saiyan Excitement R	1.00	3.00
❑ 140 Saiyan Soul Explosion R	1.00	2.00
❑ 141 Saiyan Spear R	1.00	3.00
❑ 142 Saiyan Squeeze R	1.00	2.00
❑ 143 Saiyan Vegeta's Anger Release R	1.00	2.00
❑ 144 Saiyan Vegeta's Combination Jab R	1.00	2.00
❑ 145 Saiyan Vegeta's Spinning Strike R	1.00	2.00
❑ 146 Super Android 17, the Completed R	1.00	3.00
❑ 147 Super Android 17's Absorption R	2.00	4.00
❑ 148 Super Android 17's Aerial Defense R	2.00	4.00
❑ 149 Super Android 17's Bear Crash R	1.00	2.00
❑ 150 Zarbon's Devastation R	1.00	2.00
❑ 151 Dr. Myuu, the Evil Engineer UR	15.00	35.00
❑ 152 Mark of the Dragon UR	25.00	40.00
❑ 153 Super Android 17, the Indestructible UR	30.00	55.00
❑ 154 Trunks Reconstruction UR	25.00	50.00

2004 Dragon Ball GT Shadow Dragon

Card	Low	High
Complete Set (244)	150.00	250.00
Booster Box (24 packs)	45.00	65.00
Booster Pack (10 cards)	3.00	3.75
Unlisted Commons	.10	.25
Unlisted Uncommons	.30	.75
Starter Cards (245-292)	.25	.50
*Foil: 1X to 2X Basic Cards		
❑ 167 Black Concealed Mastery R	1.00	2.00
❑ 168 Black Desperation Break R	1.00	2.00
❑ 169 Black Evil Glare R	1.00	2.00
❑ 170 Black Focal Point R	3.00	5.00
❑ 171 Black Power Abduction Drill R	1.00	2.00
❑ 172 Black Power Concussion R	2.00	4.00
❑ 173 Black Rapid Aggression R	1.00	2.00
❑ 174 Black Resourceful Drill R	1.00	2.00
❑ 175 Black Smoke Dragon Sensei R	1.00	2.00
❑ 176 Black Tunneling Technique R	1.00	2.00
❑ 177 Blue Amplified Mastery R	1.00	2.00
❑ 178 Blue Blurred Images Drill R	1.00	2.00
❑ 179 Blue Body Breakdown R	1.00	2.00
❑ 180 Blue Buried Boost Drill R	1.00	2.00
❑ 181 Blue Dragon Hammer R	1.00	2.00
❑ 182 Blue Familiar Kamehameha R	1.00	2.00
❑ 183 Blue Grieving Wish R	1.00	2.00
❑ 184 Blue Mad Dash R	2.00	4.00
❑ 185 Blue Underwear Wish R	1.00	2.00
❑ 186 Cracked Dragon Ball 5 R	1.00	2.00
❑ 187 Cracked Dragon Ball 6 R	1.00	2.00
❑ 188 Cracked Dragon Ball 7 R	1.00	2.00
❑ 189 Eis Shenron, the Backstabber R	1.00	2.00
❑ 190 Eternal Dragon Sensei R	1.00	2.00
❑ 191 Giru Sensei R	1.00	2.00
❑ 192 Gogeta, Super Saiyan 4 R	4.00	8.00
❑ 193 Goku, Super Saiyan 4 R	3.00	5.00
❑ 194 Kabito Kai Sensei R	1.00	2.00
❑ 195 Ki Depletion R	1.00	2.00
❑ 196 Nouva Shenron, Noble Fighter R	1.00	2.00
❑ 197 Nouva Shenron, Nouva Star R	1.00	2.00
❑ 198 Oceanus Shenron, Mask Unveiled R	1.00	2.00
❑ 199 Oceanus Shenron, Whirlwind Gale R	1.00	2.00
❑ 200 Omega Shenron Sensei R	1.00	2.00
❑ 201 Omega Shenron, Leader of Dragons R	1.00	2.00
❑ 202 Orange Ambush Drill R	1.00	2.00
❑ 203 Orange Approaching Darkness R	1.00	2.00
❑ 204 Orange Attack Steal R	1.00	2.00
❑ 205 Orange Breakout R	2.00	4.00
❑ 206 Orange Defensive Drill R	1.00	2.00
❑ 207 Orange Gravity Training R	1.00	2.00
❑ 208 Orange Pinpoint Mastery R	1.00	2.00
❑ 209 Orange Posture Drill R	1.00	2.00
❑ 210 Orange Training Drill R	2.00	4.00
❑ 211 Pan, the Egotistical R	2.00	4.00
❑ 212 Pan's Chasing Drill R	1.00	2.00
❑ 213 Rage Shenron, the Huge R	1.00	2.00
❑ 214 Red Chopstick-Fu R	1.00	2.00
❑ 215 Red Dragon Booster R	1.00	2.00
❑ 216 Red Energy Resonation R	2.00	4.00
❑ 217 Red Exercise Drill R	1.00	2.00
❑ 218 Red King Kai's Observation R	1.00	2.00
❑ 219 Red Mentor Mastery R	1.00	2.00
❑ 220 Red Redirect R	2.00	4.00
❑ 221 Red Secret Methods R	1.00	2.00
❑ 222 Red Wishing Drill R	1.00	2.00
❑ 223 Saiyan Blutz Abuse R	1.00	2.00
❑ 224 Saiyan Face Attack R	1.00	2.00
❑ 225 Saiyan Fortitude R	2.00	4.00
❑ 226 Saiyan Glaring Drill R	3.00	5.00
❑ 227 Saiyan Launched Attack R	1.00	2.00
❑ 228 Saiyan Outcry Drill R	1.00	2.00
❑ 229 Saiyan Rush-Down Drill R	1.00	2.00
❑ 230 Saiyan Tactical Drill R	1.00	2.00
❑ 231 Saiyan Tactical Mastery R	1.00	2.00
❑ 232 The True Face of Evil R	2.00	4.00
❑ 233 Trunks' Flying Kick R	1.00	2.00
❑ 234 Vegeta Sensei R	1.00	2.00
❑ 235 Vegeta, King of Saiyans R	1.00	3.00
❑ 236 Vegeta's Battlefield Destruction R	1.00	2.00
❑ 237 Brutal Knock-Back UR	20.00	35.00
❑ 238 Goku, the Invincible UR	50.00	75.00
❑ 239 Majin Destruction UR	20.00	40.00
❑ 240 Maniacal Blinding Slash UR	25.00	40.00
❑ 241 Moment of Distress UR	15.00	30.00
❑ 242 Omega Shenron, Unstoppable UR	30.00	50.00
❑ 243 Paparrapa!!! UR	12.00	25.00
❑ 244 Universe Spirit Bomb UR	35.00	60.00

2004 Dragon Ball GT Lost Episodes

Card	Low	High
Complete Set (155)	150.00	225.00
Booster Box (24 packs)	35.00	60.00
Booster Pack (10 cards)	3.00	3.75
*Foil: 1.5X to 3X Basic Cards		
❑ 1 A Meeting of the Minds C	.10	.25
❑ 2 Artistic Fright Drill C	.10	.25
❑ 3 Black Bear Hug C	.10	.25
❑ 4 Black Bracing Drill C	.10	.25
❑ 5 Black Capture C	.10	.25
❑ 6 Black Foul Weather C	.10	.25
❑ 7 Black Idol Discharge C	.10	.25
❑ 8 Black Overwhelming Surprise C	.10	.25
❑ 9 Black Triple Kick C	.10	.25
❑ 10 Blue Charged Energy Blast C	.10	.25
❑ 11 Blue Cower C	.10	.25
❑ 12 Blue Goku's Kamehameha C	.10	.25
❑ 13 Blue Lifting Drill C	.10	.25
❑ 14 Blue Overhead Block C	.10	.25
❑ 15 Blue Overhead Toss C	.10	.25
❑ 16 Bon Para Para C	.10	.25
❑ 17 Buried! C	.10	.25
❑ 18 Dazzle the Public C	.10	.25
❑ 19 Electrocuted C	.10	.25
❑ 20 Exploration Drill C	.10	.25
❑ 21 Glare of the Dragon C	.10	.25
❑ 22 Goku's Childish Taunt C	.10	.25
❑ 23 Goku's Left Evade C	.10	.25
❑ 24 Goku's Ride C	.10	.25
❑ 25 I've Got What You Want! C	.10	.25
❑ 26 Luud C	.10	.25
❑ 27 Mutchy C	.10	.25
❑ 28 Orange Disorientation C	.10	.25
❑ 29 Orange Emperor Pilaf's Command C	.10	.25
❑ 30 Orange Expectant Dodge C	.10	.25
❑ 31 Orange Groveling Drill C	.10	.25
❑ 32 Orange Peace Drill C	.10	.25
❑ 33 Orange Right Ki Explosion C	.10	.25
❑ 34 Orange Right Thrust C	.10	.25
❑ 35 Pan's Extreme Assailment C	.10	.25
❑ 36 Pan's Tea Time Drill C	.10	.25
❑ 37 Red Aggravated Bite C	.10	.25
❑ 38 Red Combined Blast C	.10	.25
❑ 39 Red Discovered Crouch C	.10	.25
❑ 40 Red Elusive Drill C	.10	.25
❑ 41 Red Energy Dismissal C	.10	.25
❑ 42 Red Harried Crawl C	.10	.25
❑ 43 Red Internal Ki Blast C	.10	.25
❑ 44 Red Swift Dodge C	.10	.25
❑ 45 Saiyan Amazement C	.10	.25
❑ 46 Saiyan Egged C	.10	.25
❑ 47 Saiyan Crushing Elbow C	.10	.25
❑ 48 Saiyan Pan's Foot Capture C	.10	.25
❑ 49 Saiyan Pan's Left Salvo C	.10	.25
❑ 50 Saiyan Trunks' Enraged Glare C	.10	.25
❑ 51 Saiyan Youth Aggression C	.10	.25
❑ 52 Zoonama C	.10	.25
❑ 53 Black Back Whip U	.30	.75
❑ 54 Blue Betrayal U	.30	.75
❑ 55 Black Energy Drain U	.30	.75
❑ 56 Black Excitement U	.30	.75
❑ 57 Black Pan's Energy Beam U	.30	.75
❑ 58 Black Right Energy Release U	.30	.75
❑ 59 Black Sand Blast U	.30	.75
❑ 60 Black Webbed Restraint U	.30	.75
❑ 61 Blue Doll Dress Up U	.30	.75
❑ 62 Blue Empowered Blast U	.30	.75
❑ 63 Blue Energy Thrust U	.30	.75
❑ 64 Blue Roller Coaster U	.30	.75
❑ 65 Bon Para Para, the DJ U	.30	.75
❑ 66 Cardinal Mutchy Mutchy U	.30	.75
❑ 67 Dolltaki U	.30	.75
❑ 68 Dr. Myuu U	.30	.75
❑ 69 Emperor Pilaf, the Greedy U	.30	.75
❑ 70 Extensive Eating Drill U	.30	.75
❑ 71 General Rilldo U	.30	.75
❑ 72 Orange Uppercut U	.30	.75
❑ 73 Goku's Elbow Guard U	.30	.75
❑ 74 Goku's Entrapped Drill U	.30	.75
❑ 75 Goku's Sword Catch U	.30	.75
❑ 76 Ledgic, the Fighter U	.30	.75
❑ 77 Ledgic the Weapon Masle U	.30	.75
❑ 78 Luud, the Stoic U	.30	.75
❑ 79 Luud, the Feral U	.30	.75
❑ 80 Made Over U	.30	.75
❑ 81 Mai, the Startled U	.30	.75
❑ 82 Orange Chasing Drill U	.30	.75
❑ 83 Orange Desperation Beam U	.30	.75

TCG/CCG

TCG/CCG

Card	Low	High
☐ 84 Orange Electrified Charge U	.30	.75
☐ 85 Orange Gnawing Drill U	.30	.75
☐ 86 Orange Marriage U	.30	.75
☐ 87 Orange Prepared Brace U	.30	.75
☐ 88 Preparing for Impact U	.30	.75
☐ 89 Red Criminal Intent U	.30	.75
☐ 90 Red Entranced Drill U	.30	.75
☐ 91 Red Evasive Maneuver U	.30	.75
☐ 92 Red Molar Lift U	.30	.75
☐ 93 Red Reentry U	.30	.75
☐ 94 Saiyan Restraint U	.30	.75
☐ 95 Saiyan Right Block U	.30	.75
☐ 96 Saiyan Silent Drill U	.30	.75
☐ 97 Saiyan Spying Drill U	.30	.75
☐ 98 Saiyan Taunt U	.30	.75
☐ 99 Son Para Para U	.30	.75
☐ 100 Goku U	.30	.75
☐ 101 Wanted Poster: Goku U	.30	.75
☐ 102 Wanted Poster: Pan U	.30	.75
☐ 103 Wanted Poster: Trunks U	.30	.75
☐ 104 Zoonama, the Autocrat U	.30	.75
☐ 105 The Power of the Dragon R	1.00	3.50
☐ 106 Black Blinding Beams R	1.00	3.00
☐ 107 Black Ground Hugging Drill R	1.00	2.00
☐ 108 Black Maniacal Laughter R	1.00	2.00
☐ 109 Black Reflection R	1.00	2.00
☐ 110 Black Sparring Block R	1.00	2.00
☐ 111 Blue Ball Fascination R	1.00	2.00
☐ 112 Blue Energy Deflection R	1.00	2.00
☐ 113 Blue Hostage Drill R	1.00	2.00
☐ 114 Blue Moment of Peace R	1.00	2.00
☐ 115 Blue Present R	1.00	2.00
☐ 116 Blue Trunks' Energy Discharge R	1.00	2.00
☐ 117 Bon Para Para, the Joyous R	1.00	2.00
☐ 118 Don Para Para R	1.00	2.00
☐ 119 Dragon Ball Everlasting R	1.00	3.00
☐ 120 Emperor Pilaf, the Appalled R	1.00	2.00
☐ 121 Foreshadowing R	1.00	2.00
☐ 122 Giru, the Rescuer R	1.00	2.00
☐ 123 Giru, the Fearful R	1.00	2.00
☐ 124 Goku, the Determined R	2.00	4.00
☐ 125 Gust of Wind R	1.00	3.00
☐ 126 Impressive Entrance R	1.00	2.00
☐ 127 King Kai Sensei R	1.00	2.00
☐ 128 Ledgic R	1.00	2.00
☐ 129 Mai, the Bold R	1.00	2.00
☐ 130 Orange Burst R	1.00	2.00
☐ 131 Orange Goku's Energy Volley R	1.00	3.00
☐ 132 Orange Left Ki Blast R	1.00	2.00
☐ 133 Orange Volcano R	1.00	2.00
☐ 134 Pan R	1.00	2.00
☐ 135 Pan R	1.00	2.00
☐ 136 Red Angered Search R	1.00	2.00
☐ 137 Red Debt R	1.00	2.00
☐ 138 Red Losing Battle R	1.00	3.00
☐ 139 Red Tooth Removal R	1.00	3.00
☐ 140 Red Unsuspecting Trip R	1.00	2.00
☐ 141 Saiyan Catch R	1.00	3.00
☐ 142 Saiyan Charged Attack R	1.00	2.00
☐ 143 Saiyan Chase R	2.00	4.00
☐ 144 Saiyan Goodbye R	1.00	2.00
☐ 145 Saiyan Lunge R	1.00	2.00
☐ 146 Showdown R	1.00	2.00
☐ 147 Trunks R	1.00	3.00
☐ 148 Trunks' Left Elbow Smash R	1.50	3.00
☐ 149 Trunks' Thoughts R	1.50	3.00
☐ 150 Zoonama, Discombobulated R	1.00	2.00
☐ 151 Bulma Sensei UR	15.00	30.00
☐ 152 Captured! UR	20.00	40.00
☐ 153 Trunks, Super Saiyan UR	25.00	50.00
☐ 154 Pan, the Persistent UR	20.00	40.00

2005 Dragon Ball Z Arrival

Card	Low	High
Complete Set (254)	200.00	250.00
Booster Box (12 packs)	10.00	20.00
Booster Pack (10 cards)	2.00	3.00
☐ 1 Black Arrogant Block C	.10	.20
☐ 2 Black Back Lift C	.10	.20
☐ 3 Black Chest Beam C	.10	.20
☐ 4 Black Chin Punch C	.10	.20
☐ 5 Black Dash C	.10	.20
☐ 6 Black Encouragement C	.10	.20
☐ 7 Black Face Strike C	.10	.20
☐ 8 Black Jump Kick C	.10	.20
☐ 9 Black Left Blast C	.10	.20
☐ 10 Black Moon Energy C	.10	.20
☐ 11 Black Preparation C	.10	.20
☐ 12 Black Stance C	.10	.20
☐ 13 Blue Forceful Burst C	.10	.20
☐ 14 Blue Leaping Knee C	.10	.20
☐ 15 Blue Left Blast C	.10	.20
☐ 16 Blue Left Dodge C	.10	.20
☐ 17 Blue Overhead Pound C	.10	.20
☐ 18 Blue Rage C	.10	.20
☐ 19 Blue Shielding C	.10	.20
☐ 20 Blue Shoot 'em Up C	.10	.20
☐ 21 Blue Showdown C	.10	.20
☐ 22 Blue Spit C	.10	.20
☐ 23 Blue Stalemate C	.10	.20
☐ 24 Blue Uppercut C	.10	.20
☐ 25 Chiaotzu - Energy Charged C	.10	.20
☐ 26 Chiaotzu - Silently Strong C	.10	.20
☐ 27 Earth Dragon Ball 1 C	.10	.20
☐ 28 Earth Dragon Ball 2 C	.10	.20
☐ 29 Earth Dragon Ball 3 C	.10	.20
☐ 30 Gohan - Confident Youth C	.10	.20
☐ 31 Gohan - Resolute Ally C	.10	.20
☐ 32 Gohan's Dream C	.10	.20
☐ 33 Krillin - Smiling Warrior C	.10	.20
☐ 34 Krillin's Determination C	.10	.20
☐ 35 Namekian Capture C	.10	.20
☐ 36 Namekian Charged Attack C	.10	.20
☐ 37 Namekian Concentration C	.10	.20
☐ 38 Namekian Cross Block C	.10	.20
☐ 39 Namekian Face Blast C	.10	.20
☐ 40 Namekian Finger Defense C	.10	.20
☐ 41 Namekian Focusing C	.10	.20
☐ 42 Namekian Ground Slam C	.10	.20
☐ 43 Namekian Intense Beam C	.10	.20
☐ 44 Namekian Pound C	.10	.20
☐ 45 Namekian Rear Kick C	.10	.20
☐ 46 Namekian Wrist Grab C	.10	.20
☐ 47 Nappa - Ready Saiyan C	.10	.20
☐ 48 Nappa's Protective Aura C	.10	.20
☐ 49 Orange Bite C	.10	.20
☐ 50 Orange Dinosaur Chase C	.10	.20
☐ 51 Orange Energy Clash C	.10	.20
☐ 52 Orange Energy Flare C	.10	.20
☐ 53 Orange Evade C	.10	.20
☐ 54 Orange Laughter C	.10	.20
☐ 55 Orange Mouth Beam C	.10	.20
☐ 56 Orange Power Up C	.10	.20
☐ 57 Orange Right Kick C	.10	.20
☐ 58 Orange Stomach Thrust C	.10	.20
☐ 59 Orange Shock C	.10	.20
☐ 60 Orange Surprise C	.10	.20
☐ 61 Raditz - Saiyan Invader C	.10	.20
☐ 62 Raditz - Deadly Herald C	.10	.20
☐ 63 Raditz's Triumph C	.10	.20
☐ 64 Red Cover Up C	.10	.20
☐ 65 Red Energy Dive C	.10	.20
☐ 66 Red Fingertip Shot C	.10	.20
☐ 67 Red Forceful Blast C	.10	.20
☐ 68 Red Glare C	.10	.20
☐ 69 Red Leaping Kick C	.10	.20
☐ 70 Red Leaping Thrust C	.10	.20
☐ 71 Red Left Punch C	.10	.20
☐ 72 Red Recharge C	.10	.20
☐ 73 Red Right Cross C	.10	.20
☐ 74 Red Right Kick C	.10	.20
☐ 75 Red Youth Bite C	.10	.20
☐ 76 Saibaimen - Alien Henchman C	.10	.20
☐ 77 Saibaimen - Vicious Combatant C	.10	.20
☐ 78 Saibaimen's Seeds C	.10	.20
☐ 79 Saiyan Destructive Thrust C	.10	.20
☐ 80 Saiyan Dive C	.10	.20
☐ 81 Saiyan Evasion C	.10	.20
☐ 82 Saiyan Fingertip Blast C	.10	.20
☐ 83 Saiyan Flying Kick C	.10	.20
☐ 84 Saiyan Head Crush C	.10	.20
☐ 85 Saiyan Intense Ki Ball C	.10	.20
☐ 86 Saiyan Monkey Beam C	.10	.20
☐ 87 Saiyan Shadowing C	.10	.20
☐ 88 Saiyan Sinister Smirks C	.10	.20
☐ 89 Saiyan Skull Grab C	.10	.20
☐ 90 Saiyan Unbalanced Dodge C	.10	.20
☐ 91 Tien - Prepared Z Warrior C	.10	.20
☐ 92 Tien's Help C	.10	.20
☐ 93 Vegeta's Aura C	.10	.20
☐ 94 Yamcha - Aloof Fighter C	.10	.20
☐ 95 Yamcha - Baseball Extraordinaire C	.10	.20
☐ 96 Yamcha's Stance C	.10	.20
☐ 97 Black Crying U	.20	.50
☐ 98 Black Diving Elbow U	.20	.50
☐ 99 Black Electric Tendrils U	.20	.50
☐ 100 Black Fastball U	.20	.50
☐ 101 Black Finale U	.20	.50
☐ 102 Black Power Up U	.20	.50
☐ 103 Black Quick Shot U	.20	.50
☐ 104 Black Right Block U	.20	.50
☐ 105 Black Throw U	.20	.50
☐ 106 Black Water Pound U	.20	.50
☐ 107 Blue Breakaway U	.20	.50
☐ 108 Blue Breakout U	.20	.50
☐ 109 Blue Bubble Breath U	.20	.50
☐ 110 Blue Cheer U	.20	.50
☐ 111 Blue Earth Pound U	.20	.50
☐ 112 Blue Forearm Block U	.20	.50
☐ 113 Blue Lunge U	.20	.50
☐ 114 Blue Snacks U	.20	.50
☐ 115 Blue Utility Beam U	.20	.50
☐ 116 Blue Wing Destruction U	.20	.50
☐ 117 Chaiotzu's Self Destruct U	.20	.50
☐ 118 Chiaotzu's Help U	.20	.50
☐ 119 Earth Dragon Ball 4 U	.20	.50
☐ 120 Earth Dragon Ball 5 U	.20	.50
☐ 121 Gohan's Masenko Blast U	.20	.50
☐ 122 Goku - Battle Ready U	.20	.50
☐ 123 Goku - Enraged U	.20	.50
☐ 124 Goku's Taunt U	.20	.50
☐ 125 Krillin - Serious Battler U	.20	.50
☐ 126 Krillin - Energy Blastin' U	.20	.50
☐ 127 Namekian Blinding Ray U	.20	.50
☐ 128 Namekian Braced Beam U	.20	.50
☐ 129 Namekian Confidence U	.20	.50
☐ 130 Namekian Elbow U	.20	.50
☐ 131 Namekian Evasion U	.20	.50
☐ 132 Namekian Eye Lasers U	.20	.50
☐ 133 Namekian Ki Burst U	.20	.50
☐ 134 Namekian Left Cross U	.20	.50
☐ 135 Namekian Support U	.20	.50
☐ 136 Namekian Surprise U	.20	.50
☐ 137 Nappa - Faithful Cohort U	.20	.50
☐ 138 Nappa - Ki Charged U	.20	.50
☐ 139 Orange Catch U	.20	.50
☐ 140 Orange Dance U	.20	.50
☐ 141 Orange Finger Detonation U	.20	.50
☐ 142 Orange High Knee U	.20	.50
☐ 143 Orange Lockup U	.20	.50
☐ 144 Orange Lunge U	.20	.50
☐ 145 Orange Palm Blast U	.20	.50
☐ 146 Orange Relaxation U	.20	.50
☐ 147 Orange Sacrificial Block U	.20	.50
☐ 148 Orange Sword Slice U	.20	.50
☐ 149 Piccolo - Suited For Battle U	.20	.50
☐ 150 Piccolo - Angered Namek U	.20	.50
☐ 151 Piccolo - Surprised Namek U	.20	.50
☐ 152 Piccolo's Regeneration U	.20	.50
☐ 153 Raditz - Villainous Vanguard U	.20	.50
☐ 154 Raditz - Swift to Fight U	.20	.50
☐ 155 Red Braced Attack U	.20	.50
☐ 156 Red Breakout U	.20	.50
☐ 157 Red Charged Burst U	.20	.50
☐ 158 Red Dashing Attack U	.20	.50
☐ 159 Red Electrified Attack U	.20	.50
☐ 160 Red Knee Strike U	.20	.50
☐ 161 Red Overhead Block U	.20	.50
☐ 162 Red Peace U	.20	.50
☐ 163 Red Right Hook U	.20	.50
☐ 164 Red Sword Slash U	.20	.50
☐ 165 Saibaimen's Self Destruct U	.20	.50
☐ 166 Saiyan Dashing Kick U	.20	.50
☐ 167 Saiyan Energy Gathering U	.20	.50
☐ 168 Saiyan Escaping Kick U	.20	.50
☐ 169 Saiyan Happiness U	.20	.50
☐ 170 Saiyan Ki Flare U	.20	.50
☐ 171 Saiyan Left Hit U	.20	.50
☐ 172 Saiyan Math U	.20	.50
☐ 173 Saiyan Playtime U	.20	.50
☐ 174 Saiyan Thrust U	.20	.50
☐ 175 Saiyan Triangle Burst U	.20	.50
☐ 176 Tien - Ready For Action U	.20	.50
☐ 177 Tien's Tri-Beam U	.20	.50
☐ 178 Vegeta - Rage Empowered U	.20	.50
☐ 179 Vegeta - Arrogant Prince U	.20	.50
☐ 180 Yamcha's Controlled Ki Ball U	.20	.50
☐ 181 Black Charged Ball R	1.00	2.00
☐ 182 Black Dragon Support R	1.00	2.00
☐ 183 Black Head Slam R	1.00	2.00
☐ 184 Black Huge Burst R	1.00	2.00
☐ 185 Black Overpowering Mastery R	1.00	2.00
☐ 186 Black Upward Kick R	1.00	2.00
☐ 187 Black Z Warriors' Support R	1.00	2.00
☐ 188 Blue Energy Beam R	1.00	2.00
☐ 189 Blue Forceful Mastery R	1.00	2.00
☐ 190 Blue Knee R	1.00	2.00
☐ 191 Blue Lockup R	1.00	2.00
☐ 192 Blue Lunch R	1.00	2.00
☐ 193 Blue Shout R	1.00	2.00
☐ 194 Blue Strength R	1.00	2.00
☐ 195 Blue Tail Grab R	1.00	2.00
☐ 196 Dragon Ball Radar R	1.00	2.00
☐ 197 Earth Dragon Ball 6 R	1.00	2.00
☐ 198 Earth Dragon Ball 7 R	1.00	2.00
☐ 199 Goku - Heroic Friend R	2.00	3.00
☐ 200 Goku - Desperate Savior R	2.00	3.00
☐ 201 Goku's Kamehameha R	2.00	3.00
☐ 202 Krillin - Peaceful Z Warrior R	1.00	2.00
☐ 203 Krillin's Destructo Disk R	1.00	2.00
☐ 204 Namekian Blocking Hand R	1.00	2.00
☐ 205 Namekian Conservation Mastery R	1.00	2.00
☐ 206 Namekian Defensive Stance R	1.00	2.00
☐ 207 Namekian Force Push R	1.00	2.00
☐ 208 Namekian Finger Charge R	1.00	2.00
☐ 209 Namekian Intimidation R	1.00	2.00
☐ 210 Namekian Right Jab R	1.00	2.00
☐ 211 Namekian Secret R	1.00	2.00
☐ 212 Nappa - Energy Enhanced R	1.00	2.00
☐ 213 Nappa's Bull Rush R	1.00	2.00
☐ 214 Orange Destructive Beam R	1.00	2.00
☐ 215 Orange Dinner R	1.00	2.00
☐ 216 Orange Finger Ball R	1.00	2.00
☐ 217 Orange Lookout R	2.00	3.00
☐ 218 Orange Lunging Jab R	1.00	2.00
☐ 219 Orange Rapture R	1.00	2.00
☐ 220 Orange Skillful Mastery R	1.00	2.00
☐ 221 Paid Off R	1.00	2.00
☐ 222 Piccolo - Fearless Combatant R	1.00	2.00
☐ 223 Piccolo's Special Beam Cannon R	1.00	2.00
☐ 224 Raditz's Tail Whip R	1.00	2.00
☐ 225 Red Destructive Blast R	1.00	2.00
☐ 226 Red Double Kick R	1.00	2.00
☐ 227 Red Ki Aura R	1.00	2.00
☐ 228 Red Left Kick R	1.00	2.00
☐ 229 Red Mouth Cannon R	1.00	2.00
☐ 230 Red Reversal Mastery R	1.00	2.00
☐ 231 Red Shout R	1.00	2.00
☐ 232 Refill R	1.00	2.00
☐ 233 Saiyan Aggressive Mastery R	1.00	2.00
☐ 234 Saiyan Jump R	1.00	2.00
☐ 235 Saiyan Ki Charge R	1.00	2.00
☐ 236 Saiyan Personal Ki Ball R	1.00	2.00
☐ 237 Saiyan Rest R	1.00	2.00
☐ 238 Saiyan Right Punch R	2.00	3.00
☐ 239 Saiyan Battle Armor R	1.00	2.00
☐ 240 Vegeta - Prince of All Saiyans R	2.00	3.00
☐ 241 Vegeta - Saiyan Warrior R	2.00	3.00
☐ 242 Vegeta's Gallic Gun R	2.00	3.00
☐ 243 Goku - Desperate Savior ST	1.00	2.00
☐ 244 Krillin - Peaceful Z Warrior ST	1.00	2.00
☐ 245 Nappa - Energy Enhanced ST	1.00	2.00
☐ 246 Piccolo - Fearless Combatant ST	1.00	2.00
☐ 247 Raditz - Villainous Vanguard ST	1.00	2.00
☐ 248 Vegeta - Prince of All Saiyans ST	1.00	2.00
☐ 249 Scouter Goku ST	1.00	2.00
☐ 250 Scouter Krillin ST	1.00	2.00
☐ 251 Scouter Nappa ST	1.00	2.00
☐ 252 Scouter Piccolo ST	1.00	2.00
☐ 253 Scouter Raditz ST	1.00	2.00
☐ F1 Broly - Bio-Broly P	2.50	5.00

2008 Dragon Ball Destructive Fury

Card	Low	High
Complete Set (108)	30.00	60.00
Booster Box (24 packs)	40.00	80.00
Booster Pack (10 cards)	2.50	5.00
*Foil: 1X to 2X Basic Cards		
☐ EV043 Shallow Idea C	.10	.25
☐ EV044 Return from Other World U	.20	.50
☐ EV045 New Adventure C	.10	.25
☐ EV046 Antagonism C	.10	.25
☐ EV047 Mustle Tower R	1.00	2.00
☐ EV048 Cell Game U	.20	.50
☐ EV049 The Only Aim C	.10	.25
☐ EV050 Android Project C	.10	.25
☐ EV051 Ginyu Force Gathered! R	1.00	2.00
☐ EV052 New Scanner R	1.00	2.00
☐ EV053 The Next World Martial Arts Championship U	.20	.50
☐ EV054 Saiyan's Pride C	.10	.25
☐ EV055 Appearance of a Hero U	.20	.50
☐ EV056 The Saviour? U	.20	.50
☐ EV057 Marriage C	.10	.25
☐ EV058 Comfortable Place U	.20	.50
☐ EV059 Growing Good Will C	.10	.25
☐ EV060 The Ball of Seal U	.20	.50
☐ EV061 Surprise C	.10	.25
☐ EV062 Resistance of the Majin C	.10	.25
☐ EV063 Exposure ST	.50	1.00
☐ EV064 Special Fighting Pose ST	.50	1.00
☐ TE073 Power Pole R	1.00	2.00
☐ TE074 Teleportation U	.20	.50
☐ TE075 Comrade's Assistance C	.10	.25
☐ TE076 Tri-Beam R	1.00	2.00
☐ TE077 Breaking Through the Limit R	1.00	2.00
☐ TE078 Masenko R	1.00	2.00
☐ TE079 Super Kamehameha SR	3.00	6.00
☐ TE080 Clone Jutsu U	.20	.50
☐ TE081 Powered Gun U	.20	.50
☐ TE082 Rocket Punch U	.20	.50
☐ TE083 Unexpected Counter C	.10	.25
☐ TE084 Birth of the Perfect Form R	1.00	2.00
☐ TE085 Hell Flash SR	3.00	8.00
☐ TE086 Irregular Attack C	.10	.25
☐ TE087 Battle Suit C	.10	.25
☐ TE088 Bindining Technique U	.20	.50
☐ TE089 Recoome Kick R	1.00	2.00
☐ TE090 Energy Cannon R	1.00	2.00
☐ TE091 Body Change U	.20	.50
☐ TE092 Overflowing Aura U	.20	.50
☐ TE093 Big Bang Attack SR	1.50	3.00
☐ TE094 Disguise Suit C	.10	.25
☐ TE095 Huge Difference in Power U	.20	.50
☐ TE096 Super Gravity Room U	.20	.50
☐ TE097 Emergency Stop Switch C	.10	.25
☐ TE098 Making a Deal Behind the Scenes C	.10	.25
☐ TE099 A Girl's Heart R	1.00	2.00
☐ TE100 Beginning of the Training C	.10	.25
☐ TE101 Expanding Vibration R	1.00	2.00
☐ TE102 Peculiar Space C	.10	.25
☐ TE103 Sorcery U	.20	.50
☐ TE104 Petrification U	.20	.50
☐ TE105 Pure Impulse C	.10	.25
☐ TE106 Thunder Flash R	1.00	2.00
☐ TE107 Counter Against Evil Containment Wave R	1.00	2.00
☐ TE108 Dynamic Mess Em Up Punch ST	.50	1.00
☐ TE109 Enormous Fighting Aura ST	.50	1.00
☐ WA095 Trunks C	.10	.25
☐ WA096 Goten C	.10	.25
☐ WA097 Krillin U	.20	.50
☐ WA098 Tien U	.20	.50
☐ WA099 Goku (GT) R	1.00	2.00
☐ WA100 Gohan C	.10	.25
☐ WA101 Piccolo R	1.00	2.00
☐ WA102 Trunks (Super Saiyan) SR	1.50	3.00
☐ WA103 Goku (Super Saiyan 3) SR	3.00	6.00
☐ WA104 Ninja Murasaki C	.10	.25
☐ WA105 General White C	.10	.25
☐ WA106 Colonel Violet U	.20	.50
☐ WA107 Staff Officer Black C	.10	.25
☐ WA108 Major Metallitron U	.20	.50
☐ WA109 Buyon C	.10	.25
☐ WA110 Cell Jr. R	1.00	2.00
☐ WA111 Android 16 R	1.00	2.00
☐ WA112 Cell (Perfect Form) SR	1.50	3.00
☐ WA113 West Kai U	.20	.50
☐ WA114 South Kai U	.20	.50
☐ WA115 East Kai U	.20	.50
☐ WA116 Guldo U	.20	.50
☐ WA117 Recoome C	.10	.25
☐ WA118 Burter U	.20	.50
☐ WA119 Jeice C	.10	.25
☐ WA120 Captain Ginyu R	1.00	2.00
☐ WA121 Vegeta (Brain Washed) SR	1.50	3.00
☐ WA122 Announcer C	.10	.25
☐ WA123 Launch C	.10	.25
☐ WA124 Android 8 U	.20	.50
☐ WA125 Chi-Chi C	.10	.25
☐ WA126 Videl U	.20	.50
☐ WA127 Pan R	1.00	2.00
☐ WA128 Olibu C	.10	.25
☐ WA129 Android 18 R	1.00	2.00
☐ WA130 Great Saiyaman SR	1.50	3.00
☐ WA131 Babidi C	.10	.25
☐ WA132 Bibidi C	.10	.25
☐ WA133 Piccolo Jr. U	.20	.50
☐ WA134 Pui Pui C	.10	.25
☐ WA135 Yakon C	.10	.25
☐ WA136 Pikkon R	1.00	2.00
☐ WA137 Dabura R	1.00	2.00
☐ WA138 Super Garlic Jr. R	1.00	2.00
☐ WA139 Majin Buu SR	2.00	4.00
☐ WA140 Gohan ST	.50	1.00
☐ WA141 Great Saiyaman ST	.50	1.00
☐ WA142 Vegeta ST	.50	1.00
☐ WA143 Mecha Frieza ST	.50	1.00

2008 Dragon Ball The Awakening

Card	Low	High
Complete Set (100)	30.00	60.00
Booster Box (24 packs)	30.00	60.00
Booster Pack (10 cards)	2.50	4.00
*Foil: 1X to 2X Basic Cards		
☐ EV023 Reunion C	.10	.25
☐ EV024 Outcome of the Training C	.10	.25
☐ EV025 To Planet Namek U	.20	.50
☐ EV026 Mysterious Boy from the Future R	1.00	2.00
☐ EV027 Red Ribbon Army C	.10	.25
☐ EV028 Trap in the Pilaf's Castle U	.20	.50
☐ EV029 Unleashed Threat C	.10	.25
☐ EV030 Premonition of Desperation C	.10	.25
☐ EV031 Emission of the Aura C	.10	.25
☐ EV032 Throwing the Elite Unit into the Front Line U	.20	.50
☐ EV033 All Kais Gathered! C	.10	.25
☐ EV034 Never Ending Nightmare R	1.00	2.00
☐ EV035 Love at First Sight U	.20	.50
☐ EV036 Lone Wolf C	.10	.25
☐ EV037 Prophecy of Fortuneteller Baba R	1.00	2.00
☐ EV038 Master Roshi's Full Power C	.10	.25
☐ EV039 Union of the Warriors C	.10	.25
☐ EV040 Unleashed Hidden Power C	.10	.25
☐ EV041 Avenger C	.10	.25
☐ EV042 Exhausted C	.10	.25
☐ TE038 Hermit Style Uniform C	.10	.25
☐ TE039 Wolf Fang Fist C	.10	.25
☐ TE040 Nimbus Cloud R	1.00	2.00
☐ TE041 Rapid Sword Drawing U	.20	.50
☐ TE042 Destructo Disk R	1.00	2.00
☐ TE043 Awakened by the Anger SR	1.50	3.00
☐ TE044 Spirit Bomb R	1.00	2.00
☐ TE045 Supernatural Power C	.10	.25
☐ TE046 Four Witches Technique U	.20	.50
☐ TE047 Hostage U	.20	.50
☐ TE048 Flying on a Pole C	.10	.25
☐ TE049 Absorption of Energy U	.20	.50
☐ TE050 Copied Skill R	1.00	2.00
☐ TE051 Barrier R	1.00	2.00
☐ TE052 Saibamen Capsule U	.20	.50
☐ TE053 Ruthless Blow C	.10	.25
☐ TE054 Medical Machine C	.10	.25
☐ TE055 Countdown to the Destruction U	.20	.50
☐ TE056 Gallic Gun SR	1.50	3.00
☐ TE057 Pride of Elite R	1.00	2.00
☐ TE058 Psylock Smasher R	1.00	2.00
☐ TE059 Temptation C	.10	.25
☐ TE060 Time Machine U	.20	.50
☐ TE061 Sleepy-Boy Technique C	.10	.25
☐ TE062 Momentary Battle U	.20	.50
☐ TE063 Microminiaturizer U	.20	.50
☐ TE064 Double Knock Out R	1.00	2.00
☐ TE065 Medicine from the Future R	1.00	2.00
☐ TE066 Evil Cannon C	.10	.25
☐ TE067 Healing Power C	.10	.25
☐ TE068 Black Water Mist C	.10	.25
☐ TE069 Evil Containment Wave U	.20	.50
☐ TE070 Hyperbolic Time Chamber U	.20	.50
☐ TE071 The Last Gamble SR	1.00	2.00
☐ TE072 Revival of The Shenron R	1.00	2.00
☐ WA050 Bulma U	.20	.50
☐ WA051 Dr. Brief C	.10	.25
☐ WA052 Yamcha C	.10	.25
☐ WA053 Gohan R	1.00	2.00
☐ WA054 Krillin C	.10	.25
☐ WA055 Goku U	.20	.50
☐ WA056 Trunks SR	2.00	4.00
☐ WA057 Piccolo U	.20	.50
☐ WA058 Gohan (Super Saiyan) SR	4.00	8.00
☐ WA059 Monster Carrot C	.10	.25
☐ WA060 Supreme Commander Red R	1.00	2.00
☐ WA061 Chiaotzu C	.10	.25
☐ WA062 Colonel Silver C	.10	.25
☐ WA063 General Blue U	.20	.50
☐ WA064 Tien U	.20	.50

Card	Low	High
❑ WA065 Android 19 R	1.00	2.00
❑ WA066 Android 20 R	1.00	2.00
❑ WA067 Cell (The 2nd Form) SR	5.00	10.00
❑ WA068 Saibamen C	.10	.25
❑ WA069 Bubles C	.10	.25
❑ WA070 Gregory C	.10	.25
❑ WA071 Dodoria U	.20	.50
❑ WA072 Zarbon U	.20	.50
❑ WA073 Zarbon (Transformed) R	1.00	2.00
❑ WA074 Bardock R	1.00	2.00
❑ WA075 Vegeta (Super Saiyan) SR	6.00	12.00
❑ WA076 Frieza (Full Power Form) SR	1.50	3.00
❑ WA077 Launch U	.20	.50
❑ WA078 Chi-Chi R	1.00	2.00
❑ WA079 Hercule C	.10	.25
❑ WA080 Korin U	.20	.50
❑ WA081 King Chapa C	.10	.25
❑ WA082 Ox-King C	.10	.25
❑ WA083 Mr. Popo C	.10	.25
❑ WA084 Mysterious Martial Artist R	1.00	2.00
❑ WA085 Shien SR	1.50	3.00
❑ WA086 Dende U	.20	.50
❑ WA087 Guru U	.20	.50
❑ WA088 Salt C	.10	.25
❑ WA089 Mustard C	.10	.25
❑ WA090 Vineger C	.10	.25
❑ WA091 Spice C	.10	.25
❑ WA092 Garlic Jr. R	1.00	2.00
❑ WA093 Nail R	1.00	2.00
❑ WA094 Lord Slug SR	3.00	6.00

2008 Dragon Ball The Warriors Return

Card	Low	High
Complete Set (113)	25.00	50.00
Booster Box (24 packs)	20.00	50.00
Booster Pack (9 cards)	1.25	3.00
*Foil: 1X to 2X Basic Cards		
❑ EV001 Training in the Korin Tower C	.10	.25
❑ EV002 Lesson by Master Roshi U	.20	.50
❑ EV003 Rapid Movement U	.20	.50
❑ EV004 Full Moon C	.10	.25
❑ EV005 Powerful Backup U	.20	.50
❑ EV006 Emperor Pilaf's Plot C	.10	.25
❑ EV007 No Mercy C	.10	.25
❑ EV008 Ambition of Dr. Gero U	.20	.50
❑ EV009 Crumbled Pride C	.10	.25
❑ EV010 Legendary Tribe Saiyan C	.10	.25
❑ EV011 Invasion of the Planet C	.10	.25
❑ EV012 Absolute Fear R	.75	1.50
❑ EV013 Pafu Pafu C	.10	.25
❑ EV014 Journey of Adventure C	.10	.25
❑ EV015 World Martial Arts Championship U	.20	.50
❑ EV016 Capsule Corporation C	.10	.25
❑ EV017 Threat of the Evil Tribe C	.10	.25
❑ EV018 Terrifying Plan C	.10	.25
❑ EV019 Selection of the Race R	.75	1.50
❑ EV020 Reviving Power C	.10	.25
❑ EV021 Combination ST	.50	1.00
❑ EV022 Captured ST	.50	1.00
❑ TE001 Janken-Goo U	.20	.50
❑ TE002 Spirit Ball C	.10	.25
❑ TE003 Solar Flare C	.10	.25
❑ TE004 Afterimage U	.20	.50
❑ TE005 Kamehameha R	.75	1.50
❑ TE006 One Last Attack R	.75	1.50
❑ TE007 Kaio-Ken R	.75	1.50
❑ TE008 Reversal U	.20	.50
❑ TE009 Overwhelming Power C	.10	.25
❑ TE010 Dodonpa R	.75	1.50
❑ TE011 Hyper Evolution C	.10	.25
❑ TE012 Reinforced Body C	.10	.25
❑ TE013 Merciless Attack R	.75	1.50
❑ TE014 Awakening of the Evil U	.20	.50
❑ TE015 Scanner C	.10	.25
❑ TE016 Resisting Power U	.20	.50
❑ TE017 Appearance of the Unknown Enemy C	.10	.25
❑ TE018 Stomping R	.75	1.50
❑ TE019 True Power R	.75	1.50
❑ TE020 Roar R	.75	1.50
❑ TE021 Death Ball R	.75	1.50
❑ TE022 Searching for Dragon Ball C	.10	.25
❑ TE023 Super Holy Water U	.20	.50
❑ TE024 Cross Arm Dive C	.10	.25
❑ TE025 Bankoku Bikkuri Sho C	.10	.25
❑ TE026 Senzu Beans U	.20	.50
❑ TE027 Hoipoi-Capsule R	.75	1.50
❑ TE028 Accident U	.20	.50
❑ TE029 Evil Wave Explosion U	.20	.50
❑ TE030 Giant Body Just C	.10	.25
❑ TE031 Summoning the Hidden Power U	.20	.50
❑ TE032 Absorbed Power C	.10	.25
❑ TE033 Special Beam R	.75	1.50
❑ TE034 Evil Force Organized! U	.20	.50
❑ TE035 Kami's Shrine C	.10	.25
❑ TE036 Power of the Instinct ST	.50	1.00
❑ TE037 Frieza's henchmen ST	.50	1.00
❑ WA001 Goku C	.10	.25
❑ WA002 Yamcha C	.10	.25
❑ WA003 Krillin U	.20	.50
❑ WA004 Master Roshi R	.75	1.50
❑ WA005 Tien U	.20	.50
❑ WA006 Chiaotzu C	.10	.25
❑ WA007 Gohan SR	1.50	3.00
❑ WA008 Goku (Super Saiyan) SR	2.00	4.00
❑ WA009 Giant Ape R	.75	1.50
❑ WA010 Emperor Pilaf U	.20	.50
❑ WA011 Shu C	.10	.25
❑ WA012 Mai C	.10	.25
❑ WA013 Emperor Pilaf Machine U	.20	.50
❑ WA014 Master Shen C	.10	.25
❑ WA015 Mercenary Tao R	.75	1.50
❑ WA016 Android #17 R	.75	1.50
❑ WA017 Android #18 R	.75	1.50
❑ WA018 Cell R	.75	1.50
❑ WA019 Raditz C	.10	.25
❑ WA020 Nappa C	.10	.25
❑ WA021 Vegeta SR	2.00	4.00
❑ WA022 Raspberry C	.10	.25
❑ WA023 Kyui C	.10	.25
❑ WA024 Frieza SR	1.50	3.00
❑ WA025 Frieza (The 2nd Form) R	.75	1.50
❑ WA026 Frieza (The Final Form) SR	1.50	3.00
❑ WA027 Kaio U	.20	.50
❑ WA028 Bulma U	.20	.50
❑ WA029 Oolong U	.20	.50
❑ WA030 Puar U	.20	.50
❑ WA031 Fortuneteller Baba R	.75	1.50
❑ WA032 Giran C	.10	.25
❑ WA033 Ranfan R	.75	1.50
❑ WA034 Nam U	.20	.50
❑ WA035 Jackie Chun R	.75	1.50
❑ WA036 Yajirobe C	.10	.25
❑ WA037 King Piccolo SR	2.50	5.00
❑ WA038 Piano U	.20	.50
❑ WA039 Tambourine U	.20	.50
❑ WA040 Cymbal C	.10	.25
❑ WA041 Piccolo Jr. U	.20	.50
❑ WA042 Kami R	.75	1.50
❑ WA043 Piccolo SR	1.00	2.00
❑ WA044 Yamu C	.10	.25
❑ WA045 Spopovich U	.20	.50
❑ WA046 Goku ST SR	.50	1.00
❑ WA047 Krillin ST	.30	.75
❑ WA048 Frieza ST SR	.50	1.00
❑ WA049 Frieza (The 3rd Form) ST	.30	.75
❑ WI001 Emperor Pilaf's Wish ST SR	1.00	2.00
❑ WI002 Oolong's Wish ST SR	1.00	2.00
❑ WI003 Upa's Wish ST SR	2.00	4.00
❑ WI004 Frieza's Last Wish ST SR	1.00	2.00
❑ WI005 Dende's Wish SR	1.00	2.00

2009 Dragon Ball Clash of Sagas

Card	Low	High
Complete Set (108)	40.00	80.00
Booster Box (24 packs)	40.00	80.00
Booster Pack (10 cards)	2.50	5.00
*Foil: 1X to 2X Basic Cards		
❑ EV085 Ascending to a new level R	.75	1.50
❑ EV086 Strength from loss U	.20	.50
❑ EV087 A Hero's Arrival U	.20	.50
❑ EV088 Weighted training C	.10	.25
❑ EV089 Backup has arrived C	.10	.25
❑ EV090 Roll Call U	.20	.50
❑ EV091 Base of Operations R	.75	1.50
❑ EV092 Fading Riches C	.10	.25
❑ EV093 Cold Legacy R	.75	1.50
❑ EV094 Pain and Power U	.20	.50
❑ EV095 UFO landing U	.20	.50
❑ EV096 Power Struggle R	.75	1.50
❑ EV097 Preparation for Battle U	.20	.50
❑ EV098 Unexpected Strength C	.10	.25
❑ EV099 Alternate Future SR	2.50	5.00
❑ EV100 Mystery Pots C	.10	.25
❑ EV101 Awakening of Power U	.20	.50
❑ EV102 Threat multiplied R	.75	1.50
❑ EV103 Namekian Fusion R	.75	1.50
❑ EV104 Conflict Averted C	.10	.25
❑ TE145 Super Dragon Fist SR	4.00	8.00
❑ TE146 Kamehameha R	.75	1.50
❑ TE147 Destructo Disk U	.20	.50
❑ TE148 Burning Attack C	.10	.25
❑ TE149 Spirit Bomb U	.20	.50
❑ TE150 Energy Shield R	.75	1.50
❑ TE151 Electric Attack C	.10	.25
❑ TE152 Greed is Good C	.10	.25
❑ TE153 Exploiting the weak C	.10	.25
❑ TE154 Dirty Trick C	.10	.25
❑ TE155 Power Surge R	.75	1.50
❑ TE156 Syphon of energy C	.10	.25
❑ TE157 Betrayal of Alliegence U	.20	.50
❑ TE158 Powerful Heritage U	.20	.50
❑ TE159 Energy Sword U	.20	.50
❑ TE160 Shock Wave C	.10	.25
❑ TE161 Ultimate Transformation SR	1.50	3.00
❑ TE162 Ultimate Sacrifice R	.75	1.50
❑ TE163 Tri-Beam R	.75	1.50
❑ TE164 Will of the People C	.10	.25
❑ TE165 Katana Slice C	.10	.25
❑ TE166 Sparring Match U	.20	.50
❑ TE167 Shouts of Support C	.10	.25
❑ TE168 Strategy session U	.20	.50
❑ TE169 Special Beam Cannon C	.10	.25
❑ TE170 Mouth Beam C	.10	.25
❑ TE171 Arm Stretch C	.10	.25
❑ TE172 Laser Shot R	.75	1.50
❑ TE173 Hyper Tornado U	.20	.50
❑ TE174 Regeneration of lost-limbs C	.10	.25
❑ WA190 Gohan (Super Saiyan) U	.20	.50
❑ WA191 Goku SR	1.50	3.00
❑ WA192 Future Trunks (Super Saiyan) U	.20	.50
❑ WA193 Piccolo R	.75	1.50
❑ WA194 Tien U	.20	.50
❑ WA195 Trunks C	.10	.25
❑ WA196 Goten C	.10	.25
❑ WA197 Chiatzu C	.10	.25
❑ WA198 Yamcha C	.10	.25
❑ WA199 Krillin C	.10	.25
❑ WA200 Gogeta SR	6.00	12.00
❑ WA201 Dr. Gero C	.10	.25
❑ WA202 Emperor Pilaf C	.10	.25
❑ WA203 Janemba R	.75	1.50
❑ WA204 Kogu C	.10	.25
❑ WA205 Bido U	.20	.50
❑ WA206 Bujin C	.10	.25
❑ WA207 Zangya C	.10	.25
❑ WA208 Bojack SR	3.00	6.00
❑ WA209 Dr. Wheelo C	.10	.25
❑ WA210 Super 17 SR	3.00	6.00
❑ WA211 Vegeta (Super Saiyan) R	.75	1.50
❑ WA212 Nappa C	.10	.25
❑ WA213 Daizu C	.10	.25
❑ WA214 Turles R	.75	1.50
❑ WA215 Grand Kai C	.10	.25
❑ WA216 Old Kai C	.10	.25
❑ WA217 Broly SR	7.50	15.00
❑ WA218 Kibito Kai U	.20	.50
❑ WA219 Cooler (The 3rd Form) R	.75	1.50
❑ WA220 King Cold C	.10	.25
❑ WA221 Arale C	.10	.25
❑ WA222 Dr. Brief C	.10	.25
❑ WA223 Master Roshi C	.10	.25
❑ WA224 Videl U	.20	.50
❑ WA225 Yajirobe U	.20	.50
❑ WA226 Mr. Popo U	.20	.50
❑ WA227 18 R	.75	1.50
❑ WA228 Hercule C	.10	.25
❑ WA229 Papaya Man R	.75	1.50
❑ WA230 Pan U	.20	.50
❑ WA231 Gokule R	.75	1.50
❑ WA232 Drum C	.10	.25
❑ WA233 Dr. Myu C	.10	.25
❑ WA234 Baby C	.10	.25
❑ WA235 Kami C	.10	.25
❑ WA236 Rhildo U	.20	.50
❑ WA237 Rhildo (Mecha) R	.75	1.50
❑ WA238 Kid Buu SR	2.00	4.00
❑ WA239 Pikkon U	.20	.50
❑ WA240 Buu U	.20	.50
❑ WA241 King Piccolo R	.75	1.50

2009 Dragon Ball Fusion

Card	Low	High
Complete Set (113)	30.00	60.00
Booster Box (24 packs)	30.00	60.00
Booster Pack (10 cards)	2.50	5.00
*Foil: 1X to 2X Basic Cards		
❑ EV063 Exposure ST	.50	1.00
❑ EV064 Special Fighting Pose ST	.50	1.00
❑ EV065 Flexible Way of Thinking U	.20	.50
❑ EV066 Education-Conscious Mother R	.75	1.50
❑ EV067 Training in the Other World C	.10	.25
❑ EV068 Pose Practice C	.10	.25
❑ EV069 Unreasonable Fee R	.75	1.50
❑ EV070 Invisible Opponent U	.20	.50
❑ EV071 Mysterious Android U	.20	.50
❑ EV072 Lost Pride C	.10	.25
❑ EV073 Appointment to the Force C	.10	.25
❑ EV074 Rule by the Evil U	.20	.50
❑ EV075 Quick wit of Kibito Kai R	.75	1.50
❑ EV076 Proud Clan U	.20	.50
❑ EV077 Succeeded Knowledge C	.10	.25
❑ EV078 New Pupil R	.75	1.50
❑ EV079 Wedding Dress in Flames C	.10	.25
❑ EV080 Orange Star High School C	.10	.25
❑ EV081 New Majin U	.20	.50
❑ EV082 Lottery C	.10	.25
❑ EV083 Lost Dragon Ball C	.10	.25
❑ EV084 Fear by Majin R	.75	1.50
❑ TE108 Dynamic Mess Em Up Punch ST	.50	1.00
❑ TE109 Enormous Fighting Aura ST	.50	1.00
❑ TE110 Continuous Die Die Missile R	.75	1.50
❑ TE111 Cosmic Halo U	.20	.50
❑ TE112 Unstoppable Evolution C	.10	.25
❑ TE113 Kaio-Ken X 20 R	.75	1.50
❑ TE114 Fusion R	.75	1.50
❑ TE115 Super Ghost Kamikaze Attack R	.75	1.50
❑ TE116 Potara Fusion SR	1.00	2.00
❑ TE117 Sneaking Footsteps C	.10	.25
❑ TE118 Sucking Blood U	.20	.50
❑ TE119 Hidden Weapon C	.10	.25
❑ TE120 Devilmite Beam R	.75	1.50
❑ TE121 Attack of the Androids U	.20	.50
❑ TE122 Self Explosion R	.75	1.50
❑ TE123 Super Dodonpa U	.20	.50
❑ TE124 Exceptional Power U	.20	.50
❑ TE125 Z Sword C	.10	.25
❑ TE126 Salza Blade U	.20	.50
❑ TE127 Unexpected Outcome C	.10	.25
❑ TE128 Dignity of the Conqueror R	.75	1.50
❑ TE129 Power Ball C	.10	.25
❑ TE130 Final Flash SR	1.50	3.00
❑ TE131 Clever Play C	.10	.25
❑ TE132 Sudden Change C	.10	.25
❑ TE133 Cheer From the Goddesses U	.20	.50
❑ TE134 Succeeded Talent R	.75	1.50
❑ TE135 Eight Hand Technique R	.75	1.50
❑ TE136 Bashosen U	.20	.50
❑ TE137 Buried Legacy C	.10	.25
❑ TE138 Rage R	.75	1.50
❑ TE139 Malice U	.20	.50
❑ TE140 Transformation Beam C	.10	.25
❑ TE141 Charging the Energy U	.20	.50
❑ TE142 Wipe Out Attack SR	1.00	2.00
❑ TE143 Wave Cannon C	.10	.25
❑ TE144 Super Evil Wave Explosion U	.20	.50
❑ WA140 Gohan ST	.50	1.00
❑ WA141 Great Saiyaman ST SR	.75	1.50
❑ WA142 Vegeta ST	.50	1.00
❑ WA143 Mecha Frieza ST SR	.75	1.50
❑ WA144 Ox-King C	.10	.25
❑ WA145 Dende U	.20	.50
❑ WA146 Chi-Chi C	.10	.25
❑ WA147 Goten (Super Saiyan) R	.75	1.50
❑ WA148 Trunks (Super Saiyan) R	.75	1.50
❑ WA149 Gotenks R	1.00	2.00
❑ WA150 Goku (GT Super Saiyan) R	.75	1.50
❑ WA151 Ultimate Gohan SR	1.50	3.00
❑ WA152 Vegito SR	3.00	6.00
❑ WA153 Dracula Man C	.10	.25
❑ WA154 Guard Robot U	.20	.50
❑ WA155 Mummy Man C	.10	.25
❑ WA156 Akuman R	.75	1.50
❑ WA157 Mecha Mercenary Tao U	.20	.50
❑ WA158 Android 14 R	.75	1.50
❑ WA159 Android 15 C	.10	.25
❑ WA160 Android 13 R	.75	1.50
❑ WA161 Android 13 (United) SR	2.00	4.00
❑ WA162 King Yemma U	.20	.50
❑ WA163 Captain Ginyu C	.10	.25
❑ WA164 Kibito C	.10	.25
❑ WA165 Neiz C	.10	.25
❑ WA166 Doore C	.10	.25
❑ WA167 Captain Salza R	.75	1.50
❑ WA168 Supreme Kai U	.20	.50
❑ WA169 Giant Ape (Battle Suit) R	.75	1.50
❑ WA170 Cooler (The 4th form) SR	4.00	8.00
❑ WA171 Giru C	.10	.25
❑ WA172 Upa C	.10	.25
❑ WA173 Bora R	.75	1.50
❑ WA174 Annin C	.10	.25
❑ WA175 Videl U	.20	.50
❑ WA176 Mutaito R	.75	1.50
❑ WA177 Trunks R	.75	1.50
❑ WA178 Uub SR	1.00	2.00
❑ WA179 Mighty Mask SR	1.50	3.00
❑ WA180 Lord Don Kee C	.10	.25
❑ WA181 Zoonama C	.10	.25
❑ WA182 Sansho C	.10	.25
❑ WA183 Nicky C	.10	.25
❑ WA184 Ginger C	.10	.25
❑ WA185 Ledgic U	.20	.50
❑ WA186 King Piccolo ST SR	.75	1.50
❑ WA187 Evil Majin Buu R	.75	1.50
❑ WA188 Majin Buu (Fused) SR	2.00	4.00
❑ WA189 Goku ST SR	.75	1.50
❑ WI006 Regaining the Power ST	.50	1.00
❑ WI007 Existence of Hero ST	.50	1.00
❑ WI008 Porunga of the Planet Namek ST	.50	1.00
❑ WI009 Revival of the Earth ST	.50	1.00

2004 InuYasha Tetsusaiga

Card	Low	High
BOOSTER BOX (12)	7.50	15.00
BOOSTER PACK (10)	1.00	2.00
❑ 1 Warriors C	.10	.25
❑ 2 Archers C	.10	.25
❑ 3 Ms. Ikeda C	.10	.25
❑ 4 Mayu Ikeda C	.10	.25
❑ 5 Teacher C	.10	.25
❑ 6 Wolves C	.10	.25
❑ 7 Crows C	.10	.25
❑ 8 Child Villager C	.10	.25
❑ 9 Mistress Centipede C	.10	.25
❑ 10 Bone Vulture C	.10	.25
❑ 11 Troubled Villager C	.10	.25
❑ 12 Manten's Girls C	.10	.25
❑ 13 Militia C	.10	.25
❑ 14 Kagome's Mom C	.10	.25
❑ 15 Clay Warriors C	.10	.25
❑ 16 Souls C	.10	.25
❑ 17 Builders C	.10	.25
❑ 18 Samurai C	.10	.25
❑ 19 Village Matron C	.10	.25
❑ 20 Old Villager C	.10	.25
❑ 21 High Priest C	.10	.25
❑ 22 Spider Head C	.10	.25
❑ 23 Imps C	.10	.25
❑ 24 Hurt Bandit C	.10	.25
❑ 25 Demons C	.10	.25
❑ 26 Little Vixen C	.10	.25
❑ 27 Bandits C	.10	.25
❑ 28 Village Mother C	.10	.25
❑ 29 Princess Tsuyu's Lord C	.10	.25
❑ 30 Hiyoshimaru, Nobunaga's Monkey C	.10	.25
❑ 31 Inuyasha, the Young Hanyou C	.10	.25
❑ 32 Kagome's Grandfather C	.10	.25
❑ 33 Scared Bandit C	.10	.25
❑ 34 Righteous Anger C	.10	.25
❑ 35 Protected, Yet Never Known To It's Protector C	.10	.25
❑ 36 Deadly Claws C	.10	.25
❑ 37 Evil Ritual C	.10	.25
❑ 38 Tag Team C	.10	.25
❑ 39 Enchanted Sleep C	.10	.25
❑ 40 Speed Demon C	.10	.25
❑ 41 Pulling the Strings C	.10	.25
❑ 42 You've Been a Naughty, Naughty Girl C	.10	.25
❑ 43 At What Cost C	.10	.25
❑ 44 Try Something New C	.10	.25
❑ 45 She Hit It! C	.10	.25
❑ 46 Die Stinking Toad! C	.10	.25
❑ 47 Forget Ye Differences C	.10	.25
❑ 48 Full Moon C	.10	.25
❑ 49 Priorities C	.10	.25
❑ 50 Look, I Got One! C	.10	.25
❑ 51 I'm Not Impressed C	.10	.25
❑ 52 Ambush C	.10	.25
❑ 53 Inuyasha's Destructive Path C	.10	.25
❑ 54 Call of the Wild C	.10	.25
❑ 55 Stampede C	.10	.25
❑ 56 Rioting in the Streets C	.10	.25
❑ 57 Vile Intent C	.10	.25
❑ 58 Running Engagement C	.10	.25
❑ 59 Going to the Other Side C	.10	.25
❑ 60 All You Need is the Ground C	.10	.25
❑ 61 Things to Come C	.10	.25
❑ 62 Mob Mentality C	.10	.25
❑ 63 Torches C	.10	.25
❑ 64 Sword C	.10	.25
❑ 65 The First Shard C	.10	.25
❑ 66 Spear C	.10	.25
❑ 67 School Girl Outfit C	.10	.25
❑ 68 Bow C	.10	.25
❑ 69 Pieces of the Puzzle C	.10	.25
❑ 70 Yura's Hair C	.10	.25
❑ 71 Black Pearl C	.10	.25
❑ 72 Hiten's Lightning Pike C	.10	.25
❑ 73 Yura's Sword C	.10	.25
❑ 74 Gamajiro's Shard C	.10	.25
❑ 75 Shampoo C	.10	.25
❑ 76 Manten's Shards C	.10	.25
❑ 77 Kikyo's Ashes C	.10	.25
❑ 78 Spirit Wards C	.10	.25
❑ 79 Flashlight C	.10	.25
❑ 80 Fireworks C	.10	.25
❑ 81 The Last Hut on the Left C	.10	.25
❑ 82 A Bloody Nest C	.10	.25
❑ 83 Sacred Tree C	.10	.25
❑ 84 Bone Eater's Well C	.10	.25
❑ 85 Lord Toad's Castle C	.10	.25
❑ 86 Officer U	.20	.50
❑ 87 Commanders U	.20	.50
❑ 88 Samurai Lord U	.20	.50
❑ 89 Inuyasha, Human U	.20	.50
❑ 90 Samurai, Loyal Yojimbo U	.20	.50
❑ 91 Gamajiro U	.20	.50
❑ 92 Sleeping Guard U	.20	.50
❑ 93 Beta Wolf U	.20	.50
❑ 94 Princess Tsuyu U	.20	.50
❑ 95 Sota U	.20	.50
❑ 96 Carrion Crow U	.20	.50
❑ 97 Puppet Villagers U	.20	.50
❑ 98 Steel Wasps U	.20	.50
❑ 99 Veteran Samurai U	.20	.50
❑ 100 Veteran Soldier U	.20	.50
❑ 101 Hiten, Enraged Demon U	.20	.50
❑ 102 Jaken, Sesshomaru's Pawn U	.20	.50
❑ 103 Manten, Bald Demon U	.20	.50
❑ 104 Yuka, Kagome's friend U	.20	.50
❑ 105 Kikyo U	.20	.50
❑ 106 Satoru Ikeda U	.20	.50
❑ 107 Kaede, Village Priestess U	.20	.50
❑ 108 Ayumi, Kagome's Friend U	.20	.50
❑ 109 Inuyasha's Mother U	.20	.50
❑ 110 Eri, Kagome's Friend U	.20	.50
❑ 111 Nazuna U	.20	.50
❑ 112 Kaede, the Young Brat U	.20	.50
❑ 113 Demon Carrion Crow U	.20	.50
❑ 114 Big Villager U	.20	.50
❑ 115 Buyo U	.20	.50
❑ 116 Sesshomaru's Demon U	.20	.50
❑ 117 Militia Commander U	.20	.50
❑ 118 Shippo, the Shapeshifter U	.20	.50
❑ 119 General U	.20	.50
❑ 120 Cursed Noh Mask U	.20	.50
❑ 121 Nobunaga U	.20	.50
❑ 122 Kagome Higurashi U	.20	.50
❑ 123 Great Wolf, the Alpha Male U	.20	.50
❑ 124 Boot to the Head U	.20	.50
❑ 125 Falling U	.20	.50
❑ 126 Final Strike U	.20	.50
❑ 127 Energy Whip U	.20	.50
❑ 128 Give Me My Clothes! U	.20	.50
❑ 129 Father's Legacy U	.20	.50
❑ 130 Look What I Found U	.20	.50
❑ 131 Looting U	.20	.50
❑ 132 Always Gotta Be the Nice Guy U	.20	.50
❑ 133 Preparation U	.20	.50
❑ 134 Fox Fire U	.20	.50
❑ 135 A Brother's Wrath U	.20	.50
❑ 136 The Power of Humans U	.20	.50
❑ 137 Battle Cry U	.20	.50
❑ 138 Sit!!! U	.20	.50
❑ 139 Take That! U	.20	.50
❑ 140 Sesshomaru's Poisoned Claw U	.20	.50
❑ 141 You Stinking Toad! U	.20	.50
❑ 142 Strength By Numbers U	.20	.50

☐ 143 Poison U .20 .50
☐ 144 Blades of Blood U .20 .50
☐ 145 Monkey on Your Back U .20 .50
☐ 146 See You in Hell U .20 .50
☐ 147 Caught in a Web U .20 .50
☐ 148 Destruction U .20 .50
☐ 149 Manten's Cleaver U .20 .50
☐ 150 Manten's Fox Pelt U .20 .50
☐ 151 Jewel Keychain U .20 .50
☐ 152 Sesshomaru's Robe U .20 .50
☐ 153 Shard of the Cursed Noh Mask U .20 .50
☐ 154 Kaede's Bow U .20 .50
☐ 155 Priest Garb U .20 .50
☐ 156 Hiten's Armor U .20 .50
☐ 157 Giant Cleaver U .20 .50
☐ 158 Inuyasha's Necklace U .20 .50
☐ 159 Imprisoning Chains U .20 .50
☐ 160 Sesshomaru's Armor U .20 .50
☐ 161 Hiten's Shards U .20 .50
☐ 162 Hiten's Fire Wheel Shoes U .20 .50
☐ 163 Inuyasha's Father's Tomb U .20 .50
☐ 164 Gateway to Hell U .20 .50
☐ 165 Kaede's Village U .20 .50
☐ 166 Higurashi Storage Room U .20 .50
☐ 167 Outlaw's Lair U .20 .50
☐ 168 War Camp U .20 .50
☐ 169 Wild Dog Shrine U .20 .50
☐ 170 Border of the Spirit World U .20 .50
☐ 171 Un-Mother R .75 2.00
☐ 172 Myoga R .75 2.00
☐ 173 Soul Piper, Eyes Open R .75 2.00
☐ 174 Villagers R .75 2.00
☐ 175 Kikyo, Guardian of the Jewel R .75 2.00
☐ 176 Inuyasha, Demonic Half Breed R .75 2.00
☐ 177 Kagome Outlaw Boss R .75 2.00
☐ 178 Kagome, Kikyo Reincarnated R .75 2.00
☐ 179 The Hella Nasty Crow R .75 2.00
☐ 180 Manten, Loyal Brother R .75 2.00
☐ 181 Kagome, the Archer R .75 2.00
☐ 182 Sesshomaru, Aristocratic Assassin R .75 2.00
☐ 183 Jaken R .75 2.00
☐ 184 Hiten, Demon Warrior R .75 2.00
☐ 185 Shippo, Master of Fox Fire R .75 2.00
☐ 186 Hojo R .75 2.00
☐ 187 Yura of the Demon Hair R .75 2.00
☐ 188 Kagome, the Student R .75 2.00
☐ 189 Urasue R .75 2.00
☐ 190 Head Spider Head R .75 2.00
☐ 191 Possessed Bandit Leader R .75 2.00
☐ 192 Soul Piper, Eyes Closed R .75 2.00
☐ 193 Inuyasha, Kagome's Protector R .75 2.00
☐ 194 This Human is Going to Kick Your â•¦ R .75 2.00
☐ 195 Okay Boss R .75 2.00
☐ 196 Survival of the Fittest R .75 2.00
☐ 197 Get Undressed R .75 2.00
☐ 198 I Think I Want To Touch Them R .75 2.00
☐ 199 I'll Never Let You Go R .75 2.00
☐ 200 Charge R .75 2.00
☐ 201 Blessing R .75 2.00
☐ 202 What? Broken? R .75 2.00
☐ 203 Bath Time R .75 2.00
☐ 204 Shard Shower R .75 2.00
☐ 205 Hairspray Flamethrower R .75 2.00
☐ 206 You Think He Likes You? R .75 2.00
☐ 207 Hiten's Destructive Ways R .75 2.00
☐ 208 You Tried To Kill Me! R .75 2.00
☐ 209 Defeated R .75 2.00
☐ 210 Yura's Flawless Snatch R .75 2.00
☐ 211 The Thunder Brother's Anger R .75 2.00
☐ 212 Thank You For Showing Me Mercy R .75 2.00
☐ 213 New Age Technology R .75 2.00
☐ 214 I Leave Them to You R .75 2.00
☐ 215 Kikyo's Legacy R .75 2.00
☐ 216 Where am I? R .75 2.00
☐ 217 My Power Is What it is R .75 2.00
☐ 218 Evil Things are Amidst R .75 2.00
☐ 219 Caretakers of the Shrine R .75 2.00
☐ 220 Sit! Sit! Sit! Sit! R .75 2.00
☐ 221 Caught Red Handed R .75 2.00
☐ 222 Let Go of Me R .75 2.00
☐ 223 I didn't Say Get Naked! R .75 2.00
☐ 224 Get Off Ye Duff R .75 2.00
☐ 225 Halt! R .75 2.00
☐ 226 Be as One R .75 2.00
☐ 227 Oh-Me-Oh-My! R .75 2.00
☐ 228 Yura's Comb R .75 2.00
☐ 229 Tetsusaiga R .75 2.00
☐ 230 The Cursed Noh Mask R .75 2.00
☐ 231 Staff of Two Heads R .75 2.00
☐ 232 Inuyasha's Ball R .75 2.00
☐ 233 Kagome's Backpack R .75 2.00
☐ 234 Hiten's & Manten's Thunder Cloud R .75 2.00
☐ 235 Kagome's Bow R .75 2.00
☐ 236 Shippo's Top R .75 2.00
☐ 237 Tetsusaiga's Sheath R .75 2.00
☐ 238 Medic Kit R .75 2.00
☐ 239 Kagome's Bicycle R .75 2.00
☐ 240 Robe of the Fire Rat R .75 2.00
☐ 241 Yura's Skull R .75 2.00
☐ 242 Sacred Arrow R .75 2.00
☐ 243 Urasue's Scythe R .75 2.00
☐ 244 Kagome's Birthday present R .75 2.00
☐ 245 Kikyo's Bow R .75 2.00
☐ 246 Spirit Sutra R .75 2.00
☐ 247 Resting Place R .75 2.00
☐ 248 Kagome's Junior High R .75 2.00
☐ 249 Samurai War Camp R .75 2.00
☐ 250 Hospital R .75 2.00
☐ 251 Tokyo R .75 2.00
☐ 252 Yura's Lair R .75 2.00
☐ 253 Higurashi Shrine R .75 2.00
☐ 254 Thunder Brother's Battle Ground R .75 2.00
☐ 255 Blast Land R .75 2.00
☐ 256 Inuyasha, the Feudal Warrior UR 3.00 8.00
☐ 257 Kikyo, Reborn UR 4.00 10.00
☐ 258 Sesshomaru, Transformed UR 4.00 10.00
☐ 259 Enraged UR 3.00 8.00
☐ 260 Burst of Power UR 3.00 8.00
☐ 261 Here He Comes to Save the Day! UR 3.00 8.00
☐ 262 Returning Home UR 3.00 8.00
☐ 263 Tetsusaiga, Transformed UR 3.00 8.00
☐ 264 Inuyasha, Sota's Hero PROMO 1.00 2.50
☐ 265 Iron Reaver Soul Stealer PROMO 1.00 2.50
☐ 266 Shard From the Jewel of Four Souls PROMO1.00 2.50
☐ H0 Miroku HR 10.00 20.00

2005 InuYasha Jaki

BOOSTER BOX (12) 5.00 12.00
BOOSTER PACK (10) .60 1.50

☐ 1 Flesh Eating Demon, Baby C .10 .25
☐ 2 Birds of Paradise C .10 .25
☐ 3 Naraku's Poison Insects, 2 C .10 .25
☐ 4 Flesh Eating Demon, Adult C .10 .25
☐ 5 Head of the Birds of Paradise C .10 .25
☐ 6 Inuyasha, Night of the New Moon C .10 .25
☐ 7 Jinenji's Mom C .10 .25
☐ 8 Kaijinbo, Evil Sword Smith C .10 .25
☐ 9 Koharu, Miroku's Admirer C .10 .25
☐ 10 Ginta, Member of the Wolf Demon Tribe C .10 .25
☐ 11 A-Un, Sesshomaru's Two-Headed Dragon C .10 .25
☐ 12 Totosai, Tetsusaiga's Creator C .10 .25
☐ 13 Totosai's Flying Three-Eyed Cow C .10 .25
☐ 14 Hakkaku, Member of the Wolf Demon Tribe C .10 .25
☐ 15 Bruised, Bloody and Broken C .10 .25
☐ 16 Evil Doings C .10 .25
☐ 17 Power Exit C .10 .25
☐ 18 Looking Out for You C .10 .25
☐ 19 Naraku's Cage C .10 .25
☐ 20 Taking Aim C .10 .25
☐ 21 Whatcha Getting So Angry for? C .10 .25
☐ 22 Hammer of the Armory C .10 .25
☐ 23 Koga's Jewel Shards C .10 .25
☐ 24 Mark of Onigumo C .10 .25
☐ 25 Nest of Eggs C .10 .25
☐ 26 Goshinki, Sword Breaker C .10 .25
☐ 27 Hojo, the Perfect Guy C .10 .25
☐ 28 Jinenji, the Gentle Giant C .10 .25
☐ 29 Judgmental Villagers C .10 .25
☐ 30 Kikyo's Soul Stealers C .10 .25
☐ 31 Sango, the Relentless C .10 .25
☐ 32 Samurai of Fortune C .10 .25
☐ 33 Massacre C .10 .25
☐ 34 Cat and Dog C .10 .25
☐ 35 Demonic Anger C .10 .25
☐ 36 Dragon Eyes C .10 .25
☐ 37 Holy Power C .10 .25
☐ 38 Soul Discharge C .10 .25
☐ 39 Take a Look in the Mirror C .10 .25
☐ 40 They Still Desire Her Life C .10 .25
☐ 41 Transformation C .10 .25
☐ 42 Vanquished C .10 .25
☐ 43 The Little People! C .10 .25
☐ 44 The Soul Moves On C .10 .25
☐ 45 Slayer's Heart C .10 .25
☐ 46 Koga, Speed Demon U .20 .50
☐ 47 Shippo, Master Artist U .20 .50
☐ 48 Kageromaru, Spawn of Naraku U .20 .50
☐ 49 Jaken, Evil's Comedian U .20 .50
☐ 50 How Did This Happen? U .20 .50
☐ 51 Wrath of Koga U .20 .50
☐ 52 Kagome, Innocent Warrior U .20 .50
☐ 53 Kagome, the Incarnate U .20 .50
☐ 54 They Were Dead!? U .20 .50
☐ 55 Kirara, Scared Helper U .20 .50
☐ 56 Was I Dreaming? U .20 .50
☐ 57 Miroku, Perverted Monk U .20 .50
☐ 58 Sango, Female Warrior U .20 .50
☐ 59 Evil Lurks U .20 .50
☐ 60 Sesshomaru, Wanderer U .20 .50
☐ 61 Kaede, the Counselor U .20 .50
☐ 62 Inuyasha, Master of the Wind Scar U .20 .50
☐ 63 AAAHHHH! GET IT AWAY! U .20 .50
☐ 64 Kagura, Wind Mistress U .20 .50
☐ 65 Kanna, Soul Stealer U .20 .50
☐ 66 Kanna, Spawn of Naraku U .20 .50
☐ 67 Kikyo, Wandering Soul U .20 .50
☐ 68 Kikyo, Free to Hate U .20 .50
☐ 69 Sesshomaru, Weilder of Tokijin U .20 .50
☐ 70 Naraku, Mastermind U .20 .50
☐ 71 Shippo, the Dreamer U .20 .50
☐ 72 Pull Yourself Together! U .20 .50
☐ 73 Juromaru, Spawn of Naraku U .20 .50
☐ 74 Naraku's Evil U .20 .50
☐ 75 No Rest for the Wicked U .20 .50
☐ 76 Some Things Never Change U .20 .50
☐ 77 The Birds U .20 .50
☐ 78 Things Don't Look Good for Our Hero U .20 .50
☐ 79 Den of Wolves U .20 .50
☐ 80 Kagura, Spawn of Naraku U .20 .50
☐ 81 Staff of Two Heads, Jaken's Power U .20 .50
☐ 82 Kagura's Fan U .20 .50
☐ 83 Tenseiga, the Sword of Life U .20 .50
☐ 84 Camp Site U .20 .50
☐ 85 Jenenji's Farm U .20 .50
☐ 86 Rin, Obedient Child R .75 2.00
☐ 87 He Sounds Like a Real Psycho R .75 2.00
☐ 88 Incoming! R .75 2.00
☐ 89 Nosey Little Thing R .75 2.00
☐ 90 What the Five Fingers Say R .75 2.00
☐ 91 The Wind Scar R .75 2.00
☐ 92 Koga's Rage R .75 2.00
☐ 93 I Grow Tired of These Deceptions R .75 2.00
☐ 94 Workin' the Looks R .75 2.00
☐ 95 Is That All You Got? R .75 2.00
☐ 96 To Battle! R .75 2.00
☐ 97 Our Little Secret R .75 2.00
☐ 98 Surprise R .75 2.00
☐ 99 Legendary Archers R .75 2.00
☐ 100 Where's the Party? R .75 2.00
☐ 101 That's Random R .75 2.00
☐ 102 Three's Company R .75 2.00
☐ 103 Shippo's Shroom R .75 2.00
☐ 104 Whirlwind Slice R .75 2.00
☐ 105 Moment of Compassion R .75 2.00
☐ 106 Terrorize R .75 2.00
☐ 107 What's Going On? R .75 2.00
☐ 108 Wolves Mate for Life R .75 2.00
☐ 109 It's a Lot Heavier... R .75 2.00
☐ 110 Wait... R .75 2.00
☐ 111 Totosai's Weapon Smithy R .75 2.00
☐ 112 The Miasma R .75 2.00
☐ 113 Naraku's New Castle R .75 2.00
☐ 114 Kanna's Mirror R .75 2.00
☐ 115 Bow and Arrow R .75 2.00
☐ 116 Inuyasha, the Demon Within UR 4.00 10.00
☐ 117 Naraku, Deceptive Demon UR 4.00 10.00
☐ 118 Koga, the Furious UR 4.00 10.00
☐ 119 Tokijin, the Evil Sword UR 4.00 10.00
☐ 199 I'll Never Let You Go PROMO 1.00 2.50
☐ 260 Burst of Power PROMO 1.00 2.50
☐ H1 Muso HR .75 2.00
☐ H2 Tsubaki HR .75 2.00

2005 InuYasha Jaki Shippo's Slideshow

COMPLETE SET (10) 6.00 15.00

☐ SS1 There Once Was a Dog... 1.25 3.00
☐ SS2 The Dog Was Protective of the Cat... 1.25 3.00
☐ SS3 The Wolf 1.25 3.00
☐ SS4 The Birds Hurt the Wolf... 1.25 3.00
☐ SS5 The Dog 1.25 3.00
☐ SS6 The Dog Wanted to Kill the Wolf... 1.25 3.00
☐ SS7 But the Cat Protected the Wolf... 1.25 3.00
☐ SS8 The Dog Was a REAL Jerk... 1.25 3.00
☐ SS9 The Cat 1.25 3.00
☐ SS10 So the Cat Ran Down a Well... 1.25 3.00

2005 InuYasha Kassen

BOOSTER BOX (12) 5.00 12.00
BOOSTER PACK (10) .60 1.50

☐ 1 Cat of the Panther Tribe, 1 C .10 .25
☐ 2 Cat of the Panther Tribe, 2 C .10 .25
☐ 3 Cat of the Panther Tribe, 3 C .10 .25
☐ 4 Bat Demon Tribe Member, 1 C .10 .25
☐ 5 Bat Demon Tribe Member, 2 C .10 .25
☐ 6 Bat Demon tribe member, 3 C .10 .25
☐ 7 Wolf, Koga's Companion C .10 .25
☐ 8 Torako C .10 .25
☐ 9 Kagome, Happy to be Home C .10 .25
☐ 10 Shiori's Mom C .10 .25
☐ 11 Naraku's Poison Insects, 3 C .10 .25
☐ 12 Inuyashaâ¸¢, the Little Half-Demon C .10 .25
☐ 13 Soul Collectors C .10 .25
☐ 14 Master Muso C .10 .25
☐ 15 Little Monk, Muso's Companion C .10 .25
☐ 16 Bandit General C .10 .25
☐ 17 Myoga, Enraged Flea C .10 .25
☐ 18 Kuranosuke C .10 .25
☐ 19 Enraged Villager C .10 .25
☐ 20 Royakan, Willing Helper C .10 .25
☐ 21 Bandits, Villain Soldiers C .10 .25
☐ 22 Buyo, Playful Kitty C .10 .25
☐ 23 Hachi, Raccoon Demon C .10 .25
☐ 24 Eri, Caring Friend C .10 .25
☐ 25 Yuka, Caring Friend C .10 .25
☐ 26 Bunza, Senior Apprentice C .10 .25
☐ 27 Kirara, Peaceful Companion C .10 .25
☐ 28 Totosai, Old Fool C .10 .25
☐ 29 Kaede, Village Protector C .10 .25
☐ 30 Nanafushi C .10 .25
☐ 31 Quick Slash C .10 .25
☐ 32 In Command C .10 .25
☐ 33 Prisoners of War C .10 .25
☐ 34 She is the One C .10 .25
☐ 35 What are You Thinking? C .10 .25
☐ 36 Quick Strikes C .10 .25
☐ 37 Koga's Fury C .10 .25
☐ 38 Attack of the Bat Demons of Doom C .10 .25
☐ 39 Dumbfounded C .10 .25
☐ 40 Engaged in Battle C .10 .25
☐ 41 Playing Cards C .10 .25
☐ 42 Shippo's Crayons C .10 .25
☐ 43 Stolen Shards C .10 .25
☐ 44 Smoke Bomb C .10 .25
☐ 45 Steak C .10 .25
☐ 46 Sesshomaru, Son of the Dog Leader U .20 .50
☐ 47 Inuyasha, Son of the Dog Leader U .20 .50
☐ 48 Muso, Faceless Demon U .20 .50
☐ 49 Ginta, Fierce Wolf Demon U .20 .50
☐ 50 Jaken, Imp Commander U .20 .50
☐ 51 Rin, Child Follower U .20 .50
☐ 52 No-Man U .20 .50
☐ 53 Kohaku, Slave of Naraku U .20 .50
☐ 54 Kagome, Gossiping School Girl U .20 .50
☐ 55 Miroku, the Modern Gentleman U .20 .50
☐ 56 Tsukuyomaru, Father of the Bat Demons U .20 .50
☐ 57 Miroku, Flirtatious Wandering Monk U .20 .50
☐ 58 Koga, New Leader of the Wolf Demon Tribe U .20 .50
☐ 59 Sango, Passionate Demon Slayer U .20 .50
☐ 60 Soten, Little Thunder Sister U .20 .50
☐ 61 Karan, Deva of the Panther Tribe U .20 .50
☐ 62 Shuuran, Deva of the Panther Tribe U .20 .50
☐ 63 Toran, Deva of the Panther Tribe U .20 .50
☐ 64 Kagura, Mistress of Betrayal U .20 .50
☐ 65 Naraku's Demons U .20 .50
☐ 66 Shippo, Brave Warrior U .20 .50
☐ 67 Kikyo, Forgotten Soul U .20 .50
☐ 68 Koga, Guy of Your Dreams U .20 .50
☐ 69 Koryu, Lightning Cloud Dragon U .20 .50
☐ 70 Naraku, Man of Many Demons U .20 .50
☐ 71 Wind Scar, Inuyashaâ¸¢'s Weapon U .20 .50
☐ 72 Naraku's Power U .20 .50
☐ 73 Playful Siblings U .20 .50
☐ 74 Blown Away U .20 .50
☐ 75 Wake Up U .20 .50
☐ 76 Laughing Acorns U .20 .50
☐ 77 The Bat Demons are Coming! U .20 .50
☐ 78 Walking Home U .20 .50
☐ 79 Shuffling Cards U .20 .50
☐ 80 Sudden Strike U .20 .50
☐ 81 Panther Demon Tribe's Castle U .20 .50
☐ 82 Royakan's Cave U .20 .50
☐ 83 Kagome's Bedroom U .20 .50
☐ 84 Kagome's Living Room U .20 .50
☐ 85 Well Placed Trap U .20 .50
☐ 86 Ocean U .20 .50
☐ 87 Beach Front U .20 .50
☐ 88 Country Road U .20 .50
☐ 89 Cave of the Bat Demon Tribe U .20 .50
☐ 90 Jaken, Master Thief R .75 2.00
☐ 91 Shippo, Master Duelist R .75 2.00
☐ 92 Naraku, Master of Demons R .75 2.00
☐ 93 Kikyo, Fading Soul R .75 2.00
☐ 94 Taigokumaru, Grandfather of the Bat Demons R .75 2.00
☐ 95 Shiori, Princess of the Bat Demons R .75 2.00
☐ 96 Shunran, Member of the Panther Tribe R .75 2.00
☐ 97 Power Over the Elements R .75 2.00
☐ 98 Gone Fishing R .75 2.00
☐ 99 Enter the Panther R .75 2.00
☐ 100 I'm a Genius R .75 2.00
☐ 101 Watching from Afar R .75 2.00
☐ 102 Overjoyed R .75 2.00
☐ 103 The Long Walk Home R .75 2.00
☐ 104 Loyal Followers R .75 2.00
☐ 105 True Power R .75 2.00
☐ 106 Preparing for Battle R .75 2.00
☐ 107 FINISH HIM! R .75 2.00
☐ 108 He Has Ears R .75 2.00
☐ 109 Consumed Souls R .75 2.00
☐ 110 The Heart of Onigumo R .75 2.00
☐ 111 Shikon Jewel Nearly Completed R .75 2.00
☐ 112 Blood Coral Crystal R .75 2.00
☐ 113 Tetsusaiga, Red R .75 2.00
☐ 114 City Street R .75 2.00
☐ 115 Village R .75 2.00
☐ 116 King of the Panther Tribe UR 4.00 10.00
☐ 117 Muso, Heart of Onigumo UR 4.00 10.00
☐ 118 Ready for War UR 3.00 8.00
☐ 119 Just Ask for Help UR 3.00 8.00
☐ H1 Inuyasha HR 10.00 20.00
☐ H2 Kagome HR 7.50 15.00

2005 InuYasha Kassen Legendary Foes

COMPLETE SET (10) 6.00 15.00

☐ LF1 Yura, LF 1.25 3.00
☐ LF2 Kotatsu, LF 1.25 3.00
☐ LF3 Hiten, LF 1.25 3.00
☐ LF4 Manten, LF 1.25 3.00
☐ LF5 Sesshomaru, LF 1.25 3.00
☐ LF6 Naraku, LF 1.25 3.00
☐ LF7 Juromaru, LF 1.25 3.00
☐ LF8 Kageromaru, LF 1.25 3.00
☐ LF9 Ryukotsusei, LF 1.25 3.00
☐ LF10 Demon Carrion Crow, LF 1.25 3.00

2005 InuYasha Kassen Promos

COMPLETE SET (9) 5.00 12.00

☐ KP1 Ayame, Koga's Fiancee 1.00 2.50
☐ KP2 Kagome, Protector of the Shikon Jewel 1.00 2.50
☐ KP3 Rin, Follower of Sesshomaru 1.00 2.50
☐ KP4 Kikyo, Master Archer 1.00 2.50
☐ KP5 Inuyasha, Battle Ready 1.00 2.50
☐ KP6 Rampage of Destruction 1.00 2.50
☐ KP7 One on One 1.00 2.50
☐ KP8 Karan, Soldier of the Panther Tribe 1.00 2.50
☐ KP9 Determined 1.00 2.50

2005 InuYasha Kijin

BOOSTER BOX (12) 15.00 30.00
BOOSTER PACK (10) 1.50 3.00

☐ 1 Hachi, Miroku's Friend C .10 .25
☐ 2 Taromaru C .10 .25
☐ 3 Ink Demon, 1 C .10 .25
☐ 4 Ink Demon, 2 C .10 .25
☐ 5 Jaken, Little Bundle of Evil C .10 .25
☐ 6 Kikyo, the Tragic Soul C .10 .25
☐ 7 Kohaku, the Young Demon Slayer C .10 .25
☐ 8 Miroku's Grandfather C .10 .25
☐ 9 Myoga, the Loyal Friend C .10 .25
☐ 10 Onigumo, the Helpless Foe C .10 .25
☐ 11 Villain Soldier C .10 .25
☐ 12 Oppressed Villager C .10 .25
☐ 13 Slayer, Mace and Trident C .10 .25
☐ 14 Three Eyed Wolf, Aggressive C .10 .25
☐ 15 Three Eyed Wolf, Enraged C .10 .25
☐ 16 Water God, the Evil Water Spirit C .10 .25
☐ 17 Sayo, Young Village Girl C .10 .25
☐ 18 A Girl and Her Cat C .10 .25
☐ 19 A Girl and Her Dog C .10 .25
☐ 20 Buried Alive C .10 .25
☐ 21 Defensive Stance C .10 .25
☐ 22 Hold On C .10 .25
☐ 23 I'll Be Taking That... C .10 .25
☐ 24 I'll Find Him Yet C .10 .25
☐ 25 Look What We Found! C .10 .25
☐ 26 The Group's All Here C .10 .25
☐ 27 Miroku's Wind Tunnel C .10 .25
☐ 28 On Guard C .10 .25
☐ 29 Overpowered C .10 .25
☐ 30 Quick Hands C .10 .25
☐ 31 She Hit it Again! C .10 .25
☐ 32 Shippos Everywhere C .10 .25
☐ 33 Trapped in a Shack C .10 .25
☐ 34 Tricked C .10 .25
☐ 35 What? He Stopped It? C .10 .25
☐ 36 Miroku's Staff C .10 .25
☐ 37 Monk's Ball of Dragon C .10 .25
☐ 38 Newspaper C .10 .25
☐ 39 Painting C .10 .25
☐ 40 Prayer Beads C .10 .25
☐ 41 Stolen Souls C .10 .25
☐ 42 Sutra Beads C .10 .25
☐ 43 Valuables C .10 .25
☐ 44 Shrine of the Water God C .10 .25
☐ 45 Slayers' Battleground C .10 .25
☐ 46 Ayumi, Kagome's Friend Until the End U .20 .50
☐ 47 Demon Worm Charmer U .20 .50
☐ 48 Yuka, Kagome's Friend Until the End U .20 .50
☐ 49 Kotatsu U .20 .50
☐ 50 Kaede, the Village Protector U .20 .50
☐ 51 Kagome's Grandfather, Her Personal Secretary U .20 .50
☐ 52 Kagome, Priestess in Training U .20 .50
☐ 53 Kagome, Sickly Beauty U .20 .50
☐ 54 Kirara, Sango's Companion U .20 .50
☐ 55 Kirara, Transformed U .20 .50
☐ 56 Miroku, the Cursed Monk U .20 .50
☐ 57 Mushin, the Old Drunk U .20 .50
☐ 58 Naraku's Poison Insects U .20 .50
☐ 59 Naraku, Nemesis U .20 .50
☐ 60 Villager, Battle Ready U .20 .50
☐ 61 Royakan, Protector of the Forest U .20 .50
☐ 62 Shippo, the Demon Child U .20 .50
☐ 63 Sango's Father, Demon Slayer U .20 .50
☐ 64 Axe Wielder, Slayer U .20 .50
☐ 65 Sota, Fighting Game Fanboy U .20 .50
☐ 66 The Water Goddess U .20 .50
☐ 67 Village Head Master U .20 .50
☐ 68 Weasel Demon U .20 .50
☐ 69 Eri, Kagome's Friend Until the End U .20 .50
☐ 70 Big Sit U .20 .50
☐ 71 Do You Want Him to Look? U .20 .50
☐ 72 Face-off U .20 .50
☐ 73 Kikyo's Kiss U .20 .50
☐ 74 Thinking of You U .20 .50
☐ 75 On the Run U .20 .50
☐ 76 Shippo's Item Technique U .20 .50
☐ 77 Will You Have My Children? U .20 .50
☐ 78 Hiraikotsu U .20 .50
☐ 79 Hive of Poison Insects U .20 .50
☐ 80 Miroku's Jewel Shard U .20 .50
☐ 81 Naraku's Baboon Mask U .20 .50
☐ 82 Sesshomaru's Arm U .20 .50
☐ 83 Text Books U .20 .50
☐ 84 The Mask of a Slayer U .20 .50
☐ 85 The Trident of the Water Goddess U .20 .50
☐ 86 Massacred Village U .20 .50
☐ 87 Naraku's Castle U .20 .50
☐ 88 Resting House U .20 .50
☐ 89 Rice Fields U .20 .50
☐ 90 Village by the Mountain U .20 .50
☐ 91 Inuyasha, Master of the Tetsusaiga R .75 2.00
☐ 92 Kohaku, Servant of Naraku R .75 2.00
☐ 93 Miroku, the Lady Killer R .75 2.00
☐ 94 Naraku, the Spirit of Onigumo R .75 2.00
☐ 95 Sango, the Demon Slayer R .75 2.00
☐ 96 Sesshomaru, the Evil Brother R .75 2.00
☐ 97 The Reflecting Shower R .75 2.00
☐ 98 Blush R .75 2.00
☐ 99 Brighter Days R .75 2.00
☐ 100 Child Sacrifice R .75 2.00
☐ 101 Deep Thought R .75 2.00
☐ 102 Destructive Force R .75 2.00

TCG/CCG

❑ 103 Game Over R .75 2.00
❑ 104 How Can We Thank You? R .75 2.00
❑ 105 Kikyo's Embrace R .75 2.00
❑ 106 Massive Destruction R .75 2.00
❑ 107 My Intentions Were Honorable R .75 2.00
❑ 108 Overwhelmed R .75 2.00
❑ 109 Overwhelming Odds R .75 2.00
❑ 110 She's Creeping Me Out R .75 2.00
❑ 111 Stuffed R .75 2.00
❑ 112 The Best Healing Herb R .75 2.00
❑ 113 The Most Powerful Human of Her Time R .75 2.00
❑ 114 What a Date! R .75 2.00
❑ 115 What are You Doing? R .75 2.00
❑ 116 What Strange People R .75 2.00
❑ 117 What's That Look For? R .75 2.00
❑ 118 Wolf in Your Mouth R .75 2.00
❑ 119 Barrier R .75 2.00
❑ 120 Blessed Idol R .75 2.00
❑ 121 Shikon Jewel - Half Completed R .75 2.00
❑ 122 A Field of Flowers R .75 2.00
❑ 123 Armory of the Slayers R .75 2.00
❑ 124 Cave of the Shikon Jewel R .75 2.00
❑ 125 Crater R .75 2.00
❑ 126 Field of Dead Bodies R .75 2.00
❑ 127 Hot Springs R .75 2.00
❑ 128 Lake of the Water God R .75 2.00
❑ 129 Onigumo's Cave R .75 2.00
❑ 130 Village in the Valley R .75 2.00
❑ 131 Inuyasha, Enraged Demon UR 4.00 10.00
❑ 132 A Tragic Death UR 4.00 10.00
❑ 133 Burned UR 3.00 8.00
❑ 134 On the Move UR 4.00 10.00
❑ 135 Midoriko, Creator of the Shikon Jewel PROMO1.00 2.50
❑ 136 Sango, the Scarred Warrior PROMO 1.00 2.50
❑ 137 The Eye of Naraku PROMO 1.00 2.50
❑ 138 Downtown Tokyo PROMO 1.00 2.50
❑ 182 Sesshomaru, Aristocratic Assassin PROMO 1.00 2.50
❑ 263 Tetsusaiga, Transformed PROMO 1.00 2.50
❑ H1 Koga HR 10.00 20.00
❑ H2 Kagura HR 10.00 20.00

2005 InuYasha Kijin Legends

COMPLETE SET (11) 6.00 15.00
❑ LS1 Inuyasha LEG 1.25 3.00
❑ LS2 Jaken LEG 1.25 3.00
❑ LS3 Kikyo LEG 1.25 3.00
❑ LS4 Kagome LEG 1.25 3.00
❑ LS5 Kirara LEG 1.25 3.00
❑ LS6 Kohaku LEG 1.25 3.00
❑ LS7 Miroku LEG 1.25 3.00
❑ LS8 Naraku LEG 1.25 3.00
❑ LS9 Sango LEG 1.25 3.00
❑ LS10 Sesshomaru LEG 1.25 3.00
❑ LS11 Yura LEG 1.25 3.00

2005 InuYasha Yokai

BOOSTER BOX (12) 5.00 12.00
BOOSTER PACK (10) .60 1.50
❑ 1 Inuyasha, Human at Heart C .10 .25
❑ 2 Scared Village Woman C .10 .25
❑ 3 Bandit Soldier C .10 .25
❑ 4 Village Grandpa C .10 .25
❑ 5 Serina, Young Ninja C .10 .25
❑ 6 Shippo, Shape Changing Fox C .10 .25
❑ 7 Bandit Wench C .10 .25
❑ 8 School Teacher C .10 .25
❑ 9 Kirara, House Cat C .10 .25
❑ 10 Smiling Bandit C .10 .25
❑ 11 Gatenmaru, Human C .10 .25
❑ 12 Young Village Bully C .10 .25
❑ 13 Village Wealthy Man C .10 .25
❑ 14 Lizard Demon C .10 .25
❑ 15 Demon Horde C .10 .25
❑ 16 Kikyo, the Lost Soul C .10 .25
❑ 17 Kagome's Mom, Loving Mother C .10 .25
❑ 18 Jaken, Loyal Servant C .10 .25
❑ 19 Shikigami C .10 .25
❑ 20 Shikigami Inuyasha C .10 .25
❑ 21 Shikigami Kagome C .10 .25
❑ 22 Totosai, Sword Maker C .10 .25
❑ 23 Rin, Young Follower C .10 .25
❑ 24 Demon Eye C .10 .25
❑ 25 Tsubaki's Demon C .10 .25
❑ 26 Buyo, the Fat Cat C .10 .25
❑ 27 Ninja, 1 C .10 .25
❑ 28 Ninja, 2 C .10 .25
❑ 29 Suzuna, Young Ninja Girl C .10 .25
❑ 30 Struggle C .10 .25
❑ 31 Bloody Rage C .10 .25
❑ 32 Injured During Battle C .10 .25
❑ 33 Stop Fighting C .10 .25
❑ 34 Torn Apart C .10 .25
❑ 35 Angered Beyond Belief C .10 .25
❑ 36 You'll Be Sorry C .10 .25
❑ 37 AHHHHH C .10 .25
❑ 38 Take That You Demon! C .10 .25
❑ 39 Glaring Evil C .10 .25
❑ 40 He Can't Be Dead! C .10 .25
❑ 41 Big Rolling Rock C .10 .25
❑ 42 Candle C .10 .25
❑ 43 Enchanted Bracelet C .10 .25
❑ 44 Demon Tree Fruit C .10 .25
❑ 45 Soda C .10 .25
❑ 46 Ryukotsusei, Father's Old Enemy U .20 .50
❑ 47 Tokajin, Transformed U .20 .50
❑ 48 Tokajin, Human U .20 .50
❑ 49 Kagome, #1 Student U .20 .50
❑ 50 Shippo, the Playful Fox U .20 .50
❑ 51 Kirara, Enraged Protector U .20 .50
❑ 52 Myoga, Little Bloodsucker U .20 .50
❑ 53 Satsuki, Shippo's First Love U .20 .50
❑ 54 Sango, Slayer of Demons U .20 .50
❑ 55 Hojo, a Fool in Love U .20 .50
❑ 56 Momiji, Little Priestess Girl U .20 .50
❑ 57 Miroku, Quick-Handed Monk U .20 .50
❑ 58 Kanna, Follower of Naraku U .20 .50
❑ 59 Sesshomaru, Lord of Demons U .20 .50
❑ 60 Tsubaki, Young Priestess U .20 .50
❑ 61 Botan, the Little Priestess U .20 .50
❑ 62 Koga, Wolf Leader U .20 .50
❑ 63 Miroku, Single U .20 .50
❑ 64 Kagome, Innocent U .20 .50
❑ 65 Sango, the Skilled Warrior U .20 .50
❑ 66 Coyote Demon U .20 .50
❑ 67 Kagome, Bathing Beauty U .20 .50
❑ 68 Bandit Brutality U .20 .50
❑ 69 Where are You? U .20 .50
❑ 70 Trouble Sleeping U .20 .50
❑ 71 Retreat! U .20 .50
❑ 72 Vanity U .20 .50
❑ 73 Matters of the Heart U .20 .50
❑ 74 Getting Along? U .20 .50
❑ 75 Crushed U .20 .50
❑ 76 Sake U .20 .50
❑ 77 Bath Towel U .20 .50
❑ 78 Food U .20 .50
❑ 79 Shippo's Sucker U .20 .50
❑ 80 Dried Potatoes U .20 .50
❑ 81 Tokajin's Trap U .20 .50
❑ 82 Valley Settlement U .20 .50
❑ 83 Forest Path U .20
❑ 84 Woodland Valley U .20 .50
❑ 85 Cliff Side U .20 .50
❑ 86 Ryukotsusei, Demon Awakened R .75 2.00
❑ 87 Gatenmaru, Transformed R .75 2.00
❑ 88 Naraku, Master of Deception R .75 2.00
❑ 89 Kagura, Follower of Naraku R .75 2.00
❑ 90 Tsubaki, Old Priestess R .75 2.00
❑ 91 Inuyasha, Bodyguard R .75 2.00
❑ 92 The Demon Tree R .75 2.00
❑ 93 Raging Into Battle R .75 2.00
❑ 94 Stay Rin R .75 2.00
❑ 95 Exhausted R .75 2.00
❑ 96 Sucking Your Life Away R .75 2.00
❑ 97 Unspoken Feelings R .75 2.00
❑ 98 Mind Your Own Business R .75 2.00
❑ 99 Ninja Vanish R .75 2.00
❑ 100 The Aftermath of a Legendary Battle R .75 2.00
❑ 101 Awkward Moments R .75 2.00
❑ 102 Discussing Other People's Lives R .75 2.00
❑ 103 You're Alive R .75 2.00
❑ 104 My Hero R .75 2.00
❑ 105 Tetsusaiga's Sheath, Inuyasha's Protector R .75 2.00
❑ 106 Hojo's Gift R .75 2.00
❑ 107 Bedroom R .75 2.00
❑ 108 Riverside R .75 2.00
❑ 109 The Bandit's Hideout R .75 2.00
❑ 110 Wacdnald R .75 2.00
❑ 111 Gravesite of the Slayers R .75 2.00
❑ 112 Busted R .75 2.00
❑ 113 Making Plans R .75 2.00
❑ 114 Let Me Go Home R .75 2.00
❑ 115 Evil's Awakening R .75 2.00
❑ 116 Epic Battle UR 4.00 10.00
❑ 117 Inuyasha, Demon with a Heart UR 4.00 10.00
❑ 118 Peaceful Times UR 4.00 10.00
❑ 119 Out of Control UR 3.00 8.00
❑ 183 Jaken PROMO 1.00 2.50
❑ 187 Yura, of the Demon Hair PROMO 1.00 2.50
❑ 193 Inuyasha, Kagome's Protector PROMO 1.00 2.50
❑ 261 Here He Comes to Save the Day! PROMO 1.00 2.50
❑ H1 Karan HR .75 2.00
❑ H2 Inuyasha's Father HR .75 2.00

2005 InuYasha Yokai Chibi

COMPLETE SET (10) 6.00 15.00
❑ CB1 Kagome, Chibi 1.25 3.00
❑ CB2 Shippo, Chibi 1.25 3.00
❑ CB3 Kikyo, Chibi 1.25 3.00
❑ CB4 Miroku, Chibi 1.25 3.00
❑ CB5 Sesshomaru, Chibi 1.25 3.00
❑ CB6 Inuyasha, Chibi 1.25 3.00
❑ CB7 Inuyasha, Human Chibi 1.25 3.00
❑ CB8 Sango, Chibi 1.25 3.00
❑ CB9 Sango, Slayer Chibi 1.25 3.00
❑ CB10 Koga, Wolf Chibi 1.25 3.00

2006 InuYasha Saisei

BOOSTER BOX (12) 5.00 12.00
BOOSTER PACK (10) .60 1.50
❑ 1 Naraku's Poison Insects, 4 C .10 .25
❑ 2 Kirara, Protector of Sango C .10 .25
❑ 3 Nazuna, Little Demon Hunter C .10 .25
❑ 4 Royakan, Wolf Demon C .10 .25
❑ 5 Kikyo, Forgotten Hero C .10 .25
❑ 6 Kaede, Old Warrior C .10 .25
❑ 7 Sage, Tokajin's Mentor C .10 .25
❑ 8 Muso, Ravager of Villages C .10 .25
❑ 9 Bat Demon Tribe Member, 4 C .10 .25
❑ 10 Kaede, Master Archer C .10 .25
❑ 11 Soul Piper C .10 .25
❑ 12 Mistress Centipede, Evil Demon C .10 .25
❑ 13 Cursed Noh Mask, Evil Demon C .10 .25
❑ 14 A-Un, Follower of Sesshomaru C .10 .25
❑ 15 Crows, 2 C .10 .25
❑ 16 Gamajiro, Evil Toad Demon C .10 .25
❑ 17 Sesshomaru's Demon .10 .25
Follower of Sesshomaru C
❑ 18 Torako, Bunza's Friend C .10 .25
❑ 19 Mayu Ikeda, Mischievous Soul C .10 .25
❑ 20 Shikigami, 2 C .10 .25
❑ 21 Hakkaku, Warrior of the Wolf Demon Tribe C .10 .25
❑ 22 School Teacher, Kagome's Nightmare C .10 .25
❑ 23 Ink Demon, 3 C .10 .25
❑ 24 White Wolf C .10 .25
❑ 25 Ayame, Koga's Bride to Be C .10 .25
❑ 26 Imps, 1 C .10 .25
❑ 27 Imps, 2 C .10 .25
❑ 28 Imps, 3 C .10 .25
❑ 29 Kaijimbo, Forger of Tokijin C .10 .25
❑ 30 Giant Soul Collector C .10 .25
❑ 31 Shikigami, Demon Serpent C .10 .25
❑ 32 Bunza's Father C .10 .25
❑ 33 Northern Tribe Wolf Leader C .10 .25
❑ 34 Birds of Paradise, 2 C .10 .25
❑ 35 Inuyasha, Injured C .10 .25
❑ 36 Kagome, Tender Soul C .10 .25
❑ 37 Tsubaki's Demon, Deadly Predator C .10 .25
❑ 38 Kikyo, Patient Soul C .10 .25
❑ 39 Miroku, the Thoughtful C .10 .25
❑ 40 Shippo, Little Demon Fox C .10 .25
❑ 41 Naraku, Master of Evil C .10 .25
❑ 42 Hachi, Friend of Miroku C .10 .25
❑ 43 Hair Demon C .10 .25
❑ 44 Cat of the Panther Tribe, 4 C .10 .25
❑ 45 Samurai Warrior C .10 .25
❑ 46 Inuyasha's Destructive Path C .10 .25
❑ 47 Attack of the Spirit Puppets C .10 .25
❑ 48 Don't Tell Me C .10 .25
❑ 49 Goosebumps C .10 .25
❑ 50 Family Curse C .10 .25
❑ 51 Awake C .10 .25
❑ 52 Wink C .10 .25
❑ 53 Lecher C .10 .25
❑ 54 Tender Moments C .10 .25
❑ 55 I'm Not Crying C .10 .25
❑ 56 Cursed Shikon Jewel C .10 .25
❑ 57 Slayer Weapons C .10 .25
❑ 58 Fake Jewel Shard C .10 .25
❑ 59 Alarm Clock C .10 .25
❑ 60 Stew C .10 .25
❑ 61 Inuyasha's Mother, Loving Soul U .20 .50
❑ 62 Jaken, Follower of Sesshomaru U .20 .50
❑ 63 Kohaku, Sango's Little Brother U .20 .50
❑ 64 Tokajin, Evil Mage U .20 .50
❑ 65 Muso, Soul of Onigumo U .20 .50
❑ 66 Urasue, Evil Witch U .20 .50
❑ 67 Onigumo, Future Villain U .20 .50
❑ 68 Totosai's Flying Three-Eyed Cow U .20 .50
❑ 69 Taigokumaru, Leader of the Bat Demons U .20 .50
❑ 70 Kagome, Koga's Love Interest U .20 .50
❑ 71 Koga, Protector of Kagome U .20 .50
❑ 72 Naraku's Puppet U .20 .50
❑ 73 Sesshomaru, Full Blooded Demon U .20 .50
❑ 74 Shippo, Battle Ready U .20 .50
❑ 75 Hojo, Kagome's Friend U .20 .50
❑ 76 Myoga, Terrified Flea U .20 .50
❑ 77 Koga, Hero of the Wolf Demon Tribe U .20 .50
❑ 78 Sota, Helpful Brother U .20 .50
❑ 79 Shunran, Deva of the Panther Tribe U .20 .50
❑ 80 Demon U .20 .50
❑ 81 Yura, Master of Puppets U .20 .50
❑ 82 Hachi, Shape Changing Raccoon U .20 .50
❑ 83 Totosai, Old Sword Maker U .20 .50
❑ 84 Ryukotsusei, Deadly Demon U .20 .50
❑ 85 Jaken, Critical Thinker U .20 .50
❑ 86 Tsubaki, Old Witch U .20 .50
❑ 87 Myoga, Old Friend U .20 .50
❑ 88 Policeman U .20 .50
❑ 89 Toran, Warrior of the Panther Tribe U .20 .50
❑ 90 Shuuran, Warrior of the Panther Tribe U .20 .50
❑ 91 Archery Training U .20 .50
❑ 92 Fighting Over a Girl U .20 .50
❑ 93 Goofing Around U .20 .50
❑ 94 Righteous Strike U .20 .50
❑ 95 Weakling U .20 .50
❑ 96 Coward U .20 .50
❑ 97 Deflection U .20 .50
❑ 98 We Will Protect You U .20 .50
❑ 99 Eavesdropping U .20 .50
❑ 100 Nightmares About Homework U .20 .50
❑ 101 Pinned U .20 .50
❑ 102 Famished U .20 .50
❑ 103 What Do Women Really Like??? U .20 .50
❑ 104 I Will Cause Your Demise U .20 .50
❑ 105 Generations U .20 .50
❑ 106 Priestess Traps U .20 .50
❑ 107 Sacred Saki and Charms U .20 .50
❑ 108 Iron Work Hammer U .20 .50
❑ 109 Naraku's Lair U .20 .50
❑ 110 Subway U .20 .50
❑ 111 Sango, Peaceful Traveler R .75 2.00
❑ 112 Kikyo, Supernatural Beauty R .75 2.00
❑ 113 Goshinki, Spawn of Naraku R .75 2.00
❑ 114 Inuyasha, Protector of Kagome R .75 2.00
❑ 115 Sango, Worried Sister R .75 2.00
❑ 116 Inuyasha, Sota's Hero R .75 2.00
❑ 117 Kanna, Naraku's Servant R .75 2.00
❑ 118 Naraku, the Mastermind R .75 2.00
❑ 119 Goodies R .75 2.00
❑ 120 Scissors R .75 2.00
❑ 121 Rock R .75 2.00
❑ 122 Paper R .75 2.00
❑ 123 Sucking Up R .75 2.00
❑ 124 Menacing Evil R .75 2.00
❑ 125 Learning New Techniques R .75 2.00
❑ 126 Sigh R .75 2.00
❑ 127 Enraged R .75 2.00
❑ 128 Strong Punch R .75 2.00
❑ 129 Followers R .75 2.00
❑ 130 Play Time R .75 2.00
❑ 131 Remembering Her R .75 2.00
❑ 132 I'm Honored R .75 2.00
❑ 133 The Dead Walk R .75 2.00
❑ 134 Girl Talk R .75 2.00
❑ 135 You Look Like Her R .75 2.00
❑ 136 A Deal With a Bat R .75 2.00
❑ 137 Halt! R .75 2.00
❑ 138 Scared of Not Talking R .75 2.00
❑ 139 They're so Cute R .75 2.00
❑ 140 Treasures R .75 2.00
❑ 141 Baggage R .75 2.00
❑ 142 School Hallway R .75 2.00
❑ 143 Kagome's Junior High R .75 2.00
❑ 144 Kagome's Refrigerator R .75 2.00
❑ 145 Classroom R .75 2.00
❑ 146 Graveyard R .75 2.00
❑ 147 Jealous R .75 2.00
❑ 148 Cover Up R .75 2.00
❑ 149 Down the Well R .75 2.00
❑ 150 Clash of Power R .75 2.00
❑ 151 Kagome, Traveler Through Time UR 4.00 10.00
❑ 152 Sesshomaru, Intimidating Adversary UR 4.00 10.00
❑ 153 Shunran, Panther Tribe Deva UR 4.00 10.00
❑ 154 Inuyasha, Temptress of Evil UR 5.00 12.00
❑ 155 Thank You Great Lord UR 3.00 8.00
❑ 156 You Were Worried UR 3.00 8.00
❑ 157 Tetsusaiga, Transformed UR 4.00 10.00
❑ 158 Things Never Change UR 3.00 8.00
❑ H1 The Three Sprites of the Monkey God HR 10.00 20.00
❑ H2 Kawaramaru HR 10.00 20.00

2006 InuYasha Saisei Promos

COMPLETE SET (9) 5.00 12.00
❑ P1 Inuyasha, Skilled Warrior PROMO 1.00 2.50
❑ P2 Naraku, Puppet Master PROMO 1.00 2.50
❑ P3 Sesshomaru, Diabolical Brother PROMO 1.00 2.50
❑ P4 Relaxing PROMO 1.00 2.50
❑ P5 Forward Charge PROMO 1.00 2.50
❑ P6 Kikyo, Sacred Jewel Protector PROMO 1.00 2.50
❑ P7 Meditation PROMO 1.00 2.50
❑ P8 Kagome, Guardian of the Shikon Jewel PROMO1.00 2.50
❑ P9 What Test? PROMO 1.00 2.50

2006 InuYasha Saisei Timeless Champions

COMPLETE SET (10) 6.00 15.00
❑ TC1 Inuyasha, TC 1.25 3.00
❑ TC2 Kagome, TC 1.25 3.00
❑ TC3 Miroku, TC 1.25 3.00
❑ TC4 Sango, TC 1.25 3.00
❑ TC5 Shippo, TC 1.25 3.00
❑ TC6 Kirara, TC 1.25 3.00
❑ TC7 Koga, TC 1.25 3.00
❑ TC8 Kikyo, TC 1.25 3.00
❑ TC9 Inuyasha, Human TC 1.25 3.00
❑ TC10 Kohaku, TC 1.25 3.00

2006 InuYasha Shimei

BOOSTER BOX (12) 5.00 12.00
BOOSTER PACK (10) .60 1.50
❑ 1 Rats C .10 .25
❑ 2 Tesso C .10 .25
❑ 3 Kuroro C .10 .25
❑ 4 Two-Tailed Kittens C .10 .25
❑ 5 Wolves, 2 C .10 .25
❑ 6 Clay Warriors, 2 C .10 .25
❑ 7 Gamajiro, Evil Demon C .10 .25
❑ 8 Madam Exorcist C .10 .25
❑ 9 Demon Head C .10 .25
❑ 10 Hitomi C .10 .25
❑ 11 Turtle Demon C .10 .25
❑ 12 Buyo, Happy Kitty C .10 .25
❑ 13 Mushin, the Old Monk C .10 .25
❑ 14 Angry Villagers C .10 .25
❑ 15 Hachi, as Miroku C .10 .25
❑ 16 Soldier C .10 .25
❑ 17 Surprised Outlaws C .10 .25
❑ 18 Kansuke, Mad Killer C .10 .25
❑ 19 Village Women C .10 .25
❑ 20 Myoga, Faithful Friend C .10 .25
❑ 21 Ginta, Follower of Koga C .10 .25
❑ 22 Sota, Boy in Love C .10 .25
❑ 23 Koume C .10 .25
❑ 24 Hakkaku, Follower of Koga C .10 .25
❑ 25 Kirara, Sango's Pet C .10 .25
❑ 26 Orochimaru, Evil Demon C .10 .25
❑ 27 Gyuoh, Evil Demon C .10 .25
❑ 28 Kawaramaru, Leader of the Clay Warriors C .10 .25
❑ 29 Summoned Clay Warrior C .10 .25
❑ 30 Rin, Friend of Jaken C .10 .25
❑ 31 A Friendly Conversation C .10 .25
❑ 32 Hard Strike C .10 .25
❑ 33 Tight Grip C .10 .25
❑ 34 Sneaking a Peek C .10 .25
❑ 35 Quick Reflexes C .10 .25
❑ 36 Don't Catch a Cold C .10 .25
❑ 37 Taken by Force C .10 .25
❑ 38 Stuck to a Stone C .10 .25
❑ 39 Forceful Strike C .10 .25
❑ 40 Watching Over Her C .10 .25
❑ 41 Fish C .10 .25
❑ 42 Soccer Ball C .10 .25
❑ 43 Mermaid Scale C .10 .25
❑ 44 Chips C .10 .25
❑ 45 Water Bottle C .10 .25
❑ 46 Enju, Urasue's Child U .20 .50
❑ 47 Jaken, Friend of Rin U .20 .50
❑ 48 Koga, Leader of the Wolf Demon Tribe U .20 .50
❑ 49 Onigumo, Villain U .20 .50
❑ 50 Kansuke, Aging Outlaw U .20 .50
❑ 51 The Three Sprites of the Monkey God .20 .50
Playful Kids U
❑ 52 Monkey God U .20 .50
❑ 53 Kagura, Evil Demon U .20 .50
❑ 54 Kagome, Showing the Roast U .20 .50
❑ 55 Sango, Friend of Kirara U .20 .50
❑ 56 Sango, Demon Hunter U .20 .50
❑ 57 Hachi, Friendly Raccoon U .20 .50
❑ 58 Shippo, Master Gamer U .20 .50
❑ 59 Miroku, Ready for Battle U .20 .50
❑ 60 Kagome, Master Archer U .20 .50
❑ 61 Sesshomaru, Menacing Demon U .20 .50
❑ 62 Kaede, Village Leader U .20 .50
❑ 63 Moth Demon U .20 .50
❑ 64 Naraku, Evil Demon U .20 .50
❑ 65 Inuyasha, Wearing a Hat U .20 .50
❑ 66 Inuyasha, Aggravated U .20 .50
❑ 67 Kanna, Evil Demon U .20 .50
❑ 68 Kikyo, Wandering Priestess U .20 .50
❑ 69 Fake Shikon Jewel U .20 .50
❑ 70 The Monkey God's Stone U .20 .50
❑ 71 Dagger U .20 .50
❑ 72 Beautiful Valley U .20 .50
❑ 73 Bandit Camp U .20 .50
❑ 74 Stream U .20 .50
❑ 75 Trail Into Village U .20 .50
❑ 76 Abandoned Shrine U .20 .50
❑ 77 Grassy Trail U .20 .50
❑ 78 Cliff U .20 .50
❑ 79 Cave of the Priestess U .20 .50
❑ 80 A Place to Sleep U .20 .50
❑ 81 The Night Sky U .20 .50
❑ 82 Come On U .20 .50
❑ 83 A Helping Hand U .20 .50
❑ 84 Family Dinner U .20 .50
❑ 85 All Tied Up U .20 .50
❑ 86 Promise Under the Rainbow U .20 .50
❑ 87 Relieved U .20 .50
❑ 88 Don't Be Fooled U .20 .50
❑ 89 I Was So Worried About You U .20 .50
❑ 90 Shopping U .20 .50
❑ 91 Naraku, Menacing Demon R .75 2.00
❑ 92 Sesshomaru, Silent Warrior R .75 2.00
❑ 93 Jaken, Serving Lord Sesshomaru R .75 2.00
❑ 94 Miroku, Flattering Monk R .75 2.00
❑ 95 Koga, Inuyasha's Rival R .75 2.00
❑ 96 Kawaramaru, Ruthless Leader R .75 2.00
❑ 97 Inuyasha, Master Hunter R .75 2.00
❑ 98 Following the Scent R .75 2.00
❑ 99 Overwhelmed With Happiness R .75 2.00
❑ 100 Waiting R .75 2.00
❑ 101 The Power of Prayer R .75 2.00
❑ 102 Lord Sesshomaru R .75 2.00
❑ 103 Playing With Toys R .75 2.00
❑ 104 Which One is Which? R .75 2.00
❑ 105 Keeping Warm R .75 2.00
❑ 106 Deal With It R .75 2.00
❑ 107 Determined Slayer R .75 2.00
❑ 108 I Need Help R .75 2.00
❑ 109 Deadly Poison R .75 2.00
❑ 110 Jeweled Souls R .75 2.00
❑ 111 I'm Late! R .75 2.00
❑ 112 Be Quiet R .75 2.00
❑ 113 Fake Shikon Jewel Club R .75 2.00
❑ 114 Bomb R .75 2.00
❑ 115 Swarm R .75 2.00
❑ 116 Inuyasha, Quick to Attack UR 5.00 12.00
❑ 117 Explosion UR 3.00 8.00
❑ 118 She's Just Saying That UR 3.00 8.00
❑ 119 Brute Force UR 4.00 10.00
❑ H1 Jakotsu HR 10.00 20.00
❑ H2 Bankotsu HR 10.00 20.00

2006 InuYasha Shimei Memories

COMPLETE SET (10) 6.00 15.00
❑ M1 Approaching the Well 1.25 3.00
❑ M2 He Was Here? 1.25 3.00
❑ M3 Reunited 1.25 3.00
❑ M4 A Reflection of One's Self 1.25 3.00
❑ M5 Shot in the Heart 1.25 3.00
❑ M6 Remembering the Fallen 1.25 3.00
❑ M7 Being Bashful 1.25 3.00
❑ M8 A Moment of Peace 1.25 3.00
❑ M9 Happy Birthday 1.25 3.00
❑ M10 A Special Occasion 1.25 3.00

2006 InuYasha Tousou

BOOSTER BOX (12) 5.00 12.00
BOOSTER PACK (10) .60 1.50

❑ 1 Inuyasha, Feudal Hero C .10 .25
❑ 2 Miroku, Feudal Hero C .10 .25
❑ 3 Kagome, Feudal Hero C .10 .25
❑ 4 Sango, Feudal Hero C .10 .25
❑ 5 Shippo, Feudal Hero C .10 .25
❑ 6 Kirara, Feudal Hero C .10 .25
❑ 7 Naraku, Powerful Foe C .10 .25
❑ 8 Sesshomaru, Powerful Foe C .10 .25
❑ 9 Jaken, Sesshomaru's Loyal Companion C .10 .25
❑ 10 Kikyo, Feudal Hero C .10 .25
❑ 11 Village Man C .10 .25
❑ 12 Kohaku, Naraku's Pawn C .10 .25
❑ 13 Koga, Warrior of the Wolf Demon Tribe C .10 .25
❑ 14 Kagura, Naraku's Pawn C .10 .25
❑ 15 Northern Wolf Tribe Warriors C .10 .25
❑ 16 Ayame, Princess of the Northern Wolf Tribe C .10 .25
❑ 17 Naraku's Poison Insects, 5 C .10 .25
❑ 18 Gun Battalion C .10 .25
❑ 19 Province Lord C .10 .25
❑ 20 Myoga, Traveling Flea C .10 .25
❑ 21 Koyuki, Snow Maiden C .10 .25
❑ 22 Shintaro's Sister C .10 .25
❑ 23 Cavalryman C .10 .25
❑ 24 Rin, Little Girl C .10 .25
❑ 25 Jinenji, Half Demon C .10 .25
❑ 26 Village Boy C .10 .25
❑ 27 Naraku's Poison Insects, 6 C .10 .25
❑ 28 Kanna, Naraku's Pawn C .10 .25
❑ 29 Kyokotsu, Member of the Band of Seven C .10 .25
❑ 30 Mukotsu, Member of the Band of Seven C .10 .25
❑ 31 Stay Back C .10 .25
❑ 32 Breaking the Barrier C .10 .25
❑ 33 How Dare You? C .10 .25
❑ 34 I Want Them C .10 .25
❑ 35 Off to War C .10 .25
❑ 36 Laughing Mushrooms C .10 .25
❑ 37 Keep Your Hands Off My Wolves! C .10 .25
❑ 38 Surprise Attack C .10 .25
❑ 39 Daydreaming C .10 .25
❑ 40 Wire Trap C .10 .25
❑ 41 Matchlock Rifle C .10 .25
❑ 42 Sleeping Potion C .10 .25
❑ 43 Myoga's Special Potion C .10 .25
❑ 44 Shintaro's Staff C .10 .25
❑ 45 Ointment C .10 .25
❑ 46 Wolf, 3 U .20 .50
❑ 47 Wolf Tribe Elder U .20 .50
❑ 48 Ginkotsu, Member of the Band of Seven U .20 .50
❑ 49 Kyokotsu, Warrior of the Band of Seven U .20 .50
❑ 50 Kikyo, Supernatural Priestess U .20 .50
❑ 51 Suikotsu, Good Doctor U .20 .50
❑ 52 Inuyasha, the Victor U .20 .50
❑ 53 Suikotsu, Member of the Band of Seven U .20 .50
❑ 54 Bankotsu, Member of the Band of Seven U .20 .50
❑ 55 Warlord General U .20 .50
❑ 56 Renkotsu, Member of the Band of Seven U .20 .50
❑ 57 Elder of the Northern Wolf Tribe U .20 .50
❑ 58 Battalion Leader U .20 .50
❑ 59 Kohaku, Follower of Naraku U .20 .50
❑ 60 Suikotsu, Warrior of the Band of Seven U .20 .50
❑ 61 Inuyasha, Kagome's Hero U .20 .50
❑ 62 Mukotsu, Poison Master of the Band of Seven U .20 .50
❑ 63 Guard U .20 .50
❑ 64 Sango, Last Living Slayer U .20 .50
❑ 65 Miroku, Carefree Monk U .20 .50
❑ 66 Shintaro U .20 .50
❑ 67 Kagome, Reincarnated Priestess U .20 .50
❑ 68 Ginkotsu, Warrior of the Band of Seven U .20 .50
❑ 69 Shippo, Helpful Friend U .20 .50
❑ 70 Jakotsu, Member of the Band of Seven U .20 .50
❑ 71 You're So Adorable U .20 .50
❑ 72 Die! U .20 .50
❑ 73 Surrounded U .20 .50
❑ 74 Tormented U .20 .50
❑ 75 Paralysis U .20 .50
❑ 76 I Made it Worse! U .20 .50
❑ 77 Executed U .20 .50
❑ 78 Are You Okay? U .20 .50
❑ 79 It's Not Fair U .20 .50
❑ 80 Burying the Dead U .20 .50
❑ 81 Ginkotsu's Jewel Shard U .20 .50
❑ 82 Special Restorative U .20 .50
❑ 83 Tainted Jewel Shard U .20 .50
❑ 84 Suikotsu's Claws U .20 .50
❑ 85 Mukotsu's Poison U .20 .50
❑ 86 Hijiri Island U .20 .50
❑ 87 Bamboo Forest U .20 .50
❑ 88 Tomb of the Band of Seven U .20 .50
❑ 89 Renkotsu's Workshop U .20 .50
❑ 90 Mount Hakurei U .20 .50
❑ 91 Warlord General, Military Mastermind R .75 2.00
❑ 92 Renkotsu, Tactician of the Band of Seven R .75 2.00
❑ 93 Jakotsu, Warrior of the Band of Seven R .75 2.00
❑ 94 Suikotsu, Mercenary of the Band of Seven R .75 2.00
❑ 95 Sesshomaru, Skilled Warrior R .75 2.00
❑ 96 Inuyasha, Wielder of Tetsusaiga R .75 2.00
❑ 97 Koga, Fierce Wolf Demon R .75 2.00
❑ 98 He Smelled of Corpses and Graveyard Soil R .75 2.00
❑ 99 Clash of Swords R .75 2.00
❑ 100 Sucking Out the Poison R .75 2.00
❑ 101 He Will Die... He Won't Die... R .75 2.00
❑ 102 Fun at the Hot Springs R .75 2.00
❑ 103 It's Just One Promise R .75 2.00
❑ 104 Approaching Danger R .75 2.00
❑ 105 Looking for Koga R .75 2.00
❑ 106 Abducted R .75 2.00
❑ 107 Strong Slash R .75 2.00
❑ 108 You and I Share Similar Fates R .75 2.00
❑ 109 Ginkotsu Self Destructs R .75 2.00
❑ 110 Koga's Determination R .75 2.00
❑ 111 That's Enough R .75 2.00
❑ 112 Jumping Out of the Way R .75 2.00
❑ 113 Banryu R .75 2.00
❑ 114 Jakotsuto R .75 2.00
❑ 115 Saint Hakushin's Amulet R .75 2.00
❑ 116 Bankotsu, Leader of the Band of Seven UR 4.00 10.00
❑ 117 Miroku, Warrior Monk UR 4.00 10.00
❑ 118 Saving an Old Love UR 5.00 12.00
❑ 119 Breakthrough UR 3.00 8.00
❑ H1 Saint Hakushin HR 10.00 20.00
❑ H2 Naraku, Reborn HR 10.00 20.00

2006 InuYasha Tousou Promos

COMPLETE SET (7) 3.00 8.00

❑ P1 Bankotsu, Warrior of the Band of Seven P 1.00 2.50
❑ P2 Kohaku, Tragic Soul P 1.00 2.50
❑ P3 Koga, Wolf Commander P 1.00 2.50
❑ P4 Bankotsu's Lightning Attack P 1.00 2.50
❑ P5 Sango, Fearless Warrior P 1.00 2.50
❑ P6 Clash P 1.00 2.50
❑ P7 Inuyasha, Rushing into Battle P 1.00 2.50

2006 InuYasha Tousou Weapons

COMPLETE SET (10) 6.00 15.00

❑ W1 Tetsusaiga 1.25 3.00
❑ W2 Tenseiga 1.25 3.00
❑ W3 Tokijin 1.25 3.00
❑ W4 Hiraikotsu 1.25 3.00
❑ W5 Miroku's Staff 1.25 3.00
❑ W6 Kagome's Bicycle 1.25 3.00
❑ W7 Kagome's Backpack 1.25 3.00
❑ W8 Jewel of Four Souls 1.25 3.00
❑ W9 Banryu 1.25 3.00
❑ W10 Jakotsuto 1.25 3.00

2007 InuYasha Keshin

BOOSTER BOX (12) 15.00 30.00
BOOSTER PACK (10) 1.50 3.00

❑ 1 Naraku's Demons, 2 C .10 .25
❑ 2 The Little Fox Demons C .10 .25
❑ 3 Naraku's Demons, 3 C .10 .25
❑ 4 Kohaku, Controlled by Naraku C .10 .25
❑ 5 Chokyukai's Brides C .10 .25
❑ 6 Yuka, Kagome's Classmate C .10 .25
❑ 7 Kagome's Mom, Caring Mother C .10 .25
❑ 8 Renkotsu, Warrior of the Band of Seven C .10 .25
❑ 9 Jakotsu, Soldier of the Band of Seven C .10 .25
❑ 10 Suikotsu, Maniac of the Band of Seven C .10 .25
❑ 11 Bankotsu, Strongest of the Band of Seven C .10 .25
❑ 12 Mimisenri C .10 .25
❑ 13 Kagome, Willing Helper C .10 .25
❑ 14 Sango, Feudal Warrior C .10 .25
❑ 15 Shippo, Quick Little Fox Demon C .10 .25
❑ 16 Chokyukai, Direct Descendant of Chohakkai C .10 .25
❑ 17 Sagojo, Descendant of Sagojo C .10 .25
❑ 18 Goku, Descendant of Songoku C .10 .25
❑ 19 Koga, Kagome's Protector C .10 .25
❑ 20 Kagura, Naraku's Incarnation C .10 .25
❑ 21 Kanna, Naraku's Incarnation C .10 .25
❑ 22 Kirara, Cat Demon of Two Tails C .10 .25
❑ 23 Kikyo, Powerful Priestess C .10 .25
❑ 24 Eri, Stern Director C .10 .25
❑ 25 Ayumi, Music Conductor C .10 .25
❑ 26 Sesshomaru, Inuyasha's Older Brother C .10 .25
❑ 27 Miroku, Feudal Traveler C .10 .25
❑ 28 Mizuki C .10 .25
❑ 29 Kaede, Elder Priestess C .10 .25
❑ 30 Kagome's Grandfather, Old Priest C .10 .25
❑ 31 Sins of the Past C .10 .25
❑ 32 Good Friends C .10 .25
❑ 33 May You Rest in Peace C .10 .25
❑ 34 Giving in to Temptation C .10 .25
❑ 35 Farewell Old Friend C .10 .25
❑ 36 The First Meeting C .10 .25
❑ 37 A Big Disappointment C .10 .25
❑ 38 Incinerated by the Fire Cannon C .10 .25
❑ 39 Drying Off C .10 .25
❑ 40 I Refuse to Die C .10 .25
❑ 41 Renkotsu's Blast Cannon C .10 .25
❑ 42 Robe of the Fire Rat, Inuyasha's Armor C .10 .25
❑ 43 Fire Bomb C .10 .25
❑ 44 Kanna's Mirror, Her Weapon C .10 .25
❑ 45 Groceries C .10 .25
❑ 46 Inuyasha, Kikyo's Past Love U .20 .50
❑ 47 Sango, Feudal Traveler U .20 .50
❑ 48 Naraku, Revealed U .20 .50
❑ 49 Rin, Child in Wonder U .20 .50
❑ 50 Inuyasha, Looking Sad U .20 .50
❑ 51 Shippo, the Transformer U .20 .50
❑ 52 Kagome, in a Play U .20 .50
❑ 53 Hojo, in a Play U .20 .50
❑ 54 Inuyasha, Modern U .20 .50
❑ 55 Naraku's Demons, 4 U .20 .50
❑ 56 Inuyasha, Purified U .20 .50
❑ 57 Infant, Spawn of Naraku U .20 .50
❑ 58 Miroku, Roaming Monk U .20 .50
❑ 59 Jakotsu, Band of Seven Warrior U .20 .50
❑ 60 Renkotsu .20 .50
Deceptive Member of the Band of Seven U
❑ 61 Bankotsu, Band of Seven Warrior U .20 .50
❑ 62 Yuka, the Cook U .20 .50
❑ 63 Ayumi, Strict Leader U .20 .50
❑ 64 Eri, Determined U .20 .50
❑ 65 Ginta, Koga's Companion U .20 .50
❑ 66 Hakkaku, Koga's Companion U .20 .50
❑ 67 Kagome's Grandfather, Demon Fighter U .20 .50
❑ 68 Sota, the Soul Stealer U .20 .50
❑ 69 Koga, Demon Wolf Tribe Warrior U .20 .50
❑ 70 Clumps of Flesh U .20 .50
❑ 71 Knockout Strike U .20 .50
❑ 72 New Found Power U .20 .50
❑ 73 Born Again U .20 .50
❑ 74 Holding on Tight U .20 .50
❑ 75 Cooking Class U .20 .50
❑ 76 Chokyukai's Abducted Brides U .20 .50
❑ 77 Silence U .20 .50
❑ 78 I'll Defend You U .20 .50
❑ 79 They are Both Stupid U .20 .50
❑ 80 There is Still Hope for This Child U .20 .50
❑ 81 Chinese Sutra U .20 .50
❑ 82 Necklace of Flowers U .20 .50
❑ 83 Staff U .20 .50
❑ 84 Scalpel U .20 .50
❑ 85 Naraku's Tainted Shard U .20 .50
❑ 86 Banryu, Demon Powered U .20 .50
❑ 87 Cultural Festival U .20 .50
❑ 88 Convenience Store U .20 .50
❑ 89 Chokyukai's Lair U .20 .50
❑ 90 All Knowing U .20 .50
❑ 91 Kikyo, Elegant Priestess R .75 2.00
❑ 92 Naraku, Transformed R .75 2.00
❑ 93 Chokyukai, Stealer of Women R .75 2.00
❑ 94 Infant, Controller of Hearts R .75 2.00
❑ 95 Inuyasha, the Proud R .75 2.00
❑ 96 Kagome, Feudal Traveler R .75 2.00
❑ 97 Bankotsu, Last of the Band of Seven R .75 2.00
❑ 98 Sesshomaru, Roaming Demon R .75 2.00
❑ 99 Saint Hakushin, Living Buddha R .75 2.00
❑ 100 Support from the Family R .75 2.00
❑ 101 My Lost Love R .75 2.00
❑ 102 Save Him Inuyasha! R .75 2.00
❑ 103 Thinking R .75 2.00
❑ 104 Deadly Hit R .75 2.00
❑ 105 Running Into the Windscar R .75 2.00
❑ 106 Uppercut R .75 2.00
❑ 107 Shut Your Trap! R .75 2.00
❑ 108 It's No Ones Fault But Your Own R .75 2.00
❑ 109 The Heart Scar R .75 2.00
❑ 110 I Hate You! R .75 2.00
❑ 111 At a Loss R .75 2.00
❑ 112 It's Cold R .75 2.00
❑ 113 When Will They Be Back? R .75 2.00
❑ 114 Kagome's House R .75 2.00
❑ 115 Chokyukai's Tiara R .75 2.00
❑ 116 Naraku, Master of Manipulation UR 4.00 10.00
❑ 117 Shippo, Master Fox Demon UR 4.00 10.00
❑ 118 Damn You! UR 5.00 12.00
❑ 119 An Unimaginable Loss UR 3.00 8.00
❑ H1 Sesshomaru HR 10.00 20.00
❑ H2 Sango HR 10.00 20.00

2007 InuYasha Keshin Feudal Voices Autographs

STATED PRINT RUN 170 SER. #'d SETS

❑ FV1 Inuyasha, Feudal Hero 30.00 60.00
❑ FV2 Sango, the Demon Slayer 12.00 25.00
❑ FV3 Sesshomaru, Wanderer 12.00 25.00
❑ FV4 Shippo, the Shapeshifter 12.00 25.00
❑ FV5 Miroku, Warrior Monk 12.00 25.00
❑ FV6 Koga, Protector of Kagome 12.00 25.00

2007 InuYasha Keshin Feudal Warriors

COMPLETE SET (10) 6.00 15.00

❑ FW1 Inuyasha 1.25 3.00
❑ FW2 Sesshomaru 1.25 3.00
❑ FW3 Naraku 1.25 3.00
❑ FW4 Kagome 1.25 3.00
❑ FW5 Miroku 1.25 3.00
❑ FW6 Sango 1.25 3.00
❑ FW7 Kikyo 1.25 3.00
❑ FW8 Muso 1.25 3.00
❑ FW9 Kagura 1.25 3.00
❑ FW10 Koga 1.25 3.00

2007 InuYasha Keshin Players Choice Autographs

UNPRICED DUE TO SCARCITY

❑ PC1 Inuyasha/20
❑ PC2 Koga/20
❑ PC3 Halt!/10

2007 InuYasha Keshin Promos

COMPLETE SET (7) 4.00 10.00

❑ P1 Infant, the Heart of Naraku P 1.00 2.50
❑ P2 Naraku, Master of Deception P 1.00 2.50
❑ P3 Saint Hakushin, Manipulated by Naraku P 1.00 2.50
❑ P4 Naraku, Vile Demon P 1.00 2.50
❑ P5 Shippo, in Love P 1.00 2.50
❑ P6 Miroku's Curse P 1.00 2.50
❑ P7 Sit Inuyasha! P 1.00 2.50

2007 InuYasha Tensei

BOOSTER BOX (12) 15.00 30.00
BOOSTER PACK (10) 1.50 3.00

❑ 1 Sara, Young Princess C .10 .25
❑ 2 Genbu, Ninja of the Darkness C .10 .25
❑ 3 Byakko, Ninja of the Snow C .10 .25
❑ 4 Seiryu, Ninja of the Moon C .10 .25
❑ 5 Suzaku, Ninja of the Flower C .10 .25
❑ 6 Chief Slayer C .10 .25
❑ 7 Hoshiyomi, Demon Ninja C .10 .25
❑ 8 Bird Demons, 1 C .10 .25
❑ 9 Bird Demons, 2 C .10 .25
❑ 10 Bird Demons, 3 C .10 .25
❑ 11 Hakudoshi, the Horrible C .10 .25
❑ 12 Akitoki Hojo, Hojo's Ancestor C .10 .25
❑ 13 Mezu, the Stone Gate Keeper C .10 .25
❑ 14 Gozu, the Stone Gate Keeper C .10 .25
❑ 15 Paper Thin Demon C .10 .25
❑ 16 Rengokuki, Entei's First Master C .10 .25
❑ 17 Kwannon, Salamander Demon C .10 .25
❑ 18 Entei, the Untamed C .10 .25
❑ 19 Demon Ninja Shadow Hold C .10 .25
❑ 20 The Band of Seven C .10 .25
❑ 21 Ninja Kite C .10 .25
❑ 22 Priestess Amulet C .10 .25
❑ 23 Ken Blade C .10 .25
❑ 24 Kon Blade C .10 .25
❑ 25 Byakko, Transformed U .20 .50
❑ 26 Suzaku, Flamboyant Ninja U .20 .50
❑ 27 Seiryu, Transformed U .20 .50
❑ 28 Genbu, Transformed U .20 .50
❑ 29 Saint Hijiri the Holy One U .20 .50
❑ 30 Tsubaki, Cursed Priestess U .20 .50
❑ 31 Tsukiyomi, Samurai Priestess U .20 .50
❑ 32 Shippo, Kagome's Protector U .20 .50
❑ 33 Bird Demons, 4 U .20 .50
❑ 34 Inuyasha, Protector of Kagome's Heart U .20 .50
❑ 35 Princess Abi, Princess of the Bird Demons U .20 .50
❑ 36 Kirara, Companion of Sango U .20 .50
❑ 37 Kagome, Mushin's Maid U .20 .50
❑ 38 Sango, Miroku's Love Interest U .20 .50
❑ 39 Miroku, Sentimental Monk U .20 .50
❑ 40 Sesshomaru, Master of Tenseiga U .20 .50
❑ 41 Sara, the Woman Who Loved Sesshomaru U .20 .50
❑ 42 Intoxicated U .20 .50
❑ 43 Akitoki Hojo, Protector of Kagome U .20 .50
❑ 44 Demon Ninja Doppleganger Techinque U .20 .50
❑ 45 Attack of the Bird Demons of Doom U .20 .50
❑ 46 Wounded U .20 .50
❑ 47 How Long Do You Intend to Hide? U .20 .50
❑ 48 Sack! U .20 .50
❑ 49 Shippo, the Master Fox Demon U .20 .50
❑ 50 Tomb of Inuyasha's Father U .20 .50
❑ 51 Possessed Shrine U .20 .50
❑ 52 Princess Abi, Bird Master R .75 2.00
❑ 53 Inuyasha, Heroic Champion R .75 2.00
❑ 54 Hoshiyomi, Leader of the Demon Ninja R .75 2.00
❑ 55 Entei, Raging Demon Horse R .75 2.00
❑ 56 Sesshomaru, Silent Demon R .75 2.00
❑ 57 Naraku, Wicked Demon R .75 2.00
❑ 58 Hakudoshi, Entei's Rider R .75 2.00
❑ 59 Demon Ninja Shadow Incarnation R .75 2.00
❑ 60 Preparing the Ceremony R .75 2.00
❑ 61 Naraku's Grip R .75 2.00
❑ 62 Regenerating R .75 2.00
❑ 63 He Proposed R .75 2.00
❑ 64 What Do You Want to Give Me? R .75 2.00
❑ 65 Hakudoshi R .75 2.00
❑ 66 Kikyo R .75 2.00
❑ 67 Sesshomaru, Warrior of the Feudal Era P 1.00 2.50
❑ 68 Miroku, Sango's Protector P 1.00 2.50
❑ 69 Koga, Protector of Kagome's Heart P 1.00 2.50
❑ 70 Naraku's Mark R .75 2.00
❑ 71 Could She Be? R .75 2.00
❑ 72 The Naginata of Kenkon R .75 2.00
❑ 73 Trident of Naraku's Bones R .75 2.00
❑ 74 River Bank R .75 2.00
❑ 75 Believe Us! UR 3.00 8.00
❑ 76 Princess Abi, Bird Demon Princess UR 5.00 12.00
❑ 77 Hakudoshi, Naraku's Incarnation UR 4.00 10.00
❑ 78 Kanna UR 4.00 10.00
❑ 79 The Cost of War UR 4.00 10.00
❑ 80 Tekkei UR 4.00 10.00

2007 InuYasha Tensei Classics

COMPLETE SET (10) 6.00 15.00

❑ C1 Miroku, Lecherous Monk (Saisei #IYP4) 1.25 3.00
❑ C2 Inuyasha, Helpful Friend (Saisei #OP3) 1.25 3.00
❑ C3 Kagome (Kassen #H2) 1.25 3.00
❑ C4 Sesshomaru, Rival Brother (Saisei #IYP3) 1.25 3.00
❑ C5 Rin, Follower of Sesshomaru (Kassen #KP3) 1.25 3.00
❑ C6 Yura, Master of Puppets (Saisei #81) 1.25 3.00
❑ C7 Halt! (Saisei #137) 1.25 3.00
❑ C8 Waking Up (Saisei #Op1) 1.25 3.00
❑ C9 Watching Each Others Back (Saisei #PR4) 1.25 3.00
❑ C10 Naraku's Evil Influence (Saisei #OP2) 1.25 3.00

2007 InuYasha Tensei Feudal Voices Autographs

STATED PRINT RUN 170 SER. #'d SETS

❑ FV1 Bankotsu, Band of Seven 10.00 20.00
❑ FV2 Kagura 10.00 20.00
❑ FV3 Jaken, Friend of Rin 10.00 20.00
❑ FV4 Kikyo, Legends 12.00 25.00
❑ FV5 Hakudoshi, Spawn of Naraku 10.00 20.00
❑ FV6 Naraku, Deceptive Demon 20.00 40.00

2007 InuYasha Tensei Players Choice Autographs

UNPRICED DUE TO SCARCITY

❑ PC1 Just Ask For Help/20
❑ PC2 Naraku, Reborn/20
❑ PC3 Kikyo, Fading Soul/20
❑ PC4 A Tragic Death (Kijin #104) /20
❑ PC5 Yura, Master of Puppets (Saisei #81) /20
❑ PC6 Kikyo/20
❑ PC7 You Were Worried (Saisei #156) /10
❑ PC8 Koga, the Furious (Jaki #118) /10
❑ PC9 Sesshomaru, Rival Brother (Saisei #IYP3) /10
❑ PC10 Miroku, Lecherous Monk (Saisei #IYP4) /10
❑ PC11 Inuyasha, Helpful Friend (Saisei #OP3) /10
❑ PC12 Naraku's Evil Influence (Saisei #OP2) /10
❑ PC13 Hakudoshi (Keshin #I10) /10
❑ PC14 Kanna/10

1995 Legend of the Five Rings Imperial

❑ 1 Agasha Tamori C .10 .20
❑ 2 Air Dragon R .75 2.00
❑ 3 Akodo Kage U .20 .50
❑ 4 Akodo Toturi R 3.00 8.00
❑ 5 Alhundro Cornejo U .20 .50
❑ 6 Alliance U .20 .50
❑ 7 Ambush R 2.50 6.00
❑ 8 Ancestral Sword of the Crab F 1.50 4.00
❑ 9 Ancestral Sword of the Crane F 2.50 6.00
❑ 10 Ancestral Sword of the Dragon F 3.00 8.00
❑ 11 Ancestral Sword of the Lion F 2.50 6.00
❑ 12 Ancestral Sword of the Phoenix F 2.50 6.00
❑ 13 Ancestral Sword of the Unicorn F 2.50 6.00
❑ 14 Animate the Dead U .20 .50
❑ 15 Apprentice R .60 1.50
❑ 16 Archers C .10 .20
❑ 17 Armor of Sun-Tao U .20 .50
❑ 18 Armor of the Golden Samurai U .20 .50
❑ 19 Asahina Tamako U .20 .50
❑ 20 Asahina Tomo C .10 .20
❑ 21 Asako Yasu R .40 1.00
❑ 22 Avoid Fate R 2.00 5.00
❑ 23 Barbican U .20 .50
❑ 24 Battering Ram Crew U .20 .50
❑ 25 Bayushi Kachiko R 10.00 20.00
❑ 26 Bayushi Togai R .40 1.00
❑ 27 Be Prepared to Dig Two Graves R 1.25 3.00
❑ 28 Biting Steel C .10 .20
❑ 29 Blackmail R 5.00 10.00
❑ 30 Blacksmith C .10 .20
❑ 31 Blazing Arrows U .20 .50
❑ 32 Block Supply Lines C .10 .20
❑ 33 Bloodsword C .10 .20
❑ 34 Bloom of the White Orchid R 1.25 3.00
❑ 35 Bon Festival U .20 .50
❑ 36 Bountiful Harvest R3 .75 2.00
❑ 37 Breach of Etiquette U .20 .50
❑ 38 Break Morale C .10 .20
❑ 39 Brilliant Victory C .10 .20
❑ 40 Call Upon The Wind C .10 .20
❑ 41 Careful Planning C .10 .20
❑ 42 Castle of Water C .10 .20
❑ 43 Celestial Alignment R .40 1.00
❑ 44 Charge C .10 .20
❑ 45 Chrysanthemum Festival R 1.50 4.00
❑ 46 Climbing Gear U .20 .50
❑ 47 Cloak of Night R .75 2.00
❑ 48 Contentious Terrain C .10 .20
❑ 49 Copper Mine C .10 .20
❑ 50 Counterattack U .20 .50
❑ 51 Counterspell U .20 .50
❑ 52 Crystal Katana C .10 .20
❑ 53 Daidoji Uji C .10 .20
❑ 54 Dance Troupe U .20 .50
❑ 55 Dead Walk The Earth R .60 1.50
❑ 56 Deadly Ground C .10 .20
❑ 57 Debt of Honor R .40 1.00
❑ 58 Demon-Bride of Fu Leng R 3.00 8.00
❑ 59 Diamond Mine U .20 .50
❑ 60 Dispersive Terrain C .10 .20
❑ 61 Doji Hoturi R 2.00 5.00
❑ 62 Doji Yosai C .10 .20
❑ 63 Dragon Helm U .20 .50
❑ 64 Dragon of Fire R 1.25 3.00
❑ 65 Earth Dragon R .75 2.00
❑ 66 Earthquake U .20 .50
❑ 67 Elemental Ward U .20 .50
❑ 68 Emergence of the Tortoise R .40 1.00
❑ 69 Emperor's Peace U .20 .50
❑ 70 Encircled Terrain C .10 .20
❑ 71 Energy Transference C .10 .20
❑ 72 Entrapping Terrain C .10 .20
❑ 73 Evil Feeds Upon Itself U .20 .50
❑ 74 Evil Portents R3 5.00 10.00
❑ 75 Explosives U .20 .50
❑ 76 Famous Poet C .10 .20
❑ 77 Fan of Command R .40 1.00
❑ 78 Fantastic Gardens U .20 .50
❑ 79 Feign Death R 2.50 6.00
❑ 80 Feint R .75 2.00
❑ 81 Fire Breather R .40 1.00
❑ 82 Fires of Purity U .20 .50
❑ 83 Fist of Osano-Wo R .75 2.00
❑ 84 Flight of Dragons U .20 .50
❑ 85 Focus R 2.50 6.00
❑ 86 Forest C .10 .20
❑ 87 Forgotten Tomb R .40 1.00
❑ 88 Fort On A Hill R .20 .50
❑ 89 Foxwife R 1.25 3.00

TCG/CCG

❑ 90 Frenzy U .20 .50
❑ 91 Fury of Osano-Wo C .10 .20
❑ 92 Gaijin Mercenaries R .40 1.00
❑ 93 Geisha Assassin R3 2.50 6.00
❑ 94 Ginawa C .10 .20
❑ 95 Glimpse of the Unicorn U .20 .50
❑ 96 Go Master C .10 .20
❑ 97 Goblin Chuckers C .10 .20
❑ 98 Goblin Mob C .10 .20
❑ 99 Goblin Warmonger C .10 .20
❑ 100 Gold Mine C .10 .20
❑ 101 Greater Mujina U .20 .50
❑ 102 Hawk Riders R .40 1.00
❑ 103 Hawks and Falcons C .10 .20
❑ 104 Heart of the Inferno R 2.50 6.00
❑ 105 Heavy Cavalry U .20 .50
❑ 106 Heavy Infantry U .20 .50
❑ 107 Heichi Chokei C .10 .20
❑ 108 Hida Amoro U .20 .50
❑ 109 Hida Kisada R 3.00 8.00
❑ 110 Hida Sukune C .10 .20
❑ 111 Hida Tampako C .10 .20
❑ 112 Hida Tsuru U .20 .50
❑ 113 Hida Yakamo (Crab Clan Oni) R 3.00 8.00
❑ 114 Hida Yakamo R 2.50 6.00
❑ 115 Hisa C .10 .20
❑ 116 Honorable Seppuku C .10 .20
❑ 117 Horiuchi Shoan C .10 .20
❑ 118 Hurricane U .20 .50
❑ 119 Iaijitsu Challenge C .10 .20
❑ 120 Iaijitsu Duel C .10 .20
❑ 121 Ide Tadaji R .40 1.00
❑ 122 Ikoma Ujiaki R .75 2.00
❑ 123 Immortal Steel R .75 2.00
❑ 124 Imperial Acrobats R .75 2.00
❑ 125 Imperial Gift R 3.00 8.00
❑ 126 Imperial Quest R .75 2.00
❑ 127 Inheritance R1 5.00 10.00
❑ 128 Intersecting Highways C .10 .20
❑ 129 Investigation R .75 2.00
❑ 130 Iris Festival R 2.50 6.00
❑ 131 Iron Mine C .10 .20
❑ 132 Isawa Kaede U .20 .50
❑ 133 Isawa Tadaka U .20 .50
❑ 134 Isawa Tomo U .20 .50
❑ 135 Isawa Tsuke R 2.50 6.00
❑ 136 Isawa Uona C .10 .20
❑ 137 Iuchi Daiyu U .20 .50
❑ 138 Iuchi Karasu U .20 .50
❑ 139 Iuchi Takaai R .40 1.00
❑ 140 Jade Bow C .10 .20
❑ 141 Jade Works C .10 .20
❑ 142 Kakita Toshimoko R 3.00 8.00
❑ 143 Kakita Yinobu U .20 .50
❑ 144 Kakita Yoshi R 1.25 3.00
❑ 145 Kakita Yuri U .20 .50
❑ 146 Kharmic Strike U .20 .50
❑ 147 Ki-Rin R 1.50 4.00
❑ 148 Kitsu Toju C .10 .20
❑ 149 Kitsuki Yasu R 1.50 4.00
❑ 150 Kolat Assassin U .20 .50
❑ 151 Kolat Infiltrator U .20 .50
❑ 152 Kolat Master R 2.50 6.00
❑ 153 Kolat Servant U .20 .50
❑ 154 Kuni Yori U .20 .50
❑ 155 Kyoso no Oni U .20 .50
❑ 156 Legendary Victory U .20 .50
❑ 157 Lesser Mujina C .10 .20
❑ 158 Light Cavalry C .10 .20
❑ 159 Light Infantry C .10 .20
❑ 160 Look into the Void C .10 .20
❑ 161 Market Place C .10 .20
❑ 162 Marries a Barbarian U .20 .50
❑ 163 Marsh Troll U .20 .50
❑ 164 Martyr U .20 .50
❑ 165 Mask of the Oni U .20 .50
❑ 166 Master of the Tea Ceremony R .40 1.00
❑ 167 Master Smith U .20 .50
❑ 168 Matsu Agetoki U .20 .50
❑ 169 Matsu Gohei C .10 .20
❑ 170 Matsu Hiroru U .20 .50
❑ 171 Matsu Imura U .20 .50
❑ 172 Matsu Tsuko R 5.00 10.00
❑ 173 Matsu Yojo C .10 .20
❑ 174 Meditation C .10 .20
❑ 175 Medium Cavalry C .10 .20
❑ 176 Medium Infantry C .10 .20
❑ 177 Mercy R .40 1.00
❑ 178 Mirumoto Daini C .10 .20
❑ 179 Mirumoto Hitomi C .10 .20
❑ 180 Mirumoto Sukune U .20 .50
❑ 181 Mists of Illusion U .20 .50
❑ 182 Miya Yoto U .20 .50
❑ 183 Moat C .10 .20
❑ 184 Morito C .10 .20
❑ 185 Morito Tokei C .10 .20
❑ 186 Moshi Wakiza C .10 .20
❑ 187 Moto Tsume U .20 .50
❑ 188 Naga Bowmen U .20 .50
❑ 189 Naga Bushi C .10 .20
❑ 190 Naga Shugenja C .10 .20
❑ 191 Naga Spearmen U .20 .50
❑ 192 Naga Warlord C .10 .20
❑ 193 Naginata C .10 .20
❑ 194 Naka Kuro R 2.00 5.00
❑ 195 Necromancer U .20 .50
❑ 196 Night Medallion R .40 1.00
❑ 197 Ninja Genin U .20 .50
❑ 198 Ninja Shapeshifter U .20 .50
❑ 199 Ninja Spy C .10 .20
❑ 200 Ninja Stronghold R 5.00 10.00
❑ 201 Ninja Thief U .20 .50
❑ 202 Oath of Fealty C .10 .20
❑ 203 Occult Murders U .20 .50
❑ 204 Occupied Terrain C .10 .20
❑ 205 Ogre Bushi U .20 .50
❑ 206 Oni no Akuma R 2.00 5.00
❑ 207 Oni no Shikibu U .20 .50
❑ 208 Oni no Tsuburu U .20 .50
❑ 209 Oracle of Earth R .40 1.00
❑ 210 Oracle of Fire R1 1.25 3.00
❑ 211 Oracle of Water R1 .60 1.50
❑ 212 Oracle of Wind R1 .40 1.00
❑ 213 Otaku Kamoko C .10 .20
❑ 214 Outflank C .10 .20
❑ 215 Pearl Divers C .10 .20
❑ 216 Peasant Revolt U .20 .50
❑ 217 Personal Champion R .40 1.00
❑ 218 Plague U .20 .50
❑ 219 Poisoned Weapon R 2.00 5.00
❑ 220 Port C .10 .20
❑ 221 Proposal of Peace R .60 1.50
❑ 222 Rally Troops C .10 .20
❑ 223 Rallying Cry C .10 .20
❑ 224 Ratling Bushi U .20 .50
❑ 225 Ratling Pack C .10 .20
❑ 226 Reflective Pool R .75 2.00
❑ 227 Refuse Advantage R .75 2.00
❑ 228 Remorseful Seppuku C .10 .20
❑ 229 Resist Magic R .75 2.00
❑ 230 Retired General C .10 .20
❑ 231 Retreat U .20 .50
❑ 232 Ring of Air U .20 .50
❑ 233 Ring of Earth U .20 .50
❑ 234 Ring of Fire U .20 .50
❑ 235 Ring of the Void U .20 .50
❑ 236 Ring of Water U .20 .50
❑ 237 Rise of the Phoenix R .75 2.00
❑ 238 Sacrificial Altar U .20 .50
❑ 239 Sake Works U .20 .50
❑ 240 Samurai Cavalry R .40 1.00
❑ 241 Samurai Warriors R .40 1.00
❑ 242 Sanctified Temple C .10 .20
❑ 243 Sanzo C .10 .20
❑ 244 School of Wizardry R1 3.00 8.00
❑ 245 Scout C .10 .20
❑ 246 Scribe R .40 1.00
❑ 247 Secrets on the Wind U .20 .50
❑ 248 Shadow Samurai R .40 1.00
❑ 249 Shady Dealings U .20 .50
❑ 250 Shame U .20 .50
❑ 251 Shiba Katsuda C .10 .20
❑ 252 Shiba Tsukune C .10 .20
❑ 253 Shiba Ujimitsu R 1.50 4.00
❑ 254 Shinjo Hanari U .20 .50
❑ 255 Shinjo Yasamura C .10 .20
❑ 256 Shinjo Yokatsu R 2.00 5.00
❑ 257 Shuriken of Serpents C .10 .20
❑ 258 Shuten Doji U .20 .50
❑ 259 Silver Mine C .10 .20
❑ 260 Skeletal Troops C .10 .20
❑ 261 Small Farm C .10 .20
❑ 262 Sneak Attack R3 6.00 12.00
❑ 263 Solar Eclipse R .40 1.00
❑ 264 Spearmen C .10 .20
❑ 265 Spirit Guide R 1.25 3.00
❑ 266 Stables C .10 .20
❑ 267 Star of Laramun U .20 .50
❑ 268 Strength of Purity U .20 .50
❑ 269 Summon Faeries C .10 .20
❑ 270 Summon Swamp Spirits U .20 .50
❑ 271 Summon Undead Champion R .40 1.00
❑ 272 Superior Tactics C .10 .20
❑ 273 Temple of the Ancestors U .20 .50
❑ 274 Terrible Standard of Fu Leng R .40 1.00
❑ 275 Test of Honor R 5.00 10.00
❑ 276 Test of Stone U .20 .50
❑ 277 Test of the Emerald Champion R .40 1.00
❑ 278 The Ancestral Home of the Lion .60 1.50
❑ 279 The Deafening War Drums of Fu Leng R .40 1.00
❑ 280 The Egg of P'an Ku R 5.00 10.00
❑ 281 The Esteemed House of the Crane .60 1.50
❑ 282 The Jade Hand R .60 1.50
❑ 283 The Mountain Keep of the Dragon .60 1.50
❑ 284 The Provincial Estate of the Unicorn .60 1.50
❑ 285 The Sacred Temple of the Phoenix .60 1.50
❑ 286 The War Fortress of the Crab .60 1.50
❑ 287 Togashi Hoshi R 1.50 4.00
❑ 288 Togashi Mitsu U .20 .50
❑ 289 Togashi Yokuni R 5.00 10.00
❑ 290 Togashi Yoshi U .20 .50
❑ 291 Toku C .10 .20
❑ 292 Torrential Rain R 2.50 6.00
❑ 293 Touch of Death R 1.50 4.00
❑ 294 Trade Route U .20 .50
❑ 295 Traversable Terrain C .10 .20
❑ 296 Unexpected Allies U .20 .50
❑ 297 Unscalable Walls C .10 .20
❑ 298 Void Dragon R 3.00 8.00
❑ 299 Walking the Way U .20 .50
❑ 300 Water Dragon R 1.50 4.00
❑ 301 Way of Deception U .20 .50
❑ 302 Wind Born Speed C .10 .20
❑ 303 Winds of Change U .20 .50
❑ 304 Wings of Fire C .10 .20
❑ 305 Wyrm Riders U .20 .50
❑ 306 Yasuki Taka C .10 .20
❑ 307 Yogo Junzo R 2.00 5.00
❑ 308 Yotsu Seiki C .10 .20
❑ 309 Zombie Troops U .20 .50

1996 Legend of the Five Rings Anvil of Despair

❑ 1 A Hidden Fortress U .20 .50
❑ 2 A Moment of Truth R .40 1.00
❑ 3 A Prophecy Fulfilled R .40 1.00
❑ 4 A Thunder's Sacrifice R .40 1.00
❑ 5 Agasha Koishi C .10 .20
❑ 6 Akodo Kage (Experienced) R .75 2.00
❑ 7 Ancestral Shrines of Otosan Uchi C .10 .20
❑ 8 Arrival of the Emerald Champion R 1.25 3.00
❑ 9 As the Shadow Falls U .20 .50
❑ 10 At the Last Moment C .10 .20
❑ 11 Basecamp C .10 .20
❑ 12 Battlefield of Shallow Graves C .10 .20
❑ 13 Bayushi Kachiko (Experienced) R 2.50 6.00
❑ 14 Bayushi Tangen C .10 .20
❑ 15 Benevolent Protection of Shinsei C .10 .20
❑ 16 Blood Oath C .10 .20
❑ 17 Bo Stick C .10 .20
❑ 18 Candle of the Void U .20 .50
❑ 19 Cornered C .10 .20
❑ 20 Corrupted Energies U .20 .50
❑ 21 Corrupted Silver Mine C .10 .20
❑ 22 Corruption of the Harmonies U .20 .50
❑ 23 Cremation U .20 .50
❑ 24 Daidoji Sembi C .10 .20
❑ 25 Daidoji Uji (Experienced) R .40 1.00
❑ 26 Daisho Technique C .10 .20
❑ 27 Defender From Beyond C .10 .20
❑ 28 Disarmament C .10 .20
❑ 29 Distavored R .40 1.00
❑ 30 Disrupted Resources R .40 1.00
❑ 31 Doom of Fu Leng R 1.50 4.00
❑ 32 Drum of Water U .20 .50
❑ 33 Duty to the Clan U .20 .50
❑ 34 Duty to the Empire R .40 1.00
❑ 35 Elemental Vortex U .20 .50
❑ 36 Emperor's Protection U .20 .50
❑ 37 Essence of Fire C .10 .20
❑ 38 Essence of the Void C .10 .20
❑ 39 Essence of Water C .10 .20
❑ 40 Fields of Asahina Temple C .10 .20
❑ 41 Fight to the Setting Sun C .10 .20
❑ 42 Forests of Shinomen C .10 .20
❑ 43 Fortified Coast U .20 .50
❑ 44 Fu Leng's Horde R .40 1.00
❑ 45 Garden of Purification C .10 .20
❑ 46 Golden Obi of the Sun Goddess R .75 2.00
❑ 47 Hammer of Earth U .20 .50
❑ 48 Hida Unari C .10 .20
❑ 49 Hida Yakamo (Experienced Crab Clan Oni) R 1.50 4.00
❑ 50 Hirariko U .20 .50
❑ 51 Hoseki C .10 .20
❑ 52 Hotogitsu U .20 .50
❑ 53 Ichiin C .10 .20
❑ 54 Ikoma Kimura C .10 .20
❑ 55 Imperial Honor Guard U .20 .50
❑ 56 Imperial Taxation U .20 .50
❑ 57 Inaccessible Region U .20 .50
❑ 58 Isawa Osugi U .20 .50
❑ 59 Isawa Tsuke (Experienced) R .60 1.50
❑ 60 Kaiu Pass U .20 .50
❑ 61 Kaiu Utsu U .20 .50
❑ 62 Kakita Shijin U .20 .50
❑ 63 Kamoto R .60 1.50
❑ 64 Kasuga Kyogi U .20 .50
❑ 65 Kisada's Blockade R .40 1.00
❑ 66 Kolat Instigator R 1.50 4.00
❑ 67 Kolat Interference U .20 .50
❑ 68 Kusatte Iru R .40 1.00
❑ 69 Kyojin U .20 .50
❑ 70 Lies, Lies, Lies... U .20 .50
❑ 71 Mantle of Fire U .20 .50
❑ 72 Matsu Seijuro U .20 .50
❑ 73 Mikaru C .10 .20
❑ 74 Mikio U .20 .50
❑ 75 Minor Shugenja C .10 .20
❑ 76 Monsoon U .20 .50
❑ 77 Mountain of the Seven Thunders R .60 1.50
❑ 78 Naga Guard C .10 .20
❑ 79 Night Battle C .10 .20
❑ 80 Oni no Tadaka C .10 .20
❑ 81 Otaku Baiken C .10 .20
❑ 82 Peasant Defense C .10 .20
❑ 83 Pitch and Fire C .10 .20
❑ 84 Plague Infested Region U .20 .50
❑ 85 Plague Skulls R .75 2.00
❑ 86 Political Dissent R .40 1.00
❑ 87 Possession R .40 1.00
❑ 88 Prophecy of the Hero R .40 1.00
❑ 89 Qakar U .20 .50
❑ 90 Radakast C .10 .20
❑ 91 Ratling Conjurer C .10 .20
❑ 92 Refugees C .10 .20
❑ 93 Retirement U .20 .50
❑ 94 Return of Fu Leng R 2.00 5.00
❑ 95 Rise, Brother U .20 .50
❑ 96 River Region C .10 .20
❑ 97 Scorched Earth C .10 .20
❑ 98 Shallow Victory R .40 1.00
❑ 99 Shashakar (Experienced Naga Shugenja) R .75 2.00
❑ 100 Shinjo Morito (Experienced Morito) R .60 1.50
❑ 101 Shinjo Yasoma U .20 .50
❑ 102 Shiryo no Akodo R .40 1.00
❑ 103 Shiryo no Bayushi R .40 1.00
❑ 104 Shiryo no Hiruma R .40 1.00
❑ 105 Shiryo no Isawa R .40 1.00
❑ 106 Shiryo no Kakita R .40 1.00
❑ 107 Shiryo no Shinjo R 1.25 3.00
❑ 108 Shiryo no Togashi R .40 1.00
❑ 109 Slander U .20 .50
❑ 110 Spiritual Presence C .10 .20
❑ 111 Stall Until Sunrise C .10 .20
❑ 112 Stealing the Soul U .20 .50
❑ 113 Stifling Wind C .10 .20
❑ 114 Strategic Victory U .20 .50
❑ 115 Summon Nightstalker U .20 .50
❑ 116 Suzume Mukashino C .10 .20
❑ 117 Takuan R .40 1.00
❑ 118 Tapestry of Air U .20 .50
❑ 119 Tessen C .10 .20
❑ 120 The Blood Feud R .40 1.00
❑ 121 The Bronze Gong of the Hantei R .40 1.00
❑ 122 The Celestial Pattern U .20 .50
❑ 123 The Darkest Day U .20 .50
❑ 124 The Face of Fear C .10 .20
❑ 125 The Perfect Gift R .40 1.00
❑ 126 The Tao of the Naga R .40 1.00
❑ 127 The Way of Air U .20 .50
❑ 128 The Way of Earth U .20 .50
❑ 129 The Way of Fire U .20 .50
❑ 130 The Way of Water U .20 .50
❑ 131 There is No Hope R .60 1.50
❑ 132 To Avenge Our Ancestors R .40 1.00
❑ 133 To Do What We Must U .20 .50
❑ 134 To the Last Man R 1.25 3.00
❑ 135 Togashi Kokujin R 1.25 3.00
❑ 136 Togashi Yama U .20 .50
❑ 137 Togashi Yokuni (Experienced) R 1.50 4.00
❑ 138 Tomb of Iuchiban R .40 1.00
❑ 139 Torturous Terrain C .10 .20
❑ 140 Toturi (Experienced) R 1.25 3.00
❑ 141 Toturi's Army Box .60 1.50
❑ 142 Trading Grounds C .10 .20
❑ 143 Training Grounds C .10 .20
❑ 144 Travelling Poet C .10 .20
❑ 145 Treacherous Terrain C .10 .20
❑ 146 Tsukuro R .75 2.00
❑ 147 Valley of the Shadow R .40 1.00
❑ 148 Watchtower C .10 .20
❑ 149 Wetlands C .10 .20
❑ 150 Yodin R .40 1.00
❑ 151 Yogo Ichiba U .20 .50
❑ 152 Yogo Junzo's Army Box 1.25 3.00

1996 Legend of the Five Rings Forbidden Knowledge

❑ 1 A Black Scroll is Opened U .20 .50
❑ 2 A Terrible Oath R 1.50 4.00
❑ 3 Akiyoshi C .10 .20
❑ 4 Akodo Godaigo R .60 1.50
❑ 5 An Untold Cost R .60 1.50
❑ 6 Ancestral Sword of Hantei R 2.00 5.00
❑ 7 Armor of Earth R 1.00 2.50
❑ 8 Artificer C .10 .20
❑ 9 Asako Oyo U .20 .50
❑ 10 Bandit Hideout C .10 .20
❑ 11 Battlements of Matsu Castle R .60 1.50
❑ 12 Bayushi Baku U .20 .50
❑ 13 Bayushi Shoju R 2.00 5.00
❑ 14 Beiden Pass U .20 .50
❑ 15 Black Market C .10 .20
❑ 16 Black Wind From The Soul R 1.50 4.00
❑ 17 Bog Hag C .10 .20
❑ 18 Brash Hero C .10 .20
❑ 19 Bribery U .20 .50
❑ 20 Bushi Dojo C .10 .20
❑ 21 Calling the Elements C .10 .20
❑ 22 Chasing the Wind R .40 1.00
❑ 23 Courage of the Seven Thunders U .20 .50
❑ 24 Crossroads C .10 .20
❑ 25 Crushing Attack U .20 .50
❑ 26 Dairya (Experienced) R .75 2.00
❑ 27 Dark Daughter of Fu Leng R .40 1.00
❑ 28 Dealing With Shadows U .20 .50
❑ 29 Delicate Calculations C .10 .20
❑ 30 Disharmony C .10 .20
❑ 31 Diversionary Tactics C .10 .20
❑ 32 Doji Kuwannan C .10 .20
❑ 33 Dragon Sword is Broken U .20 .50
❑ 34 Dripping Poison U .20 .50
❑ 35 Enlightenment C .10 .20
❑ 36 Family Loyalty R .40 1.00
❑ 37 Farmlands C .10 .20
❑ 38 Fearful Populace U .20 .50
❑ 39 Flatlands C .10 .20
❑ 40 Fu Leng's Steeds U .20 .50
❑ 41 Fusaki C .10 .20
❑ 42 Garotte U .20 .50
❑ 43 Goblin Berserkers C .10 .20
❑ 44 Gunsen of Water R .60 1.50
❑ 45 Hazardous Ground C .10 .20
❑ 46 Higher Ground C .10 .20
❑ 47 Ide Daikoku R .40 1.00
❑ 48 Ikoma Tsanuri U .20 .50
❑ 49 Ikoma Ujiaki (Experienced) R .40 1.00
❑ 50 Imperial Funeral U .20 .50
❑ 51 Isawa Natsune C .10 .20
❑ 52 Isawa Uona (Experienced) R .40 1.00
❑ 53 Jade Strike C .10 .20
❑ 54 Kaiu Kenru C .10 .20
❑ 55 Kaiu Suman U .20 .50
❑ 56 Kakita Foruku U .20 .50
❑ 57 Kakita Toshimoko (Experienced) R 1.50 4.00
❑ 58 Katana of Fire R .40 1.00
❑ 59 Kemmei C .10 .20
❑ 60 Kolat Saboteur R .40 1.00
❑ 61 Kolat Whisperer R .60 1.50
❑ 62 Kotaro R .40 1.00
❑ 63 Kuni Wastelands R 1.50 4.00
❑ 64 Kuni Yori (Experienced) R .40 1.00
❑ 65 Lesser Oni C .10 .20
❑ 66 Mantis Budoka U .20 .50
❑ 67 Mantis Samurai U .20 .50
❑ 68 Matsu Toshiro C .10 .20
❑ 69 Mempo of the Void R .75 2.00
❑ 70 Merchant Caravan C .10 .20
❑ 71 Mirumoto Daini (Experienced) R 1.25 3.00
❑ 72 Mountain Pass C .10 .20
❑ 73 Moving the Shadow C .10 .20
❑ 74 Nemesis U .20 .50
❑ 75 Ningyo C .10 .20
❑ 76 Ninja Kidnapper U .20 .50
❑ 77 No-Dachi C .10 .20
❑ 78 Not this Day! U .20 .50
❑ 79 Ogre Warriors R .40 1.00
❑ 80 Oni no Akeru U .20 .50
❑ 81 Oni no Jimen U .20 .50
❑ 82 Oni no Kaze U .20 .50
❑ 83 Oni no Mizu U .20 .50
❑ 84 Oni no Seiryoku U .20 .50
❑ 85 Oni no Taki-Bi U .20 .50
❑ 86 Passing on the Soul U .20 .50
❑ 87 Pearl of Wisdom R .40 1.00
❑ 88 Personal Standard C .10 .20
❑ 89 Pikemen C .10 .20
❑ 90 Plains of Otosan Uchi R 1.25 3.00
❑ 91 Purity of the Seven Thunders R .75 2.00
❑ 92 Qarash U .20 .50
❑ 93 Ramash C .10 .20
❑ 94 Reserve Movement U .20 .50
❑ 95 Return of the Fallen Lord R .75 2.00
❑ 96 Reversal of Fortunes U .20 .50
❑ 97 Ride Until Dawn R .40 1.00
❑ 98 Scorn C .10 .20
❑ 99 Seikua C .10 .20
❑ 100 Seize the Day R .40 1.00
❑ 101 Shahadet (Experienced Naga Warlord) R .60 1.50
❑ 102 Sharing the Strength of Many C .10 .20
❑ 103 Shield Wall U .20 .50
❑ 104 Shinjo Mosaku U .20 .50
❑ 105 Shinjo Sadato C .10 .20
❑ 106 Spoils of War R .40 1.00
❑ 107 Strength of the Earth U .20 .50
❑ 108 Strike at the Roots C .10 .20
❑ 109 Strike with No-Thought U .20 .50
❑ 110 Swamplands C .10 .20
❑ 111 The Arrow Knows the Way R 2.50 6.00
❑ 112 The Coward's Way U .20 .50
❑ 113 The Doji Plains U .20 .50
❑ 114 The Elements' Fury U .20 .50
❑ 115 The Emerald Armor R .75 2.00
❑ 116 The Eye of Shorihotsu U .20 .50
❑ 117 The Final Breath C .10 .20
❑ 118 The Fires That Cleanse U .20 .50
❑ 119 The First Shout C .10 .20
❑ 120 The Gates of Hida Castle R 1.25 3.00
❑ 121 The Imperial Standard R 1.50 4.00
❑ 122 The Iron Citadel R 1.50 4.00
❑ 123 The Isawa Woodlands U .20 .50
❑ 124 The Kaiu Walls U .20 .50
❑ 125 The Kakita Palisades R .40 1.00
❑ 126 The Path to Inner Peace C .10 .20
❑ 127 The People's Expense C .10 .20
❑ 128 The Price of War U .20 .50
❑ 129 The Ruined Keep of Fu Leng R .60 1.50
❑ 130 The Second Shout C .10 .20
❑ 131 The Shinjo Parade Grounds R .40 1.00
❑ 132 The Third Shout U .20 .50
❑ 133 The Togashi Bastion R .40 1.00
❑ 134 The Towers of Isawa Castle R .40 1.00
❑ 135 The Wasting Disease R 2.00 5.00
❑ 136 Those Who Stand Alone C .10 .20
❑ 137 Tides of Battle R .40 1.00
❑ 138 Togashi Mikoto C .10 .20
❑ 139 Togashi Rinjin U .20 .50
❑ 140 Tsuruchi C .10 .20
❑ 141 Unfettered Attack U .20 .50
❑ 142 Virtues of Command U .20 .50
❑ 143 Walking Horror of Fu Leng R 1.00 2.50
❑ 144 Wheel of Fate U .20 .50
❑ 145 Whispering Winds C .10 .20
❑ 146 Wind-Borne Slumbers U .20 .50

☐ 147 Yari of Air R .40 1.00
☐ 148 Yogo Asami C .10 .20
☐ 149 Yogo Junzo (Experienced) R 1.50 4.00
☐ 150 Your Life Is Mine R .75 2.00

1996 Legend of the Five Rings Shadowlands

☐ 1 A Gift of Honor R .60 1.50
☐ 2 A Stout Heart U2 .20 .50
☐ 3 Accessible Terrain C .10 .20
☐ 4 Ancient Spear of the Naga F 2.00 5.00
☐ 5 Another Time C .10 .20
☐ 6 Arrows from the Woods C .10 .20
☐ 7 Ashigaru C .10 .20
☐ 8 Ashlim U2 .20 .50
☐ 9 Balash C .10 .20
☐ 10 Bayushi Aramoro U2 .20 .50
☐ 11 Bayushi Goshiu U2 .20 .50
☐ 12 Bayushi Hisa C .10 .20
☐ 13 Bayushi Kyoto R .60 1.50
☐ 14 Bayushi Supai R .40 1.00
☐ 15 Bayushi Tomaru C/F .10 .20
☐ 16 Blood of Midnight C .10 .20
☐ 17 Call to Arms U2 .20 .50
☐ 18 Change of Loyalty R .40 1.00
☐ 19 Confusion at Court C .10 .20
☐ 20 Contemplate the Void C .10 .20
☐ 21 Corrupted Ground C .10 .20
☐ 22 Corrupted Iron Mine C .10 .20
☐ 23 Court Jester U2 .20 .50
☐ 24 Crystal Arrow C .10 .20
☐ 25 Dark Divination R 2.00 5.00
☐ 26 Dark Oracle of Air R .60 1.50
☐ 27 Dark Oracle of Earth R .60 1.50
☐ 28 Dark Oracle of Fire R .60 1.50
☐ 29 Dark Oracle of Water R 2.00 5.00
☐ 30 Darkness Feeds... R .60 1.50
☐ 31 Dashmar R .60 1.50
☐ 32 Defend Your Honor C/U1 .40 1.00
☐ 33 Desperate Measures R 2.50 6.00
☐ 34 Doji Hoturi (Experienced) R 1.50 4.00
☐ 35 Doji House Guard U2 .20 .50
☐ 36 Doom of the Crab U2 .20 .50
☐ 37 Doom of the Crane U2 .20 .50
☐ 38 Doom of the Dragon U2 .20 .50
☐ 39 Doom of the Lion U2 .20 .50
☐ 40 Doom of the Naga U2 .20 .50
☐ 41 Doom of the Phoenix U2 .20 .50
☐ 42 Doom of the Scorpion U2 .20 .50
☐ 43 Doom of the Unicorn U2 .20 .50
☐ 44 Earthworks C .10 .20
☐ 45 Enough Talk! U2 .20 .50
☐ 46 Evil Ward U2 .20 .50
☐ 47 False Alliance R .60 1.50
☐ 48 Final Charge R .40 1.00
☐ 49 Force of Will C .10 .20
☐ 50 Forced March U2 .20 .50
☐ 51 Gambling House C .10 .20
☐ 52 Garegoso no Bakemono R .60 1.50
☐ 53 Geisha House C .10 .20
☐ 54 Goblin Shaman C .10 .20
☐ 55 Gust of Wind U2 .20 .50
☐ 56 Han-Kyu U2 .20 .50
☐ 57 He's Mine! C .10 .20
☐ 58 Hida House Guard U2 .20 .50
☐ 59 Hida O-Ushi R .75 2.00
☐ 60 Himura Kage U2 .20 .50
☐ 61 His Most Favored R 2.00 5.00
☐ 62 Ikiryo C .10 .20
☐ 63 Ikoma Kaoku U2 .20 .50
☐ 64 Impassable Terrain C .10 .20
☐ 65 Imperial Levying R .75 2.00
☐ 66 Isawa Tadaka (Experienced) R .40 1.00
☐ 67 Isha C .10 .20
☐ 68 Jade Arrow U2 .20 .50
☐ 69 Jade Goblet U2 .20 .50
☐ 70 Kakita Torikago C .10 .20
☐ 71 Kakita Yogoso U2 .20 .50
☐ 72 Kitsu Motso R 1.00 2.50
☐ 73 Kolat Oyabun U2 .20 .50
☐ 74 Kumo C .10 .20
☐ 75 Levy Troops U1 .60 1.50
☐ 76 Mamoru U2 .20 .50
☐ 77 Mantis Bushi R .60 1.50
☐ 78 Mara U2 .20 .50
☐ 79 Matsu Chokoku C .10 .20
☐ 80 Matsu House Guard U2 .20 .50
☐ 81 Minor Oni Servant R .75 2.00
☐ 82 Minumoto Hitomi (Experienced) U2 .20 .50
☐ 83 Minumoto House Guard U2 .20 .50
☐ 84 Mirumoto Taki C .10 .20
☐ 85 Mountain Goblin C .10 .20
☐ 86 Nageteppo U2 .20 .50
☐ 87 New Year's Celebrations R .40 1.00
☐ 88 Obsidian Mirror R .60 1.50
☐ 89 Oni no Ogon R 1.00 2.50
☐ 90 Oni no Ogon U2 .20 .50
☐ 91 Oni no Sanru U2 .20 .50
☐ 92 Otaku Kamoko (Experienced) U2 .20 .50
☐ 93 Otaku Kojiro R .75 2.00
☐ 94 Pearl Bed C .10 .20
☐ 95 Pennaggolan C .10 .20
☐ 96 Plague Zombies C .10 .20
☐ 97 Plea of the Peasants U2 .20 .50
☐ 98 Porcelain Mask of Fu Leng R .60 1.50
☐ 99 Qamar R .60 1.50
☐ 100 Rampant Plague R .60 1.50
☐ 101 Ratling Conscripts C .10 .20
☐ 102 Ratling Scavenger C .10 .20
☐ 103 Ratling Thief U2 .20 .50
☐ 104 Setsuban Festival R .60 1.50
☐ 105 Shabura U2 .20 .50
☐ 106 Shadowlands Madmen R .40 1.00
☐ 107 Shadowlands Sickness U2 .20 .50
☐ 108 Shadowmadness U2 .20 .50
☐ 109 Shagara C .10 .20
☐ 110 Shapeshifting R 1.00 2.50
☐ 111 Shiba House Guard U2 .20 .50
☐ 112 Shiba Tetsu C .10 .20
☐ 113 Shinjo House Guard U2 .20 .50
☐ 114 Shinjo Tsuburo C .10 .20
☐ 115 Shosuro Hametsu F .60 1.50
☐ 116 Shosuro Taberu U/F .40 1.00
☐ 117 Shosuro Tage R .75 2.00
☐ 118 Skeletal Archers C .10 .20
☐ 119 Soshi Bantaro C/F .10 .20
☐ 120 Stale Wind U2 .20 .50
☐ 121 Strike at the Tail R .60 1.50
☐ 122 Suspended Terrain C .10 .20
☐ 123 Sympathetic Energies C .10 .20
☐ 124 Temple of Bishamon C .10 .20
☐ 125 Terrible Standard of Fu Leng R .40 1.00
☐ 126 Test of Might C .10 .20
☐ 127 Tetsubo C .10 .20
☐ 128 The Broken Sword of the Scorpion F 1.50 4.00
☐ 129 The Code of Bushido U2 .20 .50
☐ 130 The Falling Darkness R .40 1.00
☐ 131 The Festering Pit of Fu Leng R 1.50 4.00
☐ 132 The Fire From Within U2 .20 .50
☐ 133 The Hidden Temples of the Naga 1.00 2.50
☐ 134 The Hooded Ronin R .60 1.50
☐ 135 The Laughing Monk C .10 .20
☐ 136 The Nameless One U2 .20 .50
☐ 137 The Obsidian Hand R 1.50 4.00
☐ 138 The Rising Sun R .40 1.00
☐ 139 The Ruined Fortress of the Scorpion .20 .50
☐ 140 The Turtle's Shell U2 .20 .50
☐ 141 Threat of War R .40 1.00
☐ 142 Thunder Dragon R 1.00 2.50
☐ 143 Togashi Gaijutsu R .75 2.00
☐ 144 Tomb of Jade C .10 .20
☐ 145 Touch of Despair R .75 2.00
☐ 146 Touch of Fu Leng R .75 2.00
☐ 147 Twist of Fate R .40 1.00
☐ 148 Utter Defeat R 3.00 8.00
☐ 149 Wakizashi C .10 .20
☐ 150 Warhorses C .10 .20
☐ 151 When Darkness Draws Near R .40 1.00
☐ 152 Winning Kachiko's Favor R .75 2.00
☐ 153 Wounded in Battle C .10 .20
☐ 154 Yasuki Nokatsu C .10 .20
☐ 155 Yuki no Onna C/F .10 .20

1997 Legend of the Five Rings Crimson and Jade

☐ 1 A Glimpse of the Soul's Shadow C .10 .20
☐ 2 A Samurai's Fury R 2.00 5.00
☐ 3 A Spirit of Water C .10 .20
☐ 4 Agasha Heizo C .10 .20
☐ 5 Along the Coast at Midnight R .40 1.00
☐ 6 An Oni's Fury U .20 .50
☐ 7 Ancestral Guidance R .40 1.00
☐ 8 Ancestral Weapons of the Mantis F 1.00 2.50
☐ 9 Antidote U .20 .50
☐ 10 Architects of the Wall R .50 1.25
☐ 11 Are You With Me? U .20 .50
☐ 12 Armor of the Shadow Warrior R .60 1.50
☐ 13 Armory C1 .10 .20
☐ 14 Asahina Tomo (Experienced) R .60 1.50
☐ 15 Ashamana C .10 .20
☐ 16 Bad Kharma R .60 1.50
☐ 17 Bandit Gang C .10 .20
☐ 18 Barbarian Horde R .75 2.00
☐ 19 Bayushi Tasu U .20 .50
☐ 20 Borderland U .20 .50
☐ 21 Breaking Blow U .20 .50
☐ 22 Bridged Pass C1 .10 .20
☐ 23 Brotherhood of Shinsei .40 1.00
☐ 24 Brothers of Thunder U .20 .50
☐ 25 Carrier Pigeon C .10 .20
☐ 26 Catching the Wind's Favor C .10 .20
☐ 27 Chime of Harmony C .10 .20
☐ 28 Chinoko U .20 .50
☐ 29 Clan Banner R .60 1.50
☐ 30 Clan Heartland R 1.25 3.00
☐ 31 Corrupted Copper Mine C .10 .20
☐ 32 Counterfeit U .20 .50
☐ 33 Courier C .10 .20
☐ 34 Cowardice U .20 .50
☐ 35 Dance of the Elements U .20 .50
☐ 36 Deploy Reserves U .20 .50
☐ 37 Disrupt the Aura C .10 .20
☐ 38 Divine the Future U .20 .50
☐ 39 Doji Reju C .10 .20
☐ 40 Double Chi C .10 .20
☐ 41 Dragon's Teeth C .10 .20
☐ 42 Engineering Crew C1 .10 .20
☐ 43 Extortion R 2.00 5.00
☐ 44 Fiery Wrath R .50 1.25
☐ 45 Fight for My Favor U .20 .50
☐ 46 Fist of the Earth C .10 .20
☐ 47 Forced Alliance R .50 1.25
☐ 48 Forest of Thorns U .20 .50
☐ 49 Fresh Horse U .20 .50
☐ 50 Genzo R .60 1.50
☐ 51 Gift of the Wind C .10 .20
☐ 52 Ginawa (Experienced) R 1.25 3.00
☐ 53 Hida Yakamo (Experienced) R 1.25 3.00
☐ 54 Hiruma Yoshi C .10 .20
☐ 55 Historian C1 .10 .20
☐ 56 Hitoshi C1 .10 .20
☐ 57 Hyobe U .20 .50
☐ 58 Ikoma Ryozo U .20 .50
☐ 59 Incense of Concentration U .20 .50
☐ 60 Inner Fire U .20 .50
☐ 61 Isawa Norikazu R .60 1.50
☐ 62 Isawa Tomo (Experienced) U .20 .50
☐ 63 Island Wharf C .10 .20
☐ 64 Iuchi Daiyu (Experienced) R .60 1.50
☐ 65 Kado C .10 .20
☐ 66 Kakita Ichiro U .20 .50
☐ 67 Kanbe C1 .10 .20
☐ 68 Kenku Teacher C .10 .20
☐ 69 Kenku U .20 .50
☐ 70 Kenshin's Helm U .20 .50
☐ 71 Kitsu Motso (Experienced) R .60 1.50
☐ 72 Know Your Enemy R .50 1.25
☐ 73 Koichi C .10 .20
☐ 74 Kolat Bodyguard U .20 .50
☐ 75 Kolat's Favor U .20 .50
☐ 76 Light of the Sun Goddess U .20 .50
☐ 77 Lost Valley C1 .10 .20
☐ 78 Mantis Clan Shugenja U .20 .50
☐ 79 Masasue C .10 .20
☐ 80 Master of the Rolling River U .20 .50
☐ 81 Matsu Goemon C .10 .20
☐ 82 Mine Riots U .20 .50
☐ 83 Moto Sada C1 .10 .20
☐ 84 Moto Tsume (Experienced) R 2.00 5.00
☐ 85 Mounts C .10 .20
☐ 86 Mukami C .10 .20
☐ 87 Naming the True Evil R .60 1.50
☐ 88 Narrow Ground C .10 .20
☐ 89 New Taxes U .20 .50
☐ 90 Night of a Thousand Fires U .20 .50
☐ 91 Nobuo U .20 .50
☐ 92 Norio C .10 .20
☐ 93 Ogre Outlaw U .20 .50
☐ 94 One Koku C .10 .20
☐ 95 Oni no Chi U .20 .50
☐ 96 Oni no Genso C1 .10 .20
☐ 97 Oni Warding R .50 1.25
☐ 98 Orochi R .75 2.00
☐ 99 Osano-Wo's Breath U .20 .50
☐ 100 Pearl-Encrusted Staff R .60 1.50
☐ 101 Peasant Levies C .10 .20
☐ 102 Prayer Shrines C .10 .20
☐ 103 Robes of Shinsei U .20 .50
☐ 104 Ryosei C .10 .20
☐ 105 Secluded Ravine C1 .10 .20
☐ 106 Severed from the Emperor R 1.00 2.50
☐ 107 Shabura (Experienced) R .60 1.50
☐ 108 Shadow of the Dark God U .20 .50
☐ 109 Shalasha U .20 .50
☐ 110 Shiba Shingo C .10 .20
☐ 111 Shinjo Rojin C .10 .20
☐ 112 Shinjo Tashima U .20 .50
☐ 113 Shinsei's Shrine R .60 1.50
☐ 114 Shiryo no Agasha R .40 1.00
☐ 115 Shiryo no Doji R .60 1.50
☐ 116 Shiryo no Hida R .60 1.50
☐ 117 Shiryo no Matsu R .60 1.50
☐ 118 Shiryo no Otaku R .60 1.50
☐ 119 Shiryo no Shiba R .60 1.50
☐ 120 Shiryo no Shosuro R .60 1.50
☐ 121 Shosuro Sadato C .10 .20
☐ 122 Soshi Bantaro (Experienced) R .75 2.00
☐ 123 Stand Against the Waves C .10 .20
☐ 124 Stand Firm C .10 .20
☐ 125 Strength of My Ancestors C .10 .20
☐ 126 Strike of Flowing Water C .10 .20
☐ 127 Suana U .20 .50
☐ 128 Summons from Beyond U .20 .50
☐ 129 Sunken City R .40 1.00
☐ 130 Superior Strategist R 1.50 4.00
☐ 131 Takao U .20 .50
☐ 132 Takuni C1 .10 .20
☐ 133 Taro C .10 .20
☐ 134 Temple of Osano-Wo F .60 1.50
☐ 135 Tetsuya R .75 2.00
☐ 136 The Battle at Isawa Palace U .20 .50
☐ 137 The Death of Tsuko R .50 1.25
☐ 138 The Fault is Mine C .10 .20
☐ 139 The Great Bear R .60 1.50
☐ 140 The Hooded Ronin (Experienced) R .75 2.00
☐ 141 The Purity of Shinsei R .40 1.00
☐ 142 The Touch of Shinsei R .60 1.50
☐ 143 The Wrath of Osano-Wo C .10 .20
☐ 144 The Yasuki Estates C1 .10 .20
☐ 145 Togashi Jodome U .20 .50
☐ 146 Togashi Mitsu (Experienced) R .60 1.50
☐ 147 Tokiuji C .10 .20
☐ 148 Toturi's Fan R .75 2.00
☐ 149 Tradeposts of the Mantis C1 .10 .20
☐ 150 Tsunami U .20 .50
☐ 151 Tsuo C .10 .20
☐ 152 Tunnel System C1 .10 .20
☐ 153 Visage of the Void U .20 .50
☐ 154 Void Strike U .20 .50
☐ 155 Winter Warfare R 1.50 4.00
☐ 156 Wisdom the Wind Brings U .20 .50
☐ 157 Yasuki Kojiro U .20 .50
☐ 158 Yoritomo R 1.25 3.00
☐ 159 Yoritomo's Alliance .60 1.50
☐ 160 You Walk With Evil R 1.50 4.00
☐ 161 Yugoro R .75 2.00

1997 Legend of the Five Rings Scorpion Clan Coup Scroll 1

☐ 1 A Samurai Never Stands Alone C .10 .20
☐ 2 Agasha's Illusion U .20 .50
☐ 3 Ancestral Sword of the Scorpion U .20 .50
☐ 4 Armor of Osano-Wo C .10 .20
☐ 5 Arrival of the Unicorns C .10 .20
☐ 6 Bayushi Dozan C .10 .20
☐ 7 Bayushi Kachiko (Inexperienced) U .20 .50
☐ 8 Bayushi Shoju (Inexperienced) F 2.00 5.00
☐ 9 Bayushi Yokuan U .20 .50
☐ 10 Behind Night's Shadow U .20 .50
☐ 11 Cavalry Raiders C .10 .20
☐ 12 Daikua C .10 .20
☐ 13 Divinitory Pool C .10 .20
☐ 14 East Wall of Otosan Uchi U .20 .50
☐ 15 Flood C .10 .20
☐ 16 Freezing the Lifeblood C .10 .20
☐ 17 Garrison C .10 .20
☐ 18 Hantei the 38th U .20 .50
☐ 19 Hatsuko C .10 .20
☐ 20 Hiruma's Last Breath U .20 .50
☐ 21 Imperial Palace Guard U .20 .50
☐ 22 Isawa Tomo's Portal U .20 .50
☐ 23 Ishikawa U .20 .50
☐ 24 Iuchi Katta C .10 .20
☐ 25 Jurojin's Touch C .10 .20
☐ 26 Lieutenant Morito U .20 .50
☐ 27 Lions Attack the Crane U .20 .50
☐ 28 Musubi U .20 .50
☐ 29 Plains Above Evil C .10 .20
☐ 30 Political Distraction C .10 .20
☐ 31 Political Mistake U .20 .50
☐ 32 Robbing the Dead C .10 .20
☐ 33 Sanado U .20 .50
☐ 34 Shinjo Yokatsu U .20 .50
☐ 35 Shioda C .10 .20
☐ 36 Shosuro Ikawa C .10 .20
☐ 37 Soshi Taoshi U .20 .50
☐ 38 Soshi Ujemi U .20 .50
☐ 39 South Wall of Otosan Uchi U .20 .50
☐ 40 Storehouses C .10 .20
☐ 41 Streets of Otosan Uchi F .60 1.50
☐ 42 The 38th Hantei Falls U .20 .50
☐ 43 The Endless Well U .20 .50
☐ 44 The Exalted Ugu C .10 .20
☐ 45 The First Scroll is Opened U .20 .50
☐ 46 The Secret Entrance C .10 .20
☐ 47 The Shadow Stronghold of the Bayushi F .50 1.25
☐ 48 The Soul Goes Forth C .10 .20
☐ 49 The Unclean Cut C .10 .20
☐ 50 Through the Waterways U .20 .50
☐ 51 Toturi is Drugged U .20 .50
☐ 52 War Wagon C .10 .20
☐ 53 Yogo Shidachi C .10 .20

1997 Legend of the Five Rings Time of the Void

☐ 1 A Good Day To Die U1 .20 .50
☐ 2 A Moment of Clarity U1 .20 .50
☐ 3 A Moment of Truth R .60 1.50
☐ 4 A Soul of Thunder U .20 .50
☐ 5 A Test of Courage C1 .10 .20
☐ 6 Agasha Gennai C .10 .20
☐ 7 Agasha Tunnels C1 .10 .20
☐ 8 Akiyoshi (Experienced) U1 .20 .50
☐ 9 Akodo Tactical School R1 .75 2.00
☐ 10 al-Hazaad U1 .20 .50
☐ 11 al-Rashid C1 .10 .20
☐ 12 An Exhibition C1 .10 .20
☐ 13 Ancestral Standard of the Scorpion R1 .75 2.00
☐ 14 Ancient Armor of the Qamar R1 .75 2.00
☐ 15 As Far as the Eye Can See R1 .60 1.50
☐ 16 Asako Ishio U .20 .50
☐ 17 Asako Togama C1 .10 .20
☐ 18 Ashan C1 .10 .20
☐ 19 Augury R1 1.50 4.00
☐ 20 Battle Standard of Shinsei R1 .60 1.50
☐ 21 Battle Standard of the Mantis R1 .60 1.50
☐ 22 Battle Standard of the Naga R1 .60 1.50
☐ 23 Bayushi Goshiu (Experienced) R 1.50 4.00
☐ 24 Bayushi Hisa (Experienced) U .20 .50
☐ 25 Bayushi Kachiko (Experienced 2) R1 5.00 10.00
☐ 26 Bayushi Marumo C .10 .20
☐ 27 Bend Like A Reed C1 .10 .20
☐ 28 Berserkers C1 .10 .20
☐ 29 Bonds of Darkness R1 .50 1.25
☐ 30 Burning Your Essence R1 1.25 3.00
☐ 31 Chi Strike R .50 1.25
☐ 32 Concealed Weapon R1 .60 1.50
☐ 33 Contested Ground C1 .10 .20
☐ 34 Coordinated Fire C1 .10 .20
☐ 35 Corrupt Geisha House C .10 .20
☐ 36 Corrupt Gold Mines C .10 .20
☐ 37 Corrupt Stables C .10 .20
☐ 38 Corrupted Region C1 .10 .20
☐ 39 Counting the Lost U1 .20 .50
☐ 40 Crystal Gate C .10 .20
☐ 41 Curse of the Jackal C .10 .20
☐ 42 Dark Lord's Favor C1 .10 .20
☐ 43 Dashmar (Experienced) U1 .20 .50
☐ 44 Depth of the Void U1 .20 .50
☐ 45 Destiny Has No Secrets C1 .10 .20
☐ 46 Disenlightenment R .40 1.00
☐ 47 Distractions of the Flesh C1 .10 .20
☐ 48 Doji Chomei C .10 .20
☐ 49 Doji Hoturi (Experienced 2) R1 6.00 12.00
☐ 50 Doji Kuwanan (Experienced) U .20 .50
☐ 51 Doji Shizue C1 .10 .20
☐ 52 Doji Yosai (Experienced) R .40 1.00
☐ 53 Elite Heavy Infantry U .20 .50
☐ 54 Elite Light Infantry C1 .10 .20
☐ 55 Elite Medium Infantry C1 .10 .20
☐ 56 Enlightened Ruler R1 .60 1.50
☐ 57 Enlistment U1 .20 .50
☐ 58 Eshru C .10 .20
☐ 59 Essence of Air U1 .20 .50
☐ 60 Essence of Earth U1 .20 .50
☐ 61 Factionism R1 .60 1.50
☐ 62 Familiar Surroundings C1 .10 .20
☐ 63 Fatal Mistake R1 .60 1.50
☐ 64 Festival of Long Sticks R1 .40 1.00
☐ 65 Final Stand R .40 1.00
☐ 66 Flight of Doves U1 .20 .50
☐ 67 Flying Carpet R1 .60 1.50
☐ 68 Fog C1 .10 .20
☐ 69 For the Empire U1 .20 .50
☐ 70 Forgiveness C .10 .20
☐ 71 Gaijin Merchant U .20 .50
☐ 72 Gekkai U1 .20 .50
☐ 73 Goblin Madcaps C1 .10 .20
☐ 74 Goblin Sneaks C1 .10 .20
☐ 75 Goblin War Standard C .10 .20
☐ 76 Goblin Wizard C1 .10 .20
☐ 77 Harima U1 .20 .50
☐ 78 Heavy Mounted Infantry U .20 .50
☐ 79 Hida Amoro (Experienced) U1 .20 .50
☐ 80 Hida O-Ushi (Experienced) R 1.25 3.00
☐ 81 Hida Tadashiro C .10 .20
☐ 82 Hida War College R1 .60 1.50
☐ 83 Hida Yakamo (Experienced 2) F .60 1.50
☐ 84 Hizuka C .10 .20
☐ 85 Horde of Fu Leng C1 .10 .20
☐ 86 Horsebowmen C1 .10 .20
☐ 87 I Believed in You... C1 .10 .20
☐ 88 Ikoma Tsanuri (Experienced) R1 .50 1.25
☐ 89 In Time of War U .20 .50
☐ 90 Isawa Suma C .10 .20
☐ 91 Isawa Tadaka (Experienced 2) F 1.00 2.50
☐ 92 Isawa Uona (Experienced 2) U1 .20 .50
☐ 93 Isha (Experienced) R .40 1.00
☐ 94 Iuchi Karasu (Experienced) U .20 .50
☐ 95 Izaku Library C .10 .20
☐ 96 Jade Dragon R 1.25 3.00
☐ 97 Jiujitsu Duel U1 .20 .50
☐ 98 Junzo's Battle Standard R1 .60 1.50
☐ 99 Kage (Experienced 2 Akodo Kage) R1 .60 1.50
☐ 100 Kakita Kenjutsu School R1 .75 2.00
☐ 101 Kakita Yoshi (Experienced) U1 .20 .50
☐ 102 Kappuksu (Experienced Goblin Warmonger) U .20 .50
☐ 103 Kaze-Do C .10 .20
☐ 104 Kitsu Okura C1 .10 .20
☐ 105 Kitsu Toju (Experienced) U1 .20 .50
☐ 106 Know the School C1 .10 .20
☐ 107 Kolat Spy C1 .10 .20
☐ 108 Komaro C1 .10 .20
☐ 109 Kuni Sensin C1 .10 .20
☐ 110 Kyujutsu C1 .10 .20
☐ 111 Lady Kitsune C1 .10 .20
☐ 112 Legions of Fu Leng C .10 .20
☐ 113 Lessons from the Past C1 .10 .20
☐ 114 Light Mounted Infantry C1 .10 .20
☐ 115 Matsu Agetoki (Experienced) R .40 1.00
☐ 116 Matsu Gohei (Experienced) U .20 .50
☐ 117 Matsu Hiroru (Experienced) R1 .75 2.00
☐ 118 Matsu Turi C .10 .20
☐ 119 Mighty Protection R1 .75 2.00
☐ 120 Mikio (Experienced) U1 .20 .50
☐ 121 Mirumoto Hitomi (Experienced 2) R1 1.00 2.50
☐ 122 Mirumoto Yukihira U .20 .50
☐ 123 Moshi Wakiza (Experienced) U1 .20 .50
☐ 124 Mounted Spearmen C1 .10 .20
☐ 125 Mujina Chieftain C1 .10 .20
☐ 126 Mujina Miners U1 .20 .50
☐ 127 Mystical Terrain C .10 .20
☐ 128 Necromancer (Experienced) R 1.00 2.50
☐ 129 Ninja Stalkers U .20 .50
☐ 130 Nogolen's Bow U .20 .50
☐ 131 Obsidian Blade C .10 .20
☐ 132 Offer of Fealty C1 .10 .20
☐ 133 One With the Elements C1 .10 .20
☐ 134 Oni no Ianwa R1 .60 1.50
☐ 135 Oni no Pekkle C1 .10 .20
☐ 136 Oni no Ugulu C1 .10 .20
☐ 137 Oracle of the Void R1 .60 1.50
☐ 138 Otaku Kamoko (Experienced 2) R1 1.50 4.00
☐ 139 Plans Within Plans U1 .20 .50

TCG/CCG

❑ 140 Qamar (Experienced) R1 .40 1.00
❑ 141 Radakast (Experienced) U .20 .50
❑ 142 Rebuilding the Kaiu Walls U .20 .50
❑ 143 Regions of Rokugan U1 .20 .50
❑ 144 Rest, My Brother U .20 .50
❑ 145 River Delta U1 .20 .50
❑ 146 Ruins of the Isawa Library R1 .60 1.50
❑ 147 Ryokan's Sword C .10 .20
❑ 148 Sailors C1 .10 .20
❑ 149 Salute of the Samurai R1 .60 1.50
❑ 150 Sanctified Ground C1 .10 .20
❑ 151 Seikua (Experienced) R .40 1.00
❑ 152 Shahadet's Legion R .75 2.00
❑ 153 Shiba Tsukune (Experienced) R1 .60 1.50
❑ 154 Shinjo Hanari (Experienced) R .60 1.50
❑ 155 Shinjo Riding Stables R1 1.50 4.00
❑ 156 Shinjo Sanetama C .10 .20
❑ 157 Shinjo Shirasu C1 .10 .20
❑ 158 Shinjo Yasamura (Experienced) U1 .20 .50
❑ 159 Shinobi U1 .20 .50
❑ 160 Shiryo no Asahina R 1.00 2.50
❑ 161 Shiryo no Asako R .40 1.00
❑ 162 Shiryo no Ide R .40 1.00
❑ 163 Shiryo no Ikoma R .75 2.00
❑ 164 Shiryo no Kaiu R .60 1.50
❑ 165 Shiryo no Mirumoto R .60 1.50
❑ 166 Shiryo no Yogo R .75 2.00
❑ 167 Shiryo no Yoritomo R .40 1.00
❑ 168 Shosuro Hametsu (Experienced) U1 .20 .50
❑ 169 Stance of the Mountain C1 .10 .20
❑ 170 Strength of Osano-Wo C .10 .20
❑ 171 Strength of the Dark One U1 .20 .50
❑ 172 Strike Without Striking U1 .20 .50
❑ 173 Surrender U1 .20 .50
❑ 174 Swamp Goblins C1 .10 .20
❑ 175 Sysh C1 .10 .20
❑ 176 Taquar C1 .10 .20
❑ 177 Teeth of the Serpent U .20 .50
❑ 178 The 12th Black Scroll R1 5.00 10.00
❑ 179 The Ancestral Home of the Lion U1 .20 .50
❑ 180 The Brotherhood of Shinsei U1 .20 .50
❑ 181 The Darkest Magics R1 .75 2.00
❑ 182 The Esteemed House of the Crane U1 .20 .50
❑ 183 The Great Walls of Kaiu Box 1.50 4.00
❑ 184 The Heavy Shadow of Fear U1 .20 .50
❑ 185 The Hero's Triumph U .20 .50
❑ 186 The Hidden Heart of Iuchiban R1 1.50 4.00
❑ 187 The Hidden Temples of the Naga U1 .20 .50
❑ 188 The Light of Amaterasu C .10 .20
❑ 189 The Longest Night R1 1.25 3.00
❑ 190 The Mountain Keep of the Dragon U1 .40 1.00
❑ 191 The Path of Wisdom R 2.50 6.00
❑ 192 The Phoenix is Reborn U1 .20 .50
❑ 193 The Plains of Amaterasu U1 .20 .50
❑ 194 The Provincial Estate of the Unicorn U1 .20 .50
❑ 195 The Ruined Fortress of the Scorpion U1 .20 .50
❑ 196 The Ruins of Isawa Castle Box .60 1.50
❑ 197 The Sacred Temples of the Phoenix U1 .20 .50
❑ 198 The Scorpion's Sting R1 .75 2.00
❑ 199 The Sight of Death U .20 .50
❑ 200 The Time is Now U1 .20 .50
❑ 201 The Touch of Amaterasu U .20 .50
❑ 202 The Twelve Ronin R .75 2.00
❑ 203 The War Fortress of the Crab U1 .20 .50
❑ 204 The Yoritomo Alliance U1 .20 .50
❑ 205 To Save an Empire R1 .60 1.50
❑ 206 Today We Die R1 1.25 3.00
❑ 207 Togashi Kama C1 .10 .20
❑ 208 Togashi Testing Grounds R1 .40 1.00
❑ 209 Togashi Yokuni (Experienced 2) R 1.50 4.00
❑ 210 Togashi Yoshi (Experienced) U1 .20 .50
❑ 211 Toku (Experienced) U .20 .50
❑ 212 Toturi (Experienced 2) R1 2.00 5.00
❑ 213 Toturi's Army U1 .20 .50
❑ 214 Toturi's Battle Standard R1 .60 1.50
❑ 215 Toturi's Last Stand R1 .50 1.25
❑ 216 Toturi's Tactics R1 3.00 8.00
❑ 217 Troops from the Woods C1 .10 .20
❑ 218 Tsuyu C .10 .20
❑ 219 Unattuned U .20 .50
❑ 220 Untrustworthy U1 .20 .50
❑ 221 Warrior Monks U .20 .50
❑ 222 Wedge R1 2.50 6.00
❑ 223 Yasuki Taka (Experienced) U .20 .50
❑ 224 Yodin (Experienced) R1 .50 1.25
❑ 225 Yogo Junzo's Army U1 .20 .50
❑ 226 Yogo Oshio C1 .10 .20
❑ 227 Yoritomo (Experienced) R1 1.00 2.50
❑ 228 Yoritomo's Armor R1 .75 2.00
❑ 229 Your Last Mistake U1 .20 .50

1998 Legend of the Five Rings Scorpion Clan Coup Scroll 2

❑ 1 A Vision of Truth U .20 .50
❑ 2 Agasha Nabe C .10 .20
❑ 3 Arrival of the Unicorns C .10 .20
❑ 4 Asahina Uojin C .10 .20
❑ 5 Bayushi Dairu U .20 .50
❑ 6 Bayushi House Guard U .20 .50
❑ 7 Bayushi Kyono C .10 .20
❑ 8 Bayushi Yojiro C .10 .20
❑ 9 Defenders of the Realm C .10 .20
❑ 10 Disloyalty C .10 .20
❑ 11 Doji Satsume U .20 .50
❑ 12 Fury of the Earth C .10 .20
❑ 13 Gift of Fealty U .20 .50
❑ 14 Hasagawa C .10 .20
❑ 15 Hida Matyu C .10 .20
❑ 16 Hojatsu's Blade C .10 .20
❑ 17 Iaijutsu Art C .10 .20
❑ 18 Isawa Sze U .20 .50
❑ 19 Kappa C .10 .20
❑ 20 Kuroshin's Prayer U .20 .50
❑ 21 Led from the True Path U .20 .50
❑ 22 Lieutenant Daini U .20 .50
❑ 23 Lieutenant Uji U .20 .50
❑ 24 Matsu Hokitare C .10 .20
❑ 25 Matsu Tsuko (Inexperienced) U .20 .50
❑ 26 Monk Advisors C .10 .20
❑ 27 My Enemy's Weakness U .20 .50
❑ 28 Ninja Shapeshifter (Inexperienced) U .20 .50
❑ 29 North Wall of Otosan Uchi U .20 .50
❑ 30 One Man's Honor U .20 .50
❑ 31 Piercing the Soul C .10 .20
❑ 32 Plain of Fast Troubles C .10 .20
❑ 33 Ranbe U .20 .50
❑ 34 Rear Guard C .10 .20
❑ 35 Shazaar C .10 .20
❑ 36 Shinjo Goshi C .10 .20
❑ 37 Shoju's Armor U .20 .50
❑ 38 Soshi's Curse C .10 .20
❑ 39 The Dragon Pearl U .20 .50
❑ 40 The Face of My Enemy U .20 .50
❑ 41 The Fair Voice of Lies U .20 .50
❑ 42 The Kharmic Wheel Spins U .20 .50
❑ 43 The Moment Before the Strike C .10 .20
❑ 44 The Purity of Kitsu U .20 .50
❑ 45 The Ruby of Iuchiban U .20 .50
❑ 46 The True Lands U .20 .50
❑ 47 Touching the Soul C .10 .20
❑ 48 Trading Port C .10 .20
❑ 49 West Wall of Otosan Uchi U .20 .50
❑ 50 When Men Stand Divided C .10 .20

1998 Legend of the Five Rings Scorpion Clan Coup Scroll 3

❑ 1 A Final Duel U .20 .50
❑ 2 A Greater Destiny U .20 .50
❑ 3 Acolyte Kaede U .20 .50
❑ 4 Agasha Mumoko C .10 .20
❑ 5 Agasha's Mirror C .10 .20
❑ 6 Akodo Hari C .10 .20
❑ 7 Akodo Ikawa C .10 .20
❑ 8 Akodo Matoko U .20 .50
❑ 9 Akodo Toturi (Inexperienced) F .60 1.50
❑ 10 All Distances Are One C .10 .20
❑ 11 Asahina's Breath U .20 .50
❑ 12 Bayushi's Labyrinth U .20 .50
❑ 13 Fires of Retribution C .10 .20
❑ 14 Give Me Your Hand U .20 .50
❑ 15 Heartbeat Drummers C .10 .20
❑ 16 Hida Kisada (Inexperienced) U .20 .50
❑ 17 Hiruma Osuno C .10 .20
❑ 18 Isawa Ujina U .20 .50
❑ 19 Isawa's Helm U .20 .50
❑ 20 Jitte C .10 .20
❑ 21 Kaiu Castle U .20 .50
❑ 22 Kyudo C .10 .20
❑ 23 Lieutenant Sukune U .20 .50
❑ 24 Lieutenant Tsanuri U .20 .50
❑ 25 Mirror Image C .10 .20
❑ 26 Mirumoto Satsu U .20 .50
❑ 27 Obi of Protection U .20 .50
❑ 28 Plains of the Emerald Champion C .10 .20
❑ 29 Quarry C .10 .20
❑ 30 Shiba Kyo C .10 .20
❑ 31 Street to Street C .10 .20
❑ 32 Streets of Otosan Uchi C .10 .20
❑ 33 Subversion U .20 .50
❑ 34 Sunabe C .10 .20
❑ 35 Suru's Mempo U .20 .50
❑ 36 Swamp Spirits C .10 .20
❑ 37 Tell the Tale C .10 .20
❑ 38 The Ancient Halls of the Lion F .40 1.00
❑ 39 The Courage of Osano-Wo U .20 .50
❑ 40 The Crab Arrive C .10 .20
❑ 41 The Fog of War C .10 .20
❑ 42 The Fortune's Wisdom C .10 .20
❑ 43 The Hub Villages C .10 .20
❑ 44 The Master Painter U .20 .50
❑ 45 The People's Champion U .20 .50
❑ 46 The Shiba Fortification U .20 .50
❑ 47 The Soul of Akodo U .20 .50
❑ 48 The Soul of Shiba U .20 .50
❑ 49 The Temples of Shinsei U .20 .50
❑ 50 The World Stood Still U .20 .50
❑ 51 Whispers of the Land C .10 .20
❑ 52 Yazaki C .10 .20

1998 Legend of the Five Rings The Hidden Emperor Episode 1

❑ 1 A Time for Mortal Men C .10 .20
❑ 2 Aiki Tactics R2 .50 1.25
❑ 3 Blackened Sky U4 .20 .50
❑ 4 Broken Guard R2 .40 1.00
❑ 5 Chasing Osano-Wo C .10 .20
❑ 6 Concealed Archers C .10 .20
❑ 7 Cricket C .10 .20
❑ 8 Daidoji Rekai C .10 .20
❑ 9 Dai-kyu of Anekkusai U4 .20 .50
❑ 10 Damesh C .10 .20
❑ 11 Day and Night R3 .40 1.00
❑ 12 Elite Spearmen C .10 .20
❑ 13 Flanking Maneuver C .10 .20
❑ 14 Flee the Darkness U4 .20 .50
❑ 15 Fu Leng's Skull R 1.25 3.00
❑ 16 Grove of the Five Masters U5 .20 .50
❑ 17 Hasame C .10 .20
❑ 18 Haunted Lands C .10 .20
❑ 19 Heart of the Shinomen Forest F .40 1.00
❑ 20 Heart of the Shinomen Forest R .40 1.00
❑ 21 Hiruma Castle U5 .20 .50
❑ 22 Ikudaiu C .10 .20
❑ 23 Imperial Legion U4 .20 .50
❑ 24 Journey to the Burning Sands U4 .20 .50
❑ 25 Kakita Yoshi (Experienced 2) R3 .50 1.25
❑ 26 Kyoso no Oni (Experienced) R2 .50 1.25
❑ 27 Master's Tactics R3 .40 1.00
❑ 28 Mizu-Do C .10 .20
❑ 29 Mukami (Experienced) U5 .20 .50
❑ 30 Naga Apprentice U4 .20 .50
❑ 31 Naga Storm Mirumoto Mountain U4 .20 .50
❑ 32 Naka Kuro (Experienced) R2 .40 1.00
❑ 33 Open Fields C .10 .20
❑ 34 Otaku Tetsuko C .10 .20
❑ 35 Otomu Banu U5 .20 .50
❑ 36 Political Marriage U4 .20 .50
❑ 37 Ralish C .10 .20
❑ 38 Rebuilding the Empire U4 .20 .50
❑ 39 Scouting Team C .10 .20
❑ 40 Selection of the Chancellor U5 .20 .50
❑ 41 Shahadet (Experienced 2 Naga Warlord) F .50 1.25
❑ 42 Shinjo Yokatsu (Experienced) R2 .50 1.25
❑ 43 Shiryo no Hoturi R2 1.25 3.00
❑ 44 Shiryo no Tsuko R2 .75 2.00
❑ 45 Show Me Your Stance U5 .20 .50
❑ 46 Takuan (Experienced) R2 .75 2.00
❑ 47 The Hidden Emperor R2 .60 1.50
❑ 48 The Hiruma Dojo C .10 .20
❑ 49 The Jade Throne R .60 1.50
❑ 50 The Mountains Below Kyuden Hitomi C .10 .20
❑ 51 The People's Hero C .10 .20
❑ 52 The Scorpion Children C .10 .20
❑ 53 Tidal Land Bridge R2 1.25 3.00

1998 Legend of the Five Rings The Hidden Emperor Episode 2

❑ 1 Ancestral Duty R2 .40 1.00
❑ 2 Betrayal U5 .20 .50
❑ 3 Chitatchikkan U4 .20 .50
❑ 4 Daidoji Tsumerai C .10 .20
❑ 5 Deadly Message U4 .20 .50
❑ 6 Double Agent R3 .40 1.00
❑ 7 Doubt R2 .40 1.00
❑ 8 Drawing Fire C .10 .20
❑ 9 Flooded Pass C .10 .20
❑ 10 Ginawa (Experienced 2) R3 1.00 2.50
❑ 11 Hitomi (Experienced 3 Mirumoto Hitomi) F 1.25 3.00
❑ 12 Hitomi Akuai C .10 .20
❑ 13 Hitomi Tashima (Experienced Shinjo Tashima) U5 .20 .50
❑ 14 Hitsu-do C .10 .20
❑ 15 Imperial Ambassadorship R2 .50 1.25
❑ 16 Iuchi Shahai C .10 .20
❑ 17 Kirazo C .10 .20
❑ 18 Ki-Rin's Shrine R2 .50 1.25
❑ 19 Kisada's Funeral U5 .20 .50
❑ 20 Kitsune Diro C .10 .20
❑ 21 Kyuden Hitomi F .50 1.25
❑ 22 Kyuden Hitomi R1 .50 1.25
❑ 23 Meishodo Amulet C .10 .20
❑ 24 Mystic Ground C .10 .20
❑ 25 Ninja Mystic (Experienced Hoseki) R2 .40 1.00
❑ 26 Norikazu's Ravings U5 .20 .50
❑ 27 Palisades C .10 .20
❑ 28 Purging the House R2 .40 1.00
❑ 29 Rise Again! U4 .20 .50
❑ 30 Root the Mountain C .10 .20
❑ 31 Ryoko Owari R2 .60 1.50
❑ 32 Shinjo's Breath U4 .20 .50
❑ 33 Shinsei's Fan C .10 .20
❑ 34 Shireikan U4 .20 .50
❑ 35 Shiryo no Tadaka R2 .75 2.00
❑ 36 Shosuro Nishiko U5 .20 .50
❑ 37 Slap the Wave R2 .50 1.25
❑ 38 Sting of the Wasp C .10 .20
❑ 39 Suspicions U4 .20 .50
❑ 40 Tattered Ear Tribe C .10 .20
❑ 41 Tattoed Men R2 .60 1.50
❑ 42 Tattooing Chamber R2 .60 1.50
❑ 43 Tchickchuk C .10 .20
❑ 44 The Bayushi Provinces C .10 .20
❑ 45 The Daini (Experienced 2 Mirumoto Daini) R2 1.25 3.00
❑ 46 The Dragon's Heart R3 .50 1.25
❑ 47 The Search Begins U5 .20 .50
❑ 48 The Shinjo Stockades C .10 .20
❑ 49 The Song of Blood C .10 .20
❑ 50 Token of Jade C .10 .20
❑ 51 Veil of Shadows U4 .20 .50
❑ 52 Writ of the Magistrate U4 .20 .50
❑ 53 Yoritomo Hogosha U4 .20 .50

1998 Legend of the Five Rings The Hidden Emperor Episode 3

❑ 1 Abandoning the Fortunes U5 .20 .50
❑ 2 Aramoro (Experienced Bayushi Aramoro) U4 .20 .50
❑ 3 Ascension of the Mantis R1 .60 1.50
❑ 4 Banish All Shadows R3 2.50 6.00
❑ 5 Empty Words U4 .20 .50
❑ 6 Enlightened Tutor U5 .20 .50
❑ 7 Face of Ninube C .10 .20
❑ 8 Fields of the Morning Sun C .10 .20
❑ 9 Finding the Balance R2 .40 1.00
❑ 10 Fortified Infantry C .10 .20
❑ 11 Ginawa (Experienced) R1 1.25 3.00
❑ 12 Grasp the Earth Dragon R2 .60 1.50
❑ 13 Hitomi Kazaq C .10 .20
❑ 14 Hitomi Kokujin (Experienced) R2 2.50 6.00
❑ 15 Hold This Ground C .10 .20
❑ 16 Hoshi Eisai C .10 .20
❑ 17 Hoshi Maseru C .10 .20
❑ 18 Ikoma Ryozo (Experienced) R3 .40 1.00
❑ 19 Kamoko's Charge U4 .20 .50
❑ 20 Kobune Crew U4 .20 .50
❑ 21 Kuni Utagu C .10 .20
❑ 22 Kuni Yori (Experienced 2) R2 .50 1.25
❑ 23 Let Your Spirit Guide You R3 2.00 5.00
❑ 24 Mercy Shrouds the Earth C .10 .20
❑ 25 Monastery R2 .50 1.25
❑ 26 Moto Soro U4 .20 .50
❑ 27 Move to the Bushes R2 .40 1.00
❑ 28 Mushin C .10 .20
❑ 29 Not While I Breathe U4 .20 .50
❑ 30 Otaku Meadows C .10 .20
❑ 31 Restoring the Doji Treasury U4 .20 .50
❑ 32 Retired Wasp General C .10 .20
❑ 33 River Bridge of Kaiu C .10 .20
❑ 34 Ryoku U4 .20 .50
❑ 35 Sacrifices For Our Future U5 .20 .50
❑ 36 Seppun Kossori C .10 .20
❑ 37 Shiryo no Kisada R2 .50 1.25
❑ 38 Stand or Run U4 .20 .50
❑ 39 Suzume Yugoki U5 .20 .50
❑ 40 Takao's Jingasa C .10 .20
❑ 41 The Dark Sanctuary R2 .60 1.50
❑ 42 The Efforts of the Clan R2 .40 1.00
❑ 43 The Grey Crane (Experienced 2 Kakita Toshimoko) R2 2.00 5.00
❑ 44 The Hiruma Dojo R1 .40 1.00
❑ 45 The House of Tao F .75 2.00
❑ 46 The House of Tao R1 .75 2.00
❑ 47 The New Way C .10 .20
❑ 48 The Touch of the Lands C .10 .20
❑ 49 Togashi Hoshi (Experienced) F 1.25 3.00
❑ 50 Torii Shrine U5 .20 .50
❑ 51 Trusted Counsel U4 .20 .50
❑ 52 Tsuchi-Do C .10 .20
❑ 53 Tsuruchi's Arrow R2 .50 1.25
❑ 54 Umi Amaterasu C .10 .20
❑ 55 Where Shinsei Stood C .10 .20

1998 Legend of the Five Rings The Hidden Emperor Episode 4

❑ 1 A Dark Foretelling R .40 1.00
❑ 2 Akodo Hall of Ancestors R .40 1.00
❑ 3 Arrow from the Ranks C .10 .20
❑ 4 Asako Hosigeru C .10 .20
❑ 5 Bayushi Technique U .20 .50
❑ 6 Desperate Wager R 1.50 4.00
❑ 7 Die Tsuchi C .10 .20
❑ 8 Doji Shizue (Experienced) R 1.25 3.00
❑ 9 Doom of the Brotherhood U .20 .50
❑ 10 Festival of the River of Stars R .40 1.00
❑ 11 Flattery C .10 .20
❑ 12 Funeral Pyre C .10 .20
❑ 13 Goblin War Truck U .20 .50
❑ 14 Goldsmith C .10 .20
❑ 15 Hida Yasamura (Experienced 2 Shinjo Yasamura) R 1.25 3.00
❑ 16 Hitomi Technique U .20 .50
❑ 17 Ide Ashijun C .10 .20
❑ 18 Itako U .20 .50
❑ 19 Kitsuki Evidence C .10 .20
❑ 20 Kitsuki Kaagi U .20 .50
❑ 21 Kitsuki Kaagi's Journal U .20 .50
❑ 22 Kolat Geisha C .10 .20
❑ 23 Lay of the Land R .40 1.00
❑ 24 Lessons from Kuro R .50 1.25
❑ 25 Malekish C .10 .20
❑ 26 Matsu Ketsui R .40 1.00
❑ 27 Mujina Tricks C .10 .20
❑ 28 Ninja Saboteur R .50 1.25
❑ 29 Noble Sacrifice R .50 1.25
❑ 30 Oni no Gekido U .20 .50
❑ 31 Otaku Kamoko (Experienced 3) F 2.50 6.00
❑ 32 Otaku Xieng Chi U .20 .50
❑ 33 Philosopher C .10 .20
❑ 34 Plains of Foul Tears C .10 .20
❑ 35 Refuge of the Three Sisters U .20 .50
❑ 36 Ronin Dojo C .10 .20
❑ 37 Ryosei (Experienced) U .20 .50
❑ 38 Shinjo Groomsman R .60 1.50
❑ 39 Shinjo Technique U .20 .50
❑ 40 Shinjo Tsuburo (Experienced) R .40 1.00
❑ 41 Shiryo no Moto R .40 1.00
❑ 42 Takuan Technique U .20 .50
❑ 43 The Boundless Depths of Water U .20 .50
❑ 44 The Great Feast U .20 .50
❑ 45 The Iuchi Plains C .10 .20
❑ 46 The Kami Watch Over Me U .20 .50
❑ 47 The Naga Akasha R .40 1.00
❑ 48 The Utaku Palaces F .75 2.00
❑ 49 The Power of Incompleteness C .10 .20
❑ 50 The Price of Failure C .10 .20
❑ 51 Walk Through the Mountains C .10 .20
❑ 52 War Dogs R .50 1.25

1998 Legend of the Five Rings The Hidden Emperor Episode 5

❑ 1 A Stone Circle C6 .10 .20
❑ 2 Akodo Dagger R2 .50 1.25
❑ 3 Basher's Club U4 .20 .50
❑ 4 Battle Hardened R2 .40 1.00
❑ 5 Bayushi Aramasu U4 .20 .50
❑ 6 Bayushi Yojiro (Experienced) U5 .20 .50
❑ 7 Blade of Secrets R3 .50 1.25
❑ 8 Corrupted Jade Sliver U4 .20 .50
❑ 9 Doom of Toturi C1 .10 .20
❑ 10 Drawing Out the Darkness U4 .20 .50
❑ 11 Facing Your Devils C5 .10 .20
❑ 12 Flaming Ground U4 .20 .50
❑ 13 Hida Technique U5 .20 .50
❑ 14 Hitomi Kobai R2 .75 2.00
❑ 15 Holy Home Village C6 .10 .20
❑ 16 Imperial Edicts C5 .10 .20
❑ 17 Island Barricades U5 .20 .50
❑ 18 Island of Silk R2 .40 1.00
❑ 19 Iuchi Karasu (Experienced 2) U4 .20 .50
❑ 20 Jama Suru C6 .10 .20
❑ 21 Kouta C9 .10 .20
❑ 22 Kuni Mokuna's Guide R2 .50 1.25
❑ 23 Kyuden Yoritomo F .75 2.00
❑ 24 Large Farm C5 .10 .20
❑ 25 March of the Alliance R2 .50 1.25
❑ 26 Matsu Hiroru (Experienced 2) R2 1.25 3.00
❑ 27 Matsu Turi (Experienced) U4 .20 .50
❑ 28 Naga Pearl Guardian C6 .10 .20
❑ 29 One Life, One Destiny R2 .60 1.50
❑ 30 Out of the Shadows C6 .10 .20
❑ 31 Ratling Hordes C6 .10 .20
❑ 32 Ratling Villages C6 .10 .20
❑ 33 Salt the Earth C6 .10 .20
❑ 34 Sanzo (Experienced) R1 .40 1.00
❑ 35 Shiba Technique U4 .20 .50
❑ 36 Shiryo no Nodotai R2 .50 1.25
❑ 37 Shiryo no Osano-Wo R2 .40 1.00
❑ 38 Shrine of Osano-Wo R2 .50 1.25
❑ 39 Silk Works C5 .10 .20
❑ 40 Takao (Experienced) U4 .20 .50
❑ 41 Take the Initiative C5 .10 .20
❑ 42 The Great Silence U4 .20 .50
❑ 43 The Otaku Stables Burn R2 .50 1.25
❑ 44 The Way of Death U4 .20 .50
❑ 45 Unrequited Love C6 .10 .20
❑ 46 Wasp Archers R2 .60 1.50
❑ 47 When Dark Winds Howl U4 .20 .50
❑ 48 Yoritomo (Experienced 2) F 1.50 4.00
❑ 49 Yoritomo Nodoteki C6 .10 .20
❑ 50 Yoritomo Technique U4 .20 .50
❑ 51 Yoritomo Yukue R3 .75 2.00
❑ 52 Zokujin C5 .10 .20

1998 Legend of the Five Rings The Hidden Emperor Episode 6

❑ 1 700 Soldier Plain U5 .20 .50
❑ 2 A Pure Stroke R2 .40 1.00
❑ 3 Battle Maidens C5 .10 .20
❑ 4 Big Stink U4 .20 .50
❑ 5 Blackened Claws C6 .10 .20
❑ 6 Chi Protection C6 .10 .20
❑ 7 Cleansing Bell C6 .10 .20
❑ 8 Coordinated Strike R2 .60 1.50
❑ 9 Cultists C5 .10 .20
❑ 10 Daidoji Karasu R2 .50 1.25
❑ 11 Daisoji Osen C6 .10 .20
❑ 12 Death of the Ki-Rin R2 2.00 5.00
❑ 13 Dharma Technique U4 .20 .50
❑ 14 Doji Kuwannon (Experienced 2) F 1.50 4.00
❑ 15 Doom of the Alliance U4 .20 .50
❑ 16 Eshru (Experienced) R2 1.25 3.00
❑ 17 Haunted U4 .20 .50
❑ 18 Hida O-Ushi (Experienced 2) R2 .60 1.50
❑ 19 Hitomi Reju (Experienced Doji Reju) U4 .20 .50
❑ 20 Hoshi Wayan C6 .10 .20
❑ 21 Ikoma Technique U4 .20 .50
❑ 22 Isawa Norikazu (Experienced) R2 .50 1.25
❑ 23 Kachiko's Fan U5 .20 .50
❑ 24 Kakita Ariteko C5 .10 .20
❑ 25 Kakita Technique U4 .20 .50
❑ 26 Kansen U4 .20 .50
❑ 27 Legacy of the Dark One U4 .20 .50
❑ 28 Makashi U4 .20 .50
❑ 29 Makoto R2 .50 1.25
❑ 30 Oni no Akuma (Experienced) U4 .20 .50
❑ 31 Otaku Steed C6 .10 .20
❑ 32 Prophet's Tower U4 .20 .50
❑ 33 Ratling Nest C5 .10 .20
❑ 34 Ratling Spy C6 .10 .20
❑ 35 Shiryo no Tetsuya R2 .40 1.00
❑ 36 Shosuro Chian C6 .10 .20
❑ 37 Silk Farm C5 .10 .20
❑ 38 Speak with the Voices of the Dead R2 .40 1.00
❑ 39 Storms of War C5 .10 .20
❑ 40 Teach the Mountain R3 .40 1.00
❑ 41 The Iron Cranes C5 .10 .20
❑ 42 The Iron Fortress of the Daidoji F .75 2.00

TCG/CCG

❑ 43 The Silk Road C6 .10 .20
❑ 44 Togashi's Daisho R2 .40 1.00
❑ 45 Tohaku C5 .10 .20
❑ 46 Trapping Tactics C6 .10 .20
❑ 47 Tutor R2 .40 1.00
❑ 48 Unrelenting Terror R2 .75 2.00
❑ 49 Valley of the Two Generals R3 .50 1.25
❑ 50 War in the Shadowlands R2 .50 1.25
❑ 51 Way of Shadow U4 .20 .50
❑ 52 Wisdom Gained U4 .20 .50

1999 Legend of the Five Rings Ambition's Debt

❑ 1 A Chance Meeting U .20 .50
❑ 2 Akodo Fields U .20 .50
❑ 3 Armorer C .10 .20
❑ 4 As the Shadow Falls Foil .20 .50
❑ 5 Asahina Dorai (Experienced) R .50 1.25
❑ 6 Asahina Tsukiyoka C .10 .20
❑ 7 Ashigaru Levies C .10 .20
❑ 8 Ashlim Foil .20 .50
❑ 9 Ashlim (Experienced) R .50 1.25
❑ 10 Assault on Otosan Uchi U .20 .50
❑ 11 At'tok'tuk Sensei R 1.50 4.00
❑ 12 Baby Ki-Rin R .50 1.25
❑ 13 Bakeneko C .10 .20
❑ 14 Barracks C .10 .20
❑ 15 Bayushi Aramasu (Experienced) R .50 1.25
❑ 16 Bayushi Urei C .10 .20
❑ 17 Be the Mountain C .10 .20
❑ 18 Beiden Pass Foil .20 .50
❑ 19 Bitter Destiny R .50 1.25
❑ 20 Bloodspeaker's Deal U .20 .50
❑ 21 Bokken C .10 .20
❑ 22 Botsumoku C .10 .20
❑ 23 Bridged Pass Foil .10 .20
❑ 24 Calm Winds U .20 .50
❑ 25 Carpenter Pass U .20 .50
❑ 26 Celestial Gift U .20 .50
❑ 27 Chi Strike Foil .40 1.00
❑ 28 Concede Defeat C .10 .20
❑ 29 Corrupt Gold Mines Foil .60 1.50
❑ 30 Costly Alliance C .10 .20
❑ 31 Critical Duel C .10 .20
❑ 32 Dangerous Terrain C .10 .20
❑ 33 Dark Energy R .50 1.25
❑ 34 Darkness Within C .10 .20
❑ 35 Dead Eyes U .20 .50
❑ 36 Death of Onnotangu R .60 1.50
❑ 37 Declaration of War U .20 .50
❑ 38 Defensible Position C .10 .20
❑ 39 Den of Spies U .20 .50
❑ 40 Denying the Emperor R .50 1.25
❑ 41 Dirty Politics R 1.50 4.00
❑ 42 Disfavored Foil .40 1.00
❑ 43 Disharmony Foil .10 .20
❑ 44 Dragon Sword is Broken Foil .20 .50
❑ 45 Dragon's Strength R .40 1.00
❑ 46 Dying Effort R .50 1.25
❑ 47 Entrench U .20 .50
❑ 48 Exile's Road R .50 1.25
❑ 49 Family Shrine C .10 .20
❑ 50 Fatal Mistake Foil .50 1.25
❑ 51 Finding the Harmony U .20 .50
❑ 52 Footsteps of Madness R .50 1.25
❑ 53 Forethought R .50 1.25
❑ 54 Forgotten Lands R .60 1.50
❑ 55 Fortune's Turn C .10 .20
❑ 56 Forward, March! C .10 .20
❑ 57 Goblin Berserkers Foil .10 .20
❑ 58 Goblin Wizard Foil .10 .20
❑ 59 Goju Utsuei C .10 .20
❑ 60 Greensnake C .10 .20
❑ 61 Guardian of the Rift R .40 1.00
❑ 62 Gyosho U .20 .50
❑ 63 Hate's Heart R .50 1.25
❑ 64 Hida Amoro (Experienced 2) R .75 2.00
❑ 65 Hida Sukune Foil .10 .20
❑ 66 Hida Yakamo (Experienced 3) F .60 1.50
❑ 67 Hirariko (Experienced) R .50 1.25
❑ 68 Hiruma Sensei R .40 1.00
❑ 69 Honor, Bah! R .40 1.00
❑ 70 Honor's Cost U .20 .50
❑ 71 Hoshi Kumonosu U .20 .50
❑ 72 Ichiro Kihongo U .20 .50
❑ 73 Ikoma Ryozo (Experienced 2) F .50 1.25
❑ 74 Ikoma Sensei U .20 .50
❑ 75 Ikoma Tsanuri (Experienced 2) R 1.50 4.00
❑ 76 Ikoma Yosei U .20 .50
❑ 77 Ikudaiu (Experienced) R 1.25 3.00
❑ 78 Imperial Highway C .10 .20
❑ 79 Imperial Summons C .10 .20
❑ 80 In Search of the Future C .10 .20
❑ 81 Infantry Square C .10 .20
❑ 82 Inner Fire Foil .20 .50
❑ 83 Isawa Kaede (Experienced 2) R 1.25 3.00
❑ 84 Isawa Mitori U .20 .50
❑ 85 Issut C .10 .20
❑ 86 Judgement of Toshiken U .20 .50
❑ 87 Kage (Experienced 4 Akodo Kage) R .60 1.50
❑ 88 Kage Sensei U .20 .50
❑ 89 Kakita Aihara U .20 .50
❑ 90 Kakita Ichiro (Experienced) Foil 1.25 3.00
❑ 91 Kakita Teacher U .20 .50
❑ 92 Kitsune Diro (Experienced) R 1.25 3.00
❑ 93 Kolat Bookkeeping U .20 .50
❑ 94 Kukanchi C .10 .20
❑ 95 Kuro Sensei R .75 2.00
❑ 96 Kuro's Fire R 3.00 8.00
❑ 97 Large Shrine C .10 .20
❑ 98 Last Stand Plain C .10 .20
❑ 99 Lessons from the Past Foil .10 .20
❑ 100 Lookout Mountain C .10 .20
❑ 101 Mantis Marine Troops R .75 2.00
❑ 102 Matsu Daoquan C .10 .20
❑ 103 Matsu Mori C .10 .20
❑ 104 Moetechi C .10 .20
❑ 105 Morikage R .50 1.25
❑ 106 Moto Soro (Experienced) R .50 1.25
❑ 107 Naga Spies U .20 .50
❑ 108 Night of Three Stars C .10 .20
❑ 109 Ningyo Foil .20 .50
❑ 110 Nio Sensei R 1.25 3.00
❑ 111 Norikazu Sensei R .50 1.25
❑ 112 Nue C .10 .20
❑ 113 Oath of Courage U .20 .50
❑ 114 Obake U .20 .50
❑ 115 Olyah U .20 .50
❑ 116 Ono U .20 .50
❑ 117 Orochi C .10 .20
❑ 118 Otomo Shishi C .10 .20
❑ 119 Overconfidence C .10 .20
❑ 120 Oyuchi U .20 .50
❑ 121 Parade Ground Practice C .10 .20
❑ 122 Pikemen Foil .10 .20
❑ 123 Plague of Locusts U .20 .50
❑ 124 Plague Zombies Foil .10 .20
❑ 125 Plains of the Emerald Champion Foil .10 .20
❑ 126 Poisoned C .10 .20
❑ 127 Poisoned Honor C .10 .20
❑ 128 Political Distraction Foil .10 .20
❑ 129 Poor Health U .20 .50
❑ 130 Rattling Archers U .20 .50
❑ 131 Ravine C .10 .20
❑ 132 Recovering the True Tao U .20 .50
❑ 133 River Around the Hill C .10 .20
❑ 134 Roshungi U .20 .50
❑ 135 Ruantek C .10 .20
❑ 136 Sake Works Foil .20 .50
❑ 137 Savaged Fields U .20 .50
❑ 138 Scorpion Courtiers R .50 1.25
❑ 139 Seppun Mashita C .10 .20
❑ 140 Shadow Beast C .10 .20
❑ 141 Shakoki Dogu R .60 1.50
❑ 142 Shiba Kyukyo C .10 .20
❑ 143 Shiba Odoshi U .20 .50
❑ 144 Shinjo Shono C .10 .20
❑ 145 Shipyard C .10 .20
❑ 146 Shiryo no Kaze R .40 1.00
❑ 147 Shiryo no Takuan R .75 2.00
❑ 148 Shiryo no Yasuki R .40 1.00
❑ 149 Shiyokai U .20 .50
❑ 150 Shooting Star Strike U .20 .50
❑ 151 Shosuro Dojo R .50 1.25
❑ 152 Shosuro Yodoka U .20 .50
❑ 153 Shugenja Students U .20 .50
❑ 154 Sorrow's Path C .10 .20
❑ 155 Soshi Taoshi Foil .20 .50
❑ 156 Stand Firm Foil .10 .20
❑ 157 Storm of Arrows C .10 .20
❑ 158 Strong Words U .20 .50
❑ 159 Suana (Experienced) R .40 1.00
❑ 160 Summoning the Moon R .50 1.25
❑ 161 Suspended Terrain Foil .10 .20
❑ 162 Swifter Arrow U .20 .50
❑ 163 Sympathetic Energies Foil .20 .50
❑ 164 Tactical Maneuvers U .20 .50
❑ 165 Tangen's Lies R 1.00 2.50
❑ 166 Temple Guard U .20 .50
❑ 167 The Arrow Knows the Way Foil 2.00 5.00
❑ 168 The Damned C .10 .20
❑ 169 The Fallen Lion Fortress R .50 1.25
❑ 170 The Festering Pit of Fu Leng Foil 1.50 4.00
❑ 171 The Fire from Within Foil .40 1.00
❑ 172 The Gates to Jigoku R .50 1.25
❑ 173 The Ikoma Histories U .20 .50
❑ 174 The Kitsu Tombs F 1.00 2.50
❑ 175 The Legion of Two Thousand R 1.50 4.00
❑ 176 The New Akasha F .75 2.00
❑ 177 The Path of Akodo U .20 .50
❑ 178 The Prophecies R .50 1.25
❑ 179 The Spawning Ground F .60 1.50
❑ 180 The Sun in Shadow U .20 .50
❑ 181 To Avenge Our Ancestors Foil .40 1.00
❑ 182 Togashi Hoshi (Experienced 2) R 1.00 2.50
❑ 183 Togashi Jodome Foil .20 .50
❑ 184 Togashi Shinseken U .20 .50
❑ 185 Tohaku (Experienced) R 1.25 3.00
❑ 186 Toichi U .20 .50
❑ 187 Tonbo Toryu C .10 .20
❑ 188 Toturi's Treatise U .20 .50
❑ 189 Touching the Void U .20 .50
❑ 190 Trading Grounds Foil .20 .50
❑ 191 Troll Raiders U .20 .50
❑ 192 Troops from the Woods Foil .10 .20
❑ 193 Tsuruchi's Legion R 1.25 3.00
❑ 194 Twenty-Seven Days of Darkness U .20 .50
❑ 195 Uncertainty C .10 .20
❑ 196 Undead Cavalry C .10 .20
❑ 197 Unmaker's Shadow R .40 1.00
❑ 198 Void's Path R .50 1.25
❑ 199 War Weary U .20 .50
❑ 200 Way of the Zukojin C .10 .20
❑ 201 Woodland Reserves C .10 .20
❑ 202 Yabanjin Horsemen C .10 .20
❑ 203 Yasuki Nokatsu (Experienced) R/F .40 1.00
❑ 204 Yasuki Taka (Experienced 2) R .60 1.50
❑ 205 Yokai no Junzo F .50 1.25
❑ 206 Yokatsu (Experienced 2 Yokatsu) R .75 2.00
❑ 207 Yori Sensei R .40 1.00
❑ 208 Yoritomo Chujitsu U .20 .50
❑ 209 Yoritomo Furikae C .10 .20
❑ 210 Yoritomo Sensei U .20 .50
❑ 211 Yoshi (Experienced 2 Togashi Yoshi) R 1.25 3.00
❑ 212 Yoshi Sensei U .20 .50
❑ 213 Yosuchi C .10 .20

1999 Legend of the Five Rings Honor Bound

BOOSTER BOX (48) 100.00 200.00
BOOSTER PACK (11) 2.50 5.00
❑ 1 A New Teacher R .40 1.00
❑ 2 A Stout Heart Foil .20 .50
❑ 3 Abresax R .75 2.00
❑ 4 Akodo's Leadership R .75 2.00
❑ 5 Amnesia U .20 .50
❑ 6 An Empty Victory R .40 1.00
❑ 7 Ancient Sage C .10 .20
❑ 8 Another Time Foil .20 .50
❑ 9 Asahina Tomo Foil .10 .20
❑ 10 Asako Provinces C .10 .20
❑ 11 Awakening Shakoki Dogu C .10 .20
❑ 12 Bad Kharma Foil .50 1.25
❑ 13 Bandit Attack C .10 .20
❑ 14 Bandit Raids U .20 .50
❑ 15 Barricades C .10 .20
❑ 16 Bayushi Dozan Foil .10 .20
❑ 17 Bayushi Eiyo C .10 .20
❑ 18 Bayushi Goshiu (Experienced 2) R .75 2.00
❑ 19 Bayushi Hisa (Experienced 2) R .50 1.25
❑ 20 Bayushi Kachiko (Experienced 3) F 2.50 6.00
❑ 21 Benefices of the Emperor R .75 2.00
❑ 22 Black Pearl R .75 2.00
❑ 23 Bleeding the Elements U .20 .50
❑ 24 Blessing Upon the Lands C .10 .20
❑ 25 Bloodstrike R 2.00 5.00
❑ 26 Builders C .10 .20
❑ 27 Burn It Down C .10 .20
❑ 28 Command Staff U .20 .50
❑ 29 Court Jester Foil .20 .50
❑ 30 Curse of the Rot Within C .10 .20
❑ 31 Daidoji Kedamono C .10 .20
❑ 32 Dairya (Experienced 2) R .60 1.50
❑ 33 Dark Bargains U .20 .50
❑ 34 Darkness Beyond Darkness U .20 .50
❑ 35 Dashmar (Experienced 2) R .50 1.25
❑ 36 Deep Forest U .20 .50
❑ 37 Doji Adoka C .10 .20
❑ 38 Dragon's Claw Katana U .20 .50
❑ 39 Dragon's Teeth Foil .10 .20
❑ 40 Elite Pikemen C .10 .20
❑ 41 Energy Terrain C .10 .20
❑ 42 Extortion Foil 2.00 5.00
❑ 43 Face of the Nameless R 2.00 5.00
❑ 44 False Alliance Foil .40 1.00
❑ 45 Familiar Surroundings Foil .10 .20
❑ 46 Famine U .20 .50
❑ 47 Fear's Bane C .10 .20
❑ 48 Feydn Rafiq C .10 .20
❑ 49 Firestorm Legion R .50 1.25
❑ 50 Flameseeker C .10 .20
❑ 51 Flashing Blades U .20 .50
❑ 52 Force of Honor C .10 .20
❑ 53 Force of Will Foil .20 .50
❑ 54 Forest Fire C .10 .20
❑ 55 Forgotten Lesson R .40 1.00
❑ 56 Fortress of the Dragonfly C .10 .20
❑ 57 Ghedai C .10 .20
❑ 58 Gift of the Maker U .20 .50
❑ 59 Gohei's Daisho R .60 1.50
❑ 60 Goju Stalkers U .20 .50
❑ 61 Hasame (Experienced) R .50 1.25
❑ 62 Hassuk's Golden Bow C .10 .20
❑ 63 Hida O-Ushi (Experienced 3) F .75 2.00
❑ 64 Hida Tsuru Foil .20 .50
❑ 65 High Morale C .10 .20
❑ 66 Hiruma Yugure C .10 .20
❑ 67 Hiruma Zunguri C .10 .20
❑ 68 Hitomi Kagetora U .20 .50
❑ 69 Hitomi's Defeat U .20 .50
❑ 70 Hizuka (Experienced) R .50 1.25
❑ 71 Hojyn U .20 .50
❑ 72 Horsebowmen Foil .10 .20
❑ 73 Hoshi Wayan (Experienced) R .50 1.25
❑ 74 Hoshi's Challenge U .20 .50
❑ 75 Ikoma Ken'o U .20 .50
❑ 76 Isawa Norikazu (Experienced 2) R .75 2.00
❑ 77 Isawa Tanayama (Experienced Necromancer) R .50 1.25
❑ 78 Iuchi Shahai (Experienced) R 1.25 3.00
❑ 79 Kabuki Theater Troupe U .20 .50
❑ 80 Kaede Sensei R 3.00 8.00
❑ 81 Kaimetsu-Uo's Ono C .10 .20
❑ 82 Kakita Kaiten U .20 .50
❑ 83 Kakita's The Sword R 3.00 8.00
❑ 84 Kenshinzen R 1.25 4.00
❑ 85 Kisada Sensei U .20 .50
❑ 86 Kitsu Osen (Experienced Daidoji Osen) R .50 1.25
❑ 87 Kolat Apprentice R .50 1.25
❑ 88 Kolat Duplicate R 1.25 3.00
❑ 89 Kuni Yasashii C .10 .20
❑ 90 Kuni Yori (Experienced 3) F .75 2.00
❑ 91 Lord Moon's Bones R 2.00 5.00
❑ 92 Lord Moon's Smile R 1.00 2.50
❑ 93 Low Morale C .10 .20
❑ 94 Mantis Fleet C .10 .20
❑ 95 Master of Bushido U .20 .50
❑ 96 Master Painter Foil .20 .50
❑ 97 Matsu Morishigi C .10 .20
❑ 98 Matsu Toshiro Foil .40 1.00
❑ 99 Mercenaries C .10 .20
❑ 100 Mirumoto Uso C .10 .20
❑ 101 Mirumoto's Niten U .20 .50
❑ 102 Moment of Brilliance U .20 .50
❑ 103 Monopoly U .20 .50
❑ 104 Monsoon Season U .20 .50
❑ 105 Moto Tsume (Experienced 2) R .75 2.00
❑ 106 Moto Yesugai U .20 .50
❑ 107 Mountains of the Phoenix C .10 .20
❑ 108 Ninja Mimic U .20 .50
❑ 109 Ninja Mystic (Experienced 2 Hoseki) R .50 1.25
❑ 110 Nishiko (Experienced Shosuro Nishiko) R .60 1.50
❑ 111 Nunchaku U .20 .50
❑ 112 Oh-chi'chek C .10 .20
❑ 113 Okura is Released U .20 .50
❑ 114 One Life, One Action C .10 .20
❑ 115 Oni no Okura U .20 .50
❑ 116 Oseuth U .20 .50
❑ 117 Otomo Yayu C .10 .20
❑ 118 Palace of the Emerald Champion R .50 1.25
❑ 119 Pincer Attack C .10 .20
❑ 120 Plans Within Plans Foil 1.25 3.00
❑ 121 Porthungluin U .20 .50
❑ 122 Pressure C .10 .20
❑ 123 Return of the Kami R .40 1.00
❑ 124 Rik'tik'tichek U .20 .50
❑ 125 Rodrigo C .10 .20
❑ 126 Rugged Ground C .10 .20
❑ 127 Sabotage U .20 .50
❑ 128 Saigorei U .20 .50
❑ 129 Sanctified Ground Foil .10 .20
❑ 130 Seppun Nakao U .20 .50
❑ 131 Sepulcher of Bone F .60 1.50
❑ 132 Setsuban Festival Foil .40 1.00
❑ 133 Shadowlands Sickness Foil .20 .50
❑ 134 Shiba Kyo Foil .10 .20
❑ 135 Shiba Ningen U .20 .50
❑ 136 Shiba Raigen C .10 .20
❑ 137 Shiba Shingo Foil .20 .50
❑ 138 Shinjo's Judgement R .50 1.25
❑ 139 Shoju Sensei R 1.50 4.00
❑ 140 Shosuro Taberu (Experienced) R .75 2.00
❑ 141 Shosuro Taushui C .10 .20
❑ 142 Shurin Storms R .60 1.50
❑ 143 Silence U .20 .50
❑ 144 Silent War U .20 .50
❑ 145 Skeletal Archers Foil .20 .50
❑ 146 Slaughter of the Imperial Court R .40 1.00
❑ 147 Soshi Jomyako C .10 .20
❑ 148 Soshi Jujun C .10 .20
❑ 149 Souls of the Betrayed R .50 1.25
❑ 150 Stain Upon the Soul U .20 .50
❑ 151 Stance of the Mountain Foil .10 .20
❑ 152 Stars Scatter U .20 .50
❑ 153 Stress U .20 .50
❑ 154 Sword of the Emerald Champion R .60 1.50
❑ 155 Swordmaster C .10 .20
❑ 156 Temple of Blood C .10 .20
❑ 157 Temple to Shinsei U .20 .50
❑ 158 The Citadel of the Hiruma F .40 1.00
❑ 159 The Emperor's Lands U .20 .50
❑ 160 The Emperor's Left Hand U .20 .50
❑ 161 The Emperor's Right Hand U .20 .50
❑ 162 The Empty Pyre U .20 .50
❑ 163 The Enemy of My Enemy U .20 .50
❑ 164 The Fair Voice of Lies Foil .20 .50
❑ 165 The False Tao R .40 1.00
❑ 166 The Final Breath Foil .10 .20
❑ 167 The First Scroll is Opened Foil .20 .50
❑ 168 The Head of My Enemy R .40 1.00
❑ 169 The Kaiu Forge U .20 .50
❑ 170 The Kaiu Walls Foil .20 .50
❑ 171 The Master of Five R .60 1.50
❑ 172 The Tower of the Yogo F .60 1.50
❑ 173 The Unquiet Grave of Hida Amoro C .10 .20
❑ 174 The Wind's Truth C .10 .20
❑ 175 Thy Master's Will R .40 1.00
❑ 176 Tiger's Teeth U .20 .50
❑ 177 Tomb of Iuchiban Foil .40 1.00
❑ 178 Tomb of Jade Foil .20 .50
❑ 179 Torn From the Past U .20 .50
❑ 180 Toshimoko Sensei R 1.50 4.00
❑ 181 Toturi is Drugged Foil 1.50 4.00
❑ 182 Toturi Sensei R .60 1.50
❑ 183 Treachery and Deceit R .75 2.00
❑ 184 Trenches C .10 .20
❑ 185 Tribute to Your House R .75 2.00
❑ 186 Tunnel System Foil .20 .50
❑ 187 Uji Sensei U .20 .50
❑ 188 Uragirimono C .10 .20
❑ 189 Victory at Hiruma Castle R .40 1.00
❑ 190 Volcano R .50 1.25
❑ 191 Volturnum R .50 1.25
❑ 192 Way of the Void R .60 1.50
❑ 193 Wetlands Foil .10 .20
❑ 194 Whispers of Twilight C .10 .20
❑ 195 Whistling Arrows U .20 .50
❑ 196 Wide Terrain U .20 .50
❑ 197 Will of the Emperor C .10 .20
❑ 198 Within Your Soul C .10 .20
❑ 199 Yakamo's Funeral R .60 1.50
❑ 200 Yogo Shidachi Foil .60 1.50
❑ 201 Yokatsu Sensei R .40 1.00
❑ 202 Yokuni Sensei U .20 .50
❑ 203 Yoritomo Denkyu C .10 .20
❑ 204 Yoritomo Komori U .20 .50
❑ 205 Yoritomo Masasue (Experienced) R .50 1.25
❑ 206 Yoshun C .10 .20

1999 Legend of the Five Rings The Hidden Emperor: The Dark Journey Home

BOOSTER BOX (48) 100.00 200.00
BOOSTER PACK (11) 2.50 5.00
❑ 1 A Dark Moment C .10 .20
❑ 2 A Glimpse Beyond R .40 1.00
❑ 3 A Kolat Revealed U .20 .50
❑ 4 Agasha Gennai (Experienced) R .50 1.25
❑ 5 Agasha Kusabi U .20 .50
❑ 6 Aka Mizu-umi U .20 .50
❑ 7 Ambition R 2.00 5.00
❑ 8 Arrow of the Four Winds R .40 1.00
❑ 9 Arrowroot Tattoo U .20 .50
❑ 10 Asahina Dorai C .10 .20
❑ 11 Ashigaru Archers C .10 .20
❑ 12 Ashigaru Spearman C .10 .20
❑ 13 Assassins C .10 .20
❑ 14 Balash (Experienced) U .20 .50
❑ 15 Battlements C .10 .20
❑ 16 Bayushi Areru C .10 .20
❑ 17 Bells of the Dead C .10 .20
❑ 18 Black Finger River C .10 .20
❑ 19 Blessings of Isawa U .20 .50
❑ 20 Blood Arrows of Yajinden C .10 .20
❑ 21 Bonsai Garden C .10 .20
❑ 22 Centipede Tattoo U .20 .50
❑ 23 Chochu U .20 .50
❑ 24 Clay Horse C .10 .20
❑ 25 Contemplation C .10 .20
❑ 26 Contested Holding R 1.25 3.00
❑ 27 Crane Tattoo U .20 .50
❑ 28 Creating the Monkey Clan U .20 .50
❑ 29 Crystal Nagamaki U .20 .50
❑ 30 Daidoji Rekai (Experienced) R .50 1.25
❑ 31 Dangai C .10 .20
❑ 32 Deeds, Not Words U .20 .50
❑ 33 Disgraced U .20 .50
❑ 34 Disobedience R .40 1.00
❑ 35 Dragon Tattoo U .20 .50
❑ 36 Dragonfly Tattoo U .20 .50
❑ 37 Dragon's Tail Star U .20 .50
❑ 38 Emergence of the Masters C .10 .20
❑ 39 Eternal Halls of the Shiba F .40 1.00
❑ 40 Falling Star Strike C .10 .20
❑ 41 Final Haiku R .50 1.25
❑ 42 Firebird Falls R .50 1.25
❑ 43 Full Moon Tattoo U .20 .50
❑ 44 Glimpse of Kage U .20 .50
❑ 45 Goju Adorai F 1.25 3.00
❑ 46 Golden Sun Plain R 2.00 5.00
❑ 47 Heavy Ground C .10 .20
❑ 48 Held Terrain R .50 1.25
❑ 49 Heroic Opportunities R .50 1.25
❑ 50 Hida Rohiteki C .10 .20
❑ 51 Hidden Blade R .60 1.50
❑ 52 Hiruma Osuno (Experienced) R 1.50 4.00
❑ 53 Hitomi Dajan C .10 .20
❑ 54 Hitomi Iyojin U .20 .50
❑ 55 Hitomi Juppun U .20 .50
❑ 56 Hitomi Nakuso U .20 .50
❑ 57 Hoshi Maseru (Experienced) U .20 .50
❑ 58 Hunted U .20 .50
❑ 59 Ikoma Gunjin U .20 .50
❑ 60 Isawa Hochiu U .20 .50
❑ 61 Isawa Kaede (Experienced) R 1.50 4.00
❑ 62 Isawa Taeruko C .10 .20
❑ 63 Kage (Experienced 3 Akodo Kage) R .50 1.25
❑ 64 Kharma U .20 .50
❑ 65 Kitsu Sanako U .20 .50
❑ 66 Kitsuki Iyekao C .10 .20
❑ 67 Kitsuki's Coin R .40 1.00
❑ 68 Kolat Agent C .10 .20
❑ 69 Kolat Recruiter R 1.50 4.00
❑ 70 Let Him Escape R .60 1.50
❑ 71 Lion Tattoo U .20 .50
❑ 72 Lion's Pride R 1.25 3.00
❑ 73 Lord Moon's Blood R .75 2.00
❑ 74 Loss of Face C .10 .20
❑ 75 Magic Mud U .20 .50
❑ 76 Maho-Tsukai R .50 1.25
❑ 77 Mamoru U .20 .50
❑ 78 Mantis House Guard U .20 .50
❑ 79 Mantle of the Jade Champion R .50 1.25
❑ 80 Master of Destiny R .50 1.25

TCG/CCG

- ❑ 81 Matsu Toki U .20 .50
- ❑ 82 Moshi Hito C .10 .20
- ❑ 83 Moto Amadare C .10 .20
- ❑ 84 Moto Fanatics U .20 .50
- ❑ 85 Mountain Tattoo U .20 .50
- ❑ 86 Nightmares of Iuchiban R .50 1.25
- ❑ 87 Ninja Infiltrator (Experienced Sanado) R .60 1.50
- ❑ 88 Ninja Questioner U .20 .50
- ❑ 89 Ninja Shadow-Walker C .10 .20
- ❑ 90 Ninja Tricks U .20 .50
- ❑ 91 Ninube Ogoku C .10 .20
- ❑ 92 Osari Plains C .10 .20
- ❑ 93 Phoenix Tattoo U .20 .50
- ❑ 94 Pillaging C .10 .20
- ❑ 95 Plain of Desperate Evil U .20 .50
- ❑ 96 Poison Dartgun C .10 .20
- ❑ 97 Pride C .10 .20
- ❑ 98 Proud Words C .10 .20
- ❑ 99 Purity of Spirit C .10 .20
- ❑ 100 Ratling Scout C2 .10 .20
- ❑ 101 Rebuilding the Temples R .40 1.00
- ❑ 102 Retired Advisor R .50 1.25
- ❑ 103 Rise from the Ashes U .20 .50
- ❑ 104 River of the Dark Moon R .40 1.00
- ❑ 105 River of the Last Stand R .40 1.00
- ❑ 106 Ropp'tch'tch R .50 1.25
- ❑ 107 Seppun Toshiken R .50 1.25
- ❑ 108 Shadow Brand C .10 .20
- ❑ 109 Shadowlands Contagion R 1.25 3.00
- ❑ 110 Shadowlands Marsh U .20 .50
- ❑ 111 Shiba Gensui C .10 .20
- ❑ 112 Shiba Tetsu (Experienced) U .20 .50
- ❑ 113 Shiba Tsukune (Experienced 2) F .50 1.25
- ❑ 114 Shinko Kamiko (Experienced Pennagolan) R .50 1.25
- ❑ 115 Shiryo no Goju R .40 1.00
- ❑ 116 Shiryo no Kuni R .40 1.00
- ❑ 117 Shiryo no Yurei R .50 1.25
- ❑ 118 Shosuro (Experienced Ninja Shapeshifter) R 1.25 3.00
- ❑ 119 Shotai R .60 1.50
- ❑ 120 Siege C .10 .20
- ❑ 121 Sludge C .10 .20
- ❑ 122 Smoke and Mirrors U .20 .50
- ❑ 123 Stagnation C .10 .20
- ❑ 124 Stand Together R .50 1.25
- ❑ 125 Steep Terrain C .10 .20
- ❑ 126 Strike of Silent Waters U .20 .50
- ❑ 127 Tattooed U .20 .50
- ❑ 128 Tausha C .10 .20
- ❑ 129 Test of the Jade Champion R .40 1.00
- ❑ 130 The Agasha Join the Phoenix R .50 1.25
- ❑ 131 The Agasha Libraries C .10 .20
- ❑ 132 The Age of Man U .20 .50
- ❑ 133 The Daimyo's Command R .40 1.00
- ❑ 134 The Dark Path of Shadow F 1.25 3.00
- ❑ 135 The Edge of the Shinomen Forest C .10 .20
- ❑ 136 The Palace of Otosan-Uchi F 1.25 3.00
- ❑ 137 The Path Not Taken R 1.50 4.00
- ❑ 138 The Wave Men R .50 1.25
- ❑ 139 Threat C .10 .20
- ❑ 140 Tiger Tattoo U .20 .50
- ❑ 141 Toku (Experienced 2) R2 .75 2.00
- ❑ 142 Toritaka Genzo (Experienced Genzo) R .40 1.00
- ❑ 143 Toturi the First (Experienced 3) F 1.50 4.00
- ❑ 144 Toturi's Return U .20 .50
- ❑ 145 Touch the Lands C .10 .20
- ❑ 146 Treacherous Pass C .10 .20
- ❑ 147 Tsuruchi (Experienced) R .50 1.25
- ❑ 148 Twilight Mountains R .60 1.50
- ❑ 149 Twisting Ravine C .10 .20
- ❑ 150 Tzurui U .20 .50
- ❑ 151 Virtuous Heart C .10 .20
- ❑ 152 Warstained Fields C .10 .20
- ❑ 153 Winds and Fortunes U .20 .50
- ❑ 154 Yotsu Seou C .10 .20

2000 Legend of the Five Rings Fire and Shadow

- COMPLETE SET (220) 40.00 80.00
- BOOSTER BOX (48) 40.00 80.00
- BOOSTER PACK (11) 1.25 2.50

- ❑ 1 Agasha Fujita U .15 .40
- ❑ 2 Akui Cliffs C .10 .20
- ❑ 3 Ambush Strategist C .10 .20
- ❑ 4 Ancestors Possess the Living R .30 .75
- ❑ 5 Asako Kaushen U .15 .40
- ❑ 6 Asako Sagoten C .10 .20
- ❑ 7 Ascendence R .75 2.00
- ❑ 8 Ashalan Sandsmith C .10 .20
- ❑ 9 Assuming the Championship R .30 .75
- ❑ 10 Bayushi Aramasu (Experienced 2) R .30 .75
- ❑ 11 Bayushi Aramoro (Experienced 2) R .40 1.00
- ❑ 12 Bayushi Muraisan C .10 .20
- ❑ 13 Belyezn Rafiq U .15 .40
- ❑ 14 Bend Like A Reed Foil .40 1.00
- ❑ 15 Blade of Kaiu U .15 .40
- ❑ 16 Blood and Darkness R .30 .75
- ❑ 17 Blood of Midnight Foil .60 1.50
- ❑ 18 Bloodstained Rage C .10 .20
- ❑ 19 Bonds of Darkness Foil .60 1.50
- ❑ 20 Bridge to Jigoku R .30 .75
- ❑ 21 Brothers of Thunder Foil .60 1.50
- ❑ 22 Burden of the Word R .30 .75
- ❑ 23 Burning Your Essence Foil 2.00 5.00
- ❑ 24 Campsite U .15 .40
- ❑ 25 Capturing the Soul R 1.25 3.00
- ❑ 26 Chasing the Shadow R .40 1.00
- ❑ 27 Come One At A Time C .10 .20
- ❑ 28 Command of the Kami U .15 .40
- ❑ 29 Corrupted Dojo C .10 .20
- ❑ 30 Corrupted Ground Foil .60 1.50
- ❑ 31 Crab Cavalry R .30 .75
- ❑ 32 Crisis in Command C .10 .20
- ❑ 33 Cross-Clan Wedding R .30 .75
- ❑ 34 Crow Tattoo U .15 .40
- ❑ 35 Dakosho C .10 .20
- ❑ 36 Dangerous Choices R .30 .75
- ❑ 37 Dark Energies Run Red U .15 .40
- ❑ 38 Decoy R .30 .75
- ❑ 39 Defeat the Reserves C .10 .20
- ❑ 40 Den of Mujina U .15 .40
- ❑ 41 Disenlightenment Foil .75 2.00
- ❑ 42 Divided Loyalties R .30 .75
- ❑ 43 Djahab U .15 .40
- ❑ 44 Doji Chomei (Experienced) R .30 .75
- ❑ 45 Doji Jiro C .10 .20
- ❑ 46 Elemental Attunement R .30 .75
- ❑ 47 Emerald Magistrates R .30 .75
- ❑ 48 Emmissary of the Ivory Kingdoms U .15 .40
- ❑ 49 Eternal Darkness U .15 .40
- ❑ 50 Far From the Empire R .30 .75
- ❑ 51 Fate's Merciful Hand U .15 .40
- ❑ 52 Fearful Presence U .15 .40
- ❑ 53 Fearsome Strength U .15 .40
- ❑ 54 Feeding on Flesh R .30 .75
- ❑ 55 Fields of the Dead C .10 .20
- ❑ 56 Final Words R .30 .75
- ❑ 57 Fu Leng's Steeds Foil .75 2.00
- ❑ 58 Gift of the Emperor R .40 1.00
- ❑ 59 Goblin War Standard Foil .60 1.50
- ❑ 60 Grandfather's Jaw C .10 .20
- ❑ 61 Hanoshi C .10 .20
- ❑ 62 Hantei Sensei U .15 .40
- ❑ 63 Harsh Lessons C .10 .20
- ❑ 64 Heart of the Damned C .10 .20
- ❑ 65 Heimin Village U .15 .40
- ❑ 66 Hida Nezu U .15 .40
- ❑ 67 Hida Rohiteki (Experienced) R .30 .75
- ❑ 68 Hidden From the Empire C .10 .20
- ❑ 69 His Tsu C .10 .20
- ❑ 70 Hitomi Bujun (Experienced Mirumoto Bujun) R .30 .75
- ❑ 71 Honorable Sacrifice U .15 .40
- ❑ 72 House of Contracts C .10 .20
- ❑ 73 Hummingbird Tattoo U .15 .40
- ❑ 74 Hurricane Initiates C .10 .20
- ❑ 75 Ide Buodin C .10 .20
- ❑ 76 Ikoma Gunjin (Experienced) R .30 .75
- ❑ 77 Imperial Surveyor C .10 .20
- ❑ 78 Iron Mountain F .30 .75
- ❑ 79 Isawa Toiko C .10 .20
- ❑ 80 Jian U .15 .40
- ❑ 81 Journey to Otosan Uchi C .10 .20
- ❑ 82 Kachiko Calls to Thunder U .15 .40
- ❑ 83 Kachiko's Promises R .30 .75
- ❑ 84 Kaiu Endo C .10 .20
- ❑ 85 Kaiu Seige Engine C .10 .20
- ❑ 86 Kakita Ichiro (Experienced) R .30 .75
- ❑ 87 Kemmei Foil .60 1.50
- ❑ 88 Kitsu Gongsun U .15 .40
- ❑ 89 Kitsu Huiyuan R .30 .75
- ❑ 90 Kitsu R .30 .75
- ❑ 91 Kitsu Sensei R .30 .75
- ❑ 92 Kitsuki Mizuochi U .15 .40
- ❑ 93 Kitsune Shudo C .10 .20
- ❑ 94 Kitsune Tsuke C .10 .20
- ❑ 95 Know the Evil U .15 .40
- ❑ 96 Koichi Foil .75 2.00
- ❑ 97 Kolat Assistance R .30 .75
- ❑ 98 Kumo (Experienced) R .30 .75
- ❑ 99 Kyuden Kitsune F .30 .75
- ❑ 100 Last Refuge U .15 .40
- ❑ 101 Last Words C .10 .20
- ❑ 102 Mack'uk C .10 .20
- ❑ 103 Maintain Balance C .10 .20
- ❑ 104 Mantis Isles U .15 .40
- ❑ 105 Mara (Experienced) R .40 1.00
- ❑ 106 Masamune Katana C .10 .20
- ❑ 107 Master of the Tea Ceremony Foil .60 1.50
- ❑ 108 Matsu Suhada C .10 .20
- ❑ 109 Mine Cave-in U .15 .40
- ❑ 110 Mirumoto Songui C .10 .20
- ❑ 111 Mirumoto Sukune (Experienced) F .30 .75
- ❑ 112 Mirumoto Watanubo U .15 .40
- ❑ 113 Mirumoto Yuyake C .10 .20
- ❑ 114 Mismanaged Troops U .15 .40
- ❑ 115 Miya Yuritogen U .15 .40
- ❑ 116 Miya's Sasumata R .30 .75
- ❑ 117 Mohai U .15 .40
- ❑ 118 Moto Notu R .50 1.25
- ❑ 119 Moto Ride to the Shadowlands R .30 .75
- ❑ 120 Moto Toyotomi U .15 .40
- ❑ 121 Mountain of the Seven Thunders Foil 1.00 2.50
- ❑ 122 My Life For Yours U .15 .40
- ❑ 123 Never Yield U .15 .40
- ❑ 124 New Beginnings U .15 .40
- ❑ 125 Night Battle Foil .75 2.00
- ❑ 126 Ninja Shadow-Walker (Experienced) R .30 .75
- ❑ 127 Ninja-to R .60 1.50
- ❑ 128 Of One Mind U .15 .40
- ❑ 129 One Last Battle R .30 .75
- ❑ 130 Oni no Kamu Foil 2.00 5.00
- ❑ 131 Oni no Megada C .10 .20
- ❑ 132 Oni no Okura (Experienced) R .30 .75
- ❑ 133 Oracle of Thunder R .30 .75
- ❑ 134 Oskuda U .15 .40
- ❑ 135 Otaku Xieng Chi (Experienced) R .30 .75
- ❑ 136 Owned U .15 .40
- ❑ 137 Pearl Magic C .10 .20
- ❑ 138 Peasant Levies Foil .60 1.50
- ❑ 139 Pestilence C .10 .20
- ❑ 140 Pitfall C .10 .20
- ❑ 141 Primal Rage U .15 .40
- ❑ 142 Proud Heritage C .10 .20
- ❑ 143 Provision Storehouse C .10 .20
- ❑ 144 Purusha C .10 .20
- ❑ 145 Ranbe Foil 1.50 4.00
- ❑ 146 Ratling Youth U .15 .40
- ❑ 147 Relief C .10 .20
- ❑ 148 Remember What You Have Seen C .10 .20
- ❑ 149 Remember Your Oath R .30 .75
- ❑ 150 Return of Myth U .15 .40
- ❑ 151 Return of the True Champion U .15 .40
- ❑ 152 Rights of the Challenged C .10 .20
- ❑ 153 Road of Dust U .15 .40
- ❑ 154 Robes of Shinsei Foil .75 2.00
- ❑ 155 Run For Your Life C .10 .20
- ❑ 156 Ryosei (Experienced 2) F .30 .75
- ❑ 157 Ryoshun's First Gift C .10 .20
- ❑ 158 Sanctified Blade C .10 .20
- ❑ 159 Sanjuro C .10 .20
- ❑ 160 Satsume Sensei U .15 .40
- ❑ 161 Scrolls of Norikazu R .40 1.00
- ❑ 162 Secluded Ravine Foil 1.50 4.00
- ❑ 163 Seppun Sensei U .15 .40
- ❑ 164 Seppun Toshiken (Experienced) R .40 1.00
- ❑ 165 Shabura Foil .60 1.50
- ❑ 166 Shadowlands Madmen Foil 1.50 4.00
- ❑ 167 Shagara Foil 1.50 4.00
- ❑ 168 Shahadet's Legion Foil 1.50 4.00
- ❑ 169 Sharpest Blade R .30 .75
- ❑ 170 Shasyahkar R .30 .75
- ❑ 171 Shiba Gensui (Experienced) R .75 2.00
- ❑ 172 Shiba Katsuda Foil 1.50 4.00
- ❑ 173 Shifting Ground U .15 .40
- ❑ 174 Shi-Khan Wastes U .15 .40
- ❑ 175 Shinjo Sadato Foil 2.00 5.00
- ❑ 176 Shinobi Corruption U .15 .40
- ❑ 177 Shioda Foil .60 1.50
- ❑ 178 Shipping Lanes C .10 .20
- ❑ 179 Shokansuru U .15 .40
- ❑ 180 Shosuro Technique R .30 .75
- ❑ 181 Shrine of the Dragon Champion C .10 .20
- ❑ 182 Single Combat C .10 .20
- ❑ 183 Skeletal Elite R .40 1.00
- ❑ 184 Skirmisher's Pike C .10 .20
- ❑ 185 Slaughter of the Land U .15 .40
- ❑ 186 Sleeping Lake R .30 .75
- ❑ 187 Soul's Sacrifice U .15 .40
- ❑ 188 Spectral Guide U .15 .40
- ❑ 189 Spirit of the Bright Eye U .15 .40
- ❑ 190 Spreading the Shadow U .15 .40
- ❑ 191 Stepping Between the Cracks R .40 1.00
- ❑ 192 Stifling Wind Foil 1.50 4.00
- ❑ 193 Sunken City Foil 1.50 4.00
- ❑ 194 Sword of the Sun R .75 2.00
- ❑ 195 Taka Sensei R .30 .75
- ❑ 196 Takao (Experienced 2) F .30 .75
- ❑ 197 Tattoo of the Night Sky U .15 .40
- ❑ 198 Tax Collector C .10 .20
- ❑ 199 Temple of Divine Influence R .40 1.00
- ❑ 200 Temples of the Crow F .30 .75
- ❑ 201 The Celestial Pattern Foil 1.50 4.00
- ❑ 202 The Dark Moto Sensei R .40 1.00
- ❑ 203 The Face of Fear Foil 1.50 4.00
- ❑ 204 The Price of War Foil 1.50 4.00
- ❑ 205 The Twelve Ronin Foil 1.50 4.00
- ❑ 206 Third Mask of Iuchiban R .30 .75
- ❑ 207 Togashi Jodome (Experienced) R .40 1.00
- ❑ 208 Toritaka Kitao C .10 .20
- ❑ 209 Trade Route Foil .75 2.00
- ❑ 210 Tricked C .10 .20
- ❑ 211 Triumphant Victory R .30 .75
- ❑ 212 Tsuruchi (Experienced 2) R .40 1.00
- ❑ 213 Ujina Tomo C .10 .20
- ❑ 214 Venerable Stature C .10 .20
- ❑ 215 Warrior Monks Foil 1.50 4.00
- ❑ 216 White Shore Plain U .15 .40
- ❑ 217 Yabanjin Sorceror C .10 .20
- ❑ 218 Yoritomo Okan U .15 .40
- ❑ 219 Yoritomo Refuses the Throne U .15 .40
- ❑ 220 Yotsu Sabieru U .15 .40

2000 Legend of the Five Rings Heroes of Rokugan

- ❑ 1 Anvil of Despair F 2.00 5.00
- ❑ 2 Atarasi's Armor F 3.00 8.00
- ❑ 3 Celestial Dragon F 4.00 10.00
- ❑ 4 Cherry Blossom Festival F 1.25 3.00
- ❑ 5 Goju Yume F 1.50 4.00
- ❑ 6 Gusai F 1.50 4.00
- ❑ 7 Hida Osano-Wo F 6.00 15.00
- ❑ 8 Isawa Ijime F 1.25 3.00
- ❑ 9 Judgement F 4.00 10.00
- ❑ 10 Kakita Rensei F 4.00 10.00
- ❑ 11 Land of the Dead F .75 2.00
- ❑ 12 Matsu Hitomi F 1.50 4.00
- ❑ 13 Mirumoto Tokeru F 4.00 10.00
- ❑ 14 Miya Mashigai F .75 2.00
- ❑ 15 One Virtue and Seventy Faults F .60 1.50
- ❑ 16 Otaku Shiko F 2.00 5.00
- ❑ 17 Qatol F 3.00 8.00
- ❑ 18 Revealing the Ancient Wisdom F .75 2.00
- ❑ 19 Rezan F .75 2.00
- ❑ 20 Seppun Murayasu F .75 2.00
- ❑ 21 Shinsei's Riddle F .75 2.00
- ❑ 22 Shosuro Furuyari F 2.50 6.00
- ❑ 23 Someisa F .75 2.00
- ❑ 24 Spirit Legion F .60 1.50
- ❑ 25 The First Oni F 4.00 10.00
- ❑ 26 Warrens of the Nezumi F 1.25 3.00
- ❑ 27 Yasuki Kaneko F 3.00 8.00

2000 Legend of the Five Rings Soul of the Empire

- BOOSTER BOX (48) 50.00 100.00
- BOOSTER PACK (11) 1.50 3.00

- ❑ 1 Air Dragon (Experienced) R1 2.00 5.00
- ❑ 2 Amoro's Honor U2 .25 .60
- ❑ 3 Armor of the Ebony Samurai U2 .40 1.00
- ❑ 4 Armor of the Monkey Clan U1 .25 .60
- ❑ 5 Armor of the Twilight Mountains C1 .10 .20
- ❑ 6 Armored Steeds C1 .10 .20
- ❑ 7 Asahina Archers R2 .60 1.50
- ❑ 8 Ashida C1 .10 .20
- ❑ 9 Ashigaru C1 .40 1.00
- ❑ 10 Bayushi Aramoro (Experienced 3) R2 1.50 4.00
- ❑ 11 Bayushi Goshiu (Experienced 3) R2 2.00 5.00
- ❑ 12 Bayushi Hisa (Experienced 3) U1 1.25 3.00
- ❑ 13 Bayushi Ikita C2 .10 .20
- ❑ 14 Bayushi Meharu C1 .10 .20
- ❑ 15 Bhakarash C1 .10 .20
- ❑ 16 Bide Your Time C2 .10 .20
- ❑ 17 Blessing of the Celestial Heavens C2 .10 .20
- ❑ 18 Blood Rite R2 1.25 3.00
- ❑ 19 Bloodstained Forest U1 .25 .60
- ❑ 20 Bokatu C1 .10 .20
- ❑ 21 Brothers in Blood R2 1.25 3.00
- ❑ 22 Burning the Ashes C1 1.00 2.50
- ❑ 23 Cavalry C2 .40 1.00
- ❑ 24 Cavalry Screen C2 .10 .20
- ❑ 25 Chains of Jigoku U1 1.25 3.00
- ❑ 26 City of Empty Dreams C2 .10 .20
- ❑ 27 City of Living Flames C2 .10 .20
- ❑ 28 City of Loyalty C2 .10 .20
- ❑ 29 City of Tears C2 .10 .20
- ❑ 30 City of White Clouds C2 .10 .20
- ❑ 31 Cornering Maneuver C2 .10 .20
- ❑ 32 Daidoji Rekai (Experienced 2) R2 1.25 3.00
- ❑ 33 Daidoji Technique U2 .40 1.00
- ❑ 34 Dairya (Experienced 3) R1 1.00 2.50
- ❑ 35 Dark Plains U2 .25 .60
- ❑ 36 Deadly Fright C2 .10 .20
- ❑ 37 Death-Seeker Technique U2 .20 .50
- ❑ 38 Defenders of the Wall R2 .60 1.50
- ❑ 39 Devastation C2 .10 .20
- ❑ 40 Doji Benku C1 .10 .20
- ❑ 41 Doji Kuwannon (Experienced 2) F 1.00 2.50
- ❑ 42 Draft Notice C1 .10 .20
- ❑ 43 Dragon of Fire (Experienced) R1 1.25 3.00
- ❑ 44 Dragon's Tooth R2 .60 1.50
- ❑ 45 Earth Dragon (Experienced) R1 1.00 2.50
- ❑ 46 Elder Goju C1 .10 .20
- ❑ 47 Empty Crevasse C1 .10 .20
- ❑ 48 Eternal Halls of the Shiba U1 1.25 3.00
- ❑ 49 Eyes Shall Not See C1 .10 .20
- ❑ 50 Farmer C2 .40 1.00
- ❑ 51 Fearful Soul C2 .10 .20
- ❑ 52 Fields of Courage U2 .25 .60
- ❑ 53 Fields of the Moon U2 .25 .60
- ❑ 54 Firefly Tattoo U2 .40 1.00
- ❑ 55 For My Clan U2 .25 .60
- ❑ 56 Fortified Ground U2 .25 .60
- ❑ 57 From Broken Ground C2 .10 .20
- ❑ 58 Fulfilling My Duty C2 .10 .20
- ❑ 59 Fully Armed C2 .10 .20
- ❑ 60 Ginawa (Experienced 3) R2 .60 1.50
- ❑ 61 Glory Grounds C1 1.00 2.50
- ❑ 62 Goju Adorai (Experienced) R2 1.00 2.50
- ❑ 63 Half-Beat Strike R2 1.00 2.50
- ❑ 64 Heavy Barde R2 .60 1.50
- ❑ 65 Hida Tsuru (Experienced) R2 1.00 2.50
- ❑ 66 Hiruma Abun C1 .10 .20
- ❑ 67 Hitomi Iyojin (Experienced) R2 .60 1.50
- ❑ 68 Hoshi Eisai (Experienced) U1 .60 1.50
- ❑ 69 Hoshi Eisai (Experienced) U1 .60 1.50
- ❑ 70 Hoshi Sensei R1 .60 1.50
- ❑ 71 Hoshi Wayan (Experienced 2) R2 .60 1.50
- ❑ 72 Hoturi Sensei R2 .60 1.50
- ❑ 73 Hurlspit Goblins U2 .25 .60
- ❑ 74 Ide Tadaji (Experienced) U1 .25 .60
- ❑ 75 Imperial Wedding U2 .25 .60
- ❑ 76 Increased Production C2 .10 .20
- ❑ 77 Into the Heavens U1 .25 .60
- ❑ 78 Iron Mountain U1 1.00 2.50
- ❑ 79 Isawa Tomo (Experienced 2) U1 1.00 2.50
- ❑ 80 Jal-Pur Raiders U1 .25 .60
- ❑ 81 Jama Suru (Experienced) U1 1.00 2.50
- ❑ 82 Kaede's Tears R2 .60 1.50
- ❑ 83 Kage (Experienced 5 Akodo Kage) R1 1.00 2.50
- ❑ 84 Kakita Kryuko C2 .10 .20
- ❑ 85 Kakita Yoshi (Experienced 3) U1 1.00 2.50
- ❑ 86 Karmic Link U2 .25 .60
- ❑ 87 Katana of the Twilight Mountains C1 .10 .20
- ❑ 88 Keda C2 .10 .20
- ❑ 89 Kingdom of Ghosts C2 .10 .20
- ❑ 90 Kitsu Motso (Experienced 2) R2 1.00 2.50
- ❑ 91 Kolat Chambers U2 .25 .60
- ❑ 92 Kolat Courtiers U1 .20 .50
- ❑ 93 Kosaten Shiro F 1.25 3.00
- ❑ 94 Kosaten Shiro U1 1.25 3.00
- ❑ 95 Kyoso No Oni (Experienced 2) R2 1.25 3.00
- ❑ 96 Kyuden Kitsune U1 1.25 3.00
- ❑ 97 Lessons of Honor U2 .20 .50
- ❑ 98 Lost Souls R1 1.25 3.00
- ❑ 99 Magistrate's Blade U2 .25 .60
- ❑ 100 Master Courtier U2 1.25 3.00
- ❑ 101 Matsu Agetoki (Experienced 2) R2 1.00 2.50
- ❑ 102 Matsu Domotai C2 .10 .20
- ❑ 103 Mat'tck C1 .10 .20
- ❑ 104 Mirumoto Taki (Experienced) U1 1.00 2.50
- ❑ 105 Moon and Sun U1 .40 1.00
- ❑ 106 Moto Chargers C1 .10 .20
- ❑ 107 Moto Gaheris F 1.00 2.50
- ❑ 108 Moto Tsugi C2 .10 .20
- ❑ 109 Mujina C1 .40 1.00
- ❑ 110 Mukami (Experienced 2) R2 .60 1.50
- ❑ 111 Naga C2 .40 1.00
- ❑ 112 Naga Vipers U1 .40 1.00
- ❑ 113 Naka Kuro (Experienced 2) R2 1.25 3.00
- ❑ 114 Nature Provides C1 .10 .20
- ❑ 115 Ninja Mystic (Experienced 3 Hoseki) R2 .60 1.50
- ❑ 116 Ninja Shadow-Walker (Experienced 2) U1 1.25 3.00
- ❑ 117 Nori Farm C1 .10 .20
- ❑ 118 Norikesh C2 .10 .20
- ❑ 119 Northern Provinces of the Moto F 1.25 3.00
- ❑ 120 Northern Provinces of the Moto U1 1.25 3.00
- ❑ 121 Oni no Byoki U1 .40 1.00
- ❑ 122 Oni no Gorusei C2 .10 .20
- ❑ 123 Oni no Okura (Experienced 2) U2 1.00 2.50
- ❑ 124 Oni Podling R2 .60 1.50
- ❑ 125 Orochi Tattoo U2 .40 1.00
- ❑ 126 Otaku Kamoko (Experienced 4) R1 2.50 6.00
- ❑ 127 Otaku Sahijir C1 .10 .20
- ❑ 128 Otomo Sensei R2 .60 1.50
- ❑ 129 Otomo Towers U1 .25 .60
- ❑ 130 O-Ushi Sensei R1 1.00 2.50
- ❑ 131 O-Ushi's Hammer R1 1.00 2.50
- ❑ 132 Overwhelm C2 .10 .20
- ❑ 133 Passage of Time U2 .40 1.00
- ❑ 134 Past Glories U1 .25 .60
- ❑ 135 Political Favors C1 .10 .20
- ❑ 136 Public Ridicule U1 .25 .60
- ❑ 137 Question Without an Answer R2 .60 1.50
- ❑ 138 Rank Hath Privilege R2 1.00 2.50
- ❑ 139 Ratling Pack C1 .40 1.00
- ❑ 140 Rebirth of the Dark Daughter U2 .25 .60
- ❑ 141 Regional Travel Papers C1 .10 .20
- ❑ 142 Restoring the Age of Myth U1 .25 .60
- ❑ 143 Return of Thunder U2 .25 .60
- ❑ 144 Riding Yari U1 .20 .50
- ❑ 145 Ruined Earth R1 1.00 2.50
- ❑ 146 Ryoshun's Last Words C2 .10 .20
- ❑ 147 Seppun Toshiken (Experienced 2) R2 .60 1.50
- ❑ 148 Shadow Assassins C1 .10 .20
- ❑ 149 Shadowed Wastes U2 .25 .60
- ❑ 150 Shiba Kiku C2 .10 .20
- ❑ 151 Shiba Tsukune (Experienced 3) R2 .60 1.50
- ❑ 152 Shinjo Hanari (Experienced 2) R2 1.00 2.50
- ❑ 153 Shirasu Sensei R1 6.00 15.00
- ❑ 154 Shiryo no Chiroku R1 1.00 2.50
- ❑ 155 Shiryo no Gohei R1 1.00 2.50
- ❑ 156 Shiryo no Hantei R1 1.00 2.50
- ❑ 157 Shiryo no Kunliu R1 1.00 2.50
- ❑ 158 Shrine of the Dead C1 .10 .20
- ❑ 159 Shrines of the Emperor U1 .25 .60
- ❑ 160 Sniping U2 .40 1.00
- ❑ 161 Something Worth Dying For U2 .25 .60
- ❑ 162 Son of the Clan C2 .10 .20
- ❑ 163 Soul of the Empire U2 .25 .60
- ❑ 164 Spy Network C1 .10 .20
- ❑ 165 Steel and Iron R2 .60 1.50
- ❑ 166 Strike from Behind R2 .60 1.50
- ❑ 167 Suana (Experienced 2) R2 1.00 2.50
- ❑ 168 Swamp Marsh U2 .20 .50
- ❑ 169 Temples of the Crow U1 1.25 3.00
- ❑ 170 Temples of the New Tao C1 .10 .20
- ❑ 171 Tetsuya Sensei R2 .60 1.50
- ❑ 172 The Citadel of the Hiruma U1 2.00 5.00
- ❑ 173 The Dark Path of Shadow U1 1.25 3.00
- ❑ 174 The Emperor Returns U2 .40 1.00
- ❑ 175 The Grey Crane (Experienced 3 Kakita Toshimoko) R1 2.50 6.00
- ❑ 176 The Kitsu Tombs U1 1.25 3.00
- ❑ 177 The New Akasha U1 1.25 3.00
- ❑ 178 The Spawning Ground U1 1.25 3.00
- ❑ 179 The Sun Returns R2 1.50 4.00
- ❑ 180 The Towers of the Yogo U1 1.50 4.00
- ❑ 181 Thunder Dragon (Experienced) R1 1.25 3.00
- ❑ 182 Time of Destiny U2 .25 .60
- ❑ 183 Togashi Mitsu (Experienced 2) R1 1.00 2.50
- ❑ 184 Togashi Mitsu F .40 1.00
- ❑ 185 Togashi Senai C2 .10 .20
- ❑ 186 Toku (Experienced 3) U1 1.00 2.50
- ❑ 187 Toritaka Mariko C2 .10 .20

TCG/CCG

❑ 188 Toturi the First (Experienced 4 Toturi) F	.40	1.00
❑ 189 Travelling Caravan C1	.10	.20
❑ 190 Tsunami Legion R2	.60	1.50
❑ 191 Undead C1	.40	1.00
❑ 192 Vigilant Keep of the Monkey F	1.00	2.50
❑ 193 Vigilant Keep of the Monkey U1	1.00	2.50
❑ 194 Void Dragon (Experienced) R1	1.25	3.00
❑ 195 Void Guard U1	.25	.60
❑ 196 Water Dragon (Experienced) R1	1.00	2.50
❑ 197 When Spirits Walked U1	.25	.60
❑ 198 Where the Sun Walked R2	.60	1.50
❑ 199 Yaro C1	.10	.20
❑ 200 Yasuki Nokatsu (Experienced 2) U1	.25	.60
❑ 201 Yodin Sensei R2	.60	1.50
❑ 202 Yoritomo (Experienced 3) R2	1.00	2.50
❑ 203 Yoritomo Furukae (Experienced) U1	.25	.60
❑ 204 Yotsu Shoku C1	.10	.20
❑ 205 Z'orr'tek C1	.10	.20

2000 Legend of the Five Rings The Spirit Wars

BOOSTER BOX (36)	150.00	250.00
BOOSTER PACK (15)	5.00	10.00
❑ 1 Akodo Ginawa (Experienced 4 Ginawa) R1	2.50	6.00
❑ 2 Akodo Ijiasu U2	.30	.75
❑ 3 Akodo Quehao R2	1.25	3.00
❑ 4 Akodo Sensei U1	.30	.75
❑ 5 Amaterasu's Furnace U2	.20	.50
❑ 6 Ancestral Dictate U2	.20	.50
❑ 7 Ancestral Protection R2	.60	1.50
❑ 8 Ancient Knowledge U1	.30	.75
❑ 9 Arriving at the Imperial Gates U2	.20	.50
❑ 10 Asako Misao U2	.20	.50
❑ 11 Asako Riders R2	.60	1.50
❑ 12 Back Banner C1	.10	.20
❑ 13 Battle at White Shore Plain C2	.20	.50
❑ 14 Battle of Drowned Honor C2	.10	.20
❑ 15 Battle of Quiet Winds C2	.10	.20
❑ 16 Battle of Shallow Waters C2	.10	.20
❑ 17 Bayushi Baku (Experienced) R2	.60	1.50
❑ 18 Bayushi Paneki C2	.10	.20
❑ 19 Bayushi Yojiro (Experienced 2) R1	1.50	4.00
❑ 20 Beginning and End R2	.60	1.50
❑ 21 Birth of the Anvil R1	1.25	3.00
❑ 22 Birth of the Sword R1	1.25	3.00
❑ 23 Birth of the Wolf R1	1.00	2.50
❑ 24 Bitter R2	2.00	5.00
❑ 25 Bronze Lantern R2	.60	1.50
❑ 26 Call the Spirit R2	.60	1.50
❑ 27 Chou-Sin C2	.10	.20
❑ 28 Clay Soldiers C2	.10	.20
❑ 29 Cliff of Golden Tears U2	.20	.50
❑ 30 Crab Tattoo R2	.60	1.50
❑ 31 Cursed Ground U1	.60	1.50
❑ 32 Daidoji Hachi C1	.10	.20
❑ 33 Dark Secrets C2	.10	.20
❑ 34 Devastation of Beiden Pass C/R	.20	.50
❑ 35 Doji Kurohito U2	.20	.50
❑ 36 Doji Meihu U2	.20	.50
❑ 37 Doji Reju (Experienced 2) R1	4.00	10.00
❑ 38 Doji Reju (Experienced 2) R1	3.00	8.00
❑ 39 Dragon Dancers C1	.10	.20
❑ 40 Earthquake at Otosan Uchi R1	.60	1.50
❑ 41 East Wall of Otosan Uchi (Experienced) R1	.60	1.50
❑ 42 Elite Light Infantry F	.10	.20
❑ 43 Elite Medium Infantry F	.10	.20
❑ 44 Emperor's Under-Hand R1	4.00	10.00
❑ 45 Emperor's Favor R1	.60	1.50
❑ 46 Empress's Guard R2	1.25	3.00
❑ 47 Evil Feeds Upon Itself F	.10	.20
❑ 48 Fall of the Alliance R1	.60	1.50
❑ 49 Fall on Your Knees R2	1.50	4.00
❑ 50 Fallen Ground C2	.20	.50
❑ 51 Fallen Legion U2	.20	.50
❑ 52 Fields of Darkness C1	.10	.20
❑ 53 Fields of the Sun R1	1.25	3.00
❑ 54 Giuniko C1	.60	1.50
❑ 55 Great Crater R1	.60	1.50
❑ 56 Guard the House C2	.10	.20
❑ 57 Hantei XVI F	.30	.75
❑ 58 Hesitation U2	.20	.50
❑ 59 Hida Hio C2	.10	.20
❑ 60 Hida Kuon C2	.10	.20
❑ 61 Hida Kuroda C2	.10	.20
❑ 62 Hida Sukune (Experienced 2) R1	3.00	8.00
❑ 63 Hida Tsuneo R1	2.50	6.00
❑ 64 Hitomi's Glare R2	.60	1.50
❑ 65 Honorable R2	2.50	6.00
❑ 66 Ide Gokun U2	.20	.50
❑ 67 Ikoma Tsai C2	.10	.20
❑ 68 Imperial Census R1	2.50	6.00
❑ 69 Infantry Charge C2	.10	.20
❑ 70 Inkyo C1	.10	.20
❑ 71 Intelligence Agent U2	.30	.75
❑ 72 Interruption U2	.30	.75
❑ 73 Iron Mempo C1	.10	.20
❑ 74 Isawa Metigaru C1	.10	.20
❑ 75 Isawa Nakamuro C1	.10	.20
❑ 76 Kaiu Sensei R2	.60	1.50
❑ 77 Kakita Kaiten (Experienced) R2	.60	1.50
❑ 78 Kamoko's Constellatión R1	1.25	3.00
❑ 79 Kitsu Deijiko C2	.10	.20
❑ 80 Kitsune C1	.10	.20
❑ 81 Knowing Lands and Giving Trees U1	.30	.75
❑ 82 Kohuri C2	.10	.20
❑ 83 Kuni Utagu (Experienced) R1	2.50	6.00
❑ 84 Lady of the Forest Sensei U1	.30	.75
❑ 85 Lalesha C1	.10	.20
❑ 86 Last Gift C2	.10	.20
❑ 87 Lay the Blame C2	.10	.20
❑ 88 Let the Spirit Move You C1	.10	.20
❑ 89 Lsinyuan C1	.10	.20
❑ 90 Luring Tactics U2	.30	.75
❑ 91 Mara's Farewell C2	.10	.20
❑ 92 Master Smith Ascends C1	.10	.20
❑ 93 Matsu Goemon F	.10	.20
❑ 94 Mirumoto Ukira C2	.10	.20
❑ 95 Mirumoto Uso (Experienced) R2	.60	1.50
❑ 96 Miya Dosonu U2	.30	.75
❑ 97 Miya Sensei R2	.60	1.50
❑ 98 Miya Yemi U2	2.50	6.00
❑ 99 Mizuichi C2	.10	.20
❑ 100 Mokoto U2	.20	.50
❑ 101 Morito (Experienced 2 Morito) R1	1.25	3.00
❑ 102 Mortal Flesh U1	.20	.50
❑ 103 Moshi Shanegon U2	.30	.75
❑ 104 Moto Hideyo C1	.10	.20
❑ 105 Moto Technique R2	.60	1.50
❑ 106 Moto Vordu C2	.10	.20
❑ 107 Moving the Wind U1	.30	.75
❑ 108 Nage-yari C1	.10	.20
❑ 109 New Kimono C1	.10	.20
❑ 110 Nightmare C2	.20	.50
❑ 111 Noble Halls of the Akodo F	.30	.75
❑ 112 Noekam U2	.20	.50
❑ 113 North Wall of Otosan Uchi (Experienced) R1	.60	1.50
❑ 114 Obsidian Statues R1	.60	1.50
❑ 115 Old Debts C2	.10	.20
❑ 116 Oni no Fushiki C1	.60	1.50
❑ 117 Oni no Yamaso C1	.10	.20
❑ 118 Oni Spawn C2	.10	.20
❑ 119 Otomo Dsichi R1	1.25	3.00
❑ 120 Otomo Hoketuhime C1	.10	.20
❑ 121 Personal Sacrifice C2	.10	.20
❑ 122 Poorly Placed Garden C1	1.00	2.50
❑ 123 Quiet Tombs C1	.10	.20
❑ 124 Ratling Scroungers R2	.60	1.50
❑ 125 Return for Training U2	1.25	3.00
❑ 126 Revealing the Bastard R1	.60	1.50
❑ 127 Revering the Past R1	1.25	3.00
❑ 128 Right to Rule R1	1.25	3.00
❑ 129 Roshungi (Experienced) R2	.60	1.50
❑ 130 Ruin and Devastation U1	.20	.50
❑ 131 Saigorei (Experienced) R2	.60	1.50
❑ 132 Scaring the Masses U2	.30	.75
❑ 133 Scholarship C2	.10	.20
❑ 134 Shasyahkar (Experienced) R2	.60	1.50
❑ 135 Shaunasea U2	.20	.50
❑ 136 Shiba Aikune C2	.10	.20
❑ 137 Shiba Ningen (Experienced) R1	1.25	3.00
❑ 138 Shinjo Shono (Experienced) R2	.60	1.50
❑ 139 Shiryo no Ch'i R1	1.00	2.50
❑ 140 Shiryo no Hotei R2	.60	1.50
❑ 141 Shiryo no Nyoko R1	1.25	3.00
❑ 142 Shiryo no Rohata R1	1.25	3.00
❑ 143 Shiryo no Shoju R1	2.50	6.00
❑ 144 Shiryo no Taisa R1	1.25	3.00
❑ 145 Shiryo no Ujik-hai R1	1.25	3.00
❑ 146 Shosuro Chian (Experienced) R1	2.50	6.00
❑ 147 Shrine of the Evening Star R1	.10	.20
❑ 148 Shrine of the Spirits F	.30	.75
❑ 149 Shuriken C1	.10	.20
❑ 150 Sign of Weakness U2	.30	.75
❑ 151 Signal Corps U2	.20	.50
❑ 152 Simple Huts C1	.30	.75
❑ 153 Snow Crane Tattoo R2	1.25	3.00
❑ 154 Sodegarami C1	.10	.20
❑ 155 Soshi Angai U2	.20	.50
❑ 156 Soul Sword C1	.10	.20
❑ 157 South Wall of Otosan Uchi (Experienced) R1	1.25	3.00
❑ 158 Spirit Bells U2	.20	.50
❑ 159 Spirif Hounds C2	.10	.20
❑ 160 Star-Filled Steel U2	.20	.50
❑ 161 Sumai Match R1	1.50	4.00
❑ 162 Suzume Roshi C1	.10	.20
❑ 163 Suzume Sensei U1	.40	1.00
❑ 164 Taikon U2	.20	.50
❑ 165 Tamori Chosai C1	.10	.20
❑ 166 Tamori Shaitung U2	.20	.50
❑ 167 Te'tik'kir C1	.10	.20
❑ 168 Temptation C2	.10	.20
❑ 169 Three-Stone River U2	.30	.75
❑ 170 Through the Flames C2	.10	.20
❑ 171 Togashi Mio C1	.10	.20
❑ 172 Torii Arch C1	.10	.20
❑ 173 Torii Tattoo C2	.10	.20
❑ 174 Towers of the Asako F	.30	.75
❑ 175 Treaty U1	.30	.75
❑ 176 Tsi Yoji U2	.20	.50
❑ 177 Tsuko Sensei F	.30	.75
❑ 178 Tsuko's Heart U2	.20	.50
❑ 179 Tsuruchi Okame C1	.20	.50
❑ 180 Turn of Fate U2	.20	.50
❑ 181 Uidori U2	.20	.50
❑ 182 Undead Legion U2	.20	.50
❑ 183 Uona Sensei F	.30	.75
❑ 184 Usagi Gohei U2	.20	.50
❑ 185 Utaku Yu-Pan U2	.20	.50
❑ 186 Wall of Bones C1	.10	.20
❑ 187 War Paints R2	.60	1.50
❑ 188 Warriors of the Great Climb U2	.20	.50
❑ 189 Wasp Sensei U1	.40	1.00
❑ 190 Weapons Cache C2	.10	.20
❑ 191 West Wall of Otosan Uchi (Experienced) R1	.60	1.50
❑ 192 Where Tsanuri Fell R2	.40	1.00
❑ 193 Witch Hunt U2	.30	.75
❑ 194 Witch Hunter's Accusation U2	.30	.75
❑ 195 Wutho U2	.60	1.50
❑ 196 Yakamo's Smile R2	.60	1.50
❑ 197 Yeiseo C1	.10	.20
❑ 198 Yoee'trr U2	.60	1.50
❑ 199 Yokai no Mizushai R2	.60	1.50
❑ 200 Yoritomo Aramasu R1	4.00	10.00
❑ 201 Yoritomo Kitao C2	.10	.20
❑ 202 Yoritomo Yukue R1	1.25	3.00

2001 Legend of the Five Rings A Perfect Cut

BOOSTER BOX (48)	20.00	40.00
BOOSTER PACK (11)	1.00	2.00
❑ 1 A Desperate Act C2	.10	.20
❑ 2 A Matter of Pride U	.20	.50
❑ 3 A Plague Spreads U	.20	.50
❑ 4 Acquiring Favor U	.60	1.50
❑ 5 Advance Scout U	.20	.50
❑ 6 Akodo Setai C2	.10	.20
❑ 7 Anekkusai's Feathers C2	.10	.20
❑ 8 Asahina Handen U	.20	.50
❑ 9 Banner Guard C2	.10	.20
❑ 10 Bayushi Tai U	.20	.50
❑ 11 Bayushi Tasagore F	.75	2.00
❑ 12 Blazing Sun U	.20	.50
❑ 13 Blood Madness R	1.00	2.50
❑ 14 Breaking Concentration R	1.00	2.50
❑ 15 By Will of the Wind R	1.00	2.50
❑ 16 Cast Down the Meek C2	.10	.20
❑ 17 Command Group C4	.10	.20
❑ 18 Connecting Walls C2	.10	.20
❑ 19 Contemplation of Osano-Wo R	1.00	2.50
❑ 20 Contingency Planning R	1.00	2.50
❑ 21 Crab Recruiter R	.60	1.50
❑ 22 Crane Tradesman R	.60	1.50
❑ 23 Daidoji Megumi C2	.10	.20
❑ 24 Dairu no Shiryo R	.60	1.50
❑ 25 Dairya's Cackling Skull R	.60	1.50
❑ 26 Defensive Duty C2	.10	.20
❑ 27 Diplomatic Apprentice C2	.10	.20
❑ 28 Doji Kurohito (Experienced) F	.60	1.50
❑ 29 Elemental Shock U	.20	.50
❑ 30 Endless Deluge R	.60	1.50
❑ 31 Family Tactics C2	.10	.20
❑ 32 Fire and Air C2	.10	.20
❑ 33 Fortify U	.20	.50
❑ 34 Fukurokujin Seido U	.20	.50
❑ 35 Furious Strike R	.60	1.50
❑ 36 Guard House C2	.10	.20
❑ 37 Hida Kagore U	.20	.50
❑ 38 Hida Kuon (Experienced) F	.40	1.00
❑ 39 Hida Reiha C2	.10	.20
❑ 40 Hiruma Todori C2	.10	.20
❑ 41 Hunter C2	.10	.20
❑ 42 Hyakute no Oni U	.20	.50
❑ 43 Iaijutsu Lesson C2	.10	.20
❑ 44 Ide Michisuna R	.60	1.50
❑ 45 In Light of Darkness U	.20	.50
❑ 46 Inside Agent U	.20	.50
❑ 47 Interesting Sticks U	.25	.60
❑ 48 Isawa Hochiu (Experienced) R	.60	1.50
❑ 49 Isawa Nakamuro (Experienced) R	.60	1.50
❑ 50 Isawa Nodotai U	.25	.60
❑ 51 Kaeru Kenko U	.20	.50
❑ 52 Kaiu Hosaru U	.20	.50
❑ 53 Kakita Duelling Academy F	.60	1.50
❑ 54 Kakita Gosha U	.20	.50
❑ 55 Kayobun U	.20	.50
❑ 56 Kitsune Taro C2	.10	.20
❑ 57 Kokoro C2	.10	.20
❑ 58 Kukan-do U	.20	.50
❑ 59 Kyuden Hida F	.40	1.00
❑ 60 Lion Scout R	.60	1.50
❑ 61 Mapped Region C2	.10	.20
❑ 62 Matsu Domotai (Experienced) R	.60	1.50
❑ 63 Matsu Hyun C2	.10	.20
❑ 64 Matsu Kenji R	.60	1.50
❑ 65 Matsu Kenseiko U	.20	.50
❑ 66 Memorial C2	.10	.20
❑ 67 Mining Foreman C2	.10	.20
❑ 68 Minor Illusions R	1.00	2.50
❑ 69 Mirumoto Junnosuke U	.20	.50
❑ 70 Mirumoto Taiu C2	.10	.20
❑ 71 Miya Heikichi R	.60	1.50
❑ 72 Moto Chen R	1.00	2.50
❑ 73 Moto Reijiro U	.20	.50
❑ 74 Mujina Gang C2	.10	.20
❑ 75 Nagamaki C2	.10	.20
❑ 76 Needed at the Wall U	.20	.50
❑ 77 No One Wins U	.20	.50
❑ 78 Omoni C2	.10	.20
❑ 79 Open Arms C2	.10	.20
❑ 80 Osoreru no Oni C2	.10	.20
❑ 81 Outmaneuvered by Force U	.25	.60
❑ 82 Outmaneuvered in Court U	.25	.60
❑ 83 Persuasion R	.60	1.50
❑ 84 Phoenix Library R	.60	1.50
❑ 85 Plum Tree Training Ground U	.20	.50
❑ 86 Political Warfare U	.20	.50
❑ 87 Prepared for the Enemy C2	.10	.20
❑ 88 Preparing the Edge U	.20	.50
❑ 89 Rain of Emeralds U	.20	.50
❑ 90 Reassert One's Mettle C2	.10	.20
❑ 91 Retired Sohei C2	.10	.20
❑ 92 Returned to the Pit R	.60	1.50
❑ 93 Ronin at the Wall C2	.10	.20
❑ 94 Scorpion Distractor R	.60	1.50
❑ 95 Seppun Isei U	.20	.50
❑ 96 Shadowlands Bastion R	.60	1.50
❑ 97 Shallow Graves C2	.10	.20
❑ 98 Shiba Mirabu R	.60	1.50
❑ 99 Shiba Unasagi C2	.10	.20
❑ 100 Shinjo Sanraku C2	.10	.20
❑ 101 Shinsei's Smile R	.60	1.50
❑ 102 Shosuro Gardens F	.40	1.00
❑ 103 Shosuro Higatsuku U	.25	.60
❑ 104 Shosuro Yasuko C2	.10	.20
❑ 105 Show of Strength R	.60	1.50
❑ 106 Snowy Fields C2	.10	.20
❑ 107 Sohei R	.60	1.50
❑ 108 Soshi Tishi C2	.10	.20
❑ 109 Speed of the Waterfall U	.20	.50
❑ 110 Spyglass U	.20	.50
❑ 111 Stand as Stone U	.20	.50
❑ 112 Stand Your Ground C2	.10	.20
❑ 113 Standing Tall C2	.10	.20
❑ 114 Strong Guard U	.20	.50
❑ 115 Summoning the Gale C2	.10	.20
❑ 116 Tachi U	.20	.50
❑ 117 Taijikku U	.20	.50
❑ 118 Taiko no Shiryo R	.60	1.50
❑ 119 Tainted Bushi U	.20	.50
❑ 120 Tamori Chieko C2	.10	.20
❑ 121 Tampako no Shiryo R	.60	1.50
❑ 122 Tea House C2	.10	.20
❑ 123 Temple of the Dragon R	.60	1.50
❑ 124 The Enemy You Deserve R	.60	1.50
❑ 125 The Great Climb C2	.10	.20
❑ 126 The Greatest Cost U	.25	.60
❑ 127 The Hand of Thunder R	.60	1.50
❑ 128 The Power of Nothing R	.60	1.50
❑ 129 The Wolf Speaks R	.60	1.50
❑ 130 Thuk-Kigi's War Machine R	.60	1.50
❑ 131 Thunder Calls to Fortune R	.60	1.50
❑ 132 Togashi Iroshi U	.20	.50
❑ 133 Togashi Satsu R	.60	1.50
❑ 134 Too Much Too Soon U	.20	.50
❑ 135 Training Dojo U	.20	.50
❑ 136 Training Exercises C2	.10	.20
❑ 137 Traitor's Grove R	.60	1.50
❑ 138 Tsudao's Challenge U	.20	.50
❑ 139 Tsuno Kurushimi U	.25	.60
❑ 140 Tsuno Ravagers R	.60	1.50
❑ 141 Tsuno Squad U	.20	.50
❑ 142 Twenty Goblin Winter R	.60	1.50
❑ 143 Unavoidable Destiny R	.60	1.50
❑ 144 Unexpected Assault R	.60	1.50
❑ 145 Unexpected Confrontation R	.60	1.50
❑ 146 Unicorn Marketeer R	.60	1.50
❑ 147 Unspeakable Preparations U	.20	.50
❑ 148 Usagi Kashira C2	.10	.20
❑ 149 Utaku Mu Dan C2	.10	.20
❑ 150 While the Empire Watches U	.20	.50
❑ 151 Yasuki Heikichi C2	.10	.20
❑ 152 Yasuki Palaces R	4.00	10.00
❑ 153 Yasuki Palaces R	2.50	6.00
❑ 154 Yogoso no Shiryo R	.60	1.50
❑ 155 Yoritomo Kitao (Experienced) R	.60	1.50
❑ 156 Yoshi's Fan R	.60	1.50

2001 Legend of the Five Rings An Oni's Fury

BOOSTER BOX (48)	25.00	50.00
BOOSTER PACK (11)	1.00	2.00
❑ 1 A New Legacy R	.60	1.50
❑ 2 Aikune's Wrath R	1.00	2.50
❑ 3 Akodo Koun U	.20	.50
❑ 4 Akodo Senke C	.10	.20
❑ 5 An Error in Orders R	.60	1.50
❑ 6 Ancestral Shrine C	.10	.20
❑ 7 Armor of Shadows (Experienced Armor of the Shadow Warrior) R	.60	1.50
❑ 8 Asako Itaru U	.20	.50
❑ 9 Asako Shuntaro C	.10	.20
❑ 10 Ashigaru Barracks U	.20	.50
❑ 11 Ashigaru Hordes C	.10	.20
❑ 12 Bayushi Ambushers U	.20	.50
❑ 13 Bayushi Paneki (Experienced) R	1.25	3.00
❑ 14 Bayushi Shixiang C	.10	.20
❑ 15 Benefactor C	.10	.20
❑ 16 Blacksteel Blade C	.10	.20
❑ 17 Blue Skies C	.10	.20
❑ 18 Brightest Winter U	.20	.50
❑ 19 Burning the Tombs R	1.00	2.50
❑ 20 Carpenter Wall Falls U	.20	.50
❑ 21 Cascading Fire C	.10	.20
❑ 22 Celestial Vision U	.20	.50
❑ 23 Child of the Last Wish U	.20	.50
❑ 24 Citadel of Daigotsu F	1.25	3.00
❑ 25 City of Night R	1.00	2.50
❑ 26 Cleared Grounds U	.20	.50
❑ 27 Coastal Region U	.20	.50
❑ 28 Complications R	1.00	2.50
❑ 29 Consecrate the Land C	.10	.20
❑ 30 Daidoji Enai C	.10	.20
❑ 31 Daidoji Gudeta U	.20	.50
❑ 32 Daikyu U	.20	.50
❑ 33 Darkest Winter U	.20	.50
❑ 34 Dirty Scum! R	.60	1.50
❑ 35 Doji Yasuyo (Experienced) R	.60	1.50
❑ 36 Elegant Kimono U	.20	.50
❑ 37 Engage the Enemy R	.60	1.50
❑ 38 Everpresent Fear U	.20	.50
❑ 39 Follow the Path U	.20	.50
❑ 40 Fox Nagamaki U	.20	.50
❑ 41 Friendly Traveler Village C	.10	.20
❑ 42 Frontal Assault C	.10	.20
❑ 43 Gaijutsu no Shiryo R	.60	1.50
❑ 44 Harvest Time U	.20	.50
❑ 45 Hasty Exploitation C	.10	.20
❑ 46 Hida Sakamoto R	.60	1.50
❑ 47 Hida Sunao U	.20	.50
❑ 48 Hiruma Archers U	.20	.50
❑ 49 Hiruma Nichi C	.10	.20
❑ 50 Hitomi Akuai (Experienced) R	.60	1.50
❑ 51 Hitomi Kagetora (Experienced) F	1.00	2.50
❑ 52 Hoshi's Claw U	.20	.50
❑ 53 Hoturi's Blade U	.20	.50
❑ 54 House of the Red Lotus C	.10	.20
❑ 55 Ikoma Fudai U	.20	.50
❑ 56 Imperial Scrutiny U	.20	.50
❑ 57 Inner Wall C	.10	.20
❑ 58 Isawa Ihara R	.60	1.50
❑ 59 Iuchi Lixue R	.60	1.50
❑ 60 Kaiu Ryojiro C	.10	.20
❑ 61 Kaneka's Advance C	.10	.20
❑ 62 Kharmic Unison C	.10	.20
❑ 63 Ki-Rin's Shrine (Experienced) R	.60	1.50
❑ 64 Kitsu Dejiko (Experienced) R	1.00	2.50
❑ 65 Kitsuki Remata U	.20	.50
❑ 66 Kitsune Gohei R	.60	1.50
❑ 67 Kiyomi U	.20	.50
❑ 68 Know the Enemy R	.60	1.50
❑ 69 Know the Truth R	.60	1.50
❑ 70 Kuni Kiyoshi U	.20	.50
❑ 71 Lion Warcats U	.30	.75
❑ 72 Lobbyist C	.10	.20
❑ 73 Logistics Problem U	.20	.50
❑ 74 Lost Glories U	.20	.50
❑ 75 Mantis Raiders R	.60	1.50
❑ 76 Masume Wakizashi C	.10	.20
❑ 77 Matsu Shinya C	.10	.20
❑ 78 Mirumoto Tsuge C	.10	.20
❑ 79 Miya Hatori R	.60	1.50
❑ 80 Moment in the Sun R	.60	1.50
❑ 81 Moshi Kalani U	.20	.50
❑ 82 Moto Chagatai (Experienced) F	.60	1.50
❑ 83 Moto Vordu (Experienced) R	.60	1.50
❑ 84 Moto Wardogs U	.20	.50
❑ 85 Moto Zhijuan U	.20	.50
❑ 86 Naga Tattoo U	.20	.50
❑ 87 Naka Tokei (Experienced Morito Tokei) R	.60	1.50
❑ 88 Natsune no Shiryo R	.60	1.50
❑ 89 New Emerald Champion R	.60	1.50
❑ 90 Nezumi Technique C	.10	.20
❑ 91 Osoreru no Oni (Experienced) R	1.25	3.00
❑ 92 Otomo Motoshi C	.10	.20
❑ 93 Poetry Contest R	.60	1.50
❑ 94 Por'ee-rep C	.10	.20
❑ 95 Power C	.10	.20
❑ 96 Quench the Ashes R	.60	1.50
❑ 97 Remember the Mountain C	.10	.20
❑ 98 Rewards of Rank C	.10	.20
❑ 99 Ruins of the Kappa R	.60	1.50
❑ 100 Rumors U	.20	.50
❑ 101 Sacred Tunnels U	.20	.50
❑ 102 Sanshu Denki U	.20	.50
❑ 103 Seeking the Master R	.60	1.50
❑ 104 Seeping Darkness U	.20	.50
❑ 105 Shatter the Elements U	.20	.50
❑ 106 Shiba Aikune (Experienced) R	.60	1.50
❑ 107 Shiba Arai C	.10	.20
❑ 108 Shinjo Huang C	.10	.20
❑ 109 Shinmaki Monastery C	.10	.20
❑ 110 Shintao Library C	.10	.20
❑ 111 Shiro Ide F	1.00	2.50
❑ 112 Shiro Mirumoto F	.60	1.50
❑ 113 Show No Fear C	.10	.20
❑ 114 Slaughter the Scout C	.10	.20
❑ 115 Sleepless Nights C	.10	.20
❑ 116 Soshi Eiji U	.20	.50
❑ 117 Spider Tattoo U	.20	.50
❑ 118 Stolen Records C	.10	.20
❑ 119 Sun Kites U	.20	.50
❑ 120 Sun Tao's Tessen R	.60	1.50
❑ 121 Taking the Wall U	.20	.50
❑ 122 Tamori Hiroko C	.10	.20
❑ 123 Tetsuko no Shiryo R	.60	1.50
❑ 124 The Calm of Shinsei U	.20	.50
❑ 125 The Company You Keep C	.10	.20
❑ 126 The First Legion R	.60	1.50
❑ 127 The Jaws of Defeat C	.10	.20
❑ 128 The Jaws of Victory C	.10	.20
❑ 129 The Masters Imprisoned R	.60	1.50
❑ 130 The Oracle Awakens R	.60	1.50
❑ 131 The Price of Innocence C	.10	.20

❑ 132 The Thunder's Clap U .20 .50
❑ 133 Thunder of the Earth C .10 .20
❑ 134 Toturi Miyako C .10 .20
❑ 135 Tsukune Ascends R .60 1.50
❑ 136 Tsukune's Choice U .20 .50
❑ 137 Tsuno Attack U .20 .50
❑ 138 Tsuno Scouts U .20 .50
❑ 139 Tsuno Takuma C .10 .20
❑ 140 Usagi Ozaki R .60 1.50
❑ 141 Using the Land C .10 .20
❑ 142 Vengeance U .20 .50
❑ 143 Vordu's Discovery C .10 .20
❑ 144 Word of the Anvil R .60 1.50
❑ 145 Word of the Bastard R .60 1.50
❑ 146 Word of the Sword R .60 1.50
❑ 147 Word of the Wolf R .60 1.50
❑ 148 Written in Blood R .60 1.50
❑ 149 Yakamo's Armor R .60 1.50
❑ 150 Yasuki Hachi (Experienced) R .60 1.50
❑ 151 Yasuki Nishi U .20 .50
❑ 152 Yogo Koji C .10 .20
❑ 153 Yogo Tjeki R .60 1.50
❑ 154 Yokubo F 1.25 3.00
❑ 155 Yoritomo Katoa C .10 .20
❑ 156 Yoshimitsu no Yokai R .60 1.50

2002 Legend of the Five Rings 1,000 Years of Darkness

❑ 1 A Fallen Friend .40 1.00
❑ 2 A Wish Granted 1.25 3.00
❑ 3 Another Hero Falls 1.50 4.00
❑ 4 Aramoro's Promise 3.00 8.00
❑ 5 Asako Kinyue 1.25 3.00
❑ 6 Ashalan Blade 1.25 3.00
❑ 7 Ashura 2.00 5.00
❑ 8 Bayushi Aramoro (Experienced KYD) 3.00 8.00
❑ 9 Birth of the New Hantei 1.00 2.50
❑ 10 Bloodspeaker's Altar 1.25 3.00
❑ 11 Burial Mound .60 1.50
❑ 12 Candas 1.25 3.00
❑ 13 Chamber of the Dark Council 1.00 2.50
❑ 14 Child of Fu Leng 1.25 3.00
❑ 15 Chithith 2.00 5.00
❑ 16 Chuda Retainer 1.25 3.00
❑ 17 Daidoji Uji (Experienced 2) 3.00 8.00
❑ 18 Dark Emperor's Blessing 1.00 2.50
❑ 19 Dark Ring of Air 1.00 2.50
❑ 20 Dark Ring of Earth 1.00 2.50
❑ 21 Dark Ring of Fire 3.00 8.00
❑ 22 Dark Ring of the Void 1.00 2.50
❑ 23 Dark Ring of Water 1.25 3.00
❑ 24 Dim Mak .40 1.00
❑ 25 Everyone Dies .40 1.00
❑ 26 False Scroll .60 1.50
❑ 27 Gifts and Favors 1.00 2.50
❑ 28 Goju Hitomi (Experienced 3 Mirumoto Hitomi) 2.00 5.00
❑ 29 Hakumei 1.00 2.50
❑ 30 Hantei Kachiko (Experienced 3 Bayushi Kachiko) 10.00 25.00
❑ 31 Hantei the 39th 4.00 10.00
❑ 32 Hellbeast 1.00 2.50
❑ 33 Heroic Sacrifice 1.50 4.00
❑ 34 Hida Yakamo (Experienced 3 KYD) 8.00 20.00
❑ 35 Hitomi's Choice 1.00 2.50
❑ 36 Honzo .40 1.00
❑ 37 Horiochi Shoan (Experienced) 1.25 3.00
❑ 38 Hoturi the Heartless (Experienced 3 Doji Hoturi) 8.00 20.00
❑ 39 I Give You My Name 1.25 3.00
❑ 40 Ikoma Ujiaki (Experienced 2 KYD) 1.00 2.50
❑ 41 Importune Kami 3.00 8.00
❑ 42 Isawa Tsuke (Experienced 2) 2.50 6.00
❑ 43 Ishada 1.25 3.00
❑ 44 Island Sanctuary .40 1.00
❑ 45 Kage (Experienced 3 KYD Akodo Kage) 1.00 2.50
❑ 46 Kuni Osaku 1.00 2.50
❑ 47 Kuni Yori (Experienced 2 KYD) 1.25 3.00
❑ 48 Kuruma Date 1.00 2.50
❑ 49 Kuruma Seiro 1.00 2.50
❑ 50 Lesser of Two Evils 1.00 2.50
❑ 51 Matsu Masutaro 2.00 5.00
❑ 52 Moto Kumari .40 1.00
❑ 53 Mountain of Shadows 1.00 2.50
❑ 54 Musha 1.25 3.00
❑ 55 Obsidian and Jade .40 1.00
❑ 56 Obsidian Magistrate 1.25 3.00
❑ 57 Obsidian Mine .40 1.00
❑ 58 Oracle of Thunder (Experienced) 1.25 3.00
❑ 59 Otaku Kamoko (Experienced 3 KYD) 3.00 8.00
❑ 60 Parasitic Oni .40 1.00
❑ 61 Pick Your Battles 2.00 5.00
❑ 62 Pointless Sacrifice 1.00 2.50
❑ 63 Radakast (Experienced 2) 1.00 2.50
❑ 64 Ray of Hope .40 1.00
❑ 65 Ruins of Otosan Uchi 1.25 3.00
❑ 66 Seppun Matsuo 1.50 4.00
❑ 67 Shahai no Yokai 1.00 2.50
❑ 68 Sharp-Sharp Stick 1.00 2.50
❑ 69 Shashakar (Experienced 2) 1.25 3.00
❑ 70 Shiba Tsukune (Experienced 2 KYD) 1.25 3.00
❑ 71 Shosuro Nabukazo 1.00 2.50
❑ 72 Snak .40 1.00
❑ 73 Soul of the Grand Master .40 1.00
❑ 74 Swallowed by the Sea 1.00 2.50
❑ 75 Tadaka's Last Wish 1.00 2.50
❑ 76 Tadaka's Sacrifice 1.00 2.50
❑ 77 The Darkest Shadow 1.00 2.50
❑ 78 The Imperial Palace of Fu Leng 8.00 20.00
❑ 79 The Jade Hand (Experienced) 2.00 5.00
❑ 80 The Maw 1.25 3.00
❑ 81 The Thunders Fall 1.25 3.00
❑ 82 Togashi Mitsu (Experienced 2 KYD) 2.00 5.00
❑ 83 Togashi Sunshen 1.00 2.50
❑ 84 Togashi's Prison 1.00 2.50
❑ 85 Toku (Experienced 2 KYD) 1.00 2.50
❑ 86 Tosekiki 1.00 2.50
❑ 87 Toturi (Experienced 3 KYD) 12.00 30.00
❑ 88 Toturi's Defeat .40 1.00
❑ 89 Toturi's Grave 1.25 3.00
❑ 90 Usagi Masashi .40 1.00
❑ 91 Vengeful Kami .40 1.00
❑ 92 Yogo Junzo (Experienced 2) 3.00 8.00
❑ 93 Yoritomo (Experienced 2 KYD) 12.00 30.00
❑ 94 Zanshar .40 1.00

2002 Legend of the Five Rings Broken Blades

BOOSTER BOX (48) 20.00 40.00
BOOSTER PACK (11) 1.00 2.00

❑ 1 A Time for Action U .20 .50
❑ 2 Agasha Chieh C .10 .20
❑ 3 Akodo Fumio C .10 .20
❑ 4 Akodo Hakuseki U .20 .50
❑ 5 Akodo Yobi U .40 1.00
❑ 6 Ancient Promise U .20 .50
❑ 7 Armor of the Mountain U .20 .50
❑ 8 Asahina Sekawa (Experienced) R 1.25 3.00
❑ 9 Asako Bairei R 1.00 2.50
❑ 10 At Your Command C .10 .20
❑ 11 Badge of Purity C .10 .20
❑ 12 Banzai Charge C .10 .20
❑ 13 Bayushi Katai C .10 .20
❑ 14 Bayushi Yaro C .10 .20
❑ 15 Berserker Rage R 1.25 3.00
❑ 16 Blessed Dojo C .10 .20
❑ 17 Blessed Ward C .10 .20
❑ 18 Blood in the Shinomen U .20 .50
❑ 19 Boundless Sight R 1.25 3.00
❑ 20 Brilliant Armor C .10 .20
❑ 21 Burning Blade C .10 .20
❑ 22 Choke the Soul R 1.00 2.50
❑ 23 Chukandomo R 1.25 3.00
❑ 24 City of Gold U .20 .50
❑ 25 Conscription R 1.00 2.50
❑ 26 Consumption C .10 .20
❑ 27 Corruption's Price C .10 .20
❑ 28 Cut Them Off U .25 .60
❑ 29 Daidoji Heizo C .10 .20
❑ 30 Daidoji Merchants U .40 1.00
❑ 31 Dangerous Extremes R .60 1.50
❑ 32 Dark Oracle of Air R .60 1.50
❑ 33 Deep in Meditation R .60 1.50
❑ 34 Devout Acolyte C .10 .20
❑ 35 Dirty Fighting C .10 .20
❑ 36 Doji Akiko R .60 1.50
❑ 37 Doji Jotaro C .10 .20
❑ 38 Draw Them Out C .10 .20
❑ 39 Embargo U .20 .50
❑ 40 Entrenchment U .20 .50
❑ 41 Falcon Messengers C .10 .20
❑ 42 Field of Amaterasu C .10 .20
❑ 43 Gaheris No Shiryo R .60 1.50
❑ 44 Garen U .20 .50
❑ 45 Gunso C .10 .20
❑ 46 Harsh Winter R .60 1.50
❑ 47 Hida Advisor U .20 .50
❑ 48 Hida Kuon (Experienced 2) F .40 1.00
❑ 49 Hida Reiha (Experienced) R .60 1.50
❑ 50 Hida Tokichiro C .10 .20
❑ 51 Hiruma Ryuichi C .10 .20
❑ 52 Hitomi Eichiko U .20 .50
❑ 53 Hitomi Hogai U .40 1.00
❑ 54 Honor Is My Blade U .20 .50
❑ 55 Hound of the Lost U .20 .50
❑ 56 I Give You My Sword U .20 .50
❑ 57 Iaijutsu Technique R .60 1.50
❑ 58 Ide Sadanobu C .10 .20
❑ 59 Ikoma Otemi (Experienced) R 1.00 2.50
❑ 60 Iron Defenders U .10 .20
❑ 61 Isawa Izumi C .10 .20
❑ 62 Isawa Yoriko U .20 .50
❑ 63 Iuchi Hari U .20 .50
❑ 64 Jade Vein C .10 .20
❑ 65 Jotei R 1.25 3.00
❑ 66 Kaelung R .60 1.50
❑ 67 Katsu C .10 .20
❑ 68 Kisada's Fist R .60 1.50
❑ 69 Kisada's Shrine R .60 1.50
❑ 70 Kozue U .25 .60
❑ 71 Lady Moon's Curse C .10 .20
❑ 72 Lesser Shrine C .10 .20
❑ 73 Lobbyists U .20 .50
❑ 74 Loyal Yojimbo C .10 .20
❑ 75 Maho Bujin U .20 .50
❑ 76 Make Your Choice C .10 .20
❑ 77 Matsu Makiko C .10 .20
❑ 78 Mirumoto Shokan C .10 .20
❑ 79 Moshi Jukio R .60 1.50
❑ 80 Moth Tattoo U .20 .50
❑ 81 Moto Kubulai F 1.25 3.00
❑ 82 Muchitsujo R 1.25 3.00
❑ 83 My Father's Weapon C .10 .20
❑ 84 Mystic Dojo C .10 .20
❑ 85 No More Games, Yasuki U .20 .50
❑ 86 Ogre Hag R .60 1.50
❑ 87 Open the Waves C .10 .20
❑ 88 Open Warfare U .40 1.00
❑ 89 Overwhelmed R .60 1.50
❑ 90 Paddock U .20 .50
❑ 91 Palm Strike R .60 1.50
❑ 92 Path of the Dragon Star U .20 .50
❑ 93 Perfect Silence R .60 1.50
❑ 94 Petition Forgiveness U .20 .50
❑ 95 Pirate Wharf U .20 .50
❑ 96 Plumb the Darkness U .20 .50
❑ 97 Port Town C .10 .20
❑ 98 Private Augury U .20 .50
❑ 99 Quest for Guidance R .60 1.50
❑ 100 Ravenous Podlings R .60 1.50
❑ 101 Razor's Edge Dojo F .40 1.00
❑ 102 Relentless Assault U .20 .50
❑ 103 Rice Paddy U .20 .50
❑ 104 Righteous Protection R .60 1.50
❑ 105 Rising Sun Tattoo U .25 .60
❑ 106 Run Him Down U .25 .60
❑ 107 Sacred Gong C .10 .20
❑ 108 Sailors for Hire C .10 .20
❑ 109 Sampan C .10 .20
❑ 110 Scroll Cache R 1.25 3.00
❑ 111 Seas of Shadow R .60 1.50
❑ 112 Seductive Kansen R .60 1.50
❑ 113 Seiko No Shiryo R .60 1.50
❑ 114 Shadow Dragon U .25 .60
❑ 115 Shiba Hayoto U .20 .50
❑ 116 Shinjo Inoue C .10 .20
❑ 117 Shinjo Noriyori U .20 .50
❑ 118 Shiro Shinjo F .40 1.00
❑ 119 Shosuro Yudoka (Experienced) F .40 1.00
❑ 120 Shrine of Stone R .60 1.50
❑ 121 Slaying Fields C .10 .20
❑ 122 Solitary Engagement U .20 .50
❑ 123 Stand Aside U .20 .50
❑ 124 Tamori Shiatung (Experienced) R .60 1.50
❑ 125 Tamori Shukuen C .10 .20
❑ 126 Ten Thousand As One U .20 .50
❑ 127 The Dark Daughter's Caress R .60 1.50
❑ 128 The Importunate Vu C .10 .20
❑ 129 The Shadowed Tower of the Shosuro F .40 1.00
❑ 130 The Shogun's Fealty U .25 .60
❑ 131 The Steel Throne R .60 1.50
❑ 132 The Wolf's Proposal U .20 .50
❑ 133 Three-Pronged Assault C .10 .20
❑ 134 Time of Loyalty R .60 1.50
❑ 135 Tonfa C .10 .20
❑ 136 Toturi's Shrine R .60 1.50
❑ 137 Trade Hub C .10 .20
❑ 138 Traveling Merchants U .20 .50
❑ 139 Tsuruchi Heishiro C .10 .20
❑ 140 Tsuruchi Yutaka C .10 .20
❑ 141 Twisted Forest C .10 .20
❑ 142 Uona No Shiryo R .60 1.50
❑ 143 Veteran Bushi U .20 .50
❑ 144 We Will Have Revenge R 1.00 2.50
❑ 145 White Stag Burns R .60 1.50
❑ 146 Will of Air R .60 1.50
❑ 147 Will of Earth R .60 1.50
❑ 148 Will of Fire R .60 1.50
❑ 149 Will of Water R .60 1.50
❑ 150 Yasuki Jinn-Kuen U .20 .50
❑ 151 Yasuki Palaces R 1.25 3.00
❑ 152 Yogo Hatsumi U .20 .50
❑ 153 Yogo Tjeki (Experienced) R 1.00 2.50
❑ 154 Yoritomo Kumiko R 1.25 3.00
❑ 155 Yoritomo Soetsuko U .25 .60
❑ 156 Yoshi No Shiryo R .60 1.50

2002 Legend of the Five Rings Dark Allies

BOOSTER BOX (48) 20.00 40.00
BOOSTER PACK (11) 1.00 2.00

❑ 1 Agetoki no Shiryo R 1.00 2.50
❑ 2 Aid of the Grand Master U .40 1.00
❑ 3 Akodo Jusho U .20 .50
❑ 4 Akodo Map R .60 1.50
❑ 5 Akodo Ninsei U .20 .50
❑ 6 Asahina Keitaro U .20 .50
❑ 7 Asahina's Blessing R 1.00 2.50
❑ 8 Asako Hirariko (Experienced 2 Hirariko) F 1.25 3.00
❑ 9 Asako Misao (Experienced) R 1.00 2.50
❑ 10 Asako Yuya U .20 .50
❑ 11 Auspicious House R .60 1.50
❑ 12 Baku no Oni C .10 .20
❑ 13 Bayushi Hirono C .10 .20
❑ 14 Bayushi Norachai (Experienced) R 1.00 2.50
❑ 15 Bayushi Ogura C .10 .20
❑ 16 Bayushi Toru U 1.00 2.50
❑ 17 Be the Breeze C .10 .20
❑ 18 Bitter Vengeance R .60 1.50
❑ 19 Blackened Honor U .20 .50
❑ 20 Blade of Truths R 1.25 3.00
❑ 21 Boastful Proclamation U .20 .50
❑ 22 Break the Wave C .10 .20
❑ 23 Celestial Sword of the Mantis R 2.00 5.00
❑ 24 City of Lightning F 1.00 2.50
❑ 25 City of the Lost C .10 .20
❑ 26 Clear Water Village C .10 .20
❑ 27 Construction Crew R 1.00 2.50
❑ 28 Court Intrigue R .60 1.50
❑ 29 Cowardly Conscripts U .20 .50
❑ 30 Curse of Weakness U .20 .50
❑ 31 Deep Earth Sanctum R .60 1.50
❑ 32 Defend Yourself! U .20 .50
❑ 33 Doji Kazo R 1.00 2.50
❑ 34 Doji Midoru C .10 .20
❑ 35 Doji Okakura C .10 .20
❑ 36 Doji Seishiro U .25 .60
❑ 37 Doomsayers U .20 .50
❑ 38 Drain the Soul U .20 .50
❑ 39 Draw From Within R 1.00 2.50
❑ 40 Ebbing Strength R .60 1.50
❑ 41 Face Me! U .25 .60
❑ 42 Faith In My Clan R 1.25 3.00
❑ 43 Gale Force Winds R .60 1.50
❑ 44 Gift of the Water Dragon C .10 .20
❑ 45 Goblin Slingers C .10 .20
❑ 46 Goju Kyoden U .20 .50
❑ 47 Grim Mempo C .10 .20
❑ 48 Heavy Armor C .10 .20
❑ 49 Hida Hitoshi C .10 .20
❑ 50 Hida Kosho U .40 1.00
❑ 51 Hida Shara C .10 .20
❑ 52 Hiruma Slayers U .25 .60
❑ 53 Hitomi Maya U .20 .50
❑ 54 Honor's Lesson Dojo R .60 1.50
❑ 55 Hoshi Tadao U .20 .50
❑ 56 Hoshi Takeji C .10 .20
❑ 57 House of Fates R .60 1.50
❑ 58 Ik'krt U .25 .60
❑ 59 Ikoma Fujimaro F .25 .60
❑ 60 Ikoma Goro C .10 .20
❑ 61 Inspiration C .10 .20
❑ 62 Isawa Maasaki C .10 .20
❑ 63 It's a Trap! U .20 .50
❑ 64 Ivory Isles Mercenaries C .10 .20
❑ 65 Jagged Earth C .10 .20
❑ 66 Junnosuke (Experienced Mirumoto Junnosuke) R.60 1.50
❑ 67 Kabuki Mask R .60 1.50
❑ 68 Kaiu Namboku R .60 1.50
❑ 69 Kanbe no Shiryo R .60 1.50
❑ 70 Kaneka's Blockade R .60 1.50
❑ 71 Kaneka's Strength U .20 .50
❑ 72 Kawaru Coins R .60 1.50
❑ 73 Ki-Rin's Blessing U .20 .50
❑ 74 Kitsu Hisashi C .10 .20
❑ 75 Koan C .10 .20
❑ 76 Kobune Port C .10 .20
❑ 77 Kyojin's Blade U .20 .50
❑ 78 Kyuden Agasha F .40 1.00
❑ 79 Lies C .10 .20
❑ 80 Light a Candle C .10 .20
❑ 81 Light of the Kami C .10 .20
❑ 82 Living Death R .60 1.50
❑ 83 Lost Souls R .60 1.50
❑ 84 Make Them Pay R 1.25 3.00
❑ 85 Massive Power R .60 1.50
❑ 86 Mirumoto Zenko C .10 .20
❑ 87 Miya Gensaiken (Experienced Oni no Pekkle) R1.00 2.50
❑ 88 Moshi Junichi F .25 .60
❑ 89 Moshi Mogai F .40 1.00
❑ 90 Moto Chaozhu R .60 1.50
❑ 91 Moto Feng U .20 .50
❑ 92 Moto Quing C .10 .20
❑ 93 Moto Steed C .10 .20
❑ 94 Naishi R 1.00 2.50
❑ 95 Naseru's Strength U .20 .50
❑ 96 New Formation U .20 .50
❑ 97 Nikushimi R 1.00 2.50
❑ 98 No Failure R .60 1.50
❑ 99 No Hiding Place C .10 .20
❑ 100 Omen U .20 .50
❑ 101 One Sword C .10 .20
❑ 102 Oni Horde U .20 .50
❑ 103 Patience U .20 .50
❑ 104 Personal Sohei R .60 1.50
❑ 105 Pillaged R .60 1.50
❑ 106 Raise the Dead R .60 1.50
❑ 107 Restless Zokujin C .10 .20
❑ 108 Roaming Caravan U .20 .50
❑ 109 Ronin Village R 1.00 2.50
❑ 110 Rubble of Beiden Pass U .20 .50
❑ 111 Selecting the Chancellor U .20 .50
❑ 112 Sezaru's Mask R .60 1.50
❑ 113 Sezaru's Strength U .20 .50
❑ 114 Shackled Oni C .10 .20
❑ 115 Shiba Itami C .10 .20
❑ 116 Shiba's Shrine R .60 1.50
❑ 117 Shinjo Xushen U .20 .50
❑ 118 Shinsei's Staff C .10 .20
❑ 119 Shiro Matsu F 1.00 2.50
❑ 120 Short Season R .60 1.50
❑ 121 Shosuro Koneko U .20 .50
❑ 122 Shrieking Mujina C .10 .20
❑ 123 Shrine of Reverse Fortunes R .60 1.50
❑ 124 Soshi Kiyo U .20 .50
❑ 125 Strength in Unity C .10 .20
❑ 126 Taken Unawares C .10 .20
❑ 127 Tamori Yamabushi C .10 .20
❑ 128 Teeth of Osano-Wo R 1.25 3.00
❑ 129 Te'tik'kir (Experienced) R .60 1.50
❑ 130 The Future Laid Bare U .20 .50
❑ 131 The Wandering Monk C .10 .20
❑ 132 Thunder's Kiss C .10 .20
❑ 133 T'k C .10 .20
❑ 134 Togashi Matsuo R .60 1.50
❑ 135 Toturi Koshei U .20 .50
❑ 136 Trusted Advisor U .20 .50
❑ 137 Tsudao's Strength U .20 .50
❑ 138 Tsuno Nintai C .10 .20
❑ 139 Tsuruchi Hiro F .25 .60
❑ 140 Tsuruchi Nobumoto F .40 1.00
❑ 141 Uji no Shiryo R .60 1.50
❑ 142 Unprepared R 1.25 3.00
❑ 143 Untested Troops U .20 .50
❑ 144 Utaku Keyo C .10 .20
❑ 145 Vengeful Ronin U .20 .50
❑ 146 Veteran Samurai R 1.25 3.00
❑ 147 Violence Behind Courtliness City C .10 .20
❑ 148 Voice of the Shiryo U .20 .50
❑ 149 Wall of Steel U .20 .50
❑ 150 Wasp Tattoo U .20 .50
❑ 151 Wave Tattoo U .20 .50
❑ 152 Whistling Bulb Arrow C .10 .20
❑ 153 Wikki'thich-hie A'tck R .60 1.50
❑ 154 Yoritomo Gombei U .20 .50
❑ 155 Yoritomo Heishiro C .10 .20
❑ 156 Yoritomo Ikemoto U .20 .50
❑ 157 Yoritomo Naizen F .40 1.00
❑ 158 Yoritomo Sen F .25 .60
❑ 159 Yoritomo Sumio C .10 .20
❑ 160 Yoritomo's Kama R .60 1.50
❑ 161 You Are Weak C .10 .20

2002 Legend of the Five Rings The Fall of Otosan Uchi

❑ 1 A Champion's Strike R 1.25 3.00
❑ 2 A New Path U .20 .50
❑ 3 Agasha Oshu C .10 .20
❑ 4 Agasha Yubisaki U .20 .50
❑ 5 Aid of the Fortunes U .20 .50
❑ 6 Akodo Tsuri U .20 .50
❑ 7 Ambush Pits C .10 .20
❑ 8 Armed and Ready C .10 .20
❑ 9 Arrow of Purity C .10 .20
❑ 10 Balance in Nothingness U .40 1.00
❑ 11 Bayushi Kaukatsu (Experienced) R 1.25 3.00
❑ 12 Bayushi Seiryo C .10 .20
❑ 13 Bayushi Sharaku U .20 .50
❑ 14 Beachhead U .20 .50
❑ 15 Blood Money U .20 .50
❑ 16 Bonds of Fate C .10 .20
❑ 17 Broken Words U .20 .50
❑ 18 Carrion's Breath C .10 .20
❑ 19 Chaldera R 1.00 2.50
❑ 20 Ch'tppu'kich R .60 1.50
❑ 21 Consuming Darkness R 1.00 2.50
❑ 22 Daidoji Ekiken C .10 .20
❑ 23 Dark Eyes on the Wall R .60 1.50
❑ 24 Denkyu no Shiryo R .60 1.50
❑ 25 Dojo Raiden R .60 1.50
❑ 26 Dotanuki C .10 .20
❑ 27 Earthly Yearnings U .20 .50
❑ 28 Eye of the Needle C .10 .20
❑ 29 Far and Wide U .20 .50
❑ 30 Favor for a Favor R .60 1.50
❑ 31 Fields of Grain U .20 .50
❑ 32 Fires of the Phoenix R .60 1.50
❑ 33 Footman's Yari C .10 .20
❑ 34 Forgery R .60 1.50
❑ 35 Forward Guard C .10 .20
❑ 36 Fury of the Damned U .20 .50
❑ 37 Glick C .10 .20
❑ 38 Hand of the Shogun R .60 1.50
❑ 39 Hida Ishi U .20 .50
❑ 40 Hida Yagimaki C .10 .20
❑ 41 Hideo Spawn U .25 .60
❑ 42 Hiruma Tatsuzo R 1.00 2.50
❑ 43 Hitaka U .20 .50
❑ 44 Hoshi Chuichi F (Dragon) 1.25 3.00
❑ 45 H-Tach'ch U .20 .50
❑ 46 Hungry Ghost U .20 .50
❑ 47 Hunting Cabin R .60 1.50
❑ 48 Hurricane Tattoo U .20 .50
❑ 49 Ikoma Kyuso U .20 .50
❑ 50 Imperial Messenger U .20 .50
❑ 51 Imperial Proclamation C .10 .20
❑ 52 Inferno R .60 1.50
❑ 53 Informant R .60 1.50
❑ 54 Isawa Nodotai (Experienced) R .60 1.50
❑ 55 Iuchi Huasha U .20 .50
❑ 56 Jester R .60 1.50
❑ 57 Kaeru Contracter C .10 .20
❑ 58 Kaiu Tasuku C .10 .20
❑ 59 Kakita Instructor R .60 1.50
❑ 60 Kakita Munemori U .20 .50
❑ 61 Kakita Nakazo F (Crane) 1.00 2.50
❑ 62 Kakita Yariga C .10 .20
❑ 63 Kansen Haunting U .20 .50
❑ 64 Keen Eye U .25 .60
❑ 65 Kirei C .10 .20
❑ 66 Kiseru C .10 .20
❑ 67 Kitsu Juri R .60 1.50
❑ 68 Kjgkt R .60 1.50
❑ 69 Konetsu R 1.25 3.00
❑ 70 Kukojin (Experienced 2 Hitomi Kukojin) R .60 1.50
❑ 71 Kyofu (Experienced Hida Kuroda) R 1.25 3.00
❑ 72 Kyuden Doji F (Crane) .60 1.50
❑ 73 Kyuden Gotei F (Mantis) .60 1.50
❑ 74 Led Into Darkness C .10 .20

TCG/CCG

❑ 75 Legendary Strength C .10 .20
❑ 76 Let Courage Guide Me U .20 .50
❑ 77 Lost Ashigaru C .10 .20
❑ 78 Master Sculptor C .10 .20
❑ 79 Matsu Reishiko C .10 .20
❑ 80 Matsu Masakado C .10 .20
❑ 81 Menhari-gata R 1.00 2.50
❑ 82 Mirumoto Tachiyama U .20 .50
❑ 83 Mirumoto's Haori U .20 .50
❑ 84 Moneylender R 1.00 2.50
❑ 85 Monkey Magistrates U .20 .50
❑ 86 Moshi Hinome C .10 .20
❑ 87 Moto Sanpao C .10 .20
❑ 88 Moto Tsusung U .20 .50
❑ 89 Mystic R .60 1.50
❑ 90 Now Face Me U .20 .50
❑ 91 Ogre Hordes C .10 .20
❑ 92 Omoidasu C .10 .20
❑ 93 One Will Fall U .20 .50
❑ 94 Perfect Attunement R .60 1.50
❑ 95 Pile of Stones C .10 .20
❑ 96 Playing With Madness C .10 .20
❑ 97 Precise Orders R .60 1.50
❑ 98 Private Dojo U .25 .60
❑ 99 Pulse of the Black River U .20 .50
❑ 100 Purify C .10 .20
❑ 101 Recruiting Drive C .10 .20
❑ 102 Run For Your Lives! U .20 .50
❑ 103 Scouting Manouvers U .20 .50
❑ 104 Shahai's Fan U .20 .50
❑ 105 Shiba Takeishi C .10 .20
❑ 106 Shiba Yoma (Experienced) R .60 1.50
❑ 107 Shinjo Horsebow C .10 .20
❑ 108 Shinjo Rao C .10 .20
❑ 109 Shinjo Shono (Experienced 2) R .60 1.50
❑ 110 Shiro Tamori F (Dragon) .60 1.50
❑ 111 Shosuro Miyo C .10 .20
❑ 112 Show of Good Faith R 1.25 3.00
❑ 113 Shrine of the Moon U .20 .50
❑ 114 Shrine of the Sun U .40 1.00
❑ 115 Snake Tattoo U .20 .50
❑ 116 Song of Corruption R .60 1.50
❑ 117 Soshi Kiyo (Experienced) R .60 1.50
❑ 118 Storm Legion R .60 1.50
❑ 119 Strike at the Soul U .20 .50
❑ 120 Summon the Dead R .60 1.50
❑ 121 Superior Swordplay C .10 .20
❑ 122 Tamori Tsukiro C .10 .20
❑ 123 Tempting Kansen U .20 .50
❑ 124 Terror U .20 .50
❑ 125 The Anvil's Blessing R .60 1.50
❑ 126 The Deathless U .20 .50
❑ 127 The Seppun Temples R .60 1.50
❑ 128 The Shadow's Claw R 2.00 5.00
❑ 129 The Time Is Not Right U .20 .50
❑ 130 Third Whisker Warren C .10 .20
❑ 131 Togashi Kansuke C .10 .20
❑ 132 Togashi's Shrine R .60 1.50
❑ 133 Traveling Ronin R 1.25 3.00
❑ 134 Trickster Spirits C .10 .20
❑ 135 Tsuno Blade U .20 .50
❑ 136 Tsuno House Guard R .60 1.50
❑ 137 Tsuno Sochi C .10 .20
❑ 138 Tsuruchi Hunters C .25 .60
❑ 139 Tsuruchi Technique C .10 .20
❑ 140 Tsuruchi Terao C .10 .20
❑ 141 Tsutomo no Shiryo R .10 .20
❑ 142 Unicorn Striders C .60 1.50
❑ 143 Unquiet Spirits R .10 .20
❑ 144 Unraveling C .60 1.50
❑ 145 Using the Wish R .10 .20
❑ 146 Vengeful Dead U .60 1.50
❑ 147 Watanabe Builders C .20 .50
❑ 148 Wazinu no Yokai R .10 .20
❑ 149 Wear Him Down U .60 1.50
❑ 150 Whispers R .20 .50
❑ 151 Words Cut Like Steel R .60 1.50
❑ 152 Yasuki Yukinga U .60 1.50
❑ 153 Yokutsu no Shiryo R .20 .50
❑ 154 Yoritomo Kitilae U .60 1.50
❑ 155 Yoritomo Komori (Experienced) F (Mantis) .20 .50
❑ 156 Yoritomo Yoyonagi R .60 1.50

2003 Legend of the Five Rings Heaven and Earth

BOOSTER BOX (48) 30.00 60.00
BOOSTER PACK (11) 1.00 2.00

❑ 1 A Game of Go U .20 .50
❑ 2 A New Guardian U .20 .50
❑ 3 Accept With Honor C .10 .20
❑ 4 Akodo Rokuro C .10 .20
❑ 5 Akodo Tekkan R 1.25 3.00
❑ 6 Akodo's No-Dachi R .60 1.50
❑ 7 Ancestral Reverence R .60 1.50
❑ 8 Aramasu's Ashes R 1.25 3.00
❑ 9 Arms Merchant C .10 .20
❑ 10 Asahina Itoeko C .10 .20
❑ 11 Asako Toshi F (Phoenix) .60 1.50
❑ 12 Ashigaru Fishermen C .10 .20
❑ 13 Avalanche Tattoo U .20 .50
❑ 14 Bane of the Anvil U .20 .50
❑ 15 Bane of the Bastard U .25 .60
❑ 16 Bane of the Sword U .20 .50
❑ 17 Bane of the Wolf U .20 .50
❑ 18 Bar the Gates U .20 .50
❑ 19 Bayushi Eitarou U .20 .50
❑ 20 Bayushi Tai (Experienced) R .60 1.50
❑ 21 Blade of Slaughter U .20 .50
❑ 22 Blessed Sword C .10 .20
❑ 23 Burning Smoke C .10 .20
❑ 24 By Steel Redeemed U .20 .50
❑ 25 Celestial Imbalance U .20 .50
❑ 26 Channeling Void U .20 .50
❑ 27 Chuk'tek U .20 .50
❑ 28 Chunigo U .20 .50
❑ 29 Cove of Cursed Blades R .60 1.50
❑ 30 Crab Builders R .60 1.50
❑ 31 Critical Moment U .20 .50
❑ 32 Crude Blade C .10 .20
❑ 33 Daigotsu F (Lion, Phoenix, Shadowlands) .25 .60
❑ 34 Dark Covenant R .60 1.50
❑ 35 Dark Oracle of the Void R .60 1.50
❑ 36 Darkness Rising R .60 1.50
❑ 37 Delicate Negotiation C .10 .20
❑ 38 Deploy Scouts C .10 .20
❑ 39 Desertion U .20 .50
❑ 40 Doji Jurian U .20 .50
❑ 41 Doji Okakura (Experienced) R .60 1.50
❑ 42 Embrace the Elements R .60 1.50
❑ 43 Escape from Shadow R 1.00 2.50
❑ 44 For the Clan R .60 1.50
❑ 45 Garden of Serenity U .20 .50
❑ 46 Gargelara C .10 .20
❑ 47 Goshiu no Shiryo R .60 1.50
❑ 48 Heart of Rokugan C .10 .20
❑ 49 Hida Benjiro C .10 .20
❑ 50 Hida Hitoshi (Experienced) R .60 1.50
❑ 51 Hida War Banner C .10 .20
❑ 52 Hiruma Tsukiko C .10 .20
❑ 53 Honor's Ground C .10 .20
❑ 54 Hoshi Yoson C .10 .20
❑ 55 House of the First Stone C .10 .20
❑ 56 Ide Tang U .20 .50
❑ 57 Ikoma Fudai (Experienced) F .60 1.50
❑ 58 Ikoma Tomaru R .60 1.50
❑ 59 Introspection R 2.50 6.00
❑ 60 Isawa Junichiro C .10 .20
❑ 61 Iuchi Yue R .60 1.50
❑ 62 Jade Katana C .10 .20
❑ 63 Jade Pikemen U .20 .50
❑ 64 Jade Yari U .20 .50
❑ 65 Kaiu Waotaka U .20 .50
❑ 66 Kakita Chiyeko C .10 .20
❑ 67 Kakita Dojo U .25 .60
❑ 68 Kakita Soichi R .60 1.50
❑ 69 Kanashimi F 1.00 2.50
❑ 70 Kanji of Power U .20 .50
❑ 71 Katana of the Moon R .60 1.50
❑ 72 Kaze-no-kami's Blessing C .10 .20
❑ 73 Kikage Zumi Initiates C .20 .60
❑ 74 Kitsuki Tadashi C .10 .20
❑ 75 Kokujin's Daisho R .60 1.50
❑ 76 Kuni Rihito U .20 .50
❑ 77 Kyuden Ikoma F (Lion) .60 1.50
❑ 78 Lessons From Earth R 1.00 2.50
❑ 79 Loyalty Renewed R .60 1.50
❑ 80 Mask of the Maw 1.25 3.00
(Experienced Mask of the Oni) R
❑ 81 Master of the Bells C .10 .20
❑ 82 Matsu Watako U .20 .50
❑ 83 Military Advisor C .10 .20
❑ 84 Mirumoto Kyuzo R .60 1.50
❑ 85 Morning Glory Castle F (Phoenix) .60 1.50
❑ 86 Moto Chaozhu (Experienced) R .60 1.50
❑ 87 Nairu no Oni C .10 .20
❑ 88 Noh Theater Troupe U .20 .50
❑ 89 Observe the Enemy U .20 .50
❑ 90 Obsidian Mempo of Fu Leng R .60 1.50
❑ 91 Once and Again R .60 1.50
❑ 92 Oracle of Blood U .20 .50
❑ 93 Otomo Ambassador C .10 .20
❑ 94 Outrider R .60 1.50
❑ 95 Poison Marsh U .20 .50
❑ 96 Puppet Theater Troupe U .20 .50
❑ 97 Purification R .60 1.50
❑ 98 Ransom Hostage C .10 .20
❑ 99 Rebuilt Temple U .20 .50
❑ 100 Rekai's Harriers C .10 .20
❑ 101 Rend the Soul R 2.00 5.00
❑ 102 Righteous Conviction U .20 .50
❑ 103 Sand Garden C .10 .20
❑ 104 Shamate Pass R .60 1.50
❑ 105 Shiba Gyukudo U .20 .50
❑ 106 Shiba Mirabu (Experienced) R .60 1.50
❑ 107 Shiba Yobei C .10 .20
❑ 108 Shifting Earth C .10 .20
❑ 109 Shinjo Guan C .10 .20
❑ 110 Shinjo Slings R .60 1.50
❑ 111 Shosuro Kamatari C .10 .20
❑ 112 Shrine to Benten R 1.25 3.00
❑ 113 Shrine to Bishamon R 1.00 2.50
❑ 114 Shrine to Daikoku R 1.25 3.00
❑ 115 Shrine to Ebisu R .60 1.50
❑ 116 Shrine to Fukurokujin R 1.25 3.00
❑ 117 Shrine to Hotei R .60 1.50
❑ 118 Shrine to Jurojin U .20 .50
❑ 119 Siege Towers U .20 .50
❑ 120 Sinister Transformation C .10 .20
❑ 121 Soshi Aki R .60 1.50
❑ 122 Soshi Natsuo C .10 .20
❑ 123 Steel Fan C .10 .20
❑ 124 Stolen Relics U .20 .50
❑ 125 Stone Hand Adepts C .10 .20
❑ 126 Strange Travelers R .60 1.50
❑ 127 Subterfuge C .10 .20
❑ 128 Sunda Mizu Dojo C .10 .20
❑ 129 Superior Stance R .60 1.50
❑ 130 Sycophant C .10 .20
❑ 131 Tattoo of the Void U .20 .50
❑ 132 Tax Collection R .60 1.50
❑ 133 Tear Away the Darkness U .20 .50
❑ 134 Temple of the Ninth Kami F (Shadowlands) .60 1.50
❑ 135 Tengoku's Gates C .10 .20
❑ 136 The Demon Skull U .20 .50
❑ 137 The Mountain Does Not Move C .10 .20
❑ 138 The Topaz Armor C .10 .20
❑ 139 The White Guard U .20 .50
❑ 140 Tireless Assault C .10 .20
❑ 141 Togashi Kinuko U .20 .50
❑ 142 Togashi Tashishai U .20 .50
❑ 143 Toshimoko no Shiryo R .60 1.50
❑ 144 Tsudao's Tanto R .60 1.50
❑ 145 Tsuno Kira U .20 .50
❑ 146 Tsurayuki U .20 .50
❑ 147 Tsuruchi Ichiro R .60 1.50
❑ 148 Tsuruchi Kaii U .20 .50
❑ 149 Tsuruchi Sho C .10 .20
❑ 150 Unexpected Strike R .60 1.50
❑ 151 Unspoken Threats U .20 .50
❑ 152 Utaku Yisheng C .10 .20
❑ 153 Volcanic Fields C .10 .20
❑ 154 Wholeness of Self U .20 .50
❑ 155 Wikki'thich-hie G'ni'ch R .60 1.50
❑ 156 Yoritomo Toyozo C .10 .20
❑ 157 Zashiki Warashi U .20 .50

2003 Legend of the Five Rings Reign of Blood

BOOSTER BOX (48) 30.00 60.00
BOOSTER PACK (11) 1.00 2.00

❑ 1 Acolytes of Air C .10 .20
❑ 2 Agasha Chieh (Expecienced) F (Phoenix) 1.25 3.00
❑ 3 Akodo Ieshigi U .20 .50
❑ 4 Akodo Maiko C .10 .20
❑ 5 Asahina Nahomi C .10 .20
❑ 6 Asahina Nizomi C .10 .20
❑ 7 Asako Genjo U .20 .50
❑ 8 Asako Katsuhito C .10 .20
❑ 9 Barley Farm C .10 .20
❑ 10 Battle-Hardened C .10 .20
❑ 11 Bayushi Atsuki (Experienced Shosuro Furuyari) R1.25 3.00
❑ 12 Bayushi Shintaro U .20 .50
❑ 13 Birth and Death R .60 1.50
❑ 14 Blade of Penance R 1.25 3.00
❑ 15 Bleak Portents R 1.25 3.00
❑ 16 Blessing of the Dragon C .10 .20
❑ 17 Blood and Chaos R .60 1.50
❑ 18 Blood Armor C .10 .20
❑ 19 Blood Command R .60 1.50
❑ 20 Blood Pact C .10 .20
❑ 21 Blood-Soaked Ground R 1.00 2.50
❑ 22 Bloodspeaker Sanctum U .20 .50
❑ 23 Bloodspeaker Students C .10 .20
❑ 24 Bloodspeaker's Tools R .60 1.50
❑ 25 Bloodstained Peasants C .10 .20
❑ 26 Bones of the Fallen C .10 .20
❑ 27 Break the Line C .10 .20
❑ 28 Burning Blood C .10 .20
❑ 29 Calculate Strength U .20 .50
❑ 30 Chuda Agent C .10 .20
❑ 31 Ciphered Scroll R .60 1.50
❑ 32 City of Remembrance F (Phoenix) 1.00 2.50
❑ 33 Cloud the Soul C .10 .20
❑ 34 Corrupt Officials U .20 .50
❑ 35 Crystal Mine C .10 .20
❑ 36 Curse R .60 1.50
❑ 37 Daidoji Sabaru U .30 .75
❑ 38 Death's Caress C .10 .20
❑ 39 Ebb and Flow R .60 1.50
❑ 40 Essence of Gaki-do R .60 1.50
❑ 41 Eyc of Iuchiban R .60 1.50
❑ 42 Fan of the Grand Master U .20 .50
❑ 43 Fires of Dishonor U .20 .50
❑ 44 From Every Side C .10 .20
❑ 45 Hakai R 1.25 3.00
❑ 46 Harsh Crossing R .60 1.50
❑ 47 Harvest of Death R .60 1.50
❑ 48 Heaven's Wrath U .20 .50
❑ 49 Hero's Grave U .20 .50
❑ 50 Hida Katai C .10 .20
❑ 51 Hida Soh U .20 .50
❑ 52 Hidden Retreat C .10 .20
❑ 53 Hiruma Rikiya C .10 .20
❑ 54 Hitomi Dojo U .20 .50
❑ 55 Honor and Glory U .20 .50
❑ 56 Honor's Gift C .10 .20
❑ 57 Hope in Shadows R .60 1.50
❑ 58 Horsemaster R .60 1.50
❑ 59 Hoshi Oki C .10 .20
❑ 60 Ide Haichang C .10 .20
❑ 61 Inazuma Blade R .60 1.50
❑ 62 Inexorable March U .20 .50
❑ 63 Inkyo Teacher U .20 .50
❑ 64 Inkyo's Jingasa U .20 .50
❑ 65 Isawa Jun C .10 .20
❑ 66 Isawa Ochiai R .60 1.50
❑ 67 Iuchi Katsumi C .10 .20
❑ 68 Iuchi Tudev U .20 .50
❑ 69 Jade Shortage R .60 1.50
❑ 70 Jigoku's Rage R 1.25 3.00
❑ 71 Kakita Matabei R 1.25 3.00
❑ 72 Kakita Nichira U .20 .50
❑ 73 Kitsu Tomoe U .20 .50
❑ 74 Kouken Blade U .20 .50
❑ 75 Kuni Jiyuna U .20 .50
❑ 76 Kuroiban Advisor U .20 .50
❑ 77 Mark of the Ninth Kami R .60 1.50
❑ 78 Matsu Takenao C .10 .20
❑ 79 Matsu Taniko R .60 1.50
❑ 80 Migawari C .10 .20
❑ 81 Mirumoto Kenzo U .20 .50
❑ 82 Mirumoto Mareshi F (Dragon) 1.50 4.00
❑ 83 Moshi Kekiesu U .20 .50
❑ 84 Moto Najmudin F (Unicorn) 1.00 2.50
❑ 85 Move the Earth U .20 .50
❑ 86 Nemuranai Arms C .10 .20
❑ 87 Omen (Experienced) R .60 1.50
❑ 88 Our Darkest Hour R .60 1.50
❑ 89 Pit of Blood R .60 1.50
❑ 90 Poison the Land C .10 .20
❑ 91 Poisoned Kiss U .20 .50
❑ 92 Political Interference R 1.00 2.50
❑ 93 Purification R .60 1.50
❑ 94 Purity of the Heavens U .20 .50
❑ 95 Quarantined R .60 1.50
❑ 96 Rain of Blood R .60 1.50
❑ 97 Reflect the Spirit R .60 1.50
❑ 98 Reichin's Helm U .20 .50
❑ 99 Reinforced Cavalry U .20 .50
❑ 100 Reinforced Infantry U .20 .50
❑ 101 Reinforcements R 1.25 3.00
❑ 102 Renewed Energy U .20 .50
❑ 103 Ride the Way C .10 .20
❑ 104 Rising Shadows C .10 .20
❑ 105 Rising Terror U .20 .50
❑ 106 Search For Advantage U .20 .50
❑ 107 Sezaru's Gift R .60 1.50
❑ 108 Shadowed Terrain R .60 1.50
❑ 109 Shield of Blood R .60 1.50
❑ 110 Shinden Horiuchi F (Unicorn) .60 1.50
❑ 111 Shirasu no Shiryo F (Unicorn) .60 1.50
❑ 112 Shosuro Haru C .10 .20
❑ 113 Shrine of Fu Leng R .60 1.50
❑ 114 Shrine of Humility R .60 1.50
❑ 115 Shrine of the Eternal U .20 .50
❑ 116 Shukumei U .20 .50
❑ 117 Silence the Future R .60 1.50
❑ 118 Skub C .10 .20
❑ 119 Smite the Blood U .20 .50
❑ 120 Soshi Uidori U .20 .50
❑ 121 Speed of the Plains U .20 .50
❑ 122 Spirit Drums R .60 1.50
❑ 123 Steel on Steel C .60 1.50
❑ 124 Strange Alliance C .10 .20
❑ 125 Strategic Crossroad C .10 .20
❑ 126 Strength in Numbers U .20 .50
❑ 127 Stymied R .60 1.50
❑ 128 Suchiro no Oni C .10 .20
❑ 129 Suitengu's Uncertainty U .20 .50
❑ 130 Swift as the Wind U .20 .50
❑ 131 Taint the Land R .60 1.50
❑ 132 Talented Apprentice C .10 .20
❑ 133 Tamori Nobuyoki C .10 .20
❑ 134 Tamori's Furnace R .60 1.50
❑ 135 Tch'rikch C .10 .20
❑ 136 Temples of the Snake R .60 1.50
❑ 137 Test of Magic R .60 1.50
❑ 138 The Death of Tadaji U .20 .50
❑ 139 The Temple of Hoshi F (Dragon) 1.00 2.50
❑ 140 The Voice's Command R .60 1.50
❑ 141 Togashi Shozo U .20 .50
❑ 142 Tsuruchi Amane C .10 .20
❑ 143 Tsuruchi Fusako U .20 .50
❑ 144 Tsuruchi's Flame U .20 .50
❑ 145 Two Souls, One Destiny C .10 .20
❑ 146 Utaku Xiulian U .20 .50
❑ 147 Vigilant Witch Hunter U .20 .50
❑ 148 Way of the Willow C .10 .20
❑ 149 Where the Kami Walk U .20 .50
❑ 150 Witch Hunter's Amulet C .10 .20
❑ 151 Woodlands U .20 .50
❑ 152 Worthy Gift R .60 1.50
❑ 153 Yajinden R 2.50 6.00
❑ 154 Yasuki Trader C .10 .20
❑ 155 Yogo Hiroji C .10 .20
❑ 156 Yoritomo Kitao (Experienced 2) R 1.00 2.50
❑ 157 Yoritomo Utemaro C .10 .20

2003 Legend of the Five Rings Winds of Change

BOOSTER BOX (48) 50.00 100.00
BOOSTER PACK (11) 1.50 3.00

❑ 1 A Champion's Heart U .20 .50
❑ 2 Akodo Sarasa U .20 .50
❑ 3 Akodo Tadenori (Experienced) R 1.00 2.50
❑ 4 Akodo's Grave C .10 .20
❑ 5 Asahina Barako U .20 .50
❑ 6 Asako Shiwasu C .10 .20
❑ 7 Ashigaru Fort C .10 .20
❑ 8 Banner of Heroes R .60 1.50
❑ 9 Barren Fields C .25 .60
❑ 10 Bawaru no Oni C .10 .20
❑ 11 Baysuhi Aotora U .20 .50
❑ 12 Bayushi Kwanchi (Experienced) R 1.25 3.00
❑ 13 Bayushi Rei C .10 .20
❑ 14 Bloodied Ground R .60 1.50
❑ 15 Castle of the Wasp F (Mantis) .60 1.50
❑ 16 Chu-rochu C .10 .20
❑ 17 Clarity of Purpose C .10 .20
❑ 18 Commanding Favor R 1.25 3.00
❑ 19 Contingency Plans U .20 .50
❑ 20 Control the Field C .60 1.50
❑ 21 Corrupted Dojo U .10 .20
❑ 22 Court Chambers R .20 .50
❑ 23 Daidoji Akimasa C .60 1.50
❑ 24 Damning Evidence R .20 .50
❑ 25 Dark Soul Mask R .60 1.50
❑ 26 Dark Wings C .60 1.50
❑ 27 Defend Your Master U .10 .20
❑ 28 Dismissed U .20 .50
❑ 29 Doji Tanitsu (Experienced) R .10 .20
❑ 30 Domotai's Sacrifice R .60 1.50
❑ 31 Edict of Glory U .60 1.50
❑ 32 Edict of Judgement U .20 .50
❑ 33 Eloquence R .20 .50
❑ 34 Field of Glorious Slaughter C .10 .20
❑ 35 Fine Steed U .10 .20
❑ 36 Fruitless Combat C .20 .50
❑ 37 Gaki C .10 .20
❑ 38 Gempukku C .10 .20
❑ 39 Ghul Lord U .10 .20
❑ 40 Hachi's Legion U .20 .50
❑ 41 Hands of the Tides U .20 .50
❑ 42 Heimin Laborers U .10 .20
❑ 43 Hida Hoitsu C .20 .50
❑ 44 Hida Sozen C .10 .20
❑ 45 Hida Wukau (Experienced) F (Crab) .30 .75
❑ 46 Hiruma Tracker C .10 .20
❑ 47 Hitomi Kichi U .10 .20
❑ 48 Honored Sensei U .20 .50
❑ 49 Hospitality R .20 .50
❑ 50 Ichido no Shiryo R2 .60 1.50
❑ 51 Ik'krt (Experienced) F (Ratling) .60 1.50
❑ 52 Ikoma Korin C 1.00 2.50
❑ 53 Inspired Troops C .20 .50
❑ 54 Invasion U .10 .20
❑ 55 Isawa Fosuta R .10 .20
❑ 56 Isawa Wazuka U .60 1.50
❑ 57 Judgment of the Kami U .10 .20
❑ 58 Kaede's Fan R .10 .20
❑ 59 Kaiu Village R .60 1.50
❑ 60 Kakita Hirotada U .60 1.50
❑ 61 Kakita Rekkusu C .20 .50
❑ 62 Karo U .25 .60
❑ 63 Kharmic Vengeance R .25 .60
❑ 64 Kitsu Tanoyame U .60 1.50
❑ 65 Kitsuki Kiyushichi R .20 .50
❑ 66 Kitsuki Mizuochi R .60 1.50
❑ 67 Kitsune House Guard R .60 1.50
❑ 68 Korjagun U .10 .20
❑ 69 Koten F (Crab) .20 .50
❑ 70 Kyuden Tonbo R .20 .50
❑ 71 Mastermind U .10 .20
❑ 72 Mat'chek U .20 .50
❑ 73 Matsu Ferishi C .20 .50
❑ 74 Meditation Chamber C .10 .20
❑ 75 Mirumoto Ryosaki C .10 .20
❑ 76 Mirumoto Takeo C .10 .20
❑ 77 Miya Shoin R .10 .20
❑ 78 Monkey House Guard R .60 1.50
❑ 79 Moshi Eihime U .60 1.50
❑ 80 Moshi Yoshinaka F (Mantis) .20 .50
❑ 81 Moto Genki C 1.00 2.50
❑ 82 Moto Latomu U .10 .20
❑ 83 No Mercy R .25 .60
❑ 84 Oblivion's Gate R .20 .50
❑ 85 Officers' Council U .60 1.50
❑ 86 Official Papers U .20 .50
❑ 87 Omoni (Experienced) R .20 .50
❑ 88 Otomo Taneji C .20 .50
❑ 89 Ox House Guard R .10 .20
❑ 90 Peasant Vengeance C .60 1.50
❑ 91 Personal Librarian C .20 .50
❑ 92 Petty Insults U .10 .20
❑ 93 Poisoned Thread C .20 .50
❑ 94 Political Entanglements R .10 .20
❑ 95 Promotion to the Court R 1.25 3.00
❑ 96 Prophets C .60 1.50
❑ 97 Provincial Governor U .10 .20
❑ 98 Radiant Staff R .20 .50
❑ 99 Rage C .60 1.50
❑ 100 Reserve Commander C .20 .50
❑ 101 Retribution C .10 .20
❑ 102 Rhetoric C .10 .20
❑ 103 Ruins of Yotsu Dojo U .10 .20
❑ 104 Running Engagement C .20 .50
❑ 105 Ryouko U .10 .20
❑ 106 Sacred Grove R .40 1.00
❑ 107 Sashimono C .60 1.50
❑ 108 Seek the Path C .10 .20
❑ 109 Settozai R .10 .20

TCG/CCG

❑ 110 Sharing Strength C 1.25 3.00
❑ 111 Shiba Emiri C .10 .20
❑ 112 Shinjo Haruko U .10 .20
❑ 113 Shinjo Xushen (Experienced) R .20 .50
❑ 114 Soshi Seika U .10 .20
❑ 115 Soshi Tabito C .20 .50
❑ 116 Sound Strategy R .10 .20
❑ 117 Spearhead C 1.00 2.50
❑ 118 Stable Master U .10 .20
❑ 119 Stay Your Blade C .20 .50
❑ 120 Steadfast Bushi C .10 .20
❑ 121 Stern Reprimand U .10 .20
❑ 122 Storm Heart R .20 .50
❑ 123 Strange Politics U 2.50 6.00
❑ 124 Strike Like the Wind U .20 .50
❑ 125 Suzume House Guard R .10 .20
❑ 126 Tadaka's Children U .60 1.50
❑ 127 Tainted Dreams C .20 .50
❑ 128 Taut Bowstrings U .10 .20
❑ 129 Tch'tch Warrens F (Ratling) .20 .50
❑ 130 The Four Winds March R .60 1.50
❑ 131 The Future is Unwritten U 1.25 3.00
❑ 132 The New Order R .20 .50
❑ 133 The Outer Darkness R .60 1.50
❑ 134 The Shogun's Barracks R .60 1.50
❑ 135 The World is Empty U .60 1.50
❑ 136 Time to Pay the Price R .20 .50
❑ 137 Traitor's Reward U .20 .50
❑ 138 Treachery R .20 .50
❑ 139 Tsudao's Chambers R .60 1.50
❑ 140 Tsuruchi Tasaku C .30 .75
❑ 141 Twist the World U .10 .20
❑ 142 Untouched Temple U .20 .50
❑ 143 Utaku Qsi-Tsing C .20 .50
❑ 144 Utz! C .10 .20
❑ 145 Wait and See R .10 .20
❑ 146 Weight of the Heavens R .60 1.50
❑ 147 Well Prepared C .60 1.50
❑ 148 Wretches U .10 .20
❑ 149 Writ of Conscription U .20 .50
❑ 150 Writ of Justice R .20 .50
❑ 151 Writ of Peace U .60 1.50
❑ 152 Yasu no Shiryo R .20 .50
❑ 153 Yasuki Namika R .60 1.50
❑ 154 Yoritomo Manobu R .30 .75
❑ 155 Yoritomo Yorikane C .30 .75

2004 Legend of the Five Rings Dawn of the Empire

COMPLETE SET (108) 40.00 80.00

❑ 1 Akodo F 2.00 5.00
❑ 2 Akodo Mirotai F .40 1.00
❑ 3 Amaterasu's Blessing F .40 1.00
❑ 4 Ancient Armor F .40 1.00
❑ 5 Ancient Battlefield F 1.00 2.50
❑ 6 Ancient Sword F .40 1.00
❑ 7 Asako Moharu F .40 1.00
❑ 8 Asako Yogo F 1.00 2.50
❑ 9 A'tck F 1.25 3.00
❑ 10 Battul F 1.00 2.50
❑ 11 Bayushi F 2.00 5.00
❑ 12 Bayushi Nissho F .40 1.00
❑ 13 Bayushi's Mask F 1.00 2.50
❑ 14 Blood Calls to Blood F .40 1.00
❑ 15 Broken Sword of the Lion F 1.00 2.50
❑ 16 Call of Thunder F 1.25 3.00
❑ 17 Chamber of the Damned F .40 1.00
❑ 18 Deeds of My Ancestors F .40 1.00
❑ 19 Depths of Jigoku F .40 1.00
❑ 20 D'nir'ch F .40 1.00
❑ 21 Doji F 2.00 5.00
❑ 22 Doji Hayaku F .40 1.00
❑ 23 Doji Konishiko (Experienced 7) F 2.00 5.00
❑ 24 Eclipse F .40 1.00
❑ 25 Enmity F .40 1.00
❑ 26 Extermination F .40 1.00
❑ 27 Eye of the Emperor F .40 1.00
❑ 28 Fall from the Heavens F .40 1.00
❑ 29 Fallen Thunder F .40 1.00
❑ 30 Family Library F 1.00 2.50
❑ 31 Fu Leng F 2.00 5.00
❑ 32 Fu Leng's Sword F 2.50 6.00
❑ 33 Golden Mirror F 1.00 2.50
❑ 34 Hantei F 2.50 6.00
❑ 35 Hantei Genji F 1.25 3.00
❑ 36 Hida Atarasi (Experienced 7) F 3.00 8.00
❑ 37 Hida F 1.00 2.50
❑ 38 Hiruma F 1.25 3.00
❑ 39 Hole in the Sky F .40 1.00
❑ 40 I Can Swim F .40 1.00
❑ 41 Ide F 1.00 2.50
❑ 42 Ikoma F 1.25 3.00
❑ 43 Into the Darkness F 2.00 5.00
❑ 44 Isawa (Experienced 7) F 1.25 3.00
❑ 45 Isawa Ariminhime F .40 1.00
❑ 46 Isawa's Last Wish (Inexperienced) F .40 1.00
❑ 47 Isawa's Scrolls F .40 1.00
❑ 48 Kaimetsu-Uo F 1.00 2.50
❑ 49 Kaiu Fortress F .40 1.00
❑ 50 Kaiu Norio F .40 1.00
❑ 51 Kakita F 5.00 12.00
❑ 52 Kanashimi Toshi F 1.25 3.00
❑ 53 Kan'chek F .40 1.00
❑ 54 Kindari F .40 1.00
❑ 55 Ki-Rin's Exodus F .40 1.00
❑ 56 Legion of the Kami F .40 1.00
❑ 57 Lesson of Thunder F .40 1.00
❑ 58 Matsu (Experienced 7) F 2.00 5.00
❑ 59 Men of Cunning F .40 1.00
❑ 60 Mirumoto (Experienced 7) F 3.00 8.00
❑ 61 Mirumoto Hojatsu F 1.00 2.50
❑ 62 Mountains of Exile F .40 1.00
❑ 63 Muhomono F .40 1.00
❑ 64 Mutsuhito F 1.25 3.00
❑ 65 One Thousand Years of Peace F .40 1.00
❑ 66 Oni no Hatsu Suru F .40 1.00
❑ 67 Onnotangu's Hand (Inexperienced Obsidian Hand) F .40 1.00
❑ 68 Otaku (Experienced 7) F 1.50 4.00
❑ 69 P'an Ku F 5.00 12.00
❑ 70 Rebirth of the Dark Kami F .40 1.00
❑ 71 Sacred Arena F .40 1.00
❑ 72 Scribing the Tao F .40 1.00
❑ 73 Sculpting Flesh F .40 1.00
❑ 74 Seppun Hill F .60 1.50
❑ 75 Shiba F 4.00 10.00
❑ 76 Shinjo Bairezu F 4.00 10.00
❑ 77 Shinjo F .40 1.00
❑ 78 Shinjo's Courage F .40 1.00
❑ 79 Shinsei F 1.00 2.50
❑ 80 Shinsei's Legion F 1.00 2.50
❑ 81 Shosuro (Experienced 7) F 4.00 10.00
❑ 82 Shrine of Discussion F .40 1.00
❑ 83 Souls of the Fallen F .40 1.00
❑ 84 Spirit Made Flesh F .40 1.00
❑ 85 Standing Stones F .40 1.00
❑ 86 Student of the Tao F .40 1.00
❑ 87 Tashrak F 1.00 2.50
❑ 88 Temples of Gisei Toshi F 1.50 4.00
❑ 89 Test of the Kami F 1.00 2.50
❑ 90 The Death of Ryoshun F 4.00 10.00
❑ 91 The Emperor's Blessing F .40 1.00
❑ 92 The First Dojo F .40 1.00
❑ 93 The First Oni (Inexperienced) F 1.25 3.00
❑ 94 The First Wedding F 2.00 5.00
❑ 95 The Lying Darkness F .40 1.00
❑ 96 The Tao F .40 1.00
❑ 97 Togashi F 2.00 5.00
❑ 98 Togashi Kaiteru F .40 1.00
❑ 99 Tora F .40 1.00
❑ 100 Troll War Band F .40 1.00
❑ 101 Unmei F .40 1.00
❑ 102 Until I Understand F .40 1.00
❑ 103 Wako F .40 1.00
❑ 104 War Chariot F .40 1.00
❑ 105 Way of the Horse and Bow F .40 1.00
❑ 106 Where Gods Have Fallen F .40 1.00
❑ 107 Yobanjin Fortress F .40 1.00
❑ 108 Yogo (Experienced Asako Yogo) F 2.00 5.00

2004 Legend of the Five Rings The Hidden City

BOOSTER BOX (48) 20.00 40.00
BOOSTER PACK (11) 1.00 2.00

❑ 1 A Favor Returned C .10 .20
❑ 2 A Samurai's Anger C .10 .20
❑ 3 Akodo Dagurasu R .60 1.50
❑ 4 Akodo Dojo U .20 .50
❑ 5 Akodo Minako U .20 .50
❑ 6 Akodo Tadenori (Experienced) F (Lion) 2.00 5.00
❑ 7 Anvil of Earth R .60 1.50
❑ 8 Archer Squad U .20 .50
❑ 9 Armed Brigade U .20 .50
❑ 10 Asako Soun C .10 .20
❑ 11 Battlefield Messenger C .10 .20
❑ 12 Bayushi Adachi U .20 .50
❑ 13 Bayushi Kamnan (Experienced) R 1.25 3.00
❑ 14 Bayushi Motomu U .20 .50
❑ 15 Blade of Fury C .10 .20
❑ 16 Bleeding Grounds U .20 .50
❑ 17 Blessings of Steel R 1.00 2.50
❑ 18 Blind Honor R 1.00 2.50
❑ 19 Blocked Ground C .10 .20
❑ 20 Brilliant Soul U .20 .50
❑ 21 Brothers in Arms U .20 .50
❑ 22 Brutal Confrontation R 1.25 3.00
❑ 23 Cautious Advance R .60 1.50
❑ 24 Chee'trr C .10 .20
❑ 25 Chizuko U .20 .50
❑ 26 Ch'krit C .10 .20
❑ 27 Daidoji Kikaze R 1.00 2.50
❑ 28 Daidoji Tani C .10 .20
❑ 29 Daigotsu Dojo U .20 .50
❑ 30 Daigotsu Meguro C .20 .50
❑ 31 Daigotsu Toru U .20 .50
❑ 32 Daisho of Water R 1.50 4.00
❑ 33 Deathseeker's Oath U .20 .50
❑ 34 Delayed March C .10 .20
❑ 35 Demanding Gunso U .20 .50
❑ 36 Deranged Mujina U .20 .50
❑ 37 Desperate Conscripts C .10 .20
❑ 38 Direct Assault R 1.00 2.50
❑ 39 Disciplined Infantry C .10 .20
❑ 40 Doji Asano C .10 .20
❑ 41 Doji Yasuyo (Experienced 2) R .60 1.50
❑ 42 Drunken Mantis U .20 .50
❑ 43 Endless Horde U .20 .50
❑ 44 Er'chi-check U .20 .50
❑ 45 Essence of Yomi C .10 .20
❑ 46 Exhaustion R .60 1.50
❑ 47 Expert Archers C .10 .20
❑ 48 Explored Territory C .10 .20
❑ 49 Failure of Duty R 1.00 2.50
❑ 50 Family Token C .10 .20
❑ 51 Family War Banner R .60 1.50
❑ 52 Fire and Water C .10 .20
❑ 53 Fire in the Hidden City C .10 .20
❑ 54 Fortress of Thunder R .60 1.50
❑ 55 Fortune's Gift R .60 1.50
❑ 56 From Nowhere R .60 1.50
❑ 57 Fudoshi C .10 .20
❑ 58 Fushin R .60 1.50
❑ 59 Geisha Network U 2.50 6.00
❑ 60 Glassblower R .60 1.50
❑ 61 Gleaming Wakizashi R .60 1.50
❑ 62 Go In Disgrace U .20 .50
❑ 63 Goju Arai C .10 .20
❑ 64 Gold Buys Security R .60 1.50
❑ 65 Hada Daizu C .60 1.50
❑ 66 Hardy Infantry R .10 .20
❑ 67 Hasty Barricades C .20 .50
❑ 68 Heart of a Hero U .10 .20
❑ 69 Heart of Bushido C .60 1.50
❑ 70 Hero's Banner R .10 .20
❑ 71 Hida Enko R .60 1.50
❑ 72 Hida Sosuke C .10 .20
❑ 73 Hiruma Todori (Experienced) F (Crab) .60 1.50
❑ 74 Ichiro's Yumi C .10 .20
❑ 75 Ignominious End U .20 .50
❑ 76 Ikm'atch-tek R .60 1.50
❑ 77 Iron Pillar C .10 .20
❑ 78 Ith-ik C .10 .20
❑ 79 Iuchi Katamari U .20 .50
❑ 80 Kaiu Kamura U .20 .50
❑ 81 Kakita Kaneo U .20 .50
❑ 82 Kaneka R .60 1.50
❑ 83 Kareido no Oni U .20 .50
❑ 84 Killing Fields C .20 .50
❑ 85 Kiss of the Scorpion R .60 1.50
❑ 86 Knife in the Dark C .10 .20
❑ 87 Legacy of My Ancestors R .60 1.50
❑ 88 Lotus at Dusk R .60 1.50
❑ 89 Marching Column C .10 .20
❑ 90 Matsu Fujiwe C .10 .20
❑ 91 Matsu Ryoichi C .10 .20
❑ 92 Mirumoto Arai U .20 .50
❑ 93 Mirumoto Daisho C .10 .20
❑ 94 Mirumoto Kei U .20 .50
❑ 95 Mirumoto Satoe C .10 .20
❑ 96 Moto Gurban C .10 .20
❑ 97 Moto Taidjut C .10 .20
❑ 98 Naka Tokei (Experienced 2) R .60 1.50
❑ 99 Outer Walls C .10 .20
❑ 100 Peasant Laborers R .60 1.50
❑ 101 Pillar of Flesh R 1.00 2.50
❑ 102 Piolitical Adjunct U .20 .50
❑ 103 Purloined Letters U .20 .50
❑ 104 Quartermaster C .10 .20
❑ 105 Ratling Raider R .60 1.50
❑ 106 Retired Master U .20 .50
❑ 107 Scrutiny's Sweet Sting R .60 1.50
❑ 108 Seasoned Cavalry U .30 .75
❑ 109 Secluded Outpost R 6.00 15.00
❑ 110 Seeds of the Void R .60 1.50
❑ 111 Senpent Scimitar C .10 .20
❑ 112 Set'tchr'too U .20 .50
❑ 113 Shakuhachi of Air R .60 1.50
❑ 114 Shameless Slander U .20 .50
❑ 115 Shiba Aikune (Experienced 2) R .60 1.50
❑ 116 Shiba Koseki C .10 .20
❑ 117 Shiba Marihito U .20 .50
❑ 118 Shiba Toshiki U .20 .50
❑ 119 Shining Example U .20 .50
❑ 120 Shinjo Jinturi R .60 1.50
❑ 121 Shiranai Toshi F (Lion) 1.25 3.00
❑ 122 Shosuro Mikado C .10 .20
❑ 123 Shosuro Osamito C .10 .20
❑ 124 Shrine of Compassion R .60 1.50
❑ 125 Shrine of Courage R 1.25 3.00
❑ 126 Shrine of Duty R .60 1.50
❑ 127 S'ktcha F (Ratling) 1.25 3.00
❑ 128 Strategic Assassin C .10 .20
❑ 129 Summon Air Kami U .20 .50
❑ 130 Summon Earth Kami U .20 .50
❑ 131 Summon Fire Kami U .20 .50
❑ 132 Summon Water Kami U .20 .50
❑ 133 Tamori Minoru C .10 .20
❑ 134 Tani Hitokage F (Crab) 1.25 3.00
❑ 135 Tek'teki-tek U .20 .50
❑ 136 Ten Thousand Swords C .20 .50
❑ 137 The Iron Legion R .60 1.50
❑ 138 The Legions Charge U .30 .75
❑ 139 The Meeting Place F (Ratling) 1.25 3.00
❑ 140 The Pull of Destiny U .20 .50
❑ 141 The Shogun's Armory R .60 1.50
❑ 142 Third Whisker Mine U .20 .50
❑ 143 Togashi Tsuri R .60 1.50
❑ 144 Trade District R .60 1.50
❑ 145 Tsuruchi Arishia C .10 .20
❑ 146 Tsuruchi Mochisa U .20 .50
❑ 147 Tsuruchi Nobumoto (Experienced) R .60 1.50
❑ 148 Turn of Fortune R .60 1.50
❑ 149 Usagi Rangers C .10 .20
❑ 150 Utaku Jamaira U. .30 .75
❑ 151 War Council U .20 .50
❑ 152 We Know U .20 .50
❑ 153 Well-Tended Farm U 1.25 3.00
❑ 154 Yobanjin Wyrm R .60 1.50
❑ 155 Yoritomo Mie C .10 .20
❑ 156 Yumi of Fire R .60 1.50

2004 Legend of the Five Rings Web of Lies

BOOSTER BOX (48) 40.00 80.00
BOOSTER PACK (11) 1.25 2.50

❑ 1 Agasha Miyoshi C .10 .20
❑ 2 Akodo Kitaka C .10 .20
❑ 3 Akodo Kuemon C .10 .20
❑ 4 Akodo Rokku U .20 .50
❑ 5 Anchor the Line U .20 .50
❑ 6 Aramasu's Pride F (Mantis) .60 1.50
❑ 7 Asahina Sekawa (Experienced 2) R .60 1.50
❑ 8 Asako Hirotsugu C .10 .20
❑ 9 Asako Kinuye (Experienced) F (Phoenix) .60 1.50
❑ 10 Baraunghar Amulet U .20 .50
❑ 11 Bayushi Paneki (Experienced 2) R 1.25 3.00
❑ 12 Bayushi Shusui C .10 .20
❑ 13 Bishamon's Fury U .20 .50
❑ 14 Blade of the Master R .60 1.50
❑ 15 Blood Pearl U .20 .50
❑ 16 Brand of Fire and Thunder C .10 .20
❑ 17 Cavalry Reserves U .20 .50
❑ 18 Chirtk R .60 1.50
❑ 19 Circle of Steel C .10 .20
❑ 20 City of Blood F (Phoenix) .60 1.50
❑ 21 Cunning of Daidoji C .10 .20
❑ 22 Daidoji Setsuko U .20 .50
❑ 23 Daidoji Takihiro C .10 .20
❑ 24 Daigotsu R 1.25 3.00
❑ 25 Defining the Essence C .10 .20
❑ 26 Distant Keep U .20 .50
❑ 27 Doji Saori C .10 .20
❑ 28 Doji Takeji C .10 .20
❑ 29 False Trail R 1.25 3.00
❑ 30 Few Against Many R 2.50 6.00
❑ 31 Fields of Pyrrhic Victory R 1.50 4.00
❑ 32 Forward Sentries C .10 .20
❑ 33 Fury of Hida C .10 .20
❑ 34 Fury of Steel R .60 1.50
❑ 35 Glory of Mirumoto C .10 .20
❑ 36 Glory of the Shogun R .60 1.50
❑ 37 Gong of the Righteous Emperor U .20 .50
❑ 38 Gozoku Influence C .10 .20
❑ 39 Gozoku Pawn R 1.25 3.00
❑ 40 Gunsen-gata U .20 .50
❑ 41 Henshin's Amulet U .20 .50
❑ 42 Hida Atsumori U .20 .50
❑ 43 Hida Rikyu C .10 .20
❑ 44 Hida Shara (Experienced) R .60 1.50
❑ 45 Hiruma Oda U .20 .50
❑ 46 Hordes of the Nezumi C .10 .20
❑ 47 Hoshi Masote U .20 .50
❑ 48 House of the Spring Chrysanthemum U .20 .50
❑ 49 I Am Ready R .60 1.50
❑ 50 Ik'krt (Experienced 2) R .60 1.50
❑ 51 Ikoma Korin (Experienced) R .60 1.50
❑ 52 Invincible Legions R 1.00 2.50
❑ 53 Isawa Sachi U .20 .50
❑ 54 Isawa Sezaru R .60 1.50
❑ 55 Jade Stores U .20 .50
❑ 56 J'uma Jirushi R .60 1.50
❑ 57 Kaeru Fields R .60 1.50
❑ 58 Kaiu Kazu C .10 .20
❑ 59 Kakita Benkei R .60 1.50
❑ 60 Kanjiro U .20 .50
❑ 61 Kinuye's Garden U .20 .50
❑ 62 Kitsuku Yojimbo U .20 .50
❑ 63 Kiyune's Blood U .20 .50
❑ 64 Kobune Scout C .10 .20
❑ 65 Kuni Kiyoshi (Experienced) R .60 1.50
❑ 66 Legendary Confrontation R 2.50 6.00
❑ 67 Lessons of Pain C .10 .20
❑ 68 Living Blade Dojo R .60 1.50
❑ 69 Make Your Stand C .10 .20
❑ 70 Mak'irtch C .10 .20
❑ 71 Matsu Mieko C .10 .20
❑ 72 Mirumoto Gukochi C .10 .20
❑ 73 Mirumoto Kenzo (Experienced) R .60 1.50
❑ 74 Mirumoto Takige C .10 .20
❑ 75 Misdirection R 1.50 4.00
❑ 76 Morisue U .20 .50
❑ 77 Moshi Hinome (Experienced) R .60 1.50
❑ 78 Moto Latomu (Experienced) F (Unicorn) 1.25 3.00
❑ 79 Moto Ogedei R .60 1.50
❑ 80 Muketsu C .10 .20
❑ 81 Mura Sabishii Toshi U .25 .60
❑ 82 Natsumono U .20 .50
❑ 83 No Victory U .25 .60
❑ 84 Ogre Mage C .10 .20
❑ 85 Oni Lair U .60 1.50
❑ 86 Passion R .60 1.50
❑ 87 Peasant Defenders R .60 1.50
❑ 88 Poetry U .20 .50
❑ 89 Political Outcast R .60 1.50
❑ 90 Rage of Matsu C .10 .20
❑ 91 Rain of Death C .10 .20
❑ 92 Remember's Stick U .20 .50
❑ 93 Roadside Shrine U .20 .50
❑ 94 Ronin Swordsman R .60 1.50
❑ 95 Sapphire Strike R 1.00 2.50
❑ 96 Savagery of Moto C .10 .20
❑ 97 Secured Ground R .60 1.50
❑ 98 Seige Engine U .60 1.50
❑ 99 Shadow Harrier R .10 .20
❑ 100 Shadow of Shosuro C .60 1.50
❑ 101 Shahai (Experienced) R .60 1.50
❑ 102 Shattered Focus R .10 .20
❑ 103 Shinjo Loruko C .20 .50
❑ 104 Shinjo Suboto U .10 .20
❑ 105 Shinjo Turong C .20 .50
❑ 106 Shiny Treasure U .20 .50
❑ 107 Shore Commander U .20 .50
❑ 108 Shosuro Infiltrator U .20 .50
❑ 109 Shosuro Saemon U .20 .50
❑ 110 Shosuro Taki U .10 .20
❑ 111 Shosuro Tsuyoshi C .20 .50
❑ 112 Silent Warriors U .20 .50
❑ 113 Soul of the Clan R .60 1.50
❑ 114 Storm of Isawa C .10 .20
❑ 115 Stranglehold U .20 .50
❑ 116 Suitengu's Surge C .10 .20
❑ 117 Sword of Gales C .10 .20
❑ 118 Swordmaster Dojo U .20 .50
❑ 119 Swordmaster's Wakizashi U .20 .50
❑ 120 Tamori Watoshu U .20 .50
❑ 121 Tangen Sensei R .60 1.50
❑ 122 Tch'wik U .20 .50
❑ 123 Tears of Blood R .60 1.50
❑ 124 Tejina's Blessings U .20 .50
❑ 125 Tengoku Acolyte U .20 .50
❑ 126 The Fortunes Smile R 3.00 8.00
❑ 127 The Khol Wall F (Unicorn) .60 1.50
❑ 128 The Last Prophecy R .60 1.50
❑ 129 The Tribeless U .20 .50
❑ 130 Tik'tek C .10 .20
❑ 131 Togashi Matsuo (Experienced) R .60 1.50
❑ 132 Toturi Kurako (Experienced Akodo Kurako) R .60 1.50
❑ 133 Tsuma Dojo R .60 1.50
❑ 134 Tsuruchi Armband U .20 .50
❑ 135 Tsuruchi Etsui C .10 .20
❑ 136 Tsuruchi Iyaken C .10 .20
❑ 137 Tsuruchi Shiroko F (Mantis) .60 1.50
❑ 138 Tsuruchi's Retreat U .20 .50
❑ 139 Umasu Sensei R .60 1.50
❑ 140 Uso Sensei R .60 1.50
❑ 141 Utaku Tarako C .10 .20
❑ 142 Victory or Death R 1.25 3.00
❑ 143 Wardens C .10 .20
❑ 144 Warrior Pilgrim U .20 .50
❑ 145 Way of Sincerity U .20 .50
❑ 146 Weapon Rack C .10 .20
❑ 147 Weigh the Cost C .10 .20
❑ 148 Well-Laid Plains (sic) R .60 1.50
❑ 149 Wrath of the Storm C .10 .20
❑ 150 Writ of Commendation C .10 .20
❑ 151 Writ of Obligation C .10 .20
❑ 152 Writ of Requisition R .60 1.50
❑ 153 Yogo Rieko R .60 1.50
❑ 154 Yoritomo Matsoru U .20 .50
❑ 155 Yoritomo Tokaro C .10 .20
❑ 156 Z'chkir C .10 .20

2004 Legend of the Five Rings Wrath of the Emperor

COMPLETE SET (156)
BOOSTER BOX (48) 20.00 40.00
BOOSTER PACK (11) 1.00 2.00

❑ 1 Agasha Tomioko C .10 .20
❑ 2 Akodo Sanuro C .10 .20
❑ 3 Akodo Tsuyumi U .20 .50
❑ 4 Ambush at Sea C .10 .20
❑ 5 Ambush Duel U .20 .50
❑ 6 Archer Towers C .10 .20
❑ 7 Archer's Row U .30 .75
❑ 8 Armor of Sacrifice R .60 1.50
❑ 9 Army of Jigoku U .20 .50
❑ 10 Asako Bairei R .60 1.50
❑ 11 Asako Tsukuro U .30 .75
❑ 12 Ashigaru Armor C .10 .20
❑ 13 Bamboo Forest R .60 1.50
❑ 14 Bayushi Baku (Experienced 2) F (Scorpion) .60 1.50
❑ 15 Bayushi Muhito C .10 .20
❑ 16 Bayushi Toho U .20 .50
❑ 17 Bayushi's Knives U .20 .50
❑ 18 Beiden Shadows U .20 .50
❑ 19 Binding Kharma R 1.25 3.00
❑ 20 Blade of the Meek U .30 .75
❑ 21 Blood Frenzy U .20 .50
❑ 22 Bloodspeaker Ambush U .20 .50
❑ 23 Brother of Lighthing C .10 .20
❑ 24 Chinamire no Oni U .20 .50
❑ 25 Chuda Mishime C .10 .20
❑ 26 Companion Spirit R 2.00 5.00
❑ 27 Contagion U .20 .50
❑ 28 Courtly Sabotage R 1.00 2.50
❑ 29 Crippled Bone Runner C .10 .20
❑ 30 Crush the Unworthy C .10 .20
❑ 31 Curse of Blood R 1.00 2.50
❑ 32 Daidoji Kumi C .10 .20
❑ 33 Daidoji Ryunosuke U .20 .50
❑ 34 D'gr'n-ki C .10 .20
❑ 35 Divide and Conquer U .20 .50

TCG/CCG

TCG/CCG

❑ 36 Do Not Delay the Inevitable C .10 .20
❑ 37 Exquisite Armor C .10 .20
❑ 38 Fall Before the Master U .20 .50
❑ 39 Fierce Bushi C .10 .20
❑ 40 For the Lady C .10 .20
❑ 41 Fury of the Dark Lord R 2.00 5.00
❑ 42 Fury of the Wolf C .10 .20
❑ 43 Goemon's Ascension R .60 1.50
❑ 44 Gozoku Sensei U .30 .75
❑ 45 Hand of Vengeance U .20 .50
❑ 46 Hida Horii U .20 .50
❑ 47 Hida Sobu U .20 .50
❑ 48 Hida Tonoji U .20 .50
❑ 49 Hida's Formation U .20 .50
❑ 50 Hiruma Tokito C .10 .20
❑ 51 Hitomi Suguhara C .10 .20
❑ 52 Horiuchi Nobane C .10 .20
❑ 53 Hoshi Akiyama R 1.50 4.00
❑ 54 Hoshi Ishida U .30 .75
❑ 55 House of the Jade Princess U .20 .50
❑ 56 Ide Tang (Experienced) R .60 1.50
❑ 57 Ikoma Hasaku C .10 .20
❑ 58 Ikoma Masote U .20 .50
❑ 59 Ikoma Tsai (Experienced) R 1.00 2.50
❑ 60 Isawa Sueno U .20 .50
❑ 61 Iuchi Ryoi U .20 .50
❑ 62 Iuchiban Sensei U .20 .50
❑ 63 Iuchiban's Citadel F (Shadowlands) .60 1.50
❑ 64 Jak-ir't U .20 .50
❑ 65 Jigoku Sensei R .60 1.50
❑ 66 Kaimetsu-uo's Blade C .10 .20
❑ 67 Kakita Noritoshi (Experienced) F (Crane) 2.50 6.00
❑ 68 Kakita Tamura U .30 .75
❑ 69 Kakita Totani C .10 .20
❑ 70 Katsu F (Shadowlands) 1.25 3.00
❑ 71 Knife in the Darkness U .30 .75
❑ 72 Kuni Tansho (Experienced) R 1.25 3.00
❑ 73 Kuni Yae C .10 .20
❑ 74 Kyuden Bayushi F (Scorpion) 1.00 2.50
❑ 75 Layered Armor C .10 .20
❑ 76 Many-Temple Master U .20 .50
❑ 77 Marital Instruction R 1.25 3.00
❑ 78 Megumi (Experienced Daidoji Megumi) R .60 1.50
❑ 79 Mercy in Battle C .10 .20
❑ 80 Mihoko Sensei R .60 1.50
❑ 81 Mirumoto Kaiji U .20 .50
❑ 82 Mirumoto Narumi C .10 .20
❑ 83 Mirumoto Rosanjin (Experienced) R 1.25 3.00
❑ 84 Moshi Mogai (Experienced) R 1.00 2.50
❑ 85 Motivation R 1.25 3.00
❑ 86 Moto Chen (Experienced) R .60 1.50
❑ 87 Murder in the Streets C .10 .20
❑ 88 Musaboru no Oni C .10 .20
❑ 89 Musume Mura U 1.00 2.50
❑ 90 Ninja Mentor U .30 .75
❑ 91 One Tribe U .20 .50
❑ 92 Otomo Spokesman U .20 .50
❑ 93 Patronage C .10 .20
❑ 94 Peasant Weapons U .20 .50
❑ 95 Purge the Weak C .10 .20
❑ 96 Ratling Guide C .10 .20
❑ 97 Ratling Nameseeker C .10 .20
❑ 98 Rich Coffers C .10 .20
❑ 99 Sai no Oni R .60 1.50
❑ 100 Scroll Satchel C .10 .20
❑ 101 Setai Sensei R .60 1.50
❑ 102 Sezaru's Punishment C .10 .20
❑ 103 Shiba Hayama C .10 .20
❑ 104 Shiba Tsukimi (Experienced) R 1.00 2.50
❑ 105 Shifting Fortunes R 1.25 3.00
❑ 106 Shinjo Isuto U .20 .50
❑ 107 Shinjo Riders C .10 .20
❑ 108 Shiro Giri F (Crane) 1.00 2.50
❑ 109 Shi-Tien Yen-Wang Temple C .10 .20
❑ 110 Shosoku Sensei R .60 1.50
❑ 111 Shosuro Hokii U .20 .50
❑ 112 Shosuro Naname C .10 .20
❑ 113 Siege-Breakers C .10 .20
❑ 114 Sla'f'err U .20 .50
❑ 115 Snow-Covered Pass C .10 .20
❑ 116 Someisa Sensei R .60 1.50
❑ 117 Souls in Harmony U .20 .50
❑ 118 Spirits and Steel U .20 .50
❑ 119 Strength From Weakness U .20 .50
❑ 120 Strike and Move U .20 .50
❑ 121 Strike With No Shadow R 2.00 5.00
❑ 122 Supply Lines U .20 .50
❑ 123 Suru's Mempo (Experienced) R 1.00 2.50
❑ 124 Swamp Harriers C .10 .20
❑ 125 Tadaji Sensei R 1.00 2.50
❑ 126 Tamago R 1.25 3.00
❑ 127 Temple of Initiation R .60 1.50
❑ 128 Tenshu Sensei R 1.00 2.50
❑ 129 Te'tik'kir (Experienced 2) R 1.00 2.50
❑ 130 The Barbarian Wall R 1.00 2.50
❑ 131 The Iron Citadel (Experienced) R .60 1.50
❑ 132 The Same Old Tricks C .10 .20
❑ 133 The Tribes Gather C .10 .20
❑ 134 Tishi Sensei R 1.00 2.50
❑ 135 To the Forests U .20 .50
❑ 136 Tomorrow Sensei R 1.00 2.50
❑ 137 Touching the Elements C .10 .20
❑ 138 Tower of the Ningyo R 1.00 2.50
❑ 139 Trading House C .10 .20
❑ 140 Troublesome Bureaucrat R 1.25 3.00
❑ 141 Tsuruchi Okame (Experienced) R 1.00 2.50
❑ 142 Tsuruchi Renshi C .10 .20
❑ 143 Unleash the Demons R .60 1.50
❑ 144 Utaku Rishimaru C .10 .20
❑ 145 Veteran Spearman R .60 1.50
❑ 146 Victory of the Wolf U .20 .50
❑ 147 War on the Plains R .60 1.50
❑ 148 Wikki'thich-hie Z-ee R 1.25 3.00
❑ 149 Wrath of the Bloodspeaker R .60 1.50
❑ 150 Wrath of the Emperor R .60 1.50
❑ 151 Yasuki Hachi (Experienced 2) R 1.50 4.00
❑ 152 Yogo Baisetsu U .40 1.00
❑ 153 Yoma Sensei R .60 1.50
❑ 154 Yoritomo Egumi C .10 .20
❑ 155 Yoritomo Hotako U .20 .50
❑ 156 Yoritomo Katoa (Experienced) R 1.00 2.50

2005 Legend of the Five Rings Code of Bushido

BOOSTER BOX (48) 40.00 80.00
BOOSTER PACK (11) 1.25 2.50

❑ 1 Agasha Fumihiro R 1.00 2.50
❑ 2 Akatch C .10 .20
❑ 3 Akodo Bakin R 1.00 2.50
❑ 4 Akodo Chikafusa U .20 .50
❑ 5 Akodo Mokichi C .10 .20
❑ 6 Akodo Moromao R 1.00 2.50
❑ 7 Baraunghar Tactics R .60 1.50
❑ 8 Bayushi Bokatsu R 1.25 3.00
❑ 9 Bayushi Fujio C .10 .20
❑ 10 Bayushi Hikaru U .20 .50
❑ 11 Bayushi Kan U .20 .50
❑ 12 Bayushi Shun R 1.25 3.00
❑ 13 Bayushi's Feint U .20 .50
❑ 14 Border Skirmish U .20 .50
❑ 15 Cast Out U .20 .50
❑ 16 Chikka-tek U .20 .50
❑ 17 Chuda Isoruko C .10 .20
❑ 18 Chuda Kyuwa R 1.00 2.50
❑ 19 Chuda Ruri C .10 .20
❑ 20 Compassion R .60 1.50
❑ 21 Countermove R 1.25 3.00
❑ 22 Courage R 2.00 5.00
❑ 23 Courtesy R .60 1.50
❑ 24 Crippled Bone Blade C .10 .20
❑ 25 Czinn'tch R 1.00 2.50
❑ 26 Daidoji Nichiren U .20 .50
❑ 27 Daidoji Tae U .20 .50
❑ 28 Daidoji Teika R .60 1.50
❑ 29 Daidoji Uji (Experienced 3) R .60 1.50
❑ 30 Daigotsu Soetsu U .20 .50
❑ 31 Daigotsu Yajinden (Experienced Yajinden) R 1.00 2.50
❑ 32 Dark Fate R 1.00 2.50
❑ 33 Devoured By the Sea U .20 .50
❑ 34 Disavowed U .20 .50
❑ 35 Doji Koin U .20 .50
❑ 36 Doji Midoru F (Crane) .20 .50
❑ 37 Doji Nio C .10 .20
❑ 38 Doji Ranmaru C .10 .20
❑ 39 Doji Soh C .10 .20
❑ 40 Duty R 1.50 4.00
❑ 41 Emikek U .20 .50
❑ 42 Expanding Territory U .20 .50
❑ 43 Extended Maneuvers C .10 .20
❑ 44 Goblin Swarm U .20 .50
❑ 45 Governor's Quarters R .60 1.50
❑ 46 Guilt By Association C .10 .20
❑ 47 Hida Kosedo C .10 .20
❑ 48 Hida Renga U .20 .50
❑ 49 Hida Takuji R 1.25 3.00
❑ 50 Hida Yachi C .10 .20
❑ 51 Hiruma Hiroji U .20 .50
❑ 52 Hiruma Takaaki U .20 .50
❑ 53 Hiruma Tama C .10 .20
❑ 54 Hitomi Kobai (Experienced) R .60 1.50
❑ 55 Hitomi Morimasa R .60 1.50
❑ 56 Honesty R .60 1.50
❑ 57 Honor R .60 1.50
❑ 58 Hoshi Kaelung (Experienced Kaelung) R .60 1.50
❑ 59 Hyotaru U .20 .50
❑ 60 Ichiro Yojimbo C .10 .20
❑ 61 Ikoma Chikao F (Lion) .60 1.50
❑ 62 Ikoma Itagi U .20 .50
❑ 63 Iron Hand Strike C .10 .20
❑ 64 Isawa Eitoku U .20 .50
❑ 65 Isawa Kimi C .10 .20
❑ 66 Isawa Suzuko C .10 .20
❑ 67 Isawa Tsune C .10 .20
❑ 68 Iuchi Lixue (Experienced) R .60 1.50
❑ 69 Iuchi Umeka C .10 .20
❑ 70 Kagami no Oni C .10 .20
❑ 71 Kaimetsu-uo's Formation C .10 .20
❑ 72 Kaiu Haku R .60 1.50
❑ 73 Kaiu Sugimoto (Experienced Keeper of Earth) R.60 1.50
❑ 74 Kakita Kiyonobu R .60 1.50
❑ 75 Keep the Peace U .20 .50
❑ 76 Kensaku C .10 .20
❑ 77 Kiii C .10 .20
❑ 78 Kitsuki Hakihime C .10 .20
❑ 79 Kitsuki Nagiken R .60 1.50
❑ 80 Kitsuki Raichi C .10 .20
❑ 81 K'mee U .20 .50
❑ 82 Kobushi U .20 .50
❑ 83 Kyuden Otomo F (Crane) .60 1.50
❑ 84 Manithith R .60 1.50
❑ 85 Masahigi's Blade R .60 1.50
❑ 86 Matsu Arinori C .10 .20
❑ 87 Matsu Eishi U .20 .50
❑ 88 Matsu Okyoito C .10 .20
❑ 89 Matsu Sanraku R .60 1.50
❑ 90 Midnight Blades C .10 .20
❑ 91 Minikui no Oni R .60 1.50
❑ 92 Mirumoto Bokkai U .20 .50
❑ 93 Mirumoto Etsuya U .20 .50
❑ 94 Mirumoto Kiyohira U .20 .50
❑ 95 Moshi Hitaka R .60 1.50
❑ 96 Moto Hideyo (Experienced) R .60 1.50
❑ 97 Moto Ichezo U .20 .50
❑ 98 Moto Jippensha C .10 .20
❑ 99 Moto Kinnojo R .60 1.50
❑ 100 Moto Rumiko U .20 .50
❑ 101 Nem'tek R .60 1.50
❑ 102 Nezumi Migration U .20 .50
❑ 103 Nimm'k U .20 .50
❑ 104 Nomi U .20 .50
❑ 105 O'chin C .10 .20
❑ 106 Passage Between Worlds C .10 .20
❑ 107 Peasant Uprising C .10 .20
❑ 108 Righteous Fury C .10 .20
❑ 109 Rise of the Shogun R .60 1.50
❑ 110 Ryoken R 1.50 4.00
❑ 111 Scouring the Shadows C .10 .20
❑ 112 Seal the Way R .60 1.50
❑ 113 Shiba Denbe C .10 .20
❑ 114 Shiba Ningen (Experienced 2) R .60 1.50
❑ 115 Shiba Shinsaku U .20 .50
❑ 116 Shiba Yoshimi U .20 .50
❑ 117 Shinjo Irosuko C .10 .20
❑ 118 Shinjo Natsume U .20 .50
❑ 119 Shinjo Shria C .10 .20
❑ 120 Shiro no Soshi F (Scorpion) 1.25 3.00
❑ 121 Shiro no Yojin F (Lion) 1.25 3.00
❑ 122 Shorihotsu's Blessing C .10 .20
❑ 123 Shosuro Hisashi C .10 .20
❑ 124 Shosuro Kinji C .10 .20
❑ 125 Shosuro Madoka R .60 1.50
❑ 126 Shosuro Nakaga (Experienced Shinjo Nakaga) F (Scorpion) .60 1.50
❑ 127 Shosuro Oniji U .20 .50
❑ 128 Sincerity R .60 1.50
❑ 129 Skirt the Edge U .20 .50
❑ 130 Strike at the Head R .60 1.50
❑ 131 Sucking Mire U .20 .50
❑ 132 Sunder the Darkness R .60 1.50
❑ 133 Tactics of the Bear R .60 1.50
❑ 134 Tamafune C .10 .20
❑ 135 Tamori Konoyoe C .10 .20
❑ 136 Tasu no Oni U .20 .50
❑ 137 Tempest Island Initiate C .10 .20
❑ 138 The Emperor's Defense C .10 .20
❑ 139 The Emperor's Justice U .20 .50
❑ 140 The Lion's Roar C .10 .20
❑ 141 The Master Redeemed R 1.00 2.50
❑ 142 The Obsidian Halls of the Lost U .30 .75
❑ 143 The Wolf's Mercy U .20 .50
❑ 144 Threads of Fate C .10 .20
❑ 145 Tsuruchi Masanori C .10 .20
❑ 146 Usagi Retainer C .10 .20
❑ 147 Wayward Attack U .20 .50
❑ 148 We Stand Ready U .20 .50
❑ 149 Will of the Elements U .20 .50
❑ 150 Writ of the Anvil R .60 1.50
❑ 151 Yasuki Miliko U .20 .50
❑ 152 Yoritomo Buntaro R .60 1.50
❑ 153 Yoritomo Kaigen R .60 1.50
❑ 154 Yoritomo Kiroto U .20 .50
❑ 155 Yoritomo Kumita C .10 .20
❑ 156 Yoritomo Okitsugu U .20 .50

2005 Legend of the Five Rings Enemy of my Enemy

BOOSTER BOX (48) 40.00 80.00
BOOSTER PACK (11) 1.25 2.50

❑ 1 Advance Forces U .20 .50
❑ 2 Agasha Kushujin C .10 .20
❑ 3 Akodo Sadahige C .10 .20
❑ 4 Ancestral Standard of the Lion Clan (Experienced) R .60 1.50
❑ 5 Armor of Tengoku C .10 .20
❑ 6 Ashigaru Conscripts C .10 .20
❑ 7 Awaken the Eighth R 1.25 3.00
❑ 8 Bayushi Kaibara U .20 .50
❑ 9 Bayushi Saya C .10 .20
❑ 10 Bayushi Shinzo U .20 .50
❑ 11 Bayushi Sunetra (Experienced 2) R 1.00 2.50
❑ 12 Bayushi Tsimaru (Experienced) R .60 1.50
❑ 13 Blazing Arrow C .10 .20
❑ 14 Blight of War C .10 .20
❑ 15 Celestial Road R .60 1.50
❑ 16 Charge of the First Legion U .20 .50
❑ 17 Chi'kel U .20 .50
❑ 18 Clash of Steel R 1.00 2.50
❑ 19 Cleansing Spirit U .20 .50
❑ 20 Clumsy Ambush C .10 .20
❑ 21 Complex Maneuvers R 1.25 3.00
❑ 22 Contest of Iaijutsu C .10 .20
❑ 23 Contest of Power C .10 .20
❑ 24 Contest of Testimony C .10 .20
❑ 25 Contest of Wealth C .10 .20
❑ 26 Control the Roads U .20 .50
❑ 27 Crown of the Amethyst Champion U .20 .50
❑ 28 Curio Shop C .10 .20
❑ 29 Daidoji Armor C .10 .20
❑ 30 Daidoji Gunso C .10 .20
❑ 31 Daidoji Shihei C .10 .20
❑ 32 Darkwater Bay U .20 .50
❑ 33 Diplomatic Retreat C .10 .20
❑ 34 Doji Akiko (Experienced) R .60 1.50
❑ 35 Doji Choshi U .20 .50
❑ 36 Doji Maseru (Experienced) R .60 1.50
❑ 37 Doji Ran U .20 .50
❑ 38 Doji Reju (Experienced 3) R .60 1.50
❑ 39 Embrace the Stone U .20 .50
❑ 40 Emma-O's Amulet R .60 1.50
❑ 41 Equal Match R .60 1.50
❑ 42 Excellence R .60 1.50
❑ 43 Fire on the Sea R .60 1.50
❑ 44 Fires of Battle U .20 .50
❑ 45 Flag Messengers C .10 .20
❑ 46 Foolish Words R .60 1.50
❑ 47 Fortified Camp C .10 .20
❑ 48 Fu Leng's Tomb (Experienced Forgotten Tomb) R.60 1.50
❑ 49 Gohei Sensei R .60 1.50
❑ 50 Harmony in Chaos C .10 .20
❑ 51 Hasaiki no Oni C .10 .20
❑ 52 Hida Kisada (Experienced) R .60 1.50
❑ 53 Hida Nari U .20 .50
❑ 54 Hida Sadaharu (Experienced) F (Crab) 1.00 2.50
❑ 55 Hiruma Tokimune C .10 .20
❑ 56 Hohiro U .20 .50
❑ 57 Ide Bantu U .20 .50
❑ 58 Ikm'atch-tek (Experienced) R .60 -1.50
❑ 59 Ikoma Yasuko (Experienced Shosuro Yasuko) R.60 1.50
❑ 60 Imbue Chi C .10 .20
❑ 61 Imperial Artificer C .10 .20
❑ 62 Iron Warriors R .60 1.50
❑ 63 Isawa Jumon U .20 .50
❑ 64 Isawa Kazushi C .10 .20
❑ 65 Jade Tetsubo C .10 .20
❑ 66 Kaiu Natsukiwa C .10 .20
❑ 67 Kakita Osei C .10 .20
❑ 68 Kedamono Sensei R .60 1.50
❑ 69 Kharmic Confrontation R 1.00 2.50
❑ 70 Kitsuki Otojiro C .10 .20
❑ 71 Kr'chan C .10 .20
❑ 72 Ku'chek C .10 .20
❑ 73 Kuni Nakanu's Journals U .20 .50
❑ 74 Kuni Okichi U .20 .50
❑ 75 Legacy of Dragons U .20 .50
❑ 76 Matsu Aoiko (Experienced) R .60 1.50
❑ 77 Matsu Nanako C .10 .20
❑ 78 Matsu Robun U .25 .60
❑ 79 Matsu Takuya U .20 .50
❑ 80 Meeting the Keepers R 2.50 6.00
❑ 81 Midnight Raid U .20 .50
❑ 82 Mirumoto Hakahime C .10 .20
❑ 83 Mirumoto Hirohisa U .20 .50
❑ 84 Mirumoto Yuichi U .20 .50
❑ 85 Morale Officer C .10 .20
❑ 86 Moto Akikazu U .20 .50
❑ 87 Moto Gonnohyoe R .60 1.50
❑ 88 Moto Hanzhi (Experienced) R .60 1.50
❑ 89 Munemitsu no Oni R .60 1.50
❑ 90 Ninja Sabotage U .20 .50
❑ 91 O'kichit F (Ratling) .60 1.50
❑ 92 Oni-Daikyu R 1.50 4.00
❑ 93 Opportunists C .10 .20
❑ 94 Osaju's Lifeblood U .20 .50
❑ 95 Outmaneuvered by Tactics U .25 .60
❑ 96 Personal Assassin U .20 .50
❑ 97 Plague of Insects U .20 .50
❑ 98 Rama Singh U .25 .60
❑ 99 Ratling Trackers C .10 .20
❑ 100 Rezan (Experienced) R .60 1.50
❑ 101 Rite of Travel R .60 1.50
❑ 102 Rosoku R .60 1.50
❑ 103 Sacrifice of Pawns R 1.25 3.00
❑ 104 Sadance Contest C .10 .20
❑ 105 Sap the Spirit U .20 .50
❑ 106 Scour the Earth C .10 .20
❑ 107 Seikitsu Mountains U .20 .50
❑ 108 Sentei no Oni R 2.00 5.00
❑ 109 Seppun Toshiaki U .25 .60
❑ 110 Sezaru Returns U .20 .50
❑ 111 Shadow of Amaterasu U .20 .50
❑ 112 Shiba Naoya U .20 .50
❑ 113 Shiba Yoma (Experienced 2) R .60 1.50
❑ 114 Shining Son R .60 1.50
❑ 115 Shinjo Fuyuko C .10 .20
❑ 116 Shinjo Tsuyoshi C .10 .20
❑ 117 Shiro Kitsuki F (Dragon) 1.00 2.50
❑ 118 Shosuro Adeiko C .10 .20
❑ 119 Shrine of Thwarted Destiny C .10 .20
❑ 120 Sinister Rebirth R .60 1.50
❑ 121 Soften the Resistance C .10 .20
❑ 122 Sohei Guardian C .10 .20
❑ 123 Stagnant Ground R .60 1.50
❑ 124 Stinging Insects R .60 1.50
❑ 125 Strange Magics R .60 1.50
❑ 126 Suiteiru no Oni (Experienced) R .60 1.50
❑ 127 Tamori Shiki (Experienced) F (Dragon) .60 1.50
❑ 128 Temple of Persistence F (Crab) 1.00 2.50
❑ 129 The Bear Returns R 1.25 3.00
❑ 130 The Better Gift U .20 .50
❑ 131 The Hidden Heart of Iuchiban (Experienced) R.60 1.50
❑ 132 The Shogun's Command R .60 1.50
❑ 133 The Snake Speaks U .20 .50
❑ 134 The Steel Throne (Experienced) U .20 .50
❑ 135 Three Storms U .20 .50
❑ 136 Tighten Patrol U .20 .50
❑ 137 To Seek the Truth U .20 .50
❑ 138 Togashi Ieshigi (Experienced Akodo Ieshigi) R.60 1.50
❑ 139 Tortoise Ambassador R .60 1.50
❑ 140 Tsuruchi Risako R .60 1.50
❑ 141 Tsuruchi Shunso C .10 .20
❑ 142 Tsusung Sensei R .60 1.50
❑ 143 Unfamiliar Ground C .10 .20
❑ 144 Untested Scouts C .10 .20
❑ 145 Wandering Budoka R 6.00 15.00
❑ 146 Warrens of the One Tribe F (Ratling) 1.00 2.50
❑ 147 Writ of Command U .20 .50
❑ 148 Writ of Restriction U .20 .50
❑ 149 Yobanjin Alliance U .25 .60
❑ 150 Yojireru no Oni C .10 .20
❑ 151 Yoriki C .10 .20
❑ 152 Yoritomo Bokkai U .20 .50
❑ 153 Yoritomo Naizen (Experienced) R .60 1.50
❑ 154 Yoritomo Shumei C .10 .20
❑ 155 Yoritomo Suketsune U .20 .50
❑ 156 Zamalash U .20 .50

2006 Legend of the Five Rings Drums of War

BOOSTER BOX (48) 50.00 100.00
BOOSTER PACK (11) 1.50 3.00

❑ 1 Agasha Chisuzu U .20 .50
❑ 2 All Things Have A Price U .20 .50
❑ 3 Arms Smugglers U .50 1.25
❑ 4 Asahina Hira (Experienced Keeper of the Void) R1.00 2.50
❑ 5 Asahina Sekawa (Experienced 3) R .60 1.50
❑ 6 Asako Meisuru C .10 .20
❑ 7 Awaken the Sins U .20 .50
❑ 8 Back to Back U .20 .50
❑ 9 Bayushi Lineage U .20 .50
❑ 10 Bayushi Muhito R 1.00 2.50
❑ 11 Blade of Hubris R 2.50 6.00
❑ 12 Blessed Yumi C .10 .20
❑ 13 Border Conflict U .20 .50
❑ 14 Broad Front R 4.00 10.00
❑ 15 Broken Shinbone Warren C .10 .20
❑ 16 Buying Time U .20 .50
❑ 17 City of the Rich Frog R 1.25 3.00
❑ 18 Corrupt Jade Vein U .20 .50
❑ 19 Crane Detachment C .10 .20
❑ 20 Crippling Cut U .40 1.00
❑ 21 Crossroads of Destiny C .10 .20
❑ 22 Daigotsu Kaikou U .30 .75
❑ 23 Daigotsu Masami C .10 .20
❑ 24 Daigotsu Rekai (Experienced 3 Daidoji Rekai) R1.25 3.00
❑ 25 Dark Moto Steed U .20 .50
❑ 26 Deadly Melee R 1.25 3.00
❑ 27 Doji Chieri C .10 .20
❑ 28 Doji Lineage U .20 .50
❑ 29 Dragon's Heart Dojo F (Dragon) 1.00 2.50
❑ 30 Eager to Fight R 2.00 5.00
❑ 31 Embrace the Darkness C .10 .20
❑ 32 Exchange Destiny C .10 .20
❑ 33 Face to Face C .10 .20
❑ 34 Fields of Mercy R 1.00 2.50
❑ 35 Flying Leap C .10 .20
❑ 36 Forest Thickets C .10 .20
❑ 37 Gates of Jigoku U .20 .50
❑ 38 Goblin Healer C .10 .20
❑ 39 Goblin Sapper U .30 .75
❑ 40 Gosoku Strategies U .60 1.50
❑ 41 Gozoku Distraction R .20 .50
❑ 42 Gozoku Meddling U .20 .50
❑ 43 Grasp Destiny C .10 .20
❑ 44 Guarded by Chi R .60 1.50
❑ 45 Heigai (Experienced 5 Akodo Ginawa) F (Lion)1.25 3.00
❑ 46 Heroic Feat C .10 .20
❑ 47 Hida Daizu (Experienced) R .60 1.50
❑ 48 Hida Harou U .20 .50
❑ 49 Hida Kaihei U .20 .50
❑ 50 Hida Kengo C .10 .20
❑ 51 Hida Nichie C .10 .20
❑ 52 Hida Students R .60 1.50
❑ 53 Hitomi Mineyo C .20 .50
❑ 54 Hitomi Sugahara (Experienced) F (Dragon) 1.00 2.50
❑ 55 Hitomi Tatsumi U .20 .50
❑ 56 Hitomi Tsubo C .10 .20
❑ 57 Horiuchi Wakiza C .10 .20
❑ 58 Ichiro Kihongo (Experienced) U .20 .50
❑ 59 Ikoma Fujimaro (Experienced) R .60 1.50
❑ 60 Ikuei U .25 .60
❑ 61 Immobile Stance R 1.25 3.00
❑ 62 Isawa Aiya R .60 1.50
❑ 63 Joy of Plunder U .20 .50
❑ 64 Junghar Encampment F (Unicorn) 1.00 2.50
❑ 65 Kakita Daiki C .10 .20
❑ 66 Kakita Korihime (Experienced) U .20 .50
❑ 67 Kaneka's Conflict C .10 .20
❑ 68 Kitsu Fukashi U .20 .50
❑ 69 Kitsu Katsuko U .20 .50
❑ 70 Kitsu Lineage U .20 .50
❑ 71 Kituski Orika C .10 .20

☐ 72 Kokujin's Daisho (Experienced) R .60 1.50
☐ 73 Kyofu (Experienced 2 Hida Kuroda) R 1.25 3.00
☐ 74 Lasy Moon's Prophecy U .20 .50
☐ 75 Lateral Maneuver U .20 .50
☐ 76 Legion of the Sapphire Shrysanthemum R .60 1.50
☐ 77 Lion Detachment C .10 .20
☐ 78 Mantis Detachment U .20 .50
☐ 79 Mark of the Taine C .10 .20
☐ 80 Matsu Benika C .10 .20
☐ 81 Matsu Lineage C .10 .20
☐ 82 Matsu Yokuya C .10 .20
☐ 83 Memories of the Lost U .20 .50
☐ 84 Mockery R 2.00 5.00
☐ 85 Moto Wasaka U .20 .50
☐ 86 Municipal Roads C .10 .20
☐ 87 Naseru's Conflict C .10 .20
☐ 88 Nintai (Experienced Tsuno Nintai) R .60 1.50
☐ 89 Omoni (Experienced 2) R .60 1.50
☐ 90 Path of Jigoku U .20 .50
☐ 91 Phoenix Detachment U .20 .50
☐ 92 Porcelain Mask of Fu Leng (Experienced 2) R .60 1.50
☐ 93 Precise Strike C .10 .20
☐ 94 Reckless Pursuit C .10 .20
☐ 95 Reinforcements Arrive R 2.00 5.00
☐ 96 Relief Troops C .10 .20
☐ 97 Re-outfitting C .10 .20
☐ 98 Run or Die C .10 .20
☐ 99 Second Doom of the Lion R .60 1.50
☐ 100 Second Doom of the Phoenix R .60 1.50
☐ 101 Serene Patrol C .10 .20
☐ 102 Set'tch'chet U .25 .60
☐ 103 Sezaru's Burden R .60 1.50
☐ 104 Sezaru's Conflict U .20 .50
☐ 105 Shadow on the Court U .20 .50
☐ 106 Shadowed Path to Victory U .20 .50
☐ 107 Shamed by Valor R 1.25 3.00
☐ 108 Shattered Defenses C .10 .20
☐ 109 Shiba Arihiro U .20 .50
☐ 110 Shiba Danjuro (Experienced) R .60 1.50
☐ 111 Shiba Gyousei C .10 .20
☐ 112 Shiba's Promise R .60 1.50
☐ 113 Shinbone Pack U .25 .60
☐ 114 Shinbone Warrior C .10 .20
☐ 115 Shinjo Dun C .10 .20
☐ 116 Shinjo Shono (Experienced 3) F (Unicorn) 1.25 3.00
☐ 117 Shinsei's Crow R .60 1.50
☐ 118 Shosuro Maru (Experienced) R .60 1.50
☐ 119 Shosuro Nakako C .10 .20
☐ 120 Shosuro Rishou U .20 .50
☐ 121 Shosuro Yudoka (Experienced 2) U .20 .50
☐ 122 Shoulder to Shoulder C .10 .20
☐ 123 Silent Kill U .20 .50
☐ 124 Smuggler Agent R .60 1.50
☐ 125 Song of Steel C .10 .20
☐ 126 Soshi Shuuko C .10 .20
☐ 127 Spiked Tetsubo C .10 .20
☐ 128 Supply Smugglers C .10 .20
☐ 129 Tanuki Spirit U .20 .50
☐ 130 Tawagoto (Experienced) R .60 1.50
☐ 131 Tch'tek C .10 .20
☐ 132 The Hall of Ancestors F (Lion) 1.25 3.00
☐ 133 The Shogun's Guard R .60 1.50
☐ 134 Togashi Mitsu (Experienced 3) R .60 1.50
☐ 135 Toturi Miyako (Experienced) R .60 1.50
☐ 136 Toturi's Battle Standard (Experienced) R .60 1.50
☐ 137 Tsukuri R 6.00 15.00
☐ 138 Tsuruchi Chikuma U .25 .60
☐ 139 Tsuruchi Jougo C .10 .20
☐ 140 Turn the Tide R 1.25 3.00
☐ 141 Unexpected Resources R .60 1.50
☐ 142 Unstoppable Force R .60 1.50
☐ 143 Utaku Uzuki R .60 1.50
☐ 144 Utaku Yasuha U .20 .50
☐ 145 Vengeance Cannot Wait R .60 1.50
☐ 146 Visions of Doom U .20 .50
☐ 147 Void Dragon (Experienced 2) R .60 1.50
☐ 148 Water Is My Steed R .60 1.50
☐ 149 Weighted Yari C .10 .20
☐ 150 Yasuki Gakuto U .20 .50
☐ 151 Yoee'tr (Experienced) R .60 1.50
☐ 152 Yoritomo Bunmei C .10 .20
☐ 153 Yoritomo Hanayo U .25 .60
☐ 154 Yoritomo Kitao (Experienced 3) R .60 1.50
☐ 155 Yoritomo Yashinko R 2.50 6.00
☐ 156 Yotsu Dojo C .10 .20

2006 Legend of the Five Rings Path of Hope

BOOSTER BOX (48) 50.00 100.00
BOOSTER PACK (11) 1.50 3.00

☐ 1 A Hero's Gift U .20 .50
☐ 2 A Life for a Life R .60 1.50
☐ 3 Abandoned C .10 .20
☐ 4 Accusation U .60 1.50
☐ 5 Agasha Shaku R .60 1.50
☐ 6 Air Dragon (Experienced 2) R 1.00 2.50
☐ 7 Akodo Michio C .10 .20
☐ 8 Akodo Nariaki U .20 .50
☐ 9 Akodo Terumoto R 1.25 3.00
☐ 10 Akutenshi's Tribute C .10 .20
☐ 11 Allegiance to the Emperor C .10 .20
☐ 12 Allegiance to the Shogun C .10 .20
☐ 13 Always Ready U .20 .50
☐ 14 Arrival of the Obsidian Champion R 1.25 3.00
☐ 15 Arrogance R 1.50 4.00
☐ 16 Baraunghar Technique C .10 .20
☐ 17 Bayushi Kageki (Experienced Mad Ronin) R 1.00 2.50
☐ 18 Bayushi Kaneo C .10 .20
☐ 19 Bayushi Moyotoshi U .20 .50
☐ 20 Bayushi Shumpei U .20 .50
☐ 21 Blood and Steel U .20 .50
☐ 22 Blossoming Conflict R .60 1.50
☐ 23 Castle Gate R 1.25 3.00
☐ 24 Castle Towers C .10 .20
☐ 25 Castle Walls C .10 .20
☐ 26 Chitik R 1.50 4.00
☐ 27 Chuda Hankyu R 2.00 5.00
☐ 28 Conscriptors R 1.00 2.50
☐ 29 Conserve Your Strength C .10 .20
☐ 30 Counsel of the Keepers U .20 .50
☐ 31 Courtly Scholars U .20 .50
☐ 32 Credit Where Due C .10 .20
☐ 33 Daidoji Naito C .10 .20
☐ 34 Daigotsu Fumiaki U .10 .20
☐ 35 Daigotsu Ogiwara U .20 .50
☐ 36 Dark Feeding C .20 .50
☐ 37 Doji Fujie U .20 .50
☐ 38 Doji Jun'ai (Experienced Keeper of Water) R .20 .50
☐ 39 Doji Kazo (Experienced) U .60 1.50
☐ 40 Doji Munabu C .20 .50
☐ 41 Draw Your Blade R 8.00 20.00
☐ 42 Eyes of the Serpent C .10 .20
☐ 43 Favor to the Dragon U .20 .50
☐ 44 Favor to the Horde U .20 .50
☐ 45 Favor to the Scorpion U .20 .50
☐ 46 Favorable Terrain C .10 .20
☐ 47 Fields of Foolish Pride R 1.25 3.00
☐ 48 Flee from Tomorrow R .60 1.50
☐ 49 Forest Cleansing R 1.50 4.00
☐ 50 Forest Killer Cavern C .10 .20
☐ 51 Fortress of the Bear F (Crab) 1.25 3.00
☐ 52 Fuhao's Shadow U .20 .50
☐ 53 Golden Obi of the Sun Goddess (Experienced) R .60 1.50
☐ 54 Gr'tik-er C .10 .20
☐ 55 Heart of the Mountain U .20 .50
☐ 56 Hida Hiyao C .10 .20
☐ 57 Hida Iseki F (Crab) .40 1.00
☐ 58 Hida Takuma U .20 .50
☐ 59 Hida Uneki U .20 .50
☐ 60 Hida War Cry R .60 1.50
☐ 61 Hiruma Hino C .10 .20
☐ 62 Hiruma Hitaken R .60 1.50
☐ 63 Hisaki R .60 1.50
☐ 64 Homecoming C .10 .20
☐ 65 Honor Guard C .10 .20
☐ 66 Hoshi Masujiro U .30 .75
☐ 67 House of the White Jade Fan U .20 .50
☐ 68 Howl of the Wolf U .20 .50
☐ 69 I Know That Trick R 4.00 10.00
☐ 70 Ide Jiao U .20 .50
☐ 71 Isawa Sata U .20 .50
☐ 72 Isawa Tanaka U .20 .50
☐ 73 Isawa Tomita C .10 .20
☐ 74 Iwase C .10 .20
☐ 75 Jade Petal Tea U .20 .50
☐ 76 Kakita Tsuken .60 1.50
(Experienced Keeper of Fire) F (Crane)
☐ 77 Kharmic Struggle R .60 1.50
☐ 78 Kitsuki Ryushi R .60 1.50
☐ 79 Kitsuki Seiji C .10 .20
☐ 80 Kukojin (Experienced 3) R .60 1.50
☐ 81 Kukojin's Temptation R 1.25 3.00
☐ 82 Kuni's Eye U .20 .50
☐ 83 Kyoso's Hunters U .20 .50
☐ 84 Letter of Confession C .10 .20
☐ 85 Lone Magistrate U .20 .50
☐ 86 Matsu Hirake U .20 .50
☐ 87 Matsu Shimei C .10 .20
☐ 88 Matsu Yoshino R 1.00 2.50
☐ 89 Mirumoto Chojiro C .10 .20
☐ 90 Mirumoto Masae (Experienced Keeper of Air) R .60 1.50
☐ 91 Mishakene C .10 .20
☐ 92 Mitsu's Return R .60 1.50
☐ 93 Moshi Sayako U .20 .50
☐ 94 Moto Kang U .20 .50
☐ 95 Moto Tsume (Experienced 3) F (Shadowlands) 2.00 5.00
☐ 96 N'ck C .10 .20
☐ 97 Night Crystal Scepter C .10 .20
☐ 98 Obsidian Riders R .60 1.50
☐ 99 P-o'tch U .20 .50
☐ 100 Preparation C .10 .20
☐ 101 Proof of Dishonor U .20 .50
☐ 102 Prosperous Plains City F (Crane) 1.00 2.50
☐ 103 Rapid Deployment C .10 .20
☐ 104 Repair Crew U .20 .50
☐ 105 Righteous Doshin C .10 .20
☐ 106 Sachi's Defiance C .10 .20
☐ 107 Scrutiny of the Wasp U .20 .50
☐ 108 Second Doom of the Crab R .60 1.50
☐ 109 Second Doom of the Crane R .60 1.50
☐ 110 Secret from the Mantis U .20 .50
☐ 111 Secrets from the Ratling U .20 .50
☐ 112 Seeking Within C .10 .20
☐ 113 Selfless Courage R .60 1.50
☐ 114 Shiba Fugimori R .60 1.50
☐ 115 Shiba Riza C .10 .20
☐ 116 Shinjo Senhao R .60 1.50
☐ 117 Shinjo Wei R .60 1.50
☐ 118 Shinjo Xie C .10 .20
☐ 119 Shinjo's Arrow R .60 1.50
☐ 120 Shosuro Mikado (Experienced) R .60 1.50
☐ 121 Shosuro Toma C .10 .20
☐ 122 Shuten Doji's Fury R 2.00 5.00
☐ 123 Storm Rider Explorer R 1.25 3.00
☐ 124 Tainted Whispers C .10 .20
☐ 125 Tawagoto C .10 .20
☐ 126 Tchree U .20 .50
☐ 127 Temple of the General U .20 .50
☐ 128 Temple of the Lotus U .20 .50
☐ 129 Ten Thousand Temples U .20 .50
☐ 130 Test His Mettle C .10 .20
☐ 131 Test of Loyalty C .10 .20
☐ 132 The Bitter Shadow of Shame R 2.00 5.00
☐ 133 The Death of Akiko R .60 1.50
☐ 134 The Halls of the Damned F (Shadowlands) 1.25 3.00
☐ 135 The Kami's Blessing U .20 .50
☐ 136 The Tail Strikes U .20 .50
☐ 137 The War of Fire and Thunder R .60 1.50
☐ 138 Thunder and Steel U .20 .50
☐ 139 Togashi Razan U .20 .50
☐ 140 Tsuken's Blade C .10 .20
☐ 141 Tsuruchi Chae R .60 1.50
☐ 142 Tsuruchi Dokuo C .10 .20
☐ 143 Tsuruchi Kaya C .10 .20
☐ 144 Unexpected Testimony R .60 1.50
☐ 145 Unity of Purpose U .20 .50
☐ 146 Utaku Mihua C .10 .20
☐ 147 Valiant Stand U .20 .50
☐ 148 Wareta no Oni R .60 1.50
☐ 149 Water Dragon (Experienced 2) R .60 1.50
☐ 150 Weakened Defenses C .10 .20
☐ 151 Wisdom and Courage U .20 .50
☐ 152 Wrath of the Keepers R .60 1.50
☐ 153 Wretched Mercenary C .10 .20
☐ 154 Yoritomo Ietsuna U .20 .50
☐ 155 You Are Too Late R .60 1.50
☐ 156 Y'tchee R .60 1.50

2006 Legend of the Five Rings Rise of the Shogun

BOOSTER BOX (48) 40.00 80.00
BOOSTER PACK (11) 1.25 2.50

☐ 1 A Dragon's Caress R .60 1.50
☐ 2 Advance with Glory C .10 .20
☐ 3 Akodo Meyo C .10 .20
☐ 4 Akodo Osamu R 2.00 5.00
☐ 5 Allegiance to the Dark Lord C .30 .75
☐ 6 Ancestral Ground C .10 .20
☐ 7 Asahina Aoshi R .60 1.50
☐ 8 Asahina Beniha U .40 1.00
☐ 9 Asako Bairei (Experienced 2) R 1.25 3.00
☐ 10 Asako Makito U .20 .50
☐ 11 Assembly Grounds C .10 .20
☐ 12 Bamboo Thickets U .20 .50
☐ 13 Battle Maiden Troop R 1.50 4.00
☐ 14 Bayushi Iyona C .10 .20
☐ 15 Bayushi Kwanchi (Experienced 2) F (Scorpion) 1.50 4.00
☐ 16 Bayushi Shaiga C .10 .20
☐ 17 Bayushi Takaharu U .20 .50
☐ 18 Blackmailed Bride R 2.50 6.00
☐ 19 Bounty of the Clan U .20 .50
☐ 20 Bow Your Head! C .10 .20
☐ 21 Breeding Season U .20 .50
☐ 22 Broken Wave City F (Mantis) 1.00 2.50
☐ 23 Call Upon the Dead C .10 .20
☐ 24 Calling the East Wind R 1.25 3.00
☐ 25 Castle Barracks C .10 .20
☐ 26 Chuda Ikumi C .10 .20
☐ 27 Consumed by Five Fires C .10 .20
☐ 28 Control R 2.00 5.00
☐ 29 Crab Detachment C .10 .20
☐ 30 Daigotsu Eiya U 1.25 3.00
☐ 31 Daigotsu Makishi C .10 .20
☐ 32 Daigotsu's Discipline U .20 .50
☐ 33 Dark Harmony U .20 .50
☐ 34 Deathseeker Troop C .10 .20
☐ 35 Deeds of Honor C .10 .20
☐ 36 Delaying Column C .10 .20
☐ 37 Determination R 2.50 6.00
☐ 38 Doji Domotai (Experienced 2) R 1.25 3.00
☐ 39 Doji Ichita C .10 .20
☐ 40 Doji Otoya C .10 .20
☐ 41 Dragon Detachment U .20 .50
☐ 42 Earth Becomes Sky U .30 .75
☐ 43 East Hub Village R 1.25 3.00
☐ 44 Fan and Sword U .20 .50
☐ 45 Fields of Honor C .10 .20
☐ 46 Fire Maple Mempo U .20 .50
☐ 47 Glorious Mission C .10 .20
☐ 48 Golden Oriole Wakizashi U .20 .50
☐ 49 Hachiwari R .20 .50
☐ 50 Hida Benjiro (Experienced) R .60 1.50
☐ 51 Hida Wakou U .40 1.00
☐ 52 Hida War Drums R .60 1.50
☐ 53 Hiruma Sakimi C .10 .20
☐ 54 Hitomi Chishou C .10 .20
☐ 55 Honored Hostage U .30 .75
☐ 56 Horiushi Nobane R 1.00 2.50
☐ 57 Hunted Down C .10 .20
☐ 58 Ik'chda C .10 .20
☐ 59 Infamous Deeds C .10 .20
☐ 60 Insight R 1.50 4.00
☐ 61 Inspired Strategy U 1.00 2.50
☐ 62 Isawa Angai 2.00 5.00
(Experienced Soshi Angai) F (Phoenix)
☐ 63 Isawa Emori C .10 .20
☐ 64 Isawa Seiga C .10 .20
☐ 65 Itch'choo C .10 .20
☐ 66 Iuchi Bitomu C .10 .20
☐ 67 Jade Figurine C .10 .20
☐ 68 Kaimetsu-Ou's Lineage U .20 .50
☐ 69 Kaiu Sadao C .10 .20
☐ 70 Kakita Kaisei U .20 .50
☐ 71 K'chee R .60 1.50
☐ 72 Kisada's Banishment U .30 .75
☐ 73 Knowledge R 3.00 8.00
☐ 74 Kokujin Akae U .20 .50
☐ 75 Kokujin Konetsu R .60 1.50
☐ 76 Kuni Daigo R 1.00 2.50
☐ 77 Kuni Fumitake U .20 .50
☐ 78 Kuroiban Compound U .20 .50
☐ 79 Kyoden's Technique C .10 .20
☐ 80 Legion of Pain R 1.50 4.00
☐ 81 Lightning Strike R .60 1.50
☐ 82 Matsu Bunka U .20 .50
☐ 83 Matsu Gakuya C .10 .20
☐ 84 Matsu Yoshino (Experienced) R .60 1.50
☐ 85 Matsu Yufu U .20 .50
☐ 86 Merchant's Wagon U .60 1.50
☐ 87 Mirumoto Taishuu C .10 .20
☐ 88 Moshi Sakae U .20 .50
☐ 89 Ninube Chisai U .20 .50
☐ 90 North Hub Village R 1.50 4.00
☐ 91 Obsidian Dragon R 1.25 3.00
☐ 92 Obsidian Figurine C .10 .20
☐ 93 Oh-krch U .20 .50
☐ 94 One-Sided Melee U .20 .50
☐ 95 Oni no Akuma (Experienced 2) R 1.25 3.00
☐ 96 Pale Oak Castle F (Phoenix) .60 1.50
☐ 97 Paper Lantern Festival C .10 .20
☐ 98 Passing the Mssage U .30 .75
☐ 99 Path of Pain C .10 .20
☐ 100 Perfection R 1.25 3.00
☐ 101 Rally the Ranks C .10 .20
☐ 102 Rampage R 1.25 3.00
☐ 103 Ratling Truthseeker U .20 .50
☐ 104 Rising Tensions U .20 .50
☐ 105 River Crossing C .10 .20
☐ 106 Rosoku's Urn R .60 1.50
☐ 107 Rout C .10 .20
☐ 108 Scorpion Detachment U .20 .50
☐ 109 Second Doom of the Dragon R .60 1.50
☐ 110 Second Doom of the Scorpion R .60 1.50
☐ 111 Shadowlands Ambassador U .20 .50
☐ 112 Shiba Jouta U .20 .50
☐ 113 Shogun's Advisors R 2.50 6.00
☐ 114 Shosuro Atesharu U .30 .75
☐ 115 Slayer's Vial C .10 .20
☐ 116 Soshi Tabito (Experienced) R .60 1.50
☐ 117 South Hub Village R .60 1.50
☐ 118 Steep Slopes C .10 .20
☐ 119 Strength of the Forge R 1.50 4.00
☐ 120 Strength R .60 1.50
☐ 121 Strike of the Dragon U .30 .75
☐ 122 Stronger than Steel R .60 1.50
☐ 123 Tamori Emina R 1.00 2.50
☐ 124 Tamori Futaba U .30 .75
☐ 125 Tchik R .60 1.50
☐ 126 The City of Lies F (Scorpion) .60 1.50
☐ 127 The End is Near R .60 1.50
☐ 128 The Hammer of Kaiu C .10 .20
☐ 129 The Price of Loyalty R 2.00 5.00
☐ 130 The Rolling Tides U .20 .50
☐ 131 The Shogun's Left Hand R .60 1.50
☐ 132 The Shogun's Peace U .20 .50
☐ 133 The Shogun's Right Hand R .60 1.50
☐ 134 Tiger's Mouth C .10 .20
☐ 135 Togashi Kadoma U .30 .75
☐ 136 Togashi Satsu (Experienced 3) R 2.00 5.00
☐ 137 Tok-ik U .20 .50
☐ 138 Toku Butaku C .10 .20
☐ 139 Torii no Orochi U .20 .50
☐ 140 Tortoise Shell Armor R .60 1.50
☐ 141 Treacherous Plains R .60 1.50
☐ 142 Treacherous Sands U .60 1.50
☐ 143 Tsuruchi Chion C .10 .20
☐ 144 Tsuruchi Futoshi U .20 .50
☐ 145 Usagi Genchi C .10 .20
☐ 146 Utaku Gyonwan U .20 .50
☐ 147 Utaku Lineage U .20 .50
☐ 148 Utaku Tayoi C .10 .20
☐ 149 Utaku Wakiken U .20 .50
☐ 150 Utaku Yu-Pan (Experienced) R .60 1.50
☐ 151 West Hub Village R 1.00 2.50
☐ 152 Will R 2.50 6.00
☐ 153 Yoritomo Ryouta C .10 .20
☐ 154 Yoritomo Singh .60 1.50
(Experienced Rama Singh) F (Mantis)
☐ 155 Yoritomo Tadame R 1.25 3.00

2006 Legend of the Five Rings Test of Enlightenment

☐ 1 A Clan Divided F .75 2.00
☐ 2 A Clan United F .75 2.00
☐ 3 A Long Journey F .40 1.00
☐ 4 A Quest Abandoned F .40 1.00
☐ 5 A Sage's Counsel F .40 1.00
☐ 6 A Scorpion's Wisdom F .40 1.00
☐ 7 Achirin (Experienced) F 1.25 3.00
☐ 8 Agasha Miyoshi (Experienced) F 1.25 3.00
☐ 9 Aikido Demonstration F .75 2.00
☐ 10 Akifumi F .75 2.00
☐ 11 Akodo Anshiro (Experienced) F 1.25 3.00
☐ 12 Akodo Bakin (Experienced) F 1.25 3.00
☐ 13 Akodo Kuemon (Experienced) F 1.50 4.00
☐ 14 Akodo Natsu (Experienced) F 1.25 3.00
☐ 15 Akodo Rokuro (Experienced) F 1.50 4.00
☐ 16 Asahina Yoshino (Experienced) F 1.25 3.00
☐ 17 Asako Takakazu (Experienced) F 1.25 3.00
☐ 18 Banzai Cry F 1.25 3.00
☐ 19 Bay of Green Coral F 1.25 3.00
☐ 20 Bayushi Adachi (Experienced) F 3.00 8.00
☐ 21 Bayushi Bokatsu (Experienced) F 1.50 4.00
☐ 22 Bayushi Kan (Experienced) F 3.00 8.00
☐ 23 Bayushi Saya (Experienced) F 1.50 4.00
☐ 24 Bayushi Shinzo (Experienced) F 2.50 6.00
☐ 25 Boisterous Soldiers F 1.25 3.00
☐ 26 Brothers in Arm F 3.00 8.00
☐ 27 Cautious Escort F .75 2.00
☐ 28 Chikka-tek (Experienced) F 1.25 3.00
☐ 29 Chuda Ruri (Experienced) F 3.00 8.00
☐ 30 Curfew Declared F .75 2.00
☐ 31 Daidoji Akagi (Experienced) F 1.25 3.00
☐ 32 Daidoji Setskuo (Experienced) F 1.25 3.00
☐ 33 Daigotsu Fumiaki (Experienced) F 3.00 8.00
☐ 34 Daigotsu Soetsu (Experienced) F 3.00 8.00
☐ 35 Destined Enemies F .75 2.00
☐ 36 Diving Pool F .40 1.00
☐ 37 Doji Saori (Experienced) F 3.00 8.00
☐ 38 Doji Seo (Experienced) F 4.00 10.00
☐ 39 Eager Students F .75 2.00
☐ 40 Elemental Arrow F 1.25 3.00
☐ 41 Ep'kee (Experienced) F .40 1.00
☐ 42 Festival of Inari F .40 1.00
☐ 43 Fragrant Waters F .75 2.00
☐ 44 Gaijin Writings F .75 2.00
☐ 45 Gift of Rice F .75 2.00
☐ 46 Gran-otik (Experienced) F .75 2.00
☐ 47 Hard Pressed F .75 2.00
☐ 48 Hida Nari (Experienced) F 1.25 3.00
☐ 49 Hida Sosuke (Experienced) F 2.00 5.00
☐ 50 Hida Sozen (Experienced) F 3.00 8.00
☐ 51 Hiruma Oda (Experienced) F 4.00 10.00
☐ 52 Hitomi Kazu (Experienced) F 1.25 3.00
☐ 53 Hoshi Masote (Experienced) F 2.00 5.00
☐ 54 Ikoma Kosaku (Experienced) F 1.25 3.00
☐ 55 Inspiring Leadership F .40 1.00
☐ 56 Isawa Kimi (Experienced) F 1.25 3.00
☐ 57 Isawa Sawao (Experienced) F 1.25 3.00
☐ 58 Itsume F .40 1.00
☐ 59 Iuchi Umeka (Experienced) F 1.25 3.00
☐ 60 Journey's Beginning F .40 1.00
☐ 61 Journey's End F .40 1.00
☐ 62 Kaiu Haku (Experienced) F 1.25 3.00
☐ 63 Kakita Funaki (Experienced) F 4.00 10.00
☐ 64 K'mee (Experienced) F .75 2.00
☐ 65 Komori Junsaku F .40 1.00
☐ 66 Kuni Okichi (Experienced) F 2.00 5.00
☐ 67 Kyoso no Oni (Experienced 3) F 1.50 4.00
☐ 68 Mantle of Flame F .75 2.00
☐ 69 Mirumoto Bokkai (Experienced) F 1.25 3.00
☐ 70 Mirumoto Gonkuro (Experienced) F 3.00 8.00
☐ 71 Mirumoto Hakahime (Experienced) F 1.25 3.00
☐ 72 Monastary Classroom F .40 1.00
☐ 73 Moshangoru (Experienced) F .75 2.00
☐ 74 Moshi Amika (Experienced) F 2.00 5.00
☐ 75 Moshi Kekiesu (Experienced) F 2.00 5.00
☐ 76 Moto Akikazu (Experienced) F 1.25 3.00
☐ 77 Moto Rumiko (Experienced) F 2.00 5.00
☐ 78 Muketsu (Experienced) F 2.50 6.00
☐ 79 Mystic Waterfall F 1.25 3.00
☐ 80 Nagisa F .40 1.00
☐ 81 Partake of the Fire F 1.25 3.00
☐ 82 Qolsa F .40 1.00
☐ 83 Reckless Charge F .40 1.00
☐ 84 Rosoku Sensei F 6.00 15.00
☐ 85 Sacred Hillside F .40 1.00
☐ 86 Seeking Enlightenment F .75 2.00
☐ 87 Shiba Denbe (Experienced) F .75 2.00
☐ 88 Shiba Yoshimi (Experienced) F .75 2.00
☐ 89 Shinjo Wei (Experienced) F 1.50 4.00
☐ 90 Shosuro Dazai (Experienced) F 3.00 8.00
☐ 91 Sisters of the Elements F .75 2.00
☐ 92 Snow-Blocked Pass F .75 2.00
☐ 93 Strength of the Crab F .40 1.00
☐ 94 Strength of the Crane F .40 1.00
☐ 95 Strength of the Dragon F .40 1.00
☐ 96 Strength of the Lion F .40 1.00
☐ 97 Strength of the Mantis F .40 1.00
☐ 98 Strength of the Nezumi F .40 1.00
☐ 99 Strength of the Phoenix F .40 1.00
☐ 100 Strength of the Scorpion F .40 1.00
☐ 101 Strength of the Shadowlands F .40 1.00
☐ 102 Strength of the Unicorn F .40 1.00
☐ 103 Sumotori Arena F .40 1.00
☐ 104 Teaching Stick F .40 1.00
☐ 105 Test of Enlightenment F .40 1.00
☐ 106 The Darkened Path F .40 1.00
☐ 107 The Dragon's Talons F .40 1.00
☐ 108 The Mystic (Experienced Isawa Sezaru) F 1.50 4.00
☐ 109 The Ronin (Experienced Kaneka) F 2.00 5.00
☐ 110 The Wanderer (Experienced Emperor Toturi III) F .75 2.00
☐ 111 The Way of Will F .40 1.00
☐ 112 Togashi Nyima (Experienced) F .75 2.00
☐ 113 Tsuruchi Arishia (Experienced) F 1.50 4.00

TCG/CCG

TCG/CCG

❑ 114 Tsuruchi Terao (Experienced) F 2.00 5.00
❑ 115 Tuftuf Sake House F 1.50 4.00
❑ 116 Unexpected Find F 1.25 3.00
❑ 117 Utaku Keyo (Experienced) F 1.50 4.00
❑ 118 Utaku Tarako (Experienced) F 2.00 5.00
❑ 119 Wanderers Revealed F 1.25 3.00
❑ 120 Wandering Pilgrim F .75 2.00
❑ 121 Writ of the Elements F .40 1.00
❑ 122 Yoritomo Chimori (Experienced) F .75 2.00
❑ 123 Yoritomo Iongi (Experienced) F .75 2.00
❑ 124 Z'chkir (Experienced) F .75 2.00

2007 Legend of the Five Rings Khan's Defiance

❑ 1 A Noble End U .20 .50
❑ 2 A Soldier's Fate R 1.25 3.00
❑ 3 A Soldier's Spirit U .20 .50
❑ 4 Advance Position C .10 .20
❑ 5 Aka-Name C .10 .20
❑ 6 Akodo Hachigoro U .40 1.00
❑ 7 Akodo Shigetoshi R .50 1.25
❑ 8 Allies Become Enemies C .10 .20
❑ 9 Asahina Hideki C .10 .20
❑ 10 Asako Juro C .10 .20
❑ 11 Asako Keiki U .20 .50
❑ 12 Badge of Authority C .10 .20
❑ 13 Bayushi Hisako C .10 .20
❑ 14 Bayushi Kaukatsu (Experienced 2) R .50 1.25
❑ 15 Bayushi Maemi U .20 .50
❑ 16 Bayushi Yumita U .20 .50
❑ 17 Birth of the Blood Heir U .20 .50
❑ 18 Blade of Guile R 1.25 3.00
❑ 19 Blanketed Forest R 1.50 4.00
❑ 20 Broken Lines U .20 .50
❑ 21 Churoburo U .20 .50
❑ 22 Cool Heads Prevail U .25 .60
❑ 23 Coward! R 3.00 8.00
❑ 24 Crippled Bone Berserker U .20 .50
❑ 25 Crushing Blow U .20 .50
❑ 26 Daidoji Kikaze R .50 1.25
❑ 27 Daidoji Yaichiro U .20 .50
❑ 28 Daigotsu Rekai (Experienced 4 Daidoji Rekai) R 1.50 4.00
❑ 29 Dishonored Vassal U .20 .50
❑ 30 Dissent C .10 .20
❑ 31 Doji Doukohito C .10 .20
❑ 32 Doji Nagori (Experienced) F (Crane) 1.50 4.00
❑ 33 Doomed Intentions R 8.00 20.00
❑ 34 Fire Dragon (Experienced 2) R 1.25 3.00
❑ 35 Fist and Blade C .10 .20
❑ 36 Flanking Action R 4.00 10.00
❑ 37 Flanking Assault C .10 .20
❑ 38 Flash of Steel R 6.00 15.00
❑ 39 Frenzied Charge R 2.00 5.00
❑ 40 Gathering Darkness U .20 .50
❑ 41 Governor's Court R 8.00 20.00
❑ 42 Gutobo C .10 .20
❑ 43 Harmonious Temple U .20 .50
❑ 44 Hch-tik U .20 .50
❑ 45 Hida Dayu C .10 .20
❑ 46 Hida Ikkaku U .20 .50
❑ 47 Hida Rikyu (Experienced) F (Crab) 2.00 5.00
❑ 48 Hida Yaheiko U .40 1.00
❑ 49 Hidden Warrens C .10 .20
❑ 50 High Courts C .10 .20
❑ 51 Hitomi Shiori U .20 .50
❑ 52 Hitsu Taeruko U .20 .50
❑ 53 Hoshi Noritada C .10 .20
❑ 54 Houhou U .20 .50
❑ 55 Hunting the Prophet U .20 .50
❑ 56 Ideal Conditions C .10 .20
❑ 57 Ikoma Hanshiro C .10 .20
❑ 58 Imperial Magistrates C .10 .20
❑ 59 Impressive Resiliance R 1.25 3.00
❑ 60 Insolence Punished R 5.00 12.00
❑ 61 Iuchi Eiji U .20 .50
❑ 62 Jikagun C .10 .20
❑ 63 Kaiu Shiro F (Crab) .40 1.00
❑ 64 Kakita Noriko U .20 .50
❑ 65 Kitsu Ineko U .20 .50
❑ 66 Kitsune Tsutaro U .20 .50
❑ 67 Kumade C .10 .20
❑ 68 Lacquered Armor U .25 .60
❑ 69 Matsu Benika (Experienced) R .75 2.00
❑ 70 Matsu Yoshike C .10 .20
❑ 71 Mirumoto Rosanjin (Experienced 2) F .50 1.25
❑ 72 Mirumoto Taikishi C .10 .20
❑ 73 Moto Chagatai (Experienced 4) R 1.25 3.00
❑ 74 Moto Chen (Experienced 2) R .50 1.25
❑ 75 Mytchokan C .10 .20
❑ 76 Nairu no Oni (Experienced) R .50 1.25
❑ 77 Nezumi Vengeance U .20 .50
❑ 78 Ok'kantich C .10 .20
❑ 79 Old Alliances C .10 .20
❑ 80 One Final March C .10 .20
❑ 81 One More Sacrifice U .20 .50
❑ 82 Ordered Retreat C .75 2.00
❑ 83 Overflowing Fields R .75 2.00
❑ 84 Ox Sentry C .10 .20
❑ 85 Peaceful Discourse R 1.25 3.00
❑ 86 Pep'trchek (Experienced) F (Ratling) 1.50 4.00
❑ 87 Pincers and Tail C .10 .20
❑ 88 Purge the Unclean C .10 .20
❑ 89 Recruiting Allies R 1.25 3.00
❑ 90 Restoring Order C .10 .20
❑ 91 Reverence for Chikushudo R 2.00 5.00
❑ 92 Revolutionaries U .20 .50
❑ 93 Ruthless Advance U 1.50 4.00
❑ 94 Sachika C .30 .75
❑ 95 Sasada C .10 .20
❑ 96 Scouring the Village C .10 .20
❑ 97 Seasoned Deckhand U .30 .75
❑ 98 Second Doom of the Unicorn R .30 .75
❑ 99 Seeking the Way R 2.00 5.00
❑ 100 Seiden Sanzo R 2.50 6.00
❑ 101 Shiba Aikune (Experienced 3) R .50 1.25
❑ 102 Shiba Daizan C .10 .20
❑ 103 Shinbone Warpack R .50 1.25
❑ 104 Shinjo Isuke U .20 .50
❑ 105 Shinjo Saihan C .10 .20
❑ 106 Shizuka Toshi F (Crane) .60 1.50
❑ 107 Shosuro Aroru R .50 1.25
❑ 108 Silent Solace U .20 .50
❑ 109 Snowy Overlook C .10 .20
❑ 110 Soshi Idaurin C .10 .20
❑ 111 Soul of Battle U .20 .50
❑ 112 Soul of the Winds U .25 .60
❑ 113 Standing Fast R 1.25 3.00
❑ 114 Strength in Certainty R 2.50 6.00
❑ 115 Strike the Base R 1.25 3.00
❑ 116 Strike the Center U .40 1.00
❑ 117 Strike the Summit C .10 .20
❑ 118 Surprise Attack! C .10 .20
❑ 119 Take the Charge R 1.50 4.00
❑ 120 Tamori Nakamuro (Experienced 2 Isawa Nakamuro) R .50 1.25
❑ 121 Tamori Wotan U .20 .50
❑ 122 Temple Acolytes C .10 .20
❑ 123 Temple of Unity R 1.25 3.00
❑ 124 The Brotherhood's Influence R .50 1.25
❑ 125 The Elements' Path C .10 .20
❑ 126 The Empress' Address R 1.25 3.00
❑ 127 The General Falls U .20 .50
❑ 128 The Kami's Embrace U .20 .50
❑ 129 The Khan's Gambit U .20 .50
❑ 130 The Lesser Evil C .10 .20
❑ 131 The Portals Open U .20 .50
❑ 132 The Winter Warren F (Ratling) .25 .60
❑ 133 Togashi Tsuri (Experienced) R .75 2.00
❑ 134 Touch of Ice C .10 .20
❑ 135 Tsuruchi Ayame U .20 .50
❑ 136 Tsuruchi Etsui (Experienced) R .75 2.00
❑ 137 Tsuruchi Gidayu C .10 .20
❑ 138 Two-Front War R .50 1.25
❑ 139 Umi-Bozu U .20 .50
❑ 140 Unexpected Betrayal R 4.00 10.00
❑ 141 Unexpected News R .50 1.25
❑ 142 Unshakable R 3.00 8.00
❑ 143 Unstoppable Power U .20 .50
❑ 144 Utaku Nayan C .10 .20
❑ 145 Valley of Heroes R .50 1.25
❑ 146 Veteran Warrior C .10 .20
❑ 147 Vik-sch'tok U .20 .50
❑ 148 Watch Commander R .75 2.00
❑ 149 Wave Man U .25 .60
❑ 150 Wrath of the People R .50 1.25
❑ 151 Yasuki Jinn-Kuen (Experienced) R .50 1.25
❑ 152 Yoritomo Isoshi U .20 .50
❑ 153 Yoritomo Utemaro R .50 1.25
❑ 154 You Die With Me! C .10 .20
❑ 155 Yukari no Onna C .10 .20
❑ 156 Yuki no Onna's Wrath U .20 .50

2007 Legend of the Five Rings Samurai

❑ 1 A New Wall R 2.00 5.00
❑ 2 A Terrible Oath R .50 1.25
❑ 3 A Test of Courage C .10 .20
❑ 4 Akodo Seiichi U .25 .60
❑ 5 Akodo Shunori C .10 .20
❑ 6 Akodo Terumoto R 1.25 3.00
❑ 7 Akodo's Grave C .10 .20
❑ 8 Akuma no Oni (Experienced 2) R .50 1.25
❑ 9 Ambush R 1.00 2.50
❑ 10 Ancestral Ground F .10 .20
❑ 11 Arrival of the Emerald Champion R 1.50 4.00
❑ 12 Arrival of the Obsidian Champion R 1.25 3.00
❑ 13 Arrow of Purity C .10 .20
❑ 14 Arrows from the Woods C .10 .20
❑ 15 Asahina Beniha U .60 1.50
❑ 16 Asako Meisuru C .10 .20
❑ 17 Asako Takakazu (Experienced) R .30 .75
❑ 18 Ashigaru Conscripts C .10 .20
❑ 19 Ashigaru Spearmen C .10 .20
❑ 20 Banish All Shadows R 3.00 8.00
❑ 21 Battlefield of Shallow Graves C .10 .20
❑ 22 Bayushi Eisaku C .10 .20
❑ 23 Bayushi Hisato C .10 .20
❑ 24 Bayushi Hisoka R 1.00 2.50
❑ 25 Bayushi Iyona F .25 .60
❑ 26 Bayushi Kurumi C .10 .20
❑ 27 Bayushi Muhito U .20 .50
❑ 28 Bayushi Nomen U .20 .50
❑ 29 Bayushi Paneki (Experienced 4) F 3.00 8.00
❑ 30 Bayushi Saya C .10 .20
❑ 31 Bayushi Tsimaru (Experienced) R 1.00 2.50
❑ 32 Beiden Pass U .20 .50
❑ 33 Berserkers U .20 .50
❑ 34 Blade of Hubris R 3.00 8.00
❑ 35 Block Supply Lines C .10 .20
❑ 36 Border Skirmish U .25 .60
❑ 37 Boshanai U .25 .60
❑ 38 Brand of Fire and Thunder C .10 .20
❑ 39 Brash Hero C .10 .20
❑ 40 Brilliant Victory C .10 .20
❑ 41 Brothers in Arms (Experienced) R .10 .20
❑ 42 Brothers in Arms C 1.00 2.50
❑ 43 Burn it Down U .30 .75
❑ 44 Call of Thunder R .50 1.25
❑ 45 Castle Barracks C .10 .20
❑ 46 Castle Gate R 1.00 2.50
❑ 47 Castle of Water C .10 .20
❑ 48 Castle Walls C .10 .20
❑ 49 Ceremonial Armor U .25 .60
❑ 50 Chuda Hankyu R 1.00 2.50
❑ 51 Chuda Hiroe C .10 .20
❑ 52 Chuda Ikumi C .10 .20
❑ 53 Chuda Kyuwa R 1.50 4.00
❑ 54 Chuda Rintaro U .20 .50
❑ 55 Circle of Steel F .25 .60
❑ 56 City of the Rich Frog R 1.00 2.50
❑ 57 Cleansing Spirit U .25 .60
❑ 58 Combined Efforts F .10 .20
❑ 59 Commanding Favor R .50 1.25
❑ 60 Companion Spirit U .20 .50
❑ 61 Compassion U .25 .60
❑ 62 Concealed Archers U .25 .60
❑ 63 Consumed by Five Fires C .10 .20
❑ 64 Contested Ground C .10 .20
❑ 65 Control R 2.00 5.00
❑ 66 Control the Field C .10 .20
❑ 67 Copper Mine F .25 .60
❑ 68 Cornering Maneuver U .25 .60
❑ 69 Corrupt Adjunct U .20 .50
❑ 70 Corrupt Officials U .20 .50
❑ 71 Countermove R 1.25 3.00
❑ 72 Courage U 1.00 2.50
❑ 73 Courtesy U .30 .75
❑ 74 Crippling Cut U .25 .60
❑ 75 Crossroads Fortress F .50 1.25
❑ 76 Cut Them Off U .25 .60
❑ 77 Daidoji Akagi C .10 .20
❑ 78 Daidoji Eitoku C .10 .20
❑ 79 Daidoji Gunso F .10 .20
❑ 80 Daidoji Nagiko R .50 1.25
❑ 81 Daigotsu (Experienced 2) F 3.00 8.00
❑ 82 Daigotsu Gyoken C .10 .20
❑ 83 Daigotsu Kaikou U .40 1.00
❑ 84 Daigotsu Masami F .25 .60
❑ 85 Daigotsu Meguro C .10 .20
❑ 86 Daruma C .10 .20
❑ 87 Deception's Veil Dojo F 1.00 2.50
❑ 88 Defining the Essence C .10 .20
❑ 89 Desperate Wager R .50 1.25
❑ 90 Determination R 6.00 15.00
❑ 91 Diplomatic Apprentice F .25 .60
❑ 92 Dirty Politics R .50 1.25
❑ 93 Doji Ayano U .25 .60
❑ 94 Doji Domotai (Experienced 3) F 2.50 6.00
❑ 95 Doji Hakuseki C .10 .20
❑ 96 Doji Jotaro C .10 .20
❑ 97 Doji Jun'ai R .50 1.25
❑ 98 Doji Koin U .20 .50
❑ 99 Doji Seo F .10 .20
❑ 100 Doji Sesshu R 1.00 2.50
❑ 101 Draw Your Blade R 6.00 15.00
❑ 102 Duty U .50 1.25
❑ 103 Eager to Fight R 1.25 3.00
❑ 104 Earth Becomes Sky U .20 .50
❑ 105 Eastern Hub Port F .60 1.50
❑ 106 Encircled Terrain C .10 .20
❑ 107 Enlistment U .20 .50
❑ 108 Essence of Gaki-do R .50 1.25
❑ 109 Essence of Water F .10 .20
❑ 110 Explored Territory C .10 .20
❑ 111 Extended Maneuvers C .10 .20
❑ 112 Failure of Duty R .50 1.25
❑ 113 False Alliance R .30 .75
❑ 114 False Trail R .50 1.25
❑ 115 Family Library U .60 1.50
❑ 116 Fan of Command U .25 .60
❑ 117 Farmlands C .10 .20
❑ 118 Few Against Many R 3.00 8.00
❑ 119 First and Final Strike C .10 .20
❑ 120 Flight of Doves U .25 .60
❑ 121 Focus R .50 1.25
❑ 122 Forest Cleansing R 1.25 3.00
❑ 123 Forest Killer Cavern C .10 .20
❑ 124 Forewarning U .50 1.25
❑ 125 Fortified Camp C .10 .20
❑ 126 Frenzy F .10 .20
❑ 127 Fury of the Dark Lord R 1.00 2.50
❑ 128 Geisha House F .25 .60
❑ 129 Glory of the Shogun R .50 1.25
❑ 130 Goblin Chuckers U .20 .50
❑ 131 Gold Mine F .25 .60
❑ 132 Greater Sacrifice U .25 .60
❑ 133 Hachiwari U .25 .60
❑ 134 Heavy Infantry C .10 .20
❑ 135 Hida Daizu (Experienced) R .10 .20
❑ 136 Hida Daizu C .50 1.25
❑ 137 Hida Genichi C .10 .20
❑ 138 Hida Hiyao U .20 .50
❑ 139 Hida Kaoru C .10 .20
❑ 140 Hida Kuon (Experienced 5) F 2.50 6.00
❑ 141 Hida Sozen (Experienced) R .50 1.25
❑ 142 Hida Takuji R 1.25 3.00
❑ 143 Hired Killer U 2.50 6.00
❑ 144 Hiruma Aki U .20 .50
❑ 145 Hiruma Tama C .10 .20
❑ 146 Hitsu-do U .25 .60
❑ 147 Honesty U .25 .60
❑ 148 Honor U .25 .60
❑ 149 House of the Fallen Blossom R 1.00 2.50
❑ 150 Hunger of the Earth C .10 .20
❑ 151 I Am Ready R .50 1.25
❑ 152 Ikoma Akiyama C .10 .20
❑ 153 Ikoma Yasuko (Experienced Shosuro Yasuko) R 1.00 2.50
❑ 154 Imbue Chi C .10 .20
❑ 155 Immobile Stance R 1.00 2.50
❑ 156 Imperial Summons C .10 .20
❑ 157 Impromptu Duel C .10 .20
❑ 158 In Time of War U .20 .50
❑ 159 Inner Fire U .25 .60
❑ 160 Insight R 2.00 5.00
❑ 161 Iron Mine F .10 .20
❑ 162 Isawa Eitoku U .20 .50
❑ 163 Isawa Kyoko C .20 .50
❑ 164 Isawa Ochiai (Experienced) F .50 1.25
❑ 165 Isawa Oharu C .10 .20
❑ 166 Isawa Takesi U .25 .60
❑ 167 Isawa Umeko F .25 .60
❑ 168 Iuchi Umeka C .10 .20
❑ 169 Kabuki Theater Troupe U .20 .50
❑ 170 Kaiu Hisayuki U .20 .50
❑ 171 Kaiu Jurobei C .10 .20
❑ 172 Kaiu Sadao F .25 .60
❑ 173 Kakita Hideo C .10 .20
❑ 174 Katsu (Experienced) R 1.00 2.50
❑ 175 Kitsu Katsuko U .20 .50
❑ 176 Kitsuki Ryushi R 1.00 2.50
❑ 177 Kitsuki Taiko U .20 .50
❑ 178 Kitsune Den R 1.00 2.50
❑ 179 Kiyomi U .25 .60
❑ 180 Knife in the Darkness U .25 .60
❑ 181 Knowledge R 5.00 12.00
❑ 182 Kobune Port F .10 .20
❑ 183 Kobune Scout C .10 .20
❑ 184 Kobushi U .25 .60
❑ 185 Kodomo U .20 .50
❑ 186 Koutetsu Chikara F .50 1.25
❑ 187 Koutetsu Iyoku F .50 1.25
❑ 188 Koutetsu Kabe F .50 1.25
❑ 189 Koutetsu Kyuui F .50 1.25
❑ 190 Koutetsu Meiyo F 2.50 6.00
❑ 191 Koutetsu Mukei F 2.00 5.00
❑ 192 Koutetsu Sessou F .50 1.25
❑ 193 Koutetsu Shinri F 1.25 3.00
❑ 194 Koutetsu Unabara F .50 1.25
❑ 195 Kyoso no Oni (Experienced 3) R .20 .50
❑ 196 Kyoso no Oni U 1.50 4.00
❑ 197 Kyuden Asako F .50 1.25
❑ 198 Kyuden Ashinagabachi F 1.00 2.50
❑ 199 Kyuden Wasuremono F .40 1.00
❑ 200 Lesser Shrine U .20 .50
❑ 201 Lies, Lies, Lies... U .25 .60
❑ 202 Light Infantry C .10 .20
❑ 203 Lion's Pride U .20 .50
❑ 204 Mantis Detachment U .20 .50
❑ 205 Marketplace F .10 .20
❑ 206 Master of the Rolling River U .25 .60
❑ 207 Matsu Aoiko (Experienced) R .50 1.25
❑ 208 Matsu Benika C .10 .20
❑ 209 Matsu Bunka F .25 .60
❑ 210 Matsu Robun C .10 .20
❑ 211 Matsu Takeko C .10 .20
❑ 212 Matsu Yoshino (Experienced 2) F 2.50 6.00
❑ 213 Matsu Yufu U .20 .50
❑ 214 Menhari-gata R .75 2.00
❑ 215 Michio C .10 .20
❑ 216 Mirumoto Chojiro C .10 .20
❑ 217 Mirumoto Ichizo C .10 .20
❑ 218 Mirumoto Mareshi (Experienced) R .50 1.25
❑ 219 Mirumoto Taishuu C .25 .60
❑ 220 Misdirection R 1.00 2.50
❑ 221 Morale Officer C .10 .20
❑ 222 Moshi Amika C .10 .20
❑ 223 Moshi Euiko C .10 .20
❑ 224 Moto Akikazu C .10 .20
❑ 225 Moto Chagatai (Experienced 5) F .50 1.25
❑ 226 Moto Suren U .20 .50
❑ 227 Moto Taban U .20 .50
❑ 228 Mountain Summit Temple F .50 1.25
❑ 229 Mountains of the Phoenix C .10 .20
❑ 230 Mountain's Shadow Dojo F 1.00 2.50
❑ 231 Muketsu (Experienced) R 1.25 3.00
❑ 232 Never Stand Alone U .25 .60
❑ 233 No Hiding Place C .10 .20
❑ 234 Obsidian Dragon R 1.25 3.00
❑ 235 Ogre Warriors U .20 .50
❑ 236 Omoni (Experienced 2) R .50 1.25
❑ 237 Oni-Daikyu R .75 2.00
❑ 238 Outer Walls C .10 .20
❑ 239 Palm Strike R .50 1.25
❑ 240 Peasant Vengeance C .10 .20
❑ 241 Pekkle no Oni U .10 .20
❑ 242 Perfect Attunement R .50 1.25
❑ 243 Perfection R 1.25 3.00
❑ 244 Pokku U .25 .60
❑ 245 Political Interference R .50 1.25
❑ 246 Private Trader F .50 1.25
❑ 247 Proposal of Peace R .30 .75
❑ 248 Purge the Weak C .10 .20
❑ 249 Rapid Deployment C .10 .20
❑ 250 Raze to the Ground U .50 1.25
❑ 251 Razor of the Dawn Castle F 1.00 2.50
❑ 252 Refugees C .10 .20
❑ 253 Reinforce the Gates U .25 .60
❑ 254 Resumed Hostilities C .10 .20
❑ 255 Retribution U .25 .60
❑ 256 Rich Coffers U .25 .60
❑ 257 Righteous Doshin C .10 .20
❑ 258 Righteous Fury C .10 .20
❑ 259 Ring of Air U .25 .60
❑ 260 Ring of Earth U .25 .60
❑ 261 Ring of Fire U .25 .60
❑ 262 Ring of the Void U .25 .60
❑ 263 Ring of Water U .25 .60
❑ 264 Roshungi U .20 .50
❑ 265 Rosoku's Staff R .50 1.25
❑ 266 Rout C .10 .20
❑ 267 Ruins of Otosan Uchi R .50 1.25
❑ 268 Salute of the Samurai U .20 .50
❑ 269 Sap the Spirit U .25 .60
❑ 270 Seat of Power F .25 .60
❑ 271 Secluded Village C .10 .20
❑ 272 Secluded Waystation C .25 .60
❑ 273 Seikitsu Mountains U .20 .50
❑ 274 Severed From the Emperor R 1.25 3.00
❑ 275 Shiba Arihiro U .20 .50
❑ 276 Shiba Fugimori R 1.00 2.50
❑ 277 Shiba Ikku C .10 .20
❑ 278 Shiba Miiko C .10 .20
❑ 279 Shiba Ningen (Experienced 2) R 1.00 2.50
❑ 280 Shinjo Horsebow C .10 .20
❑ 281 Shinjo Kadonomaro U .60 1.50
❑ 282 Shinjo Meikoku C .10 .20
❑ 283 Shinjo Xushen (Experienced) R .50 1.25
❑ 284 Shinjo's Courage R 1.50 4.00
❑ 285 Shinomen Marsh F .25 .60
❑ 286 Shinsei's Last Hope U .20 .50
❑ 287 Shizuka Toshi F .60 1.50
❑ 288 Shosuro Adeiko U .25 .60
❑ 289 Shosuro Uyeda C .10 .20
❑ 290 Shout of Challenge C .10 .20
❑ 291 Shout of Defiance C .10 .20
❑ 292 Shout of Victory U .60 1.50
❑ 293 Shrine of the Sun U .25 .60
❑ 294 Shrine to Bishamon R .75 2.00
❑ 295 Shrine to Fukurokujin R 2.50 6.00
❑ 296 Shrine to Osano-Wo R 1.25 3.00
❑ 297 Shuten Doji's Fury R 1.50 4.00
❑ 298 Silence the Future R .50 1.25
❑ 299 Silver Mine F .25 .60
❑ 300 Sincerity U .25 .60
❑ 301 Skub U .25 .60
❑ 302 Sneak Attack R 2.50 6.00
❑ 303 Sorrows Path U .20 .50
❑ 304 Spearhead U .10 .20
❑ 305 Stables F .25 .60
❑ 306 Stay Your Blade C .10 .20
❑ 307 Stone Breaker R .50 1.25
❑ 308 Strength of the Forge R 3.00 8.00
❑ 309 Strength R 1.00 2.50
❑ 310 Strike of the Dragon U .25 .60
❑ 311 Superior Strategist R 2.00 5.00
❑ 312 Supply Outpost U .25 .60
❑ 313 Supply Smugglers F .25 .60
❑ 314 Sword of Victory C .10 .20
❑ 315 Tactical Advisors C .10 .20
❑ 316 Tactical Maneuvers R 1.50 4.00
❑ 317 Tamori Konoye F .10 .20
❑ 318 Temple of the Seekers F .25 .60
❑ 319 Temple to Shinsei F .25 .60
❑ 320 Temples of Gisei Toshi R 3.00 8.00
❑ 321 Test of the Emerald Champion U .20 .50
❑ 322 Test of the Jade Champion U .20 .50
❑ 323 Tetsu Kama Mura F .50 1.25
❑ 324 The Agasha Foundries F .50 1.25
❑ 325 The Arrow Knows the Way R 1.25 3.00
❑ 326 The Bitter Shadow of Shame R 2.50 6.00
❑ 327 The Crab's Strength F .30 .75
❑ 328 The Crane's Strength F .30 .75
❑ 329 The Dragon's Strength F .30 .75
❑ 330 The End is Near R .30 .75
❑ 331 The Fires that Cleanse U .25 .60
❑ 332 The Fortunes Smile R 5.00 12.00
❑ 333 The Hall of Ancestors F 1.00 2.50
❑ 334 The Kami's Blessing U .25 .60
❑ 335 The Lion's Strength F .30 .75
❑ 336 The Mantis's Strength F .30 .75
❑ 337 The Maw's Grave R 1.50 4.00
❑ 338 The Path Not Taken R .75 2.00
❑ 339 The Phoenix's Strength F .30 .75
❑ 340 The Ruined City F .50 1.25
❑ 341 The Scorpion's Strength F .60 1.50
❑ 342 The Seventh Tower F .60 1.50
❑ 343 The Shogun's Peace U .20 .50
❑ 344 The Spider's Lair F .30 .75
❑ 345 The Spider's Strength F .30 .75
❑ 346 The Temple of Death F .60 1.50
❑ 347 The Unicorn's Strength F .30 .75
❑ 348 The Utaku Plains F .60 1.50
❑ 349 Three Man Alliance Plain C .10 .20

❑ 350 Three-Stone River F	.30	.75
❑ 351 Tides of Battle F	.25	.60
❑ 352 Togashi Ieshige (Experienced Akodo Ieshige) R	.50	1.25
❑ 353 Togashi Jomei C	.10	.20
❑ 354 Togashi Kazuki U	.20	.50
❑ 355 Togashi Masujiro U	.20	.50
❑ 356 Togashi Miyoko C	.10	.20
❑ 357 Togashi Satsu (Experienced 4) F	2.50	6.00
❑ 358 Togashi's Shrine R	.50	1.25
❑ 359 Touch of Death R	2.00	5.00
❑ 360 Traveling Ronin R	.50	1.25
❑ 361 Tsi Blade C	.10	.20
❑ 362 Tsuburu no Oni U	.20	.50
❑ 363 Tsuruchi Kansuke C	.10	.20
❑ 364 Tsuruchi Kaya U	.20	.50
❑ 365 Tsuruchi Mitsuzuka C	.10	.20
❑ 366 Tsuruchi Mochisa F	.25	.60
❑ 367 Tsuruchi Nobumoto (Experienced) R	.50	1.25
❑ 368 Tsuruchi Okame (Experienced) R	.50	1.25
❑ 369 Turn of Fortune R	1.50	4.00
❑ 370 Turn the Tide R	.75	2.00
❑ 371 Unfamiliar Ground F	.25	.60
❑ 372 Unfortunate Incident C	.10	.20
❑ 373 Unrequited Love F	.25	.60
❑ 374 Unspoken Threats U	.25	.60
❑ 375 Untested Scouts C	.10	.20
❑ 376 Unwavering Assault C	.10	.20
❑ 377 Utaku Genshi R	2.50	6.00
❑ 378 Utaku Kohana C	.10	.20
❑ 379 Utaku Meadows C	.10	.20
❑ 380 Utaku Tama F	.25	.60
❑ 381 Utaku Tayoi C	.10	.20
❑ 382 Utaku Yu-Pan (Experienced) R	1.00	2.50
❑ 383 Utter Defeat R	1.50	4.00
❑ 384 Venerable Master R	1.25	3.00
❑ 385 Wako C	.10	.20
❑ 386 Walking the Way U	.60	1.50
❑ 387 Wandering Budoka R	6.00	15.00
❑ 388 Wandering Scout U	.20	.50
❑ 389 Wardens C	.10	.20
❑ 390 Wareta no Oni R	.50	1.25
❑ 391 Warrior Challenge C	.10	.20
❑ 392 We Stand Ready U	.20	.50
❑ 393 Wedge R	1.25	3.00
❑ 394 Weigh the Cost C	.10	.20
❑ 395 Well Prepared F	.10	.20
❑ 396 Will R	2.50	6.00
❑ 397 Winter Storm R	1.00	2.50
❑ 398 Winter Warfare R	1.00	2.50
❑ 399 Wisdom Gained U	.20	.50
❑ 400 Wisdom of the Keepers U	.20	.50
❑ 401 Wounded in Battle F	.10	.20
❑ 402 Wrath of Osano-Wo C	.10	.20
❑ 403 Wretched Mercenary F	.10	.20
❑ 404 Writ of Restriction U	.25	.60
❑ 405 Yobanjin Alliance U	.20	.50
❑ 406 Yobanjin Fortress R	1.00	2.50
❑ 407 Yogo Rieko R	.50	1.25
❑ 408 Yoritomo Eriko U	.20	.50
❑ 409 Yoritomo Naizen (Experienced 2) F	1.25	3.00
❑ 410 Yoritomo Okitsugu U	.20	.50
❑ 411 Yoritomo Saburo C	.10	.20
❑ 412 Yoritomo Tadame R	1.25	3.00

2007 Legend of the Five Rings Stronger Than Steel

BOOSTER BOX (48)	50.00	100.00
BOOSTER PACK (11)	1.50	3.00
❑ 1 A Gruesome Display U	.20	.50
❑ 2 A Lion's Roar U	.20	.50
❑ 3 A Matter of Honor R	.75	2.00
❑ 4 Agasha Tamaki C	.10	.20
❑ 5 Akodo Hiroyuki F	2.00	5.00
❑ 6 Akodo Katsumoto R	.75	2.00
❑ 7 Asahina Ekei R	1.25	3.00
❑ 8 Asako Bairei (Experienced 3) R	1.25	3.00
❑ 9 Asako Eichiro C	.10	.20
❑ 10 Bairei's Vigil R	.50	1.25
❑ 11 Bayushi Arunsa U	.20	.50
❑ 12 Bayushi Ryuzaburo R	.50	1.25
❑ 13 Bayushi Shinobu C	.10	.20
❑ 14 Blade of the Kansen U	.20	.50
❑ 15 Brilliant Rebirth Temple F	.75	2.00
❑ 16 Budoka's Tonfa C	.10	.20
❑ 17 Calling in Favors U	.20	.50
❑ 18 Choose Your Ground C	.10	.20
❑ 19 Chuda Genkei C	.10	.20
❑ 20 Chutaro C	.10	.20
❑ 21 City Gate C	.10	.20
❑ 22 Clan Estate U	.30	.75
❑ 23 Crosswinds Cut Style R	.75	2.00
❑ 24 Daidoji Kojima U	.20	.50
❑ 25 Daidoji Naoshige C	.10	.20
❑ 26 Daigotsu Junichi U	.20	.50
❑ 27 Daigotsu Susumu R	.60	1.50
❑ 28 Dastardly Tactics C	.10	.20
❑ 29 Datsue-ba U	.20	.50
❑ 30 Death of Virtue Style R	.75	2.00
❑ 31 Devious Explorer C	.10	.20
❑ 32 Disgraced Ronin C	.10	.20
❑ 33 Doji Armor R	.75	2.00
❑ 34 Doji Masako R	.50	1.25
❑ 35 Doji Nobuhide R	.75	2.00
❑ 36 Drawing in the Strike C	.10	.20
❑ 37 Establishing a Foothold U	.20	.50
❑ 38 Evenly Matched C	.10	.20
❑ 39 Failure to Your Daimyo U	.20	.50
❑ 40 Falling Leaf Strike C	.10	.20
❑ 41 Fight As One C	.10	.20
❑ 42 Furious Assault C	.10	.20
❑ 43 Gagoze no Oni C	.10	.20
❑ 44 Gaijin Utensil C	.10	.20
❑ 45 Goju Ryuu R	1.50	4.00
❑ 46 Gujo Odori C	.10	.20
❑ 47 Gunso Atshushi R	.75	2.00
❑ 48 Gunso Chitose R	2.50	6.00
❑ 49 Gunso Hirobumi R	.75	2.00
❑ 50 Haiku School C	.10	.20
❑ 51 Heart of the Katana Style R	.50	1.25
❑ 52 Heated Discussion U	.20	.50
❑ 53 Hida Fumetsu R	.50	1.25
❑ 54 Hida Itsuma C	.10	.20
❑ 55 Hida Kashin R	1.25	3.00
❑ 56 Hiromasa R	.60	1.50
❑ 57 Hiruma Aya R	.50	1.25
❑ 58 Hisao U	.20	.50
❑ 59 Hojatsu's Legacy Style R	.75	2.00
❑ 60 Honor is Power U	.20	.50
❑ 61 Horiuchi Yoko C	.10	.20
❑ 62 Houritsu Mura F	.75	2.00
❑ 63 Ide Eien U	.20	.50
❑ 64 Ikoma Tatsunori R	.50	1.25
❑ 65 Isawa Emori F	1.25	3.00
❑ 66 Isawa Kajibara U	.20	.50
❑ 67 Isawa's Air U	.20	.50
❑ 68 Isawa's Blood U	.20	.50
❑ 69 Isawa's Earth U	.20	.50
❑ 70 Isawa's Fire U	.20	.50
❑ 71 Isawa's Void U	.20	.50
❑ 72 Isawa's Water U	.20	.50
❑ 73 Justly Earned Victory R	4.00	10.00
❑ 74 Kafu C	.10	.20
❑ 75 Kakita Amakuni C	.10	.20
❑ 76 Kakita Kensho-in U	.20	.50
❑ 77 Katashi C	.10	.20
❑ 78 Kitsu Tenshin U	.20	.50
❑ 79 Kitsune Aiko C	.10	.20
❑ 80 Kolat Forgery U	.20	.50
❑ 81 Kuni Takaniro U	.20	.50
❑ 82 Kuni Umibe U	.20	.50
❑ 83 Kusari-Gama U	.30	.75
❑ 84 Longshoremen U	.20	.50
❑ 85 Matsu Kameko C	.10	.20
❑ 86 Matsu Sakaki U	.20	.50
❑ 87 Mirumoto Ryosaki (Experienced) R	.50	1.25
❑ 88 Mirumoto Yozo C	.30	.75
❑ 89 Moshi Taya U	.20	.50
❑ 90 Moto Chai R	.75	2.00
❑ 91 Mysterious Deaths R	1.25	3.00
❑ 92 Noburo C	.10	.20
❑ 93 O-shiken C	.10	.20
❑ 94 Overwhelming Speed U	.20	.50
❑ 95 Paper to Steel C	.20	.50
❑ 96 Paragon of Honor C	.10	.20
❑ 97 Parley C	.10	.20
❑ 98 Power of Innocence R	.75	2.00
❑ 99 Power of the Masters U	.20	.50
❑ 100 Powerful Accusation C	.10	.20
❑ 101 Private Whispers R	.60	1.50
❑ 102 Red Leaf Cut U	.40	1.00
❑ 103 Respected Mentor C	.10	.20
❑ 104 Ruthless Bandits U	.20	.50
❑ 105 Sentei no Oni U	.20	.50
❑ 106 Seppun Detachment R	.75	2.00
❑ 107 Shiba Fusaburu U	.20	.50
❑ 108 Shiba Rae R	1.25	3.00
❑ 109 Shinjo Kurimoko C	.10	.20
❑ 110 Shinjo Turong (Experienced) R	.75	2.00
❑ 111 Shosuro Kyuichi R	2.00	5.00
❑ 112 Shosuro Takuro C	.10	.20
❑ 113 Silent Movements U	.20	.50
❑ 114 Single Strike Style R	1.25	3.00
❑ 115 Soshi Ukon U	.20	.50
❑ 116 Soul Strike C	.10	.20
❑ 117 Splendid Phoenix Style R	.75	2.00
❑ 118 Storm's Eye Style R	.75	2.00
❑ 119 Strength in Shadow Style R	.75	2.00
❑ 120 Strength of Paragons C	.10	.20
❑ 121 Superior Positioning R	.60	1.50
❑ 122 Surveying the Land C	.10	.20
❑ 123 Tamori Sugi U	.20	.50
❑ 124 Temple of the Righteous Emperor C	.10	.20
❑ 125 The Heavens Are Watching U	.20	.50
❑ 126 The Hundred-Hand Strike R	3.00	8.00
❑ 127 The Rashana R	1.25	3.00
❑ 128 The Throne Stands Empty U	.20	.50
❑ 129 Tight Quarters C	.10	.20
❑ 130 Togashi Kanaye R	1.25	3.00
❑ 131 Togashi Remi C	.10	.20
❑ 132 Togashi Shichi U	.20	.50
❑ 133 Toritaka Kaiketsu C	.10	.20
❑ 134 Toshi Ranbo R	.50	1.25
❑ 135 True Strength R	.75	2.00
❑ 136 Tsuruchi Amaya R	.60	1.50
❑ 137 Tsuruchi Fuyu U	.20	.50
❑ 138 Tsuruchi Masako R	.50	1.25
❑ 139 Unbroken Blade Style R	.75	2.00
❑ 140 Unexpected Intimidation R	1.50	4.00
❑ 141 Unexpected Reinforcements C	.10	.20
❑ 142 Unproven Guardian C	.10	.20
❑ 143 Unseen Assailant U	.20	.50
❑ 144 Unseen Valor U	.20	.50
❑ 145 Use the Wind C	.10	.20
❑ 146 Utaku Etsuko R	.50	1.25
❑ 147 Utaku Saber R	1.25	3.00
❑ 148 Utaku Takai U	.10	.20
❑ 149 Vigilance Keep F	.75	2.00
❑ 150 Vision of P'an Ku U	.20	.50
❑ 151 Wasp Bow U	.30	.75
❑ 152 Watching the Battle C	.10	.20
❑ 153 Yajuu no Oni U	.20	.50
❑ 154 Yogo Honami R	.50	1.25
❑ 155 Yoritomo Daishiro F	2.00	5.00
❑ 156 Yoritomo Kane C	.10	.20

2007 Legend of the Five Rings The Emerald and Jade Champions

❑ 1 Akasha (Experienced 2) F	3.00	8.00
❑ 2 Bayushi Arashii F	.60	1.50
❑ 3 Bayushi Norachai (Experienced 2) F	2.50	6.00
❑ 4 Brisk Economy F	.60	1.50
❑ 5 Caught in the Act F	2.50	6.00
❑ 6 Daigotsu Eiya (Experienced) F	2.50	6.00
❑ 7 Daigotsu Kanpeki F	2.50	6.00
❑ 8 Daigotsu Sachio F	1.00	.25
❑ 9 Death at the Mikado F	1.25	3.00
❑ 10 Doji Toyoaki F	.60	1.50
❑ 11 Doji Yasuyo (Experienced 3) F	6.00	15.00
❑ 12 Emerald Champion's Mempo F	4.00	10.00
❑ 13 Hida Haruko F	2.00	5.00
❑ 14 Hida Sozen (Experienced 2) F	8.00	20.00
❑ 15 Hida Yagimaki (Experienced) F	1.00	2.50
❑ 16 Hiruma Todori (Experienced 2) F	2.50	6.00
❑ 17 Ikoma Otemi (Experienced 3) F	2.50	6.00
❑ 18 Isawa Kokuten F	1.25	3.00
❑ 19 Kabuki Show F	1.25	3.00
❑ 20 Kakita Noritoshi (Experienced 2) F	4.00	10.00
❑ 21 Kitsuki Iweko (Experienced) F	2.00	5.00
❑ 22 Magistrate Station F	1.50	4.00
❑ 23 Matsu Robun (Experienced) F	2.50	6.00
❑ 24 Matsu Yoshifumi F	1.50	4.00
❑ 25 Meanwhile... F	.60	1.50
❑ 26 Mikado Invitation F	1.25	3.00
❑ 27 Mirumoto Agito F	.60	1.50
❑ 28 Mirumoto Narumi (Experienced) F	2.50	6.00
❑ 29 Miya's Mercy F	.60	1.50
❑ 30 Moto Hotei F	.60	1.50
❑ 31 Night Silk Poison F	2.00	5.00
❑ 32 Ribbon of Success F	.60	1.50
❑ 33 Shiba Danjuro (Experienced 2) F	3.00	8.00
❑ 34 Shiba Yoma (Experienced 3) F	2.50	6.00
❑ 35 Shosuro Jimen (Experienced) F	3.00	8.00
❑ 36 Test of Etiquette F	.60	1.50
❑ 37 Test of Investigation F	.60	1.50
❑ 38 Test of Law F	.60	1.50
❑ 39 Test of Leadership F	.60	1.50
❑ 40 Test of Martial Ability F	.60	1.50
❑ 41 Test of Ressources F	.60	1.50
❑ 42 The Kami's Justice F	1.25	3.00
❑ 43 The Khan F	10.00	25.00
❑ 44 The Mikado F	1.25	3.00
❑ 45 The Saga of Taki F	1.25	3.00
❑ 46 Tsuruchi Etsui (Experienced 2) F	1.50	4.00
❑ 47 Tsuruchi Kaya (Experienced) F	1.50	4.00
❑ 48 Tsuruchi Ki (Experienced) F	1.25	3.00
❑ 49 Unauthorized Duel F	2.50	6.00
❑ 50 Utagawa (Experienced) F	3.00	8.00
❑ 51 Wheels within Wheels F	1.25	3.00
❑ 52 Yoritomo Kazuma F	1.25	3.00

2007 Legend of the Five Rings The Truest Test

BOOSTER BOX (48)	50.00	100.00
BOOSTER PACK (11)	1.50	3.00
❑ 1 A Legion of One C	.10	.20
❑ 2 Akegarasu U	.10	.20
❑ 3 Akodo Shinichi U	.40	1.00
❑ 4 Allegations U	.20	.50
❑ 5 Anvil of Despair (Experienced) R	.50	1.25
❑ 6 Asako Masamichi C	.10	.20
❑ 7 Assigning Blame R	5.00	12.00
❑ 8 Astonishing Resiliance R	2.00	5.00
❑ 9 Bakemono Warpack C	.10	.20
❑ 10 Bayushi Kosaku C	.10	.20
❑ 11 Bayushi Tomo C	.10	.20
❑ 12 Beginning Arbitrations C	.10	.20
❑ 13 Berserker's Charge U	.20	.50
❑ 14 Blunting the Charge C	.10	.20
❑ 15 Brand of Cowardice C	.10	.20
❑ 16 Castle Moat U	.20	.50
❑ 17 Ceremony of Planting U	.10	.20
❑ 18 Chuda Chiaki U	.30	.75
❑ 19 Chuda Eiichi U	.20	.50
❑ 20 Clan Heirloom C	.10	.20
❑ 21 Courage in Death R	2.50	6.00
❑ 22 Cowardly Rabble C	.10	.20
❑ 23 Cursed Gift U	.20	.50
❑ 24 Daidoji Gempachi R	1.25	3.00
❑ 25 Daidoji Murasaki C	.10	.20
❑ 26 Daigotsu Hidetsugu U	.20	.50
❑ 27 Daigotsu Iemitsu C	.10	.20
❑ 28 Daigotsu Yajinden (Experienced 2) F	.75	2.00
❑ 29 Da'na'tch U	.20	.50
❑ 30 Dark Inheritance U	.20	.50
❑ 31 Dawn of the Spider U	.10	.20
❑ 32 Death After Life R	1.50	4.00
❑ 33 Death Poem C	.10	.20
❑ 34 Denounced on Stage U	2.00	5.00
❑ 35 Desperate Gambit U	.20	.50
❑ 36 Devoted Yojimbo U	.20	.50
❑ 37 Doji Hitomaro C	.10	.20
❑ 38 Double Bind C	.10	.20
❑ 39 Earthen Guardians U	.20	.50
❑ 40 Echoes of Disgrace R	2.50	6.00
❑ 41 Etsushi R	1.25	3.00
❑ 42 Failure of Courage C	.10	.20
❑ 43 Fight Another Day R	.75	2.00
❑ 44 Find a Way Through It C	.10	.20
❑ 45 For the Fallen R	1.25	3.00
❑ 46 Forgotten Battleground C	.10	.20
❑ 47 Funeral Rites C	.10	.20
❑ 48 Fusami R	.60	1.50
❑ 49 Gate Guardsman U	.20	.50
❑ 50 Gift of the Lady C	.10	.20
❑ 51 Glory in Death R	1.25	3.00
❑ 52 Goju Zeshin U	.20	.50
❑ 53 Gumbai-Uchiwa C	.10	.20
❑ 54 Hashi no Oni R	.50	1.25
❑ 55 Hida Kozen U	.20	.50
❑ 56 Hida Masatari U	.20	.50
❑ 57 Hida Otoya R	1.25	3.00
❑ 58 Hida Tsuburu C	.10	.20
❑ 59 Hiruma Shotoku C	.10	.20
❑ 60 Honor in Death R	1.50	4.00
❑ 61 Honorable Rebirth R	1.25	3.00
❑ 62 Hope from Death R	.75	2.00
❑ 63 Horiuchi Rikako R	1.25	3.00
❑ 64 Ikoma Noda C	.10	.20
❑ 65 Ikoma Uchito R	.75	2.00
❑ 66 I-m'jek C	.10	.20
❑ 67 Inferno's Tooth C	.10	.20
❑ 68 Inspire Courage C	.10	.20
❑ 69 Inspire Excellence R	1.25	3.00
❑ 70 Inspire Fear C	.10	.20
❑ 71 Inspire Obediance U	.20	.50
❑ 72 Inspire Reverence U	.20	.50
❑ 73 Iron Tetsubo C	.20	.50
❑ 74 Isawa Chinatsu C	.10	.20
❑ 75 Isawa Sawao (Experienced 2) R	1.25	3.00
❑ 76 Isawa Tokiko U	.20	.50
❑ 77 Kakita Komachi U	.10	.20
❑ 78 Kan'ok'tichek (Experienced 3) R	.50	1.25
❑ 79 Kanshi U	.20	.50
❑ 80 Kazumasa R	.50	1.25
❑ 81 Kharma in Death R	.75	2.00
❑ 82 Kitsuki Berii C	.10	.20
❑ 83 K'inee (Exerpienced 2) R	1.25	3.00
❑ 84 K'mee's Jingasa U	.20	.50
❑ 85 Kokujin Buncho C	.10	.20
❑ 86 Krn'n C	.10	.20
❑ 87 Kuni Ochiyo R	1.25	3.00
❑ 88 Let Them Fight Their Dead R	1.25	3.00
❑ 89 Lion Advisor R	.50	1.25
❑ 90 Lion Mempo R	.50	1.25
❑ 91 Loyalty, Unto Death R	1.50	4.00
❑ 92 Masakazu R	.75	2.00
❑ 93 Master Saleh C	.10	.20
❑ 94 Matsu Fumiyo R	1.50	4.00
❑ 95 Matsu Ouka C	.10	.20
❑ 96 Matsu Shoken U	.10	.20
❑ 97 Merciless Death R	1.50	4.00
❑ 98 Mirumoto Jaizuru U	.20	.50
❑ 99 Mirumoto Kei (Experienced) F	2.00	5.00
❑ 100 Moshi Kiyomori U	.10	.20
❑ 101 Moshi Minami U	.20	.50
❑ 102 Moto Jin-sahn F	2.50	6.00
❑ 103 Moto Yong-tai U	.10	.20
❑ 104 Naoharu R	.75	2.00
❑ 105 Naseru's Funeral R	.60	1.50
❑ 106 Picker of Bones C	.10	.20
❑ 107 Prepared Defense U	.20	.50
❑ 108 Preparing Stockpiles C	.10	.20
❑ 109 Profit from Death R	.50	1.25
❑ 110 Purity in Death R	.75	2.00
❑ 111 Reclamation U	.20	.50
❑ 112 Redeployment U	.20	.50
❑ 113 Requisitioned Troops C	.10	.20
❑ 114 Ronin Scout U	.20	.50
❑ 115 Sake House Brawl C	.10	.20
❑ 116 Samarhad (Experienced) U	.20	.50
❑ 117 Second Doom of the Dark Lord R	.50	1.25
❑ 118 Shameful Tactics U	.20	.50
❑ 119 Share the Blame C	.10	.20
❑ 120 Shiba Sotatsu U	.10	.20
❑ 121 Shiro Usagi R	.50	1.25
❑ 122 Shosuro Jimen R	.75	2.00
❑ 123 Shosuro Maru (Experienced 2) R	.60	1.50
❑ 124 Shosuro Masanori U	.20	.50
❑ 125 Soshi Korenaga U	.20	.50
❑ 126 Soul Jar R	2.50	6.00
❑ 127 Spider Heavy Regulars C	.10	.20
❑ 128 Summon Maseru no Oni R	2.50	6.00
❑ 129 Summoned to Justice U	.75	2.00
❑ 130 Tadaka no Oni (Experienced Oni no Tadaka) R	.50	1.25
❑ 131 Tales of Battle R	1.25	3.00
❑ 132 Tempered Resurrection U	.20	.50
❑ 133 Tetsu Kama Mura F	1.25	3.00
❑ 134 The Dessicated C	.10	.20
❑ 135 The Khan's Shining Horde F	.75	2.00
❑ 136 The Price of Weakness U	.20	.50
❑ 137 The Quelsaurth R	.75	2.00
❑ 138 The Spider's Lair F	.75	2.00
❑ 139 Togashi Kisu C	.10	.20
❑ 140 Togashi Wirro U	.10	.20
❑ 141 Traveling Magistrate U	.20	.50
❑ 142 Triumph of Courage C	.10	.20
❑ 143 True Artistry U	.20	.50
❑ 144 Tsukai-sagasu R	1.25	3.00
❑ 145 Tsuruchi Ki C	.10	.20
❑ 146 Ujina Saionji C	.10	.20
❑ 147 Unicorn Wardogs U	.10	.20
❑ 148 Usagi Heiji C	.10	.20
❑ 149 Utaku Fujiko C	.10	.20
❑ 150 Utaku Remi C	.10	.20
❑ 151 Vengeful Shadows U	.20	.50
❑ 152 Wandering Sohei U	.20	.50
❑ 153 We Join the Ancestors R	1.25	3.00
❑ 154 Yoritomo Harada C	.10	.20
❑ 155 Yoritomo Kurei R	1.25	3.00
❑ 156 Yoritomo Sachina R	.75	2.00

2008 Legend of the Five Rings Honor's Veil

BOOSTER BOX (48)	50.00	100.00
BOOSTER PACK (11)	1.50	3.00
❑ 1 A Common Goal U	.20	.50
❑ 2 A Generous Offer R	1.25	3.00
❑ 3 A Lord's Compassion C	.10	.20
❑ 4 A Priest's Courtesy U	.20	.50
❑ 5 A Prophet Revealed U	.10	.20
❑ 6 A Warrior's Courtesy U	.20	.50
❑ 7 Advantageous Climate C	.10	.20
❑ 8 Akodo Bakin (Experienced 2) R	.30	.75
❑ 9 Akodo Nakama R	1.00	2.50
❑ 10 Ancestral Sword of the Ki-Rin R	.30	.75
❑ 11 Arranged Marriage C	.10	.20
❑ 12 Asako Nagami U	.10	.20
❑ 13 Asp Warriors U	.10	.20
❑ 14 Bayushi Eisaku (Experienced) F	.50	1.25
❑ 15 Bayushi Kosugi U	.10	.20
❑ 16 Bayushi Nomen (Experienced) R	1.00	2.50
❑ 17 Binding Contract U	.10	.20
❑ 18 Blessings of the Death Lords U	.10	.20
❑ 19 Borrowed Advisors C	.10	.20
❑ 20 Brute Force R	4.00	10.00
❑ 21 Clear Signals U	.20	.50
❑ 22 Consecrating the Temple R	.30	.75
❑ 23 Cornered Market U	.20	.50
❑ 24 Court Invitation C	.10	.20
❑ 25 Daidoji Takihiro (Experienced) F	.50	1.25
❑ 26 Daidoji Zoushi C	.10	.20
❑ 27 Daigotsu Hirata R	1.25	3.00
❑ 28 Daigotsu Masahiko C	.10	.20
❑ 29 Daigotsu Ryudo C	.10	.20
❑ 30 Daigotsu Sahara R	1.25	3.00
❑ 31 Daigotsu Takayasu C	.10	.20
❑ 32 Daigotsu Usharo C	.10	.20
❑ 33 Daimyo's Blade R	.60	1.50
❑ 34 Darling of the Season U	.10	.20
❑ 35 Desolate Plains U	.10	.20
❑ 36 Doji Jorihime U	.10	.20
❑ 37 Doji Tsubakita C	.10	.20
❑ 38 Duel to the Death R	1.50	4.00
❑ 39 Elaborate Preparations U	.20	.50
❑ 40 Essence of Jade Dragon C	.10	.20
❑ 41 Exchange of Hostages R	.50	1.25
❑ 42 Exchanging Civilities C	.10	.20
❑ 43 Famous Bazaar R	8.00	20.00
❑ 44 Gaining Momentum C	.10	.20
❑ 45 Gaki of Desire C	.10	.20
❑ 46 Gempukku Blade C	.10	.20
❑ 47 Gempukku Ceremony C	.10	.20
❑ 48 Gift Armor R	1.00	2.50
❑ 49 Gunso Kirita R	1.00	2.50
❑ 50 Gunso Shiraki R	1.00	2.50
❑ 51 Gunso Tabarou R	1.00	2.50
❑ 52 Hazardous Ford R	.50	1.25
❑ 53 Hida Lineage U	.20	.50
❑ 54 Hidden Dragon Temple R	.50	1.25
❑ 55 Hidden Scandal C	.10	.20
❑ 56 Hidden Sword Ronin U	.20	.50
❑ 57 Hidekazu C	.10	.20
❑ 58 High Temple of Toshi Ranbo C	.10	.20
❑ 59 Hiruma Aki (Experienced) R	1.50	4.00
❑ 60 Hiruma Ikage C	.10	.20
❑ 61 Horiuchi Meimei C	.10	.20
❑ 62 Hummingbird Wings R	2.00	5.00
❑ 63 Ide Towako U	.10	.20
❑ 64 Ide Yusuke U	.10	.20
❑ 65 Ikoma Hodota U	.10	.20
❑ 66 Impeccable Nobility C	.10	.20
❑ 67 Inspecting the Charts C	.10	.20
❑ 68 Inspiring Speech R	.50	1.25
❑ 69 Isawa Mizuhiko U	1.00	2.50
❑ 70 Isawa Shokuta C	.10	.20
❑ 71 Kaiu Genji U	.10	.20
❑ 72 Kaiu Taru R	3.00	8.00
❑ 73 Kakita Senko U	.10	.20
❑ 74 Kakita Tsukao R	1.25	3.00
❑ 75 Kata Training Grounds U	.10	.20
❑ 76 Kayomasa R	1.25	3.00
❑ 77 Kishida U	.10	.20
❑ 78 Kitsu Nariyumi C	.10	.20
❑ 79 Kitsuki Kouri U	.10	.20
❑ 80 Kitsuki Taiko (Experienced) F	1.25	3.00

TCG/CCG

Card	Low	High
❑ 81 Kitsune Mizuru C	.10	.20
❑ 82 Kitsune Ryukan (Experienced) R	.30	.75
❑ 83 Kuni Bachida C	.10	.20
❑ 84 Kyuden Kyotei F	1.25	3.00
❑ 85 Kyuden Miya R	.30	.75
❑ 86 Luxurious Gift U	.10	.20
❑ 87 Manipulation U	.20	.50
❑ 88 Martyr and Pawn U	.20	.50
❑ 89 Matsu Fukiki U	.10	.20
❑ 90 Matsu Nao C	.10	.20
❑ 91 Mirumoto Katsutoshi U	.10	.20
❑ 92 Mirumoto Satobe R	1.25	3.00
❑ 93 Mirumoto Toraizo C	.10	.20
❑ 94 Miya Anzai C	.10	.20
❑ 95 Morning Frost Castle F	1.25	3.00
❑ 96 Moto Choon-yei R	.30	.75
❑ 97 Moto Masakage C	.10	.20
❑ 98 Muddy Sandals U	.30	.75
❑ 99 My Ancestors' Strength R	.50	1.25
❑ 100 Northern Hub Village Shipwrights U	.10	.20
❑ 101 Odori Dance U	.20	.50
❑ 102 Oni Mura U	.10	.20
❑ 103 Otomo Lineage U	.20	.50
❑ 104 Passing Judgement U	.20	.50
❑ 105 Perilous Ground C	.10	.20
❑ 106 Poisoned Gift U	.10	.20
❑ 107 Pokku's Raiders C	.10	.20
❑ 108 Polite Discussion C	.10	.20
❑ 109 Puppet Master R	2.00	5.00
❑ 110 Resilient Naginata U	.10	.20
❑ 111 Respect Among Warriors C	.10	.20
❑ 112 Return to the Heavens R	.30	.75
❑ 113 Shattered Peaks C	.10	.20
❑ 114 Shiba Maroyo C	.10	.20
❑ 115 Shiba Sakishi R	.60	1.50
❑ 116 Shiba Tsukimi (Experienced 2) R	.50	1.25
❑ 117 Shikage no Oni R	.30	.75
❑ 118 Shosuro Chihiro C	.10	.20
❑ 119 Shosuro Lineage U	.20	.50
❑ 120 Shosuro Masato C	.10	.20
❑ 121 Shosuro Mizuno U	.10	.20
❑ 122 Skilled Quartermaster R	1.25	3.00
❑ 123 Snow Riders R	2.50	6.00
❑ 124 Solid Defense R	1.50	4.00
❑ 125 Solving the Riddle U	.20	.50
❑ 126 Sparrow Clan Aide C	.10	.20
❑ 127 Sun Doru R	.30	.75
❑ 128 Swift Counterattack R	2.50	6.00
❑ 129 Swift Punishment R	.50	1.25
❑ 130 Teardrop Island R	.60	1.50
❑ 131 Tempest of Osano-Wo U	.10	.20
❑ 132 The Balance Shifts U	.10	.20
❑ 133 The Champion's Guidance R	.30	.75
❑ 134 The House of False Hope F	1.00	2.50
❑ 135 The Spider's Shadow R	.30	.75
❑ 136 The Strength of Allies C	.10	.20
❑ 137 To Serve Justice C	.10	.20
❑ 138 To the Last Breath C	.10	.20
❑ 139 Togashi Keitori C	.10	.20
❑ 140 Tonfajutsu C	.10	.20
❑ 141 Torch's Flame Flickers C	.10	.20
❑ 142 Tsuruchi Takeba U	.10	.20
❑ 143 Unbiased Advice U	.20	.50
❑ 144 Under Suspicion C	.10	.20
❑ 145 Ungrateful Host R	.50	1.25
❑ 146 Utaku Keiko R	2.00	5.00
❑ 147 Versatile Army R	3.00	8.00
❑ 148 Winter Ravager C	.10	.20
❑ 149 Wolf Legion U	.10	.20
❑ 150 Wolf's Little Lesson U	.20	.50
❑ 151 Yarijutsu R	4.00	10.00
❑ 152 Yasuki Tenzo U	.10	.20
❑ 153 Yoritomo Hotako (Experienced) R	1.25	3.00
❑ 154 Yoritomo Jera U	.10	.20
❑ 155 Yoritomo Yagami C	.10	.20
❑ 156 Yoritomo Yoyonagi (Experienced) R	.30	.75

2008 Legend of the Five Rings The Heaven's Will

Card	Low	High
BOOSTER BOX (48)	50.00	100.00
BOOSTER PACK (11)	1.50	3.00
❑ 1 Adepts of Mighty Pokku C	.10	.20
❑ 2 Agasha Iwarou U	.10	.20
❑ 3 Aggressive Landing C	.10	.20
❑ 4 Akodo Hijikata R	.60	1.50
❑ 5 Akodo Shinichi (Experienced) F	1.25	3.00
❑ 6 Akodo Tadatoshi U	.10	.20
❑ 7 Armor of Light R1	1.50	4.00
❑ 8 Asako Juro (Experienced) R	.50	1.25
❑ 9 Assassin's Strike C	.10	.20
❑ 10 Bayushi Gaho C	.10	.20
❑ 11 Bayushi Irishi U	.10	.20
❑ 12 Bayushi Kasata C	.10	.20
❑ 13 Bayushi Kurumi (Experienced) R	2.50	6.00
❑ 14 Beloved of the Clan R	3.00	8.00
❑ 15 Blessed Tessen C	.10	.20
❑ 16 Blighted Region R	.50	1.25
❑ 17 Broken Reef Keep F	1.25	3.00
❑ 18 Bronze Memorial R	.75	2.00
❑ 19 Chagatai's Legion R	.50	1.25
❑ 20 Chuda Mishime (Experienced) R1	3.00	8.00
❑ 21 Chuda Shikyo U	.10	.20
❑ 22 Claiming the Throne U	.10	.20
❑ 23 Consecration R	.60	1.50
❑ 24 Daidoji Awao U	.10	.20
❑ 25 Daidoji Barashi R	1.50	4.00
❑ 26 Daigotsu Kurai C	.10	.20
❑ 27 Daigotsu Meguro (Experienced) R	.50	1.25
❑ 28 Daigotsu Sendo R	1.25	3.00
❑ 29 Daigotsu Shiraki U	.10	.20
❑ 30 Dance of the Kami U	.10	.20
❑ 31 Decisive Strike U	.10	.20
❑ 32 Decree of Peace U3	.10	.20
❑ 33 Defensive Tactics U	.20	.50
❑ 34 Deftly Wielded U3	.20	.50
❑ 35 Desperate Plea R1	1.50	4.00
❑ 36 Discretionary Valor U	.20	.50
❑ 37 Doji Hiromi U3	.10	.20
❑ 38 Dojo Applicants R	.75	2.00
❑ 39 Eku C	.10	.20
❑ 40 Entangling Terrain C	.10	.20
❑ 41 Estate Halls U	.10	.20
❑ 42 Fall of Greatness R	.50	1.25
❑ 43 Flame of Truth C3	.10	.20
❑ 44 Flanked by Nightmares R	4.00	10.00
❑ 45 Footman's Pike R	.50	1.25
❑ 46 Fortified Fields C3	.10	.20
❑ 47 Fortune's Favor U	.10	.20
❑ 48 Fubiri no Oni U	.10	.20
❑ 49 Gentle Blade of Winter U	.20	.50
❑ 50 Glukku C	.10	.20
❑ 51 Great Falls Castle F	1.25	3.00
❑ 52 Hand of Osano-Wo R	1.50	4.00
❑ 53 Hateful Curse R	.50	1.25
❑ 54 Hida Kaoru (Experienced) R	.60	1.50
❑ 55 Hida Ubogin R	1.25	3.00
❑ 56 Hiruma Moshiro C	.10	.20
❑ 57 Hiruma Tabarou U	.10	.20
❑ 58 Hold! R	.75	2.00
❑ 59 Holy Site R1	.50	1.25
❑ 60 Ideal Grounds U	.20	.50
❑ 61 Ikoma Okita C	.10	.20
❑ 62 Imperial City Guards C3	.10	.20
❑ 63 Isawa Chishaki R	.60	1.50
❑ 64 Isawa Naki C3	.10	.20
❑ 65 Isawa Ochiai (Experienced 2) R1	.50	1.25
❑ 66 Isawa Uhiko U3	.10	.20
❑ 67 Iuchi Konyo U	.10	.20
❑ 68 Kaiu Seison R	.50	1.25
❑ 69 Kakita Hideo (Experienced) R	.60	1.50
❑ 70 Kakita Hideshi C	.10	.20
❑ 71 Kakita Idzuki R	2.50	6.00
❑ 72 Kakita Toma C	.10	.20
❑ 73 Katana of Twilight R1	5.00	12.00
❑ 74 Keen Blade U3	.10	.20
❑ 75 Keeping Enemies Close U	.20	.50
❑ 76 Kimogen U	.10	.20
❑ 77 Kitsu Yutaro U	.10	.20
❑ 78 Kitsuki Rai F	2.00	5.00
❑ 79 Kitsuki Taji C	.10	.20
❑ 80 Kitsune Hisano R	1.25	3.00
❑ 81 Kuni Tanin C3	.10	.20
❑ 82 Kuri C3	.10	.20
❑ 83 Kuronada U	.40	1.00
❑ 84 Laborious Effort U3	.20	.50
❑ 85 Let Them Run C	.10	.20
❑ 86 Masu C	.10	.20
❑ 87 Matsu Hatsuyo R	1.25	3.00
❑ 88 Matsu Mikura C	.10	.20
❑ 89 Might of Paragons R	1.25	3.00
❑ 90 Mirumoto Akio R	3.00	8.00
❑ 91 Moshi Amarante U	.10	.20
❑ 92 Moshi Mareo C	.10	.20
❑ 93 Moto Soonshin R	.75	2.00
❑ 94 Musha Shugyo R1	2.00	5.00
❑ 95 My Ally's Strength C	.10	.20
❑ 96 My Enemy's Mercy R	2.00	5.00
❑ 97 No Escape U	.20	.50
❑ 98 Offered Gift R	.50	1.25
❑ 99 Old Rivalries R1	4.00	10.00
❑ 100 Only the Well-Trained Listen R	4.00	10.00
❑ 101 Ornate Armor C3	.10	.20
❑ 102 Pack Tactics C	.10	.20
❑ 103 Peaceful Interlude C3	.10	.20
❑ 104 Political Influence R	1.50	4.00
❑ 105 Powerful Blow R	4.00	10.00
❑ 106 Ramifications U	.20	.50
❑ 107 Regroup and Redeploy C	.10	.20
❑ 108 Reprimand C	.10	.20
❑ 109 Resurgence R	1.50	4.00
❑ 110 Roaring to Shake Heaven C	.10	.20
❑ 111 Sacrificial Lands U	.20	.50
❑ 112 Seeking the Path R	1.50	4.00
❑ 113 Seiko C3	.10	.20
❑ 114 Seppun Miharu R	.60	1.50
❑ 115 Shelter for Refugees U	.20	.50
❑ 116 Shiba Morihiko C	.10	.20
❑ 117 Shikibu no Oni (Experienced Oni no Shikibu) R1	1.50	4.00
❑ 118 Shinjo Aniji C	.10	.20
❑ 119 Shinjo Joyung R	.75	2.00
❑ 120 Shinjo Kirita U	.10	.20
❑ 121 Shosuro Hihiko R	4.00	10.00
❑ 122 Shosuro Kiemon U3	.10	.20
❑ 123 Silent Rot R	2.50	6.00
❑ 124 Skin of the Naga R	.50	1.25
❑ 125 Small Estate C	.10	.20
❑ 126 Stalemate R	.75	2.00
❑ 127 Stolen Blade U3	.20	.50
❑ 128 Strength in Simplicity C	.10	.20
❑ 129 Strength of my Father C3	.10	.20
❑ 130 Sublime Peacock Stance C	.10	.20
❑ 131 Subtle Reminder U	.20	.50
❑ 132 Swift Darkness U	.20	.50
❑ 133 Sword Saint Shrine C	.10	.20
❑ 134 Tamori Akeno U	.10	.20
❑ 135 The Earth's Wrath U	.10	.20
❑ 136 The Slow Death R	4.00	10.00
❑ 137 Threat of Execution U	.20	.50
❑ 138 Tiger Climbing Mountain C	.10	.20
❑ 139 Togashi Chiko U	.10	.20
❑ 140 Togashi Dai C	.10	.20
❑ 141 Togashi Miyoko (Experienced) R	.50	1.25
❑ 142 Transcendence of Flesh R	1.50	4.00
❑ 143 Traveling Smugglers C	.10	.20
❑ 144 Tsuruchi Shisuken C	.10	.20
❑ 145 Underhanded Attack U	.20	.50
❑ 146 Undermining Command U	.20	.50
❑ 147 Undignified Death R	4.00	10.00
❑ 148 Unpleasant Discovery U3	.20	.50
❑ 149 Utaku Jisoo C	.10	.20
❑ 150 Utaku Kohana (Experienced) R	.60	1.50
❑ 151 Venerable Plains of the Ikoma F	1.50	4.00
❑ 152 Veteran Advisor R	1.50	4.00
❑ 153 Victory March C	.20	.50
❑ 154 Viper Tattoo U	.20	.50
❑ 155 Wakened Dead U	.10	.20
❑ 156 Wandering Ronin R	.75	2.00
❑ 157 Ward of the Kami C	.10	.20
❑ 158 Wary Peace C	.10	.20
❑ 159 Wrack the Soul C	.10	.20
❑ 160 Yakamo's End U	.20	.50
❑ 161 Yasuki Takai U3	.10	.20
❑ 162 Yogo Koji (Experienced) R1	2.00	5.00
❑ 163 Yoritomo Joben U	.10	.20
❑ 164 Yoritomo Saburo (Experienced) R	.60	1.50
❑ 165 Yoritomo Tadame (Experienced) F	1.25	3.00
❑ 166 Yoshe C	.10	.20

2008 Legend of the Five Rings Words and Deeds

Card	Low	High
BOOSTER BOX (48)	50.00	100.00
BOOSTER PACK (11)	1.50	3.00
❑ 1 A Warrior's Patience R	1.50	4.00
❑ 2 Agasha Sanami C	.10	.20
❑ 3 Akodo Itoku R	4.00	10.00
❑ 4 Akodo Sadahige (Experienced) R	.50	1.25
❑ 5 An Act of Disdain R	1.00	2.50
❑ 6 Armor of Command C	.10	.20
❑ 7 Armor of Toshigoku U	.20	.50
❑ 8 Arrogant Dismissal C	.10	.20
❑ 9 Asahina Keitaro (Experienced) R	.50	1.25
❑ 10 Asahina Naoki R	2.50	6.00
❑ 11 Asakao Bushiken C	.10	.20
❑ 12 Bayushi Chikayo C	.10	.20
❑ 13 Bayushi Ikkou C	.10	.20
❑ 14 Bayushi Ryouya R	1.50	4.00
❑ 15 Bayushi Tenbin R	2.00	5.00
❑ 16 Bayushi Yusui U	.20	.50
❑ 17 Behind Enemy Lines C	.10	.20
❑ 18 Besieged R	1.50	4.00
❑ 19 Black and White U	.20	.50
❑ 20 Black Silk Castle F	.50	1.25
❑ 21 Blade of Awe R	1.25	3.00
❑ 22 Blade of Spirit R	1.00	2.50
❑ 23 Brink of Exhaustion R	1.25	3.00
❑ 24 Celestial Unrest U	.10	.20
❑ 25 Chuda Jinsei U	.20	.50
❑ 26 Contested Ownership C	.10	.20
❑ 27 Coordinated Movement R	1.00	2.50
❑ 28 Coronation of Jade R	.50	1.25
❑ 29 Crude Trap R	5.00	12.00
❑ 30 Customzed Armor R	1.00	2.50
❑ 31 Daidoji Teruo C	.10	.20
❑ 32 Daigotsu Gyoken (Experienced) R	2.00	5.00
❑ 33 Daigotsu Harushi C	.10	.20
❑ 34 Daigotsu Masisha U	.20	.50
❑ 35 Daimyo's Vassals R	.50	1.25
❑ 36 Darkness Unleashed U	.20	.50
❑ 37 Death Trance R	1.00	2.50
❑ 38 Demented Craftsmen U	.10	.20
❑ 39 Devastating Blow R	.50	1.25
❑ 40 Differences Between Us U	.20	.50
❑ 41 Dissolution U	.20	.50
❑ 42 Diverting the Reserves U	.20	.50
❑ 43 Doji Ayano (Experienced) R	.50	1.25
❑ 44 Doji Chitose U	.10	.20
❑ 45 Doji Sakurako U	.10	.20
❑ 46 Duel of Champions R	1.25	3.00
❑ 47 Failure of Diplomacy U	.20	.50
❑ 48 Fatina R	1.50	4.00
❑ 49 Final Sacrifice U	.20	.50
❑ 50 Follow the Flame C	.10	.20
❑ 51 Fortified Cavalry U	.20	.50
❑ 52 Glorious Path to Victory C	.10	.20
❑ 53 Gunso Hiroshi R	1.25	3.00
❑ 54 Gunso Kisho R	1.25	3.00
❑ 55 Gunso Raiden R	.60	1.50
❑ 56 Hamstrung R	4.00	10.00
❑ 57 Heaven's Fire U	.20	.50
❑ 58 Hida Bachiatari C	.20	.50
❑ 59 Hida Fubatsu U	.10	.20
❑ 60 Hida Manabu C	.10	.20
❑ 61 Hida Nichie (Experienced) R	.50	1.25
❑ 62 Hiruma Kaikawa C	.10	.20
❑ 63 Hub of Commerce C	.10	.20
❑ 64 Hurried Gempukku U	.20	.50
❑ 65 I Will Not Die Alone! U	.20	.50
❑ 66 Ikoma Asa U	.30	.75
❑ 67 Inspirational Address C	.10	.20
❑ 68 Insurmountable Obstacle U	.30	.75
❑ 69 Inu C	.10	.20
❑ 70 Isawa Kyoko (Experienced) R	.60	1.50
❑ 71 Isawa Miniko U	.10	.20
❑ 72 Isawa Wakasa R	1.00	2.50
❑ 73 Iuchi Ietsuna U	.20	.50
❑ 74 Jinako U	.20	.50
❑ 75 Kaiu Shoichi R	1.00	2.50
❑ 76 Kakita Michihiro C	.10	.20
❑ 77 Kata of the North Wind R	1.00	2.50
❑ 78 Keeping the Peace C	.10	.20
❑ 79 Kensai's Blade C	.10	.20
❑ 80 Kitsuki Mayako U	.10	.20
❑ 81 Kitsuki Nagiken (Experienced) R	.60	1.50
❑ 82 Kitsune Engo C	.10	.20
❑ 83 Kote U	.10	.20
❑ 84 Kuni Daigo (Experienced) F	1.25	3.00
❑ 85 Lightening the Load U	.20	.50
❑ 86 Maga-yari C	.20	.50
❑ 87 Masterpiece U	.20	.50
❑ 88 Masters of Steel R	1.25	3.00
❑ 89 Matsu Daichi C	.10	.20
❑ 90 Matsu Takeko (Experienced) R	.50	1.25
❑ 91 Matsu Ushio U	.10	.20
❑ 92 Matsu Yosa C	.10	.20
❑ 93 Michio (Experienced) F	2.00	5.00
❑ 94 Militia Training Ground R	1.25	3.00
❑ 95 Mirumoto Atsushi U	.10	.20
❑ 96 Mirumoto Otohiko R	.60	1.50
❑ 97 Mirumoto Toshiyuki C	.10	.20
❑ 98 Moshi Chuuya U	.10	.20
❑ 99 Moto Yong-tai (Experienced) R	.50	1.25
❑ 100 Muduro no Oni U	.20	.50
❑ 101 Mukku C	.10	.20
❑ 102 Naseru's Private Journal R	.50	1.25
❑ 103 One After Another R	.60	1.50
❑ 104 Otomo Ouga C	.20	.50
❑ 105 Patron of the Arts C	.10	.20
❑ 106 Pokku (Experienced) R	1.25	3.00
❑ 107 Prized Farmlands C	.10	.20
❑ 108 Questionable Patron C	.10	.20
❑ 109 Reckless Abandon U	.20	.50
❑ 110 Reihado Shinsei R	.60	1.50
❑ 111 Rejoining the Fight U	.20	.50
❑ 112 Remote Farms C	1.00	2.50
❑ 113 Removing the Advantage U	.20	.50
❑ 114 Rewards of Experience R	1.50	4.00
❑ 115 Rising Lava Strike U	.20	.50
❑ 116 Secret Passages C	.10	.20
❑ 117 Seized Assets C	.10	.20
❑ 118 Selfless Politics U	.20	.50
❑ 119 Shameful Injury C	.10	.20
❑ 120 Shiba Erena R	2.00	5.00
❑ 121 Shiba Ritsuo U	.20	.50
❑ 122 Shinjo Genya C	.10	.20
❑ 123 Shinjo Naota C	.10	.20
❑ 124 Shinjo Shono (Experienced 4) F	1.00	2.50
❑ 125 Shinjo T'sao U	.20	.50
❑ 126 Shiotome U	.20	.50
❑ 127 Shosuro Hirubumi C	.10	.20
❑ 128 Skilled Defense C	.10	.20
❑ 129 Song of the World R	1.25	3.00
❑ 130 Soshi Tishi (Experienced) R	.50	1.25
❑ 131 Sowing Suspicion C	.10	.20
❑ 132 Speed of the Sea C	.10	.20
❑ 133 Spider Abbot R	.60	1.50
❑ 134 Strength of Arms C	.10	.20
❑ 135 Swift Sword Cut U	.20	.50
❑ 136 Tadaka's Mirror C	.10	.20
❑ 137 Tale of Tsukuro R	10.00	25.00
❑ 138 Taoist Archer R	.10	.20
❑ 139 Tengoku's Justice C	.30	.75
❑ 140 Tetsuo C	1.50	4.00
❑ 141 The Emperor's Road R	.10	.20
❑ 142 The Fall of Shiro Moto U	.10	.20
❑ 143 The Final Wave C	1.00	2.50
❑ 144 The Great Carpenter Wall F	1.50	4.00
❑ 145 The Jackal's Kiss R	1.25	3.00
❑ 146 The Last One R	.20	.50
❑ 147 The Mountain's Feet U	5.00	12.00
❑ 148 The Third Yasuki War R	.60	1.50
❑ 149 The Western Steppes F	1.00	2.50
❑ 150 Togashi Binya C	.10	.20
❑ 151 Togashi Hogai (Experienced Hitomi Hogai) R	1.50	4.00
❑ 152 Touch of the Infinite R	.50	1.25
❑ 153 Tsuruchi Akinobu C	.10	.20
❑ 154 Tsuruchi Taiga U	.10	.20
❑ 155 Ujina Ukita C	.10	.20
❑ 156 Unwanted Mediation C	.10	.20
❑ 157 Usurpation R	3.00	8.00
❑ 158 Utaku Fusae R	.60	1.50
❑ 159 Web of Pain C	.10	.20
❑ 160 Wrist Lock U	.60	1.50
❑ 161 Ying and Yang C	.10	.20
❑ 162 Yobanjin Mercenaries C	.10	.20
❑ 163 Yoritomo Eriko (Experienced) R	.50	1.25
❑ 164 Yoritomo Fushu R	.60	1.50
❑ 165 Yoritomo Han-ku R	.50	1.25
❑ 166 Zanaru C	.10	.20

2009 Legend of the Five Rings Death at Koten

Card	Low	High
❑ 1 A False Accusation F3	1.00	2.50
❑ 2 A Magistrate's Blade F3	1.00	2.50
❑ 3 Akodo Tsudoken F1	1.25	3.00
❑ 4 Asako Fosu F1	1.50	4.00
❑ 5 Blind Rage F3	1.00	2.50
❑ 6 Cavalry Tactics F3	1.25	3.00
❑ 7 Censure of Thunder F3	.75	2.00
❑ 8 Chuda Seiki F1	2.50	6.00
❑ 9 Chugo Seido F3	2.00	5.00
❑ 10 Civil Discussion F3	.60	1.50
❑ 11 Conspiracy F1	.40	1.00
❑ 12 Court Attendants F3	.75	2.00
❑ 13 Crippling Strike F3	.60	1.50
❑ 14 Daidoji Inada F3	.40	1.00
❑ 15 Daigotsu Rasetu F3	.75	2.00
❑ 16 Dance of Flames F3	.60	1.50
❑ 17 Defensive Nature F3	1.25	3.00
❑ 18 Demonic Possession F3	.40	1.00
❑ 19 Desperate Battle F3	1.00	2.50
❑ 20 Doji Kishio F3	.40	1.00
❑ 21 Doomed Undertaking F3	.40	1.00
❑ 22 Dragon Attendants F3	.40	1.00
❑ 23 Essence of Destruction F1	1.50	4.00
❑ 24 Essence of Evil F3	.40	1.00
❑ 25 Expected Arrival F3	.60	1.50
❑ 26 Exposing Secrets F3	.60	1.50
❑ 27 Fatal Error F3	.60	1.50
❑ 28 Final Duty F3	8.00	20.00
❑ 29 Forward Camp F3	.40	1.00
❑ 30 Friendly Traveler Sake F3	.75	2.00
❑ 31 Hanayashiki F3	.40	1.00
❑ 32 Hida Hachimoto F1	1.25	3.00
❑ 33 Hida Kagura F3	.40	1.00
❑ 34 Hiruma Akio F3	.40	1.00
❑ 35 I Do Not Die So Easily! F3	.60	1.50
❑ 36 Ikoma Ryudo F3	.75	2.00
❑ 37 Imperial Adjudication F3	3.00	8.00
❑ 38 Imperial Arrival F1	.40	1.00
❑ 39 Isawa Kumai F3	.40	1.00
❑ 40 Isawa Mariko F3	.75	2.00
❑ 41 Kakita Aichiko F1	1.00	2.50
❑ 42 Kakita Tasaka F3	.40	1.00
❑ 43 Kitsuki Umibe F3	.40	1.00
❑ 44 Matsu Shunran F3	1.25	3.00
❑ 45 Matsu Youko F3	.75	2.00
❑ 46 Mirumoto Eikaru F3	.40	1.00
❑ 47 Momiji F3	.75	2.00
❑ 48 Moshi Enju F3	.75	2.00
❑ 49 Moto Rena F1	1.00	2.50
❑ 50 Moto Slhung F3	.40	1.00
❑ 51 Mutual Hatred F3	.75	2.00
❑ 52 Nosloc no Oni F3	.75	2.00
❑ 53 Order of Venom F3	.40	1.00
❑ 54 Presenting Papers F3	.40	1.00
❑ 55 Preserving Honor F3	.75	2.00
❑ 56 Ritual of Binding F3	.75	2.00
❑ 57 Ritual of Summoning F3	1.50	4.00
❑ 58 Scouting Ahead F3	1.00	2.50
❑ 59 Searching the Libraries F3	.75	2.00
❑ 60 Seppun Blade F3	6.00	15.00
❑ 61 Seppun Tashime F3	1.25	3.00
❑ 62 Shadowed Steel F1	.40	1.00
❑ 63 Shiba Kosoku F3	.60	1.50
❑ 64 Shinjo Ji-tae F3	.40	1.00
❑ 65 Shinjo Kai Ki F3	.40	1.00
❑ 66 Shosuro Takuma F3	.40	1.00
❑ 67 Suikotsu F3	1.25	3.00
❑ 68 Tamori Shaiko F1	2.00	5.00
❑ 69 The Loss of the Soul F1	1.25	3.00
❑ 70 The Second Death of Kisasda F1	.40	1.00
❑ 71 The Sensei F3	.40	1.00
❑ 72 The Student F3	.40	1.00
❑ 73 The Water Dragon's Favor F3	.40	1.00
❑ 74 Togashi Sho F3	1.00	2.50
❑ 75 Training Maneuvers F3	.75	2.00
❑ 76 Tsudo no Oni F3	1.25	3.00
❑ 77 Tsuruchi Suzuki F3	.75	2.00
❑ 78 United F3	.75	2.00
❑ 79 Unleashed Fury F3	.40	1.00
❑ 80 Veiled Menace F3	.75	2.00
❑ 81 Yasuki Tijaki F3	.40	1.00
❑ 82 Yogo Kazunori F1	5.00	12.00
❑ 83 Yoritomo Iwata (Experienced) F1	.40	1.00
❑ 84 Yoritomo Iwata F3	1.50	4.00

2009 Legend of the Five Rings Glory of the Empire

Card	Low	High
BOOSTER BOX (48)	50.00	100.00
BOOSTER PACK (11)	1.50	3.00
❑ 1 A Game of Sadane U2	.30	.75
❑ 2 A Rival Eliminated C2	.10	.20
❑ 3 Akaru no Oni C2	.10	.20
❑ 4 Akodo Hiroshi U2	.20	.50
❑ 5 Akodo Yanagi C2	.10	.20
❑ 6 An Imperial Marriage U2	.20	.50
❑ 7 Armor of the Heavens R2	4.00	10.00
❑ 8 Armor of the Ryu R1	10.00	25.00
❑ 9 Asako Kanta U2	.20	.50
❑ 10 Asako Serizawa R2	1.25	3.00
❑ 11 Asako Suda R2	1.25	3.00

❑ 12 Balanced Yari C3 .10 .20
❑ 13 Bayushi Hirose R2 5.00 12.00
❑ 14 Bayushi Ishikura R2 .75 2.00
❑ 15 Bayushi Shigeru R2 2.50 6.00
❑ 16 Buoyed by the Kami U2 .20 .50
❑ 17 Burned Village C2 .10 .20
❑ 18 Cavalry Officer C2 .10 .20
❑ 19 Certain Death C2 .10 .20
❑ 20 Changing Paths R2 2.50 6.00
❑ 21 Chrysanthemum Blossom C2 .10 .20
❑ 22 City of Tears F (Phoenix) 2.50 6.00
❑ 23 Clan Rivalries C3 .10 .20
❑ 24 Daidoji Murata U2 .20 .50
❑ 25 Daidoji Reita R2 1.50 4.00
❑ 26 Daigotsu Buroki R2 2.50 6.00
❑ 27 Daigotsu Churo C2 .10 .20
❑ 28 Daigotsu Minoko U2 .20 .50
❑ 29 Daigotsu Yuhmi R2 1.25 3.00
❑ 30 Daigotsu Zenshi R2 2.50 6.00
❑ 31 Dangerous Reconnaissance R2 2.00 5.00
❑ 32 Deadly Orders C2 .10 .20
❑ 33 Death Ravagers U3 .20 .50
❑ 34 Desperation Strikes U3 .20 .50
❑ 35 Discrete Retreat R2 3.00 8.00
❑ 36 Doji Hariya R2 2.50 6.00
❑ 37 Doji Numata C2 .10 .20
❑ 38 Doji Odaka F (Crane) 4.00 10.00
❑ 39 Endless Road C2 .10 .20
❑ 40 Eradicate All Doubt U2 .20 .50
❑ 41 First-Hand Account C2 .10 .20
❑ 42 Five Harmonies Blend U2 .20 .50
❑ 43 Fluid Formation U2 .20 .50
❑ 44 Fubatsu No-Dachi R2 .75 2.00
❑ 45 Furu no Oni R2 1.25 3.00
❑ 46 Games of Court R1 1.25 3.00
❑ 47 Goju Asagi C2 .10 .20
❑ 48 Half-Breath Strike R2 2.00 5.00
❑ 49 Hasty Exit R2 1.50 4.00
❑ 50 Hida Hikita R2 2.50 6.00
❑ 51 Hida Tatsuma R2 2.50 6.00
❑ 52 Hida Togeriso U2 .20 .50
❑ 53 Hida Yumiya U2 .20 .50
❑ 54 Hiruma Rohitsu C3 .10 .20
❑ 55 Hongo U2 .20 .50
❑ 56 Honor & Steel U2 .20 .50
❑ 57 Honor the Ancestors U3 .20 .50
❑ 58 House of Exotic Goods C2 .10 .20
❑ 59 I Carry Two Blades! C3 .10 .20
❑ 60 Ikoma Hagio R2 1.50 4.00
❑ 61 Ikoma Tomoi R2 1.25 3.00
❑ 62 Imperial Decree C2 .10 .20
❑ 63 Imperial Elite Guard C2 .10 .20
❑ 64 Imperial Intercession C2 .10 .20
❑ 65 Incredible Resilience R1 3.00 8.00
❑ 66 Inexplicable Challenge R2 5.00 12.00
❑ 67 Isawa Yutako C2 .10 .20
❑ 68 Iuchi Hotaru R2 1.50 4.00
❑ 69 Kaiu Kyoka F (Crab) 1.50 4.00
❑ 70 Kakita Omori C2 .10 .20
❑ 71 Kakita Takashima U3 .20 .50
❑ 72 Kami Unleashed R2 8.00 20.00
❑ 73 Kincho the Sixth C2 .10 .20
❑ 74 Kitsuki Kenichi C2 .10 .20
❑ 75 Kitsuki Tsuboko R2 2.00 5.00
❑ 76 Kitsune Ando U3 .20 .50
❑ 77 Kuni Sagara C2 .10 .20
❑ 78 Layered Plates R2 2.50 6.00
❑ 79 Legion of Death R2 1.25 3.00
❑ 80 Low Stance R2 10.00 25.00
❑ 81 Magistrate's Accusation U2 .20 .50
❑ 82 Malevolent Kappa C3 .10 .20
❑ 83 Matsu Ishigaki C2 .10 .20
❑ 84 Matsu Misato R2 2.50 6.00
❑ 85 Matsu Naomasa U2 .20 .50
❑ 86 Might of the Shadowlands U2 .20 .50
❑ 87 Mirumoto Ishino R2 3.00 8.00
❑ 88 Mirumoto Kuroki C3 .10 .20
❑ 89 Mirumoto Takehiro U2 .20 .50
❑ 90 Mokku C2 .20 .50
❑ 91 Moonless Riders R1 1.50 4.00
❑ 92 Moshi Awako R2 2.00 5.00
❑ 93 Moshi Nakata R2 1.25 3.00
❑ 94 Moto Juncheng C2 .10 .20
❑ 95 Moto Xiao R1 2.00 5.00
❑ 96 Mounting a Defense R2 2.00 5.00
❑ 97 Night of the Blood Moon U2 .20 .50
❑ 98 Ogre Savagery C2 .10 .20
❑ 99 Oishi R1 4.00 10.00
❑ 100 Open Shore Market C2 .10 .20
❑ 101 Oyumi R2 2.50 6.00
❑ 102 Paths of Honor & Glory R2 2.50 6.00
❑ 103 Phantom Blade Kata R2 1.50 4.00
❑ 104 Piercing the Heavens U2 .20 .50
❑ 105 Power Corrupting R2 2.50 6.00
❑ 106 Pragmatism R2 1.25 3.00
❑ 107 Public Garden R2 1.25 3.00
❑ 108 Raising Heaven's Banner C2 .10 .20
❑ 109 Reinforced Border U2 .20 .50
❑ 110 Revered Sensei U2 .20 .50
❑ 111 Riding the Clouds C3 .10 .20
❑ 112 Ronin Brotherhood R2 8.00 20.00
❑ 113 Sakarah C2 .10 .20
❑ 114 Scouring Flood C2 .10 .20
❑ 115 Seeking the Ancestors U3 .20 .50
❑ 116 Selfless Devotion C2 .10 .20
❑ 117 Servitors of Stone U2 .20 .50
❑ 118 Setting Sun Strike R2 2.00 5.00
❑ 119 Seven Fold Palace F (Crane) 2.50 6.00
❑ 120 Shattered Peaks Castle F (Crab) 2.50 6.00
❑ 121 Shiba Ikokawa F (Phoenix) 2.50 6.00
❑ 122 Shiba Raiden U2 .20 .50
❑ 123 Shiba Shigenobu C2 .10 .20
❑ 124 Shinjo Ki-Chang R2 2.50 6.00
❑ 125 Shinjo Ming-li U2 .20 .50
❑ 126 Shinjo Shinlao C3 .10 .20
❑ 127 Shisa Infestation R1 2.50 6.00
❑ 128 Shosuro Nitsu C2 .10 .20
❑ 129 Shosuro Takagi U2 .20 .50
❑ 130 Shukku U2 .20 .50
❑ 131 Siege Tactics C2 .10 .20
❑ 132 Soshi Mayumi C3 .10 .20
❑ 133 Spin the Karmic Wheel C2 .10 .20
❑ 134 Split the Reed U2 .20 .50
❑ 135 Strength of the Dead C2 .10 .20
❑ 136 Student of Ninjutsu C2 .10 .20
❑ 137 Subtle Corruption U2 .20 .50
❑ 138 Temple of Tsukune U2 .40 1.00
❑ 139 Terasaka U2 .20 .50
❑ 140 The Call of Battle C3 .10 .20
❑ 141 The Kharmic Cycle U2 .20 .50
❑ 142 The Sea's Lightning U3 .20 .50
❑ 143 The Winds' Favor R2 2.00 5.00
❑ 144 Thunder's Favor U2 .20 .50
❑ 145 Togashi Nakahara R1 1.50 4.00
❑ 146 Togashi Osawa U2 .20 .50
❑ 147 Traditions of Steel U2 .20 .50
❑ 148 Traveling Peddler R2 12.00 30.00
❑ 149 Tsuruchi Onaka C2 .10 .20
❑ 150 Undone by Truth R2 6.00 15.00
❑ 151 Unexpected Arrival R2 8.00 20.00
❑ 152 Unexplained Illness U2 .20 .50
❑ 153 Unpredictable Strategy R2 8.00 20.00
❑ 154 Unsavory Practices U2 .20 .50
❑ 155 Unworthy Rivals U2 .20 .50
❑ 156 Utaku Elite Guard U2 .20 .50
❑ 157 Utaku Yumiko U3 .20 .50
❑ 158 War Encampment C2 .10 .20
❑ 159 Winter Solstice R1 1.50 4.00
❑ 160 Winter's Embrace R1 1.50 4.00
❑ 161 Word of Fire R2 2.50 6.00
❑ 162 Word of Heaven U3 .20 .50
❑ 163 Wrath of the Elements C2 .10 .20
❑ 164 Yogo Fujitani U3 .20 .50
❑ 165 Yoritomo Kisho U2 .20 .50
❑ 166 Yoritomo Sunagawa R2 1.50 4.00

2009 Legend of the Five Rings Path of the Destroyer

COMPLETE SET (166) 40.00 80.00
BOOSTER BOX (48) 50.00 100.00
BOOSTER PACK (11) 1.50 3.00
❑ 1 Agasha Asai U .15 .40
❑ 2 Akodo Dosei C .10 .25
❑ 3 Akodo Masao C .10 .25
❑ 4 Akodo Nagataka U .15 .40
❑ 5 Akodo Shunori R .30 .75
❑ 6 Akodo's Guidance C .10 .25
❑ 7 Apprentice Shinobi U .15 .40
❑ 8 Armor of Legacy R .30 .75
❑ 9 Asako Hoshimi C .10 .25
❑ 10 Asako Misako C .10 .25
❑ 11 Assault Riders C .10 .25
❑ 12 Bare Ground C .10 .25
❑ 13 Bayushi Hisoka (Experienced) F (Scorpion) 6.00 15.00
❑ 14 Bayushi Komiya R .30 .75
❑ 15 Bayushi Minoru C .10 .25
❑ 16 Bayushi Saka U .15 .40
❑ 17 Bayushi's Guidance U .15 .40
❑ 18 Besieged Borderland C .10 .25
❑ 19 Border Ambush C .10 .25
❑ 20 Breath of the Heavens U .15 .40
❑ 21 Brothers in Harmony C .10 .25
❑ 22 Burn the Towers C .10 .25
❑ 23 Calm Before Death U .15 .40
❑ 24 Chagatai's Armor R .30 .75
❑ 25 Channeling Jigoku's Essence R .30 .75
❑ 26 Chikara (Experienced) R .30 .75
❑ 27 Cleansing the Path U .15 .40
❑ 28 Consuming the Flesh U .15 .40
❑ 29 Crushing Strength C .10 .25
❑ 30 Daidoji Kirimi C .10 .25
❑ 31 Daidoji Yorio U .15 .40
❑ 32 Daigotsu Gahseng R .30 .75
❑ 33 Daigotsu Isoroku U .15 .40
❑ 34 Daigotsu Susumu (Experienced) F (Spider) 1.00 2.50
❑ 35 Deflection R .40 1.00
❑ 36 Deployed Reinforcements U .15 .40
❑ 37 Desperate Rush R 4.00 10.00
❑ 38 Desperate Throw C .10 .25
❑ 39 Disarm U .15 .40
❑ 40 Doji Bukita R .30 .75
❑ 41 Doji Shikana C .10 .25
❑ 42 Doji Tsubota R .30 .75
❑ 43 Doji's Guidance C .10 .25
❑ 44 Dutiful Apprentice R .30 .75
❑ 45 Earth's Embrace U .15 .40
❑ 46 Eternal Armor U .15 .40
❑ 47 Expendable Resources R .30 .75
❑ 48 First to Fall C .10 .25
❑ 49 Force of Law R .30 .75
❑ 50 Forging the Gift U .15 .40
❑ 51 Fu Leng's Guidance C .10 .25
❑ 52 Gakku C .10 .25
❑ 53 Greater Good C .10 .25
❑ 54 Hand of the Jade Dragon R .30 .75
❑ 55 Hand of the Obsidian Dragon R .50 1.25
❑ 56 Hida Fosuko U .15 .40
❑ 57 Hida Ikarukani R .50 1.25
❑ 58 Hida Kitamura C .10 .25
❑ 59 Hida Suteru R .30 .75
❑ 60 Hida Tobashi R .30 .75
❑ 61 Hida's Guidance U .15 .40
❑ 62 Hidden Route R .30 .75
❑ 63 Hiruma Hidora U .15 .40
❑ 64 Ikoma Tobikuma R .30 .75
❑ 65 Impossible Force R .30 .75
❑ 66 Inspirational Victory U .15 .40
❑ 67 Isawa Fosuta (Experienced) R .30 .75
❑ 68 Isawa Mizuhiko (Experienced) R .30 .75
❑ 69 Kaiu Smithy U .15 .40
❑ 70 Kakita Kensho-in (Experienced) R .30 .75
❑ 71 Kakita Sadaka U .15 .40
❑ 72 Kata of the Concealed Blade U .15 .40
❑ 73 Kitsuki Yodo R .30 .75
❑ 74 Kitsune Iwarou U .15 .40
❑ 75 Last Stand U .15 .40
❑ 76 Laughter of the Flames C .10 .25
❑ 77 Laying in Wait R .30 .75
❑ 78 Lead By Example R .50 1.25
❑ 79 Legion of Toshigoku R .50 1.25
❑ 80 March Beyond Hope C .10 .25
❑ 81 Masserah C .10 .25
❑ 82 Master the Body R .50 1.25
❑ 83 Matsu Benika (Experienced 2) R .30 .75
❑ 84 Matsu Kasei U .15 .40
❑ 85 Might of the Kami R .30 .75
❑ 86 Mirumoto Kondo U .15 .40
❑ 87 Mirumoto Washizuka U .15 .40
❑ 88 Misleading Wasteland C .10 .25
❑ 89 Monstrous Might C .10 .25
❑ 90 Moshi Chuuna U .15 .40
❑ 91 Moto Chiang (Experienced) R .30 .75
❑ 92 Moto Jin-sahn (Experienced) F (Unicorn) 3.00 8.00
❑ 93 Moto Kang's Sword R .30 .75
❑ 94 Moto Paisei C .10 .25
❑ 95 Mountain Watch Keep F (Unicorn) 1.50 4.00
❑ 96 Nerve Strike U .15 .40
❑ 97 Nightshade Touch U .15 .40
❑ 98 One Soul's Strength U .15 .40
❑ 99 Overwhelming Pressure U .15 .40
❑ 100 Palace of Crimson Shadows F (Scorpion) 1.50 4.00
❑ 101 Pull the String R 6.00 15.00
❑ 102 Seeking the Guilty C .10 .25
❑ 103 Selfless Defense C .10 .25
❑ 104 Seven Waves Mercenaries R .30 .75
❑ 105 Sharpened Naginata C .10 .25
❑ 106 Shiba Ningen (Experienced 3) R .30 .75
❑ 107 Shiba Sakaki U .15 .40
❑ 108 Shiba Yukihito R .40 1.00
❑ 109 Shiba's Guidance C .10 .25
❑ 110 Shielded by Tempest U .15 .40
❑ 111 Shinjo Hansu R .30 .75
❑ 112 Shinjo Rina U .15 .40
❑ 113 Shinjo Scouts U .15 .40
❑ 114 Shinjo Tae-hyun C .10 .25
❑ 115 Shinjo's Guidance U .15 .40
❑ 116 Shosuro Ohba U .15 .40
❑ 117 Shosuro Sogetsu C .10 .25
❑ 118 Soshi Yoshihara R .60 1.50
❑ 119 Speed of the Blade R .30 .75
❑ 120 Spiteful Obstruction C .10 .25
❑ 121 Storm-filled Sails C .10 .25
❑ 122 Strategic Strike R 6.00 15.00
❑ 123 Strength in Honor U .15 .40
❑ 124 Strength in Terror U .15 .40
❑ 125 Suitengu's Gateway R .30 .75
❑ 126 Sympathy for the Assaulted U .15 .40
❑ 127 Synchronized Attack C .10 .25
❑ 128 Talisman of Chikushudo R .30 .75
❑ 129 Talisman of Gaki-do R .30 .75
❑ 130 Talisman of Meido R .30 .75
❑ 131 Talisman of Tengoku R .30 .75
❑ 132 Tempered No-Dachi U .15 .40
❑ 133 Test of Sincerity U .15 .40
❑ 134 The Direct Approach C .10 .25
❑ 135 The Earth Answers C .10 .25
❑ 136 The Fingers of Bone F (Spider) .75 2.00
❑ 137 The Fire Answers U .15 .40
❑ 138 The Lost Path R .40 1.00
❑ 139 Thorough Preparations C .10 .25
❑ 140 Togashi Akagi C .10 .25
❑ 141 Togashi Kazuki (Experienced) R .30 .75
❑ 142 Togashi Satsu (Experienced 5) R .30 .75
❑ 143 Togashi Shintaro C .10 .25
❑ 144 Togashi's Guidance U .15 .40
❑ 145 Torao C .10 .25
❑ 146 Tsuruchi Mochisa (Experienced) R .30 .75
❑ 147 Tsuruchi Nabeta C .10 .25
❑ 148 Udo U .15 .40
❑ 149 Unclean Sacrifice R .30 .75
❑ 150 Unshakable Resolve C .10 .25
❑ 151 Untaken C .10 .25
❑ 152 Untrained Scouts C .10 .25
❑ 153 Useful Connections R .30 .75
❑ 154 Utaku Hana U .15 .40
❑ 155 Uzaki no Oni R .40 1.00
❑ 156 Walk in Shadows R .40 1.00
❑ 157 Wall of Honor R 6.00 15.00
❑ 158 Wandering Caravan C .10 .25
❑ 159 Whispers of the Dying Moon R .30 .75
❑ 160 Whispers of the Dying Sun R .60 1.50
❑ 161 Wrath of the Thunder C .10 .25
❑ 162 Yasuki Otsuka U .15 .40
❑ 163 Yoritomo Eihiko C .10 .25
❑ 164 Yoritomo Souhiko R .30 .75
❑ 165 Yoritomo Utemaro (Experienced 2) R .30 .75
❑ 166 Yoritomo's Guidance U .15 .40

2009 Legend of the Five Rings The Imperial Gift Part 2

COMPLETE SET (82) 15.00 30.00
❑ 1 A Samurai's Soul F .40 1.00
❑ 2 Akodo Kurogane F .50 1.25
❑ 3 Arugai no Oni F 1.00 2.50
❑ 4 Back to the Front F .20 .50
❑ 5 Bayushi Kayama F .20 .50
❑ 6 Bayushi Shihaken F .20 .50
❑ 7 Bayushi Tsubaki F .20 .50
❑ 8 Breath of the Dragon F .40 1.00
❑ 9 Chuda Fukuzo F .20 .50
❑ 10 Collapsing Bridge F .20 .50
❑ 11 Daidoji Harada F .20 .50
❑ 12 Daigotsu Oki F 1.00 2.50
❑ 13 Daigotsu Shinjitsu F .50 1.25
❑ 14 Delayed Arrival F .20 .50
❑ 15 Do Not Turn Your Back! F .20 .50
❑ 16 Doji Kato F .75 2.00
❑ 17 Dutiful Yojimbo F .20 .50
❑ 18 Earthen Blade F .40 1.00
❑ 19 Elite Archers F .20 .50
❑ 20 Espionage F .20 .50
❑ 21 Fall Back! F .20 .50
❑ 22 Family Histories F .20 .50
❑ 23 Fields of Battle F .20 .50
❑ 24 For My Brothers! F .20 .50
❑ 25 Forward Reconnaissance F .50 1.25
❑ 26 Frontline Encampment F .20 .50
❑ 27 Heavy Regulars F .20 .50
❑ 28 Hida Rokurota F .30 .75
❑ 29 Hida Shinko F .30 .75
❑ 30 Hiruma Etsuro F .30 .75
❑ 31 Ikoma Igawa F .40 1.00
❑ 32 Incapacitated F .20 .50
❑ 33 Infamous Blade F .20 .50
❑ 34 Iron Fan F .20 .50
❑ 35 Isawa Reido F .20 .50
❑ 36 Isawa Tanaka F .50 1.25
❑ 37 Iuchi Kota F .40 1.00
❑ 38 Kakita Toshiro F .20 .50
❑ 39 Kitsuki Hanbei F .75 2.00
❑ 40 Kyogen F .20 .50
❑ 41 Lost Traveler Castle F .60 1.50
❑ 42 Mastery of the Blade F .20 .50
❑ 43 Midnight Assault F .20 .50
❑ 44 Military Alliance F .40 1.00
❑ 45 Mirumoto Ayabe F .40 1.00
❑ 46 Moshi Takako F .50 1.25
❑ 47 My Father's Shrine F .30 .75
❑ 48 Natsu Mansaiko F .30 .75
❑ 49 Obfuscation F .40 1.00
❑ 50 Outmatched F .40 1.00
❑ 51 Pokupo F .50 1.25
❑ 52 Prayer for Guidance F .20 .50
❑ 53 Prepared for Death F .20 .50
❑ 54 Rejuvenating Vapors F .30 .75
❑ 55 Ruthless Determination F .30 .75
❑ 56 Seppun Heavy Infantry F .30 .75
❑ 57 Shiba Nobuyuki F .20 .50
❑ 58 Shinjo Kodama F .30 .75
❑ 59 Simple Merchants F .75 2.00
❑ 60 Suitengu's Embrace F .20 .50
❑ 61 Smuggler's Port F .20 .50
❑ 62 Spearmen Legion F .20 .50
❑ 63 Straw Horse F .20 .50
❑ 64 Sunrise Keep F .10 2.50
❑ 65 Tamori Masako F .20 .50
❑ 66 The Cresting Wave F .20 .50
❑ 67 The Stone Discovered F .20 .50
❑ 68 Throwing Knives F .40 1.00
❑ 69 Thunderous Report F .40 1.00
❑ 70 Timely Assisance F .20 .50
❑ 71 Token of Destiny F .30 .75
❑ 72 Traveling Wardens F 1.00 2.50
❑ 73 Tsuruchi Oguri F .60 1.50
❑ 74 Undefended Border F .20 .50
❑ 75 Under Cover of Night F .20 .50
❑ 76 Under Seige F .20 .50
❑ 77 Utaku Yanai F .40 1.00
❑ 78 Village Guardian F .50 1.25
❑ 79 Well-Defender Border F .20 .50
❑ 80 Wrathful Defense F .20 .50
❑ 81 Yari F .20 .50
❑ 82 Yoritomo Sasake F .20 .50

2010 Legend of the Five Rings Empire at War

BOOSTER BOX (48) 50.00 100.00
BOOSTER PACK (11) 1.50 3.00
❑ 1 A Stain Cleansed R 2.50 6.00
❑ 2 Akodo Areru C .10 .25
❑ 3 Akodo Kusamoto R .50 1.25
❑ 4 Alter History R 1.50 4.00
❑ 5 Ancient Tome U .15 .40
❑ 6 Asako Ayako U .15 .40
❑ 7 Attuned to the Elements U .15 .40
❑ 8 Bakunai U .15 .40
❑ 9 Battle Fatigue R .30 .75
❑ 10 Bayushi Darisu U .15 .40
❑ 11 Bayushi Himaru C .10 .25
❑ 12 Bayushi Jutsushi (Experienced) R .30 .75
❑ 13 Bayushi Kahoku R 1.25 3.00
❑ 14 Bayushi Miyako 1.25 3.00
(Experienced 2 Toturi Miyako) Fixed
❑ 15 Bayushi Shigehiro C .10 .25
❑ 16 Bishamon's Guidance R 1.50 4.00
❑ 17 Bitter Lies Student U .15 .40
❑ 18 Blade of Perfection C .10 .25
❑ 19 Bridging the Gap C .10 .25
❑ 20 Clan Conflict C .10 .25
❑ 21 Conscript Troops C .10 .25
❑ 22 Crossing the Forbidden Sea U .15 .40
❑ 23 Daidoji Arima C .10 .25
❑ 24 Daidoji Yaichiro (Experienced) R .30 .75
❑ 25 Daigotsu Akihime U .15 .40
❑ 26 Daigotsu Hotako .40 1.00
(Experienced 2 Yoritomo Hotako) R
❑ 27 Daigotsu Shaiko (Experienced Tamori Shaiko) R .30 .75
❑ 28 Dangerous Indulgence R .30 .75
❑ 29 Death is Not the End U .15 .40
❑ 30 Distractions in Court R 2.50 6.00
❑ 31 Dockside Market C .10 .25
❑ 32 Doji Kusari R .30 .75
❑ 33 Doji Shikishi R .75 2.00
❑ 34 Doji Tajihi U .15 .40
❑ 35 Doji Umakai C .10 .25
❑ 36 Dove Tattoo U .15 .40
❑ 37 Downhill Assault U .15 .40
❑ 38 Earthen Fist C .10 .25
❑ 39 Ekichu no Oni R 3.00 8.00
❑ 40 Elemental Disciple C .10 .25
❑ 41 Endless Rain U .15 .40
❑ 42 Essence of Death C .10 .25
❑ 43 Farthest Fortress Fixed .75 2.00
❑ 44 Fearless Defense R .75 2.00
❑ 45 Feign Weakness C .10 .25
❑ 46 Fertile Plains U .15 .40
❑ 47 Final Confrontation U .15 .40
❑ 48 Fire on My Command R .40 1.00
❑ 49 Fires of the Heart U .15 .40
❑ 50 Flood the Earth U .15 .40
❑ 51 Flow of the Water C .10 .25
❑ 52 Force of Spirit R 1.00 2.50
❑ 53 Fortified Docks C .10 .25
❑ 54 Fortress of Blackened Sight Fixed 1.50 4.00
❑ 55 Fortune Favors the Bold U .15 .40
❑ 56 Fury of Suitengu U .15 .40
❑ 57 Goju Katsume C .10 .25
❑ 58 Hands of Stone U .15 .40
❑ 59 Hida Benjiro (Experienced 2) R .40 1.00
❑ 60 Hida Maruken U .15 .40
❑ 61 Hida Shikoujin R 1.00 2.50
❑ 62 Hidden Entrance U .15 .40
❑ 63 Hidden Valley U .15 .40
❑ 64 Hired Thugs C .10 .25
❑ 65 Hiroshi's Legion R .50 1.25
❑ 66 Hiruma House Guard (Experienced) R .30 .75
❑ 67 Hiruma Ikuya U .15 .40
❑ 68 Hiruma Todori (Experienced 3) R .30 .75
❑ 69 Honorable Death U .15 .40
❑ 70 Hozumi R .40 1.00
❑ 71 Ichiro Kaagi C .10 .25
❑ 72 Ikoma Hagio (Experienced) R .30 .75
❑ 73 Ikoma Toruken R .30 .75
❑ 74 Immovable Object R .30 .75
❑ 75 Imperial Orders U .15 .40
❑ 76 In the Heart of Battle C .10 .25
❑ 77 Invincible Determination U .15 .40
❑ 78 Isawa Kimi (Experienced 2) R .30 .75
❑ 79 Isawa Shioki R .30 .75
❑ 80 Isawa Takahiro U .15 .40
❑ 81 Isawa Toshio C .10 .25
❑ 82 Iuchi Jadaran C .10 .25
❑ 83 Kaiu Futaro C .10 .25
❑ 84 Kakita Mimaro U .15 .40
❑ 85 Kitsuki Nakai C .10 .25
❑ 86 Knowledge of the Land U .15 .40
❑ 87 Koji C .10 .25
❑ 88 Kuni Shikehime C .10 .25
❑ 89 Matsu Kinihara U .15 .40
❑ 90 Matsu Misuka C .10 .25
❑ 91 Matsu Otsuko U .15 .40
❑ 92 Merciless Tactics C .10 .25
❑ 93 Mirumoto Asakazu R .30 .75
❑ 94 Mirumoto Kalen U .15 .40
❑ 95 Mirumoto Kenzo (Experienced 2) Fixed 1.25 3.00
❑ 96 Mirumoto Tobushi C .10 .25
❑ 97 Moshi Yuriko U .15 .40
❑ 98 Moto Hunters R 4.00 10.00
❑ 99 Moto Munoru C .10 .25
❑ 100 Moto Shanyu U .15 .40
❑ 101 Mountainous Region C .10 .25
❑ 102 Mysterious Ailment U .15 .40
❑ 103 Night Watchers U .15 .40

❑ 104 One with the World U	.15	.40
❑ 105 Osano-Wo's Guidance R	.40	1.00
❑ 106 Otomo Seimi R	.75	2.00
❑ 107 Outsider Keep Fixed	1.00	2.50
❑ 108 Paid Off C	.10	.25
❑ 109 Perfect Aim R	.40	1.00
❑ 110 Preparing the Bodies C	.10	.25
❑ 111 Protect the Caravan C	.10	.25
❑ 112 Rekai's Yumi R	.50	1.25
❑ 113 Rus'tik'tik C	.10	.25
❑ 114 Savagery C	.10	.25
❑ 115 Secured Borders C	.10	.25
❑ 116 Shameful and Cowardly R	8.00	20.00
❑ 117 Shatter the Line C	.10	.25
❑ 118 Shiba Goto C	.10	.25
❑ 119 Shiba Morihiko (Experienced) R	.40	1.00
❑ 120 Shinjo Dun (Experienced) Fixed	.30	.75
❑ 121 Shinjo Jalair R	.30	.75
❑ 122 Shinjo's Children C	.10	.25
❑ 123 Shinran C	.10	.25
❑ 124 Shosuro Ritsuko U	.15	.40
❑ 125 Smoke Cover R	.40	1.00
❑ 126 Sought for Justice R	.60	1.50
❑ 127 Stable Ground C	.10	.25
❑ 128 Startling Attack R	.30	.75
❑ 129 Stay Put C	.10	.25
❑ 130 Stripped Armor C	.10	.25
❑ 131 Sudden Rebuke U	.15	.40
❑ 132 Sudden Strike R	.30	.75
❑ 133 Sullied Gift C	.10	.25
❑ 134 Superior Mobility R	8.00	20.00
❑ 135 Takaikabe Mura U	.15	.40
❑ 136 Talisman of Jigoku R	.30	.75
❑ 137 Tamori Kuroko U	.15	.40
❑ 138 The Art of Ninjutsu U	.15	.40
❑ 139 The Law's Strength U	.15	.40
❑ 140 The Unmaking R	1.00	2.50
❑ 141 Timely Save R	.30	.75
❑ 142 Togashi Furai R	.40	1.00
❑ 143 Travel Light C	.10	.25
❑ 144 Tsuruchi Chiko U	.15	.40
❑ 145 Tsuruchi Nobumoto (Experienced 2) R	.30	.75
❑ 146 Tsuruchi Shisuken (Experienced) R	.40	1.00
❑ 147 Tsuruchi's Legacy R	.40	1.00
❑ 148 Ugaro R	.30	.75
❑ 149 Ultimate Sacrifice R	6.00	15.00
❑ 150 Under Arrest U	.15	.40
❑ 151 Undying Warriors U	.15	.40
❑ 152 Unmoving as the Mountain C	.10	.25
❑ 153 Unnatural Flood R	.30	.75
❑ 154 Unstoppable Cut R	.60	1.50
❑ 155 Untouchable Escort U	.15	.40
❑ 156 Utaku Fujiko (Experienced) R	.50	1.25
❑ 157 Utaku Jin-lao U	.15	.40
❑ 158 Waylay the Messenger Gong Studios	.30	.75
❑ 159 Weight of Numbers R	.30	.75
❑ 160 Whirlwind U	.15	.40
❑ 161 Wooden Barricade C	.10	.25
❑ 162 Wrath R	.40	1.00
❑ 163 Yagimaki's Fist R	4.00	10.00
❑ 164 Yoritomo Kaemon C	.10	.25
❑ 165 Yoritomo Manzo R	.50	1.25
❑ 166 Yoritomo Rai C	.10	.25

2010 Legend of the Five Rings The Harbinger

COMPLETE SET (176)	30.00	60.00
BOOSTER BOX (48)	50.00	100.00
BOOSTER PACK (11)	1.50	3.00
❑ 1 A Cleansing Death U	.15	.40
❑ 2 A Paragon's Strength R	.75	2.00
❑ 3 Advanced Spellcraft U	.15	.40
❑ 4 Agasha Kusadao C	.10	.25
❑ 5 Akodo Kin C	.10	.25
❑ 6 Akodo Ryozo R	.30	.75
❑ 7 Akodo Senichi R	.30	.75
❑ 8 Akodo Senzo U2	.15	.40
❑ 9 Akodo Shigo R	.30	.75
❑ 10 Alert the Guard U2	.15	.40
❑ 11 Allure of Jigoku U	.15	.40
❑ 12 Apprehending the Villain C	.10	.25
❑ 13 Arjuna Singh U2	.15	.40
❑ 14 Arranged Guilt R	.30	.75
❑ 15 Arrows Do Not Falter U	.15	.40
❑ 16 Asahina Ekei (Experienced) R	.30	.75
❑ 17 Asako Mokichi U	.15	.40
❑ 18 Assaults Without Finesse U	.15	.40
❑ 19 Aura of Malice C	.10	.25
❑ 20 Bakemono Pups C	.10	.25
❑ 21 Banish All Doubt R	.30	.75
❑ 22 Bayushi Hikoko U	.15	.40
❑ 23 Bayushi Kindebu C	.10	.25
❑ 24 Bayushi Mago U	.15	.40
❑ 25 Bayushi Momochi C	.10	.25
❑ 26 Bayushi Suboru R	.30	.75
❑ 27 Blades of the Fallen Phoenix U	.15	.40
❑ 28 Border Pass C	.10	.25
❑ 29 Br'nn C	.10	.25
❑ 30 Burn the Village R	.30	.75
❑ 31 Chain and Sword R	.30	.75
❑ 32 Chikara C	.10	.25
❑ 33 Chuda Atsuro U2	.15	.40
❑ 34 Civility R	.40	1.00
❑ 35 Cowed by Wisdom U	.15	.40
❑ 36 Daidoji Botan C	.10	.25
❑ 37 Daidoji Yuki R	.30	.75
❑ 38 Daigotsu Azuma U	.15	.40
❑ 39 Daigotsu Koneru C	.10	.25
❑ 40 Daigotsu Yuhmi (Experienced) R	.30	.75
❑ 41 Dance of Blades R	.30	.75
❑ 42 Deceit and Subterfuge U	.15	.40
❑ 43 Determined Force R	.75	2.00
❑ 44 Doji Kazuo C	.10	.25
❑ 45 Doji Nenkai R	.30	.75
❑ 46 Dutiful Cavalry C	.10	.25
❑ 47 Elite Guard C	.10	.25
❑ 48 Emma-O's Guidance R	.30	.75
❑ 49 Enticement R	.30	.75
❑ 50 Extensive Training R	.30	.75
❑ 51 Farmlands Conscripts C	.10	.25
❑ 52 Flash of Bright Wings C	.10	.25
❑ 53 Flashy Technique C	.10	.25
❑ 54 Flawless Assassin U	.15	.40
❑ 55 Fortitude U	.15	.40
❑ 56 Fudo C	.10	.25
❑ 57 Furumaro R	.50	1.25
❑ 58 Generosity R	.30	.75
❑ 59 Groves of Stone C	.10	.25
❑ 60 Heaven's Tears R	.30	.75
❑ 61 Heavy Elite R	.50	1.25
❑ 62 Hida Harou R	.30	.75
❑ 63 Hida Hebi U	.15	.40
❑ 64 Hida Kosho (Experienced) R	.30	.75
❑ 65 Hiruma Gondo C	.10	.25
❑ 66 Hiruma Shigeo U	.15	.40
❑ 67 Hiruma Toshio R	.30	.75
❑ 68 Hold Them Off R	.30	.75
❑ 69 Hope Against Hope U	.15	.40
❑ 70 Imperial Outpost U	.15	.40
❑ 71 In Aikune's Name R	.30	.75
❑ 72 Intimidating Stance U2	.15	.40
❑ 73 Isawa Mitsuko R	.30	.75
❑ 74 Isawa Takashi R	.30	.75
❑ 75 Isawa Takino U	.15	.40
❑ 76 Junghar Legion C	.10	.25
❑ 77 Kakita Kado U	.15	.40
❑ 78 Kakita Reisei U2	.15	.40
❑ 79 Ki-Rin Tattoo U	.15	.40
❑ 80 Kitsuki Suiha U	.15	.40
❑ 81 Knowledge from Within R	1.25	3.00
❑ 82 Last Line of Defense U	.15	.40
❑ 83 Last Step Castle F (Dragon)	.40	1.00
❑ 84 Learn by Doing U	.15	.40
❑ 85 Let None Draw Near C	.10	.25
❑ 86 Masakazu (Experienced) F (Phoenix)	1.25	3.00
❑ 87 Maseru no Oni C	.10	.25
❑ 88 Matsu Akuto C	.10	.25
❑ 89 Matsu Kita U	.15	.40
❑ 90 Maws of Stone C	.10	.25
❑ 91 Mirumoto Bokusui C	.10	.25
❑ 92 Mirumoto Dakotsu U2	.15	.40
❑ 93 Mirumoto Ichizo (Experienced) R	.30	.75
❑ 94 Mirumoto Meisetsu C	.10	.25
❑ 95 Mirumoto Shiki F (Dragon)	.40	1.00
❑ 96 Morru C	.10	.25
❑ 97 Moshi Kazue C	.10	.25
❑ 98 Moshi Sayoko (Experienced) F (Mantis)	1.25	3.00
❑ 99 Moto Chuluun C	.10	.25
❑ 100 Moto Kang (Experienced) R	.30	.75
❑ 101 Moto Kushi C	.10	.25
❑ 102 Naggru C	.10	.25
❑ 103 Negotiations at Court C	.10	.25
❑ 104 Newly-Discovered Mine U	.15	.40
❑ 105 No Hope C	.10	.25
❑ 106 Offices of the Emerald Magistrates C	.10	.25
❑ 107 One with the Flame R	.30	.75
❑ 108 Oyo Seido C	.10	.25
❑ 109 Pacify C	.10	.25
❑ 110 Pawn of Corruption C	.10	.25
❑ 111 Peasant Armor C	.10	.25
❑ 112 Phantom Blade C	.10	.25
❑ 113 Pinned Down U2	.15	.40
❑ 114 Poorly Chosen Allies C	.10	.25
❑ 115 Prayer to Hotei U	.15	.40
❑ 116 Prepare for the Worst R	.30	.75
❑ 117 Preserving What Was Lost C	.10	.25
❑ 118 Reinforce the Line U	.15	.40
❑ 119 Riding in Harmony C	.10	.25
❑ 120 Roaring Sky U2	.15	.40
❑ 121 Sadamune Blade U	.15	.40
❑ 122 Saving Kazumasa C	.10	.25
❑ 123 Scout Armor C	.10	.25
❑ 124 Search for Survivors R	.30	.75
❑ 125 Senseki Province C	.10	.25
❑ 126 Seppun Tashime (Experienced) R	.30	.75
❑ 127 Shadow Plays U2	.15	.40
❑ 128 Shiba Allies C	.10	.25
❑ 129 Shiba Ikuko C	.10	.25
❑ 130 Shiba Emiko U	.15	.40
❑ 131 Shinjo Yamauchi R	.30	.75
❑ 132 Shosuro Akemi R	.30	.75
❑ 133 Sister of the Sun R	.30	.75
❑ 134 Snow-Swept Summit C	.10	.25
❑ 135 Soshi Miroki R	.30	.75
❑ 136 Spider Cultist U	.15	.40
❑ 137 Spinning Heel Kick C	.10	.25
❑ 138 Spirit of Maigo no Musha C	.10	.25
❑ 139 Stand Down! R	.30	.75
❑ 140 Stolen Property C2	.10	.25
❑ 141 Storm-Forged Blade C	.10	.25
❑ 142 Strengthening Protection U	.15	.40
❑ 143 Strike from the Shadows R	2.50	6.00
❑ 144 Subtle Sting R	.30	.75
❑ 145 Talisman of Maigo no Musha R	.30	.75
❑ 146 Talisman of Toshigoku R	.30	.75
❑ 147 Tamago (Experienced 2 Matsu Nimuro) R	2.00	5.00
❑ 148 Temporary Truce R	.30	.75
❑ 149 The Badgers Live U	.15	.40
❑ 150 The Dead Do Not Rest U	.15	.40
❑ 151 The Dread Kar R	.30	.75
❑ 152 The Eighth Legion R	.30	.75
❑ 153 The Light of Justice U	.15	.40
❑ 154 The Thriving Light R	1.50	4.00
❑ 155 The Walking Dead C	.10	.25
❑ 156 The Wrath of Kali-Ma R	.30	.75
❑ 157 Thunder Dragon Bay F (Mantis)	.40	1.00
❑ 158 Togashi Kyoshi R	.30	.75
❑ 159 Toritaka Okabe C	.10	.25
❑ 160 Travel Swiftly R	.30	.75
❑ 161 Tsuruchi Gosho U	.15	.40
❑ 162 Twin Soul Temple F (Phoenix)	1.50	4.00
❑ 163 Utaku Gunso U	.15	.40
❑ 164 Utaku Tairu R	.30	.75
❑ 165 Utaku Toshie U	.15	.40
❑ 166 Utogu no Oni C	.10	.25
❑ 167 Vigilant Eyes C	.10	.25
❑ 168 Wander Among the Stars R	.30	.75
❑ 169 Wanyudo R	.30	.75
❑ 170 Wartime Allies U	.15	.40
❑ 171 Wind-Borne Aid C	.10	.25
❑ 172 Yojimbo's Glory U	.15	.40
❑ 173 Yoritomo Eita C	.10	.25
❑ 174 Yoritomo Takara R	.30	.75
❑ 175 Yoritomo Tatsuhiko R	.30	.75
❑ 176 Yuhmi no Oni R	.30	.75

2010 Legend of the Five Rings The Plague War

BOOSTER BOX (48)	50.00	100.00
BOOSTER PACK (11)	1.50	3.00
❑ 1 A Pure Heart C2	.10	.25
❑ 2 A Tranquil Mind U2	.15	.40
❑ 3 Agasha Gifu U2	.15	.40
❑ 4 Agasha Kitsuki's Ashes R2	.50	1.25
❑ 5 Air Dragon's Guidance R2	.40	1.00
❑ 6 Akodo Kuma C2	.10	.25
❑ 7 Ao-bozu R2	.40	1.00
❑ 8 Ao-bozu's Blade C1	.10	.25
❑ 9 Asako Bairei (Experienced 4) R2	.30	.75
❑ 10 Asijin's Legacy C2	.10	.25
❑ 11 Bayushi Eiyu U4	.15	.40
❑ 12 Bayushi Keirei R2	2.50	6.00
❑ 13 Bayushi Shigeo U2	.15	.40
❑ 14 Bayushi Sorii C2	.10	.25
❑ 15 Blessings of Sky C2	.10	.25
❑ 16 Caught Unawares R2	.50	1.25
❑ 17 Choose Your Fight C2	.10	.25
❑ 18 Chuda Kanashi U2	.15	.40
❑ 19 Chuda Mishime (Experienced 2) R2	.30	.75
❑ 20 Chuda Otsu C2	.10	.25
❑ 21 Claw and Shell R2	6.00	15.00
❑ 22 Claws of the Wolf C2	.10	.25
❑ 23 Cold Hands, Stone Heart U2	.15	.40
❑ 24 Concealed Scroll R2	.40	1.00
❑ 25 Cricket Tattoo U2	.15	.40
❑ 26 Daidoji Akagi (Experienced 2) R2	.30	.75
❑ 27 Daidoji Gisei U2	.15	.40
❑ 28 Daidoji Kyorai U2	.15	.40
❑ 29 Daigotsu Arima C2	.10	.25
❑ 30 Daigotsu Setsuko (Experienced) R2	.30	.75
❑ 31 Daigotsu Shimekiri U2	.15	.40
❑ 32 Dance of the Void U2	.15	.40
❑ 33 Deathly Aura R2	2.00	5.00
❑ 34 Deception Revealed U2	.15	.40
❑ 35 Defenders of Nanashi C2	.10	.25
❑ 36 Doji Gotobo C2	.10	.25
❑ 37 Doji Hakuseki (Experienced) F (Crane)	.50	1.25
❑ 38 Doji Tadanori C2	.10	.25
❑ 39 Dutiful Cavalry C1	.10	.25
❑ 40 Earth Dragon's Guidance R2	.30	.75
❑ 41 Earthen Tetsubo C1	.10	.25
❑ 42 East Wind Riders C2	.10	.25
❑ 43 Excellent Armor U4	.15	.40
❑ 44 Farmland Conscripts C1	.10	.25
❑ 45 Feinting Position U2	.15	.40
❑ 46 Fire Blossom U4	.15	.40
❑ 47 Fire Dragon's Guidance R2	.30	.75
❑ 48 Flow of the Elements C2	.10	.25
❑ 49 Foolish Pride U4	.15	.40
❑ 50 Fortress of the Forgotten F (Crab)	.50	1.25
❑ 51 Great Hall of Records F (Lion)	1.00	2.50
❑ 52 Gotobo (Experienced) R2	.30	.75
❑ 53 Hariya's Blade C1	.10	.25
❑ 54 Hasty Evaluation C2	.10	.25
❑ 55 Heedless Assault R2	.30	.75
❑ 56 Hida Demopen R2	.30	.75
❑ 57 Hida Kichiro U2	.15	.40
❑ 58 Hida Satoshi C2	.10	.25
❑ 59 Hida Shimonai U4	.15	.40
❑ 60 Hida Tenshi C2	.10	.25
❑ 61 Hida Yaheiko (Experienced) F (Crab)	1.25	3.00
❑ 62 Hiruma Sniper U2	.15	.40
❑ 63 Honor & Strength U2	.15	.40
❑ 64 Honor's Hope C2	.10	.25
❑ 65 Hundred-Fold Cut U4	.15	.40
❑ 66 Ide Kin C2	.10	.25
❑ 67 Ikoma Satoru R2	.40	1.00
❑ 68 Imaishi R2	.30	.75
❑ 69 Impetuous Challenge C2	.10	.25
❑ 70 Inexorable Defeat U2	.15	.40
❑ 71 Infantry Follower C1	.10	.25
❑ 72 Innuendo C2	.10	.25
❑ 73 Inugami U2	.15	.40
❑ 74 Iron Gauntlet Brothers R2	.30	.75
❑ 75 Isawa Hachiko C2	.10	.25
❑ 76 Isawa Ochiai (Experienced 3) R2	.40	1.00
❑ 77 Isawa Shun U2	.15	.40
❑ 78 Iweko's Journals R2	.40	1.00
❑ 79 Karatsu C2	.10	.25
❑ 80 Kitsu Iwao U2	.15	.40
❑ 81 Kitsuki Yukari U2	.15	.40
❑ 82 Masked in Shadows R2	.30	.75
❑ 83 Matsu Haruya C2	.10	.25
❑ 84 Matsu Kenji (Experienced) R2	.30	.75
❑ 85 Matsu Mikura (Experienced) F (Lion)	.30	.75
❑ 86 Matsu Nishijo U4	.15	.40
❑ 87 Mirumoto Haru C2	.10	.25
❑ 88 Mirumoto Mori R2	1.25	3.00
❑ 89 Mountain Herd C2	.10	.25
❑ 90 Mountain Storehouse U2	.15	.40
❑ 91 Mouth of the Plague C2	.10	.25
❑ 92 Murerpus Intent C2	.10	.25
❑ 93 My Life Is Yours R2	1.50	4.00
❑ 94 Narrow Cliffs C2	.10	.25
❑ 95 Nature's Embrace C2	.10	.25
❑ 96 Nitoru C2	.10	.25
❑ 97 On All Sides U4	.15	.40
❑ 98 Only Actions Speak R2	6.00	15.00
❑ 99 Oppression C2	.10	.25
❑ 100 Order of the Wooden Blade R2	.40	1.00
❑ 101 Overpower Assault R2	2.00	5.00
❑ 102 Part the Waves C2	.10	.25
❑ 103 Patrolling the Roads U2	.15	.40
❑ 104 Plagued Terrain U2	.15	.40
❑ 105 Precious Burden C2	.10	.25
❑ 106 Proper Deference R2	.40	1.00
❑ 107 Province Assaulted U4	.15	.40
❑ 108 Questionable Charity C2	.10	.25
❑ 109 Radiant Steel U2	.15	.40
❑ 110 Reckless Confrontation U2	.15	.40
❑ 111 Relentless Conviction R2	1.00	2.50
❑ 112 Remember Their Valor C2	.10	.25
❑ 113 Rise Corrupted U2	.15	.40
❑ 114 Rising Sun Blade R2	3.00	8.00
❑ 115 Sarassa U2	.15	.40
❑ 116 Scouting Far Afield R2	1.50	4.00
❑ 117 Seawatch Castle F (Crane)	1.25	3.00
❑ 118 Selfless Yojimbo C1	.10	.25
❑ 119 Shadow's Talon R2	.75	2.00
❑ 120 Shiba Kotaro C2	.10	.25
❑ 121 Shinjo Dong-Min C2	.10	.25
❑ 122 Shinjo Hee-Young R2	.30	.75
❑ 123 Shinjo Ki-Chang (Experienced) R2	.30	.75
❑ 124 Shosuro Orikasa R2	.30	.75
❑ 125 Shosuro Rokujo C2	.10	.25
❑ 126 Shune R2	.30	.75
❑ 127 Silent Struggle U2	.15	.40
❑ 128 Simple Men C2	.10	.25
❑ 129 Spirit of Gaki-do C1	.10	.25
❑ 130 Stand as One R2	.30	.75
❑ 131 Stare Into the Void R2	.30	.75
❑ 132 Strength of Will R2	.40	1.00
❑ 133 Successful Bounty U2	.15	.40
❑ 134 Talisman of Sakkaku R2	.30	.75
❑ 135 Talisman of Yomi R2	.30	.75
❑ 136 Talisman of Yume-do R2	.30	.75
❑ 137 Tamori Shimura R2	.30	.75
❑ 138 Tennyo R2	.30	.75
❑ 139 Tetsu Kama Mine U2	.15	.40
❑ 140 Tetsubo of Earth U2	.15	.40
❑ 141 The Blessed Herd U2	.15	.40
❑ 142 The Cost of Pride R2	6.00	15.00
❑ 143 The Cursed Dead C2	.10	.25
❑ 144 The Master's Guard U2	.15	.40
❑ 145 The Oni's Footsteps C2	.10	.25
❑ 146 The Quiet Death C2	.10	.25
❑ 147 The Serpent's Deception U2	.15	.40
❑ 148 The Silent Blade U2	.15	.40
❑ 149 The Trap is Sprung! R2	.30	.75
❑ 150 The Walking Dead C1	.10	.25
❑ 151 The Wind Never Stops R2	1.00	2.50
❑ 152 Thoughtful Present C2	.10	.25
❑ 153 Thunder's Blessing C2	.10	.25
❑ 154 Togashi Kanmu U2	.15	.40
❑ 155 Togashi Konishi R2	.30	.75
❑ 156 Toshi Ranbo Guard C1	.10	.25
❑ 157 Touch of the Flames R2	.30	.75
❑ 158 Triumph Before Battle U2	.15	.40
❑ 159 Trust the Void R2	.30	.75
❑ 160 Tsai-tsu C2	.10	.25
❑ 161 Tsuruchi Gidayu (Experienced) R2	.30	.75
❑ 162 Tsuruchi Kuze C2	.10	.25
❑ 163 Tsuruchi Ogata R2	.30	.75
❑ 164 Tsuruchi Ohashi R2	.30	.75
❑ 165 Two Men At A River C2	.10	.25
❑ 166 Unexpected Sympathy C2	.10	.25
❑ 167 Unimpeachable Name U2	.15	.40
❑ 168 Unwavering Commitment U2	.15	.40
❑ 169 Utaku Kana U4	.15	.40
❑ 170 Utaku Yu-Pan (Experienced 2) R2	.30	.75
❑ 171 Void Dragon's Guidance R2	.75	2.00
❑ 172 Water Dragon's Guidance R2	.30	.75
❑ 173 Whispers of the Forgotten R2	.50	1.25
❑ 174 Yogo Rieko (Experienced) R2	.50	1.25
❑ 175 Yoritomo Chiako C2	.10	.25
❑ 176 Yoritomo Tahei U2	.15	.40

2011 Legend of the Five Rings Before the Dawn

COMPLETE SET (163)	50.00	100.00
BOOSTER BOX (48)	60.00	120.00
BOOSTER PACK (11)	2.50	4.00
❑ 1 A Champion in Court C	.10	.25
❑ 2 A Dragon's Favor U	.20	.50
❑ 3 A Gentle Word U	.20	.50
❑ 4 A Simple Yari C	.10	.25
❑ 5 Advanced Warning C	.10	.25
❑ 6 Akodo Ashiko U	.20	.50
❑ 7 Akodo Kobi (Exp) F	.75	2.00
❑ 8 Akodo Tezuka C	.10	.25
❑ 9 Amazing Feat R	.30	.75
❑ 10 Anger Management R	.30	.75
❑ 11 Asahina Nanae C	.10	.25
❑ 12 Asako Heiwa U	.20	.50
❑ 13 Asako Izuna C	.10	.25
❑ 14 Ascending the Ranks U	.20	.50
❑ 15 Ashigaru Elite R	.30	.75
❑ 16 Ashigaru Recruits C	.10	.25
❑ 17 Bayushi Ebara U	.20	.50
❑ 18 Bayushi Shibata C	.10	.25
❑ 19 Bayushi Suwabe U	.20	.50
❑ 20 Beautiful Host U	.20	.50
❑ 21 Beyond the Line C	.10	.25
❑ 22 Bird of Prey C	.10	.25
❑ 23 Brothers in Battle U	.20	.50
❑ 24 Brothers of Goemon U	.20	.50
❑ 25 Chuda Kiuchi U	.20	.50
❑ 26 Consuming Weakness C	.10	.25
❑ 27 Control the Board U	.20	.50
❑ 28 Crimson Shadow Armor C	.10	.25
❑ 29 Daidoji Masafuni U	.20	.50
❑ 30 Daigotsu Bukaro U	.20	.50
❑ 31 Daigotsu Miki C	.10	.25
❑ 32 Daigotsu Yajinden (Exp) R	.30	.75
❑ 33 Death, Defeated U	.20	.50
❑ 34 Defending Their Home C	.10	.25
❑ 35 Destructive Priorities R	3.00	8.00
❑ 36 Detained R	1.50	4.00
❑ 37 Disgraceful Conduct R	1.00	2.50
❑ 38 Dismissing the Cur R	3.00	8.00
❑ 39 Disrupting Communication C	.10	.25
❑ 40 Doji Shigeyuki U	.20	.50
❑ 41 Drawing on the Mountain U	.20	.50
❑ 42 Ebisu's Honesty R	.75	2.00
❑ 43 Ember's Final Fire U	.20	.50
❑ 44 En'you C	.10	.25
❑ 45 Erosion R	.75	2.00
❑ 46 Favors R	6.00	15.00
❑ 47 Fear Me! R	4.00	10.00
❑ 48 Firm Censure C	.10	.25
❑ 49 Fledgling Ashigaru C	.10	.25
❑ 50 Forging Destiny U	.20	.50
❑ 51 Fury of a Mob R	2.50	6.00
❑ 52 Genji's Students U	.20	.50
❑ 53 Goju Genin C	.10	.25
❑ 54 Goju Sawaki U	.20	.50
❑ 55 Headbutt U	.20	.50
❑ 56 Hida Defenders U	.20	.50
❑ 57 Hida Fujita R	.60	1.50
❑ 58 Hida Yamadera U	.20	.50
❑ 59 Hiruma Akio (Exp) F	.60	1.50
❑ 60 Horse Archers R	1.50	4.00
❑ 61 Hunger R	.30	.75
❑ 62 Ikoma Ayumu R	1.00	2.50
❑ 63 Ikoma Shinohara U	.20	.50
❑ 64 Indomitable Home C	.10	.25
❑ 65 Iron Will R	6.00	15.00
❑ 66 Isawa Kaname R	1.50	4.00
❑ 67 Isawa Sakonoko F	.40	1.00
❑ 68 Iuchi Kota (Exp) R	.30	.75
❑ 69 Iuchi Yupadi U	.20	.50
❑ 70 Kaiu Iemasa R	.30	.75
❑ 71 Kaiu Nakano U	.20	.50
❑ 72 Kakita Munemori (Exp) R	.30	.75
❑ 73 Kakita Nara R	.60	1.50
❑ 74 Kakita Yasunori U	.20	.50
❑ 75 Kitsuki Fujimura U	.20	.50
❑ 76 Komori Taruko C	.10	.25
❑ 77 Kunji C	.10	.25
❑ 78 Kyuden Hida (Exp) F	.30	.75
❑ 79 Kyuden Hida Survivor C	.10	.25
❑ 80 Matsu Kaido R	.40	1.00
❑ 81 Measure of Devotion U	.20	.50
❑ 82 Mirumoto Houken C	.10	.25
❑ 83 Mirumoto Inokuchi U	.20	.50
❑ 84 Mirumoto Yozo (Exp) R	.30	.75
❑ 85 Moshi Umiko U	.20	.50
❑ 86 Moto Hailung C	.10	.25
❑ 87 Necessary Evil R	1.50	4.00
❑ 88 Never Enough Soldiers R	.30	.75
❑ 89 Nijugun C	.10	.25
❑ 90 No Time for Games C	.10	.25

❑ 91 Oathsworn Deathseeker C .10 .25
❑ 92 Of One Instant C .10 .25
❑ 93 Omigawa C .10 .25
❑ 94 One Action, Two Strikes R 1.25 3.00
❑ 95 placeholder C .10 .25
❑ 96 Pride of the Hand C .10 .25
❑ 97 Raido no Oni C .10 .25
❑ 98 Readied Steel R 2.50 6.00
❑ 99 Reckless Rush C .10 .25
❑ 100 Record of Failure R .60 1.50
❑ 101 Revenge U .20 .50
❑ 102 Rocky Terrain C .10 .25
❑ 103 Rumormonger U .20 .50
❑ 104 Saibankan's Justice R 1.50 4.00
❑ 105 Scars of War U .20 .50
❑ 106 Seaside Bazaar R 6.00 15.00
❑ 107 Seek the Slain C .10 .25
❑ 108 Shadow Tactics C .10 .25
❑ 109 Shamate Keep F .30 .75
❑ 110 Shiba Jouta (Exp) R .30 .75
❑ 111 Shiba Ryuba U .20 .50
❑ 112 Shinjo Byung C .10 .25
❑ 113 Shinjo Dak-ho U .20 .50
❑ 114 Shosuro Toson (Exp) R .30 .75
❑ 115 Shosuro Tsuji C .10 .25
❑ 116 Show of Restraint U .20 .50
❑ 117 Sly Deciever U .20 .50
❑ 118 Soshi Komiko R 2.50 6.00
❑ 119 Spirit of the Blade C .10 .25
❑ 120 Spirit of the Shadows C .10 .25
❑ 121 Spirit of the Truth C .10 .25
❑ 122 Spirit of the Warrior C .10 .25
❑ 123 Stockpiled Resources U .20 .50
❑ 124 Stolen Merchandise R 3.00 8.00
❑ 125 Stone-Hewed Shrine U .20 .50
❑ 126 Strength of the Mountain R .30 .75
❑ 127 String of Victories U .20 .50
❑ 128 Taishuu R .30 .75
❑ 129 Takayuki C .10 .25
❑ 130 Tamori Shosei U .20 .50
❑ 131 Temple of Purity F .30 .75
❑ 132 The Agony of her Gaze R .30 .75
❑ 133 The Crimson Mark R .75 2.00
❑ 134 The Great Death R 1.00 2.50
❑ 135 The Killing Grounds C .10 .25
❑ 136 The Price of Honor R .40 1.00
❑ 137 The Red Hunger C .10 .25
❑ 138 The Second Feint R .75 2.00
❑ 139 The Sound of Thunder U .20 .50
❑ 140 The Spirit of Knowledge C .10 .25
❑ 141 The Tapestry Perceived U .20 .50
❑ 142 The World Disappears R .75 2.00
❑ 143 Thoughts of Wind C .10 .25
❑ 144 Togashi Sakata R 1.25 3.00
❑ 145 Too Close to Home U .20 .50
❑ 146 Tsi Weapon C .10 .25
❑ 147 Tsubute C .10 .25
❑ 148 Tsunami Tattoo U .20 .50
❑ 149 Tsuruchi Yashiro C .10 .25
❑ 150 Unorthodox Attack R 6.00 15.00
❑ 151 Utaku Eun-ju C .10 .25
❑ 152 Utaku Tairu (Exp) R .30 .75
❑ 153 Vigilant Riders U .20 .50
❑ 154 Visage of the Orochi C .10 .25
❑ 155 Words of Consecration R 1.50 4.00
❑ 156 Wrathful Dead C .10 .25
❑ 157 Xijki C .10 .25
❑ 158 Yasuki Dokansuto C .10 .25
❑ 159 Yoritomo Sachina (Exp) R .40 1.00
❑ 160 Yoritomo Singh (Exp) R .30 .75
❑ 161 Yoritomo Tarao U .20 .50
❑ 162 Yoritomo Zinan U .20 .50
❑ 163 Temple of the Seven Fortunes C .10 .25

2011 Legend of the Five Rings The Dead of Winter

COMPLETE SET (165) 40.00 80.00
BOOSTER BOX (48) 30.00 60.00
BOOSTER PACK (11)

❑ 1 1,000 Cuts Technique R 2.00 5.00
❑ 2 Agasha Kamarou C .10 .25
❑ 3 Agasha Kokiden U .20 .50
❑ 4 Akodo Ebiro U .20 .50
❑ 5 Akodo Raemon R .50 1.25
❑ 6 Akodo Seiichi (Exp) R .30 .75
❑ 7 All Water Flows C .10 .25
❑ 8 Ancestral Temple R .40 1.00
❑ 9 Aramasu's Vigilance F .40 1.00
❑ 10 Archery Unit C .10 .25
❑ 11 Armor of the Loyal Son R .40 1.00
❑ 12 Asahina Beniha (Exp) F 1.00 2.50
❑ 13 Asako Hitsuko R .75 2.00
❑ 14 Alone Through Life U .20 .50
❑ 15 Awed Witness R 2.00 5.00
❑ 16 Balance in Water U .20 .50
❑ 17 Bayushi Azumamoru U .20 .50
❑ 18 Bayushi Jou U .20 .50
❑ 19 Bayushi Muhito (Exp) R .30 .75
❑ 20 Bayushi Saito C .10 .25
❑ 21 Bestial Rage U .20 .50
❑ 22 Calculated Offensive C .10 .25
❑ 23 Castle of Earth C .10 .25
❑ 24 Cavalry for Hire R .30 .75
❑ 25 Chuda Inisi R .30 .75
❑ 26 Compromised U .20 .50
❑ 27 Concentrated Fire R .30 .75
❑ 28 Consumption by Fire R 1.00 2.50
❑ 29 Controlling the Seas U .20 .50
❑ 30 Corrupt Governor U .20 .50
❑ 31 Crippling Weather C .10 .25
❑ 32 Croplands C .10 .25
❑ 33 Daidoji Kagami C .10 .25
❑ 34 Daidoji Sadayori R .30 .75
❑ 35 Daigotsu Gahseng (Exp) R .30 .75
❑ 36 Daigotsu Sahara (Exp) F .30 .75
❑ 37 Daisho C .10 .25
❑ 38 Dark Oracle of Fire (Exp) R 3.00 8.00
❑ 39 Dependable Gear C .10 .25
❑ 40 Doji Nukada C .10 .25
❑ 41 Doji Shikatsu U .20 .50
❑ 42 Draw Attention U .20 .50
❑ 43 Drawing the Void C .10 .25
❑ 44 Ekibyogami's Spite R .40 1.00
❑ 45 Embassy of the Crane F 1.00 2.50
❑ 46 Endless Stamina C .10 .25
❑ 47 Favor of Artisans C .10 .25
❑ 48 Fifth Wind Cavalry R .50 1.25
❑ 49 Fosuta no Oni C .10 .25
❑ 50 Guardian of Earth U .20 .50
❑ 51 Guided by Honor U .20 .50
❑ 52 Hachigoro U .20 .50
❑ 53 Heroic Inspiration R .75 2.00
❑ 54 Hida Akeno C .10 .25
❑ 55 Hida Desora C .10 .25
❑ 56 Hida Eijiko (Exp) R .30 .75
❑ 57 Hida Tokido U .20 .50
❑ 58 Hida Yiu U .20 .50
❑ 59 Hidden in the Shadows C .10 .25
❑ 60 Hunting the Daughter R 1.50 4.00
❑ 61 Iainuki C .10 .25
❑ 62 Ieyoshi C .10 .25
❑ 63 Ignoble Demise Event U .20 .50
❑ 64 Impromptu Weapon U .20 .50
❑ 65 Inari's Blessing R .30 .75
❑ 66 Infamous Strike R 1.25 3.00
❑ 67 Inspired Devotion U .20 .50
❑ 68 Isawa Furiko R .75 2.00
❑ 69 Isawa Kumai (Exp) R .30 .75
❑ 70 Isawa Kuniki U .20 .50
❑ 71 Iuchi Katamari (Exp) R .30 .75
❑ 72 Jimen's Decree Event R .30 .75
❑ 73 Kakita Noritoshi (Exp) R .40 1.00
❑ 74 Kakita Yosuga U .20 .50
❑ 75 Karyuudo C .10 .25
❑ 76 Katahide C .10 .25
❑ 77 Khol Regulars U .20 .50
❑ 78 Kitsuki Bokuko U .20 .50
❑ 79 Know the Terrain R .30 .75
❑ 80 Kuni Kiyoshi (Exp) R .30 .75
❑ 81 Kyuden Suzume F .30 .75
❑ 82 Lack of Vigilance Event U .20 .50
❑ 83 Leaked Information U .20 .50
❑ 84 Legendary Feud R 1.00 2.50
❑ 85 Matsu Amuro U .20 .50
❑ 86 Matsu Ato C .10 .25
❑ 87 Matsu Fumiyo (Exp) R 1.00 2.50
❑ 88 Matsu Sako C .10 .25
❑ 89 Midnight Shadows C .10 .25
❑ 90 Mirumoto Hojatsu (TDoW) R .60 1.50
❑ 91 Mirumoto Kijima C .10 .25
❑ 92 Mirumoto Tsubasa U .20 .50
❑ 93 Moshi Kalani (Exp) R .50 1.25
❑ 94 Moshi Kinyo C .10 .25
❑ 95 Moto Jeng-Yun R .60 1.50
❑ 96 Muscle and Steel R 1.25 3.00
❑ 97 No Pure Breaths R .50 1.25
❑ 98 Open Emotion R .40 1.00
❑ 99 Out of Nowhere R 1.00 2.50
❑ 100 Panther Tattoo R .30 .75
❑ 101 Preparedness R 2.00 5.00
❑ 102 Preserve Your Forces C .10 .25
❑ 103 Private Farm C .10 .25
❑ 104 Public Records C .10 .25
❑ 105 Pure Breath R .30 .75
❑ 106 Rain of Justice R 2.50 6.00
❑ 107 Rally Through Sacrifice U .20 .50
❑ 108 Reach Across the World C .10 .25
❑ 109 Reckless Assault C .10 .25
❑ 110 Retired Magistrates U .20 .50
❑ 111 Second-Hand Goods R .30 .75
❑ 112 Seppun Ujifusa C .10 .25
❑ 113 Serene Brother U .20 .50
❑ 114 Shatter the Wave U .20 .50
❑ 115 Shiba Gohiko C .10 .25
❑ 116 Shinjo Chu-Yeung U .20 .50
❑ 117 Shinjo Hwarang (Exp) R .30 .75
❑ 118 Shinjo Meng-Do C .10 .25
❑ 119 Shinjo Tobasa C .10 .25
❑ 120 Shosuro Jimen (Exp) R .75 2.00
❑ 121 Shosuro Shigemasa R .60 1.50
❑ 122 Shuriken and Smoke R 1.50 4.00
❑ 123 Snow-Covered Plain C .10 .25
❑ 124 Snowy Plains C .10 .25
❑ 125 Soshi Hirotsugu C .10 .25
❑ 126 Southern Blockade R .40 1.00
❑ 127 Stand Alone Event U .20 .50
❑ 128 Stealing the Essence U .20 .50
❑ 129 Stone Guardian U .20 .50
❑ 130 Strike Quickly C .10 .25
❑ 131 Subversive Influence R .40 1.00
❑ 132 Takaharu U .20 .50
❑ 133 Tamori Wotan (Exp) R .40 1.00
❑ 134 Taxing the Scum U .20 .50
❑ 135 Temple of Redemption U .20 .50
❑ 136 Temporizing Ground C .10 .25
❑ 137 The Fires of War R 1.50 4.00
❑ 138 The Kami's Whisper R .40 1.00
❑ 139 The Shadow Court U .20 .50
❑ 140 The Testament of Fire U .20 .50
❑ 141 Togashi Okamoto C .10 .25
❑ 142 Togashi Shiori (Exp) R .40 1.00
❑ 143 Toritaka Horoiso R .50 1.25
❑ 144 Touch of Thunder R .40 1.00
❑ 145 Treacherous Defile C .10 .25
❑ 146 Tsangusuri C .10 .25
❑ 147 Tsume Spearmen C .10 .25
❑ 148 Tsuruchi Daikyu U .20 .50
❑ 149 Tsuruchi Seisha U .20 .50
❑ 150 Tsuruchi Toboro R .30 .75
❑ 151 Ujisato R .50 1.25
❑ 152 Unnatural Hunger R 1.00 2.50
❑ 153 Utaku Liu-Xeung U .20 .50
❑ 154 Vigorous Sparring U .20 .50
❑ 155 Waves Rush to the Shore U .20 .50
❑ 156 Well Scouted Target U .20 .50
❑ 157 Winter Pilgrimage C .10 .25
❑ 158 Winter Siege R .40 1.00
❑ 159 With My Last Breath C .10 .25
❑ 160 Words Have Strength U .20 .50
❑ 161 Yoritomo Ai C .10 .25
❑ 162 Yoritomo Aranai (Mantis) U .20 .50
❑ 163 Yoritomo Aranai (Spider) U .20 .50
❑ 164 Yoritomo Eihiko (Exp) F .30 .75
❑ 165 Yukataka no Onna U .20 .50

2001 Lord of the Rings The Fellowship of the Ring

COMPLETE SET (365) 50.00 100.00
BOOSTER BOX (36) 25.00 50.00
BOOSTER PACK 1.00 2.00

❑ 1C2 The One Ring, The Ruling Ring .12 .30
❑ 1C3 Axe Strike .12 .30
❑ 1C4 Battle Fury .12 .30
❑ 1C5 Cleaving Blow .12 .30
❑ 1C6 Delving .12 .30
❑ 1C7 Dwarf Guard .12 .30
❑ 1C8 Dwarven Armor .12 .30
❑ 1C9 Dwarven Axe .12 .30
❑ 1R1a The One Ring, Isildur's Bane 1.25 3.00
❑ 1R1b The One Ring, Isildur's Bane TENGWAR
❑ 1C10 Dwarven Heart .12 .30
❑ 1C11 Farin, Dwarven Emissary .12 .30
❑ 1C18 Halls of My Home .12 .30
❑ 1C19 Here Lies Balin, Son of Fundin .12 .30
❑ 1C20 Let Them Come! .12 .30
❑ 1C21 Lord of Moria .12 .30
❑ 1C24 Stairs of Khazad-dum .12 .30
❑ 1C25 Still Draws Breath .12 .30
❑ 1C26 Their Halls of Stone .12 .30
❑ 1C32 Border Defenses .12 .30
❑ 1C37 Defiance .12 .30
❑ 1C39 Elf-song .12 .30
❑ 1C41 Elven Bow .12 .30
❑ 1C42 Elven Cloak .12 .30
❑ 1C43 Far-seeing Eyes .12 .30
❑ 1C52 Lightfootedness .12 .30
❑ 1C53 Lorien Elf .12 .30
❑ 1C58 The Seen and the Unseen .12 .30
❑ 1C59 Shoulder to Shoulder .12 .30
❑ 1C61 Songs of the Blessed Realm .12 .30
❑ 1C67 Uruviel, Maid of Lorien .12 .30
❑ 1C68 The White Arrows of Lorien .12 .30
❑ 1C76 Intimidate .12 .30
❑ 1C78 Mysterious Wizard .12 .30
❑ 1C82 Risk a Little Light .12 .30
❑ 1C84 Sleep, Caradhras .12 .30
❑ 1C85 Strength of Spirit .12 .30
❑ 1C86 Treachery Deeper Than You Know .12 .30
❑ 1C92 Armor .12 .30
❑ 1R13a Gimli, Son of Gloin .60 1.50
❑ 1R13b Gimli, Son of Gloin TENGWAR
❑ 1R15 Gimli's Helm 1.00 2.50
❑ 1R16 Greatest Kingdom of My People .60 1.50
❑ 1R22 Mithril Shaft .60 1.50
❑ 1R23 Nobody Tosses a Dwarf .75 2.00
❑ 1R28 Wealth of Moria .60 1.50
❑ 1R30a Arwen, Daughter of Elrond 1.50 4.00
❑ 1R30b Arwen, Daughter of Elrond TENGWAR
❑ 1R33 Bow of the Galadhrim 1.50 4.00
❑ 1R34 Celeborn, Lord of Lorien .60 1.50
❑ 1R35 The Council of Elrond .60 1.50
❑ 1R36 Curse Their Foul Feet! .60 1.50
❑ 1R38 Double Shot 6.00 12.00
❑ 1R40 Elrond, Lord of Rivendell 1.00 2.50
❑ 1R45 Galadriel, Lady of Light .60 1.50
❑ 1R47 Gwemegil 1.00 2.50
❑ 1R49 The Last Alliance of Elves and Men 1.00 2.50
❑ 1R50a Legolas, Greenleaf 1.50 4.00
❑ 1R50b Legolas, Greenleaf TENGWAR
❑ 1R55 The Mirror of Galadriel .60 1.50
❑ 1R62 The Splendor of Their Banners .60 1.50
❑ 1R66 The Tale of Gil-galad 1.00 2.50
❑ 1R69 Albert Dreary, Entertainer From Bree .60 1.50
❑ 1R71 Durin's Secret .60 1.50
❑ 1R72a Gandalf, Friend of the Shirefolk 1.25 3.00
❑ 1R72b Gandalf, Friend of the Shirefolk TENGWAR
❑ 1R75 Glamdring .60 1.50
❑ 1R79 The Nine Walkers .60 1.50
❑ 1R80 Ottar, Man of Laketown .60 1.50
❑ 1R81 Questions That Need Answering .60 1.50
❑ 1R83a Servant of the Secret Fire 1.25 3.00
❑ 1R83b Servant of the Secret Fire TENGWAR
❑ 1R87 A Wizard Is Never Late 1.50 4.00
❑ 1R88 An Able Guide .60 1.50
❑ 1R89a Aragorn, Ranger of the North 1.25 3.00
❑ 1R89b Aragorn, Ranger of the North TENGWAR
❑ 1R90 Aragorn's Bow 1.50 4.00
❑ 1R93 Arwen's Fate .60 1.50
❑ 1R95 Blade of Gondor 1.00 2.50
❑ 1R96a Boromir, Lord of Gondor 1.25 3.00
❑ 1R96b Boromir, Lord of Gondor TENGWAR
❑ 1R99 Change of Plans .60 1.50
❑ 1U12 Gimli, Dwarf of Erebor .30 .75
❑ 1U17 Grimir, Dwarven Elder .30 .75
❑ 1U27 Thrarin, Dwarven Smith .30 .75
❑ 1U29 Ancient Enmity .30 .75
❑ 1U31 Asfaloth .30 .75
❑ 1U44 Foul Creation .30 .75
❑ 1U46 Gift of Boats .30 .75
❑ 1U48 Haldir, Elf of the Golden Wood .30 .75
❑ 1U51 Legolas, Prince of Mirkwood .30 .75
❑ 1U54 Mallorn-trees .30 .75
❑ 1U56 Orophin, Lorien Bowman .30 .75
❑ 1U57 Rumil, Elven Protector .30 .75
❑ 1U60 Silinde, Elf of Mirkwood .30 .75
❑ 1U63 Stand Against Darkness .30 .75
❑ 1U64 Support of the Last Homely House .30 .75
❑ 1U65 Swan-ship of the Galadhrim .30 .75
❑ 1U70 Barliman Butterbur, Prancing Pony Proprietor .30 .75
❑ 1U73 Gandalf's Cart .30 .75
❑ 1U74 Gandalf's Pipe .30 .75
❑ 1U77 Let Folly Be Our Cloak .30 .75
❑ 1U91 Aragorn's Pipe .30 .75
❑ 1U94 Athelas .30 .75
❑ 1U97 Boromir, Son of Denethor .30 .75
❑ 1U98 Boromir's Cloak .30 .75
❑ 1C101 Coat of Mail .12 .30
❑ 1C102 Dagger Strike .12 .30
❑ 1C103 Elendil's Valor .12 .30
❑ 1C104 Eregion's Trails .12 .30
❑ 1C106 Gondor's Vengeance .12 .30
❑ 1C107 Great Shield .12 .30
❑ 1C110 Pathfinder .12 .30
❑ 1C116 Swordarm of the White Tower .12 .30
❑ 1C117 Swordsman of the Northern Kingdom .12 .30
❑ 1C119 What Are They? .12 .30
❑ 1C121 Bred for Battle .12 .30
❑ 1C122 Breeding Pit .12 .30
❑ 1C133 Saruman's Ambition .12 .30
❑ 1C134 Saruman's Chill .12 .30
❑ 1C138 Saruman's Snows .12 .30
❑ 1C141 Their Arrows Enrage .12 .30
❑ 1C144 Uruk Bloodlust .12 .30
❑ 1C145 Uruk Brood .12 .30
❑ 1C146 Uruk Fighter .12 .30
❑ 1C149 Uruk Messenger .12 .30
❑ 1C150 Uruk Rager .12 .30
❑ 1C151 Uruk Savage .12 .30
❑ 1C152 Uruk Shaman .12 .30
❑ 1C154 Uruk Soldier .12 .30
❑ 1C156 Uruk Warrior .12 .30
❑ 1C157 Uruk-hai Armory .12 .30
❑ 1C158 Uruk-hai Raiding Party .12 .30
❑ 1C160 Uruk-hai Sword .12 .30
❑ 1C168 Drums in the Deep .12 .30
❑ 1C171 Frenzy .12 .30
❑ 1C174 Goblin Backstabber .12 .30
❑ 1C176 Goblin Marksman .12 .30
❑ 1C177 Goblin Patrol Troop .12 .30
❑ 1C179 Goblin Scavengers .12 .30
❑ 1C180 Goblin Scimitar .12 .30
❑ 1C182 Goblin Spear .12 .30
❑ 1C184 Goblin Wallcrawler .12 .30
❑ 1C185 Goblin Warrior .12 .30
❑ 1C187 Host of Thousands .12 .30
❑ 1C191 Moria Scout .12 .30
❑ 1C192 Pinned Down .12 .30
❑ 1C193 Plundered Armories .12 .30
❑ 1C196 They Are Coming .12 .30
❑ 1C197 Threat of the Unknown .12 .30
❑ 1C201 Unfamiliar Territory .12 .30
❑ 1C248 Forces of Mordor .12 .30
❑ 1C255 Mordor's Strength .12 .30
❑ 1C261 Orc Ambusher .12 .30
❑ 1C266 Orc Chieftain .12 .30
❑ 1C268 Orc Inquisitor .12 .30
❑ 1C269 Orc Scimitar .12 .30
❑ 1C271 Orc Soldier .12 .30
❑ 1C273 The Ring's Oppression .12 .30
❑ 1C277 Shadow's Reach .12 .30
❑ 1C278 Strength Born of Fear .12 .30
❑ 1C281 Under the Watching Eye .12 .30
❑ 1C283 You Bring Great Evil .12 .30
❑ 1C286 Bounder .12 .30
❑ 1C287 Extraordinary Resilience .12 .30
❑ 1C290 Frodo, Son of Drogo .12 .30
❑ 1C294 Hobbit Appetite .12 .30
❑ 1C295 Hobbit Farmer .12 .30
❑ 1C296 Hobbit Intuition .12 .30
❑ 1C297 Hobbit Party Guest .12 .30
❑ 1C298 Hobbit Stealth .12 .30
❑ 1C299 Hobbit Sword .12 .30
❑ 1C300 Longbottom Leaf .12 .30
❑ 1C303 Merry, From O'er the Brandywine .12 .30
❑ 1C304 Noble Intentions .12 .30
❑ 1C305 Old Toby .12 .30
❑ 1C306 Pippin, Friend to Frodo .12 .30
❑ 1C311 Sam, Son of Hamfast .12 .30
❑ 1C312 Sorry About Everything .12 .30
❑ 1C315 Stout and Sturdy .12 .30
❑ 1C317 There and Back Again .12 .30
❑ 1C326 Westfarthing .12 .30
❑ 1C331 Ettenmoors .12 .30
❑ 1C337 Council Courtyard .12 .30
❑ 1C346 Moria Lake .12 .30
❑ 1C349 The Bridge of Khazad-dum .12 .30
❑ 1C351 Galadriel's Glade .12 .30
❑ 1C354 Anduin Wilderland .12 .30
❑ 1C356 Anduin Banks .12 .30
❑ 1C362 Summit of Amon Hen .12 .30
❑ 1P364 Gandalf, The Grey Wizard .40 1.00
❑ 1P365 Aragorn, King in Exile .40 1.00
❑ 1R100 The Choice of Luthien .60 1.50
❑ 1R111 Pursuit Just Behind .60 1.50
❑ 1R114a The Saga of Elendil 1.00 2.50
❑ 1R114b The Saga of Elendil TENGWAR
❑ 1R115 Strength of Kings .60 1.50
❑ 1R118 Valiant Man of the West .60 1.50
❑ 1R120 Alive and Unspoiled .60 1.50
❑ 1R123 Caradhras Has Not Forgiven Us .60 1.50
❑ 1R124 Cruel Caradhras .60 1.50
❑ 1R125 Greed .60 1.50
❑ 1R127a Lurtz, Servant of Isengard .75 2.00
❑ 1R127b Lurtz, Servant of Isengard TENGWAR
❑ 1R128 Lurtz's Battle Cry
❑ 1R129 The Misadventure of Mr. Underhill .60 1.50
❑ 1R131 Orthanc Assassin .60 1.50
❑ 1R132 Parry .60 1.50
❑ 1R137 Saruman's Reach .60 1.50
❑ 1R139 Savagery to Match Their Numbers 1.25 3.00
❑ 1R140 Spies of Saruman .60 1.50
❑ 1R143 Troop of Uruk-hai .75 2.00
❑ 1R147 Uruk Guard .60 1.50
❑ 1R148 Uruk Lieutenant 1.25 3.00
❑ 1R14a Gimli's Battle Axe .60 1.50
❑ 1R14b Gimli's Battle Axe TENGWAR
❑ 1R155 Uruk Spy .60 1.50
❑ 1R163 Ancient Chieftain .60 1.50
❑ 1R165a Cave Troll of Moria, Scourge of the Black Pit 1.50 4.00
❑ 1R165b Cave Troll of Moria, Scourge of the Black Pit TENGWAR
❑ 1R166 Cave Troll's Hammer .60 1.50
❑ 1R167 Denizens Enraged .60 1.50
❑ 1R169 The End Comes .60 1.50
❑ 1R170 Fool of a Took! .60 1.50
❑ 1R172 Goblin Archer .75 2.00
❑ 1R173 Goblin Armory 5.00 10.00
❑ 1R175 Goblin Domain .60 1.50
❑ 1R183 Goblin Swarms 1.50 4.00
❑ 1R186 Guard Commander .60 1.50
❑ 1R189 Lost to the Goblins .60 1.50
❑ 1R190 Moria Axe .75 2.00
❑ 1R195 Relics of Moria .60 1.50
❑ 1R199 Troll's Keyward .75 2.00
❑ 1R200 The Underdeeps of Moria .60 1.50
❑ 1R204 All Veils Removed .60 1.50
❑ 1R205 Beauty Is Fading .60 1.50
❑ 1R206 Bent on Discovery .60 1.50
❑ 1R208 Black Steed .60 1.50
❑ 1R210 Dark Whispers .60 1.50
❑ 1R212 Fear .60 1.50
❑ 1R214 In the Ringwraith's Wake .60 1.50
❑ 1R216 Morgul Blade .60 1.50
❑ 1R217 Morgul Gates 2.50 6.00
❑ 1R221 The Pale Blade .60 1.50
❑ 1R224 Return to Its Master .75 2.00
❑ 1R228 The Twilight World .60 1.50
❑ 1R229 Ulaire Attea, Keeper of Dol Guldur 1.25 3.00
❑ 1R230 Ulaire Cantea, Lieutenant of Dol Guldur 1.50 4.00
❑ 1R236 Ulaire Toldea, Messenger of Morgul 1.25 3.00
❑ 1R237a The Witch-king, Lord of Angmar .75 2.00
❑ 1R237b The Witch-king, Lord of Angmar TENGWAR
❑ 1R240 Band of the Eye .60 1.50
❑ 1R243 Despair .60 1.50
❑ 1R244 Desperate Defense of the Ring 1.25 3.00
❑ 1R245 Desperate Measures .60 1.50
❑ 1R246 Enduring Evil .75 2.00
❑ 1R247 Enheartened Foe .60 1.50
❑ 1R250 Hate 1.50 4.00
❑ 1R252 The Irresistible Shadow .60 1.50
❑ 1R253 Journey Into Danger .60 1.50
❑ 1R254 Mordor Enraged .60 1.50
❑ 1R256a Morgul Hunter .60 1.50
❑ 1R256b Morgul Hunter TENGWAR
❑ 1R259 Morgul Warden .60 1.50
❑ 1R263 Orc Banner .60 1.50
❑ 1R264 Orc Bowmen 2.50 6.00
❑ 1R265 Orc Butchery .60 1.50
❑ 1R272 Orc War Band .60 1.50
❑ 1R276 Seeking Its Master .60 1.50
❑ 1R279 Thin and Stretched .60 1.50
❑ 1R282 The Weight of a Legacy .60 1.50
❑ 1R284 Bilbo, Retired Adventurer .60 1.50

TCG/CCG

TCG/CCG

❑ 1R288 Farmer Maggot, Chaser of Rascals .60 1.50
❑ 1R289 Frodo, Old Bilbo's Heir .75 2.00
❑ 1R291 The Gaffer, Sam's Father .60 1.50
❑ 1R302 Merry, Friend to Sam .60 1.50
❑ 1R307 Pippin, Hobbit of Some Intelligence .60 1.50
❑ 1R308 Power According to His Stature 2.50 6.00
❑ 1R310 Sam, Faithful Companion .60 1.50
❑ 1R313 Sting 1.25 3.00
❑ 1R314 Stone Trolls .60 1.50
❑ 1R318 Thror's Map .60 1.50
❑ 1U105 Foes of Mordor .30 .75
❑ 1U108 No Stranger to the Shadows .30 .75
❑ 1U109 One Whom Men Would Follow .30 .75
❑ 1U112 Ranger's Sword .30 .75
❑ 1U113 A Ranger's Versatility .30 .75
❑ 1U126 Hunt Them Down! .30 .75
❑ 1U130 No Ordinary Storm .30 .75
❑ 1U135 Saruman's Frost .30 .75
❑ 1U136 Saruman's Power .30 .75
❑ 1U142 Traitor's Voice .30 .75
❑ 1U153 Uruk Slayer .30 .75
❑ 1U159 Uruk-hai Rampage .30 .75
❑ 1U161 Wariness .30 .75
❑ 1U162 Worry .30 .75
❑ 1U164 Bitter Hatred .30 .75
❑ 1U178 Goblin Runner .30 .75
❑ 1U181 Goblin Sneak .30 .75
❑ 1U188 The Long Dark .30 .75
❑ 1U194 Relentless .30 .75
❑ 1U198 Through the Misty Mountains .30 .75
❑ 1U202 What Is This New Devilry? .30 .75
❑ 1U203 All Blades Perish .30 .75
❑ 1U207 Black Breath .30 .75
❑ 1U209 Blade Tip .30 .75
❑ 1U211 Drawn to Its Power .30 .75
❑ 1U213 Frozen by Fear .30 .75
❑ 1U215 The Master's Will .30 .75
❑ 1U218 Nazgul Sword .30 .75
❑ 1U219 The Nine Servants of Sauron .30 .75
❑ 1U220 Not Easily Destroyed .30 .75
❑ 1U222 Paths Seldom Trodden .30 .75
❑ 1U223 Relentless Charge .30 .75
❑ 1U225 Sword of Minas Morgul .30 .75
❑ 1U226 Their Power Is in Terror .30 .75
❑ 1U227 Threshold of Shadow .30 .75
❑ 1U231a Ulaire Enquea, Lieutenant of Morgul .30 .75
❑ 1U231b Ulaire Enquea, Lieutenant of Morgul TENGWAR
❑ 1U232 Ulaire Lemenya, Lieutenant of Morgul .30 .75
❑ 1U233 Ulaire Nelya, Lieutenant of Morgul .30 .75
❑ 1U234 Ulaire Nertea, Messenger of Dol Guldur .30 .75
❑ 1U235 Ulaire Otsea, Lieutenant of Morgul .30 .75
❑ 1U238 Wreathed in Shadow .30 .75
❑ 1U239 All Thought Bent on It .30 .75
❑ 1U241 Curse From Mordor .30 .75
❑ 1U242 The Dark Lord's Summons .30 .75
❑ 1U249 Gleaming Spires Will Crumble .30 .75
❑ 1U251 A Host Avails Little .30 .75
❑ 1U257 Morgul Skirmisher .30 .75
❑ 1U258 Morgul Skulker .30 .75
❑ 1U260 The Number Must Be Few .30 .75
❑ 1U262 Orc Assassin .30 .75
❑ 1U267 Orc Hunters .30 .75
❑ 1U270 Orc Scouting Band .30 .75
❑ 1U274 Sauron's Defenses .30 .75
❑ 1U275 Seeking It Always .30 .75
❑ 1U280 Tower Lieutenant .30 .75
❑ 1U285 Bilbo's Pipe .30 .75
❑ 1U292 The Gaffer's Pipe .30 .75
❑ 1U293 Halfling Deftness .30 .75
❑ 1U301 Master Proudfoot, Distant Relative of Bilbo .30 .75
❑ 1U309 Rosie Cotton, Hobbiton Lass .30 .75
❑ 1U316 A Talent for Not Being Seen .30 .75
❑ 1U319 Bag End .30 .75
❑ 1U320 East Road .30 .75
❑ 1U321 Farmer Maggot's Fields .30 .75
❑ 1U322 Green Dragon Inn .30 .75
❑ 1U323 Green Hill Country .30 .75
❑ 1U324 The Prancing Pony .30 .75
❑ 1U325 Shire Lookout Point .30 .75
❑ 1U327 Bree Gate .30 .75
❑ 1U328 Bree Streets .30 .75
❑ 1U329 Breeland Forest .30 .75
❑ 1U330 Buckleberry Ferry .30 .75
❑ 1U332 Midgewater Marshes .30 .75
❑ 1U333 Midgewater Moors .30 .75
❑ 1U334 Trollshaw Forest .30 .75
❑ 1U335 Weatherhills .30 .75
❑ 1U336 Weathertop .30 .75
❑ 1U338 Ford of Bruinen .30 .75
❑ 1U339 Frodo's Bedroom .30 .75
❑ 1U340 Rivendell Terrace .30 .75
❑ 1U341 Rivendell Valley .30 .75
❑ 1U342 Rivendell Waterfall .30 .75
❑ 1U343 Balin's Tomb .30 .75
❑ 1U344 Dwarrowdelf Chamber .30 .75
❑ 1U345 Mithril Mine .30 .75
❑ 1U347 Moria Stairway .30 .75
❑ 1U348 Pass of Caradhras .30 .75
❑ 1U350 Dimrill Dale .30 .75
❑ 1U352 Lothlorien Woods .30 .75
❑ 1U353 Anduin Confluence .30 .75
❑ 1U355 Silverlode Banks .30 .75
❑ 1U357 Brown Lands .30 .75
❑ 1U358 Pillars of the Kings .30 .75
❑ 1U359 Shores of Nen Hithoel .30 .75
❑ 1U360 Emyn Muil .30 .75
❑ 1U361 Slopes of Amon Hen .30 .75
❑ 1U363 Tol Brandir .30 .75

2002 Lord of the Rings Mines of Moria

COMPLETE SET (122) 15.00 30.00
BOOSTER BOX (36) 20.00 40.00
BOOSTER PACK 1.00 2.00

❑ 2C2 Disquiet of Our People .12 .30
❑ 2C5 Flurry of Blows .12 .30
❑ 2C6 Fror, Gimli's Kinsman .12 .30
❑ 2C9 Great Works Begun There .12 .30
❑ 2R1 Beneath the Mountains .60 1.50
❑ 2R7 Gloin, Friend to Thorin .60 1.50
❑ 2U3 Dwarven Bracers .30 .75
❑ 2U4 Endurance of Dwarves .30 .75
❑ 2U8 Golden Light on the Land .30 .75
❑ 2C10 Hand Axe .12 .30
❑ 2C14 Till Durin Wakes Again .12 .30
❑ 2C21 Erland, Advisor to Brand .12 .30
❑ 2C23 Gandalf's Wisdom .12 .30
❑ 2C24 Hugin, Emissary from Laketown .12 .30
❑ 2C26 Speak Friend and Enter .12 .30
❑ 2C29 Wizard Staff .12 .30
❑ 2C35 Natural Cover .12 .30
❑ 2C37 Sentinels of Numenor .12 .30
❑ 2C40 Demands of the Sackville-Bagginses .12 .30
❑ 2C42 Goblin Man .12 .30
❑ 2C44 No Business of Ours .12 .30
❑ 2C47 Uruk Scout .12 .30
❑ 2C51 The Balrog, Durin's Bane .12 .30
❑ 2C55 Dark Places .12 .30
❑ 2C58 Foul Tentacle .12 .30
❑ 2C60 Goblin Bowman .12 .30
❑ 2C61 Goblin Flankers .12 .30
❑ 2C62 Goblin Pursuer .12 .30
❑ 2C63 Goblin Reinforcements .12 .30
❑ 2C64 Goblin Scrabbler .12 .30
❑ 2C65 Goblin Spearman .12 .30
❑ 2C69 Old Differences .12 .30
❑ 2C88 Memory of Many Things .12 .30
❑ 2C89 Orc Scout .12 .30
❑ 2C90 Orc Taskmaster .12 .30
❑ 2C91 Southern Spies .12 .30
❑ 2C95 Vile Blade .12 .30
❑ 2C99 Deft in Their Movements .12 .30
❑ 2R11 Make Light of Burdens .60 1.50
❑ 2R12 Realm of Dwarrowdelf .60 1.50
❑ 2R15 What Are We Waiting For? .60 1.50
❑ 2R19 Release the Angry Flood .60 1.50
❑ 2R20 Secret Sentinels .60 1.50
❑ 2R22 Gandalf's Staff .60 1.50
❑ 2R25 Jarnsmid, Merchant from Dale .60 1.50
❑ 2R27 Staff Asunder .60 1.50
❑ 2R32 Flaming Brand 1.25 3.00
❑ 2R36 No Mere Ranger .60 1.50
❑ 2R38 Shield of Boromir .60 1.50
❑ 2R39 Beyond the Height of Men .60 1.50
❑ 2R43 Lurtz's Sword .60 1.50
❑ 2R45 Too Much Attention .60 1.50
❑ 2R46 Uruk Captain .60 1.50
❑ 2R49 Archer Commander .75 2.00
❑ 2R50 The Balrog's Sword .60 1.50
❑ 2R52a The Balrog, Flame of Udun .60 1.50
❑ 2R52b The Balrog, Flame of Udun TENGWAR
❑ 2R53 Cave Troll's Chain .60 1.50
❑ 2R57 Final Cry .60 1.50
❑ 2R66 Huge Tentacle .60 1.50
❑ 2R73 Watcher in the Water, Keeper of Westgate .75 2.00
❑ 2R74 Whip of Many Thongs .60 1.50
❑ 2R75 Bill Ferny, Swarthy Sneering Fellow 1.00 2.50
❑ 2R77 His Terrible Servants .60 1.50
❑ 2R80 Stricken Dumb .60 1.50
❑ 2R84 Ulaire Nelya, Ringwraith in Twilight .60 1.50
❑ 2R85 The Witch-king, Lord of the Nazgul 1.50 4.00
❑ 2R86 Wraith-world .60 1.50
❑ 2R93 Tower Assassin .60 1.50
❑ 2R94 Verily I Come .60 1.50
❑ 2R97 Consorting With Wizards .60 1.50
❑ 2U13 Tidings of Erebor .30 .75
❑ 2U16 A Blended Race .30 .75
❑ 2U17 Dismay Our Enemies .30 .75
❑ 2U18 Hosts of the Last Alliance .30 .75
❑ 2U28 Wielder of the Flame .30 .75
❑ 2U30 You Cannot Pass! .30 .75
❑ 2U31 Blood of Numenor .30 .75
❑ 2U33 Flee in Terror .30 .75
❑ 2U34 Gondor Will See It Done .30 .75
❑ 2U41 Evil Afoot .30 .75
❑ 2U48 Wizard Storm .30 .75
❑ 2U54 Dark Fire .30 .75
❑ 2U56 Fill With Fear .30 .75
❑ 2U59 Foul Things .30 .75
❑ 2U67 Moria Archer Troop .30 .75
❑ 2U68 Must Do Without Hope .30 .75
❑ 2U70 Power and Terror .30 .75
❑ 2U71 Throw Yourself in Next Time .30 .75
❑ 2U72 Troubled Mountains .30 .75
❑ 2U76 Helpless .30 .75
❑ 2U78 It Wants to be Found .30 .75
❑ 2U79 Resistance Becomes Unbearable .30 .75
❑ 2U81 They Will Find the Ring .30 .75
❑ 2U82 Ulaire Attea, The Easterling .30 .75
❑ 2U83 Ulaire Enquea, Ringwraith in Twilight .30 .75
❑ 2U87 The Eye of Sauron .30 .75
❑ 2U92 Spies of Mordor .30 .75
❑ 2U96 Bilbo, Well-spoken Gentlehobbit .30 .75
❑ 2U98 Dear Friends .30 .75
❑ 2C101 Filibert Bolger, Wily Rascal .12 .30
❑ 2C102a Frodo, Reluctant Adventurer .12 .30
❑ 2C102b Frodo, Reluctant Adventurer TENGWAR
❑ 2C104 Merry, Horticulturalist .12 .30
❑ 2C110 Pippin, Mr. Took .12 .30
❑ 2C114 Sam, Proper Poet .12 .30
❑ 2C117 Town Center .12 .30
❑ 2C119 Hollin .12 .30
❑ 2P121 Gimli, Dwarf of the Mountain-race .40 1.00
❑ 2P122 Gandalf, The Grey Pilgrim .40 1.00
❑ 2R100 Fearing the Worst .60 1.50
❑ 2R105a Mithril-coat .75 2.00
❑ 2R105b Mithril-coat TENGWAR
❑ 2R108 O Elbereth! Gilthoniel! .75 2.00
❑ 2R109 Orc-bane .60 1.50
❑ 2R112 A Promise 2.50 6.00
❑ 2R113 Red Book of Westmarch .60 1.50
❑ 2U103 Hobbit Sword-play .30 .75
❑ 2U106 Nice Imitation .30 .75
❑ 2U107 Not Feared in Sunlight .30 .75
❑ 2U111 Practically Everyone Was Invited .30 .75
❑ 2U115 Hobbiton Party Field .30 .75
❑ 2U116 Hobbiton Woods .30 .75
❑ 2U118 Great Chasm .30 .75
❑ 2U120 Valley of the Silverlode .30 .75

2002 Lord of the Rings Realms of the Elf-Lords

COMPLETE SET (122) 20.00 40.00
BOOSTER BOX (36) 20.00 40.00
BOOSTER PACK 1.00 2.00

❑ 3C6 Storm of Argument .12 .30
❑ 3R1 Book of Mazarbul .60 1.50
❑ 3R3 Mines of Khazad-Dum .60 1.50
❑ 3R8 Arwen, Lady Undomiel .60 1.50
❑ 3U2 Gimli's Pipe .30 .75
❑ 3U4 A Royal Welcome .30 .75
❑ 3U5 Song of Durin .30 .75
❑ 3U7 Arwen, Elven Rider .30 .75
❑ 3U9 Beren and Luthien .30 .75
❑ 3C11 Cast It Into the Fire! .12 .30
❑ 3C14 Erestor, Chief Advisor to Elrond .12 .30
❑ 3C16 Friends of Old .12 .30
❑ 3C22 Master of Healing .12 .30
❑ 3C28 Voice of Nimrodel .12 .30
❑ 3C30 Deep in Thought .12 .30
❑ 3C31 Depart Silently .12 .30
❑ 3C32 Fireworks .12 .30
❑ 3C33 His First Serious Check .12 .30
❑ 3C36 Unknown Perils .12 .30
❑ 3C37 Answering the Cries .12 .30
❑ 3C43 Might of Numenor .12 .30
❑ 3C48 We Must Go Warily .12 .30
❑ 3C49 Abandoning Reason for Madness .12 .30
❑ 3C51 Coming for the Ring .12 .30
❑ 3C55 Isengard Axe .12 .30
❑ 3C56 Isengard Forger .12 .30
❑ 3C59 Isengard Shaman .12 .30
❑ 3C62 Isengard Worker .12 .30
❑ 3C63 One of You Must Do This .12 .30
❑ 3C69 Saruman, Servant of the Eye .12 .30
❑ 3C70 Servants to Saruman .12 .30
❑ 3C74 Uruk Raider .12 .30
❑ 3C76 Dangerous Gamble .12 .30
❑ 3C78 Hide and Seek .12 .30
❑ 3C84 They Will Never Stop Hunting You .12 .30
❑ 3C87 The Dark Lord Advances .12 .30
❑ 3C90 Hand of Sauron .12 .30
❑ 3C94 Orc Butcher .12 .30
❑ 3C95 Orc Guard .12 .30
❑ 3C98 Orc Swordsman .12 .30
❑ 3R13 Elrond, Herald to Gil-galad 1.25 3.00
❑ 3R15 Forests of Lothlorien .60 1.50
❑ 3R17 Galadriel, Lady of the Golden Wood .60 1.50
❑ 3R19 Gift of the Evenstar .60 1.50
❑ 3R21 Long-knives of Legolas 2.00 5.00
❑ 3R23 Nenya .60 1.50
❑ 3R27 Vilya .60 1.50
❑ 3R29 Betrayal of Isengard .60 1.50
❑ 3R34 Narya 1.00 2.50
❑ 3R38 Aragorn, Heir to the White City .60 1.50
❑ 3R39 Banner of the White Tree .75 2.00
❑ 3R40 Citadel of Minas Tirith .75 2.00
❑ 3R41 Gondor Bowmen 2.00 5.00
❑ 3R42 Horn of Boromir .60 1.50
❑ 3R44 The Shards of Narsil .75 2.00
❑ 3R50 Can You Protect Me From Yourself? .60 1.50
❑ 3R52 A Fell Voice on the Air .60 1.50
❑ 3R54 Hollowing of Isengard .60 1.50
❑ 3R64 Orc Commander .60 1.50
❑ 3R65 Orc Overseer .60 1.50
❑ 3R66 Orthanc Berserker .60 1.50
❑ 3R67 The Palantir of Orthanc .60 1.50
❑ 3R68 Saruman, Keeper of Isengard .60 1.50
❑ 3R71 Tower of Orthanc .60 1.50
❑ 3R77 Depths of Moria .60 1.50
❑ 3R80 Such a Little Thing .60 1.50
❑ 3R81 Gates of the Dead City .60 1.50
❑ 3R85 Too Great and Terrible .60 1.50
❑ 3R91 His Cruelty and Malice .60 1.50
❑ 3R93 Morgul Slayer .60 1.50
❑ 3R99 Orc Trooper .60 1.50
❑ 3U10 Calaglin, Elf of Lorien .30 .75
❑ 3U12 Dinendal, Silent Scout .30 .75
❑ 3U18 Galdor, Councilor From the West .30 .75
❑ 3U20 Goradir, Councilor of Imladris .30 .75
❑ 3U24 Phial of Galadriel .30 .75
❑ 3U25 Saelbeth, Elven Councilor .30 .75
❑ 3U26 Something Draws Near .30 .75
❑ 3U35 Trust Me as You Once Did .30 .75
❑ 3U45 Some Who Resisted .30 .75
❑ 3U46 Still Sharp .30 .75
❑ 3U47 Voice of Rauros .30 .75
❑ 3U53 Hate and Anger .30 .75
❑ 3U57 Isengard Retainer .30 .75
❑ 3U58 Isengard Servant .30 .75
❑ 3U60 Isengard Smith .30 .75
❑ 3U61 Isengard Warrior .30 .75
❑ 3U72 Trapped and Alone .30 .75
❑ 3U73 The Trees Are Strong .30 .75
❑ 3U75 Uruk Ravager .30 .75
❑ 3U79 Malice .30 .75
❑ 3U82 News of Mordor .30 .75
❑ 3U83 The Ring Draws Them .30 .75
❑ 3U86 Ulaire Otsea, Ringwraith in Twilight .30 .75
❑ 3U88 Get Off the Road! .30 .75
❑ 3U89 Gleaming in the Snow .30 .75
❑ 3U92 Massing in the East .30 .75
❑ 3U96 Orc Pillager .30 .75
❑ 3U97 Orc Slayer .30 .75
❑ 3C101 Orc Warrior .12 .30
❑ 3C108 Frying Pan .12 .30
❑ 3C109 Meant to Be Alone .12 .30
❑ 3C111 Old Noakes, Purveyor of Wisdoms .12 .30
❑ 3C112 Seek and Hide .12 .30
❑ 3C114 Three Monstrous Trolls .12 .30
❑ 3C117 Gates of Argonath .12 .30
❑ 3C118 The Great River .12 .30
❑ 3P121 Legolas, Son of Thranduil .40 1.00
❑ 3P122 Boromir, Defender of Minas Tirith .40 1.00
❑ 3R102 Our List of Allies Grows Thin .60 1.50
❑ 3R103 Terrible as the Dawn .60 1.50
❑ 3R104 Tower of Barad-dur .75 2.00
❑ 3R105 Why Shouldn't I Keep It? .60 1.50
❑ 3R110 Melilot Brandybuck, Merry Dancer .60 1.50
❑ 3R113 The Shire Countryside 1.00 2.50
❑ 3U100 Orc Veteran .30 .75
❑ 3U106 Bill the Pony .30 .75
❑ 3U107 Frodo's Pipe .30 .75
❑ 3U115 Caras Galadhon .30 .75
❑ 3U116 Eregion Hills .30 .75
❑ 3U119 House of Elrond .30 .75
❑ 3U120 Wastes of Emyn Muil .30 .75

2002 Lord of the Rings The Two Towers

COMPLETE SET (365) 50.00 100.00
BOOSTER BOX (36) 25.00 50.00
BOOSTER PACK 1.00 2.00

❑ 4C2 The One Ring, The Ruling Ring .12 .30
❑ 4C3 Anger .12 .30
❑ 4C4 Band of Wild Men .12 .30
❑ 4C5 Burn Every Village .12 .30
❑ 4C7 Dark Fury .12 .30
❑ 4R1A The One Ring, Answer To All Riddles 7.50 15.00
❑ 4R1B The One Ring, Answer To All Riddles TENGWAR
❑ 4R6 Constantly Threatening .60 1.50
❑ 4U8 Death to the Strawheads .30 .75
❑ 4U9 Dunlending Arsonist .30 .75
❑ 4C10 Dunlending Brigand .12 .30
❑ 4C12 Dunlending Madman .12 .30
❑ 4C14 Dunlending Ransacker .12 .30
❑ 4C15 Dunlending Ravager .12 .30
❑ 4C16 Dunlending Robber .12 .30
❑ 4C17 Dunlending Savage .12 .30
❑ 4C18 Dunlending Warrior .12 .30
❑ 4C21 Hillman Band .12 .30
❑ 4C25 Hillman Tribe .12 .30
❑ 4C26 Iron Axe .12 .30
❑ 4C37 War Cry of Dunland .12 .30
❑ 4C42 Best Company .12 .30
❑ 4C44 Courtesy of My Hall .12 .30
❑ 4C49 Gimli, Unbidden Guest .12 .30
❑ 4C50 Here Is Good Rock .12 .30
❑ 4C51 Khazad Ai-menu .12 .30
❑ 4C56 Search Far and Wide .12 .30
❑ 4C64 Elven Sword .12 .30
❑ 4C67 Fereveldir, Son of Thandronen .12 .30
❑ 4C68 Ferevellon, Son of Thandronen .12 .30
❑ 4C70 Flashing Steel .12 .30
❑ 4C71 Haldir, Emissary of the Galadhrim .12 .30
❑ 4C74 Legolas, Elven Comrade .12 .30
❑ 4C76 Lorien Guardian .12 .30
❑ 4C78 Lorien Swordsman .12 .30
❑ 4C83 Supporting Fire .12 .30
❑ 4C85 Thandronen, Veteran Protector .12 .30
❑ 4C87 Valor .12 .30
❑ 4C90a Gandalf, The White Wizard .12 .30
❑ 4C90b Gandalf, The White Wizard TENGWAR
❑ 4C93 Have Patience .12 .30
❑ 4C97 Long I Fell .12 .30
❑ 4C98 Mithrandir, Mithrandir! .12 .30
❑ 4R19A Hides 3.00 8.00
❑ 4R19B Hides TENGWAR
❑ 4R20 Hill Chief .60 1.50
❑ 4R22 Hillman Horde .60 1.50
❑ 4R23 Hillman Mob .60 1.50
❑ 4R29 No Refuge .60 1.50
❑ 4R30 No Retreat .60 1.50
❑ 4R32 Ravage the Defeated .60 1.50
❑ 4R33 Saruman, Rabble-rouser 1.50 4.00
❑ 4R35 Wake of Destruction .60 1.50
❑ 4R39 Wild Man Raid .60 1.50
❑ 4R40 Wulf, Dunlending Chieftain .60 1.50
❑ 4R41 Axe of Erebor .75 2.00
❑ 4R45 Dwarven Foresight .60 1.50
❑ 4R46 Ever My Heart Rises .60 1.50
❑ 4R48 Gimli, Lockbearer .60 1.50
❑ 4R52 My Axe Is Notched .60 1.50
❑ 4R54 Rest by Blind Night .60 1.50
❑ 4R55 Restless Axe .60 1.50
❑ 4R58 Alliance Reforged .60 1.50
❑ 4R61 Company of Archers 1.25 3.00
❑ 4R65 Erethon, Naith Lieutenant .60 1.50
❑ 4R69 Final Count .60 1.50
❑ 4R72 Killing Field .60 1.50
❑ 4R73A Legolas, Dauntless Hunter .60 1.50
❑ 4R73B Legolas, Dauntless Hunter TENGWAR
❑ 4R75 Lembas 1.00 2.50
❑ 4R79 Night Without End .60 1.50
❑ 4R84 Sword-wall .60 1.50
❑ 4R89 Gandalf, Greyhame .75 2.00
❑ 4R91 Gandalf's Staff, Walking Stick .60 1.50
❑ 4R92 Grown Suddenly Tall .60 1.50
❑ 4R94 Hearken to Me 1.00 2.50
❑ 4R95 Into Dark Tunnels .60 1.50
❑ 4U11 Dunlending Looter .30 .75
❑ 4U13 Dunlending Pillager .30 .75
❑ 4U24 Hillman Rabble .30 .75
❑ 4U27 Living Off Rock .30 .75
❑ 4U28 No Defense .30 .75
❑ 4U31 Over the Isen .30 .75
❑ 4U34 Secret Folk .30 .75
❑ 4U36 War Club .30 .75
❑ 4U38 Wild Man of Dunland .30 .75
❑ 4U43 Come Here Lad .30 .75
❑ 4U47 From the Armory .30 .75
❑ 4U53 Quick As May Be .30 .75
❑ 4U57 Stout and Strong .30 .75
❑ 4U59 Arrow and Blade .30 .75
❑ 4U60 Blades Drawn .30 .75
❑ 4U62 Elven Bow .30 .75
❑ 4U63 Elven Brooch .30 .75
❑ 4U66 Feathered .30 .75
❑ 4U77 Lorien Is Most Welcome .30 .75
❑ 4U80 Ordulus, Young Warrior .30 .75
❑ 4U81 Pengedhel, Naith Warrior .30 .75
❑ 4U82 Strength of Arms .30 .75
❑ 4U86 Thonnas, Naith Captain .30 .75
❑ 4U88 Behold the White Rider .30 .75
❑ 4U96 Keep Your Forked Tongue .30 .75
❑ 4U99 Roll of Thunder .30 .75
❑ 4C102 Task Was Not Done .12 .30
❑ 4C104 Treebeard, Oldest Living Thing .12 .30
❑ 4C105 Under the Living Earth .12 .30
❑ 4C109 Aragorn, Heir of Elendil .12 .30
❑ 4C112 Boromir's Gauntlets .12 .30
❑ 4C113 Curse Them .12 .30
❑ 4C115 Defend It and Hope .12 .30
❑ 4C117 Faramir, Son of Denethor .12 .30
❑ 4C122 Gondorian Ranger .12 .30
❑ 4C128 New Errand .12 .30
❑ 4C129 Pathfinder .12 .30
❑ 4C130 Ranger of Ithilien .12 .30
❑ 4C131 Ranger's Bow .12 .30
❑ 4C134 Sword of Gondor .12 .30
❑ 4C135 War and Valor .12 .30
❑ 4C137 Attack on Helm's Deep .12 .30
❑ 4C141 Beyond Dark Mountains .12 .30
❑ 4C142 Broad-bladed Sword .12 .30
❑ 4C145 Cloud of Arrows .12 .30
❑ 4C151 Ferocity .12 .30
❑ 4C153 Grima, Son of Galmod .12 .30
❑ 4C156 Kill Them Now .12 .30
❑ 4C165 Orthanc Warrior .12 .30
❑ 4C175 Still They Came .12 .30
❑ 4C178 Unferth, Grima's Bodyguard .12 .30
❑ 4C180 Uruk Besieger .12 .30
❑ 4C181 Uruk Chaser .12 .30
❑ 4C183 Uruk Crossbowman .12 .30
❑ 4C184 Uruk Defender .12 .30
❑ 4C185 Uruk Fanatic .12 .30
❑ 4C187 Uruk Foot Soldier .12 .30
❑ 4C189 Uruk Plains Runner .12 .30
❑ 4C190 Uruk Pursuer .12 .30
❑ 4C191 Uruk Rear Guard .12 .30
❑ 4C192 Uruk Regular .12 .30
❑ 4C193 Uruk Runner .12 .30
❑ 4C195 Uruk Seeker .12 .30
❑ 4C196 Uruk Spear .12 .30
❑ 4C197 Uruk Stalker .12 .30
❑ 4C198 Uruk Stormer .12 .30
❑ 4C204 Uruk-hai Marauder .12 .30
❑ 4C206 Uruk-hai Patrol .12 .30
❑ 4C207 Uruk-hai Raiding Party .12 .30
❑ 4C210 We Are the Fighting Uruk-hai .12 .30
❑ 4C212 Weary .12 .30
❑ 4C221 Desert Spearman .12 .30

❑ 4C222 Desert Warrior .12 .30
❑ 4C224 Easterling Axeman .12 .30
❑ 4C226 Easterling Guard .12 .30
❑ 4C227 Easterling Infantry .12 .30
❑ 4C228 Easterling Lieutenant .12 .30
❑ 4C235 Gathering to the Summons .12 .30
❑ 4C239 Men of Rhun .12 .30
❑ 4C241 On the March .12 .30
❑ 4C248 Southron Bowman .12 .30
❑ 4C252 Southron Scout .12 .30
❑ 4C254 Southron Soldier .12 .30
❑ 4C255 Southron Spear .12 .30
❑ 4C258 Southron Wanderer .12 .30
❑ 4C260 Whirling Strike .12 .30
❑ 4C265 Elite Rider .12 .30
❑ 4C266 Eomer, Sister-son of Theoden .12 .30
❑ 4C270 Eowyn, Lady of Rohan .12 .30
❑ 4C273 Fight for the Villagers .12 .30
❑ 4C277 Guma, Plains Farmer .12 .30
❑ 4C278 Heavy Chain .12 .30
❑ 4C281 Hlafwine, Village Farmhand .12 .30
❑ 4C283 Horse of Rohan .12 .30
❑ 4C286 Rider of Rohan .12 .30
❑ 4C287 Rider's Mount .12 .30
❑ 4C288 Rider's Spear .12 .30
❑ 4C291 Sword of Rohan .12 .30
❑ 4C292 Theoden, Son of Thengel .12 .30
❑ 4C297 Work for the Sword .12 .30
❑ 4C298 Brace of Coneys .12 .30
❑ 4C302 Frodo, Tired Traveller .12 .30
❑ 4C306 Hobbit Sword .12 .30
❑ 4C308 Knocked on the Head .12 .30
❑ 4C310 Merry, Learned Guide .12 .30
❑ 4C314 Pippin, Woolly-footed Rascal .12 .30
❑ 4C316 Sam, Samwise the Brave .12 .30
❑ 4C319 Severed His Bonds .12 .30
❑ 4C321 Swiftly and Softly .12 .30
❑ 4C322 Warmed Up a Bit .12 .30
❑ 4P364A Aragorn, Wingfoot .40 1.00
❑ 4P364B Aragorn, Wingfoot TENGWAR
❑ 4P365 Theoden, Lord of the Mark .40 1.00
❑ 4R100A Shadowfax .60 1.50
❑ 4R100B Shadowfax TENGWAR
❑ 4R103A Treebeard, Earthborn .60 1.50
❑ 4R103B Treebeard, Earthborn TENGWAR
❑ 4R106 Well Met Indeed .60 1.50
❑ 4R107 Windows in a Stone Wall .60 1.50
❑ 4R111 Boromir, My Brother .60 1.50
❑ 4R116 Faramir, Captain of Gondor .60 1.50
❑ 4R118 Faramir's Bow 2.00 5.00
❑ 4R119 Faramir's Cloak .60 1.50
❑ 4R120 Forbidden Pool .60 1.50
❑ 4R121 Forests of Ithilien .60 1.50
❑ 4R124 Help in Doubt and Need .60 1.50
❑ 4R125 Henneth Annun .60 1.50
❑ 4R133 Ruins of Osgiliath .60 1.50
❑ 4R139 Banished .60 1.50
❑ 4R140 Beyond All Hope .60 1.50
❑ 4R144 Burning of Westfold .60 1.50
❑ 4R146 Come Down .60 1.50
❑ 4R149 Driven Back .60 1.50
❑ 4R150 Elite Crossbowmen .75 2.00
❑ 4R154A Grima, Wormtongue 1.25 3.00
❑ 4R154B Grima, Wormtongue TENGWAR
❑ 4R157 Leechcraft .60 1.50
❑ 4R158 Lieutenant of Orthanc .60 1.50
❑ 4R160 Mauhur, Patrol Leader .60 1.50
❑ 4R162 New Power Rising .60 1.50
❑ 4R163 No Dawn for Men .60 1.50
❑ 4R164 Orthanc Champion .75 2.00
❑ 4R166 The Palantir of Orthanc, Seventh Seeing-stone .60 1.50
❑ 4R167 Pillage of Rohan .60 1.50
❑ 4R168 Race Across the Mark .60 1.50
❑ 4R169 Ranged Commander .60 1.50
❑ 4R171 Rest While You Can .60 1.50
❑ 4R172 Rohan Is Mine .60 1.50
❑ 4R173A Saruman, Black Traitor 1.00 2.50
❑ 4R173B Saruman, Black Traitor TENGWAR
❑ 4R174 Saruman's Staff, Wizard's Device .75 2.00
❑ 4R176A Ugluk, Servant of Saruman .75 2.00
❑ 4R176B Ugluk, Servant of Saruman TENGWAR
❑ 4R177 Ugluk's Sword .60 1.50
❑ 4R179 Uruk Assault Band .60 1.50
❑ 4R186 Uruk Follower .60 1.50
❑ 4R199 Uruk Trooper .60 1.50
❑ 4R200 Uruk Vanguard .75 2.00
❑ 4R203 Uruk-hai Horde .60 1.50
❑ 4R209 Volley Fire .60 1.50
❑ 4R211 Weapons of Isengard 1.50 4.00
❑ 4R213 What Did You Discover? .60 1.50
❑ 4R214 Where Has Grima Stowed It? .60 1.50
❑ 4R215 Wounded .60 1.50
❑ 4R218 Desert Legion .75 2.00
❑ 4R219A Desert Lord 2.50 6.00
❑ 4R219B Desert Lord TENGWAR
❑ 4R223 Discovered .60 1.50
❑ 4R225A Easterling Captain .75 2.00
❑ 4R225B Easterling Captain TENGWAR
❑ 4R229 Easterling Skirmisher .60 1.50
❑ 4R231 Eastern Emyn Muil .60 1.50
❑ 4R237 Ithilien Wilderness .60 1.50
❑ 4R238 Men of Harad .60 1.50
❑ 4R240 New Fear 1.00 2.50
❑ 4R243 Rapid Fire .75 2.00
❑ 4R244 Regiment of Haradrim .60 1.50
❑ 4R245 Southron Archer .75 2.00
❑ 4R246 Southron Assassin .60 1.50
❑ 4R247 Southron Bow .75 2.00
❑ 4R251 Southron Fighter .60 1.50
❑ 4R256 Southron Troop .60 1.50
❑ 4R257 Southron Veterans .60 1.50
❑ 4R259 Vision From Afar 2.00 5.00
❑ 4R261 Wrath of Harad .60 1.50
❑ 4R262 Aldor, Soldier of Edoras .60 1.50
❑ 4R267 Eomer, Third Marshal of Riddermark 1.50 4.00
❑ 4R269 Eothain, Scout of the Mark .60 1.50
❑ 4R271 Eowyn, Sister-daughter of Theoden .60 1.50
❑ 4R272 Eowyn's Sword .75 2.00
❑ 4R274 Firefoot 1.00 2.50
❑ 4R279 Helm! Helm! .60 1.50
❑ 4R284 King's Mail .60 1.50
❑ 4R289A Simbelmyne 1.50 4.00
❑ 4R289B Simbelmyne TENGWAR
❑ 4R290 Supplies of the Mark .60 1.50
❑ 4R293 Valleys of the Mark .60 1.50
❑ 4R294 Weapon Store .75 2.00
❑ 4R299 Cliffs of Emyn Muil .75 2.00
❑ 4R300 Escape 1.00 2.50
❑ 4R301A Frodo, Courteous Halfling .60 1.50
❑ 4R301B Frodo, Courteous Halfling TENGWAR
❑ 4R303 Frodo's Cloak .60 1.50
❑ 4R304 Get On and Get Away .60 1.50
❑ 4R307 Impatient and Angry .60 1.50
❑ 4R311 Merry, Unquenchable Hobbit .60 1.50
❑ 4R313 Pippin, Just a Nuisance .60 1.50
❑ 4R315 Sam, Frodo's Gardener .60 1.50
❑ 4R317 Sam's Pack .60 1.50
❑ 4U101 Stump and Bramble .30 .75
❑ 4U108 Wizardry Indeed .30 .75
❑ 4U110 Arrows Thick in the Air .30 .75
❑ 4U114 Damrod, Ranger of Ithilien .30 .75
❑ 4U123 Hard Choice .30 .75
❑ 4U126 Ithilien Trap .30 .75
❑ 4U127 Mablung, Soldier of Gondor .30 .75
❑ 4U132 Ranger's Sword, Blade of Aragorn .30 .75
❑ 4U136 Advance Uruk Patrol .30 .75
❑ 4U138 Band of Uruk Bowmen .30 .75
❑ 4U143 Brought Back Alive .30 .75
❑ 4U147 Covering Fire .30 .75
❑ 4U148 Down to the Last Child .30 .75
❑ 4U152 Get Back .30 .75
❑ 4U155 Haunting Her Steps .30 .75
❑ 4U159 Many Riddles .30 .75
❑ 4U161 Men Will Fall .30 .75
❑ 4U170 Ranks Without Number .30 .75
❑ 4U182 Uruk Crossbow Troop .30 .75
❑ 4U188 Uruk Hunter .30 .75
❑ 4U194 Uruk Searcher .30 .75
❑ 4U201 Uruk Veteran .30 .75
❑ 4U202 Uruk-hai Band .30 .75
❑ 4U205 Uruk-hai Mob .30 .75
❑ 4U208 Vengeance .30 .75
❑ 4U216 Arrow From the South .30 .75
❑ 4U217 Desert Lancers .30 .75
❑ 4U220 Desert Soldier .30 .75
❑ 4U230 Easterling Trooper .30 .75
❑ 4U232 Elite Archer .30 .75
❑ 4U233 Fearless .30 .75
❑ 4U234 Flanking Attack .30 .75
❑ 4U236 Howl of Harad .30 .75
❑ 4U242 Raiders From the East .30 .75
❑ 4U249 Southron Commander .30 .75
❑ 4U250 Southron Explorer .30 .75
❑ 4U253 Southron Sentry .30 .75
❑ 4U263 Brego .30 .75
❑ 4U264 Ceorl, Weary Horseman .30 .75
❑ 4U268 Eomer's Spear .30 .75
❑ 4U275 Forth Eorlingas! .30 .75
❑ 4U276 Fortress Never Fallen .30 .75
❑ 4U280 Herugrim .30 .75
❑ 4U282 An Honorable Charge .30 .75
❑ 4U285 Leod, Westfold Herdsman .30 .75
❑ 4U295 Weland, Smith of the Riddermark .30 .75
❑ 4U296 Well Stored .30 .75
❑ 4U305 Good Work .30 .75
❑ 4U309 Light Shining Faintly .30 .75
❑ 4U312 Mind Your Own Affairs .30 .75
❑ 4U318 Seven We Had .30 .75
❑ 4U320 Store-room .30 .75
❑ 4U323 East Wall of Rohan .30 .75
❑ 4U324 Eastemnet Downs .30 .75
❑ 4U325 Eastemnet Gullies .30 .75
❑ 4U326 Horse-country .30 .75
❑ 4U327 Plains of Rohan .30 .75
❑ 4U328 The Riddermark .30 .75
❑ 4U329 Western Emyn Muil .30 .75
❑ 4U330 Derndingle .30 .75
❑ 4U331 Eastfold .30 .75
❑ 4U332 Fangorn Forest .30 .75
❑ 4U333 Plains of Rohan Camp .30 .75
❑ 4U334 Rohirrim Village .30 .75
❑ 4U335 Uruk Camp .30 .75
❑ 4U336 Wold of Rohan .30 .75
❑ 4U337 Barrows of Edoras .30 .75
❑ 4U338 Golden Hall .30 .75
❑ 4U339 Stables .30 .75
❑ 4U340 Streets of Edoras .30 .75
❑ 4U341 Throne Room .30 .75
❑ 4U342 Westemnet Plains .30 .75
❑ 4U343 Ered Nimrais .30 .75
❑ 4U344 Westemnet Hills .30 .75
❑ 4U345 White Mountains .30 .75
❑ 4U346 White Rocks .30 .75
❑ 4U347 Deep of Helm .30 .75
❑ 4U348 Deeping Wall .30 .75
❑ 4U349 Helm's Gate .30 .75
❑ 4U350 Hornburg Courtyard .30 .75
❑ 4U351 Hornburg Parapet .30 .75
❑ 4U352 Caves of Aglarond .30 .75
❑ 4U353 Great Hall .30 .75
❑ 4U354 Hornburg Armory .30 .75
❑ 4U355 Cavern Entrance .30 .75
❑ 4U356 Hornburg Causeway .30 .75
❑ 4U357 King's Room .30 .75
❑ 4U358 Ring of Isengard .30 .75
❑ 4U359 Wizard's Vale .30 .75
❑ 4U360 Fortress of Orthanc .30 .75
❑ 4U361 Orthanc Balcony .30 .75
❑ 4U362 Orthanc Library .30 .75
❑ 4U363 Palantir Chamber .30 .75

2003 Lord of the Rings Battle of Helm's Deep

COMPLETE SET (128) 25.00 50.00
BOOSTER BOX (36) 25.00 50.00
BOOSTER PACK 1.00 2.00

❑ 5C6 Defending the Keep .12 .30
❑ 5R3 Leaping Blaze .60 1.50
❑ 5R4 Wild Men of the Hills .60 1.50
❑ 5R5 Baruk Khazad .60 1.50
❑ 5R7 Gimli, Skilled Defender .60 1.50
❑ 5U1 Dunlending Rampager .30 .75
❑ 5U2 Dunlending Renegade .30 .75
❑ 5U8 Horn of Helm .30 .75
❑ 5U9 More to My Liking .30 .75
❑ 5C14 That Is No Orc Horn .12 .30
❑ 5C17 Forest Guardian .12 .30
❑ 5C24 Gollum, Nasty Treacherous Creature .12 .30
❑ 5C27 Poor Wretch .12 .30
❑ 5C28 Smeagol, Old Noser .12 .30
❑ 5C30 We Must Have It .12 .30
❑ 5C32 Citadel of the Stars .12 .30
❑ 5C33 City Wall .12 .30
❑ 5C35 Gondorian Knight .12 .30
❑ 5C36 Knight of Gondor .12 .30
❑ 5C37 Men of Numenor .12 .30
❑ 5C40 Take Cover .12 .30
❑ 5C43 War Must Be .12 .30
❑ 5C52 Isengard Flanker .12 .30
❑ 5C53 Isengard Rider .12 .30
❑ 5C61 Uruk Engineer .12 .30
❑ 5C62 Uruk Sapper .12 .30
❑ 5C65 Warg .12 .30
❑ 5C66 Warg-master .12 .30
❑ 5C67 Warg-rider .12 .30
❑ 5C68 Wolf-voices .12 .30
❑ 5C73 Mumak .12 .30
❑ 5C74 Southron Marcher .12 .30
❑ 5C75 Southron Runner .12 .30
❑ 5C76 Southron Traveler .12 .30
❑ 5C81 Ecglaf, Courageous Farmer .12 .30
❑ 5C83 Household Guard .12 .30
❑ 5C85 Let Us Be Swift .12 .30
❑ 5C88 Rohirrim Bow .12 .30
❑ 5C90 Rohirrim Scout .12 .30
❑ 5C91 Rohirrim Shield .12 .30
❑ 5C93 Theoden, King of the Golden Hall .12 .30
❑ 5C97 Gate Soldier .12 .30
❑ 5C98 Gate Trooper .12 .30
❑ 5C99 Gate Veteran .12 .30
❑ 5R11 Break the Charge .60 1.50
❑ 5R16 Down From the Hills .60 1.50
❑ 5R18 Fury of the White Rider .60 1.50
❑ 5R19 Lindenroot, Elder Shepherd .60 1.50
❑ 5R21 Be Back Soon .60 1.50
❑ 5R25A Gollum, Stinker 2.00 5.00
❑ 5R25B Gollum, Stinker TENGWAR
❑ 5R29A Smeagol, Slinker .60 1.50
❑ 5R29B Smeagol, Slinker TENGWAR
❑ 5R31 Alcarin, Warrior of Lamedon .60 1.50
❑ 5R39 Stone Tower .60 1.50
❑ 5R41 These Are My People .60 1.50
❑ 5R46 Berserk Savage .60 1.50
❑ 5R47 Berserk Slayer .60 1.50
❑ 5R49 Devilry of Orthanc .60 1.50
❑ 5R50 Foul Horde .60 1.50
❑ 5R51 Grima, Chief Counselor .60 1.50
❑ 5R56 Saruman, Master of Foul Folk .60 1.50
❑ 5R58 Sharku, Warg-captain .60 1.50
❑ 5R59 Sharku's Warg .75 2.00
❑ 5R69 Wolves of Isengard .60 1.50
❑ 5R70 Army of Haradrim .60 1.50
❑ 5R71 Company of Haradrim .60 1.50
❑ 5R72 Desert Stalker .60 1.50
❑ 5R78 War Mumak 1.25 3.00
❑ 5R82 Gamling, Warrior of Rohan .60 1.50
❑ 5R84 I Am Here .60 1.50
❑ 5R86 No Rest for the Weary .60 1.50
❑ 5R89 Rohirrim Helm .60 1.50
❑ 5R94 Thundering Host .60 1.50
❑ 5R95 Dead Marshes .60 1.50
❑ 5R96 Eye of Barad-Dur .60 1.50
❑ 5U10 Balglin, Elven Warrior .30 .75
❑ 5U12 Legolas' Sword .30 .75
❑ 5U13 Taurnil, Sharp-eyed Bowman .30 .75
❑ 5U15 Birchseed, Tall Statesman .30 .75
❑ 5U20 Turn of the Tide .30 .75
❑ 5U22 Evil-smelling Fens .30 .75
❑ 5U23 Follow Smeagol .30 .75
❑ 5U26 Look at Him .30 .75
❑ 5U34 Fall Back .30 .75
❑ 5U38 Rally Point .30 .75
❑ 5U42 Turgon, Man of Belfalas .30 .75
❑ 5U44 Battering Ram .30 .75
❑ 5U45 Berserk Rager .30 .75
❑ 5U48 Black Shapes Crawling .30 .75
❑ 5U54 Isengard Scimitar .30 .75
❑ 5U55 Isengard Scout Troop .30 .75
❑ 5U57 Scaling Ladder .30 .75
❑ 5U60 Siege Engine .30 .75
❑ 5U63 Uruk-hai Berserker .30 .75
❑ 5U64 War-warg .30 .75
❑ 5U77 Strength in Numbers .30 .75
❑ 5U79 Armory .30 .75
❑ 5U80 Arrow-slits .30 .75
❑ 5U87 Parapet .30 .75
❑ 5U92 Sigewulf, Brave Volunteer .30 .75
❑ 5C106 Orc Infantry .12 .30
❑ 5C108 Orc Pursuer .12 .30
❑ 5C109 Orc Runner .12 .30
❑ 5C117 You Must Help Us .12 .30
❑ 5P121 Legolas, Archer of Mirkwood .40 1.00
❑ 5P122 Eowyn, Daughter of Eomund .40 1.00
❑ 5R100A Grishnakh, Orc Captain 2.00 5.00
❑ 5R100B Grishnakh, Orc Captain TENGWAR
❑ 5R102 Morannon .60 1.50
❑ 5R103 Orc Captain .60 1.50
❑ 5R112 No Help for It .60 1.50
❑ 5R113 No Use That Way .60 1.50
❑ 5R116A Sting, Baggins Heirloom 1.50 4.00
❑ 5R116B Sting, Baggins Heirloom TENGWAR
❑ 5R123 Baruk Khazad .40 1.00
❑ 5R124 Break the Charge .40 1.00
❑ 5R125 Foul Horde .40 1.00
❑ 5R126 Army of Haradrim .40 1.00
❑ 5R127 Rohirrim Helm .40 1.00
❑ 5R128 Thundering Host .40 1.00
❑ 5U101 I'd Make You Squeak .30 .75
❑ 5U104 Orc Cutthroat .30 .75
❑ 5U105 Orc Fighter .30 .75
❑ 5U107 Orc Patrol .30 .75
❑ 5U110 Teeth of Mordor .30 .75
❑ 5U111 Frodo, Master of the Precious .30 .75
❑ 5U114 Rare Good Ballast .30 .75
❑ 5U115 Sam, Nice Sensible Hobbit .30 .75
❑ 5U118 Hornburg Wall .30 .75
❑ 5U119 Nan Curunir .30 .75
❑ 5U120 Caverns of Isengard .30 .75

2003 Lord of the Rings Ents of Fagorn

COMPLETE SET (128) 15.00 30.00
BOOSTER BOX (36) 20.00 40.00
BOOSTER PACK 1.00 2.00

❑ 6C1 Bound By Rage .12 .30
❑ 6C2 Dunlending Elder .12 .30
❑ 6C3 Dunlending Footmen .12 .30
❑ 6C4 Dunlending Headman .12 .30
❑ 6C5 Dunlending Reserve .12 .30
❑ 6R6 Hill Clan .60 1.50
❑ 6R7 Ready to Fall .75 2.00
❑ 6U8 Too Long Have These Peasants Stood .30 .75
❑ 6U9 Lend Us Your Aid .30 .75
❑ 6C10 Suspended Palaces .12 .30
❑ 6C12 Agility .12 .30
❑ 6C17 Forewarned .12 .30
❑ 6C21 Naith Longbow .12 .30
❑ 6C27 Ent Avenger .12 .30
❑ 6C29 Ent Moot .12 .30
❑ 6C33 Quickbeam, Bregalad .12 .30
❑ 6C34 Roused .12 .30
❑ 6C37 Treebeard, Guardian of the Forest .12 .30
❑ 6C38 Don't Follow the Lights .12 .30
❑ 6C40 Gollum, Old Villain .12 .30
❑ 6C42 Nasty, Foul Hobbitses .12 .30
❑ 6C43 Not Listening .12 .30
❑ 6C45 Smeagol, Poor Creature .12 .30
❑ 6C47 You're a Liar and a Thief .12 .30
❑ 6C48 Anborn, Skilled Huntsman .12 .30
❑ 6C52 Garrison of Osgiliath .12 .30
❑ 6C53 Mortal Men .12 .30
❑ 6C56 Trust .12 .30
❑ 6C59 Banner of Isengard .12 .30
❑ 6C65 Isengard Artisan .12 .30
❑ 6C67 Isengard Journeyman .12 .30
❑ 6C69 Isengard Plodder .12 .30
❑ 6C71 Isengard Tinker .12 .30
❑ 6C72 Rohirrim Traitor .12 .30
❑ 6C81 Southron Invaders .12 .30
❑ 6C95 Hrethel, Rider of Rohan .12 .30
❑ 6C97 We Left None Alive .12 .30
❑ 6C98 Banner of the Eye .12 .30
❑ 6C99 Corpse Lights .12 .30
❑ 6R11 Toss Me .60 1.50
❑ 6R15 Elrond, Keeper of Vilya .60 1.50
❑ 6R18 Galadriel, Keeper of Nenya .60 1.50
❑ 6R23 Naith Warband .60 1.50
❑ 6R26 Enraged .75 2.00
❑ 6R28 Ent Horde .60 1.50
❑ 6R30 Gandalf, Mithrandir .60 1.50
❑ 6R31 Glamdring, Lightning Brand .60 1.50
❑ 6R35 Skinbark, Fladrif .60 1.50
❑ 6R39 Don't Look at Them .75 2.00
❑ 6R41 Master Broke His Promise .60 1.50
❑ 6R44 Safe Paths .60 1.50
❑ 6R46 They Stole It .75 2.00
❑ 6R49 Ancient Roads .60 1.50
❑ 6R50 Aragorn, Defender of Free Peoples .75 2.00
❑ 6R55 Ring of Barahir .60 1.50
❑ 6R57 Agents of Orthanc .60 1.50
❑ 6R60 Berserk Butcher .60 1.50
❑ 6R62 Fires and Foul Fumes .60 1.50
❑ 6R68 Isengard Mechanics .60 1.50
❑ 6R74 Sharku, Vile Marauder .60 1.50
❑ 6R76 The Balrog, Terror of Flame and Shadow 1.25 3.00
❑ 6R77 Durin's Tower .60 1.50
❑ 6R78 Easterling Army 1.00 2.50
❑ 6R80 Southron Archer Legion .60 1.50
❑ 6R82 Trample .60 1.50
❑ 6R85 Sword of Dol Guldur .60 1.50
❑ 6R88A Ulaire Toldea, Winged Sentry 1.00 2.50
❑ 6R88B Ulaire Toldea, Winged Sentry TENGWAR
❑ 6R89 Winged and Ominous .60 1.50
❑ 6R92 Eomer, Rohirrim Captain .60 1.50
❑ 6R94 Hama, Doorward of Theoden .60 1.50
❑ 6R96 News From the Mark .60 1.50
❑ 6U13 Arwen, Evenstar of Her People .30 .75
❑ 6U14 Banner of Elbereth .30 .75
❑ 6U16 Forearmed .30 .75
❑ 6U19 Gift of Foresight .30 .75
❑ 6U20 Must Be a Dream .30 .75
❑ 6U22 Naith Troop .30 .75
❑ 6U24 Boomed and Trumpeted .30 .75
❑ 6U25 Crack Into Rubble .30 .75
❑ 6U32 Host of Fangorn .30 .75
❑ 6U36 Threw Down My Enemy .30 .75
❑ 6U51 Banner of Westernesse .30 .75
❑ 6U54 Perilous Ventures .30 .75
❑ 6U58 Assault Ladder .30 .75
❑ 6U61 Desertion .30 .75
❑ 6U63 Gnawing, Biting, Hacking, Burning .30 .75
❑ 6U64 Iron Fist of the Orc .30 .75
❑ 6U66 Isengard Builder .30 .75
❑ 6U70 Isengard Tender .30 .75
❑ 6U73 Scaffolding .30 .75
❑ 6U75 Twisted Tales .30 .75
❑ 6U79 Easterling Polearm .30 .75
❑ 6U83 Fell Beast .30 .75
❑ 6U84 Spied From Above .30 .75
❑ 6U86 Ulaire Lemenya, Winged Hunter .30 .75
❑ 6U87 Ulaire Nertea, Winged Hunter .30 .75
❑ 6U90 Banner of the Mark .30 .75
❑ 6U91 Blood Has Been Spilled .30 .75
❑ 6U93 Ever the Hope of Men .30 .75
❑ 6C100 Dead Ones .12 .30
❑ 6C102 Gate Sentry .12 .30
❑ 6C108 Wisp of Pale Sheen .12 .30
❑ 6C111 Kept Safe .12 .30
❑ 6C112 Long Slow Wrath .12 .30
❑ 6P121 Faramir, Ithilien Ranger .60 1.50
❑ 6P122 The Witch-king, Deathless Lord .60 1.50
❑ 6R101 Gate Picket .60 1.50
❑ 6R103 Gate Troll .60 1.50
❑ 6R106 Troll of Udun .60 1.50
❑ 6R109 Held .60 1.50
❑ 6R113 Merry, Impatient Hobbit .60 1.50
❑ 6R114 Pippin, Hastiest of All .60 1.50
❑ 6R123 Enraged 1.00 2.50
❑ 6R124 Skinbark, Fladrif .60 1.50
❑ 6R125 Don't Look at Them 1.50 4.00
❑ 6R126 Ancient Roads .75 2.00
❑ 6R127 Isengard Mechanics .60 1.50
❑ 6R128 Gate Troll .60 1.50
❑ 6U104 Orc Insurgent .30 .75
❑ 6U105 Peril .30 .75
❑ 6U107 Troll's Chain .30 .75
❑ 6U110 It Burns Us .30 .75
❑ 6U115 Rocks of Emyn Muil .30 .75
❑ 6U116 Westfold .30 .75
❑ 6U117 Meduseld .30 .75
❑ 6U118 Hornburg Hall .30 .75
❑ 6U119 Valley of Saruman .30 .75
❑ 6U120 Saruman's Laboratory .30 .75

2003 Lord of the Rings The Return of the King

COMPLETE SET (367) 75.00 150.00
BOOSTER BOX (36) 25.00 50.00
BOOSTER PACK 1.00 2.00

❑ 7C1 The One Ring, The Ruling Ring .12 .30
❑ 7C4 Calculated Risk .12 .30
❑ 7C6 Gimli, Faithful Companion .12 .30
❑ 7R5 Dark Ways .75 2.00
❑ 7R7 Gimli, Feared Axeman .60 1.50
❑ 7R9 Gimli's Battle Axe, Trusted Weapon 1.00 2.50
❑ 7U3 Battle Tested .30 .75
❑ 7U8 Gimli's Armor .30 .75
❑ 7C11 Out of Darkness .12 .30
❑ 7C20 Defiance .12 .30
❑ 7C23 Into the West .12 .30
❑ 7C26 Legolas, Nimble Warrior .12 .30
❑ 7C29 Still Needed .12 .30
❑ 7C30 Uncertain Paths .12 .30
❑ 7C31 All Save One .12 .30
❑ 7C34 Echoes of Valinor .12 .30
❑ 7C36 Gandalf, Defender of the West .12 .30
❑ 7C40 Have Patience .12 .30

TCG/CCG

Card	Low	High
☐ 7C41 Intimidate	.12	.30
☐ 7C46 Peace of Mind	.12	.30
☐ 7C51 Undaunted	.12	.30
☐ 7C52 Wizard Staff	.12	.30
☐ 7C53 Captured by the Ring	.12	.30
☐ 7C59 Gollum, Vile Creature	.12	.30
☐ 7C62 It's Mine	.12	.30
☐ 7C65 Never	.12	.30
☐ 7C72 Smeagol, Hurried Guide	.12	.30
☐ 7C75 Sweeter Meats	.12	.30
☐ 7C76 Very Nice Friends	.12	.30
☐ 7C81 Aragorn, Captain of Gondor	.12	.30
☐ 7C82 Cirion	.12	.30
☐ 7C83 City of Men	.12	.30
☐ 7C84 Dagger Strike	.12	.30
☐ 7C86 Denethor, Wizened Steward	.12	.30
☐ 7C89 Duty of Two	.12	.30
☐ 7C90 Faramir, Stout Captain	.12	.30
☐ 7C92 First Level	.12	.30
☐ 7C96 Gondorian Captain	.12	.30
☐ 7C99 Great Gate	.12	.30
☐ 7R10 Loyalty Unshaken	1.00	2.50
☐ 7R12 Preparations	1.00	2.50
☐ 7R16 Arwen, Fair Elf Maiden	.60	1.50
☐ 7R17 Asfaloth, Elven Steed	1.00	2.50
☐ 7R18 Bow of the Galadhrim, Gift of Galadriel	.60	1.50
☐ 7R21 Elrond, Elven Lord	.75	2.00
☐ 7R22 Hope Comes	.60	1.50
☐ 7R24 Leaving Forever	.60	1.50
☐ 7R25 Legolas, Fearless Marksman	.60	1.50
☐ 7R27 Mirkwood Bowman	.60	1.50
☐ 7R28 Shadow Between	1.25	3.00
☐ 7R2a The One Ring, Such a Weight to Carry	3.00	8.00
☐ 7R2b The One Ring, Such A Weight To Carry TENGWAR		
☐ 7R32 The Board Is Set	.60	1.50
☐ 7R33 Citadel to Gate	.60	1.50
☐ 7R37 Gandalf, Manager of Wizards	1.50	4.00
☐ 7R38 Gandalf's Staff, Focus of Power	1.25	3.00
☐ 7R39 Glamdring, Elven Blade	1.25	3.00
☐ 7R43 Light the Beacons	.60	1.50
☐ 7R44 Moment of Respite	1.25	3.00
☐ 7R48 Stay This Madness	.60	1.50
☐ 7R50 Terrible and Evil	1.50	4.00
☐ 7R56 The Dead City	.60	1.50
☐ 7R57 Fat One Wants It	.60	1.50
☐ 7R58 Gollum, Plotting Deceiver	.60	1.50
☐ 7R61 Hobbitses Are Dead	1.25	3.00
☐ 7R63 Let Her Deal With Them	1.25	3.00
☐ 7R66 No Safe Places	.60	1.50
☐ 7R67 Plotting	1.25	3.00
☐ 7R68 Scouting	.60	1.50
☐ 7R69 Secret Paths	.60	1.50
☐ 7R70 Serving the Precious	.60	1.50
☐ 7R71 Smeagol, Always Helps	1.25	3.00
☐ 7R73 Sneaking!	1.25	3.00
☐ 7R74 So Polite	.60	1.50
☐ 7R80 Anduril, King's Blade	1.00	2.50
☐ 7R85 Denethor, Steward of the City	.60	1.50
☐ 7R87 Derufin	.60	1.50
☐ 7R91 Faramir, Wizard's Pupil	.60	1.50
☐ 7R95 Gondor Still Stands	.60	1.50
☐ 7R97 Gondorian Merchant	.60	1.50
☐ 7U13 Reckless Pride	.30	.75
☐ 7U14 Slaked Thirsts	.30	.75
☐ 7U15 Ancient Blade	.30	.75
☐ 7U19 Careful Study	.30	.75
☐ 7U35 Fool's Hope	.30	.75
☐ 7U42 King's Advisor	.30	.75
☐ 7U45 Numenor's Pride	.30	.75
☐ 7U47 Sharpen Your Swords	.30	.75
☐ 7U49 Steadfast Champion	.30	.75
☐ 7U54 Clever Hobbits	.30	.75
☐ 7U55 Days Growing Dark	.30	.75
☐ 7U60 Heavy Burden	.30	.75
☐ 7U64 Nasty	.30	.75
☐ 7U77 We Hates Them	.30	.75
☐ 7U78 Where Shall We Go	.30	.75
☐ 7U88 Dervorin	.30	.75
☐ 7U93 Footman's Armor	.30	.75
☐ 7U94 Gondor Bow	.30	.75
☐ 7U98 Gondorian Sword	.30	.75
☐ 7C105 I Will Go	.12	.30
☐ 7C106 Ingold	.12	.30
☐ 7C108 Knight's Spear	.12	.30
☐ 7C111 Man the Walls	.12	.30
☐ 7C115 Ranger of Minas Tirith	.12	.30
☐ 7C116 Ranger of Osgiliath	.12	.30
☐ 7C117 Reckless Counter	.12	.30
☐ 7C118 Second Level	.12	.30
☐ 7C121 Stout Resistance	.12	.30
☐ 7C124 Targon	.12	.30
☐ 7C130 Dark Tidings	.12	.30
☐ 7C131 Desert Fighter	.12	.30
☐ 7C132 Desert Nomad	.12	.30
☐ 7C133 Desert Runner	.12	.30
☐ 7C135 Desert Sneak	.12	.30
☐ 7C137 Desert Spearman	.12	.30
☐ 7C139 Easterling Aggressor	.12	.30
☐ 7C140 Easterling Assailant	.12	.30
☐ 7C141 Easterling Attacker	.12	.30
☐ 7C142 Easterling Blademaster	.12	.30
☐ 7C144 Easterling Ransacker	.12	.30
☐ 7C149 Great Beasts	.12	.30
☐ 7C150 Harsh Tongues	.12	.30
☐ 7C153 Mumakil of the Harad	.12	.30
☐ 7C154 New Strength Came Now	.12	.30
☐ 7C155 Raider Bow	.12	.30
☐ 7C156 Raider Halberd	.12	.30
☐ 7C161 Southron Brigand	.12	.30
☐ 7C172 Troop of Haradrim	.12	.30
☐ 7C173 War Towers	.12	.30
☐ 7C184 More Unbearable	.12	.30
☐ 7C186 Morgul Axe	.12	.30
☐ 7C189 Morgul Cur	.12	.30
☐ 7C192 Morgul Hound	.12	.30
☐ 7C193 Morgul Lackey	.12	.30
☐ 7C194 Morgul Mongrel	.12	.30
☐ 7C196 Morgul Predator	.12	.30
☐ 7C198 Morgul Ruffian	.12	.30
☐ 7C199 Morgul Soldier	.12	.30
☐ 7C200 Morgul Spawn	.12	.30
☐ 7C201 Morgul Spearman	.12	.30
☐ 7C208 There Came a Cry	.12	.30
☐ 7C209 Too Late	.12	.30
☐ 7C220 War Long Planned	.12	.30
☐ 7C222 Deor	.12	.30
☐ 7C225 Elite Rider	.12	.30
☐ 7C226 Enraged Horseman	.12	.30
☐ 7C229 Eowyn, Restless Maiden	.12	.30
☐ 7C235 Guthlaf, Herald	.12	.30

Card	Low	High
☐ 7C237 His Golden Shield	.12	.30
☐ 7C240 Long Spear	.12	.30
☐ 7C243 Morning Came	.12	.30
☐ 7C246 Rohirrim Guard	.12	.30
☐ 7C247 Rohirrim Herdsman	.12	.30
☐ 7C248 Rohirrim Javelin	.12	.30
☐ 7C253 Swift Steed	.12	.30
☐ 7C256 They Sang as They Slew	.12	.30
☐ 7C257 Veteran Horseman	.12	.30
☐ 7C259 Wind in His Face	.12	.30
☐ 7C262 Above the Battlement	.12	.30
☐ 7C263 Anguish	.12	.30
☐ 7C265 Besieging Pike	.12	.30
☐ 7C273 Gorgoroth Garrison	.12	.30
☐ 7C275 Gorgoroth Pillager	.12	.30
☐ 7C276 Gorgoroth Ransacker	.12	.30
☐ 7C277 Gorgoroth Sapper	.12	.30
☐ 7C285 Mordor Defender	.12	.30
☐ 7C287 Mordor Guard	.12	.30
☐ 7C288 Mordor Regular	.12	.30
☐ 7C290 Mordor Soldier	.12	.30
☐ 7C291 Mordor Trooper	.12	.30
☐ 7C296 Orc Brood	.12	.30
☐ 7C297 Orc Butcher	.12	.30
☐ 7C298 Orc Chaser	.12	.30
☐ 7C299 Orc Destroyer	.12	.30
☐ 7C300 Orc Fanatic	.12	.30
☐ 7C303 Orc Pursuer	.12	.30
☐ 7C304 Orc Rager	.12	.30
☐ 7C312 Siegecraft	.12	.30
☐ 7C313 Some Secret Art of Flame	.12	.30
☐ 7C315 Tower Walkway	.12	.30
☐ 7C317 Frodo, Hope of Free Peoples	.12	.30
☐ 7C319 Hobbit Sword	.12	.30
☐ 7C320 Merry, Rohirrim Squire	.12	.30
☐ 7C322 Noble Intentions	.12	.30
☐ 7C323 Pippin, Sworn to Service	.12	.30
☐ 7C326 Sam, Needer of Vittles	.12	.30
☐ 7P364 Aragorn, Driven by Need	1.00	2.50
☐ 7P365 Eomer, Valiant Warchief	.40	1.00
☐ 7R100 Greatest Stronghold	.60	1.50
☐ 7R101 Guarded	.60	1.50
☐ 7R103 Hearts Raised	.75	2.00
☐ 7R104 Hidden Knowledge	.60	1.50
☐ 7R112 Noble Leaders	3.00	8.00
☐ 7R113 Pippin's Armor	.60	1.50
☐ 7R114 Pippin's Sword	.60	1.50
☐ 7R119 Seventh Level	.60	1.50
☐ 7R122 Strong and Old	.60	1.50
☐ 7R127 Vorondil	.60	1.50
☐ 7R129 Bold Men and Grim	1.00	2.50
☐ 7R143 Easterling Footman	.60	1.50
☐ 7R145 Easterling Regiment	.60	1.50
☐ 7R148 Fierce in Despair	1.00	2.50
☐ 7R152 Mumak Commander	.60	1.50
☐ 7R158 Rout	.60	1.50
☐ 7R159 Small Hope	2.00	5.00
☐ 7R163 Southron Chieftain	.60	1.50
☐ 7R164 Southron Conqueror	.60	1.50
☐ 7R165 Southron Intruder	.60	1.50
☐ 7R166 Southron Leader	.60	1.50
☐ 7R167 Southron Marksmen	.75	2.00
☐ 7R169 Surging Up	.60	1.50
☐ 7R170 Suzerain of Harad	.60	1.50
☐ 7R177 Feel His Blade	.60	1.50
☐ 7R179 Ghastly Host	.60	1.50
☐ 7R180 Gorbag, Lieutenant of Cirith Ungol	1.00	2.50
☐ 7R181 Held Ground	.60	1.50
☐ 7R182 Loathsome	.60	1.50
☐ 7R183 Mind and Body	.75	2.00
☐ 7R188 Morgul Brute	5.00	10.00
☐ 7R191 Morgul Detachment	.75	2.00
☐ 7R197 Morgul Regiment	.60	1.50
☐ 7R204 Out of Sight and Shot	1.25	3.00
☐ 7R205 Put Forth His Strength	.60	1.50
☐ 7R206 Stronghold of Minas Morgul	.75	2.00
☐ 7R210 Ulaire Attea, Wraith on Wings	1.25	3.00
☐ 7R211a Ulaire Cantea, Faster Than Winds	.75	2.00
☐ 7R211b Ulaire Cantea, Faster Than Winds TENGWAR		
☐ 7R213 Ulaire Lemenya, Assailing Minion	.60	1.50
☐ 7R215 Ulaire Nelya, Assailing Minion	.60	1.50
☐ 7R219 Ulaire Toldea, Wraith on Wings	1.00	2.50
☐ 7R221a The Witch-king, Morgul King	.75	2.00
☐ 7R221b The Witch-king, Morgul King TENGWAR		
☐ 7R223 Death They Cried	.60	1.50
☐ 7R227a Eomer, Skilled Tactician	.75	2.00
☐ 7R227b Eomer, Skilled Tactician TENGWAR		
☐ 7R228 Eowyn, Dernhelm	.60	1.50
☐ 7R230 Eowyn's Sword, Dernhelm's Blade	1.25	3.00
☐ 7R232 Firefoot, Eomer's Steed	.60	1.50
☐ 7R233 Grimbold, Marshal of Rohan	1.00	2.50
☐ 7R236 Herugrim, Sword of the Mark	.60	1.50
☐ 7R239 Leowyn	.60	1.50
☐ 7R241 Merry's Armor	.75	2.00
☐ 7R242 Merry's Sword	.75	2.00
☐ 7R249 Seeking New Foes	.60	1.50
☐ 7R250 Snowmane	.60	1.50
☐ 7R251 Stern People	.60	1.50
☐ 7R255 Theoden, Rekindled King	.60	1.50
☐ 7R260 Windfola	.60	1.50
☐ 7R261 With Strength to Fight	1.00	2.50
☐ 7R266 Breached	.60	1.50
☐ 7R267 Din of Arms	1.00	2.50
☐ 7R268 Encirclement	.60	1.50
☐ 7R269 Fires Raged Unchecked	.60	1.50
☐ 7R274 Gorgoroth Officer	.60	1.50
☐ 7R279 Gorgoroth Troop	1.25	3.00
☐ 7R283 Legions of Morgul	.60	1.50
☐ 7R284 Mordor Assassin	.60	1.50
☐ 7R286 Mordor Fighter	.60	1.50
☐ 7R306 Orc Seeker	.60	1.50
☐ 7R308 Rally the Host	.60	1.50
☐ 7R311 Siege Commander	.60	1.50
☐ 7R314 Stronghold of Cirith Ungol	.60	1.50
☐ 7R316 Troop Tower	2.00	5.00
☐ 7R318 Frodo, Wicked Masster!	.60	1.50
☐ 7R321a Merry, Swordthain	.75	2.00
☐ 7R321b Merry, Swordthain TENGWAR		
☐ 7R324a Pippin, Wearer of Black and Silver	1.00	2.50
☐ 7R324b Pippin, Wearer of Black and Silver TENGWAR		
☐ 7R325 Pressing On	.60	1.50
☐ 7R327 Sam, Resolute Halfling	.60	1.50
☐ 7R79a Anduril, Flame of the West	5.00	10.00
☐ 7R79b Anduril, Flame of the West TENGWAR		
☐ 7U102 Hasty Repairs	.30	.75
☐ 7U107 Iorlas	.30	.75
☐ 7U109 Long Prepared	.30	.75
☐ 7U110 Madril, Faramir's Aide	.30	.75
☐ 7U120 Stand to Arms	.30	.75
☐ 7U123 Support of the City	.30	.75

Card	Low	High
☐ 7U125 Third Level	.30	.75
☐ 7U126 Unexpected Visitor	.30	.75
☐ 7U128 While We Yet Live	.30	.75
☐ 7U134 Desert Scout	.30	.75
☐ 7U136 Desert Soldier	.30	.75
☐ 7U138 Desert Villain	.30	.75
☐ 7U146 Easterling Sergeant	.30	.75
☐ 7U147 Easterling Veteran	.30	.75
☐ 7U151 Hosts Still Unfought	.30	.75
☐ 7U157 Red Wrath	.30	.75
☐ 7U160 Southron Bandit	.30	.75
☐ 7U162 Southron Captain	.30	.75
☐ 7U168 Southron Thief	.30	.75
☐ 7U171 Thrice Outnumbered	.30	.75
☐ 7U174 Called	.30	.75
☐ 7U175 Corrupt	.30	.75
☐ 7U176 Disposable Servants	.30	.75
☐ 7U178 Foul Clutches	.30	.75
☐ 7U185 Morgul Answers	.30	.75
☐ 7U187 Morgul Brawler	.30	.75
☐ 7U190 Morgul Destroyer	.30	.75
☐ 7U195 Morgul on the March	.30	.75
☐ 7U202 Morgul Whelp	.30	.75
☐ 7U203 Nazgul Scimitar	.30	.75
☐ 7U207 Their Power Is in Terror	.30	.75
☐ 7U212 Ulaire Enquea, Faster Than Winds	.30	.75
☐ 7U214 Ulaire Lemenya, Wraith on Wings	.30	.75
☐ 7U216 Ulaire Nelya, Black-Mantled Wraith	.30	.75
☐ 7U217 Ulaire Nertea, Black-Mantled Wraith	.30	.75
☐ 7U218 Ulaire Otsea, Black-Mantled Wraith	.30	.75
☐ 7U224 Elfhelm, Marshal of Rohan	.30	.75
☐ 7U231 Fey He Seemed	.30	.75
☐ 7U234 Guarded Fastness	.30	.75
☐ 7U238 Knights of His House	.30	.75
☐ 7U244 Mustering for Battle	.30	.75
☐ 7U245 Riding Armor	.30	.75
☐ 7U252 Strong Arms	.30	.75
☐ 7U254 Theoden, Leader of Spears	.30	.75
☐ 7U258 White Hot Fury	.30	.75
☐ 7U264 Army of Udun	.30	.75
☐ 7U270 Gorgoroth Attacker	.30	.75
☐ 7U271 Gorgoroth Axeman	.30	.75
☐ 7U272 Gorgoroth Engineer	.30	.75
☐ 7U278 Gorgoroth Soldier	.30	.75
☐ 7U280 Great Peril of Fire	.30	.75
☐ 7U281 Great Siege-towers	.30	.75
☐ 7U282 Host of Udun	.30	.75
☐ 7U289 Mordor Savage	.30	.75
☐ 7U292 Mordor Veteran	.30	.75
☐ 7U293 Mordor Warrior	.30	.75
☐ 7U294 Orc Archer Troop	.30	.75
☐ 7U295 Orc Assault Band	.30	.75
☐ 7U301 Orc Marauder	.30	.75
☐ 7U302 Orc Officer	.30	.75
☐ 7U305 Orc Savage	.30	.75
☐ 7U307 Orc Stalker	.30	.75
☐ 7U309 Rope and Winch	.30	.75
☐ 7U310 Sauron's Hatred	.30	.75
☐ 7U328 Slow-kindled Courage	.30	.75
☐ 7U329 Dunharrow Plateau	.30	.75
☐ 7U330 Edoras Hall	.30	.75
☐ 7U331 Isengard Ruined	.30	.75
☐ 7U332 Rohirrim Road	.30	.75
☐ 7U333 Sleeping Quarters	.30	.75
☐ 7U334 Steps of Edoras	.30	.75
☐ 7U335 King's Tent	.30	.75
☐ 7U336 Rohirrim Camp	.30	.75
☐ 7U337 West Road	.30	.75
☐ 7U338 Beacon of Minas Tirith	.30	.75
☐ 7U339 Hall of the Kings	.30	.75
☐ 7U340 Tower of Ecthelion	.30	.75
☐ 7U341 Anduin Banks	.30	.75
☐ 7U342 Osgiliath Fallen	.30	.75
☐ 7U343 Pelennor Plain	.30	.75
☐ 7U344 City Gates	.30	.75
☐ 7U345 Pelennor Flat	.30	.75
☐ 7U346 Minas Tirith Fifth Circle	.30	.75
☐ 7U347 Minas Tirith First Circle	.30	.75
☐ 7U348 Minas Tirith Fourth Circle	.30	.75
☐ 7U349 Minas Tirith Second Circle	.30	.75
☐ 7U350 Minas Tirith Seventh Circle	.30	.75
☐ 7U351 Minas Tirith Sixth Circle	.30	.75
☐ 7U352 Minas Tirith Third Circle	.30	.75
☐ 7U353 Osgiliath Crossing	.30	.75
☐ 7U354 Pelennor Grassland	.30	.75
☐ 7U355 Ruined Capitol	.30	.75
☐ 7U356 Cross Roads	.30	.75
☐ 7U357 Morgul Vale	.30	.75
☐ 7U358 Morgulduin	.30	.75
☐ 7U359 Northern Ithilien	.30	.75
☐ 7U360 Dagorlad	.30	.75
☐ 7U361 Haunted Pass	.30	.75
☐ 7U362 Narchost	.30	.75
☐ 7U363 Slag Mounds	.30	.75

2004 Lord of the Rings Mount Doom

Card	Low	High
COMPLETE SET (124)	20.00	40.00
BOOSTER BOX (36)	25.00	50.00
BOOSTER PACK	1.00	2.00
☐ 10R1 Great Day, Great Hour	.60	1.50
☐ 10R3 More Yet to Come	.60	1.50
☐ 10R7 Celeborn, Lord of the Galadhrim	.60	1.50
☐ 10R8 Cirdan, The Shipwright	2.00	5.00
☐ 10U2 Memories of Darkness	.30	.75
☐ 10U4 Aegnor, Elven Escort	.30	.75
☐ 10U5 Arwen, Echo of Luthien	.30	.75
☐ 10C10 Fleet-footed	.12	.30
☐ 10C16 Gathering Wind	.12	.30
☐ 10C24 Unabated in Malice	.12	.30
☐ 10C27 Dead Man of Dunharrow	.12	.30
☐ 10C30 End of the Game	.12	.30
☐ 10C31 Every Little is a Gain	.12	.30
☐ 10C34 Last Throw	.12	.30
☐ 10C36 Cast Unto the Winds	.12	.30
☐ 10C37 Corsair Boatswain	.12	.30
☐ 10C41 Easterling Pillager	.12	.30
☐ 10C42 Far Harad Mercenaries	.12	.30
☐ 10C49 Southron Fanatic	.12	.30
☐ 10C50 Southron Savage	.12	.30
☐ 10C52 Under Foot	.12	.30
☐ 10C55 Cirith Ungol Soldier	.12	.30
☐ 10C56 Cirith Ungol Warrior	.12	.30
☐ 10C61 Houses of Lamentation	.12	.30
☐ 10C62 Morgul Banner-bearer	.12	.30
☐ 10C64 Stooping to the Kill	.12	.30
☐ 10C65 Swarming Like Beetles	.12	.30
☐ 10C66 Ten Times Outnumbered	.12	.30
☐ 10C76 Advance Marauder	.12	.30
☐ 10C77 Advance Regular	.12	.30
☐ 10C79 Barren Land	.12	.30
☐ 10C80 Beaten Back	.12	.30
☐ 10C81 Cirith Ungol Guard	.12	.30
☐ 10C84 Cirith Ungol Sentry	.12	.30
☐ 10C85 Flames Within	.12	.30
☐ 10C86 Gorgoroth Keeper	.12	.30
☐ 10C87 Gorgoroth Swarm	.12	.30
☐ 10C90 Mordor Brute	.12	.30
☐ 10C91 Mordor Fiend	.12	.30
☐ 10R11 Galadriel, Lady Redeemed	.60	1.50
☐ 10R13 Phial of Galadriel, Star-glass	.60	1.50
☐ 10R14 Borne Far Away	.60	1.50
☐ 10R17 Out of the High Airs	1.25	3.00
☐ 10R18 Treebeard, Keeper of the Watchwood	.60	1.50
☐ 10R19 A Dark Shape Sprang	.60	1.50
☐ 10R21 Gollum, Mad Thing	.60	1.50
☐ 10R23 Shelob, Her Ladyship	2.50	6.00
☐ 10R25a Aragorn, Elessar Telcontar	.75	2.00
☐ 10R25b Aragorn, Elessar Telcontar TENGWAR		
☐ 10R28 Denethor, Lord of Minas Tirith	.60	1.50
☐ 10R29 Drawing His Eye	.60	1.50
☐ 10R38 Corsair Brute	.60	1.50
☐ 10R40 Easterling Berserker	.60	1.50
☐ 10R45 Mumak Chieftain	1.25	3.00
☐ 10R46 Quelled	.60	1.50
☐ 10R48 Seasoned Leader	1.25	3.00
☐ 10R51 Stampeded	.60	1.50
☐ 10R58 Dark Swooping Shadows	.60	1.50
☐ 10R59 Gorbag, Covetous Captain	.60	1.50
☐ 10R60 Gorbag's Sword	.60	1.50
☐ 10R63 Morgul Vanguard	.60	1.50
☐ 10R67 Ulaire Cantea, Thrall of the One	.60	1.50
☐ 10R68 Ulaire Enquea, Thrall of the One	5.00	10.00
☐ 10R6a Arwen, Queen of Elves and Men	.75	2.00
☐ 10R6b Arwen, Queen of Elves and Men TENGWAR		
☐ 10R71 Ulaire Toldea, Thrall of the One	.60	1.50
☐ 10R72 Eowyn, Lady of Ithilien	.60	1.50
☐ 10R75 Advance Captain	.75	2.00
☐ 10R88a Gothmog, Lieutenant of Morgul	1.25	3.00
☐ 10R88b Gothmog, Lieutenant of Morgul TENGWAR		
☐ 10R89 Gothmog's Warg	.60	1.50
☐ 10R94 Orc Ravager	.60	1.50
☐ 10R95 Orc Slaughterer	.60	1.50
☐ 10R99 Shagrat, Captain of Cirith Ungol	.60	1.50
☐ 10R9a Elrond, Venerable Lord	.60	1.50
☐ 10R9b Elrond, Venerable Lord TENGWAR		
☐ 10U12 Glimpse of Fate	.30	.75
☐ 10U15 Brooding on Tomorrow	.30	.75
☐ 10U20 Final Strike	.30	.75
☐ 10U22 Reclaim the Precious	.30	.75
☐ 10U26 Cursed of Erech	.30	.75
☐ 10U32 Fifth Level	.30	.75
☐ 10U33 Hardy Garrison	.30	.75
☐ 10U35 Suffered Much Loss	.30	.75
☐ 10U39 Corsair Ruffian	.30	.75
☐ 10U43 Field of the Fallen	.30	.75
☐ 10U44 High Vantage	.30	.75
☐ 10U47 Rallying Call	.30	.75
☐ 10U53 Black Marshal	.30	.75
☐ 10U54 Cirith Ungol Scavenger	.30	.75
☐ 10U57 Cirith Ungol Watchman	.30	.75
☐ 10U69 Ulaire Lemenya, Thrall of the One	.30	.75
☐ 10U70 Ulaire Nelya, Thrall of the One	.30	.75
☐ 10U73 Fell Deeds Awake	.30	.75
☐ 10U74 Unyielding	.30	.75
☐ 10U78 Advance Scout	.30	.75
☐ 10U82 Cirith Ungol Patroller	.30	.75
☐ 10U83 Cirith Ungol Sentinel	.30	.75
☐ 10U92 Mordor Pillager	.30	.75
☐ 10U93 Mordor Wretch	.30	.75
☐ 10U96 Rank and File	.30	.75
☐ 10U97 The Ring is Mine!	.30	.75
☐ 10U98 Ruinous Hail	.30	.75
☐ 10C102 Uruk Axe	.12	.30
☐ 10C103 Window of the Eye	.12	.30
☐ 10C106 Chance Observation	.12	.30
☐ 10C107 Great Heart	.12	.30
☐ 10C109 Make Haste	.12	.30
☐ 10C110 A Marvel	.12	.30
☐ 10C112 Nine-fingered Frodo and the Ring of Doom	.12	.30
☐ 10C113 Orc Armor	.12	.30
☐ 10P121 Frodo, Resolute Hobbit	2.00	5.00
☐ 10P122a Sam, Great Elf Warrior	.75	2.00
☐ 10P122b Sam, Great Elf Warrior TENGWAR		
☐ 10R100 Speak No More to Me	.60	1.50
☐ 10R101 Troll of Cirith Gorgor	2.00	5.00
☐ 10R104 Birthday Present	.75	2.00
☐ 10U105 Brave and Loyal	.30	.75
☐ 10U108 A Light in His Mind	.30	.75
☐ 10U111 Narrow Escape	.30	.75
☐ 10U114 Shadowplay	.30	.75
☐ 10U115 Slunk Out of Sight	.30	.75
☐ 10U116 The Tale of the Great Ring	.30	.75
☐ 10U117 Base of Mindolluin	.30	.75
☐ 10U118 Pelennor Prairie	.30	.75
☐ 10U119 Steward's Tomb	.30	.75
☐ 10U120 Watchers of Cirith Ungol	.30	.75

2004 Lord of the Rings Reflections

Card	Low	High
COMPLETE SET (52)	40.00	80.00
BOOSTER BOX (24)	50.00	100.00
BOOSTER PACK	2.50	5.00
☐ 9R1 The One Ring, The Binding Ring	1.25	3.00
☐ 9R2 Freca, Hungry Savage	2.00	5.00
☐ 9R3 Durin III, Dwarven Lord	5.00	10.00
☐ 9R4 Gimli, Bearer of Grudges	1.50	4.00
☐ 9R5 Linnar, Dwarven Lord	.40	1.00
☐ 9R6 Ring of Accretion	.40	1.00
☐ 9R7 Ring of Fury	3.00	8.00
☐ 9R8 Ring of Guile	.40	1.00
☐ 9R9 Ring of Retribution	.40	1.00
☐ 9R10 Sindri, Dwarven Lord	.40	1.00
☐ 9R11 Uri, Dwarven Lord	.40	1.00
☐ 9R12 Aiglos	2.50	6.00
☐ 9R13 Elven Rope	.40	1.00
☐ 9R14 Galadriel, Bearer of Wisdom	1.50	4.00
☐ 9R15 Gil-galad, Elven High King	5.00	10.00
☐ 9R16 Glorfindel, Revealed in Wrath	1.25	3.00
☐ 9R17 Knife of the Galadhrim	1.25	3.00
☐ 9R18 Merry's Dagger	.40	1.00
☐ 9R19 Narya, Ring of Fire	.40	1.00
☐ 9R20 Nenya, Ring of Adamant	.40	1.00
☐ 9R21 Pippin's Dagger	.40	1.00
☐ 9R22 Strands of Elven Hair	.40	1.00
☐ 9R23 Vilya, Ring of Air	.40	1.00
☐ 9R24 Ent Draught	.40	1.00
☐ 9R25 Huorn	.40	1.00
☐ 9R26 Radagast, The Brown	5.00	10.00
☐ 9R27 Sent Back	.40	1.00
☐ 9R28 Gollum, Dark as Darkness	1.25	3.00
☐ 9R29 Slippery as Fishes	2.00	5.00

Card	Low	High
❑ 9R30 Smeagol, Bearer of Great Secrets	1.25	3.00
❑ 9R31 Boromir, Bearer of Council	2.00	5.00
❑ 9R32 Elendil, The Tall	1.00	2.50
❑ 9R33 Isildur, Bearer of Heirlooms	1.50	4.00
❑ 9R34 Narsil, Blade of the Faithful	2.00	5.00
❑ 9R35 Sapling of the White Tree	.40	1.00
❑ 9R36 Scroll of Isildur	.40	1.00
❑ 9R37 Seeing Stone of Minas Anor	.40	1.00
❑ 9R38 Seeing Stone of Orthanc	.40	1.00
❑ 9R39 Library of Orthanc	.40	1.00
❑ 9R40 Sack of the Shire	.40	1.00
❑ 9R41 Host of Moria, Legion of the Underdeeps	2.50	6.00
❑ 9R42 Ring of Asperity	.40	1.00
❑ 9R43 Ring of Ire	.75	2.00
❑ 9R44 Ring of Rancor	.40	1.00
❑ 9R45 Horn of the Mark	.40	1.00
❑ 9R46 The Red Arrow	.40	1.00
❑ 9R47 Ithil Stone	2.50	6.00
❑ 9R48 Sauron, The Lord of the Rings	5.00	10.00
❑ 9R49 Bilbo, Bearer of Things Burgled	.75	2.00
❑ 9R50 Everyone Knows	.40	1.00
❑ 9R51 Goldberry, River-daughter	.40	1.00
❑ 9R52 Tom Bombadil, The Master	.75	2.00

2004 Lord of the Rings Seige of Gondor

Card	Low	High
COMPLETE SET (122)	20.00	40.00
BOOSTER BOX (36)	25.00	50.00
BOOSTER PACK	1.00	2.00
❑ 8C1 Aggression	.12	.30
❑ 8C5 Gimli, Counter of Foes	.12	.30
❑ 8C6 Honed	.12	.30
❑ 8R2 Battle in Earnest	.60	1.50
❑ 8R3 Blood Runs Chill	2.50	6.00
❑ 8R7 Unheard of	.60	1.50
❑ 8U4 Counts But One	.30	.75
❑ 8U8 Wish For Our Kinfolk	.30	.75
❑ 8U9 A Grey Ship	.30	.75
❑ 8C10 Legolas, Elven Stalwart	.12	.30
❑ 8C14 A Fool	.12	.30
❑ 8C22 Hidden Even From Her	.12	.30
❑ 8C26 Shelob, Last Child of Ungoliant	.12	.30
❑ 8C28 Spider Poison	.12	.30
❑ 8C30 Web	.12	.30
❑ 8C31 At His Command	.12	.30
❑ 8C34 Faramir, Defender of Osgiliath	.12	.30
❑ 8C35 Fourth Level	.12	.30
❑ 8C39 Knight of Dol Amroth	.12	.30
❑ 8C40 Knight's Mount	.12	.30
❑ 8C41 Oathbreaker	.12	.30
❑ 8C47 Stronger and More Terrible	.12	.30
❑ 8C48 Swept Away	.12	.30
❑ 8C50 Black Sails of Umbar	.12	.30
❑ 8C52 Corsair Ballista	.12	.30
❑ 8C53 Corsair Buccaneer	.12	.30
❑ 8C54 Corsair Freebooter	.12	.30
❑ 8C55 Corsair Gunners	.12	.30
❑ 8C58 Corsair Plunderer	.12	.30
❑ 8C61 Haradwaith	.12	.30
❑ 8C63 Line of Defense	.12	.30
❑ 8C66 Wind That Sped Ships	.12	.30
❑ 8C74 Morgul Ambusher	.12	.30
❑ 8C75 Morgul Creeper	.12	.30
❑ 8C76 Morgul Lurker	.12	.30
❑ 8C87 Eomer, Keeper of Oaths	.12	.30
❑ 8C89 Fury of the Northmen	.12	.30
❑ 8C90 No Living Man	.12	.30
❑ 8R11 Life of the Eldar	.60	1.50
❑ 8R12 Reckless We Rode	.60	1.50
❑ 8R15a Gandalf, Leader of Men	1.25	3.00
❑ 8R15b Gandalf, Leader of Men TENGWAR		
❑ 8R20 Saved From the Fire	5.00	10.00
❑ 8R21 Shadowfax, Greatheart	.60	1.50
❑ 8R24 Promise Keeping	1.25	3.00
❑ 8R25a Shelob, Eater of Light	1.25	3.00
❑ 8R25b Shelob, Eater of Light TENGWAR		
❑ 8R27 Smeagol, Slippery Sneak	.60	1.50
❑ 8R32 Catapult	.60	1.50
❑ 8R33 Elessar's Edict	.60	1.50
❑ 8R36 Garrison of Gondor	1.50	4.00
❑ 8R37 Imrahil, Prince of Dol Amroth	.60	1.50
❑ 8R38a King of the Dead, Oathbreaker	1.25	3.00
❑ 8R38b King of the Dead, Oathbreaker TENGWAR		
❑ 8R43 Shadow Host	.75	2.00
❑ 8R49 Black Numenorean	1.50	4.00
❑ 8R51a Castamir of Umbar	1.50	4.00
❑ 8R51b Castamir of Umbar TENGWAR		
❑ 8R57a Corsair Marauder	3.00	8.00
❑ 8R57b Corsair Marauder TENGWAR		
❑ 8R62 Heavy Axeman	.60	1.50
❑ 8R65 Ships of Great Draught	3.00	8.00
❑ 8R67 Between Nazgul and Prey	2.00	5.00
❑ 8R68 Beyond All Darkness	.75	2.00
❑ 8R70 Black Flail	.75	2.00
❑ 8R72 Gothmog, Morgul Commander	1.00	2.50
❑ 8R77 Morgul Squealer	.75	2.00
❑ 8R81 Ulaire Otsea, Thrall of the One	.60	1.50
❑ 8R84 The Witch-king, Black Captain	1.00	2.50
❑ 8R88 Eowyn's Shield	.60	1.50
❑ 8R91 Rohirrim Army	.75	2.00
❑ 8R92 Theoden, Tall and Proud	1.00	2.50
❑ 8R93 Called Away	.60	1.50
❑ 8R95 Gorgoroth Assassin	1.00	2.50
❑ 8R96 Gorgoroth Berserker	.60	1.50
❑ 8U100 Gorgoroth Servitor	.30	.75
❑ 8U107 Their Marching Companies	.30	.75
❑ 8U110 Morgai Foothills	.30	.75
❑ 8U112 Song of the Shire	.30	.75
❑ 8U117 The Dimholt	.30	.75
❑ 8U118 City of the Dead	.30	.75
❑ 8U119 Crashed Gate	.30	.75
❑ 8U120 Osgiliath Channel	.30	.75
❑ 8U13 Shake Off the Shadow	.30	.75
❑ 8U16 Let Us Not Tarry	.30	.75
❑ 8U17 Mighty Steed	.30	.75
❑ 8U18 Not the First Halfling	.30	.75
❑ 8U19 On Your Doorstep	.30	.75
❑ 8U23 Larder	.30	.75
❑ 8U29 Still Far Ahead	.30	.75
❑ 8U42 A Path Appointed	.30	.75
❑ 8U44 Sixth Level	.30	.75
❑ 8U45 Sleepless Dead	.30	.75
❑ 8U46 Spectral Sword	.30	.75
❑ 8U56 Corsair Lookout	.30	.75
❑ 8U59 Corsair War Galley	.30	.75
❑ 8U60 Haradrim Marksman	.30	.75
❑ 8U64 Mumakil	.30	.75
❑ 8U69 Black Dart	.30	.75
❑ 8U71 Flung Into the Fray	.30	.75
❑ 8U73 Mastered By Madness	.30	.75
❑ 8U78 Streaming to the Field	.30	.75
❑ 8U79 Ulaire Attea, Thrall of the One	.30	.75
❑ 8U80 Ulaire Nertea, Thrall of the One	.30	.75
❑ 8U82 Unhindered	.30	.75
❑ 8U83 Winged Mount	.30	.75
❑ 8U85 Charged Headlong	.30	.75
❑ 8U86 Doom Drove Them	.30	.75
❑ 8U94 Gorgoroth Agitator	.30	.75
❑ 8U97 Gorgoroth Breaker	.30	.75
❑ 8U98 Gorgoroth Looter	.30	.75
❑ 8U99 Gorgoroth Patrol	.30	.75
❑ 8C101 Gorgoroth Stormer	.12	.30
❑ 8C102 Great Hill Troll	.12	.30
❑ 8C104 Morgai	.12	.30
❑ 8C106 Siege Troop	.12	.30
❑ 8C109 Closer and Closer He Bent	.12	.30
❑ 8C111 So Fair, So Desperate	.12	.30
❑ 8C114 Straining Towards Us	.12	.30
❑ 8C116 We Shall Meet Again Soon	.12	.30
❑ 8P121 Merry, Noble Warrior	.40	1.00
❑ 8P122 Pippin, Guard of Minas Tirith	.40	1.00
❑ 8R103a Grond, Hammer of the Underworld	1.00	2.50
❑ 8R103b Grond, Hammer of the Underworld TENGWAR		
❑ 8R105 Olog-hai of Mordor	.75	2.00
❑ 8R108 Troll of Gorgoroth, Abomination of Sauron	.75	2.00
❑ 8R113 Sting, Bane of the Eight Legs	1.25	3.00
❑ 8R115 Unheeded	.75	2.00

2004 Lord of the Rings Shadows

Card	Low	High
COMPLETE SET (266)	20.00	40.00
BOOSTER BOX (36)	20.00	40.00
BOOSTER PACK	1.00	2.00
❑ 11C4 Battle to the Last	.12	.30
❑ 11C5 Dwarven Embassy	.12	.30
❑ 11C7 Farin, Emissary of Erebor	.12	.30
❑ 11R1a The One Ring, The Ring of Rings	2.50	6.00
❑ 11R1b The One Ring, The Ring of Rings TENGWAR		
❑ 11R9 Gimli's Battle Axe, Vicious Weapon	.60	1.50
❑ 11S2 The One Ring, The Ruling Ring	.40	1.00
❑ 11U3 Axe of Khazad-dum	.30	.75
❑ 11U6 Fallen Lord	.30	.75
❑ 11U8 Gimli, Lively Combatant	.30	.75
❑ 11C13 On Guard	.12	.30
❑ 11C19 Farewell to Lorien	.12	.30
❑ 11C27 Woodland Sentinel	.12	.30
❑ 11C31 Final Account	.12	.30
❑ 11C36 Inspiration	.12	.30
❑ 11C39 Prolonged Struggle	.12	.30
❑ 11C46 Master Commands It	.12	.30
❑ 11C62 Madril, Ranger of Ithilien	.12	.30
❑ 11C63 Much-needed Rest	.12	.30
❑ 11C71 Bold and Cunning	.12	.30
❑ 11C72 Column of Easterlings	.12	.30
❑ 11C73 Corps of Harad	.12	.30
❑ 11C76 Easterling Shield Wall	.12	.30
❑ 11C79 Fearsome Dunlending	.12	.30
❑ 11C83 Force of Harad	.12	.30
❑ 11C85 Horde of Harad	.12	.30
❑ 11C86 Invading Haradrim	.12	.30
❑ 11C88 Legion of Harad	.12	.30
❑ 11C89 Long Battle Bow	.12	.30
❑ 11C93 Patroller of Haradrim	.12	.30
❑ 11C94 Pavise	.12	.30
❑ 11C98 Rampaging Easterling	.12	.30
❑ 11R10 Gimrir, Dwarven Emissary	.60	1.50
❑ 11R11 Hall of Our Fathers	.60	1.50
❑ 11R14 Well-equipped	.60	1.50
❑ 11R17 Elven Marksmanship	.60	1.50
❑ 11R22 Legolas, Woodland Emissary	.60	1.50
❑ 11R23 Legolas' Bow	.60	1.50
❑ 11R24 Might of the Elf-lords	.60	1.50
❑ 11R30 Erland, Dale Counselor	.75	2.00
❑ 11R33 Gandalf's Staff, Ash-Staff	.60	1.50
❑ 11R35 Glamdring, Foe-hammer	1.25	3.00
❑ 11R42 Gollum, Skulker	.60	1.50
❑ 11R43 Horribly Strong	.75	2.00
❑ 11R44 Incited	.60	1.50
❑ 11R48 Not Yet Vanquished	.60	1.50
❑ 11R50 Safe Passage	.60	1.50
❑ 11R51 Smeagol, Scout and Guide	.60	1.50
❑ 11R54a Aragorn, Strider	2.50	6.00
❑ 11R54b Aragorn, Strider TENGWAR		
❑ 11R57a Boromir, Hero of Osgiliath	1.25	3.00
❑ 11R57b Boromir, Hero of Osgiliath TENGWAR		
❑ 11R60 The Highest Quality	.60	1.50
❑ 11R66 Well-traveled	1.00	2.50
❑ 11R68 Armored Easterling	.60	1.50
❑ 11R70 Bloodthirsty	.60	1.50
❑ 11R75 Easterling Host	.60	1.50
❑ 11R78 Elevated Fire	1.50	4.00
❑ 11R81 Fletcher of Harad	.60	1.50
❑ 11R91 Oath Sworn	.60	1.50
❑ 11R96 Precision Targeting	.75	2.00
❑ 11S18 Elven Scout	.40	1.00
❑ 11S20 The Lady's Blessing	.40	1.00
❑ 11S21 Legolas, Companion of the Ring	.40	1.00
❑ 11S32 G for Grand	.40	1.00
❑ 11S33a Gandalf, Leader of the Company	.75	2.00
❑ 11S33b Gandalf, Leader of the Company TENGWAR		
❑ 11S53 Aragorn, Guide and Protector	.40	1.00
❑ 11S56 Battle Cry	.40	1.00
❑ 11S64 Pledge of Loyalty	.60	1.50
❑ 11S65 Ranger of Westernesse	.40	1.00
❑ 11S77 Elder of Dunland	.40	1.00
❑ 11S82 Footman of Dunland	.40	1.00
❑ 11S84 Harad Standard-bearer	.40	1.00
❑ 11S90 Man of Bree	.40	1.00
❑ 11S92 Overrun	.40	1.00
❑ 11S95 Poleaxe	.40	1.00
❑ 11S97 Raging Dunlending	.40	1.00
❑ 11U12 Mountain Homestead	.30	.75
❑ 11U15 Arwen, Staunch Defender	.30	.75
❑ 11U16 Blade of Lindon	.30	.75
❑ 11U25 Nocked	.30	.75
❑ 11U26 Uncertain Future	.30	.75
❑ 11U28 The Art of Gandalf	.30	.75
❑ 11U29 Ease the Burden	.30	.75
❑ 11U37 New Authority	.30	.75
❑ 11U38 New-awakened	.30	.75
❑ 11U40 Shadowfax, Unequaled Steed	.30	.75
❑ 11U41 Frenzied Attack	.30	.75
❑ 11U45 Led Astray	.30	.75
❑ 11U47 No End of Wickedness	.30	.75
❑ 11U49 One Good Turn Deserves Another	.30	.75
❑ 11U52 Strange and Terrible	.30	.75
❑ 11U55 Armor of the Citadel	.30	.75
❑ 11U58 Bow of Minas Tirith	.30	.75
❑ 11U59 Gondorian Blade	.30	.75
❑ 11U61 Houses of Healing	.30	.75
❑ 11U67 Archer of Harad	.30	.75
❑ 11U69 Axeman of Harad	.30	.75
❑ 11U74 Detachment of Haradrim	.30	.75
❑ 11U80 Ferocious Haradrim	.30	.75
❑ 11U87 Lathspell	.30	.75
❑ 11U99 Squad of Haradrim	.30	.75
❑ 11C101 Swarthy Bree-lander	.12	.30
❑ 11C102 Throng of Harad	.12	.30
❑ 11C103 Warrior of Dunland	.12	.30
❑ 11C107 Barbarous Orc	.12	.30
❑ 11C111 Champion Orc	.12	.30
❑ 11C113 Cutthroat Orc	.12	.30
❑ 11C120 Entrapping Orc	.12	.30
❑ 11C121 Foraging Orc	.12	.30
❑ 11C122 Frenzied Orc	.12	.30
❑ 11C125 Isengard Underling	.12	.30
❑ 11C127 Mocking Goblin	.12	.30
❑ 11C128 Mordor Scimitar	.12	.30
❑ 11C129 Mountain Orc	.12	.30
❑ 11C131 Orc Miscreant	.12	.30
❑ 11C132 Orkish Smith	.12	.30
❑ 11C136 Prowling Orc	.12	.30
❑ 11C140 Strength in Shadows	.12	.30
❑ 11C148 Hrothlac, Man of Rohan	.12	.30
❑ 11C155 Riding Like the Wind	.12	.30
❑ 11C157 Rush of Steeds	.12	.30
❑ 11C162 Crouched Down	.12	.30
❑ 11C167 Incognito	.12	.30
❑ 11C168 Merry, Loyal Companion	.12	.30
❑ 11C169 The More, The Merrier	.12	.30
❑ 11C192 Isengard Sword	.12	.30
❑ 11C195 Murderous Uruk	.12	.30
❑ 11C196 Our Foes Are Weak	.12	.30
❑ 11C198 Patrol of Uruk-hai	.12	.30
❑ 11C199 Relentless Uruk	.12	.30
❑ 11C200 Ruthless Uruk	.12	.30
❑ 11C201 Sentinel Uruk	.12	.30
❑ 11C202 Squad of Uruk-hai	.12	.30
❑ 11C203 Swarming Uruk	.12	.30
❑ 11C204 Tyrannical Uruk	.12	.30
❑ 11C206 Watchman Uruk	.12	.30
❑ 11R100 Strange-looking Men	.60	1.50
❑ 11R108 Beastly Olog-hai	1.25	3.00
❑ 11R119 Emboldened Orc	1.00	2.50
❑ 11R123a Goblin Hordes	6.00	12.00
❑ 11R123b Goblin Hordes TENGWAR		
❑ 11R133 Orkish Worker	.60	1.50
❑ 11R134 Persistent Orc	.60	1.50
❑ 11R135 Porter Troll	1.00	2.50
❑ 11R141 Undisciplined	.60	1.50
❑ 11R143 Watchful Orc	.75	2.00
❑ 11R147 Gamling, Defender of the Hornburg	.60	1.50
❑ 11R154 Riders of the Mark	.60	1.50
❑ 11R158 Sword Rack	.60	1.50
❑ 11R165 Habits of Home	.60	1.50
❑ 11R170 Pippin, Brave Decoy	.60	1.50
❑ 11R171 Salt from the Shire	.60	1.50
❑ 11R173 Sting, Weapon of Heritage	.75	2.00
❑ 11R177 Army of Uruk-hai	.60	1.50
❑ 11R179 Brawling Uruk	.60	1.50
❑ 11R181 Determined Uruk	.60	1.50
❑ 11R184 Force of Uruk-hai	.60	1.50
❑ 11R186 Furious Uruk	.60	1.50
❑ 11R194 Lurtz, Minion of the White Wizard	.75	2.00
❑ 11R205 Vigilant Uruk	.60	1.50
❑ 11R207 Dark Powers Strengthen	.60	1.50
❑ 11R211 Keening Wail	1.25	3.00
❑ 11R214 The Pale Blade, Sword of Flame	.60	1.50
❑ 11R216 A Shadow Rises	.60	1.50
❑ 11R217 Shapes Slowly Advancing	.75	2.00
❑ 11R219 Ulaire Attea, Second of the Nine Riders	.60	1.50
❑ 11R224 Ulaire Otsea, Seventh of the Nine Riders	.75	2.00
❑ 11R226a The Witch-king, Captain of the Nine Riders	3.00	8.00
❑ 11R226b The Witch-king, Captain of the Nine Riders TENGWAR		
❑ 11S112 Conquered Halls	.40	1.00
❑ 11S115 Denizen of Khazad-dum	.40	1.00
❑ 11S116 Denizen of Moria	.40	1.00
❑ 11S117 Denizen of the Black Pit	.40	1.00
❑ 11S126 Marauding Orcs	.40	1.00
❑ 11S130 Orc Hammer	.40	1.00
❑ 11S138 Skulking Goblin	.40	1.00
❑ 11S142 Unyielding Goblin	.40	1.00
❑ 11S146 Eowyn, Shieldmaiden of Rohan	.40	1.00
❑ 11S150 Rally Cry	.40	1.00
❑ 11S152 Riddermark Soldier	.40	1.00
❑ 11S153 Rider's Spear	.40	1.00
❑ 11S160 War Now Calls Us	.40	1.00
❑ 11S161 Concerning Hobbits	.40	1.00
❑ 11S164 Frodo, Protected by Many	.40	1.00
❑ 11S166 Hobbit Sword	.40	1.00
❑ 11S174 Sworn Companion	.40	1.00
❑ 11S176 Unharmed	.40	1.00
❑ 11S178 Bloodthirsty Uruk	.40	1.00
❑ 11S180 Brutality	.40	1.00
❑ 11S183 Feral Uruk	.40	1.00
❑ 11S187 Furor	.40	1.00
❑ 11S188 Hounding Uruk	.40	1.00
❑ 11S190 Invincible Uruk	.40	1.00
❑ 11S193 Lookout Uruk	.40	1.00
❑ 11S209 Drawn to its Power	.40	1.00
❑ 11S213 Moving This Way	.40	1.00
❑ 11S215 Riders in Black	.40	1.00
❑ 11S220 Ulaire Cantea, Fourth of the Nine Riders	.40	1.00
❑ 11S221 Ulaire Lemenya, Fifth of the Nine Riders	.40	1.00
❑ 11S222 Ulaire Nelya, Third of the Nine Riders	.60	1.50
❑ 11S223 Ulaire Nertea, Ninth of the Nine Riders	.40	1.00
❑ 11S225 Ulaire Toldea, Eighth of the Nine Riders	.40	1.00
❑ 11S228 Anduin Confluence	.60	1.50
❑ 11S229 Barazinbar	.40	1.00
❑ 11S230 Buckland Homestead	.40	1.00
❑ 11S231 Caras Galadhon	.40	1.00
❑ 11S232 Cavern Entrance	.40	1.00
❑ 11S233 Chamber of Mazarbul	.40	1.00
❑ 11S234 Crags of Emyn Muil	.40	1.00
❑ 11S236 East Road	.40	1.00
❑ 11S237 Ettenmoors	.40	1.00
❑ 11S238 Expanding Marshland	.40	1.00
❑ 11S239 Fangorn Glade	.40	1.00
❑ 11S240 Flats of Rohan	.40	1.00
❑ 11S241 Fortress of Orthanc	.40	1.00
❑ 11S242 Green Dragon Inn	.40	1.00
❑ 11S243 Harrowdale	.40	1.00
❑ 11S245 Helm's Gate	.40	1.00
❑ 11S247 Moria Guardroom	.40	1.00
❑ 11S248 Moria Stairway	.40	1.00
❑ 11S249 Neekerbreekers' Bog	.75	2.00
❑ 11S250 North Undeep	.40	1.00
❑ 11S251 Old Forest Road	.40	1.00
❑ 11S252 Osgiliath Reclaimed	.40	1.00
❑ 11S253 Pelennor Fields	.40	1.00
❑ 11S254 Pelennor Flat	.40	1.00
❑ 11S255 Pinnacle of Zirakzigil	.40	1.00
❑ 11S256 The Prancing Pony	.40	1.00
❑ 11S257 Rohan Uplands	.40	1.00
❑ 11S258 Slag Mounds	.40	1.00
❑ 11S259 Stables	.40	1.00
❑ 11S260 Trollshaw Forest	.40	1.00
❑ 11S261 Valley of the Silverlode	.40	1.00
❑ 11S262 Watch-tower of Cirith Ungol	.40	1.00
❑ 11S263 West Gate of Moria	.40	1.00
❑ 11S264 Westemnet Village	.40	1.00
❑ 11S265 Window on the West	.40	1.00
❑ 11S266 Woody-End	.60	1.50
❑ 11U104 Whistling Death	.30	.75
❑ 11U105 Wielding the Ring	.30	.75
❑ 11U106 Armed for Battle	.30	.75
❑ 11U109 Bladed Gauntlets	.30	.75
❑ 11U110 Bound to its Fate	.30	.75
❑ 11U114 Demoralized	.30	.75
❑ 11U118 Dread and Despair	.30	.75
❑ 11U124 Hill Orc	.30	.75
❑ 11U137 Scurrying Goblin	.30	.75
❑ 11U139 Spurred to Battle	.30	.75
❑ 11U144 Border Patrol	.30	.75
❑ 11U145 Eomer, Guardian of the Eastmark	.30	.75
❑ 11U149 Protecting the Hall	.30	.75
❑ 11U151 Riddermark Javelin	.30	.75
❑ 11U156 Rohirrim Mount	.30	.75
❑ 11U159 Theoden, King of the Eorlingas	.30	.75
❑ 11U163 Farmer Maggot, Hobbit of the Marish	.30	.75
❑ 11U172 Sam, Steadfast Friend	.30	.75
❑ 11U175 A Task Now to Be Done	.30	.75
❑ 11U182 Devastation	.30	.75
❑ 11U185 Fortitude	.30	.75
❑ 11U189 Intimidating Uruk	.30	.75
❑ 11U191 Isengard Siege Bow	.30	.75
❑ 11U197 Overpowering Uruk	.30	.75
❑ 11U208 Dark Wings	.30	.75
❑ 11U210 Hatred Stirred	.30	.75
❑ 11U212 Lost in the Woods	.30	.75
❑ 11U218 Surrounded by Wraiths	.30	.75
❑ 11U227 Anduin Banks	.30	.75
❑ 11U235 Dammed Gate-stream	.30	.75
❑ 11U244 Heights of Isengard	.30	.75
❑ 11U246 Mere of Dead Faces	.30	.75

2004 Lord of the Rings Shadows Foil

Card	Low	High
COMPLETE SET (18)	15.00	30.00
❑ 11RF1 The One Ring, The Ring of Rings (F)	2.00	5.00
❑ 11RF2 Elven Marksmanship (F)	1.25	3.00
❑ 11RF3 Legolas, Woodland Emissary (F)	.60	1.50
❑ 11RF4 Glamdring, Foe-hammer (F)	1.50	4.00
❑ 11RF5 Gollum, Skulker (F)	.60	1.50
❑ 11RF6 Smeagol, Scout and Guide (F)	.75	2.00
❑ 11RF7 Aragorn, Strider (F)	2.00	5.00
❑ 11RF8 Bloodthirsty (F)	.60	1.50
❑ 11RF9 Fletcher of Harad (F)	.75	2.00
❑ 11RF10 Porter Troll (F)	1.00	2.50
❑ 11RF11 Undisciplined (F)	.60	1.50
❑ 11RF12 Gamling, Defender of the Hornburg (F)	.60	1.50
❑ 11RF13 Sword Rack (F)	.60	1.50
❑ 11RF14 Salt from the Shire (F)	.75	2.00
❑ 11RF15 Brawling Uruk (F)	.60	1.50
❑ 11RF16 Lurtz, Minion of the White Wizard (F)	.75	2.00
❑ 11RF17 The Pale Blade, Sword of Flame (F)	.75	2.00
❑ 11RF18 The Witch-king, Captain of the Nine Riders (F)	3.00	8.00

2005 Lord of the Rings Black Rider

Card	Low	High
COMPLETE SET (194)	20.00	40.00
BOOSTER BOX (36)	20.00	40.00
BOOSTER PACK	1.00	2.00
❑ 12C4 Durability	.12	.30
❑ 12C6 Dwarven Skill	.12	.30
❑ 12C7 Dwarven Warrior	.12	.30
❑ 12C8 His Father's Charge	.12	.30
❑ 12R9 Loud and Strong	.60	1.50
❑ 12U1 Argument Ready to Hand	.30	.75
❑ 12U2 Belt of Erebor	.30	.75
❑ 12U3 A Clamour of Many Voices	.30	.75
❑ 12U5 Dwarven Bracers	.30	.75
❑ 12C16 Attunement	.12	.30
❑ 12C20 Orophin, Brother of Haldir	.12	.30
❑ 12C22 Rumil, Brother of Haldir	.12	.30
❑ 12C31 Mysterious Wizard	.12	.30
❑ 12C32 Salve	.12	.30
❑ 12C33 The Terror of His Coming	.12	.30
❑ 12C34 Traveled Leader	.12	.30
❑ 12C40 There's Another Way	.12	.30
❑ 12C44 Concealment	.12	.30
❑ 12C45 Confronting the Eye	.12	.30
❑ 12C46 Elendil's Valor	.12	.30
❑ 12C52 Tireless	.12	.30
❑ 12C53 Valorous Leader	.12	.30
❑ 12C59 Covetous Easterling	.12	.30
❑ 12C60 Crazed Hillman	.12	.30
❑ 12C61 Crooked Townsman	.12	.30
❑ 12C64 Enraged Southron	.12	.30
❑ 12C67 Goaded to War	.12	.30
❑ 12C70 Hemmed In	.12	.30
❑ 12C77 War Trident	.12	.30
❑ 12C78 Wrathful Hillman	.12	.30
❑ 12C84 Bloodstained Field	.12	.30
❑ 12C87 Goblin Aggressor	.12	.30
❑ 12C88 Great Cost	.12	.30
❑ 12C92 Orc Dreg	.12	.30
❑ 12C93 Orc Footman	.12	.30
❑ 12C95 Orc Skulker	.12	.30
❑ 12C96 Orc Spear	.12	.30
❑ 12C98 Orc Tormentor	.12	.30
❑ 12R10 No Pauses, No Spills	5.00	10.00
❑ 12R17a Elrond, Witness to History	1.25	3.00
❑ 12R17b Elrond, Witness to History TENGWAR		
❑ 12R18 Hadafang	1.25	3.00
❑ 12R19 Long-knives of Legolas	.60	1.50
❑ 12R26 Discoveries	.60	1.50
❑ 12R27 Gandalf, The White Rider	.60	1.50
❑ 12R28 Gandalf's Hat	.60	1.50
❑ 12R30 Jarnsmid, Barding Emissary	.60	1.50
❑ 12R35a Watch and Wait	1.50	4.00
❑ 12R35b Watch and Wait TENGWAR		
❑ 12R37 Come Away	.60	1.50
❑ 12R38 From Deep in Shadow	.60	1.50
❑ 12R42 Blade of Gondor, Sword of Boromir	.75	2.00
❑ 12R47 Faramir, Dunadan of Gondor	.60	1.50
❑ 12R48 Faramir's Sword	.75	2.00
❑ 12R54a Saruman, of Many Colours	.75	2.00
❑ 12R54b Saruman, of Many Colours TENGWAR		
❑ 12R56 Castamir of Umbar, Corsair Vandal	.75	2.00
❑ 12R57 Corrupted Spy	.60	1.50
❑ 12R68 Grima, Betrayer of Rohan	.60	1.50
❑ 12R69 Harrying Hillman	.60	1.50
❑ 12R72 Messenger's Mount	.60	1.50
❑ 12R74 Mumak Rider	2.00	5.00
❑ 12R75 Poisonous Words	.60	1.50
❑ 12R79 The Balrog, The Terror of Khazad-dum	1.00	2.50

TCG/CCG

❑ 12R80 Whip of Many Thongs 1.25 3.00
Weapon of Flame and Shadow
❑ 12R81 Abiding Evil .75 2.00
❑ 12R82 Barrage .75 2.00
❑ 12R83 The Beckoning Shadow .60 1.50
❑ 12R85 Cave Troll of Moria, Savage Menace 1.25 3.00
❑ 12R86 Cave Troll's Hammer, Unwieldy Cudgel .60 1.50
❑ 12R91 Orc Artisan .60 1.50
❑ 12S55 Brutal Easterling .40 1.00
❑ 12S65 Frenzied Dunlending .40 1.00
❑ 12S73a The Mouth of Sauron, Messenger of Mordor .40 1.00
❑ 12S73b The Mouth of Sauron, Messenger of Mordor TENGWAR
❑ 12U11 Nobody Tosses a Dwarf .30 .75
❑ 12U12 Proud and Able .30 .75
❑ 12U13 Sharp Defense .30 .75
❑ 12U14 Stalwart Support .30 .75
❑ 12U15 Thrarin, Smith of Erebor .30 .75
❑ 12U21 Refuge .30 .75
❑ 12U23 Seclusion .30 .75
❑ 12U24 Taking the High Ground .30 .75
❑ 12U25 Betrayal of Isengard .30 .75
❑ 12U29 Introspection .30 .75
❑ 12U36 With Doom We Come .30 .75
❑ 12U39 Not Alone .30 .75
❑ 12U41 Treacherous Little Toad .30 .75
❑ 12U43 Boromir, Defender of Minas Tirith .30 .75
❑ 12U49 Gondorian Steed .30 .75
❑ 12U50 Guardian .30 .75
❑ 12U51 Invigorated .30 .75
❑ 12U58 Countless Companies .30 .75
❑ 12U62 Dunlending Zealot .30 .75
❑ 12U63 Easterling Banner-bearer .30 .75
❑ 12U66 Gathering Strength .30 .75
❑ 12U71 Last Days .30 .75
❑ 12U76 Trail of Terror .30 .75
❑ 12U79 The Balrog .30 .75
The Terror of Khazad-dum TENGWAR
❑ 12U89 Mordor Aggressor .30 .75
❑ 12U90 Morgul Tormentor .30 .75
❑ 12U94 Orc Sapper .30 .75
❑ 12U97 Orc Strategist .30 .75
❑ 12U99 Pitiless Orc .30 .75
❑ 12C102 Scavenging Goblins .12 .30
❑ 12C106 Vile Goblin .12 .30
❑ 12C107 Aldred, Eored Soldier .12 .30
❑ 12C109 Challenging the Orc-host .12 .30
❑ 12C110 Cleaving a Path .12 .30
❑ 12C114 For the Mark .12 .30
❑ 12C115 Golden Glimmer .12 .30
❑ 12C121 Flotsam and Jetsam .12 .30
❑ 12C122 Home and Hearth .12 .30
❑ 12C123 Hope is Kindled .12 .30
❑ 12C134 Advancing Uruk .12 .30
❑ 12C137 Breeding Pit Conscript .12 .30
❑ 12C142 Merciless Uruk .12 .30
❑ 12C143 Quelling Force .12 .30
❑ 12C145 Shingle in a Storm .12 .30
❑ 12C146 Strange Device .12 .30
❑ 12C149 Uruk Common .12 .30
❑ 12C153 Uruk Pikeman .12 .30
❑ 12C159 Weapon of Opportunity .12 .30
❑ 12C160 Worthy of Mordor .12 .30
❑ 12C164 Echo of Hooves .12 .30
❑ 12C168 Nazgul Blade .12 .30
❑ 12C172 Steed of Mordor .12 .30
❑ 12C177 Ulaire Nelya, Black Hunter .12 .30
❑ 12C178 Ulaire Nertea, Black Horseman .12 .30
❑ 12C181 Unending Life .12 .30
❑ 12C182 Unimpeded .12 .30
❑ 12R100 Rallying Orc 3.00 8.00
❑ 12R101 Retribution 2.00 5.00
❑ 12R105 Troll's Keyward, Keeper of the Beast 1.00 2.50
❑ 12R108 Cast Out .60 1.50
❑ 12R111 Coil .75 2.00
❑ 12R116 Haethen, Veteran Fighter .75 2.00
❑ 12R118 The Mouth of Sauron 1.25 3.00
Lieutenant of Barad-dur
❑ 12R119 Bilbo, Melancholy Hobbit .60 1.50
❑ 12R120 Diversion .60 1.50
❑ 12R124 Long Live the Halflings .60 1.50
❑ 12R127 Pippin, Hobbit of Some Intelligence .60 1.50
❑ 12R128 A Promise 1.00 2.50
❑ 12R129 Rosie Cotton, Barmaid .75 2.00
❑ 12R139 Broken in Defeat .60 1.50
❑ 12R141 Dark Alliance .60 1.50
❑ 12R150 Uruk Decimator .60 1.50
❑ 12R154 Uruk Slaughterer .60 1.50
❑ 12R155 Uruk Zealot .60 1.50
❑ 12R156 Uruk-hai Guard .60 1.50
❑ 12R157 Uruk-hai Troop .60 1.50
❑ 12R162 Dark Approach 7.50 15.00
❑ 12R163 Dark Temptation 1.00 2.50
❑ 12R169 Sauron's Gaze .60 1.50
❑ 12R171 Shadowy Mount 1.25 3.00
❑ 12R173 Ulaire Attea, Black Predator .60 1.50
❑ 12R174a Ulaire Cantea, Black Assassin 1.50 4.00
❑ 12R174b Ulaire Cantea, Black Assassin TENGWAR
❑ 12R175 Ulaire Enquea, Black Threat .75 2.00
❑ 12R179 Ulaire Otsea, Black Specter .60 1.50
❑ 12R183 The Witch-king, Black Lord 1.25 3.00
❑ 12S113 Eored Warrior .40 1.00
❑ 12S125 Measure of Comfort .40 1.00
❑ 12S126 No Worse for Wear .40 1.00
❑ 12S133 Tolman Cotton, Farmer of Bywater .40 1.00
❑ 12S144 Saruman, Agent of the Dark Lord .40 1.00
❑ 12S151 Uruk Desecrator .40 1.00
❑ 12S152 Uruk Dominator .40 1.00
❑ 12S187 Emyn Muil .40 1.00
❑ 12S188 Hill of Sight .40 1.00
❑ 12S189 Hobbiton Market .40 1.00
❑ 12S190 Northern Pelennor .40 1.00
❑ 12U103 Storming the Ramparts .30 .75
❑ 12U104 Taunt .30 .75
❑ 12U112 Eomer, Eored Leader .30 .75
❑ 12U117 Leofric, Defender of the Mark .30 .75
❑ 12U130 Simple Living .30 .75
❑ 12U131 Stand Together .30 .75
❑ 12U132 Sudden Fury .30 .75
❑ 12U135 Barbaric Uruk .30 .75
❑ 12U136 Berserker Torch .30 .75
❑ 12U138 Broken Heirloom .30 .75
❑ 12U140 Crushing Uruk .30 .75
❑ 12U147 Suppressing Uruk .30 .75
❑ 12U148 Tempest of War .30 .75
❑ 12U158 Vicious Uruk .30 .75
❑ 12U161 Black Rider .30 .75
❑ 12U165 In the Ringwraith's Wake .30 .75
❑ 12U166 Lingering Shadow .30 .75
❑ 12U167 Minas Morgul Answers .30 .75
❑ 12U172 Sense of Obligation .30 .75
❑ 12U176 Ulaire Lemenya, Black Enemy .30 .75
❑ 12U180 Ulaire Toldea, Black Shadow .30 .75
❑ 12U184 The Witch-king's Beast, Fell Creature .30 .75
❑ 12U185 The Angle .30 .75
❑ 12U186 The Bridge of Khazad-dum .30 .75
❑ 12U191 Shores of Nen Hithoel .30 .75
❑ 12U192 Slopes of Orodruin .30 .75
❑ 12U193 Starkhorn .30 .75
❑ 12U194 Wold Battlefield .30 .75

2005 Lord of the Rings Black Rider Legends Foil

COMLETE SET (18) 20.00 40.00
❑ 12RF1 Elrond, Witness to History (F) 1.50 4.00
❑ 12RF2 Hadafang (F) 2.50 6.00
❑ 12RF3 Gandalf, The White Rider (F) .75 2.00
❑ 12RF4 Faramir, Dunadan of Gondor (F) 1.00 2.50
❑ 12RF5 Faramir's Sword (F) 1.25 3.00
❑ 12RF6 Castamir of Umbar, Corsair Vandal (F) 2.00 5.00
❑ 12RF7 Grima, Betrayer of Rohan (F) .60 1.50
❑ 12RF8 The Balrog, The Terror of Khazad-dum (F) 1.50 4.00
❑ 12RF9 Cave Troll of Moria, Savage Menace (F) 5.00 10.00
❑ 12RF10 Orc Artisan (F) 1.25 3.00
❑ 12RF11 The Mouth of Sauron 1.25 3.00
Lieutenant of Barad-dur (F)
❑ 12RF12 Bilbo, Melancholy Hobbit (F) .60 1.50
❑ 12RF13 Uruk Zealot (F) .60 1.50
❑ 12RF14 Dark Approach (F) 7.50 15.00
❑ 12RF15 Ulaire Attea, Black Predator (F) .60 1.50
❑ 12RF16 Ulaire Cantea, Black Assassin (F) 3.00 8.00
❑ 12RF17 Ulaire Enquea, Black Threat (F) 1.00 2.50
❑ 12RF18 The Witch-king, Black Lord (F) 2.50 6.00

2005 Lord of the Rings Black Rider Legends Masterworks Foil

COMPLETE SET (9) 25.00 50.00
❑ 1201 Gandalf, The White Rider (O) 5.00 10.00
❑ 1202 Faramir, Dunadan of Gondor (O) 5.00 10.00
❑ 1203 Faramir's Sword (O) 3.00 8.00
❑ 1204 The Balrog, The Terror of Khazad-dum (O) 5.00 10.00
❑ 1205 Dark Approach (O) 7.50 15.00
❑ 1206 Ulaire Attea, Black Predator (O) 3.00 8.00
❑ 1207 Ulaire Cantea, Black Assassin (O) 6.00 12.00
❑ 1208 Ulaire Enquea, Black Threat (O) 3.00 8.00
❑ 1209 The Witch-king, Black Lord (O) 7.50 15.00

2005 Lord of the Rings Bloodlines

COMPLETE SET (194) 100.00 200.00
BOOSTER BOX (36) 30.00 60.00
BOOSTER PACK 1.25 2.50
❑ 13C2 Awkward Moment .12 .30
❑ 13C6 Honoring His Kinfolk .12 .30
❑ 13C7 Sorrow Shared .12 .30
❑ 13R1 Arod, Rohirrim Steed 1.50 4.00
❑ 13R5a Gimli, Lord of the Glittering Caves 2.00 5.00
❑ 13R5b Gimli, Lord of the Glittering Caves TENGWAR
❑ 13R8 Subterranean Homestead .60 1.50
❑ 13S9 Arwen, Reflection of Luthien .40 1.00
❑ 13U3 Deep Hatred .30 .75
❑ 13U4 Dwarf-lords .30 .75
❑ 13C12 City of the Trees .12 .30
❑ 13C13 Crashing Cavalry .12 .30
❑ 13C14 Final Shot .12 .30
❑ 13C16 Inside a Song .12 .30
❑ 13C21 Many Miles .12 .30
❑ 13C23 Shrouded Elf .12 .30
❑ 13C24 Sprang Forth Nimbly .12 .30
❑ 13C25 Standing Tall .12 .30
❑ 13C29 Dasron, Merchant from Dorwinion .12 .30
❑ 13C30 Fear and Great Wonder .12 .30
❑ 13C32 For a While Less Dark .12 .30
❑ 13C35 No Colour Now .12 .30
❑ 13C39 Return to Us .12 .30
❑ 13C41 Strange Meeting .12 .30
❑ 13C47 Duality .12 .30
❑ 13C51 It's My Birthday .12 .30
❑ 13C54 Out of All Knowledge .12 .30
❑ 13C66 Faramir, Prince of Ithilien .12 .30
❑ 13C68 Guarded City .12 .30
❑ 13C69 Heirs of Gondor .12 .30
❑ 13C73 Kingsfoil .12 .30
❑ 13C77 Tradesman From Lebennin .12 .30
❑ 13C82 Bring Down the Wall .12 .30
❑ 13C83 Caravan From the South .12 .30
❑ 13C87 Driven From the Plains .12 .30
❑ 13C90 Easterling Runner .12 .30
❑ 13C96 Merciless Dunlending .12 .30
❑ 13C97 Pirate Cutthroat .12 .30
❑ 13R10 Asfaloth, Swift Blossom .60 1.50
❑ 13R11 Celeborn, The Wise 1.00 2.50
❑ 13R15 Galadriel, Sorceress of the Hidden Land .75 2.00
❑ 13R18 Legolas, of the Grey Company 1.25 3.00
❑ 13R22 Secluded Homestead .75 2.00
❑ 13R26 Take Up the Bow 1.00 2.50
❑ 13R33 Gandalf, Bearer of Obligation 2.00 5.00
❑ 13R36 The Palantir of Orthanc 1.25 3.00
Recovered Seeing Stone
❑ 13R37 Pallando, Far-travelling One 5.00 10.00
❑ 13R38 Radagast, Tender of Beasts 2.00 5.00
❑ 13R40 Shadowfax, Roaring Wind .60 1.50
❑ 13R42 Traveler's Homestead .75 2.00
❑ 13R44 Chasm's Edge 1.25 3.00
❑ 13R46a Deagol, Fateful Finder .75 2.00
❑ 13R46b Deagol, Fateful Finder TENGWAR
❑ 13R48 Fishing Boat .75 2.00
❑ 13R49 Gladden Homestead 1.25 3.00
❑ 13R57 Trap Is Sprung .75 2.00
❑ 13R58 Wild Light of Madness 1.25 3.00
❑ 13R59 Aragorn, Isildur's Heir 1.00 2.50
❑ 13R63 Brego, Loyal Steed 1.25 3.00
❑ 13R64 Denethor, Last Ruling Steward 1.00 2.50
❑ 13R65 Elendil, High-King of Gondor 6.00 12.00
❑ 13R76 Storied Homestead 1.00 2.50
❑ 13R78 Alatar Deceived .75 2.00
❑ 13R80 Radagast Deceived .60 1.50
❑ 13R81 Staff of Saruman, Fallen Istar's Stave 1.25 3.00
❑ 13R84 Corsair Champion .75 2.00
❑ 13R86 Desert Wind 1.00 2.50
❑ 13R93 Harmless 1.25 3.00
❑ 13S20 Lorien Protector .40 1.00
❑ 13S62 Boromir, Doomed Heir .40 1.00
❑ 13S74 Rally the Company .40 1.00
❑ 13S85 Cruel Dunlending .40 1.00
❑ 13S99 Stragglers .40 1.00
❑ 13U17 Kindreds Estranged .30 .75
❑ 13U19 Let Fly .30 .75
❑ 13U27 Wells of Deep Memory .30 .75
❑ 13U28 Alatar, Final Envoy .30 .75
❑ 13U31 The Flame of Anor .30 .75
❑ 13U34 Look to My Coming .30 .75
❑ 13U43 Vapour and Steam .30 .75
❑ 13U45 Cunningly Hidden .30 .75
❑ 13U50 Gollum, Her Sneak .30 .75
❑ 13U52 Little Snuffler .30 .75
❑ 13U53 Naked Waste .30 .75
❑ 13U55 Smeagol, Simple Stoor .30 .75
❑ 13U56 Softly Up Behind .30 .75
❑ 13U60 Away on the Wind .30 .75
❑ 13U61 Banners Blowing .30 .75
❑ 13U67 Guard of the White Tree .30 .75
❑ 13U70 Hope Renewed .30 .75
❑ 13U71 Isildur, Heir of Elendil .30 .75
❑ 13U72 Kings' Legacy .30 .75
❑ 13U75 Stewards' Legacy .30 .75
❑ 13U79 Pallando Deceived .30 .75
❑ 13U88 Dunlending Patriarch .30 .75
❑ 13U89 Dunlending Trapper .30 .75
❑ 13U91 Fires Brightly Burning .30 .75
❑ 13U92 Grima, Footman of Saruman .30 .75
❑ 13U94 Howdah .30 .75
❑ 13U95 Lying in Wait .30 .75
❑ 13U98 Southron Murderer .30 .75
❑ 13C102 Worn Battleaxe .12 .30
❑ 13C107 Expendable Servants .12 .30
❑ 13C111 Massing Strength .12 .30
❑ 13C113 Orc Line-breaker .12 .30
❑ 13C116 Orc Reaper .12 .30
❑ 13C119 Underdeeps Denizen .12 .30
❑ 13C120 Unforgiving Depths .12 .30
❑ 13C121 Whatever Means .12 .30
❑ 13C125 Ferthu Theoden Hal .12 .30
❑ 13C127 Freely Across Our Land .12 .30
❑ 13C129 Hamstrung .12 .30
❑ 13C132 Merchant of Westfold .12 .30
❑ 13C133 Riddermark Tactician .12 .30
❑ 13C134 Ride With Me .12 .30
❑ 13C145 Don't Let Go .12 .30
❑ 13C147 Faith in Friendship .12 .30
❑ 13C157 Westfarthing Businessman .12 .30
❑ 13C159 Assault Denizen .12 .30
❑ 13C160 Cavern Denizen .12 .30
❑ 13C161 Endless Assault .12 .30
❑ 13C162 Enemy Without Number .12 .30
❑ 13C163 Entranced Uruk .12 .30
❑ 13C164 Fearless Approach .12 .30
❑ 13C168 Uruk Aggressor .12 .30
❑ 13C172 Uruk Outrider .12 .30
❑ 13C173 Uruk Reserve .12 .30
❑ 13C175 Uruk Tactician .12 .30
❑ 13C176 War Machine .12 .30
❑ 13C184 Ulaire Nertea, Servant of the Shadow .12 .30
❑ 13R101 Voice of the Desert, Southron Troop 2.00 5.00
❑ 13R104 Chamber Patrol 1.00 2.50
❑ 13R108 Forced March .75 2.00
❑ 13R112a Orc Crusher 1.50 4.00
❑ 13R112b Orc Crusher TENGWAR
❑ 13R115 Orc Raid Commander .75 2.00
❑ 13R117 Ordnance Grunt 3.00 8.00
❑ 13R123 Eomer, Heir to Meduseld 1.00 2.50
❑ 13R126 Firefoot, Mearas of the Mark 7.50 15.00
❑ 13R136 Snowmane, Noble Mearas 1.00 2.50
❑ 13R137a Theoden, The Renowned 3.00 8.00
❑ 13R137b Theoden, The Renowned TENGWAR
❑ 13R138 Theodred, Second Marshal of the Mark 2.00 5.00
❑ 13R139 Wind-swept Homestead .60 1.50
❑ 13R140 Sauron, Dark Lord of Mordor 3.00 8.00
❑ 13R141 Sceptre of the Dark Lord 1.50 4.00
❑ 13R142 Bilbo, Aged Ring-bearer 2.00 5.00
❑ 13R143 Bill the Pony, Dearly-loved 1.00 2.50
❑ 13R149 Frodo, Frenzied Fighter 3.00 8.00
❑ 13R152 Humble Homestead 1.00 2.50
❑ 13R153 Mithril-coat, Dwarf-mail 1.00 2.50
❑ 13R155 Phial of Galadriel, The Light of Earendil 1.00 2.50
❑ 13R156a Sam, Bearer of Great Need .75 2.00
❑ 13R156b Sam, Bearer of Great Need TENGWAR
❑ 13R158 Assault Commander .75 2.00
❑ 13R169 Uruk Blitz 1.25 3.00
❑ 13R171 Uruk Invader .60 1.50
❑ 13R174a Uruk Rogue 1.00 2.50
❑ 13R174b Uruk Rogue TENGWAR
❑ 13R178 Dark Fell About Him .75 2.00
❑ 13R180 Shadow in the East .60 1.50
❑ 13R182 Ulaire Enquea, Sixth of the Nine Riders 2.00 5.00
❑ 13S100 Vicious Dunlending .40 1.00
❑ 13S109 Howling Orc .40 1.00
❑ 13S114 Orc Plains Runner .40 1.00
❑ 13S118 Picket Denizen .40 1.00
❑ 13S186 Caves of Aglarond .75 2.00
❑ 13S189 Crossroads of the Fallen Kings .75 2.00
❑ 13S191 Fords of Isen .40 1.00
❑ 13S192 The Great Gates .40 1.00
❑ 13U103 Always Threatening .30 .75
❑ 13U105 Defiled .30 .75
❑ 13U106 Enemy Upon Enemy .30 .75
❑ 13U110 Isengard Informant .30 .75
❑ 13U122 Bitter Tidings .30 .75
❑ 13U124 Eowyn, Restless Warrior .30 .75
❑ 13U128 Hama, Captain of the King's Guard .30 .75
❑ 13U130 Hurried Barrows .30 .75
❑ 13U131 King's Board .30 .75
❑ 13U135 Rider's Bow .30 .75
❑ 13U144 Daddy Twofoot, Next-door Neighbor .30 .75
❑ 13U146 Everything but My Bones .30 .75
❑ 13U148 Fates Entwined .30 .75
❑ 13U150 Frodo Gamgee, Son of Samwise .30 .75
❑ 13U151 The Gaffer, Master Gardener .30 .75
❑ 13U154 New Chapter .30 .75
❑ 13U165 Isengard Infiltrator .30 .75
❑ 13U166 New Enemy .30 .75
❑ 13U167 Signs of War .30 .75
❑ 13U170 Uruk Distractor .30 .75
❑ 13U177 Weapons of Control .30 .75
❑ 13U179 From Hideous Eyrie .30 .75
❑ 13U181 They Came From Mordor .30 .75
❑ 13U183 Ulaire Lemenya, Servant of the Shadow .30 .75
❑ 13U185 Abandoned Mine Shaft .30 .75
❑ 13U187 City of Kings .30 .75
❑ 13U188 Courtyard Parapet .30 .75
❑ 13U190 Doors of Durin .30 .75
❑ 13U193 Isenwash .30 .75
❑ 13U194 Redhorn Pass .30 .75

2005 Lord of the Rings Bloodlines Legends Foil

COMPLETE SET (18) 30.00 60.00
❑ 13RF1 Celeborn, The Wise (F) 2.00 5.00
❑ 13RF2 Galadriel, Sorceress of the Hidden Land (F) .75 2.00
❑ 13RF3 Legolas, of the Grey Company (F) 3.00 8.00
❑ 13RF4 Gandalf, Bearer of Obligation (F) 2.50 6.00
❑ 13RF5 Pallando, Far-travelling One (F) 3.00 8.00
❑ 13RF6 Deagol, Fateful Finder (F) 1.25 3.00
❑ 13RF7 Aragorn, Isildur's Heir (F) .75 2.00
❑ 13RF8 Denethor, Last Ruling Steward (F) 1.50 4.00
❑ 13RF9 Voice of the Desert, Southron Troop (F) 1.50 4.00
❑ 13RF10 Chamber Patrol (F) 1.00 2.50
❑ 13RF11 Orc Crusher (F) 1.50 4.00
❑ 13RF12 Eomer, Heir to Meduseld (F) .75 2.00
❑ 13RF13 Theoden, The Renowned (F) 1.25 3.00
❑ 13RF14 Sauron, Dark Lord of Mordor (F) 6.00 12.00
❑ 13RF15 Frodo, Frenzied Fighter (F) 3.00 8.00
❑ 13RF16 Sam, Bearer of Great Need (F) 2.50 6.00
❑ 13RF17 Uruk Blitz (F) .75 2.00
❑ 13RF18 Uruk Rogue (F) 1.50 4.00

2005 Lord of the Rings Bloodlines Legends Masterworks Foil

COMPLETE SET (9) 50.00 100.00
❑ 1301 Celeborn, The Wise (O) 7.50 15.00
❑ 1302 Galadriel, Sorceress of the Hidden Land (O) 10.00 20.00
❑ 1303 Legolas, of the Grey Company (O) 15.00 30.00
❑ 1304 Gandalf, Bearer of Obligation (O) 10.00 20.00
❑ 1305 Pallando, Far-traveling One (O) 12.00 25.00
❑ 1306 Aragorn, Isildur's Heir (O) 10.00 20.00
❑ 1307 Denethor, Last Ruling Steward (O) 7.50 15.00
❑ 1308 Eomer, Heir to Meduseld (O) 7.50 15.00
❑ 1309 Theoden, The Renowned (O) 10.00 20.00

2006 Lord of the Rings Expanded Middle-Earth

COMPLETE SET (15) 20.00 40.00
❑ 14R1 Dain Ironfoot, King Under the Mountain 2.00 5.00
❑ 14R2 Elladan, Son of Elrond 5.00 10.00
❑ 14R3 Elrohir, Son of Elrond 6.00 12.00
❑ 14R4 Gildor Inglorion, of the House of Finrod 1.25 3.00
❑ 14R5 Brand, King of Dale 2.00 5.00
❑ 14R6 Grimbeorn, Beorning Chieftain 5.00 10.00
❑ 14R7 Duilin, Ranger from Blackroot Vale 1.25 3.00
❑ 14R8 Duinhir, Tall Man of Blackroot Vale 1.25 3.00
❑ 14R9 Halbarad, Ranger of the North 2.50 6.00
❑ 14R10 Furious Hillman 1.25 3.00
❑ 14R11 Swarming Hillman 1.25 3.00
❑ 14R12 Half-troll of Far Harad 1.50 4.00
❑ 14R13 Horror of Harad 1.25 3.00
❑ 14R14 Uruk-hai Healer 1.25 3.00
❑ 14R15 Uruk-hai Scout 1.25 3.00

2006 Lord of the Rings The Hunters

BOOSTER BOX (36) 50.00 100.00
BOOSTER PACK 2.00 4.00
❑ 15C5 Gimli, Eager Hunter .12 .30
❑ 15C8 Sturdy Stock .12 .30
❑ 15R1 The One Ring, The Ring of Doom 12.00 25.00
❑ 15R6 Gloin, Son of Groin 3.00 8.00
❑ 15R9 Well-crafted Armor 1.25 3.00
❑ 15S2 The One Ring, The Ruling Ring .40 1.00
❑ 15U3 Chamber of Records .30 .75
❑ 15U4 The Fortunes of Balin's Folk .30 .75
❑ 15U7 Heavy Axe .30 .75
❑ 15C10 Whatever End .12 .30
❑ 15C13 Elven Bow .12 .30
❑ 15C14 Elven Warrior .12 .30
❑ 15C15 Focus .12 .30
❑ 15C23 Point Blank Range .12 .30
❑ 15C25 Sword of the Fallen .12 .30
❑ 15C28 Ent Avenger .12 .30
❑ 15C45 Hurry Hobbitses .12 .30
❑ 15C46 Nice Fish .12 .30
❑ 15C48 Release Them .12 .30
❑ 15C59 Dunedain of the South .12 .30
❑ 15C60a Forth the Three Hunters! DWARVEN .12 .30
❑ 15C60b Forth the Three Hunters! ELVEN .12 .30
❑ 15C60c Forth the Three Hunters! GONDOR .12 .30
❑ 15C62 Ithilien Blade .12 .30
❑ 15C65 No Quicker Path .12 .30
❑ 15C68 Ranger's Cloak .12 .30
❑ 15C69 Silent Traveler .12 .30
❑ 15C71 Unyielding Ranger .12 .30
❑ 15C73 Bold Easterling .12 .30
❑ 15C75 Courageous Easterling .12 .30
❑ 15C77 Easterling Scout .12 .30
❑ 15C80 Great Axe .12 .30
❑ 15C82 Grousing Hillman .12 .30
❑ 15C83 Hunting Herdsman .12 .30
❑ 15C91 Ravaging Wild Man .12 .30
❑ 15C93 Swarthy Hillman .12 .30
❑ 15C97 Beasts of Burden .12 .30
❑ 15R11 Arwen, She-Elf 5.00 10.00
❑ 15R12 Dinendal, Mirkwood Archer 5.00 10.00
❑ 15R19 Legolas, of the Woodland Realm 6.00 12.00
❑ 15R22 The Mirror of Galadriel, Dangerous Guide 2.00 5.00
❑ 15R24 Spied From Afar 1.25 3.00
❑ 15R29 Gandalf, Powerful Guide 7.50 15.00
❑ 15R29P Gandalf, Powerful Guide PROMO 5.00 10.00
❑ 15R30 Leaflock, Finglas 6.00 12.00
❑ 15R33 One Last Surprise 1.50 4.00
❑ 15R34 Quickbeam, Hastiest of All Ents 2.50 6.00
❑ 15R36 Shepherd of the Trees 5.00 10.00
❑ 15R38 Treebeard, Enraged Shepherd 6.00 12.00
❑ 15R40 Connected by Fate .75 2.00
❑ 15R42 Desperate Move 1.50 4.00
❑ 15R43 Gollum, Hopeless 2.50 6.00
❑ 15R47 Not This Time! 5.00 10.00
❑ 15R49 Smeagol, Wretched and Hungry 1.25 3.00
❑ 15R53 Unseen Foe 3.00 8.00
❑ 15R55 Aragorn, Thorongil 6.00 12.00
❑ 15R56 Aragorn's Bow, Ranger's Longbow 12.00 25.00
❑ 15R58 Decorated Barricade 2.00 5.00
❑ 15R64 Madril, Defender of Osgiliath 1.50 4.00
❑ 15R70 Tremendous Wall 1.00 2.50
❑ 15R72 Bill Ferny, Agent of Saruman 6.00 12.00
❑ 15R74 Chieftain of Dunland 2.00 5.00
❑ 15R76 Destroyed Homestead 1.00 2.50
❑ 15R84 Last Gasp 1.50 4.00
❑ 15R86 Mumak Commander, 6.00 12.00
Giant Among the Swertings
❑ 15R87 Primitive Savage 1.50 4.00
❑ 15R99 Black Land Chieftain 1.50 4.00
❑ 15S18 Legolas, Fleet-footed Hunter .40 1.00
❑ 15S54 Aragorn, Swift Hunter .40 1.00
❑ 15S95 Battlefield Recruit .40 1.00
❑ 15S96 Battlefield Veteran .40 1.00
❑ 15U16 Gift of the Evenstar, Blessed Light .30 .75
❑ 15U17 Haldir, Sentry of the Golden Wood .30 .75
❑ 15U20 Lorien's Blessing .30 .75
❑ 15U21 Mighty Shot .30 .75
❑ 15U26 Uruviel, Woodland Maid .30 .75
❑ 15U27 Be Gone! .30 .75
❑ 15U31 Mellon! .30 .75
❑ 15U32 Momentous Gathering .30 .75
❑ 15U35 Shadow of the Wood .30 .75
❑ 15U37 Skinbark, Elder Ent .30 .75
❑ 15U39 Called to Mordor .30 .75
❑ 15U41 Controlled by the Ring .30 .75
❑ 15U44 Herbs and Stewed Rabbit .30 .75
❑ 15U50 Something Slimy .30 .75

- 15U51 Sudden Strike .30 .75
- 15U52 Swear By the Precious .30 .75
- 15U57 Damrod, Dunadan of Gondor .30 .75
- 15U61 Gondorian Prowler .30 .75
- 15U63 Mablung, Ranger of Ithilien .30 .75
- 15U66 No Travellers In This Land .30 .75
- 15U69 Portico .30 .75
- 15U78 Engrossed Hillman .30 .75
- 15U79 Enraged Herdsman .30 .75
- 15U81 Grieving the Fallen .30 .75
- 15U85 Lying Counsel .30 .75
- 15U88 Pursuing Horde .30 .75
- 15U89 Rapid Reload .30 .75
- 15U90 Rapt Hillman .30 .75
- 15U92 Savage Southron .30 .75
- 15U94 Wandering Hillman .30 .75
- 15U98 Black Gate Sentry .30 .75
- 15C100 Black Land Commander .12 .30
- 15C101 Black Land Observer .12 .30
- 15C103 Black Land Runner .12 .30
- 15C105 Black Land Spy .12 .30
- 15C107 Desolation Orc .12 .30
- 15C108 Destructive Orc .12 .30
- 15C110 Isengard Marauder .12 .30
- 15C116 Scouting Orc .12 .30
- 15C120 Veteran War Chief .12 .30
- 15C121 Brilliant Light .12 .30
- 15C125 Eowyn, Willing Fighter .12 .30
- 15C127 Grim Trophy .12 .30
- 15C130 Horseman of the North .12 .30
- 15C131 Our Inspiration .12 .30
- 15C133 Rider's Mount .12 .30
- 15C136 Rohirrim Axe .12 .30
- 15C143 Community Living .12 .30
- 15C144 Frodo, Weary From the Journey .12 .30
- 15C145 Hobbit Sword .12 .30
- 15C147 Hobbiton Farmer, Lover of Pipeweed .12 .30
- 15C149 Merry, The Tall One .12 .30
- 15C150 No Visitors .12 .30
- 15C151 Pippin, The Short One .12 .30
- 15C156 Charging Uruk .12 .30
- 15C157 Chasing Uruk .12 .30
- 15C158 Covetous Uruk .12 .30
- 15C161 Hunting Uruk .12 .30
- 15C167 Pursuing Uruk .12 .30
- 15C169 Seeking Uruk .12 .30
- 15C176 Uruk Village Assassin .12 .30
- 15C178 Uruk Village Stormer .12 .30
- 15C179 Violent Hurl .12 .30
- 15R104 Black Land Shrieker 2.50 6.00
- 15R109 Gorbag, Filthy Rebel 2.50 6.00
- 15R112 Mountain-troll 7.50 15.00
- 15R117 Tower Troll 3.00 8.00
- 15R119 Unreasonable Choice 1.25 3.00
- 15R122 Burial Mounds 1.25 3.00
- 15R123 Eomer, Horsemaster 3.00 8.00
- 15R124 Eomer's Spear, Trusty Weapon 3.00 8.00
- 15R135 Rohan Worker 1.00 2.50
- 15R141 Sturdy Shield 1.25 3.00
- 15R146 Hobbiton Brewer, Maker of Fine Ales 5.00 10.00
- 15R148 Little Golden Flower 2.00 5.00
- 15R152 Relaxation 2.00 5.00
- 15R154 Second Breakfast 1.25 3.00
- 15R155 Advancing Horde 2.00 5.00
- 15R162 Lurtz, Now Perfected 2.00 5.00
- 15R163 Lurtz's Sword, Mighty Longsword 1.00 2.50
- 15R165 Merciless Berserker 1.25 3.00
- 15R170 Sentry Uruk 1.50 4.00
- 15R172 Ugluk, Ugly Fellow 7.50 15.00
- 15R173 Ugluk's Sword, Weapon of Command 1.50 4.00
- 15R174 Uruk Cavern Striker .75 2.00
- 15R180 With All Possible Speed 1.50 4.00
- 15R182 A Shadow Fell Over Them 1.50 4.00
- 15R184 Ulaire Attea, Desirous of Power 1.25 3.00
- 15R185 Ulaire Lemenya, Eternally Threatening 5.00 10.00
- 15R186 Ulaire Nelya, Fell Rider .75 2.00
- 15R193 Mount Doom 3.00 8.00
- 15S126 Gamling, The Old .40 1.00
- 15S138 Rohirrim Soldier .40 1.00
- 15S164 Mauhur, Relentless Hunter .40 1.00
- 15S171 Tracking Uruk .40 1.00
- 15U102 Black Land Overlord .30 .75
- 15U106 Coordinated Effort .30 .75
- 15U111 Moria Menace .30 .75
- 15U113 Orkish Camp .30 .75
- 15U114 Orkish Hunting Spear .30 .75
- 15U115 Pummeling Blow .30 .75
- 15U118 Unmistakable Omen .30 .75
- 15U128 Haleth, Son of Hama .30 .75
- 15U129 Horse of Great Stature .30 .75
- 15U132 Last Days of My House .30 .75
- 15U134 Rohan Stable Master .30 .75
- 15U137 Rohirrim Doorwarden .30 .75
- 15U139 Rohirrim Warrior .30 .75
- 15U140 Spear of the Mark .30 .75
- 15U142 Swift Stroke .30 .75
- 15U153 Sam, Innocent Traveler .30 .75
- 15U159 Defensive Rush .30 .75
- 15U160 Following Uruk .30 .75
- 15U166 Poised for Assault .30 .75
- 15U168 Searching Uruk .30 .75
- 15U175 Uruk Infantry .30 .75
- 15U177 Uruk Village Rager .30 .75
- 15U181 Later Than You Think .30 .75
- 15U183 They Feel the Precious .30 .75
- 15U187 Anduin River .30 .75
- 15U188 Breeding Pit of Isengard .30 .75
- 15U189 City Gates .30 .75
- 15U190 East Wall of Rohan .30 .75
- 15U191 Gate of Mordor .30 .75
- 15U192 Isengard Ruined .30 .75
- 15U194 Westfold Village .30 .75

2006 Lord of the Rings The Hunters Legends Foil

COMPLETE SET (18) 50.00 100.00

- 15RF1 The One Ring, The Ring of Doom (F) 30.00 60.00
- 15RF2 Well-crafted Armor (F) 2.00 5.00
- 15RF3 Legolas, of the Woodland Realm (F) 3.00 8.00
- 15RF4 The Mirror of Galadriel, Dangerous Guide (F) 1.25 3.00
- 15RF5 Gandalf, Powerful Guide (F) 7.50 15.00
- 15RF6 One Last Surprise (F) .75 2.00
- 15RF7 Quickbeam, Hastiest of All Ents (F) 5.00 10.00
- 15RF8 Smeagol, Wretched and Hungry (F) 2.50 6.00
- 15RF9 Aragorn, Thorongil (F) 10.00 20.00
- 15RF10 Madril, Defender of Osgiliath (F) 2.00 5.00
- 15RF11 Black Land Chieftain (F) 1.25 3.00
- 15RF12 Gorbag, Filthy Rebel (F) 2.00 5.00
- 15RF13 Eomer, Horsemaster (F) 3.00 8.00
- 15RF14 Sentry Uruk (F) 1.00 2.50
- 15RF15 Ulaire Attea, Desirous of Power (F) 2.50 6.00
- 15RF16 Ulaire Lemenya, Eternally Threatening (F) 5.00 10.00

Beckett LOTR price guide sponsored by wholesalegaming.com

- 15RF17 Ulaire Nelya, Fell Rider (F) 1.00 2.50
- 15RF18 Mount Doom (F) 7.50 15.00

2006 Lord of the Rings The Hunters Legends Masterworks Foil

- 1501 Legolas, of the Woodland Realm (O) 25.00 50.00
- 1502 Gandalf, Powerful Guide (O) 15.00 30.00
- 1503 Quickbeam, Hastiest of All Ents (O) 12.00 25.00
- 1504 Aragorn, Thorongil (O) 30.00 60.00
- 1505 Madril, Defender of Osgiliath (O) 15.00 30.00
- 1506 Eomer, Horsemaster (O) 10.00 20.00
- 1507 Ulaire Attea, Desirous of Power (O) 12.00 25.00
- 1508 Ulaire Lemenya, Eternally Threatening (O) 10.00 20.00
- 1509 Ulaire Nelya, Fell Rider (O) 10.00 20.00

2006 Lord of the Rings The Wraith Collection

COMPLETE SET (6) 7.50 15.00

- 16R1 Barrow-wight Stalker 1.50 4.00
- 16R2 Candle Corpses 1.50 4.00
- 16R3 Covetous Wisp 1.50 4.00
- 16R4 Dead Faces 1.50 4.00
- 16R5 Spirit of Dread 1.50 4.00
- 16R6 Undead of Angmar 1.50 4.00

2007 Lord of the Rings Rise of Saruman

- 17R2 Balin Avenged 1.50 4.00
- 17R4 Ring of Artifice 6.00 12.00
- 17R6 Thorin III, Stonehelm 6.00 12.00
- 17S7 Elven Guardian .60 1.50
- 17U1 Armor of Khazad .40 1.00
- 17U3 Dwarven Stratagem .40 1.00
- 17U5 Axe- Work .40 1.00
- 17U8 Hearth and Hall .40 1.00
- 17U9 Lothlorien Guides .40 1.00
- 17C46 Pandemonium .12 .30
- 17C51 Stampeding Madman .12 .30
- 17C53 Stampeding Savage .12 .30
- 17C54 Stampeding Shepherd .12 .30
- 17C55 Sunland Guard .12 .30
- 17C57 Sunland Skirmisher .12 .30
- 17C59 Sunland Trooper .12 .30
- 17C60 Sunland Warrior .12 .30
- 17C62 Vengeful Savage .12 .30
- 17C63 Vengeful Wild Man .12 .30
- 17C64 Vengeful Pillager .12 .30
- 17C66 Wildman's Oath .12 .30
- 17C68 Chaotic Clash .12 .30
- 17C69 Cry and Panic .12 .30
- 17C70 Feral Ride .12 .30
- 17C72 Orkish Assassin .12 .30
- 17C75 Orkish Dreg .12 .30
- 17C78 Orkish Footman .12 .30
- 17C80 Orkish Lackey .12 .30
- 17C81 Orkish Maurader .12 .30
- 17C83 Orkish Runner .12 .30
- 17C85 Orkish Traveler .12 .30
- 17C92 Vicious Warg .12 .30
- 17R13 The World Ahead 5.00 10.00
- 17R17 Gandalf, Returned 12.00 25.00
- 17R18 Glamdring, Orc Beater 2.00 5.00
- 17R20 Gwaihir, The Windlord 6.00 12.00
- 17R23 Scintillating Bird .75 2.00
- 17R24 Shadowfax, Greatest of the Mearas 6.00 12.00
- 17R27 Anduril, Sword That Was Broken 6.00 12.00
- 17R28 Faramir, Bearer of Quality 7.50 15.00
- 17R29 Faramir's Bow, Ithilien Longbow 3.00 8.00
- 17R31 Narsil, Forged by Telchar 5.00 10.00
- 17R36 Throne of Minas Tirith 5.00 10.00
- 17R37 Saruman, Instigator of Insurrection 5.00 10.00
- 17R38 Saruman, Servant of Sauron 6.00 12.00
- 17R39 Throne of Isengard 1.25 3.00
- 17R41 Ceremonial Armor 2.50 6.00
- 17R43 Easterling Sneak 1.50 4.00
- 17R44 Grima's Dagger 1.25 3.00
- 17R45 In the Wild Men's Wake 2.50 6.00
- 17R49 Stampeding Chief 3.00 8.00
- 17R52 Stampeding Ransacker 2.00 5.00
- 17R56 Sunland Scout 1.50 4.00
- 17R58 Sunland Sneak 2.00 5.00
- 17R61 Sunland Weaponmaster 5.00 10.00
- 17R65 Vengeful Primitive .75 2.00
- 17R67 A Defiled Charge 3.00 8.00
- 17R71 Grishnakh, Treacherous Captain 6.00 12.00
- 17R73 Orkish Berserker 1.25 3.00
- 17R74 Orkish Cavalry 2.50 6.00
- 17R76 Orkish Fiend 2.00 5.00
- 17R79 Orkish Invader 2.50 6.00
- 17R82 Orkish Rider 2.00 5.00
- 17R84 Orkish Scout 2.50 6.00
- 17R86 Orkish Veteran 3.00 8.00
- 17R87 Orkish Warg-master 2.50 6.00
- 17R89 Relentless Warg 6.00 12.00
- 17R93 Aragorn, Defender of Rohan 6.00 12.00
- 17R95 Eomer, Northman 6.00 12.00
- 17R96 Eowyn, Northwoman 6.00 12.00
- 17R98 Throne of the Golden Hall 3.00 8.00
- 17R99 Hama, Northman 1.50 4.00
- 17S11 Orophin, Silvan Elf .60 1.50
- 17S12 Rumil, Silvan Elf .60 1.50
- 17S30 Madril, Loyal Lieutenant .60 1.50
- 17S33 Ranger of the White Tree .60 1.50
- 17S35 Soldier's Cache .60 1.50
- 17S48 Saruman, Coldly Still .60 1.50
- 17U10 Namarie .40 1.00
- 17U14 Weapons of Lothlorien .40 1.00
- 17U15 A New Light .40 1.00
- 17U16 Barliman Butterbur, Red-Faced Landlord .40 1.00
- 17U19 Guidance of the Istari .40 1.00
- 17U21 Long-stemmed Pipe .40 1.00
- 17U22 Meneldor, Misty Mountain Eagle .40 1.00
- 17U25 The Sap is in the Bough .40 1.00
- 17U26 Woodland Onod .40 1.00
- 17U32 Nimble Attack .40 1.00
- 17U34 Spirit of the White Tree .40 1.00
- 17U40 Beast of War .40 1.00
- 17U42 Easterling Dispatcher .40 1.00
- 17U47 Primitive Brand .40 1.00
- 17U50 Stampeding Hillsman .40 1.00
- 17U77 Orkish Flanker .40 1.00
- 17U88 Orkish Warrior .40 1.00
- 17U90 Rider's Gear .40 1.00
- 17U91 Threatening Warg .40 1.00
- 17U94 Dispatched with Haste .40 1.00
- 17U97 For Death and Glory .40 1.00
- 17C113 Deathly Roar .12 .30
- 17C118 Vile Pit .12 .30
- 17C119 White Hand Aggressor .12 .30
- 17C120 White Hand Attacker .12 .30
- 17C122 White Hand Butcher .12 .30
- 17C125 White Hand Enforcer .12 .30
- 17C126 White Hand Guard .12 .30
- 17C127 White Hand Intruder .12 .30
- 17C128 White Hand Invader .12 .30
- 17C130 White Hand Scout .12 .30
- 17C131 White Hand Slayer .12 .30
- 17C133 White Hand Trooper .12 .30
- 17C134 White Hand Vanquisher .12 .30
- 17C136 White Hand Warrior .12 .30
- 17R102 Theoden, Northman, King of Rohan 1.50 4.00
- 17R105 Throne of the Dark Lord 3.00 8.00
- 17R114 Land Had Changed 2.00 5.00
- 17R116 Saruman, Master of the White Hand 3.00 8.00
- 17R121 White Hand Berserker 2.00 5.00
- 17R123 White Hand Captain 1.50 4.00
- 17R124 White Hand Destroyer 2.50 6.00
- 17R129 White Hand Legion 1.50 4.00
- 17R132 White Hand Taskmaster 2.00 5.00
- 17R135 White Hand Veteran 2.50 6.00
- 17R137 You Do Not Know Fear 5.00 10.00
- 17R139 Ulaire Cantea, Duplicitous Assassin 6.00 12.00
- 17R140 Ulaire Enquea, Duplicitous Lieutenant 3.00 8.00
- 17R141 Ulaire Otsea, Duplicitous Specter 5.00 10.00
- 17R142 Ring of Savagery 2.50 6.00
- 17R143 Ring of Terror 6.00 12.00
- 17R144 The Witch-king, Conqueror of Arthedain 3.00 8.00
- 17S115 Saruman, Curunir .60 1.50
- 17U100 Into the Caves .40 1.00
- 17U101 Soldier of Rohan .40 1.00
- 17U103 Where Now the Horse .40 1.00
- 17U104 Warrior of Rohan .40 1.00
- 17U106 Halfling Leaf .40 1.00
- 17U107 Merry, In the Bloom of Health .40 1.00
- 17U108 Hornblower Leaf .40 1.00
- 17U109 Pippin, In the Bloom of Health .40 1.00
- 17U110 Southfarthing Leaf .40 1.00
- 17U111 Southlinch Leaf .40 1.00
- 17U112 Blade of the White Hand .40 1.00
- 17U117 Spear of the White Hand .40 1.00
- 17U138 You Do Not Know Pain .40 1.00
- 17U145 Dol Guldur .40 1.00
- 17U146 Falls of Rauros .40 1.00
- 17U147 Imladris .40 1.00
- 17U148 Nurn .40 1.00

2007 Lord of the Rings Rise of Saruman Legends Foil

- 17RF1 Ring of Artifice (F) 7.50 15.00
- 17RF2 Glamdring, Orc Beater (F) 7.50 15.00
- 17RF3 Shadowfax, Greatest of the Mearas (F) 20.00 40.00
- 17RF4 Gwaihir, The Windlord (F) 10.00 20.00
- 17RF5 Anduril, Sword That Was Broken (F) 12.00 25.00
- 17RF6 Faramir, Bearer of Quality (F) 30.00 60.00
- 17RF7 Narsil, Forged by Telchar (F) 12.00 25.00
- 17RF8 Throne of Minas Tirith (F) 7.50 15.00
- 17RF9 Throne of Isengard (F) 15.00 30.00
- 17RF10 Stampeding Chief (F) 10.00 20.00
- 17RF11 Orkish Invader (F) 12.00 25.00
- 17RF12 Aragorn, Defender of Rohan (F) 10.00 20.00
- 17RF13 Throne of the Golden Hall (F) 12.00 25.00
- 17RF14 Theoden, Northman, King of Rohan (F) 15.00 30.00
- 17RF15 Throne of the Dark Lord (F) 15.00 30.00
- 17RF16 Ulaire Otsea, Duplicitous Specter (F) 15.00 30.00
- 17RF17 Ring of Savagery (F) 15.00 30.00
- 17RF18 Ring of Terror (F) 7.50 15.00

2007 Lord of the Rings Rise of Saruman Legends Masterworks Foil

UNPRICED DUE TO SCARCITY

- 1701 Shadowfax, Greatest of the Mearas (O)
- 1702 Gwaihir, The Windlord (O)
- 1703 Throne of Minas Tirith (O)
- 1704 Aragorn, Defender of Rohan (O)
- 1705 Throne of the Golden Hall (O)
- 1706 Theoden, Northman, King of Rohan (O)
- 1707 Ulaire Otsea, Duplicitous Specter (O)
- 1708 Ring of Savagery (O)
- 1709 Ring of Terror (O)

2007 Lord of the Rings Treachery and Deceit

- 18C3 Thorin's Harp .25 .60
- 18C9 Elven Defender .25 .60
- 18R1 Gimli, Sprinter 3.00 8.00
- 18R4 Arwen's Bow 3.00 8.00
- 18R5 Arwen's Dagger 3.00 8.00
- 18R6 Back to the Light 5.00 10.00
- 18R7 Celebring, Elven-smith 2.50 6.00
- 18U2 Run Until Found .40 1.00
- 18U8 Elven Armaments .40 1.00
- 18C16 Miruvore .25 .60
- 18C17 Woodhall Elf, Exile .25 .60
- 18C19 Drawn to Full Height .25 .60
- 18C20 Ents Marching .25 .60
- 18C22 Librarian, Keeper of Ancient Texts .25 .60
- 18C36 Time for Food .25 .60
- 18C39 Armor of the White City .25 .60
- 18C44 Defenses Long Held .25 .60
- 18C49 Faramir's Company .25 .60
- 18C51 For Gondor! .25 .60
- 18C56 Ranger of the South .25 .60
- 18C57 Shield of the White Tree .25 .60
- 18C65 Declined Business .25 .60
- 18C68 Harry Goatleaf .25 .60
- 18C70 Ill News Is An Ill Guest .25 .60
- 18C72 Ruffian .25 .60
- 18C73 Rough Man of the South .25 .60
- 18C74 Squint-eyed Southerner .25 .60
- 18C77 Whisper in the Dark .25 .60
- 18C84 Orkish Ax .25 .60
- 18C85 Orkish Aggressor .25 .60
- 18C87 Orkish Breeder .25 .60
- 18C88 Orkish Defender .25 .60
- 18C89 Orkish Headsman .25 .60
- 18C90 Orkish Skirmisher .25 .60
- 18C91 Orkish Sneak .25 .60
- 18C94 Cast From the Hall .25 .60
- 18R11 Galadriel's Silver Ewer 7.50 15.00
- 18R12 Gil-galad, High King of the Noldor 15.00 30.00
- 18R13 Glorfindel, Eldarin Lord 6.00 12.00
- 18R14 Haldir, Warrior Messenger 2.50 6.00
- 18R15 Lembas Bread 3.00 8.00
- 18R18 Beorning Axe 6.00 12.00
- 18R24 Our Time 3.00 8.00
- 18R26 Radagast's Herb Bag 6.00 12.00
- 18R28 Countless Cords 2.50 6.00
- 18R29 Deceit 3.00 8.00
- 18R31 It Draws Him 2.50 6.00
- 18R32 Not Easily Avoided 5.00 10.00
- 18R34 Shelob, Menace 6.00 12.00
- 18R35 Sting of Shelob 3.00 8.00
- 18R38 Aragorn, Heir to the Throne of Gondor 7.50 15.00
- 18R40 Boromir, Proud and Noble Man 6.00 12.00
- 18R41 Crown of Gondor 3.00 8.00
- 18R42 Denethor, On the Edge of Madness 2.00 5.00
- 18R43 Denethor's Sword 2.00 5.00
- 18R47 Elendil's Army 3.00 8.00
- 18R48 Faramir, Captain of Ithilien 6.00 12.00
- 18R50 The Faithful Stone 5.00 10.00
- 18R52 Gondorian Servant, Denethor's Handman 2.50 6.00
- 18R53 Horn of Boromir, The Great Horn 5.00 10.00
- 18R54 Isildur, Sword-Bearer 6.00 12.00
- 18R55 Ranger of the North 2.00 5.00
- 18R59 Watcher at Sarn Ford, Ranger of the North 3.00 8.00
- 18R66 Fleet of Corsair Ships 2.50 6.00
- 18R67 Grima, Witless Worm 6.00 12.00
- 18R69 Henchman's Dagger 2.00 5.00
- 18R71 Mumakil Commander, Bold and Grim 2.50 6.00
- 18R76 Treachery 2.50 6.00
- 18R80 Gothmog, Morgul Leader 7.50 15.00
- 18R81 Gothmog's Warg, Leader's Mount 3.00 8.00
- 18R82 Grond, Forged With Black Steel 5.00 10.00
- 18R83 Gruesome Meal 3.00 8.00
- 18R95 Eomer's Bow 2.50 6.00
- 18R96 Erkenbrand's Horn 3.00 8.00
- 18R97 Erkenbrand's Shield 6.00 12.00
- 18R98 Fall back to Helm's Deep 3.00 8.00
- 18R99 Gamling, Dutiful Marshal 2.50 6.00
- 18U10 Elven Supplies .40 1.00
- 18U21 Last Stand .40 1.00
- 18U23 One-Upsmanship .40 1.00
- 18U25 Perspective .40 1.00
- 18U27 Ship of Smoke .40 1.00
- 18U30 Enemy in Your Midst .40 1.00
- 18U33 Set Up .40 1.00
- 18U37 Trusted Promise .40 1.00
- 18U45 Dunadan's Bow .40 1.00
- 18U46 Disarmed .40 1.00
- 18U58 Soldier's Cache .40 1.00
- 18U60 Corsair Boarding Axe .40 1.00
- 18U61 Corsair Bow .40 1.00
- 18U62 Corsair Grappling Hook .40 1.00
- 18U63 Corsair Halberd .40 1.00
- 18U64 Corsair Scimitar .40 1.00
- 18U75 Ted Sandyman, Chief's Men's Ally .40 1.00
- 18U78 Destroyers and Usurpers .40 1.00
- 18U79 Frenzy of Arrows .40 1.00
- 18U86 Orkish Archer Troop .40 1.00
- 18U92 War Preparations .40 1.00
- 18U93 Wary Orc .40 1.00
- 18C101 Precise Attack .25 .60
- 18C103 Rohirrim Recruit .25 .60
- 18C106 A Dragon's Tale .25 .60
- 18C109 Make a Run For It .25 .60
- 18C116 Fury of the Evil Army .25 .60
- 18C117 Ghastly Wound .25 .60
- 18C124 White Hand Attacker .25 .60
- 18C125 White Hand Exorciser .25 .60
- 18C128 White Hand Mystic .25 .60
- 18C129 White Hand Sieger .25 .60
- 18C131 White Hand Uruk .25 .60
- 18R100 Gamling's Horn 3.00 8.00
- 18R102 Rohirrim Diadem 2.50 6.00
- 18R105 Theoden, Ednew 3.00 8.00
- 18R107 Fredegar Bolger, Fatty 5.00 10.00
- 18R112 Scouring of the Shire 7.50 15.00
- 18R113 Sting, Elven Long Knife 5.00 10.00
- 18R114 Cleaved 3.00 8.00
- 18R115 Final Triumph 3.00 8.00
- 18R118 Lurtz, Halfling Hunter 5.00 10.00
- 18R119 Lurtz's Bow, Black-Fletch Bow 5.00 10.00
- 18R122 Shagrat, Tower Captain 5.00 10.00
- 18R126 White Hand Marchers 2.00 5.00
- 18R127 White Hand Marshal 6.00 12.00
- 18R133 Pull of the Ring 2.50 6.00
- 18U104 Surrendered Weapons .40 1.00
- 18U108 Golden Perch Ale .40 1.00
- 18U110 Prized Lagan .40 1.00
- 18U111 Robin Smallburrow, Shirriff Cock-Robin .40 1.00
- 18U120 New Forges Built .40 1.00
- 18U121 Pikes Upon Pikes .40 1.00
- 18U123 Tracking the Prize .40 1.00
- 18U130 White Hand Traveler .40 1.00
- 18U132 All-Life Flees .40 1.00
- 18U134 Doorway to Doom .40 1.00
- 18U135 Foot of Mount Doom .40 1.00
- 18U136 Mithlond .40 1.00
- 18U137 Morannon Plains .40 1.00
- 18U138 Sirannon Ruins .40 1.00
- 18U139 Steward's Tomb .40 1.00
- 18U140 Streets of Bree .40 1.00

2007 Lord of the Rings Treachery and Deceit Legends Foil

- 18RF1 Arwen's Bow (F) 10.00 20.00
- 18RF2 Arwen's Dagger (F) 7.50 15.00
- 18RF3 Galadriel's Silver Ewer (F) 10.00 20.00
- 18RF4 Beorning Axe (F) 15.00 30.00
- 18RF5 Radagast's Herb Bag (F) 10.00 20.00
- 18RF6 Shelob, Menace (F) 7.50 15.00
- 18RF7 Crown of Gondor (F) 7.50 15.00
- 18RF8 Denethor's Sword (F) 7.50 15.00
- 18RF9 Watcher at Sarn Ford, Ranger of the North (F) 7.50 15.00
- 18RF10 Gothmog, Morgul Leader (F) 10.00 20.00
- 18RF11 Erkenbrand's Horn (F) 10.00 20.00
- 18RF12 Erkenbrand's Shield (F) 7.50 15.00
- 18RF13 Rohirrim Diadem (F) 7.50 15.00
- 18RF14 Theoden, Ednew (F) 7.50 15.00
- 18RF15 Fredegar Bolger, Fatty (F) 7.50 15.00
- 18RF16 Sting, Elven Long Knife (F) 10.00 20.00
- 18RF17 Shagrat, Tower Captain (F) 7.50 15.00
- 18RF18 Pull of the Ring (F) 7.50 15.00

2007 Lord of the Rings Treachery and Deceit Legends Masterworks Foil

- 1801 Beorning Axe (O) 25.00 50.00
- 1802 Radagast's Herb Bag (O) 25.00 50.00
- 1803 Crown of Gondor (O) 25.00 50.00
- 1804 Denethor's Sword (O) 25.00 50.00
- 1805 Watcher at Sarn Ford, Ranger of the North (O) 20.00 40.00
- 1806 Erkenbrand's Horn (O) 20.00 40.00
- 1807 Erkenbrand's Shield (O) 25.00 50.00
- 1808 Rohirrim Diadem (O) 20.00 40.00
- 1809 Pull of the Ring (O) 20.00 40.00

2006 Naruto Coils of the Snake

COMPLETE SET (131) 40.00 80.00
BOOSTER BOX (24) 40.00 80.00
BOOSTER PACK 2.00 4.00

- C001 Inari C .10 .25
- C002 Tazuna C .10 .25
- C003 Gato C .10 .25

TCG/CCG

❑ C004 Madam Shijimi C	.10	.25
❑ C005 Zori C	.10	.25
❑ C006 Waraji C	.10	.25
❑ J043 Shadow of the Dancing Leaf U	.20	.50
❑ J044 Windmill C	.10	.25
❑ J045 Leaf Instant Move Jutsu C	.10	.25
❑ J046 Genjutsu C	.10	.25
❑ J047 Evil Illusion: Misleading Jutsu U	.20	.50
❑ J048 Sharingan Eye R	1.00	2.50
❑ J049 Shadow Clone Jutsu U	.20	.50
❑ J050 Ninja Info Card C	.10	.25
❑ J051 Senbon R	1.25	3.00
❑ J052 Slicing Sound Wave U	.20	.50
❑ J053 Sonic Fang R	1.00	2.50
❑ J054 Wind Scythe Jutsu R	1.25	3.00
❑ J055 Puppet Master Jutsu U	.20	.50
❑ J056 The Third Eye C	.10	.25
❑ J057 Sand Shield SR	3.00	8.00
❑ J058 Stone Bullet U	.20	.50
❑ J059 Makibishi Spikes C	.10	.25
❑ J060 Cheating R	1.00	2.50
❑ J061 Shadow Clone Jutsu U	.20	.50
❑ J062 Curse Sealing U	.20	.50
❑ J063 Sharingan Eye U	.20	.50
❑ J064 Giant Shuriken U	.20	.50
❑ J065 Smoke Pellet R	1.25	3.00
❑ J066 Disguise Jutsu U	.20	.50
❑ J067 Paper Bomb U	.20	.50
❑ J068 Chakra Concentration C	.10	.25
❑ J069 Paralysis Jutsu C	.10	.25
❑ J070 String Control Jutsu C	.10	.25
❑ J071 Fire Style: Phoenix Flower Jutsu R	1.25	3.00
❑ J072 Sharingan Windmill Triple Attack C	.10	.25
❑ J073 Fire Style: Dragon Flame Jutsu SR	4.00	10.00
❑ J074 Summoning Jutsu C	.10	.25
❑ J075 Senbon Rainstorm U	.20	.50
❑ J076 Striking Shadow Snake R	1.00	2.50
❑ J077 Twin Snake Sacrifice Jutsu C	.10	.25
❑ J078 Sand Coffin U	.20	.50
❑ J079 Wind Style: Great Breakthrough R	1.25	3.00
❑ J080 Endless Path Jutsu C	.10	.25
❑ J081 Misty Follower Jutsu C	.10	.25
❑ J082 Face Stealing Jutsu U	.20	.50
❑ J083 Formation Ino-Shika-Cho U	.20	.50
❑ J084 Curse Mark Jutsu U	.20	.50
❑ M043 Combat in Extreme Conditions U	.20	.50
❑ M044 Mission Refusal C	.10	.25
❑ M045 Broken Seal R	1.00	2.50
❑ M046 Preliminary Examination C	.10	.25
❑ M047 Stay Out of This! U	.20	.50
❑ M048 Examination Rule C	.10	.25
❑ M049 Surprise Attack C	.10	.25
❑ M050 A Tool Called Ninja C	.10	.25
❑ M051 Appearance of Unknown Rivals R	1.00	2.50
❑ M052 The End of the Demon SR	3.00	8.00
❑ M053 Written Test U	.20	.50
❑ M054 Cheating Prevention U	.20	.50
❑ M055 Sharp Words C	.10	.25
❑ M056 Pass Permit U	.20	.50
❑ M057 Forbidden Technique C	.10	.25
❑ M058 Broken Heart C	.10	.25
❑ M059 First Chunin Exam R	1.25	3.00
❑ M060 Dreadful Scars C	.10	.25
❑ M061 Konohamaru Ninja Squad Appears! C	.10	.25
❑ M062 No Lunch U	.20	.50
❑ M063 All Nine Rookies Face Off U	.20	.50
❑ M064 Survival Exercise U	.20	.50
❑ M065 Picking Empty Cans C	.10	.25
❑ M066 Weeding C	.10	.25
❑ M067 Heaven Scroll C	.10	.25
❑ M068 Beyond the Goal C	.10	.25
❑ M069 Sweet Tooth C	.10	.25
❑ M070 Here Comes Second Test Proctor Anko Mitarashi! R	1.25	3.00
❑ M071 Curse Mark Out of Control R	1.00	2.50
❑ M072 Revive, Sharingan! C	.10	.25
❑ M073 Survival in the Forest of Death R	1.25	3.00
❑ M074 Striking a Deal R	1.00	2.50
❑ M075 Observer C	.10	.25
❑ M076 Image of Death C	.10	.25
❑ M077 Ninja Poem Titled Ninja Opportunity C	.10	.25
❑ M078 Lucky! C	.10	.25
❑ M079 The Fastest Ones R	1.25	3.00
❑ M080 Sakura's Decision SR	4.00	10.00
❑ M081 Earth Scroll C	.10	.25
❑ M082 Securing Food C	.10	.25
❑ M083 Promise from the Past U	.20	.50
❑ M084 Starving C	.10	.25
❑ N044 The Third Hokage SR	3.00	8.00
❑ N045 Kabuto Yakushi R	1.00	2.50
❑ N046 Naruto Uzumaki C	.10	.25
❑ N047 Sasuke Uchiha U	.20	.50
❑ N048 Sakura Haruno C	.10	.25
❑ N049 Izumo Kozuki C	.10	.25
❑ N050 Kotetsu Hagane C	.10	.25
❑ N051 Tonbo Tobitake C	.10	.25
❑ N052 Ibiki Morino R	1.25	3.00
❑ N053 Tortoise Ninja C	.10	.25
❑ N054 Crow U	.20	.50
❑ N055 Dosu Kinuta R	1.00	2.50
❑ N056 Zaku Abumi U	.20	.50
❑ N057 Kin Tsuchi C	.10	.25
❑ N058 Gaara of the Desert SR	2.00	5.00
❑ N059 Kankuro R	1.25	3.00
❑ N060 Temari R	1.50	4.00
❑ N061 Naruto Uzumaki R	1.25	3.00
❑ N062 Sasuke Uchiha R	1.25	3.00
❑ N063 Iruka Umino R	1.25	3.00
❑ N064 Kakashi Hatake SR	4.00	10.00
❑ N065 Moegi C	.10	.25
❑ N066 Udon C	.10	.25
❑ N067 Naruto Uzumaki U	.20	.50
❑ N068 Sasuke Uchiha R	1.25	3.00
❑ N069 Sakura Haruno U	.20	.50
❑ N070 Ino Yamanaka U	.20	.50
❑ N071 Shikamaru Nara U	.20	.50
❑ N072 Choji Akimichi U	.20	.50
❑ N073 Iwashi Tatami C	.10	.25
❑ N074 Mozuku C	.10	.25
❑ N075 Giant Snake U	.20	.50
❑ N076 Shigure C	.10	.25
❑ N077 Baiu C	.10	.25
❑ N078 Midare C	.10	.25
❑ N079 Oboro C	.10	.25
❑ N080 Kagari C	.10	.25
❑ N081 Mubi C	.10	.25
❑ N082 Anbu SR	2.50	6.00
❑ N083 Anko Mitarashi SR	4.00	10.00
❑ N084 Orochimaru SR	4.00	10.00

2006 Naruto Curse of the Sand

COMPLETE SET (148)	40.00	80.00
BOOSTER BOX (24)	40.00	80.00
BOOSTER PACK	2.00	4.00
❑ C008 Genzo C	.10	.25
❑ C009 Kaji ST	.40	1.00
❑ C010 Akane C	.10	.25
❑ C011 Ageha C	.10	.25
❑ C012 Himatsu C	.10	.25
❑ C013 Shizuku C	.10	.25
❑ C014 Lord of the Land of Wind ST	.40	1.00
❑ J085 Naruto Uzumaki Barrage SR	2.50	6.00
❑ J086 Primary Lotus R	.75	2.00
❑ J087 The Eight Inner Gates SR	2.50	6.00
❑ J088 Food Pills C	.10	.25
❑ J089 Ninja Art of Beast Mimicry: Man Beast Clone C	.10	.25
❑ J090 Fang over Fang U	.20	.50
❑ J091 Lions Barrage SR	3.00	8.00
❑ J092 Five-Pronged Seal R	1.00	2.50
❑ J093 Shadow Senbon C	.10	.25
❑ J094 Sound of Bells U	.20	.50
❑ J095 Chakra Absorption Jutsu C	.10	.25
❑ J096 Deformable Body U	.20	.50
❑ J097 Fog Clone Jutsu C	.10	.25
❑ J098 Earth Style: Underground Move Jutsu C	.10	.25
❑ J099 Sand Armor ST	.40	1.00
❑ J100 Sand Burial R	1.25	3.00
❑ J101 Mind Transfer Jutsu U	.20	.50
❑ J102 Human Boulder U	.20	.50
❑ J103 Gentle Fist U	.20	.50
❑ J104 Summoning Jutsu: Projectile Weapons C	.10	.25
❑ J105 Rising Twin Dragons U	.20	.50
❑ J106 Lightning Blade ST	.40	1.00
❑ J107 Silent Killing Jutsu U	.20	.50
❑ J108 Byakugan U	.20	.50
❑ J109 Summoning Jutsu U	.20	.50
❑ J110 Sexy Jutsu R	1.00	2.50
❑ J111 Hidden Lotus SR	3.00	8.00
❑ J112 Dropping a Blackboard Eraser C	.10	.25
❑ J113 A Thousand Years of Death C	.10	.25
❑ J114 Crescent Moon Dance R	1.25	3.00
❑ J115 Walking on Water Training U	.20	.50
❑ J116 Sound Reflecting Speaker U	.20	.50
❑ J117 Water Cutting Blade C	.10	.25
❑ J118 Water Wall C	.10	.25
❑ J119 Water Whip C	.10	.25
❑ J120 Hero's Water R	.75	2.00
❑ J121 Carrier Kite C	.10	.25
❑ J122 Cliff-Climbing Training C	.10	.25
❑ J123 Wind Blade ST	.40	1.00
❑ J124 Earth Style Jutsu C	.10	.25
❑ J125 Attack against Weak Spots U	.20	.50
❑ J126 Five Pronged Seal Release R	1.00	2.50
❑ M085 Quick Wit C	.10	.25
❑ M086 The Opposites Rule C	.10	.25
❑ M087 Preliminaries to the Third Exam R	.75	2.00
❑ M088 Great Ninja R	1.50	4.00
❑ M089 Make-Out Violence U	.20	.50
❑ M090 Copying Ability C	.10	.25
❑ M091 Acute Sense of Smell C	.10	.25
❑ M092 Tide of the Deadly Combat R	.75	2.00
❑ M093 Sacrifice C	.10	.25
❑ M094 Mischief of Darkness U	.20	.50
❑ M095 Forbidden Use U	.20	.50
❑ M096 Spy of the Hidden Sound Village R	.75	2.00
❑ M097 Fateful Pairings C	.10	.25
❑ M098 Situation Assessment R	.75	2.00
❑ M099 Chunin Exam Rule C	.10	.25
❑ M100 Electronic Scoreboard C	.10	.25
❑ M101 Important Advice C	.10	.25
❑ M102 Ointment C	.10	.25
❑ M103 Insightful Eye C	.10	.25
❑ M104 Main Branch and Cadet Branch U	.20	.50
❑ M105 Retailiation U	.20	.50
❑ M106 Jonins' Intervention ST	.40	1.00
❑ M107 Temptation of Power ST	.40	1.00
❑ M108 Wish ST	.40	1.00
❑ M109 Kunoichi Battle U	.20	.50
❑ M110 The Gift of Perseverance C	.10	.25
❑ M111 For someone precious to you U	.20	.50
❑ M112 Difference in Levels C	.10	.25
❑ M113 Skillful Coordination C	.10	.25
❑ M114 Four Man Squads ST	.40	1.00
❑ M115 Unhealed Wound U	.20	.50
❑ M116 Power of the Nine-Tailed Fox Spirit C	.10	.25
❑ M117 Legacy of the Hero C	.10	.25
❑ M118 Toad Sage R	.75	2.00
❑ M119 Teaching a Secret Technique R	.75	2.00
❑ M120 Complete Victory C	.10	.25
❑ M121 Continue the Mission C	.10	.25
❑ M122 Hot Spring U	.20	.50
❑ M123 Coward U	.20	.50
❑ M124 A Grain of Courage C	.10	.25
❑ M125 Secret Conspiracy R	.75	2.00
❑ M126 Double Knockdown U	.20	.50
❑ M127 Ebisu Again C	.10	.25
❑ M128 Disarmament ST	.40	1.00
❑ M129 The Hyuga Lineage U	.20	.50
❑ M130 A Flower that Carries a Wish C	.10	.25
❑ M131 Challenging Again C	.10	.25
❑ M132 Disgrace of the Village U	.20	.50
❑ N085 Naruto Uzumaki SR	3.00	8.00
❑ N086 Sasuke Uchiha R	1.50	4.00
❑ N087 Sakura Haruno R	1.50	4.00
❑ N088 Ino Yamanaka ST	.40	1.00
❑ N089 Shikamaru Nara ST	.40	1.00
❑ N090 Choji Akimichi ST	.40	1.00
❑ N091 Kiba Inuzuka ST	.40	1.00
❑ N092 Shino Aburame C	.10	.25
❑ N093 Hinata Hyuga ST	.40	1.00
❑ N094 Rock Lee R	1.00	2.50
❑ N095 Neji Hyuga U	.20	.50
❑ N096 Tenten C	.10	.25
❑ N097 Suzume U	.20	.50
❑ N098 Iyashi C	.10	.25
❑ N099 Raido Namiashi ST	.40	1.00
❑ N100 Hayate Gekko R	1.00	2.50
❑ N101 Jiraiya SR	3.00	8.00
❑ N102 Gama U	.20	.50
❑ N103 Dosu Kinuta C	.10	.25
❑ N104 Zaku Abumi C	.10	.25
❑ N105 Kin Tsuchi U	.20	.50
❑ N106 Yoroi Akado U	.20	.50
❑ N107 Misumi Tsurugi R	1.50	4.00
❑ N108 Kabuto Yakushi R	1.00	2.50
❑ N109 Kakshi Hatake R	1.00	2.50
❑ N110 Might Guy R	.75	2.00
❑ N111 Akamaru ST	.40	1.00
❑ N112 Gaara of the Desert SR	2.50	6.00
❑ N113 Kankuro R	.75	2.00
❑ N114 Temari U	.20	.50
❑ N115 Naruto Uzumaki U	.20	.50
❑ N116 Sasuke Uchiha U	.20	.50
❑ N117 Gaara of the Desert ST	.40	1.00
❑ N118 Naruto Uzumaki U	.20	.50
❑ N119 Sasuke Uchiha U	.20	.50
❑ N120 Sakura Haruno U	.20	.50
❑ N121 Ebisu R	1.50	4.00
❑ N122 Hayate Gekko R	1.50	4.00
❑ N123 Kakashi Hatake R	1.25	3.00
❑ N124 Asuma Sarutobi U	.20	.50
❑ N125 Hanabi Hyuga C	.10	.25
❑ N126 Hiashi Hyuga R	1.25	3.00
❑ N127 Jiraiya SR	3.00	8.00
❑ N128 Gamabunta SR	2.50	6.00
❑ N129 The Fourth Hokage SR	4.00	10.00
❑ N130 Baki R	1.00	2.50
❑ N131 Shibuki C	.10	.25
❑ N132 Suien U	.20	.50
❑ N133 Murasame U	.20	.50
❑ N134 Kirisame U	.20	.50
❑ N135 Hisame C	.10	.25

2006 Naruto The Path to Hokage

COMPLETE SET (127)	25.00	50.00
BOOSTER BOX (24)	30.00	60.00
BOOSTER PACK	1.50	3.00
❑ J001 Kunai C	.10	.25
❑ J002 Cross-Shaped Shuriken C	.10	.25
❑ J003 Sexy Jutsu C	.10	.25
❑ J004 Harem Jutsu U	.20	.50
❑ J005 Multi-Shadow Clone Jutsu R	.75	2.00
❑ J006 8 Trigram Divination Seal Spell Formula C	.10	.25
❑ J007 Sharingan Eye R	.75	2.00
❑ J008 Crystal Ball Jutsu ST	.40	1.00
❑ J009 A Thousand Years of Death C	.10	.25
❑ J010 Fire Style: Fire Ball Jutsu U	.20	.50
❑ J011 Shared-Instinct Assassination Jutsu ST	.40	1.00
❑ J012 Water Clone Jutsu ST	.40	1.00
❑ J013 Hidden Mist Jutsu U	.20	.50
❑ J014 Silent Killing Jutsu R	.75	2.00
❑ J015 Clone Jutsu C	.10	.25
❑ J016 Transformation Jutsu C	.10	.25
❑ J017 Substitution Jutsu C	.10	.25
❑ J018 Disguise Jutsu C	.10	.25
❑ J019 Evil Illusion: Jutsu	.40	1.00
❑ J020 Escape Jutsu C	.10	.25
❑ J021 Earth Style Jutsu	.40	1.00
❑ J022 Mind Transfer Jutsu C	.10	.25
❑ J023 Shadow Possession Jutsu ST	.40	1.00
❑ J024 Expansion Jutsu C	.10	.25
❑ J025 Shadow Clone Jutsu ST	.40	1.00
❑ J026 Leaf Hurricanes U	.20	.50
❑ J027 Leaf Whirlwind C	.10	.25
❑ J028 Ninja Art of Beast Mimicry: Jutsu	.40	1.00
❑ J029 Demon Wind Shuriken Jutsu	.40	1.00
❑ J030 Lightning Blade SR	2.50	6.00
❑ J031 Guillotine Sword ST	.40	1.00
❑ J032 Water Prison Jutsu C	.10	.25
❑ J033 Water Style: Water Dragon Jutsu C	.10	.25
❑ J034 Water Style Giant Vortex Jutsu R	1.00	2.50
❑ J035 A Thousand Needles of Death U	.20	.50
❑ J036 Crystal Ice Mirror SR	3.00	8.00
❑ J037 Shadow Shuriken Jutsu C	.10	.25
❑ J038 Sprinting in the Mist Jutsu C	.10	.25
❑ J039 Parasitic Insect Jutsu U	.20	.50
❑ J040 Tree-Climbing Training C	.10	.25
❑ J041 Summoning Earth Style: Jutsu	.40	1.00
❑ J042 Byakugan R	.75	2.00
❑ M001 Ichiraku Noodle Shop C	.10	.25
❑ M002 An Outcast's Dream C	.10	.25
❑ M003 Leaf Headband U	.20	.50
❑ M004 A Kind Teacher ST	.40	1.00
❑ M005 Disaster of the Nine-Tailed Fox Spirit SR	4.00	10.00
❑ M006 Mission Of Capturing Missing Pet Tora C	.10	.25
❑ M007 Make-Out Paradise C	.10	.25
❑ M008 An Accident U	.20	.50
❑ M009 Lone Avenger C	.10	.25
❑ M010 Exhaustion of Stamina U	.20	.50
❑ M011 Bingo Book C	.10	.25
❑ M012 The Worst Client C	.10	.25
❑ M013 Gato Transport C	.10	.25
❑ M014 Intent to Kill U	.20	.50
❑ M015 Inner Sakura U	.20	.50
❑ M016 Browsing in a Bookstore C	.10	.25
❑ M017 Three Man Squads C	.10	.25
❑ M018 One Morning R	.75	2.00
❑ M019 Failure C	.10	.25
❑ M020 Ninja Academy C	.10	.25
❑ M021 After the Battle R	.75	2.00
❑ M022 Leaf Ninja Forces C	.10	.25
❑ M023 Battle of Clones C	.10	.25
❑ M024 Oath of Pain C	.10	.25
❑ M025 The Hero Appears! U	.20	.50
❑ M026 The Most Unpredictable Ninja C	.10	.25
❑ M027 Blood of the Uchiha Clan C	.10	.25
❑ M028 Coward ST	.40	1.00
❑ M029 Seesaw Battle C	.10	.25
❑ M030 Kakashi's Foresight R	.75	2.00
❑ M031 Gathering Herbs R	.75	2.00
❑ M032 The Worst for Last U	.20	.50
❑ M033 Public Execution C	.10	.25
❑ M034 Unwanted Child C	.10	.25
❑ M035 Look for the Red Four-Leaf Clover C	.10	.25
❑ M036 Left Behind C	.10	.25
❑ M037 Specific Instruction C	.10	.25
❑ M038 Teachings of the Previous Hokage C	.10	.25
❑ M039 Small Act of Courage C	.10	.25
❑ M040 Shooting Star ST	.40	1.00
❑ M041 Manji Battle Formation C	.10	.25
❑ M042 Revival U	.20	.50
❑ N001 Naruto Uzumaki C	.10	.25
❑ N002 Sasuke Uchiha U	.20	.50
❑ N003 Sakura Haruno U	.20	.50
❑ N004 Ino Yamanaka C	.10	.25
❑ N005 Shikamaru Nara C	.10	.25
❑ N006 Choji Akimichi C	.10	.25
❑ N007 Konohamaru C	.10	.25
❑ N008 Iruka Umino C	.10	.25
❑ N009 Mizuki C	.10	.25
❑ N010 Ebisu C	.10	.25
❑ N011 Kakashi Hatake U	.20	.50
❑ N012 Asuma Sarutobi C	.10	.25
❑ N013 The Third Hokage U	.20	.50
❑ N014 The Demon Brothers Gouzu C	.10	.25
❑ N015 The Demon Brothers Meizu C	.10	.25
❑ N016 Haku ST	.40	1.00
❑ N017 Haku U	.20	.50
❑ N018 Zabuza Momochi C	.10	.25
❑ N019 Naruto Uzumaki SR	2.50	6.00
❑ N020 Sasuke Uchiha SR	3.00	8.00
❑ N021 Sakura Haruno SR	3.00	8.00
❑ N022 Iruka Umino R	.75	2.00
❑ N023 Kakashi Hatake R	.75	2.00
❑ N024 Zabuza Momochi R	.75	2.00
❑ N025 Naruto Uzumaki C	.10	.25
❑ N026 Sasuke Uchiha C	.10	.25
❑ N027 Sakura Haruno C	.10	.25
❑ N028 Kiba Inuzuka C	.10	.25
❑ N029 Shino Aburame C	.10	.25
❑ N030 Hinata Hyuga U	.20	.50
❑ N031 Rock Lee C	.10	.25
❑ N032 Tenten C	.10	.25
❑ N033 Neji Hyuga C	.10	.25
❑ N034 Konohamaru C	.10	.25
❑ N035 Kaede Ureshino C	.10	.25
❑ N036 Akamaru C	.10	.25
❑ N037 Kakashi Hatake U	.20	.50
❑ N038 Kurenai Yuhi U	.20	.50
❑ N039 Might Guy U	.20	.50
❑ N040 Zabuza Momochi U	.20	.50
❑ N041 Rock Lee R	.75	2.00
❑ N042 Neji Hyuga ST	.40	1.00
❑ N043 Haku SR	4.00	10.00

2007 Naruto Dream Legacy

COMPLETE SET (115)	40.00	80.00
BOOSTER BOX (24)	30.00	60.00
BOOSTER PACK	1.50	3.00
❑ C007 Tsunami C	.10	.25
❑ C025 Koyuki Kazahana U	.20	.50
❑ C026 Emi C	.10	.25
❑ C027 Shu C	.10	.25
❑ C028 Senta C	.10	.25
❑ C029 Bunzou C	.10	.25
❑ J173 Severe Leaf Hurricane C	.10	.25
❑ J174 Dynamic Entry R	.75	2.00
❑ J175 Toad Mouth Trap SR	2.50	6.00
❑ J176 Kaleidoscope Sharingan U	.20	.50
❑ J177 Tsukuyomi, Nightmare Realm R	.75	2.00
❑ J178 Amaterasu SR	2.50	6.00
❑ J179 Ice Style: Black Dragon Blizzard C	.10	.25
❑ J180 Ice Style: Tsubame Snowstorm C	.10	.25
❑ J181 Ice Style: Wolf-Fang Avalanche Jutsu U	.20	.50
❑ J182 Ice Style: White Whale U	.20	.50
❑ J183 Spider Web Net C	.10	.25
❑ J184 Shark Skin U	.20	.50
❑ J185 Water Style: Water Shark Bomb Jutsu ST	.40	1.00
❑ J186 Sakura Blizzard Jutsu U	.20	.50
❑ J187 Genjutsu: Sylvan Fetters C	.10	.25
❑ J188 Wind Style: Infinite Sand Storm Devastation R	.75	2.00
❑ J189 Sealing Jutsu: Fire Seal U	.20	.50
❑ J190 Chakra Control Device ST	.40	1.00
❑ J191 Ninja Fist Sword C	.10	.25
❑ J192 A Tap on the Forehead R	.75	2.00
❑ J193 Ninja Art: Needle Jizo U	.20	.50
❑ J194 Extraordinary Power R	.75	2.00
❑ J195 Fire Style: Toad Flame Bombs SR	2.50	6.00
❑ J196 Chakra Scalpel C	.10	.25
❑ J197 Coiling Around U	.20	.50
❑ J198 Tasteless and Odorless Drug U	.20	.50
❑ J199 Hidden Needles R	.75	2.00
❑ J200 Loaded Needles C	.10	.25
❑ J201 Ninja Art: Poison Fog C	.10	.25
❑ J202 Ninja Art: Mitotic Regeneration SR	2.50	6.00
❑ J203 Attack on the Nervous System R	.75	2.00
❑ J204 Summoning Jutsu C	.10	.25
❑ J205 Division C	.10	.25
❑ J206 Acid Slime U	.20	.50
❑ J207 Healing Technique U	.20	.50
❑ J208 Ground Fissure C	.10	.25
❑ J209 Earth Style: Dark Swamp C	.10	.25
❑ M174 Research Tour U	.20	.50
❑ M175 No Interest U	.20	.50
❑ M176 Too Much Baggage C	.10	.25
❑ M177 Tragic Clan U	.20	.50
❑ M178 Fratricide R	.75	2.00
❑ M179 Mysterious Small Organization C	.10	.25
❑ M180 Catch-Out ST	.40	1.00
❑ M181 Unexpected Visitor C	.10	.25
❑ M182 Huge Difference in Ability R	.75	2.00
❑ M183 Assassination of the Kazekage R	.75	2.00
❑ M184 Hex Crystal C	.10	.25
❑ M185 Coronation Ceremony C	.10	.25
❑ M186 The Adventures of Princess Gale U	.20	.50
❑ M187 3 Don'ts for Ninjas C	.10	.25
❑ M188 Unbridgeable Gap C	.10	.25
❑ M189 Recovery of the Village R	.75	2.00
❑ M190 Festival R	.75	2.00
❑ M191 Focus C	.10	.25
❑ M192 Playing Catch U	.20	.50
❑ M193 Three-Cornered Deadlock R	.75	2.00
❑ M194 Fifty-Fifty Chance R	.75	2.00
❑ M195 Request for Taking Office U	.20	.50
❑ M196 Necklace that Invites Death C	.10	.25
❑ M197 The Haze Ninja Trio C	.10	.25
❑ M198 Make-Out Bar U	.20	.50
❑ M199 Bargaining Chip C	.10	.25
❑ M200 Sign of Conspiracy R	.75	2.00
❑ M201 Unfading Affection U	.20	.50
❑ M202 Slot Machine C	.10	.25
❑ M203 Stopping the Battle C	.10	.25
❑ M204 Tea Break C	.10	.25
❑ M205 Leaf Village's Great Athletic Meet R	.75	2.00
❑ M206 Just Recovered U	.20	.50
❑ M207 Failed Jutsu ST	.40	1.00
❑ N186 Naruto Uzumaki & Iruka Umino U	.20	.50
❑ N187 Naruto Uzumaki U	.20	.50
❑ N188 Sasuke Uchiha C	.10	.25
❑ N189 Sakura Haruno U	.20	.50
❑ N190 St. Simon C	.10	.25
❑ N191 Anbu R	.75	2.00
❑ N192 Kakashi Hatake STSR	2.00	5.00
❑ N193 Might Guy R	.75	2.00
❑ N194 Asuma Sarutobi U	.20	.50
❑ N195 Kurenai Yuhi U	.20	.50
❑ N196 Tsume Inuzuka U	.20	.50
❑ N197 Kuromaru U	.20	.50
❑ N198 Ninja Toad C	.10	.25
❑ N199 Homura Mitomon R	.75	2.00
❑ N200 Koharu Utatane R	.75	2.00
❑ N201 Tsunade SR	2.50	6.00
❑ N202 Kisame Hoshigaki SR	4.00	10.00
❑ N203 Itachi Uchiha SR	5.00	12.00
❑ N204 Naruto Uzumaki & Jiraiya STSR	2.00	5.00
❑ N205 Naruto Uzumaki N-206	.40	1.00
❑ N206 Sakura Haruno & Ino Yamanaka R	.75	2.00
❑ N207 Konohamaru C	.10	.25
❑ N208 Mitate C	.10	.25
❑ N209 Nawaki U	.20	.50
❑ N210 Dan U	.20	.50
❑ N211 Shizune R	.75	2.00
❑ N212 Tonton C	.10	.25
❑ N213 Gamatatsu C	.10	.25
❑ N214 Big Brother C	.10	.25

❑ N215 Gantetsu C .10 .25
❑ N216 Kabuto Yakushi R .75 2.00
❑ N217 Orochimaru SR 3.00 8.00
❑ N218 Jiraiya R .75 2.00
❑ N219 Tsunade SR 2.50 6.00
❑ N220 Gamabunta SR 2.50 6.00
❑ N221 Manda SR 4.00 10.00
❑ N222 Katsuyu SR 2.50 6.00
❑ N223 Tsunade & Shizune SR 2.50 6.00

2007 Naruto Eternal Rivalry

COMPLETE SET (113) 40.00 80.00
BOOSTER BOX (24) 40.00 80.00
BOOSTER PACK 2.00 4.00

❑ C020 Director Makino R .75 2.00
❑ C021 Sandayu Asama U .20 .50
❑ C022 Sosetsu Kazahana U .20 .50
❑ C023 Yukie Fujikaze R .75 2.00
❑ C024 Koyuki Kazahana R .75 2.00
❑ J163 Summoning Jutsu C .10 .25
❑ J164 Toad Sword U .20 .50
❑ J165 Water Style: Liquid Bullets R .75 2.00
❑ J166 Sand Shuriken U .20 .50
❑ J167 Playing Possum Jutsu C .10 .25
❑ J168 Wind Style: Air Bullets R .75 2.00
❑ J169 Head Butt U .20 .50
❑ J170 Bring Down The House Jutsu C .10 .25
❑ J171 Chidori R .75 2.00
❑ J172 Immortality Jutsu C .10 .25
❑ M169 Special Suits U 4.00 10.00
❑ M170 Chakra Armor C .75 2.00
❑ M171 Delivery U .10 .25
❑ M172 Hidden Past U .75 2.00
❑ M173 Farewell U .75 2.00
❑ N173 Naruto Uzumaki U .10 .25
❑ N174 Sasuke Uchiha U 2.00 5.00
❑ N175 Gamakichi C .75 2.00
❑ N176 Gamabunta SR .10 .25
❑ N177 Shukaku SR .10 .25
❑ N178 Gaara of the Desert C .75 2.00
❑ N179 Gaara of the Desert Ninja .75 2.00
❑ N180 Yashamaru C .10 .25
❑ N181 Nadare Roga U .10 .25
❑ N182 Mizore Fuyukuma U .75 2.00
❑ N183 Fubuki Kakuyoku U .10 .25
❑ N184 Dotou Kazahana U .20 .50
❑ N185 Kakashi Hatake C .20 .50
❑ JUS001 Shadow Clone Jutsu SR .75 2.00
❑ JUS002 Harem Jutsu R .10 .25
❑ JUS003 Kunai C .20 .50
❑ JUS004 Primary Lotus R .10 .25
❑ JUS005 Hidden Lotus R .20 .50
❑ JUS006 Leaf Hurricane C .20 .50
❑ JUS007 Lions Barrage SR .20 .50
❑ JUS008 Sharingan Eye R .75 2.00
❑ JUS009 A Thousand Years of Death C .75 2.00
❑ JUS010 Water Clone Jutsu C .10 .25
❑ JUS011 Water Style: Water Dragon Jutsu R .75 2.00
❑ JUS012 Water Style: Water Shark Bomb Jutsu R .20 .50
❑ JUS013 Parasitic Insect Jutsu C .20 .50
❑ JUS014 Puppet Master Jutsu C .10 .25
❑ JUS015 Gigantic Fan R .10 .25
❑ JUS016 Earth Style: Headhunter Jutsu C 3.00 8.00
❑ JUS017 Shadow Possession Jutsu U .10 .25
❑ JUS018 Gentle Fist U .20 .50
❑ JUS019 8 Trigrams Palms Rotation R .75 2.00
❑ JUS020 Expansion Jutsu C .75 2.00
❑ MUS001 Unexpected Result R .20 .50
❑ MUS002 Desperate forbidden Jutsu R .75 2.00
❑ MUS003 Late!! C .20 .50
❑ MUS004 Hidden Chakra R .10 .25
❑ MUS005 Professor U .20 .50
❑ MUS006 Ambitious Eyes U .10 .25
❑ MUS007 Reliable Allies C .10 .25
❑ MUS008 Split Personality C .20 .50
❑ MUS009 Orochimaru's Forbidden Jutsu SR .20 .50
❑ MUS010 Hidden Jutsu: Immortality Jutsu C .10 .25
❑ MUS011 Two Man Squads U 4.00 10.00
❑ MUS012 The Power of Shukaku R 3.00 8.00
❑ MUS013 Tsunade's Answer R .10 .25
❑ MUS014 Internal Monster U .40 1.00
❑ MUS015 Well-Planned Mission R .10 .25
❑ MUS016 Cursed Fate U .20 .50
❑ MUS017 Rescue C .10 .25
❑ MUS018 Skillful Tactics U .20 .50
❑ MUS019 Attack from the blind spot C .20 .50
❑ MUS020 Power of the Youth C .10 .25
❑ NUS001 Naruto Uzumaki C .10 .25
❑ NUS002 Naruto Uzumaki SR 2.50 6.00
❑ NUS003 Sasuke Uchiha R .75 2.00
❑ NUS004 Sasuke Uchiha C .10 .25
❑ NUS005 Sakura Haruno U .20 .50
❑ NUS006 Sakura Haruno R .75 2.00
❑ NUS007 Sakura Haruno C .10 .25
❑ NUS008 Kakashi Hatake R .75 2.00
❑ NUS009 Kakashi Hatake R .75 2.00
❑ NUS010 Kiba Inuzuka C .10 .25
❑ NUS011 Shino Aburame C .10 .25
❑ NUS012 Hinata Hyuga C .10 .25
❑ NUS013 Ino Nakayama C .10 .25
❑ NUS014 Shikamaru Nara C .10 .25
❑ NUS015 Shikamaru Nara SR 4.00 10.00
❑ NUS016 Choji Akimichi C .10 .25
❑ NUS017 Neji Hyuga SR 4.00 10.00
❑ NUS018 Neji Hyuga C .10 .25
❑ NUS019 Rock Lee U .20 .50
❑ NUS020 Rock Lee SR 4.00 10.00
❑ NUS021 Tenten C .10 .25
❑ NUS022 Might Guy SR 2.00 5.00
❑ NUS023 Might Guy R 1.25 3.00
❑ NUS024 Gaara of the Desert R .75 2.00
❑ NUS025 Temari C .10 .25
❑ NUS026 Kankuro C .10 .25
❑ NUS027 Jiraiya R 1.50 4.00
❑ NUS028 Jiraiya U .20 .50
❑ NUS029 Tsunade U .20 .50
❑ NUS030 Orochimaru U .20 .50
❑ NUS031 The Third Hokage U .20 .50
❑ NUS032 Kabuto Yakushi R 1.25 3.00
❑ NUS033 Zabuza Momochi C .10 .25
❑ NUS034 Zabuza Momochi SR 2.00 5.00
❑ NUS035 Haku R 1.25 3.00
❑ NUS036 Haku C .10 .25
❑ NUS037 Itachi Uchiha R 1.50 4.00
❑ NUS038 Kisame Hoshigaki R 1.25 3.00
❑ NUS039 Naruto Uzumaki & Gamabunta SR 3.00 8.00
❑ NUS040 Shikamaru Nara & Asuma Sarutobi SR 4.00 10.00

2007 Naruto Quest for Power

COMPLETE SET (161) 50.00 100.00
BOOSTER BOX (24) 40.00 80.00
BOOSTER PACK 2.00 4.00

❑ C030 Boss Jirocho C .10 .25
❑ C031 Fukusuke Hikyakuya C .10 .25
❑ J210 Rasengan SR 3.00 8.00
❑ J211 Chidori SR 3.00 8.00
❑ J212 Water Style: Liquid Bullets R .75 2.00
❑ J213 Booby Trap C .10 .25
❑ J214 Application of the First Stage U .20 .50
❑ J215 Blade of the Thunder God R 1.25 3.00
❑ J216 Toothpick C .10 .25
❑ J217 String Control Jutsu U .20 .50
❑ J218 Aerial Dynamic Marking C .10 .25
❑ J219 Tunneling Fang C .10 .25
❑ J220 Earth Style Barrier: Earth Dome Prison R 1.25 3.00
❑ J221 Earth Style: Ball of Graves C .10 .25
❑ J222 Earth Style: Terra Shield C .10 .25
❑ J223 Ninja Art: Spiral Spider Web R .75 2.00
❑ J224 Ninja Art:Sticky Spider Thread C .10 .25
❑ J225 Four Black Mists Formation SR 2.00 5.00
❑ J226 Black Seal C .10 .25
❑ J227 Perimeter Barrier C .10 .25
❑ J228 Spiky Human Boulder C .10 .25
❑ J229 Partial Expansion Justu C .10 .25
❑ J230 Super Expansion Jutsu SR 3.00 8.00
❑ J231 Gentle Fist R 1.25 3.00
❑ M208 Unpredicted Clue R 2.00 5.00
❑ M209 Reunion with the Former Teacher U 2.00 5.00
❑ M210 Kakashi Sensei's True Face? C .20 .50
❑ M211 Surprise ST 1.25 3.00
❑ M212 Release from the Nightmare R .10 .25
❑ M213 Intruder C .20 .50
❑ M214 Lifelong Promise C .10 .25
❑ M215 The Will of Fire C .10 .25
❑ M216 Admonition U .20 .50
❑ M217 Supreme Order C .20 .50
❑ M218 Strength of Jutsu U .75 2.00
❑ M219 Desperate Persuasion C 1.25 3.00
❑ M220 Dedication Ceremony C .10 .25
❑ M221 Bossy Attitude C 1.25 3.00
❑ M222 My Rule C .20 .50
❑ M223 Determination to Avenge U .20 .50
❑ M224 Mind Awakening Pill R 1.00 2.50
❑ M225 Blind Corner C .75 2.00
❑ M226 Power of the Curse Mark R .10 .25
❑ M227 Game C .10 .25
❑ M228 Emergency C .20 .50
❑ M229 Sudden Encounter R .10 .25
❑ M230 The Triad Colored Pills U .20 .50
❑ M231 True Worth of the Gentle Fist C .75 2.00
❑ M232 Shikamaru's Analysis U 1.25 3.00
❑ M233 100 Times Greater Power SR .20 .50
❑ M234 Sasuke Retrieval Team R .10 .25
❑ M235 Optimum Formation ST .40 1.00
❑ N224 Naruto Uzumaki U 1.25 3.00
❑ N225 Sasuke Uchiha U .10 .25
❑ N226 Kiba Inuzuka & Akamaru C .10 .25
❑ N227 Shikamaru Nara R .10 .25
❑ N228 Choji Akimichi C .20 .50
❑ N229 Kakashi Hatake R .10 .25
❑ N230 Hinata Hyuga C .20 .50
❑ N231 Neji Hyuga U .20 .50
❑ N232 Shikamaru Nara C .10 .25
❑ N233 Naruto Uzumaki & Konohamaru U .10 .25
❑ N234 Shikamaru Nara & Choji Akimichi R .10 .25
❑ N235 Naruto Uzumaki C .20 .50
❑ N236 Sasuke Uchiha R 1.25 3.00
❑ N237 Sakura Haruno C .10 .25
❑ N238 Shikamaru Nara R .75 2.00
❑ N239 Choji Akimichi R .10 .25
❑ N240 Neji Hyuga C .20 .50
❑ N241 Kiba Inuzuka U 1.25 3.00
❑ N242 Akamaru C .20 .50
❑ N243 Genma Shiranui C .10 .25
❑ N244 Raido Namiashi C .20 .50
❑ N245 Iwashi Tatami U 2.00 5.00
❑ N246 Shizune C .75 2.00
❑ N247 The Fifth Hokage SR .40 1.00
❑ N248 Idate Morino C .20 .50
❑ N249 Aoi Rokusho U .20 .50
❑ N250 Kidomaru SR .10 .25
❑ N251 Jirobo SR .20 .50
❑ N252 Sakon SR .75 2.00
❑ N253 Tayuya SR .20 .50
❑ N254 Kimimaro SR 1.25 3.00
❑ N284 Naruto Uzumaki R 1.25 3.00
❑ N285 Sakura Haruno R .20 .50
❑ N286 Shikamaru Nara R .75 2.00
❑ N287 Gaara of the Desert R .10 .25
❑ NC001 Naruto Uzumaki U .20 .50
❑ NC002 Sasuke Uchiha C .20 .50
❑ NC003 Sakura Haruno U .20 .50
❑ NC004 Shikamaru Nara C .10 .25
❑ NC005 Rock Lee C 1.25 3.00
❑ NC006 Kakashi Hatake U .20 .50
❑ NC007 Haku U .10 .25
❑ NC008 Itachi Uchiha U .20 .50
❑ NC009 Naruto Uzumaki & Gamabunta SR .20 .50
❑ NC010 Sasuke Uchiha & Sakura Haruno R .20 .50
❑ NC011 Gaara of the Desert R .20 .50
❑ NC012 Kakashi Hatake & Iruka Umino R .10 .25
❑ NC013 Asuma Sarutobi & Kurenai Yuhi R 1.25 3.00
❑ NC014 Jiraiya & Tsunade SR .10 .25
❑ NC015 Pakkun & Tonton C 1.25 3.00
❑ NC016 Zabuza Momochi & Haku R .10 .25
❑ JUS021 Rasengan STSR .20 .50
❑ JUS022 Chidori STSR .10 .25
❑ JUS023 Water Style: Water Dragon Jutsu U .20 .50
❑ JUS024 Secret Wood Style Jutsu .75 2.00
Deep Forest Creation R
❑ JUS025 Earth Style: Dark Swamp C .10 .25
❑ JUS026 Guillotine Sword U 1.25 3.00
❑ JUS027 Ninja Art of Beast Mimicry .10 .25
Man Beast Clone C
❑ JUS028 Water Style: Giant Vortex Jutsu C 1.25 3.00
❑ JUS029 Wind Style 1.25 3.00
Infinite Sand Storm Devastation U
❑ JUS030 Wind Style: Air Bullets U .10 .25
❑ JUS031 Combined Transformation R .20 .50
❑ JUS032 Genjutsu: Infinite Darkness Jutsu R .10 .25
❑ JUS033 Research C .10 .25
❑ JUS034 Butterfly Bullet Bomb R .10 .25
❑ JUS035 Release of Chakra U .20 .50
❑ JUS036 Digital Shrapnel U .10 .25
❑ JUS037 Rasengan R 2.50 6.00
❑ JUS038 Extraordinary Power R .10 .25
❑ JUS039 Wound Healing C .20 .50
❑ JUS040 Summoning Jutsu: Blade Dance C 2.50 6.00
❑ JUS041 Flying Swallow U 2.50 6.00
❑ JUS042 High Speed Move Taijutsu C 2.50 6.00
❑ JUS043 Instant Killing U 3.00 8.00
❑ JUS044 Ninja Art: Mitotic Regeneration R 3.00 8.00
❑ MUS021 Combination U 1.25 3.00
❑ MUS022 Disappointment U 1.25 3.00
❑ MUS023 Tiny Reinforcer C 1.25 3.00
❑ MUS024 Punishment U 1.25 3.00
❑ MUS025 Pursuit R .20 .50
❑ MUS026 Anbu Days U .10 .25
❑ MUS027 Sudden Eruption R .20 .50
❑ MUS028 Solitude and Thirst R .10 .25
❑ MUS029 The Sound Ninja Five U .10 .25
❑ MUS030 Leaf Squad Organized! R .20 .50
❑ MUS031 Bravado C .20 .50
❑ MUS032 The 9th Match U .20 .50
❑ MUS033 Take it again! U 3.00 8.00
❑ MUS034 Incarnation of The Nine-Tailed Fox Spirit U1.25 3.00
❑ MUS035 Forbidden Word C 1.25 3.00
❑ MUS036 Shadow of The Nine-Tailed Fox Spirit R1.25 3.00
❑ MUS037 Pretty Please! C 1.25 3.00
❑ MUS038 Irresistible! C 2.50 6.00
❑ MUS039 Raid of Akatsuki U .10 .25
❑ MUS040 Youthful Appearance U .75 2.00
❑ NUS041 The First Hokage SR 3.00 8.00
❑ NUS042 The Second Hokage SR 3.00 8.00
❑ NUS043 Gaara of the Desert Ninja .40 1.00
❑ NUS044 Gaara of the Desert U .20 .50
❑ NUS045 Itachi Uchiha C .10 .25
❑ NUS046 Jiraiya U .20 .50
❑ NUS047 Konohamaru C .10 .25
❑ NUS048 Pakkun C .10 .25
❑ NUS049 Tsunade U .20 .50
❑ NUS050 Inochi Yamanaka & Ino Yamanaka R 1.50 4.00
❑ NUS051 Tenten C .10 .25
❑ NUS052 Temari C .10 .25
❑ NUS053 Ino Nakayama U .20 .50
❑ NUS054 Sakura Haruno U .20 .50
❑ PR005R Naruto Uzumaki U .20 .50
❑ PR006R Sasuke Uchiha U .20 .50
❑ PR007R Sakura Haruno U .20 .50
❑ PR008R Iruka Umino U .20 .50
❑ PR009R Kakashi Hatake U .20 .50
❑ PR018 The First Hokage ST .40 1.00
❑ PR019 The Second Hokage ST .40 1.00

2007 Naruto Revenge and Rebirth

COMPLETE SET (115) 40.00 80.00
BOOSTER BOX (24) 40.00 80.00
BOOSTER PACK 2.00 4.00

❑ C007 Tsunami C .10 .25
❑ C015 Ami C .10 .25
❑ C016 Teuchi C .10 .25
❑ C017 Ayame C .10 .25
❑ C018 Koji C .10 .25
❑ C019 Futaba C .10 .25
❑ J127 Kunai U .40 1.00
❑ J128 Shadow Clone Jutsu C .40 1.00
❑ J129 Release of Chakra R .20 .50
❑ J130 Sharingan Eye U .10 .25
❑ J131 Chidori SR .75 2.00
❑ J132 Palm Healing Jutsu U .20 .50
❑ J133 Dead Soul Jutsu C 4.00 10.00
❑ J134 Feather Illusion Jutsu C .20 .50
❑ J135 Four Flames Formation R .10 .25
❑ J136 Great Fan C .10 .25
❑ J137 Wind Scythe Jutsu R 1.25 3.00
❑ J138 Sand Cocoon C .10 .25
❑ J139 Sand Clone U .75 2.00
❑ J140 Shadow Possession Jutsu C .10 .25
❑ J141 Curse Mark Jutsu C .20 .50
❑ J142 Secret Mark of the Main Branch U .10 .25
❑ J143 8 Trigrams Palms Rotation R .10 .25
❑ J144 Gentle Fist Style: 8 Trigrams 64 Palms SR .20 .50
❑ J145 Naruto 2K Uzumaki Barrage SR .75 2.00
❑ J146 Clone Body Slamming U 2.50 6.00
❑ J147 Shuriken Shadow Clone Jutsu C 4.00 10.00
❑ J148 Fire Style: Dragon Flame Bombs U .20 .50
❑ J149 Reaper Death Seal SR .10 .25
❑ J150 Snake Sword R .20 .50
❑ J151 Summonin Jutsu: Reanimation SR 2.50 6.00
❑ J152 Water Style: Water Wall U .75 2.00
❑ J153 Water Style: Water Shock Wave R 2.50 6.00
❑ J154 Parasitic Insect Jutsu C .20 .50
❑ J155 Puppet Master Jutsu C .75 2.00
❑ J156 Armed Puppet U .10 .25
❑ J157 Genjutsu: Infinite Darkness Jutsu U .10 .25
❑ J158 Earth Style: Mud Wall U .20 .50
❑ J159 Secret Wood Style Jutsu .20 .50
Deep Forest Creation R
❑ J160 Mind Destruction Jutsu C .20 .50
❑ J161 Shadow Strangle Jutsu C .75 2.00
❑ J162 Expansion Jutsu C .10 .25
❑ M133 Secret Path C .10 .25
❑ M134 Pledge of Victory C .10 .25
❑ M135 Power for Change R .10 .25
❑ M136 Combo of 16 Hits U .10 .25
❑ M137 Detection C 1.25 3.00
❑ M138 High-Speed Body R .20 .50
❑ M139 Dancing Leaves...!! U .10 .25
❑ M140 Incomplete Activation C .75 2.00
❑ M141 Scheming U .20 .50
❑ M142 Abduction U .10 .25
❑ M143 Measuring the Limits U .20 .50
❑ M144 Changes in Pairings U .20 .50
❑ M145 Depression C .20 .50
❑ M146 The Final Competition Begins U .20 .50
❑ M147 Aftereffects C .10 .25
❑ M148 You Got Me! U .20 .50
❑ M149 Hidden Capacity C .10 .25
❑ M150 Caged Bird U .20 .50
❑ M151 Released Seal R .10 .25
❑ M152 Pad C .20 .50
❑ M153 Best Rival U .75 2.00
❑ M154 Stormy Battle ST .10 .25
❑ M155 Ominous Presentiment U .20 .50
❑ M156 A-Ranked Mission U .40 1.00
❑ M157 The End of the Mortal Combat R .20 .50
❑ M158 The One Who Inherits and Entrusts the Will R.20 .50
❑ M159 Research into Forbidden Jutsu U .75 2.00
❑ M160 Collapse of the Hidden Leaf Village R .75 2.00
❑ M161 Loss of All Techniques C .20 .50
❑ M162 The Name Gaara C .75 2.00
❑ M163 Basic Platoon U .10 .25
❑ M164 Holding the Enemy Back C .10 .25
❑ M165 Love C .20 .50
❑ M166 Decoy C .10 .25
❑ M167 Reason for Their Highest Renown C .10 .25
❑ M168 Another Tracker C .10 .25
❑ N136 Naruto Uzumaki U .10 .25
❑ N137 Sasuke Uchiha U .10 .25
❑ N138 Shikamaru Nara R .20 .50
❑ N139 Rock Lee C .20 .50
❑ N140 Neji Hyuga U 1.25 3.00
❑ N141 Hizashi Hyuga C .10 .25
❑ N142 Izumo Kamizuki C .20 .50
❑ N143 Kotetsu Hagane C .10 .25
❑ N144 Gemma Shiranu R .10 .25
❑ N145 Gaara of the Desert SR .10 .25
❑ N146 Temari R 1.25 3.00
❑ N147 Kazekage R 3.00 8.00
❑ N148 Kidomaru R 1.25 3.00
❑ N149 Jirobo R 1.25 3.00
❑ N150 Sakon R 1.25 3.00
❑ N151 Tayuya R 1.25 3.00
❑ N152 Kabuto Yakushi SR 1.25 3.00
❑ N153 The Nine-Tailed Fox Spirit SR 1.25 3.00
❑ N154 Naruto Uzumaki C 4.00 10.00
❑ N155 Sasuke Uchiha C 4.00 10.00
❑ N156 Shino Aburame U .10 .25
❑ N157 Adoba Yamashiro C .10 .25
❑ N158 Asuma Sarutobi U .20 .50
❑ N159 Gen Aburame U .10 .25
❑ N160 Inoichi Yamanaka R .20 .50
❑ N161 Shikaku Nara R .20 .50
❑ N162 Choza Akimichi R 1.25 3.00
❑ N163 The Third Hokage SR 1.25 3.00
❑ N164 Monkey King Enma SR 1.25 3.00
❑ N165 Pakkun C 4.00 10.00
❑ N166 Orochimaru SR 3.00 8.00
❑ N167 The First Hokage R .10 .25
❑ N168 The Second Hokage R 2.00 5.00
❑ N169 Kazekage R 1.50 4.00
❑ N170 Kankuro C 1.25 3.00
❑ N171 Crow U 1.25 3.00
❑ N172 Kakashi Hatake & Might Guy SR .10 .25
❑ EX001 Naruto Uzumaki EX .20 .50
❑ EX002 Sasuke Uchiha EX 2.50 6.00

2008 Naruto Approaching Wind

COMPLETE SET (163) 50.00 100.00
BOOSTER BOX (24) 50.00 100.00
BOOSTER PACK 2.50 5.00

❑ C043 Hikaru Tsuki C .10 .25
❑ C044 Hikaru Tsuki U .20 .50
❑ C045 Michiru Tsuki ST .40 1.00
❑ C046 Shabadaba C .10 .25
❑ J342 Double Dynamic Entry SR 4.00 10.00
❑ J343 8 Trigrams 128 Palms R .75 2.00
❑ J344 Ninja Art: Kujaku Slice C .10 .25
❑ J345 Ninja Art: Kujaku Beast C .10 .25
❑ J346 Moonlight Rasengan SR 4.00 10.00
❑ J347 Leaf Lightning Fist R .75 2.00
❑ J348 Dynamic Lightning Lotus Chain R .75 2.00
❑ J349 Money Style: Help Me Jutsu U .20 .50
❑ J350 Currency Jutsu C .10 .25
❑ J351 Face Copying Jutsu C .10 .25
❑ J352 Ninja Art: Kujaku Wing C .10 .25
❑ J353 Predation of Chakra U .20 .50
❑ J354 Chakra Rope C .10 .25
❑ J355 Ninja Art: Phantom Jutsu U .20 .50
❑ J356 Inherited Iron Arm R .75 2.00
❑ J357 Ninja Art: Shadowing C .10 .25
❑ J358 Petrifying Attack U .20 .50
❑ J359 Unusual Strength C .10 .25
❑ J360 Hundred Blooming Flowers Jutsu U .20 .50
❑ J361 Slowing Down the Reflexes U .20 .50
❑ J362 Kunai C .10 .25
❑ J363 Shadow Clone Jutsu U .20 .50
❑ J364 Summoning Jutsu U .20 .50
❑ J365 Opening the Sharingan Eye ST .40 1.00
❑ J366 Tunneling Fang C .10 .25
❑ J367 Fire Style: Fire Ball Jutsu U .20 .50
❑ J368 Hidden Mist Jutsu ST .40 1.00
❑ J369 Curse Mark Jutsu U .20 .50
❑ J370 Crystal Ice Mirror C .10 .25
❑ J371 Exercise U .20 .50
❑ J372 Energy Control R 1.25 3.00
❑ J373 Earth Style: Headhunter Jutsu U .20 .50
❑ J374 Substitution Jutsu U .20 .50
❑ J375 Shadow Possession Jutsu C .10 .25
❑ J376 Power of the Byakugan C .10 .25
❑ J377 Rasengan ST .40 1.00
❑ J378 Harem Jutsu R 1.25 3.00
❑ J379 Power of the Cursed Mark C .10 .25
❑ J380 Shuriken U .20 .50
❑ J381 Kaleidoscope Sharingan U .20 .50
❑ J382 Explosion of the Rasengan SR 4.00 10.00
❑ J383 The Eight Inner Gates SR 3.00 8.00
❑ J384 Water Style: Water Dragon Jutsu U .20 .50
❑ J385 Last Ditch Attack U .20 .50
❑ J386 Fire Style: Phoenix Flower Jutsu U .20 .50
❑ M322 Hot-Blooded Tuition SR 3.00 8.00
❑ M323 Important Promise ST .40 1.00
❑ M324 Writing Novels U .20 .50
❑ M325 A Piece of Star R .75 2.00
❑ M326 Communication U .20 .50
❑ M327 Purchasing a whole Circus U .20 .50
❑ M328 Extremely Rich U .20 .50
❑ M329 New Vessel U .20 .50
❑ M330 Temporizing Threat R .75 2.00
❑ M331 Vision of the Future R 1.50 4.00
❑ M332 Cure for the Petrification C .10 .25
❑ M333 Gas Mask U .20 .50
❑ M334 Restart C .10 .25
❑ M335 Hell Valley U .20 .50
❑ M336 Rashness C .10 .25
❑ M337 Ambush U .20 .50
❑ M338 Running to the Setting Sun C .10 .25
❑ M339 Treat R .75 2.00
❑ M340 Back to the Leaf Village! C .10 .25
❑ M341 Abandonment U .20 .50
❑ M342 Ambitious Squad U .20 .50
❑ M343 Madness U .20 .50
❑ M344 Remarkable Growth ST .40 1.00
❑ M345 Oath of Tears R .75 2.00
❑ M346 My Way of the Shinobi R .75 2.00
❑ M347 Browbeater R .75 2.00
❑ M348 Tracking by Ninja Hounds R .75 2.00
❑ M349 Quarrel R .75 2.00
❑ M350 Affected Body C .10 .25
❑ M351 Binding Destiny C .10 .25
❑ M352 Inquiry R .75 2.00
❑ M353 Being a Fool U .20 .50
❑ M354 The ones Moving in the Dark C .10 .25
❑ M355 The Final Valley U .20 .50
❑ M356 The Symbol of the Proud Clan R .75 2.00
❑ M357 Melee U .20 .50
❑ M358 Charm C .10 .25
❑ M359 Inauguration U .20 .50
❑ M360 What the Ogre has left C .10 .25
❑ M361 Eight Inner Gates U .20 .50
❑ M362 Left Alone R .75 2.00
❑ M363 Overflowing Red Chakra C .10 .25
❑ N389 Neji Hyuga U .20 .50
❑ N390 Might Guy U .20 .50
❑ N391 The Fourth Hokage & Gamabunta SR 5.00 12.00
❑ N392 Naruto Uzumaki & Rock Lee R .75 2.00

❑ N393 Naruto Uzumaki U .20 .50
❑ N394 Sakura Haruno C .10 .25
❑ N395 Rock Lee U .20 .50
❑ N396 Kakashi Hatake C .10 .25
❑ N397 Naruto Uzumaki U .20 .50
❑ N398 Sakura Haruno C .10 .25
❑ N399 Rock Lee U .20 .50
❑ N400 Kakashi Hatake U .20 .50
❑ N401 Cham U .20 .50
❑ N402 Kikki C .10 .25
❑ N403 Ishidate R .75 2.00
❑ N404 Kongo R .75 2.00
❑ N405 Karenbana R .75 2.00
❑ N406 Naruto Uzumaki & Shadow Clone STSR 5.00 12.00
❑ N407 Kunihisa C .10 .25
❑ N408 Agari Kaisen U .20 .50
❑ N409 Sumaru U .20 .50
❑ N410 Hokuto C .10 .25
❑ N411 Mizura C .10 .25
❑ N412 Natsuhi ST .40 1.00
❑ N413 Akahoshi U .20 .50
❑ N414 Sasuke Uchiha & Orochimaru SR 4.00 10.00
❑ N415 Sasuke Uchiha STSR 4.00 10.00
❑ N416 Kabuto Yakushi SR 4.00 10.00
❑ N417 Genyumaru U .20 .50
❑ N418 Naruto Uzumaki SR 5.00 12.00
❑ N419 Sakura Haruno SR 5.00 12.00
❑ N420 Shikamaru Nara U .20 .50
❑ N421 Kakashi Hatake ST .40 1.00
❑ N422 Jiraiya R 1.25 3.00
❑ N423 Tsunade R 1.00 2.50
❑ N424 Konohamaru U .20 .50
❑ N425 Naruto Uzumaki R 1.25 3.00
❑ N426 Sasuke Uchiha R 1.25 3.00
❑ N427 Kiba Inuzuka ST .40 1.00
❑ N428 Shino Aburame C .10 .25
❑ N429 Hinata Hyuga C .10 .25
❑ N430 Rock Lee C .10 .25
❑ N431 Tenten C .10 .25
❑ N432 Neji Hyuga C .10 .25
❑ N433 Ino Yamanaka U .20 .50
❑ N434 Choji Akimichi C .10 .25
❑ N435 Akamaru ST .40 1.00
❑ N436 Iruka Umino C .10 .25
❑ N437 Might Guy C .10 .25
❑ N438 Asuma Sarutobi C .10 .25
❑ N439 Hayate Gekko R 1.25 3.00
❑ N440 Anko Mitarashi R .75 2.00
❑ N441 Naruto Uzumaki & Sakura Haruno SR 4.00 10.00
❑ N442 Zaku Abumi U .20 .50
❑ N443 Dosu Kinuta ST .40 1.00
❑ N444 Haku U .20 .50
❑ N445 Zabuza Momochi SR 4.00 10.00
❑ N446 Kimimaro R 1.25 3.00
❑ N447 Orochimaru ST .40 1.00
❑ N448 Naruto Uzumaki R 1.50 4.00
❑ N449 Sakura Haruno R 1.25 3.00
❑ N450 Pakkun C .10 .25
❑ N451 Shizune U .20 .50
❑ N452 Naruto Uzumaki U .20 .50
❑ N453 Itachi Uchiha SR 4.00 10.00
❑ N454 Kisame Hoshigaki SR 4.00 10.00
❑ N455 Naruto Uzumaki & Gamabunta SR 4.00 10.00
❑ N456 Zabuza Momochi R 1.25 3.00
❑ N457 Sakon U .20 .50
❑ N458 Jirobo U .20 .50
❑ N459 Tayuya U .20 .50
❑ N460 Kidomaru U .20 .50

2008 Naruto Battle of Destiny

COMPLETE SET (151) 50.00 100.00
BOOSTER BOX (24) 40.00 80.00
BOOSTER PACK 2.00 4.00

❑ C032 Teyaki Uchiha U .20 .50
❑ C033 Uruchi Uchiha C .10 .25
❑ J232 Leaf's Severe Hurricane U .20 .50
❑ J233 Loopy Fist R .75 2.00
❑ J234 Suicidal Action C .10 .25
❑ J235 Dynamic Marking C .10 .25
❑ J236 Wolf Fang Over Fang CR .40 1.00
❑ J237 Arhat Fist U .20 .50
❑ J238 Spider Bow: Fierce Rip R .75 2.00
❑ J239 Multiple Fists Barrage C .10 .25
❑ J240 Summoning Jutsu: Rashomon U .20 .50
❑ J241 Parasitic Demon Jutsu U .20 .50
❑ J242 Summoning Jutsu C .10 .25
❑ J243 Demon Revolution U .20 .50
❑ J244 Demon Flute: Chains of Fantasia U .20 .50
❑ J245 Willow Dance C .10 .25
❑ J246 Camellia Dance C .10 .25
❑ J247 Larch Dance U .20 .50
❑ J248 Ultimate Defense: Shield of the Shukaku SR3.00 8.00
❑ J249 Puppet Show, Secret Black Move Iron Maiden C .10 .25
❑ J250 Cyclone Scythe Jutsu C .10 .25
❑ J251 Shadow Strangle Jutsu U .20 .50
❑ J252 Ninja Art: Spiral Spider Web U .20 .50
❑ J253 Clematis Dance: Flower R .75 2.00
❑ J254 Excellent Teamwork C .10 .25
❑ J255 Rasengan R 1.25 3.00
❑ J256 Chakra Threads C .10 .25
❑ J259 Chidori R 1.25 3.00
❑ J260 Fuma Ninja Sword: Horse Slayer C .10 .25
❑ J263 Demon Flute: Musical Manipulation C .10 .25
❑ J264 Bracken Dance SR 3.00 8.00
❑ J265 Fuma Ninja Art: Binding Mandala C .10 .25
❑ J266 Regenerative Healing Jutsu C .10 .25
❑ J267 Sand Shower U .20 .50
❑ J268 Sand Tsunami R 1.25 3.00
❑ J269 Giant Sand Burial R .75 2.00
❑ J270 Sand Tomb R .75 2.00
❑ J271 Ninja Art: Wind Spider U .20 .50
❑ J272 Ninja Art: Doodlebug Jutsu U .20 .50
❑ J273 Kagero Ninja Art: Bubbles U .20 .50
❑ M236 Sudden Encounter C .75 2.00
❑ M237 Fake U .10 .25
❑ M238 Handsome Devil Returns U .20 .50
❑ M239 Man-Beast Transformation Combo R .10 .25
❑ M240 Berserk U .10 .25
❑ M241 Predicament C .10 .25
❑ M242 Vessel for Dreams C .20 .50
❑ M243 Kaguya Clan R .20 .50
❑ M244 Monstrous Appearance C .10 .25
❑ M245 In the Darkness U .20 .50
❑ M246 Ally of the Leaf Village U .75 2.00
❑ M247 Busy Life C .10 .25
❑ M248 Selecting the Strongest SR .10 .25
❑ M249 Sign for Reunion C .20 .50
❑ M250 Incurable Illness U .20 .50
❑ M251 Delay in the Assault C .75 2.00
❑ M252 Concentration of Power U .20 .50
❑ M253 One-On-One Fight U .10 .25
❑ M254 Power of State 2 SR .10 .25
❑ M255 The Final Valley U 1.25 3.00
❑ M256 Visualization of Chakra U .10 .25
❑ M257 Day of Separation U .20 .50
❑ M259 Another Way R .20 .50
❑ M260 Orochimaru's Den C .10 .25
❑ M261 Repetition of the Tragedy C 2.50 6.00
❑ M262 Protean R .10 .25
❑ M263 Information Gathering U .20 .50
❑ M265 Emergency Treatment R .10 .25
❑ M266 Ugly Guinea Pig C .20 .50
❑ M267 Time for the Showdown R .20 .50
❑ N255 Orochimaru R 4.00 10.00
❑ N256 Naruto Uzumaki C .20 .50
❑ N257 Sasuke Uchiha R .20 .50
❑ N258 Rock Lee SR .20 .50
❑ N259 Itachi Uchiha SR .75 2.00
❑ N260 Fugaku Uchiha U .10 .25
❑ N261 Mikoto Uchiha C .10 .25
❑ N262 Rock Lee & Might Guy SR 1.25 3.00
❑ N263 Sasuke Uchiha & Itachi Uchiha U .20 .50
❑ N264 Shikamaru Nara & Temari SR 1.25 3.00
❑ N265 Ukon U .10 .25
❑ N266 Kimimaro R .75 2.00
❑ N267 Doki C .20 .50
❑ N268 Gaara of the Desert SR .75 2.00
❑ N269 Kankuro U 1.25 3.00
❑ N270 Temari U .75 2.00
❑ N271 Black Ant C .10 .25
❑ N272 Crow & Black Ant U .10 .25
❑ N273 Double-Headed Wolf R .75 2.00
❑ N274 Naruto Uzumaki U .10 .25
❑ N275 Kiba Inuzuka U .20 .50
❑ N276 Choji Akimichi U .75 2.00
❑ N277 Neji Hyuga R 1.25 3.00
❑ N278 Naruto Uzumaki & Shikamaru Nara SR .10 .25
❑ N279 Kimimaro SR 1.25 3.00
❑ N280 Kidomaru R 3.00 8.00
❑ N281 Jirobo R 4.00 10.00
❑ N282 Sakon R .20 .50
❑ N283 Tayuya R .10 .25
❑ N288 Naruto Uzumaki SR 4.00 10.00
❑ N289 Sasuke Uchiha SR .20 .50
❑ N290 Sakura Haruno C 4.00 10.00
❑ N291 Iruka Umino C .20 .50
❑ N292 Shizune R .75 2.00
❑ N293 Kakashi Hatake SR .10 .25
❑ N294 Jiraiya R 3.00 8.00
❑ N295 Gaara of the Desert R .20 .50
❑ N296 Sasame Fuma C .20 .50
❑ N297 Kotohime C .10 .25
❑ N298 Hanzaki C .20 .50
❑ N299 Kamikiri C .75 2.00
❑ N300 Jigumo C .20 .50
❑ N301 Kagero U .20 .50
❑ N302 Kagero R .20 .50
❑ N303 Arashi Fuma C 1.25 3.00
❑ N304 Arashi Fuma U 3.00 8.00
❑ N305 Kimimaro SR 4.00 10.00
❑ N306 Naruto Uzumaki & Sasura Haruno R 1.25 3.00
❑ JUS045 Toad Mouth Trap R 1.25 3.00
❑ JUS046 Paper Bomb C 1.25 3.00
❑ JUS047 Motto U 1.25 3.00
❑ JUS048 Rapid Movement C 4.00 10.00
❑ JUS049 Additional Blow C 4.00 10.00
❑ JUS050 Thinking Mode C .10 .25
❑ JUS051 Unexpected Attack U .10 .25
❑ JUS052 Multiple Attacks U 1.25 3.00
❑ JUS053 One Last Punch C 4.00 10.00
❑ JUS054 Fire Style: Fireball Jutsu U .75 2.00
❑ JUS055 Tsukuyomi R 1.25 3.00
❑ JUS056 Threat C .10 .25
❑ MUS041 As Equals U .10 .25
❑ MUS042 Binding Threads of the Revenge R .10 .25
❑ MUS043 Prompt Instruction R .10 .25
❑ MUS044 Temptation R .10 .25
❑ MUS045 Wrong Person C .20 .50
❑ MUS046 Prohibition of Sharingan Eye C 1.25 3.00
❑ MUS047 Announcement of the Pairing R .10 .25
❑ MUS048 Reaction of the Power C .20 .50
❑ MUS049 The Power of Hatred U 4.00 10.00
❑ MUS050 Things to Protect R 1.50 4.00
❑ NUS055 Orochimaru R 1.25 3.00
❑ NUS056 Dosu Kinuta R 1.25 3.00
❑ NUS057 Zaku Abumi U .20 .50
❑ NUS058 Neji Hyuga U .20 .50
❑ NUS059 Tsunade SR 4.00 10.00
❑ NUS060 Tsunade & Katsuyu SR 4.00 10.00
❑ NUS061 Itachi Uchiha R 1.25 3.00
❑ NUS062 Kiba Inuzuka & Akamaru R 1.25 3.00
❑ NUS063 Rock Lee U .20 .50
❑ NUS064 Shino Aburame U .20 .50
❑ NUS065 Hinata Hyuga U .20 .50

2008 Naruto Lineage of the Legends

COMPLETE SET (208) 60.00 120.00
BOOSTER BOX (24) 40.00 80.00
BOOSTER PACK 2.00 4.00

❑ C034 Kahiko U .20 .50
❑ C035 Emina C .10 .25
❑ C036 Nerugui U .20 .50
❑ C038 Sansho C .10 .25
❑ C039 Karashi U .20 .50
❑ C040 Chishima U .20 .50
❑ C041 Komei R 1.25 3.00
❑ C042 Hitode C .10 .25
❑ J257 Plasma Ball U .20 .50
❑ J258 Tornado Lightning U .20 .50
❑ J261 Power of Gelel R 1.25 3.00
❑ J262 Rising Thunder R 1.25 3.00
❑ J274 Illusion U .20 .50
❑ J275 Transformation U .20 .50
❑ J305 Clone Spinning Axe Kick C .10 .25
❑ J306 Muscle Memory C .10 .25
❑ J307 Super Excellent Great Hyper Attack C .10 .25
❑ J308 Mad Dance of Infinity R .75 2.00
❑ J309 Thunder Armor U .20 .50
❑ J310 Boulder Avalanche C .10 .25
❑ J311 Thunder Funeral: Feast of Lightning C .10 .25
❑ J312 Lightning Fangs U .20 .50
❑ J313 Lightning Ball C .10 .25
❑ J314 Thunder Dragon Tornado R .75 2.00
❑ J315 Black Tornado U .20 .50
❑ J316 Cheesecake Jutsu C .10 .25
❑ J317 Gentle Fist U .20 .50
❑ J318 Tonfa C .10 .25
❑ J319 Iron Chain U .20 .50
❑ J320 Torpedo Nail C .10 .25
❑ J321 Flying Nail Mist C .10 .25
❑ J322 Tsukuyomi U .20 .50
❑ J323 Shark Skin C .10 .25
❑ J324 Multi Shadow Clone Jutsu C .10 .25
❑ J325 Striking Shadow Snake U .20 .50
❑ J326 Released Power U .20 .50
❑ J327 Bite C .10 .25
❑ J328 Lightning Blade SR 3.00 8.00
❑ J329 Fire Style: Dragon Flame Jutsu U .20 .50
❑ J330 Deformable Body C .10 .25
❑ J331 Chakra Absorption Jutsu C .10 .25
❑ J332 Water Style: Furious Current Jutsu R 1.25 3.00
❑ J333 Water Style:Great Cannonball Jutsu U .20 .50
❑ J334 Summoning Jutsu: Sea Monster C .10 .25
❑ J335 Demon Illusion: Hellfire Jutsu U .20 .50
❑ J336 Assimilation: Sand Coffin C .10 .25
❑ J337 Assimilation: Sand Burial C .10 .25
❑ J338 Backup C .10 .25
❑ J339 Universal Assimilation Jutsu C .10 .25
❑ J340 Assimilation: Rock Tank C .10 .25
❑ J341 Three-Section Staff U .20 .50
❑ M264 Mobile Fortress C 1.25 3.00
❑ M286 Box Lunch U .10 .25
❑ M287 Curry of Life U .20 .50
❑ M288 Origin of the Legend SR .20 .50
❑ M289 Perfect Disguise? C .10 .25
❑ M290 Wounds from the Lost Battle C .10 .25
❑ M291 Leaf Village's Open Competition C .20 .50
❑ M292 No Power of Observation U .10 .25
❑ M293 False Charge C .20 .50
❑ M294 Duel at OK Temple C .20 .50
❑ M295 Visitors from the Darkness C .20 .50
❑ M296 Final Separation R .20 .50
❑ M297 Right Man for the Right Job C .20 .50
❑ M298 No Sense of Direction C .10 .25
❑ M299 Wanted Poster with a Reward R .20 .50
❑ M300 Temporary Team C .20 .50
❑ M301 Survival on Mount Takurami C .20 .50
❑ M302 Funeral of the Living C .20 .50
❑ M303 Secret Activities U .10 .25
❑ M304 Threat of the Akatsuki R .20 .50
❑ M305 Lots of Energy R .20 .50
❑ M306 Right Guess C 4.00 10.00
❑ M307 Penniless Man C .10 .25
❑ M308 Self-Sacrifice C .10 .25
❑ M309 Cooking Match! U .10 .25
❑ M310 Under a Starry Sky R .20 .50
❑ M311 Island of Mysterious Abductions C .10 .25
❑ M312 Sea Monster Panic R .10 .25
❑ M313 Ache of the Curse Mark C .10 .25
❑ M314 Blocked Memory R .75 2.00
❑ M315 Flying into the New Era R .10 .25
❑ M316 Cursed Samurai in White U .10 .25
❑ M317 False Jutsu C 1.25 3.00
❑ M318 Out-Of-Mission Activities C .10 .25
❑ M319 Clear Sky R .10 .25
❑ M320 Youths of the Land of Fire R .10 .25
❑ M321 Youths of the Land of Wind R .20 .50
❑ N344 Naruto Uzumaki C .75 2.00
❑ N345 Sakura Haruno C 1.25 3.00
❑ N346 Rock Lee C .10 .25
❑ N347 Neji Hyuga C .10 .25
❑ N348 Tenten C .10 .25
❑ N349 Might Guy R .20 .50
❑ N350 Mondai Guy U 1.25 3.00
❑ N351 Poccha Lee C .10 .25
❑ N352 Jiraiya SR .75 2.00
❑ N353 Orochimaru SR .10 .25
❑ N354 Tsunade SR .75 2.00
❑ N355 Raiga Kurosuki SR .75 2.00
❑ N356 Ranmaru C .20 .50
❑ N357 Kurosuki Gang U .10 .25
❑ N358 Sazanami R .10 .25
❑ N359 Gatsu R .75 2.00
❑ N360 Gosunkugi C 1.25 3.00
❑ N361 Konohamaru Ninja Squad C 1.25 3.00
❑ N362 Izumo Kamizuki & Kotetsu Hagane C .10 .25
❑ N363 Orochimaru & Kabuto Yakushi R .10 .25
❑ N364 Pricess Dusk U .20 .50
❑ N365 Itachi Uchiha SR .20 .50
❑ N366 Kisame Hoshigaki R .10 .25
❑ N367 Itachi Uchiha & Kisame Hoshigaki SR .20 .50
❑ N368 The First Hokage SR .75 2.00
❑ N369 The Second Hokage SR .20 .50
❑ N370 The Third Hokage SR .10 .25
❑ N371 The Fourth Hokage SR .10 .25
❑ N372 The Fifth Hokage SR .20 .50
❑ N373 Naruto Uzumaki R .20 .50
❑ N374 Shino Aburame C .10 .25
❑ N375 Ino Yamanaka C .10 .25
❑ N376 Anko Mitarashi U .20 .50
❑ N377 Kakashi Hatake SR .20 .50
❑ N378 Gamakichi & Gamatatsu C .10 .25
❑ N379 Hokushin C .20 .50
❑ N380 Nagare C .20 .50
❑ N381 Hoki U .10 .25
❑ N382 Toki R .75 2.00
❑ N383 Sasuke Uchiha R .10 .25
❑ N384 Isaribi R .20 .50
❑ N385 Amachi R .20 .50
❑ N386 Yoroi Akado U .20 .50
❑ N387 Misumi Tsurugi U .10 .25
❑ N388 Hakkaku C .10 .25
❑ JUS077 Water Style: Giant Vortex Jutsu R .10 .25
❑ JUS078 Clematis Dance: Flower C .10 .25
❑ JUS079 Paper Bomb U .10 .25
❑ JUS080 Gentle Fist Style: 8 Trigrams 64 Palms U1.25 3.00
❑ JUS081 Irregular Attack C .20 .50
❑ JUS082 Night Attack C .10 .25
❑ JUS083 Flying Knee U 4.00 10.00
❑ JUS084 Surprise Attack in the Dark C 4.00 10.00
❑ JUS085 Emergency Evacuation U 4.00 10.00
❑ JUS086 Restoration of the Memory U 5.00 12.00
❑ JUS087 Moving Under Water U .10 .25
❑ JUS088 Toad Sword U .20 .50
❑ JUS089 Sonic Speed Attack U 1.25 3.00
❑ JUS090 Armed Puppet C 1.25 3.00
❑ JUS091 Counter by the Sharingan Eye U .10 .25
❑ JUS092 Power of the Sharingan Eye U .10 .25
❑ JUS093 Smoke Pellet U .10 .25
❑ JUS094 Unguarded Moment U 1.50 4.00
❑ MUS087 Hyuga Way C .20 .50
❑ MUS088 Power of the Seven Swordsmen of the Mist C 4.00 10.00
❑ MUS089 Time Stands Still U 1.25 3.00
❑ MUS090 Unexpected Result U 4.00 10.00
❑ MUS091 Scum Recipe C 4.00 10.00
❑ MUS092 Rich Knowledge U 4.00 10.00
❑ MUS093 Ghost Panic R 4.00 10.00
❑ MUS094 Distinction U 5.00 12.00
❑ MUS095 Shadow of the Nine-Tailed Fox Spirit C4.00 10.00
❑ MUS096 Symbol of the Evil C 1.25 3.00
❑ MUS097 Organizing Teams U .10 .25
❑ MUS098 Deleted Record U .10 .25
❑ MUS099 Tragedy C .20 .50
❑ MUS100 A Vicious Reception C 4.00 10.00
❑ MUS101 World of Genjutsu U .10 .25
❑ MUS102 Toe to Toe U .10 .25
❑ MUS103 Blown in the Wind C .10 .25
❑ MUS104 Burnished Blades U .20 .50
❑ MUS105 Deep Ambition U 1.25 3.00
❑ MUS106 Repose of the Warriors C 1.25 3.00
❑ MUS107 Symbol of the Rogue Ninja R 1.25 3.00
❑ MUS108 I'm Coming to You! C .75 2.00
❑ MUS109 Curse Sealing U .20 .50
❑ MUS110 Weight Training U .20 .50
❑ MUS111 The Squad 7 U .10 .25
❑ NUS093 Temujin R 1.25 3.00
❑ NUS094 Haido U .20 .50
❑ NUS095 Haido's Soldier U .20 .50
❑ NUS096 Kamira R 1.25 3.00
❑ NUS097 Ranke R 1.25 3.00
❑ NUS098 Fugai R 1.25 3.00
❑ NUS099 Temujin U .20 .50
❑ NUS100 Haido (Transformed) R 1.25 3.00
❑ NUS101 Sasuke Uchiha U .20 .50
❑ NUS102 Ino Yamanaka C .10 .25
❑ NUS103 Shukaku SR 4.00 10.00
❑ NUS104 Naruto Uzumaki C .10 .25
❑ NUS105 Hinata Hyuga U .20 .50
❑ NUS106 Kurenai Yuhi R 1.25 3.00
❑ NUS107 Choji Akimichi C .10 .25
❑ NUS108 Haku R 1.25 3.00
❑ NUS109 The Third Hokage & Monkey King Enma R1.25 3.00
❑ NUS110 Jiraiya & Gamabunta R 1.50 4.00
❑ NUS111 Shino Aburame C .10 .25
❑ NUS112 Gaara of the Desert (Possessed Mode) R1.25 3.00
❑ NUS113 Hanabi Hyuga & Hiashi Hyuga C .10 .25
❑ NUS114 Asuma Sarutobi U .20 .50
❑ NUS115 Might Guy U .20 .50
❑ NUS116 Kakashi Hatake R 1.25 3.00
❑ NUS117 Kimimaro U .20 .50
❑ NUS118 Kankuro C .10 .25
❑ NUS119 Kakashi Hatake & Might Guy U .20 .50
❑ NUS120 Choji Akimichi C .10 .25
❑ NUS121 Temari C .10 .25
❑ NUS122 Naruto Uzumaki SR 3.00 8.00
❑ NUS123 Sasuke Uchiha SR 4.00 10.00
❑ NUS124 Kimimaro SR 3.00 8.00

2008 Naruto The Chosen

COMPLETE SET (162) 40.00 80.00
BOOSTER BOX (24) 40.00 80.00
BOOSTER PACK 2.00 4.00

❑ C037 Bikochu R .75 2.00
❑ J276 Uzumaki Formation C .20 .50
❑ J277 Information Analysis C .10 .25
❑ J278 Sealing Trap C .10 .25
❑ J279 Mad Dance of Infinity SR .10 .25
❑ J280 Falcon Drop R 2.50 6.00
❑ J281 Lightning Blade Single Slash R .75 2.00
❑ J282 Orochimaru's Secret Drug ST 1.25 3.00
❑ J283 Animalization U .40 1.00
❑ J284 Exceptional Force R .20 .50
❑ J285 Insect Attractant Jutsu C .75 2.00
❑ J286 Insect Wall Jutsu C .10 .25
❑ J287 Sand Levitation C .10 .25
❑ J288 Double Sand Blade R .10 .25
❑ J289 Mind Destruction Jutsu C .75 2.00
❑ J290 Hundred Power Palms C .10 .25
❑ J291 8 Trigrams 64 Palms for Defense R .10 .25
❑ J292 Thousand Bee Stings Jutsu C .75 2.00
❑ J293 Bee Bomb Jutsu C .10 .25
❑ J294 Honey Jutsu C .10 .25
❑ J295 Summoning Jutsu U .10 .25
❑ J296 Blazing Rasengan SR .20 .50
❑ J297 Fire Style: Flame Flower R 3.00 8.00
❑ J298 Shadow Clashing Palm Jutsu R .75 2.00
❑ J299 Heaven's Dance of Hazy White R .75 2.00
❑ J300 Last Resort: Eight Gates Assault R .75 2.00
❑ J301 Supreme Ninjutsu: One's Own Rule R .75 2.00
❑ J302 Parasitic Insects: Whirlwind R .75 2.00
❑ J303 Fire Style: Flame Rasengan R .75 2.00
❑ J304 Green Impact R .75 2.00
❑ M268 Information about Orochimaru C .75 2.00
❑ M269 Dull-Witted Brothers C .20 .50
❑ M270 Mission of Recapturing Prisoners C .10 .25
❑ M271 Screw-Up U .20 .50
❑ M272 Tsunade's Guess C .75 2.00
❑ M273 Mutual Deception C .20 .50
❑ M275 Frustrated Ambition U .75 2.00
❑ M276 Signs of Madness C .20 .50
❑ M277 Grudge about Food C 3.00 8.00
❑ M278 Becoming a Pupil C 1.25 3.00
❑ M279 Blush C 3.00 8.00
❑ M280 Gaining Time C .20 .50
❑ M281 Battle between Insect Tamers U .10 .25
❑ M282 Training in the Moonlight R .10 .25
❑ M283 Hinata in Captivity SR .75 2.00
❑ M284 Look for the Rare Bikochu C .20 .50
❑ M285 Hive with Gigantic Larvae C .20 .50
❑ N307 Naruto Uzumaki C .20 .50
❑ N308 Sasuke Uchiha C .40 1.00
❑ N309 Ino Yamanaka C .20 .50
❑ N310 Neji Hyuga C .20 .50
❑ N311 Tenten U .10 .25
❑ N312 Pakkun C .10 .25
❑ N313 Anko Mitarashi R .10 .25
❑ N314 Yugao Uzuki R .20 .50
❑ N315 Shizune R .10 .25
❑ N316 Kakashi Hatake R .10 .25
❑ N317 Might Guy C .20 .50
❑ N318 The Third Hokage SR .10 .25
❑ N319 Jiraiya R .10 .25
❑ N320 Orochimaru R .10 .25
❑ N321 Tsunade R .10 .25
❑ N322 Haku R .10 .25
❑ N323 Zabuza Momochi SR .20 .50
❑ N324 Kisame Hoshigaki R .75 2.00
❑ N325 Naruto Uzumaki C 3.00 8.00
❑ N326 Sasuke Uchiha C .10 .25
❑ N327 Sakura Haruno C .10 .25
❑ N328 Kiba Inuzuka C .20 .50
❑ N329 Shino Aburame C .20 .50
❑ N330 Hinata Hyuga R .75 2.00
❑ N331 Rock Lee U .20 .50
❑ N332 Konohamaru Ninja Squad C .20 .50
❑ N333 Kakashi Hatake U .20 .50
❑ N334 The Fifth Hokage SR .75 2.00
❑ N335 Mizuki R .75 2.00
❑ N336 Tsubaki C .10 .25
❑ N337 Fujin R .20 .50

❑ N338 Raijin R .75 2.00
❑ N339 Gaara of the Desert U .10 .25
❑ N340 Suzumebachi C .20 .50
❑ N341 Jibachi C .10 .25
❑ N342 Kurobachi C .20 .50
❑ N343 Naruto Uzumaki C .20 .50
❑ CUS001 Yukie Fujikaze U 1.25 3.00
❑ JUS057 Food Pills U .10 .25
❑ JUS058 Sexy Jutsu C .10 .25
❑ JUS059 Food Pills U .75 2.00
❑ JUS060 Attack to the Weakest Point R .10 .25
❑ JUS061 Sealing Jutsu: Fire Seal U .20 .50
❑ JUS062 Byakugan R .20 .50
❑ JUS063 Absent-Mindedness U .10 .25
❑ JUS064 8 Trigrams Palms Rotation SR .20 .50
❑ JUS065 Chidori R .10 .25
❑ JUS066 Lightning Blade SR .20 .50
❑ JUS067 Double Knock Out U .10 .25
❑ JUS068 Blade Manipulation Jutsu C .10 .25
❑ JUS069 Preparation for the Victory C .20 .50
❑ JUS070 Subjective R .20 .50
❑ JUS071 Super Genius U .20 .50
❑ JUS072 Awakening of the Monster U .10 .25
❑ JUS073 Sacrifice U .10 .25
❑ JUS074 Intake of Chakra ST .20 .50
❑ JUS075 Outsmarting the Opponent U .75 2.00
❑ JUS076 Invisible Attack U .10 .25
❑ MUS051 The Light and the Darkness U .10 .25
❑ MUS052 From the Teacher to the pupil U .10 .25
❑ MUS053 The Path to Hakage R .10 .25
❑ MUS054 Promotion to Chunin U .20 .50
❑ MUS055 The Last Bite U .10 .25
❑ MUS056 Kunoichi VS Kunoichi U .75 2.00
❑ MUS057 Absolute Obedience R .75 2.00
❑ MUS058 The Final Tournament Started! R 1.25 3.00
❑ MUS059 Elimination C .75 2.00
❑ MUS060 Rising Gate U .10 .25
❑ MUS061 No Talent Whatsoever! R 4.00 10.00
❑ MUS062 I will protect you until I die C .75 2.00
❑ MUS063 Faith Between the Teacher and the Student U 1.25 3.00
❑ MUS064 Check Book C 1.50 4.00
❑ MUS065 Millionaire U .75 2.00
❑ MUS066 Blowout U 2.50 6.00
❑ MUS067 Separation R .75 2.00
❑ MUS068 Settling the Fight C .10 .25
❑ MUS069 Legendary Sitting Duck C .10 .25
❑ MUS070 Important Things R .10 .25
❑ MUS071 Ominousness C .10 .25
❑ MUS072 Phobia U .10 .25
❑ MUS073 Overlapping Images U 1.25 3.00
❑ MUS074 Broke C .20 .50
❑ MUS075 Death U .10 .25
❑ MUS076 Putting off the Promise C .20 .50
❑ MUS077 A Shadow in the Moonlight U 3.00 8.00
❑ MUS078 Impatience C 1.50 4.00
❑ MUS079 Acquaintance C .10 .25
❑ MUS080 Deal Behind the Scenes U .75 2.00
❑ MUS081 Wipe Out U .75 2.00
❑ MUS082 Waiting for the Arrival U .20 .50
❑ MUS083 Rejection C .10 .25
❑ MUS084 Getting Scent of the Hostility C .10 .25
❑ MUS085 Stubborn U .10 .25
❑ MUS086 Just Like Drifting Clouds R .10 .25
❑ NUS066 Naruto Uzumaki & Sasuke Uchiha SR 4.00 10.00
❑ NUS067 Naruto Uzumaki & Kiba Inuzuka U .20 .50
❑ NUS068 Naruto Uzumaki & Neji Hyuga R 1.25 3.00
❑ NUS069 Gaara of the Desert U .20 .50
❑ NUS070 Gaara of the Desert STSR 2.00 5.00
❑ NUS071 Temari R .75 2.00
❑ NUS072 Gamakichi C .10 .25
❑ NUS073 Kabuto Yakushi U .20 .50
❑ NUS074 Kabuto Yakushi ST .40 1.00
❑ NUS075 Kankuro U .20 .50
❑ NUS076 Sakura Haruno ST .40 1.00
❑ NUS077 Tsunade ST .40 1.00
❑ NUS078 Kisame Hoshigaki STSR 2.00 5.00
❑ NUS079 Naruto Uzumaki & Gamakichi C .10 .25
❑ NUS080 Kimimaro U .20 .50
❑ NUS081 Itachi Uchiha R 1.50 4.00
❑ NUS082 Neji Hyuga C .10 .25
❑ NUS083 The Third Hokage SR 3.00 8.00
❑ NUS084 Neji Hyuga & Hizashi Hyuga R 1.25 3.00
❑ NUS085 Kurenai Yuhi ST .40 1.00
❑ NUS086 Dotou Kazahana U .20 .50

2009 Naruto A New Chronicle

COMPLETE SET (172) 75.00 150.00
BOOSTER BOX (24) 50.00 100.00
BOOSTER PACK 2.50 5.00

❑ J387 Sexy Jutsu R .75 2.00
❑ J388 New Pervy Ninjutsu R .75 2.00
❑ J389 Revealing the Ending C .10 .25
❑ J390 Make-Out Tactics C .10 .25
❑ J391 Brainwash Jutsu U .20 .50
❑ J392 Forbidden Word C .10 .25
❑ J393 Iron-Armed U .20 .50
❑ J394 Wind Scythe Jutsu R .75 2.00
❑ J395 Sand Shield C .10 .25
❑ J396 Leaf Rising Wind U .20 .50
❑ J397 Nunchaku C .10 .25
❑ J398 Opening the Eight Inner Gates R .75 2.00
❑ J399 Asakujaku SR 10.00 25.00
❑ J400 Giant Rasengan SR 6.00 15.00
❑ J401 Genjutsu C .10 .25
❑ J402 Mission File C .10 .25
❑ J403 Detonating Clay Eagle U .20 .50
❑ J404 Detonating Clay Bird U .20 .50
❑ J405 Detonating Clay Spider U .20 .50
❑ J406 Detonating Clay Signature Technique R 1.50 4.00
❑ J407 Cleanup U .20 .50
❑ J408 Water Style: Exploding Water Shock Wave U .20 .50
❑ J409 Water Prison Jutsu R .75 2.00
❑ J410 Shark Skin R .75 2.00
❑ J411 Impersonation Jutsu U .20 .50
❑ J412 Explosive Blade C .10 .25
❑ J413 Puppet Master Jutsu U .20 .50
❑ J414 Absolute Defense U .20 .50
❑ J415 Sand Prison U .20 .50
❑ J416 Sand Coffin SR 5.00 12.00
❑ J417 Detoxification C .10 .25
❑ J418 Deadly Poison R 1.50 4.00
❑ J419 Emission of Chakra R .75 2.00
❑ J420 Compound Jutsu C .10 .25
❑ J421 8 Trigrams Air Palm R 2.50 6.00
❑ J422 Artful Fist R .75 2.00
❑ J423 Spider Bow: Fierce Rip R .75 2.00
❑ J424 Deadly Combination Attack R .75 2.00
❑ J425 Demon Flute: Chains of Fantasia U .20 .50
❑ J426 Threat of the Puppets C .10 .25
❑ J427 Substitution by Insects C .10 .25
❑ J428 Concealed Weapon U .20 .50
❑ J429 Gentle Fist Style: 8 Trigrams 64 Palms R .75 2.00
❑ J430 Shadow Strangle Jutsu U .20 .50
❑ J431 Poison Needles U .20 .50
❑ J432 Dispatch of Anbu U .20 .50
❑ J433 Angry Fist U .20 .50
❑ J434 Striking Shadow Snake U .20 .50
❑ J435 Reaper Death Seal R .75 2.00
❑ J436 Shadow Clone Jutsu R .75 2.00
❑ J437 Summoning Jutsu C .10 .25
❑ J438 Playing Possum Jutsu C .10 .25
❑ J439 Liquid Bullets R .75 2.00
❑ J440 Air Bullets R .75 2.00
❑ J441 Sealing Jutsu: Fire Seal C .10 .25
❑ J442 Anbu Mask U .20 .50
❑ J443 Knockout Blow U .20 .50
❑ J444 Opening the Byakugan C .10 .25
❑ J445 Wolf Fang Over Fang C .10 .25
❑ J446 Larch Dance U .20 .50
❑ J447 Substitution by Puppet R .75 2.00
❑ J448 Capture C .10 .25
❑ J449 Fire Style: Fire Ball Jutsu C .10 .25
❑ M364 Dangerous Intruder U .20 .50
❑ M365 New leader of the Village U .20 .50
❑ M366 Round-Table Conference C .10 .25
❑ M367 Sending Off C .10 .25
❑ M368 Growth of the Two R .60 1.50
❑ M369 Existence of Tailed Beast U .20 .50
❑ M370 Powerful Help C .10 .25
❑ M371 Art is an explosion! R .60 1.50
❑ M372 Akatsuki Gathered C .10 .25
❑ M373 The ones who interrupt C .10 .25
❑ M374 Revenge for My Son C .10 .25
❑ M375 Sasori of the Red Sand R 3.00 8.00
❑ M376 Playing Dead U .20 .50
❑ M377 Heroic Whirl Wind R .60 1.50
❑ M378 Tyrannical Storm R .60 1.50
❑ M379 West Gate, North Gate C .10 .25
❑ M380 South Gate, East Gate C .10 .25
❑ M381 The one who lives within SR 6.00 15.00
❑ M382 Raid By Anbu U .20 .50
❑ M383 Teacher and pupils C .10 .25
❑ M384 Great Memory C .10 .25
❑ M385 A Mark U .20 .50
❑ M386 Arbitration R .60 1.50
❑ M387 Oath of Vengeance U .20 .50
❑ M388 Welling Up Red Chakra C .10 .25
❑ M389 Secret of Uchiha Clan U .20 .50
❑ M390 On the Stump C .10 .25
❑ M391 Debt R 1.25 3.00
❑ M392 A Preach C .10 .25
❑ M393 Found You! C .10 .25
❑ M394 Wonderful Days U .20 .50
❑ M395 Wager C .10 .25
❑ M396 A Gift U .20 .50
❑ M397 BBQ R 3.00 8.00
❑ M398 Preparation C .10 .25
❑ M399 Ino-Shika-Cho Trio U .20 .50
❑ M400 Inuzuka Clan U .20 .50
❑ M401 Ichiraku Noodle Shop R .60 1.50
❑ M402 Chase U .20 .50
❑ M403 Creeping Up Dark Clouds U .20 .50
❑ M404 Agony of the Strong C .10 .25
❑ M405 Numbness U .20 .50
❑ M406 Archrival U .20 .50
❑ M407 Ultimate Two-Step Program C .10 .25
❑ M408 Invitation to the Evil U .20 .50
❑ M409 Escape C .10 .25
❑ M410 Apology C .10 .25
❑ M411 Long Awaited Reinforcements R 1.50 4.00
❑ N461 Kankuro SR 12.00 30.00
❑ N462 Temari R .50 1.25
❑ N463 Yura C .10 .25
❑ N464 Baki U .20 .50
❑ N465 The Fifth Kazekage SR 8.00 20.00
❑ N466 Naruto Uzumaki U .20 .50
❑ N467 Sakura Haruno R 1.25 3.00
❑ N468 Iruka Umino U .20 .50
❑ N469 Konohamaru C .10 .25
❑ N470 Moegi C .10 .25
❑ N471 Udon C .10 .25
❑ N472 Ebisu C .10 .25
❑ N473 Kakashi Hatake SR 8.00 20.00
❑ N474 Might Guy R 1.25 3.00
❑ N475 Rock Lee R 1.25 3.00
❑ N476 Neji Hyuga U .20 .50
❑ N477 Tenten U .20 .50
❑ N478 Itachi Uchiha SR 8.00 20.00
❑ N479 Kisame Hoshigaki R 1.25 3.00
❑ N480 Deidara SR 12.00 30.00
❑ N481 Sasori SR 12.00 30.00
❑ N482 Zetsu SR 6.00 15.00
❑ N483 Gaara of the Desert U .20 .50
❑ N484 Crow U .20 .50
❑ N485 Black Ant U .20 .50
❑ N486 Salamander U .20 .50
❑ N487 Ebizo U .20 .50
❑ N488 Chiyo R 1.50 4.00
❑ N489 Cipher Corps U .20 .50
❑ N490 Naruto Uzumaki C .10 .25
❑ N491 Sakura Haruno C .10 .25
❑ N492 Rock Lee U .20 .50
❑ N493 Hinata Hyuga C .10 .25
❑ N494 Naruto Uzumaki & Gaara of the Desert SR 8.00 20.00
❑ N495 Temari & Kankuro SR 10.00 25.00
❑ N496 Sasuke Uchiha U .20 .50
❑ N497 Naruto Uzumaki U .20 .50
❑ N498 Kiba Inuzuka C .10 .25
❑ N499 Ninja Dog Squad C .10 .25
❑ N500 Hinata Hyuga & Hiashi Hyuga U .20 .50
❑ N501 Sasori & Kisame Hoshigaki SR 8.00 20.00
❑ N502 Itachi Uchiha & Deidara SR 6.00 15.00
❑ N503 Double Headed Wolf R 1.25 3.00
❑ N504 Kiba Inuzuka & Akamaru R 1.25 3.00
❑ N505 Kotetsu Hagane C .10 .25
❑ N506 Kurenai Yuhi U .20 .50
❑ N507 Genma Shiranui C .10 .25
❑ N508 Hayate Gekko U .20 .50
❑ N509 Hanabi Hyuga C .10 .25
❑ N510 Kankuro U .20 .50
❑ N511 Shino Aburame R 4.00 10.00
❑ N512 Ninja Dog Squad (All Gathered) C .10 .25
❑ N513 Neji Hyuga C .10 .25
❑ N514 Inoichi Yamanaka R 1.25 3.00
❑ N515 Shikaku Nara R 2.50 6.00
❑ N516 Choza Akimichi R 1.25 3.00
❑ N517 Gen Aburame R 1.25 3.00
❑ N518 Hiashi Hyuga R 1.25 3.00
❑ N519 Choji Akimichi C .10 .25
❑ N520 Deidara U .20 .50
❑ N521 Sasori U .20 .50

2009 Naruto Emerging Alliance

COMPLETE SET (145) 50.00 100.00
BOOSTER BOX (24) 50.00 100.00
BOOSTER PACK 2.00 5.00

❑ J496 Art of Ink Mist U .20 .50
❑ J497 Ninja Art: Super Beast Scroll R .75 2.00
❑ J498 Fire Style: Phoenix Flower Jutsu R .75 2.00
❑ J499 Self-Destruct Doppelganger R .75 2.00
❑ J500 Water Style: Water Shark Bomb Jutsu SR 10.00 25.00
❑ J501 Detonating Kunai C .10 .25
❑ J502 Sealing Jutsu: Breaking the Lions Roar SR 3.00 8.00
❑ J503 Flamethrower U .20 .50
❑ J504 Secret White Move Chikamatsu?s Ten Puppets R .75 2.00
❑ J505 Partial Expansion Jutsu U .20 .50
❑ J506 Ninja Art: Shadow Stitching SR 3.00 8.00
❑ J507 Reanimation Ninjutsu U .20 .50
❑ J508 Secret Red Move Performance of a Hundred Puppets R .75 2.00
❑ J509 Critical Wound C .10 .25
❑ J510 Getting Ready U .20 .50
❑ J511 Sense of Fear SR 4.00 10.00
❑ J512 Assimilation C .10 .25
❑ J513 Tricky Move C .10 .25
❑ J514 Ninja Art: Super Beast Scroll Rat U .20 .50
❑ J515 Wood Style Transformation C .10 .25
❑ J516 Striking Multi Shadow Snakes Jutsu U .20 .50
❑ J517 Formation! R .75 2.00
❑ J518 Revealing the True Face C .10 .25
❑ J519 Earth Style: Rending Piercing Fang SR 3.00 8.00
❑ J520 Ultimate Art U .20 .50
❑ J521 Ten Thousand Snakes Wave U .20 .50
❑ J522 Wood Style Jutsu: Wooden Lock Wall C .10 .25
❑ J523 Wood Clone Jutsu C .10 .25
❑ J524 Summoning Jutsu: Triple Rashomon R .75 2.00
❑ J525 Chakra Cannon U .20 .50
❑ J526 Thunder Funeral: Feast of Lightning U .20 .50
❑ J527 Unique Skill U .20 .50
❑ J528 Razor Chain C .10 .25
❑ J529 Sonic Attack C .10 .25
❑ J530 Super Sonic Slicing Wave C .10 .25
❑ J531 Stealing Chakra R .75 2.00
❑ J532 Twining Limbs C .10 .25
❑ J533 Bone Transformation C .10 .25
❑ J534 Bone Guard C .10 .25
❑ J535 Supplement of Energy U .20 .50
❑ J536 Wood Style Jutsu: Four Pillars Prison Jutsu U .20 .50
❑ J537 Visual Jutsu R .75 2.00
❑ J538 Giant Rasengan R .75 2.00
❑ J539 Crow Clone Jutsu R .75 2.00
❑ J540 Long Sword Shark Skin U .20 .50
❑ M455 Rules for Medical Ninjas R .75 2.00
❑ M456 Search Party C .10 .25
❑ M457 Piggyback C .10 .25
❑ M458 Filling Up the Open Spot R .75 2.00
❑ M459 100 Hot-Blooded C .10 .25
❑ M460 Fellowship C .10 .25
❑ M461 Tears for a Friend C .10 .25
❑ M462 Constricting Bind U .20 .50
❑ M463 Bad Dream R .75 2.00
❑ M464 Control by Fear C .10 .25
❑ M465 Transmitter U .20 .50
❑ M466 Lunchbox U .20 .50
❑ M467 Shake Hands U .20 .50
❑ M468 Meaning of Comrade C .10 .25
❑ M469 Tenchi Bridge C .10 .25
❑ M470 Releasing the Sealed Power U .20 .50
❑ M471 Compressed Chakra C .10 .25
❑ M472 A Sign of Revival U .20 .50
❑ M473 The best pair C .10 .25
❑ M474 Hiding U .20 .50
❑ M475 Check U .20 .50
❑ M476 Fateful Encounter C .10 .25
❑ M477 Super Bushy-Brow C .10 .25
❑ M478 Ninja Info Card R .75 2.00
❑ M479 Pressure R .75 2.00
❑ M480 Captivity R .75 2.00
❑ M481 Precious Student C .10 .25
❑ M482 The Ones Who Have the Same Eyes U .20 .50
❑ M483 Meaning of Life C .10 .25
❑ M484 Impersonation U .20 .50
❑ M485 Medical Ninja U .20 .50
❑ M486 Sealing Barrier R .75 2.00
❑ M487 A New Squad R .75 2.00
❑ M488 Surprise Training C .10 .25
❑ M489 Invitation to the Darkness U .20 .50
❑ M490 Picture Book C .10 .25
❑ M491 Discord C .10 .25
❑ M492 Secret Meeting C .10 .25
❑ M493 Commemorative Photo U .20 .50
❑ M494 Pledge under a Starry Sky C .10 .25
❑ M495 Respective Dreams C .10 .25
❑ M496 Underground Organization U .20 .50
❑ M497 Advisors U .20 .50
❑ M498 Prelude to an End U .20 .50
❑ M499 Intellectual Strategy R .75 2.00
❑ N590 Kakashi Hatake & Might Guy U .20 .50
❑ N591 Naruto Uzumaki (Tailed Beast Mode) SR 10.00 25.00
❑ N592 Naruto Uzumaki C .10 .25
❑ N593 Sakura Haruno C .10 .25
❑ N594 Sai R 1.00 2.50
❑ N595 Ino Yamanaka C .10 .25
❑ N596 Shikamaru Nara C .10 .25
❑ N597 Choji Akimichi C .10 .25
❑ N598 Yamato R .75 2.00
❑ N599 Shizune C .10 .25
❑ N600 Danzo R .75 2.00
❑ N601 Chiyo U .20 .50
❑ N602 Matsuri C .10 .25
❑ N603 Mikoshi C .10 .25
❑ N604 Tobi R 1.50 4.00
❑ N605 Sasori (Possesion Mode) R .75 2.00
❑ N606 Kabuto Yakushi SR 5.00 12.00
❑ N607 Orochimaru SR 5.00 12.00
❑ N608 Naruto Uzumaki & Sai R .75 2.00
❑ N609 Anbu (The Foundation) R .75 2.00
❑ N610 Homura Mitomon U .20 .50
❑ N611 Koharu Utatane U .20 .50
❑ N612 The First Hokage SR 5.00 12.00
❑ N613 The Second Hokage SR 5.00 12.00
❑ N614 Haku (Childhood) C .10 .25
❑ N615 Kabuto Yakushi R .75 2.00
❑ N616 Naruto Uzumaki & Yamato SR 4.00 10.00
❑ N617 Dosu Kinuta C .10 .25
❑ N618 Zaku Abumi C .10 .25
❑ N619 Kin Tsuchi C .10 .25
❑ N620 Kimimaro (Childhood) U .20 .50
❑ N621 Dosu Kinuta, Zaku Abumi & Kin Tsuchi U .20 .50
❑ N622 Anko Mitarashi C .10 .25
❑ N623 Ranmaru C .10 .25
❑ N624 Manda R .75 2.00
❑ N625 Raiga Kurosuki R .75 2.00
❑ N626 The Demon Brothers Gouzu C .10 .25
❑ N627 The Demon Brothers Meizu C .10 .25
❑ N628 Shimon Hijiri U .20 .50
❑ N629 Misumi Tsurugi C .10 .25
❑ N630 Yoroi Akado C .10 .25
❑ N631 Ino Yamanaka C .10 .25
❑ N632 Naruto Uzumaki R .75 2.00
❑ N633 Rock Lee & Tortoise Ninja U .20 .50
❑ N634 Shikamaru Nara SR 10.00 25.00
❑ N635 Choji Akimichi C .10 .25
❑ N636 Shizune & Tonton U .20 .50
❑ N637 Sasuke Uchiha C .10 .25
❑ N638 Gaara of the Desert (Possessed Mode) SR 4.00 10.00
❑ N639 Sakura Haruno & Sai R .75 2.00
❑ N640 Might Guy SR 3.00 8.00
❑ N641 Kankuro & Black Ant U .20 .50
❑ N642 Temari R .75 2.00
❑ N643 Itachi Uchiha R 1.50 4.00
❑ N644 Kisame Hoshigaki R .75 2.00

2009 Naruto Fateful Reunion

COMPLETE SET (156) 60.00 120.00
BOOSTER BOX (24) 60.00 120.00
BOOSTER PACK 3.00 6.00

❑ C047 Teuchi C .10 .25
❑ C048 Takamaru C .10 .25
❑ J450 Radio C .10 .25
❑ J451 A Thousand Years of Death R .75 2.00
❑ J452 Snatching the Weapon C .10 .25
❑ J453 Giant Shuriken U .20 .50
❑ J454 Multi Shadow Clone Taijutsu U .20 .50
❑ J455 Copy Ninjutsu C .10 .25
❑ J456 Mirror Reflection Jutsu R .75 2.00
❑ J457 Button Hook Entry C .10 .25
❑ J458 Detonating Clay Centipede C .10 .25
❑ J459 Mangekyo Sharingan SR 3.00 8.00
❑ J460 Water Style: Five Hungry Sharks SR 3.00 8.00
❑ J461 Five-Seal Barrier U .20 .50
❑ J462 Sealing Jutsu: Nine Phantom Dragons C .10 .25
❑ J463 Simultaneous Attacks U .20 .50
❑ J464 Assault Blade R .75 2.00
❑ J465 Medical Ninjutsu U .20 .50
❑ J466 Iron Sand: Scattered Showers C .10 .25
❑ J467 Iron Sand: Unleash C .10 .25
❑ J468 Body Manipulation C .10 .25
❑ J469 Concealed Weapon C .10 .25
❑ J470 Chakra Shield C .10 .25
❑ J471 Poison Smoke U .20 .50
❑ J472 Power of the Cursed Blood C .10 .25
❑ J473 8 Trigrams Palms Rotation C .10 .25
❑ J474 Scope C .10 .25
❑ J475 Fire Style: Fire Ball Jutsu U .20 .50
❑ J476 Illusion by Genjutsu U .20 .50
❑ J477 A Treasure Puppet U .20 .50
❑ J478 Continuous Firing of Poison Needles R .75 2.00
❑ J479 Hallucination by Genjutsu R .75 2.00
❑ J480 Perfect Defense R .75 2.00
❑ J481 Continuous Shuriken Attacks C .10 .25
❑ J482 Water Style: Exploding Water Shock Wave R .75 2.00
❑ J483 Clean Hit R .75 2.00
❑ J484 Clay Clone C .10 .25
❑ J485 Shadow Clone Jutsu U .20 .50
❑ J486 Genjutsu: Sylvan Fetters R .75 2.00
❑ J487 Crescent Moon Dance C .10 .25
❑ J488 Human Boulder C .10 .25
❑ J489 Genjutsu Negation U .20 .50
❑ J490 Ino-Shika-Cho Formation R .75 2.00
❑ J491 Trap C .10 .25
❑ J492 Spinning Kick C .10 .25
❑ J493 Demon Illusion: Death Mirage Jutsu R .75 2.00
❑ J494 Detonating Clay Signature Technique R .75 2.00
❑ J495 Rasengan SR 3.00 8.00
❑ M412 Mission of Capturing the Missing Pet Tora R .75 2.00
❑ M413 Lottery C .10 .25
❑ M414 Fulfilling the Quota C .10 .25
❑ M415 Buying Time R .75 2.00
❑ M416 Cruel Irony C .10 .25
❑ M417 Eliminating the Alliance U .20 .50
❑ M418 Weak Remembrance C .10 .25
❑ M419 Uncovered Trick C .10 .25
❑ M420 Control of the Nine-Tailed C .10 .25
❑ M421 Ubiquitous U .20 .50
❑ M422 Evil Spirit U .20 .50
❑ M423 Whim U .20 .50
❑ M424 Puppet Show R .75 2.00
❑ M425 Quota U .20 .50
❑ M426 The Ones Wriggling in the Dark C .10 .25
❑ M427 Messenger C .10 .25
❑ M428 Eight Ninja Dogs R .75 2.00
❑ M429 Sealing the Tailed Beast U .20 .50
❑ M430 Threat of the Tailed Beasts C .10 .25
❑ M431 Successive Kazekage U .20 .50
❑ M432 Detecting the Enemy C .10 .25
❑ M433 Unhealed Wound R .75 2.00
❑ M434 Bad Omen U .20 .50
❑ M435 Kazekage in Custody C .10 .25
❑ M436 Hidden Village of the Wind R .75 2.00
❑ M437 Long Awaited Reunion C .10 .25
❑ M438 Overflowing Fighting Spirits C .10 .25
❑ M439 New Hokage Rock C .10 .25
❑ M440 Misunderstanding U .20 .50
❑ M441 Dark Ritual U .20 .50
❑ M442 Reinforcement from Sand C .10 .25
❑ M443 Substitute R 3.00 8.00
❑ M444 Tactic against Genjutsu C .10 .25
❑ M445 Unstable Ground R .75 2.00
❑ M446 Report C .10 .25
❑ M447 4 Times Faster U .20 .50
❑ M448 Fellow and Loneliness SR 3.00 8.00
❑ M449 Losing Control of Chakra C .10 .25
❑ M450 Eternal Rivalry R .75 2.00
❑ M451 Beginning of the New Chronicle R .75 2.00
❑ M452 Corps in Black U .20 .50
❑ M453 Successive Hokage U .20 .50
❑ M454 Sleeping in the Open U .20 .50
❑ N522 Naruto Uzumaki (Tailed Beast Mode) SR 8.00 20.00
❑ N523 Sakura Haruno R .75 2.00
❑ N527 Kakashi Hatake R .75 2.00
❑ N528 Kiba Inuzuka R .75 2.00
❑ N529 Shino Aburame R .75 2.00
❑ N530 Hinata Hyuga U .20 .50
❑ N531 Ino Yamanaka U .20 .50
❑ N532 Choji Akimichi U .20 .50
❑ N533 Kotetsu Hagane U .20 .50
❑ N534 Izumo Kamizuki U .20 .50
❑ N535 Kidomaru C .10 .25
❑ N536 Jirobo C .10 .25
❑ N537 Sakon C .10 .25
❑ N538 Tayuya C .10 .25
❑ N539 Chiyo SR 5.00 12.00

TCG/CCG

❑ N540 Father and Mother U .20 .50
❑ N541 Deidara U .20 .50
❑ N542 Sasori SR 8.00 20.00
❑ N543 The 3rd Kazekage SR 6.00 15.00
❑ N544 Sasori (Puppet Mode) SR 3.00 8.00
❑ N545 Hanabi Hyuga C .10 .25
❑ N546 Neji Hyuga U .20 .50
❑ N547 Sasuke Uchiha N-548 .10 .25
❑ N548 Sasuke Uchiha SR 10.00 25.00
❑ N549 Neji Hyuga & Hinata Hyuga R .75 2.00
❑ N550 Sasuke Uchiha & Orochimaru SR 10.00 25.00
❑ N551 Shino Aburame & Kiba Inuzuka R 2.50 6.00
❑ N552 Sasori & Deidara R .75 2.00
❑ N553 Ino Yamanaka U .20 .50
❑ N554 Anko Mitarashi R .75 2.00
❑ N555 Jiraiya C .10 .25
❑ N556 Shizune R .75 2.00
❑ N557 Rock Lee N-558 .20 .50
❑ N558 Orochimaru U .20 .50
❑ N559 Naruto Uzumaki U .20 .50
❑ N560 Neji Hyuga SR 10.00 25.00
❑ N561 Hinata Hyuga U .20 .50
❑ N562 Tenten R .75 2.00
❑ N563 Naruto Uzumaki U .20 .50
❑ N564 Sasuke Uchiha U .20 .50
❑ N565 Rock Lee R .75 2.00
❑ N566 Naruto Uzumaki U .20 .50
❑ N567 Kakashi Hatake (Anbu Days) U .20 .50
❑ N568 Neji Hyuga U .20 .50
❑ N569 Temari R .75 2.00
❑ N570 Tsunade U .20 .50
❑ N571 Rock Lee U .20 .50
❑ N572 Kakashi Hatake & Might Guy R .75 2.00
❑ N573 Kakashi Hatake & Pakkun R .75 2.00
❑ N574 Kiba Inuzuka & Akamaru R 1.50 4.00
❑ N575 Naruto Uzumaki C .10 .25
❑ N576 Neji Hyuga R .75 2.00
❑ N577 Tenten U .20 .50
❑ N578 Shikamaru Nara SR 5.00 12.00
❑ N579 Sakura Haruno ST .40 1.00
❑ N580 Kakashi Hatake ST .40 1.00
❑ N581 Itachi Uchiha ST .40 1.00
❑ N582 Rock Lee ST .40 1.00
❑ N583 Ninja Dog Squad (All Gathered) ST .40 1.00
❑ N584 The 5th Kazekage ST .40 1.00
❑ N585 Jiraiya ST .40 1.00
❑ N586 The 5th Hokage ST .40 1.00
❑ N587 Orochimaru ST .40 1.00
❑ N588 Naruto Uzumaki STSR 2.00 5.00
❑ N589 Sasuke Uchiha STSR 2.00 5.00

2009 Naruto Foretold Prophecy

COMPLETE SET (177) 60.00 120.00
BOOSTER BOX (24) 40.00 80.00
BOOSTER PACK 2.00 4.00

❑ C049 Taruho U .20 .50
❑ C050 Susuki U .20 .50
❑ C051 Miroku R 1.25 3.00
❑ J541 Tongfa C .10 .25
❑ J542 Dynamic Action U .20 .50
❑ J543 Storm by Rasengan ST .40 1.00
❑ J544 Destructive Swing C .10 .25
❑ J545 Fast Capture R 1.00 2.50
❑ J546 Power of Sharingan U .20 .50
❑ J547 Fire Style: Fire Ball Jutsu C .10 .25
❑ J548 Burst of Lightning Blade U .20 .50
❑ J549 Assault of Snakes C .10 .25
❑ J550 Ecdysis C .10 .25
❑ J551 Sand Arm R 1.00 2.50
❑ J552 Giant Sand Shield C .10 .25
❑ J553 Heaven Kick of Pain U .20 .50
❑ J554 Chakra Thread C .10 .25
❑ J555 Leaf Hurricane R 1.25 3.00
❑ J556 Priestess's Bell C .10 .25
❑ J557 Chocolate Bomb!! U .20 .50
❑ J558 Hidden Lotus U .20 .50
❑ J559 Super Chakra Rasengan R 1.25 3.00
❑ J560 Shadow Mirror Body Transfer Art U .20 .50
❑ J561 Monstrous Warriors U .20 .50
❑ J562 Water Style: Surface Slicer U .20 .50
❑ J563 Combination Ninjutsu C .10 .25
❑ J564 Chakra Infusion R 1.00 2.50
❑ J565 Wind Style: Divine Down-Current C .10 .25
❑ J566 Earth Style: Petrifying Jutsu U .20 .50
❑ J567 Youth at Full Power! C .10 .25
❑ J569 Great Leaf Flash U .20 .50
❑ J570 Radiant Energy C .10 .25
❑ J571 Ninja Art: Super Beast Scroll Falcon C .10 .25
❑ J572 Ninja Art: Super Beast Scroll Snake U .20 .50
❑ J573 Snake Sword ST .40 1.00
❑ J574 Mulitple Striking Shadow Snake R 1.50 4.00
❑ J575 Chidori Stream SR 5.00 12.00
❑ J576 Sickle Chain C .10 .25
❑ J577 Weapon Control! Tensasai U .20 .50
❑ J578 Antidote C .10 .25
❑ J579 8 Trigrams Hazan Strike C .10 .25
❑ J580 Fist of Anger C .10 .25
❑ J581 Cherry Blossom Impact SR 5.00 12.00
❑ J582 Detonating Clay C .10 .25
❑ J583 Gentle Fist U .20 .50
❑ J584 Emergency Meeting U .20 .50
❑ J585 Giving Ones Best C .10 .25
❑ J586 Thousand Arms Manipulation U .20 .50
❑ J587 Wood Style: Four Pillars House Jutsu C .10 .25
❑ J588 Massive Iron Sand Attack U .20 .50
❑ J589 Kamui SR 5.00 12.00
❑ J590 8 Trigrams Air Palm C .10 .25
❑ J591 Glare of Snake U .20 .50
❑ J592 Power of the Evil C .10 .25
❑ J593 Special Power C .10 .25
❑ J594 Sealing the Evil U .20 .50
❑ J595 Ink Clone Jutsu C .10 .25
❑ J596 Running on the Water U .20 .50
❑ J597 Stock C .10 .25
❑ J598 Chakra Knife U .20 .50
❑ J599 Wood Style: Domed Wall C .10 .25
❑ J600 Revival of the Dead R 1.00 2.50
❑ J601 Interrogation C .10 .25
❑ M500 Leaf Academy U .20 .50
❑ M501 Reunion of Destiny C .10 .25
❑ M502 Betrayal R 1.25 3.00
❑ M503 Sacrifice C .10 .25
❑ M504 Target of the Vengeance C .10 .25
❑ M505 Lack of Sensitivity R 1.25 3.00
❑ M506 Luxurious Meal C .10 .25
❑ M507 Temporary Squad C .10 .25
❑ M508 The Priestess Who Seals the Evil ST .40 1.00
❑ M509 Beyond the Time C .10 .25
❑ M510 Changed Prophecy C .10 .25
❑ M511 Competition R 1.00 2.50
❑ M512 Retiring Character R 1.00 2.50
❑ M513 Surprise Attack from a Mysterious Enemy R1.00 2.50
❑ M514 Powerless C .10 .25
❑ M515 Punishment U .20 .50
❑ M516 Not Again U .20 .50
❑ M517 Cold Eyes U .20 .50
❑ M518 Heart-to-Heart Communication C .10 .25
❑ M519 Weird Picture Book U .20 .50
❑ M520 Fake Smile R 1.00 2.50
❑ M521 Internal Trouble U .20 .50
❑ M522 Secret Mission U .20 .50
❑ M523 Buddy System R 1.00 2.50
❑ M524 Search for a Member U .20 .50
❑ M525 A Tail C .10 .25
❑ M526 Necklace of the First Hokage U .20 .50
❑ M527 Master of the Weapons R 1.00 2.50
❑ M528 Inherited Kekkei Genkai C .10 .25
❑ M529 Dummy U .20 .50
❑ M530 Member List R 1.00 2.50
❑ M531 Impatient Feeling U .20 .50
❑ M532 Earth Style: Hidden Mole Jutsu C .10 .25
❑ M533 Jealousy C .10 .25
❑ M534 Bashfulness SR 6.00 15.00
❑ M535 Deep-Rooted Organization R 1.00 2.50
❑ M536 Deeply Cut Wound U .20 .50
❑ M537 Approaching Shadow of a Snake R 1.00 2.50
❑ M538 Crying in Vain R 1.00 2.50
❑ M539 The Power to Seal the Disaster U .20 .50
❑ M540 Not Another Step! R 1.00 2.50
❑ M541 Firm Union U .20 .50
❑ M542 Will of the Third Hokage C .10 .25
❑ M543 Sharpening the Blade C .10 .25
❑ M544 Big Help C .10 .25
❑ M545 Leaf Hospital SR 5.00 12.00
❑ M546 Destiny of the Clan U .20 .50
❑ M547 Approaching Showdown SR 5.00 12.00
❑ M548 Threat of the State 2 R 1.00 2.50
❑ M549 Leaf Police Force ST .40 1.00
❑ N645 Shion (Awakened) ST .40 1.00
❑ N646 Kusuna R 1.50 4.00
❑ N647 Shizuku U .20 .50
❑ N648 Setsuna U .20 .50
❑ N649 Gitai C .10 .25
❑ N650 The Nine-Tailed Fox Spirit R 1.25 3.00
❑ N651 Naruto Uzumaki C .10 .25
❑ N652 Sakura Haruno U .20 .50
❑ N653 Sasuke Uchiha R 5.00 12.00
❑ N654 Sai R 1.25 3.00
❑ N655 Yamato SR 10.00 25.00
❑ N656 Kiba Inuzuka U .20 .50
❑ N657 Shino Aburame C .10 .25
❑ N658 Hinata Hyuga U .20 .50
❑ N659 Hiashi Hyuga U .20 .50
❑ N660 Akamaru U .20 .50
❑ N661 The 5th Kazekage R 1.00 2.50
❑ N662 Kankuro R 1.00 2.50
❑ N663 Ebizo U .20 .50
❑ N664 Sasori (Childhood) U .20 .50
❑ N665 Deidara U .20 .50
❑ N666 Orochimaru SR 6.00 15.00
❑ N667 Kabuto Yakushi R 1.25 3.00
❑ N668 Sasuke Uchiha SR 10.00 25.00
❑ N669 Naruto Uzumaki STSR 2.00 5.00
❑ N670 Sasuke Uchiha STSR 2.00 5.00
❑ N671 Sai ST .40 1.00
❑ N672 Sakura Haruno C .10 .25
❑ N673 Sasori & The 3rd Kazekage R 1.25 3.00
❑ N674 Shikamaru Nara U .20 .50
❑ N675 Kakashi Hatake R 1.00 2.50
❑ N676 Itachi Uchiha ST .40 1.00
❑ N677 Yamato R 1.25 3.00
❑ N678 Baki R 3.00 8.00
❑ N679 Temari C .10 .25
❑ N680 Jiraiya ST .40 1.00
❑ N681 Tsunade C .10 .25
❑ N682 Orochimaru U .20 .50
❑ N683 Konohamaru ST .40 1.00
❑ N684 Naruto Uzumaki & Jiraiya R 2.00 5.00
❑ N685 Sakura Haruno & Tsunade SR 6.00 15.00
❑ N686 Naruto Uzumaki & Yamato C .10 .25
❑ N687 Naruto Uzumaki & Sai ST .40 1.00
❑ N688 Naruto Uzumaki & Shion R 1.25 3.00
❑ N689 Shion ST .40 1.00
❑ N690 Yomi ST .40 1.00
❑ N691 The Fourth Kazekage SR 6.00 15.00
❑ N692 Giant Ninja Toad ST .40 1.00
❑ N693 Giant Snake U .20 .50
❑ N694 Tonton C .10 .25
❑ N695 Tortoise Ninja C .10 .25
❑ N696 Giant Tiger C .10 .25
❑ N697 Kakashi Hatake (Childhood) C .10 .25
❑ N698 The Third Hokage (Childhood) U .20 .50
❑ N699 Koharu Utatane (Childhood) C .10 .25
❑ N700 Homura Mitomon (Childhood) C .10 .25
❑ N701 The Fourth Hokage (Childhood) C .10 .25
❑ N702 The Fourth Hokage (Younger Days) SR 10.00 25.00
❑ N703 Neji Hyuga (Childhood) C .10 .25
❑ N704 Tekka Uchiha ST .40 1.00
❑ N705 Inabi Uchiha ST .40 1.00
❑ N706 Yashiro Uchiha ST .40 1.00
❑ N707 Elder of Hyuga Clan U .20 .50
❑ N708 Iruka Umino (Childhood) C .10 .25

2010 Naruto Broken Promise

COMPLETE SET (157) 50.00 100.00
BOOSTER BOX (24) 50.00 100.00
BOOSTER PACK 2.50 5.00

❑ C052 Lady Haruna R .40 1.00
❑ C053 Momiji R .40 1.00
❑ C054 Chikara U .20 .50
❑ C055 Uroko U .20 .50
❑ J602 Summoning Jutsu: Ninja Dogs C .10 .25
❑ J603 Special Kunai C .10 .25
❑ J604 Chidori SR FOIL 8.00 20.00
❑ J605 White Fang's Blade C .10 .25
❑ J606 Sharingan Kunai R 1.00 2.50
❑ J607 Detonating Clay: Mysterious Bird C .10 .25
❑ J608 Tsukuyomi U .20 .50
❑ J609 Chakra Slice U .20 .50
❑ J610 Mental Fatigue R .40 1.00
❑ J611 Water Style: Water Dragon Jutsu R 1.00 2.50
❑ J612 Striking Shadow Snake R .40 1.00
❑ J613 Counter R 1.00 2.50
❑ J614 Infuriation R .40 1.00
❑ J615 Wood Style: Tree Bind Eternal Burial U .20 .50
❑ J616 Sharpness of the Weapon U .20 .50
❑ J617 Intrustion C .10 .25
❑ J618 Sharingan of Tears C .10 .25
❑ J619 Change in Chakra Form C .10 .25
❑ J620 Change in Chakra Nature R .40 1.00
❑ J621 Power of the Clones C .10 .25
❑ J622 Power of the Meteorite U .20 .50
❑ J623 Summoning Jutsu: Air Fish C .10 .25
❑ J624 Magnetic Power C .10 .25
❑ J625 Rasengan R .40 1.00
❑ J626 Genjutsu U .20 .50
❑ J627 Space Created by Genjutsu R .40 1.00
❑ J628 Canceling Tone C .10 .25
❑ J629 Dragon Eyes: Fang Release: Dark Sword U .20 .50
❑ J630 Wind Slicer C .10 .25
❑ J631 Wind Scythe Jutsu U .20 .50
❑ J632 Soaring Shot Sword C .10 .25
❑ J633 Wood Style: Great Forest Jutsu SR 3.00 8.00
❑ J634 Inflow of Chakra U .20 .50
❑ J635 Chidori Stream R 1.25 3.00
❑ J636 Water Style: Bubbling Water C .10 .25
❑ J637 Flower Shuriken .10 .25
Burning Petals and Fallen Leaves C
❑ J638 Exposing the Hideout R .40 1.00
❑ J639 High Speed Hand Signs C .10 .25
❑ J640 Fear by Genjutsu SR 12.00 30.00
❑ J641 Release of Fury SR FOIL 2.50 6.00
❑ J642 Trump card R .40 1.00
❑ J643 Beast Transformation C .10 .25
❑ J644 Beast Mimicry Ninja Art: Man Beast Clone C.10 .25
❑ M585 Succeeded Will of Fire R .40 1.00
❑ M586 Beauty and Intelligence R .40 1.00
❑ M587 Chakra Paper C .10 .25
❑ M588 Earth Style: Rampart of Flowing Soil C .10 .25
❑ M589 BBQ House "Barbe-Q" C .10 .25
❑ M590 Recollection C .10 .25
❑ M591 Restricted Jutsu U .20 .50
❑ M592 Tears of Determination R .40 1.00
❑ M593 Shogi Match SR 5.00 12.00
❑ M594 A Snake Hiding in the Dark R .40 1.00
❑ M595 Infiltration C .10 .25
❑ M596 Reconfirmation of the Mission R .40 1.00
❑ M597 Skeleton Key U .20 .50
❑ M598 Smile of the Two C .10 .25
❑ M599 Retreat C .10 .25
❑ M600 Fire Temple C .10 .25
❑ M601 Group Lesson R .75 2.00
❑ M602 Messenger Ninjas C .10 .25
❑ M603 Lullaby U .20 .50
❑ M604 Showy Entrance U .20 .50
❑ M605 Tracking Mission C .10 .25
❑ M606 Clear Tone Carries in the Sunset C .10 .25
❑ M607 Picture of Their Dreams C .10 .25
❑ M608 My First Fellow C .10 .25
❑ M609 Favor to Ask U .20 .50
❑ M610 Visiting Kakashi in the Hospital U .20 .50
❑ M611 Narrow Escape R .40 1.00
❑ M612 Seeing Through Distance U .20 .50
❑ M613 A Gift from a Friend U .20 .50
❑ M614 Pressing R .40 1.00
❑ M615 Imaginary Monster C .10 .25
❑ M616 Last Message U .20 .50
❑ M617 Efficient Training SR FOIL 5.00 12.00
❑ M618 Determination of Men SR 3.00 8.00
❑ M619 Water Style: Watefall Basin Jutsu C .10 .25
❑ M620 Reconnoitering Party C .10 .25
❑ N709 Kakashi Hatake (Boyhood) SR FOIL 10.00 25.00
❑ N710 Rin U .20 .50
❑ N711 Obito Uchiha SR FOIL 12.00 30.00
❑ N712 The Fourth Hokage SR 10.00 25.00
❑ N713 Kakkou U .20 .50
❑ N714 Taiseki C .10 .25
❑ N715 Mahiru C .10 .25
❑ N716 Zetsu U .20 .50
❑ N717 Tobi U .20 .50
❑ N718 Orochimaru (Childhood) R 1.50 4.00
❑ N719 Jiraiya (Childhood) R 1.25 3.00
❑ N720 Tsunade (Childhood) R 1.50 4.00
❑ N721 Chiriku C .10 .25
❑ N722 Hana Inuzuka U .20 .50
❑ N723 Haimaru Brothers C .10 .25
❑ N724 Yoshino Nara R 1.25 3.00
❑ N725 Shin C .10 .25
❑ N726 Naruto Uzumaki (Student) U .20 .50
❑ N727 Sasuke Uchiha (Student) U .20 .50
❑ N728 Sakura Haruno (Student) U .20 .50
❑ N729 Sakura Haruno & Hinata Hyuga R .40 1.00
❑ N730 Shikamaru Nara & Kakashi Hatake SR 5.00 12.00
❑ N731 Kakashi Hatake (Teacher) U .20 .50
❑ N732 Asuma Sarutobi C .10 .25
❑ N733 Yugito Ni'i R .40 1.00
❑ N734 Two Tails SR 5.00 12.00
❑ N735 Sasori & Zetsu U .20 .50
❑ N736 Deidara & Tobi U .20 .50
❑ N737 Itachi Uchiha SR FOIL 4.00 10.00
❑ N738 Kankuro R .75 2.00
❑ N739 Temari R .40 1.00
❑ N740 Yugao Uzuki U .20 .50
❑ N741 Kakashi Hatake C .10 .25
❑ N742 Kakashi Hatake & Pakkun C .10 .25
❑ N743 Kiba Inuzuka C .10 .25
❑ N744 Kiba Inuzuka & Akamaru C .10 .25
❑ N745 The First Hokage & Yamato R .40 1.00
❑ N746 Naruto Uzumaki U .20 .50
❑ N747 Naruto Uzumaki (Tailed Beast Form) SR FOIL4.00 10.00
❑ N748 Sasuke Uchiha U .20 .50
❑ N749 The Third Hokage C .10 .25
❑ N750 Advisor of the Sand C .10 .25
❑ N751 Rock Lee & Neji Hyuga U .20 .50
❑ N752 Ino Yamanka C .10 .25
❑ N753 Ziga C .10 .25
❑ N754 Ruiga U .20 .50
❑ N755 Renga R .40 1.00
❑ N756 Mizuki (Transformed) C .10 .25
❑ N757 Raiga Kurosuki U .20 .50
❑ N758 Ranmaru C .10 .25
❑ N759 Lord Sagi C .10 .25
❑ N760 Chishima C .10 .25
❑ N761 Amachi (Sea Monster) U .20 .50
❑ N762 Anko Mitarashi & Orochimaru U .20 .50
❑ N763 Isaribi (Sea Monster) U .20 .50
❑ N764 Rampageous Pig C .10 .25
❑ N765 Hotarubi C .10 .25
❑ N767 Natsuhi U .20 .50
❑ N768 The 3rd Hoshikage U .20 .50
❑ N769 Shiso C .10 .25
❑ N770 Yotaka C .10 .25
❑ N771 Naruto Uzumaki C .10 .25
❑ N772 Hinata Hyuga C .10 .25
❑ N773 Choji Akimichi C .10 .25
❑ N774 Ino Yamanaka U .20 .50
❑ N775 Might Guy (Afro) R .40 1.00
❑ N776 Anbu U .20 .50
❑ N777 Yakumo Kurama U .20 .50
❑ N778 Gantetsu C .10 .25
❑ N779 Menma C .10 .25
❑ N780 Hoki U .20 .50
❑ N781 Kujaku C .10 .25
❑ N782 Ryugan C .10 .25
❑ N783 Suiko C .10 .25

2010 Naruto Fangs of the Snake

COMPLETE SET (132) 50.00 100.00
BOOSTER BOX (24) 50.00 100.00
BOOSTER PACK 2.50 5.00

❑ J706 Hokage Style: Elder Jutsu R .40 1.00
❑ J707 Explosive Kunai U .20 .50
❑ J708 Summoning Jutsu: Projectile Weapons U .20 .50
❑ J709 Wood Style: Tree Bind Eternal Burial SR 5.00 12.00
❑ J710 Shikamaru's Judgement U .20 .50
❑ J711 Flying Swallow C .10 .25
❑ J712 Awakening the Byakugan U .20 .50
❑ J713 Genjutsu of Pain! R .40 1.00
❑ J714 Following the Trail C .10 .25
❑ J715 Veterinary Meds U .20 .50
❑ J716 Take Down U .20 .50
❑ J717 Backed into a Corner R .40 1.00
❑ J718 Quick Reflex U .20 .50
❑ J719 Revenge C .10 .25
❑ J720 Reading Movement U .20 .50
❑ J721 Expert Kunai C .10 .25
❑ J722 Wind Style: Toad Water Pistol U .20 .50
❑ J723 Collaboration Ninjutsu! Wind Style .40 1.00
Toad Flame Bombs! R
❑ J724 Multi Shadow Clone Jutsu U .20 .50
❑ J725 Summoning Jutsu SR 5.00 12.00
❑ J726 Collateral Damage U .20 .50
❑ J727 Clone Tactics U .20 .50
❑ J728 Snake Transformation Jutsu C .10 .25
❑ J729 Transference Ritual U .20 .50
❑ J730 Curse Mark Activation U .20 .50
❑ J731 Sword Charge C .10 .25
❑ J732 Chidori Lance U .20 .50
❑ J733 Multi Striking Shadow Snake R .40 1.00
❑ J734 Chidori Sword U .20 .50
❑ J735 Snake Bind U .20 .50
❑ J736 Elemental Defense R .40 1.00
❑ J737 Sand Cocoon U .20 .50
❑ J738 Puppet Master Jutsu U .20 .50
❑ J739 Iron-Armed Punch C .10 .25
❑ J740 Iron Sand: Unleash! R .40 1.00
❑ J741 Wind Style: Rasen Shuriken U .20 .50
❑ J742 Flamethrower U .20 .50
❑ M670 Team Asuma C .10 .25
❑ M671 Master of Weapons U .20 .50
❑ M672 Comparative Strengths C .10 .25
❑ M673 Student and Sensei R .40 1.00
❑ M674 Kakuzu's Abilities R .40 1.00
❑ M675 Shelter from the Shifting Sands R .40 1.00
❑ M676 Surprise Help R .40 1.00
❑ M677 Rapid Communication U .20 .50
❑ M678 Scouting Party R .40 1.00
❑ M679 Master of Genjutsu U .20 .50
❑ M680 Hidden Leaf Veterinary Hospital U .20 .50
❑ M681 Sync Dance U .20 .50
❑ M682 Desperate Training U .20 .50
❑ M683 Relaxation U .20 .50
❑ M684 Silent Prayer R .40 1.00
❑ M685 Well Fed U .20 .50
❑ M686 Enveloping Chakra U .20 .50
❑ M687 Animal Contract U .20 .50
❑ M688 Chakra Molding U .20 .50
❑ M689 Spread Talons U .20 .50
❑ M690 Friendship from Sorrow U .20 .50
❑ M691 Formation of Hebi R .40 1.00
❑ M692 Controlling the Curse U .20 .50
❑ M693 Sasori's Feelings U .20 .50
❑ M694 Puppet Fight: 10 VS 100! R .40 1.00
❑ M695 Kankuro's Puppet Show R .40 1.00
❑ M696 Shinobi of the Sand U .20 .50
❑ M697 Sakura's Desire R .40 1.00
❑ M698 Battle over the Barrier R .40 1.00
❑ N883 Neji Hyuga C .10 .25
❑ N884 Hanabi Hyuga C .10 .25
❑ N885 Choji Akimichi C .10 .25
❑ N886 Shikamaru Nara C .10 .25
❑ N887 Hinata Hyuga C .10 .25
❑ N888 Ino Yamanaka C .10 .25
❑ N889 Neji Hyuga R .40 1.00
❑ N890 Zetsu C .10 .25
❑ N891 Asuma Sarutobi SR 6.00 15.00
❑ N892 Yamato R .40 1.00
❑ N893 Deidara R .40 1.00
❑ N894 The First Hokage SR 6.00 15.00
❑ N895 Neji Hyuga & Hinata Hyuga R .40 1.00
❑ N896 Urushi C .10 .25
❑ N897 Guruko C .10 .25
❑ N898 Kiba Inuzuka C .10 .25
❑ N899 Sasuke Uchiha C .10 .25
❑ N900 Big Bark Bull C .10 .25
❑ N901 Obito Uchiha C .10 .25
❑ N902 Biscuit C .10 .25
❑ N903 Kotetsu Hagane C .10 .25
❑ N904 Hayate Gekko C .10 .25
❑ N905 Tobi C .10 .25
❑ N906 Kakashi Hatake (Anbu Days) SR 10.00 25.00
❑ N907 Itachi Uchiha SR 8.00 20.00
❑ N908 Gamakichi C .10 .25
❑ N909 Gamatatsu C .10 .25
❑ N910 Gamariki C .10 .25
❑ N911 Naruto Uzumaki C .10 .25
❑ N912 Gama C .10 .25
❑ N913 Rock Lee C .10 .25
❑ N914 The Fourth Hokage R .40 1.00
❑ N915 Might Guy U .20 .50
❑ N916 Sai R .40 1.00
❑ N917 Konohamaru Ninja Squad C .10 .25
❑ N918 Anko Mitarashi C .10 .25
❑ N919 Naruto Uzumaki SR 6.00 15.00
❑ N920 Kidomaru C .10 .25
❑ N921 Jirobo C .10 .25
❑ N922 Tayuya C .10 .25
❑ N923 Kabuto Yakushi SR 6.00 15.00
❑ N924 Suigetsu Hozuki R 1.50 4.00
❑ N925 Karin C .10 .25
❑ N926 Jugo C .10 .25
❑ N927 Kimimaro C .10 .25
❑ N928 Kimimaro (Childhood) C .10 .25
❑ N929 Sakon C .10 .25
❑ N930 Anko Mitarashi (Childhood) C .10 .25
❑ N931 Sasuke Uchiha R .40 1.00
❑ N932 Orochimaru (Snake Form) SR 6.00 15.00
❑ N933 Kimimaro & Jugo R .40 1.00
❑ N934 Sasuke Uchiha (State 2) SR 12.00 30.00
❑ N935 Gaara of the Desert C .10 .25
❑ N936 Kankuro C .10 .25
❑ N937 Matsuri (Childhood) C .10 .25
❑ N938 Temari C .10 .25

❑ N939 Advisor of the Sand C .10 .25
❑ N940 Sakura Haruno C .10 .25
❑ N941 Black Ant, Crow, & Salamander R .40 1.00
❑ N942 Chiyo R .40 1.00
❑ N943 Kurenai Yuhi R .40 1.00
❑ N944 Unkai Kurama U .20 .50
❑ N945 Hiruko SR 6.00 15.00
❑ N946 Katsuyu SR 6.00 15.00
❑ N947 Sasori (Puppet Mode) R .40 1.00
❑ N948 Gaara of the Desert & Temari R .40 1.00

2010 Naruto Fierce Ambitions Tin

❑ N145 Gaara of the Desert .30 .75
❑ N370 The Third Hokage .30 .75
❑ N372 The Fifth Hokage .30 .75
❑ N453 Itachi Uchiha .50 1.25
❑ N461 Kankuro .50 1.25
❑ N473 Kakashi Hatake .30 .75
❑ N480 Deidara .30 .75
❑ N495 Temari & Kankuro .30 .75
❑ NUS020 Rock Lee .50 1.25
❑ NUS040 Shikamaru Nara & Asuma Sarutobi .30 .75

2010 Naruto Path of Pain

COMPLETE SET (112) 50.00 100.00
BOOSTER BOX 50.00 100.00
BOOSTER PACK 2.50 5.00

❑ J743 Detonating Clay: C2 Dragon U .20 .50
❑ J744 Detonating Clay: Snake C .10 .25
❑ J745 Detonating Clay: Mines U .20 .50
❑ J746 Detonating Clay: C3 Ohako U .20 .50
❑ J747 Detonating Clay: C4 Karura SR 5.00 12.00
❑ J748 Clay Clone Jutsu U .20 .50
❑ J749 Lightning Blade F 2.00 5.00
❑ J750 Mangekyou Sharingan SR 6.00 15.00
❑ J751 Anticipation U .20 .50
❑ J752 Fatigue C .10 .25
❑ J753 Tracking Orders U .20 .50
❑ J754 Animal Transformation U .20 .50
❑ J755 Leaf Hurricane U .20 .50
❑ J756 Eight Inner Gates R .40 1.00
❑ J757 Primary Lotus SR 6.00 15.00
❑ J758 Severe Leaf Hurricane C .10 .25
❑ J759 Toad Mouth Trap U .20 .50
❑ J760 Piggyback R .40 1.00
❑ J761 Fire Style: Searing Migraine U .20 .50
❑ J762 Striking Shadow Snake U .20 .50
❑ J763 Striking Multi Shadow Snakes Jutsu R .40 1.00
❑ J764 Chidori C .10 .25
❑ J765 Chakra Punch C .10 .25
❑ J766 Righteous Anger U .20 .50
❑ J767 Kick of Anger U .20 .50
❑ J768 Palm Healing R .40 1.00
❑ J769 Coordination R .40 1.00
❑ J770 The Fangs of Pain U .20 .50
❑ J771 The Wings of Pain R .40 1.00
❑ J772 Rinnegan SR 5.00 12.00
❑ M699 Intellectual Strategy U .20 .50
❑ M700 Sharpened Skills R .40 1.00
❑ M701 Strategy Scroll U .20 .50
❑ M702 Rooftop Standoff U .20 .50
❑ M703 Past Lessons C .10 .25
❑ M704 Reaper Death Seal R .40 1.00
❑ M705 Sacrifice U .20 .50
❑ M706 Supervised Training U .20 .50
❑ M707 Denka & Hina U .20 .50
❑ M708 Burst of Power R .40 1.00
❑ M709 Tailed Beast Unleashed U .20 .50
❑ M710 Surprise Ability C .10 .25
❑ M711 Promise to Return U .20 .50
❑ M712 Kakashi's Test U .20 .50
❑ M713 The Great Naruto Bridge R .40 1.00
❑ M714 Suigetsu's Joy R .40 1.00
❑ M715 Power of State 2 U .20 .50
❑ M716 Pledge under a Setting Sun F 2.00 5.00
❑ M717 Barrier Preparation R .40 1.00
❑ M718 Perfect Chakra Control C .10 .25
❑ M719 Delicate Operation U .20 .50
❑ M720 Reflection R .40 1.00
❑ M721 The Time of Pain R .40 1.00
❑ M722 The City of Pain R .40 1.00
❑ N949 Detonating Clay Minion C .10 .25
❑ N950 Ino Yamanaka C .10 .25
❑ N951 Kikunojou C .10 .25
❑ N952 Yurinojou C .10 .25
❑ N953 Shikamaru Nara C .10 .25
❑ N954 Tenten U .20 .50
❑ N955 Chiriku U .20 .50
❑ N956 Yamato U .20 .50
❑ N957 Deidara SR 6.00 15.00
❑ N958 Deidara & Tobi R .40 1.00
❑ N959 Pakkun U .20 .50
❑ N960 Uhei C .10 .25
❑ N961 Shiba C .10 .25
❑ N962 Akino C .10 .25
❑ N963 Sasuke Uchiha C .10 .25
❑ N964 Kotetsu Hagane C .10 .25
❑ N965 Monkey King Enma R .40 1.00
❑ N966 Kakashi Hatake F 2.00 5.00
❑ N967 Itachi Uchiha C .10 .25
❑ N968 The Third Hokage SR 5.00 12.00
❑ N969 Might Guy R .40 1.00
❑ N970 Rock Lee & Might Guy R .40 1.00
❑ N971 Naruto Uzumaki (Taijutsu) C .10 .25
❑ N972 Izumo Kamizuki C .10 .25
❑ N973 Iruka Umino C .10 .25
❑ N974 Ninja Tortoise U .20 .50
❑ N975 Naruto Uzumaki C .10 .25
❑ N976 Naruto Uzumaki (Nine-Tail's Cloak) R .40 1.00
❑ N977 Jiraiya U .20 .50
❑ N978 The Fourth Hokage R .40 1.00
❑ N979 Doki C .10 .25
❑ N980 Karin C .10 .25
❑ N981 Tayuya (State 1) C .10 .25
❑ N982 Suigetsu Hozuki C .10 .25
❑ N983 Jugo (State 1) C .10 .25
❑ N984 Anko Mitarashi F 2.00 5.00
❑ N985 Orochimaru R .40 1.00
❑ N986 Sasuke Uchiha U .20 .50
❑ N987 Kabuto Yakushi (Possessed Mode) R .40 1.00
❑ N988 Tayuya (State 2) U .20 .50
❑ N989 Kakuzu (Soul Form) SR 6.00 15.00
❑ N990 Kamatari C .10 .25
❑ N991 Sakura Haruno C .10 .25
❑ N992 Rin C .10 .25
❑ N993 Temari C .10 .25
❑ N994 Chiyo U .20 .50
❑ N995 Shizune U .20 .50
❑ N996 Kurenai Yuhi R .40 1.00
❑ N997 Tsunade U .20 .50
❑ N998 Shukaku SR 6.00 15.00
❑ N999 Konan C .10 .25
❑ N1000 Pain (Deva Path) SR 12.00 25.00
❑ N1001 Giant Chameleon C .10 .25
❑ N1002 Giant Chimera C .10 .25
❑ N1003 Pain (Animal Path) C .10 .25
❑ N1004 Pain (Petra Path) U .20 .50
❑ N1005 Sasuke Uchiha STSR
❑ N1006 Naruto Uzumaki STSR

2010 Naruto Tournament Pack 1

COMPLETE SET (60) 40.00 80.00
BOOSTER BOX (24) 60.00 120.00
BOOSTER PACK 3.00 6.00

❑ J697 Expansion Jutsu: Super Slap! .20 .50
❑ J698 Fire Style: Fireball Jutsu .50 1.25
❑ J699 Lightning Blade Single Slash .75 2.00
❑ J700 Ninja Art: Super Beast Scroll Lion .40 1.00
❑ J701 Severe Leaf Hurricane .20 .50
❑ J702 Water Clone Jutsu .20 .50
❑ J703 Water Prison Jutsu .40 1.00
❑ J704 Medical Jutsu: Reanimation .20 .50
❑ J705 Wind Nature: Chakra Blades .40 1.00
❑ M665 Shogi Lesson .20 .50
❑ M666 Make-Out Tactics .50 1.25
❑ M667 Fierce Rivals 2.50 6.00
❑ M668 Dehydration .50 1.25
❑ M669 Bonds of Friendship 1.00 2.50
❑ N019 Naruto Uzumaki .50 1.25
❑ N024 Zabuza Momochi .50 1.25
❑ N114 Temari .10 .25
❑ N122 Hayate Gekko .10 .25
❑ N202 Kisame Hoshigaki .20 .50
❑ N209 Nawaki .20 .50
❑ N333 Kakashi Hatake .10 .25
❑ N336 Tsubaki .20 .50
❑ N371 The Fourth Hokage .10 .25
❑ N382 Toki .75 2.00
❑ N384 Isaribi .20 .50
❑ N451 Shizune .10 .25
❑ N511 Shino Aburame .40 1.00
❑ N547 Sasuke Uchiha .50 1.25
❑ N571 Rock Lee .10 .25
❑ N595 Ino Yamanaka .10 .25
❑ N600 Danzo .10 .25
❑ N622 Anko Mitarashi .10 .25
❑ N631 Ino Yamanaka .10 .25
❑ N640 Might Guy .10 .25
❑ N864 Choji Akimichi (Childhood) 2.50 6.00
❑ N865 Hinata Hyuga (Childhood) .10 .25
❑ N866 Shikamaru Nara (Childhood) .10 .25
❑ N867 Anbu (Captain) .10 .25
❑ N868 Itachi Uchiha (Anbu Days) .20 .50
❑ N869 Kiba Inuzuka (Childhood) 8.00 20.00
❑ N870 Gamabunta .10 .25
❑ N871 Konohamaru Ninja Squad 8.00 20.00
❑ N872 Rock Lee (Childhood) .10 .25
❑ N873 Giant Spider .10 .25
❑ N874 Rashomon .10 .25
❑ N875 Zabuza Momochi (Younger Days) .40 1.00
❑ N876 Ebisu 6.00 15.00
❑ N877 Gaara of the Desert (Childhood) .10 .25
❑ N878 Sasori .10 .25
❑ N879 Hinata Hyuga 25.00 50.00
❑ N880 Yamato .10 .25
❑ N881 Iruka Umino 8.00 20.00
❑ N882 Konohamaru .10 .25
❑ J696B Byakugan .10 .25
❑ NUS006 Sakura Haruno .20 .50
❑ NUS015 Shikamaru Nara 4.00 10.00
❑ NUS027 Jiraiya .20 .50
❑ NUS035 Haku .10 .25
❑ NUS072 Gamakichi .20 .50
❑ NUS106 Kurenai Yuhi .20 .50

2010 Naruto Tournament Pack 2

COMPLETE SET (64) 20.00 40.00
BOOSTER BOX 25.00 50.00
BOOSTER PACK 2.00 3.00

❑ J696 Byakugan U .20 .50
❑ J697 Expansion Jutsu: Super Slap! R .40 1.00
❑ J698 Fire Style: Fireball Jutsu R .40 1.00
❑ J699 Lightning Blade Single Slash R .40 1.00
❑ J700 Ninja Art: Super Beast Scroll Lion U .20 .50
❑ J701 Severe Leaf Hurricane U .20 .50
❑ J702 Water Clone Jutsu R .40 1.00
❑ J703 Water Prison Jutsu U .20 .50
❑ J704 Reanimation Ninjutsu R .40 1.00
❑ J705 Chakra Blades U .20 .50
❑ M665 Shogi Lesson R .40 1.00
❑ M666 Make-Out Tactics R .40 1.00
❑ M667 Fierce Rivals R .40 1.00
❑ M668 Dehydration R .40 1.00
❑ M669 Bonds of Friendship R .40 1.00
❑ N864 Choji Akimichi (Childhood) C .10 .25
❑ N865 Hinata Hyuga (Childhood) C .10 .25
❑ N866 Shikamaru Nara (Childhood) C .10 .25
❑ N867 Anbu (Captain) R .40 1.00
❑ N868 Itachi Uchiha (Anbu Days) SR 6.00 15.00
❑ N869 Kiba Inuzuka (Childhood) C .10 .25
❑ N870 Gamabunta SR 5.00 12.00
❑ N871 Konohamaru Ninja Squad U .20 .50
❑ N872 Rock Lee (Childhood) C .10 .25
❑ N873 Giant Spider C .10 .25
❑ N874 Rashomon R .40 1.00
❑ N875 Zabuza Momochi (Younger Days) SR 5.00 12.00
❑ N876 Ebisu U .20 .50
❑ N877 Gaara of the Desert (Childhood) C .10 .25
❑ N878 Sasori SR 5.00 12.00
❑ N879 Hinata Hyuga U .20 .50
❑ N880 Yamato SR 6.00 15.00
❑ N881 Iruka Umino C .10 .25
❑ N882 Konohamaru C .10 .25
❑ N1007 Neji Hyuga C .10 .25
❑ N1008 Shikamaru Nara U .20 .50
❑ N1009 Zetsu C .10 .25
❑ N1010 Deidara U .20 .50
❑ N1011 Ibiki Morino U .20 .50
❑ N1012 Shikaku Nara R .40 1.00
❑ N1013 Hidan SR 6.00 15.00
❑ N1014 Tobi C .10 .25
❑ N1015 Itachi Uchiha R .40 1.00
❑ N1016 Kiba Inuzuka U .20 .50
❑ N1017 Sasuke Uchiha C .10 .25
❑ N1018 Raido Namiashi C .10 .25
❑ N1019 Naruto Uzumaki C .10 .25
❑ N1020 Iruka Umino C .10 .25
❑ N1021 Naruto Uzumaki C .10 .25
❑ N1022 Sai R .40 1.00
❑ N1023 Ink Summon U .20 .50
❑ N1024 Jiraiya U .20 .50
❑ N1025 Kisame Hoshigaki SR 5.00 12.00
❑ N1026 Kakuzu SR 5.00 12.00
❑ N1027 Karin U .20 .50
❑ N1028 Haku C .10 .25
❑ N1029 Kimimaro R .40 1.00
❑ N1030 Sasuke Uchiha R .40 1.00
❑ N1031 Mizuki U .20 .50
❑ N1032 Shizune C .10 .25
❑ N1033 Rin C .10 .25
❑ N1034 Gaara of the Desert C .10 .25
❑ N1035 Konan R .40 1.00
❑ N1036 The Fifth Hokage R .40 1.00

2010 Naruto Untouchables Tin

❑ N086 Sasuke Uchiha .40 1.00
❑ N146 Temari .75 2.00
❑ N168 The Second Hokage 1.00 2.50
❑ N224 Naruto Uzumaki .30 .75
❑ N311 Tenten .30 .75
❑ N324 Kisame Hoshigaki .50 1.25
❑ N531 Ino Yamanaka .75 2.00
❑ N567 Kakashi Hatake (Anbu Days) 1.25 3.00
❑ PR063 Kakashi Hatake & Itachi Uchiha 1.25 3.00
❑ PR064 Naruto Uzumaki & Sasuke Uchiha 1.00 2.50
❑ PR065 Jiraiya & The Fourth Hokage 1.50 4.00
❑ NUS005 Sakura Haruno 1.00 2.50

2010 Naruto Will of Fire

COMPLETE SET (177) 60.00 120.00
BOOSTER BOX (24) 40.00 80.00
BOOSTER PACK 2.50 5.00

❑ C056 Princess Koto U .20 .50
❑ C057 Lord Owashi U .20 .50
❑ C058 Murakumo R .40 1.00
❑ C059 Giant Eagle R .40 1.00
❑ J645 Wind Style: Rasen Shuriken SR 4.00 10.00
❑ J646 Raigo! Thousand Hand Strike! U .20 .50
❑ J647 Burning Ash U .20 .50
❑ J648 Anger of the Tailed Beast U .20 .50
❑ J649 Water Style: Syrup Trap C .10 .25
❑ J650 Earth Style: Earth Pike R .40 1.00
❑ J651 Three-Bladed Scythe C .10 .25
❑ J652 Black Strings U .20 .50
❑ J653 Ritual Circle U .20 .50
❑ J654 High Speed Thinking U .20 .50
❑ J655 Shadow Possession Jutsu U .20 .50
❑ J656 Water Clone Jutsu U .20 .50
❑ J657 Howl U .20 .50
❑ J658 Scattered Thousand Birds Jutsu U .20 .50
❑ J659 Black Sword C .10 .25
❑ J660 Sharing the Pain U .20 .50
❑ J661 Shadow Stitching Jutsu U .20 .50
❑ J662 Attacking on Both Sides C .10 .25
❑ J663 Change in Chakra Nature: Rasengan U .20 .50
❑ J664 Kiss of Death U .20 .50
❑ J665 Combination Jutsu C .10 .25
❑ J666 Super Strength U .20 .50
❑ J667 Transporting the Bodies U .20 .50
❑ J668 Beast Wave: Palm Hurricane U .20 .50
❑ J669 Giant Spider U .20 .50
❑ J670 Labyrinth R .40 1.00
❑ J671 Sharingan Activated R .40 1.00
❑ J672 Illusion caused by the Poisonous Moths R .40 1.00
❑ J673 Super Expansion Jutsu U .20 .50
❑ J674 Fatal Blow U .20 .50
❑ J675 Five Pronged Seal Release C .10 .25
❑ J676 Power of the Red Chakra R .40 1.00
❑ J677 War Cry U .20 .50
❑ J678 Giant Club C .10 .25
❑ J679 Chakra Blade C .10 .25
❑ J680 Shuriken C .10 .25
❑ J681 Art of the Raging Lion's Mane U .20 .50
❑ J682 Concentration U .20 .50
❑ J683 Booby-Trap R .40 1.00
❑ J684 Kunai C .10 .25
❑ J685 Piercing Chidori SR 6.00 15.00
❑ J686 Water Style: Water Shark Bomb Jutsu U .20 .50
❑ J687 Attack from Behind U .20 .50
❑ J688 Hellfire U .20 .50
❑ J689 Exposing the Real Face U .20 .50
❑ J690 Killer Shot U .20 .50
❑ J691 Burst of Shots U .20 .50
❑ J692 Sharp Shooting U .20 .50
❑ J693 Earth Style: Stone Plate Coffin U .20 .50
❑ J694 Earth Style Revival Jutsu: Soil Bodies R .40 1.00
❑ J695 Lightning Style: Earth Slide R .40 1.00
❑ J696 Rasengan R .40 1.00
❑ M624 Bounty C .10 .25
❑ M625 Invasion of the Akatsuki R 1.25 3.00
❑ M626 Ritual R .40 1.00
❑ M627 Scream U .20 .50
❑ M628 Just Like That Hero SR 3.00 8.00
❑ M629 Tragic Destiny SR 4.00 10.00
❑ M630 The Last Moment R .40 1.00
❑ M631 The Top Priority U .20 .50
❑ M632 In the Rain C .10 .25
❑ M633 Loss R .40 1.00
❑ M634 Distraction R .40 1.00
❑ M635 Entrustment U .20 .50
❑ M636 Emergency Call-Up U .20 .50
❑ M637 Reading U .20 .50
❑ M638 The Next Target U .20 .50
❑ M639 Argument U .20 .50
❑ M640 Capture U .20 .50
❑ M641 Strong Bond C .10 .25
❑ M642 Approaching Shadow of Death R .40 1.00
❑ M643 Sudden Entry R .40 1.00
❑ M644 Strategy Meeting R .40 1.00
❑ M645 Stolen Bodies U .20 .50
❑ M646 Fierce Clash U .20 .50
❑ M647 Interruption U .20 .50
❑ M648 Present for the Promotion R .40 1.00
❑ M649 Mid-Night Shogi Match R .40 1.00
❑ M650 Under the Drifting Clouds U .20 .50
❑ M651 Farewell C .10 .25
❑ M652 Taking Over the World R .40 1.00
❑ M653 Violent Emotion U .20 .50
❑ M654 Clue U .20 .50
❑ M655 Scary Story U .20 .50
❑ M656 Rebellion U .20 .50
❑ M657 Shout of Victory U .20 .50
❑ M658 Backup C .10 .25
❑ M659 Hate U .20 .50
❑ M660 Flash Back U .20 .50
❑ M661 Hard Ones to Deal With R .40 1.00
❑ M662 Additional Team Member R .40 1.00
❑ M663 Shock R .40 1.00
❑ M664 Eight Gate Lock Up U .20 .50
❑ N784 Hidan (Cursed Mode) R .40 1.00
❑ N785 Hidan SR 10.00 25.00
❑ N786 Kakuzu SR 8.00 20.00
❑ N787 Kotetsu Hagane C .10 .25
❑ N788 Izumo Kamizuki C .10 .25
❑ N789 Sai C .10 .25
❑ N790 Kurenai Yuhi C .10 .25
❑ N791 Shikamaru Nara SR 6.00 15.00
❑ N792 Ino Yamanaka C .10 .25
❑ N793 Choji Akimichi C .10 .25
❑ N794 Naruto Uzumaki (Childhood) C .10 .25
❑ N795 Sasuke Uchiha (Childhood) C .10 .25
❑ N796 Sakura Haruno (Childhood) C .10 .25
❑ N797 Hinata Hyuga (Student) C .10 .25
❑ N798 Sora C .10 .25
❑ N799 Gozu C .10 .25
❑ N800 Guren R .40 1.00
❑ N801 Kigiri C .10 .25
❑ N802 Kihou C .10 .25
❑ N803 Nurari C .10 .25
❑ N804 Rinji C .10 .25
❑ N805 Yukimaru C .10 .25
❑ N806 Seimei R .40 1.00
❑ N807 Fudo C .10 .25
❑ N808 Fuen C .10 .25
❑ N809 Furido R .40 1.00
❑ N810 Fouka C .10 .25
❑ N811 Kazuma C .10 .25
❑ N812 Tatsuji C .10 .25
❑ N813 Roshi SR 6.00 15.00
❑ N814 Three Tails SR 5.00 12.00
❑ N815 Naruto Uzumaki C .10 .25
❑ N816 Naruto Uzumaki & Jiraiya SR 5.00 12.00
❑ N817 Rock Lee C .10 .25
❑ N818 Gaara of the Desert C .10 .25
❑ N819 Shikamaru Nara & Choji Akimichi R .40 1.00
❑ N820 Hinata Hyuga C .10 .25
❑ N821 Kisame Hoshigaki R .40 1.00
❑ N822 The Second Hokage SR 5.00 12.00
❑ N823 Asuma Sarutobi C .10 .25
❑ N824 Shino Aburame C .10 .25
❑ N825 The First Hokage SR 8.00 20.00
❑ N826 Might Guy C .10 .25
❑ N827 Jiraiya U .20 .50
❑ N828 Kabuto Yakushi R .40 1.00
❑ N829 Sasuke Uchiha C .10 .25
❑ N830 Kakashi Hatake R .40 1.00
❑ N831 Tenten C .10 .25
❑ N832 Kiba Inuzuka C .10 .25
❑ N833 Temari C .10 .25
❑ N834 Tracking Ninja C .10 .25
❑ N835 Ino Yamanaka C .10 .25
❑ N836 Anko Mitrashi C .10 .25
❑ N837 The Fifth Kazekage R .40 1.00
❑ N838 The Third Hokage R .40 1.00
❑ N839 Rock Lee C .10 .25
❑ N840 Sakura Haruno SR 4.00 10.00
❑ N841 Four Souls of Kakuzu R .40 1.00
❑ N842 Tenzo C .10 .25
❑ N843 Tsunade SR 3.00 8.00
❑ N844 Yugito Ni'i R .40 1.00
❑ N845 Fujin C .10 .25
❑ N846 Raijin C .10 .25
❑ N847 Mizuki (Childhood) C .10 .25
❑ N848 Queen Bee C .10 .25
❑ N849 Cursed Warrior C .10 .25
❑ N850 Sea Monster C .10 .25
❑ N851 Shiin C .10 .25
❑ N852 Agira R .40 1.00
❑ N853 Gensho R .40 1.00
❑ N854 Rokkaku C .10 .25
❑ N855 Yagura C .10 .25
❑ N856 Jako C .10 .25
❑ N857 Monju C .10 .25
❑ N858 Shura C .10 .25
❑ N859 Todoroki C .10 .25
❑ N860 Shikamaru Nara & Asuma Sarutobi R .40 1.00
❑ N861 Naruto Uzumaki SR 2.00 5.00
❑ N862 Sakura Haruno C .10 .25
❑ N863 Kakashi Hatake SR 1.50 4.00

2011 Naruto Invasion

COMPLETE SET (120) 40.00 80.00
BOOSTER BOX (24 PACKS) 40.00 80.00
BOOSTER PACK (10 CARDS) 2.50 4.00

❑ J865 Human Boulder U .20 .50
❑ J866 Earth Style, Mud Wall C .10 .25
❑ J867 Partial Expansion Jutsu U .20 .50
❑ J868 Smoke Pellet Kunai C .10 .25
❑ J869 Shadow Stitching R .40 1.00
❑ J870 Lightning Blade SR 2.00 5.00
❑ J871 Kamui SR 2.50 6.00
❑ J872 Fire Style, Biscuit Firing Jutsu C .10 .25
❑ J873 Fang over Fang R .40 1.00
❑ J874 Lightning Beast Running Jutsu U .20 .50
❑ J875 Sage Art, Amphibian Jutsu U .20 .50
❑ J876 Iron Chain C .10 .25
❑ J877 Lightning Style Shadow Clone R .40 1.00
❑ J878 Lightning Style, Four-Pillar Trap U .20 .50
❑ J879 Rasengan SR 10.00 25.00
❑ J880 Chakra Liquid U .20 .50
❑ J881 Water Whip ST .10 .25
❑ J882 Sticky Webbing C .10 .25
❑ J883 Ninja Art, Grudge Rain R .40 1.00
❑ J884 Wind Blade C .10 .25
❑ J885 Mind Scan C .10 .25
❑ J886 Healing Chakra Transmission R .40 1.00
❑ J887 Finishing Blow U .20 .50
❑ J888 Almighty Push SR 6.00 15.00
❑ J889 Absorption Barrier U .20 .50
❑ M817 Cornered U .20 .50
❑ M818 Information Extraction U .20 .50
❑ M819 Brooding Mood U .20 .50
❑ M820 Betrayal R .40 1.00
❑ M821 Decoding the Message R .40 1.00
❑ M822 Defensive Posture C .10 .25
❑ M823 The Man Who Died Twice U .20 .50
❑ M824 Patriarch R .40 1.00
❑ M825 Lifeflash U .20 .50
❑ M826 Final Moments U .20 .50
❑ M827 The Warhawk R .40 1.00
❑ M828 Heated Argument C .10 .25
❑ M829 Motionless R .40 1.00
❑ M830 The Sage Returns R .40 1.00
❑ M831 Ichiraku Ramen U .20 .50
❑ M832 Hero's Welcome U .20 .50
❑ M833 Feudal Lord's Treasure ST .10 .25
❑ M834 Wager U .20 .50
❑ M835 Struggle U .20 .50
❑ M836 Suspicious Characters R .40 1.00
❑ M837 Hiding C .10 .25
❑ M838 Contemplation ST .10 .25
❑ M839 Outlaws Converge U .20 .50
❑ M840 Revenge R .40 1.00
❑ M841 Floating U .20 .50

Card	Low	High
❑ M842 Regret R	.40	1.00
❑ M843 A Master's Death R	.40	1.00
❑ M844 Autopsy Report C	.10	.25
❑ M845 The Six Paths U	.20	.50
❑ M846 Invasion R	.40	1.00
❑ N1270 Shikamaru Nara C	.10	.25
❑ N1271 Choji Akimichi C	.10	.25
❑ N1272 Shiho C	.10	.25
❑ N1273 Hinata Hyuga C	.10	.25
❑ N1274 Ino Yamanaka C	.10	.25
❑ N1275 Neji Hyuga C	.10	.25
❑ N1276 Ibiki Morino U	.20	.50
❑ N1277 Tenten SR	2.00	5.00
❑ N1278 Shikamaru Nara R	.40	1.00
❑ N1279 Inoichi Yamanaka R	.40	1.00
❑ N1280 Choza Akimichi U	.20	.50
❑ N1281 Deidara SR	3.00	8.00
❑ N1282 Asuma Sarutobi R	.40	1.00
❑ N1283 Kisuke Maboroshi C	.10	.25
❑ N1284 Sasuke Uchiha (Childhood) C	.10	.25
❑ N1285 Tsukado C	.10	.25
❑ N1286 Genma Shiranui C	.10	.25
❑ N1287 Monkey King Enma C	.10	.25
❑ N1288 Tobi U	.20	.50
❑ N1289 Hidan U	.20	.50
❑ N1290 Anbu Elite R	.40	1.00
❑ N1291 Kakashi Hatake (Boyhood) R	.40	1.00
❑ N1292 Sakumo Hatake SR	2.50	6.00
❑ N1293 Kakashi Hatake R	.40	1.00
❑ N1294 Ink Leech C	.10	.25
❑ N1295 Akaboshi C	.10	.25
❑ N1296 Rock Lee C	.10	.25
❑ N1297 Ink Snake C	.10	.25
❑ N1298 Naruto Uzumaki STSR	.75	2.00
❑ N1299 Rock Lee C	.10	.25
❑ N1300 Sai U	.20	.50
❑ N1301 Shima U	.20	.50
❑ N1302 Fukasaku R	.40	1.00
❑ N1303 Killer Bee SR	2.50	6.00
❑ N1304 Might Guy ST	.10	.25
❑ N1305 Jiraiya SR	3.00	8.00
❑ N1306 Samidare C	.10	.25
❑ N1307 Jako C	.10	.25
❑ N1308 Karin C	.10	.25
❑ N1309 Jugo C	.10	.25
❑ N1310 Suigetsu Hozuki C	.10	.25
❑ N1311 Haku C	.10	.25
❑ N1312 Tayuya C	.10	.25
❑ N1313 Sasuke Uchiha STSR	.75	2.00
❑ N1314 Jirobo (State 2) R	.40	1.00
❑ N1315 Kisame Hoshigaki R	.40	1.00
❑ N1316 Kabuto Yakushi R	.40	1.00
❑ N1317 Kakuzu R	.40	1.00
❑ N1318 Orochimaru R	.40	1.00
❑ N1319 Yaoki C	.10	.25
❑ N1320 Sakura Haruno (Childhood) C	.10	.25
❑ N1321 Crow C	.10	.25
❑ N1322 Black Ant C	.10	.25
❑ N1323 Shino Aburame SR	3.00	8.00
❑ N1324 Temari C	.10	.25
❑ N1325 Salamander U	.20	.50
❑ N1326 Sakura Haruno C	.10	.25
❑ N1327 Gaara of the Desert R	.40	1.00
❑ N1328 Kankuro U	.20	.50
❑ N1329 Konan U	.20	.50
❑ N1330 Sasori (Puppet Mode) SR	4.00	10.00
❑ N1331 Giant Centipede C	.10	.25
❑ N1332 Pain (Animal Path) C	.10	.25
❑ N1333 Heretical Icon R	.40	1.00
❑ N1334 Pain (Asura Path) R	.40	1.00

2011 Naruto Shattered Truth

Card	Low	High
COMPLETE SET (120)	50.00	100.00
BOOSTER BOX	50.00	100.00
BOOSTER PACK	2.50	5.00
❑ J802 Ninja Art: Tile Shuriken C	.10	.25
❑ J803 Earth Style: Earth Dragon Bomb R	.40	1.00
❑ J804 Flying Swallow U	.20	.50
❑ J805 Self-Destructing Clay Clone R	.40	1.00
❑ J806 Headhunter Jutsu U	.20	.50
❑ J807 Fire Style: Fireball Jutsu R	.40	1.00
❑ J808 Dispatch of Anbu U	.20	.50
❑ J809 Madara's Eye U	.20	.50
❑ J810 Fire Style: Great Dragon Flame Jutsu U	.20	.50
❑ J811 Overwhelming Power U	.20	.50
❑ J812 Feral Rage R	.40	1.00
❑ J813 Wire Trap C	.10	.25
❑ J814 Kirin SR	6.00	15.00
❑ J815 Chidori R	.40	1.00
❑ J816 Snake Sword U	.20	.50
❑ J817 Water Style: Raging Waves C	.10	.25
❑ J818 Tsuchigumo Style	.20	.50
Forbidden Jutsu Release - Big Bang U		
❑ J819 Chameleon Jutsu C	.10	.25
❑ J820 Infinite Embrace R	.40	1.00
❑ J821 Bubble Barrier Jutsu R	.40	1.00
❑ J822 Poison Senbon Stream U	.20	.50
❑ J823 Amaterasu C	.10	.25
❑ J824 Tsukuyomi R	.40	1.00
❑ J825 Hologram C	.10	.25
❑ J826 Sealing Jutsu: Nine Phantom Dragons R	.40	1.00
❑ M749 Raigo's Blessing U	.20	.50
❑ M750 Clear Sky R	.40	1.00
❑ M751 Team Guy U	.20	.50
❑ M752 Senju vs. Uchiha SR	6.00	15.00
❑ M753 World of Earth R	.40	1.00
❑ M754 Anbu Assault U	.20	.50
❑ M755 World of Fire R	.40	1.00
❑ M756 Make-Out Paradise R	.40	1.00
❑ M757 Throne of the Uchiha U	.20	.50
❑ M758 Last Words U	.20	.50
❑ M759 World of Lightning R	.40	1.00
❑ M760 Baneful Gaze SR	5.00	12.00
❑ M761 Passing Fates C	.10	.25
❑ M762 Cursed Existence R	.40	1.00
❑ M763 New Members U	.20	.50
❑ M764 Rashomon's Defense U	.20	.50
❑ M765 Sasuke's Curse C	.10	.25
❑ M766 Eight-Headed Serpent Jutsu U	.20	.50
❑ M767 Orochimaru's Goal U	.20	.50
❑ M768 World of Water R	.40	1.00
❑ M769 World of Wind R	.40	1.00
❑ M770 Slug Infestation! U	.20	.50
❑ M771 Daydreaming C	.10	.25
❑ M772 Dreams of the Past C	.10	.25
❑ M773 Void World R	.40	1.00
❑ M774 Symbol of the Rogue Ninja R	.40	1.00
❑ M775 Chakra Seal U	.20	.50
❑ N1102 Choji Akimichi C	.10	.25
❑ N1103 Deidara (Younger Days) U	.20	.50
❑ N1104 Tenzo (Anbu Days) U	.20	.50
❑ N1105 Deidara (C0 Form) R	.40	1.00
❑ N1106 Denka C	.10	.25
❑ N1107 Hina C	.10	.25
❑ N1108 Anbu C	.10	.25
❑ N1109 The Thrid Hokage (Younger Days) R	.40	1.00
❑ N1110 Anbu U	.20	.50
❑ N1111 Madara Uchiha SR	5.00	12.00
❑ N1112 Kakashi Hatake (Anbu Days) U	.20	.50
❑ N1113 Itachi Uchiha R	.40	1.00
❑ N1114 Susano'o SR	5.00	12.00
❑ N1115 Sai SR	6.00	15.00
❑ N1116 Kushina Uzumaki C	.10	.25
❑ N1117 Rock Lee C	.10	.25
❑ N1118 Naruto Uzumaki U	.20	.50
❑ N1119 Jiraiya U	.20	.50
❑ N1120 Anko Mitarashi C	.10	.25
❑ N1121 Konohamaru Ninja Corp. C	.10	.25
❑ N1122 Minato Namikaze SR	5.00	12.00
❑ N1123 Naruto Uzumaki & The Fourth Hokage R	.40	1.00
❑ N1124 Karin C	.10	.25
❑ N1125 Suigetsu C	.10	.25
❑ N1126 Jugo C	.10	.25
❑ N1127 Sakon (State 1) U	.20	.50
❑ N1128 Ukon (State 1) R	.40	1.00
❑ N1129 Sasuke Uchiha SR	5.00	12.00
❑ N1130 Rashomon U	.20	.50
❑ N1131 Sakon & Ukon (State 2) R	.40	1.00
❑ N1132 Harusame C	.10	.25
❑ N1133 Utakata R	.40	1.00
❑ N1134 Hotaru Katsuragi C	.10	.25
❑ N1135 Sakura Haruno C	.10	.25
❑ N1136 Konan (Childhood) C	.10	.25
❑ N1137 Salamander C	.10	.25
❑ N1138 Temari U	.20	.50
❑ N1139 Hiruko R	.40	1.00
❑ N1140 Sasori U	.20	.50
❑ N1141 The 3rd Kazekage R	.40	1.00
❑ N1142 Sasori & Hiruko R	.40	1.00
❑ N1143 Six Tails SR	6.00	15.00
❑ N1144 Giant Panda C	.10	.25
❑ N1145 Zetsu F	2.00	5.00
❑ N1146 Tobi F	2.00	5.00
❑ N1147 Konan F	2.00	5.00
❑ N1148 Sasori F	2.00	5.00
❑ N1149 Deidara F	2.00	5.00
❑ N1150 Kisame Hoshigaki F	2.00	5.00
❑ N1151 Itachi Uchiha STSR	.40	1.00
❑ N1152 Pain (Deva Path) STSR	.40	1.00
❑ N1153 Kakuzu F	2.00	5.00
❑ N1154 Hidan F	2.00	5.00
❑ N1155 Neji Hyuga C	.10	.25
❑ N1156 Hinata Hyuga C	.10	.25
❑ N1157 Ino Yamanaka C	.10	.25
❑ N1158 Tenten C	.10	.25
❑ N1159 Shikamaru Nara U	.20	.50
❑ N1160 Yamato C	.10	.25
❑ N1161 Asuma Sarutobi C	.10	.25
❑ N1162 The 1st Hokage U	.20	.50
❑ N1163 Tsume Inuzuka C	.10	.25
❑ N1164 Kuromaru C	.10	.25
❑ N1165 Kiba Inuzuka C	.10	.25
❑ N1166 Akamaru C	.10	.25
❑ N1167 Rock Lee C	.10	.25
❑ N1168 Naruto Uzumaki C	.10	.25
❑ N1169 Might Guy U	.20	.50

2011 Naruto Tales of the Gallant Sage

Card	Low	High
COMPLETE SET (140)	50.00	100.00
BOOSTER BOX	50.00	100.00
BOOSTER PACK	2.50	5.00
❑ J773 Protective 8 Trigrams 64 Palms U	.20	.50
❑ J774 8 Trigrams Palms Rotation C	.10	.25
❑ J775 Gentle Fist Style: 8 Trigrams 64 R	.40	1.00
❑ J776 8 Trigrams Air Palm U	.20	.50
❑ J777 Detonating Kunai C	.10	.25
❑ J778 Fire Style: Dragon Flame Jutsu C	.10	.25
❑ J779 Eyes of the Betrayer U	.20	.50
❑ J780 Echoes of Pain U	.20	.50
❑ J781 Sage Art: Bath of Boiling Oil R	.40	1.00
❑ J782 Shield Block C	.10	.25
❑ J783 Toad Subjugation	.20	.50
Art of the Manipulated Shadow U		
❑ J784 Sage Art: Kebari Senbon R	.40	1.00
❑ J785 Demonic Illusion	4.00	10.00
Toad Confrontation Singing SR		
❑ J786 Snake Sword R	.40	1.00
❑ J787 Summoning Jutsu: Reanimation SR	6.00	15.00
❑ J788 Digital Phalanx Shrapnel U	.20	.50
❑ J789 Spider Bow: Fierce Rip U	.20	.50
❑ J790 Spider Armor C	.10	.25
❑ J791 Crystal Style: Burst Crystal Dragon C	.10	.25
❑ J792 Acid Shot C	.10	.25
❑ J793 First-Aid C	.10	.25
❑ J794 Ferocious Punch! U	.20	.50
❑ J795 Puppet Shield U	.20	.50
❑ J796 Puppet Summoning R	.40	1.00
❑ J797 Hydro-pump SR	4.00	10.00
❑ J798 Summoning Jutsu: Pain R	.40	1.00
❑ J799 The Eyes of Pain C	.10	.25
❑ J800 The Hand of Pain R	.40	1.00
❑ J801 The Soul of Pain U	.20	.50
❑ M723 Training in the Moonlight R	.40	1.00
❑ M724 Gentle Fist Style: Eight Trigrams U	.20	.50
❑ M725 End of the Immortal R	.40	1.00
❑ M726 Mover's Jacket C	.10	.25
❑ M727 Follower of Jashin C	.10	.25
❑ M728 Past and Future R	.40	1.00
❑ M729 Scornful Eyes U	.20	.50
❑ M730 Gathering Intel U	.20	.50
❑ M731 Another Mask... U	.20	.50
❑ M732 Doppelganger U	.20	.50
❑ M733 Mount Myoboku R	.40	1.00
❑ M734 Jiraya's Hermit Dance R	.40	1.00
❑ M735 Tale of the Gallent Jiraya C	.10	.25
❑ M736 Vessel for Dreams R	.40	1.00
❑ M737 Orochimaru's Forbidden Jutsu U	.20	.50
❑ M738 Anko's Memory C	.10	.25
❑ M739 Karin's Anger U	.20	.50
❑ M740 Monster Research R	.40	1.00
❑ M741 Katsuyu's Division R	.40	1.00
❑ M742 Ino's Tears R	.40	1.00
❑ M743 Puppet Master in Training R	.40	1.00
❑ M744 Kankuro's Tenacity U	.20	.50
❑ M745 Rash Decision U	.20	.50
❑ M746 The Ame Orphans R	.40	1.00
❑ M747 A Gift of Pain U	.20	.50
❑ M748 Chakra Paper C	.10	.25
❑ N1037 Neji Hyuga R	.40	1.00
❑ N1037 Neji Hyuga P		
❑ N1038 Hinata Hyuga U	.20	.50
❑ N1039 Ino Yamanaka P		
❑ N1039 Ino Yamanaka C	.10	.25
❑ N1040 Choji Akimichi C	.10	.25
❑ N1041 The First Hokage P		
❑ N1041 The First Hokage R	.40	1.00
❑ N1042 Asuma Sarutobi SR	6.00	15.00
❑ N1042 Asuma Sarutobi P		
❑ N1043 Shikamaru Nara (Suit) C	.10	.25
❑ N1044 Tenten C	.10	.25
❑ N1044 Tenten P		
❑ N1045 Hanabi Hyuga C	.10	.25
❑ N1046 Choji Akimichi & Shikamaru Nara R	.40	1.00
❑ N1047 Hinata Hyuga (Awakened) P		
❑ N1047 Hinata Hyuga (Awakened) C	.10	.25
❑ N1048 Hiashi Hyuga R	.40	1.00
❑ N1049 Kiba Inuzuka C	.10	.25
❑ N1050 Sasuke Uchiha C	.10	.25
❑ N1051 Hidan U	.20	.50
❑ N1051 Hidan P		
❑ N1052 Akamaru C	.10	.25
❑ N1053 Kakashi Hatake & Yamato P		
❑ N1053 Kakashi Hatake & Yamato R	.40	1.00
❑ N1054 The Third Hokage U	.20	.50
❑ N1054 The Third Hokage P		
❑ N1055 Itachi Uchiha & Sasuke Uchiha R	.40	1.00
❑ N1056 Sasuke Uchiha (Suit) C	.10	.25
❑ N1057 Kakashi Hatake R	.40	1.00
❑ N1057 Kakashi Hatake P		
❑ N1058 Itachi Uchiha U	.20	.50
❑ N1059 Kiba Inuzuka & Akamaru R	.40	1.00
❑ N1060 Kakashi Hatake & The 4th Hokage SR	5.00	12.00
❑ N1060 Kakashi Hatake & The 4th Hokage P		
❑ N1061 Naruto Uzumaki (Tailed Beast Form) R	.40	1.00
❑ N1062 Naruto Uzumaki (Four Tails) R	.40	1.00
❑ N1062 Naruto Uzumaki (Four Tails) P		
❑ N1063 Fukasaku U	.20	.50
❑ N1064 Shima C	.10	.25
❑ N1065 Gamaken C	.10	.25
❑ N1066 Great Toad Sage C	.10	.25
❑ N1067 Jiraiya (Sage Mode) P		
❑ N1067 Jiraiya (Sage Mode) SR	5.00	12.00
❑ N1068 Jiraiya P		
❑ N1068 Jiraiya U	.20	.50
❑ N1069 Rock Lee C	.10	.25
❑ N1070 Killer Bee C	.10	.25
❑ N1071 Naruto Uzumaki (Suit) C	.10	.25
❑ N1072 Sai (Suit) C	.10	.25
❑ N1073 Yahiko (Childhood) C	.10	.25
❑ N1074 Giant Spider C	.10	.25
❑ N1075 Kidomaru (State 1) P		
❑ N1075 Kidomaru (State 1) U	.20	.50
❑ N1076 Karin C	.10	.25
❑ N1077 Suigetsu Hozuki C	.10	.25
❑ N1078 Jugo C	.10	.25
❑ N1079 Kimimaro (State 1) U	.20	.50
❑ N1080 Sasuke Uchiha P		
❑ N1080 Sasuke Uchiha U	.20	.50
❑ N1081 Orochimaru SR	6.00	15.00
❑ N1082 Hanzo the Salamander R	.40	1.00
❑ N1083 Manda P		
❑ N1083 Manda U	.20	.50
❑ N1084 Kidomaru (State 2) R	.40	1.00
❑ N1085 Mini Katsuyu C	.10	.25
❑ N1086 Crow C	.10	.25
❑ N1087 Black Ant C	.10	.25
❑ N1088 Gaara of the Desert (Suit) C	.10	.25
❑ N1089 Father and Mother C	.10	.25
❑ N1090 Chiyo P		
❑ N1090 Chiyo U	.20	.50
❑ N1091 Ebizo C	.10	.25
❑ N1092 Kankuro C	.10	.25
❑ N1093 Monzaemon Chikamatsu SR	5.00	12.00
❑ N1094 Sakura Haruno R	.40	1.00
❑ N1094 Sakura Haruno P		
❑ N1095 Ino Yamanaka C	.10	.25
❑ N1096 Pain & Itachi Uchiha P		
❑ N1096 Pain & Itachi Uchiha SR	5.00	12.00
❑ N1097 Giant Rhino C	.10	.25
❑ N1098 Nagato (Childhood) C	.10	.25
❑ N1099 Pain (Human Path) U	.20	.50
❑ N1100 Pain (Naraka Path) C	.10	.25
❑ N1101 Pain (Asura Path) R	.40	1.00

2011 Naruto Tournament Pack 3

Card	Low	High
COMPLETE SET (60)	20.00	40.00
BOOSTER BOX	50.00	100.00
BOOSTER PACK	2.50	5.00
❑ J827 Tree Climbing Training U	.20	.50
❑ J828 Standing Alone U	.20	.50
❑ J829 Fire Style: Fireball Jutsu R	4.00	1.00
❑ J830 Chidori SR	5.00	12.00
❑ J831 Wind Style: Rasen Shuriken SR	4.00	10.00
❑ J832 Barrier Battle Arts R	.40	1.00
❑ J833 Deformable Body U	.20	.50
❑ J834 Blade of the Thunder God R	.40	1.00
❑ J835 Stunning Strike U	.20	.50
❑ J836 Fear of Blood R	.40	1.00
❑ J837 Chakra Manipulation Training U	.20	.50
❑ J838 Money Style: Shadow Clone Jutsu R	.40	1.00
❑ M776 Summoning Weapons R	.40	1.00
❑ M777 After the Battle R	.40	1.00
❑ M778 Old Faces, New Problems R	.40	1.00
❑ M779 Demon's Eyes R	.40	1.00
❑ M780 Clone Training U	.20	.50
❑ M781 Awkward Thinking SR	6.00	15.00
❑ M782 Low Stamina R	.40	1.00
❑ M783 Observer U	.20	.50
❑ M784 Under the Rising Moon U	.20	.50
❑ M785 Fond Memories R	.40	1.00
❑ M786 The Fool & The Elite R	.40	1.00
❑ M787 Money Style: Help Me Jutsu R	.40	1.00
❑ N1170 Hinata Hyuga C	.10	.25
❑ N1171 Shikamaru Nara C	.10	.25
❑ N1172 Neji Hyuga C	.10	.25
❑ N1173 Asuma Sarutobi C	.10	.25
❑ N1174 The 1st Hokage U	.20	.50
❑ N1175 Sasuke Uchiha C	.10	.25
❑ N1176 Kakashi Hatake C	.10	.25
❑ N1177 Itachi Uchiha U	.20	.50
❑ N1178 The 3rd Hokage R	.40	1.00
❑ N1179 Naruto Uzumaki C	.10	.25
❑ N1180 Rock Lee C	.10	.25
❑ N1181 Kushina Uzumaki C	.10	.25
❑ N1182 Killer Bee C	.10	.25
❑ N1183 Sai C	.10	.25
❑ N1184 Naruto Uzumaki (Tailed Beast Form) SR	6.00	15.00
❑ N1185 A R	.40	1.00
❑ N1186 Eight Tails U	.20	.50
❑ N1187 Suigetsu Hozuki C	.10	.25
❑ N1188 Jugo C	.10	.25
❑ N1189 Karin C	.10	.25
❑ N1190 Suigetsu Hozuki C	.10	.25
❑ N1191 Jugo C	.10	.25
❑ N1192 Sasuke Uchiha C	.10	.25
❑ N1193 Orochimaru U	.20	.50
❑ N1194 Sasuke Uchiha (State 2) R	.40	1.00
❑ N1195 Sakura Haruno C	.10	.25
❑ N1196 Gaara of the Desert C	.10	.25
❑ N1197 Kurenai Yuhi C	.10	.25
❑ N1198 Konan U	.20	.50
❑ N1199 Pain (Animal Path) C	.10	.25
❑ N1200 Pain (Preta Path) C	.10	.25
❑ N1201 Pain (Naraka Path) C	.10	.25
❑ N1202 Pain (Human Path) U	.20	.50
❑ N1203 Pain (Asura Path) U	.20	.50
❑ N1204 Pain (Deva Path) U	.20	.50
❑ N1205 Nagato SR	5.00	12.00

2011 Naruto Ultimate Battle Tin

Card	Low	High
❑ PR069 Sasori	.30	.75
❑ PR070 Deidara	.30	.75
❑ PR071 Kakashi Hatake	.30	.75
❑ PR072 Naruto Uzumaki	.30	.75
❑ PR073 Itachi Uchiha	.30	.75
❑ PR074 Sasuke Uchiha	.30	.75

2011 Naruto Weapons of War

Card	Low	High
COMPLETE SET (119)	50.00	100.00
BOOSTER BOX	50.00	100.00
BOOSTER PACK	2.50	5.00
❑ J839 Byakugan R	.40	1.00
❑ J840 Deflection C	.10	.25
❑ J841 Mind Transfer Jutsu U	.20	.50
❑ J842 Partial Expansion Jutsu R	.40	1.00
❑ J843 Shadow Possession Jutsu C	.10	.25
❑ J844 Shuriken C	.10	.25
❑ J845 Smash C	.10	.25
❑ J846 Sharingan Eye C	.10	.25
❑ J847 Mangekyo Sharingan R	.40	1.00
❑ J848 Fire Style: Dragon Flame Jutsu R	.40	1.00
❑ J849 Needle Jizo C	.10	.25
❑ J850 Double Impact U	.20	.50
❑ J851 Seven Swords Dance R	.40	1.00
❑ J852 Lariat SR	6.00	15.00
❑ J853 Chakra Cannon U	.20	.50
❑ J854 Severe Leaf Hurricane U	.20	.50
❑ J855 Water Style: Demon Wave R	.40	1.00
❑ J856 Walking on Water C	.10	.25
❑ J857 Chidori Lance R	.40	1.00
❑ J858 Snake Sword SR	8.00	20.00
❑ J859 Earth Style Barrier: Earth Dome Prison U	.20	.50
❑ J860 Parasitic Insect Jutsu R	.40	1.00
❑ J861 Mind Scour C	.10	.25
❑ J862 Finger Flick R	.40	1.00
❑ J863 Puppet Master Jutsu C	.10	.25
❑ J864 Flamethrower U	.20	.50
❑ M788 Wrath of the Two Tails U	.20	.50
❑ M789 Leaf Squad Organized! R	.40	1.00
❑ M790 Sweet Treat U	.20	.50
❑ M791 Weapons of War R	.40	1.00
❑ M792 12 Shinobi Guardians R	.40	1.00
❑ M793 Quicksand C	.10	.25
❑ M794 Pad C	.10	.25
❑ M795 Guidance U	.20	.50
❑ M796 Naruto vs. Sasuke SR	4.00	10.00
❑ M797 Hokage Rocks U	.20	.50
❑ M798 Fading Touch R	.40	1.00
❑ M799 Brotherhood R	.40	1.00
❑ M800 Sage Training R	.40	1.00
❑ M801 A Good Book U	.20	.50
❑ M802 Mad Skillz R	.40	1.00
❑ M803 Ditched C	.10	.25
❑ M804 Disaster of the Nine-Tailed Fox Spirit R	.40	1.00
❑ M805 Just Like That Hero R	.40	1.00
❑ M806 Fierce Clash U	.20	.50
❑ M807 Flashback U	.20	.50
❑ M808 Ambush C	.10	.25
❑ M809 Right of Succession SR	4.00	10.00
❑ M810 Teacher and Pupil R	.40	1.00
❑ M811 Research U	.20	.50
❑ M812 The Blank Page C	.10	.25
❑ M813 Sealing Barrier R	.40	1.00
❑ M814 Ignorance U	.20	.50
❑ M815 A Gift R	.40	1.00
❑ M816 Kage of the Leaf U	.20	.50
❑ N1206 Choji Akimichi C	.10	.25
❑ N1207 Hinata Hyuga (Kimono) C	.10	.25
❑ N1208 Tenten (Kimono) C	.10	.25
❑ N1209 Ino Yamanaka (Kimono) U	.20	.50
❑ N1210 Neji Hyuga C	.10	.25
❑ N1211 Shikamaru Nara C	.10	.25
❑ N1212 Chiriku R	.40	1.00
❑ N1213 Hinata Hyuga C	.10	.25
❑ N1214 Deidara R	.40	1.00
❑ N1215 Yamato R	.40	1.00
❑ N1216 The 1st Hokage SR	6.00	15.00
❑ N1217 Akamaru C	.10	.25
❑ N1218 Kiba Inuzuka C	.10	.25
❑ N1219 Sasuke Uchiha C	.10	.25
❑ N1220 Pakkun C	.10	.25
❑ N1221 Yugao Uzuki U	.20	.50
❑ N1222 Sasuke Uchiha C	.10	.25
❑ N1223 Obito Uchiha R	.40	1.00
❑ N1224 Tobi C	.10	.25
❑ N1225 Danzo R	.40	1.00
❑ N1226 Hidan R	.40	1.00
❑ N1227 Kakashi Hatake U	.20	.50
❑ N1228 Itachi Uchiha U	.20	.50
❑ N1229 The 3rd Hokage SR	4.00	10.00
❑ N1230 Konohamaru C	.10	.25
❑ N1231 Naruto Uzumaki C	.10	.25
❑ N1232 Ink Lion C	.10	.25
❑ N1233 Rock Lee C	.10	.25
❑ N1234 Naruto Uzumaki (Clone) C	.10	.25
❑ N1235 Iruka Umino C	.10	.25
❑ N1236 Sai R	.40	1.00
❑ N1237 Killer Bee U	.20	.50
❑ N1238 Anko Mitarashi (Kimono) U	.20	.50
❑ N1239 Might Guy R	.40	1.00
❑ N1240 Jiraiya R	.40	1.00
❑ N1241 The 4th Hokage SR	10.00	25.00
❑ N1242 Eight Tails R	.40	1.00
❑ N1243 Orochimaru C	.10	.25
❑ N1244 Sakon C	.10	.25
❑ N1245 Karin C	.10	.25
❑ N1246 Anko Mitarashi R	.40	1.00
❑ N1247 Suigetsu Hozuki U	.20	.50
❑ N1248 Jugo (State 1) U	.20	.50
❑ N1249 Zabuza Momochi SR	5.00	12.00
❑ N1250 Sasuke Uchiha SR	15.00	30.00
❑ N1251 The 2nd Hokage SR	4.00	10.00
❑ N1252 Sakura Haruno (Kimono) C	.10	.25

Card	Low	High
N1253 Kankuro C	.10	.25
N1254 Tonton C	.10	.25
N1255 Shino Aburame C	.10	.25
N1256 Sakura Haruno R	.40	1.00
N1257 Shizune (Kimono) U	.20	.50
N1258 Kurenai Yuhi R	.40	1.00
N1259 The 5th Hokage SR	4.00	10.00
N1260 Kurenai Yuhi (Kimono) R	.40	1.00
N1261 Tsunade (Kimono) R	.40	1.00
N1262 Jirobo (State 1) C	.10	.25
N1263 Kabuto Yakushi C	.10	.25
N1264 Tayuya C	.10	.25
N1265 Haku U	.20	.50
N1266 Temari C	.10	.25
N1267 Gaara of the Desert C	.10	.25
N1268 Chiyo U	.20	.50
N1269 Baki U	.20	.50

2012 Naruto Avenger's Wrath

Card	Low	High
Complete Set (120)	75.00	150.00
Booster Box (24 Packs)	40.00	80.00
Booster Pack (10 Cards)	2.50	4.00
J946 Earth Style: Hidden in Stones U	.20	.50
J947 Earth Style: Mud Wave R	.40	1.00
J948 Paper Bomb C	.10	.25
J949 Spontaneous Tree Summoning SR	12.00	30.00
J950 Narrow Dodge C	.10	.25
J951 Summoning Jutsu U	.20	.50
J952 Simulstrike R	.40	1.00
J953 Izanagi SR	8.00	20.00
J954 Taking a Hostage U	.20	.50
J955 Panic Attack C	.10	.25
J956 Art of the Raging Lion's Mane R	.40	1.00
J957 Shadow Clone Jutsu U	.20	.50
J958 Naruto Uzumaki Barrage U	.20	.50
J959 Chidori Sword R	.40	1.00
J960 Sacrifice U	.20	.50
J961 Chakra Transference C	.10	.25
J962 Mystic Fog Prison C	.10	.25
J963 Savior R	.40	1.00
J964 Wind Style: Vacuum Blade U	.20	.50
J965 Wind Style: Vacuum Bullets R	.40	1.00
J966 Enhanced Shuriken C	.10	.25
J967 Paralyzing Seal C	.10	.25
J968 Wind Style: Vacuum Blast U	.20	.50
J969 Reverse Tetragram Sealing Jutsu SR	10.00	25.00
J970 Chakra Stream U	.20	.50
J971 Unorthodox Weaponry R	.40	1.00
M914 A Quiet Day C	.10	.25
M915 Konoha's Strongest Genin SR	3.00	8.00
M916 Intriguing Story R	.40	1.00
M917 The Ultimate Weapon U	.20	.50
M918 Self Conversation U	.20	.50
M919 Desperate Power R	.40	1.00
M920 Pocket Dimension R	.40	1.00
M921 Face-off U	.20	.50
M922 The Fire Lord C	.10	.25
M923 A Rival's Challenge SR	3.00	8.00
M924 Differing Emotions C	.10	.25
M925 An Old Friend R	.40	1.00
M926 Medicinal Pills C	.20	.50
M927 Stuffed U	.20	.50
M928 Inari's Decision R	.40	1.00
M929 Moment of Weakness U	.20	.50
M930 Turn of Phrase SR	3.00	8.00
M931 Seasick U	.20	.50
M932 Skeleton Panic R	.40	1.00
M933 A Fisherman's Quarry C	.10	.25
M934 The Rogue Jinchuriki C	.10	.25
M935 Sakura's Confession SR	6.00	15.00
M936 Shameful Actions R	.40	1.00
M937 Present from Students C	.10	.25
M938 Kakashi Hatake's Date U	.20	.50
M939 Jofuku Flower R	.40	1.00
M940 Ex-Samurai R	.40	1.00
M941 Strength in Numbers U	.20	.50
M942 The Mediator R	.40	1.00
N1488 Choji Akimichi C	.10	.25
N1489 Hinata Hyuga (Childhood) C	.10	.25
N1490 Neji Hyuga C	.10	.25
N1491 Ino Yamanaka (Childhood) C	.10	.25
N1492 Chushin C	.10	.25
N1493 Tenten C	.10	.25
N1494 Shikamaru Nara U	.20	.50
N1495 Tonbei U	.20	.50
N1496 Ko Hyuga U	.20	.50
N1497 Neji Hyuga U	.20	.50
N1498 Asuma Sarutobi R	.40	1.00
N1499 Yamato R	.40	1.00
N1500 The 1st Hokage SR	8.00	20.00
N1501 Hibachi C	.10	.25
N1502 Akane C	.10	.25
N1503 Tamaki (Childhood) C	.10	.25
N1504 Kiba Inuzuka C	.10	.25
N1505 Nango C	.10	.25
N1506 Sasuke Uchiha U	.20	.50
N1507 Tobi C	.10	.25
N1508 Sasuke Uchiha R	.40	1.00
N1509 Hidan U	.20	.50
N1510 Kakashi Hatake U	.20	.50
N1511 Itachi Uchiha R	.40	1.00
N1512 Madara Uchiha SR	8.00	2.00
N1513 The 6th Hokage SR	12.00	30.00
N1514 The Sage U	.20	.50
N1515 Gameru C	.10	.25
N1516 Kusune C	.10	.25
N1517 Naruto Uzumaki C	.10	.25
N1518 Izumo Kamizuki C	.10	.25
N1519 Rock Lee U	.20	.50
N1520 Naruto Uzumaki U	.20	.50
N1521 Anko Mitarashi U	.20	.50
N1522 Sai U	.20	.50
N1523 Jiraiya R	.40	1.00
N1524 Might Guy R	.40	1.00
N1525 Might Guy and Kakashi Hatake SR	3.00	8.00
N1526 Kanabun C	.10	.25
N1527 Tanishi C	.10	.25
N1528 Karin C	.10	.25
N1529 Haku C	.10	.25
N1530 Suigetsu Hozuki U	.20	.50
N1531 Jugo U	.20	.50
N1532 Kabuto Yakushi U	.20	.50
N1533 Zabuza Momochi R	.40	1.00
N1534 Kisame Hoshigaki R	.40	1.00
N1535 Jugo (State 2) R	.40	1.00
N1536 Orochimaru R	.40	1.00
N1537 Susano'o (Sasuke) SR	25.00	50.00
N1538 Shino Aburame (Childhood) C	.10	.25
N1539 Sakura Haruno U	.20	.50
N1540 Hotaru Katsuragi C	.10	.25
N1541 Temari C	.10	.25
N1542 Gaara of the Desert C	.10	.25
N1543 Inner Sakura R	.40	1.00
N1544 Father and Mother U	.20	.50
N1545 Hiruko U	.20	.50
N1546 Kurenai Yuhi U	.20	.50
N1547 Sasori R	.40	1.00
N1548 Kurenai Yuhi and Asuma Sarutobi R	.40	1.00
N1549 Sakura Haruno and Chiyo R	.40	1.00
N1550 En no Gyoja R	.40	1.00
N1551 Samurai Warrior C	.10	.25
N1552 Mifune R	.40	1.00

2012 Naruto Hero's Ascension

Card	Low	High
Booster Box (24 Packs)	50.00	80.00
Booster Pack (10 Cards)	2.50	4.00
C060 Madara Uchiha ST	2.50	6.00
J1000 Wind Style: Rasen Shuriken ST	.40	1.00
J1001 The Mind of Pain ST	.20	.50
J972 Mind Transfer, Puppet Curse Jutsu SR	1.25	3.00
J973 Barrier Ninjutsu U	.20	.50
J974 Interrogation R	.50	1.25
J975 Overwhelming Hunger C	.10	.25
J976 Chidori R	.40	1.00
J977 Threaten C	.10	.25
J978 Body Flicker U	.20	.50
J979 Reaper Death Seal SR	2.00	5.00
J980 Backstab U	.30	.75
J981 Role Reversal R	.40	1.00
J982 Pencil Toss U	.20	.50
(Mull to Four Exclusive Preview)		
J983 Double Lariat SR	2.50	6.00
J984 Unlocking the Seal C	.10	.25
J985 Special Kunai U	.20	.50
J986 Rasengan R	1.50	4.00
J987 Water Prison Shark Dance Jutsu SR	1.25	3.00
J988 Skeletal Control U	.20	.50
J989 Summoning Jutsu: Reanimation SR	4.00	10.00
J990 Water Prison Jutsu C	.10	.25
J991 Voracious Appetite C	.10	.25
J992 Simple Disguise C	.10	.25
J993 Gigantic Fan C	.10	.25
J994 Palm Healing R	.40	1.00
J995 Fungal Power U	.20	.50
J996 Shark Skin C	.10	.25
(Pojo Exclusive Preview)		
J997 The Passion of Youth C	.10	.25
(Pojo Exclusive Preview)		
J998 Almighty Push ST	.50	1.25
J999 Eyes of the Sage ST	.20	.50
M943 Rebuilding the Village U	.20	.50
M944 Great Praise C	.10	.25
M945 The Power of the Trio R	.40	1.00
M946 A Hard Bargain R	.40	1.00
M947 The Future Hokage? U	.20	.50
M948 Out of Control Curse Mark C	.10	.25
M949 Path of the Avenger R	.40	1.00
M950 Shadow of the Leaf U	.30	.75
M951 Jonin's Intervention R	1.50	4.00
M952 Exhaustion U	.20	.50
M953 A Master's Treat U	.20	.50
M954 Disaster of the Nine-Tailed Fox Spirit R	.40	1.00
M955 A Parent's Love R	.40	1.00
M956 Unlocking the Power C	.10	.25
(Mull to Four Exclusive Preview)		
M957 The Evil Within U	.20	.50
M958 The Tailless Beast R	.40	1.00
M959 A New Master U	.20	.50
M960 Dark Aspirations R	.40	1.00
M961 Alliance of Evil U	.20	.50
M962 A Show of Power U	.20	.50
M963 Forceful Persuasion R	.40	1.00
M964 Sakura's Tears R	.40	1.00
M965 Idle Comrades U	.20	.50
M966 What Could Have Been U	.20	.50
M967 Tinker R	.40	1.00
M968 Gathering Herbs R	.40	1.00
M969 Outcast R	.40	1.00
(Pojo Exclusive Preview)		
M970 The Lord's Convene C	.10	.25
(Pojo Exclusive Preview)		
M971 Sparring U	.20	.50
(Pojo Exclusive Preview)		
M972 The Spiral of Pain ST	.40	1.00
M973 Sage's Training Ground ST	.20	.50
M974 Exhaustive Battle ST	.20	.50
M975 The Herald of Pain ST	.20	.50
N1553 Choji Akimichi C	.10	.25
N1554 Ino Yamanaka C	.10	.25
N1555 Tenten C	.10	.25
N1556 Tofu C	.10	.25
N1557 Mikage C	.10	.25
N1558 Shikamaru Nara U	.20	.50
N1559 Hinata Hyuga C	.10	.25
N1560 Zetsu U	.20	.50
N1561 Asuma Sarutobi U	.20	.50
N1562 Neji Hyuga U	.20	.50
N1563 Deidara R	.40	1.00
N1564 The 3rd Tsuchikage SR	1.50	4.00
N1565 Hanabi Hyuga C	.10	.25
N1566 Gentleman Cat C	.10	.25
N1567 Suguro C	.10	.25
N1568 Mr. Ostrich C	.10	.25
N1569 Kiba Inuzuka C	.10	.25
N1570 Sasuke Uchiha C	.10	.25
N1571 Obito Uchiha U	.20	.50
N1572 Tobi C	.10	.25
N1573 Hidan U	.20	.50
N1574 Sasuke Uchiha R	.75	2.00
N1575 Kakashi Hatake (Boyhood) U	.20	.50
N1576 Kakashi Hatake R	1.25	3.00
N1577 Itachi Uchiha R	.40	1.00
N1578 Masked Man SR	8.00	20.00
N1579 Konohamaru C	.10	.25
N1580 Naruto Uzumaki C	.10	.25
N1581 Pakkun C	.10	.25
N1582 Rock Lee U	.20	.50
(Mull to Four Exclusive Preview)		
N1583 Kushina Uzumaki R	.40	1.00
N1584 Izumo Kamizuki U	.20	.50
N1585 Sora R	.40	1.00
N1586 Naruto Uzumaki U	.20	.50
N1587 Sai U	.20	.50
N1588 Killer Bee R	.40	1.00
N1589 Killer Bee (Version 2) SR	10.00	25.00
N1590 The 4th Hokage SR	12.00	30.00
N1591 Gamabunta R	.50	1.25
N1592 Jirobo C	.10	.25
N1593 Karin C	.10	.25
N1594 Suigetsu C	.10	.25
N1595 Jugo U	.20	.50
N1596 Haku R	.40	1.00
N1597 Utakata U	.20	.50
N1598 Kabuto Yakushi U	.20	.50
N1599 Zabuza Momochi R	.40	1.00
N1600 Kisame Hoshigaki C	.10	.25
N1601 Kimimaro R	.40	1.00
N1602 Kabuto Yakushi SR	10.00	25.00
N1603 Kisame Hoshigaki SR	12.00	30.00
N1604 Gaara of the Desert C	.10	.25
N1605 Sakura Haruno C	.10	.25
N1606 Kankuro C	.10	.25
N1607 Temari C	.10	.25
N1608 Rin C	.10	.25
N1609 Shino Aburame U	.20	.50
N1610 Temari U	.20	.50
N1611 Sakura Haruno U	.20	.50
N1612 Hiruko R	.40	1.00
N1613 Chiyo U	.20	.50
N1614 Shizune R	.40	1.00
N1615 Kurenai Yuhi R	.40	1.00
N1616 Tsunade SR	3.00	8.00
N1617 Kakuzu R	.40	1.00
(Pojo Exclusive Preview)		
N1618 Naruto Uzumaki (Sage Mode) STSR	4.00	10.00
N1619 Pain (Deva Path) STSR	4.00	10.00
N1620 Jiraiya ST	.20	.50

2012 Naruto Kage Summit

Card	Low	High
Complete Set (120)	150.00	250.00
Booster Box (24)	40.00	80.00
Booster Pack (10)	2.50	4.00
J921 Sporulation Jutsu U	.20	.50
J922 Wood Style: Four Pillar Prison R	.40	1.00
J923 Lava Style: Lava Monster R	.40	1.00
J924 Golem Technique R	.40	1.00
J925 Earth Style: Weighted Boulder C	.10	.25
J926 Particle Style: Atomic Dismantling SR	6.00	15.00
J927 Danzo's Seal C	.10	.25
J928 Lightning Blade U	.20	.50
J929 Genjutsu SR	8.00	20.00
J930 Amaterasu Shield U	.20	.50
J931 Inferno Style: Flame Control R	.40	1.00
J932 Gale Style: Laser Circus R	.40	1.00
J933 Lightning Illusion: Flash Pillar C	.10	.25
J934 Liger Bomb SR	4.00	10.00
J935 Lightning Style Armor R	.40	1.00
J936 Lightning Style: Emotion Wave R	.40	1.00
J937 Water Style: Water Wall C	.10	.25
J938 Cursed Seal Chakra Blast U	.20	.50
J939 Hiramekarei Unleash: Hammer R	.40	1.00
J940 Vapor Style: Solid Fog SR	2.50	6.00
J941 Sand Shield C	.10	.25
J942 Wind Scythe Jutsu R	.40	1.00
J943 Secret Red Technique: Puppet Triad SR	6.00	15.00
J944 Sand Shower Barrage R	.40	1.00
J945 Sand Wall U	.20	.50
M884 Messengers U	.20	.50
M885 The Stone Council SR	6.00	15.00
M886 Five Kage Summit R	.40	1.00
M887 Spoils of War C	.10	.25
M888 Exhaustion R	.40	1.00
M889 Untold Destruction R	.40	1.00
M890 Battle of Attrition R	.40	1.00
M891 New Orders U	.20	.50
M892 The Leaf Council SR	6.00	15.00
M893 Tense Negotiations U	.20	.50
M894 An Honest Discussion C	.10	.25
M895 Power of Suggestion C	.10	.25
M896 Bodyguard's Protection C	.10	.25
M897 Exaggeration R	.40	1.00
M898 For Vengeance U	.20	.50
M899 The Cloud Council SR	6.00	15.00
M900 A Unique Exit U	.20	.50
M901 A Plea U	.20	.50
M902 A Dark Message C	.10	.25
M903 The Mist Council SR	3.00	8.00
M904 Massacre U	.20	.50
M905 The Kage Assassins U	.20	.50
M906 Arrogance R	.40	1.00
M907 Leader of the Bloody Mist U	.20	.50
M908 Grossed Out U	.20	.50
M909 Personal Guard R	.40	1.00
M910 The Sand Council SR	6.00	15.00
M911 Pure of Heart R	.40	1.00
M912 Sneak Attack U	.20	.50
M913 Village Heroes C	.10	.25
N1423 Neji Hyuga C	.10	.25
N1424 Ino Yamanaka C	.10	.25
N1425 Shikamaru Nara C	.10	.25
N1426 Tenten C	.10	.25
N1427 Choji Akimichi ST	.10	.25
N1428 Shikamaru Nara ST	.40	1.00
N1429 Hinata Hyuga ST	.75	2.00
N1430 Zetsu U	.20	.50
N1431 Deidara U	.20	.50
N1432 Akatsuchi R	.40	1.00
N1433 Yamato R	.40	1.00
N1434 Kurotsuchi R	.40	1.00
N1435 The 3rd Tsuchikage SR	8.00	20.00
N1436 Bartender Cat C	.10	.25
N1437 Chainya C	.10	.25
N1438 Sabiru R	.40	1.00
N1439 Sasuke Uchiha C	.10	.25
N1440 Kiba Inuzuka C	.10	.25
N1441 Tobi C	.10	.25
N1442 Hidan U	.20	.50
N1443 Sasuke Uchiha U	.20	.50
N1444 Kakashi Hatake R	.40	1.00
N1445 Itachi Uchiha R	.40	1.00
N1446 The 3rd Hokage SR	12.00	30.00
N1447 Four Tails R	.40	1.00
N1448 Io C	.10	.25
N1449 Shoseki C	.10	.25
N1450 Rock Lee C	.10	.25
N1451 Mabui U	.20	.50
N1452 Ink Mouse U	.20	.50
N1453 Naruto Uzumaki ST	.10	.25
N1454 Sai U	.20	.50
N1455 Cee U	.20	.50
N1456 Might Guy U	.20	.50
N1457 Darui R	.40	1.00
N1458 Ink Bat R	.40	1.00
N1459 The 4th Raikage SR	10.00	25.00
N1460 The Nine-Tailed Fox Spirit R	.40	1.00
N1461 Mist Anbu C	.10	.25
N1462 Suiu C	.10	.25
N1463 Jirobo C	.10	.25
N1464 Tayuya C	.10	.25
N1465 Kidomaru C	.10	.25
N1466 Sakon C	.10	.25
N1467 Jugo (State 1) C	.10	.25
N1468 Suigetsu Hozuki U	.20	.50
N1469 Chojuro U	.20	.50
N1470 Ao R	.40	1.00
N1471 The 5th Mizukage SR	15.00	40.00
N1472 Orochimaru R	.40	1.00
N1473 Zhandou C	.10	.25
N1474 Epidemic Prevention Officer C	.10	.25
N1475 Tonton C	.10	.25
N1476 Shino Aburame C	.10	.25
N1477 Sakura Haruno C	.10	.25
N1478 Temari C	.10	.25
N1479 Sand Anbu U	.20	.50
N1480 Shizune U	.20	.50
N1481 Kankuro ST	.20	.50
N1482 Scorpion R	.40	1.00
N1483 Seven Tails R	.40	1.00
N1484 Temari ST	.40	1.00
N1485 The 5th Kazekage SR	12.00	30.00
N1486 Ino Yamanaka, Shikamaru Nara, and Choji Akimichi STSR	2.00	5.00
N1487 Kankuro, Temari, and Gaara of the Desert STSR	1.50	4.00

2012 Naruto Sage's Legacy

Card	Low	High
Complete Set (120)		
Booster Box (24 Packs)		
Booster Pack (10 Cards)		
J895 Tailed Beast Sealing R	.40	1.00
J896 Gentle Fist U	.20	.50
J897 Bravery C	.10	.25
J898 Gentle Step: Twin Lion Fists SR	.40	1.00
J899 Mangekyo Sharingan R	.40	1.00
J900 Shadow Windmill C	.10	.25
J901 Crow Clone U	.20	.50
J902 Amaterasu SR	4.00	10.00
J903 Sage Art: Frog Call C	.10	.25
J904 Sage Jutsu: Rasengan Barrage R	.75	2.00
J905 Frog Kumite U	.20	.50
J906 Sage Art: Giant Rasengan R	1.00	2.50
J907 Wind Style: Rasen-Shuriken SR	4.00	10.00
J908 Chidori Lance U	.20	.50
J909 Striking Shadow Snake C	.10	.25
J910 Water Style: Exploding Water Shockwave C	.10	.25
J911 Chakra Stealing C	.10	.25
J912 Bug Shield U	.20	.50
J913 Chakra Scalpel C	.10	.25
J914 Wind Style: Pressure Damage R	.40	1.00
J915 Palm Healing U	.20	.50
J916 Pinned Down U	.20	.50
J917 Chakra Disturbance U	.20	.50
J918 Chakra Drain C	.10	.25
J919 Catastrophic Planetary Devastation SR	5.00	12.00
J920 Demonic Dragon R	.40	1.00
M855 The Hyuga Clan R	1.00	2.50
M856 Determination to Protect U	.20	.50
M857 A Matter of Love R	.40	1.00
M858 Troubling Sign U	.20	.50
M859 The Nara Clan R	.75	2.00
M860 Hyuga Training C	.10	.25
M861 The Inuzuka Clan R	.40	1.00
M862 Leader of the Cats U	.20	.50
M863 The Uchiha Clan R	.40	1.00
M864 Insanity R	.40	1.00
M865 The Strongest One R	.40	1.00
M866 Guardians of the Village R	.40	1.00
M867 Musings of a Hermit U	.20	.50
M868 Nice Guy Pose U	.20	.50
M869 Burden of Hatred C	.10	.25
M870 A Father In Dark Times U	.20	.50
M871 Shadows of the Past SR	3.00	8.00
M872 Angering the Beast R	1.00	2.50
M873 Organization of Peace R	.40	1.00
M874 An Impossible Situation R	.40	1.00
M875 Final Goodbye U	.20	.50
M876 Training in the Rain U	.20	.50
M877 Reminisce R	.75	2.00
M878 The Aburame Clan R	.40	1.00
M879 Chakra Transmission U	.20	.50
M880 Secret Book U	.20	.50
M881 Gedo: Art of Rinne Rebirth SR	3.00	8.00
M882 The True Pain U	.20	.50
M883 Awakening U	.20	.50
N1358 Choji Akimichi C	.10	.25
N1359 Shikamaru Nara C	.10	.25
N1360 Hinata Hyuga C	.10	.25
N1361 Ino Yamanaka C	.10	.25
N1362 TenTen C	.10	.25
N1363 Shikamaru Nara R	.75	2.00
N1364 Zetsu C	.10	.25
N1365 Two Tails U	.20	.50
N1366 Foo U	.20	.50
N1367 Hinata Hyuga SR	10.00	25.00
N1368 Yamato R	1.00	2.50
N1369 Deidara R	.75	2.00
N1370 The First Hokage R	.40	1.00
N1371 Cat Guard C	.10	.25
N1372 Katazu C	.10	.25
N1373 Sasuke Uchiha C	.10	.25
N1374 Kiba Inuzuka C	.10	.25
N1375 Akamaru C	.10	.25
N1376 Pakkun R	.40	1.00
N1377 Tobi C	.10	.25
N1378 Sasuke Uchiha U	.20	.50
N1379 Double Headed Wolf R	.40	1.00
N1380 Kakashi Hatake U	.20	.50
N1381 Itachi Uchiha R	.75	2.00
N1382 Hidan R	.40	1.00
N1383 The 6th Hokage SR	.40	1.00
N1384 Naruto Uzumaki C	.10	.25
N1385 Sekiei C	.10	.25
N1386 Ink Fish C	.10	.25
N1387 Konohamaru C	.10	.25
N1388 Naruto Uzumaki C	.10	.25
N1389 Karui C	.10	.25
N1390 Omoi U	.20	.50
N1391 Ink Eagle U	.20	.50
N1392 Samui R	2.00	5.00
N1393 Gamahiro R	.40	1.00
N1394 Naruto Uzumaki and Jiraiya R	1.50	4.00
N1395 Naruto Uzumaki SR	35.00	70.00
N1396 Naruto Uzumaki R	3.00	8.00
N1397 Unagi C	.10	.25
N1398 Kandachi C	.10	.25
N1399 Karin C	.10	.25
N1400 Jirobo C	.10	.25
N1401 Jugo C	.10	.25
N1402 Suigetsu C	.10	.25
N1403 Haku U	.20	.50
N1404 Five-Tails R	2.50	6.00
N1405 Kimimaro SR	4.00	10.00
N1406 Kisame Hoshigaki U	.20	.50
N1407 Zabuza Momochi U	.20	.50
N1408 Kisame Hoshigaki and Zetsu R	1.50	4.00

❑ N1409 The Second Hokage R	.40	1.00
❑ N1410 Hanare C	.10	.25
❑ N1411 Furufuki C	.10	.25
❑ N1412 Shino Aburame C	.10	.25
❑ N1413 Sakura Haruno C	.10	.25
❑ N1414 Temari C	.10	.25
❑ N1415 Father and Mother C	.10	.25
❑ N1416 Shizune C	.10	.25
❑ N1417 Torune U	.20	.50
❑ N1418 Chiyo R	.75	2.00
❑ N1419 Kurenai Yuhi R	.40	1.00
❑ N1420 Sasori R	.75	2.00
❑ N1421 Tsunade SR	6.00	15.00
❑ N1422 Pain SR	3.00	8.00

2012 Naruto Tournament Pack 4

COMPLETE SET (60)	20.00	40.00
BOOSTER BOX	40.00	80.00
BOOSTER PACK	3.00	5.00
❑ C019 Futaba C	.10	.25
❑ C032 Teyaki Uchiha U	.20	.50
❑ C048 Takamaru C	.10	.25
❑ C059 Giant Eagle R	.40	1.00
❑ J021 Earth Style: Headhunter Jutsu C	.10	.25
❑ J214 Application of the First Stage U	.20	.50
❑ J268 Sand Tsunami R	.40	1.00
❑ J462 Sealing Jutsu: Nine Phantom Dragons C	.10	.25
❑ J890 Formidable Team U	.20	.50
❑ J891 Subdue C	.10	.25
❑ J892 Taijutsu Suit U	.10	.25
❑ J893 Chakra Eater Sword U	.20	.50
❑ J894 Healing U	.20	.50
❑ M080 Sakura's Decision R	.60	1.50
❑ M092 Tide of the Deadly Combat R	.40	1.00
❑ M847 Generations U	.20	.50
❑ M848 Shikamaru's Decision R	5.00	12.00
❑ M849 Eyes of the Betrayer U	.20	.50
❑ M850 Race! C	.10	.25
❑ M851 Dango U	1.50	4.00
❑ M852 Mysterious Warrior SR	2.50	6.00
❑ M853 Twining Limbs C	.10	.25
❑ M854 Genjutsu Adept U	.20	.50
❑ N320 Orochimaru R	.40	1.00
❑ N365 Itachi Uchiha R	.40	1.00
❑ N424 Konohamaru C	.10	.25
❑ N454 Kisame Hoshigaki R	.40	1.00
❑ N488 Chiyo R	.40	1.00
❑ N560 Neji Hyuga R	.40	1.00
❑ N595 Ino Yamanaka C	.10	.25
❑ N635 Choji Akimichi C	.10	.25
❑ N657 Shino Aburame C	.10	.25
❑ N658 Hinata Hyuga C	.10	.25
❑ N675 Kakashi Hatake R	.40	1.00
❑ N711 Obito Uchiha SR	5.00	12.00
❑ N1335 Tenten C	.10	.25
❑ N1336 Neji Hyuga C	.10	.25
❑ N1337 Deidara SR	1.25	3.00
❑ N1338 Sasuke Uchiha C	.10	.25
❑ N1339 Tobi U	.20	.50
❑ N1340 Naruto Uzumaki SR	2.50	6.00
❑ N1341 Rock Lee U	.20	.50
❑ N1342 Iruka Umino C	.10	.25
❑ N1343 Sai U	.20	.50
❑ N1344 Jiraiya R	.40	1.00
❑ N1345 The 4th Hokage R	.40	1.00
❑ N1346 Yukimaru C	.10	.25
❑ N1347 Kabuto Yakushi U	.30	.75
❑ N1348 Gozu C	.10	.25
❑ N1349 Rinji C	.10	.25
❑ N1350 Guren SR	3.00	8.00
❑ N1351 Sasuke Uchiha C	.10	.25
❑ N1352 Rin C	.10	.25
❑ N1353 Utakata C	.10	.25
❑ N1354 Ebisu C	.10	.25
❑ N1355 Sakura Haruno SR	12.00	30.00
❑ N1356 Shizune U	.20	.50
❑ N1357 Gaara of the Desert R	.40	1.00
❑ JUS065 Chidori R	.40	1.00
❑ PRUS010 Sakura Haruno U	.20	.50

2013 Naruto Ultimate Ninja Storm 3

Booster Box (24 Packs)	60.00	90.00
Booster Pack (10 Cards)	3.50	4.50
❑ J1002 Golem Technique C	.10	.25
❑ J1003 Lava Style: Quicklime Congealing Jutsu C	.10	.25
❑ J1004 Particle Style: Atomic Dismantling C	.10	.25
❑ J1005 8 Trigrams 64 Palms C	.10	.25
❑ J1006 Cat Fire Bowl R	1.00	2.50
❑ J1007 Shattered Heaven SR	3.00	8.00
❑ J1008 Great Blazing Eruption R	1.00	2.50
❑ J1009 Flame Control Sword R	1.00	2.50
❑ J1010 Yasaka Magatama C	.10	.25
❑ J1011 Summoning: Gedo Statue R	.40	1.00
❑ J1012 Hirudora C	.10	.25
❑ J1013 Hell Stab: One-Finger Spear Hand U	.20	.50
❑ J1014 Tailed Beast Bomb SR	25.00	50.00
❑ J1015 Gale Style: Black Hunting C	.10	.25
❑ J1016 Bashosen's Power C	.10	.25
❑ J1017 Benihisago's Power C	.10	.25
❑ J1018 Five-Mountain Jump U	.20	.50
❑ J1019 Rough Sea Spume U	.20	.50
❑ J1020 Ninja Art: Sickle Fog Jutsu C	.10	.25
❑ J1021 Summoning: Reanimation SR	4.00	10.00
❑ J1022 Freight Bubbles U	.20	.50
❑ J1023 Phosphorus Blast U	.20	.50
❑ J1024 Sand Tsunami C	.10	.25
❑ J1025 Hidden Jutsu: Insect Bog C	.10	.25
❑ J1026 Full Blossom: Cherry Blossom Clash R	.60	1.50
❑ J1027 Spirit of the Samurai U	.20	.50
❑ J1028 Helmetsplitter's Rush C	.10	.25
❑ J1029 Fang's Rush C	.10	.25
❑ J1030 Sewing Needle's Rush U	.20	.50
❑ J1031 Master of the 7 Swords R	.75	2.00
❑ J1032 Needle Senbon C	.10	.25
❑ J1033 Spatter's Rush C	.10	.25
❑ M976 Zetsu Army C	.20	.50
❑ M977 Super Sized C	.10	.25
❑ M978 Bloodline Selection U	.20	.50
❑ M979 Masterful User R	.40	1.00
❑ M980 Digging One's Grave C	.10	.25
❑ M981 Strength of Conviction U	.20	.50
❑ M982 Destructive Duo R	.60	1.50
❑ M983 Vengeful Spirit C	.10	.25
❑ M984 Heroic Spirit C	.10	.25
❑ M985 Eight Inner Gates R	.60	1.50
❑ M986 Clash of Ideals SR	5.00	12.00
❑ M987 Lightning Speed U	.20	.50
❑ M988 Axis of Evil U	.20	.50
❑ M989 Bloodline Limit C	.10	.25
❑ M990 Hiding in the Mist U	.20	.50
❑ M991 Indomitable Strength C	.20	.50
❑ M992 Empassioned Speech R	.40	1.00
❑ M993 4 Man Squad C	.10	.25
❑ M994 Furious Tempest R	1.00	2.50
❑ M995 Tailed Beast Transformation R	.75	2.00
❑ M996 Gathering the Beasts U	.40	1.00
❑ M997 Mist's Greatest Swordsmen C	.20	.50
❑ M998 Ninja Alliance SR	3.00	8.00
❑ N1621 Choji Akimichi C	.20	.50
❑ N1622 Ino Yamanaka C	.10	.25
❑ N1623 Tenten C	.10	.25
❑ N1624 Hinata Hyuga C	.10	.25
❑ N1625 Shikamaru Nara C	.10	.25
❑ N1626 Two Tails C	.10	.25
❑ N1627 Neji Hyuga C	.10	.25
❑ N1628 Akatsuchi C	.10	.25
❑ N1629 Kurotsuchi U	.20	.50
❑ N1630 The 3rd Tsuchikage R	.50	1.25
❑ N1631 Kakashi Hatake (Boyhood) C	.20	.50
❑ N1632 Kiba Inuzuka C	.10	.25
❑ N1633 Obito Uchiha C	.10	.25
❑ N1634 Four Tails U	.20	.50
❑ N1635 Kakashi Hatake R	.50	1.25
❑ N1636 Sasuke Uchiha R	2.00	5.00
❑ N1637 Danzo U	.20	.50
❑ N1638 Tobi SR	10.00	25.00
❑ N1639 Rock Lee C	.10	.25
❑ N1640 Cee C	.10	.25
❑ N1641 Naruto Uzumaki C	.10	.25
❑ N1642 Sai C	.10	.25
❑ N1643 Killer Bee R	.50	1.25
❑ N1644 Darui U	.20	.50
❑ N1645 The 4th Raikage R	.60	1.50
❑ N1646 Naruto Uzumaki (9 Tails Cloak) SR	25.00	50.00
❑ N1647 Kabuto Yakushi R	2.00	5.00
❑ N1648 Three Tails U	.40	1.00
❑ N1649 Chojuro U	.20	.50
❑ N1650 Kisame Hoshigaki U	.20	.50
❑ N1651 Ao C	.10	.25
❑ N1652 Five Tails U	.20	.50
❑ N1653 The 5th Mizukage R	1.00	2.50
❑ N1654 Shino Aburame C	.10	.25
❑ N1655 Sakura Haruno SR	6.00	15.00
❑ N1656 Kankuro C	.10	.25
❑ N1657 Six Tails R	1.00	2.50
❑ N1658 Seven Tails R	1.25	3.00
❑ N1659 Temari U	.20	.50
❑ N1660 The 5th Kazekage R	.75	2.00
❑ N1661 Haku C	.10	.25
❑ N1662 Utakata C	.10	.25
❑ N1663 Fuu C	1.00	2.50
❑ N1664 Jinin Akebino C	.20	.50
❑ N1665 Jinpachi Munashi C	.20	.50
❑ N1666 Ameyuri Ringo C	.20	.50
❑ N1667 Kushimaru Kuriarare U	.20	.50
❑ N1668 Mangetsu Hozuki SR	8.00	20.00
❑ N1669 Zabuza Momochi U	.20	.50
❑ N1670 Fuguki Suikazan R	.40	1.00
❑ N1671 Kinkaku C	.10	.25
❑ N1672 Ginkaku C	.10	.25
❑ N1673 Asuma Sarutobi C	.10	.25
❑ N1674 Yugito Nii C	.10	.25
❑ N1675 Han C	.20	.50
❑ N1676 Roshi C	.10	.25
❑ N1677 Itachi Uchiha U	.20	.50
❑ N1678 Mifune SR	12.00	30.00
❑ N1679 The 2nd Tsuchikage U	.40	1.00
❑ N1680 The 3rd Raikage R	.75	2.00
❑ N1681 The 4th Kazekage U	.20	.50
❑ N1682 Yagura C	.20	.50
❑ N1683 Nagato SR	12.00	30.00
❑ N1684 Hanzo The Salamander U	.20	.50
❑ N1685 Madara Uchiha SR	10.00	25.00

1999 Pokemon Base 1st Edition

Complete Set (102)	125.00	250.00
Booster Box (36 ct)	350.00	700.00
Booster Pack (11 cards)	15.00	25.00
*Shadowless Border: .75X to 1.5X Base Card		
❑ 1 Alakazam (holo) (R)	15.00	30.00
❑ 2 Blastoise (holo) (R)	20.00	40.00
❑ 3 Chansey (holo) (R)	10.00	20.00
❑ 4 Charizard (holo) (R)	150.00	300.00
❑ 5 Clefairy (holo) (R)	10.00	25.00
❑ 6 Gyarados (holo) (R)	20.00	40.00
❑ 7 Hitmonchan (holo) (R)	10.00	20.00
❑ 8 Machamp (holo) (R)	3.00	8.00
❑ 9 Magneton (holo) (R)	12.00	25.00
❑ 10 Mewtwo (holo) (R)	20.00	40.00
❑ 11 Nidoking (holo) (R)	10.00	18.00
❑ 12 Ninetales (holo) (R)	18.00	25.00
❑ 13 Poliwrath (holo) (R)	12.00	22.00
❑ 14 Raichu (holo) (R)	15.00	25.00
❑ 15 Venusaur (holo) (R)	20.00	50.00
❑ 16 Zapdos (holo) (R)	15.00	22.00
❑ 17 Beedrill (R)	3.00	7.00
❑ 18 Dragonair (R)	3.00	7.00
❑ 19 Dugtrio (R)	3.00	7.00
❑ 20 Electabuzz (R)	4.00	8.00
❑ 21 Electrode (R)	3.00	6.00
❑ 22 Pidgeotto (R)	4.00	8.00
❑ 23 Arcanine (U)	1.00	2.00
❑ 24 Charmeleon (U)	1.00	2.00
❑ 25 Dewgong (U)	1.00	2.00
❑ 26 Dratini (U)	1.00	1.00
❑ 27 Farfetch'd (U)	1.00	2.00
❑ 28 Growlithe (U)	1.00	2.00
❑ 29 Haunter (U)	1.00	2.00
❑ 30 Ivysaur (U)	1.00	2.00
❑ 31 Jynx (U)	1.00	2.00
❑ 32 Kadabra (U)	1.00	2.50
❑ 33 Kakuna (UER) (U)	1.00	3.50
❑ 34 Machoke (U)	1.00	2.00
❑ 35 Magikarp (U)	1.00	2.00
❑ 36 Magmar (U)	1.00	2.00
❑ 37 Nidorino (U)	1.00	2.00
❑ 38 Poliwhirl (U)	1.00	2.00
❑ 39 Porygon (U)	1.00	2.00
❑ 40 Raticate (U)	1.00	2.00
❑ 41 Seel (U)	1.00	2.00
❑ 42 Wartortle (U)	1.00	2.00
❑ 43 Abra (C)	.30	.75
❑ 44 Bulbasaur (UER) (C)	2.00	4.00
❑ 45 Caterpie (UER) (C)	1.00	3.00
❑ 46 Charmander (C)	.30	1.00
❑ 47 Diglett (C)	.30	.75
❑ 48 Doduo (C)	.30	.75
❑ 49 Drowzee (C)	.30	.75
❑ 50 Gastly (C)	.30	.75
❑ 51 Koffing (C)	.30	.75
❑ 52 Machop (C)	.30	.75
❑ 53 Magnemite (C)	.30	.75
❑ 54 Metapod (UER) (C)	1.00	3.00
❑ 55 Nidoran (C)	.30	.75
❑ 56 Onix (C)	.30	.75
❑ 57 Pidgey (C)	.30	.75
❑ 58 Pikachu (Red cheeks Error) (C)	7.00	12.00
❑ 58 Pikachu (Yellow cheeks Corr.) (C)	2.00	4.00
❑ 59 Poliwag (C)	.30	.75
❑ 60 Ponyta (C)	.30	.75
❑ 61 Rattata (C)	.30	.75
❑ 62 Sandshrew (C)	.30	.75
❑ 63 Squirtle (C)	.30	1.00
❑ 64 Starmie (C)	.30	.75
❑ 65 Staryu (C)	.30	.75
❑ 66 Tangela (C)	.30	.75
❑ 67 Voltorb (UER) (C)	1.50	4.00
❑ 68 Vulpix (UER) (C)	1.00	2.50
❑ 69 Weedle (C)	.30	.75
❑ 70 Clefairy Doll (R)	3.00	6.00
❑ 71 Computer Search (R)	6.00	12.00
❑ 72 Devolution Spray (R)	3.00	6.00
❑ 73 Impostor Professor Oak (R)	3.00	6.00
❑ 74 Item Finder (R)	3.00	6.00
❑ 75 Lass (R)	3.00	6.00
❑ 76 Pokémon Breeder (R)	3.00	6.00
❑ 77 Pokémon Trader (R)	3.00	6.00
❑ 78 Scoop Up (R)	3.00	6.00
❑ 79 Super Energy Removal (R)	8.00	15.00
❑ 80 Defender (U)	1.00	2.00
❑ 81 Energy Retrieval (U)	1.00	2.00
❑ 82 Full Heal (U)	1.00	2.00
❑ 83 Maintenance (U)	1.00	2.00
❑ 84 Plus Power (U)	1.00	2.00
❑ 85 Pokemon Center (U)	1.00	2.00
❑ 86 Pokemon Flute (U)	1.00	2.00
❑ 87 Pokédex (U)	1.00	2.00
❑ 88 Professor Oak (U)	1.00	2.00
❑ 89 Revive (U)	1.00	2.00
❑ 90 Super Potion (U)	1.00	2.00
❑ 91 Bill (C)	.30	.75
❑ 92 Energy Removal (C)	.30	.75
❑ 93 Gust of Wind (C)	.30	.75
❑ 94 Potion (C)	.30	.75
❑ 95 Switch (C)	.30	.75
❑ 96 Double Colorless Energy (U)	.50	1.00
❑ 97 Fighting Energy	.30	.75
❑ 98 Fire Energy	.30	.75
❑ 99 Grass Energy	.30	.75
❑ 100 Lightning Energy	.30	.75
❑ 101 Psychic Energy	.30	.75
❑ 102 Water Energy	.30	.75

1999 Pokemon Base Unlimited

Complete Set (101)	65.00	118.00
Complete Set (w/Machamp) (102)	50.00	100.00
Booster Box (36 ct)	120.00	190.00
Booster Pack (11 cards)	4.00	7.00
Starter Set (60 cards)	10.00	18.00
Blackout Deck (60 cards)	6.00	12.00
Brushfire Deck (60 cards)	6.00	12.00
OverGrowth Deck (60 cards)	6.00	12.00
Zap Deck (60 cards)	6.00	12.00
*Shadowless Border: 1X to 2X Base Card		
Card 8 Machamp only in Starter Decks		
❑ 1 Alakazam (holo) (R)	3.00	6.00
❑ 2 Blastoise (holo) (R)	7.00	15.00
❑ 3 Chansey (holo) (R)	2.00	4.00
❑ 4 Charizard (holo) (R)	12.00	25.00
❑ 5 Clefairy (holo) (R)	3.00	6.00
❑ 6 Gyarados (holo) (R)	3.00	6.00
❑ 7 Hitmonchan (holo) (R)	3.00	7.00
❑ 8 Machamp (holo) (R) 1st Ed. Only	3.00	5.00
❑ 9 Magneton (holo) (R)	2.00	4.00
❑ 10 Mewtwo (holo) (R)	4.00	8.00
❑ 11 Nidoking (holo) (R)	3.00	6.00
❑ 12 Ninetales (holo) (R)	2.00	6.00
❑ 13 Poliwrath (holo) (R)	3.00	6.00
❑ 14 Raichu (holo) (R)	3.00	7.00
❑ 15 Venusaur (holo) (R)	3.00	10.00
❑ 16 Zapdos (holo) (R)	3.00	6.00
❑ 17 Beedrill (R)	1.00	2.00
❑ 18 Dragonair (R)	1.00	2.00
❑ 19 Dugtrio (R)	1.00	2.00
❑ 20 Electabuzz (R)	1.00	2.00
❑ 21 Electrode (R)	1.00	2.00
❑ 22 Pidgeotto (R)	1.00	2.00
❑ 23 Arcanine (U)	.25	1.00
❑ 24 Charmeleon (U)	.25	1.00
❑ 25 Dewgong (U)	.25	1.00
❑ 26 Dratini (U)	.25	1.00
❑ 27 Farfetch'd (U)	.25	1.00
❑ 28 Growlithe (U)	.25	1.00
❑ 29 Haunter (U)	.25	1.00
❑ 30 Ivysaur (U)	.25	1.00
❑ 31 Jynx (U)	.50	1.00
❑ 32 Kadabra (U)	.50	1.00
❑ 33 Kakuna (Length/Length Error) (U)	1.00	2.00
❑ 33 Kakuna (Length/Weight Corr.) (U)	.50	1.00
❑ 34 Machoke (U)	.50	1.00
❑ 35 Magikarp (U)	.50	1.00
❑ 36 Magmar (U)	.50	1.00
❑ 37 Nidorino (U)	.50	1.00
❑ 38 Poliwhirl (U)	.50	1.00
❑ 39 Porygon (U)	.50	1.00
❑ 40 Raticate (U)	.50	1.00
❑ 41 Seel (U)	.50	1.00
❑ 42 Wartortle (U)	.50	1.00
❑ 43 Abra (C)	.10	.30
❑ 44 Bulbasaur (Length/Weight Corr.) (C)	.25	.50
❑ 44 Bulbasaur (Length/Length Error) (C)	1.00	2.00
❑ 45 Caterpie (40 HP Corr.) (C)	.25	.50
❑ 45 Caterpie (HP 40 Error) (C)	1.00	2.00
❑ 46 Charmander (C)	.10	.30
❑ 47 Diglett (C)	.10	.30
❑ 48 Doduo (C)	.10	.30
❑ 49 Drowzee (C)	.10	.30
❑ 50 Gastly (C)	.10	.30
❑ 51 Koffing (C)	.10	.30
❑ 52 Machop (C)	.10	.30
❑ 53 Magnemite (C)	.10	.30
❑ 54 Metapod (HP 70 Error) (C)	1.00	2.00
❑ 54 Metapod (70 HP Corr.) (C)	.25	.50
❑ 55 Nidoran (C)	.10	.30
❑ 56 Onix (C)	.10	.30
❑ 57 Pidgey (C)	.10	.30
❑ 58 Pikachu (Red cheeks Error) (C)	3.00	7.00
❑ 58 Pikachu (Yellow cheeks Corr.) (C)	.50	1.00
❑ 59 Poliwag (C)	.10	.30
❑ 60 Ponyta (C)	.10	.30
❑ 61 Rattata (C)	.10	.30
❑ 62 Sandshrew (C)	.10	.30
❑ 63 Squirtle (C)	.10	.30
❑ 64 Starmie (C)	.10	.30
❑ 65 Staryu (C)	.10	.30
❑ 66 Tangela (C)	.10	.30
❑ 67 Voltorb (Monster Ball Error) (C)	1.00	2.00
❑ 67 Voltorb (Poké Ball Corr.) (C)	.25	.50
❑ 68 Vulpix (UER) (C)	.50	1.00
❑ 69 Weedle (C)	.10	.30
❑ 70 Clefairy Doll (R)	.50	1.00
❑ 71 Computer Search (R)	2.00	4.00
❑ 72 Devolution Spray (R)	.50	1.00
❑ 73 Impostor Professor Oak (R)	.50	1.00
❑ 74 Item Finder (R)	.50	1.00
❑ 75 Lass (R)	.50	1.00
❑ 76 Pokémon Breeder (R)	.50	1.00
❑ 77 Pokémon Trader (R)	.50	1.00
❑ 78 Scoop Up (R)	.50	1.00
❑ 79 Super Energy Removal (R)	.50	1.00
❑ 80 Defender (U)	.50	1.00
❑ 81 Energy Retrieval (U)	.50	1.00
❑ 82 Full Heal (U)	.50	1.00
❑ 83 Maintenance (U)	.50	1.00
❑ 84 Plus Power (U)	.50	1.00
❑ 85 Pokémon Center (U)	.50	1.00
❑ 86 Pokémon Flute (U)	.50	1.00
❑ 87 Pokédex (U)	.50	1.00
❑ 88 Professor Oak (U)	.50	1.00
❑ 89 Revive (U)	.50	1.00
❑ 90 Super Potion (U)	.50	1.00
❑ 91 Bill (C)	.10	.30
❑ 92 Energy Removal (C)	.10	.30
❑ 93 Gust of Wind (C)	.10	.30
❑ 94 Potion (C)	.10	.30
❑ 95 Switch (C)	.10	.30
❑ 96 Double Colorless Energy (U)	.50	1.00
❑ 97 Fighting Energy (C)	.10	.25
❑ 98 Fire Energy (C)	.10	.25
❑ 99 Grass Energy (C)	.10	.25
❑ 100 Lightning Energy (C)	.10	.25
❑ 101 Psychic Energy (C)	.10	.25
❑ 102 Water Energy (C)	.10	.25

1999 Pokemon Jungle 1st Edition

Complete Set (64)	75.00	100.00
Booster Box (36 ct)	85.00	128.00
Booster Pack (11 cards)	3.75	6.00
❑ 1 Clefable (holo) (R)	3.00	7.00
❑ 2 Electrode (holo) (R)	3.00	7.00
❑ 3 Flareon (holo) (R)	4.00	7.00
❑ 4 Jolteon (holo) (R)	3.00	7.00
❑ 5 Kangaskhan (holo) (R)	3.00	7.00
❑ 6 Mime (holo) (R)	3.00	7.00
❑ 7 Nidoqueen (holo) (R)	5.00	7.00
❑ 8 Pidgeot (holo) (R)	3.00	7.00
❑ 9 Pinsir (holo) (R)	3.00	7.00
❑ 10 Scyther (holo) (R)	3.00	7.00
❑ 11 Snorlax (holo) (R)	3.00	7.00
❑ 12 Vaporeon (holo) (R)	3.00	7.00
❑ 13 Venomoth (holo) (R)	3.00	7.00
❑ 14 Victreebel (holo) (R)	3.00	7.00
❑ 15 Vileplume (holo) (R)	3.00	7.00
❑ 16 Wigglytuff (holo) (R)	6.00	12.00
❑ 17 Clefable (R)	3.00	6.00
❑ 18 Electrode (UER) (R)	2.00	4.00
❑ 19 Flareon (R)	2.00	4.00
❑ 20 Jolteon (R)	2.00	4.00
❑ 21 Kangaskhan (R)	1.00	2.00
❑ 22 Mime (R)	1.00	2.00
❑ 23 Nidoqueen (R)	2.00	4.00
❑ 24 Pidgeot (R)	1.00	2.00
❑ 25 Pinsir (R)	2.00	4.00
❑ 26 Scyther (R)	2.00	4.00
❑ 27 Snorlax (R)	2.00	4.00
❑ 28 Vaporeon (R)	2.00	4.00
❑ 29 Venomoth (R)	1.00	2.00
❑ 30 Victreebel (R)	2.00	4.00
❑ 31 Vileplume (R)	2.00	2.00
❑ 32 Wigglytuff (R)	2.00	4.00
❑ 33 Butterfree ("d" Edition Error) (U)	3.00	6.00
❑ 33 Butterfree (1 Edition Corr.) (U)	2.00	5.00
❑ 34 Dodrio (U)	.30	.75
❑ 35 Exeggutor (U)	.30	.75
❑ 36 Fearow (U)	.30	.75
❑ 37 Gloom (U)	.30	.75
❑ 38 Lickitung (U)	.30	.75
❑ 39 Marowak (U)	.30	.75
❑ 40 Nidorina (U)	.30	.75
❑ 41 Parasect (U)	.30	.75
❑ 42 Persian (U)	.30	.75
❑ 43 Primeape (U)	.30	.75
❑ 44 Rapidash (U)	.30	.75
❑ 45 Rhydon (U)	.30	1.00
❑ 46 Seaking (U)	.30	.75
❑ 47 Tauros (U)	.30	.75
❑ 48 Weepinbell (U)	.30	.75
❑ 49 Bellsprout (C)	.25	.50
❑ 50 Cubone (C)	.25	.50
❑ 51 Eevee (C)	.25	.50
❑ 52 Exeggcute (C)	.25	.50
❑ 53 Goldeen (C)	.25	.50
❑ 54 Jigglypuff (C)	.25	.50
❑ 55 Mankey (C)	.25	.50
❑ 56 Meowth (C)	.25	.50
❑ 57 Nidoran-F (C)	.25	.50
❑ 58 Oddish (C)	.25	.50
❑ 59 Paras (C)	.25	.50
❑ 60 Pikachu (C)	1.00	2.00
❑ 61 Rhyhorn (C)	.25	.50
❑ 62 Spearow (C)	.25	.50
❑ 63 Venonat (C)	.25	.50
❑ 64 Trainer: Poké Ball (C)	.25	.50

1999 Pokemon Jungle Unlimited

Complete Set (64)	40.00	60.00
Booster Box (36 ct)	60.00	95.00
Booster Pack (11 cards)	2.00	3.50
Power Reserve Deck (60 cards)	8.00	13.00
Water Blast Deck (60 cards)	8.00	13.00
Holo Errors are missing Jungle Logo		
❑ 1 Clefable (holo) (R)	2.00	4.00
❑ 1 Clefable (holo) (R) (Error)	3.00	6.00
❑ 2 Electrode (holo) (R)	2.00	5.00
❑ 2 Electrode (holo) (R) (Error)	3.00	6.00
❑ 3 Flareon (holo) (R)	2.00	5.00
❑ 3 Flareon (holo) (R) (Error)	3.00	6.00
❑ 4 Jolteon (holo) (R)	2.00	5.00
❑ 4 Jolteon (holo) (R) (Error)	3.00	6.00
❑ 5 Kangaskhan (holo) (R)	2.00	4.00
❑ 5 Kangaskhan (holo) (R) (Error)	3.00	6.00
❑ 6 Mr. Mime (holo) (R)	2.00	4.00

TCG/CCG

❑ 6 Mr Mime (holo) (R) (Error)	3.00	6.00
❑ 7 Nidoqueen (holo) (R)	2.00	5.00
❑ 7 Nidoqueen (holo) (R) (Error)	3.00	6.00
❑ 8 Pidgeot (holo) (R)	2.00	4.00
❑ 8 Pidgeot (holo) (R) (Error)	3.00	6.00
❑ 9 Pinsir (holo) (R)	2.00	4.00
❑ 9 Pinsir (holo) (R) (Error)	3.00	6.00
❑ 10 Scyther (holo) (R)	2.00	4.00
❑ 10 Scyther (holo) (R) (Error)	3.00	6.00
❑ 11 Snorlax (holo) (R)	2.00	5.00
❑ 11 Snorlax (holo) (R) (Error)	3.00	6.00
❑ 12 Vaporeon (holo) (R)	2.00	4.00
❑ 12 Vaporeon (holo) (R) (Error)	3.00	6.00
❑ 13 Venomoth (holo) (R)	2.00	5.00
❑ 13 Venomoth (holo) (R) (Error)	3.00	6.00
❑ 14 Victreebel (holo) (R)	2.00	4.00
❑ 14 Victreebel (holo) (R) (Error)	3.00	6.00
❑ 15 Vileplume (holo) (R)	2.00	4.00
❑ 15 Vileplume (holo) (R) (Error)	3.00	6.00
❑ 16 Wigglytuff (holo) (R)	3.00	6.00
❑ 16 Wigglytuff (holo) (R) (Error)	4.00	8.00
❑ 17 Clefable (R)	.50	1.00
❑ 18 Electrode (R)	.50	1.00
❑ 19 Flareon (R)	.50	1.00
❑ 20 Jolteon (R)	.50	1.00
❑ 21 Kangaskhan (R)	.50	1.00
❑ 22 Mr. Mime (R)	.50	1.00
❑ 23 Nidoqueen (R)	.50	1.00
❑ 24 Pidgeot (R)	.50	1.00
❑ 25 Pinsir (R)	.50	1.00
❑ 26 Scyther (R)	.50	1.00
❑ 27 Snorlax (R)	.50	1.00
❑ 28 Vaporeon (R)	.50	1.00
❑ 29 Venomoth (R)	.50	1.00
❑ 30 Victreebel (R)	.50	1.00
❑ 31 Vileplume (R)	.50	1.00
❑ 32 Wigglytuff (R)	.50	1.00
❑ 33 Butterfree (U)	.20	.50
❑ 34 Dodrio (U)	.20	.50
❑ 35 Exeggutor (U)	.20	.50
❑ 36 Fearow (U)	.20	.50
❑ 37 Gloom (U)	.20	.50
❑ 38 Lickitung (U)	.20	.50
❑ 39 Marowak (U)	.20	.50
❑ 40 Nidorina (U)	.20	.50
❑ 41 Parasect (U)	.20	.50
❑ 42 Persian (U)	.20	.50
❑ 43 Primeape (U)	.20	.50
❑ 44 Rapidash (U)	.20	.50
❑ 45 Rhydon (U)	.20	.50
❑ 46 Seaking (U)	.20	.50
❑ 47 Tauros (U)	.20	.50
❑ 48 Weepinbell (U)	.20	.50
❑ 49 Bellsprout (C)	.10	.25
❑ 50 Cubone (C)	.10	.25
❑ 51 Eevee (C)	.10	.25
❑ 52 Exeggcute (C)	.10	.25
❑ 53 Goldeen (C)	.10	.25
❑ 54 Jigglypuff (C)	.10	.25
❑ 55 Mankey (C)	.10	.25
❑ 56 Meowth (C)	.10	.25
❑ 57 Nidoran-F (C)	.10	.25
❑ 58 Oddish (C)	.10	.25
❑ 59 Paras (C)	.10	.25
❑ 60 Pikachu (C)	.50	1.00
❑ 61 Rhyhorn (C)	.10	.25
❑ 62 Spearow (C)	.10	.25
❑ 63 Venonat (C)	.10	.25
❑ 64 Trainer: Poké Ball (C)	.10	.25

1999 Pokemon Fossil 1st Edition

Complete Set (62)	60.00	90.00
Booster Box (36 ct)	90.00	120.00
Booster Pack (11 cards)	3.00	6.00
❑ 1 Aerodactyl (holo) (R)	4.00	10.00
❑ 2 Articuno (holo) (R)	9.00	15.00
❑ 3 Ditto (holo) (R)	3.00	7.00
❑ 4 Dragonite (holo) (R)	5.00	9.00
❑ 5 Gengar (holo) (R)	3.00	7.00
❑ 6 Haunter (holo) (R)	3.00	7.00
❑ 7 Hitmonlee (holo) (R)	3.00	7.00
❑ 8 Hypno (holo) (R)	3.00	7.00
❑ 9 Kabutops (holo) (R)	5.00	10.00
❑ 10 Lapras (holo) (R)	3.00	7.00
❑ 11 Magneton (holo) (R)	2.00	5.00
❑ 12 Moltres (holo) (R)	4.00	9.00
❑ 13 Muk (holo) (R)	2.00	5.00
❑ 14 Raichu (holo) (R)	3.00	8.00
❑ 15 Zapdos (holo) (R)	4.00	7.00
❑ 16 Aerodactyl (R)	2.00	4.00
❑ 17 Articuno (R)	2.00	4.00
❑ 18 Ditto (R)	.50	1.00
❑ 19 Dragonite (R)	2.00	4.00
❑ 20 Gengar (R)	2.00	4.00
❑ 21 Haunter (R)	.50	1.00
❑ 22 Hitmonlee (R)	.50	1.00
❑ 23 Hypno (R)	.50	1.00
❑ 24 Kabutops (R)	.50	1.00
❑ 25 Lapras (R)	.50	1.00
❑ 26 Magneton (R)	.50	1.00
❑ 27 Moltres (R)	2.00	4.00
❑ 28 Muk (R)	.50	1.00
❑ 29 Raichu (R)	.50	1.00
❑ 30 Zapdos (R)	.50	1.50
❑ 31 Arbok (U)	.30	.75
❑ 32 Cloyster (U)	.30	.75
❑ 33 Gastly (U)	.30	.75
❑ 34 Golbat (U)	.30	.75
❑ 35 Golduck (U)	.30	.75
❑ 36 Golem (U)	.30	.75
❑ 37 Graveler (U)	.30	.75
❑ 38 Kingler (U)	.30	.75
❑ 39 Magmar (U)	.30	.75
❑ 40 Omastar (U)	.30	.75
❑ 41 Sandslash (U)	.30	.75
❑ 42 Seadra (U)	.30	.75
❑ 43 Slowbro (U)	.30	.75
❑ 44 Tentacruel (U)	.30	.75
❑ 45 Weezing (U)	.30	.75
❑ 46 Ekans (C)	.25	.50
❑ 47 Geodude (C)	.25	.50
❑ 48 Grimer (C)	.25	.50
❑ 49 Horsea (C)	.25	.50
❑ 50 Kabuto (C)	.25	.50
❑ 51 Krabby (C)	.25	.50
❑ 52 Omanyte (C)	.25	.50
❑ 53 Psyduck (C)	.25	.50
❑ 54 Shellder (C)	.25	.50
❑ 55 Slowpoke (C)	.25	.50
❑ 56 Tentacool (C)	.25	.50
❑ 57 Zubat (C)	.25	.50
❑ 58 Old Man Fuji (U)	.30	.75
❑ 59 Energy Search (C)	.25	.50
❑ 60 Gambler (C)	.25	.50
❑ 61 Recycle (C)	.25	.50
❑ 62 Mysterious Fossil (C)	.25	.50

1999 Pokemon Fossil Unlimited

Complete Set (62)	36.00	50.00
Booster Box (36 ct)	70.00	96.00
Booster Pack (11 cards)	3.00	4.00
Bodyguard Deck (60)	6.00	12.00
Lock Down Deck (60)	6.00	12.00
❑ 1 Aerodactyl (holo) (R)	2.00	6.00
❑ 2 Articuno (holo) (R)	4.00	10.00
❑ 3 Ditto (holo) (R)	3.00	6.00
❑ 4 Dragonite (holo) (R)	2.00	4.00
❑ 5 Gengar (holo) (R)	2.00	4.00
❑ 6 Haunter (holo) (R)	2.00	4.00
❑ 7 Hitmonlee (holo) (R)	2.00	5.00
❑ 8 Hypno (holo) (R)	2.00	4.00
❑ 9 Kabutops (holo) (R)	3.00	5.00
❑ 10 Lapras (holo) (R)	2.00	4.00
❑ 11 Magneton (holo) (R)	1.00	2.00
❑ 12 Moltres (holo) (R)	3.00	6.00
❑ 13 Muk (holo) (R)	2.00	4.00
❑ 14 Raichu (holo) (R)	2.00	5.00
❑ 15 Zapdos (holo) (R)	2.00	5.00
❑ 16 Aerodactyl (R)	1.00	2.00
❑ 17 Articuno (R)	2.00	4.00
❑ 18 Ditto (R)	.50	1.00
❑ 19 Dragonite (R)	2.00	4.00
❑ 20 Gengar (R)	1.00	2.00
❑ 21 Haunter (R)	.50	1.00
❑ 22 Hitmonlee (R)	.50	1.00
❑ 23 Hypno (R)	.50	1.00
❑ 24 Kabutops (R)	.50	1.00
❑ 25 Lapras (R)	.50	1.00
❑ 26 Magneton (R)	.50	1.00
❑ 27 Moltres (R)	2.00	4.00
❑ 28 Muk (R)	.50	1.00
❑ 29 Raichu (R)	.50	1.00
❑ 30 Zapdos (R)	.50	1.00
❑ 31 Arbok (U)	.20	.50
❑ 32 Cloyster (U)	.20	.50
❑ 33 Gastly (U)	.20	.50
❑ 34 Golbat (U)	.20	.50
❑ 35 Golduck (U)	.20	.50
❑ 36 Golem (U)	.20	.50
❑ 37 Graveler (U)	.20	.50
❑ 38 Kingler (U)	.20	.50
❑ 39 Magmar (U)	.20	.50
❑ 40 Omastar (U)	.20	.50
❑ 41 Sandslash (U)	.20	.50
❑ 42 Seadra (U)	.20	.50
❑ 43 Slowbro (U)	.20	.50
❑ 44 Tentacruel (U)	.20	.50
❑ 45 Weezing (U)	.20	.50
❑ 46 Ekans (C)	.10	.25
❑ 47 Geodude (C)	.10	.25
❑ 48 Grimer (C)	.10	.25
❑ 49 Horsea (C)	.10	.25
❑ 50 Kabuto (C)	.10	.25
❑ 51 Krabby (C)	.10	.25
❑ 52 Omanyte (C)	.10	.25
❑ 53 Psyduck (C)	.10	.25
❑ 54 Shellder (C)	.10	.25
❑ 55 Slowpoke (C)	.10	.25
❑ 56 Tentacool (C)	.10	.25
❑ 57 Zubat (C)	.10	.25
❑ 58 Old Man Fuji (U)	.20	.50
❑ 59 Energy Search (C)	.10	.25
❑ 60 Gambler (C)	.10	.25
❑ 61 Recycle (C)	.10	.25
❑ 62 Mysterious Fossil (C)	.10	.25

2000 Pokemon Base 2 Unlimited

Complete Set (130)	50.00	80.00
Booster Box (36 ct)	70.00	95.00
Booster Pack (11 cards)	2.00	4.00
Grass Chopper Deck (60)	6.00	12.00
Hot Water Deck (60)	9.00	12.00
Lightning Bug Deck (60)	6.00	10.00
Psych Out Deck (60)	9.00	12.00
❑ 1 Alakazam (holo) (R)	2.00	4.00
❑ 2 Blastoise (holo) (R)	8.00	14.00
❑ 3 Chansey (holo) (R)	2.00	4.00
❑ 4 Charizard (holo) (R)	10.00	20.00
❑ 5 Clefable (holo) (R)	1.00	3.00
❑ 6 Clefairy (holo) (R)	1.00	3.00
❑ 7 Gyarados (holo) (R)	2.00	4.00
❑ 8 Hitmonchan (holo) (R)	2.00	4.00
❑ 9 Magneton (holo) (R)	2.00	4.00
❑ 10 Mewtwo (holo) (R)	2.00	4.00
❑ 11 Nidoking (holo) (R)	2.00	4.00
❑ 12 Nidoqueen (holo) (R)	2.00	4.00
❑ 13 Ninetales (holo) (R)	2.00	4.00
❑ 14 Pidgeot (holo) (R)	2.00	4.00
❑ 15 Poliwrath (holo) (R)	2.00	4.00
❑ 16 Raichu (holo) (R)	2.00	4.00
❑ 17 Scyther (holo) (R)	2.00	4.00
❑ 18 Venusaur (holo) (R)	5.00	10.00
❑ 19 Wigglytuff (holo) (R)	2.00	4.00
❑ 20 Zapdos (holo) (R)	2.00	6.00
❑ 21 Beedrill (R)	.50	1.00
❑ 22 Dragonair (R)	.50	1.00
❑ 23 Dugtrio (R)	.50	1.00
❑ 24 Electabuzz (R)	.50	1.00
❑ 25 Electrode (R)	.50	1.00
❑ 26 Kangaskhan (R)	.50	1.00
❑ 27 Mr. Mime (R)	.50	1.00
❑ 28 Pidgeotto (R)	.50	1.00
❑ 29 Pinsir (R)	.50	1.00
❑ 30 Snorlax (R)	.50	1.00
❑ 31 Venomoth (R)	.50	1.00
❑ 32 Victreebel (R)	.50	1.00
❑ 33 Arcanine (U)	.25	.50
❑ 34 Butterfree (U)	.25	.50
❑ 35 Charmeleon (U)	.25	.50
❑ 36 Dewgong (U)	.25	.50
❑ 37 Dodrio (U)	.25	.50
❑ 38 Dratini (U)	.25	.50
❑ 39 Exeggutor (U)	.25	.50
❑ 40 Farfetch'd (U)	.25	.50
❑ 41 Fearow (U)	.25	.50
❑ 42 Growlithe (U)	.25	.50
❑ 43 Haunter (U)	.25	.50
❑ 44 Ivysaur (U)	.25	.50
❑ 45 Jynx (U)	.25	.50
❑ 46 Kadabra (U)	.25	.50
❑ 47 Kakuna (U)	.25	.50
❑ 48 Lickitung (U)	.25	.50
❑ 49 Machoke (U)	.25	.50
❑ 50 Magikarp (U)	.25	.50
❑ 51 Magmar (U)	.25	.50
❑ 52 Marowak (U)	.25	.50
❑ 53 Nidorina (U)	.25	.50
❑ 54 Nidorino (U)	.25	.50
❑ 55 Parasect (U)	.25	.50
❑ 56 Persian (U)	.25	.50
❑ 57 Poliwhirl (U)	.25	.50
❑ 58 Raticate (U)	.25	.50
❑ 59 Rhydon (U)	.25	.50
❑ 60 Seaking (U)	.25	.50
❑ 61 Seel (U)	.25	.50
❑ 62 Tauros (U)	.25	.50
❑ 63 Wartortle (U)	.25	.50
❑ 64 Weepinbell (U)	.25	.50
❑ 65 Abra (C)	.10	.25
❑ 66 Bellsprout (C)	.10	.25
❑ 67 Bulbasaur (C)	.10	.25
❑ 68 Caterpie (C)	.10	.25
❑ 69 Charmander (C)	.10	.25
❑ 70 Cubone (C)	.10	.25
❑ 71 Diglett (C)	.10	.25
❑ 72 Doduo (C)	.10	.25
❑ 73 Drowzee (C)	.10	.25
❑ 74 Exeggcute (C)	.10	.25
❑ 75 Gastly (C)	.10	.25
❑ 76 Goldeen (C)	.10	.25
❑ 77 Jigglypuff (C)	.10	.25
❑ 78 Machop (C)	.10	.25
❑ 79 Magnemite (C)	.10	.25
❑ 80 Meowth (C)	.10	.25
❑ 81 Metapod (C)	.10	.25
❑ 82 Nidoran-F (C)	.10	.25
❑ 83 Nidoran-M (C)	.10	.25
❑ 84 Onix (C)	.10	.25
❑ 85 Paras (C)	.10	.25
❑ 86 Pidgey (C)	.10	.25
❑ 87 Pikachu (C)	.50	1.00
❑ 88 Poliwag (C)	.10	.25
❑ 89 Rattata (C)	.10	.25
❑ 90 Rhyhorn (C)	.10	.25
❑ 91 Sandshrew (C)	.10	.25
❑ 92 Spearow (C)	.10	.25
❑ 93 Squirtle (C)	.10	.25
❑ 94 Starmie (C)	.10	.25
❑ 95 Staryu (C)	.10	.25
❑ 96 Tangela (C)	.10	.25
❑ 97 Venonat (C)	.10	.25
❑ 98 Voltorb (C)	.10	.25
❑ 99 Vulpix (C)	.10	.25
❑ 100 Weedle (C)	.10	.25
❑ 101 Computer Search (R)	.50	1.00
❑ 102 Imposter Professor Oak (R)	.50	1.00
❑ 103 Item Finder (R)	.50	1.00
❑ 104 Lass (R)	.50	1.00
❑ 105 Pokémon Breeder (R)	.50	1.00
❑ 106 Pokémon Trader (R)	.50	1.00
❑ 107 Scoop Up (R)	.50	1.00
❑ 108 Super Energy Removal (R)	.50	1.00
❑ 109 Defender (U)	.25	.50
❑ 110 Energy Retrieval (U)	.25	.50
❑ 111 Full Heal (U)	.25	.50
❑ 112 Maintenance (U)	.25	.50
❑ 113 PlusPower (U)	.25	.50
❑ 114 Pokémon Center (U)	.25	.50
❑ 115 Pokédex (U)	.25	.50
❑ 116 Professor Oak (U)	.25	.50
❑ 117 Super Potion (U)	.25	.50
❑ 118 Bill (C)	.10	.25
❑ 119 Energy Removal (C)	.10	.25
❑ 120 Gust of Wind (C)	.10	.25
❑ 121 Poké Ball (C)	.10	.25
❑ 122 Potion (C)	.10	.25
❑ 123 Switch (C)	.10	.25
❑ 124 Double Colorless Energy (U)	.25	.50
❑ 125 Fighting Energy (C)	.10	.25
❑ 126 Fire Energy (C)	.10	.25
❑ 127 Grass Energy (C)	.10	.25
❑ 128 Lightning Energy (C)	.10	.25
❑ 129 Psychic Energy (C)	.10	.25
❑ 130 Water Energy (C)	.10	.25

2000 Pokemon Team Rocket 1st Edition

Complete Set (82)	60.00	85.00
Complete Set w/Raichu (83)	60.00	90.00
Booster Box (36 ct)	78.00	95.00
Booster Pack (11 cards)	3.50	5.00
❑ 1 Dark Alakazam (holo) (R)	4.00	8.00
❑ 2 Dark Arbok (holo) (R) (ERR)	3.00	6.00
❑ 3 Dark Blastoise (holo) (R)	4.00	10.00
❑ 4 Dark Charizard (holo) (R)	10.00	20.00
❑ 5 Dark Dragonite (holo) (R)	5.00	12.00
❑ 6 Dark Dugtrio (holo) (R)	3.00	6.00
❑ 7 Dark Golbat (holo) (R)	3.00	6.00
❑ 8 Dark Gyarados (holo) (R)	3.00	6.00
❑ 9 Dark Hypno (holo) (R)	4.00	10.00
❑ 10 Dark Machamp (holo) (R)	4.00	10.00
❑ 11 Dark Magneton (holo) (R)	6.00	12.00
❑ 12 Dark Slowbro (holo) (R)	3.00	4.00
❑ 13 Dark Vileplume (holo) (R)	4.00	10.00
❑ 14 Dark Weezing (holo) (R)	3.00	6.00
❑ 15 Here Comes Team Rocket (holo) (R)	3.00	6.00
❑ 16 Rocket's Sneak Attack (holo) (R)	3.00	6.00
❑ 17 Rainbow Energy (holo) (R)	3.00	6.00
❑ 18 Dark Alakazam (R)	.50	1.00
❑ 19 Dark Arbok (R) (ERR)	1.00	2.00
❑ 20 Dark Blastoise (R)	1.00	2.00
❑ 21 Dark Charizard (R)	3.00	6.00
❑ 22 Dark Dragonite (R)	1.00	2.00
❑ 23 Dark Dugtrio (R)	.50	1.00
❑ 24 Dark Golbat (R)	.50	1.00
❑ 25 Dark Gyarados (R)	.50	1.00
❑ 26 Dark Hypno (R)	.50	1.00
❑ 27 Dark Machamp (R)	.50	1.00
❑ 28 Dark Magneton (R)	1.00	2.00
❑ 29 Dark Slowbro (R)	.50	1.00
❑ 30 Dark Vileplume (R)	.50	1.00
❑ 31 Dark Weezing (R)	.50	1.00
❑ 32 Dark Charmeleon (U)	.20	.50
❑ 33 Dark Dragonair (U)	.20	.50
❑ 34 Dark Electrode (U)	.20	.50
❑ 35 Dark Flareon (U)	.50	1.00
❑ 36 Dark Gloom (U)	.20	.50
❑ 37 Dark Golduck (U)	.20	.50
❑ 38 Dark Jolteon (U)	.20	.50
❑ 39 Dark Kadabra (U)	.20	.50
❑ 40 Dark Machoke (U)	.20	.50
❑ 41 Dark Muk (U)	.20	.50
❑ 42 Dark Persian (U)	.20	.50
❑ 43 Dark Primeape (U)	.20	.50
❑ 44 Dark Rapidash (U) (ERR)	.75	1.75
❑ 45 Dark Vaporeon (U)	.20	.50
❑ 46 Dark Wartortle (U)	.20	.50
❑ 47 Magikarp (U)	.20	.50
❑ 48 Porygon (U)	.20	.50
❑ 49 Abra (C)	.10	.25
❑ 50 Charmander (C)	.10	.25
❑ 51 Dark Raticate (C)	.10	.25
❑ 52 Diglett (C)	.10	.25
❑ 53 Dratini (C)	.10	.25
❑ 54 Drowzee (C)	.10	.25
❑ 55 Eevee (C)	.10	.25
❑ 56 Ekans (C)	.10	.25
❑ 57 Grimer (C)	.10	.25
❑ 58 Koffing (C)	.10	.25
❑ 59 Machop (C)	.10	.25
❑ 60 Magnemite (C)	.10	.25
❑ 61 Mankey (C)	.10	.25
❑ 62 Meowth (C)	.10	.25
❑ 63 Oddish (C)	.10	.25
❑ 64 Ponyta (C)	.10	.25
❑ 65 Psyduck (C)	.10	.25
❑ 66 Rattata (C)	.10	.25
❑ 67 Slowpoke (C)	.10	.25
❑ 68 Squirtle (C)	.10	.25
❑ 69 Voltorb (C)	.10	.25
❑ 70 Zubat (C)	.10	.25
❑ 71 Here Comes Team Rocket (R)	2.00	4.00
❑ 72 Rocket's Sneak Attack (R)	.50	1.00
❑ 73 The Boss's Way (U)	.20	.50
❑ 74 Challenge (U)	.20	.50
❑ 75 Digger (U)	.20	.50
❑ 76 Imposter Oak's Revenge (U)	.20	.50
❑ 77 Nightly Garbage Run (U)	.20	.50
❑ 78 Gas Attack (C)	.10	.25
❑ 79 Sleep (C)	.10	.25
❑ 80 Rainbow Energy (R)	.50	1.00
❑ 81 Full Heal Energy (U)	.20	.50
❑ 82 Potion Energy (U)	.20	.50
❑ 83 Dark Raichu (holo) (R) (ERR)	3.00	7.00

2000 Pokemon Team Rocket Unlimited

Complete Set (82)	40.00	55.00
Complete Set w/Raichu (83)	40.00	60.00
Booster Box (36 ct)	65.00	85.00
Booster Pack (11 cards)	2.50	3.50
Theme Deck (60 cards)	8.00	15.00
❑ 1 Dark Alakazam (holo) (R)	2.00	4.00
❑ 2 Dark Arbok (holo) (R) (ERR)	2.00	4.00
❑ 3 Dark Blastoise (holo) (R)	3.00	4.00
❑ 4 Dark Charizard (holo) (R)	6.00	12.00
❑ 5 Dark Dragonite (holo) (R)	3.00	6.00
❑ 6 Dark Dugtrio (holo) (R)	2.00	4.00
❑ 7 Dark Golbat (holo) (R)	2.00	4.00
❑ 8 Dark Gyarados (holo) (R)	1.00	4.00
❑ 9 Dark Hypno (holo) (R)	2.00	4.00
❑ 10 Dark Machamp (holo) (R)	2.00	4.00
❑ 11 Dark Magneton (holo) (R)	2.00	4.00
❑ 12 Dark Slowbro (holo) (R)	2.00	4.00
❑ 13 Dark Vileplume (holo) (R)	2.00	4.00
❑ 14 Dark Weezing (holo) (R)	2.00	4.00
❑ 15 Here Comes Team Rocket (holo) (R)	2.00	4.00
❑ 16 Rocket's Sneak Attack (holo) (R)	2.00	4.00
❑ 17 Rainbow Energy (holo) (R)	2.00	4.00
❑ 18 Dark Alakazam (R)	.50	1.00
❑ 19 Dark Arbok (R) (ERR)	.50	1.00
❑ 20 Dark Blastoise (R)	.50	1.00
❑ 21 Dark Charizard (R)	1.00	3.00
❑ 22 Dark Dragonite (R)	.50	1.00
❑ 23 Dark Dugtrio (R)	.50	1.00
❑ 24 Dark Golbat (R)	.50	1.00
❑ 25 Dark Gyarados (R)	.50	1.00
❑ 26 Dark Hypno (R)	.50	1.00
❑ 27 Dark Machamp (R)	.50	1.00
❑ 28 Dark Magneton (R)	.50	1.00
❑ 29 Dark Slowbro (R)	.50	1.00
❑ 30 Dark Vileplume (R)	.50	1.00
❑ 31 Dark Weezing (R)	.50	1.00
❑ 32 Dark Charmeleon (U)	.20	.50
❑ 33 Dark Dragonair (U)	.20	.50
❑ 34 Dark Electrode (U)	.20	.50
❑ 35 Dark Flareon (U)	.20	.50
❑ 36 Dark Gloom (U)	.20	.50
❑ 37 Dark Golduck (U)	.20	.50
❑ 38 Dark Jolteon (U)	.20	.50
❑ 39 Dark Kadabra (U)	.20	.50
❑ 40 Dark Machoke (U)	.20	.50
❑ 41 Dark Muk (U)	.20	.50
❑ 42 Dark Persian (U)	.20	.50
❑ 43 Dark Primeape (U)	.20	.50
❑ 44 Dark Rapidash (U) (ERR)	.50	1.00
❑ 45 Dark Vaporeon (U)	.20	.50
❑ 46 Dark Wartortle (U)	.20	.50
❑ 47 Magikarp (U)	.20	.50
❑ 48 Porygon (U)	.20	.50
❑ 49 Abra (C)	.10	.25
❑ 50 Charmander (C)	.10	.25
❑ 51 Dark Raticate (C)	.10	.25
❑ 52 Diglett (C)	.10	.25
❑ 53 Dratini (C)	.10	.25
❑ 54 Drowzee (C)	.10	.25
❑ 55 Eevee (C)	.10	.25
❑ 56 Ekans (C)	.10	.25
❑ 57 Grimer (C)	.10	.25
❑ 58 Koffing (C)	.10	.25
❑ 59 Machop (C)	.10	.25
❑ 60 Magnemite (C)	.10	.25
❑ 61 Mankey (C)	.10	.25
❑ 62 Meowth (C)	.10	.25
❑ 63 Oddish (C)	.10	.25
❑ 64 Ponyta (C)	.10	.25
❑ 65 Psyduck (C)	.10	.25
❑ 66 Rattata (C)	.10	.25
❑ 67 Slowpoke (C)	.10	.25
❑ 68 Squirtle (C)	.10	.25
❑ 69 Voltorb (C)	.10	.25
❑ 70 Zubat (C)	.10	.25
❑ 71 Here Comes Team Rocket (R)	.50	1.00
❑ 72 Rocket's Sneak Attack (R)	.50	1.00
❑ 73 The Boss's Way (U)	.20	.50
❑ 74 Challenge (U)	.20	.50
❑ 75 Digger (U)	.20	.50
❑ 76 Imposter Oak's Revenge (U)	.20	.50
❑ 77 Nightly Garbage Run (U)	.20	.50
❑ 78 Gas Attack (C)	.10	.25
❑ 79 Sleep (C)	.10	.25
❑ 80 Rainbow Energy (R)	.50	1.00
❑ 81 Full Heal Energy (U)	.20	.50
❑ 82 Potion Energy (U)	.20	.50
❑ 83 Dark Raichu (holo) (R) (ERR)	3.00	6.00

2000 Pokemon Gym Heroes 1st Edition

Complete Set (132)	70.00	100.00
Unopened Box (36 ct)	85.00	125.00
Unopened Pack (11 cards)	3.00	5.00
1 Blaine's Moltres (holo) (R)	3.00	7.00
2 Brock's Rhydon (holo) (R)	3.00	6.00
3 Erika's Clefable (holo) (R)	3.00	6.00
4 Erika's Dragonair (holo) (R)	3.00	6.00
5 Erika's Vileplume (holo) (R)	3.00	6.00
6 Lt. Surge's Electabuzz (holo) (R)	3.00	6.00
7 Lt. Surge's Fearow (holo) (R)	3.00	6.00
8 Lt. Surge's Magneton (holo) (R)	3.00	6.00
9 Misty's Seadra (holo) (R)	3.00	5.00
10 Misty's Tentacruel (holo) (R)	3.00	6.00
11 Rocket's Hitmonchan (holo) (R)	3.00	5.00
12 Rocket's Moltres (holo) (R)	4.00	8.00
13 Rocket's Scyther (holo) (R)	4.00	8.00
14 Sabrina's Gengar (holo) (R)	3.00	6.00
15 Brock (holo) (R)	2.00	4.00
16 Erika (holo) (R)	3.00	6.00
17 Lt. Surge (holo) (R)	3.00	6.00
18 Misty (holo) (R)	3.00	6.00
19 The Rocket's Trap (holo) (R)	3.00	6.00
20 Brock's Golem (R)	1.00	2.00
21 Brock's Onix (R)	.50	1.00
22 Brock's Rhyhorn (R)	.50	1.00
23 Brock's Sandslash (R)	.50	1.00
24 Brock's Zubat (R)	.50	1.00
25 Erika's Clefairy (R)	.50	1.00
26 Erika's Victreebel (R)	.50	1.00
27 Lt. Surge's Electabuzz (R)	.50	1.00
28 Lt. Surge's Raichu (R)	1.00	3.00
29 Misty's Cloyster (R)	.50	1.00
30 Misty's Goldeen (R)	.50	1.00
31 Misty's Poliwrath (R)	.50	1.00
32 Misty's Tentacool (R)	.50	1.00
33 Rocket's Snorlax (R)	1.00	2.00
34 Sabrina's Venomoth (R)	1.00	2.00
35 Blaine's Growlithe (U)	.20	.50
36 Blaine's Kangaskhan (U)	.20	.50
37 Blaine's Magmar (U)	.20	.50
38 Brock's Geodude (U)	.20	.50
39 Brock's Golbat (U)	.20	.50
40 Brock's Graveler (U)	.20	.50
41 Brock's Lickitung (U)	.20	.50
42 Erika's Dratini (U)	.20	.50
43 Erika's Exeggcute (U)	.20	.50
44 Erika's Exeggutor (U)	.20	.50
45 Erika's Gloom (U)	.20	.50
46 Erika's Gloom (U)	.20	.50
47 Erika's Oddish (U)	.20	.50
48 Erika's Weepinbell (U)	.20	.50
49 Erika's Weepinbell (U)	.20	.50
50 Lt. Surge's Magnemite (U)	.20	.50
51 Lt. Surge's Raticate (U)	.20	.50
52 Lt. Surge's Spearow (U)	.20	.50
53 Misty's Poliwhirl (U)	.20	.50
54 Misty's Psyduck (U)	.20	.50
55 Misty's Seaking (U)	.20	.50
56 Misty's Starmie (U)	.20	.50
57 Misty's Tentacool (U)	.20	.50
58 Sabrina's Haunter (U)	.20	.50
59 Sabrina's Jynx (U)	.20	.50
60 Sabrina's Slowbro (U)	.20	.50
61 Blaine's Charmander (C)	.10	.25
62 Blaine's Growlithe (C)	.10	.25
63 Blaine's Ponyta (C)	.10	.25
64 Blaine's Tauros (C)	.10	.25
65 Blaine's Vulpix (C)	.10	.25
66 Brock's Geodude (C)	.10	.25
67 Brock's Mankey (C)	.10	.25
68 Brock's Mankey (C)	.10	.25
69 Brock's Onix (C)	.10	.25
70 Brock's Rhyhorn (C)	.10	.25
71 Brock's Sandshrew (C)	.10	.25
72 Brock's Sandshrew (C)	.10	.25
73 Brock's Vulpix (C)	.10	.25
74 Brock's Zubat (C)	.10	.25
75 Erika's Bellsprout (C)	.10	.25
76 Erika's Bellsprout (C)	.10	.25
77 Erika's Exeggcute (C)	.10	.25
78 Erika's Oddish (C)	.10	.25
79 Erika's Tangela (C)	.10	.25
80 Lt. Surge's Magnemite (C)	.10	.25
81 Lt. Surge's Pikachu (C)	.50	1.25
82 Lt. Surge's Rattata (C)	.10	.25
83 Lt. Surge's Spearow (C)	.10	.25
84 Lt. Surge's Voltorb (C)	.10	.25
85 Misty's Goldeen (C)	.10	.25
86 Misty's Horsea (C)	.10	.25
87 Misty's Poliwag (C)	.10	.25
88 Misty's Seel (C)	.10	.25
89 Misty's Shellder (C)	.10	.25
90 Misty's Staryu (C)	.10	.25
91 Sabrina's Abra (C)	.10	.25
92 Sabrina's Drowzee (C)	.10	.25
93 Sabrina's Gastly (C)	.10	.25
94 Sabrina's Mr. Mime (C)	.10	.25
95 Sabrina's Slowpoke (C)	.10	.25
96 Sabrina's Venonat (C)	.10	.25
97 Blaine's Quiz #1 (R)	.50	1.00
98 Brock (R)	.50	1.00
99 Charity (R)	1.00	2.00
100 Erika (R)	.50	1.00
101 Lt. Surge (R)	.50	1.00
102 Misty (R)	.50	1.00
103 No Removal Gym (R)	.50	1.00
104 The Rocket's Gym (R)	1.00	2.00
105 Blaine's Last Resort (U)	.20	.50
106 Brock's Training Method (U)	.20	.50
107 Celadon City Gym (U)	.20	.50
108 Cerulean City Gym (U)	.20	.50
109 Erika's Maids (U)	.20	.50
110 Erika's Perfume (U)	.20	.50
111 Good Manners (U)	.20	.50
112 Lt. Surge's Treaty (U)	.20	.50
113 Minion of Team Rocket (U)	.20	.50
114 Misty's Wrath (U)	.20	.50
115 Pewter City Gym (U)	.20	.50
116 Recall (U)	.20	.50
117 Sabrina's ESP (U)	.20	.50
118 Secret Mission (U)	.20	.50
119 Tickling Machine (U)	.20	.50
120 Vermillion City Gym (U)	.20	.50
121 Blaine's Gamble (C)	.10	.25
122 Energy Flow (C)	.10	.25
123 Misty's Duel (C)	.10	.25
124 Narrow Gym (C)	.10	.25
125 Sabrina's Gaze (C)	.10	.25
126 Trash Exchange (C)	.10	.25
127 Fighting Energy (C)	.10	.25
128 Fire Energy (C)	.10	.25
129 Grass Energy (C)	.10	.25
130 Lightning Energy (C)	.10	.25
131 Psychic Energy (C)	.10	.25
132 Water Energy (C)	.10	.25

2000 Pokemon Gym Heroes Unlimited

Complete Set (132)	40.00	55.00
Unopened Box (36 ct)	50.00	80.00
Unopened Pack (11 cards)	2.00	4.00
1 Blaine's Moltres (holo) (R)	3.00	6.00
2 Brock's Rhydon (holo) (R)	2.00	4.00
3 Erika's Clefable (holo) (R)	2.00	4.00
4 Erika's Dragonair (holo) (R)	1.00	3.00
5 Erika's Vileplume (holo) (R)	1.00	3.00
6 Lt. Surge's Electabuzz (holo) (R)	2.00	4.00
7 Lt. Surge's Fearow (holo) (R)	2.00	4.00
8 Lt. Surge's Magneton (holo) (R)	2.00	4.00
9 Misty's Seadra (holo) (R)	2.00	4.00
10 Misty's Tentacruel (holo) (R)	2.00	4.00
11 Rocket's Hitmonchan (holo) (R)	2.00	4.00
12 Rocket's Moltres (holo) (R)	2.00	4.00
13 Rocket's Scyther (holo) (R)	2.00	4.00
14 Sabrina's Gengar (holo) (R)	2.00	4.00
15 Brock (holo) (R)	2.00	4.00
16 Erika (holo) (R)	1.00	3.00
17 Lt. Surge (holo) (R)	2.00	4.00
18 Misty (holo) (R)	1.00	4.00
19 The Rocket's Trap (holo) (R)	2.00	4.00
20 Brock's Golem (R)	.50	1.00
21 Brock's Onix (R)	.50	1.00
22 Brock's Rhyhorn (R)	.50	1.00
23 Brock's Sandslash (R)	.50	1.00
24 Brock's Zubat (R)	.50	1.00
25 Erika's Clefairy (R)	.50	1.00
26 Erika's Victreebel (R)	.50	1.00
27 Lt. Surge's Electabuzz (R)	.50	1.00
28 Lt. Surge's Raichu (R)	.50	1.00
29 Misty's Cloyster (R)	.50	1.00
30 Misty's Goldeen (R)	.50	1.00
31 Misty's Poliwrath (R)	.50	1.00
32 Misty's Tentacool (R)	.50	1.00
33 Rocket's Snorlax (R)	.50	1.00
34 Sabrina's Venomoth (R)	.50	1.00
35 Blaine's Growlithe (U)	.20	.50
36 Blaine's Kangaskhan (U)	.20	.50
37 Blaine's Magmar (U)	.20	.50
38 Brock's Geodude (U)	.20	.50
39 Brock's Golbat (U)	.20	.50
40 Brock's Graveler (U)	.20	.50
41 Brock's Lickitung (U)	.20	.50
42 Erika's Dratini (U)	.20	.50
43 Erika's Exeggcute (U)	.20	.50
44 Erika's Exeggutor (U)	.20	.50
45 Erika's Gloom (U)	.20	.50
46 Erika's Gloom (U)	.20	.50
47 Erika's Oddish (U)	.20	.50
48 Erika's Weepinbell (U)	.20	.50
49 Erika's Weepinbell (U)	.20	.50
50 Lt. Surge's Magnemite (U)	.20	.50
51 Lt. Surge's Raticate (U)	.20	.50
52 Lt. Surge's Spearow (U)	.20	.50
53 Misty's Poliwhirl (U)	.20	.50
54 Misty's Psyduck (U)	.20	.50
55 Misty's Seaking (U)	.20	.50
56 Misty's Starmie (U)	.20	.50
57 Misty's Tentacool (U)	.20	.50
58 Sabrina's Haunter (U)	.20	.50
59 Sabrina's Jynx (U)	.20	.50
60 Sabrina's Slowbro (U)	.20	.50
61 Blaine's Charmander (C)	.10	.25
62 Blaine's Growlithe (C)	.10	.25
63 Blaine's Ponyta (C)	.10	.25
64 Blaine's Tauros (C)	.10	.25
65 Blaine's Vulpix (C)	.10	.25
66 Brock's Geodude (C)	.10	.25
67 Brock's Mankey (C)	.10	.25
68 Brock's Mankey (C)	.10	.25
69 Brock's Onix (C)	.10	.25
70 Brock's Rhyhorn (C)	.10	.25
71 Brock's Sandshrew (C)	.10	.25
72 Brock's Sandshrew (C)	.10	.25
73 Brock's Vulpix (C)	.10	.25
74 Brock's Zubat (C)	.10	.25
75 Erika's Bellsprout (C)	.10	.25
76 Erika's Bellsprout (C)	.10	.25
77 Erika's Exeggcute (C)	.10	.25
78 Erika's Oddish (C)	.10	.25
79 Erika's Tangela (C)	.10	.25
80 Lt. Surge's Magnemite (C)	.10	.25
81 Lt. Surge's Pikachu (C)	.25	.50
82 Lt. Surge's Rattata (C)	.10	.25
83 Lt. Surge's Spearow (C)	.10	.25
84 Lt. Surge's Voltorb (C)	.10	.25
85 Misty's Goldeen (C)	.10	.25
86 Misty's Horsea (C)	.10	.25
87 Misty's Poliwag (C)	.10	.25
88 Misty's Seel (C)	.10	.25
89 Misty's Shellder (C)	.10	.25
90 Misty's Staryu (C)	.10	.25
91 Sabrina's Abra (C)	.10	.25
92 Sabrina's Drowzee (C)	.10	.25
93 Sabrina's Gastly (C)	.10	.25
94 Sabrina's Mr. Mime (C)	.10	.25
95 Sabrina's Slowpoke (C)	.10	.25
96 Sabrina's Venonat (C)	.10	.25
97 Blaine's Quiz #1 (R)	.50	1.00
98 Brock (R)	.50	1.00
99 Charity (R)	.50	1.00
100 Erika (R)	.50	1.00
101 Lt. Surge (R)	.50	1.00
102 Misty (R)	.50	1.00
103 No Removal Gym (R)	.50	1.00
104 The Rocket's Gym (R)	.50	1.00
105 Blaine's Last Resort (U)	.20	.50
106 Brock's Training Method (U)	.20	.50
107 Celadon City Gym (U)	.20	.50
108 Cerulean City Gym (U)	.20	.50
109 Erika's Maids (U)	.20	.50
110 Erika's Perfume (U)	.20	.50
111 Good Manners (U)	.20	.50
112 Lt. Surge's Treaty (U)	.20	.50
113 Minion of Team Rocket (U)	.20	.50
114 Misty's Wrath (U)	.20	.50
115 Pewter City Gym (U)	.20	.50
116 Recall (U)	.20	.50
117 Sabrina's ESP (U)	.20	.50
118 Secret Mission (U)	.20	.50
119 Tickling Machine (U)	.20	.50
120 Vermillion City Gym (U)	.20	.50
121 Blaine's Gamble (C)	.10	.25
122 Energy Flow (C)	.10	.25
123 Misty's Duel (C)	.10	.25
124 Narrow Gym (C)	.10	.25
125 Sabrina's Gaze (C)	.10	.25
126 Trash Exchange (C)	.10	.25
127 Fighting Energy (C)	.10	.25
128 Fire Energy (C)	.10	.25
129 Grass Energy (C)	.10	.25
130 Lightning Energy (C)	.10	.25
131 Psychic Energy (C)	.10	.25
132 Water Energy (C)	.10	.25

2000 Pokemon Gym Challenge 1st Edition

Complete Set (132)	70.00	100.00
Unopened Box (36 ct)	75.00	120.00
Unopened Pack (11 cards)	3.00	4.00
1 Blaine's Arcanine (holo) (R)	4.00	8.00
2 Blaine's Charizard (holo) (R)	6.00	12.00
3 Brock's Ninetales (holo) (R)	3.00	6.00
4 Erika's Venusaur (holo) (R)	4.00	8.00
5 Giovanni's Gyarados (holo) (R)	3.00	6.00
6 Giovanni's Machamp (holo) (R)	3.00	6.00
7 Giovanni's Nidoking (holo) (R)	3.00	6.00
8 Giovanni's Persian (holo) (R)	3.00	6.00
9 Koga's Beedrill (holo) (R)	3.00	6.00
10 Koga's Ditto (holo) (R)	3.00	6.00
11 Lt. Surge's Raichu (holo) (R)	4.00	8.00
12 Misty's Golduck (holo) (R)	3.00	6.00
13 Misty's Gyarados (holo) (R)	3.00	6.00
14 Rocket's Mewtwo (holo) (R)	4.00	8.00
15 Rocket's Zapdos (holo) (R)	3.00	5.00
16 Sabrina's Alakazam (holo) (R)	3.00	6.00
17 Blaine (holo) (R)	3.00	6.00
18 Giovanni (holo) (R)	3.00	6.00
19 Koga (holo) (R)	3.00	6.00
20 Sabrina (holo) (R)	3.00	6.00
21 Blaine's Ninetales (R)	.50	1.00
22 Brock's Dugtrio (R)	.50	1.00
23 Giovanni's Nidoqueen (R)	.50	1.00
24 Giovanni's Pinsir (R)	.50	1.00
25 Koga's Arbok (R)	.50	1.00
26 Koga's Muk (R)	.50	1.00
27 Koga's Pidgeotto (R)	.50	1.00
28 Lt. Surge's Jolteon (R)	.50	1.00
29 Sabrina's Gengar (R)	.50	1.00
30 Sabrina's Golduck (R)	.50	1.00
31 Blaine's Charmeleon (U)	.20	.50
32 Blaine's Dodrio (U)	.20	.50
33 Blaine's Rapidash (U)	.20	.50
34 Brock's Graveler (U)	.20	.50
35 Brock's Primeape (U)	.20	.50
36 Brock's Sandslash (U)	.20	.50
37 Brock's Vulpix (U)	.20	.50
38 Erika's Bellsprout (U)	.20	.50
39 Erika's Bulbasaur (U)	.20	.50
40 Erika's Clefairy (U)	.20	.50
41 Erika's Ivysaur (U)	.20	.50
42 Giovanni's Machoke (U)	.20	.50
43 Giovanni's Meowth (U)	.20	.50
44 Giovanni's Nidorina (U)	.20	.50
45 Giovanni's Nidorino (U)	.20	.50
46 Koga's Golbat (U)	.20	.50
47 Koga's Kakuna (U)	.20	.50
48 Koga's Koffing (U)	.20	.50
49 Koga's Pidgey (U)	.20	.50
50 Koga's Weezing (U)	.20	.50
51 Lt. Surge's Eevee (U)	.20	.50
52 Lt. Surge's Electrode (U)	.20	.50
53 Lt. Surge's Raticate (U)	.20	.50
54 Misty's Dewgong (U)	.20	.50
55 Sabrina's Haunter (U)	.20	.50
56 Sabrina's Hypno (U)	.20	.50
57 Sabrina's Jynx (U)	.20	.50
58 Sabrina's Kadabra (U)	.20	.50
59 Sabrina's Mr. Mime (U)	.20	.50
60 Blaine's Charmander (C)	.10	.25
61 Blaine's Doduo (C)	.10	.25
62 Blaine's Growlithe (C)	.10	.25
63 Blaine's Mankey (C)	.10	.25
64 Blaine's Ponyta (C)	.10	.25
65 Blaine's Rhyhorn (C)	.10	.25
66 Blaine's Vulpix (C)	.10	.25
67 Brock's Diglett (C)	.10	.25
68 Brock's Geodude (C)	.10	.25
69 Erika's Jigglypuff (C)	.10	.25
70 Erika's Oddish (C)	.10	.25
71 Erika's Paras (C)	.10	.25
72 Giovanni's Machop (C)	.10	.25
73 Giovanni's Magikarp (C)	.10	.25
74 Giovanni's Meowth (C)	.10	.25
75 Giovanni's Nidoran (Fem) (C)	.10	.25
76 Giovanni's Nidoran (Male) (C)	.10	.25
77 Koga's Ekans (C)	.10	.25
78 Koga's Grimer (C)	.10	.25
79 Koga's Koffing (C)	.10	.25
80 Koga's Pidgey (C)	.10	.25
81 Koga's Tangela (C)	.10	.25
82 Koga's Weedle (C)	.10	.25
83 Koga's Zubat (C)	.10	.25
84 Lt. Surge's Pikachu (C)	.25	.50
85 Lt. Surge's Rattata (C)	.10	.25
86 Lt. Surge's Voltorb (C)	.10	.25
87 Misty's Horsea (C)	.10	.25
88 Misty's Magikarp (C)	.10	.25
89 Misty's Poliwag (C)	.10	.25
90 Misty's Psyduck (C)	.10	.25
91 Misty's Seel (C)	.10	.25
92 Misty's Staryu (C)	.10	.25
93 Sabrina's Abra (C)	.10	.25
94 Sabrina's Abra (C)	.10	.25
95 Sabrina's Drowzee (C)	.10	.25
96 Sabrina's Gastly (C)	.10	.25
97 Sabrina's Gastly (C)	.10	.25
98 Sabrina's Porygon (C)	.10	.25
99 Sabrina's Psyduck (C)	.10	.25
100 Blaine (R)	.50	1.00
101 Brock's Protection (R)	.50	1.00
102 Chaos Gym (R)	.50	1.00
103 Erika's Kindness (R)	.50	1.00
104 Giovanni (R)	.50	1.00
105 Giovanni's Last Resort (R)	.50	1.00
106 Koga (R)	.50	1.00
107 Lt. Surge's Secret Plan (R)	.50	1.00
108 Misty's Wish (R)	.50	1.00
109 Resistance Gym (R)	.50	1.00
110 Sabrina (R)	.50	1.00
111 Blaine's Quiz #2 (U)	.20	.50
112 Blaine's Quiz #3 (U)	.20	.50
113 Cinnabar City Gym (U)	.20	.50
114 Fuchsia City Gym (U)	.20	.50
115 Koga's Ninja Trick (U)	.20	.50
116 Master Ball (U)	.20	.50
117 Max Revive (U)	.20	.50
118 Misty's Tears (U)	.20	.50
119 Rocket's Minefield Gym (U)	.20	.50
120 Rocket's secret Experiment (U)	.20	.50
121 Sabrina's Psychic Control (U)	.20	.50
122 Saffron City Gym (U)	.20	.50
123 Viridian City Gym (U)	.20	.50
124 Fervor (C)	.10	.25
125 Transparent Walls (C)	.10	.25
126 Warp Point (C)	.10	.25
127 Fighting Energy (C)	.10	.25
128 Fire Energy (C)	.10	.25
129 Grass Energy (C)	.10	.25
130 Lightning Energy (C)	.10	.25
131 Psychic Energy (C)	.10	.25
132 Water Energy (C)	.10	.25

2000 Pokemon Gym Challenge Unlimited

Complete Set (132)	40.00	55.00
Unopened Box (36 ct)	50.00	80.00
Unopened Pack (11 cards)	2.00	3.00
1 Blaine's Arcanine (holo) (R)	1.50	3.00
2 Blaine's Charizard (holo) (R)	5.00	10.00
3 Brock's Ninetales (holo) (R)	2.00	4.00
4 Erika's Venusaur (holo) (R)	2.00	5.00
5 Giovanni's Gyarados (holo) (R)	2.00	4.00
6 Giovanni's Machamp (holo) (R)	2.00	4.00
7 Giovanni's Nidoking (holo) (R)	2.00	4.00
8 Giovanni's Persian (holo) (R)	2.00	4.00
9 Koga's Beedrill (holo) (R)	2.00	4.00
10 Koga's Ditto (holo) (R)	2.00	4.00
11 Lt. Surge's Raichu (holo) (R)	2.00	4.00
12 Misty's Golduck (holo) (R)	2.00	4.00
13 Misty's Gyarados (holo) (R)	2.00	4.00
14 Rocket's Mewtwo (holo) (R)	2.00	4.00
15 Rocket's Zapdos (holo) (R)	2.00	4.00
16 Sabrina's Alakazam (holo) (R)	2.00	4.00
17 Blaine (holo) (R)	2.00	4.00
18 Giovanni (holo) (R)	2.00	4.00
19 Koga (holo) (R)	2.00	4.00
20 Sabrina (holo) (R)	2.00	4.00
21 Blaine's Ninetales (R)	.50	1.00
22 Brock's Dugtrio (R)	.50	1.00
23 Giovanni's Nidoqueen (R)	.50	1.00
24 Giovanni's Pinsir (R)	.50	1.00
25 Koga's Arbok (R)	.50	1.00
26 Koga's Muk (R)	.50	1.00
27 Koga's Pidgeotto (R)	.50	1.00
28 Lt. Surge's Jolteon (R)	.50	1.00
29 Sabrina's Gengar (R)	.50	1.00
30 Sabrina's Golduck (R)	.50	1.00
31 Blaine's Charmeleon (U)	.20	.50
32 Blaine's Dodrio (U)	.20	.50
33 Blaine's Rapidash (U)	.20	.50
34 Brock's Graveler (U)	.20	.50
35 Brock's Primeape (U)	.20	.50
36 Brock's Sandslash (U)	.20	.50
37 Brock's Vulpix (U)	.20	.50
38 Erika's Bellsprout (U)	.20	.50
39 Erika's Bulbasaur (U)	.20	.50
40 Erika's Clefairy (U)	.20	.50
41 Erika's Ivysaur (U)	.20	.50
42 Giovanni's Machoke (U)	.20	.50
43 Giovanni's Meowth (U)	.20	.50
44 Giovanni's Nidorina (U)	.20	.50
45 Giovanni's Nidorino (U)	.20	.50
46 Koga's Golbat (U)	.20	.50
47 Koga's Kakuna (U)	.20	.50
48 Koga's Koffing (U)	.20	.50
49 Koga's Pidgey (U)	.20	.50
50 Koga's Weezing (U)	.20	.50
51 Lt. Surge's Eevee (U)	.20	.50
52 Lt. Surge's Electrode (U)	.20	.50
53 Lt. Surge's Raticate (U)	.20	.50
54 Misty's Dewgong (U)	.20	.50
55 Sabrina's Haunter (U)	.20	.50
56 Sabrina's Hypno (U)	.20	.50
57 Sabrina's Jynx (U)	.20	.50
58 Sabrina's Kadabra (U)	.20	.50
59 Sabrina's Mr. Mime (U)	.20	.50
60 Blaine's Charmander (C)	.10	.20
61 Blaine's Doduo (C)	.10	.20
62 Blaine's Growlithe (C)	.10	.20
63 Blaine's Mankey (C)	.10	.20
64 Blaine's Ponyta (C)	.10	.20
65 Blaine's Rhyhorn (C)	.10	.20
66 Blaine's Vulpix (C)	.10	.20
67 Brock's Diglett (C)	.10	.20
68 Brock's Geodude (C)	.10	.20
69 Erika's Jigglypuff (C)	.10	.20
70 Erika's Oddish (C)	.10	.20
71 Erika's Paras (C)	.10	.20
72 Giovanni's Machop (C)	.10	.20
73 Giovanni's Magikarp (C)	.10	.20
74 Giovanni's Meowth (C)	.10	.20
75 Giovanni's Nidoran (Fem) (C)	.10	.20
76 Giovanni's Nidoran (Male) (C)	.10	.20
77 Koga's Ekans (C)	.10	.20
78 Koga's Grimer (C)	.10	.20
79 Koga's Koffing (C)	.10	.20
80 Koga's Pidgey (C)	.10	.20
81 Koga's Tangela (C)	.10	.20
82 Koga's Weedle (C)	.10	.20
83 Koga's Zubat (C)	.10	.20
84 Lt. Surge's Pikachu (C)	.25	.50
85 Lt. Surge's Rattata (C)	.10	.20
86 Lt. Surge's Voltorb (C)	.10	.20
87 Misty's Horsea (C)	.10	.20
88 Misty's Magikarp (C)	.10	.20
89 Misty's Poliwag (C)	.10	.20
90 Misty's Psyduck (C)	.10	.20
91 Misty's Seel (C)	.10	.20
92 Misty's Staryu (C)	.10	.20
93 Sabrina's Abra (C)	.10	.20
94 Sabrina's Abra (C)	.10	.20
95 Sabrina's Drowzee (C)	.10	.20
96 Sabrina's Gastly (C)	.10	.20
97 Sabrina's Gastly (C)	.10	.20
98 Sabrina's Porygon (C)	.10	.20
99 Sabrina's Psyduck (C)	.10	.20
100 Blaine (R)	.50	1.00
101 Brock's Protection (R)	.50	1.00
102 Chaos Gym (R)	.50	1.00
103 Erika's Kindness (R)	.50	1.00
104 Giovanni (R)	.50	1.00
105 Giovanni's Last Resort (R)	.50	1.00

Card	Low	High
❑ 106 Koga (R)	.50	1.00
❑ 107 Lt. Surge's Secret Plan (R)	.50	1.00
❑ 108 Misty's Wish (R)	.50	1.00
❑ 109 Resistance Gym (R)	.50	1.00
❑ 110 Sabrina (R)	.50	1.00
❑ 111 Blaine's Quiz #2 (U)	.20	.50
❑ 112 Blaine's Quiz #3 (U)	.20	.50
❑ 113 Cinnabar City Gym (U)	.20	.50
❑ 114 Fuchsia City Gym (U)	.20	.50
❑ 115 Koga's Ninja Trick (U)	.20	.50
❑ 116 Master Ball (U)	.20	.50
❑ 117 Max Revive (U)	.20	.50
❑ 118 Misty's Tears (U)	.20	.50
❑ 119 Rocket's Minefield Gym (U)	.20	.50
❑ 120 Rocket's secret Experiment (U)	.20	.50
❑ 121 Sabrina's Psychic Control (U)	.20	.50
❑ 122 Saffron City Gym (U)	.20	.50
❑ 123 Viridian City Gym (U)	.20	.50
❑ 124 Fervor (C)	.10	.20
❑ 125 Transparent Walls (C)	.10	.20
❑ 126 Warp Point (C)	.10	.20
❑ 127 Fighting Energy (C)	.10	.20
❑ 128 Fire Energy (C)	.10	.20
❑ 129 Grass Energy (C)	.10	.20
❑ 130 Lightning Energy (C)	.10	.20
❑ 131 Psychic Energy (C)	.10	.20
❑ 132 Water Energy (C)	.10	.20

2000 Pokemon Neo Genesis 1st Edition

Card	Low	High
Complete Set (111)	85.00	120.00
Booster Box (36 ct)	150.00	215.00
Booster Pack (11 cards)	5.00	7.00
❑ 1 Ampharos (holo) (R)	10.00	17.00
❑ 2 Azumarill (holo) (R)	3.00	6.00
❑ 3 Bellossom (holo) (R)	3.00	7.00
❑ 4 Feraligatr Lv.56 (holo) (R)	5.00	10.00
❑ 5 Feraligatr Lv.69 (holo) (R)	4.00	8.00
❑ 6 Heracross (holo) (R)	3.00	6.00
❑ 7 Jumpluff (holo) (R)	3.00	6.00
❑ 8 Kingdra (holo) (R)	3.00	7.00
❑ 9 Lugia (holo) (R)	12.00	20.00
❑ 10 Meganium Lv.54 (holo) (R)	3.00	6.00
❑ 11 Meganium Lv.57 (holo) (R)	10.00	17.00
❑ 12 Pichu (holo) (R)	5.00	10.00
❑ 13 Skarmory (holo) (R)	3.00	6.00
❑ 14 Slowking (holo) (R)	3.00	6.00
❑ 15 Steelix (holo) (R)	4.00	8.00
❑ 16 Togetic (holo) (R)	3.00	7.00
❑ 17 Typhlosion Lv.55 (holo) (R)	5.00	10.00
❑ 18 Typhlosion Lv.57 (holo) (R)	5.00	10.00
❑ 19 Metal Energy (holo) (R)	3.00	6.00
❑ 20 Cleffa (R)	.50	1.00
❑ 21 Donphan (R)	.50	1.00
❑ 22 Elekid (R)	1.00	1.00
❑ 23 Magby (R)	.50	1.00
❑ 24 Murkrow (R)	.50	1.00
❑ 25 Sneasel (R)	2.00	4.00
❑ 26 Aipom (U)	.20	.50
❑ 27 Ariados (U)	.20	.50
❑ 28 Bayleef Lv.22 (U)	.20	.50
❑ 29 Bayleef Lv.39 (U)	.20	.50
❑ 30 Clefairy (U)	.20	.50
❑ 31 Croconaw Lv.34 (U)	.20	.50
❑ 32 Croconaw Lv.41 (U)	.20	.50
❑ 33 Electabuzz (U)	.20	.50
❑ 34 Flaaffy (U)	.20	.50
❑ 35 Furret (U)	.20	.50
❑ 36 Gloom (U)	.20	.50
❑ 37 Granbull (U)	.20	.50
❑ 38 Lanturn (U)	.20	.50
❑ 39 Ledian (U)	.20	.50
❑ 40 Magmar (U)	.20	.50
❑ 41 Miltank (U)	.20	.50
❑ 42 Noctowl (U)	.20	.50
❑ 43 Phanpy (U)	.20	.50
❑ 44 Piloswine (U)	.20	.50
❑ 45 Quagsire (U)	.20	.50
❑ 46 Quilava Lv.28 (U)	.20	.50
❑ 47 Quilava Lv.35 (U)	.20	.50
❑ 48 Seadra (U)	.20	.50
❑ 49 Skiploom (U)	.20	.50
❑ 50 Sunflora (U)	.20	.50
❑ 51 Togepi (U)	1.00	2.00
❑ 52 Xatu (U)	.20	.50
❑ 53 Chikorita Lv.12 (C)	.10	.25
❑ 54 Chikorita Lv.19 (C)	.10	.25
❑ 55 Chinchou (C)	.10	.25
❑ 56 Cyndaquil Lv.14 (C)	.10	.25
❑ 57 Cyndaquil Lv.21 (C)	.10	.25
❑ 58 Girafarig (C)	.10	.25
❑ 59 Gligar (C)	.10	.25
❑ 60 Hoothoot (C)	.10	.25
❑ 61 Hoppip (C)	.10	.25
❑ 62 Horsea (C)	.10	.25
❑ 63 Ledyba (C)	.10	.25
❑ 64 Mantine (C)	.10	.25
❑ 65 Mareep (C)	.10	.25
❑ 66 Marill (C)	.10	.25
❑ 67 Natu (C)	.10	.25
❑ 68 Oddish (C)	.10	.25
❑ 69 Onix (C)	.10	.25
❑ 70 Pikachu (C)	.50	1.00
❑ 71 Sentret (C)	.10	.25
❑ 72 Shuckle (C)	.10	.25
❑ 73 Slowpoke (C)	.10	.25
❑ 74 Snubbull (C)	.10	.25
❑ 75 Spinarak (C)	.10	.25
❑ 76 Stantler (C)	.10	.25
❑ 77 Sudowoodo (C)	.10	.25
❑ 78 Sunkern (C)	.10	.25
❑ 79 Swinub (C)	.10	.25
❑ 80 Totodile Lv.13 (C)	.10	.25
❑ 81 Totodile Lv.20 (C)	.10	.25
❑ 82 Wooper (C)	.10	.25
❑ 83 Arcade Game (R)	.50	1.00
❑ 84 Ecogym (R)	.50	1.00
❑ 85 Energy Charge (R)	.50	1.00
❑ 86 Focus Band (R)	.50	1.00
❑ 87 Mary (R)	.50	1.00
❑ 88 PokeGear (R)	.50	1.00
❑ 89 Super Energy Retrieval (R)	.50	1.00
❑ 90 Time Capsule (R)	.50	1.00
❑ 91 Bill's Teleporter (U)	.20	.50
❑ 92 Card-Flip Game (U)	.20	.50
❑ 93 Gold Berry (U)	.20	.50
❑ 94 Miracle Berry (U)	.20	.50
❑ 95 New Pokedex (U)	.20	.50
❑ 96 Professor Elm (U)	.20	.50
❑ 97 Sprout Tower (U)	.20	.50
❑ 98 Super Scoop Up (U)	.20	.50
❑ 99 Berry (C)	.10	.25
❑ 100 Double Gust (C)	.10	.25
❑ 101 Moo-Moo Milk (C)	.10	.25
❑ 102 Pokemon March (C)	.10	.25
❑ 103 Super Rod (C)	.10	.25
❑ 104 Darkness Energy (R)	.50	1.00
❑ 105 Recycle Energy (R)	.50	1.00
❑ 106 Fighting Energy	.10	.25
❑ 107 Fire Energy	.10	.25
❑ 108 Grass Energy	.10	.25
❑ 109 Lightning Energy	.10	.25
❑ 110 Psychic Energy	.10	.25
❑ 111 Water Energy	.10	.25

2000 Pokemon Neo Genesis Unlimited

Card	Low	High
Complete Set (111)	50.00	75.00
Booster Box (36 ct)	65.00	90.00
Booster Pack (11 cards)	2.00	3.50
Hotfoot Deck (60 cards)	4.00	10.00
Cold Fusion Deck (60 cards)	4.00	10.00
❑ 1 Ampharos (holo) (R)	2.00	4.00
❑ 2 Azumarill (holo) (R)	2.00	4.00
❑ 3 Bellossom (holo) (R)	2.00	4.00
❑ 4 Feraligatr Lv.56 (holo) (R)	3.00	6.00
❑ 5 Feraligatr Lv.69 (holo) (R)	2.00	4.00
❑ 6 Heracross (holo) (R)	2.00	4.00
❑ 7 Jumpluff (holo) (R)	2.00	4.00
❑ 8 Kingdra (holo) (R)	2.00	4.00
❑ 9 Lugia (holo) (R)	12.00	16.00
❑ 10 Meganium Lv.54 (holo) (R)	2.00	4.00
❑ 11 Meganium Lv.57 (holo) (R)	4.00	8.00
❑ 12 Pichu (holo) (R)	3.00	6.00
❑ 13 Skarmory (holo) (R)	2.00	4.00
❑ 14 Slowking (holo) (R)	2.00	4.00
❑ 15 Steelix (holo) (R)	3.00	6.00
❑ 16 Togetic (holo) (R)	2.00	4.00
❑ 17 Typhlosion Lv.55 (holo) (R)	2.00	5.00
❑ 18 Typhlosion Lv.57 (holo) (R)	2.00	6.00
❑ 19 Metal Energy (holo) (R)	2.00	4.00
❑ 20 Cleffa (R)	.50	1.00
❑ 21 Donphan (R)	.50	1.00
❑ 22 Elekid (R)	.50	1.00
❑ 23 Magby (R)	.50	1.00
❑ 24 Murkrow (R)	.50	1.00
❑ 25 Sneasel (R)	1.00	2.00
❑ 26 Aipom (U)	.20	.50
❑ 27 Ariados (U)	.20	.50
❑ 28 Bayleef Lv.22 (U)	.20	.50
❑ 29 Bayleef Lv.39 (U)	.50	1.00
❑ 30 Clefairy (U)	.20	.50
❑ 31 Croconaw Lv.34 (U)	.20	.50
❑ 32 Croconaw Lv.41 (U)	.20	.50
❑ 33 Electabuzz (U)	.20	.50
❑ 34 Flaaffy (U)	.20	.50
❑ 35 Furret (U)	.20	.50
❑ 36 Gloom (U)	.20	.50
❑ 37 Granbull (U)	.20	.50
❑ 38 Lanturn (U)	.20	.50
❑ 39 Ledian (U)	.20	.50
❑ 40 Magmar (U)	.20	.50
❑ 41 Miltank (U)	.20	.50
❑ 42 Noctowl (U)	.20	.50
❑ 43 Phanpy (U)	.20	.50
❑ 44 Piloswine (U)	.20	.50
❑ 45 Quagsire (U)	.20	.50
❑ 46 Quilava Lv.28 (U)	.20	.50
❑ 47 Quilava Lv.35 (U)	.20	.50
❑ 48 Seadra (U)	.20	.50
❑ 49 Skiploom (U)	.20	.50
❑ 50 Sunflora (U)	.20	.50
❑ 51 Togepi (U)	.25	.75
❑ 52 Xatu (U)	.20	.50
❑ 53 Chikorita Lv.12 (C)	.10	.20
❑ 54 Chikorita Lv.19 (C)	.10	.20
❑ 55 Chinchou (C)	.10	.20
❑ 56 Cyndaquil Lv.14 (C)	.10	.20
❑ 57 Cyndaquil Lv.21 (C)	.10	.30
❑ 58 Girafarig (C)	.10	.20
❑ 59 Gligar (C)	.10	.20
❑ 60 Hoothoot (C)	.10	.20
❑ 61 Hoppip (C)	.10	.20
❑ 62 Horsea (C)	.10	.25
❑ 63 Ledyba (C)	.10	.20
❑ 64 Mantine (C)	.10	.20
❑ 65 Mareep (C)	.10	.20
❑ 66 Marill (C)	.10	.20
❑ 67 Natu (C)	.10	.20
❑ 68 Oddish (C)	.10	.20
❑ 69 Onix (C)	.10	.20
❑ 70 Pikachu (C)	.10	.25
❑ 71 Sentret (C)	.10	.20
❑ 72 Shuckle (C)	.10	.20
❑ 73 Slowpoke (C)	.10	.20
❑ 74 Snubbull (C)	.10	.20
❑ 75 Spinarak (C)	.10	.20
❑ 76 Stantler (C)	.10	.20
❑ 77 Sudowoodo (C)	.10	.20
❑ 78 Sunkern (C)	.10	.20
❑ 79 Swinub (C)	.10	.20
❑ 80 Totodile Lv.13 (C)	.10	.20
❑ 81 Totodile Lv.20 (C)	.10	.20
❑ 82 Wooper (C)	.10	.20
❑ 83 Arcade Game (R)	.50	1.00
❑ 84 Ecogym (R)	.50	1.00
❑ 85 Energy Charge (R)	.50	1.00
❑ 86 Focus Band (R)	.50	1.00
❑ 87 Mary (R)	.50	1.00
❑ 88 PokeGear (R)	.50	1.00
❑ 89 Super Energy Retrieval (R)	.50	1.00
❑ 90 Time Capsule (R)	.50	1.00
❑ 91 Bill's Teleporter (U)	.20	.50
❑ 92 Card-Flip Game (U)	.20	.50
❑ 93 Gold Berry (U)	.20	.50
❑ 94 Miracle Berry (U)	.20	.50
❑ 95 New Pokedex (U)	.20	.50
❑ 96 Professor Elm (U)	.20	.50
❑ 97 Sprout Tower (U)	.20	.50
❑ 98 Super Scoop Up (U)	.20	.50
❑ 99 Berry (C)	.10	.20
❑ 100 Double Gust (C)	.10	.20
❑ 101 Moo-Moo Milk (C)	.10	.20
❑ 102 Pokemon March (C)	.10	.20
❑ 103 Super Rod (C)	.10	.20
❑ 104 Darkness Energy (R)	.50	1.00
❑ 105 Recycle Energy (R)	.50	1.00
❑ 106 Fighting Energy	.10	.20
❑ 107 Fire Energy	.10	.20
❑ 108 Grass Energy	.10	.20
❑ 109 Lightning Energy	.10	.20
❑ 110 Psychic Energy	.10	.20
❑ 111 Water Energy	.10	.20

2001 Pokemon Neo Discovery 1st Edition

Card	Low	High
Complete Set (75)	65.00	100.00
Booster Box (36 ct)	100.00	170.00
Booster Pack (11 cards)	3.75	6.00
❑ 1 Espeon (holo) (R)	4.00	8.00
❑ 2 Forretress (holo) (R)	3.00	7.00
❑ 3 Hitmontop (holo) (R)	3.00	7.00
❑ 4 Houndoom (holo) (R)	3.00	7.00
❑ 5 Houndour (holo) (R)	3.00	7.00
❑ 6 Kabutops (holo) (R)	3.00	7.00
❑ 7 Magnemite (holo) (R)	3.00	7.00
❑ 8 Politoed (holo) (R)	3.00	7.00
❑ 9 Poliwrath (holo) (R)	5.00	10.00
❑ 10 Scizor (holo) (R)	3.00	7.00
❑ 11 Smeargle (holo) (R)	6.00	12.00
❑ 12 Tyranitar (holo) (R)	6.00	12.00
❑ 13 Umbreon (holo) (R)	7.00	14.00
❑ 14 Unown A (holo) (R)	3.00	6.00
❑ 15 Ursaring (holo) (R)	3.00	7.00
❑ 16 Wobbuffet (holo) (R)	3.00	7.00
❑ 17 Yanma (holo) (R)	3.00	7.00
❑ 18 Beedrill (R)	.50	1.00
❑ 19 Butterfree (R)	.50	1.00
❑ 20 Espeon (R)	1.00	2.00
❑ 21 Forretress (R)	.50	1.00
❑ 22 Hitmontop (R)	.50	1.00
❑ 23 Houndoom (R)	.50	1.00
❑ 24 Houndour (R)	.50	1.00
❑ 25 Kabutops (R)	.50	1.00
❑ 26 Magnemite (R)	.50	1.00
❑ 27 Politoed (R)	.50	1.00
❑ 28 Poliwrath (R)	.50	1.00
❑ 29 Scizor (R)	1.00	2.00
❑ 30 Smeargle (R)	.50	1.00
❑ 31 Tyranitar (R)	2.00	5.00
❑ 32 Umbreon (R)	1.00	2.00
❑ 33 Unown A (R)	.50	1.00
❑ 34 Ursaring (R)	.50	1.00
❑ 35 Wobbuffet (R)	.50	1.00
❑ 36 Yanma (R)	.50	1.00
❑ 37 Corsola (U)	.20	.50
❑ 38 Eevee (U)	.20	.50
❑ 39 Houndour (U)	.20	.50
❑ 40 Igglybuff (U)	.20	.50
❑ 41 Kakuna (U)	.20	.50
❑ 42 Metapod (U)	.20	.50
❑ 43 Omastar (U)	.20	.50
❑ 44 Poliwhirl (U)	.20	.50
❑ 45 Pupitar (U)	.20	.50
❑ 46 Scyther (U)	.20	.50
❑ 47 Unown D (U)	.20	.50
❑ 48 Unown F (U)	.20	.50
❑ 49 Unown M (U)	.20	.50
❑ 50 Unown N (U)	.20	.50
❑ 51 Unown U (U)	.20	.50
❑ 52 Xatu (U)	.20	.50
❑ 53 Caterpie (C)	.10	.25
❑ 54 Dunsparce (C)	.10	.25
❑ 55 Hoppip (C)	.10	.25
❑ 56 Kabuto (C)	.10	.25
❑ 57 Larvitar (C)	.10	.25
❑ 58 Mareep (C)	.10	.25
❑ 59 Natu (C)	.10	.25
❑ 60 Omanyte (C)	.10	.25
❑ 61 Pineco (C)	.10	.25
❑ 62 Poliwag (C)	.10	.25
❑ 63 Sentret (C)	.10	.25
❑ 64 Spinarak (C)	.10	.25
❑ 65 Teddiursa (C)	.10	.25
❑ 66 Tyrogue (C)	.10	.25
❑ 67 Unown E (C)	.10	.25
❑ 68 Unown I (C)	.10	.25
❑ 69 Unown O (C)	.10	.25
❑ 70 Weedle (C)	.10	.25
❑ 71 Wooper (C)	.10	.25
❑ 72 Trainer: Fossil Egg (U)	.20	.50
❑ 73 Trainer: Hyper Devolution Spray (U)	.20	.50
❑ 74 Trainer: Ruin Wall (U)	.20	.50
❑ 75 Trainer: Energy Ark (C)	.10	.25

2001 Pokemon Neo Discovery Unlimited

Card	Low	High
Complete Set (75)	45.00	65.00
Booster Box (36 ct)	50.00	75.00
Booster Pack (11 cards)	2.00	4.00
Brainwave Deck	4.00	10.00
Wallop Deck	4.00	10.00
❑ 1 Espeon (holo) (R)	2.00	5.00
❑ 2 Forretress (holo) (R)	2.00	4.00
❑ 3 Hitmontop (holo) (R)	1.00	4.00
❑ 4 Houndoom (holo) (R)	2.00	4.00
❑ 5 Houndour (holo) (R)	2.00	4.00
❑ 6 Kabutops (holo) (R)	2.00	4.00
❑ 7 Magnemite (holo) (R)	2.00	4.00
❑ 8 Politoed (holo) (R)	2.00	4.00
❑ 9 Poliwrath (holo) (R)	2.00	4.00
❑ 10 Scizor (holo) (R)	2.00	4.00
❑ 11 Smeargle (holo) (R)	2.00	4.00
❑ 12 Tyranitar (holo) (R)	3.00	7.00
❑ 13 Umbreon (holo) (R)	4.00	8.00
❑ 14 Unown A (holo) (R)	2.00	4.00
❑ 15 Ursaring (holo) (R)	2.00	4.00
❑ 16 Wobbuffet (holo) (R)	2.00	4.00
❑ 17 Yanma (holo) (R)	2.00	4.00
❑ 18 Beedrill (R)	.50	1.00
❑ 19 Butterfree (R)	.50	1.00
❑ 20 Espeon (R)	.50	1.00
❑ 21 Forretress (R)	.50	1.00
❑ 22 Hitmontop (R)	.50	1.00
❑ 23 Houndoom (R)	.50	1.00
❑ 24 Houndour (R)	.50	1.00
❑ 25 Kabutops (R)	.50	1.00
❑ 26 Magnemite (R)	.50	1.00
❑ 27 Politoed (R)	.50	1.00
❑ 28 Poliwrath (R)	.50	1.00
❑ 29 Scizor (R)	1.00	2.00
❑ 30 Smeargle (R)	.50	1.00
❑ 31 Tyranitar (R)	.75	2.00
❑ 32 Umbreon (R)	.50	1.00
❑ 33 Unown A (R)	.50	1.00
❑ 34 Ursaring (R)	.50	1.00
❑ 35 Wobbuffet (R)	.50	1.00
❑ 36 Yanma (R)	.50	1.00
❑ 37 Corsola (U)	.20	.50
❑ 38 Eevee (U)	.20	.50
❑ 39 Houndour (U)	.20	.50
❑ 40 Igglybuff (U)	.20	.50
❑ 41 Kakuna (U)	.20	.50
❑ 42 Metapod (U)	.20	.50
❑ 43 Omastar (U)	.20	.50
❑ 44 Poliwhirl (U)	.20	.50
❑ 45 Pupitar (U)	.20	.50
❑ 46 Scyther (U)	.20	.50
❑ 47 Unown D (U)	.20	.50
❑ 48 Unown F (U)	.20	.50
❑ 49 Unown M (U)	.20	.50
❑ 50 Unown N (U)	.20	.50
❑ 51 Unown U (U)	.20	.50
❑ 52 Xatu (U)	.20	.50
❑ 53 Caterpie (C)	.10	.20
❑ 54 Dunsparce (C)	.10	.20
❑ 55 Hoppip (C)	.10	.20
❑ 56 Kabuto (C)	.10	.20
❑ 57 Larvitar (C)	.10	.20
❑ 58 Mareep (C)	.10	.20
❑ 59 Natu (C)	.10	.20
❑ 60 Omanyte (C)	.10	.20
❑ 61 Pineco (C)	.10	.20
❑ 62 Poliwag (C)	.10	.20
❑ 63 Sentret (C)	.10	.20
❑ 64 Spinarak (C)	.10	.20
❑ 65 Teddiursa (C)	.10	.20
❑ 66 Tyrogue (C)	.10	.20
❑ 67 Unown E (C)	.10	.20
❑ 68 Unown I (C)	.10	.20
❑ 69 Unown O (C)	.10	.20
❑ 70 Weedle (C)	.10	.20
❑ 71 Wooper (C)	.10	.20
❑ 72 Trainer: Fossil Egg (U)	.20	.50
❑ 73 Trainer: Hyper Devolution Spray (U)	.20	.50
❑ 74 Trainer: Ruin Wall (U)	.20	.50
❑ 75 Trainer: Energy Ark (C)	.10	.20

2001 Pokemon Neo Revelation 1st Edition

Card	Low	High
Complete Set (66)	80.00	120.00
Booster Box (36 ct)	125.00	200.00
Booster Pack (11 cards)	4.00	7.00
❑ 1 Ampharos (holo) (R)	3.00	7.00
❑ 2 Blissey (holo) (R)	3.00	7.00
❑ 3 Celebi (holo) (R)	4.00	10.00
❑ 4 Crobat (holo) (R)	3.00	7.00
❑ 5 Delibird (holo) (R)	3.00	7.00
❑ 6 Entei (holo) (R)	4.00	8.00
❑ 7 Ho-oh (holo) (R)	7.00	15.00
❑ 8 Houndoom (holo) (R)	3.00	7.00
❑ 9 Jumpluff (holo) (R)	3.00	7.00
❑ 10 Magneton (holo) (R)	3.00	7.00
❑ 11 Misdreavus (holo) (R)	4.00	8.00
❑ 12 Porygon 2 (holo) (R)	3.00	7.00
❑ 13 Raikou (holo) (R)	3.00	7.00
❑ 14 Suicune (holo) (R)	5.00	10.00
❑ 15 Aerodactyl (R)	.50	1.00
❑ 16 Celebi (R)	1.00	2.00
❑ 17 Entei (R)	1.00	2.00
❑ 18 Ho-oh (R)	1.00	2.00
❑ 19 Kingdra (R)	.50	1.00
❑ 20 Lugia (R)	5.00	10.00
❑ 21 Raichu (R)	1.00	2.00
❑ 22 Raikou (R)	.50	1.00
❑ 23 Skarmory (R)	.50	1.00
❑ 24 Sneasel (R)	.50	1.00
❑ 25 Starmie (R)	.50	1.00
❑ 26 Sudowoodo (R)	.50	1.00
❑ 27 Suicune (R)	1.00	2.00
❑ 28 Flaaffy (U)	.20	.50
❑ 29 Golbat (U)	.20	.50
❑ 30 Graveler (U)	.20	.50
❑ 31 Jynx (U)	.20	.50
❑ 32 Lanturn (U)	.20	.50
❑ 33 Magcargo (U)	.20	.50
❑ 34 Octillery (U)	.20	.50
❑ 35 Parasect (U)	.20	.50
❑ 36 Piloswine (U)	.20	.50
❑ 37 Seaking (U)	.20	.50
❑ 38 Stantler (U)	.20	.50
❑ 39 Unown B (U)	.20	.50
❑ 40 Unown Y (U)	.20	.50
❑ 41 Aipom (C)	.10	.25
❑ 42 Chinchou (C)	.10	.25
❑ 43 Farfetch'd (C)	.10	.25
❑ 44 Geodude (C)	.10	.25
❑ 45 Goldeen (C)	.10	.25
❑ 46 Murkrow (C)	.10	.25
❑ 47 Paras (C)	.10	.25
❑ 48 Quagsire (C)	.10	.25
❑ 49 Qwilfish (C)	.10	.25
❑ 50 Remoraid (C)	.10	.25
❑ 51 Shuckle (C)	.10	.25
❑ 52 Skiploom (C)	.10	.25
❑ 53 Slugma (C)	.10	.25
❑ 54 Smoochum (C)	.10	.25
❑ 55 Snubbull (C)	.10	.25
❑ 56 Staryu (C)	.10	.25
❑ 57 Swinub (C)	.10	.25
❑ 58 Unown K (C)	.10	.25
❑ 59 Zubat (C)	.10	.25
❑ 60 Balloon Berry (U)	.20	.50
❑ 61 Healing Field (U)	.20	.50
❑ 62 Pokemon Breeder Fields (U)	.20	.50
❑ 63 Rocket's Hideout (U)	.20	.50
❑ 64 Old Rod (C)	.10	.25
❑ 65 Shining Gyarados (holo) (R)	15.00	25.00
❑ 66 Shining Magikarp (holo) (R)	5.00	10.00

2001 Pokemon Neo Revelation Unlimited

Card	Low	High
Complete Set (66)	45.00	70.00
Booster Box (36 ct)	60.00	75.00
Booster Pack (11 cards)	2.00	4.00
❑ 1 Ampharos (holo) (R)	1.00	4.00
❑ 2 Blissey (holo) (R)	2.00	4.00
❑ 3 Celebi (holo) (R)	3.00	6.00
❑ 4 Crobat (holo) (R)	2.00	4.00
❑ 5 Delibird (holo) (R)	2.00	4.00
❑ 6 Entei (holo) (R)	3.00	6.00
❑ 7 Ho-oh (holo) (R)	4.00	8.00
❑ 8 Houndoom (holo) (R)	2.00	4.00
❑ 9 Jumpluff (holo) (R)	2.00	4.00
❑ 10 Magneton (holo) (R)	2.00	4.00
❑ 11 Misdreavus (holo) (R)	2.00	4.00
❑ 12 Porygon 2 (holo) (R)	2.00	4.00
❑ 13 Raikou (holo) (R)	3.00	5.00
❑ 14 Suicune (holo) (R)	2.00	5.00
❑ 15 Aerodactyl (R)	.50	1.00
❑ 16 Celebi (R)	.50	1.00
❑ 17 Entei (R)	.50	1.00
❑ 18 Ho-oh (R)	1.00	2.00
❑ 19 Kingdra (R)	.50	1.00
❑ 20 Lugia (R)	4.00	6.00
❑ 21 Raichu (R)	.50	1.00
❑ 22 Raikou (R)	.50	1.00
❑ 23 Skarmory (R)	.50	1.00
❑ 24 Sneasel (R)	.50	1.00
❑ 25 Starmie (R)	.50	1.00

❑ 26 Sudowoodo (R)	.50	1.00
❑ 27 Suicune (R)	.50	1.00
❑ 28 Flaaffy (U)	.20	.50
❑ 29 Golbat (U)	.20	.50
❑ 30 Graveler (U)	.20	.50
❑ 31 Jynx (U)	.20	.50
❑ 32 Lanturn (U)	.20	.50
❑ 33 Magcargo (U)	.20	.50
❑ 34 Octillery (U)	.20	.50
❑ 35 Parasect (U)	.20	.50
❑ 36 Piloswine (U)	.20	.50
❑ 37 Seaking (U)	.20	.50
❑ 38 Stantler (U)	.20	.50
❑ 39 Unown B (U)	.20	.50
❑ 40 Unown Y (U)	.20	.50
❑ 41 Aipom (C)	.10	.20
❑ 42 Chinchou (C)	.10	.20
❑ 43 Farfetch'd (C)	.10	.20
❑ 44 Geodude (C)	.10	.20
❑ 45 Goldeen (C)	.10	.20
❑ 46 Murkrow (C)	.10	.20
❑ 47 Paras (C)	.10	.20
❑ 48 Quagsire (C)	.10	.20
❑ 49 Qwilfish (C)	.10	.20
❑ 50 Remoraid (C)	.10	.20
❑ 51 Shuckle (C)	.10	.20
❑ 52 Skiploom (C)	.10	.20
❑ 53 Slugma (C)	.10	.20
❑ 54 Smoochum (C)	.10	.20
❑ 55 Snubbull (C)	.10	.20
❑ 56 Staryu (C)	.10	.20
❑ 57 Swinub (C)	.10	.20
❑ 58 Unown K (C)	.10	.20
❑ 59 Zubat (C)	.10	.20
❑ 60 Balloon Berry (U)	.20	.50
❑ 61 Healing Field (U)	.20	.50
❑ 62 Pokemon Breeder Fields (U)	.20	.50
❑ 63 Rocket's Hideout (U)	.20	.50
❑ 64 Old Rod (C)	.10	.20
❑ 65 Shining Gyarados (holo) (R)	4.00	10.00
❑ 66 Shining Magikarp (holo) (R)	4.00	8.00

2002 Pokemon Neo Destiny 1st Edition

Complete Set (113)	135.00	200.00
Booster Box (36 ct)	150.00	250.00
Booster Pack (11 cards)	4.00	7.00
❑ 1 Dark Ampharos (holo) (R)	3.00	7.00
❑ 2 Dark Crobat (holo) (R)	3.00	7.00
❑ 3 Dark Donphan (holo) (R)	3.00	7.00
❑ 4 Dark Espeon (holo) (R)	6.00	10.00
❑ 5 Dark Feraligatr (holo) (R)	4.00	10.00
❑ 6 Dark Gengar (holo) (R)	3.00	7.00
❑ 7 Dark Houndoom (holo) (R)	3.00	7.00
❑ 8 Dark Porygon2 (holo) (R)	3.00	7.00
❑ 9 Dark Scizor (holo) (R)	3.00	7.00
❑ 10 Dark Typhlosion (holo) (R)	3.00	7.00
❑ 11 Dark Tyranitar (holo) (R)	4.00	8.00
❑ 12 Light Arcanine (holo) (R)	3.00	7.00
❑ 13 Light Azumarill (holo) (R)	3.00	7.00
❑ 14 Light Dragonite (holo) (R)	3.00	7.00
❑ 15 Light Togetic (holo) (R)	3.00	7.00
❑ 16 Miracle Energy (holo) (R)	3.00	7.00
❑ 17 Dark Ariados (R)	.50	1.00
❑ 18 Dark Magcargo (R)	.50	1.00
❑ 19 Dark Omastar (R)	.50	1.00
❑ 20 Dark Slowking (R)	1.00	2.00
❑ 21 Dark Ursaring (R)	.50	1.00
❑ 22 Light Dragonair (R)	.50	1.00
❑ 23 Light Lanturn (R)	.50	1.00
❑ 24 Light Ledian (R)	.50	1.00
❑ 25 Light Machamp (R)	.50	1.00
❑ 26 Light Piloswine (R)	.50	1.00
❑ 27 Unown G (R)	.50	1.00
❑ 28 Unown H (R)	.50	1.00
❑ 29 Unown W (R)	.50	1.00
❑ 30 Unown X (R)	.50	1.00
❑ 31 Chansey (U)	.20	.50
❑ 32 Dark Croconaw (U)	.20	.50
❑ 33 Dark Exeggutor (U)	.20	.50
❑ 34 Dark Flaaffy (U)	.20	.50
❑ 35 Dark Forretress (U)	.20	.50
❑ 36 Dark Haunter (U)	.20	.50
❑ 37 Dark Omanyte (U)	.20	.50
❑ 38 Dark Pupitar (U)	.20	.50
❑ 39 Dark Quilava (U)	.20	.50
❑ 40 Dark Wigglytuff (U)	.20	.50
❑ 41 Heracross (U)	.20	.50
❑ 42 Hitmonlee (U)	.20	.50
❑ 43 Houndour (U)	.20	.50
❑ 44 Jigglypuff (U)	.20	.50
❑ 45 Light Dewgong (U)	.20	.50
❑ 46 Light Flareon (U)	.20	.50
❑ 47 Light Golduck (U)	.20	.50
❑ 48 Light Jolteon (U)	.20	.50
❑ 49 Light Machoke (U)	.20	.50
❑ 50 Light Ninetales (U)	.20	.50
❑ 51 Light Slowbro (U)	.20	.50
❑ 52 Light Vaporeon (U)	.20	.50
❑ 53 Light Venomoth (U)	.20	.50
❑ 54 Light Wigglytuff (U)	.20	.50
❑ 55 Scyther (U)	.20	.50
❑ 56 Togepi (U)	.75	1.50
❑ 57 Unown C (U)	.20	.50
❑ 58 Unown P (U)	.20	.50
❑ 59 Unown Q (U)	.20	.50
❑ 60 Unown Z (U)	.20	.50
❑ 61 Cyndaquil (C)	.10	.25
❑ 62 Dark Octillery (C)	.10	.25
❑ 63 Dratini (C)	.10	.25
❑ 64 Exeggcute (C)	.10	.25
❑ 65 Gastly (C)	.10	.25
❑ 66 Girafarig (C)	.10	.25
❑ 67 Gligar (C)	.10	.25
❑ 68 Growlithe (C)	.10	.25
❑ 69 Hitmonchan (C)	.10	.25
❑ 70 Larvitar (C)	.10	.25
❑ 71 Ledyba (C)	.10	.25
❑ 72 Light Sunflora (C)	.10	.25
❑ 73 Machop (C)	.10	.25
❑ 74 Mantine (C)	.10	.25
❑ 75 Mareep (C)	.10	.25
❑ 76 Phanpy (C)	.10	.25
❑ 77 Pineco (C)	.10	.25
❑ 78 Porygon (C)	.10	.25
❑ 79 Psyduck (C)	.10	.25
❑ 80 Remoraid (C)	.10	.25
❑ 81 Seel (C)	.10	.25
❑ 82 Slugma (C)	.10	.25
❑ 83 Sunkern (C)	.10	.25
❑ 84 Swinub (C)	.10	.25
❑ 85 Totodile (C)	.10	.25
❑ 86 Unown L (C)	.10	.25
❑ 87 Unown S (C)	.10	.25
❑ 88 Unown T (C)	.10	.25
❑ 89 Unown V (C)	.10	.25
❑ 90 Venonat (C)	.10	.25
❑ 91 Vulpix (C)	.10	.25
❑ 92 Broken Ground Gym (R)	.50	1.00
❑ 93 EXP.ALL (R)	.50	1.00
❑ 94 Impostor Prof.Oak's Invent.(R)	.50	1.00
❑ 95 Radio Tower (R)	.50	1.00
❑ 96 Thought Wave Machine (R)	.50	1.00
❑ 97 Counterattack Claws (U)	.20	.50
❑ 98 Energy Amplifier (U)	.20	.50
❑ 99 Energy Stadium (U)	.20	.50
❑ 100 Lucky Stadium (U)	.20	.50
❑ 101 Pigmented Lens (U)	.20	.50
❑ 102 Pokemon Personality Test (U)	.20	.50
❑ 103 Team Rockets Evil Deeds (U)	.20	.50
❑ 104 Heal Powder (C)	.10	.25
❑ 105 Mail from Bill (C)	.10	.25
❑ 106 Shining Celebi (holo) (UR)	12.00	22.00
❑ 107 Shining Charizard (holo) (UR)	25.00	40.00
❑ 108 Shining Kabutops (holo) (UR)	10.00	20.00
❑ 109 Shining Mewtwo (holo) (UR)	12.00	25.00
❑ 110 Shining Noctowl (holo) (UR)	10.00	18.00
❑ 111 Shining Raichu (holo) (UR)	10.00	20.00
❑ 112 Shining Steelix (holo) (UR)	10.00	20.00
❑ 113 Shining Tyranitar (holo) (UR)	10.00	18.00

2002 Pokemon Neo Destiny Unlimited

Complete Set (113)	60.00	120.00
❑ 1 Dark Ampharos (holo) (R)	2.00	4.00
❑ 2 Dark Crobat (holo) (R)	2.00	4.00
❑ 3 Dark Donphan (holo) (R)	2.00	4.00
❑ 4 Dark Espeon (holo) (R)	3.00	6.00
❑ 5 Dark Feraligatr (holo) (R)	2.00	5.00
❑ 6 Dark Gengar (holo) (R)	2.00	4.00
❑ 7 Dark Houndoom (holo) (R)	2.00	4.00
❑ 8 Dark Porygon2 (holo) (R)	2.00	4.00
❑ 9 Dark Scizor (holo) (R)	2.00	4.00
❑ 10 Dark Typhlosion (holo) (R)	2.00	4.00
❑ 11 Dark Tyranitar (holo) (R)	2.00	4.00
❑ 12 Light Arcanine (holo) (R)	2.00	4.00
❑ 13 Light Azumarill (holo) (R)	2.00	4.00
❑ 14 Light Dragonite (holo) (R)	2.00	4.00
❑ 15 Light Togetic (holo) (R)	2.00	4.00
❑ 16 Miracle Energy (holo) (R)	2.00	4.00
❑ 17 Dark Ariados (R)	.50	1.00
❑ 18 Dark Magcargo (R)	.50	1.00
❑ 19 Dark Omastar (R)	.50	1.00
❑ 20 Dark Slowking (R)	.50	1.00
❑ 21 Dark Ursaring (R)	.50	1.00
❑ 22 Light Dragonair (R)	.50	1.00
❑ 23 Light Lanturn (R)	.50	1.00
❑ 24 Light Ledian (R)	.50	1.00
❑ 25 Light Machamp (R)	.50	1.00
❑ 26 Light Piloswine (R)	.50	1.00
❑ 27 Unown G (R)	.50	1.00
❑ 28 Unown H (R)	.50	1.00
❑ 29 Unown W (R)	.50	1.00
❑ 30 Unown X (R)	.50	1.00
❑ 31 Chansey (U)	.20	.50
❑ 32 Dark Croconaw (U)	.20	.50
❑ 33 Dark Exeggutor (U)	.20	.50
❑ 34 Dark Flaaffy (U)	.20	.50
❑ 35 Dark Forretress (U)	.20	.50
❑ 36 Dark Haunter (U)	.20	.50
❑ 37 Dark Omanyte (U)	.20	.50
❑ 38 Dark Pupitar (U)	.20	.50
❑ 39 Dark Quilava (U)	.20	.50
❑ 40 Dark Wigglytuff (U)	.20	.50
❑ 41 Heracross (U)	.20	.50
❑ 42 Hitmonlee (U)	.20	.50
❑ 43 Houndour (U)	.20	.50
❑ 44 Jigglypuff (U)	.20	.50
❑ 45 Light Dewgong (U)	.20	.50
❑ 46 Light Flareon (U)	.20	.50
❑ 47 Light Golduck (U)	.20	.50
❑ 48 Light Jolteon (U)	.20	.50
❑ 49 Light Machoke (U)	.20	.50
❑ 50 Light Ninetales (U)	.20	.50
❑ 51 Light Slowbro (U)	.20	.50
❑ 52 Light Vaporeon (U)	.20	.50
❑ 53 Light Venomoth (U)	.20	.50
❑ 54 Light Wigglytuff (U)	.20	.50
❑ 55 Scyther (U)	.20	.50
❑ 56 Togepi (U)	.50	1.00
❑ 57 Unown C (U)	.20	.50
❑ 58 Unown P (U)	.20	.50
❑ 59 Unown Q (U)	.20	.50
❑ 60 Unown Z (U)	.20	.50
❑ 61 Cyndaquil (C)	.10	.20
❑ 62 Dark Octillery (C)	.10	.20
❑ 63 Dratini (C)	.10	.20
❑ 64 Exeggcute (C)	.10	.20
❑ 65 Gastly (C)	.10	.20
❑ 66 Girafarig (C)	.10	.20
❑ 67 Gligar (C)	.10	.20
❑ 68 Growlithe (C)	.10	.20
❑ 69 Hitmonchan (C)	.10	.20
❑ 70 Larvitar (C)	.10	.20
❑ 71 Ledyba (C)	.10	.20
❑ 72 Light Sunflora (C)	.10	.20
❑ 73 Machop (C)	.10	.20
❑ 74 Mantine (C)	.10	.20
❑ 75 Mareep (C)	.10	.20
❑ 76 Phanpy (C)	.10	.20
❑ 77 Pineco (C)	.10	.20
❑ 78 Porygon (C)	.10	.20
❑ 79 Psyduck (C)	.10	.20
❑ 80 Remoraid (C)	.10	.20
❑ 81 Seel (C)	.10	.20
❑ 82 Slugma (C)	.10	.20
❑ 83 Sunkern (C)	.10	.20
❑ 84 Swinub (C)	.10	.20
❑ 85 Totodile (C)	.10	.20
❑ 86 Unown L (C)	.10	.20
❑ 87 Unown S (C)	.10	.20
❑ 88 Unown T (C)	.10	.20
❑ 89 Unown V (C)	.10	.20
❑ 90 Venonat (C)	.10	.20
❑ 91 Vulpix (C)	.10	.20
❑ 92 Broken Ground Gym (R)	.50	1.00
❑ 93 EXP.ALL (R)	.50	1.00
❑ 94 Impostor Prof.Oak's Invent.(R)	.50	1.00
❑ 95 Radio Tower (R)	.50	1.00
❑ 96 Thought Wave Machine (R)	.50	1.00
❑ 97 Counterattack Claws (U)	.20	.50
❑ 98 Energy Amplifier (U)	.20	.50
❑ 99 Energy Stadium (U)	.20	.50
❑ 100 Lucky Stadium (U)	.20	.50
❑ 101 Pigmented Lens (U)	.20	.50
❑ 102 Pokemon Personality Test (U)	.20	.50
❑ 103 Team Rockets Evil Deeds (U)	.20	.50
❑ 104 Heal Powder (C)	.10	.20
❑ 105 Mail from Bill (C)	.10	.20
❑ 106 Shining Celebi (holo) (UR)	7.00	15.00
❑ 107 Shining Charizard (holo) (UR)	15.00	28.00
❑ 108 Shining Kabutops (holo) (UR)	7.00	13.00
❑ 109 Shining Mewtwo (holo) (UR)	8.00	15.00
❑ 110 Shining Noctowl (holo) (UR)	5.00	10.00
❑ 111 Shining Raichu (holo) (UR)	6.00	12.00
❑ 112 Shining Steelix (holo) (UR)	5.00	12.00
❑ 113 Shining Tyranitar (holo) (UR)	6.00	12.00

2002 Pokemon Legendary Collection

Complete Set (110)	65.00	95.00
Booster Box (36 ct)	75.00	100.00
Booster Pack (11 cards)	2.00	3.50
*Box Topper 2X Regular Version		
❑ 1 Alakazam (holo) (R)	3.00	6.00
❑ 2 Articuno (holo) (R)	2.00	4.00
❑ 3 Charizard (holo) (R)	10.00	18.00
❑ 4 Dark Blastoise (holo) (R)	4.00	8.00
❑ 5 Dark Dragonite (holo) (R)	3.00	6.00
❑ 6 Dark Persian (holo) (R)	3.00	6.00
❑ 7 Dark Raichu (holo) (R)	3.00	6.00
❑ 8 Dark Slowbro (holo) (R)	2.00	4.00
❑ 9 Dark Vaporeon (holo) (R)	2.00	4.00
❑ 10 Flareon (holo) (R)	2.00	4.00
❑ 11 Gengar (holo) (R)	2.00	4.00
❑ 12 Gyarados (holo) (R)	2.00	5.00
❑ 13 Hitmonlee (holo) (R)	2.00	4.00
❑ 14 Jolteon (holo) (R)	2.00	4.00
❑ 15 Machamp (holo) (R)	2.00	4.00
❑ 16 Muk (holo) (R)	2.00	4.00
❑ 17 Ninetales (holo) (R)	2.00	4.00
❑ 18 Venusaur (holo) (R)	2.00	5.00
❑ 19 Zapdos (holo) (R)	2.00	5.00
❑ 20 Beedrill (R)	.50	1.00
❑ 21 Butterfree (R)	.50	1.00
❑ 22 Electrode (R)	.50	1.00
❑ 23 Exeggutor (R)	.50	1.00
❑ 24 Golem (R)	.50	1.00
❑ 25 Hypno (R)	.50	1.00
❑ 26 Jynx (R)	.50	1.00
❑ 27 Kabutops (R)	.50	1.00
❑ 28 Magneton (R)	.50	1.00
❑ 29 Mewtwo (R)	2.00	4.00
❑ 30 Moltres (R)	.50	1.00
❑ 31 Nidoking (R)	.50	1.00
❑ 32 Nidoqueen (R)	.50	1.00
❑ 33 Pidgeot (R)	.50	1.00
❑ 34 Pidgeotto (R)	.50	1.00
❑ 35 Rhydon (R)	.50	1.00
❑ 36 Arcanine (U)	.20	.50
❑ 37 Charmeleon (U)	.20	.50
❑ 38 Dark Dragonair (U)	.20	.50
❑ 39 Dark Wartortle (U)	.20	.50
❑ 40 Dewgong (U)	.20	.50
❑ 41 Dodrio (U)	.20	.50
❑ 42 Fearow (U)	.20	.50
❑ 43 Golduck (U)	.20	.50
❑ 44 Graveler (U)	.20	.50
❑ 45 Growlithe (U)	.20	.50
❑ 46 Haunter (U)	.20	.50
❑ 47 Ivysaur (U)	.20	.50
❑ 48 Kabuto (U)	.20	.50
❑ 49 Kadabra (U)	.20	.50
❑ 50 Kakuna (U)	.20	.50
❑ 51 Machoke (U)	.20	.50
❑ 52 Magikarp (U)	.20	.50
❑ 53 Meowth (U)	.20	.50
❑ 54 Metapod (U)	.20	.50
❑ 55 Nidorina (U)	.20	.50
❑ 56 Nidorino (U)	.20	.50
❑ 57 Omanyte (U)	.20	.50
❑ 58 Omastar (U)	.20	.50
❑ 59 Primeape (U)	.20	.50
❑ 60 Rapidash (U)	.20	.50
❑ 61 Raticate (U)	.20	.50
❑ 62 Sandslash (U)	.20	.50
❑ 63 Seadra (U)	.20	.50
❑ 64 Snorlax (U)	.20	.50
❑ 65 Tauros (U)	.20	.50
❑ 66 Tentacruel (U)	.20	.50
❑ 67 Abra (C)	.10	.20
❑ 68 Bulbasaur (C)	.10	.20
❑ 69 Caterpie (C)	.10	.20
❑ 70 Charmander (C)	.10	.20
❑ 71 Doduo (C)	.10	.20
❑ 72 Dratini (C)	.10	.20
❑ 73 Drowzee (C)	.10	.20
❑ 74 Eevee (C)	.10	.20
❑ 75 Exeggcute (C)	.10	.20
❑ 76 Gastly (C)	.10	.20
❑ 77 Geodude (C)	.10	.20
❑ 78 Grimer (C)	.10	.20
❑ 79 Machop (C)	.10	.20
❑ 80 Magnemite (C)	.10	.20
❑ 81 Mankey (C)	.10	.20
❑ 82 Nidoran (F) (C)	.10	.20
❑ 83 Nidoran (M) (C)	.10	.20
❑ 84 Onix (C)	.10	.20
❑ 85 Pidgey (C)	.10	.20
❑ 86 Pikachu (C)	.50	1.00
❑ 87 Ponyta (C)	.10	.20
❑ 88 Psyduck (C)	.10	.20
❑ 89 Rattata (C)	.10	.20
❑ 90 Rhyhorn (C)	.10	.20
❑ 91 Sandshrew (C)	.10	.20
❑ 92 Seel (C)	.10	.20
❑ 93 Slowpoke (C)	.10	.20
❑ 94 Spearow (C)	.10	.20
❑ 95 Squirtle (C)	.10	.20
❑ 96 Tentacool (C)	.10	.20
❑ 97 Voltorb (C)	.10	.20
❑ 98 Vulpix (C)	.10	.20
❑ 99 Weedle (C)	.10	.20
❑ 100 Full Heal Energy (U)	.20	.50
❑ 101 Potion Energy (U)	.20	.50
❑ 102 Pokemon Breeder (R)	.50	1.00
❑ 103 Pokemon Trader (R)	.50	1.00
❑ 104 Scoop Up (R)	.50	1.00
❑ 105 Boss's Way (U)	.20	.50
❑ 106 Challenge! (U)	.20	.50
❑ 107 Energy Retrieval (U)	.20	.50
❑ 108 Bill (C)	.10	.20
❑ 109 Mysterious Fossil (C)	.10	.20
❑ 110 Potion (C)	.10	.20

2002 Pokemon Legendary Collection Reverse Foil

Complete Set (110)	90.00	175.00
❑ 1 Alakazam (holo) (R)	6.00	12.00
❑ 2 Articuno (holo) (R)	4.00	8.00
❑ 3 Charizard (holo) (R)	15.00	30.00
❑ 4 Dark Blastoise (holo) (R)	8.00	15.00
❑ 5 Dark Dragonite (holo) (R)	6.00	12.00
❑ 6 Dark Persian (holo) (R)	6.00	12.00
❑ 7 Dark Raichu (holo) (R)	6.00	12.00
❑ 8 Dark Slowbro (holo) (R)	4.00	8.00
❑ 9 Dark Vaporeon (holo) (R)	4.00	8.00
❑ 10 Flareon (holo) (R)	4.00	8.00
❑ 11 Gengar (holo) (R)	4.00	8.00
❑ 12 Gyarados (holo) (R)	4.00	8.00
❑ 13 Hitmonlee (holo) (R)	4.00	8.00
❑ 14 Jolteon (holo) (R)	4.00	8.00
❑ 15 Machamp (holo) (R)	4.00	8.00
❑ 16 Muk (holo) (R)	4.00	8.00
❑ 17 Ninetales (holo) (R)	4.00	8.00
❑ 18 Venusaur (holo) (R)	4.00	8.00
❑ 19 Zapdos (holo) (R)	4.00	8.00
❑ 20 Beedrill (R)	1.00	2.00
❑ 21 Butterfree (R)	1.00	2.00
❑ 22 Electrode (R)	1.00	2.00
❑ 23 Exeggutor (R)	1.00	2.00
❑ 24 Golem (R)	1.00	2.00
❑ 25 Hypno (R)	1.00	2.00
❑ 26 Jynx (R)	1.00	2.00
❑ 27 Kabutops (R)	1.00	2.00
❑ 28 Magneton (R)	1.00	2.00
❑ 29 Mewtwo (R)	1.00	2.00
❑ 30 Moltres (R)	1.00	2.00
❑ 31 Nidoking (R)	1.00	2.00
❑ 32 Nidoqueen (R)	1.00	2.00
❑ 33 Pidgeot (R)	1.00	2.00
❑ 34 Pidgeotto (R)	1.00	2.00
❑ 35 Rhydon (R)	1.00	2.00
❑ 36 Arcanine (U)	.50	1.00
❑ 37 Charmeleon (U)	.50	1.00
❑ 38 Dark Dragonair (U)	.50	1.00
❑ 39 Dark Wartortle (U)	.50	1.00
❑ 40 Dewgong (U)	.50	1.00
❑ 41 Dodrio (U)	.50	1.00
❑ 42 Fearow (U)	.50	1.00
❑ 43 Golduck (U)	.50	1.00
❑ 44 Graveler (U)	.50	1.00
❑ 45 Growlithe (U)	.50	1.00
❑ 46 Haunter (U)	.50	1.00
❑ 47 Ivysaur (U)	.50	1.00
❑ 48 Kabuto (U)	.50	1.00
❑ 49 Kadabra (U)	.50	1.00
❑ 50 Kakuna (U)	.50	1.00
❑ 51 Machoke (U)	.50	1.00
❑ 52 Magikarp (U)	.50	1.00
❑ 53 Meowth (U)	.50	1.00
❑ 54 Metapod (U)	.50	1.00
❑ 55 Nidorina (U)	.50	1.00
❑ 56 Nidorino (U)	.50	1.00
❑ 57 Omanyte (U)	.50	1.00
❑ 58 Omastar (U)	.50	1.00
❑ 59 Primeape (U)	.50	1.00
❑ 60 Rapidash (U)	.50	1.00
❑ 61 Raticate (U)	.50	1.00
❑ 62 Sandslash (U)	.50	1.00
❑ 63 Seadra (U)	.50	1.00
❑ 64 Snorlax (U)	.50	1.00
❑ 65 Tauros (U)	.50	1.00
❑ 66 Tentacruel (U)	.50	1.00
❑ 67 Abra (C)	.20	.40
❑ 68 Bulbasaur (C)	.20	.40
❑ 69 Caterpie (C)	.20	.40
❑ 70 Charmander (C)	.20	.40
❑ 71 Doduo (C)	.20	.40
❑ 72 Dratini (C)	.20	.40
❑ 73 Drowzee (C)	.20	.40
❑ 74 Eevee (C)	.20	.40
❑ 75 Exeggcute (C)	.20	.40
❑ 76 Gastly (C)	.20	.40
❑ 77 Geodude (C)	.20	.40
❑ 78 Grimer (C)	.20	.40
❑ 79 Machop (C)	.20	.40
❑ 80 Magnemite (C)	.20	.40
❑ 81 Mankey (C)	.20	.40
❑ 82 Nidoran (F) (C)	.20	.40
❑ 83 Nidoran (M) (C)	.20	.40
❑ 84 Onix (C)	.20	.40
❑ 85 Pidgey (C)	.20	.40
❑ 86 Pikachu (C)	1.00	2.00
❑ 87 Ponyta (C)	.20	.40
❑ 88 Psyduck (C)	.20	.40
❑ 89 Rattata (C)	.20	.40
❑ 90 Rhyhorn (C)	.20	.40
❑ 91 Sandshrew (C)	.20	.40
❑ 92 Seel (C)	.20	.40
❑ 93 Slowpoke (C)	.20	.40
❑ 94 Spearow (C)	.20	.40
❑ 95 Squirtle (C)	.20	.40
❑ 96 Tentacool (C)	.20	.40
❑ 97 Voltorb (C)	.20	.40
❑ 98 Vulpix (C)	.20	.40
❑ 99 Weedle (C)	.20	.40
❑ 100 Full Heal Energy (U)	.50	1.00
❑ 101 Potion Energy (U)	.50	1.00
❑ 102 Pokemon Breeder (R)	1.00	2.00
❑ 103 Pokemon Trader (R)	1.00	2.00
❑ 104 Scoop Up (R)	1.00	2.00
❑ 105 Boss's Way (U)	.50	1.00
❑ 106 Challenge! (U)	.50	1.00
❑ 107 Energy Retrieval (U)	.50	1.00
❑ 108 Bill (C)	.20	.40
❑ 109 Mysterious Fossil (C)	.20	.40
❑ 110 Potion (C)	.20	.40

2002 Pokemon Expedition

Complete Set (165)	75.00	135.00
Booster Box (36 ct)	70.00	100.00
Booster Pack (11 cards)	3.00	4.00
Electric Garden Theme Deck	6.00	10.00
*Box Topper 1.5X Regular Version		
❑ 1 Alakazam (holo) (R)	3.00	6.00
❑ 2 Ampharos (holo) (R)	2.00	4.00
❑ 3 Arbok (holo) (R)	2.00	4.00
❑ 4 Blastoise (holo) (R)	4.00	8.00
❑ 5 Butterfree (holo) (R)	2.00	4.00
❑ 6 Charizard (holo) (R)	12.00	20.00
❑ 7 Clefable (holo) (R)	2.00	4.00
❑ 8 Cloyster (holo) (R)	2.00	4.00
❑ 9 Dragonite (holo) (R)	2.00	4.00
❑ 10 Dugtrio (holo) (R)	2.00	4.00
❑ 11 Fearow (holo) (R)	2.00	4.00

❑ 12 Feraligatr (holo) (R) 2.00 4.00
❑ 13 Gengar (holo) (R) 2.00 4.00
❑ 14 Golem (holo) (R) 2.00 4.00
❑ 15 Kingler (holo) (R) 1.00 3.00
❑ 16 Machamp (holo) (R) 2.00 4.00
❑ 17 Magby (holo) (R) 2.00 4.00
❑ 18 Meganium (holo) (R) 2.00 4.00
❑ 19 Mew (holo) (R) 6.00 12.00
❑ 20 Mewtwo (holo) (R) 2.00 6.00
❑ 21 Ninetales (holo) (R) 2.00 4.00
❑ 22 Pichu (holo) (R) 2.00 5.00
❑ 23 Pidgeot (holo) (R) 2.00 4.00
❑ 24 Poliwrath (holo) (R) 2.00 4.00
❑ 25 Raichu (holo) (R) 3.00 6.00
❑ 26 Rapidash (holo) (R) 2.00 4.00
❑ 27 Skarmory (holo) (R) 2.00 4.00
❑ 28 Typhlosion (holo) (R) 2.00 4.00
❑ 29 Tyranitar (holo) (R) 2.00 5.00
❑ 30 Venusaur (holo) (R) 2.00 4.00
❑ 31 Vileplume (holo) (R) 2.00 4.00
❑ 32 Weezing (holo) (R) 2.00 4.00
❑ 33 Alakazam (R) .50 1.00
❑ 34 Ampharos (R) .50 1.00
❑ 35 Arbok (R) .50 1.00
❑ 36 Blastoise (R) 1.00 2.00
❑ 37 Blastoise (R) 1.00 2.00
❑ 38 Butterfree (R) .50 1.00
❑ 39 Charizard (R) 5.00 10.00
❑ 40 Charizard (R) 8.00 15.00
❑ 41 Clefable (R) .50 1.00
❑ 42 Cloyster (R) .50 1.00
❑ 43 Dragonite (R) .50 1.00
❑ 44 Dugtrio (R) .50 1.00
❑ 45 Fearow (R) .50 1.00
❑ 46 Feraligatr (R) 1.00 2.00
❑ 47 Feraligatr (R) .50 1.00
❑ 48 Gengar (R) .50 1.00
❑ 49 Golem (R) .50 1.00
❑ 50 Kingler (R) .50 1.00
❑ 51 Machamp (R) .50 1.00
❑ 52 Magby (R) .50 1.00
❑ 53 Meganium (R) 1.00 2.00
❑ 54 Meganium (R) 1.00 2.00
❑ 55 Mew (R) 2.00 4.00
❑ 56 Mewtwo (R) 2.00 4.00
❑ 57 Ninetales (R) .50 1.00
❑ 58 Pichu (R) .50 1.00
❑ 59 Pidgeot (R) .50 1.00
❑ 60 Poliwrath (R) .50 1.00
❑ 61 Raichu (R) 2.00 4.00
❑ 62 Rapidash (R) .50 1.00
❑ 63 Skarmory (R) .50 1.00
❑ 64 Typhlosion (R) .50 1.00
❑ 65 Typhlosion (R) 1.00 2.00
❑ 66 Tyranitar (R) 2.00 4.00
❑ 67 Venusaur (R) .50 1.00
❑ 68 Venusaur (R) .50 1.00
❑ 69 Vileplume (R) .50 1.00
❑ 70 Weezing (R) .50 1.00
❑ 71 Bayleef (U) .20 .50
❑ 72 Chansey (U) .20 .50
❑ 73 Charmeleon (U) .20 .50
❑ 74 Croconaw (U) .20 .50
❑ 75 Dragonair (U) .20 .50
❑ 76 Electabuzz (U) .20 .50
❑ 77 Flaafy (U) .20 .50
❑ 78 Gloom (U) .20 .50
❑ 79 Graveler (U) .20 .50
❑ 80 Haunter (U) .20 .50
❑ 81 Hitmonlee (U) .20 .50
❑ 82 Ivysaur (U) .20 .50
❑ 83 Jynx (U) .20 .50
❑ 84 Kadabra (U) .20 .50
❑ 85 Machoke (U) .20 .50
❑ 86 Magmar (U) .20 .50
❑ 87 Metapod (U) .20 .50
❑ 88 Pidgeotto (U) .20 .50
❑ 89 Poliwhirl (U) .20 .50
❑ 90 Pupitar (U) .20 .50
❑ 91 Quilava (U) .20 .50
❑ 92 Wartortle (U) .20 .50
❑ 93 Abra (C) .10 .20
❑ 94 Bulbasaur (C) .10 .20
❑ 95 Bulbasaur (C) .10 .20
❑ 96 Caterpie (C) .10 .20
❑ 97 Charmander (C) .10 .20
❑ 98 Charmander (C) .10 .20
❑ 99 Chikorita (C) .10 .20
❑ 100 Chikorita (C) .10 .20
❑ 101 Clefairy (C) .10 .20
❑ 102 Corsola (C) .10 .20
❑ 103 Cubone (C) .10 .20
❑ 104 Cyndaquil (C) .10 .20
❑ 105 Cyndaquil (C) .10 .20
❑ 106 Diglett (C) .10 .20
❑ 107 Dratini (C) .10 .20
❑ 108 Ekans (C) .10 .20
❑ 109 Gastly (C) .10 .20
❑ 110 Geodude (C) .10 .20
❑ 111 Goldeen (C) .10 .20
❑ 112 Hoppip (C) .10 .20
❑ 113 Houndour (C) .10 .20
❑ 114 Koffing (C) .10 .20
❑ 115 Krabby (C) .10 .20
❑ 116 Larvitar (C) .10 .20
❑ 117 Machop (C) .10 .20
❑ 118 Magikarp (C) .10 .20
❑ 119 Mareep (C) .10 .20
❑ 120 Marill (C) .10 .20
❑ 121 Meowth (C) .10 .20
❑ 122 Oddish (C) .10 .20
❑ 123 Pidgey (C) .10 .20
❑ 124 Pikachu (C) .50 1.00
❑ 125 Poliwag (C) .10 .20
❑ 126 Ponyta (C) .10 .20
❑ 127 Qwilfish (C) .10 .20
❑ 128 Rattata (C) .10 .20
❑ 129 Shellder (C) .10 .20
❑ 130 Spearow (C) .10 .20
❑ 131 Squirtle (C) .10 .20
❑ 132 Squirtle (C) .10 .20
❑ 133 Tauros (C) .10 .20
❑ 134 Totodile (C) .10 .20
❑ 135 Totodile (C) .10 .20
❑ 136 Vulpix (C) .10 .20
❑ 137 Bill's Maintenance (C) .10 .20
❑ 138 Copycat (C) .10 .20
❑ 139 Dual Ball (C) .10 .20
❑ 140 Energy Removal 2 (U) .20 .50
❑ 141 Energy Restore (U) .20 .50
❑ 142 Mary's Impulse (U) .20 .50
❑ 143 Master Ball (U) .20 .50
❑ 144 Multi Technical (U) .20 .50
❑ 145 Pokemon Nurse (U) .20 .50
❑ 146 Pokemon Reversal (U) .20 .50
❑ 147 Power Charge (U) .20 .50
❑ 148 Professor Elm's (U) .20 .50
❑ 149 Professor Oak's (U) .20 .50
❑ 150 Strength Charm (U) .20 .50
❑ 151 Super Scoop Up (U) .20 .50
❑ 152 Warp Point (U) .20 .50
❑ 153 Energy Search (C) .10 .20
❑ 154 Full Heal (C) .10 .20
❑ 155 Moo-moo Milk (C) .10 .20
❑ 156 Potion (C) .10 .20
❑ 157 Switch (C) .10 .20
❑ 158 Darkness Energy (R) .50 1.00
❑ 159 Metal Energy (R) 1.00 2.00
❑ 160 Fire Energy .10 .20
❑ 161 Rock Energy .10 .20
❑ 162 Grass Energy .10 .20
❑ 163 Lightning Energy .10 .20
❑ 164 Psychic Energy .10 .20
❑ 165 Water Energy .10 .20

2002 Pokemon Expedition Reverse Foil

Complete Set (165) 90.00 175.00
❑ 1 Alakazam (holo) (R) 6.00 12.00
❑ 2 Ampharos (holo) (R) 4.00 8.00
❑ 3 Arbok (holo) (R) 4.00 8.00
❑ 4 Blastoise (holo) (R) 7.50 15.00
❑ 5 Butterfree (holo) (R) 4.00 8.00
❑ 6 Charizard (holo) (R) 20.00 40.00
❑ 7 Clefable (holo) (R) 4.00 8.00
❑ 8 Cloyster (holo) (R) 4.00 8.00
❑ 9 Dragonite (holo) (R) 4.00 8.00
❑ 10 Dugtrio (holo) (R) 4.00 8.00
❑ 11 Fearow (holo) (R) 4.00 8.00
❑ 12 Feraligatr (holo) (R) 4.00 8.00
❑ 13 Gengar (holo) (R) 4.00 8.00
❑ 14 Golem (holo) (R) 4.00 8.00
❑ 15 Kingler (holo) (R) 3.00 6.00
❑ 16 Machamp (holo) (R) 4.00 8.00
❑ 17 Magby (holo) (R) 4.00 8.00
❑ 18 Meganium (holo) (R) 4.00 8.00
❑ 19 Mew (holo) (R) 12.50 25.00
❑ 20 Mewtwo (holo) (R) 6.00 12.00
❑ 21 Ninetales (holo) (R) 4.00 8.00
❑ 22 Pichu (holo) (R) 5.00 10.00
❑ 23 Pidgeot (holo) (R) 4.00 8.00
❑ 24 Poliwrath (holo) (R) 4.00 8.00
❑ 25 Raichu (holo) (R) 6.00 12.00
❑ 26 Rapidash (holo) (R) 4.00 8.00
❑ 27 Skarmory (holo) (R) 4.00 8.00
❑ 28 Typhlosion (holo) (R) 4.00 8.00
❑ 29 Tyranitar (holo) (R) 5.00 10.00
❑ 30 Venusaur (holo) (R) 4.00 8.00
❑ 31 Vileplume (holo) (R) 4.00 8.00
❑ 32 Weezing (holo) (R) 4.00 8.00
❑ 33 Alakazam (R) 1.00 2.00
❑ 34 Ampharos (R) 1.00 2.00
❑ 35 Arbok (R) 1.00 2.00
❑ 36 Blastoise (R) 2.00 4.00
❑ 37 Blastoise (R) 2.00 4.00
❑ 38 Butterfree (R) 1.00 2.00
❑ 39 Charizard (R) 10.00 20.00
❑ 40 Charizard (R) 15.00 30.00
❑ 41 Clefable (R) 1.00 2.00
❑ 42 Cloyster (R) 1.00 2.00
❑ 43 Dragonite (R) 1.00 2.00
❑ 44 Dugtrio (R) 1.00 2.00
❑ 45 Fearow (R) 1.00 2.00
❑ 46 Feraligatr (R) 2.00 4.00
❑ 47 Feraligatr (R) 1.00 2.00
❑ 48 Gengar (R) 1.00 2.00
❑ 49 Golem (R) 1.00 2.00
❑ 50 Kingler (R) 1.00 2.00
❑ 51 Machamp (R) 1.00 2.00
❑ 52 Magby (R) 1.00 2.00
❑ 53 Meganium (R) 2.00 4.00
❑ 54 Meganium (R) 2.00 4.00
❑ 55 Mew (R) 4.00 8.00
❑ 56 Mewtwo (R) 4.00 8.00
❑ 57 Ninetales (R) 1.00 2.00
❑ 58 Pichu (R) 1.00 2.00
❑ 59 Pidgeot (R) 1.00 2.00
❑ 60 Poliwrath (R) 1.00 2.00
❑ 61 Raichu (R) 4.00 8.00
❑ 62 Rapidash (R) 1.00 2.00
❑ 63 Skarmory (R) 1.00 2.00
❑ 64 Typhlosion (R) 1.00 2.00
❑ 65 Typhlosion (R) 2.00 4.00
❑ 66 Tyranitar (R) 4.00 8.00
❑ 67 Venusaur (R) 1.00 2.00
❑ 68 Venusaur (R) 1.00 2.00
❑ 69 Vileplume (R) 1.00 2.00
❑ 70 Weezing (R) 1.00 2.00
❑ 71 Bayleef (U) .50 1.00
❑ 72 Chansey (U) .50 1.00
❑ 73 Charmeleon (U) .50 1.00
❑ 74 Croconaw (U) .50 1.00
❑ 75 Dragonair (U) .50 1.00
❑ 76 Electabuzz (U) .50 1.00
❑ 77 Flaafy (U) .50 1.00
❑ 78 Gloom (U) .50 1.00
❑ 79 Graveler (U) .50 1.00
❑ 80 Haunter (U) .50 1.00
❑ 81 Hitmonlee (U) .50 1.00
❑ 82 Ivysaur (U) .50 1.00
❑ 83 Jynx (U) .50 1.00
❑ 84 Kadabra (U) .50 1.00
❑ 85 Machoke (U) .50 1.00
❑ 86 Magmar (U) .50 1.00
❑ 87 Metapod (U) .50 1.00
❑ 88 Pidgeotto (U) .50 1.00
❑ 89 Poliwhirl (U) .50 1.00
❑ 90 Pupitar (U) .50 1.00
❑ 91 Quilava (U) .50 1.00
❑ 92 Wartortle (U) .50 1.00
❑ 93 Abra (C) .20 .40
❑ 94 Bulbasaur (C) .20 .40
❑ 95 Bulbasaur (C) .20 .40
❑ 96 Caterpie (C) .20 .40
❑ 97 Charmander (C) .20 .40
❑ 98 Charmander (C) .20 .40
❑ 99 Chikorita (C) .20 .40
❑ 100 Chikorita (C) .20 .40
❑ 101 Clefairy (C) .20 .40
❑ 102 Corsola (C) .20 .40
❑ 103 Cubone (C) .20 .40
❑ 104 Cyndaquil (C) .20 .40
❑ 105 Cyndaquil (C) .20 .40
❑ 106 Diglett (C) .20 .40
❑ 107 Dratini (C) .20 .40
❑ 108 Ekans (C) .20 .40
❑ 109 Gastly (C) .20 .40
❑ 110 Geodude (C) .20 .40
❑ 111 Goldeen (C) .20 .40
❑ 112 Hoppip (C) .20 .40
❑ 113 Houndour (C) .20 .40
❑ 114 Koffing (C) .20 .40
❑ 115 Krabby (C) .20 .40
❑ 116 Larvitar (C) .20 .40
❑ 117 Machop (C) .20 .40
❑ 118 Magikarp (C) .20 .40
❑ 119 Mareep (C) .20 .40
❑ 120 Marill (C) .20 .40
❑ 121 Meowth (C) .20 .40
❑ 122 Oddish (C) .20 .40
❑ 123 Pidgey (C) .20 .40
❑ 124 Pikachu (C) 1.00 2.00
❑ 125 Poliwag (C) .20 .40
❑ 126 Ponyta (C) .20 .40
❑ 127 Qwilfish (C) .20 .40
❑ 128 Rattata (C) .20 .40
❑ 129 Shellder (C) .20 .40
❑ 130 Spearow (C) .20 .40
❑ 131 Squirtle (C) .20 .40
❑ 132 Squirtle (C) .20 .40
❑ 133 Tauros (C) .20 .40
❑ 134 Totodile (C) .20 .40
❑ 135 Totodile (C) .20 .40
❑ 136 Vulpix (C) .20 .40
❑ 137 Bill's Maintenance (C) .20 .40
❑ 138 Copycat (C) .20 .40
❑ 139 Dual Ball (C) .20 .40
❑ 140 Energy Removal 2 (U) .50 1.00
❑ 141 Energy Restore (U) .50 1.00
❑ 142 Mary's Impulse (U) .50 1.00
❑ 143 Master Ball (U) .50 1.00
❑ 144 Multi Technical (U) .50 1.00
❑ 145 Pokemon Nurse (U) .50 1.00
❑ 146 Pokemon Reversal (U) .50 1.00
❑ 147 Power Charge (U) .50 1.00
❑ 148 Professor Elm's (U) .50 1.00
❑ 149 Professor Oak's (U) .50 1.00
❑ 150 Strength Charm (U) .50 1.00
❑ 151 Super Scoop Up (U) .50 1.00
❑ 152 Warp Point (U) .50 1.00
❑ 153 Energy Search (C) .20 .40
❑ 154 Full Heal (C) .20 .40
❑ 155 Moo-moo Milk (C) .20 .40
❑ 156 Potion (C) .20 .40
❑ 157 Switch (C) .20 .40
❑ 158 Darkness Energy (R) 1.00 2.00
❑ 159 Metal Energy (R) 2.00 4.00
❑ 160 Fire Energy .20 .40
❑ 161 Rock Energy .20 .40
❑ 162 Grass Energy .20 .40
❑ 163 Lightning Energy .20 .40
❑ 164 Psychic Energy .20 .40
❑ 165 Water Energy .20 .40

2003 Pokemon Aquapolis

Complete Set (186) 75.00 120.00
Booster Box (36 ct) 75.00 130.00
Booster Pack (11 cards) 4.00 5.00
Theme Deck 8.00 12.00
*Box Topper 2X Regular Version
❑ 1 Ampharos (R) .50 1.00
❑ 2 Arcanine (R) .50 1.00
❑ 3 Ariados (R) .50 1.00
❑ 4 Azumarill (R) .50 1.00
❑ 5 Bellossom (R) .50 1.00
❑ 6 Blissey (R) 1.00 2.00
❑ 7 Donphan (R) .50 1.00
❑ 8 Electrode (R) .50 1.00
❑ 9 Elekid (R) 1.00 2.00
❑ 10 Entei (R) 2.00 4.00
❑ 11 Espeon (R) 1.00 3.00
❑ 12 Exeggutor (R) .50 1.00
❑ 13 Exeggutor (R) .50 1.00
❑ 14 Houndoom (R) .50 1.00
❑ 15 Houndoom (R) .50 1.00
❑ 16 Hypno (R) .50 1.00
❑ 17 Jumpluff (R) .50 1.00
❑ 18 Jynx (R) .50 1.00
❑ 19 Kingdra (R) .50 1.00
❑ 20 Lanturn (R) .50 1.00
❑ 21 Lanturn (R) .50 1.00
❑ 22 Magneton (R) .50 1.00
❑ 23 Muk (R) .50 1.00
❑ 24 Nidoking (R) .50 1.00
❑ 25 Ninetales (R) .50 1.00
❑ 26 Octillery (R) .50 1.00
❑ 27 Parasect (R) .50 1.00
❑ 28 Porygon2 (R) .50 1.00
❑ 29 Primeape (R) .50 1.00
❑ 30 Quagsire (R) .50 1.00
❑ 31 Rapidash (R) .50 1.00
❑ 32 Scizor (R) .50 1.00
❑ 33 Slowbro (R) .50 1.00
❑ 34 Slowking (R) .50 1.00
❑ 35 Steelix (R) .50 1.00
❑ 36 Sudowoodo (R) .50 1.00
❑ 37 Suicune (R) 2.00 5.00
❑ 38 Tentacruel (R) .50 1.00
❑ 39 Togetic (R) .50 1.00
❑ 40 Tyranitar (R) .50 1.00
❑ 41 Umbreon (R) 1.00 2.00
❑ 42 Victreebel (R) .50 1.00
❑ 43 Vileplume (R) .50 1.00
❑ 44 Zapdos (R) 1.00 2.00
❑ 45 Bellsprout (U) .20 .50
❑ 46 Dodrio (U) .20 .50
❑ 47 Flaaffy (U) .20 .50
❑ 48 Furret (U) .20 .50
❑ 49 Gloom (U) .20 .50
❑ 50A Golduck (U) .20 .50
❑ 50B Golduck (U) .20 .50
❑ 51 Growlithe (U) .20 .50
❑ 52 Magnemite (U) .20 .50
❑ 53 Marill (U) .20 .50
❑ 54 Marowak (U) .20 .50
❑ 55 Nidorino (U) .20 .50
❑ 56 Pupitar (U) .20 .50
❑ 57 Scyther (U) .20 .50
❑ 58 Seadra (U) .20 .50
❑ 59 Seaking (U) .20 .50
❑ 60 Skiploom (U) .20 .50
❑ 61 Smoochum (U) .20 .50
❑ 62 Spinarak (U) .20 .50
❑ 63 Tyrogue (U) .20 .50
❑ 64 Voltorb (U) .20 .50
❑ 65 Weepinbell (U) .20 .50
❑ 66 Wooper (U) .20 .50
❑ 67 Aipom (C) .10 .20
❑ 68 Bellsprout (C) .10 .20
❑ 69 Chansey (C) .10 .20
❑ 70 Chinchou (C) .10 .20
❑ 71 Chinchou (C) .10 .20
❑ 72 Cubone (C) .10 .20
❑ 73 Doduo (C) .10 .20
❑ 74A Drowzee (C) .10 .20
❑ 74B Drowzee (C) .10 .20
❑ 75 Eevee (C) .10 .20
❑ 76 Exeggcute (C) .10 .20
❑ 77 Exeggcute (C) .10 .20
❑ 78 Goldeen (C) .10 .20
❑ 79 Grimer (C) .10 .20
❑ 80 Growlithe (C) .10 .20
❑ 81 Hitmonchan (C) .10 .20
❑ 82 Hitmontop (C) .10 .20
❑ 83 Hoppip (C) .10 .20
❑ 84 Horsea (C) .10 .20
❑ 85 Horsea (C) .10 .20
❑ 86 Houndour (C) .10 .20
❑ 87 Houndour (C) .10 .20
❑ 88 Kangaskhan (C) .10 .20
❑ 89 Larvitar (C) .10 .20
❑ 90 Lickitung (C) .10 .20
❑ 91 Magnemite (C) .10 .20
❑ 92 Mankey (C) .10 .20
❑ 93 Mareep (C) .10 .20
❑ 94 Miltank (C) .10 .20
❑ 95A Mr. Mime (C) .10 .20
❑ 95B Mr. Mime (C) .10 .20
❑ 96 Nidoran (C) .10 .20
❑ 97 Oddish (C) .10 .20
❑ 98 Onix (C) .10 .20
❑ 99 Paras (C) .10 .20
❑ 100 Phanpy (C) .10 .20
❑ 101 Pinsir (C) .10 .20
❑ 102 Ponyta (C) .10 .20
❑ 103A Porygon (C) .10 .20
❑ 103B Porygon (C) .10 .20
❑ 104 Psyduck (C) .10 .20
❑ 105 Remoraid (C) .10 .20
❑ 106 Scyther (C) .10 .20
❑ 107 Sentret (C) .10 .20
❑ 108 Slowpoke (C) .10 .20
❑ 109 Smeargle (C) .10 .20
❑ 110 Sneasel (C) .10 .20
❑ 111 Spinarak (C) .10 .20
❑ 112 Tangela (C) .10 .20
❑ 113 Tentacool (C) .10 .20
❑ 114 Togepi (C) .10 .25
❑ 115 Voltorb (C) .10 .20
❑ 116 Vulpix (C) .10 .20
❑ 117 Wooper (C) .10 .20
❑ 118 Apricorn Forest (R) .50 1.00
❑ 119 Darkness Cube (U) .20 .50
❑ 120 Energy Switch (U) .20 .50
❑ 121 Fighting Cube 01 (U) .20 .50
❑ 122 Fire Cube 01 (U) .20 .50
❑ 123 Forest Guardian (U) .20 .50
❑ 124 Grass Cube 01 (U) .20 .50
❑ 125 Healing Berry (U) .20 .50
❑ 126 Juggler (U) .20 .50
❑ 127 Lightning Cube 01 (U) .20 .50
❑ 128 Memory Berry (U) .20 .50
❑ 129 Metal Cube 01 (U) .20 .50
❑ 130 Pokémon Fan Club (U) .20 .50
❑ 131 Pokémon Park (U) .20 .50
❑ 132 Psychic Cube 01 (U) .20 .50
❑ 133 Seer (U) .20 .50
❑ 134 Super Energy Removal 2 (U) .20 .50
❑ 135 Time Shard (U) .20 .50
❑ 136 Town Volunteers (U) .20 .50
❑ 137 Traveling Salesman (U) .20 .50
❑ 138 Undersea Ruins (U) .20 .50
❑ 139* Power Plant (U) .20 .50
❑ 140 Water Cube 1 (U) .20 .50
❑ 141 Weakness Guard (U) .20 .50
❑ 142 Darkness Energy (R) .50 1.00
❑ 143 Metal Energy (R) .50 1.00
❑ 144 Rainbow Energy (R) .50 1.00
❑ 145 Boost Energy (U) .20 .50
❑ 146 Crystal Energy (U) .20 .50
❑ 147 Warp Energy (U) .20 .50
❑ 148 Kingdra (holo) (R) 4.00 10.00
❑ 149 Lugia (holo) (R) 15.00 25.00
❑ 150 Nidoking (holo) (R) 6.00 12.00
❑ H1 Ampharos (holo) (R) 2.00 4.00
❑ H2 Arcanine (holo) (R) 2.00 4.00
❑ H3 Ariados (holo) (R) 2.00 4.00
❑ H4 Azumarill (holo) (R) 3.00 7.00
❑ H5 Bellossom (holo) (R) 2.00 4.00
❑ H6 Blissey (holo) (R) 2.00 4.00
❑ H7 Electrode (holo) (R) 2.00 4.00
❑ H8 Entei (holo) (R) 4.00 10.00
❑ H9 Espeon (holo) (R) 2.00 6.00
❑ H10 Exeggutor (holo) (R) 2.00 4.00
❑ H11 Houndoom (holo) (R) 2.00 6.00
❑ H12 Hypno (holo) (R) 2.00 4.00
❑ H13 Jumpluff (holo) (R) 2.00 4.00
❑ H14 Kingdra (holo) (R) 2.00 4.00
❑ H15 Lanturn (holo) (R) 2.00 4.00
❑ H16 Magneton (holo) (R) 2.00 4.00
❑ H17 Muk (holo) (R) 2.00 4.00
❑ H18 Nidoking (holo) (R) 2.00 6.00
❑ H19 Ninetales (holo) (R) 2.00 6.00
❑ H20 Octillery (holo) (R) 2.00 4.00
❑ H21 Scizor (holo) (R) 2.00 6.00
❑ H22 Slowking (holo) (R) 2.00 4.00
❑ H23 Steelix (holo) (R) 2.00 4.00
❑ H24 Sudowoodo (holo) (R) 2.00 4.00
❑ H25 Suicune (holo) (R) 5.00 10.00
❑ H26 Tentacruel (holo) (R) 2.00 4.00
❑ H27 Togetic (holo) (R) 2.00 4.00
❑ H28 Tyranitar (holo) (R) 2.00 6.00
❑ H29 Umbreon (holo) (R) 7.00 15.00
❑ H30 Victreebel (holo) (R) 2.00 4.00
❑ H31 Vileplume (holo) (R) 2.00 4.00
❑ H32 Zapdos (holo) (R) 2.00 6.00

2003 Pokemon Aquapolis REVERSE FOIL

Complete Set (186) 150.00 250.00
❑ 1 Ampharos (R) 1.00 2.00
❑ 2 Arcanine (R) 1.00 2.00
❑ 3 Ariados (R) 1.00 2.00
❑ 4 Azumarill (R) 1.00 2.00
❑ 5 Bellossom (R) 1.00 2.00
❑ 6 Blissey (R) 2.00 4.00

☐ 7 Donphan (R)	1.00	2.00
☐ 8 Electrode (R)	1.00	2.00
☐ 9 Elekid (R)	1.00	2.00
☐ 10 Entei (R)	4.00	8.00
☐ 11 Espeon (R)	3.00	6.00
☐ 12 Exeggutor (R)	1.00	2.00
☐ 13 Exeggutor (R)	1.00	2.00
☐ 14 Houndoom (R)	1.00	2.00
☐ 15 Houndoom (R)	1.00	2.00
☐ 16 Hypno (R)	1.00	2.00
☐ 17 Jumpluff (R)	1.00	2.00
☐ 18 Jynx (R)	1.00	2.00
☐ 19 Kingdra (R)	1.00	2.00
☐ 20 Lanturn (R)	1.00	2.00
☐ 21 Lanturn (R)	1.00	2.00
☐ 22 Magneton (R)	1.00	2.00
☐ 23 Muk (R)	1.00	2.00
☐ 24 Nidoking (R)	1.00	2.00
☐ 25 Ninetales (R)	1.00	2.00
☐ 26 Octillery (R)	1.00	2.00
☐ 27 Parasect (R)	1.00	2.00
☐ 28 Porygon2 (R)	1.00	2.00
☐ 29 Primeape (R)	1.00	2.00
☐ 30 Quagsire (R)	1.00	2.00
☐ 31 Rapidash (R)	1.00	2.00
☐ 32 Scizor (R)	1.00	2.00
☐ 33 Slowbro (R)	1.00	2.00
☐ 34 Slowking (R)	1.00	2.00
☐ 35 Steelix (R)	1.00	2.00
☐ 36 Sudowoodo (R)	1.00	2.00
☐ 37 Suicune (R)	4.00	8.00
☐ 38 Tentacruel (R)	1.00	2.00
☐ 39 Togetic (R)	1.00	2.00
☐ 40 Tyranitar (R)	1.00	2.00
☐ 41 Umbreon (R)	1.00	2.00
☐ 42 Victreebel (R)	1.00	2.00
☐ 43 Vileplume (R)	1.00	2.00
☐ 44 Zapdos (R)	1.00	2.00
☐ 45 Bellsprout (U)	.50	1.00
☐ 46 Dodrio (U)	.50	1.00
☐ 47 Flaaffy (U)	.50	1.00
☐ 48 Furret (U)	.50	1.00
☐ 49 Gloom (U)	.50	1.00
☐ 50A Golduck (U)	.50	1.00
☐ 50B Golduck (U)	.50	1.00
☐ 51 Growlithe (U)	.50	1.00
☐ 52 Magnemite (U)	.50	1.00
☐ 53 Marill (U)	.50	1.00
☐ 54 Marowak (U)	.50	1.00
☐ 55 Nidorino (U)	.50	1.00
☐ 56 Pupitar (U)	.50	1.00
☐ 57 Scyther (U)	.50	1.00
☐ 58 Seadra (U)	.50	1.00
☐ 59 Seaking (U)	.50	1.00
☐ 60 Skiploom (U)	.50	1.00
☐ 61 Smoochum (U)	.50	1.00
☐ 62 Spinarak (U)	.50	1.00
☐ 63 Tyrogue (U)	.50	1.00
☐ 64 Voltorb (U)	.50	1.00
☐ 65 Weepinbell (U)	.50	1.00
☐ 66 Wooper (U)	.50	1.00
☐ 67 Aipom (C)	.20	.40
☐ 68 Bellsprout (C)	.20	.40
☐ 69 Chansey (C)	.20	.40
☐ 70 Chinchou (C)	.20	.40
☐ 71 Chinchou (C)	.20	.40
☐ 72 Cubone (C)	.20	.40
☐ 73 Doduo (C)	.20	.40
☐ 74A Drowzee (C)	.20	.40
☐ 74B Drowzee (C)	.20	.40
☐ 75 Eevee (C)	.20	.40
☐ 76 Exeggcute (C)	.20	.40
☐ 77 Exeggcute (C)	.20	.40
☐ 78 Goldeen (C)	.20	.40
☐ 79 Grimer (C)	.20	.40
☐ 80 Growlithe (C)	.20	.40
☐ 81 Hitmonchan (C)	.20	.40
☐ 82 Hitmontop (C)	.20	.40
☐ 83 Hoppip (C)	.20	.40
☐ 84 Horsea (C)	.20	.40
☐ 85 Horsea (C)	.20	.40
☐ 86 Houndour (C)	.20	.40
☐ 87 Houndour (C)	.20	.40
☐ 88 Kangaskhan (C)	.20	.40
☐ 89 Larvitar (C)	.20	.40
☐ 90 Lickitung (C)	.20	.40
☐ 91 Magnemite (C)	.20	.40
☐ 92 Mankey (C)	.20	.40
☐ 93 Mareep (C)	.20	.40
☐ 94 Miltank (C)	.20	.40
☐ 95A Mr. Mime (C)	.20	.40
☐ 95B Mr. Mime (C)	.20	.40
☐ 96 Nidoran (C)	.20	.40
☐ 97 Oddish (C)	.20	.40
☐ 98 Onix (C)	.20	.40
☐ 99 Paras (C)	.20	.40
☐ 100 Phanpy (C)	.20	.40
☐ 101 Pinsir (C)	.20	.40
☐ 102 Ponyta (C)	.20	.40
☐ 103A Porygon (C)	.20	.40
☐ 103B Porygon (C)	.20	.40
☐ 104 Psyduck (C)	.20	.40
☐ 105 Remoraid (C)	.20	.40
☐ 106 Scyther (C)	.20	.40
☐ 107 Sentret (C)	.20	.40
☐ 108 Slowpoke (C)	.20	.40
☐ 109 Smeargle (C)	.20	.40
☐ 110 Sneasel (C)	.20	.40
☐ 111 Spinarak (C)	.20	.40
☐ 112 Tangela (C)	.20	.40
☐ 113 Tentacool (C)	.20	.40
☐ 114 Togepi (C)	.25	.50
☐ 115 Voltorb (C)	.20	.40
☐ 116 Vulpix (C)	.20	.40
☐ 117 Wooper (C)	.20	.40
☐ 118 Apricorn Forest (R)	1.00	2.00
☐ 119 Darkness Cube (U)	.50	1.00
☐ 120 Energy Switch (U)	.50	1.00
☐ 121 Fighting Cube 01 (U)	.50	1.00
☐ 122 Fire Cube 01 (U)	.50	1.00
☐ 123 Forest Guardian (U)	.50	1.00
☐ 124 Grass Cube 01 (U)	.50	1.00
☐ 125 Healing Berry (U)	.50	1.00
☐ 126 Juggler (U)	.50	1.00
☐ 127 Lightning Cube 01 (U)	.50	1.00
☐ 128 Memory Berry (U)	.50	1.00
☐ 129 Metal Cube 01 (U)	.50	1.00
☐ 130 Pokémon Fan Club (U)	.50	1.00
☐ 131 Pokémon Park (U)	.50	1.00
☐ 132 Psychic Cube 01 (U)	.50	1.00
☐ 133 Seer (U)	.50	1.00
☐ 134 Super Energy Removal 2 (U)	.50	1.00
☐ 135 Time Shard (U)	.50	1.00
☐ 136 Town Volunteers (U)	.50	1.00
☐ 137 Traveling Salesman (U)	.50	1.00
☐ 138 Undersea Ruins (U)	.50	1.00
☐ 139 Power Plant (U)	.50	1.00
☐ 140 Water Cube 1 (U)	.50	1.00
☐ 141 Weakness Guard (U)	.50	1.00
☐ 142 Darkness Energy (R)	1.00	2.00
☐ 143 Metal Energy (R)	1.00	2.00
☐ 144 Rainbow Energy (R)	1.00	2.00
☐ 145 Boost Energy (U)	.50	1.00
☐ 146 Crystal Energy (U)	.50	1.00
☐ 147 Warp Energy (U)	.50	1.00
☐ 148 Kingdra (holo) (R)	10.00	20.00
☐ 149 Lugia (holo) (R)	20.00	40.00
☐ 150 Nidoking (holo) (R)	10.00	20.00
☐ H1 Ampharos (holo) (R)	4.00	8.00
☐ H2 Arcanine (holo) (R)	4.00	8.00
☐ H3 Ariados (holo) (R)	4.00	8.00
☐ H4 Azumarill (holo) (R)	7.50	15.00
☐ H5 Bellossom (holo) (R)	4.00	8.00
☐ H6 Blissey (holo) (R)	4.00	8.00
☐ H7 Electrode (holo) (R)	4.00	8.00
☐ H8 Entei (holo) (R)	5.00	10.00
☐ H9 Espeon (holo) (R)	4.00	8.00
☐ H10 Exeggutor (holo) (R)	4.00	8.00
☐ H11 Houndoom (holo) (R)	4.00	8.00
☐ H12 Hypno (holo) (R)	4.00	8.00
☐ H13 Jumpluff (holo) (R)	4.00	8.00
☐ H14 Kingdra (holo) (R)	4.00	8.00
☐ H15 Lanturn (holo) (R)	4.00	8.00
☐ H16 Magneton (holo) (R)	4.00	8.00
☐ H17 Muk (holo) (R)	4.00	8.00
☐ H18 Nidoking (holo) (R)	4.00	8.00
☐ H19 Ninetales (holo) (R)	4.00	8.00
☐ H20 Octillery (holo) (R)	4.00	8.00
☐ H21 Scizor (holo) (R)	4.00	8.00
☐ H22 Slowking (holo) (R)	4.00	8.00
☐ H23 Steelix (holo) (R)	4.00	8.00
☐ H24 Sudowoodo (holo) (R)	4.00	8.00
☐ H25 Suicune (holo) (R)	4.00	8.00
☐ H26 Tentacruel (holo) (R)	4.00	8.00
☐ H27 Togetic (holo) (R)	4.00	8.00
☐ H28 Tyranitar (holo) (R)	4.00	8.00
☐ H29 Umbreon (holo) (R)	10.00	20.00
☐ H30 Victreebel (holo) (R)	4.00	8.00
☐ H31 Vileplume (holo) (R)	4.00	8.00
☐ H32 Zapdos (holo) (R)	4.00	8.00

2003 Pokemon Skyridge

Regular Set (150)	50.00	100.00
Complete Set (182)	100.00	175.00
Booster Box (36 ct)	80.00	125.00
Booster Pack (11 cards)	4.00	5.00

*Jumbo Box Toppers 1.5X Regular

☐ 1 Aerodactyl (R)	.50	1.00
☐ 2 Alakazam (R)	.50	1.00
☐ 3 Arcanine (R)	.50	1.00
☐ 4 Articuno (R)	1.00	2.00
☐ 5 Beedrill (R)	.50	1.00
☐ 6 Crobat (R)	.50	1.00
☐ 7 Dewgong (R)	.50	1.00
☐ 8 Flareon (R)	.50	1.00
☐ 9 Forretress (R)	.50	1.00
☐ 10 Gengar (R)	.50	1.00
☐ 11 Gyarados (R)	1.00	2.00
☐ 12 Houndoom (R)	.50	1.00
☐ 13 Jolteon (R)	.50	1.00
☐ 14 Kabutops (R)	.50	1.00
☐ 15 Ledian (R)	.50	1.00
☐ 16 Machamp (R)	.50	1.00
☐ 17 Magcargo (R)	.50	1.00
☐ 18 Magcargo (R)	.50	1.00
☐ 19 Magneton (R)	.50	1.00
☐ 20 Magneton (R)	.50	1.00
☐ 21 Moltres (R)	.50	1.00
☐ 22 Nidoqueen (R)	.50	1.00
☐ 23 Omastar (R)	.50	1.00
☐ 24 Piloswine (R)	.50	1.00
☐ 25 Politoed (R)	.50	1.00
☐ 26 Poliwrath (R)	.50	1.00
☐ 27 Raichu (R)	1.00	2.00
☐ 28 Raikou (R)	.50	1.00
☐ 29 Rhydon (R)	.50	1.00
☐ 30 Starmie (R)	.50	1.00
☐ 31 Steelix (R)	.50	1.00
☐ 32 Umbreon (R)	.50	1.00
☐ 33 Vaporeon (R)	.50	1.00
☐ 34 Wigglytuff (R)	.50	1.00
☐ 35 Xatu (R)	.50	1.00
☐ 36 Electrode (U)	.20	.50
☐ 37 Kabuto (U)	.20	.50
☐ 38 Machoke (U)	.20	.50
☐ 39 Misdreavus (U)	.20	.50
☐ 40 Noctowl (U)	.20	.50
☐ 41 Omanyte (U)	.20	.50
☐ 42 Persian (U)	.20	.50
☐ 43 Piloswine (U)	.20	.50
☐ 44 Starmie (U)	.20	.50
☐ 45 Wobbuffet (U)	.20	.50
☐ 46 Abra (C)	.10	.20
☐ 47 Buried Fossil (C)	.10	.20
☐ 48 Cleffa (C)	.10	.20
☐ 49 Delibird (C)	.10	.20
☐ 50 Diglett (C)	.10	.20
☐ 51 Ditto (C)	.10	.20
☐ 52 Dugtrio (C)	.10	.20
☐ 53 Dunsparce (C)	.10	.20
☐ 54 Eevee (C)	.10	.20
☐ 55 Farfetch'd (C)	.10	.20
☐ 56 Forretress (C)	.10	.20
☐ 57 Gastly (C)	.10	.20
☐ 58 Girafarig (C)	.10	.20
☐ 59 Gligar (C)	.10	.20
☐ 60 Golbat (C)	.10	.20
☐ 61 Granbull (C)	.10	.20
☐ 62 Growlithe (C)	.10	.20
☐ 63 Haunter (C)	.10	.20
☐ 64 Heracross (C)	.10	.20
☐ 65 Hoothoot (C)	.10	.20
☐ 66 Houndour (C)	.10	.20
☐ 67 Igglybuff (C)	.10	.20
☐ 68 Jigglypuff (C)	.10	.20
☐ 69 Kadabra (C)	.10	.20
☐ 70 Kakuna (C)	.10	.20
☐ 71 Lapras (C)	.10	.20
☐ 72 Ledyba (C)	.10	.20
☐ 73 Ledyba (C)	.10	.20
☐ 74 Machop (C)	.10	.20
☐ 75 Magikarp (C)	.10	.20
☐ 76 Magnemite (C)	.10	.20
☐ 77 Mantine (C)	.10	.20
☐ 78 Meowth (C)	.10	.20
☐ 79 Murkrow (C)	.10	.20
☐ 80 Natu (C)	.10	.20
☐ 81 Nidoran F (C)	.10	.20
☐ 82 Nidoran F (C)	.10	.20
☐ 83 Nidorina (C)	.10	.20
☐ 84 Pikachu (C)	.10	.50
☐ 85 Pineco (C)	.10	.20
☐ 86 Pineco (C)	.10	.20
☐ 87 Poliwag (C)	.10	.20
☐ 88 Poliwhirl (C)	.10	.20
☐ 89 Raticate (C)	.10	.20
☐ 90 Rattata (C)	.10	.20
☐ 91 Rhyhorn (C)	.10	.20
☐ 92 Sandshrew (C)	.10	.20
☐ 93 Sandslash (C)	.10	.20
☐ 94 Seel (C)	.10	.20
☐ 95 Seel (C)	.10	.20
☐ 96 Shuckle (C)	.10	.20
☐ 97 Skarmory (C)	.10	.20
☐ 98 Slugma (C)	.10	.20
☐ 99 Slugma (C)	.10	.20
☐ 100 Snorlax (C)	.10	.20
☐ 101 Snubbull (C)	.10	.20
☐ 102 Stantler (C)	.10	.20
☐ 103 Staryu (C)	.10	.20
☐ 104 Staryu (C)	.10	.20
☐ 105 Sunflora (C)	.10	.20
☐ 106 Sunkern (C)	.10	.20
☐ 107 Swinub (C)	.10	.20
☐ 108 Swinub (C)	.10	.20
☐ 109 Teddiursa (C)	.10	.20
☐ 110 Ursaring (C)	.10	.20
☐ 111 Venomoth (C)	.10	.20
☐ 112 Venonat (C)	.10	.20
☐ 113 Voltorb (C)	.10	.20
☐ 114 Weedle (C)	.10	.20
☐ 115 Weedle (C)	.10	.20
☐ 116 Yanma (C)	.10	.20
☐ 117 Zubat (C)	.10	.20
☐ 118 Zubat (C)	.10	.20
☐ 119 Ancient Ruins (U)	.20	.50
☐ 120 Relic Hunter (U)	.20	.50
☐ 121 Apricorn (U)	.20	.50
☐ 122 Crystal Shard (U)	.20	.50
☐ 123 Desert Shaman (U)	.20	.50
☐ 124 Fast Ball (U)	.20	.50
☐ 125 Fisherman (U)	.20	.50
☐ 126 Friend Ball (U)	.20	.50
☐ 127 Hyper Potion (U)	.20	.50
☐ 128 Lure Ball (U)	.20	.50
☐ 129 Miracle Sphere (Alpha) (U)	.20	.50
☐ 130 Miracle Sphere (Beta) (U)	.20	.50
☐ 131 Miracle Sphere (Gamma)(U)	.20	.50
☐ 132 Mirage Stadium (U)	.20	.50
☐ 133 Mystery Plate (Alpha) (U)	.20	.50
☐ 134 Mystery Plate (Beta) (U)	.20	.50
☐ 135 Mystery Plate (Gamma) (U)	.20	.50
☐ 136 Mystery Plate (Delta) (U)	.20	.50
☐ 137 Mystery Zone (U)	.20	.50
☐ 138 Oracle (U)	.20	.50
☐ 139 Star Piece (U)	.20	.50
☐ 140 Underground Expedition (U)	.20	.50
☐ 141 Underground Lake (U)	.20	.50
☐ 142 Bounce Energy (U)	.20	.50
☐ 143 Cyclone Energy (U)	.20	.50
☐ 144 Retro Energy (U)	.20	.50
☐ 145 Celebi (holo) (R)	10.00	20.00
☐ 146 Charizard (holo) (R)	30.00	55.00
☐ 147 Crobat (holo) (R)	7.00	12.00
☐ 148 Golem (holo) (R)	7.00	12.00
☐ 149 Ho-oh (holo) (R)	10.00	18.00
☐ 150 Kabutops (holo) (R)	7.00	12.00
☐ H1 Alakazam (holo) (R)	2.00	4.00
☐ H2 Arcanine (holo) (R)	2.00	4.00
☐ H3 Articuno (holo) (R)	2.00	4.00
☐ H4 Beedrill (holo) (R)	2.00	4.00
☐ H5 Crobat (holo) (R)	2.00	4.00
☐ H6 Dewgong (holo) (R)	2.00	4.00
☐ H7 Flareon (holo) (R)	2.00	4.00
☐ H8 Forretress (holo) (R)	2.00	4.00
☐ H9 Gengar (holo) (R)	2.00	4.00
☐ H10 Gyarados (holo) (R)	2.00	4.00
☐ H11 Houndoom (holo) (R)	2.00	4.00
☐ H12 Jolteon (holo) (R)	2.00	4.00
☐ H13 Kabutops (holo) (R)	3.00	6.00
☐ H14 Ledian (holo) (R)	2.00	4.00
☐ H15 Machamp (holo) (R)	2.00	4.00
☐ H16 Magcargo (holo) (R)	2.00	4.00
☐ H17 Magcargo (holo) (R)	2.00	4.00
☐ H18 Magneton (holo) (R)	2.00	4.00
☐ H19 Magneton (holo) (R)	2.00	4.00
☐ H20 Moltres (holo) (R)	2.00	4.00
☐ H21 Nidoqueen (holo) (R)	2.00	4.00
☐ H22 Piloswine (holo) (R)	2.00	4.00
☐ H23 Politoed (holo) (R)	2.00	4.00
☐ H24 Poliwrath (holo) (R)	2.00	4.00
☐ H25 Raichu (holo) (R)	2.00	4.00
☐ H26 Raikou (holo) (R)	2.00	4.00
☐ H27 Rhydon (holo) (R)	2.00	4.00
☐ H28 Starmie (holo) (R)	2.00	4.00
☐ H29 Steelix (holo) (R)	2.00	4.00
☐ H30 Umbreon (holo) (R)	2.00	5.00
☐ H31 Vaporeon (holo) (R)	2.00	4.00
☐ H32 Xatu (holo) (R)	2.00	4.00

2003 Pokemon SkyRidge Reverse Foil

Complete Set (182)	125.00	225.00
☐ 1 Aerodactyl (R)	1.00	2.00
☐ 2 Alakazam (R)	1.00	2.00
☐ 3 Arcanine (R)	1.00	2.00
☐ 4 Articuno (R)	1.00	2.00
☐ 5 Beedrill (R)	1.00	2.00
☐ 6 Crobat (R)	1.00	2.00
☐ 7 Dewgong (R)	1.00	2.00
☐ 8 Flareon (R)	1.00	2.00
☐ 9 Forretress (R)	1.00	2.00
☐ 10 Gengar (R)	1.00	2.00
☐ 11 Gyarados (R)	1.00	2.00
☐ 12 Houndoom (R)	1.00	2.00
☐ 13 Jolteon (R)	1.00	2.00
☐ 14 Kabutops (R)	1.00	2.00
☐ 15 Ledian (R)	1.00	2.00
☐ 16 Machamp (R)	1.00	2.00
☐ 17 Magcargo (R)	1.00	2.00
☐ 18 Magcargo (R)	1.00	2.00
☐ 19 Magneton (R)	1.00	2.00
☐ 20 Magneton (R)	1.00	2.00
☐ 21 Moltres (R)	1.00	2.00
☐ 22 Nidoqueen (R)	1.00	2.00
☐ 23 Omastar (R)	1.00	2.00
☐ 24 Piloswine (R)	1.00	2.00
☐ 25 Politoed (R)	1.00	2.00
☐ 26 Poliwrath (R)	1.00	2.00
☐ 27 Raichu (R)	1.00	2.00
☐ 28 Raikou (R)	1.00	2.00
☐ 29 Rhydon (R)	1.00	2.00
☐ 30 Starmie (R)	1.00	2.00
☐ 31 Steelix (R)	1.00	2.00
☐ 32 Umbreon (R)	1.00	2.00
☐ 33 Vaporeon (R)	1.00	2.00
☐ 34 Wigglytuff (R)	1.00	2.00
☐ 35 Xatu (R)	1.00	2.00
☐ 36 Electrode (U)	.50	1.00
☐ 37 Kabuto (U)	.50	1.00
☐ 38 Machoke (U)	.50	1.00
☐ 39 Misdreavus (U)	.50	1.00
☐ 40 Noctowl (U)	.50	1.00
☐ 41 Omanyte (U)	.50	1.00
☐ 42 Persian (U)	.50	1.00
☐ 43 Piloswine (U)	.50	1.00
☐ 44 Starmie (U)	.50	1.00
☐ 45 Wobbuffet (U)	.50	1.00
☐ 46 Abra (C)	.20	.40
☐ 47 Buried Fossil (C)	.20	.40
☐ 48 Cleffa (C)	.20	.40
☐ 49 Delibird (C)	.20	.40
☐ 50 Diglett (C)	.20	.40
☐ 51 Ditto (C)	.20	.40
☐ 52 Dugtrio (C)	.20	.40
☐ 53 Dunsparce (C)	.20	.40
☐ 54 Eevee (C)	.20	.40
☐ 55 Farfetch'd (C)	.20	.40
☐ 56 Forretress (C)	.20	.40
☐ 57 Gastly (C)	.20	.40
☐ 58 Girafarig (C)	.20	.40
☐ 59 Gligar (C)	.20	.40
☐ 60 Golbat (C)	.20	.40
☐ 61 Granbull (C)	.20	.40
☐ 62 Growlithe (C)	.20	.40
☐ 63 Haunter (C)	.20	.40
☐ 64 Heracross (C)	.20	.40
☐ 65 Hoothoot (C)	.20	.40
☐ 66 Houndour (C)	.20	.40
☐ 67 Igglybuff (C)	.20	.40
☐ 68 Jigglypuff (C)	.20	.40
☐ 69 Kadabra (C)	.20	.40
☐ 70 Kakuna (C)	.20	.40
☐ 71 Lapras (C)	.20	.40
☐ 72 Ledyba (C)	.20	.40
☐ 73 Ledyba (C)	.20	.40
☐ 74 Machop (C)	.20	.40
☐ 75 Magikarp (C)	.20	.40
☐ 76 Magnemite (C)	.20	.40
☐ 77 Mantine (C)	.20	.40
☐ 78 Meowth (C)	.20	.40
☐ 79 Murkrow (C)	.20	.40
☐ 80 Natu (C)	.20	.40
☐ 81 Nidoran F (C)	.20	.40
☐ 82 Nidoran F (C)	.20	.40
☐ 83 Nidorina (C)	.20	.40
☐ 84 Pikachu (C)	.50	1.00
☐ 85 Pineco (C)	.20	.40
☐ 86 Pineco (C)	.20	.40
☐ 87 Poliwag (C)	.20	.40
☐ 88 Poliwhirl (C)	.20	.40
☐ 89 Raticate (C)	.20	.40
☐ 90 Rattata (C)	.20	.40
☐ 91 Rhyhorn (C)	.20	.40
☐ 92 Sandshrew (C)	.20	.40
☐ 93 Sandslash (C)	.20	.40
☐ 94 Seel (C)	.20	.40
☐ 95 Seel (C)	.20	.40
☐ 96 Shuckle (C)	.20	.40
☐ 97 Skarmory (C)	.20	.40
☐ 98 Slugma (C)	.20	.40
☐ 99 Slugma (C)	.20	.40
☐ 100 Snorlax (C)	.20	.40
☐ 101 Snubbull (C)	.20	.40
☐ 102 Stantler (C)	.20	.40
☐ 103 Staryu (C)	.20	.40
☐ 104 Staryu (C)	.20	.40
☐ 105 Sunflora (C)	.20	.40
☐ 106 Sunkern (C)	.20	.40
☐ 107 Swinub (C)	.20	.40
☐ 108 Swinub (C)	.20	.40
☐ 109 Teddiursa (C)	.20	.40
☐ 110 Ursaring (C)	.20	.40
☐ 111 Venomoth (C)	.20	.40
☐ 112 Venonat (C)	.20	.40
☐ 113 Voltorb (C)	.20	.40
☐ 114 Weedle (C)	.20	.40
☐ 115 Weedle (C)	.20	.40
☐ 116 Yanma (C)	.20	.40
☐ 117 Zubat (C)	.20	.40
☐ 118 Zubat (C)	.20	.40
☐ 119 Ancient Ruins (U)	.50	1.00
☐ 120 Relic Hunter (U)	.50	1.00
☐ 121 Apricorn (U)	.50	1.00
☐ 122 Crystal Shard (U)	.50	1.00
☐ 123 Desert Shaman (U)	.50	1.00
☐ 124 Fast Ball (U)	.50	1.00
☐ 125 Fisherman (U)	.50	1.00
☐ 126 Friend Ball (U)	.50	1.00
☐ 127 Hyper Potion (U)	.50	1.00
☐ 128 Lure Ball (U)	.50	1.00
☐ 129 Miracle Sphere (Alpha) (U)	.50	1.00
☐ 130 Miracle Sphere (Beta) (U)	.50	1.00
☐ 131 Miracle Sphere (Gamma)(U)	.50	1.00
☐ 132 Mirage Stadium (U)	.50	1.00
☐ 133 Mystery Plate (Alpha) (U)	.50	1.00
☐ 134 Mystery Plate (Beta) (U)	.50	1.00
☐ 135 Mystery Plate (Gamma) (U)	.50	1.00
☐ 136 Mystery Plate (Delta) (U)	.50	1.00
☐ 137 Mystery Zone (U)	.50	1.00
☐ 138 Oracle (U)	.50	1.00
☐ 139 Star Piece (U)	.50	1.00
☐ 140 Underground Expedition (U)	.50	1.00
☐ 141 Underground Lake (U)	.50	1.00
☐ 142 Bounce Energy (U)	.50	1.00
☐ 143 Cyclone Energy (U)	.50	1.00
☐ 144 Retro Energy (U)	.50	1.00
☐ 145 Celebi (holo) (R)	20.00	40.00
☐ 146 Charizard (holo) (R)	40.00	80.00
☐ 147 Crobat (holo) (R)	15.00	30.00
☐ 148 Golem (holo) (R)	8.00	15.00
☐ 149 Ho-oh (holo) (R)	6.00	12.00
☐ 150 Kabutops (holo) (R)	15.00	30.00

H1 Alakazam (holo) (R)	4.00	8.00
H2 Arcanine (holo) (R)	4.00	8.00
H3 Articuno (holo) (R)	4.00	8.00
H4 Beedrill (holo) (R)	4.00	8.00
H5 Crobat (holo) (R)	4.00	8.00
H6 Dewgong (holo) (R)	4.00	8.00
H7 Flareon (holo) (R)	4.00	8.00
H8 Forretress (holo) (R)	4.00	8.00
H9 Gengar (holo) (R)	4.00	8.00
H10 Gyarados (holo) (R)	4.00	8.00
H11 Houndoom (holo) (R)	4.00	8.00
H12 Jolteon (holo) (R)	4.00	8.00
H13 Kabutops (holo) (R)	6.00	12.00
H14 Ledian (holo) (R)	4.00	8.00
H15 Machamp (holo) (R)	4.00	8.00
H16 Magcargo (holo) (R)	4.00	8.00
H17 Magcargo (holo) (R)	4.00	8.00
H18 Magneton (holo) (R)	4.00	8.00
H19 Magneton (holo) (R)	4.00	8.00
H20 Moltres (holo) (R)	4.00	8.00
H21 Nidoqueen (holo) (R)	4.00	8.00
H22 Piloswine (holo) (R)	4.00	8.00
H23 Politoed (holo) (R)	4.00	8.00
H24 Poliwrath (holo) (R)	4.00	8.00
H25 Raichu (holo) (R)	4.00	8.00
H26 Raikou (holo) (R)	4.00	8.00
H27 Rhydon (holo) (R)	4.00	8.00
H28 Starmie (holo) (R)	4.00	8.00
H29 Steelix (holo) (R)	4.00	8.00
H30 Umbreon (holo) (R)	4.00	8.00
H31 Vaporeon (holo) (R)	4.00	8.00
H32 Xatu (holo) (R)	4.00	8.00

2003 Pokemon EX Ruby & Sapphire

Complete Set (109)	100.00	150.00
Booster Box (36 ct)	90.00	140.00
Booster Pack (9 cards)	3.00	5.00
Ruby Theme Deck	10.00	15.00
Sapphire Theme Deck	10.00	15.00
1 Aggron (holo) (R)	2.00	4.00
2 Beautifly (holo) (R)	2.00	4.00
3 Blaziken (holo) (R)	4.00	10.00
4 Camerupt (holo) (R)	2.00	4.00
5 Delcatty (holo) (R)	3.00	6.00
6 Dustox (holo) (R)	2.00	4.00
7 Gardevoir (holo) (R)	2.00	4.00
8 Hariyama (holo) (R)	2.00	4.00
9 Manectric (holo) (R)	2.00	4.00
10 Mightyena (holo) (R)	2.00	4.00
11 Sceptile (holo) (R)	2.00	4.00
12 Slaking (holo) (R)	2.00	4.00
13 Swampert (holo) (R)	2.00	4.00
14 Wailord (holo) (R)	3.00	7.00
15 Blaziken (R)	.50	1.00
16 Breloom (R)	.50	1.00
17 Donphan (R)	.50	1.00
18 Nosepass (R)	.50	1.00
19 Pelipper (R)	.50	1.00
20 Sceptile (R)	.50	1.00
21 Seaking (R)	.50	1.00
22 Sharpedo (R)	.50	1.00
23 Swampert (R)	.50	1.00
24 Weezing (R)	.50	1.00
25 Aron (U)	.20	.50
26 Cascoon (U)	.20	.50
27 Combusken (U)	.20	.50
28 Combusken (U)	.20	.50
29 Delcatty (U)	.20	.50
30 Electrike (U)	.20	.50
31 Grovyle (U)	.20	.50
32 Grovyle (U)	.20	.50
33 Hariyama (U)	.20	.50
34 Kirlia (U)	.20	.50
35 Kirlia (U)	.20	.50
36 Lairon (U)	.20	.50
37 Lairon (U)	.20	.50
38 Linoone (U)	.20	.50
39 Manectric (U)	.20	.50
40 Marshtomp (U)	.20	.50
41 Marshtomp (U)	.20	.50
42 Mightyena (U)	.20	.50
43 Silcoon (U)	.20	.50
44 Skitty (U)	.20	.50
45 Slakoth (U)	.20	.50
46 Swellow (U)	.20	.50
47 Vigoroth (U)	.20	.50
48 Wailmer (U)	.20	.50
49 Aron (C)	.10	.20
50 Aron (C)	.10	.20
51 Carvanha (C)	.10	.20
52 Electrike (C)	.10	.20
53 Electrike (C)	.10	.20
54 Koffing (C)	.10	.20
55 Goldeen (C)	.10	.20
56 Makuhita (C)	.10	.20
57 Makuhita (C)	.10	.20
58 Makuhita (C)	.10	.20
59 Mudkip (C)	.10	.20
60 Mudkip (C)	.10	.20
61 Numel (C)	.10	.20
62 Phanpy (C)	.10	.20
63 Poochyena (C)	.10	.20
64 Poochyena (C)	.10	.20
65 Poochyena (C)	.10	.20
66 Ralts (C)	.10	.20
67 Ralts (C)	.10	.20
68 Ralts (C)	.10	.20
69 Shroomish (C)	.10	.20
70 Skitty (C)	.10	.20
71 Skitty (C)	.10	.20
72 Taillow (C)	.10	.20
73 Torchic (C)	.10	.20
74 Torchic (C)	.10	.20
75 Treecko (C)	.10	.20
76 Treecko (C)	.10	.20
77 Wingull (C)	.10	.20
78 Wurmple (C)	.10	.20
79 Zigzagoon (C)	.10	.20
80 Trainer: Energy Removal 2 (U)	.20	.50
81 Trainer: Energy Restore (U)	.20	.50
82 Trainer: Energy Switch (U)	.20	.50
83 Trainer: Lady Outing (U)	.20	.50
84 Trainer: Lum Berry (U)	.20	.50
85 Trainer: Oran Berry (U)	.20	.50
86 Trainer: Poke Ball (U)	.20	.50
87 Trainer: Pokemon Reversal (U)	.20	.50
88 Trainer: PokeNav (U)	.20	.50
89 Trainer: Professor Birch (U)	.20	.50
90 Trainer: Energy Search (C)	.10	.20
91 Trainer: Potion (C)	.10	.20
92 Trainer: Switch (C)	.10	.20
93 Darkness Energy (R)	.50	1.00
94 Metal Energy (R)	.50	1.00
95 Rainbow Energy (R)	.50	1.00
96 Chansey ex (holo) (R)	2.00	5.00
97 Electabuzz ex (holo) (R)	2.00	5.00
98 Hitmonchan ex (holo) (R)	2.00	5.00
99 Lapras ex (holo) (R)	2.00	5.00
100 Magmar ex (holo) (R)	2.00	5.00
101 Mewtwo ex (holo) (R)	12.00	20.00
102 Scyther ex (holo) (R)	2.00	5.00
103 Sneasel ex (holo) (R)	2.00	6.00
104 Grass Energy (C)	.10	.20
105 Fighting Energy (C)	.10	.20
106 Water Energy (C)	.10	.20
107 Psychic Energy (C)	.10	.20
108 Fire Energy (C)	.10	.20
109 Lightning Energy (C)	.10	.20

2003 Pokemon EX Ruby & Sapphire Reverse Foil

Complete Set (109)	125.00	225.00
1 Aggron (holo) (R)	4.00	8.00
2 Beautifly (holo) (R)	4.00	8.00
3 Blaziken (holo) (R)	10.00	20.00
4 Camerupt (holo) (R)	4.00	8.00
5 Delcatty (holo) (R)	6.00	12.00
6 Dustox (holo) (R)	4.00	8.00
7 Gardevoir (holo) (R)	4.00	8.00
8 Hariyama (holo) (R)	4.00	8.00
9 Manectric (holo) (R)	4.00	8.00
10 Mightyena (holo) (R)	4.00	8.00
11 Sceptile (holo) (R)	4.00	8.00
12 Slaking (holo) (R)	4.00	8.00
13 Swampert (holo) (R)	4.00	8.00
14 Wailord (holo) (R)	7.50	15.00
15 Blaziken (R)	1.00	2.00
16 Breloom (R)	1.00	2.00
17 Donphan (R)	1.00	2.00
18 Nosepass (R)	1.00	2.00
19 Pelipper (R)	1.00	2.00
20 Sceptile (R)	1.00	2.00
21 Seaking (R)	1.00	2.00
22 Sharpedo (R)	1.00	2.00
23 Swampert (R)	1.00	2.00
24 Weezing (R)	1.00	2.00
25 Aron (U)	.50	1.00
26 Cascoon (U)	.50	1.00
27 Combusken (U)	.50	1.00
28 Combusken (U)	.50	1.00
29 Delcatty (U)	.50	1.00
30 Electrike (U)	.50	1.00
31 Grovyle (U)	.50	1.00
32 Grovyle (U)	.50	1.00
33 Hariyama (U)	.50	1.00
34 Kirlia (U)	.50	1.00
35 Kirlia (U)	.50	1.00
36 Lairon (U)	.50	1.00
37 Lairon (U)	.50	1.00
38 Linoone (U)	.50	1.00
39 Manectric (U)	.50	1.00
40 Marshtomp (U)	.50	1.00
41 Marshtomp (U)	.50	1.00
42 Mightyena (U)	.50	1.00
43 Silcoon (U)	.50	1.00
44 Skitty (U)	.50	1.00
45 Slakoth (U)	.50	1.00
46 Swellow (U)	.50	1.00
47 Vigoroth (U)	.50	1.00
48 Wailmer (U)	.50	1.00
49 Aron (C)	.20	.40
50 Aron (C)	.20	.40
51 Carvanha (C)	.20	.40
52 Electrike (C)	.20	.40
53 Electrike (C)	.20	.40
54 Koffing (C)	.20	.40
55 Goldeen (C)	.20	.40
56 Makuhita (C)	.20	.40
57 Makuhita (C)	.20	.40
58 Makuhita (C)	.20	.40
59 Mudkip (C)	.20	.40
60 Mudkip (C)	.20	.40
61 Numel (C)	.20	.40
62 Phanpy (C)	.20	.40
63 Poochyena (C)	.20	.40
64 Poochyena (C)	.20	.40
65 Poochyena (C)	.20	.40
66 Ralts (C)	.20	.40
67 Ralts (C)	.20	.40
68 Ralts (C)	.20	.40
69 Shroomish (C)	.20	.40
70 Skitty (C)	.20	.40
71 Skitty (C)	.20	.40
72 Taillow (C)	.20	.40
73 Torchic (C)	.20	.40
74 Torchic (C)	.20	.40
75 Treecko (C)	.20	.40
76 Treecko (C)	.20	.40
77 Wingull (C)	.20	.40
78 Wurmple (C)	.20	.40
79 Zigzagoon (C)	.20	.40
80 Trainer: Energy Removal 2 (U)	.50	1.00
81 Trainer: Energy Restore (U)	.50	1.00
82 Trainer: Energy Switch (U)	.50	1.00
83 Trainer: Lady Outing (U)	.50	1.00
84 Trainer: Lum Berry (U)	.50	1.00
85 Trainer: Oran Berry (U)	.50	1.00
86 Trainer: Poke Ball (U)	.50	1.00
87 Trainer: Pokemon Reversal (U)	.50	1.00
88 Trainer: PokeNav (U)	.50	1.00
89 Trainer: Professor Birch (U)	.50	1.00
90 Trainer: Energy Search (C)	.20	.40
91 Trainer: Potion (C)	.20	.40
92 Trainer: Switch (C)	.20	.40
93 Darkness Energy (R)	1.00	2.00
94 Metal Energy (R)	1.00	2.00
95 Rainbow Energy (R)	1.00	2.00
96 Chansey ex (holo) (R)	8.00	15.00
97 Electabuzz ex (holo) (R)	8.00	15.00
98 Hitmonchan ex (holo) (R)	10.00	20.00
99 Lapras ex (holo) (R)	10.00	20.00
100 Magmar ex (holo) (R)	10.00	20.00
101 Mewtwo ex (holo) (R)	15.00	30.00
102 Scyther ex (holo) (R)	15.00	30.00
103 Sneasel ex (holo) (R)	8.00	15.00
104 Grass Energy (C)	.20	.40
105 Fighting Energy (C)	.20	.40
106 Water Energy (C)	.20	.40
107 Psychic Energy (C)	.20	.40
108 Fire Energy (C)	.20	.40
109 Lightning Energy (C)	.20	.40

2003 Pokemon EX Sandstorm

Complete Set (100)	90.00	150.00
Reverse Holofoil Set (100)	150.00	200.00
Booster Box (36 ct)	90.00	140.00
Booster Pack (9 Cards)	4.00	5.00
1 Armaldo (holo) (R)	2.00	4.00
2 Cacturne (holo) (R)	2.00	4.00
3 Cradily (holo) (R)	2.00	4.00
4 Dusclops (holo) (R)	2.00	4.00
5 Flareon (holo) (R)	2.00	4.00
6 Jolteon (holo) (R)	2.00	4.00
7 Ludicolo (holo) (R)	2.00	4.00
8 Lunatone (holo) (R)	2.00	4.00
9 Mawile (holo) (R)	2.00	4.00
10 Sableye (holo) (R)	2.00	4.00
11 Seviper (holo) (R)	2.00	4.00
12 Shiftry (holo) (R)	2.00	4.00
13 Solrock (holo) (R)	3.00	6.00
14 Zangoose (holo) (R)	2.00	4.00
15 Arcanine (R)	.50	1.00
16 Espeon (R)	.50	1.00
17 Golduck (R)	.50	1.00
18 Kecleon (R)	.50	1.00
19 Omastar (R)	.50	1.00
20 Pichu (R)	.50	1.00
21 Sandslash (R)	.50	1.00
22 Shiftry (R)	.50	1.00
23 Steelix (R)	.50	1.00
24 Umbreon (R)	.50	1.00
25 Vaporeon (R)	.50	1.00
26 Wobbuffet (R)	.50	1.00
27 Anorith (U)	.20	.50
28 Anorith (U)	.20	.50
29 Arbok (U)	.20	.50
30 Azumarill (U)	.20	.50
31 Azurill (U)	.20	.50
32 Baltoy (U)	.20	.50
33 Breloom (U)	.20	.50
34 Delcatty (U)	.20	.50
35 Electabuzz (U)	.20	.50
36 Elekid (U)	.20	.50
37 Fearow (U)	.20	.50
38 Illumise (U)	.20	.50
39 Kabuto (U)	.20	.50
40 Kirlia (U)	.20	.50
41 Lairon (U)	.20	.50
42 Lileep (U)	.20	.50
43 Lileep (U)	.20	.50
44 Linoone (U)	.20	.50
45 Lombre (U)	.20	.50
46 Lombre (U)	.20	.50
47 Murkrow (U)	.20	.50
48 Nuzleaf (U)	.20	.50
49 Nuzleaf (U)	.20	.50
50 Pelipper (U)	.20	.50
51 Quilava (U)	.20	.50
52 Vigoroth (U)	.20	.50
53 Volbeat (U)	.20	.50
54 Wynaut (U)	.20	.50
55 Xatu (U)	.20	.50
56 Aron (C)	.10	.20
57 Cacnea (C)	.10	.20
58 Cacnea (C)	.10	.20
59 Cyndaquil (C)	.10	.20
60 Dunsparce (C)	.10	.20
61 Duskull (C)	.10	.20
62 Duskull (C)	.10	.20
63 Eevee (C)	.10	.20
64 Ekans (C)	.10	.20
65 Growlithe (C)	.10	.20
66 Lotad (C)	.10	.20
67 Lotad (C)	.10	.20
68 Marill (C)	.10	.20
69 Natu (C)	.10	.20
70 Omanyte (C)	.10	.20
71 Onix (C)	.10	.20
72 Pikachu (C)	.25	.50
73 Psyduck (C)	.10	.20
74 Ralts (C)	.10	.20
75 Sandshrew (C)	.10	.20
76 Seedot (C)	.10	.20
77 Seedot (C)	.10	.20
78 Shroomish (C)	.10	.20
79 Skitty (C)	.10	.20
80 Slakoth (C)	.10	.20
81 Spearow (C)	.10	.20
82 Trapinch (C)	.10	.20
83 Wailmer (C)	.10	.20
84 Wingull (C)	.10	.20
85 Zigzagoon (C)	.10	.20
86 Double Full Heal (U)	.20	.50
87 Lanette's Net Search (U)	.20	.50
88 Rare Candy (U)	2.00	5.00
89 Wally's Training (U)	.20	.50
90 Claw Fossil (C)	.10	.20
91 Mysterious Fossil (C)	.10	.20
92 Root Fossil (C)	.10	.20
93 Multi Energy (R)	.50	1.00
94 Aerodactyl ex (holo) (R)	6.00	12.00
95 Aggron ex (holo) (R)	4.00	8.00
96 Gardevoir ex (holo) (R)	4.00	8.00
97 Kabutops ex (holo) (R)	4.00	8.00
98 Raichu ex (holo) (R)	10.00	18.00
99 Typhlosion ex (holo) (R)	9.00	18.00
100 Wailord ex (holo) (R)	15.00	40.00

2003 Pokemon EX Sandstorm Reverse Foil

Complete Set (100)	150.00	250.00
1 Armaldo (holo) (R)	4.00	8.00
2 Cacturne (holo) (R)	4.00	8.00
3 Cradily (holo) (R)	4.00	8.00
4 Dusclops (holo) (R)	4.00	8.00
5 Flareon (holo) (R)	4.00	8.00
6 Jolteon (holo) (R)	4.00	8.00
7 Ludicolo (holo) (R)	4.00	8.00
8 Lunatone (holo) (R)	4.00	8.00
9 Mawile (holo) (R)	4.00	8.00
10 Sableye (holo) (R)	4.00	8.00
11 Seviper (holo) (R)	4.00	8.00
12 Shiftry (holo) (R)	4.00	8.00
13 Solrock (holo) (R)	4.00	8.00
14 Zangoose (holo) (R)	4.00	8.00
15 Arcanine (R)	1.00	2.00
16 Espeon (R)	1.00	2.00
17 Golduck (R)	1.00	2.00
18 Kecleon (R)	1.00	2.00
19 Omastar (R)	1.00	2.00
20 Pichu (R)	1.00	2.00
21 Sandslash (R)	1.00	2.00
22 Shiftry (R)	1.00	2.00
23 Steelix (R)	1.00	2.00
24 Umbreon (R)	1.00	2.00
25 Vaporeon (R)	1.00	2.00
26 Wobbuffet (R)	1.00	2.00
27 Anorith (U)	.50	1.00
28 Anorith (U)	.50	1.00
29 Arbok (U)	.50	1.00
30 Azumarill (U)	.50	1.00
31 Azurill (U)	.50	1.00
32 Baltoy (U)	.50	1.00
33 Breloom (U)	.50	1.00
34 Delcatty (U)	.50	1.00
35 Electabuzz (U)	.50	1.00
36 Elekid (U)	.50	1.00
37 Fearow (U)	.50	1.00
38 Illumise (U)	.50	1.00
39 Kabuto (U)	.50	1.00
40 Kirlia (U)	.50	1.00
41 Lairon (U)	.50	1.00
42 Lileep (U)	.50	1.00
43 Lileep (U)	.50	1.00
44 Linoone (U)	.50	1.00
45 Lombre (U)	.50	1.00
46 Lombre (U)	.50	1.00
47 Murkrow (U)	.50	1.00
48 Nuzleaf (U)	.50	1.00
49 Nuzleaf (U)	.50	1.00
50 Pelipper (U)	.50	1.00
51 Quilava (U)	.50	1.00
52 Vigoroth (U)	.50	1.00
53 Volbeat (U)	.50	1.00
54 Wynaut (U)	.50	1.00
55 Xatu (U)	.50	1.00
56 Aron (C)	.20	.40
57 Cacnea (C)	.20	.40
58 Cacnea (C)	.20	.40
59 Cyndaquil (C)	.20	.40
60 Dunsparce (C)	.20	.40
61 Duskull (C)	.20	.40
62 Duskull (C)	.20	.40
63 Eevee (C)	.20	.40
64 Ekans (C)	.20	.40
65 Growlithe (C)	.20	.40
66 Lotad (C)	.20	.40
67 Lotad (C)	.20	.40
68 Marill (C)	.20	.40
69 Natu (C)	.20	.40
70 Omanyte (C)	.20	.40
71 Onix (C)	.20	.40
72 Pikachu (C)	.50	1.00
73 Psyduck (C)	.20	.40
74 Ralts (C)	.20	.40
75 Sandshrew (C)	.20	.40
76 Seedot (C)	.20	.40
77 Seedot (C)	.20	.40
78 Shroomish (C)	.20	.40
79 Skitty (C)	.20	.40
80 Slakoth (C)	.20	.40
81 Spearow (C)	.20	.40
82 Trapinch (C)	.20	.40
83 Wailmer (C)	.20	.40
84 Wingull (C)	.20	.40
85 Zigzagoon (C)	.20	.40
86 Double Full Heal (U)	.50	1.00
87 Lanette's Net Search (U)	.50	1.00
88 Rare Candy (U)	.50	1.00
89 Wally's Training (U)	.50	1.00
90 Claw Fossil (C)	.20	.40
91 Mysterious Fossil (C)	.20	.40
92 Root Fossil (C)	.20	.40
93 Multi Energy (R)	1.00	2.00
94 Aerodactyl ex (holo) (R)	10.00	20.00
95 Aggron ex (holo) (R)	15.00	30.00
96 Gardevoir ex (holo) (R)	15.00	30.00
97 Kabutops ex (holo) (R)	12.50	25.00
98 Raichu ex (holo) (R)	25.00	50.00
99 Typhlosion ex (holo) (R)	20.00	40.00
100 Wailord ex (holo) (R)	50.00	100.00

2003 Pokemon EX Dragon

Complete Set (100)	90.00	140.00
Booster Box (36 ct)	80.00	90.00
Booster Pack (9 cards)	4.00	5.00
FireFang Deck	8.00	12.00
WindBlast Deck	8.00	12.00
1 Absol (holo) (R)	2.00	4.00
2 Altaria (holo) (R)	2.00	4.00
3 Crawdaunt (holo) (R)	1.00	4.00
4 Flygon (holo) (R)	2.00	4.00
5 Golem (holo) (R)	2.00	4.00
6 Grumpig (holo) (R)	2.00	4.00
7 Minun (holo) (R)	2.00	4.00
8 Plusle (holo) (R)	2.00	4.00
9 Roselia (holo) (R)	2.00	4.00
10 Salamence (holo) (R)	2.00	4.00
11 Shedinja (holo) (R)	2.00	4.00
12 Torkoal (holo) (R)	2.00	4.00
13 Crawdaunt (R)	.50	1.00
14 Dragonair (R)	.50	1.00
15 Flygon (R)	.50	1.00
16 Girafarig (R)	.50	1.00
17 Magneton (R)	.50	1.00
18 Ninjask (R)	.50	1.00
19 Salamence (R)	.50	1.00
20 Shelgon (R)	.50	1.00
21 Skarmory (R)	.50	1.00
22 Vibrava (R)	.50	1.00
23 Bagon (U)	.20	.50
24 Camerupt (U)	.20	.50
25 Combusken (U)	.20	.50
26 Dratini (U)	.20	.50
27 Flaaffy (U)	.20	.50
28 Forretress (U)	.20	.50
29 Graveler (U)	.20	.50
30 Graveler (U)	.20	.50
31 Grovyle (U)	.20	.50
32 Gyarados (U)	.20	.50
33 Horsea (U)	.20	.50
34 Houndoom (U)	.20	.50
35 Magneton (U)	.20	.50
36 Marshtomp (U)	.20	.50
37 Meditite (U)	.20	.50
38 Ninjask (U)	.20	.50
39 Seadra (U)	.20	.50
40 Seadra (U)	.20	.50
41 Shelgon (U)	.20	.50
42 Shelgon (U)	.20	.50
43 Shuppet (U)	.20	.50
44 Snorunt (U)	.20	.50
45 Swellow (U)	.20	.50
46 Vibrava (U)	.20	.50
47 Vibrava (U)	.20	.50
48 Whiscash (U)	.20	.50

TCG/CCG

Card	Low	High
49 Bagon (C)	.10	.20
50 Bagon (C)	.10	.20
51 Barboach (C)	.10	.20
52 Corphish (C)	.10	.20
53 Corphish (C)	.10	.20
54 Corphish (C)	.10	.20
55 Geodude (C)	.10	.20
56 Geodude (C)	.10	.20
57 Grimer (C)	.10	.20
58 Horsea (C)	.10	.20
59 Houndour (C)	.10	.20
60 Magikarp (C)	.10	.20
61 Magnemite (C)	.10	.20
62 Magnemite (C)	.10	.20
63 Magnemite (C)	.10	.20
64 Mareep (C)	.10	.20
65 Mudkip (C)	.10	.20
66 Nincada (C)	.10	.20
67 Nincada (C)	.10	.20
68 Nincada (C)	.10	.20
69 Numel (C)	.10	.20
70 Numel (C)	.10	.20
71 Pineco (C)	.10	.20
72 Slugma (C)	.10	.20
73 Spoink (C)	.10	.20
74 Spoink (C)	.10	.20
75 Swablu (C)	.10	.20
76 Taillow (C)	.10	.20
77 Torchic (C)	.10	.20
78 Trapinch (C)	.10	.20
79 Trapinch (C)	.10	.20
80 Treecko (C)	.10	.20
81 Wurmple (C)	.10	.20
82 Balloon Berry (C)	.10	.20
83 Buffer Piece (C)	.10	.20
84 Energy Recycle System (C)	.10	.20
85 High Pressure System (C)	.10	.20
86 Low Pressure System (C)	.10	.20
87 Mr. Briney's Compassion (C)	.10	.20
88 TV Reporter (C)	.10	.20
88R TV Reporter (Rev. Foil)	50.00	100.00
89 Ampharos ex (holo) (R)	2.00	5.00
90 Dragonite ex (holo) (R)	6.00	15.00
91 Golem ex (holo) (R)	10.00	20.00
92 Kingdra ex (holo) (R)	5.00	10.00
93 Latias ex (holo) (R)	10.00	20.00
94 Latios ex (holo) (R)	10.00	20.00
95 Magcargo ex (holo) (R)	4.00	8.00
96 Muk ex (holo) (R)	4.00	8.00
97 Rayquaza ex (holo) (R)	10.00	20.00
98 Charmander (holo) (R)	4.00	8.00
99 Charmeleon (holo) (R)	4.00	8.00
100 Charizard (holo) (R)	20.00	38.00

2003 Pokemon EX Dragon Reverse Foil

Card	Low	High
Complete Set (100)	200.00	300.00
1 Absol (holo) (R)	4.00	8.00
2 Altaria (holo) (R)	4.00	8.00
3 Crawdaunt (holo) (R)	4.00	8.00
4 Flygon (holo) (R)	4.00	8.00
5 Golem (holo) (R)	4.00	8.00
6 Grumpig (holo) (R)	4.00	8.00
7 Minun (holo) (R)	4.00	8.00
8 Plusle (holo) (R)	4.00	8.00
9 Roselia (holo) (R)	4.00	8.00
10 Salamence (holo) (R)	4.00	8.00
11 Shedinja (holo) (R)	4.00	8.00
12 Torkoal (holo) (R)	4.00	8.00
13 Crawdaunt (R)	1.00	2.00
14 Dragonair (R)	1.00	2.00
15 Flygon (R)	1.00	2.00
16 Girafarig (R)	1.00	2.00
17 Magneton (R)	1.00	2.00
18 Ninjask (R)	1.00	2.00
19 Salamence (R)	1.00	2.00
20 Shelgon (R)	1.00	2.00
21 Skarmory (R)	1.00	2.00
22 Vibrava (R)	1.00	2.00
23 Bagon (U)	.50	1.00
24 Camerupt (U)	.50	1.00
25 Combusken (U)	.50	1.00
26 Dratini (U)	.50	1.00
27 Flaaffy (U)	.50	1.00
28 Forretress (U)	.50	1.00
29 Graveler (U)	.50	1.00
30 Graveler (U)	.50	1.00
31 Grovyle (U)	.50	1.00
32 Gyarados (U)	.50	1.00
33 Horsea (U)	.50	1.00
34 Houndoom (U)	.50	1.00
35 Magneton (U)	.50	1.00
36 Marshtomp (U)	.50	1.00
37 Meditite (U)	.50	1.00
38 Ninjask (U)	.50	1.00
39 Seadra (U)	.50	1.00
40 Seadra (U)	.50	1.00
41 Shelgon (U)	.50	1.00
42 Shelgon (U)	.50	1.00
43 Shuppet (U)	.50	1.00
44 Snorunt (U)	.50	1.00
45 Swellow (U)	.50	1.00
46 Vibrava (U)	.50	1.00
47 Vibrava (U)	.50	1.00
48 Whiscash (U)	.50	1.00
49 Bagon (C)	.20	.40
50 Bagon (C)	.20	.40
51 Barboach (C)	.20	.40
52 Corphish (C)	.20	.40
53 Corphish (C)	.20	.40
54 Corphish (C)	.20	.40
55 Geodude (C)	.20	.40
56 Geodude (C)	.20	.40
57 Grimer (C)	.20	.40
58 Horsea (C)	.20	.40
59 Houndour (C)	.20	.40
60 Magikarp (C)	.20	.40
61 Magnemite (C)	.20	.40
62 Magnemite (C)	.20	.40
63 Magnemite (C)	.20	.40
64 Mareep (C)	.20	.40
65 Mudkip (C)	.20	.40
66 Nincada (C)	.20	.40
67 Nincada (C)	.20	.40
68 Nincada (C)	.20	.40
69 Numel (C)	.20	.40
70 Numel (C)	.20	.40
71 Pineco (C)	.20	.40
72 Slugma (C)	.20	.40
73 Spoink (C)	.20	.40
74 Spoink (C)	.20	.40
75 Swablu (C)	.20	.40
76 Taillow (C)	.20	.40
77 Torchic (C)	.20	.40
78 Trapinch (C)	.20	.40
79 Trapinch (C)	.20	.40
80 Treecko (C)	.20	.40
81 Wurmple (C)	.20	.40
82 Balloon Berry (C)	.20	.40
83 Buffer Piece (C)	.20	.40
84 Energy Recycle System (C)	.20	.40
85 High Pressure System (C)	.20	.40
86 Low Pressure System (C)	.20	.40
87 Mr. Briney's Compassion (C)	.20	.40
88 TV Reporter (C)	.20	.40
88R TV Reporter (Rev. Foil)	60.00	120.00
89 Ampharos ex (holo) (R)	12.50	25.00
90 Dragonite ex (holo) (R)	30.00	60.00
91 Golem ex (holo) (R)	20.00	40.00
92 Kingdra ex (holo) (R)	8.00	15.00
93 Latias ex (holo) (R)	20.00	40.00
94 Latios ex (holo) (R)	20.00	40.00
95 Magcargo ex (holo) (R)	8.00	15.00
96 Muk ex (holo) (R)	8.00	15.00
97 Rayquaza ex (holo) (R)	20.00	40.00
98 Charmander (holo) (R)	8.00	15.00
99 Charmeleon (holo) (R)	8.00	15.00
100 Charizard (holo) (R)	40.00	80.00

2004 Pokemon EX Team Magma Vs Team Aqua

Card	Low	High
Complete Set (97)	60.00	120.00
Booster Box (36 Packs)	250.00	400.00
Booster Pack (9 Cards)	8.00	12.00
*Reverse Foil: 1X to 2X Regular Card		
1 Team Aqua's Cacturne (holo) (R)	.75	2.00
2 Team Aqua's Crawdaunt (holo) (R)	.75	2.00
3 Team Aqua's Kyogre (holo) (R)	2.00	5.00
4 Team Aqua's Manectric (holo) (R)	1.00	2.50
5 Team Aqua's Sharpedo (holo) (R)	2.50	6.00
6 Team Aqua's Walrein (holo) (R)	.75	2.00
7 Team Magma's Aggron (holo) (R)	1.00	2.50
8 Team Magma's Claydol (holo) (R)	.75	2.00
9 Team Magma's Groudon (holo) (R)	3.00	8.00
10 Team Magma's Houndoom (holo) (R)	2.00	5.00
11 Team Magma's Rhydon (holo) (R)	.75	2.00
12 Team Magma's Torkoal (holo) (R)	.75	2.00
13 Raichu (R)	.50	1.00
14 Team Aqua's Crawdaunt (R)	.50	1.00
15 Team Aqua's Mightyena (R)	.50	1.00
16 Team Aqua's Sealeo (R)	.50	1.00
17 Team Aqua's Seviper (R)	.50	1.00
18 Team Aqua's Sharpedo (R)	.50	1.00
19 Team Magma's Camerupt (R)	.50	1.00
20 Team Magma's Lairon (R)	.50	1.00
21 Team Magma's Mightyena (R)	.50	1.00
22 Team Magma's Rhydon (R)	.50	1.00
23 Team Magma's Zangoose (R)	.50	1.00
24 Team Aqua's Cacnea (U)	.20	.50
25 Team Aqua's Carvanha (U)	.20	.50
26 Team Aqua's Corphish (U)	.20	.50
27 Team Aqua's Electrike (U)	.20	.50
28 Team Aqua's Lanturn (U)	.20	.50
29 Team Aqua's Manectric (U)	.20	.50
30 Team Aqua's Mightyena (U)	.20	.50
31 Team Aqua's Sealeo (U)	.20	.50
32 Team Magma's Baltoy (U)	.20	.50
33 Team Magma's Claydol (U)	.20	.50
34 Team Magma's Houndoom (U)	.20	.50
35 Team Magma's Houndour (U)	.20	.50
36 Team Magma's Lairon (U)	.20	.50
37 Team Magma's Mightyena (U)	.20	.50
38 Team Magma's Rhyhorn (U)	.20	.50
39 Bulbasaur (C)	.10	.20
40 Cubone (C)	.10	.20
41 Jigglypuff (C)	.10	.20
42 Meowth (C)	.10	.20
43 Pikachu (C)	.10	.20
44 Psyduck (C)	.10	.20
45 Slowpoke (C)	.10	.20
46 Squirtle (C)	.10	.20
47 Team Aqua's Carvanha (C)	.10	.20
48 Team Aqua's Carvanha (C)	.10	.20
49 Team Aqua's Chinchou (C)	.10	.20
50 Team Aqua's Corphish (C)	.10	.20
51 Team Aqua's Corphish (C)	.10	.20
52 Team Aqua's Electrike (C)	.10	.20
53 Team Aqua's Electrike (C)	.10	.20
54 Team Aqua's Poochyena (C)	.10	.20
55 Team Aqua's Poochyena (C)	.10	.20
56 Team Aqua's Spheal (C)	.10	.20
57 Team Aqua's Spheal (C)	.10	.20
58 Team Magma's Aron (C)	.10	.20
59 Team Magma's Aron (C)	.10	.20
60 Team Magma's Baltoy (C)	.10	.20
61 Team Magma's Baltoy (C)	.10	.20
62 Team Magma's Houndour (C)	.10	.20
63 Team Magma's Houndour (C)	.10	.20
64 Team Magma's Numel (C)	.10	.20
65 Team Magma's Poochyena (C)	.10	.20
66 Team Magma's Poochyena (C)	.10	.20
67 Team Magma's Rhyhorn (C)	.10	.20
68 Team Magma's Rhyhorn (C)	.10	.20
69 Team Aqua Schemer (U)	.20	.50
70 Team Magma Schemer (U)	.20	.50
71 Archie (U)	.20	.50
72 Dual Ball (U)	.20	.50
73 Maxie (U)	.20	.50
74 Strength Charm (U)	.20	.50
75 Team Aqua Ball (U)	.20	.50
76 Team Aqua Belt (U)	.20	.50
77 Team Aqua Conspirator (U)	.20	.50
78 Team Aqua Hideout (U)	.20	.50
79 Team Aqua Technical Machine 01 (U)	.20	.50
80 Team Magma Ball (U)	.20	.50
81 Team Magma Belt (U)	.20	.50
82 Team Magma Conspirator (U)	.20	.50
83 Team Magma Hideout (U)	.20	.50
84 Team Magma Tech. Machine 01 (U)	.20	.50
85 Warp Point (U)	.20	.50
86 Aqua Energy (U)	.20	.50
87 Magma Energy (U)	.20	.50
88 Double Rainbow Energy (R)	1.50	4.00
89 Blaziken ex (holo) (R)	8.00	20.00
90 Cradily ex (holo) (R)	5.00	12.00
91 Entei ex (holo) (R)	6.00	15.00
92 Raikou ex (holo) (R)	6.00	15.00
93 Sceptile ex (holo) (R)	10.00	25.00
94 Suicune ex (holo) (R)	5.00	12.00
95 Swampert ex (holo) (R)	5.00	12.00
96 Absol (holo) (R)	3.00	8.00
97 Jirachi (holo) (R)	2.00	5.00

2004 Pokemon EX Team Magma vs Team Aqua Reverse Foil

Card	Low	High
Complete Set (97)	100.00	200.00
*Reverse Foil: 1X to 2X Regular Card		
1 Team Aqua's Cacturne (holo) (R)	1.50	4.00
2 Team Aqua's Crawdaunt (holo) (R)	1.50	4.00
3 Team Aqua's Kyogre (holo) (R)	4.00	10.00
4 Team Aqua's Manectric (holo) (R)	2.00	5.00
5 Team Aqua's Sharpedo (holo) (R)	5.00	12.00
6 Team Aqua's Walrein (holo) (R)	1.50	4.00
7 Team Magma's Aggron (holo) (R)	2.00	5.00
8 Team Magma's Claydol (holo) (R)	1.50	4.00
9 Team Magma's Groudon (holo) (R)	6.00	15.00
10 Team Magma's Houndoom (holo) (R)	4.00	10.00
11 Team Magma's Rhydon (holo) (R)	1.50	4.00
12 Team Magma's Torkoal (holo) (R)	1.50	4.00
13 Raichu (R)	.75	2.00
14 Team Aqua's Crawdaunt (R)	.75	2.00
15 Team Aqua's Mightyena (R)	.75	2.00
16 Team Aqua's Sealeo (R)	.75	2.00
17 Team Aqua's Seviper (R)	.75	2.00
18 Team Aqua's Sharpedo (R)	.75	2.00
19 Team Magma's Camerupt (R)	.75	2.00
20 Team Magma's Lairon (R)	.75	2.00
21 Team Magma's Mightyena (R)	.75	2.00
22 Team Magma's Rhydon (R)	.75	2.00
23 Team Magma's Zangoose (R)	.75	2.00
24 Team Aqua's Cacnea (U)	.40	1.00
25 Team Aqua's Carvanha (U)	.40	1.00
26 Team Aqua's Corphish (U)	.40	1.00
27 Team Aqua's Electrike (U)	.40	1.00
28 Team Aqua's Lanturn (U)	.40	1.00
29 Team Aqua's Manectric (U)	.40	1.00
30 Team Aqua's Mightyena (U)	.40	1.00
31 Team Aqua's Sealeo (U)	.40	1.00
32 Team Magma's Baltoy (U)	.40	1.00
33 Team Magma's Claydol (U)	.40	1.00
34 Team Magma's Houndoom (U)	.40	1.00
35 Team Magma's Houndour (U)	.40	1.00
36 Team Magma's Lairon (U)	.40	1.00
37 Team Magma's Mightyena (U)	.40	1.00
38 Team Magma's Rhyhorn (U)	.40	1.00
71 Archie (U)	.40	1.00
72 Dual Ball (U)	.40	1.00
73 Maxie (U)	.40	1.00
74 Strength Charm (U)	.40	1.00
75 Team Aqua Ball (U)	.40	1.00
76 Team Aqua Belt (U)	.40	1.00
77 Team Aqua Conspirator (U)	.40	1.00
78 Team Aqua Hideout (U)	.40	1.00
79 Team Aqua Technical Machine 01 (U)	.40	1.00
80 Team Magma Ball (U)	.40	1.00
81 Team Magma Belt (U)	.40	1.00
82 Team Magma Conspirator (U)	.40	1.00
83 Team Magma Hideout (U)	.40	1.00
84 Team Magma Tech. Machine 01 (U)	.40	1.00
85 Warp Point (U)	.40	1.00
86 Aqua Energy (U)	.40	1.00
87 Magma Energy (U)	.40	1.00
88 Double Rainbow Energy (R)	3.00	8.00
89 Blaziken ex (holo) (R)	15.00	40.00
90 Cradily ex (holo) (R)	10.00	25.00
91 Entei ex (holo) (R)	12.00	30.00
92 Raikou ex (holo) (R)	12.00	30.00
93 Sceptile ex (holo) (R)	25.00	50.00
94 Suicune ex (holo) (R)	10.00	25.00
95 Swampert ex (holo) (R)	10.00	25.00
96 Absol (holo) (R)	6.00	15.00
97 Jirachi (holo) (R)	4.00	10.00

2004 Pokemon EX Hidden Legends

Card	Low	High
Complete Set (102)	150.00	250.00
Booster Box (36 Packs)	80.00	120.00
Booster Pack (9 Cards)	3.00	4.00
*Reverse Foil: 1X to 2X Regular Card		
1 Banette (Holo) (R)	.75	2.00
2 Claydol (Holo) (R)	.75	2.00
3 Crobat (Holo) (R)	.75	2.00
4 Dark Celebi (Holo) (R)	1.50	4.00
5 Electrode (Holo) (R)	.75	2.00
6 Exploud (Holo) (R)	.75	2.00
7 Heracross (Holo) (R)	.75	2.00
8 Jirachi (Holo) (R)	1.00	2.50
9 Machamp (Holo) (R)	.75	2.00
10 Medicham (Holo) (R)	.75	2.00
11 Metagross (Holo) (R)	.75	2.00
12 Milotic (Holo) (R)	2.00	5.00
13 Pinsir (Holo) (R)	.75	2.00
14 Shiftry (Holo) (R)	.75	2.00
15 Walrein (Holo) (R)	1.25	3.00
16 Bellossom (R)	.50	1.00
17 Chimecho (R)	.50	1.00
18 Gorebyss (R)	.50	1.00
19 Huntail (R)	.50	1.00
20 Masquerain (R)	.50	1.00
21 Metang (R)	.50	1.00
22 Ninetales (R)	.50	1.00
23 Rain Castform (R)	.50	1.00
24 Relicanth (R)	.50	1.00
25 Snow-cloud Castform (R)	.50	1.00
26 Sunny Castform (R)	.50	1.00
27 Tropius (R)	.50	1.00
28 Beldum (U)	.20	.50
29 Beldum (U)	.20	.50
30 Castform (U)	.20	.50
31 Claydol (U)	.20	.50
32 Corsola (U)	.20	.50
33 Dodrio (U)	.20	.50
34 Glalie (U)	.20	.50
35 Gloom (U)	.20	.50
36 Golbat (U)	.20	.50
37 Igglybuff (U)	.20	.50
38 Lanturn (U)	.20	.50
39 Loudred (U)	.20	.50
40 Luvdisc (U)	.20	.50
41 Machoke (U)	.20	.50
42 Medicham (U)	.20	.50
43 Metang (U)	.20	.50
44 Metang (U)	.20	.50
45 Nuzleaf (U)	.20	.50
46 Rhydon (U)	.20	.50
47 Sealeo (U)	.20	.50
48 Spinda (U)	.20	.50
49 Starmie (U)	.20	.50
50 Swalot (U)	.20	.50
51 Tentacruel (U)	.20	.50
52 Baltoy (C)	.10	.20
53 Baltoy (C)	.10	.20
54 Beldum (C)	.10	.20
55 Chikorita (C)	.10	.20
56 Chinchou (C)	.10	.20
57 Chinchou (C)	.10	.20
58 Clamperl (C)	.10	.20
59 Cyndaquil (C)	.10	.20
60 Doduo (C)	.10	.20
61 Feebas (C)	.10	.20
62 Gulpin (C)	.10	.20
63 Jigglypuff (C)	.10	.20
64 Machop (C)	.10	.20
65 Meditite (C)	.10	.20
66 Meditite (C)	.10	.20
67 Minun (C)	.10	.20
68 Oddish (C)	.10	.20
69 Plusle (C)	.10	.20
70 Rhyhorn (C)	.10	.20
71 Seedot (C)	.10	.20
72 Shuppet (C)	.10	.20
73 Snorunt (C)	.10	.20
74 Spheal (C)	.10	.20
75 Staryu (C)	.10	.20
76 Surskit (C)	.10	.20
77 Tentacool (C)	.10	.20
78 Togepi (C)	.10	.20
79 Totodile (C)	.10	.20
80 Voltorb (C)	.10	.20
81 Vulpix (C)	.10	.20
82 Whismur (C)	.10	.20
83 Zubat (C)	.10	.20
84 Ancient Technical Machine [Ice] (U)	.20	.50
85 Ancient Technical Machine [Rock] (U)	.20	.50
86 Ancient Technical Machine [Steel] (U)	.20	.50
87 Ancient Tomb (U)	.20	.50
88 Desert Ruins (U)	.20	.50
89 Island Cave (U)	.20	.50
90 Life Herb (U)	.20	.50
91 Magnetic Storm (U)	.20	.50
92 Steven's Advice (U)	.20	.50
93 Groudon ex (Holo) (R)	5.00	12.00
94 Kyogre ex (Holo) (R)	5.00	12.00
95 Metagross ex (Holo) (R)	4.00	10.00
96 Ninetales ex (Holo) (R)	8.00	20.00
97 Regice ex (Holo) (R)	5.00	12.00
98 Regirock ex (Holo) (R)	6.00	15.00
99 Registeel ex (Holo) (R)	8.00	20.00
100 Vileplume ex (Holo) (R)	5.00	12.00
101 Wigglytuff ex (Holo) (R)	3.00	8.00
102 Groudon (Holo) (R)	2.50	6.00

2004 Pokemon EX Hidden Legends Reverse Foil

*Reverse Foil: 1X to 2X Regular Card

2004 Pokemon EX Fire Red Leaf Green

Card	Low	High
Complete Set (116)	200.00	300.00
Booster Box (36 Packs)	125.00	200.00
Booster Pack (9 Cards)	6.00	9.00
*Reverse Foil: 1X to 2X Regular Card		
1 Beedrill (Holo) (R)	.75	2.00
2 Butterfree (Holo) (R)	1.00	2.50
3 Dewgong (Holo) (R)	.75	2.00
4 Ditto (Holo) (R)	1.25	3.00
5 Exeggutor (Holo) (R)	.75	2.00
6 Kangaskhan (Holo) (R)	.75	2.00
7 Marowak (Holo) (R)	.75	2.00
8 Nidoking (Holo) (R)	.75	2.00
9 Nidoqueen (Holo) (R)	.75	2.00
10 Pidgeot (Holo) (R)	1.50	4.00
11 Poliwrath (Holo) (R)	.75	2.00
12 Raichu (Holo) (R)	.75	2.00
13 Rapidash (Holo) (R)	.75	2.00
14 Slowbro (Holo) (R)	.75	2.00
15 Snorlax (Holo) (R)	2.00	5.00
16 Tauros (Holo) (R)	.75	2.00
17 Victreebel (Holo) (R)	.75	2.00
18 Arcanine (Holo) (R)	.75	2.00
19 Chansey (Holo) (R)	.75	2.00
20 Cloyster (Holo) (R)	.75	2.00
21 Dodrio (Holo) (R)	.75	2.00
22 Dugtrio (Holo) (R)	.75	2.00
23 Farfetch'd (Holo) (R)	.75	2.00
24 Fearow (Holo) (R)	.75	2.00
25 Hypno (Holo) (R)	.75	2.00
26 Kingler (Holo) (R)	.75	2.00
27 Magneton (Holo) (R)	.75	2.00
28 Primeape (Holo) (R)	.75	2.00
29 Scyther (Holo) (R)	.75	2.00
30 Tangela (Holo) (R)	.75	2.00
31 Charmeleon (U)	.20	.50
32 Drowzee (U)	.20	.50
33 Exeggcute (U)	.20	.50
34 Haunter (U)	.20	.50
35 Ivysaur (U)	.20	.50
36 Kakuna (U)	.20	.50
37 Lickitung (U)	.20	.50
38 Mankey (U)	.30	.75
39 Metapod (U)	.20	.50
40 Nidorina (U)	.20	.50
41 Nidorino (U)	.20	.50
42 Onix (U)	.30	.75
43 Parasect (U)	.20	.50
44 Persian (U)	.30	.75
45 Pidgeotto (U)	.20	.50
46 Poliwhirl (U)	.20	.50
47 Porygon (U)	.30	.75
48 Raticate (U)	.30	.75
49 Venomoth (U)	.20	.50
50 Wartortle (U)	.20	.50
51 Weepinbell (U)	.20	.50
52 Wigglytuff (U)	.20	.50
53 Bellsprout (C)	.10	.20
54 Bulbasaur (C)	.10	.20
55 Bulbasaur (C)	.10	.20
56 Caterpie (C)	.10	.20
57 Charmander (C)	.10	.20
58 Charmander (C)	.10	.20
59 Clefairy (C)	.10	.20
60 Cubone (C)	.10	.20
61 Diglett (C)	.10	.20
62 Doduo (C)	.10	.20
63 Gastly (C)	.10	.20
64 Growlithe (C)	.10	.20
65 Jigglypuff (C)	.10	.20
66 Krabby (C)	.10	.20
67 Magikarp (C)	.30	.75
68 Magnemite (C)	.10	.20
69 Meowth (C)	.10	.20
70 Nidoran F (C)	.10	.20
71 Nidoran M (C)	.10	.20
72 Paras (C)	.10	.20
73 Pidgey (C)	.10	.20
74 Pikachu (C)	.10	.20
75 Poliwag (C)	.10	.20

❑ 76 Ponyta (C) .10 .20
❑ 77 Rattata (C) .10 .20
❑ 78 Seel (C) .10 .20
❑ 79 Shellder (C) .10 .20
❑ 80 Slowpoke (C) .10 .20
❑ 81 Spearow (C) .10 .20
❑ 82 Squirtle (C) .10 .20
❑ 83 Squirtle (C) .10 .20
❑ 84 Venonat (C) .10 .20
❑ 85 Voltorb (C) .10 .20
❑ 86 Weedle (C) .10 .20
❑ 87 Bill's Maintenance (U) .20 .50
❑ 88 Celio's Network (U) .40 1.00
❑ 89 Energy Removal 2 (U) .20 .50
❑ 90 Energy Switch (U) .40 1.00
❑ 91 EXP.ALL (U) .20 .50
❑ 92 Great Ball (U) .20 .50
❑ 93 Life Herb (U) .20 .50
❑ 94 Mt. Moon (U) .30 .75
❑ 95 Poke Ball (U) .20 .50
❑ 96 PokeDex HANDY 909 (U) .20 .50
❑ 97 Pokemon Reversal (U) .20 .50
❑ 98 Professor Oak's Research (U) .20 .50
❑ 99 Super Scoop Up (U) .20 .50
❑ 100 VS Seeker (U) .20 .50
❑ 101 Potion (C) .10 .20
❑ 102 Switch (C) .10 .20
❑ 103 Multi Energy (Holo) (R) 1.50 4.00
❑ 104 Blastoise ex (Holo) (R) 12.00 30.00
❑ 105 Charizard ex (Holo) (R) 75.00 125.00
❑ 106 Clefable ex (Holo) (R) 3.00 8.00
❑ 107 Electrode ex (Holo) (R) 3.00 8.00
❑ 108 Gengar ex (Holo) (R) 6.00 15.00
❑ 109 Gyarados ex (Holo) (R) 8.00 20.00
❑ 110 Mr. Mime ex (Holo) (R) 3.00 8.00
❑ 111 Mr. Mime ex (Holo) (R) 4.00 10.00
❑ 112 Venusaur ex (Holo) (R) 10.00 25.00
❑ 113 Charmander (Holo) (R) 3.00 8.00
❑ 114 Articuno ex (Holo) (R) 8.00 20.00
❑ 115 Moltres ex (Holo) (R) 5.00 12.00
❑ 116 Zapdos ex (Holo) (R) 5.00 12.00

2004 Pokemon EX Fire Red Leaf Green Reverse Foil

*Reverse Foil: 1X to 2X Regular Card

❑ 1 Beedrill (Holo) (R) 1.50 4.00
❑ 2 Butterfree (Holo) (R) 2.00 5.00
❑ 3 Dewgong (Holo) (R) 1.50 4.00
❑ 4 Ditto (Holo) (R) 2.50 6.00
❑ 5 Exeggutor (Holo) (R) 1.50 4.00
❑ 6 Kangaskhan (Holo) (R) 1.50 4.00
❑ 7 Marowak (Holo) (R) 1.50 4.00
❑ 8 Nidoking (Holo) (R) 1.50 4.00
❑ 9 Nidoqueen (Holo) (R) 1.50 4.00
❑ 10 Pidgeot (Holo) (R) 3.00 8.00
❑ 11 Poliwrath (Holo) (R) 1.50 4.00
❑ 12 Raichu (Holo) (R) 1.50 4.00
❑ 13 Rapidash (Holo) (R) 1.50 4.00
❑ 14 Slowbro (Holo) (R) 1.50 4.00
❑ 15 Snorlax (Holo) (R) 4.00 10.00
❑ 16 Tauros (Holo) (R) 1.50 4.00
❑ 17 Victreebel (Holo) (R) 1.50 4.00
❑ 18 Arcanine (Holo) (R) 1.50 4.00
❑ 19 Chansey (Holo) (R) 1.50 4.00
❑ 20 Cloyster (Holo) (R) 1.50 4.00
❑ 21 Dodrio (Holo) (R) 1.50 4.00
❑ 22 Dugtrio (Holo) (R) 1.50 4.00
❑ 23 Farfetch'd (Holo) (R) 1.50 4.00
❑ 24 Fearow (Holo) (R) 1.50 4.00
❑ 25 Hypno (Holo) (R) 1.50 4.00
❑ 26 Kingler (Holo) (R) 1.50 4.00
❑ 27 Magneton (Holo) (R) 1.50 4.00
❑ 28 Primeape (Holo) (R) 1.50 4.00
❑ 29 Scyther (Holo) (R) 1.50 4.00
❑ 30 Tangela (Holo) (R) 1.50 4.00
❑ 103 Multi Energy (Holo) (R) 3.00 8.00
❑ 104 Blastoise ex (Holo) (R) 30.00 60.00
❑ 105 Charizard ex (Holo) (R) 100.00 200.00
❑ 106 Clefable ex (Holo) (R) 6.00 15.00
❑ 107 Electrode ex (Holo) (R) 6.00 15.00
❑ 108 Gengar ex (Holo) (R) 12.00 30.00
❑ 109 Gyarados ex (Holo) (R) 15.00 40.00
❑ 110 Mr. Mime ex (Holo) (R) 6.00 15.00
❑ 111 Mr. Mime ex (Holo) (R) 8.00 20.00
❑ 112 Venusaur ex (Holo) (R) 25.00 50.00
❑ 113 Charmander (Holo) (R) 6.00 15.00
❑ 114 Articuno ex (Holo) (R) 15.00 40.00
❑ 115 Moltres ex (Holo) (R) 10.00 25.00
❑ 116 Zapdos ex (Holo) (R) 10.00 25.00

2004 Pokemon EX Team Rocket Returns

Complete Set (111) 150.00 250.00
Booster Box (36 Packs) 200.00 300.00
Booster Pack (9 Cards) 6.00 10.00
*Reverse Foil: 1X to 2X Regular Card

❑ 1 Azumarill (Holo) (R) .75 2.00
❑ 2 Dark Ampharos (Holo) (R) 2.00 5.00
❑ 3 Dark Crobat (Holo) (R) 1.00 2.50
❑ 4 Dark Electrode (Holo) (R) .75 2.00
❑ 5 Dark Houndoom (Holo) (R) .75 2.00
❑ 6 Dark Hypno (Holo) (R) .75 2.00
❑ 7 Dark Marowak (Holo) (R) 1.00 2.50
❑ 8 Dark Octillery (Holo) (R) .75 2.00
❑ 9 Dark Slowking (Holo) (R) .75 2.00
❑ 10 Dark Steelix (Holo) (R) 1.25 3.00
❑ 11 Jumpluff (Holo) (R) .75 2.00
❑ 12 Kingdra (Holo) (R) .75 2.00
❑ 13 Piloswine (Holo) (R) .75 2.00
❑ 14 Togetic (Holo) (R) .75 2.00
❑ 15 Dark Dragonite (R) .50 1.00
❑ 16 Dark Muk (R) .50 1.00
❑ 17 Dark Raticate (R) .50 1.00
❑ 18 Dark Sandslash (R) .50 1.00
❑ 19 Dark Tyranitar (R) 1.00 2.50
❑ 20 Dark Tyranitar (R) .50 1.00
❑ 21 Delibird (R) .50 1.00
❑ 22 Furret (R) .50 1.00
❑ 23 Ledian (R) .50 1.00
❑ 24 Magby (R) .50 1.00
❑ 25 Misdreavus (R) .50 1.00
❑ 26 Quagsire (R) .50 1.00
❑ 27 Qwilfish (R) .50 1.00
❑ 28 Yanma (R) .50 1.00
❑ 29 Dark Arbok (U) .20 .50
❑ 30 Dark Ariados (U) .20 .50
❑ 31 Dark Dragonair (U) .20 .50
❑ 32 Dark Dragonair (U) .20 .50
❑ 33 Dark Flaaffy (U) .20 .50
❑ 34 Dark Golbat (U) .20 .50
❑ 35 Dark Golduck (U) .20 .50
❑ 36 Dark Gyarados (U) .20 .50
❑ 37 Dark Houndoom (U) .20 .50
❑ 38 Dark Magcargo (U) .20 .50
❑ 39 Dark Magneton (U) .20 .50
❑ 40 Dark Pupitar (U) .20 .50
❑ 41 Dark Pupitar (U) .20 .50
❑ 42 Dark Weezing (U) .20 .50
❑ 43 Heracross (U) .20 .50
❑ 44 Magmar (U) .20 .50
❑ 45 Mantine (U) .20 .50
❑ 46 Rocket's Meowth (U) .20 .50
❑ 47 Rocket's Wobbuffet (U) .20 .50
❑ 48 Seadra (U) .20 .50
❑ 49 Skiploom (U) .20 .50
❑ 50 Togepi (U) .20 .50
❑ 51 Cubone (C) .10 .20
❑ 52 Dratini (C) .10 .20
❑ 53 Dratini (C) .10 .20
❑ 54 Drowzee (C) .10 .20
❑ 55 Ekans (C) .10 .20
❑ 56 Grimer (C) .10 .20
❑ 57 Hoppip (C) .10 .20
❑ 58 Horsea (C) .10 .20
❑ 59 Houndour (C) .10 .20
❑ 60 Houndour (C) .10 .20
❑ 61 Koffing (C) .10 .20
❑ 62 Larvitar (C) .10 .20
❑ 63 Larvitar (C) .10 .20
❑ 64 Ledyba (C) .10 .20
❑ 65 Magikarp (C) .10 .20
❑ 66 Magnemite (C) .10 .20
❑ 67 Mareep (C) .10 .20
❑ 68 Marill (C) .10 .20
❑ 69 Onix (C) .10 .20
❑ 70 Psyduck (C) .10 .20
❑ 71 Rattata (C) .10 .20
❑ 72 Rattata (C) .10 .20
❑ 73 Remoraid (C) .10 .20
❑ 74 Sandshrew (C) .10 .20
❑ 75 Sentret (C) .10 .20
❑ 76 Slowpoke (C) .10 .20
❑ 77 Slugma (C) .10 .20
❑ 78 Spinarak (C) .10 .20
❑ 79 Swinub (C) .10 .20
❑ 80 Voltorb (C) .10 .20
❑ 81 Wooper (C) .10 .20
❑ 82 Zubat (C) .10 .20
❑ 83 Copycat (U) .20 .50
❑ 84 Pokemon Retriever (U) .20 .50
❑ 85 Pow! Hand Extension (U) .20 .50
❑ 86 Rocket's Admin. (U) .20 .50
❑ 87 Rocket's Hideout (U) .20 .50
❑ 88 Rocket's Mission (U) .20 .50
❑ 89 Rocket's Poké Ball (U) .20 .50
❑ 90 Rocket's Tricky Gym (U) .20 .50
❑ 91 Surprise! Time Machine (U) .20 .50
❑ 92 Swoop! Teleporter (U) 1.00 2.50
❑ 93 Venture Bomb (U) .20 .50
❑ 94 Dark Metal Energy (U) .20 .50
❑ 95 R Energy (U) .20 .50
❑ 96 Rocket's Articuno ex (Holo) (R) 10.00 25.00
❑ 97 Rocket's Entei ex (Holo) (R) 8.00 20.00
❑ 98 Rocket's Hitmonchan ex (Holo) (R) 6.00 15.00
❑ 99 Rocket's Mewtwo ex (Holo) (R) 25.00 50.00
❑ 100 Rocket's Moltres ex (Holo) (R) 6.00 15.00
❑ 101 Rocket's Scizor ex (Holo) (R) 6.00 15.00
❑ 102 Rocket's Scyther ex (Holo) (R) 8.00 20.00
❑ 103 Rocket's Sneasel ex (Holo) (R) 5.00 12.00
❑ 104 Rocket's Snorlax ex (Holo) (R) 8.00 20.00
❑ 105 Rocket's Suicune ex (Holo) (R) 12.00 30.00
❑ 106 Rocket's Zapdos ex (Holo) (R) 8.00 20.00
❑ 107 Mudkip 30.00 60.00
❑ 108 Torchic 15.00 40.00
❑ 109 Treecko 25.00 50.00
❑ 110 Charmeleon (SR) 2.00 5.00
❑ 111 Here Comes Team Rocket! (SR) 8.00 20.00

2004 Pokemon EX Team Rocket Returns Reverse Foil

Complete Set
*Reverse Foil: 1X to 2X Regular Card

❑ 1 Azumarill (Holo) (R) 1.50 4.00
❑ 2 Dark Ampharos (Holo) (R) 4.00 10.00
❑ 3 Dark Crobat (Holo) (R) 2.00 5.00
❑ 4 Dark Electrode (Holo) (R) 1.50 4.00
❑ 5 Dark Houndoom (Holo) (R) 1.50 4.00
❑ 6 Dark Hypno (Holo) (R) 1.50 4.00
❑ 7 Dark Marowak (Holo) (R) 2.00 5.00
❑ 8 Dark Octillery (Holo) (R) 1.50 4.00
❑ 9 Dark Slowking (Holo) (R) 1.50 4.00
❑ 10 Dark Steelix (Holo) (R) 2.50 6.00
❑ 11 Jumpluff (Holo) (R) 1.50 4.00
❑ 12 Kingdra (Holo) (R) 1.50 4.00
❑ 13 Piloswine (Holo) (R) 1.50 4.00
❑ 14 Togetic (Holo) (R) 1.50 4.00
❑ 15 Dark Dragonite (R) .75 2.00
❑ 16 Dark Muk (R) .75 2.00
❑ 17 Dark Raticate (R) .75 2.00
❑ 18 Dark Sandslash (R) .75 2.00
❑ 19 Dark Tyranitar (R) 2.00 5.00
❑ 20 Dark Tyranitar (R) .75 2.00
❑ 21 Delibird (R) .75 2.00
❑ 22 Furret (R) .75 2.00
❑ 23 Ledian (R) .75 2.00
❑ 24 Magby (R) .75 2.00
❑ 25 Misdreavus (R) .75 2.00
❑ 26 Quagsire (R) .75 2.00
❑ 27 Qwilfish (R) .75 2.00
❑ 28 Yanma (R) .75 2.00
❑ 29 Dark Arbok (U) .40 1.00
❑ 30 Dark Ariados (U) .40 1.00
❑ 31 Dark Dragonair (U) .40 1.00
❑ 32 Dark Dragonair (U) .40 1.00
❑ 33 Dark Flaaffy (U) .40 1.00
❑ 34 Dark Golbat (U) .40 1.00
❑ 35 Dark Golduck (U) .40 1.00
❑ 36 Dark Gyarados (U) .40 1.00
❑ 37 Dark Houndoom (U) .40 1.00
❑ 38 Dark Magcargo (U) .40 1.00
❑ 39 Dark Magneton (U) .40 1.00
❑ 40 Dark Pupitar (U) .40 1.00
❑ 41 Dark Pupitar (U) .40 1.00
❑ 42 Dark Weezing (U) .40 1.00
❑ 43 Heracross (U) .40 1.00
❑ 44 Magmar (U) .40 1.00
❑ 45 Mantine (U) .40 1.00
❑ 46 Rocket's Meowth (U) .40 1.00
❑ 47 Rocket's Wobbuffet (U) .40 1.00
❑ 48 Seadra (U) .40 1.00
❑ 49 Skiploom (U) .40 1.00
❑ 50 Togepi (U) .40 1.00
❑ 51 Cubone (C) .15 .40
❑ 52 Dratini (C) .15 .40
❑ 53 Dratini (C) .15 .40
❑ 54 Drowzee (C) .15 .40
❑ 55 Ekans (C) .15 .40
❑ 56 Grimer (C) .15 .40
❑ 57 Hoppip (C) .15 .40
❑ 58 Horsea (C) .15 .40
❑ 59 Houndour (C) .15 .40
❑ 60 Houndour (C) .15 .40
❑ 61 Koffing (C) .15 .40
❑ 62 Larvitar (C) .15 .40
❑ 63 Larvitar (C) .15 .40
❑ 64 Ledyba (C) .15 .40
❑ 65 Magikarp (C) .15 .40
❑ 66 Magnemite (C) .15 .40
❑ 67 Mareep (C) .15 .40
❑ 68 Marill (C) .15 .40
❑ 69 Onix (C) .15 .40
❑ 70 Psyduck (C) .15 .40
❑ 71 Rattata (C) .15 .40
❑ 72 Rattata (C) .15 .40
❑ 73 Remoraid (C) .15 .40
❑ 74 Sandshrew (C) .15 .40
❑ 75 Sentret (C) .15 .40
❑ 76 Slowpoke (C) .15 .40
❑ 77 Slugma (C) .15 .40
❑ 78 Spinarak (C) .15 .40
❑ 79 Swinub (C) .15 .40
❑ 80 Voltorb (C) .15 .40
❑ 81 Wooper (C) .15 .40
❑ 82 Zubat (C) .15 .40
❑ 83 Copycat (U) .40 1.00
❑ 84 Pokemon Retriever (U) .40 1.00
❑ 85 Pow! Hand Extension (U) .40 1.00
❑ 86 Rocket's Admin. (U) .40 1.00
❑ 87 Rocket's Hideout (U) .40 1.00
❑ 88 Rocket's Mission (U) .40 1.00
❑ 89 Rocket's Poké Ball (U) .40 1.00
❑ 90 Rocket's Tricky Gym (U) .40 1.00
❑ 91 Surprise! Time Machine (U) .40 1.00
❑ 92 Swoop! Teleporter (U) 2.00 5.00
❑ 93 Venture Bomb (U) .40 1.00
❑ 94 Dark Metal Energy (U) .40 1.00
❑ 95 R Energy (U) .40 1.00
❑ 96 Rocket's Articuno ex (Holo) (R) 25.00 50.00
❑ 97 Rocket's Entei ex (Holo) (R) 15.00 40.00
❑ 98 Rocket's Hitmonchan ex (Holo) (R) 12.00 30.00
❑ 99 Rocket's Mewtwo ex (Holo) (R) 40.00 80.00
❑ 100 Rocket's Moltres ex (Holo) (R) 12.00 30.00
❑ 101 Rocket's Scizor ex (Holo) (R) 12.00 30.00
❑ 102 Rocket's Scyther ex (Holo) (R) 15.00 40.00
❑ 103 Rocket's Sneasel ex (Holo) (R) 10.00 25.00
❑ 104 Rocket's Snorlax ex (Holo) (R) 15.00 40.00
❑ 105 Rocket's Suicune ex (Holo) (R) 30.00 60.00
❑ 106 Rocket's Zapdos ex (Holo) (R) 15.00 40.00
❑ 107 Shining Mudkip 50.00 100.00
❑ 108 Shining Torchic 40.00 80.00
❑ 109 Shining Treecko 40.00 80.00
❑ 110 Charmeleon (SR) 4.00 10.00
❑ 111 Here Comes Team Rocket! (SR) 15.00 40.00

2004 Pokemon EX Trainer Kit

Complete Set (60) 7.00 12.00
Common Card (not listed) (C) .10 .20

❑ 2 Latios (holo) (R) 2.00 5.00
❑ 4 Latias (holo) (R) 2.00 5.00

2005 Pokemon EX Deoxys

Booster Box (36 Packs) 125.00 200.00
Booster Pack (9 Cards) 4.00 6.00

❑ 1 Altaria (Holo) (R) 2.00 4.00
❑ 2 Beautifly (Holo) (R) 3.00 6.00
❑ 3 Breloom (Holo) (R) 3.00 6.00
❑ 4 Camerupt (Holo) (R) 3.00 6.00
❑ 5 Claydol (Holo) (R) 3.00 6.00
❑ 6 Crawdaunt (Holo) (R) 3.00 6.00
❑ 7 Dusclops (Holo) (R) 3.00 6.00
❑ 8 Gyarados (Holo) (R) 4.00 8.00
❑ 9 Jirachi (Holo) (R) 3.00 6.00
❑ 10 Ludicolo (Holo) (R) 2.00 4.00
❑ 11 Metagross (Holo) (R) 5.00 10.00
❑ 12 Mightyena (Holo) (R) 3.00 6.00
❑ 13 Ninjask (Holo) (R) 3.00 6.00
❑ 14 Shedinja (Holo) (R) 3.00 6.00
❑ 15 Slaking (Holo) (R) 3.00 6.00
❑ 16 Deoxys (Normal) (R) .50 1.00
❑ 17 Deoxys (Attack) (R) 1.00 2.00
❑ 18 Deoxys (Defense) (R) .50 1.00
❑ 19 Ludicolo (R) .50 1.00
❑ 20 Magcargo (R) .50 1.00
❑ 21 Pelipper (R) .50 1.00
❑ 22 Rayquaza (R) 1.00 2.00
❑ 23 Sableye (R) .50 1.00
❑ 24 Seaking (R) .50 1.00
❑ 25 Shiftry (R) .50 1.00
❑ 26 Skarmory (R) .50 1.00
❑ 27 Tropius (R) .50 1.00
❑ 28 Whiscash (R) .50 1.00
❑ 29 Xatu (R) .50 1.00
❑ 30 Donphan (U) .20 .50
❑ 31 Golbat (U) .20 .50
❑ 32 Grumpig (U) .20 .50
❑ 33 Lombre (U) .20 .50
❑ 34 Lombre (U) .20 .50
❑ 35 Lotad (U) .20 .50
❑ 36 Lunatone (U) .20 .50
❑ 37 Magcargo (U) .20 .50
❑ 38 Manectric (U) .20 .50
❑ 39 Masquerain (U) .20 .50
❑ 40 Metang (U) .20 .50
❑ 41 Minun (U) .20 .50
❑ 42 Nosepass (U) .20 .50
❑ 43 Nuzleaf (U) .20 .50
❑ 44 Plusle (U) .20 .50
❑ 45 Shelgon (U) .20 .50
❑ 46 Silcoon (U) .20 .50
❑ 47 Solrock (U) .20 .50
❑ 48 Starmie (U) .20 .50
❑ 49 Swellow (U) .20 .50
❑ 50 Vigoroth (U) .20 .50
❑ 51 Weezing (U) .20 .50
❑ 52 Bagon (C) .10 .20
❑ 53 Baltoy (C) .10 .20
❑ 54 Barboach (C) .10 .20
❑ 55 Beldum (C) .10 .20
❑ 56 Carvanha (C) .10 .20
❑ 57 Corphish (C) .10 .20
❑ 58 Duskull (C) .10 .20
❑ 59 Electrike (C) .10 .20
❑ 60 Electrike (C) .10 .20
❑ 61 Goldeen (C) .10 .20
❑ 62 Koffing (C) .10 .20
❑ 63 Lotad (C) .10 .20
❑ 64 Magikarp (C) .10 .20
❑ 65 Makuhita (C) .10 .20
❑ 66 Natu (C) .10 .20
❑ 67 Nincada (C) .10 .20
❑ 68 Numel (C) .10 .20
❑ 69 Phanpy (C) .10 .20
❑ 70 Poochyena (C) .10 .20
❑ 71 Seedot (C) .10 .20
❑ 72 Shroomish (C) .10 .20
❑ 73 Slakoth (C) .10 .20
❑ 74 Slugma (C) .10 .20
❑ 75 Slugma (C) .10 .20
❑ 76 Spoink (C) .10 .20
❑ 77 Staryu (C) .10 .20
❑ 78 Surskit (C) .10 .20
❑ 79 Swablu (C) .10 .20
❑ 80 Taillow (C) .10 .20
❑ 81 Wingull (C) .10 .20
❑ 82 Wurmple (C) .10 .20
❑ 83 Zubat (C) .10 .20
❑ 84 Balloon Berry .10 .20
❑ 85 Crystal Shard .10 .20
❑ 86 Energy Charge .10 .20
❑ 87 Lady Outing .10 .20
❑ 88 Master Ball .10 .20
❑ 89 Meteor Falls .10 .20
❑ 90 Professor Cozmo's Discovery .10 .20
❑ 91 Space Center .10 .20
❑ 92 Strength Charm .10 .20
❑ 93 Boost Energy .10 .20
❑ 94 Healing Energy .10 .20
❑ 95 Scramble Energy .10 .20
❑ 96 Crobat ex (Holo) (R) 4.00 10.00
❑ 97 Deoxys ex (Normal) (Holo) (R) 5.00 12.00
❑ 98 Deoxys ex (Attack) (Holo) (R) 6.00 15.00
❑ 99 Deoxys ex (Defense) (Holo) (R) 4.00 10.00
❑ 100 Hariyama ex (Holo) (R) 4.00 10.00
❑ 101 Manectric ex (Holo) (R) 3.00 8.00
❑ 102 Rayquaza ex (Holo) (R) 8.00 20.00
❑ 103 Salamence ex (Holo) (R) 10.00 25.00
❑ 104 Sharpedo ex (Holo) (R) 6.00 15.00
❑ 105 Latias (Holo) (R) 40.00 80.00
❑ 106 Latios (Holo) (R) 40.00 80.00
❑ 107 Rayquaza (Holo) (R) 60.00 120.00
❑ 108 Rocket's Raikou ex (Holo) (R) 6.00 15.00

2005 Pokemon EX Deoxys Reverse Foil

Complete Set (108) 150.00 250.00
*Reverse Foil: 1X to 2X Basic Card

2005 Pokemon EX Emerald

Complete Set (107) 125.00 175.00
Booster Box (36 Packs) 90.00 150.00
Booster Pack (9 Cards) 3.50 5.00
*Reverse Foil: 1X to 2X Basic Card

❑ 1 Blaziken (Holo) (R) 2.00 4.00
❑ 2 Deoxys (Holo) (R) 2.00 4.00
❑ 3 Exploud (Holo) (R) 2.00 4.00
❑ 4 Gardevoir (Holo) (R) 2.00 4.00
❑ 5 Groudon (Holo) (R) 2.00 4.00
❑ 6 Kyogre (Holo) (R) 3.00 6.00
❑ 7 Manectric (Holo) (R) 2.00 4.00
❑ 8 Milotic (Holo) (R) 3.00 6.00
❑ 9 Rayquaza (Holo) (R) 3.00 6.00
❑ 10 Sceptile (Holo) (R) 2.00 4.00
❑ 11 Swampert (Holo) (R) 2.00 4.00
❑ 12 Chimecho (R) .50 1.00
❑ 13 Glalie (R) .50 1.00
❑ 14 Groudon (R) .50 1.00
❑ 15 Kyogre (R) .50 1.00
❑ 16 Manectric (R) .50 1.00
❑ 17 Nosepass (R) .50 1.00
❑ 18 Relicanth (R) .50 1.00
❑ 19 Rhydon (R) .50 1.00
❑ 20 Seviper (R) .50 1.00
❑ 21 Zangoose (R) .50 1.00
❑ 22 Breloom (U) .20 .50
❑ 23 Camerupt (U) .20 .50
❑ 24 Claydol (U) .20 .50
❑ 25 Combusken (U) .20 .50
❑ 26 Dodrio (U) .20 .50
❑ 27 Electrode (U) .20 .50
❑ 28 Grovyle (U) .20 .50
❑ 29 Grumpig (U) .20 .50
❑ 30 Grumpig (U) .20 .50
❑ 31 Hariyama (U) .20 .50
❑ 32 Illumise (U) .20 .50
❑ 33 Kirlia (U) .20 .50
❑ 34 Linoone (U) .20 .50
❑ 35 Loudred (U) .20 .50
❑ 36 Marshtomp (U) .20 .50
❑ 37 Minun (U) .20 .50
❑ 38 Ninetales (U) .20 .50
❑ 39 Plusle (U) .20 .50
❑ 40 Swalot (U) .20 .50
❑ 41 Swellow (U) .20 .50
❑ 42 Volbeat (U) .20 .50
❑ 43 Baltoy (C) .10 .20
❑ 44 Cacnea (C) .10 .20
❑ 45 Doduo (C) .10 .20
❑ 46 Duskull (C) .10 .20
❑ 47 Electrike (C) .10 .20
❑ 48 Electrike (C) .10 .20
❑ 49 Feebas (C) .10 .20
❑ 50 Feebas (C) .10 .20
❑ 51 Gulpin (C) .10 .20
❑ 52 Larvitar (C) .10 .20
❑ 53 Luvdisc (C) .10 .20
❑ 54 Makuhita (C) .10 .20
❑ 55 Meditite (C) .10 .20
❑ 56 Mudkip (C) .10 .20
❑ 57 Numel (C) .10 .20
❑ 58 Numel (C) .10 .20
❑ 59 Pichu (C) .10 .20
❑ 60 Pikachu (C) .10 .20
❑ 61 Ralts (C) .10 .20
❑ 62 Rhyhorn (C) .10 .20
❑ 63 Shroomish (C) .10 .20
❑ 64 Snorunt (C) .10 .20
❑ 65 Spoink (C) .10 .20
❑ 66 Spoink (C) .10 .20
❑ 67 Swablu (C) .10 .20
❑ 68 Taillow (C) .10 .20
❑ 69 Torchic (C) .10 .20
❑ 70 Treecko (C) .10 .20
❑ 71 Voltorb (C) .10 .20
❑ 72 Vulpix (C) .10 .20
❑ 73 Whismur (C) .10 .20
❑ 74 Zigzagoon (C) .10 .20
❑ 75 Battle Frontier (U) .20 .50
❑ 76 Double Full Heal (U) .20 .50

□ 77 Lanette's Net Search (U) .20 .50
□ 78 Lum Berry (U) .20 .50
□ 79 Mr. Stone's Project (U) .20 .50
□ 80 Oran Berry (U) .20 .50
□ 81 Pokenav (U) .20 .50
□ 82 Professor Birch (U) .20 .50
□ 83 Rare Candy (U) .20 .50
□ 84 Scott (U) .20 .50
□ 85 Wally's Training (U) .20 .50
□ 86 Darkness Energy (R) .50 1.00
□ 87 Double Rainbow Energy (R) .50 1.00
□ 88 Metal Energy (R) .50 1.00
□ 89 Mutli Energy (R) .50 1.00
□ 90 Altaria ex (Holo) (R) 4.00 10.00
□ 91 Cactürne ex (Holo) (R) 5.00 12.00
□ 92 Camerupt ex (Holo) (R) 6.00 15.00
□ 93 Deoxys ex (Holo) (R) 6.00 15.00
□ 94 Dusclops ex (Holo) (R) 4.00 10.00
□ 95 Medicham ex (Holo) (R) 4.00 10.00
□ 96 Milotic ex (Holo) (R) 10.00 20.00
□ 97 Raichu ex (Holo) (R) 6.00 15.00
□ 98 Regice ex (Holo) (R) 5.00 12.00
□ 99 Regirock (Holo) (R) 10.00 20.00
□ 100 Registeel (Holo) (R) 5.00 12.00
□ 101 Grass Energy (Holo) 1.00 2.00
□ 102 Fire Energy (Holo) 1.00 2.00
□ 103 Water Energy (Holo) 1.00 2.00
□ 104 Lightning Energy (Holo) 1.00 2.00
□ 105 Psychic Energy (Holo) 1.00 2.00
□ 106 Fighting Energy (Holo) 1.00 2.00
□ 107 Farfetch'd (Holo) (R) 2.00 5.00

2005 Pokemon EX Emerald Reverse Foil

Complete Set 150.00 250.00
*Reverse Foil: 1X to 2X Basic Card

2005 Pokemon EX Unseen Forces

Complete Set (117) 120.00 200.00
Booster Box (36 ct) 75.00 90.00
Booster Pack (9 cards) 3.50 4.00

□ 1 Ampharos (Holo) (R) 3.00 6.00
□ 2 Ariados (Holo) (R) 3.00 5.00
□ 3 Bellossom (Holo) (R) 3.00 5.00
□ 4 Feraligatr (Holo) (R) 3.50 6.00
□ 5 Flareon (Holo) (R) 3.00 6.00
□ 6 Forretress (Holo) (R) 3.00 6.00
□ 7 Houndoom (Holo) (R) 3.00 6.00
□ 8 Jolteon (Holo) (R) 3.00 6.00
□ 9 Meganium (Holo) (R) 3.00 6.00
□ 10 Octillery (Holo) (R) 3.00 5.00
□ 11 Poliwrath (Holo) (R) 3.00 5.00
□ 12 Porygon 2 (Holo) (R) 3.00 6.00
□ 13 Slowbro (Holo) (R) 2.00 4.00
□ 14 Slowking (Holo) (R) 2.00 4.00
□ 15 Sudowoodo (Holo) (R) 3.00 5.00
□ 16 Sunflora (Holo) (R) 3.00 5.00
□ 17 Typhlosion (Holo) (R) 3.50 5.00
□ 18 Ursaring (Holo) (R) 3.00 5.00
□ 19 Vaporeon (Holo) (R) 3.00 5.00
□ 20 Chansey (R) .50 1.00
□ 21 Cleffa (R) .50 1.00
□ 22 Electabuzz (R) .50 1.00
□ 23 Elekid (R) .50 1.00
□ 24 Hitmonchan (R) .50 1.00
□ 25 Hitmonlee (R) .50 1.00
□ 26 Hitmontop (R) .50 1.00
□ 27 Ho-Oh (R) 1.00 2.00
□ 28 Jynx (R) .50 1.00
□ 29 Lugia (R) 3.00 6.00
□ 30 Murkrow (R) .50 1.00
□ 31 Smoochum (R) .50 1.00
□ 32 Stantler (R) .50 1.00
□ 33 Tyrogue (R) .50 1.00
□ 34 Aipom (U) .20 .50
□ 35 Bayleef (U) .20 .50
□ 36 Clefable (U) .20 .50
□ 37 Corsola (U) .20 .50
□ 38 Croconaw (U) .20 .50
□ 39 Granbull (U) .20 .50
□ 40 Lanturn (U) .20 .50
□ 41 Magcargo (U) .20 .50
□ 42 Miltank (U) .20 .50
□ 43 Noctowl (U) .20 .50
□ 44 Quagsire (U) .20 .50
□ 45 Quilava (U) .20 .50
□ 46 Scyther (U) .20 .50
□ 47 Shuckle (U) .20 .50
□ 48 Smeargle (U) .20 .50
□ 49 Xatu (U) .20 .50
□ 50 Yanma (U) .20 .50
□ 51 Chikorita (C) .10 .20
□ 52 Chinchou (C) .10 .20
□ 53 Clefairy (C) .10 .20
□ 54 Cyndaquil (C) .10 .20
□ 55 Eevee (C) .10 .20
□ 56 Flaaffy (C) .10 .20
□ 57 Gligar (C) .10 .20
□ 58 Gloom (C) .10 .20
□ 59 Hoothoot (C) .10 .20
□ 60 Houndour (C) .10 .20
□ 61 Larvitar (C) .10 .20
□ 62 Mareep (C) .10 .20
□ 63 Natu (C) .10 .20
□ 64 Oddish (C) .10 .20
□ 65 Onix (C) .10 .20
□ 66 Pineco (C) .10 .20
□ 67 Poliwag (C) .10 .20
□ 68 Poliwhirl (C) .10 .20
□ 69 Porygon (C) .10 .20
□ 70 Pupitar (C) .10 .20
□ 71 Remoraid (C) .10 .20
□ 72 Slowpoke (C) .10 .20
□ 73 Slugma (C) .10 .20
□ 74 Snubbull (C) .10 .20
□ 75 Spinarak (C) .10 .20
□ 76 Sunkern (C) .10 .20
□ 77 Teddiursa (C) .10 .20
□ 78 Totodile (C) .10 .20
□ 79 Wooper (C) .10 .20
□ 80 Curse Powder (U) .20 .50
□ 81 Energy Recycle System (U) .20 .50
□ 82 Energy Removal 2 (U) .20 .50
□ 83 Energy Root (U) .20 .50
□ 84 Energy Switch (U) .20 .50
□ 85 Fluffy Berry (U) .20 .50
□ 86 Mary's Request (U) .20 .50
□ 87 Poke Ball (U) .20 .50
□ 88 Pokemon Reversal (U) .20 .50
□ 89 Professor Elm's Training Method (U) .20 .50
□ 90 Protective Orb (U) .20 .50
□ 91 Sitrus Berry (U) .20 .50
□ 92 Solid Rage (U) .20 .50
□ 93 Warp Point (U) .20 .50
□ 94 Energy Search (C) .10 .20
□ 95 Potion (C) .10 .20
□ 96 Darkness Energy (R) .50 1.00
□ 97 Metal Energy (R) .50 1.00
□ 98 Boost Energy (U) .20 .50
□ 99 Cyclone Energy (U) .20 .50
□ 100 Warp Energy (U) .20 .50
□ 101 Blissey EX (UR) Holo 8.00 16.00
□ 102 Espeon EX (UR) Holo 8.00 16.00
□ 103 Feraligatr EX (UR) Holo 8.00 16.00
□ 104 Ho-Oh EX (UR) Holo 10.00 20.00
□ 105 Lugia EX (UR) Holo 20.00 35.00
□ 106 Meganium EX (UR) Holo 8.00 18.00
□ 107 Politoed EX (UR) Holo 8.00 18.00
□ 108 Scizor EX (UR) Holo 8.00 16.00
□ 109 Steelix EX (UR) Holo 10.00 20.00
□ 110 Typhlosion EX (UR) Holo 8.00 18.00
□ 111 Tyranitar EX (UR) Holo 10.00 20.00
□ 112 Umbreon EX (UR) Holo 8.00 16.00
□ 113 Entei Star (UR) 12.00 22.00
□ 114 Raikou Star (UR) 15.00 25.00
□ 115 Suicune Star (UR) 15.00 25.00
□ 116 Rocket's Persian EX (Box Topper) 5.00 12.00
□ 117 Celebi EX (SCR) 10.00 25.00

2005 Pokemon EX Unseen Forces Reverse Foil

*Reverse Foil: 1X to 2X Regular Card

□ 1 Ampharos (R) Holo 6.00 12.00
□ 2 Ariados (R) Holo 5.00 10.00
□ 3 Bellossom (R) Holo 5.00 10.00
□ 4 Feraligatr (R) Holo 6.00 12.00
□ 5 Flareon (R) Holo 6.00 12.00
□ 6 Forretress (R) Holo 6.00 12.00
□ 7 Houndoom (R) Holo 6.00 12.00
□ 8 Jolteon (R) Holo 6.00 12.00
□ 9 Meganium (R) Holo 6.00 12.00
□ 10 Octillery (R) Holo 5.00 10.00
□ 11 Poliwrath (R) Holo 5.00 10.00
□ 12 Porygon 2 (R) Holo 6.00 12.00
□ 13 Slowbro (R) Holo 4.00 8.00
□ 14 Slowking (R) Holo 4.00 8.00
□ 15 Sudowoodo (R) Holo 5.00 10.00
□ 16 Sunflora (R) Holo 5.00 10.00
□ 17 Typhlosion (R) Holo 5.00 10.00
□ 18 Ursaring (R) Holo 5.00 10.00
□ 19 Vaporeon (R) Holo 5.00 10.00
□ 20 Chansey (R) 1.00 2.00
□ 21 Cleffa (R) 1.00 2.00
□ 22 Electabuzz (R) 1.00 2.00
□ 23 Elekid (R) 1.00 2.00
□ 24 Hitmonchan (R) 1.00 2.00
□ 25 Hitmonlee (R) 1.00 2.00
□ 26 Hitmontop (R) 1.00 2.00
□ 27 Ho-Oh (R) 2.00 4.00
□ 28 Jynx (R) 1.00 2.00
□ 29 Lugia (R) 6.00 12.00
□ 30 Murkrow (R) 1.00 2.00
□ 31 Smoochum (R) 1.00 2.00
□ 32 Stantler (R) 1.00 2.00
□ 33 Tyrogue (R) 1.00 2.00
□ 34 Aipom (U) .50 1.00
□ 35 Bayleef (U) .50 1.00
□ 36 Clefable (U) .50 1.00
□ 37 Corsola (U) .50 1.00
□ 38 Croconaw (U) .50 1.00
□ 39 Granbull (U) .50 1.00
□ 40 Lanturn (U) .50 1.00
□ 41 Magcargo (U) .50 1.00
□ 42 Miltank (U) .50 1.00
□ 43 Noctowl (U) .50 1.00
□ 44 Quagsire (U) .50 1.00
□ 45 Quilava (U) .50 1.00
□ 46 Scyther (U) .50 1.00
□ 47 Shuckle (U) .50 1.00
□ 48 Smeargle (U) .50 1.00
□ 49 Xatu (U) .50 1.00
□ 50 Yanma (U) .50 1.00
□ 51 Chikorita (C) .20 .40
□ 52 Chinchou (C) .20 .40
□ 53 Clefairy (C) .20 .40
□ 54 Cyndaquil (C) .20 .40
□ 55 Eevee (C) .20 .40
□ 56 Flaafy (C) .20 .40
□ 57 Gligar (C) .20 .40
□ 58 Gloom (C) .20 .40
□ 59 Hoothoot (C) .20 .40
□ 60 Houndour (C) .20 .40
□ 61 Larvitar (C) .20 .40
□ 62 Mareep (C) .20 .40
□ 63 Natu (C) .20 .40
□ 64 Oddish (C) .20 .40
□ 65 Onix (C) .20 .40
□ 66 Pineco (C) .20 .40
□ 67 Poliwag (C) .20 .40
□ 68 Poliwhirl (C) .20 .40
□ 69 Porygon (C) .20 .40
□ 70 Pupitar (C) .20 .40
□ 71 Remoraid (C) .20 .40
□ 72 Slowpoke (C) .20 .40
□ 73 Slugma (C) .20 .40
□ 74 Snubbull (C) .20 .40
□ 75 Spinarak (C) .20 .40
□ 76 Sunkern (C) .20 .40
□ 77 Teddiursa (C) .20 .40
□ 78 Totodile (C) .20 .40
□ 79 Wooper (C) .20 .40
□ 80 Curse Powder (U) .50 1.00
□ 81 Energy Recycle System (U) .50 1.00
□ 82 Energy Removal 2 (U) .50 1.00
□ 83 Energy Root (U) .50 1.00
□ 84 Energy Switch (U) .50 1.00
□ 85 Fluffy Berry (U) .50 1.00
□ 86 Mary's Request (U) .50 1.00
□ 87 Poke Ball (U) .50 1.00
□ 88 Pokemon Reversal (U) .50 1.00
□ 89 Professor Elm's Training Method (U) .50 1.00
□ 90 Protective Orb (U) .50 1.00
□ 91 Sitrus Berry (U) .50 1.00
□ 92 Solid Rage (U) .50 1.00
□ 93 Warp Point (U) .50 1.00
□ 94 Energy Search (C) .20 .40
□ 95 Potion (C) .20 .40
□ 96 Darkness Energy (R) 1.00 2.00
□ 97 Metal Energy (R) 1.00 2.00
□ 98 Boost Energy (U) .50 1.00
□ 99 Cyclone Energy (U) .50 1.00
□ 100 Warp Energy (U) .50 1.00
□ 101 Blissey EX (UR) Holo 15.00 30.00
□ 102 Espeon EX (UR) Holo 15.00 30.00
□ 103 Feraligatr EX (UR) Holo 15.00 30.00
□ 104 Ho-Oh EX (UR) Holo 20.00 40.00
□ 105 Lugia EX (UR) Holo 35.00 70.00
□ 106 Meganium EX (UR) Holo 20.00 40.00
□ 107 Politoed EX (UR) Holo 20.00 40.00
□ 108 Scizor EX (UR) Holo 15.00 30.00
□ 109 Steelix EX (UR) Holo 20.00 40.00
□ 110 Typhlosion EX (UR) Holo 20.00 40.00
□ 111 Tyranitar EX (UR) Holo 20.00 40.00
□ 112 Umbreon EX (UR) Holo 15.00 30.00
□ 113 Entei Star (UR) 20.00 40.00
□ 114 Raikou Star (UR) 25.00 50.00
□ 115 Suicune Star (UR) 25.00 50.00
□ 116 Rocket's Persian EX Box Topper 12.50 25.00
□ 117 Celebi EX (SCR) 25.00 50.00

2005 Pokemon EX Unseen Forces Unown

COMPLETE SET (28) 30.00 60.00

□ A Unown 2.00 5.00
□ B Unown 2.00 5.00
□ C Unown 2.00 5.00
□ D Unown 2.00 5.00
□ E Unown 2.00 5.00
□ F Unown 2.00 5.00
□ G Unown 2.00 5.00
□ H Unown 2.00 5.00
□ I Unown 2.00 5.00
□ J Unown 2.00 5.00
□ K Unown 2.00 5.00
□ L Unown 2.00 5.00
□ M Unown 2.00 5.00
□ N Unown 2.00 5.00
□ O Unown 2.00 5.00
□ P Unown 2.00 5.00
□ Q Unown 2.00 5.00
□ R Unown 2.00 5.00
□ S Unown 2.00 5.00
□ T Unown 2.00 5.00
□ U Unown 2.00 5.00
□ V Unown 2.00 5.00
□ W Unown 2.00 5.00
□ X Unown 2.00 5.00
□ Y Unown 2.00 5.00
□ Z Unown 2.00 5.00
□ EP Unown 2.00 5.00
□ QM Unown 2.00 5.00

2005 Pokemon EX Delta Species

Complete Set (113) 60.00 100.00
Booster Box (36 Packs) 75.00 100.00
Booster Pack (9 Cards) 3.00 4.00

□ 1 Beedrill DS (Holo) (R) 3.00 6.00
□ 2 Crobat DS (Holo) (R) 3.00 6.00
□ 3 Dragonite DS (Holo) (R) 4.00 8.00
□ 4 Espeon DS (Holo) (R) 3.00 6.00
□ 5 Flareon DS (Holo) (R) 3.00 6.00
□ 6 Gardevoir DS (Holo) (R) 4.00 8.00
□ 7 Jolteon DS (Holo) (R) 4.00 8.00
□ 8 Latias DS (Holo) (R) 4.00 8.00
□ 9 Latios (holo) (R) 4.00 8.00
□ 10 Marowak DS (Holo) (R) 2.00 5.00
□ 11 Metagross DS (Holo) (R) 3.00 6.00
□ 12 Mewtwo DS (Holo) (R) 6.00 12.00
□ 13 Rayquaza DS (Holo) (R) 4.00 8.00
□ 14 Salamence DS (Holo) (R) 4.00 8.00
□ 15 Starmie DS (Holo) (R) 3.00 5.00
□ 16 Tyranitar DS (Holo) (R) 4.00 8.00
□ 17 Umbreon DS (Holo) (R) 3.00 6.00
□ 18 Vaporeon DS (Holo) (R) 4.00 8.00
□ 19 Azumarill DS (R) .50 1.00
□ 20 Azurill (R) .50 1.00
□ 21 Holon's Electrode (R) .50 1.00
□ 22 Holon's Magneton (R) .50 1.00
□ 23 Hypno (R) .50 1.00
□ 24 Mightyena DS (R) .50 1.00
□ 25 Porygon2 (R) .50 1.00
□ 26 Rain Castform (R) .50 1.00
□ 27 Sandslash DS (R) .50 1.00
□ 28 Slowking (R) .50 1.00
□ 29 Snow-cloud Castform (R) .50 1.00
□ 30 Starmie DS (R) .50 1.00
□ 31 Sunny Castform (R) .50 1.00
□ 32 Swellow (R) .50 1.00
□ 33 Weezing (R) .50 1.00
□ 34 Castform (U) .20 .50
□ 35 Ditto (U) .20 .50
□ 36 Ditto (U) .20 .50
□ 37 Ditto (U) .20 .50
□ 38 Ditto (U) .20 .50
□ 39 Ditto (U) .20 .50
□ 40 Ditto (U) .20 .50
□ 41 Dragonair DS (U) .20 .50
□ 42 Dragonair DS (U) .20 .50
□ 43 Golbat (U) .20 .50
□ 44 Hariyama (U) .20 .50
□ 45 Illumise (U) .20 .50
□ 46 Kakuna (U) .20 .50
□ 47 Kirlia (U) .20 .50
□ 48 Magneton (U) .20 .50
□ 49 Metang DS (U) .20 .50
□ 50 Persian (U) .20 .50
□ 51 Pupitar DS (U) .20 .50
□ 52 Rapidash (U) .20 .50
□ 53 Shelgon DS (U) .20 .50
□ 54 Shelgon DS (U) .20 .50
□ 55 Skarmory (U) .20 .50
□ 56 Volbeat (U) .20 .50
□ 57 Bagon DS (C) .10 .20
□ 58 Bagon DS (C) .10 .20
□ 59 Beldum DS (C) .10 .20
□ 60 Cubone (C) .10 .20
□ 61 Ditto (C) .10 .20
□ 62 Ditto (C) .10 .20
□ 63 Ditto (C) .10 .20
□ 64 Ditto (C) .10 .20
□ 65 Dratini DS (C) .10 .20
□ 66 Dratini DS (C) .10 .20
□ 67 Drowzee (C) .10 .20
□ 68 Eevee DS (C) .10 .20
□ 69 Eevee (C) .10 .20
□ 70 Holon's Magnemite (C) .10 .20
□ 71 Holon's Voltorb (C) .10 .20
□ 72 Koffing (C) .10 .20
□ 73 Larvitar DS (C) .10 .20
□ 74 Magnemite (C) .10 .20
□ 75 Makuhita (C) .10 .20
□ 76 Marill (C) .10 .20
□ 77 Meowth (C) .10 .20
□ 78 Ponyta (C) .10 .20
□ 79 Poochyena (C) .10 .20
□ 80 Porygon (C) .10 .20
□ 81 Ralts (C) .10 .20
□ 82 Sandshrew (C) .10 .20
□ 83 Slowpoke (C) .10 .20
□ 84 Staryu (C) .10 .20
□ 85 Staryu (C) .10 .20
□ 86 Taillow (C) .10 .20
□ 87 Weedle (C) .10 .20
□ 88 Zubat (C) .10 .20
□ 89 Dual Ball (U) .20 .50
□ 90 Great Ball (U) .20 .50
□ 91 Holon Farmer (U) .20 .50
□ 92 Holon Lass (U) .20 .50
□ 93 Holon Mentor (U) .20 .50
□ 94 Holon Research Tower (U) .20 .50
□ 95 Holon Researcher (U) .20 .50
□ 96 Holon Ruins (U) .20 .50
□ 97 Holon Scientist (U) .20 .50
□ 98 Holon Transceiver (U) 3.00 6.00
□ 99 Master Ball (U) .20 .50
□ 100 Super Scoop Up (U) .20 .50
□ 101 Potion (C) .10 .20
□ 102 Switch (C) .10 .20
□ 103 Darkness Energy (R) .50 1.00
□ 104 Holon Energy FF (R) .50 1.00
□ 105 Holon Energy GL (R) .50 1.00
□ 106 Holon Energy WP (R) .50 1.00
□ 107 Metal Energy (R) .50 1.00
□ 108 Flareon ex (Holo) (R) 8.00 15.00
□ 109 Jolteon ex (Holo) (R) 8.00 15.00
□ 110 Vaporeon ex (Holo) (R) 7.00 15.00
□ 111 Groudon [star] (Holo) (R) 15.00 25.00
□ 112 Kyogre [star] (Holo) (R) 12.00 25.00
□ 113 Metagross [star] (Holo) (R) 10.00 20.00
□ 114 Azumarill (Holo) (R) 2.00 4.00

2005 Pokemon EX Delta Species Reverse Foil

Complete Set 150.00 250.00
*Reverse Foil: 1X to 2X Basic Card

2006 Pokemon EX Legend Maker

Complete Set (93) 75.00 100.00
Booster Box (36 ct) 80.00 90.00
Booster Pack (9 cards) 3.00 4.00

□ 1 Aerodactyl (Holo) (R) 2.00 5.00
□ 2 Aggron (Holo) (R) 2.00 4.00
□ 3 Cradily (Holo) (R) 2.00 4.00
□ 4 Delcatty (Holo) (R) 2.00 4.00
□ 5 Gengar (Holo) (R) 2.00 4.00
□ 6 Golem (Holo) (R) 2.00 5.00
□ 7 Kabutops (Holo) (R) 3.00 6.00
□ 8 Lapras (Holo) (R) 2.00 4.00
□ 9 Machamp (Holo) (R) 2.00 5.00
□ 10 Mew (Holo) (R) 4.00 8.00
□ 11 Muk (Holo) (R) 2.00 4.00
□ 12 Shiftry (Holo) (R) 2.00 4.00
□ 13 Victreebel (Holo) (R) 2.00 4.00
□ 14 Wailord (Holo) (R) 3.00 8.50
□ 15 Absol (R) .50 1.00
□ 16 Girafarig (R) .50 1.00
□ 17 Gorebyss (R) .50 1.00
□ 18 Huntail (R) .50 1.00
□ 19 Lanturn (R) .50 1.00
□ 20 Lunatone (R) .50 1.00
□ 21 Magmar (R) .50 1.00
□ 22 Magneton (R) .50 1.00
□ 23 Omastar (R) .50 1.00
□ 24 Pinsir (R) .50 1.00
□ 25 Solrock (R) .50 1.00
□ 26 Spinda (R) .50 1.00
□ 27 Torkoal (R) .50 1.00
□ 28 Wobbuffet (R) .50 1.00
□ 29 Anorith (U) .20 .50
□ 30 Cascoon (U) .20 .50
□ 31 Dunsparce (U) .20 .50
□ 32 Electrode (U) .20 .50
□ 33 Furret (U) .20 .50
□ 34 Graveler (U) .20 .50
□ 35 Haunter (U) .20 .50
□ 36 Kabuto (U) .20 .50
□ 37 Kecleon (U) .20 .50
□ 38 Lairon (U) .20 .50
□ 39 Machoke (U) .20 .50
□ 40 Misdreavus (U) .20 .50
□ 41 Nuzleaf (U) .20 .50
□ 42 Roselia (U) .20 .50
□ 43 Sealeo (U) .20 .50
□ 44 Tangela (U) .20 .50
□ 45 Tentacruel (U) .20 .50
□ 46 Vibrava (U) .20 .50
□ 47 Weepinbell (U) .20 .50
□ 48 Aron (C) .10 .20
□ 49 Bellsprout (C) .10 .20
□ 50 Chinchou (C) .10 .20
□ 51 Clamperl (C) .10 .20
□ 52 Gastly (C) .10 .20
□ 53 Geodude (C) .10 .20
□ 54 Grimer (C) .10 .20
□ 55 Growlithe (C) .10 .20
□ 56 Lileep (C) .10 .20
□ 57 Machop (C) .10 .20
□ 58 Magby (C) .10 .20
□ 59 Magnemite (C) .10 .20
□ 60 Omanyte (C) .10 .20
□ 61 Seedot (C) .10 .20
□ 62 Sentret (C) .10 .20
□ 63 Shuppet (C) .10 .20
□ 64 Skitty (C) .10 .20
□ 65 Spheal (C) .10 .20
□ 66 Tentacool (C) .10 .20
□ 67 Trapinch (C) .10 .20
□ 68 Voltorb (C) .10 .20
□ 69 Wailmer (C) .10 .20
□ 70 Wurmple (C) .10 .20
□ 71 Wynaut (C) .10 .20
□ 72 Cursed Stone (U) .20 .50
□ 73 Fieldworker (U) .20 .50
□ 74 Full Flame (U) .20 .50
□ 75 Giant Stump (U) .20 .50
□ 76 Power Tree (U) .20 .50
□ 77 Strange Cave (U) .20 .50
□ 78 Claw Fossil (C) .10 .20
□ 79 Mysterious Fossil (C) .10 .20
□ 80 Root Fossil (C) .10 .20
□ 81 Rainbow Energy (R) .50 1.00
□ 82 React Energy (U) .20 .50
□ 83 Arcanine ex (Holo) (R) 7.00 14.00
□ 84 Armaldo ex (Holo) (R) 7.00 14.00
□ 85 Banette ex (Holo) (R) 6.00 12.00
□ 86 Dustox ex (Holo) (R) 10.00 20.00
□ 87 Flygon ex (Holo) (R) 7.00 14.00
□ 88 Mew ex (Holo) (R) 10.00 20.00

Card	Low	High
☐ 89 Walrein ex (Holo) (R)	8.00	15.00
☐ 90 Regice [star] (Holo) (R)	18.00	25.00
☐ 91 Regirock [star] (Holo) (R)	15.00	30.00
☐ 92 Registeel [star] (Holo) (R)	10.00	20.00
☐ 93 Pikachu (Holo) (R)	3.00	5.00

2006 Pokemon EX Legend Maker Reverse Foil

Card	Low	High
Complete Set (93)	125.00	225.00
*Reverse Foil: 1X to 2X Basic Cards		
☐ 1 Aerodactyl (Holo) (R)	5.00	10.00
☐ 2 Aggron (Holo) (R)	4.00	8.00
☐ 3 Cradily (Holo) (R)	4.00	8.00
☐ 4 Delcatty (Holo) (R)	4.00	8.00
☐ 5 Gengar (Holo) (R)	4.00	8.00
☐ 6 Golem (Holo) (R)	5.00	10.00
☐ 7 Kabutops (Holo) (R)	6.00	12.00
☐ 8 Lapras (Holo) (R)	4.00	8.00
☐ 9 Machamp (Holo) (R)	5.00	10.00
☐ 10 Mew (Holo) (R)	7.50	15.00
☐ 11 Muk (Holo) (R)	4.00	8.00
☐ 12 Shiftry (Holo) (R)	4.00	8.00
☐ 13 Victreebel (Holo) (R)	4.00	8.00
☐ 14 Wailord (Holo) (R)	10.00	20.00
☐ 15 Absol (R)	1.00	2.00
☐ 16 Girafarig (R)	1.00	2.00
☐ 17 Gorebyss (R)	1.00	2.00
☐ 18 Huntail (R)	1.00	2.00
☐ 19 Lanturn (R)	1.00	2.00
☐ 20 Lunatone (R)	1.00	2.00
☐ 21 Magmar (R)	1.00	2.00
☐ 22 Magneton (R)	1.00	2.00
☐ 23 Omastar (R)	1.00	2.00
☐ 24 Pinsir (R)	1.00	2.00
☐ 25 Solrock (R)	1.00	2.00
☐ 26 Spinda (R)	1.00	2.00
☐ 27 Torkoal (R)	1.00	2.00
☐ 28 Wobbuffet (R)	1.00	2.00
☐ 29 Anorith (U)	.50	1.00
☐ 30 Cascoon (U)	.50	1.00
☐ 31 Dunsparce (U)	.50	1.00
☐ 32 Electrode (U)	.50	1.00
☐ 33 Furret (U)	.50	1.00
☐ 34 Graveler (U)	.50	1.00
☐ 35 Haunter (U)	.50	1.00
☐ 36 Kabuto (U)	.50	1.00
☐ 37 Kecleon (U)	.50	1.00
☐ 38 Lairon (U)	.50	1.00
☐ 39 Machoke (U)	.50	1.00
☐ 40 Misdreavus (U)	.50	1.00
☐ 41 Nuzleaf (U)	.50	1.00
☐ 42 Roselia (U)	.50	1.00
☐ 43 Sealeo (U)	.50	1.00
☐ 44 Tangela (U)	.50	1.00
☐ 45 Tentacruel (U)	.50	1.00
☐ 46 Vibrava (U)	.50	1.00
☐ 47 Weepinbell (U)	.50	1.00
☐ 48 Aron (C)	.20	.40
☐ 49 Bellsprout (C)	.20	.40
☐ 50 Chinchou (C)	.20	.40
☐ 51 Clamperl (C)	.20	.40
☐ 52 Gastly (C)	.20	.40
☐ 53 Geodude (C)	.20	.40
☐ 54 Grimer (C)	.20	.40
☐ 55 Growlithe (C)	.20	.40
☐ 56 Lileep (C)	.20	.40
☐ 57 Machop (C)	.20	.40
☐ 58 Magby (C)	.20	.40
☐ 59 Magnemite (C)	.20	.40
☐ 60 Omanyte (C)	.20	.40
☐ 61 Seedot (C)	.20	.40
☐ 62 Sentret (C)	.20	.40
☐ 63 Shuppet (C)	.20	.40
☐ 64 Skitty (C)	.20	.40
☐ 65 Spheal (C)	.20	.40
☐ 66 Tentacool (C)	.20	.40
☐ 67 Trapinch (C)	.20	.40
☐ 68 Voltorb (C)	.20	.40
☐ 69 Wailmer (C)	.20	.40
☐ 70 Wurmple (C)	.20	.40
☐ 71 Wynaut (C)	.20	.40
☐ 72 Cursed Stone (U)	.50	1.00
☐ 73 Fieldworker (U)	.50	1.00
☐ 74 Full Flame (U)	.50	1.00
☐ 75 Giant Stump (U)	.50	1.00
☐ 76 Power Tree (U)	.50	1.00
☐ 77 Strange Cave (U)	.50	1.00
☐ 78 Claw Fossil (C)	.20	.40
☐ 79 Mysterious Fossil (C)	.20	.40
☐ 80 Root Fossil (C)	.20	.40
☐ 81 Rainbow Energy (R)	1.00	2.00
☐ 82 React Energy (U)	.50	1.00
☐ 83 Arcanine ex (Holo) (R)	15.00	30.00
☐ 84 Armaldo ex (Holo) (R)	15.00	30.00
☐ 85 Banette ex (Holo) (R)	12.50	25.00
☐ 86 Dustox ex (Holo) (R)	20.00	40.00
☐ 87 Flygon ex (Holo) (R)	15.00	30.00
☐ 88 Mew ex (Holo) (R)	20.00	40.00
☐ 89 Walrein ex (Holo) (R)	15.00	30.00
☐ 90 Regice [star] (Holo) (R)	25.00	50.00
☐ 91 Regirock [star] (Holo) (R)	30.00	60.00
☐ 92 Registeel [star] (Holo) (R)	20.00	40.00
☐ 93 Pikachu (Holo) (R)	5.00	10.00

2006 Pokemon EX Holon Phantoms

Card	Low	High
Complete Set (111)	100.00	150.00
Booster Box (36 ct)	70.00	90.00
Booster Pack (9 cards)	3.75	4.00
Theme Deck	7.00	10.00
☐ 1 Armaldo (Holo) (R)	2.00	4.00
☐ 2 Cradily (Holo) (R)	2.00	4.00
☐ 3 Deoxys (Attack) (Holo) (R)	2.00	5.00
☐ 4 Deoxys (Defense) (Holo) (R)	2.00	5.00
☐ 5 Deoxys (Normal) (Holo) (R)	3.00	7.00
☐ 6 Deoxys (Speed) (Holo) (R)	2.00	5.00
☐ 7 Flygon (Holo) (R)	2.00	4.00
☐ 8 Gyarados (Holo) (R)	4.00	8.00
☐ 9 Kabutops (Holo) (R)	2.00	4.00
☐ 10 Kingdra (Holo) (R)	2.00	5.00
☐ 11 Latias (Holo) (R)	3.00	6.00
☐ 12 Latios (Holo) (R)	3.00	5.00
☐ 13 Omastar (Holo) (R)	2.00	4.00
☐ 14 Pidgeot (Holo) (R)	2.00	4.00
☐ 15 Raichu (Holo) (R)	3.00	5.00
☐ 16 Rayquaza (Holo) (R)	3.00	6.00
☐ 17 Vileplume (Holo) (R)	2.00	4.00
☐ 18 Absol (R)	.50	1.00
☐ 19 Bellossom (R)	.50	1.00
☐ 20 Blaziken (R)	.50	1.00
☐ 21 Latias (R)	.50	1.00
☐ 22 Latios (R)	.50	1.00
☐ 23 Mawile (R)	.50	1.00
☐ 24 Mewtwo (R)	2.00	4.00
☐ 25 Nosepass (R)	.50	1.00
☐ 26 Rayquaza (R)	1.00	2.00
☐ 27 Regice (R)	.50	1.00
☐ 28 Regirock (R)	1.00	2.00
☐ 29 Registeel (R)	1.00	2.00
☐ 30 Relicanth (R)	.50	1.00
☐ 31 Sableye (R)	.50	1.00
☐ 32 Seviper (R)	.50	1.00
☐ 33 Torkoal (R)	.50	1.00
☐ 34 Zangoose (R)	.50	1.00
☐ 35 Aerodactyl (U)	.20	.50
☐ 36 Camerupt (U)	.20	.50
☐ 37 Chimecho (U)	.20	.50
☐ 38 Claydol (U)	.20	.50
☐ 39 Combusken (U)	.20	.50
☐ 40 Donphan (U)	.20	.50
☐ 41 Exeggutor (U)	.20	.50
☐ 42 Gloom (U)	.20	.50
☐ 43 Golduck (U)	.20	.50
☐ 44 Holon's Castform (U)	.50	1.50
☐ 45 Lairon (U)	.20	.50
☐ 46 Manectric (U)	.20	.50
☐ 47 Masquerain (U)	.20	.50
☐ 48 Persian (U)	.20	.50
☐ 49 Pidgeotto (U)	.20	.50
☐ 50 Primeape (U)	.20	.50
☐ 51 Raichu (U)	.20	.50
☐ 52 Seadra (U)	.20	.50
☐ 53 Sharpedo (U)	.20	.50
☐ 54 Vibrava (U)	.20	.50
☐ 55 Whiscash (U)	.20	.50
☐ 56 Wobbuffet (U)	.20	.50
☐ 57 Anorith (C)	.10	.20
☐ 58 Aron (C)	.10	.20
☐ 59 Baltoy (C)	.10	.20
☐ 60 Barboach (C)	.10	.20
☐ 61 Carvanha (C)	.10	.20
☐ 62 Corphish (C)	.10	.20
☐ 63 Corphish (C)	.10	.20
☐ 64 Electrike (C)	.10	.20
☐ 65 Exeggcute (C)	.10	.20
☐ 66 Horsea (C)	.10	.20
☐ 67 Kabuto (C)	.10	.20
☐ 68 Lileep (C)	.10	.20
☐ 69 Magikarp (C)	.10	.20
☐ 70 Mankey (C)	.10	.20
☐ 71 Meowth (C)	.10	.20
☐ 72 Numel (C)	.10	.20
☐ 73 Oddish (C)	.10	.20
☐ 74 Omanyte (C)	.10	.20
☐ 75 Phanpy (C)	.10	.20
☐ 76 Pichu (C)	.20	.50
☐ 77 Pidgey (C)	.10	.20
☐ 78 Pikachu (C)	.20	.50
☐ 79 Pikachu (C)	.20	.50
☐ 80 Poochyena (C)	.10	.20
☐ 81 Psyduck (C)	.10	.20
☐ 82 Surskit (C)	.10	.20
☐ 83 Torchic (C)	.10	.20
☐ 84 Trapinch (C)	.10	.20
☐ 85 Holon Adventurer (U)	.20	.50
☐ 86 Holon Fossil (U)	.20	.50
☐ 87 Holon Lake (U)	.20	.50
☐ 88 Mr. Stone's Project (U)	.20	.50
☐ 89 Professor Cozmo's Discovery (U)	.20	.50
☐ 90 Rare Candy (U)	3.00	5.00
☐ 91 Claw Fossil (C)	.10	.20
☐ 92 Mysterious Fossil (C)	.10	.20
☐ 93 Root Fossil (C)	.10	.20
☐ 94 Darkness Energy (R)	.50	1.00
☐ 95 Metal Energy (R)	.50	1.00
☐ 96 Multi Energy (R)	.50	1.00
☐ 97 d Rainbow Energy (U)	.20	.50
☐ 98 Dark Metal Energy (U)	.20	.50
☐ 99 Crawdaunt ex (Holo) (R)	6.00	10.00
☐ 100 Mew ex (Holo) (R)	9.00	18.00
☐ 101 Mightyena ex (Holo) (R)	4.00	12.00
☐ 102 Gyarados (Shining Holo)	17.00	30.00
☐ 103 Mewtwo (Shining Holo)	15.00	32.00
☐ 104 Pikachu (Shining Holo)	15.00	25.00
☐ 105 Grass Energy	.10	.20
☐ 106 Fire Energy	.10	.20
☐ 107 Water Energy	.10	.20
☐ 108 Lightning Energy	.10	.20
☐ 109 Psychic Energy	.10	.20
☐ 110 Fighting Energy	.10	.20
☐ 111 Mew (Holo) (R)	2.00	4.00

2006 Pokemon EX Holon Phantoms Reverse Foil

Card	Low	High
Complete Set (111)	150.00	250.00
*Reverse Foil: 1X to 2X Basic Cards		
☐ 1 Armaldo (Holo) (R)	4.00	8.00
☐ 2 Cradily (Holo) (R)	4.00	8.00
☐ 3 Deoxys (Attack) (Holo) (R)	5.00	10.00
☐ 4 Deoxys (Defense) (Holo) (R)	5.00	10.00
☐ 5 Deoxys (Normal) (Holo) (R)	7.50	15.00
☐ 6 Deoxys (Speed) (Holo) (R)	5.00	10.00
☐ 7 Flygon (Holo) (R)	4.00	8.00
☐ 8 Gyarados (Holo) (R)	7.50	15.00
☐ 9 Kabutops (Holo) (R)	4.00	8.00
☐ 10 Kingdra (Holo) (R)	5.00	10.00
☐ 11 Latias (Holo) (R)	6.00	12.00
☐ 12 Latios (Holo) (R)	5.00	10.00
☐ 13 Omastar (Holo) (R)	4.00	8.00
☐ 14 Pidgeot (Holo) (R)	4.00	8.00
☐ 15 Raichu (Holo) (R)	5.00	10.00
☐ 16 Rayquaza (Holo) (R)	6.00	12.00
☐ 17 Vileplume (Holo) (R)	4.00	8.00
☐ 18 Absol (R)	1.00	2.00
☐ 19 Bellossom (R)	1.00	2.00
☐ 20 Blaziken (R)	1.00	2.00
☐ 21 Latias (R)	1.00	2.00
☐ 22 Latios (R)	1.00	2.00
☐ 23 Mawile (R)	1.00	2.00
☐ 24 Mewtwo (R)	4.00	8.00
☐ 25 Nosepass (R)	1.00	2.00
☐ 26 Rayquaza (R)	2.00	4.00
☐ 27 Regice (R)	1.00	2.00
☐ 28 Regirock (R)	2.00	4.00
☐ 29 Registeel (R)	2.00	4.00
☐ 30 Relicanth (R)	1.00	2.00
☐ 31 Sableye (R)	1.00	2.00
☐ 32 Seviper (R)	1.00	2.00
☐ 33 Torkoal (R)	1.00	2.00
☐ 34 Zangoose (R)	1.00	2.00
☐ 35 Aerodactyl (U)	.50	1.00
☐ 36 Camerupt (U)	.50	1.00
☐ 37 Chimecho (U)	.50	1.00
☐ 38 Claydol (U)	.50	1.00
☐ 39 Combusken (U)	.50	1.00
☐ 40 Donphan (U)	.50	1.00
☐ 41 Exeggutor (U)	.50	1.00
☐ 42 Gloom (U)	.50	1.00
☐ 43 Golduck (U)	.50	1.00
☐ 44 Holon's Castform (U)	1.50	3.00
☐ 45 Lairon (U)	.50	1.00
☐ 46 Manectric (U)	.50	1.00
☐ 47 Masquerain (U)	.50	1.00
☐ 48 Persian (U)	.50	1.00
☐ 49 Pidgeotto (U)	.50	1.00
☐ 50 Primeape (U)	.50	1.00
☐ 51 Raichu (U)	.50	1.00
☐ 52 Seadra (U)	.50	1.00
☐ 53 Sharpedo (U)	.50	1.00
☐ 54 Vibrava (U)	.50	1.00
☐ 55 Whiscash (U)	.50	1.00
☐ 56 Wobbuffet (U)	.50	1.00
☐ 57 Anorith (C)	.20	.40
☐ 58 Aron (C)	.20	.40
☐ 59 Baltoy (C)	.20	.40
☐ 60 Barboach (C)	.20	.40
☐ 61 Carvanha (C)	.20	.40
☐ 62 Corphish (C)	.20	.40
☐ 63 Corphish (C)	.20	.40
☐ 64 Electrike (C)	.20	.40
☐ 65 Exeggcute (C)	.20	.40
☐ 66 Horsea (C)	.20	.40
☐ 67 Kabuto (C)	.20	.40
☐ 68 Lileep (C)	.20	.40
☐ 69 Magikarp (C)	.20	.40
☐ 70 Mankey (C)	.20	.40
☐ 71 Meowth (C)	.20	.40
☐ 72 Numel (C)	.20	.40
☐ 73 Oddish (C)	.20	.40
☐ 74 Omanyte (C)	.20	.40
☐ 75 Phanpy (C)	.20	.40
☐ 76 Pichu (C)	.50	1.00
☐ 77 Pidgey (C)	.20	.40
☐ 78 Pikachu (C)	.50	1.00
☐ 79 Pikachu (C)	.50	1.00
☐ 80 Poochyena (C)	.20	.40
☐ 81 Psyduck (C)	.20	.40
☐ 82 Surskit (C)	.20	.40
☐ 83 Torchic (C)	.20	.40
☐ 84 Trapinch (C)	.20	.40
☐ 85 Holon Adventurer (U)	.50	1.00
☐ 86 Holon Fossil (U)	.50	1.00
☐ 87 Holon Lake (U)	.50	1.00
☐ 88 Mr. Stone's Project (U)	.50	1.00
☐ 89 Professor Cozmo's Discovery (U)	.50	1.00
☐ 90 Rare Candy (U)	5.00	10.00
☐ 91 Claw Fossil (C)	.20	.40
☐ 92 Mysterious Fossil (C)	.20	.40
☐ 93 Root Fossil (C)	.20	.40
☐ 94 Darkness Energy (R)	1.00	2.00
☐ 95 Metal Energy (R)	1.00	2.00
☐ 96 Multi Energy (R)	1.00	2.00
☐ 97 d Rainbow Energy (U)	.50	1.00
☐ 98 Dark Metal Energy (U)	.50	1.00
☐ 99 Crawdaunt ex (Holo) (R)	10.00	20.00
☐ 100 Mew ex (Holo) (R)	20.00	40.00
☐ 101 Mightyena ex (Holo) (R)	12.50	25.00
☐ 102 Gyarados (Shining Holo)	30.00	60.00
☐ 103 Mewtwo (Shining Holo)	30.00	60.00
☐ 104 Pikachu (Shining Holo)	25.00	50.00
☐ 105 Grass Energy	.20	.40
☐ 106 Fire Energy	.20	.40
☐ 107 Water Energy	.20	.40
☐ 108 Lightning Energy	.20	.40
☐ 109 Psychic Energy	.20	.40
☐ 110 Fighting Energy	.20	.40
☐ 111 Mew (Holo) (R)	4.00	8.00

2006 Pokemon EX Crystal Guardians

Card	Low	High
Complete Set (100)	125.00	200.00
Booster Box (36 ct)	70.00	90.00
Booster Pack (9 cards)	3.75	4.00
☐ 1 Banette (Holo) (R)	3.00	6.00
☐ 2 Blastoise DS (Holo) (R)	4.00	12.00
☐ 3 Camerupt (Holo) (R)	3.00	6.00
☐ 4 Charizard DS (Holo) (R)	12.50	23.00
☐ 5 Dugtrio (Holo) (R)	3.00	6.00
☐ 6 Ludicolo DS (Holo) (R)	3.00	6.00
☐ 7 Luvdisc (Holo) (R)	3.00	6.00
☐ 8 Manectric (Holo) (R)	3.00	6.00
☐ 9 Mawile (Holo) (R)	3.00	6.00
☐ 10 Sableye (Holo) (R)	3.00	6.00
☐ 11 Swalot (Holo) (R)	3.00	5.00
☐ 12 Tauros (Holo) (R)	3.00	6.00
☐ 13 Wigglytuff (Holo) (R)	3.00	6.00
☐ 14 Blastoise (R)	1.00	2.00
☐ 15 Cacturne DS (R)	.50	1.00
☐ 16 Combusken (R)	.50	1.00
☐ 17 Dusclops (R)	.50	1.00
☐ 18 Fearow DS (R)	.50	1.00
☐ 19 Grovyle DS (R)	.50	1.00
☐ 20 Grumpig (R)	.50	1.00
☐ 21 Igglybuff (R)	.50	1.00
☐ 22 Kingler DS (R)	.50	1.00
☐ 23 Loudred (R)	.50	1.00
☐ 24 Marshtomp (R)	.50	1.00
☐ 25 Medicham (R)	.50	1.00
☐ 26 Pelipper DS (R)	.50	1.00
☐ 27 Swampert (R)	.50	1.00
☐ 28 Venusaur (R)	.50	1.00
☐ 29 Charmeleon (U)	.20	.50
☐ 30 Charmeleon DS (U)	.20	.50
☐ 31 Combusken (U)	.20	.50
☐ 32 Grovyle (U)	.20	.50
☐ 33 Gulpin (U)	.20	.50
☐ 34 Ivysaur (U)	.20	.50
☐ 35 Ivysaur (U)	.20	.50
☐ 36 Lairon (U)	.20	.50
☐ 37 Lombre (U)	.20	.50
☐ 38 Marshtomp (U)	.20	.50
☐ 39 Nuzleaf (U)	.20	.50
☐ 40 Shuppet (U)	.20	.50
☐ 41 Skitty (U)	.20	.50
☐ 42 Wartortle (U)	.20	.50
☐ 43 Wartortle (U)	.20	.50
☐ 44 Aron (C)	.10	.20
☐ 45 Bulbasaur (C)	.10	.20
☐ 46 Bulbasaur (C)	.10	.20
☐ 47 Cacnea (C)	.10	.20
☐ 48 Charmander (C)	.10	.20
☐ 49 Charmander DS (C)	.10	.20
☐ 50 Diglett (C)	.10	.20
☐ 51 Duskull (C)	.10	.20
☐ 52 Electrike (C)	.10	.20
☐ 53 Jigglypuff (C)	.10	.20
☐ 54 Krabby (C)	.10	.20
☐ 55 Lotad (C)	.10	.20
☐ 56 Meditite (C)	.10	.20
☐ 57 Mudkip (C)	.10	.20
☐ 58 Mudkip (C)	.10	.20
☐ 59 Numel (C)	.10	.20
☐ 60 Seedot (C)	.10	.20
☐ 61 Spearow (C)	.10	.20
☐ 62 Spoink (C)	.10	.20
☐ 63 Squirtle (C)	.10	.20
☐ 64 Squirtle (C)	.10	.20
☐ 65 Torchic (C)	.10	.20
☐ 66 Torchic (C)	.10	.20
☐ 67 Treecko (C)	.10	.20
☐ 68 Treecko DS (C)	.10	.20
☐ 69 Whismur (C)	.10	.20
☐ 70 Wingull (C)	.10	.20
☐ 71 Bill's Maintenance (U)	.20	.50
☐ 72 Castaway (U)	.20	.50
☐ 73 Celio's Network (U)	.20	.50
☐ 74 Cessation Crystal (U)	.20	.50
☐ 75 Crystal Beach (U)	.20	.50
☐ 76 Crystal Shard (U)	.20	.50
☐ 77 Double Full Heal (U)	.20	.50
☐ 78 Dual Ball (U)	.20	.50
☐ 79 Holon Circle (U)	.20	.50
☐ 80 Memory Berry (U)	.20	.50
☐ 81 Mysterious Shard (U)	.20	.50
☐ 82 Poke Ball (U)	.20	.50
☐ 83 PokeNav (U)	.20	.50
☐ 84 Warp Point (U)	.20	.50
☐ 85 Windstorm (U)	.20	.50
☐ 86 Energy Search (C)	.10	.20
☐ 87 Potion (C)	.10	.20
☐ 88 Double Rainbow Energy (R)	3.00	5.00
☐ 89 Aggron ex (Holo) (R)	5.00	15.00
☐ 90 Blaziken ex (Holo) (R)	10.00	20.00
☐ 91 Delcatty ex (Holo) (R)	5.00	9.00
☐ 92 Exploud ex (Holo) (R)	5.00	9.00
☐ 93 Groudon ex (Holo) (R)	10.00	18.00
☐ 94 Jirachi ex (Holo) (R)	7.00	15.00
☐ 95 Kyogre ex (Holo) (R)	7.00	15.00
☐ 96 Sceptile ex DS (Holo) (R)	7.00	15.00
☐ 97 Shiftry ex (Holo) (R)	5.00	9.00
☐ 98 Swampert ex (Holo) (R)	7.00	15.00
☐ 99 Alakazam Shining (Holo) (R)	15.00	20.00
☐ 100 Celebi Shining (Holo) (R)	10.00	20.00

2006 Pokemon EX Crystal Guardians Reverse Foil

Card	Low	High
Complete Set (100)	150.00	250.00
*Reverse Foils: 1X to 2X Basic Cards		
☐ 1 Banette (Holo) (R)	6.00	12.00
☐ 2 Blastoise DS (Holo) (R)	12.50	25.00
☐ 3 Camerupt (Holo) (R)	6.00	12.00
☐ 4 Charizard DS (Holo) (R)	25.00	50.00
☐ 5 Dugtrio (Holo) (R)	6.00	12.00
☐ 6 Ludicolo DS (Holo) (R)	6.00	12.00
☐ 7 Luvdisc (Holo) (R)	6.00	12.00
☐ 8 Manectric (Holo) (R)	6.00	12.00
☐ 9 Mawile (Holo) (R)	6.00	12.00
☐ 10 Sableye (Holo) (R)	6.00	12.00
☐ 11 Swalot (Holo) (R)	5.00	10.00
☐ 12 Tauros (Holo) (R)	6.00	12.00
☐ 13 Wigglytuff (Holo) (R)	6.00	12.00
☐ 14 Blastoise (R)	2.00	4.00
☐ 15 Cacturne DS (R)	1.00	2.00
☐ 16 Combusken (R)	1.00	2.00
☐ 17 Dusclops (R)	1.00	2.00
☐ 18 Fearow DS (R)	1.00	2.00
☐ 19 Grovyle DS (R)	1.00	2.00
☐ 20 Grumpig (R)	1.00	2.00
☐ 21 Igglybuff (R)	1.00	2.00
☐ 22 Kingler DS (R)	1.00	2.00
☐ 23 Loudred (R)	1.00	2.00
☐ 24 Marshtomp (R)	1.00	2.00
☐ 25 Medicham (R)	1.00	2.00
☐ 26 Pelipper DS (R)	1.00	2.00
☐ 27 Swampert (R)	1.00	2.00
☐ 28 Venusaur (R)	1.00	2.00
☐ 29 Charmeleon (U)	.50	1.00
☐ 30 Charmeleon DS (U)	.50	1.00
☐ 31 Combusken (U)	.50	1.00
☐ 32 Grovyle (U)	.50	1.00
☐ 33 Gulpin (U)	.50	1.00
☐ 34 Ivysaur (U)	.50	1.00
☐ 35 Ivysaur (U)	.50	1.00
☐ 36 Lairon (U)	.50	1.00
☐ 37 Lombre (U)	.50	1.00
☐ 38 Marshtomp (U)	.50	1.00
☐ 39 Nuzleaf (U)	.50	1.00
☐ 40 Shuppet (U)	.50	1.00
☐ 41 Skitty (U)	.50	1.00
☐ 42 Wartortle (U)	.50	1.00
☐ 43 Wartortle (U)	.50	1.00
☐ 44 Aron (C)	.20	.40
☐ 45 Bulbasaur (C)	.20	.40
☐ 46 Bulbasaur (C)	.20	.40
☐ 47 Cacnea (C)	.20	.40
☐ 48 Charmander (C)	.20	.40
☐ 49 Charmander DS (C)	.20	.40
☐ 50 Diglett (C)	.20	.40
☐ 51 Duskull (C)	.20	.40
☐ 52 Electrike (C)	.20	.40
☐ 53 Jigglypuff (C)	.20	.40
☐ 54 Krabby (C)	.20	.40
☐ 55 Lotad (C)	.20	.40
☐ 56 Meditite (C)	.20	.40
☐ 57 Mudkip (C)	.20	.40
☐ 58 Mudkip (C)	.20	.40
☐ 59 Numel (C)	.20	.40
☐ 60 Seedot (C)	.20	.40
☐ 61 Spearow (C)	.20	.40
☐ 62 Spoink (C)	.20	.40
☐ 63 Squirtle (C)	.20	.40
☐ 64 Squirtle (C)	.20	.40
☐ 65 Torchic (C)	.20	.40
☐ 66 Torchic (C)	.20	.40
☐ 67 Treecko (C)	.20	.40
☐ 68 Treecko DS (C)	.20	.40
☐ 69 Whismur (C)	.20	.40
☐ 70 Wingull (C)	.20	.40
☐ 71 Bill's Maintenance (U)	.50	1.00
☐ 72 Castaway (U)	.50	1.00
☐ 73 Celio's Network (U)	.50	1.00
☐ 74 Cessation Crystal (U)	.50	1.00
☐ 75 Crystal Beach (U)	.50	1.00
☐ 76 Crystal Shard (U)	.50	1.00
☐ 77 Double Full Heal (U)	.50	1.00
☐ 78 Dual Ball (U)	.50	1.00
☐ 79 Holon Circle (U)	.50	1.00
☐ 80 Memory Berry (U)	.50	1.00
☐ 81 Mysterious Shard (U)	.50	1.00

TCG/CCG

☐ 82 Poke Ball (U) .50 1.00
☐ 83 PokeNav (U) .50 1.00
☐ 84 Warp Point (U) .50 1.00
☐ 85 Windstorm (U) .50 1.00
☐ 86 Energy Search (C) .20 .40
☐ 87 Potion (C) .20 .40
☐ 88 Double Rainbow Energy (R) 5.00 10.00
☐ 89 Aggron ex (Holo) (R) 15.00 30.00
☐ 90 Blaziken ex (Holo) (R) 20.00 40.00
☐ 91 Delcatty ex (Holo) (R) 10.00 20.00
☐ 92 Exploud ex (Holo) (R) 10.00 20.00
☐ 93 Groudon ex (Holo) (R) 20.00 40.00
☐ 94 Jirachi ex (Holo) (R) 15.00 30.00
☐ 95 Kyogre ex (Holo) (R) 15.00 30.00
☐ 96 Sceptile ex DS (Holo) (R) 15.00 30.00
☐ 97 Shiftry ex (Holo) (R) 10.00 20.00
☐ 98 Swampert ex (Holo) (R) 15.00 30.00
☐ 99 Alakazam Shining (Holo) (R) 20.00 40.00
☐ 100 Celebi Shining (Holo) (R) 20.00 40.00

2006 Pokemon EX Dragon Frontiers

Complete Set (101) 70.00 100.00
Booster Box (36 ct) 75.00 90.00
Booster Pack (9 cards) 3.00 4.00
Theme Deck 10.00 14.00

☐ 1 Ampharos DS (Holo) (R) 3.00 6.00
☐ 2 Feraligatr DS (Holo) (R) 3.00 7.00
☐ 3 Heracross DS (Holo) (R) 3.00 6.00
☐ 4 Meganium DS (Holo) (R) 3.00 6.00
☐ 5 Milotic DS (Holo) (R) 4.00 8.00
☐ 6 Nidoking DS (Holo) (R) 3.00 6.00
☐ 7 Nidoqueen DS (Holo) (R) 3.00 6.00
☐ 8 Ninetales DS (Holo) (R) 3.00 7.00
☐ 9 Pinsir DS (Holo) (R) 3.00 7.00
☐ 10 Snorlax DS (Holo) (R) 3.00 6.00
☐ 11 Togetic DS (Holo) (R) 3.00 7.00
☐ 12 Typhlosion DS (Holo) (R) 3.00 7.00
☐ 13 Arbok DS (R) .50 1.00
☐ 14 Cloyster DS (R) .50 1.00
☐ 15 Dewgong DS (R) .50 1.00
☐ 16 Gligar DS (R) .50 1.00
☐ 17 Jynx DS (R) .50 1.00
☐ 18 Ledian DS (R) .50 1.00
☐ 19 Lickitung DS (R) .50 1.00
☐ 20 Mantine DS (R) .50 1.00
☐ 21 Quagsire DS (R) .50 1.00
☐ 22 Seadra DS (R) .50 1.00
☐ 23 Tropius DS (R) .50 1.00
☐ 24 Vibrava DS (R) .50 1.00
☐ 25 Xatu DS (R) .50 1.00
☐ 26 Bayleef DS (U) .20 .50
☐ 27 Croconaw DS (U) .20 .50
☐ 28 Dragonair DS (U) .20 .50
☐ 29 Electabuzz DS (U) .20 .75
☐ 30 Flaaffy DS (U) .20 .50
☐ 31 Horsea DS (U) .20 .50
☐ 32 Kirlia (U) .20 .50
☐ 33 Kirlia DS (U) .20 .50
☐ 34 Nidorina DS (U) .20 .50
☐ 35 Nidorino DS (U) .20 .50
☐ 36 Quilava DS (U) .20 .50
☐ 37 Seadra DS (U) .20 .50
☐ 38 Shelgon DS (U) .20 .50
☐ 39 Smeargle DS (U) .20 .50
☐ 40 Swellow DS (U) .20 .50
☐ 41 Togepi DS (U) .20 .50
☐ 42 Vibrava DS (U) .20 .50
☐ 43 Bagon DS (C) .10 .20
☐ 44 Chikorita DS (C) .10 .20
☐ 45 Cyndaquil DS (C) .10 .20
☐ 46 Dratini DS (C) .10 .20
☐ 47 Ekans DS (C) .10 .20
☐ 48 Elekid DS (C) .10 .20
☐ 49 Feebas DS (C) .10 .20
☐ 50 Horsea DS (C) .10 .20
☐ 51 Larvitar (C) .10 .20
☐ 52 Larvitar DS (C) .10 .20
☐ 53 Ledyba DS (C) .10 .20
☐ 54 Mareep DS (C) .10 .20
☐ 55 Natu DS (C) .10 .20
☐ 56 Nidoran DS (C) .10 .20
☐ 57 Nidoran DS (C) .10 .20
☐ 58 Pupitar (C) .10 .20
☐ 59 Pupitar DS .10 .20
☐ 60 Ralts (C) .10 .20
☐ 61 Ralts DS (C) .10 .20
☐ 62 Seel DS (C) .10 .20
☐ 63 Shellder DS (C) .10 .20
☐ 64 Smoochum DS (C) .10 .20
☐ 65 Swablu DS (C) .10 .20
☐ 66 Taillow DS (C) .10 .20
☐ 67 Totodile DS (C) .10 .20
☐ 68 Trapinch DS (C) .10 .20
☐ 69 Trapinch DS (C) .10 .20
☐ 70 Vulpix DS (C) .10 .20
☐ 71 Wooper DS (C) .10 .20
☐ 72 Buffer Piece (U) .20 .50
☐ 73 Copycat (U) .20 .50
☐ 74 Holon Legacy (U) .20 .50
☐ 75 Holon Mentor (U) .20 .50
☐ 76 Island Hermit (U) .20 .50
☐ 77 Mr. Stone's Project (U) .20 .50
☐ 78 Old Rod (U) .20 .50
☐ 79 Professor Elm's Training Method (U) .20 .50
☐ 80 Professor Oak's Research (U) .20 .50
☐ 81 Strength Charm (U) .20 .50
☐ 82 TV Reporter (U) .20 .50
☐ 83 Switch (C) .10 .20
☐ 84 Holon Energy FF (R) .50 1.00
☐ 85 Holon Energy GL (R) .50 1.00
☐ 86 Holon Energy WP (R) .50 1.00
☐ 87 Boost Energy (U) .20 .50
☐ 88 Rainbow Energy (U) .20 .50
☐ 89 Scramble Energy (U) .20 .50
☐ 90 Altaria ex DS (Holo) (R) 7.00 14.00
☐ 91 Dragonite ex DS (R) 8.00 15.00
☐ 92 Flygon ex DS (R) 12.00 20.00
☐ 93 Gardevoir ex DS (R) 7.00 15.00
☐ 94 Kingdra ex DS (R) 8.00 15.00
☐ 95 Latias ex DS (R) 10.00 18.00
☐ 96 Latios ex DS (R) 8.00 15.00
☐ 97 Rayquaza ex DS (R) 12.00 20.00
☐ 98 Salamence ex DS (R) 8.00 25.00
☐ 99 Tyranitar ex DS (R) 7.00 15.00
☐ 100 Charizard DS (Holo) (R) 25.00 42.00
☐ 101 Mew DS (Holo) (R) 15.00 30.00

2006 Pokemon EX Dragon Frontiers Reverse Foil

Complete Set (101) 200.00 300.00
*Reverse Foils: 1X to 2X Basic Cards

☐ 1 Ampharos DS (Holo) (R) 6.00 12.00
☐ 2 Feraligatr DS (Holo) (R) 7.50 15.00
☐ 3 Heracross DS (Holo) (R) 6.00 12.00
☐ 4 Meganium DS (Holo) (R) 6.00 12.00
☐ 5 Milotic DS (Holo) (R) 7.50 15.00
☐ 6 Nidoking DS (Holo) (R) 6.00 12.00
☐ 7 Nidoqueen DS (Holo) (R) 6.00 12.00
☐ 8 Ninetales DS (Holo) (R) 7.50 15.00
☐ 9 Pinsir DS (Holo) (R) 7.50 15.00
☐ 10 Snorlax DS (Holo) (R) 6.00 12.00
☐ 11 Togetic DS (Holo) (R) 7.50 15.00
☐ 12 Typhlosion DS (Holo) (R) 7.50 15.00
☐ 13 Arbok DS (R) 1.00 2.00
☐ 14 Cloyster DS (R) 1.00 2.00
☐ 15 Dewgong DS (R) 1.00 2.00
☐ 16 Gligar DS (R) 1.00 2.00
☐ 17 Jynx DS (R) 1.00 2.00
☐ 18 Ledian DS (R) 1.00 2.00
☐ 19 Lickitung DS (R) 1.00 2.00
☐ 20 Mantine DS (R) 1.00 2.00
☐ 21 Quagsire DS (R) 1.00 2.00
☐ 22 Seadra DS (R) 1.00 2.00
☐ 23 Tropius DS (R) 1.00 2.00
☐ 24 Vibrava DS (R) 1.00 2.00
☐ 25 Xatu DS (R) 1.00 2.00
☐ 26 Bayleef DS (U) .50 1.00
☐ 27 Croconaw DS (U) .50 1.00
☐ 28 Dragonair DS (U) .50 1.00
☐ 29 Electabuzz DS (U) .75 1.50
☐ 30 Flaaffy DS (U) .50 1.00
☐ 31 Horsea DS (U) .50 1.00
☐ 32 Kirlia (U) .50 1.00
☐ 33 Kirlia DS (U) .50 1.00
☐ 34 Nidorina DS (U) .50 1.00
☐ 35 Nidorino DS (U) .50 1.00
☐ 36 Quilava DS (U) .50 1.00
☐ 37 Seadra DS (U) .50 1.00
☐ 38 Shelgon DS (U) .50 1.00
☐ 39 Smeargle DS (U) .50 1.00
☐ 40 Swellow DS (U) .50 1.00
☐ 41 Togepi DS (U) .50 1.00
☐ 42 Vibrava DS (U) .50 1.00
☐ 43 Bagon DS (C) .20 .40
☐ 44 Chikorita DS (C) .20 .40
☐ 45 Cyndaquil DS (C) .20 .40
☐ 46 Dratini DS (C) .20 .40
☐ 47 Ekans DS (C) .20 .40
☐ 48 Elekid DS (C) .20 .40
☐ 49 Feebas DS (C) .20 .40
☐ 50 Horsea DS (C) .20 .40
☐ 51 Larvitar (C) .20 .40
☐ 52 Larvitar DS (C) .20 .40
☐ 53 Ledyba DS (C) .20 .40
☐ 54 Mareep DS (C) .20 .40
☐ 55 Natu DS (C) .20 .40
☐ 56 Nidoran DS (C) .20 .40
☐ 57 Nidoran DS (C) .20 .40
☐ 58 Pupitar (C) .20 .40
☐ 59 Pupitar DS .20 .40
☐ 60 Ralts (C) .20 .40
☐ 61 Ralts DS (C) .20 .40
☐ 62 Seel DS (C) .20 .40
☐ 63 Shellder DS (C) .20 .40
☐ 64 Smoochum DS (C) .20 .40
☐ 65 Swablu DS (C) .20 .40
☐ 66 Taillow DS (C) .20 .40
☐ 67 Totodile DS (C) .20 .40
☐ 68 Trapinch DS (C) .20 .40
☐ 69 Trapinch DS (C) .20 .40
☐ 70 Vulpix DS (C) .20 .40
☐ 71 Wooper DS (C) .20 .40
☐ 72 Buffer Piece (U) .50 1.00
☐ 73 Copycat (U) .50 1.00
☐ 74 Holon Legacy (U) .50 1.00
☐ 75 Holon Mentor (U) .50 1.00
☐ 76 Island Hermit (U) .50 1.00
☐ 77 Mr. Stone's Project (U) .50 1.00
☐ 78 Old Rod (U) .50 1.00
☐ 79 Professor Elm's Training Method (U) .50 1.00
☐ 80 Professor Oak's Research (U) .50 1.00
☐ 81 Strength Charm (U) .50 1.00
☐ 82 TV Reporter (U) .50 1.00
☐ 83 Switch (C) .20 .40
☐ 84 Holon Energy FF (R) 1.00 2.00
☐ 85 Holon Energy GL (R) 1.00 2.00
☐ 86 Holon Energy WP (R) 1.00 2.00
☐ 87 Boost Energy (U) .50 1.00
☐ 88 Rainbow Energy (U) .50 1.00
☐ 89 Scramble Energy (U) .50 1.00
☐ 90 Altaria ex DS (Holo) (R) 15.00 30.00
☐ 91 Dragonite ex DS (R) 15.00 30.00
☐ 92 Flygon ex DS (R) 20.00 40.00
☐ 93 Gardevoir ex DS (R) 15.00 30.00
☐ 94 Kingdra ex DS (R) 15.00 30.00
☐ 95 Latias ex DS (R) 20.00 40.00
☐ 96 Latios ex DS (R) 15.00 30.00
☐ 97 Rayquaza ex DS (R) 20.00 40.00
☐ 98 Salamence ex DS (R) 25.00 50.00
☐ 99 Tyranitar ex DS (R) 15.00 30.00
☐ 100 Charizard DS (Holo) (R) 40.00 80.00
☐ 101 Mew DS (Holo) (R) 30.00 60.00

2007 Pokemon EX Power Keepers

Complete Set (108) 70.00 120.00
Booster Box (36 ct) 70.00 85.00
Booster Pack (9 cards) 3.00 3.75

☐ 1 Aggron Holo (R) 3.00 6.00
☐ 2 Altaria Holo (R) 2.00 4.00
☐ 3 Armaldo Holo (R) 3.00 6.00
☐ 4 Banette Holo (R) 3.00 6.00
☐ 5 Blaziken Holo (R) 3.00 6.00
☐ 6 Charizard Holo (R) 9.00 15.00
☐ 7 Cradily Holo (R) 2.00 4.00
☐ 8 Delcatty Holo (R) 2.00 4.00
☐ 9 Gardevoir Holo (R) 3.00 6.00
☐ 10 Kabutops Holo (R) 2.00 4.00
☐ 11 Machamp Holo (R) 2.00 4.00
☐ 12 Raichu Holo (R) 2.00 4.00
☐ 13 Slaking Holo (R) 1.00 4.00
☐ 14 Dusclops (R) .50 1.00
☐ 15 Lanturn (R) .50 1.00
☐ 16 Magneton (R) .50 1.00
☐ 17 Mawile (R) .50 1.00
☐ 18 Mightyena (R) .50 1.00
☐ 19 Ninetales (R) .50 1.00
☐ 20 Omastar (R) .50 1.00
☐ 21 Pichu (R) .50 1.00
☐ 22 Sableye (R) .50 1.00
☐ 23 Seviper (R) .50 1.00
☐ 24 Wobbuffet (R) .50 1.00
☐ 25 Zangoose (R) .50 1.00
☐ 26 Anorith (U) .20 .50
☐ 27 Cacturne (U) .20 .50
☐ 28 Charmeleon (U) .20 .50
☐ 29 Combusken (U) .20 .50
☐ 30 Glalie (U) .20 .50
☐ 31 Kirlia (U) .20 .50
☐ 32 Lairon (U) .20 .50
☐ 33 Machoke (U) .20 .50
☐ 34 Medicham (U) .20 .50
☐ 35 Metang (U) .20 .50
☐ 36 Nuzleaf (U) .20 .50
☐ 37 Sealeo (U) .20 .50
☐ 38 Sharpedo (U) .20 .50
☐ 39 Shelgon (U) .20 .50
☐ 40 Vibrava (U) .20 .50
☐ 41 Vigoroth (U) .20 .50
☐ 42 Aron (C) .10 .20
☐ 43 Bagon (C) .10 .20
☐ 44 Baltoy (C) .10 .20
☐ 45 Beldum (C) .10 .20
☐ 46 Cacnea (C) .10 .20
☐ 47 Carvanha (C) .10 .20
☐ 48 Charmander (C) .10 .20
☐ 49 Chinchou (C) .10 .20
☐ 50 Duskull (C) .10 .20
☐ 51 Kabuto (C) .10 .20
☐ 52 Lileep (C) .10 .20
☐ 53 Machop (C) .10 .20
☐ 54 Magnemite (C) .10 .20
☐ 55 Meditite (C) .10 .20
☐ 56 Omanyte (C) .10 .20
☐ 57 Pikachu (C) .10 .20
☐ 58 Poochyena (C) .10 .20
☐ 59 Ralts (C) .10 .20
☐ 60 Seedot (C) .10 .20
☐ 61 Shuppet (C) .10 .20
☐ 62 Skitty (C) .10 .20
☐ 63 Slakoth (C) .10 .20
☐ 64 Snorunt (C) .10 .20
☐ 65 Spheal (C) .10 .20
☐ 66 Swablu (C) .10 .20
☐ 67 Torchic (C) .10 .20
☐ 68 Trapinch (C) .10 .20
☐ 69 Vulpix (C) .10 .20
☐ 70 Wynaut (C) .10 .20
☐ 71 Battle Frontier (U) .20 .50
☐ 72 Drake's Stadium (U) .20 .50
☐ 73 Energy Recycle System (U) .20 .50
☐ 74 Energy Removal 2 (U) .20 .50
☐ 75 Energy Switch (U) .20 .50
☐ 76 Glacia's Stadium (U) .20 .50
☐ 77 Great Ball (U) .20 .50
☐ 78 Master Ball (U) .20 .50
☐ 79 Phoebe's Stadium (U) .20 .50
☐ 80 Professor Birch (U) .20 .50
☐ 81 Scott (U) .20 .50
☐ 82 Sidney's Stadium (U) .20 .50
☐ 83 Steven's Advice (U) .20 .50
☐ 84 Claw Fossil (C) .10 .20
☐ 85 Mysterious Fossil (C) .10 .20
☐ 86 Root Fossil (C) .10 .20
☐ 87 Darkness Energy (R) .50 1.00
☐ 88 Metal Energy (R) .50 1.00
☐ 89 Multi Energy (R) .50 1.00
☐ 90 Cyclone Energy (U) .20 .50
☐ 91 Warp Energy (U) .20 .50
☐ 92 Absol ex (Holo) (R) 8.00 18.00
☐ 93 Claydol ex (Holo) (R) 8.00 15.00
☐ 94 Flygon ex (Holo) (R) 8.00 16.00
☐ 95 Metagross ex (Holo) (R) 6.00 12.00
☐ 96 Salamence ex (Holo) (R) 10.00 20.00
☐ 97 Shiftry ex (Holo) (R) 8.00 16.00
☐ 98 Skarmory ex (Holo) (R) 8.00 16.00
☐ 99 Walrein ex (Holo) (R) 6.00 16.00
☐ 100 Flareon [star] (Holo) (R) 12.00 25.00
☐ 101 Jolteon [star] (Holo) (R) 10.00 20.00
☐ 102 Vaporeon [star] (Holo) (R) 15.00 20.00
☐ 103 Grass Energy Holo (R) .50 1.00
☐ 104 Fire Energy Holo (R) .50 1.00
☐ 105 Water Energy Holo (R) .50 1.00
☐ 106 Lightning Energy Holo (R) .50 1.00
☐ 107 Psychic Energy Holo (R) .50 1.00
☐ 108 Fighting Energy Holo (R) .50 1.00

2007 Pokemon EX Power Keepers Reverse Foil

Complete Set (108) 150.00 250.00
*Reverse Foil: 1X to 2X Basic Cards

☐ 1 Aggron Holo (R) 6.00 12.00
☐ 2 Altaria Holo (R) 4.00 8.00
☐ 3 Armaldo Holo (R) 6.00 12.00
☐ 4 Banette Holo (R) 6.00 12.00
☐ 5 Blaziken Holo (R) 6.00 12.00
☐ 6 Charizard Holo (R) 15.00 30.00
☐ 7 Cradily Holo (R) 4.00 8.00
☐ 8 Delcatty Holo (R) 4.00 8.00
☐ 9 Gardevoir Holo (R) 6.00 12.00
☐ 10 Kabutops Holo (R) 4.00 8.00
☐ 11 Machamp Holo (R) 4.00 8.00
☐ 12 Raichu Holo (R) 4.00 8.00
☐ 13 Slaking Holo (R) 4.00 8.00
☐ 14 Dusclops (R) 1.00 2.00
☐ 15 Lanturn (R) 1.00 2.00
☐ 16 Magneton (R) 1.00 2.00
☐ 17 Mawile (R) 1.00 2.00
☐ 18 Mightyena (R) 1.00 2.00
☐ 19 Ninetales (R) 1.00 2.00
☐ 20 Omastar (R) 1.00 2.00
☐ 21 Pichu (R) 1.00 2.00
☐ 22 Sableye (R) 1.00 2.00
☐ 23 Seviper (R) 1.00 2.00
☐ 24 Wobbuffet (R) 1.00 2.00
☐ 25 Zangoose (R) 1.00 2.00
☐ 26 Anorith (U) .50 1.00
☐ 27 Cacturne (U) .50 1.00
☐ 28 Charmeleon (U) .50 1.00
☐ 29 Combusken (U) .50 1.00
☐ 30 Glalie (U) .50 1.00
☐ 31 Kirlia (U) .50 1.00
☐ 32 Lairon (U) .50 1.00
☐ 33 Machoke (U) .50 1.00
☐ 34 Medicham (U) .50 1.00
☐ 35 Metang (U) .50 1.00
☐ 36 Nuzleaf (U) .50 1.00
☐ 37 Sealeo (U) .50 1.00
☐ 38 Sharpedo (U) .50 1.00
☐ 39 Shelgon (U) .50 1.00
☐ 40 Vibrava (U) .50 1.00
☐ 41 Vigoroth (U) .50 1.00
☐ 42 Aron (C) .20 .40
☐ 43 Bagon (C) .20 .40
☐ 44 Baltoy (C) .20 .40
☐ 45 Beldum (C) .20 .40
☐ 46 Cacnea (C) .20 .40
☐ 47 Carvanha (C) .20 .40
☐ 48 Charmander (C) .20 .40
☐ 49 Chinchou (C) .20 .40
☐ 50 Duskull (C) .20 .40
☐ 51 Kabuto (C) .20 .40
☐ 52 Lileep (C) .20 .40
☐ 53 Machop (C) .20 .40
☐ 54 Magnemite (C) .20 .40
☐ 55 Meditite (C) .20 .40
☐ 56 Omanyte (C) .20 .40
☐ 57 Pikachu (C) .20 .40
☐ 58 Poochyena (C) .20 .40
☐ 59 Ralts (C) .20 .40
☐ 60 Seedot (C) .20 .40
☐ 61 Shuppet (C) .20 .40
☐ 62 Skitty (C) .20 .40
☐ 63 Slakoth (C) .20 .40
☐ 64 Snorunt (C) .20 .40
☐ 65 Spheal (C) .20 .40
☐ 66 Swablu (C) .20 .40
☐ 67 Torchic (C) .20 .40
☐ 68 Trapinch (C) .20 .40
☐ 69 Vulpix (C) .20 .40
☐ 70 Wynaut (C) .20 .40
☐ 71 Battle Frontier (U) .50 1.00
☐ 72 Drake's Stadium (U) .50 1.00
☐ 73 Energy Recycle System (U) .50 1.00
☐ 74 Energy Removal 2 (U) .50 1.00
☐ 75 Energy Switch (U) .50 1.00
☐ 76 Glacia's Stadium (U) .50 1.00
☐ 77 Great Ball (U) .50 1.00
☐ 78 Master Ball (U) .50 1.00
☐ 79 Phoebe's Stadium (U) .50 1.00
☐ 80 Professor Birch (U) .50 1.00
☐ 81 Scott (U) .50 1.00
☐ 82 Sidney's Stadium (U) .50 1.00
☐ 83 Steven's Advice (U) .50 1.00
☐ 84 Claw Fossil (C) .20 .40
☐ 85 Mysterious Fossil (C) .20 .40
☐ 86 Root Fossil (C) .20 .40
☐ 87 Darkness Energy (R) 1.00 2.00
☐ 88 Metal Energy (R) 1.00 2.00
☐ 89 Multi Energy (R) 1.00 2.00
☐ 90 Cyclone Energy (U) .50 1.00
☐ 91 Warp Energy (U) .50 1.00
☐ 92 Absol ex Holo (R) 20.00 40.00
☐ 93 Claydol ex Holo (R) 15.00 30.00
☐ 94 Flygon ex Holo (R) 15.00 30.00
☐ 95 Metagross ex Holo (R) 12.50 25.00
☐ 96 Salamence ex Holo (R) 20.00 40.00
☐ 97 Shiftry ex Holo (R) 15.00 30.00
☐ 98 Skarmory ex Holo (R) 15.00 30.00
☐ 99 Walrein ex Holo (R) 15.00 30.00
☐ 100 Flareon Holo (R) "star" 25.00 50.00
☐ 101 Jolteon Holo (R) "star" 20.00 40.00
☐ 102 Vaporeon Holo (R) "star" 20.00 40.00
☐ 103 Grass Energy Holo (R) 1.00 2.00
☐ 104 Fire Energy Holo (R) 1.00 2.00
☐ 105 Water Energy Holo (R) 1.00 2.00
☐ 106 Lightning Energy Holo (R) 1.00 2.00
☐ 107 Psychic Energy Holo (R) 1.00 2.00
☐ 108 Fighting Energy Holo (R) 1.00 2.00

2007 Pokemon Diamond & Pearl

Complete Set (130) 75.00 130.00
Booster Box (36 ct) 70.00 90.00
Booster Pack (9 cards) 3.50 4.00
Collector's Tin 18.00 22.00

☐ 1 Dialga (Holo) (R) 8.00 15.00
☐ 2 Dusknoir (Holo) (R) 2.00 6.00
☐ 3 Electivire (Holo) (R) 4.00 11.00
☐ 4 Empoleon (Holo) (R) 3.00 6.00
☐ 5 Infernape (Holo) (R) 6.00 12.00
☐ 6 Lucario (Holo) (R) 10.00 20.00
☐ 7 Luxray (Holo) (R) 2.00 6.00
☐ 8 Magnezone (Holo) (R) 4.00 8.00
☐ 9 Manaphy (Holo) (R) 2.00 6.00
☐ 10 Mismagius (Holo) (R) 2.00 5.00
☐ 11 Palkia (Holo) (R) 8.00 15.00
☐ 12 Rhyperior (Holo) (R) 6.00 12.00
☐ 13 Roserade (Holo) (R) 3.00 6.00
☐ 14 Shiftry (Holo) (R) 2.00 5.00
☐ 15 Skuntank (Holo) (R) 2.00 5.00
☐ 16 Staraptor (Holo) (R) 3.00 6.00
☐ 17 Torterra (Holo) (R) 4.00 8.00
☐ 18 Azumarill (R) .50 1.00
☐ 19 Beautifly (R) .50 1.00
☐ 20 Bibarel (R) .50 1.00
☐ 21 Carnivine (R) .50 1.00
☐ 22 Clefable (R) .50 1.00
☐ 23 Drapion (R) .50 1.00
☐ 24 Drifblim (R) .50 1.00
☐ 25 Dustox (R) .50 1.00
☐ 26 Floatzel (R) 1.00 1.00
☐ 27 Gengar (R) .50 1.50
☐ 28 Heracross (R) .50 1.00
☐ 29 Hippowdon (R) 1.00 1.00
☐ 30 Lopunny (R) .50 1.00
☐ 31 Machamp (R) .50 1.00
☐ 32 Medicham (R) .50 1.00
☐ 33 Munchlax (R) .50 1.00
☐ 34 Noctowl (R) .50 1.00
☐ 35 Pachirisu (R) 1.00 2.00
☐ 36 Purugly (R) .50 1.00
☐ 37 Snorlax (R) .50 1.00
☐ 38 Steelix (R) .50 1.00
☐ 39 Vespiquen (R) .50 1.00
☐ 40 Weavile (R) .50 1.00
☐ 41 Wobbuffet (R) .50 1.50
☐ 42 Wynaut (R) .50 1.00
☐ 43 Budew (U) .10 .20
☐ 44 Cascoon (U) .20 .50
☐ 45 Cherrim (U) .20 .50
☐ 46 Drifloon (U) .20 .50
☐ 47 Dusclops (U) .20 .50
☐ 48 Elekid (U) .20 .50
☐ 49 Grotle (U) .20 .50
☐ 50 Haunter (U) .20 .50
☐ 51 Hippopotas (U) .20 .50
☐ 52 Luxio (U) .20 .50
☐ 53 Machoke (U) .20 .50
☐ 54 Magneton (U) .20 .50
☐ 55 Mantyke (U) .20 .50
☐ 56 Monferno (U) .20 .50
☐ 57 Nuzleaf (U) .20 .50
☐ 58 Prinplup (U) .20 .50
☐ 59 Rapidash (U) .20 .50
☐ 60 Rhydon (U) .50 1.00

TCG/CCG

□ 61 Riolu (U) .20 .50
□ 62 Seaking (U) .20 .50
□ 63 Silcoon (U) .20 .50
□ 64 Staravia (U) .20 .50
□ 65 Unown A (U) .20 .50
□ 66 Unown B (U) .20 .50
□ 67 Unown C (U) .20 .50
□ 68 Unown D (U) .20 .50
□ 69 Azurill (C) .10 .20
□ 70 Bidoof (C) .10 .20
□ 71 Bonsly (C) .10 .20
□ 72 Buizel (C) .10 .20
□ 73 Buneary (C) .10 .20
□ 74 Chatot (C) .10 .20
□ 75 Cherubi (C) .10 .20
□ 76 Chimchar (C) .10 .50
□ 77 Clefairy (C) .10 .20
□ 78 Cleffa (C) .10 .20
□ 79 Combee (C) .10 .20
□ 80 Duskull (C) .10 .20
□ 81 Electabuzz (C) .10 .20
□ 82 Gastly (C) .10 .20
□ 83 Glameow (C) .10 .20
□ 84 Goldeen (C) .10 .20
□ 85 Hoothoot (C) .10 .20
□ 86 Machop (C) .10 .20
□ 87 Magnemite (C) .10 .20
□ 88 Marill (C) .10 .20
□ 89 Meditite (C) .10 .20
□ 90 Mime Jr. (C) .10 .20
□ 91 Misdreavus (C) .10 .20
□ 92 Onix (C) .10 .20
□ 93 Piplup (C) .10 .50
□ 94 Ponyta (C) .10 .20
□ 95 Rhyhorn (C) .10 .20
□ 96 Roselia (C) .10 .20
□ 97 Seedot (C) .10 .20
□ 98 Shinx (C) .10 .20
□ 99 Skorupi (C) .10 .20
□ 100 Sneasel (C) .10 .20
□ 101 Starly (C) .10 .20
□ 102 Stunky (C) .10 .20
□ 103 Turtwig (C) .10 .50
□ 104 Wurmple (C) .10 .20
□ 105 Double Full Heal (U) .20 .50
□ 106 Energy Restore (U) .20 .50
□ 107 Energy Switch (U) .20 .50
□ 108 Night Pokemon Center (U) .20 .50
□ 109 PlusPower (U) .20 .50
□ 110 Poke Ball (U) .20 .50
□ 111 Pokedex HANDY910s (U) .20 .50
□ 112 Professor Rowan (U) .20 .50
□ 113 Rival (U) .20 .50
□ 114 Speed Stadium (U) .20 .50
□ 115 Super Scoop Up (U) .20 .50
□ 116 Warp Point (U) .20 .50
□ 117 Energy Search (C) .10 .20
□ 118 Potion (C) .10 .20
□ 119 Switch (C) .10 .20
□ 120 Empoleon Lv.X (Holo) (R) 8.00 15.00
□ 121 Infernape Lv.X (Holo) (R) 7.00 15.00
□ 122 Torterra Lv.X (Holo) (R) 7.00 15.00
□ 123 Grass Energy .10 .20
□ 124 Fire Energy .10 .20
□ 125 Water Energy .10 .20
□ 126 Lightning Energy .10 .20
□ 127 Fighting Energy .10 .20
□ 128 Psychic Energy .10 .20
□ 129 Darkness Energy .10 .20
□ 130 Metal Energy .10 .20

2007 Pokemon DP Mysterious Treasures

Complete Set (124) 90.00 140.00
□ 1 Aggron (Holo) (R) 2.00 5.00
□ 2 Alakazam (Holo) (R) 2.00 5.00
□ 3 Ambipom (Holo) (R) 4.00 8.00
□ 4 Azelf (Holo) (R) 5.00 8.00
□ 5 Blissey (Holo) (R) 5.00 10.00
□ 6 Bronzong (Holo) (R) 3.00 6.00
□ 7 Celebi (Holo) (R) 5.00 10.00
□ 8 Feraligatr (Holo) (R) 3.00 6.00
□ 9 Garchomp (Holo) (R) 5.00 8.00
□ 10 Honchkrow (Holo) (R) 3.00 6.00
□ 11 Lumineon (Holo) (R) 2.00 4.00
□ 12 Magmortar (Holo) (R) 4.00 8.00
□ 13 Meganium (Holo) (R) 4.00 9.00
□ 14 Mesprit (Holo) (R) 3.00 7.00
□ 15 Raichu (Holo) (R) 3.00 7.00
□ 16 Typhlosion (Holo) (R) 3.00 6.00
□ 17 Tyranitar (Holo) (R) 3.00 6.00
□ 18 Uxie (Holo) (R) 2.00 5.00
□ 19 Abomasnow (R) .50 1.00
□ 20 Ariados (R) .50 1.00
□ 21 Bastiodon (R) 1.00 2.00
□ 22 Chimecho (R) .50 1.00
□ 23 Crobat (R) .50 1.00
□ 24 Exeggutor (R) .50 1.00
□ 25 Glalie (R) .50 1.00
□ 26 Gyarados (R) .50 1.00
□ 27 Kricketune (R) .50 1.00
□ 28 Manectric (R) .50 1.00
□ 29 Mantine (R) .50 1.00
□ 30 Mr. Mime (R) .50 1.00
□ 31 Nidoqueen (R) .50 1.00
□ 32 Ninetales (R) .50 1.00
□ 33 Rampardos (R) 1.00 2.00
□ 34 Slaking (R) .50 1.00
□ 35 Sudowoodo (R) .50 1.00
□ 36 Toxicroak (R) .50 1.00
□ 37 Unown (R) .50 1.00
□ 38 Ursaring (R) .50 1.00
□ 39 Walrein (R) .50 1.00
□ 40 Whiscash (R) .50 1.00
□ 41 Bayleef (U) .20 .50
□ 42 Chingling (U) .20 .50
□ 43 Cranidos (U) .20 .50
□ 44 Croconaw (U) .20 .50
□ 45 Dewgong (U) .20 .50
□ 46 Dodrio (U) .20 .50
□ 47 Dunsparce (U) .20 .50
□ 48 Gabite (U) .20 .50
□ 49 Girafarig (U) .20 .50
□ 50 Golbat (U) .20 .50
□ 51 Graveler (U) .20 .50
□ 52 Happiny (U) .20 .50
□ 53 Lairon (U) .20 .50
□ 54 Magmar (U) .20 .50
□ 55 Masquerain (U) .20 .50
□ 56 Nidorina (U) .20 .50
□ 57 Octillery (U) .20 .50
□ 58 Parasect (U) .20 .50
□ 59 Pupitar (U) .20 .50
□ 60 Quilava (U) .20 .50
□ 61 Sandslash (U) .20 .50
□ 62 Sealeo (U) .20 .50
□ 63 Shieldon (U) .20 .50
□ 64 Tropius (U) .20 .50
□ 65 Unown E (U) .20 .50
□ 66 Unown M (U) .20 .50
□ 67 Unown T (U) .20 .50
□ 68 Vigoroth (U) .20 .50
□ 69 Abra (C) .10 .20
□ 70 Aipom (C) .10 .20
□ 71 Aron (C) .10 .20
□ 72 Barboach (C) .10 .20
□ 73 Bidoof (C) .10 .20
□ 74 Bronzor (C) .10 .20
□ 75 Buizel (C) .10 .20
□ 76 Chansey (C) .10 .20
□ 77 Chikorita (C) .10 .20
□ 78 Croagunk (C) .10 .20
□ 79 Cyndaquil (C) .10 .20
□ 80 Doduo (C) .10 .20
□ 81 Electrike (C) .10 .20
□ 82 Exeggcute (C) .10 .20
□ 83 Finneon (C) .10 .20
□ 84 Geodude (C) .10 .20
□ 85 Gible (C) .10 .20
□ 86 Kricketot (C) .10 .20
□ 87 Larvitar (C) .10 .20
□ 88 Magby (C) .10 .20
□ 89 Magikarp (C) .10 .20
□ 90 Murkrow (C) .10 .20
□ 91 Nidoran (C) .10 .20
□ 92 Paras (C) .10 .20
□ 93 Pichu (C) .20 .50
□ 94 Pikachu (C) .20 .50
□ 95 Remoraid (C) .10 .20
□ 96 Sandshrew (C) .10 .20
□ 97 Seel (C) .10 .20
□ 98 Shinx (C) .10 .20
□ 99 Slakoth (C) .10 .20
□ 100 Snorunt (C) .10 .20
□ 101 Snover (C) .10 .20
□ 102 Spheal (C) .10 .20
□ 103 Spinarak (C) .10 .20
□ 104 Surskit (C) .10 .20
□ 105 Teddiursa (C) .10 .20
□ 106 Totodile (C) .10 .20
□ 107 Vulpix (C) .10 .20
□ 108 Zubat (C) .10 .20
□ 109 Bebe's Search (U) .20 .50
□ 110 Dusk Ball (U) .20 .50
□ 111 Fossil Excavator (U) .20 .50
□ 112 Lake Boundary (U) .20 .50
□ 113 Night Maintenance (U) .20 .50
□ 114 Quick Ball (U) .20 .75
□ 115 Team Galactic's Wager (U) .20 .50
□ 116 Armor Fossil (C) .10 .20
□ 117 Skull Fossil (C) .10 .20
□ 118 Multi Energy (R) .50 1.00
□ 119 Darkness Energy (U) .20 .50
□ 120 Metal Energy (U) .20 .50
□ 121 Electivire Lv.X (Holo) (R) 5.00 10.00
□ 122 Lucario Lv.X (Holo) (R) 7.00 12.00
□ 123 Magmortar Lv.X (Holo) (R) 6.00 12.00
□ 124 Time Space Distortion (Holo) (SCR) 10.00 20.00

2007 Pokemon DP Mysterious Treasures Reverse Foil

*Rev.Foil: 1X to 2X Basic Cards

2007 Pokemon DP Secret Wonders

Complete Set (132) 90.00 130.00
□ 1 Ampharos (Holo) (R) 3.00 7.00
□ 2 Blastoise (Holo) (R) 4.00 7.00
□ 3 Charizard (Holo) (R) 7.00 15.00
□ 4 Entei (Holo) (R) 3.00 6.00
□ 5 Flygon (Holo) (R) 3.00 6.00
□ 6 Gallade (Holo) (R) 4.00 8.00
□ 7 Gardevoir (Holo) (R) 4.00 8.00
□ 8 Gastrodon East Sea (Holo) (R) 3.00 6.00
□ 9 Gastrodon West Sea (Holo) (R) 3.00 6.00
□ 10 Ho-Oh (Holo) (R) 3.00 6.00
□ 11 Jumpluff (Holo) (R) 3.00 6.00
□ 12 Lickilicky (Holo) (R) 3.00 5.00
□ 13 Ludicolo (Holo) (R) 3.00 5.00
□ 14 Lugia (Holo) (R) 5.00 10.00
□ 15 Mew (Holo) (R) 4.00 8.00
□ 16 Raikou (Holo) (R) 3.00 5.00
□ 17 Roserade (Holo) (R) 3.00 5.00
□ 18 Salamence (Holo) (R) 4.00 9.00
□ 19 Suicune (Holo) (R) 5.00 10.00
□ 20 Venusaur (Holo) (R) 3.00 6.00
□ 21 Absol (R) 1.00 2.00
□ 22 Arcanine (R) .50 1.00
□ 23 Banette (R) .50 1.00
□ 24 Dugtrio (R) .50 1.00
□ 25 Electivire (R) 1.00 2.00
□ 26 Electrode (R) .50 1.00
□ 27 Furret (R) .50 1.00
□ 28 Golduck (R) .50 1.00
□ 29 Golem (R) .50 1.00
□ 30 Jynx (R) .50 1.00
□ 31 Magmortar (R) .50 1.00
□ 32 Minun (R) .50 1.00
□ 33 Mothim (R) .50 1.00
□ 34 Nidoking (R) .50 1.50
□ 35 Pidgeot (R) .50 1.00
□ 36 Plusle (R) .50 1.00
□ 37 Sharpedo (R) .50 1.00
□ 38 Sunflora (R) .50 1.00
□ 39 Unown S (R) .50 1.00
□ 40 Weavile (R) .50 1.00
□ 41 Wormadam Plant Cloak (R) .50 1.00
□ 42 Wormadam Sandy Cloak (R) .50 1.00
□ 43 Wormadam Trash Cloak (R) .50 1.00
□ 44 Xatu (R) .50 1.00
□ 45 Breloom (U) .20 .50
□ 46 Charmeleon (U) .20 .50
□ 47 Cloyster (U) .20 .50
□ 48 Donphan (U) .20 .50
□ 49 Farfetch'd (U) .20 .50
□ 50 Flaaffy (U) .20 .50
□ 51 Ivysaur (U) .20 .50
□ 52 Kecleon (U) .20 .50
□ 53 Kirlia (U) .20 .50
□ 54 Lombre (U) .20 .50
□ 55 Miltank (U) .20 .50
□ 56 Muk (U) .20 .50
□ 57 Nidorino (U) .20 .50
□ 58 Pidgeotto (U) .20 .50
□ 59 Pinsir (U) .20 .50
□ 60 Quagsire (U) .20 .50
□ 61 Raticate (U) .20 .50
□ 62 Roselia (U) .20 .50
□ 63 Sableye (U) .20 .50
□ 64 Shelgon (U) .20 .50
□ 65 Skiploom (U) .20 .50
□ 66 Smeargle (U) .20 .50
□ 67 Smoochum (U) .20 .50
□ 68 Unown K (U) .20 .50
□ 69 Unown N (U) .20 .50
□ 70 Unown O (U) .20 .50
□ 71 Unown X (U) .20 .50
□ 72 Unown Z (U) .20 .50
□ 73 Venomoth (U) .20 .50
□ 74 Vibrava (U) .20 .50
□ 75 Wartortle (U) .20 .50
□ 76 Bagon (C) .10 .20
□ 77 Bulbasaur (C) .10 .20
□ 78 Burmy Plant Cloak (C) .10 .20
□ 79 Burmy Sandy Cloak (C) .10 .20
□ 80 Burmy Trash Cloak (C) .10 .20
□ 81 Carvanha (C) .10 .20
□ 82 Charmander (C) .10 .20
□ 83 Clefairy (C) .10 .20
□ 84 Corsola (C) .10 .20
□ 85 Diglett (C) .10 .20
□ 86 Duskull (C) .10 .20
□ 87 Electabuzz (C) .10 .20
□ 88 Grimer (C) .10 .20
□ 89 Growlithe (C) .10 .20
□ 90 Hoppip (C) .10 .20
□ 91 Lickitung (C) .10 .20
□ 92 Lotad (C) .10 .20
□ 93 Magmar (C) .10 .20
□ 94 Mareep (C) .10 .20
□ 95 Murkrow (C) .10 .20
□ 96 Natu (C) .10 .20
□ 97 Nidoran (C) .10 .20
□ 98 Phanpy (C) .10 .20
□ 99 Pidgey (C) .10 .20
□ 100 Psyduck (C) .10 .20
□ 101 Qwilfish (C) .10 .20
□ 102 Ralts (C) .10 .20
□ 103 Rattata (C) .10 .20
□ 104 Sentret (C) .10 .20
□ 105 Shellder (C) .10 .20
□ 106 Shellos East Sea (C) .10 .30
□ 107 Shellos West Sea (C) .10 .30
□ 108 Shroomish (C) .10 .20
□ 109 Shuckle (C) .10 .20
□ 110 Shuppet (C) .10 .20
□ 111 Spinda (C) .10 .20
□ 112 Squirtle (C) .10 .20
□ 113 Stantler (C) .10 .20
□ 114 Sunkern (C) .10 .20
□ 115 Trapinch (C) .10 .20
□ 116 Venonat (C) .10 .20
□ 117 Voltorb (C) .10 .20
□ 118 Wooper (C) .10 .20
□ 119 Bebe's Search (U) .20 .50
□ 120 Night Maintenance (U) .20 .50
□ 121 PlusPower (U) .25 .75
□ 122 Professor Oak's Visit (U) .20 .50
□ 123 Professor Rowan (U) .20 .50
□ 124 Rival (U) .20 .50
□ 125 Roseanne's Research (U) 2.00 5.00
□ 126 Team Galactic's Mars (U) .20 .50
□ 127 Potion (C) .10 .20
□ 128 Switch (C) .10 .20
□ 129 Darkness Energy (U) .20 .50
□ 130 Metal Energy (U) .20 .50
□ 131 Gardevoir LV.X (Holo) (R) 10.00 20.00
□ 132 Honchkrow LV.X (Holo) (R) 8.00 15.00

2007 Pokemon DP Secret Wonders Reverse Foil

*Reverse Foil: 1X to 2X Basic Cards

2008 Pokemon DP Great Encounters

Complete Set (106) 75.00 150.00
Booster Box (36 ct) 90.00 100.00
Booster Pack (10 cards) 3.50 4.00
□ 1 Blaziken (Holo) (R) 3.00 7.00
□ 2 Cresselia (Holo) (R) 3.00 7.00
□ 3 Darkrai (Holo) (R) 3.00 10.00
□ 4 Darkrai (Holo) (R) 3.00 6.00
□ 5 Pachirisu (Holo) (R) 3.00 7.00
□ 6 Porygon-Z (Holo) (R) 3.00 6.00
□ 7 Rotom (Holo) (R) 3.00 6.00
□ 8 Sceptile (Holo) (R) 3.00 6.00
□ 9 Swampert (Holo) (R) 3.00 6.00
□ 10 Tangrowth (Holo) (R) 3.00 6.00
□ 11 Togekiss (Holo) (R) 3.00 7.00
□ 12 Altaria (R) .50 1.00
□ 13 Beedrill (R) .50 1.00
□ 14 Butterfree (R) .50 1.00
□ 15 Claydol (R) 8.00 16.00
□ 16 Dialga (R) 2.00 4.00
□ 17 Exploud (R) .50 1.00
□ 18 Houndoom (R) 1.00 1.00
□ 19 Hypno (R) .50 1.00
□ 20 Kingler (R) .50 1.00
□ 21 Lapras (R) .50 1.00
□ 22 Latias (R) .50 1.50
□ 23 Latios (R) .50 1.50
□ 24 Mawile (R) .50 1.00
□ 25 Milotic (R) .50 1.00
□ 26 Palkia (R) 1.00 2.00
□ 27 Primeape (R) .50 1.00
□ 28 Slowking (R) .50 1.00
□ 29 Unown H (R) .50 1.00
□ 30 Wailord (R) 5.00 10.00
□ 31 Weezing (R) .50 1.00
□ 32 Wigglytuff (R) .50 1.00
□ 33 Arbok (U) .20 .50
□ 34 Cacturne (U) .20 .50
□ 35 Combusken (U) .20 .50
□ 36 Delibird (U) .20 .50
□ 37 Floatzel (U) .20 .50
□ 38 Gorebyss (U) .20 .50
□ 39 Granbull (U) .20 .50
□ 40 Grovyle (U) .20 .50
□ 41 Hariyama (U) .20 .50
□ 42 Huntail (U) .20 .50
□ 43 Linoone (U) .20 .50
□ 44 Loudred (U) .20 .50
□ 45 Magcargo (U) .20 .50
□ 46 Marshtomp (U) .20 .50
□ 47 Metapod (U) .20 .50
□ 48 Pelipper (U) .20 .50
□ 49 Porygon2 (U) .20 .50
□ 50 Purugly (U) .20 .50
□ 51 Relicanth (U) .20 .50
□ 52 Seviper (U) .20 .50
□ 53 Skarmory (U) .20 .50
□ 54 Slowbro (U) .20 .50
□ 55 Togetic (U) .20 .50
□ 56 Unown F (U) .20 .50
□ 57 Unown G (U) 3.00 6.00
□ 58 Wailmer (U) .20 .50
□ 59 Zangoose (U) .20 .50
□ 60 Baltoy (C) .10 .20
□ 61 Buizel (C) .10 .20
□ 62 Cacnea (C) .10 .20
□ 63 Caterpie (C) .10 .20
□ 64 Clamperl (C) .10 .20
□ 65 Drowzee (C) .10 .20
□ 66 Ekans (C) .10 .20
□ 67 Feebas (C) .10 .20
□ 68 Glameow (C) .10 .20
□ 69 Houndour (C) .10 .20
□ 70 Igglybuff (C) .10 .20
□ 71 Illumise (C) .10 .20
□ 72 Jigglypuff (C) .10 .20
□ 73 Kakuna (C) .10 .20
□ 74 Koffing (C) .10 .20
□ 75 Krabby (C) .10 .20
□ 76 Lunatone (C) .10 .20
□ 77 Luvdisc (C) .10 .20
□ 78 Makuhita (C) .10 .20
□ 79 Mankey (C) .10 .20
□ 80 Mudkip (C) .10 .20
□ 81 Porygon (C) .10 .20
□ 82 Slowpoke (C) .10 .20
□ 83 Slugma (C) .10 .20
□ 84 Snubbull (C) .10 .20
□ 85 Solrock (C) .10 .20
□ 86 Swablu (C) .10 .20
□ 87 Tangela (C) .10 .20
□ 88 Togepi (C) .10 .20
□ 89 Torchic (C) .10 .20
□ 90 Treecko (C) .10 .20
□ 91 Unown L (C) .10 .20
□ 92 Volbeat (C) .10 .20
□ 93 Weedle (C) .10 .20
□ 94 Whismur (C) .10 .20
□ 95 Wingull (C) .10 .20
□ 96 Zigzagoon (C) .10 .20
□ 97 Amulet Coin (U) .20 .50
□ 98 Felicity's Drawing (U) .20 .50
□ 99 Leftovers (U) .20 .50
□ 100 Moonlight Stadium (U) .20 .50
□ 101 Premier Ball (U) .20 .50
□ 102 Rare Candy (U) 4.00 7.00
□ 103 Cresselia LV.X (Holo) (R) 10.00 20.00
□ 104 Darkrai LV.X (Holo) (R) 10.00 18.00
□ 105 Dialga LV.X (Holo) (R) 12.00 20.00
□ 106 Palkia LV.X (Holo) (R) 10.00 20.00

2008 Pokemon DP Great Encounters Reverse Foil

*Reverse Foil: 1X to 2X Basic Cards

2008 Pokemon DP Majestic Dawn

Complete Set (100) 85.00 150.00
Booster Box (36 ct) 75.00 95.00
Booster Pack (10 cards) 3.00 4.00
□ 1 Articuno (Holo) (R) 3.00 7.00
□ 2 Cresselia (Holo) (R) 2.00 4.00
□ 3 Darkrai (Holo) (R) 3.00 7.00
□ 4 Dialga (Holo) (R) 4.00 9.00
□ 5 Glaceon (Holo) (R) 4.00 8.00
□ 6 Kabutops (Holo) (R) 2.00 4.00
□ 7 Leafeon (Holo) (R) 5.00 10.00
□ 8 Manaphy (Holo) (R) 3.00 6.00
□ 9 Mewtwo (Holo) (R) 4.00 9.00
□ 10 Moltres (Holo) (R) 6.00 12.00
□ 11 Palkia (Holo) (R) 4.00 8.00
□ 12 Phione (Holo) (R) 5.00 9.00
□ 13 Rotom (Holo) (R) 2.00 4.00
□ 14 Zapdos (Holo) (R) 4.00 8.00
□ 15 Aerodactyl (R) .50 1.00
□ 16 Bronzong (R) 1.00 2.00
□ 17 Empoleon (R) 3.00 6.00
□ 18 Espeon (R) .50 1.00
□ 19 Flareon (R) .50 1.00
□ 20 Glaceon (R) 2.00 4.00
□ 21 Hippowdon (R) .50 1.00
□ 22 Infernape (R) 2.00 4.00
□ 23 Jolteon (R) 1.00 1.00
□ 24 Leafeon (R) 2.00 4.00
□ 25 Minun (R) .50 1.00
□ 26 Omastar (R) .50 1.00
□ 27 Phione (R) 1.00 2.00
□ 28 Plusle (R) .50 1.00
□ 29 Scizor (R) .50 1.00
□ 30 Torterra (R) 2.00 4.00
□ 31 Toxicroak (R) .50 1.00
□ 32 Umbreon (R) 1.00 2.00
□ 33 Unown P (R) .50 1.00
□ 34 Vaporeon (R) 2.00 4.00
□ 35 Ambipom (U) .20 .50
□ 36 Fearow (U) .20 .50
□ 37 Grotle (U) .20 .50
□ 38 Kangaskhan (U) .20 .50
□ 39 Lickitung (U) .20 .50
□ 40 Manectric (U) .20 .50
□ 41 Monferno (U) .20 .50
□ 42 Mothim (U) .20 .50
□ 43 Pachirisu (U) .30 .75
□ 44 Prinplup (U) .30 .75
□ 45 Raichu (U) .50 1.00
□ 46 Scyther (U) .20 .50
□ 47 Staravia (U) .20 .50
□ 48 Sudowoodo (U) .20 .50
□ 49 Unown Q (U) .20 .50
□ 50 Aipom (C) .10 .20
□ 51 Aipom (C) .10 .20
□ 52 Bronzor (C) .10 .20
□ 53 Buneary (C) .10 .20
□ 54 Burmy Sand Cloak (C) .10 .20
□ 55 Chatot (C) .10 .20
□ 56 Chimchar (C) .10 .20
□ 57 Chimchar (C) .10 .20
□ 58 Chingling (C) .10 .20
□ 59 Combee (C) .10 .20
□ 60 Croagunk (C) .10 .20
□ 61 Drifloon (C) .10 .20
□ 62 Eevee (C) .10 .20
□ 63 Eevee (C) .10 .20
□ 64 Electrike (C) .10 .20
□ 65 Glameow (C) .10 .25
□ 66 Hippopotas (C) .10 .20
□ 67 Kabuto (C) .10 .20
□ 68 Munchlax (C) .10 .25
□ 69 Omanyte (C) .10 .20

TCG/CCG

❑ 70 Pikachu (C) .20 .50
❑ 71 Piplup (C) .10 .20
❑ 72 Piplup (C) .10 .25
❑ 73 Shellos East Sea (C) .10 .20
❑ 74 Spearow (C) .10 .20
❑ 75 Starly (C) .10 .20
❑ 76 Stunky (C) .10 .20
❑ 77 Turtwig (C) .10 .20
❑ 78 Turtwig (C) .10 .20
❑ 79 Dawn Stadium (U) .20 .50
❑ 80 Dusk Ball (U) .20 .50
❑ 81 Energy Restore (U) .20 .50
❑ 82 Fossil Excavator (U) .20 .50
❑ 83 Mom's Kindness (U) .20 .50
❑ 84 Old Amber (U) .20 .50
❑ 85 Poke Ball (U) .20 .50
❑ 86 Quick Ball (U) .20 .50
❑ 87 Super Scoop Up (U) .25 .75
❑ 88 Warp Point (C) .10 .20
❑ 89 Dome Fossil (C) .10 .20
❑ 90 Energy Search (C) .10 .20
❑ 91 Helix Fossil (C) .10 .20
❑ 92 Call Energy (U) 1.00 2.00
❑ 93 Darkness Energy (U) .20 .50
❑ 94 Health Energy (U) .20 .50
❑ 95 Metal Energy (U) .20 .50
❑ 96 Recover Energy (U) .20 .50
❑ 97 Garchomp Lv X (Holo) (R) 10.00 20.00
❑ 98 Glaceon Lv X (Holo) (R) 12.00 22.00
❑ 99 Leafeon Lv X (Holo) (R) 22.00 30.00
❑ 100 Porygon Lv X (Holo) (R) 7.00 14.00

2008 Pokemon DP Majestic Dawn Reverse Foil

*Reverse Foil: 1X to 2X Basic Cards

2008 Pokemon DP Legends Awakened

Complete Set (146) 175.00 250.00
Booster Box (36 ct) 75.00 95.00
Booster Pack (10 cards) 3.00 4.00

❑ 1 Deoxys Normal Form (Holo) (R) 3.00 6.00
❑ 2 Dragonite (Holo) (R) 3.00 6.00
❑ 3 Froslass (Holo) (R) 5.00 10.00
❑ 4 Giratina (Holo) (R) 5.00 10.00
❑ 5 Gliscor (Holo) (R) 2.00 5.00
❑ 6 Heatran (Holo) (R) 3.00 6.00
❑ 7 Kingdra (Holo) (R) 5.00 10.00
❑ 8 Luxray (Holo) (R) 3.00 6.00
❑ 9 Mamoswine (Holo) (R) 2.00 4.00
❑ 10 Metagross (Holo) (R) 3.00 6.00
❑ 11 Mewtwo (Holo) (R) 3.00 10.00
❑ 12 Politoed (Holo) (R) 2.00 4.00
❑ 13 Probopass (Holo) (R) 2.00 5.00
❑ 14 Rayquaza (Holo) (R) 4.00 9.00
❑ 15 Regigigas (Holo) (R) 6.00 12.00
❑ 16 Spiritomb (Holo) (R) 3.00 6.00
❑ 17 Yanmega (Holo) (R) 2.00 4.00
❑ 18 Armaldo (R) 1.00 2.00
❑ 19 Azelf (R) 2.50 3.00
❑ 20 Bellossom (R) .50 1.00
❑ 21 Cradily (R) .50 1.00
❑ 22 Crawdaunt (R) .50 1.00
❑ 23 Delcatty (R) .50 1.00
❑ 24 Deoxys Attack Form (R) .50 1.00
❑ 25 Deoxys Defense Forme (R) .50 1.00
❑ 26 Deoxys Speed Form (R) 1.00 2.00
❑ 27 Ditto (R) .50 1.00
❑ 28 Forretress (R) .50 1.00
❑ 29 Groudon (R) 2.00 3.00
❑ 30 Heatran (R) .50 1.00
❑ 31 Jirachi (R) 1.00 3.00
❑ 32 Kyogre (R) 1.00 2.00
❑ 33 Lopunny (R) .50 1.00
❑ 34 Mesprit (R) 1.00 3.00
❑ 35 Poliwrath (R) .50 1.00
❑ 36 Regice (R) .50 1.00
❑ 37 Regigigas (R) 1.00 3.00
❑ 38 Regirock (R) 1.00 2.00
❑ 39 Registeel (R) 1.00 3.00
❑ 40 Shedinja (R) .50 1.00
❑ 41 Torkoal (R) .50 1.00
❑ 42 Unown ! (R) .50 1.00
❑ 43 Uxie (R) 4.00 20.00
❑ 44 Victreebel (R) .50 1.00
❑ 45 Vileplume (R) .50 1.00
❑ 46 Anorith (U) .20 .50
❑ 47 Camerupt (U) .20 .50
❑ 48 Castform (U) .20 .50
❑ 49 Castform Rain Form (U) .20 .50
❑ 50 Castform Snow-Cloud Form (U) .20 .50
❑ 51 Castform Sunny Form (U) .20 .50
❑ 52 Dragonair (U) .20 .50
❑ 53 Drifblim (U) .20 .50
❑ 54 Exeggutor (U) .20 .50
❑ 55 Gliscor (U) .20 .50
❑ 56 Grumpig (U) .20 .50
❑ 57 Houndoom (U) .20 .50
❑ 58 Lanturn (U) .20 .50
❑ 59 Lanturn (U) .20 .50
❑ 60 Ledian (U) .20 .50
❑ 61 Lucario (U) .20 .50
❑ 62 Luxio (U) .20 .50
❑ 63 Marowak (U) .20 .50
❑ 64 Metang (U) .20 .50
❑ 65 Metang (U) .20 .50
❑ 66 Mightyena (U) .20 .50
❑ 67 Ninjask (U) .20 .50
❑ 68 Persian (U) .20 .50
❑ 69 Piloswine (U) .20 .50
❑ 70 Seadra (U) .20 .50
❑ 71 Starmie (U) .20 .50
❑ 72 Swalot (U) .20 .50
❑ 73 Swellow (U) .20 .50
❑ 74 Tauros (U) .20 .50
❑ 75 Tentacruel (U) .20 .50
❑ 76 Unown J (U) .20 .50
❑ 77 Unown R (U) .20 .50
❑ 78 Unown U (U) .20 .50
❑ 79 Unown V (U) .20 .50
❑ 80 Unown W (U) .20 .50
❑ 81 Unown Y (U) .20 .50
❑ 82 Unown ? (U) .20 .50
❑ 83 Beldum (C) .10 .20
❑ 84 Beldum (C) .10 .20
❑ 85 Bellsprout (C) .10 .20
❑ 86 Buneary (C) .10 .20
❑ 87 Chinchou (C) .10 .20
❑ 88 Chinchou (C) .10 .20
❑ 89 Corphish (C) .10 .20
❑ 90 Cubone (C) .10 .20
❑ 91 Dratini (C) .10 .20
❑ 92 Drifloon (C) .10 .20
❑ 93 Exeggcute (C) .10 .20
❑ 94 Gligar (C) .10 .20
❑ 95 Gligar (C) .10 .20
❑ 96 Gloom (C) .10 .20
❑ 97 Gloom (C) .10 .20
❑ 98 Gulpin (C) .10 .20
❑ 99 Hitmonchan (C) .10 .20
❑ 100 Hitmonlee (C) .10 .20
❑ 101 Hitmontop (C) .10 .20
❑ 102 Horsea (C) .10 .20
❑ 103 Houndour (C) .10 .20
❑ 104 Ledyba (C) .10 .20
❑ 105 Lileep (C) .10 .20
❑ 106 Meowth (C) .10 .20
❑ 107 Misdreavus (C) .10 .20
❑ 108 Nincada (C) .10 .20
❑ 109 Nosepass (C) .10 .20
❑ 110 Numel (C) .10 .20
❑ 111 Oddish (C) .10 .20
❑ 112 Oddish (C) .10 .20
❑ 113 Pineco (C) .10 .20
❑ 114 Poliwag (C) .10 .20
❑ 115 Poliwhirl (C) .10 .20
❑ 116 Poochyena (C) .10 .20
❑ 117 Riolu (C) .10 .20
❑ 118 Shinx (C) .10 .20
❑ 119 Skitty (C) .10 .20
❑ 120 Sneasel (C) .10 .20
❑ 121 Spoink (C) .10 .20
❑ 122 Staryu (C) .10 .20
❑ 123 Swinub (C) .10 .20
❑ 124 Taillow (C) .10 .20
❑ 125 Tentacool (C) .10 .20
❑ 126 Tyrogue (C) .10 .20
❑ 127 Weepinbell (C) .10 .20
❑ 128 Yanma (C) .10 .20
❑ 129 Bubble Coat (U) .20 .50
❑ 130 Buck's Training (U) .20 .50
❑ 131 Cynthia's Feelings (U) .20 .50
❑ 132 Energy Pickup (U) .20 .50
❑ 133 Poké Radar (U) .20 .50
❑ 134 Snowpoint Temple (U) .20 .50
❑ 135 Stark Mountain (U) .20 .50
❑ 136 Technical Machine TS-1 (U) .20 .50
❑ 137 Technical Machine TS-2 (U) .20 .50
❑ 138 Claw Fossil (C) .10 .20
❑ 139 Root Fossil (C) .10 .20
❑ 140 Azelf LV.X (Holo) (R) 10.00 20.00
❑ 141 Gliscor LV.X (Holo) (R) 10.00 20.00
❑ 142 Magnezone LV.X (Holo) (R) 10.00 20.00
❑ 143 Mesprit LV.X (Holo) (R) 10.00 20.00
❑ 144 Mewtwo LV.X (Holo) (R) 10.00 20.00
❑ 145 Rhyperior LV.X (Holo) (R) 7.00 15.00
❑ 146 Uxie LV.X (Holo) (R) 10.00 20.00

2008 Pokemon DP Stormfront

Complete Set (103) 100.00 150.00
Booster Box (36 ct) 75.00 95.00
Booster Pack (10 cards) 3.00 4.00

❑ 1 Dusknoir (Holo)(R) 2.00 5.00
❑ 2 Empoleon (Holo)(R) 3.00 7.00
❑ 3 Infernape (Holo)(R) 2.00 5.00
❑ 4 Lumineon (Holo)(R) 2.00 5.00
❑ 5 Magnezone (Holo)(R) 2.00 5.00
❑ 6 Magnezone (Holo)(R) 2.00 5.00
❑ 7 Mismagius (Holo)(R) 2.00 5.00
❑ 8 Raichu (Holo)(R) 3.00 7.00
❑ 9 Regigigas (Holo)(R) 4.00 8.00
❑ 10 Sceptile (Holo)(R) 3.00 6.00
❑ 11 Torterra (Holo)(R) 2.00 5.00
❑ 12 Abomasnow (R) 1.00 2.00
❑ 13 Bronzong (R) .50 1.00
❑ 14 Cherrim (R) .50 1.00
❑ 15 Drapion (R) .50 1.00
❑ 16 Drifblim (R) .50 1.00
❑ 17 Dusknoir (R) 1.00 2.00
❑ 18 Gengar (R) 3.00 7.00
❑ 19 Gyarados (R) 2.00 4.00
❑ 20 Machamp (R) 1.50 3.00
❑ 21 Mamoswine (R) .50 1.00
❑ 22 Rapidash (R) .50 1.00
❑ 23 Roserade (R) .50 1.00
❑ 24 Salamence (R) 2.00 3.50
❑ 25 Scizor (R) .50 1.00
❑ 26 Skuntank (R) .50 1.00
❑ 27 Staraptor (R) .50 1.00
❑ 28 Steelix (R) 1.00 2.00
❑ 29 Tangrowth (R) .75 1.50
❑ 30 Tyranitar (R) .50 1.00
❑ 31 Vespiquen (R) .50 1.00
❑ 32 Bibarel (U) .20 .50
❑ 33 Budew (U) .20 .50
❑ 34 Dusclops (U) .20 .50
❑ 35 Dusclops (U) .20 .50
❑ 36 Electrode (U) .20 .50
❑ 37 Electrode (U) .20 .50
❑ 38 Farfetch'd (U) .20 .50
❑ 39 Grovyle (U) .20 .50
❑ 40 Haunter (U) .20 .50
❑ 41 Machoke (U) .20 .50
❑ 42 Magneton (U) .20 .50
❑ 43 Magneton (U) .20 .50
❑ 44 Miltank (U) .20 .50
❑ 45 Pichu (U) .20 .50
❑ 46 Piloswine (U) .20 .50
❑ 47 Pupitar (U) .20 .50
❑ 48 Sableye (U) .20 .50
❑ 49 Scyther (U) .20 .50
❑ 50 Shelgon (U) .20 .50
❑ 51 Skarmory (U) .20 .50
❑ 52 Staravia (U) .20 .50
❑ 53 Bagon (C) .10 .20
❑ 54 Bidoof (C) .10 .20
❑ 55 Bronzor (C) .10 .20
❑ 56 Cherubi (C) .10 .20
❑ 57 Combee (C) .10 .20
❑ 58 Drifloon (C) .10 .20
❑ 59 Duskull (C) .10 .20
❑ 60 Duskull (C) .10 .20
❑ 61 Finneon (C) .10 .20
❑ 62 Gastly (C) .10 .20
❑ 63 Larvitar (C) .10 .20
❑ 64 Machop (C) .10 .20
❑ 65 Magikarp (C) .10 .20
❑ 66 Magnemite (C) .10 .20
❑ 67 Magnemite (C) .10 .20
❑ 68 Misdreavus (C) .10 .20
❑ 69 Onix (C) .10 .20
❑ 70 Pikachu (C) .25 .50
❑ 71 Ponyta (C) .10 .20
❑ 72 Roselia (C) .10 .20
❑ 73 Skorupi (C) .10 .20
❑ 74 Snover (C) .10 .20
❑ 75 Starly (C) .10 .20
❑ 76 Stunky (C) .10 .20
❑ 77 Swinub (C) .10 .20
❑ 78 Tangela (C) .10 .20
❑ 79 Treecko (C) .10 .20
❑ 80 Voltorb (C) .10 .20
❑ 81 Voltorb (C) .10 .20
❑ 82 Conductive Quarry (U) .20 .50
❑ 83 Energy Link (U) .20 .50
❑ 84 Energy Switch (U) .20 .50
❑ 85 Great Ball (U) .20 .50
❑ 86 Luxury Ball (U) .20 .50
❑ 87 Marley's Request (U) .20 .50
❑ 88 Poké Blower (U) .30 1.00
❑ 89 Poké Drawer (U) .20 .50
❑ 90 Poké Healer (U) .20 .50
❑ 91 Premier Ball (U) .20 .50
❑ 92 Potion (C) .10 .20
❑ 93 Switch (C) .10 .20
❑ 94 Cyclone Energy (U) .20 .50
❑ 95 Warp Energy (U) .20 .50
❑ 96 Dusknoir LV.X (Holo)(R) 8.00 15.00
❑ 97 Heatran LV.X (Holo)(R) 10.00 16.00
❑ 98 Machamp LV.X (Holo)(R) 10.00 20.00
❑ 99 Raichu LV.X (Holo)(R) 10.00 18.00
❑ 100 Regigigas LV.X (Holo)(R) 6.00 12.00
❑ 101 Charmander (Holo)(R) 3.00 7.00
❑ 102 Charmeleon (Holo)(R) 5.00 10.00
❑ 103 Charizard (Holo)(R) 8.00 15.00
❑ SH1 Drifloon 3.00 6.00
❑ SH2 Duskull 4.00 8.00
❑ SH3 Voltorb 4.00 8.00

2008 Pokemon DP Stormfront Reverse Foil

*Reverse Foil: 1X to 2X Basic Cards

2009 Pokemon Platinum

Complete Set

❑ 1 Ampharos (Holo) (R) 1.50 4.00
❑ 2 Blastoise (Holo) (R) 1.50 4.00
❑ 3 Blaziken (Holo) (R) 1.50 4.00
❑ 4 Delcatty (Holo) (R) .75 2.00
❑ 5 Dialga (Holo) (R) .75 2.00
❑ 6 Dialga (Holo) (R) .75 2.00
❑ 7 Dialga G (Holo) (R) 2.00 5.00
❑ 8 Gardevoir (Holo) (R) .75 2.00
❑ 9 Giratina (Holo) (R) .75 2.00
❑ 10 Giratina (Holo) (R) 1.25 3.00
❑ 11 Manectric (Holo) (R) .75 2.00
❑ 12 Palkia G (Holo) (R) 1.50 4.00
❑ 13 Rampardos (Holo) (R) 1.25 3.00
❑ 14 Shaymin (Holo) (R) .75 2.00
❑ 15 Shaymin (Holo) (R) .75 2.00
❑ 16 Slaking (Holo) (R) .75 2.00
❑ 17 Weavile G (Holo) (R) 1.25 3.00
❑ 18 Altaria (R) .50 1.00
❑ 19 Banette (R) .50 1.00
❑ 20 Bastiodon (R) .50 1.00
❑ 21 Beautifly (R) .50 1.00
❑ 22 Blissey (R) .50 1.00
❑ 23 Dialga (R) .50 1.00
❑ 24 Dugtrio (R) .50 1.00
❑ 25 Dustox (R) .50 1.00
❑ 26 Empoleon (R) .50 1.00
❑ 27 Giratina (R) .50 1.00
❑ 28 Giratina (R) .50 1.00
❑ 29 Golduck (R) .50 1.00
❑ 30 Gyarados G (R) .50 1.00
❑ 31 Infernape (R) .50 1.00
❑ 32 Kricketune (R) .50 1.00
❑ 33 Lickilicky (R) .50 1.00
❑ 34 Ludicolo (R) .50 1.00
❑ 35 Luvdisc (R) .50 1.00
❑ 36 Ninetales (R) .50 1.00
❑ 37 Palkia (R) .50 1.00
❑ 38 Shaymin (R) .50 1.00
❑ 39 Torterra (R) .50 1.00
❑ 40 Toxicroak G (R) .50 1.00
❑ 41 Bronzong G (U) .20 .50
❑ 42 Cacturne (U) .20 .50
❑ 43 Carnivine (U) .20 .50
❑ 44 Cascoon (U) .20 .50
❑ 45 Combusken (U) .20 .50
❑ 46 Cranidos (U) .20 .50
❑ 47 Crobat G (U) .20 .50
❑ 48 Flaaffy (U) .20 .50
❑ 49 Grotle (U) .20 .50
❑ 50 Houndoom G (U) .20 .50
❑ 51 Kirlia (U) .20 .50
❑ 52 Lombre (U) .20 .50
❑ 53 Lucario (U) .20 .50
❑ 54 Mightyena (U) .20 .50
❑ 55 Mismagius (U) .20 .50
❑ 56 Monferno (U) .20 .50
❑ 57 Muk (U) .20 .50
❑ 58 Octillery (U) .20 .50
❑ 59 Prinplup (U) .20 .50
❑ 60 Probopass (U) .20 .50
❑ 61 Seviper (U) .20 .50
❑ 62 Shieldon (U) .20 .50
❑ 63 Silcoon (U) .20 .50
❑ 64 Vigoroth (U) .20 .50
❑ 65 Wartortle (U) .20 .50
❑ 66 Zangoose (U) .20 .50
❑ 67 Cacnea (C) .10 .20
❑ 68 Carnivine (C) .10 .20
❑ 69 Chansey (C) .10 .20
❑ 70 Chimchar (C) .10 .20
❑ 71 Combee (C) .10 .20
❑ 72 Diglett (C) .10 .20
❑ 73 Dunsparce (C) .10 .20
❑ 74 Electrike (C) .10 .20
❑ 75 Grimer (C) .10 .20
❑ 76 Happiny (C) .10 .20
❑ 77 Honchkrow G (C) .10 .20
❑ 78 Kricketot (C) .10 .20
❑ 79 Lapras (C) .10 .20
❑ 80 Lickitung (C) .10 .20
❑ 81 Lotad (C) .10 .20
❑ 82 Mareep (C) .10 .20
❑ 83 Misdreavus (C) .10 .20
❑ 84 Nosepass (C) .10 .20
❑ 85 Piplup (C) .10 .20
❑ 86 Poochyena (C) .10 .20
❑ 87 Psyduck (C) .10 .20
❑ 88 Purugly G (C) .10 .20
❑ 89 Ralts (C) .10 .20
❑ 90 Remoraid (C) .10 .20
❑ 91 Riolu (C) .10 .20
❑ 92 Shuppet (C) .10 .20
❑ 93 Skitty (C) .10 .20
❑ 94 Skuntank G (C) .10 .20
❑ 95 Slakoth (C) .10 .20
❑ 96 Squirtle (C) .10 .20
❑ 97 Swablu (C) .10 .20
❑ 98 Tauros (C) .10 .20
❑ 99 Torchic (C) .10 .20
❑ 100 Torkoal (C) .10 .20
❑ 101 Turtwig (C) .10 .20
❑ 102 Vulpix (C) .10 .20
❑ 103 Wurmple (C) .10 .20
❑ 104 Broken Time-Space (U) .20 .50
❑ 105 Cyrus's Conspiracy (U) .20 .50
❑ 106 Galactic HQ (U) .20 .50
❑ 107 Level Max (U) .20 .50
❑ 108 Life Herb (U) .20 .50
❑ 109 Looker's Investigation (U) .20 .50
❑ 110 Memory Berry (U) .20 .50
❑ 111 Miasma Valley (U) .20 .50
❑ 112 Pluspower (U) .20 .50
❑ 113 Poke Ball (U) .20 .50
❑ 114 Pokedex Handy 910s (U) .20 .50
❑ 115 Pokemon Rescue (U) .20 .50
❑ 116 Energy Gain (U) .20 .50
❑ 117 Power Spray (U) .20 .50
❑ 118 Poke Turn (U) .20 .50
❑ 119 Armor Fossil (C) .10 .20
❑ 120 Skull Fossil (C) .10 .20
❑ 121 Rainbow Energy (U) .20 .50
❑ 122 Dialga G LV.X (Holo) (R) 3.00 8.00
❑ 123 Drapion LV.X (Holo) (R) 2.50 6.00
❑ 124 Giratina LV.X (Holo) (R) 3.00 8.00
❑ 125 Palkia G LV.X (Holo) (R) 2.00 5.00
❑ 126 Shaymin LV.X (Holo) (R) 5.00 12.00
❑ 127 Shaymin LV.X (Holo) (R) 3.00 8.00
❑ 128 Electabuzz (Holo) (R) .75 2.00
❑ 129 Hitmonchan (Holo) (R) .75 2.00
❑ 130 Scyther (Holo) (R) 1.25 3.00
❑ SH4 Lotad (Holo) (R) 1.25 3.00
❑ SH5 Swablu (Holo) (R) 1.50 4.00
❑ SH6 Vulpix (Holo) (R) 4.00 10.00

2009 Pokemon Platinum Rising Rivals

Complete Set (114) 150.00 200.00
Booster Box (36 Packs) 70.00 100.00
Booster Pack (10 Cards) 3.50 4.00

❑ 1 Arcanine (Holo) (R) 2.00 5.00
❑ 2 Bastiodon GL (Holo) (R) 2.00 4.00
❑ 3 Darkrai G (Holo) (R) 3.00 6.00
❑ 4 Floatzel GL (Holo) (R) 3.00 6.00
❑ 5 Flygon (Holo) (R) 5.00 10.00
❑ 6 Froslass GL (Holo) (R) 2.00 4.00
❑ 7 Jirachi (Holo) (R) 3.00 6.00
❑ 8 Lucario GL (Holo) (R) 4.00 8.00
❑ 9 Luxray GL (Holo) (R) 4.00 7.00
❑ 10 Mismagius GL (Holo) (R) 2.00 4.00
❑ 11 Rampardos GL (Holo) (R) 2.00 4.00
❑ 12 Roserade GL (Holo) (R) 2.00 4.00
❑ 13 Shiftry (Holo) (R) 2.00 5.00
❑ 14 Aggron (R) .50 1.00
❑ 15 Beedrill (R) .50 1.50
❑ 16 Bronzong 4 (R) .50 1.00
❑ 17 Drapion 4 (R) .50 1.00
❑ 18 Espeon 4 (R) .50 1.00
❑ 19 Flareon (R) .50 1.00
❑ 20 Gallade 4 (R) 2.00 4.00
❑ 21 Gastrodon East Sea (R) .50 1.00
❑ 22 Gastrodon West Sea (R) .50 1.00
❑ 23 Golem 4 (R) .50 1.00
❑ 24 Heracross 4 (R) .50 1.00
❑ 25 Hippowdon (R) .50 1.00
❑ 26 Jolteon (R) 1.00 2.00
❑ 27 Mamoswine GL (R) .50 1.00
❑ 28 Mr. Mime 4 (R) .50 1.00
❑ 29 Nidoking (R) 1.00 3.00
❑ 30 Nidoqueen (R) .50 1.00
❑ 31 Raichu GL (R) .50 1.50
❑ 32 Rhyperior 4 (R) .50 1.00
❑ 33 Snorlax (R) .50 1.00
❑ 34. Vaporeon (R) .50 1.00
❑ 35 Vespiquen 4 (R) 1.00 2.00
❑ 36 Walrein (R) .50 1.00
❑ 37 Yanmega 4 (R) .50 1.00
❑ 38 Alakazam 4 (U) 1.00 2.00
❑ 39 Electrode G (U) .20 .50
❑ 40 Gengar GL (U) .20 .50
❑ 41 Glaceon (U) 1.00 3.00
❑ 42 Hippowdon 4 (U) .25 .75
❑ 43 Infernape 4 (U) 1.00 2.00
❑ 44 Lairon (U) .20 .50
❑ 45 Leafeon (U) .20 .50
❑ 46 Machamp GL (U) .20 .50
❑ 47 Rapidash 4 (U) .20 .50
❑ 48 Scizor 4 (U) .20 .50
❑ 49 Sharpedo (U) .20 .50
❑ 50 Starmie (U) .20 .50
❑ 51 Steelix GL (U) .20 .50
❑ 52 Tropius (U) .20 .50
❑ 53 Vibrava (U) .20 .50
❑ 54 Whiscash 4 (U) .20 .50
❑ 55 Aerodactyl GL (C) .10 .20
❑ 56 Ambipom G (C) .10 .20
❑ 57 Aron (C) .10 .20
❑ 58 Carvanha (C) .10 .20
❑ 59 Eevee (C) .10 .20
❑ 60 Flareon 4 (C) .10 .20
❑ 61 Forretress G (C) .10 .20
❑ 62 Gliscor 4 (C) .10 .20
❑ 63 Growlithe (C) .10 .20
❑ 64 Hippopotas (C) .10 .20
❑ 65 Houndoom 4 (C) .10 .20
❑ 66 Kakuna (C) .10 .20
❑ 67 Kecleon (C) .10 .20
❑ 68 Koffing (C) .10 .20
❑ 69 Munchlax (C) .10 .20
❑ 70 Munchlax (C) .10 .20
❑ 71 Nidoran F (C) .10 .20
❑ 72 Nidoran M (C) .10 .20
❑ 73 Nidorina (C) .10 .20
❑ 74 Nidorino (C) .10 .20
❑ 75 Nuzleaf (C) .10 .20
❑ 76 Quagsire GL (C) .10 .20
❑ 77 Sealeo (C) .10 .20
❑ 78 Seedot (C) .10 .20
❑ 79 Shellos East Sea (C) .10 .20
❑ 80 Shellos West Sea (C) .10 .20
❑ 81 Snorlax (C) .10 .20
❑ 82 Spheal (C) .10 .20

TCG/CCG

❑ 83 Staryu (C) .10 .20
❑ 84 Trapinch (C) .10 .20
❑ 85 Turtwig GL (C) .10 .20
❑ 86 Weedle (C) .10 .20
❑ 87 Weezing (C) .10 .20
❑ 88 Aaron's Collection (U) .20 .50
❑ 89 Bebe's Search (U) .50 1.00
❑ 90 Bertha's Warmth (U) .20 .50
❑ 91 Flint's Willpower (U) .20 .50
❑ 92 Lucian's Assignment (U) .20 .50
❑ 93 Pokemon Contest Hall (U) 1.00 2.00
❑ 94 Sunyshore City Gym (U) .20 .50
❑ 95 Technical Machine G (U) .20 .50
❑ 96 SP-Radar (U) .20 .50
❑ 97 Underground Expedition (U) .20 .50
❑ 98 Volkner's Philosophy (U) 2.00 4.00
❑ 99 Darkness Energy (U) .20 .50
❑ 100 Metal Energy (U) .20 .50
❑ 101 SP Energy (U) .20 .50
❑ 102 Upper Energy (U) 1.00 2.00
❑ 103 Alakazam 4 LV.X (Holo) (R) 10.00 15.00
❑ 104 Floatzel GL LV.X (Holo) (R) 8.00 15.00
❑ 105 Flygon LV.X (Holo) (R) 20.00 30.00
❑ 106 Gallade 4 LV.X (Holo) (R) 12.00 20.00
❑ 107 Hippowdon LV.X (Holo) (R) 8.00 15.00
❑ 108 Infernape 4 LV.X (Holo) (R) 10.00 18.00
❑ 109 Luxray GL LV.X (Holo) (R) 50.00 90.00
❑ 110 Mismagius GL LV.X (Holo) (R) 7.00 15.00
❑ 111 Snorlax LV.X (Holo) (R) 12.00 20.00
❑ 112 Pikachu (Holo) (R) 3.00 6.00
❑ 113 Flying Pikachu (Holo) (R) 3.00 6.00
❑ 114 Surfing Pikachu (Holo) (R) 3.00 6.00
❑ RT1 Fan Rotom 3.00 6.00
❑ RT2 Frost Rotom 3.00 6.00
❑ RT3 Heat Rotom 3.00 6.00
❑ RT4 Mow Rotom 3.00 6.00
❑ RT5 Wash Rotom 3.00 6.00
❑ RT6 Charons Choice 5.00 10.00

2009 Pokemon Platinum Rising Rivals Reverse Foil

*Reverse Foil: 1X to 2X Basic Cards

2009 Pokemon Platinum Supreme Victors

Complete Set (150) 175.00 250.00
Booster Box (36 Packs) 80.00 100.00
Booster Pack (10 Cards) 3.50 4.00
*Reverse Foil: 1X to 2X Basic Cards

❑ 1 Absol G (Holo) (R) 2.00 4.00
❑ 2 Blaziken FB (Holo) (R) 2.00 4.00
❑ 3 Drifblim FB (Holo) (R) 2.00 4.00
❑ 4 Electivire FB (Holo) (R) 2.00 4.00
❑ 5 Garchomp (Holo) (R) 2.00 5.00
❑ 6 Magmortar (Holo) (R) 2.00 4.00
❑ 7 Metagross (Holo) (R) 2.00 4.00
❑ 8 Rayquaza C (Holo) (R) 3.00 5.00
❑ 9 Regigigas FB (Holo) (R) 2.00 4.00
❑ 10 Rhyperior (Holo) (R) 2.00 4.00
❑ 11 Staraptor FB (Holo) (R) 2.00 4.00
❑ 12 Swampert (Holo) (R) 2.00 4.00
❑ 13 Venusaur (Holo) (R) 2.00 5.00
❑ 14 Yanmega (Holo) (R) 2.00 4.00
❑ 15 Arcanine G (R) .50 1.00
❑ 16 Articuno (R) .50 1.00
❑ 17 Butterfree FB (R) .50 1.00
❑ 18 Camerupt (R) .50 1.00
❑ 19 Camerupt G (R) .50 1.00
❑ 20 Charizard (R) 2.00 4.00
❑ 21 Chimecho (R) .50 1.00
❑ 22 Claydol (R) 1.00 2.00
❑ 23 Crawdaunt (R) .50 1.00
❑ 24 Dewgong (R) .50 1.00
❑ 25 Dodrio (R) .50 1.00
❑ 26 Dusknoir FB (R) .50 1.00
❑ 27 Empoleon FB (R) 1.00 1.00
❑ 28 Exploud (R) .50 1.50
❑ 29 Honchkrow (R) .50 1.00
❑ 30 Lickilicky C (R) .50 1.00
❑ 31 Lucario C (R) 1.00 2.00
❑ 32 Lunatone (R) .50 1.00
❑ 33 Mawile (R) .50 1.00
❑ 34 Medicham (R) .50 1.00
❑ 35 Milotic C (R) .50 1.00
❑ 36 Moltres (R) 1.00 2.00
❑ 37 Mr. Mime (R) .50 1.00
❑ 38 Parasect (R) .50 1.00
❑ 39 Primeape (R) .50 1.00
❑ 40 Roserade C (R) .50 1.00
❑ 41 Sableye (R) .50 1.00
❑ 42 Sandslash (R) .50 1.00
❑ 43 Seaking (R) .50 1.00
❑ 44 Shedinja (R) .50 1.00
❑ 45 Solrock (R) .50 1.00
❑ 46 Spinda (R) .50 1.00
❑ 47 Wailord (R) 2.00 4.00
❑ 48 Zapdos (R) .50 1.00
❑ 49 Altaria C (U) .20 .50
❑ 50 Arcanine (U) .20 .50
❑ 51 Bibarel (U) .20 .50
❑ 52 Breloom (U) .20 .50
❑ 53 Carnivine (U) .20 .50
❑ 54 Chatot G (U) .20 .50
❑ 55 Cherrim (U) .20 .50
❑ 56 Dragonite FB (U) .20 .50
❑ 57 Drifblim (U) .20 .50
❑ 58 Floatzel (U) .20 .50
❑ 59 Gabite (U) .20 .50
❑ 60 Garchomp C (U) .50 1.00
❑ 61 Hippopotas (U) .20 .50
❑ 62 Ivysaur (U) .20 .50
❑ 63 Lopunny (U) .20 .50
❑ 64 Loudred (U) .20 .50
❑ 65 Magmar (U) .20 .50
❑ 66 Manectric G (U) .20 .50
❑ 67 Marshtomp (U) .20 .50
❑ 68 Masquerain (U) .20 .50
❑ 69 Metang (U) .20 .50
❑ 70 Milotic (U) .20 .50
❑ 71 Minun (U) .20 .50
❑ 72 Murkrow (U) .20 .50
❑ 73 Ninjask (U) .20 .50
❑ 74 Numel (U) .20 .50
❑ 75 Pinsir (U) .20 .50
❑ 76 Plusle (U) .20 .50
❑ 77 Raichu (U) .50 1.00
❑ 78 Raticate (U) .20 .50
❑ 79 Relicanth (U) .20 .50
❑ 80 Rhydon (U) .20 .50
❑ 81 Roserade (U) .20 .50
❑ 82 Rotom (U) .20 .50
❑ 83 Skarmory (U) .20 .50
❑ 84 Spiritomb (U) .20 .50
❑ 85 Staravia (U) .20 .50
❑ 86 Togekiss C (U) .20 .50
❑ 87 Wailmer (U) .20 .50
❑ 88 Yanma (U) .20 .50
❑ 89 Baltoy (C) .10 .20
❑ 90 Beldum (C) .10 .20
❑ 91 Bidoof (C) .10 .20
❑ 92 Buizel (C) .10 .20
❑ 93 Bulbasaur (C) .10 .20
❑ 94 Buneary (C) .10 .20
❑ 95 Chatot (C) .10 .20
❑ 96 Cherubi (C) .10 .20
❑ 97 Chimchar (C) .10 .20
❑ 98 Chingling (C) .10 .20
❑ 99 Combee (C) .10 .20
❑ 100 Corphish (C) .10 .20
❑ 101 Croagunk (C) .10 .20
❑ 102 Doduo (C) .10 .20
❑ 103 Drifloon (C) .10 .20
❑ 104 Feebas (C) .10 .20
❑ 105 Geodude (C) .10 .20
❑ 106 Gible (C) .10 .20
❑ 107 Goldeen (C) .10 .20
❑ 108 Growlithe (C) .10 .20
❑ 109 Kricketot (C) .10 .20
❑ 110 Magikarp (C) .10 .20
❑ 111 Magnemite (C) .10 .20
❑ 112 Mankey (C) .10 .20
❑ 113 Meditite (C) .10 .20
❑ 114 Meowth (C) .10 .20
❑ 115 Mime Jr (C) .10 .20
❑ 116 Mudkip (C) .10 .20
❑ 117 Nincada (C) .10 .20
❑ 118 Pachirisu (C) .10 .20
❑ 119 Paras (C) .10 .20
❑ 120 Pikachu (C) .20 .50
❑ 121 Piplup (C) .20 .50
❑ 122 Rhyhorn (C) .10 .20
❑ 123 Roselia (C) .10 .20
❑ 124 Sandshrew (C) .10 .20
❑ 125 Seel (C) .10 .20
❑ 126 Shinx (C) .10 .20
❑ 127 Shroomish (C) .10 .20
❑ 128 Skorupi (C) .10 .20
❑ 129 Starly (C) .10 .20
❑ 130 Surskit (C) .10 .20
❑ 131 Turtwig (C) .10 .20
❑ 132 Whismur (C) .10 .20
❑ 133 Zubat (C) .10 .20
❑ 134 Battle Tower (U) .20 .50
❑ 135 Champion Room (U) .20 .50
❑ 136 Cynthia's Guidance (U) .20 .50
❑ 137 Cyrus's Initiative (U) .20 .50
❑ 138 Night Teleporter (U) .20 .50
❑ 139 Palmer's Contribution (U) .20 .50
❑ 140 VS. Seeker (U) .20 .50
❑ 141 Absol G LV.X (Holo) (R) 7.00 15.00
❑ 142 Blaziken FB LV.X (Holo) (R) 12.00 20.00
❑ 143 Charizard G LV.X (Holo) (R) 12.00 20.00
❑ 144 Electivire FB LV.X (Holo) (R) 7.00 15.00
❑ 145 Garchomp C LV.X (Holo) (R) 10.00 18.00
❑ 146 Rayquaza C LV.X (Holo) (R) 12.00 23.00
❑ 147 Staraptor FB LV.X (Holo) (R) 9.00 18.00
❑ 148 Articuno (Holo) (R) 3.00 6.00
❑ 149 Moltres (Holo) (R) 3.00 6.00
❑ 150 Zapdos (Holo) (R) 4.00 7.00
❑ SH7 Milotic (R) 3.00 6.00
❑ SH8 Yanma (R) 3.00 6.00
❑ SH9 Relicanth (R) 3.00 6.00

2009 Pokemon Platinum Supreme Victors Reverse Foil

*Reverse Foil: 1X to 2X Basic Cards

2009 Pokemon Platinum Arceus

Complete Set (99) 150.00 200.00
Booster Box (36 Packs) 80.00 100.00
Booster Pack (10 Cards) 3.50 4.00

❑ 1 Charizard (Holo) (R) 5.00 8.00
❑ 2 Froslass (Holo) (R) 2.00 4.00
❑ 3 Heatran (Holo) (R) 2.00 4.00
❑ 4 Kabutops (Holo) (R) 2.00 4.00
❑ 5 Luxray (Holo) (R) 2.00 4.00
❑ 6 Mothim (Holo) (R) 2.00 4.00
❑ 7 Probopass (Holo) (R) 2.00 4.00
❑ 8 Salamence (Holo) (R) 2.00 4.00
❑ 9 Swalot (Holo) (R) 2.00 4.00
❑ 10 Tangrowth (Holo) (R) 2.00 4.00
❑ 11 Toxicroak (Holo) (R) 2.00 4.00
❑ 12 Zapdos (Holo) (R) 2.00 5.00
❑ 13 Aerodactyl (R) .50 1.00
❑ 14 Bronzong (R) .50 1.00
❑ 15 Cherrim (R) .50 1.00
❑ 16 Gengar (R) .50 1.00
❑ 17 Gengar (R) .50 1.00
❑ 18 Glalie (R) .50 1.00
❑ 19 Golem (R) .50 1.00
❑ 20 Hariyama (R) .50 1.00
❑ 21 Lopunny (R) .50 1.00
❑ 22 Manectric (R) .50 1.00
❑ 23 Omastar (R) .50 1.00
❑ 24 Pelipper (R) .50 1.00
❑ 25 Pichu (R) .50 1.00
❑ 26 Porygon Z (R) .50 1.00
❑ 27 Raichu (R) .50 1.00
❑ 28 Rapidash (R) .50 1.00
❑ 29 Raticate (R) .50 1.00
❑ 30 Sceptile (R) .50 1.00
❑ 31 Sceptile (R) .50 1.00
❑ 32 Spiritomb (R) .50 1.00
❑ 33 Bronzong (U) .20 .50
❑ 34 Bronzor (U) .20 .50
❑ 35 Charmeleon (U) .20 .50
❑ 36 Gastly (U) .20 .50
❑ 37 Graveler (U) .20 .50
❑ 38 Grovyle (U) .20 .50
❑ 39 Grovyle (U) .20 .50
❑ 40 Gulpin (U) .20 .50
❑ 41 Haunter (U) .20 .50
❑ 42 Haunter (U) .20 .50
❑ 43 Luxio (U) .20 .50
❑ 44 Manectric (U) .20 .50
❑ 45 Pelipper (U) .20 .50
❑ 46 Ponyta (U) .20 .50
❑ 47 Rapidash (U) .20 .50
❑ 48 Shelgon (U) .20 .50
❑ 49 Wormadam (U) .20 .50
❑ 50 Wormadam (U) .20 .50
❑ 51 Wormadam (U) .20 .50
❑ 52 Bagon (C) .10 .20
❑ 53 Beedrill (C) .10 .20
❑ 54 Bronzor (C) .10 .20
❑ 55 Buneary (C) .10 .20
❑ 56 Burmy (C) .10 .20
❑ 57 Burmy (C) .10 .20
❑ 58 Burmy (C) .10 .20
❑ 59 Charmander (C) .10 .20
❑ 60 Cherubi (C) .10 .20
❑ 61 Croagunk (C) .10 .20
❑ 62 Electrike (C) .10 .20
❑ 63 Electrike (C) .10 .20
❑ 64 Gastly (C) .10 .20
❑ 65 Geodude (C) .10 .20
❑ 66 Gulpin (C) .10 .20
❑ 67 Kabuto (C) .10 .20
❑ 68 Makuhita (C) .10 .20
❑ 69 Nosepass (C) .10 .20
❑ 70 Omanyte (C) .10 .20
❑ 71 Pikachu (C) .20 .50
❑ 72 Ponyta (C) .10 .20
❑ 73 Rattata (C) .10 .20
❑ 74 Shinx (C) .10 .20
❑ 75 Snorunt (C) .10 .20
❑ 76 Tangela (C) .10 .20
❑ 77 Tangela (C) .10 .20
❑ 78 Treecko (C) .10 .20
❑ 79 Treecko (C) .10 .20
❑ 80 Wingull (C) .10 .20
❑ 81 Wingull (C) .10 .20
❑ 82 Beginning Door (U) .20 .50
❑ 83 Bench Shield (U) .20 .50
❑ 84 Buffer Piece (U) .20 .50
❑ 85 Department Store Girl (U) .20 .50
❑ 86 Energy Restore (U) .20 .50
❑ 87 Expert Belt (U) .20 .50
❑ 88 Lucky Egg (U) .20 .50
❑ 89 Old Amber (U) .20 .50
❑ 90 Professor Oak's Visit (U) .20 .50
❑ 91 Ultimate Zone (U) .20 .50
❑ 92 Dome Fossil (C) .10 .20
❑ 93 Helix Fossil (C) .10 .20
❑ 94 Arceus LV X (Holo) (R) 7.00 15.00
❑ 95 Arceus LV X (Holo) (R) 5.00 10.00
❑ 96 Arceus LV X (Holo) (R) 7.00 15.00
❑ 97 Gengar LV X (Holo) (R) 7.00 15.00
❑ 98 Salamence LV X (Holo) (R) 5.00 10.00
❑ 99 Tangrowth LV X (Holo) (R) 7.00 15.00
❑ SH10 Bagon (Rev H) (R) 2.00 4.00
❑ SH11 Ponyta (Rev H) (R) 2.00 4.00
❑ SH12 Shinx (Rev H) (R) 3.00 5.00
❑ AR1 Arceus (Holo) (R) 4.00 8.00
❑ AR2 Arceus (Holo) (R) 4.00 8.00
❑ AR3 Arceus (Holo) (R) 3.00 6.00
❑ AR4 Arceus (Holo) (R) 4.00 8.00
❑ AR5 Arceus (Holo) (R) 4.00 8.00
❑ AR6 Arceus (Holo) (R) 3.00 6.00
❑ AR7 Arceus (Holo) (R) 3.00 6.00
❑ AR8 Arceus (Holo) (R) 4.00 8.00
❑ AR9 Arceus (Holo) (R) 3.00 6.00

2009 Pokemon Platinum Arceus Reverse Foil

*Reverse Foil: 1X to 2X Basic Cards

2010 Pokemon HeartGold SoulSilver

Booster Box 85.00 100.00
Booster Pack 3.50 4.00
*Reverse Foil: 1X to 2X Regular Card

❑ 1 Arcanine (Holo) (R) 2.00 4.00
❑ 2 Azumarill (Holo) (R) 2.00 4.00
❑ 3 Clefable (Holo) (R) 2.00 4.00
❑ 4 Gyarados (Holo) (R) 2.00 5.00
❑ 5 Hitmontop (Holo) (R) 2.00 4.00
❑ 6 Jumpluff (Holo) (R) 4.00 8.00
❑ 7 Ninetales (Holo) (R) 2.00 4.00
❑ 8 Noctowl (Holo) (R) 2.00 4.00
❑ 9 Quagsire (Holo) (R) 2.00 4.00
❑ 10 Raichu (Holo) (R) 2.00 5.00
❑ 11 Shuckle (Holo) (R) 2.00 4.00
❑ 12 Slowking (Holo) (R) 2.00 4.00
❑ 13 Wobbuffet (Holo) (R) 2.00 4.00
❑ 14 Ampharos (R) .50 1.00
❑ 15 Ariados (R) .50 1.00
❑ 16 Butterfree (R) .50 1.00
❑ 17 Cleffa (R) .50 1.00
❑ 18 Exeggutor (R) .50 1.00
❑ 19 Farfetch'd (R) .50 1.00
❑ 20 Feraligatr (R) .50 1.00
❑ 21 Furret (R) .50 1.00
❑ 22 Granbull (R) .50 1.00
❑ 23 Hypno (R) .50 1.00
❑ 24 Lapras (R) .50 1.00
❑ 25 Ledian (R) .50 1.00
❑ 26 Meganium (R) .50 1.00
❑ 27 Persian (R) .50 1.00
❑ 28 Pichu (R) .50 1.00
❑ 29 Sandslash (R) .50 1.00
❑ 30 Smoochum (R) .50 1.00
❑ 31 Sunflora (R) .50 1.00
❑ 32 Typhlosion (R) .50 1.00
❑ 33 Tyrogue (R) .50 1.00
❑ 34 Weezing (R) .50 1.00
❑ 35 Bayleef (U) .20 .50
❑ 36 Blissey (U) .20 .50
❑ 37 Corsola (U) .20 .50
❑ 38 Croconaw (U) .20 .50
❑ 39 Delibird (U) .20 .50
❑ 40 Donphan (U) .20 .50
❑ 41 Dunsparce (U) .20 .50
❑ 42 Flaaffy (U) .20 .50
❑ 43 Heracross (U) .20 .50
❑ 44 Igglybuff (U) .20 .50
❑ 45 Mantine (U) .20 .50
❑ 46 Metapod (U) .20 .50
❑ 47 Miltank (U) .20 .50
❑ 48 Parasect (U) .20 .50
❑ 49 Quilava (U) .20 .50
❑ 50 Qwilfish (U) .20 .50
❑ 51 Skiploom (U) .20 .50
❑ 52 Slowbro (U) .20 .50
❑ 53 Starmie (U) .20 .50
❑ 54 Unown (U) .20 .50
❑ 55 Unown (U) .20 .50
❑ 56 Wigglytuff (U) .20 .50
❑ 57 Caterpie (C) .10 .25
❑ 58 Chansey (C) .10 .25
❑ 59 Chikorita (C) .10 .25
❑ 60 Clefairy (C) .10 .25
❑ 61 Cyndaquil (C) .10 .25
❑ 62 Drowzee (C) .10 .25
❑ 63 Exeggcute (C) .10 .25
❑ 64 Girafarig (C) .10 .25
❑ 65 Growlithe (C) .10 .25
❑ 66 Hoothoot (C) .10 .25
❑ 67 Hoppip (C) .10 .25
❑ 68 Jigglypuff (C) .10 .25
❑ 69 Jynx (C) .10 .25
❑ 70 Koffing (C) .10 .25
❑ 71 Ledyba (C) .10 .25
❑ 72 Magikarp (C) .10 .25
❑ 73 Mareep (C) .10 .25
❑ 74 Marill (C) .10 .25
❑ 75 Meowth (C) .10 .25
❑ 76 Paras (C) .10 .25
❑ 77 Phanpy (C) .10 .25
❑ 78 Pikachu (C) .10 .25
❑ 79 Sandshrew (C) .10 .25
❑ 80 Sentret (C) .10 .25
❑ 81 Slowpoke (C) .10 .25
❑ 82 Snubbull (C) .10 .25
❑ 83 Spinarak (C) .10 .25
❑ 84 Staryu (C) .10 .25
❑ 85 Sunkern (C) .10 .25
❑ 86 Totodile (C) .10 .25
❑ 87 Vulpix (C) .10 .25
❑ 88 Wooper (C) .10 .25
❑ 89 Bill (U) .20 .50
❑ 90 Copycat (U) .20 .50
❑ 91 Energy Switch (U) 1.00 2.00
❑ 92 Fisherman (U) .20 .50
❑ 93 Full Heal (U) .20 .50
❑ 94 Moomoo Milk (U) .20 .50
❑ 95 Poke Ball (U) .20 .50
❑ 96 Pokegear 3.0 (U) .20 .50
❑ 97 Pokemon Collector (U) .20 .50
❑ 98 Pokemon Communication (U) 1.00 2.00
❑ 99 Pokemon Reversal (U) .20 .50
❑ 100 Professor Elm's Training Method (U) .20 .50
❑ 101 Professor Oak's New Theory (U) .20 .50
❑ 102 Switch (U) .20 .50
❑ 103 Double Colorless Energy (U) 4.00 8.00
❑ 104 Rainbow Energy (U) 1.00 2.00
❑ 105 Ampharos (Prime) (Holo) (R) 6.00 12.00
❑ 106 Blissey (Prime) (Holo) (R) 2.00 4.00
❑ 107 Donphan (Prime) (Holo) (R) 10.00 15.00
❑ 108 Feraligatr (Prime) (Holo) (R) 4.00 8.00
❑ 109 Meganium (Prime) (Holo) (R) 4.00 8.00
❑ 110 Typhlosion (Prime) (Holo) (R) 4.00 8.00
❑ 111 Ho-Oh LEGEND (Top) (Holo) (R) 10.00 20.00
❑ 112 Ho-Oh LEGEND (Bottom) (Holo) (R) 10.00 20.00
❑ 113 Lugia LEGEND (Top) (Holo) (R) 10.00 20.00
❑ 114 Lugia LEGEND (Bottom) (Holo) (R) 10.00 20.00
❑ 115 Grass Energy (C) .10 .25
❑ 116 Fire Energy (C) .10 .25
❑ 117 Water Energy (C) .10 .25
❑ 118 Lightning Energy (C) .10 .25
❑ 119 Psychic Energy (C) .10 .25
❑ 120 Fighting Energy (C) .10 .25
❑ 121 Darkness Energy (C) .10 .25
❑ 122 Metal Energy (C) .10 .25
❑ 123 Gyarados (Holo) (R) 7.00 15.00
❑ 124 Alph Lithograph 10.00 20.00

2010 Pokemon HeartGold SoulSilver Reverse Foil

*Reverse Foil: 1X to 2X Basic Cards

2010 Pokemon HS Triumphant

Complete Set (103) 75.00 125.00
Booster Box 75.00 100.00
Booster Pack 3.00 4.00
*Reverse Foil: 1X to 2X Regular Card

❑ 1 Aggron (Holo) (R) 1.50 4.00
❑ 2 Altaria (Holo) (R) 1.50 4.00
❑ 3 Celebi (Holo) (R) 1.50 4.00
❑ 4 Drapion (Holo) (R) 1.50 4.00
❑ 5 Mamoswine (Holo) (R) 1.50 4.00
❑ 6 Nidoking (Holo) (R) 1.50 4.00
❑ 7 Porygon-Z (Holo) (R) 1.50 4.00
❑ 8 Rapidash (Holo) (R) 1.50 4.00
❑ 9 Solrock (Holo) (R) 1.50 4.00
❑ 10 Spiritomb (Holo) (R) 1.50 4.00
❑ 11 Venomoth (Holo) (R) 1.50 4.00
❑ 12 Victreebel (Holo) (R) 1.50 4.00
❑ 13 Ambipom (R) .40 1.00
❑ 14 Banette (R) .40 1.00
❑ 15 Bronzong (R) .40 1.00
❑ 16 Carnivine (R) .40 1.00
❑ 17 Ditto (R) .40 1.00
❑ 18 Dragonite (R) .40 1.00
❑ 19 Dugtrio (R) .40 1.00
❑ 20 Electivire (R) .40 1.00
❑ 21 Elekid (R) .40 1.00
❑ 22 Golduck (R) .40 1.00
❑ 23 Grumpig (R) .40 1.00
❑ 24 Kricketune (R) .40 1.00
❑ 25 Lunatone (R) .40 1.00
❑ 26 Machamp (R) .40 1.00
❑ 27 Magmortar (R) .40 1.00
❑ 28 Nidoqueen (R) .40 1.00
❑ 29 Pidgeot (R) .40 1.00
❑ 30 Sharpedo (R) .40 1.00
❑ 31 Wailord (R) .40 1.00
❑ 32 Dragonair (U) .20 .50
❑ 33 Electabuzz (U) .20 .50
❑ 34 Electrode (U) .20 .50
❑ 35 Haunter (U) .20 .50
❑ 36 Kangaskhan (U) .20 .50
❑ 37 Lairon (U) .20 .50
❑ 38 Lickilicky (U) .20 .50
❑ 39 Luvdisc (U) .20 .50
❑ 40 Machoke (U) .20 .50
❑ 41 Magby (U) .20 .50
❑ 42 Magmar (U) .20 .50
❑ 43 Magneton (U) .20 .50
❑ 44 Marowak (U) .20 .50
❑ 45 Nidorina (U) .20 .50
❑ 46 Nidorino (U) .20 .50
❑ 47 Pidgeotto (U) .20 .50
❑ 48 Piloswine (U) .20 .50
❑ 49 Porygon2 (U) .20 .50
❑ 50 Tentacruel (U) .20 .50
❑ 51 Unown (U) .20 .50
❑ 52 Wailmer (U) .20 .50
❑ 53 Weepinbell (U) .20 .50
❑ 54 Yanmega (U) .20 .50
❑ 55 Aipom (C) .10 .25
❑ 56 Aron (C) .10 .25
❑ 57 Bellsprout (C) .10 .25
❑ 58 Bronzor (C) .10 .25
❑ 59 Carvanha (C) .10 .25
❑ 60 Cubone (C) .10 .25
❑ 61 Diglett (C) .10 .25
❑ 62 Dratini (C) .10 .25
❑ 63 Gastly (C) .10 .25
❑ 64 Illumise (C) .10 .25

TCG/CCG

❑ 65 Kricketot (C) .10 .25
❑ 66 Lickitung (C) .10 .25
❑ 67 Machop (C) .10 .25
❑ 68 Magnemite (C) .10 .25
❑ 69 Nidoran F (C) .10 .25
❑ 70 Nidoran M (C) .10 .25
❑ 71 Pidgey (C) .10 .25
❑ 72 Ponyta (C) .10 .25
❑ 73 Porygon (C) .10 .25
❑ 74 Psyduck (C) .10 .25
❑ 75 Shuppet (C) .10 .25
❑ 76 Skorupi (C) .10 .25
❑ 77 Spoink (C) .10 .25
❑ 78 Swablu (C) .10 .25
❑ 79 Swinub (C) .10 .25
❑ 80 Tentacool (C) .10 .25
❑ 81 Venonat (C) .10 .25
❑ 82 Volbeat (C) .10 .25
❑ 83 Voltorb (C) .10 .25
❑ 84 Yanma (C) .10 .25
❑ 85 Black Belt (U) .20 .50
❑ 86 Indigo Plateau (U) .20 .50
❑ 87 Junk Arm (U) .20 .50
❑ 88 Seeker (U) .20 .50
❑ 89 Twins (U) .20 .50
❑ 90 Rescue Energy (U) .20 .50
❑ 91 Absol (Holo) (R) 3.00 8.00
❑ 92 Celebi (Holo) (R) 5.00 12.00
❑ 93 Electrode (Holo) (R) 2.00 5.00
❑ 94 Gengar (Holo) (R) 5.00 12.00
❑ 95 Machamp (Holo) (R) 4.00 10.00
❑ 96 Magnezone (Holo) (R) 4.00 10.00
❑ 97 Mew (Holo) (R) 5.00 12.00
❑ 98 Yanmega (Holo) (R) 3.00 8.00
❑ 99 Darkrai & Cresselia LEGEND (R) 4.00 10.00
❑ 100 Darkrai & Cresselia LEGEND (R) 4.00 10.00
❑ 101 Palkia & Dialga LEGEND (R) 5.00 12.00
❑ 102 Palkia & Dialga LEGEND (R) 5.00 12.00
❑ SP Alph Lithograph (Holo) (R) 3.00 8.00

2010 Pokemon HS Triumphant Reverse Foil

*Reverse Foil: 1X to 2X Basic Cards

2010 Pokemon HS Unleashed

Complete Set (96) 80.00 120.00
Booster Box 75.00 90.00
Booster Pack 3.00 4.00
*Reverse Foil: 1X to 2X Regular Card

❑ 1 Jirachi (Holo) (R) 2.00 4.00
❑ 2 Magmortar (Holo) (R) 2.00 4.00
❑ 3 Manaphy (Holo) (R) 2.00 4.00
❑ 4 Metagross (Holo) (R) 2.00 4.00
❑ 5 Mismagius (Holo) (R) 2.00 4.00
❑ 6 Octillery (Holo) (R) 2.00 4.00
❑ 7 Politoed (Holo) (R) 2.00 4.00
❑ 8 Shaymin (Holo) (R) 2.00 4.00
❑ 9 Sudowoodo (Holo) (R) 2.00 4.00
❑ 10 Torterra (Holo) (R) 2.00 4.00
❑ 11 Xatu (Holo) (R) 2.00 4.00
❑ 12 Beedrill (R) .40 1.00
❑ 13 Blastoise (R) .40 1.00
❑ 14 Crobat (R) .40 1.00
❑ 15 Fearow (R) .40 1.00
❑ 16 Floatzel (R) .40 1.00
❑ 17 Kingdra (R) .40 1.00
❑ 18 Lanturn (R) .40 1.00
❑ 19 Lucario (R) .40 1.00
❑ 20 Ninetales (R) .40 1.00
❑ 21 Poliwrath (R) .40 1.00
❑ 22 Primeape (R) .40 1.00
❑ 23 Roserade (R) .40 1.00
❑ 24 MetalSteelix (R) .40 1.00
❑ 25 Torkoal (R) .40 1.00
❑ 26 Tyranitar (R) .40 1.00
❑ 27 Ursaring (R) .40 1.00
❑ 28 Cherrim (U) .20 .50
❑ 29 Dunsparce (U) .20 .50
❑ 30 Golbat (U) .20 .50
❑ 31 Grotle (U) .20 .50
❑ 32 Kakuna (U) .20 .50
❑ 33 Metang (U) .20 .50
❑ 34 Minun (U) .20 .50
❑ 35 Numel (U) .20 .50
❑ 36 Plusle (U) .20 .50
❑ 37 Poliwhirl (U) .20 .50
❑ 38 Pupitar (U) .20 .50
❑ 39 Pupitar (U) .20 .50
❑ 40 Seadra (U) .20 .50
❑ 41 Tauros (U) .20 .50
❑ 42 Wartortle (U) .20 .50
❑ 43 Aipom (C) .10 .25
❑ 44 Beldum (C) .10 .25
❑ 45 Buizel (C) .10 .25
❑ 46 Carnivine (C) .10 .25
❑ 47 Cherubi (C) .10 .25
❑ 48 Chinchou (C) .10 .25
❑ 49 Horsea (C) .10 .25
❑ 50 Larvitar (C) .10 .25
❑ 51 Larvitar (C) .10 .25
❑ 52 Magmar (C) .10 .25
❑ 53 Mankey (C) .10 .25
❑ 54 Misdreavus (C) .10 .25
❑ 55 Natu (C) .10 .25
❑ 56 Onix (C) .10 .25
❑ 57 Onix (C) .10 .25
❑ 58 Poliwag (C) .10 .25
❑ 59 Remoraid (C) .10 .25
❑ 60 Riolu (C) .10 .25
❑ 61 Roselia (C) .10 .25
❑ 62 Spearow (C) .10 .25
❑ 63 Squirtle (C) .10 .25
❑ 64 Stantler (C) .10 .25
❑ 65 Teddiursa (C) .10 .25
❑ 66 Tropius (C) .10 .25
❑ 67 Turtwig (C) .10 .25
❑ 68 Vulpix (C) .10 .25
❑ 69 Weedle (C) .10 .25
❑ 70 Zubat (C) .10 .25
❑ 71 Cheerleader's Cheer (U) .20 .50
❑ 72 Dual Ball (U) .20 .50
❑ 73 Emcee's Chatter (U) .20 .50
❑ 74 Energy Returner (U) .20 .50
❑ 75 Engineer's Adjustments (U) .20 .50
❑ 76 Good Rod (U) .20 .50
❑ 77 Interviewer's Questions (U) .20 .50
❑ 78 Judge (U) .20 .50
❑ 79 Life Herb (U) .20 .50
❑ 80 Plus Power (U) .20 .50
❑ 81 Pokemon Circulator (U) .20 .50
❑ 82 Rare Candy (U) 2.00 4.00
❑ 83 Super Scoop Up (U) .20 .50
❑ 84 Crobat (Prime) (Holo) (R) 6.00 12.00
❑ 85 Kingdra (Prime) (Holo) (R) 6.00 12.00
❑ 86 Lanturn (Prime) (Holo) (R) 6.00 12.00
❑ 87 Steelix (Prime) (Holo) (R) 6.00 12.00
❑ 88 Tyranitar (Prime) (Holo) (R) 8.00 15.00
❑ 89 Ursaring (Prime) (Holo) (R) 6.00 12.00
❑ 90 Entei & Raikou LEGEND (Holo) (R) 6.00 12.00
❑ 91 Entei & Raikou LEGEND (Holo) (R) 10.00 20.00
❑ 92 Raikou & Suicune LEGEND (Holo) (R) 6.00 12.00
❑ 93 Raikou & Suicune LEGEND (Holo) (R) 6.00 12.00
❑ 94 Suicune & Entei LEGEND (Holo) (R) 5.00 10.00
❑ 95 Suicune & Entei LEGEND (Holo) (R) 5.00 10.00
❑ 96 Alph Lithograph (R) 5.00 10.00

2010 Pokemon HS Unleashed Reverse Foil

*Reverse Foil: 1X to 2X Basic Cards

2010 Pokemon HS Undaunted

Complete Set (91) 75.00 125.00
Booster Box 75.00 100.00
Booster Pack 3.00 5.00
*Reverse Foil: 1X to 2X Regular Card

❑ 1 Bellossom (Holo) (R) 2.00 4.00
❑ 2 Espeon (Holo) (R) 2.00 4.00
❑ 3 Forretress (Holo) (R) 2.00 4.00
❑ 4 Gliscor (Holo) (R) 2.00 4.00
❑ 5 Houndoom (Holo) (R) 2.00 4.00
❑ 6 Magcargo (Holo) (R) 2.00 4.00
❑ 7 Scizor (Holo) (R) 2.00 4.00
❑ 8 Smeargle (Holo) (R) 2.00 4.00
❑ 9 Togekiss (Holo) (R) 2.00 4.00
❑ 10 Umbreon (Holo) (R) 2.00 4.00
❑ 11 Dodrio (R) .40 1.00
❑ 12 Drifblim (R) .40 1.00
❑ 13 Forretress (R) .40 1.00
❑ 14 Hariyama (R) .40 1.00
❑ 15 Honchkrow (R) .40 1.00
❑ 16 Honchkrow (R) .40 1.00
❑ 17 Leafeon (R) .40 1.00
❑ 18 Metagross (R) .40 1.00
❑ 19 Mismagius (R) .40 1.00
❑ 20 Rotom (R) .40 1.00
❑ 21 Skarmory (R) .40 1.00
❑ 22 Tropius (R) .40 1.00
❑ 23 Vespiquen (R) .40 1.00
❑ 24 Vileplume (R) .40 1.00
❑ 25 Weavile (R) .40 1.00
❑ 26 Flareon (U) .20 .50
❑ 27 Gloom (U) .20 .50
❑ 28 Jolteon (U) .20 .50
❑ 29 Lairon (U) .20 .50
❑ 30 Metang (U) .20 .50
❑ 31 Muk (U) .20 .50
❑ 32 Pinsir (U) .20 .50
❑ 33 Raichu (U) .20 .50
❑ 34 Raticate (U) .20 .50
❑ 35 Sableye (U) .20 .50
❑ 36 Scyther (U) .20 .50
❑ 37 Skuntank (U) .20 .50
❑ 38 Slowbro (U) .20 .50
❑ 39 Togetic (U) .20 .50
❑ 40 Unown (U) .20 .50
❑ 41 Vaporeon (U) .20 .50
❑ 42 Aron (C) .10 .25
❑ 43 Beldum (C) .10 .25
❑ 44 Combee (C) .10 .25
❑ 45 Doduo (C) .10 .25
❑ 46 Drifloon (C) .10 .25
❑ 47 Eevee (C) .10 .25
❑ 48 Eevee (C) .10 .25
❑ 49 Gligar (C) .10 .25
❑ 50 Grimer (C) .10 .25
❑ 51 Hitmonchan (C) .10 .25
❑ 52 Hitmonlee (C) .10 .25
❑ 53 Houndour (C) .10 .25
❑ 54 Houndour (C) .10 .25
❑ 55 Makuhita (C) .10 .25
❑ 56 Mawile (C) .10 .25
❑ 57 Misdreavus (C) .10 .25
❑ 58 Murkrow (C) .10 .25
❑ 59 Murkrow (C) .10 .25
❑ 60 Oddish (C) .10 .25
❑ 61 Pikachu (C) .10 .25
❑ 62 Pineco (C) .10 .25
❑ 63 Pineco (C) .10 .25
❑ 64 Rattata (C) .10 .25
❑ 65 Scyther (C) .10 .25
❑ 66 Slowpoke (C) .10 .25
❑ 67 Slugma (C) .10 .25
❑ 68 Sneasel (C) .10 .25
❑ 69 Stunky (C) .10 .25
❑ 70 Togepi (C) .10 .25
❑ 71 Burned Tower (U) .20 .50
❑ 72 Defender (U) .20 .50
❑ 73 Energy Exchanger (U) .20 .50
❑ 74 Flower Shop Lady (U) .20 .50
❑ 75 Legend Box (U) .20 .50
❑ 76 Ruins of Alph (U) .20 .50
❑ 77 Sage's Training (U) .20 .50
❑ 78 Team Rocket's Trickery (U) .20 .50
❑ 79 Darkness Energy (U) .20 .50
❑ 80 Metal Energy (U) .20 .50
❑ 81 Espeon (Holo) (R) 3.00 6.00
❑ 82 Houndoom (Holo) (R) 3.00 6.00
❑ 83 Raichu (Holo) (R) 2.50 5.00
❑ 84 Scizor (Holo) (R) 4.00 8.00
❑ 85 Slowking (Holo) (R) 2.50 5.00
❑ 86 Umbreon (Holo) (R) 4.00 10.00
❑ 87 Kyogre & Groudon LEGEND (Holo) (R) 5.00 12.00
❑ 88 Kyogre & Groudon LEGEND (Holo) (R) 5.00 12.00
❑ 89 Rayquaza & Deoxys LEGEND (Holo) (R) 5.00 12.00
❑ 90 Rayquaza & Deoxys LEGEND (Holo) (R) 5.00 12.00
❑ SP Alph Lithograph (Holo) (R) 2.50 5.00

2010 Pokemon HS Undaunted Reverse Foil

*Reverse Foil: 1X to 2X Basic Cards

2011 Pokemon Black and White

Complete Set (115) 50.00 100.00
Booster Box (36 Packs)
Booster Pack (10 Cards)

❑ 1 Snivy (C) .10 .25
❑ 2 Snivy (C) .10 .25
❑ 3 Servine (U) .20 .50
❑ 4 Servine (U) .20 .50
❑ 5 Serperior (Holo) (R) 1.50 4.00
❑ 6 Serperior (Holo) (R) 1.50 4.00
❑ 7 Pansage (C) .10 .25
❑ 8 Simisage (U) .20 .50
❑ 9 Petilil (C) .10 .25
❑ 10 Lilligant (R) .40 1.00
❑ 11 Maractus (U) .20 .50
❑ 12 Maractus (R) .40 1.00
❑ 13 Deerling (C) .10 .25
❑ 14 Sawsbuck (R) .40 1.00
❑ 15 Tepig (C) .10 .25
❑ 16 Tepig (C) .10 .25
❑ 17 Pignite (U) .20 .50
❑ 18 Pignite (U) .20 .50
❑ 19 Emboar (Holo) (R) 2.00 5.00
❑ 20 Emboar (Holo) (R) 10.00 20.00
❑ 21 Pansear (C) .10 .25
❑ 22 Simisear (U) .20 .50
❑ 23 Darumaka (C) .10 .25
❑ 24 Darumaka (U) .20 .50
❑ 25 Darmanitan (R) .40 1.00
❑ 26 Reshiram (Holo) (R) 3.00 8.00
❑ 27 Oshawott (C) .10 .25
❑ 28 Oshawott (C) .10 .25
❑ 29 Dewott (U) .20 .50
❑ 30 Dewott (U) .20 .50
❑ 31 Samurott (Holo) (R) 1.50 4.00
❑ 32 Samurott (Holo) (R) 2.00 5.00
❑ 33 Panpour (C) .10 .25
❑ 34 Simipour (U) .20 .50
❑ 35 Basculin (U) .20 .50
❑ 36 Ducklett (C) .10 .25
❑ 37 Swanna (R) .40 1.00
❑ 38 Alomomola (U) .20 .50
❑ 39 Alomomola (R) .40 1.00
❑ 40 Blitzle (C) .10 .25
❑ 41 Blitzle (C) .10 .25
❑ 42 Zebstrika (U) .20 .50
❑ 43 Zebstrika (R) .40 1.00
❑ 44 Joltik (C) .10 .25
❑ 45 Joltik (C) .10 .25
❑ 46 Galvantula (R) .40 1.00
❑ 47 Zekrom (Holo) (R) 1.50 4.00
❑ 48 Munna (U) .20 .50
❑ 49 Musharna (R) .40 1.00
❑ 50 Woobat (C) .10 .25
❑ 51 Swoobat (U) .20 .50
❑ 52 Venipede (C) .10 .25
❑ 53 Whirlipede (U) .20 .50
❑ 54 Scolipede (R) .40 1.00
❑ 55 Solosis (C) .10 .25
❑ 56 Duosion (U) .20 .50
❑ 57 Reuniclus (Holo) (R) 1.50 4.00
❑ 58 Timburr (C) .10 .25
❑ 59 Timburr (C) .10 .25
❑ 60 Gurdurr (U) .20 .50
❑ 61 Throh (R) .40 1.00
❑ 62 Sawk (R) .40 1.00
❑ 63 Sandile (C) .10 .25
❑ 64 Krokorok (U) .20 .50
❑ 65 Krookodile (Holo) (R) 1.50 4.00
❑ 66 Purrloin (C) .10 .25
❑ 67 Liepard (R) .40 1.00
❑ 68 Scraggy (C) .10 .25
❑ 69 Scrafty (R) .40 1.00
❑ 70 Zorua (C) .10 .25
❑ 71 Zoroark (Holo) (R) 3.00 8.00
❑ 72 Vullaby (C) .10 .25
❑ 73 Mandibuzz (R) .40 1.00
❑ 74 Klink (C) .10 .25
❑ 75 Klang (U) .20 .50
❑ 76 Klinklang (Holo) (R) 1.50 4.00
❑ 77 Patrat (C) .10 .25
❑ 78 Patrat (C) .10 .25
❑ 79 Watchog (U) .20 .50
❑ 80 Lillipup (C) .10 .25
❑ 81 Lillipup (C) .10 .25
❑ 82 Herdier (U) .20 .50
❑ 83 Stoutland (R) .40 1.00
❑ 84 Pidove (C) .10 .25
❑ 85 Tranquill (U) .20 .50
❑ 86 Unfezant (R) .40 1.00
❑ 87 Audino (U) .20 .50
❑ 88 Minccino (C) .10 .25
❑ 89 Cinccino (R) .40 1.00
❑ 90 Bouffalant (U) .20 .50
❑ 91 Bouffalant (R) .40 1.00
❑ 92 Energy Retrieval (U) .20 .50
❑ 93 Energy Search (C) .10 .25
❑ 94 Energy Switch (U) .20 .50
❑ 95 Full Heal (U) .20 .50
❑ 96 PlusPower (U) .20 .50
❑ 97 Poke Ball (U) .20 .50
❑ 98 Pokedex (U) .20 .50
❑ 99 Pokemon Communication (U) .20 .50
❑ 100 Potion (C) .10 .25
❑ 101 Professor Juniper (U) .20 .50
❑ 102 Revive (U) .20 .50
❑ 103 Super Scoop Up (U) .20 .50
❑ 104 Switch (U) .20 .50
❑ 105 Grass Energy (C) .10 .25
❑ 106 Fire Energy (C) .10 .25
❑ 107 Water Energy (C) .10 .25
❑ 108 Lightning Energy (C) .10 .25
❑ 109 Psychic Energy (C) .10 .25
❑ 110 Fighting Energy (C) .10 .25
❑ 111 Darkness Energy (C) .10 .25
❑ 112 Metal Energy (C) .10 .25
❑ 113 Reshiram (Holo) (SR) 10.00 20.00
❑ 114 Zekrom (Holo) (SR) 10.00 20.00
❑ 115 Pikachu (UR) 10.00 20.00

2011 Pokemon Black and White Reverse Foil

*Rev.Foil: .8X to 2X Basic Cards

2011 Pokemon Black and White Emerging Powers

Complete Set (98) 40.00 100.00
Booster Box (36 Packs)
Booster Pack (10 Cards)

❑ 1 Pansage (C) .10 .25
❑ 2 Simisage (R) .40 1.00
❑ 3 Sewaddle (C) .10 .25
❑ 4 Sewaddle (C) .10 .25
❑ 5 Swadloon (U) .20 .50
❑ 6 Swadloon (U) .20 .50
❑ 7 Leavanny (R) .75 2.00
❑ 8 Leavanny (R) .75 2.00
❑ 9 Cottonee (C) .10 .25
❑ 10 Cottonee (C) .10 .25
❑ 11 Whimsicott (U) .20 .50
❑ 12 Whimsicott (R) .40 1.00
❑ 13 Petilil (C) .10 .25
❑ 14 Lilligant (U) .20 .50
❑ 15 Deerling (C) .10 .25
❑ 16 Sawsbuck (R) .40 1.00
❑ 17 Virizion (Holo) (R) 2.00 5.00
❑ 18 Pansear (C) .10 .25
❑ 19 Simisear (R) .40 1.00
❑ 20 Darumaka (C) .10 .25
❑ 21 Darmanitan (R) .60 1.50
❑ 22 Panpour (C) .10 .25
❑ 23 Simipour (R) .40 1.00
❑ 24 Basculin (C) .10 .25
❑ 25 Basculin (U) .20 .50
❑ 26 Ducklett (C) .10 .25
❑ 27 Swanna (R) .40 1.00
❑ 28 Cubchoo (C) .10 .25
❑ 29 Cubchoo (C) .10 .25
❑ 30 Beartic (Holo) (R) 3.00 8.00
❑ 31 Beartic (R) .75 2.00
❑ 32 Emolga (C) .10 .25
❑ 33 Joltik (C) .10 .25
❑ 34 Galvantula (U) .20 .50
❑ 35 Thundurus (Holo) (R) 2.00 5.00
❑ 36 Woobat (C) .10 .25
❑ 37 Swoobat (R) .40 1.00
❑ 38 Venipede (C) .10 .25
❑ 39 Whirlipede (U) .20 .50
❑ 40 Scolipede (R) .40 1.00
❑ 41 Sigilyph (U) .20 .50
❑ 42 Sigilyph (U) .20 .50
❑ 43 Gothita (C) .10 .25
❑ 44 Gothita (C) .10 .25
❑ 45 Gothorita (U) .20 .50
❑ 46 Gothorita (U) .20 .50
❑ 47 Gothitelle (Holo) (R) 1.50 4.00
❑ 48 Gothitelle (R) .40 1.00
❑ 49 Roggenrola (C) .10 .25
❑ 50 Roggenrola (C) .10 .25
❑ 51 Boldore (U) .20 .50
❑ 52 Boldore (U) .20 .50
❑ 53 Gigalith (R) .40 1.00
❑ 54 Drilbur (U) .20 .50
❑ 55 Drilbur (C) .10 .25
❑ 56 Excadrill (Holo) (R) 1.25 3.00
❑ 57 Excadrill (R) 1.50 4.00
❑ 58 Throh (U) .20 .50
❑ 59 Sawk (U) .20 .50
❑ 60 Sandile (C) .10 .25
❑ 61 Krokorok (U) .20 .50
❑ 62 Krookodile (R) .60 1.50
❑ 63 Terrakion (Holo) (R) 1.00 2.50
❑ 64 Purrloin (C) .10 .25
❑ 65 Liepard (R) 1.50 4.00
❑ 66 Zorua (U) .20 .50
❑ 67 Zoroark (Holo) (R) 1.25 3.00
❑ 68 Vullaby (C) .10 .25
❑ 69 Mandibuzz (R) .60 1.50
❑ 70 Ferroseed (C) .10 .25
❑ 71 Ferroseed (C) .10 .25
❑ 72 Ferrothorn (R) .40 1.00
❑ 73 Ferrothorn (U) .20 .50
❑ 74 Klink (C) .10 .25
❑ 75 Klang (U) .20 .50
❑ 76 Klinklang (R) .75 2.00
❑ 77 Cobalion (Holo) (R) 2.00 5.00
❑ 78 Patrat (C) .10 .25
❑ 79 Watchog (U) .20 .50
❑ 80 Pidove (C) .10 .25
❑ 81 Tranquill (U) .20 .50
❑ 82 Unfezant (R) .60 1.50
❑ 83 Audino (U) .20 .50
❑ 84 Minccino (C) .10 .25
❑ 85 Cinccino (U) .20 .50
❑ 86 Rufflet (C) .10 .25
❑ 87 Rufflet (C) .10 .25
❑ 88 Braviary (Holo) (R) 1.25 3.00
❑ 89 Tornadus (Holo) (R) 1.25 3.00
❑ 90 Bianca (U) .50 1.25
❑ 91 Cheren (U) .20 .50
❑ 92 Crushing Hammer (U) .20 .50
❑ 93 Great Ball (U) .20 .50
❑ 94 Max Potion (U) 2.00 5.00
❑ 95 Pokemon Catcher (U) 8.00 20.00
❑ 96 Recycle (U) .20 .50
❑ 97 Thundurus (Holo) (SR) 4.00 10.00
❑ 98 Tornadus (Holo) (SR) 3.00 8.00

2011 Pokemon Black and White Emerging Powers Reverse Foil

*Reverse Foil: .8X to 2X Basic Cards

2011 Pokemon Black and White Noble Victories

Complete Set (102) 75.00 125.00
Booster Box (36 Packs)
Booster Pack (10 Cards)

❑ 1 Sewaddle (C) .10 .25
❑ 2 Swadloon (U) .20 .50
❑ 3 Leavanny (Holo) (R) .40 1.00
❑ 4 Petilil (C) .10 .25
❑ 5 Lilligant (R) .40 1.00
❑ 6 Dwebble (C) .10 .25
❑ 7 Crustle (U) .20 .50
❑ 8 Karrablast (C) .10 .25
❑ 9 Foongus (C) .10 .25
❑ 10 Amoonguss (U) .20 .50
❑ 11 Shelmet (C) .10 .25
❑ 12 Accelgor (R) 1.25 3.00
❑ 13 Virizion (Holo) (R) 3.00 8.00
❑ 14 Victini (Holo) (R) 5.00 12.00
❑ 15 Victini (Holo) (R) 4.00 10.00
❑ 16 Pansear (C) .10 .25
❑ 17 Simisear (U) .20 .50
❑ 18 Heatmor (U) .20 .50
❑ 19 Larvesta (C) .10 .25
❑ 20 Larvesta (C) .10 .25
❑ 21 Volcarona (R) 1.25 3.00
❑ 22 Tympole (C) .10 .25
❑ 23 Palpitoad (U) .20 .50
❑ 24 Seismitoad (R) .60 1.50
❑ 25 Tirtouga (U) .20 .50
❑ 26 Carracosta (R) 1.50 4.00
❑ 27 Vanillite (C) .10 .25
❑ 28 Vanillish (U) .20 .50
❑ 29 Vanilluxe (R) 2.50 6.00
❑ 30 Frillish (C) .10 .25
❑ 31 Jellicent (R) .75 2.00
❑ 32 Cryogonal (U) .20 .50
❑ 33 Cryogonal (R) 1.00 2.50
❑ 34 Kyurem (Holo) (R) 8.00 20.00
❑ 35 Blitzle (C) .10 .25
❑ 36 Zebstrika (R) .40 1.00
❑ 37 Emolga (U) .20 .50
❑ 38 Tynamo (C) .10 .25
❑ 39 Tynamo (C) .10 .25
❑ 40 Eelektrik (U) .20 .50
❑ 41 Eelektross (Holo) (R) 1.50 4.00

❑ 42 Stunfisk (C) .10 .25
❑ 43 Victini (R) 3.00 8.00
❑ 44 Yamask (C) .10 .25
❑ 45 Yamask (C) .10 .25
❑ 46 Cofagrigus (R) .40 1.00
❑ 47 Cofagrigus (R) .40 1.00
❑ 48 Trubbish (C) .10 .25
❑ 49 Garbodor (U) .20 .50
❑ 50 Solosis (C) .10 .25
❑ 51 Duosion (U) .20 .50
❑ 52 Reuniclus (R) .40 1.00
❑ 53 Reuniclus (R) .40 1.00
❑ 54 Elgyem (C) .10 .25
❑ 55 Elgyem (C) .10 .25
❑ 56 Beheeyem (R) .40 1.00
❑ 57 Litwick (C) .10 .25
❑ 58 Litwick (C) .10 .25
❑ 59 Lampent (U) .20 .50
❑ 60 Chandelure (R) 3.00 8.00
❑ 61 Gigalith (R) .75 2.00
❑ 62 Timburr (C) .10 .25
❑ 63 Gurdurr (U) .20 .50
❑ 64 Conkeldurr (Holo) (R) 1.50 4.00
❑ 65 Conkeldurr (R) .75 2.00
❑ 66 Archen (U) .20 .50
❑ 67 Archeops (R) 2.00 5.00
❑ 68 Stunfisk (U) .20 .50
❑ 69 Mienfoo (C) .10 .25
❑ 70 Mienshao (U) .20 .50
❑ 71 Golett (C) .10 .25
❑ 72 Golurk (R) .40 1.00
❑ 73 Terrakion (Holo) (R) 2.00 5.00
❑ 74 Landorus (Holo) (R) 4.00 10.00
❑ 75 Pawniard (C) .10 .25
❑ 76 Bisharp (U) .20 .50
❑ 77 Deino (C) .10 .25
❑ 78 Zweilous (U) .20 .50
❑ 79 Hydreigon (Holo) (R) 5.00 12.00
❑ 80 Escavalier (R) .60 1.50
❑ 81 Pawniard (C) .10 .25
❑ 82 Bisharp (Holo) (R) 2.00 5.00
❑ 83 Durant (U) .20 .50
❑ 84 Cobalion (Holo) (R) 4.00 10.00
❑ 85 Audino (U) .20 .50
❑ 86 Axew (C) .10 .25
❑ 87 Fraxure (U) .20 .50
❑ 88 Haxorus (Holo) (R) 2.50 6.00
❑ 89 Druddigon (R) 1.50 4.00
❑ 90 Cover Fossil (U) .20 .50
❑ 91 Eviolite (U) .20 .50
❑ 92 N (U) .20 .50
❑ 93 Plume Fossil (U) .20 .50
❑ 94 Rocky Helmet (U) .20 .50
❑ 95 Super Rod (U) .20 .50
❑ 96 Xtransceiver (U) .20 .50
❑ 97 Virizion (Holo) (SR) 8.00 20.00
❑ 98 Victini (Holo) (SR) 10.00 25.00
❑ 99 Terrakion (Holo) (SR) 8.00 20.00
❑ 100 Cobalion (Holo) (SR) 10.00 25.00
❑ 101 N (Holo) (SR) 10.00 25.00
❑ 102 Meowth (SR) 6.00 15.00

2011 Pokemon Black and White Noble Victories Reverse Foil

*Reverse Foil: .8X to 2X Basic Cards

2011 Pokemon Call of Legends

Complete Set 40.00 80.00

❑ 1 Clefable (Holo) (R) .40 1.00
❑ 2 Deoxys (Holo) (R) .40 1.00
❑ 3 Dialga (Holo) (R) .40 1.00
❑ 4 Espeon (Holo) (R) .50 1.25
❑ 5 Forretress (Holo) (R) .40 1.00
❑ 6 Groudon (Holo) (R) 1.50 4.00
❑ 7 Gyarados (Holo) (R) .40 1.00
❑ 8 Hitmontop (Holo) (R) .40 1.00
❑ 9 Ho-Oh (Holo) (R) 1.50 4.00
❑ 10 Houndoom (Holo) (R) .40 1.00
❑ 11 Jirachi (Holo) (R) .40 1.00
❑ 12 Kyogre (Holo) (R) .60 1.50
❑ 13 Leafeon (Holo) (R) .60 1.50
❑ 14 Lucario (Holo) (R) .50 1.25
❑ 15 Lugia (Holo) (R) 2.00 5.00
❑ 16 Magmortar (Holo) (R) .40 1.00
❑ 17 Ninetales (Holo) (R) .60 1.50
❑ 18 Pachirisu (Holo) (R) .40 1.00
❑ 19 Palkia (Holo) (R) .40 1.00
❑ 20 Rayquaza (Holo) (R) 1.50 4.00
❑ 21 Smeargle (Holo) (R) .60 1.50
❑ 22 Umbreon (Holo) (R) .60 1.50
❑ 23 Ampharos (R) .30 .75
❑ 24 Cleffa (R) .40 1.00
❑ 25 Feraligatr (R) .30 .75
❑ 26 Granbull (R) .30 .75
❑ 27 Meganium (R) .30 .75
❑ 28 Mismagius (R) .30 .75
❑ 29 Mr. Mime (R) .30 .75
❑ 30 Pidgeot (R) .30 .75
❑ 31 Skarmory (R) .30 .75
❑ 32 Slowking (R) .30 .75
❑ 33 Snorlax (R) .30 .75
❑ 34 Tangrowth (R) .30 .75
❑ 35 Typhlosion (R) .30 .75
❑ 36 Tyrogue (R) .30 .75
❑ 37 Ursaring (R) .30 .75
❑ 38 Weezing (R) .30 .75
❑ 39 Zangoose (R) .30 .75
❑ 40 Bayleef (U) .20 .50
❑ 41 Croconaw (U) .20 .50
❑ 42 Donphan (U) .20 .50
❑ 43 Flaaffy (U) .20 .50
❑ 44 Flareon (U) .20 .50
❑ 45 Jolteon (U) .20 .50
❑ 46 Magby (U) .20 .50
❑ 47 Mime Jr. (U) .20 .50
❑ 48 Pidgeotto (U) .20 .50
❑ 49 Quilava (U) .20 .50
❑ 50 Riolu (U) .20 .50
❑ 51 Seviper (U) .20 .50
❑ 52 Vaporeon (U) .20 .50
❑ 53 Chikorita (C) .10 .25
❑ 54 Clefairy (C) .10 .25
❑ 55 Cyndaquil (C) .10 .25
❑ 56 Eevee (C) .10 .25
❑ 57 Hitmonchan (C) .10 .25
❑ 58 Hitmonlee (C) .10 .25
❑ 59 Houndour (C) .10 .25
❑ 60 Koffing (C) .10 .25
❑ 61 Magikarp (C) .10 .25
❑ 62 Magmar (C) .10 .25
❑ 63 Mareep (C) .10 .25
❑ 64 Mawile (C) .10 .25
❑ 65 Misdreavus (C) .10 .25
❑ 66 Phanpy (C) .10 .25
❑ 67 Pidgey (C) .10 .25
❑ 68 Pineco (C) .10 .25
❑ 69 Relicanth (C) .10 .25
❑ 70 Slowpoke (C) .10 .25
❑ 71 Snubbull (C) .10 .25
❑ 72 Tangela (C) .10 .25
❑ 73 Teddiursa (C) .10 .25
❑ 74 Totodile (C) .10 .25
❑ 75 Vulpix (C) .10 .25
❑ 76 Cheerleader's Cheer (U) .20 .50
❑ 77 Copycat (U) .20 .50
❑ 78 Dual Ball (U) .20 .50
❑ 79 Interviewer's Questions (U) .20 .50
❑ 80 Lost Remover (U) .20 .50
❑ 81 Lost World (U) .20 .50
❑ 82 Professor Elm's Training Method (U) .20 .50
❑ 83 Professor Oak's New Theory (U) .60 1.50
❑ 84 Research Record (U) .20 .50
❑ 85 Sage's Training (U) .20 .50
❑ 86 Darkness Energy (U) .20 .50
❑ 87 Metal Energy (U) .20 .50
❑ 88 Grass Energy (C) 1.00 2.50
❑ 89 Fire Energy (C) 2.00 5.00
❑ 90 Water Energy (C) 3.00 8.00
❑ 91 Lightning Energy (C) 2.00 5.00
❑ 92 Psychic Energy (C) 2.50 6.00
❑ 93 Fighting Energy (C) 2.00 5.00
❑ 94 Darkness Energy (C) 3.00 8.00
❑ 95 Metal Energy (C) 2.50 6.00

2011 Pokemon Call of Legends Reverse Foil

*Reverse Foil: .8X to 2X Basic Cards

2011 Pokemon Call of Legends Shiny

Complete Set (11) 40.00 80.00

❑ SL1 Deoxys (Holo) (R) 3.00 8.00
❑ SL2 Dialga (Holo) (R) 4.00 10.00
❑ SL3 Entei (Holo) (R) 3.00 8.00
❑ SL4 Groudon (Holo) (R) 4.00 10.00
❑ SL5 Ho-Oh (Holo) (R) 6.00 15.00
❑ SL6 Kyogre (Holo) (R) 4.00 10.00
❑ SL7 Lugia (Holo) (R) 5.00 12.00
❑ SL8 Palkia (Holo) (R) 3.00 8.00
❑ SL9 Raikou (Holo) (R) 3.00 8.00
❑ SL10 Rayquaza (Holo) (R) 6.00 15.00
❑ SL11 Suicune (Holo) (R) 4.00 10.00

2012 Pokemon Black and White Boundaries Crossed

❑ 1 Oddish (C) .10 .25
❑ 2 Gloom (U) .20 .50
❑ 3 Vileplume (Holo) (R) .75 2.00
❑ 4 Bellossom (R) .30 .75
❑ 5 Tangela (C) .10 .25
❑ 6 Tangrowth (Holo) (R) .60 1.50
❑ 7 Scyther (C) .10 .25
❑ 8 Heracross (U) .20 .50
❑ 9 Celebi-EX (Holo) (R) 3.00 8.00
❑ 10 Shaymin (R) .30 .75
❑ 11 Snivy (C) .10 .25
❑ 12 Servine (U) .20 .50
❑ 13 Serperior (Holo) (R) .60 1.50
❑ 14 Cottonee (C) .10 .25
❑ 15 Whimsicott (R) .30 .75
❑ 16 Petilil (U) .20 .50
❑ 17 Lilligant (R) .30 .75
❑ 18 Charmander (C) .10 .25
❑ 19 Charmeleon (U) .20 .50
❑ 20 Charizard (Holo) (R) 3.00 8.00
❑ 21 Numel (C) .10 .25
❑ 22 Camerupt (R) .30 .75
❑ 23 Victini (R) .40 1.00
❑ 24 Tepig (C) .10 .25
❑ 25 Pignite (U) .20 .50
❑ 26 Emboar (Holo) (R) .60 1.50
❑ 27 Darumaka (C) .10 .25
❑ 28 Darmanitan (U) .20 .50
❑ 29 Squirtle (C) .10 .25
❑ 30 Wartortle (U) .20 .50
❑ 31 Blastoise (Holo) (R) 6.00 15.00
❑ 32 Psyduck (C) .10 .25
❑ 33 Psyduck (C) .10 .25
❑ 34 Golduck (U) .20 .50
❑ 35 Golduck (R) .30 .75
❑ 36 Marill (C) .10 .25
❑ 37 Azumarill (U) .20 .50
❑ 38 Delibird (U) .20 .50
❑ 39 Oshawott (C) .10 .25
❑ 40 Dewott (U) .20 .50
❑ 41 Samurott (Holo) (R) .60 1.50
❑ 42 Ducklett (C) .10 .25
❑ 43 Swanna (U) .20 .50
❑ 44 Frillish (C) .10 .25
❑ 45 Jellicent (R) .30 .75
❑ 46 Cryogonal (U) .20 .50
❑ 47 Keldeo (Holo) (R) 1.00 2.50
❑ 48 Keldeo (R) .30 .75
❑ 49 Keldeo-EX (Holo) (R) 10.00 25.00
❑ 50 Pikachu (C) .10 .25
❑ 51 Voltorb (C) .10 .25
❑ 52 Electrode (U) .20 .50
❑ 53 Electabuzz (C) .10 .25
❑ 54 Electivire (Holo) (R) .60 1.50
❑ 55 Chinchou (C) .10 .25
❑ 56 Blitzle (C) .10 .25
❑ 57 Zebstrika (Holo) (R) .60 1.50
❑ 58 Wobbuffet (U) .20 .50
❑ 59 Spoink (C) .10 .25
❑ 60 Grumpig (R) .30 .75
❑ 61 Duskull (C) .10 .25
❑ 62 Dusclops (U) .20 .50
❑ 63 Dusknoir (Holo) (R) 2.00 5.00
❑ 64 Croagunk (C) .10 .25
❑ 65 Croagunk (U) .20 .50
❑ 66 Toxicroak (R) .30 .75
❑ 67 Cresselia-EX (Holo) (R) 4.00 10.00
❑ 68 Munna (U) .20 .50
❑ 69 Musharna (R) .30 .75
❑ 70 Woobat (C) .10 .25
❑ 71 Swoobat (R) .30 .75
❑ 72 Venipede (C) .10 .25
❑ 73 Whirlipede (U) .20 .50
❑ 74 Scolipede (Holo) (R) .60 1.50
❑ 75 Gothita (C) .10 .25
❑ 76 Gothorita (U) .20 .50
❑ 77 Meloetta (Holo) (R) 1.50 4.00
❑ 78 Sandshrew (C) .10 .25
❑ 79 Sandslash (U) .20 .50
❑ 80 Gligar (C) .10 .25
❑ 81 Gliscor (Holo) (R) .60 1.50
❑ 82 Makuhita (C) .10 .25
❑ 83 Trapinch (C) .10 .25
❑ 84 Dwebble (C) .10 .25
❑ 85 Crustle (Holo) (R) .60 1.50
❑ 86 Mienfoo (C) .10 .25
❑ 87 Mienfoo (U) .20 .50
❑ 88 Mienshao (U) .20 .50
❑ 89 Landorus-EX (Holo) (R) 12.00 30.00
❑ 90 Purrloin (C) .10 .25
❑ 91 Liepard (Holo) (R) .60 1.50
❑ 92 Vullaby (C) .10 .25
❑ 93 Mandibuzz (U) .20 .50
❑ 94 Scizor (Holo) (R) .60 1.50
❑ 95 Skarmory (U) .20 .50
❑ 96 Skarmory (U) .20 .50
❑ 97 Klink (U) .20 .50
❑ 98 Vibrava (U) .20 .50
❑ 99 Flygon (Holo) (R) 1.00 2.50
❑ 100 Black Kyurem (R) .40 1.00
❑ 101 Black Kyurem-EX (Holo) (R) 6.00 15.00
❑ 102 White Kyurem (R) .40 1.00
❑ 103 White Kyurem-EX (Holo) (R) 5.00 12.00
❑ 104 Rattata (C) .10 .25
❑ 105 Raticate (U) .20 .50
❑ 106 Meowth (C) .10 .25
❑ 107 Farfetch'd (U) .20 .50
❑ 108 Ditto (Holo) (R) 2.00 5.00
❑ 109 Snorlax (U) .20 .50
❑ 110 Togepi (C) .10 .25
❑ 111 Dunsparce (C) .10 .25
❑ 112 Taillow (C) .10 .25
❑ 113 Skitty (C) .10 .25
❑ 114 Delcatty (U) .20 .50
❑ 115 Spinda (C) .10 .25
❑ 116 Buneary (C) .10 .25
❑ 117 Lopunny (U) .20 .50
❑ 118 Patrat (C) .10 .25
❑ 119 Watchog (U) .20 .50
❑ 120 Lillipup (C) .10 .25
❑ 121 Herdier (U) .20 .50
❑ 122 Stoutland (Holo) (R) .60 1.50
❑ 123 Pidove (C) .10 .25
❑ 124 Tranquill (U) .20 .50
❑ 125 Unfezant (R) .30 .75
❑ 126 Audino (R) .30 .75
❑ 127 Aspertia City Gym (U) .20 .50
❑ 128 Energy Search (C) .10 .25
❑ 129 Great Ball (U) .20 .50
❑ 130 Hugh (U) .20 .50
❑ 131 Poke Ball (C) .10 .25
❑ 132 Potion (C) .10 .25
❑ 133 Rocky Helmet (U) .20 .50
❑ 134 Skyla (U) 1.25 3.00
❑ 135 Switch (C) .10 .25
❑ 136 Town Map (U) .20 .50
❑ 137 Computer Search (Holo) (R) 8.00 20.00
❑ 138 Crystal Edge (Holo) (R) .75 2.00
❑ 139 Crystal Wall (Holo) (R) .75 2.00
❑ 140 Gold Potion (Holo) (R) 3.00 8.00
❑ 141 Celebi-EX (Holo) (SR) 6.00 15.00
❑ 142 Keldeo-EX (Holo) (SR) 20.00 40.00
❑ 143 Cresselia-EX (Holo) (SR) 6.00 15.00
❑ 144 Landorus-EX (Holo) (SR) 20.00 40.00
❑ 145 Black Kyurem-EX (Holo) (SR) 10.00 25.00
❑ 146 White Kyurem-EX (Holo) (SR) 10.00 25.00
❑ 147 Bianca (Holo) (SR) 12.00 30.00
❑ 148 Cheren (Holo) (SR) 10.00 25.00
❑ 149 Skyla (Holo) (SR) 15.00 40.00
❑ 150 Golurk (UR) 5.00 12.00
❑ 151 Terrakion (UR) 8.00 20.00
❑ 152 Altaria (UR) 6.00 15.00
❑ 153 Rocky Helmet (UR) 5.00 12.00

2012 Pokemon Black and White Boundaries Crossed Reverse Foil

*Reverse Foil: .8X to 2X Basic Cards

2012 Pokemon Black and White Dark Explorers

Complete Set

❑ 1 Bulbasaur (C) .10 .25
❑ 2 Ivysaur (U) .20 .50
❑ 3 Venusaur (Holo) (R) 1.50 4.00
❑ 4 Scyther (U) .20 .50
❑ 5 Carnivine (R) 1.00 2.50
❑ 6 Leafeon (R) 1.00 2.50
❑ 7 Dwebble (C) .10 .25
❑ 8 Crustle (U) .20 .50
❑ 9 Karrablast (C) .10 .25
❑ 10 Shelmet (C) .10 .25
❑ 11 Accelgor (R) .40 1.00
❑ 12 Flareon (U) .20 .50
❑ 13 Entei EX (Holo) (R) 8.00 20.00
❑ 14 Torchic (C) .10 .25
❑ 15 Torchic (C) .10 .25
❑ 16 Combusken (U) .20 .50
❑ 17 Blaziken (Holo) (R) 1.50 4.00
❑ 18 Torkoal (U) .20 .50
❑ 19 Heatmor (R) .40 1.00
❑ 20 Larvesta (C) .10 .25
❑ 21 Larvesta (C) .10 .25
❑ 22 Volcarona (Holo) (R) 1.00 2.50
❑ 23 Slowpoke (C) .10 .25
❑ 24 Slowbro (U) .20 .50
❑ 25 Vaporeon (U) .20 .50
❑ 26 Kyogre EX (Holo) (R) 8.00 20.00
❑ 27 Piplup (C) .10 .25
❑ 28 Prinplup (U) .20 .50
❑ 29 Empoleon (Holo) (R) 3.00 8.00
❑ 30 Glaceon (R) .40 1.00
❑ 31 Tympole (C) .10 .25
❑ 32 Palpitoad (U) .20 .50
❑ 33 Vanillite (C) .10 .25
❑ 34 Vanillish (U) .20 .50
❑ 35 Ducklett (C) .10 .25
❑ 36 Swanna (R) .40 1.00
❑ 37 Jolteon (U) .20 .50
❑ 38 Raikou EX (Holo) (R) 10.00 25.00
❑ 39 Plusle (C) .10 .25
❑ 40 Minun (C) .10 .25
❑ 41 Joltik (C) .10 .25
❑ 42 Joltik (C) .10 .25
❑ 43 Galvantula (R) .40 1.00
❑ 44 Tynamo (C) .10 .25
❑ 45 Tynamo (C) .10 .25
❑ 46 Eelektrik (U) .20 .50
❑ 47 Eelektross (Holo) (R) 1.50 4.00
❑ 48 Espeon (R) 1.50 4.00
❑ 49 Slowking (R) .40 1.00
❑ 50 Woobat (C) .10 .25
❑ 51 Yamask (U) .20 .50
❑ 52 Cofagrigus (R) 1.00 2.50
❑ 53 Aerodactyl (R) 1.00 2.50
❑ 54 Groudon EX (Holo) (R) 12.00 30.00
❑ 55 Drilbur (C) .10 .25
❑ 56 Excadrill (R) .40 1.00
❑ 57 Excadrill (R) .40 1.00
❑ 58 Timburr (C) .10 .25
❑ 59 Gurdurr (U) .20 .50
❑ 60 Umbreon (U) .20 .50
❑ 61 Umbreon (U) .20 .50
❑ 62 Sableye (U) .20 .50
❑ 63 Darkrai EX (Holo) (R) 40.00 80.00
❑ 64 Sandile (C) .10 .25
❑ 65 Krokorok (U) .20 .50
❑ 66 Krookodile (Holo) (R) 2.00 5.00
❑ 67 Scraggy (C) .10 .25
❑ 68 Scrafty (R) 1.00 2.50
❑ 69 Zorua (C) .10 .25
❑ 70 Zorua (C) .10 .25
❑ 71 Zoroark (R) 3.00 8.00
❑ 72 Bisharp (R) 1.50 4.00
❑ 73 Vullaby (U) .20 .50
❑ 74 Escavalier (R) .40 1.00
❑ 75 Klink (C) .10 .25
❑ 76 Klang (U) .20 .50
❑ 77 Klinklang (Holo) (R) 1.25 3.00
❑ 78 Pawniard (C) .10 .25
❑ 79 Bisharp (R) 1.50 4.00
❑ 80 Chansey (C) .10 .25
❑ 81 Chansey (C) .10 .25
❑ 82 Blissey (Holo) (R) 1.00 2.50
❑ 83 Eevee (C) .10 .25
❑ 84 Eevee (C) .10 .25
❑ 85 Chatot (U) .20 .50
❑ 86 Lillipup (C) .10 .25
❑ 87 Herdier (U) .20 .50
❑ 88 Stoutland (R) 1.50 4.00
❑ 89 Haxorus (Holo) (R) 1.50 4.00
❑ 90 Tornadus EX (Holo) (R) 20.00 40.00
❑ 91 Cheren (U) .20 .50
❑ 92 Dark Claw (U) .20 .50
❑ 93 Dark Patch (U) .20 .50
❑ 94 Enhanced Hammer (U) .20 .50
❑ 95 Hooligans Jim & Cas (U) .20 .50
❑ 96 N (U) .20 .50
❑ 97 Old Amber Aerodactyl (U) .20 .50
❑ 98 Professor Juniper (U) .20 .50
❑ 99 Random Receiver (U) .20 .50
❑ 100 Rare Candy (U) .20 .50
❑ 101 Twist Mountain (U) .20 .50
❑ 102 Ultra Ball (U) .20 .50
❑ 103 Entei EX (Holo) (SR) 12.00 30.00
❑ 104 Kyogre EX (Holo) (SR) 10.00 25.00
❑ 105 Raikou EX (Holo) (SR) 20.00 40.00
❑ 106 Groudon EX (Holo) (SR) 20.00 40.00
❑ 107 Darkrai EX (Holo) (SR) 50.00 100.00
❑ 108 Tornadus EX (Holo) (SR) 25.00 50.00
❑ 109 Gardevoir (UR) 10.00 25.00
❑ 110 Archeops (UR) 10.00 25.00
❑ 111 Pokemon Catcher (UR) 30.00 60.00

2012 Pokemon Black and White Dark Explorers Reverse Foil

*Reverse Foil: .8X to 2X Basic Cards

2012 Pokemon Black and White Dragons Exalted

❑ 1 Hoppip (C) .10 .25
❑ 2 Skiploom (U) .20 .50
❑ 3 Jumpluff (R) .30 .75
❑ 4 Yanma (C) .10 .25
❑ 5 Yanmega (R) .30 .75
❑ 6 Wurmple (C) .10 .25
❑ 7 Silcoon (U) .20 .50
❑ 8 Beautifly (R) .30 .75
❑ 9 Cascoon (U) .20 .50
❑ 10 Nincada (C) .10 .25
❑ 11 Ninjask (U) .20 .50
❑ 12 Roselia (U) .20 .50
❑ 13 Roselia (C) .10 .25
❑ 14 Roserade (U) .20 .50
❑ 15 Roserade (R) .30 .75
❑ 16 Maractus (U) .20 .50
❑ 17 Foongus (C) .10 .25
❑ 18 Vulpix (C) .10 .25
❑ 19 Ninetales (Holo) (R) 1.00 2.50
❑ 20 Magmar (C) .10 .25
❑ 21 Magmortar (R) .30 .75
❑ 22 Ho-Oh EX (Holo) (R) 6.00 15.00
❑ 23 Magikarp (C) .10 .25
❑ 24 Gyarados (R) .30 .75
❑ 25 Wailmer (U) .20 .50
❑ 26 Wailord (Holo) (R) .60 1.50
❑ 27 Feebas (C) .10 .25
❑ 28 Milotic (Holo) (R) .60 1.50
❑ 29 Spheal (C) .10 .25
❑ 30 Sealeo (U) .20 .50
❑ 31 Walrein (R) .30 .75
❑ 32 Buizel (C) .10 .25
❑ 33 Floatzel (U) .20 .50
❑ 34 Tympole (C) .10 .25
❑ 35 Palpitoad (U) .20 .50
❑ 36 Seismitoad (R) .30 .75
❑ 37 Alomomola (R) .30 .75
❑ 38 Mareep (C) .10 .25
❑ 39 Flaaffy (U) .20 .50
❑ 40 Ampharos (Holo) (R) .60 1.50
❑ 41 Electrike (C) .10 .25
❑ 42 Electrike (C) .10 .25
❑ 43 Manectric (R) .30 .75
❑ 44 Manectric (R) .30 .75
❑ 45 Emolga (U) .20 .50
❑ 46 Mew EX (Holo) (R) 8.00 20.00
❑ 47 Dustox (R) .30 .75
❑ 48 Shedinja (R) .30 .75
❑ 49 Drifloon (C) .10 .25
❑ 50 Drifloon (C) .10 .25
❑ 51 Drifblim (R) .30 .75
❑ 52 Sigilyph (Holo) (R) 3.00 8.00
❑ 53 Trubbish (C) .10 .25
❑ 54 Garbodor (Holo) (R) 1.50 4.00
❑ 55 Gothita (C) .10 .25
❑ 56 Gothorita (U) .20 .50
❑ 57 Gothitelle (R) .30 .75
❑ 58 Golett (C) .10 .25
❑ 59 Golurk (Holo) (R) .60 1.50
❑ 60 Cubone (C) .10 .25
❑ 61 Marowak (R) .30 .75
❑ 62 Nosepass (C) .10 .25
❑ 63 Baltoy (C) .10 .25

TCG/CCG

- □ 64 Claydol (R) .30 .75
- □ 65 Roggenrola (C) .10 .25
- □ 66 Boldore (U) .20 .50
- □ 67 Gigalith (Holo) (R) .60 1.50
- □ 68 Throh (U) .20 .50
- □ 69 Sawk (U) .20 .50
- □ 70 Stunfisk (U) .20 .50
- □ 71 Terrakion EX (Holo) (R) 6.00 15.00
- □ 72 Murkrow (C) .10 .25
- □ 73 Honchkrow (R) .30 .75
- □ 74 Houndour (C) .10 .25
- □ 75 Houndoom (R) .30 .75
- □ 76 Stunky (C) .10 .25
- □ 77 Skuntank (U) .20 .50
- □ 78 Aron (C) .10 .25
- □ 79 Lairon (U) .20 .50
- □ 80 Aggron (Holo) (R) .60 1.50
- □ 81 Registeel EX (Holo) (R) 6.00 15.00
- □ 82 Probopass (R) .30 .75
- □ 83 Durant (U) .20 .50
- □ 84 Altaria (Holo) (R) 1.00 2.50
- □ 85 Rayquaza EX (Holo) (R) 5.00 12.00
- □ 86 Gible (C) .10 .25
- □ 87 Gible (C) .10 .25
- □ 88 Gabite (U) .20 .50
- □ 89 Gabite (U) .20 .50
- □ 90 Garchomp (Holo) (R) 2.50 6.00
- □ 91 Garchomp (R) .30 .75
- □ 92 Giratina EX (Holo) (R) 6.00 15.00
- □ 93 Deino (C) .10 .25
- □ 94 Deino (C) .10 .25
- □ 95 Zweilous (U) .20 .50
- □ 96 Zweilous (U) .20 .50
- □ 97 Hydreigon (Holo) (R) 4.00 10.00
- □ 98 Hydreigon (R) .30 .75
- □ 99 Aipom (C) .10 .25
- □ 100 Ambipom (R) .30 .75
- □ 101 Slakoth (C) .10 .25
- □ 102 Vigoroth (U) .20 .50
- □ 103 Slaking (Holo) (R) .60 1.50
- □ 104 Swablu (C) .20 .50
- □ 105 Swablu (C) .10 .25
- □ 106 Bidoof (C) .10 .25
- □ 107 Bibarel (U) .20 .50
- □ 108 Audino (U) .20 .50
- □ 109 Minccino (C) .10 .25
- □ 110 Bouffalant (U) .20 .50
- □ 111 Rufflet (C) .10 .25
- □ 112 Braviary (R) .30 .75
- □ 113 Devolution Spray (U) .20 .50
- □ 114 Giant Cape (U) .20 .50
- □ 115 Rescue Scarf (U) .20 .50
- □ 116 Tool Scrapper (U) .20 .50
- □ 117 Blend Energy GFPD (U) .60 1.50
- □ 118 Blend Energy WLFM (U) .40 1.00
- □ 119 Ho-Oh (Holo) (SR) 10.00 25.00
- □ 120 Mew (Holo) (SR) 12.00 30.00
- □ 121 Terrakion (Holo) (SR) 8.00 20.00
- □ 122 Registeel (Holo) (SR) 8.00 20.00
- □ 123 Rayquaza (Holo) (SR) 10.00 25.00
- □ 124 Giratina (Holo) (SR) 8.00 20.00
- □ 125 Serperior (UR) 6.00 15.00
- □ 126 Reuniclus (UR) 6.00 15.00
- □ 127 Krookodile (UR) 8.00 20.00
- □ 128 Rayquaza (UR) 12.00 30.00

2012 Pokemon Black and White Dragons Exalted Reverse Foil

*Reverse Foil: .8X to 2X Basic Cards

2012 Pokemon Black and White Next Destinies

- □ 1 Pinsir (R) .40 1.00
- □ 2 Seedot (C) .10 .25
- □ 3 Kricketot (C) .10 .25
- □ 4 Kricketune (U) .20 .50
- □ 5 Shaymin EX (Holo) (R) 6.00 15.00
- □ 6 Pansage (C) .10 .25
- □ 7 Simisage (R) .40 1.00
- □ 8 Foongus (C) .10 .25
- □ 9 Amoonguss (R) .40 1.00
- □ 10 Growlithe (C) .10 .25
- □ 11 Growlithe (C) .10 .25
- □ 12A Arcanine (R) .40 1.00
- □ 12B Arcanine STAFF 10.00 20.00
- □ 13 Arcanine (U) .20 .50
- □ 14 Moltres (Holo) (R) .75 2.00
- □ 15 Pansear (C) .10 .25
- □ 16 Simisear (R) .40 1.00
- □ 17 Darumaka (C) .10 .25
- □ 18 Litwick (C) .10 .25
- □ 19 Lampent (U) .20 .50
- □ 20 Chandelure (Holo) (R) 2.50 6.00
- □ 21 Reshiram (R) 1.50 4.00
- □ 22 Reshiram EX (Holo) (R) 5.00 12.00
- □ 23 Staryu (C) .10 .25
- □ 24 Starmie (U) .20 .50
- □ 25 Lapras (R) .40 1.00
- □ 26 Lapras (U) .20 .50
- □ 27 Articuno (Holo) (R) .75 2.00
- □ 28 Panpour (C) .10 .25
- □ 29 Simipour (R) .40 1.00
- □ 30 Basculin (U) .20 .50
- □ 31 Vanillite (C) .10 .25
- □ 32 Vanillish (U) .20 .50
- □ 33 Vanilluxe (Holo) (R) 2.50 6.00
- □ 34 Frillish (U) .20 .50
- □ 35 Jellicent (R) .40 1.00
- □ 36 Cubchoo (C) .10 .25
- □ 37 Beartic (R) .40 1.00
- □ 38 Kyurem EX (Holo) (R) 6.00 15.00
- □ 39 Pikachu (C) .10 .25
- □ 40 Raichu (U) .20 .50
- □ 41 Zapdos (Holo) (R) 1.50 4.00
- □ 42 Shinx (C) .10 .25
- □ 43 Shinx (C) .10 .25
- □ 44 Luxio (U) .20 .50
- □ 45 Luxio (U) .20 .50
- □ 46 Luxray (Holo) (R) 1.50 4.00
- □ 47 Blitzle (C) .10 .25
- □ 48 Zebstrika (R) .40 1.00
- □ 49 Emolga (U) .20 .50
- □ 50 Zekrom (R) 2.00 5.00
- □ 51 Zekrom EX (Holo) (R) 6.00 15.00
- □ 52 Grimer (C) .10 .25
- □ 53 Muk (R) .40 1.00
- □ 54A Mewtwo EX (Holo) (R) 12.00 30.00
- □ 54B Mewtwo EX (Holo) JUMBO 4.00 10.00
- □ 55 Ralts (C) .10 .25
- □ 56 Kirlia (U) .20 .50
- □ 57 Gardevoir (Holo) (R) 4.00 10.00
- □ 58 Munna (C) .10 .25
- □ 59 Musharna (R) .75 2.00
- □ 60 Darmanitan (R) 1.25 3.00
- □ 61 Elgyem (C) .10 .25
- □ 62 Beheeyem (R) .40 1.00
- □ 63 Riolu (C) .10 .25
- □ 64 Lucario (Holo) (R) 2.00 5.00
- □ 65 Hippopotas (C) .10 .25
- □ 66 Hippowdon (U) .20 .50
- □ 67 Mienfoo (C) .10 .25
- □ 68 Mienshao (U) .20 .50
- □ 69 Sneasel (C) .10 .25
- □ 70 Weavile (R) 1.00 2.50
- □ 71 Nuzleaf (U) .20 .50
- □ 72 Shiftry (R) .75 2.00
- □ 73 Scraggy (U) .20 .50
- □ 74 Scrafty (Holo) (R) .75 2.00
- □ 75 Bronzor (C) .10 .25
- □ 76 Bronzong (R) .40 1.00
- □ 77 Ferroseed (C) .10 .25
- □ 78 Jigglypuff (U) .20 .50
- □ 79 Wigglytuff (R) .40 1.00
- □ 80 Meowth (C) .10 .25
- □ 81 Persian (R) .40 1.00
- □ 82 Regigigas EX (Holo) (R) 10.00 25.00
- □ 83 Pidove (C) .10 .25
- □ 84 Minccino (U) .20 .50
- □ 85 Cinccino (Holo) (R) 1.00 2.50
- □ 86 Cilan (U) .20 .50
- □ 87 Exp. Share (U) .20 .50
- □ 88 Heavy Ball (U) .20 .50
- □ 89 Level Ball (U) .20 .50
- □ 90 Pokemon Center (U) .20 .50
- □ 91 Skyarrow Bridge (U) .20 .50
- □ 92 Double Colorless Energy (U) .20 .50
- □ 93 Prism Energy (U) .20 .50
- □ 94 Shaymin EX (Holo) (SR) 15.00 40.00
- □ 95 Reshiram EX (Holo) (SR) 12.00 30.00
- □ 96 Kyurem EX (Holo) (SR) 12.00 30.00
- □ 97 Zekrom EX (Holo) (SR) 12.00 30.00
- □ 98 Mewtwo EX (Holo) (SR) 35.00 70.00
- □ 99 Regigigas EX (Holo) (SR) 15.00 40.00
- □ 100 Emboar (UR) 10.00 25.00
- □ 101 Chandelure (UR) 12.00 30.00
- □ 102 Zoroark (UR) 10.00 25.00
- □ 103 Hydreigon (UR) 15.00 40.00

2012 Pokemon Black and White Next Destinies Reverse Foil

*Reverse Foil: .8X to 2X Basic Cards

2012 Pokemon Dragon Vault

Complete Set (No Promos) 20.00 40.00

Promo Cards issued one per blister pack

- □ 1 Dratini .15 .40
- □ 2 Dratini .15 .40
- □ 3 Dragonair .15 .40
- □ 4 Dragonair .15 .40
- □ 5 Dragonite .40 1.00
- □ 6 Bagon .15 .40
- □ 7 Shelgon .15 .40
- □ 8 Salamence .40 1.00
- □ 9a Latias .40 1.00
- □ 9b Latias PROMO .75 2.00
- (DRAGON VAULT printed on image)
- □ 10a Latios .40 1.00
- □ 10b Latios PROMO .75 2.00
- (DRAGON VAULT printed on image)
- □ 11a Rayquaza 3.00 8.00
- □ 11b Rayquaza PROMO 2.00 5.00
- (DRAGON VAULT printed on image)
- □ 12 Axew .15 .40
- □ 13 Axew .15 .40
- □ 14 Fraxure .15 .40
- □ 15 Fraxure .15 .40
- □ 16b Haxorus .40 1.00
- □ 16a Haxorus PROMO .75 2.00
- (DRAGON VAULT printed on image)
- □ 17b Druddigon .40 1.00
- □ 17a Druddigon PROMO .75 2.00
- (DRAGON VAULT printed on image)
- □ 18 Exp. Share .15 .40
- □ 19 First Ticket 2.00 5.00
- □ 20 Super Rod .60 1.50
- □ 21 Kyurem 8.00 20.00
- □ NNO Code Card 1.50 4.00

2013 Pokemon Black and White Plasma Blast

- □ 1 Surskit (C) .10 .25
- □ 2 Masquerain (R) .25 .60
- □ 3 Lileep (U) .15 .40
- □ 4 Cradily (R) .25 .60
- □ 5 Tropius (U) .15 .40
- □ 6 Karrablast (C) .10 .25
- □ 7 Shelmet (C) .10 .25
- □ 8 Accelgor (R) .25 .60
- □ 9 Virizion-EX (Holo) (R) 12.00 30.00
- □ 10 Genesect (R) .25 .60
- □ 11 Genesect-EX (Holo) (R) 12.00 30.00
- □ 12 Larvesta (C) .10 .25
- □ 13 Volcarona (R) .25 .60
- □ 14 Squirtle (C) .10 .25
- □ 15 Wartortle (U) .15 .40
- □ 16 Blastoise (Holo) (R) 2.00 5.00
- □ 17 Lapras (C) .10 .25
- □ 18 Remoraid (C) .10 .25
- □ 19 Octillery (U) .15 .40
- □ 20 Suicune (R) .50 1.25
- □ 21 Snorunt (C) .10 .25
- □ 22 Glalie (U) .15 .40
- □ 23 Froslass (R) .25 .60
- □ 24 Relicanth (U) .15 .40
- □ 25 Snover (C) .10 .25
- □ 26 Abomasnow (U) .15 .40
- □ 27 Tirtouga (U) .15 .40
- □ 28 Carracosta (R) .25 .60
- □ 29 Ducklett (C) .10 .25
- □ 30 Kyurem-EX (Holo) (R) 3.00 8.00
- □ 31 Tynamo (C) .10 .25
- □ 32 Eelektrik (U) .15 .40
- □ 33 Eelektross (Holo) (R) .25 .60
- □ 34 Drifloon (C) .10 .25
- □ 35 Drifblim (R) .25 .60
- □ 36 Uxie (R) .25 .60
- □ 37 Mesprit (Holo) (R) .40 1.00
- □ 38 Azelf (R) .25 .60
- □ 39 Munna (C) .10 .25
- □ 40 Musharna (U) .15 .40
- □ 41 Sigilyph (Holo) (R) 2.00 5.00
- □ 42 Solosis (C) .10 .25
- □ 43 Duosion (U) .15 .40
- □ 44 Reuniclus (R) .25 .60
- □ 45 Golett (C) .10 .25
- □ 46 Golurk (Holo) (R) .25 .60
- □ 47 Machop (C) .10 .25
- □ 48 Machoke (U) .15 .40
- □ 49 Machamp (Holo) (R) .25 .60
- □ 50 Machamp (R) .25 .60
- □ 51 Throh (C) .10 .25
- □ 52 Sawk (C) .10 .25
- □ 53 Archen (U) .15 .40
- □ 54 Archeops (Holo) (R) .25 .60
- □ 55 Houndour (C) .10 .25
- □ 56 Houndoom (Holo) (R) .25 .60
- □ 57 Aron (C) .10 .25
- □ 58 Lairon (U) .15 .40
- □ 59 Aggron (R) .25 .60
- □ 60 Jirachi-EX (Holo) (R) 3.00 8.00
- □ 61 Escavalier (R) .25 .60
- □ 62 Bagon (C) .10 .25
- □ 63 Shelgon (U) .15 .40
- □ 64 Salamence (Holo) (R) .60 1.50
- □ 65 Dialga-EX (Holo) (R) 2.50 6.00
- □ 66 Palkia-EX (Holo) (R) 3.00 8.00
- □ 67 Axew (C) .10 .25
- □ 68 Fraxure (U) .15 .40
- □ 69 Haxorus (Holo) (R) .75 2.00
- □ 70 Druddigon (C) .10 .25
- □ 71 Kangaskhan (C) .10 .25
- □ 72 Porygon (C) .10 .25
- □ 73 Porygon2 (U) .15 .40
- □ 74 Porygon-Z (Holo) (R) .25 .60
- □ 75 Teddiursa (C) .10 .25
- □ 76 Ursaring (U) .15 .40
- □ 77 Chatot (U) .15 .40
- □ 78 Caitlin (U) .15 .40
- □ 79 Cover Fossil (U) .15 .40
- □ 80 Energy Retrieval (U) .15 .40
- □ 81 Iris (U) .15 .40
- □ 82 Plume Fossil (U) .15 .40
- □ 83 Pokémon Catcher (U) 2.00 5.00
- □ 84 Professor Juniper (U) .15 .40
- □ 85 Rare Candy (U) .75 2.00
- □ 86 Reversal Trigger (U) .15 .40
- □ 87 Root Fossil Lileep (U) .15 .40
- □ 88 Silver Bangle (U) .40 1.00
- □ 89 Silver Mirror (U) .25 .60
- □ 90 Ultra Ball (U) .75 2.00
- □ 91 Plasma Energy (U) .15 .40
- □ 92 G Booster (Holo) (R) 2.00 5.00
- □ 93 G Scope (Holo) (R) 1.00 2.50
- □ 94 Master Ball (Holo) (R) 2.00 5.00
- □ 95 Scoop Up Cyclone (Holo) (R) 1.50 4.00
- □ 96 Virizion-EX (Holo) (SR) 15.00 40.00
- □ 97 Genesect-EX (Holo) (SR) 15.00 40.00
- □ 98 Jirachi-EX (Holo) (SR) 5.00 12.00
- □ 99 Dialga-EX (Holo) (SR) 5.00 12.00
- □ 100 Palkia-EX (Holo) (SR) 5.00 12.00
- □ 101 Iris (Holo) (SR) 8.00 20.00
- □ 102 Exeggcute (UR) 6.00 15.00
- □ 103 Virizion (UR) 6.00 15.00
- □ 104 Dusknoir (UR) 6.00 15.00
- □ 105 Rare Candy (UR) 12.00 30.00

2013 Pokemon Black and White Plasma Blast Reverse Foil

*Reverse Foil: .8X to 2X Basic Cards

2013 Pokemon Black and White Plasma Freeze

- □ 1 Weedle (C) .10 .25
- □ 2 Kakuna (U) .15 .40
- □ 3 Beedrill (R) .25 .60
- □ 4 Exeggcute (U) .15 .40
- □ 5 Exeggutor (R) .25 .60
- □ 6 Treecko (C) .10 .25
- □ 7 Grovyle (U) .15 .40
- □ 8 Sceptile (Holo) (R) .40 1.00
- □ 9 Cacnea (C) .10 .25
- □ 10 Cacturne (R) .25 .60
- □ 11 Leafeon (R) .25 .60
- □ 12 Flareon (U) .15 .40
- □ 13 Heatran-EX (Holo) (R) 3.00 8.00
- □ 14 Litwick (C) .10 .25
- □ 15 Lampent (U) .15 .40
- □ 16 Chandelure (Holo) (R) .60 1.50
- □ 17 Reshiram (Holo) (R) .40 1.00
- □ 18 Horsea (C) .10 .25
- □ 19 Seadra (U) .15 .40
- □ 20 Vaporeon (U) .15 .40
- □ 21 Wooper (C) .10 .25
- □ 22 Quagsire (R) .25 .60
- □ 23 Glaceon (R) .25 .60
- □ 24 Tympole (C) .10 .25
- □ 25 Palpitoad (U) .15 .40
- □ 26 Seismitoad (R) .25 .60
- □ 27 Vanillite (C) .10 .25
- □ 28 Vanillish (U) .15 .40
- □ 29 Vanilluxe (R) .25 .60
- □ 30 Cryogonal (U) .15 .40
- □ 31 Kyurem (Holo) (R) 4.00 10.00
- □ 32 Voltorb (C) .10 .25
- □ 33 Electrode (Holo) (R) .40 1.00
- □ 34 Jolteon (U) .15 .40
- □ 35 Chinchou (C) .10 .25
- □ 36 Lanturn (U) .15 .40
- □ 37 Pachirisu (C) .10 .25
- □ 38 Thundurus-EX (Holo) (R) 15.00 35.00
- □ 39 Zekrom (Holo) (R) .40 1.00
- □ 40 Nidoran F (C) .10 .25
- □ 41 Nidorina (U) .15 .40
- □ 42 Nidoqueen (R) .25 .60
- □ 43 Nidoran M (C) .10 .25
- □ 44 Nidorino (U) .15 .40
- □ 45 Grimer (C) .10 .25
- □ 46 Muk (R) .25 .60
- □ 47 Mr. Mime (R) .25 .60
- □ 48 Espeon (U) .15 .40
- □ 49 Sableye (R) .25 .60
- □ 50 Beldum (C) .10 .25
- □ 51 Metang (U) .15 .40
- □ 52 Metagross (Holo) (R) .30 .75
- □ 53 Deoxys-EX (Holo) (R) 20.00 50.00
- □ 54 Yamask (C) .10 .25
- □ 55 Yamask (C) .10 .25
- □ 56 Cofagrigus (Holo) (R) .30 .75
- □ 57 Cofagrigus (R) .25 .60
- □ 58 Nidoking (R) .25 .60
- □ 59 Mankey (C) .10 .25
- □ 60 Primeape (C) .10 .25
- □ 61 Onix (U) .15 .40
- □ 62 Makuhita (C) .10 .25
- □ 63 Hariyama (R) .25 .60
- □ 64 Umbreon (Holo) (R) .60 1.50
- □ 65 Sneasel (C) .10 .25
- □ 66 Weavile (R) .30 .75
- □ 67 Absol (Holo) (R) 1.25 3.00
- □ 68 Sandile (C) .10 .25
- □ 69 Krokorok (U) .15 .40
- □ 70 Krookodile (R) .25 .60
- □ 71 Pawniard (C) .10 .25
- □ 72 Pawniard (C) .10 .25
- □ 73 Bisharp (R) .25 .60
- □ 74 Bisharp (U) .15 .40
- □ 75 Deino (C) .10 .25
- □ 76 Deino (C) .10 .25
- □ 77 Zweilous (U) .15 .40
- □ 78 Hydreigon (Holo) (R) .30 .75
- □ 79 Steelix (R) .25 .60
- □ 80 Mawile (U) .15 .40
- □ 81 Dratini (C) .10 .25
- □ 82 Dragonair (U) .15 .40
- □ 83 Dragonite (Holo) (R) .60 1.50
- □ 84 Kingdra (Holo) (R) .60 1.50
- □ 85 Latias-EX (Holo) (R) 5.00 12.00
- □ 86 Latios-EX (Holo) (R) 4.00 10.00
- □ 87 Rattata (C) .10 .25
- □ 88 Raticate (R) .25 .60
- □ 89 Eevee (C) .10 .25
- □ 90 Eevee (C) .10 .25
- □ 91 Hoothoot (C) .10 .25
- □ 92 Noctowl (U) .15 .40
- □ 93 Miltank (U) .15 .40
- □ 94 Kecleon (R) .25 .60
- □ 95 Starly (C) .10 .25
- □ 96 Staravia (U) .15 .40
- □ 97 Staraptor (R) .25 .60
- □ 98 Tornadus-EX (Holo) (R) 5.00 12.00
- □ 99 Float Stone (U) .30 .75
- □ 100 Frozen City (U) .15 .40
- □ 101 Ghetsis (Holo) (R) 1.50 4.00
- □ 102 Shadow Triad (U) .15 .40
- □ 103 Superior Energy Retrieval (U) .30 .75
- □ 104 Team Plasma Badge (U) .15 .40
- □ 105 Team Plasma Ball (U) .30 .75
- □ 106 Plasma Energy (U) .15 .40
- □ 107 Life Dew (Holo) (R) 1.00 2.50
- □ 108 Rock Guard (Holo) (R) 1.00 2.50
- □ 109 Heatran-EX (Holo) (SR) 6.00 15.00
- □ 110 Thundurus-EX (Holo) (SR) 15.00 40.00
- □ 111 Deoxys-EX (Holo) (SR) 20.00 50.00
- □ 112 Latias-EX (Holo) (SR) 8.00 20.00
- □ 113 Latios-EX (Holo) (SR) 8.00 20.00
- □ 114 Tornadus-EX (Holo) (SR) 8.00 20.00
- □ 115 Ghetsis (Holo) (SR) 8.00 20.00
- □ 116 Professor Juniper (Holo) (SR) 20.00 40.00
- □ 117 Empoleon (UR) 10.00 25.00
- □ 118 Sigilyph (UR) 10.00 25.00
- □ 119 Garbodor (UR) 8.00 20.00
- □ 120 Garchomp (UR) 10.00 25.00
- □ 121 Max Potion (UR) 10.00 25.00
- □ 122 Ultra Ball (UR) 25.00 50.00

2013 Pokemon Black and White Plasma Freeze Reverse Foil

*Reverse Foil: .8X to 2X Basic Cards

2013 Pokemon Black and White Plasma Storm

- □ 1 Turtwig (C) .10 .25
- □ 2 Grotle (U) .20 .50
- □ 3 Torterra (R) .30 .75
- □ 4 Combee (C) .10 .25
- □ 5 Vespiquen (R) .30 .75
- □ 6 Cherubi (C) .10 .25
- □ 7 Cherrim (R) .30 .75
- □ 8 Sewaddle (C) .10 .25
- □ 9 Swadloon (U) .20 .50
- □ 10 Leavanny (R) .30 .75
- □ 11 Maractus (U) .20 .50
- □ 12 Foongus (C) .10 .25
- □ 13 Amoonguss (U) .20 .50
- □ 14 Moltres-EX (Holo) (R) 4.00 10.00
- □ 15 Chimchar (C) .10 .25
- □ 16 Monferno (U) .20 .50
- □ 17 Infernape (Holo) (R) .75 2.00
- □ 18 Victini-EX (Holo) (R) 6.00 15.00
- □ 19 Pansear (C) .10 .25
- □ 20 Simisear (U) .20 .50
- □ 21 Litwick (C) .10 .25
- □ 22 Lampent (U) .20 .50
- □ 23 Heatmor (U) .20 .50
- □ 24 Squirtle (C) .10 .25
- □ 25 Articuno-EX (Holo) (R) 6.00 15.00
- □ 26 Swinub (C) .10 .25
- □ 27 Piloswine (U) .20 .50
- □ 28 Mamoswine (R) .30 .75
- □ 29 Lotad (C) .10 .25
- □ 30 Lombre (U) .20 .50
- □ 31 Ludicolo (R) .30 .75
- □ 32 Carvanha (C) .10 .25
- □ 33 Sharpedo (R) .30 .75
- □ 34 Manaphy (Holo) (R) .60 1.50
- □ 35 Vanillite (C) .10 .25
- □ 36 Vanillish (U) .20 .50
- □ 37 Vanilluxe (R) .30 .75
- □ 38 Frillish (C) .10 .25
- □ 39 Jellicent (R) .30 .75
- □ 40 Cubchoo (C) .10 .25
- □ 41 Beartic (R) .30 .75
- □ 42 Magnemite (C) .10 .25
- □ 43 Magnemite (C) .10 .25
- □ 44 Magneton (U) .20 .50
- □ 45 Magneton (U) .20 .50
- □ 46 Magnezone (Holo) (R) 1.50 4.00
- □ 47 Magnezone (R) .30 .75
- □ 48 Zapdos-EX (Holo) (R) 5.00 12.00
- □ 49 Rotom (U) .20 .50
- □ 50 Joltik (C) .10 .25
- □ 51 Galvantula (U) .20 .50
- □ 52 Zubat (C) .10 .25
- □ 53 Zubat (C) .10 .25
- □ 54 Golbat (U) .20 .50
- □ 55 Crobat (Holo) (R) .75 2.00
- □ 56 Koffing (C) .10 .25
- □ 57 Koffing (U) .20 .50
- □ 58 Weezing (Holo) (R) .60 1.50
- □ 59 Ralts (C) .10 .25
- □ 60 Kirlia (U) .20 .50
- □ 61 Gallade (Holo) (R) .60 1.50
- □ 62 Giratina (R) .40 1.00
- □ 63 Trubbish (U) .20 .50
- □ 64 Trubbish (C) .10 .25
- □ 65 Trubbish (C) .10 .25

Card	Low	High
❑ 66 Garbodor (Holo) (R)	.40	1.00
❑ 67 Garbodor (R)	.30	.75
❑ 68 Elgyem (C)	.10	.25
❑ 69 Elgyem (U)	.20	.50
❑ 70 Beheeyem (R)	.30	.75
❑ 71 Phanpy (C)	.10	.25
❑ 72 Donphan (U)	.20	.50
❑ 73 Lunatone (U)	.20	.50
❑ 74 Solrock (U)	.20	.50
❑ 75 Riolu (C)	.10	.25
❑ 76 Riolu (C)	.10	.25
❑ 77 Lucario (U)	.20	.50
❑ 78 Lucario (Holo) (R)	.60	1.50
❑ 79 Timburr (C)	.10	.25
❑ 80 Gurdurr (U)	.20	.50
❑ 81 Conkeldurr (R)	.30	.75
❑ 82 Purrloin (C)	.10	.25
❑ 83 Purrloin (C)	.10	.25
❑ 84 Liepard (R)	.30	.75
❑ 85 Scraggy (C)	.10	.25
❑ 86 Scrafty (R)	.30	.75
❑ 87 Skarmory (R)	.30	.75
❑ 88 Klink (C)	.10	.25
❑ 89 Klang (U)	.20	.50
❑ 90 Klinklang (Holo) (R)	1.50	4.00
❑ 91 Durant (U)	.20	.50
❑ 92 Durant (U)	.20	.50
❑ 93 Cobalion-EX (Holo) (R)	8.00	20.00
❑ 94 Druddigon (R)	.30	.75
❑ 95 Black Kyurem-EX (Holo) (R)	10.00	25.00
❑ 96 White Kyurem-EX (Holo) (R)	4.00	10.00
❑ 97 Clefairy (C)	.10	.25
❑ 98 Clefable (R)	.30	.75
❑ 99 Doduo (C)	.10	.25
❑ 100 Dodrio (R)	.30	.75
❑ 101 Snorlax (R)	.40	1.00
❑ 102 Togepi (C)	.10	.25
❑ 103 Togetic (U)	.20	.50
❑ 104 Togekiss (Holo) (R)	.60	1.50
❑ 105 Whismur (C)	.10	.25
❑ 106 Loudred (U)	.20	.50
❑ 107 Exploud (R)	.30	.75
❑ 108 Lugia-EX (Holo) (R)	10.00	25.00
❑ 109 Skitty (C)	.10	.25
❑ 110 Patrat (C)	.10	.25
❑ 111 Patrat (C)	.10	.25
❑ 112 Watchog (U)	.20	.50
❑ 113 Watchog (R)	.30	.75
❑ 114 Bouffalant (R)	.30	.75
❑ 115 Rufflet (C)	.10	.25
❑ 116 Braviary (R)	.30	.75
❑ 117 Bicycle (U)	.30	.75
❑ 118 Colress (U)	.75	2.00
❑ 119 Colress Machine (U)	.50	1.25
❑ 120 Escape Rope (U)	.30	.75
❑ 121 Ether (U)	.30	.75
❑ 122 Eviolite (U)	.40	1.00
❑ 123 Hypnotoxic Laser (U)	2.00	5.00
❑ 124 Plasma Frigate (U)	.20	.50
❑ 125 Team Plasma Grunt (U)	.20	.50
❑ 126 Virbank City Gym (U)	.75	2.00
❑ 127 Plasma Energy (U)	.40	1.00
❑ 128 Dowsing Machine (Holo) (R)	2.50	6.00
❑ 129 Scramble Switch (Holo) (R)	3.00	8.00
❑ 130 Victory Piece (Holo) (R)	.75	2.00
❑ 131 Victini-EX (Holo) (SR)	8.00	20.00
❑ 132 Articuno-EX (Holo) (SR)	8.00	20.00
❑ 133 Cobalion-EX (Holo) (SR)	10.00	25.00
❑ 134 Lugia-EX (Holo) (SR)	12.00	30.00
❑ 135 Colress (Holo) (SR)	8.00	20.00
❑ 136 Charizard (UR)	25.00	50.00
❑ 137 Blastoise (UR)	20.00	40.00
❑ 138 Random Receiver (UR)	6.00	15.00

2013 Pokemon Black and White Plasma Storm Reverse Foil

*Reverse Foil: .8X to 2X Basic Cards

2004 Pokemon Organized Play Series 1

Released in Sept. 2004

Card	Low	High
Booster Pack (2 cards)	2.00	3.00
❑ 1 Blaziken (R)	.50	1.00
❑ 2 Metagross (R)	.50	1.00
❑ 3 Rayquaza (R)	.50	1.00
❑ 4 Sceptile (R)	.50	1.00
❑ 5 Swampert (R)	.50	1.00
❑ 6 Beautifly (U)	.20	.50
❑ 7 Masquerain (U)	.20	.50
❑ 8 Murkrow (U)	.20	.50
❑ 9 Pupitar (U)	.20	.50
❑ 10 Torkoal (U)	.20	.50
❑ 11 Larvitar (C)	.10	.20
❑ 12 Minun (C)	.10	.20
❑ 13 Plusle (C)	.20	.50
❑ 14 Surskit (C)	.10	.50
❑ 15 Swellow (C)	.10	.20
❑ 16 Armaldo ex (R)	4.00	10.00
❑ 17 Tyranitar ex (R)	5.00	10.00

2005 Pokemon Organized Play Series 2

Card	Low	High
Booster Pack (2 cards)	2.00	3.00
Released in Aug. 2005		
❑ 1 Entei (R)	.50	1.00
❑ 2 Pidgeot (R)	.50	1.00
❑ 3 Raikou (R)	.50	1.00
❑ 4 Suicune (R)	1.00	2.00
❑ 5 Tauros (R)	.50	1.00
❑ 6 Venusaur (R)	2.00	2.00
❑ 7 Ivysaur (U)	.20	.50
❑ 8 Mr. Briney's Compassion (U)	.20	.50
❑ 9 Multi Technical Machine 01 (U)	.20	.50
❑ 10 Pokémon Park (U)	.20	.50
❑ 11 TV Reporter (U)	.20	.50
❑ 12 Bulbasaur (C)	.10	.20
❑ 13 Cacnea (C)	.10	.20
❑ 14 Luvdisc (C)	.10	.20
❑ 15 Phanpy (C)	.10	.20
❑ 16 Pikachu (C)	.20	.50
❑ 17 Celebi ex (R)	4.00	8.00

2006 Pokemon Organized Play Series 3

Card	Low	High
Booster Pack (2 cards)	2.00	3.00
Released in April 2006		
❑ 1 Blastoise (Holo) (R)	10.00	20.00
❑ 1 Blastoise (R)	1.00	2.00
❑ 2 Flareon (Holo) (R)	4.00	10.00
❑ 2 Flareon (R)	1.00	2.00
❑ 3 Jolteon (Holo) (R)	4.00	10.00
❑ 3 Jolteon (R)	.50	1.00
❑ 4 Minun (R)	1.00	2.00
❑ 4 Minun (Holo) (R)	4.00	10.00
❑ 5 Plusle (Holo) (R)	4.00	10.00
❑ 5 Plusle (R)	1.00	2.00
❑ 6 Vaporeon (Holo) (R)	4.00	10.00
❑ 6 Vaporeon (R)	1.00	2.00
❑ 7 Combusken (U)	.20	.50
❑ 8 Donphan (U)	.20	.50
❑ 9 Forretress (U)	.20	.50
❑ 10 High Pressure System (U)	.20	.50
❑ 11 Low Pressure System (U)	.20	.50
❑ 12 Ditto (Mr. Mime) (C)	.10	.20
❑ 13 Eevee (C)	.10	.20
❑ 14 Ivysaur (C)	.10	.20
❑ 15 Marshtomp (C)	.10	.20
❑ 16 Pichu Bros. (C)	2.00	4.00
❑ 17 Ho-oh EX (Holo) (R)	5.00	12.00
❑ 17 Ho-oh EX (R)	1.00	2.00

2006 Pokemon Organized Play Series 4

Card	Low	High
Booster pack (2 cards)	2.00	3.00
Released in August 2006		
❑ 1 Chimecho (R)	1.00	2.00
❑ 2 Deoxys (R)	1.00	2.00
❑ 2 Deoxys (Holo) (R)	4.00	10.00
❑ 3 Flygon (Holo) (R)	3.00	6.00
❑ 3 Flygon (R)	1.00	2.00
❑ 4 Mew (R)	1.00	2.00
❑ 4 Mew (Holo) (R)	4.00	10.00
❑ 5 Sceptile (R)	1.00	2.00
❑ 6 Combusken (Holo) (R)	3.00	6.00
❑ 6 Combusken (U)	.20	.50
❑ 7 Grovyle (U)	.20	.50
❑ 8 Heal Energy (U)	.20	.50
❑ 9 Pokémon Fan Club (U)	.20	.50
❑ 10 Scramble Energy (U)	.20	.50
❑ 11 Mudkip (Holo) (R)	3.00	7.00
❑ 11 Mudkip (C)	.10	.20
❑ 12 Pidgey (C)	.10	.20
❑ 13 Pikachu (C)	.50	1.00
❑ 13 Pikachu (Holo) (R)	4.00	10.00
❑ 14 Squirtle (C)	.10	.20
❑ 15 Treecko (C)	.10	.20
❑ 16 Wobbuffet (C)	.10	.20
❑ 16 Wobbuffet (Holo) (R)	3.00	6.00
❑ 17 Deoxys EX (R)	1.00	2.00

2007 Pokemon Organized Play Series 5

Card	Low	High
Booster Pack (2 cards)	2.00	3.00
Released in March 2007		
❑ 1 Ho-Oh (R)	1.00	2.00
❑ 1 Ho-Oh (Holo) (R)	7.00	15.00
❑ 2 Lugia (R)	1.00	2.00
❑ 2 Lugia (Holo) (R)	7.00	15.00
❑ 3 Mew (R)	1.00	2.00
❑ 3 Mew (Holo) (R)	4.00	10.00
❑ 4 Double Rainbow Energy (R)	.50	1.00
❑ 5 Charmeleon (U)	.20	.50
❑ 6 Bill's Maintenance (U)	.20	.50
❑ 7 Rare Candy (U)	1.00	2.00
❑ 8 Boost Energy (U)	.20	.50
❑ 9 Delta Rainbow Energy (U)	.20	.50
❑ 10 Charmander (C)	.10	.20
❑ 11 Meowth (C)	.10	.20
❑ 12 Pikachu (C)	.50	1.00
❑ 12 Pikachu (Holo) (R)	4.00	10.00
❑ 13 Pikachu (C)	.50	1.00
❑ 14 Pelipper (C)	.10	.20
❑ 14 Pelipper (Holo) (R)	3.00	6.00
❑ 15 Zangoose (C)	.10	.20
❑ 15 Zangoose (Holo) (R)	3.00	6.00
❑ 16 Espeon (R)	9.00	15.00
❑ 17 Umbreon (R)	4.00	8.00

2007 Pokemon Organized Play Series 6

Card	Low	High
Booster Pack	2.00	3.00
Released in Sept. 2007		
❑ 1 Bastiodon (R)	1.00	2.00
❑ 2 Lucario (R)	1.00	2.00
❑ 3 Manaphy (R)	.50	1.00
❑ 3 Manaphy (Holo) (R)	3.00	6.00
❑ 4 Pachirisu (R)	1.00	2.00
❑ 5 Rampardos (R)	.50	1.00
❑ 6 Drifloon (U)	.20	.50
❑ 7 Gible (Holo) (R)	3.00	6.00
❑ 7 Gible (U)	.20	.50
❑ 8 Riolu (Holo) (R)	3.00	6.00
❑ 8 Riolu (U)	.20	.50
❑ 9 Pikachu (U)	.20	.50
❑ 9 Pikachu (Holo) (R)	4.00	10.00
❑ 10 Staravia (U)	.20	.50
❑ 11 Bidoof (C)	.10	.20
❑ 12 Buneary (C)	.10	.20
❑ 13 Cherubi (C)	.10	.20
❑ 14 Chimchar (Holo) (R)	4.00	8.00
❑ 14 Chimchar (C)	.10	.20
❑ 15 Piplup (Holo) (R)	5.00	10.00
❑ 15 Piplup (C)	.10	.20
❑ 16 Starly (C)	.10	.20
❑ 17 Turtwig (C)	.10	.20

2008 Pokemon Organized Play Series 7

Card	Low	High
Booster Pack (2 cards)	2.00	3.00
Released in Feb. 2008		
❑ 1 Ampharos (R)	2.00	5.00
❑ 2 Gallade (R)	4.00	8.00
❑ 3 Latias (R)	2.00	5.00
❑ 4 Latios (R)	2.00	4.00
❑ 5 Mothim (R)	2.00	4.00
❑ 6 Delibird (U)	.20	.50
❑ 7 Flaaffy (U)	.20	.50
❑ 8 Kirlia (U)	.20	.50
❑ 8 Kirlia (Holo) (R)	5.00	10.00
❑ 9 Stantler (U)	.20	.50
❑ 10 Wormadam (U)	.20	.50
❑ 11 Burmy (C)	.20	.50
❑ 12 Burmy (C)	.10	.20
❑ 13 Corsola (C)	.10	.20
❑ 14 Mareep (C)	.20	.50
❑ 15 Ralts (C)	.20	.50
❑ 16 Sentret (C)	.20	.50
❑ 17 Spinda (C)	.20	.50

2008 Pokemon Organized Play Series 8

Card	Low	High
❑ 1 Heatran (R)	2.00	4.00
❑ 2 Lucario (R)	5.00	10.00
❑ 3 Luxray (Holo) (R)	4.00	8.00
❑ 4 Probopass (Holo) (R)	4.00	8.00
❑ 5 Yanmega (R)	2.00	4.00
❑ 6 Cherrim (U)	.20	.50
❑ 7 Carnivine (U)	.20	.50
❑ 8 Luxio (U)	.20	.50
❑ 9 Night Maintenance (U)	.20	.50
❑ 10 Rare Candy (U)	2.00	4.00
❑ 11 Roseanne's Research (U)	2.00	4.00
❑ 12 Chimchar (C)	.10	.20
❑ 13 Croagunk (C)	.10	.20
❑ 14 Happiny (C)	.10	.20
❑ 15 Piplup (C)	.10	.20
❑ 16 Riolu (C)	.10	.20
❑ 17 Turtwig (C)	.10	.20

2009 Pokemon Organized Play Series 9

Card	Low	High
❑ 1 Garchomp	2.00	4.00
❑ 2 Manaphy	.20	.50
❑ 3 Raichu	.50	1.00
❑ 4 Regigigas	1.00	2.00
❑ 5 Rotom (Holo)	5.00	10.00
❑ 6 Buizel	.20	.50
❑ 7 Croagunk	.20	.50
❑ 8 Gabite	.20	.50
❑ 9 Lopunny	.20	.50
❑ 10 Pachirisu	.50	1.00
❑ 11 Pichu	.20	.50
❑ 12 Buneary	.20	.50
❑ 13 Chimchar	.20	.50
❑ 14 Gible	.20	.50
❑ 15 Pikachu	.50	1.00
❑ 16 Piplup	.20	.50
❑ 17 Turtwig	.20	.50

2008 Pokemon DP Promos

Card	Low	High
❑ DP1 Turtwig (Holo) (R)	5.00	10.00
❑ DP2 Chimchar (Holo) (R)	5.00	10.00
❑ DP3 Piplup (Holo) (R)	5.00	10.00
❑ DP4 Pachirisu (Holo) (R)	5.00	10.00
❑ DP5 Qtr Finalist Stamped	200.00	400.00
❑ DP5 Top 16 Stamped		
❑ DP5 Tropical Wind (WORLDS)	100.00	200.00
❑ DP5 No.1 Trainer		
❑ DP5 Staff Stamped	20.00	40.00
❑ DP5 No.3 Trainer (Holo) (R)		
❑ DP6 Buneary (Holo) (R)	3.00	6.00
❑ DP7 Cranidos (Holo) (R)	3.00	6.00
❑ DP8 Sheldon (Holo) (R)	3.00	6.00
❑ DP9 Torterra Lv. X (Holo) (R)	10.00	20.00
❑ DP10 Infernape Lv.X (Holo) (R)	10.00	20.00
❑ DP11 Empoleon Lv.X (Holo) (R)	5.00	10.00
❑ DP12 Lucario Lv.X (Holo) (R)	5.00	10.00
❑ DP13 Buizel (Holo) (R)	3.00	6.00
❑ DP14 Chatot (Holo) (R)	3.00	6.00
❑ DP15 Shinx (Holo) (R)	3.00	6.00
❑ DP16 Pikachu (Holo) (R)	20.00	30.00
❑ DP17 Dialga Lv.X (Holo) (R)	5.00	10.00
❑ DP18 Palkia Lv.X (Holo) (R)	5.00	10.00
❑ DP19 Darkrai Lv.X (Holo) (R)	5.00	10.00
❑ DP20 Magmortar (Holo) (R)	3.00	6.00
❑ DP21 Raichu (Holo) (R)	4.00	8.00
❑ DP22 Mime Jr (Holo) (R)	10.00	20.00
❑ DP23 Glameow (Holo) (R)	12.00	22.00
❑ DP24 Darkrai (Holo) (R)	5.00	8.00
❑ DP28 Mewtwo (Holo) (R)	4.00	5.00
❑ DP29 Rhyperior (Holo) (R)	6.00	12.00
❑ DP30 Regigigas (Holo) (R)	4.00	9.00
❑ DP31 Heatran (Holo) (R)	3.00	6.00
❑ DP32 Magnezone (Holo) (R)	1.00	3.00
❑ DP33 Dusknoir (Holo) (R)	1.00	3.00
❑ DP34 Drifblim (Holo) (R)	1.00	3.00
❑ DP35 Porygon Z (Holo) (R)	3.00	7.00
❑ DP36 Gliscor (Holo) (R)	5.00	10.00
❑ DP37 Dialga (Holo) (R)	5.00	10.00
❑ DP38 Giratina (Holo) (R)	8.00	16.00
❑ DP39 Shaymin (Holo) (R)	8.00	16.00
❑ DP40 Regigigas	3.00	6.00
❑ DP44 Magnezone	2.00	4.00

2008 Pokemon Burger King

Card	Low	High
Card Set (12)	12.00	20.00
Toy Set (12)	10.00	20.00
Toys (individually)	1.00	2.00
❑ 6 Lucario	1.00	2.00
❑ 9 Manaphy	1.00	3.00
❑ 35 Pachirisu	.50	1.00
❑ 49 Grotle	2.00	4.00
❑ 52 Happiny	.50	1.00
❑ 56 Monferno	.50	1.00
❑ 58 Prinplup	.50	1.00
❑ 76 Chimchar	.50	1.00
❑ 93 Piplup	.50	1.00
❑ 94 Pikachu	1.00	2.00
❑ 98 Shinx	.50	1.00
❑ 103 Turtwig	.50	1.00

2009 Pokemon Burger King Platinum

Card	Low	High
❑ 1 Chimchar	.25	.50
❑ 2 Dialga	1.00	2.00
❑ 3 Eevee	.25	.50
❑ 4 Giratina	1.00	2.00
❑ 5 Glaceon	.50	1.00
❑ 6 Leafeon	1.00	2.00
❑ 7 Meowth	.25	.50
❑ 8 Palkia	1.00	2.00
❑ 9 Pichu	.25	.50
❑ 10 Pikachu	.50	1.00
❑ 11 Piplup	.25	.50
❑ 12 Turtwig	.25	.50

1996 Pokemon Base Japanese

Card	Low	High
Complete Set (102)	60.00	85.00
Booster Box (60 ct)	40.00	80.00
Booster Pack (10 cards)	2.00	4.00
Starter Set (60 cards)	15.00	20.00
❑ 1 Bulbasaur (C)	.50	1.00
❑ 2 Ivysaur (U)	.75	2.00
❑ 3 Venusaur (holo) (R)	6.00	12.00
❑ 4 Charmander (C)	.50	1.00
❑ 5 Charmeleon (U)	1.00	2.00
❑ 6 Charizard (holo) (R)	12.00	20.00
❑ 7 Squirtle (C)	.50	1.00
❑ 8 Wartortle (U)	1.00	2.00
❑ 9 Blastoise (holo) (R)	6.00	10.00
❑ 10 Caterpie (C)	.25	.50
❑ 11 Metapod (C)	.25	.50
❑ 13 Weedle (C)	.25	.50
❑ 14 Kakuna (U)	.25	.50
❑ 15 Beedrill (R)	3.00	5.00
❑ 16 Pidgey (C)	.25	.50
❑ 17 Pidgeotto (R)	2.00	4.00
❑ 19 Rattata (C)	.25	.50
❑ 20 Raticate (U)	.50	1.00
❑ 25 Pikachu (C)	.50	1.50
❑ 26 Raichu (holo) (R)	4.00	8.00
❑ 27 Sandshrew (C)	.25	.50
❑ 32 Nidoran-M (C)	.25	.50
❑ 33 Nidorino (U)	.50	1.00
❑ 34 Nidoking (holo) (R)	3.00	6.00
❑ 35 Clefairy (holo) (R)	4.00	8.00
❑ 37 Vulpix (C)	.25	.50
❑ 38 Ninetales (holo) (R)	3.00	6.00
❑ 50 Diglett (C)	.25	.50
❑ 51 Dugtrio (R)	3.00	5.00
❑ 58 Growlithe (U)	.50	1.00
❑ 59 Arcanine (U)	.50	1.00
❑ 60 Poliwag (C)	.25	.50
❑ 61 Poliwhirl (U)	.50	1.00
❑ 62 Poliwrath (holo) (R)	2.00	4.00
❑ 63 Abra (C)	.25	.75
❑ 64 Kadabra (U)	.50	1.00
❑ 65 Alakazam (holo) (R)	4.00	8.00
❑ 66 Machop (C)	.25	.50
❑ 67 Machoke (U)	.50	1.00
❑ 68 Machamp (holo) (R)	4.00	7.00
❑ 77 Ponyta (C)	.25	.50
❑ 81 Magnemite (C)	.25	.50
❑ 82 Magneton (holo) (R)	3.00	6.00
❑ 83 Farfetch'd (U)	.50	1.00
❑ 84 Doduo (C)	.25	.50
❑ 86 Seel (U)	.50	1.00
❑ 87 Dewgong (U)	.50	1.00
❑ 92 Gastly (C)	.25	.50
❑ 93 Haunter (U)	.50	1.00
❑ 95 Onix (C)	.25	.50
❑ 96 Drowzee (C)	.25	.50
❑ 100 Voltorb (C)	.25	.50
❑ 101 Electrode (R)	2.00	5.00
❑ 107 Hitmonchan (holo) (R)	4.00	8.00
❑ 109 Koffing (C)	.25	.50
❑ 113 Chansey (holo) (R)	5.00	8.00
❑ 114 Tangela (C)	.25	.50
❑ 120 Staryu (C)	.25	.50
❑ 121 Starmie (C)	.25	.50
❑ 124 Jynx (U)	.50	1.00
❑ 125 Electabuzz (R)	3.00	5.00
❑ 126 Magmar (U)	1.00	2.00
❑ 129 Magikarp (U)	.50	1.00
❑ 130 Gyarados (holo) (R)	4.00	8.00
❑ 137 Porygon (U)	.50	1.00
❑ 145 Zapdos (holo) (R)	4.00	8.00
❑ 147 Dratini (U)	.50	1.00
❑ 148 Dragonair (R)	3.00	5.00
❑ 150 Mewtwo (holo) (R)	4.00	8.00
❑ NNO Trainer: Computer Search (R)	1.00	3.00
❑ NNO Trainer: Energy Retrieval (C)	.25	.50
❑ NNO Trainer: Item Finder (R)	1.00	3.00
❑ NNO Trainer: Pokédex (U)	.50	1.00
❑ NNO Trainer: Pokémon Trader (R)	2.00	4.00
❑ NNO Trainer: Scoop Up (R)	1.00	3.00
❑ NNO Trainer: Bill (C)	.25	.50
❑ NNO Trainer: Devolution Spray (R)	1.00	3.00
❑ NNO Trainer: Gust of Wind (C)	.25	.50
❑ NNO Trainer: Maintenance (U)	.50	1.00
❑ NNO Trainer: Pokémon Center (U)	1.00	2.00
❑ NNO Trainer: Professor Oak (U)	1.50	3.00
❑ NNO Trainer: Super Potion (U)	.50	1.00
❑ NNO Trainer: Clefairy Doll (R)	2.00	4.00
❑ NNO Trainer: Energy Removal (C)	.25	.50
❑ NNO Trainer: Imposter Prof. Oak (R)	1.00	3.00
❑ NNO Trainer: Plus Power (U)	.50	1.00
❑ NNO Trainer: Pokémon Flute (U)	1.00	2.00
❑ NNO Trainer: Revive (U)	.50	1.00
❑ NNO Trainer: Switch (C)	.50	1.00
❑ NNO Energy: Double Colorless (U)	.50	1.00
❑ NNO Trainer: Defender (U)	.50	1.00
❑ NNO Trainer: Full Heal (U)	.50	1.00
❑ NNO Trainer: Lass (R)	1.00	3.00
❑ NNO Trainer: Pokémon Breeder (R)	1.00	3.00
❑ NNO Trainer: Potion (C)	.25	.50
❑ NNO Trainer: Super Energy Removal (R)	1.00	3.00

1997 Pokemon Jungle Japanese

Card	Low	High
Complete Set (48)	40.00	65.00
Booster Box (60 ct)	50.00	90.00
Booster Pack (10 cards)	2.00	3.00
❑ 12 Butterfree (U)	.50	1.00
❑ 18 Pidgeot (holo) (R)	2.00	4.00
❑ 21 Spearow (C)	.25	.50
❑ 22 Fearow (U)	.50	1.00
❑ 25 Pikachu (C)	.75	1.50
❑ 29 Nidoran-F (C)	.25	.50
❑ 30 Nidorina (U)	.50	1.00
❑ 31 Nidoqueen (holo) (R)	2.00	4.00
❑ 36 Clefable (holo) (R)	2.00	4.00
❑ 39 Jigglypuff (C)	.50	1.00
❑ 40 Wigglytuff (holo) (R)	2.00	4.00
❑ 43 Oddish (C)	.25	.50
❑ 44 Gloom (U)	.50	1.00
❑ 45 Vileplume (holo) (R)	2.00	4.00
❑ 46 Paras (C)	.25	.50
❑ 47 Parasect (U)	.50	1.00
❑ 48 Venonat (C)	.25	.50
❑ 49 Venomoth (holo) (R)	2.00	4.00
❑ 52 Meowth (C)	.25	.50
❑ 53 Persian (U)	1.00	2.00
❑ 56 Mankey (C)	.25	.50
❑ 57 Primeape (U)	.50	1.00
❑ 69 Bellsprout (C)	.25	.50
❑ 70 Weepinbell (U)	.75	1.50
❑ 71 Victreebel (holo) (R)	2.00	4.00
❑ 78 Rapidash (U)	.75	1.50
❑ 85 Dodrio (U)	.75	1.50
❑ 101 Electrode (holo) (R)	2.00	4.00
❑ 102 Exeggcute (C)	.25	.50
❑ 103 Exeggutor (U)	.75	1.50
❑ 104 Cubone (C)	.25	.50
❑ 105 Marowak (U)	.50	1.50
❑ 108 Lickitung (U)	.75	1.50
❑ 111 Rhyhorn (C)	.25	.50
❑ 112 Rhydon (U)	.50	1.25
❑ 115 Kangaskhan (holo) (R)	2.00	4.00
❑ 118 Goldeen (C)	.25	.50
❑ 119 Seaking (U)	.50	1.25
❑ 122 Mime (holo) (R)	2.00	4.00
❑ 123 Scyther (holo) (R)	2.00	5.00
❑ 127 Pinsir (holo) (R)	2.00	4.00
❑ 128 Tauros (U)	.50	1.00
❑ 133 Eevee (C)	.25	.75
❑ 134 Vaporeon (holo) (R)	2.00	4.00
❑ 135 Jolteon (holo) (R)	2.00	4.00
❑ 136 Flareon (holo) (R)	2.00	4.00
❑ 143 Snorlax (holo) (R)	2.00	4.00
❑ NNO Trainer: Poké Ball (C)	.25	.50

1997 Pokemon Fossil Japanese

Card	Low	High
Complete Set (48)	50.00	65.00
Booster Box (60 ct)	75.00	100.00
Booster Pack (10 cards)	2.25	4.00

TCG/CCG

❑ 23 Ekans (C)	.25	.75
❑ 24 Arbok (U)	1.00	2.00
❑ 26 Raichu (holo) (R)	2.00	5.00
❑ 28 Sandslash (U)	.50	1.00
❑ 41 Zubat (C)	.25	.50
❑ 42 Golbat (U)	.50	1.50
❑ 54 Psyduck (C)	.25	.50
❑ 55 Golduck (U)	.50	1.00
❑ 72 Tentacool (C)	.25	.50
❑ 73 Tentacruel (U)	.50	1.00
❑ 74 Geodude (C)	.25	.50
❑ 75 Graveler (U)	.75	1.50
❑ 76 Golem (U)	.75	1.50
❑ 79 Slowpoke (C)	.25	.50
❑ 80 Slowbro (U)	.50	1.00
❑ 82 Magneton (holo) (R)	2.00	4.00
❑ 88 Grimer (C)	.25	.50
❑ 89 Muk (holo) (R)	2.00	4.00
❑ 90 Shellder (C)	.25	.50
❑ 91 Cloyster (U)	.50	1.00
❑ 92 Gastly (U)	.50	1.25
❑ 93 Haunter (holo) (R)	2.00	4.00
❑ 94 Gengar (holo) (R)	2.00	4.00
❑ 97 Hypno (holo) (R)	2.00	4.00
❑ 98 Krabby (C)	.25	.50
❑ 99 Kingler (U)	.50	1.00
❑ 106 Hitmonlee (holo) (R)	2.00	4.00
❑ 110 Weezing (U)	.50	1.25
❑ 116 Horsea (C)	.25	.50
❑ 117 Seadra (U)	1.00	2.00
❑ 126 Magmar (U)	1.00	2.00
❑ 131 Lapras (holo) (R)	2.00	4.00
❑ 132 Ditto (holo) (R)	2.00	4.00
❑ 138 Omanyte (C)	.25	.50
❑ 139 Omastar (U)	.50	1.00
❑ 140 Kabuto (C)	.25	.50
❑ 141 Kabutops (holo) (R)	2.00	4.00
❑ 142 Aerodactyl (holo) (R)	2.00	4.00
❑ 144 Articuno (holo) (R)	2.00	5.00
❑ 145 Zapdos (holo) (R)	2.00	4.00
❑ 146 Moltres (holo) (R)	2.00	5.00
❑ 149 Dragonite (holo) (R)	2.00	5.00
❑ 151 Mew (holo) (R)	7.00	15.00
❑ NNO Trainer: Fuji Old Man (U)	.50	1.00
❑ NNO Trainer: Energy Transfer (C)	.25	.50
❑ NNO Trainer: Mysterious Fossil (C)	.25	.50
❑ NNO Trainer: Gambler (Dice) (C)	.25	.50
❑ NNO Trainer: Recycle (C)	.25	.50

1997 Pokemon Team Rocket Japanese

Complete Set (65)	40.00	65.00
Booster Box (60 ct)	50.00	90.00
Booster Pack (10 cards)	1.00	3.00
❑ 4 Charmander (C)	.50	1.00
❑ 5 Charmeleon (U)	.50	1.00
❑ 6 Evil Charizard (holo) (R)	5.00	10.00
❑ 7 Squirtle (C)	.50	1.00
❑ 8 Evil Wartortle (U)	.50	1.00
❑ 9 Evil Blastoise (holo) (R)	3.00	6.00
❑ 19 Rattata (C)	.25	.50
❑ 20 Evil Raticate (C)	.25	.50
❑ 23 Ekans (C)	.25	.50
❑ 24 Evil Arbok (holo) (R)	2.00	4.00
❑ 41 Zubat (C)	.25	.50
❑ 42 Evil Golbat (holo) (R)	2.00	4.00
❑ 43 Oddish (C)	.25	.50
❑ 44 Evil Gloom (U)	.50	1.00
❑ 45 Evil Vileplume (holo) (R)	2.00	4.00
❑ 50 Diglett (C)	.25	.50
❑ 51 Evil Dugtrio (holo) (R)	2.00	4.00
❑ 52 Meowth (C)	.25	.75
❑ 53 Evil Persian (C)	.25	.75
❑ 54 Psyduck (C)	.25	.50
❑ 55 Evil Golduck (U)	.50	1.00
❑ 56 Mankey (C)	.25	.50
❑ 57 Evil Primeape (U)	.50	1.50
❑ 63 Abra (C)	.25	.50
❑ 64 Evil Kadabra (U)	1.00	2.00
❑ 65 Evil Alakazam (holo) (R)	2.00	4.00
❑ 66 Machop (C)	.25	.50
❑ 67 Evil Machoke (U)	.50	1.25
❑ 68 Evil Machamp (holo) (R)	2.00	4.00
❑ 77 Ponyta (C)	.25	.50
❑ 78 Evil Rapidash (C)	.25	.75
❑ 79 Slowpoke (C)	.25	.50
❑ 80 Evil Slowbro (holo) (R)	2.00	4.00
❑ 81 Magnemite (C)	.25	.50
❑ 82 Evil Magneton (holo) (R)	2.00	4.00
❑ 88 Grimer (C)	.25	.50
❑ 89 Evil Muk (U)	.50	1.00
❑ 96 Drowzee (C)	.25	.50
❑ 97 Evil Hypno (holo) (R)	2.00	4.00
❑ 100 Voltorb (C)	.25	.50
❑ 101 Evil Electrode (U)	.50	1.00
❑ 109 Koffing (C)	.25	.50
❑ 110 Evil Weezing (holo) (R)	2.00	4.00
❑ 129 Magikarp (C)	.25	.50
❑ 130 Evil Gyarados (holo) (R)	4.00	5.00
❑ 133 Eevee (C)	.25	.50
❑ 134 Evil Vaporeon (U)	.50	1.00
❑ 135 Evil Jolteon (U)	.50	1.00
❑ 136 Evil Flareon (U)	.50	1.00
❑ 137 Porygon (C)	.25	.50
❑ 147 Dratini (C)	.25	.50
❑ 148 Dragonair (U)	1.00	2.00
❑ 149 Evil Dragonite (holo) (R)	2.00	5.00
❑ NNO Trainer: Fumigation (C)	.25	.50
❑ NNO Trainer: Hitmonlee's Foot (U)	.75	1.50
❑ NNO Energy: Rainbow (holo) (R)	2.00	4.00
❑ NNO Trainer: Giovanni (U)	.75	2.00
❑ NNO Trainer: Landmines (C)	.25	.50
❑ NNO Energy: Super Potion (C)	.25	.50
❑ NNO T: Here Comes Team Rocket (holo) (R)	12.00	20.00
❑ NNO Trainer: Sleep! Sleep! (C)	.25	.50
❑ NNO Trainer: TR's Little Sister (holo.) (R)	3.00	6.00
❑ NNO Energy: Full Heal (C)	.25	.50
❑ NNO Trainer: Garbage Collection (C)	.25	.50
❑ NNO Trainer: Impostor Oak's Gang (U)	1.00	2.00

1998 Pokemon Gym Leaders 1 Japanese

Complete set (96)	40.00	80.00
Booster Box (60 ct)	60.00	95.00
Booster Pack (10 cards)	2.00	4.00
Nivi City Gym Deck #1 (Brock)	10.00	20.00
Hanada Gym Deck #2 (Misty)	8.00	16.00
Kuchiba Gym Deck #3 (Lt.Surge)	10.00	20.00
Tamamushi Gym Deck #4 (Erika)	10.00	20.00
Yamabuki Gym Deck #5 (Sabrina)	8.00	16.00
Gurne Gym Deck #6 (Blaine)	10.00	20.00
❑ 1 Bulbasaur (U)	1.00	2.00
❑ 19 Rattata (C)	.25	.50
❑ 20 Raticate (U)	.50	1.00
❑ 21 Spearow (C)	.25	.50
❑ 22 Fearow (holo) (R)	2.00	4.00
❑ 25 Pikachu (C)	.50	1.00
❑ 27 Sandshrew (C)	.25	.50
❑ 28 Sandslash (U)	.50	1.00
❑ 35 Clefairy (U)	.75	2.00
❑ 36 Clefable (holo) (R)	2.00	4.00
❑ 37 Vulpix (C)	.25	.50
❑ 37 Vulpix (U)	.50	2.00
❑ 38 Ninetales (holo) (R)	2.00	4.00
❑ 39 Jigglypuff (C)	.25	.50
❑ 41 Zubat (C)	.25	.50
❑ 42 Golbat (U)	.50	1.00
❑ 43 Oddish (C) Level 10	.25	.50
❑ 43 Oddish (C) Level 15	.25	.50
❑ 44 Gloom (U)	.50	2.00
❑ 45 Vileplume (holo) (R)	2.00	4.00
❑ 46 Paras (C)	.25	.50
❑ 50 Diglett (C)	.25	.50
❑ 54 Psyduck (C)	.25	.50
❑ 55 Golduck (holo) (R)	2.00	4.00
❑ 56 Mankey (C)	.25	.50
❑ 57 Primeape (U)	.50	1.00
❑ 60 Poliwag (C)	.25	.50
❑ 61 Poliwhirl (U)	1.00	2.00
❑ 69 Bellsprout (C)	.50	1.00
❑ 69 Bellsprout (U)	.50	1.50
❑ 70 Weepinbell (U)	.50	1.00
❑ 71 Victreebel (R)	1.00	2.00
❑ 72 Tentacool (U)	.50	1.00
❑ 73 Tentacruel (holo) (R)	2.00	4.00
❑ 74 Geodude (C) Level 13	.25	.50
❑ 74 Geodude (C) Level 15	.25	.50
❑ 75 Graveler (U)	1.00	2.00
❑ 76 Golem (R)	1.00	2.00
❑ 81 Magnemite (C)	.25	.50
❑ 81 Magnemite (U)	.50	1.00
❑ 82 Magneton (holo) (R)	2.00	4.00
❑ 86 Seel (C)	.25	.50
❑ 87 Dewgong (U)	.50	1.00
❑ 95 Onix (C)	.25	.50
❑ 100 Voltorb (C)	.25	.50
❑ 102 Exeggcute (U)	1.00	2.00
❑ 103 Exeggutor (U)	1.00	2.00
❑ 107 Hitmonchan (holo) (R)	2.00	5.00
❑ 108 Lickitung (U)	1.00	2.00
❑ 111 Rhyhorn (C)	.25	.50
❑ 112 Rhydon (holo) (R)	2.00	4.00
❑ 114 Tangela (C)	.25	.50
❑ 116 Horsea (C) Level 16	.25	.50
❑ 116 Horsea (C) Level 10	.25	.50
❑ 117 Seadra (holo) (R)	2.00	4.00
❑ 118 Goldeen (C)	.25	.50
❑ 120 Staryu (C)	.25	.50
❑ 123 Scyther (holo) (R)	3.00	6.00
❑ 125 Electabuzz (holo) (R)	2.00	4.00
❑ 129 Magikarp (C)	.25	.50
❑ 130 Gyarados (holo) (R)	2.00	4.00
❑ 133 Eevee (U)	1.00	2.00
❑ 135 Jolteon (R)	1.00	2.00
❑ 146 Moltres (holo) (R)	2.00	4.00
❑ 147 Dratini (U)	1.00	2.00
❑ 148 Dragonair (holo) (R)	2.00	5.00
❑ NNO Trainer: Brock Fighting Badge (R)	2.00	4.00
❑ NNO Trainer: Brock's Number One (R)	1.00	2.00
❑ NNO Trainer: Brock's Onix (U)	.50	1.00
❑ NNO Trainer: Energy Vortex (C)	.25	.50
❑ NNO Trainer: Erika w/Grass Badge (R)	1.00	2.00
❑ NNO Trainer: Erika Kneeling (U)	.50	1.00
❑ NNO Trainer: Erika's Perfume (U)	.50	1.00
❑ NNO Trainer: Erika's Servants (U)	.50	1.00
❑ NNO Trainer: Erika Thinking (R)	1.00	2.00
❑ NNO Trainer: Erika's Umbrella (R)	1.00	2.00
❑ NNO Trainer: Flare (R)	1.00	2.00
❑ NNO Trainer: Garden (U)	.50	1.00
❑ NNO Trainer: Laser (U)	.50	1.00
❑ NNO Trainer: Lt.Surge's Aim (R)	1.00	2.00
❑ NNO Trainer: Lt.Surge's Handshake (U)	.50	1.00
❑ NNO Trainer: Lt.Surge w/Lightning (R)	1.00	2.00
❑ NNO Trainer: Lt.Surge w/Raichu (U)	.50	1.00
❑ NNO Trainer: Misty's Anger w/Psyduck (U)	.50	1.00
❑ NNO Trainer: Misty's Heal w/Staryu (C)	.25	.50
❑ NNO Trainer: Misty's Love w/hearts (R)	1.00	2.00
❑ NNO Trainer: Misty's Peace (C)	.25	.50
❑ NNO Trainer: Misty w/Water Badge (R)	1.00	2.00
❑ NNO Trainer: No Energy Removal (R)	1.00	2.00
❑ NNO Trainer: Prison (R)	1.00	2.00
❑ NNO Trainer: Slowpoke's Brain (U)	.50	1.00
❑ NNO Trainer: Small Stadium (C)	.25	.50
❑ NNO Trainer: Stadium Psychedelic (R)	1.00	2.00
❑ NNO Trainer: Stadium Rock (U)	.50	1.00
❑ NNO Trainer: Rocket Girl Pointing (holo.) (R)	1.00	2.00
❑ NNO Trainer: Water (U)	.50	1.00

1998 Pokemon Gym Leaders 2 Japanese

Complete set (98)	40.00	60.00
Booster Box (60 ct)	55.00	85.00
Booster Pack (10 cards)	2.00	3.00
❑ 2 Ivysaur (U)	1.00	2.00
❑ 3 Venusaur (holo) (R)	3.00	6.00
❑ 4 Charmander (C)	.50	1.00
❑ 5 Charmeleon (U)	1.00	2.00
❑ 6 Charizard (holo) (R)	6.00	12.00
❑ 13 Weedle (C)	.25	.50
❑ 14 Kakuna (U)	1.00	2.00
❑ 15 Beedrill (holo) (R)	2.00	4.00
❑ 16 Pidgey Level 15 (C)	.25	.50
❑ 16 Pidgey Level 9 (U)	1.00	2.00
❑ 17 Pidgeotto (R)	1.00	2.00
❑ 23 Ekans (C)	.25	.50
❑ 24 Arbok (R)	1.00	2.00
❑ 26 Raichu (holo) (R)	2.00	5.00
❑ 29 Nidoran-F (C)	.25	.50
❑ 30 Nidorina (U)	.50	1.00
❑ 31 Nidoqueen (R)	1.00	2.00
❑ 32 Nidoran-M (C)	.25	.50
❑ 33 Nidorino (U)	.50	1.00
❑ 34 Nidoking (holo) (R)	2.00	4.00
❑ 37 Vulpix (C)	.25	.50
❑ 38 Ninetales (R)	1.00	2.00
❑ 41 Zubat (C)	.25	.50
❑ 42 Golbat (U)	.50	1.25
❑ 48 Venonat (C)	.25	.50
❑ 49 Venomoth (R)	1.00	2.00
❑ 51 Dugtrio (R)	1.00	2.00
❑ 52 Meowth Level 12 (U)	1.00	2.00
❑ 52 Meowth Level 17 (C)	.25	.50
❑ 53 Persian (holo) (R)	2.00	4.00
❑ 54 Psyduck (C)	.25	.50
❑ 55 Golduck (R)	1.00	2.00
❑ 56 Mankey (C)	.25	.50
❑ 58 Growlithe (C)	.25	.50
❑ 59 Arcanine (holo) (R)	2.00	4.00
❑ 62 Poliwrath (R)	1.00	2.00
❑ 63 Abra (C)	.25	.50
❑ 64 Kadabra (U)	1.00	2.00
❑ 65 Alakazam (holo) (R)	2.00	4.00
❑ 66 Machop (C)	.25	.50
❑ 67 Machoke (U)	.50	1.00
❑ 68 Machamp (holo) (R)	2.00	4.00
❑ 77 Ponyta (C)	.25	.50
❑ 78 Rapidash (U)	.50	1.25
❑ 79 Slowpoke (C)	.25	.50
❑ 80 Slowbro (U)	.50	1.00
❑ 84 Doduo Level 15 (R)(White Star)	5.00	12.00
❑ 84 Doduo Level 17 (C)	.25	.50
❑ 88 Grimer (C)	.25	.50
❑ 89 Muk (R)	2.00	4.00
❑ 92 Gastly (U)	.50	1.00
❑ 93 Haunter (U)	.50	1.00
❑ 94 Gengar (holo) (R)	2.00	4.00
❑ 96 Drowzee (C)	.25	.50
❑ 97 Hypno (U)	.50	1.00
❑ 109 Koffing Level 10 (C)	.25	.50
❑ 109 Koffing Level 15 (U)	.50	1.00
❑ 110 Weezing (U)	.50	1.00
❑ 111 Rhyhorn (C)	.25	.50
❑ 113 Chansey (U) (White Diamond)	5.00	12.00
❑ 114 Tangela (C)	.25	.50
❑ 115 Kangaskhan (U)	1.00	2.00
❑ 122 Mr. Mime (C)	.25	.75
❑ 124 Jynx (U)	.50	1.00
❑ 126 Magmar (U)	1.00	2.00
❑ 127 Pinsir (R)	1.00	2.00
❑ 128 Tauros (C)	.25	.50
❑ 129 Magikarp (C)	.25	.50
❑ 130 Gyarados (holo) (R)	2.00	4.00
❑ 132 Ditto (holo) (R)	2.00	4.00
❑ 137 Porygon (C)	.25	.75
❑ 143 Snorlax (R)	2.00	4.00
❑ 145 Zapdos (holo) (R)	3.00	6.00
❑ 146 Moltres (holo) (R)	3.00	6.00
❑ 150 Mewtwo (holo) (R)	4.00	8.00
❑ NNO Trainer: Blaine's Stare (U)	.50	1.00
❑ NNO Trainer: Blaine's Dice (C)	.25	.50
❑ NNO Trainer: Blaine's Fire Badge (R)	1.00	2.00
❑ NNO Trainer: Blaine's Poke Ball (U)	.50	1.00
❑ NNO Trainer: Cinnabar Island (U)	.50	1.00
❑ NNO Trainer: Contract Golbat/Koga's Skill (U)	8.00	20.00
❑ NNO Trainer: Fuschia City Gym (U)	.50	1.00
❑ NNO Trainer: Giovanni (holo) (R)	2.00	4.00
❑ NNO Trainer: Giovanni's Trump/Nidoking (R)	1.00	2.00
❑ NNO Trainer: Koga Badge (R)	1.00	2.00
❑ NNO Trainer: Phasing Unseen Wall (C)	.25	.50
❑ NNO Trainer: Pool Warp Point (C)	.25	.50
❑ NNO Trainer: Rocket's Test Potion (U)	.50	1.00
❑ NNO Trainer: Sabrina (R)	1.00	2.00
❑ NNO Trainer: Sabrina's Poke Ball (C)	.25	.50
❑ NNO Trainer: Sabrina's ESP (U)	.50	1.00
❑ NNO Trainer: Sabrina's Psychic Control (U)	.50	1.00
❑ NNO Trainer: Saffron City Gym (U)	.50	1.00
❑ NNO Trainer: Team Rocket Member (U)	.50	1.00
❑ NNO Trainer: Tickle Machine (U)	.50	1.00
❑ NNO Trainer: Trash Exchange (C)	.25	.50
❑ NNO Trainer: TR's Exploding Gym (U)	.50	1.00
❑ NNO Trainer: Viridian City (R)	1.00	2.00

2000 Pokemon Neo Japanese

Complete Set (96)	60.00	100.00
Booster Box (60 ct)	50.00	75.00
Booster Pack (10 cards)	3.00	4.00
Starter Set (60)	20.00	25.00
❑ 25 Pikachu (C)	.50	1.25
❑ 35 Clefairy (U)	.50	1.00
❑ 43 Oddish (C)	.25	.50
❑ 44 Gloom (U)	.50	1.00
❑ 79 Slowpoke (C)	.25	.50
❑ 95 Onix (C)	.25	.50
❑ 116 Horsea (C)	.25	.50
❑ 117 Seadra (U)	.50	1.00
❑ 125 Electabuzz (U)	.50	1.50
❑ 126 Magmar (U)	.50	1.00
❑ 152 Chikorita (C)	.50	1.00
❑ 153 Bayleef (U)	.50	2.00
❑ 154 Meganium (holo) (R)	2.00	4.00
❑ 155 Cyndaquil (C)	.25	.50
❑ 156 Quilava (U)	.50	1.00
❑ 157 Typhlosion (holo) (R)	2.00	4.00
❑ 158 Totodile (C)	.50	1.00
❑ 159 Croconaw (U)	.75	2.00
❑ 160 Feraligatr (holo) (R)	3.00	6.00
❑ 161 Sentret (C)	.25	.50
❑ 162 Furret (U)	.50	1.00
❑ 163 Hoothoot (C)	.50	1.00
❑ 164 Noctowl (U)	.50	1.00
❑ 165 Ledyba (C)	.25	.75
❑ 166 Ledian (U)	.50	1.00
❑ 167 Spinarak (C)	.25	.50
❑ 168 Ariados (U)	.50	1.00
❑ 170 Chinchou (C)	.25	.50
❑ 171 Lanturn (U)	.50	1.00
❑ 172 Pichu (holo) (R)	4.00	8.00
❑ 173 Cleffa (R)	2.00	4.00
❑ 175 Togepi (U)	1.00	2.00
❑ 176 Togetic (holo) (R)	2.00	4.00
❑ 177 Natu (C)	.25	.50
❑ 178 Xatu (U)	.50	1.00
❑ 179 Mareep (C)	.25	.50
❑ 180 Flaaffy (U)	.50	1.00
❑ 181 Ampharos (holo) (R)	2.00	4.00
❑ 182 Bellossom (holo) (R)	2.00	4.00
❑ 183 Marril (C)	1.50	3.00
❑ 184 Azumarill (holo) (R)	2.00	4.00
❑ 185 Sudowoodo (C)	.25	.50
❑ 187 Hoppip (C)	.25	.50
❑ 188 Skiploom (U)	.50	1.25
❑ 189 Jumpluff (holo) (R)	2.00	4.00
❑ 190 Aipom (U)	.50	1.00
❑ 191 Sunkern (C)	.25	.50
❑ 192 Sunflora (U)	.50	1.00
❑ 194 Wooper (C)	.75	1.50
❑ 195 Quagsire (U)	.50	1.00
❑ 198 Murkrow (R)	2.00	4.00
❑ 199 Slowking (holo) (R)	2.00	4.00
❑ 203 Girafarig(C)	.25	.50
❑ 207 Gligar (C)	.25	.50
❑ 208 Steelix (holo) (R)	2.00	4.00
❑ 209 Snubbull (C)	1.00	1.50
❑ 210 Granbull (U)	.75	1.75
❑ 213 Shuckle (C)	.25	.50
❑ 214 Heracross (holo) (R)	2.00	4.00
❑ 215 Sneasel (R)	2.00	4.00
❑ 220 Swinub (C)	.25	.50
❑ 221 Piloswine (U)	.50	1.00
❑ 226 Mantine (C)	.25	.50
❑ 227 Skarmory (holo) (R)	2.00	4.00
❑ 230 Kingdra (holo) (R)	2.00	4.00
❑ 231 Phanpy (U)	.50	1.00
❑ 232 Donphan (R)	1.00	2.00
❑ 234 Stantler (C)	.25	.50
❑ 239 Elekid (R)	1.00	2.00
❑ 240 Magby (R)	1.00	2.00
❑ 241 Miltank (U)	.50	1.00
❑ 249 Lugia (holo) (R)	6.00	12.00
❑ NNO Evil Energy (R)	1.00	2.00
❑ NNO Recycle Energy (R)	1.00	2.00
❑ NNO Steel Energy (holo) (R)	2.00	4.00
❑ NNO Trainer: Acorn (C)	.25	.50
❑ NNO Trainer: Bellsprout Tower (U)	.50	1.00
❑ NNO T: Bill's Transfer Device (U)	.50	1.00
❑ NNO Trainer: Card Machine (U)	.50	1.00
❑ NNO Trainer: Ekoro Gym (R)	1.00	2.00
❑ NNO Trainer: Energy Charge (R)	1.00	2.00
❑ NNO T: Fighting Spirit Headband (R)	1.00	2.00
❑ NNO Trainer: Golden Acorn (U)	.50	1.00
❑ NNO Trainer: Kurumi (radio) (R)	1.00	2.00
❑ NNO Trainer: Miracle Acorn (U)	.50	1.00
❑ NNO Trainer: Moo Moo Milk (C)	.25	.50
❑ NNO Trainer: New Pokédex (U)	.50	1.00
❑ NNO Trainer: Poké Gear (R)	1.00	2.00
❑ NNO Trainer: Pokémon Town (C)	.25	.50
❑ NNO Trainer: Professor Utsugi (U)	.50	1.00
❑ NNO T: Reverse Nomination (C)	.25	.50
❑ NNO Trainer: Slot Machine (R)	1.00	2.00
❑ NNO T: Super Energy Retrieval (R)	1.00	2.00
❑ NNO Trainer: Super Rod (C)	.25	.50
❑ NNO Trainer: Super Scoop Up (U)	.50	1.00
❑ NNO Trainer: Time Capsule (R)	1.00	2.00

2000 Pokemon Neo 2 Japanese

Complete Set (57)	30.00	50.00
Unopened Box (60 ct)	40.00	60.00
Unopened Pack (10 cards)	2.00	4.00
❑ 10 Caterpie (C)	.25	.50
❑ 11 Metapod (U)	.50	1.00
❑ 12 Butterfree (holo) (R)	2.00	4.00
❑ 13 Weedle (C)	.25	.50
❑ 14 Kakuna (U)	.50	1.00
❑ 15 Beedrill (holo) (R)	2.00	4.00
❑ 26 Dark Raichu (holo) (R)	3.00	6.00
❑ 60 Poliwag (C)	.25	.50
❑ 61 Poliwhirl (U)	.50	1.00
❑ 62 Poliwrath (holo) (R)	2.00	4.00
❑ 81 Magnemite (holo) (R)	2.00	4.00
❑ 123 Scyther (U)	.50	1.00
❑ 133 Eevee (U)	.50	1.00
❑ 138 Omanyte (C)	.25	.50
❑ 139 Omastar (U)	.50	1.00
❑ 140 Kabuto (C)	.25	.50
❑ 141 Kabutops (holo) (R)	2.00	4.00
❑ 161 Sentret (C)	.10	.25
❑ 167 Spinarak (C)	.25	.50
❑ 174 Igglybuff (U)	.50	1.00
❑ 177 Natu (C)	.25	.50
❑ 178 Xatu (U)	.50	1.00
❑ 179 Mareep (C)	.25	.50
❑ 186 Politoed (holo) (R)	2.00	4.00
❑ 187 Hoppip (C)	.25	.50
❑ 193 Yanma (holo) (R)	2.00	4.00
❑ 194 Wooper (C)	.25	.50
❑ 196 Espeon (holo) (R)	3.00	6.00
❑ 197 Umbreon (holo) (R)	2.00	4.00
❑ 201 Unown I (C)	.25	.75
❑ 201 Unown F (U)	1.00	2.00
❑ 201 Unown D (U)	.75	1.50
❑ 201 Unown U (U)	2.00	3.00
❑ 201 Unown A (holo) (R)	2.00	4.00
❑ 201 Unown M (U)	.50	1.00
❑ 202 Wobbuffet (holo) (R)	2.00	4.00
❑ 204 Pineco (C)	.25	.50
❑ 205 Forretress (holo) (R)	2.00	4.00
❑ 206 Dunsparce (C)	.25	.50
❑ 212 Scizor (holo) (R)	3.00	6.00
❑ 216 Teddiursa (C)	.25	.50
❑ 217 Ursaring (holo) (R)	2.00	4.00
❑ 222 Corsola (U)	.50	1.00
❑ 228 Houndour (U)	.50	1.25
❑ 228 Houndour (holo) (R)	3.00	6.00
❑ 229 Houndoom (holo) (R)	3.00	6.00
❑ 235 Smeargle (holo) (R)	2.00	4.00
❑ 236 Tyrogue (C)	.25	.50
❑ 237 Hitmontop (holo) (R)	2.00	4.00
❑ 246 Larvitar (C)	.25	.50
❑ 247 Pupitar (U)	.50	1.00
❑ 248 Tyranitar (holo) (R)	3.00	6.00
❑ NNO Trainer: Egg (U)	.50	1.00
❑ NNO Trainer: Energy Ark (C)	.50	1.00
❑ NNO Trainer: Hyper Spray (U)	.50	1.00
❑ NNO Trainer: Ruin Wall Pikachu (U)	1.00	2.00
❑ NNO Trainer: Ruin Wall Raichu (U)	.75	1.50

2001 Pokemon Neo 3 Japanese

Complete Set (57)	35.00	60.00
Unopened Box (60 ct)	40.00	60.00
Unopened Pack (10 cards)	1.00	2.00
❑ 26 Raichu (U)	.50	1.25
❑ 41 Zubat (C)	.25	.50
❑ 42 Golbat (C)	.25	.50
❑ 46 Paras (C)	.25	.50
❑ 47 Parasect (U)	.50	1.00
❑ 74 Geodude (C)	.25	.50
❑ 75 Graveler (U)	.50	1.00
❑ 82 Magneton (holo) (R)	2.00	4.00
❑ 83 Farfetch'd (C)	.25	.50
❑ 118 Goldeen (C)	.25	.50
❑ 119 Seaking (U)	.50	1.00
❑ 120 Staryu (C)	.25	.50
❑ 121 Starmie (holo) (R)	2.00	4.00
❑ 124 Jynx (U)	.50	1.00
❑ 129 Magikarp (holo) (UR)	6.00	12.00
❑ 130 Gyarados (holo) (UR)	6.00	12.00
❑ 142 Aerodactyl (holo) (R)	2.00	4.00
❑ 169 Crobat (holo) (R)	2.00	4.00
❑ 170 Chinchou (C)	.25	.50
❑ 171 Lanturn (U)	.50	1.00
❑ 180 Flaaffy (U)	.50	1.00
❑ 181 Ampharos (holo) (R)	2.00	4.00
❑ 188 Skiploom (C)	.25	.50
❑ 189 Jumpluff (holo) (R)	2.00	4.00
❑ 190 Aipom (C)	.25	.50

TCG/CCG

❑ 195 Quagsire (C) .25 .50
❑ 198 Murkrow (C) .25 .50
❑ 200 Misdreavus (holo) (R) 2.00 4.00
❑ 201 Unown K (C) 2.00 4.00
❑ 201 Unown B (U) 1.50 3.00
❑ 201 Unown Y (U) 1.50 3.00
❑ 209 Snubbull (C) .25 .50
❑ 211 Qwilfish (C) .25 .50
❑ 213 Shuckle (U) .50 1.00
❑ 218 Slugma (C) .25 .50
❑ 219 Magcargo (U) .50 1.00
❑ 220 Swinub (C) .25 .50
❑ 221 Piloswine (U) .50 1.00
❑ 223 Remoraid (C) .25 .50
❑ 224 Octillery (U) .50 1.00
❑ 225 Delibird (holo) (R) 2.00 4.00
❑ 229 Houndoom (holo) (R) 3.00 4.00
❑ 230 Kingdra (holo) (R) 2.00 4.00
❑ 233 Porygon2 (holo) (R) 2.00 4.00
❑ 234 Stantler (U) .50 1.00
❑ 238 Smoochum (C) .25 .50
❑ 242 Blissey (holo) (R) 2.00 4.00
❑ 243 Raikou (holo) (R) 2.00 4.00
❑ 244 Entei (holo) (R) 2.00 4.00
❑ 245 Suicune (holo) (R) 3.00 5.00
❑ 250 Ho-oh (holo) (R) 3.00 5.00
❑ 251 Celebi (holo) (R) 3.00 5.00
❑ NNO Trainer: Rocket's Gengar R (U) .50 1.00
❑ NNO Trainer: Dragonite (U) .50 1.00
❑ NNO Trainer: Old Fishing Rod (C) .25 .50
❑ NNO Trainer: Seed (U) .50 1.00
❑ NNO Trainer: Stadium (U) .50 1.00

2001 Pokemon Neo 4 Japanese

Complete Set (113) 100.00 200.00
Unopened Box (60 ct) 75.00 125.00
Unopened Pack (10 cards) 2.00 4.00

❑ 6 Charizard (foil) (UR) 10.00 20.00
❑ 26 Raichu (foil) (UR) 5.00 10.00
❑ 37 Vulpix (C) .25 .50
❑ 38 Ninetales (U) .50 1.00
❑ 39 Jigglypuff (C) .25 .50
❑ 40 Wigglytuff Lv.33 (U) .50 1.00
❑ 40 Wigglytuff Lv.24 (U) .50 1.00
❑ 48 Venonat (C) .25 .50
❑ 49 Venomoth (U) .50 1.00
❑ 54 Psyduck (C) .25 .50
❑ 55 Golduck (U) .50 1.00
❑ 58 Growlithe (C) .25 .50
❑ 59 Arcanine (holo) (R) 3.00 6.00
❑ 66 Machop (C) .25 .50
❑ 67 Machoke (U) .50 1.00
❑ 68 Machamp (R) 1.00 2.00
❑ 80 Slowbro (U) .50 1.00
❑ 86 Seel (C) .25 .50
❑ 87 Dewgong (U) .50 1.00
❑ 92 Gastly (C) .25 .50
❑ 93 Haunter (U) .50 1.00
❑ 94 Gengar (holo) (R) 3.00 6.00
❑ 102 Exeggcute (C) .25 .50
❑ 103 Exeggutor (U) .25 .50
❑ 106 Hitmonlee (U) .50 1.00
❑ 107 Hitmonchan (C) .25 .50
❑ 113 Chansey (U) .50 1.00
❑ 123 Scyther (U) .50 1.00
❑ 134 Vaporeon (U) .50 1.00
❑ 135 Jolteon (U) .50 1.00
❑ 136 Flareon (U) .50 1.00
❑ 137 Porygon (C) .25 .50
❑ 138 Omanyte (C) .25 .50
❑ 139 Omastar (R) 1.00 2.00
❑ 141 Kabutops (foil) (UR) 5.00 10.00
❑ 147 Dratini (C) .25 .50
❑ 148 Dragonair (R) 1.00 2.00
❑ 149 Dragonite (holo) (R) 3.00 6.00
❑ 150 Mewtwo (foil) (UR) 8.00 12.00
❑ 155 Cyndaquil (C) .25 .50
❑ 156 Quilava (U) .50 1.00
❑ 157 Typhlosion (holo) (R) 3.00 5.00
❑ 158 Totodile (C) .25 .50
❑ 159 Croconaw (U) .25 .50
❑ 160 Feraligatr (holo) (R) 3.00 5.00
❑ 164 Noctowl (foil) (UR) 8.00 12.00
❑ 165 Ledyba (C) .25 .50
❑ 166 Ledian (R) 1.00 2.00
❑ 168 Ariados (R) 1.00 2.00
❑ 169 Crobat (holo) (R) 2.00 5.00
❑ 171 Lanturn (R) .50 1.00
❑ 175 Togepi (C) .25 .50
❑ 176 Togetic (holo) (R) 2.00 5.00
❑ 179 Mareep (C) .25 .50
❑ 180 Flaffy (U) .50 1.00
❑ 181 Ampharos (holo) (R) 2.00 5.00
❑ 184 Azumarill (holo) (R) 2.00 4.00
❑ 191 Sunkern (C) .25 .50
❑ 192 Sunflora (C) .25 .50
❑ 196 Espeon (holo) (R) 3.00 6.00
❑ 199 Slowking (R) 1.00 2.00
❑ 201 Unown H (R) 1.00 2.00
❑ 201 Unown S (R) 1.00 2.00
❑ 201 Unown X (R) 1.00 2.00
❑ 201 Unown G (R) 1.00 2.00
❑ 201 Unown Q (U) 2.00 4.00
❑ 201 Unown W (R) 2.00 4.00
❑ 201 Unown L (C) 1.00 3.00
❑ 201 Unown T (R) 1.00 2.00
❑ 201 Unown Z (U) 3.00 5.00
❑ 201 Unown C (U) 3.00 5.00
❑ 201 Unown P (U) 2.00 4.00
❑ 201 Unown V (C) 1.00 3.00
❑ 203 Girafarig (C) .25 .50
❑ 204 Pineco (C) .25 .50
❑ 205 Forretress (U) .50 1.00
❑ 207 Gligar (C) .25 .50
❑ 208 Steelix (foil) (UR) 3.00 6.00
❑ 212 Scizor (holo) (R) 3.00 7.00
❑ 214 Heracross (U) .50 1.00
❑ 217 Ursaring (R) 1.00 2.00
❑ 218 Slugma (C) .25 .50
❑ 219 Magcargo (R) 1.00 2.00
❑ 220 Swinub (C) .25 .50
❑ 221 Piloswine (R) 1.00 2.00
❑ 223 Remoraid (C) .25 .50
❑ 224 Octillery (U) .50 1.00
❑ 226 Mantine (C) .25 .50
❑ 228 Houndour (C) .25 .50
❑ 229 Houndoom (holo) (R) 3.00 6.00
❑ 231 Phanpy (C) .25 .50
❑ 232 Donphan (holo) (R) 3.00 6.00
❑ 233 Porygon2 (holo) (R) 3.00 6.00
❑ 246 Larvitar (C) .25 .50
❑ 247 Pupitar (U) .50 1.00
❑ 248 Tyranitar (foil) (UR) 6.00 10.00
❑ 248 Tyranitar (holo) (R) 4.00 8.00
❑ 251 Celebi (foil) (UR) 5.00 10.00
❑ NNO Trainer: Energy Stadium (U) .50 1.00
❑ NNO Trainer: Experience Share (R) 1.00 2.00
❑ NNO Trainer: Rocket's Secret Machine (R) 1.00 2.00
❑ NNO Trainer: Impostor Oak's Invention (R) 1.00 2.00
❑ NNO Trainer: Bumpy Gym (R) 1.00 2.00
❑ NNO Trainer: Bill's Mail (C) .25 .50
❑ NNO Trainer: All-Purpose Powder (C) .25 .50
❑ NNO Miracle Energy (holo) (R) 2.00 4.00
❑ NNO Trainer: Counter Claw (U) .50 1.00
❑ NNO Trainer: Energy Amplifier (U) .50 1.00
❑ NNO Trainer: Team Rocket's Secret Maneuvers (U) .50 1.00
❑ NNO Trainer: Radio Tower (R) 1.00 2.00
❑ NNO Trainer: Scope Lens (U) .50 1.00
❑ NNO Trainer: Determine Personality (U) 1.00 2.00
❑ NNO Trainer: Lucky Stadium (U) .50 1.00

2001 Pokemon VS 1st Edition Japanese

Complete Set (144) 150.00 300.00
Fire/Water Booster Box (10 ct.) 60.00 100.00
Grass/Lightning Booster Box (10 ct.) 60.00 100.00
Psychic/Fighting Booster Box (10 ct.) 60.00 100.00
Fire/Water Pack (30 cards) 8.00 12.00
Grass/Lightning Pack (30 cards) 8.00 12.00
Psychic/Fighting Pack (30 cards) 8.00 12.00

❑ 1 Pidgeot (C) .50 1.00
❑ 2 Fearow (C) .75 1.50
❑ 3 Farfetch'd (C) .50 1.00
❑ 4 Dodrio (C) .50 1.00
❑ 5 Togetic (C) .50 1.00
❑ 6 Delibird (C) .50 1.00
❑ 7 Skarmory (holo) (R) 3.00 6.00
❑ 8 Butterfree (C) .50 1.00
❑ 9 Beedrill (C) 1.00 2.00
❑ 10 Pinsir (C) 1.00 2.00
❑ 11 Ledian (C) 1.00 2.00
❑ 12 Yanma (C) .50 1.00
❑ 13 Scizor (holo) (R) 3.00 6.00
❑ 14 Clefable (C) .50 1.00
❑ 15 Wigglytuff (C) .50 1.00
❑ 16 Persian (C) .50 1.00
❑ 17 Lickitung (C) .50 1.00
❑ 18 Furret (C) .50 1.00
❑ 19 Miltank (C) .50 1.00
❑ 20 Ninetails (C) .50 1.00
❑ 21 Gengar (C) .50 1.00
❑ 22 Hypno (C) .50 1.00
❑ 23 Marowak (C) .50 1.00
❑ 24 Noctowl (C) .50 1.00
❑ 25 Murkrow (holo) (R) 3.00 6.00
❑ 26 Misdreavus (C) .50 1.00
❑ 27 Raichu (C) 1.00 2.00
❑ 28 Magneton (C) .50 1.00
❑ 29 Electabuzz (C) .50 1.00
❑ 30 Jolteon (C) .50 1.00
❑ 31 Ampharos (C) .50 1.00
❑ 32 Steelix (C) .50 1.00
❑ 33 Primeape (C) .50 1.00
❑ 34 Poliwrath (C) .50 1.00
❑ 35 Rhydon (C) .50 1.00
❑ 36 Tauros (C) .50 1.00
❑ 37 Granbull (C) .50 1.00
❑ 38 Donphan (C) 1.00 2.00
❑ 39 Dewgong (C) .50 1.00
❑ 40 Cloyster (C) 1.00 2.00
❑ 41 Lapras (C) .50 1.00
❑ 42 Articuno (C) .50 1.00
❑ 43 Sneasel (holo) (R) 3.00 6.00
❑ 44 Piloswine (C) .50 1.00
❑ 45 Delibird (C) .50 1.00
❑ 46 Blastoise (C) 1.00 2.00
❑ 47 Jynx (C) .50 1.00
❑ 48 Gyarados (C) .50 1.00
❑ 49 Dragonite (C) .50 1.00
❑ 50 Politoed (C) .50 1.00
❑ 51 Mantine (C) .50 1.00
❑ 52 Kingdra (C) .50 1.00
❑ 53 Raichu (C) .75 1.50
❑ 54 Lanturn (C) .50 1.00
❑ 55 Xatu (C) .50 1.00
❑ 56 Espeon (C) .75 1.50
❑ 57 Lapras (C) .50 1.00
❑ 58 Quagsire (C) .50 1.00
❑ 59 Bellossom (C) .50 1.00
❑ 60 Jumpluff (C) .50 1.00
❑ 61 Beedrill (C) .50 1.00
❑ 62 Arbok (C) .50 1.00
❑ 63 Venomoth (C) .50 1.00
❑ 64 Weezing (C) .50 1.00
❑ 65 Ariados (C) .50 1.00
❑ 66 Crobat (C) .50 1.00
❑ 67 Shuckle (C) .50 1.00
❑ 68 Omastar (C) .50 1.00
❑ 69 Kabutops (C) .50 1.00
❑ 70 Typhlosion (C) .50 1.00
❑ 71 Slugma (C) .50 1.00
❑ 72 Slowbro (C) .50 1.00
❑ 73 Exeggutor (C) .50 1.00
❑ 74 Jynx (C) .50 1.00
❑ 75 Xatu (C) .50 1.00
❑ 76 Espeon (C) 1.00 2.00
❑ 77 Slowking (C) .50 1.00
❑ 78 Girafarig (C) 1.00 2.00
❑ 79 Crobat (C) .50 1.00
❑ 80 Forretress (C) .50 1.00
❑ 81 Machamp (C) .50 1.00
❑ 82 Hitmonlee (C) .50 1.00
❑ 83 Hitmonchan (C) .50 1.00
❑ 84 Steelix (holo) (R) 3.00 6.00
❑ 85 Ursaring (C) .50 1.00
❑ 86 Hitmontop (C) .50 1.00
❑ 87 Rapidash (C) 1.00 2.00
❑ 88 Magmar (C) .50 1.00
❑ 89 Flareon (C) .50 1.00
❑ 90 Tyranitar (holo) (R) 4.00 8.00
❑ 91 Umbreon (holo) (R) 2.00 5.00
❑ 92 Houndoom (C) 2.00 4.00
❑ 93 Wobbuffet (holo) (R) 2.00 4.00
❑ 94 Raikou (holo) (R) 2.00 4.00
❑ 95 Entei (holo) (R) 3.00 7.00
❑ 96 Suicune (holo) (R) 3.00 6.00
❑ 97 Charizard (C) 2.00 4.00
❑ 98 Gyarados (C) .75 1.50
❑ 99 Aerodactyl (C) .75 1.50
❑ 100 Dragonite (C) .75 1.50
❑ 101 Ampharos (C) .75 1.50
❑ 102 Kingdra (C) .75 1.50
❑ 103 Trainer: Falkner's TM 01 (U) .75 1.50
❑ 104 Trainer: Falkner's TM 02 (U) 1.00 2.00
❑ 105 Trainer: Bugsy's TM 01 (U) 1.00 2.00
❑ 106 Trainer: Bugsy's TM 02 (U) .75 1.50
❑ 107 Trainer: Whitney's TM 01 (U) 1.00 2.00
❑ 108 Trainer: Whitney's TM 02 (U) 2.00 4.00
❑ 109 Trainer: Morty's TM 01 (U) .75 1.50
❑ 110 Trainer: Morty's TM 02 (U) .75 1.50
❑ 111 Trainer: Jasmine's TM 01 (U) 1.00 2.00
❑ 112 Trainer: Jasmine's TM 02 (U) 1.00 2.00
❑ 113 Trainer: Chuck's TM 01 (U) 1.00 2.00
❑ 114 Trainer: Chuck's TM 02 (U) .75 1.50
❑ 115 Trainer: Pryce's TM 01 (U) .75 1.50
❑ 116 Trainer: Pryce's TM 02 (U) .75 1.50
❑ 117 Trainer: Clair's TM 01 (U) 1.00 2.00
❑ 118 Trainer: Clair's TM 02 (U) .75 1.50
❑ 119 Trainer: Janine's TM 01 (U) 1.00 2.00
❑ 120 Trainer: Janine's TM 02 (U) 1.00 2.00
❑ 121 Trainer: Will's TM 01 (U) .75 1.50
❑ 122 Trainer: Will's TM 02 (U) .75 1.50
❑ 123 Trainer: Bruno's TM 01 (U) .75 1.50
❑ 124 Trainer: Bruno's TM 02 (U) 1.00 2.00
❑ 125 Trainer: Karen's TM 01 (U) 1.00 2.00
❑ 126 Trainer: Karen's TM 02(U) .75 1.50
❑ 127 Trainer: Team Rocket's TM 01 (U) .75 1.50
❑ 128 Trainer: Lance's TM 01 (U) 1.00 2.00
❑ 129 Trainer: Lance's TM 02 (U) 1.00 2.00
❑ 130 Trainer: Potion (C) .50 1.00
❑ 131 Trainer: Moo-Moo Milk (C) .50 1.00
❑ 132 Trainer: Full Heal (C) .75 1.50
❑ 133 Trainer: Pokemon Reverse (C) .75 1.50
❑ 134 Trainer: Switch (C) .50 1.00
❑ 135 Trainer: Warp Point (C) .50 1.00
❑ 136 Trainer: Super Scoop Up (C) .50 1.00
❑ 137 Trainer: Energy Flow (C) .75 1.50
❑ 138 Trainer: Super Energy Retrieval (C) .75 1.50
❑ 139 Trainer: Energy Ark (C) .75 1.50
❑ 140 Trainer: Energy Revive (C) .75 1.50
❑ 141 Trainer: Master Ball (C) .50 1.00
❑ NNO Dark Energy (holo) 2.00 4.00
❑ NNO Metal Energy (holo) 2.00 4.00
❑ NNO Rainbow Energy (holo) 2.00 4.00

2001 Pokemon E Cards Series 1 Japanese

Complete Set (128) 125.00 180.00
Booster Box (40 ct) 75.00 120.00
Booster Pack (5 cards) 3.00 6.00

❑ 1 Koffing (C) .25 .50
❑ 2 Hoppop (C) .25 .50
❑ 3 Caterpie (C) .25 .50
❑ 4 Ekans (C) .25 .50
❑ 5 Oddish (C) .25 .50
❑ 6 Vulpix (C) .25 .50
❑ 7 Ponyta (C) .25 .50
❑ 8 Poliwag (C) .25 .50
❑ 9 Shellder (C) .25 .50
❑ 10 Krabby (C) .25 .50
❑ 11 Goldeen (C) .25 .50
❑ 12 Magikarp (C) .25 .50
❑ 13 Marill (C) .25 .50
❑ 14 Quilfish (C) .25 .50
❑ 15 Corsola (C) .25 .50
❑ 16 Pikachu (C) .50 1.00
❑ 17 Mareep (C) .25 .50
❑ 18 Abra (C) .25 .50
❑ 19 Gastly (C) .25 .50
❑ 20 Diglett (C) .25 .50
❑ 21 Machop (C) .25 .50
❑ 22 Geodude (C) .25 .50
❑ 23 Cubone (C) .25 .50
❑ 24 Larvitar (C) .25 .50
❑ 25 Pidgey (C) .25 .50
❑ 26 Rattata (C) .25 .50
❑ 27 Spearow (C) .25 .50
❑ 28 Clefairy (C) .25 .50
❑ 29 Meowth (C) .25 .50
❑ 30 Tauros (C) .25 .50
❑ 31 Dratini (C) .25 .50
❑ 32 Houndour (C) .25 .50
❑ 33 Metapod (U) .50 1.00
❑ 34 Gloom (U) .50 1.00
❑ 35 Magmar (U) .50 1.00
❑ 36 Poliwhirl (U) .50 1.00
❑ 37 Jynx (U) .50 1.00
❑ 38 Electabuzz (U) .50 1.00
❑ 39 Flaaffy (U) .50 1.00
❑ 40 Kadabra (U) .50 1.00
❑ 41 Haunter (U) .50 1.00
❑ 42 Machoke (U) .50 1.00
❑ 43 Graveler (U) .50 1.00
❑ 44 Hitmonlee (U) .75 1.25
❑ 45 Pupitar (U) .50 1.00
❑ 46 Pidgeotto (U) .50 1.00
❑ 47 Chansey (U) .50 1.00
❑ 48 Dragonair (U) .75 1.25
❑ 49 Trainer: Totodile (U) .50 1.00
❑ 50 Trainer: Energy (U) .50 1.00
❑ 51 Trainer: Super Energy Retrieval (U) .50 1.00
❑ 52 Trainer: Marill (U) .50 1.00
❑ 53 Trainer: (U) .50 1.00
❑ 54 Trainer: Film Crew (U) .50 1.00
❑ 55 Trainer: Super Scoop Up (U) .50 1.00
❑ 56 Trainer: Necklace (U) .50 1.00
❑ 57 Trainer: Pokeball (U) .50 1.00
❑ 58 Trainer: Wooper (U) .50 1.00
❑ 59 Trainer: Pokemon Reverse (U) .50 1.00
❑ 60 Trainer: Electronics (U) .50 1.00
❑ 61 Trainer: Master Ball (U) .50 1.00
❑ 62 Trainer: (U) .50 1.00
❑ 63 Trainer: (U) .50 1.00
❑ 64 Trainer: Warp Point (U) .50 1.00
❑ 65 Venusaur (R) 1.00 3.00
❑ 66 Butterfree (R) 1.00 2.00
❑ 67 Arbok (R) 1.00 2.00
❑ 68 Vileplume (R) 1.00 2.00
❑ 69 Weezing (R) 1.00 2.00
❑ 70 Meganium (R) 1.00 3.00
❑ 71 Charizard (R) 2.00 5.00
❑ 72 Ninetales (R) 1.00 2.00
❑ 73 Rapidash (R) 1.00 2.00
❑ 74 Typhlosion (R) 1.50 3.00
❑ 75 Magby (R) 1.00 2.00
❑ 76 Blastoise (R) 1.50 3.00
❑ 77 Poliwrath (R) 1.00 2.00
❑ 78 Cloyster (R) 1.00 2.00
❑ 79 Kingler (R) 1.00 2.00
❑ 80 Feraligatr (R) 1.50 3.00
❑ 81 Raichu (R) 1.50 3.00
❑ 82 Pichu (R) 1.50 4.00
❑ 83 Ampharos (R) 1.00 2.00
❑ 84 Alakazam (R) 1.00 2.00
❑ 85 Gengar (R) 1.00 2.00
❑ 86 Mewtwo (R) 1.50 3.00
❑ 87 Mew (R) 1.50 3.50
❑ 88 Dugtrio (R) 1.00 2.00
❑ 89 Machamp (R) 1.00 2.00
❑ 90 Golem (R) 1.00 2.00
❑ 91 Pidgeot (R) 1.00 2.00
❑ 92 Fearow (R) 1.00 2.00
❑ 93 Clefable (R) 1.00 2.00
❑ 94 Dragonite (R) 1.00 2.00
❑ 95 Tyranitar (R) 1.50 3.00
❑ 96 Skarmory (R) 1.00 2.00
❑ 97 Venusaur (holo) (R) 3.00 6.00
❑ 98 Butterfree (holo) (R) 2.00 4.00
❑ 99 Arbok (holo) (R) 2.00 4.00
❑ 100 Vileplume (holo) (R) 2.00 4.00
❑ 101 Weezing (holo) (R) 2.00 4.00
❑ 102 Meganium (holo) (R) 2.00 4.00
❑ 103 Charizard (holo) (R) 10.00 18.00
❑ 104 Ninetales (holo) (R) 2.00 4.00
❑ 105 Rapidash (holo) (R) 2.00 4.00
❑ 106 Typhlosion (holo) (R) 2.00 5.00
❑ 107 Magby (holo) (R) 2.00 4.00
❑ 108 Blastoise (holo) (R) 4.00 8.00
❑ 109 Poliwrath (holo) (R) 2.00 4.00
❑ 110 Cloyster (holo) (R) 2.00 4.00
❑ 111 Kingler (holo) (R) 2.00 4.00
❑ 112 Feraligatr (holo) (R) 2.00 5.00
❑ 113 Raichu (holo) (R) 2.00 4.00
❑ 114 Pichu (holo) (R) 3.00 6.00
❑ 115 Ampharos (holo) (R) 2.00 4.00
❑ 116 Alakazam (holo) (R) 2.00 4.00
❑ 117 Gengar (holo) (R) 2.00 4.00
❑ 118 Mewtwo (holo) (R) 4.00 8.00
❑ 119 Mew (holo) (R) 4.00 8.00
❑ 120 Dugtrio (holo) (R) 2.00 4.00
❑ 121 Machamp (holo) (R) 2.00 4.00
❑ 122 Golem (holo) (R) 2.00 4.00
❑ 123 Pidgeot (holo) (R) 2.00 4.00
❑ 124 Fearow (holo) (R) 2.00 4.00
❑ 125 Clefable (holo) (R) 2.00 4.00
❑ 126 Dragonite (holo) (R) 2.00 5.00
❑ 127 Tyranitar (holo) (R) 2.00 5.00
❑ 128 Skarmory (holo) (R) 2.00 4.00

1996-02 Pokemon Coro Coro Comics Japanese

Note: Also spelled as Koro Koro.

❑ 0 Abra 5.00 10.00
❑ 0 Blastoise 5.00 10.00
❑ 0 Celebi (Jumbo VS) 25.00 40.00
❑ 0 Charizard (Jumbo size) 20.00 35.00
❑ 0 Cubone 5.00 10.00
❑ 0 Dratini 5.00 10.00
❑ 0 Entei (Jumbo) 5.00 10.00
❑ 0 Electabuzz 5.00 10.00
❑ 0 Farfetch'd 5.00 10.00
❑ 0 Growlithe 5.00 10.00
❑ 0 Ho-oh 6.00 12.00
❑ 0 Jigglypuff 25.00 50.00
❑ 0 Jolteon 5.00 10.00
❑ 0 Legendary Birds (Jumbo Size) 20.00 30.00
❑ 0 Mankey 5.00 10.00
❑ 0 Marill (also known as Pikablu) 5.00 10.00
❑ 0 Meowth (Team Rocket) 5.00 10.00
❑ 0 Meowth GB 5.00 10.00
❑ 0 Mew on Lily Pad (Glossy) 10.00 20.00
❑ 0 Mew (Shiny)(holo) 8.00 16.00
❑ 0 Mewtwo 20.00 40.00
❑ 0 Mewtwo vs. Mew (Jumbo size) 25.00 50.00
❑ 0 Nidoking 5.00 10.00
❑ 0 Onix 5.00 10.00
❑ 0 Cleffa 5.00 10.00
❑ 0 Pichu, Pikachu (Jumbo) 10.00 20.00
❑ 0 Pikachu Flying Balloons 15.00 30.00
❑ 0 Pikachu In Ivy 20.00 40.00
❑ 0 Pikachu, Jigglypuff, Clefairy (Jumbo) 20.00 40.00
❑ 0 Pikachu Surfing 15.00 30.00
❑ 0 Pikachu swimming (Jumbo) 20.00 40.00
❑ 0 Scizor 5.00 10.00
❑ 0 Slowking 5.00 10.00
❑ 0 Staryu 5.00 10.00
❑ 0 Smoochum 5.00 10.00
❑ 0 Togepi 10.00 20.00
❑ 0 Unown R 5.00 10.00
❑ 0 Wooper 5.00 10.00
❑ 0 Trainer: Imakuni 5.00 10.00
❑ 0 Trainer: Koffing 5.00 10.00
❑ 0 Trainer: Legendary birds (Jumbo size) 10.00 20.00
❑ 0 Trainer: Pikachu and friends 35.00 50.00
❑ 0 Trainer: Pokemon Island 10.00 20.00

2001 Pokemon CD Promos Japanese

Complete Set (10) 15.00 30.00

❑ 3 Venusaur (holo) (lightning bolt) 3.00 6.00
❑ 6 Charizard (holo) (lightning bolt) 6.00 12.00
❑ 9 Blastoise (holo) (lightning bolt) 4.00 8.00
❑ 59 Arcanine 1.00 2.00
❑ 137 Porygon (holo) 3.00 6.00
❑ 143 Snorlax (holo) 1.00 3.00
❑ 150 Mewtwo (glossy) (Poké Ball) 5.00 10.00
❑ 151 Mew (glossy) (Poké Ball) 4.00 8.00
❑ NNO Trainer Card .75 2.00
❑ NNO Trainer Card with Onix 1.00 3.00

1997 Pokemon Meiji Set 1 Japanese

❑ 0 Ash 60.00 100.00
❑ 0 Blastoise 20.00 40.00
❑ 0 Brock 40.00 70.00
❑ 0 Caterpie 5.00 10.00
❑ 0 Charizard 50.00 100.00
❑ 0 Charmander 12.00 25.00
❑ 0 Dragonair 5.00 12.00
❑ 0 Electabuzz 5.00 10.00
❑ 0 Ekans 25.00 50.00
❑ 0 Giovanni 35.00 70.00
❑ 0 Golem 5.00 10.00
❑ 0 Hitmonlee 5.00 10.00
❑ 0 James 50.00 75.00
❑ 0 Jesse 40.00 70.00
❑ 0 Jolteon 5.00 12.00
❑ 0 Jynx 5.00 10.00
❑ 0 Kabutops 5.00 10.00
❑ 0 Kadabra 5.00 10.00
❑ 0 Koffing 5.00 10.00
❑ 0 Meowth 5.00 10.00
❑ 0 Mew 15.00 35.00
❑ 0 Mewtwo 50.00 80.00
❑ 0 Nidoking 12.00 20.00
❑ 0 Nidoqueen 12.00 20.00
❑ 0 Persian 20.00 30.00
❑ 0 Pidgey 5.00 10.00
❑ 0 Pikachu 50.00 90.00

❑ 0 Prof. Oak 20.00 30.00
❑ 0 Raticate 5.00 10.00
❑ 0 Spearow 5.00 10.00
❑ 0 Squirtle 15.00 25.00
❑ 0 Staryu 5.00 10.00
❑ 0 Vaporeon 5.00 10.00
❑ 0 Weepinbell 5.00 10.00
❑ 0 Weezing 20.00 30.00
❑ 0 Wigglypuff 5.00 10.00
❑ 0 Zapdos 15.00 30.00

1998 Pokemon Meiji Set 2 Japanese

Complete Set (48) 450.00 600.00

❑ 1 Mewtwo 20.00 40.00
❑ 2 Scientist 2.00 5.00
❑ 3 Ancient Mew 100.00 200.00
❑ 4 Mewtwo in armor 25.00 40.00
❑ 5 Mewtwo close-up 25.00 35.00
❑ 6 Pirate Trainer 3.00 6.00
❑ 7 Dragonite 10.00 22.00
❑ 8 Nurse Joy holograph 3.00 7.00
❑ 9 Officer Jenny 4.00 10.00
❑ 10 Pidgeot 3.00 7.00
❑ 11 Ms.Boija 3.00 5.00
❑ 12 Nurse Joy 4.00 8.00
❑ 13 Brock 5.00 10.00
❑ 14 Mew flying 18.00 30.00
❑ 15 Pokémon Trainer 2.00 6.00
❑ 16 Pokémon Trainer 2.00 5.00
❑ 17 Mewtwo's machine 2.00 5.00
❑ 18 Team Rocket 10.00 20.00
❑ 19 Meowth and James 5.00 11.00
❑ 20 Venusaur 12.00 20.00
❑ 21 Charizard & Blastoise 15.00 30.00
❑ 22 Mewtwo & Evil Pokémon 20.00 40.00
❑ 23 Charizard battle 20.00 30.00
❑ 24 Mewtwo 25.00 35.00
❑ 25 Psyducks 10.00 15.00
❑ 26 Pikachu 20.00 30.00
❑ 27 Meowth 10.00 18.00
❑ 28 Sad Pikachu 10.00 17.00
❑ 29 Misty and Brock 12.00 20.00
❑ 30 Mew 22.00 40.00
❑ 31 Gyarados battle 10.00 20.00
❑ 32 Happy Mew 25.00 60.00
❑ 33 Pokémon Island 2.00 5.00
❑ 34 Charizard and others 15.00 22.00
❑ 35 Togepi 20.00 30.00
❑ 36 Togepi crying 18.00 35.00
❑ 37 Funny face Pikachu 15.00 25.00
❑ 38 Pikachu, Squirtle and Bulbasaur 10.00 20.00
❑ 39 Pikachu & Togepi 10.00 20.00
❑ 40 Pikachu & Raichu battle 15.00 30.00
❑ 41 Pikachu & Raichu Cheek to cheek 25.00 40.00
❑ 42 Pikachu & Raichu Cheek to cheek 18.00 30.00
❑ 43 Pikachu & Raichu get squashed 10.00 20.00
❑ 44 Pikachu and others 25.00 45.00
❑ 45 Charizard & Squirtle 20.00 30.00
❑ 46 Swinging Pikachu 30.00 50.00
❑ 47 Togepi & Vulpix 15.00 25.00
❑ 48 Happy Pikachu 20.00 40.00

1999 Pokemon Meiji 3 Japanese

Complete Set (24) 30.00 60.00

❑ NNO Alakazam (Foodin) 3.00 5.00
❑ NNO Arcanine (Windie) 2.00 4.00
❑ NNO Articuno (Freezer) 3.00 6.00
❑ NNO Blastoise (Kamex) 4.00 7.00
❑ NNO Bulbasaur (Fushigidane) 3.00 5.00
❑ NNO Chansey (Lucky) 2.00 4.00
❑ NNO Charizard (Lizardon) 10.00 20.00
❑ NNO Dragonite (Kairyu) 3.00 5.00
❑ NNO Eevee (Eievui) 2.00 4.00
❑ NNO Gengar (Gangar) 2.00 4.00
❑ NNO Jigglypuff (Purin) 3.00 5.00
❑ NNO Lapras (Laplace) 3.00 5.00
❑ NNO Meowth (Nyarth) 3.00 5.00
❑ NNO Mew 5.00 10.00
❑ NNO Mewtwo 3.00 5.00
❑ NNO Moltres (Fire) 3.00 5.00
❑ NNO Pikachu 3.00 6.00
❑ NNO Raichu 3.00 5.00
❑ NNO Squirtle (Zenigame) 3.00 5.00
❑ NNO Togepi (Togepy) 3.00 6.00
❑ NNO Venusaur (Fushigibana) 3.00 5.00
❑ NNO Zapdos (Thunder) 3.00 5.00
❑ NNO Ash & Misty (Satoshi & Kasumi) 3.00 5.00
❑ NNO Team Rocket (Rocket-Dan) 1.00 3.00

2000 Pokemon Meiji 4 Japanese

Complete Set (16) 20.00 40.00

❑ NNO Herakurosa 3.00 5.00
❑ NNO Lugia 5.00 12.00
❑ NNO Otachi 3.00 5.00
❑ NNO Totodile 3.00 5.00
❑ NNO Hapinasu 3.00 5.00
❑ NNO Bellossom 3.00 5.00
❑ NNO Odoshishi 3.00 5.00
❑ NNO Togepi 4.00 8.00
❑ NNO Chikorita 3.00 5.00
❑ NNO Cyndaquil 4.00 8.00
❑ NNO Marill 5.00 10.00
❑ NNO Elekid 3.00 5.00
❑ NNO Hoothoot 3.00 5.00
❑ NNO Mr. Mime 3.00 5.00
❑ NNO Ledyba 3.00 5.00
❑ NNO Pikachu 4.00 8.00

2000 Pokemon Meiji Blue 5 Japanese

Complete Set (16) 10.00 20.00

❑ 0 Aipom 3.00 5.00
❑ 0 Entei 2.00 4.00
❑ 0 Espeon 3.00 5.00
❑ 0 Hitmontop 3.00 5.00
❑ 0 Ho-oh 2.00 4.00
❑ 0 Hoppip 3.00 5.00
❑ 0 Houndour 3.00 5.00
❑ 0 Pichu 2.00 4.00
❑ 0 Pikachu 3.00 6.00
❑ 0 Phanpy 3.00 5.00
❑ 0 Raikou 3.00 5.00
❑ 0 Slowking 3.00 5.00
❑ 0 Smeargle 3.00 5.00
❑ 0 Sudowoodo 3.00 5.00
❑ 0 Suicune 3.00 5.00
❑ 0 Togetic 3.00 5.00

2001 Pokemon Meiji Silver Set 6 Japanese

Complete Set (18) 12.00 25.00

❑ 0 Bayleaf 2.00 4.00
❑ 0 Blissey 2.00 4.00
❑ 0 Celebi 3.00 6.00
❑ 0 Chikorita 2.00 4.00
❑ 0 Cyndaquil 3.00 5.00
❑ 0 Delibird 2.00 4.00
❑ 0 Entei 2.00 4.00
❑ 0 Feraligatr 2.00 4.00
❑ 0 Ho-oh 2.00 4.00
❑ 0 Lugia 4.00 8.00
❑ 0 Marill 2.00 4.00
❑ 0 Meowth 2.00 4.00
❑ 0 Pichu 2.00 4.00
❑ 0 Pikachu 4.00 8.00
❑ 0 Quilava 3.00 5.00
❑ 0 Raikou 2.00 4.00
❑ 0 Suicune 2.00 4.00
❑ 0 Totodile 2.00 4.00

2002 Pokemon Meiji Set 7 Japanese

Complete Set (16) 20.00 35.00
Common Card 1.00 2.00

❑ 0 Charizard vs. Lugia 5.00 10.00

2000 Pokemon Neo Promos Japanese

Complete Set (9) 10.00 15.00

❑ 152 Chikorita 1.00 2.00
❑ 153 Bayleef 1.00 2.00
❑ 154 Meganium (holo) 2.00 4.00
❑ 155 Cyndaquil 1.00 2.00
❑ 156 Quilava 1.00 2.00
❑ 157 Typhlosion (holo) 2.00 4.00
❑ 158 Totodile 1.00 2.00
❑ 159 Croconaw 1.00 2.00
❑ 160 Ferligatr (holo) 2.00 4.00

2000 Pokemon Neo 2 Promos Japanese

Complete Set (9) 15.00 30.00

❑ 6 Charizard (holo) 8.00 15.00
❑ 133 Eevee 1.00 2.00
❑ 172 Pichu (holo) 3.00 6.00
❑ 196 Espeon 1.00 2.00
❑ 197 Umbreon 1.00 2.00
❑ 201 Unown N .75 1.50
❑ 201 Unown O .75 1.50
❑ 201 Unown E .75 1.50
❑ 244 Entei (holo) 3.00 6.00

2001 Pokemon Neo 3 Promos Japanese

Complete Set (9) 15.00 30.00

❑ 185 Sudowoodo 1.00 3.00
❑ 215 Sneasel 1.00 3.00
❑ 227 Skarmory 1.00 3.00
❑ 243 Raikou 3.00 6.00
❑ 244 Entei 3.00 6.00
❑ 245 Suicune 3.00 6.00
❑ 249 Lugia 6.00 10.00
❑ 250 Ho-oh 3.00 6.00
❑ 251 Celebi (holo) 6.00 12.00

2001 Pokemon VS Promos Japanese

❑ 0 Celebi (Fan Club Booklet) 8.00 16.00
❑ 0 Ho-oh (Coro Coro Comics) 8.00 15.00
❑ 0 Lapras (card game booklet) 10.00 15.00
❑ 0 Larvitar (ANA airlines promo) 12.00 20.00
❑ 0 Pikachu (ANA airlines promo) 12.00 20.00
❑ 0 Rapidash (Coro Coro Comics) 6.00 12.00
❑ 0 Scizor (fan club booklet) 6.00 12.00
❑ 0 Sneasel (Coro Coro promo) 10.00 20.00
❑ 0 Tyranitar (movie promo set) 15.00 30.00

2001-02 Pokemon E Card Promos Japanese

❑ 0 Celebi (Spaceworld 2001) 15.00 30.00
❑ 0 Kakureon (movie promo) 20.00 30.00
❑ 0 Latias,Latios (Jumbo Movie) 12.00 20.00
❑ 0 Pichu Brothers (movie promo) 20.00 30.00
❑ 0 Pikachu (McDonalds promo) 15.00 30.00
❑ 0 Suicune (Celebi DVD) 15.00 35.00
❑ 0 Tyrogue (McDonalds promo) 8.00 12.00
❑ 0 Umbreon (McDonalds promo) 20.00 40.00
❑ 0 Wooper (McDonalds promo) 5.00 10.00
❑ 0 Zapdos (McDonalds promo) 5.00 10.00
❑ 38P Pikachu (PokeFest 02) 20.00 40.00
❑ 39P Crystal Energy (PokeFest 02) 10.00 20.00
❑ 40P Boost Energy (PokeFest 02) 10.00 20.00
❑ 41P Warp Energy (PokeFest 02) 10.00 20.00
❑ 42P Pikachu (PokeFest 02) 5.00 10.00
❑ 43P Pichu (PokeFest 02) 5.00 10.00
❑ 44P Mewtwo (PokeFest 02) 5.00 10.00
❑ 45P Lugia (PokeFest 02) 5.00 10.00
❑ 46P Celebi (PokeFest 02) 6.00 12.00
❑ 47P Entei (Railroad promo) 6.00 12.00

1998 Pokemon Quick Starters Green Japanese

Green (Olive) Set (60) 35.00 75.00
Pokemon cards (not listed) 1.00 2.00

❑ 1 Bulbasaur 2.00 4.00
❑ 4 Charmander 2.00 4.00
❑ 10 Caterpie 3.00 5.00
❑ 11 Metapod 3.00 6.00
❑ 19 Rattata 3.00 6.00
❑ 29 Nidoran-F 3.00 6.00
❑ 32 Nidoran-M 3.00 6.00
❑ 35 Clefairy 2.00 4.00
❑ 37 Vulpix 3.00 6.00
❑ 58 Growlithe 3.00 6.00
❑ 63 Abra 3.00 6.00
❑ 64 Kadabra 6.00 10.00
❑ 77 Ponyta 3.00 6.00
❑ 78 Rapidash 3.00 6.00
❑ 92 Gastly 3.00 6.00
❑ 93 Haunter 3.00 6.00
❑ 113 Chansey 2.00 4.00
❑ 115 Kangaskhan 2.00 4.00
❑ 122 Mime 2.00 4.00
❑ 123 Scyther (holo) 12.00 20.00
❑ 126 Magmar 3.00 6.00
❑ 127 Pinsir 3.00 6.00
❑ 137 Porygon 3.00 6.00
❑ 144 Articuno (holo) 10.00 20.00
❑ 150 Mewtwo 4.00 8.00
❑ NNO Trainer: Poké Ball (holo) 4.00 8.00
❑ NNO Trainers or Energies .10 .25

1998 Pokemon Quick Starters Red Japanese

Red (Pink) Set (60) 60.00 100.00
Pokemon cards (not listed) 2.00 4.00

❑ 7 Squirtle 2.00 4.00
❑ 25 Pikachu (Level13) 10.00 20.00
❑ 25 Pikachu (Level 5) 10.00 20.00
❑ 26 Raichu 2.00 5.00
❑ 27 Sandshrew 3.00 6.00
❑ 28 Sandslash 3.00 6.00
❑ 60 Poliwag 3.00 6.00
❑ 61 Poliwhirl 3.00 6.00
❑ 62 Poliwrath 3.00 6.00
❑ 66 Machop 3.00 6.00
❑ 67 Machoke 3.00 6.00
❑ 81 Magnemite 2.00 4.00
❑ 82 Magneton 3.00 6.00
❑ 84 Doduo 3.00 6.00
❑ 86 Seel 3.00 6.00
❑ 87 Dewgong 2.00 4.00
❑ 95 Onix 3.00 6.00
❑ 100 Voltorb 3.00 6.00
❑ 107 Hitmonlee 2.00 5.00
❑ 108 Lickitung 3.00 6.00
❑ 124 Jynx 3.00 6.00
❑ 131 Lapras 2.00 5.00
❑ 143 Snorlax 2.00 5.00
❑ 145 Zapdos (holo) 12.00 20.00
❑ 146 Moltres (holo) 10.00 20.00
❑ NNO Trainers or Energies .10 .25
❑ NNO Trainer: Poké Ball (holo) 4.00 8.00

1999 Pokemon Southern Islands Japanese

Complete set (18) 12.00 20.00
Rainbow Collection (9) 6.00 10.00
Tropical Island Collection (9) 6.00 10.00

❑ 2 Ivysaur (Rainbow) 2.00 4.00
❑ 8 Wartortle (Tropical) 2.00 4.00
❑ 12 Butterfree (Rainbow) 2.00 4.00
❑ 18 Pidgeot (Rainbow) 2.00 4.00
❑ 20 Raticate (Rainbow) 2.00 4.00
❑ 39 Jigglypuff (Rainbow) 2.00 4.00
❑ 45 Vileplume (holo) (Tropical) 3.00 6.00
❑ 57 Primeape (Tropical) 2.00 4.00
❑ 73 Tentacruel (Tropical) 2.00 4.00
❑ 95 Onix (Rainbow) 2.00 4.00
❑ 103 Exeggutor (Tropical) 2.00 4.00
❑ 108 Lickitung (Tropical) 1.00 3.00
❑ 131 Lapras (Tropical) 2.00 4.00
❑ 151 Mew (holo) (Rainbow) 3.00 6.00
❑ NNO Marill (holo) (Tropical) 3.00 6.00
❑ NNO Ledyba (holo) (Rainbow) 3.00 6.00
❑ NNO Togepi (holo) (Rainbow) 3.00 6.00
❑ NNO Slowking (holo) (Tropical) 3.00 6.00

1999 Pokemon Sweepstakes Japanese

Complete Set 1 (3) 25.00 50.00
Complete Set 2 (3) 25.00 50.00

❑ 0 Blastoise (set 1) 12.00 20.00
❑ 0 Charizard (set 1) 15.00 30.00
❑ 0 Venusaur (set 1) 5.00 10.00
❑ 0 Feraligatr (set 2) 10.00 20.00
❑ 0 Meganium (set 2) 10.00 20.00
❑ 0 Typhlosion (set 2) 10.00 20.00

2001 Pokemon Vending Series One Japanese

Series One set (36) 40.00 60.00
Vending Sheets 5.00 15.00

❑ 1 Bulbasaur 5.00 8.00
❑ 4 Charmander 5.00 8.00
❑ 7 Squirtle 4.00 8.00
❑ 10 Caterpie 2.00 4.00
❑ 11 Metapod 3.00 4.00
❑ 13 Weedle 2.00 4.00
❑ 14 Kakuna 2.00 4.00
❑ 16 Pidgey 2.00 4.00
❑ 19 Rattata 2.00 4.00
❑ 25 Pikachu 8.00 16.00
❑ 29 Nidoran-F 2.00 4.00
❑ 32 Nidoran-M 2.00 4.00
❑ 35 Clefairy 5.00 8.00
❑ 40 Wigglytuff 3.00 5.00
❑ 41 Zubat 2.00 4.00
❑ 42 Golbat 2.00 4.00
❑ 46 Paras 2.00 4.00
❑ 47 Parasect 2.00 4.00
❑ 60 Poliwag 2.00 4.00
❑ 61 Poliwhirl 3.00 5.00
❑ 62 Poliwrath 3.00 5.00
❑ 63 Abra 3.00 5.00
❑ 74 Geodude 2.00 4.00
❑ 78 Rapidash 3.00 5.00
❑ 84 Doduo 2.00 4.00
❑ 85 Dodrio 2.00 4.00
❑ 108 Lickitung 2.00 4.00
❑ 113 Chansey 4.00 7.00
❑ 122 Mime 4.00 7.00
❑ 127 Pinsir 2.00 4.00
❑ 133 Eevee 3.00 5.00
❑ 137 Porygon 2.00 4.00
❑ 143 Snorlax 3.00 5.00
❑ 150 Mewtwo 8.00 15.00
❑ NNO Trainer: Glowing Moon 2.00 4.00
❑ NNO Trainer: Mine Shaft 2.00 4.00

2001 Pokemon Vending Series Two Japanese

Series Two set (36) 35.00 60.00
Vending Sheets 10.00 20.00

❑ 21 Spearow 2.00 4.00
❑ 22 Fearow 2.00 4.00
❑ 26 Raichu 5.00 10.00
❑ 27 Sandshrew 2.00 4.00
❑ 49 Venomoth 3.00 5.00
❑ 66 Machop 2.00 4.00
❑ 67 Machoke 2.00 4.00
❑ 75 Graveller 2.00 4.00
❑ 81 Magnemite 2.00 4.00
❑ 82 Magneton 2.00 4.00
❑ 86 Seel 2.00 4.00
❑ 87 Dewgong 2.00 4.00
❑ 88 Grimer 2.00 4.00
❑ 90 Shellder 2.00 4.00
❑ 95 Onix 2.00 4.00
❑ 98 Krabby 2.00 4.00
❑ 100 Voltorb 3.00 5.00
❑ 105 Marowak 3.00 5.00
❑ 106 Hitmonlee 5.00 8.00
❑ 107 Hitmonchan 3.00 5.00
❑ 109 Koffing 2.00 4.00
❑ 114 Tangela 2.00 4.00
❑ 124 Jynx 2.00 4.00
❑ 125 Electabuzz 3.00 6.00
❑ 131 Lapras 3.00 5.00
❑ 132 Ditto 2.00 4.00
❑ 138 Omanyte 3.00 5.00
❑ 140 Kabuto 2.00 4.00
❑ 142 Aerodactyl 5.00 10.00
❑ 144 Articuno 5.00 10.00
❑ 145 Zapdos 5.00 10.00
❑ 146 Moltres 4.00 8.00
❑ NNO Trainer: Floating Crystal 2.00 4.00
❑ NNO Trainer: Glowing Poké Ball 2.00 4.00
❑ NNO Trainer: Hitmonlee in crystal 3.00 5.00
❑ NNO Trainer: Lots of Digletts 3.00 5.00

2001 Pokemon Vending Series Three Japanese

Series Three set (45) 30.00 60.00
Vending Sheets 5.00 15.00

❑ 17 Pidgeotto 2.00 4.00
❑ 24 Arbok 2.00 4.00
❑ 28 Sandslash 2.00 4.00
❑ 30 Nidorina 2.00 4.00
❑ 33 Nidorino 2.00 4.00
❑ 37 Vulpix 2.00 4.00
❑ 48 Venonat 2.00 4.00
❑ 55 Golduck 2.00 4.00
❑ 58 Growlithe 2.00 4.00
❑ 64 Kadabra (#1 & #2) 3.00 5.00
❑ 67 Machoke 3.00 4.00
❑ 69 Bellsprout 3.00 4.00
❑ 70 Weepinbell 3.00 5.00
❑ 75 Graveller 3.00 5.00
❑ 77 Ponyta 2.00 4.00
❑ 80 Slowbro 2.00 4.00
❑ 93 Haunter (#1 & #2) 3.00 5.00
❑ 97 Hypno 2.00 4.00
❑ 99 Kingler 2.00 4.00
❑ 104 Cubone 2.00 4.00
❑ 110 Weezing 2.00 4.00
❑ 112 Rhydon 2.00 4.00
❑ 115 Kangaskhan 3.00 6.00
❑ 116 Horsea 2.00 5.00
❑ 117 Seadra 2.00 4.00
❑ 120 Staryu 2.00 4.00
❑ 123 Scyther 4.00 8.00
❑ 126 Magmar 2.00 4.00
❑ 128 Tauros 2.00 4.00
❑ 138 Omanyte 2.00 4.00
❑ 150 Mewtwo 6.00 12.00
❑ NNO Trainer: Mankey w/Poke Balls 2.00 4.00
❑ NNO Trainer: Tower at Night 2.00 4.00
❑ NNO WB Checklists 1.00 2.00
❑ NNO WB Extra Rule: 6 Decks 3.00 6.00
❑ NNO WB Extra Rule: 6 Players 4.00 8.00
❑ NNO WB Extra Rule: Deck Swap 3.00 6.00
❑ NNO WB Extra Rule: Girl & Boy 4.00 8.00
❑ NNO WB Extra Rule: Meowth 4.00 7.00
❑ NNO WB Pass Card 2.00 4.00
❑ NNO WB Pikachu 10.00 15.00
❑ NNO WB Pokemon Machine 2.00 4.00
❑ NNO WB Red Guy in Hole 1.00 2.00
❑ NNO WB Red Guy Rules 1.00 2.00
❑ NNO WB Red Guy Trainer 1.00 2.00

2001 Pokemon Vending Series Three Mail-in Japanese

Complete Set (5) 50.00 100.00

❑ 0 Alakazam (holo) 15.00 30.00
❑ 0 Gengar (holo) 15.00 30.00
❑ 0 Golem (holo) 15.00 30.00
❑ 0 Machamp (holo) 15.00 30.00
❑ 0 Omastar (holo) 15.00 30.00

2001 Pokemon Vending Series Double Zero Japanese

Complete Set (3) 30.00 50.00

❑ 0 Mew (with bubbles) 10.00 20.00
❑ 0 Mewtwo 10.00 20.00
❑ 0 Pikachu (lightning bolt) 10.00 20.00

2001 Pokemon Video Starter Japanese

Complete Set (82) 14.00 30.00
Energy Cards (not listed) .20 .50

❑ 0 Blastoise (holo) (SD) 8.00 12.00
❑ 0 Venusaur (holo) (BD) 8.00 12.00
❑ 1 Bulbasaur (BD) 1.50 3.00
❑ 1 Growlithe (SD) 1.00 2.00
❑ 2 Diglett (SD) 1.00 2.00
❑ 2 Drowzee (BD) 1.00 2.00
❑ 3 Raichu (BD) 1.50 3.00
❑ 3 Wartortle (SD) 1.00 2.00
❑ 9 Poliwag (SD) 1.00 2.00
❑ 10 Wartortle (SD) 1.00 2.00
❑ 13 Pikachu (BD) 2.00 5.00
❑ 13 Spearow (SD) 1.00 2.00
❑ 14 Jigglypuff (SD) 1.00 3.00
❑ 16 Squirtle (SD) 2.00 4.00
❑ 16 Meowth (BD) 1.00 2.00
❑ 18 Squirtle (SD) 2.00 4.00
❑ 18 Bulbasaur (BD) 1.50 3.00
❑ 22 Ivysaur (BD) 1.50 3.00
❑ 23 Double Colorless Energy (BD) .50 1.00
❑ 25 Double Colorless Energy (SD) .50 1.00
❑ 26 Growlithe (SD) 1.00 2.00
❑ 26 Electabuzz (BD) 1.00 2.00
❑ 29 Bulbasaur (BD) 1.50 3.00
❑ 30 Doduo (BD) 1.00 2.00
❑ 32 Ivysaur (BD) 1.50 3.00
❑ 32 Arcanine (SD) 2.00 4.00
❑ 35 Bulbasaur (BD) 1.50 3.00
❑ 35 Machop (SD) 1.00 2.00
❑ 37 Squirtle (SD) 2.00 4.00
❑ 37 Jynx (BD) 1.00 2.00
❑ 39 Koffing (BD) 1.00 2.00
❑ 39 Magmar (SD) 1.00 2.00
❑ 40 Pikachu (BD) 3.00 6.00
❑ 40 Squirtle (SD) 2.00 4.00

1998 Japanese Pokemon Web Set

Complete Set (48) 40.00 75.00
Sealed Pack 3.00 7.00

❑ 1 Ivysaur (C) .25 .50
❑ 2 Nidoran (M) (C) .25 .50
❑ 3 Venonat (C) .25 .50
❑ 4 Exeggcute (C) .25 .50
❑ 5 Tangela (C) .25 .50
❑ 6 Growlithe (C) .25 .50
❑ 7 Charmeleon (C) .25 .50
❑ 8 Vulpix (C) .25 .50
❑ 9 Wartortle (C) .25 .50
❑ 10 Marill (C) .25 .50
❑ 11 Voltorb (C) .25 .50
❑ 12 Slowpoke (C) .25 .50
❑ 13 Diglett (C) .25 .50
❑ 14 Hitmonlee (C) .25 .50
❑ 15 Trainer: Bill's Teleporter (C) .50 1.00
❑ 16 Trainer: New Pokedex (C) .50 1.00
❑ 17 Dark Ivysaur (U) .50 1.00
❑ 18 Nidorino (U) .50 1.00
❑ 19 Venomoth (U) .50 1.00
❑ 20 Exeggutor (U) .50 1.00

❑ 21 Dark Weezing (U) .50 1.00
❑ 22 Dark Charmeleon (U) .75 1.50
❑ 23 Arcanine (U) 1.00 2.00
❑ 24 Dark Wartortle (U) .75 1.50
❑ 25 Pikachu (U) .75 1.50
❑ 26 Electrode (U) .50 1.00
❑ 27 Dark Kadabra (U) .50 1.00
❑ 28 Dark Slowbro (U) .50 1.00
❑ 29 Dugtrio (U) 1.00 2.00
❑ 30 Trainer: Crystal (U) .75 1.50
❑ 31 Trainer: Hyper Devolution Spray (U) .50 1.00
❑ 32 Trainer: Primeape Poke Ball (U) .50 1.00
❑ 33 Nidoking (R) 1.00 2.00
❑ 34 Ninetails (R) 1.00 2.00
❑ 35 Magikarp (R) 2.00 4.00
❑ 36 Raichu (R) 2.00 4.00
❑ 37 Dark Alakazam (R) 2.00 4.00
❑ 38 Dragonite (R) 2.00 4.00
❑ 39 Meowth (R) 1.00 2.00
❑ 40 Trainer: Rocket's Sneak Attack (R) 1.00 2.00
❑ 41 Dark Venusaur (holo) (R) 3.00 6.00
❑ 42 Dark Charizard (holo) (R) 10.00 20.00
❑ 43 Moltres (holo) (R) 3.00 6.00
❑ 44 Dark Blastoise (holo) (R) 4.00 8.00
❑ 45 Articuno (holo) (R) 3.00 6.00
❑ 46 Zapdos (holo) (R) 3.00 6.00
❑ 47 Gengar (holo) (R) 3.00 6.00
❑ 48 Machamp (holo) (R) 3.00 6.00

1999-02 Pokemon Promo Star Wizards of the Coast

❑ 1 Pikachu (Pokemon League) 4.00 8.00
❑ 1 Pikachu 1st Edition (Jungle packs) 60.00 120.00
❑ 2 Electabuzz (First Movie) 2.00 4.00
❑ 3 Mewtwo (First Movie) 3.00 6.00
❑ 4 Pikachu (First Movie) 5.00 10.00
❑ 5 Dragonite (First Movie) 3.00 6.00
❑ 6 Arcanine (Pokemon League) 4.50 8.00
❑ 7 Jigglypuff (Cassette Mail-in) 2.00 4.00
❑ 8 Mew (Pokemon League) .50 2.00
❑ 9 Mew (holo) (Pokemon League) 2.00 4.00
❑ 10 Meowth (holo) (TCG Game Boy) 6.00 10.00
❑ 11 Eevee (Pokemon League) 1.00 3.00
❑ 12 Mewtwo (Nintendo Magazine) 15.00 25.00
❑ 13 Venusaur (Strategy Guide) 4.00 10.00
❑ 14 Mewtwo (Movie Video) 2.00 4.00
❑ 15 Cool Porygon (Stadium Bundle) 5.00 10.00
❑ 16 Computer Error (Pokemon League) 1.00 3.00
❑ 17 Dark Persian (Nintendo Mag.) (Err) 50.00 80.00
❑ 17 Dark Persian (Nintendo Mag.) 5.00 10.00
❑ 18 TR's Meowth (Pokemon League) 1.00 3.00
❑ 19 Sabrina's Abra (Nintendo Mag.) 4.00 8.00
❑ 20 Psyduck (Pokemon League) 1.00 3.00
❑ 21 Moltres (Movie 2000) 2.00 5.00
❑ 22 Articuno (Movie 2000) 1.00 3.00
❑ 23 Zapdos (Movie 2000) 2.00 5.00
❑ 24 Birthday Pikachu (holo)/ (Pokemon League) 8.00 12.00
❑ 25 Flying Pikachu 2.00 4.00
❑ 26 Pikachu (Snap) 4.00 8.00
❑ 27 Pikachu (Movie 2000 Video) 8.00 16.00
❑ 28 Surfing Pikachu 3.00 7.00
❑ 29 Marill (Neo Genesis) 3.00 6.00
❑ 30 Togepi 3.00 7.00
❑ 31 Cleffa 1.00 2.00
❑ 32 Smeargle 1.00 3.00
❑ 33 Scizor (holo) 1.00 2.00
❑ 34 Entei (holo) (Movie 2001) 3.00 6.00
❑ 35 Pichu (holo) (Pokemon Lea.) 5.00 10.00
❑ 36 Igglybuff 2.00 4.00
❑ 37 Hitmontop .50 1.00
❑ 38 Unown J 3.00 6.00
❑ 39 Misdreavus 1.00 2.00
❑ 40 Trainer: Pokemon Center 5.00 10.00
❑ 41 Trainer: Lucky Stadium 3.00 6.00
❑ 42 Trainer: Pokemon Tower 3.00 6.00
❑ 43 Machamp 1.00 2.00
❑ 44 Magmar 1.00 2.00
❑ 45 Scyther 1.00 3.00
❑ 46 Electabuzz 1.00 3.00
❑ 47 Mew (Lilypad) 1.00 3.00
❑ 48 Articuno 4.00 8.00
❑ 49 Snorlax 2.00 5.00
❑ 50 Celebi (movie promo) 3.00 6.00
❑ 51 Rapidash 3.00 6.00
❑ 52 Ho-oh 8.00 12.00
❑ 53 Suicune 3.00 7.00

1999-02 Pokemon American Promos - Wizards of the Coast

❑ 0 Aerodactyl (Fossil) (Pre-release) 6.00 10.00
❑ 0 Ancient Mew (holo) (Movie 2000) 1.00 2.00
❑ 0 Articuno,Moltres,Zapdos (Jumbo) 8.00 20.00
❑ 0 Brock's Vulpix W gold 2.00 4.00
❑ 0 Cletable (Jungle) (Pre-release) 14.00 27.00
❑ 0 Dark Arbok W gold stamp 2.00 4.00
❑ 0 Dark Charmeleon W gold stamp 5.00 10.00
❑ 0 Dark Gyarados (holo) (Pre-rel.) 3.00 6.00
❑ 0 Exeggutor (Bilingual) 10.00 25.00
❑ 0 Hoppip (2002 E3) 5.00 12.00
❑ 0 Kabuto W gold stamped (TopDeck) 2.00 4.00
❑ 0 Meowth gold border 8.00 15.00
❑ 0 Misty's Psyduck W gold stamp 6.00 9.00
❑ 0 Misty's Seadra (Pre-release) 1.00 3.00
❑ 0 Pichu (2002 E3) 3.00 10.00
❑ 0 Pikachu E3 gold stamped 5.00 12.00
❑ 0 Pikachu E3 gold (Red Cheeks) 50.00 100.00
❑ 0 Pikachu Jumbo Size (TopDeck) 3.00 6.00
❑ 0 Pikachu PokeTour 1999 gold stamped 20.00 30.00
❑ 0 Pikachu W gold stamped (Duelist) 8.00 12.00
❑ 0 Professor Elm (Best) (holo) 10.00 18.00
❑ 0 Wartortle W gold (TopDeck) 4.00 8.00
❑ 0 Gyarados (Pre-release) 3.00 6.00
❑ 0 Wartortle (Pre-release) 4.00 8.00

2002-04 Pokemon USA Promo Cards

❑ 0 Bagon (Gencon) 10.00 20.00
❑ 0 Bagon (Inquest Magazine) 4.00 8.00
❑ 0 Bagon (Scrye Magazine) 4.00 8.00
❑ 0 Blastoise (Nat.Chmpship) 15.00 30.00
❑ 0 Chansey (ERR) 20.00 40.00
❑ 0 Gastly 30.00 60.00
❑ 0 Hoppip (2002 E3) 20.00 40.00
❑ 0 Pichu (2002 E3) 20.00 40.00
❑ 0 Shadow Lugia (jumbo) 10.00 20.00
❑ 1 Kyogre ex (Promo Star) 10.00 20.00
❑ 2 Groudon ex (Promo Star) 10.00 20.00
❑ 3 Treecko 4.00 10.00
❑ 4 Grovyle 4.00 8.00
❑ 5 Mudkip (H) (UK Promo) 5.00 10.00
❑ 6 Torchic (H) (UK Promo) 5.00 10.00
❑ 7 Treecko (H) 5.00 10.00
❑ 8 Torchic 4.00 9.00
❑ 9 Combusken 8.00 16.00
❑ 10 Mudkip (H) 4.00 10.00
❑ 11 Marshtomp 4.00 10.00
❑ 12 Pikachu (H) (Collector Tin) 8.00 12.00
❑ 13 Meowth (H) (Collector Tin) 2.00 5.00
❑ 14 Latias (Heroes Movie) 3.00 7.00
❑ 15 Latios (Heroes Movie) 3.00 7.00
❑ 16A Treecko (H) (EX Deck Tin) 1.00 2.00
❑ 16B Treecko (Target Stores) 1.00 2.00
❑ 17B Torchic (Target Stores) 1.00 2.00
❑ 17A Torchic (H) (EX Deck Tin) 1.00 2.00
❑ 18A Mudkip (Target Stores) 1.00 2.00
❑ 18B Mudkip (H) (EX Deck Tin) 1.00 2.00
❑ 19B Whismur (H) (EX Deck Tin) 1.00 2.00
❑ 19A Whismur (Target Stores) 1.00 2.00
❑ 20 Ludicolo (H) (EX Value Pack 1) 1.00 2.00
❑ 21 Jirachi (Jirachi: Wish Maker DVD) 1.00 2.00
❑ 22 Beldum (e-League June 2004) 1.00 2.00
❑ 23 Metang (Stadium Challenge 2004) 2.00 4.00
❑ 24 Chimecho (e-League July 2004) 30.00 60.00
❑ 25 Flygon (e-League August 2004) 10.00 20.00
❑ 26B Tropical Wind T (Worlds 2004) 1.00 2.00
❑ 26A Tropical Wind (2007) 200.00 300.00
❑ 27 Tropical Tidal Wave T (Worlds 2005) 1.00 2.00
❑ 28 Championship Arena T (Worlds 2005) 1.00 2.00
❑ 29 Celebi (H) (EX VP 2/EX Collector's Carry Tin)1.00 2.00
❑ 30 Suicune (H) (EX VP 2/EX Collector's Carry Tin)1.00 2.00
❑ 31 Moltres ex (H) (EX Collector's Tin 2) 1.00 2.00
❑ 32 Articuno ex (H) (EX Collector's Tin 2) 1.00 2.00
❑ 33 Zapdos ex (H) (EX Collector's Tin 2) 1.00 2.00
❑ 34 Typhlosion (H) (EX Value Pack 5) 1.00 2.00
❑ 35 Pikachu (H) (EX Value Pack 4) 1.00 2.00
❑ 36 Tropical Tidal Wave (Worlds) 1.00 2.00
❑ 37 Kyogre ex (H) (EX Collector's Tin 3) 1.00 2.00
❑ 38 Groudon ex (H) (EX Collector's Tin 3) 1.00 2.00
❑ 39 Rayquaza ex (H) (EX Collector's Tin 3) 1.00 2.00
❑ 40A Darkness Energy 10.00 20.00
❑ 40B Mew (H) 6.00 12.00

1999 Pokemon Best Winner Promos

Complete Set (8) 20.00 30.00
❑ 1 Electabuzz (holo) 3.00 6.00
❑ 2 Hitmonchan (holo) 3.00 6.00
❑ 3 Professor Elm (holo) 3.00 6.00
❑ 4 Rocket's Sizor 1.00 2.00
❑ 5 Rocket's Sneasel 1.00 2.00
❑ 6 Dark Ivysaur 1.00 2.00
❑ 7 Dark Venusaur 1.00 2.00
❑ 8 Rocket's Mewtwo (holo) 3.00 6.00

2011 Pokemon McDonald's Promos

Complete Set 4.00 10.00

2012 Pokemon McDonald's Promos

Complete Set 10.00 25.00
❑ 1 Servine 1.25 3.00
❑ 2 Pansage 1.00 2.50
❑ 3 Dwebble 3.00 8.00
❑ 4 Pignite 2.50 6.00
❑ 5 Dewott 2.50 6.00
❑ 6 Emolga 1.50 4.00
❑ 7 Woobat 1.25 3.00
❑ 8 Drilbur 2.00 5.00
❑ 9 Purrloin 2.00 5.00
❑ 10 Scraggy 1.25 3.00
❑ 11 Klang 1.50 4.00
❑ 12 Axew 1.25 3.00

1996-02 Pokemon Promos Japanese

❑ 0 Ancient Mew (holo.) (Err.Nintedo) 40.00 60.00
❑ 0 Ancient Mew (holo.) (Corr.Nintendo) 15.00 25.00
❑ 0 Articuno (ANA airlines) 12.00 25.00
❑ 0 Black Energy (card game booklet) 3.00 10.00
❑ 0 Dragonite (ANA airlines) 10.00 20.00
❑ 0 Dragonite (Game Boy insert) 20.00 40.00
❑ 0 Eevee (Trophy Fan Club) 100.00 200.00
❑ 0 Hitmontop (Movie Giveaway) 10.00 20.00
❑ 0 Igglybuff (Movie) 12.00 25.00
❑ 0 Jigglypuff (Kado Book) 20.00 50.00
❑ 0 Jynx (Pokemon Book) 12.00 20.00
❑ 0 Kangaskhan (League Prize) 500.00 900.00
❑ 0 Lugia (holo) (Game Boy 2) 20.00 30.00
❑ 0 Mankey (Glossy) (Pokemon mag) 10.00 20.00
❑ 0 Marill (ANA airlines 2000) 10.00 20.00
❑ 0 Meowth (Japan Rail 2000) 35.00 75.00
❑ 0 Meowth (Meowth's Party CD) 18.00 25.00
❑ 0 Mew on Lily Pad (Japan Railroad Rally) 50.00 80.00
❑ 0 Mewtwo (holo) (Game Boy 2) 20.00 35.00
❑ 0 Misdrevus (Japenese Mag Insert) 8.00 15.00
❑ 0 Moltres (ANA airlines) 10.00 20.00
❑ 0 Moltres (Poke Ball logo) 12.00 20.00
❑ 0 Murkrow (card game booklet) 7.00 15.00
❑ 0 Persian (Fan Club Mag.) 10.00 20.00
❑ 0 Pikachu Level 11 (ANA airlines) 25.00 45.00
❑ 0 Pikachu Level 12 (ANA airlines) 30.00 60.00
❑ 0 Pikachu Birthday (2nd Anv.) (White Star) 30.00 60.00
❑ 0 Pikachu Illustrator (paintbrush) 1000.00 2000.00
❑ 0 Pikachu Mt.Fuji (Japan Railroad Rally) 100.00 250.00
❑ 0 Pikachu Promo Star (Pokemon League)
❑ 0 Pikachu Promo Star (1st Edition)
❑ 0 Pikachu Snap (mag insert) 20.00 30.00
❑ 0 Porygon (holo) (Pokemon League) 50.00 100.00
❑ 0 Psyduck question mark (Poke mag) 15.00 30.00
❑ 0 Smeargle (Pokemon Book) 12.00 22.00
❑ 0 Steelix (Pokemon mag.) 4.00 8.00
❑ 0 Special Card Celebi 20.00 40.00
❑ 0 Togepi (ANA Airlines 2000) 15.00 30.00
❑ 0 Venusaur (Japanese Game Boy) 12.00 20.00
❑ 0 Unown J (Japanese mag insert) 10.00 20.00
❑ 0 Zapdos (ANA airlines giveaway) 10.00 20.00
❑ 0 Zapdos (Poke Ball logo) 15.00 25.00
❑ 0 Trainer: Golden Acorn (Champion 2000) 25.00 50.00
❑ 0 Trainer: Grand Party (holo) (Poke League) 20.00 60.00
❑ 0 Trainer: Imakuni (CD) 15.00 25.00
❑ 0 Trainer: Lucky Stadium Chubu (Zapdos) 20.00 45.00
❑ 0 Trainer: Lucky Stadium Chugoku (Gyarados) 30.00 40.00
❑ 0 Trainer: Lucky Stadium Hokkaido (Pikachu) 25.00 40.00
❑ 0 Trainer: Lucky Stadium (Mew) 25.00 40.00
❑ 0 Trainer: Lucky Stadium Kyoto (Moltres) 25.00 40.00
❑ 0 Trainer: Lucky Stadium Kanto (Lugia) 20.00 40.00
❑ 0 Trainer: Lucky Stadium Kyushu (Onix) 30.00 40.00
❑ 0 Trainer: Lucky Stadium Tohoku (Diglett) 20.00 40.00
❑ 0 Trainer: Miracle Acorn (Champion 2000) 25.00 50.00
❑ 0 Trainer: Misty and Lapras 15.00 25.00
❑ 0 Trainer: New Touch 10.00 30.00
❑ 0 Trainer No.3 (Tournament giveaway)
❑ 0 Trainer: Pikachu with Bronze Trophy 500.00 1000.00
❑ 0 Trainer: Pikachu with Silver Trophy 700.00 1500.00
❑ 0 Trainer: Pikachu with Gold Trophy 1000.00 2000.00
❑ 0 Trainer: Touch (a.k.a. Picasso) 6.00 15.00
❑ 0 Trainer: Trading Please (holo.back) 75.00 125.00
❑ 0 Trainer: Tropical Mega Battle 200.00 500.00
❑ 0 Trainer E Card Imakuni 10.00 25.00

2000 Pokemon Pikachu World Collection

Complete set (9) 12.00 22.00
❑ 0 Base Set Pikachu (Korean) 2.00 4.00
❑ 0 Birthday Pikachu (English) 6.00 12.00
❑ 0 First Movie Pikachu (Dutch) 2.00 4.00
❑ 0 Flying Pikachu (German) 4.00 8.00
❑ 0 Ivy Pikachu (Portuguese) 3.00 5.00
❑ 0 Jungle Pikachu (Chinese) 3.00 5.00
❑ 0 Snap Pikachu (Spanish) 2.00 4.00
❑ 0 Surfing Pikachu (French) 4.00 8.00
❑ 0 Vending Pikachu (Italian) 2.00 4.00

1999 Pokemon Southern Island

Complete Set (18) 12.00 25.00
❑ 1 Mew (holo) 2.00 5.00
❑ 2 Pidgeot 1.00 2.00
❑ 3 Onix 1.00 2.00
❑ 4 Togepi (holo) 3.00 6.00
❑ 5 Ivysaur 1.00 2.00
❑ 6 Raticate 1.00 2.00
❑ 7 Ledyba (holo) 2.00 4.00
❑ 8 Jigglypuff 1.00 2.00
❑ 9 Butterfree 1.00 2.00
❑ 10 Tentacruel 1.00 2.00
❑ 11 Marill (holo) 4.00 8.00
❑ 12 Lapras 1.00 2.00
❑ 13 Exeggutor 1.00 2.00
❑ 14 Slowking (holo) 2.00 4.00
❑ 15 Wartortle 1.00 2.00
❑ 16 Lickitung 1.00 2.00
❑ 17 Vileplume (holo) 2.00 4.00
❑ 18 Primeape 1.00 2.00

1994 Star Trek Premiere Black Border

BOOSTER BOX (36 PACKS) 50.00 100.00
BOOSTER PACK (15 CARDS) 2.00 4.00
❑ 1 Albert Einstein R 1.25 3.00
❑ 2 Alexander Rozhenko U .20 .50
❑ 3 Alidar Jarok R .40 1.00
❑ 4 Alien Abduction U .20 .50
❑ 5 Alien Groupie R .40 1.00
❑ 6 Alien Parasites U .20 .50
❑ 7 Alien Probe U .20 .50
❑ 8 Alynna Nechayev R .40 1.00
❑ 9 Alyssa Ogawa U .20 .50
❑ 10 Amanda Rogers U .20 .50
❑ 11 Amarie U .20 .50
❑ 12 Anaphasic Organism C .10 .25
❑ 13 Ancient Computer R .40 1.00
❑ 14 Anti-Time Anomaly R .75 2.00
❑ 15 Archer C .10 .25
❑ 16 Armus - Skin of Evil R .40 1.00
❑ 17 Asteroid Sanctuary C .10 .25
❑ 18 Atmospheric Ionization C .10 .25
❑ 19 Auto-Destruct Sequence U .20 .50
❑ 20 Avert Disaster R .40 1.00
❑ 21 Ba'el U .20 .50
❑ 22 Baran U .20 .50
❑ 23 Barclay's Protomorphosis Disease R .40 1.00
❑ 24 Batrell C .10 .25
❑ 25 Benjamin Maxwell U .20 .50
❑ 26 Betazoid Gift Box R .40 1.00
❑ 27 B'Etor R .60 1.50
❑ 28 Beverly Crusher R .60 1.50
❑ 29 B'iJik C .10 .25
❑ 30 Birth of Junior U .20 .50
❑ 31 Bochra U .20 .50
❑ 32 Bok U .20 .50
❑ 33 Borg Ship R 1.50 4.00
❑ 34 Bynars Weapon Enhancement R .60 1.50
❑ 35 Calloway C .10 .25
❑ 36 Chalnoth U .20 .50
❑ 37 Christopher Hobson C .10 .25
❑ 38 Cloaked Mission U .20 .50
❑ 39 Combat Vessel C .10 .25
❑ 40 Cosmic String Fragment U .20 .50
❑ 41 Covert Installation C .10 .25
❑ 42 Covert Rescue U .20 .50
❑ 43 Crosis R 1.25 3.00
❑ 44 Crystalline Entity R .40 1.00
❑ 45 Cultural Observation R .40 1.00
❑ 46 Cytherians R .40 1.00
❑ 47 Darian Wallace C .10 .25
❑ 48 Data R 2.00 5.00
❑ 49 D'deridex C .10 .25
❑ 50 Deanna Troi R 2.00 5.00
❑ 51 Devinoni Ral U .20 .50
❑ 52 Devoras R .75 2.00
❑ 53 Diplomacy Mission U .20 .50
❑ 54 Disruptor Overload C .10 .25
❑ 55 Distortion Field U .20 .50
❑ 56 Distortion of Space/Time Continuum U .20 .50
❑ 57 Divok C .10 .25
❑ 58 Dr. Farek C .10 .25
❑ 59 Dr. LaForge R .40 1.00
❑ 60 Dr. Leah Brahms R .60 1.50
❑ 61 Dr. Reyga U .20 .50
❑ 62 Dr. Selar U .20 .50
❑ 63 Dukath C .10 .25
❑ 64 Duras R .40 1.00
❑ 65 El-Adrel Creature U .20 .50
❑ 66 Emergency Transporter Armbands C .10 .25
❑ 67 Energy Vortex U .20 .50
❑ 68 Engineering Kit C .10 .25
❑ 69 Engineering PADD C .10 .25
❑ 70 Eric Pressman U .20 .50
❑ 71 Escape Pod C .10 .25
❑ 72 Espionage: Federation on Klingon C .10 .25
❑ 73 Espionage: Klingon on Federation C .10 .25
❑ 74 Espionage: Romulan on Federation C .10 .25
❑ 75 Espionage: Romulan on Klingon C .10 .25
❑ 76 Etana Jol U .20 .50
❑ 77 Evacuation U .20 .50
❑ 78 Evaluate Terraforming R .40 1.00
❑ 79 Evek U .20 .50
❑ 80 Excavation C .10 .25
❑ 81 Exocomp U .20 .50
❑ 82 Explore Black Cluster R .40 1.00
❑ 83 Explore Dyson Sphere R .40 1.00
❑ 84 Explore Typhone Expanse R .40 1.00
❑ 85 Expose Covert Supply U .20 .50
❑ 86 Extraction R .40 1.00
❑ 87 Federation Outpost C .10 .25
❑ 88 Federation PADD C .10 .25
❑ 89 Fek'lhr U .20 .50
❑ 90 Female's Love Interest C .10 .25
❑ 91 Fever Emergency C .10 .25
❑ 92 Firestorm U .20 .50
❑ 93 First Contact U .20 .50
❑ 94 Fleet Admiral Shanthi U .20 .50
❑ 95 Full Planet Scan U .20 .50
❑ 96 Galathon C .10 .25
❑ 97 Gaps in Normal Space U .20 .50
❑ 98 Genetronic Replicator U .20 .50
❑ 99 Geordi LaForge R 3.00 8.00
❑ 100 Giusti C .10 .25
❑ 101 Goddess of Empathy R .40 1.00
❑ 102 Gorath C .10 .25
❑ 103 Gorta C .10 .25
❑ 104 Gowron R .40 1.00
❑ 105 Gravitic Mine U .20 .50
❑ 106 Haakona R .60 1.50
❑ 107 Hannah Bates U .20 .50
❑ 108 Hologram Ruse U .20 .50
❑ 109 Holo-Projectors U .20 .50
❑ 110 Honor Challenge R .40 1.00
❑ 111 Horga'hn R .75 2.00
❑ 112 Hugh R .40 1.00
❑ 113 Hunt for DNA Program R .40 1.00
❑ 114 Husnock Ship U .20 .50
❑ 115 Hyper-Aging U .20 .50
❑ 116 I.K.C. Bortas R .40 1.00
❑ 117 I.K.C. Buruk R .40 1.00
❑ 118 I.K.C. Hegh'ta R .40 1.00
❑ 119 I.K.C. K'Vort C .10 .25
❑ 120 I.K.C. Pagh R .40 1.00
❑ 121 I.K.C. Qu'Vat R .40 1.00
❑ 122 I.K.C. Vor'Cha C .10 .25
❑ 123 I.K.C. Vorn U .20 .50
❑ 124 Iconia Investigation R .40 1.00
❑ 125 Iconian Computer Weapon C .10 .25
❑ 126 Impassable Door C .10 .25
❑ 127 Incoming Message - Federation U .20 .50
❑ 128 Incoming Message - Klingon U .20 .50
❑ 129 Incoming Message - Romulan U .20 .50
❑ 130 Interphase Generator R .40 1.00
❑ 131 Investigate Shattered Space R .40 1.00
❑ 132 Investigate Alien Probe R .40 1.00
❑ 133 Investigate Anomaly C .10 .25
❑ 134 Investigate Disappearance R .40 1.00
❑ 135 Investigate Disturbance R .40 1.00
❑ 136 Investigate Massacre R .40 1.00
❑ 137 Investigate Raid R .40 1.00
❑ 138 Investigate Rogue Comet R .60 1.50
❑ 139 Investigate Sighting R .40 1.00
❑ 140 Investigate Time Continuum R .60 1.50
❑ 141 Ishara Yar U .20 .50
❑ 142 Jaglom Shrek - Information Broker R .40 1.00
❑ 143 Jaron C .10 .25
❑ 144 J'Dan C .10 .25
❑ 145 Jean-Luc Picard R 5.00 10.00
❑ 146 Jenna D'Sora U .20 .50
❑ 147 Jera C .10 .25
❑ 148 Jo'Bril U .20 .50
❑ 149 Kahless R .40 1.00
❑ 150 Kareel Odan U .20 .50
❑ 151 Kargan R .40 1.00
❑ 152 K'Ehleyr R .40 1.00
❑ 153 Kell U .20 .50
❑ 154 Kevin Uxbridge U .20 .50
❑ 155 Khazara R .40 1.00
❑ 156 Khitomer Research R .40 1.00
❑ 157 Kivas Fajo - Collector U .20 .50
❑ 158 Klag C .10 .25
❑ 159 Kle'eg C .10 .25
❑ 160 Klingon Death Yell R .40 1.00
❑ 161 Klingon Disruptor C .10 .25
❑ 162 Klingon Outpost C .10 .25
❑ 163 Klingon PADD C .10 .25
❑ 164 Klingon Right of Vengeance C .10 .25
❑ 165 K'mpec U .20 .50
❑ 166 Konmel U .20 .50
❑ 167 Koral U .20 .50
❑ 168 Koroth U .20 .50
❑ 169 Korris U .20 .50
❑ 170 Krios Suppression U .20 .50
❑ 171 Kromm C .10 .25
❑ 172 K'Tal U .20 .50
❑ 173 Ktarian Game R .40 1.00
❑ 174 K'Tesh C .10 .25
❑ 175 Kurak R .60 1.50
❑ 176 Kurlan Naiskos R .60 1.50
❑ 177 Kurn R .40 1.00
❑ 178 K'Vada U .20 .50
❑ 179 Leah Brahms R .40 1.00
❑ 180 Life Form Scan U .20 .50
❑ 181 Linda Larson C .10 .25
❑ 182 L'Kor U .20 .50
❑ 183 Long-Range Scan C .10 .25
❑ 184 Lore Returns R .40 1.00
❑ 185 Lore's Fingernail R .40 1.00
❑ 186 Loss of Orbital Stability C .10 .25
❑ 187 Lursa R .40 1.00
❑ 188 Lwaxanna Troi R .75 2.00
❑ 189 Male's Love Interest C .10 .25
❑ 190 Masaka Transformations U .20 .50
❑ 191 Matriarchal Society U .20 .50
❑ 192 McKnight C .10 .25
❑ 193 Medical Kit C .10 .25
❑ 194 Medical Relief R .40 1.00
❑ 195 Medical Tricorder C .10 .25
❑ 196 Mendak R .40 1.00
❑ 197 Mendon C .10 .25
❑ 198 Menthar Booby Trap C .10 .25
❑ 199 Mercenary Ship C .10 .25
❑ 200 Metaphasic Shields U .20 .50
❑ 201 Microbiotic Colony C .10 .25
❑ 202 Microvirus C .10 .25
❑ 203 Mirok U .20 .50
❑ 204 Morag U .20 .50
❑ 205 Morgan Bateson R .60 1.50
❑ 206 Mot the Barber U .20 .50
❑ 207 Movar U .20 .50
❑ 208 Nagilum R .40 1.00
❑ 209 Nanites U .20 .50
❑ 210 Narik C .10 .25
❑ 211 Nausicaans U .20 .50
❑ 212 Near Warp Transport U .20 .50
❑ 213 Neela Daren R .40 1.00
❑ 214 Neral U .20 .50
❑ 215 Neural Servo Device U .20 .50
❑ 216 New Contact R .40 1.00
❑ 217 Nikolai Rozhenko U .20 .50
❑ 218 Nitrium Metal Parasites U .20 .50
❑ 219 Norah Satie U .20 .50
❑ 220 Nu'Daq U .20 .50
❑ 221 Null Space U .20 .50
❑ 222 Nutational Shields U .20 .50
❑ 223 N'Vek U .20 .50

TCG/CCG

- ❑ 224 Ocett U .20 .50
- ❑ 225 Palor Toff - Alien Trader C .10 .25
- ❑ 226 Palteth C .10 .25
- ❑ 227 Pardek U .20 .50
- ❑ 228 Parem U .20 .50
- ❑ 229 Particle Fountain C .10 .25
- ❑ 230 Pattern Enhancers C .10 .25
- ❑ 231 Pegasus Search R .40 1.00
- ❑ 232 Phased Matter C .10 .25
- ❑ 233 Pi R .40 1.00
- ❑ 234 Plasma Fire C .10 .25
- ❑ 235 Plunder Site U .20 .50
- ❑ 236 Portal Guard U .20 .50
- ❑ 237 Q R 1.50 4.00
- ❑ 238 Q2 U .20 .50
- ❑ 239 Q-Net C .10 .25
- ❑ 240 Radioactive Garbage Scow U .20 .50
- ❑ 241 Raise The Stakes U .20 .50
- ❑ 242 Rebel Encounter U .20 .50
- ❑ 243 Red Alert! C .10 .25
- ❑ 244 Reginald Barclay R .40 1.00
- ❑ 245 Relief Mission C .10 .25
- ❑ 246 REM Fatigue Hallucinations U .20 .50
- ❑ 247 Repair Mission C .10 .25
- ❑ 248 Res-Q C .10 .25
- ❑ 249 Restore Errant Moon U .20 .50
- ❑ 250 Richard Galen R .40 1.00
- ❑ 251 Riva U .20 .50
- ❑ 252 Ro Laren R .40 1.00
- ❑ 253 Roga Danar R 2.00 5.00
- ❑ 254 Rogue Borg Mercenaries C .10 .25
- ❑ 255 Romulan Disruptor C .10 .25
- ❑ 256 Romulan Outpost C .10 .25
- ❑ 257 Romulan PADD C .10 .25
- ❑ 258 Runabout C .10 .25
- ❑ 259 Sarek R .75 2.00
- ❑ 260 Sarjenka R .75 2.00
- ❑ 261 Sarthong Plunder R .40 1.00
- ❑ 262 Satelk R .40 1.00
- ❑ 263 Scan C .10 .25
- ❑ 264 Science Vessel C .10 .25
- ❑ 265 Scout Vessel C .10 .25
- ❑ 266 Secret Salvage U .20 .50
- ❑ 267 Seek Life-Form R .40 1.00
- ❑ 268 Sela R .40 1.00
- ❑ 269 Selok C .10 .25
- ❑ 270 Shaka, When the Walls Fell U .20 .50
- ❑ 271 Shelby R .40 1.00
- ❑ 272 Ship Seizure C .10 .25
- ❑ 273 Simon Tarses C .10 .25
- ❑ 274 Sir Isaac Newton R 1.25 3.00
- ❑ 275 Sirna Kolrami U .20 .50
- ❑ 276 Sito Jaxa C .10 .25
- ❑ 277 Soren U .20 .50
- ❑ 278 Spacedock C .10 .25
- ❑ 279 Starfleet Type II Phaser C .10 .25
- ❑ 280 Static Warp Bubble C .10 .25
- ❑ 281 Strategic Diversion U .20 .50
- ❑ 282 Study Hole in Space R .40 1.00
- ❑ 283 Study Lonka Pulsar R .40 1.00
- ❑ 284 Study Nebula R .40 1.00
- ❑ 285 Study Plasma Streamer C .10 .25
- ❑ 286 Study Stellar Collision C .10 .25
- ❑ 287 Subspace Interference C .10 .25
- ❑ 288 Subspace Schism U .20 .50
- ❑ 289 Subspace Warp Rift C .10 .25
- ❑ 290 Supernova R .75 2.00
- ❑ 291 Survey Mission R .40 1.00
- ❑ 292 Tachyon Detection Grid C .10 .25
- ❑ 293 Taibak U .20 .50
- ❑ 294 Taitt C .10 .25
- ❑ 295 Takket C .10 .25
- ❑ 296 Tallus C .10 .25
- ❑ 297 Tam Elbrun R 1.25 3.00
- ❑ 298 Tarellian Plague Ship U .20 .50
- ❑ 299 Tarus C .10 .25
- ❑ 300 Tasha Yar R 2.00 5.00
- ❑ 301 Taul C .10 .25
- ❑ 302 Taurik C .10 .25
- ❑ 303 Tebok U .20 .50
- ❑ 304 Telepathic Alien Kidnappers U .20 .50
- ❑ 305 Temporal Causality Loop R .40 1.00
- ❑ 306 Temporal Rift U .20 .50
- ❑ 307 Test Mission C .10 .25
- ❑ 308 Tetryon Field C .10 .25
- ❑ 309 The Devil R .40 1.00
- ❑ 310 The Juggler U .20 .50
- ❑ 311 The Traveler: Transcendence U .20 .50
- ❑ 312 Thei C .10 .25
- ❑ 313 Thomas Riker R 1.50 4.00
- ❑ 314 Thought Maker R .40 1.00
- ❑ 315 Time Travel Pod R .40 1.00
- ❑ 316 Toby Russell U .20 .50
- ❑ 317 Tokath U .20 .50
- ❑ 318 Tomalak R .40 1.00
- ❑ 319 Tomek C .10 .25
- ❑ 320 Toq U .20 .50
- ❑ 321 Torak U .20 .50
- ❑ 322 Toral U .20 .50
- ❑ 323 Toreth R .40 1.00
- ❑ 324 Torin C .10 .25
- ❑ 325 Tox Uthat R .60 1.50
- ❑ 326 T'Pan U .20 .50
- ❑ 327 Transwarp Conduit U .20 .50
- ❑ 328 Treaty: Federation/Klingon C .10 .25
- ❑ 329 Treaty: Federation/Romulan C .10 .25
- ❑ 330 Treaty: Romulan/Klingon C .10 .25
- ❑ 331 Tricorder C .10 .25
- ❑ 332 Tsiolkovsky Infection R .40 1.00
- ❑ 333 Two-Dimensional Creatures U .20 .50
- ❑ 334 Type VI Shuttlecraft C .10 .25
- ❑ 335 U.S.S. Brittain R .40 1.00
- ❑ 336 U.S.S. Enterprise R 4.00 10.00
- ❑ 337 U.S.S. Excelsior C .10 .25
- ❑ 338 U.S.S. Galaxy C .10 .25
- ❑ 339 U.S.S. Hood R .40 1.00
- ❑ 340 U.S.S. Miranda C .10 .25
- ❑ 341 U.S.S. Nebula C .10 .25
- ❑ 342 U.S.S. Oberth C .10 .25
- ❑ 343 U.S.S. Phoenix R .40 1.00
- ❑ 344 U.S.S. Sutherland U .20 .50
- ❑ 345 U.S.S. Yamato R .40 1.00
- ❑ 346 Vagh U .20 .50
- ❑ 347 Varel C .10 .25
- ❑ 348 Varon-T Disruptor R .40 1.00
- ❑ 349 Vash R .40 1.00
- ❑ 350 Vekma C .10 .25
- ❑ 351 Vekor C .10 .25
- ❑ 352 Vulcan Mindmeld U .20 .50
- ❑ 353 Vulcan Stone of Gol R .40 1.00
- ❑ 354 Warp Core Breach R .40 1.00
- ❑ 355 Wesley Crusher R 1.25 3.00
- ❑ 356 Where No One Has Gone Before C .10 .25
- ❑ 357 William T. Riker R 3.00 8.00
- ❑ 358 Wind Dancer R .40 1.00
- ❑ 359 Worf R 2.00 5.00
- ❑ 360 Wormhole C .10 .25
- ❑ 361 Wormhole Negotiations R .60 1.50
- ❑ 362 Yridian Shuttle C .10 .25
- ❑ 363 Zibalian Transport C .10 .25

1995 Star Trek Alternate Universe

- BOOSTER BOX (36) 15.00 30.00
- BOOSTER PACK (15) 1.00 1.50
- ❑ 1 Ajur U .20 .50
- ❑ 2 Alien Labyrinth C .10 .25
- ❑ 3 Alternate Universe Door C .10 .25
- ❑ 4 Anti-Matter Spread C .10 .25
- ❑ 5 Barclay's Transporter Phobia U .20 .50
- ❑ 6 Baryon Buildup C .10 .25
- ❑ 7 Berlingoff Rasmussen R 1.25 3.00
- ❑ 8 Beverly Picard R 2.00 5.00
- ❑ 9 Boratus U .20 .50
- ❑ 10 Brain Drain U .20 .50
- ❑ 11 Brute Force R .75 2.00
- ❑ 12 Captain's Log U .20 .50
- ❑ 13 Cardassian Trap U .20 .50
- ❑ 14 Coalescent Organism R .75 2.00
- ❑ 15 Commander Tomalak R 2.00 5.00
- ❑ 16 Compromised Mission R 1.50 4.00
- ❑ 17 Conundrum C .10 .25
- ❑ 18 Countermanda C .10 .25
- ❑ 19 Cryosatellite R 1.25 3.00
- ❑ 20 Data's Head R 1.50 4.00
- ❑ 21 Dathon R .75 2.00
- ❑ 22 Dead in Bed U .20 .50
- ❑ 23 Decius R .75 2.00
- ❑ 24 Destroy Radioactive Garbage Scow C .10 .25
- ❑ 25 Devidian Door R 1.50 4.00
- ❑ 26 Devidian Foragers C .10 .25
- ❑ 27 Diplomatic Conference R .75 2.00
- ❑ 28 D'Tan U .20 .50
- ❑ 29 Echo Papa 607 Killer Drone R 1.50 4.00
- ❑ 30 Edo Probe U .20 .50
- ❑ 31 Edo Vessel R .75 2.00
- ❑ 32 Empathic Echo C .10 .25
- ❑ 33 Engage Shuttle Operations U .20 .50
- ❑ 34 Eyes in the Dark C .10 .25
- ❑ 35 Ferengi Attack C .10 .25
- ❑ 36 FGC-47 Research R .75 2.00
- ❑ 37 Fire Sculptor C .10 .25
- ❑ 38 Fissure Research R .75 2.00
- ❑ 39 Frame of Mind U .20 .50
- ❑ 40 Future Enterprise UR 30.00 60.00
- ❑ 41 Gomtuu R .75 2.00
- ❑ 42 Governor Worf R 1.25 3.00
- ❑ 43 Hail C .10 .25
- ❑ 44 Hidden Entrance C .10 .25
- ❑ 45 Howard Heirloom Candle C .10 .25
- ❑ 46 Humuhumunukunukuapua'a C .10 .25
- ❑ 47 Hunter Gangs C .10 .25
- ❑ 48 I.K.C. Fek'lhr R .75 2.00
- ❑ 49 I.K.C. K'Ratak C .10 .25
- ❑ 50 I.P. Scanner C .10 .25
- ❑ 51 Ian Andrew Troi R 1.25 3.00
- ❑ 52 Iconian Gateway R .75 2.00
- ❑ 53 Incoming Message: Attack Authorization U .20 .50
- ❑ 54 Interphasic Plasma Creatures C .10 .25
- ❑ 55 Interrogation R .75 2.00
- ❑ 56 Intruder Force Field U .20 .50
- ❑ 57 Isabella U .20 .50
- ❑ 58 Jack Crusher R 1.25 3.00
- ❑ 59 Jamaharon C .10 .25
- ❑ 60 Kevin Uxbridge: Convergence C .10 .25
- ❑ 61 Klim Dokachin U .20 .50
- ❑ 62 K'mtar R .75 2.00
- ❑ 63 LaForge Maneuver U .20 .50
- ❑ 64 Lakanta U .20 .50
- ❑ 65 Latinum Payoff C .10 .25
- ❑ 66 Lower Decks U .20 .50
- ❑ 67 Lt. (j.g.) Picard U .20 .50
- ❑ 68 Major Rakal R 1.25 3.00
- ❑ 69 Malfunctioning Door C .10 .25
- ❑ 70 Maman Picard U .20 .50
- ❑ 71 Maques U .20 .50
- ❑ 72 Mickey D. U .20 .50
- ❑ 73 Montgomery Scott C .10 .25
- ❑ 74 Mot's Advice U .20 .50
- ❑ 75 Neutral Outpost C .10 .25
- ❑ 76 Ophidian Cane R .75 2.00
- ❑ 77 Outpost Raid C .10 .25
- ❑ 78 Parallel Romance U .20 .50
- ❑ 79 Particle Scattering Field C .10 .25
- ❑ 80 Paul Rice U .20 .50
- ❑ 81 Phaser Burns C .10 .25
- ❑ 82 Punishment Zone C .10 .25
- ❑ 83 Qualor II Rendezvous U .20 .50
- ❑ 84 Quantum Singularity Lifeforms U .20 .50
- ❑ 85 Quash Conspiracy R .75 2.00
- ❑ 86 Rachel Garrett R 1.50 4.00
- ❑ 87 Rascals U .20 .50
- ❑ 88 Receptacle Stones R .75 2.00
- ❑ 89 Rescue Captives U .20 .50
- ❑ 90 Ressikan Flute R .75 2.00
- ❑ 91 Reunion R .75 2.00
- ❑ 92 Revolving Door R .75 2.00
- ❑ 93 Richard Castillo U .20 .50
- ❑ 94 Risa Shore Leave R .75 2.00
- ❑ 95 Rishon Uxbridge C .10 .25
- ❑ 96 Romulan Ambush U .20 .50
- ❑ 97 Royale Casino: Blackjack U .20 .50
- ❑ 98 Samuel Clemens' Pocketwatch R 1.25 3.00
- ❑ 99 Security Sacrifice C .10 .25
- ❑ 100 Seize Wesley R .75 2.00
- ❑ 101 Senior Staff Meeting U .20 .50
- ❑ 102 Stefan DeSeve R .75 2.00
- ❑ 103 Tama U .20 .50
- ❑ 104 Targ C .10 .25
- ❑ 105 Tasha Yar - Alternate R 1.50 4.00
- ❑ 106 Temporal Narcosis U .20 .50
- ❑ 107 The Charybdis U .20 .50
- ❑ 108 The Gatherers C .10 .25
- ❑ 109 The Higher... The Fewer U .20 .50
- ❑ 110 The Mask of Korgano C .10 .25
- ❑ 111 Thermal Deflectors U .20 .50
- ❑ 112 Thine Own Self C .10 .25
- ❑ 113 Thought Fire C .10 .25
- ❑ 114 U.S.S. Enterprise-C R 1.50 4.00
- ❑ 115 Vorgon Raiders R .75 2.00
- ❑ 116 Vulcan Nerve Pinch C .10 .25
- ❑ 117 Warped Space R 1.25 3.00
- ❑ 118 Wartime Conditions R .75 2.00
- ❑ 119 Wolf U .20 .50
- ❑ 120 Worshiper C .10 .25
- ❑ 121 Yellow Alert C .10 .25
- ❑ 122 Zaldan U .20 .50

1995 Star Trek Premiere White Border

- ❑ 1 Albert Einstein R 1.25 3.00
- ❑ 2 Alexander Rozhenko U .20 .50
- ❑ 3 Alidar Jarok R .40 1.00
- ❑ 4 Alien Abduction U .20 .50
- ❑ 5 Alien Groupie R .40 1.00
- ❑ 6 Alien Parasites U .20 .50
- ❑ 7 Alien Probe U .20 .50
- ❑ 8 Alynna Nechayev R .40 1.00
- ❑ 9 Alyssa Ogawa U .20 .50
- ❑ 10 Amanda Rogers U .20 .50
- ❑ 11 Amarie U .20 .50
- ❑ 12 Anaphasic Organism C .10 .25
- ❑ 13 Ancient Computer R .40 1.00
- ❑ 14 Anti-Time Anomaly R .75 2.00
- ❑ 15 Archer C .10 .25
- ❑ 16 Armus - Skin of Evil R .40 1.00
- ❑ 17 Asteroid Sanctuary C .10 .25
- ❑ 18 Atmospheric Ionization C .10 .25
- ❑ 19 Auto-Destruct Sequence U .20 .50
- ❑ 20 Avert Disaster R .40 1.00
- ❑ 21 Ba'el U .20 .50
- ❑ 22 Baran U .20 .50
- ❑ 23 Barclay's Protomorphosis Disease R .40 1.00
- ❑ 24 Batrell C .10 .25
- ❑ 25 Benjamin Maxwell U .20 .50
- ❑ 26 Betazoid Gift Box R .40 1.00
- ❑ 27 B'Etor R .60 1.50
- ❑ 28 Beverly Crusher R .60 1.50
- ❑ 29 B'iJik C .10 .25
- ❑ 30 Birth of Junior U .20 .50
- ❑ 31 Bochra U .20 .50
- ❑ 32 Bok U .20 .50
- ❑ 33 Borg Ship R 1.50 4.00
- ❑ 34 Bynars Weapon Enhancement R .60 1.50
- ❑ 35 Calloway C .10 .25
- ❑ 36 Chalnoth U .20 .50
- ❑ 37 Christopher Hobson C .10 .25
- ❑ 38 Cloaked Mission U .20 .50
- ❑ 39 Combat Vessel C .10 .25
- ❑ 40 Cosmic String Fragment U .20 .50
- ❑ 41 Covert Installation C .10 .25
- ❑ 42 Covert Rescue U .20 .50
- ❑ 43 Crosis R 1.25 3.00
- ❑ 44 Crystalline Entity R .40 1.00
- ❑ 45 Cultural Observation R .40 1.00
- ❑ 46 Cytherians R .40 1.00
- ❑ 47 Darian Wallace C .10 .25
- ❑ 48 Data R 2.00 5.00
- ❑ 49 D'deridex C .10 .25
- ❑ 50 Deanna Troi R 2.00 5.00
- ❑ 51 Devinoni Ral U .20 .50
- ❑ 52 Devoras R .75 2.00
- ❑ 53 Diplomacy Mission U .20 .50
- ❑ 54 Disruptor Overload C .10 .25
- ❑ 55 Distortion Field U .20 .50
- ❑ 56 Distortion of Space/Time Continuum U .20 .50
- ❑ 57 Divok C .10 .25
- ❑ 58 Dr. Farek C .10 .25
- ❑ 59 Dr. LaForge R .40 1.00
- ❑ 60 Dr. Leah Brahms R .60 1.50
- ❑ 61 Dr. Reyga U .20 .50
- ❑ 62 Dr. Selar U .20 .50
- ❑ 63 Dukath C .10 .25
- ❑ 64 Duras R .40 1.00
- ❑ 65 El-Adrel Creature U .20 .50
- ❑ 66 Emergency Transporter Armbands C .10 .25
- ❑ 67 Energy Vortex U .20 .50
- ❑ 68 Engineering Kit C .10 .25
- ❑ 69 Engineering PADD C .10 .25
- ❑ 70 Eric Pressman U .20 .50
- ❑ 71 Escape Pod C .10 .25
- ❑ 72 Espionage: Federation on Klingon C .10 .25
- ❑ 73 Espionage: Klingon on Federation C .10 .25
- ❑ 74 Espionage: Romulan on Federation C .10 .25
- ❑ 75 Espionage: Romulan on Klingon C .10 .25
- ❑ 76 Etana Jol U .20 .50
- ❑ 77 Evacuation U .20 .50
- ❑ 78 Evaluate Terraforming R .40 1.00
- ❑ 79 Evek U .20 .50
- ❑ 80 Excavation C .10 .25
- ❑ 81 Exocomp U .20 .50
- ❑ 82 Explore Black Cluster R .40 1.00
- ❑ 83 Explore Dyson Sphere R .40 1.00
- ❑ 84 Explore Typhone Expanse R .40 1.00
- ❑ 85 Expose Covert Supply U .20 .50
- ❑ 86 Extraction R .40 1.00
- ❑ 87 Federation Outpost C .10 .25
- ❑ 88 Federation PADD C .10 .25
- ❑ 89 Fek'lhr U .20 .50
- ❑ 90 Female's Love Interest C .10 .25
- ❑ 91 Fever Emergency C .10 .25
- ❑ 92 Firestorm U .20 .50
- ❑ 93 First Contact U .20 .50
- ❑ 94 Fleet Admiral Shanthi U .20 .50
- ❑ 95 Full Planet Scan U .20 .50
- ❑ 96 Galathon C .10 .25
- ❑ 97 Gaps in Normal Space U .20 .50
- ❑ 98 Genetronic Replicator U .20 .50
- ❑ 99 Geordi LaForge R 3.00 8.00
- ❑ 100 Giusti C .10 .25
- ❑ 101 Goddess of Empathy R .40 1.00
- ❑ 102 Gorath C .10 .25
- ❑ 103 Gorta C .10 .25
- ❑ 104 Gowron R .40 1.00
- ❑ 105 Gravitic Mine U .20 .50
- ❑ 106 Haakona R .60 1.50
- ❑ 107 Hannah Bates U .20 .50
- ❑ 108 Hologram Ruse U .20 .50
- ❑ 109 Holo-Projectors U .20 .50
- ❑ 110 Honor Challenge R .40 1.00
- ❑ 111 Horga'hn R .75 2.00
- ❑ 112 Hugh R .40 1.00
- ❑ 113 Hunt for DNA Program R .40 1.00
- ❑ 114 Husnock Ship U .20 .50
- ❑ 115 Hyper-Aging U .20 .50
- ❑ 116 I.K.C. Bortas R .40 1.00
- ❑ 117 I.K.C. Buruk R .40 1.00
- ❑ 118 I.K.C. Hegh'ta R .40 1.00
- ❑ 119 I.K.C. K'Vort C .10 .25
- ❑ 120 I.K.C. Pagh R .40 1.00
- ❑ 121 I.K.C. Qu'Vat R .40 1.00
- ❑ 122 I.K.C. Vor'Cha C .10 .25
- ❑ 123 I.K.C. Vorn U .20 .50
- ❑ 124 Iconia Investigation R .40 1.00
- ❑ 125 Iconian Computer Weapon C .10 .25
- ❑ 126 Impassable Door C .10 .25
- ❑ 127 Incoming Message - Federation U .20 .50
- ❑ 128 Incoming Message - Klingon U .20 .50
- ❑ 129 Incoming Message - Romulan U .20 .50
- ❑ 130 Interphase Generator R .40 1.00
- ❑ 131 Investigate Shattered Space R .40 1.00
- ❑ 132 Investigate Alien Probe R .40 1.00
- ❑ 133 Investigate Anomaly C .10 .25
- ❑ 134 Investigate Disappearance R .40 1.00
- ❑ 135 Investigate Disturbance R .40 1.00
- ❑ 136 Investigate Massacre R .40 1.00
- ❑ 137 Investigate Raid R .40 1.00
- ❑ 138 Investigate Rogue Comet R .60 1.50
- ❑ 139 Investigate Sighting R .40 1.00
- ❑ 140 Investigate Time Continuum R .60 1.50
- ❑ 141 Ishara Yar U .20 .50
- ❑ 142 Jaglom Shrek - Information Broker R .40 1.00
- ❑ 143 Jaron C .10 .25
- ❑ 144 J'Dan C .10 .25
- ❑ 145 Jean-Luc Picard R 5.00 10.00
- ❑ 146 Jenna D'Sora U .20 .50
- ❑ 147 Jera C .10 .25
- ❑ 148 Jo'Bril U .20 .50
- ❑ 149 Kahless R .40 1.00
- ❑ 150 Kareel Odan U .20 .50
- ❑ 151 Kargan R .40 1.00
- ❑ 152 K'Ehleyr R .40 1.00
- ❑ 153 Kell U .20 .50
- ❑ 154 Kevin Uxbridge U .20 .50
- ❑ 155 Khazara R .40 1.00
- ❑ 156 Khitomer Research R .40 1.00
- ❑ 157 Kivas Fajo - Collector U .20 .50
- ❑ 158 Klag C .10 .25
- ❑ 159 Kle'eg C .10 .25
- ❑ 160 Klingon Death Yell R .40 1.00
- ❑ 161 Klingon Disruptor C .10 .25
- ❑ 162 Klingon Outpost C .10 .25
- ❑ 163 Klingon PADD C .10 .25
- ❑ 164 Klingon Right of Vengeance C .10 .25
- ❑ 165 K'mpec U .20 .50
- ❑ 166 Konmel U .20 .50
- ❑ 167 Koral U .20 .50
- ❑ 168 Koroth U .20 .50
- ❑ 169 Korris U .20 .50
- ❑ 170 Krios Suppression U .20 .50
- ❑ 171 Kromm C .10 .25
- ❑ 172 K'Tal U .20 .50
- ❑ 173 Ktarian Game R .40 1.00
- ❑ 174 K'Tesh C .10 .25
- ❑ 175 Kurak R .60 1.50
- ❑ 176 Kurlan Naiskos R .60 1.50
- ❑ 177 Kurn R .40 1.00
- ❑ 178 K'Vada U .20 .50
- ❑ 179 Leah Brahms R .40 1.00
- ❑ 180 Life Form Scan U .20 .50
- ❑ 181 Linda Larson C .10 .25
- ❑ 182 L'Kor U .20 .50
- ❑ 183 Long-Range Scan C .10 .25
- ❑ 184 Lore Returns R .40 1.00
- ❑ 185 Lore's Fingernail R .40 1.00
- ❑ 186 Loss of Orbital Stability C .10 .25
- ❑ 187 Lursa R .40 1.00
- ❑ 188 Lwaxanna Troi R .75 2.00
- ❑ 189 Male's Love Interest C .10 .25
- ❑ 190 Masaka Transformations U .20 .50
- ❑ 191 Matriarchal Society U .20 .50
- ❑ 192 McKnight C .10 .25
- ❑ 193 Medical Kit C .10 .25
- ❑ 194 Medical Relief R .40 1.00
- ❑ 195 Medical Tricorder C .10 .25
- ❑ 196 Mendak R .40 1.00
- ❑ 197 Mendon C .10 .25
- ❑ 198 Menthar Booby Trap C .10 .25
- ❑ 199 Mercenary Ship C .10 .25
- ❑ 200 Metaphasic Shields U .20 .50
- ❑ 201 Microbiotic Colony C .10 .25
- ❑ 202 Microvirus C .10 .25
- ❑ 203 Mirok U .20 .50
- ❑ 204 Morag U .20 .50
- ❑ 205 Morgan Bateson R .60 1.50
- ❑ 206 Mot the Barber U .20 .50
- ❑ 207 Movar U .20 .50
- ❑ 208 Nagilum R .40 1.00
- ❑ 209 Nanites U .20 .50
- ❑ 210 Narik C .10 .25
- ❑ 211 Nausicaans U .20 .50
- ❑ 212 Near Warp Transport U .20 .50
- ❑ 213 Neela Daren R .40 1.00
- ❑ 214 Neral U .20 .50
- ❑ 215 Neural Servo Device U .20 .50
- ❑ 216 New Contact R .40 1.00
- ❑ 217 Nikolai Rozhenko U .20 .50
- ❑ 218 Nitrium Metal Parasites U .20 .50
- ❑ 219 Norah Satie U .20 .50
- ❑ 220 Nu'Daq U .20 .50
- ❑ 221 Null Space U .20 .50
- ❑ 222 Nutational Shields U .20 .50
- ❑ 223 N'Vek U .20 .50
- ❑ 224 Ocett U .20 .50
- ❑ 225 Palor Toff - Alien Trader C .10 .25
- ❑ 226 Palteth C .10 .25
- ❑ 227 Pardek U .20 .50
- ❑ 228 Parem U .20 .50
- ❑ 229 Particle Fountain C .10 .25
- ❑ 230 Pattern Enhancers C .10 .25
- ❑ 231 Pegasus Search R .40 1.00
- ❑ 232 Phased Matter C .10 .25
- ❑ 233 Pi R .40 1.00
- ❑ 234 Plasma Fire C .10 .25
- ❑ 235 Plunder Site U .20 .50
- ❑ 236 Portal Guard U .20 .50
- ❑ 237 Q R 1.50 4.00
- ❑ 238 Q2 U .20 .50
- ❑ 239 Q-Net C .10 .25
- ❑ 240 Radioactive Garbage Scow U .20 .50
- ❑ 241 Raise The Stakes U .20 .50
- ❑ 242 Rebel Encounter U .20 .50
- ❑ 243 Red Alert! C .10 .25
- ❑ 244 Reginald Barclay R .40 1.00
- ❑ 245 Relief Mission C .10 .25
- ❑ 246 REM Fatigue Hallucinations U .20 .50
- ❑ 247 Repair Mission C .10 .25
- ❑ 248 Res-Q C .10 .25
- ❑ 249 Restore Errant Moon U .20 .50
- ❑ 250 Richard Galen R .40 1.00
- ❑ 251 Riva U .20 .50
- ❑ 252 Ro Laren R .40 1.00
- ❑ 253 Roga Danar R 2.00 5.00

❑ 254 Rogue Borg Mercenaries C .10 .25
❑ 255 Romulan Disruptor C .10 .25
❑ 256 Romulan Outpost C .10 .25
❑ 257 Romulan PADD C .10 .25
❑ 258 Runabout C .10 .25
❑ 259 Sarek R .75 2.00
❑ 260 Sarjenka R .75 2.00
❑ 261 Sarthong Plunder R .40 1.00
❑ 262 Satelk R .40 1.00
❑ 263 Scan C .10 .25
❑ 264 Science Vessel C .10 .25
❑ 265 Scout Vessel C .10 .25
❑ 266 Secret Salvage U .20 .50
❑ 267 Seek Life-Form R .40 1.00
❑ 268 Sela R .40 1.00
❑ 269 Selok C .10 .25
❑ 270 Shaka, When the Walls Fell U .20 .50
❑ 271 Shelby R .40 1.00
❑ 272 Ship Seizure C .10 .25
❑ 273 Simon Tarses C .10 .25
❑ 274 Sir Isaac Newton R 1.25 3.00
❑ 275 Sirna Kolrami U .20 .50
❑ 276 Sito Jaxa C .10 .25
❑ 277 Soren U .20 .50
❑ 278 Spacedock C .10 .25
❑ 279 Starfleet Type II Phaser C .10 .25
❑ 280 Static Warp Bubble C .10 .25
❑ 281 Strategic Diversion U .20 .50
❑ 282 Study Hole in Space R .40 1.00
❑ 283 Study Lonka Pulsar R .40 1.00
❑ 284 Study Nebula R .40 1.00
❑ 285 Study Plasma Streamer C .10 .25
❑ 286 Study Stellar Collision C .10 .25
❑ 287 Subspace Interference C .10 .25
❑ 288 Subspace Schism U .20 .50
❑ 289 Subspace Warp Rift C .10 .25
❑ 290 Supernova R .75 2.00
❑ 291 Survey Mission R .40 1.00
❑ 292 Tachyon Detection Grid C .10 .25
❑ 293 Taibak U .20 .50
❑ 294 Taitt C .10 .25
❑ 295 Takket C .10 .25
❑ 296 Tallus C .10 .25
❑ 297 Tam Elbrun R 1.25 3.00
❑ 298 Tarellian Plague Ship U .20 .50
❑ 299 Tarus C .10 .25
❑ 300 Tasha Yar R 2.00 5.00
❑ 301 Taul C .10 .25
❑ 302 Taurik C .10 .25
❑ 303 Tebok U .20 .50
❑ 304 Telepathic Alien Kidnappers U .20 .50
❑ 305 Temporal Causality Loop R .40 1.00
❑ 306 Temporal Rift U .20 .50
❑ 307 Test Mission C .10 .25
❑ 308 Tetryon Field C .10 .25
❑ 309 The Devil R .40 1.00
❑ 310 The Juggler U .20 .50
❑ 311 The Traveler: Transcendence U .20 .50
❑ 312 Thei C .10 .25
❑ 313 Thomas Riker R 1.50 4.00
❑ 314 Thought Maker R .40 1.00
❑ 315 Time Travel Pod R .40 1.00
❑ 316 Toby Russell U .20 .50
❑ 317 Tokath U .20 .50
❑ 318 Tomalak R .40 1.00
❑ 319 Tomek C .10 .25
❑ 320 Toq U .20 .50
❑ 321 Torak U .20 .50
❑ 322 Toral U .20 .50
❑ 323 Toreth R .40 1.00
❑ 324 Torin C .10 .25
❑ 325 Tox Uthat R .60 1.50
❑ 326 T'Pan U .20 .50
❑ 327 Transwarp Conduit U .20 .50
❑ 328 Treaty: Federation/Klingon C .10 .25
❑ 329 Treaty: Federation/Romulan C .10 .25
❑ 330 Treaty: Romulan/Klingon C .10 .25
❑ 331 Tricorder C .10 .25
❑ 332 Tsiolkovsky Infection R .40 1.00
❑ 333 Two-Dimensional Creatures U .20 .50
❑ 334 Type VI Shuttlecraft C .10 .25
❑ 335 U.S.S. Brittain R .40 1.00
❑ 336 U.S.S. Enterprise R 4.00 10.00
❑ 337 U.S.S. Excelsior C .10 .25
❑ 338 U.S.S. Galaxy C .10 .25
❑ 339 U.S.S. Hood R .40 1.00
❑ 340 U.S.S. Miranda C .10 .25
❑ 341 U.S.S. Nebula C .10 .25
❑ 342 U.S.S. Oberth C .10 .25
❑ 343 U.S.S. Phoenix R .40 1.00
❑ 344 U.S.S. Sutherland U .20 .50
❑ 345 U.S.S. Yamato R .40 1.00
❑ 346 Vagh U .20 .50
❑ 347 Varel C .10 .25
❑ 348 Varon-T Disruptor R .40 1.00
❑ 349 Vash R .40 1.00
❑ 350 Vekma C .10 .25
❑ 351 Vekor C .10 .25
❑ 352 Vulcan Mindmeld U .20 .50
❑ 353 Vulcan Stone of Gol R .40 1.00
❑ 354 Warp Core Breach R .40 1.00
❑ 355 Wesley Crusher R 1.25 3.00
❑ 356 Where No One Has Gone Before C .10 .25
❑ 357 William T. Riker R 3.00 8.00
❑ 358 Wind Dancer R .40 1.00
❑ 359 Worf R 2.00 5.00
❑ 360 Wormhole C .10 .25
❑ 361 Wormhole Negotiations R .60 1.50
❑ 362 Yridian Shuttle C .10 .25
❑ 363 Zibalian Transport C .10 .25

1996 Star Trek Q Continuum

COMPLETE SET (121) 15.00 30.00
BOOSTER BOX (36) 20.00 40.00
BOOSTER PACK (18) 1.00 2.00

❑ 1 Aldebaran Serpent C .10 .25
❑ 2 Amanda's Parents C .10 .25
❑ 3 Android Nightmares U .20 .50
❑ 4 Anti-Matter Pod C .10 .25
❑ 5 Arbiter of Succession R .75 2.00
❑ 6 Are These Truly Your Friends, Brother? C .10 .25
❑ 7 Barber Pole U .20 .50
❑ 8 Bendii Syndrome R .75 2.00
❑ 9 Blade of Tkon R .75 2.00
❑ 10 Brainwash R .75 2.00
❑ 11 Calamarain R .75 2.00
❑ 12 Canar R .75 2.00
❑ 13 Chinese Finger Puzzle C .10 .25
❑ 14 Colony C .10 .25
❑ 15 Data's Body R 1.25 3.00
❑ 16 Data's Medals C .10 .25

Beckett Star Trek price guide sponsored by wholesalegaming.com

❑ 17 Discommendation U .20 .50
❑ 18 Door-Net U .20 .50
❑ 19 Doppelganger R 1.25 3.00
❑ 20 Dr. Q, Medicine Entity C .10 .25
❑ 21 Drag Net R .75 2.00
❑ 22 Drought Tree C .10 .25
❑ 23 End Transmission C .10 .25
❑ 24 Frigid U .20 .50
❑ 25 Galen R 1.25 3.00
❑ 26 Gibson C .10 .25
❑ 27 Gift of the Tormentor C .10 .25
❑ 28 Go Back Whence thou Camest C .10 .25
❑ 29 Guilty - Provisionally U .20 .50
❑ 30 Heisenberg Compensators U .20 .50
❑ 31 His Honor, the High Sheriff of Notthingam U .20 .50
❑ 32 I am not a Merry Man R .75 2.00
❑ 33 I.K.C. Maht-H'a R .75 2.00
❑ 34 I.K.C. T'ong U .20 .50
❑ 35 Immortal Again U .20 .50
❑ 36 Incoming Message - The Continuum C .10 .25
❑ 37 Into the Breach C .10 .25
❑ 38 Investigate Legend R .75 2.00
❑ 39 Ira Graves R .75 2.00
❑ 40 Jealous Amanda C .10 .25
❑ 41 Jenice Manheim U .20 .50
❑ 42 John Doe U .20 .50
❑ 43 Juliana Tainer R 1.25 3.00
❑ 44 Kahlest U .20 .50
❑ 45 Kareen Brianon U .20 .50
❑ 46 Katherine Pulaski R 1.25 3.00
❑ 47 K'chiQ U .20 .50
❑ 48 Keiko O'Brien R 1.25 3.00
❑ 49 Kitrik U .20 .50
❑ 50 Klingon Civil War R .75 2.00
❑ 51 Klingon Painstik U .20 .50
❑ 52 K'nera U .20 .50
❑ 53 Kova Tholl U .20 .50
❑ 54 Lal R 1.25 3.00
❑ 55 Lemon-Aid C .10 .25
❑ 56 Madam Guinan R 1.25 3.00
❑ 57 Madred R .75 2.00
❑ 58 Mandarin Bailiff C .10 .25
❑ 59 Manheim's Dimensional Door R .75 2.00
❑ 60 Marouk U .20 .50
❑ 61 Military Privilege C .10 .25
❑ 62 Mirasta Yale U .20 .50
❑ 63 Mona Lisa R .75 2.00
❑ 64 Mordock U .20 .50
❑ 65 Mortal Q R 1.50 4.00
❑ 66 Mr. Homm R .75 2.00
❑ 67 Nebula C .10 .25
❑ 68 Nick Locarno R .75 2.00
❑ 69 Off Switch C .10 .25
❑ 70 Parallax Arguers C .10 .25
❑ 71 Paul Manheim R .75 2.00
❑ 72 Paxan Wormhole R .75 2.00
❑ 73 Penalty Box U .20 .50
❑ 74 Plague Planet R .75 2.00
❑ 75 Pla-Net C .10 .25
❑ 76 Plasmadyne Relay C .10 .25
❑ 77 Plexing C .10 .25
❑ 78 Q-Flash C .10 .25
❑ 79 Q's Planet U .20 .50
❑ 80 Q's Tent C .10 .25
❑ 81 Q's Vicious Animal Things U .20 .50
❑ 82 Rager U .20 .50
❑ 83 Robin Lefler U .20 .50
❑ 84 Royale Casino: Craps U .20 .50
❑ 85 Sakkath U .20 .50
❑ 86 Samaritan Snare R .75 2.00
❑ 87 Samuel Clemens U .20 .50
❑ 88 Scottish Setter C .10 .25
❑ 89 Security Precautions C .10 .25
❑ 90 Sirol U .20 .50
❑ 91 Sonya Gomez U .20 .50
❑ 92 Soong-type Android C .10 .25
❑ 93 Space C .10 .25
❑ 94 Subsection Q, Paragraph 10 C .10 .25
❑ 95 System Wide Cascade Failure R .75 2.00
❑ 96 Tarchannen Study R .75 2.00
❑ 97 Taris R .75 2.00
❑ 98 Tarmin R .75 2.00
❑ 99 Telak U .20 .50
❑ 100 Terix R .75 2.00
❑ 101 Terraforming Station R .75 2.00
❑ 102 The Higher…the Q-er C .10 .25
❑ 103 The Issue is Patriotism U .20 .50
❑ 104 The Naked Truth C .10 .25
❑ 105 The Sheliak R .75 2.00
❑ 106 Tijuana Crass C .10 .25
❑ 107 Timicin U .20 .50
❑ 108 T'Pau U .20 .50
❑ 109 Transfiguration U .20 .50
❑ 110 Trust Me C .10 .25
❑ 111 T'Shanik U .20 .50
❑ 112 U.S.S. Stargazer R 1.50 4.00
❑ 113 Ves Alkar U .20 .50
❑ 114 Wesley Gets the Point U .20 .50
❑ 115 Where's Guinan? U .20 .50
❑ 116 Wrong Door U .20 .50
❑ 117 You Will in Time C .10 .25
❑ 118 Yuta R 1.25 3.00
❑ 119 Zalkonian Storage Capsule R .75 2.00
❑ 120 Zalkonian Vessel C .10 .25
❑ 121 Zon R .75 2.00

1997 Star Trek First Anthology

❑ 1 Dr. Telek R'Mor PV 2.00 5.00
❑ 2 Ensign Tuvok PV 2.00 5.00
❑ 3 Garak PV 2.00 5.00
❑ 4 Orb of Prophecy and Change PV 2.00 5.00
❑ 5 Quark Son of Keldar PV 2.00 5.00
❑ 6 Thomas Paris PV 2.00 5.00

1997 Star Trek First Contact

❑ 1 A Change of Plans C .10 .25
❑ 2 Abandon Mission R .60 1.50
❑ 3 Activate Subcommands C .10 .25
❑ 4 Adapt: Modulate Shields U .20 .50
❑ 5 Adapt: Negate Obstruction C .10 .25
❑ 6 Admiral Hayes R .75 2.00
❑ 7 Alas, Poor Queen R .60 1.50
❑ 8 Alyssa Ogawa R .75 2.00
❑ 9 Android Headlock R .60 1.50
❑ 10 Antique Machine Gun R .60 1.50
❑ 11 Assign Mission Specialists C .10 .25
❑ 12 Assimilate Counterpart U .20 .50
❑ 13 Assimilate Homeworld R 1.00 2.50
❑ 14 Assimilate Planet C .10 .25
❑ 15 Assimilate Starship U .20 .50
❑ 16 Assimilate This! R .60 1.50
❑ 17 Assimilation Table U .20 .50
❑ 18 Assimilation Tubules U .20 .50
❑ 19 Awaken C .10 .25
❑ 20 Balancing Act U .20 .50
❑ 21 Beverly Crusher R 1.50 4.00
❑ 22 Blended U .20 .50
❑ 23 Borg Cube C .10 .25
❑ 24 Borg Kiss R .60 1.50
❑ 25 Borg Neuroprocessor R .60 1.50
❑ 26 Borg Outpost C .10 .25
❑ 27 Borg Queen R .75 2.00
❑ 28 Borg Scout Vessel C .10 .25
❑ 29 Borg Servo U .20 .50
❑ 30 Borg Sphere C .10 .25
❑ 31 Build Interplexing Beacon R .60 1.50
❑ 32 Data R 2.00 5.00
❑ 33 Deactivation C .10 .25
❑ 34 Dead End U .20 .50
❑ 35 Deanna Troi R 1.25 3.00
❑ 36 Disengage Safety Protocols U .20 .50
❑ 37 Don't Call Me Ahab U .20 .50
❑ 38 Dr. Royse C .10 .25
❑ 39 E.M.H. Program U .20 .50
❑ 40 Eight of Nineteen C .10 .25
❑ 41 Eighteen of Nineteen C .10 .25
❑ 42 Eleven of Nineteen C .10 .25
❑ 43 Eliminate Starship U .20 .50
❑ 44 Espionage Mission R .75 2.00
❑ 45 Establish Gateway C .10 .25
❑ 46 Fifteen of Seventeen C .10 .25
❑ 47 Five of Eleven C .10 .25
❑ 48 Four of Eleven C .10 .25
❑ 49 Fractal Encryption Code U .20 .50
❑ 50 Geordi LaForge R 1.50 4.00
❑ 51 Hawk U .20 .50
❑ 52 He Will Make an Excellent Drone U .20 .50
❑ 53 I'm a Doctor, Not a Doorstop U .20 .50
❑ 54 Inge Eiger C .10 .25
❑ 55 Intermix Ratio U .20 .50
❑ 56 Jean-Luc Picard R 2.00 5.00
❑ 57 Joseph Travis C .10 .25
❑ 58 Kathleen Tonell U .20 .50
❑ 59 Lack of Preparation C .10 .25
❑ 60 Launch Portal U .20 .50
❑ 61 Lightner U .20 .50
❑ 62 Lily Sloane R .75 2.00
❑ 63 Lisa Azar U .20 .50
❑ 64 Magic Carpet Ride OCD R .60 1.50
❑ 65 Maglock C .10 .25
❑ 66 Mercy Kill U .20 .50
❑ 67 Mirror Image U .20 .50
❑ 68 Mission Debriefing U .20 .50
❑ 69 Montana Missile Complex R .60 1.50
❑ 70 My First Raygun R .60 1.50
❑ 71 Nine of Eleven C .10 .25
❑ 72 Nine of Seventeen C .10 .25
❑ 73 Obarakeh C .10 .25
❑ 74 Ocular Implants R .60 1.50
❑ 75 One of Eleven C .10 .25
❑ 76 Ooby Dooby R .60 1.50
❑ 77 Patrol Neutral Zone C .10 .25
❑ 78 Paul Porter R .60 1.50
❑ 79 Phoenix R .75 2.00
❑ 80 Planet C .10 .25
❑ 81 Prepare Assault Teams U .20 .50
❑ 82 Primitive Culture R 1.00 2.50
❑ 83 Queen's Borg Cube R 1.50 4.00
❑ 84 Queen's Borg Sphere R .75 2.00
❑ 85 Ready Room Door U .20 .50
❑ 86 Regenerate R 2.00 5.00
❑ 87 Reginald Barclay R .75 2.00
❑ 88 Remodulation U .20 .50
❑ 89 Retask R 1.00 2.50
❑ 90 Richard Wilkins C .10 .25
❑ 91 Salvage Starship R .60 1.50
❑ 92 Scorched Hand U .20 .50
❑ 93 Scout Encounter R 1.00 2.50
❑ 94 Sense the Borg U .20 .50
❑ 95 Sevek U .20 .50
❑ 96 Shipwreck R .75 2.00
❑ 97 Shot in the Back C .10 .25
❑ 98 Six of Eleven C .10 .25
❑ 99 Six of Seventeen C .10 .25
❑ 100 Sixteen of Nineteen C .10 .25
❑ 101 Solkar R .60 1.50
❑ 102 Starfleet Type III Phaser Rifle U .20 .50
❑ 103 Stop First Contact R .75 2.00
❑ 104 Strict Dress Code R .75 2.00
❑ 105 Temporal Vortex U .20 .50
❑ 106 Temporal Wake R .60 1.50
❑ 107 Ten of Nineteen C .10 .25
❑ 108 The Line Must Be Drawn Here C .10 .25
❑ 109 Theta-Radiation Poisoning R .75 2.00
❑ 110 Thirteen of Nineteen C .10 .25
❑ 111 Thomas McClure U .20 .50
❑ 112 Three of Nineteen C .10 .25
❑ 113 Three-Dimensional Thinking R .60 1.50
❑ 114 Tommygun U .20 .50
❑ 115 Transwarp Network Gateway C .10 .25
❑ 116 T'Shonra U .20 .50
❑ 117 Two of Eleven C .10 .25
❑ 118 Two of Nineteen C .10 .25
❑ 119 Two of Seventeen C .10 .25
❑ 120 U.S.S. Bozeman U .20 .50
❑ 121 U.S.S. Enterprise-E R 3.00 8.00
❑ 122 Undetected Beam-In R .75 2.00
❑ 123 Visit Cochrane Memorial R .75 2.00
❑ 124 Vulcan Lander U .20 .50
❑ 125 Wall of Ships R 1.00 2.50
❑ 126 Weak Spot R .60 1.50
❑ 127 William T. Riker R 1.50 4.00
❑ 128 Worf R 1.50 4.00
❑ 129 Zefram Cochrane R 1.00 2.50
❑ 130 Zefram Cochrane's Telescope R .60 1.50

1997 Star Trek The Fajo Collection

COMPLETE SET (18) 30.00 60.00

❑ 1 1962 Roger Maris Baseball Card SR 2.00 5.00
❑ 2 Black Hole SR 2.00 5.00
❑ 3 Dixon Hill's Business Card SR 2.00 5.00
❑ 4 DNA Metamorphosis SR 2.00 5.00
❑ 5 Dr. Soong SR 2.00 5.00
❑ 6 Guinan SR 2.00 5.00
❑ 7 I.K.C. Chang SR 2.00 5.00
❑ 8 Kivas Fajo SR 2.00 5.00
❑ 9 Locutus of Borg SR 2.00 5.00
❑ 10 Lore SR 2.00 5.00
❑ 11 Miles O'Brien SR 2.00 5.00
❑ 12 Persistence of Memory SR 2.00 5.00
❑ 13 Picard's Artificial Heart SR 2.00 5.00
❑ 14 Qapla'! SR 2.00 5.00
❑ 15 Sisters of Duras SR 2.00 5.00
❑ 16 Spot SR 2.00 5.00
❑ 17 Tallera SR 2.00 5.00
❑ 18 U.S.S. Pasteur SR 2.00 5.00

1998 Star Trek Deep Space Nine

COMPLETE SET (277)
BOOSTER BOX (30)
BOOSTER PACK (9)

❑ 1 Aamin Marritza R .60 1.50
❑ 2 Access Relay Station R .40 1.00
❑ 3 Acquire Illicit Explosives S .20 .50
❑ 4 Activate Tractor Beam C .10 .25
❑ 5 Aid Fugitives R .40 1.00
❑ 6 Airlock R .60 1.50
❑ 7 Aldara R .60 1.50
❑ 8 Alien Gambling Device R .40 1.00
❑ 9 Alter Records U .20 .50
❑ 10 Altonian Brain Teaser U .20 .50
❑ 11 Altovar R .60 1.50
❑ 12 Amaros C .10 .25
❑ 13 Anara C .10 .25
❑ 14 Angry Mob C .10 .25
❑ 15 Aphasia Device C .10 .25
❑ 16 Ari C .10 .25
❑ 17 Arms Deal U .20 .50
❑ 18 Assassin's Blade C .10 .25
❑ 19 Assault Vessel C .10 .25
❑ 20 Automated Security System R .75 2.00
❑ 21 Bajoran Civil War R 1.00 2.50
❑ 22 Bajoran Freighter C .10 .25
❑ 23 Bajoran Interceptor U .20 .50
❑ 24 Bajoran Outpost C .10 .25
❑ 25 Bajoran PADD C .10 .25
❑ 26 Bajoran Phaser C .10 .25
❑ 27 Bajoran Phaser Rifle U .20 .50
❑ 28 Bajoran Scout Vessel U .20 .50
❑ 29 Bajoran Wormhole U .20 .50
❑ 30 Bareil Antos R .75 2.00
❑ 31 Baseball R .75 2.00
❑ 32 Benjamin Sisko R 2.00 5.00
❑ 33 Beware of Q C .10 .25
❑ 34 Boheeka R .60 1.50
❑ 35 Borad R .60 1.50
❑ 36 Bo'Rak R .60 1.50
❑ 37 Brief Romance C .10 .25
❑ 38 Camping Trip R .60 1.50
❑ 39 Cardassian Disruptor C .10 .25
❑ 40 Cardassian Disruptor Rifle U .20 .50
❑ 41 Cardassian Outpost C .10 .25
❑ 42 Cardassian PADD C .10 .25
❑ 43 Cardassian Shuttle C .10 .25
❑ 44 Central Command R .75 2.00
❑ 45 Cha'Joh R 1.00 2.50
❑ 46 Chamber of Ministers R .60 1.50
❑ 47 Changeling Research R .60 1.50
❑ 48 Characterize Neutrino Emissions S .20 .50
❑ 49 Clan People C .10 .25
❑ 50 Colonel Day R .60 1.50
❑ 51 Colony Preparations U .20 .50
❑ 52 Commander's Office U .20 .50
❑ 53 Common Thief C .10 .25
❑ 54 Computer Crash U .20 .50
❑ 55 Coutu C .10 .25
❑ 56 Cure Blight R .60 1.50
❑ 57 Dakol C .10 .25
❑ 58 Dal'Rok U .20 .50
❑ 59 Danar R .75 2.00
❑ 60 Deep Space Nine / Terok Nor R 6.00 15.00
❑ 61 Defiant Dedication Plaque R 1.25 3.00
❑ 62 Deliver Supplies S .20 .50
❑ 63 Derell C .10 .25
❑ 64 D'Ghor R .60 1.50
❑ 65 DNA Clues R .60 1.50
❑ 66 Docking Pads U .20 .50
❑ 67 Docking Ports C .10 .25
❑ 68 Docking Procedures C .10 .25
❑ 69 Docking Pylons U .20 .50
❑ 70 Dr. Nydom C .10 .25
❑ 71 Dropping In U .20 .50
❑ 72 Dukat R 2.00 5.00
❑ 73 Duonetic Field Generator U .20 .50
❑ 74 Duranja R .60 1.50
❑ 75 Elim Garak R 2.00 5.00
❑ 76 Eliminate Virus S .20 .50
❑ 77 Enabran Tain R 1.00 2.50
❑ 78 Engineering Tricorder C .10 .25
❑ 79 Entek R .60 1.50
❑ 80 Espionage: Bajoran on Cardassian U .20 .50
❑ 81 Espionage: Cardassian on Bajoran U .20 .50
❑ 82 Espionage: Cardassian on Federation U .20 .50
❑ 83 Espionage: Cardassian on Klingon U .20 .50
❑ 84 Espionage: Romulan on Bajoran U .20 .50
❑ 85 Espionage: Romulan on Cardassian U .20 .50
❑ 86 Establish Landing Protocols C .10 .25
❑ 87 Establish Station S .20 .50
❑ 88 Establish Tractor Lock R .60 1.50
❑ 89 E'Tyshra U .20 .50
❑ 90 Explore Gamma Quadrant U .20 .50
❑ 91 Extradition U .20 .50
❑ 92 Extraordinary Methods U .20 .50
❑ 93 Fightin' Words U .20 .50
❑ 94 File Mission Report U .20 .50
❑ 95 Flaxian Assassin U .20 .50
❑ 96 Flaxian Scout Vessel C .10 .25
❑ 97 Framed for Murder U .20 .50
❑ 98 Galor C .10 .25
❑ 99 Garak Has Some Issues R 1.00 2.50
❑ 100 Garak's Tailor Shop R .60 1.50
❑ 101 Garanian Bolites C .10 .25
❑ 102 General Krim R .60 1.50
❑ 103 Ghoren C .10 .25
❑ 104 Gilora Rejal R .60 1.50
❑ 105 Going to the Top R 2.00 5.00
❑ 106 Graham Davis C .10 .25
❑ 107 Grilka R 1.00 2.50
❑ 108 Groumall R .75 2.00
❑ 109 Guest Quarters U .20 .50
❑ 110 Harvester Virus R .75 2.00
❑ 111 Hate Crime U .20 .50
❑ 112 Hidden Fighter U .20 .50
❑ 113 Hogue C .10 .25
❑ 114 HQ: Defensive Measures U .20 .50
❑ 115 HQ: Return Orb to Bajor R 1.00 2.50
❑ 116 HQ: Secure Homeworld U .20 .50
❑ 117 HQ: War Room U .20 .50

TCG/CCG

❑ 118 Hypospray U .20 .50
❑ 119 I Tried to Warn You U .20 .50
❑ 120 I.K.C. Toh'Kaht R 1.00 2.50
❑ 121 Incoming Message - Bajoran U .20 .50
❑ 122 Incoming Message - Cardassian U .20 .50
❑ 123 Infirmary U .20 .50
❑ 124 Intercept Maquis S .20 .50
❑ 125 Intercept Renegade S .20 .50
❑ 126 Investigate Rumors R .60 1.50
❑ 127 Isolinear Puzzle C .10 .25
❑ 128 Jabara U .20 .50
❑ 129 Jace Michaels C .10 .25
❑ 130 Jadzia Dax R 2.00 5.00
❑ 131 Jaheel C .10 .25
❑ 132 Jake and Nog R 1.50 4.00
❑ 133 Jaro Essa R .60 1.50
❑ 134 Jasad U .20 .50
❑ 135 Julian Bashir R 2.00 5.00
❑ 136 Jural C .10 .25
❑ 137 Kai Opaka R .60 1.50
❑ 138 Kalita C .10 .25
❑ 139 Kallis Ven C .10 .25
❑ 140 Karen Loews C .10 .25
❑ 141 Karina R .75 2.00
❑ 142 Kidnappers C .10 .25
❑ 143 Kira Nerys R 1.50 4.00
❑ 144 Klaestron Outpost C .10 .25
❑ 145 Korinas R .75 2.00
❑ 146 Kotran Pa'Dar U .20 .50
❑ 147 Kovat R .75 2.00
❑ 148 Kressari Rendezvous S .20 .50
❑ 149 Lenaris Holem R .60 1.50
❑ 150 Lethean Telepathic Attack U .20 .50
❑ 151 Li Nalas R .60 1.50
❑ 152 Lockbox C .10 .25
❑ 153 Lojal C .10 .25
❑ 154 Magnentic North U .20 .50
❑ 155 Makbar R 1.00 2.50
❑ 156 Martus Mazur R .60 1.50
❑ 157 Medical PADD U .20 .50
❑ 158 Military Freighter U .20 .50
❑ 159 Minister Rozahn C .10 .25
❑ 160 Miradorn Raider C .10 .25
❑ 161 Misguided Activist C .10 .25
❑ 162 Mora Pol R .60 1.50
❑ 163 Morka R .60 1.50
❑ 164 Mysterious Orb R .75 2.00
❑ 165 Nalan Bal C .10 .25
❑ 166 Natima Lang R .75 2.00
❑ 167 Navigate Plasma Storms U .20 .50
❑ 168 Neela R .75 2.00
❑ 169 No Loose Ends R .60 1.50
❑ 170 None Shall Pass C .10 .25
❑ 171 Nor C .10 .25
❑ 172 Odo R 2.00 5.00
❑ 173 Odo's Cousin U .20 .50
❑ 174 Ooli U .20 .50
❑ 175 Ops C .10 .25
❑ 176 Orb Experience U .20 .50
❑ 177 Orb Fragment R .60 1.50
❑ 178 Orb Negotiations U .20 .50
❑ 179 Ore Processing Unit U .20 .50
❑ 180 Orren Ran C .10 .25
❑ 181 Pallra R .60 1.50
❑ 182 Parn C .10 .25
❑ 183 Paxton Reese C .10 .25
❑ 184 Perak C .10 .25
❑ 185 Plain, Simple Garak R 1.00 2.50
❑ 186 Plans of the Obsidian Order R .75 2.00
❑ 187 Plans of the Tal Shiar R .75 2.00
❑ 188 Prakesh R .60 1.50
❑ 189 Preparation U .20 .50
❑ 190 Process Ore U .20 .50
❑ 191 Promenade Shops U .20 .50
❑ 192 Protouniverse R .60 1.50
❑ 193 Prylar Mond C .10 .25
❑ 194 Punishment Box U .20 .50
❑ 195 Pup R .60 1.50
❑ 196 Rano Dake C .10 .25
❑ 197 Rase Norvan C .10 .25
❑ 198 Rax'Na C .10 .25
❑ 199 Razka Karn R .60 1.50
❑ 200 Reaction Control Thrusters C .10 .25
❑ 201 Reclamation C .10 .25
❑ 202 Recruit Mercenaries R .60 1.50
❑ 203 Refuse Immigration S .20 .50
❑ 204 Reignite Dead Star S .20 .50
❑ 205 Rekelen C .10 .25
❑ 206 Relocate Settlers S .20 .50
❑ 207 Renewal Scroll U .20 .50
❑ 208 Rescue Personnel R .60 1.50
❑ 209 Rescue Prisoners S .20 .50
❑ 210 Retaya R .60 1.50
❑ 211 Rethorical Question U .20 .50
❑ 212 Rigelian Freighter C .10 .25
❑ 213 Rinnak Pire C .10 .25
❑ 214 Rionoj C .10 .25
❑ 215 Risky Business U .20 .50
❑ 216 Ruwon R .60 1.50
❑ 217 Sakonna R .60 1.50
❑ 218 Saltah'na Clock R .60 1.50
❑ 219 Science Kit C .10 .25
❑ 220 Science Lab U .20 .50
❑ 221 Science PADD U .20 .50
❑ 222 Search and Rescue S .20 .50
❑ 223 Search for Survivors S .20 .50
❑ 224 Secret Compartment R .60 1.50
❑ 225 Security Office U .20 .50
❑ 226 Seismic Quake R .60 1.50
❑ 227 Selveth R .60 1.50
❑ 228 Shakaar Edon R .60 1.50
❑ 229 Sharat U .20 .50
❑ 230 Skullduggery C .10 .25
❑ 231 Smoke Bomb U .20 .50
❑ 232 Sorus R .60 1.50
❑ 233 Study Badlands U .20 .50
❑ 234 Study Plasma Storm S .20 .50
❑ 235 Subspace Seaweed U .20 .50
❑ 236 Surmak Ren R .75 2.00
❑ 237 Survey Star System U .20 .50
❑ 238 Symbiont Diagnosis R .60 1.50
❑ 239 System 5 Disruptors R .60 1.50
❑ 240 Tahna Los R .60 1.50
❑ 241 Taylor Moore C .10 .25
❑ 242 Tekeny Ghemor R .75 2.00
❑ 243 The Three Vipers R .60 1.50
❑ 244 The Walls Have Ears R 1.00 2.50
❑ 245 Time To Reconsider U .20 .50
❑ 246 T'Kar U .20 .50
❑ 247 T'Lor C .10 .25
❑ 248 Tora Ziyal R .60 1.50
❑ 249 Toran R .60 1.50
❑ 250 Trauma R .60 1.50
❑ 251 Trazko U .20 .50
❑ 252 Treaty: Bajoran/Klingon U .20 .50
❑ 253 Treaty: Federation/Bajoran C .10 .25
❑ 254 Treaty: Federation/Cardassian C .10 .25
❑ 255 Treaty: Romulan/Cardassian U .20 .50
❑ 256 Turrel R .60 1.50
❑ 257 Ty Kajada C .10 .25
❑ 258 U.S.S. Danube C .10 .25
❑ 259 U.S.S. Yangtzee Kiang R .60 1.50
❑ 260 Ulani Belor C .10 .25
❑ 261 Unnatural Causes U .20 .50
❑ 262 Untrustworthy Associate U .20 .50
❑ 263 Vakis R .75 2.00
❑ 264 Vantika's Neural Pathways C .10 .25
❑ 265 Varis Sul U .20 .50
❑ 266 Vedek Sorad C .10 .25
❑ 267 Vedek Winn R .60 1.50
❑ 268 Vendetta C .10 .25
❑ 269 Verify Evidence S .20 .50
❑ 270 Vole Infestation C .10 .25
❑ 271 Weapons Locker C .10 .25
❑ 272 Weld Ram C .10 .25
❑ 273 Wormhole Navigation Schematic U .20 .50
❑ 274 Xepolite Freighter C .10 .25
❑ 275 Yeto R .60 1.50
❑ 276 Zef'Nor R .60 1.50
❑ 277 U.S.S. Defiant PREVIEW 6.00 15.00

1998 Star Trek Official Tournament Sealed Deck

❑ 1 Abandon Ship! P 1.00 2.00
❑ 2 Armus - Sticky Situation P 1.00 2.00
❑ 3 Darmok P 1.00 2.00
❑ 4 Establish Relations P 1.00 2.00
❑ 5 Explore Interstellar Matter P 1.00 2.00
❑ 6 Hide and Seek P 1.00 2.00
❑ 7 Hippocratic Oath P 1.00 2.00
❑ 8 Husnock Outpost P 1.00 2.00
❑ 9 Impose Order P 1.00 2.00
❑ 10 Investigate Incursion P 1.00 2.00
❑ 11 Make Us Go P 1.00 2.00
❑ 12 Mineral Survey P 1.00 2.00
❑ 13 Open Diplomatic Relations P 1.00 2.00
❑ 14 Reflection Therapy P 1.00 2.00
❑ 15 Space Door P 1.00 2.00
❑ 16 Space Time Portal P 1.00 2.00
❑ 17 Suna P 1.00 2.00
❑ 18 Test Propulsion Systems P 1.00 2.00
❑ 19 Treaty: Federation/Romulan/Klingon P 1.00 2.00
❑ 20 Unscientific Method P 1.00 2.00

1998 Star Trek Starter Deck II

❑ 1 Botanical Research P 1.00 2.00
❑ 2 Ferengi Trading Post P 1.00 2.00
❑ 3 Geological Survey P 1.00 2.00
❑ 4 Memory Wipe P 1.00 2.00
❑ 5 Military Exercises P 1.00 2.00
❑ 6 Search for Weapons P 1.00 2.00
❑ 7 Study Cometary Cloud P 1.00 2.00
❑ 8 Study Pulsar P 1.00 2.00

1999 Star Trek Blaze of Glory

❑ 1 A Good Day to Live R .60 1.50
❑ 2 Access Denied U .20 .50
❑ 3 Admiral Ross R .75 2.00
❑ 4 Alpha Attack Ship U .20 .50
❑ 5 Ambassador Tomalak R .60 1.50
❑ 6 Attack Pattern Delta U .20 .50
❑ 7 Attack Wing C .10 .25
❑ 8 Bat'leth Tournament U .20 .50
❑ 9 Bat'leth U .20 .50
❑ 10 Battle Bridge Door C .10 .25
❑ 11 Blood Oath R .75 2.00
❑ 12 Boone Impersonator R .60 1.50
❑ 13 Borg Cutting Beam R .60 1.50
❑ 14 Captured U .20 .50
❑ 15 Chart Stellar Cluster R .60 1.50
❑ 16 Chief O'Brien R 1.25 3.00
❑ 17 Chula: The Abyss R .60 1.50
❑ 18 Chula: The Lights C .10 .25
❑ 19 Commandeer Ship U .20 .50
❑ 20 Counterintelligence U .20 .50
❑ 21 Crimson Forcefield U .20 .50
❑ 22 Defense System Upgrade U .20 .50
❑ 23 Dial Martok for Murder U .20 .50
❑ 24 D'K tahg C .10 .25
❑ 25 Dolak U .20 .50
❑ 26 Donald Varley R .60 1.50
❑ 27 Dr. Koramar U .20 .50
❑ 28 Drumhead U .20 .50
❑ 29 Duran'Adar C .10 .25
❑ 30 D'Vin C .10 .25
❑ 31 E-Band Emissions R .75 2.00
❑ 32 Elim R 1.00 2.50
❑ 33 Engage Shuttle Operations: Dominion U .20 .50
❑ 34 Enrique Muniz R .60 1.50
❑ 35 Evasive Maneuvers C .10 .25
❑ 36 Examine Singularity U .20 .50
❑ 37 Fajo's Gallery R .60 1.50
❑ 38 Ferengi Ingenuity U .20 .50
❑ 39 Full Phaser Spread C .10 .25
❑ 40 Furel U .20 .50
❑ 41 Gelnon R .60 1.50
❑ 42 Goraxus R .60 1.50
❑ 43 Gravimetric Distortion C .10 .25
❑ 44 Gul Madred R .60 1.50
❑ 45 Hazardous Duty C .10 .25
❑ 46 Holding Cell Door C .10 .25
❑ 47 Hon'Tihl U .20 .50
❑ 48 I.K.C. Koraga R 1.00 2.50
❑ 49 I.K.C. Lukara R 1.00 2.50
❑ 50 I.K.C. Negh'Var R 1.00 2.50
❑ 51 Ilon Tandro R .60 1.50
❑ 52 Impersonate Captive R .75 2.00
❑ 53 Inside Operation R .60 1.50
❑ 54 Intruder Alert! U .20 .50
❑ 55 Ixtana'Rax R .60 1.50
❑ 56 Jadzia Dax R 1.50 4.00
❑ 57 Kang R .60 1.50
❑ 58 Kar'takin U .20 .50
❑ 59 Kavok R .60 1.50
❑ 60 Keldon C .10 .25
❑ 61 Klingon Disruptor Rifle U .20 .50
❑ 62 Koloth R .75 2.00
❑ 63 Kor R .75 2.00
❑ 64 Kraxon R .60 1.50
❑ 65 Kudak'Etan R .60 1.50
❑ 66 La Forge Impersonator R .60 1.50
❑ 67 Lamat'Ukan U .20 .50
❑ 68 Locutus' Borg Cube R 1.25 3.00
❑ 69 Long Live the Queen R .75 2.00
❑ 70 Lupaza U .20 .50
❑ 71 Maximum Firepower R 1.50 4.00
❑ 72 Mek'leth C .10 .25
❑ 73 Miles O'Brien R 1.50 4.00
❑ 74 Mopak C .10 .25
❑ 75 Navok C .10 .25
❑ 76 New Essentialists C .10 .25
❑ 77 N'Garen C .10 .25
❑ 78 Odo Founder R .75 2.00
❑ 79 Oken'alak C .10 .25
❑ 80 Outgunned R .60 1.50
❑ 81 Parthok R .60 1.50
❑ 82 Phased Polaron Beam C .10 .25
❑ 83 Phaser Array Power Cell C .10 .25
❑ 84 Phaser Banks C .10 .25
❑ 85 Photon Torpedo C .10 .25
❑ 86 Picard Maneuver R .75 2.00
❑ 87 Plasma Torpedo C .10 .25
❑ 88 Prepare The Prisoner U .20 .50
❑ 89 Primary Energy Weapon C .10 .25
❑ 90 Prisoner Escort C .10 .25
❑ 91 Prisoner Exchange U .20 .50
❑ 92 Pulse Disruptor C .10 .25
❑ 93 Pulse Phaser Cannons C .10 .25
❑ 94 Quantum Torpedo C .10 .25
❑ 95 Quark Son of Keldar R .75 2.00
❑ 96 Riker Wil R .75 2.00
❑ 97 R'Mal C .10 .25
❑ 98 Ro Laren R .75 2.00
❑ 99 Romulan Disruptor Rifle U .20 .50
❑ 100 Romulan Shuttle C .10 .25
❑ 101 Sarita Carson C .10 .25
❑ 102 Scanner Interference U .20 .50
❑ 103 Security Holding Cell U .20 .50
❑ 104 Senator Letant R .60 1.50
❑ 105 Sniper U .20 .50
❑ 106 Spiral-Wave Disruptor C .10 .25
❑ 107 Starfleet Type I Phaser C .10 .25
❑ 108 Stellar Flare U .20 .50
❑ 109 Strafing Run C .10 .25
❑ 110 Sword of Kahless R .75 2.00
❑ 111 Tamarith U .20 .50
❑ 112 Target Engines C .10 .25
❑ 113 Target Shields C .10 .25
❑ 114 Target These Coordinates R 1.25 3.00
❑ 115 Target Weapons C .10 .25
❑ 116 Tharket U .20 .50
❑ 117 The Albino R .60 1.50
❑ 118 The Big Picture U .20 .50
❑ 119 The Guardian U .20 .50
❑ 120 The Wake of the Borg U .20 .50
❑ 121 Torture R .75 2.00
❑ 122 U.S.S. Thunderchild R 1.25 3.00
❑ 123 Ultimatum U .20 .50
❑ 124 Umal'Adan U .20 .50
❑ 125 Under Fire U .20 .50
❑ 126 Victory is Life C .10 .25
❑ 127 Voktak C .10 .25
❑ 128 Wo'Din C .10 .25
❑ 129 Worf Son of Mogh R 1.25 3.00
❑ 130 Zetal C .10 .25

1999 Star Trek Blaze of Glory Foil

❑ 1 Borg Cutting Beam VRF 1.50 4.00
❑ 2 Elim URF 6.00 15.00
❑ 3 Fajo's Gallery VRF 1.50 4.00
❑ 4 Goraxus VRF 1.50 4.00
❑ 5 I.K.C. Negh'Var VRF 1.50 4.00
❑ 6 Inside Operation VRF 1.50 4.00
❑ 7 Jadzia Dax URF 6.00 15.00
❑ 8 Kang VRF 1.50 4.00
❑ 9 Koloth VRF 1.50 4.00
❑ 10 Kor SRF 3.00 8.00
❑ 11 Kraxon VRF 1.50 4.00
❑ 12 La Forge Impersonator SRF 3.00 8.00
❑ 13 Locutus' Borg Cube URF 6.00 15.00
❑ 14 Maximum Firepower SRF 3.00 8.00
❑ 15 Odo Founder SRF 3.00 8.00
❑ 16 Riker Wil URF 6.00 15.00
❑ 17 Sword of Kahless SRF 3.00 8.00
❑ 18 U.S.S. Thunderchild SRF 3.00 8.00

1999 Star Trek Enhanced First Contact

❑ 1 Add Distinctiveness P 2.00 5.00
❑ 2 Bareil of Borg P 2.00 5.00
❑ 3 Dukat of Borg P 2.00 5.00
❑ 4 Eleven of Seventeen P 2.00 5.00
❑ 5 Gowron of Borg P 2.00 5.00
❑ 6 Nightmare P 2.00 5.00
❑ 7 Population 9 Billion - All Borg P 2.00 5.00
❑ 8 Service the Collective P 2.00 5.00
❑ 9 Six of Nineteen P 2.00 5.00
❑ 10 Sphere Encounter P 2.00 5.00
❑ 11 Tomalak of Borg P 2.00 5.00
❑ 12 We are the Borg P 2.00 5.00
❑ 13 Assimilated Counterpart OVERLAY 2.00 5.00
❑ 14 Communication Drone P OVERLAY 2.00 5.00
❑ 15 Defense Drone P OVERLAY 2.00 5.00
❑ 16 Navigation Drone P OVERLAY 2.00 5.00

1999 Star Trek Rules of Acquisition

COMPLETE SET (130) 20.00 40.00
BOOSTER BOX (30) 15.00 30.00
BOOSTER PACK (9) 1.00 1.50

❑ 1 1st Rule of Acquisition C .10 .25
❑ 2 6th Rule of Acquisition C .10 .25
❑ 3 33rd Rule of Acquisition U .20 .50
❑ 4 34th Rule of Acquisition U .20 .50
❑ 5 47th Rule of Acquisition U .20 .50
❑ 6 59th Rule of Acquisition U .20 .50
❑ 7 75th Rule of Acquisition U .20 .50
❑ 8 211th Rule of Acquisition C .10 .25
❑ 9 Aluura R 1.25 3.00
❑ 10 Ambassador Krajensky U .20 .50
❑ 11 Apnex R 1.25 3.00
❑ 12 Arandis R 1.25 3.00
❑ 13 Benil U .20 .50
❑ 14 Berik U .20 .50
❑ 15 Birta U .20 .50
❑ 16 Bodyguards U .20 .50
❑ 17 Bractor R .60 1.50
❑ 18 Breen CRM114 R .60 1.50
❑ 19 B'rel C .10 .25
❑ 20 Bribery C .10 .25
❑ 21 Brunt R 1.25 3.00
❑ 22 Calandra C .10 .25
❑ 23 Cargo Bay C .10 .25
❑ 24 Center of Attention U .20 .50
❑ 25 Chula: Crossroads C .10 .25
❑ 26 Chula: The Door R .75 2.00
❑ 27 Collect Sample C .10 .25
❑ 28 Continuing Committee R .75 2.00
❑ 29 Dabo U .20 .50
❑ 30 Dangerous Liaisons C .10 .25
❑ 31 Deliver Message U .20 .50
❑ 32 Deyos R .75 2.00
❑ 33 D'Kora Marauder C .10 .25
❑ 34 D'Kora Transport C .10 .25
❑ 35 Dr. Borts C .10 .25
❑ 36 Edan'Atal C .10 .25
❑ 37 Elizabeth Lense R 1.00 2.50
❑ 38 Emergency Evacuation C .10 .25
❑ 39 Establish Trade Route C .10 .25
❑ 40 Ferengi Bug U .20 .50
❑ 41 Ferengi Conference C .10 .25
❑ 42 Ferengi Disruptor C .10 .25
❑ 43 Ferengi Disruptor Rifle U .20 .50
❑ 44 Ferengi Energy Weapon C .10 .25
❑ 45 Ferengi Outpost C .10 .25
❑ 46 Ferengi PADD C .10 .25
❑ 47 Ferengi Shuttle U .20 .50
❑ 48 Forced Labor Camp U .20 .50
❑ 49 Frool C .10 .25
❑ 50 Gaila R 1.00 2.50
❑ 51 George Primmin R 1.00 2.50
❑ 52 Gold-Pressed Latinum U .20 .50
❑ 53 Goss U .20 .50
❑ 54 Gral R .75 2.00
❑ 55 Grand Nagus Gint R 1.25 3.00
❑ 56 Grand Nagus Zek R 1.25 3.00
❑ 57 Gunrunning U .20 .50
❑ 58 Hagath R 1.00 2.50
❑ 59 Hanok U .20 .50
❑ 60 HQ: Ferengi Credit Exchange U .20 .50
❑ 61 Ikat'Ika R .75 2.00
❑ 62 In the Pale Moonlight U .20 .50
❑ 63 Incoming Message - Ferengi C .10 .25
❑ 64 Inglatu C .10 .25
❑ 65 Ishka R .75 2.00
❑ 66 It's Only a Game U .20 .50
❑ 67 Jovis R .60 1.50
❑ 68 Karemman Vessel C .10 .25
❑ 69 Kasidy Yates R .75 2.00
❑ 70 Kazago U .20 .50
❑ 71 Krajensky Founder R .75 2.00
❑ 72 Krax U .20 .50
❑ 73 Krayton R .60 1.50
❑ 74 Kreechta R .60 1.50
❑ 75 Krozh C .10 .25
❑ 76 Krunk C .10 .25
❑ 77 Kukalaka R .75 2.00
❑ 78 Leck R .60 1.50
❑ 79 Leeta R 1.25 3.00
❑ 80 Lemec R .60 1.50
❑ 81 Letek C .10 .25
❑ 82 Lurin R .60 1.50
❑ 83 Maihar'du R 1.00 2.50
❑ 84 Mardah U .20 .50
❑ 85 Margh R 1.00 2.50
❑ 86 Market Research C .10 .25
❑ 87 Morn R .75 2.00
❑ 88 Morta U .20 .50
❑ 89 Naprem R 1.00 2.50
❑ 90 Nava C .10 .25
❑ 91 Nibor U .20 .50
❑ 92 Nilva C .10 .25
❑ 93 Nog R 1.25 3.00
❑ 94 Omag R .60 1.50
❑ 95 Orb of Wisdom R .60 1.50
❑ 96 Orion Syndicate Bomb R .75 2.00
❑ 97 Par Lenor U .20 .50
❑ 98 Patahk R .60 1.50
❑ 99 Patrol Ship C .10 .25
❑ 100 Pel U .20 .50
❑ 101 Phased Cloaking Device R .60 1.50
❑ 102 Plasma Energy Burst U .20 .50
❑ 103 Prak C .10 .25
❑ 104 Protection Racket R .60 1.50
❑ 105 Purchase Moon U .20 .50
❑ 106 Qol C .10 .25
❑ 107 Quark R 2.50 6.00
❑ 108 Quark's Bar R 1.25 3.00
❑ 109 Quark's Isolinear Rods R .60 1.50
❑ 110 Quark's Treasure R .75 2.00
❑ 111 Reactor Overload U .20 .50
❑ 112 Rom R 1.25 3.00
❑ 113 Runabout Search U .20 .50
❑ 114 Scepter of the Grand Nagus R .60 1.50
❑ 115 Scientific Method C .10 .25
❑ 116 Senator Cretak R 1.25 3.00
❑ 117 Small Cloaking Devive U .20 .50
❑ 118 Solok C .10 .25
❑ 119 Sovak U .20 .50
❑ 120 Starry Night R .60 1.50
❑ 121 Strange Bedfellows U .20 .50
❑ 122 Taar C .10 .25
❑ 123 The Ferengi Rules of Acquisition U .20 .50
❑ 124 Tog U .20 .50
❑ 125 Tol U .20 .50
❑ 126 Tower of Commerce R .60 1.50
❑ 127 Tulaberry Wine Negotiations U .20 .50
❑ 128 U.S.S. Sao Paulo R 1.25 3.00
❑ 129 Vacuum-Desiccated Remains C .10 .25
❑ 130 Writ of Accountability R .75 2.00

1999 Star Trek The Dominion

COMPLETE SET (130) 50.00 100.00
BOOSTER BOX (30) 50.00 100.00
BOOSTER PACK (9) 2.50 5.00

❑ 1 10 and 01 R .75 2.00
❑ 2 Admiral Leyton R .60 1.50
❑ 3 Amat'igan R .60 1.50
❑ 4 Anya U .20 .50
❑ 5 Arak'Taral U .20 .50
❑ 6 Archanis Dispute U .20 .50
❑ 7 Atul U .20 .50
❑ 8 Azet'izan C .10 .25
❑ 9 Berserk Changeling U .20 .50
❑ 10 Betazed Invasion R .60 1.50
❑ 11 Bioweapon Ruse U .20 .50
❑ 12 Borath R .60 1.50
❑ 13 Caught Red-Handed C .10 .25
❑ 14 Ch'Pok R .60 1.50
❑ 15 Chula: Pick One to Save Two U .20 .50
❑ 16 Chula: The Chandra R .60 1.50
❑ 17 Chula: The Dice C .10 .25
❑ 18 Construct Depot C .10 .25
❑ 19 Crew Reassignment U .20 .50
❑ 20 Crisis C .10 .25

❑ 21 Croden's Key R .60 1.50
❑ 22 Damar R .60 1.50
❑ 23 Daro U .20 .50
❑ 24 D'deridex Advanced R 1.50 4.00
❑ 25 Dejar U .20 .50
❑ 26 Dominion PADD C .10 .25
❑ 27 Empok Nor R .75 2.00
❑ 28 Engage Cloak U .20 .50
❑ 29 Eris C .10 .25
❑ 30 Espionage: Dominion on Federation U .20 .50
❑ 31 Espionage: Dominion on Klingon U .20 .50
❑ 32 Espionage: Dominion on Romulan U .20 .50
❑ 33 Establish Dominion Foothold U .20 .50
❑ 34 Fair Play U .20 .50
❑ 35 Flight of the Intruder U .20 .50
❑ 36 Founder Leader R .75 2.00
❑ 37 Founder Secret R .60 1.50
❑ 38 Founder U .20 .50
❑ 39 Friendly Fire C .10 .25
❑ 40 Garak R .60 1.50
❑ 41 General Hazar C .10 .25
❑ 42 Goran'Agar R .75 2.00
❑ 43 Gurat'urak C .10 .25
❑ 44 I.K.C. Rotarran R .75 2.00
❑ 45 In the Bag C .10 .25
❑ 46 Install Autonomic Systems Parasite U .20 .50
❑ 47 Intelligence Operation U .20 .50
❑ 48 Invasive Beam-In C .10 .25
❑ 49 Investigate Coup U .20 .50
❑ 50 Issue Secret Orders R .60 1.50
❑ 51 Jaresh-Inyo R .60 1.50
❑ 52 Jem'Hadar Attack Ship C .10 .25
❑ 53 Jem'Hadar Birthing Chamber C .10 .25
❑ 54 Jem'Hadar Disruptor C .10 .25
❑ 55 Jem'Hadar Disruptor Rifle U .20 .50
❑ 56 Jem'Hadar Sacrifice C .10 .25
❑ 57 Jem'Hadar Warship U .20 .50
❑ 58 Kai Winn R .60 1.50
❑ 59 Keevan R .60 1.50
❑ 60 Keeve Falor C .10 .25
❑ 61 Keldon Advanced R 1.25 3.00
❑ 62 Keogh R .60 1.50
❑ 63 Ketracel-White C .10 .25
❑ 64 Kilana R .60 1.50
❑ 65 Kira Founder R .75 2.00
❑ 66 Koret'alak C .10 .25
❑ 67 Leyton Founder R .60 1.50
❑ 68 Limara'Son C .10 .25
❑ 69 Lovok Founder R .60 1.50
❑ 70 Lovok R .60 1.50
❑ 71 Macet U .20 .50
❑ 72 Makla'Gor C .10 .25
❑ 73 Martok Founder R .75 2.00
❑ 74 Martok R 1.50 4.00
❑ 75 Meso'Clan U .20 .50
❑ 76 Michael Eddington R .75 2.00
❑ 77 Mining Survey U .20 .50
❑ 78 Mission Fatigue U .20 .50
❑ 79 Navigational Hazards C .10 .25
❑ 80 O'Brien Founder R .75 2.00
❑ 81 Office of the President R .75 2.00
❑ 82 Office of the Proconsul R .75 2.00
❑ 83 Omet'iklan R .60 1.50
❑ 84 Operate Wormhole Relays U .20 .50
❑ 85 Orb of Prophecy and Change R .60 1.50
❑ 86 Ornithar C .10 .25
❑ 87 Orta U .20 .50
❑ 88 Post Garrison U .20 .50
❑ 89 Primary Supply Depot C .10 .25
❑ 90 Protect Shipment U .20 .50
❑ 91 Quest for the Sword U .20 .50
❑ 92 Remata'Klan R .60 1.50
❑ 93 Remote Supply Depot U .20 .50
❑ 94 Rescue Founder U .20 .50
❑ 95 Salia R .60 1.50
❑ 96 Security Briefing U .20 .50
❑ 97 Senator Vreenak R .60 1.50
❑ 98 Shape-Shift U .20 .50
❑ 99 Silaran Prin U .20 .50
❑ 100 Sisko 197 Subroutine U .20 .50
❑ 101 Sleeper Trap R .60 1.50
❑ 102 Soto U .20 .50
❑ 103 Strike Three C .10 .25
❑ 104 Subjugate Planet U .20 .50
❑ 105 Surprise Assault C .10 .25
❑ 106 Tactical Console U .20 .50
❑ 107 Talak'talan R .60 1.50
❑ 108 Telle C .10 .25
❑ 109 Temo'Zuma C .10 .25
❑ 110 The Earring of Li Nalas R .60 1.50
❑ 111 The Great Hall R .75 2.00
❑ 112 The Great Link R .75 2.00
❑ 113 Toman'torax R .60 1.50
❑ 114 Trager R .60 1.50
❑ 115 Treaty: Bajoran/Dominion C .10 .25
❑ 116 Treaty: Cardassian/Dominion C .10 .25
❑ 117 Treaty: Romulan/Dominion C .10 .25
❑ 118 T'Rul U .20 .50
❑ 119 U.S.S. Defiant R 3.00 8.00
❑ 120 U.S.S. Odyssey U .20 .50
❑ 121 U.S.S. Rio Grande R .60 1.50
❑ 122 Uncover DNA Clues U .20 .50
❑ 123 Virak'kara C .10 .25
❑ 124 Weyoun R 1.25 3.00
❑ 125 Yak'Talon C .10 .25
❑ 126 Yelgren R .60 1.50
❑ 127 You Dirty Rat U .20 .50
❑ 128 Young Jem'Hadar C .10 .25
❑ 129 Zayra R .60 1.50
❑ 130 Zyree C .10 .25

1999 Star Trek The Dominion Previews

❑ 1 Admiral Riker PV 6.00 15.00
❑ 2 Captain Kirk PV 6.00 15.00
❑ 3 Seven of Nine PV 6.00 15.00
❑ 4 Worf Son of Mogh PV 6.00 15.00

2000 Star Trek Enhanced Premiere

❑ 1 Beverly and Will P 2.00 5.00
❑ 2 Data and Geordi P 2.00 5.00
❑ 3 Data and Picard P 2.00 5.00
❑ 4 Jean-Luc and Beverly P 2.00 5.00
❑ 5 Sons of Mogh P 2.00 5.00
❑ 6 The Trois P 2.00 5.00
❑ 7 Alien Parasites and REM Fatigue Hallucinations P 2.00 5.00
❑ 8 Anaphasic Organism and Nagilum P 2.00 5.00
❑ 9 Ancient Computer and Microvirus P 2.00 5.00
❑ 10 Iconian Computer Weapon and Hyper-Aging P 2.00 5.00
❑ 11 Female's Love Interest and Radioactive Garbage Scow P 2.00 5.00
❑ 12 Male's Love Interest and Tarellian Plague Ship P 2.00 5.00
❑ 13 Covert Installation II P 2.00 5.00
❑ 14 Excavation II P 2.00 5.00
❑ 15 Explore Black Cluster II P 2.00 5.00
❑ 16 Explore Typhon Expanse II P 2.00 5.00
❑ 17 Investigate Anomaly II P 2.00 5.00
❑ 18 Investigate Sighting II P 2.00 5.00
❑ 19 Relief Mission II P 2.00 5.00
❑ 20 Secret Salvage II P 2.00 5.00
❑ 21 Test Mission II P 2.00 5.00

2000 Star Trek Mirror Mirror

COMPLETE SET (131) 30.00 60.00
BOOSTER BOX (30) 20.00 40.00
BOOSTER PACK (11) 1.00 2.00

❑ 1 Tantalus Field R .60 1.50
❑ 2 A Fast Ship Would be Nice R .75 2.00
❑ 3 Artillery Attack R .60 1.50
❑ 4 Chula: The Game U .20 .50
❑ 5 Denevan Neural Parasites R .60 1.50
❑ 6 Distraction U .20 .50
❑ 7 Emergency Conversion C .10 .25
❑ 8 Gorn Encounter U .20 .50
❑ 9 Horta R .60 1.50
❑ 10 Kelvan Show of Force R .75 2.00
❑ 11 Quantum Fissure U .20 .50
❑ 12 Royale Casino: Slots C .10 .25
❑ 13 Bajoran Wormhole: Mirror Universe U .20 .50
❑ 14 The Guardian of Forever R .75 2.00
❑ 15 Agonizer U .20 .50
❑ 16 Classic Disruptor C .10 .25
❑ 17 Ferengi Whip U .20 .50
❑ 18 Mirror Dagger C .10 .25
❑ 19 Multidimensional Transporter Device C .10 .25
❑ 20 Romulan Cloaking Device U .20 .50
❑ 21 Self-Sealing Stem Bolts C .10 .25
❑ 22 Stolen Cloaking Device U .20 .50
❑ 23 35th Rule of Acquisition U .20 .50
❑ 24 Blood Screening U .20 .50
❑ 25 Treaty: Federation/Dominion C .10 .25
❑ 26 Alliance Nor C .10 .25
❑ 27 Mirror Terok Nor (Front) | (Reverse) R+ 2.00 5.00
❑ 28 Terran Outpost C .10 .25
❑ 29 Terran Rebellion HQ R .75 2.00
❑ 30 Klingon Empire Outpost C .10 .25
❑ 31 Agony Booth U .20 .50
❑ 32 Crossover C .10 .25
❑ 33 Emblem of The Alliance C .10 .25
❑ 34 Emblem of the Empire C .10 .25
❑ 35 Hostage Trade C .10 .25
❑ 36 No Way Out U .20 .50
❑ 37 The Art of Diplomacy R .60 1.50
❑ 38 Transporter Mixup U .20 .50
❑ 39 I'm a Doctor, Not a Bricklayer! U .20 .50
❑ 40 Vulcan Death Grip U .20 .50
❑ 41 Disrupt Alliance U .20 .50
❑ 42 Feldomite Rush U .20 .50
❑ 43 Historical Research U .20 .50
❑ 44 Mine Dilithium U .20 .50
❑ 45 Search for Rebels U .20 .50
❑ 46 Construct Starship R .75 2.00
❑ 47 For Cardassia! U .20 .50
❑ 48 The Emperor's New Cloak U .20 .50
❑ 49 Bareil R+ 1.25 3.00
❑ 50 Commander Leeta R .60 1.50
❑ 51 Gantt C .10 .25
❑ 52 Javek Len C .10 .25
❑ 53 Overseer Odo R+ 1.50 4.00
❑ 54 Romara Cal C .10 .25
❑ 55 Taymar Bern C .10 .25
❑ 56 The Intendant R+ 1.25 3.00
❑ 57 Weyoun of Borg R+ 1.50 4.00
❑ 58 Aramax C .10 .25
❑ 59 Dorza C .10 .25
❑ 60 Overseer Mardel U .20 .50
❑ 61 Security Chief Garak R+ 1.50 4.00
❑ 62 Thrax U .20 .50
❑ 63 Luaran R .60 1.50
❑ 64 Captain Bashir R+ 1.25 3.00
❑ 65 Captain Dax R+ 1.25 3.00
❑ 66 Chief Engineer Scott R+ 1.25 3.00
❑ 67 Chief Navigator Chekov R+ 1.25 3.00
❑ 68 Chief Surgeon McCoy R+ 1.25 3.00
❑ 69 Comm Officer Uhura R+ 1.25 3.00
❑ 70 Crewman Wilson C .10 .25
❑ 71 Dr. Farallon R .60 1.50
❑ 72 Ensign Davis C .10 .25
❑ 73 Ensign Gaffney C .10 .25
❑ 74 First Officer Spock UR 20.00 40.00
❑ 75 Jake Sisko R+ 1.25 3.00
❑ 76 James Tiberius Kirk R+ 2.00 5.00
❑ 77 Lt. Kyle U .20 .50
❑ 78 Lt. Moreau U .20 .50
❑ 79 Marauder C .10 .25
❑ 80 Marlena Moreau R+ 1.25 3.00
❑ 81 Mr. Andrews C .10 .25
❑ 82 Mr. Tuvok R 1.00 2.50
❑ 83 Nurse Chapel R+ 1.25 3.00
❑ 84 Prot U .20 .50
❑ 85 Security Chief Sulu R+ 1.25 3.00
❑ 86 Smiley R+ 1.25 3.00
❑ 87 Transporter Chief Kyle U .20 .50
❑ 88 Mr. Brunt R+ 1.25 3.00
❑ 89 Mr. Nog R+ 1.25 3.00
❑ 90 Mr. Quark R+ 1.25 3.00
❑ 91 Mr. Rom R+ 1.25 3.00
❑ 92 Korvek C .10 .25
❑ 93 Loreva C .10 .25
❑ 94 Regent Worf R+ 1.25 3.00
❑ 95 Rinox U .20 .50
❑ 96 Rukor U .20 .50
❑ 97 T'Vor C .10 .25
❑ 98 Telok U .20 .50
❑ 99 Vartog C .10 .25
❑ 100 Balok U .20 .50
❑ 101 Dr. Roger Korby U .20 .50
❑ 102 Ezri R+ 1.25 3.00
❑ 103 Fontaine R+ 1.25 3.00
❑ 104 Mr. Sisko R+ 1.50 4.00
❑ 105 Professor Sisko R+ 1.25 3.00
❑ 106 Ruk R .60 1.50
❑ 107 Thomas Paris R .75 2.00
❑ 108 Wyatt Earp U .20 .50
❑ 109 Commander Charvanek R+ 1.25 3.00
❑ 110 D'vano C .10 .25
❑ 111 Gorrus C .10 .25
❑ 112 Subcommander Tal U .20 .50
❑ 113 Tagus C .10 .25
❑ 114 Alliance Interceptor C .10 .25
❑ 115 Bajoran Warship R .75 2.00
❑ 116 Alliance Galor C .10 .25
❑ 117 Enhanced Attack Ship U .20 .50
❑ 118 Defiant R+ 2.00 5.00
❑ 119 I.S.S. Constitution C .10 .25
❑ 120 I.S.S. Enterprise R+ 1.50 4.00
❑ 121 Rebel Interceptor C .10 .25
❑ 122 Type 18 Shuttlepod U .20 .50
❑ 123 Mirror Ferengi Shuttle U .20 .50
❑ 124 Alliance K'Vort C .10 .25
❑ 125 Alliance Vor'Cha C .10 .25
❑ 126 I.K.C. Ki'tang U .20 .50
❑ 127 Regency 1 R .75 2.00
❑ 128 Fesarius R .60 1.50
❑ 129 Battle Cruiser C .10 .25
❑ 130 Ops: Mirror Universe C .10 .25
❑ 131 Halkan Council R .60 1.50

2000 Star Trek Reflections

BOOSTER BOX (36) 40.00 80.00
BOOSTER PACK (18) 2.00 4.00

❑ 1 Borg Queen URF 25.00 50.00
❑ 2 D'deridex Advanced SRF 2.00 5.00
❑ 3 Keldon Advanced SRF 2.00 5.00
❑ 4 10 and 01 SRF 1.25 3.00
❑ 5 100,000 Tribbles (Clone) BTF 3.00 8.00
❑ 6 Admiral Riker BTF 6.00 15.00
❑ 7 Alas, Poor Queen VRF .40 1.00
❑ 8 Armus - Skin of Evil VRF .40 1.00
❑ 9 Assimilate Homeworld VRF .40 1.00
❑ 10 Barclay's Protomorphosis Disease SRF 1.00 2.50
❑ 11 Bareil Antos VRF .40 1.00
❑ 12 Benjamin Sisko SRF 3.00 8.00
❑ 13 Betazoid Gift Box VRF .40 1.00
❑ 14 B'Etor SRF 1.25 3.00
❑ 15 Beverly Crusher SRF 2.00 5.00
❑ 16 Beverly Picard SRF 1.50 4.00
❑ 17 Borg Ship SRF 2.50 6.00
❑ 18 Bynars Weapon Enhancement SRF 1.50 4.00
❑ 19 Central Command SRF 1.00 2.50
❑ 20 Cha'Joh VRF .40 1.00
❑ 21 Chamber of Ministers SRF 1.25 3.00
❑ 22 Cryosatellite VRF .40 1.00
❑ 23 Crystalline Entity VRF .40 1.00
❑ 24 Cytherians SRF 1.00 2.50
❑ 25 Damar VRF .40 1.00
❑ 26 Data SRF 2.50 6.00
❑ 27 Data's Head SRF 1.00 2.50
❑ 28 Dathon SRF 1.00 2.50
❑ 29 Deanna Troi SRF 2.50 6.00
❑ 30 Decius VRF .40 1.00
❑ 31 Devidian Door SRF 2.00 5.00
❑ 32 DNA Clues VRF .40 1.00
❑ 33 Dr. Telek R'Mor BTF 2.50 6.00
❑ 34 Dukat SRF 2.00 5.00
❑ 35 Elim Garak SRF 1.00 2.50
❑ 36 Espionage Mission SRF 1.00 2.50
❑ 37 Founder Leader SRF 1.00 2.50
❑ 38 Future Enterprise URF 50.00 100.00
❑ 39 Galen SRF 1.25 3.00
❑ 40 Garak VRF .40 1.00
❑ 41 Geordi La Forge SRF 1.50 4.00
❑ 42 Gomtuu VRF .40 1.00
❑ 43 Governor Worf SRF 1.00 2.50
❑ 44 Gowron SRF 1.00 2.50
❑ 45 Gowron of Borg BTF 2.50 6.00
❑ 46 Horga'hn SRF 1.00 2.50
❑ 47 I.K.C. Bortas VRF .40 1.00
❑ 48 I.K.C. Fek'lhr VRF .40 1.00
❑ 49 I.K.C. Hegh'ta VRF .40 1.00
❑ 50 I.K.C. Rotarran VRF .40 1.00
❑ 51 Interrogation VRF .40 1.00
❑ 52 Investigate Shattered Space VRF .40 1.00
❑ 53 Investigate Rumors VRF .40 1.00
❑ 54 Jadzia Dax SRF 2.00 5.00
❑ 55 Jean-Luc Picard URF 30.00 60.00
❑ 56 Julian Bashir SRF 2.00 5.00
❑ 57 Kahless VRF .40 1.00
❑ 58 Khazara VRF .40 1.00
❑ 59 Kira Founder VRF .40 1.00
❑ 60 Kira Nerys SRF 2.50 6.00
❑ 61 Klingon Death Yell VRF .40 1.00
❑ 62 Kurlan Naiskos SRF 1.00 2.50
❑ 63 Kurn VRF .40 1.00
❑ 64 Lursa SRF 1.00 2.50
❑ 65 Madam Guinan SRF 1.00 2.50
❑ 66 Magic Carpet Ride OCD VRF .40 1.00
❑ 67 Major Rakal SRF 1.00 2.50
❑ 68 Martok SRF 1.50 4.00
❑ 69 Montana Missile Complex VRF .40 1.00
❑ 70 O'Brien Founder VRF .40 1.00
❑ 71 Ocular Implants VRF .40 1.00
❑ 72 Odo SRF 1.50 4.00
❑ 73 Office of the President SRF 1.00 2.50
❑ 74 Office of the Proconsul SRF 1.00 2.50
❑ 75 Pegasus Search VRF .40 1.00
❑ 76 Plans of the Tal Shiar VRF .40 1.00
❑ 77 Prakesh VRF .40 1.00
❑ 78 Q SRF 1.00 2.50
❑ 79 Queen's Borg Cube SRF 1.25 3.00
❑ 80 Regenerate SRF 1.25 3.00
❑ 81 Ressikan Flute VRF .40 1.00
❑ 82 Retask VRF .40 1.00
❑ 83 Revolving Door VRF .40 1.00
❑ 84 Roga Danar SRF 1.00 2.50
❑ 85 Scout Encounter VRF .40 1.00
❑ 86 Sela SRF 1.00 2.50
❑ 87 Seven of Nine CTF 4.00 10.00
❑ 88 Study Nebula VRF .40 1.00
❑ 89 Supernova VRF .40 1.00
❑ 90 System 5 Disruptors VRF .40 1.00
❑ 91 Taris VRF .40 1.00
❑ 92 Tasha Yar-Alternate SRF 1.25 3.00
❑ 93 The Great Hall SRF 1.00 2.50
❑ 94 The Great Link SRF 1.00 2.50
❑ 95 The Sheliak VRF .40 1.00
❑ 96 Toreth VRF .40 1.00
❑ 97 U.S.S Defiant URF 20.00 40.00
❑ 98 U.S.S. Enterprise SRF 1.25 3.00
❑ 99 U.S.S. Enterprise-C VRF .40 1.00
❑ 100 Wall of Ships VRF .40 1.00
❑ 101 Weyoun SRF 1.50 4.00
❑ 102 William T. Riker SRF 1.50 4.00
❑ 103 Worf SRF 1.00 2.50
❑ 104 Wormhole Negotiations VRF .40 1.00
❑ 105 Yuta VRF .40 1.00

2000 Star Trek Second Anthology

❑ 1 Bashir Founder P .75 2.00
❑ 2 Jodmos P .75 2.00
❑ 3 Koval P .75 2.00
❑ 4 Legate Damar P .75 2.00
❑ 5 Luther Sloan P .75 2.00
❑ 6 Vedek Dax P .75 2.00

2000 Star Trek The Trouble With Tribbles

COMPLETE SET (141) 30.00 60.00
BOOSTER BOX (30) 20.00 40.00
BOOSTER PACK (11) 1.00 2.00

❑ 1 Orb of Time R .60 1.50
❑ 2 Chula: The Drink R .60 1.50
❑ 3 Chula: The Way Home C .10 .25
❑ 4 Executive Authorization R .75 2.00
❑ 5 Ferengi Infestation R .60 1.50
❑ 6 Lineup C .10 .25
❑ 7 Oops! C .10 .25
❑ 8 Palukoo U .20 .50
❑ 9 Q Gets the Point C .10 .25
❑ 10 Storage Compartment Door C .10 .25
❑ 11 Classic Communicator C .10 .25
❑ 12 Classic Medical Tricorder U .20 .50
❑ 13 Classic Tricorder U .20 .50
❑ 14 Classic Type II Phaser C .10 .25
❑ 15 VR Headset U .20 .50
❑ 16 62nd Rule of Acquisition C .10 .25
❑ 17 Organian Peace Treaty C .10 .25
❑ 18 Subspace Transporter C .10 .25
❑ 19 Temporal Investigations C .10 .25
❑ 20 Treaty: Cardassian/Bajoran C .10 .25
❑ 21 Treaty: Romulan/Bajoran C .10 .25
❑ 22 Deep Space Station K-7 R .75 2.00
❑ 23 Chain Reaction Ricochet R .60 1.50
❑ 24 Homefront U .20 .50
❑ 25 HQ: Orbital Weapons Platform R .60 1.50
❑ 26 Make It So R .60 1.50
❑ 27 Obelisk of Masaka U .20 .50
❑ 28 Panel Overload C .10 .25
❑ 29 Q the Referee U .20 .50
❑ 30 Resistance is Futile R .60 1.50
❑ 31 Tribble Bomb U .20 .50
❑ 32 We Look for Things U .20 .50
❑ 33 Burial Ground U .20 .50
❑ 34 Live Long and Prosper C .10 .25
❑ 35 Obedience Brings Victory U .20 .50
❑ 36 Scan Cycle Check C .10 .25
❑ 37 Suicidal Attack C .10 .25
❑ 38 Agricultural Assessment U .20 .50
❑ 39 Assign Support Personnel C .10 .25
❑ 40 Council of Warriors R .75 2.00
❑ 41 Defend Homeworld U .20 .50
❑ 42 Hero of the Empire U .20 .50
❑ 43 First Minister Shakaar R+ 1.25 3.00
❑ 44 Sarish Rez U .20 .50
❑ 45 Six of Thirteen C .10 .25
❑ 46 Third of Five R+ 1.25 3.00
❑ 47 Broca U .20 .50
❑ 48 Kira R+ 1.50 4.00
❑ 49 Amet'alox C .10 .25
❑ 50 Lam C .10 .25
❑ 51 Thot Gor R+ 1.25 3.00
❑ 52 Thot Pran U .20 .50
❑ 53 Varat'idan C .10 .25
❑ 54 B.G. Robinson U .20 .50
❑ 55 Captain Kirk R+ 2.00 5.00
❑ 56 Dr. McCoy UR 2.50 6.00
❑ 57 Dulmer R+ 1.25 3.00
❑ 58 Ensign Checkov R+ 1.50 4.00
❑ 59 Ensign O'Brien R+ 1.25 3.00
❑ 60 Lt. Bailey R+ 1.25 3.00
❑ 61 Lt. Bashir R+ 1.50 4.00
❑ 62 Lt. D'Amato U .20 .50
❑ 63 Lt. Dax R+ 1.50 4.00
❑ 64 Lt. Grant C .10 .25
❑ 65 Lt. Nagata U .20 .50
❑ 66 Lt. Sisko P .40 1.00
❑ 67 Lt. Sulu R+ 1.50 4.00
❑ 68 Lt. Uhura R+ 1.50 4.00
❑ 69 Lt. Watley U .20 .50
❑ 70 Lucsly R+ 1.25 3.00
❑ 71 Mr. Scott R+ 1.50 4.00
❑ 72 Mr. Spock R+ 2.00 5.00
❑ 73 Nilz Baris U .20 .50
❑ 74 Falar U .20 .50
❑ 75 Lumba R+ 1.25 3.00
❑ 76 Mordoc C .10 .25
❑ 77 Arne Darvin R+ 1.25 3.00
❑ 78 Captain Koloth P .40 1.00
❑ 79 Daval C .10 .25
❑ 80 Kered C .10 .25
❑ 81 Korax U .20 .50
❑ 82 Kras U .20 .50
❑ 83 Thopok U .20 .50
❑ 84 Tumek U .20 .50
❑ 85 Barry Waddle R+ 1.25 3.00
❑ 86 Danderdag C .10 .25
❑ 87 Gem U .20 .50
❑ 88 Grebnedlog R+ 1.25 3.00
❑ 89 Liam Bilby U .20 .50
❑ 90 Odo R+ 1.25 3.00
❑ 91 Reginod U .20 .50
❑ 92 Worf R+ 1.25 3.00
❑ 93 Yint C .10 .25
❑ 94 Jenok C .10 .25
❑ 95 Kalenna U .20 .50
❑ 96 Keras R+ 1.25 3.00
❑ 97 The Centurion R+ 1.25 3.00
❑ 98 Velal R+ 1.25 3.00
❑ 99 Q-Type Android U .20 .50
❑ 100 Bajoran Raider U .20 .50
❑ 101 Bok'Nor U .20 .50
❑ 102 Stolen Attack Ship R 1.00 2.50
❑ 103 Breen Warship R 1.00 2.50
❑ 104 Dominion Battleship R 1.00 2.50
❑ 105 Weyoun's Warship R 1.00 2.50
❑ 106 Columbus C .10 .25
❑ 107 Starship Constitution C .10 .25
❑ 108 Starship Enterprise R+ 2.00 5.00
❑ 109 Brunt's Shuttle R .60 1.50
❑ 110 I.K.C. Gr'oth R+ 1.25 3.00
❑ 111 I.K.C. Ning'tao R .75 2.00
❑ 112 Mondor U .20 .50
❑ 113 Gal Gath'thong R .60 1.50
❑ 114 Bajoran Shrine U .20 .50
❑ 115 Bajoran Phaser Banks C .10 .25
❑ 116 Breen Disruptor Burst C .10 .25
❑ 117 Breen Energy-Dampening Weapon R 1.00 2.50
❑ 118 Chain Reaction Pulsar U .20 .50
❑ 119 Sherman's Peak U .20 .50
❑ 120 1 Tribble (Bonus) C .10 .25
❑ 121 1 Tribble (Discard) C .10 .25
❑ 122 1 Tribble (Go) C .10 .25
❑ 123 10 Tribbles (Bonus) U .20 .50
❑ 124 10 Tribbles (Go) U .20 .50
❑ 125 10 Tribbles (Poison) U .20 .50
❑ 126 100 Tribbles (Bonus) U .20 .50
❑ 127 100 Tribbles (Poison) U .20 .50
❑ 128 100 Tribbles (Rescue) U .20 .50
❑ 129 1,000 Tribbles (Bonus) R* .60 1.50
❑ 130 1,000 Tribbles (Discard) R* .60 1.50
❑ 131 1,000 Tribbles (Rescue) R* .60 1.50

TCG/CCG

☐ 132 10,000 Tribbles (Go) R+ .75 2.00
☐ 133 10,000 Tribbles (Poison) R+ .75 2.00
☐ 134 10,000 Tribbles (Rescue) R+ .75 2.00
☐ 135 100,000 Tribbles (Clone) R+ .75 2.00
☐ 136 100,000 Tribbles (Discard) R+ .75 2.00
☐ 137 100,000 Tribbles (Rescue) R+ .75 2.00
☐ 138 ...in the Engine Room C .10 .25
☐ 139 ...in the Transporters C .10 .25
☐ 140 ...on the Bridge C .10 .25
☐ 141 ...on the Station C .10 .25

2000 Star Trek The Trouble With Tribbles Federation Starter Deck

☐ 1 Alyssa Ogawa (FC) R .75 2.00
☐ 2 Archer (Prem) C .10 .25
☐ 3 Chula: The Abyss (BoG) R .60 1.50
☐ 4 Chula: The Lights (BoG) C .10 .25
☐ 5 Fleet Admiral Shanthi (Prem) U .20 .50
☐ 6 Hazardous Duty (BoG) C .10 .25
☐ 7 Male's Love Interest (Prem) C .10 .25
☐ 8 Medical Kit (Prem) C .10 .25
☐ 9 Montgomery Scott (AU) C .10 .25
☐ 10 Plasmadyne Relay (QC) C .10 .25
☐ 11 Security Precautions (QC) C .10 .25
☐ 12 Starfleet Type I Phaser (BoG) C .10 .25
☐ 13 Thomas McClure (FC) U .20 .50

2000 Star Trek The Trouble With Tribbles Klingon Starter Deck

☐ 1 Alternate Universe Door (AU) C .10 .25
☐ 2 Anaphasic Organism (Prem) C .10 .25
☐ 3 Bat'leth (BoG) U .20 .50
☐ 4 Lack of Preparation (FC) C .10 .25
☐ 5 Malfunctioning Door (AU) C .10 .25
☐ 6 Matriarchal Society (Prem) U .20 .50
☐ 7 Medical Tricorder (Prem) C .10 .25
☐ 8 Microvirus (Prem) C .10 .25
☐ 9 Morka (DS9) R 1.00 2.50
☐ 10 Primitive Culture (FC) R 1.00 2.50
☐ 11 Res-Q (Prem) C .10 .25
☐ 12 Scientific Method (RoA) C .10 .25
☐ 13 Vekor (Prem) C .10 .25
☐ 14 Wo'Din (BoG) C .10 .25

2000 Star Trek Voyager

BOOSTER BOX (30) 25.00 50.00
BOOSTER PACK (11) 1.25 2.50

☐ 1 Aggressive Behavior R .60 1.50
☐ 2 Assassin's Blade S .20 .50
☐ 3 Astral Eddy R .60 1.50
☐ 4 Balancing Act U .20 .50
☐ 5 Civil Unrest C .10 .25
☐ 6 Common Thief S .20 .50
☐ 7 Crisis S .20 .50
☐ 8 Female's Love Interest S .20 .50
☐ 9 Flash Plasma Storm U .20 .50
☐ 10 Gravimetric Distortion S .20 .50
☐ 11 Hanonian Land Eel R .60 1.50
☐ 12 Hazardous Duty S .20 .50
☐ 13 Hull Breach R .75 2.00
☐ 14 Implication C .10 .25
☐ 15 Kazon Bomb C .10 .25
☐ 16 Komar Possession U .20 .50
☐ 17 Lack of Preparation S .20 .50
☐ 18 Macrovirus R .60 1.50
☐ 19 Male's Love Interest S .20 .50
☐ 20 Matriarchal Society S .20 .50
☐ 21 Navigational Hazards S .20 .50
☐ 22 Radioactive Garbage Scow S .20 .50
☐ 23 Spatial Rift C .10 .25
☐ 24 Subspace Fracture R .60 1.50
☐ 25 The Cloud R .60 1.50
☐ 26 The Swarm R .60 1.50
☐ 27 Trabe Grenade C .10 .25
☐ 28 Twisted U .20 .50
☐ 29 Volcanic Eruption R .60 1.50
☐ 30 Barzan Wormhole R 1.25 3.00
☐ 31 Ready Room Door U .20 .50
☐ 32 Temporal Micro-Wormhole C .10 .25
☐ 33 Bio-Neural Gel Pack C .10 .25
☐ 34 Engineering Kit S .20 .50
☐ 35 Engineering Tricorder S .20 .50
☐ 36 Kazon Disruptor C .10 .25
☐ 37 Kazon Disruptor Rifle U .20 .50
☐ 38 Medical Kit S .20 .50
☐ 39 Medical PADD S .20 .50
☐ 40 Mobile Holo-Emitter U .20 .50
☐ 41 Science PADD S .20 .50
☐ 42 Starfleet Type II Phaser S .20 .50
☐ 43 Starfleet Type III Phaser Rifle U .20 .50
☐ 44 Transporter Control Module C .10 .25
☐ 45 Vidiian Harvester U .20 .50
☐ 46 Ancestral Vision R .60 1.50
☐ 47 Captain's Log U .20 .50
☐ 48 Fair Play U .20 .50
☐ 49 Kal-Toh U .20 .50
☐ 50 Lower Decks U .20 .50
☐ 51 Mission Debriefing U .20 .50
☐ 52 The Big Picture U .20 .50
☐ 53 The Next Emanation C .10 .25
☐ 54 Villagers With Torches C .10 .25
☐ 55 Kazon Outpost C .10 .25
☐ 56 Nekrit Supply Depot P .20 .50
☐ 57 Vidiian Outpost C .10 .25
☐ 58 Blue Alert C .10 .25
☐ 59 Caretaker's Array R .75 2.00
☐ 60 Containment Field C .10 .25
☐ 61 Delta Quadrant Spatial Scission C .10 .25
☐ 62 Handshake U .20 .50
☐ 63 Home Away From Home C .10 .25
☐ 64 The Kazon Collective C .10 .25
☐ 65 The Vidiian Sodality C .10 .25
☐ 66 Vidiian Boarding Claw R .75 2.00
☐ 67 War Council R .75 2.00
☐ 68 Auto-Destruct Sequence U .20 .50
☐ 69 Beyond the Subatomic C .10 .25
☐ 70 Distortion of Space/Time Continuum U .20 .50
☐ 71 Escape Pod C .10 .25
☐ 72 Mutation U .20 .50
☐ 73 Nanoprobe Resuscitation C .10 .25
☐ 74 Quinn R 1.25 3.00
☐ 75 The Gift U .20 .50
☐ 76 The Phage C .10 .25
☐ 77 The Power C .10 .25
☐ 78 Acquire Technology U .20 .50
☐ 79 Aftermath U .20 .50
☐ 80 Ambush Ship U .20 .50
☐ 81 Answer Distress Signal U .20 .50
☐ 82 Assist Cooperative U .20 .50
☐ 83 Catalog Phenomena C .10 .25
☐ 84 Combat Training U .20 .50
☐ 85 Contact Resistance C .10 .25
☐ 86 Cure Deadly Virus R .60 1.50
☐ 87 Expose Plot U .20 .50
☐ 88 Heal Life-Form U .20 .50
☐ 89 Inversion Mystery U .20 .50
☐ 90 Investigate Quantum Singularity R .60 1.50
☐ 91 Kazon Conference U .20 .50
☐ 92 Liberation U .20 .50
☐ 93 Prevent Annihilation U .20 .50
☐ 94 Prison Break U .20 .50
☐ 95 Reinitialize Warp Reaction U .20 .50
☐ 96 Research Phage U .20 .50
☐ 97 Restock Supplies U .20 .50
☐ 98 Restore Victims R .60 1.50
☐ 99 Return Life-form U .20 .50
☐ 100 Revive Settlers U .20 .50
☐ 101 Salvage Operation U .20 .50
☐ 102 Stop Bombardment U .20 .50
☐ 103 Study Interment Site C .10 .25
☐ 104 Study Interstellar Colony U .20 .50
☐ 105 Tak Tak Negotiation C .10 .25
☐ 106 Unseat Dictator U .20 .50
☐ 107 Assign Mission Specialists C .10 .25
☐ 108 Boarding Party U .20 .50
☐ 109 Commandeer Ship U .20 .50
☐ 110 Divert Power U .20 .50
☐ 111 Organ Theft U .20 .50
☐ 112a Tabor BLUE R 1.25 3.00
☐ 112b Tabor PLUM R 1.25 3.00
☐ 113a Seska DK RED R 1.25 3.00
☐ 113b Seska PURPLE R 1.25 3.00
☐ 114a Ayala BLUE C .10 .25
☐ 114b Ayala GOLD C .10 .25
☐ 115a B'Elanna Torres BLUE R 3.00 8.00
☐ 115b B'Elanna Torres GOLD R 3.00 8.00
☐ 116 Cavit C .10 .25
☐ 117a Chakotay BLUE R 3.00 8.00
☐ 117b Chakotay GOLD R 3.00 8.00
☐ 118a Chell BLUE U .20 .50
☐ 118b Chell GOLD U .20 .50
☐ 119 Dr. Fitzgerald C .10 .25
☐ 120 Harry Kim R 1.50 4.00
☐ 121 Joseph Carey C .10 .25
☐ 122 Kathryn Janeway R 2.50 6.00
☐ 123a Lon Suder BLUE R 2.00 5.00
☐ 123b Lon Suder GOLD R 2.00 5.00
☐ 124a Mariah Henley BLUE C .10 .25
☐ 124b Mariah Henley GOLD C .10 .25
☐ 125a Marla Gilmore BLUE U .20 .50
☐ 125b Marla Gilmore GOLD U .20 .50
☐ 126a Maxwell Burke BLUE R 2.00 5.00
☐ 126b Maxwell Burke GOLD R 2.00 5.00
☐ 127 Mitchell U .20 .50
☐ 128 Mortimer Harren U .20 .50
☐ 129a Noah Lessing BLUE U .20 .50
☐ 129b Noah Lessing GOLD U .20 .50
☐ 130 Rollins U .20 .50
☐ 131a Rudolph Ransom BLUE R 2.00 5.00
☐ 131b Rudolph Ransom GOLD R 2.00 5.00
☐ 132 Samantha Wildman R .75 2.00
☐ 133 Stadi C .10 .25
☐ 134 The Doctor R 1.50 4.00
☐ 135a Thompson BLUE C .10 .25
☐ 135b Thompson GOLD C .10 .25
☐ 136 Tom Paris R 1.50 4.00
☐ 137 Tuvok R 1.50 4.00
☐ 138 Vorik R .75 2.00
☐ 139 William Telfer C .10 .25
☐ 140 Dr. Arridor R .60 1.50
☐ 141 Kol R .60 1.50
☐ 142 Corez C .10 .25
☐ 143 Culluh R .75 2.00
☐ 144 Haliz U .20 .50
☐ 145 Halok U .20 .50
☐ 146 Haron R .60 1.50
☐ 147 Jabin U .20 .50
☐ 148 Karden R 1.25 3.00
☐ 149 Loran U .20 .50
☐ 150 Maniz C .10 .25
☐ 151 Minnis R .60 1.50
☐ 152 Narret C .10 .25
☐ 153 Rabek C .10 .25
☐ 154 Razik R .60 1.50
☐ 155 Rettick U .20 .50
☐ 156 Ril C .10 .25
☐ 157 Saldin C .10 .25
☐ 158 Tersa U .20 .50
☐ 159 Tierna R .60 1.50
☐ 160 Valek U .20 .50
☐ 161 Arturis R .60 1.50
☐ 162 Dr. Ma'Bor Jetrel R .60 1.50
☐ 163 Dr. Neria U .20 .50
☐ 164a Kes BLUE R 1.50 4.00
☐ 164b Kes GOLD R 1.50 4.00
☐ 165 Kurros R .60 1.50
☐ 166 Magistrate Drang S .20 .50
☐ 167a Neelix BLUE R 1.50 4.00
☐ 167b Neelix GOLD R 1.50 4.00
☐ 168 Nimira S .20 .50
☐ 169 Paxim C .10 .25
☐ 170 Penk R 1.25 3.00
☐ 171a Seven of Nine BLUE R 6.00 15.00
☐ 171b Seven of Nine GOLD R 6.00 51.00
☐ 172 Tanis R .60 1.50
☐ 173 The Pendari Champion UR 15.00 30.00
☐ 174 Dr. Telek R'Mor R .75 2.00
☐ 175 Nevala R .60 1.50
☐ 176 Rekar R .60 1.50
☐ 177 Danara Pel R .60 1.50
☐ 178 Dereth R .60 1.50
☐ 179 Drenol C .10 .25
☐ 180 Hophalin C .10 .25
☐ 181 Losarus C .10 .25
☐ 182 Motura R .60 1.50
☐ 183 Nadirum C .10 .25
☐ 184 Nirata C .10 .25
☐ 185 Sethis C .10 .25
☐ 186 Sorum C .10 .25
☐ 187 Sulan R .60 1.50
☐ 188 Telari C .10 .25
☐ 189 Thaden C .10 .25
☐ 190 Delta Flyer R .60 1.50
☐ 191 Type 9 Shuttlecraft C .10 .25
☐ 192a U.S.S. Equinox BLUE R 1.25 3.00
☐ 192b U.S.S. Equinox GOLD R 1.25 3.00
☐ 193 U.S.S. Intrepid C .10 .25
☐ 194 U.S.S. Voyager R 2.50 6.00
☐ 195 Kazon Raider C .10 .25
☐ 196 Kazon Shuttle C .10 .25
☐ 197 Kazon Warship R 1.25 3.00
☐ 198 Bothan Vessel U .20 .50
☐ 199 Vidiian Cruiser R 1.25 3.00
☐ 200 Vidiian Interceptor C .10 .25
☐ 201 Vidiian Scout Vessel C .10 .25

2001 Star Trek Holodeck Adventures

BOOSTER BOX (30) 25.00 50.00
BOOSTER PACK (11) 1.25 2.50

☐ 1 The City Of B'hala R .60 1.50
☐ 2 Alice C .10 .25
☐ 3 Chula: Echoes C .10 .25
☐ 4 Chula: Trickery U .20 .50
☐ 5 Cytoplasmic Life-Form U .20 .50
☐ 6 Dejaren C .10 .25
☐ 7 Emergent Life-Form U .20 .50
☐ 8 Primitive Humanoids C .10 .25
☐ 9 Talosian Cage U .20 .50
☐ 10 The Clown: Guillotine U .20 .50
☐ 11 The Clown: Playing Doctor R .60 1.50
☐ 12 Your Galaxy is Impure R .75 2.00
☐ 13 Holodeck Door U .20 .50
☐ 14 '45 Dom Perignon C .10 .25
☐ 15 Ablative Armor C .10 .25
☐ 16 Satan's Robot U .20 .50
☐ 17 Bynars Data Transfer U .20 .50
☐ 18 Dominion War Efforts C .10 .25
☐ 19 Ferengi Financial Data Net R .60 1.50
☐ 20 Holo-projectors U .20 .50
☐ 21 Oo-mox C .10 .25
☐ 22 Transwarp Hub R .60 1.50
☐ 23 Children of Light C .10 .25
☐ 24 Clone Machine R .60 1.50
☐ 25 Cybernetics Expertise C .10 .25
☐ 26 Holoprogram: 221B Baker Street C .10 .25
☐ 27 Holoprogram: Deadwood C .10 .25
☐ 28 Holoprogram: Noah's Mountain Retreat C .10 .25
☐ 29 Holoprogram: The Fortress of Doom C .10 .25
☐ 30 Holoprogram: The Office of Dixon Hill C .10 .25
☐ 31 In the Zone C .10 .25
☐ 32 Jem'hadar Shrouding C .10 .25
☐ 33 Tongo R .60 1.50
☐ 34 White Deprivation C .10 .25
☐ 35 All Threes U .20 .50
☐ 36 Data, Keep Dealing U .20 .50
☐ 37 I'm a doctor, not a Bartender C .10 .25
☐ 38 I've Been Waiting for You U .20 .50
☐ 39 Remember The Alamo C .10 .25
☐ 40 Small Oversight C .10 .25
☐ 41 Establish Home Planet U .20 .50
☐ 42 Mine Gallicite C .10 .25
☐ 43 Repair Memorial U .20 .50
☐ 44 Seal Rift U .20 .50
☐ 45 Study Protonebula U .20 .50
☐ 46 Transport Colonists C .10 .25
☐ 47 Bajoran Resistance Cell U .20 .50
☐ 48 Hunting Group C .10 .25
☐ 49 Orbital Bombardment R .60 1.50
☐ 50 Els Renora U .20 .50
☐ 51a Iden DK BLUE R+ 2.50 6.00
☐ 51b Iden PLUM R+ 2.50 6.00
☐ 52 Teero Anaydis R .60 1.50
☐ 53 Crell Moset R+ .75 2.00
☐ 54a Doran DK BLUE C .10 .25
☐ 54b Doran PURPLE C .10 .25
☐ 55 Ekoor U .20 .50
☐ 56a Harath DK BLUE C .10 .25
☐ 56b Harath PURPLE C .10 .25
☐ 57a Kejal DK BLUE R+ 2.50 6.00
☐ 57b Kejal PURPLE R+ 2.50 6.00
☐ 58 Mila U .20 .50
☐ 59 Rusot U .20 .50
☐ 60 Seskal U .20 .50
☐ 61 Vornar C .10 .25
☐ 62a Dar BROWN C .10 .25
☐ 62b Dar DK BLUE C .10 .25
☐ 63a Wodek'idan BROWN C .10 .25
☐ 63b Wodek'idan DK BLUE C .10 .25
☐ 64 Admiral J.P. Hanson R+ .75 2.00
☐ 65 Boothby R+ 1.25 3.00
☐ 66 E.M.H. - Mark II U .20 .50
☐ 67 Edward Jellico R+ .75 2.00
☐ 68 Ezri Dax R+ 2.00 5.00
☐ 69 Lewis Zimmerman R+ .75 2.00
☐ 70 Naomi Wildman U .20 .50
☐ 71 Sam Lavelle C .10 .25
☐ 72a Sumek BLUE C .10 .25
☐ 72b Sumek DK BLUE C .10 .25
☐ 73 The E.C.H. R+ .75 2.00
☐ 74a Weiss BLUE R+ 2.50 6.00
☐ 74b Weiss DK BLUE R+ 2.50 6.00
☐ 75 Rulat U .20 .50
☐ 76 B'Elanna Daughter of Miral R+ 1.25 3.00
☐ 77 Chancellor Gowron R+ .75 2.00
☐ 78 Kar'meth C .10 .25
☐ 79 Nirok U .20 .50
☐ 80 Ah-Kel and Ro-Kel R .60 1.50
☐ 81 Anastasia Komananov R+ 1.25 3.00
☐ 82 Arachnia R+ 1.25 3.00
☐ 83 Barash R .60 1.50
☐ 84 Buster Kincaid R .75 2.00
☐ 85 Captain Proton R+ 1.25 3.00
☐ 86 Carlos R .60 1.50
☐ 87 Chaotica R .75 2.00
☐ 88 Cravic Unit 122 U .20 .50
☐ 89 Cyrus Redblock U .20 .50
☐ 90 Deputy Rozhenko U .20 .50
☐ 91 Dixon Hill UR 25.00 50.00
☐ 92 Dr. Noah R+ 1.25 3.00
☐ 93 Duchamps R+ 1.25 3.00
☐ 94 Durango R+ .75 2.00
☐ 95 Eli Hollander U .20 .50
☐ 96 Falcon R+ 1.25 3.00
☐ 97 Felix Leech U .20 .50
☐ 98 Frank Hollander R+ .75 2.00
☐ 99 John Watson R+ 1.25 3.00
☐ 100 Leonardo da Vinci R .75 2.00
☐ 101 Lily R .60 1.50
☐ 102 Lonzak U .20 .50
☐ 103 Madam Pulaski U .20 .50
☐ 104 Minuet R .60 1.50
☐ 105 Mona Luvsitt R .60 1.50
☐ 106 Mr. Garak R+ .75 2.00
☐ 107 Nicki the Nose U .20 .50
☐ 108 Pralor Unit 3947 U .20 .50
☐ 109 Pralor Unit 6263 C .10 .25
☐ 110 Professor Honey Bare R+ 1.50 4.00
☐ 111 Professor Moriarty R+ .75 2.00
☐ 112 Regina Barthalomew U .20 .50
☐ 113 Secret Agent Julian Bashir R+ 1.25 3.00
☐ 114 Sheriff Worf R+ 1.25 3.00
☐ 115 Sherlock Holmes R+ 1.25 3.00
☐ 116 Sigmund Freud R .60 1.50
☐ 117 The President of Earth R .60 1.50
☐ 118 The Twin Mistresses of Evil U .20 .50
☐ 119 Vic Fontaine R+ .75 2.00
☐ 120a Garren DK BLUE C .10 .25
☐ 120b Garren GREEN C .10 .25
☐ 121 Praetor Neral R+ .75 2.00
☐ 122 Maleth C .10 .25
☐ 123 Ar-Q-ologist C .10 .25
☐ 124 Q's Fantasy Women C .10 .25
☐ 125 Quandary C .10 .25
☐ 126 Trullux U .20 .50
☐ 127 Baxial U .20 .50
☐ 128 Cravic Warship U .20 .50
☐ 129a Olarra DK BLUE R+ 6.00 15.00
☐ 129b Olarra GOLD R+ 6.00 15.00
☐ 130 Pralor Warship U .20 .50
☐ 131 Holosuite C .10 .25

2001 Star Trek The Borg

BOOSTER BOX (30) 15.00 30.00
BOOSTER PACK (11) 1.00 1.50

☐ 1 Ankari Spirits R .60 1.50
☐ 2 Impressive Trophies U .20 .50
☐ 3 Invasive Procedures U .20 .50
☐ 4 Photonic Energy Being U .20 .50
☐ 5 Replicator Accident R .60 1.50
☐ 6 Sabotaged Negotiations U .20 .50
☐ 7 The Clown: Beneath the Mask U .20 .50
☐ 8 The Clown: My Festival R .60 1.50
☐ 9 The Weak Will Perish R .75 2.00
☐ 10 Transwarp Network Gateway C .10 .25
☐ 11 Borg Data Node U .20 .50
☐ 12 Borg Nanoprobes U .20 .50
☐ 13 Borg Vinculum C .10 .25
☐ 14 Hirogen Disruptor Rifle U .20 .50
☐ 15 Hirogen Talon C .10 .25
☐ 16 Maturation Chamber U .20 .50
☐ 17 Activate Subcommands C .10 .25
☐ 18 Alas, Poor Drone U .20 .50
☐ 19 Cranial Transceiver Implant C .10 .25
☐ 20 Meditation U .20 .50
☐ 21 Omega Particle U .20 .50
☐ 22 Quantum Slipstream Drive C .10 .25
☐ 23 Borg Outpost C .10 .25
☐ 24 Unicomplex R+ .75 2.00
☐ 25 Hirogen Outpost C .10 .25
☐ 26 Cortical Node Implant C .10 .25
☐ 27 Feedback Surge U .20 .50
☐ 28 Hirogen Hunt C .10 .25
☐ 29 Relics of the Chase U .20 .50
☐ 30 Rituals of the Hunt C .10 .25
☐ 31 Adapt: Modulate Shields U .20 .50
☐ 32 Adapt: Negate Obstruction C .10 .25
☐ 33 Awaken C .10 .25
☐ 34 Multivector Assault Mode U .20 .50
☐ 35 Narrow Escape U .20 .50
☐ 36 Corner Enemy Ship U .20 .50
☐ 37 Establish Settlement U .20 .50
☐ 38 Hunt Alien U .20 .50
☐ 39 Maintenance Overhaul U .20 .50
☐ 40 Repair Null Space Catapult U .20 .50
☐ 41 Secure Station C .10 .25
☐ 42 Assimilate Planet C .10 .25
☐ 43 Assimilate Species R .60 1.50
☐ 44 Assimilate Starship U .20 .50
☐ 45 Eliminate Starship U .20 .50
☐ 46 Establish Gateway C .10 .25
☐ 47 Harness Particle 010 R .60 1.50
☐ 48 Omega Directive U .20 .50
☐ 49 Reassimilate Lost Drone U .20 .50
☐ 50 Borg Queen R+ 3.00 8.00
☐ 51 Eight of Eighteen C .10 .25
☐ 52 Eight of Fifteen C .10 .25
☐ 53 Eleven of Eighteen C .10 .25
☐ 54 Eleven of Twelve C .10 .25
☐ 55 Fifth R+ .75 2.00
☐ 56 First R+ .75 2.00
☐ 57 Four of Nine R+ .75 2.00
☐ 58 Nine of Fifteen C .10 .25
☐ 59 Nine of Twelve C .10 .25
☐ 60 Second R+ .75 2.00
☐ 61 Seven of Nine R+ 1.50 4.00
☐ 62 Seventeen of Eighteen C .10 .25
☐ 63 Six of Twelve C .10 .25
☐ 64 Third and Fourth R+ .75 2.00
☐ 65 Three of Nine R+ .75 2.00
☐ 66 Two of Nine R+ .75 2.00
☐ 67 Two of Twelve C .10 .25
☐ 68a Angelo Tassoni BLUE C .10 .25
☐ 68b Angelo Tassoni GOLD C .10 .25
☐ 69 Deanna Troi R+ 1.25 3.00
☐ 70a Equinox Doctor BLUE R+ 3.00 8.00
☐ 70b Equinox Doctor GOLD R+ 3.00 8.00
☐ 71a Hogan BLUE C .10 .25
☐ 71b Hogan GOLD C .10 .25
☐ 72 Reginald Barclay UR 10.00 20.00
☐ 73 Gegis R .60 1.50
☐ 74 Nunk U .20 .50
☐ 75 Yeggie U .20 .50
☐ 76 Davar C .10 .25
☐ 77 Decaren R .60 1.50
☐ 78 Donik R+ .75 2.00
☐ 79 Gann R .60 1.50
☐ 80a Hajur DK BLUE R+ 3.00 8.00
☐ 80b Hajur GOLD R+ 3.00 8.00
☐ 81 Harkan C .10 .25
☐ 82 Idrin R .60 1.50
☐ 83 Jetarn C .10 .25
☐ 84 Jorik R .60 1.50
☐ 85 Karon R .60 1.50
☐ 86 Karr R+ .75 2.00
☐ 87 Konuric C .10 .25
☐ 88 Netek R+ 1.00 2.50
☐ 89 Ranjen C .10 .25
☐ 90 Takirac U .20 .50
☐ 91 Turanj U .20 .50
☐ 92 Vurond C .10 .25
☐ 93 Lagren U .20 .50
☐ 94 Surat R .60 1.50
☐ 95 Tanar C .10 .25
☐ 96 Ch'Regha U .20 .50
☐ 97 Kamok C .10 .25
☐ 98 Kohlar R .60 1.50
☐ 99 Morak U .20 .50
☐ 100 T'Greth U .20 .50
☐ 101 B'Elanna R+ 1.25 3.00
☐ 102 Captain Chakotay R+ 1.25 3.00
☐ 103 Fennim R .60 1.50

❑ 104a Icheb BLUE R+ 2.00 5.00
❑ 104b Icheb GOLD R+ 2.00 5.00
❑ 105 Kes R+ .75 2.00
❑ 106 Lansor U .20 .50
❑ 107 Mabus U .20 .50
❑ 108a Marika BLUE R+ 1.50 4.00
❑ 108b Marika GOLD R+ 1.50 4.00
❑ 109a Mezoti BLUE R+ 1.50 4.00
❑ 109b Mezoti GOLD R+ 1.50 4.00
❑ 110 One R+ 1.00 2.50
❑ 111a Orum GOLD R+ 2.00 5.00
❑ 111b Orum GREEN R+ 2.00 5.00
❑ 112 P'Chan U .20 .50
❑ 113a Rebi and Azan BLUE R+ 1.50 4.00
❑ 113b Rebi and Azan GOLD R+ 1.50 4.00
❑ 114a Riley Frasier BLUE R+ 1.50 4.00
❑ 114b Riley Frasier GOLD R+ 1.50 4.00
❑ 115 Sullin R .60 1.50
❑ 116 The Artificial Intelligence U .20 .50
❑ 117 Thenelak C .10 .25
❑ 118 Dilanum C .10 .25
❑ 119 Sinaren C .10 .25
❑ 120 Borg Cube U .20 .50
❑ 121 Borg Probe C .10 .25
❑ 122 Borg Queen's Ship R .75 2.00
❑ 123 Borg Tactical Cube R .75 2.00
❑ 124a U.S.S. Prometheus BLUE R+ 10.00 20.00
❑ 124b U.S.S. Prometheus GREEN R+ 10.00 20.00
❑ 125 Hunting Vessel C .10 .25
❑ 126 Venatic Hunter R .60 1.50
❑ 127 Kazon Fighter U .20 .50
❑ 128 I.K.C. Voq'leng R+ .75 2.00
❑ 129 Liberty R+ .75 2.00
❑ 130 The Think Tank's Ship R .60 1.50
❑ 131a U.S.S. Dauntless BLUE R+ 6.00 15.00
❑ 131b U.S.S. Dauntless GOLD R+ 6.00 15.00

2002 Star Trek The Motion Pictures

BOOSTER BOX (30) 100.00 200.00
BOOSTER PACK (11) 4.00 8.00

❑ 1 The Genesis Device R .60 1.50
❑ 2 Engine Imbalance U .20 .50
❑ 3 God R .60 1.50
❑ 4 Hero Worship R .60 1.50
❑ 5 I Hate You C .10 .25
❑ 6 Linguistic Legerdemain C .10 .25
❑ 7 Now Would Be A Good Time U .20 .50
❑ 8 Subspace Shock Wave C .10 .25
❑ 9 The Whale Probe R .60 1.50
❑ 10 V'Ger R .60 1.50
❑ 11 The Nexus U .20 .50
❑ 12 Transport Inhibitor C .10 .25
❑ 13 Transporter Drones U .20 .50
❑ 14 Duj Saq C .10 .25
❑ 15 Fal-tor-pan C .10 .25
❑ 16 I Just Love Scanning for Life-forms R .60 1.50
❑ 17 Isomagnetic Disintegrator U .20 .50
❑ 18 To Be Or Not To Be U .20 .50
❑ 19 Ceti Eel C .10 .25
❑ 20 Release This Pain C .10 .25
❑ 21 I Do Not Take Orders From You! U .20 .50
❑ 22 Lure of the Nexus C .10 .25
❑ 23 No, Kirk... The Game's Not Over C .10 .25
❑ 24 Prefix Code Transmission C .10 .25
❑ 25 Smooth as an Android's BottomU .20 .50
❑ 26 The Needs of the Many... C .10 .25
❑ 27 What Does God Need With A StarshipR .75 2.00
❑ 28 Analyze Radiation C .10 .25
❑ 29 Insurrection C .10 .25
❑ 30 Observe Ritual C .10 .25
❑ 31 The Discovery of Sha Ka Ree C .10 .25
❑ 32 Collect Metaphasic Particles U .20 .50
❑ 33 Revenge is a Dish Best Served Cold U .20 .50
❑ 34 Admiral Cartwright U .20 .50
❑ 35 Admiral Kirk R+ 3.00 8.00
❑ 36 Amanda Grayson R+ .75 2.00
❑ 37 Ambassador Sarek R+ .75 2.00
❑ 38 Captain Spock R+ 1.50 4.00
❑ 39 Captain Styles U .20 .50
❑ 40 Captain Sulu R+ 1.25 3.00
❑ 41 Carol Marcus R .75 2.00
❑ 42 Clark Terrell U .20 .50
❑ 43 Commander Chekov R+ 1.25 3.00
❑ 44 Commander Rand R .60 1.50
❑ 45 Commander Uhura R+ 1.25 3.00
❑ 46 David Marcus R .75 2.00
❑ 47 Demora Sulu U .20 .50
❑ 48 Dmitri Valtane U .20 .50
❑ 49 Dr. Chapel R+ 1.25 3.00
❑ 50 Dr. McCoy R+ 1.25 3.00
❑ 51 Ensign Tuvok R .75 2.00
❑ 52 Henreid C .10 .25
❑ 53 Ilia U .20 .50
❑ 54 J.T. Esteban U .20 .50
❑ 55 Jacobson C .10 .25
❑ 56 James T. Kirk UR 30.00 60.00
❑ 57 John Harriman R+ .75 2.00
❑ 58 Lojur C .10 .25
❑ 59 Mark Tobiaston C .10 .25
❑ 60 Matthew Dougherty U .20 .50
❑ 61 Mr. Scott R+ 1.25 3.00
❑ 62 Saavik R+ 1.25 3.00
❑ 63 St. John Talbot U .20 .50
❑ 64 T'Lar U .20 .50
❑ 65 Tahglio C .10 .25
❑ 66 Valeris R .60 1.50
❑ 67 Voight C .10 .25
❑ 68 Willard Decker R+ .75 2.00
❑ 69 Azetbur U .20 .50
❑ 70 Brigadier Kerla R .60 1.50
❑ 71 Captain Kang R+ 1.25 3.00
❑ 72 Ch'dak C .10 .25
❑ 73 Chancellor Gorkon R+ .75 2.00
❑ 74 Colonel Worf R+ 1.25 3.00
❑ 75 General Chang R+ 1.50 4.00
❑ 76 General Korrd U .20 .50
❑ 77 Kamarag U .20 .50
❑ 78 Karnog C .10 .25
❑ 79 Klaa U .20 .50
❑ 80 Komal C .10 .25
❑ 81 Kor'choth C .10 .25
❑ 82 Koth U .20 .50
❑ 83 Krase R+ .75 2.00
❑ 84 Kruge R+ .75 2.00
❑ 85 Maltz U .20 .50
❑ 86 Regnor C .10 .25
❑ 87 Torg R .60 1.50
❑ 88 Valkris U .20 .50
❑ 89 Vixis U .20 .50
❑ 90 Wotein C .10 .25
❑ 91 Gracie and George U .20 .50
❑ 92a Dr. Gillian Taylor BLUE R+ 10.00 20.00
❑ 92b Dr. Gillian Taylor GOLD R+ 10.00 20.00
❑ 93 Dr. Tolian Soran R+ 1.25 3.00
❑ 94 Gallatin R .60 1.50
❑ 95 J'Onn U .20 .50
❑ 96 Joachim R .60 1.50
❑ 97 Khan R+ 1.50 4.00
❑ 98 Martia U .20 .50
❑ 99 Mas'ud C .10 .25
❑ 100 Pa'rena C .10 .25
❑ 101 Rae'alin C .10 .25
❑ 102 Ru'afo R+ 1.25 3.00
❑ 103 Sam'po C .10 .25
❑ 104 Sarod C .10 .25
❑ 105 Sharic C .10 .25
❑ 106 Sybok U .20 .50
❑ 107 Wajahut C .10 .25
❑ 108 Caithlin Dar U .20 .50
❑ 109 Nanclus R .60 1.50
❑ 110a H.M.S. Bounty BLUE R+ 15.00 30.00
❑ 110b H.M.S. Bounty RED R+ 15.00 30.00
❑ 111 Starship Constitution C .10 .25
❑ 112 Starship Enterprise R+ 1.50 4.00
❑ 113 Starship Excelsior R+ 1.25 3.00
❑ 114 U.S.S. Enterprise-A R+ 1.50 4.00
❑ 115 U.S.S. Enterprise-B U .20 .50
❑ 116 I.K.C. Amar R .60 1.50
❑ 117 I.K.C. Chontay U .20 .50
❑ 118 I.K.C. K'elric U .20 .50
❑ 119 I.K.C. K't'inga C .10 .25
❑ 120 I.K.C. Kla'Diyus R+ 1.25 3.00
❑ 121 Kronos One R+ 1.25 3.00
❑ 122 Injector Assembly One U .20 .50
❑ 123 Li'seria U .20 .50
❑ 124 Son'a Battleship R .60 1.50
❑ 125 Son'a Shuttle C .10 .25
❑ 126a U.S.S. Reliant BLUE R+ 20.00 40.00
❑ 126b U.S.S. Reliant GOLD R+ 20.00 40.00
❑ 127 Isolytic Burst U .20 .50
❑ 128 Riker Maneuver U .20 .50
❑ 129 Target Warp Field Coils C .10 .25
❑ 130 Camp Khitomer R .60 1.50
❑ 131 Cetacean Institute C .10 .25

2003 Star Trek Call To Arms

BOOSTER BOX (30) 25.00 50.00
BOOSTER PACK (11) 1.25 2.50

❑ 3C1 A Bad End (1E) .10 .20
❑ 3C3 Close Call (1E) .10 .20
❑ 3C4 Confined to Quarters (1E) .10 .20
❑ 3C6 Depression .10 .20
❑ 3C8 Don't Let It End This Way (1E) .10 .20
❑ 3R5 Dangerous Climb (1E) .40 1.00
❑ 3S2 An Old Debt .20 .50
❑ 3S7 DNA Analysis (1E) .20 .50
❑ 3U9 Dressing Down .20 .50
❑ 3C13 Graviton Wave (1E) .10 .20
❑ 3C14 History Repeats Itself (1E) .10 .20
❑ 3C17 Miner Disagreement .10 .20
❑ 3C18 Murder Investigation (1E) .10 .20
❑ 3C24 Rock People (1E) .10 .20
❑ 3C27 Sheer Lunacy .10 .20
❑ 3C29 So Many Enemies (1E) .10 .20
❑ 3C33 A Second Chance at Life (1E) .10 .20
❑ 3C41 Dispensing the White .10 .20
❑ 3C43 Enemy in your Midst .10 .20
❑ 3C45 Jem'Hadar Ambush (1E) .10 .20
❑ 3C50 Quite a Coincidence (1E) .10 .20
❑ 3C51 Regeneration Alcoves .10 .20
❑ 3C55 Severed Link .10 .20
❑ 3C58 Stir Crazy .10 .20
❑ 3C67 Vorta Cloning (1E) .10 .20
❑ 3C71 Cultist Attack (1E) .10 .20
❑ 3C78 The Founder Is Wise .10 .20
❑ 3C79 We're Everywhere .10 .20
❑ 3R11 Forsaken (1E) .75 2.00
❑ 3R12 Gomtuu Shock Wave (1E) 1.25 3.00
❑ 3R19 Overwhelmed .75 2.00
❑ 3R22 Quantum Filament (1E) .40 1.00
❑ 3R31 The Demands of Duty (1E) .40 1.00
❑ 3R34 Abduction .40 1.00
❑ 3R37 Bred For Battle (1E) .40 1.00
❑ 3R38 Building a Bridge (1E) .40 1.00
❑ 3R39 Cavalry Raid 1.00 2.50
❑ 3R44 I Don't Like to Lose .40 1.00
❑ 3R46 Jem'Hadar Birthing Chamber .40 1.00
❑ 3R49 Psychological Pressure (1E) 1.25 3.00
❑ 3R54 Set Up (1E) .75 2.00
❑ 3R56 Sluggo .40 1.00
❑ 3R57 Steeled By Loss .40 1.00
❑ 3R59 The Blight .40 1.00
❑ 3R60 The Crystalline Entity .40 1.00
❑ 3R61 The Enterprise Incident .40 1.00
❑ 3R62 The Manheim Effect .40 1.00
❑ 3R72 Founder Trap .60 1.50
❑ 3R74 Our Death is Glory To the Founders 1.50 4.00
❑ 3R75 Parting Shot .40 1.00
❑ 3R76 Pseudopod 1.50 4.00
❑ 3S10 Failure To Communicate (1E) .20 .50
❑ 3S15 Inside Collaborators (1E) .20 .50
❑ 3S16 Justice or Vengeance (1E) .20 .50
❑ 3S21 Psycho-Kinetic Attack (1E) .20 .50
❑ 3S30 Sokath, His Eyes Uncovered .20 .50
❑ 3S36 Borg Cutting Beam .20 .50
❑ 3S70 Analyze .20 .50
❑ 3S82 Assault On Species 8472 .20 .50
❑ 3S83 Battle Reconnaissance (1E) .20 .50
❑ 3S86 Destroy Iconian Gateway (1E) .20 .50
❑ 3S92 Founders' Homeworld, Home of the Great Link .20 .50
❑ 3S94 Hunt Alien .20 .50
❑ 3U20 Psychic Receptacle (1E) .20 .50
❑ 3U23 Restricted Area (1E) .20 .50
❑ 3U25 Rogue Borg Ambush .20 .50
❑ 3U26 Secret Identity (1E) .20 .50
❑ 3U28 Skeleton Crew (1E) .20 .50
❑ 3U32 Jem'Hadar Disruptor Pistol .20 .50
❑ 3U35 Adding to Our Perfection .20 .50
❑ 3U40 Changeling Sabotage .20 .50
❑ 3U42 Dissolving the Senate .20 .50
❑ 3U47 Jem'Hadar Strike Force (1E) .20 .50
❑ 3U48 One With the Borg .20 .50
❑ 3U52 Sabotage Program .20 .50
❑ 3U53 Sensing a Trap .20 .50
❑ 3U63 The Trial Never Ended .20 .50
❑ 3U64 The Will of the Collective .20 .50
❑ 3U65 Trial of Faith (1E) .20 .50
❑ 3U66 Under Suspicion .20 .50
❑ 3U68 We're Mutants .20 .50
❑ 3U69 Adapt .20 .50
❑ 3U73 Insult .20 .50
❑ 3U77 Security Sweep (1E) .20 .50
❑ 3U80 You Could Be Invaluable (1E) .20 .50
❑ 3U81 Archanis Dispute .20 .50
❑ 3U84 Camping Trip .20 .50
❑ 3U85 Clash at Chin'toka (1E) .20 .50
❑ 3U87 Destroy Transwarp Hub .20 .50
❑ 3U88 Evade Borg Vessel .20 .50
❑ 3U89 Evade Dominion Squadron (1E) .20 .50
❑ 3U90 Expose Changeling Influence .20 .50
❑ 3U91 Extract Defector .20 .50
❑ 3U93 Harness Omega Particle .20 .50
❑ 3U95 Instruct Advanced Drone .20 .50
❑ 3U96 Mouth of the Wormhole, Terok Nor .20 .50
❑ 3U97 Pacify Warring Factions .20 .50
❑ 3U98 Peaceful Contact .20 .50
❑ 3U99 Plot Invasion .20 .50
❑ 3C111 Jorem .10 .20
❑ 3C117 Yelsar .10 .20
❑ 3C118 Acclimation Drone .10 .20
❑ 3C119 Allocation Drone .10 .20
❑ 3C120 Appraisal Drone .10 .20
❑ 3C121 Archival Drone .10 .20
❑ 3C125 Cartography Drone .10 .20
❑ 3C126 Computation Drone (1E) .10 .20
❑ 3C127 Continuity Drone .10 .20
❑ 3C128 Evaluation Drone .10 .20
❑ 3C129 Guidance Drone .10 .20
❑ 3C130 Information Drone .10 .20
❑ 3C131 Invasive Drone .10 .20
❑ 3C133 Negation Drone .10 .20
❑ 3C134 Opposition Drone .10 .20
❑ 3C135 Preservation Drone .10 .20
❑ 3C137 Research Drone .10 .20
❑ 3C140 Transwarp Drone .10 .20
❑ 3C142 Davin (1E) .10 .20
❑ 3C145 Magren (1E) .10 .20
❑ 3C147 Nerot .10 .20
❑ 3C148 Thorel (1E) .10 .20
❑ 3C152 Founder Councilor .10 .20
❑ 3C156 Imat'Korex (1E) .10 .20
❑ 3C164 Odera'Klen (1E) .10 .20
❑ 3C165 Rak'tazan (1E) .10 .20
❑ 3C167 Tholun (1E) .10 .20
❑ 3C168 Tozara'Kesh (1E) .10 .20
❑ 3C169 Varen'agor (1E) .10 .20
❑ 3C189 E'Tyshra .10 .20
❑ 3C190 Jakin (1E) .10 .20
❑ 3C192 Nydrom .10 .20
❑ 3C193 Sharat .10 .20
❑ 3C195 Mullen .10 .20
❑ 3C198 Borg Cube .10 .20
❑ 3C201 Modern Galor (1E) .10 .20
❑ 3C203 Jem'Hadar Warship .10 .20
❑ 3R112 Kira Nerys, Reformed Collaborator (1E) .75 2.00
❑ 3R113 Odo, Wayward Link (1E) .60 1.50
❑ 3R114 Porta, Advisor to the Emissary .40 1.00
❑ 3R116 Yassim, Zealous Protester .40 1.00
❑ 3R123 Borg Queen, Guardian of the Hive 1.50 4.00
❑ 3R132 Locutus, Voice of the Borg 1.50 4.00
❑ 3R138 Seven of Nine, Part of the Greater Whole 1.50 4.00
❑ 3R141 Damar, Useful Adjutant .40 1.00
❑ 3R143 Dukat, Liberator and Protector (1E) .60 1.50
❑ 3R149 Tora Ziyal, Beloved Daughter (1E) 1.25 3.00
❑ 3R150 Bashir Founder, Nefarious Saboteur .40 1.00
❑ 3R151 Borath, Psychological Researcher .40 1.00
❑ 3R155 Ikat'ika, Honorable Warrior (1E) 1.25 3.00
❑ 3R159 Kira Founder, Examiner 1.00 2.50
❑ 3R166 Remata'Klan, Unit Leader (1E) .60 1.50
❑ 3R171 Weyoun, Loyal Subject of the Dominion (1E) .75 2.00
❑ 3R173 Yelgrun, Blunt Negotiator .40 1.00
❑ 3R174 B'Elanna Torres, Creative Engineer (1E) .75 2.00
❑ 3R175 Jack, Maladjusted Misfit (1E) .60 1.50
❑ 3R176 Lauren, Seductress .40 1.00
❑ 3R177 Michael Eddington, Traitor to Starfleet (1E) 1.25 3.00
❑ 3R180 Reginald Barclay, Reclusive Engineer .60 1.50
❑ 3R182 Quark, Resistance Informant (1E) .75 2.00
❑ 3R183 Rom, Undercover Spy (1E) .60 1.50
❑ 3R184 Alexander Rozhenko, Good Luck Charm (1E) .40 1.00
❑ 3R185 Darok, Martok's Aide .40 1.00
❑ 3R186 Kor, Noble Warrior to the End .40 1.00
❑ 3R191 Kasidy Yates, Maquis Smuggler .40 1.00
❑ 3R196 Pardek, Betrayer (1E) .40 1.00
❑ 3R197 Ruwon, Intelligence Analyst (1E) .40 1.00
❑ 3R200 Locutus' Borg Cube 1.25 3.00
❑ 3R204 Tenak'talar, Weyoun's Warship (1E) 1.50 4.00
❑ 3R205 U.S.S. Defiant, Stolen Warship 2.00 5.00
❑ 3R206 I.K.S. Pagh (1E) .40 1.00
❑ 3R207 Xhosa .40 1.00
❑ 3R208 Soterus (1E) .60 1.50
❑ 3S101 Rescue Prisoners of War .20 .50
❑ 3S103 Salvage Borg Ship (1E) .20 .50
❑ 3S104 Salvage Dominion Ship .20 .50
❑ 3S108 Survey Star System .20 .50
❑ 3S110 Unicomplex, Root of the Hive Mind .20 .50
❑ 3S122 Borg Queen, Bringer of Order .40 1.00
❑ 3S124 Calibration Drone (1E) .40 1.00
❑ 3S139 Seven of Nine .40 1.00
Representative of the Hive (1E)
❑ 3S154 Founder Leader, Forbidding Judge .20 .50
❑ 3S158 Kilana, Dissembling Envoy (1E) .20 .50
❑ 3S162 Martok Founder, Poison of the Empire .20 .50
❑ 3S163 Noret'ikar (1E) .20 .50
❑ 3S199 Borg Sphere .40 1.00
❑ 3S202 Jem'Hadar Attack Ship .20 .50
❑ 3U100 Political Intrigue .20 .50
❑ 3U102 Restock Ketracel-White .20 .50
❑ 3U105 Signal for Rescue (1E) .20 .50
❑ 3U106 Stage Bombardment .20 .50
❑ 3U107 Study Rare Phenomenon (1E) .20 .50
❑ 3U109 The Siege of AR-558 (1E) .20 .50
❑ 3U115 Tahna Los, Voice of the Kohn-ma (1E) .20 .50
❑ 3U136 Reclamation Drone (1E) .20 .50
❑ 3U144 Elim Garak, Plain, Simple Taylor (1E) .20 .50
❑ 3U146 Mavek, Science Officer (1E) .20 .50
❑ 3U153 Founder Leader, Beguiling Teacher (1E) .20 .50
❑ 3U157 Keevan, Conniving Liar (1E) .20 .50
❑ 3U160 Limara'Son, Fierce Soldier .20 .50
❑ 3U161 Lovok Founder, Puppet Master .20 .50
❑ 3U170 Weyoun, Instrument of the Founders .20 .50
❑ 3U172 Yak'Talon, Deadly Patroller .20 .50
❑ 3U178 Norah Satie, Starfleet Investigator .20 .50
❑ 3U179 Patrick, Idiot Savant (1E) .20 .50
❑ 3U181 Sarina Douglas, Catatonic Conundrum (1E) .20 .50
❑ 3U187 Larg, Piece of Baktag (1E) .20 .50
❑ 3U188 Martok, Leader of Destiny (1E) .20 .50
❑ 3U194 Karina, Intelligence Analyst (1E) .20 .50

2003 Star Trek Energize

BOOSTER BOX (30) 100.00 200.00
BOOSTER PACK (11) 4.00 8.00

❑ 2C4 Dedication to Duty (1E) .10 .20
❑ 2C5 Disgraceful Assault (1E) .10 .20
❑ 2C6 Disruptor Accident (1E) .10 .20
❑ 2C7 DNA Security Scan (1E) .10 .20
❑ 2R2 Casualties of War .50 1.25
❑ 2R9 Face to Face (1E) .75 2.00
❑ 2U1 A Klingon Matter .20 .50
❑ 2U3 Crippling Attack (1E) .20 .50
❑ 2U8 Exposed Power Relay (1E) .20 .50
❑ 2C13 Houdini Mines .10 .20
❑ 2C14 Meaningless Words (1E) .10 .20
❑ 2C15 Memory Invasion (1E) .10 .20
❑ 2C16 Nausicaans Pirates (1E) .10 .20
❑ 2C20 Racial Tension (1E) .10 .20
❑ 2C21 Sorting Things Out (1E) .10 .20
❑ 2C23 Subspace Accident (1E) .10 .20
❑ 2C24 Telepathic Deception (1E) .10 .20
❑ 2C25 Timescape .10 .20
❑ 2C27 Traitor Exposed (1E) .10 .20
❑ 2C28 Unexpected (1E) .10 .20
❑ 2C29 Bat'leth .10 .20
❑ 2C34 Cargo Run (1E) .10 .20
❑ 2C39 Crowd Control .10 .20
❑ 2C43 For the Cause .10 .20
❑ 2C45 Heart of Glory (1E) .10 .20
❑ 2C47 Legal Proceedings (1E) .10 .20
❑ 2C48 Life Support .10 .20
❑ 2C52 Personal Forcefield (1E) .10 .20
❑ 2C54 Pickpocket .10 .20
❑ 2C56 Power to the Weapons (1E) .10 .20
❑ 2C57 Rash Aggression (1E) .10 .20
❑ 2C58 Reconfiguration (1E) .10 .20
❑ 2C60 Salvaging the Wreckage .10 .20
❑ 2C69 Unexpected Difficulties .10 .20
❑ 2C75 Coordinated Attack .10 .20
❑ 2C78 Emergency Treatment .10 .20
❑ 2C79 Fresh Tactic .10 .20
❑ 2C88 Team of Ambassadors (1E) .10 .20
❑ 2C89 The Prophets' Guidance (1E) .10 .20
❑ 2C90 The Truth of War .10 .20
❑ 2C92 Vision of Violence (1E) .10 .20
❑ 2R11 Head to Head (1E) .50 1.25
❑ 2R26 Training Accident .50 1.25
❑ 2R30 Ak'voh .50 1.25
❑ 2R31 Assassination Plot (1E) 1.25 3.00
❑ 2R35 Common Ground .50 1.25
❑ 2R36 Complications .50 1.25
❑ 2R37 Confessions in the Pale Moonlight .50 1.25
❑ 2R38 Conscription .50 1.25
❑ 2R40 Deep Roots .50 1.25
❑ 2R41 Disable Sensors (1E) 1.00 2.50
❑ 2R49 Machinations .50 1.25
❑ 2R59 Retaliation .50 1.25
❑ 2R61 Shadow Operation .50 1.25
❑ 2R65 Straying from the Path (1E) .50 1.25
❑ 2R67 The Text of the Kosst Amojan .50 1.25
❑ 2R68 Under Scrutiny (1E) .50 1.25
❑ 2R72 Visionary (1E) .50 1.25
❑ 2R81 If Wishes Were Horses .50 1.25
❑ 2R82 Ja'chuq 1.25 3.00
❑ 2R83 Powerful Example .50 1.25
❑ 2R85 Relentless .75 2.00
❑ 2R91 Vile Deception .50 1.25
❑ 2U10 Flim-Flam Artist (1E) .20 .50
❑ 2U12 Hired Muscle (1E) .20 .50
❑ 2U17 Picking Up the Pieces (1E) .20 .50
❑ 2U18 Plasma Shock (1E) .20 .50
❑ 2U19 Quaint Technology (1E) .20 .50
❑ 2U22 Stolen Computer Core .20 .50
❑ 2U32 Born for Conquest (1E) .20 .50
❑ 2U33 Brief Reunion .20 .50
❑ 2U42 Ferocity (1E) .20 .50
❑ 2U44 For the Sisko (1E) .20 .50
❑ 2U46 Kotra (1E) .20 .50
❑ 2U50 Mental Discipline (1E) .20 .50
❑ 2U51 Peldor Joi .20 .50
❑ 2U53 Picking Up the Basics .20 .50
❑ 2U55 Political Leverage (1E) .20 .50
❑ 2U62 Sickbay (1E) .20 .50
❑ 2U63 Smuggling Run .20 .50
❑ 2U64 Staunch Determination .20 .50
❑ 2U66 Temba, His Arms Wide .20 .50
❑ 2U70 Unseen Manipulations .20 .50
❑ 2U71 Vast Resources .20 .50
❑ 2U73 We Will Not Surrender (1E) .20 .50
❑ 2U74 Bank Heist .20 .50
❑ 2U76 Diplomatic Masquerade .20 .50
❑ 2U77 Discreet Inquiry .20 .50
❑ 2U80 Honorable Death .20 .50
❑ 2U84 Precautionary Measures (1E) .20 .50
❑ 2U86 Shared Delicacy (1E) .20 .50
❑ 2U87 Stricken Dumb .20 .50
❑ 2U93 We Are Klingon .20 .50
❑ 2U94 Well-Crafted Lure .20 .50
❑ 2U95 Aid Clone Colony .20 .50
❑ 2U96 Athos IV, Maquis Base .20 .50
❑ 2U97 Avert Danger .20 .50
❑ 2U98 Brute Force .20 .50
❑ 2U99 Cargo Haul .20 .50
❑ 2C109 Ro Laren, Maquis Sympathizer (1E) .10 .20
❑ 2C116 Jural .10 .20
❑ 2C126 Kelly, Relief Tactical Officer (1E) .10 .20
❑ 2C129 Niles .10 .20
❑ 2C133 Bregath .10 .20
❑ 2C134 Divok .10 .20
❑ 2C140 Khar .10 .20
❑ 2C141 Khos (1E) .10 .20
❑ 2C143 Koral, Dour Smuggler (1E) .10 .20
❑ 2C145 Losta (1E) .10 .20
❑ 2C148 Arctus Baran, Mercenary Captain .10 .20
❑ 2C149 Harana .10 .20
❑ 2C150 Jaglom Shrek (1E) .10 .20
❑ 2C151 Kobb .10 .20
❑ 2C152 Liam Bilby, Family Man .10 .20
❑ 2C153 Macius (1E) .10 .20
❑ 2C154 Maques, Cairn Delegate (1E) .10 .20
❑ 2C155 Narik (1E) .10 .20
❑ 2C159 Sark (1E) .10 .20
❑ 2C160 Vekor .10 .20
❑ 2C164 Palteth .10 .20
❑ 2C167 Toraan .10 .20
❑ 2C172 Maquis Raider (1E) .10 .20
❑ 2C176 Mercenary Ship .10 .20
❑ 2R104 Borum, Selfless Hero (1E) .50 1.25
❑ 2R105 Jaro Essa, Leader of the Circle .50 1.25
❑ 2R106 Kira Nerys, Impassioned Major (1E) 1.25 3.00
❑ 2R107 Kurn, Bajoran Security Officer (1E) .50 1.25
❑ 2R108 Leeta, Dabo Girl (1E) 1.25 3.00
❑ 2R112 Winn Adami, Devious Manipulator .50 1.25
❑ 2R114 Enabran Tain, Retired Mastermind (1E) .50 1.25
❑ 2R115 Evek, Harsh Interrogator (1E) .50 1.25
❑ 2R120 Chakotay, Freedom Fighter 1.25 3.00
❑ 2R121 Ezri Dax, Station Counselor .75 2.00

TCG/CCG

❑ 2R122 Jake Sisko, Temporal Anchor .50 1.25
❑ 2R125 Keiko O'Brien, School Teacher .50 1.25
❑ 2R127 Michael Eddington, Noble Hero (1E) .75 2.00
❑ 2R128 Miles O'Brien, Transporter Chief .75 2.00
❑ 2R130 Rebecca Sullivan, Resistance Fighter (1E) 1.50 4.00
❑ 2R131 Thomas Riker, Defiant Leader (1E) 1.00 2.50
❑ 2R135 Drex, Arrogant Warrior .50 1.25
❑ 2R136 K'mpec, Klingon Supreme Commander .50 1.25
❑ 2R138 Kahless, The Unforgettable .50 1.25
❑ 2R139 Kargan, Rash Captain (1E) .50 1.25
❑ 2R142 Konmel, Renegade Warrior .50 1.25
❑ 2R144 Korris, Renegade Captain (1E) .50 1.25
❑ 2R157 Roga Danar, Decorated Subhadar .75 2.00
❑ 2R158 Sakonna, Gunrunner (1E) .50 1.25
❑ 2R161 Galathon, Steadfast Rival .75 2.00
❑ 2R163 Neral, Senate Proconsul .50 1.25
❑ 2R165 Sirol, Diplomatic Adversary (1E) .50 1.25
❑ 2R168 Toreth, Cautious Commander (1E) .50 1.25
❑ 2R169 Kitara (1E) 1.00 2.50
❑ 2R170 Aldara (1E) .75 2.00
❑ 2R173 Valjean .60 1.50
❑ 2R174 I.K.S. Qam-Chee (1E) .75 2.00
❑ 2R175 Fortune .50 1.25
❑ 2R178 Khazara (1E) .75 2.00
❑ 2R179 Terix (1E) .75 2.00
❑ 2R180 Trolarak (1E) .75 2.00
❑ 2U100 Investigate Maquis Activity (1E) .20 .50
❑ 2U101 Mine Nebula .20 .50
❑ 2U102 Treat Plague Ship (1E) .20 .50
❑ 2U103 Akorem Laan, Revered Poet (1E) .20 .50
❑ 2U110 The Sirah, The Storyteller .20 .50
❑ 2U111 Varis Sul, Tetrarch of the Paqu (1E) .20 .50
❑ 2U113 Boheeka, Clandestine Connection .20 .50
❑ 2U117 Natima Lang .20 .50
Professor of Political Ethics (1E)
❑ 2U118 Benjamin Sisko, Man of Resolve (1E) .20 .50
❑ 2U119 Cal Hudson .20 .50
Attache to the Demilitarized Zone
❑ 2U123 Joseph Sisko, Creole Chef (1E) .20 .50
❑ 2U124 Julian Bashir, Unnatural Freak .20 .50
❑ 2U132 William Patrick Samuels .20 .50
Maquis Saboteur (1E)
❑ 2U137 Kahless .20 .50
The Greatest Warrior of Them All (1E)
❑ 2U146 M'vil .20 .50
❑ 2U147 Amaros, Earnest Vanguard .20 .50
❑ 2U156 Raimus, Criminal Master .20 .50
❑ 2U162 Mirok, Interphase Researcher (1E) .20 .50
❑ 2U166 T'Rul, Curt Subcommander (1E). .20 .50
❑ 2U171 Guingouin (1E) .20 .50
❑ 2U177 Tama (1E) .20 .50

2004 Star Trek Fractured Time

❑ 5P1 Temporal Misalignment .75 2.00
❑ 5P2 The Clown: Bitter Medicine (1E) 1.50 4.00
❑ 5P3 Tragic Turn 5.00 10.00
❑ 5P4 Cardassian Protectorate 1.25 3.00
❑ 5P6 Heightened Perception .75 2.00
❑ 5P7 Medical Teams .75 2.00
❑ 5P8 Noble Cause (1E) .75 2.00
❑ 5P9 Out of Options (1E) .75 2.00
❑ 5R5 Expand the Collective 1.25 3.00
❑ 5P10 Quantum Incursions (1E) 1.25 3.00
❑ 5P11 Quarantine .75 2.00
❑ 5P12 Security Drills (1E) 1.50 4.00
❑ 5P13 Spreading Fear (1E) .75 2.00
❑ 5P14 Tampering With Time .75 2.00
❑ 5P15 Temporal Test Subject (1E) .75 2.00
❑ 5P16 The Edge of Forever .75 2.00
❑ 5P17 The Play's the Thing .75 2.00
❑ 5P18 Unyielding 2.00 5.00
❑ 5P19 Explicit Orders (1E) 1.50 4.00
❑ 5P20 Fitting In (1E) 2.00 5.00
❑ 5P21 Collapse Anti-Time Anomaly .75 2.00
❑ 5P22 Kira Nerys, The Intendant 1.25 3.00
❑ 5P23 Kira Taban, Husband and Father (1E) .75 2.00
❑ 5P24 Dukat, Prefect of Bajor 1.25 3.00
❑ 5P25 Elim Garak, First Officer of Terok Nor 1.25 3.00
❑ 5P26 Borath, Subconscious Projection .75 2.00
❑ 5P27 Founder Agitator, Elusive Assassin .75 2.00
❑ 5P28 James T. Kirk, Living Legend 2.00 5.00
❑ 5P29 Tasha Yar, Tactical Officer 1.50 4.00
❑ 5P30 Worf, First Officer 1.50 4.00
❑ 5P31 Korath, Duplicitous Tinkerer 1.25 3.00
❑ 5P32 Worf, Regent of the Alliance 1.50 4.00
❑ 5P33 Benjamin Sisko, Outlaw (1E) 1.50 4.00
❑ 5P34 Daniels, Temporal Enforcers 1.25 3.00
❑ 5P35 Miles O'Brien, Smiley 2.50 6.00
❑ 5P36 The Traveler, Transcendent Explorer (1E) .75 2.00
❑ 5P37 Tomalak, Irate Commander (1E) .75 2.00
❑ 5P38 B'tanay (1E) .75 2.00
❑ 5P39 Sphere 634 2.00 5.00
❑ 5P40 U.S.S. Enterprise-D, Personal Flagship 3.00 8.00

2004 Star Trek Necessary Evil

BOOSTER BOX (30) 200.00 300.00
BOOSTER PACK (11) 6.00 12.00

❑ 4C1 A Devil Scorned .10 .20
❑ 4C2 A Pleasant Surprise (1E) .10 .20
❑ 4C3 A Royal Hunt .10 .20
❑ 4C4 Alluring Spy .10 .20
❑ 4C5 B'omar Stipulations (1E) .10 .20
❑ 4C6 Back Room Dealings (1E) .10 .20
❑ 4R7 Biochemical Hyperacceleration 1.50 4.00
❑ 4R9 Broken Captive (1E) 1.25 3.00
❑ 4U8 Bleeding to Death (1E) .20 .50
❑ 4C13 Echo Papa Stasis Field (1E) .10 .20
❑ 4C15 Guess Who's Coming to Dinner? (1E) .10 .20
❑ 4C17 In the Way (1E) .10 .20
❑ 4C19 Lack of Preparation .10 .20
❑ 4C20 Language Barrier .10 .20
❑ 4C21 On Foreign Ground .10 .20
❑ 4C26 Test of Wisdom .10 .20
❑ 4C31 Your Moment is Fading .10 .20
❑ 4C32 Emergency Transport Unit (1E) .10 .20
❑ 4C43 Captain on the Bridge .10 .20
❑ 4C45 Collateral Damage .10 .20
❑ 4C46 Deep Hatred .10 .20
❑ 4C56 Gunboat Diplomacy (1E) .10 .20
❑ 4C57 Hollow Pleasantries .10 .20
❑ 4C58 Holographic Hoax .10 .20
❑ 4C63 Mutual Advantage .10 .20
❑ 4C64 No Escape .10 .20
❑ 4C66 Party Atmosphere .10 .20
❑ 4C69 Pulling the Strings .10 .20
❑ 4C72 Shared Problems .10 .20
❑ 4C73 Standing Your Ground .10 .20
❑ 4C77 The Key to Victory .10 .20
❑ 4C81 VIP Welcome .10 .20
❑ 4C82 We Are Back .10 .20
❑ 4C87 Chance Observation .10 .20
❑ 4C96 The First of Many (1E) .10 .20
❑ 4C97 The Order of Things .10 .20
❑ 4C99 Anneli (1E) .10 .20
❑ 4R11 Counterinsurgency Program 1.25 3.00
❑ 4R18 In Training 1.25 3.00
❑ 4R25 Talosian Trial 1.25 3.00
❑ 4R27 The Dreamer and the Dream 1.50 4.00
❑ 4R28 Tsiolkovsky Infection 2.00 5.00
❑ 4R30 Whisper in the Dark 1.25 3.00
❑ 4R34 The Sword of Kahless 1.25 3.00
❑ 4R35 Accepting the Past 1.50 4.00
❑ 4R36 All-Out War 3.00 8.00
❑ 4R37 Anything or Anyone 3.00 8.00
❑ 4R40 At What Cost? 6.00 12.00
❑ 4R44 Caught in the Act 2.00 5.00
❑ 4R49 Endangered 3.00 8.00
❑ 4R51 Far-Seeing Eyes 2.50 6.00
❑ 4R52 Field Studies 1.25 3.00
❑ 4R59 Militia Patrol (1E) 1.25 3.00
❑ 4R65 Organized Terrorist Activities 7.50 15.00
❑ 4R68 Prison Compound (1E) 2.50 6.00
❑ 4R70 Ressikan Flute 2.50 6.00
❑ 4R71 Running a Tight Ship 1.25 3.00
❑ 4R74 Storage Compartment 2.00 5.00
❑ 4R78 The Perfect Tool 1.25 3.00
❑ 4R79 Thought Maker 2.50 6.00
❑ 4R83 You've Always Been My Favorite 5.00 10.00
❑ 4R85 Allies on the Inside 2.50 6.00
❑ 4R86 Brainwashing 1.25 3.00
❑ 4R89 Knowledge and Experience 1.25 3.00
❑ 4R94 Outlining the Stakes 1.25 3.00
❑ 4R98 The Rite of Emergence 1.25 3.00
❑ 4U10 Cave-In .20 .50
❑ 4U12 Dealing With Pressure .20 .50
❑ 4U14 Formal Hearing .20 .50
❑ 4U16 Harsh Conditions .20 .50
❑ 4U22 Renegade Ambush .20 .50
❑ 4U23 Short Circuit (1E) .20 .50
❑ 4U24 Side by Side (1E) .20 .50
❑ 4U29 Ungracious Hosts (1E) .20 .50
❑ 4U33 The Stone of Gol .20 .50
❑ 4U38 Apprehended .20 .50
❑ 4U39 At An Impasse .20 .50
❑ 4U41 Battle Lust .20 .50
❑ 4U42 Biological Distinctiveness .20 .50
❑ 4U47 Deploy the Fleet .20 .50
❑ 4U48 Desperate Sacrifice .20 .50
❑ 4U50 Escaping Detection .20 .50
❑ 4U53 Forcing Their Hand (1E) .20 .50
❑ 4U54 Forever Linked (1E) .20 .50
❑ 4U55 Getting Under Your Skin (1E) .20 .50
❑ 4U60 Misdirection (1E) .20 .50
❑ 4U61 Mission Accomplished (1E) .20 .50
❑ 4U62 More Than Meets the Eye .20 .50
❑ 4U67 Power Shift .20 .50
❑ 4U75 Targeted for Assimilation .20 .50
❑ 4U76 Tempted By Flesh .20 .50
❑ 4U80 Undercover Resource .20 .50
❑ 4U84 Your Fear Will Destroy You .20 .50
❑ 4U88 Indomitable .20 .50
❑ 4U90 Lying in Wait .20 .50
❑ 4U91 Natural Instincts .20 .50
❑ 4U92 One-Upmanship .20 .50
❑ 4U93 Operational Necessity .20 .50
❑ 4U95 Reborn .20 .50
❑ 4C105 Kulan, Militia Soldier .10 .20
❑ 4C107 Razka Karn, Scavenger (1E) .10 .20
❑ 4C110 Treyam, Militia Soldier .10 .20
❑ 4C111 Defragmentation Drone .10 .20
❑ 4C112 Examination Drone .10 .20
❑ 4C118 Hogue, Student of Political Ethics .10 .20
❑ 4C125 Amar'itak .10 .20
❑ 4C127 Leyton Founder, Hostile Operative .10 .20
❑ 4C136 Dorian Collins .10 .20
Acting Chief Petty Officer (1E)
❑ 4C142 Karen Farris, Rigorous Leader (1E) .10 .20
❑ 4C145 Riley Shepard, Confident Cadet (1E) .10 .20
❑ 4C146 Seth Matthews, Red Squad Cadet (1E) .10 .20
❑ 4C147 Tamal, Technician (1E) .10 .20
❑ 4C153 K'Tal, Senior Council Member .10 .20
❑ 4C156 Aaron Conor, Born Leader .10 .20
❑ 4C160 Hannah Bates, Biosphere Expert (1E) .10 .20
❑ 4C162 Martin Benbeck, Strict Interpreter .10 .20
❑ 4C163 Morik .10 .20
❑ 4C164 Reide (1E) .10 .20
❑ 4C167 Kell, Romulan Accomplice .10 .20
❑ 4C170 Mareth .10 .20
❑ 4C172 Relam .10 .20
❑ 4C174 Selok, Deep Cover Operative .10 .20
❑ 4C175 Setek .10 .20
❑ 4C177 Taul .10 .20
❑ 4R100 Bareil Antos, Opaka's Protector 1.25 3.00
❑ 4R102 Dukat, Anjohl Tennan 1.50 4.00
❑ 4R103 Kira Meru, Comfort Woman (1E) 1.50 4.00
❑ 4R104 Krim, Thoughtful Tactician 1.25 3.00
❑ 4R106 Leeta, Rebel Supporter (1E) 2.00 5.00
❑ 4R108 Solbor, Faithful Attendant (1E) 2.00 5.00
❑ 4R119 Kira Nerys, Iliana Ghemor 2.00 5.00
❑ 4R121 Odo, Impartial Investigator 2.00 5.00
❑ 4R124 Toran, Ambitious Brute (1E) 1.25 3.00
❑ 4R126 Founder Architect (1E) 1.50 4.00
❑ 4R130 Odo Founder, Adept Imposter 1.50 4.00
❑ 4R131 Rodak'koden (1E) 1.25 3.00
❑ 4R133 Beverly Crusher, Chief Physician (1E) 2.50 6.00
❑ 4R134 Data, Pinocchio (1E) 2.50 6.00
❑ 4R138 Guinan, Listener 1.50 4.00
❑ 4R139 Jadzia Dax, Problem Solver (1E) 3.00 8.00
❑ 4R140 Jake Sisko, Reporter Behind the Lines 3.00 8.00
❑ 4R149 William T. Riker, First Officer (1E) 2.50 6.00
❑ 4R150 Worf, Conn Officer 2.50 6.00
❑ 4R151 B'Etor, Ambitious Renegade 1.25 3.00
❑ 4R152 Jadzia Dax, Sworn Ally (1E) 2.50 6.00
❑ 4R154 Lursa, Ambitious Renegade 1.25 3.00
❑ 4R155 William T. Riker, Exchange Officer 2.00 5.00
❑ 4R157 Crosis, Fanatical Lieutenant 1.25 3.00
❑ 4R158 Data, Loyal Brother (1E) 1.25 3.00
❑ 4R161 Lore, The One 2.50 6.00
❑ 4R165 B'Etor, Romulan Conspirator 1.25 3.00
❑ 4R168 Koval, Chairman of the Tal Shiar 1.25 3.00
❑ 4R169 Lursa, Romulan Conspirator 1.25 3.00
❑ 4R173 Sela, Devious Schemer (1E) 1.25 3.00
❑ 4R180 I.K.S. Ning'tao 2.50 6.00
❑ 4U101 Day Kannu .20 .50
❑ 4U109 Surmak Ren, Medical Administrator .20 .50
❑ 4U113 Facilitation Drone .20 .50
❑ 4U114 Five of Twelve .20 .50
Secondary Adjunct of Trimatrix 942
❑ 4U115 Reconnaissance Drone (1E) .20 .50
❑ 4U116 Aamin Marritza, Honorable Patriot (1E) .20 .50
❑ 4U117 Broca, Groveling Lackey .20 .50
❑ 4U120 Mila, Trusted Confidante .20 .50
❑ 4U122 Rusot, Proud Nationalist (1E) .20 .50
❑ 4U123 Seskal, Comrade in Arms .20 .50
❑ 4U128 Luaran, Cautious Inspector .20 .50
❑ 4U129 O'Brien Founder, Agent Provocateur .20 .50
❑ 4U132 Weyoun, Warship Commander .20 .50
❑ 4U135 Deanna Troi, Ship's Counselor (1E) .20 .50
❑ 4U137 Geordi La Forge, Conn Officer (1E) .20 .50
❑ 4U141 Kalita, Maquis Pilot .20 .50
❑ 4U143 Lenara Kahn, Wormhole Theorist (1E) .20 .50
❑ 4U144 Miles O'Brien, Repair Chief .20 .50
❑ 4U148 Tim Watters, Valiant Captain (1E) .20 .50
❑ 4U159 Goval, Follower of the One .20 .50
❑ 4U166 Bochra, Loyal Centurion .20 .50
❑ 4U171 Parem, Special Security (1E) .20 .50
❑ 4U176 Tamarith, Reformist (1E) .20 .50
❑ 4U178 Talnot .20 .50
❑ 4U179 U.S.S. Valiant, Red Squad Training Ship (1E) .20 .50

2004 Star Trek Necessary Evil Foil

❑ 4R28 Tsiolkovsky Infection 12.00 25.00
❑ 4R30 Whisper in the Dark 12.00 25.00
❑ 4R36 All-Out War 12.00 25.00
❑ 4R37 Anything or Anyone 12.00 25.00
❑ 4R74 Storage Compartment 12.00 25.00
❑ 4R83 You've Always Been My Favorite 12.00 25.00
❑ 4R89 Knowledge and Experience 12.00 25.00
❑ 4R102 Dukat, Anjohl Tennan 12.00 25.00
❑ 4R119 Kira Nerys, Iliana Ghemor 12.00 25.00
❑ 4R121 Odo, Impartial Investigator 12.00 25.00
❑ 4R130 Odo Founder, Adept Imposter 12.00 25.00
❑ 4R138 Guinan, Listener 12.00 25.00
❑ 4R139 Jadzia Dax, Problem Solver (1E) 20.00 40.00
❑ 4R155 William T. Riker Exchange Officer (1E) 20.00 40.00
❑ 4R157 Crosis, Fanatical Lieutenant 12.00 25.00
❑ 4R161 Lore, The One 12.00 25.00
❑ 4R165 B'Etor, Romulan Conspirator 12.00 25.00
❑ 4R169 Lursa, Romulan Conspirator 12.00 25.00

1995 Star Wars Premiere

COMPLETE SET (324) 75.00 150.00
BOOSTER BOX (36 PACKS) 75.00 150.00
BOOSTER PACK 3.00 6.00

❑ 1 2X-3KPR (Tooex) U1 .30 .75
❑ 2 5D6-RA-7 (Fivedesix) R1 1.25 3.00
❑ 3 A Disturbance In The Force U1 .30 .75
❑ 4 A Few Maneuvers C2 .12 .30
❑ 5 A Tremor In The Force U1 .30 .75
❑ 6 Admiral Motti R2 .75 2.00
❑ 7 Affect Mind R1 1.25 3.00
❑ 8 Alderaan DARK R1 1.25 3.00
❑ 9 Alderaan LIGHT U2 .75 2.00
❑ 10 Alter DARK U1 .30 .75
❑ 11 Alter LIGHT U1 .30 .75
❑ 12 Assault Rifle R2 .75 2.00
❑ 13 Baniss Keeg C2 .12 .30
❑ 14 Bantha U2 .30 .75
❑ 15 Beggar R1 1.25 3.00
❑ 16 Beru Lars U2 .30 .75
❑ 17 Beru Stew U2 .30 .75
❑ 18 Biggs Darklighter R2 .75 2.00
❑ 19 Black 2 R1 2.50 6.00
❑ 20 Black 3 U1 .30 .75
❑ 21 Blast Door Controls U2 .30 .75
❑ 22 Blaster C2 .12 .30
❑ 23 Blaster Rack U1 .30 .75
❑ 24 Blaster Rifle LIGHT C1 .12 .30
❑ 25 Blaster Rifle DARK C2 .12 .30
❑ 26 Blaster Scope U1 .30 .75
❑ 27 Boosted TIE Cannon U1 .30 .75
❑ 28 Boring Conversation Anyway R1 1.25 3.00
❑ 29 BoShek U1 .30 .75
❑ 30 C-3PO (See-Threepio) R1 3.00 8.00
❑ 31 Caller DARK U2 .30 .75
❑ 32 Caller LIGHT U2 .30 .75
❑ 33 Cantina Brawl R1 1.25 3.00
❑ 34 Charming To The Last R2 .75 2.00
❑ 35 Chief Bast U1 .30 .75
❑ 36 Collateral Damage C2 .12 .30
❑ 37 Collision! C2 .12 .30
❑ 38 Colonel Wulff Yularen U1 .30 .75
❑ 39 Combined Attack C2 .12 .30
❑ 40 Comlink C1 .12 .30
❑ 41 Commander Praji U2 .30 .75
❑ 42 Corellian Corvette U2 .40 1.00
❑ 43 Counter Assault C1 .12 .30
❑ 44 Crash Site Memorial U1 .30 .75
❑ 45 CZ-3 (Seezee-Three) C1 .12 .30
❑ 46 Dantooine DARK U1 .30 .75
❑ 47 Dantooine LIGHT U1 .30 .75
❑ 48 Dark Collaboration R1 1.25 3.00
❑ 49 Dark Hours U2 .30 .75
❑ 50 Dark Jedi Lightsaber U1 .40 1.00
❑ 51 Dark Jedi Presence R1 4.00 10.00
❑ 52 Dark Maneuvers C2 .12 .30
❑ 53 Darth Vader R1 10.00 25.00
❑ 54 Dathcha U1 .30 .75
❑ 55 Dead Jawa C2 .12 .30
❑ 56 Death Star Plans R1 1.25 3.00
❑ 57 Death Star Sentry U1 .30 .75
❑ 58 Death Star Trooper C2 .12 .30
❑ 59 Death Star: Central Core U2 .30 .75
❑ 60 Death Star: Detention Block Control Room U2 .30 .75
❑ 61 Death Star: Detention Block Corridor C1 .12 .30
❑ 62 Death Star: Docking Bay 327 DARK C2 .12 .30
❑ 63 Death Star: Docking Bay 327 LIGHT C2 .12 .30
❑ 64 Death Star: Level 4 Military Corridor U1 .30 .75
❑ 65 Death Star: Trash Compactor U1 .30 .75
❑ 66 Death Star: War Room U2 .30 .75
❑ 67 Demotion R2 .75 2.00
❑ 68 Devastator R1 2.50 6.00
❑ 69 Dice Ibegon R2 .75 2.00
❑ 70 Disarmed DARK R1 1.25 3.00
❑ 71 Disarmed LIGHT R1 1.25 3.00
❑ 72 Djas Puhr R2 .75 2.00
❑ 73 Don't Get Cocky R1 1.25 3.00
❑ 74 Don't Underestimate Our Chances C1 .12 .30
❑ 75 Dr. Evazan R2 .75 2.00
❑ 76 Droid Detector C2 .12 .30
❑ 77 Droid Shutdown C2 .12 .30
❑ 78 DS-61-2 U1 .30 .75
❑ 79 DS-61-3 R1 3.00 8.00
❑ 80 Dutch R1 2.50 6.00
❑ 81 EG-6 (Eegee-Six) U2 .30 .75
❑ 82 Electrobinoculars C2 .12 .30
❑ 83 Elis Helrot U2 .30 .75
❑ 84 Ellorrs Madak C2 .12 .30
❑ 85 Emergency Deployment U1 .30 .75
❑ 86 Escape Pod U2 .30 .75
❑ 87 Evacuate? U2 .30 .75
❑ 88 Expand The Empire R1 1.25 3.00
❑ 89 Eyes In The Dark U1 .30 .75
❑ 90 Fear Will Keep Them In Line R2 .75 2.00
❑ 91 Feltipern Trevagg U1 .30 .75
❑ 92 Figrin D'an U2 .30 .75
❑ 93 Friendly Fire C2 .12 .30
❑ 94 Full Scale Alert U2 .30 .75
❑ 95 Full Throttle R2 .75 2.00
❑ 96 Fusion Generator Supply Tanks DARK C2 .12 .30
❑ 97 Fusion Generator Supply Tanks LIGHT C2 .12 .30
❑ 98 Gaderffii Stick C2 .12 .30
❑ 99 Garindan R2 .75 2.00
❑ 100 General Dodonna U1 .30 .75
❑ 101 General Tagge R2 .75 2.00
❑ 102 Gift Of The Mentor R1 1.25 3.00
❑ 103 Gold 1 R2 .75 2.00
❑ 104 Gold 5 R2 .75 2.00
❑ 105 Grand Moff Tarkin R1 3.00 8.00
❑ 106 Gravel Storm U2 .30 .75
❑ 107 Han Seeker R2 .75 2.00
❑ 108 Han Solo R1 5.00 12.00
❑ 109 Han's Back U2 .30 .75
❑ 110 Han's Dice C2 .12 .30
❑ 111 Han's Heavy Blaster Pistol R2 .75 2.00
❑ 112 Hear Me Baby, Hold Together C2 .12 .30
❑ 113 Help Me Obi-Wan Kenobi R1 1.25 3.00
❑ 114 How Did We Get Into This Mess? U2 .30 .75
❑ 115 Hydroponics Station U2 .30 .75
❑ 116 Hyper Escape C2 .12 .30
❑ 117 I Find Your Lack Of Faith Disturbing R1 1.25 3.00
❑ 118 I Have You Now R2 .75 2.00
❑ 119 I've Got A Bad Feeling About This C2 .12 .30
❑ 120 I've Got A Problem Here C2 .12 .30
❑ 121 I've Lost Artoo! U1 .30 .75
❑ 122 Imperial Barrier DARK C2 .12 .30
❑ 123 Imperial Blaster LIGHT C2 .12 .30
❑ 124 Imperial Code Cylinder C2 .12 .30
❑ 125 Imperial Pilot C2 .12 .30
❑ 126 Imperial Reinforcements C1 .12 .30
❑ 127 Imperial Trooper Guard C2 .12 .30
❑ 128 Imperial-Class Star Destroyer U1 .75 2.00
❑ 129 Into The Garbage Chute, Flyboy R2 .75 2.00
❑ 130 Ion Cannon U1 .30 .75
❑ 131 It Could Be Worse C2 .12 .30
❑ 132 It's Worse C2 .12 .30
❑ 133 Jawa DARK C2 .12 .30
❑ 134 Jawa LIGHT C2 .12 .30
❑ 135 Jawa Pack U1 .30 .75
❑ 136 Jawa Siesta U1 .30 .75
❑ 137 Jedi Lightsaber U1 .30 .75
❑ 138 Jedi Presence R1 1.25 3.00
❑ 139 Jek Porkins U1 .30 .75
❑ 140 Juri Juice R2 .75 2.00
❑ 141 K'lor'slug R1 1.25 3.00
❑ 142 Kabe U1 .30 .75
❑ 143 Kal'Falnl C'ndros R1 1.25 3.00
❑ 144 Kessel Run R2 .75 2.00
❑ 145 Kessel DARK U2 .30 .75
❑ 146 Kessel LIGHT U2 .30 .75
❑ 147 Ket Maliss C2 .12 .30
❑ 148 Kintan Strider C1 .12 .30
❑ 149 Kitik Keed'kak R1 1.25 3.00
❑ 150 Krayt Dragon Howl R1 1.25 3.00
❑ 151 Labria R2 .75 2.00
❑ 152 Laser Projector U2 .30 .75
❑ 153 Lateral Damage R2 .75 2.00
❑ 154 Leesub Sirln R2 .75 2.00
❑ 155 Leia Organa R1 4.00 10.00
❑ 156 Leia's Back U2 .30 .75
❑ 157 Leia's Sporting Blaster U1 .30 .75
❑ 158 Lieutenant Tanbris U2 .30 .75
❑ 159 Lift Tube DARK C2 .12 .30
❑ 160 Lift Tube LIGHT C2 .12 .30
❑ 161 Light Repeating Blaster Rifle R1 1.25 3.00
❑ 162 Lightsaber Proficiency R1 1.25 3.00
❑ 163 Limited Resources U2 .30 .75
❑ 164 LIN-V8K (Elleyein-Veeatekay) C1 .12 .30
❑ 165 LIN-V8M (Elleyein-Veeateemm) C1 .12 .30
❑ 166 Local Trouble R1 1.25 3.00
❑ 167 Lone Pilot R2 .75 2.00
❑ 168 Lone Warrior R2 .75 2.00
❑ 169 Look Sir, Droids R1 1.25 3.00
❑ 170 Luke Seeker R2 .75 2.00
❑ 171 Luke Skywalker R1 6.00 15.00
❑ 172 Luke? Luuuuke! U1 .30 .75
❑ 173 Luke's Back U2 .30 .75
❑ 174 Luke's X-34 Landspeeder U1 .30 .75
❑ 175 M'iiyoom Onith U2 .30 .75
❑ 176 Macroscan C2 .12 .30
❑ 177 Mantellian Savrip R2 .75 2.00
❑ 178 Millenium Falcon R1 3.00 8.00
❑ 179 Molator R1 1.25 3.00
❑ 180 Momaw Nadon U2 .30 .75
❑ 181 Moment Of Triumph R2 .75 2.00
❑ 182 Move Along... R1 1.25 3.00
❑ 183 MSE-6 'Mouse' Droid U1 .30 .75
❑ 184 Myo R2 .75 2.00
❑ 185 Nabrun Leids U2 .30 .75
❑ 186 Narrow Escape C2 .12 .30
❑ 187 Nevar Yalnal R2 .75 2.00
❑ 188 Nightfall U1 .30 .75
❑ 189 Noble Sacrifice R2 .75 2.00
❑ 190 Obi-Wan Kenobi R1 4.00 10.00
❑ 191 Obi-Wan's Cape R1 1.25 3.00
❑ 192 Obi-Wan's Lightsaber R1 2.50 6.00
❑ 193 Observation Holocam U2 .30 .75
❑ 194 Old Ben C2 .12 .30
❑ 195 Ommni Box C2 .12 .30
❑ 196 On The Edge R2 .75 2.00
❑ 197 Organa's Ceremonial Necklace R1 1.25 3.00
❑ 198 Our Most Desperate Hour R1 1.25 3.00
❑ 199 Out Of Nowhere U2 .30 .75
❑ 200 Overload C2 .12 .30
❑ 201 Owen Lars U1 .30 .75
❑ 202 Panic U1 .30 .75
❑ 203 Physical Choke R1 1.25 3.00
❑ 204 Plastoid Armor U2 .30 .75
❑ 205 Ponda Baba U1 .30 .75
❑ 206 Pops U1 .30 .75
❑ 207 Precise Attack C2 .12 .30
❑ 208 Presence Of The Force R1 1.25 3.00
❑ 209 Prophetess U1 .30 .75
❑ 210 Proton Torpedoes C2 .12 .30
❑ 211 Quad Laser Cannon U1 .30 .75
❑ 212 R1-G4 (Arone-Geefour) C2 .12 .30
❑ 213 R2-X2 (Artoo-Extoo) C2 .12 .30
❑ 214 R4-E1 (Arfour-Eeone) C2 .12 .30
❑ 215 R4-M9 (Arfour-Emmnine) C2 .12 .30
❑ 216 Radar Scanner C2 .12 .30
❑ 217 Reactor Terminal U2 .30 .75
❑ 218 Rebel Barrier C2 .12 .30

☐ 219 Rebel Guard C2 .12 .30
☐ 220 Rebel Pilot C2 .12 .30
☐ 221 Rebel Planners R2 .75 2.00
☐ 222 Rebel Reinforcements C1 .12 .30
☐ 223 Rebel Trooper C3 .12 .30
☐ 224 Red 1 U1 .30 .75
☐ 225 Red 3 R2 .75 2.00
☐ 226 Red Leader R1 2.50 6.00
☐ 227 Restraining Bolt DARK C2 .12 .30
☐ 228 Restraining Bolt LIGHT C2 .12 .30
☐ 229 Restricted Deployment U1 .30 .75
☐ 230 Return Of A Jedi U2 .30 .75
☐ 231 Revolution R1 1.25 3.00
☐ 232 Rycar Ryjerd U1 .30 .75
☐ 233 Sai'torr Kal Fas C2 .12 .30
☐ 234 Sandcrawler DARK R2 .75 2.00
☐ 235 Sandcrawler LIGHT R2 .75 2.00
☐ 236 Scanning Crew C2 .12 .30
☐ 237 Scomp Link Access C2 .12 .30
☐ 238 Send A Detachment Down R1 1.25 3.00
☐ 239 Sense DARK U1 .30 .75
☐ 240 Sense LIGHT U1 .30 .75
☐ 241 Set For Stun C2 .12 .30
☐ 242 Shistavanen Wolfman C2 .12 .30
☐ 243 Skywalkers R1 1.25 3.00
☐ 244 Solo Han R2 .75 2.00
☐ 245 SoroSuub V-35 Landspeeder C2 .12 .30
☐ 246 Spaceport Speeders U2 .30 .75
☐ 247 Special Modifications U1 .30 .75
☐ 248 Stormtrooper C3 .12 .30
☐ 249 Stormtrooper Backpack C2 .12 .30
☐ 250 Stormtrooper Utility Belt C2 .12 .30
☐ 251 Sunsdown U1 .30 .75
☐ 252 Surprise Assault C1 .12 .30
☐ 253 Tactical Re-Call R2 .75 2.00
☐ 254 Tagge Seeker R2 .75 2.00
☐ 255 Takeel C2 .12 .30
☐ 256 Tallon Roll C2 .12 .30
☐ 257 Talz C2 .12 .30
☐ 258 Targeting Computer U1 .30 .75
☐ 259 Tarkin Seeker R2 .75 2.00
☐ 260 Tatooine DARK C2 .12 .30
☐ 261 Tatooine LIGHT C2 .12 .30
☐ 262 Tatooine Utility Belt C2 .12 .30
☐ 263 Tatooine: Cantina DARK R2 .75 2.00
☐ 264 Tatooine: Cantina LIGHT R2 .75 2.00
☐ 265 Tatooine: Docking Bay 94 DARK C2 .12 .30
☐ 266 Tatooine: Docking Bay 94 LIGHT C2 .12 .30
☐ 267 Tatooine: Dune Sea C1 .12 .30
☐ 268 Tatooine: Jawa Camp DARK C1 .12 .30
☐ 269 Tatooine: Jawa Camp LIGHTC1 .12 .30
☐ 270 Tatooine: Jundland Wastes C1 .12 .30
☐ 271 Tatooine: Lars' Moisture Farm LIGHT C1 .12 .30
☐ 272 Tatooine: Lars' Moisture Farm DARK U2 .30 .75
☐ 273 Tatooine: Mos Eisley DARK C1 .12 .30
☐ 274 Tatooine: Mos Eisley LIGHT U2 .30 .75
☐ 275 Tatooine: Obi-Wan's Hut R1 1.25 3.00
☐ 276 Thank The Maker R2 .75 2.00
☐ 277 The Bith Shuffle C2 .12 .30
☐ 278 The Circle Is Now Complete R1 1.25 3.00
☐ 279 The Empire's Back U1 .30 .75
☐ 280 The Force Is Strong With This One R2 .75 2.00
☐ 281 This Is All Your Fault U1 .30 .75
☐ 282 TIE Advanced x1 U2 .30 .75
☐ 283 TIE Fighter C2 .12 .30
☐ 284 TIE Scout C2 .12 .30
☐ 285 Timer Mine DARK C2 .12 .30
☐ 286 Timer Mine LIGHT C2 .12 .30
☐ 287 Tonnika Sisters R1 1.25 3.00
☐ 288 Traffic Control U2 .30 .75
☐ 289 Trinto Duaba U1 .30 .75
☐ 290 Trooper Charge U2 .30 .75
☐ 291 Turbolaser Battery R2 .75 2.00
☐ 292 Tusken Breath Mask U1 .30 .75
☐ 293 Tusken Raider C2 .12 .30
☐ 294 Tusken Scavengers C2 .12 .30
☐ 295 Ubrikkian 9000 Z001 C2 .12 .30
☐ 296 Utinni! DARK R1 1.25 3.00
☐ 297 Utinni! LIGHT R1 1.25 3.00
☐ 298 Vader's Custom TIE R1 4.00 10.00
☐ 299 Vader's Eye R1 1.25 3.00
☐ 300 Vader's Lightsaber R1 3.00 8.00
☐ 301 Vaporator C2 .12 .30
☐ 302 Warrior's Courage R2 .75 2.00
☐ 303 We're All Gonna Be A Lot Thinner! R1 1.25 3.00
☐ 304 We're Doomed C2 .12 .30
☐ 305 WED15-1662 'Treadwell' Droid R2 .75 2.00
☐ 306 WED-9-M1 'Bantha' Droid R2 .75 2.00
☐ 307 Wioslea U1 .30 .75
☐ 308 Wrong Turn U1 .30 .75
☐ 309 Wuher U2 .30 .75
☐ 310 X-wing C2 .12 .30
☐ 311 Yavin 4 DARK C2 .12 .30
☐ 312 Yavin 4 LIGHT C2 .12 .30
☐ 313 Yavin 4: Docking Bay DARK C2 .12 .30
☐ 314 Yavin 4: Docking Bay LIGHT C2 .12 .30
☐ 315 Yavin 4: Jungle LIGHT C1 .12 .30
☐ 316 Yavin 4: Jungle DARK U2 .30 .75
☐ 317 Yavin 4: Massassi Throne Room R1 1.25 3.00
☐ 318 Yavin 4: Massassi War Room U2 .30 .75
☐ 319 Yavin Sentry U2 .30 .75
☐ 320 Yerka Mig U1 .30 .75
☐ 321 You Overestimate Their Chances C1 .12 .30
☐ 322 Your Eyes Can Deceive You U1 .30 .75
☐ 323 Your Powers Are Weak, Old Man R1 1.25 3.00
☐ 324 Y-wing C2 .12 .30

1996 Star Wars A New Hope

COMPLETE SET (162) 50.00 100.00
BOOSTER BOX (36) 50.00 100.00
BOOSTER PACK 2.00 4.00

☐ 1 Advance Preparation U1 .40 1.00
☐ 2 Advosze C2 .12 .30
☐ 3 Alternatives To Fighting U1 .40 1.00
☐ 4 Arcona C2 .12 .30
☐ 5 Astromech Shortage U2 .40 1.00
☐ 6 Attack Run R2 1.25 3.00
☐ 7 Besieged R2 1.25 3.00
☐ 8 Bespin Motors Void Spider THX 1138 C2 .12 .30
☐ 9 Black 4 U2 .40 1.00
☐ 10 Blast The Door, Kid! C2 .12 .30
☐ 11 Blue Milk C2 .12 .30
☐ 12 Bowcaster R2 1.25 3.00
☐ 13 Brainiac R1 2.50 6.00
☐ 14 Captain Khurgee U1 .40 1.00
☐ 15 Cell 2187 R1 1.25 3.00
☐ 16 Chewbacca R2 6.00 15.00
☐ 17 Clak'dor VII R2 1.25 3.00
☐ 18 Come With Me C2 .12 .30
☐ 19 Commander Evram Lajaie C1 .12 .30
☐ 20 Commander Vanden Willard U2 .40 1.00
☐ 21 Commence Primary Ignition R2 1.25 3.00
☐ 22 Commence Recharging R2 1.25 3.00
☐ 23 Conquest R1 4.00 10.00
☐ 24 Corellia R1 1.25 3.00
☐ 25 Corellian C2 .12 .30
☐ 26 Corellian Slip C2 .12 .30
☐ 27 Dannik Jerriko R1 1.25 3.00
☐ 28 Danz Borin U2 .40 1.00
☐ 29 Dark Waters R2 1.25 3.00
☐ 30 Death Star Gunner C1 .12 .30
☐ 31 Death Star R2 4.00 10.00
☐ 32 Death Star Tractor Beam R2 1.25 3.00
☐ 33 Death Star: Conference Room U1 .40 1.00
☐ 34 Death Star: Trench R2 1.25 3.00
☐ 35 Defel C2 .12 .30
☐ 36 Dejarik Hologameboard R1 1.25 3.00
☐ 37 Dianoga R2 1.25 3.00
☐ 38 Doikk Na'ts U2 .40 1.00
☐ 39 Double Agent R2 1.25 3.00
☐ 40 DS-61-4 R2 1.25 3.00
☐ 41 Eject! Eject! C2 .12 .30
☐ 42 Enhanced TIE Laser Cannon C2 .12 .30
☐ 43 Evader U1 .40 1.00
☐ 44 Fire Extinguisher U2 .40 1.00
☐ 45 Garouf Lafoe U2 .40 1.00
☐ 46 Ghhhk C2 .12 .30
☐ 47 Gold 2 U1 .40 1.00
☐ 48 Grappling Hook C2 .12 .30
☐ 49 Greedo R1 3.00 8.00
☐ 50 Grimtaash C2 .12 .30
☐ 51 Hem Dazon R1 1.25 3.00
☐ 52 Het Nkik U2 .40 1.00
☐ 53 Houjix C2 .12 .30
☐ 54 Hunchback R1 1.25 3.00
☐ 55 Hyperwave Scan U1 .40 1.00
☐ 56 Hypo R1 1.25 3.00
☐ 57 I Have A Very Bad Feeling About This C2 .12 .30
☐ 58 I'm Here To Rescue You U1 .40 1.00
☐ 59 I'm On The Leader R1 1.25 3.00
☐ 60 Ickabel G'ont U2 .40 1.00
☐ 61 Imperial Commander C2 .12 .30
☐ 62 Imperial Holotable R1 1.25 3.00
☐ 63 Imperial Justice C2 .12 .30
☐ 64 Imperial Squad Leader C3 .12 .30
☐ 65 Incom T-16 Skyhopper C2 .12 .30
☐ 66 Informant U1 .40 1.00
☐ 67 IT-O (Eyetee-Oh) R1 1.25 3.00
☐ 68 Jawa Blaster C2 .12 .30
☐ 69 Jawa Ion Gun C2 .12 .30
☐ 70 Kashyyyk DARK C1 .12 .30
☐ 71 Kashyyyk LIGHTC1 .12 .30
☐ 72 Kiffex R1 1.25 3.00
☐ 73 Krayt Dragon Bones U1 .40 1.00
☐ 74 Laser Gate U2 .40 1.00
☐ 75 Leia Seeker R2 1.25 3.00
☐ 76 Let The Wookiee Win R1 5.00 12.00
☐ 77 Lirin Car'n U2 .40 1.00
☐ 78 Logistical Delay U2 .40 1.00
☐ 79 Lt. Pol Treidum C1 .12 .30
☐ 80 Lt. Shann Childsen U1 .40 1.00
☐ 81 Luke's Cape R1 1.25 3.00
☐ 82 Luke's Hunting Rifle U1 .40 1.00
☐ 83 Magnetic Suction Tube DARK R2 1.25 3.00
☐ 84 Magnetic Suction Tube LIGHT R2 1.25 3.00
☐ 85 Maneuver Check R2 1.25 3.00
☐ 86 Merc Sunlet C2 .12 .30
☐ 87 M-HYD 'Binary' Droid U1 .40 1.00
☐ 88 Mobquet A-1 Deluxe Floater C2 .12 .30
☐ 89 Monnok C2 .12 .30
☐ 90 Mosep U2 .40 1.00
☐ 91 Motti Seeker R2 1.25 3.00
☐ 92 Nalan Cheel U2 .40 1.00
☐ 93 Ng'ok C2 .12 .30
☐ 94 Officer Evax C1 .12 .30
☐ 95 Oo-ta Goo-ta, Solo? C2 .12 .30
☐ 96 Out Of Commission U2 .40 1.00
☐ 97 Program Trap U1 .40 1.00
☐ 98 Quite A Mercenary C2 .12 .30
☐ 99 R2-D2 (Artoo-Detoo) R2 6.00 15.00
☐ 100 R2-Q2 (Artoo-Kyootoo) C2 .12 .30
☐ 101 R3-T6 (Arthree-Teesix) R1 1.25 3.00
☐ 102 R5-A2 (Arfive-Aytoo) C2 .12 .30
☐ 103 R5-D4 (Arfive-Defour) C2 .12 .30
☐ 104 RA-7 (Aray-Seven) C2 .12 .30
☐ 105 Ralltiir DARK C1 .12 .30
☐ 106 Ralltiir LIGHT C1 .12 .30
☐ 107 Rebel Commander C2 .12 .30
☐ 108 Rebel Squad Leader C3 .12 .30
☐ 109 Rebel Tech C1 .12 .30
☐ 110 Rectenna C2 .12 .30
☐ 111 Red 2 R1 1.25 3.00
☐ 112 Red 5 R1 3.00 8.00
☐ 113 Red 6 U1 .40 1.00
☐ 114 Reegesk U2 .40 1.00
☐ 115 Remote C2 .12 .30
☐ 116 Reserve Pilot U1 .40 1.00
☐ 117 Retract the Bridge R1 1.25 3.00
☐ 118 Rodian C2 .12 .30
☐ 119 Rogue Bantha U1 .40 1.00
☐ 120 Sabotage U1 .40 1.00
☐ 121 Sandcrawler: Droid Junkheap R1 1.25 3.00
☐ 122 Sandcrawler: Loading Bay R1 1.25 3.00
☐ 123 Saurin C2 .12 .30
☐ 124 Scanner Techs U1 .40 1.00
☐ 125 Sensor Panel U1 .40 1.00
☐ 126 Sniper U1 .40 1.00
☐ 127 Solomahal C2 .12 .30
☐ 128 Sorry About The Mess U1 .40 1.00
☐ 129 Spice Mines Of Kessel R1 1.25 3.00
☐ 130 Stunning Leader C2 .12 .30
☐ 131 Superlaser R2 2.00 5.00
☐ 132 SW-4 Ion Cannon R2 1.25 3.00
☐ 133 Swilla Corey C2 .12 .30
☐ 134 Tantive IV R1 4.00 10.00
☐ 135 Tatooine: Bluffs R1 1.25 3.00
☐ 136 Tech Mo'r U2 .40 1.00
☐ 137 Tentacle C2 .12 .30
☐ 138 There'll Be Hell To Pay U2 .40 1.00
☐ 139 They're On Dantooine R1 1.25 3.00
☐ 140 This Is Some Rescue! U1 .40 1.00
☐ 141 TIE Assault Squadron U1 .40 1.00
☐ 142 TIE Vanguard C2 .12 .30
☐ 143 Tiree U2 .40 1.00
☐ 144 Tractor Beam U1 .40 1.00
☐ 145 Trooper Davin Felth R2 1.25 3.00
☐ 146 Tzizvvt R2 1.25 3.00
☐ 147 U-3PO (Yoo-Threepio) R1 1.25 3.00
☐ 148 Undercover DARK U2 .40 1.00
☐ 149 Undercover LIGHT U2 .40 1.00
☐ 150 URoRRuR'R'R U2 .40 1.00
☐ 151 URoRRuR'R'R's Hunting Rifle U1 .40 1.00
☐ 152 Victory-Class Star Destroyer U1 .40 1.00
☐ 153 We Have A Prisoner C2 .12 .30
☐ 154 WED15-I7 'Septoid' Droid U2 .40 1.00
☐ 155 Wedge Antilles R1 6.00 15.00
☐ 156 What're You Tryin' To Push On Us? U2 .40 1.00
☐ 157 Wookiee Roar R1 1.25 3.00
☐ 158 Yavin 4: Briefing Room U1 .40 1.00
☐ 159 Yavin 4: Massassi Ruins U1 .40 1.00
☐ 160 You're All Clear Kid! R1 1.25 3.00
☐ 161 Y-wing Assault Squadron U1 .40 1.00
☐ 162 Zutton C1 .12 .30

1996 Star Wars Hoth

COMPLETE SET (163) 50.00 100.00
BOOSTER BOX (36 PACKS) 50.00 100.00
BOOSTER PACK 2.00 4.00

☐ 1 2-1B (Too-Onebee) R1 1.25 3.00
☐ 2 A Dark Time For The Rebellion C1 .12 .30
☐ 3 Admiral Ozzel R1 1.25 3.00
☐ 4 Anakin's Lightsaber R1 6.00 15.00
☐ 5 Artillery Remote R2 1.25 3.00
☐ 6 AT-AT Cannon U1 .40 1.00
☐ 7 AT-AT Driver C2 .12 .30
☐ 8 Atgar Laser Cannon U2 .40 1.00
☐ 9 Attack Pattern Delta U1 .40 1.00
☐ 10 Bacta Tank R2 2.00 5.00
☐ 11 Blizzard 1 R1 2.50 6.00
☐ 12 Blizzard 2 R2 1.25 3.00
☐ 13 Blizzard Scout 1 R1 2.50 6.00
☐ 14 Blizzard Walker U2 .40 1.00
☐ 15 Breached Defenses U2 .40 1.00
☐ 16 Cal Alder U2 .40 1.00
☐ 17 Captain Lennox U1 .40 1.00
☐ 18 Captain Piett R2 1.25 3.00
☐ 19 Cold Feet C2 .12 .30
☐ 20 Collapsing Corridor R2 1.25 3.00
☐ 21 Commander Luke Skywalker R1 6.00 15.00
☐ 22 ComScan Detection C2 .12 .30
☐ 23 Concussion Grenade R1 1.25 3.00
☐ 24 Crash Landing U1 .40 1.00
☐ 25 Dack Ralter R2 1.25 3.00
☐ 26 Dark Dissension R1 1.25 3.00
☐ 27 Death Mark R1 1.25 3.00
☐ 28 Death Squadron U1 .40 1.00
☐ 29 Debris Zone R2 1.25 3.00
☐ 30 Deflector Shield Generators U2 .40 1.00
☐ 31 Derek 'Hobbie' Klivian U1 .40 1.00
☐ 32 Direct Hit U1 .40 1.00
☐ 33 Disarming Creature R1 1.25 3.00
☐ 34 Dual Laser Cannon U1 .40 1.00
☐ 35 Echo Base Operations R2 1.25 3.00
☐ 36 Echo Base Trooper C3 .12 .30
☐ 37 Echo Base Trooper Officer C1 .12 .30
☐ 38 Echo Trooper Backpack C2 .12 .30
☐ 39 EG-4 (Eegee-Four) C1 .12 .30
☐ 40 Electro-Rangefinder U1 .40 1.00
☐ 41 Evacuation Control U1 .40 1.00
☐ 42 E-web Blaster C1 .12 .30
☐ 43 Exhaustion U2 .40 1.00
☐ 44 Exposure U1 .40 1.00
☐ 45 Fall Back! C2 .12 .30
☐ 46 Frostbite DARK C2 .12 .30
☐ 47 Frostbite LIGHT C2 .12 .30
☐ 48 Frozen Dinner R1 1.25 3.00
☐ 49 Furry Fury R2 1.25 3.00
☐ 50 FX-10 (Effex-ten) C2 .12 .30
☐ 51 FX-7 (Effex-Seven) C2 .12 .30
☐ 52 General Carlist Rieekan R2 1.25 3.00
☐ 53 General Veers R1 3.00 8.00
☐ 54 Golan Laser Battery U1 .40 1.00
☐ 55 He Hasn't Come Back Yet C2 .12 .30
☐ 56 High Anxiety R1 1.25 3.00
☐ 57 Hoth Survival Gear C2 .12 .30
☐ 58 Hoth DARK U2 .40 1.00
☐ 59 Hoth LIGHT U2 .40 1.00
☐ 60 Hoth: Defensive Perimeter DARK C2 .12 .30
☐ 61 Hoth: Defensive Perimeter LIGHT C2 .12 .30
☐ 62 Hoth: Echo Command Center (War Room) DARK U2 .40 1.00
☐ 63 Hoth: Echo Command Center (War Room) LIGHT U2 .40 1.00
☐ 64 Hoth: Echo Corridor LIGHT C2 .12 .30
☐ 65 Hoth: Echo Corridor DARK U2 .40 1.00
☐ 66 Hoth: Echo Docking Bay DARK C2 .12 .30
☐ 67 Hoth: Echo Docking Bay LIGHT C2 .12 .30
☐ 68 Hoth: Echo Med Lab C2 .12 .30
☐ 69 Hoth: Ice Plains C2 .12 .30
☐ 70 Hoth: Main Power Generators U2 .40 1.00
☐ 71 Hoth: North Ridge DARK C2 .12 .30
☐ 72 Hoth: North Ridge LIGHT C2 .12 .30
☐ 73 Hoth: Snow Trench C2 .12 .30
☐ 74 Hoth: Wampa Cave R2 1.25 3.00
☐ 75 I Thought They Smelled Bad On The Outside R11.25 3.00
☐ 76 I'd Just As Soon Kiss A Wookiee C2 .12 .30
☐ 77 Ice Storm DARK U1 .40 1.00
☐ 78 Ice Storm LIGHT U1 .40 1.00
☐ 79 Image Of The Dark Lord R2 1.25 3.00
☐ 80 Imperial Domination U1 .40 1.00
☐ 81 Imperial Gunner C2 .12 .30
☐ 82 Imperial Supply C1 .12 .30
☐ 83 Infantry Mine DARK C2 .12 .30
☐ 84 Infantry Mine LIGHT C2 .12 .30
☐ 85 It Can Wait C2 .12 .30
☐ 86 Jeroen Webb U1 .40 1.00
☐ 87 K-3PO (Kay-Threepio) R1 1.25 3.00
☐ 88 Lieutenant Cabbel U2 .40 1.00
☐ 89 Lightsaber Deficiency U1 .40 1.00
☐ 90 Lucky Shot U1 .40 1.00
☐ 91 Major Bren Derlin R2 1.25 3.00
☐ 92 Medium Repeating Blaster Cannon C1 .12 .30
☐ 93 Medium Transport U2 .40 1.00
☐ 94 Meteor Impact? R1 1.25 3.00
☐ 95 Mournful Roar R1 1.25 3.00
☐ 96 Nice Of You Guys To Drop By C2 .12 .30
☐ 97 Oh, Switch Off C2 .12 .30
☐ 98 One More Pass U1 .40 1.00
☐ 99 Ord Mantell DARK C2 .12 .30
☐ 100 Ord Mantell LIGHT U2 .40 1.00
☐ 101 Our First Catch Of The Day C2 .12 .30
☐ 102 Perimeter Scan C2 .12 .30
☐ 103 Planet Defender Ion Cannon R2 1.25 3.00
☐ 104 Portable Fusion Generator C2 .12 .30
☐ 105 Power Harpoon U1 .40 1.00
☐ 106 Probe Antennae U2 .40 1.00
☐ 107 Probe Droid C2 .12 .30
☐ 108 Probe Droid Laser U2 .40 1.00
☐ 109 Probe Telemetry C2 .12 .30
☐ 110 R2 Sensor Array C2 .12 .30
☐ 111 R-3PO (Ar-Threepio) DARK R2 1.25 3.00
☐ 112 R-3PO (Ar-Threepio) LIGHT R2 1.25 3.00
☐ 113 R5-M2 (Arfive-Emmtoo) C2 .12 .30
☐ 114 Rebel Scout C1 .12 .30
☐ 115 Responsibility Of Command R1 1.25 3.00
☐ 116 Rogue 1 R1 2.50 6.00
☐ 117 Rogue 2 R2 1.25 3.00
☐ 118 Rogue 3 R1 2.50 6.00
☐ 119 Rogue Gunner C2 .12 .30
☐ 120 Romas Lock Navander U2 .40 1.00
☐ 121 Rug Hug R1 1.25 3.00
☐ 122 Scruffy-Looking Nerf Herder R2 1.25 3.00
☐ 123 Self-Destruct Mechanism U1 .40 1.00
☐ 124 Shawn Valdez U1 .40 1.00
☐ 125 Silence Is Golden U2 .40 1.00
☐ 126 Snowspeeder U2 .40 1.00
☐ 127 Snowtrooper C3 .12 .30
☐ 128 Snowtrooper Officer C1 .12 .30
☐ 129 Stalker R1 4.00 10.00
☐ 130 Stop Motion C2 .12 .30
☐ 131 Surface Defense Cannon R2 1.25 3.00
☐ 132 Tactical Support R2 1.25 3.00
☐ 133 Tamizander Rey U2 .40 1.00
☐ 134 Target The Main Generator R2 1.25 3.00
☐ 135 Tauntaun Bones U1 .40 1.00
☐ 136 Tauntaun C2 .12 .30
☐ 137 Tauntaun Handler C2 .12 .30
☐ 138 That's It, The Rebels Are There! U2 .40 1.00
☐ 139 The First Transport Is Away! R1 1.25 3.00
☐ 140 The Shield Doors Must Be Closed U1 .40 1.00
☐ 141 This Is Just Wrong R1 1.25 3.00
☐ 142 Tigran Jamiro U1 .40 1.00
☐ 143 Too Cold For Speeders U1 .40 1.00
☐ 144 Toryn Farr U1 .40 1.00
☐ 145 Trample R1 1.25 3.00
☐ 146 Turn It Off! Turn It Off! C1 .12 .30
☐ 147 Tyrant R1 3.00 8.00
☐ 148 Under Attack U1 .40 1.00
☐ 149 Vehicle Mine DARK C2 .12 .30
☐ 150 Vehicle Mine LIGHT C2 .12 .30
☐ 151 Walker Barrage U1 .40 1.00
☐ 152 Walker Sighting U2 .40 1.00
☐ 153 Wall Of Fire U1 .40 1.00
☐ 154 Wampa R2 1.25 3.00
☐ 155 Weapon Malfunction R1 1.25 3.00
☐ 156 WED-1016 'Techie' Droid C1 .12 .30
☐ 157 Wes Janson R2 1.25 3.00
☐ 158 Who's Scruffy-Looking? R1 1.25 3.00
☐ 159 Wyron Serper U2 .40 1.00
☐ 160 Yaggle Gakkle R2 1.25 3.00
☐ 161 You Have Failed Me For The Last Time R1 1.25 3.00
☐ 162 You Will Go To The Dagobah System R1 1.25 3.00
☐ 163 Zev Senesca R2 1.25 3.00

1996 Star Wars Jedi Pack

COMPLETE SET (11) 3.00 8.00

☐ 1 Hyperoute Navigation Chart PM .40 1.00
☐ 2 Dark Forces PM .40 1.00
☐ 3 Eriadu PM .40 1.00
☐ 4 For Luck PM .40 1.00
☐ 5 Gravity Shadow PM .40 1.00
☐ 6 Han PM .40 1.00
☐ 7 Leia PM .40 1.00
☐ 8 Luke's T-16 Skyhopper PM .40 1.00
☐ 9 Motti PM .40 1.00
☐ 10 Tarkin PM .40 1.00
☐ 11 Tedn Dahai PM .40 1.00

1997 Star Wars Cloud City

COMPLETE SET (180) 50.00 100.00
BOOSTER BOX (30) 50.00 100.00
BOOSTER PACK 2.00 4.00

☐ 1 Ability, Ability, Ability C .12 .30
☐ 2 Abyss U .40 1.00
☐ 3 Access Denied C .12 .30
☐ 4 Advantage R 1.25 3.00
☐ 5 Aiiii! Aaa! Agggggggggg! R 1.25 3.00
☐ 6 All My Urchins R 1.25 3.00
☐ 7 All Too Easy R 1.25 3.00
☐ 8 Ambush R 1.25 3.00
☐ 9 Armed And Dangerous U .40 1.00
☐ 10 Artoo, Come Back At Once! R 1.25 3.00
☐ 11 As Good As Gone C .12 .30
☐ 12 Atmospheric Assault R 1.25 3.00
☐ 13 Beldon's Eye R 1.25 3.00
☐ 14 Bespin DARK U .40 1.00
☐ 15 Bespin LIGHT U .40 1.00
☐ 16 Bespin: Cloud City DARK U .40 1.00
☐ 17 Bespin: Cloud City LIGHT U .40 1.00
☐ 18 Binders C .12 .30
☐ 19 Bionic Hand R 1.25 3.00
☐ 20 Blasted Droid C .12 .30
☐ 21 Blaster Proficiency C .12 .30
☐ 22 Boba Fett R 8.00 20.00
☐ 23 Boba Fett's Blaster Rifle R 3.00 8.00
☐ 24 Bounty C .12 .30
☐ 25 Brief Loss Of Control R 1.25 3.00
☐ 26 Bright Hope R 1.25 3.00
☐ 27 Captain Bewil R 1.25 3.00
☐ 28 Captain Han Solo R 8.00 20.00
☐ 29 Captive Fury U .40 1.00
☐ 30 Captive Pursuit C .12 .30
☐ 31 Carbon-Freezing U .40 1.00
☐ 32 Carbonite Chamber Console U .40 1.00
☐ 33 Chasm U .40 1.00
☐ 34 Chief Retwin R 1.25 3.00
☐ 35 Civil Disorder C .12 .30
☐ 36 Clash Of Sabers U .40 1.00
☐ 37 Cloud Car DARK C .12 .30
☐ 38 Cloud Car LIGHT C .12 .30
☐ 39 Cloud City Blaster DARK C .12 .30
☐ 40 Cloud City Blaster LIGHT C .12 .30
☐ 41 Cloud City Engineer C .12 .30
☐ 42 Cloud City Sabacc DARK U .40 1.00
☐ 43 Cloud City Sabacc LIGHT U .40 1.00
☐ 44 Cloud City Technician C .12 .30
☐ 45 Cloud City Trooper DARK C .12 .30
☐ 46 Cloud City Trooper LIGHT C .12 .30
☐ 47 Cloud City: Carbonite Chamber DARK U .40 1.00
☐ 48 Cloud City: Carbonite Chamber LIGHT U .40 1.00
☐ 49 Cloud City: Chasm Walkway DARK C .12 .30
☐ 50 Cloud City: Chasm Walkway LIGHT C .12 .30
☐ 51 Cloud City: Dining Room R 1.25 3.00
☐ 52 Cloud City: East Platform (Docking Bay) C .12 .30
☐ 53 Cloud City: Guest Quarters R 1.25 3.00
☐ 54 Cloud City: Incinerator DARK C .12 .30
☐ 55 Cloud City: Incinerator LIGHT C .12 .30
☐ 56 Cloud City: Lower Corridor DARK U .40 1.00
☐ 57 Cloud City: Lower Corridor LIGHT U .40 1.00
☐ 58 Cloud City: Platform 327 (Docking Bay) C .12 .30
☐ 59 Cloud City: Security Tower C .12 .30
☐ 60 Cloud City: Upper Plaza Corridor DARK C .12 .30
☐ 61 Cloud City: Upper Plaza Corridor LIGHT U .40 1.00
☐ 62 Clouds DARK C .12 .30

TCG/CCG

❑ 63 Clouds LIGHT C .12 .30
❑ 64 Commander Desanne U .40 1.00
❑ 65 Computer Interface C .12 .30
❑ 66 Courage Of A Skywalker R 1.25 3.00
❑ 67 Crack Shot U .40 1.00
❑ 68 Cyborg Construct U .40 1.00
❑ 69 Dark Approach R 1.25 3.00
❑ 70 Dark Deal R 1.25 3.00
❑ 71 Dark Strike C .12 .30
❑ 72 Dash C .12 .30
❑ 73 Despair R 1.25 3.00
❑ 74 Desperate Reach U .40 1.00
❑ 75 Dismantle On Sight R 1.25 3.00
❑ 76 Dodge C .12 .30
❑ 77 Double Back U .40 1.00
❑ 78 Double-Crossing, No-Good Swindler C .12 .30
❑ 79 E Chu Ta C .12 .30
❑ 80 E-3P0 R 1.25 3.00
❑ 81 End This Destructive Conflict R 1.25 3.00
❑ 82 Epic Duel R 2.00 5.00
❑ 83 Fall Of The Empire U .40 1.00
❑ 84 Fall Of The Legend U .40 1.00
❑ 85 Flight Escort R 1.25 3.00
❑ 86 Focused Attack R 1.25 3.00
❑ 87 Force Field R 1.25 3.00
❑ 88 Forced Landing R 1.25 3.00
❑ 89 Frozen Assets R 1.25 3.00
❑ 90 Gambler's Luck R 1.25 3.00
❑ 91 Glancing Blow R 1.25 3.00
❑ 92 Haven R 1.25 3.00
❑ 93 He's All Yours, Bounty Hunter R 1.25 3.00
❑ 94 Heart Of The Chasm U .40 1.00
❑ 95 Hero Of A Thousand Devices U .40 1.00
❑ 96 Higher Ground R 1.25 3.00
❑ 97 Hindsight R 1.25 3.00
❑ 98 Hopping Mad R 1.25 3.00
❑ 99 Human Shield C .12 .30
❑ 100 I Am Your Father R 1.25 3.00
❑ 101 I Don't Need Their Scum, Either R 1.25 3.00
❑ 102 I Had No Choice R 1.25 3.00
❑ 103 Imperial Decree U .40 1.00
❑ 104 Imperial Trooper Guard Dainsom U .40 1.00
❑ 105 Impressive, Most Impressive R 1.25 3.00
❑ 106 Innocent Scoundrel U .40 1.00
❑ 107 Interrogation Array R 1.25 3.00
❑ 108 Into The Ventilation Shaft, Lefty R 1.25 3.00
❑ 109 It's A Trap! U .40 1.00
❑ 110 Kebyc U .40 1.00
❑ 111 Keep Your Eyes Open C .12 .30
❑ 112 Lando Calrissian DARK R 5.00 12.00
❑ 113 Lando Calrissian LIGHT R 5.00 12.00
❑ 114 Lando's Wrist Comlink U .40 1.00
❑ 115 Leia Of Alderaan R 2.00 5.00
❑ 116 Levitation Attack U .40 1.00
❑ 117 Lieutenant Cecius U .40 1.00
❑ 118 Lieutenant Sheckil R 1.25 3.00
❑ 119 Lift Tube Escape C .12 .30
❑ 120 Lobot R 2.50 6.00
❑ 121 Luke's Blaster Pistol R 1.25 3.00
❑ 122 Mandalorian Armor R 2.00 5.00
❑ 123 Mostly Armless R 1.25 3.00
❑ 124 NOOOOOOOOOOOO! R 1.25 3.00
❑ 125 Obsidian 7 R 2.00 5.00
❑ 126 Obsidian 8 R 2.00 5.00
❑ 127 Off The Edge R 1.25 3.00
❑ 128 Old Pirates R 1.25 3.00
❑ 129 Out Of Somewhere U .40 1.00
❑ 130 Path Of Least Resistance C .12 .30
❑ 131 Point Man R 1.25 3.00
❑ 132 Prepare The Chamber U .40 1.00
❑ 133 Princess Leia R 4.00 10.00
❑ 134 Projective Telepathy U .40 1.00
❑ 135 Protector R 1.25 3.00
❑ 136 Punch It! R 1.25 3.00
❑ 137 Put That Down C .12 .30
❑ 138 Redemption R 2.50 6.00
❑ 139 Release Your Anger R 1.25 3.00
❑ 140 Rendezvous Point On Tatooine R 1.25 3.00
❑ 141 Rescue In The Clouds C .12 .30
❑ 142 Restricted Access C .12 .30
❑ 143 Rite Of Passage C .12 .30
❑ 144 Shattered Hope U .40 1.00
❑ 145 Shocking Information C .12 .30
❑ 146 Shocking Revelation C .12 .30
❑ 147 Slave I R 4.00 10.00
❑ 148 Slip Sliding Away R 1.25 3.00
❑ 149 Smoke Screen R 1.25 3.00
❑ 150 Somersault C .12 .30
❑ 151 Sonic Bombardment U .40 1.00
❑ 152 Special Delivery C .12 .30
❑ 153 Surprise R 1.25 3.00
❑ 154 Surreptitious Glance R 1.25 3.00
❑ 155 Swing-And-A-Miss U .40 1.00
❑ 156 The Emperor's Prize R 1.25 3.00
❑ 157 This Is Even Better R 1.25 3.00
❑ 158 This Is Still Wrong R 1.25 3.00
❑ 159 Tibanna Gas Miner DARK C .12 .30
❑ 160 Tibanna Gas Miner LIGHT C .12 .30
❑ 161 TIE Sentry Ships C .12 .30
❑ 162 Treva Horme U .40 1.00
❑ 163 Trooper Assault C .12 .30
❑ 164 Trooper Jerrol Blendin U .40 1.00
❑ 165 Trooper Utris M'toc U .40 1.00
❑ 166 Ugloste R 1.25 3.00
❑ 167 Ugnaught C .12 .30
❑ 168 Uncontrollable Fury R 1.25 3.00
❑ 169 Vader's Bounty R 1.25 3.00
❑ 170 Vader's Cape R 1.25 3.00
❑ 171 We'll Find Han R 1.25 3.00
❑ 172 We're The Bait R 1.25 3.00
❑ 173 Weapon Levitation U .40 1.00
❑ 174 Weapon Of An Ungrateful Son U .40 1.00
❑ 175 Weather Vane DARK U .40 1.00
❑ 176 Weather Vane LIGHT U .40 1.00
❑ 177 Why Didn't You Tell Me? R 1.25 3.00
❑ 178 Wiorkettle U .40 1.00
❑ 179 Wookiee Strangle R 1.25 3.00
❑ 180 You Are Beaten U .40 1.00

1997 Star Wars Dagobah

COMPLETE SET (181) 50.00 100.00
BOOSTER BOX (60 PACKS) 50.00 100.00
BOOSTER PACK 1.50 3.00

❑ 1 3,720 To 1 C .12 .30
❑ 2 4-LOM R 2.50 6.00
❑ 3 4-LOM's Concussion Rifle R 2.00 5.00
❑ 4 A Dangerous Time C .12 .30
❑ 5 A Jedi's Strength U .40 1.00
❑ 6 Anger, Fear, Aggression C .12 .30
❑ 7 Anoat DARK U .40 1.00
❑ 8 Anoat LIGHT U .40 1.00
❑ 9 Apology Accepted C .12 .30
❑ 10 Asteroid Field DARK C .12 .30
❑ 11 Asteroid Field LIGHT C .12 .30
❑ 12 Asteroid Sanctuary C .12 .30
❑ 13 Asteroids Do Not Concern Me R 1.25 3.00
❑ 14 Astroid Sanctuary C .12 .30
❑ 15 Astromech Translator C .12 .30
❑ 16 At Peace R 1.25 3.00
❑ 17 Avenger R 4.00 10.00
❑ 18 Away Put Your Weapon U .40 1.00
❑ 19 Awwww, Cannot Get Your Ship Out C .12 .30
❑ 20 Bad Feeling Have I R 1.25 3.00
❑ 21 Big One DARK U .40 1.00
❑ 22 Big One LIGHT U .40 1.00
❑ 23 Big One: Asteroid Cave or Space Slug Belly DARK U .40 1.00
❑ 24 Big One: Asteroid Cave or Space Slug Belly LIGHT U .40 1.00
❑ 25 Blasted Varmints C .12 .30
❑ 26 Bog-wing DARK C .12 .30
❑ 27 Bog-wing LIGHT C .12 .30
❑ 28 Bombing Run R 1.25 3.00
❑ 29 Bossk R 3.00 8.00
❑ 30 Bossk's Mortar Gun R 2.00 5.00
❑ 31 Broken Concentration R 1.25 3.00
❑ 32 Captain Needa R 2.00 5.00
❑ 33 Close Call C .12 .30
❑ 34 Closer?! U .40 1.00
❑ 35 Comm Chief C .12 .30
❑ 36 Commander Brandei U .40 1.00
❑ 37 Commander Gherant U .40 1.00
❑ 38 Commander Nemet U .40 1.00
❑ 39 Control DARK U .40 1.00
❑ 40 Control LIGHT U .40 1.00
❑ 41 Corporal Derdram U .40 1.00
❑ 42 Corporal Vandolay U .40 1.00
❑ 43 Corrosive Damage R 1.25 3.00
❑ 44 Dagobah U .40 1.00
❑ 45 Dagobah: Bog Clearing R 1.25 3.00
❑ 46 Dagobah: Cave R 1.25 3.00
❑ 47 Dagobah: Jungle U .40 1.00
❑ 48 Dagobah: Swamp U .40 1.00
❑ 49 Dagobah: Training Area C .12 .30
❑ 50 Dagobah: Yoda's Hut R 2.00 5.00
❑ 51 Defensive Fire C .12 .30
❑ 52 Dengar R 1.25 3.00
❑ 53 Dengar's Blaster Carbine R 1.25 3.00
❑ 54 Descent Into The Dark R 1.25 3.00
❑ 55 Do, Or Do Not C .12 .30
❑ 56 Domain Of Evil U .40 1.00
❑ 57 Dragonsnake R 1.25 3.00
❑ 58 Droid Sensorscope C .12 .30
❑ 59 Effective Repairs R 1.25 3.00
❑ 60 Egregious Pilot Error R 1.25 3.00
❑ 61 Encampment C .12 .30
❑ 62 Executor R 8.00 20.00
❑ 63 Executor: Comm Station U .40 1.00
❑ 64 Executor: Control Station U .40 1.00
❑ 65 Executor: Holotheatre R 1.25 3.00
❑ 66 Executor: Main Corridor C .12 .30
❑ 67 Executor: Meditation Chamber R 1.25 3.00
❑ 68 Failure At The Cave R 1.25 3.00
❑ 69 Fear C .12 .30
❑ 70 Field Promotion R 1.25 3.00
❑ 71 Flagship R 1.25 3.00
❑ 72 Flash Of Insight U .40 1.00
❑ 73 Found Someone You Have U .40 1.00
❑ 74 Frustration R 1.25 3.00
❑ 75 Great Warrior C .12 .30
❑ 76 Grounded Starfighter U .40 1.00
❑ 77 Han's Toolkit R 1.25 3.00
❑ 78 He Is Not Ready C .12 .30
❑ 79 Hiding In The Garbage R 1.25 3.00
❑ 80 HoloNet Transmission U .40 1.00
❑ 81 Hound's Tooth R 2.50 6.00
❑ 82 I Have A Bad Feeling About This R 1.25 3.00
❑ 83 I Want That Ship R 1.25 3.00
❑ 84 IG-2000 R 2.00 5.00
❑ 85 IG-88 R 4.00 10.00
❑ 86 IG-88's Neural Inhibitor R 2.00 5.00
❑ 87 IG-88's Pulse Cannon R 2.00 5.00
❑ 88 Imbalance U .40 1.00
❑ 89 Imperial Helmsman C .12 .30
❑ 90 Ineffective Maneuver U .40 1.00
❑ 91 It Is The Future You See R 1.25 3.00
❑ 92 Jedi Levitation R 1.25 3.00
❑ 93 Knowledge And Defense C .12 .30
❑ 94 Landing Claw R 1.25 3.00
❑ 95 Lando System? R 1.25 3.00
❑ 96 Levitation U .40 1.00
❑ 97 Lieutenant Commander Ardan U .40 1.00
❑ 98 Lieutenant Suba R 1.25 3.00
❑ 99 Lieutenant Venka U .40 1.00
❑ 100 Light Maneuvers R 1.25 3.00
❑ 101 Location, Location, Location R 1.25 3.00
❑ 102 Lost In Space R 1.25 3.00
❑ 103 Lost Relay C .12 .30
❑ 104 Luke's Backpack R 1.25 3.00
❑ 105 Mist Hunter R 2.00 5.00
❑ 106 Moving To Attack Position C .12 .30
❑ 107 Much Anger In Him R 1.25 3.00
❑ 108 Mynock DARK C .12 .30
❑ 109 Mynock LIGHT C .12 .30
❑ 110 Never Tell Me The Odds C .12 .30
❑ 111 No Disintegrations! R 1.25 3.00
❑ 112 Nudj C .12 .30
❑ 113 Obi-Wan's Apparition R 1.25 3.00
❑ 114 Order To Engage R 1.25 3.00
❑ 115 Polarized Negative Power Coupling R 1.25 3.00
❑ 116 Portable Fusion Generator C .12 .30
❑ 117 Precision Targeting U .40 1.00
❑ 118 Proton Bombs U .40 1.00
❑ 119 Punishing One R 2.00 5.00
❑ 120 Quick Draw C .12 .30
❑ 121 Raithal DARK R 1.25 3.00
❑ 122 Raithal LIGHT U .40 1.00
❑ 123 Rebel Flight Suit C .12 .30
❑ 124 Recoil In Fear C .12 .30
❑ 125 Reflection R 1.25 3.00
❑ 126 Report To Lord Vader R 1.25 3.00
❑ 127 Res Luk Ra'auf R 1.25 3.00
❑ 128 Retractable Arm C .12 .30
❑ 129 Rogue Asteroid DARK C .12 .30
❑ 130 Rogue Asteroid LIGHT C .12 .30
❑ 131 Rycar's Run R 1.25 3.00
❑ 132 Scramble U .40 1.00
❑ 133 Shoo! Shoo! U .40 1.00
❑ 134 Shot In The Dark U .40 1.00
❑ 135 Shut Him Up Or Shut Him Down U .40 1.00
❑ 136 Size Matters Not R 1.25 3.00
❑ 137 Sleen C .12 .30
❑ 138 Smuggler's Blues R 1.25 3.00
❑ 139 Something Hit Us! U .40 1.00
❑ 140 Son of Skywalker R 8.00 20.00
❑ 141 Space Slug DARK R 1.25 3.00
❑ 142 Space Slug LIGHT U .40 1.00
❑ 143 Star Destroyer: Launch Bay C .12 .30
❑ 144 Starship Levitation U .40 1.00
❑ 145 Stone Pile R 1.25 3.00
❑ 146 Sudden Impact U .40 1.00
❑ 147 Take Evasive Action C .12 .30
❑ 148 The Dark Path R 1.25 3.00
❑ 149 The Professor R 1.25 3.00
❑ 150 There Is No Try C .12 .30
❑ 151 They'd Be Crazy To Follow Us C .12 .30
❑ 152 This Is More Like It R 1.25 3.00
❑ 153 This Is No Cave R 1.25 3.00
❑ 154 Those Rebels Won't Escape Us C .12 .30
❑ 155 Through The Force Things You Will See R 1.25 3.00
❑ 156 TIE Avenger C .12 .30
❑ 157 TIE Bomber U .40 1.00
❑ 158 Tight Squeeze R 1.25 3.00
❑ 159 Transmission Terminated U .40 1.00
❑ 160 Tunnel Vision U .40 1.00
❑ 161 Uncertain Is The Future C .12 .30
❑ 162 Unexpected Interruption R 1.25 3.00
❑ 163 Vine Snake DARK C .12 .30
❑ 164 Vine Snake LIGHT C .12 .30
❑ 165 Visage Of The Emperor R 1.25 3.00
❑ 166 Visored Vision C .12 .30
❑ 167 Voyeur C .12 .30
❑ 168 Warrant Officer M'Kae U .40 1.00
❑ 169 Wars Not Make One Great U .40 1.00
❑ 170 We Can Still Outmaneuver Them R 1.25 3.00
❑ 171 We Don't Need Their Scum R 1.25 3.00
❑ 172 WHAAAAAAAAAOOOOW! R 1.25 3.00
❑ 173 What Is Thy Bidding, My Master? R 1.25 3.00
❑ 174 Yoda R 8.00 20.00
❑ 175 Yoda Stew U .40 1.00
❑ 176 Yoda, You Seek Yoda R 1.25 3.00
❑ 177 Yoda's Gimer Stick R 1.25 3.00
❑ 178 Yoda's Hope U .40 1.00
❑ 179 You Do Have Your Moments U .40 1.00
❑ 180 Zuckuss R 2.00 5.00
❑ 181 Zuckuss' Snare Rifle R 1.25 3.00

1997 Star Wars First Anthology

COMPLETE SET (6) 3.00 8.00

❑ 1 Boba Fett PV .75 2.00
❑ 2 Commander Wedge Antilles PV .75 2.00
❑ 3 Death Star Assault Squadron PV .75 2.00
❑ 4 Hit And Run PV .75 2.00
❑ 5 Jabba's Influence PV .75 2.00
❑ 6 X-wing Assault Squadron PV .75 2.00

1997 Star Wars Rebel Leaders

COMPLETE SET (2) 1.25 3.00

❑ 1 Gold Leader In Gold 1 PM 1.00 2.50
❑ 2 Red Leader In Red 1 PM 1.00 2.50

1998 Star Wars Enhanced Premiere

COMPLETE SET (6) 3.00 8.00

❑ 1 Boba Fett With Blaster Rifle PM .75 2.00
❑ 2 Darth Vader With Lightsaber PM .75 2.00
❑ 3 Han With Heavy Blaster Pistol PM .75 2.00
❑ 4 Leia With Blaster Rifle PM .75 2.00
❑ 5 Luke With Lightsaber PM .75 2.00
❑ 6 Obi-Wan With Lightsaber PM .75 2.00

1998 Star Wars Jabba's Palace

COMPLETE SET (180) 40.00 80.00
BOOSTER BOX (60 PACKS) 40.00 80.00
BOOSTER PACK 1.00 2.00

❑ 1 8D8 R 1.25 3.00
❑ 2 A Gift U .40 1.00
❑ 3 Abyssin C .12 .30
❑ 4 Abyssin Ornament U .40 1.00
❑ 5 All Wrapped Up U .40 1.00
❑ 6 Amanaman R 1.25 3.00
❑ 7 Amanin C .12 .30
❑ 8 Antipersonnel Laser Cannon U .40 1.00
❑ 9 Aqualish C .12 .30
❑ 10 Arc Welder U .40 1.00
❑ 11 Ardon Vapor Crell R 1.25 3.00
❑ 12 Artoo R 3.00 8.00
❑ 13 Artoo, I Have A Bad Feeling About This U .40 1.00
❑ 14 Attark R 1.25 3.00
❑ 15 Aved Luun R 1.25 3.00
❑ 16 B'omarr Monk C .12 .30
❑ 17 Bane Malar R 1.25 3.00
❑ 18 Bantha Fodder C .12 .30
❑ 19 Barada R 1.25 3.00
❑ 20 Baragwin C .12 .30
❑ 21 Bargaining Table U .40 1.00
❑ 22 Beedo R 1.25 3.00
❑ 23 BG-J38 R 1.25 3.00
❑ 24 Bib Fortuna R 1.25 3.00
❑ 25 Blaster Deflection R 1.25 3.00
❑ 26 Bo Shuda U .40 1.00
❑ 27 Bubo U .40 1.00
❑ 28 Cane Adiss U .40 1.00
❑ 29 Chadra-Fan C .12 .30
❑ 30 Chevin C .12 .30
❑ 31 Choke C .12 .30
❑ 32 Corellian Retort U .40 1.00
❑ 33 CZ-4 C .12 .30
❑ 34 Den Of Thieves U .40 1.00
❑ 35 Dengar's Modified Riot Gun R 1.25 3.00
❑ 36 Devaronian C .12 .30
❑ 37 Don't Forget The Droids C .12 .30
❑ 38 Double Laser Cannon R 1.25 3.00
❑ 39 Droopy McCool R 1.25 3.00
❑ 40 Dune Sea Sabacc DARK U .40 1.00
❑ 41 Dune Sea Sabacc LIGHT U .40 1.00
❑ 42 Elom C .12 .30
❑ 43 Ephant Mon R 1.25 3.00
❑ 44 EV-9D9 R 1.25 3.00
❑ 45 Fallen Portal U .40 1.00
❑ 46 Flom Lamproid C .12 .30
❑ 47 Fozec R 1.25 3.00
❑ 48 Gailid R 1.25 3.00
❑ 49 Gamorrean Ax C .12 .30
❑ 50 Gamorrean Guard C .12 .30
❑ 51 Garon Nas Tal R 1.25 3.00
❑ 52 Geezum R 1.25 3.00
❑ 53 Ghoel R 1.25 3.00
❑ 54 Giran R 1.25 3.00
❑ 55 Gran C .12 .30
❑ 56 H'nemthe C .12 .30
❑ 57 Herat R 1.25 3.00
❑ 58 Hermi Odle R 1.25 3.00
❑ 59 Hidden Compartment U .40 1.00
❑ 60 Hidden Weapons U .40 1.00
❑ 61 Holoprojector U .40 1.00
❑ 62 Hutt Bounty R 1.25 3.00
❑ 63 Hutt Smooch U .40 1.00
❑ 64 I Must Be Allowed To Speak R 1.25 3.00
❑ 65 Information Exchange U .40 1.00
❑ 66 Ishi Tib C .12 .30
❑ 67 Ithorian C .12 .30
❑ 68 J'Quille R 1.25 3.00
❑ 69 Jabba the Hutt R 4.00 10.00
❑ 70 Jabba's Palace Sabacc DARK U .40 1.00
❑ 71 Jabba's Palace Sabacc LIGHT U .40 1.00
❑ 72 Jabba's Palace: Audience Chamber DARK U .40 1.00
❑ 73 Jabba's Palace: Audience Chamber LIGHT U .40 1.00
❑ 74 Jabba's Palace: Droid Workshop U .40 1.00
❑ 75 Jabba's Palace: Dungeon U .40 1.00
❑ 76 Jabba's Palace: Entrance Cavern DARK U .40 1.00
❑ 77 Jabba's Palace: Entrance Cavern LIGHT U .40 1.00
❑ 78 Jabba's Palace: Rancor Pit U .40 1.00
❑ 79 Jabba's Sail Barge R 2.50 6.00
❑ 80 Jabba's Sail Barge: Passenger Deck R 1.25 3.00
❑ 81 Jedi Mind Trick R 1.25 3.00
❑ 82 Jess R 1.25 3.00
❑ 83 Jet Pack U .40 1.00
❑ 84 Kalit R 1.25 3.00
❑ 85 Ke Chu Ke Kakuta? C .12 .30
❑ 86 Kiffex R 1.25 3.00
❑ 87 Kirdo III R 1.25 3.00
❑ 88 Kithaba R 1.25 3.00
❑ 89 Kitonak C .12 .30
❑ 90 Klaatu R 1.25 3.00
❑ 91 Klatooinian Revolutionary C .12 .30
❑ 92 Laudica R 1.25 3.00
❑ 93 Leslomy Tacema R 1.25 3.00
❑ 94 Life Debt R 1.25 3.00
❑ 95 Loje Nella R 1.25 3.00
❑ 96 Malakili R 1.25 3.00
❑ 97 Mandalorian Mishap U .40 1.00
❑ 98 Max Rebo R 1.25 3.00
❑ 99 Mos Eisley Blaster DARK C .12 .30
❑ 100 Mos Eisley Blaster LIGHT C .12 .30
❑ 101 Murttoc Yine R 1.25 3.00
❑ 102 Nal Hutta R 1.25 3.00
❑ 103 Nar Shaddaa Wind Chimes U .40 1.00
❑ 104 Nikto C .12 .30
❑ 105 Nizuc Bek R 1.25 3.00
❑ 106 None Shall Pass C .12 .30
❑ 107 Nysad R 1.25 3.00
❑ 108 Oola R 1.25 3.00
❑ 109 Ortolan C .12 .30
❑ 110 Ortugg R 1.25 3.00
❑ 111 Palejo Reshad R 1.25 3.00
❑ 112 Pote Snitkin R 1.25 3.00
❑ 113 Princess Leia Organa R 3.00 8.00
❑ 114 Projection Of A Skywalker U .40 1.00
❑ 115 Pucumir Thryss R 1.25 3.00
❑ 116 Quarren C .12 .30
❑ 117 Quick Reflexes C .12 .30
❑ 118 R'kik D'nec, Hero Of The Dune Sea R 1.25 3.00
❑ 119 Rancor R 2.50 6.00
❑ 120 Rayc Ryjerd R 1.25 3.00
❑ 121 Ree-Yees R 1.25 3.00
❑ 122 Rennek R 1.25 3.00
❑ 123 Resistance U .40 1.00
❑ 124 Revealed U .40 1.00
❑ 125 Saelt-Marae R 1.25 3.00
❑ 126 Salacious Crumb R 1.25 3.00
❑ 127 Sandwhirl DARK U .40 1.00
❑ 128 Sandwhirl LIGHT U .40 1.00
❑ 129 Scum And Villainy R 1.25 3.00
❑ 130 Sergeant Doallyn R 1.25 3.00
❑ 131 Shasa Tiel R 1.25 3.00
❑ 132 Sic-Six C .12 .30
❑ 133 Skiff DARK C .12 .30
❑ 134 Skiff LIGHT C .12 .30
❑ 135 Skrilling C .12 .30
❑ 136 Skull U .40 1.00
❑ 137 Snivvian C .12 .30
❑ 138 Someone Who Loves You U .40 1.00
❑ 139 Strangle R 1.25 3.00
❑ 140 Tamtel Skreej R 2.50 6.00
❑ 141 Tanus Spijek R 1.25 3.00
❑ 142 Tatooine: Desert DARK C .12 .30
❑ 143 Tatooine: Desert LIGHT C .12 .30
❑ 144 Tatooine: Great Pit Of Carkoon U .40 1.00
❑ 145 Tatooine: Hutt Canyon U .40 1.00
❑ 146 Tatooine: Jabba's Palace U .40 1.00
❑ 147 Taym Dren-garen R 1.25 3.00
❑ 148 Tessek R 1.25 3.00
❑ 149 The Signal C .12 .30
❑ 150 Thermal Detonator R 2.00 5.00
❑ 151 Thul Fain R 1.25 3.00
❑ 152 Tibrin R 1.25 3.00
❑ 153 Torture C .12 .30
❑ 154 Trandoshan C .12 .30
❑ 155 Trap Door U .40 1.00
❑ 156 Twi'lek Advisor C .12 .30
❑ 157 Ultimatum U .40 1.00
❑ 158 Unfriendly Fire R 1.25 3.00
❑ 159 Vedain R 1.25 3.00
❑ 160 Velken Tezeri R 1.25 3.00
❑ 161 Vibro-Ax DARK C .12 .30
❑ 162 Vibro-Ax LIGHT C .12 .30
❑ 163 Vizam R 1.25 3.00
❑ 164 Vul Tazaene R 1.25 3.00
❑ 165 Weapon Levitation U .40 1.00
❑ 166 Weequay Guard C .12 .30
❑ 167 Weequay Hunter C .12 .30
❑ 168 Weequay Marksman U .40 1.00
❑ 169 Weequay Skiff Master C .12 .30
❑ 170 Well Guarded U .40 1.00
❑ 171 Whiphid C .12 .30
❑ 172 Wittin R 1.25 3.00
❑ 173 Wooof R 1.25 3.00
❑ 174 Worrt U .40 1.00
❑ 175 Wounded Wookiee U .40 1.00
❑ 176 Yarkora C .12 .30
❑ 177 Yarna d'al' Gargan U .40 1.00
❑ 178 You Will Take Me To Jabba Now C .12 .30
❑ 179 Yoxgit R 1.25 3.00
❑ 180 Yuzzum C .12 .30

1998 Star Wars Official Tournament Sealed Deck

COMPLETE SET (18) 4.00 10.00

❑ 1 Arleil Schous PM .40 1.00
❑ 2 Black Squadron TIE PM .40 1.00
❑ 3 Chall Bekan PM .40 1.00
❑ 4 Corulag DARK PM .40 1.00
❑ 5 Corulag LIGHT PM .40 1.00
❑ 6 Dreadnaught-Class Heavy Cruiser PM .40 1.00

❑ 7 Faithful Service PM .40 1.00
❑ 8 Forced Servitude PM .40 1.00
❑ 9 Gold Squadron Y-wing PM .40 1.00
❑ 10 It's a Hit! PM .40 1.00
❑ 11 Obsidian Squadron TIE PM .40 1.00
❑ 12 Rebel Trooper Recruit PM .40 1.00
❑ 13 Red Squadron X-wing PM .40 1.00
❑ 14 Stormtrooper Cadet PM .40 1.00
❑ 15 Tarkin's Orders PM .40 1.00
❑ 16 Tatooine: Jundland Wastes PM .40 1.00
❑ 17 Tatooine: Tusken Canyon PM .40 1.00
❑ 18 Z-95 Headhunter PM .40 1.00

1998 Star Wars Second Anthology

COMPLETE SET (6) 4.00 10.00
❑ 1 Flagship Operations PV 1.00 2.50
❑ 2 Mon Calamari Star Cruiser PV 1.00 2.50
❑ 3 Mon Mothma PV 1.00 2.50
❑ 4 Rapid Deployment PV 1.00 2.50
❑ 5 Sarlacc PV 1.00 2.50
❑ 6 Thunderflare PV 1.00 2.50

1998 Star Wars Special Edition

COMPLETE SET (324) 75.00 150.00
BOOSTER BOX (30) 60.00 120.00
BOOSTER PACK 3.00 6.00
❑ 1 ISB Operations / Empire's Sinister Agents R 1.00 2.50
❑ 2 2X-7KPR (Tooex) C .12 .30
❑ 3 A Bright Center To The Universe U .40 1.00
❑ 4 A Day Long Remembered U .40 1.00
❑ 5 A Real Hero R 1.00 2.50
❑ 6 Air-2 Racing Swoop C .12 .30
❑ 7 Ak-rev U .40 1.00
❑ 8 Alderaan Operative C .12 .30
❑ 9 Alert My Star Destroyer! C .12 .30
❑ 10 All Power To Weapons C .12 .30
❑ 11 All Wings Report In R 1.00 2.50
❑ 12 Anoat Operative DARK C .12 .30
❑ 13 Anoat Operative LIGHT C .12 .30
❑ 14 Antilles Maneuver C .12 .30
❑ 15 ASP-707 (Ayesspee) F .60 1.50
❑ 16 Balanced Attack U .40 1.00
❑ 17 Bantha Herd R .75 2.00
❑ 18 Barquin D'an U .40 1.00
❑ 19 Ben Kenobi R 2.00 5.00
❑ 20 Blast Points C .12 .30
❑ 21 Blown Clear U .40 1.00
❑ 22 Boba Fett R 1.50 4.00
❑ 23 Boelo R 1.00 2.50
❑ 24 Bossk In Hound's Tooth R 1.00 2.50
❑ 25 Bothan Spy C .12 .30
❑ 26 Bothawui F .60 1.50
❑ 27 Bothawui Operative C .12 .30
❑ 28 Brangus Glee R .75 2.00
❑ 29 Bren Quersey U .40 1.00
❑ 30 Bron Burs R .75 2.00
❑ 31 B-wing Attack Fighter F .60 1.50
❑ 32 Camie R 1.00 2.50
❑ 33 Carbon Chamber Testing 1.00 2.50
My Favorite Decoration R
❑ 34 Chyler U .40 1.00
❑ 35 Clak'dor VII Operative U .40 1.00
❑ 36 Cloud City Celebration R 1.00 2.50
❑ 37 Cloud City Occupation R 1.25 3.00
❑ 38 Cloud City: Casino DARK U .40 1.00
❑ 39 Cloud City: Casino LIGHT U .40 1.00
❑ 40 Cloud City: Core Tunnel U .40 1.00
❑ 41 Cloud City: Downtown Plaza DARK R 1.00 2.50
❑ 42 Cloud City: Downtown Plaza LIGHT R 1.00 2.50
❑ 43 Cloud City: Interrogation Room C .12 .30
❑ 44 Cloud City: North Corridor C .12 .30
❑ 45 Cloud City: Port Town District U .40 1.00
❑ 46 Cloud City: Upper Walkway C .12 .30
❑ 47 Cloud City: West Gallery DARK C .12 .30
❑ 48 Cloud City: West Gallery LIGHT C .12 .30
❑ 49 Colonel Feyn Gospic R 1.00 2.50
❑ 50 Combat Cloud Car F .60 1.50
❑ 51 Come Here You Big Coward! C .12 .30
❑ 52 Commander Wedge Antilles R 1.00 2.50
❑ 53 Coordinated Attack C .12 .30
❑ 54 Corellia Operative U .40 1.00
❑ 55 Corellian Engineering Corporation R 1.00 2.50
❑ 56 Corporal Grenwick R .75 2.00
❑ 57 Corporal Prescott U .40 1.00
❑ 58 Corulag Operative C .12 .30
❑ 59 Coruscant Celebration R .75 2.00
❑ 60 Coruscant DARK R 2.50 6.00
❑ 61 Coruscant LIGHT R 1.00 2.50
❑ 62 Coruscant: Docking Bay C .12 .30
❑ 63 Coruscant: Imperial City U .40 1.00
❑ 64 Coruscant: Imperial Square R 1.25 3.00
❑ 65 Counter Surprise Assault R 1.00 2.50
❑ 66 Dagobah U .40 1.00
❑ 67 Dantooine Base Operations .75 2.00
More Dangerous Than You Realize R
❑ 68 Dantooine Operative C .12 .30
❑ 69 Darklighter Spin C .12 .30
❑ 70 Darth Vader, Dark Lord Of The Sith R 6.00 15.00
❑ 71 Death Squadron Star Destroyer R 1.00 2.50
❑ 72 Death Star Assault Squadron R 1.00 2.50
❑ 73 Death Star R 1.25 3.00
❑ 74 Death Star: Detention Block Control Room C .12 .30
❑ 75 Death Star: Detention Block Corridor C .12 .30
❑ 76 Debnoli R 1.00 2.50
❑ 77 Desert DARK F .60 1.50
❑ 78 Desert LIGHT F .60 1.50
❑ 79 Desilijic Tattoo U .40 1.00
❑ 80 Desperate Tactics C .12 .30
❑ 81 Destroyed Homestead R 1.00 2.50
❑ 82 Dewback C .12 .30
❑ 83 Direct Assault C .12 .30
❑ 84 Disruptor Pistol DARK F .60 1.50
❑ 85 Disruptor Pistol LIGHT F .60 1.50
❑ 86 Docking And Repair Facilities R 1.00 2.50
❑ 87 Dodo Bodonawieedo U .40 1.00
❑ 88 Don't Tread On Me R 1.00 2.50
❑ 89 Down With The Emperor! U .40 1.00
❑ 90 Dr. Evazan's Sawed-off Blaster U .40 1.00
❑ 91 Draw Their Fire U .40 1.00
❑ 92 Dreaded Imperial Starfleet R 1.25 3.00
❑ 93 Droid Merchant C .12 .30
❑ 94 Dune Walker R 1.25 3.00
❑ 95 Echo Base Trooper Rifle C .12 .30
❑ 96 Elyhek Rue U .40 1.00
❑ 97 Entrenchment R .75 2.00
❑ 98 Eriadu Operative C .12 .30
❑ 99 Executor: Docking Bay U .40 1.00
❑ 100 Farm F .60 1.50
❑ 101 Fellpern Trevagg's Stun Rifle U .40 1.00
❑ 102 Firepower C .12 .30
❑ 103 Firin Morett U .40 1.00
❑ 104 First Aid F .60 1.50
❑ 105 First Strike U .40 1.00
❑ 106 Flare-S Racing Swoop C .12 .30
❑ 107 Flawless Marksmanship C .12 .30
❑ 108 Floating Refinery C .12 .30
❑ 109 Fondor U .40 1.00
❑ 110 Forest DARK F .60 1.50
❑ 111 Forest LIGHT F .60 1.50
❑ 112 Gela Yeens U .40 1.00
❑ 113 General McQuarrie R .75 2.00
❑ 114 Gold 3 U .40 1.00
❑ 115 Gold 4 U .40 1.00
❑ 116 Gold 6 U .40 1.00
❑ 117 Goo Nee Tay R 1.00 2.50
❑ 118 Greeata U .40 1.00
❑ 119 Grondorn Muse R .75 2.00
❑ 120 Harc Seff U .40 1.00
❑ 121 Harvest R 1.25 3.00
❑ 122 Heavy Fire Zone C .12 .30
❑ 123 Heroes Of Yavin R .75 2.00
❑ 124 Heroic Sacrifice U .40 1.00
❑ 125 Hidden Base 1.50 4.00
Systems Will Slip Through Your Fingers R
❑ 126 Hit And Run R .75 2.00
❑ 127 Hol Okand U .40 1.00
❑ 128 Homing Beacon R 1.00 2.50
❑ 129 Hoth Sentry U .40 1.00
❑ 130 Hunt Down And Destroy The Jedi 1.50 4.00
Their Fire Has Gone Out Of The Universe R
❑ 131 Hunting Party R 1.00 2.50
❑ 132 I Can't Shake Him! C .12 .30
❑ 133 Iasa, The Traitor Of Jawa Canyon R .75 2.00
❑ 134 IM4-099 F .60 1.50
❑ 135 Imperial Atrocity R 3.00 8.00
❑ 136 Imperial Occupation / Imperial Control R 1.00 2.50
❑ 137 Imperial Propaganda R 3.00 8.00
❑ 138 In Range C .12 .30
❑ 139 Incom Corporation R .75 2.00
❑ 140 InCom Engineer C .12 .30
❑ 141 Intruder Missile DARK F .60 1.50
❑ 142 Intruder Missile LIGHT F .60 1.50
❑ 143 It's Not My Fault! F .60 1.50
❑ 144 Jabba R 1.00 2.50
❑ 145 Jabba's Influence R .75 2.00
❑ 146 Jabba's Space Cruiser R 1.25 3.00
❑ 147 Jabba's Through With You U .40 1.00
❑ 148 Jabba's Twerps U .40 1.00
❑ 149 Joh Yowza R .75 2.00
❑ 150 Jungle DARK F .60 1.50
❑ 151 Jungle LIGHT F .60 1.50
❑ 152 Kalit's Sandcrawler R 1.00 2.50
❑ 153 Kashyyyk Operative DARK U .40 1.00
❑ 154 Kashyyyk Operative LIGHT U .40 1.00
❑ 155 Kessel Operative U .40 1.00
❑ 156 Ketwol R .75 2.00
❑ 157 Kiffex Operative DARK U .40 1.00
❑ 158 Kiffex Operative LIGHT U .40 1.00
❑ 159 Kirdo III Operative C .12 .30
❑ 160 Koensayr Manufacturing R 1.00 2.50
❑ 161 Krayt Dragon R 1.00 2.50
❑ 162 Kuat Drive Yards R 1.25 3.00
❑ 163 Kuat U .40 1.00
❑ 164 Lando's Blaster Rifle R 1.00 2.50
❑ 165 Legendary Starfighter C .12 .30
❑ 166 Leia's Blaster Rifle R 1.00 2.50
❑ 167 Lieutenant Lepira U .40 1.00
❑ 168 Lieutenant Naytaan U .40 1.00
❑ 169 Lieutenant Tarn Mison R 1.00 2.50
❑ 170 Lobel C .12 .30
❑ 171 Lobot R 1.00 2.50
❑ 172 Local Defense U .40 1.00
❑ 173 Local Uprising / Liberation R 1.00 2.50
❑ 174 Lyn Me U .40 1.00
❑ 175 Major Palo Torshan R 1.00 2.50
❑ 176 Makurth F .60 1.50
❑ 177 Maneuvering Flaps C .12 .30
❑ 178 Masterful Move C .12 .30
❑ 179 Mechanical Failure R .75 2.00
❑ 180 Meditation R 1.25 3.00
❑ 181 Medium Bulk Freighter U .40 1.00
❑ 182 Melas R 1.00 2.50
❑ 183 Mind What You Have Learned 1.25 3.00
Save You It Can R
❑ 184 Moisture Farmer C .12 .30
❑ 185 Nal Hutta Operative C .12 .30
❑ 186 Neb Dulo U .40 1.00
❑ 187 Nebit R 1.00 2.50
❑ 188 Niado Duegad U .40 1.00
❑ 189 Nick Of Time U .40 1.00
❑ 190 No Bargain U .40 1.00
❑ 191 Old Times R .75 2.00
❑ 192 On Target C .12 .30
❑ 193 One-Arm R 1.00 2.50
❑ 194 Oppressive Enforcement U .40 1.00
❑ 195 Ord Mantell Operative C .12 .30
❑ 196 Organized Attack C .12 .30
❑ 197 OS-72-1 In Obsidian 1 R 1.00 2.50
❑ 198 OS-72-10 R 1.00 2.50
❑ 199 OS-72-2 In Obsidian 2 R 1.00 2.50
❑ 200 Outer Rim Scout R 1.50 4.00
❑ 201 Overwhelmed C .12 .30
❑ 202 Patrol Craft DARK C .12 .30
❑ 203 Patrol Craft LIGHT C .12 .30
❑ 204 Planetary Subjugation U .40 1.00
❑ 205 Ponda Baba's Hold-out Blaster U .40 1.00
❑ 206 Portable Scanner C .12 .30
❑ 207 Power Pivot C .12 .30
❑ 208 Precise Hit C .12 .30
❑ 209 Pride Of The Empire C .12 .30
❑ 210 Princess Organa R 1.25 3.00
❑ 211 Put All Sections On Alert C .12 .30
❑ 212 R2-A5 (Artoo-Ayfive) U .40 1.00
❑ 213 R3-A2 (Arthree-Aytoo) U .40 1.00
❑ 214 R3-T2 (Arthree-Teetoo) R 1.00 2.50
❑ 215 Ralthal Operative C .12 .30
❑ 216 Ralltiir Freighter Captain F .60 1.50
❑ 217 Ralltiir Operations 1.50 4.00
In The Hands Of The Empire R
❑ 218 Ralltiir Operative C .12 .30
❑ 219 Rapid Fire C .12 .30
❑ 220 Rappertunie U .40 1.00
❑ 221 Rebel Ambush C .12 .30
❑ 222 Rebel Base Occupation R .75 2.00
❑ 223 Rebel Fleet R 1.00 2.50
❑ 224 Red 10 U .40 1.00
❑ 225 Red 7 U .40 1.00
❑ 226 Red 8 U .40 1.00
❑ 227 Red 9 U .40 1.00
❑ 228 Relentless Pursuit C .12 .30
❑ 229 Rendezvous Point R 1.00 2.50
❑ 230 Rendili F .60 1.50
❑ 231 Rendili StarDrive R .75 2.00
❑ 232 Rescue The Princess 1.00 2.50
Sometimes I Amaze Even Myself R
❑ 233 Return To Base R 1.00 2.50
❑ 234 Roche U .40 1.00
❑ 235 Rock Wart F .60 1.50
❑ 236 Rogue 4 R 1.50 4.00
❑ 237 Ronto DARK C .12 .30
❑ 238 Ronto LIGHT C .12 .30
❑ 239 RR'uruurrr R 1.00 2.50
❑ 240 Ryle Torsyn U .40 1.00
❑ 241 Rystall R 1.50 4.00
❑ 242 Sacrifice F .60 1.50
❑ 243 Sandspeeder F .60 1.50
❑ 244 Sandtrooper F .60 1.50
❑ 245 Sarlacc R 1.00 2.50
❑ 246 Scrambled Transmission U .40 1.00
❑ 247 Scurrier F .60 1.50
❑ 248 Secret Plans U .40 1.00
❑ 249 Sentinel-Class Landing Craft F .60 1.50
❑ 250 Sergeant Edian U .40 1.00
❑ 251 Sergeant Hollis R 1.00 2.50
❑ 252 Sergeant Major Bursk U .40 1.00
❑ 253 Sergeant Major Enfield R .75 2.00
❑ 254 Sergeant Merril U .40 1.00
❑ 255 Sergeant Narthax R 1.00 2.50
❑ 256 Sergeant Torent R 1.00 2.50
❑ 257 S-Foils C .12 .30
❑ 258 SFS L-s9.3 Laser Cannons C .12 .30
❑ 259 Short-Range Fighters R 1.00 2.50
❑ 260 Sienar Fleet Systems R 1.00 2.50
❑ 261 Slayn and Korpil Facilities R .75 2.00
❑ 262 Slight Weapons Malfunction C .12 .30
❑ 263 Soth Petikkin R .75 2.00
❑ 264 Spaceport City DARK F .60 1.50
❑ 265 Spaceport City LIGHT F .60 1.50
❑ 266 Spaceport Docking Bay DARK F .60 1.50
❑ 267 Spaceport Docking Bay LIGHT F .60 1.50
❑ 268 Spaceport Prefect's Office F .60 1.50
❑ 269 Spaceport Street DARK F .60 1.50
❑ 270 Spaceport Street LIGHT F .60 1.50
❑ 271 Spiral R 1.25 3.00
❑ 272 Star Destroyer! R 1.00 2.50
❑ 273 Stay Sharp! U .40 1.00
❑ 274 Steady Aim C .12 .30
❑ 275 Strategic Reserves R 1.00 2.50
❑ 276 Suppressive Fire C .12 .30
❑ 277 Surface Defense R 1.00 2.50
❑ 278 Swamp DARK F .60 1.50
❑ 279 Swamp LIGHT F .60 1.50
❑ 280 Swoop Mercenary F .60 1.50
❑ 281 Sy Snootles R 1.00 2.50
❑ 282 T-47 Battle Formation R 1.00 2.50
❑ 283 Tarkin's Bounty U .40 1.00
❑ 284 Tatooine Celebration R 1.25 3.00
❑ 285 Tatooine Occupation R 1.50 4.00
❑ 286 Tatooine: Anchorhead F .60 1.50
❑ 287 Tatooine: Beggar's Canyon R .75 2.00
❑ 288 Tatooine: Jabba's Palace C .12 .30
❑ 289 Tatooine: Jawa Canyon DARK U .40 1.00
❑ 290 Tatooine: Jawa Canyon LIGHT U .40 1.00
❑ 291 Tatooine: Krayt Dragon Pass F .60 1.50
❑ 292 Tatooine: Tosche Station C .12 .30
❑ 293 Tauntaun Skull C .12 .30
❑ 294 Tawss Khaa R .75 2.00
❑ 295 The Planet That It's Farthest From U .40 1.00
❑ 296 Thedit R 1.00 2.50
❑ 297 Theron Nett U .40 1.00
❑ 298 They're Coming In Too Fast! C .12 .30
❑ 299 They're Tracking Us C .12 .30
❑ 300 They've Shut Down The Main Reactor C .12 .30
❑ 301 Tibrin Operative C .12 .30
❑ 302 TIE Defender Mark I F .60 1.50
❑ 303 TK-422 R 1.00 2.50
❑ 304 Trooper Sabacc DARK F .60 1.50
❑ 305 Trooper Sabacc LIGHT F .60 1.50
❑ 306 Uh-oh! U .40 1.00
❑ 307 Umpass-stay R .75 2.00
❑ 308 Ur'Ru'r R 1.00 2.50
❑ 309 URoRRuR'R'R's Bantha R 1.00 2.50
❑ 310 Uutkik R 1.00 2.50
❑ 311 Vader's Personal Shuttle R 1.00 2.50
❑ 312 Vengeance R 1.00 2.50
❑ 313 Wakeelmui U .40 1.00
❑ 314 Watch Your Back! C .12 .30
❑ 315 Weapons Display C .12 .30
❑ 316 Wise Advice U .40 1.00
❑ 317 Wittin's Sandcrawler R 1.00 2.50
❑ 318 Womp Rat C .12 .30
❑ 319 Wookiee F .60 1.50
❑ 320 Wrist Comlink C .12 .30
❑ 321 X-wing Assault Squadron R 1.00 2.50
❑ 322 X-wing Laser Cannon C .12 .30
❑ 323 Yavin 4 Trooper F .60 1.50
❑ 324 Yavin 4: Massassi Headquarters R 1.00 2.50

1999 Star Wars Endor

COMPLETE SET (180) 75.00 150.00
BOOSTER BOX (30) 75.00 150.00
BOOSTER PACK 3.50 7.00
❑ 1 A280 Sharpshooter Rifle R 2.50 6.00
❑ 2 Accelerate C .12 .30
❑ 3 Aim High R 1.00 2.50
❑ 4 Always Thinking With Your Stomach R 2.50 6.00
❑ 5 An Entire Legion Of My Best Troops U .40 1.00
❑ 6 Aratech Corporation R 1.00 2.50
❑ 7 AT-ST Dual Cannon R 6.00 15.00
❑ 8 AT-ST Pilot C .12 .30
❑ 9 Battle Order U .40 1.00
❑ 10 Battle Plan U .40 1.00
❑ 11 Biker Scout Gear U .40 1.00
❑ 12 Biker Scout Trooper C .12 .30
❑ 13 BlasTech E-11B Blaster Rifle C .12 .30
❑ 14 Captain Yutani U .40 1.00
❑ 15 Careful Planning C .12 .30
❑ 16 Carida U .40 1.00
❑ 17 Chandrila U .40 1.00
❑ 18 Chewbacca of Kashyyyk R .75 2.00
❑ 19 Chewbacca's Bowcaster R 2.50 6.00
❑ 20 Chewie's AT-ST R 3.00 8.00
❑ 21 Chief Chirpa R 1.00 2.50
❑ 22 Closed Door R .75 2.00
❑ 23 Colonel Dyer R 1.25 3.00
❑ 24 Combat Readiness C .12 .30
❑ 25 Commander Igar R 1.25 3.00
❑ 26 Commando Training C .12 .30
❑ 27 Compact Firepower C .12 .30
❑ 28 Corporal Avarik U .40 1.00
❑ 29 Corporal Beezer U .40 1.00
❑ 30 Corporal Delevar U .40 1.00
❑ 31 Corporal Drazin U .40 1.00
❑ 32 Corporal Drelosyn R 1.25 3.00
❑ 33 Corporal Janse U .40 1.00
❑ 34 Corporal Kensaric R 1.25 3.00
❑ 35 Corporal Misik R 1.00 2.50
❑ 36 Corporal Oberk R 1.25 3.00
❑ 37 Count Me In R .75 2.00
❑ 38 Counterattack R .75 2.00
❑ 39 Covert Landing U .40 1.00
❑ 40 Crossfire R 3.00 8.00
❑ 41 Daughter of Skywalker R 10.00 20.00
❑ 42 Deactivate The Shield Generator R 1.25 3.00
❑ 43 Dead Ewok C .12 .30
❑ 44 Don't Move! C .12 .30
❑ 45 Dresselian Commando C .12 .30
❑ 46 Early Warning Network R .75 2.00
❑ 47 Eee Chu Wawa! C .12 .30
❑ 48 Elite Squadron Stormtrooper C .12 .30
❑ 49 Empire's New Order R .75 2.00
❑ 50 Endor Celebration R .75 2.00
❑ 51 Endor Occupation R .75 2.00
❑ 52 Endor Operations / Imperial Outpost R 2.50 6.00
❑ 53 Endor Scout Trooper C .12 .30
❑ 54 Endor DARK U .40 1.00
❑ 55 Endor LIGHT U .40 1.00
❑ 56 Endor: Ancient Forest U .40 1.00
❑ 57 Endor: Back Door DARK U .40 1.00
❑ 58 Endor: Back Door LIGHT U .40 1.00
❑ 59 Endor: Bunker DARK U .40 1.00
❑ 60 Endor: Bunker LIGHT U .40 1.00
❑ 61 Endor: Chief Chirpa's Hut R 3.00 8.00
❑ 62 Endor: Dark Forest R 2.50 6.00
❑ 63 Endor: Dense Forest DARK C .12 .30
❑ 64 Endor: Dense Forest LIGHT C .12 .30
❑ 65 Endor: Ewok Village DARK U .40 1.00
❑ 66 Endor: Ewok Village LIGHT U .40 1.00
❑ 67 Endor: Forest Clearing U .40 1.00
❑ 68 Endor: Great Forest DARK C .12 .30
❑ 69 Endor: Great Forest LIGHT C .12 .30
❑ 70 Endor: Hidden Forest Trail U .40 1.00
❑ 71 Endor: Landing Platform (Docking Bay) DARK C .12 .30
❑ 72 Endor: Landing Platform (Docking Bay) LIGHT C .12 .30
❑ 73 Endor: Rebel Landing Site (Forest) R 2.50 6.00
❑ 74 Establish Secret Base R 1.50 4.00
❑ 75 Ewok And Roll C .12 .30
❑ 76 Ewok Bow C .12 .30
❑ 77 Ewok Catapult U .40 1.00
❑ 78 Ewok Glider C .12 .30
❑ 79 Ewok Log Jam C .12 .30
❑ 80 Ewok Rescue C .12 .30
❑ 81 Ewok Sentry C .12 .30
❑ 82 Ewok Spear C .12 .30
❑ 83 Ewok Spearman C .12 .30
❑ 84 Ewok Tribesman C .12 .30
❑ 85 Explosive Charge U .40 1.00
❑ 86 Firefight C .12 .30
❑ 87 Fly Casual R .75 2.00
❑ 88 Free Ride U .40 1.00
❑ 89 Freeze! U .40 1.00
❑ 90 General Crix Madine R 1.00 2.50
❑ 91 General Solo R .75 2.00
❑ 92 Get Alongside That One U .40 1.00
❑ 93 Go For Help! C .12 .30
❑ 94 Graak R .75 2.00
❑ 95 Here We Go Again R .75 2.00
❑ 96 High-speed Tactics U .40 1.00
❑ 97 Hot Pursuit C .12 .30
❑ 98 I Have A Really Bad Feeling About This C .12 .30
❑ 99 I Hope She's All Right U .40 1.00
❑ 100 I Know R 1.25 3.00
❑ 101 I Wonder Who They Found U .40 1.00
❑ 102 Imperial Academy Training C .12 .30
❑ 103 Imperial Arrest Order U .40 1.00
❑ 104 Imperial Tyranny C .12 .30
❑ 105 Insurrection U .40 1.00
❑ 106 It's An Older Code R .75 2.00
❑ 107 Kazak R 1.00 2.50
❑ 108 Lambda-class Shuttle C .12 .30
❑ 109 Lieutenant Arnet U .40 1.00
❑ 110 Lieutenant Greeve R .75 2.00
❑ 111 Lieutenant Grond U .40 1.00
❑ 112 Lieutenant Page R 1.50 4.00
❑ 113 Lieutenant Renz R .75 2.00
❑ 114 Lieutenant Watts R 1.25 3.00
❑ 115 Logray R .75 2.00
❑ 116 Lost In The Wilderness R .75 2.00
❑ 117 Lumat U .40 1.00
❑ 118 Main Course U .40 1.00
❑ 119 Major Hewex R .75 2.00
❑ 120 Major Marquand R 1.50 4.00
❑ 121 Mon Mothma R 1.25 3.00
❑ 122 Navy Trooper C .12 .30
❑ 123 Navy Trooper Fenson R 1.00 2.50
❑ 124 Navy Trooper Shield Technician C .12 .30
❑ 125 Navy Trooper Vesden U .40 1.00
❑ 126 Ominous Rumors R .75 2.00
❑ 127 Orrimaarko R .75 2.00
❑ 128 Outflank C .12 .30
❑ 129 Paploo U .40 1.00
❑ 130 Perimeter Patrol R 1.00 2.50
❑ 131 Pinned Down U .40 1.00
❑ 132 Pitiful Little Band C .12 .30
❑ 133 Rabin U .40 1.00
❑ 134 Rapid Deployment R .75 2.00
❑ 135 Rebel Strike Team / Garrison Destroyed R 1.25 3.00
❑ 136 Relentless Tracking R .75 2.00
❑ 137 Romba R .75 2.00
❑ 138 Scout Blaster C .12 .30
❑ 139 Scout Recon C .12 .30
❑ 140 Search And Destroy U .40 1.00
❑ 141 Security Precautions R 2.50 6.00
❑ 142 Sergeant Barich R 2.00 5.00
❑ 143 Sergeant Brooks Carlson R .75 2.00
❑ 144 Sergeant Bruckman R .75 2.00
❑ 145 Sergeant Elsek U .40 1.00
❑ 146 Sergeant Irol R 1.50 4.00
❑ 147 Sergeant Junkin U .40 1.00
❑ 148 Sergeant Tarl U .40 1.00
❑ 149 Sergeant Wallen R 1.50 4.00
❑ 150 Sneak Attack C .12 .30
❑ 151 Sound The Attack C .12 .30
❑ 152 Speeder Bike DARK C .12 .30
❑ 153 Speeder Bike LIGHT C .12 .30
❑ 154 Speeder Bike Cannon U .40 1.00
❑ 155 Surprise Counter Assault R .75 2.00
❑ 156 Take The Initiative C .12 .30
❑ 157 Teebo R .75 2.00
❑ 158 Tempest 1 R .75 2.00
❑ 159 Tempest Scout 1 R 1.00 2.50
❑ 160 Tempest Scout 2 R 2.00 5.00
❑ 161 Tempest Scout 3 R .75 2.00
❑ 162 Tempest Scout 4 R 2.50 6.00
❑ 163 Tempest Scout 5 R 2.00 5.00
❑ 164 Tempest Scout 6 R 2.50 6.00
❑ 165 Tempest Scout U .40 1.00

TCG/CCG

❑ 166 That's One R .75 2.00
❑ 167 This Is Absolutely Right R .75 2.00
❑ 168 Threepio R 1.25 3.00
❑ 169 Throw Me Another Charge U .40 1.00
❑ 170 Tydirium R 1.25 3.00
❑ 171 Well-earned Command R .75 2.00
❑ 172 Were You Looking For Me? R 4.00 10.00
❑ 173 Wicket R .75 2.00
❑ 174 Wokling R 6.00 15.00
❑ 175 Wookiee Guide C .12 .30
❑ 176 Wounded Warrior R 1.50 4.00
❑ 177 Wuta U .40 1.00
❑ 178 You Rebel Scum R 1.00 2.50
❑ 179 YT-1300 Transport C .12 .30
❑ 180 Yub Yub! C .12 .30

1999 Star Wars Enhanced Cloud City

❑ 1 4-LOM With Concussion Rifle PM 1.50 4.00
❑ 2 Any Methods Necessary PM 2.00 5.00
❑ 3 Boba Fett in Slave I PM 1.00 2.50
❑ 4 Chewie With Blaster Rifle PM 1.00 2.50
❑ 5 Crush The Rebellion PM 1.25 3.00
❑ 6 Dengar In Punishing One PM 1.00 2.50
❑ 7 IG-88 With Riot Gun PM 3.00 8.00
❑ 8 Lando In Millennium Falcon PM 1.00 2.50
❑ 9 Lando With Blaster Pistol PM 1.00 2.50
❑ 10 Quiet Mining Colony / Independent Operation PM1.00 2.50
❑ 11 This Deal Is Getting Worse All The Time 1.00 2.50
Pray I Don't Alter It Any Further
❑ 12 Z-95 Bespin Defense Fighter PM 1.00 2.50

1999 Star Wars Enhanced Jabba's Palace

❑ 1 Bossk With Mortar Gun PM 1.00 2.50
❑ 2 Boushh PM 1.25 3.00
❑ 3 Court Of The Vile Gangster 1.00 2.50
I Shall Enjoy Watching You Die PM
❑ 4 Dengar With Blaster Carbine PM 1.00 2.50
❑ 5 IG-88 In IG-2000 PM 1.00 2.50
❑ 6 Jodo Kast PM 1.50 4.00
❑ 7 Mara Jade, The Emperor's Hand PM 10.00 20.00
❑ 8 Mara Jade's Lightsaber PM 1.50 4.00
❑ 9 Master Luke PM 2.50 6.00
❑ 10 See-Threepio PM 1.00 2.50
❑ 11 You Can Either Profit By This... 1.00 2.50
Or Be Destroyed PM
❑ 12 Zuckuss In Mist Hunter PM 1.25 3.00

2000 Star Wars Death Star II

COMPLETE SET (182) 200.00 300.00
BOOSTER BOX (36) 150.00 250.00
BOOSTER PACK 5.00 9.00

❑ 1 Accuser R 1.25 3.00
❑ 2 Admiral Ackbar XR 1.25 3.00
❑ 3 Admiral Chiraneau R 1.50 4.00
❑ 4 Admiral Piett XR 1.00 2.50
❑ 5 Anakin Skywalker R 1.00 2.50
❑ 6 Aquaris C .12 .30
❑ 7 A-wing C .12 .30
❑ 8 A-wing Cannon C .12 .30
❑ 9 Baron Soontir Fel R 1.50 4.00
❑ 10 Battle Deployment R 1.25 3.00
❑ 11 Black 11 R 1.00 2.50
❑ 12 Blue Squadron 5 U .40 1.00
❑ 13 Blue Squadron B-wing R 1.50 4.00
❑ 14 Bring Him Before Me / Take Your Father's Place R1.00 2.50
❑ 15 B-wing Attack Squadron R 1.00 2.50
❑ 16 B-wing Bomber C .12 .30
❑ 17 Capital Support R 1.00 2.50
❑ 18 Captain Godherdt U .40 1.00
❑ 19 Captain Jonus U .40 1.00
❑ 20 Captain Sarkli R 1.00 2.50
❑ 21 Captain Verrack U .40 1.00
❑ 22 Captain Yorr U .40 1.00
❑ 23 Chimaera R 2.50 6.00
❑ 24 Close Air Support C .12 .30
❑ 25 Colonel Cracken R 1.00 2.50
❑ 26 Colonel Davod Jon U .40 1.00
❑ 27 Colonel Jendon R 1.00 2.50
❑ 28 Colonel Salm U .40 1.00
❑ 29 Combat Response C .12 .30
❑ 30 Combined Fleet Action R 1.00 2.50
❑ 31 Commander Merrejk R 1.25 3.00
❑ 32 Concentrate All Fire R 1.00 2.50
❑ 33 Concussion Missiles DARK C .12 .30
❑ 34 Concussion Missiles LIGHT C .12 .30
❑ 35 Corporal Marmor U .40 1.00
❑ 36 Corporal Midge U .40 1.00
❑ 37 Critical Error Revealed C .12 .30
❑ 38 Darth Vader's Lightsaber R 1.00 2.50
❑ 39 Death Star II R 1.25 3.00
❑ 40 Death Star II: Capacitors C .12 .30
❑ 41 Death Star II: Coolant Shaft C .12 .30
❑ 42 Death Star II: Docking Bay C .12 .30
❑ 43 Death Star II: Reactor Core C .12 .30
❑ 44 Death Star II: Throne Room R 1.00 2.50
❑ 45 Defiance R 1.25 3.00
❑ 46 Desperate Counter C .12 .30
❑ 47 Dominator R 1.00 2.50
❑ 48 DS-181-3 U .40 1.00
❑ 49 DS-181-4 U .40 1.00
❑ 50 Emperor Palpatine UR 30.00 60.00
❑ 51 Emperor's Personal Shuttle R 1.00 2.50
❑ 52 Emperor's Power U .40 1.00
❑ 53 Endor Shield U .40 1.00
❑ 54 Enhanced Proton Torpedoes C .12 .30
❑ 55 Fighter Cover R 2.00 5.00
❑ 56 Fighters Coming In R 1.00 2.50
❑ 57 First Officer Thaneespi R 1.00 2.50
❑ 58 Flagship Executor R 1.25 3.00
❑ 59 Flagship Operations R 1.00 2.50
❑ 60 Force Lightning R 2.00 5.00
❑ 61 Force Pike C .12 .30
❑ 62 Gall C .12 .30
❑ 63 General Calrissian R 1.00 2.50
❑ 64 General Walex Blissex U .40 1.00
❑ 65 Gold Squadron 1 R 1.00 2.50
❑ 66 Gray Squadron 1 U .40 1.00
❑ 67 Gray Squadron 2 U .40 1.00
❑ 68 Gray Squadron Y-wing Pilot C .12 .30
❑ 69 Green Leader R 1.00 2.50
❑ 70 Green Squadron 1 R 1.00 2.50
❑ 71 Green Squadron 3 R 1.00 2.50
❑ 72 Green Squadron A-wing R 1.25 3.00
❑ 73 Green Squadron Pilot C .12 .30
❑ 74 Head Back To The Surface C .12 .30
❑ 75 Heading For The Medical Frigate C .12 .30
❑ 76 Heavy Turbolaser Battery DARK C .12 .30
❑ 77 Heavy Turbolaser Battery LIGHT C .12 .30
❑ 78 Home One R 4.00 10.00
❑ 79 Home One: Docking Bay C .12 .30
❑ 80 Home One: War Room R 1.25 3.00
❑ 81 Honor Of The Jedi U .40 1.00
❑ 82 I Feel The Conflict U .40 1.00
❑ 83 I'll Take The Leader R 2.50 6.00
❑ 84 I'm With You Too R 1.50 4.00
❑ 85 Imperial Command R 4.00 10.00
❑ 86 Inconsequential Losses C .12 .30
❑ 87 Independence R 1.25 3.00
❑ 88 Insertion Planning C .12 .30
❑ 89 Insignificant Rebellion U .40 1.00
❑ 90 Intensify The Forward Batteries R 1.00 2.50
❑ 91 Janus Greejatus R 1.00 2.50
❑ 92 Judicator R 1.50 4.00
❑ 93 Karie Neth U .40 1.00
❑ 94 Keir Santage U .40 1.00
❑ 95 Kin Kian U .40 1.00
❑ 96 Launching The Assault R 1.00 2.50
❑ 97 Leave Them To Me C .12 .30
❑ 98 Let's Keep A Little Optimism Here C .12 .30
❑ 99 Liberty R 1.25 3.00
❑ 100 Lieutenant Blount R 1.00 2.50
❑ 101 Lieutenant Endicott U .40 1.00
❑ 102 Lieutenant Hebsly U .40 1.00
❑ 103 Lieutenant s'Too Vees U .40 1.00
❑ 104 Lieutenant Telsij U .40 1.00
❑ 105 Lord Vader R 10.00 20.00
❑ 106 Luke Skywalker, Jedi Knight UR 30.00 60.00
❑ 107 Luke's Lightsaber R 1.50 4.00
❑ 108 Luminous U .40 1.00
❑ 109 Major Haash'n U .40 1.00
❑ 110 Major Mianda U .40 1.00
❑ 111 Major Olander Brit U .40 1.00
❑ 112 Major Panno U .40 1.00
❑ 113 Major Rhymer U .40 1.00
❑ 114 Major Turr Phennir U .40 1.00
❑ 115 Masanya R 1.50 4.00
❑ 116 Menace Fades C .12 .30
❑ 117 Mobilization Points C .12 .30
❑ 118 Moff Jerjerrod R 1.00 2.50
❑ 119 Mon Calamari DARK C .12 .30
❑ 120 Mon Calamari LIGHT C .12 .30
❑ 121 Mon Calamari Star Cruiser R 1.25 3.00
❑ 122 Myn Kyneugh R 1.00 2.50
❑ 123 Nebulon-B Frigate U .40 1.00
❑ 124 Nien Nunb R 1.25 3.00
❑ 125 Obsidian 10 U .40 1.00
❑ 126 Onyx 1 R 1.25 3.00
❑ 127 Onyx 2 U .40 1.00
❑ 128 Operational As Planned C .12 .30
❑ 129 Orbital Mine C .12 .30
❑ 130 Our Only Hope U .40 1.00
❑ 131 Overseeing It Personally R 1.00 2.50
❑ 132 Prepared Defenses C .12 .30
❑ 133 Rebel Leadership R 3.00 8.00
❑ 134 Red Squadron 1 R 1.00 2.50
❑ 135 Red Squadron 4 U .40 1.00
❑ 136 Red Squadron 7 U .40 1.00
❑ 137 Rise, My Friend R 1.00 2.50
❑ 138 Royal Escort C .12 .30
❑ 139 Royal Guard C .12 .30
❑ 140 Saber 1 R 6.00 15.00
❑ 141 Saber 2 U .40 1.00
❑ 142 Saber 3 U .40 1.00
❑ 143 Saber 4 U .40 1.00
❑ 144 Scimitar 1 U .40 1.00
❑ 145 Scimitar 2 U .40 1.00
❑ 146 Scimitar Squadron TIE C .12 .30
❑ 147 Scythe 1 U .40 1.00
❑ 148 Scythe 3 U .40 1.00
❑ 149 Scythe Squadron TIE C .12 .30
❑ 150 SFS L-s7.2 TIE Cannon C .12 .30
❑ 151 Sim Aloo R 1.00 2.50
❑ 152 Something Special Planned For Them C .12 .30
❑ 153 Squadron Assignments C .12 .30
❑ 154 Staging Areas C .12 .30
❑ 155 Strike Planning R 1.00 2.50
❑ 156 Strikeforce C .12 .30
❑ 157 Sullust DARK C .12 .30
❑ 158 Sullust LIGHT C .12 .30
❑ 159 Superficial Damage C .12 .30
❑ 160 Superlaser Mark II U .40 1.00
❑ 161 Taking Them With Us R 1.25 3.00
❑ 162 Tala 1 R 1.00 2.50
❑ 163 Tala 2 R 1.00 2.50
❑ 164 Ten Numb R 1.00 2.50
❑ 165 That Thing's Operational R 1.00 2.50
❑ 166 The Emperor's Shield R 1.00 2.50
❑ 167 The Emperor's Sword R 1.00 2.50
❑ 168 The Time For Our Attack Has Come C .12 .30
❑ 169 The Way Of Things U .40 1.00
❑ 170 There Is Good In Him / I Can Save Him R 1.00 2.50
❑ 171 Thunderflare R 1.00 2.50
❑ 172 TIE Interceptor C .12 .30
❑ 173 Twilight Is Upon Me R 1.00 2.50
❑ 174 Tycho Celchu R 1.25 3.00
❑ 175 Visage R 1.00 2.50
❑ 176 We're In Attack Position Now R 2.50 6.00
❑ 177 Wedge Antilles, Red Squadron Leader R 1.50 4.00
❑ 178 You Cannot Hide Forever U .40 1.00
❑ 179 You Must Confront Vader R 1.50 4.00
❑ 180 Young Fool R 1.00 2.50
❑ 181 Your Destiny C .12 .30
❑ 182 Your Insight Serves You Well U .40 1.00

2000 Star Wars Jabba's Palace Sealed Deck

❑ 1 Agents In The Court / No Love For The Empire PM.40 1.00
❑ 2 Hutt Influence PM .40 1.00
❑ 3 Jabba's Palace: Antechamber PM .40 1.00
❑ 4 Jabba's Palace: Lower Passages PM .40 1.00
❑ 5 Lando With Vibro-Ax PM .40 1.00
❑ 6 Let Them Make The First Move / My Kind Of Scum .40 1.00
Fearless And Inventive PM
❑ 7 Mercenary Pilot PM .40 1.00
❑ 8 Mighty Jabba PM .40 1.00
❑ 9 No Escape PM .40 1.00
❑ 10 Ounee Ta PM .40 1.00
❑ 11 Palace Raider PM .40 1.00
❑ 12 Power Of The Hutt PM .40 1.00
❑ 13 Racing Skiff DARK PM .40 1.00
❑ 14 Racing Skiff LIGHT PM .40 1.00
❑ 15 Seeking An Audience PM .40 1.00
❑ 16 Stun Blaster DARK PM .40 1.00
❑ 17 Stun Blaster LIGHT PM .40 1.00
❑ 18 Tatooine: Desert Heart PM .40 1.00
❑ 19 Tatooine: Hutt Trade Route (Desert) PM .40 1.00
❑ 20 Underworld Contacts PM .40 1.00

2000 Star Wars Reflections II

BOOSTER BOX (30) 150.00 250.00
BOOSTER PACK 5.00 10.00

❑ 1 There Is No Try and Oppressive Enforcement PM.60 1.50
❑ 2 Abyssin Ornament and Wounded Wookiee PM .40 1.00
❑ 3 Agents Of Black Sun .40 1.00
Vengence Of The Dark Prince PM
❑ 4 Alter and Collateral Damage PM .60 1.50
❑ 5 Alter and Friendly Fire PM .60 1.50
❑ 6 Arica PM 2.00 5.00
❑ 7 Artoo and Threepio PM .60 1.50
❑ 8 Black Sun Fleet PM .40 1.00
❑ 9 Captain Gilad Pellaeon PM .60 1.50
❑ 10 Chewbacca, Protector PM .60 1.50
❑ 11 Control and Set For Stun PM .60 1.50
❑ 12 Control and Tunnel Vision PM 1.00 2.50
❑ 13 Corran Horn PM 1.50 4.00
❑ 14 Dark Maneuvers and Tallon Roll PM 1.00 2.50
❑ 15 Dash Rendar PM 1.25 3.00
❑ 16 Defensive Fire and Hutt Smooch PM .40 1.00
❑ 17 Do, Or Do Not and Wise Advice PM .40 1.00
❑ 18 Dr Evazan and Ponda Baba PM .40 1.00
❑ 19 Evader and Monnok PM .60 1.50
❑ 20 Ghhhk and Those Rebels Won't Escape Us PM.40 1.00
❑ 21 Grand Admiral Thrawn PM 2.50 6.00
❑ 22 Guri PM 1.25 3.00
❑ 23 Houjix and Out Of Nowhere PM .60 1.50
❑ 24 Jabba's Prize PM .40 1.00
❑ 25 Kir Kanos PM .40 1.00
❑ 26 LE-BO2D9 [Leebo] PM .40 1.00
❑ 27 Luke Skywalker, Rebel Scout PM 1.00 2.50
❑ 28 Mercenary Armor PM .40 1.00
❑ 29 Mirax Terrik PM .60 1.50
❑ 30 Nar Shaddaa Wind .40 1.00
Chimes and Out Of Somewhere PM
❑ 31 No Questions Asked PM .40 1.00
❑ 32 Obi-Wan's Journal PM .40 1.00
❑ 33 Ommni Box and It's Worse PM .40 1.00
❑ 34 Out of Commission and 1.00 2.50
Transmission Terminated PM
❑ 35 Outrider PM .60 1.50
❑ 36 Owen Lars and Beru Lars PM .40 1.00
❑ 37 Path Of Least Resistance and Revealed PM .40 1.00
❑ 38 Prince Xizor PM 1.50 4.00
❑ 39 Pulsar Skate PM .40 1.00
❑ 40 Sense and Recoil In Fear PM .60 1.50
❑ 41 Sense and Uncertain Is The Future PM .60 1.50
❑ 42 Shocking Information and Grimtaash PM .40 1.00
❑ 43 Sniper and Dark Strike PM .40 1.00
❑ 44 Snoova PM 1.00 2.50
❑ 45 Sorry About The Mess and .60 1.50
Blaster Proficiency PM
❑ 46 Slinger PM .40 1.00
❑ 47 Sunsdown and Too Cold For Speeders PM .40 1.00
❑ 48 Talon Karrde PM .60 1.50
❑ 49 The Bith Shuffle and Desperate Reach PM .40 1.00
❑ 50 The Emperor PM 1.50 4.00
❑ 51 Vigo PM 1.50 4.00
❑ 52 Virago PM .40 1.00
❑ 53 Watch Your Step .40 1.00
This Place Can Be A Little Rough PM
❑ 54 Yoda Stew and You Do Have Your Moments PM.40 1.00

2000 Star Wars Third Anthology

COMPLETE SET (6) 4.00 10.00

❑ 1 A New Secret Base PM 1.00 2.50
❑ 2 Artoo-Detoo In Red 5 PM 1.00 2.50
❑ 3 Echo Base Garrison PM 1.00 2.50
❑ 4 Massassi Base Operations// One In A Million PM1.00 2.50
❑ 5 Prisoner 2187 PM 1.00 2.50
❑ 6 Set Your Course For Alderaan 1.00 2.50
The Ultimate Power In The Universe PM

2001 Star Wars Coruscant

❑ 1 A Tragedy Has Occurred U .40 1.00
❑ 2 A Vergence In The Force U .40 1.00
❑ 3 Accepting Trade Federation Control U .40 1.00
❑ 4 Aks Moe R 1.25 3.00
❑ 5 All Wings Report In and Darklighter Spin R 6.00 15.00
❑ 6 Allegations Of Corruption U .40 1.00
❑ 7 Alter DARK U .40 1.00
❑ 8 Alter LIGHT U .40 1.00
❑ 9 Another Pathetic Lifeform U .40 1.00
❑ 10 Are You Brain Dead?! R 1.50 4.00
❑ 11 Ascertaining The Truth U .40 1.00
❑ 12 Baseless Accusations C .12 .30
❑ 13 Baskol Yeesrim U .40 1.00
❑ 14 Battle Droid Blaster Rifle C .12 .30
❑ 15 Battle Order and First Strike R 1.00 2.50
❑ 16 Battle Plan and Draw Their Fire R 1.50 4.00
❑ 17 Begin Landing Your Troops U .40 1.00
❑ 18 Blockade Flagship: Bridge R 3.00 8.00
❑ 19 Captain Madakor R 1.00 2.50
❑ 20 Captain Panaka R 1.00 2.50
❑ 21 Chokk U .40 1.00
❑ 22 Control DARK U .40 1.00
❑ 23 Control LIGHT U .40 1.00
❑ 24 Coruscant DARK C .12 .30
❑ 25 Coruscant LIGHT C .12 .30
❑ 26 Coruscant Guard DARK C .12 .30
❑ 27 Coruscant Guard LIGHT C .12 .30
❑ 28 Coruscant: Docking Bay DARK C .12 .30
❑ 29 Coruscant: Docking Bay LIGHT C .12 .30
❑ 30 Coruscant: Galactic Senate DARK C .12 .30
❑ 31 Coruscant: Galactic Senate LIGHT C .12 .30
❑ 32 Coruscant: Jedi Council Chamber R 3.00 8.00
❑ 33 Credits Will Do Fine C .12 .30
❑ 34 Darth Maul, Young Apprentice R 15.00 30.00
❑ 35 Daultay Dofine R 1.25 3.00
❑ 36 Depa Billaba R 1.25 3.00
❑ 37 Destroyer Droid R 12.00 25.00
❑ 38 Dioxis R 1.00 2.50
❑ 39 Do They Have A Code Clearance? R 1.00 2.50
❑ 40 Droid Starfighter C .12 .30
❑ 41 Drop! U .40 1.00
❑ 42 Edcel Bar Gane C .12 .30
❑ 43 Enter The Bureaucrat U .40 1.00
❑ 44 Establish Control U .40 1.00
❑ 45 Free Ride and Endor Celebration R 1.50 4.00
❑ 46 Freon Drevan U .40 1.00
❑ 47 Gardulla The Hutt U .40 1.00
❑ 48 Graxol Kelvyyn U .40 1.00
❑ 49 Grotto Werribee R 1.25 3.00
❑ 50 Gungan Warrior C .12 .30
❑ 51 Horox Ryyder C .12 .30
❑ 52 I Will Not Defer U .40 1.00
❑ 53 I've Decided To Go Back C .12 .30
❑ 54 Imperial Arrest Order and Secret Plans R 3.00 8.00
❑ 55 Imperial Artillery R 3.00 8.00
❑ 56 Inconsequential Barriers C .12 .30
❑ 57 Insurrection and Aim High R 2.50 6.00
❑ 58 Jawa DARK C .12 .30
❑ 59 Jawa LIGHT C .12 .30
❑ 60 Keder The Black R 1.00 2.50
❑ 61 Ki-Adi-Mundi U .40 1.00
❑ 62 Kill Them Immediately C .12 .30
❑ 63 Lana Dobreed U .40 1.00
❑ 64 Laser Cannon Battery U .40 1.00
❑ 65 Liana Merian U .40 1.00
❑ 66 Lieutenant Williams U .40 1.00
❑ 67 Little Real Power C .12 .30
❑ 68 Lott Dod R 1.25 3.00
❑ 69 Mace Windu R 10.00 20.00
❑ 70 Malastare DARK U .40 1.00
❑ 71 Malastare LIGHT U .40 1.00
❑ 72 Mas Amedda U .40 1.00
❑ 73 Master Qui-Gon R 3.00 8.00
❑ 74 Masterful Move and Endor Occupation R 2.00 5.00
❑ 75 Maul Strikes R 2.00 5.00
❑ 76 Maul's Sith Infiltrator R 3.00 8.00
❑ 77 Might Of The Republic R 2.50 6.00
❑ 78 Mind Tricks Don't Work On Me U .40 1.00
❑ 79 Mindful Of The Future C .12 .30
❑ 80 Motion Supported U .40 1.00
❑ 81 Murr Danod R 1.00 2.50
❑ 82 My Lord, Is That Legal? / I Will Make It Legal U.40 1.00
❑ 83 My Loyal Bodyguard U .40 1.00
❑ 84 Naboo Blaster C .12 .30
❑ 85 Naboo Blaster Rifle DARK C .12 .30
❑ 86 Naboo Blaster Rifle LIGHT C .12 .30
❑ 87 Naboo Defense Fighter C .12 .30
❑ 88 Naboo Fighter Pilot C .12 .30
❑ 89 Naboo Security Officer Blaster C .12 .30
❑ 90 Naboo DARK U .40 1.00
❑ 91 Naboo LIGHT U .40 1.00
❑ 92 Naboo: Battle Plains DARK C .12 .30
❑ 93 Naboo: Battle Plains LIGHT C .12 .30
❑ 94 Naboo: Swamp DARK C .12 .30
❑ 95 Naboo: Swamp LIGHT C .12 .30
❑ 96 Naboo: Theed Palace Courtyard DARK C .12 .30
❑ 97 Naboo: Theed Palace Courtyard LIGHT C .12 .30
❑ 98 Naboo: Theed Palace Docking Bay DARK C .12 .30
❑ 99 Naboo: Theed Palace Docking Bay LIGHT C .12 .30
❑ 100 Naboo: Theed Palace Throne Room DARK C .12 .30
❑ 101 Naboo: Theed Palace Throne Room LIGHT C .12 .30
❑ 102 Neimoidian Advisor U .40 1.00
❑ 103 Neimoidian Pilot C .12 .30
❑ 104 New Leadership Is Needed C .12 .30
❑ 105 No Civility, Only Politics C .12 .30
❑ 106 No Money, No Parts .40 1.00
No Deal! / You're A Slave? U
❑ 107 Nute Gunray R 1.00 2.50
❑ 108 Odin Nesloor U .40 1.00
❑ 109 On The Payroll Of The Trade Federation C .12 .30
❑ 110 Orn Free Taa C .12 .30
❑ 111 Our Blockade Is Perfectly Legal U .40 1.00
❑ 112 P-59 R 3.00 8.00
❑ 113 P-60 R 1.50 4.00
❑ 114 Panaka's Blaster R 1.25 3.00
❑ 115 Passel Argente C .12 .30
❑ 116 Phylo Gandish R 1.50 4.00
❑ 117 Plea To The Court U .40 1.00
❑ 118 Plead My Case To The Senate .40 1.00
Sanity And Compassion U
❑ 119 Plo Koon R 3.00 8.00
❑ 120 Queen Amidala, Ruler Of Naboo R 5.00 10.00
❑ 121 Queen's Royal Starship R 1.25 3.00
❑ 122 Radiant VII R 1.50 4.00
❑ 123 Rebel Artillery R 3.00 8.00
❑ 124 Republic Cruiser C .12 .30
❑ 125 Reveal Ourselves To The Jedi C .12 .30
❑ 126 Ric Olie R 1.00 2.50
❑ 127 Rune Haako R 1.00 2.50
❑ 128 Sabe R 1.25 3.00
❑ 129 Sache U .40 1.00
❑ 130 Secure Route U .40 1.00
❑ 131 Security Battle Droid C .12 .30
❑ 132 Security Control U .40 1.00
❑ 133 Sei Taria U .40 1.00
❑ 134 Senator Palpatine (head and shoulders) R 3.00 8.00
❑ 135 Senator Palpatine (head shot) R 15.00 30.00
❑ 136 Sense DARK U .40 1.00
❑ 137 Sense LIGHT U .40 1.00
❑ 138 Short Range Fighters and Watch Your Back! R2.50 6.00
❑ 139 Speak With The Jedi Council R 3.00 8.00
❑ 140 Squabbling Delegates R 1.25 3.00
❑ 141 Stay Here, Where It's Safe C .12 .30
❑ 142 Supreme Chancellor Valorum R 1.00 2.50
❑ 143 Tatooine DARK U .40 1.00
❑ 144 Tatooine LIGHT U .40 1.00
❑ 145 Tatooine: Marketplace DARK C .12 .30
❑ 146 Tatooine: Marketplace LIGHT C .12 .30
❑ 147 Tatooine: Mos Espa Docking Bay DARK C .12 .30
❑ 148 Tatooine: Mos Espa Docking Bay LIGHT C .12 .30
❑ 149 Tatooine: Watto's Junkyard DARK C .12 .30
❑ 150 Tatooine: Watto's Junkyard LIGHT C .12 .30
❑ 151 TC-14 R 1.00 2.50
❑ 152 Televan Koreyy R 1.00 2.50
❑ 153 Tendau Bendon U .40 1.00
❑ 154 Tey How U .40 1.00
❑ 155 The Gravest Of Circumstances U .40 1.00
❑ 156 The Hyperdrive Generator's Gone .40 1.00
We'll Need A New One U
❑ 157 The Phantom Menace R 5.00 10.00
❑ 158 The Point Is Conceded C .12 .30
❑ 159 They Will Be No Match For You R 1.00 2.50
❑ 160 They're Still Coming Through! U .40 1.00
❑ 161 This Is Outrageous! U .40 1.00
❑ 162 Thrown Back C .12 .30
❑ 163 Tikkes C .12 .30
❑ 164 Toonbuck Toora U .40 1.00
❑ 165 Trade Federation Battleship U .40 1.00
❑ 166 Trade Federation Droid Control Ship R 1.25 3.00
❑ 167 Tusken Raider C .12 .30
❑ 168 Vote Now! DARK R 1.00 2.50
❑ 169 Vote Now! LIGHT R 1.25 3.00
❑ 170 We Must Accelerate Our Plans R 10.00 20.00
❑ 171 We Wish To Board At Once R 2.00 5.00
❑ 172 We're Leaving C .12 .30
❑ 173 Wipe Them Out, All Of Them U .40 1.00
❑ 174 Yade M'rak U .40 1.00
❑ 175 Yané U .40 1.00
❑ 176 Yarua U .40 1.00
❑ 177 Yeb Yeb Adem'thorn C .12 .30
❑ 178 Yoda, Senior Council Member R 2.50 6.00
❑ 179 You Cannot Hide Forever and 2.50 6.00
Mobilization Points R
❑ 180 You've Got A Lot Of Guts Coming Here R 1.25 3.00
❑ 181 Your Insight Serves 1.00 2.50
You Well and Staging Areas R
❑ 182 Coruscant Dark Side List 1 .12 .30
❑ 183 Coruscant Dark Side List 2 .12 .30
❑ 184 Coruscant Light Side List 1 .12 .30
❑ 185 Coruscant Light Side List 2 .12 .30
❑ 186 Coruscant Rule Card 1 .12 .30
❑ 187 Coruscant Rule Card 2 .12 .30
❑ 188 Coruscant Rule Card 3 .12 .30

TCG/CCG

2001 Star Wars Reflections III

BOOSTER BOX (30) 250.00 350.00
BOOSTER PACK 7.50 15.00

❏ 1 A Close Race PM 1.00 2.50
❏ 2 A Remote Planet PM 1.00 2.50
❏ 3 A Tragedy Has Occured PM 1.25 3.00
❏ 4 A Useless Gesture PM 1.00 2.50
❏ 5 Aim High PM 1.25 3.00
❏ 6 Allegations of Coruption PM 1.00 2.50
❏ 7 An Unusual Amount Of Fear PM 1.00 2.50
❏ 8 Another Pathetic Lifeform PM 1.00 2.50
❏ 9 Armament Dismantled PM 1.00 2.50
❏ 10 Battle Order PM 1.00 2.50
❏ 11 Battle Plan PM 1.25 3.00
❏ 12 Bib Fortuna PM 1.00 2.50
❏ 13 Blizzard 4 PM 2.00 5.00
❏ 14 Blockade Flagship: Hallway PM 1.00 2.50
❏ 15 Blow Parried PM 1.00 2.50
❏ 16 Boba Fett, Bounty Hunter PM 6.00 12.00
❏ 17 Chewie, Enraged PM 1.50 4.00
❏ 18 Clinging To The Edge PM 1.00 2.50
❏ 19 Colo Claw Fish DARK PM 1.00 2.50
❏ 20 Colo Claw Fish LIGHT PM 1.00 2.50
❏ 21 Come Here You Big Coward PM 1.25 3.00
❏ 22 Conduct Your Search PM 1.25 3.00
❏ 23 Crossfire PM 1.00 2.50
❏ 24 Dark Rage PM 1.00 2.50
❏ 25 Darth Maul's Demise PM 1.00 2.50
❏ 26 Deep Hatred PM 1.00 2.50
❏ 27 Desperate Times PM 1.00 2.50
❏ 28 Diversionary Tactics PM 1.00 2.50
❏ 29 Do They Have A Code Clearance? PM 1.25 3.00
❏ 30 Do, Or Do Not PM 1.00 2.50
❏ 31 Don't Do That Again PM 1.00 2.50
❏ 32 Echo Base Sensors PM 1.25 3.00
❏ 33 Energy Walls DARK PM 1.00 2.50
❏ 34 Energy Walls LIGHT PM 1.00 2.50
❏ 35 Ewok Celebration PM 1.00 2.50
❏ 36 Fall Of A Jedi PM 1.00 2.50
❏ 37 Fanfare PM 1.00 2.50
❏ 38 Fear Is My Ally PM 1.00 2.50
❏ 39 Force Push PM 1.25 3.00
❏ 40 Han, Chewie, and The Falcon PM 6.00 12.00
❏ 41 He Can Go About His Business PM 1.00 2.50
❏ 42 Horace Vancil PM 1.00 2.50
❏ 43 Inner Strength PM 1.00 2.50
❏ 44 Jabba Desilijic Tiure PM 1.00 2.50
❏ 45 Jar Jar's Electropole PM 1.00 2.50
❏ 46 Jedi Leap PM 1.00 2.50
❏ 47 Lando Calrissian, Scoundrel PM 2.00 5.00
❏ 48 Lando's Not A System, He's A Man PM 1.00 2.50
❏ 49 Leave them to Me PM 1.00 2.50
❏ 50 Leia, Rebel Princess PM 2.50 6.00
❏ 51 Let's Keep A Little Optimism Here PM 1.00 2.50
❏ 52 Lord Maul PM 7.50 15.00
❏ 53 Maul's Double-Bladed Lightsaber PM 2.00 5.00
❏ 54 Naboo: Theed Palace Generator Core DARK PM1.00 2.50
❏ 55 Naboo: Theed Palace Generator Core LIGHT PM1.00 2.50
❏ 56 Naboo: Theed Palace Generator DARK PM 1.00 2.50
❏ 57 Naboo: Theed Palace Generator LIGHT PM 1.00 2.50
❏ 58 No Escape PM 1.00 2.50
❏ 59 No Match For A Sith PM 1.00 2.50
❏ 60 Obi-Wan Kenobi, Jedi Knight PM 1.50 4.00
❏ 61 Obi-Wan's Lightsaber PM 1.00 2.50
❏ 62 Only Jedi Carry That Weapon PM 1.00 2.50
❏ 63 Opee Sea Killer DARK PM 1.00 2.50
❏ 64 Opee Sea Killer LIGHT PM 1.00 2.50
❏ 65 Oppressive Enforcement PM 1.00 2.50
❏ 66 Ounee Ta PM 1.00 2.50
❏ 67 Planetary Defenses PM 1.00 2.50
❏ 68 Prepare For A Surface Attack PM 1.00 2.50
❏ 69 Qui-Gon Jinn, Jedi Master PM 2.50 6.00
❏ 70 Qui-Gon's End PM 1.25 3.00
❏ 71 Reistance PM 1.00 2.50
❏ 72 Sando Aqua Monster DARK PM 1.00 2.50
❏ 73 Sando Aqua Monster LIGHT PM 1.00 2.50
❏ 74 Secret Plans PM 1.00 2.50
❏ 75 Sio Bibble PM 1.00 2.50
❏ 76 Stormtrooper Garrison PM 5.00 10.00
❏ 77 Strike Blockaded PM 1.00 2.50
❏ 78 The Ebb Of Battle PM 1.00 2.50
❏ 79 The Hutts Are Gangsters PM 1.00 2.50
❏ 80 There Is No Try PM 1.25 3.00
❏ 81 They Must Never Again Leave This City PM 1.00 2.50
❏ 82 Thok and Thug PM 1.00 2.50
❏ 83 Through The Corridor PM 1.00 2.50
❏ 84 Ultimatum PM 1.00 2.50
❏ 85 Unsalvageable PM 1.00 2.50
❏ 86 We'll Let Fate-a Decide, Huh? PM 1.00 2.50
❏ 87 Weapon Of A Fallen Mentor PM 1.00 2.50
❏ 88 Weapon Of A Sith PM 1.00 2.50
❏ 89 Where Are Those Droidekas?! PM 1.00 2.50
❏ 90 Wipe Them Out, All Of Them PM 1.00 2.50
❏ 91 Wise Advice PM 1.00 2.50
❏ 92 Yoda, Master Of The Force PM 5.00 10.00
❏ 93 You Cannot Hide Forever PM 1.00 2.50
❏ 94 You've Never Won A Race? PM 1.00 2.50
❏ 95 Your Insight Serves You Well PM 1.00 2.50
❏ 96 Your Ship? PM 1.25 3.00

2001 Star Wars Tatooine

BOOSTER BOX (30) 50.00 100.00
BOOSTER PACK 2.50 5.00

❏ 1 A Jedi's Concentration C .12 .30
❏ 2 A Jedi's Focus C .12 .30
❏ 3 A Jedi's Patience C .12 .30
❏ 4 A Jedi's Resilience U .40 1.00
❏ 5 A Million Voices Crying Out R .75 2.00
❏ 6 A Step Backward U .40 1.00
❏ 7 Anakin's Podracer R .75 2.00
❏ 8 Aurra Sing R 1.50 4.00
❏ 9 Ben Quadinaros' Podracer C .12 .30
❏ 10 Boonta Eve Podrace DARK R .75 2.50
❏ 11 Boonta Eve Podrace LIGHT R .75 2.00
❏ 12 Brisky Morning Munchen R .75 2.00
❏ 13 Caldera Righim C .12 .30
❏ 14 Changing The Odds C .12 .30
❏ 15 Daroe R .75 2.00
❏ 16 Darth Maul R 1.50 4.00
❏ 17 Deneb Both U .40 1.00
❏ 18 Don't Do That Again C .12 .30
❏ 19 Dud Bolt's Podracer C .12 .30
❏ 20 Either Way, You Win U .40 1.00
❏ 21 End Of A Reign R .75 2.00
❏ 22 Entering The Arena U .40 1.00
❏ 23 Eopie C .12 .30
❏ 24 Eventually You'll Lose U .40 1.00
❏ 25 Fanfare C .12 .30
❏ 26 Gamall Wironicc U .40 1.00
❏ 27 Ghana Gleemort U .40 1.00
❏ 28 Gragra U .40 1.00
❏ 29 Great Shot, Kid! R .75 2.00
❏ 30 Grugnak U .40 1.00
❏ 31 His Name Is Anakin C .12 .30
❏ 32 Hit Racer U .40 1.00
❏ 33 I Can't Believe He's Gone C .12 .30
❏ 34 I Did It! R .75 2.00
❏ 35 I Will Find Them Quickly, Master R .75 2.00
❏ 36 I'm Sorry R .75 2.00
❏ 37 If The Trace Was Correct U .40 1.00
❏ 38 Jar Jar Binks R .75 2.00
❏ 39 Jedi Escape C .12 .30
❏ 40 Join Me! U .40 1.00
❏ 41 Keeping The Empire Out Forever R .75 2.00
❏ 42 Lathe U .40 1.00
❏ 43 Lightsaber Parry C .12 .30
❏ 44 Loci Rosen U .40 1.00
❏ 45 Losing Track C .12 .30
❏ 46 Maul's Electrobinoculars C .12 .30
❏ 47 Maul's Lightsaber R .75 2.00
❏ 48 Neck And Neck U .40 1.00
❏ 49 Ni Chuba Na?? C .12 .30
❏ 50 Obi-wan Kenobi, Padawan Learner R 1.00 2.50
❏ 51 Padme Naberrie R 2.00 5.00
❏ 52 Pit Crews U .40 1.00
❏ 53 Pit Droid C .12 .30
❏ 54 Podrace Prep U .40 1.00
❏ 55 Podracer Collision U .40 1.00
❏ 56 Quietly Observing U .40 1.00
❏ 57 Qui-Gon Jinn R 1.50 4.00
❏ 58 Qui-Gon Jinn's Lightsaber R 1.00 2.50
❏ 59 Rachalt Hyst U .40 1.00
❏ 60 Sebulba R .75 2.00
❏ 61 Sebulba's Podracer R .75 2.00
❏ 62 Shmi Skywalker R .75 2.00
❏ 63 Sith Fury C .12 .30
❏ 64 Sith Probe Droid R 1.00 2.50
❏ 65 Start Your Engines! U .40 1.00
❏ 66 Tatooine: City Outskirts U .40 1.00
❏ 67 Tatooine: Desert Landing Site R .75 2.00
❏ 68 Tatooine: Mos Espa DARK C .12 .30
❏ 69 Tatooine: Mos Espa LIGHT C .12 .30
❏ 70 Tatooine: Podrace Arena DARK C .12 .30
❏ 71 Tatooine: Podrace Arena LIGHT C .12 .30
❏ 72 Tatooine: Podracer Bay C .12 .30
❏ 73 Tatooine: Slave Quarters U .40 1.00
❏ 74 Teemto Pagalies' Podracer C .12 .30
❏ 75 The Camp C .12 .30
❏ 76 The Shield Is Down! R .75 2.00
❏ 77 There Is No Conflict C .12 .30
❏ 78 Threepio With His Parts Showing R 1.25 3.00
❏ 79 Too Close For Comfort U .40 1.00
❏ 80 Vader's Anger C .12 .30
❏ 81 Watto R 1.25 3.00
❏ 82 Watto's Box C .12 .30
❏ 83 Watto's Chance Cube U .40 1.00
❏ 84 We Shall Double Our Efforts! R .75 2.00
❏ 85 What Was It U .40 1.00
❏ 86 Yotts Orren U .40 1.00
❏ 87 You May Start Your Landing R .75 2.00
❏ 88 You Swindled Me! U .40 1.00
❏ 89 You Want This, Don't You? C .12 .30
❏ 90 You'll Find I'm Full Of Surprises U .40 1.00
❏ 91 Tatooine Dark Side List .12 .30
❏ 92 Tatooine Light Side List .12 .30
❏ 93 Tatooine Rule Card 1 .12 .30
❏ 94 Tatooine Rule Card 2 .12 .30
❏ 95 Tatooine Rule Card 3 .12 .30

2001 Star Wars Theed Palace

❏ 1 3B3-10 U .30 .75
❏ 2 3B3-1204 U .30 .75
❏ 3 3B3-21 U .30 .75
❏ 4 3B3-888 U .30 .75
❏ 5 AAT Assault Leader R 1.00 2.50
❏ 6 AAT Laser Cannon U .30 .75
❏ 7 Activate The Droids C .12 .30
❏ 8 After Her! R .75 2.00
❏ 9 Amidala's Blaster R .75 2.00
❏ 10 Armored Attack Tank U .30 .75
❏ 11 Artoo, Brave Little Droid R 1.50 4.00
❏ 12 Ascension Guns U .30 .75
❏ 13 At Last We Are Getting Results C .12 .30
❏ 14 Battle Droid Officer C .12 .30
❏ 15 Battle Droid Pilot C .12 .30
❏ 16 Big Boomers! C .12 .30
❏ 17 Blockade Flaghip R 1.50 4.00
❏ 18 Blockade Flagship: Docking Bay DARK U .30 .75
❏ 19 Blockade Flagship: Docking Bay LIGHT U .30 .75
❏ 20 Bok Askol U .30 .75
❏ 21 Booma C .12 .30
❏ 22 Boss Nass R 1.25 3.00
❏ 23 Bravo 1 R .75 2.00
❏ 24 Bravo 2 U .30 .75
❏ 25 Bravo 3 U .30 .75
❏ 26 Bravo 4 U .30 .75
❏ 27 Bravo 5 U .30 .75
❏ 28 Bravo Fighter R .75 2.00
❏ 29 Captain Tarpals R .75 2.00
❏ 30 Captain Tarpals' Electropole C .12 .30
❏ 31 Captian Daultay Dofine R .75 2.00
❏ 32 Cease Fire! C .12 .30
❏ 33 Corporal Rushing U .30 .75
❏ 34 Dams Denna U .30 .75
❏ 35 Darth Maul With Lightsaber R 12.00 25.00
❏ 36 Darth Sidious R 25.00 50.00
❏ 37 DFS Squadron Starfighter C .12 .30
❏ 38 DFS-1015 U .30 .75
❏ 39 DFS-1308 R .75 2.00
❏ 40 DFS-327 C .12 .30
❏ 41 Droid Racks R 1.25 3.00
❏ 42 Droid Starfighter Laser Cannons C .12 .30
❏ 43 Drop Your Weapons C .12 .30
❏ 44 Electropole C .12 .30
❏ 45 Energy Shell Launchers C .12 .30
❏ 46 Fambaa C .12 .30
❏ 47 Fighters Straight Ahead U .30 .75
❏ 48 General Jar Jar R 1.25 3.00
❏ 49 Get To Your Ships! C .12 .30
❏ 50 Gian Speeder C .12 .30
❏ 51 Gimme A Lift! R .75 2.00
❏ 52 Gungan Energy Shield C .12 .30
❏ 53 Gungan General C .12 .30
❏ 54 Gungan Guard C .12 .30
❏ 55 Halt! C .12 .30
❏ 56 I'll Try Spinning R .75 2.00
❏ 57 Infantry Battle Droid C .12 .30
❏ 58 Invasion / In Complete Control U .30 .75
❏ 59 It's On Automatic Pilot C .12 .30
❏ 60 Jerus Jannick U .30 .75
❏ 61 Kaadu C .12 .30
❏ 62 Let's Go Left R .75 2.00
❏ 63 Lieutenant Arven Wendik U .30 .75
❏ 64 Lieutenant Chamberlyn U .30 .75
❏ 65 Lieutenant Rya Kirsch U .30 .75
❏ 66 Mace Windu, Jedi Master R 7.50 15.00
❏ 67 Master, Destroyers! R 1.00 2.50
❏ 68 Multi Troop Transport U .30 .75
❏ 69 Naboo Celebration R .75 2.00
❏ 70 Naboo Occupation R 1.00 2.50
❏ 71 Naboo: Boss Nass's Chambers U .30 .75
❏ 72 Naboo: Otoh Gunga Entrance U .30 .75
❏ 73 Naboo: Theed Palace Hall U .30 .75
❏ 74 Naboo: Theed Palace Hallway U .30 .75
❏ 75 No Giben Up, General Jar Jar! R .75 2.00
❏ 76 Nothing Can Get Through Are Shield R 1.00 2.50
❏ 77 Nute Gunray, Neimoidian Viceroy R 2.00 5.00
❏ 78 Officer Dolphe U .30 .75
❏ 79 Officer Ellberger U .30 .75
❏ 80 Officer Perosei U .30 .75
❏ 81 OOM-9 U .30 .75
❏ 82 Open Fire! C .12 .30
❏ 83 OWO-1 With Backup R 1.25 3.00
❏ 84 Panaka, Protector Of The Queen R 2.50 6.00
❏ 85 Proton Torpedoes C .12 .30
❏ 86 Queen Amidala R 10.00 20.00
❏ 87 Qui-Gon Jinn With Lightsaber R 7.50 15.00
❏ 88 Rayno Vaca U .30 .75
❏ 89 Rep Been U .30 .75
❏ 90 Ric Olie, Bravo Leader R .75 2.00
❏ 91 Rolling, Rolling, Rolling R 1.00 2.50
❏ 92 Royal Naboo Security Officer C .12 .30
❏ 93 Rune Haako, Legal Counsel R 1.25 3.00
❏ 94 Senate Hovercam DARK R 1.00 2.50
❏ 95 Senate Hovercam LIGHT R 1.00 2.50
❏ 96 Sil Unch U .30 .75
❏ 97 Single Trooper Aerial Platform C .12 .30
❏ 98 SSA-1015 U .30 .75
❏ 99 SSA-306 U .30 .75
❏ 100 SSA-719 R 1.25 3.00
❏ 101 STAP Blaster Cannons C .12 .30
❏ 102 Steady, Steady C .12 .30
❏ 103 Take Them Away C .12 .30
❏ 104 Take This! C .12 .30
❏ 105 Tank Commander C .12 .30
❏ 106 The Deflector Shield Is Too Strong R .75 2.00
❏ 107 There They Are! U .30 .75
❏ 108 They Win This Round R .75 2.00
❏ 109 This Is Not Good C .12 .30
❏ 110 Trade Federation Landing Craft C .12 .30
❏ 111 TT-6 R 1.00 2.50
❏ 112 TT-9 R .75 2.00
❏ 113 We Didn't Hit It C .12 .30
❏ 114 We Don't Have Time For This R 1.00 2.50
❏ 115 We Have A Plan .12 .30
They Will Be Lost And Confused C
❏ 116 We're Hit Artoo C .12 .30
❏ 117 Wesa Gotta Grand Army C .12 .30
❏ 118 Wesa Ready To Do Our-sa Part C .12 .30
❏ 119 Whoooo! C .12 .30
❏ 120 Theed Palace Dark Side List .12 .30
❏ 121 Theed Palace Light Side List .12 .30

2002 Star Wars A New Hope

*FOIL: .8X TO 2X BASIC CARDS
BOOSTER BOX (36 PACKS) 25.00 50.00
BOOSTER PACK (11 CARDS) 1.50 3.00

❏ 1 Admiral Motti (A) R .60 1.50
❏ 2 Beru Lars (A) R .60 1.50
❏ 3 Blaster Barrage R .60 1.50
❏ 4 Capture the Falcon R .60 1.50
❏ 5 Contingency Plan R .60 1.50
❏ 6 Dannik Jerriko (A) R .60 1.50
❏ 7 Darth Vader (A) R 1.25 3.00
❏ 8 Desperate Confrontation R .75 2.00
❏ 9 Destroy Alderaan R .60 1.50
❏ 10 Dianoga (A) R .60 1.50
❏ 11 Disturbance in the Force R .60 1.50
❏ 12 It's Not Over Yet R .60 1.50
❏ 13 EG-6 Power Droid R .60 1.50
❏ 14 Elite Stormtrooper Squad R .60 1.50
❏ 15 Figrin D'an (A) R .75 2.00
❏ 16 Greedo (A) R .60 1.50
❏ 17 Hold 'Em Off R .60 1.50
❏ 18 Imperial Blockade R .60 1.50
❏ 19 Imperial Navy Helmsman R .60 1.50
❏ 20 Imperial Sentry Droid R .60 1.50
❏ 21 IT-0 Interrogator Droid R .75 2.00
❏ 22 Jawa Leader R .60 1.50
❏ 23 Krayt Dragon R .60 1.50
❏ 24 Leia's Kiss R .60 1.50
❏ 25 Luke Skywalker (B) R .60 1.50
❏ 26 Luke Skywalker (A) R .60 1.58
❏ 27 Luke's Speeder (A) R .60 1.50
❏ 28 Luke's X-Wing (A) R .60 1.50
❏ 29 Momaw Nadon (A) R 1.00 2.50
❏ 30 Most Desperate Hour R .60 1.50
❏ 31 No Escape R .60 1.50
❏ 32 Obi-Wan Kenobi (E) R .60 1.50
❏ 33 Obi-Wan's Prowess R .60 1.50
❏ 34 Obi-Wan's Task R .60 1.50
❏ 35 Our Only Hope R .60 1.50
❏ 36 Owen Lars (A) R .60 1.50
❏ 37 Plan of Attack R .60 1.50
❏ 38 Princess Leia (A) R .60 1.50
❏ 39 Protection of the Master R .60 1.50
❏ 40 R5-D4 (A) R .60 1.50
❏ 41 Rebel Crew Chief R .60 1.50
❏ 42 Rebel Lieutenant R .60 1.50
❏ 43 Regroup on Yavin R .60 1.50
❏ 44 Sandtrooper R .60 1.50
❏ 45 Starfighter's End R .60 1.50
❏ 46 Stormtrooper TK-421 R .60 1.50
❏ 47 Strategy Session R .60 1.50
❏ 48 Strike Me Down R .60 1.50
❏ 49 Surprise Attack R .60 1.50
❏ 50 Tantive IV (A) R .60 1.50
❏ 51 Tarkin's Stench R .60 1.50
❏ 52 TIE Fighter Elite Pilot U .20 .50
❏ 53 Tiree (A) R .60 1.50
❏ 54 Tractor Beam R .60 1.50
❏ 55 URoRRuR'R'R (A) R .60 1.50
❏ 56 Imperial Manipulation R .60 1.50
❏ 57 Vader's Leadership R .60 1.50
❏ 58 Vader's TIE Fighter (A) R .60 1.50
❏ 59 Wedge Antilles (A) R .60 1.50
❏ 60 Yavin 4 Hangar Base R .60 1.50
❏ 61 Astromech Assistance U .20 .50
❏ 62 Benefits of Training U .20 .50
❏ 63 Biggs Darklighter (A) U .20 .50
❏ 64 C-3PO (C) U .20 .50
❏ 65 Commander Praji (A) U .20 .50
❏ 66 Tatooine Sandcrawler U .20 .50
❏ 67 Darth Vader (B) U .20 .50
❏ 68 Death Star Hangar Bay U .20 .50
❏ 69 Death Star Plans U .20 .50
❏ 70 Death Star Scanning Technician U .20 .50
❏ 71 Death Star Superlaser Gunner U .20 .50
❏ 72 Death Star Turbolaser Gunner U .20 .50
❏ 73 Demonstration of Power U .20 .50
❏ 74 Devastator (A) U .20 .50
❏ 75 Dissolve the Senate U .20 .50
❏ 76 Error in Judgment U .20 .50
❏ 77 Fate of the Dragon U .20 .50
❏ 78 General Dodonna (A) U .20 .50
❏ 79 General Tagge (A) U .20 .50
❏ 80 Han's Courage U .20 .50
❏ 81 Imperial Control Station U .20 .50
❏ 82 Imperial Navy Lieutenant U .20 .50
❏ 83 Insignificant Power U .20 .50
❏ 84 Into the Garbage Chute C .10 .25
❏ 85 Jawa U .20 .50
❏ 86 Jawa Collection Team U .20 .50
❏ 87 Jedi Extinction U .20 .50
❏ 88 Jon Dutch Vander (A) U .20 .50
❏ 89 Learning the Force U .20 .50
❏ 90 Lieutenant Tanbris (A) U .20 .50
❏ 91 LIN Demolitionmech U .20 .50
❏ 92 Luke Skywalker (C) U .20 .50
❏ 93 Luke's Warning U .20 .50
❏ 94 Mounted Stormtrooper U .20 .50
❏ 95 Mouse Droid U .20 .50
❏ 96 Obi-Wan Kenobi (F) U .20 .50
❏ 97 Oil Bath U .20 .50
❏ 98 Princess Leia (B) U .20 .50
❏ 99 R2-D2 (C) U .20 .50
❏ 100 Rebel Blockade Runner U .20 .50
❏ 101 Rebel Control Officer U .20 .50
❏ 102 Rebel Control Post U .20 .50
❏ 103 Rebel Marine U .20 .50
❏ 104 Rebel Surrender U .20 .50
❏ 105 Rebel Trooper U .20 .50
❏ 106 Remote Seeker Droid U .20 .50
❏ 107 Press the Advantage U .20 .50
❏ 108 Stabilize Deflectors U .20 .50
❏ 109 Star Destroyer Commander U .20 .50
❏ 110 Stormtrooper Charge U .20 .50
❏ 111 Stormtrooper DV-692 U .20 .50
❏ 112 Stormtrooper Squad Leader U .20 .50
❏ 113 Stormtrooper TK-119 U .20 .50
❏ 114 Support in the Senate U .20 .50
❏ 115 Disrupt the Power System U .20 .50
❏ 116 Tatooine Speeder U .20 .50
❏ 117 Tusken Sharpshooter U .20 .50
❏ 118 Vader's Interference U .20 .50
❏ 119 Vader's TIE Fighter (B) U .60 1.50
❏ 120 Wuher (A) U .20 .50
❏ 121 Air Cover C .10 .25
❏ 122 Precise Blast C .10 .25
❏ 123 Stay Sharp C .10 .25
❏ 124 Carrack Cruiser C .10 .25
❏ 125 Darth Vader (C) C .10 .25
❏ 126 Death Star Cannon Tower C .10 .25
❏ 127 Death Star Guard Squad C .10 .25
❏ 128 Domesticated Bantha C .10 .25
❏ 129 Flare-S Swoop C .10 .25
❏ 130 Ground Support C .10 .25
❏ 131 Imperial Detention Block C .10 .25
❏ 132 Imperial Star Destroyer C .10 .25
❏ 133 Incom T-16 Skyhopper C .10 .25
❏ 134 Into Hiding C .10 .25
❏ 135 Jawa Squad C .10 .25
❏ 136 Jawa Supply Trip C .10 .25
❏ 137 Jump to Lightspeed C .10 .25
❏ 138 Luke Skywalker (D) C .10 .25
❏ 139 Luke's Repairs C .10 .25
❏ 140 Moisture Farm C .10 .25
❏ 141 Planetary Defense Turret C .10 .25
❏ 142 Nowhere to Run C .10 .25
❏ 143 Obi-Wan Kenobi (G) C .10 .25
❏ 144 Jedi Intervention C .10 .25
❏ 145 Obi-Wan's Plan C .10 .25
❏ 146 Penetrate the Shields C .10 .25
❏ 147 Preemptive Shot C .10 .25
❏ 148 Princess Leia (C) C .10 .25
❏ 149 Rebel Fighter Wing C .10 .25
❏ 150 Rebel Honor Company C .10 .25
❏ 151 Rebel Marine Squad C .10 .25
❏ 152 Rebel Pilot C .10 .25
❏ 153 Rebel Squad C .10 .25
❏ 154 Rescue C .10 .25
❏ 155 Slipping Through C .10 .25
❏ 156 SoruSuub V-35 Courier C .10 .25
❏ 157 Synchronized Assault C .10 .25
❏ 158 Stormtrooper Assault Team C .10 .25
❏ 159 Stormtrooper DV-523 C .10 .25
❏ 160 Stormtrooper Patrol C .10 .25
❏ 161 Stormtrooper Squad C .10 .25
❏ 162 TIE Fighter DS-3-12 C .10 .25
❏ 163 TIE Fighter DS-73-3 C .10 .25
❏ 164 TIE Fighter DS-55-6 C .10 .25
❏ 165 TIE Fighter DS-61-9 C .10 .25
❏ 166 TIE Fighter Pilot C .10 .25
❏ 167 TIE Fighter Squad C .10 .25
❏ 168 Tusken Squad C .10 .25
❏ 169 Vader's Grip U .10 .25
❏ 170 Victory-Class Star Destroyer C .10 .25
❏ 171 Well-Aimed Shot C .10 .25
❏ 172 X-wing Red One C .10 .25
❏ 173 X-wing Red Three C .10 .25
❏ 174 X-wing Red Two C .10 .25
❏ 175 X-wing Attack Formation C .10 .25
❏ 176 Y-wing Gold One C .10 .25
❏ 177 Y-wing Gold Squadron C .10 .25
❏ 178 YT-1300 Transport C .10 .25
❏ 179 YV-664 Light Freighter C .10 .25
❏ 180 Z-95 Headhunter C .10 .25

2002 Star Wars A New Hope Foil

❏ 1 Admiral Motti (A) R 1.25 3.00
❏ 2 Beru Lars (A) R 1.25 3.00
❏ 3 Blaster Barrage R 1.25 3.00
❏ 4 Capture the Falcon R 1.25 3.00
❏ 5 Contingency Plan R 1.25 3.00
❏ 6 Dannik Jerriko (A) R 1.25 3.00
❏ 7 Darth Vader (A) R 2.50 6.00
❏ 8 Desperate Confrontation R 1.50 4.00
❏ 9 Destroy Alderaan R 1.25 3.00
❏ 10 Dianoga (A) R 1.25 3.00
❏ 11 Disturbance in the Force R 1.25 3.00
❏ 12 It's Not Over Yet R 1.25 3.00
❏ 13 EG-6 Power Droid R 1.25 3.00
❏ 14 Elite Stormtrooper Squad R 1.25 3.00
❏ 15 Figrin D'an (A) R 1.50 4.00
❏ 16 Greedo (A) R 1.25 3.00
❏ 17 Hold 'Em Off R 1.25 3.00

Card	Low	High
❑ 18 Imperial Blockade R	1.25	3.00
❑ 19 Imperial Navy Helmsman R	1.25	3.00
❑ 20 Imperial Sentry Droid R	1.25	3.00
❑ 21 IT-0 Interrogator Droid R	1.50	4.00
❑ 22 Jawa Leader R	1.25	3.00
❑ 23 Krayt Dragon R	1.25	3.00
❑ 24 Leia's Kiss R	1.25	3.00
❑ 25 Luke Skywalker (B) R	1.25	3.00
❑ 26 Luke Skywalker (A) R	1.25	3.00
❑ 27 Luke's Speeder (A) R	1.25	3.00
❑ 28 Luke's X-Wing (A) R	1.25	3.00
❑ 29 Momaw Nadon (A) R	2.00	5.00
❑ 30 Most Desperate Hour R	1.25	3.00
❑ 31 No Escape R	1.25	3.00
❑ 32 Obi-Wan Kenobi (E) R	1.25	3.00
❑ 33 Obi-Wan's Prowess R	1.25	3.00
❑ 34 Obi-Wan's Task R	1.25	3.00
❑ 35 Our Only Hope R	1.25	3.00
❑ 36 Owen Lars (A) R	1.25	3.00
❑ 37 Plan of Attack R	1.25	3.00
❑ 38 Princess Leia (A) R	1.25	3.00
❑ 39 Protection of the Master R	1.25	3.00
❑ 40 R5-D4 (A) R	1.25	3.00
❑ 41 Rebel Crew Chief R	1.25	3.00
❑ 42 Rebel Lieutenant R	1.25	3.00
❑ 43 Regroup on Yavin R	1.25	3.00
❑ 44 Sandtrooper R	1.25	3.00
❑ 45 Starfighter's End R	1.25	3.00
❑ 46 Stormtrooper TK-421 R	1.25	3.00
❑ 47 Strategy Session R	1.25	3.00
❑ 48 Strike Me Down R	1.25	3.00
❑ 49 Surprise Attack R	1.25	3.00
❑ 50 Tantive IV (A) R	1.25	3.00
❑ 51 Tarkin's Stench R	1.25	3.00
❑ 52 TIE Fighter Elite Pilot U	.40	1.00
❑ 53 Tiree (A) R	1.25	3.00
❑ 54 Tractor Beam R	1.25	3.00
❑ 55 URoRRuR'R'R (A) R	1.25	3.00
❑ 56 Imperial Manipulation R	1.25	3.00
❑ 57 Vader's Leadership R	1.25	3.00
❑ 58 Vader's TIE Fighter (A) R	1.25	3.00
❑ 59 Wedge Antilles (A) R	1.25	3.00
❑ 60 Yavin 4 Hangar Base R	1.25	3.00
❑ 61 Astromech Assistance U	.40	1.00
❑ 62 Benefits of Training U	.40	1.00
❑ 63 Biggs Darklighter (A) U	.40	1.00
❑ 64 C-3PO (C) U	.40	1.00
❑ 65 Commander Praji (A) U	.40	1.00
❑ 66 Tatooine Sandcrawler U	.40	1.00
❑ 67 Darth Vader (B) U	.40	1.00
❑ 68 Death Star Hangar Bay U	.40	1.00
❑ 69 Death Star Plans U	.40	1.00
❑ 70 Death Star Scanning Technician U	.40	1.00
❑ 71 Death Star Superlaser Gunner U	.40	1.00
❑ 72 Death Star Turbolaser Gunner U	.40	1.00
❑ 73 Demonstration of Power U	.40	1.00
❑ 74 Devastator (A) U	.40	1.00
❑ 75 Dissolve the Senate U	.40	1.00
❑ 76 Error in Judgment U	.40	1.00
❑ 77 Fate of the Dragon U	.40	1.00
❑ 78 General Dodonna (A) U	.40	1.00
❑ 79 General Tagge (A) U	.40	1.00
❑ 80 Han's Courage U	.40	1.00
❑ 81 Imperial Control Station U	.40	1.00
❑ 82 Imperial Navy Lieutenant U	.40	1.00
❑ 83 Insignificant Power U	.40	1.00
❑ 84 Into the Garbage Chute C	.20	.50
❑ 85 Jawa U	.40	1.00
❑ 86 Jawa Collection Team U	.40	1.00
❑ 87 Jedi Extinction U	.40	1.00
❑ 88 Jon Dutch Vander (A) U	.40	1.00
❑ 89 Learning the Force U	.40	1.00
❑ 90 Lieutenant Tanbris (A) U	.40	1.00
❑ 91 LIN Demolitionmech U	.40	1.00
❑ 92 Luke Skywalker (C) U	.40	1.00
❑ 93 Luke's Warning U	.40	1.00
❑ 94 Mounted Stormtrooper U	.40	1.00
❑ 95 Mouse Droid U	.40	1.00
❑ 96 Obi-Wan Kenobi (F) U	.40	1.00
❑ 97 Oil Bath U	.40	1.00
❑ 98 Princess Leia (B) U	.40	1.00
❑ 99 R2-D2 (C) U	.40	1.00
❑ 100 Rebel Blockade Runner U	.40	1.00
❑ 101 Rebel Control Officer U	.40	1.00
❑ 102 Rebel Control Post U	.40	1.00
❑ 103 Rebel Marine U	.40	1.00
❑ 104 Rebel Surrender U	.40	1.00
❑ 105 Rebel Trooper U	.40	1.00
❑ 106 Remote Seeker Droid U	.40	1.00
❑ 107 Press the Advantage U	.40	1.00
❑ 108 Stabilize Deflectors U	.40	1.00
❑ 109 Star Destroyer Commander U	.40	1.00
❑ 110 Stormtrooper Charge U	.40	1.00
❑ 111 Stormtrooper DV-692 U	.40	1.00
❑ 112 Stormtrooper Squad Leader U	.40	1.00
❑ 113 Stormtrooper TK-119 U	.40	1.00
❑ 114 Support in the Senate U	.40	1.00
❑ 115 Disrupt the Power System U	.40	1.00
❑ 116 Tatooine Speeder U	.40	1.00
❑ 117 Tusken Sharpshooter U	.40	1.00
❑ 118 Vader's Interference U	.40	1.00
❑ 119 Vader's TIE Fighter (B) U	1.25	3.00
❑ 120 Wuher (A) U	.40	1.00
❑ 121 Air Cover C	.20	.50
❑ 122 Precise Blast C	.20	.50
❑ 123 Stay Sharp C	.20	.50
❑ 124 Carrack Cruiser C	.20	.50
❑ 125 Darth Vader (C) C	.20	.50
❑ 126 Death Star Cannon Tower C	.20	.50
❑ 127 Death Star Guard Squad C	.20	.50
❑ 128 Domesticated Bantha C	.20	.50
❑ 129 Flare-S Swoop C	.20	.50
❑ 130 Ground Support C	.20	.50
❑ 131 Imperial Detention Block C	.20	.50
❑ 132 Imperial Star Destroyer C	.20	.50
❑ 133 Incom T-16 Skyhopper C	.20	.50
❑ 134 Into Hiding C	.20	.50
❑ 135 Jawa Squad C	.20	.50
❑ 136 Jawa Supply Trip C	.20	.50
❑ 137 Jump to Lightspeed C	.20	.50
❑ 138 Luke Skywalker (D) C	.20	.50
❑ 139 Luke's Repairs C	.20	.50
❑ 140 Moisture Farm C	.20	.50
❑ 141 Planetary Defense Turret C	.20	.50
❑ 142 Nowhere to Run C	.20	.50
❑ 143 Obi-Wan Kenobi (G) C	.20	.50
❑ 144 Jedi Intervention C	.20	.50
❑ 145 Obi-Wan's Plan C	.20	.50
❑ 146 Penetrate the Shields C	.20	.50
❑ 147 Preemptive Shot C	.20	.50
❑ 148 Princess Leia (C) C	.20	.50

Card	Low	High
❑ 149 Rebel Fighter Wing C	.20	.50
❑ 150 Rebel Honor Company C	.20	.50
❑ 151 Rebel Marine Squad C	.20	.50
❑ 152 Rebel Pilot C	.20	.50
❑ 153 Rebel Squad C	.20	.50
❑ 154 Rescue C	.20	.50
❑ 155 Slipping Through C	.20	.50
❑ 156 SoruSuub V-35 Courier C	.20	.50
❑ 157 Synchronized Assault C	.20	.50
❑ 158 Stormtrooper Assault Team C	.20	.50
❑ 159 Stormtrooper DV-523 C	.20	.50
❑ 160 Stormtrooper Patrol C	.20	.50
❑ 161 Stormtrooper Squad C	.20	.50
❑ 162 TIE Fighter DS-3-12 C	.20	.50
❑ 163 TIE Fighter DS-73-3 C	.20	.50
❑ 164 TIE Fighter DS-55-6 C	.20	.50
❑ 165 TIE Fighter DS-61-9 C	.20	.50
❑ 166 TIE Fighter Pilot C	.20	.50
❑ 167 TIE Fighter Squad C	.20	.50
❑ 168 Tusken Squad C	.20	.50
❑ 169 Vader's Grip U	.20	.50
❑ 170 Victory-Class Star Destroyer C	.20	.50
❑ 171 Well-Aimed Shot C	.20	.50
❑ 172 X-wing Red One C	.20	.50
❑ 173 X-wing Red Three C	.20	.50
❑ 174 X-wing Red Two C	.20	.50
❑ 175 X-wing Attack Formation C	.20	.50
❑ 176 Y-wing Gold One C	.20	.50
❑ 177 Y-wing Gold Squadron C	.20	.50
❑ 178 YT-1300 Transport C	.20	.50
❑ 179 YV-664 Light Freighter C	.20	.50
❑ 180 Z-95 Headhunter C	.20	.50

2002 Star Wars Attack of the Clones

Card	Low	High
BOOSTER BOX (36)	20.00	40.00
BOOSTER PACK	1.00	1.50
❑ 1 Anakin Skywalker (A) R	.60	1.50
❑ 2 Anakin Skywalker (B) R	.60	1.50
❑ 3 Assassin Droid ASN-121 (A) R	.60	1.50
❑ 4 Bail Organa (A) R	.60	1.50
❑ 5 Battle Fatigue R	.60	1.50
❑ 6 Boba Fett (A) R	.60	1.50
❑ 7 Captain Typho (A) R	.60	1.50
❑ 8 Clear the Skies R	.60	1.50
❑ 9 Clone Officer R	.60	1.50
❑ 10 Dark Rendezvous R	.60	1.50
❑ 11 Dark Side's Command R	.60	1.50
❑ 12 Dark Side's Compulsion R	.60	1.50
❑ 13 Darth Sidious (A) R	.60	1.50
❑ 14 Darth Tyranus (A) R	.60	1.50
❑ 15 Destruction of Hope R	.60	1.50
❑ 16 Dexter Jettster (A) R	.60	1.50
❑ 17 Geonosian Sentry R	.60	1.50
❑ 18 Hero's Duty R	.60	1.50
❑ 19 Hero's Flaw R	.60	1.50
❑ 20 Interference in the Senate R	.60	1.50
❑ 21 Jango Fett (A) R	.60	1.50
❑ 22 Jango Fett (B) R	.60	1.50
❑ 23 Jar Jar Binks (A) R	.60	1.50
❑ 24 Jedi Call for Help R	.60	1.50
❑ 25 Jedi Council Summons R	.60	1.50
❑ 26 Jedi Knight's Deflection R	.60	1.50
❑ 27 Lama Su (A) R	.60	1.50
❑ 28 Luxury Airspeeder U	.20	.50
❑ 29 A Moment's Rest R	.60	1.50
❑ 30 Naboo Defense Station R	.60	1.50
❑ 31 Obi-Wan Kenobi (A) R	.60	1.50
❑ 32 Obi-Wan's Starfighter (A) R	.60	1.50
❑ 33 Order Here R	.60	1.50
❑ 34 Padmé Amidala (A) R	.60	1.50
❑ 35 Padmé Amidala (B) R	.60	1.50
❑ 36 Padmé's Yacht (A) R	.60	1.50
❑ 37 Plo Koon (A) R	.60	1.50
❑ 38 Plot the Secession R	.60	1.50
❑ 39 Power Dive R	.60	1.50
❑ 40 Queen Jamillia (A) R	.60	1.50
❑ 41 R2-D2 (A) R	.60	1.50
❑ 42 San Hill (A) U	.20	.50
❑ 43 Second Effort R	.60	1.50
❑ 44 Seek the Council's Wisdom R	.60	1.50
❑ 45 Shu Mai (A) U	.20	.50
❑ 46 Slave I (A) R	.60	1.50
❑ 47 Spirit of the Fallen R	.60	1.50
❑ 48 Target the Senator R	.60	1.50
❑ 49 Taun We (A) R	.60	1.50
❑ 50 Trade Federation Battleship Core R	.60	1.50
❑ 51 Tyranus's Edict R	.60	1.50
❑ 52 Tyranus's Geonosian Speeder (A) R	.60	1.50
❑ 53 Tyranus's Solar Sailer (A) R	.60	1.50
❑ 54 Tyranus's Wrath R	.60	1.50
❑ 55 War Will Follow R	.60	1.50
❑ 56 Ward of the Jedi R	.60	1.50
❑ 57 Windu's Solution R	.60	1.50
❑ 58 Yoda (A) R	.60	1.50
❑ 59 Yoda's Intervention R	.60	1.50
❑ 60 Zam Wesell (A) R	.60	1.50
❑ 61 Acklay U	.20	.50
❑ 62 Anakin Skywalker (C) U	.20	.50
❑ 63 Anakin's Inspiration U	.20	.50
❑ 64 AT-TE Walker 23X U	.20	.50
❑ 65 AT-TE Walker 71E R	.60	1.50
❑ 66 Attract Enemy Fire U	.20	.50
❑ 67 C-3PO (A) U	.20	.50
❑ 68 Capture Obi-Wan U	.20	.50
❑ 69 Chancellor Palpatine (A) R	.60	1.50
❑ 70 Chase the Villain U	.20	.50
❑ 71 Cheat the Game U	.20	.50
❑ 72 Cliegg Lars (A) U	.20	.50
❑ 73 Clone Warrior 4/163 U	.20	.50
❑ 74 Clone Warrior 5/373 U	.20	.50
❑ 75 Commerce Guild Droid Platoon U	.20	.50
❑ 76 Cordé (A) U	.20	.50
❑ 77 Coruscant Freighter AA-9 (A) U	.20	.50
❑ 78 Dark Speed U	.20	.50
❑ 79 Darth Tyranus (B) U	.20	.50
❑ 80 Departure Time U	.20	.50
❑ 81 Destroyer Droid, P Series U	.20	.50
❑ 82 Down in Flames U	.20	.50
❑ 83 Droid Control Ship U	.20	.50
❑ 84 Elan Sleazebaggano (A) R	.60	1.50
❑ 85 Geonosian Guard U	.20	.50
❑ 86 Geonosian Warrior U	.20	.50
❑ 87 Go to the Temple U	.20	.50
❑ 88 Infantry Battle Droid, B1 Series U	.20	.50
❑ 89 Jango Fett (C) U	.20	.50
❑ 90 Jawa Sandcrawler U	.20	.50
❑ 91 Jedi Patrol U	.20	.50
❑ 92 Kaminoan Guard U	.20	.50
❑ 93 Kit Fisto (A) U	.20	.50
❑ 94 Master and Apprentice U	.20	.50
❑ 95 Naboo Security Guard U	.20	.50
❑ 96 Naboo Spaceport U	.20	.50
❑ 97 Nexu U	.20	.50
❑ 98 Nute Gunray (A) U	.20	.50
❑ 99 Obi-Wan Kenobi (B) U	.20	.50
❑ 100 Padmé Amidala (C) U	.20	.50
❑ 101 Poggle the Lesser (A) U	.20	.50
❑ 102 Reek U	.20	.50
❑ 103 Republic Assault Ship U	.20	.50
❑ 104 Republic Cruiser C	.10	.25
❑ 105 Shaak Ti (A) U	.20	.50
❑ 106 Ship Arrival U	.20	.50
❑ 107 Splinter the Republic U	.20	.50
❑ 108 Strength of Hate U	.20	.50
❑ 109 Subtle Assassination U	.20	.50
❑ 110 Super Battle Droid 8EX U	.20	.50
❑ 111 Trade Federation Battleship U	.20	.50
❑ 112 Trade Federation C-9979 U	.20	.50
❑ 113 Tyranus's Gift U	.20	.50
❑ 114 Underworld Connections U	.20	.50
❑ 115 Wat Tambor (A) U	.20	.50
❑ 116 Watto (A) U	.20	.50
❑ 117 Weapon Response U	.20	.50
❑ 118 Wedding of Destiny U	.20	.50
❑ 119 Yoda (B) U	.20	.50
❑ 120 Zam's Airspeeder (A) U	.20	.50
❑ 121 Anakin Skywalker (D) C	.10	.25
❑ 122 Battle Droid Squad C	.10	.25
❑ 123 Bravo N-1 Starfighter C	.10	.25
❑ 124 Chancellor's Guard Squad C	.10	.25
❑ 125 Clone Platoon C	.10	.25
❑ 126 Clone Squad C	.10	.25
❑ 127 Commerce Guild Droid 81 C	.10	.25
❑ 128 Commerce Guild Starship C	.10	.25
❑ 129 Corellian Star Shuttle C	.10	.25
❑ 130 Darth Tyranus (C) C	.10	.25
❑ 131 Destroyer Droid Squad C	.10	.25
❑ 132 Droid Starfighter DFS-4CT C	.10	.25
❑ 133 Droid Starfighter Squadron C	.10	.25
❑ 134 Droid Starfighter Wing C	.10	.25
❑ 135 Elite Jedi Squad C	.10	.25
❑ 136 Flying Geonosian Squad C	.10	.25
❑ 137 Geonosian Defense Platform C	.10	.25
❑ 138 Geonosian Fighter C	.10	.25
❑ 139 Geonosian Squad C	.10	.25
❑ 140 Gozanti Cruiser C	.10	.25
❑ 141 Hatch a Clone C	.10	.25
❑ 142 Hero's Dodge C	.10	.25
❑ 143 High-Force Dodge C	.10	.25
❑ 144 Hyperdrive Ring C	.10	.25
❑ 145 InterGalactic Banking Clan Starship C	.10	.25
❑ 146 Jango Fett (D) C	.10	.25
❑ 147 Jedi Starfighter 3R3 C	.10	.25
❑ 148 Knockdown C	.10	.25
❑ 149 Lost in the Asteroids C	.10	.25
❑ 150 Lull in the Fighting C	.10	.25
❑ 151 Mending C	.10	.25
❑ 152 N-1 Starfighter C	.10	.25
❑ 153 Naboo Cruiser C	.10	.25
❑ 154 Naboo Royal Starship C	.10	.25
❑ 155 Naboo Senatorial Escort C	.10	.25
❑ 156 Naboo Starfighter Squadron C	.10	.25
❑ 157 Obi-Wan Kenobi (C) C	.10	.25
❑ 158 Padawan's Deflection C	.10	.25
❑ 159 Padmé Amidala (D) C	.10	.25
❑ 160 Patrol Speeder C	.10	.25
❑ 161 Peace on Naboo C	.10	.25
❑ 162 Pilot's Dodge C	.10	.25
❑ 163 Recon Speeder U	.10	.25
❑ 164 Republic Attack Gunship UH-478 C	.10	.25
❑ 165 Repulsorlift Malfunction C	.10	.25
❑ 166 Return to Spaceport C	.10	.25
❑ 167 Rickshaw C	.10	.25
❑ 168 Slumming on Coruscant C	.10	.25
❑ 169 Sonic Shockwave C	.10	.25
❑ 170 Speeder Bike Squadron C	.10	.25
❑ 171 Starship Refit C	.10	.25
❑ 172 Surge of Power C	.10	.25
❑ 173 Swoop Bike C	.10	.25
❑ 174 Take the Initiative C	.10	.25
❑ 175 Target Locked C	.10	.25
❑ 176 Taylander Shuttle C	.10	.25
❑ 177 Techno Union Starship C	.10	.25
❑ 178 Trade Federation War Freighter C	.10	.25
❑ 179 Walking Droid Fighter C	.10	.25
❑ 180 Zam Wesell (B) C	.10	.25

2002 Star Wars Attack of the Clones Foil

Card	Low	High
❑ 1 Anakin Skywalker (A) R	1.25	3.00
❑ 2 Anakin Skywalker (B) R	1.25	3.00
❑ 3 Assassin Droid ASN-121 (A) R	1.25	3.00
❑ 4 Bail Organa (A) R	1.25	3.00
❑ 5 Battle Fatigue R	1.25	3.00
❑ 6 Boba Fett (A) R	1.25	3.00
❑ 7 Captain Typho (A) R	1.25	3.00
❑ 8 Clear the Skies R	1.25	3.00
❑ 9 Clone Officer R	1.25	3.00
❑ 10 Dark Rendezvous R	1.25	3.00
❑ 11 Dark Side's Command R	1.25	3.00
❑ 12 Dark Side's Compulsion R	1.25	3.00
❑ 13 Darth Sidious (A) R	1.25	3.00
❑ 14 Darth Tyranus (A) R	1.25	3.00
❑ 15 Destruction of Hope R	1.25	3.00
❑ 16 Dexter Jettster (A) R	1.25	3.00
❑ 17 Geonosian Sentry R	1.25	3.00
❑ 18 Hero's Duty R	1.25	3.00
❑ 19 Hero's Flaw R	1.25	3.00
❑ 20 Interference in the Senate R	1.25	3.00
❑ 21 Jango Fett (A) R	1.25	3.00
❑ 22 Jango Fett (B) R	1.25	3.00
❑ 23 Jar Jar Binks (A) R	1.25	3.00
❑ 24 Jedi Call for Help R	1.25	3.00
❑ 25 Jedi Council Summons R	1.25	3.00
❑ 26 Jedi Knight's Deflection R	1.25	3.00
❑ 27 Lama Su (A) R	1.25	3.00
❑ 28 Luxury Airspeeder U	.40	1.00
❑ 29 A Moment's Rest R	1.25	3.00
❑ 30 Naboo Defense Station R	1.25	3.00
❑ 31 Obi-Wan Kenobi (A) R	1.25	3.00
❑ 32 Obi-Wan's Starfighter (A) R	1.25	3.00
❑ 33 Order Here R	1.25	3.00
❑ 34 Padmé Amidala (A) R	1.25	3.00
❑ 35 Padmé Amidala (B) R	1.25	3.00
❑ 36 Padmé's Yacht (A) R	1.25	3.00
❑ 37 Plo Koon (A) R	1.25	3.00
❑ 38 Plot the Secession R	1.25	3.00
❑ 39 Power Dive R	1.25	3.00
❑ 40 Queen Jamillia (A) R	1.25	3.00
❑ 41 R2-D2 (A) R	1.25	3.00
❑ 42 San Hill (A) U	.40	1.00
❑ 43 Second Effort R	1.25	3.00
❑ 44 Seek the Council's Wisdom R	1.25	3.00
❑ 45 Shu Mai (A) U	.40	1.00
❑ 46 Slave I (A) R	1.25	3.00
❑ 47 Spirit of the Fallen R	1.25	3.00
❑ 48 Target the Senator R	1.25	3.00
❑ 49 Taun We (A) R	1.25	3.00
❑ 50 Trade Federation Battleship Core R	1.25	3.00
❑ 51 Tyranus's Edict R	1.25	3.00
❑ 52 Tyranus's Geonosian Speeder (A) R	1.25	3.00
❑ 53 Tyranus's Solar Sailer (A) R	1.25	3.00
❑ 54 Tyranus's Wrath R	1.25	3.00
❑ 55 War Will Follow R	1.25	3.00
❑ 56 Ward of the Jedi R	1.25	3.00
❑ 57 Windu's Solution R	1.25	3.00
❑ 58 Yoda (A) R	1.25	3.00
❑ 59 Yoda's Intervention R	1.25	3.00
❑ 60 Zam Wesell (A) R	1.25	3.00
❑ 61 Acklay U	.40	1.00
❑ 62 Anakin Skywalker (C) U	.40	1.00
❑ 63 Anakin's Inspiration U	.40	1.00
❑ 64 AT-TE Walker 23X U	.40	1.00
❑ 65 AT-TE Walker 71E R	1.25	3.00
❑ 66 Attract Enemy Fire U	.40	1.00
❑ 67 C-3PO (A) U	.40	1.00
❑ 68 Capture Obi-Wan U	.40	1.00
❑ 69 Chancellor Palpatine (A) R	1.25	3.00
❑ 70 Chase the Villain U	.40	1.00
❑ 71 Cheat the Game U	.40	1.00
❑ 72 Cliegg Lars (A) U	.40	1.00
❑ 73 Clone Warrior 4/163 U	.40	1.00
❑ 74 Clone Warrior 5/373 U	.40	1.00
❑ 75 Commerce Guild Droid Platoon U	.40	1.00
❑ 76 Cordé (A) U	.40	1.00
❑ 77 Coruscant Freighter AA-9 (A) U	.40	1.00
❑ 78 Dark Speed U	.40	1.00
❑ 79 Darth Tyranus (B) U	.40	1.00
❑ 80 Departure Time U	.40	1.00
❑ 81 Destroyer Droid, P Series U	.40	1.00
❑ 82 Down in Flames U	.40	1.00
❑ 83 Droid Control Ship U	.40	1.00
❑ 84 Elan Sleazebaggano (A) R	1.25	3.00
❑ 85 Geonosian Guard U	.40	1.00
❑ 86 Geonosian Warrior U	.40	1.00
❑ 87 Go to the Temple U	.40	1.00
❑ 88 Infantry Battle Droid, B1 Series U	.40	1.00
❑ 89 Jango Fett (C) U	.40	1.00
❑ 90 Jawa Sandcrawler U	.40	1.00
❑ 91 Jedi Patrol U	.40	1.00
❑ 92 Kaminoan Guard U	.40	1.00
❑ 93 Kit Fisto (A) U	.40	1.00
❑ 94 Master and Apprentice U	.40	1.00
❑ 95 Naboo Security Guard U	.40	1.00
❑ 96 Naboo Spaceport U	.40	1.00
❑ 97 Nexu U	.40	1.00
❑ 98 Nute Gunray (A) U	.40	1.00
❑ 99 Obi-Wan Kenobi (B) U	.40	1.00
❑ 100 Padmé Amidala (C) U	.40	1.00
❑ 101 Poggle the Lesser (A) U	.40	1.00
❑ 102 Reek U	.40	1.00
❑ 103 Republic Assault Ship U	.40	1.00
❑ 104 Republic Cruiser C	.20	.50
❑ 105 Shaak Ti (A) U	.40	1.00
❑ 106 Ship Arrival U	.40	1.00
❑ 107 Splinter the Republic U	.40	1.00
❑ 108 Strength of Hate U	.40	1.00
❑ 109 Subtle Assassination U	.40	1.00
❑ 110 Super Battle Droid 8EX U	.40	1.00
❑ 111 Trade Federation Battleship U	.40	1.00
❑ 112 Trade Federation C-9979 U	.40	1.00
❑ 113 Tyranus's Gift U	.40	1.00
❑ 114 Underworld Connections U	.40	1.00
❑ 115 Wat Tambor (A) U	.40	1.00
❑ 116 Watto (A) U	.40	1.00
❑ 117 Weapon Response U	.40	1.00
❑ 118 Wedding of Destiny U	.40	1.00
❑ 119 Yoda (B) U	.40	1.00
❑ 120 Zam's Airspeeder (A) U	.40	1.00
❑ 121 Anakin Skywalker (D) C	.20	.50
❑ 122 Battle Droid Squad C	.20	.50
❑ 123 Bravo N-1 Starfighter C	.20	.50
❑ 124 Chancellor's Guard Squad C	.20	.50
❑ 125 Clone Platoon C	.20	.50
❑ 126 Clone Squad C	.20	.50
❑ 127 Commerce Guild Droid 81 C	.20	.50
❑ 128 Commerce Guild Starship C	.20	.50
❑ 129 Corellian Star Shuttle C	.20	.50
❑ 130 Darth Tyranus (C) C	.20	.50
❑ 131 Destroyer Droid Squad C	.20	.50
❑ 132 Droid Starfighter DFS-4CT C	.20	.50
❑ 133 Droid Starfighter Squadron C	.20	.50
❑ 134 Droid Starfighter Wing C	.20	.50
❑ 135 Elite Jedi Squad C	.20	.50
❑ 136 Flying Geonosian Squad C	.20	.50
❑ 137 Geonosian Defense Platform C	.20	.50
❑ 138 Geonosian Fighter C	.20	.50
❑ 139 Geonosian Squad C	.20	.50
❑ 140 Gozanti Cruiser C	.20	.50
❑ 141 Hatch a Clone C	.20	.50
❑ 142 Hero's Dodge C	.20	.50
❑ 143 High-Force Dodge C	.20	.50
❑ 144 Hyperdrive Ring C	.20	.50
❑ 145 InterGalactic Banking Clan Starship C	.20	.50
❑ 146 Jango Fett (D) C	.20	.50
❑ 147 Jedi Starfighter 3R3 C	.20	.50
❑ 148 Knockdown C	.20	.50
❑ 149 Lost in the Asteroids C	.20	.50
❑ 150 Lull in the Fighting C	.20	.50
❑ 151 Mending C	.20	.50
❑ 152 N-1 Starfighter C	.20	.50
❑ 153 Naboo Cruiser C	.20	.50
❑ 154 Naboo Royal Starship C	.20	.50
❑ 155 Naboo Senatorial Escort C	.20	.50
❑ 156 Naboo Starfighter Squadron C	.20	.50
❑ 157 Obi-Wan Kenobi (C) C	.20	.50
❑ 158 Padawan's Deflection C	.20	.50
❑ 159 Padmé Amidala (D) C	.20	.50
❑ 160 Patrol Speeder C	.20	.50
❑ 161 Peace on Naboo C	.20	.50
❑ 162 Pilot's Dodge C	.20	.50
❑ 163 Recon Speeder U	.20	.50
❑ 164 Republic Attack Gunship UH-478 C	.20	.50
❑ 165 Repulsorlift Malfunction C	.20	.50
❑ 166 Return to Spaceport C	.20	.50
❑ 167 Rickshaw C	.20	.50
❑ 168 Slumming on Coruscant C	.20	.50
❑ 169 Sonic Shockwave C	.20	.50
❑ 170 Speeder Bike Squadron C	.20	.50

Card	Low	High
❑ 171 Starship Refit C	.20	.50
❑ 172 Surge of Power C	.20	.50
❑ 173 Swoop Bike C	.20	.50
❑ 174 Take the Initiative C	.20	.50
❑ 175 Target Locked C	.20	.50
❑ 176 Taylander Shuttle C	.20	.50
❑ 177 Techno Union Starship C	.20	.50
❑ 178 Trade Federation War Freighter C	.20	.50
❑ 179 Walking Droid Fighter C	.20	.50
❑ 180 Zam Wesell (B) C	.20	.50

2004 Vs System DC Origins

Card	Low	High
COMPLETE SET (165)	30.00	60.00
BOOSTER BOX (24)	15.00	30.00
❑ 1 Alfred Pennyworth, Faithful Friend R	2.00	5.00
❑ 2 Azrael, Jean Paul Valley C	.10	.25
❑ 3 Barbara Gordon Oracle, Information Network R	1.25	3.00
❑ 4 Batman, Caped Crusader C	.10	.25
❑ 5 Batman, The Dark Knight R	2.00	5.00
❑ 6 Batman, World's Greatest Detective U	.20	.50
❑ 7 Cassandra Cain Batgirl, Martial Artist C	.10	.25
❑ 8 Catwoman, Selina Kyle C	.10	.25
❑ 9 Commissioner Gordon, James Gordon U	.20	.50
❑ 10 Dick Grayson Nightwing, High-Flying Acrobat R	2.00	4.00
❑ 11 Dick Grayson Nightwing Defender of Bludhaven C	.10	.25
❑ 12 Dick Grayson Robin, Sidekick R	1.25	3.00
❑ 13 Dinah Laurel Lance Black Canary, Canary Cry C	.10	.25
❑ 14 GCPD Officer, Army C	.10	.25
❑ 15 Harvey Bullock, GCPD Detective U	.20	.50
❑ 16 Huntress, Helena Rosa Bertinelli C	.10	.25
❑ 17 Lady Shiva, Sandra Woosan C	.10	.25
❑ 18 Lucius Fox, Wayne Enterprises Executive R	.40	1.00
❑ 19 Spoiler, Stephanie Brown U	.20	.50
❑ 20 Superman, Big Blue Boy Scout R	2.50	6.00
❑ 21 Tim Drake Robin, Young Detective C	.10	.25
❑ 22 Batarang U	.20	.50
❑ 23 Batcave R	.75	2.00
❑ 24 Batmobile R	1.25	3.00
❑ 25 Batplane U	.20	.50
❑ 26 Bat-Signal U	.20	.50
❑ 27 Clocktower C	.10	.25
❑ 28 Dynamic Duo U	.20	.50
❑ 29 Fizzle R	2.00	5.00
❑ 30 GCPD Headquarters U	.20	.50
❑ 31 Utility Belt U	.20	.50
❑ 32 Wayne Enterprises R	.40	1.00
❑ 33 Wayne Manor U	.20	.50
❑ 34 Bart Allen Kid Flash, Speedster C	.10	.25
❑ 35 Beast Boy, Garfield Logan R	.40	1.00
❑ 36 Cassie Sandsmark Wonder Girl Zeus's Chosen C	.10	.25
❑ 37 Connor Kent Superboy, Tactile Telekinetic C	.10	.25
❑ 38 Dick Grayson Nightwing, Titan Leader C	.10	.25
❑ 39 Donna Troy Wonder Girl, Amazon Warrior R	1.50	4.00
❑ 40 Dawn Granger Dove, Agent of Order C	.10	.25
❑ 41 Garth Tempest, Atlantean Sorcerer R	2.00	5.00
❑ 42 Hank Hall Hawk, Agent of Chaos C	.10	.25
❑ 43 Kole, Kole Weathers U	.20	.50
❑ 44 Koriand'r Starfire, Alien Princess C	.10	.25
❑ 45 Mirage, Miriam Delgado U	.20	.50
❑ 46 Omen, Lilith Clay R	.40	1.00
❑ 47 Pantha, Subject X-24 C	.10	.25
❑ 48 Phantasm, Danny Chase R	.75	2.00
❑ 49 Raven, Daughter of Trigon R	1.25	3.00
❑ 50 Red Star, Leonid Kovar U	.20	.50
❑ 51 Roy Harper Arsenal, Sharpshooter C	.10	.25
❑ 52 Terra, Tara Markov R	1.00	2.50
❑ 53 Tim Drake Robin, The Boy Wonder C	.10	.25
❑ 54 Vic Stone Cyborg, Human Machine C	.10	.25
❑ 55 Circle Defense U	.20	.50
❑ 56 Heroic Sacrifice R	.75	2.00
❑ 57 Liberty Island Base U	.20	.50
❑ 58 Optitron R	.75	2.00
❑ 59 Tamaran U	.20	.50
❑ 60 Teen Titans Go! C	.10	.25
❑ 61 Titans Tower U	.20	.50
❑ 62 T-Jet U	.20	.50
❑ 63 USS Argus R	.40	1.00
❑ 64 Bane, The Man Who Broke the Bat C	.10	.25
❑ 65 Charaxes, Drury Walker C	.10	.25
❑ 66 Firefly, Garfield Lynns R	.60	1.50
❑ 67 Harley Quinn, Dr. Harleen Quinzel C	.10	.25
❑ 68 Killer Croc, Waylon Jones C	.10	.25
❑ 69 Mad Hatter, Jervis Tetch R	.60	1.50
❑ 70 Man-Bat, Dr. Robert Langstrom C	.10	.25
❑ 71 Matt Hagen Clayface, Man of Clay C	.10	.25
❑ 72 Mr. Freeze, Dr. Victor Fries C	.10	.25
❑ 73 Mr. Zsasz, Victor Zsasz R	.60	1.50
❑ 74 Poison Ivy, Pamela Isley R	.75	2.00
❑ 75 Professor Hugo Strange, Psycho-Analyst C	.10	.25
❑ 76 Query and Echo, Double Trouble U	.20	.50
❑ 77 Ratcatcher, Otis Flannegan U	.20	.50
❑ 78 Scarecrow, Professor Jonathan Crane R	1.00	2.50
❑ 79 The Joker, Joker's Wild R	1.50	4.00
❑ 80 The Joker, Laughing Lunatic C	.10	.25
❑ 81 The Joker, The Clown Prince of Crime R	1.25	3.00
❑ 82 The Penguin, Oswald Chesterfield Cobblepot C	.10	.25
❑ 83 The Riddler, Edward Nygma U	.20	.50
❑ 84 Two-Face, Harvey Dent U	.20	.50
❑ 85 Ventriloquist Scarface, Arnold Wesker R	.60	1.50
❑ 86 Arkham Asylum U	.20	.50
❑ 87 Blackgate Prison R	.60	1.50
❑ 88 Cracking the Vault R	.40	1.00
❑ 89 Fear and Confusion C	.10	.25
❑ 90 Kidnapping U	.20	.50
❑ 91 No Man's Land U	.20	.50
❑ 92 Paralyzing Kiss U	.20	.50
❑ 93 Prison Break U	.20	.50
❑ 94 Riddle Me This U	.20	.50
❑ 95 Rigged Elections R	.60	1.50
❑ 96 Assassin Initiate, Army C	.10	.25
❑ 97 Bane, Ubu C	.10	.25
❑ 98 Dr. Tzin-Tzin, Master of Hypnosis C	.10	.25
❑ 99 Hassim, Loyal Retainer U	.20	.50
❑ 100 Josef Witschi, Talia's Assistant U	.20	.50
❑ 101 Kyle Abbot, Wolf in Man's Clothing C	.10	.25
❑ 102 Lady Shiva, Master Assassin R	.60	1.50
❑ 103 Malaq, Money Man U	.20	.50
❑ 104 Ra's al Ghul, Immortal Villain C	.10	.25
❑ 105 Ra's al Ghul, Master Swordsman C	.10	.25
❑ 106 Ra's al Ghul, The Demon's Head R	.60	1.50
❑ 107 Talia, Daughter of the Demon's Head R	.60	1.50
❑ 108 Thuggee, Army C	.10	.25
❑ 109 Ubu, Ra's al Ghul's Bodyguard C	.10	.25
❑ 110 Whisper A'Daire, Cold-Blooded Manipulator C	.10	.25
❑ 111 Clench Virus U	.20	.50
❑ 112 Dual Nature R	.40	1.00
❑ 113 Flying Fortress U	.20	.50
❑ 114 Lazarus Pit C	.10	.25
❑ 115 Mountain Stronghold U	.20	.50
❑ 116 Remake the World R	.40	1.00
❑ 117 The Shrike R	.40	1.00
❑ 118 Tower of Babel R	.60	1.50
❑ 119 Wheel of Plagues R	.40	1.00
❑ 120 Dr. Light, Arthur Light U	.20	.50
❑ 121 Gizmo, Mikron O'Jeneus U	.20	.50
❑ 122 Jinx, Elemental Sorceress U	.20	.50
❑ 123 Mammoth, Baran Flinders R	.40	1.00
❑ 124 Neutron, Nat Tryon R	.40	1.00
❑ 125 Psimon, Dr. Simon Jones R	.40	1.00
❑ 126 Shimmer, Selinda Flinders U	.20	.50
❑ 127 The Underworld Star U	.20	.50
❑ 128 Deathstroke the Terminator, Slade Wilson R	.75	2.00
❑ 129 Black Mask, Roman Sionis U	.20	.50
❑ 130 Blackfire, Komand'r R	.40	1.00
❑ 131 Brother Blood, Leader of the Church of Blood C	.10	.25
❑ 132 Ferak, Army C	.10	.25
❑ 133 King Snake, Sir Edmund Dorrance U	.20	.50
❑ 134 Lady Vic, Lady Elaine Marsh-Morton U	.20	.50
❑ 135 Lightning, Travis Williams U	.20	.50
❑ 136 Lockup, Lyle Bolton U	.20	.50
❑ 137 The Demon, Jason Blood R	.60	1.50
❑ 138 The Demon, Etrigan R	.60	1.50
❑ 139 Thunder, Gan Williams U	.20	.50
❑ 140 Trigon, The Terrible R	.40	1.00
❑ 141 Wildebeest, Army C	.10	.25
❑ 142 A Death in the Family R	.40	1.00
❑ 143 Airborne Assault U	.20	.50
❑ 144 Break You C	.10	.25
❑ 145 Combat Reflexes C	.10	.25
❑ 146 Concrete Jungle R	.40	1.00
❑ 147 Crossbow C	.10	.25
❑ 148 Escrima Sticks U	.20	.50
❑ 149 Fast Getaway C	.10	.25
❑ 150 From the Shadows C	.10	.25
❑ 151 Gone But Not Forgotten U	.20	.50
❑ 152 GothCorp R	.40	1.00
❑ 153 Have a Blast! R	1.25	3.00
❑ 154 Hidden Surveillance R	.40	1.00
❑ 155 Home Surgery U	.20	.50
❑ 156 Last Laugh U	.20	.50
❑ 157 Mega-Blast C	.10	.25
❑ 158 Museum Heist R	.40	1.00
❑ 159 My Beloved U	.20	.50
❑ 160 Shape Change U	.20	.50
❑ 161 Tag Team C	.10	.25
❑ 162 The Brave and the Bold U	.20	.50
❑ 163 Total Anarchy R	.40	1.00
❑ 164 Twin Firearms U	.20	.50
❑ 165 World's Finest C	.10	.25

2004 Vs System DC Origins Foil

Card	Low	High
COMPLETE SET (165)	60.00	120.00

*FOIL: .8X TO 2X BASIC CARDS

2004 Vs System Marvel Origins

Card	Low	High
COMPLETE SET (220)	40.00	80.00
BOOSTER BOX (24)	20.00	40.00
❑ 1 Archangel, Warren Worthington III C	.10	.25
❑ 2 Banshee, Sean Cassidy C	.10	.25
❑ 3 Beast, Dr. Henry McCoy U	.20	.50
❑ 4 Bishop, Lucas Bishop C	.10	.25
❑ 5 Colossus, Peter Rasputin C	.10	.25
❑ 6 Cyclops, Scott Summers C	.10	.25
❑ 7 Cyclops, Slim C	.10	.25
❑ 8 Dazzler, Alison Blaire C	.10	.25
❑ 9 Forge, Cheyenne Mystic R	.40	1.00
❑ 10 Gambit, Remy LeBeau U	.20	.50
❑ 11 Havok, Alex Summers R	.40	1.00
❑ 12 Iceman, Bobby Drake U	.20	.50
❑ 13 Jean Grey, Marvel Girl C	.10	.25
❑ 14 Jean Grey, Phoenix Force R	1.00	2.50
❑ 15 Longshot, Rebel Freedom Fighter R	.75	2.00
❑ 16 Moira MacTaggert, World-Renowned Geneticist R	.40	1.00
❑ 17 Nightcrawler, Fuzzy Elf R	1.00	2.50
❑ 18 Nightcrawler, Kurt Wagner U	.20	.50
❑ 19 Professor X, Charles Xavier C	.10	.25
❑ 20 Professor X, World's Most Powerful Telepath R	.50	1.25
❑ 21 Psylocke, Betsy Braddock C	.10	.25
❑ 22 Rogue, Power Absorption R	.75	2.00
❑ 23 Rogue, Powerhouse U	.20	.50
❑ 24 Shadowcat, Kitty Pryde C	.10	.25
❑ 25 Storm, Ororo Munroe C	.10	.25
❑ 26 Storm, Weather Witch R	1.25	3.00
❑ 27 Wolverine, Berserker Rage R	1.00	2.50
❑ 28 Wolverine, James Howlett U	.20	.50
❑ 29 Wolverine, Logan C	.10	.25
❑ 30 Cerebro R	1.00	2.50
❑ 31 Children of the Atom R	.75	2.00
❑ 32 Danger Room U	.20	.50
❑ 33 Fastball Special U	.20	.50
❑ 34 Muir Island U	.20	.50
❑ 35 Professor Xavier's Mansion R	.50	1.25
❑ 36 The Blackbird R	.40	1.00
❑ 37 X-Corporation U	.20	.50
❑ 38 Xavier's Dream R	.50	1.25
❑ 39 Xavier's School for Gifted Youngsters U	.20	.50
❑ 40 Alicia Masters, Blind Sculptress R	.40	1.00
❑ 41 Ant Man, Scott Lang C	.10	.25
❑ 42 Crystal, Inhuman C	.10	.25
❑ 43 Frankie Raye, Herald of Galactus U	.20	.50
❑ 44 Franklin Richards, Child Prodigy R	.50	1.25
❑ 45 Ghost Rider, New Fantastic Four R	1.00	2.50
❑ 46 Hulk, New Fantastic Four R	1.00	2.50
❑ 47 Human Torch, Johnny Storm C	.10	.25
❑ 48 Human Torch, Hotshot R	.60	1.50
❑ 49 Human Torch, Super Nova U	.20	.50
❑ 50 Invisible Woman, The Invisible Girl U	.20	.50
❑ 51 Invisible Woman, Sue Storm C	.10	.25
❑ 52 Invisible Woman, Sue Richards R	.40	1.00
❑ 53 Luke Cage, Hero for Hire U	.20	.50
❑ 54 Medusa, Inhuman C	.10	.25
❑ 55 Mr. Fantastic, Reed Richards C	.10	.25
❑ 56 Mr. Fantastic, Stretch U	.20	.50
❑ 57 Mr. Fantastic, Scientific Genius R	.75	2.00
❑ 58 She-Hulk, Jennifer Walters U	.20	.50
❑ 59 She-Hulk, Green Jeans C	.10	.25
❑ 60 She-Thing, Sharon Ventura C	.10	.25
❑ 61 Spider-Man, New Fantastic Four R	1.00	2.50
❑ 62 Thing, Ben Grimm C	.10	.25
❑ 63 Thing, Heavy Hitter R	1.00	2.50
❑ 64 Thing, The Ever-Lovin' Blue-Eyed Thing U	.20	.50
❑ 65 Wolverine, New Fantastic Four R	1.25	3.00
❑ 66 A Child Named Valeria R	.40	1.00
❑ 67 Antarctic Research Base R	.40	1.00
❑ 68 Baxter Building U	.20	.50
❑ 69 Cosmic Radiation R	.50	1.25
❑ 70 Fantasticar R	.50	1.25
❑ 71 Four Freedoms Plaza R	.40	1.00
❑ 72 It's Clobberin' Time! R	1.50	4.00
❑ 73 Signal Flare R	.40	1.00
❑ 74 The Pogo Plane R	.40	1.00
❑ 75 Yancy Street U	.20	.50
❑ 76 Avalanche, Dominic Petros U	.20	.50
❑ 77 Blob, Fred Dukes C	.10	.25
❑ 78 Destiny, Irene Adler C	.10	.25
❑ 79 Lorelei, Savage Land Mutate C	.10	.25
❑ 80 Magneto, Eric Lehnsherr U	.20	.50
❑ 81 Magneto, Master of Magnetism R	1.00	2.50
❑ 82 Magneto, Lord Magnus R	1.00	2.50
❑ 83 Mastermind, Jason Wyngarde U	.20	.50
❑ 84 Mystique, Raven Darkholme U	.20	.50
❑ 85 Mystique, Shape-Changing Assassin C	.10	.25
❑ 86 Phantazia, Eileen Harsaw C	.10	.25
❑ 87 Pyro, St. John Allerdyce C	.10	.25
❑ 88 Quicksilver, Pietro Maximoff C	.10	.25
❑ 89 Quicksilver, Speed Demon R	.75	2.00
❑ 90 Rogue, Anna Raven C	.10	.25
❑ 91 Sabretooth, Feral Rage R	.50	1.25
❑ 92 Sabretooth, Victor Creed C	.10	.25
❑ 93 Sauron, Dr. Karl Lykos C	.10	.25
❑ 94 Scarlet Witch, Wanda Maximoff C	.10	.25
❑ 95 Toad, Mortimer Toynbee C	.10	.25
❑ 96 Unus, Angelo Unuscione U	.20	.50
❑ 97 Asteroid M U	.20	.50
❑ 98 Avalon Space Station U	.20	.50
❑ 99 Genosha R	1.00	2.50
❑ 100 Global Domination R	.40	1.00
❑ 101 Lost City U	.20	.50
❑ 102 Mutant Supremacy R	.50	1.25
❑ 103 Savage Land U	.20	.50
❑ 104 The Mutant Menace U	.20	.50
❑ 105 The New Brotherhood U	.20	.50
❑ 106 War On Humanity U	.20	.50
❑ 107 Boris, Personal Servant of Dr. Doom R	1.50	4.00
❑ 108 Darkoth, Major Desmund Pitt U	.20	.50
❑ 109 Doom Guards, Army C	.10	.25
❑ 110 Doom-Bot, Army U	.40	1.00
❑ 111 Dr. Doom, Diabolic Genius U	.20	.50
❑ 112 Dr. Doom, Victor Von Doom C	.10	.25
❑ 113 Dr. Doom, Lord of Latveria R	1.25	3.00
❑ 114 Dragon Man, Experimental Monster C	.10	.25
❑ 115 Kristoff Von Doom The Boy Who Would Be Doom U	.20	.50
❑ 116 Rama-Tut, Pharaoh from the 30th Century R	.40	1.00
❑ 117 Robot Destroyer, Army R	.40	1.00
❑ 118 Robot Enforcer, Army C	.10	.25
❑ 119 Robot Seeker, Army C	.10	.25
❑ 120 Robot Sentry, Army C	.10	.25
❑ 121 Sub-Mariner, Ally of Doom R	.75	2.00
❑ 122 Tibetan Monks, Army C	.10	.25
❑ 123 Titania, Mary MacPherran C	.10	.25
❑ 124 Victor Von Doom II, Son of Doom U	.20	.50
❑ 125 Volcana, Marsha Rosenberg U	.20	.50
❑ 126 Bitter Rivals U	.20	.50
❑ 127 Doom Triumphant R	.50	1.25
❑ 128 Doom's Throne Room R	.20	.50
❑ 129 Doomstadt C	.10	.25
❑ 130 Faces of Doom U	.20	.50
❑ 131 Latveria R	.40	1.00
❑ 132 Micro-Size C	.10	.25
❑ 133 Mystical Paralysis U	.20	.50
❑ 134 Power Compressor R	.40	1.00
❑ 135 Reign of Terror R	.50	1.25
❑ 136 The Power Cosmic R	.50	1.25
❑ 137 Bastion, Leader of Operation: Zero Tolerance R	.75	2.00
❑ 138 Boliver Trask, Creator of the Sentinel Program R	.75	2.00
❑ 139 Master Mold, Sentinel Supreme R	.75	2.00
❑ 140 Nimrod, Mutant Hunter U	.20	.50
❑ 141 Senator Kelly, Anti-Mutant Advocate U	.20	.50
❑ 142 Sentinel Mark I, Army C	.10	.25
❑ 143 Sentinel Mark II, Army C	.10	.25
❑ 144 Sentinel Mark IV, Army U	.20	.50
❑ 145 Wild Sentinel, Army C	.10	.25
❑ 146 Combat Protocols U	.20	.50
❑ 147 Micro-Sentinels R	.50	1.25
❑ 148 Orbital Sentinel Base U	.20	.50
❑ 149 Primary Directive R	.40	1.00
❑ 150 Prime Sentinels U	.20	.50
❑ 151 Project: Wide Awake U	.20	.50
❑ 152 Reconstruction Program C	.10	.25
❑ 153 Search and Destroy U	.20	.50
❑ 154 South American Sentinel Base U	.20	.50
❑ 155 Underground Sentinel Base R	.50	1.25
❑ 156 Annihilus, Destroyer of Life R	.40	1.00
❑ 157 Blastaar, King of Baluur R	.50	1.25
❑ 158 Negative Zone U	.20	.50
❑ 159 Skrull Soldier, Army C	.10	.25
❑ 160 Super Skrull, Engineered Super-Soldier R	.75	2.00
❑ 161 Apocalypse, En Sabah Nur R	1.00	2.50
❑ 162 Arcade, Master of Murderworld U	.20	.50
❑ 163 Black Tom, Thomas Cassidy C	.10	.25
❑ 164 Dark Phoenix, Cosmic Entity R	2.00	5.00
❑ 165 Juggernaut, Cain Marko R	1.25	3.00
❑ 166 Lady Deathstrike, Yuriko Oyama R	.50	1.25
❑ 167 Mojo, Ruler of Mojoworld U	.20	.50
❑ 168 Mr. Sinister, Dr. Nathaniel Essex R	.75	2.00
❑ 169 Onslaught Psionic Spawn of Xavier and Magneto R	1.25	3.00
❑ 170 Puppet Master, Philip Masters C	.10	.25
❑ 171 Random Punks, Army C	.10	.25
❑ 172 Spiral, Ricochet Rita C	.10	.25
❑ 173 Acrobatic Dodge C	.10	.25
❑ 174 Advanced Hardware C	.10	.25
❑ 175 Backfire C	.10	.25
❑ 176 Base of Operations C	.10	.25
❑ 177 Betrayal R	.50	1.25
❑ 178 Blind Sided R	.40	1.00
❑ 179 Borrowed Blade C	.10	.25
❑ 180 Burn Rubber C	.10	.25
❑ 181 Charge! U	.20	.50
❑ 182 Common Enemy U	.20	.50
❑ 183 Cover Fire C	.10	.25
❑ 184 Dual Sidearms C	.10	.25
❑ 185 Entangle U	.20	.50
❑ 186 Fall Back! U	.20	.50
❑ 187 Finishing Move C	.10	.25
❑ 188 Flame Trap R	.60	1.50
❑ 189 Flying Kick C	.10	.25
❑ 190 Focused Blast U	.20	.50
❑ 191 Foiled R	.75	2.00
❑ 192 Friendly Fire U	.20	.50
❑ 193 Gamma Bomb R	.50	1.25
❑ 194 Greater of Two Evils R	.50	1.25
❑ 195 Heroes United U	.20	.50
❑ 196 Ka-Boom! R	1.25	3.00
❑ 197 Kevlar Body Armor U	.20	.50
❑ 198 Last Stand C	.10	.25
❑ 199 Marvel Team-Up U	.20	.50
❑ 200 Medical Attention C	.10	.25
❑ 201 Mutant Nation U	.20	.50
❑ 202 Nasty Surprise C	.10	.25
❑ 203 Night Vision U	.20	.50
❑ 204 Not So Fast U	.20	.50
❑ 205 One-Two Punch C	.10	.25
❑ 206 Overload U	.20	.50
❑ 207 Overpowered U	.20	.50
❑ 208 Personal Force Field U	.20	.50
❑ 209 Political Pressure R	.50	1.25
❑ 210 Press the Attack U	.20	.50
❑ 211 Reconnaissance U	.20	.50
❑ 212 Relocation R	.50	1.25
❑ 213 Salvage R	.60	1.50
❑ 214 Savage Beatdown R	4.00	10.00
❑ 215 Surprise Attack C	.10	.25
❑ 216 Swift Escape U	.20	.50
❑ 217 Team Tactics C	.10	.25
❑ 218 Tech Upgrade C	.10	.25
❑ 219 Unlikely Allies U	.20	.50
❑ 220 Unstable Molecules C	.10	.25

2004 Vs System Marvel Origins Foil

Card	Low	High
COMPLETE SET (220)	80.00	160.00

*FOIL: .8X TO 2X BASIC CARDS

2004 Vs System Superman Man of Steel

Card	Low	High
COMPLETE SET (165)	20.00	40.00
BOOSTER BOX (24)	15.00	30.00
❑ 1 Alpha Centurion, Marcus Aelius C	.10	.25
❑ 2 Cir-El Supergirl, Daughter of Tomorrow C	.10	.25
❑ 3 Connor Kent Superboy, Kon-El U	.20	.50
❑ 4 Dubbilex, DNAlien U	.20	.50
❑ 5 Eradicator, Soul of Krypton C	.10	.25
❑ 6 Gangbuster, Jose Delgado C	.10	.25
❑ 7 Girl 13, Traci Thirteen U	.20	.50
❑ 8 Jimmy Olsen, Superman's Pal U	.20	.50
❑ 9 John Henry Irons Steel, Peerless Engineer C	.10	.25
❑ 10 Kara Zor-El Supergirl, Last Daughter of Krypton C	.10	.25
❑ 11 Krypto, Superdog R	.40	1.00
❑ 12 Lana Lang, Smallville Sweetheart U	.20	.50
❑ 13 Linda Danvers Supergirl, Matrix R	.75	2.00
❑ 14 Lois Lane, Star Reporter U	.20	.50
❑ 15 Perry White, Chief R	.60	1.50
❑ 16 Professor Emil Hamilton, Garrulous Genius C	.10	.25
❑ 17 Rose Thorn, Rose Forrest U	.20	.50
❑ 18 Scorn, Ceritak C	.10	.25
❑ 19 Strange Visitor, Sharon Vance R	.40	1.00
❑ 20 Superman, Blue R	.10	.25
❑ 21 Superman, Clark Kent C	.40	1.00
❑ 22 Superman, Kal-El U	1.50	4.00
❑ 23 Superman, Man of Steel R	.10	.25
❑ 24 Superman, Red C	.10	.25
❑ 25 Superman, Robots Army C	1.25	3.00
❑ 26 Cadmus Labs U	.20	.50
❑ 27 Daily Planet R	.60	1.50
❑ 28 Entropy Aegis Armor R	.40	1.00
❑ 29 Fortress of Solitude U	.20	.50
❑ 30 Kandor R	.40	1.00
❑ 31 Last Son of Krypton R	.60	1.50
❑ 32 Man of Tomorrow U	.20	.50
❑ 33 Super Speed U	.20	.50
❑ 34 X-Ray Vision R	.60	1.50
❑ 35 Beautiful Dreamer, Forever People U	.20	.50
❑ 36 Big Barda, Barda Free C	.10	.25
❑ 37 Big Bear, Forever People C	.10	.25
❑ 38 Fastbak, Sky Scorcher C	.10	.25
❑ 39 Forager, Bug Warrior C	.10	.25
❑ 40 Himon, Enigmatic Researcher U	.20	.50
❑ 41 Infinity Man, Drax R	.40	1.00
❑ 42 Izaya Highfather, The Inheritor C	.10	.25
❑ 43 Lightray, Solis C	.10	.25
❑ 44 Lonar, Explorer U	.20	.50
❑ 45 Mark Moonrider, Forever People C	.10	.25
❑ 46 Metron, Time Traveler C	.10	.25
❑ 47 Orion, Dog of War R	.40	1.00
❑ 48 Orion, True Son of Darkseid C	.10	.25
❑ 49 Scott Free Mister Miracle, Escape Artist R	.60	1.50
❑ 50 Serifan, Forever People C	.10	.25
❑ 51 Takion Highfather, Josh Saunders R	.40	1.00
❑ 52 Vykin, Forever People U	.20	.50
❑ 53 Astro Force R	.75	2.00
❑ 54 Dog of War U	.20	.50
❑ 55 Escape Artist U	.20	.50
❑ 56 Forever People R	.75	2.00
❑ 57 New Genesis R	.75	2.00
❑ 58 Supercycle U	.20	.50
❑ 59 The Prophecy Fulfilled R	.60	1.50
❑ 60 The Source R	2.00	5.00
❑ 61 Atomic Skull, Joe Martin U	.20	.50
❑ 62 Bizarro, Imperfect Duplicate R	1.00	2.50
❑ 63 Brainiac 2.5, Vrill Dox C	.10	.25
❑ 64 Dominus, Tuoni R	.60	1.50
❑ 65 Doomsday, Armageddon Creature R	.40	1.00
❑ 66 Encantadora, Lourdes Lucero C	.10	.25
❑ 67 Eradicator, Doctor David Connor C	.10	.25
❑ 68 General Zod, Ruler of Pokolistan R	.40	1.00
❑ 69 Gog, Nemesis C	.10	.25
❑ 70 Hank Henshaw Cyborg, Evil Imposter R	.60	1.50
❑ 71 Hope, Amazon Bodyguard U	.20	.50
❑ 72 Intergang, Army U	.20	.50
❑ 73 Lex Luthor, Power Armor C	.10	.25
❑ 74 Lex Luthor, President Luthor R	1.00	2.50
❑ 75 Massacre, Alien Bounty Hunter U	.20	.50
❑ 76 Mercy, Amazon Bodyguard C	.10	.25
❑ 77 Metallo, John Corben C	.10	.25
❑ 78 Mongal, Ruler of Almerac C	.10	.25
❑ 79 Mongul, Tyrant of Warworld C	.10	.25
❑ 80 Mr. Mxyzptlk, Fifth Dimension Imp U	.20	.50
❑ 81 Parasite, Rudy Jones C	.10	.25
❑ 82 Prankster, Oswald Loomis U	.20	.50
❑ 83 Satanus, Evil Incarnate R	.40	1.00
❑ 84 Silver Banshee, Siobhan McDougal C	.10	.25
❑ 85 Talia, LexCorp CEO U	.20	.50
❑ 86 Winslow Schott Toyman, Crooked Craftsman U	.20	.50
❑ 87 Bizarro World R	.40	1.00
❑ 88 Brainiac's Ship R	.60	1.50
❑ 89 Feeding Time! U	.20	.50
❑ 90 Kryptonite R	.60	1.50
❑ 91 LexCorp U	.20	.50
❑ 92 Revenge Pact R	.60	1.50
❑ 93 State of the Union R	.40	1.00
❑ 94 Suicide Slums U	.20	.50
❑ 95 Toy Soldiers U	.20	.50
❑ 96 Warworld R	.40	1.00
❑ 97 Amazing Grace, Manipulator R	.40	1.00
❑ 98 Bernadeth, Leader of Female Furies C	.10	.25
❑ 99 Brimstone, Engine of Destruction R	.40	1.00
❑ 100 Darkseid, Lord of Apokolips R	1.00	2.50
❑ 101 Darkseid, Uxas U	.20	.50
❑ 102 Desaad, Royal Torturer C	.10	.25
❑ 103 Devilance, The Pursuer C	.10	.25
❑ 104 Glorious Godfrey, Persuader U	.20	.50
❑ 105 Gole, Deep Six U	.20	.50
❑ 106 Granny Goodness, Everyone's Favorite Granny C	.10	.25
❑ 107 Hunger Dogs, Army U	.20	.50

❑ 108 Jaffar, Deep Six U .20 .50
❑ 109 Kalibak, Unworthy Son C .10 .25
❑ 110 Kanto, Darkseid's Assassin C .10 .25
❑ 111 Kurin, Deep Six U .20 .50
❑ 112 Shaligo, Deep Six C .10 .25
❑ 113 Slig, Deep Six C .10 .25
❑ 114 Steppenwolf, Darkseid's General C .10 .25
❑ 115 Superman, False Son R .20 .50
❑ 116 Topkick, Parademon Drill Instructor U .20 .50
❑ 117 Trok, Deep Six C .10 .25
❑ 118 Anti-Life Equation R .40 1.00
❑ 119 Apokolips R .40 1.00
❑ 120 Armagetto U .20 .50
❑ 121 Beta Club U .20 .50
❑ 122 Firepits of Apokolips U .20 .50
❑ 123 Granny Loves You U .20 .50
❑ 124 Happiness Home R .40 1.00
❑ 125 Hordes of Apokolips U .20 .50
❑ 126 Omega Beams R .40 1.00
❑ 127 Ride of the Black Racer R .40 1.00
❑ 128 Blood Feud U .20 .50
❑ 129 Phantom Zone U .20 .50
❑ 130 The Exchange R .40 1.00
❑ 131 Barbara Gordon Batgirl, Guardian of Gotham R.75 2.00
❑ 132 Jason Todd Robin, Crime Fighter R .75 2.00
❑ 133 Spoiler Robin, The Girl Wonder U .20 .50
❑ 134 Detective Work R 1.00 2.50
❑ 135 Donna Troy Troia, Child of Myth R .75 2.00
❑ 136 Roy Harper Speedy, Mercurial Marksman R .40 1.00
❑ 137 Wally West Kid Flash, Fastest Teen Alive R .40 1.00
❑ 138 New Teen Titans R 1.00 2.50
❑ 139 Blockbuster, Roland Desmond U .20 .50
❑ 140 Maxie Zeus, God Complex U .20 .50
❑ 141 The Joker, Emperor Joker R .75 2.00
❑ 142 Smiles, Everyone! R .40 1.00
❑ 143 Bronze Tiger, Benjamin Turner U .20 .50
❑ 144 Merlyn, Deadly Archer U .20 .50
❑ 145 Pit of Madness R .40 1.00
❑ 146 The Demon's Head R .40 1.00
❑ 147 Charger, Power Conduit U .20 .50
❑ 148 Deuce, Miss Perception U .20 .50
❑ 149 Imperiex, The Beginning and The End R .40 1.00
❑ 150 Back to Back C .10 .25
❑ 151 Boom Tube C .10 .25
❑ 152 Female Furies C .10 .25
❑ 153 Heat Vision C .10 .25
❑ 154 I Hate Magic! C .10 .25
❑ 155 Men of Steel C .10 .25
❑ 156 Metropolis C .10 .25
❑ 157 Mother Box U .20 .50
❑ 158 Narrow Escape C .10 .25
❑ 159 Path of Destruction C .10 .25
❑ 160 Phantom Zone Projector U .20 .50
❑ 161 Play Time C .10 .25
❑ 162 Royal Decree U .20 .50
❑ 163 Stopped Cold C .10 .25
❑ 164 Super Strength C .10 .25
❑ 165 Up, Up, and Away C .10 .25

2004 Vs System Superman Man of Steel Foil

COMPLETE SET (165) 40.00 80.00
*FOIL: .8X TO 2X BASIC CARDS

2004 Vs System Web of Spider-Man

COMPLETE SET (165) 25.00 50.00
BOOSTER BOX (24) 20.00 40.00

❑ 1 Black Cat, Felicia Hardy C .10 .25
❑ 2 Daredevil, The Man Without Fear C .10 .25
❑ 3 Madame Web, Cassandra Webb C .10 .25
❑ 4 Prowler, Hobie Brown C .10 .25
❑ 5 Punisher, Vigilante U .20 .50
❑ 6 Solo, James Bourne C .10 .25
❑ 7 Spider-Man, Friendly Neighborhood Spider-Man C.10 .25
❑ 8 Spider-Man, The Amazing Spider-Man R 1.25 3.00
❑ 9 Nova, Richard Rider U .20 .50
❑ 10 Daily Bugle U .20 .50
❑ 11 ESU Science Lab U .20 .50
❑ 12 Spider Senses U .20 .50
❑ 13 Twist of Fate U .20 .50
❑ 14 Dr. Octopus, Doc Ock R 1.25 3.00
❑ 15 Dr. Octopus, Otto Octavius C .10 .25
❑ 16 Electro, Maxwell Dillon U .20 .50
❑ 17 Green Goblin, Norman Osborn C .10 .25
❑ 18 Kraven the Hunter, Sergei Kravinoff C .10 .25
❑ 19 Lizard, Dr. Curtis Connors C .10 .25
❑ 20 Rhino, Alex O'Hirn C .10 .25
❑ 21 Venom, Eddie Brock U .20 .50
❑ 22 Vulture, Adrian Toomes C .10 .25
❑ 23 Doc Ock's Lab U .20 .50
❑ 24 Osborn Industries U .20 .50
❑ 25 Sadistic Choice U .20 .50
❑ 26 Sinister Salvo U .20 .50
❑ 27 Alley-Oop! C .10 .25
❑ 28 Crushing Blow C .10 .25
❑ 29 Jetpack C .10 .25
❑ 30 No Fear C .10 .25
❑ 31 Smoke Screen C .10 .25
❑ 32 Aunt May, May Parker U .20 .50
❑ 33 Black Cat, Master Thief U .20 .50
❑ 34 Cardiac, Elias Wirtham U .20 .50
❑ 35 Cloak, Tyrone Johnson C .10 .25
❑ 36 Dagger, Tandy Bowen U .20 .50
❑ 37 Dusk, Cassie St. Commons C .10 .25
❑ 38 Ezekiel, Spirit of the Spider C .10 .25
❑ 39 Firestar, Hot Stuff R .50 1.25
❑ 40 Hornet, Eddie McDonough C .10 .25
❑ 41 Human Torch, Friendly Rival C .10 .25
❑ 42 Iceman, Cool Customer C .10 .25
❑ 43 Jessica Drew Spider-Woman, Venom Blast U .20 .50
❑ 44 Julia Carpenter Spider-Woman, Web Weaver R.75 2.00
❑ 45 Mary Jane Watson, MJ R 1.25 3.00
❑ 46 Mattie Franklin Spider-Woman, Gift of Power U.20 .50
❑ 47 Prodigy, Richie Gilmore C .10 .25
❑ 48 Puma, Thomas Fireheart C .10 .25
❑ 49 Ricochet, Johnny Gallo C .10 .25
❑ 50 Rocket Racer, Robert Farrell C .10 .25
❑ 51 Scarlet Spider, Ben Reilly C .10 .25
❑ 52 Silver Sable, Silver Sablinova C .10 .25
❑ 53 Spider-Man, Alien Symbiote C .10 .25
❑ 54 Spider-Man, Cosmic Spider-Man R 2.50 6.00
❑ 55 Wild Pack, Army C .10 .25
❑ 56 Will O' The Wisp, Jackson Arvad R .50 1.25
❑ 57 Ace Reporter R .50 1.25
❑ 58 Armored Spider Suit U .20 .50
❑ 59 Costume Change U .20 .50
❑ 60 Fun and Games R .50 1.25
❑ 61 Going My Way? U .20 .50
❑ 62 Midtown High School C .10 .25
❑ 63 My Hero U .20 .50
❑ 64 Nice Try! R .50 1.25
❑ 65 Spider-Tracer R .50 1.25
❑ 66 Sticky Situation U .20 .50
❑ 67 Tragic Loss U .20 .50
❑ 68 Unexpected Mutation U .20 .50
❑ 69 Alistair Smythe, Ultimate Spider Slayer R .50 1.25
❑ 70 Beetle, Abner Jenkins C .10 .25
❑ 71 Boomerang, Fred Myers C .10 .25
❑ 72 Carnage, Cletus Kasady R 1.00 2.50
❑ 73 Chameleon, Dmitri Smerdyakov C .10 .25
❑ 74 Green Goblin, Altered Ego C .10 .25
❑ 75 Hammerhead, Gangster C .10 .25
❑ 76 Hobgoblin, Roderick Kingsley C .10 .25
❑ 77 Hydro-Man, Morris Bench C .10 .25
❑ 78 Jackal, Dr. Miles Warren C .10 .25
❑ 79 Kaine, Imperfect Clone C .10 .25
❑ 80 Kingpin, Crime Boss R 1.00 2.50
❑ 81 Man-Wolf, John Jameson C .10 .25
❑ 82 Morbius, Dr. Michael Morbius R 1.00 2.50
❑ 83 Mysterio, Quentin Beck R .50 1.25
❑ 84 Sandman, William Baker R 1.00 2.50
❑ 85 Scorpion, MacDonald Gargan C .10 .25
❑ 86 Shocker, Herman Schultz C .10 .25
❑ 87 Shriek, Frances Barrison U .20 .50
❑ 88 Silvermane, Silvio Manfredi C .10 .25
❑ 89 Speed Demon, James Sanders C .10 .25
❑ 90 The Rose, Richard Fisk R .50 1.25
❑ 91 Tinkerer, Phineas Mason R .50 1.25
❑ 92 Tombstone, Lonnie Lincoln R .75 2.00
❑ 93 Venom, Alien Symbiote R 2.00 5.00
❑ 94 Dangerous Experiment R .75 2.00
❑ 95 Fisk Towers R .50 1.25
❑ 96 Get Him My Petsss R .50 1.25
❑ 97 Goblin Glider U .20 .50
❑ 98 Hired Goons C .10 .25
❑ 99 Lion's Den C .10 .25
❑ 100 Oscorp Board Room U .20 .50
❑ 101 Rejuvenation U .20 .50
❑ 102 Spider Slayers U .20 .50
❑ 103 Archangel, Angel of Death U .20 .50
❑ 104 Emma Frost 1.50 4.00
Headmistress of Xavier's Academy R
❑ 105 John Proudstar Thunderbird, Apache Warrior U.20 .50
❑ 106 Shadowcat, Pride of the X-Men U .20 .50
❑ 107 Sunfire, Shiro Yoshida R .50 1.25
❑ 108 Aerial Supremacy U .20 .50
❑ 109 Bamf! R 1.25 3.00
❑ 110 Madripoor U .20 .50
❑ 111 Power Nexus R .75 2.00
❑ 112 Siege Perilous R .50 1.25
❑ 113 Ultimate Sacrifice R 1.25 3.00
❑ 114 Silver Surfer, Norrin Radd R 2.50 6.00
❑ 115 Wyatt Wingfoot, Keewazi Adventurer U .20 .50
❑ 116 Marvel's First Family R .75 2.00
❑ 117 Pier 4 R .50 1.25
❑ 118 Supernova U .20 .50
❑ 119 Mimic, Calvin Rankin R 1.00 2.50
❑ 120 Post, Kevin Tremain R .50 1.25
❑ 121 Thornn, Feral Hunter U .20 .50
❑ 122 Insignificant Threat R .50 1.25
❑ 123 Misappropriation U .20 .50
❑ 124 Rise to Power R .75 2.00
❑ 125 Volcanic Base R .50 1.25
❑ 126 Dr. Hauptmann, Diabolic Inventor U .20 .50
❑ 127 Purple Man, Zebediah Killgrave U .20 .50
❑ 128 Terrax, Tyros R .50 1.25
❑ 129 Decoy Program R .50 1.25
❑ 130 Devil's Due R .75 2.00
❑ 131 Latverian Embassy R .50 1.25
❑ 132 Mark II, Number II, Leader Unit R 1.00 2.50
❑ 133 Sentinel Mark V, Army C .10 .25
❑ 134 Sentinel Mark III, Army C .10 .25
❑ 135 Tri-Sentinel, Super Sentinel R .50 1.25
❑ 136 Next Generation Technology R .75 2.00
❑ 137 Termination Sequence R .75 2.00
❑ 138 Wave of Sentinels R .75 2.00
❑ 139 Lyja, The Lazerfist U .20 .50
❑ 140 Deathlok, Luther Manning R 1.00 2.50
❑ 141 J. Jonah Jameson, Sensationalist R .75 2.00
❑ 142 Mole Man, Leader of the Moloids U .20 .50
❑ 143 Bad Press R .50 1.25
❑ 144 Big Bully C .10 .25
❑ 145 Breaking Story U .20 .50
❑ 146 Clone Saga U .20 .50
❑ 147 Com Link U .20 .50
❑ 148 Crowd Control C .10 .25
❑ 149 Fight to the Finish U .20 .50
❑ 150 Flamethrower R .50 1.25
❑ 151 Forced Allegiance U .20 .50
❑ 152 Grounded C .10 .25
❑ 153 Mojoverse C .10 .25
❑ 154 Murderworld R 1.00 2.50
❑ 155 Pinned U .20 .50
❑ 156 Pleasant Distraction U .20 .50
❑ 157 Rapier U .20 .50
❑ 158 Rise from the Grave R .50 1.25
❑ 159 Sinister Six U .20 .50
❑ 160 Sonic Gun U .20 .50
❑ 161 Sucker Punch U .20 .50
❑ 162 Surrounded C .10 .25
❑ 163 Thinking Outside the Box R .50 1.25
❑ 164 Time Platform R .50 1.25
❑ 165 Unmasked U .20 .50

2004 Vs System Web of Spider-Man Foil

COMPLETE SET (165) 50.00 100.00
*FOIL: .8X TO 2X BASIC CARDS

2005 Vs System Green Lantern Corps

COMPLETE SET (220) 30.00 60.00
BOOSTER BOX (24) 30.00 60.00

❑ 1 Abin Sur, Green Lantern of Ungara U .20 .50
❑ 2 Alan Scott, Keeper of the Starheart C .10 .25
❑ 3 Arisia, Green Lantern of Graxos IV U .20 .50
❑ 4 Boodikka, Green Lantern of Bellatrix C .10 .25
❑ 5 Brik, Green Lantern of Dryad U .20 .50
❑ 6 Ch'p, Green Lantern of H'ven C .10 .25
❑ 7 G'Nort, Green Lantern of G'Newt C .10 .25
❑ 8 Guy Gardner, Strong Arm of the Corps C .10 .25
❑ 9 Hal Jordan, Green Lantern of Earth C .10 .25
❑ 10 Hal Jordan, Green Lantern of Sector 2814 R 1.50 4.00
❑ 11 Hal Jordan, Reborn R 1.00 2.50
❑ 12 Jack T. Chance, Green Lantern of Garnet U .20 .50
❑ 13 Jade, Jennifer-Lynn Hayden C .10 .25
❑ 14 John Stewart, Green Lantern of Earth C .10 .25
❑ 15 Katma Tui, Green Lantern of Korugar C .10 .25
❑ 16 Kilowog, Green Lantern of Bolovax Vik C .10 .25
❑ 17 Kreon, Green Lantern of Tebis C .10 .25
❑ 18 Kyle Rayner, Green Lantern of the Universe C .10 .25
❑ 19 Kyle Rayner, Ion R 1.00 2.50
❑ 20 Kyle Rayner, Last Green Lantern U .20 .50
❑ 21 Olapet, Green Lantern of Southern Goldstar C .10 .25
❑ 22 Rot Lop Fan .10 .25
F-Sharp Bell of the Obsidian Deeps C
❑ 23 Salakk, Green Lantern of Slyggia U .20 .50
❑ 24 Sinestro, Green Lantern of Korugar R 2.00 5.00
❑ 25 Tomar Re, Green Lantern of Xudar U .20 .50
❑ 26 Tomar Tu, Green Lantern of Xudar C .10 .25
❑ 27 Central Power Battery C .10 .25
❑ 28 Emerald City, Construct R .10 .25
❑ 29 Force Sphere, Construct C .10 .25
❑ 30 Green Lantern Ring U .20 .50
❑ 31 Guardians Reborn U .20 .50
❑ 32 Jackhammer, Construct C .10 .25
❑ 33 Mean Green Machine, Construct U .20 .50
❑ 34 Mogo R .50 1.25
❑ 35 Oa R 1.25 3.00
❑ 36 Reciting the Oath U .20 .50
❑ 37 Appa Ali Apsa, Mad God R .30 .75
❑ 38 Black Hand, Dark-Hearted Villain C .10 .25
❑ 39 Carol Ferris Star Sapphire, Beloved Enemy C .10 .25
❑ 40 Dr. Light, Master of Holograms U .20 .50
❑ 41 Dr. Polaris, Dr. Neal Emerson C .10 .25
❑ 42 Dr. Ub'X, Galactic Conqueror C .10 .25
❑ 43 Evil Star, Servant of the Star-Band R .75 2.00
❑ 44 Fatality, Yrra Cynril R .30 .75
❑ 45 Goldface, Keith Kenyon C .10 .25
❑ 46 Grayven, Son of Darkseid C .10 .25
❑ 47 Hal Jordan, Parallax R 1.50 4.00
❑ 48 Hector Hammond, Super-Futuristic Mind C .10 .25
❑ 49 Henry King Jr. Brainwave, Psionic Manipulator U.20 .50
❑ 50 Invisible Destroyer, Subconscious Entity C .10 .25
❑ 51 Krona, Creator of the Anti-Matter Universe C .10 .25
❑ 52 Legion, He Who Is Many C .10 .25
❑ 53 Major Disaster, Paul Booker U .20 .50
❑ 54 Major Force, Clifford Zmeck C .10 .25
❑ 55 Malvolio, Lord of the Green Flame C .10 .25
❑ 56 Myrwhydden, Mightiest of Mages C .10 .25
❑ 57 Remoni-Notra Star Sapphire .10 .25
Obsessed Warrior Princess C
❑ 58 Sinestro, Enemy of the Corps R 1.25 3.00
❑ 59 Sonar, Dastardly Discord C .10 .25
❑ 60 Starlings, Army U .20 .50
❑ 61 Tattooed Man, Abel Tarrant U .20 .50
❑ 62 The Shark, T. S. Smith C .10 .25
❑ 63 Battered and Broken U .20 .50
❑ 64 Damsel in Distress, Construct C .10 .25
❑ 65 Emerald Twilight U .20 .50
❑ 66 Empire of Tears U .20 .50
❑ 67 Femme Fatality U .20 .50
❑ 68 Golden Death C .10 .25
❑ 69 In Darkest Night U .20 .50
❑ 70 Korugar R .30 .75
❑ 71 Prison Planet R .30 .75
❑ 72 Prisoner of a Mad God R .30 .75
❑ 73 Sinestro Defiant C .10 .25
❑ 74 Anti-Green Lantern, Army C .10 .25
❑ 75 Anti-Monitor, Architect of Destruction R .75 2.00
❑ 76 Dead-Eye, Qwardian Conglomerate U .20 .50
❑ 77 Elasti-Man, Qwardian Conglomerate C .10 .25
❑ 78 Element Man, Qwardian Conglomerate C .10 .25
❑ 79 Fiero, Qwardian Conglomerate C .10 .25
❑ 80 Frostbite, Qwardian Conglomerate C .10 .25
❑ 81 Gnaxos, Arena Robot C .10 .25
❑ 82 Johnny Quick, Crime Syndicate R 1.00 2.50
❑ 83 Kiman, Chief Weaponer U .20 .50
❑ 84 Nero, Qwardian Puppet R .75 2.00
❑ 85 Owlman, Crime Syndicate C .10 .25
❑ 86 Power Ring, Crime Syndicate C .10 .25
❑ 87 Qwardian Watchdog, Gatekeeper U .20 .50
❑ 88 Qwardians, Army C .10 .25
❑ 89 Scarab, Qwardian Conglomerate U .20 .50
❑ 90 Shadow Creatures, Army U .20 .50
❑ 91 Sinestro, Lantern in Exile C .10 .25
❑ 92 Slipstream, Qwardian Conglomerate C .10 .25
❑ 93 St'nlli, Super-Qwardian C .10 .25
❑ 94 Superwoman, Crime Syndicate C .10 .25
❑ 95 Ultraman, Crime Syndicate C .10 .25
❑ 96 Weaponers of Qward, Army C .10 .25
❑ 97 Xallarap, Anti-Green Lantern Corps C .10 .25
❑ 98 Yokal, The Atrocious U .20 .50
❑ 99 Anti-Matter Cannon R 1.00 2.50
❑ 100 Anti-Matter Universe R .50 1.25
❑ 101 Banished to the Anti-Matter Universe U .20 .50
❑ 102 From Qward With Hate R .30 .75
❑ 103 In the Hands of Qward R .30 .75
❑ 104 Nero Unleashed C .10 .25
❑ 105 Q Energy U .20 .50
❑ 106 Q Field C .10 .25
❑ 107 Qward R .30 .75
❑ 108 Qwardian Council Hall R .30 .75
❑ 109 Thunderous Onslaught C .10 .25
❑ 110 Yellow Power Ring U .20 .50
❑ 111 Governor Tozad, Planetary Commander U .20 .50
❑ 112 Grandmaster, Manhunter Leader R .30 .75
❑ 113 Harlequin, Molly Mayne-Scott C .10 .25
❑ 114 Highmaster, Supreme Leader C .10 .25
❑ 115 Lana Lang, Manhunter Sleeper U .20 .50
❑ 116 Manhunter Engineer, Army C .10 .25
❑ 117 Manhunter Excavator, Army C .10 .25
❑ 118 Manhunter Giant, Army C .10 .25
❑ 119 Manhunter Guardsman, Army C .10 .25
❑ 120 Manhunter Infiltrator, Army C .10 .25
❑ 121 Manhunter Lantern, Power Ring Thief C .10 .25
❑ 122 Manhunter Protector, Army C .10 .25
❑ 123 Manhunter Sniper, Army C .10 .25
❑ 124 Manhunter Soldier, Army C .10 .25
❑ 125 Mark Shaw, Manhunter C .10 .25
❑ 126 Pan, Manhunter Duplicate R .30 .75
❑ 127 Rocket Red, Manhunter Sleeper C .10 .25
❑ 128 Sleeper Agent, Manhunter Sleeper C .10 .25
❑ 129 Supermanhunter, Kryptonite Armor C .10 .25
❑ 130 Council of Power R .30 .75
❑ 131 Fire Support C .10 .25
❑ 132 Manhunter Science C .10 .25
❑ 133 Manhunter Spacecraft R .50 1.25
❑ 134 Manhunter Transphere C .10 .25
❑ 135 Only a Friend Can Betray You C .10 .25
❑ 136 Orinda R .50 1.25
❑ 137 Plans Within Plans C .10 .25
❑ 138 Rebellion on Oa R .75 2.00
❑ 139 The Fall of Oa R .75 2.00
❑ 140 The Manhunters are a Myth R .50 1.25
❑ 141 Underground Complex U .20 .50
❑ 142 Superman, Returned U .20 .50
❑ 143 House of El U .20 .50
❑ 144 S.T.A.R. Labs R .50 1.25
❑ 145 The Kent Farm R .75 2.00
❑ 146 Commander, Military Leader of New Genesis R.50 1.25
❑ 147 Soldiers of New Genesis, Army U .20 .50
❑ 148 Sturmer, War Dog R .30 .75
❑ 149 Children of Forever R .30 .75
❑ 150 Power Armor Elite, Army U .20 .50
❑ 151 Death of Superman R 1.25 3.00
❑ 152 Fifth Dimension R .50 1.25
❑ 153 Hostage Situation R .30 .75
❑ 154 Dr. Bedlam, Psionic Being R .30 .75
❑ 155 Parademons, Army U .20 .50
❑ 156 Virman Vundabar .20 .50
Military Leader of Apokolips U
❑ 157 Apokoliptian Hospitality U .20 .50
❑ 158 Darkseid Undenied R .50 1.25
❑ 159 Azrael Batman, Knightfall U .20 .50
❑ 160 Ragman, Rory Regan R .50 1.25
❑ 161 Blood in the Dark U .20 .50
❑ 162 Bart Allen Impulse, Hyper-Accelerated U .20 .50
❑ 163 Garth Aqualad, Atlantean Ambassador U .20 .50
❑ 164 Jericho, Joseph Wilson R .30 .75
❑ 165 Hush, Mystery Man R .30 .75
❑ 166 Two-Face, Split Personality R .50 1.25
❑ 167 Bat's Belfry R .50 1.25
❑ 168 Dr. Ebenezer Darrk, .20 .50
Original Leader of the League U
❑ 169 Sensei, Martial Arts Master U .20 .50
❑ 170 Shadows of the Past R .30 .75
❑ 171 Reign of Terra R .50 1.25
❑ 172 Fists of the Guardians, Oan Enforcers U .20 .50
❑ 173 Ganthet, Last Guardian C .10 .25
❑ 174 Guy Gardner, Warrior C .10 .25
❑ 175 Hal Jordan Spectre, Mortal Avatar R 1.25 3.00
❑ 176 Light Brigade, Construct C .10 .25
❑ 177 Mouse Trap, Construct U .20 .50
❑ 178 Solomon Grundy, Born on a Monday C .10 .25
❑ 179 Space Bears, Construct C .10 .25
❑ 180 Armies of Qward R .30 .75
❑ 181 Battle of Wills C .10 .25
❑ 182 Birthing Chamber U .20 .50
❑ 183 Book of Oa C .10 .25
❑ 184 Breaking Ground, Construct R .30 .75
❑ 185 Catcher's Mitt, Construct C .10 .25
❑ 186 Chopping Block, Construct C .10 .25
❑ 187 Coast City C .10 .25
❑ 188 Cosmic Conflict C .10 .25
❑ 189 Dimming of the Starheart C .10 .25
❑ 190 Emerald Dawn U .20 .50
❑ 191 Hard-Traveling Heroes C .10 .25
❑ 192 Helping Hand, Construct C .10 .25
❑ 193 In Evil Star's Evil Clutches C .10 .25
❑ 194 In Remembrance C .10 .25
❑ 195 Jailbird, Construct R .30 .75
❑ 196 Lantern's Light C .10 .25
❑ 197 Lanterns in Love, Construct C .10 .25
❑ 198 Light Armor, Construct C .10 .25
❑ 199 Living Ink, Construct C .10 .25
❑ 200 Locked in Combat C .10 .25
❑ 201 Millennium C .10 .25
❑ 202 Mosaic World C .10 .25
❑ 203 No Evil Shall Escape Our Sight, Construct C .10 .25
❑ 204 No Man Escapes the Manhunters C .10 .25
❑ 205 Ole!, Construct C .10 .25
❑ 206 Pest Control, Construct C .10 .25
❑ 207 Power Surge U .20 .50
❑ 208 Qwardian Pincer C .10 .25
❑ 209 Rain of Acorns, Construct U .20 .50
❑ 210 Recharging the Ring C .10 .25
❑ 211 Sector 2814 U .20 .50
❑ 212 Shock Troops C .10 .25
❑ 213 Stealing the Light C .10 .25
❑ 214 Sweeping Up, Construct C .10 .25
❑ 215 The Ring Has Chosen U .20 .50
❑ 216 Trapped in the Sciencells U .20 .50
❑ 217 Uppercut, Construct C .10 .25
❑ 218 Willworld R .30 .75
❑ 219 Yellow Impurity C .10 .25
❑ 220 Zero Hour R 1.00 2.50

2005 Vs System Green Lantern Corps Foil

COMPLETE SET (220) 60.00 120.00
*FOIL: .8X TO 2X BASIC CARDS

2005 Vs System Justice League of America

COMPLETE SET (220) 25.00 50.00
BOOSTER BOX (24) 25.00 50.00

❑ 1 Aquaman, Arthur Curry C .10 .25
❑ 2 Aquaman, King of the Seven Seas U .20 .50
❑ 3 Barry Allen The Flash, Scarlet Speedster R .30 .75
❑ 4 Batman, Avatar of Justice C .10 .25
❑ 5 Connor Hawke Green Arrow, Son of the Archer U.20 .50
❑ 6 Dinah Laurel Lance Black Canary .10 .25
Blonde Bombshell C
❑ 7 Elongated Man, Ralph Dibny C .10 .25
❑ 8 Faith, The Fat Lady U .20 .50
❑ 9 Firestorm, The Nuclear Man U .20 .50
❑ 10 Gypsy, Cynthia Reynolds C .10 .25
❑ 11 Hal Jordan, Hard-Traveling Hero C .10 .25
❑ 12 John Henry Irons Steel, Steel-Drivin' Man C .10 .25
❑ 13 John Stewart, Emerald Architect C .10 .25
❑ 14 Katar Hol Hawkman, Thanagarian Enforcer C .10 .25
❑ 15 Martian Manhunter, Manhunter from Mars R .30 .75
❑ 16 Oliver Queen Green Arrow, Hard-Traveling Hero C.10 .25
❑ 17 Plastic Man, Eel O'Brian R .30 .75
❑ 18 Ray Palmer The Atom, World's Smallest Hero R.30 .75
❑ 19 Red Tornado, John Smith C .10 .25
❑ 20 Shayera Thal Hawkwoman .10 .25
Thanagarian Enforcer C
❑ 21 Snapper Carr, Cool Daddy-O U .20 .50
❑ 22 Superman, Avatar of Peace R 1.25 3.00
❑ 23 Wonder Woman, Princess Diana C .10 .25
❑ 24 Wonder Woman, Avatar of Truth R .40 1.00
❑ 25 Zatanna, Zatanna Zatara R .40 1.00
❑ 26 Zauriel, Guardian Angel C .10 .25
❑ 27 Disband the League U .20 .50
❑ 28 Field of Honor U .20 .50
❑ 29 Hero's Welcome R .40 1.00
❑ 30 Monitor Womb Station R .30 .75
❑ 31 New Era R .30 .75
❑ 32 Reform the League C .10 .25
❑ 33 Roll Call! C .10 .25
❑ 34 Satellite HQ C .10 .25
❑ 35 Secret Sanctuary U .20 .50
❑ 36 Teleport Tube R .30 .75
❑ 37 Wall of Will, Construct C .10 .25
❑ 38 The Watchtower R .40 1.00
❑ 39 Batman, Hidden Crusader C .10 .25
❑ 40 Bluejay, Jay Abrams C .10 .25
❑ 41 Booster Gold, Michael Jon Carter C .10 .25
❑ 42 Captain Atom, Nathaniel Adam C .10 .25
❑ 43 Captain Marvel, Billy Batson R .30 .75
❑ 44 Catherine Cobert, Embassy Chief U .20 .50
❑ 45 Crimson Fox, Vivian and Constance D'Aramis U.20 .50
❑ 46 Dinah Laurel Lance Black Canary, Pretty Bird C.10 .25
❑ 47 Dr. Fate, Kent Nelson R .30 .75
❑ 48 Fire, Beatriz DaCosta C .10 .25
❑ 49 Guy Gardner, Egomaniac C .10 .25
❑ 50 Ice, Tora Olafsdotter C .10 .25
❑ 51 Joseph Jones General Glory .10 .25
Lady Liberty's Champion C
❑ 52 Kimiyo Hoshi Dr. Light, Starlight Sentinel C .10 .25

TCG/CCG

❑ 53 L-Ron, Robot Companion U .20 .50
❑ 54 Martian Manhunter, J'onn J'onzz U .20 .50
❑ 55 Maxwell Lord, Financier C .10 .25
❑ 56 Metamorpho, Rex Mason C .10 .25
❑ 57 Oberon, Micro Manager U .20 .50
❑ 58 Power Girl, Karen Starr R .30 .75
❑ 59 Rocket Red #4, Dmitri Pushkin C .10 .25
❑ 60 Scott Free Mister Miracle .20 .50
Man of a Thousand Escapes U
❑ 61 Silver Sorceress, Laura Cynthia Neilsen C .10 .25
❑ 62 Sue Dibny, Charismatic Coordinator C .10 .25
❑ 63 Tasmanian Devil, Hugh Dawkins C .10 .25
❑ 64 Ted Kord Blue Beetle, Heir of the Scarab C .10 .25
❑ 65 BWA HA-HA HA HA! R 1.00 2.50
❑ 66 The Castle U .20 .50
❑ 67 JLI Embassy C .10 .25
❑ 68 Justice League Task Force, Team-Up C .10 .25
❑ 69 Kooey Kooey Kooey R 1.00 2.50
❑ 70 Plasma Blast C .10 .25
❑ 71 Running Interference U .20 .50
❑ 72 Safety in Numbers U .20 .50
❑ 73 Staged Attack C .10 .25
❑ 74 UN General Assembly R .40 1.00
❑ 75 UN Recognition C .10 .25
❑ 76 Abra Kadabra, Citizen Abra U .20 .50
❑ 77 Captain Boomerang, George Harkness C .10 .25
❑ 78 Circe, Immortal Sorceress C .10 .25
❑ 79 Creeping Doom, Army C .10 .25
❑ 80 David Clinton Chronos, The Time Thief C .10 .25
❑ 81 Dr. Light, Light Shaper R .30 .75
❑ 82 Evan McCulloch Mirror Master .10 .25
Smoke and Mirrors C
❑ 83 Floronic Man, Alien Hybrid U .20 .50
❑ 84 The General, Wade Eiling R .30 .75
❑ 85 Illusionary Warriors, Army C .10 .25
❑ 86 Infernal Minions, Army C .10 .25
❑ 87 Insectoid Troopers, Army C .10 .25
❑ 88 IQ, Ira Quimby C .10 .25
❑ 89 The Joker, Headline Stealer C .10 .25
❑ 90 Lex Luthor, Nefarious Philanthropist U .20 .50
❑ 91 Lex Luthor, Evil Incorporated C .10 .25
❑ 92 Libra, Alien Conqueror R .30 .75
❑ 93 Ocean Master, Son of Atlan C .10 .25
❑ 94 Poison Ivy, Deadly Rose R 1.25 3.00
❑ 95 Prometheus, Darker Knight C .10 .25
❑ 96 Sam Scudder Mirror Master, Reflective Rogue U .20 .50
❑ 97 Scarecrow, Psycho Psychologist C .10 .25
❑ 98 Shadow-Thief, Carl Sands C .10 .25
❑ 99 The Shark, Karshon C .10 .25
❑ 100 Tattooed Man, Living Ink C .10 .25
❑ 101 Zazzala Queen Bee, Royal Genetrix C .10 .25
❑ 102 All Too Easy C .10 .25
❑ 103 Criminal Mastermind C .10 .25
❑ 104 Gang-Up, Team-Up C .10 .25
❑ 105 Hard-Light Storage Tank R .50 1.25
❑ 106 Infestation U .20 .50
❑ 107 Injustice Gang Satellite R .30 .75
❑ 108 Philosopher's Stone R .30 .75
❑ 109 Power Siphon R .75 2.00
❑ 110 Royal Egg-Matrix U .20 .50
❑ 111 Secret Files C .10 .25
❑ 112 World War III R .30 .75
❑ 113 Captain Boomerang, Digger U .20 .50
❑ 114 Captain Cold, Leonard Snart U .20 .50
❑ 115 Charaxes, Killer Moth C .10 .25
❑ 116 Copperhead, Slithering Assassin C .10 .25
❑ 117 Crystal Frost Killer Frost, Cold-Hearted Killer U .20 .50
❑ 118 Darkseid, Heart of Darkness C .10 .25
❑ 119 Deadshot, Floyd Lawton R .30 .75
❑ 120 Dr. Sivana, Thaddeus Bodog Sivana C .10 .25
❑ 121 Floronic Man, Jason Woodrue C .10 .25
❑ 122 Funky Flashman, Salesman Supreme U .20 .50
❑ 123 Gorilla Grodd, Simian Mastermind C .10 .25
❑ 124 Hector Hammond, Mind Over Matter C .10 .25
❑ 125 Henry King Brainwave, Sinister Psionic C .10 .25
❑ 126 James Jesse Trickster, Giovanni Giuseppe C .10 .25
❑ 127 Lex Luthor, Criminal Genius R .30 .75
❑ 128 Manhunter Clone, Clone of Paul Kirk C .10 .25
❑ 129 Mark Desmond Blockbuster, Mindless Brute U .20 .50
❑ 130 The Mist, Jonathan Smythe C .10 .25
❑ 131 Poison Ivy, Kiss of Death C .10 .25
❑ 132 Psycho-Pirate, Roger Hayden R .30 .75
❑ 133 Quakemaster, Robert Coleman U .20 .50
❑ 134 Remoni-Notra Star Sapphire .20 .50
Zamoran Champion U
❑ 135 Scarecrow, Fearmonger C .10 .25
❑ 136 Sinestro, Corrupted by the Ring R .30 .75
❑ 137 Solomon Grundy, Buried on Sunday R .30 .75
❑ 138 Ultra-Humanite, Evolutionary Antecedent C .10 .25
❑ 139 The Wizard, William Zard C .10 .25
❑ 140 Attend or Die! R .30 .75
❑ 141 Divided We Fall R .30 .75
❑ 142 Funky's Big Rat Code, Team-Up C .10 .25
❑ 143 Gorilla City C .10 .25
❑ 144 Mysterious Benefactor U .20 .50
❑ 145 The Plunder Plan C .10 .25
❑ 146 Quadromobile U .20 .50
❑ 147 Sinister Citadel U .20 .50
❑ 148 Slaughter Swamp C .10 .25
❑ 149 Sorcerer's Treasure R .30 .75
❑ 150 Straight to the Grave R 2.50 6.00
❑ 151 With Prejudice C .10 .25
❑ 152 Justice League Signal Device C .10 .25
❑ 153 Magnificent Seven C .10 .25
❑ 154 World's Greatest Heroes, Team-Up C .10 .25
❑ 155 Amazo, Ivo's Android R .30 .75
❑ 156 Despero, Master of the Third Eye C .10 .25
❑ 157 Dr. Destiny, John Dee C .10 .25
❑ 158 Felix Faust, Infernal Dealmaker U .20 .50
❑ 159 Kanjar Ro, Kylaq Defense Minister C .10 .25
❑ 160 Mageddon, Weapon of Universal Destruction R .30 .75
❑ 161 Neron, Soul Collector R .30 .75
❑ 162 Professor Ivo, Anthony Ivo C .10 .25
❑ 163 Queen of Fables, Wickedest Witch C .10 .25
❑ 164 Rama Khan, Elemental Magician C .10 .25
❑ 165 Starro the Conqueror, Intergalactic Starfish R .30 .75
❑ 166 T.O. Morrow, Thomas Oscar Morrow U .20 .50
❑ 167 Tomorrow Woman, Trojan Telepath R .30 .75
❑ 168 Air Strike C .10 .25
❑ 169 Atlantean Trident U .20 .50
❑ 170 Balance of Power C .10 .25
❑ 171 Bulletproof C .10 .25
❑ 172 Counterstrike C .10 .25
❑ 173 Counterterrorism U .20 .50
❑ 174 Crisis on Infinite Earths, Team-Up R 1.50 4.00
❑ 175 Death Times Five C .10 .25
❑ 176 Death Trap C .10 .25
❑ 177 Funeral For a Friend U .20 .50
❑ 178 Glass Jaw C .10 .25
❑ 179 High-Tech Flare Gun U .20 .50
❑ 180 H'ronmeer's Curse R .30 .75
❑ 181 Identity Crisis R .30 .75
❑ 182 Lair of the Mastermind C .10 .25
❑ 183 Lead by Example C .10 .25
❑ 184 Membership Drive C .10 .25
❑ 185 Midnight Cravings C .10 .25
❑ 186 Not on My Watch U .20 .50
❑ 187 Nth Metal C .10 .25
❑ 188 Rallying Cry! C .10 .25
❑ 189 Resistance is Useless C .10 .25
❑ 190 Secret Origins R .75 2.00
❑ 191 Shake it Off C .10 .25
❑ 192 S.T.A.R. Labs Orbital Platform C .10 .25
❑ 193 Token Resistance C .10 .25
❑ 194 Trial by Fire C .10 .25
❑ 195 UN Building, Team-Up C .10 .25
❑ 196 Vicarious Living U .20 .50
❑ 197 Wheel of Misfortune U .20 .50
❑ 198 Mogo, The Living Planet R .30 .75
❑ 199 Oliver Queen Green Arrow, Emerald Archer U .20 .50
❑ 200 Recharge the Sun R .30 .75
❑ 201 Controller Sanction U .20 .50
❑ 202 Fatality, Emerald Assassin R .30 .75
❑ 203 Chomin, Qwardian Spy U .20 .50
❑ 204 General Fabrikant, Qwardian General U .20 .50
❑ 205 Matter Convergence R .30 .75
❑ 206 Conscription R .30 .75
❑ 207 Manhunter Conqueror, Grandmaster U .20 .50
❑ 208 War Without End R .30 .75
❑ 209 Kelex, Faithful Servant U .20 .50
❑ 210 Look-Alike Squad R 1.00 2.50
❑ 211 Bizarro Ray U .20 .50
❑ 212 Maxima, Empress of Almerac R .30 .75
❑ 213 Mobius Chair U .20 .50
❑ 214 Valkyra, Valkyrie of New Genesis U .20 .50
❑ 215 Die for Darkseid! U .20 .50
❑ 216 Mantis, Power Parasite R .30 .75
❑ 217 Justice League of Arkham, Team-Up U .20 .50
❑ 218 The Creeper, Jack Ryder R .75 2.00
❑ 219 Poisoned! U .20 .50
❑ 220 Bumblebee, Karen Beecher-Duncan U .20 .50

2005 Vs System Justice League of America Foil

COMPLETE SET (220) 50.00 100.00
*FOIL: .8X TO 2X BASIC CARDS

2005 Vs System Marvel Knights

COMPLETE SET (220) 25.00 50.00
BOOSTER BOX (24) 15.00 30.00
❑ 1 Blade, Eric Brooks R .50 1.25
❑ 2 Brother Voodoo, Jericho Drumm C .10 .25
❑ 3 Caretaker, Nomadic Mentor C .10 .25
❑ 4 Cloak, Child of Darkness C .10 .25
❑ 5 Dagger, Child of Light U .20 .50
❑ 6 Daredevil, Guardian Devil C .10 .25
❑ 7 Daredevil, Matt Murdock R 1.00 2.50
❑ 8 Daredevil, Protector of Hell's Kitchen C .10 .25
❑ 9 Dr. Strange, Stephen Strange R .40 1.00
❑ 10 Elektra, Assassin U .20 .50
❑ 11 Elektra, Elektra Natchios C .10 .25
❑ 12 Ghost Rider, Danny Ketch R .60 1.50
❑ 13 Ghost Rider, Johnny Blaze C .10 .25
❑ 14 Hannibal King, Occult Investigator C .10 .25
❑ 15 Iron Fist, Danny Rand C .10 .25
❑ 16 Iron Fist, Living Weapon C .10 .25
❑ 17 Luke Cage, Power Man R .40 1.00
❑ 18 Luke Cage, Street Enforcer C .10 .25
❑ 19 Micro-Chip, Linus Lieberman C .10 .25
❑ 20 Mikado and Mosha, Angels of Destruction C .10 .25
❑ 21 Moon Knight, Marc Spector C .10 .25
❑ 22 Natasha Romanoff Black Widow, KGB Killer U .20 .50
❑ 23 Punisher, Executioner C .10 .25
❑ 24 Punisher, Judge R .40 1.00
❑ 25 Punisher, Jury U .20 .50
❑ 26 Shang Chi, Master of Kung Fu U .20 .50
❑ 27 Spider-Man, The Spectacular Spider-Man C .10 .25
❑ 28 Stick, Leader of the Chaste U .20 .50
❑ 29 Yelena Belova Black Widow, Enemy Agent R .40 1.00
❑ 30 Blind Justice R .40 1.00
❑ 31 Bring the Pain C .10 .25
❑ 32 Crime and Punishment C .10 .25
❑ 33 Deposed C .10 .25
❑ 34 Head Shot C .10 .25
❑ 35 Hell's Kitchen U .20 .50
❑ 36 Judge, Jury, and Executioner C .10 .25
❑ 37 Midnight Sons C .10 .25
❑ 38 Penance Stare U .20 .50
❑ 39 Punisher's Armory U .20 .50
❑ 40 Quentin Carnival U .20 .50
❑ 41 Quick Kill C .10 .25
❑ 42 Swan Dive U .20 .50
❑ 43 Titanium Sword U .20 .50
❑ 44 War Wagon C .10 .25
❑ 45 Wild Ride R 2.50 6.00
❑ 46 Anarchist, Man of the People R .40 1.00
❑ 47 Anarchist, Tike Alicar U .20 .50
❑ 48 Battering Ram, Short-Lived Strongman C .10 .25
❑ 49 Bloke, Mickey Tork U .20 .50
❑ 50 Coach, Manipulative Mentor C .10 .25
❑ 51 Corkscrew, Twisted Trainee C .10 .25
❑ 52 Dead Girl, Crafty Cadaver C .10 .25
❑ 53 Doop, Forward Observer C .10 .25
❑ 54 Doop, Ultimate Weapon R .40 1.00
❑ 55 El Guapo, Robbie Rodriguez U .20 .50
❑ 56 Gin Genie, Beckah Parker C .10 .25
❑ 57 La Nuit, Pierre Truffaut C .10 .25
❑ 58 Mysterious Fan Boy, Arthur Lundberg C .10 .25
❑ 59 Orphan, Good Guy C .10 .25
❑ 60 Orphan, Guy Smith C .10 .25
❑ 61 Orphan, Mr. Sensitive R .40 1.00
❑ 62 Phat, William Reilly R .40 1.00
❑ 63 Plazm, Protoplasmic Protagonist C .10 .25
❑ 64 Saint Anna, Sympathetic Healer C .10 .25
❑ 65 Sluk, Byron Spencer C .10 .25
❑ 66 The Spike, Angry Young Mutant C .10 .25
❑ 67 U-Go-Girl, Eddie Sawyer U .20 .50
❑ 68 U-Go-Girl, Tragic Teleporter U .20 .50
❑ 69 Venus Dee Milo, Dee Milo R .40 1.00
❑ 70 Venus Dee Milo, Telegenic Teleporter U .20 .50
❑ 71 Vivisector, Lunatic Lycanthrope C .10 .25
❑ 72 Vivisector, Myles Alfred C .10 .25
❑ 73 Zeitgeist, Axel Cluney C .10 .25
❑ 74 Dead Weight U .20 .50
❑ 75 Doop Cam C .10 .25
❑ 76 Failing Stars C .10 .25
❑ 77 Glory Hound C .10 .25
❑ 78 Go in Swinging U .20 .50
❑ 79 Grandstanding U .20 .50
❑ 80 Mind Over Matter U .20 .50
❑ 81 Missed Drop C .10 .25
❑ 82 Nerve Strike C .10 .25
❑ 83 Never Give Up! U .20 .50
❑ 84 Overexposed C .10 .25
❑ 85 Spin Doctoring R .75 2.00
❑ 86 Star of the Show R .60 1.50
❑ 87 Supporting Role C .10 .25
❑ 88 Training Theatre U .20 .50
❑ 89 X-Statix Cafe C .10 .25
❑ 90 X-Statix HQ R .40 1.00
❑ 91 Bullseye, Deadly Marksman R .50 1.25
❑ 92 Bullseye, Master of Murder C .10 .25
❑ 93 Carbone's Assassins, Army C .10 .25
❑ 94 Cobra, Klaus Vorhees C .10 .25
❑ 95 Deadpool, Wade Wilson R .50 1.25
❑ 96 Death-Stalker, Phillip Sterling C .10 .25
❑ 97 Echo, Maya Lopez C .10 .25
❑ 98 Jaime Ortiz Damage, Cybernetic Enforcer C .10 .25
❑ 99 Jester, Jonathan Powers U .20 .50
❑ 100 Jigsaw, Billy Russo U .20 .50
❑ 101 Kingpin, The Kingpin of Crime R .40 1.00
❑ 102 Kingpin, Wilson Fisk C .10 .25
❑ 103 Kirigi, Master Assassin U .20 .50
❑ 104 Masked Marauder, Frank Farnum C .10 .25
❑ 105 Mr. Code, Masked Malcontent U .20 .50
❑ 106 Mr. Fear, Zoltan Drago C .10 .25
❑ 107 Mr. Hyde, Calvin Zabo C .10 .25
❑ 108 Nuke, Renegade Super Soldier C .10 .25
❑ 109 Owl, Leland Owlsley R .50 1.25
❑ 110 Roscoe Sweeny, Fixer U .20 .50
❑ 111 Saracen, Muzzafar Lambert C .10 .25
❑ 112 Sniper, Rich van Burian C .10 .25
❑ 113 Stilt-Man, Wilbur Day R .40 1.00
❑ 114 The Hand, Army C .10 .25
❑ 115 The Rose, Shadowy Lieutenant U .20 .50
❑ 116 The Russian, Contract Killer C .10 .25
❑ 117 Typhoid Mary, Mary Walker R .40 1.00
❑ 118 Vanessa Fisk, Mob Matron C .10 .25
❑ 119 Armed Escort C .10 .25
❑ 120 Boss of Bosses U .20 .50
❑ 121 Drive-by Shooting C .10 .25
❑ 122 Face the Master U .20 .50
❑ 123 Geraci Family Estate U .20 .50
❑ 124 Good Night, Sweet Prince C .10 .25
❑ 125 Hand Dojo U .20 .50
❑ 126 King Takes Knight R .40 1.00
❑ 127 Made Men C .10 .25
❑ 128 Marked for Death U .20 .50
❑ 129 No Rest for the Wicked C .10 .25
❑ 130 Rough House C .10 .25
❑ 131 Shakedown C .10 .25
❑ 132 Sold Out R .40 1.00
❑ 133 The Family C .10 .25
❑ 134 Untouchable R .40 1.00
❑ 135 Uprising U .20 .50
❑ 136 Anton Hellgate, Thanatologist C .10 .25
❑ 137 Asmodeus, Duke of Hell U .20 .50
❑ 138 Blackheart, Son of Mephisto C .10 .25
❑ 139 Blackout, Master of Darkness U .20 .50
❑ 140 Centurious, The Soulless Man C .10 .25
❑ 141 Deacon Frost, Vampire Master R .50 1.25
❑ 142 Dracula, Lord of the Damned C .10 .25
❑ 143 Dracula, Vlad Dracula R .50 1.25
❑ 144 Lilith, Daughter of Dracula R .40 1.00
❑ 145 Marie Laveau, Voodoo Priestess U .40 1.00
❑ 146 Mephisto, Father of Lies R .40 1.00
❑ 147 Mephisto, Soulstealer U .20 .50
❑ 148 Morbius, The Living Vampire C .10 .25
❑ 149 Nekra, Nekra Sinclair U .20 .50
❑ 150 New Blood, Army C .10 .25
❑ 151 Nightmare, Dark Lord of Dreams C .10 .25
❑ 152 Orb, Drake Shannon R .60 1.50
❑ 153 Reaper, Vampire Armageddon C .10 .25
❑ 154 Shelob, Queen of Spiders U .20 .50
❑ 155 Skinner, Psychotic Shredder C .10 .25
❑ 156 Steel Wind, Cyborg Cyclist C .10 .25
❑ 157 Suicide, Chris Daniels C .10 .25
❑ 158 Tryks, Army C .10 .25
❑ 159 Varnae, First Vampire R .40 1.00
❑ 160 Vengeance, Michael Badilino C .10 .25
❑ 161 Werewolf by Night, Jack Russell C .10 .25
❑ 162 Zarathos, Spirit of Vengeance C .10 .25
❑ 163 Zodiak, Norman Harrison C .10 .25
❑ 164 Black Magic C .10 .25
❑ 165 Blood Hunt R .40 1.00
❑ 166 Children of the Night C .10 .25
❑ 167 Dark Embrace R .40 1.00
❑ 168 Dracula's Castle U .20 .50
❑ 169 Evil Awakens U .20 .50
❑ 170 Gravesite U .20 .50
❑ 171 Hypnotic Charms C .10 .25
❑ 172 Infernal Gateway U .20 .50
❑ 173 Mist Form U .20 .50
❑ 174 Shadow Step C .10 .25
❑ 175 Strength of the Grave C .10 .25
❑ 176 The Darkhold C .10 .25
❑ 177 Club Dead C .10 .25
❑ 178 Wake the Dead U .20 .50
❑ 179 Witching Hour R .40 1.00
❑ 180 Blade, The Daywalker C .10 .25
❑ 181 Professor X, Mutant Mentor R .50 1.25
❑ 182 Elektra, Agent of the Hand C .10 .25
❑ 183 Deathwatch, Unrepentant Killer C .10 .25
❑ 184 Moving Target C .10 .25
❑ 185 Hell's Fury C .10 .25
❑ 186 Day of the Dead C .10 .25
❑ 187 Blown to Pieces C .10 .25
❑ 188 Team X-change R .40 1.00
❑ 189 Coalition of Heroes R .40 1.00
❑ 190 Honor Among Thieves R .40 1.00
❑ 191 Professor X, Mental Master R .50 1.25
❑ 192 Outback Stronghold R .40 1.00
❑ 193 Valeria, Daughter of Doom R .40 1.00
❑ 194 Lockjaw, Inhuman U .20 .50
❑ 195 Scarlet Witch, Eldritch Enchantress R .40 1.00
❑ 196 Monument to a Madman R .40 1.00
❑ 197 Diplomatic Immunity R .40 1.00
❑ 198 Hounds of Ahab, Army U .20 .50
❑ 199 Mekanix R .40 1.00
❑ 200 Frog Man, Eugene Patilio U .20 .50
❑ 201 Scarlet Spider Spider-Man, Successor R .50 1.25
❑ 202 Swing into Action R .40 1.00
❑ 203 The Slingers R .40 1.00
❑ 204 Web Shooters R .40 1.00
❑ 205 Carrion, Cadaverous Clone U .20 .50
❑ 206 Mendel Stromm, Robot Master R .40 1.00
❑ 207 Scorpia, Elaine Colls U .20 .50
❑ 208 Inside Job R .40 1.00
❑ 209 Lacuna, Media Darling C .10 .25
❑ 210 Sharon Ginsberg, Corrupt Counsel C .10 .25
❑ 211 Advance Recon C .10 .25
❑ 212 Marvel Team-Up C .10 .25
❑ 213 Medallion of Power R .40 1.00
❑ 214 Meltdown C .10 .25
❑ 215 Mystic Chain R .50 1.25
❑ 216 Mystical Sigil U .20 .50
❑ 217 Out of the Darkness C .10 .25
❑ 218 Psychoville C .10 .25
❑ 219 Team Spirit U .20 .50
❑ 220 Weapon of Choice R .50 1.25

2005 Vs System Marvel Knights Foil

COMPLETE SET (220) 50.00 100.00
*FOIL: .8X TO 2X BASIC CARDS

2005 Vs System The Avengers

COMPLETE SET (220) 25.00 50.00
BOOSTER BOX (24) 20.00 40.00
❑ 1 Beast, Furry Blue Scientist C .10 .25
❑ 2 Black Panther, T'challa U .20 .50
❑ 3 Captain America, Steve Rogers C .10 .25
❑ 4 Captain America, Super Soldier R 1.00 2.50
❑ 5 Carol Danvers Warbird, Galactic Adventurer C .10 .25
❑ 6 Dane Whitman Black Knight, Heroic Paladin C .10 .25
❑ 7 Falcon, Sam Wilson C .10 .25
❑ 8 Hank Pym Ant Man, Diminutive Hero C .10 .25
❑ 9 Hank Pym Giant Man, Towering Titan U .20 .50
❑ 10 Hank Pym Goliath, Giant Genius C .10 .25
❑ 11 Hank Pym Yellowjacket, Pym Particle Creator C .10 .25
❑ 12 Hawkeye, Clinton Barton C .10 .25
❑ 13 Hercules, Son of Zeus U .20 .50
❑ 14 Hulk, Gamma Rage R .50 1.25
❑ 15 Iron Man, Invincible C .10 .25
❑ 16 Iron Man, Tony Stark C .10 .25
❑ 17 Jarvis, Honorary Avenger R 1.00 2.50
❑ 18 Monica Rambeau Captain Marvel, Lady of Light R 1.00 2.50
❑ 19 Natasha Romanoff Black Widow, Super Spy U .20 .50
❑ 20 Quicksilver, Mutant Avenger C .10 .25
❑ 21 Rick Jones, A Hero's Best Friend U .20 .50
❑ 22 Scarlet Witch, Mistress of Chaos Magic C .10 .25
❑ 23 She-Hulk, Gamma Bombshell C .10 .25
❑ 24 Thor, God of Thunder R 1.50 4.00
❑ 25 Thor, Odinson R 1.50 4.00
❑ 26 Vision, Synthetic Humanoid C .10 .25
❑ 27 Wasp, Janet Van Dyne-Pym C .10 .25
❑ 28 Wonder Man, Simon Williams U .20 .50
❑ 29 Avengers Assemble! R 2.00 5.00
❑ 30 Avengers Mansion R 1.00 2.50
❑ 31 Call Down the Lightning C .10 .25
❑ 32 Chaos Magic R .40 1.00
❑ 33 Earth's Mightiest Heroes R 1.25 3.00
❑ 34 Legendary Battles C .10 .25
❑ 35 Mjolnir R .50 1.25
❑ 36 Playroom C .10 .25
❑ 37 Pym Laboratories U .20 .50
❑ 38 Quinjet C .10 .25
❑ 39 Repel Attack C .10 .25
❑ 40 Repulsor Ray C .10 .25
❑ 41 Two Worlds, Team-Up C .10 .25
❑ 42 Walk Through Walls R .40 1.00
❑ 43 Albert Gaines Nuke, Atomic Powerhouse C .10 .25
❑ 44 Amphibian, Kingsley Rice R .40 1.00
❑ 45 Ape X, Xina C .10 .25
❑ 46 Arcanna, Arcanna Jones C .10 .25
❑ 47 Blue Eagle, James Dore Jr. C .10 .25
❑ 48 Doctor Decibel, Anton Decibel C .10 .25
❑ 49 Doctor Spectrum, Joe Ledger R .50 1.25
❑ 50 Foxfire, Olivia Underwood U .20 .50
❑ 51 Golden Archer, Wyatt McDonald C .10 .25
❑ 52 Haywire, Harold Danforth C .10 .25
❑ 53 Hyperion, Mark Milton C .10 .25
❑ 54 Hyperion, Sun God R .40 1.00
❑ 55 Inertia, Edith Freiberg C .10 .25
❑ 56 Lady Lark, Linda Lewis U .20 .50
❑ 57 Lamprey, Donald McQuiggan C .10 .25
❑ 58 Moonglow, Melissa Hanover C .10 .25
❑ 59 Nighthawk, Kyle Richmond C .10 .25
❑ 60 Power Princess, The Last Utopian R .40 1.00
❑ 61 Power Princess, Zarda C .10 .25
❑ 62 Quagmire, Jerome Meyers U .20 .50
❑ 63 Redstone, Michael Redstone U .20 .50
❑ 64 Shape, Malleable Mutant U .20 .50
❑ 65 Skymax, Skrullian Skymaster C .10 .25
❑ 66 Thermite, Sam Yurimoto C .10 .25
❑ 67 Tom Thumb, Thomas Thompson C .10 .25
❑ 68 Whizzer, Stanley Stewart U .20 .50
❑ 69 AIDA R .40 1.00
❑ 70 Airskimmer C .10 .25
❑ 71 Answer the Call C .10 .25
❑ 72 Behavior Modification Device, Team-Up C .10 .25
❑ 73 Eldritch Power C .10 .25
❑ 74 Hibernaculum C .10 .25
❑ 75 Other-Earth R .50 1.25
❑ 76 Panacea Potion U .20 .50
❑ 77 Peace in Our Time U .20 .50
❑ 78 Project Utopia R .40 1.00
❑ 79 Rocket Central R .40 1.00
❑ 80 Squadron City R .40 1.00
❑ 81 Supply Line U .20 .50
❑ 82 Utopia Isle U .20 .50
❑ 83 Beetle Mach 1, Reluctant Hero C .10 .25
❑ 84 Beetle Mach 2, Matthew Davis C .10 .25
❑ 85 Beetle Mach 3, Repentant Villain U .20 .50
❑ 86 Beetle Mach 4, New Team Leader C .10 .25
❑ 87 Blizzard, Donny Gill C .10 .25
❑ 88 Charcoal, Charles Burlingame C .10 .25
❑ 89 Dallas Riordan, Mayoral Aide C .10 .25
❑ 90 Dallas Riordan Vantage, Ionic Inheritor C .10 .25
❑ 91 Erik Josten Atlas, Ionic Powerhouse R .40 1.00
❑ 92 Erik Josten Atlas, Kosmos Convict U .20 .50
❑ 93 Genis-Vell Captain Marvel, Son of Mar-Vell R .50 1.25
❑ 94 Hawkeye, Leader by Example R .60 1.50
❑ 95 Helmut Zemo Citizen V, Tactician C .10 .25
❑ 96 Helmut Zemo Citizen V, Warmonger C .10 .25
❑ 97 Iron Man Cobalt Man, Avenger in Disguise C .10 .25
❑ 98 Jolt, Helen Takahama C .10 .25
❑ 99 Joystick, Janice Yanizesh U .20 .50
❑ 100 Karla Sofen Meteorite, Celestial Power R .40 1.00
❑ 101 Karla Sofen Meteorite, Twin Moonstones R .40 1.00
❑ 102 Melissa Gold Songbird, Heroine Unbound C .10 .25
❑ 103 Melissa Gold Songbird, Sonic Carapace U .20 .50
❑ 104 Ogre, Weaponsmith U .20 .50
❑ 105 Paul Ebersol Techno, Gadgeteer C .10 .25
❑ 106 Paul Ebersol Techno, Man of Metal C .10 .25
❑ 107 Plant Man Blackheath, Samuel Smithers C .10 .25
❑ 108 Radioactive Man, Reformed Renegade U .20 .50
❑ 109 Speed Demon, Second Chance Speedster U .20 .50
❑ 110 A Second Chance U .20 .50
❑ 111 Biomodem Satellite U .20 .50
❑ 112 Combat Maneuvers C .10 .25
❑ 113 Deadly Conspiracy C .10 .25
❑ 114 Justice, Like Lightning C .10 .25
❑ 115 Marvel's Most Wanted R .40 1.00
❑ 116 Mt. Charteris R .40 1.00
❑ 117 New Identity R 1.25 3.00
❑ 118 Project Liberator R .40 1.00
❑ 119 Stormfront-1, Team-Up C .10 .25
❑ 120 Thunder Jet C .10 .25
❑ 121 Thunderbolts Plaza R .40 1.00

TCG/CCG

122 V-Wing U .20 .50
123 Win-Lose Deal U .20 .50
124 Beetle, Armorsmith C .10 .25
125 Bulldozer, Wrecking Crew C .10 .25
126 Egghead, Elihas Starr C .10 .25
127 Enchantress, Amora C .10 .25
128 Erik Josten Goliath, Growing Menace C .10 .25
129 Executioner, Scourge of Jotunheim R .40 1.00
130 Grey Gargoyle, Paul Pierre Duval U .20 .50
131 Heinrich Zemo Baron Zemo, Baron of Zeulniz C .10 .25
132 Helmut Zemo Baron Zemo, Uber Enemy U .20 .50
133 Karla Sofen Moonstone, Master Manipulator U .20 .50
134 Klaw, Ulysses Klaw R .50 1.25
135 Marcus Daniels Blackout, Darkbringer C .10 .25
136 Melissa Gold Screaming Mimi .10 .25
Mimi Schwartz C
137 Melter, Bruno Horgan C .10 .25
138 Mr. Hyde, Engine of Destruction C .10 .25
139 Nathan Garrett Black Knight, Corrupt Crusader C .10 .25
140 Paul Ebersol Fixer, Problem Solver R .40 1.00
141 Piledriver, Wrecking Crew C .10 .25
142 Radioactive Man, Chen Lu C .10 .25
143 Scorpion, Fatal Sting U .20 .50
144 Shocker, Vibro-Shock Villain R .40 1.00
145 The Wrecker, Wrecking Crew C .10 .25
146 Thunderball, Wrecking Crew C .10 .25
147 Tiger Shark, Todd Arliss C .10 .25
148 Titania, Vengeful Vixen C .10 .25
149 Ultron Crimson Cowl, Dark Disguise U .20 .50
150 Ultron Ultron 5, Ultimate Evil R .40 1.00
151 Whirlwind, David Cannon U .20 .50
152 Yellowjacket, Rita DeMara C .10 .25
153 Adhesive X U .20 .50
154 Crime Spree C .10 .25
155 Evil Reborn C .10 .25
156 Hard Sound Construct, Construct R .50 1.25
157 Hero's Demise R .50 1.25
158 Mystic Summons C .10 .25
159 Sonic Disruption C .10 .25
160 Stolen Power C .10 .25
161 The Wrecking Crew C .10 .25
162 Under Siege R .40 1.00
163 Unfair Advantage C .10 .25
164 Amenhotep, Dark Pharaoh U .20 .50
165 Baltag, Hand of the Conqueror C .10 .25
166 Growing Man, Kinetic Stimuloid U .20 .50
167 Kang Kross-roads U .20 .50
168 Kang, Earth Mesozoic-24 U .20 .50
169 Kang, Immortus R .40 1.00
170 Kang, Kang Cobra C .10 .25
171 Kang, Kang Kong R .40 1.00
172 Kang, Kang Ransom R .50 1.25
173 Kang, Lord Kang R .40 1.00
174 Kang, Lord of Limbo C .10 .25
175 Kang, Master of Time C .10 .25
176 Kang, Rama Tut U .20 .50
177 Kang, The Conqueror R .40 1.00
178 Kang's Guards, Army U .20 .50
179 Macrobots, Army C .10 .25
180 Tempus, Menace out of Time C .10 .25
181 Game of the Galaxy R .40 1.00
182 Kang, Ultimate Kang C .10 .25
183 Null Time Zone R 1.00 2.50
184 Psyche-Globe U .20 .50
185 Spheres of Solitude U .20 .50
186 The Time Keepers C .10 .25
187 Faces of Evil, Team-Up C .10 .25
188 Justice for All, Team-Up C .10 .25
189 Supreme Sanction, Team-Up C .10 .25
190 A Day Unlike Any Other, Team-Up C .10 .25
191 Avengers Disassembled R .40 1.00
192 Call to Arms C .10 .25
193 Force Field Belt C .10 .25
194 Heroes in Reserve C .10 .25
195 Insect Swarm C .10 .25
196 Might Makes Right C .10 .25
197 Prismatic Shield, Construct C .10 .25
198 Seek Cover C .10 .25
199 Shrink U .20 .50
200 System Failure R .75 2.00
201 United We Stand C .10 .25
202 War of Attrition R .40 1.00
203 Windstorm C .10 .25
204 Polaris, Lorna Dane U .20 .50
205 Framistat U .20 .50
206 Mammomax, Elephant Boy U .20 .50
207 Zorba, Deposed Leader of Latveria R .40 1.00
208 Ahab, Houndkeeper U .20 .50
209 Spider-Man, Peter Parker R 1.25 3.00
210 White Tiger, Hector Ayala U .20 .50
211 Basilisk, Basil Elks U .20 .50
212 Vermin, Sewer Rat U .20 .50
213 Lady Punisher, Lynn Michaels U .20 .50
214 Bring Down the House R .40 1.00
215 Phat, Liv'n Large U .20 .50
216 Mutant of the Year R .50 1.25
217 Hitman, Burt Kenyon U .20 .50
218 Hired Hit R .50 1.25
219 Mortician, Toussaint Morrow U .20 .50
220 Spirits of Vengeance R .40 1.00

2005 Vs System The Avengers Foil

COMPLETE SET (220) 50.00 100.00
*FOIL: .8X TO 2X BASIC CARDS

2006 Vs System Heralds of Galactus

COMPLETE SET (220) 35.00 75.00
BOOSTER BOX (24) 25.00 50.00
1 Air-Walker, Gabriel Lan R 2.50 6.00
2 Air-Walker, Harbinger of Despair U .20 .50
3 Destroyer, Soulless Juggernaut C .10 .25
4 Destroyer, Harbinger of Devastation C .10 .25
5 Firelord, Pyreus Kril C .10 .25
6 Firelord, Harbinger of Havoc C .10 .25
7 Frankie Raye Nova, Optimistic Youth C .10 .25
8 Frankie Raye Nova, Soul Searcher C .10 .25
9 Frankie Raye Nova, Harbinger of Death C .10 .25
10 Galactus, The Maker U .20 .50
11 Galactus, Devourer of Worlds R 3.00 8.00
12 Galan, Famished C .10 .25
13 Human Torch, The Invisible Man C .10 .25
14 Morg, Slayer C .10 .25
15 Morg, Corrupt Destroyer C .10 .25
16 Morg, Harbinger of Extinction C .10 .25
17 Plasma, Replacement Herald C .10 .25
18 Red Shift, Rift Walker R 2.00 5.00
19 Silver Surfer, Skyrider of the Spaceways U .75 2.00
20 Silver Surfer, Righteous Protector C .10 .25
21 Silver Surfer, Harbinger of Oblivion R 1.50 4.00
22 Stardust, Merciless Warrior C .10 .25
23 Terrax, The Tamer R .60 1.50
24 Terrax, Harbinger of Ruin R .50 1.25
25 The Fallen One, The Forgotten C .10 .25
26 The Punishers, Army C .10 .25
27 Tyrant, The Original Herald U .20 .50
28 Absorba Shield R .75 2.00
29 Cosmic Necessity U .20 .50
30 Creation of a Herald R 3.00 8.00
31 Elemental Battle C .10 .25
32 Elemental Converters U .20 .50
33 I Hunger R .60 1.50
34 I Must Obey R .40 1.00
35 Inspiring Demise R 1.50 4.00
36 Kindred Spirits U .20 .50
37 Pacification U .20 .50
38 Relentless Onslaught C .10 .25
39 Taa II R .40 1.00
40 The Herald Ordeal, Team-Up C .10 .25
41 The Power Cosmic Unleashed C .10 .25
42 Ultimate Nullifier R .50 1.25
43 Worldeater Apparatus U .20 .50
44 Worldship U .20 .50
45 Admiral Galen Kor, Lunatic Legion C .10 .25
46 Bron Char, Lunatic Legion R .50 1.25
47 Captain Att-Lass, Starforce C .10 .25
48 Clumsy Foulup, Puppet Dictator C .10 .25
49 Colonel Yon-Rogg, Commander of the Helion R .60 1.50
50 Commander Dylon Clr, Lunatic Legion C .10 .25
51 Dr. Minerva, Starforce C .10 .25
52 Korath the Pursuer, Starforce C .10 .25
53 Kree Commandos, Army U .20 .50
54 Kree Public Accusers, Army U .20 .50
55 Kree Soldiers, Army U .20 .50
56 Lieutenant Kona Lor, Lunatic Legion C .10 .25
57 Lunatic Legionnaires, Army U .20 .50
58 Mar-Vell Captain Marvel, Soldier of the Empire C .10 .25
59 Mar-Vell Captain Marvel, Enemy of the Empire C .10 .25
60 Nenora, Skrull Usurper C .10 .25
61 Ronan the Accuser, Starforce C .10 .25
62 Ronan the Accuser, Supreme Public Accuser R .40 1.00
63 Ruul Warrior, Army C .10 .25
64 Sentry #459, Advance Guard C .10 .25
65 Shatterax, Starforce C .10 .25
66 Sintariis, High Kronamaster R .40 1.00
67 Supreme Intelligence, Kree Collective R .40 1.00
68 Supremor, Starforce C .10 .25
69 Talla Ron, Lunatic Legion C .10 .25
70 Ultimus, Starforce C .10 .25
71 Conquered Planet C .10 .25
72 Enemy of the Empire U .20 .50
73 Genetic Destiny U .20 .50
74 Hala C .10 .25
75 Improper Burial U .20 .50
76 Live Kree . . . or Die! U .20 .50
77 Nega-Bands U .20 .50
78 Nega-Bomb R .40 1.00
79 Penal Colony C .10 .25
80 Planet Weapon R .60 1.50
81 Pressed into Service, Team-Up C .10 .25
82 Remnant Fleet C .10 .25
83 Starforce Strike C .10 .25
84 Stargate R 2.50 6.00
85 Strategic Retreat R .40 1.00
86 The Infamous Seven U .20 .50
87 The Lunatic Legion U .20 .50
88 Universal Weapon C .10 .25
89 Ahura, Heir to Attilan C .10 .25
90 Alaris, The Outgoing One C .10 .25
91 Alpha Primitives, Army C .10 .25
92 Black Bolt, Illuminati C .10 .25
93 Black Bolt, King of the Inhumans C .10 .25
94 Black Bolt, Devastating Decree R .50 1.25
95 Crystal, Elementelle C .10 .25
96 Dewoz, Dark Reflection C .10 .25
97 Dinu, Face of Terror C .10 .25
98 Franklin Richards, Creator of Counter-Earth C .10 .25
99 Gorgon, Thundering Hooves R .40 1.00
100 Human Torch, Sparky C .10 .25
101 Invisible Woman, Flame On! C .10 .25
102 Jolen, The Treacherous One U .20 .50
103 Karnak, The Shatterer R .75 2.00
104 Lockjaw, Inhuman's Best Friend U .75 2.00
105 Luna Maximoff, Only Human C .10 .25
106 Maximus the Mad, Mental Manipulator C .10 .25
107 Medusa, Queen of the Inhumans U .20 .50
108 Mr. Fantastic, Illuminati U .20 .50
109 Nahrees, The Negative One C .10 .25
110 Quicksilver, Inhuman by Marriage C .10 .25
111 San, The Alienated One C .10 .25
112 Thing, Rockhead C .10 .25
113 Tonaja, The Responsible One C .10 .25
114 Triton, Aquatic Ambassador R .40 1.00
115 Attilan R .75 2.00
116 Blue Area of the Moon C .10 .25
117 Exploiting the Flaw R .50 1.25
118 Extended Family, Team-Up C .10 .25
119 Final Decree R .40 1.00
120 Himalayan Enclave C .10 .25
121 It's Clobberin' Time! C .10 .25
122 Power Struggle U .20 .50
123 Terrigenesis U .20 .50
124 The Great Refuge R 3.00 8.00
125 The Outside World C .10 .25
126 The Royal Guard R 1.50 4.00
127 The Substructure C .10 .25
128 Waking the Ancestors C .10 .25
129 Divinity, Vampiric General U .20 .50
130 Doom-Bot Dr. Doom, Cosmic Thief C .10 .25
131 Doom-Bot Corps, Army C .10 .25
132 Dorma, Atlantean General C .10 .25
133 Dr. Doom, Richards's Rival C .10 .25
134 Dr. Doom, Sorcerous Savant C .10 .25
135 Dr. Doom, Latverian Monarch R .60 1.50
136 Elite Doom Guards, Army C .10 .25
137 Invisible Woman, Baroness Von Doom C .10 .25
138 Iron Man, Illuminati C .10 .25
139 Kang, One of Many U .20 .50
140 Kang, Destiny Warrior R .75 2.00
141 Klaw, Sonic Construct R .40 1.00
142 Lancer, Samantha Dunbar C .10 .25
143 Magneto, Acts of Vengeance C .10 .25
144 Mole Man, Moloid Master U .20 .50
145 Molecule Man, Owen Reece R .40 1.00
146 Moloids, Army C .10 .25
147 Mr. Fantastic, Doom's Adversary U .20 .50
148 Purple Man, Subtle Manipulator U .20 .50
149 Shakti, Mage General C .10 .25
150 Sub-Mariner, Illuminati C .10 .25
151 Technarx, Cyborg General C .10 .25
152 Titania, Temper Tantrum C .10 .25
153 Ultron Ultron 11, Army C .10 .25
154 Valeria Von Doom, Heir to Latveria C .10 .25
155 Armies of Doom U .20 .50
156 Arsenal of Doom C .10 .25
157 Astral Suppression U .20 .50
158 Doom Needs Only Doom C .10 .25
159 Doomed Earth R 1.50 4.00
160 Doomstadt, Castle Doom R 1.25 3.00
161 Expendable Ally R 1.25 3.00
162 For the Glory of Doom!, Team-Up C .10 .25
163 Lust for Power R .40 1.00
164 Mask of Doom U .20 .50
165 Master of Puppets U .20 .50
166 Super-Genius C .10 .25
167 The Devil We Know C .10 .25
168 The Enemy Within R .40 1.00
169 Time Thief R 3.00 8.00
170 Unthinkable R .40 1.00
171 Adam Warlock, Protector of the Soul Gem U .20 .50
172 Drax the Destroyer .40 1.00
Protector of the Power Gem R
173 Gamora, Protector of the Time Gem U .20 .50
174 Moondragon, Protector of the Mind Gem C .10 .25
175 Pip the Troll, Protector of the Space Gem U .20 .50
176 Thanos, Protector of the Reality Gem R .40 1.00
177 Gathering the Watch U .20 .50
178 Mind Gem, Infinity Gem C .10 .25
179 Power Gem, Infinity Gem C .10 .25
180 Reality Gem, Infinity Gem R 1.50 4.00
181 Soul Gem, Infinity Gem U .20 .50
182 Soul World U .20 .50
183 Space Gem, Infinity Gem U .20 .50
184 The Infinity Gauntlet R .50 1.25
185 Time Gem, Infinity Gem R .50 1.25
186 Captain America, Skrull Impostor U .20 .50
187 Ethan Edwards, Visitor from Another World C .10 .25
188 Paibok, The Power Skrull C .10 .25
189 Rogue, Total Transformation R .50 1.25
190 Titannus, Alien Conqueror C .10 .25
191 Warskrull, Skrull Infiltrator U .20 .50
192 Wolverine, Skrunucklehead C .10 .25
193 Act of Defiance, Team-Up C .10 .25
194 Alien Insurrection C .10 .25
195 Interstellar Offensive C .10 .25
196 Armageddon R .75 2.00
197 Assault and Battery U .20 .50
198 Barbaric Brawl C .10 .25
199 Battleworld C .10 .25
200 Cannibal Tech C .10 .25
201 Cosmic Order C .10 .25
202 Ego the Living Planet R .40 1.00
203 Intergalactic Summit C .10 .25
204 Sworn Enemies C .10 .25
205 The Kyln C .10 .25
206 The Rapture U .20 .50
207 The Uni-Power C .10 .25
208 Thanos, Alpha and Omega R .40 1.00
209 Barnacle, Acolyte U .20 .50
210 Negative Zone, Shadow Dimension U .20 .50
211 Syphonn, Energy Leech R .50 1.25
212 Carnage, Symbiote Surfer R .60 1.50
213 Dr. Strange, Illuminati U .20 .50
214 Mephisto, Lord of Hell U .20 .50
215 Taskmaster, Mnemonic Assassin U .20 .50
216 O-Force R .40 1.00
217 Katrina Luisa Van Horne Amazon .20 .50
Unrepentant Hero U
218 Haywire, Suicidal Lover R .60 1.50
219 Litterbug, Killer Cockroach U .20 .50
220 Mr. Sinister, Supreme Geneticist U .20 .50

2006 Vs System Heralds of Galactus Foil

COMPLETE SET (220) 75.00 150.00
*FOIL: .8X TO 2X BASIC CARDS

2006 Vs System Infinite Crisis

COMPLETE SET (220) 25.00 50.00
BOOSTER BOX (24) 20.00 40.00
1 Alan Scott Sentinel, Golden Age Guardian R .40 1.00
2 Atom Smasher, Al Rothstein U .20 .50
3 Batman, Earth 2 C .10 .25
Golden Age Academic U
4 Black Adam, Ruthless Hero C .10 .25
5 Captain Marvel, Earth's Mightiest Mortal R .40 1.00
6 Carter Hall Hawkman, Eternal Champion C .10 .25
7 Charles McNider Dr. Mid-Nite .20 .50
8 Chay-Ara Hawkgirl, Eternal Companion C .10 .25
9 Dr. Fate, Lord of Order R .40 1.00
10 Hourman III Hourman, Time Machine U .20 .50
11 Huntress, Earth 2 C .10 .25
12 Jakeem Williams, JJ Thunder U .20 .50
13 Jay Garrick The Flash, Golden Age Speedster R .40 1.00
14 Katar Hol Hawkman, Eternal Hero C .10 .25
15 Kate Spencer Manhunter, Fearless Renegade U .20 .50
16 Kendra Saunders Hawkgirl, Eternal Heroine C .10 .25
17 Michael Holt Mr. Terrific, Renaissance Man C .10 .25
18 Power Girl, Earth 2 C .10 .25
19 Prince Khufu Hawkman, Eternal Warrior C .10 .25
20 Rex Tyler Hourman, Inventor of Miraclo R .40 1.00
21 Richard Tyler Hourman, Man of the Hour U .20 .50
22 Sand, Sanderson Hawkins C .10 .25
23 Stargirl, Courtney Whitmore C .10 .25
24 Superman, Earth 2 C .10 .25
25 Ted Grant Wildcat, Golden Age Pugilist C .10 .25
26 Terry Sloane Mr. Terrific .10 .25
Golden Age Gold Medalist C
27 The Phantom Stranger, Wandering Hero U .20 .50
28 Thunderbolt, Yz R .40 1.00
29 Wesley Dodds The Sandman .20 .50
Golden Age Gunman U
30 Wonder Woman, Earth 2 C .10 .25
31 A Moment of Crisis C .10 .25
32 Advance Warning R .40 1.00
33 Allied Against the Dark C .10 .25
34 Brothers in Arms U .20 .50
35 Double Play U .20 .50
36 Heroic Rescue C .10 .25
37 JSA Headquarters R .40 1.00
38 Justice United, Team-Up C .10 .25
39 Living Legacy U .20 .50
40 Taking Up the Mantle C .10 .25
41 The Rock of Eternity R .75 2.00
42 T-Spheres C .10 .25
43 Black Alice, Lori Zechlin U .20 .50
44 Blackbriar Thorn, Druid of Cymru U .20 .50
45 Blue Devil, Dan Cassidy C .10 .25
46 Blue Devil, Big Blue C .10 .25
47 Captain Marvel, Champion of Magic R .40 1.00
48 Detective Chimp, Bobo T. Chimpanzee C .10 .25
49 Detective Chimp, Shoeless Gumshoe R .40 1.00
50 Dr. Fate, Hector Hall C .10 .25
51 Dr. Occult, Richard Occult C .10 .25
52 Ibis, Prince Amentep C .10 .25
53 June Moon Enchantress, Good Witch R .40 1.00
54 June Moon Enchantress, Bad Witch R .40 1.00
55 Madame Xanadu, Cartomancer U .20 .50
56 Manitou Dawn, Spirit Shaman C .10 .25
57 Nightmaster, Jim Rook C .10 .25
58 Nightmaster, Demon Slayer R .40 1.00
59 Nightshade, Eve Eden C .10 .25
60 Nightshade, Shadow Siren C .10 .25
61 Ragman, Patchmonger U .20 .50
62 Ragman, Redeemer of Souls C .10 .25
63 Rose Psychic, Ghost Detective C .10 .25
64 Shazam, The Sorcerer R .40 1.00
65 The Phantom Stranger, Fallen Angel C .10 .25
66 Witchfire, Rebecca Carstairs C .10 .25
67 Zatanna, Magical Manipulator C .10 .25
68 Zatanna, Showstopper C .10 .25
69 Abjuration, Magic U .20 .50
70 Chimp Detective Agency R .40 1.00
71 Collecting Souls, Magic C .10 .25
72 Conjuration, Magic R .40 1.00
73 Divination, Magic C .10 .25
74 Magical Conduit, Magic U .20 .50
75 Mystical Binding, Magic C .10 .25
76 Spectral Slaughter, Magic R .40 1.00
77 Slepping Between Worlds, Magic C .10 .25
78 The Conclave, Magic R 1.25 3.00
79 The Oblivion Bar U .20 .50
80 True Name, Magic C .10 .25
81 Adrian Chase Vigilante, Street Justice R .40 1.00
82 Ahmed Samsarra, White King U .20 .50
83 Amanda Waller, Queen C .10 .25
84 Annihilation Protocol OMAC Robot, Army C .10 .25
85 Arthur Kendrick, Knight C .10 .25
86 Aspiring Pawn, Army C .10 .25
87 Black Thorn, Elizabeth Thorne U .20 .50
88 Christopher Smith Peacemaker .20 .50
Obsessed Outlaw U
89 Connie Webb, Knight U .20 .50
90 Elimination Protocol OMAC Robot, Army C .10 .25
91 Graziella Reza, Knight C .10 .25
92 Harry Stein, King in Check U .20 .50
93 Huntress, Reluctant Queen C .10 .25
94 Jacob Lee, Knight U .20 .50
95 Maxwell Lord, Black King R .40 1.00
96 Neutralization Protocol OMAC Robot, Army C .10 .25
97 Retrieval Protocol OMAC Robot, Army C .10 .25
98 Roy Harper Arsenal, Knight C .10 .25
99 Sarge Steel, Knight U .20 .50
100 Sasha Bordeaux, Knight C .10 .25
101 Sasha Bordeaux, Autonomous Prototype C .10 .25
102 Surveillance Pawn, Army C .10 .25
103 Valentina Vostok Negative Woman, Bishop C .10 .25
104 Brother Eye U .20 .50
105 Brother I Satellite U .20 .50
106 Check and Mate! R .40 1.00
107 Checkmate Armory C .10 .25
108 Checkmate Safe House, Team-Up C .10 .25
109 Knight Armor U .20 .50
110 Knightmare Scenario U .20 .50
111 Knights' Gambit R .40 1.00
112 Laser Watch C .10 .25
113 Pawn of the Black King R .40 1.00
114 Rook Control U .20 .50
115 Secret Checkmate HQ C .10 .25
116 Target Acquired C .10 .25
117 Threat Neutralized U .20 .50
118 Traitor to the Cause C .10 .25
119 Alexander Luthor, Duplicitous Doppelganger U .20 .50
120 Alexander Luthor, Insidious Impostor R .40 1.00
121 Alexander Luthor, Diabolical Double C .10 .25
122 Bizarro, ME AM BIZARRO #1 C .10 .25
123 Black Adam, Teth-Adam C .10 .25
124 Black Adam, Lord of Kahndaq R .40 1.00
125 Cheetah, Feral Feline C .10 .25
126 Count Vertigo, Werner Vertigo C .10 .25
127 Deathstroke the Terminator, Lethal Weapon C .10 .25
128 Deathstroke the Terminator, Ultimate Assassin R .40 1.00
129 Dr. Polaris, Force of Nature C .10 .25
130 Dr. Light, Furious Flashpoint U .20 .50
131 Dr. Psycho, Mental Giant C .10 .25
132 Dr. Psycho, Twisted Telepath C .10 .25
133 Fatality, Flawless Victory R .40 1.00
134 Hunter Zolomon Professor Zoom .40 1.00
Sinister Speedster R
135 Ishmael Gregor Sabbac, Malevolent Marvel C .10 .25
136 Mr. Freeze, Brutal Blizzard C .10 .25
137 Sinestro, Villain Reborn C .10 .25
138 Talia, Beloved Betrayer U .20 .50
139 Talia, Daughter of Madness R .40 1.00
140 The Calculator, Noah Kuttler C .10 .25
141 The Calculator, Evil Oracle C .10 .25
142 The Calculator, Crime Broker C .10 .25
143 Weather Wizard, Mark Mardon C .10 .25
144 Zazzala Queen Bee, Mistress of the Hive C .10 .25
145 3 . . . 2 . . . 1 . . . R .40 1.00
146 Arms Deal R .40 1.00
147 Baddest of the Bad U .20 .50
148 Coercion, Team-Up C .10 .25
149 Grand Gesture C .10 .25
150 Join Us or Die U .20 .50
151 No Hope R .40 1.00
152 No Mercy C .10 .25
153 Return Fire! C .10 .25
154 Systematic Torture C .10 .25
155 The Science Spire R .75 2.00
156 Catman, Thomas Blake C .10 .25
157 Cheshire, Jade C .10 .25
158 Deadshot, Dead Aim C .10 .25
159 Fiddler, Isaac Bowin C .10 .25
160 Lex Luthor Mockingbird, Evil Exile U .20 .50
161 Parademon, Apokoliptian Ally C .10 .25
162 Ragdoll, Resilient Rogue C .10 .25
163 Scandal, Savage Spawn C .10 .25
164 Dodge the Bullet R .40 1.00
165 Help Wanted, Team-Up U .20 .50
166 House of Secrets U .20 .50
167 It's Not Over Yet U .20 .50
168 Secret Six Victorious R .40 1.00
169 Harbinger, Multiverse Messenger R .40 1.00
170 Pariah, Herald of Doom R .40 1.00
171 Superboy, Earth Prime R .40 1.00
172 The Monitor, Guardian of the Multiverse R .40 1.00
173 Bart Allen The Flash, Impulsive Speedster R .40 1.00
174 Amulet of Nabu, Fate Artifact C .10 .25
175 Cloak of Nabu, Fate Artifact C .10 .25
176 Helm of Nabu, Fate Artifact C .10 .25
177 Dr. Fate's Tower U .20 .50
178 Fate Has Spoken, Magic R .40 1.00
179 Eclipso, Jean Loring R .40 1.00
180 Jaime Reyes Blue Beetle, High-Tech Hero U .20 .50
181 Mordru, Dark Lord C .10 .25
182 The Spectre, Soulless R .40 1.00
183 Absolute Dominance R .40 1.00

TCG/CCG

❑ 184 Blinding Rage R 1.00 2.50
❑ 185 Burning Gaze C .10 .25
❑ 186 Death from Above C .10 .25
❑ 187 Defend Yourself! C .10 .25
❑ 188 Deflection C .10 .25
❑ 189 End of All That Is R .40 1.00
❑ 190 Epic Battle C .10 .25
❑ 191 Forbidden Loyalties, Team-Up C .10 .25
❑ 192 I Still Hate Magic! C .10 .25
❑ 193 Magical Lobotomy, Magic U .20 .50
❑ 194 Multiverse Power Battery U .20 .50
❑ 195 Rann C .10 .25
❑ 196 Relentless Pursuit C .10 .25
❑ 197 Removed from Continuity R .40 1.00
❑ 198 Revitalize C .10 .25
❑ 199 Thanagar C .10 .25
❑ 200 Thanagarian Invasion C .10 .25
❑ 201 Transmutation, Magic R .40 1.00
❑ 202 Tricked-Out Sports Car C .10 .25
❑ 203 Watch the Birdie! C .10 .25
❑ 204 Barbara Gordon Oracle, Data Broker R .40 1.00
❑ 205 Leslie Thompkins's Clinic U .20 .50
❑ 206 Mourn for the Lost U .20 .50
❑ 207 Return of Donna Troy U .20 .50
❑ 208 Amadeus Arkham, Architect of Insanity U .20 .50
❑ 209 The Joker, Permanent Vacation R .60 1.50
❑ 210 The Penguin, Arms Merchant U .20 .50
❑ 211 Seiobo's Garden R .40 1.00
❑ 212 Lois Lane, Earth 2 U .20 .50
❑ 213 Lex Luthor, Champion of the Common Man U .20 .50
❑ 214 Kilowog, Drill Sergeant U .20 .50
❑ 215 Brainiac, Earth 2 U .20 .50
❑ 216 Obsidian, Todd James Rice U .20 .50
❑ 217 Adam Strange, Champion of Rann R .40 1.00
❑ 218 Animal Man, Buddy Baker U .20 .50
❑ 219 Mr. Mxyzptlk, Troublesome Trickster R .40 1.00
❑ 220 Ultra-Humanite, Metahuman Manipulator R .40 1.00

2006 Vs System Infinite Crisis Foil

COMPLETE SET (220) 50.00 100.00
*FOIL: .8X TO 2X BASIC CARDS

2006 Vs System Legion of Super-Heroes

COMPLETE SET (220) 30.00 60.00
BOOSTER BOX (24) 25.00 50.00
❑ 1 Andromeda, Laurel Gand C .10 .25
❑ 2 Apparition, Tinya Wazzo C .10 .25
❑ 3 Bouncing Boy, Chuck Taine C .10 .25
❑ 4 Brainiac 5.1, Querl Dox R .75 2.00
❑ 5 Chameleon, Reep Daggle U .20 .50
❑ 6 Colossal Boy Leviathan, Gim Allon C .10 .25
❑ 7 Cosmic Boy, Rokk Krinn R .75 2.00
❑ 8 Dream Girl, Nura Nal R 1.00 2.50
❑ 9 Element Lad, Jan Arrah C .10 .25
❑ 10 Ferro Lad, Andrew Nolan C .10 .25
❑ 11 Jazmin Cullen Kid Quantum, Hero of Xanthu C .10 .25
❑ 12 Kara Zor-El Supergirl, Lost in Time U .20 .50
❑ 13 Karate Kid, Val Armorr C .10 .25
❑ 14 Kinetix, Zoe Saugin C .10 .25
❑ 15 Live Wire, Garth Ranzz C .10 .25
❑ 16 Mon-el Valor, Lar Gand R .40 1.00
❑ 17 R.J. Brande, Philanthropist U .20 .50
❑ 18 Saturn Girl, Imra Ardeen R .60 1.50
❑ 19 Sensor, Jeka Wynzorr U .20 .50
❑ 20 Shrinking Violet Leviathan, Salu Digby U .20 .50
❑ 21 Spark, Ayla Ranzz C .10 .25
❑ 22 Star Boy, Thom Kallor C .10 .25
❑ 23 Sun Boy, Dirk Morgna C .10 .25
❑ 24 Timber Wolf, Brin Londo C .10 .25
❑ 25 Triad, Luornu Durgo U .20 .50
❑ 26 Ultra Boy, Jo Nah U .20 .50
❑ 27 Umbra, Tasmia Mallor C .10 .25
❑ 28 Wildfire, Drake Burroughs C .10 .25
❑ 29 XS, Jenni Ognats C .10 .25
❑ 30 Celebrity Status R .60 1.50
❑ 31 Flight Ring C .10 .25
❑ 32 Foiled Assassination U .20 .50
❑ 33 Legion Headquarters C .10 .25
❑ 34 Legion of Super-Pets C .10 .25
❑ 35 Legion World C .10 .25
❑ 36 Let's Go, Legionnaires! C .10 .25
❑ 37 Long Live the Legion U .20 .50
❑ 38 Many Worlds C .10 .25
❑ 39 New Recruits R .75 2.00
❑ 40 Past, Present, and Future, Team-Up C .10 .25
❑ 41 Science Police Central R .60 1.50
❑ 42 Terror Incognita R .75 2.00
❑ 43 We Are Legion U .20 .50
❑ 44 Youth of Tomorrow, Team-Up C .10 .25
❑ 45 Atrophos, Chief Blight Scientist U .20 .50
❑ 46 Brainiac 4, Dark Circle Leader C .10 .25
❑ 47 Composite Man, Living Weapon R .40 1.00
❑ 48 Computo, Rogue Program C .10 .25
❑ 49 Computo Mr. Venge, Hidden File C .10 .25
❑ 50 Cosmic King, Legion of Super Villains C .10 .25
❑ 51 Daxamites, Army C .10 .25
❑ 52 Dominators, Alien Invaders C .10 .25
❑ 53 Emerald Empress, Fatal Five U .20 .50
❑ 54 Emerald Eye, Sentient Artifact C .10 .25
❑ 55 Glorith, Seductive Sorceress C .10 .25
❑ 56 Lightning Lord, Legion of Super Villains C .10 .25
❑ 57 Mano, Fatal Five C .10 .25
❑ 58 Mordru, The Merciless C .10 .25
❑ 59 Ol-Vir, Legion of Super Villains C .10 .25
❑ 60 Ra's al Ghul, Engine of Change C .10 .25
❑ 61 Ra's al Ghul Leland McCauley, U.P. President C .10 .25
❑ 62 Saturn Queen, Legion of Super Villains C .10 .25
❑ 63 Shrinking Violet Emerald Empress, Emerald Vi C .10 .25
❑ 64 Starfinger, Char Burrane R .75 2.00
❑ 65 Tarik the Mute, Legion of Super Villains C .10 .25
❑ 66 Tharok, Fatal Five C .10 .25
❑ 67 The Blight, Army U .20 .50
❑ 68 The Persuader, Fatal Five R 1.00 2.50
❑ 69 Time Trapper, Temporal Manipulator R 1.25 3.00
❑ 70 Universo, Vidar R .75 2.00
❑ 71 Validus, Fatal Five C .10 .25
❑ 72 Altered History C .10 .25
❑ 73 Asteroid JS-1967 U .20 .50
❑ 74 Chain Lightning C .10 .25
❑ 75 Dark Circle Rising U .20 .50
❑ 76 Dominated R .40 1.00
❑ 77 Earth Enslaved U .20 .50
❑ 78 Fatal Five Hundred C .10 .25
❑ 79 Five Against One C .10 .25
❑ 80 For Khundia! C .10 .25
❑ 81 Khundian Warship U .20 .50
❑ 82 Legion of the Damned C .10 .25
❑ 83 Mutual Enemies U .20 .50
❑ 84 Return of the Demon's Head R 1.25 3.00
❑ 85 Sorcerous Suppression C .10 .25
❑ 86 Tempus Fugit U .20 .50
❑ 87 The Sun-Eater R .60 1.50
❑ 88 Apokoliptian Zealots, Army C .10 .25
❑ 89 Bernadeth, Female Fury U .20 .50
❑ 90 Dark Champion, Mockery C .10 .25
❑ 91 Dark Firestorm, Mockery C .10 .25
❑ 92 Dark Kryptonian Dark Superboy, Mockery R .75 2.00
❑ 93 Dark Lantern, Mockery C .10 .25
❑ 94 Dark Martian, Mockery C .10 .25
❑ 95 Dark Superboy, Mockery R .75 2.00
❑ 96 Dark Thanagarian, Mockery C .10 .25
❑ 97 Dark Warrior, Mockery C .10 .25
❑ 98 Darkseid, 8th Century C .10 .25
❑ 99 Darkseid, Apokolips Now R .75 2.00
❑ 100 Darkseid, Apokoliptian Oppressor C .10 .25
❑ 101 Darkseid, Evil Reborn C .10 .25
❑ 102 Darkseid, Nemesis R .75 2.00
❑ 103 Gillotina, Female Fury C .10 .25
❑ 104 Kara Zor-El Supergirl, Female Fury C .10 .25
❑ 105 Knockout, Female Fury C .10 .25
❑ 106 Lashina, Female Fury C .10 .25
❑ 107 Mad Harriet, Female Fury C .10 .25
❑ 108 Malice Vundabar, Female Fury C .10 .25
❑ 109 Parademon Elite, Army C .10 .25
❑ 110 Speed Queen, Female Fury C .10 .25
❑ 111 Stompa, Female Fury R .60 1.50
❑ 112 31st Century Apokolips R .50 1.25
❑ 113 All Hail Darkseid! U .20 .50
❑ 114 Ancient Evils, Team-Up C .10 .25
❑ 115 Ancient Throne U .20 .50
❑ 116 Created from Hate R 2.50 6.00
❑ 117 Curse of Darkness R .40 1.00
❑ 118 Dark Fury C .10 .25
❑ 119 Dark Matter Drain R .40 1.00
❑ 120 Joining the Darkseid, Team-Up C .10 .25
❑ 121 No Match for Darkseid R .75 2.00
❑ 122 Omega Effect C .10 .25
❑ 123 Price of Treason C .10 .25
❑ 124 Prophetic Battle C .10 .25
❑ 125 Servants of Darkness C .10 .25
❑ 126 Shock and Awe U .20 .50
❑ 127 Unravel Reality U .20 .50
❑ 128 Bart Allen Kid Flash, Heir to the Mantle U .20 .50
❑ 129 Bart Allen The Flash, Titans Tomorrow West U .20 .50
❑ 130 Beast Boy, Party Animal C .10 .25
❑ 131 Beast Boy Animal Man, Titans Tomorrow West C .10 .25
❑ 132 Bette Kane Batwoman, Titans Tomorrow East U .20 .50
❑ 133 Bumblebee, Titans Tomorrow East C .10 .25
❑ 134 Cassie Sandsmark Wonder Girl .10 .25
Ares's Chosen C
❑ 135 Cassie Sandsmark Wonder Woman .10 .25
Titans Tomorrow West C
❑ 136 Connor Kent Superboy .10 .25
Inspiration to the Legion C
❑ 137 Connor Kent Superman .40 1.00
Titans Tomorrow West R
❑ 138 Dawn Granger Dove, Avatar of Order C .10 .25
❑ 139 Duela Dent Harlequin, The Joker's Daughter C .10 .25
❑ 140 Freddy Freeman Captain Marvel .10 .25
Titans Tomorrow East C
❑ 141 Holly Granger Hawk, Avatar of Chaos C .10 .25
❑ 142 Kid Devil, Eddie Bloomberg C .10 .25
❑ 143 Koriand'r Starfire, Tamaranian Princess C .10 .25
❑ 144 Lorena Marquez Aquawoman .50 1.25
Titans Tomorrow West R
❑ 145 Mia Dearden Speedy, Deadly Aim C .10 .25
❑ 146 Raven, Rachel Roth R .50 1.25
❑ 147 Raven Dark Raven, Titans Tomorrow West R .75 2.00
❑ 148 Rose Wilson The Ravager .40 1.00
Daughter of Deathstroke R
❑ 149 Rose Wilson The Ravager .20 .50
Titans Tomorrow East U
❑ 150 Terra, Titans Tomorrow East U .20 .50
❑ 151 The Herald, Malcolm Duncan C .10 .25
❑ 152 Tim Drake Batman, Titans Tomorrow West U .20 .50
❑ 153 Tim Drake Robin, Sidekick No More C .10 .25
❑ 154 Vic Stone Cyborg, Titans Veteran C .10 .25
❑ 155 Vic Stone Cyborg 2.0, Titans Tomorrow East U .20 .50
❑ 156 Born of Blood U .20 .50
❑ 157 Clash of the Titans C .10 .25
❑ 158 First Date C .10 .25
❑ 159 Generation Next, Team-Up C .10 .25
❑ 160 Hall of Mentors U .20 .50
❑ 161 Now You See Me R .40 1.00
❑ 162 Order and Chaos U .20 .50
❑ 163 Pour It On R 1.00 2.50
❑ 164 Tamaranian Garden R .40 1.00
❑ 165 Titans Communicator C .10 .25
❑ 166 Titans Memorial U .20 .50
❑ 167 Titans, Together! R .50 1.25
❑ 168 T-Jet, Tamaranian Fighter U .20 .50
❑ 169 Donna Troy, Born Again C .10 .25
❑ 170 Superboy, Yellow Sun Armor U .20 .50
❑ 171 Jason Todd Red Hood, Revived R .40 1.00
❑ 172 31st Century Metropolis, Team-Up C .10 .25
❑ 173 Awestruck C .10 .25
❑ 174 Blinding Light C .10 .25
❑ 175 Busted Knee C .10 .25
❑ 176 Contact! U .20 .50
❑ 177 Cosmic Tuning Fork R 1.50 4.00
❑ 178 Death of a Legionnaire C .10 .25
❑ 179 Earth 2 U .20 .50
❑ 180 Forged in Crisis U .20 .50
❑ 181 Furious Assault C .10 .25
❑ 182 Furnace of Apokolips C .10 .25
❑ 183 Girls' Night Out C .10 .25
❑ 184 Legion Lost C .10 .25
❑ 185 Level 12 Intelligence R 1.25 3.00
❑ 186 Lost in Translation U .20 .50
❑ 187 Mobilize R 12.00 30.00
❑ 188 Need for Speed R 1.00 2.50
❑ 189 Ravaged! U .20 .50
❑ 190 Steely Resolve R .40 1.00
❑ 191 Substitute Heroes C .10 .25
❑ 192 The Future Is Changing C .10 .25
❑ 193 Titans of Tomorrow U .20 .50
❑ 194 United Planets HQ, Team-Up C .10 .25
❑ 195 Crimson Avenger, Jill Carlyle U .20 .50
❑ 196 Jack Knight Starman, Knight Past U .20 .50
❑ 197 Power Girl, Child of Crisis R 1.25 3.00
❑ 198 S.T.R.I.P.E., Pat Dugan U .20 .50
❑ 199 Alan Scott, White King U .20 .50
❑ 200 Director Bones, D.E.O. U .20 .50
❑ 201 Fire, Knight U .20 .50
❑ 202 Girl 13 Traci Thirteen, Hex and the City R .40 1.00
❑ 203 Mary Marvel, World's Mightiest Girl U .20 .50
❑ 204 Otherworldly Battle, Magic R .40 1.00
❑ 205 Blüdhaven Destroyed R .40 1.00
❑ 206 Chemo, Chemical Golem U .20 .50
❑ 207 High Society C .10 .25
❑ 208 Harvey Bullock, Bishop R .75 2.00
❑ 209 The Riddler, Brain Teaser R .40 1.00
❑ 210 Nyssa Raatko, Daughter of the Demon R .60 1.50
❑ 211 Solar Powered R 1.00 2.50
❑ 212 Brainiac 2.5, Future Intelligence R .60 1.50
❑ 213 Shiloh Norman Mister Miracle .50 1.25
Soldier of Victory R
❑ 214 Kyle Rayner Ion, Torch Bearer R 1.50 4.00
❑ 215 Mongul, Intergalactic Menace R .40 1.00
❑ 216 Alexander Luthor, Earth 3 U .20 .50
❑ 217 Kate Spencer Manhunter, Vigilante Justice U .20 .50
❑ 218 Wally West The Flash, The Fastest Man Alive R .60 1.50
❑ 219 Peter Merkel Ragdoll, Malleable Miscreant U .20 .50
❑ 220 Owen Mercer Captain Boomerang .20 .50
Digger's Son U

2006 Vs System X-Men

COMPLETE SET (220) 30.00 60.00
BOOSTER BOX (24) 30.00 60.00
❑ 1 Archangel, Angel C .10 .25
❑ 2 Beast, Feline Geneticist U .20 .50
❑ 3 Bishop, XSE Commando C .10 .25
❑ 4 Cannonball, Blast Field C .10 .25
❑ 5 Changeling, Kevin Sidney R .40 1.00
❑ 6 Colossus, Organic Steel U .20 .50
❑ 7 Cyclops, Blue Leader C .10 .25
❑ 8 Dazzler, Rock Star C .10 .25
❑ 9 Emma Frost, Friend or Foe R 1.00 2.50
❑ 10 Gambit, Ragin' Cajun U .20 .50
❑ 11 Havok, Critical Mass C .10 .25
❑ 12 Iceman, Deep Freeze C .10 .25
❑ 13 Jean Grey, Red R .40 1.00
❑ 14 Jubilee, Jubilation Lee U .20 .50
❑ 15 Juggernaut, The Unstoppable U .75 2.00
❑ 16 Lockheed, Saurian Sidekick C .10 .25
❑ 17 Longshot, Hero of Mojoworld U .20 .50
❑ 18 Nightcrawler, Swashbuckler C .10 .25
❑ 19 Professor X, Headmaster R 1.50 4.00
❑ 20 Psylocke, Armored Empath C .10 .25
❑ 21 Rachel Summers Phoenix .40 1.00
Phoenix of the Future R
❑ 22 Rogue, Anna Marie C .10 .25
❑ 23 Sage, Xavier's Secret Weapon C .10 .25
❑ 24 Shadowcat, Katya C .10 .25
❑ 25 Storm, Gold Leader C .10 .25
❑ 26 Wolverine, The Best at What He Does C .10 .25
❑ 27 Xorn, Shen Xorn C .10 .25
❑ 28 Angel of Mercy U .20 .50
❑ 29 Blackbird Blue U .20 .50
❑ 30 Harry's Hideaway U .20 .50
❑ 31 Phoenix Rising R .40 1.00
❑ 32 Rebirth C .10 .25
❑ 33 SNIKT! R .60 1.50
❑ 34 Time Breach R .40 1.00
❑ 35 Turnabout C .10 .25
❑ 36 Worthington Industries, X-Corp R 1.25 3.00
❑ 37 X-Corp: Amsterdam, X-Corp C .10 .25
❑ 38 X-Corp: Hong Kong, X-Corp C .10 .25
❑ 39 X-Corp: Paris, X-Corp C .10 .25
❑ 40 X-Men United, Team-Up C .10 .25
❑ 41 X-Treme Maneuver U .20 .50
❑ 42 Angel Dust, Adrenaline Junkie U .20 .50
❑ 43 Annalee, Mother Hen C .10 .25
❑ 44 Ape, Metamorph R .40 1.00
❑ 45 Artie, Arthur Maddicks C .10 .25
❑ 46 Blow Hard, Windbag U .20 .50
❑ 47 Caliban, Mutant Bloodhound C .10 .25
❑ 48 Callisto, Morlock Queen C .10 .25
❑ 49 Cybelle, Meltdown R .40 1.00
❑ 50 Electric Eve, Live Wire C .10 .25
❑ 51 Erg, Electric Eye C .10 .25
❑ 52 Feral, Maria Callasantos C .10 .25
❑ 53 Healer, Life Giver C .10 .25
❑ 54 Hemingway, Gene Nation C .10 .25
❑ 55 Hump, Servant of Masque U .20 .50
❑ 56 Leech, Inhibitor U .20 .50
❑ 57 Marrow, Gene Nation C .10 .25
❑ 58 Masque, Flesh Shaper U .20 .50
❑ 59 Mikhail Rasputin, Morlock Messiah R .40 1.00
❑ 60 Piper, Rat Charmer C .10 .25
❑ 61 Plague, Deathwalker C .10 .25
❑ 62 Postman, Memory Thief U .20 .50
❑ 63 Scaleface, Dragon Lady C .10 .25
❑ 64 Storm, Leader of the Morlocks C .10 .25
❑ 65 Sunder, Callisto's Enforcer C .10 .25
❑ 66 Tar Baby, Adhesive Ally C .10 .25
❑ 67 The Beautiful Dreamer, Dreamweaver C .10 .25
❑ 68 Thornn, Lucia Callasantos R .40 1.00
❑ 69 Tommy, Runaway C .10 .25
❑ 70 Backs Against the Wall R .40 1.00
❑ 71 Bloodhound U .20 .50
❑ 72 Bum's Rush C .10 .25
❑ 73 Good Samaritan R .40 1.00
❑ 74 Morlock Justice U .20 .50
❑ 75 Neutralized C .10 .25
❑ 76 Retribution C .10 .25
❑ 77 Sewer System U .20 .50
❑ 78 Shrapnel Blast U .20 .50
❑ 79 Subterranean Sanctuary R .40 1.00
❑ 80 The Alley U .20 .50
❑ 81 The Forsaken, Team-Up C .10 .25
❑ 82 The Hill C .10 .25
❑ 83 Amelia Voght, Acolyte R .75 2.00
❑ 84 Anne-Marie Cortez, Acolyte C .10 .25
❑ 85 Avalanche, Freedom Force R .40 1.00
❑ 86 Blob, Freedom Force C .10 .25
❑ 87 Chrome, Acolyte C .10 .25
❑ 88 Colossus, Acolyte U .20 .50
❑ 89 Crimson Commando, Freedom Force C .10 .25
❑ 90 Destiny, Freedom Force C .10 .25
❑ 91 Exodus, Acolyte C .10 .25
❑ 92 Fabian Cortez, Acolyte U .20 .50
❑ 93 Harry Delgado, Acolyte C .10 .25
❑ 94 Joanna Cargill, Acolyte C .10 .25
❑ 95 Julia Carpenter, Freedom Force C .10 .25
❑ 96 Kleinstock Brothers, Acolyte U .20 .50
❑ 97 Magneto, Ruler of Avalon R .50 1.25
❑ 98 Mystique, Freedom Force U .20 .50
❑ 99 Polaris, Acolyte C .10 .25
❑ 100 Pyro, Freedom Force C .10 .25
❑ 101 Rem-Ram, Acolyte C .10 .25
❑ 102 Sabretooth, Savage Killer R .50 1.25
❑ 103 Scanner, Acolyte C .10 .25
❑ 104 Senyaka, Acolyte C .10 .25
❑ 105 Silver Sabre, Freedom Force C .10 .25
❑ 106 Spiral, Freedom Force R .40 1.00
❑ 107 Spoor, Acolyte C .10 .25
❑ 108 Stonewall, Freedom Force U .20 .50
❑ 109 Toad, Hopalong C .10 .25
❑ 110 Unuscione, Acolyte U .20 .50
❑ 111 Acolyte Body Armor U .20 .50
❑ 112 Boot to the Head R .50 1.25
❑ 113 Freedom Force C .10 .25
❑ 114 Go Down Fighting C .10 .25
❑ 115 Hellhound U .20 .50
❑ 116 Kill the Flatscans U .20 .50
❑ 117 Lying in Wait C .10 .25
❑ 118 Planet X, Team-Up C .10 .25
❑ 119 Ruins of Avalon R .40 1.00
❑ 120 Shake, Rattle, and Roll R .40 1.00
❑ 121 Sovereign Superior U .20 .50
❑ 122 The Acolytes R .40 1.00
❑ 123 Wundagore Citadel C .10 .25
❑ 124 Beef, Hellion C .10 .25
❑ 125 Bevatron, Hellion C .10 .25
❑ 126 Catseye, Hellion U .20 .50
❑ 127 Courtney Ross, Once and Future Queen U .20 .50
❑ 128 Dark Phoenix, Alien Life Force R .50 1.25
❑ 129 Donald Pierce, White Bishop C .10 .25
❑ 130 Emma Frost, White Queen C .10 .25
❑ 131 Empath, Hellion C .10 .25
❑ 132 Firestar, Hellion C .10 .25
❑ 133 Friedrich Von Roehm, Black Rook C .10 .25
❑ 134 Harry Leland, Black Bishop R .40 1.00
❑ 135 Hellfire Club Initiate, Army C .10 .25
❑ 136 Hellfire Club Mercenary, Army C .10 .25
❑ 137 James Proudstar Thunderbird, Hellion R .40 1.00
❑ 138 Jetstream, Hellion C .10 .25
❑ 139 Madelyne Pryor, Black Rook C .10 .25
❑ 140 Magneto, Black Lord R .40 1.00
❑ 141 Mastermind, Dark Dreamer C .10 .25
❑ 142 Roberto Da Costa, Heir to the Throne C .10 .25
❑ 143 Roulette, Hellion R .40 1.00
❑ 144 Sage, Tessa C .10 .25
❑ 145 Sebastian Shaw, Black King R .40 1.00
❑ 146 Selene, Black Queen C .10 .25
❑ 147 Shinobi Shaw, White King C .10 .25
❑ 148 Tarot, Hellion C .10 .25
❑ 149 Trevor Fitzroy, White Rook R .40 1.00
❑ 150 Viper, White Warrior Princess C .10 .25
❑ 151 Absolute Power U .20 .50
❑ 152 Army of One C .10 .25
❑ 153 Cardinal Law C .10 .25
❑ 154 Deadly Game R .40 1.00
❑ 155 Eminent Domain R .40 1.00
❑ 156 Evil Alliance, Team-Up C .10 .25
❑ 157 Inner Circle R .40 1.00
❑ 158 Join the Club! U .20 .50
❑ 159 Massachusetts Academy U .20 .50
❑ 160 Power and Wealth R .75 2.00
❑ 161 Power Play R .40 1.00
❑ 162 Raising Hell C .10 .25
❑ 163 Shaw Industries U .20 .50
❑ 164 The Hellfire Club C .10 .25
❑ 165 Above and Below, Team-Up U .20 .50
❑ 166 Blow the Man Down R .50 1.25
❑ 167 Chill Out! R .40 1.00
❑ 168 Drain Essence C .10 .25
❑ 169 Feel the Burn C .10 .25
❑ 170 Magnetic Force U .20 .50
❑ 171 The Evil Eye C .10 .25
❑ 172 Phase Shift C .10 .25
❑ 173 Memory Probe C .10 .25
❑ 174 Mental Domination U .20 .50
❑ 175 Mind Control C .10 .25
❑ 176 Psi-Link R .40 1.00
❑ 177 Psionic Storm C .10 .25
❑ 178 Psychic Armor C .10 .25
❑ 179 Psychic Struggle R .40 1.00
❑ 180 Immovable C .10 .25
❑ 181 Kidney Punch C .10 .25
❑ 182 Kill or be Killed C .10 .25
❑ 183 Mob Mentality R .40 1.00
❑ 184 Momentary Distraction R .40 1.00
❑ 185 Pack Tactics C .10 .25
❑ 186 Special Delivery U .20 .50
❑ 187 Krakoa, Island Monster C .10 .25
❑ 188 Multiple Man Jamie Madrox, Army U 1.50 4.00
❑ 189 Wolverine, Patch R .40 1.00
❑ 190 X-23, Laura Kinney R .50 1.25
❑ 191 Alter Density C .10 .25
❑ 192 Brave New World, Team-Up C .10 .25
❑ 193 District X U. .20 .50
❑ 194 Enemy of My Enemy R 10.00 25.00
❑ 195 Homo Superior C .10 .25
❑ 196 Image Inducer C .10 .25
❑ 197 Leadership Challenge C .10 .25
❑ 198 Mindtap Mechanism U .20 .50
❑ 199 Mutant Massacre U .20 .50
❑ 200 Mutopia, Team-Up C .10 .25
❑ 201 Super Hero Showdown C .10 .25
❑ 202 Teamwork U .20 .50
❑ 203 Franklin Richards, Trapped in Time R .40 1.00
❑ 204 Kristoff Von Doom, Pretender to the Throne R .40 1.00
❑ 205 Sentinel Mark VI, Army U .20 .50
❑ 206 Toxin, Patrick Mulligan U .20 .50
❑ 207 Man-Bull, William Taurens R .40 1.00
❑ 208 Black Panther, King of Wakanda U .20 .50
❑ 209 Henrietta Hunter, X-Celebrity U .20 .50
❑ 210 Doctor Sun, Creator of Project: Mind R .40 1.00
❑ 211 Witch Woman, Linda Littletrees U .20 .50
❑ 212 Doctor Druid, Anthony Druid U .20 .50
❑ 213 Sub-Mariner, Namor U .20 .50
❑ 214 Lady Lark, Skylark R .40 1.00
❑ 215 Mysterium, Joseph Lightner R .40 1.00
❑ 216 Genis-Vell Photon, Transformed U .20 .50
❑ 217 Mech Bay R .40 1.00
❑ 218 Absorbing Man, Carl Creel R .40 1.00
❑ 219 Gargantua, Edward Cobert R .40 1.00
❑ 220 Kang, Scarlet Centurion U .20 .50

2006 Vs System X-Men Foil

COMPLETE SET (220) 60.00 120.00
*FOIL: .8X TO 2X BASIC CARDS

2007 Vs System DC Legends

COMPLETE SET (273) 50.00 100.00
BOOSTER BOX (24) 50.00 100.00
❑ 1 Aquaman, Founding Member C .10 .25
❑ 2 Aquaman, Lord of Atlantis U .20 .50
❑ 3 Aztek, Champion of Quetzalcoatl C .10 .25
❑ 4 Barry Allen The Flash, Crimson Tornado R 3.00 8.00
❑ 5 Barry Allen The Flash, Founding Member R 1.25 3.00
❑ 6 Batman, Founding Member R 5.00 12.00
❑ 7 Batman, Justice's Shadow C .10 .25
❑ 8 Big Barda, Furious Fatale C .10 .25
❑ 9 Black Lightning, Energetic Hero U .20 .50
❑ 10 Dinah Laurel Lance Black Canary, New Wings C .10 .25
❑ 11 Elongated Man, Stretchable Sleuth U .20 .50
❑ 12 Firehawk, Flaming Justice C .10 .25
❑ 13 Firestorm, Ronnie Raymond U .20 .50
❑ 14 Hal Jordan, Founding Member R 3.00 8.00
❑ 15 Hal Jordan, Fearless R 2.50 6.00
❑ 16 John Henry Irons Steel, Working Man C .10 .25
❑ 17 John Stewart, The Master Builder C .10 .25
❑ 18 Katar Hol Hawkman, Death from Above C .10 .25
❑ 19 Kendra Saunders Hawkgirl .10 .25
Thanagarian Heroine C
❑ 20 Kyle Rayner, Guardian of the Universe U .20 .50

❑ 21 Martian Manhunter, Founding Member C .10 .25
❑ 22 Martian Manhunter, The Last Martian R 1.25 3.00
❑ 23 Oliver Queen Green Arrow, Bullseye C .10 .25
❑ 24 Plastic Man, Plastic Fantastic U .20 .50
❑ 25 Ray Palmer The Atom, World's Smallest Hero R.40 1.00
❑ 26 Red Tornado, Elemental Android C .10 .25
❑ 27 Roy Harper Red Arrow, Coming of Age R .75 2.00
❑ 28 Superman, Metropolis Marvel R 2.00 5.00
❑ 29 Superman, Founding Member R 1.50 4.00
❑ 30 Vixen, Tantu Totem C .10 .25
❑ 31 Wally West The Flash, Keystone Cop C .10 .25
❑ 32 Wonder Woman, Ambassador of Peace R 2.00 5.00
❑ 33 Wonder Woman, Founding Member C .10 .25
❑ 34 Zatanna, Sucoh Sucop! C .10 .25
❑ 35 Sea Creatures, Army R 1.50 4.00
❑ 36 Lasso of Truth R .50 1.25
❑ 37 Batcomputer, Criminal Database U .20 .50
❑ 38 Cadmus Labs U .20 .50
❑ 39 Hall of Justice U .20 .50
❑ 40 Keystone City U .20 .50
❑ 41 Poseidonis R .75 2.00
❑ 42 The Watchtower R .40 1.00
❑ 43 Atomize R .75 2.00
❑ 44 Battle Training C .10 .25
❑ 45 Crisis Averted C .10 .25
❑ 46 Emerald Rebirth U .20 .50
❑ 47 Fearless R .60 1.50
❑ 48 From the Darkness R 3.00 8.00
❑ 49 Full Throttle R 1.25 3.00
❑ 50 Fury of the Amazons R 1.25 3.00
❑ 51 Indestructible R 4.00 10.00
❑ 52 Intangible R .40 1.00
❑ 53 Magnificent Seven C .10 .25
❑ 54 Mightiest Heroes R 4.00 10.00
❑ 55 New Era R .40 1.00
❑ 56 Recharge! R 1.25 3.00
❑ 57 Reform the League C .10 .25
❑ 58 Stalwart Defense U .20 .50
❑ 59 Telepathic Link R .40 1.00
❑ 60 Terminal Velocity R 1.00 2.50
❑ 61 Truth, Justice, and Peace R .75 2.00
❑ 62 Argent, Toni Monetti C .10 .25
❑ 63 Bart Allen Kid Flash, Generation Fourth U .20 .50
❑ 64 Beast Boy, Garfield Logan R .75 2.00
❑ 65 Beast Boy, Freak of Nature C .10 .25
❑ 66 Bette Kane Flamebird, Reflex Action C .10 .25
❑ 67 Bumblebee, Sonic Sting U .20 .50
❑ 68 Cassie Sandsmark Wonder Girl, Might of Atlas C.10 .25
❑ 69 Dawn Granger Dove, Terataya's Chosen C .10 .25
❑ 70 Dick Grayson Nightwing, Going it Alone C .10 .25
❑ 71 Donna Troy Wonder Girl, Amazon Warrior R .40 1.00
❑ 72 Freddy Freeman Captain Marvel Jr. .10 .25
Third in Line C
❑ 73 Holly Granger Hawk, T'Charr's Chosen U .20 .50
❑ 74 Hot Spot, Isaiah Crockett C .10 .25
❑ 75 Jericho, Contact! R .40 1.00
❑ 76 Kid Devil, Teen Hellion C .10 .25
❑ 77 Koriand'r Starfire, Fiery Temper U .20 .50
❑ 78 Koriand'r Starfire, X'Hal's Fury R 4.00 10.00
❑ 79 Mia Dearden Speedy, Archer's Apprentice C .10 .25
❑ 80 Miss Martian, M'gann M'orzz R 1.25 3.00
❑ 81 Pantha, Subject X-24 C .10 .25
❑ 82 Raven, Demon Spawn C .10 .25
❑ 83 Ray Palmer The Atom, Tiny Titan C .10 .25
❑ 84 Red Star, Russian Roulette C .10 .25
❑ 85 Rose Wilson The Ravager, Redemption Earned U.20 .50
❑ 86 Roy Harper Speedy, Mercurial Marksman R .40 1.00
❑ 87 Roy Harper Arsenal, Additional Firepower R 1.25 3.00
❑ 88 Tim Drake Robin, Titan in Command U .20 .50
❑ 89 Tim Drake Robin, Leader of the Pack R .75 2.00
❑ 90 Vic Stone Cyborg, Mechanized Mentor C .10 .25
❑ 91 Vic Stone Cyborg, Titans Warhorse U .20 .50
❑ 92 Zatara, Teen Magician U .20 .50
❑ 93 Cybernetic Laser U .20 .50
❑ 94 T-Jet, Unique * Titans Transport R .40 1.00
❑ 95 Weapon Upgrade R .40 1.00
❑ 96 Optitron R .40 1.00
❑ 97 Solar Tower C .10 .25
❑ 98 Titans Tower U .20 .50
❑ 99 Best Friends Forever R .40 1.00
❑ 100 Call of the Wild U .20 .50
❑ 101 Cunning Strategy R .60 1.50
❑ 102 Follow the Leader U .20 .50
❑ 103 Graduation Day U .20 .50
❑ 104 Headstrong Charge R .40 1.00
❑ 105 More Than Just Sidekicks C .10 .25
❑ 106 Prodigies U .20 .50
❑ 107 Starbolts R .50 1.25
❑ 108 Teen Titans Go! C .10 .25
❑ 109 Abra Kadabra, Magical Rogue C .10 .25
❑ 110 Agamemno, Interplanetary Conqueror R .40 1.00
❑ 111 Barracuda, Earth 3 C .10 .25
❑ 112 Black Manta, Deepwater Denizen C .10 .25
❑ 113 Captain Boomerang, George Harkness C .10 .25
❑ 114 Catwoman, Cat o' Nine Tails C .10 .25
❑ 115 Circe, Evil Enchantress C .10 .25
❑ 116 David Clinton Chronos, Timetwister R .40 1.00
❑ 117 Dr. Light, Blinding Flash R .40 1.00
❑ 118 Felix Faust, Soulless Mystic C .10 .25
❑ 119 Jemm, Son of Saturn U .20 .50
❑ 120 Johnny Quick, Earth 3 C .10 .25
❑ 121 The Joker, Headline Stealer C .10 .25
❑ 122 The Joker, Killer Smile R .75 2.00
❑ 123 Lex Luthor, Megalomaniac R 1.50 4.00
❑ 124 Lex Luthor, Metropolis Mogul C .10 .25
❑ 125 Lex Luthor, The Everyman R .40 1.00
❑ 126 Ocean Master, Son of Atlan C .10 .25
❑ 127 Owlman, Earth 3 C .10 .25
❑ 128 The Penguin, Gentleman of Crime C .10 .25
❑ 129 Power Ring, Earth 3 C .10 .25
❑ 130 Prometheus, New Year's Evil U .20 .50
❑ 131 Scarecrow, Chiroptophobic R .75 2.00
❑ 132 The Shade, Ageless Enigma U .20 .50
❑ 133 Sinestro, Korugaran Despot C .10 .25
❑ 134 Superwoman, Earth 3 C .10 .25
❑ 135 Tattooed Man, Art Imitates Life R .40 1.00
❑ 136 Ultraman, Earth 3 C .10 .25
❑ 137 Vandal Savage, Cro-Magnon Man R .40 1.00
❑ 138 White Martian, Earth 3 C .10 .25
❑ 139 Zazzala Queen Bee, H.I.V.E. Monarch R .60 1.50
❑ 140 Laughing Gas U .20 .50
❑ 141 Earth 3 U .20 .50
❑ 142 Injustice Gang Satellite R .40 1.00
❑ 143 All Too Easy C .10 .25
❑ 144 Crime Syndicate of Amerika R 1.50 4.00
❑ 145 Criminal Mastermind C .10 .25
❑ 146 Evil Genius U .20 .50
❑ 147 Gang-Up, Team-Up C .10 .25
❑ 148 Injustice for All R .40 1.00
❑ 149 The Joke's on You! R .50 1.25
❑ 150 Power Siphon R .40 1.00
❑ 151 Research and Development R .40 1.00
❑ 152 Secret Files C .10 .25
❑ 153 Sunburst R .50 1.25
❑ 154 Amazo, Power Duplication C .10 .25
❑ 155 Basil Karlo Clayface, Slimy Shapeshifter U .20 .50
❑ 156 Bizarro, Dark Mirror U .20 .50
❑ 157 Black Manta, Underwater Marauder R 1.25 3.00
❑ 158 The Calculator, Q.E.D. C .10 .25
❑ 159 Charaxes, Moth Monster R 2.00 5.00
❑ 160 Cheetah, Barbara Minerva U .20 .50
❑ 161 Chemo, Toxic Waste R 2.50 6.00
❑ 162 Darkseid, Destroyer of Life C .10 .25
❑ 163 Darkseid, Dark God R 1.50 4.00
❑ 164 Deadshot, Floyd Lawton R .40 1.00
❑ 165 Deathstroke the Terminator, Killing Machine C.10 .25
❑ 166 Desaad, Dark Side Therapy R .50 1.25
❑ 167 Doomsday, Engine of Destruction R .50 1.25
❑ 168 Dr. Polaris, Polar Opposite C .10 .25
❑ 169 Dr. Psycho, Demented Dwarf C .10 .25
❑ 170 Dr. Sivana, Mad Scientist C .10 .25
❑ 171 Fatality, Okaaran Warrior R 1.00 2.50
❑ 172 Felix Faust, Dark Bargain U .20 .50
❑ 173 Floronic Man, Jason Woodrue C .10 .25
❑ 174 Giganta, Rampaging U .20 .50
❑ 175 Gorilla Grodd, Grodd Awful C .10 .25
❑ 176 Gorilla Grodd, Psionic Simian C .10 .25
❑ 177 Ishmael Gregor Sabbac, Deadly Sin R .40 1.00
❑ 178 King Shark, Jaws of Death R 1.00 2.50
❑ 179 Mark Desmond Blockbuster, Mindless Brute U.20 .50
❑ 180 Mr. Freeze, Cold Blooded R .75 2.00
❑ 181 Poison Ivy, Intoxicating U .20 .50
❑ 182 Psycho-Pirate, Medusa Mask C .10 .25
❑ 183 The Riddler, Riddle Me This R 1.25 3.00
❑ 184 Shadow-Thief, Umbral Burglar C .10 .25
❑ 185 Sinestro, Yellow Lantern R 1.25 3.00
❑ 186 Solomon Grundy, Died on a Saturday R .60 1.50
❑ 187 Gorilla City C .10 .25
❑ 188 Hidden HQ R 1.00 2.50
❑ 189 Remote Facility, Non-Unique C .10 .25
❑ 190 Acceptable Loss C .10 .25
❑ 191 Anger and Hate R .75 2.00
❑ 192 Anti-Life R .60 1.50
❑ 193 Coup d'Etat R .40 1.00
❑ 194 Endgame R .50 1.25
❑ 195 Forced Conscription C .10 .25
❑ 196 Going Ape U .20 .50
❑ 197 Lord of Apokolips U .20 .50
❑ 198 Maleficent Meeting C .10 .25
❑ 199 Master Plan U .20 .50
❑ 200 Monkey See, Monkey Do R .75 2.00
❑ 201 Shadow Strike C .10 .25
❑ 202 Straight to the Grave R 1.00 2.50
❑ 203 Unnatural Selection U .20 .50
❑ 204 Cassandra Cain, Daughter of Shiva U .20 .50
❑ 205 David Cain, World Class Assassin R .40 1.00
❑ 206 Hassim, Loyal Retainer U .20 .50
❑ 207 Lady Shiva, Master Assassin R .40 1.00
❑ 208 The Mad Dog, Rabid Killer C .10 .25
❑ 209 Merlyn, Direct Hit Man R 1.00 2.50
❑ 210 Novice Assassin, Army C .10 .25
❑ 211 Nyssa Raatko, Maiden of Death C .10 .25
❑ 212 Ra's al Ghul, Demon's Head Rising C .10 .25
❑ 213 Ra's al Ghul, The Demon's Head R 1.25 3.00
❑ 214 Shadow Assassin, Army C .10 .25
❑ 215 Shrike, Boone C .10 .25
❑ 216 Talia, Heir Apparent C .10 .25
❑ 217 Ubu, Ra's al Ghul's Bodyguard C .10 .25
❑ 218 The Demon's Quarters R .40 1.00
❑ 219 Flying Fortress U .20 .50
❑ 220 Lazarus Pit, Non-Unique * Death's Door R .60 1.50
❑ 221 Mountain Stronghold, Non-Unique U .20 .50
❑ 222 Plague Zone, Non-Unique U .20 .50
❑ 223 The Demon's Head R .40 1.00
❑ 224 Demonfang C .10 .25
❑ 225 Divide and Conquer R .50 1.25
❑ 226 Harsh Judgment R .40 1.00
❑ 227 Tower of Babel R .40 1.00
❑ 228 The Chief, Niles Caulder U .20 .50
❑ 229 Elasti-Girl, Rita Farr R .60 1.50
❑ 230 Mento, Steve Dayton U .20 .50
❑ 231 Negative Man, Larry Trainor U .20 .50
❑ 232 Robotman, Cliff Steele C .10 .25
❑ 233 Dayton Manor R 1.00 2.50
❑ 234 Freak Out R .60 1.50
❑ 235 Misfits R .50 1.25
❑ 236 Strange Days R .40 1.00
❑ 237 Captain Atom, Quantum Energy R .40 1.00
❑ 238 The Demon, Etrigan R .50 1.25
❑ 239 Imperiex, The Beginning and The End R .40 1.00
❑ 240 Lobo, The Main Man R 1.50 4.00
❑ 241 Supernova, Daniel Carter R 1.00 2.50
❑ 242 Terra, Earth Mover R .50 1.25
❑ 243 Twin Firearms U .20 .50
❑ 244 Nth Metal C .10 .25
❑ 245 Birthing Chamber U .20 .50
❑ 246 Coast City C .10 .25
❑ 247 Metropolis Reborn, Non-Unique * Team-Up C.10 .25
❑ 248 A Better World, Team-Up C .10 .25
❑ 249 Blind Sided R 1.25 3.00
❑ 250 Blinding Rage R 1.00 2.50
❑ 251 Break You C .10 .25
❑ 252 Changing Minds, Team-Up C .10 .25
❑ 253 Chaos and Villainy, Team-Up C .10 .25
❑ 254 Combat Reflexes C .10 .25
❑ 255 Death Trap C .10 .25
❑ 256 Dirty Tricks R .40 1.00
❑ 257 Duty Calls C .10 .25
❑ 258 From the Shadows C .10 .25
❑ 259 Have a Blast! R 1.00 2.50
❑ 260 Hero's Best Friend C .10 .25
❑ 261 Heroes of Two Worlds R 2.50 6.00
❑ 262 Heroic Effort C .10 .25
❑ 263 Home Surgery C .10 .25
❑ 264 Judgment Day R .40 1.00
❑ 265 Mirror Image R .50 1.25
❑ 266 The Multiverse, Team-Up C .10 .25
❑ 267 Nasty Surprise C .10 .25
❑ 268 Overwhelming Odds C .10 .25
❑ 269 Path of Destruction C .10 .25
❑ 270 Shape Change U .20 .50
❑ 271 Tag Team C .10 .25
❑ 272 Total Anarchy R .40 1.00
❑ 273 Total Recall, Team-Up U .20 .50

2007 Vs System DC Legends Foil

COMPLETE SET (273) 100.00 200.00
*FOIL: .8X TO 2X BASIC CARDS

2007 Vs System Marvel Legends

COMPLETE SET (273) 50.00 100.00
BOOSTER BOX (24) 30.00 60.00
❑ 1 Archangel, Aeroballistic C .10 .25
❑ 2 Beast, Bookworm R .75 2.00
❑ 3 Bishop, Time Cop C .10 .25
❑ 4 Blink, Exile C .10 .25
❑ 5 Cable, Nathan Summers C .10 .25
❑ 6 Cable, Askani'Son U .20 .50
❑ 7 Colossus, Tin Man C .10 .25
❑ 8 Cyclops, Fearless Leader C .10 .25
❑ 9 Domino, Neena Thurman R 1.50 4.00
❑ 10 Emma Frost, Ice Queen R 2.50 6.00
❑ 11 Forge, Inventor Extraordinaire U .20 .50
❑ 12 Gambit, Swamp Rat U .20 .50
❑ 13 Havok, Unstable Son C .10 .25
❑ 14 Iceman, Frosty C .10 .25
❑ 15 Jean Grey, Teen Telepath C .10 .25
❑ 16 Jean Grey, Phoenix Rising C .10 .25
❑ 17 Jean Grey, Phoenix Force R .60 1.50
❑ 18 Jubilee, Mallrat C .10 .25
❑ 19 Mimic, Exile R 1.00 2.50
❑ 20 Morph, Exile U .20 .50
❑ 21 Multiple Man, Army MadroX C .10 .25
❑ 22 Nightcrawler, Man of the Cloth C .10 .25
❑ 23 Professor X, Idealistic Dreamer C .10 .25
❑ 24 Professor X, World's Most Powerful Telepath R.60 1.50
❑ 25 Psylocke, Second Skin C .10 .25
❑ 26 Rogue, Power Absorption R 1.00 2.50
❑ 27 Shadowcat, Phase Shifter R 1.25 3.00
❑ 28 Storm, Elemental Goddess C .10 .25
❑ 29 Sunfire, Rising Sun C .10 .25
❑ 30 Wolverine, Logan C .10 .25
❑ 31 Wolverine, Bub R 2.00 5.00
❑ 32 Wolverine, Bloodlust U .20 .50
❑ 33 X-Man, Nate Grey C .10 .25
❑ 34 Cerebro R .40 1.00
❑ 35 Muir Island U .20 .50
❑ 36 Xavier's Institute of Higher Learning R 4.00 10.00
❑ 37 Adamantium Claws R 3.00 8.00
❑ 38 Battle Tactics C .10 .25
❑ 39 Berserker Rage R 4.00 10.00
❑ 40 Bodyslide R 3.00 8.00
❑ 41 Children of the Atom R .75 2.00
❑ 42 Cleansing Flame R .75 2.00
❑ 43 Commanding Nature C .10 .25
❑ 44 Fastball Special U .20 .50
❑ 45 Healing Factor U .20 .50
❑ 46 Sneak Attack R 1.25 3.00
❑ 47 Splintering Consciousness U .20 .50
❑ 48 Telepathic Suppression R .75 2.00
❑ 49 To Me, My X-Men! R 1.25 3.00
❑ 50 Turnabout C .10 .25
❑ 51 Avalanche, Earthmover R .60 1.50
❑ 52 Black Tom, Callous Opportunist C .10 .25
❑ 53 Blob, Fred Dukes C .10 .25
❑ 54 Blob, Immovable Object U .20 .50
❑ 55 Dark Beast, Sinister Reflection R .75 2.00
❑ 56 Destiny, Doomsday Diarist U .20 .50
❑ 57 Exodus, Bennet du Paris C .10 .25
❑ 58 Juggernaut, Champion of Cyttorak C .10 .25
❑ 59 Juggernaut, Walking Disaster U .20 .50
❑ 60 Juggernaut, Weapon of Mass Destruction R .75 2.00
❑ 61 Magneto, Mutant Terrorist C .10 .25
❑ 62 Magneto, Mutant Supreme R 1.25 3.00
❑ 63 Magneto, Master of Magnetism R .50 1.25
❑ 64 Mammomax, Maximus Jensen C .10 .25
❑ 65 Mystique, Shapely Shifter U .20 .50
❑ 66 Mystique, Shape-Changing Assassin C .10 .25
❑ 67 Nocturne, Talia Wagner R 1.00 2.50
❑ 68 Phantazia, Eileen Harsaw C .10 .25
❑ 69 Post, Harbinger of Onslaught C .10 .25
❑ 70 Pyro, St. John Allerdyce C .10 .25
❑ 71 Quicksilver, Mercurial Speedster C .10 .25
❑ 72 Quicksilver, Speed Demon R .75 2.00
❑ 73 Random, Marshall Evan Stone III R 1.00 2.50
❑ 74 Rogue, Southern Belle C .10 .25
❑ 75 Sabretooth, Genocidal Savage C .10 .25
❑ 76 Sabretooth, Feral Rage R .75 2.00
❑ 77 Sauron, Mutant Vampire R .75 2.00
❑ 78 Scarlet Witch, Mistress of Magic C .10 .25
❑ 79 Scarlet Witch, Brotherhood Sister C .10 .25
❑ 80 Sentinel Mark VII, Repurposed R 1.25 3.00
❑ 81 Toad, Court Jester C .10 .25
❑ 82 Unus, Angelo Unuscione U .20 .50
❑ 83 Xorn, Champion of Mutantkind R .75 2.00
❑ 84 Juggernaut's Helmet U .20 .50
❑ 85 Asteroid M U .20 .50
❑ 86 Genosha R 1.00 2.50
❑ 87 Underground Resistance R 2.50 6.00
❑ 88 A Human Juggernaut R .60 1.50
❑ 89 Avalanched! C .10 .25
❑ 90 Betrayal Most Foul R .50 1.25
❑ 91 Eviscerate C .10 .25
❑ 92 Immovable Object C .10 .25
❑ 93 Insignificant Threat R .60 1.50
❑ 94 Iron Extraction R 1.25 3.00
❑ 95 Metallic Assault R .60 1.50
❑ 96 Pecking Order U .20 .50
❑ 97 Sibling Support C .10 .25
❑ 98 The Next Brotherhood R 2.50 6.00
❑ 99 Unstoppable R 1.50 4.00
❑ 100 Xorn's Takeover R .40 1.00
❑ 101 Black Cat, Thrillseeker C .10 .25
❑ 102 Black Panther, Silent Stalker C .10 .25
❑ 103 Black Widow, Femme Fatale R 1.25 3.00
❑ 104 Blade, Vampire Slayer R 1.25 3.00
❑ 105 Captain America, Loyal Patriot R 2.00 5.00
❑ 106 Cloak, Shadowmaster R .50 1.25
❑ 107 Dagger, Lightbringer C .10 .25
❑ 108 Daredevil, Fearless Survivor C .10 .25
❑ 109 Daredevil, Hornhead C .10 .25
❑ 110 Deadgirl, Dead Again? U .20 .50
❑ 111 Dr. Strange, Master of the Mystic Arts C .10 .25
❑ 112 Echo, Masterless Samurai R 1.00 2.50
❑ 113 Elektra, Masterless Assassin R 2.50 6.00
❑ 114 Ghost Rider, The Devil's Rider C .10 .25
❑ 115 Ghost Rider, Spirit of Vengeance U .20 .50
❑ 116 Ghost Rider, Danny Ketch R .75 2.00
❑ 117 Hulk, Savage Hulk R 1.50 4.00
❑ 118 Iron Fist, Hired Hero C .10 .25
❑ 119 Luke Cage, Hired Hero C .10 .25
❑ 120 Marvel Boy, Noh-Varr U .20 .50
❑ 121 Moon Knight, Knight of Khonshu C .10 .25
❑ 122 Morbius, Biochemical Bloodsucker U .20 .50
❑ 123 Nick Fury, Col. Nicholas Fury R 1.00 2.50
❑ 124 Punisher, Suicide Run C .10 .25
❑ 125 Punisher, Guns Blazing U .20 .50
❑ 126 Punisher, Angel of Death R 2.00 5.00
❑ 127 Shang Chi, Martial Master R .50 1.25
❑ 128 Spider-Man, Webhead C .10 .25
❑ 129 Spider-Man, Outlaw C .10 .25
❑ 130 The Sentry, Forgotten Hero U .20 .50
❑ 131 Vengeance, Spirit of Vengeance C .10 .25
❑ 132 White Tiger, Angela Del Toro C .10 .25
❑ 133 Wolverine, Covert Predator C .10 .25
❑ 134 Brass Grill C .10 .25
❑ 135 Desert Eagle C .10 .25
❑ 136 M60s U .20 .50
❑ 137 Scattergun R .75 2.00
❑ 138 Wheels of Vengeance R .75 2.00
❑ 139 Dark Alley C .10 .25
❑ 140 Anguish of the Innocent R .60 1.50
❑ 141 Bring the Pain C .10 .25
❑ 142 Chain of Vengeance U .20 .50
❑ 143 Defensive Formation R 1.00 2.50
❑ 144 Encircle R .75 2.00
❑ 145 Neighborhood Watch, Team-Up C .10 .25
❑ 146 Penance Stare U .20 .50
❑ 147 Quick Kill C .10 .25
❑ 148 Reload R .75 2.00
❑ 149 Sniper Shot R 1.25 3.00
❑ 150 Wild Ride R 2.00 5.00
❑ 151 Ant-Man, King of the Hill C .10 .25
❑ 152 Crystal, Inhuman Elemental C .10 .25
❑ 153 Dr. Strange, Ally of The Four R 1.25 3.00
❑ 154 Frankie Raye, Johnny's Flame C .10 .25
❑ 155 Franklin Richards, Child of the Cosmos C .10 .25
❑ 156 Ghost Rider, Rider on the Storm C .10 .25
❑ 157 H.E.R.B.I.E., Robot Nanny R .75 2.00
❑ 158 Hulk, The Fantastic Hulk C .10 .25
❑ 159 Human Torch, Matchstick U .20 .50
❑ 160 Human Torch, Nova Blast C .10 .25
❑ 161 Human Torch, Flame On! R .75 2.00
❑ 162 Invisible Woman, Walking on Air C .10 .25
❑ 163 Invisible Woman .10 .25
First Lady of the Fantastic Four C
❑ 164 Invisible Woman, Sight Unseen U .20 .50
❑ 165 Invisible Woman, Shield of The Four R .75 2.00
❑ 166 Luke Cage, Steel-Hard Skin R 1.25 3.00
❑ 167 Luke Cage, Paid in Full C .10 .25
❑ 168 Lyja, Mrs. Johnny Storm R .60 1.50
❑ 169 Medusa, Red R .75 2.00
❑ 170 Mr. Fantastic, Stringbean C .10 .25
❑ 171 Mr. Fantastic, Critical Thinker U .20 .50
❑ 172 Mr. Fantastic, Dimensional Explorer C .10 .25
❑ 173 Namorita, Atlantean Warrior Princess R .75 2.00
❑ 174 Nathaniel Richards, Temporal Traveler R .75 2.00
❑ 175 She-Hulk, Single Green Lawyer C .10 .25
❑ 176 Silver Surfer, Norrin Radd R .75 2.00
❑ 177 Spider-Man, Power and Responsibility U .20 .50
❑ 178 Sub-Mariner, Uncertain Ally U .20 .50
❑ 179 Thing, Idol O'Millions C .10 .25
❑ 180 Thing, Heavy Hitter R .50 1.25
❑ 181 Thing, The Ever-Lovin' Blue-Eyed Thing U .20 .50
❑ 182 Uatu the Watcher , He Who Watches U .20 .50
❑ 183 Valeria Richards , Child of Light and Darkness U.20 .50
❑ 184 Fantasticar 2.0 R .60 1.50
❑ 185 Future Technology R .60 1.50
❑ 186 Unstable Molecular Suit C .10 .25
❑ 187 Four Freedoms Plaza R .75 2.00
❑ 188 Pier 4 R .50 1.25
❑ 189 Clobberin' Pine! R .75 2.00
❑ 190 Eureka! R .60 1.50
❑ 191 Family of Four R 1.25 3.00
❑ 192 Firewall U .20 .50
❑ 193 Force Field Projection R 1.50 4.00
❑ 194 Heat Wave R .75 2.00
❑ 195 Invisibility U .20 .50
❑ 196 It's Clobberin' Time! R .75 2.00
❑ 197 Reed and Sue C .10 .25
❑ 198 Signal Flare R .75 2.00
❑ 199 Stretch Out U .20 .50
❑ 200 Torch and Thing C .10 .25
❑ 201 Boris, Personal Servant of Dr. Doom R 1.00 2.50
❑ 202 Doom-Bot, Army U .20 .50
❑ 203 Doom-Bot II, Army C .10 .25
❑ 204 Dr. Doom, Diabolic Genius U .20 .50
❑ 205 Dr. Doom, Gypsy King C .10 .25
❑ 206 Dr. Doom, Fearsome Monarch U .20 .50
❑ 207 Dr. Doom, Lord of Latveria R .50 1.25
❑ 208 Dragon Man, Experimental Monster C .10 .25
❑ 209 Dreadnought Tank, Arsenal of Doom R .75 2.00
❑ 210 Pacifier Robot, Army C .10 .25
❑ 211 Puppet Master, Overprotective Father R .75 2.00
❑ 212 Swarm Bots, Army C .10 .25
❑ 213 Ultron, Army C .10 .25
❑ 214 Armor of Doom R .75 2.00
❑ 215 Faces of Doom U .20 .50
❑ 216 Fervent Research R 1.25 3.00
❑ 217 Mystical Paralysis U .20 .50
❑ 218 Robotic Offensive U .20 .50
❑ 219 Sacrificial Pawn C .10 .25
❑ 220 Supersize C .10 .25
❑ 221 The Power Cosmic R .40 1.00
❑ 222 Gladiator, Praetor of the Imperial Guard R .50 1.25
❑ 223 Lilandra, Majestrix of the Shi'ar R .75 2.00
❑ 224 Shi'ar Soldier, Army C .10 .25
❑ 225 Apocalypse, The Fittest R .75 2.00
❑ 226 Bullseye, #1 with a Bullet U .20 .50
❑ 227 Deadpool, Interminable Terminator U .20 .50
❑ 228 Holocaust, Nemesis R .75 2.00
❑ 229 Mr. Sinister, Visionary Geneticist U .20 .50
❑ 230 Omega Red, Cold War Commando R .75 2.00
❑ 231 Onslaught .75 2.00
Psionic Spawn of Xavier and Magneto R
❑ 232 Random Punks, Army C .10 .25
❑ 233 Stryfe, X-Cutioner C .10 .25
❑ 234 Frag Grenade C .10 .25
❑ 235 Katana C .10 .25
❑ 236 Mandroid Prototype R .50 1.25
❑ 237 Med Kit U .20 .50
❑ 238 Steel Girder R .75 2.00
❑ 239 Three-Ton Boulder R .40 1.00
❑ 240 Construction Site C .10 .25
❑ 241 Evil Lair U .20 .50
❑ 242 Research Facility C .10 .25
❑ 243 Unstable Ground R .50 1.25
❑ 244 Assorted Aliases R 1.25 3.00
❑ 245 Burn Rubber C .10 .25
❑ 246 Combat Veteran U .20 .50
❑ 247 Crushing Blow C .10 .25
❑ 248 Dealing with the Devil, Team-Up U .20 .50
❑ 249 Devastating Blow C .10 .25
❑ 250 Finishing Move C .10 .25
❑ 251 For Great Justice! C .10 .25
❑ 252 Fortify C .10 .25
❑ 253 Forward Assault C .10 .25
❑ 254 Gamma Bomb R .40 1.00
❑ 255 Heroes of the City, Team-Up C .10 .25
❑ 256 Marvel Crossover, Team-Up C .10 .25
❑ 257 Mental Blast C .10 .25
❑ 258 Mobilize R 6.00 15.00
❑ 259 Monkey Business R 1.25 3.00
❑ 260 New and Improved R 2.00 5.00
❑ 261 New Mutations U .75 2.00

Card	Low	High
262 Only Human R	2.50	6.00
263 Overwhelming Force U	.75	2.00
264 RAT-TAT-TAT R	.50	1.25
265 Reset R	1.50	4.00
266 Rigged Explosives R	1.25	3.00
267 Savage Beatdown R	5.00	12.00
268 Secret Identity R	1.00	2.50
269 Shrink U	.20	.50
270 Strange Bedfellows, Team-Up U	.20	.50
271 Swift Escape U	.20	.50
272 The 198, Team-Up C	.10	.25
273 The Greater Threat, Team-Up C	.10	.25

2007 Vs System Marvel Legends Foil

COMPLETE SET (273) 100.00 200.00
*FOIL: .8X TO 2X BASIC CARDS

2007 Vs System Marvel Team-Up

Card	Low	High
COMPLETE SET (220)	30.00	60.00
BOOSTER BOX (24)	20.00	40.00
1 Aunt May, Golden Oldie U	.20	.50
2 Black Cat, Nine Lives C	.10	.25
3 Blade, Nightstalker U	.20	.50
4 Captain America, Heroic Paragon C	.10	.25
5 Daredevil, New Kingpin C	.10	.25
6 Darkhawk, Chris Powell C	.10	.25
7 Elektra, Leader of the Hand C	.10	.25
8 Frank Drake, Nightstalker C	.10	.25
9 Ka-Zar, Lord Kevin Plunder C	.10	.25
10 Luke Cage, Neighborhood Watch C	.10	.25
11 Man-Thing, Theodore Sallis U	.20	.50
12 Mattie Franklin, Reserve Webhead C	.10	.25
13 Michael Collins Deathlok Schizophrenic Cyborg C	.10	.25
14 Night Thrasher, Dwayne Michael Taylor C	.10	.25
15 Phil Urich Green Goblin, Lunatic Laugh U	.20	.50
16 Punisher, Frank Castle U	.20	.50
17 The Sentry, Golden Guardian of Good R	.40	1.00
18 Shanna the She-Devil, Shanna O'Hara Plunder C	.10	.25
19 Sleepwalker, Rick Sheridan R	.40	1.00
20 Speedball, Robert Baldwin C	.10	.25
21 Spider-Man, Stark's Protege R	1.25	3.00
22 Spider-Man, The Sensational Spider-Man R	.75	2.00
23 Spider-Man, Parasitic Host C	.10	.25
24 Spider-Man, Spider-Hulk C	.10	.25
25 Spider-Man, The Amazing Bag-Man C	.10	.25
26 Venom, Lethal Protector C	.10	.25
27 Wolverine, Canucklehead C	.10	.25
28 Zabu, Constant Companion C	.10	.25
29 Catch You Later! U	.20	.50
30 Down, but Not Out U	.20	.50
31 Drink This! R	.40	1.00
32 Empire State University R	1.25	3.00
33 Feminine Wiles U	.20	.50
34 Gift Wrapped R	1.50	4.00
35 Indebted R	1.50	4.00
36 Need a Lift? U	.20	.50
37 Ring of Fire U	.20	.50
38 Spider-Sense Tingling! C	.10	.25
39 Spider-Signal U	.20	.50
40 Spider-Mobile, Unique C	.10	.25
41 Stark Tower, Team-Up C	.10	.25
42 Target Practice C	.10	.25
43 Trial by Jury R	.50	1.25
44 Archangel, New Defender C	.10	.25
45 Beast, New Defender U	.20	.50
46 Brunnhilde Valkyrie, Barbara Norriss C	.10	.25
47 Devil-Slayer, Eric Simon Payne R	.40	1.00
48 Dr. Strange, Founding Father R	.75	2.00
49 Dr. Strange, Sorcerer Supreme R	.60	1.50
50 Gargoyle, Isaac Christians C	.10	.25
51 Hawkeye, Loud Mouth R	.60	1.50
52 Hellcat, Patsy Walker C	.10	.25
53 Howard the Duck, Master of Quack-Fu C	.10	.25
54 Hulk, Grumpy Green Goliath C	.10	.25
55 Hulk, Strongest One There Is R	.50	1.25
56 Iceman, New Defender U	.20	.50
57 Jack of Hearts, Jack Hart C	.10	.25
58 John Walker U.S. Agent, Loose Cannon C	.10	.25
59 Johnny Blaze Ghost Rider, Damned C	.10	.25
60 Kyle Richmond Nighthawk, Heart of the Team C	.10	.25
61 Professor X, Illuminati C	.10	.25
62 Richard Rider Nova, Xandarian Nova Corps C	.10	.25
63 Samantha Parrington Valkyrie Chooser of the Slain R	1.50	4.00
64 Silver Surfer, Prodigal Herald U	.20	.50
65 Silver Surfer, Earthbound C	.10	.25
66 Sub-Mariner, Neptune's Fist C	.10	.25
67 Sub-Mariner, King of Atlantis C	.10	.25
68 Tania Belinskya Red Guardian, Cold Warrior C	.10	.25
69 Wendell Vaughn Quasar Protector of the Universe C	.10	.25
70 Wong, Mystical Manservant R	1.50	4.00
71 Astral Projection U	.20	.50
72 Banished to the Abyss U	.20	.50
73 The Arrival R	2.00	5.00
74 The Book of the Vishanti U	.20	.50
75 Consulting the Orb U	.20	.50
76 Crimson Bands of Cyttorak R	.50	1.25
77 Defenders Defend! U	.20	.50
78 Eye of Agamotto, Unique R	.40	1.00
79 Imperius Rex! C	.10	.25
80 One-Man Rampage R	.50	1.25
81 The Order R	.75	2.00
82 Sanctum Sanctorum U	.20	.50
83 Secret Defenders, Team-Up C	.10	.25
84 Soul Survival U	.20	.50
85 Star-Crossed C	.10	.25
86 Teleportation Ring, Unique C	.10	.25
87 Zzzax Attax! C	.10	.25
88 Albert Malik Red Skull, Axis of Evil C	.10	.25
89 Answer, Aaron Nicholson R	.75	2.00
90 Black Tarantula, Carlos LaMuerto U	.20	.50
91 Bullseye, Assassin for Hire C	.10	.25
92 Carnage, Psychopath R	.75	2.00
93 Chameleon, Man of Many Faces C	.10	.25
94 Dr. Octopus, Master of Evil R	.60	1.50
95 Electro, Shock Jock U	.20	.50
96 Francis Klum Mysterio, Mutant Magician C	.10	.25
97 Fusion, Markley C	.10	.25
98 Gog, Alien Menace R	.40	1.00
99 Harry Osborn Green Goblin, Unfortunate Son C	.10	.25
100 Jason Macendale Hobgoblin Possessed Lunatic C	.10	.25
101 Lizard, Voracious Predator R	.60	1.50
102 Maguire Beck Mad Jack, Jack o' Lantern C	.10	.25
103 Nitro, Robert Hunter R	.40	1.00
104 Razorfist, Sociopathic Mercenary C	.10	.25
105 Rhino, Unstoppable Force C	.10	.25
106 Slyde, Jalome Beacher C	.10	.25
107 Spider-Man Robot, Timespinner C	.10	.25
108 Spider-Slayer V.X., Arachnid Hunter C	.10	.25
109 Spot, Dr. Jonathan Ohnn C	.10	.25
110 Swarm, Fritz von Meyer U	.20	.50
111 Trapster, Peter Petruski C	.10	.25
112 Venom, Mac Gargan C	.10	.25
113 Venom, The Hunger C	.10	.25
114 Vulture, Aerial Stalker C	.10	.25
115 Alien Symbiote, Unique C	.10	.25
116 Breakout U	.20	.50
117 The Contract, Team-Up C	.10	.25
118 Demonic Association U	.20	.50
119 The Enforcers R	.40	1.00
120 Gotcha! C	.10	.25
121 The Great Game U	.20	.50
122 Hidden Cache R	.40	1.00
123 Legacy of Evil U	.20	.50
124 Legion of Losers C	.10	.25
125 Planet of the Symbiotes U	.20	.50
126 Ravencroft Institute R	.40	1.00
127 Sand Trap U	.20	.50
128 Spider Hunt R	.60	1.50
129 Suffocation C	.10	.25
130 The Vault U	.20	.50
131 Baron Mordo, Karl Amadeus Mordo C	.10	.25
132 Black Rose, Roxanne Simpson U	.20	.50
133 Blackheart, Black King R	.60	1.50
134 Chthon, Demon of the Darkhold U	.20	.50
135 Doppelganger, Killer Clone C	.10	.25
136 Dormammu, Dread Dormammu C	.10	.25
137 The Dwarf, Soul Broker U	.20	.50
138 Dweller-in-Darkness, Fear Lord C	.10	.25
139 Ebenezer Laughton Scarecrow Undead Lunatic C	.10	.25
140 Illyana Rasputin Magik, Queen of Limbo C	.10	.25
141 Madelyne Pryor, Goblyn Queen U	.20	.50
142 Meatmarket, Lilin C	.10	.25
143 Mephisto, pheles C	.10	.25
144 The Mindless Ones, Army C	.10	.25
145 Modred the Mystic, Servant of Chthon C	.10	.25
146 Morlun, Totem Hunter C	.10	.25
147 N'astirh, Liege of Limbo C	.10	.25
148 The N'Garai, Army C	.10	.25
149 Noble Kale, Lord of Hell R	.40	1.00
150 Pilgrim, Lilin C	.10	.25
151 Queen Lilith, Den Mother C	.10	.25
152 Satana, Hellstrom C	.10	.25
153 Shathra, Sharon Keller C	.10	.25
154 Shuma-Gorath He Who Sleeps but Shall Awake R	.40	1.00
155 Thanos, Courting Death R	.40	1.00
156 Umar, Sorceress Sublime R	.40	1.00
157 Zarathos, Demon of Fire C	.10	.25
158 Book of Cagliostro U	.20	.50
159 Dark Bargain R	.40	1.00
160 Dark Designs C	.10	.25
161 The Dark Dimension, Non-Unique C	.10	.25
162 Death's Embrace R	1.50	4.00
163 Demonic Embryo C	.10	.25
164 Dimensional Rift R	.60	1.50
165 In Limbo U	.20	.50
166 Mausoleum, Non-Unique C	.10	.25
167 Midnight Massacre R	.50	1.25
168 Netherworld Gift U	.20	.50
169 Ritual Sacrifice, Team-Up C	.10	.25
170 Siege of Darkness C	.10	.25
171 Strange Love U	.20	.50
172 Surtur's Anvil U	.20	.50
173 Transformation C	.10	.25
174 Undead Legions R	.50	1.25
175 Battlestar, Lemar Hoskins R	.40	1.00
176 Chen, Amy Chen C	.10	.25
177 Crippler, Carl Striklan C	.10	.25
178 Dominic Fortune, Soldier of Fortune U	.20	.50
179 Fin, Intruders C	.10	.25
180 Man-Eater, Intruders C	.10	.25
181 Paladin, Intruders R	.40	1.00
182 Powell, Southern Charm U	.20	.50
183 Quentino, Raul Quentino U	.20	.50
184 Sandman, Intruders U	.20	.50
185 Silver Sable, World's Deadliest Mercenary R	.40	1.00
186 Wild Pack Recruit, Army U	.20	.50
187 Bounty Hunt U	.20	.50
188 Capture Net U	.20	.50
189 Stealthcraft, Team-Up C	.10	.25
190 Alyosha Kravinoff, Son of Kraven C	.10	.25
191 Deadpool, Merc With a Mouth R	.60	1.50
192 Demogoblin, Disembodied Demon C	.10	.25
193 Dr. Doom, Just Reward R	.40	1.00
194 Hellstorm, Son of Satan C	.10	.25
195 Moon Knight, Fist of Khonshu C	.10	.25
196 Morbius, Shadow of the Vampire R	.40	1.00
197 Against All Odds R	.75	2.00
198 Big Leagues R	4.00	10.00
199 Burns at the Touch C	.10	.25
200 He Who Watches U	.20	.50
201 The Illuminati C	.10	.25
202 Justice Is Served! C	.10	.25
203 Marvel Crossover, Team-Up C	.10	.25
204 Poker Night C	.10	.25
205 Rabbit Fire C	.10	.25
206 We Had a Team-Up, Team-Up C	.10	.25
207 What Are Friends For? C	.10	.25
208 Cassandra Nova, Genocidal Tendencies U	.20	.50
209 Damocles Base R	1.00	2.50
210 Dark Beast, McCoy U	.20	.50
211 Ego Gem, Unique ? Infinity Gem U	.20	.50
212 Hulk, Joe Fixit U	.20	.50
213 Monster Island R	.40	1.00
214 New Baxter Building U	.20	.50
215 Quicksilver, Terrigenesis Rebirth U	.20	.50
216 Ronan the Accuser, Exiled U	.20	.50
217 Super Skrull, Kl'rt R	.40	1.00
218 The B Team R	.40	1.00
219 The Annihilation Wave R	.40	1.00
220 The Void, Robert Reynolds R	.40	1.00

2007 Vs System Marvel Team-Up Foil

COMPLETE SET (220) 60.00 120.00
*FOIL: .8X TO 2X BASIC CARDS

2007 Vs System World's Finest

Card	Low	High
COMPLETE SET (220)	30.00	60.00
BOOSTER BOX (24)	40.00	80.00
1 Bibbo Bibbowski, Barroom Brawler U	.20	.50
2 Brahma, Supermen of America C	.10	.25
3 The Guardian, Jim Harper U	.20	.50
4 Hiro Okamura Toyman, Whiz-Kid C	.10	.25
5 John Henry Irons Steel, Armor Aura C	.10	.25
6 John Henry Irons Steel, Steel Works U	.20	.50
7 Kara Zor-El Flamebird, Kandorian Vigilante C	.10	.25
8 Kara Zor-El Supergirl, Claire Connors R	1.00	2.50
9 Kelex, Caretaker of the Fortress C	.10	.25
10 Krypto, Guard Dog of El C	.10	.25
11 Lois Lane, Reporter Extraordinaire U	.20	.50
12 Loser, Supermen of America C	.10	.25
13 Maximum, Supermen of America C	.10	.25
14 Natasha Irons Steel, Unlikely Alloy C	.10	.25
15 The Newsboy Legion, Army C	.10	.25
16 Outburst, Supermen of America C	.10	.25
17 Power Girl Nightwing, Kandorian Vigilante C	.10	.25
18 Pyrogen, Supermen of America R	.75	2.00
19 Superman, Man of Tomorrow C	.10	.25
20 Superman, Deterrent Force R	2.00	5.00
21 Superman, Last Son of Krypton R	2.00	5.00
22 Superman, Bulletproof R	1.25	3.00
23 Vartox, Hero of Tynola U	.20	.50
24 White Lotus, Supermen of America C	.10	.25
25 Wonder Woman, Deflection Diva R	.75	2.00
26 City of Tomorrow, Team-Up C	.10	.25
27 Kandor, City in a Bottle U	.20	.50
28 Smallville U	.20	.50
29 Desperate Sacrifice U	.20	.50
30 Double Team C	.10	.25
31 Early Edition R	.60	1.50
32 For the Man Who Has Everything R	.60	1.50
33 Future Friends C	.10	.25
34 Good Boy! C	.10	.25
35 Home Sweet Home U	.20	.50
36 Impervious U	.20	.50
37 Iron Will C	.10	.25
38 Soaring to New Heights C	.10	.25
39 Alfred Pennyworth, Faithful Friend R	.60	1.50
40 Batman, Problem Solver U	.20	.50
41 Batman, Twilight Vigilante C	.10	.25
42 Bat-Mite, #1 Fan R	.75	2.00
43 Batmobile, Burn Rubber U	.20	.50
44 Commissioner Gordon, Gotham Central U	.20	.50
45 Crispus Allen, Gotham Central C	.10	.25
46 Gotham Central S.W.A.T., Army C	.10	.25
47 Harvey Bullock, Gotham Central C	.10	.25
48 Kate Kane Batwoman, Katherine the Younger R	1.00	2.50
49 Maggie Sawyer, Gotham Central C	.10	.25
50 The Question, Victor Sage U	.20	.50
51 Renee Montoya, Gotham Central U	.20	.50
52 Tim Drake Robin, Flying Solo C	.10	.25
53 Two-Face, Jekyll and Hyde C	.10	.25
54 Batman and the Outsiders R	1.25	3.00
55 Bat-Signal U	.20	.50
56 Batman, Cape and Cowl R	.75	2.00
57 Gotham Central U	.20	.50
58 Bat Got Your Tongue? R	.60	1.50
59 Batcave, Crime-Fighting Lab U	.20	.50
60 Good Cop, Good Cop C	.10	.25
61 The Hook-Up, Team-Up C	.10	.25
62 Interrogate R	.60	1.50
63 Nine Lives U	.20	.50
64 Taking Aim R	.60	1.50
65 Barbara Gordon Oracle, Hacker Elite C	.10	.25
66 Barbara Gordon Oracle, Inside Information U	.20	.50
67 Cassandra Cain, Death's Daughter C	.10	.25
68 Catwoman, Feline Fatale C	.10	.25
69 Dinah Laurel Lance Black Canary Cry in the Dark C	.10	.25
70 Gypsy, Illusionary Operative U	.20	.50
71 Huntress, Vicious Vigilante C	.10	.25
72 Lady Blackhawk, Zinda Blake R	.60	1.50
73 Lady Shiva, Jade Canary C	.10	.25
74 Savant, Brian Durlin C	.10	.25
75 Ted Grant Wildcat, Nine Lives C	.10	.25
76 Vixen, Mari Jiwe McCabe C	.10	.25
77 Aerie One U	.20	.50
78 Birds of a Feather C	.10	.25
79 Cry for Blood C	.10	.25
80 Black Lightning, Jefferson Pierce C	.10	.25
81 Dick Grayson Nightwing, Renegade C	.10	.25
82 Dick Grayson Nightwing, Rough Justice U	.20	.50
83 Faust, Sebastian Faust U	.20	.50
84 Freddy Freeman Captain Marvel Jr., CM3 C	.10	.25
85 Geo-Force, Brion Markov C	.10	.25
86 Grace, Grace Choi C	.10	.25
87 Grace, The Bouncer U	.20	.50
88 Halo, Gabrielle Doe C	.10	.25
89 Huntress, Harsh Mistress C	.10	.25
90 Indigo, Paranoid Android C	.10	.25
91 Jade, Emerald Beacon C	.10	.25
92 Katana, Tatsu Yamashiro U	.20	.50
93 Katana, Soultaker R	.60	1.50
94 Kimiyo Hoshi Dr. Light, Sunburst R	.75	2.00
95 Koriand'r Starfire, Royal Temper C	.10	.25
96 Looker, Emily Briggs C	.10	.25
97 Metamorpho, The Element Man C	.10	.25
98 Owen Mercer Captain Boomerang Jr. Prodigal Son C	.10	.25
99 Roy Harper Arsenal, Ladies' Man C	.10	.25
100 Shift, Knockoff R	.60	1.50
101 Technocrat, Geoffrey Barron C	.10	.25
102 Terra, Little Sis R	1.00	2.50
103 Thunder, Anissa Pierce C	.10	.25
104 Thunder, Heavy Duty C	.10	.25
105 Wylde, Charlie Wylde C	.10	.25
106 Pequod, Unique U	.20	.50
107 Brooklyn HQ R	.60	1.50
108 Markovia U	.20	.50
109 Optitron Corporation U	.20	.50
110 Batman, Dark Knight Returned U	.20	.50
111 Betrayal of Trust U	.20	.50
112 Booze Elementals C	.10	.25
113 Fighting the Liar C	.10	.25
114 Get It Done U	.20	.50
115 Hell Breaks Loose C	.10	.25
116 Incognito C	.10	.25
117 The Insiders, Team-Up C	.10	.25
118 Recruiting Drive R	.75	2.00
119 Scorched Earth C	.10	.25
120 Soul Slicer U	.20	.50
121 Taking Out the Trash U	.20	.50
122 Anarky, Lonnie Machin U	.20	.50
123 Basil Karlo Ultimate Clayface, Mud Pack R	.60	1.50
124 Batarang, Cutting Edge R	1.00	2.50
125 Batzarro, World's Worst Detective U	.20	.50
126 Calendar Man, Julian Gregory Day U	.20	.50
127 Catwoman, Jewel Thief C	.10	.25
128 Charaxes, Drury Walker C	.10	.25
129 Crime Doctor, Bradford Thorne C	.10	.25
130 Firefly, Burning Desire C	.10	.25
131 Great White, Warren White C	.10	.25
132 Harley Quinn, Mr. J's Girl C	.10	.25
133 The Joker, Crazy for You R	.75	2.00
134 The Joker, Out of His Mind R	1.25	3.00
135 The Joker Red Hood, The Man Who Laughs U	.20	.50
136 KGBeast, Anatoli Knyazev C	.10	.25
137 Killer Croc, Cannibal C	.10	.25
138 Mad Hatter, Mad as a Hatter U	.20	.50
139 Matt Hagen Clayface, Mud Pack C	.10	.25
140 Mr. Freeze, Cold Shoulder C	.10	.25
141 Mr. Zsasz, Scar Tissue C	.10	.25
142 The Penguin, Crime's Early Bird C	.10	.25
143 Poison Ivy, Venomous Vixen C	.10	.25
144 The Riddler, Multiple Choice U	.20	.50
145 Scarecrow, Fear and Loathing R	.60	1.50
146 Sondra Fuller Clayface, Mud Pack C	.10	.25
147 Tally Man, Tax Time R	.60	1.50
148 Two-Face, Heads or Tails C	.10	.25
149 Arkham Asylum, Team-Up R	.60	1.50
150 Blackgate Prison, Maximum Security U	.20	.50
151 All Locked Up C	.10	.25
152 Beside Myself R	.60	1.50
153 Burn Baby Burn C	.10	.25
154 Hush Baby C	.10	.25
155 It's a Hard Life R	.60	1.50
156 Money Talks R	.60	1.50
157 Pick a Card R	.75	2.00
158 Usual Suspects U	.20	.50
159 Alexandra Allston Parasite, Power Drain C	.10	.25
160 Atomic Skull, Cursed R	.60	1.50
161 Bizarro, Bizarro World's Finest R	.75	2.00
162 Brainiac 12, Upgrade Complete C	.10	.25
163 Brainiac 13, B-13 C	.10	.25
164 Darkseid, The Omega U	.20	.50
165 Doomsday, Evolution Advanced C	.10	.25
166 Hank Henshaw Cyborg Manhunter Grandmaster U	.20	.50
167 Indigo, Brainiac 8 R	.75	2.00
168 Kryptonite Man, K. Russell Abernathy C	.10	.25
169 Lex Luthor, Master Manipulator R	1.25	3.00
170 Lex Luthor, Sinister Scientist C	.10	.25
171 Livewire, Leslie Willis C	.10	.25
172 Manchester Black, Union Jack C	.10	.25
173 Maxima, Warrior Queen C	.10	.25
174 Metallo, Kryptonite Heart C	.10	.25
175 Mongul, Son of the Tyrant C	.10	.25
176 Mr. Mxyzptlk, Felonious Fiend R	.60	1.50
177 Natasha Irons Starlight, Everyman Project U	.20	.50
178 Preus, Citizen's Patrol C	.10	.25
179 Professor Emil Hamilton Ruin, Power Suit R	.60	1.50
180 Satanus, Colin Thornton U	.20	.50
181 Solaris, Tyrant Sun R	1.00	2.50
182 Terra-Man, Toby Manning C	.10	.25
183 Ultraman, Despot of Kandor C	.10	.25
184 Winslow Schott Toyman, Child's Play C	.10	.25
185 Graveyard of Solitude U	.20	.50
186 Battle for Metropolis U	.20	.50
187 Bizarro Brawl R	.60	1.50
188 Dimensional Deal, Team-Up C	.10	.25
189 Executive Privilege R	.75	2.00
190 Fatal Weakness R	1.00	2.50
191 Future Shock C	.10	.25
192 Hidden Agenda R	.60	1.50
193 Hostile Takeover C	.10	.25
194 Imprisoned in the Source R	.60	1.50
195 Knowledge Is Power U	.20	.50
196 Never-Ending Battle C	.10	.25
197 Obey or Die! R	.75	2.00
198 World's Worstest, Team-Up C	.10	.25
199 At Their Finest R	.60	1.50
200 Best of the Best R	1.25	3.00
201 Brains and Brawn R	1.00	2.50
202 Phantom Zone U	.20	.50
203 Power Armor C	.10	.25
204 Stryker's Island R	.60	1.50
205 Batter Up! C	.10	.25
206 Batzarro Beatdown R	.60	1.50
207 Certifiable R	.60	1.50
208 Chilly Reception R	.60	1.50
209 Crackshot C	.10	.25
210 Engine of Change U	.20	.50
211 Gorilla Warfare C	.10	.25
212 Jack-in-the-Box R	.75	2.00
213 SKREEEEEEE! C	.10	.25
214 Spirit of Nabu, Magic U	.20	.50
215 Standoff U	.20	.50
216 Tied Down C	.10	.25
217 Training Day, Team-Up C	.10	.25
218 Truth and Justice, Team-Up C	.10	.25
219 Matter-Eater Lad, Tenzil Kem U	.20	.50
220 Deathstroke the Terminator Wolf in Bat's Clothing U	.20	.50

2007 Vs System World's Finest Foil

COMPLETE SET (220) 60.00 120.00
*FOIL: .8X TO 2X BASIC CARDS

2008 Vs System Marvel Universe

Card	Low	High
COMPLETE SET (330)	50.00	100.00
BOOSTER BOX (24)	30.00	60.00
1 Bill Foster Goliath, Secret Avenger R	.75	2.00
2 Black Panther, Secret Avenger C	.10	.25
3 Cable, Secret Avenger R	.75	2.00
4 Captain America, The Patriot - Secret Avenger C	.10	.25
5 Captain America, Champion License R	2.00	5.00
6 Captain America, Living Legend R	1.50	4.00
7 Captain America, Sentinel of Liberty R	1.50	4.00
8 Cloak, Secret Avenger U	.20	.50
9 Dagger, Secret Avenger C	.10	.25
10 Dr. Strange, Secret Avenger R	1.50	4.00
11 Echo Ronin, Secret Avenger C	.10	.25
12 Falcon, Secret Avenger C	.10	.25
13 Hawkeye Ronin, Secret Avenger U	.20	.50
14 Hercules, Secret Avenger C	.10	.25
15 Hulkling, Teddy Altman - Young Avenger C	.10	.25
16 Human Torch, Secret Avenger C	.10	.25
17 Invisible Woman, Secret Avenger C	.10	.25
18 Iron Fist Daredevil, Imposter - Secret Avenger U	.20	.50
19 Iron Fist, Secret Avenger C	.10	.25
20 Jessica Drew Spider-Woman, Secret Avenger U	.20	.50
21 Kate Bishop Hawkeye, Young Avenger R	.75	2.00
22 Luke Cage, Secret Avenger U	.20	.50
23 Patriot, Elijah Bradley - Young Avenger C	.10	.25
24 Punisher, Secret Avenger R	1.00	2.50
25 Speed, Thomas Shepard - Young Avenger U	.20	.50
26 Spider-Man, Secret Avenger R	1.50	4.00
27 Stature, Cassandra Lang - Young Avenger U	.20	.50
28 Storm, Secret Avenger C	.10	.25
29 Vision, Young Avenger R	.75	2.00
30 Wiccan, William Kaplan - Young Avenger U	.20	.50
31 Wolverine, Secret Avenger R	1.50	4.00
32 Captain America's Shield, Null R	1.50	4.00
33 Electron Scrambler, Null R	.75	2.00
34 Safe House No. 23, Team-Up U	.20	.50
35 Above the Law, Null U	.20	.50
36 Atlantis, Null R	.75	2.00
37 Avengers Forever, Null U	.20	.50
38 Avengers Reassembled, Null R	2.00	5.00
39 The Big Three, Null C	.10	.25
40 Charging Star, Null R	1.50	4.00
41 Final Justice, Null U	.20	.50
42 Hard to Kill, Null C	.10	.25

TCG/CCG

☐ 43 Liberating Number 42, Null C .10 .25
☐ 44 Reckless Youth, Null R .75 2.00
☐ 45 Secret Avengers, Team-Up C .10 .25
☐ 46 Shield Slash, Null C .10 .25
☐ 47 Stars and Stripes, Null U .20 .50
☐ 48 Switching Sides, Null U .20 .50
☐ 49 Thou Art No Thor!, Null R .75 2.00
☐ 50 Young Avengers, Null C .10 .25
☐ 51 Beetle Mach, Discharged C .10 .25
☐ 52 Blizzard, Frosty Friend U .20 .50
☐ 53 Bullseye, Lester R 1.25 3.00
☐ 54 Bullseye, Closer to God R 1.25 3.00
☐ 55 Genis-Vell Photon, Cosmic Threat C .10 .25
☐ 56 Green Goblin, Insanity Unleashed C .10 .25
☐ 57 Green Goblin, Director of the Thunderbolts C .10 .25
☐ 58 Helmut Zemo Baron Zemo .75 2.00
Master of the Moonstones R
☐ 59 Joystick, Fun and Games U .20 .50
☐ 60 Karla Sofen Moonstone, Uncertain Loyalty C .10 .25
☐ 61 Karla Sofen Moonstone, Field Commander U .20 .50
☐ 62 Lady Deathstrike, Opportunistic Killer C .10 .25
☐ 63 Melissa Gold Songbird, Caged Angel C .10 .25
☐ 64 Radioactive Man, Containment Suit R 1.00 2.50
☐ 65 Radioactive Man, Sheep in Wolf's Clothing U .20 .50
☐ 66 Speed Demon, Whizzer U .20 .50
☐ 67 Speedball Penance, Pain Monger C .10 .25
☐ 68 Speedball Penance, Repentant Masochist R .75 2.00
☐ 69 Swordsman, Andreas Von Strucker C .10 .25
☐ 70 Taskmaster, Super Hero Trainer C .10 .25
☐ 71 Venom, Faithless Monster U .20 .50
☐ 72 Venom, Brain-Eater C .10 .25
☐ 73 The T-Wagon, Null U .20 .50
☐ 74 The Zeus, Unique R .75 2.00
☐ 75 Thunderbolts Mountain, Null R .75 2.00
☐ 76 Collect Them All!, Null R 1.00 2.50
☐ 77 Dangerous Liason, Null R .75 2.00
☐ 78 Faith In Monsters, Null U .20 .50
☐ 79 Ruthless Agression, Null C .10 .25
☐ 80 Sanctioned Killers, Team-Up C .10 .25
☐ 81 Speedball Is Dead, Null U .20 .50
☐ 82 Unregistered Combatants, Null R .75 2.00
☐ 83 The Wrong Stuff, Team-Up C .10 .25
☐ 84 Ares, Mighty Avenger R 1.00 2.50
☐ 85 Bishop, Agent of S.H.I.E.L.D. U .20 .50
☐ 86 Blade, Independant Contractor U .20 .50
☐ 87 Cape-Killers Unit, Army - Agent of S.H.I.E.L.D. U .20 .50
☐ 88 Carol Danvers Ms. Marvel, Mighty Avenger C .10 .25
☐ 89 Daisy Johnson, Agent of S.H.I.E.L.D. C .10 .25
☐ 90 Deadpool, Independant Contractor C .10 .25
☐ 91 Doc Samson, Agent of S.H.I.E.L.D. C .10 .25
☐ 92 Dum-Dum Dugan, Howling Commando C .10 .25
☐ 93 Eric O'Grady Ant Man, Fugitive at Large C .10 .25
☐ 94 Hank Pym Yellowjacket, Initiative Instructor U .20 .50
☐ 95 Iron Man, Mighty Avenger R 2.00 5.00
☐ 96 Iron Man, Director of S.H.I.E.L.D. U .20 .50
☐ 97 Jessica Drew Spider-Woman .10 .25
Agent of S.H.I.E.L.D. - HYDRA C
☐ 98 Justice, Vance Astrovik C .10 .25
☐ 99 Life Model Decoy, More Human Than Human R 1.00 2.50
☐ 100 Maria Hill, Deputy Commander of S.H.I.E.L.D. C .10 .25
☐ 101 Mar-Vell Captain Marvel .10 .25
Warden of Prison Alpha C
☐ 102 Mr. Fantastic, Haunted Genius C .10 .25
☐ 103 Natasha Romanoff Black Widow .20 .50
Mighty Avenger U
☐ 104 Nick Fury, Director of S.H.I.E.L.D. R 1.00 2.50
☐ 105 S.H.I.E.L.D. Agents, Army .10 .25
Agent of S.H.I.E.L.D. C
☐ 106 Sentinel Squad O*N*E*, Army U .20 .50
☐ 107 The Sentry, Mighty Avenger R .75 2.00
☐ 108 Sharon Carter, Agent 13 .10 .25
Agent of S.H.I.E.L.D. C
☐ 109 She-Hulk, Agent of S.H.I.E.L.D. C .10 .25
☐ 110 Spider-Man, Unmasked R 1.00 2.50
☐ 111 Squirrel Girl, Doreen Green U .20 .50
☐ 112 Thing, Conscientious Objector R .75 2.00
☐ 113 Thor, Cyborg Clone R .75 2.00
☐ 114 Tigra, Greer Grant Nelson C .10 .25
☐ 115 War Machine, Director of the Initiative C .10 .25
☐ 116 Wasp, Mighty Avenger U .20 .50
☐ 117 Wolverine, Agent of S.H.I.E.L.D. - HYDRA U .20 .50
☐ 118 Wonder Man, Mighty Avenger R .75 2.00
☐ 119 Yelena Belova Black Widow .75 2.00
Agent of S.H.I.E.L.D. - HYDRA R
☐ 120 Extremis Upgrade, Null U .20 .50
☐ 121 Hulkbuster Armor, Null R 1.00 2.50
☐ 122 Power Dampeners, Null U .20 .50
☐ 123 S.H.I.E.L.D. Flying Car, Null U .20 .50
☐ 124 Godseye Satellite, Null U .20 .50
☐ 125 Negative Zone, Non-Unique - Prison Alpha R .75 2.00
☐ 126 S.H.I.E.L.D. Helicarrier, Null R 1.00 2.50
☐ 127 Stark Armory, Null R .75 2.00
☐ 128 Company of Heroes, Null U .20 .50
☐ 129 I'm a Futurist, Null R .75 2.00
☐ 130 The Initiative, Team-Up C .10 .25
☐ 131 License to Kill, Null R .75 2.00
☐ 132 Out for Justice, Null C .10 .25
☐ 133 S.T.A.R. Squad, Null U .20 .50
☐ 134 Scarlet Spiders, Null U .20 .50
☐ 135 Secret War, Team-Up C .10 .25
☐ 136 Security Clearance, Null R .75 2.00
☐ 137 You're Under Arrest!, Null R .75 2.00
☐ 138 A.I.M. Agents, Army - A.I.M. C .10 .25
☐ 139 Arnim Zola, The Bio-Fanatic Raid U .20 .50
☐ 140 Baron Strucker, Baron Wolfgang Von Strucker .10 .25
HYDRA C
☐ 141 Crossbones, Brock Rumlow - Raid C .10 .25
☐ 142 Doctor Faustus, Johann Fennhoff - Raid U .20 .50
☐ 143 Elektra, Pawn of the Gorgon - HYDRA U .20 .50
☐ 144 The Gorgon, Tomi Shishido - HYDRA R .75 2.00
☐ 145 The Hand, Army - HYDRA U .20 .50
☐ 146 Head Case, Sean Madigan - A.I.M. R .75 2.00
☐ 147 The Hood, Prince of Pistols C .10 .25
☐ 148 HYDRA Recruit, Army - HYDRA C .10 .25
☐ 149 James Barnes Winter Soldier 1.00 2.50
Communist Puppet - Raid R
☐ 150 Kingpin, War Profiteer - HYDRA U .20 .50
☐ 151 M.O.D.O.K. .10 .25
Mobile Organism Designed Only for Killing - A.I.M. C
☐ 152 Mandarin, Tem Borjigan R .75 2.00
☐ 153 Master Man, Max Lohmer - Raid U .20 .50
☐ 154 MODOC Squad, Army - A.I.M. C .10 .25
☐ 155 Red Skull, Aleksander Lukin - Raid C .10 .25
☐ 156 Red Skull, Johann Shmidt - HYDRA C .10 .25
☐ 157 Red Skull, Master of Creation C .10 .25
☐ 158 Scientist Supreme .20 .50
Monica Rappaccini - A.I.M. U
☐ 159 Silver Samurai, Kenuichio Harada - HYDRA R .75 2.00
☐ 160 Sin, Synthia Schmidt - Raid C .10 .25
☐ 161 The Sleeper, Doomsday Device - Raid R .75 2.00
☐ 162 Viper, Madame Hydra - HYDRA U .20 .50
☐ 163 Cosmic Cube, Null R .75 2.00
☐ 164 Death Warrant, Null R 1.00 2.50
☐ 165 Satan Claw, Null U .20 .50
☐ 166 Fortress Yashida, Null U .20 .50
☐ 167 HYDRA Armageddon Carrier, Null R .75 2.00
☐ 168 Underground Laboratory, Null R .75 2.00
☐ 169 Acts of Vengeance, Null U .20 .50
☐ 170 Assault on Hellicarrier 13, Null U .20 .50
☐ 171 Cold Storage, Null R .75 2.00
☐ 172 Cut Off One Head..., Null R .75 2.00
☐ 173 Double Agent!, Team-Up C .10 .25
☐ 174 Enemies of the State, Null C .10 .25
☐ 175 Hail Hydra!, Team-Up C .10 .25
☐ 176 New King in Town, Null U .20 .50
☐ 177 Ninjas! Ninjas! Ninjas!, Null R .75 2.00
☐ 178 Radically Advanced, Null U .20 .50
☐ 179 Archangel, Champion U .20 .50
☐ 180 Brood, Brood Creature 2 of 6 C .10 .25
☐ 181 Caiera, The Oldstrong U .20 .50
☐ 182 Elloe Kaifi, Slave of the Empire U .20 .50
☐ 183 Hiroim, The Shamed C .10 .25
☐ 184 Hulk, Exile C .10 .25
☐ 185 Hulk, Green Scar R 1.50 4.00
☐ 186 Hulk, Gladiator C .10 .25
☐ 187 Hulk, The Green King C .10 .25
☐ 188 Hulk, Sakaar'Son C .10 .25
☐ 189 Hulk, Worldbreaker R 1.00 2.50
☐ 190 Korg, Kronan Warrior U .20 .50
☐ 191 Mastermind Excello, Amadeus Cho R 1.00 2.50
☐ 192 Miek, The Unhived C .10 .25
☐ 193 Rick Jones, Monster's Best Friend C .10 .25
☐ 194 The Great Arena, Null R .75 2.00
☐ 195 Imperial Dreadnaught, Null C .10 .25
☐ 196 Sakaar, Null R .75 2.00
☐ 197 Bloodsport, Null U .20 .50
☐ 198 The End of the World, Null R .75 2.00
☐ 199 Fight or Die!, Null U .20 .50
☐ 200 Hulk Red, Null U .20 .50
☐ 201 Hulk Smash, Null R 5.00 12.00
☐ 202 Righteous Anger, Null R .75 2.00
☐ 203 The Strongest One There Is, Null U .20 .50
☐ 204 Warbound to the End, Null R 1.00 2.50
☐ 205 World War Hulk, Team-Up .20 .50
☐ 206 Annihilus, Anti-Matter Master C .10 .25
☐ 207 Annihilus, The Living Death That Walks R .75 2.00
☐ 208 Blastaar, The Living Bomb Burst R .75 2.00
☐ 209 The Centurians, Army C .10 .25
☐ 210 Currs, Army U .20 .50
☐ 211 Ravenous, Steward of Annihilus U .20 .50
☐ 212 Seekers, Army C .10 .25
☐ 213 Skreet, Chaos Mite C .10 .25
☐ 214 Thanos, The Mad Titan R 1.00 2.50
☐ 215 Cosmic Control Rod, Unique U .20 .50
☐ 216 Negative Zone, Non-Unique - Gateway R .75 2.00
☐ 217 Negative Zone, Non-Unique .10 .25
Harvester of Sorrows C
☐ 218 Negative Zone, Non-Unique .10 .25
Seat of Annihilation C
☐ 219 Gift for Death, Null R .75 2.00
☐ 220 Swarm of Annihilus, Null R .75 2.00
☐ 221 Wave of Destruction, Null R .75 2.00
☐ 222 Beta Ray Bill, Simon Walters - Omega Flight R 1.50 4.00
☐ 223 John Walker U.S. Agent, Omega Flight R .75 2.00
☐ 224 Julia Carpenter Arachne, Omega Flight C .10 .25
☐ 225 Sasquatch, Walter Langrowski - Omega Flight C .10 .25
☐ 226 Talisman, Elizabeth Twoyoungmen .10 .25
Omega Flight C
☐ 227 Weapon Omega, Michael Pointer .75 2.00
Omega Flight R
☐ 228 Alpha Flight: Reborn, Null R 1.25 3.00
☐ 229 Omega Flight, Team-Up C .10 .25
☐ 230 Black Bolt, Protector of the Space Gem U .20 .50
☐ 231 Dr. Strange, Protector of the Soul Gem U .20 .50
☐ 232 Iron Man, Protector of the Reality Gem U .20 .50
☐ 233 Mr. Fantastic, Protector of the Power Gem C .10 .25
☐ 234 Professor X, Protector of the Mind Gem U .20 .50
☐ 235 Sub-Mariner, Protector of the Time Gem U .20 .50
☐ 236 Atlantis Attacks!, Null C .10 .25
☐ 237 Undisclosed Location, Non-Unique U .20 .50
☐ 238 The 100 Ideas, Null U .20 .50
☐ 239 Clandestine Operations, Null R 1.50 4.00
☐ 240 The Elektra Situation, Null R 1.00 2.50
☐ 241 Essence of Zom, Null R .75 2.00
☐ 242 The Infinity Gauntlet, Null R 1.00 2.50
☐ 243 Realm of the Mind, Null U .20 .50
☐ 244 Secret Government, Null U .20 .50
☐ 245 Silent War, Null R .75 2.00
☐ 246 Loki, Loki Laufeyson R .75 2.00
☐ 247 Thor, Donald Blake R .75 2.00
☐ 248 The Reckoning, Null U .20 .50
☐ 249 Sub-Mariner, The Avenging Son U .20 .50
☐ 250 Atlantean Warriors, Army U .20 .50
☐ 251 Magneto, House of M C .10 .25
☐ 252 Quicksilver, House of M R 1.00 2.50
☐ 253 Scarlet Witch, House of M R .75 2.00
☐ 254 Dr. Doom, Future Perfect U .20 .50
☐ 255 Torture Chamber, Null U .20 .50
☐ 256 I Am Doom, Null C .10 .25
☐ 257 Silver Surfer, The Silver Savage U .20 .50
☐ 258 Black Bolt, Enemy Within C .10 .25
☐ 259 James Barnes Bucky, Kid Commando R 1.00 2.50
☐ 260 Kang, Non-Unique - Time Warrior U .20 .50
☐ 261 Kang Iron Lad, Non-Unique - Young Avenger R .75 2.00
☐ 262 Punisher, Captain America R 1.00 2.50
☐ 263 Aaron Stack, Hater of Fleshy Ones U .20 .50
☐ 264 The Captain, Can't Remember His Real Name U .20 .50
☐ 265 Elsa Bloodstone, Foulmouthed Bombshell U .20 .50
☐ 266 Monica Rambeau, I Was An Avenger U .20 .50
☐ 267 Tabitha Smith, Zomg! U .20 .50
☐ 268 Ultron, Ultron Prime R .75 2.00
☐ 269 Spider-Girl, Daughter of Spider-Man U .20 .50
☐ 270 Cammi, Annoying Sidekick U .20 .50
☐ 271 Drax the Destroyer, Titan Slayer U .20 .50
☐ 272 Phyla-Vell Quasar, Protector of the Universe C .10 .25
☐ 273 Richard Rider Nova Centurion .20 .50
Keeper of the Worldmind U
☐ 274 Ronan the Accuser, Kree Emporer U .20 .50
☐ 275 Star-Lord, Peter Quill R .75 2.00
☐ 276 Super Skrull, Noble Sacrifice U .20 .50
☐ 277 Maverick, Christoph Nord R .75 2.00
☐ 278 Sabretooth, Government Assassin U .20 .50
☐ 279 Wolverine, Weapon 10 U .20 .50
☐ 280 Professor X, Mutant Benefactor U .20 .50
☐ 281 Abomination, Emil Blonsky U .20 .50
☐ 282 Adam Warlock, Savior of the Universe R .75 2.00
☐ 283 Aegis, Lady of All Sorrows R .75 2.00
☐ 284 The Beyonder, Inhuman R .75 2.00
☐ 285 Death, The Second Force of the Universe R .75 2.00
☐ 286 Fin Fang Foom .75 2.00
He Whose Limbs Shatter Mountains R
☐ 287 James Barnes Captain America .20 .50
Legacy Reborn U
☐ 288 James Barnes Winter Soldier, Out in the Cold R 1.00 2.50
☐ 289 Layla Miller, She Knows Stuff U .20 .50
☐ 290 Nick Fury, Off the Grid U .20 .50
☐ 291 Skaar, Son of Hulk U .20 .50
☐ 292 Tenebrous, Of the Darkness R .75 2.00
☐ 293 Quantum Bands, Unique C .10 .25
☐ 294 Alias Investigations, Null U .20 .50
☐ 295 Asgard, Null C .10 .25
☐ 296 The Raft, Null U .20 .50
☐ 297 Agents of H.A.T.E., Null C .10 .25
☐ 298 Annihilating Conquest, Null U .20 .50
☐ 299 Carrying the Torch, Null R 2.00 5.00
☐ 300 Casualty of War, Null U .20 .50
☐ 301 Code White, Null U .20 .50
☐ 302 Collateral Damage, Null C .10 .25
☐ 303 Death of the Dream, Null U .20 .50
☐ 304 Empire's End, Null U .20 .50
☐ 305 Flattened, Null C .10 .25
☐ 306 Frog of Thunder, Null R .75 2.00
☐ 307 Grudge Match, Null C .10 .25
☐ 308 Heroes for Hire, Team-Up C .10 .25
☐ 309 House of M, Null C .10 .25
☐ 310 Hunt for Nitro, Null C .10 .25
☐ 311 I Got 'Em All, Null R .75 2.00
☐ 312 Invasion Plans, Null C .10 .25
☐ 313 Lay Down With Dogs, Null U .20 .50
☐ 314 Losing the Argument, Null C .10 .25
☐ 315 Messiah Complex, Null C .10 .25
☐ 316 My Name is Peter Parker..., Null R 1.50 4.00
☐ 317 No Retreat, No Surrender, Null C .10 .25
☐ 318 Now I'm Fighting Dirty, Null C .10 .25
☐ 319 Outmatched, Null C .10 .25
☐ 320 Public Outcry, Null C .10 .25
☐ 321 Rogue Squadron, Null U .20 .50
☐ 322 She-Hulk Smash!, Null U .20 .50
☐ 323 Sleeper Cells, Null R .75 2.00
☐ 324 Slobberknocker, Null C .10 .25
☐ 325 The Stamford Incident, Null U .20 .50
☐ 326 Superhuman Registration Act, Team-Up R 2.00 5.00
☐ 327 Trouble With Dinosaurs, Null R 1.00 2.50
☐ 328 Uncertain Legacy, Null R 1.00 2.50
☐ 329 Underground Movement, Team-Up R .75 2.00
☐ 330 What If?, Team-Up C .10 .25

2008 Vs System Marvel Universe Foil

COMPLETE SET (330) 100.00 200.00
*FOIL: .8X TO 2X BASIC CARDS

2006 World of Warcraft Heroes of Azeroth

COMPLETE SET (361)
BOOSTER BOX (24)
☐ 1 Boris Brightbeard U .20 .50
☐ 2 Dizdemona U .20 .50
☐ 3 Elendril U .20 .50
☐ 4 Graccus U .20 .50
☐ 5 Litori Frostburn U .20 .50
☐ 6 Moonshadow U .20 .50
☐ 7 Timmo Shadestep U .20 .50
☐ 8 Warrax U .20 .50
☐ 9 Gorebelly U .20 .50
☐ 10 Grennan Stormspeaker U .20 .50
☐ 11 Kayleitha U .20 .50
☐ 12 Omedus the Punisher U .20 .50
☐ 13 Radak Doombringer U .20 .50
☐ 14 Sen'zir Beastwalker U .20 .50
☐ 15 Ta'zo U .20 .50
☐ 16 Thangal U .20 .50
☐ 17 Bash U .20 .50
☐ 18 Bear Form U .20 .50
☐ 19 Circle of Life R 1.00 2.00
☐ 20 Entangling Roots C .10 .20
☐ 21 Feral Rage R 1.00 2.00
☐ 22 Healing Touch U .20 .50
☐ 23 Innervate R 3.00 6.00
☐ 24 Mark of the Wild C .10 .20
☐ 25 Maul U .20 .50
☐ 26 Natural Defenses R 1.00 2.00
☐ 27 Natural Selection C .10 .20
☐ 28 Nature's Swiftness R 1.00 2.00
☐ 29 Predatory Strikes R 4.00 8.00
☐ 30 Primal Mending U .20 .50
☐ 31 Starfire R 1.00 2.00
☐ 32 Aimed Shot R 5.00 10.00
☐ 33 Arcane Shot C .10 .20
☐ 34 Aspect of the Hawk R 1.00 2.00
☐ 35 Bestial Wrath R 2.00 4.00
☐ 36 Bloodclaw C .10 .20
☐ 37 Eagle Eye U .20 .50
☐ 38 Fury R 6.00 12.00
☐ 39 Marked for Death U .20 .50
☐ 40 Master of the Hunt R 4.00 8.00
☐ 41 Multi-Shot R 2.00 4.00
☐ 42 Old Bones U .20 .50
☐ 43 Rapid Fire R 2.00 4.00
☐ 44 Ravenous Bite C .10 .20
☐ 45 Rayder U .20 .50
☐ 46 Track Humanoids U .20 .50
☐ 47 Arcane Intellect U .20 .50
☐ 48 Blink C .10 .20
☐ 49 Brain Freeze R 1.00 2.00
☐ 50 Cold Snap R 1.00 2.00
☐ 51 Counterspell R 4.00 8.00
☐ 52 Fire Blast C .10 .20
☐ 53 Fireball U .20 .50
☐ 54 Flamestrike R 1.00 2.00
☐ 55 Frost Nova R 5.00 10.00
☐ 56 Frostbolt U .20 .50
☐ 57 Mana Agate U .20 .50
☐ 58 Polymorph C .10 .20
☐ 59 Pyroblast R 1.00 2.00
☐ 60 Winter's Grasp U .20 .50
☐ 61 World in Flames R 1.00 2.00
☐ 62 Blessing of Might U .20 .50
☐ 63 Blessing of Protection U .20 .50
☐ 64 Blessing of Wisdom R 4.00 8.00
☐ 65 Cleanse U .20 .50
☐ 66 Devotion Aura R 1.00 2.00
☐ 67 Divine Shield R 5.00 10.00
☐ 68 Hammer of Justice C .10 .20
☐ 69 Holy Light C .10 .20
☐ 70 Holy Shield R 1.00 2.00
☐ 71 Retribution Aura R 1.00 2.00
☐ 72 Sacred Duty C .10 .20
☐ 73 Seal of Light U .20 .50
☐ 74 Seal of Wisdom R 1.00 2.00
☐ 75 Touched by Light U .20 .50
☐ 76 Chastise U .20 .50
☐ 77 Dispel Magic U .20 .50
☐ 78 Flash Heal C .10 .20
☐ 79 Heal U .20 .50
☐ 80 Mind Blast R 1.00 2.00
☐ 81 Mind Control R 1.00 2.00
☐ 82 Mind Spike C .10 .20
☐ 83 Power Word: Fortitude C .10 .20
☐ 84 Prayer of Healing U .20 .50
☐ 85 Psychic Scream R 1.00 2.00
☐ 86 Resurrection R 1.00 2.00
☐ 87 Shadow Word: Pain U .20 .50
☐ 88 Shadowform R 1.00 2.00
☐ 89 Smite R 1.00 2.00
☐ 90 Spiritual Healing R 1.00 2.00
☐ 91 Backstab R 1.00 2.00
☐ 92 Cold Blood R 1.00 2.00
☐ 93 Coup de Grace C .10 .20
☐ 94 Crippling Poison U .20 .50
☐ 95 Deadly Poison U .20 .50
☐ 96 Dismantle U .20 .50
☐ 97 Eviscerate R 1.00 2.00
☐ 98 Expose Armor R 1.00 2.00
☐ 99 Gouge C .10 .20
☐ 100 Lobotomize R 1.00 2.00
☐ 101 Premeditation R 1.00 2.00
☐ 102 Sinister Strike C .10 .20
☐ 103 Stealth U .20 .50
☐ 104 Veil of Night R 1.00 2.00
☐ 105 Waylay U .20 .50
☐ 106 Chain Lightning R 3.00 6.00
☐ 107 Earthbind Totem U .20 .50
☐ 108 Elemental Focus R 1.00 2.00
☐ 109 Frost Shock C .10 .20
☐ 110 Ghost Wolf U .20 .50
☐ 111 Healing Stream Totem U .20 .50
☐ 112 Healing Wave C .10 .20
☐ 113 Lightning Bolt C .10 .20
☐ 114 Purge U .20 .50
☐ 115 Rockbiter Weapon R 1.00 2.00
☐ 116 Searing Totem U .20 .50
☐ 117 Totemic Call R .20 .50
☐ 118 Windfury Totem R 1.00 2.00
☐ 119 Windfury Weapon R 1.00 2.00
☐ 120 Corruption U .20 .50
☐ 121 Curse of Agony R 2.00 4.00
☐ 122 Dark Pact R 1.00 2.00
☐ 123 Fear C .10 .20
☐ 124 Forbidden Knowledge R 1.00 2.00
☐ 125 Grimdron U .20 .50
☐ 126 Helwen R 1.00 2.00
☐ 127 Infernal R 1.00 2.00
☐ 128 Life Tap U .20 .50
☐ 129 Rain of Fire R 1.00 2.00
☐ 130 Sarmoth C .10 .20
☐ 131 Sever the Cord C .10 .20
☐ 132 Shadow Bolt U .20 .50
☐ 133 Soul Link R 1.00 2.00
☐ 134 Steal Essence U .20 .50
☐ 135 Battle Shout C .10 .20
☐ 136 Berserker Stance R 1.00 2.00
☐ 137 Charge U .20 .50
☐ 138 Cleave R 1.00 2.00
☐ 139 Defensive Stance R 1.00 2.00
☐ 140 Demoralizing Shout U .20 .50
☐ 141 Execute C .10 .20
☐ 142 Heroic Strike U .20 .50
☐ 143 Last Stand R 1.00 2.00
☐ 144 Mocking Blow R 1.00 2.00
☐ 145 Mortal Strike R 1.00 2.00
☐ 146 Rend C .10 .20
☐ 147 Shield Bash R 1.00 2.00
☐ 148 Stalwart Protector U .20 .50
☐ 149 Sunder Armor U .20 .50
☐ 150 Face Smash C .10 .20
☐ 151 From the Shadows R 1.00 2.00
☐ 152 Sneak C .10 .20
☐ 153 Into the Fray C .10 .20
☐ 154 Lust for Battle R 1.00 2.00
☐ 155 Skewer C .10 .20
☐ 156 Burn Away C .10 .20
☐ 157 Call the Spirit C .10 .20
☐ 158 Caught Off-Guard C .10 .20
☐ 159 Exhaustion C .10 .20
☐ 160 Fall Back C .10 .20
☐ 161 Guard Duty C .10 .20
☐ 162 Interest You in a Pint? C .10 .20
☐ 163 Lie In Wait C .10 .20
☐ 164 On Your Feet C .10 .20
☐ 165 Quick Strike C .10 .20
☐ 166 Rally the Troops C .10 .20
☐ 167 Rise to the Challenge E 5.00 10.00
☐ 168 Shattering Blow C .10 .20
☐ 169 Spirit Healer E 5.00 10.00
☐ 170 Sudden Reversal C .10 .20
☐ 171 Vanquish C .10 .20
☐ 172 Withdraw C .10 .20
☐ 173 Acolyte Demia U .20 .50
☐ 174 Adept Breton U .20 .50
☐ 175 Anika Berlyn C .10 .20
☐ 176 Apprentice Teep C .10 .20
☐ 177 Augustus Corpsemonger R 1.00 2.00
☐ 178 Bizzik Sparkcog U .20 .50
☐ 179 Braxiss the Sleeper U .20 .50
☐ 180 Crazy Igvand C .10 .20
☐ 181 Donna Callister U .20 .50
☐ 182 Dorric the Martyr C .10 .20
☐ 183 Freya Lightsworn C .10 .20
☐ 184 Galahandra, Keeper of the Silent Grove C .10 .20
☐ 185 Galway Steamwhistle U .20 .50
☐ 186 Grint Sundershot C .10 .20
☐ 187 Hannah the Unstoppable C .10 .20
☐ 188 Ironforge Guards C .10 .20
☐ 189 Kailis Truearc R 1.00 2.00
☐ 190 Kena Shadowbrand C .10 .20
☐ 191 King Magni Bronzebeard E 10.00 20.00
☐ 192 Kor Cinderveín C .10 .20
☐ 193 Kryton Barleybeard U .20 .50
☐ 194 Lady Courtney Noel C .10 .20
☐ 195 Lady Jaina Proudmoore E 5.00 10.00
☐ 196 Lafiel C .10 .20
☐ 197 Latro Abiectus C .10 .20
☐ 198 Leeroy Jenkins E 15.00 30.00
☐ 199 Lhurg Venomblade R 1.00 2.00
☐ 200 Liba Wobblebonk C .10 .20
☐ 201 Lord Grayson Shadowbreaker E 5.00 10.00
☐ 202 Lorekeeper Darian R 1.00 2.00
☐ 203 LtCommander Dudefella R 1.00 2.00
☐ 204 Maxum Ironbrew C .10 .20
☐ 205 Medoc Spiritwarden U .20 .50
☐ 206 Melgwy Pingzot U .20 .50
☐ 207 Mezzik Darkspark U .20 .50
☐ 208 Milo the Unmerciful C .10 .20
☐ 209 Moira Darkheart C .10 .20
☐ 210 Nerra Lifeboon C .10 .20
☐ 211 Nightbloom R 1.00 2.00

❑ 212 Parvink C	.10	.20
❑ 213 Randipan U	.20	.50
❑ 214 Ryn Dreamstrider C	.10	.20
❑ 215 Sentry Gwynn R	1.00	2.00
❑ 216 Seva Shadowdancer R	1.00	2.00
❑ 217 Sha'lin Nightwind C	.10	.20
❑ 218 Stylean Silversteel C	.10	.20
❑ 219 Tracker Gallen C	.10	.20
❑ 220 Treesong U	.20	.50
❑ 221 Tristan Rapidstrike C	.10	.20
❑ 222 Warden Tonarin C	.10	.20
❑ 223 Wilba R	1.00	2.00
❑ 224 Wyneth Harridan R	1.00	2.00
❑ 225 Arnold Flem U	.20	.50
❑ 226 Bala Silentblade C	.10	.20
❑ 227 Barak the Shamed R	1.00	2.00
❑ 228 Benethor Draigo C	.10	.20
❑ 229 Besh'iah C	.10	.20
❑ 230 Blood Guard Mal'wani C	.10	.20
❑ 231 Brigg C	.10	.20
❑ 232 Confessor Mildred C	.10	.20
❑ 233 Dark Cleric Jocasta U	.20	.50
❑ 234 Deacon Johanna U	.20	.50
❑ 235 Elder Moorf U	.20	.50
❑ 236 Fa'tafi C	.10	.20
❑ 237 Fianna Spellbinder E	3.00	6.00
❑ 238 Garlok Skullsplitter C	.10	.20
❑ 239 Gellrin of the Gallows R	3.00	6.00
❑ 240 Guardian Steelhorn C	.10	.20
❑ 241 Halnar Stands-Alone R	1.00	2.00
❑ 242 Hierophant Caydiem U	.20	.50
❑ 243 Hur Shieldsmasher C	.10	.20
❑ 244 Jin'tak Nightfang C	.10	.20
❑ 245 Kaal Soulreaper E	5.00	10.00
❑ 246 Kagra of the Crossroads C	.10	.20
❑ 247 Karkas Deathhowl C	.10	.20
❑ 248 Ka'tali Stonetusk C	.10	.20
❑ 249 Kulan Earthguard C	.10	.20
❑ 250 Masten Everspirit R	1.00	2.00
❑ 251 Mias the Putrid C	.10	.20
❑ 252 Moko Hunts-at-Dawn U	.20	.50
❑ 253 Ophelia Barrows C	.10	.20
❑ 254 Orgrimmar Grunts C	.10	.20
❑ 255 Panax the Unstable R	1.00	2.00
❑ 256 Pugg U	.20	.50
❑ 257 Rak Skyfury U	.20	.50
❑ 258 Samuel Grey U	.20	.50
❑ 259 Skorn, Mistress of Shadow R	1.00	2.00
❑ 260 Taz'dingo C	.10	.20
❑ 261 Tewa Wildmane R	6.00	12.00
❑ 262 Vaerik Proudhoof C	.10	.20
❑ 263 Valthak Spiritdrinker R	1.00	2.00
❑ 264 Vesh'ral C	.10	.20
❑ 265 Vexra Darkfall U	.20	.50
❑ 266 Voss Treebender C	.10	.20
❑ 267 Warchief Thrall E	5.00	10.00
❑ 268 Warlord Goretooth E	2.00	4.00
❑ 269 Watcher Mal'wi C	.10	.20
❑ 270 Wazzuli Wildmender C	.10	.20
❑ 271 Windseer Tarus U	.20	.20
❑ 272 Wormwood U	.20	.20
❑ 273 Ya'mon R	1.00	2.00
❑ 274 Zorm Stonefury C	.10	.20
❑ 275 Zygore Bladebreaker C	.10	.20
❑ 276 Zy'lah Manslayer R	5.00	10.00
❑ 277 Chromie E	4.00	8.00
❑ 278 Landro Longshot R	1.00	2.00
❑ 279 Saltwater Snapjaw R	2.00	4.00
❑ 280 Thunderhead Hippogryph R	5.00	10.00
❑ 281 Bad Mojo Mask R	1.00	2.00
❑ 282 Chromatic Cloak U	.20	.50
❑ 283 Deathdealer Breastplate R	3.00	6.00
❑ 284 Devilsaur Leggings U	.20	.50
❑ 285 Draconian Deflector U	.20	.50
❑ 286 Edgemaster's Handguards U	.20	.50
❑ 287 Eye of Flame R	1.00	2.00
❑ 288 Eye of Rend U	.20	.50
❑ 289 Girdle of Uther R	2.00	4.00
❑ 290 Golem Skull Helm U	.20	.50
❑ 291 Green Whelp Armor U	.20	.50
❑ 292 Helm of Fire R	1.00	2.00
❑ 293 Herod's Shoulder R	2.00	4.00
❑ 294 Hide of the Wild U	.20	.50
❑ 295 Horns of Eranikus R	1.00	2.00
❑ 296 Invulnerable Mail E	5.00	10.00
❑ 297 Lionheart Helm U	.20	.50
❑ 298 Mooncloth Robe R	1.00	2.00
❑ 299 Skullflame Shield E	5.00	10.00
❑ 300 Stronghold Gauntlets E	5.00	10.00
❑ 301 Truesilver Breastplate U	.20	.50
❑ 302 Wall of the Dead E	5.00	10.00
❑ 303 Whitemane's Chapeau U	.20	.20
❑ 304 Barov Peasant Caller R	1.00	2.00
❑ 305 Hearthstone E	5.00	10.00
❑ 306 Lei of Lilies E	3.00	6.00
❑ 307 Masons Fraternity Ring U	.20	.50
❑ 308 Myrmidon's Signet U	.20	.50
❑ 309 Noggenfogger Elixir R	1.00	2.00
❑ 310 Piccolo of the Flaming Fire R	1.00	2.00
❑ 311 Ancient Bone Bow U	.20	.50
❑ 312 Annihilator U	.20	.50
❑ 313 Arcanite Reaper R	1.00	2.00
❑ 314 Argent Crusader R	1.00	2.00
❑ 315 Barman Shanker U	.20	.50
❑ 316 Brain Hacker U	.20	.50
❑ 317 The Cruel Hand of Timmy R	2.00	4.00
❑ 318 Destiny E	3.00	6.00
❑ 319 Dwarven Hand Cannon E	3.00	6.00
❑ 320 Fang of the Crystal Spider R	1.00	2.00
❑ 321 Flame Wrath R	1.00	2.00
❑ 322 Gift of the Elven Magi R	1.00	2.00
❑ 323 The Hammer of Grace U	.20	.50
❑ 324 Hand of Edward the Odd E	3.00	6.00
❑ 325 Headmaster's Charge E	5.00	10.00
❑ 326 Heartseeker U	.20	.50
❑ 327 Hypnotic Blade R	1.00	2.00
❑ 328 Iceblade Hacker U	.20	.50
❑ 329 Illusionary Rod U	.20	.50
❑ 330 Inventor's Focal Sword R	1.00	2.00
❑ 331 Kol Blade U	.20	.50
❑ 332 Rod of the Ogre Magi U	.20	.50
❑ 333 Scarlet Kris U	.20	.50
❑ 334 The Shatterer U	.20	.50
❑ 335 Teebu's Blazing Longsword E	5.00	10.00
❑ 336 Thrash Blade R	1.00	2.00
❑ 337 Truesilver Champion R	2.00	4.00
❑ 338 Twig of the World Tree R	3.00	6.00
❑ 339 Wraith Scythe R	1.00	2.00
❑ 340 The Defias Brotherhood C	.10	.20
❑ 341 Dragonkin Menace U	.20	.50
❑ 342 The Missing Diplomat U	.20	.50
❑ 343 Counterattack U	.20	.50
❑ 344 For the Horde! U	.20	.50
❑ 345 Torek's Assault C	.10	.20
❑ 346 Are We There, Yeti? U	.20	.50
❑ 347 Battle of Darrowshire C	.10	.20
❑ 348 Big Game Hunter C	.10	.20
❑ 349 Blueleaf Tubers C	.10	.20
❑ 350 Chasing A-Me 01 C	.10	.20
❑ 351 A Donation of Wool C	.10	.20
❑ 352 In Dreams C	.10	.20
❑ 353 Into the Maw of Madness C	.10	.20
❑ 354 It's a Secret to Everybody C	.10	.20
❑ 355 Kibler's Exotic Pets C	.10	.20
❑ 356 The Love Potion C	.10	.20
❑ 357 The Princess Trapped C	.10	.20
❑ 358 Sunken Treasure C	.10	.20
❑ 359 Tooga's Quest R	2.00	4.00
❑ 360 Your Fortune Awaits You C	.10	.20
❑ 361 Zapped Giants C	.10	.20

2006 World of Warcraft Heroes of Azeroth Loot

❑ 1 Landro Longshot	15.00	30.00
❑ 2 Thunderhead HippoGryph	35.00	70.00
❑ 3 Saltwater Snapjaw	100.00	160.00

2007 World of Warcraft Fires of Outland

COMPLETE SET (246)	100.00	175.00
❑ 1 Deacon Markus Hallow U	.20	.50
❑ 2 Fillet, Kneecapper Extraordinaire U	.20	.50
❑ 3 Kana Nassis U	.20	.50
❑ 4 Mazar U	.20	.50
❑ 5 Moala Stonebinder U	.20	.50
❑ 6 Ozzati U	.20	.50
❑ 7 Rotun Daggerhand U	.20	.50
❑ 8 Thalia Truthbringer U	.20	.60
❑ 9 Yanna Dai'shalan U	.20	.50
❑ 10 Cul Rendhoof U	.20	.50
❑ 11 Exaura the Cryptkeeper U	.20	.50
❑ 12 Harrigan Soulsunder U	.20	.50
❑ 13 Indalamar U	.20	.50
❑ 14 Mojo Shaper Ojo'mon U	.20	.50
❑ 15 Nathadan U	.20	.50
❑ 16 Ona Skyshot U	.20	.50
❑ 17 Raesa Morningstar U	.20	.50
❑ 18 Zomm Hopeslayer U	.20	.50
❑ 19 Call of the Wild C	.10	.20
❑ 20 Demoralizing Roar R	1.00	2.00
❑ 21 Flight Form U	.20	.50
❑ 22 Force of Nature R	3.00	6.00
❑ 23 Lifebloom C	.10	.20
❑ 24 Moonfire R	6.00	12.00
❑ 25 Prowl U	.20	.50
❑ 26 Tree of Life R	4.00	8.00
❑ 27 Zephyr C	.10	.20
❑ 28 Aspect of the Monkey U	.20	.50
❑ 29 Freezing Trap C	.10	.20
❑ 30 Kill Command U	.20	.50
❑ 31 Misdirection R	1.00	2.00
❑ 32 Nightfire R	1.00	2.00
❑ 33 Readiness R	1.00	2.00
❑ 34 Shelly C	.10	.20
❑ 35 Silencing Shot R	1.00	2.00
❑ 36 Take the Shot C	.10	.20
❑ 37 Amplify Magic U	.20	.50
❑ 38 Arcane Blast C	.10	.20
❑ 39 Dragon's Breath R	1.00	2.00
❑ 40 Fizzle U	.20	.50
❑ 41 Frost Funnel C	.10	.20
❑ 42 Mana Jade C	.10	.20
❑ 43 Megamorph R	1.00	2.00
❑ 44 Molten Armor R	1.00	2.00
❑ 45 Slow R	3.00	6.00
❑ 46 Avenger's Shield R	2.00	4.00
❑ 47 Blessing of Divinity C	.10	.20
❑ 48 Divine Illumination R	1.00	2.00
❑ 49 Guarded by the Light C	.10	.20
❑ 50 Hammer of the Righteous C	.10	.20
❑ 51 Redemption U	.20	.50
❑ 52 Righteous Defense U	.20	.50
❑ 53 Seal of Blood R	.20	.50
❑ 54 Seal of Vengeance R	1.00	2.00
❑ 55 Binding Heal C	.10	.20
❑ 56 Holy Fire U	.20	.50
❑ 57 Mass Dispel U	.20	.50
❑ 58 Mind Soothe C	.10	.20
❑ 59 Pact of Shadow R	1.00	2.00
❑ 60 Pain Suppression R	1.00	2.00
❑ 61 Shadowfiend R	1.00	2.00
❑ 62 Soul Rend C	.10	.20
❑ 63 Vampiric Touch R	2.00	4.00
❑ 64 Anesthetic Poison C	.10	.20
❑ 65 Deadly Brew U	.20	.50
❑ 66 Envenom R	1.00	2.00
❑ 67 Filthy Tricks R	1.00	2.00
❑ 68 Garrote U	.20	.50
❑ 69 Jackknife C	.10	.20
❑ 70 Mutilate R	1.00	2.00
❑ 71 Pick Pocket C	.10	.20
❑ 72 Surprise Attacks R	1.00	2.00
❑ 73 Bloodlust U	.20	.50
❑ 74 Chain Heal C	.10	.20
❑ 75 Earth Shield R	1.00	2.00
❑ 76 Earth Shock R	1.00	2.00
❑ 77 Fire Elemental Totem C	.10	.20
❑ 78 Heroism U	.20	.50
❑ 79 Life Arc C	.10	.20
❑ 80 Shamanistic Rage R	1.00	2.00
❑ 81 Tremor Totem R	1.00	2.00
❑ 82 Angrida C	.10	.20
❑ 83 Death Coil U	.20	.50
❑ 84 Hukkath R	2.00	4.00
❑ 85 Immolate C	.10	.20
❑ 86 Incinerate U	.20	.50
❑ 87 Jar Soul C	.10	.20
❑ 88 Shadowfury R	4.00	8.00
❑ 89 Soulshatter R	1.00	2.00
❑ 90 Unstable Affliction R	4.00	8.00
❑ 91 Berserker Rage R	1.00	2.00
❑ 92 Devastate R	1.00	2.00
❑ 93 Hamstring C	.10	.20
❑ 94 Intervene C	.10	.20
❑ 95 Rallying Shout U	.20	.50
❑ 96 Rampage R	1.00	2.00
❑ 97 Spell Reflection U	.20	.50
❑ 98 Strength of Arms R	1.00	2.00
❑ 99 Victory Rush C	.10	.20
❑ 100 Battle Preparations U	.20	.50
❑ 101 A Break in the Action U	.20	.50
❑ 102 Corpse Run E	4.00	8.00
❑ 103 Defensive Breach C	.10	.20
❑ 104 Explosions C	.10	.20
❑ 105 Goblin Gumbo R	1.00	2.00
❑ 106 Gone Fishin' R	1.00	2.00
❑ 107 Greed Before Need E	4.00	8.00
❑ 108 Treasure Chest U	.20	.50
❑ 109 Ultimate Triumph C	.10	.20
❑ 110 Andiss Butcherson U	.20	.50
❑ 111 Bitties U	.20	.50
❑ 112 Breanna Greenmother R	1.00	2.00
❑ 113 Caddrick Von Styler R	1.00	2.00
❑ 114 Celee Cogfreeze R	1.00	2.00
❑ 115 Christopher the Devout C	.10	.20
❑ 116 Enfea Contha R	1.00	2.00
❑ 117 Exodar Peacekeepers C	.10	.20
❑ 118 Fugu R	1.00	2.00
❑ 119 Guruvan U	.20	.50
❑ 120 Hailey Goodchilde C	.10	.20
❑ 121 He Who Has No Life E	5.00	10.00
❑ 122 Izza Spindleflame C	.10	.20
❑ 123 Jewelcrafter Zanaz C	.10	.20
❑ 124 Josiah King C	.10	.20
❑ 125 Jubilee Arcspark R	4.00	8.00
❑ 126 Krenig Soulguard C	.10	.20
❑ 127 Kulvo Jadefist C	.10	.20
❑ 128 Magraff Sparroweye Ironhammer U	.20	.50
❑ 129 Marilyn of the Sacred Vows C	.10	.20
❑ 130 Miandra R	1.00	2.00
❑ 131 Nalkas C	.10	.20
❑ 132 Narmak Doomratchet R	1.00	2.00
❑ 133 Neeka C	.10	.20
❑ 134 Nesmend Darkbreaker U	.20	.50
❑ 135 Norrund Grovewalker C	.10	.20
❑ 136 Parren Shadowshot U	.10	.20
❑ 137 Porto C	.10	.20
❑ 138 Prophet Velen E	5.00	10.00
❑ 139 Ranthus Adler C	.10	.20
❑ 140 Rodrigo C	.10	.20
❑ 141 Sal Grimstalker C	.10	.20
❑ 142 Savina Greysky C	.10	.20
❑ 143 Shadowmistress Jezebel Hawke U	.20	.50
❑ 144 Tinkmaster Overspark E	4.00	8.00
❑ 145 Tomadae the Magnificent U	.20	.50
❑ 146 Trogun Smith C	.10	.20
❑ 147 Tyler Falconbridge U	.20	.50
❑ 148 Ubel Sternbrow U	.20	.50
❑ 149 Unen Rataan C	.10	.20
❑ 150 Vindicator Borovon R	2.00	4.00
❑ 151 Archdruid Hamuul Runetotem E	3.00	6.00
❑ 152 Ash'ergi C	.10	.20
❑ 153 Borlis Brode U	.20	.50
❑ 154 Broan Charges-the-Fight U	.20	.50
❑ 155 Drusenna the Vigilant U	.20	.50
❑ 156 Erytheis C	.10	.20
❑ 157 E'sad U	.20	.50
❑ 158 Ez'trin U	.20	.50
❑ 159 Faesha Firestalker U	.20	.50
❑ 160 Gahrunt Foulfang U	.20	.50
❑ 161 Garell Strout U	.20	.50
❑ 162 Gor'gar R	1.00	2.00
❑ 163 Hurlorn Battlechaser C	.10	.20
❑ 164 Jazmin Bloodlove C	.10	.20
❑ 165 Jon Reaver C	.10	.20
❑ 166 Kagella Shadowmark C	.10	.20
❑ 167 Karrok Scarrend C	.10	.20
❑ 168 Kelvor Valorshine C	.10	.20
❑ 169 Kiani De'nara R	1.00	2.00
❑ 170 Lessa the Awakener R	1.00	2.00
❑ 171 Lor'themar Theron E	7.00	15.00
❑ 172 Magistrix Maelnerana U	.20	.50
❑ 173 Malistra the Demonmistress U	.20	.50
❑ 174 Manthos the Recently Sewn U	.20	.50
❑ 175 Mordotz E	3.00	6.00
❑ 176 Morlug Soulslaver R	1.00	2.00
❑ 177 Mustang Sally C	.10	.20
❑ 178 Najan Spiritbender C	.10	.20
❑ 179 Nala Stalks-the-Night U	.20	.50
❑ 180 Nalonae C	.10	.20
❑ 181 One-Thousand-Battles C	.10	.20
❑ 182 Rek'gar C	.10	.20
❑ 183 Shawn of the Dead R	2.00	4.00
❑ 184 Silvermoon Sentinels C	.10	.20
❑ 185 Snarl Hellwind U	.20	.50
❑ 186 Snig Feralsnout C	.10	.20
❑ 187 Sus'vayin C	.10	.20
❑ 188 Tempest, Son-of-Storms R	1.00	2.00
❑ 189 Tez Tez the Patchmonger C	.10	.20
❑ 190 Uglund Duskrider C	.10	.20
❑ 191 Vorden the Shadowbringer R	1.00	2.00
❑ 192 Chen Stormstout E	3.00	6.00
❑ 193 Spectral Tiger R	7.00	15,00
❑ 194 Aldori Legacy Defender U	.20	.50
❑ 195 Doomplate Legguards E	6.00	12.00
❑ 196 Emerald-Scale Greaves R	1.00	2.00
❑ 197 Faith Healer's Boots E	3.00	6.00
❑ 198 Gauntlets of Vindication R	4.00	8.00
❑ 199 Mana-Etched Pantaloons R	1.00	2.00
❑ 200 Master Cannoneer Boots U	.20	.50
❑ 201 Moonstrider Boots C	.10	.20
❑ 202 Pauldrons of the Crimson Flight E	3.00	6.00
❑ 203 Predatory Gloves R	3.00	6.00
❑ 204 Sky-Hunter Swift Boots U	.20	.50
❑ 205 Spellbreaker's Buckler R	1.00	2.00
❑ 206 Sun-Gilded Shouldercaps U	.20	.50
❑ 207 Warpwood Binding R	1.00	2.00
❑ 208 Abacus of Violent Odds E	1.00	2.00
❑ 209 Band of the Ranger-General R	1.00	2.00
❑ 210 Burst of Knowledge R	1.00	2.00
❑ 211 Choker of Fluid Thought R	1.00	2.00
❑ 212 Elemental Focus Band R	1.00	2.00
❑ 213 Greatsword of Forlorn Visions R	1.00	2.00
❑ 214 Hammer of the Grand Crusader U	.20	.50
❑ 215 Latro's Shifting Sword U	.20	.50
❑ 216 Masterwork Stormhammer R	1.00	2.00
❑ 217 Reaver of the Infinites E	3.00	6.00
❑ 218 Serpentcrest Life-Staff U	.20	.50
❑ 219 Sonic Spear U	.20	.50
❑ 220 Staff of the Ruins U	.20	.50
❑ 221 Stellaris U	.20	.50
❑ 222 Sunfury Bow of the Phoenix U	.20	.50
❑ 223 Sword of a Thousand Truths E	7.00	15.00
❑ 224 Telescopic Sharprifle R	1.00	2.00
❑ 225 Timeslicer U	.20	.50
❑ 226 Warp Splinter's Thorn U	.20	.50
❑ 227 Corki's Ransom C	.10	.20
❑ 228 Totem of Coo C	.10	.20
❑ 229 Standards and Practices C	.10	.20
❑ 230 Swift Discipline C	.10	.20
❑ 231 Brother Against Brother U	.20	.50
❑ 232 A Donation of Mageweave C	.10	.20
❑ 233 The Fare of Lar'korwi R	1.00	2.00
❑ 234 The Flawless Flame C	.10	.20
❑ 235 Gahz'ridian C	.10	.20
❑ 236 In Case of Emergency R	1.00	2.00
❑ 237 Kodo Roundup C	.10	.20
❑ 238 Leader of the Bloodscale C	.10	.20
❑ 239 Lost R	1.00	2.00
❑ 240 One Draenei's Junk C	.10	.20
❑ 241 Timbermaw Ally U	.20	.50
❑ 242 To Serve Kum'isha C	.10	.20
❑ 243 The Ultimate Bloodsport R	1.00	2.00
❑ 244 Voidwalkers Gone Wild U	.20	.50
❑ 245 What's Wrong at Cenarion Thicket? C	.10	.20
❑ 246 When Smokey Sings, I Get Violent R	.20	.50

2007 World of Warcraft Fires of Outland Loot

❑ 1 Goblin Gumbo L	15.00	30.00
❑ 2 Gone Fishin' L	50.00	100.00
❑ 3 Spectral Tiger L	650.00	900.00

2007 World of Warcraft March of the Legion

COMPLETE SET (319)	30.00	60.00
BOOSTER BOX (24)		
❑ 1 Arktos U	.10	.20
❑ 2 Bildros Nullvoid U	.20	.50
❑ 3 Blaize Brightspark U	.20	.50
❑ 4 Chaigon Steelsight U	.10	.20
❑ 5 Dralor U	.20	.50
❑ 6 Halavar U	.20	.50
❑ 7 Keegana Silvershield U	.20	.50
❑ 8 Kintara Wintermoon U	.20	.50
❑ 9 Memri the Channeler U	.20	.50
❑ 10 Bloody Mary U	.20	.50
❑ 11 Bo'ja, Arcanist Absolute U	.20	.50
❑ 12 Chancellor Velora U	.20	.50
❑ 13 Forang Deathrattle U	.20	.50
❑ 14 Hekto Starspire U	.20	.50
❑ 15 Kassandra Flameheart U	.10	.20
❑ 16 Taheo Skyspeaker U	.20	.50
❑ 17 Urrth U	.20	.50
❑ 18 Zag'zil U	.20	.50
❑ 19 Barkskin R	2.00	5.00
❑ 20 Dreamstate R	4.00	8.00
❑ 21 Druid Training U	.20	.50
❑ 22 Earth and Sky C	.10	.20
❑ 23 Feral Instinct R	2.00	5.00
❑ 24 Gift of the Wild R	1.00	2.00
❑ 25 Invigorating Touch U	.10	.20
❑ 26 Natural Genesis R	1.00	2.00
❑ 27 Shred C	.10	.20
❑ 28 Strangling Roots C	.10	.20
❑ 29 Sustain or Reclaim U	.20	.50
❑ 30 Swipe C	.10	.20
❑ 31 Aspect of the Cheetah R	1.00	2.00
❑ 32 Bestial Swiftness R	1.00	2.00
❑ 33 Blinky R	1.00	2.00
❑ 34 Bloody Welcome C	.10	.20
❑ 35 Crippling Shot C	.10	.20
❑ 36 Double Barrel U	.20	.50
❑ 37 Hunter Training U	.20	.50
❑ 38 Ripper U	.10	.20
❑ 39 Scraps C	.10	.20
❑ 40 Serpent Sting C	.10	.20
❑ 41 Thrill of the Hunt R	.1.00	2.00
❑ 42 Track Demons R	1.00	2.00
❑ 43 Arcane Brilliance U	.20	.50
❑ 44 Arcane Explosion R	3.00	6.00
❑ 45 Cold Front C	.10	.20
❑ 46 Fire Power R	4.00	8.00
❑ 47 Fuel for the Fire R	1.00	2.00
❑ 48 Mage Training U	.20	.50
❑ 49 Magma Spike C	.10	.20
❑ 50 Nether Fracture C	.10	.20
❑ 51 Portal R	10.00	20.00
❑ 52 Touch of Ice U	.20	.50
❑ 53 Touch of the Arcane C	.10	.20
❑ 54 Wand Specialization R	1.00	2.00
❑ 55 Ardent Defender R	1.00	2.00
❑ 56 Blessed Protector C	.20	.50
❑ 57 Exorcism U	.20	.50
❑ 58 Judgement of Light R	1.00	2.00
❑ 59 Judgement of Wisdom R	1.00	2.00
❑ 60 The Light's Largess C	.10	.20
❑ 61 Martyr's Mending R	1.00	2.00
❑ 62 Paladin Training U	.10	.20
❑ 63 Reclusion C	.10	.20
❑ 64 Sacred Purification C	.10	.20
❑ 65 Sanctity Aura R	4.00	8.00
❑ 66 Sheath of Light U	.20	.50
❑ 67 Absorb Magic C	.10	.20
❑ 68 Chasten C	.10	.20
❑ 69 Heartening Arrival U	.20	.50
❑ 70 Holy Nova R	5.00	10.00
❑ 71 Infusion of Fortitude C	.10	.20
❑ 72 Kindred Spirits R	1.00	2.00
❑ 73 Mental Anguish C	.10	.20
❑ 74 Prayer of Fortitude R	1.00	2.00
❑ 75 Priest Training U	.10	.20
❑ 76 Shadow Weaving R	10.00	20.00
❑ 77 Touch of Darkness U	.20	.50
❑ 78 Twist of Faith R	1.00	2.00
❑ 79 Adrenaline Rush R	1.00	2.00
❑ 80 Blind R	3.00	6.00
❑ 81 Cheat Death R	2.00	5.00
❑ 82 Head Trauma C	.10	.20
❑ 83 Hide and Stab C	.10	.20
❑ 84 Obfuscate C	.10	.20
❑ 85 On the Brink C	.10	.20
❑ 86 Rogue Training U	.10	.20
❑ 87 Sprint U	.20	.50
❑ 88 Thick as Thieves R	1.00	2.00
❑ 89 Unfair Advantage R	1.00	2.00
❑ 90 Wound Poison U	.20	.50
❑ 91 Chill C	.10	.20
❑ 92 Eathrend Weapon R	1.00	2.00
❑ 93 Earth's Bounty C	.10	.20
❑ 94 Echo of the Elements R	2.00	4.00
❑ 95 Elements' Fury C	.10	.20
❑ 96 Mana Spring Totem U	.20	.50
❑ 97 Reincarnation R	2.00	4.00
❑ 98 Sentry Totem U	.20	.50
❑ 99 Shaman Training U	.20	.50
❑ 100 Stoneclaw Totem C	.10	.20
❑ 101 Totem of Wrath R	1.00	2.00
❑ 102 Totemic Focus R	1.00	2.00
❑ 103 Banish U	.20	.50
❑ 104 Curse of Contagion C	.10	.20
❑ 105 Drain Mana R	4.00	8.00
❑ 106 Fel Pact R	1.00	2.00
❑ 107 Haaroon R	2.00	5.00
❑ 108 Invoke the Nether R	2.00	4.00
❑ 109 Rulrin U	.20	.50
❑ 110 Siphon Life R	5.00	10.00
❑ 111 Soul Inversion C	.10	.20
❑ 112 Swallow Soul C	.10	.20
❑ 113 Thulthun C	.10	.20
❑ 114 Warlock Training U	.20	.50
❑ 115 Gear Upgrade R	3.00	6.00

❑ 116 Intensify Rage C .10 .20
❑ 117 Piercing Howl R 2.00 4.00
❑ 118 Puncture C .10 .20
❑ 119 Retaliation R 1.00 2.00
❑ 120 Safeguard C .10 .20
❑ 121 Salt the Wounds C .10 .20
❑ 122 Two-Handed Weapon Specialization R 1.00 2.00
❑ 123 Unrelenting Assault R 1.00 2.00
❑ 124 Warrior Training U .20 .50
❑ 125 Withering Shout U .20 .50
❑ 126 Wreck U .20 .50
❑ 127 Bling R 1.00 2.00
❑ 128 Kiting R .10 .20
❑ 129 Meeting Stone E 5.00 10.00
❑ 130 Paper Airplane R 1.00 2.00
❑ 131 Thundering Footsteps R 1.00 2.00
❑ 132 Aldana U .20 .50
❑ 133 Alhas C .10 .20
❑ 134 Anders Blankheart U .20 .50
❑ 135 Archbishop Benedictus E .10 .20
❑ 136 Arlek Stonehilt U .20 .50
❑ 137 Bakaar U .20 .50
❑ 138 Blizzazz C .10 .20
❑ 139 Blademistress Lyss U .20 .50
❑ 140 Caretaker Devonar C .10 .20
❑ 141 Caretaker Heartwing C .10 .20
❑ 142 Caretaker Mooncrier C .10 .20
❑ 143 Champion Zosimus R 1.00 2.00
❑ 144 Cookie McWeaksauce E 5.00 10.00
❑ 145 The Darkeater R 1.00 2.00
❑ 146 Durae Crystalshield C .10 .20
❑ 147 Force Commander Danath Trollbane E 5.00 10.00
❑ 148 Gabble C .10 .20
❑ 149 Gareth Ironshot C .10 .20
❑ 150 Givon U .10 .20
❑ 151 Hanaga Silvervein C .10 .20
❑ 152 Hoxie Mettlemelt R 1.00 2.00
❑ 153 Ingrid Shadowstorm C .10 .20
❑ 154 Jav Stonewall C .10 .20
❑ 155 Kiki Sparkbottom U .20 .50
❑ 156 Kyla Duskrider C .10 .20
❑ 157 Magdeline Prideheart C .10 .20
❑ 158 Marnie Moonlight U .20 .50
❑ 159 Miner Harshdin U .20 .50
❑ 160 Miner Stonedeep R 1.00 2.00
❑ 161 Piana C .10 .20
❑ 162 Rahn Grimstaff C .10 .20
❑ 163 Routeen C .10 .20
❑ 164 Sharial U .20 .50
❑ 165 Shem Reznict R 1.00 2.00
❑ 166 Syluri C .10 .20
❑ 167 Tarwila Gladespring C .10 .20
❑ 168 Tracker Pardo C .10 .20
❑ 169 Waldo the Decoy U .20 .50
❑ 170 Weeble C .10 .20
❑ 171 Zandar Shadesprocket C .10 .20
❑ 172 Acid Hands McGillicutty C .10 .20
❑ 173 Arnerus Brightsteppe U .20 .50
❑ 174 Blood Knight Tarae U .20 .50
❑ 175 Bloodblade C .10 .20
❑ 176 Bloodeye C .10 .20
❑ 177 Bloodsoul C .10 .20
❑ 178 Bolan Earthmend C .10 .20
❑ 179 Captain Swash C .10 .20
❑ 180 Cholda Wildbloom C .10 .20
❑ 181 Doshura Risestrider U .20 .50
❑ 182 Ezra Phoenix C .10 .20
❑ 183 Fungus Face McGillicutty C .10 .20
❑ 184 Golas Swiftwind U .10 .20
❑ 185 Grandma Deadsie R 1.00 2.00
❑ 186 Groundshaker Earnheart C .10 .20
❑ 187 Gurzuk C .10 .20
❑ 188 Hota the Bloodsoaked C .10 .20
❑ 189 Imp Mistress Noali R 1.00 2.00
❑ 190 Instructor Antheol E 5.00 10.00
❑ 191 Jaedan Sunshot C .10 .20
❑ 192 Ja'zoona C .10 .20
❑ 193 Jurpak C .10 .20
❑ 194 Kallas Sunflame R 1.00 2.00
❑ 195 Marka Addington U .20 .50
❑ 196 Nazgrel, Advisor to Thrall E 5.00 10.00
❑ 197 Osha Shadowdrinker R 1.00 2.00
❑ 198 Ossandran, Crematorium Master C .10 .20
❑ 199 Poison Tongue McGillicutty U .10 .20
❑ 200 Ruala the Spotter U .20 .50
❑ 201 Seamus Somerset U .10 .20
❑ 202 Shadala C .10 .20
❑ 203 Silea Dawnwalker C .10 .20
❑ 204 Spider Legs McGillicutty C .10 .20
❑ 205 Trytha Darksun U .20 .50
❑ 206 Tyrennius Scratheblade C .10 .20
❑ 207 Varimathras E 5.00 10.00
❑ 208 Volin Netherburn U .20 .50
❑ 209 Wysko U .20 .50
❑ 210 Yellowspine C .10 .20
❑ 211 Zul'that Steeltusk R 1.00 2.00
❑ 212 Adyen the Lightwarden E 5.00 10.00
❑ 213 Anchorite Alonora C .10 .20
❑ 214 Anchorite Jaliah U .20 .50
❑ 215 Anchorite Viluaa C .10 .20
❑ 216 Darynus C .10 .20
❑ 217 Ishanah, High Priestess of the Aldor E 20.00 40.00
❑ 218 Marksman Boriz U .20 .50
❑ 219 Neophyte Morandi C .10 .20
❑ 220 Vindicator Belian C .10 .20
❑ 221 Vindicator Dindro U .20 .50
❑ 222 Vindicator Kaldel C .10 .20
❑ 223 Vindicator Khorin R 1.00 2.00
❑ 224 Vindicator Melina C .10 .20
❑ 225 Vindicator Trytan C .10 .20
❑ 226 Vindicator Zalreth R 1.00 2.00
❑ 227 Xavar the Resourceful C .10 .20
❑ 228 Zaistor the Vigilant C .10 .20
❑ 229 Arcane Guardian C .10 .20
❑ 230 Arcanist Avelena C .10 .20
❑ 231 Arcanist Raith C .10 .20
❑ 232 Arcanist Tian C .10 .20
❑ 233 Magister Ashi C .10 .20
❑ 234 Magister Lashan U .20 .50
❑ 235 Magistrix Fyalenn E 5.00 10.00
❑ 236 Magistrix Oleinas R 1.00 2.00
❑ 237 Magistrix Tibrana U .20 .50
❑ 238 Retainer Jitaen C .10 .20
❑ 239 Retainer Kedryn C .10 .20
❑ 240 Retainer Khorbus U .10 .20
❑ 241 Retainer Mythras R 1.00 2.00
❑ 242 Retainer Nealos C .10 .20
❑ 243 Retainer Salvan C .10 .20
❑ 244 Retainer Zaelan C .10 .20
❑ 245 Voren'thal the Seer E 5.00
❑ 246 A'dal E 5.00 10.00
❑ 247 Arazzius the Cruel R 1.00 2.00
❑ 248 Doom Lord Kazzak E 7.00 15.00
❑ 249 Fel Cannon U .20 .50
❑ 250 Razorsaw R 1.00 2.00
❑ 251 Robotic Homing Chicken R 1.00 2.00
❑ 252 Shattrath City Peacekeeper C .10 .20
❑ 253 Sironas R 1.00 2.00
❑ 254 Warbringer Arix'amal U .20 .50
❑ 255 Abyss Walker's Boots U .10 .20
❑ 256 Bloodstained Ravager Gauntlets R 1.00 2.00
❑ 257 Demon Hide Spaulders U .20 .50
❑ 258 Demonfang Ritual Helm R 1.00 2.00
❑ 259 Devil-Stiched Leggings U .20 .50
❑ 260 Doomplate Chestguard U .20 .50
❑ 261 Fel Leather Gloves U .20 .50
❑ 262 Gauntlets of the Skullsplitter U .20 .50
❑ 263 Hauberk of Desolation U .20 .50
❑ 264 Mana-Etched Vestments U .20 .50
❑ 265 Manaspark Gloves R 1.00 2.00
❑ 266 Platinum Shield of the Valorous U .10 .20
❑ 267 Shadowstalker's Sash U 1.00 2.00
❑ 268 Stormshield of Renewal U .20 .50
❑ 269 Wastewalker Tunic U .20 .50
❑ 270 Bladefist's Breadth U .20 .50
❑ 271 Freezing Band E 10.00 20.00
❑ 272 Ring of Flowing Light U .10 .20
❑ 273 Vengeance of the Illidari U .20 .50
❑ 274 Axe of the Legion U .20 .50
❑ 275 Blade of Unquenched Thirst R 1.00 2.00
❑ 276 Braxxis' Staff of Slumber R 1.00 2.00
❑ 277 The Bringer of Death R 1.00 2.00
❑ 278 Crimson Shocker U .20 .50
❑ 279 Crystalfire Staff U .20 .50
❑ 280 Demonblood Eviscerator R 1.00 2.00
❑ 281 Demonslayer E 5.00 10.00
❑ 282 The Essence Focuser U .20 .50
❑ 283 Greatsword of Horrid Dreams R 4.00 8.00
❑ 284 Hemet's Elekk Gun R 1.00 2.00
❑ 285 Hungering Bone Cudgel U .10 .20
❑ 286 Nexus Torch U .10 .20
❑ 287 Runesong Dagger U .10 .20
❑ 288 Scepter of the Unholy R 1.00 2.00
❑ 289 Singing Crystal Axe E 5.00 10.00
❑ 290 Skyfire Hawk-Bow U .10 .20
❑ 291 Terokk's Quill R 1.00 2.00
❑ 292 Wand of Eternal Light U .20 .50
❑ 293 Whispering Blade of Slaying U .20 .50
❑ 294 Against the Legion C .10 .20
❑ 295 The Blood is Life C .10 .20
❑ 296 Buying Time U .10 .20
❑ 297 Demonic Contamination C .10 .20
❑ 298 Dousing the Flames of Protection C .10 .20
❑ 299 Falling to Corruption C .10 .20
❑ 300 A Final Blow C .10 .20
❑ 301 Forces of Jaedenar C .10 .20
❑ 302 Forge Camp: Annihilated C .10 .20
❑ 303 The Formation of Felbane U .20 .50
❑ 304 Gurok the Usurper U .20 .50
❑ 305 Hellfire Fortifications C .10 .20
❑ 306 Levixus the Soul Caller C .10 .20
❑ 307 Mission: The Abyssal Shelf R 1.00 2.00
❑ 308 The Name of the Beast C .10 .20
❑ 309 Natural Remedies C .10 .20
❑ 310 An OOX of Your Own R 1.00 2.00
❑ 311 Pride of the Fel Horde C .10 .20
❑ 312 Retribution of the Light C .10 .20
❑ 313 The Root of All Evil C .10 .20
❑ 314 The Spirit Polluted C .10 .20
❑ 315 Survey the Land C .10 .20
❑ 316 Toxic Horrors C .10 .20
❑ 317 A Traitor Among Us C .10 .20
❑ 318 Wanted: Durn the Hungerer C .10 .20
❑ 319 You Are Rakh'likh, Demon C .10 .20

2007 World of Warcraft March of the Legion Loot

❑ 1 Paper Airplane L 10.00 20.00
❑ 2 Robotic Homing Chicken L 50.00 100.00
❑ 3 Kiting L 75.00 150.00

2007 World of Warcraft Through the Dark Portal

COMPLETE SET (319)
BOOSTER BOX (24)

❑ 1 Anchorite Kalinna U .20 .50
❑ 2 Grumpherys U .20 .50
❑ 3 Nathressa Darkstrider U .20 .50
❑ 4 Phadalus the Enlightened U .20 .50
❑ 5 Ruby Gemsparkle U .20 .50
❑ 6 Savin Lightguard U .20 .50
❑ 7 Telrander U .20 .50
❑ 8 Victoria Jaton U .20 .50
❑ 9 Zenith Shadowforce U .20 .50
❑ 10 Aleyah Dawnborn U .20 .50
❑ 11 Azarak Wolfsblood U .20 .50
❑ 12 Bulkas Wildhorn U .20 .50
❑ 13 Daspien Bladedancer U .20 .60
❑ 14 Haruka Skycaller U .20 .50
❑ 15 Mojo Mender Ja'nah U .20 .50
❑ 16 Morganis Blackvein U .20 .50
❑ 17 Morova of the Sands U .20 .50
❑ 18 Pagatha Soulbinder U .20 .50
❑ 19 Cat Form C .10 .20
❑ 20 Claw U .20 .50
❑ 21 Cyclone C .10 .20
❑ 22 Heart of the Wild R 1.00 2.00
❑ 23 Moonkin Form R 1.00 2.00
❑ 24 Nature of the Beast U .20 .50
❑ 25 Nature's Majesty C .10 .20
❑ 26 Rake U .20 .50
❑ 27 Swiftshift R 1.00 2.00
❑ 28 Thorns R 1.00 2.00
❑ 29 Travel Form R 1.00 2.00
❑ 30 Wrath C .10 .20
❑ 31 Aspect of the Viper R 1.00 2.00
❑ 32 Chops U .20 .50
❑ 33 Frost Trap R 5.00 10.00
❑ 34 Hootie C .10 2.00
❑ 35 Immolation Trap U .20 .50
❑ 36 Lightning Reflexes R 2.00 4.00
❑ 37 Point Blank C .10 .20
❑ 38 Protect the Master U .20 .50
❑ 39 Spirit Bond R 2.00 4.00
❑ 40 Trophy Kill C .10 .20
❑ 41 Venomstrike R 4.00 8.00
❑ 42 Wing Clip C .10 .20
❑ 43 Arcane Missiles C .10 .20
❑ 44 Arcane Power R 1.00 2.00
❑ 45 Arc of Flame C .10 .20
❑ 46 Blistering Fire C .10 .20
❑ 47 Conjured Sparkling Water U .20 .50
❑ 48 Dampen Magic U .20 .50
❑ 49 Deep Freeze C .10 .20
❑ 50 Evocation R 1.00 2.00
❑ 51 Ice Block R 4.00 8.00
❑ 52 Mana Shield R 1.00 2.00
❑ 53 Scorch U .20 .50
❑ 54 Spellsteal R 2.00 4.00
❑ 55 Blessing of Freedom C .10 .20
❑ 56 Blessing of Sacrifice R 1.00 2.00
❑ 57 Consecration R 1.00 2.00
❑ 58 Hammer of Wrath C .10 .20
❑ 59 Illumination R 1.00 2.00
❑ 60 Infusion of Light C .10 .20
❑ 61 Lay on Hands R 5.00 10.00
❑ 62 Righteous Vengeance C .10 .20
❑ 63 Seal of Command R 2.00 4.00
❑ 64 Seal of the Crusader U .20 .50
❑ 65 Spiritual Attunement U .20 .50
❑ 66 Undaunted Defense U .20 .50
❑ 67 Brainwash R 1.00 2.00
❑ 68 Clarity of Thought U .20 .50
❑ 69 Convalescence C .10 .20
❑ 70 Greater Heal U .20 .50
❑ 71 Inner Fire R 1.00 2.00
❑ 72 Inner Focus R 1.00 2.00
❑ 73 Lightwell R 1.00 2.00
❑ 74 Mana Burn R 2.00 4.00
❑ 75 Mind Vision C .10 .20
❑ 76 Power Word: Shield C .10 .20
❑ 77 Renew U .20 .50
❑ 78 Shadow Word: Death C .10 .20
❑ 79 Ambush R 6.00 12.00
❑ 80 Blade Flurry R 3.00 6.00
❑ 81 Distract C .10 .20
❑ 82 Kick R 6.00 12.00
❑ 83 Master of Deception R 2.00 4.00
❑ 84 Mind-numbing Poison U .20 .50
❑ 85 Prey on the Weak C .10 .20
❑ 86 Purloin C .10 .20
❑ 87 Shiv C .10 .20
❑ 88 Slaughter from the Shadows R 4.00 8.00
❑ 89 Slice and Dice U .20 .50
❑ 90 Vanish U .20 .60
❑ 91 Ancestral Spirit C .10 .20
❑ 92 Earth Elemental Totem R 2.00 4.00
❑ 93 Fire Nova Totem U .20 .50
❑ 94 Flame Shock C .10 .20
❑ 95 Flametongue Weapon U .20 .50
❑ 96 Grace of Air Totem R 1.00 2.00
❑ 97 Lightning Shield R 1.00 2.00
❑ 98 Lightning Storm U .20 .50
❑ 99 Mana Tide Totem R 1.00 2.00
❑ 100 Shock and Soothe C .10 .20
❑ 101 Stormstrike R 2.00 4.00
❑ 102 Surge of Life C .10 .20
❑ 103 Curse of Tongues U .20 .50
❑ 104 Doomguard R 1.00 2.00
❑ 105 Eye of Kilrogg C .10 .20
❑ 106 Fel Armor R 1.00 2.00
❑ 107 Fel Domination R 1.00 2.00
❑ 108 Hellfire R 4.00 8.00
❑ 109 Morfiel U .20 .50
❑ 110 Mortal Delights U .20 .50
❑ 111 Piztog C .10 .20
❑ 112 Ritual Sacrifice C .10 .20
❑ 113 Shadowburn R 5.00 10.00
❑ 114 Shred Soul C .10 .20
❑ 115 Anger Management R 1.00 2.00
❑ 116 Bloodrage R 1.00 2.00
❑ 117 Challenging Shout U .20 .50
❑ 118 Commanding Shout C .10 .20
❑ 119 Cruelty R 1.00 2.00
❑ 120 Crushing Blow C .10 .20
❑ 121 Intercept C .10 .20
❑ 122 Killing Spree R 2.00 4.00
❑ 123 Revenge U .20 .50
❑ 124 Slam U .20 .50
❑ 125 Thunder Clap R 4.00 8.00
❑ 126 Vigilance C .10 .20
❑ 127 Dual Wield U .20 .50
❑ 128 Diplomacy U .20 .60
❑ 129 Escape Artist U .20 .50
❑ 130 Heroic Presence U .20 .50
❑ 131 Shadowmeld U .20 .50
❑ 132 Stoneform U .20 .50
❑ 133 Arcane Torrent U .20 .50
❑ 134 Berserking U .20 .50
❑ 135 Blood Fury U .20 .50
❑ 136 Cannibalize U .20 .50
❑ 137 War Stomp U .20 .50
❑ 138 Boat to Booty Bay E 4.00 8.00
❑ 139 Desperate Block C .10 .20
❑ 140 Echoes of the Shifting Sands E 3.00 6.00
❑ 141 First to Fall C .10 .20
❑ 142 Flash of Steel C .10 .20
❑ 143 Fortune Telling R 1.00 2.00
❑ 144 Furious Resolve C .10 .20
❑ 145 Legend of Mount Hyjal R 1.00 2.00
❑ 146 Lessons in Lurking C .10 .20
❑ 147 Malfunction C .10 .20
❑ 148 Rest and Relaxation R 1.00 2.00
❑ 149 Swift Assault C .10 .20
❑ 150 Turn Aside C .10 .20
❑ 151 Unraveled Plans C .10 .20
❑ 152 Unwelcome Visitor C .10 .20
❑ 153 Apprentice Merry C .10 .20
❑ 154 Avanthera C .10 .20
❑ 155 Barnathrum, Lord of Pain C .10 .20
❑ 156 Bretander of the Claw C .10 .20
❑ 157 Brother Rhone C .10 .20
❑ 158 Bubula del Kissel C .10 .20
❑ 159 Cerwyn C .10 .20
❑ 160 Chipper Ironbane C .10 .20
❑ 161 Darnassus Sentinels C .10 .20
❑ 162 Durdin Hammerhand C .10 .20
❑ 163 Field Commander Olinnae U .20 .50
❑ 164 Gertha, The Old Crone U .20 .50
❑ 165 Goldenmoon U .20 .50
❑ 166 Gustaf Trueshot R 1.00 2.00
❑ 167 High Priestess Tyrande Whisperwind E 6.00 12.00
❑ 168 Ilandre Moonspear R 1.00 2.00
❑ 169 Ivus the Forest Lord E 7.00 15.00
❑ 170 Jeleane Nightbreeze C .10 .20
❑ 171 Kal'ai the Uplifting R 1.00 2.00
❑ 172 Kallipssa U .20 .50
❑ 173 Kavai the Wanderer C .10 .20
❑ 174 Korthas Greybeard C .10 .20
❑ 175 Lady Kath U .20 .50
❑ 176 Lilnas the Calm C .10 .20
❑ 177 Lowdown Luppo Shadefizzle R 1.00 2.00
❑ 178 Lynda Steele C .10 .20
❑ 179 Margaret Fowl C .10 .20
❑ 180 Marshal Reginald Windsor E 5.00 10.00
❑ 181 Master Mathia Shaw E 7.00 15.00
❑ 182 Meekway Humzinger U .20 .50
❑ 183 Miner Moggun C .10 .20
❑ 184 Mya, Dragonling Wrangler C .10 .20
❑ 185 Pithran Mithrilshot U .20 .50
❑ 186 Primalist Naseth U .20 .50
❑ 187 Raul Fingers Maldren C .10 .20
❑ 188 Reverend Tobias C .10 .20
❑ 189 Scaramanga C .10 .20
❑ 190 Seraph the Exalted R 1.00 2.00
❑ 191 Steelsmith Joseph Carroll U .20 .50
❑ 192 Tim C .10 .20
❑ 193 Valanos C .10 .20
❑ 194 Vestia Abiectus C .10 .20
❑ 195 Vindicator Enkallus C .10 .20
❑ 196 Warden Ravella C .10 .20
❑ 197 Wisp U .20 .50
❑ 198 Araelun C .10 .20
❑ 199 Bhenn Checks-the-Sky C .10 .20
❑ 200 Bluffwatchers C .10 .20
❑ 201 Boneshanks C .10 .20
❑ 202 Branu Wildbloom C .10 .20
❑ 203 Clara Graves U .20 .50
❑ 204 Dark Cleric Ismantal U .20 .50
❑ 205 Dayna Cousin-to-Sun C .10 .20
❑ 206 Debros Cousin-to-Moon C .10 .20
❑ 207 Dramla Lifebender R 1.00 3.00
❑ 208 Elithys Firestorm C .10 .20
❑ 209 Gamon U .20 .50
❑ 210 Ghank C .10 .20
❑ 211 Greefer C .10 .20
❑ 212 Grunt Baranka C .10 .20
❑ 213 Guardian Steppestrider C .10 .20
❑ 214 High Overlord Saurfang E 10.00 20.00
❑ 215 Ja'zaron C .10 .20
❑ 216 Julia Graves C .10 .20
❑ 217 Kalnuf Eagleheart C .10 .20
❑ 218 Katsin Bloodoath C .10 .20
❑ 219 Koringar the Heavy U .20 .50
❑ 220 Kralnor U .20 .50
❑ 221 Leeza, Tomb Robber C .10 .20
❑ 222 Lokholar the Ice Lord E 7.00 15.00
❑ 223 Magran Proudstep C .10 .20
❑ 224 Morik C .10 .20
❑ 225 Naolin Sunsurge R 1.00 2.00
❑ 226 Nyn'jah C .10 .20
❑ 227 Outrider Zarg C .10 .20
❑ 228 Plagueborn Meatwall U .20 .50
❑ 229 Queen Sylvanas Windrunner E 7.00 15.00
❑ 230 Ra'chee C .10 .20
❑ 231 Rexxar E 10.00 20.00
❑ 232 Scout Omerrta C .10 .20
❑ 233 Sister Rot C .10 .20
❑ 234 Stone Guard Rashun R 1.00 2.00
❑ 235 Tanwa the Marksman U .20 .50
❑ 236 Thysta Spiritlasher U .20 .50
❑ 237 Tiril Dawnrider C .10 .20
❑ 238 Tyrus Sheynathren U .20 .50
❑ 239 Vanda Skydaughter C .10 .20
❑ 240 Warcaller Zin'bawa R 1.00 2.00
❑ 241 Warmaster Hork R 1.00 2.00
❑ 242 Waz'luk C .10 8.00
❑ 243 Field Repair Bot 74A U .20 .50
❑ 244 King Mukla R 2.00 4.00
❑ 245 Overseer Oilfist C .10 .20
❑ 246 Stitches E 5.00 10.00
❑ 247 Aegis of the Blood God E 5.00 10.00
❑ 248 Argent Defender U .20 .50
❑ 249 Belt of the Archmage R 1.00 2.00
❑ 250 Bracers of the Eclipse R 1.00 2.00
❑ 251 Crimson Felt Hat U .20 .50
❑ 252 Crown of Destruction R 1.00 2.00
❑ 253 Elven Chain Boots U .20 .50
❑ 254 The Immovable Object U .20 .50
❑ 255 Magiskull Cuffs U .20 .50
❑ 256 Mugger's Belt U .20 .50
❑ 257 Observer's Shield U .20 .50
❑ 258 Onslaught Girdle R 2.00 4.00
❑ 259 Ornate Adamantium Breastplate U .20 .50
❑ 260 Pads of the Dread Wolf U .20 .50
❑ 261 Vambraces of the Sadist U .20 .50
❑ 262 Wristguards of True Flight U .20 .50
❑ 263 Jin'do's Bag of Whammies R 1.00 2.00
❑ 264 Jin'do's Evil Eye R .10 .20
❑ 265 Major Healing Potion U .20 .50
❑ 266 Penelope's Rose U .20 .50
❑ 267 Ramstein's Lightning Bolts U .20 .50
❑ 268 Ring of the Unliving E 4.00 8.00
❑ 269 Trance Stone U .20 .50
❑ 270 Anathema R 2.00 4.00
❑ 271 Blackcrow U .20 .50
❑ 272 Fel Iron Hatchet U .20 .50
❑ 273 Felstriker E 10.00 20.00
❑ 274 Gurubashi Dwarf Destroyer R 1.00 2.00
❑ 275 Halberd of Smiting U .20 .50
❑ 276 Hellreaver U .20 .50
❑ 277 Jin'do's Judgement R 1.00 2.00
❑ 278 The Lobotomizer U .20 .50
❑ 279 Lok'delar, Stave of the Ancient Keepers R 1.00 2.00
❑ 280 Scimitar of the Nexus Stalkers U .20 .50
❑ 281 Silent Fang U .20 .50
❑ 282 Staff of Dominance R 1.00 2.00
❑ 283 Thunderfury, Blessed Blade of the Windseeker E15.00 25.00
❑ 284 Touch of Chaos R 1.00 2.00
❑ 285 The Unstoppable Force U .20 .50
❑ 286 Viking Warhammer U .20 .50
❑ 287 Will of Arlokk U .20 .50
❑ 288 Zin'rokh, Destroyer of Worlds E 6.00 12.00
❑ 289 Crown of the Earth C .10 .20
❑ 290 Inoculation C .10 .20
❑ 291 Manhunt C .10 .20
❑ 292 Operation Recombobulation R 1.00 2.00
❑ 293 The Perfect Stout C .10 .20
❑ 294 Raene's Cleansing C .10 .20
❑ 295 A Refugee's Quandary C .10 .20
❑ 296 The Relics of Wakening R 1.00 2.00
❑ 297 Rescue the Survivors R 1.00 2.00
❑ 298 Tundra MacGrann's Stolen Stash R 2.00 4.00
❑ 299 Wanted: Hogger R 2.00 4.00
❑ 300 Felendren the Banished R 2.00 4.00
❑ 301 The Haunted Mills R 3.00 6.00
❑ 302 Hidden Enemies C .10 .20
❑ 303 Lazy Peons C .10 .20
❑ 304 A New Plague C .10 .20
❑ 305 Poison Water C .10 .20
❑ 306 Rite of Vision R 2.00 4.00
❑ 307 Solanian's Belongings C .10 .20
❑ 308 Test of Faith C .10 .20
❑ 309 Thwarting Kolkar Aggression C .10 .20
❑ 310 Zalazane R 1.00 2.00
❑ 311 Alas, Andorhal U .20 .50

❑ 312 As the Crow Flies C .10 .20
❑ 313 Divino-matic Rod C .10 .20
❑ 314 A Donation of Silk C .10 .20
❑ 315 The Dying Balance C .10 .20
❑ 316 Finkle Einhorn, At Your Service C .10 .20
❑ 317 The Green Hills of Stranglethorn C .10 .20
❑ 318 Samophlange U .20 .50
❑ 319 The Scourge Cauldrons C .10 .20

2007 World of Warcraft Through the Dark Portal Loot

COMPLETE SET (3)

❑ 1 Rest and Relaxation 10.00 25.00
❑ 2 King Mukla 40.00 75.00
❑ 3 Fortune Telling 40.00 75.00

2008 World of Warcraft Drums of War

COMPLETE SET (268)
BOOSTER BOX (24)

❑ 1 Grand Marshall Goldensword U .20 .50
❑ 2 Lord Benjamin Tremendouson U .20 .50
❑ 3 Martiana the Mindwrench U .20 .50
❑ 4 Oakenclaw U .20 .50
❑ 5 Pidge Filthfinder U .20 .50
❑ 6 Shaii, Strategist Supreme U .20 .50
❑ 7 Spellweaver Jihan U .20 .50
❑ 8 Umbrage U .20 .50
❑ 9 Zorin of the Thunderhead U .20 .50
❑ 10 Boarguts the Impaler U .20 .50
❑ 11 Justice Blindburn U .20 .50
❑ 12 The Longeye U .20 .50
❑ 13 Maleo the Blur U .20 .50
❑ 14 Shalju Stormshatter U .20 .50
❑ 15 Sinthya Flabberghast U .20 .50
❑ 16 Spiritualist Sunshroud U .20 .50
❑ 17 Turane Soulpact U .20 .50
❑ 18 Velindra Sepulchre U .20 .50
❑ 19 Aquatic Form R .50 1.00
❑ 20 Celestial Communion U .20 .50
❑ 21 Cower U .20 .50
❑ 22 Feral Charge R 2.00 4.00
❑ 23 Hibernate C .10 .20
❑ 24 Life of the Land R .50 1.00
❑ 25 Master Instinct C .10 .20
❑ 26 Moonflare U .20 .50
❑ 27 Empty the Stables R .50 1.00
❑ 28 Hissy R .50 1.00
❑ 29 Hunter's Mark U .20 .50
❑ 30 Resourcefulness R .50 1.00
❑ 31 Snipe C .10 .20
❑ 32 Sudden Shot U .20 .50
❑ 33 Turn the Blade C .10 .20
❑ 34 Zip U .20 .50
❑ 35 Conjured Cinnamon Roll U .20 .50
❑ 36 Ice Lance C .10 .20
❑ 37 Mystic Denial R 3.00 6.00
❑ 38 Presence of Mind R .50 1.00
❑ 39 Pyroclastic Consumption R .50 1.00
❑ 40 Spell Suppression C .10 .20
❑ 41 Temporary Dissipation U .20 .50
❑ 42 Transfigure U .20 .50
❑ 43 Aura of Accuracy R .50 1.00
❑ 44 Blessing of Trials U .20 .50
❑ 45 Crusader Strike R .50 1.00
❑ 46 Inspiring Light C .10 .20
❑ 47 Penance R .50 1.00
❑ 48 Reprisal U .20 .50
❑ 49 Seal of Justice U .20 .50
❑ 50 Seal of Righteousness C .10 .20
❑ 51 Dawn's Grace U .20 .50
❑ 52 Equalize R 3.00 6.00
❑ 53 Exasperate U .20 .50
❑ 54 Misery R 2.00 4.00
❑ 55 Precognition R .50 1.00
❑ 56 Shadow Word: Anguish C .10 .20
❑ 57 Sublimate U .20 .50
❑ 58 Vampiric Tendrils C .10 .20
❑ 59 Deathblow U .20 .50
❑ 60 Detect Traps R 2.00 4.00
❑ 61 Gang Up C .10 .20
❑ 62 Nerves of Steel R 1.00 2.00
❑ 63 Pernicious Poison U .20 .50
❑ 64 Ransack R .50 1.00
❑ 65 Slay the Feeble C .10 .20
❑ 66 Surge of Adrenaline U .20 .50
❑ 67 Energized C .10 .20
❑ 68 Greater Chain Lightning R .50 1.00
❑ 69 Grounding Totem U .20 .50
❑ 70 Lightning Overload R .50 1.00
❑ 71 Natural Conduit C .10 .20
❑ 72 Primal Totem U .20 .50
❑ 73 Water Breathing R .50 1.00
❑ 74 Winterstorm Totem U .20 .50
❑ 75 Curse of Fatigue U .20 .50
❑ 76 Drain Will C .10 .20
❑ 77 Enslaved Abyssal R .50 1.00
❑ 78 Gakmat U .20 .50
❑ 79 Rain of Shadow U .20 .50
❑ 80 Suspended Curse C .10 .20
❑ 81 Unending Breath R .50 1.00
❑ 82 Unholy Power R .50 1.00
❑ 83 Absolute Poise U .20 .50
❑ 84 Battle Tactics R .50 1.00
❑ 85 Behead C .10 .20
❑ 86 Enduring Shout U .20 .50
❑ 87 Menace C .10 .20
❑ 88 Taunt U .20 .50
❑ 89 War of Attrition R .50 1.00
❑ 90 Weapon Mastery R .50 1.00
❑ 91 Arcane Spikes C .10 .20
❑ 92 Bloody Ritual C .10 .20
❑ 93 Courageous Defense C .10 .20
❑ 94 Creeping Shadow C .10 .20
❑ 95 Demolish C .10 .20
❑ 96 Eagle Sight C .10 .20
❑ 97 Engulfing Blaze C .10 .20
❑ 98 Fire and Ice C .10 .20
❑ 99 Immobilize C .10 .20
❑ 100 Lose Control C .10 .20
❑ 101 Natural Disaster C .10 .20
❑ 102 Nature Unleashed C .10 .20
❑ 103 Revitalize C .10 .20
❑ 104 Revival Stone C .10 .20
❑ 105 Spell Ricochet C .10 .20
❑ 106 Sphere of Divinity C .10 .20
❑ 107 Thud C .10 .20
❑ 108 Topple C .10 .20
❑ 109 Owned R .50 1.00
❑ 110 Pandamonium R .50 1.00
❑ 111 Slashdance U .20 .50
❑ 112 Al'lanora U .20 .50
❑ 113 Angur Frostbeard C .10 .20
❑ 114 Braeden Nightblade C .10 .20
❑ 115 Brelnor Mindbender U .20 .50
❑ 116 Catarina Clark C .10 .20
❑ 117 Chief Researcher Kartos R .50 1.00
❑ 118 Consul Rhys Lorgrand R 2.00 4.00
❑ 119 Cymbre Shadowdrifter C .10 .20
❑ 120 Daniel Soortan C .10 .20
❑ 121 Durgrin Ironedge C .10 .20
❑ 122 Elementalist Psyrin C .10 .20
❑ 123 Envoy Aiden LeNoir C .10 .20
❑ 124 Envoy Samantha Dillon C .10 .20
❑ 125 Errzig Cogflicker C .10 .20
❑ 126 Falcore C .10 .20
❑ 127 Gryth Thurden, Gryphon Master U .20 .50
❑ 128 The Hammerhand Brothers C .10 .20
❑ 129 Helena Demonfire R .50 1.00
❑ 130 High Tinker Mekkatorque E 3.00 6.00
❑ 131 Keward Rocksalt C .10 .20
❑ 132 Kinivus C .10 .20
❑ 133 Lanthus of the Forest C .10 .20
❑ 134 Lolly the Unsuspecting R .50 1.00
❑ 135 Loraala C .10 .20
❑ 136 Magnus Longbarrel C .10 .20
❑ 137 Meganna Callaghan C .10 .20
❑ 138 Mollie Brightheart C .10 .20
❑ 139 Ninoo of the Light C .10 .20
❑ 140 Rayne Savageboon C .10 .20
❑ 141 Ryno the Short C .10 .20
❑ 142 Swordsmith Hanso C .10 .20
❑ 143 Tinker Art Seaclock C .10 .20
❑ 144 Tinker Bixy Blue C .10 .20
❑ 145 Tinker Burnfizzle C .10 .20
❑ 146 Tinker Casey Springlock C .10 .20
❑ 147 Tonks the Tenacious C .10 .20
❑ 148 Treewarden Tolven C .10 .20
❑ 149 Tully Fiddlewit U .20 .50
❑ 150 Virkaltor C .10 .20
❑ 151 Weldon Barov E 12.00 20.00
❑ 152 Woodsie Leafsong C .10 .20
❑ 153 Wyler Surestrike C .10 .20
❑ 154 Zempre, Grace of Elune R 2.00 4.00
❑ 155 Zophos C .10 .20
❑ 156 Alamo R .50 1.00
❑ 157 Alexi Barov E 4.00 8.00
❑ 158 Boum Headshot C .10 .20
❑ 159 Cairne Bloodhoof E 4.00 8.00
❑ 160 Centurion Addisyn C .10 .20
❑ 161 Chief Researcher Amereldine R .50 1.00
❑ 162 Cromarius Blackfist C .10 .20
❑ 163 Darbun Steppeheart C .10 .20
❑ 164 Defender Kaniya C .10 .20
❑ 165 Doomsayer Din'ju R .50 1.00
❑ 166 Elizabeth Crowley C .10 .20
❑ 167 Erindae Firestrider C .10 .20
❑ 168 Gatlin Clouds-the-Sky C .10 .20
❑ 169 Geoffrey Kimble C .10 .20
❑ 170 Himul Longstrider C .10 .20
❑ 171 Horkin Figluster C .10 .20
❑ 172 Jack Coor C .10 .20
❑ 173 Jee'zee C .10 .20
❑ 174 Jil'ti U .20 .50
❑ 175 Johnny Rotten U .20 .50
❑ 176 Kileana Darkblaze C .10 .20
❑ 177 Kirga Earthguard C .10 .20
❑ 178 Kray'zin Firetusk R .50 1.00
❑ 179 Lifemender Dorn C .10 .20
❑ 180 Logor Blackfist C .10 .20
❑ 181 Malicious Mallina U .20 .50
❑ 182 Michael Garrett, Bat Handler U .20 .50
❑ 183 Mistress Naila Flameburst C .10 .20
❑ 184 Mortok C .10 .20
❑ 185 Munkin Blackfist C .10 .20
❑ 186 Nok'tal the Savage C .10 .20
❑ 187 Orion C .10 .20
❑ 188 Quakelord Razek Warhoof R 2.00 4.00
❑ 189 Rensarth Shadowsun C .10 .20
❑ 190 Roktar Blackfist C .10 .20
❑ 191 Rula Blackfist C .10 .20
❑ 192 Sanva C .10 .20
❑ 193 Sarn Earthtrembler C .10 .20
❑ 194 Sepirion U .20 .50
❑ 195 Skumm Bag'go C .10 .20
❑ 196 Sorga the Swift C .10 .20
❑ 197 Tormentor Emek C .10 .20
❑ 198 Zari'zari C .10 .20
❑ 199 Zi'mo C .10 .20
❑ 200 Dagg'um Ty'gor U .20 .50
❑ 201 The Red Bearon R 1.00 2.00
❑ 202 Vixton Pinchwhistle E 3.00 6.00
❑ 203 Amani Mask of Death R .50 1.00
❑ 204 Blue Suede Shoes U .20 .50
❑ 205 Boots of the Resilient U .20 .50
❑ 206 Cloak of Subjugated Power R .50 1.00
❑ 207 Forest Stalker's Bracers U .20 .50
❑ 208 Girdle of the Blasted Reaches U .20 .50
❑ 209 Gladiator's Regalia E 4.00 7.00
❑ 210 Masquerade Gown R .50 1.00
❑ 211 Merciless Gladiator's Battlegear E 3.00 6.00
❑ 212 Mok'Nathal Wildercloak U .20 .50
❑ 213 Nyn'jah's Tabi Boots R .50 1.00
❑ 214 Scaled Breastplate of Carnage R .50 1.00
❑ 215 Vengeful Gladiator's Vestments E 4.00 8.00
❑ 216 Arcanite Dragonling U .20 .50
❑ 217 Rune of Metamorphosis U .20 .50
❑ 218 Veteran's Pendant R .50 1.00
❑ 219 Medallion of the Alliance U .20 .50
❑ 220 Medallion of the Horde U .20 .50
❑ 221 Black Amnesty R 2.00 4.00
❑ 222 Bloodseeker R .50 1.00
❑ 223 Blue Diamond Witchwand U .20 .50
❑ 224 Cold Forged Hammer R .50 1.00
❑ 225 Continuum Blade R .50 1.00
❑ 226 Frostguard U .20 .50
❑ 227 Gladiator's Spellblade R .50 1.00
❑ 228 Ice Barbed Spear R .50 1.00
❑ 229 Light's Justice U .20 .50
❑ 230 Lohn'goron, Bow of the Torn-heart U .20 .50
❑ 231 Merciless Gladiator's Greatsword R .50 1.00
❑ 232 Netherbane U .20 .50
❑ 233 The Oathkeeper E 3.00 6.00
❑ 234 The Staff of Twin Worlds E 4.00 8.00
❑ 235 Vengeful Gladiator's Bonecracker R .50 1.00
❑ 236 Wand of Biting Cold U .20 .50
❑ 237 Electrified Dagger U .20 .50
❑ 238 Glacial Blade U .20 .50
❑ 239 Establishing New Outposts C .10 .20
❑ 240 In Defense of Halaa C .10 .20
❑ 241 Order Must Be Restored C .10 .20
❑ 242 Bolstering Our Defenses C .10 .20
❑ 243 Enemies, Old and New C .10 .20
❑ 244 The Final Message to the Wildhammer C .10 .20
❑ 245 Arena Master C .10 .20
❑ 246 Corruption of Earth and Seed C .10 .20
❑ 247 The Last Barov C .10 .20
❑ 248 Oshu'gun Crystal Powder C .10 .20
❑ 249 Outland Sucks C .10 .20
❑ 250 A Rare Bean C .10 .20
❑ 251 Revenge is Tasty C .10 .20
❑ 252 Scouring the Desert C .10 .20
❑ 253 Someone Else's Hard Work Pays Off R .50 1.00
❑ 254 Soup for the Soul C .10 .20
❑ 255 Spirits of Auchindoun C .10 .20
❑ 256 Super Hot Stew C .10 .20
❑ 257 Damassus R .50 1.00
❑ 258 Southshore U .20 .50
❑ 259 Stormwind City R 3.00 6.00
❑ 260 Sen'jin Village R .50 1.00
❑ 261 Tarren Mill U .20 .50
❑ 262 Thunder Bluff R .50 1.00
❑ 263 Auchindoun Spirit Towers U .20 .50
❑ 264 Halaa U .20 .50
❑ 265 Hellfire Citadel C .10 .20
❑ 266 Silithus R .50 1.00
❑ 267 Towers of Eastern Plaguelands C .10 .20
❑ 268 Twin Spire Ruins C .10 .20

2008 World of Warcraft Drums of War Loot

❑ 1 Slashdance 2.00 4.00
❑ 2 Owned 30.00 60.00
❑ 3 The Red Bearon 100.00 200.00

2008 World of Warcraft Hunt for Illidan

COMPLETE SET (252)
BOOSTER BOX (24)

❑ 1 Black Ice Fizzlefreeze U .20 .50
❑ 2 Blaine Roberts U .20 .50
❑ 3 Durga Gravestone U .20 .50
❑ 4 Elumeria Wildershot U .20 .50
❑ 5 Eriun Moonglow U .20 .50
❑ 6 Kamboozle, Bringer of Doom U .20 .50
❑ 7 Marta Spires U .20 .50
❑ 8 Vakeron U .20 .50
❑ 9 Zaritha U .20 .50
❑ 10 Grindel Hellbringer U .20 .50
❑ 11 Joren the Martyr U .20 .50
❑ 12 Koth, Caller of the Hunt U .20 .50
❑ 13 Phosphus the Everburning U .20 .50
❑ 14 Ravenna U .20 .50
❑ 15 Ringleader Kuma U .20 .50
❑ 16 Tahanu Brinkrunner U .10 .20
❑ 17 Valterus U .20 .50
❑ 18 Warmaster Bo'jo U .20 .50
❑ 19 Kurzon the False U .20 .50
❑ 20 Famish the Binder U .20 .50
❑ 21 Imp Lord Pinprik U .20 .50
❑ 22 Mother Misery U .20 .50
❑ 23 Obliveron U .20 .50
❑ 24 Xia, Queen of Suffering U .20 .50
❑ 25 Brace or Mace U .20 .50
❑ 26 Energize C .10 .20
❑ 27 Feral Energy R .50 1.00
❑ 28 Ferociousness C .10 .20
❑ 29 Furor R .50 1.00
❑ 30 Insect Swarm R 2.00 5.00
❑ 31 Rebirth U .20 .50
❑ 32 Rotten to the Spore R .50 1.00
❑ 33 Stormfire C .10 .20
❑ 34 Typhoon U .20 .50
❑ 35 Bait the Trap U .20 .50
❑ 36 The Beast Within R .10 .20
❑ 37 Ice Trap C .10 .20
❑ 38 Patient Shot C .10 .20
❑ 39 Shadow C .10 .20
❑ 40 Stable Master U .20 .50
❑ 41 Trueshot Aura R 2.00 4.00
❑ 42 Viper Sting R .50 1.00
❑ 43 Webster R .50 1.00
❑ 44 Wipe or Snipe U .20 .50
❑ 45 Arcane Research C .10 .20
❑ 46 Astral Grief C .10 .20
❑ 47 Blast Wave R 5.00 10.00
❑ 48 Brain Lock C .10 .20
❑ 49 Flickers from the Past R .50 1.00
❑ 50 Mage Armor U .20 .50
❑ 51 The More, the Scarier R .50 1.00
❑ 52 Smoke or Croak U .20 .50
❑ 53 Supernova U .20 .50
❑ 54 Water Elemental R 7.00 15.00
❑ 55 Blessing of Salvation U .20 5.00
❑ 56 Blessing of Sanctuary R 1.50 3.00
❑ 57 Crusader's Sweep C .10 .20
❑ 58 Divine Plea R .50 1.00
❑ 59 Exemplar's Shield U .20 .50
❑ 60 Full Circle R .50 1.00
❑ 61 Holy Shock R 5.00 10.00
❑ 62 Righteousness Aura C .10 .20
❑ 63 Seal of Retribution C .10 .20
❑ 64 Shield or Wield U .20 .50
❑ 65 Circle of Healing R .50 1.00
❑ 66 Divine Spirit R 2.00 5.00
❑ 67 Equal Opportunity C .10 .20
❑ 68 Faces from the Past R 1.00 2.00
❑ 69 Lesser Heal C .10 .20
❑ 70 Levitate C .10 .20
❑ 71 Mana Burst U .20 .50
❑ 72 Mindflip R 1.50 3.00
❑ 73 Shadow Word: Agony U .20 .50
❑ 74 Woe or Grow U .20 .50
❑ 75 Dirty Work R 1.00 2.00
❑ 76 Disassemble C .10 .20
❑ 77 Feint C .10 .20
❑ 78 Fight or Blight U .20 .50
❑ 79 Knock Out U .20 .50
❑ 80 Massacre U .20 .50
❑ 81 Overkill R .50 1.00
❑ 82 Sap C .10 .20
❑ 83 Shadowstep R .50 1.00
❑ 84 Vigor R 2.00 4.00
❑ 85 Crackling Purge U .20 5.00
❑ 86 Exemplar's Blades U .20 .50
❑ 87 Far Sight C .10 .20
❑ 88 Gifts from the Past R .50 1.00
❑ 89 Lightning Arc C .10 .20
❑ 90 Magma Totem C .10 .20
❑ 91 Mend or End U .20 .50
❑ 92 Raise from the Ashes R .50 1.00
❑ 93 Spirit Weapons R .50 1.00
❑ 94 Totemic Mastery R .50 1.00
❑ 95 Aftermath R .50 1.00
❑ 96 Clinging Curse C .10 .20
❑ 97 Crush Soul C .10 .20
❑ 98 Curse of Exhaustion R .50 1.00
❑ 99 Demon Armor U .20 .50
❑ 100 Enslave Demon U .20 .50
❑ 101 Rain or Pain U .20 .50
❑ 102 Sarlia R .50 1.00
❑ 103 Velnoth C .10 .20
❑ 104 Vicious Circle R 1.50 3.00
❑ 105 Disarm C .10 .20
❑ 106 Duty Bound U .20 .50
❑ 107 Finishing Shout U .20 .50
❑ 108 Infuriate R .50 1.00
❑ 109 Pummel R 2.00 5.00
❑ 110 Slay or Stay U .20 .50
❑ 111 Sweeping Strikes R .20 .50
❑ 112 Taste for Blood C .10 .20
❑ 113 Taunting Blows C .10 .20
❑ 114 Vitality R .50 1.00
❑ 115 Disco Inferno R 1.00 2.00
❑ 116 The Footsteps of Illidan U .10 .20
❑ 117 Acolyte Kemistra U .20 .50
❑ 118 Alamira Grovetender C .10 .20
❑ 119 Bimble Blackout U .20 .50
❑ 120 Brodien U .20 .50
❑ 121 Dashel Stonefist U .20 .50
❑ 122 Defender Nagalaas C .10 .20
❑ 123 Elaar R .50 1.00
❑ 124 First Responder Avaressa C .10 .20
❑ 125 First Responder Margan C .10 .20
❑ 126 Harnum Firebelly C .10 .20
❑ 127 High Inspector Campbell R 1.50 3.00
❑ 128 Kathia the Quick C .10 .20
❑ 129 Kindara Mindflayer C .10 .20
❑ 130 Kurdran Wildhammer E 1.50 3.00
❑ 131 Liandra Rustshadow C .10 .20
❑ 132 Lord Cindervein C .10 .20
❑ 133 Luumon C .10 .20
❑ 134 Madison Alters U .20 .50
❑ 135 Master Marksman McGee R .50 1.00
❑ 136 Ol' Stonewall C .10 .20
❑ 137 Raena the Unpredictable C .10 .20
❑ 138 Ripley Spellfizzle C .10 .20
❑ 139 Scrapper Ironbane C .10 .20
❑ 140 Spirit of Stormrage E 3.00 6.00
❑ 141 Talian Bladebender C .20 .50
❑ 142 Wildwatcher Elandra C .10 .20
❑ 143 Wimbly Tinkerton U .20 .50
❑ 144 Zorus the Judicator R .50 1.00
❑ 145 Alecia Hall C .10 .20
❑ 146 Blood Guard Gulmok E 1.50 3.00
❑ 147 Blood Knight Kyria C .10 .20
❑ 148 Brok Bloodcaller U .20 .50
❑ 149 Chief Apothecary Hildagard E 2.00 4.00
❑ 150 Dawn Ravensdale C .10 .20
❑ 151 Deathgrip Jones C .10 .20
❑ 152 Elder Huntsman Swiftshot R .50 1.00
❑ 153 Eyeball Jones U .20 .50
❑ 154 Flame Bender Ta'jin U .20 .50
❑ 155 Forager Cloudbloom U .20 .50
❑ 156 Forager Hoofbeat C .10 .20
❑ 157 Illia the Bitter C .10 .20
❑ 158 Kaelos Sunscream C .10 .20
❑ 159 Kam'pah C .10 .20
❑ 160 Lu'ka de Wall C .10 .20
❑ 161 Natasha Hutchins C .10 .20
❑ 162 Offender Gora U .20 .50
❑ 163 Overlord Or'barokh R .50 1.00
❑ 164 The Painsaw C 1.50 3.00
❑ 165 Ra'waza Stonetusk C .10 .20
❑ 166 Roger Mortis C .10 .20
❑ 167 Roon Plainswalker C .10 .20
❑ 168 Skronk Skullseeker C .10 .20
❑ 169 The Soul Conductor R .10 .20
❑ 170 Tusk U .20 .50
❑ 171 Xela the Tormentor R .50 1.00
❑ 172 Ya'za the Vandal C .10 .20
❑ 173 Anchorite Ceyla R .50 1.00
❑ 174 Anchorite Kilandra C .10 .20
❑ 175 Exarch Onaala E 4.00 8.00
❑ 176 Instructor Giralo C .10 .20
❑ 177 Thief Catcher Norun C .10 .20
❑ 178 Vindicator Aluumen R .50 1.00
❑ 179 Vindicator Falaan R .50 1.00
❑ 180 Vindicator Javlo C .10 .20
❑ 181 Vindicator Kentho U .20 .50
❑ 182 Vindicator Lorin U .20 .50
❑ 183 Vindicator Vasha U .20 .50
❑ 184 Arcanist Bartis C .10 .20
❑ 185 Arcanist Renaan C .10 .20
❑ 186 Arcanist Thelis R .50 1.00
❑ 187 Battlemage Vyara R .50 1.00
❑ 188 Historian Firana C .10 .20
❑ 189 Magistrix Valthin U .20 .50
❑ 190 Retainer Alashon R .50 1.00
❑ 191 Retainer Faryn U .20 .50
❑ 192 Retainer Kai C .10 .20
❑ 193 Retainer Marcus U .10 .20
❑ 194 Varen the Reclaimer E 1.50 3.00
❑ 195 Akama E 5.00 10.00
❑ 196 Ambassador Jerrikar R .50 1.00
❑ 197 Azaloth E 5.00 10.00
❑ 198 Collidus the Warp-Watcher E 3.00 6.00
❑ 199 Doomwalker E 3.00 6.00
❑ 200 Edward the Odd E 2.00 4.00
❑ 201 Ethereal Plunderer R 1.00 2.00
❑ 202 Maiev Shadowsong E 6.00 12.00
❑ 203 Xi'ri E 3.00 6.00
❑ 204 Akama's Sash R .50 1.00
❑ 205 Ar'tor's Mainstay R .50 1.00
❑ 206 Borak's Belt of Bravery U .20 .50
❑ 207 Coif of the Wicked R .50 1.00
❑ 208 Doomplate Shoulderguards U .20 .50
❑ 209 Gloves of the High Magus E 5.00 10.00
❑ 210 Greaves of Desolation R .50 1.00
❑ 211 The Hands of Fate R .20 .50
❑ 212 Hauberk of Karabor R .50 1.00
❑ 213 Mana-Etched Spaulders U .20 .50
❑ 214 Naaru Belt of Precision R .50 1.00
❑ 215 Netherwing Protector's Shield U .20 .50
❑ 216 Pauldrons of Desolation R .50 1.00
❑ 217 Wastewalker Shoulderpads U .20 .50
❑ 218 Band of the Inevitable R 3.00 6.00
❑ 219 Lightwarden's Band R 2.00 4.00
❑ 220 Medallion of the Lightbearer U .20 .50
❑ 221 Scryer's Bloodgem U .20 .50
❑ 222 Seer's Signet R .50 1.00
❑ 223 Ashtongue Blade U .20 .50
❑ 224 Bloodwarder's Rifle R .50 1.00
❑ 225 Felstel Whisper Knives R 1.50 3.00
❑ 226 Hammer of the Naaru E 6.00 12.00
❑ 227 Illidari-Bane Mageblade U .20 .50
❑ 228 Lucky Strike Axe R .50 1.00
❑ 229 Staff of the Ashtongue Deathsworn R .50 1.00
❑ 230 Tirisfal Wand of Ascendancy U .20 .50
❑ 231 Vindicator's Brand R 2.00 4.00
❑ 232 Retainer's Blade R 4.00 8.00
❑ 233 Return to the Aldor C .10 .20

❑ 234 Return to the Scryers C .10 .20
❑ 235 Against the Illidari C .10 .20
❑ 236 Akama's Promise C .10 .20
❑ 237 Bane of the Illidari C .10 .20
❑ 238 Battle of the Crimson Watch C .10 .20
❑ 239 The Cipher of Damnation C .50 1.00
❑ 240 The Deathforge U .10 .20
❑ 241 The Fel and the Furious C .20 .50
❑ 242 I Was a Lot of Things C .10 .20
❑ 243 The Lexicon Demonica R .50 1.00
❑ 244 Minions of the Shadow Council R 3.00 6.00
❑ 245 The Path of Conquest C .10 .20
❑ 246 Reclaiming Holy Grounds U .20 .50
❑ 247 The Secret Compromised C .10 .20
❑ 248 Skywing R .50 1.00
❑ 249 The Summoning Chamber U .50 1.00
❑ 250 Tabards of the Illidari C .50 1.00
❑ 251 Teron Gorefiend, I Am C .10 .20
❑ 252 What Illidan Wants, Illidan Gets U .20 .50

2008 World of Warcraft Hunt for Illidan Loot

❑ 1 The Footsteps of Illidan 3.00 6.00
❑ 2 Disco Inferno 30.00 60.00
❑ 3 Ethereal Plunderer 150.00 300.00

2008 World of Warcraft Servants of the Betrayer

COMPLETE SET (264)
BOOSTER BOX (24)

❑ 1 Commander Michael Goodchilde U .20 .50
❑ 2 Fallingstar U .20 .50
❑ 3 Ixamos the Redeemed U .20 .50
❑ 4 Marlowe Christophers U .20 .50
❑ 5 Mythen of the Wild U .20 .50
❑ 6 Obora the Wise U .20 .50
❑ 7 Ressa Shadeshine U .20 .50
❑ 8 Sharpshooter Nally U .20 .50
❑ 9 Sister Remba U .20 .50
❑ 10 Crusader Michael Goodchilde U .20 .50
❑ 11 Fallenstar U .20 .50
❑ 12 Ixamos the Corrupted U .20 .50
❑ 13 Marlowe the Felsworn U .20 .50
❑ 14 Mythen of the Fang U .20 .50
❑ 15 Obora the Mad U .20 .50
❑ 16 Ressa the Leper Queen U .20 .50
❑ 17 Seadog Nally U .20 .50
❑ 18 Remba, Abbess of Ash U .20 .50
❑ 19 Jonas White U .20 .50
❑ 20 Kil'zin of the Darkspear U .20 .50
❑ 21 Lelora Sunlancer U .20 .50
❑ 22 Lionar, Unbound U .20 .50
❑ 23 Morn Walks-the-Path U .20 .50
❑ 24 Plague Fleshbane U .20 .50
❑ 25 Runetusk U .20 .50
❑ 26 Vor'na the Disciplined U .20 .50
❑ 27 Warden Stormclaw U .20 .50
❑ 28 Jonas the Red U .20 .50
❑ 29 Kil'zin of the Bloodscalp U .20 .50
❑ 30 Lelora the Dawnslayer U .20 .50
❑ 31 Lionar the Blood Cursed U .20 .50
❑ 32 Morn Salts-the-Land U .20 .50
❑ 33 Plague Demonsoul U .20 .50
❑ 34 Bloodtusk U .20 .50
❑ 35 Vor'na the Wretched U .20 .50
❑ 36 Desecrator Stormclaw U .20 .50
❑ 37 Chew Toy U .20 .50
❑ 38 Earth Mother's Blessing C .10 .20
❑ 39 Form of the Serpent R 5.00 10.00
❑ 40 Gift of Nature R .50 1.00
❑ 41 King of the Jungle R .50 1.00
❑ 42 Lacerate C .10 .20
❑ 43 The Natural Order C .10 .20
❑ 44 Savage Fury R .50 1.00
❑ 45 Tainted Earth U .20 .50
❑ 46 Tranquility U .20 .50
❑ 47 Bogspike C .10 .20
❑ 48 Death Trap R .50 1.00
❑ 49 Feeding Frenzy U .20 .50
❑ 50 Feign Death R 3.00 6.00
❑ 51 King Khan U .20 .50
❑ 52 Rain of Arrows C .10 .20
❑ 53 Ranged Weapon Specialization R 1.50 3.00
❑ 54 Run to Ground C .10 .20
❑ 55 Snake Trap U .20 .50
❑ 56 Survival Instincts R 1.00 2.00
❑ 57 Arcane Focus R .50 1.00
❑ 58 Blaze C .10 .20
❑ 59 Frost Armor U .20 .50
❑ 60 Frostbite R .50 1.00
❑ 61 Invisibility U .20 .50
❑ 62 Invocation R 1.00 2.00
❑ 63 Living Pyre C .10 .20
❑ 64 Metamorph C .10 .20
❑ 65 Murderous Torment U .20 .50
❑ 66 Tomb of Ice R .50 1.00
❑ 67 Aura of Fanaticism U .20 .50
❑ 68 Avenging Wrath U .20 .50
❑ 69 Blessed Life R 1.00 2.00
❑ 70 Blessing of the Martyr C .10 .20
❑ 71 Crusade R .50 1.00
❑ 72 Divine Riposte U .20 .50
❑ 73 Flash of Light C .10 .20
❑ 74 Seal of Betrayal R 1.50 3.00
❑ 75 Seal of Redemption C .10 .20
❑ 76 Wrath of Turalyon R .50 1.00
❑ 77 Castigate U .20 .50
❑ 78 Darkness R .50 1.00
❑ 79 Eclipse U .20 .50
❑ 80 Enlightenment R .50 1.00
❑ 81 Fade U .20 .50
❑ 82 Melt Face C .10 .20
❑ 83 Prayer of Mending C .10 .20
❑ 84 Salvation C .10 .20
❑ 85 Shadow Silhouettes R .50 1.00
❑ 86 Spiritual Domination R 1.50 3.00
❑ 87 Blade Twisting R .50 1.00
❑ 88 Cloak of Shadows C .10 .20
❑ 89 Cut to the Chase U .20 .50
❑ 90 Diversion C .10 .20
❑ 91 Evasion R .50 1.00
❑ 92 Find Weakness R .50 1.00
❑ 93 Gut Shot R .50 1.00
❑ 94 Pilfer U .20 .50
❑ 95 Sacrificial Poison U .20 .50
❑ 96 Unbalance C .10 .20
❑ 97 Death Shock U .20 .50
❑ 98 Elemental Precision R .50 1.00
❑ 99 Life Cycle C .10 .20
❑ 100 Maelstrom Weapon C .10 .20
❑ 101 Shamanistic Dual Wield R 1.00 2.00
❑ 102 Stoneskin Totem U .20 .50
❑ 103 Storm Shock C .10 .20
❑ 104 Totemic Recovery R .50 1.00
❑ 105 Totem of Decay R .50 1.00
❑ 106 Water Shield U .20 .50
❑ 107 Apocanon U .20 .50
❑ 108 Banish to the Nether C .10 .20
❑ 109 Curse of Frenzy U .20 .50
❑ 110 Demonic Knowledge R .50 1.00
❑ 111 Dread Infernal R 2.00 4.00
❑ 112 Fel Fire C .10 .20
❑ 113 Gobloz C .10 .20
❑ 114 Ripped through the Portal R 4.00 8.00
❑ 115 Ritual of Souls U .20 .50
❑ 116 Shadow and Flame R .10 .20
❑ 117 Armed to the Teeth C .10 .20
❑ 118 Bloodbath R .50 1.00
❑ 119 Champion Stance C .10 .20
❑ 120 Deafening Shout R .50 1.00
❑ 121 Shield Slam R .50 1.00
❑ 122 Smash C .20 .50
❑ 123 Sudden Death U .20 .50
❑ 124 Titan's Grip U .20 .50
❑ 125 Unbridled Wrath R .50 1.00
❑ 126 Whirlwind U .20 .50
❑ 127 Papa Hummel's Old-Fashioned Pet Biscuit U .20 .50
❑ 128 Personal Weather Maker R .50 1.00
❑ 129 Angelista C .10 .20
❑ 130 Antikron the Unyielding U .20 .50
❑ 131 Barous the Storm Baron R 1.00 2.00
❑ 132 Bearlady Brala R .50 1.00
❑ 133 Breen Toestubber C .10 .20
❑ 134 Domona the Ever-Watchful U .20 .50
❑ 135 Falana of the Glen C .10 .20
❑ 136 Highlord Bolvar Fordragon E 2.50 5.00
❑ 137 Horace Shadowfall R .50 1.00
❑ 138 Inventor Dorbin Callus E 2.50 5.00
❑ 139 Jezbella of Karabor C .10 .20
❑ 140 Justicar Brace U .20 .50
❑ 141 Kronore R .50 1.00
❑ 142 Llyras Keeneye C .10 .20
❑ 143 Lunen the Moon Baron R .50 1.00
❑ 144 Miner Steelwhiskers C .10 .20
❑ 145 Myriam Starcaller C .10 .20
❑ 146 Narthadus C .10 .20
❑ 147 Orderkeeper Callister C .10 .20
❑ 148 Orderkeeper Henley C .10 .20
❑ 149 Orderkeeper Vesra U .20 .50
❑ 150 Quigley Slipshade C .10 .20
❑ 151 Rames the Purifier C .10 .20
❑ 152 Razak Ironsides E 4.00 8.00
❑ 153 Roke the Ice Baron R .50 1.00
❑ 154 Rysa the Earthcaller C .10 .20
❑ 155 Sampron the Banisher R .50 1.00
❑ 156 Stella Forgebane C .10 .20
❑ 157 Aesadonna Al'mere R .50 1.00
❑ 158 Alchemist Norrin'thal C .10 .20
❑ 159 Cerrik Blooddawn C .10 .20
❑ 160 David Smythe C .10 .20
❑ 161 Delrach the Vile C .10 .20
❑ 162 Gok Stormhammer R .50 1.00
❑ 163 Hulok Trailblazer C .10 .20
❑ 164 Icemistress Gal'ha R .50 1.00
❑ 165 Jae'va the Relentless C .10 .20
❑ 166 Jessup Smythe C .10 .20
❑ 167 Leoroxx E 3.00 6.00
❑ 168 Lifemistress Tanagra R .50 1.00
❑ 169 Lilith Smythe C .10 .20
❑ 170 Matalo Trailfinder U .20 .50
❑ 171 Mojo Doctor Zin'tar U .20 .50
❑ 172 Ras'tari Bloodfrenzy U .20 .50
❑ 173 Roena Trailmaker C .10 .20
❑ 174 Rogg Dreadnock U .20 .50
❑ 175 Saurfang the Younger E 1.50 3.00
❑ 176 Scholar Krosiss C .10 .20
❑ 177 Sek Grimlash R .50 1.00
❑ 178 Sha'kar C .50 1.00
❑ 179 Skymistress Taranna R .50 1.00
❑ 180 Tarn Darkwalker C .10 .20
❑ 181 Tatulla the Reclaimer C .10 .20
❑ 182 Ulrac Bloodshadow R .50 1.00
❑ 183 Vexmaster Nar'jo C .10 .20
❑ 184 Anchorite Fareena U .20 .50
❑ 185 Anchorite Karja E 1.00 2.00
❑ 186 Anchorite Onkoth U .20 .50
❑ 187 Atani of the Watch C .15 .20
❑ 188 Bulvai of the Watch C .10 .20
❑ 189 Exarch Orelis E 2.00 4.00
❑ 190 Marksman Eowan U .20 .50
❑ 191 Marksman Glous R 12.00 20.00
❑ 192 Niyore of the Watch R 2.50 5.00
❑ 193 Vindicator Agran C .10 .20
❑ 194 Vindicator Ostakron C .10 .20
❑ 195 Xanata the Lightsworn U .20 .50
❑ 196 Arcanist Alathana U .20 .50
❑ 197 Arcanist Atikan R .50 1.00
❑ 198 Arcanist Dayvana U .20 .50
❑ 199 Arcanist Lyronia C .10 .20
❑ 200 Magistrix Dianas C .10 .20
❑ 201 Magistrix Larynna E 2.50 5.00
❑ 202 Retainer Athan U .20 .50
❑ 203 Retainer Cara C .10 .20
❑ 204 Retainer Eteron R .50 1.00
❑ 205 Retainer Ryn U .20 .50
❑ 206 Retainer Zian C .10 .20
❑ 207 Spymaster Thalodien E 3.00 6.00
❑ 208 Coilfang Myrmidon C .10 .20
❑ 209 Lady Katrana Prestor E 2.00 4.00
❑ 210 Lady Vashj E 5.00 10.00
❑ 211 Millhouse Manastorm E 1.50 3.00
❑ 212 Pathaleon the Calculator R .50 1.00
❑ 213 Prince Kael'thas Sunstrider E 6.00 12.00
❑ 214 Sunseeker Astromage C .10 .20
❑ 215 Warlord Kalithresh R .50 1.00
❑ 216 X-51 Nether-Rocket R .50 1.00
❑ 217 Arcanium Signet Bands U .20 .50
❑ 218 Armwraps of Disdain U .20 .50
❑ 219 Azure-Shield of Coldarra R .50 1.00
❑ 220 Barbaric Legstraps U .20 .50
❑ 221 Doomplate Warhelm U .20 .50
❑ 222 Fanblade Pauldrons U .20 .50
❑ 223 Helm of Desolation U .20 .50
❑ 224 Legguards of the Shattered Hand R .50 1.00
❑ 225 Mana-Etched Crown R .50 1.00
❑ 226 Mana-Sphere Shoulderguards R .10 .20
❑ 227 Wastewalker Helm U .20 .50
❑ 228 Wastewalker Leggings R 1.50 3.00
❑ 229 Choker of Vile Intent R .50 1.00
❑ 230 Hourglass of the Unraveller R .50 1.00
❑ 231 Quagmirran's Eye R 1.50 3.00
❑ 232 Ring of the Shadow Deeps U .20 .50
❑ 233 Ring of the Silver Hand R .50 1.00
❑ 234 Blade of Wizardry E 5.00 10.00
❑ 235 Bloodskull Destroyer U .20 .40
❑ 236 Essence Gatherer U .20 .50
❑ 237 Plasma Rat's Hyper-Scythe U .20 .50
❑ 238 Quantum Blade E 2.50 5.00
❑ 239 Reflex Blades U .20 .50
❑ 240 Terokk's Shadowstaff R 1.00 2.00
❑ 241 Vileblade of the Betrayer R .50 1.00
❑ 242 Voidfire Wand R 6.00 12.00
❑ 243 Wand of the Seer R .50 1.00
❑ 244 Wrathtide Longbow U .20 .50
❑ 245 Marks of Kil'jaeden C .10 .20
❑ 246 Sunfury Briefings C .10 .20
❑ 247 Firewing Signets C .10 .20
❑ 248 Manaforge B'naar C .50 1.00
❑ 249 Deep Sea Salvage C .10 .20
❑ 250 Dr. Boom C .10 .20
❑ 251 An Improper Burial C .10 .20
❑ 252 Information Gathering C .10 .20
❑ 253 Kim'jael Indeed U .20 .50
❑ 254 Leader of the Darkcrest C .10 .20
❑ 255 Meeting with the Master C .10 .20
❑ 256 Needs More Cowbell R 1.00 2.00
❑ 257 Orders From Lady Vashj C .10 .20
❑ 258 Potential Energy Source U .20 .50
❑ 259 Preparing for War C .10 .20
❑ 260 Shutting Down Manaforge Ara C .10 .20
❑ 261 The Sigil of Krasus C .10 .20
❑ 262 The Unending Invasion C .10 .20
❑ 263 A Warm Welcome R 1.00 2.00
❑ 264 You, Robot U .20 .50

2008 World of Warcraft Servants of the Betrayer Loot

❑ 1 Papa Hummel's Old-Fashioned Pet Biscuit 5.00 10.00
❑ 2 Personal Weather Maker 50.00 100.00
❑ 3 X-51 Nether-Rocket 250.00 350.00

2009 World of Warcraft Blood of Gladiators

BOOSTER BOX (24 packs) 30.00 60.00
BOOSTER PACK (19 cards) 1.50 3.00

❑ 1 Bronson Greatwhisker U .20 .50
❑ 2 Chloe Mithrilbolt U .20 .50
❑ 3 Feera Quickshot U .20 .50
❑ 4 Gwon Strongbark U .20 .50
❑ 5 Gyro of the Ring U .20 .50
❑ 6 Kalatine Carmichael U .20 .50
❑ 7 Kristoff Manchester U .20 .50
❑ 8 Nicholas Merrick U .20 .50
❑ 9 Statia the Preserver U .20 .50
❑ 10 Andarius the Damned U .20 .50
❑ 11 Bonewall Simms U .20 .50
❑ 12 Brahu Starsear U .20 .50
❑ 13 Cerripha Sunstreak U .20 .50
❑ 14 Savitir Skullsmasher U .20 .50
❑ 15 Sharpeye Yan'ja U .20 .50
❑ 16 Thoros the Savior U .20 .50
❑ 17 Tribemother Torra U .20 .50
❑ 18 Witch Doctor Koo'zar U .20 .50
❑ 19 Friends in High Places C .10 .20
❑ 20 Nature's Reach R .60 1.50
❑ 21 Reforestation U .20 .50
❑ 22 The Sowing of Seeds U .20 .50
❑ 23 Starshot C .10 .20
❑ 24 Tiger's Fury R .40 1.00
❑ 25 Utopia R .40 1.00
❑ 26 The Aim of Eagles U .20 .50
❑ 27 Bolton U .20 .50
❑ 28 Clutch Shot C .10 .20
❑ 29 Improvised Weaponry R .40 1.00
❑ 30 Quickdraw C .10 .20
❑ 31 Scatter Shot R .60 1.50
❑ 32 Volley R .60 1.50
❑ 33 Blizzard R .40 1.00
❑ 34 Combustion R .40 1.00
❑ 35 Heartburn C .10 .20
❑ 36 Mana Ruby R .40 1.00
❑ 37 Meltdown U .20 .50
❑ 38 Sear C .10 .20
❑ 39 The Taste of Arcana U .20 .50
❑ 40 Atonement C .10 .20
❑ 41 Divine Favor R .60 1.50
❑ 42 Divine Justice C .10 .20
❑ 43 Glimmer of Hope U .20 .50
❑ 44 Reckoning of the Light R .60 1.50
❑ 45 The Rewards of Faith U .20 .50
❑ 46 Sacred Moment R .60 1.50
❑ 47 Darkest Before the Light R .40 1.00
❑ 48 Disperse Magic C .10 .20
❑ 49 Focused Will R .40 1.00
❑ 50 Horrify C .10 .20
❑ 51 The Omens of Terror U .20 .50
❑ 52 Power Word: Restore U .20 .50
❑ 53 Splinter Mind R .40 1.00
❑ 54 Deadliness R .40 1.00
❑ 55 The Depth of Shadows U .20 .50
❑ 56 Intuition C .10 .20
❑ 57 Slash and Dash C .10 .20
❑ 58 Stab in the Dark U .20 .50
❑ 59 Surgical Strikes R .40 1.00
❑ 60 Yoink! R .60 1.50
❑ 61 The Crash of Tides U .20 .50
❑ 62 Echo Totem R .40 1.00
❑ 63 Fork Lightning C .10 .20
❑ 64 Greater Chain Heal U .20 .50
❑ 65 Strength of Earth Totem C .10 .20
❑ 66 Tidal Mastery R .60 1.50
❑ 67 Tremor Shock R 1.25 3.00
❑ 68 Curse of Endless Suffering C .10 .20
❑ 69 Curse of Midnight U .20 .50
❑ 70 Dark Justice C .10 .20
❑ 71 Grim Reach R .75 2.00
❑ 72 Kreedom R .60 1.50
❑ 73 The Promises of Darkness U .20 .50
❑ 74 Ritual of Summoning R .40 1.00
❑ 75 The Benefits of Practice U .20 .50
❑ 76 Cowering Shout C .10 .20
❑ 77 Defiance R .40 1.00
❑ 78 A Final Sacrifice C .10 .20
❑ 79 A Flawless Advance R .40 1.00
❑ 80 Pulverize U .20 .50
❑ 81 Shield Wall R .60 1.50
❑ 82 Blessing of the Heavens C .10 .20
❑ 83 Burly Bellow C .10 .20
❑ 84 Disappear C .10 .20
❑ 85 Double Time C .10 .20
❑ 86 Optimize C .10 .20
❑ 87 Phase Hound C .10 .20
❑ 88 Poof! C .10 .20
❑ 89 Recall from the Brink C .10 .20
❑ 90 Victimize C .10 .20
❑ 91 Center of Attention R .40 1.00
❑ 92 Foam Sword Rack R .40 1.00
❑ 93 Anduin Wrynn E 1.25 3.00
❑ 94 Chillhands Spigotgulp U .20 .50
❑ 95 Cracklehands Spigotgulp C .10 .20
❑ 96 Elder Achillia C .10 .20
❑ 97 Elder Tomas C .10 .20
❑ 98 Elder Valdar of the Exodar C .10 .20
❑ 99 Elder Zeez C .10 .20
❑ 100 Gladiator Katianna C .10 .20
❑ 101 Gladiator Keward C .10 .20
❑ 102 Gladiator Kinivus C .10 .20
❑ 103 Gladiator Lanthus C .10 .20
❑ 104 Gladiator Loraala C .10 .20
❑ 105 Gladiator Magnus C .10 .20
❑ 106 Gladiator Meganna C .10 .20
❑ 107 Gladiator Ryno C .10 .20
❑ 108 Gladiator Zophos C .10 .20
❑ 109 Huntress Xenia C .10 .20
❑ 110 Kristina Soulcinder C .10 .20
❑ 111 Kurdoc Greybeard U .20 .50
❑ 112 Mikael the Blunt U .20 .50
❑ 113 Miranda McMiserson R .40 1.00
❑ 114 Ossus the Ancient R 1.50 4.00
❑ 115 Pappy Ironbane U .20 .50
❑ 116 Quickhands Spigotgulp C .10 .20
❑ 117 Trakas C .10 .20
❑ 118 Tyrus Lionheart C .10 .20
❑ 119 Wynnd the Spry C .10 .20
❑ 120 Aknot Whetstone C .10 .20
❑ 121 Canissa the Shadow C .10 .20
❑ 122 Edward Hack Robinson C .10 .20
❑ 123 Furious Kalla U .20 .50
❑ 124 Gladiator Addisyn C .10 .20
❑ 125 Gladiator Boum C .10 .20
❑ 126 Gladiator Dorn C .10 .20
❑ 127 Gladiator Emek C .10 .20
❑ 128 Gladiator Kaniya C .10 .20
❑ 129 Gladiator Kileana C .10 .20
❑ 130 Gladiator Sepirion C .10 .20
❑ 131 Gladiator Skumm C .10 .20
❑ 132 Gladiator Zi'mo C .10 .20
❑ 133 Grismare U .20 .50
❑ 134 Hex Doctor No'jin C .10 .20
❑ 135 Karina of Silvermoon C .10 .20
❑ 136 Karta Foultongue C .10 .20
❑ 137 Kazamon Steelskin R 5.00 10.00
❑ 138 Kino the Cold C .10 .20
❑ 139 Melissa Gerrard C .10 .20
❑ 140 Naliss the Silencer R .60 1.50
❑ 141 Nea Sunmark C .10 .20
❑ 142 Rorga Trueshot C .10 .20
❑ 143 Thomas Slash Robinson C .10 .20
❑ 144 Tor'gor Darkfire U .20 .50
❑ 145 Vol'jin E .75 2.00
❑ 146 Voltrinnia U .20 .50
❑ 147 Broll Bearmantle E .75 2.00
❑ 148 Lo'Gosh E 1.00 2.50
❑ 149 Rehgar Earthfury E 5.00 10.00
❑ 150 Valeera Sanguinar E 1.00 2.50
❑ 151 Krixel Pinchwhistle R .40 1.00
❑ 152 Mogor R .60 1.50
❑ 153 Sandbox Tiger U .20 .50
❑ 154 Short John Mithril R .60 1.50
❑ 155 Skarr the Unbreakable R .40 1.00
❑ 156 Amice of Brilliant Light U .20 .50
❑ 157 Antonidas's Aegis of Rapt Concentration R 2.00 5.00
❑ 158 Bloodsea Brigand's Vest U .20 .50
❑ 159 Cloak of the Shrouded Mists R .40 1.00
❑ 160 Cowl of the Guiltless U .20 .50
❑ 161 Cuffs of Devastation U .20 .50
❑ 162 Fists of Mukoa U .20 .50
❑ 163 Gladiator's Aegis E .75 2.00
❑ 164 Merciless Gladiator's Pursuit E .75 2.00
❑ 165 Quickstrider Moccasins R .40 1.00
❑ 166 Slayer's Waistguard U .20 .50
❑ 167 Vengeful Gladiator's Felshroud E 2.50 6.00
❑ 168 Band of Vile Aggression R .40 1.00
❑ 169 The Seal of Danzalar R .60 1.50
❑ 170 Talisman of the Alliance U .20 .50
❑ 171 Talisman of the Horde U .20 .50
❑ 172 Battle Mage's Baton R .60 1.50
❑ 173 Boggspine Knuckles U .20 .50
❑ 174 Boundless Agony R .40 1.00
❑ 175 The Decapitator R .60 1.50
❑ 176 Emerald Ripper R .60 1.50
❑ 177 Gladiator's Salvation R .60 1.50
❑ 178 Gorehowl E 2.00 5.00
❑ 179 King's Defender U .20 .50
❑ 180 Merciless Gladiator's Crossbow of the Phoenix R .40 1.00
❑ 181 Mogor's Anointing Club R .40 1.00
❑ 182 Nethershard R .60 1.50
❑ 183 Seth's Graphite Fishing Pole R .40 1.00
❑ 184 Shuriken of Negation R 1.00 2.50
❑ 185 Tempest of Chaos R .60 1.50
❑ 186 Twinblade of the Phoenix R 2.00 5.00
❑ 187 Vengeful Gladiator's Piercing Touch R .40 1.00
❑ 188 Wand of the Forgotten Star U .20 .50
❑ 189 World Breaker R .60 1.50
❑ 190 Arena Grandmaster C .10 .20
❑ 191 The Challenge C .10 .20
❑ 192 Mark V Is Alive! R .40 1.00
❑ 193 A Question of Gluttony C .10 .20
❑ 194 The Ring of Blood: The Blue Brothers C .10 .20
❑ 195 The Ring of Blood: Brokentoe C .10 .20
❑ 196 The Ring of Blood: The Final Challenge C .10 .20
❑ 197 The Ring of Blood: Rokdar the Sundered Lord C .10 .20
❑ 198 The Ring of Blood: Skra'gath C .10 .20
❑ 199 The Ring of Blood: The Warmaul Champion C .10 .20
❑ 200 Uncatalogued Species C .10 .20
❑ 201 Gurubashi Arena U .20 .50
❑ 202 The Ring of Blood U .20 .50
❑ 203 The Circle of Blood C .10 .20
❑ 204 Ring of Trials C .10 .20
❑ 205 The Ruins of Lordaeron C .10 .20
❑ 206 The Exodar R .40 1.00
❑ 207 Orgrimmar R 5.00 10.00
❑ 208 Silvermoon City R 2.50 6.00

2009 World of Warcraft Blood of Gladiators Loot

❑ 1 Sandbox Tiger 2.00 5.00
❑ 2 Center of Attention 25.00 50.00
❑ 3 Foam Sword Rack 40.00 80.00

2009 World of Warcraft Fields of Honor

COMPLETE SET (208)
BOOSTER BOX (24 packs) 40.00 80.00
BOOSTER PACK (19 cards) 2.00 4.00

❑ 1 Katianna the Shrouded U .20 .50
❑ 2 Keward the Ravager U .20 .50
❑ 3 Kinivus the Focused U .20 .50
❑ 4 Lanthus the Restorer U .20 .50
❑ 5 Loraala the Frigid U .20 .50
❑ 6 Magnus the Depriver U .20 .50

TCG/CCG

❑ 7 Meganna the Stalker U .20 .50
❑ 8 Ryno the Wicked U .20 .50
❑ 9 Zophos the Vengeful U .20 .50
❑ 10 Addisyn the Untouchable U .20 .50
❑ 11 Boum the Bloodseeker U .20 .50
❑ 12 Dorn the Tranquil U .20 .50
❑ 13 Emek the Equalizer U .20 .50
❑ 14 Kaniya the Steadfast U .20 .50
❑ 15 Kileana the Inferno U .20 .50
❑ 16 Sepirion the Poised U .20 .50
❑ 17 Skumm the Pillager U .20 .50
❑ 18 Zi'mo the Empowered U .20 .50
❑ 19 Celestial Shard U .20 .50
❑ 20 Convocation R .40 1.00
❑ 21 Grizzly Defender R .40 1.00
❑ 22 Omen of Clarity R .40 1.00
❑ 23 Pack Tactics U .20 .50
❑ 24 Regrowth C .10 .20
❑ 25 Tanglevine C .10 .20
❑ 26 Crusty C .10 .20
❑ 27 Dundee R .40 1.00
❑ 28 Explosive Trap U .20 .50
❑ 29 Intimidation R .40 1.00
❑ 30 Planned Assault R .40 1.00
❑ 31 Reload U .20 .50
❑ 32 Track Hidden C .10 .20
❑ 33 Brittilize C .10 .20
❑ 34 Everlasting Cold C .10 .20
❑ 35 Ice Barbs R .40 1.00
❑ 36 Icy Veins R .40 1.00
❑ 37 Nether Fissure U .20 .50
❑ 38 Roaring Blaze U .20 .50
❑ 39 Set Ablaze R .40 1.00
❑ 40 Blessed Defense C .10 .20
❑ 41 Blessing of Kings R .40 1.00
❑ 42 Concentration Aura U .20 .50
❑ 43 Convert U .20 .50
❑ 44 Holy Strike C .10 .20
❑ 45 Resolute Aura R .40 1.00
❑ 46 Uplifting Prayer R .40 1.00
❑ 47 Blind Faith R .40 1.00
❑ 48 Mist of Corrosion C .10 .20
❑ 49 Searing Light R .40 1.00
❑ 50 A Taste of Divinity R .40 1.00
❑ 51 Tithe U .20 .50
❑ 52 United Front C .10 .20
❑ 53 Vampiric Dominance U .20 .50
❑ 54 Burgle R .40 1.00
❑ 55 Carnage U .20 .50
❑ 56 Hidden Weaponry C .10 .20
❑ 57 Kidney Shot R .40 1.00
❑ 58 Lead Astray C .10 .20
❑ 59 Rupture U .20 .50
❑ 60 Ruthlessness R .40 1.00
❑ 61 Chain Purge U .20 .50
❑ 62 Earthen Flurry C .10 .20
❑ 63 Elemental Weapons R .40 1.00
❑ 64 Hatchet Totem R .40 1.00
❑ 65 Spark U .20 .50
❑ 66 Wavestorm Totem C .10 .20
❑ 67 Windfury Infusion R .40 1.00
❑ 68 Backlash R .40 1.00
❑ 69 Cremate C .10 .20
❑ 70 Curse of the Elements R .40 1.00
❑ 71 Curse of Weakness C .10 .20
❑ 72 Dominate U .20 .50
❑ 73 Hesriana E 5.00 10.00
❑ 74 Soulstone U .20 .50
❑ 75 Bleed C .10 .20
❑ 76 Blood Frenzy R .40 1.00
❑ 77 Collateral Damage U .20 .50
❑ 78 Keys to the Armory R .40 1.00
❑ 79 Overpower R .40 1.00
❑ 80 Reckless Abandon U .20 .50
❑ 81 Split Open C .10 .20
❑ 82 Arcane Warding C .10 .20
❑ 83 Celerity C .10 .20
❑ 84 Essence of Mending C .10 .20
❑ 85 Fortifying Shout C .10 .20
❑ 86 Frigid Winds C .10 .20
❑ 87 No Man's Land C .10 .20
❑ 88 Pin C .10 .20
❑ 89 Sacrificial Vengeance C .10 .20
❑ 90 Screeching Shot C .10 .20
❑ 91 Path of Cenarius U .20 .50
❑ 92 Adam Eternum R .40 1.00
❑ 93 Baelgond Soulgrace U .20 .50
❑ 94 Bladehands Spigotgulp C .10 .20
❑ 95 Corvus Promaethon C .10 .20
❑ 96 Darok Steelstrike C .10 .20
❑ 97 Dimzer the Prestidigitator R .40 1.00
❑ 98 Durgle Wizzledab C .10 .20
❑ 99 Endina the Hunted C .10 .20
❑ 100 Gromble the Apt U .20 .50
❑ 101 Grudum, Trove Guardian C .10 .20
❑ 102 Illiyana Moonblaze E .75 2.00
❑ 103 Iravar U .20 .50
❑ 104 Jonas Targan C .10 .20
❑ 105 Lairin the Grounded C .10 .20
❑ 106 Larrington Zarus R .40 1.00
❑ 107 Maeryl Leafstrike C .10 .20
❑ 108 Marundal the Kindred R .40 1.00
❑ 109 Mayla Finksputter C .10 .20
❑ 110 Modric Sternbeard C .10 .20
❑ 111 Naan the Selfless C .10 .20
❑ 112 Noxel Shroudhaggle C .10 .20
❑ 113 Orlund C .10 .20
❑ 114 Quenlan Lifeboon C .10 .20
❑ 115 Royal Guardian Jameson R .40 1.00
❑ 116 Skaduzzle C .10 .20
❑ 117 Spelunker Maddocks R .40 1.00
❑ 118 Vanndar Stormpike E 2.00 5.00
❑ 119 Vurkeran C .10 .20
❑ 120 Zumbly Fiddlespark C .10 .20
❑ 121 Blood Knight Haeleth C .10 .20
❑ 122 Bloodwatcher Denissa C .10 .20
❑ 123 Charkov C .10 .20
❑ 124 Dannon Spellsurge C .10 .20
❑ 125 Dark Archon Farrum U .20 .50
❑ 126 Deathstalker Leanna C .10 .20
❑ 127 Dethvir The Malignant R .40 1.00
❑ 128 Drek'Thar E 1.50 4.00
❑ 129 Elder Narando C .10 .20
❑ 130 Grugthar Sharpblade C .10 .20
❑ 131 Iku'tak C .10 .20
❑ 132 Keldor the Lost R .40 1.00
❑ 133 Kelm Hargunth E 1.25 3.00
❑ 134 Mojo Masher Shakko C .10 .20
❑ 135 Mojo Masher Ven'dango C .10 .20
❑ 136 Morkad Sharptooth C .10 .20
❑ 137 Nathaniel Voran C .10 .20
❑ 138 Nazguk Sharptongue R .40 1.00
❑ 139 Plainsrunner Marun C .10 .20
❑ 140 Plainswatcher Taro R .40 1.00
❑ 141 Rakasa Mournewind C .10 .20
❑ 142 Samuel Harrison C .10 .20
❑ 143 Scout Kurgo C .10 .20
❑ 144 Sergeant Pugg U .20 .50
❑ 145 Siaranna the Fickle R .40 1.00
❑ 146 Sivandra Darklust C .10 .20
❑ 147 Windstriker Larun R .40 1.00
❑ 148 Yula the Fair U .20 .50
❑ 149 Zalan Ragewind C .10 .20
❑ 150 Backstab Bindo E 1.50 4.00
❑ 151 El Pollo Grande R .40 1.00
❑ 152 Treebole E 1.25 3.00
❑ 153 Berserker Bracers R .40 1.00
❑ 154 Bonefist Gauntlets U .20 .50
❑ 155 Bulwark of the Amani Empire R .40 1.00
❑ 156 Don Alejandro's Money Belt R .40 1.00
❑ 157 Dryad's Wrist Bindings U .20 .50
❑ 158 Gladiator's Sanctuary E 1.25 3.00
❑ 159 Grips of Damnation U .20 .50
❑ 160 Marksman's Legguards U .20 .50
❑ 161 Merciless Gladiator's Raiment E 1.50 4.00
❑ 162 Vengeful Gladiator's Earthshaker E 1.25 3.00
❑ 163 Veteran's Dreadweave Belt R .40 1.00
❑ 164 Windtalker's Wristguards R .40 1.00
❑ 165 Bangle of Endless R .40 1.00
❑ 166 Pinata R .40 1.00
❑ 167 Stormpike Insignia U .20 .50
❑ 168 Frostwolf Insignia U .20 .50
❑ 169 Apostle of Argus U .20 .50
❑ 170 Arcanite Steam-Pistol U .20 .50
❑ 171 Blackout Truncheon R .40 1.00
❑ 172 Firemaul of Destruction U .20 .50
❑ 173 Gladiator's Maul R .40 1.00
❑ 174 Heartless U .20 .50
❑ 175 Heartrazor U .20 .50
❑ 176 Hope Ender R .40 1.00
❑ 177 Jin'rohk, The Great Apocalypse E 7.50 15.00
❑ 178 Merciless Gladiator's Gavel R .40 1.00
❑ 179 Steelhawk Crossbow R .40 1.00
❑ 180 Vengeful Gladiator's Cleaver R .40 1.00
❑ 181 Wand of Prismatic Focus U .20 .50
❑ 182 Wub's Cursed Hexblade R .40 1.00
❑ 183 Crackling Staff U .20 .50
❑ 184 Hellforged Halberd R .40 1.00
❑ 185 Blackened Spear R .40 1.00
❑ 186 Whiteout Staff U .20 .50
❑ 187 Call to Arms: Alterac Valley C .10 .20
❑ 188 Call to Arms: Arathi Basin C .10 .20
❑ 189 Call to Arms: Eye of the Storm C .10 .20
❑ 190 Call to Arms: Warsong Gulch C .10 .20
❑ 191 Capture a Mine C .10 .20
❑ 192 Defusing the Threat C .10 .20
❑ 193 The Eye of Command C .10 .20
❑ 194 In Nightmares U .20 .50
❑ 195 Legendary Heroes C .10 .20
❑ 196 Proving Grounds C .10 .20
❑ 197 Rise and Be Recognized C .10 .20
❑ 198 Showdown R .40 1.00
❑ 199 Towers and Bunkers C .10 .20
❑ 200 Concerted Efforts C .10 .20
❑ 201 For Great Honor C .10 .20
❑ 202 Alterac Valley C .10 .20
❑ 203 Arathi Basin C .10 .20
❑ 204 Eye of the Storm C .10 .20
❑ 205 Warsong Gulch C .10 .20
❑ 206 Gnomeregan R .40 1.00
❑ 207 Ironforge R .40 1.00
❑ 208 Undercity R .40 1.00

2009 World of Warcraft Fields of Honor Loot

❑ 1 Path of Cenarius 2.50 6.00
❑ 2 Pinata 20.00 40.00
❑ 3 El Pollo Grande 150.00 250.00

2009 World of Warcraft Scourgewar

Booster Box (24 Packs) 50.00 100.00
Booster Pack (19 Cards) 3.00 5.00

❑ 1 Aurnya the Lightsworn U .20 .50
❑ 2 Bordrak Barrelblast U .20 .50
❑ 3 Erondra Frostmoon U .20 .50
❑ 4 Felbender Lara U .20 .50
❑ 5 Ivan, Bladewind Brute U .20 .50
❑ 6 Nylaith, Guardian of the Wild U .20 .50
❑ 7 Prometha U .20 .50
❑ 8 Riley Sizzleswitch U .20 .50
❑ 9 Rordag the Sly U .20 .50
❑ 10 Xerandaal, Shade Servitor U .20 .50
❑ 11 Blythe the Pyromaniac U .20 .50
❑ 12 Emerson Zantides U .20 .50
❑ 13 Kaerie, Defender of the Sunwell U .20 .50
❑ 14 Levander of the Sanguine Shot U .20 .50
❑ 15 Maloduri U .20 .50
❑ 16 Souldrinker Bogmara U .20 .50
❑ 17 Teina Cloudstalker U .20 .50
❑ 18 Triton the Sacrilegious U .20 .50
❑ 19 Zagrun Wolfeye U .20 .50
❑ 20 Zorak'tul U .20 .50
❑ 21 Kel'Thuzad E 5.00 10.00
❑ 22 Army of the Dead R 1.25 4.00
❑ 23 Corpse Explosion R 1.25 3.00
❑ 24 Death and Decay U .20 .50
❑ 25 Deathcharger R 1.25 3.00
❑ 26 Death Pact U .20 .50
❑ 27 Icy Torment C .10 .20
❑ 28 Obliterate C .10 .20
❑ 29 Suffocating Grip C .10 .20
❑ 30 Unholy Presence C .10 .20
❑ 31 Unholy Rune C .10 .20
❑ 32 Berserk R .40 1.00
❑ 33 Blessing of Cenarius C .10 .20
❑ 34 Call of the Grove U .20 .50
❑ 35 Feline Grace C .10 .20
❑ 36 Hurricane R 2.00 5.00
❑ 37 Natural Repossession U .20 .50
❑ 38 Nature's Focus C .10 .20
❑ 39 Nourish R .75 2.00
❑ 40 Ursoc's Fury C .10 .20
❑ 41 Bombard R .75 2.00
❑ 42 Buzz U .20 .50
❑ 43 Chimera Shot R .40 1.00
❑ 44 Conflagration Trap C .10 .20
❑ 45 Fang C .10 .20
❑ 46 Master's Call U .20 .50
❑ 47 Raptor Strike C .10 .20
❑ 48 Scorpid Sting C .10 .20
❑ 49 Spoils of the Hunt R .40 1.00
❑ 50 Arcane Burst C .10 .20
❑ 51 Arcane Tactics C .10 .20
❑ 52 Astral Denial U .20 .50
❑ 53 Freeze U .20 .50
❑ 54 Living Bomb R .40 1.00
❑ 55 Mana Sapphire R .60 1.50
❑ 56 Mirror Image R .40 1.00
❑ 57 Polymorph: Penguin C .10 .20
❑ 58 Smoldering Blast C .10 .20
❑ 59 Blessing of Liberty U .20 .50
❑ 60 Boon of Light C .10 .20
❑ 61 Divine Storm R .40 1.00
❑ 62 Hammer of the Divine R .60 1.50
❑ 63 Seal of Divinity R .40 1.00
❑ 64 Shadow Resistance Aura C .10 .20
❑ 65 Stifling Decree C .10 .20
❑ 66 Vengeance of the Light U .20 .50
❑ 67 Vindictive Strike C .10 .20
❑ 68 Dark Penance C .10 .20
❑ 69 Delusions of Grandeur C .10 .20
❑ 70 Devouring Plague R .60 1.50
❑ 71 Dispersion R .60 1.50
❑ 72 Gathering of Wits R .40 1.00
❑ 73 Power Word: Sanctuary U .20 .50
❑ 74 Power Word: Vigor C .10 .20
❑ 75 Prayer of Shadow Protection U .20 .50
❑ 76 Shadow Word: Chaos C .10 .20
❑ 77 Aggressive Infiltration C .10 .20
❑ 78 Belligerence U .20 .50
❑ 79 Dead Weight C .10 .20
❑ 80 Deadly Throw R .40 1.00
❑ 81 Disarm Trap C .10 .20
❑ 82 Enveloping Shadows R .40 1.00
❑ 83 Perforation Poison C .10 .20
❑ 84 Plunder R .40 1.00
❑ 85 Sinister Set-up C .10 .20
❑ 86 Feral Spirit R 2.00 5.00
❑ 87 Incendiary Totem U .20 .50
❑ 88 Mass Purge C .10 .20
❑ 89 Soothing Wave C .10 .20
❑ 90 Squall Totem R 2.50 6.00
❑ 91 Surge of Lightning C .10 .20
❑ 92 Tidal Infusion C .10 .20
❑ 93 Water Walking U .20 .50
❑ 94 Wind Shear R 1.25 3.00
❑ 95 Detonate Soul R .60 1.50
❑ 96 Dreadsteed R 1.25 3.00
❑ 97 Haunt R 1.25 3.00
❑ 98 Jek'kresh U .20 .50
❑ 99 Offering to the Nether C .10 .20
❑ 100 Rhuunom C .10 .20
❑ 101 Shadow Burst C .10 .20
❑ 102 Shadow Ward C .10 .20
❑ 103 Terrifying Visage C .10 .20
❑ 104 Death Wish R 1.00 2.50
❑ 105 Debilitating Shout U .20 .50
❑ 106 Gushing Wound C .10 .20
❑ 107 Human Shield C .10 .20
❑ 108 Provoke C .10 .20
❑ 109 Recklessness R .40 1.00
❑ 110 Reconstruct R .75 2.00
❑ 111 Ruination C .10 .20
❑ 112 Shield Block C .10 .20
❑ 113 Tuskarr Kite U .20 .50
❑ 114 Bloody Grip U .20 .50
❑ 115 Crippling Strike U .20 .50
❑ 116 Frost Burst U .20 .50
❑ 117 Galvanize U .20 .50
❑ 118 Putrefying Poison U .20 .50
❑ 119 Shadows of Death U .20 .50
❑ 120 Shield of Distortion U .20 .50
❑ 121 Staunch Reprisal U .20 .50
❑ 122 Word of Blight U .20 .50
❑ 123 Next Stop, Menethil Harbor! C .10 .20
❑ 124 All Aboard for Undercity! C .10 .20
❑ 125 Anarchist Bladewalker U .20 .50
❑ 126 Anduros Silversong C .10 .20
❑ 127 Archduke Franklin Pearce C .10 .20
❑ 128 Corruptor Mimi Whippleshade U .20 .50
❑ 129 Danyssa Stillheart C .10 .20
❑ 130 Earthshaper Javuun C .10 .20
❑ 131 Ferandus Duskfall C .10 .20
❑ 132 Field Commander Foggo C .10 .20
❑ 133 Flint Shadowmore E 3.00 8.00
❑ 134 Great Elekk R .60 1.50
❑ 135 Gregory Flamewaker C .10 .20
❑ 136 High Magus Euli C .10 .20
❑ 137 Horatio Plaguetouch C .10 .20
❑ 138 Hulstom, Servant of the Light C .10 .20
❑ 139 Justicar Andaer Ragepaw U .20 .50
❑ 140 Justicar Broxlo Frostnuggle U .20 .50
❑ 141 Justicar Gavin Shadesticker U .20 .50
❑ 142 Justicar Maxwell Forthright U .20 .50
❑ 143 Kaale C .10 .20
❑ 144 King Varian Wrynn E 2.50 6.00
❑ 145 Mardun Valorhearth C .10 .20
❑ 146 Mioma Shadowflint C .10 .20
❑ 147 Mooncaller Jynalla Nightpath U .20 .50
❑ 148 Myrodan Silversong C .10 .20
❑ 149 Nakistis, Exodar Armorer C .10 .20
❑ 150 Olaf Steelbreaker C .10 .20
❑ 151 Petreus Roffe C .10 .20
❑ 152 Plasu C .10 .20
❑ 153 Skaala of the Somber Watch C .10 .20
❑ 154 Soulseeker Huulo C .10 .20
❑ 155 Starli C .10 .20
❑ 156 Swift Nightsaber R .40 1.00
❑ 157 Swift Ram R .40 1.00
❑ 158 Trixie Boltclunker C .10 .20
❑ 159 Varah, Fury of the Stars C .10 .20
❑ 160 Vesperia Silversong C .10 .20
❑ 161 Voidmaven Christie Noone U .20 .50
❑ 162 Zealot Kalinov R .40 1.00
❑ 163 Azamoth Deathfang C .10 .20
❑ 164 Besora Galefeather C .10 .20
❑ 165 Broderick Langforth R 10.00 20.00
❑ 166 Claemora Amberglare C .10 .20
❑ 167 Conqueror Gurzom U .20 .50
❑ 168 Conqueror Jarano U .20 .50
❑ 169 Conqueror Neusuada U .20 .50
❑ 170 Conqueror Yun'zon U .20 .50
❑ 171 Drandus the Deathcaller U .20 .50
❑ 172 Emelia Darkhand C .10 .20
❑ 173 Farander Shadesurge C .10 .20
❑ 174 Firewarden Wyland Kaslinth C .10 .20
❑ 175 Garrosh Hellscream E 1.50 4.00
❑ 176 Ginza Darktusk C .10 .20
❑ 177 Great Kodo R .40 1.00
❑ 178 Grovemender Ash'lon C .10 .20
❑ 179 Haranto Darkstrider C .10 .20
❑ 180 Huro'shal Gutwrench C .10 .20
❑ 181 Huzrula C .10 .20
❑ 182 Jaroth Lightguard C .10 .20
❑ 183 Kurao Stormheart C .10 .20
❑ 184 Makta the Rumbler U .20 .50
❑ 185 Mojo Mistress Zurania C .10 .20
❑ 186 Nathanos Blightcaller E 5.00 10.00
❑ 187 Raztu'jor C .10 .20
❑ 188 Rukdara Dreadhand C .10 .20
❑ 189 Sindo'zur the Toxifier U .20 .50
❑ 190 Swift Raptor R 1.00 2.50
❑ 191 Tanzuri C .10 .20
❑ 192 Teresa Voidheart C .10 .20
❑ 193 Thag Big Bounty Cragshot C .10 .20
❑ 194 Thurgood Steelwall C .10 .20
❑ 195 Twilight Vanquisher Knolan R .60 1.50
❑ 196 Verzuk Bloodfist C .10 .20
❑ 197 Vindron the Impure U .20 .50
❑ 198 Whitney Gravecaller C .10 .20
❑ 199 Winston Duskhaven C .10 .20
❑ 200 Alard Schmied R .40 1.00
❑ 201 Azjol-anak Acidslinger C .10 .20
❑ 202 Azjol-anak Acidspewer C .10 .20
❑ 203 Azjol-anak Battleguard C .10 .20
❑ 204 Azjol-anak Broodguard C .10 .20
❑ 205 Azjol-anak Webspinner C .10 .20
❑ 206 Azjol-anak Webweaver C .10 .20
❑ 207 Charles Worth R .40 1.00
❑ 208 Diane Cannings R .40 1.00
❑ 209 Kilix the Unraveler R .40 1.00
❑ 210 Klannoc Macleod E .60 1.50
❑ 211 Lord Darion Mograine E .60 1.50
❑ 212 Lord Jorach Ravenholdt E 1.00 2.50
❑ 213 Mor'zul Bloodbringer E .60 1.50
❑ 214 Spectral Kitten R .75 2.00
❑ 215 Tiny U .20 .50
❑ 216 Bloodbane's Fall C .10 .20
❑ 217 Boots of the Whirling Mist R .40 1.00
❑ 218 Breastplate of Undeath U .20 .50
❑ 219 The Darkspeaker's Footpads C .10 .20
❑ 220 Greaves of Ancient Evil R .60 1.50
❑ 221 Incursion Vestments R .40 1.00
❑ 222 King Dred's Helm R .40 1.00
❑ 223 Riot Shield U .20 .50
❑ 224 Shoulderpads of Fleshwerks C .10 .20
❑ 225 Spaulders of Lost Secrets C .10 .20
❑ 226 Vengeance Wrap U .20 .50
❑ 227 Oracle Talisman of Ablution U .20 .50
❑ 228 Dragonflight Great-Ring E .75 2.00
❑ 229 Extract of Necromantic Power R 1.25 3.00
❑ 230 Mighty Shadow Protection Potion C .10 .20
❑ 231 Arm Blade of Augelmir U .20 .50
❑ 232 Blade of the Empty Void R .40 1.00
❑ 233 Crimson Cranium Crusher R .40 1.00
❑ 234 Dagger of Betrayal R .40 1.00
❑ 235 Edge of Oblivion R .75 2.00
❑ 236 Encrusted Zombie Finger R .40 1.00
❑ 237 Fleshwerk Throwing Glaive R .40 1.00
❑ 238 Gavel of the Fleshcrafter U .20 .50
❑ 239 Life-Staff of the Web Lair R .40 1.00
❑ 240 Netherbreath Spellblade R .60 1.50
❑ 241 Reanimator's Hacker U .20 .50
❑ 242 Reaper of Dark Souls U .20 .50
❑ 243 Saliva Corroded Pike U .20 .50
❑ 244 Staff of Sinister Claws U .20 .50
❑ 245 Touch of Unlife U .20 .50
❑ 246 Trapper's Rifle R .40 1.00
❑ 247 Trophy Gatherer U .20 .50
❑ 248 Unearthed Broadsword C .10 .20
❑ 249 Death to the Traitor King C .10 .20
❑ 250 A Voice in the Dark C .10 .20
❑ 251 Brothers in Death U .20 .50
❑ 252 Culling the Damned C .10 .20
❑ 253 Dark Horizon C .10 .20
❑ 254 Death's Gaze C .10 .20
❑ 255 Defiling the Defilers C .10 .20
❑ 256 Dreadsteed of Xoroth U .20 .50
❑ 257 Junkboxes Needed U .20 .50
❑ 258 Pure Evil C .10 .20
❑ 259 Sacrifices Must Be Made C .10 .20
❑ 260 Scourge Tactics C .10 .20
❑ 261 Tales of Destruction C .10 .20
❑ 262 The Overseer's Shadow C .10 .20
❑ 263 The Restless Dead C .10 .20
❑ 264 Under the Shadow C .10 .20
❑ 265 Unfit for Death C .10 .20
❑ 266 Whirlwind Weapon U .20 .50
❑ 267 World of Shadows C .10 .20
❑ 268 Legendary Leathers, Dalaran R .40 1.00
❑ 269 Talismanic Textiles, Dalaran R .40 1.00
❑ 270 Tanks for Everything, Dalaran R .40 1.00

2009 World of Warcraft Scourgewar Loot

❑ 1 Tiny 3.00 8.00
❑ 2 Tuskarr Kite 50.00 100.00
❑ 3 Spectral Kitten 100.00 175.00

2010 World of Warcraft Scourgewar Icecrown

Booster Box (24 Packs) 50.00 100.00
Booster Pack (19 Cards) 3.00 5.00

❑ 1 Arch Druid Lilliandra U .20 .50
❑ 2 Argent Confessor Paletress U .20 .50
❑ 3 Eadric the Pure U .20 .50
❑ 4 Rimblat Earthshatter U .20 .50
❑ 5 Dalronn the Controller U .20 .50
❑ 6 General Lightsbane U .20 .50
❑ 7 Overseer Savryn U .20 .50
❑ 8 Queen Angerboda U .20 .50
❑ 9 Syreian the Bonecarver U .20 .50
❑ 10 Thane Ufrang the Mighty U .20 .50
❑ 11 Turov the Risen U .20 .50
❑ 12 Askalti Darksteel U .20 .50
❑ 13 Blood Lord Vorath U .20 .50
❑ 14 Deathseer Zuk'raj U .20 .50
❑ 15 Kjaran the Callous U .20 .50
❑ 16 Lich King, The E 10.00 20.00
❑ 17 Arctic Blast C .10 .25
❑ 18 Blood Plague C .10 .25
❑ 19 Death Gate R .40 1.00
❑ 20 Entomb C .10 .25
❑ 21 Frost Rune U .20 .50
❑ 22 Frost Strike R .40 1.00
❑ 23 Mark of Undeath U .20 .50
❑ 24 Rune Strike C .10 .25
❑ 25 Feral Dominance U .20 .50
❑ 26 Gale Winds R .40 1.00
❑ 27 Mark of Life C .10 .25
❑ 28 Natural Reclamation R .40 1.00
❑ 29 Predatory Sense C .10 .25
❑ 30 Ravage C .10 .25
❑ 31 Savage Roar U .20 .50
❑ 32 Bestial Resurgence U .20 .50
❑ 33 Cold Bones C .10 .25
❑ 34 Deuce R 2.00 5.00
❑ 35 Freezing Arrow C .10 .25
❑ 36 Penetrating Shots R .40 1.00
❑ 37 Primal Focus U .20 .50
❑ 38 Sharp Eye C .10 .25

TCG/CCG

Card	Low	High
39 Arcane Binding R	.40	1.00
40 Arcane Essence U	.20	.50
41 Cone of Cold C	.10	.25
42 Fingers of Frost R	.40	1.00
43 Flame Burst C	.10	.25
44 Frost Ward C	.10	.25
45 Whiteout U	.20	.50
46 Blessing of the Templar R	.75	2.00
47 Deliberate Heal C	.10	.25
48 Deliberate Vengeance C	.10	.25
49 Frost Resistance Aura C	.10	.25
50 Reckoning R	.40	1.00
51 Restitution U	.20	.50
52 Seal of Purity U	.20	.50
53 Desperate Condemnation C	.10	.25
54 Desperate Plea C	.10	.25
55 Mind Sear U	.20	.50
56 Power Infusion R	.40	1.00
57 Prayer of Spirit U	.20	.50
58 Prayer of Vitality C	.10	.25
59 Psychic Shriek R	.40	1.00
60 Butcher U	.20	.50
61 Close Quarters Combat R	.40	1.00
62 Divert C	.10	.25
63 Fan of Knives R	2.00	5.00
64 Instant Poison C	.10	.25
65 Paralyze U	.20	.50
66 Poach C	.10	.25
67 Colossal Totem U	.20	.50
68 Elemental Shield C	.10	.25
69 Frost Resistance Totem U	.20	.50
70 Hex C	.10	.25
71 Lava Burst C	.10	.25
72 Spiritual Awakening R	.40	1.00
73 Thunderstorm R	.75	2.00
74 Demonic Accord C	.10	.25
75 Embrace of the Nether C	.10	.25
76 Fel Fury U	.20	.50
77 Fel Infernal U	.20	.50
78 Jaktip C	.10	.25
79 Metamorphosis R	.40	1.00
80 Nether Rift R	.40	1.00
81 Command Decision C	.10	.25
82 Conquering Shout C	.10	.25
83 Fit of Rage R	.75	2.00
84 Heroic Throw U	.20	.50
85 Payment of Blood U	.20	.50
86 Pierce C	.10	.25
87 Warbringer R	.40	1.00
88 Bloody Slaughter U	.20	.50
89 Boundless Concentration U	.20	.50
90 Embolism U	.20	.50
91 Fortify U	.20	.50
92 Frost Surge U	.20	.50
93 Inner Rage U	.20	.50
94 Necessary Sacrifice U	.20	.50
95 Primal Taming U	.20	.50
96 Torment of Shadows U	.20	.50
97 Paint Bomb U	.20	.50
98 Akiko the Alert U	.20	.50
99 Ashnaar, Frost Herald R	10.00	20.00
100 Bronwyn Lightborn C	.10	.25
101 Cynthia Masters C	.10	.25
102 Darktwister Kern C	.10	.25
103 Hazlow Mudshuggle C	.10	.25
104 Jaina, Lady of Theramore E	10.00	20.00
105 Justicar Andra Goldblast U	.20	.50
106 Justicar Johanna Rastol U	.20	.50
107 Justicar Nordar Stonegrave U	.20	.50
108 Kylanda the Harmonious U	.20	.50
109 Kysa Shadowstalker C	.10	.25
110 Lissie Spizfrat C	.10	.25
111 Madrea Bluntbrew C	.10	.25
112 Pathfinder Fansal R	.40	1.00
113 Phantrich C	.10	.25
114 Rhyllor of the Glade C	.10	.25
115 Sparkington the Abrupt U	.20	.50
116 Swift Palomino R	.40	1.00
117 Tani Bixtix C	.10	.25
118 Thassarian R	.40	1.00
119 Vanora Moonshot C	.10	.25
120 Vishala C	.10	.25
121 Vylar Whitepaw C	.10	.25
122 Wesley Shadowsworn C	.10	.25
123 Adenda Lighthaven C	.10	.25
124 Bradford the Frozen U	.20	.50
125 Buma Sharpstride C	.10	.25
126 Conqueror Edge U	.20	.50
127 Conqueror Nairi U	.20	.50
128 Conqueror Tristos U	.20	.50
129 Deathlord Jones R	2.00	5.00
130 Doom C	.10	.25
131 Frostweaver Dakar'sith R	.75	2.00
132 Hansi Wildcoat C	.10	.25
133 Indauma Bloodfire C	.10	.25
134 Jasmine von Ludrow C	.10	.25
135 Koltira Deathweaver R	.40	1.00
136 Kozik Skullcracker C	.10	.25
137 Kuz'vun C	.10	.25
138 Loate Grimtusk C	.10	.25
139 Savuka the Acute U	.20	.50
140 Skeletal Warhorse R	.40	1.00
141 Stephen Hathrow C	.10	.25
142 Thrall, Warchief of the Horde E	20.00	40.00
143 Torashu Stronghoof C	.10	.25
144 Treewatcher Kursha U	.20	.50
145 Uh'gali the Elementalist U	.20	.50
146 Vukora Netherflame C	.10	.25
147 Zaduru C	.10	.25
148 Banshee Soulclaimer C	.10	.25
149 Crypt Fiend C	.10	.25
150 Hulking Abomination U	.20	.50
151 King Ymiron R	.40	1.00
152 Malefic Necromancer C	.10	.25
153 Marauding Geist C	.10	.25
154 Orbaz Bloodbane R	.40	1.00
155 Overlord Drakuru R	.40	1.00
156 Plague Eruptor U	.20	.50
157 Shade of Arugal R	.75	2.00
158 Sindragosa, the Frost Queen E	4.00	10.00
159 Stonespine Gargoyle C	.10	.25
160 Underking Talonox R	.40	1.00
161 Ymirheim Chosen Warrior C	.10	.25
162 Azjol-anak Deathwatcher R	.40	1.00
163 Azjol-anak Skirmisher U	.20	.50
164 Alchemist Finklestein U	.20	.50
165 Babagahnoosh the Grumpy E	4.00	10.00
166 Bath'rah the Windwatcher E	3.00	8.00
167 Hemet Nesingwary E	2.00	5.00
168 Rhonin E	.40	1.00
169 Wooly White Rhino R	.40	1.00
170 Bitter Cold Armguards C	.10	.25
171 Frost-bound Chain Bracers R	.40	1.00
172 Gloves of the Frozen Glade R	.40	1.00
173 Hero's Surrender R	.75	2.00
174 Iceshear Mantle C	.10	.25
175 Icy Scale Chestguard C	.10	.25
176 Legplates of the Endless Void R	.40	1.00
177 Shawl of Haunted Memories R	.75	2.00
178 Winter's Icy Embrace C	.10	.25
179 Flare of the Heavens R	.40	1.00
180 Frostbridge Orb R	.40	1.00
181 Frostweave Bandage U	.20	.50
182 Glacial Bag R	.40	1.00
183 Portal Stone R	.40	1.00
184 Sigil of the Vengeful Heart R	.40	1.00
185 Soul of the Dead R	.40	1.00
186 Super Simian Sphere R	.75	2.00
187 Titan-forged Rune of Cruelty R	.75	2.00
188 Totem of Splintering R	.40	1.00
189 Avalanche R	.40	1.00
190 Black Ice U	.20	.50
191 Chilly Slobberknocker R	.40	1.00
192 Hailstorm R	2.00	5.00
193 Iceshrieker's Touch U	.20	.50
194 Journey's End R	.40	1.00
195 Kel'Thuzad's Reach E	.75	2.00
196 Kingsbane R	.40	1.00
197 Nesingwary 4000 U	.20	.50
198 Spinning Fate R	1.50	4.00
199 Stormstrike Mace R	.40	1.00
200 Stormtip R	.40	1.00
201 Val'anyr, Hammer of Ancient Kings E	2.00	5.00
202 Voldrethar, Dark Blade of Oblivion R	.75	2.00
203 Proper String, A U	.20	.50
204 Rituals of Power U	.20	.50
205 Spirit Totem U	.20	.50
206 Army of the Damned C	.10	.25
207 All Things in Good Time U	.20	.50
208 Tirion's Gambit U	.20	.50
209 Boon of A'dal, The C	.10	.25
210 Boon of Alexstrasza, The C	.10	.25
211 Boon of Remulos, The C	.10	.25
212 Cold Hearted C	.10	.25
213 Everfrost C	.10	.25
214 Hero's Burden, A C	.10	.25
215 Last Line of Defense, The C	.10	.25
216 Rider of Frost, The C	.10	.25
217 Storm King's Vengeance, The C	.10	.25
218 That's Abominable! C	.10	.25
219 Orgrim's Hammer R	.40	1.00
220 Skybreaker, The R	.40	1.00

2010 World of Warcraft Scourgewar Icecrown Loot

Card	Low	High
1 Paint Bomb	1.00	2.50
2 Portal Stone	25.00	50.00
3 Wooly White Rhino	125.00	200.00

2010 World of Warcraft Scourgewar Wrathgate

Card	Low	High
Booster Box (24 Packs)	50.00	100.00
Booster Pack (19 Cards)	3.00	5.00
1 Archmage Barstow U	.20	.50
2 Durzion, Champion of A'dal U	.20	.50
3 Earthmender Vaaki U	.20	.50
4 Esonea U	.20	.50
5 Gramm Thunderjaw U	.20	.50
6 Krunkle Deadspark U	.20	.50
7 Lunira Swiftbreath U	.20	.50
8 Rinni Gloomtrik U	.20	.50
9 Sarina the Immaculate U	.20	.50
10 Tysandri Duskstrike U	.20	.50
11 Crusader Farisa U	.20	.50
12 Harona Proudmane U	.20	.50
13 Jeremiah Karvok U	.20	.50
14 Krog the Deathfist U	.20	.50
15 Kungen the Thunderer U	.20	.50
16 Mojo Master Zandum U	.20	.50
17 Nuvon Dawnfury U	.20	.50
18 Spiritwalker Kavi'je U	.20	.50
19 Sunstalker Andora U	.20	.50
20 Thaka Deadeye U	.20	.50
21 Highlord Tirion Fordring E	15.00	30.00
22 Anti-Magic Shell U	.20	.50
23 Blood Rune U	.20	.50
24 Dark Command C	.10	.25
25 Frost Fever C	.10	.25
26 Hysteria R	.60	1.50
27 Lesson of the Grave C	.10	.25
28 Pestilence R	.40	1.00
29 Surge of Blood C	.10	.25
30 Blustering Winds C	.10	.25
31 Dire Bear Form U	.20	.50
32 Gift of the Earthmother R	2.50	6.00
33 Lesson of the Wild C	.10	.25
34 Nature's Vengeance R	.40	1.00
35 Scent of Nature C	.10	.25
36 Stranglevine U	.20	.50
37 Banzai U	.20	.50
38 Explosive Shot R	2.00	5.00
39 Eyes of the Beast U	.20	.50
40 Hail of Arrows R	.40	1.00
41 Lesson of the Beast C	.10	.25
42 Mongoose Bite C	.10	.25
43 Mothra C	.10	.25
44 Explosive Flames C	.10	.25
45 Flash of Brilliance R	.40	1.00
46 Frozen Solid U	.20	.50
47 Ice Nova U	.20	.50
48 Lesson of the Arcane C	.10	.25
49 Netherwind Presence R	.40	1.00
50 Scald C	.10	.25
51 Charger R	.60	1.50
52 Holy Fury C	.10	.25
53 Lesson of the Divine C	.10	.25
54 Presence of the Divine U	.20	.50
55 Seal of Sanctity U	.20	.50
56 Shelter C	.10	.25
57 Unyielding Faith R	.40	1.00
58 Dementia U	.20	.50
59 Fright C	.10	.25
60 Holy Guardian R	.40	1.00
61 Lesson of the Light C	.10	.25
62 Power Word: Faith C	.10	.25
63 Sacred Circle U	.20	.50
64 Spirit of Redemption R	.40	1.00
65 Flesh Eating Poison U	.20	.50
66 Annihilate U	.20	.50
67 Lesson of the Shadow C	.10	.25
68 Master Poisoner R	.40	1.00
69 Pick Lock C	.10	.25
70 Raze R	.40	1.00
71 Weakening Poison U	.20	.50
72 Ancestral Awakening R	1.50	4.00
73 Astral Recall R	1.50	4.00
74 Fusion Totem U	.20	.50
75 Gushing Totem U	.20	.50
76 Infusion of Earth C	.10	.25
77 Lesson of the Elements C	.10	.25
78 Surge of Life C	.10	.25
79 Curse of Doom U	.20	.50
80 Devastation R	.40	1.00
81 Drain Essence C	.10	.25
82 Dread Doomguard R	.40	1.00
83 Lesson of the Nether C	.10	.25
84 Lynxia U	.20	.50
85 Void Pact C	.10	.25
86 Expertise of Steel R	.40	1.00
87 Flawless Defense U	.20	.50
88 Impede U	.20	.50
89 Lesson of the Call C	.10	.25
90 Mortal Slash C	.10	.25
91 Requite C	.10	.25
92 Wrecking Crew R	.40	1.00
93 Bestial Rage U	.20	.50
94 Feast of Flame U	.20	.50
95 Gift of the Pious U	.20	.50
96 Hit and Run U	.20	.50
97 Holy Barrier U	.20	.50
98 Kick Thinking U	.20	.50
99 Master's Stable U	.20	.50
100 Nurturing Spirit U	.20	.50
101 Strength of Battle U	.20	.50
102 Landro's Gift U	.20	.50
103 Tubs Klankbopple C	.10	.25
104 Antyr C	.10	.25
105 Arlen the Untamed U	.20	.50
106 Armored Snowy Gryphon R	.60	1.50
107 Ayluro Nightwind C	.10	.25
108 Bantham, Jadefist Apprentice C	.10	.25
109 Blazemistress Lindsey C	.10	.25
110 Bolvar, Highlord of Fordragon Hold E	1.00	2.50
111 Bronthea the Resolute U	.20	.50
112 Burly Berta R	5.00	12.00
113 Devona Berkshire R	.40	1.00
114 Grumdur Bladebane C	.10	.25
115 High Commander Halford Wyrmbane E	1.50	4.00
116 Hurdan the Everlasting U	.20	.50
117 Ixiya the Attuned C	.10	.25
118 Justicar Drathnea U	.20	.50
119 Justicar Nimzi Banedrizzle U	.20	.50
120 Justicar Ularu U	.20	.50
121 Kaelyn Vineminder C	.10	.25
122 Lady Bancroft C	.10	.25
123 Lyshala Ravenshot C	.10	.25
124 Mithran the Sniper C	.10	.25
125 Nethermaven Donna Chastain C	.10	.25
126 Nurgle Tinkfrost C	.10	.25
127 Swift Mechanostrider R	.40	1.00
128 Wyndarr Shadefist C	.10	.25
129 Armored Blue Wind Rider R	.40	1.00
130 Astani Dawngrace C	.10	.25
131 Bluffstalker Honovi C	.10	.25
132 Cedric Darwin C	.10	.25
133 Conqueror Hashkon U	.20	.50
134 Conqueror Vun'jin U	.20	.50
135 Conqueror Zaala U	.20	.50
136 Daralis the Sanctifier U	.20	.50
137 Dhoros Ravestrike C	.10	.25
138 Dorzok Shadowhand C	.10	.25
139 Goru Thornmane C	.10	.25
140 Hanthal Lightward C	.10	.25
141 Katoka Dreadblade R	.40	1.00
142 Murphy Watson C	.10	.25
143 Muruna the Savage U	.20	.50
144 Rpanauk Icemist E	.60	1.50
145 Roshen the Oathsworn U	.20	.50
146 Saurfang the Younger, Kor'kron Warlord E	10.00	25.00
147 Soram Wildbark C	.10	.25
148 Sullivan Holmes C	.10	.25
149 Sunguard Cersie C	.10	.25
150 Swift Hawkstrider R	2.00	5.00
151 Swift Timber Wolf R	.60	1.50
152 Tuskmender Jan'zu C	.10	.25
153 Uruka the Cutthroat R	4.00	10.00
154 Vuz'din C	.10	.25
155 Zugra, Windseer Apprentice C	.10	.25
156 Blazing Hippogryph R	.40	1.00
157 Brother Keltan U	.20	.50
158 Commander Falstaav C	.10	.25
159 Crusade Commander Entari R	.40	1.00
160 Crusade Engineer Spitzpatrick C	.10	.25
161 Crusader Lord Dalfors C	.10	.25
162 Eitrigg E	.40	1.00
163 Father Gustav C	.10	.25
164 Sister Colleen Tulley C	.10	.25
165 Veteran Crusader Aliocha Segard C	.10	.25
166 Azjol-anak Champion R	3.00	8.00
167 Aurius E	2.00	5.00
168 Eris Havenfire E	.60	1.50
169 Keeper Remulos E	.60	1.50
170 Boots of the Renewed Flight U	.20	.50
171 Cloak of the Shadowed Sun R	.40	1.00
172 Gloves of Token Respect R	.40	1.00
173 Helm of Vital Protection R	.40	1.00
174 Hood of the Exodus R	.40	1.00
175 Leggings of the Honored U	.20	.50
176 Protective Barricade of the Light R	.40	1.00
177 Sun-Emblazoned Chestplate R	.40	1.00
178 Sympathy U	.20	.50
179 Upstanding Spaulders R	.40	1.00
180 Gigantique Bag R	.40	1.00
181 Idol of the Shooting Star R	.40	1.00
182 Libram of Radiance R	.40	1.00
183 Life-Binder's Locket R	.40	1.00
184 Platinum Disks of Swiftness R	.40	1.00
185 Statue Generator R	.40	1.00
186 Angry Dread C	.10	.25
187 Colossal Skull-Clad Cleaver U	.20	.50
188 Fading Glow C	.10	.25
189 Final Voyage R	.40	1.00
190 Fist of the Deity R	.40	1.00
191 Haunting Call R	.40	1.00
192 Life and Death R	.40	1.00
193 Lifeblade of Belgaristrasz R	.40	1.00
194 Nerubian Conqueror R	.40	1.00
195 Silent Crusader R	.60	1.50
196 Spire of Sunset R	.40	1.00
197 Staff of Trickery C	.10	.25
198 Sword of Justice R	.40	1.00
199 Torch of Holy Fire R	.40	1.00
200 Wraith Spear R	.40	1.00
201 No Mere Dream U	.20	.50
202 Paladin Training U	.20	.50
203 The Ichor of Undeath U	.20	.50
204 The Call of the Crusade C	.10	.25
205 Apply This Twice Daily C	.10	.25
206 Conversing With the Depths C	.10	.25
207 Cycle of Life C	.10	.25
208 I'm Not Dead Yet! R	.40	1.00
209 Light Within the Darkness C	.10	.25
210 No One to Save You C	.10	.25
211 On Ruby Wings R	.40	1.00
212 Planning for the Future C	.10	.25
213 Really Big Worm C	.10	.25
214 Return to Angrathar C	.10	.25
215 Seeds of the Lashers C	.10	.25
216 A Tale of Valor C	.10	.25
217 Wanton Warlord C	.10	.25
218 Fordragon Hold R	1.00	2.50
219 Kor'kron Vanguard R	4.00	10.00
220 Angrathar the Wrathgate E	.60	1.50

2010 World of Warcraft Scourgewar Wrathgate Loot

Card	Low	High
1 Landro's Gift	15.00	30.00
2 Statue Generator	20.00	40.00
3 Blazing Hippogryph	300.00	450.00

2010 World of Warcraft World Breaker

Card	Low	High
Booster Box (24 Packs)	40.00	80.00
Booster Pack (19 Cards)	3.00	4.00
1 Amaria Kelsur U	.20	.50
2 Arturius Hathrow U	.20	.50
3 Bragvi Stormstein U	.20	.50
4 Caleb Pavish U,	.20	.50
5 Haedis U	.20	.50
6 Jaenel U	.20	.50
7 Kadus Frosthand U	.20	.50
8 Peter Hottelet U	.20	.50
9 Tilly Fiddlelight U	.20	.50
10 Victor Baltus U	.20	.50
11 Ayaka Winterhoof U	.20	.50
12 Grizlik Sparkhex U	.20	.50
13 Jai Dawnsteel U	.20	.50
14 Jumo'zin U	.20	.50
15 Malaxia Wizwhirl U	.20	.50
16 Rekwa Proudhorn U	.20	.50
17 Suvok Frozeneye U	.20	.50
18 Valerie Worfield U	.20	.50
19 Vorix Zorbuzz U	.20	.50
20 Yuna Sunridge U	.20	.50
21 Alexstrasza the Life-Binder E	6.00	15.00
22 Ysera the Dreamer E	6.00	15.00
23 Black Blood C	.10	.25
24 Blood Chill C	.10	.25
25 Chains of Ice R	.60	1.50
26 Dancing Rune Weapon R	.40	1.00
27 Frenzy U	.20	.50
28 Grip of the Damned C	.10	.25
29 Path of Frost C	.10	.25
30 Strangulate U	.20	.50
31 Unholy Ground R	.75	2.00
32 Withering Decay U	.20	.50
33 Earth and Moon R	1.00	2.50
34 Entangling Growth C	.10	.25
35 Faerie Fire U	.20	.50
36 Flourish U	.20	.50
37 Mark of the Untamed U	.20	.50
38 Nature's Fury R	.60	1.50
39 Reawakening R	.40	1.00
40 Rejuvenation C	.10	.25
41 Savage Bear Form C	.10	.25
42 Wrath C	.10	.25
43 Aspect of the Wild R	1.50	4.00
44 Blast Trap U	.20	.50
45 Boomer R	2.00	5.00
46 Detect Prey U	.20	.50
47 Flare C	.10	.25
48 Steady Shot U	.20	.50
49 Tesla C	.10	.25
50 Track Dragonkin C	.10	.25
51 Wing Clip C	.10	.25
52 Wyvern Sting R	.40	1.00
53 Enduring Winter R	.40	1.00
54 Extinguish U	.20	.50
55 Fire Blast C	.10	.25
56 Frost Wave C	.10	.25
57 Frostfire Bolt U	.20	.50
58 Frozen Nerves C	.10	.25
59 Mana Diamond R	.40	1.00
60 Mana Shift R	.40	1.00
61 Ripple U	.20	.50
62 Unstable Infusion C	.10	.25
63 Blessing of Defense C	.10	.25
64 Blessing of the Kindred R	.40	1.00
65 Blessing of Virtue U	.20	.50
66 Censure C	.10	.25
67 Divine Cleansing U	.20	.50
68 Holy Light C	.10	.25
69 Repentance R	.40	1.00
70 Sacred Shield U	.20	.50
71 Seal of Wrath R	.40	1.00
72 Stasis C	.10	.25
73 Dark Extortion R	.40	1.00
74 Divine Fury R	.75	2.00
75 Divine Hymn U	.20	.50
76 Flash Heal C	.10	.25
77 Oppress C	.10	.25
78 Power Word: Preservation C	.10	.25
79 Power Word: Shelter U	.20	.50
80 Psychic Wail U	.20	.50
81 Seeping Shadows R	.40	1.00
82 Spiritual Harmony C	.10	.25
83 Aggressive Exploitation C	.10	.25
84 Bully C	.10	.25
85 Contagious Poison R	.40	1.00
86 Daze U	.20	.50
87 Draining Poison U	.20	.50
88 Excessive Force C	.10	.25
89 Gouge C	.10	.25
90 Incapacitate U	.20	.50
91 Seal Fate R	.60	1.50
92 Steal Steel R	.40	1.00
93 Ancestral Purge C	.10	.25
94 Breath of the Elements R	.40	1.00
95 Earthen Blast U	.20	.50
96 Earthen Embrace C	.10	.25
97 Elemental Vision C	.10	.25
98 Lightning Bolt C	.10	.25
99 Nature Resistance Totem U	.20	.50
100 Rolling Thunder R	.40	1.00
101 Spiritual Return R	.60	1.50
102 Thunderstrike Weapon U	.20	.50
103 Demonic Reclamation U	.20	.50
104 Demonic Soulstone C	.10	.25
105 Fear C	.10	.25

Card	Low	High
❑ 106 Fel Blaze U	.20	.50
❑ 107 Jhuunash R	1.00	2.50
❑ 108 Muddle U	.20	.50
❑ 109 Nether Inversion C	.10	.25
❑ 110 Sardok C	.10	.25
❑ 111 Searing Pain R	1.00	2.50
❑ 112 Summoning Portal R	1.00	2.50
❑ 113 Chaotic Rush U	.20	.50
❑ 114 Crushing Strike C	.10	.25
❑ 115 Defender's Vigil C	.10	.25
❑ 116 Execute C	.10	.25
❑ 117 Heroic Impulse C	.10	.25
❑ 118 Juggernaut R	.60	1.50
❑ 119 Onslaught R	.40	1.00
❑ 120 Raging Shout U	.20	.50
❑ 121 Stance Mastery R	.40	1.00
❑ 122 Thunderous Challenge U	.20	.50
❑ 123 Avatar of the Wild E	10.00	25.00
❑ 124 Vigil of the Light E	2.50	6.00
❑ 125 Viciousness U	.20	.50
❑ 126 Rocket Barrage U	.20	.50
❑ 127 Adrienne the Inspiring U	.20	.50
❑ 128 Aileen the Thunderblessed R	.40	1.00
❑ 129 Alador Stonebrew C	.10	.25
❑ 130 Alister Cooper C	.10	.25
❑ 131 Andrew Ulric C	.10	.25
❑ 132 Aresha Thorncaller U	.20	.50
❑ 133 Arisa Sarum U	.20	.50
❑ 134 Bayner Cogbertson C	.10	.25
❑ 135 Bella Wilder C	.10	.25
❑ 136 Fenton Guardmont C	.10	.25
❑ 137 Furan Rookbane C	.10	.25
❑ 138 Garet Vice C	.10	.25
❑ 139 Gerana Sparkfist C	.10	.25
❑ 140 Hira C	.10	.25
❑ 141 Jarrod Gravon U	.20	.50
❑ 142 Jinie Swizzleshade C	.10	.25
❑ 143 Kalek Deepearth C	.10	.25
❑ 144 Kentro Slade R	.40	1.00
❑ 145 King Genn Greymane E	6.00	15.00
❑ 146 Kirjen Fizzgar C	.10	.25
❑ 147 Koeus C	.10	.25
❑ 148 Laenthor Shademoon C	.10	.25
❑ 149 Loriam Argos C	.10	.25
❑ 150 Magni, the Mountain King E	4.00	10.00
❑ 151 Marcus Dominar C	.10	.25
❑ 152 Marius Jator U	.20	.50
❑ 153 Nami Dabpox C	.10	.25
❑ 154 Nightstalker Austen C	.10	.25
❑ 155 Pixia Darkmist C	.10	.25
❑ 156 Pyromancer Davins R	.40	1.00
❑ 157 Rolan Phoenix R	2.50	6.00
❑ 158 Savis Cindur C	.10	.25
❑ 159 Shanis Bladefall C	.10	.25
❑ 160 Terina Calin C	.10	.25
❑ 161 Varandas Silverleaf U	.20	.50
❑ 162 Watchman Visi C	.10	.25
❑ 163 Wazix Blonktop C	.10	.25
❑ 164 Zuur C	.10	.25
❑ 165 Boki Earthgaze C	.10	.25
❑ 166 Cadon Thundershade C	.10	.25
❑ 167 Cairne, Earthmother's Chosen E	6.00	15.00
❑ 168 Ceraka U	.20	.50
❑ 169 Dorladris Spellfire C	.10	.25
❑ 170 Drizzle Steelslam C	.10	.25
❑ 171 Exxi the Windshaper R	.60	1.50
❑ 172 Frek Snipelix U	.20	.50
❑ 173 Gispax the Mixologist R	.40	1.00
❑ 174 Gorz Blazefist C	.10	.25
❑ 175 Grazzle Grubhook C	.10	.25
❑ 176 Guardian Steelhoof C	.10	.25
❑ 177 Huruk Lightvow C	.10	.25
❑ 178 Jezziki Shinebog C	.10	.25
❑ 179 Kerzok Plixboom U	.20	.50
❑ 180 Kistix Shockvat C	.10	.25
❑ 181 Kloxx Dedrix C	.10	.25
❑ 182 Landon Dunavin C	.10	.25
❑ 183 Mahna Lightsky U	.20	.50
❑ 184 Neboz Tombwex U	.20	.50
❑ 185 Onnekra Bloodfang C	.10	.25
❑ 186 Orkahn of Orgrimmar U	.20	.50
❑ 187 Oruk Starstorm C	.10	.25
❑ 188 Rosalyne von Erantor U	.20	.50
❑ 189 Ruon Wildhoof C	.10	.25
❑ 190 Sava'gin the Reckless R	2.00	5.00
❑ 191 Sura Lightningheart C	.10	.25
❑ 192 Telor Sunsurge C	.10	.25
❑ 193 Thrandis the Venomous R	.40	1.00
❑ 194 Toz'jun C	.10	.25
❑ 195 Trade Prince Gallywix E	3.00	8.00
❑ 196 Traxel Emberklik C	.10	.25
❑ 197 Vala Carville C	.10	.25
❑ 198 Veline Bladestar C	.10	.25
❑ 199 Zakis Trickstab C	.10	.25
❑ 200 Zerzu C	.10	.25
❑ 201 Zulanji C	.10	.25
❑ 202 Zulbraka C	.10	.25
❑ 203 Emerald Acidspewer C	.10	.25
❑ 204 Emerald Captain C	.10	.25
❑ 205 Emerald Emissary U	.20	.50
❑ 206 Emerald Lifewarden U	.20	.50
❑ 207 Emerald Soldier C	.10	.25
❑ 208 Emerald Tree Warder C	.10	.25
❑ 209 Emerald Wanderer C	.10	.25
❑ 210 Eranikus R	.60	1.50
❑ 211 Korialstrasz R	.40	1.00
❑ 212 Ruby Blazewing U	.20	.50
❑ 213 Ruby Emissary U	.20	.50
❑ 214 Ruby Enforcer C	.10	.25
❑ 215 Ruby Flameblade C	.10	.25
❑ 216 Ruby Protector C	.10	.25
❑ 217 Ruby Skyrazor C	.10	.25
❑ 218 Ruby Stalker C	.10	.25
❑ 219 Mottled Drake E	.75	2.00
❑ 220 Landro's Lil' XT U	.20	.50
❑ 221 Etched Dragonbone Girdle U	.20	.50
❑ 222 Polished Breastplate of Valor R	.40	1.00
❑ 223 Prized Beastmaster's Mantle R	.40	1.00
❑ 224 Robe of the Waking Nightmare U	.20	.50
❑ 225 Skinned Whelp Shoulders U	.20	.50
❑ 226 Stained Shadowcraft Tunic R	.40	1.00
❑ 227 Tattered Dreadmist Mantle R	.40	1.00
❑ 228 Wyrmwing Treads U	.20	.50
❑ 229 Discerning Eye of the Beast U	.20	.50
❑ 230 Dread Pirate Ring U	.20	.50
❑ 231 Grim Campfire R	.40	1.00
❑ 232 Swift Hand of Justice U	.20	.50
❑ 233 Abomination Knuckles C	.10	.25
❑ 234 Abracadaver R	.40	1.00
❑ 235 Balanced Heartseeker R	.40	1.00
❑ 236 Bloodied Arcanite Reaper R	.40	1.00
❑ 237 Charmed Ancient Bone Bow R	.40	1.00
❑ 238 Citadel Enforcer's Claymore C	.10	.25
❑ 239 Devout Aurastone Hammer R	.40	1.00
❑ 240 Dignified Headmaster's Charge R	.40	1.00
❑ 241 Gutbuster R	.40	1.00
❑ 242 Hersir's Greatspear U	.20	.50
❑ 243 Lockjaw U	.20	.50
❑ 244 Ramaladni's Blade of Culling R	.40	1.00
❑ 245 Repurposed Lava Dredger R	.40	1.00
❑ 246 Stakethrower U	.20	.50
❑ 247 Troggbane, Axe of the Frostborne King E	1.00	2.50
❑ 248 Venerable Mass of McGowan R	.40	1.00
❑ 249 Wand of Ruby Claret C	.10	.25
❑ 250 Warmace of Menethil R	.40	1.00
❑ 251 Leader of the Pack R	.40	1.00
❑ 252 Warchief's Revenge R	.40	1.00
❑ 253 Challenge to the Black Flight C	.10	.25
❑ 254 Cleansing Witch Hill C	.10	.25
❑ 255 Corrosion Prevention C	.10	.25
❑ 256 Counting Out Time C	.10	.25
❑ 257 Crystals of Power C	.10	.25
❑ 258 Essence of Enmity, The C	.10	.25
❑ 259 Finding the Source C	.10	.25
❑ 260 Grimtotem Weapon, The C	.10	.25
❑ 261 Key to Freedom, The C	.10	.25
❑ 262 Locked Away C	.10	.25
❑ 263 Matter of Time, A C	.10	.25
❑ 264 Mighty U'cha, The C	.10	.25
❑ 265 Mystery Goo C	.10	.25
❑ 266 Torch of Retribution, The C	.10	.25
❑ 267 What's Haunting Witch Hill? C	.10	.25
❑ 268 Witch's Bane, The C	.10	.25
❑ 269 Gilneas R	.60	1.50
❑ 270 Lost Isles R	.40	1.00

2010 World of Warcraft World Breaker Loot

Card	Low	High
❑ 1 Landro's Lil' XT	3.00	8.00
❑ 2 Grim Campfire	8.00	20.00
❑ 3 Mottled Drake	125.00	200.00

2011 World of Warcraft Throne of the Tides

Card	Low	High
Complete Set (263)		
Booster Box (36 Packs)	50.00	100.00
Booster Pack (16 Cards)	3.00	4.00
❑ 1 Anaka the Light's Bulwark U	.20	.50
❑ 2 Barathex, Undeath's Hand U	.20	.50
❑ 3 High Magus Olvek U	.20	.50
❑ 4 Janvaru the Thunderspeaker U	.20	.50
❑ 5 Master Sniper Simon McKey U	.20	.50
❑ 6 Sana the Black Blade U	.20	.50
❑ 7 Skodis the Nethertwister C	.10	.25
❑ 8 Steelguard Adamson U	.20	.50
❑ 9 Tinker Priest Cassie U	.20	.50
❑ 10 Wildseer Varel U	.20	.50
❑ 11 Drazul the Molten U	.20	.50
❑ 12 Fama'sin the Lifeseer U	.20	.50
❑ 13 Gaxtro, Bilgewater Marksman U	.20	.50
❑ 14 Ghoulmaster Kalisa U	.20	.50
❑ 15 High Priestess Neeri U	.20	.50
❑ 16 Jak the Bilgewater Bruiser U	.20	.50
❑ 17 Joleera U	.20	.50
❑ 18 Rohashu, Zealot of the Sun U	.20	.50
❑ 19 Samaku, Hand of the Tempest U	.20	.50
❑ 20 Voidbringer Jindal'an U	.20	.50
❑ 21 Deathbringer Kor'ush C	.10	.25
❑ 22 Grglmrgl U	.20	.50
❑ 23 Lady Sira'kess U	.20	.50
❑ 24 Rawrbrgle U	.20	.50
❑ 25 Neptulon E	6.00	15.00
❑ 26 Brittle Bones R	1.25	3.00
❑ 27 Claws of the Dead U	.20	.50
❑ 28 Death's Duo R	.60	1.50
❑ 29 Infestation U	.20	.50
❑ 30 Monstrous Essence R	1.25	3.00
❑ 31 Plagued Mind U	.20	.50
❑ 32 Skullchewer U	.20	.50
❑ 33 Boundless Wild R	.75	2.00
❑ 34 Fungal Growth R	.60	1.50
❑ 35 Mark of Goldrinn C	.10	.25
❑ 36 Stalwart Bear Form U	.20	.50
❑ 37 Verdant Boon U	.20	.50
❑ 38 Wild Roots U	.20	.50
❑ 39 Bestial Revival R	2.00	5.00
❑ 40 Chompers U	.20	.50
❑ 41 Clamps C	.10	.25
❑ 42 Concussive Barrage R	3.00	8.00
❑ 43 Monstrous Mark R	1.00	2.50
❑ 44 Roar of the Beast U	.20	.50
❑ 45 Track Enemy U	.20	.50
❑ 46 Char R	.60	1.50
❑ 47 Focus Magic R	.75	2.00
❑ 48 Glacial Tomb C	.10	.25
❑ 49 Molten Scorch U	.20	.50
❑ 50 Monstrous Frostbolt Volley R	1.00	2.50
❑ 51 Touch of Brilliance U	.20	.50
❑ 52 Vortex U	.20	.50
❑ 53 Blessing of the Light C	.10	.25
❑ 54 Blessing of the Righteous U	.20	.50
❑ 55 Boundless Might R	.60	1.50
❑ 56 Grand Crusader R	6.00	15.00
❑ 57 Hammer of the Zealot U	.20	.50
❑ 58 Righteous Cleanse U	.20	.50
❑ 59 Boundless Shadows R	1.00	2.50
❑ 60 Chakra R	.75	2.00
❑ 61 Power Word: Purity C	.10	.25
❑ 62 Power Word: Vitality U	.20	.50
❑ 63 Psychic Screech U	.20	.50
❑ 64 Tendrils of Darkness U	.20	.50
❑ 65 Disorienting Blow U	.20	.50
❑ 66 Distraction Technique U	.20	.50
❑ 67 Poison Bomb R	.60	1.50
❑ 68 Sleeping Poison R	.60	1.50
❑ 69 Vendetta R	.60	1.50
❑ 70 Boundless Life R	1.00	2.50
❑ 71 Earthen Might C	.10	.25
❑ 72 Lava Shock U	.20	.50
❑ 73 Shock of the Elements C	.10	.25
❑ 74 Spark of Life R	1.25	3.00
❑ 75 Windguard Totem U	.20	.50
❑ 76 Fel Summon U	.20	.50
❑ 77 Grimnar U	.20	.50
❑ 78 Hellisa C	.10	.25
❑ 79 Nether Balance R	.60	1.50
❑ 80 Soul Cleave U	.20	.50
❑ 81 Soul Swap R	.75	2.00
❑ 82 Armsman U	.20	.50
❑ 83 Augment Steel R	1.00	2.50
❑ 84 Bloodsurge R	.60	1.50
❑ 85 Furious Strike U	.20	.50
❑ 86 Monstrous Cleave U	.20	.50
❑ 87 Rallying Swarm R	.60	1.50
❑ 88 Monstrous Strike C	.10	.25
❑ 89 Monstrous Upheaval C	.10	.25
❑ 90 RwlRwlRwlRwl! U	.20	.50
❑ 91 Unleash the Swarm! U	.20	.50
❑ 92 Face of Fear C	.10	.25
❑ 93 Rallying Cry of the Dragonslayer C	.10	.25
❑ 94 Strength of Will C	.10	.25
❑ 95 Surge of Power R	.75	2.00
❑ 96 Arcanomage Misti R	.75	2.00
❑ 97 Ardon Almastor C	.10	.25
❑ 98 Balrak Stoutstone C	.10	.25
❑ 99 Braeo Darkpaw C	.10	.25
❑ 100 Burdok Brewshot C	.10	.25
❑ 101 Corin Stallnorth C	.10	.25
❑ 102 Dastrin Bowman C	.10	.25
❑ 103 Davius, Herald of Nature U	.20	.50
❑ 104 Dradam Chillblade C	.10	.25
❑ 105 Dulvar, Hand of the Light E	4.00	10.00
❑ 106 Evaax, Herald of Death U	.20	.50
❑ 107 Faenis the Tranquil R	1.50	4.00
❑ 108 Faithseer Jasmina R	1.50	4.00
❑ 109 Fumdol Mountainfrost C	.10	.25
❑ 110 Funken Fusemissile C	.10	.25
❑ 111 Grumdak, Herald of the Hunt U	.20	.50
❑ 112 Hadrack the Devoted R	.60	1.50
❑ 113 Hunrik Blackiron C	.10	.25
❑ 114 Jaema, Herald of the Light R	.60	1.50
❑ 115 Kaelon, Herald of the Flame U	.20	.50
❑ 116 Kara Vesstal C	.10	.25
❑ 117 Kieron the Loaner R	.60	1.50
❑ 118 Laetho Moonbranch C	.10	.25
❑ 119 Larrisa Valorshield C	.10	.25
❑ 120 Lodur, Herald of the Elements U	.20	.50
❑ 121 Malar Silverfrost U	.20	.50
❑ 122 Maloc, Herald of Trickery C	.10	.25
❑ 123 Mekkatorque, King of the Gnomes E	5.00	12.00
❑ 124 Militia Commander Balor R	.60	1.50
❑ 125 Sebastian Malak C	.10	.25
❑ 126 Shania, Herald of Faith C	.10	.25
❑ 127 Shaylith Swiftblade U	.20	.50
❑ 128 Tallie Sprinklelight C	.10	.25
❑ 129 Trista, Herald of the Fel U	.20	.50
❑ 130 Vaakia C	.10	.25
❑ 131 Valak the Vortex R	1.25	3.00
❑ 132 Vandos, Herald of War U	.20	.50
❑ 133 Vindicator Saaris R	.60	1.50
❑ 134 Wuzlo Grindergear C	.10	.25
❑ 135 Xuurvis C	.10	.25
❑ 136 Zintix the Frostbringer R	.75	2.00
❑ 137 Akasi, Herald of Nature U	.20	.50
❑ 138 Alana the Woebringer R	1.25	3.00
❑ 139 Alethia Brightsong C	.10	.25
❑ 140 Amano, Herald of the Sun U	.20	.50
❑ 141 Anastina, Herald of the Fel U	.20	.50
❑ 142 Asoren Darksnout C	.10	.25
❑ 143 Baxtan, Herald of the Flame U	.20	.50
❑ 144 Daroka Venomfist C	.10	.25
❑ 145 Deatheater Stroud U	.20	.50
❑ 146 Draga'zal C	.10	.25
❑ 147 Eralysa Sunshot C	.10	.25
❑ 148 Hagtrix the Mindsifter R	.60	1.50
❑ 149 Hesawa Stormwalker C	.10	.25
❑ 150 Izzy Quizfiz C	.10	.25
❑ 151 Jagrok, Herald of Trickery U	.20	.50
❑ 152 Jaron, Herald of the Hunt U	.20	.50
❑ 153 Jex'ali C	.10	.25
❑ 154 Jumahko Thundersky C	.10	.25
❑ 155 Kalam'ti R	1.25	3.00
❑ 156 Kazbaz C	.10	.25
❑ 157 Keleaa Ashford C	.10	.25
❑ 158 Kinza, Mistress of the Elements R	.75	2.00
❑ 159 Krezza the Explosive R	.60	1.50
❑ 160 Kromdar, Herald of War U	.20	.50
❑ 161 Lordann the Bloodreaver R	5.00	12.00
❑ 162 Mazu'kon E	25.00	50.00
❑ 163 Moro Wildmesa C	.10	.25
❑ 164 Nazuk Darkblood C	.10	.25
❑ 165 Parexia, Herald of the Shadows U	.20	.50
❑ 166 Prazo Whiptrick C	.10	.25
❑ 167 Runzik Shrapnelwhiz C	.10	.25
❑ 168 Samantha Galvington C	.10	.25
❑ 169 Shala'zum R	.60	1.50
❑ 170 Treespeaker Onaha R	.75	2.00
❑ 171 Vol'jin, Darkspear Chieftain E	2.50	6.00
❑ 172 Vuza'jin C	.10	.25
❑ 173 Yana'mi C	.10	.25
❑ 174 Zarixx, Herald of Death U	.20	.50
❑ 175 Zizzlix Drizzledrill C	.10	.25
❑ 176 Zudzo, Herald of the Elements U	.20	.50
❑ 177 Gilblin Bully C	.10	.25
❑ 178 Gilblin Deathscrounger R	3.00	8.00
❑ 179 Gilblin Hoarder U	.20	.50
❑ 180 Gilblin Plunderer U	.20	.50
❑ 181 Gilblin Trickster U	.20	.50
❑ 182 Bobbler U	.20	.50
❑ 183 Brighteye C	.10	.25
❑ 184 Bubblegil U	.20	.50
❑ 185 Chumly U	.20	.50
❑ 186 Crabbyfin U	.20	.50
❑ 187 Gobbler R	1.00	2.50
❑ 188 Murloc Coastrunner C	.10	.25
❑ 189 Nibbler C	.10	.25
❑ 190 Slippyfist R	.60	1.50
❑ 191 Snurky C	.10	.25
❑ 192 Swarmtooth U	.20	.50
❑ 193 Buldrug C	.10	.25
❑ 194 Drugush the Crusher C	.10	.25
❑ 195 Neph'lahim R	.60	1.50
❑ 196 Tar'gak the Felcrazed U	.20	.50
❑ 197 Thrug the Hurler U	.20	.50
❑ 198 Zor'chal the Shadowseer U	.20	.50
❑ 199 Commander Ulthok E	10.00	20.00
❑ 200 Faceless Sapper C	.10	.25
❑ 201 Faceless Watcher R	2.00	5.00
❑ 202 Deep Subjugator U	.20	.50
❑ 203 Mindbender Ghur'sha R	1.50	4.00
❑ 204 Idra'kess Enchantress U	.20	.50
❑ 205 Idra'kess Mistress U	.20	.50
❑ 206 Lady Naz'jar E	3.00	8.00
❑ 207 Naz'jar Harpooner C	.10	.25
❑ 208 Naz'jar Myrmidon C	.10	.25
❑ 209 Naz'jar Sorceress C	.10	.25
❑ 210 Sira'kess Tide Priestess U	.20	.50
❑ 211 Abyssal Seahorse R	.60	1.50
❑ 212 Gnash R	.75	2.00
❑ 213 Kolorath E	1.00	2.50
❑ 214 Nespirah R	.60	1.50
❑ 215 Ozumat E	6.00	15.00
❑ 216 Revenant of Neptulon U	.20	.50
❑ 217 Servant of Neptulon U	.20	.50
❑ 218 Unstable Corruption R	1.50	4.00
❑ 219 Wasteland Tallstrider E	4.00	10.00
❑ 220 Bloat the Bubble Fish U	.20	.50
❑ 221 Erunak Stonespeaker R	4.00	10.00
❑ 222 Toshe Chaosrender R	2.00	5.00
❑ 223 Periwinkle Cloak U	.20	.50
❑ 224 Shroud of Cooperation U	.20	.50
❑ 225 Triton Legplates R	.75	2.00
❑ 226 Wentletrap Vest C	.10	.25
❑ 227 Big Cauldron of Battle R	.60	1.50
❑ 228 Blessing of the Old God C	.10	.25
❑ 229 Bottled Cunning C	.10	.25
❑ 230 Bottled Death C	.10	.25
❑ 231 Bottled Elements C	.10	.25
❑ 232 Bottled Knowledge C	.10	.25
❑ 233 Bottled Life C	.10	.25
❑ 234 Bottled Light C	.10	.25
❑ 235 Bottled Mind C	.10	.25
❑ 236 Bottled Rage C	.10	.25
❑ 237 Bottled Spite C	.10	.25
❑ 238 Bottled Void C	.10	.25
❑ 239 Bottled Wild C	.10	.25
❑ 240 Nautilus Ring U	.20	.50
❑ 241 Ring of the Great Whale U	.20	.50
❑ 242 Severed Visionary Tentacle U	.20	.50
❑ 243 Throwing Starfish R	.75	2.00
❑ 244 Breathstone-Infused Longbow U	.20	.50
❑ 245 Cerith Spire Staff R	.75	2.00
❑ 246 Dawnblaze Blade U	.20	.50
❑ 247 Dirk's Command C	.10	.25
❑ 248 Downfall Hammer U	.20	.50
❑ 249 Eel Cutter C	.10	.25
❑ 250 Lightning Whelk Axe C	.10	.25
❑ 251 Polentate's Letter Opener U	.20	.50
❑ 252 Sorrow's End R	1.00	2.50
❑ 253 Throat Slasher C	.10	.25
❑ 254 The Culmination of Our Efforts C	.10	.25
❑ 255 The Last Living Lorekeeper C	.10	.25
❑ 256 Reoccupation U	.20	.50
❑ 257 Rescue the Earthspeaker! C	.10	.25
❑ 258 Seeds of Their Demise C	.10	.25
❑ 259 Setting an Example C	.10	.25
❑ 260 Wake of Destruction U	.20	.50
❑ 261 Waking the Beast C	.10	.25
❑ 262 Waters of Elune C	.10	.25
❑ 263 Throne of the Tides R	.60	1.50

2011 World of Warcraft Throne of the Tides Loot

Card	Low	High
❑ 1 Bloat the Bubble Fish	3.00	8.00
❑ 2 Throwing Starfish	8.00	20.00
❑ 3 Wasteland Tallstrider	75.00	150.00

2011 World of Warcraft Twilight of the Dragons

Card	Low	High
Booster Box (24 packs)	40.00	80.00
Booster Pack (19 cards)	3.00	4.00
❑ 1 Auralyn the Light of Dawn U	.20	.50
❑ 2 Bladesinger Alyssa U	.20	.50
❑ 3 Deragor the Earthsworn U	.20	.50
❑ 4 Jasmia, Nature's Chosen U	.20	.50
❑ 5 Kavar the Bloodthirsty U	.20	.50
❑ 6 Nomak the Blazingclaw U	.20	.50
❑ 7 Soul-Eater Morgania U	.20	.50
❑ 8 Trilik the Light's Spark U	.20	.50
❑ 9 Vad of the Four Winds U	.20	.50
❑ 10 Zane the Sniper U	.20	.50
❑ 11 Amah the Sun's Grace U	.20	.50
❑ 12 Amaxi the Cruel U	.20	.50
❑ 13 Dar'thael the Bloodsworn U	.20	.50
❑ 14 Dragonslayer Drux U	.20	.50
❑ 15 Earthseer Nakza U	.20	.50
❑ 16 Flame Keeper Rizzli U	.20	.50
❑ 17 Samael the Bloodpoint U	.20	.50
❑ 18 Sumi'jin, Guardian of Cenarius U	.20	.50
❑ 19 Suncaller Haruh U	.20	.50
❑ 20 Zazel the Greedy U	.20	.50
❑ 21 Deathwing the Destroyer E	10.00	25.00
❑ 22 Black Death U	.20	.50
❑ 23 Dark Simulacrum R	.40	1.00
❑ 24 Favor of Undeath C	.10	.25
❑ 25 Frozen Core C	.10	.25
❑ 26 Glacial Strike C	.10	.25
❑ 27 Hungering Cold R	.60	1.50
❑ 28 Necrotic Strike U	.20	.50
❑ 29 Twisted Death Pact U	.20	.50
❑ 30 Favor of Nature C	.10	.25
❑ 31 Fierce Cat Form U	.20	.50
❑ 32 Living Roots C	.10	.25
❑ 33 Rebirth U	.20	.50
❑ 34 Tears of Aessina C	.10	.25
❑ 35 Twisted Wrath U	.20	.50
❑ 36 Wild Growth R	.40	1.00
❑ 37 Wild Mushroom R	.40	1.00
❑ 38 Camouflage R	.40	1.00
❑ 39 Cinder C	.10	.25
❑ 40 Disengage C	.10	.25
❑ 41 Explosive Hunt U	.20	.50
❑ 42 Favor of the Hunt C	.10	.25
❑ 43 Immolation Trap U	.20	.50
❑ 44 Master Marksman R	.60	1.50
❑ 45 Nag the Twisted U	.20	.50
❑ 46 Blazing Debris C	.10	.25
❑ 47 Favor of the Arcane C	.10	.25
❑ 48 Fireball U	.20	.50
❑ 49 Flame Orb R	.60	1.50
❑ 50 Glaciate C	.10	.25
❑ 51 Pyromaniac R	.75	2.00
❑ 52 Ring of Frost U	.20	.50
❑ 53 Twisted Arcana U	.20	.50
❑ 54 Beacon of Light R	1.00	2.50
❑ 55 Blessing of Might U	.20	.50
❑ 56 Favor of the Light C	.10	.25
❑ 57 Guardian of Ancient Kings R	2.00	5.00
❑ 58 Hammer of Retribution C	.10	.25
❑ 59 Hand of Protection C	.10	.25
❑ 60 Twisted Light U	.20	.50
❑ 61 Word of Glory U	.20	.50
❑ 62 Favor of Spirit C	.10	.25
❑ 63 Heal U	.20	.50
❑ 64 Holy Blaze U	.20	.50
❑ 65 Inner Will R	.40	1.00
❑ 66 Power Word: Absorb C	.10	.25
❑ 67 Power Word: Barrier R	.75	2.00
❑ 68 Psychic Melt C	.10	.25
❑ 69 Twisted Mind Spike U	.20	.50
❑ 70 Break Steel C	.10	.25
❑ 71 Favor of Mischief C	.10	.25
❑ 72 Mind-Numbing Poison U	.20	.50
❑ 73 Revealing Strike R	1.00	2.50
❑ 74 Smoke Bomb R	.75	2.00
❑ 75 Swindle U	.20	.50
❑ 76 Twisted Massacre U	.20	.50
❑ 77 Vicious Strike C	.10	.25
❑ 78 Burning Winds R	.40	1.00
❑ 79 Cleanse Spirit C	.10	.25
❑ 80 Favor of the Elements C	.10	.25

Card	Low	High
☐ 81 Flametongue Weapon U	.20	.50
☐ 82 Inferno Totem U	.20	.50
☐ 83 Primal Strike C	.10	.25
☐ 84 Riptide R	1.00	2.50
☐ 85 Twisted Fire Nova U	.20	.50
☐ 86 Chaos Bolt R	1.50	4.00
☐ 87 Demonic Corruption R	2.50	6.00
☐ 88 Favor of the Nether C	.10	.25
☐ 89 Fel Immolation C	.10	.25
☐ 90 Incinerate U	.20	.50
☐ 91 Selora C	.10	.25
☐ 92 Twisted Infernal U	.20	.50
☐ 93 Void Rip U	.20	.50
☐ 94 Colossus Smash R	.40	1.00
☐ 95 Demoralizing Strike C	.10	.25
☐ 96 Executioner's Mark C	.10	.25
☐ 97 Favor of Steel C	.10	.25
☐ 98 Heroic Leap U	.20	.50
☐ 99 Shockwave R	.60	1.50
☐ 100 Slam U	.20	.50
☐ 101 Twisted Rampage U	.20	.50
☐ 102 Frozen Frenzy E	2.00	5.00
☐ 103 Council of Three Hammers E	2.50	6.00
☐ 104 Fool's Gold R	.60	1.50
☐ 105 Abbie Whizzleblade C	.10	.25
☐ 106 Alrak Stonecrack C	.10	.25
☐ 107 Brel Blazebeard C	.10	.25
☐ 108 Chandra Marlight C	.10	.25
☐ 109 Frizzle Stumbleshade C	.10	.25
☐ 110 Gardos Gravefang U	.20	.50
☐ 111 Haratha Hammerflame C	.10	.25
☐ 112 Javeer C	.10	.25
☐ 113 Jerrak Krandle U	.20	.50
☐ 114 Jessa the Lifebound U	.20	.50
☐ 115 Kalan Howland C	.10	.25
☐ 116 Kelsa Wildfire C	.10	.25
☐ 117 Knight Karia C	.10	.25
☐ 118 Lord Darius Crowley U	.20	.50
☐ 119 Lyrana of Eldre'Thalas R	.40	1.00
☐ 120 Maurice Steelson U	.20	.50
☐ 121 Prince Anduin Wrynn E	2.50	6.00
☐ 122 Roger Ulric C	.10	.25
☐ 123 Stacia Markton U	.20	.50
☐ 124 Stargazer Ronal C	.10	.25
☐ 125 Tania Falan U	.20	.50
☐ 126 Vakus the Inferno R	6.00	15.00
☐ 127 Windspeaker Nuvu C	.10	.25
☐ 128 Abysswalker Rakau U	.20	.50
☐ 129 Azami'tal the Flamebender R	.60	1.50
☐ 130 Azizi Daggerflick C	.10	.25
☐ 131 Banok Sunrock C	.10	.25
☐ 132 Blood Knight Adrenna U	.20	.50
☐ 133 Commander Molotov R	.40	1.00
☐ 134 Dagax the Butcher R	5.00	12.00
☐ 135 Falixia Frizzleblast C	.10	.25
☐ 136 Flamebringer Gaxix U	.20	.50
☐ 137 Gavin Haverston C	.10	.25
☐ 138 Gerwixicks C	.10	.25
☐ 139 Gollom Skybang C	.10	.25
☐ 140 Gordash Firetooth C	.10	.25
☐ 141 High Chieftain Baine Bloodhoof E	2.00	5.00
☐ 142 High Guard Braxx C	.10	.25
☐ 143 Jaga'zul the Wild's Fury R	.75	2.00
☐ 144 Kraxos Chizzlecoin U	.20	.50
☐ 145 Kyroth Steelspite C	.10	.25
☐ 146 Rakala Deathsmash C	.10	.25
☐ 147 Sahama Brighthorn C	.10	.25
☐ 148 Shade Emissary Vaxxod U	.20	.50
☐ 149 Warchief Garrosh Hellscream E	4.00	10.00
☐ 150 Wildweaver Masa'zun C	.10	.25
☐ 151 Yazli Earthspark C	.10	.25
☐ 152 Zor'dul Deathbinder C	.10	.25
☐ 153 Nefarian U	.20	.50
☐ 154 Obsidia R	.40	1.00
☐ 155 Obsidian Drakonid C	.10	.25
☐ 156 Obsidian Drudge C	.10	.25
☐ 157 Obsidian Enforcer C	.10	.25
☐ 158 Obsidian Pyrewing C	.10	.25
☐ 159 Obsidian Skyterror C	.10	.25
☐ 160 Sinestra R	2.00	5.00
☐ 161 Twilight Corruptor U	.20	.50
☐ 162 Twilight Drake U	.20	.50
☐ 163 Twilight Emissary U	.20	.50
☐ 164 Twilight Shadowdrake U	.20	.50
☐ 165 Twilight Wyrmkiller U	.20	.50
☐ 166 Caelestrasz R	1.50	4.00
☐ 167 Merithra R	.40	1.00
☐ 168 Arygos R	1.00	2.50
☐ 169 Anachronos R	.40	1.00
☐ 170 Ignacious R	.40	1.00
☐ 171 Feludius R	.40	1.00
☐ 172 Arion R	.60	1.50
☐ 173 Terrastra R	.40	1.00
☐ 174 Cho'gall E	1.50	4.00
☐ 175 Amani Dragonhawk E	2.50	6.00
☐ 176 Nightsaber Cub U	.20	.50
☐ 177 Thrall, Guardian of the Elements E	3.00	8.00
☐ 178 Battleplate of the Apocalypse U	.20	.50
☐ 179 Double Attack Handguards U	.20	.50
☐ 180 Flame Pillar Leggings C	.10	.25
☐ 181 Polished Helm of Valor R	.60	1.50
☐ 182 Proto-Handler's Gauntlets C	.10	.25
☐ 183 Stained Shadowcraft Cap R	.75	2.00
☐ 184 Tarnished Raging Berserker's Helm R	.60	1.50
☐ 185 Tattered Dreadmist Mask R	.60	1.50
☐ 186 Corrupted Egg Shell U	.20	.50
☐ 187 Darkmoon Card: Hurricane R	.75	2.00
☐ 188 Akirus the Worm-Breaker R	2.00	5.00
☐ 189 Axe of the Eclipse U	.20	.50
☐ 190 Blade of the Burning Sun R	.40	1.00
☐ 191 Blade of the Witching Hour C	.10	.25
☐ 192 Chelley's Staff of Dark Mending R	.75	2.00
☐ 193 Claws of Torment C	.10	.25
☐ 194 Cookie's Stirring Rod R	.40	1.00
☐ 195 Crul'korak, the Lightning's Arc R	2.50	6.00
☐ 196 Darklight Torch U	.20	.50
☐ 197 Dragonheart Piercer U	.20	.50
☐ 198 Elementium Poleaxe U	.20	.50
☐ 199 Lava Spine U	.20	.50
☐ 200 Obsidium Executioner C	.10	.25
☐ 201 Organic Lifeform Inverter U	.20	.50
☐ 202 Shalug'doom, the Axe of Unmaking E	3.00	8.00
☐ 203 Twilight's Hammer R	1.50	4.00
☐ 204 Volatile Thunderstick U	.20	.50
☐ 205 Battle of Life and Death C	.10	.25
☐ 206 Blackout U	.20	.50
☐ 207 The Crucible of Carnage: The Twilight Terror C	.10	.25
☐ 208 Devoured C	.10	.25
☐ 209 Enter the Dragon Queen C	.10	.25
☐ 210 Far from the Nest C	.10	.25
☐ 211 Fire the Cannon C	.10	.25
☐ 212 A Fiery Reunion C	.10	.25
☐ 213 Last of Her Kind C	.10	.25
☐ 214 The Maw of Iso'rath C	.10	.25
☐ 215 Mercy for the Bound C	.10	.25
☐ 216 Mr. Goldmine's Wild Ride C	.10	.25
☐ 217 Twilight Extermination C	.10	.25
☐ 218 Unbinding C	.10	.25
☐ 219 The Worldbreaker R	.75	2.00
☐ 220 Twilight Citadel R	20.00	40.00

2011 World of Warcraft Twilight of the Dragons Loot

Card	Low	High
☐ 1 Nightsaber Cub	6.00	15.00
☐ 2 Fool's Gold	10.00	25.00
☐ 3 Amani Dragonhawk	125.00	200.00

2011 World of Warcraft War of the Elements

Card	Low	High
Booster Box (24 Packs)	40.00	80.00
Booster Pack (19 Cards)	3.00	4.00
☐ 1 Almia Moonwhisper U	.20	.50
☐ 2 Aric Stonejack U	.20	.50
☐ 3 Edwin Blademark U	.20	.50
☐ 4 Grayson Steelworth U	.20	.50
☐ 5 Gundek Hammerguard U	.20	.50
☐ 6 Huntsman Gorwal U	.20	.50
☐ 7 Merissa Firebrew U	.20	.50
☐ 8 Olivia Demascas U	.20	.50
☐ 9 Thira Anvilash U	.20	.50
☐ 10 Vanira Raventhorne U	.20	.50
☐ 11 Baxxel Geartooth U	.20	.50
☐ 12 Fraznak the Furious U	.20	.50
☐ 13 Jinxy Blastwheel U	.20	.50
☐ 14 Kanga the Primal U	.20	.50
☐ 15 Mindtwister Quimtrix U	.20	.50
☐ 16 Sunwalker Nahano U	.20	.50
☐ 17 Tazrik Crankrust U	.20	.50
☐ 18 Uzak'zim U	.20	.50
☐ 19 Zimzi the Trickster U	.20	.50
☐ 20 Zin'sul U	.20	.50
☐ 21 Kalecgos E	6.00	15.00
☐ 22 Nozdormu the Timeless E	4.00	10.00
☐ 23 Blight Bringers C	.10	.20
☐ 24 Command of Undeath C	.10	.20
☐ 25 Death Strike U	.20	.50
☐ 26 Frozen Blight U	.20	.50
☐ 27 Gargoyle R	6.00	15.00
☐ 28 Horn of Winter C	.10	.20
☐ 29 Outbreak R	.40	1.00
☐ 30 Sanguine Presence R	.40	1.00
☐ 31 Brutal Bear Form U	.20	.50
☐ 32 Celestial Moonfire R	1.50	4.00
☐ 33 Healing Touch U	.20	.50
☐ 34 Maim C	.10	.20
☐ 35 Moonshard C	.10	.20
☐ 36 Rend and Tear R	.75	2.00
☐ 37 Savage Cat Form C	.10	.20
☐ 38 Starburst R	2.00	5.00
☐ 39 Arcane Shot C	.10	.20
☐ 40 Cobra Shot R	.75	2.00
☐ 41 Donatello C	.10	.20
☐ 42 Loque R	2.00	5.00
☐ 43 Noxious Trap R	.75	2.00
☐ 44 Warning Shot C	.10	.20
☐ 45 Widow Venom U	.20	.50
☐ 46 Wild Fervor U	.20	.50
☐ 47 Arcane Barrage R	4.00	10.00
☐ 48 Arcane Foresight C	.10	.20
☐ 49 Arcane Inferno R	.40	1.00
☐ 50 Arcane Missiles C	.10	.20
☐ 51 Draconic Flames U	.20	.50
☐ 52 Flash Freeze C	.10	.20
☐ 53 Mystical Refreshment R	.40	1.00
☐ 54 Tidal Elemental U	.20	.50
☐ 55 Blessing of Faith U	.20	.50
☐ 56 Flash of Light C	.10	.20
☐ 57 Holy Vengeance R	.40	1.00
☐ 58 Holy Wrath R	.40	1.00
☐ 59 Inquisition C	.10	.20
☐ 60 Light of Reckoning C	.10	.20
☐ 61 Shield of the Righteous R	.40	1.00
☐ 62 Vengeful Crusader Strike U	.20	.50
☐ 63 Dark Embrace R	.40	1.00
☐ 64 Expel C	.10	.20
☐ 65 Focused Dispel C	.10	.20
☐ 66 Hymn of Hope U	.20	.50
☐ 67 Leap of Faith R	3.00	8.00
☐ 68 Mind Melt R	1.50	4.00
☐ 69 Power Word: Endurance U	.20	.50
☐ 70 Shadow Word: Death C	.10	.20
☐ 71 Agonizing Poison U	.20	.50
☐ 72 Coated Blades R	.40	1.00
☐ 73 Infiltrate C	.10	.20
☐ 74 Invigorate U	.20	.50
☐ 75 Sap C	.10	.20
☐ 76 Shadow Dance R	2.00	5.00
☐ 77 Tormenting Gouge C	.10	.20
☐ 78 Tricksters Gambit R	2.00	5.00
☐ 79 Ancestral Recovery C	.10	.20
☐ 80 Blazing Elemental Totem U	.20	.50
☐ 81 Chain Heal C	.10	.20
☐ 82 Elemental Flames C	.10	.20
☐ 83 Primal Dexterity U	.20	.50
☐ 84 Tempest Totem R	1.00	2.50
☐ 85 Totemic Vigor R	.40	1.00
☐ 86 Unleash Elements R	2.00	5.00
☐ 87 Dread Touch C	.10	.20
☐ 88 Everlasting Affliction R	1.50	4.00
☐ 89 Fel Covenant C	.10	.20
☐ 90 Fel Flame R	1.50	4.00
☐ 91 Grimdron U	.20	.50
☐ 92 Grim Harvest R	.40	1.00
☐ 93 Maazhum C	.10	.20
☐ 94 Seed of Corruption U	.20	.50
☐ 95 Burning Rage R	.40	1.00
☐ 96 Dauntless Defender C	.10	.20
☐ 97 Enraged Regeneration R	.40	1.00
☐ 98 Intercept C	.10	.20
☐ 99 Merciless Strikes U	.20	.50
☐ 100 Peerless Guard C	.10	.20
☐ 101 Shattering Throw U	.20	.50
☐ 102 Intensify E	3.00	8.00
☐ 103 To Arms! E	4.00	10.00
☐ 104 Firelord's Gift, The U	.20	.50
☐ 105 Stonemother's Gift, The U	.20	.50
☐ 106 Tidehunter's Gift, The U	.20	.50
☐ 107 Windlord's Gift, The U	.20	.50
☐ 108 Arvos Jadestone C	.10	.20
☐ 109 Axar C	.10	.20
☐ 110 Brimi Tinkerblade C	.10	.20
☐ 111 Cadric Talworth C	.10	.20
☐ 112 Dagin Bootzap C	.10	.20
☐ 113 Dominic Kandor C	.10	.20
☐ 114 Elmira Moonsurge R	.40	1.00
☐ 115 Erama C	.10	.20
☐ 116 Gully Rustinax C	.10	.20
☐ 117 Jeniva Prescott C	.10	.20
☐ 118 Jerrick Valder C	.10	.20
☐ 119 Kane the Arcanist U	.20	.50
☐ 120 Nathar Wilderson C	.10	.20
☐ 121 Nessera Gildenrose C	.10	.20
☐ 122 Patricia Potter C	.10	.20
☐ 123 Rufus Claybourne R	4.00	10.00
☐ 124 Shadowseer Calista U	.20	.50
☐ 125 Shaytha Lumenira U	.20	.50
☐ 126 Stevrona Forgemender R	.75	2.00
☐ 127 Tidus the Relentless R	2.00	5.00
☐ 128 Vincent Brayden C	.10	.20
☐ 129 Xeris C	.10	.20
☐ 130 Zooti Fizzlefury U	.20	.50
☐ 131 Burom Bladeseer C	.10	.20
☐ 132 Caera Sunforge C	.10	.20
☐ 133 Drax Felfuse C	.10	.20
☐ 134 Hanu Skyhorn U	.20	.50
☐ 135 Kark Baneblood C	.10	.20
☐ 136 Kizzli Grinderstub C	.10	.20
☐ 137 Korlix Grimvik C	.10	.20
☐ 138 Kuatha Mornhoof C	.10	.20
☐ 139 Lena Naville C	.10	.20
☐ 140 Maxie the Blaster R	.40	1.00
☐ 141 Nikka Blastbor C	.10	.20
☐ 142 Rakzi the Earthgraced R	.75	2.00
☐ 143 Razo'jun U	.20	.50
☐ 144 Rumu Moonhaze C	.10	.20
☐ 145 Shaera Strikewing C	.10	.20
☐ 146 Talaan Solaras C	.10	.20
☐ 147 Timriv the Enforcer C	.10	.20
☐ 148 Tharuk Foulblade U	.20	.50
☐ 149 Tol'zin R	2.00	5.00
☐ 150 Valytha Colton C	.10	.20
☐ 151 Yoza'tsu C	.10	.20
☐ 152 Zarvix the Tormentor R	.40	1.00
☐ 153 Zeni'vun U	.20	.50
☐ 154 Azure Captain C	.10	.20
☐ 155 Azure Drake C	.10	.20
☐ 156 Azure Emissary U	.20	.50
☐ 157 Azure Enforcer C	.10	.20
☐ 158 Azure Magus C	.10	.20
☐ 159 Azure Skyrazor U	.20	.50
☐ 160 Tyrygosa R	1.50	4.00
☐ 161 Bronze Drake C	.10	.20
☐ 162 Bronze Drakonid U	.20	.50
☐ 163 Bronze Emissary U	.20	.50
☐ 164 Bronze Guardian C	.10	.20
☐ 165 Bronze Skyrazor C	.10	.20
☐ 166 Bronze Warden C	.10	.20
☐ 167 Soridormi R	1.50	4.00
☐ 168 Al'Akir the Windlord E	3.00	8.00
☐ 169 Bound Vortex U	.20	.50
☐ 170 Bound Rumbler U	.20	.50
☐ 171 Therazane the Stonemother E	2.50	6.00
☐ 172 Bound Inferno U	.20	.50
☐ 173 Ragnaros the Firelord E	2.50	6.00
☐ 174 Bound Torrent U	.20	.50
☐ 175 Neptulon the Tidehunter E	2.50	6.00
☐ 176 Landro's Lichling U	.20	.50
☐ 177 Malfurion Stormrage E	4.00	10.00
☐ 178 Savage Raptor E	2.50	6.00
☐ 179 Champions Deathdealer Breastplate R	.75	2.00
☐ 180 Crown of Chelonian Freedom U	.20	.50
☐ 181 God Grinding Grips U	.20	.50
☐ 182 Helm of Terrorizing Fangs R	.40	1.00
☐ 183 Leggings of the Vanquished Usurper U	.20	.50
☐ 184 Polished Spaulders of Valor R	.40	1.00
☐ 185 Stained Shadowcraft Spaulders R	.40	1.00
☐ 186 Tattered Dreadmist Robe R	.75	2.00
☐ 187 Wildlife Defender R	.40	1.00
☐ 188 Darkmoon Card: Volcano R	.40	1.00
☐ 189 Landros Hitching Post R	.40	1.00
☐ 190 Axe of Grounded Flame R	.40	1.00
☐ 191 Barnacle Coated Greataxe R	.40	1.00
☐ 192 Blacksoul Polearm R	.40	1.00
☐ 193 Crusher of Bonds C	.10	.20
☐ 194 Fire Etched Dagger U	.20	.50
☐ 195 Glyphtrace Ritual Knife R	1.50	4.00
☐ 196 Kickback 5000 R	.40	1.00
☐ 197 Lightningflash U	.20	.50
☐ 198 Lordbane Scepter R	.40	1.00
☐ 199 Poisonfire Greatsword R	.40	1.00
☐ 200 Perforator, The R	.40	1.00
☐ 201 Wild Hammer R	.40	1.00
☐ 202 Aessina's Miracle C	.10	.20
☐ 203 All That Rises C	.10	.20
☐ 204 Bird In Hand, A C	.10	.20
☐ 205 Breaking the Bonds C	.10	.20
☐ 206 Defending the Rift C	.10	.20
☐ 207 Dragon, Unchained C	.10	.20
☐ 208 Elemental Energy C	.10	.20
☐ 209 End of the Supply Line C	.10	.20
☐ 210 Entrenched C	.10	.20
☐ 211 Forged of Shadow and Flame C	.10	.20
☐ 212 Head-Full of Wind, A U	.20	.50
☐ 213 Lightning in a Bottle C	.10	.20
☐ 214 Putting the Pieces Together U	.20	.50
☐ 215 Sea Legs U	.20	.50
☐ 216 Something That Burns U	.20	.50
☐ 217 Abyssal Maw R	1.50	4.00
☐ 218 Deepholm R	.75	2.00
☐ 219 Firelands R	2.00	5.00
☐ 220 Skywall R	1.00	2.50

2011 World of Warcraft War of the Elements Loot

Card	Low	High
☐ 1 Landro's Lichling	3.00	8.00
☐ 2 War Party Hitching Post	15.00	40.00
☐ 3 Savage Raptor	125.00	200.00

2012 World of Warcraft Crown of the Heavens

Card	Low	High
Complete Set (198)		
Booster Box (36 Packs)		
Booster Pack (16 Cards)		
☐ 1 Arisella, Daughter of Cenarius U	.20	.50
☐ 2 Iso'rath U	.20	.50
☐ 3 Tyrus Blackhorn U	.20	.50
☐ 4 Warlord Grok'thol U	.20	.50
☐ 5A Cenarius, Lord of the Forest E	2.00	5.00
☐ 5B Cenarius, Lord of the Forest	4.00	10.00
☐ 6 Crimson Guard C	.10	.25
☐ 7 Dark Transformation R	.60	1.50
☐ 8 Despair of Undeath U	.20	.50
☐ 9 Leeching Fever U	.20	.50
☐ 10 Vampiric Siphon R	.60	1.50
☐ 11 Ferocious Cat Form U	.20	.50
☐ 12 Malfurion's Gift R	.60	1.50
☐ 13 Mark of Elderlimb U	.20	.50
☐ 14 Mark of the Ancients C	.10	.25
☐ 15 Monstrous Boon R	1.50	4.00
☐ 16 Wild Cascade R	.40	1.00
☐ 17 McCloud the Fox C	.10	.25
☐ 18 Quick Trap U	.20	.50
☐ 19 Sniper Training R	1.00	2.50
☐ 20 Yertle R	4.00	10.00
☐ 21 Flame Lance C	.10	.25
☐ 22 Frost Blast U	.20	.50
☐ 23 Ice Barrier R	6.00	15.00
☐ 24 Overload U	.20	.50
☐ 25 Shroud of the Archmage R	2.00	5.00
☐ 26 The Art of War R	.40	1.00
☐ 27 Blessing of the Devoted C	.10	.25
☐ 28 Divine Bulwark R	.40	1.00
☐ 29 Light of the Naaru U	.20	.50
☐ 30 Vindicator's Shock U	.20	.50
☐ 31 Borrowed Time R	1.50	4.00
☐ 32 Faithful Heat U	.20	.50
☐ 33 Shadow Word: Despair U	.20	.50
☐ 34 Shroud of the High Priest R	.40	1.00
☐ 35 Spiritual Imbalance C	.10	.25
☐ 36 Assassin's Strike C	.10	.25
☐ 37 Boundless Thievery R	1.00	2.50
☐ 38 Hemorrhage R	.40	1.00
☐ 39 Poison the Well U	.20	.50
☐ 40 Earthquake R	.40	1.00
☐ 41 Frost Arc C	.10	.25
☐ 42 Monstrous Totem R	1.00	2.50
☐ 43 Rage of the Elements U	.20	.50
☐ 44 Tidal Totem U	.20	.50
☐ 45 Unleash Inferno R	1.25	3.00
☐ 46 Banish Soul U	.20	.50
☐ 47 Fire and Brimstone R	1.00	2.50
☐ 48 Gakuri U	.20	.50
☐ 49 Monstrous Void R	1.25	3.00
☐ 50 Shaafun C	.10	.25
☐ 51 Shroud of the Nethermancer R	.60	1.50
☐ 52 Bladestorm R	3.00	8.00
☐ 53 Boundless Rage R	1.00	2.50
☐ 54 Brutal Strike C	.10	.25
☐ 55 Destructive Disarm U	.20	.50
☐ 56 Infectious Brutality U	.20	.50
☐ 57 Hexamorph U	.20	.50
☐ 58 The Light's Gaze U	.20	.50
☐ 59 Master's Embrace U	.20	.50
☐ 60 Overwhelm U	.20	.50
☐ 61 Paralyzing Strike U	.20	.50
☐ 62 Essence of Aggression U	.20	.50
☐ 63 Essence of Defense U	.20	.50
☐ 64 Essence of Focus U	.20	.50
☐ 65 Essence of Light U	.20	.50
☐ 66 Essence of Rage U	.20	.50
☐ 67 Essence of War U	.20	.50
☐ 68 Bark and Bite R	.60	1.50
☐ 69 Bash and Slash R	1.25	3.00
☐ 70 Fear and Loathing R	.40	1.00
☐ 71 Preserve and Protect R	1.50	4.00
☐ 72 Rime and Freezin' R	1.50	4.00
☐ 73 Aeshia Moonstreak C	.10	.25
☐ 74 Aleksei Brandal U	.20	.50
☐ 75 Anathel the Eagle-Eye R	1.25	3.00
☐ 76 Andrews the Just C	.10	.25
☐ 77 Archdruid Malfurion Stormrage E	2.50	6.00
☐ 78 Bromor the Shadowblade R	.40	1.00
☐ 79 Dar the Beastmaster C	.10	.25
☐ 80 Emree U	.20	.50
☐ 81 Esala U	.20	.50
☐ 82 Father Charles C	.10	.25
☐ 83 Flamesinger Zara C	.10	.25
☐ 84 Frimzy Fuzzbum U	.20	.50
☐ 85 Gerrunge the Sadist R	.40	1.00
☐ 86 Graddis Battlebeard R	.40	1.00
☐ 87 Grovewarden Daviak U	.20	.50
☐ 88 Jeishal U	.40	1.00
☐ 89 Kalam Blacksteel C	.10	.25
☐ 90 Kaldric Stoutwhisker U	.20	.50
☐ 91 Lucy Elizabeth C	.10	.25
☐ 92 Shalyssa Groveshaper C	.10	.25
☐ 93 Targus Roughblade C	.10	.25
☐ 94 Thadrus, Shield of Teldrassil R	3.00	8.00
☐ 95 Tharal Wildbreeze C	.10	.25
☐ 96 Tommi Spazzratchet C	.10	.25
☐ 97 Tyrande, High Priestess of Elune E	4.00	10.00
☐ 98 Velkin Gray U	.20	.50
☐ 99 Wendy Anne C	.10	.25
☐ 100 Zazzo Dizzleflame R	1.00	2.50
☐ 101 Abasha Windstorm U	.20	.50
☐ 102 Alyna Sunshower C	.10	.25
☐ 103 Baru Gravehorn U	.20	.50
☐ 104 Drotara the Bloodpoint C	.10	.25
☐ 105 Elderguard Brennan U	.20	.50
☐ 106 Grak Foulblade C	.10	.25
☐ 107 Gravelord Adams R	1.00	2.50
☐ 108 Hamuul Runetotem E	1.00	2.50
☐ 109 Horngrim U	.20	.50
☐ 110 Ian Lanstrick U	.20	.50
☐ 111 Icaros the Sunward C	.10	.25
☐ 112 Kraznix Smolderpain C	.10	.25
☐ 113 Lazarus Marrowbane C	.10	.25
☐ 114 Moharu the Skyseer R	.40	1.00
☐ 115 Muluno Sunbreath U	.20	.50
☐ 116 Nox the Lifedrainer R	.40	1.00
☐ 117 Raezi C	.10	.25
☐ 118 Soulde the Earthshaker R	1.25	3.00
☐ 119 Sylvanas, Queen of the Forsaken E	2.00	5.00
☐ 120 Thespius Bloodblaze C	.10	.25
☐ 121 Thunderpetal U	.20	.50
☐ 122 Tor Earthwalker C	.10	.25
☐ 123 Tristani the Sunblade R	.40	1.00
☐ 124 Vazu'jin C	.10	.25
☐ 125 Vizo Arctwister C	.10	.25
☐ 126 Vor'zun C	.10	.25
☐ 127 Witch Doctor Ka'booma R	3.00	8.00
☐ 128 Zaza'jun U	.20	.50
☐ 129 Brogre U	.20	.50
☐ 130 Deathsmasher Mogdar C	.10	.25
☐ 131 Drak'narr C	.10	.25
☐ 132 Dro'gash R	.40	1.00
☐ 133 Grag'tok C	.10	.25
☐ 134 Grug the Bonecrusher C	.10	.25
☐ 135 High Warlord Zogar E	2.50	6.00
☐ 136 Krogar the Colossal R	3.00	8.00
☐ 137 Krum'shal U	.20	.50
☐ 138 Throk the Conqueror C	.10	.25
☐ 139 Torr'nag U	.20	.50
☐ 140 Trag'ush C	.10	.25
☐ 141 Jadefire Felsworn U	.20	.50
☐ 142 Jadefire Hellcaller C	.10	.25
☐ 143 Jadefire Rogue U	.20	.50
☐ 144 Jadefire Satyr C	.10	.25
☐ 145 Jadefire Scout C	.10	.25
☐ 146 Jadefire Trickster C	.10	.25

❑ 147 Prince Xavalis E	5.00	12.00
❑ 148 Vylokx R	2.50	6.00
❑ 149 Baby Murloc U	1.00	2.50
❑ 150 Bubblesmash C	.10	.25
❑ 151 Gutfin C	.10	.25
❑ 152 King Bagurgle, Terror of the Tides E	3.00	8.00
❑ 153 Splashtooth C	.10	.25
❑ 154 Keeper Alinar C	.10	.25
❑ 155 Keeper Balos C	.10	.25
❑ 156 Keeper Sharus R	4.00	10.00
❑ 157 Remulos, Son of Cenarius R	2.50	6.00
❑ 158 Ashroot, Ancient of Lore U	.20	.50
❑ 159 Stonebranch, Ancient of War U	.20	.50
❑ 160 High Prophet Barim R	.40	1.00
❑ 161 Neferset Darkcaster C	.10	.25
❑ 162 Aessina R	.40	1.00
❑ 163 Gronn Skullcracker R	2.50	6.00
❑ 164 Harpy Matriarch C	.10	.25
❑ 165 Vicious Grell U	.20	.50
❑ 166 Corrupted Hippogryph E	1.00	2.50
❑ 167 Farseer Nobundo R	.40	1.00
❑ 168 Hyjal Stag C	.10	.25
❑ 169 Muln Earthfury R	1.50	4.00
❑ 170 Belt of Absolute Zero C	.10	.25
❑ 171 Crown of the Ogre King R	2.00	5.00
❑ 172 Gravitational Pull R	1.50	4.00
❑ 173 Power Generator Hood C	.10	.25
❑ 174 Spaulders of the Scarred Lady U	.20	.50
❑ 175 Magical Ogre Idol R	1.50	4.00
❑ 176 Miniature Voodoo Mask R	5.00	12.00
❑ 177 Vial of Stolen Memories R	1.50	4.00
❑ 178 Brainsplinter U	.20	.50
❑ 179 Branch of Nordrassil R	.40	1.00
❑ 180 Dragonwrath, Tarecgosa's Rest E	1.50	4.00
❑ 181 Gurubashi Punisher U	.20	.50
❑ 182 Irontree Knives U	.20	.50
❑ 183 Legacy of Arlokk U	.20	.50
❑ 184 Lumbering Ogre Axe C	.10	.25
❑ 185 Maimgor's Bite R	1.50	4.00
❑ 186 Mandible of Beth'tilac C	.10	.25
❑ 187 Mandokir's Tribute U	.20	.50
❑ 188 Reclaimed Ashkandi R	1.50	4.00
❑ 189 Skullstealer Greataxe C	.10	.25
❑ 190 Sulfuras, The Extinguished Hand R	1.25	3.00
❑ 191 An Ancient Awakens C	.10	.25
❑ 192 As Hyjal Burns C	.10	.25
❑ 193 The Battle Is Won, the War Goes On C	.10	.25
❑ 194 Black Heart of Flame C	.10	.25
❑ 195 Cleaning House C	.10	.25
❑ 196 If You're Not Against Us... C	.10	.25
❑ 197 Signed in Blood C	.10	.25
❑ 198 Nordrassil, the World Tree R	1.50	4.00

2012 World of Warcraft Crown of the Heavens Loot

❑ 1 Vicious Grell	5.00	12.00
❑ 2 Magical Ogre Idol	15.00	40.00
❑ 3 Corrupted Hippogryph	100.00	200.00

2012 World of Warcraft Tomb of the Forgotten

Complete Set (202)
Booster Box (36 Packs)
Booster Pack (16 Cards)

❑ 1 Dark Pharaoh Tekahn U	.20	.50
❑ 2 The Forgotten U	.20	.50
❑ 3 Nexus-Thief Asar U	.20	.50
❑ 4 Augh U	.20	.50
❑ 5 High Guardian Malosun U	.20	.50
❑ 6 Jasani, Shrine Keeper U	.20	.50
❑ 7 Mistress Nesala U	.20	.50
❑ 8 Mogdar the Frozenheart U	.20	.50
❑ 9 Thrall the Earth-Warder E	4.00	10.00
❑ 9EA Thrall the Earth-Warder E (Extended Art)		
❑ 10 Blood Parasite R	1.50	4.00
❑ 11 Boundless Winter R	.40	1.00
❑ 12 Frozen Strength U	.20	.50
❑ 13 Raise the Dead C	.10	.25
❑ 14 Siphon of Undeath U	.20	.50
❑ 15 Mark of Restoration U	.20	.50
❑ 16 Natural Purification R	.75	2.00
❑ 17 Primal Madness R	1.00	2.50
❑ 18 Wild Rejuvenation U	.20	.50
❑ 19 Wild Wrath C	.10	.25
❑ 20 Cobra Sting R	.40	1.00
❑ 21 Hunter's Focus C	.10	.25
❑ 22 Interfering Shot U	.20	.50
❑ 23 Obliterating Trap U	.20	.50
❑ 24 Ubersrc R	.75	2.00
❑ 25 Boundless Magic R	1.00	2.50
❑ 26 Firestarter R	.60	1.50
❑ 27 Polymorph: Pig U	.20	.50
❑ 28 Spark of Brilliance C	.10	.25
❑ 29 Wildfire U	.20	.50
❑ 30 Blessing of Resolution U	.20	.50
❑ 31 Divine Redemption R	.40	1.00
❑ 32 Hammer of Vengeance U	.20	.50
❑ 33 Hand of Devotion U	.20	.50
❑ 34 Monstrous Vengeance R	.75	2.00
❑ 35 Tower of Radiance R	1.00	2.50
❑ 36 Faithful Dispel U	.20	.50
❑ 37 Mind Shatter C	.10	.25
❑ 38 Monstrous Intervention R	.40	1.00
❑ 39 Power Word: Resurrection R	.40	1.00
❑ 40 Shadow Word: Corruption U	.20	.50
❑ 41 Shadowy Apparition R	3.00	8.00
❑ 42 Decisive Strike C	.10	.25
❑ 43 Extortion U	.20	.50
❑ 44 Monstrous Rush R	1.25	3.00
❑ 45 Restless Blades R	1.50	4.00
❑ 46 Slaughter R	1.00	2.50
❑ 47 Trickster's Reflex U	.20	.50
❑ 48 Ancestral Revival R	.75	2.00
❑ 49 Arc Heal U	.20	.50
❑ 50 Call of Lightning U	.20	.50
❑ 51 Force of Earth C	.10	.25
❑ 52 Unleashed Rage R	1.00	2.50
❑ 53 Boundless Hellfire R	4.00	10.00
❑ 54 Dark Intent U	.20	.50
❑ 55 Drain Soul C	.10	.25
❑ 56 Frenzied Doomguard U	.20	.50
❑ 57 Hand of Gul'dan R	.40	1.00
❑ 58 Champion's Shout R	.40	1.00
❑ 59 Concussion Blow R	.40	1.00
❑ 60 Fearless Strike U	.20	.50
❑ 61 Guardian's Endurance U	.20	.50
❑ 62 Terrifying Shout C	.10	.25
❑ 63 Thrall's Desire R	.40	1.00
❑ 64 Thrall's Doubt R	.40	1.00
❑ 65 Thrall's Fury R	.40	1.00
❑ 66 Thrall's Patience R	.40	1.00
❑ 67 Courage C	.10	.25
❑ 68 Monstrous Heal C	.10	.25

Beckett Vs System price guide sponsored by wholesalegaming.com

❑ 69 Monstrous Regeneration C	.10	.25
❑ 70 Monstrous Strength C	.10	.25
❑ 71 Power C	.10	.25
❑ 72 Wisdom C	.10	.25
❑ 73 Aaron Goodchilde R	1.50	4.00
❑ 74 Alaria the Huntress C	.10	.25
❑ 75 Ashton Barstow C	.10	.25
❑ 76 Baradis Darkstone C	.10	.25
❑ 77 Bishop Ketodo C	.10	.25
❑ 78 Crankston Deathspark C	.10	.25
❑ 79 Darkstalker Soran E	2.50	6.00
❑ 80 Earthseer Dambrak R	.40	1.00
❑ 81 Elementalist Arax U	.20	.50
❑ 82 Goetia C	.10	.25
❑ 83 Gretta Grindstone U	.20	.50
❑ 84 Jaelen the Ripper R	1.50	4.00
❑ 85 Jarius Blackwood U	.20	.50
❑ 86 Kalaan C	.10	.25
❑ 87 Kedan Burstbeard C	.10	.25
❑ 88 Kraven the Gravebound U	.20	.50
❑ 89 Naasi C	.10	.25
❑ 90 Philosopher Kirlenko U	.20	.50
❑ 91 Renzo Soulfang R	.75	2.00
❑ 92 Sergeant Corsetti C	.10	.25
❑ 93 Shadowseer Thraner U	.20	.50
❑ 94 Taliax the Ironjaw R	.40	1.00
❑ 95 Velen, Prophet of the Naaru E	1.50	4.00
❑ 96 Zalabar the Dark Tinkerer R	.40	1.00
❑ 97 Amara Kells C	.10	.25
❑ 98 Brulu Breaks-the-Land U	.20	.50
❑ 99 Daedak the Graveborne R	10.00	25.00
❑ 100 Dakturak C	.10	.25
❑ 101 Deathguard Ashleigh R	.60	1.50
❑ 102 Galvano the Beast Lord E	2.50	6.00
❑ 103 Grok Goreblade C	.10	.25
❑ 104 Harudu Cloudshot C	.10	.25
❑ 105 Ishael Bloodlight C	.10	.25
❑ 106 Kaelzin C	.10	.25
❑ 107 Lor'themar Theron, Regent Lord E	4.00	10.00
❑ 108 Nadina the Red R	2.50	6.00
❑ 109 Raso'jin U	.20	.50
❑ 110 Seraxa Brightmix R	1.00	2.50
❑ 111 Sludgelauncher Krillzix R	.40	1.00
❑ 112 Soulstealer Adams U	.20	.50
❑ 113 Sunstalker Maelan C	.10	.25
❑ 114 Thanu Sunhorn U	.20	.50
❑ 115 Trickster Tesslah C	.10	.25
❑ 116 Veliana Felblood U	.20	.50
❑ 117 Wrex C	.10	.25
❑ 118 Yunzo the Hexer U	.20	.50
❑ 119 Zanrix Steelboot C	.10	.25
❑ 120 Zindalan R	.40	1.00
❑ 121 General Husam E	12.00	30.00
❑ 122 Harbinger Sefu R	1.00	2.50
❑ 123 High Oracle Naseem R	.75	2.00
❑ 124 Neferset Bladelord C	.10	.25
❑ 125 Neferset Champion C	.10	.25
❑ 126 Neferset Darkcaster C	.10	.25
❑ 127 Neferset Frostbringer C	.10	.25
❑ 128 Neferset Runecaster C	.10	.25
❑ 129 Neferset Scorpid Keeper C	.10	.25
❑ 130 Neferset Sentry U	.20	.50
❑ 131 Neferset Shadowlancer C	.10	.25
❑ 132 Neferset Shadowstalker U	.20	.50
❑ 133 Neferset Shieldguard U	.20	.50
❑ 134 Okumet, Herald of the Light U	.20	.50
❑ 135 Taluret, Herald of Faith U	.20	.50
❑ 136 Dun'zarg C	.10	.25
❑ 137 Gorlash, Herald of the Elements U	.20	.50
❑ 138 Korbash the Devastator R	.40	1.00
❑ 139 Mok'drul U	.20	.50
❑ 140 Zog, Herald of Death U	.20	.50
❑ 141 Zores, Herald of War U	.20	.50
❑ 142 Zuglisch C	.10	.25
❑ 143 Frizzlight C	.10	.25
❑ 144 Nargle, Fang of the Swarm E	1.50	4.00
❑ 145 Ragespike C	.10	.25
❑ 146 Shiverspine U	.20	.50
❑ 147 Slimefin U	.20	.50
❑ 148 Swifteye R	.75	2.00
❑ 149 Kresss, Herald of the Hunt U	.20	.50
❑ 150 Pythisss, Herald of Frost U	.20	.50
❑ 151 Araxian, Herald of Trickery U	.20	.50
❑ 152 Bazul, Herald of the Fel U	.20	.50
❑ 153 Akhet R	.40	1.00
❑ 154 Lockmaw R	.75	2.00
❑ 155 Obsidian Colossus R	1.25	3.00
❑ 156 Pygmy Firebreather C	.10	.25
❑ 157 Pygmy Pyramid E	25.00	50.00
❑ 158 Renshol, Herald of Nature U	.20	.50
❑ 159 Siamat, Lord of the South Wind E	1.50	4.00
❑ 160 Sand Scarab U	.20	.50
❑ 161 Aggra R	3.00	8.00
❑ 162 Harrison Jones R	.40	1.00
❑ 163 White Camel E	1.50	4.00
❑ 164 Anraphet's Regalia C	.10	.25
❑ 165 Bulwark of the Primordial Mound U	.20	.50
❑ 166 Flickering Cowl U	.20	.50
❑ 167 Flickering Shoulders C	.10	.25
❑ 168 Gloves of Dissolving Smoke U	.20	.50
❑ 169 Helm of Blazing Glory R	.40	1.00
❑ 170 Helm of Setesh U	.20	.50
❑ 171 Mantle of Master Cho U	.20	.50
❑ 172 Pauldrons of Roaring Flame C	.10	.25
❑ 173 Poison Fang Bracers U	.20	.50
❑ 174 Scalp of the Bandit Prince R	.75	2.00
❑ 175 Ammunae, Construct of Life R	.40	1.00
❑ 176 Isiset, Construct of Magic R	.40	1.00
❑ 177 Rajh, Construct of the Sun R	.75	2.00
❑ 178 Setesh, Construct of Destruction R	.75	2.00
❑ 179 Apparatus of Khaz'goroth C	.10	.25
❑ 180 Rune of Zeth C	.10	.25
❑ 181 Spurious Sarcophagus R	.40	1.00
❑ 182 Variable Pulse Lightning Capacitor R	1.25	3.00
❑ 183 Barim's Main Cauche U	.20	.50
❑ 184 Bitling Wind U	.20	.50
❑ 185 Fandral's Flamescythe C	.10	.25
❑ 186 Feeding Frenzy R	1.50	4.00
❑ 187 Hammer of Sparks U	.20	.50
❑ 188 Ko'gun, Hammer of the Firelord R	.75	2.00
❑ 189 Lava Bolt Crossbow U	.20	.50
❑ 190 Obsidium Cleaver C	.10	.25
❑ 191 Overpowered Chicken Splitter C	.10	.25
❑ 192 Ruthless Gladiator's Decapitator R	.40	1.00
❑ 193 Scepter of Power U	.20	.50
❑ 194 Spire of Scarlet Pain U	.20	.50
❑ 195 Zoid's Firelit Greatsword U	.20	.50
❑ 196 The Defense of Nahom C	.10	.25
❑ 197 The Fall of Neferst City C	.10	.25
❑ 198 Gnomebliteration C	.10	.25
❑ 199 Tailgunner C	.10	.25
❑ 200 Thieving Little Pluckers C	.10	.25
❑ 201 Traitors! C	.10	.25
❑ 202 Uldum R	.40	1.00

2012 World of Warcraft Tomb of the Forgotten Loot

❑ 1 Sand Scarab	3.00	8.00
❑ 2 Spurious Sarcophagus	8.00	20.00
❑ 3 White Camel	50.00	100.00

2012 World of Warcraft War of the Ancients

Complete Set (240)
Booster Box (36 packs)
Booster Pack (15 cards)

❑ 1 Malorne the White Stag E	2.50	6.00
❑ 1EA Malorne the White Stag (Extended Art)	10.00	25.00
❑ 2 Beyond the Grave R	.60	1.50
❑ 3 Crushing Death U	.20	.50
❑ 4 Death's Decree U	.20	.50
❑ 5 Despair of Winter R	1.50	4.00
❑ 6 Ebon Plague R	1.25	3.00
❑ 7 Festering Disease U	.20	.50
❑ 8 Frigid Frailty C	.10	.25
❑ 9 Ancient Bear Form U	.20	.50
❑ 10 Euphoria R	.60	1.50
❑ 11 Lions, Tigers, and Bears R	.60	1.50
❑ 12 Mark of Growth U	.20	.50
❑ 13 Mark of Malorne C	.10	.25
❑ 14 Wild Attunement R	.60	1.50
❑ 15 Wild Seeds U	.20	.50
❑ 16 Arrowstorm C	.10	.25
❑ 17 Bear Trap U	.20	.50
❑ 18 Beast Mastery R	2.00	5.00
❑ 19 Endure R	.60	1.50
❑ 20 Furious George U	.20	.50
❑ 21 Skitter R	.60	1.50
❑ 22 Arcane Potency R	2.50	6.00
❑ 23 Arcane Unraveling U	.20	.50
❑ 24 Conjure Elementals R	.60	1.50
❑ 25 Firestorm U	.20	.50
❑ 26 Ice Prison C	.10	.25
❑ 27 Manaflow R	.60	1.50
❑ 28 Reckless Fireball U	.20	.50
❑ 29 Blessing of Vigilance U	.20	.50
❑ 30 Crusader's Might R	.60	1.50
❑ 31 Divinity R	.60	1.50
❑ 32 Guardian of the Light R	.75	2.00
❑ 33 Hammer of Sanctity U	.20	.50
❑ 34 Holy Ground U	.20	.50
❑ 35 Shield of Light C	.10	.25
❑ 36 Gifted Heal U	.20	.50
❑ 37 Guardian Spirit R	.60	1.50
❑ 38 Mind Crush U	.20	.50
❑ 39 Power Word: Tenacity R	.60	1.50
❑ 40 Redeeming Dispel C	.10	.25
❑ 41 Shadow Word: Devour R	.60	1.50
❑ 42 Spirit Shield U	.20	.50
❑ 43 Devious Dismantle U	.20	.50
❑ 44 Guise of the Stalker U	.20	.50
❑ 45 Hands of Deceit R	.75	2.00
❑ 46 Hidden Strike C	.10	.25
❑ 47 Kiss of Death R	.75	2.00
❑ 48 Opportunity R	.60	1.50
❑ 49 Volatile Poison U	.20	.50
❑ 50 Elemental Echo R	.60	1.50
❑ 51 Elemental Purge U	.20	.50
❑ 52 Gale Force C	.10	.25
❑ 53 Lava Strike U	.20	.50
❑ 54 Scalding Totem U	.20	.50
❑ 55 Spark of Rage R	.60	1.50
❑ 56 Spirit Link Totem R	.60	1.50
❑ 57 Call the Void U	.20	.50
❑ 58 Demonic Infusion U	.20	.50
❑ 59 Gaktai C	.10	.25
❑ 60 Netherpocalypse R	.75	2.00
❑ 61 Nightfall R	2.00	5.00
❑ 62 Nimanda R	.60	1.50
❑ 63 Soul Trap U	.20	.50
❑ 64 Blind Rage U	.20	.50
❑ 65 Bloodthirsty Shout C	.10	.25
❑ 66 Combat Stance R	.75	2.00
❑ 67 Decimate U	.20	.50
❑ 68 Raging Blow R	.60	1.50
❑ 69 Ruthless Execution U	.20	.50
❑ 70 Strife R	1.50	4.00
❑ 71 Blitz C	.10	.25
❑ 72 Focused Heal C	.10	.25
❑ 73 Legacy of Stormrage E	2.00	5.00
❑ 74 Legacy of the Legion E	20.00	40.00
❑ 75 Vigilant Guard C	.10	.25
❑ 76 Glory to the Alliance! C	.10	.25
❑ 77 Blood and Thunder! C	.10	.25
❑ 78 Burn Away C	.10	.25
❑ 79 Elune's Blessing C	.10	.25
❑ 80 Shattering Blow C	.10	.25
❑ 81 Strike C	.10	.25
❑ 82 Alpha Prime R	.60	1.50
❑ 83 Ansem, Timewalker Deathblade R	1.00	2.50
❑ 84 Bolin Moonflare U	.20	.50
❑ 85 Darkshire Deathsworn C	.10	.25
❑ 86 Darlon Blacksoul U	.20	.50
❑ 87 Darnassus Mooncaller C	.10	.25
❑ 88 Darnassus Shadowblade C	.10	.25
❑ 89 Darnassus Warrior C	.10	.25
❑ 90 Delinar Silvershot U	.20	.50
❑ 91 Eldre'Thalas Sorceress C	.10	.25
❑ 92 Elysa Lockewood U	.20	.50
❑ 93 Fimlet Sparklight U	.20	.50
❑ 94 Hugh Mann U	.20	.50
❑ 95 Ian Barus U	.20	.50
❑ 96 Jaal U	.20	.50
❑ 97 Jarod Shadowsong R	1.50	4.00
❑ 98 Lady Bancroft C	.10	.25
❑ 99 Lara, Timewalker Commander R	.60	1.50
❑ 100 Lexie Silverblade U	.20	.50
❑ 101EA Lord Kur'talos Ravencrest (Extended Art)	30.00	60.00
❑ 101 Lord Kur'talos Ravencrest E	20.00	40.00
❑ 102 Nalisa Nightbreeze U	.20	.50
❑ 103 Northshire Cleric C	.10	.25
❑ 104 Northshire Crusader C	.10	.25
❑ 105 Nyala Shadefury U	.20	.50
❑ 106 Rhonin the Time-Lost E	4.00	10.00
❑ 107 Shadowglen Stalker C	.10	.25
❑ 108 Shandris Feathermoon R	2.00	5.00
❑ 109 SI:7 Assassin C	.10	.25
❑ 110 Stella Bellamy U	.20	.50
❑ 111 Stormwind Summoner C	.10	.25
❑ 112 Tarwila Gladespring C	.10	.25
❑ 113 Teldrassil Tracker C	.10	.25
❑ 114 Teldrassil Wildguard C	.10	.25
❑ 115 Tessa Black E	3.00	8.00
❑ 116 Timewalker Guard C	.10	.25
❑ 117 Timewalker Lightsworn C	.10	.25
❑ 118 Timewalker Sentinel C	.10	.25
❑ 119 Toraan, Eye of O'ros R	.60	1.50
❑ 120 Virgil, Timewalker Marshal R	.60	1.50
❑ 121 Ahul Moonspeaker U	.20	.50
❑ 122 Baine, Son of Cairne E	1.25	3.00
❑ 123 Belmaril, Timewalker Bloodmage R	.60	1.50
❑ 124 Bhenn Checks-the-Sky C	.10	.25
❑ 125 Bloodsoul C	.10	.25
❑ 126 Dawnhoof Brightcaller C	.10	.25
❑ 127 Drom'kor, Timewalker Necrolyte R	.60	1.50
❑ 128 Durotar Flamecaster C	.10	.25
❑ 129 Durotar Frostblade C	.10	.25
❑ 130 Ellen Burroughs U	.20	.50
❑ 131 Garrosh, Son of Grom E	8.00	20.00
❑ 131EA Garrosh, Son of Grom (Extended Art)	30.00	60.00
❑ 132 Garyk Stormcrier U	.20	.50
❑ 133 Jevan Grimtotem R	.60	1.50
❑ 134 Kahul the Sunseer R	3.00	8.00
❑ 135 Klandark U	.20	.50
❑ 136 Mulgore Deathwalker C	.10	.25
❑ 137 Mulgore Guardian C	.10	.25
❑ 138 Orgrimmar Heartstriker C	.10	.25
❑ 139 Orgrimmar Killblade C	.10	.25
❑ 140 Orgrimmar Marksman C	.10	.25
❑ 141 Orox Darkhorn U	.20	.50
❑ 142 Razor Hill Assassin C	.10	.25
❑ 143 Razor Hill Spiritseer C	.10	.25
❑ 144 Ror Tramplehoof U	.20	.50
❑ 145 Shaka Deadmark U	.20	.50
❑ 146 Soulrender Keldah U	.20	.50
❑ 147 Stafa'jul U	.20	.50
❑ 148 Takara, Timewalker Warlord R	2.50	6.00
❑ 149 Thunder Bluff Spiritwalker C	.10	.25
❑ 150 Thunder Bluff Steelsnout C	.10	.25
❑ 151 Thunder Bluff Sunwalker C	.10	.25
❑ 152 Thunder Bluff Wildheart C	.10	.25
❑ 153 Tilu Plainstalker U	.20	.50
❑ 154 Timewalker Grunt C	.10	.25
❑ 155 Timewalker Sunguard C	.10	.25
❑ 156 Toho Bloomhorn U	.20	.50
❑ 157 Torzuk Soulfang E	8.00	20.00
❑ 158 Vorgo, Timewalker Stormlord R	2.00	5.00
❑ 159 Xarantaur R	.60	1.50
❑ 160 Zarim Redskull U	.20	.50
❑ 161 Agamaggan R	.60	1.50
❑ 162 Aviana the Reborn R	.60	1.50
❑ 163 Azgalor the Pit Lord E	2.50	6.00
❑ 164 Azzinoth R	.60	1.50
❑ 165 Blazing Infernal C	.10	.25
❑ 166 Child of Agamaggan C	.10	.25
❑ 167 Child of Aviana C	.10	.25
❑ 168 Child of Goldrinn C	.10	.25
❑ 169 Child of Tortolla C	.10	.25
❑ 170 Child of Ursoc C	.10	.25
❑ 171 Child of Ursol C	.10	.25
❑ 172 Corrupted Furbolg U	.20	.50
❑ 173 Eye of the Legion C	.10	.25
❑ 174 Feldrake R	1.25	3.00
❑ 175 Felguard Marauder C	.10	.25
❑ 176 Frenzied Felhound C	.10	.25
❑ 177 Frenzyfin U	.20	.50
❑ 178 Furbolg Avenger C	.10	.25
❑ 179 Furbolg Chieftain U	.20	.50
❑ 180 Furbolg Firecaller C	.10	.25
❑ 181 Goldrinn R	1.00	2.50
❑ 182 Hulking Helboar C	.10	.25
❑ 183 Jadefire Netherseer U	.20	.50
❑ 184 Jadefire Soulstealer U	.20	.50
❑ 185 Keening Shivarra U	.20	.50
❑ 186 Keeper Yarashal C	.10	.25
❑ 187 Leafbeard, Ancient of Lore U	.20	.50
❑ 188 Legion Fel Reaver U	.20	.50
❑ 189 Mo'arg Doomsmith U	.20	.50
❑ 190 Monstrous Terrorguard U	.20	.50
❑ 191 Mossbark, Ancient of War C	.10	.25
❑ 192 Neltharion the Earth-Warder E	2.00	5.00
❑ 193 Peroth'arn R	.60	1.50
❑ 194 Rampaging Furbolg C	.10	.25
❑ 195 Scheming Dreadlord C	.10	.25
❑ 196 Sinister Watcher C	.10	.25
❑ 197 Strongroot, Ancient of War U	.20	.50
❑ 198 Tortolla R	.75	2.00
❑ 199 Trogg Earthrager C	.10	.25
❑ 200 Unstoppable Abyssal C	.10	.25
❑ 201 Ursoc the Mighty R	.60	1.50
❑ 202 Ursol the Wise R	.60	1.50
❑ 203 Void Terror C	.10	.25
❑ 204 Volatile Terrorfiend U	.20	.50
❑ 205 Warmaul Ogre C	.10	.25
❑ 206 Dungard Ironcutter R	.60	1.50
❑ 207 Earthen Crusher C	.10	.25
❑ 208 Girdle of the Queen's Champion C	.10	.25
❑ 209 Helm of Thorns C	.10	.25
❑ 210 Historian's Sash U	.20	.50
❑ 211 Legguards of the Legion R	.75	2.00
❑ 212 Spaulders of Eternity C	.10	.25
❑ 213 Darnassus Tabard U	.20	.50
❑ 214 Demon Hunter's Aspect U	.20	.50
❑ 215 Grand Marshal's Tome of Power U	.20	.50
❑ 216 Orgrimmar Tabard U	.20	.50
❑ 217 Signet of the Timewalker U	.20	.50
❑ 218 Stormwind Tabard U	.20	.50
❑ 219 Tabard of the Legion U	.20	.50
❑ 220 Thunder Bluff Tabard U	.20	.50
❑ 221 Arathar, the Eye of Flame U	.20	.50
❑ 222 Axe of Cenarius E	3.00	8.00
❑ 223 Axe of the Tauren Chieftains C	.10	.25
❑ 224 Crescent Wand R	.60	1.50
❑ 225 Gavel of Peroth'arn R	.60	1.50
❑ 226 High Warlord's Cleaver U	.20	.50
❑ 227 Pit Lord's Destroyer C	.10	.25
❑ 228 Scepter of Azshara R	.60	1.50
❑ 229 Stalk of Corruption U	.20	.50
❑ 230 Trickster's Edge R	.60	1.50
❑ 231 Wand of the Demonsoul C	.10	.25
❑ 232 Archival Purposes C	.10	.25
❑ 233 The Caverns of Time U	.20	.50
❑ 234 Documenting the Timeways C	.10	.25
❑ 235 The End Time U	.20	.50
❑ 236 In Unending Numbers U	.20	.50
❑ 237 The Path to the Dragon Soul C	.10	.25
❑ 238 The Vainglorious C	.10	.25
❑ 239 The Well of Eternity C	.10	.25

❑ 240 Zin-Azshari R .60 1.50
❑ T1 Human Warrior TOKEN .10 .25
❑ T2 Orc Warrior TOKEN .10 .25

2012 World of Warcraft War of the Ancients Loot

❑ 1 Eye of the Legion 3.00 8.00
❑ 2 Demon Hunter's Aspect 12.00 30.00
❑ 3 Feldrake 150.00 250.00

2013 World of Warcraft Betrayal of the Guardian

Complete Set (202)
Booster Box (36 Packs)
Booster Pack (16 Cards)

❑ 1 Aegwynn, Guardian of Tirisfal E 1.50 4.00
❑ 1EA Aegwynn, Guardian of Tirisfal (Extended Art) 10.00 25.00
❑ 2 Bone Shield R .60 1.50
❑ 3 Corruption of the Ages R .75 2.00
❑ 4 Grim Touch R .40 1.00
❑ 5 Hand of Dread C .10 .25
❑ 6 Soul Pox U .20 .50
❑ 7 Timeless Undeath U .20 .50
❑ 8 Ancient Moonkin Form R 1.25 3.00
❑ 9 Feral Prowess C .10 .25
❑ 10 Living Seed R .50 1.25
❑ 11 Roar of the Ages R .75 2.00
❑ 12 Thorns of Nordrassil U .20 .50
❑ 13 Timeless Bounty U .20 .50
❑ 14 Biley C .10 .25
❑ 15 Gahz'rilla E 6.00 15.00
❑ 16 Intervening Shot U .20 .50
❑ 17 Piercing Shots R 2.00 5.00
❑ 18 Timeless Aim U .20 .50
❑ 19 Wrath of the Ages R .50 1.25
❑ 20 Arcane Shock U .20 .50
❑ 21 Critical Mass R .75 2.00
❑ 22 Flame Volley C .10 .25
❑ 23 Frost Stasis R 1.50 4.00
❑ 24 Secrets of the Ages R .50 1.25
❑ 25 Timeless Arcana U .20 .50
❑ 26 Blessing of the Pure C .10 .25
❑ 27 Crusade of Kings R 1.50 4.00
❑ 28 Guardian of the Ages R .60 1.50
❑ 29 Light of Dawn R .75 2.00
❑ 30 Light's Vengeance U .20 .50
❑ 31 Timeless Light U .20 .50
❑ 32 Dark Deliverance C .10 .25
❑ 33 Holy Word: Hope U .20 .50
❑ 34 Power Word: Spirit R .75 2.00
❑ 35 Prayer of the Ages R .50 1.25
❑ 36 Psychic Horror R .40 1.00
❑ 37 Timeless Agony U .20 .50
❑ 38 Fast-Acting Poison U .20 .50
❑ 39 No Mercy R 1.25 3.00
❑ 40 Timeless Deception U .20 .50
❑ 41 Venomous Wounds R .40 1.00
❑ 42 Cloudburst R .50 1.25
❑ 43 Freezing Rain Totem U .20 .50
❑ 44 Magma Blast C .10 .25
❑ 45 Static Shock R 1.00 2.50
❑ 46 Storm of the Ages R .50 1.25
❑ 47 Timeless Winds U .20 .50
❑ 48 Curse of the Fel R .75 2.00
❑ 49 Demonic Rebirth R .60 1.50
❑ 50 Fel Inversion C .10 .25
❑ 51 Ritual of the Ages R .50 1.25
❑ 52 Thoglos U .20 .50
❑ 53 Timeless Shadow U .20 .50
❑ 54 Bastion of Defense R 1.25 3.00
❑ 55 Brutal Steel R .50 1.25
❑ 56 Fortified Defenses U .20 .50
❑ 57 Fury of the Ages R .40 1.00
❑ 58 Timeless Resilience U .20 .50
❑ 59 Legacy of Betrayal E 20.00 50.00
❑ 60 More Work? C .10 .25
❑ 61 Sigil of the Legion C .10 .25
❑ 62 Archdruid Fandral Staghelm R 8.00 20.00
❑ 63 Belthira the Black Thorn E 10.00 25.00
❑ 64 Danath Trollbane R 1.50 4.00
❑ 65 Darris Leafshade U .20 .50
❑ 66 Dwarf Demolitionist U .20 .50
❑ 67 Elistari Silverwind U .20 .50
❑ 68 General Turalyon E 2.50 6.00
❑ 69 Gnomish Flying Machine U .20 .50
❑ 70 Human Darkweaver C .10 .25
❑ 71 Human Footman C .10 .25
❑ 72 Human Knight C .10 .25
❑ 73 Human Operative C .10 .25
❑ 74 Human Peasant C .10 .25
❑ 75 Human Sniper C .10 .25
❑ 76 Khadgar R .75 2.00
❑ 77 Lady Voltaire R .40 1.00
❑ 78 Loremaster Pooth R .50 1.25
❑ 79 Myro Lumastis U .20 .50
❑ 80 Night Elf Arcanist C .10 .25
❑ 81 Night Elf Bladedancer C .10 .25
❑ 82 Night Elf Grovewalker C .10 .25
❑ 83 Night Elf Moon Priestess C .10 .25
❑ 84 Night Elf Ranger C .10 .25
❑ 85 Night Elf Swiftblade C .10 .25
❑ 86 Thane Kurdran Wildhammer R .40 1.00
❑ 87 Virendra Moonglow U .20 .50
❑ 88 Xander Blackcrow U .20 .50
❑ 89 Blood Knight Lynesta R .40 1.00
❑ 90 Chora Cloudspeaker U .20 .50
❑ 91 Dohna Darksky U .20 .50
❑ 92 Draka R 2.50 6.00
❑ 93 Durotan R .50 1.25
❑ 94 Farseer Horgath R .40 1.00
❑ 95 Goblin Sapper U .20 .50
❑ 96 Korah Icefang U .20 .50
❑ 97 Korgen Skullcleaver U .20 .50
❑ 98 Magatha Grimtotem R .40 1.00
❑ 99 Makuna Hatada E 8.00 20.00
❑ 100 Orc Blackblade C .10 .25
❑ 101 Orc Flamecaller C .10 .25
❑ 102 Orc Grunt C .10 .25
❑ 103 Orc Necrolyte C .10 .25
❑ 104 Orc Peon C .10 .25
❑ 105 Orgrim Doomhammer E 2.00 5.00
❑ 106 Tauren Deathwalker C .10 .25
❑ 107 Tauren Lightcaller C .10 .25
❑ 108 Tauren Mystic C .10 .25
❑ 109 Tauren Plainsrider C .10 .25
❑ 110 Tauren Sunhoof C .10 .25
❑ 111 Tauren Tracker C .10 .25
❑ 112 Tauren Wildmender C .10 .25
❑ 113 Troll Axethrower U .20 .50
❑ 114 Zafira Ragebolt U .20 .50
❑ 115 Zul'jin R 2.50 6.00
❑ 116 Blanca, Timewalker Mage U .20 .50
❑ 117 Enabrin, Timewalker Druid U .20 .50
❑ 118 Lyra, Timewalker Embermage U .20 .50
❑ 119 Moro, Timewalker Druid U .20 .50
❑ 120 Nazzik, Timewalker Trickster R .40 1.00
❑ 121 Nehru, Timewalker Hunter U .20 .50
❑ 122 Timewalker Juggernaut C .10 .25
❑ 123 Timewalker Shadowseer C .10 .25
❑ 124 Timewalker Smasher C .10 .25
❑ 125 Timewalker Vanguard C .10 .25
❑ 126 Watsun, Timewalker Lightshield R 2.00 5.00
❑ 127 Zor'ka, Timewalker Shaman U .20 .50
❑ 128 Arcane Anomaly C .10 .25
❑ 129 Arcane Protector U .20 .50
❑ 130 The Big Bad Wolf R .60 1.50
❑ 131 Bigbelly, Furbolg Chieftain R .75 2.00
❑ 132 Blackfang Tarantula C .10 .25
❑ 133 Darkwater Crocolisk C .10 .25
❑ 134 Doom Commander Zaakuul E 5.00 12.00
❑ 135 Doomguard Soldier C .10 .25
❑ 136 Durnholde Tracking Hound C .10 .25
❑ 137 Enslaved Red Dragon U .20 .50
❑ 138 Eredar Deathbringer C .10 .25
❑ 139 Ethereal Spellfilcher U .20 .50
❑ 140 Ethereal Thief U .20 .50
❑ 141 Felguard Annihilator C .10 .25
❑ 142 Frostwolf C .10 .25
❑ 143 Furbolg Shaman C .10 .25
❑ 144 Ghostly Charger R .50 1.25
❑ 145 Greater Fleshbeast C .10 .25
❑ 146 Highland Lion C .10 .25
❑ 147 Karazhan Concubine C .10 .25
❑ 148 Kil'rek R .75 2.00
❑ 149 Moroes R 4.00 10.00
❑ 150 Nightbane E 2.00 5.00
❑ 151 Prince Malchezaar E 4.00 10.00
❑ 152 Ravenous Furbolg C .10 .25
❑ 153 Servant of Terestian C .10 .25
❑ 154 Shade of Aran R 4.00 10.00
❑ 155 Shadowmoon Mage C .10 .25
❑ 156 Shivarra Deathspeaker C .10 .25
❑ 157 Snappyfin R .50 1.25
❑ 158 Spawn of Hyakiss U .20 .50
❑ 159 Spawn of Rokad U .20 .50
❑ 160 Spawn of Shadikith U .20 .50
❑ 161 Terestian Illhoof R .75 2.00
❑ 162 Vile Watcher C .10 .25
❑ 163 Voidshrieker C .10 .25
❑ 164 Wildhammer Gryphon U .20 .50
❑ 165 Wrathguard Defender C .10 .25
❑ 166 Floating Spellbook C .10 .25
❑ 167 Don Carlos' Famous Hat U .20 .50
❑ 168 Durotan's Battle Harness U .20 .50
❑ 169 Gauntlets of the Ancient Frostwolf U .20 .50
❑ 170 Khadgar's Kilt of Abjuration U .20 .50
❑ 171 Mantle of Abrahmis R 2.00 5.00
❑ 172 Royal Crest of Lordaeron R .40 1.00
❑ 173 VanCleef's Boots R 1.25 3.00
❑ 174 Dark Portal Hearthstone U .20 .50
❑ 175 Time-Bending Gem C .10 .25
❑ 176 Moroes' Lucky Pocket Watch U .20 .50
❑ 177 Atiesh, Greatstaff of the Guardian E 3.00 8.00
❑ 178 Bloodfire Greatstaff C .10 .25
❑ 179 Despair R .40 1.00
❑ 180 Fool's Bane R 1.50 4.00
❑ 181 Hellscream Slicer U .20 .50
❑ 182 Lothar's Edge U .20 .50
❑ 183 Millennium Blade C .10 .25
❑ 184 Quel'Serrar C .10 .25
❑ 185 Riftmaker R .75 2.00
❑ 186 Shard of the Virtuous U .20 .50
❑ 187 Staff of Infinite Mysteries R .40 1.00
❑ 188 Time-Shifted Dagger C .10 .25
❑ 189 Vagaries of Time C .10 .25
❑ 190 Warglaive of Azzinoth E 8.00 20.00
❑ 191 Windrunner's Bow R 1.25 3.00
❑ 192 Assault on Blackrock Spire U .20 .50
❑ 193 The Fall of Lordaeron U .20 .50
❑ 194 The Black Morass C .10 .25
❑ 195 A Demonic Presence U .20 .50
❑ 196 Escape from Durnholde C .10 .25
❑ 197 The Master's Touch C .10 .25
❑ 198 Medivh's Journal C .10 .25
❑ 199 The Opening of the Dark Portal C .10 .25
❑ 200 Taretha's Diversion C .10 .25
❑ 201 Capital City, Lordaeron R .75 2.00
❑ 202 Blackrock Spire R 1.50 4.00

2013 World of Warcraft Betrayal of the Guardian Loot

❑ 1 Floating Spellbook 4.00 10.00
❑ 2 Dark Portal Hearthstone 15.00 40.00
❑ 3 Ghostly Charger 150.00 250.00

2013 World of Warcraft Reign of Fire

Complete Set (197)
Booster Box (36 Packs)
Booster Pack (16 Cards)

❑ 1 Medivh the Prophet E 3.00 8.00
❑ 1EA Medivh the Prophet (Extended Art) 6.00 15.00
❑ 2 Kil'jaeden the Deceiver E 2.00 5.00
❑ 3 Gravebound C .10 .25
❑ 4 Howling Blast R 2.50 6.00
❑ 5 Numbing Cold U .15 .40
❑ 6 Rune of Vengeance R .30 .75
❑ 7 Vilegut R 1.50 4.00
❑ 8 Will from Beyond U .15 .40
❑ 9 Agile Cat Form U .15 .40
❑ 10 Blood in the Water R .40 1.00
❑ 11 Lunar Barrage R .75 2.00
❑ 12 Nurture R .60 1.50
❑ 13 Snare from Beyond U .15 .40
❑ 14 Wild Harmony C .10 .25
❑ 15 Counterattack R .40 1.00
❑ 16 Dakota R 1.00 2.50
❑ 17 Disrupting Shot U .15 .40
❑ 18 Ravenous Frenzy C .10 .25
❑ 19 Track from Beyond U .15 .40
❑ 20 Unleash the Beasts R .30 .75
❑ 21 Arcane Breach U .15 .40
❑ 22 Flames from Beyond U .15 .40
❑ 23 Mass Teleport R .30 .75
❑ 24 Permafrost R .30 .75
❑ 25 Phoenix R 1.50 4.00
❑ 26 Temporal Shift C .10 .25
❑ 27 Blaze of Light C .10 .25
❑ 28 Blessing from Beyond U .15 .40
❑ 29 Blinding Word R 2.00 5.00
❑ 30 Heroic Bulwark U .15 .40
❑ 31 Mass Redemption R .30 .75
❑ 32 Zealotry R .40 1.00
❑ 33 Lightlance U .15 .40
❑ 34 Power Word: Bravery R .30 .75
❑ 35 Shadows from Beyond U .15 .40
❑ 36 Soul Warding R .60 1.50
❑ 37 Splintered Thought R .75 2.00
❑ 38 Spook C .10 .25
❑ 39 Bounty Hunt C .10 .25
❑ 40 Malice From Beyond U .15 .40
❑ 41 Savage Combat R .60 1.50
❑ 42 Smoke Screen U .15 .40
❑ 43 Torturous Poison R .30 .75
❑ 44 Ancestral Renewal R .30 .75
❑ 45 Feedback R .40 1.00
❑ 46 Lust for Battle C .10 .25
❑ 47 Magnetic Totem R .75 2.00
❑ 48 Tempest Elemental U .15 .40
❑ 49 Totem from Beyond U .25 .60
❑ 50 Curse from Beyond U .15 .40
❑ 51 Havoc R .40 1.00
❑ 52 Life Drain C .10 .25
❑ 53 Nether Rip R 1.00 2.50
❑ 54 Soulbond U .15 .40
❑ 55 Zhar'doom R 1.00 2.50
❑ 56 Bladewhirl R .40 1.00
❑ 57 Blade Strike U .15 .40
❑ 58 Howl from Beyond C .10 .25
❑ 59 Impale R .30 .75
❑ 60 Tactical Mastery R .30 .75
❑ 61 Thundercrash C .10 .25
❑ 62 Call of C'Thun R .30 .75
❑ 63 Call of Yogg-Saron R .30 .75
❑ 64 Dodge C .10 .25
❑ 65 Legacy of the Horde E 3.00 8.00
❑ 66 Legacy of Lordaeron E 1.50 4.00
❑ 67 Savage Beatdown C .10 .25
❑ 68 Alana the Hopebringer E 1.50 4.00
❑ 69 Alethar the Blightspreader R 1.00 2.50
❑ 70 Ashenvale Acolyte C .10 .25
❑ 71 Ashenvale Archer C .10 .25
❑ 72 Ashenvale Illusionist C .10 .25
❑ 73 Daniel Darkheart U .15 .40
❑ 74 Disciple of the Light C .10 .25
❑ 75 Druid of the Talon U .15 .40
❑ 76 Elwynn Burglar C .10 .25
❑ 77 Elwynn Huntsman C .10 .25
❑ 78 Emora Delwin U .15 .40
❑ 79 Felwood Grovestalker C .10 .25
❑ 80 Goran, Timewalker Lavacaller U .15 .40
❑ 81 Grand Admiral Daelin Proudmoore R .50 1.25
❑ 82 Huntress C .10 .25
❑ 83 Jaina, Apprentice of Antonidas R .75 2.00
❑ 84 Johnny B. Goode U .15 .40
❑ 85 Komma, Timewalker Graveguard U .15 .40
❑ 86 Ky'lai Darkblood U .15 .40
❑ 87 Lunaris Silverfrost U .15 .40
❑ 88 Mias the Fair C .10 .25
❑ 89 Muradin, Bronzebeard Adventurer R .75 2.00
❑ 90 Naisha R 3.00 8.00
❑ 91 Stormwind Recruit C .10 .25
❑ 92 Warden Maiev E 4.00 10.00
❑ 93 The Widow Deadsie R .40 1.00
❑ 94 Adonal Brokenhoof U .15 .40
❑ 95 Blackrock Shooter C .10 .25
❑ 96 Blurg Firekin U .15 .40
❑ 97 Bor Breakfist U .15 .40
❑ 98 Dawnstrider Sunward C .10 .25
❑ 99 Drek'Thar, Frostwolf General R .30 .75
❑ 100 Grom Hellscream R .40 1.00
❑ 101 Haro Setting-Sun U .15 .40
❑ 102 High Chieftain Cairne Bloodhoof E 1.25 3.00
❑ 103 High Warlord Gorebelly E 4.00 10.00
❑ 104 Joru the Blinding Light R 1.50 4.00
❑ 105 Kurala Deadshot U .15 .40
❑ 106 Nuada Windwaker U .15 .40
❑ 107 Orc Raider C .10 .25
❑ 108 Orc Shaman C .10 .25
❑ 109 Rokhan R .50 1.25
❑ 110 Roza the Star-Mother R .30 .75
❑ 111 Runetotem Guardian C .10 .25
❑ 112 Seres, Timewalker Assassin U .15 .40
❑ 113 Shattered Hand Cutthroat C .10 .25
❑ 114 Sixto the Earth-Blessed R 1.50 4.00
❑ 115 Sunwalker Lighthorn C .10 .25
❑ 116 Thunderhorn Windwalker C .10 .25
❑ 117 Valik, Timewalker Sharpshooter U .15 .40
❑ 118 Warsong Deadblade C .10 .25
❑ 119 Winterhoof Frostheart C .10 .25
❑ 120 Abomination U .15 .40
❑ 121 Anub'arak, The Traitor King E 4.00 10.00
❑ 122 Banshee U .15 .40
❑ 123 Blackhorn Fearmonger C .10 .25
❑ 124 Bleakheart Hellcaller C .10 .25
❑ 125 Brood Mother R .30 .75
❑ 126 Cult Master Kel'Thuzad R .75 2.00
❑ 127 Cunning Crypt Fiend C .10 .25
❑ 128 Darkflame Dreadlord C .10 .25
❑ 129 Doomguard Invader C .10 .25
❑ 130 Dreadhound C .10 .25
❑ 131 Eredar Chaosbringer U .15 .40
❑ 132 Eredar Strategist U .25 .60
❑ 133 Fel Imp U .15 .40
❑ 134 Felguard Basher C .10 .25
❑ 135 Frost Wyrm R .40 1.00
❑ 136 Furbolg Champion U .15 .40
❑ 137 Furbolg Spiritbinder C .10 .25
❑ 138 Hateful Darkweaver U .15 .40
❑ 139 Hateful Fiend U .15 .40
❑ 140 Hateful Infernal U .15 .40
❑ 141 Hateful Seductress U .15 .40
❑ 142 Hungry Ghoul C .10 .25
❑ 143 Mal'Ganis E 2.00 5.00
❑ 144 Mo'arg Punisher C .10 .25
❑ 145 Naga Royal Guard U .15 .40
❑ 146 Naga Siren U .15 .40
❑ 147 Necromancer U .15 .40
❑ 148 Priestess of Horror C .10 .25
❑ 149 Priestess of Ruin C .10 .25
❑ 150 Quillbeast C .10 .25
❑ 151 Savage Wrathguard C .10 .25
❑ 152 Scheming Watcher C .10 .25
❑ 153 Sister of Seduction C .10 .25
❑ 154 Sogoridon the Savage R .40 1.00
❑ 155 Terror Hound C .10 .25
❑ 156 Terrorguard Detonator C .10 .25
❑ 157 Thunder Hawk C .10 .25
❑ 158 Torrid Abyssal C .10 .25
❑ 159 Varimathras, Dreadlord Insurgent R 2.00 5.00
❑ 160 Void Brute C .10 .25
❑ 161 Zalekor the Ferocious R .60 1.50
❑ 162 Bloodmage Kael'thas R .30 .75
❑ 163 Goblin Tinkerer R .50 1.25
❑ 164 Pandaren Brewmaster R .75 2.00
❑ 165 Rexxar the Wanderer R 1.25 3.00
❑ 166 Belt of Giant Strength R .40 1.00
❑ 167 Boots of Quel'Thalas U .15 .40
❑ 168 Boots of Speed U .15 .40
❑ 169 Circlet of Nobility C .10 .25
❑ 170 Cloak of Flames U .15 .40
❑ 171 Mask of Death U .15 .40
❑ 172 Robe of the Magi R .30 .75
❑ 173 Amulet of Spell Shield U .15 .40
❑ 174 Anti-magic Potion C .10 .25
❑ 175 Glyph of Omniscience C .10 .25
❑ 176 Healing Wards U .15 .40
❑ 177 Health Stone C .10 .25
❑ 178 Orb of Darkness U .15 .40
❑ 179 Ring of Protection C .10 .25
❑ 180 Scroll of Town Portal C .10 .25
❑ 181 Claws of Attack R .30 .75
❑ 182 Corrupted Ashbringer R .40 1.00
❑ 183 Doomhammer E 1.25 3.00
❑ 184 Frostmourne E 2.50 6.00
❑ 185 Kelen's Dagger of Escape C .10 .25
❑ 186 Rod of Necromancy R .30 .75
❑ 187 Staff of Silence U .15 .40
❑ 188 Wand of Mana Stealing U .15 .40
❑ 189 Eternity's End U .15 .40
❑ 190 The Founding of Durotar U .15 .40
❑ 191 The Invasion of Kalimdor C .10 .25
❑ 192 Legacy of the Damned C
❑ 193 Path of the Damned C .10 .25
❑ 194 The Scourge of Lordaeron C .10 .25
❑ 195 Terror of the Tides C .10 .25
❑ 196 Ashenvale R 5.00 12.00
❑ 197 Mulgore R .30 .75

1999 Young Jedi Menace of Darth Maul

COMPLETE SET (140) 10.00 25.00
BOOSTER BOX (30 PACKS) 15.00 30.00

❑ 1 Obi-Wan Kenobi, Young Jedi R 2.00 5.00
❑ 2 Qui-Gon Jinn, Jedi Master R 1.50 4.00
❑ 3 Jar Jar Binks, Gungan Chuba Thief R 1.00 2.50
❑ 4 Anakin Skywalker, Podracer Pilot R .75 2.00
❑ 5 Padme Naberrie, Handmaiden R 1.25 3.00
❑ 6 Captain Panaka, Protector of the Queen R .75 2.00
❑ 7 Mace Windu, Jedi Master R 1.00 2.50
❑ 8 Queen Amidala, Ruler of Naboo R 1.25 3.00
❑ 9 Queen Amidala, Royal Leader R 1.25 3.00
❑ 10 Yoda, Jedi Master R 1.25 3.00
❑ 11 R2-D2, Astromech Droid R 1.00 2.50
❑ 12 C-3PO, Anakin's Creation R 1.00 2.50
❑ 13 Boss Nass, Leader of the Gungans U .30 .75
❑ 14 Ric Olie, Ace Pilot U .30 .75
❑ 15 Captain Tarpals, Gungan Guard U .30 .75
❑ 16 Rabe, Handmaiden U .30 .75
❑ 17 Rep Been, Gungan U .30 .75
❑ 18 Mas Amedda, Vice Chancellor U .30 .75
❑ 19 Naboo Officer, Battle Planner U .30 .75
❑ 20 Naboo Security, Guard C .10 .25
❑ 21 Bravo Pilot, Veteran Flyer C .10 .25
❑ 22 Gungan Official, Bureaucrat C .10 .25
❑ 23 Gungan Soldier, Scout C .10 .25
❑ 24 Gungan Guard C .10 .25
❑ 25 Gungan Warrior, Infantry C .10 .25
❑ 26 Gungan Soldier, Veteran C .10 .25
❑ 27 Ishi Tib, Warrior C .10 .25
❑ 28 Ithorian, Merchant C .10 .25
❑ 29 Jawa, Thief C .10 .25
❑ 30 Jawa, Bargainer S .10 .25
❑ 31 Royal Guard, Leader C .10 .25
❑ 32 Royal Guard, Veteran C .10 .25
❑ 33 Obi-Wan Kenobi, Jedi Padawan S .10 .25
❑ 34 Obi-Wan Kenobi's Lightsaber R 1.00 2.50
❑ 35 Jedi Lightsaber, Constructed by Ki-Adi-Mundi U .30 .75
❑ 36 Anakin Skywalker's Podracer R .75 2.00
❑ 37 Captain Panaka's Blaster C .10 .25
❑ 38 Jar Jar Binks' Electropole U .30 .75
❑ 39 Electropole C .10 .25
❑ 40 Eopie C .10 .25
❑ 41 Kaadu C .10 .25
❑ 42 Flash Speeder C .10 .25
❑ 43 Jawa Ion Blaster C .10 .25
❑ 44 Naboo Blaster C .10 .25
❑ 45 Blaster C .10 .25
❑ 46 Blaster Rifle C .10 .25
❑ 47 Anakin Skywalker, Meet Obi-Wan Kenobi U .30 .75
❑ 48 Are You An Angel? U .30 .75
❑ 49 Cha Skrunee Da Pat, Sleemo C .10 .25
❑ 50 Counterparts U .30 .75
❑ 51 Da Beings Hereabouts Cawazy C .10 .25
❑ 52 Enough Of This Pretense U .30 .75
❑ 53 Fear Attracts The Fearful U .30 .75
❑ 54 Gungan Curiosity C .10 .25
❑ 55 He Was Meant To Help You U .30 .75
❑ 56 I Have A Bad Feeling About This U .30 .75
❑ 57 I've Been Trained In Defense U .30 .75
❑ 58 Security Volunteers C .10 .25
❑ 59 Shmi's Pride U .30 .75
❑ 60 The Federation Has Gone Too Far C .10 .25
❑ 61 The Negotiations Were Short C .10 .25
❑ 62 The Queen's Plan C .10 .25
❑ 63 We're Not In Trouble Yet U .30 .75
❑ 64 Yousa Guys Bombad! R .60 1.50
❑ 65 Tatooine Podrace Arena S .10 .25
❑ 66 Coruscant Capital City S .10 .25
❑ 67 Naboo Theed Palace S .10 .25
❑ 68 Bravo 1, Naboo Starfighter U .30 .75
❑ 69 Naboo Starfighter C .10 .25
❑ 70 Republic Cruiser, Transport C .10 .25
❑ 71 Darth Maul, Sith Apprentice R 2.50 6.00
❑ 72 Darth Sidious, Sith Master R 1.50 4.00
❑ 73 Sebulba, Bad-Tempered Dug R 1.00 2.50
❑ 74 Watto, Slave Owner R .75 2.00
❑ 75 Aurra Sing, Bounty Hunter R 1.25 3.00
❑ 76 Jabba the Hutt, Vile Crime Lord R 1.00 2.50
❑ 77 Gardulla the Hutt, Crime Lord U .30 .75
❑ 78 Destroyer Droid Squad, Security Division R .60 1.50
❑ 79 Battle Droid Squad, Assault Unit R .75 2.00
❑ 80 Ben Quadinaros, Podracer Pilot U .30 .75
❑ 81 Gasgano, Podracer Pilot U .30 .75
❑ 82 Mawhonic, Podracer Pilot U .30 .75
❑ 83 Teemto Pagalies, Podracer Pilot U .30 .75
❑ 84 Bib Fortuna, Twi'lek Advisor U .30 .75
❑ 85 Ann and Tann Gella, Sebulba's Attendants U .30 .75
❑ 86 Gragra, Chuba Peddler C .10 .25
❑ 87 Passel Argente, Senator C .10 .25
❑ 88 Trade Federation Tank, Armored Division R .75 2.00
❑ 89 Destroyer Droid, Wheel Droid C .10 .25
❑ 90 Destroyer Droid, Defense Droid C .10 .25
❑ 91 Sith Probe Droid, Spy Drone C .10 .25
❑ 92 Pit Droid, Engineer C .10 .25
❑ 93 Pit Droid, Heavy Lifter C .10 .25
❑ 94 Pit Droid, Mechanic C .10 .25
❑ 95 Tusken Raider, Nomad C .10 .25
❑ 96 Tusken Raider, Marksman C .10 .25
❑ 97 Battle Droid: Pilot, MTT Division C .10 .25
❑ 98 Battle Droid: Security, MTT Division C .10 .25

TCG/CCG

Card	Low	High
❑ 99 Battle Droid: Infantry, MTT Division C	.10	.25
❑ 100 Battle Droid: Officer, MTT Division C	.10	.25
❑ 101 Battle Droid: Pilot, AAT Division C	.10	.25
❑ 102 Battle Droid: Security, AAT Division C	.10	.25
❑ 103 Battle Droid: Infantry, AAT Division C	.10	.25
❑ 104 Battle Droid: Officer, AAT Division C	.10	.25
❑ 105 Neimoidian, Trade Federation Pilot S	.10	.25
❑ 106 Darth Maul, Sith Lord S	.40	1.00
❑ 107 Sith Lightsaber R	.75	2.00
❑ 108 Aurra Sing's Blaster Rifle R	.60	1.50
❑ 109 Sebulba's Podracer R	.60	1.50
❑ 110 Ben Quadinaros' Podracer U	.30	.75
❑ 111 Gasgano's Podracer U	.30	.75
❑ 112 Mawhonic's Podracer U	.30	.75
❑ 113 Teemto Pagalies' Podracer U	.30	.75
❑ 114 Trade Federation Tank Laser Cannon U	.30	.75
❑ 115 Multi Troop Transport U	.30	.75
❑ 116 STAP U	.30	.75
❑ 117 Tatooine Thunder Rifle C	.10	.25
❑ 118 Battle Droid Blaster Rifle C	.10	.25
❑ 119 Blaster C	.10	.25
❑ 120 Blaster Rifle C	.10	.25
❑ 121 At Last We Will Have Revenge R	.60	1.50
❑ 122 Begin Landing Your Troops C	.10	.25
❑ 123 Boonta Eve Podrace U	.30	.75
❑ 124 Grueling Contest U	.30	.75
❑ 125 In Complete Control C	.10	.25
❑ 126 Kaa Bazza Kundee Hodrudda! U	.30	.75
❑ 127 Opee Sea Killer C	.10	.25
❑ 128 Podrace Preparation U	.30	.75
❑ 129 Sandstorm C	.10	.25
❑ 130 Sniper C	.10	.25
❑ 131 The Invasion Is On Schedule C	.10	.25
❑ 132 Vile Gangsters U	.30	.75
❑ 133 Watto's Wager U	.30	.75
❑ 134 You Have Been Well Trained R	.60	1.50
❑ 135 Tatooine Desert Landing Site S	.10	.25
❑ 136 Coruscant Jedi Council Chamber S	.10	.25
❑ 137 Naboo Gungan Swamp S	.10	.25
❑ 138 Darth Maul's Starfighter, Sith Infiltrator R	1.00	2.50
❑ 139 Droid Starfighter C	.10	.25
❑ 140 Battleship, Trade Federation Transport C	.10	.25

1999 Young Jedi Menace of Darth Maul Foil

Card	Low	High
COMPLETE SET (18)	6.00	15.00
❑ F1 Obi-Wan Kenobi, Young Jedi R	2.50	6.00
❑ F2 Jar-Jar Binks, Gungan Chuba Thief R	1.25	3.00
❑ F3 Mace Windu, Jedi Master U	1.25	3.00
❑ F4 Queen Amidala, Ruler of Naboo U	2.00	5.00
❑ F5 C-3PO, Anakin's Creation U	1.25	3.00
❑ F6 Obi-Wan Kenobi's Lightsaber C	1.00	2.50
❑ F7 Anakin Skywalker's Podracer C	.75	2.00
❑ F8 Bravo 1, Naboo Starfighter C	.40	1.00
❑ F9 Republic Cruiser, Transport C	.40	1.00
❑ F10 Darth Maul, Sith Apprentice R	3.00	8.00
❑ F11 Darth Sidious, Sith Master R	2.00	5.00
❑ F12 Destroyer Droid Squad, Security Division U	.60	1.50
❑ F13 Battle Droid Squad, Assault Unit U	.60	1.50
❑ F14 Sebulba's Podracer U	.60	1.50
❑ F15 Ben Quadinaros' Podracer C	.40	1.00
❑ F16 Gasgano's Podracer C	.40	1.00
❑ F17 Mawhonic's Podracer C	.40	1.00
❑ F18 Teemto Pagalies' Podracer C	.40	1.00

1999 Young Jedi The Jedi Council

Card	Low	High
COMPLETE SET (140)	8.00	20.00
BOOSTER BOX (30 PACKS)	10.00	20.00
❑ 1 Obi-Wan Kenobi, Jedi Apprentice R	1.50	4.00
❑ 2 Qui-Gon Jinn, Jedi Protector R	1.25	3.00
❑ 3 Jar Jar Binks, Gungan Outcast R	.75	2.00
❑ 4 Anakin Skywalker, Child of Prophecy R	.75	2.00
❑ 5 Padme Naberrie, Queen's Handmaiden R	1.00	2.50
❑ 6 Captain Panaka, Amidala's Bodyguard R	.60	1.50
❑ 7 Mace Windu, Senior Jedi Council Member R	.75	2.00
❑ 8 Queen Amidala, Representative of Naboo R	1.00	2.50
❑ 9 Queen Amidala, Voice of Her People R	1.00	2.50
❑ 10 Yoda, Jedi Council Member R	1.00	2.50
❑ 11 R2-D2, Loyal Droid R	.75	2.00
❑ 12 Ki-Adi-Mundi, Cerean Jedi Knight R	.75	2.00
❑ 13 Adi Gallia, Corellian Jedi Master U	.30	.75
❑ 14 Depa Billaba, Jedi Master U	.30	.75
❑ 15 Eeth Koth, Zabrak Jedi Master U	.30	.75
❑ 16 Even Piell, Lannik Jedi Master U	.30	.75
❑ 17 Oppo Rancisis, Jedi Master U	.30	.75
❑ 18 Plo Koon, Jedi Master U	.30	.75
❑ 19 Saesee Tiin, Iktotchi Jedi Master U	.30	.75
❑ 20 Yaddle, Jedi Master U	.30	.75
❑ 21 Yarael Poof, Quermian Jedi Master U	.30	.75
❑ 22 Boss Nass, Gungan Leader U	.30	.75
❑ 23 Ric Olié, Chief Pilot U	.30	.75
❑ 24 Captain Tarpals, Gungan Battle Leader U	.30	.75
❑ 25 Eirtae, Handmaiden U	.30	.75
❑ 26 Valorum, Supreme Chancellor C	.10	.25
❑ 27 Sci Taria, Chancellor's Aide C	.10	.25
❑ 28 Naboo Officer, Liberator C	.10	.25
❑ 29 Bravo Pilot, Naboo Volunteer C	.10	.25
❑ 30 Naboo Security, Amidala's Guard C	.10	.25
❑ 31 Republic Captain, Officer C	.10	.25
❑ 32 Republic Pilot, Veteran C	.10	.25
❑ 33 Coruscant Guard, Coruscant Detachment C	.10	.25
❑ 34 Coruscant Guard, Peacekeeper C	.10	.25
❑ 35 Coruscant Guard, Officer C	.10	.25
❑ 36 Coruscant Guard, Chancellor's Guard C	.10	.25
❑ 37 Wookiee Senator, Representative C	.10	.25
❑ 38 Galactic Senator, Delegate S	.10	.25
❑ 39 Obi-Wan Kenobi, Jedi Warrior S	.10	.25
❑ 40 Qui-Gon Jinn's Lightsaber R	.60	1.50
❑ 41 Amidala's Blaster R	.60	1.50
❑ 42 Adi Gallia's Lightsaber U	.30	.75
❑ 43 Coruscant Guard Blaster Rifle U	.30	.75
❑ 44 Ascension Gun C	.10	.25
❑ 45 Electropole C	.10	.25
❑ 46 Kaadu C	.10	.25
❑ 47 Flash Speeder C	.10	.25
❑ 48 Gian Speeder C	.10	.25
❑ 49 Naboo Blaster C	.10	.25
❑ 50 Blaster C	.10	.25
❑ 51 Blaster Rifle C	.10	.25
❑ 52 Balance To The Force U	.30	.75
❑ 53 Brave Little Droid U	.30	.75
❑ 54 Dos Mackineeks No Comen Here! C	.10	.25
❑ 55 Galactic Chancellor C	.10	.25
❑ 56 Hate Leads To Suffering U	.30	.75
❑ 57 I Will Not Cooperate U	.30	.75
❑ 58 Invasion! C	.10	.25
❑ 59 May The Force Be With You C	.10	.25
❑ 60 Senator Palpatine C	.10	.25
❑ 61 The Might Of The Republic C	.10	.25
❑ 62 We Don't Have Time For This C	.10	.25
❑ 63 We Wish To Board At Once C	.10	.25
❑ 64 Wisdom Of The Council R	.60	1.50
❑ 65 Tatooine Mos Espa S	.10	.25
❑ 66 Coruscant Jedi Council Chamber S	.10	.25
❑ 67 Naboo Gungan Swamp S	.10	.25
❑ 68 Bravo 2, Naboo Starfighter U	.30	.75
❑ 69 Naboo Starfighter C	.10	.25
❑ 70 Radiant VII, Republic Cruiser Transport C	.10	.25
❑ 71 Darth Maul, Master of Evil R	2.00	5.00
❑ 72 Darth Sidious, Lord of the Sith R	1.25	3.00
❑ 73 Sebulba, Podracer Pilot R	.75	2.00
❑ 74 Watto, Junk Merchant R	.60	1.50
❑ 75 Jabba the Hutt, Gangster R	.75	2.00
❑ 76 Nute Gunray, Neimoidian Viceroy R	.60	1.50
❑ 77 Rune Haako, Neimoidian Advisor R	.60	1.50
❑ 78 Destroyer Droid Squad, Defense Division R	.60	1.50
❑ 79 Battle Droid Squad, Escort Unit R	.60	1.50
❑ 80 Trade Federation Tank, Assault Division R	.60	1.50
❑ 81 Lott Dod, Neimoidian Senator R	.60	1.50
❑ 82 Fode and Beed, Podrace Announcer R	.60	1.50
❑ 83 Clegg Holdfast, Podracer Pilot U	.30	.75
❑ 84 Dud Bolt, Podracer Pilot U	.30	.75
❑ 85 Mars Guo, Podracer Pilot U	.30	.75
❑ 86 Ody Mandrell, Podracer Pilot U	.30	.75
❑ 87 Ratts Tyerell, Podracer Pilot U	.30	.75
❑ 88 Aks Moe, Senator C	.10	.25
❑ 89 Horox Ryyder, Senator C	.10	.25
❑ 90 Edcel Bar Gane, Roona Senator C	.10	.25
❑ 91 Galactic Delegate, Representative C	.10	.25
❑ 92 Destroyer Droid, Assault Droid C	.10	.25
❑ 93 Destroyer Droid, Battleship Security C	.10	.25
❑ 94 Sith Probe Droid, Hunter Droid C	.10	.25
❑ 95 Rodian, Mercenary C	.10	.25
❑ 96 Battle Droid: Pilot, Assault Division C	.10	.25
❑ 97 Battle Droid: Security, Assault Division C	.10	.25
❑ 98 Battle Droid: Infantry, Assault Division C	.10	.25
❑ 99 Battle Droid: Officer, Assault Division C	.10	.25
❑ 100 Battle Droid: Pilot, Guard Division C	.10	.25
❑ 101 Battle Droid: Security, Guard Division C	.10	.25
❑ 102 Battle Droid: Infantry, Guard Division C	.10	.25
❑ 103 Battle Droid: Officer, Guard Division C	.10	.25
❑ 104 Neimoidian Aide, Trade Federation Delegate S	.10	.25
❑ 105 Darth Maul, Sith Warrior S	.10	.25
❑ 106 Darth Maul's Lightsaber R	.60	1.50
❑ 107 Darth Maul's Sith Speeder R	.60	1.50
❑ 108 Clegg Holdfast's Podracer U	.30	.75
❑ 109 Dud Bolt's Podracer U	.30	.75
❑ 110 Mars Guo's Podracer U	.30	.75
❑ 111 Ody Mandrell's Podracer U	.30	.75
❑ 112 Ratts Tyerell's Podracer U	.30	.75
❑ 113 Trade Federation Tank Laser Cannon U	.30	.75
❑ 114 Multi Troop Transport U	.30	.75
❑ 115 STAP U	.30	.75
❑ 116 Thermal Detonator U	.30	.75
❑ 117 Battle Droid Blaster Rifle C	.10	.25
❑ 118 Blaster C	.10	.25
❑ 119 Blaster Rifle C	.10	.25
❑ 120 I Object! C	.10	.25
❑ 121 I Will Deal With Them Myself C	.10	.25
❑ 122 Let Them Make The First Move R	.60	1.50
❑ 123 Move Against The Jedi First C	.10	.25
❑ 124 Open Fire! U	.30	.75
❑ 125 Seal Off The Bridge U	.30	.75
❑ 126 Start Your Engines! U	.30	.75
❑ 127 Switch To Bio C	.10	.25
❑ 128 Take Them To Camp Four C	.10	.25
❑ 129 Very Unusual C	.10	.25
❑ 130 Vote Of No Confidence C	.10	.25
❑ 131 We Are Meeting No Resistance C	.10	.25
❑ 132 We Have Them On The Run U	.30	.75
❑ 133 Yoka To Bantha Poodoo C	.10	.25
❑ 134 Your Little Insurrection Is At An End U	.30	.75
❑ 135 Tatooine Podrace Arena S	.10	.25
❑ 136 Coruscant Galactic Senate S	.10	.25
❑ 137 Naboo Battle Plains S	.10	.25
❑ 138 Sith Infiltrator, Starfighter U	.30	.75
❑ 139 Droid Starfighter C	.10	.25
❑ 140 Battleship, Trade Federation Transport C	.10	.25

1999 Young Jedi The Jedi Council Foil

Card	Low	High
COMPLETE SET (18)	4.00	10.00
❑ F1 Obi-Wan Kenobi, Jedi Apprentice UR	2.00	5.00
❑ F2 Qui-Gon Jinn, Jedi Protector SR	.75	2.00
❑ F3 Padmé Naberrie, Queen's Handmaiden SR	.75	2.00
❑ F4 Captain Panaka, Amidala's Bodyguard SR	.60	1.50
❑ F5 Mace Windu, Senior Jedi Council Member SR	1.00	2.50
❑ F6 Queen Amidala, Representative of Naboo VR	1.25	3.00
❑ F7 R2-D2, Loyal Droid VR	1.25	3.00
❑ F8 Qui-Gon Jinn's Lightsaber VR	.40	1.00
❑ F9 Amidala's Blaster VR	.40	1.00
❑ F10 Darth Maul, Master of Evil UR	2.00	5.00
❑ F11 Darth Sidious, Lord of the Sith UR	1.25	3.00
❑ F12 Watto, Junk Merchant SR	.60	1.50
❑ F13 Jabba the Hutt, Gangster SR	.60	1.50
❑ F14 Nute Gunray, Neimoidian Viceroy SR	.60	1.50
❑ F15 Rune Haako, Neimoidian Advisor VR	.40	1.00
❑ F16 Lott Dod, Neimoidian Senator VR	.40	1.00
❑ F17 Darth Maul's Lightsaber VR	.40	1.00
❑ F18 Darth Maul's Sith Speeder VR	.40	1.00

2000 Young Jedi Battle of Naboo

Card	Low	High
COMPLETE SET (140)	8.00	20.00
BOOSTER BOX (30 PACKS)	15.00	30.00
❑ 1 Obi-Wan Kenobi, Jedi Knight R	1.50	4.00
❑ 2 Qui-Gon Jinn, Jedi Ambassador R	1.25	3.00
❑ 3 Jar Jar Binks, Bombad Gungan General R	.75	2.00
❑ 4 Anakin Skywalker, Padawan R	.75	2.00
❑ 5 Padme Naberrie, Amidala's Handmaiden R	1.00	2.50
❑ 6 Captain Panaka, Veteran Leader R	.60	1.50
❑ 7 Mace Windu, Jedi Speaker R	.75	2.00
❑ 8 Queen Amidala, Resolute Negotiator R	1.00	2.50
❑ 9 Queen Amidala, Keeper of the Peace R	1.00	2.50
❑ 10 Yoda, Jedi Elder R	1.00	2.50
❑ 11 R2-D2, The Queen's Hero R	.75	2.00
❑ 12 Boss Nass, Gungan Chief U	.30	.75
❑ 13 Ric Olie, Bravo Leader U	.30	.75
❑ 14 Captain Tarpals, Gungan Officer U	.30	.75
❑ 15 Sio Bibble, Governor of Naboo U	.30	.75
❑ 16 Sabe, Handmaiden Decoy Queen U	.30	.75
❑ 17 Sache, Handmaiden U	.30	.75
❑ 18 Yane, Handmaiden U	.30	.75
❑ 19 Naboo Officer, Squad Leader U	.30	.75
❑ 20 Naboo Officer, Commander C	.10	.25
❑ 21 Naboo Bureaucrat, Official C	.10	.25
❑ 22 Naboo Security, Trooper C	.10	.25
❑ 23 Naboo Security, Defender C	.10	.25
❑ 24 Bravo Pilot, Ace Flyer C	.10	.25
❑ 25 Coruscant Guard, Chancellor's Escort C	.10	.25
❑ 26 Alderaan Diplomat, Senator C	.10	.25
❑ 27 Council Member, Naboo Governor C	.10	.25
❑ 28 Gungan Warrior, Veteran C	.10	.25
❑ 29 Gungan Guard, Lookout C	.10	.25
❑ 30 Gungan General, Army Leader C	.10	.25
❑ 31 Gungan Soldier, Infantry C	.10	.25
❑ 32 Rep Officer, Gungan Diplomat S	.10	.25
❑ 33 Obi-Wan Kenobi, Jedi Negotiator S	.10	.25
❑ 34 Mace Windu's Lightsaber R	.60	1.50
❑ 35 Eeth Koth's Lightsaber U	.30	.75
❑ 36 Captain Tarpals' Electropole U	.30	.75
❑ 37 Planetary Shuttle C	.10	.25
❑ 38 Fambaa C	.10	.25
❑ 39 Electropole C	.10	.25
❑ 40 Kaadu C	.10	.25
❑ 41 Flash Speeder C	.10	.25
❑ 42 Blaster C	.10	.25
❑ 43 Heavy Blaster C	.10	.25
❑ 44 Capture The Viceroy C	.10	.25
❑ 45 Celebration C	.10	.25
❑ 46 Guardians Of The Queen U	.30	.75
❑ 47 Gunga City C	.10	.25
❑ 48 Gungan Battle Cry U	.30	.75
❑ 49 How Wude! U	.30	.75
❑ 50 I Will Take Back What Is Ours C	.10	.25
❑ 51 Jedi Force Push U	.30	.75
❑ 52 Meeeesa Lika Dis! C	.10	.25
❑ 53 NOOOOOOOOOOO! R	.60	1.50
❑ 54 Thanks, Artoo! U	.30	.75
❑ 55 The Chancellor's Ambassador U	.30	.75
❑ 56 The Will Of The Force R	.60	1.50
❑ 57 Young Skywalker U	.30	.75
❑ 58 Your Occupation Here Has Ended C	.10	.25
❑ 59 Bombad General U	.30	.75
❑ 60 Kiss Your Trade Franchise Goodbye U	.30	.75
❑ 61 There's Always A Bigger Fish C	.10	.25
❑ 62 Uh-Oh! C	.10	.25
❑ 63 We Wish To Form An Alliance C	.10	.25
❑ 64 Tatooine Desert Landing Site S	.10	.25
❑ 65 Coruscant Galactic Senate S	.10	.25
❑ 66 Naboo Battle Plains S	.10	.25
❑ 67 Amidala's Starship, Royal Transport R	.60	1.50
❑ 68 Bravo 3, Naboo Starfighter U	.30	.75
❑ 69 Naboo Starfighter C	.10	.25
❑ 70 Republic Cruiser, Transport C	.10	.25
❑ 71 Darth Maul, Dark Lord of the Sith R	2.00	5.00
❑ 72 Darth Sidious, Sith Manipulator R	1.25	3.00
❑ 73 Sebulba, Dangerous Podracer Pilot R	.60	1.50
❑ 74 Watto, Toydarian Gambler R	.60	1.50
❑ 75 Aurra Sing, Mercenary R	.75	2.00
❑ 76 Jabba The Hutt, Crime Lord R	.60	1.50
❑ 77 Nute Gunray, Neimoidian Despot R	.60	1.50
❑ 78 Rune Haako, Neimoidian Deputy R	.60	1.50
❑ 79 Destroyer Droid Squad, Guard Division R	.60	1.50
❑ 80 Battle Droid Squad, Guard Unit R	.60	1.50
❑ 81 Trade Federation Tank, Guard Division R	.60	1.50
❑ 82 Trade Federation Tank, Patrol Division R	.60	1.50
❑ 83 P-59, Destroyer Droid Commander U	.30	.75
❑ 84 OOM-9, Battle Droid Commander U	.30	.75
❑ 85 Daultay Dofine, Neimoidian Attendant U	.30	.75
❑ 86 Diva Shaliqua, Singer U	.30	.75
❑ 87 Diva Funquita, Dancer U	.30	.75
❑ 88 Bith, Musician U	.30	.75
❑ 89 Quarren, Smuggler U	.30	.75
❑ 90 Toonbuck Toora, Senator U	.30	.75
❑ 91 Aqualish, Galactic Senator C	.10	.25
❑ 92 Twi'lek Diplomat, Senator C	.10	.25
❑ 93 Weequay, Enforcer C	.10	.25
❑ 94 Nikto, Slave C	.10	.25
❑ 95 Pacithhip, Prospector C	.10	.25
❑ 96 Destroyer Droid, Vanguard Droid C	.10	.25
❑ 97 Destroyer Droid, MTT Infantry C	.10	.25
❑ 98 Sith Probe Droid, Remote Tracker C	.10	.25
❑ 99 Battle Droid: Pilot, Patrol Division C	.10	.25
❑ 100 Battle Droid: Security, Patrol Division C	.10	.25
❑ 101 Battle Droid: Infantry, Patrol Division C	.10	.25
❑ 102 Battle Droid: Officer, Patrol Division C	.10	.25
❑ 103 Battle Droid: Pilot, Defense Division C	.10	.25
❑ 104 Battle Droid: Security, Defense Division C	.10	.25
❑ 105 Battle Droid: Infantry, Defense Division C	.10	.25
❑ 106 Battle Droid: Officer, Defense Division C	.10	.25
❑ 107 Neimoidian Advisor, Bureaucrat S	.10	.25
❑ 108 Darth Maul, Evil Sith Lord S	.10	.25
❑ 109 Darth Maul's Lightsaber R	.75	2.00
❑ 110 Sith Lightsaber R	.60	1.50
❑ 111 Darth Maul's Electrobinoculars U	.30	.75
❑ 112 Trade Federation Tank Laser Cannon U	.30	.75
❑ 113 Multi Troop Transport U	.30	.75
❑ 114 STAP U	.30	.75
❑ 115 Battle Droid Blaster Rifle C	.10	.25
❑ 116 Blaster C	.10	.25
❑ 117 Blaster Rifle C	.10	.25
❑ 118 A Thousand Terrible Things C	.10	.25
❑ 119 Armored Assault C	.10	.25
❑ 120 Death From Above C	.10	.25
❑ 121 Don't Spect A Werm Welcome C	.10	.25
❑ 122 I Will Make It Legal C	.10	.25
❑ 123 Not For A Sith R	.60	1.50
❑ 124 Now There Are Two Of Them U	.30	.75
❑ 125 Sith Force Push U	.30	.75
❑ 126 The Phantom Menace U	.30	.75
❑ 127 They Win This Round C	.10	.25
❑ 128 We Are Sending All Troops C	.10	.25
❑ 129 After Her! C	.10	.25
❑ 130 Da Dug Chaaa! U	.30	.75
❑ 131 Sando Aqua Monster C	.10	.25
❑ 132 They Will Not Stay Hidden For Long C	.10	.25
❑ 133 This Is Too Close! U	.30	.75
❑ 134 Tatooine Mos Espa S	.10	.25
❑ 135 Coruscant Capital City S	.10	.25
❑ 136 Naboo Theed Palace S	.10	.25
❑ 137 Droid Control Ship Trade Federation Transport U	.30	.75
❑ 138 Sith Infiltrator, Starfighter U	.30	.75
❑ 139 Droid Starfighter C	.10	.25
❑ 140 Battleship, Trade Federation Transport C	.10	.25

2000 Young Jedi Battle of Naboo Foil

Card	Low	High
COMPLETE SET (18)	4.00	10.00
❑ F1 Obi-Wan Kenobi, Jedi Knight UR	1.50	4.00
❑ F2 Qui-Gon Jinn, Jedi Ambassador UR	.75	2.00
❑ F3 Queen Amidala, Keeper of the Peace SR	.75	2.00
❑ F4 Yoda, Jedi Elder SR	.75	2.00
❑ F5 R2-D2, The Queen's Hero SR	.75	2.00
❑ F6 Queen Amidala, Resolute Negotiator VR	.60	1.50
❑ F7 Mace Windu's Lightsaber VR	.40	1.00
❑ F8 The Will Of The Force VR	.40	1.00
❑ F9 Amidala's Starship, Royal Transport VR	.40	1.00
❑ F10 Darth Maul, Dark Lord of the Sith UR	1.50	4.00
❑ F11 Aurra Sing, Mercenary UR	.75	2.00
❑ F12 Nute Gunray, Neimoidian Despot SR	.60	1.50
❑ F13 Destroyer Droid Squad, Guard Division SR	.60	1.50
❑ F14 Trade Federation Tank, Guard Division SR	.60	1.50
❑ F15 Battle Droid Squad, Guard Unit VR	.40	1.00
❑ F16 Trade Federation Tank, Patrol Division VR	.40	1.00
❑ F17 Darth Maul's Lightsaber VR	.40	1.00
❑ F18 Not For A Sith VR	.40	1.00

2000 Young Jedi Duel of the Fates

Card	Low	High
COMPLETE SET (60)	5.00	12.00
BOOSTER BOX (30 PACKS)	10.00	25.00
❑ 1 Obi-Wan Kenobi, Jedi Student R	1.50	4.00
❑ 2 Qui-Gon Jinn, Jedi Mentor UR	1.25	3.00
❑ 3 Anakin Skywalker, Rookie Pilot R	.75	2.00
❑ 4 Captain Panaka, Security Commander R	.60	1.50
❑ 5 Mace Windu, Jedi Councilor R	.75	2.00
❑ 6 Queen Amidala, Young Leader R	1.00	2.50
❑ 7 Yoda, Jedi Philosopher R	1.00	2.50
❑ 8 R2-D2, Repair Droid R	.75	2.00
❑ 9 Ric Olie, Starship Pilot R	.60	1.50
❑ 10 Bravo Pilot, Flyer C	.10	.25
❑ 11 Valorum, Leader of the Senate C	.10	.25
❑ 12 Qui-Gon Jinn's Lightsaber Wielded by Obi-Wan Kenobi R	.60	1.50
❑ 13 Booma U	.30	.75
❑ 14 A Powerful Opponent C	.10	.25
❑ 15 Come On, Move! U	.30	.75
❑ 16 Critical Confrontation C	.10	.25
❑ 17 Gungan Mounted Troops U	.30	.75
❑ 18 Naboo Fighter Attack C	.10	.25
❑ 19 Qui-Gon's Final Stand C	.10	.25
❑ 20 Run The Blockade C	.10	.25
❑ 21 Twist Of Fate C	.10	.25
❑ 22 You Are Strong With The Force U	.30	.75
❑ 23 Gungan Energy Shield U	.30	.75
❑ 24 He Can See Things Before They Happen U	.30	.75
❑ 25 Jedi Meditation U	.30	.75
❑ 26 Jedi Training U	.30	.75
❑ 27 Naboo Royal Security Forces U	.30	.75
❑ 28 Pounded Unto Death C	.10	.25
❑ 29 Senate Guard C	.10	.25
❑ 30 Naboo Starfighter C	.10	.25
❑ 31 Darth Maul, Student of the Dark Side UR	1.50	4.00
❑ 32 Darth Sidious, Master of the Dark Side R	1.00	2.50
❑ 33 Aurra Sing, Trophy Collector R	.75	2.00
❑ 34 Tey How, Neimoidian Command Officer R	.60	1.50
❑ 35 OWO-1, Battle Droid Command Officer R	.60	1.50
❑ 36 Rayno Vaca, Taxi Driver R	.60	1.50
❑ 37 Baskol Yeesrim, Gran Senator R	.60	1.50
❑ 38 Starfighter Droid, DFS-327 R	.60	1.50
❑ 39 Starfighter Droid, DFS-1104 R	.60	1.50
❑ 40 Starfighter Droid, DFS-1138 R	.60	1.50
❑ 41 Jedi Lightsaber, Stolen by Aurra Sing U	.30	.75
❑ 42 Coruscant Taxi U	.30	.75
❑ 43 Neimoidian Viewscreen C	.10	.25
❑ 44 Battle Droid Patrol U	.30	.75
❑ 45 Change In Tactics C	.10	.25
❑ 46 Dangerous Encounter C	.10	.25
❑ 47 Darth Maul Defiant C	.10	.25
❑ 48 Impossible! C	.10	.25
❑ 49 It's A Standoff! U	.30	.75
❑ 50 Mobile Assassin U	.30	.75
❑ 51 Power Of The Sith C	.10	.25
❑ 52 Starfighter Screen C	.10	.25
❑ 53 To The Death C	.10	.25
❑ 54 Use Caution U	.30	.75
❑ 55 Blockade U	.30	.75
❑ 56 End This Pointless Debate U	.30	.75
❑ 57 The Duel Begins U	.30	.75
❑ 58 The Jedi Are Involved U	.30	.75
❑ 59 Where Are Those Droidekas? U	.30	.75
❑ 60 Droid Starfighter C	.10	.25

2001 Young Jedi Boonta Eve Podrace

Card	Low	High
COMPLETE SET (63)	4.00	10.00
BOOSTER BOX (30 PACKS)	10.00	20.00
❑ 1 Anakin Skywalker, Boonta Eve Podracer Pilot UR	.75	2.00
❑ 2 Yoda, Jedi Instructor R	1.00	2.50
❑ 3 C-3PO, Human-Cyborg Relations Droid R	.75	2.00
❑ 4 Jira, Pallie Vendor R	.60	1.50
❑ 5 Kitster, Anakin's Friend R	.60	1.50
❑ 6 Wald, Anakin's Friend R	.60	1.50
❑ 7 Seek, Anakin's Friend U	.30	.75
❑ 8 Amee, Anakin's Friend U	.30	.75
❑ 9 Melee, Anakin's Friend U	.30	.75
❑ 10 Captain Tarpals, Gungan Leader R	.60	1.50
❑ 11 Boles Roor, Podracer Pilot U	.30	.75
❑ 12 Elan Mak, Podracer Pilot U	.30	.75
❑ 13 Neva Kee, Podracer Pilot U	.30	.75
❑ 14 Wan Sandage, Podracer Pilot U	.30	.75
❑ 15 Shmi Skywalker, Anakin's Mother R	.60	1.50
❑ 16 Boles Roor's Podracer U	.30	.75
❑ 17 Elan Mak's Podracer U	.30	.75
❑ 18 Neva Kee's Podracer U	.30	.75
❑ 19 Wan Sandage's Podracer U	.30	.75
❑ 20 Comlink C	.10	.25
❑ 21 Hold-Out Blaster C	.10	.25
❑ 22 Dis Is Nutsen C	.10	.25
❑ 23 Masquerade C	.10	.25
❑ 24 No Giben Up, General Jar Jar C	.10	.25
❑ 25 What Does Your Heart Tell You? C	.10	.25
❑ 26 All-Out Defense U	.30	.75
❑ 27 Bravo Squadron C	.10	.25
❑ 28 Hologram Projector C	.10	.25
❑ 29 Boonta Eve Classic R	.60	1.50
❑ 30 Amidala's Starship R	.60	1.50
❑ 31 Sebulba, Dug Podracer Pilot UR	.60	1.50
❑ 32 Watto, Podrace Sponsor R	.60	1.50
❑ 33 Aurra Sing, Formidable Adversary R	.75	2.00
❑ 34 Jabba The Hutt, O Grandio Lust R	.60	1.50
❑ 35 TC-14, Protocol Droid R	.60	1.50
❑ 36 Orr'UrRuuR'R, Tusken Raider Leader Rare R	.60	1.50
❑ 37 UrrOr'RuuR, Tusken Raider Warrior U	.30	.75
❑ 38 RuuR'Ur, Tusken Raider Sniper C	.10	.25
❑ 39 Sil Unch, Neimoidian Comm Officer U	.30	.75
❑ 40 Graxol Kelvyyn and Shakka U	.30	.75
❑ 41 Corix Venne, Bith Musician C	.10	.25
❑ 42 Reike Th'san, Arms Smuggler R	.60	1.50
❑ 43 Meddun, Nikto Mercenary U	.30	.75
❑ 44 Rum Sleg, Bounty Hunter R	.60	1.50
❑ 45 Aehrrley Rue, Freelance Pilot U	.30	.75
❑ 46 Jedwar Seelah, Explorer Scout U	.30	.75
❑ 47 Chokk, Klatooinian Explosives Expert C	.10	.25
❑ 48 Tatooine Backpack C	.10	.25
❑ 49 Gaderffii Stick C	.10	.25
❑ 50 Hold-Out Blaster C	.10	.25
❑ 51 Watto's Datapad U	.30	.75
❑ 52 Colo Claw Fish C	.10	.25
❑ 53 He Always Wins! C	.10	.25
❑ 54 Bounty Hunter C	.10	.25
❑ 55 Two-Pronged Attack C	.10	.25
❑ 56 All-Out Attack U	.30	.75
❑ 57 Eventually You'll Lose U	.30	.75
❑ 58 Gangster's Paradise U	.30	.75
❑ 59 Boonta Eve Classic R	.60	1.50
❑ 60 Viceroy's Battleship R	.60	1.50
❑ R1 Rule Card 1	.08	.20
❑ R2 Rule Card 2	.08	.20
❑ R3 Rule Card 3	.08	.20

HOW TO USE

What's Listed
Products listed in the Price Guide typically: 1) are produced by licensed manufacturers, 2) are widely available and 3) have market activity on single items.

What the Columns Mean
The LO and HI columns reflect current retail selling ranges. The HI column on the right generally represents the full retail selling price. The LO column on the left generally represents the lowest price one would expect to find with extensive shopping.

Quality
All figures in the Price Guide are based on undamaged figures. Damaged figures are generally sold for 25 to 75 percent of Mint value.

Currency
This Price Guide is intended to reflect the entire North American market. All listed prices are in U.S. dollars.

Legend
Rarity structure can vary greatly across different games; a full description of the rarity structure in every game is beyond the scope of this book. Below are some of the most commonly used rarity abbreviations, which we've tried to incorporate in our listings.

F - Fixed figure, typically found in starter packs.

C - Common figure.

U - Uncommon figure.

R - Rare figure.

SR/UR/VR - Super/Ultra/Very Rare figure. Rarity may vary, but is typically found in one of every X (3, 6, 12, 24, etc.) packs.

CH, LE - Chase/Limited Edition figure. As with SR/UR designation, typcially found in one of every X packs.

E - Epic rarity figure (World of Warcraft).

PR - Promo figure.

Pre-2006, HeroClix used an alternate rarity designation for its figures, based on that figure's "rank" in the game:

R - Rookie (roughly analagous to Common)

E - Experienced (roughly analagous to Uncommon)

V - Veteran (roughly analagous to Rare)

U - Unique (roughly analagous to Super/Ultra Rare)

Note: Beckett does not sell individual cards, for any game.

2003 Dungeons and Dragons Dragoneye Miniatures

❑ 1 Cleric of Moradin U	1.00	2.00
❑ 2 Dwarven Defender R	7.50	15.00
❑ 3 Gnome Fighter C	.50	1.00
❑ 4 Gold Champion (Half-Dragon) R	7.50	15.00
❑ 5 Human Crossbowman C	.50	1.00
❑ 6 Lion Falcon Monk R	7.50	15.00
❑ 7 Purple Dragon Knight R	7.50	15.00
❑ 8 Stalwart Paladin U	1.00	2.00
❑ 9 Stonechild C	.50	1.00
❑ 10 Dwarven Werebear (Hybrid Form) U	1.00	2.00
❑ 11 Dire Lion R	7.50	15.00
❑ 12 Regdar, Human Fighter U	1.00	2.00
❑ 13 Bladesinger R	7.50	15.00
❑ 14 Brass Dragon (Young) R	10.00	20.00
❑ 15 Copper Samurai U	1.00	2.00
❑ 16 Daring Rogue U	1.00	2.00
❑ 17 Drunken Master U	1.00	2.00
❑ 18 Dwarf Barbarian C	.50	1.00
❑ 19 Elf Spearguard C	.50	1.00
❑ 20 Half-Elf Sorcerer U	1.00	2.00
❑ 21 Halfling Outrider R	7.50	15.00
❑ 22 Kerwyn, Human Rogue U	1.00	2.00
❑ 23 Medium Air Elemental U	1.00	2.00
❑ 24 Silver Sorcerer (Half-Dragon) R	12.50	25.00
❑ 25 Barbarian Mercenary C	.50	1.00
❑ 26 Dire Ape R	10.00	20.00
❑ 27 Druid of Obad-Hai U	1.00	2.00
❑ 28 Baaz Draconian C	.50	1.00
❑ 29 Blue Wyrmling U	1.00	2.00
❑ 30 Cleric of Nerull U	1.00	2.00
❑ 31 Goblin Skirmisher C	.50	1.00
❑ 32 Goblin Warrior C	.50	1.00
❑ 33 Hobgoblin Warrior C	.50	1.00
❑ 34 Kapak Draconian U	1.00	2.00
❑ 35 Kobold Skirmisher C	.50	1.00
❑ 36 Medium Water Elemental U	1.00	2.00
❑ 37 Salamander R	7.50	15.00
❑ 38 Thayan Knight R	7.50	15.00
❑ 39 Urthok the Vicious U	1.00	2.00
❑ 40 Wererat (Hybrid Form) U	1.00	2.00
❑ 41 Carrion Crawler R	7.50	15.00
❑ 42 Grimlock C	.50	1.00
❑ 43 Abyssal Maw C	.50	1.00
❑ 44 Black Dragon (Young) R	10.00	20.00
❑ 45 Bright Naga R	7.50	15.00
❑ 46 Bugbear C	.50	1.00
❑ 47 Chitine U	1.00	2.00
❑ 48 Dretch C	.50	1.00
❑ 49 Drow Warrior U	1.00	2.00
❑ 50 Drow Wizard U	1.00	2.00
❑ 51 Eye of Gruumsh R	10.00	20.00
❑ 52 Gargoyle U	1.00	2.00
❑ 53 Harpy U	1.00	2.00
❑ 54 Large Monstrous Spider R	15.00	30.00
❑ 55 Large Red Dragon Young R	15.00	30.00
❑ 56 Ogre Ravager R	12.50	25.00
❑ 57 Orc Druid R	7.50	15.00
❑ 58 Red Samurai U	1.00	2.00
❑ 59 Small White Dragon (Very Young) U	1.00	2.00
❑ 60 Troglodyte C	.50	1.00

2003 Dungeons and Dragons Harbinger Miniatures

❑ 1 Cleric of Order U	1.00	2.00
❑ 2 Cleric of Yondalla U	1.00	2.00
❑ 3 Dwarf Axefighter C	.50	1.00
❑ 4 Ember, Human Monk U	1.00	2.00
❑ 5 Evoker's Apprentice U	1.00	2.00
❑ 6 Halfling Veteran U	1.00	2.00
❑ 7 Hound Archon R	15.00	30.00
❑ 8 Human Commoner C	.50	1.00
❑ 9 Large Earth Elemental R	12.50	25.00
❑ 10 Man-at-Arms C	.50	1.00
❑ 11 Sun Soul Initiate U	1.00	2.00
❑ 12 Sword of Heironeous R	15.00	30.00
❑ 13 Tordek, Dwarf Fighter U	1.00	2.00
❑ 14 Jozan, Cleric of Pelor U	1.00	2.00
❑ 15 Arcane Archer R	12.50	25.00
❑ 16 Axe Sister U	1.00	2.00
❑ 17 Centaur R	12.50	25.00
❑ 18 Cleric of Corellon Larethian R	15.00	30.00
❑ 19 Crested Felldrake C	.50	1.00
❑ 20 Devis, Half-Elf Bard U	1.00	2.00
❑ 21 Elf Archer C	.50	1.00
❑ 22 Elf Pyromancer R	15.00	30.00
❑ 23 Elf Ranger U	1.00	2.00
❑ 24 Gnome Recruit C	.50	1.00
❑ 25 Human Wanderer U	1.00	2.00
❑ 26 Krusk, Half-Orc Barbarian U	1.00	2.00
❑ 27 Lidda, Halfling Rogue U	1.00	2.00
❑ 28 Nebin, Gnome Illusionist U	1.00	2.00
❑ 29 Vadania, Half-Elf Druid R	15.00	30.00
❑ 30 Wild Elf Barbarian U	1.00	2.00
❑ 31 Wood Elf Skirmisher U	1.00	2.00
❑ 32 Azer Raider U	1.00	2.00
❑ 33 Half-Orc Monk U	1.00	2.00
❑ 34 Dire Boar R	15.00	30.00
❑ 35 Lizardfolk U	1.00	2.00
❑ 36 Shambling Mound R	15.00	30.00
❑ 37 Wolf C	.50	1.00
❑ 38 Thri-Kreen Ranger R	12.50	25.00
❑ 39 Barghest R	12.50	25.00
❑ 40 Bearded Devil R	25.00	40.00
❑ 41 Displacer Beast R	15.00	30.00
❑ 42 Goblin Sneak C	.50	1.00
❑ 43 Half-Orc Fighter C	.50	1.00
❑ 44 Hell Hound C	.50	1.00
❑ 45 Human Blackguard R	15.00	30.00
❑ 46 Human Executioner U	1.00	2.00
❑ 47 Human Thug U	1.00	2.00
❑ 48 Kobold Warrior C	.50	1.00
❑ 49 Medusa R	12.50	25.00
❑ 50 Mind Flayer R	15.00	30.00
❑ 51 Mummy R	10.00	20.00
❑ 52 Wight U	1.00	2.00
❑ 53 Wraith R	15.00	30.00
❑ 54 Owlbear R	15.00	30.00
❑ 55 Skeleton C	.50	1.00
❑ 56 Troglodyte Zombie U	1.00	2.00
❑ 57 Wolf Skeleton C	.50	1.00
❑ 58 Zombie C	.50	1.00
❑ 59 Cleric of Gruumsh R	15.00	30.00
❑ 60 Drow Archer U	1.00	2.00
❑ 61 Drow Cleric of Lolth R	25.00	40.00
❑ 62 Drow Fighter U	1.00	2.00
❑ 63 Ghoul C	.50	1.00
❑ 64 Gnoll U	1.00	2.00
❑ 65 Half-Orc Assassin U	1.00	2.00
❑ 66 Human Bandit C	.50	1.00
❑ 67 Hyena C	.50	1.00
❑ 68 Kuo-Toa C	.50	1.00
❑ 69 Large Fire Elemental R	15.00	30.00
❑ 70 Minotaur R	15.00	30.00
❑ 71 Ogre R	15.00	30.00
❑ 72 Orc Archer U	1.00	2.00
❑ 73 Orc Berserker U	1.00	2.00
❑ 74 Orc Spearfighter C	.50	1.00
❑ 75 Orc Warrior C	.50	1.00
❑ 76 Tiefling Captain U	1.00	2.00
❑ 77 Troll R	15.00	30.00
❑ 78 Umber Hulk R	15.00	30.00
❑ 79 Werewolf U	1.00	2.00
❑ 80 Worg U	1.00	2.00

2004 Dungeons and Dragons Aberrations Miniatures

❑ 1 Alusair Obarskyr R	7.50	15.00
❑ 2 Anvil of Thunder U	1.00	2.00
❑ 3 Celestial Black Bear C	.50	1.00
❑ 4 Cleric of St. Cuthbert U	1.00	2.00
❑ 5 Dragon Samurai R	7.50	15.00
❑ 6 Exorcist of the Silver Flame R	7.50	15.00
❑ 7 Hill Dwarf Warrior C	.50	1.00
❑ 8 Man-at-Arms C	.50	1.00
❑ 9 Rhek U	1.00	2.00
❑ 10 Warforged Hero R	7.50	15.00
❑ 11 Aasimar Favored Soul U	1.00	2.00
❑ 12 Adventuring Wizard R	7.50	15.00
❑ 13 Bariaur Ranger U	1.00	2.00
❑ 14 Cleric of Garl Glittergold U	1.00	2.00
❑ 15 Crow Shaman R	10.00	20.00
❑ 16 Elf Warrior C	.50	1.00
❑ 17 Frenzied Berserker R	7.50	15.00
❑ 18 Half-Elf Bow Initiate R	7.50	15.00
❑ 19 Longtooth Barbarian U	1.00	2.00
❑ 20 Sharn Cutthroat (Changeling) U	1.00	2.00
❑ 21 Valenar Commander R	7.50	15.00
❑ 22 Formian Warrior U	1.00	2.00
❑ 23 Ethereal Filcher U	1.00	2.00
❑ 24 Ryld Argith (Drow) R	10.00	20.00
❑ 25 Wyvern R	7.50	15.00
❑ 26 Achaierai R	7.50	15.00
❑ 27 Bladebearer Hobgoblin U	1.00	2.00
❑ 28 Dekanter Goblin C	.50	1.00
❑ 29 Destrachan U	1.00	2.00
❑ 30 Emerald Claw Soldier C	.50	1.00
❑ 31 Fiendish Dire Weasel C	.50	1.00
❑ 32 Green Dragon (very young) R	10.00	20.00
❑ 33 Half-Elf Hexblade U	1.00	2.00
❑ 34 Half-Illithid Lizardfolk U	1.00	2.00
❑ 35 Hook Horror R	7.50	15.00
❑ 36 Iron Cobra U	1.00	2.00
❑ 37 Kobold Champion C	.50	1.00
❑ 38 Kobold Sorcerer U	1.00	2.00
❑ 39 Mind Flayer Telepath R	10.00	20.00
❑ 40 Mongrelfolk C	.50	1.00
❑ 41 Myconid Guard C	.50	1.00
❑ 42 Sahuagin Ranger U	1.00	2.00
❑ 43 Silent Wolf Goblin C	.50	1.00
❑ 44 Skullsplitter R	6.00	12.00
❑ 45 Flesh Golem R	7.50	15.00
❑ 46 Carrion Tribe Barbarian C	.50	1.00
❑ 47 Choker U	1.00	2.00
❑ 48 Chuul R	7.50	15.00
❑ 49 Fiendish Giant Praying Mantis R	7.50	15.00
❑ 50 Gibbering Mouther R	7.50	15.00
❑ 51 Gnoll C	.50	1.00
❑ 52 Gnoll Skeleton C	.50	1.00
❑ 53 Ice Troll R	7.50	15.00
❑ 54 Mad Slasher U	1.00	2.00
❑ 55 Mountain Orc C	.50	1.00
❑ 56 Ogre Zombie R	7.50	15.00
❑ 57 Orc Sergeant U	1.00	2.00
❑ 58 Taer C	.50	1.00
❑ 59 Yuan-Ti Abomination R	7.50	15.00
❑ 60 Yuan-Ti Halfblood U	1.00	2.00

2004 Dungeons and Dragons Archfiends Miniatures

❑ 1 Cleric of Lathander U	1.00	2.00
❑ 2 Dalelands Militia C	.50	1.00
❑ 3 Gold Dwarf Fighter U	1.00	2.00
❑ 4 Human Dragonslayer U	1.00	2.00
❑ 5 Large Silver Dragon R	25.00	40.00
❑ 6 Medium Earth Elemental U	1.00	2.00
❑ 7 Paladin of Torm R	10.00	20.00
❑ 8 Soldier of Cormyr C	.50	1.00
❑ 9 Healer U	1.00	2.00
❑ 10 Mialee, Elf Wizard U	1.00	2.00
❑ 11 Catfolk C	.50	1.00
❑ 12 Champion of Eilistraee R	15.00	30.00
❑ 13 Cleric of Kord U	1.00	2.00
❑ 14 Drizzt, Drow Ranger R	30.00	50.00
❑ 15 Evermeet Wizard U	1.00	2.00
❑ 16 Graycloak Ranger C	.50	1.00
❑ 17 Halfling Ranger U	1.00	2.00
❑ 18 Halfling Wizard U	1.00	2.00
❑ 19 Ialdabode, Human Psion U	1.00	2.00
❑ 20 Moon Elf Fighter U	1.00	2.00
❑ 21 Ragnara, Psychic Warrior U	1.00	2.00
❑ 22 Unicorn R	12.50	25.00
❑ 23 Githzerai C	.50	1.00
❑ 24 Sage C	.50	1.00
❑ 25 Clay Golem R	12.50	25.00
❑ 26 Half-Orc Barbarian U	1.00	2.00
❑ 27 Wereboar U	1.00	2.00
❑ 28 Aspect of Bane R	10.00	20.00
❑ 29 Bone Devil R	10.00	20.00
❑ 30 Dark Moon Monk U	1.00	2.00
❑ 31 Dread Guard C	.50	1.00
❑ 32 Duergar Warrior C	.50	1.00
❑ 33 Erinyes R	10.00	20.00
❑ 34 Gauth R	12.50	25.00
❑ 35 Human Cleric of Bane R	10.00	20.00
❑ 36 Nothic U	1.00	2.00
❑ 37 Red Wizard R	12.50	25.00
❑ 38 Snig the Axe C	.50	1.00
❑ 39 Xill U	1.00	2.00
❑ 40 Zhentarim Fighter C	.50	1.00

❑ 41 Gravehound C .50 1.00
❑ 42 Ochre Jelly R 12.50 25.00
❑ 43 Warrior Skeleton C .50 1.00
❑ 44 Abyssal Eviscerator U 1.00 2.00
❑ 45 Aspect of Demogorgon R 12.50 25.00
❑ 46 Aspect of Lolth R 15.00 30.00
❑ 47 Aspect of Orcus R 12.50 25.00
❑ 48 Cultist of the Dragon C .50 1.00
❑ 49 Cursed Spirit C .50 1.00
❑ 50 Drow Sergeant U 1.00 2.00
❑ 51 Githyanki Fighter U 1.00 2.00
❑ 52 Gnoll Archer C .50 1.00
❑ 53 Hill Giant R 12.50 25.00
❑ 54 Medium Fire Elemental U 1.00 2.00
❑ 55 Orc Champion R 12.50 25.00
❑ 56 Orc Raider C .50 1.00
❑ 57 Vampire Aristocrat R 12.50 25.00
❑ 58 Vrock R 12.50 25.00
❑ 59 Young Minotaur U 1.00 2.00
❑ 60 Yuan-Ti Pureblood U 1.00 2.00

2004 Dungeons and Dragons Giants of Legend Miniatures

❑ 1 Bronze Wyrmling U 1.00 2.00
❑ 2 Dwarf Sergeant U 1.00 2.00
❑ 3 Standardbearer U 1.00 2.00
❑ 4 Stone Golem R 10.00 20.00
❑ 5 Sword of Glory U 1.00 2.00
❑ 6 Warforged Fighter U 1.00 2.00
❑ 7 Warmage U 1.00 2.00
❑ 8 Young Master R 7.50 15.00
❑ 9 Aramil, Adventurer U 1.00 2.00
❑ 10 Eberk, Adventurer U 1.00 2.00
❑ 11 Protectar U 1.00 2.00
❑ 12 Regdar, Adventurer U 1.00 2.00
❑ 13 Basilisk U 1.00 2.00
❑ 14 Deepshadow Elf C .50 1.00
❑ 15 Fire Genasi Dervish R 7.50 15.00
❑ 16 Githyanki Renegade R 7.50 15.00
❑ 17 Half-Giant Psychic Warrior R 7.50 15.00
❑ 18 Inspiring Marshal R 7.50 15.00
❑ 19 Lidda, Adventurer U 1.00 2.00
❑ 20 Medium Astral Construct C .50 1.00
❑ 21 War Chanter R 7.50 15.00
❑ 22 Xeph Soulknife U 1.00 2.00
❑ 23 City Guard C .50 1.00
❑ 24 Crucian U 1.00 2.00
❑ 25 Dire Wolf R 7.50 15.00
❑ 26 Mordenkainen the Mage R 12.50 25.00
❑ 27 Otyugh R 7.50 15.00
❑ 28 Bladeling Fighter C .50 1.00
❑ 29 Blue C .50 1.00
❑ 30 Dire Rat C .50 1.00
❑ 31 Fire Giant R 12.50 25.00
❑ 32 Hobgoblin Sergeant C .50 1.00
❑ 33 King Snurre R 10.00 20.00
❑ 34 Lemure C .50 1.00
❑ 35 Lizardfolk Rogue C .50 1.00
❑ 36 Lord Soth R 15.00 30.00
❑ 37 Manticore R 7.50 15.00
❑ 38 Rakshasa R 10.00 20.00
❑ 39 Scarlet Brotherhood Monk U 1.00 2.00
❑ 40 Zombie C .50 1.00
❑ 41 Blue Slaad R 10.00 20.00
❑ 42 Bugbear Footpad C .50 1.00
❑ 43 Displacer Serpent C .50 1.00
❑ 44 Drider Sorcerer R 10.00 20.00
❑ 45 Drow Fighter U 1.00 2.00
❑ 46 Drow Rogue U 1.00 2.00
❑ 47 Ettercap C .50 1.00
❑ 48 Frost Giant R 12.50 25.00
❑ 49 Ghast C .50 1.00
❑ 50 Gnoll Sergeant U 1.00 2.00
❑ 51 Grick C .50 1.00
❑ 52 Lareth the Beautiful R 7.50 15.00
❑ 53 Lich Necromancer R 12.50 25.00
❑ 54 Minotaur R 10.00 20.00
❑ 55 Minotaur Skeleton R 7.50 15.00
❑ 56 Orc Brute C .50 1.00
❑ 57 Quasit U 1.00 2.00
❑ 58 Red Wyrmling R 7.50 15.00
❑ 59 Tanarukk C .50 1.00
❑ 60 Werewolf U 1.00 2.00
❑ 61 Huge Gold Dragon R .50
❑ 62 Cloud Giant U 1.00 2.00
❑ 63 Storm Giant R 12.50 25.00
❑ 64 Treant U 1.00 2.00
❑ 65 Warforged Titan R 15.00 30.00
❑ 66 Behir R 15.00 30.00
❑ 67 Bulette U 1.00 2.00
❑ 68 Fiendish Tyrannosaurus U 1.00 2.00
❑ 69 Fomorian U 1.00 2.00
❑ 70 Glabrezu R 20.00 35.00
❑ 71 Huge Red Dragon R 35.00 60.00
❑ 72 Nightwalker U 1.00 2.00

2005 Dungeons and Dragons Angelfire Miniatures

❑ 1 Caravan Guard C .50 1.00
❑ 2 Cleric of Dol Arrah U 1.00 2.00
❑ 3 Dwarf Raider C .50 1.00
❑ 4 Dwarf Wizard U 1.00 2.00
❑ 5 Justice Archon U 1.00 2.00
❑ 6 Mounted Paladin R 10.00 20.00
❑ 7 Spiker Champion U 1.00 2.00
❑ 8 Stone Giant R 7.50 15.00
❑ 9 Sword Archon R 6.00 12.00
❑ 10 Trumpet Archon R 6.00 12.00
❑ 11 Ulmo Lightbringer R 6.00 12.00
❑ 12 Village Priest U 1.00 2.00
❑ 13 Werebear U 1.00 2.00
❑ 14 Archmage R 7.50 15.00
❑ 15 Celestial Pegasus R 6.00 12.00
❑ 16 Divine Crusader of Corellon R 6.00 12.00
❑ 17 Djinni R 7.50 15.00
❑ 18 Elf Swashbuckler U 1.00 2.00
❑ 19 Ghaele Eladrin R 6.00 12.00
❑ 20 Large Air Elemental U 1.00 2.00
❑ 21 Large Copper Dragon R 10.00 20.00
❑ 22 Longstrider Ranger U 1.00 2.00
❑ 23 Phoelarch R 6.00 12.00
❑ 24 Talenta Halfling U 1.00 2.00
❑ 25 Thorn U 1.00 2.00
❑ 26 Thri-Kreen Barbarian R 7.50 15.00
❑ 27 Wand Expert U 1.00 2.00
❑ 28 Weretiger U 1.00 2.00
❑ 29 Wild Elf Raider C .50 1.00
❑ 30 Xeph Warrior C .50 1.00
❑ 31 Dwarf Mercenary C .50 1.00
❑ 32 Blackscale Lizardfolk U 1.00 2.00
❑ 33 Red Slaad R 7.50 15.00
❑ 34 Scorpion Clan Drow Fighter U 1.00 2.00
❑ 35 Barbed Devil R 6.00 12.00
❑ 36 Chain Devil R 7.50 15.00
❑ 37 Chraal U 1.00 2.00
❑ 38 Direguard C .50 1.00
❑ 39 Efreeti R 7.50 15.00
❑ 40 Flamebrother Salamander U 1.00 2.00
❑ 41 Ghostly Consort R 6.00 12.00
❑ 42 Hobgoblin Impaler C .50 1.00
❑ 43 Imp U 1.00 2.00
❑ 44 Kobold Soldier C .50 1.00
❑ 45 Mina, Dark Cleric R 7.50 15.00
❑ 46 Ogre Mage R 6.00 12.00
❑ 47 Orog Warlord R 6.00 12.00
❑ 48 Steel Predator R 6.00 12.00
❑ 49 Vargouille U 1.00 2.00
❑ 50 Skeletal Archer C .50 1.00
❑ 51 Abyssal Skulker C .50 1.00
❑ 52 Bugbear Champion of Erythnul U 1.00 2.00
❑ 53 Feral Minotaur U 1.00 2.00
❑ 54 Fiendish Dire Wolverine U 1.00 2.00
❑ 55 Hezrou R 7.50 15.00
❑ 56 Magmin U 1.00 2.00
❑ 57 Ophidian C .50 1.00
❑ 58 Orc Wolf Shaman R 6.00 12.00
❑ 59 Troll Slasher U 1.00 2.00
❑ 60 Wrackspawn C .50 1.00

2005 Dungeons and Dragons Deathknell Miniatures

❑ 1 Champion of Yondalla R 7.50 15.00
❑ 2 Couatl R 10.00 20.00
❑ 3 Dwarf Artificer U 1.00 2.00
❑ 4 Dwarf Caver U 1.00 2.00
❑ 5 Dwarf Phalanx Soldier U 1.00 2.00
❑ 6 Dwarf Samurai R 7.50 15.00
❑ 7 Gold Dragon R 10.00 20.00
❑ 8 Skullclan Hunter U 1.00 2.00
❑ 9 Soldier of Thrane U 1.00 2.00
❑ 10 Valorous Prince R 7.50 15.00
❑ 11 Warforged Wizard U 1.00 2.00
❑ 12 Whirling Steel Monk U 1.00 2.00
❑ 13 Celestial Dire Badger C .50 1.00
❑ 14 Catfolk Wilder U 1.00 2.00
❑ 15 Centaur Hero R 7.50 15.00
❑ 16 Dark Traveler U 1.00 2.00
❑ 17 Dragonblade Ninja U 1.00 2.00
❑ 18 Goliath Barbarian R 7.50 15.00
❑ 19 Greenfang Druid R 7.50 15.00
❑ 20 Griffon R 7.50 15.00
❑ 21 Ibixian C .50 1.00
❑ 22 Rask, Half-Orc Chainfighter R 7.50 15.00
❑ 23 Renegade Warlock U 1.00 2.00
❑ 24 Undying Soldier U 1.00 2.00
❑ 25 Voice of Battle U 1.00 2.00
❑ 26 Dire Bear U 1.00 2.00
❑ 27 Timber Wolf C .50 1.00
❑ 28 Giant Frog C .50 1.00
❑ 29 Wood Woad U 1.00 2.00
❑ 30 Ambush Drake R 7.50 15.00
❑ 31 Aspect of Nerull R 10.00 20.00
❑ 32 Beholder R 25.00 40.00
❑ 33 Death Knight R 7.50 15.00
❑ 34 Goblin Adept C .50 1.00
❑ 35 Grell U 1.00 2.00
❑ 36 Grim Necromancer U 1.00 2.00
❑ 37 Kruthik Hatchling C .50 1.00
❑ 38 Large Blue Dragon R 10.00 20.00
❑ 39 Mummy Lord R 7.50 15.00
❑ 40 Skeletal Dwarf C .50 1.00
❑ 41 Skullcrusher Ogre U 1.00 2.00
❑ 42 Spectre R 7.50 15.00
❑ 43 Spellstitched Hobgoblin Zombie C .50 1.00
❑ 44 Thaskor R 7.50 15.00
❑ 45 Warpriest of Hextor R 7.50 15.00
❑ 46 Bloodhulk Fighter U 1.00 2.00
❑ 47 Boneclaw R 7.50 15.00
❑ 48 Bullywug Thug C .50 1.00
❑ 49 Burning Skeleton U 1.00 2.00
❑ 50 Deathlock C .50 1.00
❑ 51 Dolgrim U 1.00 2.00
❑ 52 Ettin Skirmisher R 7.50 15.00
❑ 53 Fiendish Monstrous Scorpion R 7.50 15.00
❑ 54 Flind Captain U 1.00 2.00
❑ 55 Forest Troll U 1.00 2.00
❑ 56 Kenku Sneak C .50 1.00
❑ 57 Orc Savage C .50 1.00
❑ 58 Ravenous Vampire R 7.50 15.00
❑ 59 Vampire Spawn U 1.00 2.00
❑ 60 Zombie White Dragon R 12.50 25.00

2005 Dungeons and Dragons Underdark Miniatures

❑ 1 Battle Plate Marshal R 6.00 12.00
❑ 2 Dwarf Ancestor R 6.00 12.00
❑ 3 Earth Shugenja U 1.00 2.00
❑ 4 Githzerai Monk U 1.00 2.00
❑ 5 Gold Dwarf Soldier C .50 1.00
❑ 6 Half-Orc Paladin U 1.00 2.00
❑ 7 Lantern Bearer U 1.00 2.00
❑ 8 Loyal Earth Elemental U 1.00 2.00
❑ 9 Marut R 6.00 12.00
❑ 9 Epic Marut R 7.50 15.00
❑ 10 Medium Silver Dragon R 12.50 25.00
❑ 11 Royal Guard C .50 1.00
❑ 12 Slayer of Domiel R 6.00 12.00
❑ 13A Aspect of Kord R 6.00 12.00
❑ 13B Epic Aspect of Kord R 6.00 12.00
❑ 14 Dromite Wilder R 6.00 12.00
❑ 15 Elf Stalker U 1.00 2.00
❑ 16A Elminster of Shadowdale R 12.50 25.00
❑ 16B Epic Elminster of Shadowdale R 6.00 12.00
❑ 17 Guenhwyvar U 1.00 2.00
❑ 18 Half-Ogre Barbarian U 1.00 2.00
❑ 19 Halfling Sneak C .50 1.00
❑ 20 Nentyar Hunter U 1.00 2.00
❑ 21A Epic Rikka, Angelic Avenger R 6.00 12.00
❑ 21B Rikka, Angelic Avenger R 7.50 15.00
❑ 22 Satyr U 1.00 2.00
❑ 23 Spirit Folk Fighter C .50 1.00
❑ 24 Wizard Tactician U 1.00 2.00
❑ 25A Epic Iron Golem R 6.00 12.00
❑ 25B Iron Golem R 7.50 15.00
❑ 26A Epic Justicator R 6.00 12.00
❑ 26B Justicator R 6.00 12.00
❑ 27 Mercenary Sergeant C .50 1.00
❑ 28 Xorn U 1.00 2.00
❑ 29 Monitor Lizard C .50 1.00
❑ 30 Ankheg U 1.00 2.00
❑ 31 Xen'drik Champion R 6.00 12.00
❑ 32A Artemis Entreri R 10.00 20.00
❑ 32B Epic Artemis Entreri R 6.00 12.00
❑ 33 Dark Naga U 1.00 2.00
❑ 34 Dolgaunt Monk U 1.00 2.00
❑ 35 Duergar Champion U 1.00 2.00
❑ 36 Half-Orc Executioner U 1.00 2.00
❑ 37 Helmed Horror R 6.00 12.00
❑ 38 Kobold Miner C .50 1.00
❑ 39 Skeletal Equiceph U 1.00 2.00
❑ 40 Troglodyte Captain U 1.00 2.00
❑ 41A Balor R 15.00 30.00
❑ 41B Epic Balor R 6.00 12.00
❑ 42 Dark Creeper C .50 1.00
❑ 43A Death Slaad R 6.00 12.00
❑ 43B Epic Death Slaad R 6.00 12.00
❑ 44 Dire Bat U 1.00 2.00
❑ 45 Draegloth R 6.00 12.00
❑ 46 Drow Arachnomancer R 7.50 15.00
❑ 47 Drow Arcane Guard U 1.00 2.00
❑ 48 Gray Render R 6.00 12.00
❑ 49 Grimlock Barbarian U 1.00 2.00
❑ 50 Half-Fiend Ogre R 6.00 12.00
❑ 51 Hunched Giant R 6.00 12.00
❑ 52 Large Deep Dragon R 10.00 20.00
❑ 53 Lolth's Sting C .50 1.00
❑ 54 Mounted Drow Patrol R 7.50 15.00
❑ 55 Orc Skeleton C .50 1.00
❑ 56 Roper R 6.00 12.00
❑ 57 Spider of Lolth C .50 1.00
❑ 58 Swarm of Spiders U 1.00 2.00
❑ 59 Troglodyte Barbarian C .50 1.00
❑ 60 Winter Wolf U 1.00 2.00

2006 Dungeons and Dragons Blood War Miniatures

❑ 1 Arcadian Hippogriff R 6.00 12.00
❑ 2 Celestial Giant Stag Beetle U 1.00 2.00
❑ 3 Dwarf Sniper U 1.00 2.00
❑ 4 Elf Dragonkith R 6.00 12.00
❑ 5 Elf Warmage U 1.00 2.00
❑ 6 Half-Orc Spy U 1.00 2.00
❑ 7 Hammerer C .50 1.00
❑ 8 Harmonium Guard C .50 1.00
❑ 9 Kolyarut R 6.00 12.00
❑ 10 Solar R 7.50 15.00
❑ 11 Soldier of Bytopia C .50 1.00
❑ 12 Thundertusk Cavalry R 6.00 12.00
❑ 13 Air Genasi Swashbuckler R 6.00 12.00
❑ 14 Bralani Eladrin R 6.00 12.00
❑ 15 Centaur War Hulk R 6.00 12.00
❑ 16 Free League Ranger C .50 1.00
❑ 17 Gnome Trickster U 1.00 2.00
❑ 18 Hero of Valhalla C .50 1.00
❑ 19 Lillend R 6.00 12.00
❑ 20 Medium Copper Dragon U 1.00 2.00
❑ 21 Phoera U 1.00 2.00
❑ 22 Shadowdancer U 1.00 2.00
❑ 23 Storm Silverhand R 7.50 15.00
❑ 24 Valenar Nomad Charger R 6.00 12.00
❑ 25 Dragonmark Heir of Deneith U 1.00 2.00
❑ 26 Maug U 1.00 2.00
❑ 27 Living Flaming Sphere U 1.00 2.00
❑ 28 Acheron Goblin C .50 1.00
❑ 29 Blood of Vol Cultist C .50 1.00
❑ 30 Bluespawn Stormlizard U 1.00 2.00
❑ 31 Fire Giant Forgepriest R 7.50 15.00
❑ 32 Greenspawn Sneak C .50 1.00
❑ 33 Hellcat R 6.00 12.00
❑ 34 Horned Devil R 10.00 20.00
❑ 35 Ice Devil R 7.50 15.00
❑ 36 Karsite Fighter U 1.00 2.00
❑ 37 Kobold Monk C .50 1.00
❑ 38 Large Water Elemental U 1.00 2.00
❑ 39 Lord of Blades R 6.00 12.00
❑ 40 Mercykiller U 1.00 2.00
❑ 41 Mezzoloth U 1.00 2.00
❑ 42 Pit Fiend R 10.00 20.00
❑ 43 Red Hand War Sorcerer U 1.00 2.00
❑ 44 Soulknife Infiltrator U 1.00 2.00
❑ 45 Chasme R 6.00 12.00
❑ 46 Demonic Gnoll Priestess U 6.00 12.00
❑ 47 Doomguard C .50 1.00
❑ 48 Earth Element Gargoyle U 1.00 2.00
❑ 49 Ethereal Marauder U 1.00 2.00
❑ 50 Fiendish Snake C .50 1.00
❑ 51 Githyanki Dragon Knight R 6.00 12.00
❑ 52 Gnoll Barbarian U 1.00 2.00
❑ 53 Green Slaad U 1.00 2.00
❑ 54 Howler R 6.00 12.00
❑ 55 Marilith R 7.50 15.00
❑ 56 Orc Wizard U 1.00 2.00
❑ 57 Owlbear Rager R 6.00 12.00
❑ 58 Skeletal Reaper C .50 1.00
❑ 59 Succubus R 6.00 12.00
❑ 60 Vlaakith the Lich Queen R 7.50 15.00

2006 Dungeons and Dragons War Drums Miniatures

❑ 1 Arcane Ballista R 6.00 12.00
❑ 2 Arcanix Guard C .50 1.00
❑ 3 Aspect of Moradin R 7.50 15.00
❑ 4 Axe Soldier C .50 1.00
❑ 5 Combat Medic U 1.00 2.00
❑ 6 Elemental Wall U 1.00 2.00
❑ 7 Large Bronze Dragon R 10.00 20.00
❑ 8 Sacred Watcher U 1.00 2.00
❑ 9 Sand Giant R 6.00 12.00
❑ 10 Shieldwall Soldier C .50 1.00
❑ 11 Warforged Bodyguard U 1.00 2.00
❑ 12 Warforged Captain U 1.00 2.00
❑ 13 Warforged Scout U 1.00 2.00
❑ 14 Warpriest of Moradin U 1.00 2.00
❑ 15 Brass Samurai U 1.00 2.00
❑ 16 Dragon Totem Hero R 6.00 12.00
❑ 17 Dragonne R 6.00 12.00
❑ 18 Halfling Slinger C .50 1.00
❑ 19 Hunting Cougar C .50 1.00
❑ 20 Lion of Talisid U 1.00 2.00
❑ 21 Mephling Pyromancer U 1.00 2.00
❑ 22 Steelheart Archer U 1.00 2.00
❑ 23 Warbound Impaler R 6.00 12.00
❑ 24 Warforged Barbarian R 6.00 12.00
❑ 25 Wemic Barbarian R 6.00 12.00
❑ 26 Wood Elf Ranger C .50 1.00
❑ 27 Gulgar R 6.00 12.00
❑ 28 Aspect of Hextor R 7.50 15.00
❑ 29 Flameskull U 1.00 2.00
❑ 30 Goblin Blackblade C .50 1.00
❑ 31 Goblin Underboss U 1.00 2.00
❑ 32 Hobgoblin Archer C .50 1.00
❑ 33 Inspired Lieutenant U 1.00 2.00
❑ 34 Karrnathi Zombie U 1.00 2.00
❑ 35 Khumat R 6.00 12.00
❑ 36 Large Duergar U 1.00 2.00
❑ 37 Night Hag R 6.00 12.00
❑ 38 Shuluth, Archvillain R 6.00 12.00
❑ 39 Skeletal Legionnaire C .50 1.00
❑ 40 Snig, Worg Rider R 6.00 12.00
❑ 41 Terror Wight C .50 1.00
❑ 42 War Troll R 7.50 15.00
❑ 43 Zakya Rakshasa R 6.00 12.00
❑ 44 Blood Ghost Berserker U 1.00 2.00
❑ 45 Chimera R 6.00 12.00
❑ 46 Derro C .50 1.00
❑ 47 Fiendish Girallon U 1.00 2.00
❑ 48 Frost Dwarf U 1.00 2.00
❑ 49 Hill Giant Barbarian U 1.00 2.00
❑ 50 Hill Giant Chieftain R 6.00 12.00
❑ 51 Horde Zombie C .50 1.00
❑ 52 Howling Orc C .50 1.00
❑ 53 King Obould Many-Arrows R 6.00 12.00
❑ 54 Ogre War Hulk R 6.00 12.00
❑ 55 Orc Mauler C .50 1.00
❑ 56 Orc Wardrummer R 6.00 12.00
❑ 57 Quaggoth Slave C .50 1.00
❑ 58 Tiefling Blademaster U 1.00 2.00
❑ 59 Troglodyte Thug C .50 1.00
❑ 60 Warduke R 7.50 15.00

2006 Dungeons and Dragons War of the Dragon Queen Miniatures

❑ 1 Aasimar Fighter C .50 1.00
❑ 2 Epic Aspect of Bahamut R 12.50 25.00
❑ 3 Cleric of Syreth U 1.00 2.00
❑ 4 Dragonborn Fighter R 5.00 10.00
❑ 5 Golden Protector R 5.00 10.00
❑ 6 Meepo, Dragonlord R 5.00 10.00
❑ 7A Epic Slaughterstone Eviscerator R 5.00 10.00
❑ 7B Slaughterstone Eviscerator R 5.00 10.00
❑ 8A Epic Tordek, Dwarf Champion R 5.00 10.00
❑ 8B Tordek, Dwarf Champion R 5.00 10.00
❑ 9 War Weaver R 5.00 10.00
❑ 10 Bonded Fire Summoner U 1.00 2.00
❑ 11 Clawfoot Rider R 5.00 10.00
❑ 12 Goliath Cleric of Kavaki R 5.00 10.00
❑ 13A Epic Griffon Cavalry R 5.00 10.00
❑ 13B Griffon Cavalry R 7.50 15.00
❑ 14 Small Copper Dragon U 1.00 2.00
❑ 15 Spellscale Sorcerer R 5.00 10.00
❑ 16 Storm Archer U 1.00 2.00
❑ 17 Tavern Brawler C .50 1.00
❑ 18 Warden of the Wood U 1.00 2.00
❑ 19 Azer Fighter C .50 1.00
❑ 20 Epic Huge Fire Elemental U 1.00 2.00
❑ 21 Epic Purple Worm U 1.00 2.00
❑ 22 War Ape C .50 1.00
❑ 23 Wizened Elder Watcher R 5.00 10.00
❑ 24 Epic Aspect of Tiamat R 15.00 30.00
❑ 25A Blackguard on Nightmare R 7.50 15.00
❑ 25B Epic Blackguard on Nightmare R 5.00 10.00
❑ 26 Epic Bluespawn Godslayer U 1.00 2.00
❑ 27 Cadaver Collector R 7.50 15.00
❑ 28 Diseased Dire Rat C .50 1.00
❑ 29 Epic Displacer Beast Pack Lord U 1.00 2.00
❑ 30 Doom Fist Monk C .50 1.00
❑ 31 Epic Dracolich R 12.50 25.00
❑ 32 Dragonwrought Kobold U 1.00 2.00
❑ 33 Dread Warrior C .50 1.00
❑ 34 Epic Eldritch Giant R 6.00 12.00
❑ 35 Greenspawn Razorfiend U 1.00 2.00
❑ 36 Hobgoblin Talon of Tiamat R 5.00 10.00
❑ 37 Kobold Zombie C .50 1.00
❑ 38 Large Green Dragon R 10.00 20.00
❑ 39 Wererat Rogue U 1.00 2.00
❑ 40 Poison Dusk Lizardfolk U 1.00 2.00
❑ 41 Witchknife C .50 1.00
❑ 42 Blackspawn Exterminator U 1.00 2.00
❑ 43 Cleric of Laogzed C .50 1.00
❑ 44 Cloudreaver C .50 1.00
❑ 45 Demonic Gnoll Archer U 1.00 2.00
❑ 46 Epic Huge Fiendish Spider U 1.00 2.00
❑ 47 Hunting Hyena C .50 1.00
❑ 48 Large Fang Dragon R 7.50 15.00
❑ 49 Magma Hurler R 5.00 10.00
❑ 50 Epic Mountain Troll U 1.00 2.00
❑ 51 Ogre Skirmisher U 1.00 2.00
❑ 52 Redspawn Firebelcher R 5.00 10.00
❑ 53 Small Black Dragon U 1.00 2.00
❑ 54 Small Fire Elemental U 1.00 2.00
❑ 55 Epic Sorcerer on Black Dragon R 10.00 20.00
❑ 56 Stirge U 1.00 2.00
❑ 57 Epic Tundra Scout R 7.50 15.00
❑ 58 Twig Blight C .50 1.00
❑ 59 Whitespawn Hordeling C .50 1.00
❑ 60 Yuan-Ti Halfblood Sorcerer U 1.00 2.00

2007 Dungeons and Dragons Desert of Desolation Miniatures

❑ 1 Angel of Vengeance R 7.50 15.00
❑ 2 Animated Statue C .50 1.00
❑ 3 Dwarf Brawler U 1.00 2.00
❑ 4 Dwarf Maulfighter U 1.00 2.00
❑ 5 Human Cleric of Bahamut U 1.00 2.00
❑ 6 Macetail Behemoth R 7.50 15.00
❑ 7 Militia Archer C .50 1.00

❑ 8 Sphinx R 7.50 15.00
❑ 9 Thundertusk Boar U 1.00 2.00
❑ 10 Bruenor Battlehammer R 7.50 15.00
❑ 11 Farmer C .50 1.00
❑ 12 Merchant Guard C .50 1.00
❑ 13 Warhorse U 1.00 2.00
❑ 14 Black Woods Dryad C .50 1.00
❑ 15 Cliffwalk Archer U 1.00 2.00
❑ 16 Elf Conjurer R 7.50 15.00
❑ 17 Eternal Blade U 1.00 2.00
❑ 18 Halfling Enchanter U 1.00 2.00
❑ 19 Halfling Rogue U 1.00 2.00
❑ 20 Gelatinous Cube R 7.50 15.00
❑ 21 Mercenary General R 7.50 15.00
❑ 22 Visejaw Crocodile U 1.00 2.00
❑ 23 Capricious Copper Dragon R 12.50 25.00
❑ 24 Tiefling Cleric U 1.00 2.00
❑ 25 Tiefling Rogue U 1.00 2.00
❑ 26 Astral Stalker U 1.00 2.00
❑ 27 Blood of Vol Fanatic C .50 1.00
❑ 28 Guardian Mummy U 1.00 2.00
❑ 29 Manticore Sniper R 7.50 15.00
❑ 30 Nightmare R 7.50 15.00
❑ 31 Osyluth R 7.50 15.00
❑ 32 Rot Scarab Swarm C .50 1.00
❑ 33 Sahuagin U 1.00 2.00
❑ 34 Sahuagin Baron R 7.50 15.00
❑ 35 Shakar-Kai Assassin U 1.00 2.00
❑ 36 Shadow Mastiff U 1.00 2.00
❑ 37 Spined Devil U 1.00 2.00
❑ 38 Blade Spider R 7.50 15.00
❑ 39 Boneshard Skeleton C .50 1.00
❑ 40 Cyclops R 7.50 15.00
❑ 41 Demonweb Swarm C .50 1.00
❑ 42 Flame Snake C .50 1.00
❑ 43 Naga R 7.50 15.00
❑ 44 Bar-Lgura R 7.50 15.00
❑ 45 Drider R 10.00 20.00
❑ 46 Drow Blademaster C .50 1.00
❑ 47 Drow Spider Priestess U 1.00 2.00
❑ 48 Ettercap Webspinner U 1.00 2.00
❑ 49 Feral Troll R 7.50 15.00
❑ 50 Fire Archon R 7.50 15.00
❑ 51 Large Fire Elemental U 1.00 2.00
❑ 52 Ogre Brute R 7.50 15.00
❑ 53 Rage Drake R 7.50 15.00
❑ 54 Ravenous Ghoul U 1.00 2.00
❑ 55 Shrieking Harpy U 1.00 2.00
❑ 56 Snaketongue Cultist C .50 1.00
❑ 57 Umber Hulk Delver R 10.00 20.00
❑ 58 Werewolf Champion R 7.50 15.00
❑ 59 Yuan-Ti Champion of Zehir R 7.50 15.00
❑ 60 Yuan-Ti Malison U 1.00 2.00

2007 Dungeons and Dragons Night Below Miniatures

❑ 1 Arcadian Avenger U 1.00 2.00
❑ 2 Brass Golem U 1.00 2.00
❑ 3 Champion of Dol Dorn U 1.00 2.00
❑ 4 Deep Legionnaire C .50 1.00
❑ 5 Delver Sergeant C .50 1.00
❑ 6 Earth Mephit U 1.00 2.00
❑ 7 Guard of Mithral Hall C .50 1.00
❑ 8 Guardian Naga R 7.50 15.00
❑ 9 Kalashtar Bodyguard U 1.00 2.00
❑ 10A Epic Large Gold Dragon R 7.50 15.00
❑ 10B Large Gold Dragon R 10.00 20.00
❑ 11 Shadowbane Inquisitor U 1.00 2.00
❑ 12 Valiant Cavalry R 7.50 15.00
❑ 13 Greyhawk City Militia Sergeant C .50 1.00
❑ 14 Raistlin Majere R 12.50 25.00
❑ 15 Darkmantle C .50 1.00
❑ 16 Digester U 1.00 2.00
❑ 17 Dire Tiger R 7.50 15.00
❑ 18 Giant Eagle U 1.00 2.00
❑ 19 Greater Basilisk R 7.50 15.00
❑ 20 Halfling Tombseeker U 1.00 2.00
❑ 21 Hierophant of the Seventh Wind R 7.50 15.00
❑ 22 Verdant of the Reaver U 1.00 2.00
❑ 23 Warpriest of Vandria U 1.00 2.00
❑ 24 Wild Mage U 1.00 2.00
❑ 25 Epic Wulfgar R 7.50 15.00
❑ 25 Wulfgar R 7.50 15.00
❑ 26 Aspect of Loviatar R 7.50 15.00
❑ 27 Assassin R 7.50 15.00
❑ 28 Bluespawn Ambusher C .50 1.00
❑ 29 Dread Wraith R 7.50 15.00
❑ 30 Exarch of Tyranny R 7.50 15.00
❑ 31 Greater Barghest R 5.00 10.00
❑ 32 Greenspawn Zealot U 1.00 2.00
❑ 33 Hobgoblin Marshal C .50 1.00
❑ 34 Ice Mephit U 1.00 2.00
❑ 35 Kobold Trapmaker C .50 1.00
❑ 36 Lady Vol R 7.50 15.00
❑ 37 Medusa Archer U 1.00 2.00
❑ 38 Mind Flayer Lich R 7.50 15.00
❑ 39 Noble Salamander R 7.50 15.00
❑ 40 Prisoner C .50 1.00
❑ 41 Skeletal Courser R 7.50 15.00
❑ 42 Trained Carrion Crawler U 1.00 2.00
❑ 43 Krenshar U 1.00 2.00
❑ 44 Lifeleech Otyugh R 7.50 15.00
❑ 45 Babau U 1.00 2.00
❑ 46 Berserk Flesh Golem R 7.50 15.00
❑ 47 Carnage Demon C .50 1.00
❑ 48 Cerebrilith U 1.00 2.00
❑ 49 Clawborn Scorrow R 7.50 15.00
❑ 50 Dracotaur Rager R 7.50 15.00
❑ 51 Drow Enforcer U 1.00 2.00
❑ 52 Frost Giant Jarl R 7.50 15.00
❑ 53 Gnoll Claw Fighter C .50 1.00
❑ 54 Kuo-Toa Hunter C .50 1.00
❑ 55 Kuo-Toa Whip U 1.00 2.00
❑ 56 Large Chaos Beast U 1.00 2.00
❑ 57 Large Shadow Dragon R 10.00 20.00
❑ 58 Large White Dragon R 10.00 20.00
❑ 59 Orc Banebreak Rider R 7.50 15.00
❑ 60 Shadow U 1.00 2.00

2008 Dungeons and Dragons Against the Giants Miniatures

❑ 1 Shocktroop Devil R 7.50 15.00
❑ 2 Voracious Ice Devil R 7.50 15.00
❑ 3 Deathpriest of Orcus U 1.00 2.00
❑ 4 Degenerate Cultist of Orcus C .50 1.00
❑ 5 Gnaw Demon C .50 1.00
❑ 6 Efreeti Flamestrider R 7.50 15.00
❑ 7 Visceral Devourer U 1.00 2.00
❑ 8 Doresain, the Ghoul King R 6.00 12.00
❑ 9 Thunderblast Cyclone U 1.00 2.00
❑ 10 Yuan-Ti Anathema R 7.50 15.00
❑ 11 Elder Red Dragon R 15.00 30.00
❑ 12 Fire Titan R 10.00 20.00
❑ 13 Armored Gulvorg U 1.00 2.00
❑ 14 Bugbear Lancebreaker U 1.00 2.00
❑ 15 Dragonborn Defender R 7.50 15.00
❑ 16 Dragonborn Myrmidon R 6.00 12.00
❑ 17 Dwarf Warsword U 1.00 2.00
❑ 18 Feybound Halfling U 1.00 2.00
❑ 19 Fire Giant Raider R 7.50 15.00
❑ 20 Fist of Moradin U 1.00 2.00
❑ 21 Goblin Runner C .50 1.00
❑ 22 Hobgoblin Guard C .50 1.00
❑ 23 Mighty Blademaster R 6.00 12.00
❑ 24 Skullcleave Warrior R 6.00 12.00
❑ 25 Tiefling Gladiator R 6.00 12.00
❑ 26 Fire Bat U 1.00 2.00
❑ 27 Orc Zombie C .50 1.00
❑ 28 Plaguechanged Ghoul U 1.00 2.00
❑ 29 Shadow Hulk R 10.00 20.00
❑ 30 Xorn Ravager U 1.00 2.00
❑ 31 Cave Bear U 1.00 2.00
❑ 32 Cockatrice U 1.00 2.00
❑ 33 Earth Titan U 1.00 2.00
❑ 34 Flamescorched Kobold C .50 1.00
❑ 35 Furious Owlbear R 6.00 12.00
❑ 36 Galeb Duhr C .50 1.00
❑ 37 Lizardfolk Raider U 1.00 2.00
❑ 38 Shifter Claw Adept U 1.00 2.00
❑ 39 Storm Giant Thunderer R 7.50 15.00
❑ 40 Angel of Retribution R 6.00 12.00
❑ 41 Captain of the Watch U 1.00 2.00
❑ 42 Chain Golem U 1.00 2.00
❑ 43 Cloaktrick Rogue R 6.00 12.00
❑ 44 Half-Elf Assassin U 1.00 2.00
❑ 45 Eladrin Pyromancer U 1.00 2.00
❑ 46 Golden Wyvern Initiate U 1.00 2.00
❑ 47 Tomebound Arcanist R 6.00 12.00
❑ 48 Blazing Skeleton U 1.00 2.00
❑ 49 Boneclaw Impaler R 6.00 12.00
❑ 50 Death Titan R 10.00 20.00
❑ 51 Lurking Wraith U 1.00 2.00
❑ 52 Young Adamantine Dragon R 7.50 15.00
❑ 53 Blackroot Treant U 1.00 2.00
❑ 54 Enormous Carrion Crawler U 1.00 2.00
❑ 55 Hellwasp U 1.00 2.00
❑ 56 Ochre Jelly C .50 1.00
❑ 57 Ravenous Dire Rat C .50 1.00
❑ 58 Roper R 6.00 12.00
❑ 59 Elder White Dragon R 15.00 30.00
❑ 60 Elf Arcane Archer U 1.00 2.00

2008 Dungeons and Dragons Dungeons of Dread Miniatures

❑ 1 Dwarf Warlord U 1.00 2.00
❑ 2 Angel of Valor R 6.00 12.00
❑ 3 Cleric of Pelor U 1.00 2.00
❑ 4 Halfling Paladin U 1.00 2.00
❑ 5 Young Silver Dragon R 10.00 20.00
❑ 6 Elf Archer C .50 1.00
❑ 7 Death Knight R 7.50 15.00
❑ 8 Orc Raider C .50 1.00
❑ 9 Young Red Dragon R 10.00 20.00
❑ 10 Gargoyle U 1.00 2.00
❑ 11 Oni R 6.00 12.00
❑ 12 Chillborn C .50 1.00
❑ 13 Drow Spiderguard U 1.00 2.00
❑ 14 Eye of Flame R 10.00 20.00
❑ 15 Immolith R 6.00 12.00
❑ 16 Shadow Demon U 1.00 2.00
❑ 17 Warrior Wight U 1.00 2.00
❑ 18 Howling Hag U 1.00 2.00
❑ 19 Magma Brute U 1.00 2.00
❑ 20 Vrock R 6.00 12.00
❑ 21 Ascendant Hellsword R 6.00 12.00
❑ 22 Rakshasa Baron R 6.00 12.00
❑ 23 Vampire Spawn C .50 1.00
❑ 24 Champion of Baphomet R 6.00 12.00
❑ 25 Balhannoth R 6.00 12.00
❑ 26 Mind Flayer Scourge R 7.50 15.00
❑ 27 Troglodyte Bonecrusher C .50 1.00
❑ 28 Vampire Vizier R 7.50 15.00
❑ 29 Ice Archon U 1.00 2.00
❑ 30 Lamia R 6.00 12.00
❑ 31 Gnoll Marauder U 1.00 2.00
❑ 32 Bugbear Headreaver U 1.00 2.00
❑ 33 Dwarf Shieldmaiden U 1.00 2.00
❑ 34 Goblin Picador C .50 1.00
❑ 35 Human Fighter U 1.00 2.00
❑ 36 Iron Defender C .50 1.00
❑ 37 Dire Wolf U 1.00 2.00
❑ 38 Eltin Jack-of-Irons R 6.00 12.00
❑ 39 Everfrost Ranger U 1.00 2.00
❑ 40 Griffon R 6.00 12.00
❑ 41 Kobold Archer C .50 1.00
❑ 42 Wyvern R 7.50 15.00
❑ 43 Defiant Rake U 1.00 2.00
❑ 44 Emerald Orb Wizard R 6.00 12.00
❑ 45 Grick C .50 1.00
❑ 46 Spectral Magelord R 6.00 12.00
❑ 47 Tiefling Warlock U 1.00 2.00
❑ 48 Warforged Infiltrator U 1.00 2.00
❑ 49 Runecarved Eidolon R 6.00 12.00
❑ 50 Drow Wand Mage U 1.00 2.00
❑ 51 Shade Knight U 1.00 2.00
❑ 52 Skeletal Tomb Guardian R 6.00 12.00
❑ 53 Bulette U 1.00 2.00
❑ 54 Deathjump Spider C .50 1.00
❑ 55 Fen Hydra R 7.50 15.00
❑ 56 Giant Centipede C .50 1.00
❑ 57 Hook Horror U 1.00 2.00
❑ 58 Shadowhunter Bat U 1.00 2.00
❑ 59 Spectral Panther U 1.00 2.00
❑ 60 Bralani R 6.00 12.00

2003 DC Heroclix Cosmic Justice Miniatures

Complete Set (96) 150.00 225.00
Booster Pack 5.00 7.00

❑ 1 Easy Company Soldier R .25 .50
❑ 2 Easy Company Soldier E .50 .75
❑ 3 Easy Company Soldier V .75 1.00
❑ 4 Easy Company Medic R .25 .50
❑ 5 Easy Company Medic E .50 .75
❑ 6 Easy Company Medic V .75 1.00
❑ 7 Parademon Scout R .25 .50
❑ 8 Parademon Scout E .50 .75
❑ 9 Parademon Scout V .75 1.00
❑ 10 Parademon Warrior R .25 .50
❑ 11 Parademon Warrior E .50 .75
❑ 12 Parademon Warrior V .75 1.00
❑ 13 Lex Corp. Security R .25 .50
❑ 14 Lex Corp. Security E .50 .75
❑ 15 Lex Corp. Security V .75 1.00
❑ 16 Lex Corp. Battlesuit R .25 .50
❑ 17 Lex Corp. Battlesuit E .50 .75
❑ 18 Lex Corp. Battlesuit V .75 1.00
❑ 19 Sgt. Rock R .25 .50
❑ 20 Sgt. Rock E .50 .75
❑ 21 Sgt. Rock V 1.00 2.00
❑ 22 Penguin R .50 1.00
❑ 23 Penguin E 1.00 2.00
❑ 24 Penguin V 2.00 3.00
❑ 25 Manhunter R .25 .50
❑ 26 Manhunter E .50 .75
❑ 27 Manhunter V .75 1.00
❑ 28 Fury R .25 .50
❑ 29 Fury E .50 .75
❑ 30 Fury V 1.00 2.00
❑ 31 Poison Ivy R .50 .75
❑ 32 Poison Ivy E .75 1.00
❑ 33 Poison Ivy V 1.00 2.00
❑ 34 Black Canary R .25 .50
❑ 35 Black Canary E .50 .75
❑ 36 Black Canary V .75 1.00
❑ 37 Green Arrow R .75 1.50
❑ 38 Green Arrow E 1.00 3.00
❑ 39 Green Arrow V 5.00 8.00
❑ 40 Troia R .25 .50
❑ 41 Troia E .50 .75
❑ 42 Troia V .75 1.00
❑ 43 Cosmic Boy R .25 .50
❑ 44 Cosmic Boy E .50 .75
❑ 45 Cosmic Boy V .75 1.00
❑ 46 Live Wire R .25 .50
❑ 47 Live Wire E .50 .75
❑ 48 Live Wire V 1.00 2.00
❑ 49 Saturn Girl R .25 .50
❑ 50 Saturn Girl E .50 .75
❑ 51 Saturn Girl V .75 1.00
❑ 52 Fatality R .25 .50
❑ 53 Fatality E .50 .75
❑ 54 Fatality V 1.00 2.00
❑ 55 Zatanna R .25 .50
❑ 56 Zatanna E .50 .75
❑ 57 Zatanna V 1.00 2.00
❑ 58 Lady Shiva R .25 .50
❑ 59 Lady Shiva E .50 .75
❑ 60 Lady Shiva V 1.00 2.00
❑ 61 Starfire R .75 2.00
❑ 62 Starfire E 2.00 4.00
❑ 63 Starfire V 3.00 6.00
❑ 64 Starman R .75 2.00
❑ 65 Starman E 2.00 4.00
❑ 66 Starman V 3.00 6.00
❑ 67 Firestorm R 2.00 4.00
❑ 68 Firestorm E 3.00 6.00
❑ 69 Firestorm V 5.00 8.00
❑ 70 Cheetah R .70 1.00
❑ 71 Cheetah E 1.00 3.00
❑ 72 Cheetah V 2.00 4.00
❑ 73 Deathstroke R .50 1.00
❑ 74 Deathstroke E 1.00 3.00
❑ 75 Deathstroke V 2.00 4.00
❑ 76 Wonder Woman R .50 1.00
❑ 77 Wonder Woman E 2.00 3.00
❑ 78 Wonder Woman V 3.00 6.00
❑ 79 Circe R .50 1.00
❑ 80 Circe E 1.00 3.00
❑ 81 Circe V 3.00 5.00
❑ 82 Green Lantern R 1.00 2.00
❑ 83 Green Lantern E 2.00 4.00
❑ 84 Green Lantern V 3.00 7.00
❑ 85 Martian Manhunter U 30.00 45.00
❑ 86 Bizarro U 18.00 30.00
❑ 87 Brother Blood U 9.00 12.00
❑ 88 Amazo U 20.00 35.00
❑ 89 Lex Luthor U 15.00 20.00
❑ 90 Eclipso U 15.00 20.00
❑ 91 Despero U 15.00 20.00
❑ 92 Modru U 15.00 20.00
❑ 93 Catgirl U 7.00 13.00
❑ 94 Batgirl U 15.00 20.00
❑ 95 Batman U 15.00 22.00
❑ 96 Superman U 30.00 45.00
❑ 201 Easy Co. (Little Sure Shot) LE 6.00 10.00
❑ 202 Easy Co. Medic (Four Eyes) LE 2.00 5.00
❑ 203 Parademon Scout (Pharzoot) LE 4.00 10.00
❑ 204 Parademon Warrior (Valinus) LE 4.00 7.00
❑ 205 Lex Corp. Security (Hope) LE 4.00 7.00
❑ 206 Lex Corp. Battlesuit (Eddie Carlin) LE 4.00 7.00
❑ 207 Sgt. Rock (General Frank Rock) LE 3.00 6.00
❑ 208 Penguin (Oswald Cobblepot) LE 5.00 10.00
❑ 209 Manhunter (Manhunter 2.0) LE 4.00 8.00
❑ 210 Fury (Hippolyta Trevor-Hall) LE 3.00 6.00
❑ 211 Poison Ivy (Pamela Isley) LE 3.00 7.00
❑ 212 Black Canary (Dinah Lance) LE 2.00 5.00
❑ 213 Green Arrow (Oliver Queen) LE 8.00 15.00
❑ 214 Troia (Donna Troy) LE 3.00 6.00
❑ 215 Live Wire (Garth Ranzz) LE 3.00 5.00
❑ 216 Cosmic Boy (Rokk Krinn) LE 5.00 10.00
❑ 217 Satrun Girl (Irma Ardeen) LE 4.00 7.00
❑ 218 Fatality (Yrra Cynril) LE 12.00 20.00
❑ 219 Zatanna Zatara LE 7.00 12.00
❑ 220 Lady Shiva (Sandra Wu-San) LE 3.00 7.00
❑ 221 Green Lantern (Phasing) LE 8.00 12.00
❑ 222 Atom LE 15.00 25.00
❑ 223 Plastic Man (Mailbox) LE 15.00 20.00

2004 DC Heroclix Unleashed Miniatures

Complete Set (97) 175.00 250.00
Booster Pack 5.00 7.00

❑ 1 DEO Agent R .50 .75
❑ 2 DEO Agent E .75 1.00
❑ 3 DEO Agent V 1.00 1.50
❑ 4 HDC Trooper R .50 .75
❑ 5 HDC Trooper E .75 1.00
❑ 6 HDC Trooper V 1.00 1.50
❑ 7 Gotham Undercover R .50 .75
❑ 8 Gotham Undercover E .75 1.00
❑ 9 Gotham Undercover V 1.00 1.50
❑ 10 Science Police R .50 .75
❑ 11 Science Police E .75 1.00
❑ 12 Science Police V 1.00 1.50
❑ 13 Kobra Fanatic R .50 .75
❑ 14 Kobra Fanatic E .75 1.00
❑ 15 Kobra Fanatic V 1.00 1.50
❑ 16 Hawkgirl R .50 .75
❑ 17 Hawkgirl E .75 1.00
❑ 18 Hawkgirl V 1.00 1.50
❑ 19 Brainiac 5 R .50 .75
❑ 20 Brainiac 5 E .75 1.00
❑ 21 Brainiac 5 V 1.00 1.50
❑ 22 Scarecrow R .50 .75
❑ 23 Scarecrow E .75 1.00
❑ 24 Scarecrow V 1.00 1.50
❑ 25 Deadshot R .50 .75
❑ 26 Deadshot E .75 1.00
❑ 27 Deadshot V 1.00 1.50
❑ 28 Two-Face R .50 .75
❑ 29 Two-Face E .75 1.00
❑ 30 Two-Face V 1.00 2.00
❑ 31 Cheshire R .50 .75
❑ 32 Cheshire E .75 1.00
❑ 33 Cheshire V 1.00 1.50
❑ 34 Rocket Red R .50 .75
❑ 35 Rocket Red E .75 1.00
❑ 36 Rocket Red V 1.00 1.50
❑ 37 Chameleon R .50 .75
❑ 38 Chameleon E .75 1.00
❑ 39 Chameleon V 1.00 2.00
❑ 40 Kobra R .50 .75
❑ 41 Kobra E .75 1.00
❑ 42 Kobra V 1.00 1.50
❑ 43 Killer Croc R .50 .75
❑ 44 Killer Croc E .75 1.00
❑ 45 Killer Croc V 1.00 2.00
❑ 46 Killer Frost R .50 .75
❑ 47 Killer Frost E .75 1.00
❑ 48 Killer Frost V 1.00 1.50
❑ 49 Batgirl R .50 .75
❑ 50 Batgirl E .75 1.00
❑ 51 Batgirl V 2.00 4.00
❑ 52 Cyborg R .50 .75
❑ 53 Cyborg E .75 1.00
❑ 54 Cyborg V 1.00 1.50
❑ 55 Queen Bee R .50 .75
❑ 56 Queen Bee E .75 1.00
❑ 57 Queen Bee V 1.00 1.50
❑ 58 Big Barda R .50 .75
❑ 59 Big Barda E .75 1.00
❑ 60 Big Barda V 1.00 1.50
❑ 61 Shade R .50 1.00
❑ 62 Shade E 1.00 2.00
❑ 63 Shade V 2.00 3.00
❑ 64 Raven R .50 .75
❑ 65 Raven E 1.00 2.00
❑ 66 Raven V 2.00 3.00
❑ 67 Jesse Quick R .50 .75
❑ 68 Jesse Quick E .75 1.00
❑ 69 Jesse Quick V 1.00 1.50
❑ 70 Dr. Fate R .50 1.00
❑ 71 Dr. Fate E 1.00 2.00
❑ 72 Dr. Fate V 4.00 8.00
❑ 73 Maxima R .50 1.00
❑ 74 Maxima E 1.00 2.00
❑ 75 Maxima V 2.00 4.00
❑ 76 Supergirl R 1.00 1.50
❑ 77 Supergirl E 2.00 3.00
❑ 78 Supergirl V 3.00 4.00
❑ 79 Black Adam R 1.00 2.00
❑ 80 Black Adam E 2.00 3.00
❑ 81 Black Adam V 4.00 8.00
❑ 82 Green Lantern R 2.00 4.00
❑ 83 Green Lantern E 3.00 6.00
❑ 84 Green Lantern V 6.00 12.00
❑ 85 Metallo U 18.00 22.00
❑ 86 The General U 15.00 18.00
❑ 87 Kilowog U 20.00 25.00
❑ 88 Shazam! U 25.00 35.00
❑ 89 Ultrahumanite U 6.00 12.00
❑ 90 Silver Swan U 10.00 18.00
❑ 91 Nu'bia U 5.00 12.00
❑ 92 Mr. Bones U 10.00 15.00
❑ 93 Wonder Woman U 22.00 30.00
❑ 94 Batman U 25.00 40.00
❑ 95 Superman U 40.00 60.00
❑ 96 Magog U 20.00 30.00
❑ 97 Bat Sentry U 20.00 30.00
❑ 201 DEO Agent (Cameron Chase) LE 6.00 10.00
❑ 202 HDC Trooper (Montgomery Kelley) LE 6.00 10.00
❑ 203 Gotham Undercover (Matches Malone) LE 3.00 7.00
❑ 204 Science Police (Shvaugh Erin) LE 3.00 7.00
❑ 205 Kobra (Jason Burr) LE 5.00 10.00
❑ 206 Hawkgirl (Kendra Saunders) LE 10.00 16.00
❑ 207 Brainiac 5 (Querl Dox) LE 10.00 16.00
❑ 208 Scarecrow (Jonathan Crane) LE 10.00 20.00
❑ 210 Two-Face (Harvey Dent) LE 10.00 20.00
❑ 211 Cheshire (Jade) LE 10.00 16.00
❑ 212 Rocket Red (Dmitri Pushkin) LE 10.00 20.00
❑ 215 Jesse Quick (Jesse Chambers) LE 12.00 25.00
❑ 216 Dr. Fate (Hector Hall) LE 12.00 20.00
❑ 217 Maxima (Maxima of Almerac) LE 10.00 18.00
❑ 218 Supergirl (Kara Zor-El) LE 10.00 18.00
❑ 219 Black Adam (Teth-Adam) LE 6.00 12.00
❑ 220 Green Lantern (Hal Jordan) LE 30.00 55.00
❑ 221 Shazam! (Kingdom Come) LE 12.00 20.00
❑ 222 Catwoman LE 15.00 25.00

2005 DC Heroclix Hypertime Miniatures

Item	Low	High
Complete Set (130)	175.00	235.00
Booster Pack	4.00	7.00
Starter Set	8.00	15.00
❑ 1 Gotham Policeman R	.25	.35
❑ 2 Gotham Policeman E	.50	.75
❑ 3 Gotham Policeman V	1.00	1.50
❑ 4 Metropolis S.C.U R	.25	.35
❑ 5 Metropolis S.C.U E	.50	.75
❑ 6 Metropolis S.C.U V	1.00	1.50
❑ 7 Checkmate Agent R	.25	.35
❑ 8 Checkmate Agent E	.50	.75
❑ 9 Checkmate Agent V	1.00	2.00
❑ 10 Checkmate Medic R	.25	.35
❑ 11 Checkmate Medic E	.50	.75
❑ 12 Checkmate Medic V	1.00	1.50
❑ 13 Intergang Agent R	.25	.35
❑ 14 Intergang Agent E	.50	.75
❑ 15 Intergang Agent V	1.00	2.00
❑ 16 Intergang Medic R	.25	.35
❑ 17 Intergang Medic E	.50	.75
❑ 18 Intergang Medic V	1.00	2.00
❑ 19 Lackey R	.25	.35
❑ 20 Lackey E	.50	.75
❑ 21 Lackey V	1.00	2.50
❑ 22 Criminal R	.25	.35
❑ 23 Criminal E	.50	.75
❑ 24 Criminal V	.75	1.00
❑ 25 Huntress R	.25	.35
❑ 26 Huntress E	.50	.75
❑ 27 Huntress V	.75	1.00
❑ 28 Robin R	.25	.35
❑ 29 Robin E	.50	.75
❑ 30 Robin V	1.00	2.00
❑ 31 Hawkman R	.25	.35
❑ 32 Hawkman E	.50	.75
❑ 33 Hawkman V	1.00	2.00
❑ 34 Harley Quinn R	.75	1.50
❑ 35 Harley Quinn E	1.00	2.00
❑ 36 Harley Quinn V	2.00	4.00
❑ 37 Catwoman R	.25	.50
❑ 38 Catwoman E	.75	1.00
❑ 39 Catwoman V	1.00	2.00
❑ 40 Man-Bat R	.25	.35
❑ 41 Man-Bat E	.50	.75
❑ 42 Man-Bat V	.75	1.00
❑ 43 Riddler R	.50	1.00
❑ 44 Riddler E	1.00	2.00
❑ 45 Riddler V	2.00	4.00
❑ 46 Mad Hatter R	.25	.35
❑ 47 Mad Hatter E	.50	.75
❑ 48 Mad Hatter V	1.00	1.50
❑ 49 T.O. Morrow R	.25	.35
❑ 50 T.O. Morrow E	.50	.75
❑ 51 T.O. Morrow V	1.00	1.50
❑ 52 Aquaman R	1.00	1.50
❑ 53 Aquaman E	1.50	2.50
❑ 54 Aquaman V	2.00	4.00
❑ 55 Blue Beetle R	.25	.35
❑ 56 Blue Beetle E	.50	.75
❑ 57 Blue Beetle V	1.00	1.50
❑ 58 Booster Gold R	.25	.35
❑ 59 Booster Gold E	.50	.75
❑ 60 Booster Gold V	1.00	1.50
❑ 61 Nightwing R	.75	1.00
❑ 62 Nightwing E	1.00	2.00
❑ 63 Nightwing V	3.00	5.00
❑ 64 Changeling R	.25	.35
❑ 65 Changeling E	.50	.75
❑ 66 Changeling V	1.00	1.50
❑ 67 Steel R	.30	.50
❑ 68 Steel E	1.00	2.00
❑ 69 Steel V	2.00	3.00
❑ 70 Gorilla Grodd R	.50	1.00
❑ 71 Gorilla Grodd E	1.00	2.00
❑ 72 Gorilla Grodd V	2.00	4.00
❑ 73 Soloman Grundy R	.50	1.00
❑ 74 Soloman Grundy E	1.00	2.00
❑ 75 Soloman Grundy V	2.00	4.00
❑ 76 Black Manta R	.50	1.00
❑ 77 Black Manta E	1.00	2.00
❑ 78 Black Manta V	2.00	4.00
❑ 79 Weather Wizard R	.50	1.00
❑ 80 Weather Wizard E	1.00	2.00
❑ 81 Weather Wizard V	2.00	4.00
❑ 82 Clayface III R	.50	1.00
❑ 83 Clayface III E	1.00	2.00
❑ 84 Clayface III V	2.00	4.00
❑ 85 Hawk R	.50	1.00
❑ 86 Hawk E	1.00	2.00
❑ 87 Hawk V	2.00	4.00
❑ 88 Dove R	1.00	2.00
❑ 89 Dove E	2.00	5.00
❑ 90 Dove V	5.00	8.00
❑ 91 Bane R	1.00	2.00
❑ 92 Bane E	2.00	3.00
❑ 93 Bane V	3.00	5.00
❑ 94 Doomsday R	.50	1.50
❑ 95 Doomsday E	1.00	2.00
❑ 96 Doomsday V	2.00	4.00
❑ 97 Joker R	1.00	2.00
❑ 98 Joker E	2.00	4.00
❑ 99 Joker V	5.00	8.00
❑ 100 Plastic Man R	.50	1.00
❑ 101 Plastic Man E	1.00	2.00
❑ 102 Plastic Man V	3.00	5.00
❑ 103 Flash R	1.00	2.00
❑ 104 Flash E	3.00	5.00
❑ 105 Flash V	4.00	8.00
❑ 106 Batman R	.75	1.50
❑ 107 Batman E	1.00	2.50
❑ 108 Batman V	6.00	11.00
❑ 109 Superman R	1.00	2.00
❑ 110 Superman E	2.00	3.00
❑ 111 Superman V	4.00	6.00
❑ 112 Arcane R	1.00	2.00
❑ 113 Arcane E	2.00	4.00
❑ 114 Arcane V	3.00	6.00
❑ 115 Swamp Thing R	1.00	2.00
❑ 116 Swamp Thing E	2.00	4.00
❑ 117 Swamp Thing V	3.00	7.00
❑ 118 Braniac 13 R	.50	1.00
❑ 119 Braniac 13 E	1.00	2.00
❑ 120 Braniac 13 V	2.00	4.00
❑ 121 Parasite U	4.00	8.00
❑ 122 Desaad U	8.00	15.00
❑ 123 Darkseid U	10.00	18.00
❑ 124 Commissioner Gordon U	8.00	12.00
❑ 125 The Key U	4.00	8.00
❑ 126 Joker U	8.00	20.00
❑ 127 Catwoman U	10.00	20.00
❑ 128 Flash U	15.00	20.00
❑ 129 Batman U	20.00	30.00
❑ 130 Superman U	15.00	25.00
❑ 131 Hawkman (Carter Hall) LE	8.00	10.00
❑ 132 Harley Quinn (Harleen Quinzel) LE	6.00	8.00
❑ 133 Catwoman (Selina Kyle) LE	10.00	15.00
❑ 134 Man-Bat (Kirk Langstrom) LE	5.00	7.00
❑ 135 Riddler (Eddie Nashton) LE	5.00	8.00
❑ 136 Mad Hatter (Jervis Tetch) LE	3.00	5.00
❑ 137 T.O. Morrow (TO Morrow) LE	3.00	5.00
❑ 138 Aquaman (Arthur Curry) LE	7.00	12.00
❑ 139 Blue Beetle (Ted Kord) LE	6.00	12.00
❑ 140 Booster Gold (Michael Jon Carter) LE	8.00	12.00
❑ 141 Superman (OWAW) LE	12.00	20.00

2005 DC Heroclix Icons Miniatures

Item	Low	High
Booster Pack	6.00	8.00
Bystander Cards (B1-B6)	.50	1.00
Infiltration Cards (IBF1-IBF9)	.50	1.00
Rookie	.25	.50
Experienced	.50	1.00
Veteran	1.00	2.00
❑ 1 Batman E	1.00	2.00
❑ 2 Robin E	.50	1.00
❑ 3 Hawkgirl E	.25	.50
❑ 4 The Joker E	1.00	2.00
❑ 5 Harley Quinn E	.30	1.00
❑ 6 Man-Bat E	.25	.50
❑ 7 Scarecrow R	.25	.50
❑ 8 Scarecrow E	.50	1.00
❑ 9 Scarecrow V	1.00	2.00
❑ 10 Beast Boy R	.25	.50
❑ 11 Changeling E	.50	1.00
❑ 12 Beast Boy V	1.00	2.00
❑ 13 Robin R	.50	1.00
❑ 14 Robin E	1.00	2.00
❑ 15 Robin V	2.00	4.00
❑ 16 Cheetah R	.25	.50
❑ 17 Cheetah E	.50	1.00
❑ 18 Cheetah V	1.00	2.00
❑ 19 Blackfire R	.25	.50
❑ 20 Blackfire E	.50	1.00
❑ 21 Blackfire V	1.00	2.00
❑ 22 Starfire R	.25	.50
❑ 23 Starfire E	.50	1.00
❑ 24 Starfire V	1.00	2.00
❑ 25 Aquaman R	.50	1.00
❑ 26 Aquaman E	1.00	2.00
❑ 27 Aquaman V	2.00	4.00
❑ 28 Raven R	.25	.50
❑ 29 Raven E	.50	1.00
❑ 30 Raven V	1.00	2.00
❑ 31 Wonder Woman R	.50	1.00
❑ 32 Wonder Woman E	1.00	2.00
❑ 33 Wonder Woman V	2.00	4.00
❑ 34 Bizarro R	.50	1.00
❑ 35 Bizarro E	1.00	2.00
❑ 36 Bizarro V	2.00	4.00
❑ 37 The Joker R	.50	1.00
❑ 38 The Joker E	1.00	2.00
❑ 39 The Joker V	3.00	5.00
❑ 40 Batman R	.50	1.00
❑ 41 Batman E	1.00	2.00
❑ 42 Batman V	3.00	5.00
❑ 43 Darkseid R	.25	.50
❑ 44 Darkseid E	.50	1.00
❑ 45 Darkseid V	1.00	2.00
❑ 46 Superman R	.50	1.00
❑ 47 Superman E	1.00	2.00
❑ 48 Superman V	3.00	5.00
❑ 49 Ra's al-Ghul U	10.00	15.00
❑ 50 Brainiac U	20.00	30.00
❑ 51 Lex Luthor U	15.00	25.00
❑ 52 Terra U	12.00	18.00
❑ 53 Cyborg U	12.00	16.00
❑ 54 The Flash U	15.00	25.00
❑ 201 Dr. Jonathan Crane U	3.00	5.00
❑ 202 Gar Logan U	15.00	20.00
❑ 203 Tim Drake U	15.00	20.00
❑ 204 Barbara Ann Minerva U	15.00	20.00
❑ 205 Princess Komand'r U	15.00	20.00
❑ 206 Princess Koriand'r U	15.00	20.00
❑ 207 Dark Knight Detective U	15.00	20.00
❑ 208 Batman E (Promo)	1.00	1.00
❑ 209 Professor Zoom U	15.00	20.00
❑ B7 Speed Saunders U	15.00	20.00

2005 DC Heroclix Legacy Miniatures

Item	Low	High
Complete Set (97)	250.00	350.00
Booster Pack	6.00	8.00
Feats Cards (F1-F8)	1.00	2.00
Battlefield Cards (BF1-BF6)	.50	1.00
Tokens (B1-B7)	.50	1.00
❑ 1 Spoiler R	.50	.75
❑ 2 Spoiler E	.75	1.50
❑ 3 Spoiler V	1.00	2.00
❑ 4 Hyena R	.50	.75
❑ 5 Hyena E	.75	1.50
❑ 6 Hyena V	1.00	2.00
❑ 7 Enchantress R	.50	.75
❑ 8 Enchantress E	.75	1.50
❑ 9 Enchantress V	1.00	2.00
❑ 10 Talia R	.50	.75
❑ 11 Talia E	.75	1.50
❑ 12 Talia V	1.00	2.00
❑ 13 Hourman R	.50	.75
❑ 14 Hourman E	.75	1.50
❑ 15 Hourman V	1.00	2.00
❑ 16 Mr. Terrific R	.50	.75
❑ 17 Mr. Terrific E	.75	1.50
❑ 18 Mr. Terrific V	1.00	2.00
❑ 19 Star-Spangled Kid R	.50	.75
❑ 20 Star-Spangled Kid E	.75	1.50
❑ 21 Stargirl V	1.00	2.00
❑ 22 Ravager R	.50	.75
❑ 23 Ravager E	.75	1.50
❑ 24 Ravager V	1.00	2.00
❑ 25 Power Girl R	.50	.75
❑ 26 Power Girl E	.75	1.50
❑ 27 Power Girl V	1.00	2.00
❑ 28 Impulse R	.50	.75
❑ 29 Impulse E	.75	1.50
❑ 30 Kid Flash V	2.00	4.00
❑ 31 Kid Quantum R	.50	.75
❑ 32 Kid Quantum E	.75	1.50
❑ 33 Kid Quantum V	1.00	2.00
❑ 34 Jinx R	.50	.75
❑ 35 Jinx E	.75	1.50
❑ 36 Jinx V	1.00	2.00
❑ 37 Mr. Freeze R	1.00	2.00
❑ 38 Mr. Freeze E	2.00	4.00
❑ 39 Mr. Freeze V	3.00	6.00
❑ 40 Speedy R	.50	.75
❑ 41 Arsenal E	.75	1.50
❑ 42 Arsenal V	1.00	2.00
❑ 43 Wildfire R	.50	.75
❑ 44 Wildfire E	.75	1.50
❑ 45 Wildfire V	1.00	2.00
❑ 46 Superwoman R	.50	.75
❑ 47 Superwoman E	.75	1.50
❑ 48 Superwoman V	1.00	2.00
❑ 49 The Demon R	.50	.75
❑ 50 The Demon E	.75	1.50
❑ 51 The Demon V	2.00	4.00
❑ 52 Obsidian R	.50	.75
❑ 53 Obsidian E	.75	1.50
❑ 54 Obsidian V	1.00	2.00
❑ 55 Jade R	.50	.75
❑ 56 Jade E	.75	1.50
❑ 57 Jade V	2.00	4.00
❑ 58 Sinestro R	1.00	2.00
❑ 59 Sinestro E	2.00	4.00
❑ 60 Sinestro V	4.00	8.00
❑ 61 Blockbuster R	.50	.75
❑ 62 Blockbuster E	.75	1.50
❑ 63 Blockbuster V	1.00	2.00
❑ 64 Superboy R	1.00	2.00
❑ 65 Superboy E	2.00	4.00
❑ 66 Superboy V	3.00	6.00
❑ 67 Persuader R	.50	.75
❑ 68 Persuader E	.75	1.50
❑ 69 Persuader V	1.00	2.00
❑ 70 Captain Atom R	.50	.75
❑ 71 Captain Atom E	.75	1.50
❑ 72 Captain Atom V	1.00	2.00
❑ 73 Major Force R	.50	.75
❑ 74 Major Force E	.75	1.50
❑ 75 Major Force V	1.00	2.00
❑ 76 Ra's al-Ghul R	.50	.75
❑ 77 Ra's al-Ghul E	.75	1.50
❑ 78 Ra's al-Ghul V	1.00	2.00
❑ 79 The Joker R	2.00	3.00
❑ 80 The Joker E	3.00	5.00
❑ 81 The Joker V	4.00	8.00
❑ 82 Batman R	2.00	3.00
❑ 83 Batman E	3.00	5.00
❑ 84 Batman V	4.00	8.00
❑ 85 Oracle U	15.00	25.00
❑ 86 Hush U	12.00	18.00
❑ 87 Wonder Woman U	20.00	30.00
❑ 88 Ares U	10.00	12.00
❑ 89 Ultraman U	12.00	15.00
❑ 90 General Zod U	12.00	15.00
❑ 91 Prometheus U	8.00	10.00
❑ 92 Mongul U	8.00	10.00
❑ 93 Hawkman U	8.00	10.00
❑ 94 Red Robin U	15.00	20.00
❑ 95 Flash U	20.00	25.00
❑ 96 Green Lantern U	40.00	60.00
❑ 97 Steel E	15.00	20.00
❑ 201 Victor Fries U	12.00	18.00
❑ 202 Roy Harper, Jr. U	10.00	18.00
❑ 203 Drake Burroughs U	10.00	18.00
❑ 204 Lois Lane U	12.00	20.00
❑ 205 Etrigan U	10.00	18.00
❑ 206 Todd Rice U	10.00	18.00
❑ 207 Jennifer-Lynn Hayden U	10.00	18.00
❑ 208 Sinestro of Korugar U	12.00	20.00
❑ 209 Roland Desmond U	10.00	18.00
❑ 210 Connor Kent U	12.00	20.00
❑ 211 Nyeun Chun Ti U	10.00	18.00
❑ 212 Capt. Nathaniel Adam U	12.00	20.00
❑ 213 Clifford Zmeck U	10.00	18.00
❑ 214 The Demon's Head U	10.00	18.00
❑ 215 The Red Hood U	10.00	18.00
❑ 216 Bruce Wayne U	20.00	30.00
❑ 221 Mr. Freeze U	12.00	18.00

2007 DC Heroclix Justice League Miniatures

Item	Low	High
❑ 1 Batman V	4.00	10.00
❑ 2 Aquaman R	.20	.50
❑ 3 Creeper E	.40	1.00
❑ 4 Firehawk E	.40	1.00
❑ 5 Mento V	2.00	5.00
❑ 6 Heat Wave E	.40	1.00
❑ 7 Icicle R	.20	.50
❑ 8 Lex Luthor V	2.00	5.00
❑ 9 The Joker U	4.00	10.00
❑ 10 Bulleteer R	.20	.50
❑ 11 Black Canary E	.40	1.00
❑ 12 Crimson Fox R	.20	.50
❑ 13 Doctor Light E	.40	1.00
❑ 14 Green Arrow E	.40	1.00
❑ 15 Gypsy E	.40	1.00
❑ 16 Bouncing Boy E	.40	1.00
❑ 17 Parasite U	4.00	10.00
❑ 18 Firestorm R	.20	.50
❑ 19 Merlyn E	.40	1.00
❑ 20 Black Hand E	.40	1.00
❑ 21 King Shark E	.40	1.00
❑ 22 Professor Ivo V	2.00	5.00
❑ 23 Toyman R	.20	.50
❑ 24 Chronos V	2.00	5.00
❑ 25 Dr. Alchemy E	.40	1.00
❑ 26 Captain Boomerang V	2.00	5.00
❑ 27 The Flash U	4.00	10.00
❑ 28 Zatanna E	.40	1.00
❑ 29 Zauriel R	.20	.50
❑ 30 Plastic Man V	2.00	5.00
❑ 31 Tharok E	.40	1.00
❑ 32 Bronze Tiger E	.40	1.00
❑ 33 Vigilante R	.20	.50
❑ 34 August General in Iron R	.20	.50
❑ 35 Deadman U	4.00	10.00
❑ 36 Granny Goodness U	4.00	10.00
❑ 37 Wonder Woman E	.40	1.00
❑ 38 Batman and Robin U	4.00	10.00
❑ 39 Batzarro R	.20	.50
❑ 40 Hector Hammond E	.40	1.00
❑ 41 Mr. Mxyzptlk U	4.00	10.00
❑ 42 Abra Kadabra V	2.00	5.00
❑ 43 Dr. Polaris V	2.00	5.00
❑ 44 Major Disaster V	2.00	5.00
❑ 45 Aztek R	.20	.50
❑ 46 Superman E	.40	1.00
❑ 47 Hourman R	.20	.50
❑ 48 Dream Girl R	.20	.50
❑ 49 Shining Knight R	.20	.50
❑ 50 Power Ring U	4.00	10.00
❑ 51 Lobo U	15.00	30.00
❑ 52 Amazo U	4.00	10.00
❑ 53 Big Barda and Mr. Miracle U	4.00	10.00
❑ 54 Doomsday U	15.00	30.00
❑ 55 Green Lantern V	2.00	5.00
❑ 56 Time Trapper E	.40	1.00
❑ 57 The Flash E	.40	1.00
❑ 58 Batman V	2.00	5.00
❑ 59 Wonder Woman E	.40	1.00
❑ 60 Superman V	2.00	5.00
❑ 61 Phantom Stranger U	4.00	10.00

2007 DC Heroclix Legion of Superheroes Miniatures

Item	Low	High
❑ 1 Lightning Lad E	.75	2.00
❑ 2 Saturn Girl E	.75	2.00
❑ 3 Cosmic Boy E	.75	2.00
❑ 4 Timber Wolf E	.75	2.00
❑ 5 Phantom Girl R	.75	2.00
❑ 6 Ultra Boy R	.75	2.00
❑ 7 Young Superman R	.75	2.00
❑ 8 Shrinking Violet E	.75	2.00

2008 DC Heroclix Arkham Asylum Miniatures

Item	Low	High
❑ 1 White Martian V	3.00	8.00
❑ 2 Manhunter R	.20	.50
❑ 3 Multiplex E	.40	1.00
❑ 4 The Question R	.20	.50
❑ 5 Floronic Man E	.40	1.00
❑ 6 Gotham City Detective V	3.00	8.00
❑ 7 Two-Face V	3.00	8.00
❑ 8 Street Thug R	.20	.50
❑ 9 Kid Devil R	.20	.50
❑ 10 Gorilla Grodd V	3.00	8.00
❑ 11 The Riddler V	3.00	8.00
❑ 12 Amanda Waller R	.20	.50
❑ 13 Human Bomb R	.20	.50
❑ 14 Scandal Savage E	.40	1.00
❑ 15 Plasmus R	.20	.50
❑ 16 Batman R	.20	.50
❑ 17 Man-Bat Assassin R	.20	.50
❑ 18 Solomon Grundy E	.40	1.00
❑ 19 Lashina U	8.00	20.00
❑ 20 Anarky E	.40	1.00
❑ 21 Miss Martian R	.20	.50
❑ 22 Hitman V	3.00	8.00
❑ 23 Wonder Woman V	3.00	8.00
❑ 24 Count Vertigo V	3.00	8.00
❑ 25 Johnny Sorrow U	8.00	20.00
❑ 26 Nightshade E	.40	1.00
❑ 27 Firefly E	.40	1.00
❑ 28 Arkillo E	.40	1.00
❑ 29 Per Degaton U	8.00	20.00
❑ 30 Amon Sur R	.20	.50
❑ 31 Captain Gordon E	.40	1.00
❑ 32 Lightning Lord V	3.00	8.00
❑ 33 Thinker U	8.00	20.00
❑ 34 Robin V	3.00	8.00
❑ 35 Ghost Fox Killer E	.40	1.00
❑ 36 Zoom U	8.00	20.00
❑ 37 Element Lad R	.20	.50
❑ 38 The Penguin V	3.00	8.00
❑ 39 Cosmic King V	3.00	8.00
❑ 40 Doctor Destiny U	8.00	20.00
❑ 41 Frankenstein V	3.00	8.00
❑ 42 Ventriloquist E	.40	1.00
❑ 43 Calculator U	8.00	20.00
❑ 44 Yellow Lantern R	.20	.50
❑ 45 Circe U	8.00	20.00
❑ 46 Lyssa Drak E	.40	1.00
❑ 47 Ultra-Humanite V	3.00	8.00
❑ 48 Bizarro #1 V	3.00	8.00
❑ 49 Black Manta V	3.00	8.00
❑ 50 Metron U	8.00	20.00
❑ 51 Mad Hatter V	3.00	8.00
❑ 52 Batgirl E	.40	1.00
❑ 53 The Top V	3.00	8.00
❑ 54 Despero U	8.00	20.00
❑ 55 Sabbac R	.20	.50
❑ 56 The Flash U	8.00	20.00
❑ 57 Saturn Queen V	3.00	8.00
❑ 58 Chang Tzu U	8.00	20.00
❑ 59 The Joker U	8.00	20.00
❑ 60 Superman Prime U	20.00	40.00
❑ 61 Clown Prince of Crime U	20.00	40.00
❑ 99 Batman U	75.00	100.00
❑ 100 Batman U	75.00	100.00
❑ 101 Crispus Allen U	8.00	20.00
❑ 102 Harvey Dent U	6.00	15.00
❑ 103 Henchman U	6.00	15.00
❑ 104 Grodd E	.40	1.00
❑ 105 Edward Nigma U	6.00	15.00

2008 DC Heroclix Batman Alpha Miniatures

Item	Low	High
❑ 1 Batman SE	8.00	20.00
❑ 2 The Caped Crusader SE	8.00	20.00
❑ 3 The Masked Manhunter SE	8.00	20.00
❑ 4 Batman SE	8.00	20.00
❑ 5 Robin C	.20	.50
❑ 6 Harley Quinn C	.20	.50
❑ 7 Penguin C	.20	.50
❑ 8 Poison Ivy C	.20	.50
❑ 9 Clayface C	.20	.50

❑ 10 Scarecrow C .20 .50
❑ 11 Huntress C .20 .50
❑ 12 Bane C .20 .50
❑ 13 Mad Hatter C .20 .50
❑ 14 Alfred C .20 .50
❑ 15 Gotham City P.D. C .20 .50
❑ 16 Riddler C .20 .50
❑ 17 Killer Croc C .20 .50
❑ 18 Talia C .20 .50
❑ 19 Joker U .40 1.00
❑ 20 Commissioner Gordon U .40 1.00
❑ 21 Two-Face U .40 1.00
❑ 22 Ra's Al Ghul U .40 1.00
❑ 23 Mr. Freeze U .40 1.00
❑ 24 Batgirl U .40 1.00
❑ 25 Oracle U .40 1.00
❑ 26 Catwoman U .40 1.00
❑ 27 Clown Prince of Crime R 3.00 8.00
❑ 28 Boy Wonder R 3.00 8.00
❑ 29 Nightwing R 3.00 8.00
❑ 30 Dynamic Duo R 3.00 8.00
❑ 31 Batman SE 8.00 20.00

2008 DC Heroclix Crisis Miniatures

❑ 1 Robin R .20 .50
❑ 2 Kid Flash R .20 .50
❑ 3 Wonder Girl R .20 .50
❑ 4 Aqualad R .20 .50
❑ 5 Speedy R .20 .50
❑ 6 Shimmer E .40 1.00
❑ 7 Jericho E .40 1.00
❑ 8 Mercury E .40 1.00
❑ 9 Gold E .40 1.00
❑ 10 Liberty Belle V 3.00 8.00
❑ 11 Klarion R .20 .50
❑ 12 Supernova E .40 1.00
❑ 13 Robin V 3.00 8.00
❑ 14 Batgirl E .40 1.00
❑ 15 Iron E .40 1.00
❑ 16 Ace R .20 .50
❑ 17 Red Hood E .40 1.00
❑ 18 Red Arrow V 3.00 8.00
❑ 19 Batwoman R .20 .50
❑ 20 Dr. Sivana U 8.00 20.00
❑ 21 Rip Hunter U 8.00 20.00
❑ 22 Dawnstar E .40 1.00
❑ 23 Green Lantern V 3.00 8.00
❑ 24 Karate Kid V 3.00 8.00
❑ 25 Jack and Ten R .20 .50
❑ 26 Green Arrow V 3.00 8.00
❑ 27 Trickster and Pied Piper V 3.00 8.00
❑ 28 Deathstroke U 8.00 20.00
❑ 29 Nightwing V 3.00 8.00
❑ 30 Blue Beetle V 3.00 8.00
❑ 31 Mammoth E .40 1.00
❑ 32 Hawk and Dove R .20 .50
❑ 33 Psimon E .40 1.00
❑ 34 Lead and Tin E .40 1.00
❑ 35 Uncle Sam U 8.00 20.00
❑ 36 The Chief R .20 .50
❑ 37 Kyle Rayner V 3.00 8.00
❑ 38 Wonder Girl V 3.00 8.00
❑ 39 Harbinger R .20 .50
❑ 40 Forerunner E .40 1.00
❑ 41 Mary Marvel V 3.00 8.00
❑ 42 Mordru U 8.00 20.00
❑ 43 Monarch E .40 1.00
❑ 44 Accomplished Perfect Physician R .20 .50
❑ 45 Trigon U 8.00 20.00
❑ 46 Star Sapphire V 3.00 8.00
❑ 47 Tempest V 3.00 8.00
❑ 48 Darkseid V 6.00 15.00
❑ 49 Will Magnus and Platinum E .40 1.00
❑ 50 Captain Marvel, Jr. E .40 1.00
❑ 51 King and Queen R .20 .50
❑ 52 Psycho-Pirate V 3.00 8.00
❑ 53 Black Adam U 15.00 30.00
❑ 54 Alex Luthor U 8.00 20.00
❑ 55 Sinestro V 30.00 60.00
❑ 56 Supergirl V 8.00 20.00
❑ 57 The Flash U 15.00 30.00
❑ 58 Nightwing and Starfire E .40 1.00
❑ 59 The Spectre U 15.00 30.00
❑ 60 Monitor V 3.00 8.00
❑ 61 World's Finest U 8.00 20.00
❑ 100 Superman U 8.00 20.00
❑ 105 Superman U 8.00 20.00

2010 DC Heroclix Blackest Night Miniatures

COMPLETE SET 10.00 25.00
❑ 1 Mera 2.00 5.00
❑ 2 Lex Luthor 2.00 5.00
❑ 3 Scarecrow 2.00 5.00
❑ 4 Green Lantern 2.00 5.00
❑ 5 Flash 2.00 5.00
❑ 6 Atom 2.00 5.00
❑ 7 Wonder Woman 2.00 5.00

2010 DC Heroclix Brightest Day Action Pack Miniatures

COMPLETE SET 10.00 25.00
❑ 1 Martian Manhunter 2.00 5.00
❑ 2 Firestorm 2.00 5.00
❑ 3 Deadman 2.00 5.00
❑ 4 Hawkgirl 2.00 5.00
❑ 5 Captain Boomerang 2.00 5.00
❑ 6 Aquaman 2.00 5.00
❑ 7 Osiris 2.00 5.00

2010 DC Heroclix Brave and the Bold Miniatures

❑ 1 Bruce Wayne C .20 .50
❑ 2 Clark Kent C .20 .50
❑ 3 Diana Prince C .20 .50
❑ 4 League Assassin C .20 .50
❑ 5 Amazon C .20 .50
❑ 6 Checkmate Pawn (W) C .20 .50
❑ 7 Checkmate Knight (W) C .20 .50
❑ 8 Parademon Grunt C .20 .50
❑ 9 The Atom and Hawkman C .20 .50
❑ 10 Jason Blood C .20 .50
❑ 11 League Elite C .20 .50
❑ 12 Amazon of Bana-Mighdall C .20 .50
❑ 13 Checkmate Pawn (B) C .20 .50
❑ 14 Checkmate Knight (B) C .20 .50
❑ 15 Parademon Drill Sergeant C .20 .50
❑ 16 Batman U U .50 1.00
❑ 17 Superman U .50 1.00
❑ 18 Wonder Woman U .50 1.00
❑ 19 Talia U .50 1.00
❑ 20 Damian Wayne U .50 1.00
❑ 21 The Holiday Killer U .50 1.00
❑ 22 Cave Carson U .50 1.00
❑ 23 Max Mercury U .50 1.00
❑ 24 Mikron O'Jeneus U .50 1.00
❑ 25 Goodness and Mercy U .50 1.00
❑ 26 The Sensei U .50 1.00
❑ 27 Phillipus U .50 1.00
❑ 28 Pawn 502 U .50 1.00
❑ 29 Mademoiselle Marie U .50 1.00
❑ 30 The Parademon U .50 1.00
❑ 31 Brainiac R 2.00 5.00
❑ 32 Kryptonite Man R 2.00 5.00
❑ 33 Metallo R 2.00 5.00
❑ 34 Ra's Al Ghul R 2.00 5.00
❑ 35 Power Girl R 2.00 5.00
❑ 36 Martian Manhunter R 2.00 5.00
❑ 37 Extant R 2.00 5.00
❑ 38 Inertia R 2.00 5.00
❑ 39 Etrigan R 2.00 5.00
❑ 40 Lex Luthor and Brainiac R 2.00 5.00
❑ 41 Talia al Ghul R 2.00 5.00
❑ 42 Robin R 2.00 5.00
❑ 43 Kid Zoom R 2.00 5.00
❑ 44 Black Flash R 2.00 5.00
❑ 45 The Wizard Shazam! R 2.00 5.00
❑ 46 Batman and Green Arrow SR 8.00 20.00
❑ 47 The Flashes SR 8.00 20.00
❑ 48 Flash and Green Lantern SR 8.00 20.00
❑ 49 Superman and the Flash SR 8.00 20.00
❑ 50 Fire and Ice SR 8.00 20.00
❑ 51 Green Lantern and Green Arrow SR 8.00 20.00
❑ 52 Blue Beetle and Booster Gold SR 8.00 20.00
❑ 53 Poison Ivy and Harley Quinn SR 8.00 20.00
❑ 54 Mister Miracle and Oberon SR 8.00 20.00
❑ 55 Shazam and Black Adam SR 10.00 25.00
❑ 56 Black Hand CH 50.00 75.00
❑ 57 Martian Manhunter CH 50.00 75.00
❑ 58 Kal-L CH 75.00 125.00
❑ 59 Nekron CH 50.00 75.00
❑ 100 Batman and Catwoman LE 15.00 30.00
❑ 101 Bruce Wayne LE 15.00 30.00
❑ 102 Clark Kent LE 15.00 30.00
❑ 103 Diana Prince LE 15.00 30.00

2010 DC Heroclix Jonah Hex Battle Pack Miniatures

❑ 1 Jonah Hex 1.00 2.50
❑ 2 Quentin Turnbull 1.00 2.50
❑ 3 Lilah 1.00 2.50

2010 DC Heroclix 75th Anniversary Miniatures

❑ 1 Easy Company Soldier C .20 .50
❑ 2 Zamaron C .20 .50
❑ 3 Dominator C .20 .50
❑ 4 Gorilla City Warrior C .20 .50
❑ 5 Deadshot C .20 .50
❑ 6 Donna Troy C .20 .50
❑ 7 Ice C .20 .50
❑ 8 Crimson Avenger C .20 .50
❑ 9 Bart Allen C .20 .50
❑ 10 Johnny Quick C .20 .50
❑ 11 Mr. Terrific C .20 .50
❑ 12 The Atom C .20 .50
❑ 13 Green Arrow C .20 .50
❑ 14 Beast Boy C .20 .50
❑ 15 Beast Boy (Rear) C .20 .50
❑ 16 Beast Boy (Cheetah) C .20 .50
❑ 17 Sgt. Rock U .40 1.00
❑ 18 Queen Aga'po U .40 1.00
❑ 19 Ruling Caste Dominator U .40 1.00
❑ 20 Solovar U .40 1.00
❑ 21 Warlord U .40 1.00
❑ 22 Nightmaster U .40 1.00
❑ 23 Osiris U .40 1.00
❑ 24 Detective Chimp U .40 1.00
❑ 25 Sargon the Sorcerer U .40 1.00
❑ 26 Superboy U .40 1.00
❑ 27 Ocean Master U .40 1.00
❑ 28 Mera U .40 1.00
❑ 29 Aquaman U .40 1.00
❑ 30 Wonder Woman U .40 1.00
❑ 31 Batman U .40 1.00
❑ 32 Superman U .40 1.00
❑ 33 Isis R 2.00 5.00
❑ 34 Black Alice R 2.00 5.00
❑ 35 Ragdoll R 2.00 5.00
❑ 36 Animal Man R 2.00 5.00
❑ 37 Captain Comet R 2.00 5.00
❑ 38 Kyle Rayner R 2.00 5.00
❑ 39 Guy Gardner R 2.00 5.00
❑ 40 Saint Walker R 2.00 5.00
❑ 41 Inigo - 1 R 2.00 5.00
❑ 42 Atrocitus R 2.00 5.00
❑ 43 Larfleeze R 2.00 5.00
❑ 44 Mongul R 2.00 5.00
❑ 45 Scar R 2.00 5.00
❑ 46 John Stewart R 2.00 5.00
❑ 47 Carol Ferris R 2.00 5.00
❑ 48 Ganthet R 2.00 5.00
❑ 49 Green Lantern SR 15.00 30.00
❑ 50 Superman SR 10.00 25.00
❑ 51 Wonder Woman SR 10.00 25.00
❑ 52 Batman SR 10.00 25.00
❑ 53 Hal Jordan SR 15.00 30.00
❑ 54 Barry Allen SR 10.00 25.00
❑ 55 Beast Boy (T-Rex) SR 10.00 25.00
❑ 56 Doomsday SR 10.00 25.00
❑ 57 Bane SR 20.00 40.00
❑ 58 Ares SR 10.00 25.00
❑ 59 Wonder Twins SR 10.00 25.00
❑ 60 Sinestro SR 25.00 50.00
❑ 100 Sinestro 25.00 50.00
❑ 101 Grodd LE 5.00 12.00
❑ 102 Gleek LE 6.00 15.00
❑ 103 Troia LE 4.00 10.00
❑ 104 Impulse LE 4.00 10.00
❑ 105 Ice Maiden LE 5.00 12.00
❑ 200 Green Lantern (FCBD) LE 2.00 5.00
❑ 201 Wonder Woman (Conv) LE 75.00 150.00
❑ W-1 Ice CH 25.00 50.00
❑ W-2 Bart Allen CH 25.00 50.00
❑ W-3 Donna Troy CH 30.00 60.00
❑ W-4 Hal Jordan CH 60.00 120.00
❑ W-5 Animal Man CH 30.00 60.00
❑ W-6 Superman CH 40.00 80.00
❑ W-7 Flash CH 50.00 100.00
❑ W-8 Wonder Woman CH 30.00 60.00
❑ W-9 Superboy CH 25.00 50.00
❑ W-10 Green Arrow CH 40.00 80.00

2010 DC Heroclix Watchmen Miniatures

❑ 1 Rorschach 6.00 15.00
❑ 2 Silk Spectre 6.00 15.00
❑ 3 Nite Owl 6.00 15.00
❑ 4 Ozymandias 6.00 15.00
❑ 5 Dr. Manhattan 6.00 15.00
❑ 6 The Comedian 1.50 4.00
❑ 7 Hooded Justice 1.50 4.00
❑ 8 Captain Metropolis 1.50 4.00
❑ 9 The Comedian 1.50 4.00
❑ 10 Silk Spectre 1.50 4.00
❑ 11 Dr. Manhattan 1.50 4.00
❑ 12 Nite Owl 1.50 4.00
❑ 13 Walter Kovacs 1.50 4.00
❑ 14 Mask-Killer 1.50 4.00
❑ 15 Bubastis 1.50 4.00
❑ 16 Knot Top Leader 1.50 4.00
❑ 17 Knot Top 1.50 4.00
❑ 18 Moloch the Mystic 1.50 4.00
❑ 19 Big Figure 1.50 4.00
❑ 20 Larry and Mike 1.50 4.00
❑ 21 The Comedian and Nite Owl 1.50 4.00
❑ 22 Silk Spectre and Dr. Manhattan 1.50 4.00
❑ 23 Ozymandias and Bubastis 1.50 4.00
❑ 24 Nite Owl and Rorschach 1.50 4.00
❑ 25 Dr. Manhattan 1.50 4.00
❑ NNO Dr. Manhattan (SDCC promo) 70.00 100.00

2011 DC Heroclix Green Lantern Fast Forces Miniatures

Complete Set 8.00 20.00
❑ 1 Green Lantern .60 1.50
❑ 2 Kilowog .60 1.50
❑ 3 Tomar Re .40 1.00
❑ 4 Sinestro .75 2.00
❑ 5 Guardian of the Universe 3.00 8.00
❑ 6 Abin Sur .75 2.00

2011 DC Heroclix Green Lantern Gravity Feed Miniatures

❑ 1 Green Lantern .75 2.00
❑ 2 Hal Jordan .60 1.50
❑ 3 Kilowog 1.25 3.00
❑ 4 Tomar Re .40 1.00
❑ 5 Sinestro .75 2.00
❑ 6 Ganthet 1.50 4.00
❑ 7 Abin Sur .75 2.00
❑ 8 R'Amey Holl 1.00 2.50
❑ 9 Salaak 2.50 6.00
❑ 10 Boodikka 1.00 2.50

2011 DC Heroclix Superman Miniatures

❑ 1 Superman C 1.50 4.00
❑ 2 Kryptonian Soldier C .20 .50
❑ 3 Kryptonian Infiltrator C .20 .50
❑ 4 Intergang Underboss C .20 .50
❑ 5 Seven Deadly Brothers C .60 1.50
❑ 6 All-Star Bizarro C .20 .50
❑ 7 Starboy C .20 .50
❑ 8 Brainiac 5 C .20 .50
❑ 9 Lois Lane, Superwoman C .20 .50
❑ 10 Supergirl C .75 2.00
❑ 11 Gangbuster C .20 .50
❑ 12 Livewire C .20 .50
❑ 13 Maxwell Lord C .20 .50
❑ 14 Mercy Graves C .20 .50
❑ 15 Lex Luthor C .20 .50
❑ 16 Element Woman C .20 .50
❑ 17 Superboy U .40 1.00
❑ 18 Steel U .50 1.25
❑ 19 Magog U .40 1.00
❑ 20 Bruno Mannheim U .40 1.00
❑ 21 Human Target U .40 1.00
❑ 22 Sun Boy U .40 1.00
❑ 23 Earth Man U .40 1.00
❑ 24 Invisible Kid U .40 1.00
❑ 25 Matter-Eater Lad U .40 1.00
❑ 26 Lucy Lane, Superwoman U .50 1.25
❑ 27 Parasite U .40 1.00
❑ 28 Manchester Black U .40 1.00
❑ 29 Silver Banshee U .60 1.50
❑ 30 Hope Taya U .40 1.00
❑ 31 Non U .50 1.25
❑ 32 Project: Superman U .40 1.00
❑ 33 Eradicator R 2.50 6.00
❑ 34 Cyborg Superman R 1.50 4.00
❑ 35 Magog KC R .40 1.00
❑ 36 Composite Superman R .75 2.00
❑ 37 Libra R .40 1.00
❑ 38 Princess Projectra R .40 1.00
❑ 39 Wildfire R .40 1.00
❑ 40 Maxwell Lord R .40 1.00
❑ 41 Starman R .40 1.00
❑ 42 Lobo R 2.00 5.00
❑ 43 Doomsday R 1.00 2.50
❑ 44 Ursa R .60 1.50
❑ 45 Wonder Woman SR 3.00 8.00
❑ 46 The Bat-Man (Batman) SR 3.00 8.00
❑ 47 The Flash SR 4.00 10.00
❑ 48 Aquaman SR 4.00 10.00
❑ 49 Queen of Fables SR 2.50 6.00
❑ 50 Imperiex SR 3.00 8.00
❑ 51 Swamp Thing SR 3.00 8.00
❑ 52 Darkseid SR 8.00 20.00
❑ 53 Zod SR 3.00 8.00
❑ 54 Black Adam SR 10.00 25.00
❑ 55 Superman (Earth One) CH 8.00 20.00
❑ 56 Superman (Son of Darkseid) CH 12.00 30.00
❑ 57 Superman CH 8.00 20.00
❑ 58 Kal CH 5.00 12.00
❑ 101 Commander El 1.50 4.00
❑ 102 Manhunter Grandmaster 3.00 8.00
❑ 103 Bizarro-Girl 2.50 6.00
❑ 104 Zibarro 1.50 4.00
❑ 105 Superman Beyond 4.00 10.00

2011 DC Heroclix Superman Fast Forces Battle For Smallville Miniatures

❑ 1 Superman 6.00 15.00
❑ 2 Supergirl 2.50 6.00
❑ 3 Steel .75 2.00
❑ 4 Lex Luthor 1.50 4.00
❑ 5 Kryptonian Renegade 3.00 8.00
❑ 6 Bizarro 1.50 4.00

2012 DC Heroclix 10th Anniversary Miniatures

❑ 1 Batman C 1.25 3.00
❑ 2 Wonder Woman C .40 1.00
❑ 3 John Jones C .40 1.00
❑ 4 Green Lantern C 1.25 3.00
❑ 5 Brainiac C .40 1.00
❑ 6 Batgirl C .75 2.00
❑ 7 Nightwing C 2.50 6.00
❑ 8 Catwoman C .40 1.00
❑ 9 Blue Beetle C 2.00 5.00
❑ 10 The Flash U 2.50 6.00
❑ 11 Green Lantern U 1.25 3.00
❑ 12 Brainiac U 2.00 5.00
❑ 13 Lex Luthor U .40 1.00
❑ 14 Robin U .40 1.00
❑ 15 Catwoman U 1.50 4.00
❑ 16 Blue Beetle U 1.00 2.50
❑ 17 Oracle R 6.00 15.00
❑ 18 The Flash R 3.00 8.00
❑ 19 Martian Manhunter R 3.00 8.00
❑ 20 Lex Luthor R 6.00 15.00
❑ 21 Superman R 5.00 12.00
❑ 22 Black Lantern Wonder Woman CH 10.00 25.00
❑ 23 Black Lantern Batman CH 12.00 30.00
❑ 24 Black Lantern Superman CH 12.00 30.00

2012 DC Heroclix Batman Miniatures

❑ 1 Batman C .60 1.50
❑ 2 Bruce Wayne C .40 1.00
❑ 3 Arkham Asylum Guard C .60 1.50
❑ 4 The Joker Thug C .60 1.50
❑ 5 Beast Boy C .40 1.00
❑ 6 Hired Henchman C .60 1.50
❑ 7a Catwoman C .40 1.00
❑ 7b Selina Kyle C 2.50 6.00
❑ 8 Nightwing C .40 1.00
❑ 9 Red Robin C .40 1.00
❑ 10 Blackbat C .40 1.00
❑ 11 Katana C .40 1.00
❑ 12 Grifter C .40 1.00
❑ 13 The Joker C .40 1.00
❑ 14 Harley Quinn C .50 1.25
❑ 15 Nightrunner C .40 1.00
❑ 16 Batgirl C .40 1.00
❑ 17 Robin U .40 1.00
❑ 18 Aaron Cash U .40 1.00
❑ 19 Beast Boy U .40 1.00
❑ 20 KGBeast U .40 1.00
❑ 21 Thunder U .40 1.00
❑ 22 Two-Face U .40 1.00
❑ 23a Sasha Bordeaux U .40 1.00
❑ 23b Black Queen U 2.00 5.00
❑ 24 Maul U .40 1.00
❑ 25 Batgirl U .50 1.25
❑ 26 Roy Raymond, Jr. U .40 1.00
❑ 27 Dick Grayson U .40 1.00
❑ 28 Zealot U .40 1.00
❑ 29 Godiva U .40 1.00
❑ 30 El Gaucho U .40 1.00
❑ 31 Alfred Pennyworth U .75 2.00
❑ 32 Big Barda R 2.50 6.00
❑ 33 Bad Samaritan R .40 1.00
❑ 34 Poison Ivy R .75 2.00
❑ 35 Rocket Red R .40 1.00
❑ 36 Batwoman R .50 1.25
❑ 37a Hush R 1.50 4.00
❑ 37b Bruce Wayne R 8.00 20.00
❑ 38 August General in Iron R .40 1.00
❑ 39 Hugo Strange R .60 1.50
❑ 40 Halo R .40 1.00
❑ 41 Lucius Fox R .40 1.00
❑ 42 Batwing R .40 1.00
❑ 43 Warblade R .60 1.50
❑ 44 Mr. Unknown R .40 1.00
❑ 45 Black Lightning SR 2.50 6.00
❑ 46 Geo-Force SR 2.50 6.00
❑ 47 Doctor Phosphorus SR 2.00 5.00
❑ 48 Mr. Freeze SR 6.00 15.00
❑ 49 Socialist Red Guardsman SR 1.50 4.00
❑ 50 Remac SR 1.50 4.00
❑ 51 Rex Mason SR 2.00 5.00
❑ 52 Booster Gold SR 4.00 10.00
❑ 53a Batman SR 6.00 15.00
❑ 53b The Caped Crusader SR 30.00 60.00
❑ 54 Voodoo SR 5.00 12.00
❑ 55 The Insider CH 6.00 15.00
❑ 56 Batman CH 8.00 20.00
❑ 57 Omega Batman CH 10.00 25.00
❑ 58 Batman CH 25.00 50.00
❑ 59 Batman CH 8.00 20.00
❑ 99a Flock of Bats (Black) C 1.25 3.00
❑ 99b Flock of Bats (Brown) C 2.50 6.00
❑ 99c Flock of Bats (Grey) C 4.00 10.00
❑ 100 Nightwing and Batgirl M .40 1.00
❑ V001 Batmobile SR 12.00 30.00
❑ V002 Batwing SR 6.00 15.00
❑ V003 Invisible Jet SR 6.00 15.00
❑ V004 GCPD Cruiser SR 10.00 25.00
❑ V005 Military Tank SR 6.00 15.00
❑ V006 Haunted Tank SR 12.00 30.00
❑ V007 The Bug SR 30.00 60.00

2012 DC Heroclix Batman Fast Forces Miniatures

❑ 1 Batman 2.00 5.00
❑ 2 Damian Wayne .75 2.00
❑ 3 Nightwing 2.50 6.00
❑ 4 Red Robin 1.00 2.50
❑ 5 Alfred Pennyworth 2.50 6.00
❑ 6 Batgirl 1.25 3.00

MINIATURES

2012 DC Heroclix Batman Gravity Feed Miniatures

Item	Low	High
☐ 201 Batman	1.50	4.00
☐ 202 Bruce Wayne	2.00	5.00
☐ 203 Hired Goon	1.50	4.00
☐ 204 Catwoman	2.00	5.00
☐ 205 Nightwing	.40	1.00
☐ 206 Red Robin	.40	1.00
☐ 207 The Joker	1.50	4.00
☐ 208 Harley Quinn	2.00	5.00
☐ 209 Batgirl	2.00	5.00
☐ 210 Two-Face	.60	1.50

2012 DC Heroclix Batman Streets of Gotham Miniatures

Item	Low	High
☐ 1 GCPD Officer C	1.50	4.00
☐ 2 Lady Blackhawk C	.40	1.00
☐ 3 Black Canary C	.40	1.00
☐ 4 GCPD Detective C	1.00	2.50
☐ 5 GCPD Sergeant C	1.25	3.00
☐ 6 Blue Beetle C	.40	1.00
☐ 7 False Facer C	.40	1.00
☐ 8 Fire C	.50	1.25
☐ 9 Dove C	.50	1.25
☐ 10 Black Glove Demon C	.75	2.00
☐ 11 Dr. Hurt C	.40	1.00
☐ 12 Robin C	.40	1.00
☐ 13 Batman C	1.25	3.00
☐ 14 Huntress U	1.00	2.50
☐ 15a Renee Montoya U	1.50	4.00
☐ 15b The Question U	6.00	15.00
☐ 16 Harvey Bullock U	.75	2.00
☐ 17 Ice U	1.25	3.00
☐ 18 Hawk U	.40	1.00
☐ 19 Red Hood U	3.00	8.00
☐ 20 Calendar Man U	1.25	3.00
☐ 21 Killer Croc U	2.50	6.00
☐ 22 Harvey Dent U	.40	1.00
☐ 23 Scarecrow U	2.00	5.00
☐ 24 Mr. Zsasz R	3.00	8.00
☐ 25 Omac R	2.00	5.00
☐ 26 Commissioner Gordon R	2.50	6.00
☐ 27 Guy Gardner R	8.00	20.00
☐ 28 Vixen R	2.50	6.00
☐ 29 Onomatopoeia R	2.50	6.00
☐ 30 Black Mask R	2.50	6.00
☐ 31 The Architect R	1.25	3.00
☐ 32 Batman SR	2.00	5.00
☐ 33 Superman SR	3.00	8.00
☐ 34 Wonder Woman SR	2.00	5.00
☐ 35 Void SR	6.00	15.00
☐ 36 Spartan Warrior Spirit SR	3.00	8.00
☐ 37 Emp SR	2.50	6.00
☐ 38 David Cain SR	3.00	8.00
☐ 39 Lady Shiva SR	4.00	10.00
☐ 40 Deathstroke SR	6.00	15.00
☐ 41 Black Canary SR	1.50	4.00
☐ 42 Starling SR	2.00	5.00
☐ 43 Katana SR	2.00	5.00
☐ 44 Starfire SR	5.00	12.00
☐ 45 Arsenal SR	2.00	5.00
☐ 46 Crux SR	1.25	3.00
☐ 47 Batman SR	2.00	5.00
☐ 48 Robin SR	.75	2.00
☐ 49 GCPD Motor Officer SR	2.00	5.00
☐ 50 Batman CH	10.00	25.00
☐ 51 Batman CH	10.00	25.00
☐ 52 Batman CH	12.00	30.00
☐ 100 Batman of the Future LE	2.00	5.00
☐ V001 Batcycle SR	8.00	20.00
☐ V002 Robincycle SR	2.50	6.00
☐ V003 GCPD Motorcycle SR	4.00	10.00

2012 DC Heroclix Batman Streets of Gotham Fast Forces Miniatures

Item	Low	High
☐ 1 Oracle	4.00	10.00
☐ 2 Lady Blackhawk	.40	1.00
☐ 3 Huntress	1.25	3.00
☐ 4 Black Canary	.75	2.00
☐ 5 Hawk	.60	1.50
☐ 6 Dove	.40	1.00

2012 DC Heroclix Justice League New 52 Miniatures

Item	Low	High
☐ 1 Superman C	3.00	8.00
☐ 2 Batman C	2.00	5.00
☐ 3 Wonder Woman C	2.00	5.00
☐ 4 Green Lantern C	1.50	4.00
☐ 5 Aquaman C	2.00	5.00
☐ 6 Cyborg C	1.25	3.00
☐ 7 Green Arrow C	5.00	12.00
☐ 8 Mera C	.50	1.25
☐ 9 Firestorm C	.75	2.00
☐ 10 Firestorm C	.60	1.50
☐ 11 Hawkman U	3.00	8.00
☐ 12 Shade the Changing Man U	.50	1.25
☐ 13 Deadman U	1.25	3.00
☐ 14 Zatanna U	2.50	6.00
☐ 15 Mindwarp U	.75	2.00
☐ 16 Enchantress U	8.00	20.00
☐ 17 The Flash R	4.00	10.00
☐ 18 Madame Xanadu R	4.00	10.00
☐ 19 John Constantine R	10.00	25.00
☐ 20 Deathstroke R	8.00	20.00
☐ 21 Fury R	3.00	8.00

2012 DC Heroclix Justice League New 52 Fast Forces Miniatures

Item	Low	High
☐ 1 Cyborg	.75	2.00
☐ 2 Superman	2.50	6.00
☐ 3 Batman	2.00	5.00
☐ 4 Wonder Woman	4.00	10.00
☐ 5 The Flash	5.00	12.00
☐ 6 Green Lantern	1.50	4.00

2012 DC Heroclix The Dark Knight Rises Miniatures

Item	Low	High
☐ 1 The Dark Knight C	2.00	5.00
☐ 2 Shadow Assassin C	2.00	5.00
☐ 3 Bruce Wayne C	.75	2.00
☐ 4 Arkham Asylum Inmate C	1.25	3.00
☐ 5 GCPD Officer C	2.00	5.00
☐ 6 Catwoman C	.75	2.00
☐ 7 The Joker's Henchman C	.75	2.00
☐ 8 Mercenary C	1.50	4.00
☐ 9 Two-Face C	.40	1.00
☐ 10 Falcone Bodyguard C	1.25	3.00
☐ 11 GCPD Riot Officer C	2.00	5.00
☐ 12 Miranda Tate U	.60	1.50
☐ 13 Alfred Pennyworth U	2.50	6.00
☐ 14 Bane U	2.00	5.00
☐ 15 Master Bruce Wayne U	.75	2.00
☐ 16 Salvatore Maroni U	.75	2.00
☐ 17 Harvey Dent U	2.00	5.00
☐ 18 Rachel Dawes U	1.25	3.00
☐ 19 The Joker's Henchman U	3.00	8.00
☐ 20 The Joker as Sgt. U	1.25	3.00
☐ 21 Lt. Gordon U	6.00	15.00
☐ 22 Ra's Al-Ghul R	3.00	8.00
☐ 23 Henri Ducard R	5.00	12.00
☐ 24 Carmine Falcone R	1.50	4.00
☐ 25 Scarecrow R	5.00	12.00
☐ 26 Lucius Fox R	4.00	10.00
☐ 27 Commissioner Gordon R	5.00	12.00
☐ 28 The Joker R	10.00	25.00
☐ 29 The Batman R	6.00	15.00
☐ 100 Batman LE	1.50	4.00
☐ 101 Batman F	1.50	4.00
☐ 102 Catwoman F	.60	1.50
☐ 103 Bane F	4.00	10.00
☐ 104 The Joker F	4.00	10.00
☐ 105 Harvey Two-Face F	.40	1.00
☐ 106 Sgt. Gordon F	1.00	2.50

2012 DC Heroclix The Dark Knight Rises Gravity Feed Miniatures

Item	Low	High
☐ 201 Batman	2.50	6.00
☐ 202 Bruce Wayne	.60	1.50
☐ 203 Catwoman	1.50	4.00
☐ 204 Bane	1.25	3.00
☐ 205 Rachel Dawes	1.25	3.00
☐ 206 John Blake	6.00	15.00
☐ 207 The Joker's Henchman #3	3.00	8.00
☐ 208 The Joker's Henchman #4	4.00	10.00
☐ 209 The Joker	4.00	10.00
☐ 210 Arkham Asylum Escapee	1.50	4.00

2013 DC Heroclix Teen Titans Miniatures

Item	Low	High
☐ 1 Robin C	.20	.50
☐ 2 Kid Flash C	.20	.50
☐ 3 Fairchild C	.20	.50
☐ 4 Psion C	.20	.50
☐ 5a Gordanian C	.40	1.00
☐ 5b Beast Boy (In Gordanian Form) C	3.00	8.00
☐ 6 Arrowette C	.20	.50
☐ 7 Jinx C	.40	1.00
☐ 8 Wonder Girl C	.40	1.00
☐ 9 N.O.W.H.E.R.E. Soldier C	.50	1.25
☐ 10 Brother Blood Acolyte C	.20	.50
☐ 11 Mammoth C	.20	.50
☐ 12 Red Star C	.20	.50
☐ 13 Solstice C	.20	.50
☐ 14 Osiris C	.20	.50
☐ 15 Aquaman C	.50	1.25
☐ 16 Grymm C	.20	.50
☐ 17a Li'l Lobo U	.60	1.50
☐ 17b Slobo U	3.00	8.00
☐ 18 Red Robin U	.20	.50
☐ 19 Beast Boy U	.20	.50
☐ 20 Fairchild U	.20	.50
☐ 21 Beast Boy (Tiger) U	.40	1.00
☐ 22 Nightwing U	.40	1.00
☐ 23 Red Hood U	.40	1.00
☐ 24 Lightning U	.20	.50
☐ 25 Cyborg U	.60	1.50
☐ 26 Superboy U	.75	2.00
☐ 27 Centerhall U	.20	.50
☐ 28 Empress U	.20	.50
☐ 29 Shimmer U	.20	.50
☐ 30 Rose Wilson U	.20	.50
☐ 31 Leash U	.20	.50
☐ 32 Dr. Light U	.40	1.00
☐ 33 Green Lantern R	2.00	5.00
☐ 34 Grunge R	.40	1.00
☐ 35 Terra R	.20	.50
☐ 36 Arsenal R	1.25	3.00
☐ 37a Deathstroke R	5.00	12.00
☐ 37b Ravager R	8.00	20.00
☐ 38 Changeling R	.75	2.00
☐ 39 Kid Flash R	.60	1.50
☐ 40 Secret R	.40	1.00
☐ 41 Thunder R	.40	1.00
☐ 42 Indigo R	.60	1.50
☐ 43 Ridge R	.40	1.00
☐ 44 Gizmo R	.75	2.00
☐ 45 Static R	.50	1.25
☐ 46 Red Tornado SR	8.00	20.00
☐ 47a Starfire SR	20.00	40.00
☐ 47b Blackfire SR	25.00	50.00
☐ 48 Skitter SR	2.50	6.00
☐ 49 Bunker SR	3.00	8.00
☐ 50 The Flash SR	12.00	30.00
☐ 51 Brother Blood SR	2.50	6.00
☐ 52 Psimon SR	4.00	10.00
☐ 53 Omen SR	3.00	8.00
☐ 54 The Ray SR	3.00	8.00
☐ 55 Warblade SR	4.00	10.00
☐ 56 Harvest SR	6.00	15.00
☐ 57 Headcase CH	10.00	25.00
☐ 58 Sun Girl CH	12.00	30.00
☐ 59 Inertia CH	12.00	30.00
☐ 60 Persuader CH	10.00	25.00
☐ 61 Zookeeper CH	10.00	25.00
☐ 62 Superboy Prime CH	35.00	70.00
☐ 63 Cyborg SR	2.50	6.00
☐ 64 Raven SR	12.00	30.00
☐ 65 Wonder Girl SR	3.00	8.00
☐ 66 Superman SR	10.00	25.00
☐ 67 Batman SR	10.00	25.00
☐ 68 Wonder Woman SR	6.00	15.00
☐ 69 Cinder SR	2.50	6.00
☐ 70 Cheshire SR	6.00	15.00
☐ 71 Tattooed Man SR	3.00	8.00
☐ 72 Burnout SR	3.00	8.00
☐ 73 Sarah Rainmaker SR	5.00	12.00
☐ 74 Freefall SR	5.00	12.00
☐ 75 Aqualad SR	2.00	5.00
☐ 76 Wonder Girl SR	3.00	8.00
☐ 77 Starfire SR	10.00	25.00
☐ G001 Trigon SR		
☐ T001 New Teen Titans SR	5.00	12.00
☐ T002 Justice League SR	15.00	40.00
☐ T003 Titans: Villains For Hire SR	3.00	8.00
☐ T004 Gen13 SR	5.00	12.00
☐ T005 Teen Titans SR	2.50	6.00
☐ T006 Outlaws SR	6.00	15.00

2013 DC Heroclix Teen Titans Fast Forces Miniatures

Item	Low	High
☐ 1 Fairchild	.50	1.25
☐ 2 Beast Boy	.40	1.00
☐ 3 Terra	.40	1.00
☐ 4 Lightning	.75	2.00
☐ 5 Thunder	.75	2.00
☐ 6 Ridge	.75	2.00

2013 DC Heroclix Teen Titans Gravity Feed Miniatures

Item	Low	High
☐ 201 Red Robin	1.00	2.50
☐ 202 Superboy	2.50	6.00
☐ 203 Wonder Girl	.75	2.00
☐ 204 Red Hood	2.50	6.00
☐ 205 N.O.W.H.E.R.E. Soldier	2.50	6.00
☐ 206 Brother Blood Acolyte	1.25	3.00
☐ 207 Solstice	.75	2.00
☐ 208 Rose Wilson	1.50	4.00
☐ 209 Leash	.50	1.25
☐ 210 Grymm	.40	1.00

2003 Indy Heroclix Miniatures

Item	Low	High
Complete Set (120)	100.00	175.00
Booster Pack	5.00	7.00
☐ 1 Ashleigh R	.30	.50
☐ 2 Ashleigh E	.50	1.00
☐ 3 Ashleigh V	1.00	2.00
☐ 4 Tomoe R	.30	.50
☐ 5 Tomoe E	.50	1.00
☐ 6 Tomoe V	1.00	2.00
☐ 7 Saurian Trooper R	.30	.50
☐ 8 Saurian Trooper E	.50	1.00
☐ 9 Saurian Trooper V	1.00	2.00
☐ 10 Scarab R	.30	.50
☐ 11 Scarab E	.50	1.00
☐ 12 Scarab V	1.00	2.00
☐ 13 Tiger Lilly R	.30	.50
☐ 14 Tiger Lilly E	.50	1.00
☐ 15 Tiger Lilly V	1.00	2.00
☐ 16 Sydney Savage R	.30	.50
☐ 17 Sydney Savage E	.50	1.00
☐ 18 Sydney Savage V	1.00	2.00
☐ 19 Johnny Alpha R	.30	.50
☐ 20 Johnny Alpha E	.50	1.00
☐ 21 Johnny Alpha V	1.00	2.00
☐ 22 Judge Hershey R	.30	.50
☐ 23 Judge Hershey E	.50	1.00
☐ 24 Judge Hershey V	1.00	2.00
☐ 25 Aphrodite IX R	.30	.50
☐ 26 Aphrodite IX E	.50	1.00
☐ 27 Aphrodite IX V	1.00	2.00
☐ 28 Magdalena R	.30	.50
☐ 29 Magdalena E	.50	1.00
☐ 30 Magdalena V	1.00	2.00
☐ 31 Arashi R	.30	.50
☐ 32 Arashi E	.50	1.00
☐ 33 Arashi V	1.00	2.00
☐ 34 Lobster Johnson R	.30	.50
☐ 35 Lobster Johnson E	.50	1.00
☐ 36 Lobster Johnson V	1.00	2.00
☐ 37 Arwyn R	.30	.50
☐ 38 Arwyn E	.50	1.00
☐ 39 Arwyn V	1.00	2.00
☐ 40 Boon R	.30	.50
☐ 41 Boon E	.50	1.00
☐ 42 Boon V	1.00	2.00
☐ 43 Ian Nottingham R	.30	.50
☐ 44 Ian Nottingham E	.50	1.00
☐ 45 Ian Nottingham V	1.00	2.00
☐ 46 The Darkness R	.30	.50
☐ 47 The Darkness E	.50	1.00
☐ 48 The Darkness V	1.00	2.00
☐ 49 Natalia Kassle R	.30	.50
☐ 50 Natalia Kassle E	.50	1.00
☐ 51 Natalia Kassle V	1.00	2.00
☐ 52 Major Maxim R	.30	.50
☐ 53 Major Maxim E	.50	1.00
☐ 54 Major Maxim V	1.00	2.00
☐ 55 Bron R	.30	.50
☐ 56 Bron E	.50	1.00
☐ 57 Bron V	1.00	2.00
☐ 58 Shi R	.30	.50
☐ 59 Shi E	.50	1.00
☐ 60 Shi V	1.00	2.00
☐ 61 Yukio R	.30	.50
☐ 62 Yukio E	.50	1.00
☐ 63 Yukio V	1.00	2.00
☐ 64 Witchblade R	.30	.50
☐ 65 Witchblade E	.50	1.00
☐ 66 Witchblade V	1.00	2.00
☐ 67 Hellboy R	.50	1.00
☐ 68 Hellboy E	1.00	2.00
☐ 69 Hellboy V	3.00	5.00
☐ 70 Judge Dredd R	.30	.50
☐ 71 Judge Dredd E	.50	1.00
☐ 72 Judge Dredd V	1.00	2.00
☐ 73 Abbey Chase R	.30	.50
☐ 74 Abbey Chase E	.50	1.00
☐ 75 Abbey Chase V	1.00	2.00
☐ 76 Kabuki R	.30	.50
☐ 77 Kabuki E	.50	1.00
☐ 78 Kabuki V	1.00	2.00
☐ 79 Death Demon R	.30	.50
☐ 80 Death Demon E	.50	1.00
☐ 81 Death Demon V	1.00	2.00
☐ 82 Rasputin R	.30	.50
☐ 83 Rasputin E	.50	1.00
☐ 84 Rasputin V	1.00	2.00
☐ 85 Samandhal Rey U	8.00	12.00
☐ 86 Arwyn U	10.00	15.00
☐ 87 Hellboy U	20.00	30.00
☐ 88 Hecate U	10.00	15.00
☐ 89 Shi U	10.00	15.00
☐ 90 Abbey Chase U	10.00	15.00
☐ 91 Judge Anderson U	10.00	18.00
☐ 92 Judge Death U	10.00	18.00
☐ 93 Witchblade U	10.00	18.00
☐ 94 Angelus U	10.00	15.00
☐ 95 Siamese U	8.00	12.00
☐ 96 Cyblade U	8.00	12.00
☐ 97 Brit City Judge R	.30	.50
☐ 98 Brit City Judge E	.50	1.00
☐ 99 Brit City Judge V	1.00	2.00
☐ 100 Stix R	.30	.50
☐ 101 Stix E	.50	1.00
☐ 102 Stix V	1.00	2.00
☐ 103 Wulf Sternhammer R	.30	.50
☐ 104 Wulf Sternhammer E	.50	1.00
☐ 105 Wulf Sternhammer V	1.00	2.00
☐ 106 Torquemada R	.30	.50
☐ 107 Torquemada E	.50	1.00
☐ 108 Torquemada V	1.00	2.00
☐ 109 Nemesis R	.30	.50
☐ 110 Nemesis E	.50	1.00
☐ 111 Nemesis V	1.00	2.00
☐ 112 Judge Fire R	.30	.50
☐ 113 Judge Fire E	.50	1.00
☐ 114 Judge Fire V	1.00	2.00
☐ 115 Judge Mortis R	.30	.50
☐ 116 Judge Mortis E	.50	1.00
☐ 117 Judge Mortis V	1.00	2.00
☐ 118 Judge Fear R	.30	.50
☐ 119 Judge Fear E	.50	1.00
☐ 120 Judge Fear V	1.00	2.00
☐ 201 Ashleigh (Princess Ashleigh) LE	10.00	15.00
☐ 202 Tomoe (Tomoe Gozan) LE	8.00	12.00
☐ 203 Saurian Trooper (Bajounte-Ka) LE	8.00	12.00
☐ 204 Scarab (Keiko) LE	8.00	12.00
☐ 205 Tiger Lilly (Akemi) LE	8.00	12.00
☐ 206 Sydney Savage (Spec Ops Savage) LE	8.00	12.00
☐ 207 Johnny Alpha (Search/Destroy Agent Alpha) LE	8.00	15.00
☐ 208 Judge Hershey (Barbara Hershey) LE	12.00	18.00
☐ 209 Aphrodite IX (Aphrodite) LE	8.00	12.00
☐ 210 Magdalena (Sister Magdalena) LE	8.00	12.00
☐ 211 Arashi (Masahiro Arashi) LE	8.00	12.00
☐ 212 Lobster Johnson (Lobster Johnson) LE	8.00	12.00
☐ 221 Witchblade (Scrye) LE	12.00	20.00
☐ 222 Boon (Inquest) LE	8.00	12.00
☐ 223 Arwyn	8.00	12.00
☐ P1 Johnny Alpha PROMO		

2011 Indy Heroclix Gears of War Miniatures

Item	Low	High
COMPLETE SET	30.00	60.00
☐ 1 Marcus Fenix	3.00	8.00
☐ 2 Dominic Santiago	3.00	8.00
☐ 3 Augustus Cole	3.00	8.00
☐ 4 Damon Baird	3.00	8.00
☐ 5 Anya Stroud	3.00	8.00
☐ 6 Mauler	3.00	8.00
☐ 7 Locust Drone	3.00	8.00
☐ 8 Kantus	3.00	8.00
☐ 9 General RAAM	3.00	8.00
☐ 10 Skorge	3.00	8.00

2011 Indy Heroclix Street Fighter Miniatures

Item	Low	High
BOOSTER BOX	4.00	8.00
☐ 1 Ken C	3.00	6.00
☐ 2 Ryu C	3.00	6.00
☐ 3 Blanka C	.50	1.00
☐ 3B Blanka CH	25.00	40.00
☐ 4 Dhalsim C	.50	1.00
☐ 5 Zangief C	1.00	2.00
☐ 5B Zangief CH	20.00	30.00
☐ 6 E. Honda C	1.00	2.00
☐ 7 Guile C	1.00	2.00
☐ 8 Chun-Li C	.50	1.00
☐ 8B Chun-Li CH	25.00	40.00
☐ 9 Cammy C	1.00	2.00
☐ 9B Cammy CH	30.00	50.00
☐ 10 Dee Jay C	1.00	2.00
☐ 11 Fei Long U	3.00	8.00
☐ 12 T. Hawk U	2.00	5.00
☐ 13 Balrog U	3.00	8.00
☐ 14 Vega U	6.00	15.00
☐ 15 Sagat U	3.00	8.00
☐ 16 Ken U	5.00	10.00
☐ 17 Dhalsim U	2.00	5.00
☐ 18 Guile U	5.00	10.00
☐ 19 M. Bison R	15.00	30.00
☐ 20 Ryu R	10.00	20.00
☐ 21 Ken R	10.00	20.00
☐ 22 Akuma R	15.00	30.00
☐ 23 Evil Ryu R	10.00	20.00
☐ 101 Ryu F	3.00	6.00
☐ 102 Blanka F	3.00	6.00
☐ 103 Dhalsim F	3.00	6.00
☐ 104 Chun-Li F	3.00	6.00
☐ 105 Guile F	3.00	6.00
☐ 106 Ken F	3.00	6.00

2002 Marvel Heroclix Clobberin Time Miniatures

Item	Low	High
Complete Set (96)	200.00	275.00
Booster Pack	8.00	12.00
☐ 1 S.H.I.E.L.D. Trooper R	.30	.50
☐ 2 S.H.I.E.L.D. Trooper E	.50	.75
☐ 3 S.H.I.E.L.D. Trooper V	1.00	2.00
☐ 4 S.H.I.E.L.D. Sniper R	.30	.50
☐ 5 S.H.I.E.L.D. Sniper E	.50	.75
☐ 6 S.H.I.E.L.D. Sniper V	1.00	2.00
☐ 7 Mandroid Armor R	.30	.50
☐ 8 Mandroid Armor E	.50	.75
☐ 9 Mandroid Armor V	1.00	2.00
☐ 10 A.I.M. Agent R	.30	.50
☐ 11 A.I.M. Agent E	.50	.75
☐ 12 A.I.M. Agent V	1.00	2.00
☐ 13 A.I.M. Medic R	.30	.50
☐ 14 A.I.M. Medic E	.50	.75
☐ 15 A.I.M. Medic V	1.00	2.00
☐ 16 Skrull Commando R	.30	.50
☐ 17 Skrull Commando E	.50	.75
☐ 18 Skrull Commando V	1.00	2.00
☐ 19 Vampire Lackey R	.30	.50
☐ 20 Vampire Lackey E	.50	.75
☐ 21 Vampire Lackey V	1.00	2.00
☐ 22 Black Cat R	.30	.50
☐ 23 Black Cat E	.50	.75

MINIATURES

❑ 24 Black Cat V 1.00 2.00
❑ 25 Yellowjacket R .30 .50
❑ 26 Yellowjacket E .50 .75
❑ 27 Yellowjacket V 1.00 2.00
❑ 28 Doombot R 1.00 2.00
❑ 29 Doombot E 2.00 3.00
❑ 30 Doombot V 4.00 6.00
❑ 31 Avalanche R .30 .50
❑ 32 Avalanche E .50 .75
❑ 33 Avalanche V 1.00 2.00
❑ 34 Blob R .30 .50
❑ 35 Blob E .50 .75
❑ 36 Blob V 1.00 2.00
❑ 37 Toad R .30 .50
❑ 38 Toad E .50 .75
❑ 39 Toad V 1.00 2.00
❑ 40 Elektra R .30 .50
❑ 41 Elektra E .50 .75
❑ 42 Elektra V 1.00 2.00
❑ 43 Invisible Girl R 5.00 10.00
❑ 44 Invisible Girl E 10.00 15.00
❑ 45 Invisible Woman V 15.00 25.00
❑ 46 Thing R 4.00 7.00
❑ 47 Thing E 5.00 10.00
❑ 48 Thing V 10.00 20.00
❑ 49 Human Torch R 4.00 7.00
❑ 50 Human Torch E 5.00 10.00
❑ 51 Human Torch V 15.00 20.00
❑ 52 Hawkeye R .30 .50
❑ 53 Hawkeye E .50 .75
❑ 54 Hawkeye V 1.00 2.00
❑ 55 Black Widow R .30 .50
❑ 56 Black Widow E .50 .75
❑ 57 Black Widow V 1.00 2.00
❑ 58 Blastaar R .30 .50
❑ 59 Blastaar E .50 .75
❑ 60 Blastaar V 1.00 2.00
❑ 61 Thor R 6.00 10.00
❑ 62 Thor E 10.00 15.00
❑ 63 Thor V 15.00 25.00
❑ 64 Sandman R .30 .50
❑ 65 Sandman E .50 .75
❑ 66 Sandman V 1.00 2.00
❑ 67 Logan R 1.00 2.00
❑ 68 Logan E 3.00 5.00
❑ 69 Logan V 6.00 10.00
❑ 70 Mr. Fantastic R 4.00 8.00
❑ 71 Mr. Fantastic E 8.00 12.00
❑ 72 Mr. Fantastic V 10.00 20.00
❑ 73 Dr. Doom R 6.00 10.00
❑ 74 Dr. Doom E 10.00 20.00
❑ 75 Dr. Doom V 20.00 35.00
❑ 76 Dr. Octopus R 3.00 6.00
❑ 77 Dr. Octopus E 4.00 8.00
❑ 78 Dr. Octopus V 7.00 12.00
❑ 79 White Queen R 3.00 5.00
❑ 80 White Queen E 4.00 8.00
❑ 81 White Queen V 7.00 12.00
❑ 82 She-Hulk R 1.00 2.00
❑ 83 She-Hulk E 3.00 5.00
❑ 84 She-Hulk V 5.00 10.00
❑ 85 Nightcrawler U 55.00 90.00
❑ 86 Nick Fury U 25.00 40.00
❑ 87 Moondragon U 15.00 30.00
❑ 88 Spider-Man U 20.00 30.00
❑ 89 Mojo U 18.00 30.00
❑ 90 Super Skrull U 18.00 30.00
❑ 91 Red Skull U 20.00 30.00
❑ 92 Spiral U 20.00 40.00
❑ 93 Titania U 15.00 25.00
❑ 94 Mr. Fix-It U 18.00 30.00
❑ 95 Medusa U 15.00 25.00
❑ 96 Enchantress U 15.00 25.00
❑ 101 S.H.I.E.L.D. Trooper (Clay Quartermain) LE 10.00 15.00
❑ 102 S.H.I.E.L.D. Sniper (Laura Brown) LE 12.00 18.00
❑ 103 Mandroid Armor (Agent Beaulieu) LE 12.00 18.00
❑ 104 AIM Agent (George Tarleton) LE 10.00 15.00
❑ 105 AIM Agent (Scientist Supreme) LE 12.00 18.00
❑ 106 Skrull Commando (Paibok) LE 8.00 15.00
❑ 107 Vampire Lackey (Rachel Van Helsing) LE 12.00 18.00
❑ 108 Black Cat (Felicia Hardy) LE 12.00 18.00
❑ 109 Yellowjacket (Rita DeMara) LE 15.00 25.00
❑ 110 Dr. Doom (Dr. Doom) LE 25.00 35.00
❑ 111 Avalanche (Dominic Petros) LE 10.00 15.00
❑ 112 Blob (Fred J. Dukes) LE 15.00 22.00
❑ 113 Toad (Mortimer Toynbee) LE 12.00 18.00
❑ 114 Elektra (Elektra Natchios) LE 10.00 15.00
❑ 115 Invisible Woman (Sue Storm) LE 20.00 25.00
❑ 116 Thing (Benjamin J. Grimm) LE 20.00 30.00
❑ 117 Human Torch (Johnny Storm) LE 20.00 30.00
❑ 118 Hawkeye (Clint Barton) LE 18.00 25.00
❑ 119 Black Widow (Natasha Romanov) LE 60.00 90.00
❑ 120 Blastaar (Blastaar of Baluur) LE 20.00 40.00

2002 Marvel Heroclix Infinity Challenge Miniatures

Complete Set (150) 125.00 200.00
Booster Pack 3.00 5.00

❑ 1 S.H.I.E.L.D. Agent R .25 .40
❑ 2 S.H.I.E.L.D. Agent E .30 .60
❑ 3 S.H.I.E.L.D. Agent V 1.00 1.50
❑ 4 S.H.I.E.L.D. Medic R .25 .40
❑ 5 S.H.I.E.L.D. Medic E .30 .60
❑ 6 S.H.I.E.L.D. Medic V 1.00 2.00
❑ 7 Hydra Operative R .25 .40
❑ 8 Hydra Operative E .30 .60
❑ 9 Hydra Operative V 1.00 1.50
❑ 10 Hydra Medic R .25 .40
❑ 11 Hydra Medic E .30 .60
❑ 12 Hydra Medic V 1.00 1.50
❑ 13 Thug R .25 .40
❑ 14 Thug E .30 .60
❑ 15 Thug V 1.00 1.50
❑ 16 Henchman R .25 .40
❑ 17 Henchman E .30 .60
❑ 18 Henchman V 1.00 1.50
❑ 19 Skrull Agent R .25 .40
❑ 20 Skrull Agent E .30 .60
❑ 21 Skrull Agent V 1.00 3.00
❑ 22 Skrull Warrior R .25 .40
❑ 23 Skrull Warrior E .30 .60
❑ 24 Skrull Warrior V 1.00 3.00
❑ 25 Blade R .25 .40
❑ 26 Blade E .30 .60
❑ 27 Blade V 1.50 2.00
❑ 28 Wolfsbane R .25 .40
❑ 29 Wolfsbane E .30 .60
❑ 30 Wolfsbane V 1.50 2.00
❑ 31 Elektra R .25 .40
❑ 32 Elektra E .30 .60
❑ 33 Elektra V 1.50 2.00
❑ 34 Wasp R .25 .40
❑ 35 Wasp E .30 .60
❑ 36 Wasp V 1.00 1.50
❑ 37 Constrictor R .25 .40
❑ 38 Constrictor E .30 .60
❑ 39 Constrictor V 1.00 1.50
❑ 40 Boomerang R .25 .40
❑ 41 Boomerang E .30 .60
❑ 42 Boomerang V 1.00 1.50
❑ 43 Kingpin R .25 .50
❑ 44 Kingpin E .40 .75
❑ 45 Kingpin V 1.00 2.00
❑ 46 Vulture R .50 .75
❑ 47 Vulture E 1.00 1.50
❑ 48 Vulture V 1.50 2.00
❑ 49 Jean Grey R 1.00 1.50
❑ 50 Jean Grey E 2.00 3.00
❑ 51 Jean Grey V 3.00 4.00
❑ 52 Hobgoblin R .50 .75
❑ 53 Hobgoblin E .75 1.00
❑ 54 Hobgoblin V 1.00 2.50
❑ 55 Sabretooth R .50 .75
❑ 56 Sabretooth E .75 1.00
❑ 57 Sabretooth V 2.00 3.00
❑ 58 Hulk R 1.00 1.50
❑ 59 Hulk E 2.00 3.00
❑ 60 Hulk V 5.00 8.00
❑ 61 Puppet Master R .25 .40
❑ 62 Puppet Master E .30 .60
❑ 63 Puppet Master V 1.00 1.50
❑ 64 Annihilus R .25 .40
❑ 65 Annihilus E .30 .60
❑ 66 Annihilus V 1.00 3.00
❑ 67 Captain America R 2.00 3.00
❑ 68 Captain America E 3.00 5.00
❑ 69 Captain America V 5.00 7.00
❑ 70 Spider-Man R 2.00 2.50
❑ 71 Spider-Man E 3.00 4.00
❑ 72 Spider-Man V 5.00 6.00
❑ 73 Wolverine R 3.00 4.00
❑ 74 Wolverine E 4.00 5.00
❑ 75 Wolverine V 5.00 8.00
❑ 76 Professor Xavier R 1.00 1.50
❑ 77 Professor Xavier E 2.00 2.50
❑ 78 Professor Xavier V 3.00 5.00
❑ 79 Juggernaut R 1.00 2.00
❑ 80 Juggernaut E 2.00 3.00
❑ 81 Juggernaut V 4.00 6.00
❑ 82 Cyclops R 1.00 1.50
❑ 83 Cyclops E 2.00 3.00
❑ 84 Cyclops V 3.00 5.00
❑ 85 Black Panther R 1.00 2.00
❑ 86 Black Panther E 2.00 2.50
❑ 87 Black Panther V 3.00 5.00
❑ 88 Blizzard R .25 .40
❑ 89 Blizzard E .30 .60
❑ 90 Blizzard V 1.00 2.00
❑ 91 Pyro R .50 1.00
❑ 92 Pyro E 1.00 2.00
❑ 93 Pyro V 3.00 4.00
❑ 94 Whirlwind R .25 .40
❑ 95 Whirlwind E .30 .60
❑ 96 Whirlwind V 1.00 1.50
❑ 97 Daredevil R .50 .75
❑ 98 Daredevil E 1.00 1.50
❑ 99 Daredevil V 2.00 3.00
❑ 100 Bullseye R .75 1.00
❑ 101 Bullseye E 1.00 2.00
❑ 102 Bullseye V 3.00 5.00
❑ 103 Scarlet Witch R 1.00 1.50
❑ 104 Scarlet Witch E 1.50 2.00
❑ 105 Scarlet Witch V 3.00 4.00
❑ 106 Quicksilver R 1.00 1.50
❑ 107 Quicksilver E 1.50 2.00
❑ 108 Quicksilver V 3.00 5.00
❑ 109 Mr. Hyde R .25 .40
❑ 110 Mr. Hyde E .30 .60
❑ 111 Mr. Hyde V 1.00 1.50
❑ 112 Klaw R .25 .40
❑ 113 Klaw E .30 .60
❑ 114 Klaw V 1.00 2.00
❑ 115 Controller R .25 .40
❑ 116 Controller E .30 .60
❑ 117 Controller V 2.00 3.00
❑ 118 Hercules R .50 .75
❑ 119 Hercules E 1.00 1.50
❑ 120 Hercules V 3.00 4.00
❑ 121 Rogue R 1.00 2.00
❑ 122 Rogue E 2.00 3.00
❑ 123 Rogue V 5.00 8.00
❑ 124 Dr. Strange R 1.00 2.00
❑ 125 Dr. Strange E 2.00 3.50
❑ 126 Dr. Strange V 4.00 7.00
❑ 127 Magneto R 2.00 3.00
❑ 128 Magneto E 4.00 6.00
❑ 129 Magneto V 7.00 12.00
❑ 130 Kang R .75 1.00
❑ 131 Kang E 1.00 2.00
❑ 132 Kang V 2.00 3.00
❑ 133 Ultron R 1.00 1.50
❑ 134 Ultron E 2.00 3.00
❑ 135 Ultron V 3.00 5.00
❑ 136 Firelord R 1.00 2.00
❑ 137 Firelord E 2.00 3.00
❑ 138 Firelord V 4.00 6.00
❑ 139 Vision U 15.00 20.00
❑ 140 Quasar U 9.00 15.00
❑ 141 Thanos U 15.00 20.00
❑ 142 Nightmare U 10.00 15.00
❑ 143 Wasp U 8.00 12.00
❑ 144 Elektra U 8.00 12.00
❑ 145 Professor Xavier U 10.00 15.00
❑ 146 Juggernaut U 10.00 15.00
❑ 147 Cyclops U 8.00 12.00
❑ 148 Captain America U 10.00 15.00
❑ 149 Wolverine U 10.00 20.00
❑ 150 Spider-Man U 12.00 20.00
❑ 151 S.H.I.E.L.D. Agent (Gabriel Jones) LE 10.00 14.00
❑ 152 S.H.I.E.L.D. Medic (Tia Senyaka) LE 10.00 18.00
❑ 153 Hydra Operative (Operative #128) LE 7.00 12.00
❑ 154 Hydra Medic (Medic #519) LE 7.00 12.00
❑ 155 Thug (Knuckles) LE 7.00 12.00
❑ 156 Thug (Joey the Snake) LE 7.00 12.00
❑ 157 Skrull Agent (Nenora) LE 10.00 12.00
❑ 158 Skrull Warrior (Raksor) LE 9.00 15.00
❑ 159 Blade (Blade) LE 9.00 15.00
❑ 160 Wolfsbane (Rahne Sinclair) LE 8.00 12.00
❑ 161 Constrictor (Frank Schlichting) LE 8.00 12.00
❑ 162 Boomerang (Fred Myers) LE 15.00 20.00
❑ 163 Kingpin (Wilson Fisk) LE 10.00 15.00
❑ 164 Vulture (Adrian Toomes) LE 10.00 15.00
❑ 165 Jean Grey LE 15.00 30.00
❑ 166 Hobgoblin (Ned Leeds) LE 15.00 25.00
❑ 167 Sabretooth (Victor Creed) LE 30.00 60.00
❑ 168 Hulk (Bruce Banner) LE 30.00 50.00
❑ 169 Puppet Master (Phillip Masters) LE 10.00 18.00
❑ 170 Annihilus LE 30.00 60.00
❑ 171 Wolverine (Bezerker) LE 10.00 20.00
❑ 172 Yellowjacket LE 15.00 20.00
❑ 173 Ant-Man LE 20.00 25.00
❑ 199 Hulk (Playstation) LE 25.00 35.00
❑ BF1 Sentinel (Big Figure) 25.00 40.00
❑ PR Spider-man (Promo) 5.00 10.00

2003 Marvel Heroclix Critical Mass Miniatures

Complete Set (96) 175.00 275.00
Booster Pack 5.00 8.00

❑ 1 Moloid R .30 .50
❑ 2 Moloid E .50 .75
❑ 3 Moloid V 1.00 2.00
❑ 4 Brood Warrior R .30 .50
❑ 5 Brood Warrior E .50 .75
❑ 6 Brood Warrior V 1.00 2.00
❑ 7 Kree Warrior R .30 .50
❑ 8 Kree Warrior E .50 .75
❑ 9 Kree Warrior V 1.00 2.00
❑ 10 SWAT Heavy Weapons R .30 .50
❑ 11 SWAT Heavy Weapons E .50 .75
❑ 12 SWAT Heavy Weapons V 1.00 2.00
❑ 13 Dreadnought R .30 .50
❑ 14 Dreadnought E .50 .75
❑ 15 Dreadnought V 1.00 2.00
❑ 16 Hepzibah R .30 .50
❑ 17 Hepzibah E .50 .75
❑ 18 Hepzibah V 1.00 2.00
❑ 19 Marrow R .30 .50
❑ 20 Marrow E .50 .75
❑ 21 Marrow V 1.00 2.00
❑ 22 Corsair R .30 .50
❑ 23 Corsair E .50 .75
❑ 24 Corsair V 1.00 2.00
❑ 25 Moon Knight R .30 .50
❑ 26 Moon Knight E .50 1.00
❑ 27 Moon Knight V 1.00 3.00
❑ 28 Calypso R .30 .50
❑ 29 Calypso E .50 .75
❑ 30 Calypso V 1.00 2.00
❑ 31 Elektra R .50 1.00
❑ 32 Elektra E 1.00 2.00
❑ 33 Elektra V 2.00 4.00
❑ 34 Daredevil R 1.00 2.00
❑ 35 Daredevil E 2.00 3.00
❑ 36 Daredevil V 3.00 5.00
❑ 37 Magick R .30 .50
❑ 38 Magick E .50 .75
❑ 39 Magick V 1.00 2.00
❑ 40 Archangel R .30 .50
❑ 41 Archangel E .50 .75
❑ 42 Archangel V 3.00 5.00
❑ 43 Kraven R .30 .50
❑ 44 Kraven E .50 .75
❑ 45 Kraven V 1.00 2.00
❑ 46 Rhino R .30 .50
❑ 47 Rhino E .50 .75
❑ 48 Rhino V 1.00 2.00
❑ 49 Mole Man R .30 .50
❑ 50 Mole Man E .50 .75
❑ 51 Mole Man V 1.00 2.00
❑ 52 Nebula R .30 .50
❑ 53 Nebula E .50 .75
❑ 54 Nebula V 1.00 2.00
❑ 55 Moonstone R .30 .50
❑ 56 Meteorite E .50 .75
❑ 57 Meteorite V 1.00 2.00
❑ 58 Brood Queen R .30 .50
❑ 59 Brood Queen E .50 .75
❑ 60 Brood Queen V 1.00 2.00
❑ 61 Patch R .30 .50
❑ 62 Patch E .50 .75
❑ 63 Patch V 1.00 2.00
❑ 64 Diablo R .30 .50
❑ 65 Diablo E .50 .75
❑ 66 Diablo V 1.00 2.00
❑ 67 Spider-Man R 1.00 2.00
❑ 68 Spider-Man E 2.00 3.00
❑ 69 Spider-Man V 3.00 6.00
❑ 70 Venom R 1.00 2.00
❑ 71 Venom E 2.00 4.00
❑ 72 Venom V 3.00 6.00
❑ 73 Ulik R .30 .50
❑ 74 Ulik E .50 .75
❑ 75 Ulik V 1.00 2.00
❑ 76 Umar R .30 .50
❑ 77 Umar E .50 .75
❑ 78 Umar V 1.00 2.00
❑ 79 Black Queen R .30 .50
❑ 80 Selene E .50 .75
❑ 81 Selene V 1.00 2.00
❑ 82 Absorbing Man R 1.00 2.00
❑ 83 Absorbing Man E 2.00 3.00
❑ 84 Absorbing Man V 3.00 6.00
❑ 85 Warbird U 8.00 12.00
❑ 86 Captain Marvel U 8.00 12.00
❑ 87 Adam Warlock U 10.00 18.00
❑ 88 Ronan the Accuser U 8.00 15.00
❑ 89 Sersi U 8.00 12.00
❑ 90 Morgan Le Fay U 8.00 12.00
❑ 91 Terrax U 15.00 20.00
❑ 92 Dormammu U 8.00 12.00
❑ 93 Nova U 10.00 15.00
❑ 94 Beta Ray Bill U 10.00 15.00
❑ 95 Hulk U 20.00 30.00
❑ 96 Silver Surfer U 30.00 40.00
❑ 201 Moloid (Val-Or) LE 15.00 25.00
❑ 202 Brood Warrior (Dive Bomber) LE 10.00 15.00
❑ 203 Kree Warrior (Captain Mar-vell) LE 12.00 18.00
❑ 204 SWAT Heavy Arms (Roger Falcone) LE 10.00 15.00
❑ 206 Hepzibah (Hepzibah) LE 10.00 15.00
❑ 207 Marrow (Sarah) LE 10.00 15.00
❑ 208 Corsair (Major Christopher Summers) LE 10.00 18.00
❑ 209 Moon Knight (Marc Spector) LE 12.00 15.00
❑ 210 Calypso (Calypso Ezili) LE 7.00 15.00
❑ 211 Elektra (Elektra Natchios) LE 10.00 15.00
❑ 212 Daredevil (Matt Murdock) LE 15.00 25.00
❑ 214 Archangel (Warren Worthington III) LE 25.00 40.00
❑ 215 Kraven (Sergei Kravinov) LE 10.00 15.00
❑ 216 Rhino (Alex O'Hirn) LE 15.00 25.00
❑ 217 Mole Man (Rupert) LE 20.00 30.00
❑ 218 Nebula (Nebula) LE 10.00 15.00
❑ 219 Meteorite (Dr. Karla Sofen) LE 20.00 30.00
❑ 220 Brood Queen (Professor Xavier) LE 15.00 20.00
❑ 221 Silver Surfer (Chromed) LE 25.00 40.00
❑ 222 Invisible Woman (Dial Only) LE 20.00 30.00
❑ G1 Galactus (Big Figure) 125.00 200.00

2003 Marvel Heroclix Xplosion Miniatures

Complete Set (96) 175.00 225.00
Booster Pack 4.00 6.00

❑ 1 Con Artist R .30 .50
❑ 2 Con Artist E .50 .75
❑ 3 Con Artist V 1.00 2.00
❑ 4 Hand Ninja Katana R .30 .50
❑ 5 Hand Ninja Katana E .50 .75
❑ 6 Hand Ninja Katana V 1.00 2.00
❑ 7 Hand Ninja Nunchuks R .30 .50
❑ 8 Hand Ninja Nunchuks E .50 .75
❑ 9 Hand Ninja Nunchuks V 1.00 2.00
❑ 10 SWAT Officer R .30 .50
❑ 11 SWAT Officer E .50 .75
❑ 12 SWAT Officer V 1.00 2.00
❑ 13 SWAT Specialist R .30 .50
❑ 14 SWAT Specialist E .50 .75
❑ 15 SWAT Specialist V 1.00 2.00
❑ 16 Paramedic R .30 .50
❑ 17 Paramedic E .50 .75
❑ 18 Paramedic V 1.00 2.00
❑ 19 Typhoid Mary R .30 .50
❑ 20 Typhoid Mary E .50 .75
❑ 21 Typhoid Mary V 1.00 2.00
❑ 22 Destiny R .30 .50
❑ 23 Destiny E .50 .75
❑ 24 Destiny V 1.00 2.00
❑ 25 Boom Boom R .30 .50
❑ 26 Boom Boom E .50 .75
❑ 27 Meltdown V 1.00 2.00
❑ 28 Mystique R .30 .50
❑ 29 Mystique E .50 .75
❑ 30 Mystique V 1.00 2.00
❑ 31 Viper R .30 .50
❑ 32 Viper E .50 .75
❑ 33 Viper V 1.00 2.00
❑ 34 Shadowcat R .30 .50
❑ 35 Shadowcat E .50 .75
❑ 36 Shadowcat V 1.00 2.00
❑ 37 Iceman R .30 .50
❑ 38 Iceman E .50 .75
❑ 39 Iceman V 1.00 2.00
❑ 40 Madame Masque R .30 .50
❑ 41 Madame Masque E .50 .75
❑ 42 Madame Masque V 1.00 2.00
❑ 43 Doc Samson R .30 .50
❑ 44 Doc Samson E .50 .75
❑ 45 Doc Samson V 1.00 2.00
❑ 46 Scorpion R .30 .50
❑ 47 Scorpion E .50 .75
❑ 48 Scorpion V 1.00 2.00
❑ 49 Abomination R .30 .50
❑ 50 Abomination E .50 .75
❑ 51 Abomination V 2.00 4.00
❑ 52 Crimson Dynamo R .30 .50
❑ 53 Crimson Dynamo E .50 .75
❑ 54 Crimson Dynamo V 1.00 2.00
❑ 55 Beast R .50 1.00
❑ 56 Beast E 1.00 2.00
❑ 57 Beast V 2.00 3.00
❑ 58 Psylocke R .30 .50
❑ 59 Psylocke E .50 .75
❑ 60 Psylocke V 1.00 2.00
❑ 61 Daredevil R .50 1.00
❑ 62 Daredevil E 2.00 3.00
❑ 63 Daredevil V 3.00 5.00
❑ 64 Taskmaster R .30 .50
❑ 65 Taskmaster E .50 .75
❑ 66 Taskmaster V 1.00 2.00
❑ 67 Silver Samurai R .30 .50
❑ 68 Silver Samurai E .50 .75
❑ 69 Silver Samurai V 1.00 2.00
❑ 70 Gambit R .50 1.00
❑ 71 Gambit E 1.00 2.00
❑ 72 Gambit V 2.00 3.00
❑ 73 Mandarin R .30 .50
❑ 74 Mandarin E .50 .75
❑ 75 Mandarin V 1.00 2.00
❑ 76 Iron Man R 1.00 2.00
❑ 77 Iron Man E 2.00 4.00
❑ 78 Iron Man V 3.00 6.00
❑ 79 Colossus R .30 .50
❑ 80 Colossus E .50 .75
❑ 81 Colossus V 1.00 2.00
❑ 82 Storm R .50 1.00
❑ 83 Storm E 1.00 2.00
❑ 84 Storm V 2.00 3.00
❑ 85 Shadowcat U 10.00 15.00
❑ 86 Elektra U 15.00 20.00
❑ 87 Deathbird U 10.00 15.00
❑ 88 Apocalypse U 15.00 25.00
❑ 89 Green Goblin U 20.00 30.00
❑ 90 The Leader U 12.00 18.00
❑ 91 Sauron U 12.00 18.00
❑ 92 Lady Deathstrike U 15.00 20.00
❑ 93 Spider-Man U 25.00 35.00

☐ 94 Hulk (Savage) U 20.00 30.00
☐ 95 Phoenix U 20.00 25.00
☐ 96 Weapon X U 18.00 25.00
☐ 201 Con Artist (Sarah St. John) LE 10.00 18.00
☐ 202 Hand Ninja (Kirigi) LE 10.00 15.00
☐ 203 Hand Ninja (Elektra) LE 15.00 20.00
☐ 204 SWAT Specialist (Sammy Liebman) LE 12.00 15.00
☐ 205 SWAT Officer (Frank Gunzer) LE 12.00 15.00
☐ 206 Paramedic (Jane Foster) LE 40.00 60.00
☐ 207 Typhoid Mary (Mary Walker) LE 10.00 15.00
☐ 208 Destiny (Irene Adler) LE 40.00 65.00
☐ 209 Boom-Boom (Tabitha Smith) LE 10.00 15.00
☐ 210 Mystique (Raven Darkholme) LE 12.00 18.00
☐ 211 Viper (Madame Hydra) LE 10.00 15.00
☐ 212 Shadowcat (Kitty Pryde) LE 15.00 25.00
☐ 213 Iceman (Bobby Drake) LE 20.00 30.00
☐ 214 Madame Masque (Whitney Frost) LE 12.00 15.00
☐ 215 Doc Samson (Leonard Samson) LE 18.00 25.00
☐ 216 Scorpion (Mac Gargan) LE 15.00 25.00
☐ 217 Abomination (Emil Blonsky) LE 12.00 18.00
☐ 218 Crimson Dynamo (Dimitri Bulkharin) LE 15.00 30.00
☐ 219 Beast (Hank McCoy) LE 20.00 30.00
☐ 220 Psylocke (Betsy Braddock) LE 18.00 25.00

2004 Marvel Heroclix Mutant Mayhem Miniatures

Complete Set (97) 150.00 200.00
Booster Pack 4.00 7.00
☐ 1 U-Men R .30 .50
☐ 2 U-Men E .50 .75
☐ 3 U-Men V 1.00 2.00
☐ 4 Vanisher R .30 .50
☐ 5 Vanisher E .50 .75
☐ 6 Vanisher V 1.00 2.00
☐ 7 Skullbuster R .30 .50
☐ 8 Skullbuster E .50 .75
☐ 9 Skullbuster V 1.00 2.00
☐ 10 Harpoon R .30 .50
☐ 11 Harpoon E .50 .75
☐ 12 Harpoon V 1.00 2.00
☐ 13 Vertigo R .30 .50
☐ 14 Vertigo E .50 .75
☐ 15 Vertigo V 1.00 2.00
☐ 16 Arclight R .30 .50
☐ 17 Arclight E .50 .75
☐ 18 Arclight V 1.00 2.00
☐ 19 Wild Child R .30 .50
☐ 20 Wildheart E .50 .75
☐ 21 Wild Child V 1.00 2.00
☐ 22 Blade R .50 1.00
☐ 23 Blade E 1.00 2.00
☐ 24 Blade V 2.00 4.00
☐ 25 Puck R .30 .50
☐ 26 Puck E .50 .75
☐ 27 Puck V 1.00 2.00
☐ 28 Domino R .30 .50
☐ 29 Domino E .50 .75
☐ 30 Domino V 1.00 2.00
☐ 31 Polaris R .30 .50
☐ 32 Polaris E .50 .75
☐ 33 Polaris V 1.00 2.00
☐ 34 Silver Sable R .30 .50
☐ 35 Silver Sable E .50 .75
☐ 36 Silver Sable V 1.00 2.00
☐ 37 Havok R .30 .50
☐ 38 Havok E .50 .75
☐ 39 Havok V 1.00 2.00
☐ 40 Wonder Man R .30 .50
☐ 41 Wonder Man E .50 .75
☐ 42 Wonder Man V 1.00 2.00
☐ 43 Firestar R .30 .50
☐ 44 Firestar E .50 .75
☐ 45 Firestar V 1.00 2.00
☐ 46 Cloak R .30 .50
☐ 47 Cloak E .50 .75
☐ 48 Cloak V 1.00 2.00
☐ 49 Dagger R .30 .50
☐ 50 Dagger E .50 .75
☐ 51 Dagger V 1.00 2.00
☐ 52 Bishop R .50 1.00
☐ 53 Bishop E 1.00 2.00
☐ 54 Bishop V 2.00 4.00
☐ 55 Blink R .30 .50
☐ 56 Blink E .50 .75
☐ 57 Blink V 1.00 2.00
☐ 58 Spider-Man R 1.00 2.00
☐ 59 Spider-Man E 2.00 3.00
☐ 60 Spider-Man V 4.00 6.00
☐ 61 Man-Thing R .30 .50
☐ 62 Man-Thing E .50 .75
☐ 63 Man-Thing V 1.00 2.00
☐ 64 Snowbird R .30 .50
☐ 65 Snowbird E .50 .75
☐ 66 Snowbird V 3.00 5.00
☐ 67 Northstar R .30 .50
☐ 68 Northstar E .50 .75
☐ 69 Northstar V 1.00 2.00
☐ 70 Sasquatch R .30 .50
☐ 71 Sasquatch E .50 .75
☐ 72 Tanaraq V 1.00 2.00
☐ 73 Cable R .30 .50
☐ 74 Cable E .50 .75
☐ 75 Soldier X V 3.00 5.00
☐ 76 Deadpool R .30 .50
☐ 77 Deadpool E .50 .75
☐ 78 Deadpool V 1.00 3.00
☐ 79 Wolverine R 1.00 2.00
☐ 80 Wolverine E 2.00 3.00
☐ 81 Wolverine V 4.00 7.00
☐ 82 Hulk R 1.00 2.00
☐ 83 Hulk E 2.00 3.00
☐ 84 Hulk V 3.00 6.00
☐ 85 Longshot U 10.00 15.00
☐ 86 Mimic U 10.00 15.00
☐ 87 Fantomex U 10.00 15.00
☐ 88 Donald Pierce U 10.00 15.00
☐ 89 Bastion U 9.00 12.00
☐ 90 M.O.D.O.K. U 10.00 15.00
☐ 91 Gladiator U 12.00 18.00
☐ 92 Black Queen U 9.00 12.00
☐ 93 Shadow King U 10.00 15.00
☐ 94 N'astirh U 10.00 15.00
☐ 95 Count Nefaria U 10.00 18.00
☐ 96 Loki U 10.00 18.00
☐ 97 Giant-Man E 18.00 25.00
☐ 201 Alex Summers U 10.00 15.00
☐ 202 Simon Williams U 10.00 15.00
☐ 203 Angelica Jones U 10.00 15.00
☐ 204 Tyrone Johnson U 10.00 15.00
☐ 205 Tandy Bowen U 10.00 15.00
☐ 206 Bishop of XSE U 10.00 15.00
☐ 207 Clarice Ferguson U 10.00 15.00
☐ 208 Peter Parker U 18.00 25.00
☐ 209 Ted Sallis U 10.00 15.00
☐ 210 Narya U 10.00 15.00
☐ 211 Jean-Paul Beaubier U 10.00 15.00
☐ 212 Walter Langkowski U 10.00 15.00
☐ 213 Nathaniel Summers U 10.00 15.00
☐ 214 Wade Wilson U 10.00 15.00
☐ 215 Logan U 12.00 20.00
☐ 216 Dr. Bruce Banner U 12.00 20.00
☐ 217 Polaris U 10.00 15.00
☐ 218 Hulk U 20.00 25.00
☐ 220 Dark Phoenix R 35.00 60.00
☐ 220 Dark Phoenix E 35.00 65.00
☐ 220 Dark Phoenix V 35.00 65.00
☐ 221 Nova U 20.00 30.00
☐ 222 Hulk U 20.00 25.00

2004 Marvel Heroclix Ultimates Miniatures

Complete Set (96) 200.00 275.00
Booster Pack 5.00 8.00
☐ 1 Morlock R .30 .50
☐ 2 Morlock E .50 .75
☐ 3 Morlock V 1.00 2.00
☐ 4 Hellfire Guard R .30 .50
☐ 5 Hellfire Guard E .50 .75
☐ 6 Hellfire Guard V 1.00 2.00
☐ 7 Scourge R .30 .50
☐ 8 Scourge E .50 .75
☐ 9 Scourge V 1.00 2.00
☐ 10 Sentinel Trooper R .30 .50
☐ 11 Sentinel Trooper E .50 .75
☐ 12 Sentinel Trooper V 1.00 2.00
☐ 13 Lizard R .30 .50
☐ 14 Lizard E .50 .75
☐ 15 Lizard V 1.00 2.00
☐ 16 Princess Python R .30 .50
☐ 17 Princess Python E .50 .75
☐ 18 Princess Python V 1.00 2.00
☐ 19 Calisto R .30 .50
☐ 20 Calisto E .50 .75
☐ 21 Calisto V 1.00 2.00
☐ 22 Sidewinder R .30 .50
☐ 23 Sidewinder E .50 .75
☐ 24 Sidewinder V 1.00 2.00
☐ 25 Black Widow R .30 .50
☐ 26 Black Widow E .50 .75
☐ 27 Black Widow V 1.00 2.00
☐ 28 Storm R .50 1.00
☐ 29 Storm E 1.00 2.00
☐ 30 Storm V 2.00 4.00
☐ 31 Anaconda R .30 .50
☐ 32 Anaconda E .50 .75
☐ 33 Anaconda V 1.00 2.00
☐ 34 Hawkeye R .30 .50
☐ 35 Hawkeye E .50 .75
☐ 36 Hawkeye V 1.00 2.00
☐ 37 Hellcat R .30 .50
☐ 38 Hellcat E .50 .75
☐ 39 Hellcat V 1.00 2.00
☐ 40 Spider-Man R 1.00 2.00
☐ 41 Spider-Man E 2.00 3.00
☐ 42 Spider-Man V 3.00 5.00
☐ 43 Beast R .50 1.00
☐ 44 Beast E 1.00 2.00
☐ 45 Beast V 2.00 4.00
☐ 46 Wolverine R 1.00 2.00
☐ 47 Wolverine E 2.00 4.00
☐ 48 Wolverine V 4.00 8.00
☐ 49 Mysterio R .30 .50
☐ 50 Mysterio E .50 .75
☐ 51 Mysterio V 1.00 2.00
☐ 52 Punisher R .50 1.00
☐ 53 Punisher E 1.00 2.00
☐ 54 Punisher V 2.00 4.00
☐ 55 Electro R .30 .50
☐ 56 Electro E .50 .75
☐ 57 Electro V 1.00 2.00
☐ 58 Ghost Rider R 1.00 2.00
☐ 59 Ghost Rider E 2.00 3.00
☐ 60 Ghost Rider V 3.00 5.00
☐ 61 Cyclops R 1.00 2.00
☐ 62 Cyclops E 2.00 3.00
☐ 63 Cyclops V 3.00 5.00
☐ 64 Captain America R 1.00 2.00
☐ 65 Captain America E 2.00 3.00
☐ 66 Captain America V 4.00 7.00
☐ 67 Sabretooth R 1.00 2.00
☐ 68 Sabretooth E 2.00 3.00
☐ 69 Sabretooth V 3.00 5.00
☐ 70 Doctor Octopus R 1.00 2.00
☐ 71 Doctor Octopus E 2.00 3.00
☐ 72 Doctor Octopus V 4.00 6.00
☐ 73 Colossus R 1.00 2.00
☐ 74 Colossus E 2.00 3.00
☐ 75 Colossus V 3.00 5.00
☐ 76 Marvel Girl R .30 .50
☐ 77 Marvel Girl E .50 .75
☐ 78 Marvel Girl V 1.00 2.00
☐ 79 Wrecker R .30 .50
☐ 80 Wrecker E .50 .75
☐ 81 Wrecker V 1.00 2.00
☐ 82 Captain Britain R .30 .50
☐ 83 Captain Britain E .50 .75
☐ 84 Captain Britain V 3.00 5.00
☐ 85 Xorn U 15.00 20.00
☐ 86 Baron Zemo U 10.00 15.00
☐ 87 Carnage U 20.00 28.00
☐ 88 Vindicator U 10.00 15.00
☐ 89 Iron Man U 20.00 30.00
☐ 90 Mr. Sinister U 12.00 20.00
☐ 91 Crimson Cowl U 10.00 15.00
☐ 92 Magneto U 15.00 22.00
☐ 93 Phoenix U 15.00 25.00
☐ 94 Goblin Queen U 10.00 18.00
☐ 95 Hulk U 20.00 30.00
☐ 96 Thor U 25.00 45.00
☐ 200 Magneto LE 20.00 30.00
☐ 201 Morlock (Jonny Ell) LE 12.00 20.00
☐ 202 Hellfire Guard (Wade Cole) LE 12.00 20.00
☐ 203 Scourge (Justice is Served) LE 10.00 15.00
☐ 204 Sentinel Trooper (Sentinel Captain LE 10.00 15.00
☐ 205 Dr. Curtis Connors LE 10.00 18.00
☐ 206 Princess Python (Zelda Dubois) LE 10.00 15.00
☐ 207 Morlock Leader LE 10.00 18.00
☐ 208 Seth Voelker LE 10.00 18.00
☐ 209 Natasha Romanova LE 10.00 18.00
☐ 210 Ororo Munroe LE 10.00 18.00
☐ 211 Blanche Sitznski LE 10.00 18.00
☐ 212 Clint Barton LE 10.00 18.00
☐ 213 Hellcat (Patsy Walker) LE 10.00 15.00
☐ 214 Peter Parker (Spider-Man) LE 18.00 25.00
☐ 215 Beast (Hank McCoy) LE 12.00 18.00
☐ 216 Wolverine (James Howlett) LE 12.00 20.00
☐ 217 Electro (Quentin Beck) LE 10.00 15.00
☐ 218 Punisher (Frank Castle) LE 10.00 15.00
☐ 219 Electro (Maxwell Dillon) LE 10.00 18.00
☐ 220 Ghost Rider (Danny Ketch) LE 12.00 20.00
☐ 221 Doc Ock (Dr.Otto Octavius) 20.00 25.00

2004 Marvel Heroclix Universe Miniatures

Complete Set (126) 300.00 400.00
Booster Pack 2.50 4.00
☐ 1 Spider-Man E 1.00 2.00
☐ 2 Wolverine E 1.00 2.00
☐ 3 Wasp E .50 .75
☐ 4 Hobgoblin E 1.00 2.00
☐ 5 Sabretooth E 1.00 2.00
☐ 6 Elektra E 1.00 2.00
☐ 7 Con Artist R .30 .50
☐ 8 Con Artist E .50 .75
☐ 9 Con Artist V 1.00 2.00
☐ 10 Hand Ninja Katana R .30 .50
☐ 11 Hand Ninja Katana E .50 .75
☐ 12 Hand Ninja Katana V 1.00 2.00
☐ 13 Hand Ninja Nunchuks R .30 .50
☐ 14 Hand Ninja Nunchuks E .50 .75
☐ 15 Hand Ninja Nunchuks V 1.00 2.00
☐ 16 SWAT Officer R .30 .50
☐ 17 SWAT Officer E .50 .75
☐ 18 SWAT Officer V 1.00 2.00
☐ 19 SWAT Specialist R .30 .50
☐ 20 SWAT Specialist E .50 .75
☐ 21 SWAT Specialist V 1.00 2.00
☐ 22 Paramedic R .30 .50
☐ 23 Paramedic E .50 .75
☐ 24 Paramedic V 1.00 2.00
☐ 25 Typhoid Mary R .30 .50
☐ 26 Typhoid Mary E .50 .75
☐ 27 Typhoid Mary V 1.00 2.00
☐ 28 Destiny R .30 .50
☐ 29 Destiny E .50 .75
☐ 30 Destiny V 1.00 2.00
☐ 31 Boom Boom R .30 .50
☐ 32 Boom Boom E .50 .75
☐ 33 Meltdown V 1.00 2.00
☐ 34 Mystique R .30 .50
☐ 35 Mystique E .50 .75
☐ 36 Mystique V 2.00 4.00
☐ 37 Viper R .30 .50
☐ 38 Viper E .50 .75
☐ 39 Viper V 1.00 2.00
☐ 40 Shadowcat R .30 .50
☐ 41 Shadowcat E .50 .75
☐ 42 Shadowcat V 1.00 2.00
☐ 43 Daredevil R .50 1.00
☐ 44 Daredevil E 1.00 2.00
☐ 45 Daredevil V 2.00 4.00
☐ 46 Taskmaster R .30 .50
☐ 47 Taskmaster E .50 .75
☐ 48 Taskmaster V 1.00 2.00
☐ 49 Silver Samurai R .30 .50
☐ 50 Silver Samurai E .50 .75
☐ 51 Silver Samurai V 1.00 2.00
☐ 52 Gambit R 1.00 2.00
☐ 53 Gambit E 2.00 3.00
☐ 54 Gambit V 3.00 5.00
☐ 55 Mandarin R .30 .50
☐ 56 Mandarin E .50 .75
☐ 57 Mandarin V 1.00 2.00
☐ 58 Iron Man R 1.00 2.00
☐ 59 Iron Man E 2.00 4.00
☐ 60 Iron Man V 4.00 7.00
☐ 61 Colossus R 1.00 2.00
☐ 62 Colossus E 2.00 3.00
☐ 63 Colossus V 3.00 5.00
☐ 64 Storm R 1.00 2.00
☐ 65 Storm E 2.00 3.00
☐ 66 Storm V 3.00 5.00
☐ 67 Kingpin R .30 .50
☐ 68 Kingpin E .50 .75
☐ 69 Kingpin V 1.00 2.00
☐ 70 Vulture R .30 .50
☐ 71 Vulture E .50 .75
☐ 72 Vulture V 2.00 4.00
☐ 73 Jean Grey R .50 1.00
☐ 74 Jean Grey E 1.00 2.00
☐ 75 Jean Grey V 2.00 4.00
☐ 76 Hobgoblin R .30 .50
☐ 77 Hobgoblin E .50 .75
☐ 78 Hobgoblin V 1.00 2.00
☐ 79 Sabretooth R .50 1.00
☐ 80 Sabretooth E 1.00 2.00
☐ 81 Sabretooth V 2.00 4.00
☐ 82 Hulk R .50 1.00
☐ 83 Hulk E 1.00 2.00
☐ 84 Hulk V 2.00 4.00
☐ 85 Puppet Master R .30 .50
☐ 86 Puppet Master E .50 .75
☐ 87 Puppet Master V 1.00 2.00
☐ 88 Annihilus R .30 .50
☐ 89 Annihilus E .50 .75
☐ 90 Annihilus V 1.00 2.00
☐ 91 Captain America R 1.00 2.00
☐ 92 Captain America E 2.00 3.00
☐ 93 Captain America V 3.00 5.00
☐ 94 Spider-Man R 1.00 2.00
☐ 95 Spider-Man E 2.00 3.00
☐ 96 Spider-Man V 3.00 6.00
☐ 97 Wolverine R 1.00 2.00
☐ 98 Wolverine E 2.00 4.00
☐ 99 Wolverine V 4.00 7.00
☐ 100 Professor Xavier R .50 1.00
☐ 101 Professor Xavier E 1.00 2.00
☐ 102 Professor Xavier V 2.00 4.00
☐ 103 Cyclops R 1.00 2.00
☐ 104 Cyclops E 2.00 3.00
☐ 105 Cyclops V 3.00 5.00
☐ 106 Black Panther R .30 .50
☐ 107 Black Panther E .50 .75
☐ 108 Black Panther V 1.00 2.00
☐ 109 Pyro R .30 .50
☐ 110 Pyro E .50 .75
☐ 111 Pyro V 1.00 2.00
☐ 112 Bullseye R .30 .50
☐ 113 Bullseye E .50 .75
☐ 114 Bullseye V 1.00 2.00
☐ 115 Vision U 8.00 12.00
☐ 116 Quasar U 8.00 10.00
☐ 117 Thanos U 12.00 20.00
☐ 118 Nightmare U 10.00 12.00
☐ 119 Wasp U 10.00 12.00
☐ 120 Elektra U 8.00 10.00
☐ 121 Professor Xavier U 8.00 12.00
☐ 122 Juggernaut U 8.00 10.00
☐ 123 Cyclops U 8.00 10.00
☐ 124 Captain America U 10.00 12.00
☐ 125 Wolverine U 15.00 18.00
☐ 126 Spider-Man U 15.00 20.00

2005 Marvel Heroclix Armor Wars Miniatures

Complete Set (114)
☐ 1 Firebrand R .20 .50
☐ 2 Firebrand E .40 1.00
☐ 3 Firebrand V .75 2.00
☐ 4 Paladin R .20 .50
☐ 5 Paladin E .40 1.00
☐ 6 Paladin V 1.00
☐ 7 Lorelei R .20 .50
☐ 8 Lorelei E .40 1.00
☐ 9 Lorelei V 1.00
☐ 10 Diamond Lil R .20 .50
☐ 11 Diamond Lil E .40 1.00
☐ 12 Diamond Lil V .75 2.00
☐ 13 Echo R .20 .50
☐ 14 Echo E .40 1.00
☐ 15 Echo V 1.00
☐ 16 Killer Shrike R .20 .50
☐ 17 Killer Shrike E .40 1.00
☐ 18 Killer Shrike V .75 2.00
☐ 19 Thunderbird R .20 .50
☐ 20 Thunderbird E .40 1.00
☐ 21 Warpath V .75 2.00
☐ 22 Banshee R .20 .50
☐ 23 Banshee E .40 1.00
☐ 24 Banshee V .75 2.00
☐ 25 Spymaster R .20 .50
☐ 26 Spymaster E .40 1.00
☐ 27 Spymaster V .75 2.00
☐ 28 Ghost R .20 .50
☐ 29 Ghost E .40 1.00
☐ 30 Ghost V .75 2.00
☐ 31 Magma R .20 .50
☐ 32 Magma E .40 1.00
☐ 33 Magma V .75 2.00
☐ 34 Marrina R .20 .50
☐ 35 Marrina E .40 1.00
☐ 36 Marrina V .75 2.00
☐ 37 Thunderball R .20 .50
☐ 38 Thunderball E .40 1.00
☐ 39 Thunderball V .75 2.00
☐ 40 Aurora R .20 .50
☐ 41 Aurora E .40 1.00
☐ 42 Aurora V .75 2.00
☐ 43 Cannonball R .20 .50
☐ 44 Cannonball E .40 1.00
☐ 45 Cannonball V .75 2.00
☐ 46 Wendigo R .20 .50
☐ 47 Wendigo E .40 1.00
☐ 48 Wendigo V .75 2.00
☐ 49 Shaman R .20 .50
☐ 50 Shaman E .40 1.00
☐ 51 Shaman V .75 2.00
☐ 52 Quicksilver R .20 .50
☐ 53 Quicksilver E .40 1.00
☐ 54 Quicksilver V .75 2.00
☐ 55 Psylocke R .20 .50
☐ 56 Psylocke E .40 1.00
☐ 57 Psylocke V .75 2.00
☐ 58 Sunrise R .20 .50
☐ 59 Sunrise E .40 1.00
☐ 60 Sunrise V .75 2.00
☐ 61 Dazzler R .20 .50
☐ 62 Dazzler E .40 1.00
☐ 63 Dazzler V .75 2.00
☐ 64 Executioner R .20 .50
☐ 65 Executioner E .40 1.00
☐ 66 Executioner V .75 2.00
☐ 67 War Machine R .20 .50
☐ 68 War Machine E .40 1.00
☐ 69 War Machine V .75 2.00
☐ 70 Crimson Dynamo R .20 .50
☐ 71 Crimson Dynamo E .40 1.00
☐ 72 Crimson Dynamo V .75 2.00
☐ 73 Titanium Man R .20 .50
☐ 74 Titanium Man E .40 1.00
☐ 75 Titanium Man V .75 2.00
☐ 76 Iron Man R .20 .50
☐ 77 Iron Man E .40 1.00
☐ 78 Iron Man V .75 2.00
☐ 79 Captain America R .20 .50
☐ 80 Captain America E .40 1.00
☐ 81 Captain America V 2.00 5.00
☐ 82 Ultron-5 R .20 .50
☐ 83 Ultron-11 E .40 1.00
☐ 84 Ultron-16 V .75 2.00
☐ 85 Crystal U 3.00 8.00
☐ 86 Shathra U 3.00 8.00
☐ 87 Jocasta U 3.00 8.00
☐ 88 Iron Man U 3.00 8.00
☐ 89 Black King U 3.00 8.00

Card	Low	High
❑ 90 Iron Monger U	3.00	8.00
❑ 91 Sentry U	3.00	8.00
❑ 92 Spider-Woman U	3.00	8.00
❑ 93 Spider-Man U	3.00	8.00
❑ 94 Mystique U	3.00	8.00
❑ 95 Wolverine U	3.00	8.00
❑ 96 Magneto U	3.00	8.00
❑ 201 Eliot Franklin LE	6.00	15.00
❑ 202 Jeanne-Marie Beaubier LE	6.00	15.00
❑ 203 Sam Guthrie LE	6.00	15.00
❑ 204 Georges Baptiste LE	6.00	15.00
❑ 205 Talisman LE	6.00	15.00
❑ 206 Sir Pietro Maximoff LE	6.00	15.00
❑ 207 Captain Britain LE	6.00	15.00
❑ 208 Shiro Yoshida LE	6.00	15.00
❑ 209 Ali Blair LE	6.00	15.00
❑ 210 Skurge LE	6.00	15.00
❑ 211 James Rhodes LE	6.00	15.00
❑ 212 Gennady Gavrilov LE	6.00	15.00
❑ 213 The Gremlin LE	6.00	15.00
❑ 214 Tony Stark LE	6.00	15.00
❑ 215 John Walker LE	6.00	15.00
❑ 216 Ultron-13 LE	6.00	15.00
❑ 217 Jessica Drew LE	6.00	15.00
❑ 218 Anthony Stark LE	6.00	15.00

2005 Marvel Heroclix Fantastic Forces Miniatures

Card	Low	High
Complete Set (96)	250.00	300.00
Booster Pack	5.00	7.00
Battlefield Cards (BF1-BF6)	.50	1.00
Feats Cards (F1-F8)	1.00	2.00
Token Cards (B1-B6)	.50	1.00
❑ 1 Lockjaw R	.30	.50
❑ 2 Lockjaw E	.50	.75
❑ 3 Lockjaw V	1.00	2.00
❑ 4 Black Knight R	.30	.50
❑ 5 Black Knight E	.50	.75
❑ 6 Black Knight V	1.00	2.00
❑ 7 Mirage R	.30	.50
❑ 8 Moonstar E	.50	.75
❑ 9 Moonstar V	1.00	2.00
❑ 10 Hawkeye R	.30	.50
❑ 11 Hawkeye E	.50	.75
❑ 12 Hawkeye V	1.00	2.00
❑ 13 Awesome Android R	.30	.50
❑ 14 Awesome Android E	.50	.75
❑ 15 Awesome Andy V	1.00	2.00
❑ 16 Goliath R	.30	.50
❑ 17 Atlas E	.50	.75
❑ 18 Atlas V	1.00	2.00
❑ 19 Yellowjacket R	.30	.50
❑ 20 Yellowjacket E	.50	.75
❑ 21 Yellowjacket V	2.00	3.00
❑ 22 Ghost Rider R	.50	1.00
❑ 23 Ghost Rider E	1.00	2.00
❑ 24 Ghost Rider V	2.00	3.00
❑ 25 Asp R	.30	.50
❑ 26 Asp E	.50	.75
❑ 27 Asp V	1.00	2.00
❑ 28 Shocker R	.30	.50
❑ 29 Shocker E	.50	.75
❑ 30 Shocker V	2.00	4.00
❑ 31 Tigra R	.30	.50
❑ 32 Tigra E	.50	.75
❑ 33 Tigra V	2.00	4.00
❑ 34 Jolt R	.30	.50
❑ 35 Jolt E	.50	.75
❑ 36 Jolt V	1.00	2.00
❑ 37 Karma R	.30	.50
❑ 38 Karma E	.50	.75
❑ 39 Karma V	1.00	2.00
❑ 40 Vulture R	.30	.50
❑ 41 Vulture E	.50	.75
❑ 42 Vulture V	3.00	5.00
❑ 43 Songbird R	.30	.50
❑ 44 Songbird E	.50	.75
❑ 45 Songbird V	1.00	2.00
❑ 46 Iron Fist R	.30	.50
❑ 47 Iron Fist E	1.00	2.00
❑ 48 Iron Fist V	3.00	5.00
❑ 49 Power Man R	.30	.50
❑ 50 Power Man E	1.00	2.00
❑ 51 Cage V	2.00	3.00
❑ 52 Scarlet Witch R	.30	.50
❑ 53 Scarlet Witch E	1.00	2.00
❑ 54 Scarlet Witch V	2.00	4.00
❑ 55 Rogue R	.30	.50
❑ 56 Rogue E	.50	.75
❑ 57 Rogue V	1.00	2.00
❑ 58 Dr. Strange R	.50	1.00
❑ 59 Dr. Strange E	1.00	2.00
❑ 60 Dr. Strange V	3.00	5.00
❑ 61 Green Goblin R	1.00	2.00
❑ 62 Green Goblin E	2.00	3.00
❑ 63 Green Goblin V	3.00	5.00
❑ 64 Juggernaut R	1.00	2.00
❑ 65 Juggernaut E	2.00	3.00
❑ 66 Juggernaut V	4.00	6.00
❑ 67 Sub-Mariner R	2.00	3.00
❑ 68 Sub-Mariner E	3.00	4.00
❑ 69 Sub-Mariner V	4.00	6.00
❑ 70 Human Torch R	1.00	2.00
❑ 71 Human Torch E	2.00	3.00
❑ 72 Human Torch V	3.00	5.00
❑ 73 Invisible Woman R	1.00	2.00
❑ 74 Invisible Woman E	2.00	3.00
❑ 75 Invisible Woman V	4.00	7.00
❑ 76 The Thing R	1.00	2.00
❑ 77 The Thing E	2.00	3.00
❑ 78 The Thing V	3.00	6.00
❑ 79 Mr. Fantastic R	1.00	2.00
❑ 80 Mr. Fantastic E	2.00	3.00
❑ 81 Mr. Fantastic V	3.00	6.00
❑ 82 Nightcrawler R	1.00	2.00
❑ 83 Nightcrawler E	2.00	3.00
❑ 84 Nightcrawler V	3.00	6.00
❑ 85 Volcana U	10.00	15.00
❑ 86 Mad Thinker U	12.00	18.00
❑ 87 Arnim Zola U	10.00	15.00
❑ 88 Baron Mordo U	10.00	15.00
❑ 89 Baron Blood U	10.00	15.00
❑ 90 Nimrod U	20.00	40.00
❑ 91 Orphan U	10.00	15.00
❑ 92 Wolverine U	12.00	20.00
❑ 93 Warlock U	12.00	20.00
❑ 94 Professor Xavier U	18.00	25.00
❑ 95 Dr. Doom U	10.00	18.00
❑ 96 Spider-Man U	20.00	30.00
❑ 201 Norman Osborn U	15.00	25.00
❑ 202 Cain Marko U	20.00	25.00
❑ 203 Namor U	15.00	25.00
❑ 204 Johnny Storm U	15.00	20.00

2006 Marvel Heroclix 2099 Miniatures

Card	Low	High
❑ 1 Hulk U	8.00	20.00
❑ 2 Ravage E	4.00	10.00
❑ 3 Punisher V	4.00	10.00
❑ 4 Ghost Rider E	6.00	15.00
❑ 5 Meanstreak E	4.00	10.00
❑ 6 Junkpile V	4.00	10.00
❑ 7 Doom U	6.00	15.00

2006 Marvel Heroclix Danger Room Miniatures

Card	Low	High
❑ 1 Cyclops V	1.00	2.50
❑ 2 Colossus V	1.00	2.50
❑ 3 Angel V	3.00	8.00
❑ 4 Jean Grey V	1.00	2.50
❑ 5 Beast V	1.00	2.50
❑ 6 Storm V	1.00	2.50

2006 Marvel Heroclix Sinister Miniatures

Card	Low	High
❑ 1 HYDRA Footsoldier R	.20	.50
❑ 2 HYDRA Technician E	.40	1.00
❑ 3 HYDRA Officer V	2.00	5.00
❑ 4 SHIELD Trooper R	.20	.50
❑ 5 SHIELD Sniper E	.40	1.00
❑ 6 SHIELD Agent V	2.00	5.00
❑ 7 Swordsman R	.20	.50
❑ 8 Swordsman E	.40	1.00
❑ 9 Swordsman V	2.00	5.00
❑ 10 Hydro Man R	.20	.50
❑ 11 Hydro Man E	.40	1.00
❑ 12 Hydro Man V	2.00	5.00
❑ 13 Paste Pot Pete R	.20	.50
❑ 14 Trapster E	.40	1.00
❑ 15 Trapster V	2.00	5.00
❑ 16 Mockingbird R	.20	.50
❑ 17 Mockingbird E	.40	1.00
❑ 18 Mockingbird V	2.00	5.00
❑ 19 Jewel R	.20	.50
❑ 20 Jessica Jones E	.40	1.00
❑ 21 Jessica Jones V	2.00	5.00
❑ 22 Beetle R	.20	.50
❑ 23 Beetle E	.40	1.00
❑ 24 Beetle V	2.00	5.00
❑ 25 Wingless Wizard R	.20	.50
❑ 26 Wizard E	.40	1.00
❑ 27 Wizard V	2.00	5.00
❑ 28 Electro R	.20	.50
❑ 29 Electro E	.40	1.00
❑ 30 Electro V	2.00	5.00
❑ 31 Fixer R	.20	.50
❑ 32 Techno E	.40	1.00
❑ 33 Fixer V	2.00	5.00
❑ 34 Jack O'Lantern R	.20	.50
❑ 35 Jack O'Lantern E	.40	1.00
❑ 36 Jack O'Lantern V	2.00	5.00
❑ 37 Sprite R	.20	.50
❑ 38 Shadowcat E	.40	1.00
❑ 39 Shadowcat V	2.00	5.00
❑ 40 MACH-1 R	.20	.50
❑ 41 MACH-3 E	.40	1.00
❑ 42 MACH-4 V	2.00	5.00
❑ 43 Nighthawk R	.20	.50
❑ 44 Nighthawk E	.40	1.00
❑ 45 Nighthawk V	2.00	5.00
❑ 46 Valkyrie R	.20	.50
❑ 47 Valkyrie E	.40	1.00
❑ 48 Valkyrie V	2.00	5.00
❑ 49 Multiple Man R	.20	.50
❑ 50 Multiple Man E	.40	1.00
❑ 51 Madrox V	2.00	5.00
❑ 52 Deathlok R	.20	.50
❑ 53 Deathlok E	.40	1.00
❑ 54 Deathlok V	2.00	5.00
❑ 55 Falcon R	.20	.50
❑ 56 Falcon E	.40	1.00
❑ 57 Falcon V	2.00	5.00
❑ 58 Spider-Man R	.20	.50
❑ 59 Spider-Man E	.40	1.00
❑ 60 Spider-Man V	2.00	5.00
❑ 61 Radioactive Man R	.20	.50
❑ 62 Radioactive Man E	.40	1.00
❑ 63 Radioactive Man V	2.00	5.00
❑ 64 Captain Marvel R	.20	.50
❑ 65 Photon E	.40	1.00
❑ 66 Pulsar V	2.00	5.00
❑ 67 Rhino R	.20	.50
❑ 68 Rhino E	.40	1.00
❑ 69 Rhino V	2.00	5.00
❑ 70 Whizzer R	.20	.50
❑ 71 Speed Demon E	.40	1.00
❑ 72 Speed Demon V	2.00	5.00
❑ 73 Daredevil R	.20	.50
❑ 74 Daredevil E	.40	1.00
❑ 75 Daredevil V	2.00	5.00
❑ 76 Meggan R	.20	.50
❑ 77 Meggan E	.40	1.00
❑ 78 Meggan V	2.00	5.00
❑ 79 Bullseye R	.20	.50
❑ 80 Bullseye E	.40	1.00
❑ 81 Bullseye V	4.00	10.00
❑ 82 Kraven R	.20	.50
❑ 83 Kraven E	.40	1.00
❑ 84 Kraven V	2.00	5.00
❑ 85 Forge U	4.00	10.00
❑ 86 Purple Man U	4.00	10.00
❑ 87 Maximus U	4.00	10.00
❑ 88 Baron Strucker U	4.00	10.00
❑ 89 Charcoal U	4.00	10.00
❑ 90 Wolverine U	15.00	30.00
❑ 91 Nick Fury U	4.00	10.00
❑ 92 Arkon U	4.00	10.00
❑ 93 Ka-Zar U	4.00	10.00
❑ 94 Scarlet Spider U	4.00	10.00
❑ 95 Stilt Man U	6.00	15.00
❑ 96 Black Bolt U	15.00	30.00
❑ 201 Soulsword Wielder U	4.00	10.00
❑ 202 Abner Jenkins U	4.00	10.00
❑ 203 Kyle Richmond U	4.00	10.00
❑ 204 Brunnhilde U	4.00	10.00
❑ 205 James Madrox U	4.00	10.00
❑ 206 Michael Roth U	4.00	10.00
❑ 207 Sam Wilson U	4.00	10.00
❑ 208 Symbiote U	4.00	10.00
❑ 209 Dr. Chen Lu U	4.00	10.00
❑ 210 Monica Rambeau U	4.00	10.00
❑ 211 Aleksei Mikhailovich U	4.00	10.00
❑ 212 James Sanders U	4.00	10.00
❑ 213 Kingpin of Hell's Kitchen U	4.00	10.00
❑ 214 Goblin Princess U	4.00	10.00
❑ 215 Lester U	4.00	10.00
❑ 216 Kraven the Spider U	4.00	10.00
❑ 217 Spider-Man U	4.00	10.00
❑ 218 Venom U	15.00	30.00
❑ 219 Snap Wilson U	4.00	10.00

2006 Marvel Heroclix Supernova Miniatures

Card	Low	High
❑ 1 Kree Warrior R	.20	.50
❑ 2 Kree Captain E	.40	1.00
❑ 3 Kree Colonel V	2.00	5.00
❑ 4 Skrull Infiltrator R	.20	.50
❑ 5 Skrull Warrior E	.40	1.00
❑ 6 Skrull General V	2.00	5.00
❑ 7 Shi'ar Warrior R	.20	.50
❑ 8 Shi'ar Borderer E	.40	1.00
❑ 9 Shi'ar Admiral V	2.00	5.00
❑ 10 Badoon Warrior R	.20	.50
❑ 11 Badoon Guard E	.40	1.00
❑ 12 Badoon Commander V	2.00	5.00
❑ 13 Night Thrasher R	.20	.50
❑ 14 Night Thrasher E	.40	1.00
❑ 15 Night Thrasher V	2.00	5.00
❑ 16 Jubilee R	.20	.50
❑ 17 Jubilee E	.40	1.00
❑ 18 Jubilee V	2.00	5.00
❑ 19 Super-Apes: Igor R	.20	.50
❑ 20 Super-Apes: Mikhlo E	.40	1.00
❑ 21 Super-Apes: Peotor V	2.00	5.00
❑ 22 Raza R	.20	.50
❑ 23 Raza E	.40	1.00
❑ 24 Raza V	2.00	5.00
❑ 25 Sunspot R	.20	.50
❑ 26 Sunspot E	.40	1.00
❑ 27 Sunspot V	2.00	5.00
❑ 28 Marvel Boy R	.20	.50
❑ 29 Justice E	.40	1.00
❑ 30 Justice V	2.00	5.00
❑ 31 Tessa R	.20	.50
❑ 32 Sage E	.40	1.00
❑ 33 Sage V	2.00	5.00
❑ 34 Nocturne R	.20	.50
❑ 35 Nocturne E	.40	1.00
❑ 36 Nocturne V	2.00	5.00
❑ 37 Nova R	.20	.50
❑ 38 Kid Nova E	.40	1.00
❑ 39 Nova V	2.00	5.00
❑ 40 Bulldozer R	.20	.50
❑ 41 Bulldozer E	.40	1.00
❑ 42 Bulldozer V	2.00	5.00
❑ 43 Aleta R	.20	.50
❑ 44 Aleta E	.40	1.00
❑ 45 Starhawk V	2.00	5.00
❑ 46 Kang R	.20	.50
❑ 47 Kang E	.40	1.00
❑ 48 Kang the Conqueror V	2.00	5.00
❑ 49 Ant-Man R	.20	.50
❑ 50 Ant-Man E	.40	1.00
❑ 51 Ant-Man V	2.00	5.00
❑ 52 Weapon Alpha R	.20	.50
❑ 53 Guardian E	.40	1.00
❑ 54 Vindicator V	2.00	5.00
❑ 55 She-Hulk R	.20	.50
❑ 56 She-Hulk E	.40	1.00
❑ 57 She-Hulk V	2.00	5.00
❑ 58 Vance Astro R	.20	.50
❑ 59 Vance Astro E	.40	1.00
❑ 60 Major Victory V	2.00	5.00
❑ 61 Vision R	.20	.50
❑ 62 Vision E	.40	1.00
❑ 63 Vision V	2.00	5.00
❑ 64 Drax the Destroyer R	.20	.50
❑ 65 Drax the Destroyer E	.40	1.00
❑ 66 Drax V	2.00	5.00
❑ 67 Mantis R	.20	.50
❑ 68 Mantis E	.40	1.00
❑ 69 Mantis V	2.00	5.00
❑ 70 Doctor Spectrum R	.20	.50
❑ 71 Doctor Spectrum E	.40	1.00
❑ 72 Doctor Spectrum V	2.00	5.00
❑ 73 Hyperion R	.20	.50
❑ 74 Hyperion E	.40	1.00
❑ 75 Hyperion V	2.00	5.00
❑ 76 Silver Surfer R	.20	.50
❑ 77 Silver Surfer E	.40	1.00
❑ 78 Silver Surfer V	6.00	15.00
❑ 79 Legacy R	.20	.50
❑ 80 Captain Marvel E	.40	1.00
❑ 81 Photon V	4.00	10.00
❑ 82 Thor R	.20	.50
❑ 83 Thor E	.40	1.00
❑ 84 Thor V	2.00	5.00
❑ 85 Majestrix Lilandra U	4.00	10.00
❑ 86 Red Ghost U	4.00	10.00
❑ 87 Machine Man U	4.00	10.00
❑ 88 Karnak U	4.00	10.00
❑ 89 Power Princess U	4.00	10.00
❑ 90 Jack of Hearts U	4.00	10.00
❑ 91 Super Skrull U	4.00	10.00
❑ 92 Korvac U	4.00	10.00
❑ 93 Captain Mar-Vell U	4.00	10.00
❑ 94 Binary U	4.00	10.00
❑ 95 Graviton U	4.00	10.00
❑ 96 Thanos U	6.00	15.00
❑ 201 Super-Nova U	4.00	10.00
❑ 202 Henry Camp U	4.00	10.00
❑ 203 One-Who-Knows U	4.00	10.00
❑ 204 Nathaniel Richards U	4.00	10.00
❑ 205 Dr. Hank Pym U	4.00	10.00
❑ 206 James MacDonald Hudson U	4.00	10.00
❑ 207 Jennifer Walters, Esq. U	4.00	10.00
❑ 208 Vance Astrovik U	4.00	10.00
❑ 209 Victor Shade U	4.00	10.00
❑ 210 Arthur Douglas U	4.00	10.00
❑ 211 Celestial Madonna U	4.00	10.00
❑ 212 Joe Ledger U	4.00	10.00
❑ 213 King Hyperion U	4.00	10.00
❑ 214 Norrin Radd U	6.00	15.00
❑ 215 Genis-Vell U	4.00	10.00
❑ 216 Dr. Donald Blake U	4.00	10.00
❑ 217 Iron Man U	4.00	10.00
❑ 218 Doom U	6.00	15.00
❑ 219 Skymax U	4.00	10.00
❑ 220 Spider-Man U	4.00	10.00
❑ 221 Colonel America U	4.00	10.00
❑ 222 Wolverine U	4.00	10.00
❑ 223 Hulk U	4.00	10.00
❑ 224 The Mighty Thor U	4.00	10.00

2007 Marvel Heroclix Avengers Miniatures

Card	Low	High
❑ 1 Captain America R	.20	.50
❑ 2 Iron Man U	8.00	20.00
❑ 3 Captain Britain R	.20	.50
❑ 4 Gargoyle V	4.00	10.00
❑ 5 Guardsman V	4.00	10.00
❑ 6 Moon Knight V	4.00	10.00
❑ 7 Crossbones E	.40	1.00
❑ 8 Wonder Man V	4.00	10.00
❑ 9 Hulkling R	.20	.50
❑ 10 Patriot R	.20	.50
❑ 11 Stature R	.20	.50
❑ 12 Shang-Chi E	.40	1.00
❑ 13 Piledriver E	.40	1.00
❑ 14 Stingray R	.20	.50
❑ 15 US Agent V	4.00	10.00
❑ 16 Luke Cage V	4.00	10.00
❑ 17 Living Laser V	4.00	10.00
❑ 18 Blazing Skull V	4.00	10.00
❑ 19 Darkhawk R	.20	.50
❑ 20 Dragon Man E	.40	1.00
❑ 21 Toro R	.20	.50
❑ 22 Iron Widow E	.40	1.00
❑ 23 Lionheart R	.20	.50
❑ 24 Black Panther R	.20	.50
❑ 25 Quicksilver R	.20	.50
❑ 26 Scarlet Witch R	.20	.50
❑ 27 Vision R	.20	.50
❑ 28 Wasp E	.40	1.00
❑ 29 Taskmaster U	8.00	20.00
❑ 30 Iron Lad R	.20	.50
❑ 31 Ronin R	.20	.50
❑ 32 Red Skull U	8.00	20.00
❑ 33 Abomination R	.20	.50
❑ 34 Baron Zemo V	4.00	10.00
❑ 35 Bucky R	.20	.50
❑ 36 Falcon E	.40	1.00
❑ 37 Thin Man V	4.00	10.00
❑ 38 Giant Man R	.20	.50
❑ 39 Spitfire V	4.00	10.00
❑ 40 Namor U	8.00	20.00
❑ 41 Union Jack E	.40	1.00
❑ 42 Starfox E	.40	1.00
❑ 43 Molecule Man U	8.00	20.00
❑ 44 Grim Reaper V	4.00	10.00
❑ 45 Thunderstrike R	.20	.50
❑ 46 Namorita E	.40	1.00
❑ 47 Wiccan R	.20	.50
❑ 48 Yondu V	4.00	10.00
❑ 49 Two-Gun Kid V	4.00	10.00
❑ 50 Winter Soldier V	4.00	10.00
❑ 51 Spider-Man V	8.00	20.00
❑ 52 Citizen V V	4.00	10.00
❑ 53 The Colonel R	.20	.50
❑ 54 Ares U	8.00	20.00
❑ 55 Hulk U	8.00	20.00
❑ 56 Hawkeye U	8.00	20.00
❑ 57 Scarlet Witch R	.20	.50
❑ 58 Quicksilver R	.20	.50
❑ 59 Wasp R	.20	.50
❑ 60 Cap and Bucky U	8.00	20.00
❑ 61 Mandarin U	8.00	20.00
❑ 100 Silver Surfer U	8.00	20.00
❑ 101 Terrax the Tamer U	8.00	20.00
❑ 102 Firelord U	8.00	20.00
❑ 103 Stardust U	8.00	20.00

2007 Marvel Heroclix Mutations and Monsters Miniatures

Card	Low	High
❑ 1 Marvel Girl C	.20	.50
❑ 2 Cyclops C	.20	.50
❑ 3 Beast C	.20	.50
❑ 4 Iceman C	.20	.50
❑ 5 Strong Guy C	.20	.50
❑ 6 Pete Wisdom C	.20	.50
❑ 7 Brood C	.20	.50
❑ 8 Box C	.20	.50
❑ 9 Cuckoo C	.20	.50
❑ 10 Maverick C	.20	.50
❑ 11 Dazzler C	.20	.50
❑ 12 Colossus C	.20	.50
❑ 13 Agent Brand C	.20	.50
❑ 14 Bishop C	.20	.50
❑ 15 The Hood C	.20	.50
❑ 16 Miek C	.20	.50
❑ 17 Hulk U	.40	1.00
❑ 18 Korg U	.40	1.00
❑ 19 Absorbing Man U	.40	1.00
❑ 20 Morph U	.40	1.00
❑ 21 Mimic U	.40	1.00
❑ 22 Gorgon U	.40	1.00
❑ 23 Cyclops U	.40	1.00
❑ 24 Shatterstar U	.40	1.00
❑ 25 Zzzax U	.40	1.00
❑ 26 Chamber U	.40	1.00
❑ 27 Beast U	.40	1.00
❑ 28 Giant-Man U	.40	1.00
❑ 29 Iceman U	.40	1.00
❑ 30 X-23 U	.40	1.00
❑ 31 Professor X U	.40	1.00
❑ 32 Gambit U	.40	1.00
❑ 33 Green Scar R	6.00	15.00
❑ 34 Archangel R	4.00	10.00

❑ 35 Ahab R	4.00	10.00
❑ 36 Fabian Cortez R	4.00	10.00
❑ 37 Jean Grey R	4.00	10.00
❑ 38 Omegaed R	4.00	10.00
❑ 39 Danger R	4.00	10.00
❑ 40 Devil Dinosaur & Moon Boy R	4.00	10.00
❑ 41 Spider-Man R	4.00	10.00
❑ 42 Unus theUntouchable R	4.00	10.00
❑ 43 Black Tom Cassidy R	4.00	10.00
❑ 44 The Leader R	4.00	10.00
❑ 45 High Evolutionary R	4.00	10.00
❑ 46 Arcade R	4.00	10.00
❑ 47 Super-Adaptoid R	4.00	10.00
❑ 48 Wrecker R	4.00	10.00
❑ 49 Cassandra Nova SR	6.00	15.00
❑ 50 Hulkbuster SR	15.00	30.00
❑ 51 Silver Savage SR	6.00	15.00
❑ 52 Mastermind SR	6.00	15.00
❑ 53 Emma Frost SR	15.00	30.00
❑ 54 Living Monolith SR	6.00	15.00
❑ 55 Iron Man SR	6.00	15.00
❑ 56 Wolverine SR	8.00	20.00
❑ 57 Storm SR	6.00	15.00
❑ 58 Warskrull SR	6.00	15.00
❑ 59 Apocalypse SR	15.00	30.00
❑ 60 Maestro SR	6.00	15.00
❑ 61 Dark Beast LE	8.00	20.00
❑ 62 Rampaging Hulk LE	8.00	20.00
❑ 101 Esme Cuckoo LE	8.00	20.00
❑ 102 Incredible Hulk LE	8.00	20.00
❑ 103 Proteus LE	8.00	20.00
❑ 104 Charles Xavier LE	10.00	25.00

2007 Marvel Heroclix Secret Invasion Miniatures

❑ 1 Spider-Man C	.20	.50
❑ 2 Moloid C	.20	.50
❑ 3 Tombstone C	.20	.50
❑ 4 Iron Fist C	.20	.50
❑ 5 Sharon Carter C	.20	.50
❑ 6 Yellowjacket C	.20	.50
❑ 7 Atlantean Warrior C	.20	.50
❑ 8 Ms. Marvel C	.20	.50
❑ 9 Gravity C	.20	.50
❑ 10 Grey Gargoyle C	.20	.50
❑ 11 Arachne C	.20	.50
❑ 12 Gee C	.20	.50
❑ 13 Lightspeed C	.20	.50
❑ 14 Massmaster C	.20	.50
❑ 15 Energizer C	.20	.50
❑ 16 Hercules C	.20	.50
❑ 17 Human Torch U	.40	1.00
❑ 18 Clea U	.40	1.00
❑ 19 Captain America U	.40	1.00
❑ 20 Immortus U	.40	1.00
❑ 21 Iron Man U	.40	1.00
❑ 22 Goliath U	.40	1.00
❑ 23 Hawkeye U	.40	1.00
❑ 24 Spider-Slayer U	.40	1.00
❑ 25 She-Thing U	.40	1.00
❑ 26 Kristoff U	.40	1.00
❑ 27 Tarantula U	.40	1.00
❑ 28 Attuma U	.40	1.00
❑ 29 Morbius U	.40	1.00
❑ 30 Punisher U	.40	1.00
❑ 31 Mole Man U	.40	1.00
❑ 32 Dum Dum Dugan U	.40	1.00
❑ 33 Dr. Strange R	2.00	5.00
❑ 34 Dr. Octopus R	2.00	5.00
❑ 35 Howard the Duck R	2.00	5.00
❑ 36 Malice R	2.00	5.00
❑ 37 Triton R	2.00	5.00
❑ 38 Speedball R	2.00	5.00
❑ 39 Cloak and Dagger R	2.00	5.00
❑ 40 Doom R	2.00	5.00
❑ 41 Spider-Girl R	2.00	5.00
❑ 42 Captain Mar-Vell R	2.00	5.00
❑ 43 Psycho-Man R	2.00	5.00
❑ 44 Super-Skrull: X-Men R	2.00	5.00
❑ 45 Namor R	2.00	5.00
❑ 46 Thor Girl R	2.00	5.00
❑ 47 Adam Warlock R	2.00	5.00
❑ 48 Elektra R	2.00	5.00
❑ 49 Ringmaster SR	8.00	20.00
❑ 50 Magus SR	8.00	20.00
❑ 51 Nick Fury SR	8.00	20.00
❑ 52 Impossible Man SR	8.00	20.00
❑ 53 Skrull Emperor SR	8.00	20.00
❑ 54 Gamora SR	8.00	20.00
❑ 55 Mephisto SR	8.00	20.00
❑ 56 Annihilus SR	8.00	20.00
❑ 57 Jarvis SR	8.00	20.00
❑ 58 Power Man and Iron Fist SR	8.00	20.00
❑ 59 Sentry SR	8.00	20.00
❑ 60 Super-Skrull: Avengers SR	8.00	20.00
❑ 100 Spider-Woman CH	30.00	60.00
❑ 199 Susan Richards CH	25.00	50.00

2009 Marvel Heroclix Hammer of Thor Miniatures

❑ 1 Bug C	.20	.50
❑ 2 Kingpin C	.20	.50
❑ 3 Hand Ninja C	.20	.50
❑ 4 Rock Troll C	.20	.50
❑ 5 Jimmy Woo C	.20	.50
❑ 6 Pip the Troll C	.20	.50
❑ 7 Marvel Boy C	.20	.50
❑ 8 Phalanx Soldier C	.20	.50
❑ 9 Malakith C	.20	.50
❑ 10 M-11 C	.20	.50
❑ 11 Enchantress C	.20	.50
❑ 12 Valkyrie C	.20	.50
❑ 13 Bi-Beast C	.20	.50
❑ 14 Asguardian Warrior C	.20	.50
❑ 15 Fire Demon C	.20	.50
❑ 16 Thor C	.20	.50
❑ 17 Balder U	.40	1.00
❑ 18 Fandril U	.40	1.00
❑ 19 Chase Stein U	.40	1.00
❑ 20 Karnilla U	.40	1.00
❑ 21 Ulik U	.40	1.00
❑ 22 Moonstone U	.40	1.00
❑ 23 Beta Ray Bill U	.40	1.00
❑ 24 Namora U	.40	1.00
❑ 25 Starlord U	.40	1.00
❑ 26 Pluto U	.40	1.00
❑ 27 Moondragon U	.40	1.00
❑ 28 Rocket Raccoon U	.40	1.00
❑ 29 Gorilla Man U	.40	1.00
❑ 30 Owl U	.40	1.00
❑ 31 Ronan the Accuser U	.40	1.00
❑ 32 Daredevil U	.40	1.00
❑ 33 Sif R	4.00	10.00
❑ 34 Hogun R	4.00	10.00
❑ 35 Loki R	15.00	30.00
❑ 36 Heimdall R	4.00	10.00
❑ 37 Songbird R	4.00	10.00
❑ 38 Venom R	4.00	10.00
❑ 39 Destroyer R	4.00	10.00
❑ 40 Captain America R	15.00	30.00
❑ 41 Molly Hayes R	4.00	10.00
❑ 42 Phyl-vell R	4.00	10.00
❑ 43 Penance R	4.00	10.00
❑ 44 Air-Walker R	4.00	10.00
❑ 45 Karolina R	4.00	10.00
❑ 46 Fenris Wolf R	4.00	10.00
❑ 47 Nico Minoru R	4.00	10.00
❑ 48 Spider-Man R	8.00	20.00
❑ 49 Ultron SR	20.00	40.00
❑ 50 Hela SR	4.00	10.00
❑ 51 Odin SR	8.00	20.00
❑ 52 Venus SR	4.00	10.00
❑ 53 Seth SR	4.00	10.00
❑ 54 Loki SR	8.00	20.00
❑ 55 Valkyrie SR	15.00	30.00
❑ 56 Surtur SR	4.00	10.00
❑ 57 Thor and Loki SR	15.00	30.00
❑ 58 Gertrude Yorkes and Old Lace SR	8.00	20.00
❑ 59 Volstagg SR	20.00	40.00
❑ 60 Kurse SR	8.00	20.00
❑ 61 Thor's Mighty Chariot CH	15.00	30.00
❑ 99 Thorbuster CH	30.00	60.00
❑ 100 Thor, Frog of Thunder LE	30.00	60.00
❑ 101 Samantha Parrington LE	15.00	30.00
❑ 102 Skill-Brother LE	15.00	30.00
❑ 103 Gharskygt LE	15.00	30.00
❑ 104 Son of Surtur LE	15.00	30.00
❑ 105 Thor, the Reigning LE	15.00	30.00
❑ 201 Ragnarok Surtur CH	15.00	30.00

2010 Marvel Heroclix Web of Spider-Man Miniatures

❑ 1 H.A.M.M.E.R. Agent C	.20	.50
❑ 2 Symbiote C	.20	.50
❑ 3 Reseacher C	.20	.50
❑ 4 Nurse C	.20	.50
❑ 5 Code: Blue Officer C	.20	.50
❑ 6 Mugger C	.20	.50
❑ 7 Spider-Man C	.20	.50
❑ 8 Peter Parker C	.20	.50
❑ 9 Venom C	.20	.50
❑ 10 Eddie Brock C	.20	.50
❑ 11 Prowler C	.20	.50
❑ 12 Puma C	.20	.50
❑ 13 Will-O'-the-Wisp C	.20	.50
❑ 14 Iron Man C	.20	.50
❑ 15 Molten Man C	.20	.50
❑ 16 Ironclad C	.20	.50
❑ 17 H.A.M.M.E.R. Elite U	.40	1.00
❑ 18 Carnage U	.40	1.00
❑ 19 Chameleon U	.40	1.00
❑ 20 Firestar U	.40	1.00
❑ 21 Lt. Marcus Stone U	.40	1.00
❑ 22 Spider-Man U	.40	1.00
❑ 23 Norman Osborn U	.40	1.00
❑ 24 Ben Rielly U	.40	1.00
❑ 25 Anti-Venom U	.40	1.00
❑ 26 Black Cat U	.40	1.00
❑ 27 X-23 U	.40	1.00
❑ 28 Warpath U	.40	1.00
❑ 29 Wolfsbane U	.40	1.00
❑ 30 Mary Jane Watson U	.40	1.00
❑ 31 Daken U	.40	1.00
❑ 32 Vector U	.40	1.00
❑ 33 Menace R	4.00	10.00
❑ 34 Victor Mancha R	4.00	10.00
❑ 35 J. Jonah Jameson R	4.00	10.00
❑ 36 Vermin R	4.00	10.00
❑ 37 Scorpion R	4.00	10.00
❑ 38 Noh-Varr R	4.00	10.00
❑ 39 Iron Patriot R	4.00	10.00
❑ 40 Scarlet Spider R	4.00	10.00
❑ 41 Cardiac R	4.00	10.00
❑ 42 Bullseye R	4.00	10.00
❑ 43 Wolverine R	4.00	10.00
❑ 44 Rocket Racer R	4.00	10.00
❑ 45 Solo R	4.00	10.00
❑ 46 Jackal R	4.00	10.00
❑ 47 Nightcrawler R	6.00	15.00
❑ 48 X-Ray R	4.00	10.00
❑ 49 Groot SR	6.00	15.00
❑ 50 Red Hulk SR	25.00	50.00
❑ 51 The Spot SR	6.00	15.00
❑ 52 Morlun SR	6.00	15.00
❑ 53 Red She-Hulk SR	8.00	20.00
❑ 54 Doctor Octopus SR	6.00	15.00
❑ 55 Sandman SR	6.00	15.00
❑ 56 Mysterio SR	6.00	15.00
❑ 57 Deadpool SR	25.00	50.00
❑ 58 Green Goblin SR	10.00	25.00
❑ 59 Iron Man/War Machine SR	20.00	40.00
❑ 60 Vapor SR	6.00	15.00
❑ 61 Spider-Hulk SR	10.00	25.00
❑ 62 Doppleganger CH	15.00	30.00
❑ 63 Bombastic Bag-Man CH	15.00	30.00
❑ 64 Cosmic Spider-Man LE	25.00	50.00
❑ 100 Spider-Man LE	8.00	20.00
❑ 101 Venom LE	8.00	20.00
❑ 102 Night Nurse LE	8.00	20.00
❑ 103 Toxin LE	8.00	20.00
❑ 104 Daken LE	8.00	20.00
❑ 105 The Burglar LE	8.00	20.00

2011 Marvel Heroclix Captain America Miniatures

❑ 1 Captain America C	.40	1.00
❑ 2 Howling Commando C	.40	1.00
❑ 3 Hydra Agent C	.75	2.00
❑ 4 S.H.I.E.L.D. Specialist C	.40	1.00
❑ 5 S.H.I.E.L.D. Agent C	.40	1.00
❑ 6 Black Widow C	.20	.50
❑ 7 Adaptoid C	.20	.50
❑ 8 Stonewall C	.20	.50
❑ 9 Slingshot C	.20	.50
❑ 10 Mentallo C	.20	.50
❑ 11 Jack Flag C	.20	.50
❑ 12 Diamondback C	.20	.50
❑ 13 Mister Hyde C	.20	.50
❑ 14 Luke Cage C	.20	.50
❑ 15 Red Guardian C	.20	.50
❑ 16 Nomad C	.20	.50
❑ 17 Richard Fisk U	.20	.50
❑ 18 Maria Hill U	.20	.50
❑ 19 Yelena Belova U	.20	.50
❑ 20 Super-Adaptoid U	.20	.50
❑ 21 Phobos U	.20	.50
❑ 22 Hardball U	.20	.50
❑ 23 Nick Fury U	.40	1.00
❑ 24 Doorman U	.30	.75
❑ 25 Sin U	.20	.50
❑ 26 Viper U	.40	1.00
❑ 27 Nightshade U	.20	.50
❑ 28 Batroc U	.30	.75
❑ 29 Klaw U	.20	.50
❑ 30 Falcon U	.30	.75
❑ 31 Steve Rogers U	.40	1.00
❑ 32 Scorpion U	.20	.50
❑ 33 Scientist Supreme R	.30	.75
❑ 34 Quake R	.40	1.00
❑ 35 Hellfire R	.20	.50
❑ 36 Armadillo R	.40	1.00
❑ 37 Black Panther R	1.25	3.00
❑ 38 Cobra R	.40	1.00
❑ 39 Eel R	.40	1.00
❑ 40 Captain America R	3.00	8.00
❑ 41 Mr. Immortal R	.30	.75
❑ 42 Crimson Dynamo R	.75	2.00
❑ 43 Darkstar R	1.00	2.50
❑ 44 Ursa Major R	.60	1.50
❑ 45 Fixer R	.50	1.25
❑ 46 Gorgon R	.75	2.00
❑ 47 Dirk Anger R	.40	1.00
❑ 48 Quasar SR	4.00	10.00
❑ 49 Maelstorm SR	3.00	8.00
❑ 50 MODOK SR	10.00	25.00
❑ 51 Scorpio SR	2.50	6.00
❑ 52 Red Skull SR	4.00	10.00
❑ 53 Baron Strucker SR	3.00	8.00
❑ 54 Baron Zemo SR	3.00	8.00
❑ 55 Kitty Pryde SR	4.00	10.00
❑ 56 Squirrel Girl SR	6.00	15.00
❑ 57 Invisible Woman SR	8.00	20.00
❑ 58 Human Torch SR	8.00	20.00
❑ 59 Weapon X CH	20.00	40.00
❑ 60 Captain America CH	15.00	30.00
❑ 61 Capworlf CH	20.00	40.00
❑ 62 The Captain CH	25.00	50.00
❑ 63 Rojhaz CH	6.00	15.00
❑ 100 Life Model Decoy LMD	3.00	6.00
❑ 101 Red Guardian LE	.75	2.00
❑ 102 Bob, Agent of Hydra LE	2.50	6.00
❑ 103 Gabe Jones LE	1.00	2.50
❑ 104 Successful Dirk Anger LE	1.25	3.00
❑ 105 Madame Hydra LE	2.50	6.00
❑ 201 Howling Commando	3.00	8.00
❑ 202 Hydra Officer	2.00	5.00
❑ 203 S.H.I.E.L.D. Field Agent	2.00	5.00
❑ 204 S.H.I.E.L.D. Sentry	1.50	4.00
❑ 205 Captain America	1.25	3.00
❑ 206 Black Widow	.60	1.50
❑ 207 Nick Fury	.75	2.00
❑ 208 Red Skull	2.50	6.00
❑ 209 Sin	1.25	3.00
❑ 210 Klaw	2.00	5.00

2011 Marvel Heroclix Giant Size X-Men Miniatures

❑ 1 Madrox C	1.50	4.00
❑ 2 Purifier C	.20	.50
❑ 3 Omega Prime Sentinel C	1.00	2.50
❑ 4 Hellfire Club Guard C	1.25	3.00
❑ 5 Mindless One C	2.50	6.00
❑ 6 Skullbuster C	.20	.50
❑ 7 Pretty Boy C	.20	.50
❑ 8 Cyclops C	2.50	6.00
❑ 9 Wolverine C	3.00	8.00
❑ 10 Beast C	.60	1.50
❑ 11 Emma Frost C	.75	2.00
❑ 12 Cypher C	.60	1.50
❑ 13 Empath C	.20	.50
❑ 14 Roullette C	.40	1.00
❑ 15 Tabitha Smith C	.20	.50
❑ 16 Aaron Stack C	.20	.50
❑ 17 Domino C	1.50	4.00
❑ 18 Caliban U	.30	.75
❑ 19 William Stryker U	.30	.75
❑ 20 Harry Leland U	.30	.75
❑ 21 Tarot U	.40	1.00
❑ 22 Cannonball U	.20	.50
❑ 23 Psylocke U	3.00	8.00
❑ 24 Gideon U	.30	.75
❑ 25 Elixir U	.40	1.00
❑ 26 Leech U	.60	1.50
❑ 27 Siryn U	.30	.75
❑ 28 Elsa Bloodstone U	1.00	2.50
❑ 29 Monica Rambeau U	.30	.75
❑ 30 Rogue U	2.00	5.00
❑ 31 Angel U	1.25	3.00
❑ 32 Ch'od U	.20	.50
❑ 33 Blob U	1.50	4.00
❑ 34 Pyro R	3.00	8.00
❑ 35 Mystique R	4.00	10.00
❑ 36 Professor X R	8.00	20.00
❑ 37 Gatecrasher R	.20	.50
❑ 38 Iceman R	2.00	5.00
❑ 39 Lockheed R	4.00	10.00
❑ 40 Sabretooth R	6.00	15.00
❑ 41 Stryfe R	1.25	3.00
❑ 42 Predator X R	2.50	6.00
❑ 43 Trevor Fitzroy R	.75	2.00
❑ 44 Bonebreaker R	.75	2.00
❑ 45 Vulcan R	2.00	5.00
❑ 46 Juggernaut SR	25.00	50.00
❑ 47 Phoenix SR	20.00	40.00
❑ 48 Storm SR	15.00	30.00
❑ 49 Archangel SR	10.00	25.00
❑ 50 Armor SR	6.00	15.00
❑ 51 Hulk SR	10.00	25.00
❑ 52 Wolverine SR	8.00	20.00
❑ 53 Magneto SR	40.00	75.00
❑ 54 The Captain SR	4.00	10.00
❑ 55 Cable & Deadpool CH	15.00	30.00
❑ 56 Colossus & Wolverine CH	15.00	30.00
❑ 57 Cyclops & Phoenix CH	10.00	20.00
❑ 58 Gambit & Rogue CH	8.00	20.00
❑ 100 Jamie Madrox	.75	2.00
❑ 101 Psylocke LE	2.50	6.00
❑ 102 Cable LE	15.00	30.00
❑ 103 Deadpool LE	20.00	40.00
❑ 104 Archangel LE	15.00	30.00
❑ 105 Karima LE	1.50	4.00
❑ 201 Pestilence LE	20.00	40.00
❑ 202 War LE	25.00	50.00
❑ 203 Famine LE	3.00	6.00
❑ G01 Sentinel Mark II	10.00	25.00
❑ G02 Sentinel Mark V	8.00	20.00
❑ G03 Apocalypse	15.00	30.00
❑ G04 Onslaught	25.00	50.00
❑ G05 Nemesis	8.00	20.00
❑ G06 Frost Giant	10.00	25.00
❑ G07 Apocalypse	15.00	30.00
❑ G08 Sentinel Mark II	15.00	30.00
❑ G09 Sentinel Mark V	8,00	20.00
❑ M001 Moonstone LE		

2011 Marvel Heroclix Hammer of Thor Fast Forces Miniatures

COMPLETE SET (6)	10.00	20.00
❑ 1 Fandral	2.00	5.00
❑ 2 Hogun	2.00	5.00
❑ 3 Volstagg	2.00	5.00
❑ 4 Asguardian Brawler	2.00	5.00
❑ 5 Thor	5.00	10.00
❑ 6 Loki	5.00	10.00

2012 Marvel Heroclix The Incredible Hulk Miniatures

❑ 1 Hulk C	.60	1.50
❑ 2 Bruce Banner C	.20	.50
❑ 3 A.I.M. AIM Agent C	.60	1.50
❑ 4 Hulkbuster Soldier C	.40	1.00
❑ 5 Humanoid C	.40	1.00
❑ 6 Hulk Robot C	.20	.50
❑ 7 She-Hulk C	.40	1.00
❑ 8 John Jameson C	.20	.50
❑ 9 Man-Wolf C	.20	.50
❑ 10 Punisher C	.20	.50
❑ 11 Punisher C	.30	.75
❑ 12 Thundra C	.20	.50
❑ 13 Abomination C	.20	.50
❑ 14 The Leader C	.20	.50
❑ 15 Skaar U	.40	1.00
❑ 16 Lyra U	.20	.50
❑ 17 A.I.M. Renegade U	.60	1.50
❑ 18 A.I. Marine U	.40	1.00
❑ 19 Black Tarantula U	.40	1.00
❑ 20 White Tiger U	.20	.50
❑ 21 Daredevil U	.20	.50
❑ 22 Matt Murdock U	.20	.50
❑ 23 Punisher U	.20	.50
❑ 24 Jigsaw U	.20	.50
❑ 25 Rick Jones U	.20	.50
❑ 26 Hercules U	.40	1.00
❑ 27 Amadeus Cho R	.75	2.00
❑ 28 Red Hulk R	2.00	5.00
❑ 29 General Thunderbolt Ross R	.20	.50
❑ 30 Doc Samson R	.20	.50
❑ 31 Daredevil R	.50	1.25
❑ 32 Shanna R	.20	.50
❑ 33 Tiger Shark R	.60	1.50
❑ 34 Man-Beast R	.20	.50
❑ 35 Wolverine R	.40	1.00
❑ 36 Joe Fixit R	.40	1.00
❑ 37 Ghost Rider SR	6.00	15.00
❑ 38 Spider-Man SR	4.00	10.00
❑ 39 Caiera SR	4.00	10.00
❑ 40 A-Bomb SR	2.50	6.00
❑ 41 Ka-Zar SR	2.00	5.00
❑ 42 Black Bolt SR	8.00	20.00
❑ 43 Hulk SR	5.00	12.00
❑ 44 Red King SR	3.00	8.00
❑ 45 Cosmic Hulk SR	5.00	12.00
❑ 46 Winter Hulk CH	10.00	25.00
❑ 47 Hulklops CH	8.00	20.00
❑ 48 Icehulk CH	8.00	20.00
❑ 49 Hulkmariner CH	6.00	15.00
❑ 50 Mighty Thorr CH	10.00	25.00
❑ 51 Wolverine CH	10.00	25.00
❑ 100 A.I. Marine Hulk LE	.75	2.00
❑ 101 Bruce Banner LE	1.50	4.00
❑ 102 Major Glenn Talbot LE	1.25	3.00
❑ 103 Daredevil LE	1.50	4.00
❑ 104 Black Bolt LE	3.00	8.00
❑ S101 Gamma Bomb	5.00	12.00
❑ S102 Globe of Ultimate Knowledge	.75	2.00

2012 Marvel Heroclix The Incredible Hulk Fast Forces Miniatures

❑ 1 Hulk	.75	2.00
❑ 2 Hulkbuster Wrangler	1.00	2.50
❑ 3 She-Hulk	1.50	4.00
❑ 4 Abomination	.60	1.50
❑ 5 General Thunderbolt Ross	.40	1.00
❑ 6 The Leader	.40	1.00

2012 Marvel Heroclix The Incredible Hulk Gravity Feed Miniatures

❑ 201 Hulk	1.25	3.00
❑ 202 Bruce Banner	.40	1.00
❑ 203 Hulkbuster Squad Leader	.75	2.00
❑ 204 She-Hulk	1.50	4.00
❑ 205 Punisher	2.00	5.00
❑ 206 Abomination	.75	2.00
❑ 207 Skaar	.75	2.00
❑ 208 General Thunderbolt Ross	1.00	2.50

- ❑ 209 The Leader .40 1.00
- ❑ 210 Red Hulk 3.00 8.00

2012 Marvel Heroclix 10th Anniversary Miniatures

- ❑ 1 Captain America C .75 2.00
- ❑ 2 Hulk C .75 2.00
- ❑ 3 Thing C .75 2.00
- ❑ 4 Green Goblin C 1.25 3.00
- ❑ 5 Thor C 2.00 5.00
- ❑ 6 Marvel Girl C 1.25 3.00
- ❑ 7 Storm C 1.50 4.00
- ❑ 8 White Queen C 1.25 3.00
- ❑ 9 Iron Man C 4.00 10.00
- ❑ 10 Weapon X U 1.00 2.50
- ❑ 11 Thing U .75 2.00
- ❑ 12 Iron Man U 1.25 3.00
- ❑ 13 Hulk U 8.00 20.00
- ❑ 14 Emma Frost U 3.00 8.00
- ❑ 15 Magneto U 1.50 4.00
- ❑ 16 Thor U 2.50 6.00
- ❑ 17 Spider-Man U 6.00 15.00
- ❑ 18 Green Goblin R 8.00 20.00
- ❑ 19 Magneto R 12.00 30.00
- ❑ 20 Storm R 8.00 20.00
- ❑ 21 Dark Phoenix R 25.00 50.00
- ❑ 22 Skrull Wolverine CH 12.00 30.00
- ❑ 23 Skrull Captain America CH 10.00 25.00
- ❑ 24 Skrull Spider-Man CH 12.00 30.00

2012 Marvel Heroclix Avengers Movie Miniatures

- ❑ 1 Captain America C 1.25 3.00
- ❑ 2 Hydra Soldier C 1.50 4.00
- ❑ 3 Agent of S.H.I.E.L.D. C .75 2.00
- ❑ 4 Thor C 1.50 4.00
- ❑ 5 Frost Giant C 2.00 5.00
- ❑ 6 Iron Man C 1.50 4.00
- ❑ 7 Black Widow C 1.25 3.00
- ❑ 8 Skrull Commando C 1.25 3.00
- ❑ 9 Hawkeye C 1.50 4.00
- ❑ 10 S.H.I.E.L.D. Commando C 1.25 3.00
- ❑ 11 Maria Hill U .75 2.00
- ❑ 12 Sif U .75 2.00
- ❑ 13 Bruce Banner U .40 1.00
- ❑ 14 Hulk U 1.50 4.00
- ❑ 15 Loki U 2.50 6.00
- ❑ 16 Red Skull U 1.25 3.00
- ❑ 17 Bucky Barnes U .75 2.00
- ❑ 18 Captain America R 2.50 6.00
- ❑ 19 Iron Man R 1.50 4.00
- ❑ 20 Thor R 2.00 5.00
- ❑ 21 Howard Stark R 1.25 3.00
- ❑ 22 Destroyer R 6.00 15.00
- ❑ 23 Volstagg SR 1.25 3.00
- ❑ 24 Hogun SR 1.25 3.00
- ❑ 25 Fandral SR 1.25 3.00
- ❑ 26 Dum Dum Dugan SR 2.50 6.00
- ❑ 27 Gabe Jones SR 1.25 3.00
- ❑ 28 Captain America SR 3.00 8.00
- ❑ 29 Loki SR 3.00 8.00
- ❑ 30 Laufey SR 4.00 10.00
- ❑ 31 Frost Giant Champion SR 3.00 8.00
- ❑ 32 Skrull General SR 2.50 6.00
- ❑ 33 Skrull Saboteur SR 1.50 4.00
- ❑ 34 Skrull Warrior SR 2.00 5.00
- ❑ 35 Nick Fury SR 3.00 8.00
- ❑ 36 Black Widow SR 2.00 5.00
- ❑ 37 S.H.I.E.L.D. Enforcer SR 2.50 6.00
- ❑ 38 Johann Schmidt SR .75 2.00
- ❑ 39 Hydra Footsoldier SR 2.50 6.00
- ❑ 40 Hydra Technician SR 5.00 12.00
- ❑ 41 Red Skull CH 6.00 15.00
- ❑ 42 Odin CH 8.00 20.00

2012 Marvel Heroclix Avengers Movie Gravity Feed Miniatures

- ❑ 201 Thor 2.50 6.00
- ❑ 202 Hulk 12.00 30.00
- ❑ 203 Nick Fury 2.00 5.00
- ❑ 204 Captain America 3.00 8.00
- ❑ 205 Iron Man 2.00 5.00
- ❑ 206 Agent Coulson 8.00 20.00
- ❑ 207 Skrull Infiltrator 3.00 8.00
- ❑ 208 Hawkeye 3.00 8.00
- ❑ 209 Tony Stark 2.00 5.00
- ❑ 210 Heimdall 3.00 8.00
- ❑ 211 Loki 15.00 40.00

2012 Marvel Heroclix Avengers Movie Starter Set Miniatures

- ❑ 1 The Mighty Avenger 1.00 2.50
- ❑ 2 The First Avenger 2.00 5.00
- ❑ 3 The Armored Avenger .60 1.50
- ❑ 4 The Covert Avenger .75 2.00
- ❑ 5 The Sharpshooting Avenger 2.00 5.00
- ❑ 6 The Incredible Avenger 1.25 3.00

2012 Marvel Heroclix Chaos War Miniatures

- ❑ 1 Captain America C .20 .50
- ❑ 2 Iron Man Drone C .75 2.00
- ❑ 3 Ultron Drone C .40 1.00
- ❑ 4 Egghead C .20 .50
- ❑ 5 Sentinel C 1.25 3.00
- ❑ 6 Space Phantom C .20 .50
- ❑ 7 Masque Duplicate C .20 .50
- ❑ 8 Lava Man C .20 .50
- ❑ 9 Shadow Council Soldier C .40 1.00
- ❑ 10 Donald Blake C .40 1.00
- ❑ 11 Tony Stark C .20 .50
- ❑ 12 Dinah Soar C .20 .50
- ❑ 13 Vision C .20 .50
- ❑ 14 Hank Pym C .20 .50
- ❑ 15 Ant-Man C .30 .75
- ❑ 16 Wasp U .20 .50
- ❑ 17 Madame Masque U .20 .50
- ❑ 18 Jinku U .20 .50
- ❑ 19 Max Fury U .20 .50
- ❑ 20 Black Knight U .20 .50
- ❑ 21 Speed U .20 .50
- ❑ 22 Sharon Carter U .20 .50
- ❑ 23 Ms. Marvel U .40 1.00
- ❑ 24 Iron Man U .75 2.00
- ❑ 25 Nitro U .20 .50
- ❑ 26 Ant-Man U .20 .50
- ❑ 27 Genis-Vell U .30 .75
- ❑ 28 Wonder Man U .20 .50
- ❑ 29 Wolverine U 1.25 3.00
- ❑ 30 Wasp R 1.25 3.00
- ❑ 31 Black Knight R .60 1.50
- ❑ 32 Quicksilver R .75 2.00
- ❑ 33 Victoria Hand R .40 1.00
- ❑ 34 Ares R .75 2.00
- ❑ 35 Sentry R 1.00 2.50
- ❑ 36 Tigra R .40 1.00
- ❑ 37 Spider-Woman R .40 1.00
- ❑ 38 Thor R 1.25 3.00
- ❑ 39 Hawkeye R 4.00 10.00
- ❑ 40 Nick Fury R .60 1.50
- ❑ 41 Baron Zemo R .75 2.00
- ❑ 42 Loki SR 3.00 8.00
- ❑ 43 Binary SR 2.50 6.00
- ❑ 44 Crystal SR 5.00 12.00
- ❑ 45 Void SR 6.00 15.00
- ❑ 46 The Unspoken SR 3.00 8.00
- ❑ 47 Mr. Sinister SR 10.00 25.00
- ❑ 48 Taskmaster SR 8.00 20.00
- ❑ 49 Morgan Le Fay SR 6.00 15.00
- ❑ 50 Kang SR 6.00 15.00
- ❑ 51 Chaos King SR 6.00 15.00
- ❑ 52 Lockjaw and Hairball SR 2.50 6.00
- ❑ 53 Ant-Man and Wasp CH 10.00 25.00
- ❑ 54 Hawkeye and Mockingbird CH 8.00 20.00
- ❑ 55 Vision and Scarlet Witch CH 6.00 15.00
- ❑ 56 Scarlet Witch and Wonder Man CH 6.00 15.00
- ❑ 57 Sentry and Void CH 35.00 70.00
- ❑ 58 Dr. Doom and Kang CH 12.00 30.00
- ❑ 59 Thor and Hercules CH 10.00 25.00
- ❑ 60 Avengers Prime CH 35.00 70.00
- ❑ 100 Vision LE 2.50 6.00
- ❑ 101 Mr. Fantastic LE 3.00 8.00
- ❑ 102 Invisible Woman LE 4.00 10.00
- ❑ 103 Thing LE 2.50 6.00
- ❑ 104 Spider-Man LE 5.00 12.00

2012 Marvel Heroclix Chaos War Fast Forces Miniatures

- ❑ 1 Iron Man 1.25 3.00
- ❑ 2 Thor 1.25 3.00
- ❑ 3 Captain America 1.25 3.00
- ❑ 4 Wasp 1.25 3.00
- ❑ 5 Mockingbird 4.00 10.00
- ❑ 6 Scarlet Witch 30.00 60.00

2012 Marvel Heroclix Galactic Guardians Miniatures

- ❑ 1 Nova Prime C .40 1.00
- ❑ 2 Nova Corps Recruit C .40 1.00
- ❑ 3 Cardinal of the UCT C .40 1.00
- ❑ 4 Skrull Rebel C .20 .50
- ❑ 5 Annihilation Seeker C .20 .50
- ❑ 6 Doombot C .75 2.00
- ❑ 7 Blood Brother C .20 .50
- ❑ 8 Nebula C .20 .50
- ❑ 9 Namor C .20 .50
- ❑ 10 Adam Warlock C .20 .50
- ❑ 11 Drax C .20 .50
- ❑ 12 Charlie-27 C .20 .50
- ❑ 13 Hollywood C .20 .50
- ❑ 14 Astral Dr. Strange U 2.00 5.00
- ❑ 15 Nova Corps Centurion U .30 .75
- ❑ 16 Cardinal Raker U .20 .50
- ❑ 17 Lyja the Laserfist U .20 .50
- ❑ 18 Ravenous U .20 .50
- ❑ 19 Dr. Doom U 1.25 3.00
- ❑ 20 Magus U .30 .75
- ❑ 21 Red Shift U .20 .50
- ❑ 22 Xavin U .20 .50
- ❑ 23 Blastaar U .20 .50
- ❑ 24 Nikki U .20 .50
- ❑ 25 Martinex U .20 .50
- ❑ 26 Mole Man U 1.25 3.00
- ❑ 27 Hulk R .75 2.00
- ❑ 28 Dr. Strange R 1.25 3.00
- ❑ 29 Morg R .75 2.00
- ❑ 30 Fallen One R .40 1.00
- ❑ 31 Captain Marvel R 1.00 2.50
- ❑ 32 Adam Warlock R .60 1.50
- ❑ 33 Gamora R .40 1.00
- ❑ 34 Super-Skrull R .50 1.25
- ❑ 35 Replica R .30 .75
- ❑ 36 Silver Surfer R 2.00 5.00
- ❑ 37 Mr. Fantastic SR 4.00 10.00
- ❑ 38 The Thing SR 5.00 12.00
- ❑ 39 Cosmo SR 6.00 15.00
- ❑ 40 Gladiator SR 3.00 8.00
- ❑ 41 Lord Mar-Vell SR 3.00 8.00
- ❑ 42 Medusa SR 4.00 10.00
- ❑ 43 Stranger SR 2.50 6.00
- ❑ 44 Mistress Death SR 8.00 20.00
- ❑ 45 Thanos SR 10.00 25.00
- ❑ 46 Dr. Doom CH 12.00 30.00
- ❑ 47 Mr. Fantastic CH 8.00 20.00
- ❑ 48 Keeper CH 8.00 20.00
- ❑ 49 Thanos CH 40.00 80.00
- ❑ 100 Super Nova LE 1.25 3.00
- ❑ 101 Iron Man LE 5.00 12.00
- ❑ 102 Hulk LE 2.00 5.00
- ❑ 103 Wolverine LE 5.00 12.00
- ❑ 104 Spider-Man LE 4.00 10.00
- ❑ S101 Nova Helmet .75 2.00
- ❑ S102 Cosmic Cube 2.00 5.00

2012 Marvel Heroclix Galactic Guardians Fast Forces Miniatures

- ❑ 1 Nova C 1.25 3.00
- ❑ 2 Silver Surfer C 2.50 6.00
- ❑ 3 Gladiator C 2.50 6.00
- ❑ 4 Quasar C 3.00 8.00
- ❑ 5 Beta Ray Bill C 6.00 15.00
- ❑ 6 Ronan the Accuser C 3.00 8.00

2012 Marvel Heroclix Galactic Guardians Giant Miniatures

- ❑ G1 Galactus SR 40.00 80.00
- ❑ G2 Ziran the Tester SR 12.00 30.00
- ❑ G3 Master Gold SR 15.00 40.00
- ❑ G4 Giganto, The Mole Monster SR 12.00 30.00
- ❑ G5 Uatu, The Watcher SR 15.00 40.00
- ❑ G6 Dormammu SR 25.00 50.00

2012 Marvel Heroclix Galactic Guardians Gravity Feed Miniatures

- ❑ 201 Nova C .40 1.00
- ❑ 202 Skrull Assassin C .75 2.00
- ❑ 203 Namor C .60 1.50
- ❑ 204 Drax C .40 1.00
- ❑ 205 Dr. Doom C 2.00 5.00
- ❑ 206 Dr. Strange C 3.00 8.00
- ❑ 207 Hulk C 1.25 3.00
- ❑ 208 Super Skrull C .75 2.00
- ❑ 209 Silver Surfer C 2.00 5.00
- ❑ 210 Nova Corps Denarian C 1.25 3.00

2013 Marvel Heroclix Amazing Spider-Man Miniatures

- ❑ 1A Spider-Man (green) C 1.25 3.00
- ❑ 1B Spider-Man (red) C .75 2.00
- ❑ 1B Spider-Man (blue) C .75 2.00
- ❑ 2 Shocker C .20 .50
- ❑ 3 Dagger C .20 .50
- ❑ 4 Blade C .30 .75
- ❑ 5 Dr. Strange C .30 .75
- ❑ 6 Zuvembie C 1.25 3.00
- ❑ 7 Johnny Blaze C .20 .50
- ❑ 8 Doctor Druid C .20 .50
- ❑ 9 Daimon Hellstrom C .20 .50
- ❑ 10 Frankenstein's Monster C .20 .50
- ❑ 11 Living Mummy C .20 .50
- ❑ 12 Vampire C .40 1.00
- ❑ 13A Frank Drake C .20 .50
- ❑ 13B Hannibal King C .75 2.00
- ❑ 14 Werewolf C .60 1.50
- ❑ 15 Werewolf By Night C .40 1.00
- ❑ 16 Dracula C .40 1.00
- ❑ 17A Dr. Voodoo U .60 1.50
- ❑ 17B Brother Voodoo U 8.00 20.00
- ❑ 18 Scarlet Spider U .60 1.50
- ❑ 19 Vulture U .20 .50
- ❑ 20 Rhino U .40 1.00
- ❑ 21 Electro U .40 1.00
- ❑ 22 Cloak U .30 .75
- ❑ 23 Wong U .30 .75
- ❑ 24 Spider-Man U .40 1.00
- ❑ 25 Manphibian U .40 1.00
- ❑ 26 Mysterio U 2.00 5.00
- ❑ 27 Spider-Girl U .20 .50
- ❑ 28 Morbius R .75 2.00
- ❑ 29 Demogoblin R .75 2.00
- ❑ 30 Lizard R 1.25 3.00
- ❑ 31A Kraven the Hunter R 2.00 5.00
- ❑ 31B Alyosha Kraven R 8.00 20.00
- ❑ 32 Moon Knight R .75 2.00
- ❑ 33 Man-Thing R 1.25 3.00
- ❑ 34 Satana Hellstrom R .40 1.00
- ❑ 35 Jennifer Kale R .40 1.00
- ❑ 36 Kaine R .40 1.00
- ❑ 37 Ancient One R .75 2.00
- ❑ 38 Carrion R .30 .75
- ❑ 39 Spider-Man R .60 1.50
- ❑ 40 Blackheart SR 5.00 12.00
- ❑ 41A Hobgoblin SR 4.00 10.00
- ❑ 41B Hobgoblin SR 12.00 30.00
- ❑ 42 Nightmare SR 5.00 12.00
- ❑ 43 Baron Mordo SR 3.00 8.00
- ❑ 44 Colleen Wing and Misty Knight SR 3.00 8.00
- ❑ 45 Terrax SR 5.00 12.00
- ❑ 46 Ghost Rider SR 15.00 40.00
- ❑ 47 Man-Thing and Howard the Duck SR 3.00 8.00
- ❑ 48 Madame Web SR 4.00 10.00
- ❑ 49 Spider-Man 2099 SR 8.00 20.00
- ❑ 50 Hornet CH 6.00 15.00
- ❑ 51 Ricochet CH 6.00 15.00
- ❑ 52 Dusk CH 8.00 20.00
- ❑ 53 Prodigy CH 6.00 15.00
- ❑ 54 Spider-Man CH 8.00 20.00
- ❑ 55 Spider-Man CH 10.00 25.00
- ❑ 56 Iron Spider CH 15.00 40.00
- ❑ 57 Spider-Man CH 12.00 30.00

2013 Marvel Heroclix Amazing Spider-Man Gravity Feed Miniatures

- ❑ 201 Spider-Man C 2.50 6.00
- ❑ 202 Cloak C 1.25 3.00
- ❑ 203 Dagger C 1.25 3.00
- ❑ 204 Rhino C 1.00 2.50
- ❑ 205 Electro C .60 1.50
- ❑ 206 Mysterio C 1.50 4.00
- ❑ 207 Blade C 1.25 3.00
- ❑ 208 Shocker C 1.25 3.00
- ❑ 209 Scarlet Spider C .75 2.00
- ❑ 210 Spider-Girl C .60 1.50

2013 Marvel Heroclix Wolverine and the X-Men Miniatures

- ❑ 1 Wolverine C .40 1.00
- ❑ 2 Colossus C .40 1.00
- ❑ 3 Shadowcat C .20 .50
- ❑ 4 Mirage C .20 .50
- ❑ 5 Oracle C .20 .50
- ❑ 6 Toad C .20 .50
- ❑ 7 Shi'ar Soldier C .40 1.00
- ❑ 8 Dazzler C .30 .75
- ❑ 9 Longshot C .40 1.00
- ❑ 10 Shatterstar C .20 .50
- ❑ 11A Deathlok C .20 .50
- ❑ 11B Deathlok C 5.00 12.00
- ❑ 12 Strong Guy C .20 .50
- ❑ 13 Multiple Man C 2.00 5.00
- ❑ 14 Rictor C .20 .50
- ❑ 15 Cyber C .20 .50
- ❑ 16 Cyclops U .60 1.50
- ❑ 17 Jean Grey U .40 1.00
- ❑ 18 Sunspot U .20 .50
- ❑ 19 Starbolt U .20 .50
- ❑ 20 White King U .30 .75
- ❑ 21 Flatman U .20 .50
- ❑ 22 Korvus U .30 .75
- ❑ 23A Deathbird U .20 .50
- ❑ 23B Cerise U 5.00 12.00
- ❑ 24 Havok U .75 2.00
- ❑ 25 Polaris U .75 2.00
- ❑ 26 Layla Miller U .30 .75
- ❑ 27 Husk U .30 .75
- ❑ 28 Kid Omega U .20 .50
- ❑ 29 Sauron U .40 1.00
- ❑ 30 Lady Deathstrike U .40 1.00
- ❑ 31 Gambit R 2.50 6.00
- ❑ 32 Bishop R 1.50 4.00
- ❑ 33 Forge R 1.25 3.00
- ❑ 34 Magik R 1.25 3.00
- ❑ 35 Black King R 1.50 4.00
- ❑ 36 Smasher R .40 1.00
- ❑ 37A Magneto R 6.00 15.00
- ❑ 37B Magneto R 15.00 40.00
- ❑ 38 Legion R .75 2.00
- ❑ 39 Big Bertha R 1.00 2.50
- ❑ 40 Hope Summers R 1.50 4.00
- ❑ 41 Spiral R 4.00 10.00
- ❑ 42 Fantomex R 2.00 5.00
- ❑ 43 Shadow King R 1.25 3.00
- ❑ 44 Silver Samurai R 1.50 4.00
- ❑ 45 Phoenix SR 10.00 25.00
- ❑ 46 Warlock SR 6.00 15.00
- ❑ 47A Jubilee SR 12.00 30.00
- ❑ 47B Jubilee SR 25.00 50.00
- ❑ 48 Warstar SR 6.00 15.00
- ❑ 49 Black Queen SR 8.00 20.00
- ❑ 50 Mojo SR 4.00 10.00
- ❑ 51 X-Man SR 6.00 15.00
- ❑ 52 Lilandra SR 4.00 10.00
- ❑ 53 Professor X and Magneto SR 6.00 15.00
- ❑ 54 M SR 5.00 12.00
- ❑ 55 Mikhail Rasputin SR 3.00 8.00
- ❑ 56 Exodus SR 6.00 15.00
- ❑ 57 Cyclops CH 30.00 60.00
- ❑ 58 Namor CH 30.00 60.00
- ❑ 59 Colossus CH 30.00 60.00
- ❑ 60 Emma Frost CH 30.00 60.00
- ❑ 61 Magik CH 30.00 60.00
- ❑ 62 Beast SB 8.00 20.00
- ❑ 63 Psylocke SB 10.00 25.00
- ❑ 64 Rogue SB 10.00 25.00
- ❑ 65 Storm SB 6.00 15.00
- ❑ 66 Iceman SB 8.00 20.00
- ❑ 67 Archangel SB 8.00 20.00
- ❑ 68 Captain Britain SB 8.00 20.00
- ❑ 69 Meggan SB 3.00 8.00
- ❑ 70 Nightcrawler SB 12.00 30.00
- ❑ 71 Cannonball SB 6.00 15.00
- ❑ 72 Wolfsbane SB 5.00 12.00
- ❑ 73 Magma SB 5.00 12.00
- ❑ 74 Gladiator SB 8.00 20.00
- ❑ 75 Manta SB 10.00 25.00
- ❑ 76 Hussar SB 8.00 20.00
- ❑ 77 White Queen SB 8.00 20.00
- ❑ 78 Quicksilver SB 6.00 15.00
- ❑ 79 Scarlet Witch SB 6.00 15.00
- ❑ 80 Lockheed SB 3.00 8.00
- ❑ T001 X-Men: Blue Strike Force SB 8.00 20.00
- ❑ T002 X-Men: Gold Strike Force SB 8.00 20.00
- ❑ T003 Excalibur SB 5.00 12.00
- ❑ T004 New Mutants SB 5.00 12.00
- ❑ T005 Shi'ar Imperial Guard SB 8.00 20.00
- ❑ T006 Hellfire Club SB 6.00 15.00
- ❑ T007 Brotherhood of Mutants SB 8.00 20.00

2013 Marvel Heroclix Wolverine and the X-Men Gravity Feed Miniatures

- ❑ 201 Wolverine C 2.00 5.00
- ❑ 202 Colossus C 1.50 4.00
- ❑ 203 Havok C 1.25 3.00
- ❑ 204 Shadowcat C 1.25 3.00
- ❑ 205 Multiple Man C 2.00 5.00
- ❑ 206 Shi'ar Guard C 1.50 4.00
- ❑ 207 Toad C 1.25 3.00
- ❑ 208 Cyber C 1.25 3.00
- ❑ 209 Jean Grey C 1.50 4.00
- ❑ 210 Lady Deathstrike C 1.50 4.00

2004 Star Wars Clone Strike Miniatures

- ❑ 1 48 Super Battle Droid U .60 1.50
- ❑ 2 Aayla Secura VR 12.00 20.00
- ❑ 3 Aerial Clone Trooper Captain R 6.00 12.00
- ❑ 4 Agen Kolar R 6.00 12.00
- ❑ 5 Anakin Skywalker VR 15.00 25.00
- ❑ 6 Aqualish Spy C .30 .75
- ❑ 7 ARC Trooper U .60 1.50
- ❑ 8 Asajj Ventress R 6.00 12.00
- ❑ 9 Aurra Sing VR 20.00 35.00
- ❑ 10 Battle Droid C .30 .75
- ❑ 11 Battle Droid C .30 .75
- ❑ 12 Battle Droid C .30 .75
- ❑ 13 Battle Droid Officer U .60 1.50
- ❑ 14 Battle Droid on STAP R 6.00 12.00
- ❑ 15 Captain Typho R 6.00 12.00
- ❑ 16 Clone Trooper C .30 .75
- ❑ 17 Clone Trooper C .30 .75
- ❑ 18 Clone Trooper Commander U .60 1.50
- ❑ 19 Clone Trooper Grenadier C .30 .75
- ❑ 20 Clone Trooper Sergeant C .30 .75
- ❑ 21 Count Dooku VR 15.00 25.00
- ❑ 22 Dark Side Acolyte U .60 1.50
- ❑ 23 Darth Maul VR 18.00 30.00
- ❑ 24 Darth Sidious VR 15.00 25.00
- ❑ 25 Destroyer Droid R 6.00 12.00
- ❑ 26 Devaronian Bounty Hunter C .30 .75
- ❑ 27 Durge R 6.00 12.00
- ❑ 28 Dwarf Spider Droid R 6.00 12.00
- ❑ 29 General Grievous VR 18.00 30.00
- ❑ 30 General Kenobi R 6.00 12.00
- ❑ 31 Geonosian Drone C .30 .75
- ❑ 32 Geonosian Overseer U .60 1.50
- ❑ 33 Geonosian Picador on Orray R 6.00 12.00
- ❑ 34 Geonosian Soldier U .60 1.50
- ❑ 35 Gran Raider C .30 .75
- ❑ 36 Gungan Cavalry on Kaadu R 6.00 12.00
- ❑ 37 Gungan Infantry C .30 .75
- ❑ 38 Ishi Tib Scout U .60 1.50
- ❑ 39 Jango Fett R 6.00 12.00
- ❑ 40 Jedi Guardian U .60 1.50
- ❑ 41 Ki-Adi-Mundi R 6.00 12.00
- ❑ 42 Kit Fisto R 6.00 12.00
- ❑ 43 Klatooinian Enforcer C .30 .75
- ❑ 44 Luminara Unduli R 6.00 12.00
- ❑ 45 Mace Windu VR 15.00 25.00

❑ 46 Naboo Soldier U .60 1.50
❑ 47 Nikto Soldier C .30 .75
❑ 48 Padme Amidala VR 12.00 20.00
❑ 49 Plo Koon R 6.00 12.00
❑ 50 Quarren Raider U .60 1.50
❑ 51 Qui-Gon Jinn VR 12.00 20.00
❑ 52 Quinlan Vos VR 12.00 20.00
❑ 53 Rodian Mercenary U .60 1.50
❑ 54 Saesee Tiin R 6.00 12.00
❑ 55 Security Battle Droid C .30 .75
❑ 56 Super Battle Droid U .60 1.50
❑ 57 Weequay Mercenary C .30 .75
❑ 58 Wookiee Commando U .60 1.50
❑ 59 Yoda VR 18.00 30.00
❑ 60 Zam Wesell R 6.00 12.00

2004 Star Wars Rebel Storm Miniatures

❑ 1 4-LOM R 5.00 10.00
❑ 2 Bespin Guard C .30 .75
❑ 3 Boba Fett VR 15.00 40.00
❑ 4 Bossk R 5.00 10.00
❑ 5 Bothan Spy U .60 1.50
❑ 6 C-3PO R 5.00 10.00
❑ 7 Chewbacca R 6.00 12.00
❑ 8 Commando on Speeder Bike VR 15.00 25.00
❑ 9 Darth Vader, Dark Jedi R 6.00 12.00
❑ 10 Darth Vader, Sith Lord VR 12.50 25.00
❑ 11 Dengar R 5.00 10.00
❑ 12 Duros Mercenary U .60 1.50
❑ 13 Elite Hoth Trooper U .60 1.50
❑ 14 Elite Rebel Trooper C .30 .75
❑ 15 Elite Snowtrooper U .60 1.50
❑ 16 Elite Stormtrooper U .60 1.50
❑ 17 Emperor Palpatine VR 15.00 30.00
❑ 18 Ewok C .30 .75
❑ 19 Gamorrean Guard U .60 1.50
❑ 20 General Veers R 5.00 10.00
❑ 21 Grand Moff Tarkin R 5.00 10.00
❑ 22 Greedo R 5.00 10.00
❑ 23 Han Solo R 5.00 10.00
❑ 24 Heavy Stormtrooper U .60 1.50
❑ 25 Hoth Trooper C .30 .75
❑ 26 IG-88 R 5.00 10.00
❑ 27 Imperial Officer U .60 1.50
❑ 28 Ithorian Scout U .60 1.50
❑ 29 Jabba the Hutt VR 12.50 25.00
❑ 30 Jawa C .30 .75
❑ 31 Lando Calrissian R 5.00 10.00
❑ 32 Luke Skywalker, Jedi Knight VR 18.00 30.00
❑ 33 Luke Skywalker, Rebel R 6.00 12.00
❑ 34 Mara Jade Emperor's Hand R 5.00 10.00
❑ 35 Mon Calamari Mercenary C .30 .75
❑ 36 Obi-Wan Kenobi VR 12.50 25.00
❑ 37 Princess Leia, Captive VR 12.50 25.00
❑ 38 Princess Leia, Senator R 6.00 12.00
❑ 39 Probe Droid VR 10.00 20.00
❑ 40 Quarren Assassin U .60 1.50
❑ 41 R2-D2 R 6.00 12.00
❑ 42 Rebel Commando U .60 1.50
❑ 43 Rebel Officer U .60 1.50
❑ 44 Rebel Pilot C .30 .75
❑ 45 Rebel Trooper C .30 .75
❑ 46 Rebel Trooper C .30 .75
❑ 47 Royal Guard U .60 1.50
❑ 48 Sandtrooper on Dewback VR 10.00 20.00
❑ 49 Scout Trooper on Bike VR 10.00 20.00
❑ 50 Scout Trooper U .60 1.50
❑ 51 Snowtrooper C .30 .75
❑ 52 Stormtrooper C .30 .75
❑ 53 Stormtrooper C .30 .75
❑ 54 Stormtrooper C .30 .75
❑ 55 Stormtrooper Officer U .60 1.50
❑ 56 Tusken Raider C .30 .75
❑ 57 Twi'lek Bodyguard U .60 1.50
❑ 58 Twi'lek Scoundrel C .30 .75
❑ 59 Wampa VR 10.00 20.00
❑ 60 Wookiee Soldier C .30 .75

2005 Star Wars Bounty Hunters Miniatures

❑ 1 4-LOM, Bounty Hunter R 6.00 12.00
❑ 2 Aqualish Assassin C .30 .75
❑ 3 Ayy Vida R 6.00 12.00
❑ 4 Basilisk War Droid U .60 1.50
❑ 5 Bib Fortuna R 6.00 12.00
❑ 6 Bith Black Sun Vigo U .60 1.50
❑ 7 Boba Fett, Bounty Hunter VR 15.00 40.00
❑ 8 BoShek R 6.00 12.00
❑ 9 Bossk, Bounty Hunter R 7.50 15.00
❑ 10 Boushh R 6.00 12.00
❑ 11 Calo Nord R 6.00 12.00
❑ 12 Chewbacca w/C-3PO VR 10.00 18.00
❑ 13 Commerce Guild Homing Spider Droid U .60 1.50
❑ 14 Corellian Pirate U .60 1.50
❑ 15 Corporate Alliance Tank Droid U .60 1.50
❑ 16 Dannik Jerriko VR 7.50 15.00
❑ 17 Dark Hellion Marauder on Swoop Bike U .60 1.50
❑ 18 Dark Hellion Swoop Gang Member C .30 .75
❑ 19 Defel Spy C .30 .75
❑ 20 Dengar, Bounty Hunter R 7.50 15.00
❑ 21 Djas Puhr R 6.00 12.00
❑ 22 Droid Starfighter in Walking Mode R 7.50 15.00
❑ 23 E522 Assassin Droid U .60 1.50
❑ 24 Gamorrean Thug C .30 .75
❑ 25 Garindan R 6.00 12.00
❑ 26 Han Solo, Scoundrel VR 7.50 15.00
❑ 27 Huge Crab Droid U .60 1.50
❑ 28 Human Blaster-for-Hire C .30 .75
❑ 29 IG-88, Bounty Hunter VR 15.00 25.00
❑ 30 ISP Speeder R 6.00 12.00
❑ 31 Jango Fett, Bounty Hunter VR 15.00 30.00
❑ 32 Klatooinian Hunter C .30 .75
❑ 33 Komari Vosa R 7.50 15.00
❑ 34 Lord Vader VR 10.00 20.00
❑ 35 Luke Skywalker of Dagobah R 7.50 15.00
❑ 36 Mandalore the Indomitable VR 12.50 25.00
❑ 37 Mandalorian Blademaster U .60 1.50
❑ 38 Mandalorian Commander U .60 1.50
❑ 39 Mandalorian Soldier C .30 .75
❑ 40 Mandalorian Supercommando C .30 .75
❑ 41 Mandalorian Warrior C .30 .75
❑ 42 Mistryl Shadow Guard U .60 1.50
❑ 43 Mustafarian Flea Rider R 6.00 12.00
❑ 44 Mustafarian Soldier C .30 .75
❑ 45 Nikto Gunner on Desert Skiff VR 10.00 20.00
❑ 46 Nym VR 7.50 15.00
❑ 47 Princess Leia, Hoth Commander R 7.50 15.00
❑ 48 Quarren Bounty Hunter C .30 .75
❑ 49 Rebel Captain U .60 1.50
❑ 50 Rebel Heavy Trooper U .60 1.50
❑ 51 Rebel Snowspeeder U .60 1.50
❑ 52 Rodian Hunt Master U .60 1.50
❑ 53 Talon Karrde VR 7.50 15.00
❑ 54 Tamtel Skreej VR 7.50 15.00
❑ 55 Tusken Raider Sniper C .30 .75
❑ 56 Utapaun on Dactillion VR 7.50 15.00
❑ 57 Weequay Leader U .60 1.50
❑ 58 Weequay Thug C .30 .75
❑ 59 Young Krayt Dragon VR 10.00 20.00
❑ 60 Zuckuss R 7.50 15.00

2005 Star Wars Revenge of the Sith Miniatures

❑ 1 49 Nautolan Soldier C .30 .75
❑ 2 Agen Kolar, Jedi Master R 6.00 12.00
❑ 3 Alderaan Trooper U .75 1.50
❑ 4 Anakin Skywalker, Jedi Knight R 6.00 12.00
❑ 5 Anakin Skywalker Sith Apprentice VR 15.00 25.00
❑ 6 AT-RT VR 15.00 25.00
❑ 7 Bail Organa VR 10.00 20.00
❑ 8 Battle Droid C .30 .75
❑ 9 Battle Droid C .30 .75
❑ 10 Boba Fett, Young Mercenary R 6.00 12.00
❑ 11 Bodyguard Droid U .75 1.50
❑ 12 Bodyguard Droid U .75 1.50
❑ 13 Captain Antilles R 6.00 12.00
❑ 14 Chagrian Mercenary Commander U .75 1.50
❑ 15 Chewbacca of Kashyyk VR 15.00 25.00
❑ 16 Clone Trooper C .30 .75
❑ 17 Clone Trooper C .30 .75
❑ 18 Clone Trooper Commander U .75 1.50
❑ 19 Clone Trooper Gunner C .30 .75
❑ 20 Dark Side Adept U .75 1.50
❑ 21 Darth Tyranus R 6.00 12.00
❑ 22 Darth Vader VR 18.00 30.00
❑ 23 Destroyer Droid R 6.00 12.00
❑ 24 Devaronian Soldier C .30 .75
❑ 25 Emperor Palpatine, Sith Lord VR 18.00 30.00
❑ 26 General Grievous, Jedi Hunter VR 18.00 30.00
❑ 27 General Grievous, Supreme Commander R 6.00 12.00
❑ 28 Gotal Fringer U .75 1.50
❑ 29 Grievous Wheel Bike VR 15.00 25.00
❑ 30 Human Mercenary U .75 1.50
❑ 31 Ikotchi Tech Specialist U .75 1.50
❑ 32 Jedi Knight U .75 1.50
❑ 33 Mace Windu, Jedi Master VR 18.00 30.00
❑ 34 Medical Droid R 6.00 12.00
❑ 35 Mon Mothma VR 10.00 20.00
❑ 36 Muun Guard U .75 1.50
❑ 37 Neimoidian Soldier U .75 1.50
❑ 38 Neimoidian Soldier U .75 1.50
❑ 39 Obi-Wan Kenobi, Jedi Master R 6.00 12.00
❑ 40 Polis Massa Medic C .30 .75
❑ 41 R2-D2, Astromech Droid VR 15.00 25.00
❑ 42 Royal Guard U .75 1.50
❑ 43 San Hill R 6.00 12.00
❑ 44 Senate Guard U .75 1.50
❑ 45 Separatist Commando C .30 .75
❑ 46 Shaak Ti R 6.00 12.00
❑ 47 Sly Moore R 6.00 12.00
❑ 48 Stass Allie R 6.00 12.00
❑ 49 Super Battle Droid C .30 .75
❑ 50 Super Battle Droid C .30 .75
❑ 51 Tarfful R 6.00 12.00
❑ 52 Tion Medon R 6.00 12.00
❑ 53 Utapaun Soldier C .30 .75
❑ 54 Utapaun Soldier C .30 .75
❑ 55 Utapaun Soldier C .30 .75
❑ 56 Wat Tambor R 6.00 12.00
❑ 57 Wookiee Berserker C .30 .75
❑ 58 Wookiee Scout U .75 1.50
❑ 59 Yoda, Jedi Master R 7.50 15.00
❑ 60 Yuzzem C .30 .75
❑ 61 Zabrak Fringer C .30 .75

2005 Star Wars Universe Miniatures

❑ 1 Abyssin Black Sun Thug C .30 .75
❑ 2 Acklay U .75 1.50
❑ 3 Admiral Ackbar VR 10.00 20.00
❑ 4 ASP-7 U .75 1.50
❑ 5 AT-ST R 7.50 15.00
❑ 6 B'omarr Monk R 7.50 15.00
❑ 7 Baron Fel VR 18.00 30.00
❑ 8 Battle Droid U .75 1.50
❑ 9 Battle Droid U .75 1.50
❑ 10 Bith Rebel C .30 .75
❑ 11 Chewbacca, Rebel Hero R 7.50 15.00
❑ 12 Clone Trooper C .30 .75
❑ 13 Clone Trooper on BARC Speeder R 10.00 20.00
❑ 14 Dark Side Marauder U .75 1.50
❑ 15 Dark Trooper Phase III U .75 1.50
❑ 16 Darth Maul on Speeder VR 12.50 25.00
❑ 17 Darth Vader, Jedi Hunter R 7.50 15.00
❑ 18 Dash Rendar R 7.50 15.00
❑ 19 Dr. Evazan VR 10.00 20.00
❑ 20 Dressellian Commando C .30 .75
❑ 21 Elite Clone Trooper U .75 1.50
❑ 22 Flash Speeder U .75 1.50
❑ 23 Gonk Power Droid C .30 .75
❑ 24 Grand Admiral Thrawn VR 18.00 30.00
❑ 25 Guri R 7.50 15.00
❑ 26 Hailfire Droid U .75 1.50
❑ 27 Han Solo, Rebel Hero R 7.50 15.00
❑ 28 Kaminoan Ascetic C .30 .75
❑ 29 Kyle Katarn VR 10.00 20.00
❑ 30 Lando Calrissian, Hero of Taanab R 7.50 15.00
❑ 31 Lobot R 6.00 12.00
❑ 32 Luke Skywalker on Tauntaun R 10.00 20.00
❑ 33 Luke Skywalker, Jedi Master VR 18.00 30.00
❑ 34 New Republic Commander U .75 1.50
❑ 35 New Republic Trooper C .30 .75
❑ 36 Nexu U .75 1.50
❑ 37 Nien Nunb R 6.00 12.00
❑ 38 Nightsister Sith Witch U .75 1.50
❑ 39 Noghri U .75 1.50
❑ 40 Nom Anor R 7.50 15.00
❑ 41 Nute Gunray R 6.00 12.00
❑ 42 Obi-Wan on Boga VR 12.50 25.00
❑ 43 Ponda Baba R 6.00 12.00
❑ 44 Prince Xizor VR 10.00 20.00
❑ 45 Princess Leia, Rebel Hero VR 10.00 20.00
❑ 46 Rancor VR 20.00 35.00
❑ 47 Reek U .75 1.50
❑ 48 Rodian Black Sun Vigo U .75 1.50
❑ 49 Shistavanen Pilot U .75 1.50
❑ 50 Stormtrooper C .30 .75
❑ 51 Stormtrooper Commander U .75 1.50
❑ 52 Super Battle Droid C .30 .75
❑ 53 Super Battle Droid Commander U .75 1.50
❑ 54 Tusken Raider on Bantha U .75 1.50
❑ 55 Vornskr C .30 .75
❑ 56 Warmaster Tsavong Lah VR 15.00 25.00
❑ 57 Wedge Antilles R 7.50 15.00
❑ 58 X-1 Viper Droid U .75 1.50
❑ 59 Young Jedi Knight C .30 .75
❑ 60 Yuuzhan Vong Subaltern U .75 1.50
❑ 61 Yuuzhan Vong Warrior C .30 .75

2006 Star Wars Champions of the Force Miniatures

❑ 1 Arcona Smuggler C .30 .75
❑ 2 Barriss Offee R 6.00 12.00
❑ 3 Bastila Shan VR 10.00 20.00
❑ 5 Clone Commander Bacara R 6.00 12.00
❑ 6 Clone Commander Cody R 7.50 15.00
❑ 7 Clone Commander Gree R 6.00 12.00
❑ 8 Corran Horn R 6.00 12.00
❑ 9 Coruscant Guard C .30 .75
❑ 10 Crab Droid U .60 1.50
❑ 11 Dark Jedi U .60 1.50
❑ 12 Dark Jedi Master U .60 1.50
❑ 13 Dark Side Enforcer U .60 1.50
❑ 14 Dark Trooper Phase I C .30 .75
❑ 15 Dark Trooper Phase II U .60 1.50
❑ 16 Dark Trooper Phase II VR 10.00 20.00
❑ 17 Darth Bane VR 12.50 25.00
❑ 18 Darth Malak VR 12.50 25.00
❑ 19 Darth Maul, Champion of the Sith R 7.50 15.00
❑ 20 Darth Nihilus VR 10.00 20.00
❑ 21 Darth Sidious, Dark Lord of the Sith R 6.00 12.00
❑ 22 Depa Billaba R 6.00 12.00
❑ 23 Even Piell R 6.00 12.00
❑ 24 Exar Kun VR 12.50 25.00
❑ 25 General Windu R 6.00 12.00
❑ 26 Gundark Fringe U .60 1.50
❑ 27 HK-47 VR 10.00 20.00
❑ 28 Hoth Trooper with Atgar Cannon R 6.00 12.00
❑ 29 Jacen Solo VR 10.00 20.00
❑ 30 Jaina Solo VR 10.00 20.00
❑ 31 Jedi Consular U .60 1.50
❑ 32 Jedi Guardian U .60 1.50
❑ 33 Jedi Padawan U .60 1.50
❑ 34 Jedi Sentinel U .60 1.50
❑ 35 Jedi Weapon Master C .30 .75
❑ 36 Kashyyyk Trooper C .30 .75
❑ 37 Luke Skywalker, Young Jedi VR 12.50 25.00
❑ 38 Mas Amedda R 7.50 15.00
❑ 39 Massassi Sith Mutant U .60 1.50
❑ 41 Octuparra Droid R 6.00 12.00
❑ 42 Old Republic Commander U .60 1.50
❑ 43 Old Republic Trooper U .60 1.50
❑ 44 Old Republic Trooper C .30 .75
❑ 45 Queen Amidala R 6.00 12.00
❑ 46 Qui-Gon Jinn, Jedi Master R 7.50 15.00
❑ 47 R5 Astromech Droid C .30 .75
❑ 48 Republic Commando Boss U .60 1.50
❑ 49 Republic Commando Fixer C .30 .75
❑ 50 Republic Commando Scorch C .30 .75
❑ 51 Republic Commando Sev C .30 .75
❑ 52 Saleucami Trooper C .30 .75
❑ 53 Sandtrooper C .30 .75
❑ 54 Sith Assault Droid U .60 1.50
❑ 55 Sith Trooper C .30 .75
❑ 56 Sith Trooper C .30 .75
❑ 57 Sith Trooper Commander U .60 1.50
❑ 58 Snowtrooper with E-Web Blaster R 6.00 12.00
❑ 59 Ugnaught Demolitionist C .30 .75
❑ 60 Ulic Qel-Droma VR 7.50 15.00
❑ 61 Utapau Trooper C .30 .75
❑ 62 Varactyl Wrangler C .30 .75
❑ 63 Yoda of Dagobah VR 12.50 25.00

2007 Star Wars Alliance and Empire Miniatures

❑ 1 Admiral Piett R 5.00 10.00
❑ 2 Advance Agent, Officer U .60 1.50
❑ 3 Advance Scout C .30 .75
❑ 4 Aurra Sing, Jedi Hunter VR 10.00 20.00
❑ 5 Biggs Darklighter VR 7.50 15.00
❑ 6 Boba Fett, Enforcer VR 12.50 25.00
❑ 7 C-3PO and R2-D2 R 5.00 10.00
❑ 8 Chadra-Fan Pickpocket U .60 1.50
❑ 9 Chewbacca, Enraged Wookiee R 5.00 10.00
❑ 10 Darth Vader, Imperial Commander VR 12.50 25.00
❑ 11 Death Star Gunner U .60 1.50
❑ 12 Death Star Trooper C .30 .75
❑ 13 Duros Explorer C .30 .75
❑ 14 Elite Hoth Trooper C .30 .75
❑ 15 Ephant Mon VR 7.50 15.00
❑ 16 Ewok Hang Glider R 5.00 10.00
❑ 17 Ewok Warrior C .30 .75
❑ 18 Gamorrean Guard C .30 .75
❑ 19 Han Solo in Stormtrooper Armor R 5.00 10.00
❑ 20 Han Solo on Tauntaun VR 10.00 20.00
❑ 21 Han Solo Rogue R 5.00 10.00
❑ 22 Heavy Stormtrooper U .60 1.50
❑ 23 Human Force Adept C .30 .75
❑ 24 Imperial Governor Tarkin R 5.00 10.00
❑ 25 Imperial Officer U .60 1.50
❑ 26 Ithorian Commander U .60 1.50
❑ 27 Jabba, Crime Lord VR 7.50 15.00
❑ 28 Jawa on Ronto VR 7.50 15.00
❑ 29 Jawa Trader U .60 1.50
❑ 30 Lando Calrissian, Dashing Scoundrel R 5.00 10.00
❑ 31 Luke Skywalker, Champion of the Force VR 12.50 25.00
❑ 32 Luke Skywalker, Hero of Yavin R 5.00 10.00
❑ 33 Luke's Landspeeder VR 7.50 15.00
❑ 34 Mara Jade, Jedi R 5.00 10.00
❑ 35 Mon Calamari Tech Specialist C .30 .75
❑ 36 Nikto Soldier C .30 .75
❑ 37 Obi-Wan Kenobi, Force Spirit VR 7.50 15.00
❑ 38 Princess Leia R 5.00 10.00
❑ 39 Quinlan Vos, Infiltrator VR 10.00 20.00
❑ 40 Rampaging Wampa VR 7.50 15.00
❑ 41 Rebel Commando C .30 .75
❑ 42 Rebel Commando Strike Leader U .60 1.50
❑ 43 Rebel Leader U .60 1.50
❑ 44 Rebel Pilot C .30 .75
❑ 45 Rebel Trooper U .60 1.50
❑ 46 Rodian Scoundrel U .60 1.50
❑ 47 Scout Trooper U .60 1.50
❑ 48 Snivvian Fringer C .30 .75
❑ 49 Snowtrooper C .30 .75
❑ 50 Storm Commando R 5.00 10.00
❑ 51 Stormtrooper C .30 .75
❑ 52 Stormtrooper Officer U .60 1.50
❑ 53 Stormtrooper on Repulsor Sled VR 10.00 20.00
❑ 54 Talz Spy Fringe U .60 1.50
❑ 55 Trandoshan Mercenary U .60 1.50
❑ 56 Tusken Raider C .30 .75
❑ 57 Twi'lek Rebel Agent U .60 1.50
❑ 58 Wicket R 5.00 10.00
❑ 59 Wookiee Freedom Fighter C .30 .75
❑ 60 Yomin Carr R 6.00 12.00

2008 World of Warcraft Miniatures

❑ 1 Aleyah Dawnborn C 1.00 2.00
❑ 2 Amalar Ironhoof R 2.50 6.00
❑ 3 Amon Darkheart C 1.00 2.00
❑ 4 Archmage Arugal E 12.50 25.00
❑ 5 Azarak Wolfsblood R 2.00 5.00
❑ 6 Bleakheart Hellcaller R 2.00 5.00
❑ 7 Blindlight Murloc C 1.00 2.00
❑ 8 Bloodscale Wavecaller R 2.00 5.00
❑ 9 Bog Elemental C 1.00 2.00
❑ 10 Boris Brightbeard C 1.00 2.00
❑ 11 Boulderfist Warrior C 1.00 2.00
❑ 12 Celenias Firemane C 1.00 2.00
❑ 13 Chen Stormstout R 2.50 6.00
❑ 14 Crushridge Ogre R 2.00 5.00
❑ 15 Daelas Firewing R 2.00 5.00
❑ 16 Delyn Darksun C 1.00 2.00
❑ 17 Dizdemona R 2.50 6.00
❑ 18 Dralor R 2.00 5.00
❑ 19 Elendril C 1.00 2.00
❑ 20 Enraged Fire Spirit R 2.50 6.00
❑ 21 Fillet Kneecapper Extraordinaire R 2.50 6.00
❑ 22 Frostmane Troll R 2.00 5.00
❑ 23 Frostsaber Prowler C 1.00 2.00
❑ 24 Goblin Shredder R 3.00 8.00
❑ 25 Gorebelly C 1.25 3.00
❑ 26 Graccus C 1.00 2.00
❑ 27 Grumpherys R 2.00 5.00
❑ 28 Haruka Skycaller R 3.00 8.00
❑ 29 Harvest Golem C 1.00 2.00
❑ 30 Helwen C 1.25 3.00
❑ 31 High Priestess Tyrande Whisperwind E 15.00 30.00
❑ 32 Highlord Bolvar Fordragon E 12.50 25.00
❑ 33 Irana R 2.50 6.00
❑ 34 Ji'lan C 1.00 2.00
❑ 35 Kayleitha C 1.00 2.00
❑ 36 Leeroy Jenkins R 3.00 8.00
❑ 37 Litori Frostburn C 1.00 2.00
❑ 38 Loriai Risingmoon C 1.00 2.00
❑ 39 Lotherin C 1.00 2.50
❑ 40 Magistrix Kiala R 2.50 6.00
❑ 41 Marsh Murloc R 2.50 6.00
❑ 42 Mojo Mender Ja'nah C 1.00 2.00
❑ 43 Mojo Shaper Ojo'mon C 1.00 2.00
❑ 44 Moonshadow C 1.00 2.50
❑ 45 Morganis Blackvein C 1.00 2.00
❑ 46 Namrah R 3.00 8.00
❑ 47 Nathressa Darkstrider R 3.00 8.00
❑ 48 Omedus the Punisher R 2.00 5.00
❑ 49 Ona Skyshot R 2.50 6.00
❑ 50 Phadalus the Enlightened C 1.00 2.00
❑ 51 Radak Doombringer C 1.00 2.00
❑ 52 Ras Frostwhisper E 12.50 25.00
❑ 53 Rethilgore C 1.00 2.00
❑ 54 Roria R 2.00 5.00
❑ 55 Ruby Gemsparkle C 1.00 2.50
❑ 56 Sarmoth C 1.25 3.00
❑ 57 Savin Lightguard R 2.50 6.00
❑ 58 Skeletal Priest R 3.00 8.00
❑ 59 Slitherblade Tidehunter C 1.00 2.00

2009 World of Warcraft Spoils of War Miniatures

❑ 1 Anchorite Cristia R 2.00 5.00
❑ 2 Beren Embersbane C 1.00 2.00
❑ 3 Bogstrok Razorclaw R 2.00 5.00
❑ 4 Cairne Bloodhoof E 15.00 30.00
❑ 5 Champion Shadowsun R 2.00 5.00
❑ 6 Chancellor Velora C 1.00 2.00
❑ 7 Conqueror Aluna R 2.00 5.00
❑ 8 Crashing Wave-Spirit C 1.00 2.00
❑ 9 Dagg'um Ty'gor R 2.00 5.00
❑ 10 Daspien Bladedancer R 2.00 5.00
❑ 11 Daxin Firesworn C 1.00 2.00
❑ 12 Deathwhisperer R 2.00 5.00
❑ 13 Drokkar of the Four Boars C 1.00 2.00
❑ 14 Elanna Starbreeze C 1.00 2.00
❑ 15 Elizabetha Cairnwillow R 2.00 5.00
❑ 16 Ethereal Crypt Raider C 1.00 2.00
❑ 17 Ethereal Priest C 1.00 2.00
❑ 18 Felguard Legionnaire C 1.00 2.00
❑ 19 Grimdron R 2.00 5.00
❑ 20 Harnum Firebelly C 1.00 2.00
❑ 21 Hulok Trailblazer C 1.00 2.00
❑ 22 Illiana Sunshield R 2.50 6.00
❑ 23 Ironfur Bear C 1.00 2.00
❑ 24 Ixamos the Redeemed R 2.50 6.00
❑ 25 Lady Jaina Proudmoore E 12.50 25.00
❑ 26 Lady Vashj E 20.00 40.00
❑ 27 Magdeline Prideheart R 2.00 5.00
❑ 28 Magistrix Enaria R 2.00 5.00
❑ 29 Marlowe Christophers C 1.00 2.00
❑ 30 Morova of the Sands R 2.50 6.00
❑ 31 Najan Spiritbinder C 1.00 2.00
❑ 32 Parvink R 2.00 5.00
❑ 33 Prince Kael'thas Sunstrider E 12.50 25.00
❑ 34 Prophet Velen E 12.50 25.00
❑ 35 Razaani Nexus Stalker R 2.00 5.00
❑ 36 Rexxar E 12.50 25.00
❑ 37 Ryno the Short R 3.00 8.00
❑ 38 Sethekk Talon Lord C 1.00 2.00
❑ 39 Sha'do R 2.00 5.00
❑ 40 Shienor Sorcerer R 2.00 5.00
❑ 41 Sidian Morningblade C 1.00 2.00

MODERN ERA NON-SPORTS

HOW TO USE

What's Listed

Products listed in the Price Guide typically: 1) are produced by licensed manufacturers, 2) are widely available and 3) have market activity on single items.

What the Columns Mean

The LO and HI columns reflect current retail selling ranges. The HI column on the right generally represents the full retail selling price. The LO column on the left generally represents the lowest price one would expect to find with extensive shopping.

Grading

All cards in the Price Guide are based on NrMint to Mint condition. Damaged cards are generally sold for 25 to 75 percent of Mint value. Toy prices are based on mint condition. Toys that are loose (out of package), are generally sold for 50 percent of the listed price.

Currency

This Price Guide is intended to reflect the entire North American market. All listed prices are in U.S. dollars.

1975 Comic Book Heroes Stickers

Card	LO	HI
COMPLETE SET (41)	25.00	50.00
COMMON CARD (1-41)	.60	1.50
❑ 1 Black Widow	.60	1.50
❑ 2 Captain America 1	.60	1.50
❑ 3 Captain America 2	.60	1.50
❑ 4A Captain Marvel (Which Way to the John?)	.60	1.50
❑ 4B Captain Marvel (Fly the Friendly Skys of United!)	.60	1.50
❑ 5 Checklist	.60	1.50
❑ 6 Conan	.60	1.50
❑ 7 Daredevil	.60	1.50
❑ 8 Dr. Doom	.60	1.50
❑ 9 Dr. Octopus	.60	1.50
❑ 10 Dr. Strange	.60	1.50
❑ 11 Dracula 1	.60	1.50
❑ 12 Dracula 2	.60	1.50
❑ 13 Frankenstein's Monster	.60	1.50
❑ 14 Ghost Rider	.60	1.50
❑ 15 Hawkeye	.60	1.50
❑ 16 Hulk 1	.60	1.50
❑ 17 Hulk 2	.60	1.50
❑ 18 Human Torch 1	.60	1.50
❑ 19 Human Torch 2	.60	1.50
❑ 20 Iron Fist	.60	1.50
❑ 21 Iron Man	.60	1.50
❑ 22 Ka Zar	.60	1.50
❑ 23 Kull	.60	1.50
❑ 24 Luke Cage	.60	1.50
❑ 25 Man Thing	.60	1.50
❑ 26 Medusa	.60	1.50
❑ 27 Morbius Living Vampire	.60	1.50
❑ 28 Mr. Fantastic	.60	1.50
❑ 29 Shang Li Kung Fu	.60	1.50
❑ 30 Spiderman 1	.60	1.50
❑ 31A Spiderman 2 (Bug Off!)	.60	1.50
❑ 31B Spiderman 2 (You Drive Me Up a Wall!)	.60	1.50
❑ 32 Sub Mariner	.60	1.50
❑ 33 The Falcon	.60	1.50
❑ 34 The Living Mummy	.60	1.50
❑ 35 The Son of Satan	.60	1.50
❑ 36 The Thing 1	.60	1.50
❑ 37 The Thing 2	.60	1.50
❑ 38 The Valkyrie	.60	1.50
❑ 39 Thor 1	.60	1.50
❑ 40 Thor 2	.60	1.50
❑ 41 Werewolf	.60	1.50
❑ CL1 Checklist Puzzle Top Left Corner	.75	2.00
❑ CL2 Checklist Puzzle Top Center	.75	2.00
❑ CL3 Checklist Puzzle Top Right Corner	.75	2.00
❑ CL4 Checklist Puzzle Middle Left	.75	2.00
❑ CL5 Checklist Puzzle Middle Center	.75	2.00
❑ CL6 Checklist Puzzle Middle Right	.75	2.00
❑ CL7A Checklist Puzzle Bottom Left Corner (w/Copyright)	.75	2.00
❑ CL7B Checklist Puzzle Bottom Left Corner (w/o Copyright)	.75	2.00
❑ CL8 Checklist Puzzle Bottom Center	.75	2.00
❑ CL9A Checklist Puzzle Bottom Right Corner (w/Copyright)	.75	2.00
❑ CL9B Checklist Puzzle Bottom Right Corner (w/o Copyright)	.75	2.00

1976 Marvel Super Heroes Stickers

Card	LO	HI
COMPLETE SET (46)	25.00	50.00
COMPLETE CL SET (9)	3.00	8.00
❑ 1 Black Goliath	.60	1.50
❑ 2 Blade	.60	1.50
❑ 3 Bucky	.60	1.50
❑ 4 Captain America	.60	1.50
❑ 5 Conan Hold the Pickle Or Else!	.60	1.50
❑ 6 Conan Shall We Dance?	.60	1.50
❑ 7 Cyclops	.60	1.50
❑ 8 Daredevil	.60	1.50
❑ 9 Deathlok	.60	1.50
❑ 10 Dr. Doom	.60	1.50
❑ 11 Dr. Strange	.60	1.50
❑ 12 Dracula	.60	1.50
❑ 13 Galactus	.60	1.50
❑ 14 Goliath	.60	1.50
❑ 15 Hercules Like My Nail Polish?	.60	1.50
❑ 16 Hercules Look, I Have a Hang Nail!	.60	1.50
❑ 17 Howard the Duck	.60	1.50
❑ 18 Ice Man	.60	1.50
❑ 19 Invisible Girl	.60	1.50
❑ 20 Iron Man	.60	1.50
❑ 21 Kid Colt	.60	1.50
❑ 22 Killraven	.60	1.50
❑ 23 Loki What an Awful Case of Ear Wax!	.60	1.50
❑ 24 Loki Who Says I'm Bull-Headed?	.60	1.50
❑ 25 Luke Cage Like My Denture Work?	.60	1.50
❑ 26 Luke Cage Two All Beef Patties Please	.60	1.50
❑ 27 Peter Parker	.60	1.50
❑ 28 Red Skull	.60	1.50
❑ 29 Red Sonja	.60	1.50
❑ 30 Sgt. Fury	.60	1.50
❑ 31 Silver Surfer	.60	1.50
❑ 32 Son of Satan	.60	1.50
❑ 33 Spider-Man	.60	1.50
❑ 34 The Angel	.60	1.50
❑ 35 The Hulk Can Anyone Make Cuffs Right?	.60	1.50
❑ 36 The Hulk Help Cure Athlete's Feet	.60	1.50
❑ 37 The Human Torch	.60	1.50
❑ 38 The Punisher	.60	1.50
❑ 39 The Thing	.60	1.50
❑ 40 The Vision	.60	1.50
❑ 41 The Watcher	.60	1.50
❑ 42 Thor	.60	1.50
❑ 43 Tigra	.60	1.50
❑ 44 Volstagg Fat is Beautiful!	.60	1.50
❑ 45 Volstagg I was a 980 Pound Weakling!	.60	1.50
❑ 46 Warlock	.60	1.50
❑ CL1 Checklist Puzzle Bottom Center	.40	1.00
❑ CL2 Checklist Puzzle Bottom Left	.40	1.00
❑ CL3 Checklist Puzzle Bottom Right	.40	1.00
❑ CL4 Checklist Puzzle Middle Center	.40	1.00
❑ CL5 Checklist Puzzle Middle Left	.40	1.00
❑ CL6 Checklist Puzzle Middle Right	.40	1.00
❑ CL7 Checklist Puzzle Top Center	.40	1.00
❑ CL8 Checklist Puzzle Top Left	.40	1.00
❑ CL9 Checklist Puzzle Top Right	.40	1.00

1976 Star Trek

Card	LO	HI
COMPLETE SET (88)	75.00	150.00
❑ 1 The U.S.S. Enterprise	1.50	4.00
❑ 2 Captain James T. Kirk	1.00	2.50
❑ 3 Dr. Bones McCoy	1.00	2.50
❑ 4 Science Officer Spock	1.00	2.50
❑ 5 Engineer Scott	1.00	2.50
❑ 6 Lieutenant Uhura	1.00	2.50
❑ 7 Ensign Chekov	1.00	2.50
❑ 8 The Phaser	1.00	2.50
❑ 9 The Shuttle Craft	1.00	2.50
❑ 10 Opponents	1.00	2.50
❑ 11 Energize	1.00	2.50
❑ 12 The Alien Mr. Spock	1.00	2.50
❑ 13 Men of the Enterprise	1.00	2.50
❑ 14 Story of Voyage One	1.00	2.50
❑ 15 Live Long and Prosper	1.00	2.50
❑ 16 View From the Bridge	1.00	2.50
❑ 17 Toward the Unknown	1.00	2.50
❑ 18 Enterprise Orbiting Earth	1.00	2.50
❑ 19 The Purple Barrier	1.00	2.50
❑ 20 Outwitting a God	1.00	2.50
❑ 21 Planet Delta Vega	1.00	2.50
❑ 22 Charlie's Law	1.00	2.50
❑ 23 Mysterious Cube	1.00	2.50
❑ 24 Dwarfed by the Enemy	1.00	2.50
❑ 25 Balok's Alter-Ego	1.00	2.50
❑ 26 Last of It's Kind	1.00	2.50
❑ 27 Frozen World	1.00	2.50
❑ 28 Spock Loses Control	1.00	2.50
❑ 29 The Naked Time	1.00	2.50
❑ 30 The Demon Within	1.00	2.50
❑ 31 My Enemy My Self	1.00	2.50
❑ 32 Monster Android	1.00	2.50
❑ 33 Korby's Folly	1.00	2.50
❑ 34 The Duplicate Man	1.00	2.50
❑ 35 Balance of Terror	1.00	2.50
❑ 36 Attacked by Spores	1.00	2.50
❑ 37 Spock Unwinds	1.00	2.50
❑ 38 Duel at Gothos	1.00	2.50
❑ 39 Timeship at Lazarus	1.00	2.50
❑ 40 Dagger of the Mind	1.00	2.50
❑ 41 The Lawgivers	1.00	2.50
❑ 42 Hunting the Tunnel Monster	1.00	2.50
❑ 43 Battling the Horta	1.00	2.50
❑ 44 Strange Communication	1.00	2.50
❑ 45 A Startling Discovery	1.00	2.50
❑ 46 McCoy Insane	1.00	2.50
❑ 47 The Guardian of Forever	1.00	2.50
❑ 48 Visit to a Hostile City	1.00	2.50
❑ 49 Mystery at Star Base	1.00	2.50
❑ 50 Fate of Captain Pike	1.00	2.50
❑ 51 The Talosians	1.00	2.50
❑ 52 Ordeal of Rigel Seven	1.00	2.50
❑ 53 Capturing the Keeper	1.00	2.50
❑ 54 Blasted by the Enemy	1.00	2.50
❑ 55 Trapped by the Lizard Creature	1.00	2.50
❑ 56 The Gorn Strikes	1.00	2.50
❑ 57 Earthman's Triumph	1.00	2.50
❑ 58 Specimen Unknown	1.00	2.50
❑ 59 Mirror, Mirror	1.00	2.50
❑ 60 Spock's Wedding	1.00	2.50
❑ 61 Strangled by Mr. Spock	1.00	2.50
❑ 62 Grasp of the Gods	1.00	2.50
❑ 63 The Monster Called Nomad	1.00	2.50
❑ 64 The Companion	1.00	2.50
❑ 65 Journey to Babel	1.00	2.50
❑ 66 Death Ship	1.00	2.50
❑ 67 The Tholian Web	1.00	2.50
❑ 68 The Architects of Pain	1.00	2.50
❑ 69 The Mugato	1.00	2.50
❑ 70 The Deadly Years	1.00	2.50
❑ 71 Ancient Rome Revisited	1.00	2.50
❑ 72 The Melkotian	1.00	2.50
❑ 73 The Vulcan Mind Meld	1.00	2.50
❑ 74 Possessed by Zargon	1.00	2.50
❑ 75 Creation of a Humanoid	1.00	2.50
❑ 76 Captured by Romulans	1.00	2.50
❑ 77 A War of Worlds	1.00	2.50
❑ 78 Space of Brains	1.00	2.50
❑ 79 I Yarneg	1.00	2.50
❑ 80 Death in a Single Cell	1.00	2.50
❑ 81 The Uninvited	1.00	2.50
❑ 82 The Lights of Zetar	1.00	2.50
❑ 83 Invaded by Alien Energy	1.00	2.50
❑ 84 Kirk's Deadliest Foe	1.00	2.50
❑ 85 The Trouble with Tribbles	1.00	2.50
❑ 86 The Nazi Planet	1.00	2.50
❑ 87 The Starship Eater	1.00	2.50
❑ 88 Star Trek Lives	1.50	4.00

1976 Star Trek Stickers

Card	LO	HI
COMPLETE SET (22)	50.00	100.00
❑ 1 James Kirk	3.00	8.00
❑ 2 Mr. Spock-- Unearthly!	2.50	6.00
❑ 3 Spock of Vulcan	2.50	6.00
❑ 4 Dr. Bones Mccoy	2.50	6.00
❑ 5 Engineer Scott	2.50	6.00
❑ 6 Lieutenant Uhura	2.50	6.00
❑ 7 Ensign Chekov	2.50	6.00
❑ 8 The Starship Enterprise	2.50	6.00
❑ 9 Kirk Beaming Up!	2.50	6.00
❑ 10 Star Trek Lives!	2.50	6.00
❑ 11 Highly Illogical!	2.50	6.00
❑ 12 The Keeper	2.50	6.00
❑ 13 Commander Balok	2.50	6.00
❑ 14 The Mugato	2.50	6.00
❑ 15 Lal, the Interrogator	2.50	6.00
❑ 16 The Parallel Spock	2.50	6.00
❑ 17 Ambassador Gav	2.50	6.00
❑ 18 Alien Possession!	2.50	6.00
❑ 19 Spock Lives!	2.50	6.00
❑ 20 Evil Klingon Kang	2.50	6.00
❑ 21 Spock Forever!	2.50	6.00
❑ 22 The Romulan Vessel	2.50	6.00

1978 Battlestar Galactica

Card	LO	HI
COMPLETE SET (132)	12.50	30.00
❑ 1 Lorne Greene Is Commander Adama	.15	.40
❑ 2 Dirk Benedict Is Lt. Starbuck	.15	.40
❑ 3 Richard Hatch Is Captain Apollo	.15	.40
❑ 4 Lew Ayres Is The Colony President	.15	.40
❑ 5 A Day Of Peace Or Betrayal	.15	.40
❑ 6 Preparing To Blast A Battlestar	.15	.40
❑ 7 For The Love Of Gold Cubits	.15	.40
❑ 8 Sneak Attack	.15	.40
❑ 9 President Adar Endangered	.15	.40
❑ 10 Blasting The Planet Caprica	.15	.40
❑ 11 A World In Flames	.15	.40
❑ 12 They're Bombing The City	.15	.40
❑ 13 Adar's Final Moments	.15	.40
❑ 14 The President's Council Destroyed	.15	.40
❑ 15 Panic In Caprica Mall	.15	.40
❑ 16 Doomsday On Caprica	.15	.40
❑ 17 Blasted By The Cylon Warships	.15	.40
❑ 18 Caught In The Middle Of A Star Battle	.15	.40
❑ 19 Annihilation Of The Human Colonies	.15	.40
❑ 20 The Cylon Centurions	.15	.40
❑ 21 The Imperious Leader	.15	.40
❑ 22 Fate Of The Traitor Baltar	.15	.40
❑ 23 Serina Survives The Onslaught	.15	.40
❑ 24 Leveling A Planet	.15	.40
❑ 25 The Escape Plan	.15	.40
❑ 26 Adama's Dream	.15	.40
❑ 27 The Colonial Battlestars	.15	.40
❑ 28 Charting The Exodus	.15	.40
❑ 29 Laurette Spang Is Cassiopea	.15	.40
❑ 30 Fleet Of Colonial Vipers	.15	.40
❑ 31 Adama	.15	.40
❑ 32 Galactica Under Fire	.15	.40
❑ 33 The Commander and His Daughter	.15	.40
❑ 34 Muffit 2	.15	.40
❑ 35 Boxey's New Daggit	.15	.40
❑ 36 Boosting Boxey's Morale	.15	.40
❑ 37 Destination: Earth	.15	.40
❑ 38 The Planet Carillon	.15	.40
❑ 39 Speeding Toward Carillon	.15	.40
❑ 40 Starbuck's Landram	.15	.40
❑ 41 The Big Bash On Carillon	.15	.40
❑ 42 Pig-Faced Tourist	.15	.40
❑ 43 Chamber Of The Imperious	.15	.40
❑ 44 At The Gambling Casino	.15	.40
❑ 45 Carillon A Nice Place To Visit	.15	.40
❑ 46 Intergalactic Gambler	.15	.40
❑ 47 Bizarre Wonderland	.15	.40
❑ 48 Boxey Attacked By Alien Creatures	.15	.40
❑ 49 The Ovion Insectoids	.15	.40
❑ 50 Ovion Guards Escort Boxey	.15	.40
❑ 51 Boxey And Muffit Are Reunited	.15	.40
❑ 52 Captured By Ovion Warriors	.15	.40
❑ 53 One Of Lotay's Musicians	.15	.40
❑ 54 Lotay	.15	.40
❑ 55 Coferring With Seetol	.15	.40
❑ 56 The Colonists and The Insectoids	.15	.40
❑ 57 Escape From Fiery Death	.15	.40
❑ 58 Bridge Of The Galactica	.15	.40
❑ 59 An Ovlon Warrior	.15	.40
❑ 60 Profile Of An Ovion	.15	.40
❑ 61 An Elaborate Party For The Colonists	.15	.40
❑ 62 The Space Supremes	.15	.40
❑ 63 Trio Of Tucanas	.15	.40
❑ 64 Where The Elite Meet	.15	.40
❑ 65 Jane Seymour Is Serina	.15	.40
❑ 66 Serina Arrives At The Carillon Bash	.15	.40
❑ 67 Maren Jensen Is Athena	.15	.40
❑ 68 Flamboyant Lovers	.15	.40
❑ 69 The War Of The Wiles	.15	.40
❑ 70 Hitting Outrageously High Notes	.15	.40
❑ 71 The Lord Of Galactica	.15	.40
❑ 72 Galacticans Discuss Their Dilemma	.15	.40
❑ 73 Lotay And Her Centurion Allies	.15	.40
❑ 74 Nourishment For Newborn Ovions	.15	.40
❑ 75 Brood Of The Insectoids	.15	.40
❑ 76 Starbuck And Boxey To The Rescue	.15	.40
❑ 77 Lt. Starbuck Posed For Action	.15	.40
❑ 78 Metallic Monster	.15	.40
❑ 79 Attack Of The Cyclons	.15	.40
❑ 80 Shoot-Out In The Ovion Catacombs	.15	.40
❑ 81 My Blaster Is Quick	.15	.40
❑ 82 Inside The Chosen Chamber	.15	.40
❑ 83 Creatures Of Destruction	.15	.40
❑ 84 A Narrow Escape	.15	.40
❑ 85 Covered by Lt. Boomer	.15	.40
❑ 86 The Human Exterminators	.15	.40
❑ 87 Army Of Evil	.15	.40
❑ 88 Destroying The Human Refuse	.15	.40
❑ 89 Unstoppable Invaders	.15	.40
❑ 90 Night Of The Metal Monsters	.15	.40
❑ 91 Clipped By A Laser Blast	.15	.40
❑ 92 Seetol's Fate	.15	.40
❑ 93 The Colonist's Counterattack	.15	.40
❑ 94 Don't Mess With Starbuck	.15	.40
❑ 95 Centurions On The March	.15	.40
❑ 96 The Cylon War Machine	.15	.40
❑ 97 The Destructors	.15	.40
❑ 98 Emissaries Of Hate	.15	.40
❑ 99 Attacking Our Heroes	.15	.40
❑ 100 Destroy The Human Vermin	.15	.40
❑ 101 A Planet In Peril	.15	.40
❑ 102 Fantastic Weapons Of The Cylons	.15	.40
❑ 103 Holding The Enemy At Bay	.15	.40
❑ 104 Man Of Destiny	.15	.40
❑ 105 Everything's A-Ok	.15	.40
❑ 106 Flight To Oblivion	.15	.40
❑ 107 Preparing The Colonial Ships	.15	.40
❑ 108 The Moment Of Truth	.15	.40
❑ 109 Colonial Star Pilots	.15	.40
❑ 110 Facing Incredible Odds	.15	.40
❑ 111 The Cylon Supreme Star Force	.15	.40
❑ 112 Blasted By The Enemy	.15	.40
❑ 113 The Destroying Ray	.15	.40

❑ 114 The Fate Of Humankind Before Them .15 .40
❑ 115 Cylon Warships Closing In .15 .40
❑ 116 A Direct Hit .15 .40
❑ 117 Athena On Galactica .15 .40
❑ 118 The Battlestar Quakes .15 .40
❑ 119 Monitoring The Battle .15 .40
❑ 120 Athena In Action .15 .40
❑ 121 Troubled Colonial Elder .15 .40
❑ 122 A Day Of Deliverance .15 .40
❑ 123 Landrams To The Rescue .15 .40
❑ 124 The Battle Is Ours .15 .40
❑ 125 Picking Up The Last Stranded Colonists .15 .40
❑ 126 The Odyssey Of Battlestar Galactica .15 .40
❑ 127 Stars Dirk Benedict .15 .40
Richard Hatch
❑ 128 Dirk Benedict Portrait Shot .15 .40
❑ 129 A Boy And His Err Daggit .15 .40
❑ 130 Self-Reliant Athena .15 .40
❑ 131 Lovely Jane Seymour Takes A Breather .15 .40
❑ 132 Photographing A Colonial Viper .15 .40

1978 Battlestar Galactica Stickers

COMPLETE SET (22) 3.00 8.00
❑ 1 Commander Adama .20 .50
❑ 2 Lt. Starbuck .20 .50
❑ 3 Captain Apollo .20 .50
❑ 4 Lt. Boomer .20 .50
❑ 5 Athena .20 .50
❑ 6 An Ovion Warrior .20 .50
❑ 7 The Imperious Leader .20 .50
❑ 8 Casino Patron .20 .50
❑ 9 President Adar .20 .50
❑ 10 Serina .20 .50
❑ 11 Android Sister .20 .50
❑ 12 Cylons On The March .20 .50
❑ 13 Carillon .20 .50
Survivor Of Carillon
❑ 14 Alien Warrior .20 .50
❑ 15 Cassiopea .20 .50
❑ 16 Cylon Centurion .20 .50
❑ 17 Dirk Benedict .20 .50
Starbuck
❑ 18 Galactican Warrior .20 .50
❑ 19 Boxey .20 .50
❑ 20 Space Warrior .20 .50
❑ 21 Galactican Elder .20 .50
❑ 22 Spirit Of Salvation .20 .50

1978 Superman The Movie

COMPLETE SET (165) 15.00 40.00
❑ 1 Christopher Reeve as The Man of Steel .15 .40
❑ 2 Christopher Reeve as Clark Kent .15 .40
❑ 3 Margot Kidder as Lois Lane .15 .40
❑ 4 Zooming Across The Sky .15 .40
❑ 5 Valerie Perrine as Eve .15 .40
❑ 6 Ned Beatty as Otis .15 .40
❑ 7 Jackie Cooper as Perry White .15 .40
❑ 8 Editor and Staff of the Daily Planet .15 .40
❑ 9 Susannah York as Lara .15 .40
❑ 10 Marc McClure as Jimmy Olsen .15 .40
❑ 11 Glenn Ford as Jonathan Kent .15 .40
❑ 12 The Majestic Planet Krypton .15 .40
❑ 13 Incredible Laboratory of Jor-El .15 .40
❑ 14 Lois Lane In a Jam .15 .40
❑ 15 A Study in Villainy .15 .40
❑ 16 Arch Criminals On Trial .15 .40
❑ 17 Briefing Military Police of Krypton .15 .40
❑ 18 A World Torn Asunder... .15 .40
❑ 19 The Spaceship Blasts Off .15 .40
❑ 20 Protector of the Peace .15 .40
❑ 21 The Might of Superman .15 .40
❑ 22 A Final Farewell from Lara .15 .40
❑ 23 the Death Throes of Planet Krypton .15 .40
❑ 24 Clark Kent, Ace Reporter .15 .40
❑ 25 Destruction of a World in Space .15 .40
❑ 26 Aerial Adventure .15 .40
❑ 27 Escape from Destruction .15 .40
❑ 28 Journey Across the Gulf of Space .15 .40
❑ 29 Superbaby arrives on Earth .15 .40
❑ 30 Observing Landing of a Spaceship .15 .40
❑ 31 Adopting a Space Child .15 .40
❑ 32 Young Clark Kent and his Foster Dad .15 .40
❑ 33 The Passing of Jonathan Kent .15 .40
❑ 34 The Youthful Lois Lane and her Parents .15 .40
❑ 35 Superman Makes the Headlines .15 .40
❑ 36 Paying a Call on Lois Lane .15 .40
❑ 37 Night Flight .15 .40
❑ 38 Flight Ov er Metropolis .15 .40
❑ 39 Perils of The Big City .15 .40
❑ 40 The Man Of Steel In Flight .15 .40
❑ 41 Panic In the Sky .15 .40
❑ 42 Amazing Strength of the Star Child .15 .40
❑ 43 Sole Survivor of Krypton .15 .40
❑ 44 Preparing to Leap Skyward .15 .40
❑ 45 Facing Incredible Odds .15 .40
❑ 46 Trial By Fire .15 .40
❑ 47 On the Trail of Lex Luthor .15 .40
❑ 48 The Icy Peril .15 .40
❑ 49 Ready for Action .15 .40
❑ 50 Heroic Stranger from the Stars .15 .40
❑ 51 The Amazing Man of Steel .15 .40
❑ 52 Interview with Superman .15 .40
❑ 53 The incredible Scoop of Lois Lane .15 .40
❑ 54 Superman Leaps Into Action .15 .40
❑ 55 Superman To The Rescue .15 .40
❑ 56 A Daring Rescue .15 .40
❑ 57 Lois Lane thanks Superman .15 .40
❑ 58 Rescued by the Man of Steel .15 .40
❑ 59 Superman .15 .40
❑ 60 Confronting the Arch-Criminal Lex Luthor .15 .40
❑ 61 Portrait of a Hero .15 .40
❑ 62 Protector of Truth and Justice .15 .40
❑ 63 All-American Hero .15 .40
❑ 64 First Appearance In the Comics .15 .40
❑ 65 Soaring Above The City .15 .40
❑ 66 Landing of the Spaceship .15 .40
❑ 67 Nefarious Plan of Lex Luthor .15 .40
❑ 68 The Scheme to Destroy Superman .15 .40
❑ 69 Marlon Brando as Jor-El .15 .40
❑ 70 Jor-El and Lara... Their Final Moments .15 .40
❑ 71 The Projection of Jor-El .15 .40
❑ 72 Doomsday On Krypton .15 .40
❑ 73 Life-Saving Spaceship of Jor-El .15 .40
❑ 74 The Infant Son of Jor-El .15 .40
❑ 75 Lex Luthor and Eve... Companions in Villainy.15 .40
❑ 76 Gene Hackman as Lex Luthor .15 .40
❑ 77 Conversing With The Elders .15 .40
❑ 78 Rushing to the Rescue .15 .40
❑ 79 Phyllis Thaxter plays Martha Kent .15 .40
❑ 80 Sunset in Smallville .15 .40
❑ 81 Fabulous Lair of Lex Luthor .15 .40
❑ 82 The Villains Discuss their Plan .15 .40
❑ 83 Christopher Reeve plays Superman .15 .40
❑ 84 A Razzled Lois Lane .15 .40
❑ 85 Inside the Fortress of Solitude .15 .40
❑ 86 A Low Moment for Clark Kent .15 .40
❑ 87 Ace Bumbler Otis .15 .40
❑ 88 The Dynamic Duo of Villainy .15 .40
❑ 89 Lovely Lois Lane .15 .40
❑ 90 Clinging to Life .15 .40
❑ 91 Clark Kent as a Young Man .15 .40
❑ 92 The Family of Jor-El on Krypton .15 .40
❑ 93 Superman in a Pensive Mood .15 .40
❑ 94 Sarah Douglas plays Ursa .15 .40
❑ 95 Eve's Part in the Lex Luthor Plan .15 .40
❑ 96 Clark Kent of the Daily Planet .15 .40
❑ 97 Director Richard Donner .15 .40
❑ 98 Christopher Reeve plays Clark Kent .15 .40
❑ 99 Accident On the Road .15 .40
❑ 100 Ned Beatty plays Otis .15 .40
❑ 101 Saved by the Man of Steel .15 .40
❑ 102 Marc McClure plays Jimmy Olsen .15 .40
❑ 103 Face Of Anger .15 .40
❑ 104 Farewell to Smallville .15 .40
❑ 105 Glenn Ford plays Jonathan Kent .15 .40
❑ 106 And Who, Disguised as Clark Kent . . . .15 .40
❑ 107 Superman Visits the Fortress of Solitude .15 .40
❑ 108 Maria Schell plays Vond-Ah .15 .40
❑ 109 Incredible Display of Strength .15 .40
❑ 110 Jack O'Halloran plays Non .15 .40
❑ 111 Spotting the Man of Steel .15 .40
❑ 112 Destruction of the Dam .15 .40
❑ 113 The Chamber of the Council of Elders .15 .40
❑ 114 Fleeing the Destruction of Krypton .15 .40
❑ 115 Superman In Metropolis .15 .40
❑ 116 The One-And-Only Lois Lane .15 .40
❑ 117 Jonathan Kent In Smallville .15 .40
❑ 118 Repairing the Twisted Train Rails .15 .40
❑ 119 Terence Stamp plays General Zod .15 .40
❑ 120 Mysterious Hunt for Lex Luthor .15 .40
❑ 121 The World's Most Diabolical Villain .15 .40
❑ 122 Lex Luthor wants YOU .15 .40
❑ 123 Time For a Quick Change .15 .40
❑ 124 200 Feet Below Grand Central Station .15 .40
❑ 125 Cub Reporter Jimmy Olsen .15 .40
❑ 126 Flight Around Metropolis .15 .40
❑ 127 Condemned to the Phantom Zone .15 .40
❑ 128 Eve Teschmacher : Dizzy, .15 .40
Devious and Delightful
❑ 129 Our Hero In Civilian Clothes .15 .40
❑ 130 Clark Kent Transforms Into Superman .15 .40
❑ 131 Jor-El in the Trial Chamber .15 .40
❑ 132 Jackie Cooper plays Perry White .15 .40
❑ 133 The Incredible Scheme Begins .15 .40
❑ 134 Eve and her Mentor, Lex Luthor .15 .40
❑ 135 John Barry, Master of Illusion .15 .40
❑ 136 Amazing Hearing Powers of Superman .15 .40
❑ 137 Ursa - Villainess Supreme .15 .40
❑ 138 Might of the Man of Steel .15 .40
❑ 139 Valerie Perrine plays Eve .15 .40
❑ 140 Lovers from Different Worlds .15 .40
❑ 141 Susannah York plays Lara .15 .40
❑ 142 Gene Hackman plays Lex Luthor .15 .40
❑ 143 Vond-Ah and Jor-El .15 .40
❑ 144 Valerie Perrine, featured as Eve .15 .40
❑ 145 The Farm of Jonathan Kent in Smallville .15 .40
❑ 146 The Stupendous Man of Steel .15 .40
❑ 147 Young Clark Kent and the Mysterious Crystal.15 .40
❑ 148 Superman Spots a Crime .15 .40
❑ 149 Can This Be the End of Lois Lane? .15 .40
❑ 150 Night Heist .15 .40
❑ 151 Flying Over the Dam .15 .40
❑ 152 The Movie Set for Krypton .15 .40
❑ 153 A Cowardly Blow from Behind .15 .40
❑ 154 Mission for a Bumbler .15 .40
❑ 155 Visitor from Another Planet .15 .40
❑ 156 Lex Luthor : Madman or Brilliant Scientist?.15 .40
❑ 157 Deceiving His Military Foes .15 .40
❑ 158 Soaring to New Heights .15 .40
❑ 159 'Copter Atop the Daily Planet .15 .40
❑ 160 Death of an Exotic World .15 .40
❑ 161 How did you know the exact .15 .40
contents of my purse
❑ 162 Threatened By a Mugger .15 .40
❑ 163 On His Way to the Lair of Lex Luthor .15 .40
❑ 164 The Objective of Lex Luthor .15 .40
❑ 165 Saving a Power Plant .15 .40

1979 Star Trek the Motion Picture

COMPLETE SET (88) 12.50 30.00
❑ 1 Star Trek the Motion Picture .15 .40
❑ 2 Toward the Unknown .15 .40
❑ 3 Space Intruder .15 .40
❑ 4 Fate of the Klingons .15 .40
❑ 5 Warning from Space .15 .40
❑ 6 Our Starcrafts Annihilated .15 .40
❑ 7 Enterprise in Drydock .15 .40
❑ 8 Rebuilding the Enterprise .15 .40
❑ 9 Filming Drydock Sequence .15 .40
❑ 10 James T. Kirk .15 .40
❑ 11 Captain Kirk's Mission .15 .40
❑ 12 Dr. Bones McCoy .15 .40
❑ 13 Executive Officer Decker .15 .40
❑ 14 Navigator Ilia .15 .40
❑ 15 Uhura .15 .40
❑ 16 Helmsman Sulu .15 .40
❑ 17 Engineer Scott .15 .40
❑ 18 Security Chief Chekov .15 .40
❑ 19 Dr. Christine Chapel .15 .40
❑ 20 Janice Rand .15 .40
❑ 21 The Vulcan Mr. Spock .15 .40
❑ 22 Spock on the Planet Vulcan .15 .40
❑ 23 The UFP Assembled .15 .40
❑ 24 Being from Beyond .15 .40
❑ 25 The Face of Terror .15 .40
❑ 26 Lizardlike Diplomat .15 .40
❑ 27 Not of this Earth .15 .40
❑ 28 Alien Insectoid .15 .40
❑ 29 The Unearthly .15 .40
❑ 30 The Andorians .15 .40
❑ 31 Advanced Life Form .15 .40
❑ 32 Betel's Attendant .15 .40
❑ 33 Andorian Close-Up .15 .40
❑ 34 The U.S.S. Enterprise .15 .40
❑ 35 Back in Operation .15 .40
❑ 36 Refurbished Starship .15 .40
❑ 37 Enterprise Rear View .15 .40
❑ 38 Return to the Bridge .15 .40
❑ 39 The Senior Officers .15 .40
❑ 40 View from the Bridge .15 .40
❑ 41 Scotty's Domain .15 .40
❑ 42 Fantastic New Devices .15 .40
❑ 43 The Engineering Deck .15 .40
❑ 44 Investigating a Malfunction .15 .40
❑ 45 Heart of the Starship .15 .40
❑ 46 Incredible Explosion .15 .40
❑ 47 Starship Under Attack .15 .40
❑ 48 Assault on Chekov .15 .40
❑ 49 Half Human .15 .40
❑ 50 Spock's Fight for Life .15 .40
❑ 51 Into the Nameless Void .15 .40
❑ 52 Terror in the Transporter Room .15 .40
❑ 53 The Surak Craft .15 .40
❑ 54 Transporter Malfunction .15 .40
❑ 55 Zero Gravity Adventure .15 .40
❑ 56 Symbol of Her People .15 .40
❑ 57 Exotically Beautiful Ilia .15 .40
❑ 58 Spock's Discovery .15 .40
❑ 59 The Phaser Battle .15 .40
❑ 60 Ilia in Sick Bay .15 .40
❑ 61 Stamina of the Alien .15 .40
❑ 62 Filming the Shuttlecraft .15 .40
❑ 63 Star Explorer .15 .40
❑ 64 Alien Menace .15 .40
❑ 65 Star Challengers .15 .40
❑ 66 Beam Me Down Scotty .15 .40
❑ 67 The Landing Party .15 .40
❑ 68 Portrait of a Vulcan .15 .40
❑ 69 Beyond Infinity .15 .40
❑ 70 The Encounter .15 .40
❑ 71 It's Secret Revealed .15 .40
❑ 72 On Spock's Native World .15 .40
❑ 73 Spectacular Starship .15 .40
❑ 74 Welcoming Dr. McCoy Aboard .15 .40
❑ 75 Kirk's Last Stand .15 .40
❑ 76 Landscape of Vulcan .15 .40
❑ 77 Klingon Warship Rearview .15 .40
❑ 78 The Final Frontiersman .15 .40
❑ 79 Klingon Warship .15 .40
❑ 80 Vulcan Starship Overhead View .15 .40
❑ 81 Pride of the Starfleet .15 .40
❑ 82 Janice Rand .15 .40
❑ 83 The Unearthly Mr. Spock .15 .40
❑ 84 Women from Planet Delta .15 .40
❑ 85 New Starfleet Uniforms .15 .40
❑ 86 Men With a Mission .15 .40
❑ 87 The Deltan Beauty .15 .40
❑ 88 Klingon Commander .15 .40

1979 Star Trek the Motion Picture Stickers

COMPLETE SET (22) 3.00 8.00
❑ 1 Engineer Scott .20 .50
❑ 2 Janice Rand .20 .50
❑ 3 On Spock's Native World .20 .50
❑ 4 Security Chief Chekov .20 .50
❑ 5 Navigator Ilia .20 .50
❑ 6 Helmsman Sulu .20 .50
❑ 7 Star Explorer .20 .50
❑ 8 Dr. Christine Chapel .20 .50
❑ 9 Portrait of a Vulcan .20 .50
❑ 10 Dr. Bones McCoy .20 .50
❑ 11 Uhura .20 .50
❑ 12 The Deltan Beauty .20 .50
❑ 13 The Face of Terror .20 .50
❑ 14 Being from Beyond .20 .50
❑ 15 Advanced Life Form .20 .50
❑ 16 Executive Officer Decker .20 .50
❑ 17 Betel's Attendant .20 .50
❑ 18 Lizardlike Diplomat .20 .50
❑ 19 Pride of the Starfleet .20 .50
❑ 20 Klingon Warship .20 .50
❑ 21 The Surak Craft .20 .50
❑ 22 Spectacular Starship .20 .50

1984 Star Trek III The Search for Spock

COMPLETE SET (60) 7.50 20.00
❑ 1 Wm. Shatner as Adm. James T. Kirk .15 .40
❑ 2 Leonard Nimoy as Cpt. Spock .15 .40
❑ 3 DeForest Kelley as Dr. Leonard McCoy .15 .40
❑ 4 James Doohan as Chief Eng. Montgomery Scott.15 .40
❑ 5 George Takei as Cpt. Hikaru Sulu .15 .40
❑ 6 Walter Koenig as Comm. Pavel Chekov .15 .40
❑ 7 Nichelle Nichols as Uhura .15 .40
❑ 8 Robin Curtis as Lt. Saavik .15 .40
❑ 9 Mark Lenard as Amb. Sarek .15 .40
❑ 10 Dame Judith Anderson as Vulcan .15 .40
High Priestess
❑ 11 Robert Hooks as Starfleet Comm. Morrow .15 .40
❑ 12 Christopher Lloyd as Klingon Comm. Kruge.15 .40
❑ 13 Kruge's Pet, Warrigul .15 .40
❑ 14 Enterprise Returning Home for Repairs .15 .40
❑ 15 Enterprise Next to Escelsior Spacedock .15 .40
❑ 16 Sarek Mind-Melds with Kirk .15 .40
❑ 17 Kirk Replaying Flight Records .15 .40
❑ 18 Kirk Reviewing Tape .15 .40
❑ 19 Morrow Tells Kirk the Bad News .15 .40
❑ 20 Conspirators in Conference .15 .40
❑ 21 Visiting Bones in Prison .15 .40
❑ 22 Liberating Bones from Prison .15 .40
❑ 23 Sabotaging Communication's Console .15 .40
❑ 24 Kirk and Crew Find Saavik and Spock .15 .40
❑ 25 Commander Chekov at the Helm .15 .40
❑ 26 Lt. Saavik and Dr. David Marcus .15 .40
❑ 27 Dr. Marcus Arrives on His Creation .15 .40
❑ 28 Locating Spock's Torpedo Tube Coffin .15 .40
❑ 29 Spock's Burial Robe, But No Body .15 .40
❑ 30 What Could Have Happened to Spock's Body?.15 .40
❑ 31 Tracing Spock? .15 .40
❑ 32 The Spock Child Lost in the Snow .15 .40
❑ 33 Rescuing the Spock Child .15 .40
❑ 34 Uncloaking Itself .15 .40
❑ 35 The Spock Child Resting .15 .40
❑ 36 Klingon Landing Party .15 .40
❑ 37 Kruge Subduing a Genesis Mutation .15 .40
❑ 38 Kruge Planning His Next Strategy .15 .40
❑ 39 Deadly Enemies .15 .40
❑ 40 Scotty and Chekov Worrying .15 .40
❑ 41 Young Spock in Agony .15 .40
❑ 42 Saavik Soothing Young Spock .15 .40
❑ 43 Spock, A Young Adult .15 .40
❑ 44 Which One Shall I Execute? .15 .40
❑ 45 David Attracts the Klingon's Fatal Hand .15 .40
❑ 46 Turning Certain Death .15 .40
❑ 47 Watching the Starship Enterprise .15 .40
❑ 48 Kruge in Rage After Kirk Outwits Him .15 .40
❑ 49 Kirk and Kruge Duel as Genesis Convulses .15 .40
❑ 50 Fighting on the Brink of Destruction .15 .40
❑ 51 The Death Throes of Genesis .15 .40
❑ 52 Kirk Bargaining for the Lives of His Crew .15 .40
❑ 53 Escaping the Exploding Genesis Planet .15 .40
❑ 54 The Enterprise Crew .15 .40
❑ 55 The Enterprise Crew .15 .40
❑ 56 Sarek, At the Foot of Mount Seleya .15 .40
❑ 57 McCoy's Friendship for Spock .15 .40
❑ 58 L'Tar Performs the Ritual .15 .40
❑ 59 Spock and Kirk Face to Face .15 .40
❑ 60 Spock's Memories Restored .15 .40

1985 Garbage Pail Kids

COMMON CARD (1a-41b) 2.00 5.00
COMMON CARD (42a-83b) .60 1.50
❑ 1A Nasty Nick 15.00 30.00
❑ 1B Evil Eddie 15.00 30.00
❑ 2A Junkfood John 2.00 5.00
❑ 2B Ray Decay 2.00 5.00
❑ 3A Up Chuck 2.00 5.00
❑ 3B Heavin' Steven 2.00 5.00
❑ 4A Fryin' Brian 2.00 5.00
❑ 4B Electric Bill 2.00 5.00
❑ 5A Dead Ted 2.00 5.00
❑ 5B Jay Decay 2.00 5.00
❑ 6A Art Apart 2.00 5.00
❑ 6B Busted Bob 2.00 5.00
❑ 7A Stormy Heather 2.00 5.00
❑ 7B April Showers 2.00 5.00
❑ 8A Adam Bomb 15.00 30.00
❑ 8B Blasted Billy 10.00 25.00
❑ 9A Boozin' Bruce 2.00 5.00
❑ 9B Drunk Ken 2.00 5.00
❑ 10A Tee-Vee Stevie 2.00 5.00
❑ 10B Geeky Gary 2.00 5.00
❑ 11A Itchy Ritchie 2.00 5.00
❑ 11B Bugged Bert 2.00 5.00
❑ 12A Furry Fran 2.00 5.00
❑ 12B Hairy Mary 2.00 5.00
❑ 13A Ashcan Andy 2.00 5.00
❑ 13B Spacey Stacy 2.00 5.00
❑ 14A Potty Scotty 2.00 5.00
❑ 14B Jason Basin 2.00 5.00
❑ 15A Ailin' Al 2.00 5.00
❑ 15B Mauled Paul 2.00 5.00
❑ 16A Weird Wendy 2.00 5.00
❑ 16B Haggy Maggie 2.00 5.00
❑ 17A Wacky Jackie 2.00 5.00
❑ 17B Loony Lenny 2.00 5.00
❑ 18A Cranky Frankie 2.00 5.00
❑ 18B Bad Brad 2.00 5.00
❑ 19A Corroded Carl 2.00 5.00
❑ 19B Crater Chris 2.00 5.00
❑ 20A Swell Mel 2.00 5.00
❑ 20B Dressy Jesse 2.00 5.00
❑ 21A Virus Iris 2.00 5.00
❑ 21B Sicky Vicky 2.00 5.00
❑ 22A Junky Jeff 2.00 5.00
❑ 22B Stinky Stan 2.00 5.00
❑ 23A Drippy Dan 2.00 5.00
❑ 23B Leaky Lou 2.00 5.00
❑ 24A Nervous Rex 2.00 5.00
❑ 24B Nerdy Norm 2.00 5.00
❑ 25A Creepy Carol 2.00 5.00
❑ 25B Scary Carrie 2.00 5.00
❑ 26A Slobby Robbie 2.00 5.00
❑ 26B Fat Matt 2.00 5.00
❑ 27A Brainy Janie 2.00 5.00
❑ 27B Jenny Genius 2.00 5.00
❑ 28A Oozy Suzy 2.00 5.00
❑ 28B Meltin' Melissa 2.00 5.00
❑ 29A Bony Joanie 2.00 5.00
❑ 29B Thin Lynn 2.00 5.00
❑ 30A New Wave Dave 2.00 5.00
❑ 30B Graffiti Petey 2.00 5.00
❑ 31A Run Down Rhoda 2.00 5.00
❑ 31B Flat Pat 2.00 5.00
❑ 32A Frigid Bridget 2.00 5.00
❑ 32B Chilly Millie 2.00 5.00
❑ 33A Mad Mike 2.00 5.00
❑ 33B Savage Stuart 2.00 5.00
❑ 34A Kim Kong 2.00 5.00
❑ 34B Anna Banana 2.00 5.00
❑ 35A Wrinkly Randy 2.00 5.00
❑ 35B Rockin' Robert 2.00 5.00
❑ 36A Wrappin' Ruth 2.00 5.00
❑ 36B Tommy Tomb 2.00 5.00
❑ 37A Guillo Tina 2.00 5.00
❑ 37B Cindy Lopper 2.00 5.00
❑ 38A Slimy Sam 2.00 5.00
❑ 38B Lizard Liz 2.00 5.00
❑ 39A Buggy Betty 2.00 5.00
❑ 39B Green Jean 2.00 5.00
❑ 40A Unstitched Mitch 2.00 5.00
❑ 40B Damaged Don 2.00 5.00
❑ 41A Mean Gene 2.00 5.00
❑ 41B Joltin' Joe 2.00 5.00
❑ 42A Patty Putty .60 1.50
❑ 42B Muggin' Megan .60 1.50
❑ 43A Smelly Kelly .60 1.50
❑ 43B Doug Plug .60 1.50
❑ 44A Sy Clops .60 1.50
❑ 44B One-Eyed Jack .60 1.50
❑ 45A Leaky Lindsay .60 1.50
❑ 45B Messy Tessie .60 1.50
❑ 46A Rappin' Ron .60 1.50
❑ 46B Ray Gun .60 1.50
❑ 47A Disgustin' Justin .60 1.50
❑ 47B Vile Kyle .60 1.50
❑ 48A Tongue Tied Tim .60 1.50
❑ 48B Marty Mouthful .60 1.50
❑ 49A Double Heather .60 1.50
❑ 49B-1 Fran Fran 2.00 5.00
❑ 49B-2 Schizo Fran 2.00 5.00
❑ 50A Mad Donna .60 1.50
❑ 50B Nutty Nicole .60 1.50
❑ 51A Russell Muscle .60 1.50
❑ 51B Brett Sweat .60 1.50
❑ 52A Dirty Harry .60 1.50
❑ 52B Rob Slob .60 1.50
❑ 53A Jolted Joel .60 1.50
❑ 53B Live Mike .60 1.50
❑ 54A Fryin' Ryan .60 1.50
❑ 54B Charred Chad .60 1.50
❑ 55A Hairy Gary .60 1.50
❑ 55B Brutal Brad .60 1.50
❑ 56A Hairy Carrie .60 1.50
❑ 56B Brutal Bridget .60 1.50
❑ 57A Tommy Gun .60 1.50
❑ 57B Dead Fred .60 1.50
❑ 58A Cracked Jack .60 1.50
❑ 58B Soft Boiled Sam .60 1.50
❑ 59A Clogged Duane .60 1.50
❑ 59B Bye Bye Bobby .60 1.50
❑ 60A Prickly Rick .60 1.50
❑ 60B Cactus Carol .60 1.50
❑ 61A Jolly Roger .60 1.50
❑ 61B Pegleg Peter .60 1.50
❑ 62A Greaser Greg .60 1.50
❑ 62B Chris Hiss .60 1.50
❑ 63A Spacey Stacy .60 1.50
❑ 63B Janet Planet .60 1.50
❑ 64A Hot Scott .60 1.50
❑ 64B Luke Warm .60 1.50
❑ 65A Shrunken Ed .60 1.50
❑ 65B Cheeky Charles .60 1.50
❑ 66A Matt Ratt .60 1.50
❑ 66B Rachel Rodent .60 1.50
❑ 67A Phony Lisa .60 1.50
❑ 67B Mona Loser .60 1.50
❑ 68A Oliver Twisted .60 1.50
❑ 68B Dizzy Dave .60 1.50
❑ 69A Jenny Jelly .60 1.50
❑ 69B Sara Slime .60 1.50
❑ 70A Bad Breath Seth .60 1.50
❑ 70B Foul Phil .60 1.50
❑ 71A Odd Todd .60 1.50
❑ 71B Bent Ben .60 1.50
❑ 72A Mad Max .60 1.50
❑ 72B Brainy Brian .60 1.50
❑ 73A Gorgeous George .60 1.50
❑ 73B Dollar Bill .60 1.50
❑ 74A Mark Bark .60 1.50
❑ 74B Kennel Kenny .60 1.50
❑ 75A Off-The-Wall Paul .60 1.50
❑ 75B Zach Plaque .60 1.50
❑ 76A Bonnie Bunnie .60 1.50
❑ 76B Pourin' Lauren .60 1.50
❑ 77A Ghastly Ashley .60 1.50
❑ 77B Acne Amy .60 1.50
❑ 78A Wrinkled Rita .60 1.50
❑ 78B Ancient Annie .60 1.50
❑ 79A Sewer Sue .60 1.50
❑ 79B Michelle Muck .60 1.50
❑ 80A Tattoo Lou .60 1.50
❑ 80B Art Gallery .60 1.50
❑ 81A Split Kit .60 1.50
❑ 81B Mixed-Up Mitch .60 1.50
❑ 82A Slain Wayne .60 1.50
❑ 82B Ventilated Vinnie .60 1.50
❑ 83A Ugh Lee .60 1.50
❑ 83B Sumo Sid .60 1.50

1985 Garbage Pail Kids Matte Back

*MATTE BACK: SAME PRICE AS BASIC CARDS
❑ 1A Nasty Nick 15.00 30.00
❑ 1B Evil Eddie 15.00 30.00
❑ 2A Junkfood John 2.00 5.00
❑ 2B Ray Decay 2.00 5.00
❑ 3A Up Chuck 2.00 5.00
❑ 3B Heavin' Steven 2.00 5.00
❑ 4A Fryin' Brian 2.00 5.00
❑ 4B Electric Bill 2.00 5.00
❑ 5A Dead Ted 2.00 5.00
❑ 5B Jay Decay 2.00 5.00
❑ 6A Art Apart 2.00 5.00
❑ 6B Busted Bob 2.00 5.00
❑ 7A Stormy Heather 2.00 5.00
❑ 7B April Showers 2.00 5.00
❑ 8A Adam Bomb 15.00 30.00
❑ 8B Blasted Billy 10.00 25.00
❑ 9A Boozin' Bruce 2.00 5.00
❑ 9B Drunk Ken 2.00 5.00
❑ 10A Tee-Vee Stevie 2.00 5.00
❑ 10B Geeky Gary 2.00 5.00
❑ 11A Itchy Ritchie 2.00 5.00
❑ 11B Bugged Bert 2.00 5.00
❑ 12A Furry Fran 2.00 5.00
❑ 12B Hairy Mary 2.00 5.00
❑ 13A Ashcan Andy 2.00 5.00
❑ 13B Spacey Stacy 2.00 5.00
❑ 14A Potty Scotty 2.00 5.00
❑ 14B Jason Basin 2.00 5.00
❑ 15A Ailin' Al 2.00 5.00
❑ 15B Mauled Paul 2.00 5.00
❑ 16A Weird Wendy 2.00 5.00
❑ 16B Haggy Maggie 2.00 5.00
❑ 17A Wacky Jackie 2.00 5.00
❑ 17B Loony Lenny 2.00 5.00
❑ 18A Cranky Frankie 2.00 5.00
❑ 18B Bad Brad 2.00 5.00
❑ 19A Corroded Carl 2.00 5.00
❑ 19B Crater Chris 2.00 5.00
❑ 20A Swell Mel 2.00 5.00
❑ 20B Dressy Jesse 2.00 5.00
❑ 21A Virus Iris 2.00 5.00
❑ 21B Sicky Vicky 2.00 5.00
❑ 22A Junky Jeff 2.00 5.00
❑ 22B Stinky Stan 2.00 5.00
❑ 23A Drippy Dan 2.00 5.00
❑ 23B Leaky Lou 2.00 5.00
❑ 24A Nervous Rex 2.00 5.00
❑ 24B Nerdy Norm 2.00 5.00
❑ 25A Creepy Carol 2.00 5.00
❑ 25B Scary Carrie 2.00 5.00
❑ 26A Slobby Robbie 2.00 5.00
❑ 26B Fat Matt 2.00 5.00
❑ 27A Brainy Janie 2.00 5.00
❑ 27B Jenny Genius 2.00 5.00
❑ 28A Oozy Suzy 2.00 5.00
❑ 28B Meltin' Melissa 2.00 5.00
❑ 29A Bony Joanie 2.00 5.00
❑ 29B Thin Lynn 2.00 5.00
❑ 30A New Wave Dave 2.00 5.00
❑ 30B Graffiti Petey 2.00 5.00
❑ 31A Run Down Rhoda 2.00 5.00
❑ 31B Flat Pat 2.00 5.00
❑ 32A Frigid Bridget 2.00 5.00
❑ 32B Chilly Millie 2.00 5.00
❑ 33A Mad Mike 2.00 5.00
❑ 33B Savage Stuart 2.00 5.00
❑ 34A Kim Kong 2.00 5.00
❑ 34B Anna Banana 2.00 5.00
❑ 35A Wrinkly Randy 2.00 5.00
❑ 35B Rockin' Robert 2.00 5.00
❑ 36A Wrappin' Ruth 2.00 5.00
❑ 36B Tommy Tomb 2.00 5.00
❑ 37A Guillo Tina 2.00 5.00
❑ 37B Cindy Lopper 2.00 5.00
❑ 38A Slimy Sam 2.00 5.00
❑ 38B Lizard Liz 2.00 5.00
❑ 39A Buggy Betty 2.00 5.00
❑ 39B Green Jean 2.00 5.00
❑ 40A Unstitched Mitch 2.00 5.00
❑ 40B Damaged Don 2.00 5.00
❑ 41A Mean Gene 2.00 5.00
❑ 41B Joltin' Joe 2.00 5.00

1986 Garbage Pail Kids

- COMPLETE SET (334)
- COMPLETE SERIES 3 (82) 10.00 25.00
- COMPLETE SERIES 4 (84) 10.00 25.00
- COMPLETE SERIES 5 (80) 10.00 25.00
- COMPLETE SERIES 6 (88) 10.00 25.00

- ❑ 84A Joe Blow .15 .40
- ❑ 84B Rod Wad .15 .40
- ❑ 85A Stuck Chuck .15 .40
- ❑ 85B Pinned Lynn .15 .40
- ❑ 86A Horsey Henry .15 .40
- ❑ 86B Galloping Glen .15 .40
- ❑ 87A Hot Head Harvey .15 .40
- ❑ 87B Roy Bot .15 .40
- ❑ 88A Dinah Saur .15 .40
- ❑ 88B Farrah Fossil .15 .40
- ❑ 89A Hurt Curt .15 .40
- ❑ 89B Pat Splat .15 .40
- ❑ 90A Stoned Sean .15 .40
- ❑ 90B Thick Vic .15 .40
- ❑ 91A Blake Flake .15 .40
- ❑ 91B Hippie Skippy .15 .40
- ❑ 92A Marvin Gardens .15 .40
- ❑ 92B Spittin' Spencer .15 .40
- ❑ 93A Drew Blood .15 .40
- ❑ 93B Bustin' Dustin .15 .40
- ❑ 94A Bruised Lee .15 .40
- ❑ 94B Karate Kate .15 .40
- ❑ 95A Grim Jim .15 .40
- ❑ 95B Beth Death .15 .40
- ❑ 96A Distorted Dot .15 .40
- ❑ 96B Mirror Imogene .15 .40
- ❑ 97A Punchy Perry .15 .40
- ❑ 97B Creamed Keith .15 .40
- ❑ 98A Charlotte Web .15 .40
- ❑ 98B Didi T. .15 .40
- ❑ 99A Beaky Becky .15 .40
- ❑ 99B Picky Mickey .15 .40
- ❑ 100A Ali Gator .15 .40
- ❑ 100B Marshy Marshall .15 .40
- ❑ 101A Mushy Marsha .15 .40
- ❑ 101B Basking Robin .15 .40
- ❑ 102A Mugged Marcus .15 .40
- ❑ 102B Kayo'd Cody .15 .40
- ❑ 103A Wriggley Rene .15 .40
- ❑ 103B Curly Carla .15 .40
- ❑ 104A Silent Sandy .15 .40
- ❑ 104B Barren Aaron .15 .40
- ❑ 105A Juicy Jessica .15 .40
- ❑ 105B Green Dean .15 .40
- ❑ 106A Fowl Raoul .15 .40
- ❑ 106B Mack Quack .15 .40
- ❑ 107A Totem Paula .15 .40
- ❑ 107B Tatum Pole .15 .40
- ❑ 108A Smelly Sally .15 .40
- ❑ 108B Fishy Phyllis .15 .40
- ❑ 109A Toady Terry .15 .40
- ❑ 109B Croakin' Colin .15 .40
- ❑ 110A Snooty Sam .15 .40
- ❑ 110B U.S. Arnie .15 .40
- ❑ 111A Target Margaret .15 .40
- ❑ 111B Bullseye Barry .15 .40
- ❑ 112A Frank N. Stein .15 .40
- ❑ 112B Undead Jed .15 .40
- ❑ 113A Alice Island .15 .40
- ❑ 113B Liberty Libby .15 .40
- ❑ 114A Starin' Darren .15 .40
- ❑ 114B Peepin' Tom .15 .40
- ❑ 115A Warmin' Norman .15 .40
- ❑ 115B Well Done Sheldon .15 .40
- ❑ 116A Eerie Eric .15 .40
- ❑ 116B Berserk Kirk .15 .40
- ❑ 117A Rocky N. Roll .15 .40
- ❑ 117B Les Vegas .15 .40
- ❑ 118A Half-Nelson .15 .40
- ❑ 118B Glandular Angela .15 .40
- ❑ 119A Ned Head .15 .40
- ❑ 119B Still Jill .15 .40
- ❑ 120A Babbling Brooke .15 .40
- ❑ 120B Jelly Kelly .15 .40
- ❑ 121A Apple Cory .15 .40
- ❑ 121B Dwight Bite .15 .40
- ❑ 122A Broad Maud .15 .40
- ❑ 122B Large Marge .15 .40
- ❑ 123A Glooey Gabe .15 .40
- ❑ 123B Sticky Rick .15 .40
- ❑ 124A Hugh Mungous .15 .40
- ❑ 124B King-Size Kevin .15 .40
- ❑ 125A Holly Wood .15 .40
- ❑ 125B1 Woody Alan (1st Print Run) .25 .60
- ❑ 125B2 Oak Kay (2nd Print Run) .40 1.00
- ❑ 126A Armpit Britt .15 .40
- ❑ 126B Shaggy Aggie .15 .40
- ❑ 127A Travellin' Travis .15 .40
- ❑ 127B Flat Tyler .15 .40
- ❑ 128A Sloshed Josh .15 .40
- ❑ 128B Low Cal .15 .40
- ❑ 129A Second Hand Rose .15 .40
- ❑ 129B Trashed Tracy .15 .40
- ❑ 130A Nicky Hickey .15 .40
- ❑ 130B Hank E. Panky .15 .40
- ❑ 131A Stuffed Stephen .15 .40
- ❑ 131B Rutherford B. Hay .15 .40
- ❑ 132A Bony Tony .15 .40
- ❑ 132B Unzipped Zack .15 .40
- ❑ 133A Furry Murray .15 .40
- ❑ 133B Foxy Francis .15 .40
- ❑ 134A Hip Kip .15 .40
- ❑ 134B Walt Witless .15 .40
- ❑ 135A Rock E. Horror .15 .40
- ❑ 135B Marty Gras .15 .40
- ❑ 136A Swollen Sue Ellen .15 .40
- ❑ 136B Bloated Blair .15 .40
- ❑ 137A Max Axe .15 .40
- ❑ 137B Deadly Dudley .15 .40
- ❑ 138A Alien Ian .15 .40
- ❑ 138B Outerspace Chase .15 .40
- ❑ 139A Double Iris .15 .40
- ❑ 139B 4-Eyed Ida .15 .40
- ❑ 140A Mouth Phil .15 .40
- ❑ 140B Tooth Les .15 .40
- ❑ 141A Ashley Can .15 .40
- ❑ 141B Greta Garbage .15 .40
- ❑ 142A Bruce Moose .15 .40
- ❑ 142B Hunted Hunter .15 .40
- ❑ 143A Melba Toast .15 .40
- ❑ 143B Hy Rye .15 .40
- ❑ 144A Horny Hal .15 .40
- ❑ 144B Ruby Toot .15 .40
- ❑ 145A Dale Snail .15 .40
- ❑ 145B Crushed Shelly .15 .40
- ❑ 146A Baked Jake .15 .40
- ❑ 146B Dry Guy .15 .40
- ❑ 147A Amazin' Grace .15 .40
- ❑ 147B Muscular Molly .15 .40
- ❑ 148A Turned-On Tara .15 .40
- ❑ 148B Tiffany Lamp .15 .40
- ❑ 149A1 Reese Pieces (1st Print Run) .25 .60
- ❑ 149A2 Puzzled Paul (2nd Print Run) .40 1.00
- ❑ 149B Incomplete Pete .15 .40
- ❑ 150A Hairy Harriet .15 .40
- ❑ 150B Bushy Bernice .15 .40
- ❑ 151A Losing Faith .15 .40
- ❑ 151B Dyin' Dinah .15 .40
- ❑ 152A Whisperin' Woody .15 .40
- ❑ 152B Van Triloquist .15 .40
- ❑ 153A Jack O. Lantern .15 .40
- ❑ 153B Duncan Pumpkin .15 .40
- ❑ 154A Basket Casey .15 .40
- ❑ 154B Dribblin' Derek .15 .40
- ❑ 155A Spikey Mikey .15 .40
- ❑ 155B Nailed Neil .15 .40
- ❑ 156A Warrin' Warren .15 .40
- ❑ 156B Brett Vet .15 .40
- ❑ 157A Larry Lips .15 .40
- ❑ 157B Distortin' Morton .15 .40
- ❑ 158A Meltin' Elton .15 .40
- ❑ 158B1 Crystal Gale (1st Print Run) .25 .60
- ❑ 158B2 Ig Lou (2nd Print Run) .40 1.00
- ❑ 159A Catty Kathy .15 .40
- ❑ 159B Kitty Litter .15 .40
- ❑ 160A Decapitated Hedy .15 .40
- ❑ 160B Formalde Heidi .15 .40
- ❑ 161A Shorned Sean .15 .40
- ❑ 161B Hy Gene .15 .40
- ❑ 162A Yicchy Mickey .15 .40
- ❑ 162B Barfin' Bart .15 .40
- ❑ 163A Trish Squish .15 .40
- ❑ 163B Ruby Cube .15 .40
- ❑ 164A Teddy Bear .15 .40
- ❑ 164B1 Salvatore Dolly (1st Print Run) .25 .60
- ❑ 164B2 Battered Brad (2nd Print Run) .40 1.00
- ❑ 165A Dana Druff .15 .40
- ❑ 165B Flakey Fay .15 .40
- ❑ 166A Cored Gordon .15 .40
- ❑ 166B No Way Jose .15 .40
- ❑ 167A Mick Dagger .15 .40
- ❑ 167B Slayed Slade .15 .40
- ❑ 168A Handy Randy .15 .40
- ❑ 168B Jordan Nuts .15 .40
- ❑ 169A Dee Faced .15 .40
- ❑ 169B Terri Cloth .15 .40
- ❑ 170A Richie Retch .15 .40
- ❑ 170B Luke Puke .15 .40
- ❑ 171A Willie Wipe-Out .15 .40
- ❑ 171B Spencer Dispenser .15 .40
- ❑ 172A Nat Nerd .15 .40
- ❑ 172B Clark Can't .15 .40
- ❑ 173A Menaced Dennis .15 .40
- ❑ 173B Wormy Shermy .15 .40
- ❑ 174A Fred Thread .15 .40
- ❑ 174B Repaired Rex .15 .40
- ❑ 175A Windy Winston .15 .40
- ❑ 175B Johnny One-Note .15 .40
- ❑ 176A Condo Minnie .15 .40
- ❑ 176B Bill Ding .15 .40
- ❑ 177A Meltin' Milton .15 .40
- ❑ 177B Lazy Louie .15 .40
- ❑ 178A Earl Painting .15 .40
- ❑ 178B Blue-Boy George .15 .40
- ❑ 179A Moe Skeeto .15 .40
- ❑ 179B Sting Ray .15 .40
- ❑ 180A Haunted Hollis .15 .40
- ❑ 180B Batty Barney .15 .40
- ❑ 181A Cliff Hanger .15 .40
- ❑ 181B Neck Ty .15 .40
- ❑ 182A Sprayed Wade .15 .40
- ❑ 182B Tagged Tad .15 .40
- ❑ 183A Diaper Dan .15 .40
- ❑ 183B Pinned Penny .15 .40
- ❑ 184A Upside Down Donald .15 .40
- ❑ 184B Hugh Turn .15 .40
- ❑ 185A Fran Furter .15 .40
- ❑ 185B Hot Doug .15 .40
- ❑ 186A Iron-Jaw Aaron .15 .40
- ❑ 186B Jean Machine .15 .40
- ❑ 187A Ginger Snapped .15 .40
- ❑ 187B Edible Ernie .15 .40
- ❑ 188A Mel Meal .15 .40
- ❑ 188B Ross Roast .15 .40
- ❑ 189A Brenda Blender .15 .40
- ❑ 189B Juicy Lucy .15 .40
- ❑ 190A Gory Rory .15 .40
- ❑ 190B Gil Grill .15 .40
- ❑ 191A Ben Bolt .15 .40
- ❑ 191B Fried Franklin .15 .40
- ❑ 192A Delicate Tess .15 .40
- ❑ 192B Hamburger Pattie .15 .40
- ❑ 193A Shattered Shelby .15 .40
- ❑ 193B Cracked Craig .15 .40
- ❑ 194A Nasty Nancy .15 .40
- ❑ 194B Razzin' Roslyn .15 .40
- ❑ 195A Lucas Mucus .15 .40
- ❑ 195B Dotty Dribble .15 .40
- ❑ 196A Dangling Dolly .15 .40
- ❑ 196B Surreal Neal .15 .40
- ❑ 197A Doughy Joey .15 .40
- ❑ 197B Starchy Archie .15 .40
- ❑ 198A Gore May .15 .40
- ❑ 198B Connie Sewer .15 .40
- ❑ 199A Ruptured Rupert .15 .40
- ❑ 199B Gassy Gus .15 .40
- ❑ 200A Flouride Floyd .15 .40
- ❑ 200B Dental Daniel .15 .40
- ❑ 201A Michael Mutant .15 .40
- ❑ 201B Zeke Freak .15 .40
- ❑ 202A Ultra Violet .15 .40
- ❑ 202B Tanya Hide .15 .40
- ❑ 203A Toothie Ruthie .15 .40
- ❑ 203B Dental Flossie .15 .40
- ❑ 204A Jules Drools .15 .40
- ❑ 204B Kit Spit .15 .40
- ❑ 205A Hot Rod .15 .40
- ❑ 205B Bud Buggy .15 .40
- ❑ 206A Deaf Geoff .15 .40
- ❑ 206B Audio Augie .15 .40
- ❑ 207A Over Flo .15 .40
- ❑ 207B Moist Joyce .15 .40
- ❑ 208A Joel Hole .15 .40
- ❑ 208B Teed-Off Tom .15 .40
- ❑ 209A Whacked-Up Wally .15 .40
- ❑ 209B Paddlin' Madeline .15 .40
- ❑ 210A Intense Payne .15 .40
- ❑ 210B First Ada .15 .40
- ❑ 211A See More Seymour .15 .40
- ❑ 211B Coy Roy .15 .40
- ❑ 212A Upliftin' Clifton .15 .40
- ❑ 212B Air-Head Jed .15 .40
- ❑ 213A Otto Whack .15 .40
- ❑ 213B Elliot Mess .15 .40
- ❑ 214A Off-Color Clara .15 .40
- ❑ 214B Brushed-Off Brends .15 .40
- ❑ 215A Gnawing Nora .15 .40
- ❑ 215B Nervous Nellie .15 .40
- ❑ 216A Tiny Tim .15 .40
- ❑ 216B Small Saul .15 .40
- ❑ 217A Trashy Trudy .15 .40
- ❑ 217B Rose Dispose .15 .40
- ❑ 218A Tom Thumb .15 .40
- ❑ 218B Bridget Digit .15 .40
- ❑ 219A George Washingdone .15 .40
- ❑ 219B Pressed Preston .15 .40
- ❑ 220A Joan Clone .15 .40
- ❑ 220B Warty Ward .15 .40
- ❑ 221A Cracked Crystal .15 .40
- ❑ 221B Shrill Jill .15 .40
- ❑ 222A Troy Toy .15 .40
- ❑ 222B Loose Spring .15 .40
- ❑ 223A Lolly Poppy .15 .40
- ❑ 223B Lily Popped .15 .40
- ❑ 224A Monte Zuma .15 .40
- ❑ 224B Pagan Megan .15 .40
- ❑ 225A Nasal Hazel .15 .40
- ❑ 225B Snotty Lottie .15 .40
- ❑ 226A Pierced Pearl .15 .40
- ❑ 226B Cheap Jewel .15 .40
- ❑ 227A Bea Sting .15 .40
- ❑ 227B Screaming Mimi .15 .40
- ❑ 228A Casper Gasper .15 .40
- ❑ 228B Uncool Carl .15 .40
- ❑ 229A Clair Stare .15 .40
- ❑ 229B Bloodshot Scott .15 .40
- ❑ 230A Manuel Labor .15 .40
- ❑ 230B Handy Andy .15 .40
- ❑ 231A Ashley Tray .15 .40
- ❑ 231B Bernie Burns .15 .40
- ❑ 232A Pam Hame .15 .40
- ❑ 232B Cole Cut .15 .40
- ❑ 233A Wes Mess .15 .40
- ❑ 233B Trash-Can Ken .15 .40
- ❑ 234A Harry Canary .15 .40
- ❑ 234B Burt Cage .15 .40
- ❑ 235A Ugly Hans .15 .40
- ❑ 235B Jan Hand .15 .40
- ❑ 236A Trina Cleaner .15 .40
- ❑ 236B Suckin' Sybil .15 .40
- ❑ 237A Totaled Todd .15 .40
- ❑ 237B Towin' Owen .15 .40
- ❑ 238A Marc Spark .15 .40
- ❑ 238B Cherry Bomb .15 .40
- ❑ 239A Jerry Atric .15 .40
- ❑ 239B Abraham Wrinklin' .15 .40
- ❑ 240A Radar Ray .15 .40
- ❑ 240B Eve Droppin' .15 .40
- ❑ 241A Old Gloria Checklist .15 .40
- ❑ 241B Jose Can You See .15 .40
- ❑ 242A Clean Maureen .15 .40
- ❑ 242B Dryin' Ryan .15 .40
- ❑ 243A Lee Tree .15 .40
- ❑ 243B Sherwood Forest .15 .40
- ❑ 244A Welcome Matt .15 .40
- ❑ 244B Muddy Maude .15 .40
- ❑ 245A Shish K. Bob .15 .40
- ❑ 245B Barbie Q. .15 .40
- ❑ 246A John John .15 .40
- ❑ 246B Flushing Floyd .15 .40
- ❑ 247A Rusty Heap .15 .40
- ❑ 247B Rustin' Justin .15 .40
- ❑ 248A Hector Collector .15 .40
- ❑ 249A Many Lenny .15 .40
- ❑ 249B Lotta Carlotta .15 .40
- ❑ 250A Newly-Dead Ed .15 .40
- ❑ 250B Dyna Mike .15 .40

1987 Garbage Pail Kids

- COMPLETE SET (416)
- COMPLETE SERIES 7 (84) 10.00 25.00
- COMPLETE SERIES 8 (84) 10.00 25.00
- COMPLETE SERIES 9 (88) 10.00 25.00
- COMPLETE SERIES 10 (78) 10.00 25.00
- COMPLETE SERIES 11 (84) 10.00 25.00

- ❑ 251A Barfin' Barbara .15 .40
- ❑ 251B Valerie Vomit .15 .40
- ❑ 252A Milky Wayne .15 .40
- ❑ 252B Dairy Cari .15 .40
- ❑ 253A1 Russ Pus (puzzle center back) .15 .40
- ❑ 253A2 Russ Pus (puzzle corner back) .15 .40
- ❑ 253B1 Louise Squeeze (puzzle center back) .15 .40
- ❑ 253B2 Louise Squeeze (puzzle corner back) .15 .40
- ❑ 254A Chris Mess .15 .40
- ❑ 254B Sandy Clod .15 .40
- ❑ 255A On The Mark .15 .40
- ❑ 255B Bull's Ira .15 .40
- ❑ 256A Jack Pot .15 .40
- ❑ 256B Monte Carlo .15 .40
- ❑ 257A Cut-Up Carmen .15 .40
- ❑ 257B Dotted Lionel .15 .40
- ❑ 258A Mickey Mouths .15 .40
- ❑ 258B Oral Laurel .15 .40
- ❑ 259A Grilled Gil .15 .40
- ❑ 259B Well Don .15 .40
- ❑ 260A Adam Boom .15 .40
- ❑ 260B1 Blasted Billy II (blue header) .15 .40
- ❑ 260B2 Blasted Billy II (purple header) 3.00 8.00
- ❑ 261A Gooey Huey .15 .40
- ❑ 261B1 Bobbi Booger (blue header) .15 .40
- ❑ 261B2 Bobbi Booger (purple header) 3.00 8.00
- ❑ 262A Brainless Bryan .15 .40
- ❑ 262B Jughead Ted .15 .40
- ❑ 263A Vincent Van Gone .15 .40
- ❑ 263B Modern Art .15 .40
- ❑ 264A Pete Seat .15 .40
- ❑ 264B Noel Bowl .15 .40
- ❑ 265A1 Curly Shirley (puzzle center back) .15 .40
- ❑ 265A2 Curly Shirley (puzzle side back) .15 .40
- ❑ 265B1 Blown Joan (puzzle center back) .15 .40
- ❑ 265B2 Blown Joan (puzzle side back) .15 .40
- ❑ 266A Roy L. Flush .15 .40
- ❑ 266B Shuffled Sherman .15 .40
- ❑ 267A Tongue Tied Tina .15 .40
- ❑ 267B Braided Brandy .15 .40
- ❑ 268A Phil Grim .15 .40
- ❑ 268B William Penned .15 .40
- ❑ 269A Sharpened Sheena .15 .40
- ❑ 269B Cranky Kristin .15 .40
- ❑ 270A Cannibal Stu .15 .40
- ❑ 270B Brewin' Bruno .15 .40
- ❑ 271A Bratty Maddy .15 .40
- ❑ 271B Dirty Birdie .15 .40
- ❑ 272A Elastic Elwood .15 .40
- ❑ 272B Fletcher Stretcher .15 .40
- ❑ 273A Haunted Forrest .15 .40
- ❑ 273B Sappy Sarah .15 .40
- ❑ 274A Reptilian Lillian .15 .40
- ❑ 274B Jay Prey .15 .40
- ❑ 275A Wheel Barry .15 .40
- ❑ 275B Rollin' Roland .15 .40
- ❑ 276A Vanessa Undresser .15 .40
- ❑ 276B Banana Anna .15 .40
- ❑ 277A Reuben Cube .15 .40
- ❑ 277B Blockhead Blake .15 .40
- ❑ 278A Have A Nice Dave .15 .40
- ❑ 278B Miles Smiles .15 .40
- ❑ 279A Short Mort .15 .40
- ❑ 279B Noah Body .15 .40
- ❑ 280A Shut-Up Sherwin .15 .40
- ❑ 280B Filled Up Philip .15 .40
- ❑ 281A Soured Howard .15 .40
- ❑ 281B Paul Bunion .15 .40
- ❑ 282A Screwey Dewey .15 .40
- ❑ 282B Bent Brent .15 .40
- ❑ 283A Alien Alan .15 .40
- ❑ 283B Martian Marcia .15 .40
- ❑ 284A Manny Heads .15 .40
- ❑ 284B Max Stacks .15 .40
- ❑ 285A Wind Sheila .15 .40
- ❑ 285B Hit N' Ronni .15 .40
- ❑ 286A Haley Comet .15 .40
- ❑ 286B June Moon .15 .40
- ❑ 287A Christine Vaccine .15 .40
- ❑ 287B Medi Kate .15 .40
- ❑ 288A Grant Ant .15 .40
- ❑ 288B Sticky Nikki .15 .40
- ❑ 289A Stair Casey .15 .40
- ❑ 289B1 Alexander The Grate (black card number) .15 .40
- ❑ 289B2 Alexander The Grate (white card number) 3.00 8.00
- ❑ 290A Busted Armand .15 .40
- ❑ 290B Jim Nauseum .15 .40
- ❑ 291A Homer Runt .15 .40
- ❑ 291B Screwball Lew .15 .40
- ❑ 292A Staple Gunther .15 .40
- ❑ 292B Clipped Claude .15 .40
- ❑ 293A Explorin' Norman .15 .40
- ❑ 293B Drillin' Dylan .15 .40
- ❑ 294A Weird Wendell .15 .40
- ❑ 294B Luke At Me .15 .40
- ❑ 295A Charlie Horse .15 .40
- ❑ 295B Amusement Parker .15 .40
- ❑ 296A Plucked Daisy .15 .40
- ❑ 296B Wiltin' Milton .15 .40
- ❑ 297A Yul Tied .15 .40
- ❑ 297B Murray Christmas .15 .40
- ❑ 298A1 Bloody Mary (puzzle center back) .15 .40
- ❑ 298A2 Bloody Mary (puzzle corner back) .15 .40
- ❑ 298B1 Donna Donor (puzzle center back) .15 .40
- ❑ 298B2 Donna Donor (puzzle corner back) .15 .40
- ❑ 299A Buck Puck .15 .40
- ❑ 299B Lowell Goal .15 .40
- ❑ 300A Corrina Corona .15 .40
- ❑ 300B Smokey Joe .15 .40
- ❑ 301A Bowling Elaine .15 .40
- ❑ 301B Mike Strike .15 .40
- ❑ 302A Mixed-Up Mick .15 .40
- ❑ 302B Artificial Mitchell .15 .40
- ❑ 303A Hung Up Hank .15 .40
- ❑ 303B Coat Rack Zack .15 .40
- ❑ 304A Rubbin' Robyn .15 .40
- ❑ 304B Soapy Opie .15 .40
- ❑ 305A Grate Scott .15 .40
- ❑ 305B Reggie Veggie .15 .40
- ❑ 306A Midge Fridge .15 .40
- ❑ 306B Leftover Grover .15 .40
- ❑ 307A Divin' Ivan .15 .40
- ❑ 307B Walter Sport .15 .40
- ❑ 308A Fritz Spritz .15 .40
- ❑ 308B Ella P. Record .15 .40
- ❑ 309A Heartless Hal .15 .40
- ❑ 309B Bowen Arrow .15 .40
- ❑ 310A Stinkin' Stella .15 .40
- ❑ 310B Smellin' Helen .15 .40
- ❑ 311A Stu Spew .15 .40
- ❑ 311B Slimin' Simon .15 .40
- ❑ 312A Moe Bile .15 .40
- ❑ 312B Dang Len .15 .40
- ❑ 313A Graham Bell .15 .40
- ❑ 313B Death Neil .15 .40
- ❑ 314A Shifting Sandy .15 .40
- ❑ 314B Grainy Janey .15 .40
- ❑ 315A Messy Bessie .15 .40
- ❑ 315B Unclean Helene .15 .40
- ❑ 316A Flowin' Owen .15 .40
- ❑ 316B Russell Spout .15 .40
- ❑ 317A James Flames .15 .40
- ❑ 317B Burnin' Vernon .15 .40
- ❑ 318A1 Haley's Vomit (puzzle center back) .15 .40
- ❑ 318A2 Haley's Vomit (puzzle side back) .15 .40
- ❑ 318B1 Inter Stella (puzzle center back) .15 .40
- ❑ 318B2 Inter Stella (puzzle side back) .15 .40
- ❑ 319A Chopped Susie .15 .40
- ❑ 319B Shana Saw .15 .40
- ❑ 320A Pumping Aaron .15 .40
- ❑ 320B Will Explode .15 .40
- ❑ 321A Squashed Josh .15 .40
- ❑ 321B Squoze Rose .15 .40
- ❑ 322A K.O.'d Karl .15 .40
- ❑ 322B Sparrin' Warren .15 .40
- ❑ 323A Piece O' Lisa .15 .40
- ❑ 323B Wedding Bella .15 .40
- ❑ 324A Waffle Ira .15 .40
- ❑ 324B Griddled Greta .15 .40
- ❑ 325A Marcel Parcel .15 .40
- ❑ 325B Handle With Caren .15 .40
- ❑ 326A Leather Heather .15 .40
- ❑ 326B Chained Shane .15 .40
- ❑ 327A Needled Nina .15 .40
- ❑ 327B Knittin' Brittany .15 .40
- ❑ 328A Glowing Amber .15 .40
- ❑ 328B Bright Dwight .15 .40
- ❑ 329A Lem Phlegm .15 .40
- ❑ 329B Gezundt Heidi .15 .40
- ❑ 330A Lotta Lotta .15 .40
- ❑ 330B Dupli-Kit .15 .40
- ❑ 331A Page Cage .15 .40
- ❑ 331B Tommy Ache .15 .40
- ❑ 332A Sling Scott .15 .40
- ❑ 332B Teddy Aim Fire .15 .40
- ❑ 333A Ortho Donny .15 .40
- ❑ 333B Ruth Canal .15 .40
- ❑ 334A Ashley To Ashes .15 .40
- ❑ 334B Dustin To Dust .15 .40
- ❑ 335A Cute Tippi .15 .40
- ❑ 335B Waxy Wendy .15 .40
- ❑ 336A Laser Ray .15 .40
- ❑ 336B Sizzlin' Sid .15 .40
- ❑ 337A Early Bert .15 .40
- ❑ 337B Rotten Robin .15 .40
- ❑ 338A See-Sawyer .15 .40
- ❑ 338B Teeter Todd .15 .40
- ❑ 339A Snot Rope Hope .15 .40
- ❑ 339B Drippy Debbie .15 .40
- ❑ 340A Half-Baked Betty .15 .40
- ❑ 340B Rollin' Rolanda .15 .40
- ❑ 341A Juicy Bruce .15 .40
- ❑ 341B Fruity Rudy .15 .40
- ❑ 342A Jim Equipment .15 .40
- ❑ 342B Buddy Builder .15 .40
- ❑ 343A Con Vic .15 .40
- ❑ 343B Al Catraz .15 .40
- ❑ 344A Perry Chute .15 .40
- ❑ 344B Rip Cord .15 .40
- ❑ 345A Cyril Bowl .15 .40
- ❑ 345B Soggy Oggie .15 .40
- ❑ 346A Peeled Paul .15 .40
- ❑ 346B Skin Les .15 .40
- ❑ 347A Dam Dan .15 .40
- ❑ 347B Mike Dike .15 .40
- ❑ 348A Plane Jane .15 .40
- ❑ 348B Woody Shop .15 .40
- ❑ 349A Polluted Percy .15 .40
- ❑ 349B Barnacle Bill .15 .40
- ❑ 350A Misty Suds .15 .40
- ❑ 350B Amelia Airhead .15 .40
- ❑ 351A Cheryl Peril .15 .40
- ❑ 351B Deflatin' Nathan .15 .40
- ❑ 352A Herman Hormone .15 .40
- ❑ 352B Turned-On Ron .15 .40
- ❑ 353A Bazooka Joanne .15 .40
- ❑ 353B Bubbly Babs .15 .40
- ❑ 354A Clark Shark .15 .40
- ❑ 354B Manny Eater .15 .40
- ❑ 355A Beasty Boyd .15 .40
- ❑ 355B1 Semi Colin (no card number) 100.00 200.00
- ❑ 355B2 Semi Colin (w card number) .15 .40
- ❑ 356A Momma Mia .15 .40
- ❑ 356B Electric Shari .15 .40
- ❑ 357A 3-Dee .15 .40
- ❑ 357B Blurry Blair .15 .40
- ❑ 358A Mac The Knife .15 .40
- ❑ 358B Wade Blade .15 .40
- ❑ 359A Kerosene Kerry .15 .40
- ❑ 359B Blazin' Blake .15 .40
- ❑ 360A Marcus Mucus .15 .40
- ❑ 360B Gun Beryl .15 .40
- ❑ 361A Diced Brice .15 .40
- ❑ 361B Chopped Chet .15 .40
- ❑ 362A Doug Food .15 .40
- ❑ 362B Nick Yick .15 .40
- ❑ 363A Slidin' Sloan .15 .40
- ❑ 363B Flamin' Damon .15 .40
- ❑ 364A Sticky Ricky .15 .40
- ❑ 364B Gooey Louie .15 .40
- ❑ 365A Shrap Nell .15 .40
- ❑ 365B Hanna Grenade .15 .40
- ❑ 366A Low-Life Lola .15 .40
- ❑ 366B Sis Pool .15 .40
- ❑ 367A Dent Al .15 .40
- ❑ 367B Fluoride Ida .15 .40
- ❑ 368A Nat Splat .15 .40
- ❑ 368B Jugglin' Jud .15 .40
- ❑ 369A Scalped Ralph .15 .40
- ❑ 369B Bone-Head Fred .15 .40
- ❑ 370A Cementin' Quentin .15 .40
- ❑ 370B Minus Hans .15 .40
- ❑ 371A Grippin' Griffin .15 .40
- ❑ 371B Ren Wrench .15 .40
- ❑ 372A Jack Frost .15 .40
- ❑ 372B Window Payne .15 .40
- ❑ 373A Desi Island .15 .40
- ❑ 373B Marooned Maureen .15 .40
- ❑ 374A Swiss Kris .15 .40
- ❑ 374B Cheesy Chandra .15 .40
- ❑ 375A Trap Dora .15 .40
- ❑ 375B Rear View Myra .15 .40
- ❑ 376A Retchin' Gretchen .15 .40
- ❑ 376B Ill Jill .15 .40
- ❑ 377A Closet Clyde .15 .40
- ❑ 377B Hooked Howie .15 .40
- ❑ 378A Empty Emmy .15 .40
- ❑ 378B Ragged Aggie .15 .40
- ❑ 379A1 Locked Dorian (puzzle preview back) .15 .40
- ❑ 379A2 Locked Dorian (blue Garbage Gang header) .15 .40
- ❑ 379A3 Locked Dorian (red Garbage Gang header) .15 .40
- ❑ 379B1 Sidney Kidney (puzzle preview back) .15 .40
- ❑ 379B2 Sidney Kidney (blue Garbage Gang header) .15 .40
- ❑ 379B3 Sidney Kidney (red Garbage Gang header) .15 .40
- ❑ 380A Vermin Herman .15 .40
- ❑ 380B Gullivered Travis .15 .40
- ❑ 381A Ground Chuck .15 .40
- ❑ 381B Lean Jean .15 .40
- ❑ 382A Good-Bye Hy .15 .40
- ❑ 382B Farewell Mel .15 .40
- ❑ 383A Itchy Mitch .15 .40
- ❑ 383B Raked Jake .15 .40
- ❑ 384A1 Flamin' Raymond (white square under banner) .15 .40
- ❑ 384A2 Flamin' Raymond (no white square under banner) .15 .40
- ❑ 384B1 Hot Toddy (white square under banner) .15 .40
- ❑ 384B2 Hot Toddy (no white square under banner) .15 .40
- ❑ 385A1 Phil 'Er Up (blue Garbage Gang header) .15 .40
- ❑ 385A2 Phil 'Er Up (red Garbage Gang header, die-cut runs through "PEEL HERE") .15 .40
- ❑ 385A3 Phil 'Er Up (red Garbage Gang header, correct die-cut) .15 .40
- ❑ 385B1 Chuckin' Charlie (blue Garbage Gang header) .15 .40
- ❑ 385B2 Chuckin' Charlie (red Garbage Gang header, die-cut runs through "PEEL HERE") .15 .40
- ❑ 385B3 Chuckin' Charlie (red Garbage Gang header, correct die-cut) .15 .40
- ❑ 386A Snotty Dotty .15 .40
- ❑ 386B Frozen Flo .15 .40
- ❑ 387A Fatty Maddie .15 .40
- ❑ 387B Cora Corset .15 .40

❑ 388A Facey Tracie .15 .40
❑ 388B Heads Upton .15 .40
❑ 389A Dire Rita .15 .40
❑ 389B Overflow Joe .15 .40
❑ 390A Connecting Dots .15 .40
❑ 390B Twinny Vinnie .15 .40
❑ 391A Glass Isaac .15 .40
❑ 391B False Iris .15 .40
❑ 392A Ann Chovie .15 .40
❑ 392B Sardine Candice .15 .40
❑ 393A Jess Express .15 .40
❑ 393B Choo-Choo Trina .15 .40
❑ 394A Barb Wire .15 .40
❑ 394B Play Penny .15 .40
❑ 395A Paved Dave .15 .40
❑ 395B Run-Over Grover .15 .40
❑ 396A Creamed Gene .15 .40
❑ 396B Clobbered Bob .15 .40
❑ 397A Cleaned Up Clint .15 .40
❑ 397B Sucked Up Stefan .15 .40
❑ 398A Skin' Ian .15 .40
❑ 398B Sheared Sherwood .15 .40
❑ 399A Dirty Flora .15 .40
❑ 399B Gina Cleaner .15 .40
❑ 400A Varicose Wayne .15 .40
❑ 400B Elaine Vein .15 .40
❑ 401A Viv E. Section .15 .40
❑ 401B Disect Ed .15 .40
❑ 402A1 Lunchpail Gail .15 .40
(die-cut runs through "PEEL HERE")
❑ 402A2 Lunchpail Gail (correct die-cut) .15 .40
❑ 402B1 Lunchbox Stu .15 .40
(die-cut runs through "PEEL HERE")
❑ 402B2 Lunchbox Stu (correct die-cut) .15 .40
❑ 403A Hunter Punter .15 .40
❑ 403B Fractured Francis .15 .40
❑ 404A Airy Mary .15 .40
❑ 404B Hissy Missie .15 .40
❑ 405A Over-Ripe Melanie .15 .40
❑ 405B Walter Melon .15 .40
❑ 406A Shopping Carter .15 .40
❑ 406B Super Marcus .15 .40
❑ 407A Cracked Sheldon .15 .40
❑ 407B Wally Walnut .15 .40
❑ 408A1 Lickin' Leon (blue Garbage Gang header) .15 .40
❑ 408A2 Lickin' Leon (red Garbage Gang header) .15 .40
❑ 408B1 Rat-Sucker Randall .15 .40
(blue Garbage Gang header)
❑ 408B2 Rat-Sucker Randall .15 .40
(red Garbage Gang header)
❑ 409A Tiltin' Milton .15 .40
❑ 409B Amazing Mason .15 .40
❑ 410A Scratching Pole Paul .15 .40
❑ 410B Clawed Claude .15 .40
❑ 411A Van Pire .15 .40
❑ 411B Bud Sucker .15 .40
❑ 412A Mixed-Up Trixie .15 .40
❑ 412B Doughy Chloe .15 .40
❑ 413A Barnyard Barney .15 .40
❑ 413B Dick Hick .15 .40
❑ 414A Umbilical Courtney .15 .40
❑ 414B Yo Yolanda .15 .40
❑ 415A Erased Erica .15 .40
❑ 415B Wiped Out Winnie .15 .40
❑ 416A Shootin' Newton .15 .40
❑ 416B Sherman Tank .15 .40
❑ 417A Hangin' Harriet .15 .40
❑ 417B Swingin' Sophie .15 .40
❑ 418A Lucy Lock-It .15 .40
❑ 418B Shut Up Shirley .15 .40
❑ 419A Meg-A-Volt .15 .40
❑ 419B Charged Marge .15 .40
❑ 420A Spanked Hank .15 .40
❑ 420B Spikey Sondra .15 .40
❑ 421A Groovy Greg .15 .40
❑ 421B Combin' Harry .15 .40
❑ 422A Sheri Cola .15 .40
❑ 422B All Night Dinah .15 .40
❑ 423A Hungry Ivan .15 .40
❑ 423B Sy Sly .15 .40
❑ 424A Rainy Storm .15 .40
❑ 424B Lightning Linda .15 .40
❑ 425A Denny Saur .15 .40
❑ 425B Rip Tile .15 .40
❑ 426A Quenching Quincy .15 .40
❑ 426B Squirtin' Burton .15 .40
❑ 427A Ripped Fletch .15 .40
❑ 427B Taped Tate .15 .40
❑ 428A Lotta Litter .15 .40
❑ 428B Garbage Mouth Gilbert .15 .40
❑ 429A Laundry Matt .15 .40
❑ 429B Drip-Dry Dru .15 .40
❑ 430A Taste Bud .15 .40
❑ 430B Salivatin' Sal .15 .40
❑ 431A Pollutin' Newton .15 .40
❑ 431B Empty Head Jed .15 .40
❑ 432A Packed Mac .15 .40
❑ 432B Sue Case .15 .40
❑ 433A Porcelain Lynn .15 .40
❑ 433B Arlene Latrine .15 .40
❑ 434A Holly Daze .15 .40
❑ 434B Joyous Noel .15 .40
❑ 435A London Bridget .15 .40
❑ 435B Toxic Wes .15 .40
❑ 436A Scaldin' Alden .15 .40
❑ 436B Steamy Mimi .15 .40
❑ 437A Sliced Brad .15 .40
❑ 437B Dead Lee .15 .40
❑ 438A Hallie Ween .15 .40
❑ 438B Trick Or Tricia .15 .40
❑ 439A Jack Splat .15 .40
❑ 439B Abstract Art .15 .40
❑ 440A Bert Squirt .15 .40
❑ 440B Fritzie Zits .15 .40
❑ 441A Loose Leif .15 .40
❑ 441B Composition Booker .15 .40
❑ 442A Rugged Roy .15 .40
❑ 442B Bare Barry .15 .40
❑ 443A Wet Whit .15 .40
❑ 443B Wee-Wee Willie .15 .40
❑ 444A Fairy Tale Dale .15 .40
❑ 444B Nose Drip Skip .15 .40
❑ 445A Colette Coldcut .15 .40
❑ 445B Ellie Deli .15 .40
❑ 446A Mean Marlene .15 .40
❑ 446B Punk Rocky .15 .40
❑ 447A Gushing Garfield .15 .40
❑ 447B Drained Blaine .15 .40
❑ 448A Touch Toni .15 .40
❑ 448B Phoney Joni .15 .40
❑ 449A Bert Food .15 .40
❑ 449B Gutsy Gus .15 .40
❑ 450A Ike Spike .15 .40
❑ 450B Mason Mace .15 .40
❑ 451A Destroyed Lloyd .15 .40
❑ 451B Tinsel Tim .15 .40
❑ 452A Impaled Gail .15 .40
❑ 452B Magic Wanda .15 .40
❑ 453A Dead End Kit .15 .40
❑ 453B Slidin' Clyde .15 .40
❑ 454A Lynched Lyndon .15 .40
❑ 454B Bruce Noose .15 .40
❑ 455A Charred Cole .15 .40
❑ 455B Deviled Egbert .15 .40
❑ 456A Split Cord .15 .40
❑ 456B William Won't Tell .15 .40
❑ 457A Sally Suction .15 .40
❑ 457B Teethin' Trina .15 .40
❑ 458A Dental Hy Gene .15 .40
❑ 458B Rudy Canal .15 .40
❑ 459A1 Vomited (light yellow checklist) .15 .40
❑ 459A2 Vomited (dark yellow checklist) .15 .40
❑ 459B1 Juicy Jules (light yellow checklist) .15 .40
❑ 459B2 Juicy Jules (dark yellow checklist) .15 .40

1988 Garbage Pail Kids

COMPLETE SET (322)
COMPLETE SERIES 12 (82) 12.00 30.00
COMPLETE SERIES 13 (80) 12.00 30.00
COMPLETE SERIES 14 (80) 12.00 30.00
COMPLETE SERIES 15 (80) 15.00 40.00

❑ 460A Ball 'n Shane .20 .50
❑ 460B Hard Rocky .20 .50
❑ 461A Mara Thon .20 .50
❑ 461B Racy Lacey .20 .50
❑ 462A Half Price .20 .50
❑ 462B Checked-Out Chet .20 .50
❑ 463A Phooey To Huey .20 .50
❑ 463B Razzin' Ross .20 .50
❑ 464A Tongue Tied Teddy .20 .50
❑ 464B Dressed To Killian .20 .50
❑ 465A Upsy Daisys .20 .50
❑ 465B Barfy Barbies .20 .50
❑ 466A Seasick Cecil .20 .50
❑ 466B Dinner At Eytan .20 .50
❑ 467A Tongue In Chico .20 .50
❑ 467B Nick Lick .20 .50
❑ 468A Mummified Clyde .20 .50
❑ 468B Twyla Paper .20 .50
❑ 469A1 Upset Tommy (checklist) .20 .50
❑ 469A2 Upset Tommy (Garbage Gang) .20 .50
❑ 469B1 Tub O' Lars (checklist) .20 .50
❑ 469B2 Tub O' Lars (Garbage Gang) .20 .50
❑ 470A Quick Sandy .20 .50
❑ 470B Abraham Sinkin' .20 .50
❑ 471A Freestyle Kyle .20 .50
❑ 471B Rad Rod .20 .50
❑ 472A1 Walter Fall (Garbage Gang) .20 .50
❑ 472A2 Walter Fall (puzzle preview) .20 .50
❑ 472B1 Ronny Nose (Garbage Gang) .20 .50
❑ 472B2 Ronny Nose (puzzle preview) .20 .50
❑ 473A Heavy Meryl .20 .50
❑ 473B One-Night Stan .20 .50
❑ 474A Sole Food Sol .20 .50
❑ 474B Gooey Stuey .20 .50
❑ 475A Road-Kill Will .20 .50
❑ 475B Stop Sy .20 .50
❑ 476A Barf Band Ben .20 .50
❑ 476B Off Key Lee .20 .50
❑ 477A Ingrid Inc. .20 .50
❑ 477B Smokestack Zach .20 .50
❑ 478A Bizarre Lamar .20 .50
❑ 478B Rearranged Raymond .20 .50
❑ 479A Gulpin' Gabe .20 .50
❑ 479B Over Eatin' Ethan .20 .50
❑ 480A Robby Rubbish .20 .50
❑ 480B Garbage Pail Kitty .20 .50
❑ 481A Car-Stick Karla (Garbage Gang) .20 .50
❑ 481A Car-Stick Karla (puzzle preview) .20 .50
❑ 481B Cruisin' Susan (puzzle preview) .20 .50
❑ 481B Cruisin' Susan (Garbage Gang) .20 .50
❑ 482A Lickin' Leo .20 .50
❑ 482B Lappin' Lenny .20 .50
❑ 483A Seedy Sydney .20 .50
❑ 483B Fertile Myrtle .20 .50
❑ 484A Tim Can .20 .50
❑ 484B Rusty Bolts .20 .50
❑ 485A 12 O'Clock Hy .20 .50
❑ 485B Midnight Dwight .20 .50
❑ 486A Chiseler Chad .20 .50
❑ 486B Julius Sneezer .20 .50
❑ 487A Dead Letter Debbie .20 .50
❑ 487B Maimed Mamie .20 .50
❑ 488A Telly Scope .20 .50
❑ 488B Peek-A-Boo Beau .20 .50
❑ 489A Irate Ira .20 .50
❑ 489B Angry Annie .20 .50
❑ 490A Kinky Kristine .20 .50
❑ 490B Knot The Norm .20 .50
❑ 491A Sunken Trevor .20 .50
❑ 491B Anchored Hank .20 .50
❑ 492A Cory On The Cob .20 .50
❑ 492B Hot Buttered Corinne .20 .50
❑ 493A Peanut Butter 'n Kelly .20 .50
❑ 493B Out-To-Lunch Lance .20 .50
❑ 494A Mitch Match .20 .50
❑ 494B Hot Dot .20 .50
❑ 495A Gloppy Glen .20 .50
❑ 495B Slop Top Todd .20 .50
❑ 496A Allison Waterland .20 .50
❑ 496B Jon Pond .20 .50
❑ 497A Lame Lem .20 .50
❑ 497B Edward Hopper .20 .50
❑ 498A Rolls Royce .20 .50
❑ 498B Piston Pete .20 .50
❑ 499A Abandoned Amanda .20 .50
❑ 499B Please Give Me A Homer .20 .50
❑ 500A Winkless Wally .20 .50
❑ 500B Sight Les .20 .50
❑ 501A Missing Marcia .20 .50
❑ 501B Hidden Heidi .20 .50
❑ 502A Gory Laurie .20 .50
❑ 502B Undead Ned .20 .50
❑ 503A Louise Trapeze .20 .50
❑ 503B 3-Ring Cyril .20 .50
❑ 504A Cooper Scooper .20 .50
❑ 504B Jess Desserts .20 .50
❑ 505A Sucked Chuck .20 .50
❑ 505B Unsani-Terry .20 .50
❑ 506A Tire Jack .20 .50
❑ 506B Crankin' Franklin .20 .50
❑ 507A1 Target Prentice (Garbage Gang) .20 .50
❑ 507A2 Target Prentice (puzzle preview) .20 .50
❑ 507B1 Blow Hardy (Garbage Gang) .20 .50
❑ 507B2 Blow Hardy (puzzle preview) .20 .50
❑ 508A Barry Bomber .20 .50
❑ 508B Hi-Flyin' Brian .20 .50
❑ 509A Misfortune Cookie .20 .50
❑ 509B Chow Maynard .20 .50
❑ 510A Grim Kim .20 .50
❑ 510B Taffy Pull .20 .50
❑ 511A Puffy Buffy .20 .50
❑ 511B Busty Dusty .20 .50
❑ 512A Seymour Barf .20 .50
❑ 512B Kent Stand It .20 .50
❑ 513A Repeatin' Pete .20 .50
❑ 513B Round Robyns .20 .50
❑ 514A Ampu-Ted .20 .50
❑ 514B Hans Off .20 .50
❑ 515A Wretched Richard .20 .50
❑ 515B Billy Ache .20 .50
❑ 516A Bubblin' Lynn .20 .50
❑ 516B Heavin' Heather .20 .50
❑ 517A Chester Drawers .20 .50
❑ 517B Natty Dresser .20 .50
❑ 518A1 Barfin' Marvin (blue Garbage Gang header) .20 .50
❑ 518A2 Barfin' Marvin .20 .50
(yellow Garbage Gang header)
❑ 518B1 Over Etan (blue Garbage Gang header) .20 .50
❑ 518B2 Over Etan (yellow Garbage Gang header) .20 .50
❑ 519A Paddlin' Adeline .20 .50
❑ 519B Rikki Racket .20 .50
❑ 520A Sprinkling Jose .20 .50
❑ 520B Jay Spray .20 .50
❑ 521A Dee Odorant .20 .50
❑ 521B Stan Can .20 .50
❑ 522A Bloody Murray .20 .50
❑ 522B Juan For The Road .20 .50
❑ 523A Meltdown Meryl .20 .50
❑ 523B Steamed Piper .20 .50
❑ 524A Pop Connie .20 .50
❑ 524B Poppy Corn .20 .50
❑ 525A Cocktail Dale .20 .50
❑ 525B Party-Pooper Patty .20 .50
❑ 526A Ripped Kip .20 .50
❑ 526B Torn Shaun .20 .50
❑ 527A Toilet Bo .20 .50
❑ 527B Butt-Bit Brandon .20 .50
❑ 528A Daniel Prune .20 .50
❑ 528B Dried-Fruit Newt .20 .50
❑ 529A Corkscrewed Drew .20 .50
❑ 529B Champ-Pain Dwayne .20 .50
❑ 530A Fun Gus .20 .50
❑ 530B Warty Morty .20 .50
❑ 531A Stormy Skye .20 .50
❑ 531B Claude Burst .20 .50
❑ 532A Fertile Liza .20 .50
❑ 532B Horace Manure .20 .50
❑ 533A Jiggley Jennifer .20 .50
❑ 533B Spooned June .20 .50
❑ 534A1 Jayne Drain (checklist) .20 .50
❑ 534A2 Jayne Drain (Garbage Gang) .20 .50
❑ 534B1 Eda Mouthful (checklist) .20 .50
❑ 534B2 Eda Mouthful (Garbage Gang) .20 .50
❑ 535A Howie Hanging .20 .50
❑ 535B Rush Hour Russ .20 .50
❑ 536A Scrambled Aggie .20 .50
❑ 536B Sonny Side Up .20 .50
❑ 537A Miriam Migraine .20 .50
❑ 537B Head Buster .20 .50
❑ 538A1 Cat-Cradled Cathy (Garbage Gang) .20 .50
❑ 538A2 Cat-Cradled Cathy (puzzle preview) .20 .50
❑ 538B1 Gooey Gwen (Garbage Gang) .20 .50
❑ 538B2 Gooey Gwen (puzzle preview) .20 .50
❑ 539A John John .20 .50
❑ 539B All Wet Walt .20 .50
❑ 540A Ill Windsor .20 .50
❑ 540B Horatio Hornblower .20 .50
❑ 541A1 Rocco Socko (Garbage Gang) .20 .50
❑ 541A2 Rocco Socko (puzzle preview) .20 .50
❑ 541B1 Destroyed Boyd (Garbage Gang) .20 .50
❑ 541B2 Destroyed Boyd (puzzle preview) .20 .50
❑ 542A Jugglin' Julian .20 .50
❑ 542B Up In The Aaron .20 .50
❑ 543A Undersea Lee .20 .50
❑ 543B Sailin' Waylon .20 .50
❑ 544A Zipped Kip .20 .50
❑ 544B Jack Tracks .20 .50
❑ 545A Artie Party .20 .50
❑ 545B Driftin' Clifton .20 .50
❑ 546A Modern Marlise .20 .50
❑ 546B Abstract Abby .20 .50
❑ 547A Cuckoo Clark .20 .50
❑ 547B Bile Lyle .20 .50
❑ 548A1 Walt To Wall (checklist) .20 .50
❑ 548A2 Walt To Wall (Garbage Gang) .20 .50
❑ 548B1 Nailed Noel (checklist) .20 .50
❑ 548B2 Nailed Noel (Garbage Gang) .20 .50
❑ 549A Shannon Cannon .20 .50
❑ 549B Bomb Shelly .20 .50
❑ 550A Violent Viola .20 .50
❑ 550B Sawin' Susan .20 .50
❑ 551A Rah Rah Roni .20 .50
❑ 551B Sis Boom Bonnie .20 .50
❑ 552A Half Whit .20 .50
❑ 552B Lead-Head Ned .20 .50
❑ 553A Cold Sore Lenore .20 .50
❑ 553B Kissy Missy .20 .50
❑ 554A Rufus Refuse .20 .50
❑ 554B Cleaned Up Parker .20 .50
❑ 555A Alien Ed .20 .50
❑ 555B Phone Homer .20 .50
❑ 556A Mothy Martha .20 .50
❑ 556B Nailed Natalie .20 .50
❑ 557A Stu Brew .20 .50
❑ 557B Empty Ken .20 .50
❑ 558A Hans Off .20 .50
❑ 558B Numb Nate .20 .50
❑ 559A Dwayne Stain .20 .50
❑ 559B Spilled Gil .20 .50
❑ 560A Lappin' Larry .20 .50
❑ 560B Guzzlin' Guy .20 .50
❑ 561A Marsh Room .20 .50
❑ 561B Todd Stool .20 .50
❑ 562A1 Post No Bill (blue Garbage Gang header) .20 .50
❑ 562A2 Post No Bill (yellow Garbage Gang header) .20 .50
❑ 562B1 Bulletin Boris (blue Garbage Gang header) .20 .50
❑ 562B2 Bulletin Boris .20 .50
(yellow Garbage Gang header)
❑ 563A Potato Chip .20 .50
❑ 563B Dick Tater .20 .50
❑ 564A Millie Meter .20 .50
❑ 564B Asa Rule .20 .50
❑ 565A Easter Bonnie .20 .50
❑ 565B Hard-Boiled Meg .20 .50
❑ 566A Swarmin' Armin .20 .50
❑ 566B Infested Lester .20 .50
❑ 567A Doomsday Dom .20 .50
❑ 567B A-Bomb Tom .20 .50
❑ 568A Glut Tony .20 .50
❑ 568B Phil Swill .20 .50
❑ 569A Cut Curt .20 .50
❑ 569B Electric Fanny .20 .50
❑ 570A Ava Shaver .20 .50
❑ 570B Holly Hormone .20 .50
❑ 571A Rubber Robert .20 .50
❑ 571B Inside Otto .20 .50
❑ 572A Fake Jake .20 .50
❑ 572B Sham Sam .20 .50
❑ 573A1 Snotwich Sandra (Garbage Gang) .20 .50
❑ 573A2 Snotwich Sandra (puzzle preview) .20 .50
❑ 573B1 Hedda Spreader (Garbage Gang) .20 .50
❑ 573B2 Hedda Spreader (puzzle preview) .20 .50
❑ 574A Shattered Shell .20 .50
❑ 574B Fractured Frank .20 .50
❑ 575A Brain Drain Brian .20 .50
❑ 575B Pick A Winnie .20 .50
❑ 576A Croaked Kaye .20 .50
❑ 576B Sporty Morty .20 .50
❑ 577A Sown Sonya .20 .50
❑ 577B Stitchin' Tyne .20 .50
❑ 578A Dial-A-Twyla .20 .50
❑ 578B Phone Bella .20 .50
❑ 579A Judd Cud .20 .50
❑ 579B Spearmint Mindy .20 .50
❑ 580A Burnt-Out Brett .20 .50
❑ 580B Burne Toast .20 .50
❑ 581A1 Shel Game (checklist) .25 .60
❑ 581A2 Shel Game (Garbage Gang) .25 .60
❑ 581B1 3-Card Monte (checklist) .25 .60
❑ 581B2 3-Card Monte (Garbage Gang) .25 .60
❑ 582A1 Take-Out Dinah (Garbage Gang) .25 .60
❑ 582A2 Take-Out Dinah (puzzle) .25 .60
❑ 582B1 Chow Mame (Garbage Gang) .25 .60
❑ 582B2 Chow Mame (puzzle) .25 .60
❑ 583A1 Lyle Tile (puzzle piece) .25 .60
❑ 583A2 Lyle Tile (puzzle preview) .25 .60
❑ 583B1 Harry Glyph (puzzle piece) .25 .60
❑ 583B2 Harry Glyph (puzzle preview) .25 .60
❑ 584A1 Slimy Hymie (puzzle piece) .25 .60
❑ 584A2 Slimy Hymie (puzzle preview) .25 .60
❑ 584B1 Crawlin' Rollin (puzzle piece) .25 .60
❑ 584B2 Crawlin' Rollin (puzzle preview) .25 .60
❑ 585A Picky Nick .25 .60
❑ 585B Beulah Ghoul .25 .60
❑ 586A Peter Cheater .25 .60
❑ 586B Dean List .25 .60
❑ 587A Cornelia Flake .25 .60
❑ 587B Mala Nutrition .25 .60
❑ 588A Yo! Gert .25 .60
❑ 588B Ice Cream Connie .25 .60
❑ 589A Ecch Benedict .25 .60
❑ 589B Brain Les .25 .60
❑ 590A Little Leak Len .25 .60
❑ 590B Snot-Ball Saul .25 .60
❑ 591A Frank Footer .25 .60
❑ 591B Dog Bites Boyd .25 .60
❑ 592A Extra Dexter .25 .60
❑ 592B Flabby Abby .25 .60
❑ 593A Footloose Fred .25 .60
❑ 593B Lucky Lew .25 .60
❑ 594A Tied Di .25 .60
❑ 594B Knotty Lottie .25 .60
❑ 595A Mal Practice .25 .60
❑ 595B Intensive Carrie .25 .60
❑ 596A Sani Klaus .25 .60
❑ 596B Sick Nick .25 .60
❑ 597A Harry Armpits .25 .60
❑ 597B Under Arnie .25 .60
❑ 598A Vise Guy .25 .60
❑ 598B Hugh Fix-It .25 .60
❑ 599A Bern-Out .25 .60
❑ 599B Dim-Bulb Bob .25 .60
❑ 600A Vendo-Matt .25 .60
❑ 600B Doug Slug .25 .60
❑ 601A Losin' Wade .25 .60
❑ 601B Hy Cholesterol .25 .60
❑ 602A Upside Donna .25 .60
❑ 602B Two-Fer Juan .25 .60
❑ 603A Mitch Mitt .25 .60
❑ 603B Foul Bill .25 .60
❑ 604A Sandi Box .25 .60
❑ 604B Cat Litter .25 .60
❑ 605A Windy Mindy .25 .60
❑ 605B Birthday Kate .25 .60
❑ 606A Foul-Towel Raoul .25 .60
❑ 606B Muddy Buddy .25 .60
❑ 607A Kit Video .25 .60
❑ 607B Ham Actor .25 .60
❑ 608A Fairy Mary .25 .60
❑ 608B Stinker Belle .25 .60
❑ 609A Dewy Dewey .25 .60
❑ 609B Dank Frank .25 .60
❑ 610A Beau Constricted .25 .60
❑ 610B Coiled Carl .25 .60
❑ 611A Acid Wayne .25 .60
❑ 611B Polluted Paul .25 .60
❑ 612A Shoe Lacey .25 .60
❑ 612B Weird Walker .25 .60
❑ 613A Bag Piper .25 .60
❑ 613B Great Scott .25 .60
❑ 614A Fillin' Dylan .25 .60
❑ 614B Cutting Juan .25 .60
❑ 615A Preston Change-O .25 .60
❑ 615B Sleight Of Hans .25 .60
❑ 616A Alec Gator .25 .60
❑ 616B Croco-Dale .25 .60
❑ 617A Claude Flesh .25 .60
❑ 617B Slasher Asher .25 .60
❑ 618A Paper Dolly .25 .60
❑ 618B Catie Cut-Up .25 .60
❑ 619A V.C. Arnie .25 .60
❑ 619B Cassette Casey .25 .60
❑ 620A Ada Bomb .25 .60
❑ 620B1 Blasted Betty (w/ "eyelash" on top border) 4.00 10.00
❑ 620B2 Blasted Betty (no "eyelash" on top border) .25 .60

1988 The Punisher

COMPLETE SET (50) 6.00 15.00

❑ 1 Checklist .30 .75
❑ 2 Circle of Blood .30 .75
❑ 3 The Files .30 .75
❑ 4 Attacked .30 .75
❑ 5 Jigsaw .30 .75
❑ 6 Prepare to Escape .30 .75
❑ 7 Saved .30 .75
❑ 8 Prison Break .30 .75
❑ 9 Plan Two .30 .75
❑ 10 The Offer .30 .75
❑ 11 Forced Revenge .30 .75
❑ 12 Back to the War .30 .75
❑ 13 Get Kingpin .30 .75
❑ 14 The Trap .30 .75
❑ 15 BOOM! .30 .75
❑ 16 Rescued .30 .75
❑ 17 Alaric .30 .75
❑ 18 Set Up .30 .75
❑ 19 Ambushed .30 .75
❑ 20 Face to Face .30 .75
❑ 21 Angela's Secret .30 .75
❑ 22 Slaughterday .30 .75
❑ 23 Santiago .30 .75
❑ 24 The New Driver .30 .75
❑ 25 Don't Snivel .30 .75
❑ 26 You're Not Mob .30 .75
❑ 27 Lookalike .30 .75
❑ 28 One Down .30 .75
❑ 29 Hello Marcus .30 .75
❑ 30 Angela?! .30 .75
❑ 31 Not you, too .30 .75
❑ 32 Final Solution .30 .75
❑ 33 Surprise Visit .30 .75
❑ 34 Dead Aide .30 .75
❑ 35 Packing it in .30 .75
❑ 36 Drive On .30 .75
❑ 37 Jigsaw or Punisher .30 .75
❑ 38 Showdown .30 .75
❑ 39 Come with Me .30 .75
❑ 40 Down the Hatch .30 .75
❑ 41 In the Chamber .30 .75
❑ 42 Final Solution II .30 .75
❑ 43 Strategy Time .30 .75
❑ 44 Vapor Lock .30 .75
❑ 45 Breakout .30 .75
❑ 46 Strike Back .30 .75
❑ 47 Off Guard .30 .75
❑ 48 Do it, or Else .30 .75
❑ 49 Enough, Tony .30 .75
❑ 50 Do Nothing .30 .75

1989 Batman Movie (O-Pee-Chee)

COMPLETE SET (308) 10.00 25.00
COMP. SER. ONE (154) 6.00 15.00
COMP. SER. TWO (154) 6.00 15.00

❑ 1 Introduction .10 .25
❑ 2 Darknight Detective .10 .25
❑ 3 Bruce Wayne .10 .25
❑ 4 The Clown Prince of Crime .10 .25
❑ 5 Jack Napier .10 .25
❑ 6 Vicki Vale .10 .25
❑ 7 Alexander Knox .10 .25
❑ 8 Commissioner Gordon .10 .25
❑ 9 Alfred the Butler .10 .25
❑ 10 D.A. Harvey Dent .10 .25
❑ 11 Crime Boss Carl Grissom .10 .25
❑ 12 Alicia Hunt .10 .25
❑ 13 Gotham City After Dark .10 .25
❑ 14 Mugged .10 .25
❑ 15 Rooftop Rendezvous .10 .25
❑ 16 Night of the Bat .10 .25
❑ 17 Nailed by the Dark Avenger .10 .25
❑ 18 Who...What Are You .10 .25
❑ 19 Gotham City's Dark Knight .10 .25
❑ 20 The New D.A. .10 .25
❑ 21 Knox on the Job .10 .25
❑ 22 The Set-Up .10 .25
❑ 23 Bruce in Wayne Manor .10 .25
❑ 24 Meeting Their Host .10 .25
❑ 25 View from the Batcave .10 .25
❑ 26 The Axis Chemical Factory .10 .25
❑ 27 Mysterious Manhunter .10 .25
❑ 28 Batman's Weapon .10 .25
❑ 29 Toxic Flood .10 .25
❑ 30 In the Batman's Clutches .10 .25
❑ 31 Commissioner Gordon--Hostage .10 .25
❑ 32 Holding Batman at Bay .10 .25
❑ 33 Hero and the Horror .10 .25
❑ 34 Jack Loses His Grip .10 .25
❑ 35 Plunge into Toxic Oblivion .10 .25
❑ 36 Rising Above It All .10 .25
❑ 37 Spotted by Commissioner Gordon .10 .25
❑ 38 Front Page Story .10 .25
❑ 39 Ghastly Revelation .10 .25
❑ 40 Back from the Dead .10 .25
❑ 41 No Deals, Grissom .10 .25
❑ 42 Call Me ... Joker .10 .25
❑ 43 Grissom's Gruesome Demise .10 .25
❑ 44 Wait'll They Get a Load of Me .10 .25
❑ 45 Hi Honey .10 .25
❑ 46 The New Crime Boss .10 .25
❑ 47 Gotham City's Crime Lords .10 .25
❑ 48 Joy-Buzzed to Death .10 .25
❑ 49 Evil of the Joker .10 .25
❑ 50 Fried Alive .10 .25
❑ 51 I'm in Charge Now .10 .25
❑ 52 A Final Farewell .10 .25
❑ 53 Lord of Wayne Manor .10 .25
❑ 54 Outside City Hall .10 .25
❑ 55 The Mime of Mayhem .10 .25
❑ 56 Funny Meeting You Here .10 .25
❑ 57 City Hall Massacre .10 .25
❑ 58 Outrageous Assault .10 .25
❑ 59 Who's the Wildest One of All .10 .25
❑ 60 The Joker's Lair .10 .25
❑ 61 Vicki's Most Devoted Fan .10 .25
❑ 62 Keep Up the Bad Work .10 .25
❑ 63 Smylex Attack .10 .25
❑ 64 The Joker Conquers TV .10 .25
❑ 65 Love that Joker .10 .25
❑ 66 Let's Go Shopping .10 .25
❑ 67 At the Flugelheim .10 .25
❑ 68 The Art of Crime .10 .25
❑ 69 A Date with Vicki .10 .25
❑ 70 You Light Up My Life .10 .25
❑ 71 Alicia's New Look .10 .25
❑ 72 No No I'm Melting .10 .25
❑ 73 Crash .10 .25
❑ 74 The Rescue .10 .25
❑ 75 Swing to Safety .10 .25
❑ 76 A Daring Escape .10 .25
❑ 77 The Batmobile .10 .25
❑ 78 Fantastic Chase .10 .25
❑ 79 The Batmobile Tears Away .10 .25
❑ 80 Cocooned .10 .25
❑ 81 Is It Halloween .10 .25

- ❑ 82 How Much Do You Weigh .10 .25
- ❑ 83 Death-Defying Duo .10 .25
- ❑ 84 Hang On, Vicki .10 .25
- ❑ 85 Batman Overpowered .10 .25
- ❑ 86 The Challenge .10 .25
- ❑ 87 Urban Warriors .10 .25
- ❑ 88 Slashing Assault .10 .25
- ❑ 89 Photographed by Vicki .10 .25
- ❑ 90 Friend ... Or Mad Vigilated .10 .25
- ❑ 91 Within the Batcave .10 .25
- ❑ 92 Vicki in a Jam .10 .25
- ❑ 93 The Joker Is Wild .10 .25
- ❑ 94 Haunting Memory .10 .25
- ❑ 95 Fate of the Wayne Family .10 .25
- ❑ 96 Gearing Up for Danger .10 .25
- ❑ 97 Knight Patrol .10 .25
- ❑ 98 Sabotage .10 .25
- ❑ 99 The Axis Fireball .10 .25
- ❑ 100 Escape from Flaming Death .10 .25
- ❑ 101 The Master of Disaster .10 .25
- ❑ 102 Bicentennial Nightmare .10 .25
- ❑ 103 Twisted Terrorists .10 .25
- ❑ 104 Flight of the Batwing .10 .25
- ❑ 105 Batwing Cockpit .10 .25
- ❑ 106 The Joker's Secret Weapon .10 .25
- ❑ 107 Taking Aim at the Batwing .10 .25
- ❑ 108 Super-Sleek Craft .10 .25
- ❑ 109 Crash Dive .10 .25
- ❑ 110 Vicki to the Rescue .10 .25
- ❑ 111 The Joker Takes a Hostage .10 .25
- ❑ 112 Batman Lives .10 .25
- ❑ 113 Grim Vendetta .10 .25
- ❑ 114 In Danger's Domain .10 .25
- ❑ 115 Watch Out Behind You .10 .25
- ❑ 116 Assault on the Caped Fury .10 .25
- ❑ 117 Desperate Struggle .10 .25
- ❑ 118 Grip of Death .10 .25
- ❑ 119 Perilous Plunge .10 .25
- ❑ 120 Batman in Action .10 .25
- ❑ 121 No Match for Batman .10 .25
- ❑ 122 Bruised But Not Beaten .10 .25
- ❑ 123 The Joker's Final Stand .10 .25
- ❑ 124 Dance of Death .10 .25
- ❑ 125 Vicki Imperiled .10 .25
- ❑ 126 The Titans Clash .10 .25
- ❑ 127 Batman vs. Madman .10 .25
- ❑ 128 The Dark Knight Triumphs .10 .25
- ❑ 129 The Joker--Over the Edge .10 .25
- ❑ 130 He Who Laughs Last .10 .25
- ❑ 131 The Bat-Signal .10 .25
- ❑ 132 The Guardian of Gotham City .10 .25
- ❑ 133 Batman .10 .25
- ❑ 134 Batman logo .10 .25
- ❑ 135 Vicki Vale .10 .25

Bruce Wayne

- ❑ 136 Batmobile .10 .25
- ❑ 137 Joker .10 .25
- ❑ 138 Joker's gang .10 .25
- ❑ 139 Batman .10 .25

Joker

- ❑ 140 Batmobile .10 .25
- ❑ 141 Three Joker heads .10 .25
- ❑ 142 Joker .10 .25
- ❑ 143 Batman .10 .25
- ❑ 144 Batman statue .10 .25
- ❑ 145 Batplane .10 .25
- ❑ 146 Batplane .10 .25
- ❑ 147 Joker .10 .25
- ❑ 148 Joker .10 .25
- ❑ 149 Batman .10 .25
- ❑ 150 Joker .10 .25
- ❑ 151 Batman .10 .25
- ❑ 152 Batman .10 .25
- ❑ 153 Joker .10 .25
- ❑ 154 Vicki Vale .10 .25
- ❑ 155 Batman--The 2nd Series .10 .25
- ❑ 156 The Man and His Quarry .10 .25
- ❑ 157 Hand of Vengeance .10 .25
- ❑ 158 Parked in the Batcave .10 .25
- ❑ 159 Fistfuls of Funny Money .10 .25
- ❑ 160 Onward, To His Fate .10 .25
- ❑ 161 Doppelganger .10 .25
- ❑ 162 Time to Die, Grissom .10 .25
- ❑ 163 Armadillo Effect .10 .25
- ❑ 164 The Last of Eckhardt .10 .25
- ❑ 165 Leer of the Clown Prince .10 .25
- ❑ 166 I've Got to Work Tonight .10 .25
- ❑ 167 Leap from the Belltower .10 .25
- ❑ 168 March of the Misfits .10 .25
- ❑ 169 Meltingly Beautiful .10 .25
- ❑ 170 You Know Who I Mean .10 .25
- ❑ 171 Power of the Batmobile .10 .25
- ❑ 172 Flugelheim Aftermath .10 .25
- ❑ 173 Alley Bat .10 .25
- ❑ 174 Aiming To Kill .10 .25
- ❑ 175 News of the Battle .10 .25
- ❑ 176 The Wayne Manor Party .10 .25
- ❑ 177 Of Mimes and Memories .10 .25
- ❑ 178 Danger in the Streets .10 .25
- ❑ 179 The Oddest Couple .10 .25
- ❑ 180 Knight and the Damsel .10 .25
- ❑ 181 Hanging On For Life .10 .25
- ❑ 182 Murder...Just for Laughs .10 .25
- ❑ 183 Twisted Pitchman .10 .25
- ❑ 184 Copter Escape .10 .25
- ❑ 185 Instructions for Alfred .10 .25
- ❑ 186 Gotham City Landscape .10 .25
- ❑ 187 Flugelheim Museum Interior .10 .25
- ❑ 188 Elevated Subway Exterior .10 .25
- ❑ 189 Flugelheim Museum Exterior .10 .25
- ❑ 190 Grissom's Office .10 .25
- ❑ 191 Their Final Bow .10 .25
- ❑ 192 The Batmobile--Head On .10 .25
- ❑ 193 Dangling Devil .10 .25
- ❑ 194 See Rotelli Roast .10 .25
- ❑ 195 The Defeat of Batman .10 .25
- ❑ 196 Sneaking Up Behind Jack .10 .25
- ❑ 197 Festival of Madness .10 .25
- ❑ 198 Battered But Unbowed .10 .25
- ❑ 199 Mission Accomplished .10 .25
- ❑ 200 Retreat Into Darkness .10 .25
- ❑ 201 You Want To Get Nuts .10 .25
- ❑ 202 The Master's Mimes .10 .25
- ❑ 203 Knox Chats with Alfred .10 .25
- ❑ 204 Savage Sneak Attack .10 .25
- ❑ 205 Madness Wears a Smile .10 .25
- ❑ 206 The Batmobile Escapes .10 .25
- ❑ 207 Jack and Alicia .10 .25
- ❑ 208 Trick or Treat .10 .25
- ❑ 209 The Field Flies High .10 .25
- ❑ 210 His Card... .10 .25
- ❑ 211 Silent But Deadly .10 .25
- ❑ 212 The Phantom Avengers .10 .25
- ❑ 213 A New Mad Plan .10 .25
- ❑ 214 Friends and Lovers .10 .25
- ❑ 215 Fiery Finale .10 .25
- ❑ 216 Another Man Down .10 .25
- ❑ 217 The Batwing Soars .10 .25
- ❑ 218 The Joker by Tim Burton .10 .25
- ❑ 219 Batman Costume Design .10 .25
- ❑ 220 The Joker Costume Design .10 .25
- ❑ 221 Batman Design Concept .10 .25
- ❑ 222 Metal Walkway .10 .25
- ❑ 223 Tugging the Line .10 .25
- ❑ 224 The Hanging Hood .10 .25
- ❑ 225 Over the Gantry .10 .25
- ❑ 226 The Joker Knocked Backwards .10 .25
- ❑ 227 Danger Directly Ahead .10 .25
- ❑ 228 Clearing the Trigger .10 .25
- ❑ 229 Preparing for an Assault .10 .25
- ❑ 230 Cathedral Dead Ahead .10 .25
- ❑ 231 Goons in Hot Pursuit .10 .25
- ❑ 232 Mysterious Millionaire .10 .25
- ❑ 233 Alleys of Gotham City .10 .25
- ❑ 234 The Villain Supreme .10 .25
- ❑ 235 Who Is Jack Napier .10 .25
- ❑ 236 The Joke's on Alicia .10 .25
- ❑ 237 Weapon Against Evil .10 .25
- ❑ 238 His Foul and Fiendish Grin .10 .25
- ❑ 239 Armor Inspiration .10 .25
- ❑ 240 Grotesque Reflections .10 .25
- ❑ 241 A Gift for Vicki .10 .25
- ❑ 242 The Night Is His Again .10 .25
- ❑ 243 Kids Playing Batman .10 .25
- ❑ 244 Brains + Beauty = Vicki .10 .25
- ❑ 245 Everyone Needs a Hobby .10 .25
- ❑ 246 Throttling a Punk .10 .25
- ❑ 247 An Artist Most Bizarre .10 .25
- ❑ 248 Batman's Public Service .10 .25
- ❑ 249 A Goon and His Tune .10 .25
- ❑ 250 City of Light and Danger .10 .25
- ❑ 251 Heroic Escape .10 .25
- ❑ 252 How the Joker Lives .10 .25
- ❑ 253 Batman in the Belfrey .10 .25
- ❑ 254 Classic First Issue .10 .25
- ❑ 255 Directing Grissom's Murder .10 .25
- ❑ 256 The Clown and the Clapboard .10 .25
- ❑ 257 The Director's Vision .10 .25
- ❑ 258 Maniacal Murderer .10 .25
- ❑ 259 Knox Takes a Shot at Heroism .10 .25
- ❑ 260 What Tim Burton Wants .10 .25
- ❑ 261 Getting the Worst from Grissom .10 .25
- ❑ 262 Directing Helicopter Escape .10 .25
- ❑ 263 Special Advice for Batman .10 .25
- ❑ 264 Directing Michael Keaton .10 .25
- ❑ 265 Flight of the Dark Avenger .10 .25
- ❑ 266 Interviewed by Knox .10 .25
- ❑ 267 Tim Burton, Filmmaker .10 .25
- ❑ 268 Alicia--Exquisite .10 .25
- ❑ 269 Presenting the Batmobile .10 .25
- ❑ 270 Relaxing with Key Players .10 .25
- ❑ 271 Filming the Dance Macabre .10 .25
- ❑ 272 Shooting the Rescue Scene .10 .25
- ❑ 273 Dining at Wayne Manor .10 .25
- ❑ 274 Secret Life of Bruce Wayne .10 .25
- ❑ 275 City Street Miniature .10 .25
- ❑ 276 At the Nerve Center .10 .25
- ❑ 277 Computerized SFX .10 .25
- ❑ 278 Fantastic Miniature Set .10 .25
- ❑ 279 Trail of the Mystery Man .10 .25
- ❑ 280 Directing Jack Nicholson .10 .25
- ❑ 281 Dance of the Deranged .10 .25
- ❑ 282 From Burton to Batman .10 .25
- ❑ 283 Batman's Revenge .10 .25
- ❑ 284 Gruesome Grimace .10 .25
- ❑ 285 Buildings of Gotham City .10 .25
- ❑ 286 The Killer Clown's In Town .10 .25
- ❑ 287 Joker .10 .25

Batman

- ❑ 288 Batman .10 .25
- ❑ 289 Joker .10 .25
- ❑ 290 Batman .10 .25
- ❑ 291 Joker .10 .25
- ❑ 292 Batman .10 .25
- ❑ 293 Joker .10 .25
- ❑ 294 Batman .10 .25
- ❑ 295 Joker .10 .25
- ❑ 296 Batman .10 .25
- ❑ 297 Joker .10 .25
- ❑ 298 Batman .10 .25
- ❑ 299 Batman .10 .25
- ❑ 300 Bruce Wayne .10 .25
- ❑ 301 Joker .10 .25
- ❑ 302 Batman logo .10 .25
- ❑ 303 Batman .10 .25
- ❑ 304 Joker .10 .25
- ❑ 305 Batman .10 .25
- ❑ 306 Batman .10 .25

Vicki Vale

- ❑ 307 Joker .10 .25
- ❑ 308 Batmobile .10 .25

1989 Batman Movie (Topps)

COMPLETE SET (264) 10.00 25.00
COMP. SER. ONE (132) 6.00 15.00
COMP. SER. TWO (132) 6.00 15.00

- ❑ 1 Introduction .10 .25
- ❑ 2 Darknight Detective .10 .25
- ❑ 3 Bruce Wayne .10 .25
- ❑ 4 The Clown Prince of Crime .10 .25
- ❑ 5 Jack Napier .10 .25
- ❑ 6 Vicki Vale .10 .25
- ❑ 7 Alexander Knox .10 .25
- ❑ 8 Commissioner Gordon .10 .25
- ❑ 9 Alfred the Butler .10 .25
- ❑ 10 D.A. Harvey Dent .10 .25
- ❑ 11 Crime Boss Carl Grissom .10 .25
- ❑ 12 Alicia Hunt .10 .25
- ❑ 13 Gotham City After Dark .10 .25
- ❑ 14 Mugged .10 .25
- ❑ 15 Rooftop Rendezvous .10 .25
- ❑ 16 Night of the Bat .10 .25
- ❑ 17 Nailed by the Dark Avenger .10 .25
- ❑ 18 Who...What Are You .10 .25
- ❑ 19 Gotham City's Dark Knight .10 .25
- ❑ 20 The New D.A. .10 .25
- ❑ 21 Knox on the Job .10 .25
- ❑ 22 The Set-Up .10 .25
- ❑ 23 Bruce in Wayne Manor .10 .25
- ❑ 24 Meeting Their Host .10 .25
- ❑ 25 View from the Batcave .10 .25
- ❑ 26 The Axis Chemical Factory .10 .25
- ❑ 27 Mysterious Manhunter .10 .25
- ❑ 28 Batman's Weapon .10 .25
- ❑ 29 Toxic Flood .10 .25
- ❑ 30 In the Batman's Clutches .10 .25
- ❑ 31 Commissioner Gordon--Hostage .10 .25
- ❑ 32 Holding Batman at Bay .10 .25
- ❑ 33 Hero and the Horror .10 .25
- ❑ 34 Jack Loses His Grip .10 .25
- ❑ 35 Plunge into Toxic Oblivion .10 .25
- ❑ 36 Rising Above It All .10 .25
- ❑ 37 Spotted by Commissioner Gordon .10 .25
- ❑ 38 Front Page Story .10 .25
- ❑ 39 Ghastly Revelation .10 .25
- ❑ 40 Back from the Dead .10 .25
- ❑ 41 No Deals, Grissom .10 .25
- ❑ 42 Call Me ... Joker .10 .25
- ❑ 43 Grissom's Gruesome Demise .10 .25
- ❑ 44 Wait'll They Get a Load of Me .10 .25
- ❑ 45 Hi Honey .10 .25
- ❑ 46 The New Crime Boss .10 .25
- ❑ 47 Gotham City's Crime Lords .10 .25
- ❑ 48 Joy-Buzzed to Death .10 .25
- ❑ 49 Evil of the Joker .10 .25
- ❑ 50 Fried Alive .10 .25
- ❑ 51 I'm in Charge Now .10 .25
- ❑ 52 A Final Farewell .10 .25
- ❑ 53 Lord of Wayne Manor .10 .25
- ❑ 54 Outside City Hall .10 .25
- ❑ 55 The Mime of Mayhem .10 .25
- ❑ 56 Funny Meeting You Here .10 .25
- ❑ 57 City Hall Massacre .10 .25
- ❑ 58 Outrageous Assault .10 .25
- ❑ 59 Who's the Wildest One of All .10 .25
- ❑ 60 The Joker's Lair .10 .25
- ❑ 61 Vicki's Most Devoted Fan .10 .25
- ❑ 62 Keep Up the Bad Work .10 .25
- ❑ 63 Smylex Attack .10 .25
- ❑ 64 The Joker Conquers TV .10 .25
- ❑ 65 Love that Joker .10 .25
- ❑ 66 Let's Go Shopping .10 .25
- ❑ 67 At the Flugelheim .10 .25
- ❑ 68 The Art of Crime .10 .25
- ❑ 69 A Date with Vicki .10 .25
- ❑ 70 You Light Up My Life .10 .25
- ❑ 71 Alicia's New Look .10 .25
- ❑ 72 No No I'm Melting .10 .25
- ❑ 73 Crash .10 .25
- ❑ 74 The Rescue .10 .25
- ❑ 75 Swing to Safety .10 .25
- ❑ 76 A Daring Escape .10 .25
- ❑ 77 The Batmobile .10 .25
- ❑ 78 Fantastic Chase .10 .25
- ❑ 79 The Batmobile Tears Away .10 .25
- ❑ 80 Cocooned .10 .25
- ❑ 81 Is It Halloween .10 .25
- ❑ 82 How Much Do You Weigh .10 .25
- ❑ 83 Death-Defying Duo .10 .25
- ❑ 84 Hang On, Vicki .10 .25
- ❑ 85 Batman Overpowered .10 .25
- ❑ 86 The Challenge .10 .25
- ❑ 87 Urban Warriors .10 .25
- ❑ 88 Slashing Assault .10 .25
- ❑ 89 Photographed by Vicki .10 .25
- ❑ 90 Friend ... Or Mad Vigilated .10 .25
- ❑ 91 Within the Batcave .10 .25
- ❑ 92 Vicki in a Jam .10 .25
- ❑ 93 The Joker Is Wild .10 .25
- ❑ 94 Haunting Memory .10 .25
- ❑ 95 Fate of the Wayne Family .10 .25
- ❑ 96 Gearing Up for Danger .10 .25
- ❑ 97 Knight Patrol .10 .25
- ❑ 98 Sabotage .10 .25
- ❑ 99 The Axis Fireball .10 .25
- ❑ 100 Escape from Flaming Death .10 .25
- ❑ 101 The Master of Disaster .10 .25
- ❑ 102 Bicentennial Nightmare .10 .25
- ❑ 103 Twisted Terrorists .10 .25
- ❑ 104 Flight of the Batwing .10 .25
- ❑ 105 Batwing Cockpit .10 .25
- ❑ 106 The Joker's Secret Weapon .10 .25
- ❑ 107 Taking Aim at the Batwing .10 .25
- ❑ 108 Super-Sleek Craft .10 .25
- ❑ 109 Crash Dive .10 .25
- ❑ 110 Vicki to the Rescue .10 .25
- ❑ 111 The Joker Takes a Hostage .10 .25
- ❑ 112 Batman Lives .10 .25
- ❑ 113 Grim Vendetta .10 .25
- ❑ 114 In Danger's Domain .10 .25
- ❑ 115 Watch Out Behind You .10 .25
- ❑ 116 Assault on the Caped Fury .10 .25
- ❑ 117 Desperate Struggle .10 .25
- ❑ 118 Grip of Death .10 .25
- ❑ 119 Perilous Plunge .10 .25
- ❑ 120 Batman in Action .10 .25
- ❑ 121 No Match for Batman .10 .25
- ❑ 122 Bruised But Not Beaten .10 .25
- ❑ 123 The Joker's Final Stand .10 .25
- ❑ 124 Dance of Death .10 .25
- ❑ 125 Vicki Imperiled .10 .25
- ❑ 126 The Titans Clash .10 .25
- ❑ 127 Batman vs. Madman .10 .25
- ❑ 128 The Dark Knight Triumphs .10 .25
- ❑ 129 The Joker--Over the Edge .10 .25
- ❑ 130 He Who Laughs Last .10 .25
- ❑ 131 The Bat-Signal .10 .25
- ❑ 132 The Guardian of Gotham City .10 .25
- ❑ 133 Batman--The 2nd Series .10 .25
- ❑ 134 The Man and His Quarry .10 .25
- ❑ 135 Hand of Vengeance .10 .25
- ❑ 136 Parked in the Batcave .10 .25
- ❑ 137 Fistfuls of Funny Money .10 .25
- ❑ 138 Onward, To His Fate .10 .25
- ❑ 139 Doppelganger .10 .25
- ❑ 140 Time to Die, Grissom .10 .25
- ❑ 141 Armadillo Effect .10 .25
- ❑ 142 The Last of Eckhardt .10 .25
- ❑ 143 Leer of the Clown Prince .10 .25
- ❑ 144 I've Got to Work Tonight .10 .25
- ❑ 145 Leap from the Belltower .10 .25
- ❑ 146 March of the Misfits .10 .25
- ❑ 147 Meltingly Beautiful .10 .25
- ❑ 148 You Know Who I Mean .10 .25
- ❑ 149 Power of the Batmobile .10 .25
- ❑ 150 Flugelheim Aftermath .10 .25
- ❑ 151 Alley Bat .10 .25
- ❑ 152 Aiming To Kill .10 .25
- ❑ 153 News of the Battle .10 .25
- ❑ 154 The Wayne Manor Party .10 .25
- ❑ 155 Of Mimes and Memories .10 .25
- ❑ 156 Danger in the Streets .10 .25
- ❑ 157 The Oddest Couple .10 .25
- ❑ 158 Knight and the Damsel .10 .25
- ❑ 159 Hanging On For Life .10 .25
- ❑ 160 Murder...Just for Laughs .10 .25
- ❑ 161 Twisted Pitchman .10
- ❑ 162 Copter Escape .10 .25
- ❑ 163 Instructions for Alfred .10 .25
- ❑ 164 Gotham City Landscape .10 .25
- ❑ 165 Flugelheim Museum Interior .10 .25
- ❑ 166 Elevated Subway Exterior .10 .25
- ❑ 167 Flugelheim Museum Exterior .10 .25
- ❑ 168 Grissom's Office .10 .25
- ❑ 169 Their Final Bow .10 .25
- ❑ 170 The Batmobile--Head On .10 .25
- ❑ 171 Dangling Devil .10 .25
- ❑ 172 See Rotelli Roast .10 .25
- ❑ 173 The Defeat of Batman .10 .25
- ❑ 174 Sneaking Up Behind Jack .10 .25
- ❑ 175 Festival of Madness .10 .25
- ❑ 176 Battered But Unbowed .10 .25
- ❑ 177 Mission Accomplished .10 .25
- ❑ 178 Retreat Into Darkness .10 .25
- ❑ 179 You Want To Get Nuts .10 .25
- ❑ 180 The Master's Mimes .10 .25
- ❑ 181 Knox Chats with Alfred .10 .25
- ❑ 182 Savage Sneak Attack .10 .25
- ❑ 183 Madness Wears a Smile .10 .25
- ❑ 184 The Batmobile Escapes .10 .25
- ❑ 185 Jack and Alicia .10 .25
- ❑ 186 Trick or Treat .10 .25
- ❑ 187 The Field Flies High .10 .25
- ❑ 188 His Card... .10 .25
- ❑ 189 Silent But Deadly .10 .25
- ❑ 190 The Phantom Avengers .10 .25
- ❑ 191 A New Mad Plan .10 .25
- ❑ 192 Friends and Lovers .10 .25
- ❑ 193 Fiery Finale .10 .25
- ❑ 194 Another Man Down .10 .25
- ❑ 195 The Batwing Soars .10 .25
- ❑ 196 The Joker by Tim Burton .10 .25
- ❑ 197 Batman Costume Design .10 .25
- ❑ 198 The Joker Costume Design .10 .25
- ❑ 199 Batman Design Concept .10 .25
- ❑ 200 Metal Walkway .10 .25
- ❑ 201 Tugging the Line .10 .25
- ❑ 202 The Hanging Hood .10 .25
- ❑ 203 Over the Gantry .10 .25
- ❑ 204 The Joker Knocked Backwards .10 .25
- ❑ 205 Danger Directly Ahead .10 .25
- ❑ 206 Clearing the Trigger .10 .25
- ❑ 207 Preparing for an Assault .10 .25
- ❑ 208 Cathedral Dead Ahead .10 .25
- ❑ 209 Goons in Hot Pursuit .10 .25
- ❑ 210 Mysterious Millionaire .10 .25
- ❑ 211 Alleys of Gotham City .10 .25
- ❑ 212 The Villain Supreme .10 .25
- ❑ 213 Who Is Jack Napier .10 .25
- ❑ 214 The Joke's on Alicia .10 .25
- ❑ 215 Weapon Against Evil .10 .25
- ❑ 216 His Foul and Fiendish Grin .10 .25
- ❑ 217 Armor Inspiration .10 .25
- ❑ 218 Grotesque Reflections .10 .25
- ❑ 219 A Gift for Vicki .10 .25
- ❑ 220 The Night Is His Again .10 .25
- ❑ 221 Kids Playing Batman .10 .25
- ❑ 222 Brains + Beauty = Vicki .10 .25
- ❑ 223 Everyone Needs a Hobby .10 .25
- ❑ 224 Throttling a Punk .10 .25
- ❑ 225 An Artist Most Bizarre .10 .25
- ❑ 226 Batman's Public Service .10 .25
- ❑ 227 A Goon and His Tune .10 .25
- ❑ 228 City of Light and Danger .10 .25
- ❑ 229 Heroic Escape .10 .25
- ❑ 230 How the Joker Lives .10 .25
- ❑ 231 Batman in the Belfrey .10 .25
- ❑ 232 Classic First Issue .10 .25
- ❑ 233 Directing Grissom's Murder .10 .25
- ❑ 234 The Clown and the Clapboard .10 .25
- ❑ 235 The Director's Vision .10 .25
- ❑ 236 Maniacal Murderer .10 .25
- ❑ 237 Knox Takes a Shot at Heroism .10 .25
- ❑ 238 What Tim Burton Wants .10 .25
- ❑ 239 Getting the Worst from Grissom .10 .25
- ❑ 240 Directing Helicopter Escape .10 .25
- ❑ 241 Special Advice for Batman .10 .25
- ❑ 242 Directing Michael Keaton .10 .25
- ❑ 243 Flight of the Dark Avenger .10 .25
- ❑ 244 Interviewed by Knox .10 .25
- ❑ 245 Tim Burton, Filmmaker .10 .25
- ❑ 246 Alicia--Exquisite .10 .25
- ❑ 247 Presenting the Batmobile .10 .25
- ❑ 248 Relaxing with Key Players .10 .25
- ❑ 249 Filming the Dance Macabre .10 .25
- ❑ 250 Shooting the Rescue Scene .10 .25
- ❑ 251 Dining at Wayne Manor .10 .25
- ❑ 252 Secret Life of Bruce Wayne .10 .25
- ❑ 253 City Street Miniature .10 .25
- ❑ 254 At the Nerve Center .10 .25
- ❑ 255 Computerized SFX .10 .25
- ❑ 256 Fantastic Miniature Set .10 .25
- ❑ 257 Trail of the Mystery Man .10 .25
- ❑ 258 Directing Jack Nicholson .10 .25
- ❑ 259 Dance of the Deranged .10 .25
- ❑ 260 From Burton to Batman .10 .25
- ❑ 261 Batman's Revenge .10 .25
- ❑ 262 Gruesome Grimace .10 .25
- ❑ 263 Buildings of Gotham City .10 .25
- ❑ 264 The Killer Clown's In Town .10 .25

1989 Batman Movie Collector's Edition

COMPLETE SET (264) 10.00 25.00
COMP. SER. ONE (132) 6.00 15.00
COMP. SER. ONE FACT. SET (165) 8.00 20.00
COMP. SER. TWO (132) 6.00 15.00
COMP. SER. TWO FACT. SET (165) 8.00 20.00

1989 Batman Movie Collector's Edition Bonus

COMPLETE SET (22) 3.00 8.00
COMP. SER. ONE SET (11) 2.00 5.00
COMP. SER. TWO SET (11) 2.00 5.00

- ❑ A Batman in Batwing Cockpit .30 .75
- ❑ B The Batwing Swoops Down .30 .75
- ❑ C Canyons of Gotham City .30 .75
- ❑ D Zeroing in on The Joker .30 .75
- ❑ E Setting the Missile Sights .30 .75
- ❑ F Hitting the Switch .30 .75
- ❑ G Firing Away .30 .75
- ❑ H The Joker Avoids the Onslaught .30 .75
- ❑ I The Dark Knight Reacts .30 .75
- ❑ J The Batwing Bounces .30 .75
- ❑ K Cathedral Directly Ahead .30 .75
- ❑ L Grappling Hook .30 .75
- ❑ M Batarang .30 .75
- ❑ N Darkly Humorous Pistols .30 .75
- ❑ O Batman's Time Bomb .30 .75
- ❑ P Smoke Capsules .30 .75
- ❑ Q Handset and Tracer .30 .75
- ❑ R Batmobile Communicator .30 .75
- ❑ S Cocooned Batmobile .30 .75
- ❑ T Acid-Squirting Flower .30 .75
- ❑ U Batman's Gauntlet .30 .75
- ❑ V Utility Belt, Body Armor .30 .75

1989 Batman Movie Stickers

COMPLETE SET (44) 4.00 10.00
COMP. SER. ONE (22) 2.50 6.00
COMP. SER. TWO (22) 2.50 6.00
STATED ODDS ONE PER PACK

- ❑ 1 Batman .20 .50
- ❑ 2 Batman logo .20 .50
- ❑ 3 Vicki Vale .20 .50

Bruce Wayne

- ❑ 4 Batmobile .20 .50
- ❑ 5 Joker .20 .50
- ❑ 6 Joker's gang .20 .50
- ❑ 7 Batman .20 .50

Joker

- ❑ 8 Batmobile .20 .50
- ❑ 9 Three Joker heads .20 .50
- ❑ 10 Joker .20 .50
- ❑ 11 Batman .20 .50
- ❑ 12 Batman statue .20 .50
- ❑ 13 Batplane .20 .50
- ❑ 14 Batplane .20 .50
- ❑ 15 Joker .20 .50
- ❑ 16 Joker .20 .50
- ❑ 17 Batman .20 .50
- ❑ 18 Joker .20 .50
- ❑ 19 Batman .20 .50
- ❑ 20 Batman .20 .50
- ❑ 21 Joker .20 .50
- ❑ 22 Vicki Vale .20 .50
- ❑ 23 Joker .20 .50

Batman

- ❑ 24 Batman .20 .50
- ❑ 25 Joker .20 .50
- ❑ 26 Batman .20 .50
- ❑ 27 Joker .20 .50
- ❑ 28 Batman .20 .50
- ❑ 29 Joker .20 .50
- ❑ 30 Batman .20 .50
- ❑ 31 Joker .20 .50
- ❑ 32 Batman .20 .50
- ❑ 33 Joker .20 .50
- ❑ 34 Batman .20 .50
- ❑ 35 Batman .20 .50
- ❑ 36 Bruce Wayne .20 .50
- ❑ 37 Joker .20 .50
- ❑ 38 Batman logo .20 .50
- ❑ 39 Batman .20 .50
- ❑ 40 Joker .20 .50
- ❑ 41 Batman .20 .50
- ❑ 42 Batman .20 .50

Vicki Vale

- ❑ 43 Joker .20 .50
- ❑ 44 Batmobile .20 .50

1990 Marvel Universe

COMPLETE SET (162) 12.00 30.00

- ❑ 1 Captain America .15 .40
- ❑ 2 Spider-Man .15 .40
- ❑ 3 Hulk .15 .40
- ❑ 4 Daredevil .15 .40
- ❑ 5 Nick Fury .15 .40
- ❑ 6 Thing .15 .40
- ❑ 7 Professor X .15 .40
- ❑ 8 Cyclops .15 .40
- ❑ 9 Marvel Girl .15 .40
- ❑ 10 Wolverine .15 .40
- ❑ 11 Phoenix .15 .40
- ❑ 12 Power Man .15 .40
- ❑ 13 Dazzler .15 .40
- ❑ 14 Dagger .15 .40
- ❑ 15 Quasar .15 .40
- ❑ 16 Sub-Mariner .15 .40
- ❑ 17 Hulk .15 .40
- ❑ 18 Thor .15 .40
- ❑ 19 Mister Fantastic .15 .40
- ❑ 20 Black Panther .15 .40
- ❑ 21 Archangel .15 .40
- ❑ 22 Iceman .15 .40
- ❑ 23 Wolverine .15 .40
- ❑ 24 Storm .15 .40
- ❑ 25 Shadowcat .15 .40
- ❑ 26 Moon Knight .15 .40
- ❑ 27 Lockheed .15 .40
- ❑ 28 Aunt May .15 .40
- ❑ 29 Spider-Man .15 .40
- ❑ 30 Spider-Man .15 .40
- ❑ 31 Captain America .15 .40
- ❑ 32 Silver Surfer .15 .40
- ❑ 33 Human Torch .15 .40
- ❑ 34 Doctor Strange .15 .40
- ❑ 35 Havok .15 .40
- ❑ 36 Colossus .15 .40
- ❑ 37 Wolverine .15 .40
- ❑ 38 Nightcrawler .15 .40
- ❑ 39 She-Hulk .15 .40
- ❑ 40 Captain Britain .15 .40
- ❑ 41 Rogue .15 .40
- ❑ 42 Iron Man .15 .40
- ❑ 43 Invisible Woman .15 .40
- ❑ 44 Punisher .15 .40
- ❑ 45 Longshot .15 .40
- ❑ 46 Beast .15 .40
- ❑ 47 Punisher .15 .40
- ❑ 48 Storm .15 .40
- ❑ 49 Elektra .15 .40
- ❑ 50 Cloak .15 .40
- ❑ 51 Wasp .15 .40
- ❑ 52 Kingpin .15 .40
- ❑ 53 Baron Zemo .15 .40
- ❑ 54 Loki .15 .40
- ❑ 55 Juggernaut .15 .40
- ❑ 56 Nightmare .15 .40
- ❑ 57 Sabretooth .15 .40
- ❑ 58 Electro .15 .40
- ❑ 59 Doctor Octopus .15 .40
- ❑ 60 Doctor Doom .15 .40
- ❑ 61 Ultron .15 .40
- ❑ 62 Enchantress .15 .40
- ❑ 63 Magneto .15 .40

MODERN ERA NON-SPORTS

- ❑ 64 Bullseye .15 .40
- ❑ 65 Mister Sinister .15 .40
- ❑ 66 Sandman .15 .40
- ❑ 67 Lizard .15 .40
- ❑ 68 Mole Man .15 .40
- ❑ 69 Dormammu .15 .40
- ❑ 70 Leader .15 .40
- ❑ 71 Blob .15 .40
- ❑ 72 Black Cat .15 .40
- ❑ 73 Venom .15 .40
- ❑ 74 Green Goblin .15 .40
- ❑ 75 Galactus .15 .40
- ❑ 76 Mandarin .15 .40
- ❑ 77 High Evolutionary .15 .40
- ❑ 78 Mephisto .15 .40
- ❑ 79 Thanos .15 .40
- ❑ 80 Apocalypse .15 .40
- ❑ 81 Red Skull .15 .40
- ❑ 82 Ghost Rider .15 .40
- ❑ 83 Deathlok .15 .40
- ❑ 84 Guardians of the Galaxy .15 .40
- ❑ 85 New Warriors .15 .40
- ❑ 86 Nomad .15 .40
- ❑ 87 Foolkiller .15 .40
- ❑ 88 Thing vs. Hulk .15 .40
- ❑ 89 Fantastic Four vs. Galctus .15 .40
- ❑ 90 Fantastic Four vs. Doctor Doom .15 .40
- ❑ 91 Thor vs. Surtur .15 .40
- ❑ 92 Spider-Man vs. Kraven .15 .40
- ❑ 93 Spider-Man vs. Dr. Octopus .15 .40
- ❑ 94 Daredevil vs. Bullseye .15 .40
- ❑ 95 Daredevil vs. Kingpin .15 .40
- ❑ 96 Silver Surfer vs. Mephisto .15 .40
- ❑ 97 Captain America vs. Red Skull .15 .40
- ❑ 98 Dark Phoenix Saga .15 .40
- ❑ 99 X-Men vs. Avengers .15 .40
- ❑ 100 X-Men vs. Magneto .15 .40
- ❑ 101 X-Men vs. Fantastic Four .15 .40
- ❑ 102 Fall of the Mutants .15 .40
- ❑ 103 Evolutionary War .15 .40
- ❑ 104 Atlantis Attacks .15 .40
- ❑ 105 Acts of Vengeance .15 .40
- ❑ 106 Spider-Man vs. Venom .15 .40
- ❑ 107 Nick Fury vs. Hydra .15 .40
- ❑ 108 Armor Wars I .15 .40
- ❑ 109 Daredevil vs. Wolverine .15 .40
- ❑ 110 Daredevil vs. Punisher .15 .40
- ❑ 111 Spider-Man vs. Green Goblin .15 .40
- ❑ 112 Spider-Man vs. Hobgoblin .15 .40
- ❑ 113 Hulk vs. Wolverine .15 .40
- ❑ 114 Hulk vs. Spider-Man .15 .40
- ❑ 115 Captain America vs. Wolverine .15 .40
- ❑ 116 Silver Surfer vs. Thanos .15 .40
- ❑ 117 X-Factor vs. Apocalypse .15 .40
- ❑ 118 X-Men vs. Freedom Force .15 .40
- ❑ 119 Wolverine vs. Sabretooth .15 .40
- ❑ 120 X-Men in the Savage Land .15 .40
- ❑ 121 Iron Man vs. Titanium Man .15 .40
- ❑ 122 Thor vs. Loki .15 .40
- ❑ 123 First Kree Skrull War .15 .40
- ❑ 124 Fantastic Four #1 .15 .40
- ❑ 125 X-Men #1 .15 .40
- ❑ 126 Amazing Fantasy #15 .15 .40
- ❑ 127 The Punisher Vol. 2 #1 .15 .40
- ❑ 128 Journey into Mystery #83 .15 .40
- ❑ 129 Amazing Spider-Man #129 .15 .40
- ❑ 130 Avengers #1 .15 .40
- ❑ 131 Amazing Spider-Man #1 .15 .40
- ❑ 132 Giant-Size X-Men #1 .15 .40
- ❑ 133 Wolverine Limited Series #1 .15 .40
- ❑ 134 Incredible Hulk #181 .15 .40
- ❑ 135 Tales of Suspense #39 .15 .40
- ❑ 136 Avengers #4 .15 .40
- ❑ 137 Fantastic Four .15 .40
- ❑ 138 Avengers .15 .40
- ❑ 139 X-Men .15 .40
- ❑ 140 X-Men .15 .40
- ❑ 141 Cloak and Dagger .15 .40
- ❑ 142 New Mutants .15 .40
- ❑ 143 X-Factor .15 .40
- ❑ 144 Excalibur .15 .40
- ❑ 145 Brotherhood of Evil Mutants .15 .40
- ❑ 146 Sinister Six .15 .40
- ❑ 147 Hellfire Club .15 .40
- ❑ 148 Alpha Flight .15 .40
- ❑ 149 Spider-Man .15 .40
- ❑ 150 Doctor Doom .15 .40
- ❑ 151 Doctor Octopus .15 .40
- ❑ 152 The Hulk .15 .40
- ❑ 153 Silver Surfer .15 .40
- ❑ 154 Thor .15 .40
- ❑ 155 Punisher .15 .40
- ❑ 156 Magneto .15 .40
- ❑ 157 Captain America .15 .40
- ❑ 158 Doctor Strange .15 .40
- ❑ 159 Iron Man .15 .40
- ❑ 160 Wolverine .15 .40
- ❑ 161 Stan Lee: Mr. Marvel .15 .40
- ❑ 162 Marvel 1990 Checklist .15 .40

1990 Marvel Universe Holograms

COMPLETE SET (5) 12.00 30.00

- ❑ MH1 Cosmic Spider-Man 3.00 8.00
- ❑ MH2 Magneto 3.00 8.00
- ❑ MH3 Silver Surfer 3.00 8.00
- ❑ MH4 Wolverine 3.00 8.00
- ❑ MH5 Spider-Man vs. Green Goblin 3.00 8.00

1990 The Simpsons

COMPLETE SET (88) 6.00 15.00

- ❑ 1 Don't Forget Your Lunches .20 .50
- ❑ 2 Suck .20 .50
- ❑ 3 I'm Lisa Simpson - I'm Above Domestic Cleaning .20 .50
- ❑ 4 I'm Bart Seemp-seau, Famous Underwater Explorer .20 .50
- ❑ 5 No More Television - for All Eternity .20 .50
- ❑ 6 I have an Announcement to Make: I'm Bored .20 .50
- ❑ 7 Marge - You're My Wife, but Cupcakes are My Mistress .20 .50
- ❑ 8 Calm Down, Boy! It Was Just a Nightmare .20 .50
- ❑ 9 Comics are for Kids, Boy .20 .50
- ❑ 10 Time for Our Favorite Cartoon, Itchy and Scratchy .20 .50
- ❑ 11 The Family That Mambos Together, Stays Together .20 .50
- ❑ 12 Bart! Uh, Oh .20 .50
- ❑ 13 Are We at Weenie Barn Yet .20 .50
- ❑ 14 We're the Grown-Ups and You're the Children .20 .50
- ❑ 15 Help! I'm a Fully Developed Female .20 .50
- ❑ 16 Suck! Suck .20 .50
- ❑ 17 Now Get in There and Clean Up That Mess .20 .50
- ❑ 18 Come Back Here, You Little Smartass .20 .50
- ❑ 19 Tolstoy Schmolstoy! Space Mutants II is What I Call .20 .50
- ❑ 20 I'm No Supervising Technician .20 .50
- ❑ 21 All Right! America's Most Armed and Dangerous .20 .50
- ❑ 22 Ha! Ha! Ha! Ha .20 .50
- ❑ 23 Suck! Suck! Suck .20 .50
- ❑ 24 Homework is Society's Way of Torturing Their Young .20 .50
- ❑ 25 No Reststops for the Next 16 Hours .20 .50
- ❑ 26 Zee Brave Undair Sea Exploraire Wrestles .20 .50
- ❑ 27 Look Homer, Clean as a Whistle .20 .50
- ❑ 28 We Can Never Let Him Down. He'll Kill Us .20 .50
- ❑ 29 Don't Bug Me, I'm Studying, Man .20 .50
- ❑ 30 And Don't Come Out Till You Sparkle, Boy .20 .50
- ❑ 31 Maggie? Lisa? You in There .20 .50
- ❑ 32 Should I Turn On the TV .20 .50
- ❑ 33 Don't Have a Cow, Man .20 .50
- ❑ 34 Bart! Get Back Here .20 .50
- ❑ 35 Anybody Seen Maggie .20 .50
- ❑ 36 Marge, Let's Run Away From Home .20 .50
- ❑ 37 She's Such an Adorable Infant .20 .50
- ❑ 38 It's the Bart Simpson Show Starring Bart Simpson .20 .50
- ❑ 39 Quiet! Genius at Work, Man .20 .50
- ❑ 40 Shut Up Back There, You Little Smart Alecks .20 .50
- ❑ 41 Bart! Did You Eat All the Pork Rinds .20 .50
- ❑ 42 What'll it Be Tonight, Marge? .20 .50
- ❑ 43 Suck! Suck! Suck .20 .50
- ❑ 44 March Your Butts Straight Up to Bed .20 .50
- ❑ 45 Happy Father's Day, Dad. They Were 12 for a Dollar .20 .50
- ❑ 46 Stand Back, Comrades! .20 .50
- ❑ 47 There's Nothing More Disheartening .20 .50
- ❑ 48 Right On, Dude .20 .50
- ❑ 49 Who Do You Think You Are, Thomas Edison .20 .50
- ❑ 50 This Looks Like the Work of One Bartholomew J. Simpson .20 .50
- ❑ 51 You Said Left. I Said Right .20 .50
- ❑ 52 It's Quiet. Yeah, Too Quiet .20 .50
- ❑ 53 Kids Out There in T.V. Land - You're Being Duped .20 .50
- ❑ 54 There's Only So Much One Hell Raisin' Kid Can Take, Man .20 .50
- ❑ 55 It's Amazing How Much Beauty .20 .50
- ❑ 56 Aaauuughhh .20 .50
- ❑ 57 Who Ate My Cookies .20 .50
- ❑ 58 Back Off, Homer. I Happen to Be .20 .50
- ❑ 59 I Said, Knock It Off .20 .50
- ❑ 60 Don't Blame Us, Dad! We're Merely .20 .50
- ❑ 61 Go to Bed! Go to Bed! Right Now .20 .50
- ❑ 62 There's Only One Cookie Left! .20 .50
- ❑ 63 I Didn't Do It. Nobody Saw Me Do It. .20 .50
- ❑ 64 Gangway, Man .20 .50
- ❑ 65 Which One of You Ate My Last Donut .20 .50
- ❑ 66 Bart? Uh Oh Gotta Hide .20 .50
- ❑ 67 Last One to the Breakfast Table is a Wimp, Man .20 .50
- ❑ 68 God Jelp Me .20 .50
- ❑ 69 Bart, You're Such a Dimwit .20 .50
- ❑ 70 I'm Bart Simpson, Who the Hell are You .20 .50
- ❑ 71 Your Father's Chasing After Bart Because He Loves Him. .20 .50
- ❑ 72 Bbaarrtttt .20 .50
- ❑ 73 I Can't Wait to See the Happy Little Elves .20 .50
- ❑ 74 Why You Little!!!! Lets Break for a Commercial .20 .50
- ❑ 75 For the Last Time, I'm the Parent and You're the Children .20 .50
- ❑ 76 I Think It's Time to Go Down to The Dairy Den .20 .50
- ❑ 77 Let's Take Turns Yelling Into the Canyon .20 .50
- ❑ 78 Marge! Where's the Personals Section of Today's Paper .20 .50
- ❑ 79 We Have No Idea Who Made This Mess .20 .50
- ❑ 80 This is the Life, Man .20 .50
- ❑ 81 Me, Bartunga! Me, Leesumba .20 .50
- ❑ 82 Unga, Bunga, Yunga, Ho .20 .50
- ❑ 83 There is Justice in the World, Maggie .20 .50
- ❑ 84 Suck, suck, suck, suck, suck .20 .50
- ❑ 85 Uh, Oh .20 .50
- ❑ 86 Another Day of Parental Oppression .20 .50
- ❑ 87 Aye Carumba .20 .50
- ❑ 88 Apple Polisher! Thank You Very Much .20 .50

1991 Marvel 1st Covers II

COMPLETE SET (100) 8.00 20.00

- ❑ 1 Beware .20 .50
- ❑ 2 Giant-Size Chillers - Curse of Dracula .20 .50
- ❑ 3 The Spectacular Spider-Man .20 .50
- ❑ 4 The Human Fly .20 .50
- ❑ 5 The Marvel No-Prize Book .20 .50
- ❑ 6 Marvel Superhero - Contest of Champions (Limited Series) .20 .50
- ❑ 7 Hercules (Limited Series) .20 .50
- ❑ 8 Wolverine (Limited Series) .40 1.00
- ❑ 9 Vision and The Scarlet Witch (Limited Series) .20 .50
- ❑ 10 The Uncanny X-Men at the State Fair of Texas .20 .50
- ❑ 11 Marvel Age .20 .50
- ❑ 12 Obnoxio the Clown vs. The X-Men .20 .50
- ❑ 13 The Saga of Crystar - Crystal Warrior .20 .50
- ❑ 14 Hawkeye (Limited Series) .20 .50
- ❑ 15 Cloak & Dagger (Limited Series) .20 .50
- ❑ 16 Marvel Tails - Starring Peter Porker - The Spectacular Spider-Ham .20 .50
- ❑ 17 The Falcon (Limited Series) .20 .50
- ❑ 18 Magik (Limited Series) .20 .50
- ❑ 19 The Jack of Hearts (Limited Series) .20 .50
- ❑ 20 The X-Men and the Micronauts .20 .50
- ❑ 21 Secret Wars (Limited Series) .20 .50
- ❑ 22 Power Pack .20 .50
- ❑ 23 West Coast Avengers (Limited Series) .20 .50
- ❑ 24 Machine Man (Limited Series) .20 .50
- ❑ 25 Web of Spider-Man .20 .50
- ❑ 26 Moon Knight .20 .50
- ❑ 27 Cloak and Dagger .20 .50
- ❑ 28 Secret Wars II (Limited Series) .20 .50
- ❑ 29 The Life of Captain Marvel .20 .50
- ❑ 30 Longshot (Limited Series) .20 .50
- ❑ 31 Squadron Supreme (Limited Series) .20 .50
- ❑ 32 The Vision and The Scarlet Witch (Limited Series) .20 .50
- ❑ 33 Nightcrawler (Limited Series) .20 .50
- ❑ 34 Marvel Saga - The Official History of the Marvel Universe .20 .50
- ❑ 35 X-Men and Alpha Flight (Limited Series) .20 .50
- ❑ 36 The Punisher (Limited Series) .40 1.00
- ❑ 37 X-Factor .20 .50
- ❑ 38 Classic X-Men .20 .50
- ❑ 39 Strikeforce: Morituri .20 .50
- ❑ 40 The Nam .20 .50
- ❑ 41 The Comet Man .20 .50
- ❑ 42 Fallen Angels (Limited Series) .20 .50
- ❑ 43 Strange Tales .20 .50
- ❑ 44 The X-Men vs. The Avengers (Limited Series) .20 .50
- ❑ 45 Silver Surfer .20 .50
- ❑ 46 The Punisher .20 .50
- ❑ 47 Solo Adventures Starring Hawkeye and Mockingbird .20 .50
- ❑ 48 Marvel Comics Presents Wolverine .20 .50
- ❑ 49 Spellbound (Limited Series) .20 .50
- ❑ 50 Nick Fury vs. S.H.I.E.L.D. .20 .50
- ❑ 51 Black Panther (Limited Series) .20 .50
- ❑ 52 What the ?! .20 .50
- ❑ 53 Wolfpack (Limited Series) .20 .50
- ❑ 54 Excalibur .20 .50
- ❑ 55 X-Terminators .20 .50
- ❑ 56 The Saga of The Sub-Mariner (Limited Series) .20 .50
- ❑ 57 The Punisher War Journal .20 .50
- ❑ 58 Wolverine .40 1.00
- ❑ 59 Semper Fi' .20 .50
- ❑ 60 Fred Hembeck Destroys the Marvel Universe .20 .50
- ❑ 61 What If ... .20 .50
- ❑ 62 Solarman .20 .50
- ❑ 63 Damage Control (Limited Series) .20 .50
- ❑ 64 The Sensational She-Hulk .20 .50
- ❑ 65 Marc Spector - Moon Knight .20 .50
- ❑ 66 Nth Man - The Ultimate Ninja .20 .50
- ❑ 67 Nick Fury, Agent of S.H.I.E.L.D. .20 .50
- ❑ 68 Power Pachyderms .20 .50
- ❑ 69 The Wolverine Saga .20 .50
- ❑ 70 Quasar .20 .50
- ❑ 71 Shadow Masters (Limited Series) .20 .50
- ❑ 72 The War .20 .50
- ❑ 73 Damage Control (Limited Series) .20 .50
- ❑ 74 Open Space .20 .50
- ❑ 75 The Punisher: No Escape .20 .50
- ❑ 76 The Thanos Quest .20 .50
- ❑ 77 X-Men Spotlight On ... Starjammers (Limited Series) .20 .50
- ❑ 78 Namor, The Sub-Mariner .20 .50
- ❑ 79 The Saga of the Original Human Torch (Limited Series) .20 .50
- ❑ 80 Ghost Rider .20 .50
- ❑ 81 Marvel Superheroes - Spring Special .20 .50
- ❑ 82 Black Knight (Limited Series) .20 .50
- ❑ 83 Guardians of the Galaxy .20 .50
- ❑ 84 Deathlok (Limited Series) .20 .50
- ❑ 85 The New Warriors .20 .50
- ❑ 86 The Punisher Armory .20 .50
- ❑ 87 Spider-Man .20 .50
- ❑ 88 Fool Killer (Limited Series) .20 .50
- ❑ 89 Nomad .20 .50
- ❑ 90 Black Panther: Panther's Prey (Limited Series) .20 .50
- ❑ 91 Punisher P.O.V. (Limited Series) .20 .50
- ❑ 92 Darkhawk .20 .50
- ❑ 93 Nightcat .20 .50
- ❑ 94 Sweet Sixteen .20 .50
- ❑ 95 The Deadly Foes of Spider-Man (Limited Series) .20 .50
- ❑ 96 Damage Control Vol. III .20 .50
- ❑ 97 Sleepwalker .20 .50
- ❑ 98 Deathlok .20 .50
- ❑ 99 The Infinity Gauntlet (Limited Series) .20 .50
- ❑ 100 Checklist .20 .50

1991 Marvel Universe

COMPLETE SET (162) 12.00 30.00

- ❑ 1 Spider-Man .15 .40
- ❑ 2 Daredevil .15 .40
- ❑ 3 Thing .15 .40
- ❑ 4 Marvel Girl .15 .40
- ❑ 5 Phoenix .15 .40
- ❑ 6 Sub-Mariner .15 .40
- ❑ 7 Mister Fantastic .15 .40
- ❑ 8 Iceman .15 .40
- ❑ 9 Shadowcat .15 .40
- ❑ 10 Human Torch .15 .40
- ❑ 11 Nightcrawler .15 .40
- ❑ 12 Captain Britain .15 .40
- ❑ 13 Iron Man .15 .40
- ❑ 14 Punisher .15 .40
- ❑ 15 Cable .15 .40
- ❑ 16 Deathlok .15 .40
- ❑ 17 Gambit .15 .40
- ❑ 18 Psylocke .15 .40
- ❑ 19 Vision .15 .40
- ❑ 20 Hawkeye .15 .40
- ❑ 21 Silver Sable .15 .40
- ❑ 22 Night Thrasher .15 .40
- ❑ 23 Puck .15 .40
- ❑ 24 Union Jack .15 .40
- ❑ 25 Quicksilver .15 .40
- ❑ 26 Scarlet Witch .15 .40
- ❑ 27 Havok .15 .40
- ❑ 28 Iron Fist .15 .40
- ❑ 29 Adam Warlock .15 .40
- ❑ 30 Wonder Man .15 .40
- ❑ 31 Sasquatch .15 .40
- ❑ 32 Firestar .15 .40
- ❑ 33 Death's Head .15 .40
- ❑ 34 Speedball .15 .40
- ❑ 35 USAgent .15 .40
- ❑ 36 Banshee .15 .40
- ❑ 37 Meggan .15 .40
- ❑ 38 Jubilee .15 .40
- ❑ 39 Ghost Rider .15 .40
- ❑ 40 Beast .15 .40
- ❑ 41 Invisible Woman .15 .40
- ❑ 42 Rogue .15 .40
- ❑ 43 She-Hulk .15 .40
- ❑ 44 Dr. Strange .15 .40
- ❑ 45 Silver Surfer .15 .40
- ❑ 46 Storm .15 .40
- ❑ 47 Archangel .15 .40
- ❑ 48 Thor .15 .40
- ❑ 49 Quasar .15 .40
- ❑ 50 Wolverine .15 .40
- ❑ 51 Cyclops .15 .40
- ❑ 52 Nick Fury .15 .40
- ❑ 53 Hulk .15 .40
- ❑ 54 Captain America .15 .40
- ❑ 55 Kingpin .15 .40
- ❑ 56 Sabretooth .15 .40
- ❑ 57 Magneto .15 .40
- ❑ 58 Venom .15 .40
- ❑ 59 Galactus .15 .40
- ❑ 60 Mandarin .15 .40
- ❑ 61 Chameleon .15 .40
- ❑ 62 Super Skrull .15 .40
- ❑ 63 Grim Reaper .15 .40
- ❑ 64 Mojo .15 .40
- ❑ 65 Fin Fang Foom .15 .40
- ❑ 66 Jigsaw .15 .40
- ❑ 67 Tombstone .15 .40
- ❑ 68 Ulik .15 .40
- ❑ 69 Baron Strucker .15 .40
- ❑ 70 Mysterio .15 .40
- ❑ 71 Sauron .15 .40
- ❑ 72 Annihilus .15 .40
- ❑ 73 Rhino .15 .40
- ❑ 74 Absorbing Man .15 .40
- ❑ 75 Doctor Octopus .15 .40
- ❑ 76 Baron Mordo .15 .40
- ❑ 77 Saracen .15 .40
- ❑ 78 Nebula .15 .40
- ❑ 79 Puma .15 .40
- ❑ 80 Deathwatch .15 .40
- ❑ 81 Kang .15 .40
- ❑ 82 Blackout .15 .40
- ❑ 83 Calypso .15 .40
- ❑ 84 Ultron .15 .40
- ❑ 85 Thanos .15 .40
- ❑ 86 Hobgoblin .15 .40
- ❑ 87 Lizard .15 .40
- ❑ 88 Doctor Doom .15 .40
- ❑ 89 Loki .15 .40
- ❑ 90 Red Skull .15 .40
- ❑ 91 Spider-Man vs. Venom .15 .40
- ❑ 92 Fantastic Four vs. Skrulls .15 .40
- ❑ 93 Wolverine vs. Sabretooth .15 .40
- ❑ 94 Silver Surfer vs. Galactus .15 .40
- ❑ 95 Daredevil vs. Elektra .15 .40
- ❑ 96 Avengers vs. Kang .15 .40
- ❑ 97 Human Torch vs. Sub-Mariner .15 .40
- ❑ 98 Spider-Man vs. Hobgoblin .15 .40
- ❑ 99 Captain America vs. Baron Zemo .15 .40
- ❑ 100 Punisher vs. Jigsaw .15 .40
- ❑ 101 X-Factor vs. Apocalypse .15 .40
- ❑ 102 Punisher vs. Kingpin .15 .40
- ❑ 103 Thing vs. Hulk .15 .40
- ❑ 104 Daredevil vs. Bullseye .15 .40
- ❑ 105 Spider-Man vs. Doctor Octopus .15 .40
- ❑ 106 X-Men vs. Sentinels .15 .40
- ❑ 107 Fantastic Four vs. Galctus .15 .40
- ❑ 108 Wolverine vs. Hulk .15 .40
- ❑ 109 Ghost Rider vs. Deathwatch .15 .40
- ❑ 110 Dr. Strange vs. Baron Mordo .15 .40
- ❑ 111 Nick Fury vs. Baron Strucker .15 .40
- ❑ 112 Spider-Man vs. Lizard .15 .40
- ❑ 113 Silver Surfer vs. Thanos .15 .40
- ❑ 114 Avengers vs. Ultron .15 .40
- ❑ 115 Captain America vs. Red Skull .15 .40
- ❑ 116 Daredevil vs. Punisher .15 .40
- ❑ 117 X-Men vs. Marauders .15 .40
- ❑ 118 Iron Man vs. Mandarin .15 .40
- ❑ 119 Hulk vs. Leader .15 .40
- ❑ 120 Thor vs. Loki .15 .40
- ❑ 121 Spider-Man vs. J. Jonah Jameson .15 .40
- ❑ 122 Thor vs. Ulik .15 .40
- ❑ 123 Silver Surfer vs. Mephisto .15 .40
- ❑ 124 Fantastic Four vs. Doctor Doom .15 .40
- ❑ 125 X-Men vs. Magneto .15 .40
- ❑ 126 Daredevil vs. Kingpin .15 .40
- ❑ 127 Captain America's Shield .15 .40
- ❑ 128 Thor's Hammer .15 .40
- ❑ 129 Daredevil's Billy Club .15 .40
- ❑ 130 Ultimate Nullifier .15 .40
- ❑ 131 Spider-Man's Web-Shooters .15 .40
- ❑ 132 Punisher's Arsenal .15 .40
- ❑ 133 Iron Man's Armor .15 .40
- ❑ 134 Infinity Gauntlet .15 .40
- ❑ 135 Quasar's Quantum Bands .15 .40
- ❑ 136 Dr. Octopus's Arms .15 .40
- ❑ 137 Mandarin's Rings .15 .40
- ❑ 138 Wolverine's Claws .15 .40
- ❑ 139 Captain Marvel .15 .40
- ❑ 140 Bucky .15 .40
- ❑ 141 Green Goblin .15 .40
- ❑ 142 Original Ghost Rider .15 .40
- ❑ 143 Kraven .15 .40
- ❑ 144 Dark Phoenix .15 .40
- ❑ 145 Darkhawk .15 .40
- ❑ 146 Sleepwalker .15 .40
- ❑ 147 Rage .15 .40
- ❑ 148 X-Force .15 .40
- ❑ 149 New Fantastic Four .15 .40
- ❑ 150 Fantastic Four .15 .40
- ❑ 151 Avengers .15 .40
- ❑ 152 Avengers West Coast .15 .40
- ❑ 153 X-Men .15 .40
- ❑ 154 X-Factor .15 .40
- ❑ 155 Excalibur .15 .40
- ❑ 156 New Warriors .15 .40
- ❑ 157 Masters of Evil .15 .40
- ❑ 158 Marauders .15 .40
- ❑ 159 Strength .15 .40
- ❑ 160 Agility .15 .40
- ❑ 161 Durability .15 .40
- ❑ 162 Marvel 1991 Checklist .15 .40

1991 Marvel Universe Holograms

COMPLETE SET (5) 12.00 30.00

- ❑ H1 Spider-Man 3.00 8.00
- ❑ H2 Hulk 3.00 8.00
- ❑ H3 Punisher 3.00 8.00
- ❑ H4 Doctor Doom 3.00 8.00
- ❑ H5 Fantastic Four (Mole Man 3.00 8.00
- ❑ H1AU Spider-Man Stan Lee AU

1991 Star Trek

COMPLETE SET (310) 12.50 30.00
COMP.FACTORY TIN (310) 50.00 100.00

- ❑ 1 Where No Man Has Gone Before .15 .40
- ❑ 2 The Last Outpost .15 .40
- ❑ 3 Space Seed .15 .40
- ❑ 4 Where No One Has Gone Before .15 .40
- ❑ 5 The Corbomite Maneuver .15 .40
- ❑ 6 Haven .15 .40
- ❑ 7 Mudd's Women .15 .40
- ❑ 8 Code of Honor .15 .40
- ❑ 9 The Enemy Within .15 .40
- ❑ 10 The Naked Now .15 .40
- ❑ 11 The Man Trap .15 .40
- ❑ 12 Encounter at Farpoint .15 .40
- ❑ 13 The Naked Time .15 .40
- ❑ 14 Lonely Among Us .15 .40
- ❑ 15 Charlie X .15 .40
- ❑ 16 Justice .15 .40
- ❑ 17 Balance of Terror .15 .40
- ❑ 18 The Battle .15 .40
- ❑ 19 What Are Little Girls Made Of? .15 .40
- ❑ 20 Hide and Q .15 .40
- ❑ 21 Dagger of the Mind .15 .40
- ❑ 22 Too Short a Season .15 .40
- ❑ 23 Miri .15 .40
- ❑ 24 The Big Goodbye .15 .40
- ❑ 25 Conscience of the King .15 .40
- ❑ 26 Datalore .15 .40
- ❑ 27 The Galileo Seven .15 .40
- ❑ 28 Symbiosis .15 .40
- ❑ 29 Court Martial .15 .40
- ❑ 30 We'll Always Have Paris .15 .40
- ❑ 31 The Menagerie .15 .40
- ❑ 32 The Neutral Zone .15 .40
- ❑ 33 Shore Leave .15 .40
- ❑ 34 Where Silence Has Lease .15 .40
- ❑ 35 The Square of Gothos .15 .40
- ❑ 36 Conspiracy .15 .40
- ❑ 37 Arena .15 .40
- ❑ 38 Elementary, Dear Data .15 .40
- ❑ 39 The Alternative Factor .15 .40
- ❑ 40 The Outrageous Okona .15 .40
- ❑ 41 Tomorrow is Yesterday .15 .40
- ❑ 42 The Schizoid Man .15 .40
- ❑ 43 The Return of the Archons .15 .40
- ❑ 44 The Measure of a Man .15 .40
- ❑ 45 A Taste of Armageddon .15 .40
- ❑ 46 The Dauphin .15 .40
- ❑ 47 This Side of Paradise .15 .40
- ❑ 48 Contagion .15 .40
- ❑ 49 The Devil in the Dark .15 .40
- ❑ 50 The Arsenal of Freedom .15 .40
- ❑ 51 Errand of Mercy .15 .40
- ❑ 52 Skin of Evil .15 .40
- ❑ 53 The City on the Edge of Forever .15 .40
- ❑ 54 Heart of Glory .15 .40
- ❑ 55 Operation Annihilate! .15 .40
- ❑ 56 Coming of Age .15 .40
- ❑ 57 Catspaw .15 .40
- ❑ 58 When the Bough Breaks .15 .40
- ❑ 59 Metamorphosis .15 .40
- ❑ 60 Home Soil .15 .40
- ❑ 61 Friday's Child .15 .40
- ❑ 62 11001001 .15 .40
- ❑ 63 Who Mourns for Adonais? .15 .40
- ❑ 64 Angel One .15 .40
- ❑ 65 Amok Time .15 .40
- ❑ 66 Loud As a Whisper .15 .40
- ❑ 67 The Doomsday Machine .15 .40
- ❑ 68 Unnatural Selection .15 .40
- ❑ 69 Wolf in the Fold .15 .40
- ❑ 70 A Matter of Honor .15 .40
- ❑ 71 The Changeling .15 .40
- ❑ 72 The Royale .15 .40
- ❑ 73 Mirror, Mirror .15 .40
- ❑ 74 The Child .15 .40
- ❑ 75 The Deadly Years .15 .40
- ❑ 76 Pen Pals .15 .40
- ❑ 77 The Trouble with Tribbles .15 .40
- ❑ 78 Times Squared .15 .40
- ❑ 79 Bread and Circuses .15 .40
- ❑ 80 The Icarus Factor .15 .40
- ❑ 81 The Apple .15 .40
- ❑ 82 Warp Drive .15 .40
- ❑ 83 Transporter .15 .40
- ❑ 84 The Continuing Voyages .15 .40
- ❑ 85 Tribbles .15 .40
- ❑ 86 A Place for Families .15 .40
- ❑ 87 Communications .15 .40
- ❑ 88 The Prime Directive .15 .40
- ❑ 89 Communicators .15 .40
- ❑ 90 U.S.S. Enterprise .15 .40
- ❑ 91 Tricorder .15 .40
- ❑ 92 U.S.S. Enterprise .15 .40
- ❑ 93 Phasers .15 .40
- ❑ 94 Dilithium Crystals .15 .40
- ❑ 95 Spock .15 .40
- ❑ 96 TenForward .15 .40
- ❑ 97 James T. Kirk .15 .40
- ❑ 98 Transporter .15 .40
- ❑ 99 Pavel Chekov, Navigator .15 .40
- ❑ 100 Shuttlecraft .15 .40
- ❑ 101 Sulu, Chief Helmsman .15 .40
- ❑ 102 Diagnostic Bed .15 .40
- ❑ 103 Montgomery Scott, Chief Engineer .15 .40
- ❑ 104 Defensive Shields .15 .40
- ❑ 105 Uhura, Communications .15 .40
- ❑ 106 Holodeck .15 .40
- ❑ 107 Leonard McCoy, Physician .15 .40
- ❑ 108 Medical Tricorder .15 .40
- ❑ 109 Vulcan .15 .40
- ❑ 110 Lieutenant Worf .15 .40
- ❑ 111 Klingons .15 .40
- ❑ 112 Geordi LaForge, Lt. Comm. .15 .40
- ❑ 113 Gorn .15 .40
- ❑ 114 Deanna Troi, Counselor .15 .40
- ❑ 115 Talosians .15 .40
- ❑ 116 Dr. Beverly Crusher, Physician .15 .40
- ❑ 117 Captain James T. Kirk .15 .40
- ❑ 118 The Ferengi .15 .40
- ❑ 119 Commander Spock .15 .40
- ❑ 120 Wesley Crusher, Ensign .15 .40
- ❑ 121 Montgomery Scott .15 .40
- ❑ 122 Guinan .15 .40
- ❑ 123 Dr. Leonard McCoy .15 .40
- ❑ 124 Captain JeanLuc Picard .15 .40
- ❑ 125 Andorians .15 .40
- ❑ 126 Commander William T. Riker .15 .40
- ❑ 127 Uhura .15 .40
- ❑ 128 Romulans .15 .40
- ❑ 129 Pavel Andreievich Chekov .15 .40
- ❑ 130 Patrick Stewart .15 .40
- ❑ 131 Worldsinger .15 .40
- ❑ 132 Jonathan Frakes .15 .40
- ❑ 133 Enemy Unseen .15 .40
- ❑ 134 Michael Dorn .15 .40
- ❑ 135 Argon Affair .15 .40
- ❑ 136 Marina Sirtis .15 .40
- ❑ 137 Fast Friends .15 .40
- ❑ 138 Levar Burton .15 .40
- ❑ 139 Gone! .15 .40
- ❑ 140 Brent Spiner .15 .40
- ❑ 141 A Piece of the Action .15 .40
- ❑ 142 Wil Wheaton .15 .40
- ❑ 143 The Pandora Principle .15 .40
- ❑ 144 Gates McFadden .15 .40
- ❑ 145 Amok Time .15 .40
- ❑ 146 Doomsday World .15 .40
- ❑ 147 Journey to Bebel .15 .40
- ❑ 148 The Derelict .15 .40
- ❑ 149 Phasers .15 .40

MODERN ERA NON-SPORTS

❑ 150 The Gift .15 .40
❑ 151 The Devil in the Dark .15 .40
❑ 152 The Weapon .15 .40
❑ 153 Beaming Down .15 .40
❑ 154 Contamination .15 .40
❑ 155 GhostWalker .15 .40
❑ 156 The Eyes of the Beholders .15 .40
❑ 157 Home is the Hunter .15 .40
❑ 158 Exiles .15 .40
❑ 159 Checklist .15 .40
❑ 160 Checklist .15 .40
❑ 161 I, Mudd .15 .40
❑ 162 Q Who .15 .40
❑ 163 Journey to Babel .15 .40
❑ 164 The Samaritan Snare .15 .40
❑ 165 A Private Little War .15 .40
❑ 166 Up the Long Ladder .15 .40
❑ 167 The Gamesters of Triskelion .15 .40
❑ 168 Manhunt .15 .40
❑ 169 Obsession .15 .40
❑ 170 The Emissary .15 .40
❑ 171 The Immunity Syndrome .15 .40
❑ 172 Peak Performance .15 .40
❑ 173 A Piece of the Action .15 .40
❑ 174 Shades of Gray .15 .40
❑ 175 By Any Other Name .15 .40
❑ 176 The Ensigns of Command .15 .40
❑ 177 Return to Tomorrow .15 .40
❑ 178 Evolution .15 .40
❑ 179 Patterns of Force .15 .40
❑ 180 The Survivors .15 .40
❑ 181 The Ultimate Computer .15 .40
❑ 182 Who Watches the Watchers .15 .40
❑ 183 The Omega Glory .15 .40
❑ 184 The Bonding .15 .40
❑ 185 Assignment Earth .15 .40
❑ 186 Booby Trap .15 .40
❑ 187 Elaan of Troyius .15 .40
❑ 188 The Enemy .15 .40
❑ 189 Spectre of the Gun .15 .40
❑ 190 The Price .15 .40
❑ 191 The Paradise Syndrome .15 .40
❑ 192 The Vengeance Factor .15 .40
❑ 193 The Enterprise Incident .15 .40
❑ 194 The Defector .15 .40
❑ 195 And the Children Shall Lead .15 .40
❑ 196 The Hunted .15 .40
❑ 197 Spock's Brain .15 .40
❑ 198 The High Ground .15 .40
❑ 199 Is There In Truth No Beauty? .15 .40
❑ 200 Deja Q .15 .40
❑ 201 The Empath .15 .40
❑ 202 A Matter of Perspective .15 .40
❑ 203 The Tholian Web .15 .40
❑ 204 Yesterday's Enterprise .15 .40
❑ 205 For the World is Hollow and I Have Touched the Sky .15 .40
❑ 206 The Offspring .15 .40
❑ 207 The Day of the Dove .15 .40
❑ 208 Sins of the Father .15 .40
❑ 209 Plato's Stepchildren .15 .40
❑ 210 Allegiance .15 .40
❑ 211 Wink of An Eye .15 .40
❑ 212 Captain's Holiday .15 .40
❑ 213 That Which Survives .15 .40
❑ 214 Tin Man .15 .40
❑ 215 Let That Be Your Last Battlefield .15 .40
❑ 216 Hollow Pursuits .15 .40
❑ 217 Whom Gods Destroy .15 .40
❑ 218 The Most Toys .15 .40
❑ 219 The Mark of Gideon .15 .40
❑ 220 Sarek .15 .40
❑ 221 The Lights of Zetar .15 .40
❑ 222 Menage A Troi .15 .40
❑ 223 The Cloudminders .15 .40
❑ 224 Transfigurations .15 .40
❑ 225 The Way to Eden .15 .40
❑ 226 The Best of Both Worlds, Part I .15 .40
❑ 227 Requiem for Methuselah .15 .40
❑ 228 The Best of Both Worlds, Part II .15 .40
❑ 229 The Savage Curtain .15 .40
❑ 230 Suddenly Human .15 .40
❑ 231 All Our Yesterdays .15 .40
❑ 232 Brothers .15 .40
❑ 233 Turnabout Intruder .15 .40
❑ 234 Family .15 .40
❑ 235 U.S.S. Enterprise One of the Vanguard .15 .40
❑ 236 Remember Me .15 .40
❑ 237 Deck : The Bridge .15 .40
❑ 238 Legacy .15 .40
❑ 239 Bridge: Main Viewscreen .15 .40
❑ 240 Reunion .15 .40
❑ 241 Transporter Room .15 .40
❑ 242 Future Imperfect .15 .40
❑ 243 Transporter Controls .15 .40
❑ 244 Final Mission .15 .40
❑ 245 Corridor .15 .40
❑ 246 The Loss .15 .40
❑ 247 Shuttlecraft .15 .40
❑ 248 Data's Day .15 .40
❑ 249 Shuttlecraft Hangar Deck .15 .40
❑ 250 The Mission Continues .15 .40
❑ 251 Engineering Plans of U.S.S. Enterprise .15 .40
❑ 252 Turbolift .15 .40
❑ 253 NCC .15 .40
❑ 254 Battle Section .15 .40
❑ 255 Hypospray .15 .40
❑ 256 Ship's Computer .15 .40
❑ 257 Command Insignia .15 .40
❑ 258 Technology Unchained .15 .40
❑ 259 Sciences Insignia .15 .40
❑ 260 The Main Bridge:Command Area .15 .40
❑ 261 Engineering Insignia .15 .40
❑ 262 The Main Bridge:Forward Stations .15 .40
❑ 263 William Shatner .15 .40
❑ 264 The Main Bridge:Aft Stations .15 .40
❑ 265 Leonard Nimoy .15 .40
❑ 266 The Dress Uniform .15 .40
❑ 267 DeForest Kelley .15 .40
❑ 268 Picard and Riker .15 .40
❑ 269 James Doohan .15 .40
❑ 270 Picard and Q .15 .40
❑ 271 Nichelle Nichols .15 .40
❑ 272 Riker and Troi .15 .40
❑ 273 George Takei .15 .40
❑ 274 Picard and Troi .15 .40
❑ 275 Walter Koenig .15 .40
❑ 276 Riker and Geordi .15 .40
❑ 277 The Origins of Star Trek .15 .40
❑ 278 Picard and Wesley .15 .40
❑ 279 TV Credit Card #1 .15 .40
❑ 280 Riker and Data .15 .40
❑ 281 TV Credit Card #2 .15 .40
❑ 282 Picard and Data .15 .40
❑ 283 TV Credit Card #3 .15 .40
❑ 284 Troi and Dr. Crusher .15 .40
❑ 285 TV Credit Card #4 .15 .40
❑ 286 Picard and Sarek .15 .40
❑ 287 TV Credit Card #5 .15 .40
❑ 288 Picard and Worf .15 .40
❑ 289 TV Credit Card #6 .15 .40
❑ 290 Picard and Dr. Crusher .15 .40
❑ 291 Nacelles .15 .40
❑ 292 Picard and Guinan .15 .40
❑ 293 United Federation of Planets .15 .40
❑ 294 Data .15 .40
❑ 295 Neutral Zone .15 .40
❑ 296 The Borg .15 .40
❑ 297 Environmental Suit .15 .40
❑ 298 Dr. Kate Pulaski .15 .40
❑ 299 Vulcan Lyrette .15 .40
❑ 300 Dr. Leah Brahms .15 .40
❑ 301 The Melkot .15 .40
❑ 302 K'Ehleyr .15 .40
❑ 303 Harcourt Fenton Mudd .15 .40
❑ 304 Vash .15 .40
❑ 305 Horta .15 .40
❑ 306 Armus .15 .40
❑ 307 Cpt. Christopher Pike .15 .40
❑ 308 Gene Roddenberry and Crew .15 .40
❑ 309 Star Trek Checklist .15 .40
❑ 310 Star Trek:The Next Generation Checklist .15 .40
❑ NNO HOLOGRAM 6.00 15.00

1991 Terminator II

COMPLETE SET (140) 5.00 12.00
COMP.FACTORY SET 12.50 30.00
HOLOGRAM FOUND IN FACTORY SETS

❑ 1 The Cyborg Returns .15 .40
❑ 2 Terminator 2: Judgment Day .15 .40
❑ 3 Terminator's Creator .15 .40
❑ 4 On the Battlefield .15 .40
❑ 5 Score One for the Resistance .15 .40
❑ 6 Armed and Ready .15 .40
❑ 7 I Can't Let you Take the Man's Bike, Son .15 .40
❑ 8 What Terminator Wants, Terminator Gets .15 .40
❑ 9 Terminator Begins his Mission .15 .40
❑ 10 The Unstoppable T-1000 .15 .40
❑ 11 John Connor, Not So Average American Kid .15 .40
❑ 12 Sarah Connor, Former Waitress .15 .40
❑ 13 Observing a Mental Patient .15 .40
❑ 14 Dreams Meet Reality for Kyle and Sarah .15 .40
❑ 15 I Feel Much Better Now .15 .40
❑ 16 You Have to Let Me See My Son .15 .40
❑ 17 Officer X Stalks Its Prey .15 .40
❑ 18 Hunting for John .15 .40
❑ 19 Terminator Carries Roses for his Date .15 .40
❑ 20 If John Thinks This Game is Intense, Just Wait .15 .40
❑ 21 The T-1000 Closes in on John .15 .40
❑ 22 Terminator Explodes Through the Shop Window .15 .40
❑ 23 A Rough Landing .15 .40
❑ 24 Terminator Gets Back Up .15 .40
❑ 25 Exiting the Parking Garage .15 .40
❑ 26 Dir. James Cameron Stages a Scene .15 .40
❑ 27 How Fast Can This Bike Go? .15 .40
❑ 28 Terminator Searches for John .15 .40
❑ 29 700 Pounds of Airborne Harley .15 .40
❑ 30 Too Hot To Handle? .15 .40
❑ 31 Terminator and John Escape Again .15 .40
❑ 32 When Cops are Everywhere, It's Easy to Blend In .15 .40
❑ 33 Who is this Guy I'm Riding With? .15 .40
❑ 34 Terminator .15 .40
❑ 35 Terminator and John Infiltrate Pescadero .15 .40
❑ 36 You Have to do What I Say? .15 .40
❑ 37 You Can't Just go Around Killing People .15 .40
❑ 38 Talk To Us, Don't You Care? .15 .40
❑ 39 The Pescadero State Hospital .15 .40
❑ 40 The T-1000 Dispatches Lewis the Guard .15 .40
❑ 41 The Face of Sarah's Worst Nightmare .15 .40
❑ 42 Come With Me If You Want to Live .15 .40
❑ 43 The Escape is Almost Complete .15 .40
❑ 44 Go, Run! .15 .40
❑ 45 Firing at Point-Blank Range .15 .40
❑ 46 A Close Call .15 .40
❑ 47 John Stares at the Unstoppable T-1000 .15 .40
❑ 48 Terminator Sews up Sarah's Wound .15 .40
❑ 49 Does It Hurt? .15 .40
❑ 50 Terminator's Switch is Reset to Learn .15 .40
❑ 51 Resetting Terminator's Computer Chip .15 .40
❑ 52 Keeping Watch .15 .40
❑ 53 Miles Dyson, Computer Genius .15 .40
❑ 54 Sunday Morning at the Home of Miles Dyson .15 .40
❑ 55 James Cameron Directs at the Compound .15 .40
❑ 56 Going for Guns .15 .40
❑ 57 Oye, Big John. Who's Your Large Friend .15 .40
❑ 58 Enrique Salceda's Compound .15 .40
❑ 59 Drop by Anytime .15 .40
❑ 60 High-Five .15 .40
❑ 61 Ready for War .15 .40
❑ 62 Ready to Cruise .15 .40
❑ 63 No Fate .15 .40
❑ 64 Sarah Takes Aim at Dyson .15 .40
❑ 65 Mom? You Okay? .15 .40
❑ 66 James Cameron Directs Schwarzenegger .15 .40
❑ 67 Terminator is Prepared to go to Extremes .15 .40
❑ 68 The Truth is Revealed .15 .40
❑ 69 Maybe This Will Convince Dyson to Help .15 .40
❑ 70 We Have to Destroy Everything .15 .40
❑ 71 Evening, Paul. These Are Friends of Mine .15 .40
❑ 72 Are These Authorized Personnel? .15 .40
❑ 73 Let Me Try Mine .15 .40
❑ 74 Armed and Dangerous .15 .40
❑ 75 Can They Change the World's Fate? .15 .40
❑ 76 Will the Destruction of Cyberdyne Save the World? .15 .40
❑ 77 Give Me That Thing a Second .15 .40
❑ 78 John's Auto-Teller Experience Pays Off .15 .40
❑ 79 Filming the Siege of Cyberdyne .15 .40
❑ 80 Cyberdyne is Under Siege .15 .40
❑ 81 Human Casualties: 0 .15 .40
❑ 82 The Vault is Opened .15 .40
❑ 83 Handing Over the Evidence .15 .40
❑ 84 Sarah Confronts the Swat Team .15 .40
❑ 85 Go, Dyson Tells Sarah .15 .40
❑ 86 For Miles Dyson, The End is Near .15 .40
❑ 87 Termination Override .15 .40
❑ 88 The Swats Can't Stop Him .15 .40
❑ 89 I'll Be Back .15 .40
❑ 90 A Total Rout .15 .40
❑ 91 The Swat Van Crashes into the Lobby .15 .40
❑ 92 Airborne Kawasaki .15 .40
❑ 93 Inside a Rolling Armory .15 .40
❑ 94 The T-1000 Prepares to Fire Again .15 .40
❑ 95 Sarah Fires on the T-1000's Chopper .15 .40
❑ 96 Come On, Mom, We Gotta Keep Moving .15 .40
❑ 97 T-1000 Commandeers a Tanker .15 .40
❑ 98 Faster, He's Right On Us .15 .40
❑ 99 Drive For a Minute .15 .40
❑ 100 The T-1000 Borrows a Tanker Truck .15 .40
❑ 101 Terminator Rides the Tanker .15 .40
❑ 102 Hasta La Vista, Baby .15 .40
❑ 103 The T-1000 Reforms Once More .15 .40
❑ 104 Come On, Mom, You Can Do It .15 .40
❑ 105 The T-1000 Sticks to Its Mission .15 .40
❑ 106 The Gun Points Right at the Audience .15 .40
❑ 107 Steel Fingers Aim the M-79 .15 .40
❑ 108 The Battle is Joined .15 .40
❑ 109 John Finds his Mother Among the Machines .15 .40
❑ 110 Terminator Frees Himself from the Machine's Jaws .15 .40
❑ 111 Terminator Goes After the T-1000 .15 .40
❑ 112 Sarah Shoots the T-1000 .15 .40
❑ 113 The Stiletto Goes In .15 .40
❑ 114 The T-1000 Skewers Sarah .15 .40
❑ 115 Will This Stop the T-1000? .15 .40
❑ 116 The T-1000 Strikes Back .15 .40
❑ 117 The T-1000 Hammers Terminator .15 .40
❑ 118 The Eye Servo Glares Red .15 .40
❑ 119 Terminator Drags Himself After the T-1000 .15 .40
❑ 120 The Real Sarah Connoer Seals Her Fate .15 .40
❑ 121 The Grenade Explodes Inside the T-1000 .15 .40
❑ 122 The End of the T-1000 .15 .40
❑ 123 It's Over .15 .40
❑ 124 The T-1000 Meets a Fiery Fate .15 .40
❑ 125 Director and Actor Confer .15 .40
❑ 126 Please Don't Go
❑ 127 I Know Now Why You Cry .15 .40
❑ 128 The Final Good-Bye .15 .40
❑ 129 Are You Afraid? .15 .40
❑ 130 The Endoskeleton Shows Through
❑ 131 Into The Fire .15 .40
❑ 132 Mission Completed .15 .40
❑ 133 Producer-Director James Cameron .15 .40
❑ 134 Arnold Schwarzenegger .15 .40
❑ 135 Linda Hamilton .15 .40
❑ 136 Edward Furlong .15 .40
❑ 137 Robert Patrick .15 .40
❑ 138 Credits .15 .40
❑ 139 Checklist .15 .40
❑ 140 Checklist .15 .40
❑ NNO HOLOGRAM 7.50 20.00

1991 Wolverine From Then Til Now

COMPLETE SET (45) 8.00 20.00

❑ 1 Wolverine .30 .75
❑ 2 Wendigo .30 .75
❑ 3 Spider-Man .30 .75
❑ 4 Bloodlust .30 .75
❑ 5 Attacked .30 .75
❑ 6 Come On .30 .75
❑ 7 Android .30 .75
❑ 8 The Blues .30 .75
❑ 9 Pull Me Up .30 .75
❑ 10 Blood .30 .75
❑ 11 4 of Us .30 .75
❑ 12 Brood .30 .75
❑ 13 New Warriors .30 .75
❑ 14 Patch .30 .75
❑ 15 The Team .30 .75
❑ 16 Hulk .30 .75
❑ 17 Come ON .30 .75
❑ 18 Ghost Rider .30 .75
❑ 19 Cable .30 .75
❑ 20 Logan .30 .75
❑ 21 Meltdown .30 .75
❑ 22 otha .30 .75
❑ 23 A-A-A-H .30 .75
❑ 24 The Beast .30 .75
❑ 25 Webbed .30 .75
❑ 26 Metamorphosis .30 .75
❑ 27 Crucified .30 .75
❑ 28 Buried .30 .75
❑ 29 Deathstrike .30 .75
❑ 30 Surrounded .30 .75
❑ 31 Mad as .30 .75
❑ 32 Werewolf .30 .75
❑ 33 In the Dark .30 .75
❑ 34 Trio .30 .75
❑ 35 X-Men .30 .75
❑ 36 Jubilee .30 .75
❑ 37 Hodge .30 .75
❑ 38 X-tinction .30 .75
❑ 39 Archangel .30 .75
❑ 40 Help Me .30 .75
❑ 41 Weapon X .30 .75
❑ 42 Sedated .30 .75
❑ 43 Rage! .30 .75
❑ 44 Massacre .30 .75
❑ 45 Checklist .30 .75
❑ NNO Header .10 .25

1991 X-Force

COMPLETE SET (90) 6.00 15.00

❑ 1 New Mutants .15 .40
❑ 2 The Vulture .15 .40
❑ 3 The Plan .15 .40
❑ 4 Escape .15 .40
❑ 5 Nitro .15 .40
❑ 6 Freedom Force .15 .40
❑ 7 Rusty and Skids .15 .40
❑ 8 Cable .15 .40
❑ 9 The M.L.F. .15 .40
❑ 10 Dark Valkyrie .15 .40
❑ 11 Going Home .15 .40
❑ 12 I'm Slaying .15 .40
❑ 13 All Aboard .15 .40
❑ 14 Stryfe .15 .40
❑ 15 Gunfire .15 .40
❑ 16 Break-Out .15 .40
❑ 17 Captured .15 .40
❑ 18 Join Us .15 .40
❑ 19 X-Factor .15 .40
❑ 20 Mystique .15 .40
❑ 21 Fight .15 .40
❑ 22 Defense .15 .40
❑ 23 New Leader .15 .40
❑ 24 Sabretooth .15 .40
❑ 25 Caliban .15 .40
❑ 26 Rictor .15 .40
❑ 27 To the Death .15 .40
❑ 28 Snap .15 .40
❑ 29 Skrulls .15 .40
❑ 30 Sunfire .15 .40
❑ 31 Sleet .15 .40
❑ 32 Poison .15 .40
❑ 33 Uh Oh .15 .40
❑ 34 Wolverine .15 .40
❑ 35 The Bold .15 .40
❑ 36 Captured .15 .40
❑ 37 Whoa .15 .40
❑ 38 Pals .15 .40
❑ 39 Free .15 .40
❑ 40 Dropping In .15 .40
❑ 41 Get Out .15 .40
❑ 42 A Hero Falls .15 .40
❑ 43 Hodge .15 .40
❑ 44 Let's Move .15 .40
❑ 45 Stop .15 .40
❑ 46 Beast .15 .40
❑ 47 Genosha .15 .40
❑ 48 Jubilee .15 .40
❑ 49 Archangel .15 .40
❑ 50 Mutate .15 .40
❑ 51 Gambit .15 .40
❑ 52 What-to-do .15 .40
❑ 53 Restored .15 .40
❑ 54 Rahne .15 .40
❑ 55 Changes .15 .40
❑ 56 Gideon .15 .40
❑ 57 Dad .15 .40
❑ 58 Get Rahne .15 .40
❑ 59 Assassin .15 .40
❑ 60 Deadpool .15 .40
❑ 61 Stopped .15 .40
❑ 62 Domino .15 .40
❑ 63 The End .15 .40
❑ 64 Feral .15 .40
❑ 65 Tunnels .15 .40
❑ 66 Proudstar .15 .40
❑ 67 Deceit .15 .40
❑ 68 Revenge .15 .40
❑ 69 So .15 .40
❑ 70 Good-bye .15 .40
❑ 71 Stranger .15 .40
❑ 72 The New .15 .40
❑ 73 Shatterstar .15 .40
❑ 74 Found .15 .40
❑ 75 Protectorate .15 .40
❑ 76 Offense .15 .40
❑ 77 Teamwork .15 .40
❑ 78 Ferocious .15 .40
❑ 79 Blood .15 .40
❑ 80 Warrior .15 .40
❑ 81 Masque .15 .40
❑ 82 Decisions .15 .40
❑ 83 Unmasked .15 .40
❑ 84 X-Force .15 .40
❑ 85 Pursuit .15 .40
❑ 86 Wildside .15 .40
❑ 87 Terrorist .15 .40
❑ 88 Reaper .15 .40
❑ 89 War .15 .40
❑ 90 Checklist .15 .40

1991 X-Men

COMPLETE SET (90) 8.00 20.00

❑ 1 The X-Men .20 .50
❑ 2 The Reavers .20 .50
❑ 3 The Mandarin .20 .50
❑ 4 Betsy .20 .50
❑ 5 Slaymaster .20 .50
❑ 6 Lady Mandarin .20 .50
❑ 7 Patch .20 .50
❑ 8 Accommodation .20 .50
❑ 9 The Beast .20 .50
❑ 10 Games .20 .50
❑ 11 My Turn .20 .50
❑ 12 #1 Fan .20 .50
❑ 13 Harriers .20 .50
❑ 14 Magistrates .20 .50
❑ 15 Lian .20 .50
❑ 16 Storm .20 .50
❑ 17 Gambit .20 .50
❑ 18 Nanny .20 .50
❑ 19 Orphanmaker .20 .50
❑ 20 Partners .20 .50
❑ 21 Together Again .20 .50
❑ 22 Captain America .20 .50
❑ 23 Friend .20 .50
❑ 24 My Turf .20 .50
❑ 25 Black Widow .20 .50
❑ 26 To the Rescue .20 .50
❑ 27 Conflict .20 .50
❑ 28 Cyborgs .20 .50
❑ 29 Ms. Marvel .20 .50
❑ 30 Savage Land .20 .50
❑ 31 Shadow King .20 .50
❑ 32 Drained .20 .50
❑ 33 Magneto .20 .50
❑ 34 First Strike .20 .50
❑ 35 Danger Room .20 .50
❑ 36 Our Turn .20 .50
❑ 37 Pathfinders .20 .50
❑ 38 Strikeforce .20 .50
❑ 39 Flight .20 .50
❑ 40 Powerless .20 .50
❑ 41 Warlock .20 .50
❑ 42 Take 'Em Out .20 .50
❑ 43 Psylocke .20 .50
❑ 44 Cameron .20 .50
❑ 45 Havok .20 .50
❑ 46 Mutate #20 .20 .50
❑ 47 On Trial .20 .50
❑ 48 Hodge .20 .50
❑ 49 Cable .20 .50
❑ 50 Match .20 .50
❑ 51 Restored .20 .50
❑ 52 Final Strike .20 .50
❑ 53 What's Next .20 .50
❑ 54 Allies .20 .50
❑ 55 Assault .20 .50
❑ 56 Zaladane .20 .50
❑ 57 Teleported .20 .50
❑ 58 Deathbird .20 .50
❑ 59 Starjammers .20 .50
❑ 60 Imperial Fleet .20 .50
❑ 61 Manacle .20 .50
❑ 62 Fair Game .20 .50
❑ 63 Lilandra .20 .50
❑ 64 Conquered .20 .50
❑ 65 Rejoined .20 .50
❑ 66 Airborne .20 .50
❑ 67 Revenge .20 .50
❑ 68 Brainchild .20 .50
❑ 69 Draining .20 .50
❑ 70 Repowered .20 .50
❑ 71 Mentor .20 .50
❑ 72 The Dungeons .20 .50
❑ 73 My Wings .20 .50
❑ 74 Execution .20 .50
❑ 75 We're Back .20 .50
❑ 76 War Skrull .20 .50
❑ 77 Aboard .20 .50
❑ 78 In Space .20 .50
❑ 79 Remember Us .20 .50
❑ 80 One-on-One .20 .50
❑ 81 Professor X .20 .50
❑ 82 Colossus .20 .50
❑ 83 Testing .20 .50
❑ 84 Old Times .20 .50
❑ 85 Whoa .20 .50
❑ 86 Watch It .20 .50
❑ 87 On the Move .20 .50
❑ 88 Homo Superiors .20 .50
❑ 89 Omega Red .20 .50
❑ 90 Checklist .20 .50
❑ NNO Jim Lee Autograph 75.00 150.00

1992 Batman Returns (O-Pee-Chee)

COMPLETE SET (89) 4.00 10.00

❑ 1 A Recipe for Success .12 .30
❑ 2 The Dark Knight of Gotham City .12 .30
❑ 3 Introducing the Penguin .12 .30
❑ 4 Introducing Catwoman .12 .30
❑ 5 Evil Prince of the City .12 .30
❑ 6 Nightmare as a Child .12 .30
❑ 7 Master of the Lower Depths .12 .30
❑ 8 Peering Out of the Darkness .12 .30
❑ 9 Addressing Gotham City .12 .30
❑ 10 A Secretary Named Selina .12 .30
❑ 11 Watching from Wayne Manor .12 .30
❑ 12 What in the Name Of .12 .30
❑ 13 A Ghoulish Gift .12 .30
❑ 14 A Giant Surprise Package .12 .30
❑ 15 All Hell Breaks Loose .12 .30
❑ 16 Roar of the Batmobile .12 .30
❑ 17 Plowing Into Peril .12 .30
❑ 18 Cycling Psychos .12 .30
❑ 19 Terror in Gotham Square .12 .30
❑ 20 Scene of the Crime .12 .30
❑ 21 In the Clown's Clutches .12 .30
❑ 22 Let Her Go .12 .30
❑ 23 Human Flame Thrower .12 .30
❑ 24 Counterattack .12 .30
❑ 25 The Fire Breather Aflame .12 .30
❑ 26 Icy Lair .12 .30
❑ 27 Sultan of the Sewers .12 .30
❑ 28 Unholy Alliance .12 .30
❑ 29 Shreck's Way .12 .30
❑ 30 Through a Window Harshly .12 .30
❑ 31 Revived by Feline Friends .12 .30
❑ 32 Birth of Catwoman .12 .30
❑ 33 An Acrobatic Surprise .12 .30
❑ 34 Gotham's Unlikely Hero .12 .30
❑ 35 In Search of His Roots .12 .30
❑ 36 The List of Oswald Cobblepot .12 .30
❑ 37 Cemetery Pilgrimage .12 .30
❑ 38 Destiny of the Cobblepots .12 .30
❑ 39 Hizzoner... The Penguin .12 .30
❑ 40 Feline on the Prowl .12 .30
❑ 41 Night Watchers .12 .30
❑ 42 Meow .12 .30
❑ 43 Cat Challenges Bat .12 .30
❑ 44 Sinful, Sinuous Catwoman .12 .30
❑ 45 Only Eight Lives Left .12 .30
❑ 46 Burn, Baby, Burn .12 .30
❑ 47 The Plan to Destroy Batman .12 .30
❑ 48 Bruce and Selina Unmasked .12 .30
❑ 49 Rescuing the Ice Princess .12 .30
❑ 50 What Do You Want .12 .30
❑ 51 Sabotaging the Batmobile .12 .30
❑ 52 Innocent Victim .12 .30
❑ 53 A Long Way Down .12 .30
❑ 54 Over the Edge .12 .30
❑ 55 Wild Batmobile .12 .30
❑ 56 Gordon Against Him .12 .30
❑ 57 Flight of the Batmissile .12 .30
❑ 58 Cop Car Catastrophe .12 .30
❑ 59 A Penguin Scorned .12 .30
❑ 60 On the Campaign Trail .12 .30
❑ 61 Oswald Outwitted .12 .30
❑ 62 Turning on the Crowd .12 .30
❑ 63 Back to the Depths .12 .30
❑ 64 The Max-squerade .12 .30
❑ 65 Bruce Wayne In Costume .12 .30
❑ 66 Crashing the Party .12 .30
❑ 67 The Penguin's Revenge .12 .30
❑ 68 Fearsome Felon .12 .30
❑ 69 The Time Is At Hand .12 .30
❑ 70 The Kiddie Express .12 .30
❑ 71 Rallying His Troops .12 .30
❑ 72 Penguins on the March .12 .30
❑ 73 Missiles Away .12 .30
❑ 74 Invading Gotham City .12 .30
❑ 75 Gliding Gladiator .12 .30
❑ 76 Battered by Batman .12 .30
❑ 77 The Dark Knight Triumphant .12 .30
❑ 78 Batskiboat Attack .12 .30
❑ 79 Fury of the Penguin .12 .30
❑ 80 When Titans Collide .12 .30
❑ 81 The Penguin's Plunge .12 .30
❑ 82 Vengeance Is Hers .12 .30
❑ 83 Don't Interfere, Batman .12 .30
❑ 84 Shreck's Final Stand .12 .30
❑ 85 Lashing Out .12 .30
❑ 86 No Escape for Shreck .12 .30
❑ 87 Destroying His Life Support .12 .30
❑ 88 Farewell, Penguin .12 .30
❑ 89 Checklist .12 .30

1992 Batman Returns (Stadium Club)

COMPLETE SET (100) 5.00 12.00

❑ 1 Director Tim Burton gives Michelle Pfeiffer .15 .40
❑ 2 Director Tim Burton found working .15 .40
❑ 3 The chemistry between Michael Keaton .15 .40
❑ 4 I've always found Michael Keaton .15 .40
❑ 5 Has success spoiled Tim Burton .15 .40
❑ 6 Michelle Pfeiffer lends both her lustrous tale .15 .40
❑ 7 Alfred Pennyworth .15 .40
❑ 8 In the first Batman movie .15 .40
❑ 9 In what has become something of a tradition .15 .40
❑ 10 Actor Michael Keaton .15 .40
❑ 11 Batman has his hands full .15 .40

❑ 12 Once a submissive secretary .15 .40
❑ 13 Catwoman is brought to life .15 .40
❑ 14 A warped genius .15 .40
❑ 15 Reflecting Tim Burton's stylized approach .15 .40
❑ 16 With an act of shocking violence .15 .40
❑ 17 On the set of Batman Returns .15 .40
❑ 18 Tim Burton directs actors .15 .40
❑ 19 Batman (Michael Keaton) confronts .15 .40
❑ 20 The elite party animals who attend .15 .40
❑ 21 Batman is a relevant character .15 .40
❑ 22 Director Tim Burton gives mayoral candidate .15 .40
❑ 23 Parallels between hero and villain .15 .40
❑ 24 A consultant on Batman Returns .15 .40
❑ 25 The creation of the enormous .15 .40
❑ 26 Tim Burton directs Christopher Walken .15 .40
❑ 27 There are many differences .15 .40
❑ 28 Director Tim Burton enjoys creating .15 .40
❑ 29 The streets and rooftops of Gotham .15 .40
❑ 30 Raised in the suburban Southern California .15 .40
❑ 31 Just as Batman has a Batcave .15 .40
❑ 32 Most of the characters .15 .40
❑ 33 With his portrayal of the malevolent Penguin .15 .40
❑ 34 Selina's apartment very much reflects .15 .40
❑ 35 The oppressive Shreck Building .15 .40
❑ 36 It was a partnership made in hell .15 .40
❑ 37 Unlike her counterpart .15 .40
❑ 38 When The Penguin visits Gotham Cemetery .15 .40
❑ 39 Adjustments are made .15 .40
❑ 40 Tim Burton was determined .15 .40
❑ 41 Batman Returns has fun .15 .40
❑ 42 Just as apes raised young Tarzan .15 .40
❑ 43 One of the biggest thrills .15 .40
❑ 44 Batman Returns is even more .15 .40
❑ 45 At Max Shreck's eccentric Maxsquerade .15 .40
❑ 46 The rooftops are an important element .15 .40
❑ 47 Directing Selina Kyle .15 .40
❑ 48 Director Tim Burton prepares Danny DeVito .15 .40
❑ 49 Both Batman movies reflect .15 .40
❑ 50 Selina Kyle (Michelle Pfeiffer) relaxes .15 .40
❑ 51 Penguins, penguins everywhere .15 .40
❑ 52 The Batmobile is prepared .15 .40
❑ 53 Just as Batman has his Batmobile .15 .40
❑ 54 Director Tim Burton shoots Max Shreck .15 .40
❑ 55 Production designer Bo Welch .15 .40
❑ 56 Catwoman and The Penguin .15 .40
❑ 57 Cinematographer Stefan Czapsky .15 .40
❑ 58 Selina Kyle's murderer .15 .40
❑ 59 Bruce Wayne (Michael Keaton) is hard .15 .40
❑ 60 Batman's remarkable Batskiboat .15 .40
❑ 61 The Penguin running for Mayor .15 .40
❑ 62 Why is Batman such a popular .15 .40
❑ 63 A portrait of two celebrated fantasy .15 .40
❑ 64 A massive explosion .15 .40
❑ 65 Masked or unmasked .15 .40
❑ 66 The style and technological capabilities .15 .40
❑ 67 Mechanical effects supervisor Chuck Gaspar .15 .40
❑ 68 After blasting out .15 .40
❑ 69 Although a memorable villain .15 .40
❑ 70 Tim Burton directs Danny DeVito .15 .40
❑ 71 Another view of Batman's spectacular .15 .40
❑ 72 He's making a list and checking it twice .15 .40
❑ 73 The Shreck Building under construction .15 .40
❑ 74 As the Batmobile blasts into town .15 .40
❑ 75 Inside his secret headquarters .15 .40
❑ 76 During the climax of Batman Returns .15 .40
❑ 77 Portrait of the villainous Red Triangle Circus .15 .40
❑ 78 Tim Burton directs the exciting Max-squerade .15 .40
❑ 79 Bruce Wayne (Michael Keaton) .15 .40
❑ 80 Battling the evil Red Triangle Circus Gang .15 .40
❑ 81 The first Batman movie .15 .40
❑ 82 A rendering of Batman .15 .40
❑ 83 Tim Burton is a rarity .15 .40
❑ 84 Michelle Pfeiffer plays Selina Kyle .15 .40
❑ 85 Director Tim Burton guides Danny DeVito .15 .40
❑ 86 The grinning, distantly sinister Shreck .15 .40
❑ 87 Director Tim Burton grew up in Burbank .15 .40
❑ 88 One of the new thrills of Batman Returns .15 .40
❑ 89 Batman Returns director Tim Burton .15 .40
❑ 90 Some finished Batman cowls .15 .40
❑ 91 In Batman Returns, Michael Gough .15 .40
❑ 92 The air conditioning system .15 .40
❑ 93 Under Tim Burton's supervision .15 .40
❑ 94 Much of the tricky special effects .15 .40
❑ 95 Burton and Batman .15 .40
❑ 96 In the exciting climax of Batman Returns .15 .40
❑ 97 Can Batman and Catwoman .15 .40
❑ 98 The pram-prison, hurled into icy waters .15 .40
❑ 99 Enraged Gothamites chase .15 .40
❑ 100 As in the first Batman movie .15 .40

1992 Batman Returns (Topps)

COMPLETE SET (88) 4.00 10.00
❑ 1 A Recipe for Success .12 .30
❑ 2 The Dark Knight of Gotham City .12 .30
❑ 3 Introducing the Penguin .12 .30
❑ 4 Introducing Catwoman .12 .30
❑ 5 Evil Prince of the City .12 .30
❑ 6 Nightmare as a Child .12 .30
❑ 7 Master of the Lower Depths .12 .30
❑ 8 Peering Out of the Darkness .12 .30
❑ 9 Addressing Gotham City .12 .30
❑ 10 A Secretary Named Selina .12 .30
❑ 11 Watching from Wayne Manor .12 .30
❑ 12 What in the Name Of .12 .30
❑ 13 A Ghoulish Gift .12 .30
❑ 14 A Giant Surprise Package .12 .30
❑ 15 All Hell Breaks Loose .12 .30
❑ 16 Roar of the Batmobile .12 .30
❑ 17 Plowing Into Peril .12 .30
❑ 18 Cycling Psychos .12 .30
❑ 19 Terror in Gotham Square .12 .30
❑ 20 Scene of the Crime .12 .30
❑ 21 In the Clown's Clutches .12 .30
❑ 22 Let Her Go .12 .30
❑ 23 Human Flame Thrower .12 .30
❑ 24 Counterattack .12 .30
❑ 25 The Fire Breather Aflame .12 .30
❑ 26 Icy Lair .12 .30
❑ 27 Sultan of the Sewers .12 .30
❑ 28 Unholy Alliance .12 .30
❑ 29 Shreck's Way .12 .30
❑ 30 Through a Window Harshly .12 .30
❑ 31 Revived by Feline Friends .12 .30
❑ 32 Birth of Catwoman .12 .30
❑ 33 An Acrobatic Surprise .12 .30
❑ 34 Gotham's Unlikely Hero .12 .30
❑ 35 In Search of His Roots .12 .30
❑ 36 The List of Oswald Cobblepot .12 .30
❑ 37 Cemetery Pilgrimage .12 .30
❑ 38 Destiny of the Cobblepots .12 .30
❑ 39 Hizzoner... The Penguin .12 .30
❑ 40 Feline on the Prowl .12 .30
❑ 41 Night Watchers .12 .30
❑ 42 Meow .12 .30
❑ 43 Cat Challenges Bat .12 .30
❑ 44 Sinful, Sinuous Catwoman .12 .30
❑ 45 Only Eight Lives Left .12 .30
❑ 46 Burn, Baby, Burn .12 .30
❑ 47 The Plan to Destroy Batman .12 .30
❑ 48 Bruce and Selina Unmasked .12 .30
❑ 49 Rescuing the Ice Princess .12 .30
❑ 50 What Do You Want .12 .30
❑ 51 Sabotaging the Batmobile .12 .30
❑ 52 Innocent Victim .12 .30
❑ 53 A Long Way Down .12 .30
❑ 54 Over the Edge .12 .30
❑ 55 Wild Batmobile .12 .30
❑ 56 Gordon Against Him .12 .30
❑ 57 Flight of the Batmissile .12 .30
❑ 58 Cop Car Catastrophe .12 .30
❑ 59 A Penguin Scorned .12 .30
❑ 60 On the Campaign Trail .12 .30
❑ 61 Oswald Outwitted .12 .30
❑ 62 Turning on the Crowd .12 .30
❑ 63 Back to the Depths .12 .30
❑ 64 The Max-squerade .12 .30
❑ 65 Bruce Wayne In Costume .12 .30
❑ 66 Crashing the Party .12 .30
❑ 67 The Penguin's Revenge .12 .30
❑ 68 Fearsome Felon .12 .30
❑ 69 The Time Is At Hand .12 .30
❑ 70 The Kiddie Express .12 .30
❑ 71 Rallying His Troops .12 .30
❑ 72 Penguins on the March .12 .30
❑ 73 Missiles Away .12 .30
❑ 74 Invading Gotham City .12 .30
❑ 75 Gliding Gladiator .12 .30
❑ 76 Battered by Batman .12 .30
❑ 77 The Dark Knight Triumphant .12 .30
❑ 78 Batskiboat Attack .12 .30
❑ 79 Fury of the Penguin .12 .30
❑ 80 When Titans Collide .12 .30
❑ 81 The Penguin's Plunge .12 .30
❑ 82 Vengeance Is Hers .12 .30
❑ 83 Don't Interfere, Batman .12 .30
❑ 84 Shreck's Final Stand .12 .30
❑ 85 Lashing Out .12 .30
❑ 86 No Escape for Shreck .12 .30
❑ 87 Destroying His Life Support .12 .30
❑ 88 Farewell, Penguin .12 .30

1992 Batman Returns Stadium Club Inserts

COMPLETE SET (10) 2.00 5.00
STATED ODDS ONE PER PACK
❑ A Batman Blows It .40 1.00
❑ B Director Tim Burton enjoys .40 1.00
❑ C As part of the Penguin Catwoman .40 1.00
❑ D Once a submissive secretary .40 1.00
❑ E Penguins, penguins everywhere .40 1.00
❑ F Director Tim Burton found .40 1.00
❑ G Why is Batman such a popular .40 1.00
❑ H When the Penguin visits .40 1.00
❑ I Director Tim Burton gives .40 1.00
❑ J Introducing The Batmissile .40 1.00

1992 DC Cosmic

COMPLETE SET (180) 6.00 15.00
❑ 1 Vitamin 2-X .12 .30
❑ 2 The Blue Beetle's Magic Scarab .12 .30
❑ 3 Blue Beetle's Bug .12 .30
❑ 4 The Flash's Winged Helmet .12 .30
❑ 5 The Flash's Ring and Costume .12 .30
❑ 6 Flash's Special Police Band Radio Receivers .12 .30
❑ 7 Alan Scott's Power Ring .12 .30
❑ 8 Hal Jordan's Power Ring and Battery .12 .30
❑ 9 The Guardians of the Universe .12 .30
❑ 10 Hawkman's Mace and Cestus .12 .30
❑ 11 Hawkman's Starship .12 .30
❑ 12 Hawkman's Blaster .12 .30
❑ 13 The Brazier Used to Summon Shazam .12 .30
❑ 14 Whiz-TV .12 .30
❑ 15 The Gift of the Elders .12 .30
❑ 16 The Daily Star .12 .30
❑ 17 Superman's Arctic Fortress of Solitude .12 .30
❑ 18 The Doomed Planet Krypton .12 .30
❑ 19 Paradise Island, Home of the Amazons .12 .30
❑ 20 The Invisible Robot Plane .12 .30
❑ 21 The Magic Lasso .12 .30
❑ 22 The Cheetah's Dagger .12 .30
❑ 23 The Cheetah's Razor-Tipped Gloves .12 .30
❑ 24 Minerva's Cheetah Elixir .12 .30
❑ 25 The Powerstone .12 .30
❑ 26 Lex Luthor's Lab .12 .30
❑ 27 Lex Luthor's Kryptonite Ring .12 .30
❑ 28 Mr. Mxyztplk's Derby .12 .30
❑ 29 The Fifth Dimension .12 .30
❑ 30 An Example of Mxyztplk's Magic .12 .30
❑ 31 Animal Man's Alien Benefactors .12 .30
❑ 32 Atlantis, Aqualad's Home .12 .30
❑ 33 The Lighthouse Where Aquaman was Raised .12 .30
❑ 34 Black Condor's Dagger .12 .30
❑ 35 Black Lightning's Power Belt .12 .30
❑ 36 Blackhawk's Plane, The Grumman X-F5F Skyrocket .12 .30
❑ 37 Blue Devil's Rocket-Powered Trident .12 .30
❑ 38 Booster Gold's Wrist Blasters and Power Rods .12 .30
❑ 39 Bronze Tiger's Original Mask .12 .30
❑ 40 The Logans' Experimental Ray .12 .30
❑ 41 The Creeper's Transformation Device .12 .30
❑ 42 Crimson Fox's Steel Claws .12 .30
❑ 43 Cyborg's Arsenal .12 .30
❑ 44 Deathstroke's Power Staff .12 .30
❑ 45 Dr. Light's Laboratory .12 .30
❑ 46 Terataya .12 .30
❑ 47 Gingold, Elongated Man's Secret Stretching Elixir .12 .30
❑ 48 The Pyroplasm Ray .12 .30
❑ 49 The Machine That Created Firehawk .12 .30
❑ 50 Hudson Nuclear Power Plant .12 .30
❑ 51 Gangbuster's Nunchaks and Taser .12 .30
❑ 52 Prince Brion's Home Country of Markovia .12 .30
❑ 53 The Guardian's Shield .12 .30
❑ 54 Guy Gardner's Library .12 .30
❑ 55 T'Charr .12 .30
❑ 56 Hawkwoman's Wings and Anti-Gravity Belt .12 .30
❑ 57 Hourman's Strength-Augmenting Skin Patches .12 .30
❑ 58 The Dome, Former Global Guardians Headquarters .12 .30
❑ 59 Jade's Power Pulse .12 .30
❑ 60 Stewart's Current Home, The Planet Oa .12 .30
❑ 61 Soultaker, Katana's Sword .12 .30
❑ 62 The Orb of Ra, Metamorpho's Sole Weakness .12 .30
❑ 63 Infinity, Inc. Headquarters .12 .30
❑ 64 The Nightshade Dimension .12 .30
❑ 65 Nightwing's Stun Disks and Gas Mask .12 .30
❑ 66 The Lost City of Feithera .12 .30
❑ 67 Nuklon's Exercise Equipment .12 .30
❑ 68 Pantha's Claws .12 .30
❑ 69 Peacemaker's Cybernetic Helmet, Jetpack, and Belt .12 .30
❑ 70 Phantom Lady's Holographic Jewel and Wrist Taser .12 .30
❑ 71 Karen Starr's Company, Starrware, Inc. .12 .30
❑ 72 Rags 'n' Tatters, Rory Regan's Junk Shop .12 .30
❑ 73 Raven's Soul-Self .12 .30
❑ 74 Rocket Red's Electro Net .12 .30
❑ 75 Speedy's Bow and Arrows .12 .30
❑ 76 New Chronos .12 .30
❑ 77 Vixen's Tantu Totem .12 .30
❑ 78 Grant's Gym .12 .30
❑ 79 Amazo's Creation Matrix .12 .30
❑ 80 Big Sir's Energy Mace .12 .30
❑ 81 Black Manta's Undersea Craft .12 .30
❑ 82 Roland Desmond's Blockbuster Serum .12 .30
❑ 83 Bolt's Power Glove .12 .30
❑ 84 Brainiac's Spaceship .12 .30
❑ 85 Captain Boomerang's Sonic and Explosive Boomerangs .12 .30
❑ 86 Professor Norton, Chemo's Creator .12 .30
❑ 87 Chronos's Time-Wise Weaponry .12 .30
❑ 88 Copperhead's Venomous Fangs .12 .30
❑ 89 Vertigo's Inner-Ear Implant .12 .30
❑ 90 Deadline's Energy Rifle and Anti-Gravity Disks .12 .30
❑ 91 Deadshot's Wrist Magnum .12 .30
❑ 92 Dr. Light's Strobe Ray and Teleportation Gun .12 .30
❑ 93 Dr. Polaris' Magno-Gun .12 .30
❑ 94 Eclipso's Black Diamond .12 .30
❑ 95 Goldface's Gold Gun .12 .30
❑ 96 Gorilla City .12 .30
❑ 97 Houngan's Voodoo Doll .12 .30
❑ 98 Jericho's Wildebeest Glove .12 .30
❑ 99 Druspa Tau, Kestrel's Homerealm .12 .30
❑ 100 Monarch's Space Station .12 .30
❑ 101 Ocean Master's Oxygen-Filtering Helmet .12 .30
❑ 102 The Toxic Waste that Transformed Parasite .12 .30
❑ 103 A Sample of Phobia's Illusions .12 .30
❑ 104 General Zahl's Laboratory .12 .30
❑ 105 The Medusa Mask .12 .30
❑ 106 The Shadow Field Generator .12 .30
❑ 107 Silver Swan's Sonic Power .12 .30
❑ 108 Sonar's Sonic Pistol .12 .30
❑ 109 Toyman's Deadly Arsenal .12 .30
❑ 110 The Source of Savage's Immortality .12 .30
❑ 111 Warp's Dimensional Portal .12 .30
❑ 112 Adam Strange's Blaster and Rocket Pack .12 .30
❑ 113 The Green Lantern Corps' Earth Headquarters .12 .30
❑ 114 Barda's Mega-Rod .12 .30
❑ 115 The Black Racer's Skis of Death .12 .30
❑ 116 Fastbak's Aeropads .12 .30
❑ 117 G'nort's Custom-Designed Power Ring .12 .30
❑ 118 Kilowog's Lab .12 .30
❑ 119 Supertown, New Genesis .12 .30
❑ 120 Lobo's Intergalacticycle .12 .30
❑ 121 The Planet Mars .12 .30
❑ 122 Metron's Mobius Chair .12 .30
❑ 123 Mr. Miracle's Aero Disks and Multi-Cube .12 .30
❑ 124 Orion's Mother Box and Astro-Glider .12 .30
❑ 125 Starfire's Gordanian Captors .12 .30
❑ 126 The Mace and Hammer of Ares .12 .30
❑ 127 Tamaran .12 .30
❑ 128 The Planet Apokolips .12 .30
❑ 129 Desaad's Killing Gloves .12 .30
❑ 130 Despero's Deadly Chessboard .12 .30
❑ 131 Godfrey's Mind Control Helmets .12 .30
❑ 132 Granny's Punishment Club .12 .30
❑ 133 Kalibak's Beta-Club .12 .30
❑ 134 The Planet Thanagar .12 .30
❑ 135 The Cluster .12 .30
❑ 136 Maxima's Starship .12 .30
❑ 137 The Nebulamobile .12 .30
❑ 138 Sinestro's Power Ring .12 .30
❑ 139 Starro's Starship .12 .30
❑ 140 Steppenwolf's Electro-Axe .12 .30
❑ 141 The Promethean Galaxy, Yuga Khan's Prison .12 .30
❑ 142 Crisis on Earths One & Two .12 .30
❑ 143 Crisis on Earths One & Two .12 .30
❑ 144 Crisis on Earths One & Two .12 .30
❑ 145 Crisis on Infinite Earths .12 .30
❑ 146 Crisis on Infinite Earths .12 .30
❑ 147 Crisis on Infinite Earths .12 .30
❑ 148 Legends .12 .30
❑ 149 Legends .12 .30
❑ 150 Legends .12 .30
❑ 151 Millennium .12 .30
❑ 152 Millennium .12 .30
❑ 153 Millennium .12 .30
❑ 154 Invasion .12 .30
❑ 155 Invasion .12 .30
❑ 156 Invasion .12 .30
❑ 157 Cosmic Odyssey .12 .30
❑ 158 Cosmic Odyssey .12 .30
❑ 159 Cosmic Odyssey .12 .30
❑ 160 The Great Darkness Saga .12 .30
❑ 161 The Great Darkness Saga .12 .30
❑ 162 The Great Darkness Saga .12 .30
❑ 163 Armageddon 2001 .12 .30
❑ 164 Armageddon 2001 .12 .30
❑ 165 Armageddon 2001 .12 .30
❑ 166 War of the Gods .12 .30
❑ 167 War of the Gods .12 .30
❑ 168 War of the Gods .12 .30
❑ 169 Action Comics #1 .12 .30
❑ 170 All-American Comics #16 .12 .30
❑ 171 All Star Comics #3 .12 .30
❑ 172 The Brave and the Bold #34 .12 .30
❑ 173 New Gods #1 .12 .30
❑ 174 Sensation Comics #1 .12 .30
❑ 175 Showcase #22 .12 .30
❑ 176 Showcase #34 .12 .30
❑ 177 Superman #1 .12 .30
❑ 178 Wonder Woman #1 .12 .30
❑ 179 Checklist One .12 .30
❑ 180 Checklist Two .12 .30

1992 DC Cosmic Holograms

COMPLETE SET (10) 12.00 30.00
STATED ODDS 1:10
❑ DCH1 Clark Kent Lois Lane 2.50 6.00
❑ DCH2 Darkseid 2.50 6.00
❑ DCH3 Deathstroke the Terminator 2.50 6.00
❑ DCH4 Flash 2.50 6.00
❑ DCH5 Green Lantern 2.50 6.00
❑ DCH6 Hawkman 2.50 6.00
❑ DCH7 Lobo 2.50 6.00
❑ DCH8 Superman 2.50 6.00
❑ DCH9 Wonder Woman 2.50 6.00
❑ DCH10 Waverider 2.50 6.00

1992 Ghost Rider II

COMPLETE SET (80) 4.00 10.00
❑ 1 Blood Signs .12 .30
❑ 2 Zodiak .12 .30
❑ 3 Possessed .12 .30
❑ 4 Asleep .12 .30
❑ 5 Zarathos .12 .30
❑ 6 Dr. Strange .12 .30
❑ 7 Captured .12 .30
❑ 8 Snowblind .12 .30
❑ 9 Johnny Blaze .12 .30
❑ 10 The Original .12 .30
❑ 11 Old Times .12 .30
❑ 12 Control .12 .30
❑ 13 Freedom .12 .30
❑ 14 Confrontation .12 .30
❑ 15 Hellfire .12 .30
❑ 16 Shot .12 .30
❑ 17 Wounded .12 .30
❑ 18 No Escape .12 .30
❑ 19 Stop It .12 .30
❑ 20 Scarred .12 .30
❑ 21 Exhausted .12 .30
❑ 22 Team-Up .12 .30
❑ 23 Hobgoblin .12 .30
❑ 24 Spider-Man .12 .30
❑ 25 Fire Power .12 .30
❑ 26 Styge .12 .30
❑ 27 Bare Bones .12 .30
❑ 28 In Between .12 .30
❑ 29 Suicide .12 .30
❑ 30 Mephisto .12 .30
❑ 31 Death .12 .30
❑ 32 Punishment .12 .30
❑ 33 Penance Stare .12 .30
❑ 34 Ninjas .12 .30
❑ 35 Buried .12 .30
❑ 36 Deathwatch .12 .30
❑ 37 Hag and Troll .12 .30
❑ 38 Final Conflict .12 .30
❑ 39 You Will Die .12 .30
❑ 40 Revenge .12 .30
❑ 41 Dan's Death .12 .30
❑ 42 Nightmare .12 .30
❑ 43 New Orleans .12 .30
❑ 44 Frenzy .12 .30
❑ 45 Hot Heads .12 .30
❑ 46 Undead .12 .30
❑ 47 Hearts of Darkness .12 .30
❑ 48 Blackheart .12 .30
❑ 49 Sleepwalker .12 .30
❑ 50 Deathlock .12 .30
❑ 51 Moon Knight .12 .30
❑ 52 Daredevil .12 .30
❑ 53 Fear .12 .30
❑ 54 Fantastic Four .12 .30
❑ 55 Four of Us .12 .30
❑ 56 The Midnight Sons .12 .30
❑ 57 Lilith's Motive .12 .30
❑ 58 Lilith .12 .30
❑ 59 Morbius .12 .30
❑ 60 Duo .12 .30
❑ 61 Nightstalkers .12 .30
❑ 62 Mistaken I.D. .12 .30
❑ 63 Darkhold .12 .30
❑ 64 Spirits of Vengeance .12 .30
❑ 65 Partners .12 .30
❑ 66 Teacher .12 .30
❑ 67 Vendetta .12 .30
❑ 68 First Mission .12 .30
❑ 69 Demon .12 .30
❑ 70 Transformation .12 .30
❑ 71 Emblem .12 .30
❑ 72 The Chain .12 .30
❑ 73 Powers and Abilities .12 .30
❑ 74 Pain .12 .30
❑ 75 Taking a Human Life .12 .30
❑ 76 First Series .12 .30
❑ 77 The Start .12 .30
❑ 78 The Champions .12 .30
❑ 79 Restarted .12 .30
❑ 80 Checklist .12 .30

1992 Ghost Rider II Glow in the Dark

COMPLETE SET (10) 2.50 6.00
❑ G1 Illuminating .40 1.00
❑ G2 Vigilantes .40 1.00
❑ G3 My Arsenal .40 1.00
❑ G4 Power Source .40 1.00
❑ G5 Wolverine .40 1.00
❑ G6 The Flames .40 1.00
❑ G7 Punisher .40 1.00
❑ G8 Hot Air .40 1.00
❑ G9 Cable .40 1.00
❑ G10 Grin and Bear It .40 1.00

1992 Marvel Masterpieces

COMPLETE SET (100) 10.00 25.00
❑ 1 Blob .30 .75
❑ 2 Blaze .30 .75
❑ 3 Black Widow .30 .75
❑ 4 Black Panther .30 .75
❑ 5 Black Cat .30 .75
❑ 6 Bishop .30 .75
❑ 7 Beast .30 .75
❑ 8 Archangel .30 .75
❑ 9 Apocalypse .30 .75
❑ 10 Adam Warlock .30 .75
❑ 11 Darkhawk .30 .75
❑ 12 Daredevil .30 .75
❑ 13 Cyclops .30 .75
❑ 14 Colossus .30 .75
❑ 15 Captain Britain .30 .75
❑ 16 Captain America .30 .75
❑ 17 Cage .30 .75
❑ 18 Cable .30 .75
❑ 19 Bullseye .30 .75
❑ 20 Dazzler .30 .75
❑ 21 Enchantress .30 .75
❑ 22 Elektra .30 .75
❑ 23 Electro .30 .75
❑ 24 Dr. Strange .30 .75
❑ 25 Dr. Octopus .30 .75
❑ 26 Dr. Doom .30 .75
❑ 27 Dormammu .30 .75
❑ 28 Deathlok .30 .75
❑ 29 Gambit .30 .75
❑ 30 Galactus .30 .75
❑ 31 Human Torch .30 .75
❑ 32 Hulk .30 .75
❑ 33 Hobgoblin .30 .75
❑ 34 Hawkeye .30 .75
❑ 35 Havok .30 .75
❑ 36 Green Goblin .30 .75
❑ 37 Ghost Rider .30 .75
❑ 38 Iron Man .30 .75
❑ 39 Invisible Woman .30 .75
❑ 40 Iceman .30 .75
❑ 41 Lizard .30 .75
❑ 42 Leader .30 .75
❑ 43 Kingpin .30 .75
❑ 44 Kang .30 .75
❑ 45 Juggernaut .30 .75
❑ 46 Jean Grey .30 .75
❑ 47 Mandarin .30 .75
❑ 48 Major Victory .30 .75
❑ 49 Magneto .30 .75
❑ 50 Loki .30 .75
❑ 51 Moon Knight .30 .75
❑ 52 Mole Man .30 .75
❑ 53 Mojo .30 .75
❑ 54 Mephisto .30 .75
❑ 55 Meggan .30 .75
❑ 56 Namorita .30 .75
❑ 57 Namor .30 .75
❑ 58 Mr. Sinister .30 .75
❑ 59 Mr. Fantastic .30 .75
❑ 60 Morbius .30 .75
❑ 61 Nightmare .30 .75
❑ 62 Nightcrawler .30 .75
❑ 63 Night Thrasher .30 .75
❑ 64 Nick Fury .30 .75
❑ 65 Psylocke .30 .75
❑ 66 Professor X .30 .75
❑ 67 Phoenix .30 .75
❑ 68 Nova .30 .75
❑ 69 Northstar .30 .75
❑ 70 Nomad .30 .75
❑ 71 Quicksilver .30 .75
❑ 72 Quasar .30 .75
❑ 73 Punisher .30 .75
❑ 74 Shatterstar .30 .75
❑ 75 Shadowcat .30 .75
❑ 76 Sauron .30 .75
❑ 77 Sandman .30 .75
❑ 78 Sabretooth .30 .75
❑ 79 Rogue .30 .75
❑ 80 Red Skull .30 .75
❑ 81 Silver Sable .30 .75
❑ 82 She-Hulk .30 .75
❑ 83 Thanos .30 .75
❑ 84 Super Skrull .30 .75
❑ 85 Strong Guy .30 .75
❑ 86 Storm .30 .75
❑ 87 Spider-Man .30 .75
❑ 88 Speedball .30 .75
❑ 89 Sleepwalker .30 .75
❑ 90 Silver Surfer .30 .75
❑ 91 Thing .30 .75
❑ 92 Thor .30 .75
❑ 93 Wonder Man .30 .75
❑ 94 Wolverine .30 .75
❑ 95 White Queen .30 .75
❑ 96 Weapon Omega .30 .75
❑ 97 Venom .30 .75
❑ 98 Ultron .30 .75
❑ 99 Tombstone .30 .75
❑ 100 Checklist .30 .75

1992 Marvel Masterpieces Battle Spectra

COMPLETE SET (5) 8.00 20.00
❑ 1D Thing vs. Hulk 2.00 5.00
❑ 2D Silver Surfer vs. Thanos 2.00 5.00
❑ 3D Wolverine vs. Sabretooth 2.00 5.00
❑ 4D Spider-Man vs. Venom 2.00 5.00
❑ 5D Captain America vs. Red Skull 2.00 5.00

1992 Marvel Masterpieces Lost Marvel Bonus

COMPLETE SET (5) 12.00 30.00
❑ LM1 Scarlet Witch 3.00 8.00
❑ LM2 Feral 3.00 8.00
❑ LM3 Deathbird 3.00 8.00
❑ LM4 Typhoid Mary 3.00 8.00
❑ LM5 Jubilee 3.00 8.00

1992 Marvel Masterpieces Prototypes

❑ 36 Hulk
❑ 86 Spider-Man
❑ 98 Wolverine

1992 Marvel Universe

COMPLETE SET (201) 12.00 30.00
❑ 1 Spider-Man .15 .40
❑ 2 Quasar .15 .40
❑ 3 Sleepwalker .15 .40
❑ 4 Gambit .15 .40
❑ 5 Cannonball .15 .40
❑ 6 Beast .15 .40
❑ 7 Quicksilver .15 .40
❑ 8 Weapon Omega .15 .40
❑ 9 Doctor Strange .15 .40
❑ 10 Major Victory .15 .40
❑ 11 Phoenix .15 .40
❑ 12 Black Widow .15 .40
❑ 13 Hulk .15 .40
❑ 14 Sunfire .15 .40
❑ 15 Silver Surfer .15 .40
❑ 16 She-Hulk .15 .40
❑ 17 Captain Britain .15 .40
❑ 18 Cage .15 .40
❑ 19 Domino .15 .40
❑ 20 Daredevil .15 .40
❑ 21 Morbius .15 .40
❑ 22 Nightcrawler .15 .40
❑ 23 Black Panther .15 .40
❑ 24 Ant-Man .15 .40
❑ 25 Ghost Rider .15 .40
❑ 26 Darkhawk .15 .40
❑ 27 Iceman .15 .40
❑ 28 Punisher .15 .40
❑ 29 Wolfsbane .15 .40
❑ 30 Storm .15 .40
❑ 31 Wonder Man .15 .40
❑ 32 Moon Knight .15 .40
❑ 33 Mr. Fantastic .15 .40
❑ 34 Invisible Woman .15 .40

MODERN ERA NON-SPORTS

❑ 35 Shadowcat .15 .40
❑ 36 Warlock .15 .40
❑ 37 Captain America .15 .40
❑ 38 Wolverine .15 .40
❑ 39 Namor .15 .40
❑ 40 Nick Fury .15 .40
❑ 41 Professor X .15 .40
❑ 42 Shatterstar .15 .40
❑ 43 Multiple Man .15 .40
❑ 44 Blaze .15 .40
❑ 45 Deathlok .15 .40
❑ 46 Colossus .15 .40
❑ 47 Meggan .15 .40
❑ 48 Thor .15 .40
❑ 49 Namorita .15 .40
❑ 50 Cable .15 .40
❑ 51 Psylocke .15 .40
❑ 52 Warpath .15 .40
❑ 53 Nomad .15 .40
❑ 54 Polaris .15 .40
❑ 55 Charlie-27 .15 .40
❑ 56 Thing .15 .40
❑ 57 Longshot .15 .40
❑ 58 Human Torch .15 .40
❑ 59 Night Thrasher .15 .40
❑ 60 Siryn .15 .40
❑ 61 Nova .15 .40
❑ 62 Iron Man .15 .40
❑ 63 Archangel .15 .40
❑ 64 Rogue .15 .40
❑ 65 Silver Sable .15 .40
❑ 66 Jean Grey .15 .40
❑ 67 Feral .15 .40
❑ 68 Cyclops .15 .40
❑ 69 Starhawk .15 .40
❑ 70 Havok .15 .40
❑ 71 Spider-Man Human Torch .15 .40
❑ 72 Spider-Man Ghost Rider .15 .40
❑ 73 Spider-Man Punisher .15 .40
❑ 74 Spider-Man Wolverine .15 .40
❑ 75 Wolverine Captain America .15 .40
❑ 76 Wolverine Hulk .15 .40
❑ 77 Wolverine Cable .15 .40
❑ 78 Magneto Dr. Doom .15 .40
❑ 79 Ghost Rider Blaze .15 .40
❑ 80 Captain America Nomad .15 .40
❑ 81 Spider-Man Darkhawk .15 .40
❑ 82 Iceman Human Torch .15 .40
❑ 83 Captain America U.S. Agent .15 .40
❑ 84 Wolverine Daredevil .15 .40
❑ 85 Vision Scarlet Witch .15 .40
❑ 86 Punisher Deathlok .15 .40
❑ 87 Thor Corps .15 .40
❑ 88 Wolverine Ghost Rider/Punisher .15 .40
❑ 89 Wonder Man Beast .15 .40
❑ 90 Ghost Rider Daredevil .15 .40
❑ 91 Wolverine Havok .15 .40
❑ 92 Punisher Daredevil .15 .40
❑ 93 Daredevil Black Widow .15 .40
❑ 94 Punisher Captain America .15 .40
❑ 95 Spider-Man Sleepwalker .15 .40
❑ 96 Power Man Iron Fist .15 .40
❑ 97 Spider-Man Daredevil .15 .40
❑ 98 Hulk Thing .15 .40
❑ 99 Red Skull Baron Zemo .15 .40
❑ 100 Juggernaut Black Tom .15 .40
❑ 101 Abomination .15 .40
❑ 102 Zodiak .15 .40
❑ 103 Apocalypse .15 .40
❑ 104 Sphinx .15 .40
❑ 105 Destroyer .15 .40
❑ 106 Red Skull .15 .40
❑ 107 Puppet Master .15 .40
❑ 108 Venom .15 .40
❑ 109 Diablo .15 .40
❑ 110 The Rose .15 .40
❑ 111 Doctor Doom .15 .40
❑ 112 Magneto .15 .40
❑ 113 Necrom .15 .40
❑ 114 Green Goblin .15 .40
❑ 115 Dracula .15 .40
❑ 116 Sauron .15 .40
❑ 117 Cyber .15 .40
❑ 118 Mephisto .15 .40
❑ 119 Mad Thinker .15 .40
❑ 120 Carnage .15 .40
❑ 121 Hobgoblin .15 .40
❑ 122 Gideon .15 .40
❑ 123 White Queen .15 .40
❑ 124 Omega Red .15 .40
❑ 125 Maelstrom .15 .40
❑ 126 Thanos .15 .40
❑ 127 Zarrko .15 .40
❑ 128 Magus .15 .40
❑ 129 Sabretooth .15 .40
❑ 130 Kingpin .15 .40
❑ 131 Silvermane .15 .40
❑ 132 Cardiac .15 .40
❑ 133 Blackheart .15 .40
❑ 134 Terrax .15 .40
❑ 135 Mr. Sinister .15 .40
❑ 136 Slug .15 .40
❑ 137 Hate-Monger .15 .40
❑ 138 Crossbones .15 .40
❑ 139 Shiva .15 .40
❑ 140 Blackout .15 .40
❑ 141 Pantheon .15 .40
❑ 142 Slapstick .15 .40
❑ 143 Cerise .15 .40
❑ 144 Darkhold Redeemers .15 .40
❑ 145 Strong Guy .15 .40
❑ 146 Bishop .15 .40
❑ 147 Silhouette .15 .40
❑ 148 Kylun .15 .40
❑ 149 Talon .15 .40
❑ 150 Collector .15 .40
❑ 151 Galactus .15 .40
❑ 152 Watcher .15 .40
❑ 153 Living Tribunal .15 .40
❑ 154 Ego .15 .40
❑ 155 Eternity .15 .40
❑ 156 Celestials .15 .40
❑ 157 Death .15 .40
❑ 158 Stranger .15 .40
❑ 159 In-Betweener .15 .40
❑ 160 Epoch .15 .40
❑ 161 Hulk .15 .40
❑ 162 Spider-Man .15 .40
❑ 163 Silver Surfer .15 .40
❑ 164 Wolverine .15 .40
❑ 165 Iron Man .15 .40
❑ 166 Captain America .15 .40
❑ 167 Ghost Rider .15 .40
❑ 168 Daredevil .15 .40
❑ 169 Fantastic Four .15 .40
❑ 170 Thor .15 .40
❑ 171 Avengers .15 .40
❑ 172 X-Force .15 .40
❑ 173 X-Factor .15 .40
❑ 174 New Warriors .15 .40
❑ 175 Alpha Flight .15 .40
❑ 176 Avengers West Coast .15 .40
❑ 177 Nightstalkers .15 .40
❑ 178 Guardians of the Galaxy .15 .40
❑ 179 X-Men (Gold) .15 .40
❑ 180 Excalibur .15 .40
❑ 181 Fantastic Four .15 .40
❑ 182 X-Men (Blue) .15 .40
❑ 183 Serpent Society .15 .40
❑ 184 X-tinction Agenda .15 .40
❑ 185 Evolutionary War .15 .40
❑ 186 Operation Galactic Storm .15 .40
❑ 187 Secret Wars .15 .40
❑ 188 Inferno .15 .40
❑ 189 Infinity Gauntlet .15 .40
❑ 190 Kree vs. Skrull War .15 .40
❑ 191 Atlantis Attacks .15 .40
❑ 192 I Married a Skrull .15 .40
❑ 193 Days of Future Past .15 .40
❑ 194 All Hulks Unite .15 .40
❑ 195 Dark Phoenix Saga .15 .40
❑ 196 The Coming of Galactus .15 .40
❑ 197 Death of Gwen Stacy .15 .40
❑ 198 Fall of the Kingpin .15 .40
❑ 199 Wedding of Spider-Man .15 .40
❑ 200A Checklist (no border on back of card) .15 .40
❑ 200B Checklist (white border on back of card) .15 .40

1992 Marvel Universe Holograms

COMPLETE SET (5) 8.00 20.00
❑ H1 Hulk 2.00 5.00
❑ H2 Thing 2.00 5.00
❑ H3 Wolverine 2.00 5.00
❑ H4 Venom 2.00 5.00
❑ H5 Ghost Rider 2.00 5.00

1992 The Punisher Guts and Gunpowder

COMPLETE SET (90) 6.00 15.00
❑ 1 Creating .15 .40
❑ 2 First Appearance .15 .40
❑ 3 Spider-Man .15 .40
❑ 4 Bugged .15 .40
❑ 5 Similar Pasts .15 .40
❑ 6 Training .15 .40
❑ 7 Soldier .15 .40
❑ 8 The Catalyst .15 .40
❑ 9 AWOL .15 .40
❑ 10 Rage .15 .40
❑ 11 Retribution .15 .40
❑ 12 Punisher .15 .40
❑ 13 Journal .15 .40
❑ 14 Justice .15 .40
❑ 15 Mornings .15 .40
❑ 16 Preparation .15 .40
❑ 17 Weapons .15 .40
❑ 18 Arsenal .15 .40
❑ 19 Maggia .15 .40
❑ 20 Says Who .15 .40
❑ 21 Punishment .15 .40
❑ 22 Mercy .15 .40
❑ 23 Daredevil .15 .40
❑ 24 Hornhead .15 .40
❑ 25 Anti-Hero .15 .40
❑ 26 Indepth .15 .40
❑ 27 Prison .15 .40
❑ 28 Defense .15 .40
❑ 29 Crime .15 .40
❑ 30 Captain America .15 .40
❑ 31 Kingpin .15 .40
❑ 32 Fisk .15 .40
❑ 33 Jigsaw .15 .40
❑ 34 Microchip .15 .40
❑ 35 Microchip, Jr .15 .40
❑ 36 A Father's Loss .15 .40
❑ 37 The Board .15 .40
❑ 38 Aides .15 .40
❑ 39 To Die For .15 .40
❑ 40 Sniper .15 .40
❑ 41 Illusions .15 .40
❑ 42 Ghost Rider .15 .40
❑ 43 Vigilantes .15 .40
❑ 44 Darkhawk .15 .40
❑ 45 Wolverine .15 .40
❑ 46 Africa .15 .40
❑ 47 Bushwacker .15 .40
❑ 48 Triple Threat .15 .40
❑ 49 Van .15 .40
❑ 50 Transport .15 .40
❑ 51 Aloha! .15 .40
❑ 52 Not Ready .15 .40
❑ 53 Concealment .15 .40
❑ 54 Inspirations .15 .40
❑ 55 Group of One .15 .40
❑ 56 Submerged .15 .40
❑ 57 Practice .15 .40
❑ 58 Shadowmasters .15 .40
❑ 59 Kevlar .15 .40
❑ 60 Disguises .15 .40
❑ 61 Reflection .15 .40
❑ 62 Doctor Doom .15 .40
❑ 63 Deathlok .15 .40
❑ 64 Moonknight .15 .40
❑ 65 Dead Man's Hand .15 .40
❑ 66 Blood & Glory .15 .40
❑ 67 Hulk .15 .40
❑ 68 Mr. Fixit .15 .40
❑ 69 Reality .15 .40
❑ 70 Undressed .15 .40
❑ 71 Uzi .15 .40
❑ 72 Colt .45 .15 .40
❑ 73 War Zone .15 .40
❑ 74 Johnny Tower .15 .40
❑ 75 User .15 .40
❑ 76 Shotgun .15 .40
❑ 77 Double-Crossed .15 .40
❑ 78 Discovered .15 .40
❑ 79 Countdown .15 .40
❑ 80 Open Fire .15 .40
❑ 81 Shark Island .15 .40
❑ 82 Toxic .15 .40
❑ 83 Cleaning .15 .40
❑ 84 Fun .15 .40
❑ 85 Favorite Gun .15 .40
❑ 86 Hostages .15 .40
❑ 87 Love .15 .40
❑ 88 Black Widow .15 .40
❑ 89 Punisher 2099 .15 .40
❑ 90 Checklist .15 .40

1992 The Punisher Guts and Gunpowder Prisms

COMPLETE SET (3) 5.00 12.00
STATED ODDS 1:48
❑ 1 Defense Mechanism 2.50 6.00
❑ 2 Popularity 2.50 6.00
❑ 3 Deathwish 2.50 6.00

1992 The Punisher Guts and Gunpowder Scratch and Sniff

COMPLETE SET (3) 4.00 10.00
STATED ODDS 1:24
❑ 1 Preparation 4.00 10.00
❑ 2 Stunts 2.00 5.00
❑ 3 The Actor

1992 Spider-Man The Todd McFarlane Era

COMPLETE SET (90) 6.00 15.00
❑ 1 The Beginning .15 .40
❑ 2 Uptown .15 .40
❑ 3 Arachknight .15 .40
❑ 4 Arise .15 .40
❑ 5 Married Life .15 .40
❑ 6 The Lizard .15 .40
❑ 7 Friendly, Neighborhood .15 .40
❑ 8 Connors .15 .40
❑ 9 A Spider .15 .40
❑ 10 Spider-Sense .15 .40
❑ 11 Attacked .15 .40
❑ 12 Poison .15 .40
❑ 13 Fatality .15 .40
❑ 14 Alone .15 .40
❑ 15 Resurrection .15 .40
❑ 16 The Hunter .15 .40
❑ 17 Rooftop .15 .40
❑ 18 Trashed .15 .40
❑ 19 Dazed .15 .40
❑ 20 The Past .15 .40
❑ 21 Drugged .15 .40
❑ 22 Kraven .15 .40
❑ 23 The Witch .15 .40
❑ 24 Once Again .15 .40
❑ 25 Explosion .15 .40
❑ 26 Crawling Out .15 .40
❑ 27 Voodoo .15 .40
❑ 28 Last Time .15 .40
❑ 29 Death .15 .40
❑ 30 Home .15 .40
❑ 31 Another Time .15 .40
❑ 32 Dark Days .15 .40
❑ 33 Hobgoblin .15 .40
❑ 34 Heading Out .15 .40
❑ 35 Tuning In .15 .40
❑ 36 Ghost Rider .15 .40
❑ 37 The Kid .15 .40
❑ 38 Team Up .15 .40
❑ 39 Busting In .15 .40
❑ 40 Spirit of Vengeance .15 .40
❑ 41 Ready .15 .40
❑ 42 Fire Creature .15 .40
❑ 43 Stop This .15 .40
❑ 44 Perceptions .15 .40
❑ 45 Folklore .15 .40
❑ 46 Hanging Out .15 .40
❑ 47 J.J. Jameson .15 .40
❑ 48 Murder .15 .40
❑ 49 Wolverine .15 .40
❑ 50 The Mystery .15 .40
❑ 51 Gotcha .15 .40
❑ 52 The Hunter .15 .40
❑ 53 The Myth .15 .40
❑ 54 Investigation .15 .40
❑ 55 Shot .15 .40
❑ 56 Into the Woods .15 .40
❑ 57 Wounded .15 .40
❑ 58 Wendigo .15 .40
❑ 59 Primal .15 .40
❑ 60 Time To Go .15 .40
❑ 61 Crime Fighters .15 .40
❑ 62 Evidence .15 .40
❑ 63 Parker .15 .40
❑ 64 Hurt .15 .40
❑ 65 The Bullet .15 .40
❑ 66 Pondering .15 .40
❑ 67 Together .15 .40
❑ 68 Stay Here .15 .40
❑ 69 Masked .15 .40
❑ 70 Trapped .15 .40
❑ 71 Set-Up .15 .40
❑ 72 Sub-City .15 .40
❑ 73 Keever .15 .40
❑ 74 Web-Slinger .15 .40
❑ 75 Black Costume .15 .40
❑ 76 Morbius .15 .40
❑ 77 Spotted .15 .40
❑ 78 Vampire .15 .40
❑ 79 Down Under .15 .40
❑ 80 Too Many .15 .40
❑ 81 Male Bonding .15 .40
❑ 82 Mouthful .15 .40
❑ 83 Bad Ones .15 .40
❑ 84 I'm Gone .15 .40
❑ 85 X-Force .15 .40
❑ 86 Juggernaut .15 .40
❑ 87 Young Ones .15 .40
❑ 88 Cable .15 .40
❑ 89 Join Together .15 .40
❑ 90 Checklist .15 .40

1992 Spider-Man The Todd McFarlane Era Prisms

COMPLETE SET (6) 15.00 30.00
STATED ODDS 1:16
❑ P1 Thirty Years 4.00 10.00
❑ P2 Dynamic 4.00 10.00
❑ P3 Number One 4.00 10.00
❑ P4 Impact 4.00 10.00
❑ P5 Image 4.00 10.00
❑ P6 Red and Blue 4.00 10.00

1992 Spider-Man II 30th Anniversary

COMPLETE SET (90) 6.00 15.00
❑ 1 September, 1962 .15 .40
❑ 2 6 Years Old .15 .40
❑ 3 The Exhibition .15 .40
❑ 4 Human Spider .15 .40
❑ 5 Reflexes .15 .40
❑ 6 Wall Climber .15 .40
❑ 7 Spider-Sense .15 .40
❑ 8 Web-Shooters .15 .40
❑ 9 Web Fluid .15 .40
❑ 10 Equipment .15 .40
❑ 11 Wrestling .15 .40
❑ 12 Irony .15 .40
❑ 13 A Hero is Born .15 .40
❑ 14 Amazing Spider-Man .15 .40
❑ 15 The Chameleon .15 .40
❑ 16 J. J. Jameson .15 .40
❑ 17 Bad Press .15 .40
❑ 18 John Jameson .15 .40
❑ 19 Fantastic Four .15 .40
❑ 20 Shutter-Bug .15 .40
❑ 21 Duel to the Death .15 .40
❑ 22 The Vulture .15 .40
❑ 23 The Tinkerer .15 .40
❑ 24 Doctor Octopus .15 .40
❑ 25 First Defeat .15 .40
❑ 26 Sandman .15 .40
❑ 27 Doctor Doom .15 .40
❑ 28 The Lizard .15 .40
❑ 29 Four Eyes .15 .40
❑ 30 Electro .15 .40
❑ 31 Betty Brant .15 .40
❑ 32 The Enforcers .15 .40
❑ 33 Mysterio .15 .40
❑ 34 Green Goblin .15 .40
❑ 35 Break-Up .15 .40
❑ 36 Big Shoes .15 .40
❑ 37 The Hulk .15 .40
❑ 38 Kraven .15 .40
❑ 39 The Ringmaster .15 .40
❑ 40 Daredevil .15 .40
❑ 41 Sinister Six .15 .40
❑ 42 The Scorpion .15 .40
❑ 43 Spider-Slayer .15 .40
❑ 44 Molten Man .15 .40
❑ 45 The Rhino .15 .40
❑ 46 The Test .15 .40
❑ 47 The X-Men .15 .40
❑ 48 The Shocker .15 .40
❑ 49 Captain Stacy .15 .40
❑ 50 The Prowler .15 .40
❑ 51 Drug Abuse .15 .40
❑ 52 Morbius .15 .40
❑ 53 Man-Wolf .15 .40
❑ 54 Gwen Stacy .15 .40
❑ 55 Gwen's Death .15 .40
❑ 56 Green Goblin's Death .15 .40
❑ 57 The Jackal .15 .40
❑ 58 The Punisher .15 .40
❑ 59 Vigilante .15 .40
❑ 60 Seeing Green .15 .40
❑ 61 Black Cat .15 .40
❑ 62 The Burglar .15 .40
❑ 63 Hydro-Man .15 .40
❑ 64 Hobgoblin .15 .40
❑ 65 Kingpin .15 .40
❑ 66 Secret Wars .15 .40
❑ 67 The Suit .15 .40
❑ 68 Bad Luck .15 .40
❑ 69 The Rose .15 .40
❑ 70 The Symbiote .15 .40
❑ 71 The Avengers .15 .40
❑ 72 Venom .15 .40
❑ 73 Unmasked .15 .40
❑ 74 Marriage .15 .40
❑ 75 Buried Alive .15 .40
❑ 76 Vermin .15 .40
❑ 77 Universal Powers .15 .40
❑ 78 Captured .15 .40
❑ 79 Issue #300 .15 .40
❑ 80 Silver Sable .15 .40
❑ 81 Arrogance .15 .40
❑ 82 Spider-Man #1 .15 .40
❑ 83 Heroes .15 .40
❑ 84 Spawn .15 .40
❑ 85 New Rose .15 .40
❑ 86 New Warriors .15 .40
❑ 87 Soul of the Hunter .15 .40
❑ 88 Parents .15 .40
❑ 89 Spider-Man 2099 .15 .40
❑ 90 Checklist .15 .40

1992 Spider-Man II 30th Anniversary Prisms

COMPLETE SET (6) 8.00 20.00
STATED ODDS 1:16
❑ P7 Assistant Needed 2.50 6.00
❑ P8 Stan the Man 2.50 6.00
❑ P9 Promoted 2.50 6.00
❑ P10 Creating 2.50 6.00
❑ P11 Insectman 2.50 6.00
❑ P12 Moving On 2.50 6.00

1992 Star Trek The Next Generation

COMPLETE SET (120) 5.00 12.00
HOLOGRAM ODDS 1:18
❑ 1 Where No One Has Gone Before .15 .40
❑ 2 Fifth Season Commemorative .15 .40
❑ 3 Gene Roddenberry .15 .40
❑ 4 Jean-Luc Picard .15 .40
❑ 5 William Riker .15 .40
❑ 6 Data .15 .40
❑ 7 Worf .15 .40
❑ 8 Geordi LaForge .15 .40
❑ 9 Deanna Troi .15 .40
❑ 10 Beverly Crusher .15 .40
❑ 11 Guinan .15 .40
❑ 12 Wesley Crusher .15 .40
❑ 13 Miles O'Brien .15 .40
❑ 14 Keiko O'Brien .15 .40
❑ 15 Reginald Barclay .15 .40
❑ 16 Ro Laren .15 .40
❑ 17 Lwaxana Troi .15 .40
❑ 18 Tasha Yar .15 .40
❑ 19 Sergey & Helena Rozhenko .15 .40
❑ 20 Alexander Rozhenko .15 .40
❑ 21 K'ehleyr .15 .40
❑ 22 Dr. Kate Pulaski .15 .40
❑ 23 Sarek .15 .40
❑ 24 The Traveler .15 .40
❑ 25 Lore .15 .40
❑ 26 The Q .15 .40
❑ 27 The Borg .15 .40
❑ 28 Sela .15 .40
❑ 29 Livingston .15 .40
❑ 30 Locutus .15 .40
❑ 31 Klingon Bird-of-Prey .15 .40
❑ 32 Klingon K'T'Inga Class Battle Cruiser .15 .40
❑ 33 Klingon Vor'Cha Class Attack Cruiser .15 .40
❑ 34 Romulan Warbird .15 .40
❑ 35 Romulan Scout Ship .15 .40
❑ 36 Ferengi Marauder .15 .40
❑ 37 Borg Ship .15 .40
❑ 38 Cardassian Galor Warship .15 .40
❑ 39 UFP Ambassador Class Starship .15 .40
❑ 40 UFP Excelsior Class Starship .15 .40
❑ 41 UFP Miranda Class Starship .15 .40
❑ 42 UFP Constellation Class Starship .15 .40
❑ 43 U.S.S. Enterprise .15 .40
❑ 44 Enterprise History .15 .40
❑ 45 Ship Schematic .15 .40
❑ 46 Ship Schematic .15 .40
❑ 47 Galaxy Class Development Project .15 .40
❑ 48 Commissioning Plaque .15 .40
❑ 49 Warp Engines .15 .40
❑ 50 Impulse Engines .15 .40
❑ 51 Main Bridge .15 .40
❑ 52 Battle Bridge .15 .40
❑ 53 Sickbay .15 .40
❑ 54 Main Engineering .15 .40
❑ 55 Tractor Beams .15 .40
❑ 56 Ship's Phasers .15 .40
❑ 57 Photon Torpedoes .15 .40
❑ 58 Shuttlepods .15 .40
❑ 59 Transporter .15 .40
❑ 60 Food Replicators .15 .40
❑ 61 Three-Dimensional Chess .15 .40
❑ 62 Ten-Forward .15 .40
❑ 63 Holodecks .15 .40
❑ 64 Corridors & Turbolifts .15 .40
❑ 65 Communicator .15 .40
❑ 66 Phaser Type I .15 .40
❑ 67 Phaser Type II .15 .40
❑ 68 Phaser Rifle .15 .40
❑ 69 Tricorder .15 .40
❑ 70 Medical Tricorder .15 .40
❑ 71 Hypospray .15 .40
❑ 72 Personal Access Display Device .15 .40
❑ 73 Isolinear Optical Chip .15 .40
❑ 74 U.S.S. Enterprise Signage .15 .40
❑ 75 Starfleet Uniforms .15 .40
❑ 76 Starfleet Rank Insignia .15 .40
❑ 77 Seal of the United Federation of Planets .15 .40
❑ 78 Starfleet Emblem .15 .40
❑ 79 Symbol of the Klingon Empire .15 .40
❑ 80 Symbol of the Romulan Star Empire .15 .40
❑ 81 Symbol of the Ferengi Alliance .15 .40
❑ 82 Symbol of the Borg .15 .40
❑ 83 Make-Up .15 .40
❑ 84 Wardrobe .15 .40
❑ 85 Art & Design .15 .40
❑ 86 Prosthetics Creature Shop .15 .40
❑ 87 Set Construction .15 .40
❑ 88 Special Effects: Lighting & Props .15 .40
❑ 89 Special Effects: Digital Composition .15 .40
❑ 90 Principal Photography .15 .40
❑ 91 Filming & Post-Production .15 .40
❑ 92 Inertial Damping System .15 .40
❑ 93 Saucer Module Separation Systems .15 .40
❑ 94 Emergency Landing of Saucer Module .15 .40
❑ 95 External & Internal Coord. System .15 .40
❑ 96 Flight Information Input .15 .40
❑ 97 Flight Control .15 .40
❑ 98 Operations Management .15 .40
❑ 99 Tactical Systems .15 .40
❑ 100 Main Bridge AFT Stations .15 .40
❑ 101 Ship's Computer .15 .40
❑ 102 Warp Propulsion System .15 .40
❑ 103 Dilithium Crystals .15 .40
❑ 104 Warp Drive Nacelles .15 .40
❑ 105 Bussard Ramscoop .15 .40
❑ 106 Navigational Deflector Systems .15 .40
❑ 107 Transporter Theory & Operation .15 .40
❑ 108 Holodeck Environment Simulation Theory .15 .40
❑ 109 Artificial Gravity Generation .15 .40
❑ 110 Shuttlecraft Classifications .15 .40
❑ 111 Captain's Yacht .15 .40
❑ 112 Data Trivia .15 .40
❑ 113 Q Trivia .15 .40
❑ 114 Captain Jean-Luc Picard Trivia .15 .40
❑ 115 U.S.S. Enterprise Trivia .15 .40
❑ 116 Klingon Trivia .15 .40
❑ 117 Alien Trivia .15 .40
❑ 118 Behind-the-Scenes Trivia .15 .40
❑ 119 Checklist .15 .40
❑ 120 Checklist .15 .40
❑ H1 Klingon Hologram 3.00 8.00
❑ H2 Klingon Hologram 3.00 8.00
❑ H3 Warbird Hologram 3.00 8.00
❑ H4 Ferengi Hologram 3.00 8.00
❑ H5 Galaxy Class Starship 3.00 8.00

1992 The Uncanny X-Men

Card	Low	High
COMPLETE SET (100)	8.00	20.00
❑ 1 Beast	.20	.50
❑ 2 Wolverine	.20	.50
❑ 3 Havok	.20	.50
❑ 4 Iceman	.20	.50
❑ 5 Phoenix	.20	.50
❑ 6 Nightcrawler	.20	.50
❑ 7 Cannonball	.20	.50
❑ 8 Wolfsbane	.20	.50
❑ 9 Siryn	.20	.50
❑ 10 Lockheed	.20	.50
❑ 11 Professor X	.20	.50
❑ 12 Psylocke	.20	.50
❑ 13 Domino	.20	.50
❑ 14 Storm	.20	.50
❑ 15 Meggan	.20	.50
❑ 16 Feral	.20	.50
❑ 17 Cyclops	.20	.50
❑ 18 Gambit	.20	.50
❑ 19 Cable	.20	.50
❑ 20 Archangel	.20	.50
❑ 21 Banshee	.20	.50
❑ 22 Shadowcat	.20	.50
❑ 23 Kylun	.20	.50
❑ 24 Jean Grey	.20	.50
❑ 25 Colossus	.20	.50
❑ 26 Warpath	.20	.50
❑ 27 Polaris	.20	.50
❑ 28 Boom Boom	.20	.50
❑ 29 Jubilee	.20	.50
❑ 30 Shatterstar	.20	.50
❑ 31 Strong Guy	.20	.50
❑ 32 Captain Britain	.20	.50
❑ 33 Forge	.20	.50
❑ 34 Multiple Man	.20	.50
❑ 35 Quicksilver	.20	.50
❑ 36 Rogue	.20	.50
❑ 37 Widget	.20	.50
❑ 38 Bishop	.20	.50
❑ 39 Maverick	.20	.50
❑ 40 Cerise	.20	.50
❑ 41 Magneto	.20	.50
❑ 42 Mr. Sinister	.20	.50
❑ 43 Deadpool	.20	.50
❑ 44 Proteus	.20	.50
❑ 45 Mojo II	.20	.50
❑ 46 Juggernaut	.20	.50
❑ 47 Sentinels	.20	.50
❑ 48 Gideon	.20	.50
❑ 49 Masque	.20	.50
❑ 50 Shiva	.20	.50
❑ 51 Apocalypse	.20	.50
❑ 52 Sabretooth	.20	.50
❑ 53 Mojo	.20	.50
❑ 54 Caliban	.20	.50
❑ 55 Gatecrasher	.20	.50
❑ 56 Brood	.20	.50
❑ 57 Blob	.20	.50
❑ 58 Stryfe	.20	.50
❑ 59 Warwolves	.20	.50
❑ 60 Omega Red	.20	.50
❑ 61 Black Tom	.20	.50
❑ 62 Mystique	.20	.50
❑ 63 Sauron	.20	.50
❑ 64 Saturnyne	.20	.50
❑ 65 Toad	.20	.50
❑ 66 Shadow King	.20	.50
❑ 67 White Queen	.20	.50
❑ 68 Mastermind	.20	.50
❑ 69 Deathbird	.20	.50
❑ 70 Lady Deathstrike	.20	.50
❑ 71 X-Men (Gold)	.20	.50
❑ 72 X-Men (Blue)	.20	.50
❑ 73 X-Factor	.20	.50
❑ 74 X-Force	.20	.50
❑ 75 Excalibur	.20	.50
❑ 76 Hellfire Club	.20	.50
❑ 77 Mutant Liberation Front	.20	.50
❑ 78 Brotherhood of Evil Mutants	.20	.50
❑ 79 Upstarts	.20	.50
❑ 80 Technet	.20	.50
❑ 81 Sunspot	.20	.50
❑ 82 Dark Phoenix	.20	.50
❑ 83 Longshot	.20	.50
❑ 84 Magik	.20	.50
❑ 85 Dazzler	.20	.50
❑ 86 Starjammers	.20	.50
❑ 87 Imperial Guard	.20	.50
❑ 88 Lilandra	.20	.50
❑ 89 W.H.O.	.20	.50
❑ 90 Roma	.20	.50
❑ 91 Nightcrawler	.20	.50
❑ 92 Archangel	.20	.50
❑ 93 Storm	.20	.50
❑ 94 Gambit	.20	.50
❑ 95 Wolverine	.20	.50
❑ 96 Shatterstar	.20	.50
❑ 97 Cyclops	.20	.50
❑ 98 Cable	.20	.50
❑ 99 Colossus	.20	.50
❑ 100 Cerebro	.20	.50

1992 The Uncanny X-Men Holograms

Card	Low	High
COMPLETE SET (5)	8.00	20.00
❑ XH1 Wolverine	4.00	10.00
❑ XH2 Cable	3.00	8.00
❑ XH3 Gambit	3.00	8.00
❑ XH4 Magneto	3.00	8.00
❑ XH5 X-Men	3.00	8.00

1992 Unity

Card	Low	High
COMPLETE SET (90)	4.00	10.00
❑ 1 Unity #0	.12	.30
❑ 2 From the Black Hole	.12	.30
❑ 3 Discovering the Body	.12	.30
❑ 4 The Lost Land	.12	.30
❑ 5 Solar Lends a Hand	.12	.30
❑ 6 The Heroes Gather	.12	.30
❑ 7 The Mothergod	.12	.30
❑ 8 Eternal Warrior #1	.12	.30
❑ 9 Gilad Enters the Battle	.12	.30
❑ 10 Archer and Armstrong #1	.12	.30
❑ 11 The Heroes Scatter	.12	.30
❑ 12 Archer's Future	.12	.30
❑ 13 Armstrong Takes a Hit	.12	.30
❑ 14 The Speakeasy	.12	.30
❑ 15 Magnusw Robot Fighter #15	.12	.30
❑ 16 Mothergod's Tower	.12	.30
❑ 17 X-O Manowar #7	.12	.30
❑ 18 Pterodactyl Peril	.12	.30
❑ 19 X-O Frees the Slaves	.12	.30
❑ 20 Shadowman #4	.12	.30
❑ 21 Shadowman's Arrival	.12	.30
❑ 22 Erica is Forewarned	.12	.30
❑ 23 Solar Attacks	.12	.30
❑ 24 Shadowman Burns	.12	.30
❑ 25 Solar is Contained	.12	.30
❑ 26 Rai #6	.12	.30
❑ 27 Japan Falls	.12	.30
❑ 28 Harbinger #8	.12	.30
❑ 29 The War Goes Badly	.12	.30
❑ 30 Sting is Enraged	.12	.30
❑ 31 Erica Reacts	.12	.30
❑ 32 Solar, Man of the Atom #12	.12	.30
❑ 33 Eternal Warrior #2	.12	.30
❑ 34 The Two Gilads	.12	.30
❑ 35 Too Late	.12	.30
❑ 36 Archer and Armstrong #2	.12	.30
❑ 37 For Every Mother's Child	.12	.30
❑ 38 Mothergod Awakes	.12	.30
❑ 39 Now Comes Turok	.12	.30
❑ 40 A Hot Shot	.12	.30
❑ 41 A Change of Heart	.12	.30
❑ 42 Magnus Robot Fighter #16	.12	.30
❑ 43 The Baby is Born	.12	.30
❑ 44 X-O Manowar #8	.12	.30
❑ 45 Close to Finish	.12	.30
❑ 46 The Peace Treaty	.12	.30
❑ 47 Erica's Treachery	.12	.30
❑ 48 Jaws of Death	.12	.30
❑ 49 The Good Skin Returns	.12	.30
❑ 50 X-O Fights Back	.12	.30
❑ 51 Shadowman #5	.12	.30
❑ 52 Regeneration	.12	.30
❑ 53 Thwart the Mission	.12	.30
❑ 54 The Truth Revealed	.12	.30
❑ 55 Serve the Demon ... Pay the Price	.12	.30
❑ 56 Rai #7	.12	.30
❑ 57 Last of His Kind	.12	.30
❑ 58 The Plan is Finalized	.12	.30
❑ 59 Entering the Complex	.12	.30
❑ 60 The Last Stand	.12	.30
❑ 61 Mothergod Attacks	.12	.30
❑ 62 First Fatality	.12	.30
❑ 63 A Hero Falls	.12	.30
❑ 64 Albert's Revenge	.12	.30
❑ 65 Harbinger #9	.12	.30
❑ 66 The Containment Center	.12	.30
❑ 67 The Wormhole	.12	.30
❑ 68 Solar's Remains	.12	.30
❑ 69 Escape	.12	.30
❑ 70 The Beginning of the End	.12	.30
❑ 71 The Hand of Destiny	.12	.30
❑ 72 Solar, Man of the Atom #13	.12	.30
❑ 73 Albert Takes His Shot	.12	.30
❑ 74 Solar Returns	.12	.30
❑ 75 The Final Battle	.12	.30
❑ 76 Triumphant	.12	.30
❑ 77 Unity #1	.12	.30
❑ 78 Judgment	.12	.30
❑ 79 Trapped For Eternity	.12	.30
❑ 80 Self-Destruct	.12	.80
❑ 81 Looking For Elya	.12	.30
❑ 82 Magnus Fights On	.12	.30
❑ 83 Just Desserts	.12	.30
❑ 84 X-O the Conqueror	.12	.30
❑ 85 From Little Acorn	.12	.30
❑ 86 Suddenly... a Black Hole	.12	.30
❑ 87 Solar Saves the Day	.12	.30
❑ 88 The Lost Land Destroyed	.12	.30
❑ 89 3975 A.D.	.12	.30
❑ 90 Checklist	.12	.30

1992 Unity Chromium

Card	Low	High
COMPLETE SET (6)	3.00	8.00
STATED ODDS 1:6		
❑ 1 Bloodshot	1.00	2.50
❑ 2 Hotshot	1.00	2.50
❑ 3 Rai	1.00	2.50
❑ 4 Rai and the Future Force	1.00	2.50
❑ 5 Screen	1.00	2.50
❑ 6 Turok	1.00	2.50

1992 Wolverine From Then Til Now II

Card	Low	High
COMPLETE SET (90)	5.00	12.00
❑ 1 Wolverine	.15	.40
❑ 2 Change	.15	.40
❑ 3 Mutation	.15	.40
❑ 4 Fox-Like	.15	.40
❑ 5 Aging	.15	.40
❑ 6 S.H.I.E.L.D.	.15	.40
❑ 7 Logan	.15	.40
❑ 8 Project X	.15	.40
❑ 9 Professor	.15	.40
❑ 10 Dr. A. B. Cornelius	.15	.40
❑ 11 Wild Beast	.15	.40
❑ 12 Helmet	.15	.40
❑ 13 I Like Him	.15	.40
❑ 14 Shiva	.15	.40
❑ 15 Triggers	.15	.40
❑ 16 Mutant Powers	.15	.40
❑ 17 Ferocious	.15	.40
❑ 18 Adamantium	.15	.40
❑ 19 Claws	.15	.40
❑ 20 Hunting	.15	.40
❑ 21 Berserk	.15	.40
❑ 22 Discipline	.15	.40
❑ 23 Wild Beast	.15	.40
❑ 24 Animalistic	.15	.40
❑ 25 Department H	.15	.40
❑ 26 First Mission	.15	.40
❑ 27 First Defeat	.15	.40
❑ 28 Weapon Alpha	.15	.40
❑ 29 In Search Of	.15	.40
❑ 30 New X-Men	.15	.40
❑ 31 Krakoa	.15	.40
❑ 32 Teammates	.15	.40
❑ 33 Just Kidding	.15	.40
❑ 34 Resentment	.15	.40
❑ 35 Magneto	.15	.40
❑ 36 Costume	.15	.40
❑ 37 Phoenix	.15	.40
❑ 38 Mariko	.15	.40
❑ 39 Alpha Flight	.15	.40
❑ 40 Hellfire Club	.15	.40
❑ 41 Slice and Dice	.15	.40
❑ 42 Old Ties	.15	.40
❑ 43 Disgrace	.15	.40
❑ 44 New Threads	.15	.40
❑ 45 The Brood	.15	.40
❑ 46 Shadowcat	.15	.40
❑ 47 Fastball Special	.15	.40
❑ 48 Vindicator	.15	.40
❑ 49 Mutant Massacre	.15	.40
❑ 50 Grey Hulk	.15	.40
❑ 51 Resurrection	.15	.40
❑ 52 Patch	.15	.40
❑ 53 Genosha	.15	.40
❑ 54 Donald Pierce	.15	.40
❑ 55 Reavers	.15	.40
❑ 56 Jubilation Lee	.15	.40
❑ 57 1941	.15	.40
❑ 58 The X-Men	.15	.40
❑ 59 Psylocke	.15	.40
❑ 60 Gambit	.15	.40
❑ 61 Popularity	.15	.40
❑ 62 Cable	.15	.40
❑ 63 Scorpio	.15	.40
❑ 64 Appeal	.15	.40
❑ 65 Lady Deathstrike	.15	.40
❑ 66 Cylla	.15	.40
❑ 67 Punisher	.15	.40
❑ 68 Buried Alive	.15	.40
❑ 69 Deadly Imitator	.15	.40
❑ 70 Elsie Dee	.15	.40
❑ 71 Matsuo	.15	.40
❑ 72 Flashback	.15	.40
❑ 73 Maverick	.15	.40
❑ 74 Resurrected	.15	.40
❑ 75 Omega Red	.15	.40
❑ 76 Carbonadium	.15	.40
❑ 77 Honor	.15	.40
❑ 78 Sabretooth	.15	.40
❑ 79 Silver Fox	.15	.40
❑ 80 Reiko	.15	.40
❑ 81 Heavy Metal	.15	.40
❑ 82 Escape	.15	.40
❑ 83 Barbaric	.15	.40
❑ 84 Rip and Tear	.15	.40
❑ 85 Ghost Rider	.15	.40
❑ 86 Cyber	.15	.40
❑ 87 Venom	.15	.40
❑ 88 The End	.15	.40
❑ 89 The Future	.15	.40
❑ 90 Checklist	.15	.40

1992 Wolverine From Then Til Now II Prisms

Card	Low	High
COMPLETE SET (6)	8.00	20.00
STATED ODDS 1:16		
❑ P1 Archetypal	2.00	5.00
❑ P2 Away	2.00	5.00
❑ P3 Attitude	2.00	5.00
❑ P4 Healing	2.00	5.00
❑ P5 Languages	2.00	5.00
❑ P6 Memories	2.00	5.00

1992 Youngblood

Card	Low	High
COMPLETE SET (90)	4.00	10.00
❑ 1 Youngblood	.12	.30
❑ 2 Evolution	.12	.30
❑ 3 1985	.12	.30
❑ 4 The Beginning	.12	.30
❑ 5 Teflon Team	.12	.30
❑ 6 Media	.12	.30
❑ 7 Superheroes	.12	.30
❑ 8 Employees	.12	.30
❑ 9 Nine to Five	.12	.30
❑ 10 Terms	.12	.30
❑ 11 Flip Format	.12	.30
❑ 12 Home and Away	.12	.30
❑ 13 Duel Teams	.12	.30
❑ 14 Shaft	.12	.30
❑ 15 Leader	.12	.30
❑ 16 Diversion	.12	.30
❑ 17 Shelly	.12	.30
❑ 18 Assassin	.12	.30
❑ 19 Ballpoint	.12	.30
❑ 20 Bullseye	.12	.30
❑ 21 Alert	.12	.30
❑ 22 Bedrock	.12	.30
❑ 23 Warm-hearted	.12	.30
❑ 24 Lunch	.12	.30
❑ 25 Duty Calls	.12	.30
❑ 26 Diehard	.12	.30
❑ 27 Top Secret	.12	.30
❑ 28 Underground	.12	.30
❑ 29 Unbeatable	.12	.30
❑ 30 Chapel	.12	.30
❑ 31 Killing Time	.12	.30
❑ 32 Bearing Arms	.12	.30
❑ 33 Vogue	.12	.30
❑ 34 Unobedient	.12	.30
❑ 35 Photon	.12	.30
❑ 36 Cover-Up	.12	.30
❑ 37 Unsure	.12	.30
❑ 38 Switch Hitters	.12	.30
❑ 39 S.O.S.	.12	.30
❑ 40 Strongarm	.12	.30
❑ 41 Gage	.12	.30
❑ 42 Escape	.12	.30
❑ 43 Vendetta	.12	.30
❑ 44 Freedom	.12	.30
❑ 45 Payback	.12	.30
❑ 46 Overseas	.12	.30
❑ 47 Task Force	.12	.30
❑ 48 Air Attack	.12	.30
❑ 49 Dropping In	.12	.30
❑ 50 Sentinel	.12	.30
❑ 51 Tailored	.12	.30
❑ 52 Power	.12	.30
❑ 53 Above	.12	.30
❑ 54 Responsibilities	.12	.30
❑ 55 Warrior	.12	.30
❑ 56 Agreement	.12	.30
❑ 57 War Play	.12	.30
❑ 58 The Kill	.12	.30
❑ 59 Cat People	.12	.30
❑ 60 Taboo Love	.12	.30
❑ 61 Half-Breed	.12	.30
❑ 62 Cougar	.12	.30
❑ 63 Target Ahead	.12	.30
❑ 64 Riptide	.12	.30
❑ 65 Unegar	.12	.30
❑ 66 Oversized	.12	.30
❑ 67 Brahma	.12	.30
❑ 68 Powerhouse	.12	.30
❑ 69 Shocked	.12	.30
❑ 70 Unaffected	.12	.30
❑ 71 Psi-Fire	.12	.30
❑ 72 On Parole	.12	.30
❑ 73 Far Away	.12	.30
❑ 74 Long Distance	.12	.30
❑ 75 Little By Little	.12	.30
❑ 76 Within	.12	.30
❑ 77 For the Fun of It	.12	.30
❑ 78 Too Late	.12	.30
❑ 79 Let's Go	.12	.30
❑ 80 Prophet	.12	.30
❑ 81 Hand-to-Hand	.12	.30
❑ 82 Creating	.12	.30
❑ 83 The Image	.12	.30
❑ 84 Independent	.12	.30
❑ 85 Image Comics	.12	.30
❑ 86 Years Ago	.12	.30
❑ 87 Berserkers	.12	.30
❑ 88 Cross	.12	.30
❑ 89 Shadowhawk	.12	.30
❑ NNO Checklist	.12	.30

1992 Youngblood Prisms

Card	Low	High
COMPLETE SET (6)	3.00	8.00
STATED ODDS 1:16		
❑ P1 Sentinel	1.00	2.50
❑ P2 Photon and Combat	1.00	2.50
❑ P3 Diehard	1.00	2.50
❑ P4 Shaft	1.00	2.50
❑ P5 Cougar	1.00	2.50
❑ P6 New Titans	1.00	2.50

1993 DC Bloodlines

Card	Low	High
COMPLETE SET (81)	5.00	12.00
❑ 1 Deadly Genesis	.12	.30
❑ 2 Lobo Out for Blood	.12	.30
❑ 3 Lobo and Layla - Bad to the Bone	.12	.30
❑ 4 The Demonseed's Arrival	.12	.30
❑ 5 The Man of Steel	.12	.30
❑ 6 Battle on the Edge	.12	.30
❑ 7 Glonth's Abattoir	.12	.30
❑ 8 Flash and Argus - Race to Action	.12	.30
❑ 9 Linked in Blood	.12	.30
❑ 10 Blood Magic	.12	.30
❑ 11 Assault on the Innocent	.12	.30
❑ 12 Titans Clash	.12	.30
❑ 13 Gemir's Primal Hunger	.12	.30
❑ 14 The Man of Tomorrow	.12	.30
❑ 15 To Save Her Soul	.12	.30
❑ 16 Lissik's Blood Passion	.12	.30
❑ 17 Green Lantern and Nightblade	.12	.30
❑ 18 Nightblade's Retribution	.12	.30
❑ 19 Lionheart - Battleground Zero	.12	.30
❑ 20 Cry for Blood	.12	.30
❑ 21 Knights and Warriors	.12	.30
❑ 22 Loose Cannon Rages	.12	.30
❑ 23 The Last Son of Krypton	.12	.30
❑ 24 Against Cannon Fire	.12	.30
❑ 25 Storm of Blood and Anger	.12	.30
❑ 26 Valor in a Jamm	.12	.30
❑ 27 Jamm Jams	.12	.30
❑ 28 Lust's Deadly Arrow	.12	.30
❑ 29 The Hook and Green Arrow	.12	.30
❑ 30 Lissik Is Hooked	.12	.30
❑ 31 The Ray Unleashed	.12	.30
❑ 32 Plague of the Terrorsmith	.12	.30
❑ 33 Amazon Fury	.12	.30
❑ 34 In Blood's Rapture	.12	.30
❑ 35 Superboy	.12	.30
❑ 36 Sparx Fly	.12	.30
❑ 37 The Sky Rains Blood	.12	.30
❑ 38 Mongrel's Frenzy	.12	.30
❑ 39 Hawkman versus Mongrel	.12	.30
❑ 40 Lock and Load	.12	.30
❑ 41 The Heat of Gunfire	.12	.30
❑ 42 Deathstroke and Gunfire	.12	.30
❑ 43 Devils Face Off	.12	.30
❑ 44 The Rage King	.12	.30
❑ 45 Prism's Light	.12	.30
❑ 46 Slay the Beast	.12	.30
❑ 47 Hitman versus The Demon	.12	.30
❑ 48 Demon's Ire	.12	.30
❑ 49 Experience Chimera	.12	.30
❑ 50 Warriors United	.12	.30
❑ 51 A New Horror Is Born	.12	.30
❑ 52 Pax Brings the War Home	.12	.30
❑ 53 Parasites from the Stars	.12	.30
❑ 54 Death World	.12	.30
❑ 55 Layla	.12	.30
❑ 56 Edge	.12	.30
❑ 57 Argus	.12	.30
❑ 58 Anima	.12	.30
❑ 59 Myriad	.12	.30
❑ 60 Nightblade	.12	.30
❑ 61 Lionheart	.12	.30
❑ 62 Loose Cannon	.12	.30
❑ 63 Jamm	.12	.30
❑ 64 The Hook	.12	.30
❑ 65 Terrorsmith	.12	.30
❑ 66 Sparx	.12	.30
❑ 67 Mongrel	.12	.30
❑ 68 Gunfire	.12	.30
❑ 69 Prism	.12	.30
❑ 70 Hitman	.12	.30
❑ 71 Chimera	.12	.30
❑ 72 Pax	.12	.30
❑ 73 Pritor	.12	.30
❑ 74 Angon	.12	.30
❑ 75 Lissik	.12	.30
❑ 76 Glonth	.12	.30
❑ 77 Gemir	.12	.30
❑ 78 Venev	.12	.30
❑ 79 Slodd	.12	.30
❑ 80 Checklist A	.12	.30
❑ 81 Checklist B	.12	.30

1993 DC Bloodlines Embossed Foil

Card	Low	High
COMPLETE SET (5)	12.00	30.00
COMPLETE SET w/o SP (4)	8.00	20.00
STATED ODDS 1:18		
SP STATED ODDS 1:72		
❑ S1 The Man of Steel	3.00	8.00
❑ S2 The Man of Tomorrow	3.00	8.00
❑ S3 The Last Son of Krypton	3.00	8.00
❑ S4 Superboy	3.00	8.00
❑ S5 Superman Redemption SP	8.00	20.00

1993 DC Cosmic Teams

Card	Low	High
COMPLETE SET (150)	6.00	15.00
❑ 1 Justice League America	.15	.40
❑ 2 Justice League America	.15	.40
❑ 3 Justice League America	.15	.40
❑ 4 Justice League International	.15	.40
❑ 5 Justice League International	.15	.40
❑ 6 Justice League International	.15	.40
❑ 7 Justice Society of America	.15	.40
❑ 8 Justice Society of America	.15	.40
❑ 9 Justice Society of America	.15	.40
❑ 10 New Titans	.15	.40
❑ 11 New Titans	.15	.40
❑ 12 New Titans	.15	.40
❑ 13 Team Titans	.15	.40
❑ 14 Team Titans	.15	.40
❑ 15 Team Titans	.15	.40
❑ 16 L.E.G.I.O.N.	.15	.40
❑ 17 L.E.G.I.O.N.	.15	.40
❑ 18 L.E.G.I.O.N.	.15	.40
❑ 19 Legionnaires	.15	.40
❑ 20 Legionnaires	.15	.40
❑ 21 Legionnaires	.15	.40
❑ 22 Green Lantern Corps	.15	.40
❑ 23 Green Lantern Corps	.15	.40
❑ 24 Green Lantern Corps	.15	.40
❑ 25 Worlds of Magic	.15	.40
❑ 26 Worlds of Magic	.15	.40
❑ 27 Worlds of Magic	.15	.40
❑ 28 Foes of the Justice League	.15	.40
❑ 29 Foes of the Justice League	.15	.40
❑ 30 Foes of the Justice League	.15	.40
❑ 31 Society of Sin	.15	.40
❑ 32 Society of Sin	.15	.40
❑ 33 Society of Sin	.15	.40
❑ 34 Foes of Superman	.15	.40
❑ 35 Foes of Superman	.15	.40
❑ 36 Foes of Superman	.15	.40
❑ 37 Justice League America	.15	.40
❑ 38 Justice League America	.15	.40
❑ 39 Justice League America	.15	.40
❑ 40 Justice League America	.15	.40
❑ 41 Justice League America	.15	.40
❑ 42 Justice League America	.15	.40
❑ 43 Justice League America	.15	.40
❑ 44 Justice League International	.15	.40
❑ 45 Justice League International	.15	.40
❑ 46 Justice League International	.15	.40
❑ 47 Justice League International	.15	.40
❑ 48 Justice League International	.15	.40
❑ 49 Justice League International	.15	.40
❑ 50 Justice League International	.15	.40
❑ 51 Justice Society of America	.15	.40
❑ 52 Justice Society of America	.15	.40
❑ 53 Justice Society of America	.15	.40
❑ 54 Justice Society of America	.15	.40
❑ 55 Justice Society of America	.15	.40
❑ 56 Justice Society of America	.15	.40
❑ 57 Justice Society of America	.15	.40
❑ 58 Justice Society of America	.15	.40
❑ 59 New Titans	.15	.40
❑ 60 New Titans	.15	.40
❑ 61 New Titans	.15	.40
❑ 62 New Titans	.15	.40
❑ 63 New Titans	.15	.40
❑ 64 New Titans	.15	.40
❑ 65 Team Titans	.15	.40
❑ 66 Team Titans	.15	.40
❑ 67 Team Titans	.15	.40
❑ 68 Team Titans	.15	.40
❑ 69 Team Titans	.15	.40
❑ 70 Team Titans	.15	.40
❑ 71 Team Titans	.15	.40
❑ 72 L.E.G.I.O.N.	.15	.40
❑ 73 L.E.G.I.O.N.	.15	.40
❑ 74 L.E.G.I.O.N.	.15	.40
❑ 75 L.E.G.I.O.N.	.15	.40
❑ 76 L.E.G.I.O.N.	.15	.40
❑ 77 L.E.G.I.O.N.	.15	.40
❑ 78 L.E.G.I.O.N.	.15	.40
❑ 79 L.E.G.I.O.N.	.15	.40
❑ 80 L.E.G.I.O.N.	.15	.40
❑ 81 L.E.G.I.O.N.	.15	.40
❑ 82 Legionnaires	.15	.40
❑ 83 Legionnaires	.15	.40
❑ 84 Legionnaires	.15	.40
❑ 85 Legionnaires	.15	.40
❑ 86 Legionnaires	.15	.40
❑ 87 Legionnaires	.15	.40
❑ 88 Legionnaires	.15	.40
❑ 89 Legionnaires	.15	.40
❑ 90 Legionnaires	.15	.40
❑ 91 Legionnaires	.15	.40
❑ 92 Legionnaires	.15	.40
❑ 93 Legionnaires	.15	.40
❑ 94 Legionnaires	.15	.40
❑ 95 Legionnaires	.15	.40
❑ 96 Legionnaires	.15	.40
❑ 97 Legionnaires	.15	.40
❑ 98 Legionnaires	.15	.40
❑ 99 Legionnaires	.15	.40
❑ 100 Legionnaires	.15	.40
❑ 101 Legionnaires	.15	.40
❑ 102 Legionnaires	.15	.40
❑ 103 Green Lantern Corps	.15	.40
❑ 104 Green Lantern Corps	.15	.40
❑ 105 Green Lantern Corps	.15	.40
❑ 106 Green Lantern Corps	.15	.40
❑ 107 Green Lantern Corps	.15	.40
❑ 108 Green Lantern Corps	.15	.40
❑ 109 Green Lantern Corps	.15	.40
❑ 110 Green Lantern Corps	.15	.40
❑ 111 Green Lantern Corps	.15	.40
❑ 112 Worlds of Magic	.15	.40
❑ 113 Worlds of Magic	.15	.40
❑ 114 Worlds of Magic	.15	.40
❑ 115 Worlds of Magic	.15	.40
❑ 116 Worlds of Magic	.15	.40
❑ 117 Worlds of Magic	.15	.40
❑ 118 Worlds of Magic	.15	.40
❑ 119 Worlds of Magic	.15	.40
❑ 120 Worlds of Magic	.15	.40
❑ 121 Foes of the Justice League	.15	.40
❑ 122 Foes of the Justice League	.15	.40
❑ 123 Foes of the Justice League	.15	.40
❑ 124 Foes of the Justice League	.15	.40
❑ 125 Foes of the Justice League	.15	.40
❑ 126 Society of Sin	.15	.40
❑ 127 Society of Sin	.15	.40
❑ 128 Society of Sin	.15	.40
❑ 129 Society of Sin	.15	.40
❑ 130 Society of Sin	.15	.40
❑ 131 Foes of Superman	.15	.40
❑ 132 Foes of Superman	.15	.40
❑ 133 Foes of Superman	.15	.40
❑ 134 Foes of Superman	.15	.40
❑ 135 Foes of Superman	.15	.40
❑ 136 Foes of Superman	.15	.40
❑ 137 Foes of Superman	.15	.40
❑ 138 Foes of Superman	.15	.40
❑ 139 Foes of Superman	.15	.40

Card	Low	High
140 Foes of Superman	.15	.40
141 The New Breed	.15	.40
142 The New Breed	.15	.40
143 The New Breed	.15	.40
144 The New Breed	.15	.40
145 The New Breed	.15	.40
146 The New Breed	.15	.40
147 The New Breed	.15	.40
148 The New Breed	.15	.40
149 Checklist A	.15	.40
150 Checklist B	.15	.40

1993 DC Cosmic Teams Holograms

Card	Low	High
COMPLETE SET (6)	6.00	15.00
DCH11 Captain Marvel	2.00	5.00
DCH12 Hawkman	2.00	5.00
DCH13 Lobo	2.00	5.00
DCH14 The Spectre	2.00	5.00
DCH15 Superman	2.00	5.00
DCH16 Swamp Thing	2.00	5.00

1993 Marvel Masterpieces

Card	Low	High
COMPLETE SET (90)	12.00	30.00
1 Hulk	.30	.75
2 Human Torch	.30	.75
3 Thor	.30	.75
4 Iron Man	.30	.75
5 Spider-Man	.30	.75
6 Wolverine	.30	.75
7 Cyclops	.30	.75
8 Doctor Strange	.30	.75
9 Namor	.30	.75
10 Storm	.30	.75
11 Silver Surfer	.30	.75
12 Vision	.30	.75
13 Ghost Rider	.30	.75
14 Thing	.30	.75
15 Captain America	.30	.75
16 Archangel	.30	.75
17 Beast	.30	.75
18 Cable	.30	.75
19 Carnage	.30	.75
20 Hulk 2099	.30	.75
21 Doctor Doom	.30	.75
22 Daredevil	.30	.75
23 Iron Fist	.30	.75
24 Psylocke	.30	.75
25 Morbius	.30	.75
26 Punisher	.30	.75
27 Rogue	.30	.75
28 Sabretooth	.30	.75
29 Forge	.30	.75
30 She-Hulk	.30	.75
31 Gambit	.30	.75
32 U.S.Agent	.30	.75
33 Spider-Woman	.30	.75
34 Stryfe	.30	.75
35 Thanos	.30	.75
36 Blade	.30	.75
37 Adam Warlock	.30	.75
38 Colossus	.30	.75
39 Magneto	.30	.75
40 Vulture	.30	.75
41 Spider-Man 2099	.30	.75
42 Punisher 2099	.30	.75
43 Doom 2099	.30	.75
44 Ravage 2099	.30	.75
45 Venom	.30	.75
46 Domino	.30	.75
47 Annihilus	.30	.75
48 Rhino	.30	.75
49 Puma	.30	.75
50 Cannonball	.30	.75
51 Polaris	.30	.75
52 Longshot	.30	.75
53 Cyber	.30	.75
54 Omega Red	.30	.75
55 Deadpool	.30	.75
56 Kingpin	.30	.75
57 Bishop	.30	.75
58 Absorbing Man	.30	.75
59 Darkhawk	.30	.75
60 Mystique	.30	.75
61 Abomination	.30	.75
62 Wasp	.30	.75
63 Scorpion	.30	.75
64 Captain Britain	.30	.75
65 Black Knight	.30	.75
66 Sasquatch	.30	.75
67 Black Widow	.30	.75
68 Typhoid Mary	.30	.75
69 War Machine	.30	.75
70 Hawkeye	.30	.75
71 Deathlok	.30	.75
72 Nightcrawler	.30	.75
73 Thunderstrike	.30	.75
74 Vengeance	.30	.75
75 Jean Grey	.30	.75
76 Shatterstar	.30	.75
77 Beta Ray Bill	.30	.75
78 Night Thrasher	.30	.75
79 Red Skull	.30	.75
80 Lilith	.30	.75
81 Falcon	.30	.75
82 Hercules	.30	.75
83 Nova	.30	.75
84 Havok	.30	.75
85 Phoenix	.30	.75
86 Crystal	.30	.75
87 Drax	.30	.75
88 Terrax	.30	.75
89 Vulture 2099	.30	.75
90 Checklist	.30	.75

1993 Marvel Masterpieces Spectra Etch

Card	Low	High
COMPLETE SET (8)	8.00	20.00
S1 Meanstreak	1.25	3.00
S2 Cerebra	1.25	3.00
S3 Krystalin	1.25	3.00
S4 Metalhead	1.25	3.00
S5 Serpentina	1.25	3.00
S6 Bloodhawk	1.25	3.00
S7 Skullfire	1.25	3.00
S8 Xi'an	1.25	3.00

1993 Marvel Universe

Card	Low	High
COMPLETE SET (180)	10.00	25.00
1 Hulk	.10	.30
2 Moon Knight	.10	.30
3 Siege	.10	.30
4 Deadzone	.10	.30
5 Wild Pack	.10	.30
6 Silver Sable	.10	.30
7 Doc Samson	.10	.30
8 Deathlok	.10	.30
9 Moses Magnum	.10	.30
10 Warlock	.10	.30
11 Silver Surfer	.10	.30
12 Quasar	.10	.30
13 Starhawk	.10	.30
14 Galactus	.10	.30
15 Goddess	.10	.30
16 Thanos	.10	.30
17 Morg	.10	.30
18 Drax	.10	.30
19 Nova	.10	.30
20 Firestar	.10	.30
21 Cardinal	.10	.30
22 Namorita	.10	.30
23 Speedball	.10	.30
24 Turbo	.10	.30
25 Rage	.10	.30
26 Night Thrasher	.10	.30
27 Darkhawk	.10	.30
28 Deadpool	.10	.30
29 Cannonball	.10	.30
30 Slayback	.10	.30
31 Sabretooth	.10	.30
32 Shatterstar	.10	.30
33 Apocalypse	.10	.30
34 Mr. Sinister	.10	.30
35 Cable	.10	.30
36 Stryfe	.10	.30
37 Guardian	.10	.30
38 Micromax	.10	.30
39 Wildheart	.10	.30
40 Captain Britain	.10	.30
41 Phoenix	.10	.30
42 Nightcrawler	.10	.30
43 Havok	.10	.30
44 Psylocke	.10	.30
45 Strong Guy	.10	.30
46 Dr. Strange	.10	.30
47 Dormammu	.10	.30
48 Beta Ray Bill	.10	.30
49 Loki	.10	.30
50 Cobweb	.10	.30
51 Blackheart	.10	.30
52 Sleepwalker	.10	.30
53 Thor	.10	.30
54 Hellstorm	.10	.30
55 Venom	.10	.30
56 Demogoblin	.10	.30
57 Carnage	.10	.30
58 Hobgoblin	.10	.30
59 Spider-Man	.10	.30
60 Cardiac	.10	.30
61 Rhino	.10	.30
62 Shock	.10	.30
63 Daredevil	.10	.30
64 Scarlet Witch	.10	.30
65 Spider-Woman	.10	.30
66 Splice	.10	.30
67 Iron Man	.10	.30
68 Wonder Man	.10	.30
69 War Machine	.10	.30
70 Namor	.10	.30
71 Tiger Shark	.10	.30
72 U.S. Agent	.10	.30
73 Mr. Fantastic	.10	.30
74 Invisible Woman	.10	.30
75 Human Torch	.10	.30
76 Lyja	.10	.30
77 Occulus	.10	.30
78 Molecule Man	.10	.30
79 Dr. Doom	.10	.30
80 Thing	.10	.30
81 Klaw	.10	.30
82 She-Hulk	.10	.30
83 Punisher	.10	.30
84 Falcon	.10	.30
85 Hardcore	.10	.30
86 Nomad	.10	.30
87 Terror, Inc.	.10	.30
88 Iron Fist	.10	.30
89 Cage	.10	.30
90 Scarecrow	.10	.30
91 Black Knight	.10	.30
92 Crystal	.10	.30
93 Sersi	.10	.30
94 Thunderstrike	.10	.30
95 Captain America	.10	.30
96 Hercules	.10	.30
97 Bloodaxe	.10	.30
98 Red Skull	.10	.30
99 Proctor	.10	.30
100 Deathwatch	.10	.30
101 Lilith	.10	.30
102 Heart Attack	.10	.30
103 Blaze	.10	.30
104 Basilisk	.10	.30
105 Ghost Rider	.10	.30
106 Darkhold Redeemers	.10	.30
107 Morbius	.10	.30
108 Nightstalkers	.10	.30
109 Storm	.10	.30
110 Archangel	.10	.30
111 Beast	.10	.30
112 Rogue	.10	.30
113 Magneto	.10	.30
114 Gambit	.10	.30
115 Cyclops	.10	.30
116 Wolverine	.10	.30
117 Bishop	.10	.30
118 Ovoids	.10	.30
119 Brood	.10	.30
120 Titans	.10	.30
121 Badoon	.10	.30
122 Asgardians	.10	.30
123 Skrulls	.10	.30
124 Shi'ar	.10	.30
125 Kree	.10	.30
126 Rigellians	.10	.30
127 Black Axe	.10	.30
128 Techno Wizards	.10	.30
129 Motormouth	.10	.30
130 Bloodseed	.10	.30
131 Dark Angel	.10	.30
132 Wild Thing	.10	.30
133 Die-Cut	.10	.30
134 Death's Head II	.10	.30
135 Death Metal	.10	.30
136 The Origin of Wolverine	.10	.30
137 The Origin of Cable	.10	.30
138 The Face of Darkhawk	.10	.30
139 The Origin of Ghost Rider	.10	.30
140 The Fate of the X-Men	.10	.30
141 The Face of Doctor Doom	.10	.30
142 The Sixth Member of the Infinity Watch	.10	.30
143 The Secret of Spider-Man's Parents	.10	.30
144 The Origin of Nightcrawler	.10	.30
145 Spider-Man vs Carnage	.10	.30
146 Cable vs Stryfe	.10	.30
147 Ghost Rider vs Lilith	.10	.30
148 Silver Surfer vs Morg	.10	.30
149 Wolverine vs Sabretooth	.10	.30
150 Thor vs Loki	.10	.30
151 War Machine	.10	.30
152 Spider-Man vs Venom	.10	.30
153 Punisher vs Thorn	.10	.30
154 X-Cutioner's Song	.10	.30
155 Spider-Man vs Sinister Six	.10	.30
156 Infinity War	.10	.30
157 Spirits of Venom	.10	.30
158 Hulk vs Leader	.10	.30
159 Ghost Rider vs Blackout	.10	.30
160 Dr. Strange vs Dormammu	.10	.30
161 Wolverine vs Cyber	.10	.30
162 Captain America vs Crossbones	.10	.30
163 Punisher vs Jigsaw	.10	.30
164 Wolverine vs Venom	.10	.30
165 Spider-Man vs Juggernaut	.10	.30
166 Darkhawk vs Evilhawk	.10	.30
167 X-Force vs Brotherhood of Evil Mutants	.10	.30
168 Daredevil vs Typhoid Mary	.10	.30
169 Spider-Man vs Kingpin	.10	.30
170 Thor vs Bloodaxe	.10	.30
171 Warlock vs Man-Beast	.10	.30
172 Ghost Rider vs Blaze	.10	.30
173 Hulk vs Hulk	.10	.30
174 Fantastic Four vs Secret Defenders	.10	.30
175 Spider-Man vs Cardiac	.10	.30
176 Punisher vs Ghost Rider	.10	.30
177 Wolverine vs Omega Red	.10	.30
178 Cable vs Deadpool	.10	.30
179 Hulk vs X-Factor	.10	.30
180 Checklist	.10	.30
HIV Spider-Man vs. Venom HOLO	10.00	25.00

1993 Marvel Universe Red Foil

Card	Low	High
COMPLETE SET (9)	8.00	20.00
1 Doom 2099	1.00	2.50
2 Vulture 2099	1.00	2.50
3 Ravage 2099	1.00	2.50
4 Fearmaster	1.00	2.50
5 Spider-Man 2099	1.00	2.50
6 Punisher 2099	1.00	2.50
7 Specialist	1.00	2.50
8 Dethstryk	1.00	2.50
9 Tiger Wylde	1.00	2.50

1993 Star Trek TNG Behind the Scenes

Card	Low	High
COMPLETE SET (39)	5.00	12.00
1 Behind the Scenes	.15	.40
2 Key Grip	.15	.40
3 Co-Producer	.15	.40
4 Scenic Art Supervisor Technical Consultant	.15	.40
5 Production Sound Mixer	.15	.40
6 Stunt Coordinator	.15	.40
7 Story Editor	.15	.40
8 Senior Illustrator Technical Consultant	.15	.40
9 Visual Effects Supervisor	.15	.40
10 Set Designer	.15	.40
11 Unit Production Manager	.15	.40
12 Prop Master	.15	.40
13 Co-Executive Producer	.15	.40
14 Mechanical Effects Coordinator	.15	.40
15 First Assistant Director	.15	.40
16 Set Security Officer	.15	.40
17 Costume Designer	.15	.40
18 First Assistant Director	.15	.40
19 Co-Producer	.15	.40
20 Director of Photography	.15	.40
21 Producer	.15	.40
22 Visual Effects Supervisor	.15	.40
23 Production Designer	.15	.40
24 Property Master	.15	.40
25 Composer	.15	.40
26 Vendor Miniatures	.15	.40
27 Sript Supervisor	.15	.40
28 Executive Producer	.15	.40
29 Script Coordinator Pre-Production Associate	.15	.40
30 Chief Lighting Technician	.15	.40
31 Key Second Assistant Director	.15	.40
32 Set Decorator	.15	.40
33 Composer	.15	.40
34 Co-Producer	.15	.40
35 Associate Producer	.15	.40
36 Make-Up Supervisor and Designer	.15	.40
37 Executive Producer	.15	.40
38 Fifth Season Credits	.15	.40
39 Checklist	.02	.10

1994 Amazing Spider-Man

Card	Low	High
COMPLETE SET (150)	6.00	15.00
1 Wall-Crawling	.15	.40
2 Web-Shooting	.15	.40
3 Web-Slinging	.15	.40
4 Spider-Tracers	.15	.40
5 Spider-Agility	.15	.40
6 Spider-Signal	.15	.40
7 Spider-Strength	.15	.40
8 Spider-Leap	.15	.40
9 Spider-Sense	.15	.40
10 Vulnerable to Sonics	.15	.40
11 Web-Shooting	.15	.40
12 Spider-Agility	.15	.40
13 Living Costume	.15	.40
14 Disguise	.15	.40
15 Fearsome	.15	.40
16 Vulnerable to Fire	.15	.40
17 Immune to Spider-Sense	.15	.40
18 Super Strength	.15	.40
19 Black Costume	.15	.40
20 Captain Universe	.15	.40
21 Spider-Lizard	.15	.40
22 Man-Spider	.15	.40
23 Extra Arms	.15	.40
24 Spider-Clone	.15	.40
25 Spider-Hulk	.15	.40
26 Doppelganger	.15	.40
27 Shrinking Spidey	.15	.40
28 Tarantula	.15	.40
29 Spider-Slayer	.15	.40
30 Jackal	.15	.40
31 Puma	.15	.40
32 Spider-Man	.15	.40
33 Cardiac	.15	.40
34 Chance	.15	.40
35 Styx and Stone	.15	.40
36 Tombstone	.15	.40
37 Sandstorm	.15	.40
38 Demogoblin	.15	.40
39 Silvermane	.15	.40
40 Hammerhead	.15	.40
41 Spider-Man	.15	.40
42 Man-Wolf	.15	.40
43 Warrant	.15	.40
44 Blood Rose	.15	.40
45 Calypso	.15	.40
46 Green Goblin	.15	.40
47 Spider-Man	.15	.40
48 The Jury	.15	.40
49 Carrion	.15	.40
50 Vermin	.15	.40
51 Shocker	.15	.40
52 Kingpin	.15	.40
53 Sin-Eater	.15	.40
54 Rhino	.15	.40
55 Beetle	.15	.40
56 Solo	.15	.40
57 Boomerang	.15	.40
58 Hydro-Man	.15	.40
59 Scorpion	.15	.40
60 Speed Demon	.15	.40
61 Kraven	.15	.40
62 Spider-Man	.15	.40
63 Chameleon	.15	.40
64 Doctor Octopus	.15	.40
65 Vulture	.15	.40
66 Carnage	.15	.40
67 Venom	.15	.40
68 Spider-Man	.15	.40
69 Electro	.15	.40
70 Lizard	.15	.40
71 Hobgoblin	.15	.40
72 Mysterio	.15	.40
73 Black Cat	.15	.40
74 Nightwatch	.15	.40
75 Spider-Man	.15	.40
76 Sandman	.15	.40
77 Molten Man	.15	.40
78 Cloak and Dagger	.15	.40
79 Silver Sable	.15	.40
80 Prowler	.15	.40
81 Annex	.15	.40
82 Spider-Man & Wolverine	.15	.40
83 Spider-Man & Daredevil	.15	.40
84 Spider-Man & Punisher	.15	.40
85 Spider-Man & Avengers	.15	.40
86 Spider-Man & Green Goblin	.15	.40
87 Spider-Man & Ghost Rider	.15	.40
88 Spider-Man & X-Men	.15	.40
89 Spider-Man & Venom	.15	.40
90 Spider-Man & Captain America	.15	.40
91 Spider-Man & Doctor Strange	.15	.40
92 Spider-Man & Silver Sable	.15	.40
93 Spider-Man & Human Torch	.15	.40
94 Spider-Man & Nova	.15	.40
95 Spider-Man & New Warriors	.15	.40
96 Spider-Man & Darkhawk	.15	.40
97 Spider-Man vs. Venom	.15	.40
98 Spider-Man vs. Carnage	.15	.40
99 Spider-Man vs. Hobgoblin	.15	.40
100 Spider-Man vs. Green Goblin	.15	.40
101 Spider-Man vs. Doctor Octopus	.15	.40
102 Spider-Man vs. Lizard	.15	.40
103 Spider-Man vs. Firelord	.15	.40
104 Spider-Man vs. Silver Surfer	.15	.40
105 Spider-Man vs. Tombstone	.15	.40
106 Spider-Man vs. Rhino	.15	.40
107 Spider-Man vs. Hulk	.15	.40
108 Spider-Man vs. Electro	.15	.40
109 Spider-Man vs. Kraven	.15	.40
110 Spider-Man vs. Mysterio	.15	.40
111 Spider-Man vs. Kingpin	.15	.40
112 Spider-Man vs. Vulture	.15	.40
113 Spider-Man vs. Doctor Doom	.15	.40
114 Spider-Man vs. Puma	.15	.40
115 Spider-Man vs. Black Cat	.15	.40
116 Spider-Man vs. Juggernaut	.15	.40
117 Spider-Man vs. Vermin	.15	.40
118 Spider-Man vs. Scorpion	.15	.40
119 Spider-Man vs. Red Skull	.15	.40
120 Spider-Man vs. Sabretooth	.15	.40
121 Spider-Man vs. Morbius	.15	.40
122 Mary Jane	.15	.40
123 Flash Thompson	.15	.40
124 J. Jonah Jameson	.15	.40
125 Aunt May	.15	.40
126 Joe Robbie Robertson	.15	.40
127 Peter Parker	.15	.40
128 The Spider's Bite!	.15	.40
129 Powers for Profit!	.15	.40
130 Not My Job!	.15	.40
131 To Catch a Thief!	.15	.40
132 A Graveside Vow!	.15	.40
133 Maximum Carnage	.15	.40
134 Round Robin	.15	.40
135 Return of the Sinister Six	.15	.40
136 Revenge of the Sinister Six	.15	.40
137 The Child Within	.15	.40
138 Spirits of Venom	.15	.40
139 Fearful Symmetry	.15	.40
140 Assassin Nation Plot	.15	.40
141 Death of Gwen Stacy	.15	.40
142 The Wedding of Peter and Mary Jane	.15	.40
143 Invasion of the Spider-Slayers	.15	.40
144 The Osborn Legacy	.15	.40
145 The Return of Peter Parker's Parents	.15	.40
146 The Black Costume Saga	.15	.40
147 Return of the Burglar	.15	.40
148 Funeral Arrangements	.15	.40
149 Eye of the Puma	.15	.40
150 Checklist	.15	.40

1994 Amazing Spider-Man Gold-Web

Card	Low	High
COMPLETE SET (6) RANDOM INSERT IN JUMBO PACKS	6.00	15.00
1 Venom	2.00	5.00
2 Mary Jane	2.00	5.00
3 Spider-Man	2.00	5.00
4 Chameleon	2.00	5.00
5 Hobgoblin	2.00	5.00
6 Carnage	2.00	5.00

1994 Amazing Spider-Man Gold-Web Wal-Mart

Card	Low	High
COMPLETE SET (6) STATED ODDS 1:7 WAL-MART PACKS	6.00	15.00
1 Spider-Man	2.00	5.00
2 Lizard	2.00	5.00
3 Black Cat	2.00	5.00
4 Vulture	2.00	5.00
5 Doctor Octopus	2.00	5.00
6 Spider-Man	2.00	5.00

1994 Amazing Spider-Man Holograms

Card	Low	High
COMPLETE SET (4) STATED ODDS 1:18	15.00	40.00
1 Carnage	6.00	15.00
2 Spider-Man	6.00	15.00
3 Venom	6.00	15.00
4 Spider-Man	6.00	15.00

1994 Amazing Spider-Man Masterprints

Card	Low	High
COMPLETE SET (9) STATED ODDS ONE PER CASE	15.00	40.00
1 Allies	4.00	10.00
2 Enemies I	4.00	10.00
3 Enemies II	4.00	10.00
4 Enemies III	4.00	10.00
5 Enemies IV	4.00	10.00
6 Enemies V	4.00	10.00
7 Powers	4.00	10.00
8 Strangest Transformations	4.00	10.00
9 Venom	4.00	10.00

1994 Amazing Spider-Man Suspended Animation

Card	Low	High
COMPLETE SET (12) STATED ODDS 1:4 HOBBY	10.00	25.00
1 Spider-Man	1.50	4.00
2 Mary Jane	1.50	4.00
3 Chameleon	1.50	4.00
4 Venom	1.50	4.00
5 Carnage	1.50	4.00
6 Hobgoblin	1.50	4.00
7 Spider-Man	1.50	4.00
8 Vulture	1.50	4.00
9 Doctor Octopus	1.50	4.00
10 Spider-Man	1.50	4.00
11 Black Cat	1.50	4.00
12 Lizard	1.50	4.00

1994 Batman Saga of the Dark Knight

Card	Low	High
COMPLETE SET (100) SD1 STATED ODDS 1:240	6.00	15.00
1 Saga of the Dark Knight	.15	.40
2 The Cave	.15	.40
3 The Permanent Nightmare	.15	.40
4 Training Abroad	.15	.40
5 Shaman	.15	.40
6 Crime Alley	.15	.40
7 The Omen	.15	.40
8 Two Sides of the Same Coin	.15	.40
9 Face to Face	.15	.40
10 Falsely Accused	.15	.40
11 Feline Fatale	.15	.40
12 Finding a Friend	.15	.40
13 Birth of the Joker	.15	.40
14 First Impressions	.15	.40
15 Partners in Crime	.15	.40
16 Not... Strong... Enough	.15	.40
17 The Power of Venom	.15	.40
18 Withdrawal	.15	.40
19 Dick Grayson	.15	.40
20 Robin Retires	.15	.40
21 Nightwing	.15	.40
22 Jason Todd	.15	.40
23 Out of Line	.15	.40
24 A Death in the Family	.15	.40
25 Tim Drake	.15	.40
26 Uneasy Alliance	.15	.40
27 Severed Ties	.15	.40
28 A Sacred Trust	.15	.40
29 Partners	.15	.40
30 Demon's Head	.15	.40
31 My Father's Killer	.15	.40
32 Equal Justice	.15	.40
33 The Cult	.15	.40
34 Proving Ground	.15	.40
35 Rite of Passage	.15	.40
36 Seduction of the Gun	.15	.40
37 That's It	.15	.40
38 Freedom of Madness	.15	.40
39 The Search	.15	.40
40 Missile Deal	.15	.40
41 Reunion	.15	.40
42 Betrayal	.15	.40
43 Mourning Time	.15	.40
44 Ultimate Joke	.15	.40
45 Two-Minute Warning	.15	.40
46 The Joker	.15	.40
47 Catwoman	.15	.40
48 Two-Face	.15	.40
49 The Penguin	.15	.40
50 Ra's Al Ghul	.15	.40
51 The Scarecrow	.15	.40
52 The Mudpack	.15	.40
53 The Riddler/Poison Ivy	.15	.40
54 Killer Croc/Scarface	.15	.40
55 Consumed by Guilt	.15	.40
56 Am I Mad	.15	.40
57 Homecoming	.15	.40
58 Confrontation	.15	.40
59 Double Jeopardy	.15	.40
60 Reunited	.15	.40
61 Only a Boy	.15	.40
62 Never Again	.15	.40
63 Initiation	.15	.40
64 Inheritance	.15	.40
65 Lehah	.15	.40
66 Knight of St. Dumas	.15	.40
67 Hostage	.15	.40
68 Savior	.15	.40
69 Trial by Fire	.15	.40
70 Birth	.15	.40
71 Transfusion	.15	.40
72 Hunt	.15	.40
73 Arkham Breakout	.15	.40
74 One Down	.15	.40

❑ 75 Behemoth .15 .40
❑ 76 Meet Mr. Zsasz .15 .40
❑ 77 Tipping the Scale .15 .40
❑ 78 Bloodlust .15 .40
❑ 79 Inferno .15 .40
❑ 80 The Vixen of Vines .15 .40
❑ 81 Clueless .15 .40
❑ 82 Fear Equals Rage .15 .40
❑ 83 Face Me .15 .40
❑ 84 The Broken Bat .15 .40
❑ 85 Accept the Cowl .15 .40
❑ 86 Bad Blood .15 .40
❑ 87 Anarchy/Law .15 .40
❑ 88 Claws for Bane .15 .40
❑ 89 The Vision .15 .40
❑ 90 King of Gotham .15 .40
❑ 91 The Crusade .15 .40
❑ 92 Back Off .15 .40
❑ 93 Charades .15 .40
❑ 94 Prince of Fools .15 .40
❑ 95 Corrosion .15 .40
❑ 96 No Deals .15 .40
❑ 97 Off the Deep End .15 .40
❑ 98 Dehumanized .15 .40
❑ 99 Kinghtsend .15 .40
❑ 100 Checklist .15 .40
❑ SD1 Batman Skydisc 8.00 20.00

1994 Batman Saga of the Dark Knight Spectra Etch Portraits

COMPLETE SET (5) 6.00 15.00
STATED ODDS 1:18
❑ B1 Batman 2.50 6.00
❑ B2 Batman 2.50 6.00
❑ B3 Batman 2.50 6.00
❑ B4 Batman 2.50 6.00
❑ B5 Batman 2.50 6.00

1994 DC Master Series

COMPLETE SET (90) 6.00 15.00
SD2 STATED ODDS 1:240
❑ 1 Superman .15 .40
❑ 2 Supergirl .15 .40
❑ 3 Superboy .15 .40
❑ 4 Steel .15 .40
❑ 5 Cyborg .15 .40
❑ 6 Lex Luthor II .15 .40
❑ 7 The Eradicator .15 .40
❑ 8 Mongul .15 .40
❑ 9 Doomsday .15 .40
❑ 10 Glorith .15 .40
Mordru
❑ 11 Valor .15 .40
❑ 12 Emerald Dragon .15 .40
❑ 13 Live Wire .15 .40
❑ 14 Saturn Girl .15 .40
❑ 15 Cosmic Boy .15 .40
❑ 16 Virus .15 .40
Pulse
❑ 17 Andromeda .15 .40
❑ 18 Polestar .15 .40
❑ 19 Vril Dox .15 .40
❑ 20 Captain Atom .15 .40
❑ 21 Mirage .15 .40
❑ 22 Martian Manhunter .15 .40
❑ 23 Nightwing .15 .40
❑ 24 Geo-Force .15 .40
❑ 25 Battalion .15 .40
❑ 26 Arsenal .15 .40
❑ 27 Ferrin Colos .15 .40
❑ 28 Batman .15 .40
❑ 29 Robin .15 .40
❑ 30 Azreal - Batman .15 .40
❑ 31 Bane .15 .40
❑ 32 Oracle .15 .40
❑ 33 The Joker .15 .40
❑ 34 Ra's Al Ghul .15 .40
❑ 35 Catwoman .15 .40
❑ 36 Two-Face .15 .40
❑ 37 Monarch .15 .40
❑ 38 Vandal Savage .15 .40
❑ 39 Raven .15 .40
❑ 40 Poison Ivy .15 .40
❑ 41 Black Adam .15 .40
❑ 42 Darkseid .15 .40
❑ 43 Brimstone .15 .40
❑ 44 Doctor Polaris .15 .40
❑ 45 Blaze .15 .40
❑ 46 Green Lantern .15 .40
❑ 47 Alan Scott .15 .40
❑ 48 Guy Gardner: Warrior .15 .40
❑ 49 Sinestro .15 .40
❑ 50 Hal Jordon .15 .40
❑ 51 Guardians of the Universe .15 .40
❑ 52 Impulse .15 .40
❑ 53 The Flash .15 .40
❑ 54 Max Mercury .15 .40
❑ 55 The Spectre .15 .40
❑ 56 The Demon .15 .40
❑ 57 Phantom Stranger .15 .40
❑ 58 Deadman .15 .40
❑ 59 Eclipso .15 .40
❑ 60 Dr. Fate .15 .40
❑ 61 Orion .15 .40
❑ 62 Lobo .15 .40
❑ 63 Deathstroke, The Terminator .15 .40
❑ 64 Green Arrow .15 .40
❑ 65 Gypsy .15 .40
❑ 66 Changling .15 .40
❑ 67 Crimson Fox .15 .40
❑ 68 Metamorpho .15 .40
❑ 69 Maxima .15 .40
❑ 70 Aquaman .15 .40
❑ 71 Huntress .15 .40
❑ 72 The Atom .15 .40
❑ 73 Damage .15 .40
❑ 74 Anima .15 .40
❑ 75 Argus .15 .40
❑ 76 Triumph .15 .40
❑ 77 Technocrat .15 .40
Wylde
❑ 78 The Ray .15 .40
❑ 79 Starman .15 .40
❑ 80 Gunfire .15 .40
❑ 81 Faust .15 .40
❑ 82 Hawkman .15 .40
❑ 83 Hawkwoman .15 .40
❑ 84 The Guardian .15 .40
❑ 85 Wonder Woman .15 .40
❑ 86 Blue Beetle .15 .40
Booster Gold
❑ 87 Black Canary .15 .40
❑ 88 Power Girl .15 .40
❑ 89 Shazam .15 .40
❑ 90 Checklist .15 .40
❑ SD2 Superman Skydisc Redemption 20.00 50.00

1994 DC Master Series Double-Sided Spectra

COMPLETE SET (5) 30.00 75.00
STATED ODDS 1:36
❑ DS1 Green Lantern 8.00 20.00
Hal Jordon
❑ DS2 Batman 8.00 20.00
The Joker
❑ DS3a Superman 8.00 20.00
Doomsday/ (S in card number is backwards)
❑ DS3b Superman 8.00 20.00
Doomsday/ (S in card number is correct)
❑ DS4 Flash 8.00 20.00
Reverse Flash
❑ DS5 Lobo 8.00 20.00
Lobo

1994 DC Master Series Foil

COMPLETE SET (4) 8.00 20.00
STATED ODDS 1:18
❑ F1 Wonder Woman 2.50 6.00
❑ F2 Aquaman 2.50 6.00
❑ F3 Green Arrow 2.50 6.00
❑ F4 Hawkman 2.50 6.00

1994 Mars Attacks Archives

COMPLETE SET (99) 15.00 40.00
❑ 1 The Invasion Begins .20 .50
❑ 2 Martians Approaching .20 .50
❑ 3 Attacking an Army Base .20 .50
❑ 4 Saucers Blast Our Jets .20 .50
❑ 5 Washington in Flames .20 .50
❑ 6 Burning Navy Ships .20 .50
❑ 7 Destroying the Bridge .20 .50
❑ 8 Terror in Times Square .20 .50
❑ 9 The Human Torch .20 .50
❑ 10 The Skyscraper Tumbles .20 .50
❑ 11 Destroy the City .20 .50
❑ 12 Death in the Cockpit .20 .50
❑ 13 Watching from Mars .20 .50
❑ 14 Charred by Martians .20 .50
❑ 15 Saucers Invade China .20 .50
❑ 16 Panic in Parliament .20 .50
❑ 17 Beast and the Beauty .20 .50
❑ 18 A Soldier Fights Back .20 .50
❑ 19 Burning Flesh .20 .50
❑ 20 Crushed to Death .20 .50
❑ 21 Prize Captive .20 .50
❑ 22 Burning Cattle .20 .50
❑ 23 The Frost Ray .20 .50
❑ 24 The Shrinking Ray .20 .50
❑ 25 Capturing a Martian .20 .50
❑ 26 The Tidal Wave .20 .50
❑ 27 The Giant Flies .20 .50
❑ 28 Helpless Victim .20 .50
❑ 29 Death in the Shelter .20 .50
❑ 30 Trapped .20 .50
❑ 31 The Monster Reaches In .20 .50
❑ 32 Robot Terror .20 .50
❑ 33 Removing the Victims .20 .50
❑ 34 Terror in the Railroad .20 .50
❑ 35 The Flame Throwers .20 .50
❑ 36 Destroying a Dog .20 .50
❑ 37 Creeping Menace .20 .50
❑ 38 Victims of the Bug .20 .50
❑ 39 Army of Giant Insects .20 .50
❑ 40 High Voltage Execution .20 .50
❑ 41 Horror in Paris .20 .50
❑ 42 Hairy Fiend .20 .50
❑ 43 Blasting the Bug .20 .50
❑ 44 Battle in the Air .20 .50
❑ 45 Fighting Giant Insects .20 .50
❑ 46 Blast Off for Mars .20 .50
❑ 47 Earth Bombs Mars .20 .50
❑ 48 Earthmen Land on Mars .20 .50
❑ 49 The Earthmen Charge .20 .50
❑ 50 Smashing the Enemy .20 .50
❑ 51 Crushing the Martians .20 .50
❑ 52 Giant Robot .20 .50
❑ 53 Martian City in Ruins .20 .50
❑ 54 Mars Explodes .20 .50
❑ 55 Mars Attacks Checklist .20 .50
❑ 56 The Garden of Peace .20 .50
❑ 57 Late Night Discovery .20 .50
❑ 58 The Last Picture Show .20 .50
❑ 59 Blasted into Oblivion .20 .50
❑ 60 Unspeakable Experiments .20 .50
❑ 61 Flight of the Doomed .20 .50
❑ 62 Last Licks .20 .50
❑ 63 Common Cause .20 .50
❑ 64 Slaughter in the Suburbs .20 .50
❑ 65 Naked and the Dead .20 .50
❑ 66 Earth Triumphant .20 .50
❑ 67 Mars Attacks No. 1 .20 .50
❑ 68 Mars Attacks No. 2 .20 .50
❑ 69 Mars Attacks No. 3 .20 .50
❑ 70 Mars Attacks No. 4 .20 .50
❑ 71 Mars Attacks No. 5 .20 .50
❑ 72 Mars Attacks No. 1 .20 .50
❑ 73 Mars Attacks No. 2 .20 .50
❑ 74 Mars Attacks No. 3 .20 .50
❑ 75 Mars Attacks No. 4 .20 .50
❑ 76 Mars Attacks No. 5 .20 .50
❑ 77 Martian saucers .20 .50
Insectoid designs
❑ 78 American soldiers .20 .50
Evolution of a Martian
❑ 79 Martian and victim .20 .50
Human guinea pigs
❑ 80 Woman blasts Martian .20 .50
Tied to rocket tubes
❑ 81 Mars needs women .20 .50
Spider and woman
❑ 82 Tormented soul .20 .50
New York
❑ 83 Bloated beetle .20 .50
Moscow
❑ 84 War pod .20 .50
Earthlings to smithereens
❑ 85 Force field bubble .20 .50
Impalement
❑ 86 Wet t-shirt contest .20 .50
Large Martian
❑ 87 Infant's pram .20 .50
War under the sea
❑ 88 Portrait of a Martian .20 .50
Giant robots
❑ 89 Concentration camp .20 .50
More robots
❑ 90 Marine resistance .20 .50
Martian tanks
❑ 91 Martian religion .20 .50
Invasion begins
❑ 92 Profile in courage .20 .50
Third eye Martians
❑ 93 When worlds collide .20 .50
Attacking a base
❑ 94 Martians as insects .20 .50
Burning flesh
❑ 95 Apocalyptic destruction .20 .50
Atomic bullets
❑ 96 Training the Bugs .20 .50
Original wrapper
❑ 97 Chainsaw Massacre .20 .50
Original box
❑ 98 Jarred heads .20 .50
Attack from Space
❑ 99 Norm Saunders: A Self-Portrait .20 .50

1994 Mars Attacks Archives First Day Issue

COMPLETE SET (55) 125.00 250.00
*FIRST DAY: 4X TO 10X BASE CARDS 2.00 5.00
STATED ODDS 1:9

1994 Marvel Annual

COMPLETE SET (150) 20.00 50.00
❑ 1 The Thing .25 .60
❑ 2 The Incredible Hulk .25 .60
❑ 3 With Great Power .25 .60
❑ 4 God of Thunder .25 .60
❑ 5 Spider-Man .25 .60
❑ 6 Iron Man UER/ (card incorrectly #'d 8) .25 .60
❑ 7 Hulk vs Thing .25 .60
❑ 8 Vulture vs Spider-Man .25 .60
❑ 9 Dr. Octopus .25 .60
❑ 10 Xavier .25 .60
❑ 11 Avengers .25 .60
❑ 12 Dr. Strange .25 .60
❑ 13 Quicksilver .25 .60
❑ 14 Man without Fear .25 .60
❑ 15 Scorpion vs Spider-Man .25 .60
❑ 16 Captain America .25 .60
❑ 17 Daredevil vs Submariner .25 .60
❑ 18 Invisible Woman .25 .60
❑ 19 Sentinels .25 .60
❑ 20 Coming of Galactus .25 .60
❑ 21 The Power Cosmic .25 .60
❑ 22 Spider-Man vs Green Goblin .25 .60
❑ 23 Rhino vs Spider-Man .25 .60
❑ 24 Mary Jane .25 .60
❑ 25 Dr. Doom .25 .60
❑ 26 Warlock .25 .60
❑ 27 Behold the Vision .25 .60
❑ 28 Mephisto .25 .60
❑ 29 Morbius .25 .60
❑ 30 The Original Ghost Rider .25 .60
❑ 31 Thanos .25 .60
❑ 32 Death of Gwen Stacy .25 .60
❑ 33 The Punisher .25 .60
❑ 34 Wolverine vs Hulk .25 .60
❑ 35 The Scarlet Witch .25 .60
❑ 36 Invaders .25 .60
❑ 37 The Black Cat .25 .60
❑ 38 White Queen .25 .60
❑ 39 She Hulk .25 .60
❑ 40 Moon Knight .25 .60
❑ 41 Days of Future Past .25 .60
❑ 42 Elektra .25 .60
❑ 43 Death of Elektra .25 .60
❑ 44 Hobgoblin .25 .60
❑ 45 Northstar .25 .60
❑ 46 Beta Ray Bill .25 .60
❑ 47 The Trial of Mr. Fantastic .25 .60
❑ 48 The Black Costume .25 .60
❑ 49 Puma vs Spidey .25 .60
❑ 50 Silver Sable Inc. .25 .60
❑ 51 Iceman .25 .60
❑ 52 Apocalypse Now .25 .60
❑ 53 Deadly Enemies .25 .60
❑ 54 Nightcrawler .25 .60
❑ 55 Creation of Archangel .25 .60
❑ 56 Mr. Sinister .25 .60
❑ 57 The Wedding .25 .60
❑ 58 Jubilee .25 .60
❑ 59 Armor Wars .25 .60
❑ 60 Tombstone .25 .60
❑ 61 Venom .25 .60
❑ 62 Typhoid Mary .25 .60
❑ 63 Mr. Fix-It .25 .60
❑ 64 Speedball .25 .60
❑ 65 Cap vs Cap .25 .60
❑ 66 Quasar .25 .60
❑ 67 Cosmic Spider-Man .25 .60
❑ 68 Nomad .25 .60
❑ 69 Thanos .25 .60
❑ 70 Bodyslide .25 .60
❑ 71 New Ghost Rider .25 .60
❑ 72 Creation of Deathlok .25 .60
❑ 73 The New Nova .25 .60
❑ 74 Cable vs Wolverine .25 .60
❑ 75 Gambit .25 .60
❑ 76 X-Tinction Agenda .25 .60
❑ 77 The new Hulk .25 .60
❑ 78 Deadpool .25 .60
❑ 79 Shatterstar .25 .60
❑ 80 X-Force .25 .60
❑ 81 Johnny Blaze .25 .60
❑ 82 Child of the Future .25 .60
❑ 83 X-Factor .25 .60
❑ 84 Blue & Gold .25 .60
❑ 85 Bishop .25 .60
❑ 86 Omega Red vs Wolverine .25 .60
❑ 87 Punisher vs the Mob .25 .60
❑ 88 Carnage .25 .60
❑ 89 Cage .25 .60
❑ 90 War Machine .25 .60
❑ 91 Death of Mariko .25 .60
❑ 92 Spider Slayers .25 .60
❑ 93 Nightstalkers .25 .60
❑ 94 Spider-Man 2099 .25 .60
❑ 95 Hulk Leads the Pantheon .25 .60
❑ 96 Stryfe .25 .60
❑ 97 Mirror Images .25 .60
❑ 98 Wonder Man .25 .60
❑ 99 Doom 2099 .25 .60
❑ 100 Lethal Protector .25 .60
❑ 101 Punisher 2099 .25 .60
❑ 102 Green Goblin .25 .60
❑ 103 Alternate Visions .25 .60
❑ 104 Maximum Carnage .25 .60
❑ 105 Namor .25 .60
❑ 106 Random .25 .60
❑ 107 Psylocke .25 .60
❑ 108 Psi-Lord .25 .60
❑ 109 Thunderstrike .25 .60
❑ 110 Infinity Crusade .25 .60
❑ 111 Hulk 2099 .25 .60
❑ 112 Cable Returns .25 .60
❑ 113 The Death of Illyana .25 .60
❑ 114 Gambit & Rogue .25 .60
❑ 115 Vengeance .25 .60
❑ 116 Daredevil .25 .60
❑ 117 The New Ravage .25 .60
❑ 118 Wolverine Defeated .25 .60
❑ 119 Bone Claws .25 .60
❑ 120 Magneto Returns .25 .60
❑ 121 Xavier vs Magneto .25 .60
❑ 122 Colossus Defects .25 .60
❑ 123 Exodus .25 .60
❑ 124 Bloodhawk .25 .60
❑ 125 Zarathos .25 .60
❑ 126 Final Conflict .25 .60
❑ 127 Centurious .25 .60
❑ 128 The Thor Corps. .25 .60
❑ 129 Sabretooth Surrenders .25 .60
❑ 130 Venom: The Madness .25 .60
❑ 131 Strange .25 .60
❑ 132 Suicide Run .25 .60
❑ 133 Legacy .25 .60
❑ 134 Justice .25 .60
❑ 135 Carnage .25 .60
❑ 136 Venom .25 .60
❑ 137 Spider-Demon .25 .60
❑ 138 Shriek .25 .60
❑ 139 Spider-Man .25 .60
❑ 140 Venom Lives .25 .60
❑ 141 Cyclops .25 .60
❑ 142 Jean Grey .25 .60
❑ 143 Bishop .25 .60
❑ 144 Warpath .25 .60
❑ 145 Rogue .25 .60
❑ 146 Domino .25 .60
❑ 147 Boom! Boom .25 .60
❑ 148 Wolverine .25 .60
❑ 149 Havok .25 .60
❑ 150 Checklist .25 .60

1994 Marvel Annual FlairPrint

COMPLETE SET (10) 10.00 25.00
STATED ODDS ONE PER CASE
❑ 1 Cable 2.00 5.00
❑ 2 Cyclops 2.00 5.00
❑ 3 Ghost Rider 2.00 5.00
❑ 4 Iron Man 2.00 5.00
❑ 5 Magneto 2.00 5.00
❑ 6 Phoenix 2.00 5.00
❑ 7 Punisher 2.00 5.00
❑ 8 Storm 2.00 5.00
❑ 9 Venom 2.00 5.00
❑ 10 Wolverine 2.00 5.00

1994 Marvel Annual PowerBlast

COMPLETE SET (18) 6.00 15.00
STATED ODDS 1:2
❑ 1 Cable .50 1.25
❑ 2 Cyclops .50 1.25
❑ 3 Iron Man .50 1.25
❑ 4 Magneto .50 1.25
❑ 5 Phoenix .50 1.25
❑ 6 Storm .50 1.25
❑ 7 Venom .50 1.25
❑ 8 Wolverine .50 1.25
❑ 9 Ghost Rider .50 1.25
❑ 10 Punisher .50 1.25
❑ 11 Captain America .50 1.25
❑ 12 Gambit .50 1.25
❑ 13 Thor .50 1.25
❑ 14 Silver Surfer .50 1.25
❑ 15 Spider-Man .50 1.25
❑ 16 Deadpool .50 1.25
❑ 17 Invisible Woman .50 1.25
❑ 18 Dr. Doom .50 1.25

1994 Marvel Masterpieces

COMPLETE SET (140) 10.00 25.00
❑ 1 Apocalypse .25 .60
❑ 2 Archangel .25 .60
❑ 3 Beast .25 .60
❑ 4 Bishop .25 .60
❑ 5 Blaco Bolt .25 .60
❑ 6 Black Cat .25 .60
❑ 7 Black Knight .25 .60
❑ 8 Black Panther .25 .60
❑ 9 Black Widow .25 .60
❑ 10 Blackout .25 .60
❑ 11 Blackwulf .25 .60
❑ 12 Blade .25 .60
❑ 13 Blaze .25 .60
❑ 14 Blood Wraith .25 .60
❑ 15 Bloodaxe .25 .60
❑ 16 Bloodhawk .25 .60
❑ 17 Cable .25 .60
❑ 18 Captain America .25 .60
❑ 19 Captain Universe .25 .60
❑ 20 Carnage .25 .60
❑ 21 Century .25 .60
❑ 22 Cerebra .25 .60
❑ 23 Chamber .25 .60
❑ 24 Colossus .25 .60
❑ 25 Cyclops .25 .60
❑ 26 Daredevil .25 .60
❑ 27 Darkhawk .25 .60
❑ 28 Deadpool .25 .60
❑ 29 Deathlok .25 .60
❑ 30 Demogoblin .25 .60
❑ 31 Dr. Doom .25 .60
❑ 32 Domino .25 .60
❑ 33 Doom 2099 .25 .60
❑ 34 Elektra .25 .60
❑ 35 Evilhawk .25 .60
❑ 36 Exodus .25 .60
❑ 37 Fin Fang Foom .25 .60
❑ 38 Firestar .25 .60
❑ 39 Nick Fury .25 .60
❑ 40 Galactus .25 .60
❑ 41 Gambit .25 .60
❑ 42 Ghost Rider .25 .60
❑ 43 Ghost Rider 2099 .25 .60
❑ 44 Green Goblin .25 .60
❑ 45 Jean Grey .25 .60
❑ 46 Grim Reaper .25 .60
❑ 47 Guardian .25 .60
❑ 48 Havok .25 .60
❑ 49 Hawkeye .25 .60
❑ 50 Hulk .25 .60
❑ 51 Hulk 2099 .25 .60
❑ 52 Human Torch .25 .60
❑ 53 Husk .25 .60
❑ 54 Iceman .25 .60
❑ 55 Invisible Woman .25 .60
❑ 56 Iron Man .25 .60
❑ 57 Jack of Hearts .25 .60
❑ 58 Jubilee .25 .60
❑ 59 Juggernaut .25 .60
❑ 60 Junkpile .25 .60
❑ 61 Justice .25 .60
❑ 62 Kingpin .25 .60
❑ 63 Klaw .25 .60
❑ 64 Krystalin .25 .60
❑ 65 Kymaera .25 .60
❑ 66 Legacy .25 .60
❑ 67 Lilith .25 .60
❑ 68 Loki .25 .60
❑ 69 M .25 .60
❑ 70 Magneto .25 .60
❑ 71 Mandarin .25 .60
❑ 72 Meanstreak .25 .60
❑ 73 Medusa .25 .60
❑ 74 Mephisto .25 .60
❑ 75 Metalhead .25 .60
❑ 76 Mr. Fantastic .25 .60
❑ 77 Mr. Hyde .25 .60
❑ 78 Mondo .25 .60
❑ 79 Morbius .25 .60
❑ 80 Morg .25 .60
❑ 81 Namor .25 .60
❑ 82 Nebula .25 .60
❑ 83 Night Thrasher .25 .60
❑ 84 Nightcrawler .25 .60
❑ 85 Nightwatch .25 .60
❑ 86 Nova .25 .60
❑ 87 Odin .25 .60
❑ 88 Penance .25 .60
❑ 89 Phoenix .25 .60
❑ 90 Professor X .25 .60
❑ 91 Prowler .25 .60
❑ 92 Psi-Lord .25 .60
❑ 93 Psylocke .25 .60
❑ 94 Punisher .25 .60
❑ 95 Punisher 2099 .25 .60
❑ 96 Quasar .25 .60
❑ 97 Random .25 .60
❑ 98 Ravage 2099 .25 .60
❑ 99 Red Skull .25 .60
❑ 100 Rhino .25 .60
❑ 101 Rogue .25 .60
❑ 102 Sabretooth .25 .60
❑ 103 Sauron .25 .60
❑ 104 Scarecrow .25 .60
❑ 105 Scarlet Witch .25 .60
❑ 106 Shadowcat .25 .60
❑ 107 Shatterstar .25 .60
❑ 108 She-Hulk .25 .60
❑ 109 Siege .25 .60
❑ 110 Silver Sable .25 .60
❑ 111 Silver Surfer .25 .60
❑ 112 Skin .25 .60
❑ 113 Skullfire .25 .60
❑ 114 Solo .25 .60
❑ 115 Spider-Man .25 .60
❑ 116 Spider-Man 2099 .25 .60
❑ 117 Spider-Woman .25 .60
❑ 118 Storm .25 .60
❑ 119 Strange .25 .60
❑ 120 Synch .25 .60
❑ 121 Terrax .25 .60
❑ 122 Thanos .25 .60
❑ 123 Thing .25 .60
❑ 124 Thor .25 .60
❑ 125 Thunderstrike .25 .60
❑ 126 Typhoid Mary .25 .60
❑ 127 Tyrant .25 .60
❑ 128 Ulik .25 .60
❑ 129 U.S. Agent .25 .60
❑ 130 Vengeance .25 .60
❑ 131 Venom .25 .60
❑ 132 Vision .25 .60
❑ 133 War Machine .25 .60
❑ 134 Warlock .25 .60
❑ 135 Werewolf .25 .60
❑ 136 White Queen .25 .60
❑ 137 Wolverine .25 .60
❑ 138 Wrecker .25 .60
❑ 139 Xi'an .25 .60
❑ 140 Checklist .25 .60

1994 Marvel Masterpieces Holofoil Silver

COMPLETE SET (10) 8.00 20.00
❑ 1 Captain America 1.00 2.50
❑ 2 Carnage 1.00 2.50
❑ 3 Daredevil 1.00 2.50
❑ 4 Hulk 1.00 2.50
❑ 5 Iron Man 1.00 2.50
❑ 6 Punisher 1.00 2.50
❑ 7 Scarlet Witch 1.00 2.50
❑ 8 Spider-Man 1.00 2.50
❑ 9 Venom 1.00 2.50
❑ 10 War Machine 1.00 2.50

1994 Marvel Masterpieces Holofoil Bronze

COMPLETE SET (10) 15.00 40.00
❑ 1 Captain America 2.00 5.00
❑ 2 Carnage 2.00 5.00
❑ 3 Daredevil 2.00 5.00
❑ 4 Hulk 2.00 5.00
❑ 5 Iron Man 2.00 5.00
❑ 6 Punisher 2.00 5.00
❑ 7 Scarlet Witch 2.00 5.00
❑ 8 Spider-Man 2.00 5.00
❑ 9 Venom 2.00 5.00
❑ 10 War Machine 2.00 5.00

1994 Marvel Masterpieces Holofoil Gold

COMPLETE SET (10) 10.00 25.00
❑ 1 Captain America 1.25 3.00
❑ 2 Carnage 1.25 3.00
❑ 3 Daredevil 1.25 3.00
❑ 4 Hulk 1.25 3.00
❑ 5 Iron Man 1.25 3.00
❑ 6 Punisher 1.25 3.00
❑ 7 Scarlet Witch 1.25 3.00

❑ 8 Spider-Man 1.25 3.00
❑ 9 Venom 1.25 3.00
❑ 10 War Machine 1.25 3.00

1994 Marvel Masterpieces Masterprints

COMPLETE SET (10) 12.00 30.00
❑ 1 Capt. America 1.50 4.00
❑ 2 Gambit 1.50 4.00
❑ 3 Human Torch 1.50 4.00
❑ 4 Psylocke 1.50 4.00
❑ 5 Rogue 1.50 4.00
❑ 6 Silver Surfer 1.50 4.00
❑ 7 Thing 1.50 4.00
❑ 8 Venom 1.50 4.00
❑ 9 War Machine 1.50 4.00
❑ 10 Wolverine 1.50 4.00

1994 Marvel Masterpieces PowerBlast

COMPLETE SET (9) 8.00 20.00
❑ PB1 Apocalypse 1.00 2.50
❑ PB2 Archangel 1.00 2.50
❑ PB3 Cable 1.00 2.50
❑ PB4 Cyclops 1.00 2.50
❑ PB5 Gambit 1.00 2.50
❑ PB6 Magneto 1.00 2.50
❑ PB7 Rogue 1.00 2.50
❑ PB8 Sabretooth 1.00 2.50
❑ PB9 Wolverine 1.00 2.50

1994 Marvel Universe

COMPLETE SET (200) 10.00 25.00
❑ 1 Spider-Man .10 .30
❑ 2 Venom .10 .30
❑ 3 Punisher .10 .30
❑ 4 Wolverine .10 .30
❑ 5 Gambit .10 .30
❑ 6 Silver Surfer .10 .30
❑ 7 Rogue .10 .30
❑ 8 Iron Man .10 .30
❑ 9 Ghost Rider .10 .30
❑ 10 Exodus .10 .30
Cannonball
❑ 11 Siryn .10 .30
Shatterstar
❑ 12 Wolverine .10 .30
Rogue
❑ 13 Rictor .10 .30
Warpath/Boomer/Feral
❑ 14 Magneto .10 .30
❑ 15 Bishop .10 .30
Colossus
❑ 16 Cable .10 .30
Sunspot
❑ 17 Gambit .10 .30
Quicksilver
❑ 18 Professor X .10 .30
Jean Grey
❑ 19 Captain America .10 .30
❑ 20 Firestar .10 .30
Carnage
❑ 21 Demogoblin .10 .30
Cloak/Nightwatch
❑ 22 Shriek .10 .30
Doppelganger
❑ 23 Spider-Man .10 .30
❑ 24 Dagger .10 .30
Morbius/Deathlok
❑ 25 Black Cat .10 .30
❑ 26 Iron Fist .10 .30
❑ 27 Venom .10 .30
❑ 28 Rogue .10 .30
Iceman
❑ 29 Crystal .10 .30
Cyclops/Psylocke
❑ 30 Exodus .10 .30
Black Night
❑ 31 U.S. Agent .10 .30
❑ 32 Gambit .10 .30
Professor X
❑ 33 Beast .10 .30
❑ 34 Sersi .10 .30
Captain America
❑ 35 Quicksilver .10 .30
Fabian Cortez
❑ 36 War Machine .10 .30
❑ 37 Sister Nil .10 .30
❑ 38 Strange .10 .30
❑ 39 Victoria Montesi .10 .30
❑ 40 Morbius .10 .30
❑ 41 Dr. Strange .10 .30
❑ 42 Ghost Rider .10 .30
❑ 43 Blade .10 .30
❑ 44 Blaze .10 .30
❑ 45 Vengeance .10 .30
❑ 46 Hitman .10 .30
❑ 47 Desmond Kline .10 .30
❑ 48 Punisher .10 .30
❑ 49 Rapido .10 .30
❑ 50 Payback .10 .30
❑ 51 Outlaw .10 .30
❑ 52 Lynn Michaels .10 .30
❑ 53 V.I.G.I.L. .10 .30
❑ 54 Yuppunisher .10 .30
❑ 55 Dr. Strange .10 .30
❑ 56 Moondragon .10 .30
❑ 57 Maxam .10 .30
Pip the Troll
❑ 58 Silver Surfer .10 .30
❑ 59 Thor .10 .30
❑ 60 Warlock .10 .30
❑ 61 Thanos .10 .30
❑ 62 Gamora .10 .30
❑ 63 Drax .10 .30
❑ 64 Venom .10 .30
❑ 65 Siege .10 .30
❑ 66 Morbius .10 .30
❑ 67 Crippler .10 .30
Silver Sable
❑ 68 Snakeroot .10 .30
❑ 69 Erynys .10 .30
John Garrett
❑ 70 Hellspawn .10 .30
❑ 71 Elektra .10 .30
Daredevil
❑ 72 Stone .10 .30
Eddit Passim
❑ 73 Rage .10 .30
Firestar
❑ 74 Nova .10 .30
❑ 75 Iron Man .10 .30
Hulkbuster
❑ 76 Thunderstrike .10 .30
❑ 77 Venom .10 .30
❑ 78 Hulk .10 .30
❑ 79 Speedball .10 .30
Night Thrasher
❑ 80 Iron Man .10 .30
❑ 81 Deathlok .10 .30
❑ 82 Spider-Man 2099 .10 .30
❑ 83 Thor 2099 .10 .30
❑ 84 Ravage 2099 .10 .30
❑ 85 Bloodhawk .10 .30
Krystalin/Meanstreak
❑ 86 Heimdall 2099 .10 .30
❑ 87 Punisher 2099 .10 .30
❑ 88 Loki 2099 .10 .30
❑ 89 Doom 2099 .10 .30
❑ 90 Hela 2099 .10 .30
❑ 91 Banshee .10 .30
❑ 92 Beast .10 .30
❑ 93 Bishop .10 .30
❑ 94 Cable .10 .30
❑ 95 Chamber .10 .30
❑ 96 Colossus .10 .30
❑ 97 Cyclops .10 .30
❑ 98 Deadpool .10 .30
❑ 99 Exodus .10 .30
❑ 100 Gambit .10 .30
❑ 101 Gamesmaster .10 .30
❑ 102 Haven .10 .30
❑ 103 Husk .10 .30
❑ 104 Jubilee .10 .30
❑ 105 Juggernaut .10 .30
❑ 106 M .10 .30
❑ 107 Mondo .10 .30
❑ 108 Mystique .10 .30
❑ 109 Penance .10 .30
❑ 110 Phoenix .10 .30
❑ 111 Polaris .10 .30
❑ 112 Psylocke .10 .30
❑ 113 Random .10 .30
❑ 114 Rogue .10 .30
❑ 115 Sabretooth .10 .30
❑ 116 Shadowcat .10 .30
❑ 117 Shatterstar .10 .30
❑ 118 Siena Blaze .10 .30
❑ 119 Skin .10 .30
❑ 120 Storm .10 .30
❑ 121 Synch .10 .30
❑ 122 Warpath .10 .30
❑ 123 White Queen .10 .30
❑ 124 Wolverine .10 .30
❑ 125 Carnage .10 .30
❑ 126 Chameleon .10 .30
❑ 127 Hobgoblin .10 .30
❑ 128 Nightwatch .10 .30
❑ 129 Solo .10 .30
❑ 130 Spider-Man .10 .30
❑ 131 Venom .10 .30
❑ 132 Vulture .10 .30
❑ 133 Warrant .10 .30
❑ 134 Punisher .10 .30
❑ 135 Blade .10 .30
❑ 136 Blaze .10 .30
❑ 137 Ghost Rider .10 .30
❑ 138 Morbius .10 .30
❑ 139 Salome .10 .30
❑ 140 Strange .10 .30
❑ 141 Vengeance .10 .30
❑ 142 Zarathos .10 .30
❑ 143 Black Knight .10 .30
❑ 144 Black Widow .10 .30
❑ 145 Captain America .10 .30
❑ 146 Crystal .10 .30
❑ 147 Giant-Man .10 .30
❑ 148 Hawkeye .10 .30
❑ 149 Quicksilver .10 .30
❑ 150 Thor .10 .30
❑ 151 Thunderstrike .10 .30
❑ 152 Vision .10 .30
❑ 153 Legacy .10 .30
❑ 154 Morg .10 .30
❑ 155 Silver Surfer .10 .30
❑ 156 Terrax .10 .30
❑ 157 Thanos .10 .30
❑ 158 Tyrant .10 .30
❑ 159 Warlock .10 .30
❑ 160 Century .10 .30
❑ 161 Iron Man .10 .30
❑ 162 Scarlet Witch .10 .30
❑ 163 U.S. Agent .10 .30
❑ 164 War Machine .10 .30
❑ 165 Darkhawk .10 .30
❑ 166 Justice .10 .30
❑ 167 Kymaera .10 .30
❑ 168 Night Thrasher .10 .30
❑ 169 Nova .10 .30
❑ 170 Sphinx .10 .30
❑ 171 Bloodhawk .10 .30
❑ 172 Brimstone Love .10 .30
❑ 173 Cerebra .10 .30
❑ 174 Doom 2099 .10 .30
❑ 175 Ghost Rider 2099 .10 .30
❑ 176 Hulk 2099 .10 .30
❑ 177 Junkpile .10 .30
❑ 178 Krystalin .10 .30
❑ 179 Meanstreak .10 .30
❑ 180 Metalhead .10 .30
❑ 181 Punisher 2099 .10 .30
❑ 182 Ravage 2099 .10 .30
❑ 183 Skullfire .10 .30
❑ 184 Spider-Man 2099 .10 .30
❑ 185 Xi'an .10 .30
❑ 186 Abomination .10 .30
❑ 187 Blackwulf .10 .30
❑ 188 Daredevil .10 .30
❑ 189 Elektra .10 .30
❑ 190 Hulk .10 .30
❑ 191 Human Torch .10 .30
❑ 192 Invisible Woman .10 .30
❑ 193 Lyja .10 .30
❑ 194 Namor .10 .30
❑ 195 Psi-Lord .10 .30
❑ 196 Silver Sable .10 .30
❑ 197 Thing .10 .30
❑ 198 Trauma .10 .30
❑ 199 Typhoid Mary .10 .30
❑ 200 Checklist .10 .30

1994 Marvel Universe Holograms

COMPLETE SET (4) 25.00 50.00
❑ 1 Spider-Man 6.00 15.00
❑ 2 Wolverine 6.00 15.00
❑ 3 War Machine 6.00 15.00
❑ 4 Silver Surfer 6.00 15.00

1994 Marvel Universe Power Blast Rainbow

COMPLETE SET (9) 10.00 25.00
❑ 1 Carnage 1.25 3.00
❑ 2 Punisher 1.25 3.00
❑ 3 Ghost Rider 1.25 3.00
❑ 4 Gambit 1.25 3.00
❑ 5 Hulk 1.25 3.00
❑ 6 Spider-Man 1.25 3.00
❑ 7 Iron Man 1.25 3.00
❑ 8 Cyclops 1.25 3.00
❑ 9 Thing 1.25 3.00

1994 Marvel Universe Power Blast Gold

COMPLETE SET (9) 12.00 30.00
❑ 1 Carnage 1.50 4.00
❑ 2 Punisher 1.50 4.00
❑ 3 Ghost Rider 1.50 4.00
❑ 4 Gambit 1.50 4.00
❑ 5 Hulk 1.50 4.00
❑ 6 Spider-Man 1.50 4.00
❑ 7 Iron Man 1.50 4.00
❑ 8 Cyclops 1.50 4.00
❑ 9 Thing 1.50 4.00

1994 Marvel Universe Power Blast Silver

COMPLETE SET (9) 10.00 25.00
❑ 1 Carnage 1.25 3.00
❑ 2 Punisher 1.25 3.00
❑ 3 Ghost Rider 1.25 3.00
❑ 4 Gambit 1.25 3.00
❑ 5 Hulk 1.25 3.00
❑ 6 Spider-Man 1.25 3.00
❑ 7 Iron Man 1.25 3.00
❑ 8 Cyclops 1.25 3.00
❑ 9 Thing 1.25 3.00

1994 Marvel Universe Suspended Animation

COMPLETE SET (10) 12.00 30.00
❑ 1 Gambit 1.50 4.00
❑ 2 Human Torch 1.50 4.00
❑ 3 Invisible Woman 1.50 4.00
❑ 4 Iron Man 1.50 4.00
❑ 5 Silver Surfer 1.50 4.00
❑ 6 Spider-Man 1.50 4.00
❑ 7 Thing 1.50 4.00
❑ 8 Venom 1.50 4.00
❑ 9 War Machine 1.50 4.00
❑ 10 Wolverine 1.50 4.00

1994 Marvel Universe Suspended Animation Jumbo

COMPLETE SET (6) 12.00 30.00
❑ 1 Gambit 2.50 6.00
❑ 2 Iron Man 2.50 6.00
❑ 3 Spider-Man 2.50 6.00
❑ 4 Thing 2.50 6.00
❑ 5 Venom 2.50 6.00
❑ 6 Wolverine 2.50 6.00

1995 Batman Forever (Fleer)

COMPLETE SET (120) 5.00 12.00
❑ 1 Batman .12 .30
❑ 2 Bruce Wayne .12 .30
❑ 3 Man Behind The Mask .12 .30
❑ 4 Scaling New Heights .12 .30
❑ 5 Gotham's Defender .12 .30
❑ 6 Criminals Beware .12 .30
❑ 7 Robin .12 .30
❑ 8 Dick Grayson .12 .30
❑ 9 Solid Ally .12 .30
❑ 10 Striking Back .12 .30
❑ 11 Ready For Duty .12 .30
❑ 12 Poised To Strike .12 .30
❑ 13 Two-Face .12 .30
❑ 14 Harvey Dent .12 .30
❑ 15 Double Trouble .12 .30
❑ 16 Trust Me .12 .30
❑ 17 Escape Artist .12 .30
❑ 18 The Riddler .12 .30
❑ 19 Edward Nygma .12 .30
❑ 20 Brilliant Madman .12 .30
❑ 21 Take Your Chances .12 .30
❑ 22 Mad For Revenge .12 .30
❑ 23 Insane Partners .12 .30
❑ 24 Chase Meridian .12 .30
❑ 25 Thrill Of the chase .12 .30
❑ 26 Right-Hand Man .12 .30
❑ 27 Commissioner Gordon .12 .30
❑ 28 Sugar .12 .30
❑ 29 Sugar And Spice .12 .30
❑ 30 Triple Threat .12 .30
❑ 31 Criminal At Large .12 .30
❑ 32 You're My Idol .12 .30
❑ 33 Nygma's Brainchild .12 .30
❑ 34 Rejection .12 .30
❑ 35 Lair Of The Bat .12 .30
❑ 36 Aiming To Kill .12 .30
❑ 37 A Bat Trap .12 .30
❑ 38 The Law Arrives .12 .30
❑ 39 Instant Attraction .12 .30
❑ 40 Burn, Batty, Burn .12 .30
❑ 41 Serving Justice .12 .30
❑ 42 Hitching A Ride .12 .30
❑ 43 Two-Face Splits .12 .30
❑ 44 Deadly Demonstration .12 .30
❑ 45 Brain Drain .12 .30
❑ 46 Doomed To Die .12 .30
❑ 47 Dream Terror .12 .30
❑ 48 Edward Resigns .12 .30
❑ 49 Dead Man's Farewell .12 .30
❑ 50 Puzzling It Out .12 .30
❑ 51 Off The Deep End .12 .30
❑ 52 A Trip To The Doctor .12 .30
❑ 53 A Case For Chase .12 .30
❑ 54 The Flying Graysons .12 .30
❑ 55 Star Performer .12 .30
❑ 56 Where Is Batman .12 .30
❑ 57 Center Stage .12 .30
❑ 58 Bruce Makes An Offer .12 .30
❑ 59 Thinking It Over .12 .30
❑ 60 Headline Tragedy .12 .30
❑ 61 Clear Signals .12 .30
❑ 62 Man And Machine .12 .30
❑ 63 Engine Of Vengeance .12 .30
❑ 64 Sweet Temptation .12 .30
❑ 65 Spice Of Life .12 .30
❑ 66 Guess Who .12 .30
❑ 67 Brain Blast .12 .30
❑ 68 Home Sweet Hideout .12 .30
❑ 69 What A Rush .12 .30
❑ 70 The Riddler Debuts .12 .30
❑ 71 Jackpot .12 .30
❑ 72 Boxing Lesson .12 .30
❑ 73 Victorious .12 .30
❑ 74 Sneaking A Peek .12 .30
❑ 75 Plagued By The Past .12 .30
❑ 76 Nygma Goes Public .12 .30
❑ 77 Right Of Passage .12 .30
❑ 78 Food For Thought .12 .30
❑ 79 Examination .12 .30
❑ 80 An Opportune Moment .12 .30
❑ 81 Cave Of Wonders .12 .30
❑ 82 Mystery Man .12 .30
❑ 83 Freak Attack .12 .30
❑ 84 Stealing A Kiss .12 .30
❑ 85 Birds Of A Feather .12 .30
❑ 86 Grand Entrance .12 .30
❑ 87 Success At Last .12 .30
❑ 88 Making The Scene .12 .30
❑ 89 Toast To A Twosome .12 .30
❑ 90 Crashing The Party .12 .30
❑ 91 Double Whammy .12 .30
❑ 92 Ready, Aim, Blast .12 .30
❑ 93 In Too Deep .12 .30
❑ 94 A Helping Hand .12 .30
❑ 95 Aftermath .12 .30
❑ 96 Man Of Shadow .12 .30
❑ 97 Bad News .12 .30
❑ 98 Double-Cross .12 .30
❑ 99 Mind Over Madness .12 .30
❑ 100 Deadly Duo .12 .30
❑ 101 No Simple Man .12 .30
❑ 102 Joy Of Crooking .12 .30
❑ 103 Bye-Bye Batcave .12 .30
❑ 104 Gleeful Destruction .12 .30
❑ 105 Clean-Up Crew .12 .30
❑ 106 Nighty-Night, Chase .12 .30
❑ 107 Facing The Fear .12 .30
❑ 108 New And Improved .12 .30
❑ 109 Robin Takes Flight .12 .30
❑ 110 Coming To Terms .12 .30
❑ 111 Partners .12 .30
❑ 112 To the Rescue .12 .30
❑ 113 Alone No More .12 .30
❑ 114 Hit And Miss .12 .30
❑ 115 Ready To Pounce .12 .30
❑ 116 Robin Under Glass .12 .30
❑ 117 Too Far Gone .12 .30
❑ 118 The Last Laugh .12 .30
❑ 119 Legends Forever .12 .30
❑ 120 Checklist .12 .30

1995 Batman Forever (Ultra)

COMPLETE SET (120) 6.00 15.00
❑ 1 Batman .12 .30
❑ 2 Bruce Wayne .12 .30
❑ 3 Man Behind The Mask .12 .30
❑ 4 Scaling New Heights .12 .30
❑ 5 Gotham's Defender .12 .30
❑ 6 Criminals Beware .12 .30
❑ 7 Robin .12 .30
❑ 8 Dick Grayson .12 .30
❑ 9 Solid Ally .12 .30
❑ 10 Striking Back .12 .30
❑ 11 Ready For Duty .12 .30
❑ 12 Poised To Strike .12 .30
❑ 13 Two-Face .12 .30
❑ 14 Harvey Dent .12 .30
❑ 15 Double Trouble .12 .30
❑ 16 Trust Me .12 .30
❑ 17 Escape Artist .12 .30
❑ 18 The Riddler .12 .30
❑ 19 Edward Nygma .12 .30
❑ 20 Brilliant Madman .12 .30
❑ 21 Take Your Chances .12 .30
❑ 22 Mad For Revenge .12 .30
❑ 23 Insane Partners .12 .30
❑ 24 Chase Meridian .12 .30
❑ 25 Thrill Of the chase .12 .30
❑ 26 Right-Hand Man .12 .30
❑ 27 Commissioner Gordon .12 .30
❑ 28 Sugar .12 .30
❑ 29 Sugar And Spice .12 .30
❑ 30 Triple Threat .12 .30
❑ 31 Criminal At Large .12 .30
❑ 32 You're My Idol .12 .30
❑ 33 Nygma's Brainchild .12 .30
❑ 34 Rejection .12 .30
❑ 35 Lair Of The Bat .12 .30
❑ 36 Aiming To Kill .12 .30
❑ 37 A Bat Trap .12 .30
❑ 38 The Law Arrives .12 .30
❑ 39 Instant Attraction .12 .30
❑ 40 Burn, Batty, Burn .12 .30
❑ 41 Serving Justice .12 .30
❑ 42 Hitching A Ride .12 .30
❑ 43 Two-Face Splits .12 .30
❑ 44 Deadly Demonstration .12 .30
❑ 45 Brain Drain .12 .30
❑ 46 Doomed To Die .12 .30
❑ 47 Dream Terror .12 .30
❑ 48 Edward Resigns .12 .30
❑ 49 Dead Man's Farewell .12 .30
❑ 50 Puzzling It Out .12 .30
❑ 51 Off The Deep End .12 .30
❑ 52 A Trip To The Doctor .12 .30
❑ 53 A Case For Chase .12 .30
❑ 54 The Flying Graysons .12 .30
❑ 55 Star Performer .12 .30
❑ 56 Where Is Batman .12 .30
❑ 57 Center Stage .12 .30
❑ 58 Bruce Makes An Offer .12 .30
❑ 59 Thinking It Over .12 .30
❑ 60 Headline Tragedy .12 .30
❑ 61 Clear Signals .12 .30
❑ 62 Man And Machine .12 .30
❑ 63 Engine Of Vengeance .12 .30
❑ 64 Sweet Temptation .12 .30
❑ 65 Spice Of Life .12 .30
❑ 66 Guess Who .12 .30
❑ 67 Brain Blast .12 .30
❑ 68 Home Sweet Hideout .12 .30
❑ 69 What A Rush .12 .30
❑ 70 The Riddler Debuts .12 .30
❑ 71 Jackpot .12 .30
❑ 72 Boxing Lesson .12 .30
❑ 73 Victorious .12 .30
❑ 74 Sneaking A Peek .12 .30
❑ 75 Plagued By The Past .12 .30
❑ 76 Nygma Goes Public .12 .30
❑ 77 Right Of Passage .12 .30
❑ 78 Food For Thought .12 .30
❑ 79 Examination .12 .30
❑ 80 An Opportune Moment .12 .30
❑ 81 Cave Of Wonders .12 .30
❑ 82 Mystery Man .12 .30
❑ 83 Freak Attack .12 .30
❑ 84 Stealing A Kiss .12 .30
❑ 85 Birds Of A Feather .12 .30
❑ 86 Grand Entrance .12 .30
❑ 87 Success At Last .12 .30
❑ 88 Making The Scene .12 .30
❑ 89 Toast To A Twosome .12 .30
❑ 90 Crashing The Party .12 .30
❑ 91 Double Whammy .12 .30
❑ 92 Ready, Aim, Blast .12 .30
❑ 93 In Too Deep .12 .30
❑ 94 A Helping Hand .12 .30
❑ 95 Aftermath .12 .30
❑ 96 Man Of Shadow .12 .30
❑ 97 Bad News .12 .30
❑ 98 Double-Cross .12 .30
❑ 99 Mind Over Madness .12 .30
❑ 100 Deadly Duo .12 .30
❑ 101 No Simple Man .12 .30
❑ 102 Joy Of Crooking .12 .30
❑ 103 Bye-Bye Batcave .12 .30
❑ 104 Gleeful Destruction .12 .30
❑ 105 Clean-Up Crew .12 .30
❑ 106 Nighty-Night, Chase .12 .30
❑ 107 Facing The Fear .12 .30
❑ 108 New And Improved .12 .30
❑ 109 Robin Takes Flight .12 .30
❑ 110 Coming To Terms .12 .30
❑ 111 Partners .12 .30
❑ 112 To the Rescue .12 .30
❑ 113 Alone No More .12 .30
❑ 114 Hit And Miss .12 .30
❑ 115 Ready To Pounce .12 .30
❑ 116 Robin Under Glass .12 .30
❑ 117 Too Far Gone .12 .30
❑ 118 The Last Laugh .12 .30
❑ 119 Legends Forever .12 .30
❑ 120 Checklist .12 .30
❑ A1 Batman PROMO

1995 Batman Forever Acclaim Video Game Tips (Ultra)

COMPLETE SET (2) 1.00 2.50
STATED ODDS 1:18
❑ G1 Somewhere Hidden .75 2.00
❑ G2 Robin Needs to Eliminate .75 2.00

1995 Batman Forever Animaction (Ultra)

COMPLETE SET (10) 5.00 12.00
STATED ODDS 1:4
❑ 1 Batman 1.00 2.50
❑ 2 Sugar/Two-Face/Spice 1.00 2.50
❑ 3 The Riddler 1.00 2.50
❑ 4 Robin 1.00 2.50
❑ 5 Dr. Chase Meridian 1.00 2.50
❑ 6 Batman and Robin 1.00 2.50
❑ 7 Edward Nygma 1.00 2.50
❑ 8 The Riddler 1.00 2.50
❑ 9 Batman 1.00 2.50
❑ 10 Two-Face and The Riddler 1.00 2.50

1995 Batman Forever Holograms (Ultra)

COMPLETE SET (36) 5.00 12.00
STATED ODDS ONE PER PACK
❑ 1 Eyes of the Law .30 .75
❑ 2 Double Features .30 .75
❑ 3 Ed Nygma .30 .75
❑ 4 The Riddler .30 .75
❑ 5 Dr. Chase Meridian .30 .75
❑ 6 Robin .30 .75
❑ 7 Sugar .30 .75
❑ 8 Fists of Fury .30 .75
❑ 9 Towers of Power .30 .75
❑ 10 Ooo... Good One .30 .75
❑ 11 Batman .30 .75
❑ 12 Commissioner Gordon .30 .75
❑ 13 Mad Scientist .30 .75
❑ 14 Success at Last .30 .75
❑ 15 Million Dollar Smile .30 .75
❑ 16 In Your Two-Face .30 .75
❑ 17 Two-Timing .30 .75
❑ 18 Partners .30 .75
❑ 19 Clogged Brain Drain .30 .75
❑ 20 The Caped Crusader .30 .75
❑ 21 Criminal Genius .30 .75
❑ 22 The Doctor is In .30 .75
❑ 23 A Double Take .30 .75
❑ 24 The Boy Wonder .30 .75
❑ 25 Introducing the Future .30 .75
❑ 26 Dress to Thrill .30 .75
❑ 27 Sugar and Spice .30 .75
❑ 28 Everything Nice .30 .75
❑ 29 Cheap Haircut .30 .75
❑ 30 Lending a Hand .30 .75
❑ 31 Built for Speed .30 .75
❑ 32 I Said, Limbo .30 .75
❑ 33 Up To No Good .30 .75
❑ 34 Pearl Pilfering .30 .75
❑ 35 Power Trip .30 .75
❑ 36 I Am Batmaaan .30 .75

1995 Batman Forever Metal

COMPLETE SET (100) 8.00 20.00
A1 STATED ODDS 1:18
❑ 1 Batman .20 .50
❑ 2 Commissioner Gordon .20 .50
❑ 3 Breakdown .20 .50
❑ 4 Back-Up .20 .50
❑ 5 By Hook or Crook .20 .50
❑ 6 Making Up His Minds .20 .50
❑ 7 Unconventional Cure .20 .50
❑ 8 Swinging into Action .20 .50
❑ 9 Justice on the Wing .20 .50
❑ 10 Edward Nygma .20 .50
❑ 11 True Genius .20 .50
❑ 12 Power Play .20 .50
❑ 13 Batboat .20 .50
❑ 14 Riddle Me This .20 .50
❑ 15 Surprise Package .20 .50
❑ 16 A Question of Power .20 .50

❑ 17 Brain Power .20 .50
❑ 18 Full Loon Rising .20 .50
❑ 19 New Math .20 .50
❑ 20 Common Ground .20 .50
❑ 21 Cat and Mouse .20 .50
❑ 22 High and Mighty .20 .50
❑ 23 First Strike .20 .50
❑ 24 Playing the Game .20 .50
❑ 25 Don't Look Now .20 .50
❑ 26 Knock Out .20 .50
❑ 27 Classified Information .20 .50
❑ 28 Cave Dweller .20 .50
❑ 29 Alfred Pennyworth .20 .50
❑ 30 Forever Marked .20 .50
❑ 31 Perfect Fit .20 .50
❑ 32 Controlled Fury .20 .50
❑ 33 Pole Position .20 .50
❑ 34 Guardian .20 .50
❑ 35 The Dark Night .20 .50
❑ 36 Arsenal .20 .50
❑ 37 Fly By Night .20 .50
❑ 38 Night Watch .20 .50
❑ 39 Against the Wall .20 .50
❑ 40 Grappling for Justice .20 .50
❑ 41 Built for Speed .20 .50
❑ 42 Sentinel .20 .50
❑ 43 Fugitive .20 .50
❑ 44 Which Came First .20 .50
❑ 45 Pushing the Limits .20 .50
❑ 46 Double or Nothing .20 .50
❑ 47 Double Burden .20 .50
❑ 48 Friendship's Price .20 .50
❑ 49 Power Struggle .20 .50
❑ 50 Night's Ally .20 .50
❑ 51 Split Personality .20 .50
❑ 52 Chase Meridian .20 .50
❑ 53 Double Jeopardy .20 .50
❑ 54 Joke's on You .20 .50
❑ 55 A Moth to a Flame .20 .50
❑ 56 Two-Time Loser .20 .50
❑ 57 Plotting to Split .20 .50
❑ 58 Escape .20 .50
❑ 59 Body Double .20 .50
❑ 60 Parting Shot .20 .50
❑ 61 Man in the Mirror .20 .50
❑ 62 Double Kings .20 .50
❑ 63 Doubles .20 .50
❑ 64 Moving Target .20 .50
❑ 65 Armed and Dangerous .20 .50
❑ 66 Sure Footing .20 .50
❑ 67 Robin .20 .50
❑ 68 Starting Again .20 .50
❑ 69 Hunting .20 .50
❑ 70 Teamwork .20 .50
❑ 71 Grace Under Pressure .20 .50
❑ 72 Trap Shooting .20 .50
❑ 73 Up In Smoke .20 .50
❑ 74 City Escape .20 .50
❑ 75 Beneath the Surface .20 .50
❑ 76 Partnership .20 .50
❑ 77 Look Out, Riddler .20 .50
❑ 78 From Shadows Above .20 .50
❑ 79 Need a Lift .20 .50
❑ 80 Dangerous Heights .20 .50
❑ 81 Creatures of the Night .20 .50
❑ 82 Head's Up .20 .50
❑ 83 Eyes in the Night .20 .50
❑ 84 Strategy .20 .50
❑ 85 Target Ahead .20 .50
❑ 86 Perfect 10 .20 .50
❑ 87 Stand-Off .20 .50
❑ 88 Fun's Over! .20 .50
❑ 89 Red Alert .20 .50
❑ 90 A Closer Look .20 .50
❑ 91 Gotham's Best .20 .50
❑ 92 Fearless .20 .50
❑ 93 Over the Edge .20 .50
❑ 94 On the Prowl .20 .50
❑ 95 Defenders .20 .50
❑ 96 Two of a Kind .20 .50
❑ 97 Code Red .20 .50
❑ 98 Urban Legends .20 .50
❑ 99 Look Out Below .20 .50
❑ 100 Checklist .20 .50
❑ A1 Video Game Preview 1.00 2.50

1995 Batman Forever Metal Silver Flasher
COMPLETE SET 15.00 40.00
STATED ODDS ONE PER PACK

1995 Batman Forever Metal Gold Blaster
COMPLETE SET (10) 5.00 12.00
STATED ODDS 1:3

❑ 1 Batman 1.00 2.50
❑ 2 Robin 1.00 2.50
❑ 3 Batman and Robin 1.00 2.50
❑ 4 The Riddler 1.00 2.50
❑ 5 Two-Face 1.00 2.50
❑ 6 The Dark Knight 1.00 2.50
❑ 7 Robin 1.00 2.50
❑ 8 Batman and Robin 1.00 2.50
❑ 9 The Riddler 1.00 2.50
❑ 10 Two-Face 1.00 2.50

1995 Batman Forever Metal Holograms
COMPLETE SET (4) 8.00 20.00
STATED ODDS 1:18

❑ H1 Batman 4.00 10.00
❑ H2 Two-Face 4.00 10.00
❑ H3 The Riddler 4.00 10.00
❑ H4 Robin 4.00 10.00

1995 Batman Forever Metal Movie Preview
COMPLETE SET (8) 5.00 12.00
STATED ODDS 1:6

❑ 1 Batman 1.25 3.00
❑ 2 Two-Face 1.25 3.00
❑ 3 Edward Nygma 1.25 3.00
❑ 4 The Riddler 1.25 3.00
❑ 5 Behold The Riddler 1.25 3.00
❑ 6 Dr. Chase Meridian 1.25 3.00
❑ 7 Robin 1.25 3.00
❑ 8 Sugar 1.25 3.00

1995 Batman Master Series
COMPLETE SET (90) 8.00 20.00

❑ 1 Gotham .20 .50
❑ 2 Arkham Asylum for the Criminally Insane .20 .50
❑ 3 Bulletin .20 .50
❑ 4 Pier 13 .20 .50
❑ 5 Stacked Deck .20 .50
❑ 6 Ghost of a Ghost .20 .50
❑ 7 He was Real! .20 .50
❑ 8 Death of a Dark Legend .20 .50
❑ 9 I Did It! .20 .50
❑ 10 Headquarters .20 .50
❑ 11 The Log of Commissioner Gordon .20 .50
❑ 12 Sgt. Harvey Bullock .20 .50
❑ 13 Officer Renee Montoya .20 .50
❑ 14 Lietenant Lawrence Kitch .20 .50
❑ 15 Sgt. Mackenzie Hardback Bock .20 .50
❑ 16 Friends .20 .50
❑ 17 Lt. Sarah Gordon .20 .50
❑ 18 Deathtrap .20 .50
❑ 19 Wayne Manor .20 .50
❑ 20 The Journal of Alfred Pennyworth .20 .50
❑ 21 Destiny .20 .50
❑ 22 Inspiration .20 .50
❑ 23 Year One .20 .50
❑ 24 Killing Joke .20 .50
❑ 25 Secret Passage .20 .50
❑ 26 The Cave .20 .50
❑ 27 Target Practice .20 .50
❑ 28 Three Robins .20 .50
❑ 29 Dick Grayson .20 .50
❑ 30 Jason Todd .20 .50
❑ 31 Death in the Family .20 .50
❑ 32 Tim Drake .20 .50
❑ 33 Wild Joker .20 .50
❑ 34 Suspects .20 .50
❑ 35 More than Trophies .20 .50
❑ 36 Laughing Batty .20 .50
❑ 37 Catwoman .20 .50
❑ 38 Black Mask .20 .50
❑ 39 Lady Shiva .20 .50
❑ 40 Ras al Ghul .20 .50
❑ 41 Talia .20 .50
❑ 42 The Penguin .20 .50
❑ 43 Poison Ivy .20 .50
❑ 44 The Riddler .20 .50
❑ 45 Solitary Madness .20 .50
❑ 46 Hard Copy .20 .50
❑ 47 Bane .20 .50
❑ 48 Mad Hatter .20 .50
❑ 49 Two Face .20 .50
❑ 50 Killer Croc .20 .50
❑ 51 Man-Bat .20 .50
❑ 52 Scarecrow .20 .50
❑ 53 Red-Handed .20 .50
❑ 54 Clown Prince of Crime Detection .20 .50
❑ 55 Kitty Killer .20 .50
❑ 56 Masks of Black .20 .50
❑ 57 Double-Mug .20 .50
❑ 58 Did the Demon Do It .20 .50
❑ 59 Gone with the Demon's Daughter .20 .50
❑ 60 Birdbrained Bumbershooter .20 .50
❑ 61 An Itch Too Far .20 .50
❑ 62 The Question Is .20 .50
❑ 63 Sherlock Jokes Strikes Out .20 .50
❑ 64 Dark Angel .20 .50
❑ 65 Crocodile Tears .20 .50
❑ 66 By Zeus! .20 .50
❑ 67 Pulling Strings .20 .50
❑ 68 Tweedledee and Dumber .20 .50
❑ 69 Strange Analysis .20 .50
❑ 70 Master of Fear .20 .50
❑ 71 Keeping Scar .20 .50
❑ 72 Worlds of Madness .20 .50
❑ 73 Uncivil War .20 .50
❑ 74 Jack's Whack .20 .50
❑ 75 Sacred Scare .20 .50
❑ 76 Whodunit Houdini .20 .50
❑ 77 Past Master of the Future .20 .50
❑ 78 Blunder Gods .20 .50
❑ 79 It's Dead! .20 .50
❑ 80 Teething .20 .50
❑ 81 Secret Ceremony .20 .50
❑ 82 Digging Batty .20 .50
❑ 83 Unrest in Peace .20 .50
❑ 84 Shadow of the Bat .20 .50
❑ 85 The Bat Is Dead, Long Live the Bat .20 .50
❑ 86 Snapped Trap .20 .50
❑ 87 Accomplices .20 .50
❑ 88 Back to Arkham .20 .50
❑ 89 Creature of the Night .20 .50
❑ 90 Checklist .20 .50

1995 Batman Master Series Artist's Proof
COMPLETE SET 20.00 50.00
STATED ODDS ONE PER PACK

1995 Batman Master Series Chromium
COMPLETE SET (2) 6.00 15.00
STATED ODDS 1:24

❑ 1 Batman 4.00 10.00
❑ 2 The Joker 4.00 10.00

1995 Batman Master Series Clearchrome
COMPLETE SET (2) 20.00 40.00
STATED ODDS 1:120

❑ 1 Batman 10.00 25.00
❑ 2 The Joker 10.00 25.00

1995 Batman Master Series Master Villains
COMPLETE SET (10) 10.00 25.00
STATED ODDS 1:10

❑ 1 Black Mask 2.00 5.00
❑ 2 Two-Face 2.00 5.00
❑ 3 Catwoman 2.00 5.00
❑ 4 The Riddler 2.00 5.00
❑ 5 The Penguin 2.00 5.00
❑ 6 Poison Ivy 2.00 5.00
❑ 7 Ras al Ghul 2.00 5.00
❑ 8 Scarecrow 2.00 5.00
❑ 9 Bane 2.00 5.00
❑ 10 The Joker 2.00 5.00

1995 Batman Master Series Spectra Etch
COMPLETE SET (6) 5.00 12.00
STATED ODDS 1:6

❑ 1 Batman 1.25 3.00
Ken Kelly
❑ 2 Batman 1.25 3.00
Vincent DiFate
❑ 3 Batman 1.25 3.00
Joe DeVito
❑ 4 Batman 1.25 3.00
Romas
❑ 5 Batman 1.25 3.00
Nick Jainschigg
❑ 6 Batman 1.25 3.00
James Warhola

1995 DC Power Chrome Legends
COMPLETE SET (150) 8.00 20.00

❑ 1 Superman .15 .40
❑ 2 Wonder Woman .15 .40
❑ 3 The Power of Shazam .15 .40
❑ 4 Batman .15 .40
❑ 5 Hawkman .15 .40
❑ 6 Aquaman .15 .40
❑ 7 Green Arrow .15 .40
❑ 8 Flash .15 .40
❑ 9 Green Lantern .15 .40
❑ 10 Superman .15 .40
❑ 11 Metamorpho .15 .40
❑ 12 Crimson Fox .15 .40
❑ 13 Nuklon .15 .40
❑ 14 Fire .15 .40
❑ 15 Obsidian .15 .40
❑ 16 Ice Maiden .15 .40
❑ 17 Atom .15 .40
❑ 18 Power Girl .15 .40
❑ 19 Hawkwoman .15 .40
❑ 20 The Power of Shazam .15 .40
❑ 21 Superboy .15 .40
❑ 22 Supergirl .15 .40
❑ 23 Geo-Force .15 .40
❑ 24 Steel .15 .40
❑ 25 Wonder Woman .15 .40
❑ 26 Arsenal .15 .40
❑ 27 Donna Troy .15 .40
❑ 28 Mirage .15 .40
❑ 29 Terra .15 .40
❑ 30 Minion .15 .40
❑ 31 Bloodwynd .15 .40
❑ 32 Green Arrow .15 .40
❑ 33 Green Arrow II .15 .40
❑ 34 Mr. Miracle .15 .40
❑ 35 Artemis .15 .40
❑ 36 Fate .15 .40
❑ 37 Batman .15 .40
❑ 38 Robin .15 .40
❑ 39 Nightwing .15 .40
❑ 40 Huntress .15 .40
❑ 41 Black Canary .15 .40
❑ 42 Azrael .15 .40
❑ 43 Loose Cannon .15 .40
❑ 44 Guy Gardner, Warrior .15 .40
❑ 45 Lobo .15 .40
❑ 46 Demon .15 .40
❑ 47 Deathstroke .15 .40
❑ 48 Spectre .15 .40
❑ 49 Black Lightning .15 .40
❑ 50 Hawkman .15 .40
❑ 51 Martian Manhunter .15 .40
❑ 52 Triumph .15 .40
❑ 53 Despero .15 .40
❑ 54 Gypsy .15 .40
❑ 55 Ray .15 .40
❑ 56 Golden Age Ray .15 .40
❑ 57 Vril Dox .15 .40
❑ 58 Strata .15 .40
❑ 59 Phase .15 .40
❑ 60 Stealth .15 .40
❑ 61 Borb Borbb .15 .40
❑ 62 Telepath .15 .40
❑ 63 Garv .15 .40
❑ 64 Flash .15 .40
❑ 65 Captain Atom .15 .40
❑ 66 Booster Gold .15 .40
❑ 67 Blue Beetle .15 .40
❑ 68 Amazing Man .15 .40
❑ 69 Maxima .15 .40
❑ 70 Firestorm .15 .40
❑ 71 Max Mercury .15 .40
❑ 72 Impulse .15 .40
❑ 73 Jesse Quick .15 .40
❑ 74 Damage .15 .40
❑ 75 Iron Munro .15 .40
❑ 76 Wyldheart .15 .40
❑ 77 Manhunter .15 .40
❑ 78 Gunfire .15 .40
❑ 79 Argus .15 .40
❑ 80 Starman .15 .40
❑ 81 Anima .15 .40
❑ 82 Doomsday .15 .40
❑ 83 Lex Luthor .15 .40
❑ 84 The Cyborg .15 .40
❑ 85 Lord Satanus .15 .40
❑ 86 Brainiac .15 .40
❑ 87 Black Adam .15 .40
❑ 88 Blaze .15 .40
❑ 89 Bane .15 .40
❑ 90 Poison Ivy .15 .40
❑ 91 The Riddler .15 .40
❑ 92 The Joker .15 .40
❑ 93 Black Spider .15 .40
❑ 94 The Penguin .15 .40
❑ 95 Two-Face .15 .40
❑ 96 Wild Huntsman .15 .40
❑ 97 New Mist .15 .40
❑ 98 Man-Bat .15 .40
❑ 99 Cheetah .15 .40
❑ 100 White Magician .15 .40
❑ 101 Circe .15 .40
❑ 102 Death Masque .15 .40
❑ 103 Doctor Polaris .15 .40
❑ 104 Monarch .15 .40
❑ 105 Vandal Savage .15 .40
❑ 106 Count Viper .15 .40
❑ 107 Kobra .15 .40
❑ 108 Brimstone .15 .40
❑ 109 The Baron .15 .40
❑ 110 Lyrl Dox .15 .40
❑ 111 Darkseid .15 .40
❑ 112 Parallax .15 .40
❑ 113 Changeling .15 .40
❑ 114 Raven .15 .40
❑ 115 Catwoman .15 .40
❑ 116 Maitresse .15 .40
❑ 117 Ocean Master .15 .40
❑ 118 Aquaman .15 .40
❑ 119 Aqualab .15 .40
❑ 120 Dolphin .15 .40
❑ 121 Meridian .15 .40
❑ 122 Claw .15 .40
❑ 123 Black Condor .15 .40
❑ 124 Red Tornado .15 .40
❑ 125 Willpower .15 .40
❑ 126 Jack O'Lantern .15 .40
❑ 127 Golem .15 .40
❑ 128 Green Lantern .15 .40
❑ 129 Sentinel .15 .40
❑ 130 Ferrin Colos .15 .40
❑ 131 Cosmic Boy .15 .40
❑ 132 Saturn Girl .15 .40
❑ 133 Live Wire .15 .40
Spark
❑ 134 Shrinking Violet .15 .40
❑ 135 Brainiac 5 .15 .40
❑ 136 Chameleon .15 .40
❑ 137 XS .15 .40
❑ 138 Invisible Kid .15 .40
❑ 139 Ultra Boy .15 .40
❑ 140 Kinetix .15 .40
❑ 141 Leviathan .15 .40
❑ 142 Cascade .15 .40
❑ 143 Rampart .15 .40
❑ 144 Cruiser .15 .40
❑ 145 Network .15 .40
❑ 146 Reflex .15 .40
❑ 147 Indigo .15 .40
❑ 148 Finale .15 .40
❑ 149 Checklist A .15 .40
❑ 150 Checklist B .15 .40

1995 DC Power Chrome Legends Battlezone
COMPLETE SET (6) 8.00 20.00
STATED ODDS 1:11

❑ B1 Superman 2.00 5.00
The Cyborg
❑ B2 Batman 2.00 5.00
Gotham's Worst
❑ B3 Wonder Woman 2.00 5.00
Para-Demon
❑ B4 Flash 2.00 5.00
Razer
❑ B5 Green Lantern 2.00 5.00
Parallax
❑ B6 Aquaman 2.00 5.00
Thanatos

1995 DC Power Chrome Legends Hard Hitters
COMPLETE SET (18) 6.00 15.00
STATED ODDS 1:2

❑ H1 Superman .75 2.00
❑ H2 Batman .75 2.00
❑ H3 Wonder Woman .75 2.00
❑ H4 Green Lantern .75 2.00
❑ H5 Flash .75 2.00
❑ H6 Hawkman .75 2.00
❑ H7 Aquaman .75 2.00
❑ H8 Robin .75 2.00
❑ H9 Lobo .75 2.00
❑ H10 Superman .75 2.00
❑ H11 Batman .75 2.00
❑ H12 Wonder Woman .75 2.00
❑ H13 Green Lantern .75 2.00
❑ H14 Flash .75 2.00
❑ H15 Hawkman .75 2.00
❑ H16 Aquaman .75 2.00
❑ H17 Robin .75 2.00
❑ H18 Lobo .75 2.00

1995 DC Power Chrome Legends Legacy
COMPLETE SET (3) 12.00 30.00
STATED ODDS 1:36

❑ L1 Superman 6.00 15.00
❑ L2 Batman 6.00 15.00
❑ L3 Wonder Woman 6.00 15.00

1995 DC Versus Marvel
COMPLETE SET (100) 8.00 20.00

❑ 1 Superman .15 .40
Hulk
❑ 2 Captain America .15 .40
❑ 3 Elektra .15 .40
❑ 4 Hulk .15 .40
❑ 5 Jubilee .15 .40
❑ 6 Namor .15 .40
❑ 7 Quicksilver .15 .40
❑ 8 Sabretooth .15 .40
❑ 9 Silver Surfer .15 .40
❑ 10 Silver Surfer .15 .40
Green Lantern
❑ 11 Spider-Man .15 .40
❑ 12 Storm .15 .40
❑ 13 Thor .15 .40
❑ 14 Wolverine .15 .40
❑ 15 Aquaman .15 .40
❑ 16 Azrael .15 .40
❑ 17 Batman .15 .40
❑ 18 Captain Marvel .15 .40
❑ 19 Captain Marvel .15 .40
Thor
❑ 20 Catwoman .15 .40
❑ 21 Flash .15 .40
❑ 22 Green Lantern .15 .40
❑ 23 Lobo .15 .40
❑ 24 Robin .15 .40
❑ 25 Superboy .15 .40
❑ 26 Superman .15 .40
❑ 27 Wonder Woman .15 .40
❑ 28 Quicksilver .15 .40
Flash
❑ 29 Abomination .15 .40
❑ 30 Bullseye .15 .40
❑ 31 Doctor Doom .15 .40
❑ 32 Galactus .15 .40
❑ 33 Green Goblin .15 .40
❑ 34 Juggernaut .15 .40
❑ 35 Kingpin .15 .40
❑ 36 Lizard .15 .40
❑ 37 Wonder Woman .15 .40
Storm
❑ 38 Magneto .15 .40
❑ 39 Thanos .15 .40
❑ 40 Bane .15 .40
❑ 41 Black Adam .15 .40
❑ 42 Circe .15 .40
❑ 43 Darkseid .15 .40
❑ 44 Doctor Polaris .15 .40
❑ 45 The Joker .15 .40
❑ 46 Aquaman .15 .40
Namor
❑ 47 Kadabra .15 .40
❑ 48 Killer Croc .15 .40
❑ 49 Lex Luthor .15 .40
❑ 50 Penguin .15 .40
❑ 51 Archangel .15 .40
Hawkman
❑ 52 Azrael .15 .40
Sabretooth
❑ 53 Black Widow .15 .40
Black Canary
❑ 54 Blue Beetle .15 .40
Spider-Woman
❑ 55 Wolverine .15 .40
Lobo
❑ 56 Capt. Marvel .15 .40
Capt. Marvel
❑ 57 Cable .15 .40
Captain Atom
❑ 58 Deathstroke .15 .40
Punisher
❑ 59 Ghost Rider .15 .40
Demon
❑ 60 Nightwing .15 .40
Gambit
❑ 61 Human Torch .15 .40
Firestorm
❑ 62 Steel .15 .40
Iron Man
❑ 63 Hawkeye .15 .40
Green Arrow
❑ 64 Robin .15 .40
Jubilee
❑ 65 Venom .15 .40
Lobo
❑ 66 The Ray .15 .40
Nova
❑ 67 Thor .15 .40
Wonder Woman
❑ 68 Warrior .15 .40
War Machine
❑ 69 Captain America .15 .40
Bane
❑ 70 Batman .15 .40
Bullseye
❑ 71 Electro .15 .40
Black Lightning
❑ 72 Riddler .15 .40
Daredevil
❑ 73 Spider-Man .15 .40
Superboy
❑ 74 Green Lantern .15 .40
Green Goblin
❑ 75 Jigsaw .15 .40
Deathstroke
❑ 76 Killer Croc .15 .40
Hulk
❑ 77 Doctor Doom .15 .40
Capt. Marvel
❑ 78 The Joker .15 .40
Spider-Man
❑ 79 Galactus vs.Spectre .15 .40
❑ 80 Superman .15 .40
Juggernaut
❑ 81 Absorbing Man .15 .40
Steel
❑ 82 Catwoman .15 .40
Elektra
❑ 83 Thing .15 .40
Solomon Grundy
❑ 84 Killer Croc .15 .40
Abomination
❑ 85 Arcade .15 .40
Riddler
❑ 86 Black Adam .15 .40
Mandarin
❑ 87 Bullseye .15 .40
Deadshot
❑ 88 Poison Ivy vs.Black Cat .15 .40
❑ 89 Enchantress .15 .40
Circe
❑ 90 Dr. Polaris .15 .40
Magneto
❑ 91 Captain America .15 .40
Batman
❑ 92 Darkseid .15 .40
Thanos
❑ 93 Doctor Doom .15 .40
Cyborg
❑ 94 Two-Face .15 .40
Jigsaw
❑ 95 Green Goblin .15 .40
The Joker
❑ 96 Man-Bat .15 .40
Lizard
❑ 97 Kingpin .15 .40
Lex Luthor
❑ 98 Scarecrow .15 .40
Scarecrow
❑ 99 Mole Man .15 .40
Penguin
❑ 100 Checklist .15 .40

1995 DC Versus Marvel Amalgam Preview
COMPLETE SET (4) 1.00 2.50
STATED ODDS ONE PER PACK

❑ 1 Dark Claw .40 1.00
❑ 2 Spider-Boy .40 1.00
❑ 3 Dark Claw .40 1.00
❑ 4 Spider-Boy .40 1.00

1995 DC Versus Marvel Holo F/X
COMPLETE SET (12) 10.00 25.00
STATED ODDS 1:8

❑ 1 Sabretooth 1.50 4.00
Azrael
❑ 2 Aquaman 1.50 4.00
Namor
❑ 3 Captain America 1.50 4.00
Batman
❑ 4 Catwoman 1.50 4.00
Elektra
❑ 5 Quicksilver 1.50 4.00
Flash
❑ 6 Superman 1.50 4.00
Hulk
❑ 7 Silver Surfer 1.50 4.00
Green Lantern
❑ 8 Robin 1.50 4.00
Jubilee
❑ 9 Wolverine 1.50 4.00
Lobo
❑ 10 Captain Marvel 1.50 4.00
Thor
❑ 11 Spider-Man 1.50 4.00
Superboy
❑ 12 Wonder Woman 1.50 4.00
Storm

1995 DC Versus Marvel Impact
COMPLETE SET (18) 10.00 25.00
STATED ODDS 1:2

MODERN ERA NON-SPORTS

Card	Low	High
❑ 1 Thor	1.25	3.00
❑ 2 Metamorpho	1.25	3.00
❑ 3 Iron Man	1.25	3.00
❑ 4 Crimson Fox	1.25	3.00
❑ 5 Wonder Woman	1.25	3.00
Black Widow		
❑ 6 Hawkman	1.25	3.00
❑ 7 Quicksilver	1.25	3.00
❑ 8 Flash	1.25	3.00
❑ 9 Hawkeye	1.25	3.00
❑ 10 Gambit	1.25	3.00
❑ 11 Supergirl	1.25	3.00
❑ 12 Beast	1.25	3.00
❑ 13 Split	1.25	3.00
❑ 14 Cyclops	1.25	3.00
Nightwing		
❑ 15 The Atom	1.25	3.00
❑ 16 Rogue	1.25	3.00
❑ 17 Impulse	1.25	3.00
❑ 18 Wolverine	1.25	3.00

1995 DC Versus Marvel Mirage

Card	Low	High
COMPLETE SET (2)	60.00	120.00
STATED ODDS 1:360		
❑ 1 Superboy	40.00	80.00
Spider-Man/Spider-Boy		
❑ 2 Wolverine	40.00	80.00
Batman/Dark Claw		

1995 DC Villains The Dark Judgement

Card	Low	High
COMPLETE SET (90)	6.00	15.00
SM1 STATED ODDS 1:180		
❑ 1 DC Villains	.15	.40
❑ 2 Cheshire	.15	.40
❑ 3 Deadline	.15	.40
❑ 4 Shrapnel	.15	.40
❑ 5 Copperhead	.15	.40
❑ 6 KGBeast	.15	.40
❑ 7 Scarth	.15	.40
❑ 8 Major Force	.15	.40
❑ 9 Captain Boomerang	.15	.40
❑ 10 Black Mask	.15	.40
❑ 11 Black Manta	.15	.40
❑ 12 Ocean Master	.15	.40
❑ 13 The Mist	.15	.40
❑ 14 Metallo	.15	.40
❑ 15 Black Adam	.15	.40
❑ 16 Psimon	.15	.40
❑ 17 The Ravager	.15	.40
❑ 18 The Parasite	.15	.40
❑ 19 Ventriloquist	.15	.40
Scarface		
❑ 20 Toyman	.15	.40
❑ 21 Hellhound	.15	.40
❑ 22 Cheetah	.15	.40
❑ 23 Two-Face	.15	.40
❑ 24 Parallax	.15	.40
❑ 25 Cyborg	.15	.40
❑ 26 Dr. Polaris	.15	.40
❑ 27 Lyrl Dox	.15	.40
❑ 28 The Joker	.15	.40
❑ 29 White Lotus	.15	.40
❑ 30 The Shade	.15	.40
❑ 31 Talia	.15	.40
❑ 32 Catwoman	.15	.40
❑ 33 Knockout	.15	.40
❑ 34 Lady Shiva	.15	.40
❑ 35 Man-Bat	.15	.40
❑ 36 Lobo	.15	.40
❑ 37 Bizarro	.15	.40
❑ 38 Poison Ivy	.15	.40
❑ 39 The Riddler	.15	.40
❑ 40 Gunhawk	.15	.40
❑ 41 Weather Wizard	.15	.40
❑ 42 The Trickster	.15	.40
❑ 43 Captain Cold	.15	.40
❑ 44 Mirror Master	.15	.40
❑ 45 Scarecrow	.15	.40
❑ 46 The Penguin	.15	.40
❑ 47 Mudpack	.15	.40
❑ 48 Anarky	.15	.40
❑ 49 Killer Croc	.15	.40
❑ 50 Abra Kadabra	.15	.40
❑ 51 Changeling	.15	.40
❑ 52 King Shark	.15	.40
❑ 53 Charnelle	.15	.40
❑ 54 Mr. Mxyzptlk	.15	.40
❑ 55 Crimelord	.15	.40
❑ 56 King Snake	.15	.40
❑ 57 Bane	.15	.40
❑ 58 Count Viper	.15	.40
❑ 59 Order of St. Dumas	.15	.40
❑ 60 Female Furies	.15	.40
❑ 61 Blackfire	.15	.40
❑ 62 Darkseid's Elite	.15	.40
❑ 63 Monarch	.15	.40
❑ 64 Solomon Grundy	.15	.40
❑ 65 Felix Faust	.15	.40
❑ 66 Kingdom	.15	.40
❑ 67 The Demon	.15	.40
❑ 68 Circe	.15	.40
❑ 69 Wild Huntsman	.15	.40
❑ 70 Silver Banshee	.15	.40
❑ 71 Ares	.15	.40
❑ 72 Dementor	.15	.40
❑ 73 Kobra	.15	.40
❑ 74 Dr. Sivana	.15	.40
❑ 75 Raven	.15	.40
❑ 76 Vandal Savage	.15	.40
❑ 77 Ra's Al Ghul	.15	.40
❑ 78 Lord Havok	.15	.40
❑ 79 Death Masque	.15	.40
❑ 80 The Baron	.15	.40
❑ 81 Lex Luthor	.15	.40
❑ 82 Brimstone	.15	.40
❑ 83 The Controllers	.15	.40
❑ 84 The Dominators	.15	.40
❑ 85 Brainiac	.15	.40
❑ 86 Mongul	.15	.40
❑ 87 Darkseid	.15	.40
❑ 88 Doomsday	.15	.40
❑ 89 Unknown	.15	.40
❑ 90 Checklist	.15	.40
❑ SM1 Two-Face Redemption	8.00	20.00

1995 DC Villains The Dark Judgement Gathering of Evil

Card	Low	High
COMPLETE SET (9)	6.00	15.00
STATED ODDS 1:7		
❑ GE1 Lex Luthor	1.25	3.00
❑ GE2 Doomsday	1.25	3.00
❑ GE3 The Joker	1.25	3.00
❑ GE4 Darkseid	1.25	3.00
❑ GE5 Parallax	1.25	3.00
❑ GE6 Bane	1.25	3.00
❑ GE7 Mongul	1.25	3.00
❑ GE8 Brainiac	1.25	3.00
❑ GE9 Circe	1.25	3.00

1995 DC Villains The Dark Judgement Villains Attack

Card	Low	High
COMPLETE SET (3)	8.00	20.00
STATED ODDS 1:30		
❑ CC1 Knightfall	4.00	10.00
❑ CC2 The Death of Superman	4.00	10.00
❑ CC3 Zero Hour	4.00	10.00

1995 Marvel Annual

Card	Low	High
COMPLETE SET (150)	20.00	50.00
❑ 1 Jean Grey	.20	.50
❑ 2 Nightcrawler	.20	.50
❑ 3 Psylocke	.20	.50
❑ 4 Gambit	.20	.50
❑ 5 Storm	.20	.50
❑ 6 Iceman	.20	.50
❑ 7 Colossus	.20	.50
❑ 8 Beast	.20	.50
❑ 9 Cyclops	.20	.50
❑ 10 Sabretooth	.20	.50
❑ 11 Synch	.20	.50
❑ 12 Emma Frost	.20	.50
❑ 13 Jubilee	.20	.50
❑ 14 Skin	.20	.50
❑ 15 Legion	.20	.50
❑ 16 X-Treme	.20	.50
❑ 17 Cable	.20	.50
❑ 18 Omega Red	.20	.50
❑ 19 D'spayre	.20	.50
❑ 20 Nimrod	.20	.50
❑ 21 Shatterstar	.20	.50
❑ 22 Phalanx	.20	.50
❑ 23 Random	.20	.50
❑ 24 Wolfsbane	.20	.50
❑ 25 Multiple Man	.20	.50
❑ 26 Polaris	.20	.50
❑ 27 Mr. Sinister	.20	.50
❑ 28 Havok	.20	.50
❑ 29 Forge	.20	.50
❑ 30 Guido vs. Blob	.20	.50
❑ 31 Mystique	.20	.50
❑ 32 Phoenix	.20	.50
❑ 33 Britanic	.20	.50
❑ 34 Douglock	.20	.50
❑ 35 Legacy Virus	.20	.50
❑ 36 Kitty Pryde	.20	.50
❑ 37 Tapestry	.20	.50
❑ 38 Lady Deathstrike	.20	.50
❑ 39 Broken Claws	.20	.50
❑ 40 Final Sanction	.20	.50
❑ 41 Healing Factor	.20	.50
❑ 42 Rogue	.20	.50
❑ 43 Belladonna	.20	.50
❑ 44 Nathan Dayspring	.20	.50
❑ 45 Apocalypse	.20	.50
❑ 46 Bishop	.20	.50
❑ 47 Deadpool	.20	.50
❑ 48 Juggernaut	.20	.50
❑ 49 Spider-Man	.20	.50
❑ 50 Lifetheft	.20	.50
❑ 51 Pursuit	.20	.50
❑ 52 Hobgoblin	.20	.50
❑ 53 Bloody Mary	.20	.50
❑ 54 Facade	.20	.50
❑ 55 Mary Jane	.20	.50
❑ 56 Demogoblin	.20	.50
❑ 57 The Shrieking	.20	.50
❑ 58 Green Goblin	.20	.50
❑ 59 Grim Hunter	.20	.50
❑ 60 Scarlet Spider	.20	.50
❑ 61 Power & Responsibility	.20	.50
❑ 62 Judas Traveller	.20	.50
❑ 63 Puma	.20	.50
❑ 64 Vulture	.20	.50
❑ 65 Scarlet Spider vs. Venom	.20	.50
❑ 66 Venom	.20	.50
❑ 67 Nights of Vengeance	.20	.50
❑ 68 Separation Anxiety	.20	.50
❑ 69 Shroud	.20	.50
❑ 70 Nightwatch	.20	.50
❑ 71 Black Cat	.20	.50
❑ 72 Annex	.20	.50
❑ 73 Solo	.20	.50
❑ 74 Elektra	.20	.50
❑ 75 Daredevil	.20	.50
❑ 76 Invisible Woman	.20	.50
❑ 77 Galactus	.20	.50
❑ 78 Dark Raider	.20	.50
❑ 79 Human Torch	.20	.50
❑ 80 Franklin Richards	.20	.50
❑ 81 Thing	.20	.50
❑ 82 Hulk	.20	.50
❑ 83 Loss of a Friend	.20	.50
❑ 84 Savage Hulk	.20	.50
❑ 85 Namor	.20	.50
❑ 86 Darkhawk	.20	.50
❑ 87 Blackwulf	.20	.50
❑ 88 Llyron	.20	.50
❑ 89 Silver Sable	.20	.50
❑ 90 Dr. Druid	.20	.50
❑ 91 Moon Knight	.20	.50
❑ 92 Clan Destine	.20	.50
❑ 93 Thor 2099	.20	.50
❑ 94 Punisher 2099	.20	.50
❑ 95 Ravage 2099	.20	.50
❑ 96 Spider-Man 2099	.20	.50
❑ 97 Ghost Rider 2099	.20	.50
❑ 98 Xi'an	.20	.50
❑ 99 Warewolf	.20	.50
❑ 100 Vendetta	.20	.50
❑ 101 Skullfire	.20	.50
❑ 102 Bloodhawk	.20	.50
❑ 103 The Specialist	.20	.50
❑ 104 Metalhead	.20	.50
❑ 105 Doom 2099	.20	.50
❑ 106 Hulk 2099	.20	.50
❑ 107 Captain America	.20	.50
❑ 108 Americop	.20	.50
❑ 109 Free Spirit	.20	.50
❑ 110 Baron Zemo	.20	.50
❑ 111 Thor	.20	.50
❑ 112 Bloodaxe	.20	.50
❑ 113 Thunderstrike	.20	.50
❑ 114 Quicksilver	.20	.50
❑ 115 Hercules	.20	.50
❑ 116 Giant Man	.20	.50
❑ 117 Vision	.20	.50
❑ 118 Strange	.20	.50
❑ 119 Salome'	.20	.50
❑ 120 Dr. Strange	.20	.50
❑ 121 Morbius	.20	.50
❑ 122 Vengeance	.20	.50
❑ 123 Ghost Rider	.20	.50
❑ 124 Blackout	.20	.50
❑ 125 Scarecrow	.20	.50
❑ 126 Blade	.20	.50
❑ 127 Blaze	.20	.50
❑ 128 Thanos	.20	.50
❑ 129 Starblast	.20	.50
❑ 130 Silver Surfer	.20	.50
❑ 131 Quasar	.20	.50
❑ 132 Tyrant	.20	.50
❑ 133 Iron Man	.20	.50
❑ 134 Spider-Woman	.20	.50
❑ 135 Crash & Burn	.20	.50
❑ 136 Wonder Man	.20	.50
❑ 137 Century	.20	.50
❑ 138 Hawkeye	.20	.50
❑ 139 War Machine	.20	.50
❑ 140 Mandarin	.20	.50
❑ 141 U.S. Agent	.20	.50
❑ 142 Punisher	.20	.50
❑ 143 Pariah	.20	.50
❑ 144 Nova	.20	.50
❑ 145 Justice	.20	.50
❑ 146 Kymaera	.20	.50
❑ 147 Sphinx	.20	.50
❑ 148 Shatterforce	.20	.50
❑ 149 Night Thrasher	.20	.50
❑ 150 Checklist	.20	.50

1995 Marvel Annual Chromium

Card	Low	High
COMPLETE SET (12)	6.00	15.00
STATED ODDS 1:2		
❑ 1 Spider-Man	.75	2.00
❑ 2 Carnage	.75	2.00
❑ 3 Iron Man	.75	2.00
❑ 4 Thing	.75	2.00
❑ 5 Hulk	.75	2.00
❑ 6 Ghost Rider	.75	2.00
❑ 7 Gambit	.75	2.00
❑ 8 Cyclops	.75	2.00
❑ 9 Punisher	.75	2.00
❑ 10 Bishop	.75	2.00
❑ 11 Juggernaut	.75	2.00
❑ 12 Colossus	.75	2.00

1995 Marvel Annual DuoBlast

Card	Low	High
COMPLETE SET (3)	4.00	10.00
STATED ODDS 1:6		
❑ 1 Spider-Man	2.00	5.00
(Scarlet Spider		
❑ 2 Punisher 2099	2.00	5.00
(Vendetta		
❑ 3 Iron Man	2.00	5.00
(War Machine		

1995 Marvel Annual FlairPrint

Card	Low	High
COMPLETE SET (10)	10.00	25.00
STATED ODDS ONE PER CASE		
❑ 1 Carnage	2.00	5.00
❑ 2 Cyclops	2.00	5.00
❑ 3 Gambit	2.00	5.00
❑ 4 Iron Man	2.00	5.00
❑ 5 Jean Grey	2.00	5.00
❑ 6 Namor	2.00	5.00
❑ 7 Spider-Man	2.00	5.00
❑ 8 Storm	2.00	5.00
❑ 9 Thing	2.00	5.00
❑ 10 Wolverine	2.00	5.00

1995 Marvel Annual HoloBlast

Card	Low	High
COMPLETE SET (12)	12.00	30.00
STATED ODDS 1:3		
❑ 1 Wolverine vs. Cyber	1.50	4.00
❑ 2 Deadpool vs. Juggernaut	1.50	4.00
❑ 3 Spider-Man vs. Scarlet Spider	1.50	4.00
❑ 4 Cable vs. Nimrod	1.50	4.00
❑ 5 Iron Man vs. Mandarin	1.50	4.00
❑ 6 Venom vs. Demogoblin	1.50	4.00
❑ 7 Hulk vs. Trauma	1.50	4.00
❑ 8 Punisher 2099 vs. Public Enemy	1.50	4.00
❑ 9 Banshee vs. Phalanx	1.50	4.00
❑ 10 Ghost Rider vs. Scarecrow	1.50	4.00
❑ 11 Namor vs. Llyron	1.50	4.00
❑ 12 Gambit vs. Sabretooth	1.50	4.00

1995 Marvel Annual PowerBlast

Card	Low	High
COMPLETE SET (24)	10.00	25.00
STATED ODDS ONE PER PACK		
❑ 1 Wolverine	.60	1.50
❑ 2 Silver Surfer	.60	1.50
❑ 3 Venom	.60	1.50
❑ 4 Rogue	.60	1.50
❑ 5 Storm	.60	1.50
❑ 6 Daredevil	.60	1.50
❑ 7 Jean Grey	.60	1.50
❑ 8 Jubilee	.60	1.50
❑ 9 Sabretooth	.60	1.50
❑ 10 Morbius	.60	1.50
❑ 11 Apocalypse	.60	1.50
❑ 12 Beast	.60	1.50
❑ 13 Human Torch	.60	1.50
❑ 14 Captain America	.60	1.50
❑ 15 Cable	.60	1.50
❑ 16 Archangel	.60	1.50
❑ 17 Deadpool	.60	1.50
❑ 18 Iceman	.60	1.50
❑ 19 Professor X	.60	1.50
❑ 20 Thor	.60	1.50
❑ 21 Thanos	.60	1.50
❑ 22 Mandarin	.60	1.50
❑ 23 Demogoblin	.60	1.50
❑ 24 Phalanx	.60	1.50

1995 Marvel Masterpieces

Card	Low	High
COMPLETE SET (151)	25.00	60.00
❑ 1 Apocalypse	.30	.75
❑ 2 Apocalypse	.30	.75
❑ 3 Apocalypse	.30	.75
❑ 4 Archangel	.30	.75
❑ 5 Archangel	.30	.75
❑ 6 Archangel	.30	.75
❑ 7 Beast	.30	.75
❑ 8 Beast	.30	.75
❑ 9 Beast	.30	.75
❑ 10 Bishop	.30	.75
❑ 11 Bishop	.30	.75
❑ 12 Bishop	.30	.75
❑ 13 Cable	.30	.75
❑ 14 Cable	.30	.75
❑ 15 Cable	.30	.75
❑ 16 Captain America	.30	.75
❑ 17 Captain America	.30	.75
❑ 18 Captain America	.30	.75
❑ 19 Carnage	.30	.75
❑ 20 Carnage	.30	.75
❑ 21 Carnage	.30	.75
❑ 22 Cyclops	.30	.75
❑ 23 Cyclops	.30	.75
❑ 24 Cyclops	.30	.75
❑ 25 Daredevil	.30	.75
❑ 26 Daredevil	.30	.75
❑ 27 Daredevil	.30	.75
❑ 28 Dr. Doom	.30	.75
❑ 29 Dr. Doom	.30	.75
❑ 30 Dr. Doom	.30	.75
❑ 31 Galactus	.30	.75
❑ 32 Galactus	.30	.75
❑ 33 Galactus	.30	.75
❑ 34 Gambit	.30	.75
❑ 35 Gambit	.30	.75
❑ 36 Gambit	.30	.75
❑ 37 Ghost Rider	.30	.75
❑ 38 Ghost Rider	.30	.75
❑ 39 Ghost Rider	.30	.75
❑ 40 Hulk	.30	.75
❑ 41 Hulk	.30	.75
❑ 42 Hulk	.30	.75
❑ 43 Human Torch	.30	.75
❑ 44 Human Torch	.30	.75
❑ 45 Human Torch	.30	.75
❑ 46 Iceman	.30	.75
❑ 47 Iceman	.30	.75
❑ 48 Iceman	.30	.75
❑ 49 Invisible Woman	.30	.75
❑ 50 Invisible Woman	.30	.75
❑ 51 Invisible Woman	.30	.75
❑ 52 Iron Man	.30	.75
❑ 53 Iron Man	.30	.75
❑ 54 Iron Man	.30	.75
❑ 55 Jean Grey	.30	.75
❑ 56 Jean Grey	.30	.75
❑ 57 Jean Grey	.30	.75
❑ 58 Jubilee	.30	.75
❑ 59 Jubilee	.30	.75
❑ 60 Jubilee	.30	.75
❑ 61 Magneto	.30	.75
❑ 62 Magneto	.30	.75
❑ 63 Magneto	.30	.75
❑ 64 Mandarin	.30	.75
❑ 65 Mandarin	.30	.75
❑ 66 Mandarin	.30	.75
❑ 67 Mr. Sinister	.30	.75
❑ 68 Mr. Sinister	.30	.75
❑ 69 Mr. Sinister	.30	.75
❑ 70 Namor	.30	.75
❑ 71 Namor	.30	.75
❑ 72 Namor	.30	.75
❑ 73 Professor X	.30	.75
❑ 74 Professor X	.30	.75
❑ 75 Professor X	.30	.75
❑ 76 Psylocke	.30	.75
❑ 77 Psylocke	.30	.75
❑ 78 Psylocke	.30	.75
❑ 79 Punisher	.30	.75
❑ 80 Punisher	.30	.75
❑ 81 Punisher	.30	.75
❑ 82 Rogue	.30	.75
❑ 83 Rogue	.30	.75
❑ 84 Rogue	.30	.75
❑ 85 Sabretooth	.30	.75
❑ 86 Sabretooth	.30	.75
❑ 87 Sabretooth	.30	.75
❑ 88 Silver Surfer	.30	.75
❑ 89 Silver Surfer	.30	.75
❑ 90 Silver Surfer	.30	.75
❑ 91 Spider-Man	.30	.75
❑ 92 Spider-Man	.30	.75
❑ 93 Spider-Man	.30	.75
❑ 94 Storm	.30	.75
❑ 95 Storm	.30	.75
❑ 96 Storm	.30	.75
❑ 97 Thanos	.30	.75
❑ 98 Thanos	.30	.75
❑ 99 Thanos	.30	.75
❑ 100 Thing	.30	.75
❑ 101 Thing	.30	.75
❑ 102 Thing	.30	.75
❑ 103 Thor	.30	.75
❑ 104 Thor	.30	.75
❑ 105 Thor	.30	.75
❑ 106 Venom	.30	.75
❑ 107 Venom	.30	.75
❑ 108 Venom	.30	.75
❑ 109 War Machine	.30	.75
❑ 110 War Machine	.30	.75
❑ 111 War Machine	.30	.75
❑ 112 Wolverine	.30	.75
❑ 113 Wolverine	.30	.75
❑ 114 Wolverine	.30	.75
❑ 115 Black Cat	.30	.75
❑ 116 Black Panther	.30	.75
❑ 117 Blaze	.30	.75
❑ 118 Colossus	.30	.75
❑ 119 Cyber	.30	.75
❑ 120 Deadpool	.30	.75
❑ 121 Deathlok	.30	.75
❑ 122 Domino	.30	.75
❑ 123 Dr. Octopus	.30	.75
❑ 124 Elektra	.30	.75
❑ 125 Emplate	.30	.75
❑ 126 Green Goblin	.30	.75
❑ 127 Hobgoblin	.30	.75
❑ 128 Juggernaut	.30	.75
❑ 129 Kingpin	.30	.75
❑ 130 Lizard	.30	.75
❑ 131 Loki	.30	.75
❑ 132 Mephisto	.30	.75
❑ 133 Modok	.30	.75
❑ 134 Mojo	.30	.75
❑ 135 Mr. Fantastic	.30	.75
❑ 136 Mystique	.30	.75
❑ 137 Nightcrawler	.30	.75
❑ 138 Omega Red	.30	.75
❑ 139 Penance	.30	.75
❑ 140 Red Skull	.30	.75
❑ 141 Rhino	.30	.75
❑ 142 Sauron	.30	.75
❑ 143 Scarlet Spider	.30	.75
❑ 144 Shatterstar	.30	.75
❑ 145 She-Hulk	.30	.75
❑ 146 Skin	.30	.75
❑ 147 Spider-Man 2099	.30	.75
❑ 148 Strong Guy	.30	.75
❑ 149 Tyrant	.30	.75
❑ 150 Vision	.30	.75
❑ 151 Marvel Masterpieces	.30	.75

1995 Marvel Masterpieces Canvas

Card	Low	High
COMPLETE SET (22)	15.00	40.00
STATED ODDS 1:2		
❑ 1 Archangel	1.25	3.00
❑ 2 Beast	1.25	3.00
❑ 3 Bishop	1.25	3.00
❑ 4 Cable	1.25	3.00
❑ 5 Daredevil	1.25	3.00
❑ 6 Galactus	1.25	3.00
❑ 7 Gambit	1.25	3.00
❑ 8 Ghost Rider	1.25	3.00
❑ 9 Human Torch	1.25	3.00
❑ 10 Ice Man	1.25	3.00
❑ 11 Invisible Woman	1.25	3.00
❑ 12 Jubilee	1.25	3.00
❑ 13 Magneto	1.25	3.00
❑ 14 Namor	1.25	3.00
❑ 15 Professor X	1.25	3.00
❑ 16 Psylocke	1.25	3.00
❑ 17 Punisher	1.25	3.00
❑ 18 Rogue	1.25	3.00
❑ 19 Silver Surfer	1.25	3.00
❑ 20 Spider-Man	1.25	3.00
❑ 21 Thing	1.25	3.00
❑ 22 War Machine	1.25	3.00

1995 Marvel Masterpieces E-Motion

Card	Low	High
COMPLETE SET (150)	100.00	200.00
*EMOTION: 1.2X TO 3X BASIC CARDS		

1995 Marvel Masterpieces Holoflash

Card	Low	High
COMPLETE SET (8)	100.00	200.00
STATED ODDS 1:12		
❑ 1 Apocalypse	10.00	25.00
❑ 2 Carnage	10.00	25.00
❑ 3 Dr. Doom	10.00	25.00
❑ 4 Mandarin	10.00	25.00
❑ 5 Mr. Sinister	10.00	25.00
❑ 6 Sabretooth	10.00	25.00
❑ 7 Thanos	10.00	25.00
❑ 8 Venom	10.00	25.00

1995 Marvel Masterpieces Mirage

Card	Low	High
STATED ODDS 1:360		
❑ 1 Classic Avengers	150.00	250.00
❑ 2 X-Men	150.00	250.00

1995 Marvel Metal

Card	Low	High
COMPLETE SET (138)	25.00	60.00
❑ 1 Beast	.30	.75
❑ 2 Bishop	.30	.75
❑ 3 Cyclops	.30	.75
❑ 4 Gambit	.30	.75
❑ 5 Holocaust	.30	.75
❑ 6 Jean Grey	.30	.75
❑ 7 Nightcrawler	.30	.75
❑ 8 Sunfire	.30	.75
❑ 9 Weapon X	.30	.75
❑ 10 Black Widow	.30	.75
❑ 11 Captain America	.30	.75
❑ 12 Giant Man	.30	.75
❑ 13 Thor	.30	.75
❑ 14 Thunderstrike	.30	.75
❑ 15 Vision	.30	.75
❑ 16 Galactus	.30	.75
❑ 17 Nebula	.30	.75
❑ 18 Silver Surfer	.30	.75
❑ 19 Thanos	.30	.75
❑ 20 Tyrant	.30	.75
❑ 21 Warlock	.30	.75
❑ 22 Hawkeye	.30	.75
❑ 23 Iron Man	.30	.75
❑ 24 Mandarin	.30	.75
❑ 25 Scarlet Witch	.30	.75
❑ 26 Spider-Woman	.30	.75
❑ 27 War Machine	.30	.75
❑ 28 Daredevil	.30	.75
❑ 29 Deathlok	.30	.75
❑ 30 Elektra	.30	.75
❑ 31 Hulk	.30	.75
❑ 32 Human Torch	.30	.75
❑ 33 Invisible Woman	.30	.75
❑ 34 Mephisto	.30	.75
❑ 35 Modok	.30	.75
❑ 36 Mr. Fantastic	.30	.75
❑ 37 Namor	.30	.75
❑ 38 Puppet Master	.30	.75
❑ 39 She-Hulk	.30	.75
❑ 40 Silver Sable	.30	.75
❑ 41 Super Skrull	.30	.75
❑ 42 Thing	.30	.75
❑ 43 Bloodhawk	.30	.75
❑ 44 Brimstone Love	.30	.75
❑ 45 Doom 2099	.30	.75
❑ 46 Ghost Rider 2099	.30	.75
❑ 47 Hulk 2099	.30	.75
❑ 48 Junkpile	.30	.75
❑ 49 Meanstreak	.30	.75
❑ 50 Punisher 2099	.30	.75
❑ 51 Ravage 2099	.30	.75
❑ 52 Skullfire	.30	.75
❑ 53 Spider-Man 2099	.30	.75
❑ 54 Vendetta	.30	.75
❑ 55 Xi'an	.30	.75
❑ 56 Blade	.30	.75
❑ 57 Blaze	.30	.75
❑ 58 Dr. Strange	.30	.75
❑ 59 Ghost Rider	.30	.75
❑ 60 Morbius	.30	.75
❑ 61 Strange	.30	.75
❑ 62 Vengeance	.30	.75
❑ 63 Firestar	.30	.75
❑ 64 Justice	.30	.75
❑ 65 Kymaera	.30	.75
❑ 66 Night Thrasher	.30	.75
❑ 67 Nova	.30	.75
❑ 68 Rage	.30	.75
❑ 69 Punisher	.30	.75
❑ 70 Black Cat	.30	.75

Card	Low	High
❑ 71 Carnage	.30	.75
❑ 72 Dr. Octopus	.30	.75
❑ 73 Judas Traveller	.30	.75
❑ 74 Rhino	.30	.75
❑ 75 Scarlet Spider	.30	.75
❑ 76 Scorpion	.30	.75
❑ 77 Shocker	.30	.75
❑ 78 Spider-Man	.30	.75
❑ 79 Stunner	.30	.75
❑ 80 Venom	.30	.75
❑ 81 Vulture	.30	.75
❑ 82 Apocalypse	.30	.75
❑ 83 Archangel	.30	.75
❑ 84 Banshee	.30	.75
❑ 85 Beast	.30	.75
❑ 86 Bishop	.30	.75
❑ 87 Boomer	.30	.75
❑ 88 Cable	.30	.75
❑ 89 Chamber	.30	.75
❑ 90 Colossus	.30	.75
❑ 91 Cyclops	.30	.75
❑ 92 Deadpool	.30	.75
❑ 93 Domino	.30	.75
❑ 94 Gambit	.30	.75
❑ 95 Cannonball	.30	.75
❑ 96 Iceman	.30	.75
❑ 97 Jean Grey	.30	.75
❑ 98 Jubilee	.30	.75
❑ 99 Juggernaut	.30	.75
❑ 100 Lady Deathstrike	.30	.75
❑ 101 Omega Red	.30	.75
❑ 102 Longshot	.30	.75
❑ 103 M	.30	.75
❑ 104 Magneto	.30	.75
❑ 105 Mondo	.30	.75
❑ 106 Mr. Sinister	.30	.75
❑ 107 Mystique	.30	.75
❑ 108 Nightcrawler	.30	.75
❑ 109 Penance	.30	.75
❑ 110 Phoenix	.30	.75
❑ 111 Professor X	.30	.75
❑ 112 Psylocke	.30	.75
❑ 113 Random	.30	.75
❑ 114 Rogue	.30	.75
❑ 115 Sabretooth	.30	.75
❑ 116 Sauron	.30	.75
❑ 117 Shadowcat	.30	.75
❑ 118 Skin	.30	.75
❑ 119 Storm	.30	.75
❑ 120 Strong Guy	.30	.75
❑ 121 Stryfe	.30	.75
❑ 122 Synch	.30	.75
❑ 123 Warpath	.30	.75
❑ 124 White Queen	.30	.75
❑ 125 Wolverine	.30	.75
❑ 126 Beast Continues to Mutate	.30	.75
❑ 127 Cable Kills the X-Men	.30	.75
❑ 128 Dr. Doom, the Hero	.30	.75
❑ 129 The Fantastic Four Lose the Trial of Galactus	.30	.75
❑ 130 Iron Man in the Time of King Arthur	.30	.75
❑ 131 Kraven Kills Spider-Man	.30	.75
❑ 132 Rogue Acquires the Power of Thor	.30	.75
❑ 133 Silver Surfer Dons the Infinity Gauntlet	.30	.75
❑ 134 Spider-Man Keeps His Six Arms	.30	.75
❑ 135 Storm: The Thief	.30	.75
❑ 136 Venom Possesses the Punisher	.30	.75
❑ 137 Wolverine Becomes Lord of the Vampires	.30	.75
❑ 138 Checklist	.30	.75

1995 Marvel Metal Blaster

Card	Low	High
COMPLETE SET (18)	10.00	25.00
STATED ODDS 1:2 HOBBY, 2:3 JUMBO		
❑ 1 Cable	.75	2.00
❑ 2 Captain America	.75	2.00
❑ 3 Cyclops	.75	2.00
❑ 4 Gambit	.75	2.00
❑ 5 Hulk	.75	2.00
❑ 6 Human Torch	.75	2.00
❑ 7 Iron Man	.75	2.00
❑ 8 Jean Grey	.75	2.00
❑ 9 Punisher	.75	2.00
❑ 10 Rogue	.75	2.00
❑ 11 Silver Surfer	.75	2.00
❑ 12 Spider-Man	.75	2.00
❑ 13 Storm	.75	2.00
❑ 14 Thing	.75	2.00
❑ 15 Thor	.75	2.00
❑ 16 Venom	.75	2.00
❑ 17 War Machine	.75	2.00
❑ 18 Wolverine	.75	2.00

1995 Marvel Metal Blaster Gold

Card	Low	High
COMPLETE SET (18)	15.00	40.00
STATED ODDS 1:3		
❑ 1 Cable	1.25	3.00
❑ 2 Captain America	1.25	3.00
❑ 3 Cyclops	1.25	3.00
❑ 4 Gambit	1.25	3.00
❑ 5 Hulk	1.25	3.00
❑ 6 Human Torch	1.25	3.00
❑ 7 Iron Man	1.25	3.00
❑ 8 Jean Grey	1.25	3.00
❑ 9 Punisher	1.25	3.00
❑ 10 Rogue	1.25	3.00
❑ 11 Silver Surfer	1.25	3.00
❑ 12 Spider-Man	1.25	3.00
❑ 13 Storm	1.25	3.00
❑ 14 Thing	1.25	3.00
❑ 15 Thor	1.25	3.00
❑ 16 Venom	1.25	3.00
❑ 17 War Machine	1.25	3.00
❑ 18 Wolverine	1.25	3.00

1995 Marvel Metal Prints

Card	Low	High
COMPLETE SET (10)	12.00	30.00
STATED ODDS ONE PER CASE		
❑ 1 Bishop	1.50	4.00
❑ 2 Carnage	1.50	4.00
❑ 3 Human Torch	1.50	4.00
❑ 4 Iron Man	1.50	4.00
❑ 5 Jubilee	1.50	4.00
❑ 6 Mr. Sinister	1.50	4.00
❑ 7 Spider-Man	1.50	4.00
❑ 8 Storm	1.50	4.00
❑ 9 Thing	1.50	4.00
❑ 10 Wolverine	1.50	4.00

1995 Marvel Metal Silver Flasher

Card	Low	High
COMPLETE SET (137)	100.00	200.00

1995 Star Trek Thirty Years of Star Trek Phase One

Card	Low	High
COMPLETE SET (100)	6.00	15.00
❑ 1 U.S.S. Enterprise NCC-1701	.15	.40
❑ 2 U.S.S. Enterprise NCC-1701-A	.15	.40
❑ 3 U.S.S. Enterprise NCC-1701-B	.15	.40
❑ 4 U.S.S. Enterprise NCC-1701-C	.15	.40
❑ 5 U.S.S. Enterprise NCC-1701-D	.15	.40
❑ 6 Future U.S.S. Enterprise	.15	.40
❑ 7 Fesarius	.15	.40
❑ 8 Romulan Bird-of-Prey	.15	.40
❑ 9 Galileo NCC-1701/7	.15	.40
❑ 10 Lazarus' Ship	.15	.40
❑ 11 S.S. Botany Bay	.15	.40
❑ 12 Woden	.15	.40
❑ 13 U.S.S. Constellation	.15	.40
❑ 14 23rd Century Fleet	.15	.40
❑ 15 Melkotian Marker Buoy	.15	.40
❑ 16 Tholian Vessel	.15	.40
❑ 17 Yonanda	.15	.40
❑ 18 Aurora	.15	.40
❑ 19 S.S. Huron	.15	.40
❑ 20 Orion Pirate Ship	.15	.40
❑ 21 Klingon Vessels of the 23rd Century	.15	.40
❑ 22 Vulcan Shuttle	.15	.40
❑ 23 U.S.S. Reliant	.15	.40
❑ 24 U.S.S. Grissom	.15	.40
❑ 25 U.S.S. Excelsior NCC-2000	.15	.40
❑ 26 U.S.S. Saratoga	.15	.40
❑ 27 Ferengi Marauder	.15	.40
❑ 28 U.S.S. Stargazer	.15	.40
❑ 29 Batris	.15	.40
❑ 30 Sanction	.15	.40
❑ 31 Borg Vessel	.15	.40
❑ 32 U.S.S. Hood: NCC-42296	.15	.40
❑ 33 Romulan Scout Ship	.15	.40
❑ 34 Tin Man	.15	.40
❑ 35 Talarian Observation Craft	.15	.40
❑ 36 U.S.S. Phoenix	.15	.40
❑ 37 U.S.S. Brattain	.15	.40
❑ 38 Klingon Vessels of the 24th Century	.15	.40
❑ 39 U.S.S. Sutherland	.15	.40
❑ 40 U.S.S. Merrimac	.15	.40
❑ 41 U.S.S. Jenolen: NCC-2010	.15	.40
❑ 42 Romulan Warbird	.15	.40
❑ 43 U.S.S. Gorkon	.15	.40
❑ 44 U.S.S. Pegasus	.15	.40
❑ 45 U.S.S. Pasteur	.15	.40
❑ 46 Deep Space Nine	.15	.40
❑ 47 Cardassian Warship	.15	.40
❑ 48 U.S.S. Orinoco	.15	.40
❑ 49 U.S.S. Odyssey	.15	.40
❑ 50 U.S.S. Defiant	.15	.40
❑ 51 Bajoran Sailing Vessel	.15	.40
❑ 52 Maquis Ship	.15	.40
❑ 53 U.S.S. Voyager	.15	.40
❑ 54 Kazon Vessels	.15	.40
❑ 55 Laser Cannon	.15	.40
❑ 56 Personal Ear Receiver	.15	.40
❑ 57 Phaser	.15	.40
❑ 58 Astrogator	.15	.40
❑ 59 Replicator	.15	.40
❑ 60 Korby's Android Replicator	.15	.40
❑ 61 Neural Neutralizer	.15	.40
❑ 62 Transmuter	.15	.40
❑ 63 Universal Translator	.15	.40
❑ 64 Nomad	.15	.40
❑ 65 Agony Booth	.15	.40
❑ 66 Collar of Obedience	.15	.40
❑ 67 M-5 Computer	.15	.40
❑ 68 Asteroid Deflector	.15	.40
❑ 69 Portable Cerebral Stabilizer	.15	.40
❑ 70 Atavachron	.15	.40
❑ 71 EVA Suits	.15	.40
❑ 72 Perscan Device	.15	.40
❑ 73 Photon Torpedo	.15	.40
❑ 74 Genesiss Torpedo	.15	.40
❑ 75 Antigravity Boots	.15	.40
❑ 76 VISOR	.15	.40
❑ 77 Hypospray	.15	.40
❑ 78 Dilithium Crystals	.15	.40
❑ 79 Nanites	.15	.40
❑ 80 UV Light Source	.15	.40
❑ 81 Tractor Beam	.15	.40
❑ 82 Romulan Disruptor	.15	.40
❑ 83 Deflector Shields	.15	.40
❑ 84 Transporter	.15	.40
❑ 85 Particle Fountain	.15	.40
❑ 86 Pattern Enhancer	.15	.40
❑ 87 Holodeck	.15	.40
❑ 88 Phasing Cloak	.15	.40
❑ 89 PADD	.15	.40
❑ 90 M-113 Creature	.15	.40
❑ 91 Balok	.15	.40
❑ 92 Tellarite	.15	.40
❑ 93 Andorian	.15	.40
❑ 94 Lieutenant Arex	.15	.40
❑ 95 Borg	.15	.40
❑ 96 Bolian	.15	.40
❑ 97 Bajoran	.15	.40
❑ 98 Cardassian	.15	.40
❑ 99 Checklist A	.15	.40
❑ 100 Checklist B	.15	.40

1995 Star Trek Thirty Years of Star Trek Phase One Die-Cut Technology

Card	Low	High
COMPLETE SET (3)	5.00	12.00
STATED ODDS 1:36		
❑ D1 Klingon Knife	3.00	8.00
❑ D2 Starfleet Phaser	3.00	8.00
❑ D3 Romulan/Klingon Disruptor	3.00	

1995 Star Trek Thirty Years of Star Trek Phase One Evolution of Technology

Card	Low	High
COMPLETE SET (9)	5.00	12.00
STATED ODDS 1:12		
❑ E1 Mid-23rd Century Phaser	1.25	3.00
❑ E2 Late 23rd Century Phaser	1.25	3.00
❑ E3 24th Century Phaser	1.25	3.00
❑ E4 Mid-23rd Century Communicator	1.25	3.00
❑ E5 Late 23rd Century Communicator	1.25	3.00
❑ E6 24th Century Communicator	1.25	3.00
❑ E7 Mid-23rd Century Tricorder	1.25	3.00
❑ E8 Late 23rd Century Tricorder	1.25	3.00
❑ E9 24th Century Tricorder	1.25	3.00

1995 Star Trek Thirty Years of Star Trek Phase One Registry Plaques

Card	Low	High
STATED ODDS 1:72		
❑ R1 U.S.S. Enterprise	8.00	20.00
❑ R2 NCC 1701-A	8.00	20.00
❑ R3 NCC 1701-B	8.00	20.00
❑ R4 NCC-1701-D	8.00	20.00
❑ R5 U.S.S. Excelsior	8.00	20.00
❑ R6 U.S.S. Stargazer	8.00	20.00
❑ R7 U.S.S. Brattain	8.00	20.00
❑ R8 U.S.S. Sutherland NCC-72015	8.00	20.00
❑ R9 U.S.S. Voyager	8.00	20.00

1995 Star Trek Thirty Years of Star Trek Phase One Skymotion

Card	Low	High
STATED ODDS 1:180		
OVERSIZE CARD AVAILABLE VIA MAIL ORDER		
❑ 1 U.S.S. Enterprise	10.00	25.00
❑ 2 U.S.S. Enterprise OVERSIZE		
❑ 3 Skymotion Exchange		

1995 Star Trek Voyager Series 1

Card	Low	High
COMPLETE SET (98)	5.00	12.00
❑ 1 Outlaws	.15	.40
❑ 2 Desperate Flight	.15	.40
❑ 3 Evasive Maneuvers	.15	.40
❑ 4 Phenomena	.15	.40
❑ 5 Rehabilitation	.15	.40
❑ 6 A Second Chance	.15	.40
❑ 7 Reporting for Duty	.15	.40
❑ 8 Deep Space Rendezvous	.15	.40
❑ 9 About Ferengi	.15	.40
❑ 10 No Sale	.15	.40
❑ 11 Contrasting Receptions	.15	.40
❑ 12 Farewells	.15	.40
❑ 13 Departures	.15	.40
❑ 14 Destination: Badlands	.15	.40
❑ 15 You Say Tomato	.15	.40
❑ 16 Confession	.15	.40
❑ 17 Missing in Action	.15	.40
❑ 18 Wave Front	.15	.40
❑ 19 Swept Away	.15	.40
❑ 20 The Array	.15	.40
❑ 21 Medical Emergency	.15	.40
❑ 22 Holographic Help	.15	.40
❑ 23 Microfracture	.15	.40
❑ 24 Complications	.15	.40
❑ 25 Doctored Exit	.15	.40
❑ 26 Questionable Manners	.15	.40
❑ 27 Homespun Mystery	.15	.40
❑ 28 Barnyard Clue	.15	.40
❑ 29 Pitched Standoff	.15	.40
❑ 30 Behind the Barn	.15	.40
❑ 31 Invasive Procedure	.15	.40
❑ 32 Strategic Alliance	.15	.40
❑ 33 Maquis Rebel	.15	.40
❑ 34 Second Visit	.15	.40
❑ 35 Old Debts	.15	.40
❑ 36 Awakening	.15	.40
❑ 37 Klingon Blood	.15	.40
❑ 38 Captain's Log	.15	.40
❑ 39 Logical Counsel	.15	.40
❑ 40 Unsuspected Ally	.15	.40
❑ 41 Eccentric Guide	.15	.40
❑ 42 Beamed Aboard	.15	.40
❑ 43 Starfleet and Maquis	.15	.40
❑ 44 Explanations	.15	.40
❑ 45 City of Care	.15	.40
❑ 46 A New Experience	.15	.40
❑ 47 Rough Surface	.15	.40
❑ 48 Detoured	.15	.40
❑ 49 Bad Manners	.15	.40
❑ 50 Watered Down	.15	.40
❑ 51 Reunion	.15	.40
❑ 52 Escape Route	.15	.40
❑ 53 Returning the Favor	.15	.40
❑ 54 Underground Allies	.15	.40
❑ 55 Obstacles	.15	.40
❑ 56 Change in Plans	.15	.40
❑ 57 On the Run	.15	.40
❑ 58 Rescue Party	.15	.40
❑ 59 Underground Trap	.15	.40
❑ 60 Ironic Rescue	.15	.40
❑ 61 Red Alert	.15	.40
❑ 62 Kazon Encounter	.15	.40
❑ 63 Crossfire	.15	.40
❑ 64 Tandem Strategy	.15	.40
❑ 65 Unpaid Debts	.15	.40
❑ 66 A Greater Challenge	.15	.40
❑ 67 Great Sacrifice	.15	.40
❑ 68 Collision Course	.15	.40
❑ 69 Natural State	.15	.40
❑ 70 The Greater Good	.15	.40
❑ 71 New Assignments	.15	.40
❑ 72 Where No One Has Gone Before	.15	.40
❑ 73 Mural Card 1	.15	.40
❑ 74 Mural Card 2	.15	.40
❑ 75 Mural Card 3	.15	.40
❑ 76 Mural Card 4	.15	.40
❑ 77 Mural Card 5	.15	.40
❑ 78 Mural Card 6	.15	.40
❑ 79 Mural Card 7	.15	.40
❑ 80 Mural Card 8	.15	.40
❑ 81 Mural Card 9	.15	.40
❑ 82 Neelix and Kes	.15	.40
❑ 83 The Two in Command	.15	.40
❑ 84 Lunch Break	.15	.40
❑ 85 A Desert Rehearsal	.15	.40
❑ 86 Standing By	.15	.40
❑ 87 Planet of Ocampas	.15	.40
❑ 88 High Overhead	.15	.40
❑ 89 On Your Mark	.15	.40
❑ 90 The Ocampan Desert	.15	.40
❑ 91 Warp Engines	.15	.40
❑ 92 Desktop Display Terminal	.15	.40
❑ 93 Medical Hologram	.15	.40
❑ 94 Control Display Panels	.15	.40
❑ 95 Matter Anti-Matter Reactor	.15	.40
❑ 96 Navigational Deflector	.15	.40
❑ 97 Checklist A	.15	.40
❑ 98 Checklist B	.15	.40

1995 Star Trek Voyager Series 1 Crew

Card	Low	High
COMPLETE SET (9)	7.50	20.00
❑ 1 Capt. Janeway	1.25	3.00
❑ 2 Chakotay	1.25	3.00
❑ 3 Tuvok	1.25	3.00
❑ 4 Paris	1.25	3.00
❑ 5 Torres	1.25	3.00
❑ 6 Ensign Kim	1.25	3.00
❑ 7 The Doctor	1.25	3.00
❑ 8 Neelix	1.25	3.00
❑ 9 Kes	1.25	3.00

1995 Star Trek Voyager Series 2

Card	Low	High
COMPLETE SET (90)	5.00	12.00
❑ 1 Mission Chronology	.15	.40
❑ 2 Mission Chronology	.15	.40
❑ 3 Mission Chronology	.15	.40
❑ 4 Mission Chronology	.15	.40
❑ 5 Mission Chronology	.15	.40
❑ 6 Mission Chronology	.15	.40
❑ 7 Mission Chronology	.15	.40
❑ 8 Mission Chronology	.15	.40
❑ 9 Mission Chronology	.15	.40
❑ 10 Caretaker	.15	.40
❑ 11 Caretaker	.15	.40
❑ 12 Caretaker	.15	.40
❑ 13 Caretaker	.15	.40
❑ 14 Caretaker	.15	.40
❑ 15 Caretaker	.15	.40
❑ 16 Parallax	.15	.40
❑ 17 Parallax	.15	.40
❑ 18 Parallax	.15	.40
❑ 19 Time and Again	.15	.40
❑ 20 Time and Again	.15	.40
❑ 21 Time and Again	.15	.40
❑ 22 Phage	.15	.40
❑ 23 Phage	.15	.40
❑ 24 Phage	.15	.40
❑ 25 The Cloud	.15	.40
❑ 26 The Cloud	.15	.40
❑ 27 The Cloud	.15	.40
❑ 28 Eye of the Needle	.15	.40
❑ 29 Eye of the Needle	.15	.40
❑ 30 Eye of the Needle	.15	.40
❑ 31 Ex Post Facto	.15	.40
❑ 32 Ex Post Facto	.15	.40
❑ 33 Ex Post Facto	.15	.40
❑ 34 Emanations	.15	.40
❑ 35 Emanations	.15	.40
❑ 36 Emanations	.15	.40
❑ 37 Prime Factors	.15	.40
❑ 38 Prime Factors	.15	.40
❑ 39 Prime Factors	.15	.40
❑ 40 State of Flux	.15	.40
❑ 41 State of Flux	.15	.40
❑ 42 State of Flux	.15	.40
❑ 43 Heroes and Demons	.15	.40
❑ 44 Heroes and Demons	.15	.40
❑ 45 Heroes and Demons	.15	.40
❑ 46 Cathexis	.15	.40
❑ 47 Cathexis	.15	.40
❑ 48 Cathexis	.15	.40
❑ 49 Faces	.15	.40
❑ 50 Faces	.15	.40
❑ 51 Faces	.15	.40
❑ 52 Jetrel	.15	.40
❑ 53 Jetrel	.15	.40
❑ 54 Jetrel	.15	.40
❑ 55 Learning Curve	.15	.40
❑ 56 Learning Curve	.15	.40
❑ 57 Learning Curve	.15	.40
❑ 58 Question One of Six	.15	.40
❑ 59 Question Two of Six	.15	.40
❑ 60 Question Three of Six	.15	.40
❑ 61 Question Four of Six	.15	.40
❑ 62 Question Five of Six	.15	.40
❑ 63 Question Six of Six	.15	.40
❑ 64 Akoonah	.15	.40
❑ 65 Sims Beacon	.15	.40
❑ 66 Vidiian Organ Remover	.15	.40
❑ 67 Memory Engrams	.15	.40
❑ 68 Transporter Test Cylinder	.15	.40
❑ 69 Cenotaph	.15	.40
❑ 70 Spatial Trajector	.15	.40
❑ 71 Metreon Regenerative Fusion	.15	.40
❑ 72 Bio-Neural Gel Pack	.15	.40
❑ 73 Quantum Singularity	.15	.40
❑ 74 The Cloud	.15	.40
❑ 75 Phage Mirror Asteroid	.15	.40
❑ 76 Tractor Beam	.15	.40
❑ 77 Telek	.15	.40
❑ 78 Grendel	.15	.40
❑ 79 Rinax	.15	.40
❑ 80 Gathorel Labin	.15	.40
❑ 81 Cosmic Antibodies	.15	.40
❑ 82 Kazon Desert	.15	.40
❑ 83 Ocampan Underground	.15	.40
❑ 84 Time and Again Planet	.15	.40
❑ 85 Vidiian Asteroid	.15	.40
❑ 86 Banean Homeworld	.15	.40
❑ 87 State of Flux Planet	.15	.40
❑ 88 Cast	.15	.40
❑ 89 Checklist	.15	.40
❑ 90 Checklist	.02	.10

1995 Star Trek Voyager Series 2 Crew

Card	Low	High
COMPLETE SET (9)	15.00	40.00
ONE PER WALMART PACK		
❑ E1 Captain Janeway	2.00	5.00
❑ E2 Chakotay	2.00	5.00
❑ E3 Tuvok	2.00	5.00
❑ E4 B'Elanna Torres	2.00	5.00
❑ E5 Tom Paris	2.00	5.00
❑ E6 Harry Kim	2.00	5.00
❑ E7 The Doctor	2.00	5.00
❑ E8 Kes	2.00	5.00
❑ E9 Neelix	2.00	5.00

1995 Star Trek Voyager Series 2 Recipes

Card	Low	High
COMPLETE SET (6)	10.00	25.00
STATED ODDS 1:18		
❑ R1 Vulcan Plomeek Soup	2.00	5.00
❑ R2 Laurelian Blue Pudding	2.00	5.00
❑ R3 Takar Loggerhead Eggs	2.00	5.00
❑ R4 Proteinaceous Coffee Cocktail	2.00	5.00
❑ R5 Macaroni & Brill Cheese	2.00	5.00
❑ R6 Spinach Shake with Pear	2.00	5.00

1995 Star Trek Voyager Series 2 Xenobio

Card	Low	High
COMPLETE SET (9)	20.00	50.00
STATED ODDS 1:12		
❑ S1 Seska	3.00	8.00
❑ S2 Telek	3.00	8.00
❑ S3 Gathorel Labin	3.00	8.00
❑ S4 Dr. Neria	3.00	8.00
❑ S5 Sulan	3.00	8.00
❑ S6 Jetrel	3.00	8.00
❑ S7 Jabin	3.00	8.00
❑ S9 Lidell	3.00	8.00
❑ S9 Toscat	3.00	8.00

1995 The X-Files

Card	Low	High
COMPLETE SET (72)	5.00	12.00
❑ 1 Title Card Mulder and Scully	.15	.40
❑ 2 Introduction	.15	.40
❑ 3 Introduction	.15	.40
❑ 4 Mulder, Fox	.15	.40
❑ 5 Scully, Dana Katherine	.15	.40
❑ 6 Deep Throat	.15	.40
❑ 7 The Cigarette Smoking Man	.15	.40
❑ 8 Skinner, Walter S.	.15	.40
❑ 9 The Lone Gunmen	.15	.40
❑ 10 Pilot Episode	.15	.40
❑ 11 Deep Throat	.15	.40
❑ 12 Squeeze	.15	.40
❑ 13 Conduit	.15	.40
❑ 14 The Jersey Devil	.15	.40
❑ 15 Shadows	.15	.40
❑ 16 Ghost in the Machine	.15	.40
❑ 17 Ice	.15	.40
❑ 18 Space	.15	.40
❑ 19 Fallen Angel	.15	.40
❑ 20 Eve	.15	.40
❑ 21 Fire	.15	.40
❑ 22 Beyond the Sea	.15	.40
❑ 23 Genderbender	.15	.40
❑ 24 Lazarus	.15	.40
❑ 25 Young at Heart	.15	.40
❑ 26 E.B.E.	.15	.40
❑ 27 Miracle Man	.15	.40
❑ 28 Shapes	.15	.40
❑ 29 Darkness Falls	.15	.40
❑ 30 Tooms	.15	.40
❑ 31 Born Again	.15	.40
❑ 32 Roland	.15	.40
❑ 33 The Erlenmeyer Flask	.15	.40
❑ 34 UFO	.15	.40
❑ 35 Face of Fear	.15	.40
❑ 36 Paranormal Terror	.15	.40
❑ 37 Homunculus	.15	.40
❑ 38 Eugene Tooms	.15	.40
❑ 39 The Jersey Devil	.15	.40
❑ 40 Parasitic Worms	.15	.40
❑ 41 The Face of Mars	.15	.40
❑ 42 Cecil L'Ively	.15	.40
❑ 43 Manitou	.15	.40
❑ 44 Prehistoric Insects	.15	.40
❑ 45 Alien Fetus	.15	.40
❑ 46 Anti-Gravity Aircraft	.15	.40
❑ 47 UFO Concept Design	.15	.40
❑ 48 Runway Encounter	.15	.40
❑ 49 Government UFO	.15	.40
❑ 50 Caught in the Beam	.15	.40
❑ 51 The UFO Above	.15	.40
❑ 52 Tooms Scales the Wall	.15	.40
❑ 53 Unearthly Elongation	.15	.40
❑ 54 Tooms Squeezes into Chimney	.15	.40
❑ 55 Tooms Storyboards	.15	.40
❑ 56 Jersey Devil Concept Designs	.15	.40
❑ 57 Parasitic Worms	.15	.40
❑ 58 Invaded Host	.15	.40
❑ 59 Fallen Angel Concept Designs	.15	.40
❑ 60 Salamander Hand	.15	.40
❑ 61 Serial Killer John Barnett	.15	.40
❑ 62 Skeletal Remains	.15	.40
❑ 63 Alien Embryos	.15	.40
❑ 64 Promotional Illustration	.15	.40
❑ 65 Poster Graphic	.15	.40
❑ 66 Episode: Ice	.15	.40
❑ 67 Episode: Shadows	.15	.40
❑ 68 Episode: Fallen Angel	.15	.40
❑ 69 Episode: Shapes	.15	.40
❑ 70 Episode: Space	.15	.40
❑ 71 Episode: Trust No One	.15	.40
❑ 72 Checklist	.02	.10

1995 The X-Files Foil

Card	Low	High
COMPLETE SET (72)	30.00	80.00
*FOIL: 1.5X TO 4X BASE CARDS	.60	1.50

1995 The X-Files Chromium Finest

Card	Low	High
COMPLETE SET (4)	12.50	30.00
❑ X1 Agents Mulder and Scully	5.00	12.00
❑ X2 The Erlenmeyer Flask	5.00	12.00
❑ X3 Fox Mulder	5.00	12.00
❑ X4 Dana Scully	5.00	12.00

1995 The X-Files Etched

Card	Low	High
COMPLETE SET (6)	15.00	40.00
❑ I1 I1-Do Not Open Until X-mas	4.00	10.00
❑ I2 I2-A Dismemberance of Things Past	4.00	10.00
❑ I3 I3-The Return	4.00	10.00
❑ I4 I4-Firebird Part One: Khobka's Lament	4.00	10.00
❑ I5 I5-Firebird Part Two: Crescit Eundo	4.00	10.00
❑ I6 I6-Firebird Part Three: A Brief Authority	4.00	10.00

1996 DC Outburst Firepower

Card	Low	High
COMPLETE SET (80)	5.00	12.00
❑ 1 Superman	.15	.40
❑ 2 Azrael	.15	.40
❑ 3 Batman	.15	.40
❑ 4 Martian Manhunter	.15	.40
❑ 5 Wonder Woman	.15	.40
❑ 6 Flash	.15	.40
❑ 7 Fire	.15	.40
❑ 8 Metamorpho	.15	.40
❑ 9 Spectre	.15	.40
❑ 10 Lobo	.15	.40
❑ 11 Maxima	.15	.40
❑ 12 Bane	.15	.40
❑ 13 The Ray	.15	.40
❑ 14 Superman	.15	.40
❑ 15 Captain Marvel	.15	.40
❑ 16 Steel	.15	.40
❑ 17 Captain Atom	.15	.40
❑ 18 Supergirl	.15	.40
❑ 19 Superboy	.15	.40
❑ 20 Booster Gold	.15	.40
❑ 21 Robin	.15	.40
❑ 22 Black Canary	.15	.40
❑ 23 Hawkman	.15	.40
❑ 24 Man-Bat	.15	.40
❑ 25 Batman	.15	.40
❑ 26 Huntress	.15	.40
❑ 27 Nightwing	.15	.40
❑ 28 Green Lantern	.15	.40
❑ 29 Arsenal	.15	.40
❑ 30 Starman	.15	.40
❑ 31 Fate	.15	.40
❑ 32 Aquaman	.15	.40
❑ 33 Orion	.15	.40

Card	Low	High
34 Green Arrow	.15	.40
35 Blue Beetle	.15	.40
36 Deathstroke	.15	.40
37 Catwoman	.15	.40
38 Two-Face	.15	.40
39 Darkseid	.15	.40
40 Cyborg	.15	.40
41 The Joker	.15	.40
42 Mr. Freeze	.15	.40
43 The Riddler	.15	.40
44 Chronos	.15	.40
45 Neron	.15	.40
46 Parallax	.15	.40
47 Poison Ivy	.15	.40
48 Black Adam	.15	.40
49 Ra's Al Ghul	.15	.40
50 Lex Luthor	.15	.40
51 Circe	.15	.40
52 Dr. Polaris	.15	.40
53 Kobra	.15	.40
54 Brainiac	.15	.40
55 Superman	.15	.40
56 Superboy	.15	.40
57 Wonder Woman	.15	.40
58 Hawkman	.15	.40
59 Green Lantern	.15	.40
60 Robin	.15	.40
61 Batman	.15	.40
62 Captain Marvel	.15	.40
63 Aquaman	.15	.40
64 Nightwing	.15	.40
65 Catwoman	.15	.40
66 Aquaman	.15	.40
67 Black Canary	.15	.40
68 Flash	.15	.40
69 Robin	.15	.40
70 Mr. Miracle	.15	.40
71 Impulse	.15	.40
72 Hawkman	.15	.40
73 Superman	.15	.40
74 Flash	.15	.40
75 Martian Manhunter	.15	.40
76 Warrior	.15	.40
77 Batman	.15	.40
78 Green Lantern	.15	.40
79 Wonder Woman	.15	.40
80 Checklist	.15	.40

1996 DC Outburst Firepower Holoburst

Card	Low	High
COMPLETE SET (2)	5.00	12.00
STATED ODDS 1:36		
1 Superman to the Rescue	3.00	8.00
2 Batman Swings into Action	3.00	8.00

1996 DC Outburst Firepower Maximum Fire-power

Card	Low	High
COMPLETE SET (20)	6.00	15.00
STATED ODDS 2:3		
1 Batman Sounds the Alarm	.60	1.50
2 Oracle Leads the Way	.60	1.50
3 Superman Turns Up the Heat	.60	1.50
4 Hawkman Hits from Above	.60	1.50
5 Flash Clears the Blast Zone	.60	1.50
6 Make Way for Superman	.60	1.50
7 Two Heroes Triumph	.60	1.50
8 Lava Meets Lantern's Light	.60	1.50
9 An Amazon Calls the Shots	.60	1.50
10 Flash Beats Back an Army	.60	1.50
11 Green Lantern Holds the Line	.60	1.50
12 A Shock to the System	.60	1.50
13 Flash Breaks the Barrier	.60	1.50
14 Down for the Count	.60	1.50
15 Parallax in Command	.60	1.50
16 Superman Takes a Hit	.60	1.50
17 Parallax Escapes	.60	1.50
18 Batman's Last Chance	.60	1.50
19 One Shot at Success	.60	1.50
20 United They Stand	.60	1.50

1996 Marvel Masterpieces

Card	Low	High
COMPLETE SET (100)	300.00	500.00
1 Archangel	3.00	8.00
2 Beast	3.00	8.00
3 Bishop	3.00	8.00
4 Black Cat	3.00	8.00
5 Black Widow	3.00	8.00
6 Cable	3.00	8.00
7 Captain America	3.00	8.00
8 Carnage	3.00	8.00
9 Crystal	3.00	8.00
10 Cyclops	3.00	8.00
11 Domino	3.00	8.00
12 Dr. Doom	3.00	8.00
13 Dr. Strange	3.00	8.00
14 Elektra	3.00	8.00
15 Gambit	3.00	8.00
16 Ghost Rider	3.00	8.00
17 Green Goblin	3.00	8.00
18 Hawkeye	3.00	8.00
19 Holocaust	3.00	8.00
20 Hulk	3.00	8.00
21 Human Torch	3.00	8.00
22 Iceman	3.00	8.00
23 Invisible Woman	3.00	8.00
24 Iron Man	3.00	8.00
25 Jackal	3.00	8.00
26 Jean Grey	3.00	8.00
27 Kymaera	3.00	8.00
28 Lizard	3.00	8.00
29 Mystique	3.00	8.00
30 Namor	3.00	8.00
31 Omega Red	3.00	8.00
32 Onslaught	3.00	8.00
33 Professor X	3.00	8.00
34 Psi-Lord	3.00	8.00
35 Psylocke	3.00	8.00
36 Punisher	3.00	8.00
37 Quicksilver	3.00	8.00
38 Rogue	3.00	8.00
39 Sabretooth	3.00	8.00
40 Scarlet Witch	3.00	8.00
41 Shadowcat	3.00	8.00
42 She-Hulk	3.00	8.00
43 Silver Sable	3.00	8.00
44 Silver Surfer	3.00	8.00
45 Spider-Man	3.00	8.00
46 Spider-Woman	3.00	8.00
47 Storm	3.00	8.00
48 Thanos	3.00	8.00
49 Thing	3.00	8.00
50 Thor	3.00	8.00
51 Venom	3.00	8.00
52 War Machine	3.00	8.00
53 Warlock	3.00	8.00
54 White Queen	3.00	8.00
55 Cable	3.00	8.00
56 Stryfe	3.00	8.00
57 Genesis	3.00	8.00
58 X-Man	3.00	8.00
59 Dark Beast	3.00	8.00
60 Random	3.00	8.00
61 Apocalypse	3.00	8.00
62 Angel	3.00	8.00
63 Archangel	3.00	8.00
64 Spider-Man	3.00	8.00
65 Dr. Octopus	3.00	8.00
66 Dr. Octopus	3.00	8.00
67 Iron Man	3.00	8.00
68 Fin Fang Foom	3.00	8.00
69 War Machine	3.00	8.00
70 Phoenix	3.00	8.00
71 Magneto	3.00	8.00
72 Phoenix	3.00	8.00
73 Captain America	3.00	8.00
74 Red Skull	3.00	8.00
75 U.S.Agent	3.00	8.00
76 Ghost Rider	3.00	8.00
77 Blackout	3.00	8.00
78 Vengeance	3.00	8.00
79 Venom	3.00	8.00
80 Spider-Man	3.00	8.00
81 Carnage	3.00	8.00
82 Thor	3.00	8.00
83 Loki	3.00	8.00
84 Thunderstrike	3.00	8.00
85 Spider-Man	3.00	8.00
86 Scarlet Spider	3.00	8.00
87 Spider-Man	3.00	8.00
88 Ant Man	3.00	8.00
89 Yellowjacket	3.00	8.00
90 Giant-Man	3.00	8.00
91 Weapon X	3.00	8.00
92 Wolverine	3.00	8.00
93 Wolverine	3.00	8.00
94 Daredevil	3.00	8.00
95 Daredevil	3.00	8.00
96 Daredevil	3.00	8.00
97 Hulk	3.00	8.00
98 Hulk	3.00	8.00
99 Hulk	3.00	8.00
100 Checklist	3.00	8.00

1996 Marvel Masterpieces Artwork Redemption

UNPRICED ARTWORK PRINT RUN 1

- 1 Beast
- 2 Elektra
- 3 Gambit
- 4 Human Torch
- 5 Silver Surfer
- 6 Spider-Man
- 7 Storm
- 8 Venom
- 9 Wolverine

1996 Marvel Masterpieces Double Impact

Card	Low	High
COMPLETE SET (6)	300.00	500.00
STATED ODDS 1:4		
1 Bishop / Beast	50.00	100.00
2 Punisher / Psylocke	50.00	100.00
3 Rogue / Human Torch/Rogue	50.00	100.00
4 Silver Surfer / Captain America	50.00	100.00
5 Storm / Spider-Man	50.00	100.00
6 Wolverine / Venom	50.00	100.00

1996 Marvel Masterpieces Gallery

Card	Low	High
COMPLETE SET (6)	75.00	150.00
STATED ODDS 1:3		
1 Cyclops	15.00	30.00
2 Hulk	15.00	30.00
3 Magneto	15.00	30.00
4 Sabretooth	15.00	30.00
5 Spider-Man	15.00	30.00
6 Wolverine	15.00	30.00

1996 Marvel Onslaught

Card	Low	High
COMPLETE SET (100)	10.00	25.00
1 Archangel	.20	.50
2 Beast	.20	.50
3 Bishop	.20	.50
4 Cannonball	.20	.50
5 Cyclops	.20	.50
6 Gambit	.20	.50
7 Iceman	.20	.50
8 Phoenix	.20	.50
9 Psylocke	.20	.50
10 Rogue	.20	.50
11 Storm	.20	.50
12 Wolverine	.20	.50
13 Dark Beast	.20	.50
14 Fatale	.20	.50
15 Havok	.20	.50
16 Holocaust	.20	.50
17 Onslaught	.20	.50
18 Post	.20	.50
19 Random	.20	.50
20 Sentinels	.20	.50
21 Black Widow	.20	.50
22 Captain America	.20	.50
23 Crystal	.20	.50
24 Giant-Man	.20	.50
25 Hawkeye	.20	.50
26 Iron Man	.20	.50
27 Quicksilver	.20	.50
28 Scarlet Witch	.20	.50
29 Thor	.20	.50
30 Vision	.20	.50
31 Wasp	.20	.50
32 Cable	.20	.50
33 Caliban	.20	.50
34 Domino	.20	.50
35 Meltdown	.20	.50
36 Shatterstar	.20	.50
37 Siryn	.20	.50
38 Sunspot	.20	.50
39 Warpath	.20	.50
40 X-Man	.20	.50
41 Human Torch	.20	.50
42 Invisible Woman	.20	.50
43 Mr. Fantastic	.20	.50
44 Thing	.20	.50
45 Forge	.20	.50
46 Mystique	.20	.50
47 Sabretooth	.20	.50
48 Shard	.20	.50
49 Wild Child	.20	.50
50 Colossus	.20	.50
51 Nightcrawler	.20	.50
52 Shadowcat	.20	.50
53 Apocalypse	.20	.50
54 Bastion	.20	.50
55 Dr. Doom	.20	.50
56 Gateway	.20	.50
57 Juggernaut	.20	.50
58 Magneto	.20	.50
59 Mr. Sinister	.20	.50
60 Black Panther	.20	.50
61 Daredevil	.20	.50
62 Dr. Strange	.20	.50
63 Elektra	.20	.50
64 Charlie & Franklin	.20	.50
65 Hulk	.20	.50
66 Punisher	.20	.50
67 Spider-Man	.20	.50
68 Coming of Onslaught	.20	.50
69 Onslaught Revealed	.20	.50
70 Avengers Assemble!	.20	.50
71 Day of the Sentinels	.20	.50
72 Onslaught Absorbs Franklin Richards	.20	.50
73 Onslaught Sheds Xavier	.20	.50
74 X-Man No More	.20	.50
75 Assault on Onslaught	.20	.50
76 The Ultimate Sacrifice	.20	.50
77 Nuclear Holocaust	.20	.50
78 A World Without Heroes	.20	.50
79 A New Beginning	.20	.50
80 Black Bolt	.20	.50
81 Black Panther	.20	.50
82 Bucky	.20	.50
83 Captain America	.20	.50
84 Dr. Doom	.20	.50
85 Falcon	.20	.50
86 Galactus	.20	.50
87 Hawkeye	.20	.50
88 Human Torch	.20	.50
89 Invisible Girl	.20	.50
90 Iron Man	.20	.50
91 Master Man	.20	.50
92 Mr. Fantastic	.20	.50
93 Namor	.20	.50
94 Red Skull	.20	.50
95 Scarlet Witch	.20	.50
96 Silver Surfer	.20	.50
97 Swordsman	.20	.50
98 Thing	.20	.50
99 Vision	.20	.50
100 Checklist	.20	.50

1996 Marvel Onslaught Autographs

COMPLETE SET (4)
STATED ODDS 1:4500

- 1 Mr. Fantastic / Jim Lee
- 2 Captain America / Rob Liefeld
- 3 Silver Surfer / Stan Lee
- 4 Iron Man / Stan Lee

1996 Marvel Onslaught Mirage

Card	Low	High
COMPLETE SET (3)	20.00	50.00
STATED ODDS 1:36		
1 Avengers	10.00	25.00
2 Fantastic Four	10.00	25.00
3 Onslaught	10.00	25.00

1996 Marvel Onslaught Overpower Hero

Card	Low	High
COMPLETE SET (4)	4.00	10.00
STATED ODDS 1:9		
1 Dark Beast	2.00	5.00
2 Holocaust	2.00	5.00
3 Onslaught	2.00	5.00
4 Post	2.00	5.00

1996 Marvel Onslaught Overpower Mission

Card	Low	High
COMPLETE SET (7)	8.00	20.00
STATED ODDS 1:9		
1 Unity in Chaos	2.00	5.00
2 Incredible Forces	2.00	5.00
3 Child of the Future	2.00	5.00
4 Display of Power	2.00	5.00
5 Sphere of Influence	2.00	5.00
6 Desperate Reunion	2.00	5.00
7 Ground Zero	2.00	5.00

1996 Star Trek First Contact

Card	Low	High
COMPLETE SET (60)	4.00	10.00
SPINER AUTO ODDS 1:3,600		
1 A Dedicated Vessel	.15	.40
2 The Nightmare	.15	.40
3 The Neutral Zone	.15	.40
4 U.S.S. Defiant, Off-Line	.15	.40
5 Borg Sphere	.15	.40
6 Unto the Breach	.15	.40
7 Zefram and Lily	.15	.40
8 Borg Meteor	.15	.40
9 Historic Date	.15	.40
10 21st Century Civilians	.15	.40
11 Lily Opens Fire	.15	.40
12 Lily Faints	.15	.40
13 The Phoenix	.15	.40
14 Heating Up	.15	.40
15 Sickbay Goes Dead	.15	.40
16 Please State the Nature	.15	.40
17 Drinking With Zefram	.15	.40
18 The Hive	.15	.40
19 Firefight	.15	.40
20 Lietenant Commander Data Captured	.15	.40
21 Assimilated	.15	.40
22 Captain Jean-Luc Picard and Lily	.15	.40
23 Borg Drones	.15	.40
24 Talk of the Future	.15	.40
25 View From the Stars	.15	.40
26 Borg Queen	.15	.40
27 Real Skin	.15	.40
28 Borgified Starship	.15	.40
29 The Return of Dixon Hill	.15	.40
30 Nightclub Entrance	.15	.40
31 A Ruby Kiss	.15	.40
32 Borg in the Night	.15	.40
33 Missile Complex	.15	.40
34 Barclay meets a Legend	.15	.40
35 Reports of My Assimilation	.15	.40
36 Lily Meets Lt. Commander Worf	.15	.40
37 Lost in the Woods	.15	.40
38 Suiting up for Zero G	.15	.40
39 Lietenant Commander Data the Rebel	.15	.40
40 Pain and Pleasure	.15	.40
41 Interplexing Spires	.15	.40
42 Hull Fight	.15	.40
43 Deflector Separation	.15	.40
44 True Motives	.15	.40
45 Objection Noted	.15	.40
46 Lost Friend	.15	.40
47 Phoenix Launches	.15	.40
48 Databorg	.15	.40
49 Captain Jean-Luc Picard Faces the Queen	.15	.40
50 The Return of Locutus	.15	.40
51 Sacrifice	.15	.40
52 Target Phoenix	.15	.40
53 Phoenix Hits Warp	.15	.40
54 Hive Collapse	.15	.40
55 Close Encounter	.15	.40
56 First Contact	.15	.40
57 Back on Duty	.15	.40
58 New Friends	.15	.40
59 U.S.S. Enterprise Crew	.15	.40
60 Checklist	.15	.40
NNO Brent Spiner AU		

1996 Star Trek First Contact Behind the Scenes

Card	Low	High
COMPLETE SET (10)	4.00	10.00
STATED ODDS 1:6		
BS1 Jonathon Frakes the Director	1.00	2.50
BS2 Directing a Klingon	1.00	2.50
BS3 With Friends Like These	1.00	2.50
BS4 On Location	1.00	2.50
BS5 Give That Borg a Hand	1.00	2.50
BS6 Made for the Job	1.00	2.50
BS7 Fit for a Queen	1.00	2.50
BS8 It's Easier in Space	1.00	2.50
BS9 Lt. Commander Data and the Borg Queen	1.00	2.50
BS10 A Man Amongst Borg	1.00	2.50

1996 Star Trek First Contact Blueprint Posters

COMPLETE SET (3)
STATED ODDS 1:36

- S1 U.S.S. Enterprise
- S2 Borg Cube
- S3 Phoenix

1996 Star Trek First Contact Characters

Card	Low	High
COMPLETE SET (10)	8.00	20.00
STATED ODDS 1:9		
C1 Captain Jean-Luc Picard	1.50	4.00
C2 Lieutenant Commander Data	1.50	4.00
C3 Lieutenant Commander Geordi La Forge	1.50	4.00
C4 Commander William T. Riker	1.50	4.00
C5 Lieutenant Deanna Troi	1.50	4.00
C6 Dr. Beverly Crusher	1.50	4.00
C7 Lieutenant Commander Worf	1.50	4.00
C8 Lieutenant Hawk	1.50	4.00
C9 Zefram Cochrane	1.50	4.00
C10 Lily Sloane	1.50	4.00

1996 Star Trek First Contact Enterprise

Card	Low	High
COMPLETE SET (6)	4.00	10.00
STATED ODDS 1:8		
E1 Bridge	1.50	4.00
E2 Main Engineering	1.50	4.00
E3 Ready Room	1.50	4.00
E4 Sickbay	1.50	4.00
E5 Evacuation Corridor	1.50	4.00
E6 Observation Lounge	1.50	4.00

1996 Star Trek First Contact Techno-Cel Borg

Card	Low	High
COMPLETE SET (12)	10.00	25.00
STATED ODDS 1:8		
B1 Star Trek: The Next Generation Borg	2.00	5.00
B2 Star Trek: First Contact Borg	2.00	5.00
B3 Locutus	2.00	5.00
B4 Klingon Borg	2.00	5.00
B5 Bolian Borg	2.00	5.00
B6 Cardassian Borg	2.00	5.00
B7 Borg Queen	2.00	5.00
B8 Borg Alcove	2.00	5.00
B9 Borgified Engineering	2.00	5.00
B10 Star Trek: First Contact Borg	2.00	5.00
B11 Star Trek: First Contact Borg	2.00	5.00
B12 Borg Symbol	2.00	5.00

1996 Star Trek Voyager Profiles Autographs

Card	Low	High
COMPLETE SET (20)	400.00	800.00
RANDOM INSERTS IN PACKS		
1 Kate Mulgrew	40.00	80.00
2 Robert Beltran	20.00	40.00
3 Harry Kim	20.00	40.00
4 Tim Russ	20.00	40.00
5 Roxann Dawson	20.00	40.00
6 Robert D.McNeill	20.00	40.00
7 Jeri Ryan	75.00	150.00
8 Robert Picardo	30.00	60.00
9 Ethan Phillips	20.00	40.00
10 Jennifer Lien	30.00	60.00
11 John DeLancie	20.00	40.00
12 Dwight Schultz	20.00	40.00
13 Henry Darrow	20.00	40.00
14 Alex Enberg	20.00	40.00
15 Tony Todd	20.00	40.00
16 Leland Orser	20.00	40.00
17 Michael McKean	20.00	40.00
18 Josh Clark	20.00	40.00
19 John Rhys-Davies	20.00	40.00
20 George Takei	25.00	50.00

1996 The X-Files Season Three

Card	Low	High
COMPLETE SET (72)	5.00	12.00
1 Title Card	.15	.40
2 Introduction	.15	.40
3 Fox Mulder	.15	.40
4 Dana Scully	.15	.40
5 Walter Skinner	.15	.40
6 The Cigarette-Smoking Man	.15	.40
7 X	.15	.40
8 The Lone Gunmen	.15	.40
9 The Well-Manicured Man	.15	.40
10 The Blessing Way	.15	.40
11 Paper Clip	.15	.40
12 D.P.O.	.15	.40
13 Clyde Bruckman's Final Repose	.15	.40
14 The List	.15	.40
15 2Shy	.15	.40
16 The Walk	.15	.40
17 Oubliette	.15	.40
18 Nisei	.15	.40
19 731	.15	.40
20 Revelations	.15	.40
21 War of the Coprophages	.15	.40
22 Syzygy	.15	.40
23 Grotesque	.15	.40
24 Piper Maru	.15	.40
25 Apocrypha	.15	.40
26 Pusher	.15	.40
27 Teso Dos Bichos	.15	.40
28 Hell Money	.15	.40
29 Jose Chung's 'From Outer Space	.15	.40
30 Avatar	.15	.40
31 Quagmire	.15	.40
32 Wetwired	.15	.40
33 Talitha Cumi	.15	.40
34 More Secrets of the X-Files	.15	.40
35 The X-Files on Video	.15	.40
36 The X-Files on Video II	.15	.40
37 Lightning Boy	.15	.40
38 Reincarnated For Revenge	.15	.40
39 The Monster Called Madness	.15	.40
40 Genetically Different Human	.15	.40
41 Unwitting Victim	.15	.40
42 Lethal Aparition	.15	.40
43 Emulsified Remains	.15	.40
44 Inhuman Interests	.15	.40
45 Embittered Veteran	.15	.40
46 Demonic Madman's Fall	.15	.40
47 Victim of Vengeance	.15	.40
48 Insect Perspective	.15	.40
49 Alien Autopsy Subject	.15	.40
50 Extraterrestrial Abduction	.15	.40
51 The Man With the Power	.15	.40
52 Robotic Insect	.15	.40
53 Decapitation Sculptings	.15	.40
54 Bruckman's Decomposition	.15	.40
55 Alien Ooze Appliance	.15	.40
56 Cockroach Crossing	.15	.40
57 Cyclopean Alien	.15	.40
58 731 Extraterrestrials	.15	.40
59 Liquefied Corpse	.15	.40
60 Grotesque Sculpting	.15	.40
61 Awaken The Sleep of Reason	.15	.40
62 A System of Secret Files	.15	.40
63 Prophecy of Death for Mulder	.15	.40
64 Monsters Begetting Monsters	.15	.40
65 An Apology for the Truth	.15	.40
66 Smart is Sexy	.15	.40
67 At the Center of a Cosmic G-Spot	.15	.40
68 An Exchange of Information	.15	.40
69 The Truths Are Out There	.15	.40
70 Guardian Angel	.15	.40
71 A Miraculous Individual	.15	.40
72 Checklist	.02	.10

1996 The X-Files Season Three Foil

Card	Low	High
COMPLETE SET	10.00	25.00
STATED ODDS ONE PER PACK		

1996 The X-Files Season Three Etched Foil

Card	Low	High
COMPLETE SET (6)	10.00	20.00
STATED ODDS 1:12		
i1 One Player Only	2.00	5.00
i2 Falling	2.00	5.00
i3 Home of the Brave, Part One: The New World	2.00	5.00
i4 Home of the Brave, Part Two: A Question of Ownership	2.00	5.00
i5 Thin Air	2.00	5.00
i6 Night Lights, Part One	2.00	5.00

1996 The X-Files Season Three Holograms

Card	Low	High
COMPLETE SET (2)	3.00	8.00
STATED ODDS 1:18		
X1 Fox Mulder	2.00	5.00
X2 Mulder/Scully	2.00	5.00

1996 The X-Files Season Three Paranormals Finest

Card	Low	High
COMPLETE SET (2)	3.00	8.00
STATED ODDS 1:18		
X3PF1 Episode 3X04	2.00	5.00
X3PF2 Episode 3X10	2.00	5.00

1996 The X-Files Season Three Promos

Card	Low	High
P1 Scully/Mulder	.75	2.00
P2 Scully/Mulder	.75	2.00
P3 Dead Alien	1.50	4.00
P4 Two Guys Fighting	1.25	3.00
P5 Scully/Mulder	8.00	20.00

1997 Batman and Robin

Card	Low	High
COMPLETE SET (70)	5.00	12.00
1 A New Battle Begins	.15	.40
2 Call To Arms	.15	.40
3 Cold-Hearted Thief	.15	.40
4 Crashing the Scene	.15	.40
5 Heist Hockey	.15	.40
6 Face-Off to Lift-Off	.15	.40
7 A Venomous Relationship	.15	.40
8 A Tragic Genesis	.15	.40
9 A Monstrous Partner	.15	.40
10 Surprise Visit	.15	.40
11 Taking the Bait	.15	.40
12 Man in the Spotlight	.15	.40
13 Gorilla My Dreams	.15	.40
14 A Mesmerizing Beauty	.15	.40
15 Dueling Passions	.15	.40
16 Winter on Wheels	.15	.40
17 Cold Encounters	.15	.40
18 Nice Try, Vine Lady	.15	.40
19 A Change of Plans	.15	.40
20 Pulling Rank	.15	.40
21 Capture and Control	.15	.40
22 Mr. Freeze on Ice	.15	.40
23 The Cold Hard Facts	.15	.40
24 House Hunting	.15	.40
25 Midnight Madness	.15	.40
26 Sis to the Rescue	.15	.40
27 Let's Make a Deal	.15	.40
28 Cruel Manipulations	.15	.40
29 Planning an Ice Age	.15	.40

Card	Low	High
30 Adam and Evil	.15	.40
31 Sending Clear Signals	.15	.40
32 The Real Party Begins	.15	.40
33 Sweet, Sweet Poison	.15	.40
34 Battle of Titans	.15	.40
35 Global Warning	.15	.40
36 Batman	.15	.40
37 Mr. Freeze	.15	.40
38 Robin	.15	.40
39 Robin	.15	.40
40 Batman	.15	.40
41 Pamela Isley	.15	.40
42 Mr. Freeze	.15	.40
43 Robin	.15	.40
44 Mr. Freeze	.15	.40
45 Robin	.15	.40
46 Bruce	.15	.40
47 Mr. Freeze	.15	.40
48 Dick	.15	.40
49 Julie/Bruce	.15	.40
50 Robin	.15	.40
51 Ivy	.15	.40
52 Poison Ivy	.15	.40
53 Batman	.15	.40
54 Poison Ivy	.15	.40
55 Bruce	.15	.40
56 Poison Ivy	.15	.40
57 Mr. Freeze	.15	.40
58 Batgirl	.15	.40
59 Batman	.15	.40
60 Mr. Freeze	.15	.40
61 Batgirl	.15	.40
62 Poison Ivy	.15	.40
63 Batman	.15	.40
64 Alfred	.15	.40
65 Posion Ivey	.15	.40
66 Batman	.15	.40
67 Alfred	.15	.40
68 Batman	.15	.40
69 Batman	.15	.40
70 Checklist	.15	.40

1997 Batman and Robin Autographs

STATED ODDS 1:720

Card	Low	High
1 Alicia Silverstone as Batgirl	40.00	80.00
2 Arnold Schwarzenegger as Mr. Freeze	150.00	250.00
3 Chris O'Donnell as Robin	20.00	40.00
4 George Clooney as Batman	200.00	300.00
5 Joel Schumacher		
6 Uma Thurman as Poison Ivy	250.00	350.00

1997 Batman and Robin Celluloid Action

Card	Low	High
COMPLETE SET (6)	10.00	25.00
STATED ODDS 1:24		
1 Batman and Robin	3.00	8.00
2 Freezemobile	3.00	8.00
3 Poison Ivy	3.00	8.00
4 Batgirl	3.00	8.00
5 Bane	3.00	8.00
6 Batman	3.00	8.00

1997 Batman and Robin Mini-Posters

Card	Low	High
COMPLETE SET (5)	2.50	6.00
STATED ODDS 1:6		
1 Batgirl	1.00	2.50
2 Batman	1.00	2.50
3 Freeze	1.00	2.50
4 Poison Ivy	1.00	2.50
5 Robin	1.00	2.50

1997 Batman and Robin Profiles

Card	Low	High
COMPLETE SET (12)	4.00	10.00
STATED ODDS 1:3		
P1 Batman	.75	2.00
P2 Batman	.75	2.00
P3 Batman	.75	2.00
P4 Mr. Freeze	.75	2.00
P5 Mr. Freeze	.75	2.00
P6 Mr. Freeze	.75	2.00
P7 Robin	.75	2.00
P8 Robin	.75	2.00
P9 Poison Ivy	.75	2.00
P10 Poison Ivy	.75	2.00
P11 Batgirl	.75	2.00
P12 Bane	.75	2.00

1997 Batman and Robin Storyboard

Card	Low	High
COMPLETE SET (24)	6.00	15.00
STATED ODDS ONE PER PACK		
S1 Vaulting over ice	.50	1.25
S2 Vaulting over ice	.50	1.25
S3 Vaulting over ice	.50	1.25
S4 Vaulting over ice	.50	1.25
S5 Vaulting over ice	.50	1.25
S6 Vaulting over ice	.50	1.25
S7 Battle on the ice	.50	1.25
S8 Battle on the ice	.50	1.25
S9 Battle on the ice	.50	1.25
S10 Battle on the ice	.50	1.25
S11 Battle on the ice	.50	1.25
S12 Battle on the ice	.50	1.25
S13 Escape from Arkham Asylum	.50	1.25
S14 Escape from Arkham Asylum	.50	1.25
S15 Escape from Arkham Asylum	.50	1.25
S16 Escape from Arkham Asylum	.50	1.25
S17 Escape from Arkham Asylum	.50	1.25
S18 Escape from Arkham Asylum	.50	1.25
S19 Doomed to thaw	.50	1.25
S20 Doomed to thaw	.50	1.25
S21 Doomed to thaw	.50	1.25
S22 Doomed to thaw	.50	1.25
S23 Doomed to thaw	.50	1.25
S24 Doomed to thaw	.50	1.25

1997 Marvel Premium QFX

Card	Low	High
COMPLETE SET (72)	5.00	12.00
1 Marvel Premium QFX	.15	.40
2 Beast	.15	.40
3 Silver Surfer	.15	.40
4 Bullseye	.15	.40
5 Captain America	.15	.40
6 Carnage	.15	.40
7 Cyclops	.15	.40
8 Daredevil	.15	.40
9 Dr. Doom	.15	.40
10 Dr. Octopus	.15	.40
11 Elektra	.15	.40
12 Ghost Rider	.15	.40
13 Hobgoblin	.15	.40
14 Hulk	.15	.40
15 Human Torch	.15	.40
16 Iceman	.15	.40
17 Invisible Woman	.15	.40
18 Iron Man	.15	.40
19 Juggernaut	.15	.40
20 Kingpin	.15	.40
21 Lizard	.15	.40
22 Magneto	.15	.40
23 Namor	.15	.40
24 Punisher	.15	.40
25 Rhino	.15	.40
26 Thor	.15	.40
27 Venom	.15	.40
28 Wolverine	.15	.40
29 Black Bolt	.15	.40
30 Black Panther	.15	.40
31 Black Widow	.15	.40
32 Chamber	.15	.40
33 Deathlok	.15	.40
34 Dr. Strange	.15	.40
35 Jubilee	.15	.40
36 Ka-Zar	.15	.40
37 Leech with Artie	.15	.40
38 Mephisto	.15	.40
39 Moon Knight	.15	.40
40 Psylocke	.15	.40
41 Rogue	.15	.40
42 Sabretooth	.15	.40
43 Storm	.15	.40
44 Thanos	.15	.40
45 Typhoid Mary	.15	.40
46 Ant-Man	.15	.40
47 Devil Dinosaur & Moonboy	.15	.40
48 Hellstorm	.15	.40
49 Howard the Duck	.15	.40
50 Impossible Man	.15	.40
51 J. Jonah Jameson	.15	.40
52 Man-Thing	.15	.40
53 Nomad	.15	.40
54 Squirrel Girl	.15	.40
55 Gambit	.15	.40
56 Giant-Man	.15	.40
57 Mr. Fantastic	.15	.40
58 Random	.15	.40
59 Red Skull	.15	.40
60 Scarlet Witch	.15	.40
61 Spider-Man	.15	.40
62 Thing	.15	.40
63 Wolverine	.15	.40
64 The Coming of Galactus	.15	.40
65 Magneto vs. the U.N.	.15	.40
66 Storm Battles Callisto	.15	.40
67 The Death of Gwen Stacy	.15	.40
68 Birth of the Phoenix	.15	.40
69 Ghost Rider Reborn	.15	.40
70 The Origin of Daredevil	.15	.40
71 Origin of the Punisher	.15	.40
72 Maximum Carnage	.15	.40

1997 Marvel Premium QFX LazerBlast

Card	Low	High
COMPLETE SET (4)	5.00	12.00
STATED ODDS 1:9		
1 Wolverine	2.00	5.00
2 Spider-Man	2.00	5.00
3 Hulk	2.00	5.00
4 Punisher	2.00	5.00

1997 Marvel Premium QFX PhotoGrafix

Card	Low	High
COMPLETE SET (9)	8.00	20.00
STATED ODDS 1:6		
1 Bucky	1.50	4.00
2 Captain America	1.50	4.00
3 Hulk	1.50	4.00
4 Red Skull	1.50	4.00
5 Dr. Doom	1.50	4.00
6 Iron Man	1.50	4.00
7 Mr. Fantastic	1.50	4.00
8 Thing	1.50	4.00
9 Thor	1.50	4.00

1997 Men In Black

Card	Low	High
COMPLETE SET (90)	4.00	10.00
CUNNINGHAM AUTO RANDOM INSERT IN PACKS		
1 Men In Black	.10	.25
2 Border Crossing	.10	.25
3 Illegal Alien	.10	.25
4 Alien Ex-Con	.10	.25
5 Mikey Attacks	.10	.25
6 Cover-Up Cavalry	.10	.25
7 Retirement	.10	.25
8 New York Chase	.10	.25
9 Freeze	.10	.25
10 End of the Line	.10	.25
11 I Believe You	.10	.25
12 Pawn Shop	.10	.25
13 I'm Going to Count to Three	.10	.25
14 Blown Away	.10	.25
15 Ever See One of These	.10	.25
16 Farm Encounter	.10	.25
17 Edgar Returns	.10	.25
18 Moving Crew	.10	.25
19 Best of the Best	.10	.25
20 Written Exam	.10	.25
21 Shooting Gallery	.10	.25
22 Eye Exam	.10	.25
23 History Lesson	.10	.25
24 Who Drank all the Cream	.10	.25
25 In or Out	.10	.25
26 Exterminated	.10	.25
27 MiB HQ	.10	.25
28 Alien Immigration	.10	.25
29 New Technology	.10	.25
30 Observation	.10	.25
31 Initiation	.10	.25
32 Erasure	.10	.25
33 Jay	.10	.25
34 Zed's Office	.10	.25
35 Traffic Stop	.10	.25
36 Congratulations It's a Squid	.10	.25
37 The Hot Sheets	.10	.25
38 Edgar in Pursuit	.10	.25
39 Farmhouse Interview	.10	.25
40 Bea's Story	.10	.25
41 Cover Story	.10	.25
42 We Have a Bug	.10	.25
43 Summit Meeting	.10	.25
44 Assassination	.10	.25
45 The Morgue	.10	.25
46 Alien Autopsy	.10	.25
47 Unlike Anything I've Ever Seen	.10	.25
48 Splitting Head	.10	.25
49 Cryptic Message	.10	.25
50 Neuralyzed	.10	.25
51 Coffee Break	.10	.25
52 Towed	.10	.25
53 The Chase is On	.10	.25
54 Level Four	.10	.25
55 Frank the Pug	.10	.25
56 Information Shakedown	.10	.25
57 Orion's Belt	.10	.25
58 Bug Off	.10	.25
59 Hidden Danger	.10	.25
60 Hostage Situation	.10	.25
61 Prelude to War	.10	.25
62 World's Fair	.10	.25
63 MiB Express	.10	.25
64 Showdown	.10	.25
65 Lift Off	.10	.25
66 Crash Landing	.10	.25
67 Edgar No More	.10	.25
68 Face Off	.10	.25
69 Exterminated	.10	.25
70 Mission Accomplished	.10	.25
71 Good-Bye	.10	.25
72 The Newest Agent	.10	.25
73 Kay	.10	.25
74 Jay	.10	.25
75 Elle	.10	.25
76 Zed	.10	.25
77 Dee	.10	.25
78 Headquarters	.10	.25
79 Immigration	.10	.25
80 Arsenal	.10	.25
81 Toy Shop	.10	.25
82 Samarians	.10	.25
83 Lysians	.10	.25
84 The Squats	.10	.25
85 Vyrmidians	.10	.25
86 The Homarid	.10	.25
87 The Pug	.10	.25
88 Erragnians	.10	.25
89 Bugs	.10	.25
90 Checklist	.10	.25
NNO Lowell Cunningham AU	6.00	15.00

1997 Men In Black Alien Profiles

Card	Low	High
COMPLETE SET (5)	2.50	6.00
STATED ODDS 1:11		
P1 Mikey	.75	2.00
P2 Yin and Yang	.75	2.00
P3 Skulk Brothers	.75	2.00
P4 Rosenberg	.75	2.00
P5 Edgar	.75	2.00

1997 Men In Black Cards In Black

Card	Low	High
COMPLETE SET (2)	10.00	20.00
STATED ODDS 1:54		
B1 Jay	6.00	15.00
B2 Kay	6.00	15.00

1997 Men In Black Foilworks

Card	Low	High
COMPLETE SET (5)	6.00	15.00
STATED ODDS 1:24		
S1 Alien Technology	2.00	5.00
S2 Cover-Ups	2.00	5.00
S3 Neuralyzer	2.00	5.00
S4 Aliens	2.00	5.00
S5 Men in Black Mythos	2.00	5.00

1997 Sliders

Card	Low	High
COMPLETE SET (72)	5.00	12.00
1 Sliders Title Card	.15	.40
2 The First Season	.15	.40
3 The Second Season	.15	.40
4 It Gets Better	.15	.40
5 We're Buds, Right?	.15	.40
6 I Don't have a Dog	.15	.40
7 We're Not in Kansas	.15	.40
8 Call Me Comrade	.15	.40
9 Hygienically Approved	.15	.40
10 Some Unexpected Help	.15	.40
11 Age Before Beauty	.15	.40
12 Bennish's Solution	.15	.40
13 The Atomic Genie	.15	.40
14 Dinner By Candlelight	.15	.40
15 A King's Ransom	.15	.40
16 Tune In, Turn On, Turn Over	.15	.40
17 Just Think It	.15	.40
18 Breakfast Of Champions	.15	.40
19 Vote Arturo!	.15	.40
20 The Undisputed King	.15	.40
21 Double Vision	.15	.40
22 Another Lucky Winner!	.15	.40
23 Run For It!	.15	.40
24 A Rare Breed	.15	.40
25 Patriots!	.15	.40
26 See Me!	.15	.40
27 Dead-Eye	.15	.40
28 Target Practice	.15	.40
29 The Buddy System	.15	.40
30 We, the People	.15	.40
31 Danger: Predators!	.15	.40
32 Almost Home	.15	.40
33 Wade's Death	.15	.40
34 Bond, Derek Bond	.15	.40
35 The Incorruptibles	.15	.40
36 One Cool Cat	.15	.40
37 Prayin To Jesus	.15	.40
38 An Explosive Situation	.15	.40
39 Jump Right In	.15	.40
40 Who Killed Q.R.?	.15	.40
41 Kromaggs Rule!	.15	.40
42 Inside a Manta	.15	.40
43 The Trackers	.15	.40
44 Caught!	.15	.40
45 Time's Arrow	.15	.40
46 Armada	.15	.40
47 Harvest Time	.15	.40
48 Rapture	.15	.40
49 Damnation	.15	.40
50 Fissions of the Soul	.15	.40
51 Dimensional Shadows	.15	.40
52 Soul Survivors	.15	.40
53 Narcotica	.15	.40
54 Blood & Splendor	.15	.40
55 Paint it Red!	.15	.40
56 The New Ice Age	.15	.40
57 Fish Out of Water	.15	.40
58 Too Cool! Too Bad	.15	.40
59 Mrs. President	.15	.40
60 The Secrets Of Sorcery	.15	.40
61 Trouble in the Rubble	.15	.40
62 Just Desserts	.15	.40
63 A Big Bite	.15	.40
64 The Third Season	.15	.40
65 Rules of the Game	.15	.40
66 Double Cross	.15	.40
67 Electric Twister Acid Test	.15	.40
68 Quinn Mallorhy	.15	.40
69 Wade Wells	.15	.40
70 Maximillian Arturo	.15	.40
71 Rembrandt Brown	.15	.40
72 Checklist	.15	.40
NNO Dealer Issue Promo Card	2.00	5.00

1997 Sliders Embossed

Card	Low	High
COMPLETE SET (9)	7.50	20.00
STATED ODDS 1:12		
1 Welcome to level one	1.25	3.00
2 Stay alive	1.25	3.00
3 See you at the beach	1.25	3.00
4 Welcome to San Angeles	1.25	3.00
5 Max?	1.25	3.00
6 The dark side	1.25	3.00
7 The haven	1.25	3.00
8 Outcasts	1.25	3.00
9 Redemption	1.25	3.00

1997 Sliders Foilworks

Card	Low	High
COMPLETE SET (6)	7.50	20.00
STATED ODDS 1:18		
1 The Ancient Kromagg Homeworld	1.50	4.00
2 The Ancient Kromagg Homeworld	1.50	4.00
3 The Ancient Kromagg Homeworld	1.50	4.00
4 The Kromagg Homeworld Forests	1.50	4.00
5 The Kromagg Homeworld City-states	1.50	4.00
6 The Kromagg Homeworld Even Today	1.50	4.00

1997 Star Trek DS9 Profiles

Card	Low	High
COMPLETE SET (82)	5.00	12.00
1 Sisko	.15	.40
2 Sisko	.15	.40
3 The Emissary I & II	.15	.40
4 The Maquis I & II	.15	.40
5 Through the Looking Glass	.15	.40
6 Paradise Lost	.15	.40
7 Kai Opaka's Memoirs of Sisko	.15	.40
8 Kasidy Yates Memoirs of Sisko	.15	.40
9 Joseph Sisko's Memoirs of Sisko	.15	.40
10 Worf	.15	.40
11 Worf	.15	.40
12 Way of the Warrior I & II	.15	.40
13 The Sword of Kahless	.15	.40
14 The Sons of Mogh	.15	.40
15 Let He Who is Without Sin	.15	.40
16 Kor's Memoirs of Worf	.15	.40
17 Gowron's Memoirs of Worf	.15	.40
18 Dax's Memoirs of Worf	.15	.40
19 Kira	.15	.40
20 Kira	.15	.40
21 Duet	.15	.40
22 Second Skin	.15	.40
23 Life Support	.15	.40
24 The Begotten	.15	.40
25 Shakaar's Memoirs of Kira	.15	.40
26 Kai Winn's Memoirs of Kira	.15	.40
27 Gul Dukat's Memoirs of Kira	.15	.40
28 Dax	.15	.40
29 Dax	.15	.40
30 Dax	.15	.40
31 Invasive Procedures	.15	.40
32 Facets	.15	.40
33 Rejoined	.15	.40
34 Worf's Memoirs of Dax	.15	.40
35 Arjin's Memoirs of Dax	.15	.40
36 Sisko's Memoirs of Dax	.15	.40
37 Odo	.15	.40
38 Odo	.15	.40
39 Necessary Evil	.15	.40
40 The Alternate	.15	.40
41 The Search II	.15	.40
42 The Begotten	.15	.40
43 Lwaxana's Memoirs of Odo	.15	.40
44 Changeling's Memoirs of Odo	.15	.40
45 Edagran Tain's Memoirs of Odo	.15	.40
46 Bashir	.15	.40
47 Bashir	.15	.40
48 The Wire	.15	.40
49 Distant Voices	.15	.40
50 Hippocratic Oath	.15	.40
51 Our Man Bashir	.15	.40
52 Garak's Memoirs of Bashir	.15	.40
53 O'Brien's Memoirs of Bashir	.15	.40
54 Melora's Memoirs of Bashir	.15	.40
55 O'Brien	.15	.40
56 O'Brien	.15	.40
57 Captive Pursuit	.15	.40
58 The Storyteller	.15	.40
59 Tribunal	.15	.40
60 The Assignment	.15	.40
61 Keiko's Memoirs of O'Brien	.15	.40
62 Bashir's Memoirs of O'Brien	.15	.40
63 O'Brien's Memoirs of O'Brien	.15	.40
64 Quark	.15	.40
65 Quark	.15	.40
66 Prophet Motive	.15	.40
67 House of Quark	.15	.40
68 Little Green Men	.15	.40
69 Body Parts	.15	.40
70 Rom's Memoirs of Quark	.15	.40
71 Ishka's Memoirs of Quark	.15	.40
72 Grilka's Memoirs of Quark	.15	.40
73 Jake	.15	.40
74 Jake	.15	.40
75 Explorers	.15	.40
76 The Visitor	.15	.40
77 The Muse	.15	.40
78 Nor the Battle to the Strong	.15	.40
79 Mardah's Memoirs of Jake	.15	.40
80 Nog's Memoirs of Jake	.15	.40
81 Jennifer Sisko's Memoirs of Jake	.15	.40
82 Checklist	.15	.40

1997 Star Trek DS9 Profiles Autographs

Card	Low	High
COMPLETE SET (3)	150.00	250.00
RANDOM INSERTS IN PACKS		
NNO Rene Auberjonois	50.00	100.00
NNO Armin Shimerman	50.00	100.00
NNO Terry Farrell	50.00	100.00

1997 Star Trek DS9 Profiles Latinum Profiles

Card	Low	High
COMPLETE SET (9)	25.00	60.00
STATED ODDS 1:6		
1 Sisko	3.00	8.00
2 Worf	3.00	8.00
3 Kira	3.00	8.00
4 Dax	3.00	8.00
5 Odo	3.00	8.00
6 Bashir	3.00	8.00
7 O'Brien	3.00	8.00
8 Quark	3.00	8.00
9 Jake	3.00	8.00

1997 Star Trek DS9 Profiles Quark's Bar

Card	Low	High
COMPLETE SET (9)	7.50	20.00
STATED ODDS 1:3		
QB1 Never Place Friendship Above Profit	1.25	3.00
QB2 No Good Deed Ever Goes Unpunished	1.25	3.00
QB3 Good Customers Are as Rare as Latinum - Treasure Them	1.25	3.00
QB4 Latinum Lasts Longer than Lust	1.25	3.00
QB5 Beware the Man Who Doesn't Make Time for Oomox	1.25	3.00
QB6 Never Allow Family to Stand in the Way of Opportunity	1.25	3.00
QB7 There is No Honor in Poverty	1.25	3.00
QB8 The Justification for Profit is Profit	1.25	3.00
QB9 A Ferengi without Profit is No Ferengi at All	1.25	3.00

1997 Star Trek DS9 Profiles Trials and Tribbleations

Card	Low	High
COMPLETE SET (9)	10.00	25.00
STATED ODDS 1:6		
TT1 Kirk, Uhura, Sisko	1.50	4.00
TT2 Bashir, Tribbles, Bartender	1.50	4.00
TT3 Odo, Uhura, Chekov	1.50	4.00
TT4 Sisko, Dax	1.50	4.00
TT5 Sisko, Dax, Kirk, Spock	1.50	4.00
TT6 Dax, Kirk	1.50	4.00
TT7 O'Brien, Bashir, Kirk	1.50	4.00
TT8 Worf, Darvin, Odo	1.50	4.00
TT9 Quark, Tribbles	1.50	4.00

1997 Star Trek The Next Generation Season Six

Card	Low	High
COMPLETE SET (108)	6.00	15.00
529 46001.3 - 46041.1	.15	.40
530 46071.6 - 46154.2	.15	.40
531 46192.3 - 46235.7	.15	.40
532 46271.5 - 46357.4	.15	.40
533 46360.8 - 46519.1	.15	.40
534 46578.4 - 46579.2	.15	.40
535 46682.4 - 46731.5	.15	.40
536 46778.1 - 46852.2	.15	.40
537 46915.2 - 46982.1	.15	.40
538 Time's Arrow Part II	.15	.40
539 Time's Arrow Part II	.15	.40
540 Time's Arrow Part II	.15	.40
541 Realm Of Fear	.15	.40
542 Realm Of Fear	.15	.40
543 Realm Of Fear	.15	.40
544 Man of the People	.15	.40
545 Man of the People	.15	.40
546 Man of the People	.15	.40
547 Relics	.15	.40
548 Relics	.15	.40
549 Relics	.15	.40
550 Schisms	.15	.40
551 Schisms	.15	.40
552 Schisms	.15	.40
553 True Q	.15	.40
554 True Q	.15	.40
555 True Q	.15	.40
556 Rascals	.15	.40
557 Rascals	.15	.40
558 Rascals	.15	.40
559 A Fistful of Datas	.15	.40
560 A Fistful of Datas	.15	.40
561 A Fistful of Datas	.15	.40
562 The Quality Of Life	.15	.40
563 The Quality Of Life	.15	.40
564 The Quality Of Life	.15	.40
565 Chain of Command Part I	.15	.40
566 Chain of Command Part I	.15	.40
567 Chain of Command Part I	.15	.40
568 Chain of Command Part II	.15	.40
569 Chain of Command Part II	.15	.40
570 Chain of Command Part II	.15	.40
571 Ship in A Bottle	.15	.40
572 Ship in A Bottle	.15	.40
573 Ship in A Bottle	.15	.40
574 Aquiel	.15	.40
575 Aquiel	.15	.40
576 Aquiel	.15	.40
577 Face of the Enemy	.15	.40
578 Face of the Enemy	.15	.40
579 Face of the Enemy	.15	.40
580 Tapestry	.15	.40
581 Tapestry	.15	.40
582 Tapestry	.15	.40
583 Birthright Part I	.15	.40
584 Birthright Part I	.15	.40
585 Birthright Part I	.15	.40
586 Birthright Part II	.15	.40
587 Birthright Part II	.15	.40
588 Birthright Part II	.15	.40
589 Starship Mine	.15	.40
590 Starship Mine	.15	.40
591 Starship Mine	.15	.40
592 Lessons	.15	.40
593 Lessons	.15	.40
594 Lessons	.15	.40
595 The Chase	.15	.40
596 The Chase	.15	.40
597 The Chase	.15	.40
598 Frame of Mind	.15	.40
599 Frame of Mind	.15	.40
600 Frame of Mind	.15	.40
601 Suspicions	.15	.40
602 Suspicions	.15	.40
603 Suspicions	.15	.40
604 Rightful Heir	.15	.40
605 Rightful Heir	.15	.40
606 Rightful Heir	.15	.40
607 Second Chances	.15	.40
608 Second Chances	.15	.40
609 Second Chances	.15	.40
610 Timescape	.15	.40
611 Timescape	.15	.40
612 Timescape	.15	.40

❑ 613 Descent Part I .15 .40
❑ 614 Descent Part I .15 .40
❑ 615 Descent Part I .15 .40
❑ 616 Checklist A .15 .40
❑ 617 Checklist B .15 .40
❑ 618 Cast and Production Credits .15 .40
❑ 619 Chief Miles O'Brien .15 .40
❑ 620 Chief Miles O'Brien .15 .40
❑ 621 Chief Miles O'Brien .15 .40
❑ 622 Chief Miles O'Brien .15 .40
❑ 623 Chief Miles O'Brien .15 .40
❑ 624 Chief Miles O'Brien .15 .40
❑ 625 Chief Miles O'Brien .15 .40
❑ 626 Chief Miles O'Brien .15 .40
❑ 627 Chief Miles O'Brien .15 .40
❑ 628 Q .15 .40
❑ 629 Q .15 .40
❑ 630 Q .15 .40
❑ 631 Q .15 .40
❑ 632 Q .15 .40
❑ 633 Q .15 .40
❑ 634 Q .15 .40
❑ 635 Q .15 .40
❑ 636 Q .15 .40

1997 Star Trek The Next Generation Season Six Embossed Characters

COMPLETE SET (3) 10.00 20.00
STATED ODDS 1:24
❑ S34 Scotty 4.00 10.00
❑ S35 Alexander 4.00 10.00
❑ S36 Lore 4.00 10.00

1997 Star Trek The Next Generation Season Six Holograms

COMPLETE SET (2) 20.00 40.00
STATED ODDS 1:90
❑ H11 O'Brien 12.00 30.00
❑ H12 Q 12.00 30.00

1997 Star Trek The Next Generation Season Six Skymotion

COMPLETE SET (2) 8.00 20.00
❑ SM1 Amanda Rogers 8.00 20.00
(issued as case topper)
❑ SM2 Timescape 4.00 10.00
(issued as box topper)

1997 Star Trek Voyager Season Two

COMPLETE SET (112) 40.00 80.00
191-193 STATED ODDS 1:12
194-196 STATED ODDS 1:12
197-199 STATED ODDS 1:18
200-202 STATED ODDS 1:48
❑ 91 Timeline Mural .15 .40
❑ 92 Timeline Mural .15 .40
❑ 93 Timeline Mural .15 .40
❑ 94 Timeline Mural .15 .40
❑ 95 Timeline Mural .15 .40
❑ 96 Timeline Mural .15 .40
❑ 97 Timeline Mural .15 .40
❑ 98 Timeline Mural .15 .40
❑ 99 Timeline Mural .15 .40
❑ 100 The 37's .15 .40
❑ 101 The 37's .15 .40
❑ 102 The 37's .15 .40
❑ 103 Initiations .15 .40
❑ 104 Initiations .15 .40
❑ 105 Initiations .15 .40
❑ 106 Projections .15 .40
❑ 107 Projections .15 .40
❑ 108 Projections .15 .40
❑ 109 Elogium .15 .40
❑ 110 Elogium .15 .40
❑ 111 Elogium .15 .40
❑ 112 Non Sequitur .15 .40
❑ 113 Non Sequitur .15 .40
❑ 114 Non Sequitur .15 .40
❑ 115 Twisted .15 .40
❑ 116 Twisted .15 .40
❑ 117 Twisted .15 .40
❑ 118 Parturition .15 .40
❑ 119 Parturition .15 .40
❑ 120 Parturition .15 .40
❑ 121 Persistence of Vision .15 .40
❑ 122 Persistence of Vision .15 .40
❑ 123 Persistence of Vision .15 .40
❑ 124 Tattoo .15 .40
❑ 125 Tattoo .15 .40
❑ 126 Tattoo .15 .40
❑ 127 Cold Fire .15 .40
❑ 128 Cold Fire .15 .40
❑ 129 Cold Fire .15 .40
❑ 130 Maneuvers .15 .40
❑ 131 Maneuvers .15 .40
❑ 132 Maneuvers .15 .40
❑ 133 Resistance .15 .40
❑ 134 Resistance .15 .40
❑ 135 Resistance .15 .40
❑ 136 Prototype .15 .40
❑ 137 Prototype .15 .40
❑ 138 Prototype .15 .40
❑ 139 Alliances .15 .40
❑ 140 Alliances .15 .40
❑ 141 Alliances .15 .40
❑ 142 Threshold .15 .40
❑ 143 Threshold .15 .40
❑ 144 Threshold .15 .40
❑ 145 Meld .15 .40
❑ 146 Meld .15 .40
❑ 147 Meld .15 .40
❑ 148 Dreadnought .15 .40
❑ 149 Dreadnought .15 .40
❑ 150 Dreadnought .15 .40
❑ 151 Death Wish .15 .40
❑ 152 Death Wish .15 .40
❑ 153 Death Wish .15 .40
❑ 154 Lifesigns .15 .40
❑ 155 Lifesigns .15 .40
❑ 156 Lifesigns .15 .40
❑ 157 Investigations .15 .40
❑ 158 Investigations .15 .40
❑ 159 Investigations .15 .40
❑ 160 Deadlock .15 .40
❑ 161 Deadlock .15 .40
❑ 162 Deadlock .15 .40
❑ 163 Innocence .15 .40
❑ 164 Innocence .15 .40
❑ 165 Innocence .15 .40
❑ 166 The Thaw .15 .40
❑ 167 The Thaw .15 .40
❑ 168 The Thaw .15 .40
❑ 169 Tuvix .15 .40
❑ 170 Tuvix .15 .40
❑ 171 Tuvix .15 .40
❑ 172 Resolutions .15 .40
❑ 173 Resolutions .15 .40
❑ 174 Resolutions .15 .40
❑ 175 Basics, Part 1 .15 .40
❑ 176 Basics, Part 1 .15 .40
❑ 177 Basics, Part 1 .15 .40
❑ 178 Checklist .15 .40
❑ 179 Checklist .15 .40
❑ 180 Production Credits .15 .40
❑ 181 Fan Club Card .15 .40
❑ 182 U.S.S Voyager .15 .40
❑ 183 Libby .15 .40
❑ 184 Lt. Reginald Barclay .15 .40
❑ 185 Admiral Paris .15 .40
❑ 186 Amelia Earhart .15 .40
❑ 187 Commander Wm. Riker .15 .40
❑ 188 Mark .15 .40
❑ 189 Sir Isaac Newton .15 .40
❑ 190 Q .15 .40
❑ 191 Bothan 1.25 3.00
❑ 192 Repto-Humanoid 1.25 3.00
❑ 193 Trabe 1.25 3.00
❑ 194 Landing Struts 1.25 3.00
❑ 195 3947 1.25 3.00
❑ 196 Hibernation Pods 1.25 3.00
❑ 197 Hanon IV 1.25 3.00
❑ 198 Sobras 1.25 3.00
❑ 199 Planet from Tattoo 1.25 3.00
❑ 200 Janeway as Lucie 5.00 12.00
❑ 201 Chakotay and Paris 5.00 12.00
❑ 202 The Doctor 5.00 12.00

1997 The X-Files Showcase

COMPLETE SET (72) 6.00 15.00
❑ 1X0101 Deep Throat .20 .50
❑ 1X0102 Deep Throat .20 .50
❑ 1X0103 Deep Throat .20 .50
❑ 1X0104 Deep Throat .20 .50
❑ 1X0105 Deep Throat .20 .50
❑ 1X0106 Deep Throat .20 .50
❑ 1X0107 Deep Throat .20 .50
❑ 1X0108 Deep Throat .20 .50
❑ 1X0109 Deep Throat .20 .50
❑ 1X0110 Deep Throat .20 .50
❑ 1X0111 Deep Throat .20 .50
❑ 1X0112 Deep Throat .20 .50
❑ 1X0201 Squeeze .20 .50
❑ 1X0202 Squeeze .20 .50
❑ 1X0203 Squeeze .20 .50
❑ 1X0204 Squeeze .20 .50
❑ 1X0205 Squeeze .20 .50
❑ 1X0206 Squeeze .20 .50
❑ 1X0207 Squeeze .20 .50
❑ 1X0208 Squeeze .20 .50
❑ 1X0209 Squeeze .20 .50
❑ 1X0210 Squeeze .20 .50
❑ 1X0211 Squeeze .20 .50
❑ 1X0212 Squeeze .20 .50
❑ 1X0701 Ice .20 .50
❑ 1X0702 Ice .20 .50
❑ 1X0703 Ice .20 .50
❑ 1X0704 Ice .20 .50
❑ 1X0705 Ice .20 .50
❑ 1X0706 Ice .20 .50
❑ 1X0707 Ice .20 .50
❑ 1X0708 Ice .20 .50
❑ 1X0709 Ice .20 .50
❑ 1X0710 Ice .20 .50
❑ 1X0711 Ice .20 .50
❑ 1X0712 Ice .20 .50
❑ 1X0901 Fallen Angel .20 .50
❑ 1X0902 Fallen Angel .20 .50
❑ 1X0903 Fallen Angel .20 .50
❑ 1X0904 Fallen Angel .20 .50
❑ 1X0905 Fallen Angel .20 .50
❑ 1X0906 Fallen Angel .20 .50
❑ 1X0907 Fallen Angel .20 .50
❑ 1X0908 Fallen Angel .20 .50
❑ 1X0909 Fallen Angel .20 .50
❑ 1X0910 Fallen Angel .20 .50
❑ 1X0911 Fallen Angel .20 .50
❑ 1X0912 Fallen Angel .20 .50
❑ 1X2301 The Erlenmeyer Flask .20 .50
❑ 1X2302 The Erlenmeyer Flask .20 .50
❑ 1X2303 The Erlenmeyer Flask .20 .50
❑ 1X2304 The Erlenmeyer Flask .20 .50
❑ 1X2305 The Erlenmeyer Flask .20 .50
❑ 1X2306 The Erlenmeyer Flask .20 .50
❑ 1X2307 The Erlenmeyer Flask .20 .50
❑ 1X2308 The Erlenmeyer Flask .20 .50
❑ 1X2309 The Erlenmeyer Flask .20 .50
❑ 1X2310 The Erlenmeyer Flask .20 .50
❑ 1X2311 The Erlenmeyer Flask .20 .50
❑ 1X2312 The Erlenmeyer Flask .20 .50
❑ 1X7901 The X-Files Pilot .20 .50
❑ 1X7902 The X-Files Pilot .20 .50
❑ 1X7903 The X-Files Pilot .20 .50
❑ 1X7904 The X-Files Pilot .20 .50
❑ 1X7905 The X-Files Pilot .20 .50
❑ 1X7906 The X-Files Pilot .20 .50
❑ 1X7907 The X-Files Pilot .20 .50
❑ 1X7908 The X-Files Pilot .20 .50
❑ 1X7909 The X-Files Pilot .20 .50
❑ 1X7910 The X-Files Pilot .20 .50
❑ 1X7911 The X-Files Pilot .20 .50
❑ 1X7912 The X-Files Pilot .20 .50

1997 The X-Files Showcase Laser

COMPLETE SET (6) 6.00 15.00
❑ L1 The X-Files Pilot 2.00 5.00
❑ L2 Deep Throat 2.00 5.00
❑ L3 Squeeze 2.00 5.00
❑ L4 Ice 2.00 5.00
❑ L5 Fallen Angel 2.00 5.00
❑ L6 The Erlenmeyer Flask 2.00 5.00

1997 The X-Files Showcase Promos

❑ FC Investigate Membership Kit #2
❑ P1 Pilot Episode 1X79P1 .60 1.50

1997 The X-Files Showcase X-Effect

COMPLETE SET (6) 5.00 12.00
❑ E1 The X-Files Pilot 1.50 4.00
❑ E2 Deep Throat 1.50 4.00
❑ E3 Squeeze 1.50 4.00
❑ E4 Ice 1.50 4.00
❑ E5 Fallen Angel 1.50 4.00
❑ E6 The Erlenmeyer Flask 1.50 4.00

1998 Alien Legacy

COMPLETE SET (90) 5.00 12.00
RE1 STATED ODDS 1:108
❑ 1 Alien Legacy .15 .40
❑ 2 The Nostromo Crew Awakened .15 .40
❑ 3 Entering the Derelict Spacecraft .15 .40
❑ 4 The Space Jockey .15 .40
❑ 5 The Face Hugger .15 .40
❑ 6 The Chest Burster .15 .40
❑ 7 Death from On High .15 .40
❑ 8 The Skull Smasher .15 .40
❑ 9 Lambert's Final Moments .15 .40
❑ 10 Ripley Strikes Back .15 .40
❑ 11 Blasted into Space .15 .40
❑ 12 Unwanted Return .15 .40
❑ 13 The New Mission .15 .40
❑ 14 A Colony Invaded .15 .40
❑ 15 Discovering Newt .15 .40
❑ 16 Catacombs of Death .15 .40
❑ 17 Kill Me .15 .40
❑ 18 Aliens Attack .15 .40
❑ 19 Emergency Retreat .15 .40
❑ 20 No Escape .15 .40
❑ 21 Newt Imperiled .15 .40
❑ 22 Destroying the Nest .15 .40
❑ 23 Rampaging Queen .15 .40
❑ 24 Bishop Ripped Apart .15 .40
❑ 25 The Titans Clash .15 .40
❑ 26 Jaws of a Queen .15 .40
❑ 27 Battle to the Death .15 .40
❑ 28 Sole Survivor .15 .40
❑ 29 Creature on the Prowl .15 .40
❑ 30 Curious about Ripley .15 .40
❑ 31 Old Friends Reunited .15 .40
❑ 32 Death from Above .15 .40
❑ 33 Counterattack .15 .40
❑ 34 Monster in the Maze .15 .40
❑ 35 Slaying the Dragon .15 .40
❑ 36 Ripley's Sacrifice .15 .40
❑ 37 Life after Death .15 .40
❑ 38 Ripley Reborn .15 .40
❑ 39 The Mercenaries .15 .40
❑ 40 Alien On Board .15 .40
❑ 41 Ordeal .15 .40
❑ 42 Underwater Assault .15 .40
❑ 43 Trapped in the Egg Chamber .15 .40
❑ 44 Queen and the Newborn .15 .40
❑ 45 Kindred .15 .40
❑ 46 The Nostromo .15 .40
❑ 47 The Space Derelict .15 .40
❑ 48 Cheyenne Utility Dropship .15 .40
❑ 49 Armored Personnel Carrier .15 .40
❑ 50 Firepower .15 .40
❑ 51 Powerloader .15 .40
❑ 52 Above the Prison Planet .15 .40
❑ 53 The Aurica Docking Bay .15 .40
❑ 54 Waste Tank Cocooning Area .15 .40
❑ 55 Surreal Surroundings .15 .40
❑ 56 Face Hugger .15 .40
❑ 57 Alien Soldier .15 .40
❑ 58 Queen vs. Ripley .15 .40
❑ 59 The Protecting Drone .15 .40
❑ 60 Future Vision .15 .40
❑ 61 Operation Alien .15 .40
❑ 62 Nightmare Asylum .15 .40
❑ 63 The Female War .15 .40
❑ 64 The Classic Alien Soldier .15 .40
❑ 65 An Extraterrestrial Jaws .15 .40
❑ 66 Creature Featured .15 .40
❑ 67 Shuttle Stowaway .15 .40
❑ 68 Blasted by Ripley .15 .40
❑ 69 The Aliens Warrior .15 .40
❑ 70 The Queen's Egg Sack .15 .40
❑ 71 Fury of the Queen .15 .40
❑ 72 Queen: Front View .15 .40
❑ 73 A New Breed of Alien .15 .40
❑ 74 In the Blast Furnace .15 .40
❑ 75 Lucifer Descending .15 .40
❑ 76 Captured Warriors .15 .40
❑ 77 Aliens Underwater .15 .40
❑ 78 The Queen Defiant .15 .40
❑ 79 Newborn Nightmare .15 .40
❑ 80 Wall of the Newborn .15 .40
❑ 81 Head of Horror .15 .40
❑ 82 Ellen Ripley .15 .40
❑ 83 Nostromo's Chief Officers .15 .40
❑ 84 Robots .15 .40
❑ 85 Colonial Marines .15 .40
❑ 86 Ripley's Loved Ones .15 .40
❑ 87 Three Tough Hombres .15 .40
❑ 88 Can They Be Trusted .15 .40
❑ 89 Xenomorph .15 .40
❑ 90 Checklist .15 .40
❑ RE1 Alien Acid Bath SP 6.00 15.00

1998 Alien Legacy DVD Collection

COMPLETE SET (9) 4.00 10.00
ISSUED IN ALIEN DVD COLLECTION
❑ AU1 The Alien Legacy .75 2.00
❑ AU2 Alien: The Story .75 2.00
❑ AU3 Alien: The Film .75 2.00
❑ AU4 Aliens: The Story .75 2.00
❑ AU5 Aliens: The Film .75 2.00
❑ AU6 Alien 3: The Story .75 2.00
❑ AU7 Alien 3: The Film .75 2.00
❑ AU8 Alien Resurrection: The Story .75 2.00
❑ AU9 Alien Resurrection: The Film .75 2.00

1998 Alien Legacy Evolution of Ripley

COMPLETE SET (4) 5.00 12.00
STATED ODDS 1:27
❑ C21 Alien 2.00 5.00
❑ C22 Aliens 2.00 5.00
❑ C23 Alien3 2.00 5.00
❑ C24 Alien Resurrection 2.00 5.00

1998 Alien Legacy K-Mart Video

COMPLETE SET (9) 4.00 10.00
ISSUED IN K-MART ALIEN COLLECTION
❑ A1 The Alien Legacy .75 2.00
❑ A2 Alien: The Story .75 2.00
❑ A3 Alien: The Film .75 2.00
❑ A4 Aliens: The Story .75 2.00
❑ A5 Aliens: The Film .75 2.00
❑ A6 Alien 3: The Story .75 2.00
❑ A7 Alien 3: The Film .75 2.00
❑ A8 Alien Resurrection: The Story .75 2.00
❑ A9 Alien Resurrection: The Film .75 2.00

1998 Alien Legacy Poster Gallery

COMPLETE SET (9) 5.00 12.00
STATED ODDS 1:17
❑ CP1 The original teaser poster 1.00 2.50
❑ CP2 When time came to finalize 1.00 2.50
❑ CP3 This original foreign poster 1.00 2.50
❑ CP4 The first official Alien movie poster 1.00 2.50
❑ CP5 The original Aliens poster 1.00 2.50
❑ CP6 This original poster design 1.00 2.50
❑ CP7 A monstrous Alien fetus 1.00 2.50
❑ CP8 An original teaser poster 1.00 2.50
❑ CP9 The US one-sheet poster 1.00 2.50

1998 Babylon 5 Season Five

COMPLETE SET (81) 5.00 12.00
❑ 1 Title Card .15 .40
❑ 2 No Compromises .15 .40
❑ 3 The Very Long Night of Londo Mollari .15 .40
❑ 4 The Paragon of Animals .15 .40
❑ 5 A View from the Gallery .15 .40
❑ 6 Learning Curve .15 .40
❑ 7 Strange Relations .15 .40
❑ 8 Secrets of the Soul .15 .40
❑ 9 In the Kingdom of the Blind .15 .40
❑ 10 A Tragedy of Telepaths .15 .40
❑ 11 Phoenix Rising .15 .40
❑ 12 Day of the Dead .15 .40
❑ 13 The Ragged Edge .15 .40
❑ 14 The Corps Is Mother, The Corps Is Father .15 .40
❑ 15 Meditations on the Abyss .15 .40
❑ 16 Darkness Ascending .15 .40
❑ 17 And All My Dreams, Torn Asunder .15 .40
❑ 18 Movements of Fire and Shadow .15 .40
❑ 19 The Fall of Centauri Prime .15 .40
❑ 20 The Wheel of Fire .15 .40
❑ 21 Objects in Motion .15 .40
❑ 22 Objects at Rest .15 .40
❑ 23 New Regime .15 .40
❑ 24 New Regime .15 .40
❑ 25 New Regime .15 .40
❑ 26 New Regime .15 .40
❑ 27 New Regime .15 .40
❑ 28 Lochley Takes Captains Chair .15 .40
❑ 29 Lochley Takes Captains Chair .15 .40
❑ 30 Lochley Takes Captains Chair .15 .40
❑ 31 Lochley Takes Captains Chair .15 .40
❑ 32 Lochley Takes Captains Chair .15 .40
❑ 33 Lochley Takes Captains Chair .15 .40
❑ 34 Lochley Takes Captains Chair .15 .40
❑ 35 Lochley Takes Captains Chair .15 .40
❑ 36 Lochley Takes Captains Chair .15 .40
❑ 37 G'Kar .15 .40
❑ 38 G'Kar .15 .40
❑ 39 G'Kar .15 .40
❑ 40 G'Kar .15 .40
❑ 41 G'Kar .15 .40
❑ 42 G'Kar .15 .40
❑ 43 G'Kar .15 .40
❑ 44 G'Kar .15 .40
❑ 45 G'Kar .15 .40
❑ 46 What Happened to Mr. Garibaldi? .15 .40
❑ 47 What Happened to Mr. Garibaldi? .15 .40
❑ 48 What Happened to Mr. Garibaldi? .15 .40
❑ 49 What Happened to Mr. Garibaldi? .15 .40
❑ 50 What Happened to Mr. Garibaldi? .15 .40
❑ 51 What Happened to Mr. Garibaldi? .15 .40
❑ 52 What Happened to Mr. Garibaldi? .15 .40
❑ 53 What Happened to Mr. Garibaldi? .15 .40
❑ 54 What Happened to Mr. Garibaldi? .15 .40
❑ 55 Telepaths .15 .40
❑ 56 Telepaths .15 .40
❑ 57 Telepaths .15 .40
❑ 58 Telepaths .15 .40
❑ 59 Telepaths .15 .40
❑ 60 Telepaths .15 .40
❑ 61 Telepaths .15 .40
❑ 62 Telepaths .15 .40
❑ 63 Telepaths .15 .40
❑ 64 Fall of Centauri Prime .15 .40
❑ 65 Fall of Centauri Prime .15 .40
❑ 66 Fall of Centauri Prime .15 .40
❑ 67 Fall of Centauri Prime .15 .40
❑ 68 Fall of Centauri Prime .15 .40
❑ 69 Fall of Centauri Prime .15 .40
❑ 70 Fall of Centauri Prime .15 .40
❑ 71 Fall of Centauri Prime .15 .40
❑ 72 Fall of Centauri Prime .15 .40
❑ 73 The Alliance .15 .40
❑ 74 The Alliance .15 .40
❑ 75 The Alliance .15 .40
❑ 76 The Alliance .15 .40
❑ 77 The Alliance .15 .40
❑ 78 The Alliance .15 .40
❑ 79 The Alliance .15 .40
❑ 80 The Alliance .15 .40
❑ 81 Checklist .15 .40

1998 Babylon 5 Season Five Autographs

COMPLETE SET (22) 400.00 700.00
RANDOM INSERTS IN PACKS
❑ A1 Bruce Boxleitner 30.00 60.00
❑ A2 Tracy Scoggins 25.00 50.00
❑ A3 Walter Koenig 25.00 50.00
❑ A4 Ray O'Connor 8.00 20.00
❑ A5 Marj. Monaghan 20.00 40.00
❑ A6 Dex E. Sanders 8.00 20.00
❑ A7 Denise Gentile 20.00 40.00
❑ A8 Ian Ogilvy 10.00 25.00
❑ A9 Bridget Flanery 10.00 25.00
❑ A10 P.Tallman 30.00 60.00
Willerth
❑ A11 Maria Marshall 10.00 25.00
❑ A12 Wayne Alexander 8.00 20.00
❑ A13 Wayne Alexander 8.00 20.00
❑ A14 Julie C. Brown 20.00 40.00
❑ A15 Joshua Cox 8.00 20.00
❑ A16 Penn & Teller 25.00 50.00
❑ A17 Ed Wasser 25.00 50.00
❑ A18 Patricia Tallman 25.00 50.00
❑ A19 Fabiano Udenio 10.00 25.00
❑ A20 John Copeland 20.00 40.00
❑ A21 Robin A. Downes 20.00 40.00
❑ A22 Joshua Cox 8.00 20.00

1998 Babylon 5 Season Five One Exit

COMPLETE SET (6) 5.00 12.00
❑ E1 Lennier 1.25 3.00
❑ E2 Londo 1.25 3.00
❑ E3 G'Kar & Lyta 1.25 3.00
❑ E4 Garibaldi 1.25 3.00
❑ E5 Franklin 1.25 3.00
❑ E6 Delenn & Sheridan 1.25 3.00

1998 Babylon 5 Season Five River of Souls

COMPLETE SET (9) 6.00 15.00
RANDOM INSERTS IN PACKS
❑ R1 The Vault of Souls .75 2.00
❑ R2 Introducing Dr. Bryson .75 2.00
❑ R3 Love Bat .75 2.00
❑ R4 First Contact .75 2.00
❑ R5 Holobrothel Tech .75 2.00
❑ R6 Soul Hunter .75 2.00
❑ R7 The Truth of Ralga .75 2.00
❑ R8 Another Lochley .75 2.00
❑ R9 Supreme Sacrifice .75 2.00

1998 Babylon 5 Season Five Sleeping Light

COMPLETE SET (9) 10.00 25.00
RANDOM INSERTS IN PACKS
❑ S1 General Ivanova 1.50 4.00
❑ S2 Emperor Vir Cotto 1.50 4.00
❑ S3 Franklin and Garibaldi 1.50 4.00
❑ S4 The Banquet 1.50 4.00
❑ S5 Good-Bye 1.50 4.00
❑ S6 One Last Visit 1.50 4.00
❑ S7 Sleeping in Light 1.50 4.00
❑ S8 Lights Out 1.50 4.00
❑ S9 In Memory Still Bright 1.50 4.00

1998 Babylon 5 Season Five Thirdspace

COMPLETE SET (9) 10.00 25.00
RANDOM INSERTS IN PACKS
❑ T1 The Discovery 1.50 4.00
❑ T2 And So it Begins 1.50 4.00
❑ T3 Dark Runes 1.50 4.00
❑ T4 Bots Are Drawn 1.50 4.00
❑ T5 The Dark Tower 1.50 4.00
❑ T6 Thirdspace 1.50 4.00
❑ T7 Anti-Life Itself 1.50 4.00
❑ T8 The Battle 1.50 4.00
❑ T9 A Dark Guardian 1.50 4.00

1998 Buffy the Vampire Slayer Season One

COMPLETE SET (72) 12.50 30.00
❑ 1 Buffy The Vampire Slayer .20 .50
❑ 2 New Girl .20 .50
❑ 3 I Got Hungry .20 .50
❑ 4 Who Are You? .20 .50
❑ 5 Amen .20 .50
❑ 6 In The Beginning .20 .50
❑ 7 First Reaction .20 .50
❑ 8 The Prophecy .20 .50
❑ 9 Be Afraid .20 .50
❑ 10 Release The Unworthy .20 .50
❑ 11 Take Her! .20 .50
❑ 12 Catherine, The Great .20 .50
❑ 13 Sweet Dreams .20 .50
❑ 14 The Substitute .20 .50
❑ 15 It Just Bugs Me .20 .50
❑ 16 Instant Chemistry .20 .50
❑ 17 A Fairly Slim Lead .20 .50
❑ 18 You Killed My Date! .20 .50
❑ 19 Absolutely No Admittance .20 .50
❑ 20 Leader Of The Pack .20 .50
❑ 21 An Act Of Agression .20 .50
❑ 22 First Aid .20 .50
❑ 23 I Better Go .20 .50
❑ 24 I Miss Him .20 .50
❑ 25 Betrayal .20 .50
❑ 26 Lets Get It Done .20 .50
❑ 27 Where Am I .20 .50
❑ 28 This Is Very Bad .20 .50
❑ 29 You Have Mail .20 .50
❑ 30 The Digital Circle .20 .50
❑ 31 She's The Last .20 .50
❑ 32 I Got It .20 .50
❑ 33 He's Coming, Right .20 .50
❑ 34 Fear .20 .50
❑ 35 Send In The Clown .20 .50
❑ 36 No More Hiding .20 .50
❑ 37 Queen Cordelia .20 .50
❑ 38 You're The Lesson .20 .50
❑ 39 This Is A Sign .20 .50
❑ 40 Apocalypse Stuff .20 .50
❑ 41 Think It'll Hurt? .20 .50
❑ 42 A Child Shall Lead Them .20 .50
❑ 43 I Like Your Dress .20 .50
❑ 44 I Have No Breath .20 .50
❑ 45 Welcome Back .20 .50
❑ 46 Buffy Summers .20 .50
❑ 47 Rupert Giles .20 .50
❑ 48 Willow Rosenberg .20 .50
❑ 49 Xander Harris .20 .50
❑ 50 Angel .20 .50
❑ 51 Cordelia .20 .50
❑ 52 Vampyr .20 .50
❑ 53 Daemons .20 .50
❑ 54 Lycanthropes .20 .50
❑ 55 Becoming A Vampire .20 .50
❑ 56 Dating .20 .50
❑ 57 Starting Over .20 .50
❑ 58 Privacy .20 .50
❑ 59 Rivals .20 .50
❑ 60 Helping Others .20 .50
❑ 61 Knowledge .20 .50
❑ 62 Decorating .20 .50
❑ 63 Strategy .20 .50
❑ 64 The Master .20 .50
❑ 65 Luke .20 .50
❑ 66 Darla .20 .50
❑ 67 Thomas .20 .50
❑ 68 The Witch .20 .50
❑ 69 Moloch, The Corruptor .20 .50
❑ 70 The Anointed One .20 .50
❑ 71 The Birthday Clown .20 .50
❑ 72 Checklist .20 .50
❑ BL1 Season Two Promo 2.00 5.00
❑ NNO How To Kill A Vampire 5.00 12.00

1998 Buffy the Vampire Slayer Season One Autographs

COMPLETE SET (4) 700.00 1200.00
RANDOM INSERTS IN PACKS
❑ A1 Joss Whedon 75.00 150.00
❑ A2 David Boreanaz 200.00 400.00
❑ A3 Alyson Hannigan 300.00 500.00
❑ A4 Mark Metcalf 150.00 250.00

1998 Buffy the Vampire Slayer Season One Promos
COMPLETE SET (3) 4.00 10.00
❑ BP1 Buffy the Vampire Slayer 2.00 5.00
❑ BP2 Buffy the Vampire Slayer 2.00 5.00
❑ MS1 Buffy the Vampire Slayer 2.00 5.00

1998 Buffy the Vampire Slayer Season One Slayer Kit
COMPLETE SET (6) 40.00 100.00
STATED ODDS 1:27
❑ S1 Wooden Stake 7.50 20.00
❑ S2 Cross 7.50 20.00
❑ S3 Holy Water 7.50 20.00
❑ S4 Garlic 7.50 20.00
❑ S5 Crossbow 7.50 20.00
❑ S6 Sword 7.50 20.00

1998 Buffy the Vampire Slayer Season One The Chosen One
COMPLETE SET (9) 30.00 75.00
STATED ODDS 1:11
❑ C1 The Chosen One 4.00 10.00
❑ C2 The Chosen One 4.00 10.00
❑ C3 The Chosen One 4.00 10.00
❑ C4 The Chosen One 4.00 10.00
❑ C5 The Chosen One 4.00 10.00
❑ C6 The Chosen One 4.00 10.00
❑ C7 The Chosen One 4.00 10.00
❑ C8 The Chosen One 4.00 10.00
❑ C9 The Chosen One 4.00 10.00

1998 Lost In Space The Movie
COMPLETE SET (90) 5.00 12.00
J1 STATED ODDS 1:108
❑ 1 Lost in Space .15 .40
❑ 2 Eagle One .15 .40
❑ 3 Sedition Raider .15 .40
❑ 4 Moving Day .15 .40
❑ 5 Monkey Business .15 .40
❑ 6 Meet the Press .15 .40
❑ 7 Launch Dome .15 .40
❑ 8 A Boy's World .15 .40
❑ 9 Saboteur .15 .40
❑ 10 Welcome Aboard .15 .40
❑ 11 One Last Detail .15 .40
❑ 12 Betrayed .15 .40
❑ 13 Cryosuits .15 .40
❑ 14 Powering Main Systems .15 .40
❑ 15 On Your Command .15 .40
❑ 16 Destroy .15 .40
❑ 17 Disable Program .15 .40
❑ 18 Berserker .15 .40
❑ 19 Leap to Safety .15 .40
❑ 20 Power Down .15 .40
❑ 21 Certain Doom .15 .40
❑ 22 The Life I Save... .15 .40
❑ 23 Anywhere But Here .15 .40
❑ 24 Alien Stars .15 .40
❑ 25 You're Lucky .15 .40
❑ 26 The Proteus .15 .40
❑ 27 Hostile Environment .15 .40
❑ 28 Captain's Log .15 .40
❑ 29 An Onboard Jungle .15 .40
❑ 30 Don't Evolve .15 .40
❑ 31 Robot Defense .15 .40
❑ 32 Armed & Dangerous .15 .40
❑ 33 Let's Move .15 .40
❑ 34 Hang On .15 .40
❑ 35 Blawp .15 .40
❑ 36 Can I Keep Her? .15 .40
❑ 37 Pretty Girl .15 .40
❑ 38 Star Light, Star Bright .15 .40
❑ 39 In Control .15 .40
❑ 40 I'm Coming Back .15 .40
❑ 41 Come Home .15 .40
❑ 42 Still Scheming... .15 .40
❑ 43 Danger, Will Robinson .15 .40
❑ 44 You're a Doctor .15 .40
❑ 45 Repairs .15 .40
❑ 46 Cool .15 .40
❑ 47 Smith's Discovery .15 .40
❑ 48 Blawp, Come Back .15 .40
❑ 49 When Are We? .15 .40
❑ 50 We're Turned Around .15 .40
❑ 51 Indeed .15 .40
❑ 52 This Can't Be .15 .40
❑ 53 I'm Your Son .15 .40
❑ 54 Rescue Party .15 .40
❑ 55 No Two Alike .15 .40
❑ 56 Where Are We? .15 .40
❑ 57 I'll Change History .15 .40
❑ 58 A Brief Lesson .15 .40
❑ 59 Never Fear... .15 .40
❑ 60 Matter of Survival .15 .40
❑ 61 ... Smith Is Here .15 .40
❑ 62 Kill Them All .15 .40
❑ 63 I Am a God .15 .40
❑ 64 Halt .15 .40
❑ 65 Robot Will Save .15 .40
❑ 66 He's Still Breathing .15 .40
❑ 67 Jump .15 .40
❑ 68 Evil's True Form .15 .40
❑ 69 A Close Call .15 .40
❑ 70 No Choice At All .15 .40
❑ 71 Come with Us .15 .40
❑ 72 Don't Forget Me .15 .40
❑ 73 Set Design .15 .40
❑ 74 The Line of Fire .15 .40
❑ 75 Danger .15 .40
❑ 76 A Perfect Fit .15 .40
❑ 77 It Takes Six .15 .40
❑ 78 All Grown Up .15 .40
❑ 79 Hangin' Around .15 .40
❑ 80 Just Relax .15 .40
❑ 81 In Between Takes .15 .40
❑ 82 Professor John Robinson .15 .40
❑ 83 Maureen Robinson .15 .40
❑ 84 Dr. Judy Robinson .15 .40
❑ 85 Penny Robinson .15 .40
❑ 86 Will Robinson .15 .40
❑ 87 Major Don West .15 .40
❑ 88 Dr. Zachary Smith .15 .40
❑ 89 Mission Robot .15 .40
❑ 90 Checklist .15 .40
❑ J1 Jupiter 2 4.00 10.00

1998 Lost In Space The Movie Autographs
RANDOM INSERT IN PACKS
❑ A1 Mimi Rogers 10.00 25.00
❑ A2 Lacey Chabert 30.00 60.00
❑ A3 Jack Johnson 6.00 15.00

1998 Lost In Space The Movie Double Feature
COMPLETE SET (9) 5.00 12.00
STATED ODDS 1:11
❑ DF1 John Robinson 1.00 2.50
❑ DF2 Maureen Robinson 1.00 2.50
❑ DF3 Judy Robinson 1.00 2.50
❑ DF4 Penny Robinson 1.00 2.50
❑ DF5 Will Robinson 1.00 2.50
❑ DF6 Major Don West 1.00 2.50
❑ DF7 Zachary Smith 1.00 2.50
❑ DF8 Mission Robot 1.00 2.50
❑ DF9 Blawp 1.00 2.50
Debbie

1998 Lost In Space The Movie War Of The Robots
COMPLETE SET (4) 8.00 20.00
STATED ODDS 1:24
❑ R1 The Mission's Robot 3.00 8.00
❑ R2 Will's Robot 3.00 8.00
❑ R3 B-9 3.00 8.00
❑ R4 Robot Ancestry 3.00 8.00

1998 Small Soldiers
COMPLETE SET (90) 4.00 10.00
S1 STATED ODDS 1:108
❑ 1 Title Card .08 .25
❑ 2 The Presentation .08 .25
❑ 3 Don't Forget .08 .25
❑ 4 Delivery .08 .25
❑ 5 I Owe You One .08 .25
❑ 6 Sworn Enemies .08 .25
❑ 7 I've Seen You Around .08 .25
❑ 8 Way Cool! .08 .25
❑ 9 The New Display .08 .25
❑ 10 I Am Archer .08 .25
❑ 11 Chip Breaks Out .08 .25
❑ 12 Fall In .08 .25
❑ 13 Home .08 .25
❑ 14 Armed And Dangerous .08 .25
❑ 15 Frag Em All .08 .25
❑ 16 The War Zone .08 .25
❑ 17 Who Did This .08 .25
❑ 18 Clean Up .08 .25
❑ 19 Recon .08 .25
❑ 20 Command Post .08 .25
❑ 21 Hold On .08 .25
❑ 22 There's A Problem .08 .25
❑ 23 The Trap .08 .25
❑ 24 The Interrogator .08 .25
❑ 25 Into The Pit .08 .25
❑ 26 Medic .08 .25
❑ 27 A Packed Arsenal .08 .25
❑ 28 I'm Messed Up .08 .25
❑ 29 Where Are They .08 .25
❑ 30 You In There .08 .25
❑ 31 What Was That .08 .25
❑ 32 We Fixed Him .08 .25
❑ 33 Age Five...And Up .08 .25
❑ 34 What Is Cristy .08 .25
❑ 35 A Complete Collection .08 .25
❑ 36 Wire Tap .08 .25
❑ 37 Move Out .08 .25
❑ 38 You Can Talk .08 .25
❑ 39 P.O.W. .08 .25
❑ 40 Bombshells, Sir .08 .25
❑ 41 You'll Live On .08 .25
❑ 42 Reporting For Duty .08 .25
❑ 43 Attack .08 .25
❑ 44 Hi! You're Cute .08 .25
❑ 45 Are You Scared .08 .25
❑ 46 The Wind .08 .25
❑ 47 Search Complete .08 .25
❑ 48 Surrender .08 .25
❑ 49 Behind Enemy Lines .08 .25
❑ 50 The Rescue .08 .25
❑ 51 Roll Out .08 .25
❑ 52 Christy Fights Back .08 .25
❑ 53 Expect No Mercy .08 .25
❑ 54 Interlock .08 .25
❑ 55 There's Still A Way .08 .25
❑ 56 Home At Last .08 .25
❑ 57 You're Alive .08 .25
❑ 58 Oh, No .08 .25
❑ 59 Negotiations .08 .25
❑ 60 Reinforcements .08 .25
❑ 61 Ready To Detonate .08 .25
❑ 62 We Must Help Alan .08 .25
❑ 63 We Will Lose .08 .25
❑ 64 Insaniac's Charge .08 .25
❑ 65 Freakenstein Fires .08 .25
❑ 66 Go .08 .25
❑ 67 The Chopper .08 .25
❑ 68 No Prisoners .08 .25
❑ 69 High Voltage .08 .25
❑ 70 Do You Smell Smoke .08 .25
❑ 71 Are You Okay .08 .25
❑ 72 We Won .08 .25
❑ 73 Archer .08 .25
❑ 74 Insaniac .08 .25
❑ 75 Slamfist .08 .25
❑ 76 Punch-It .08 .25
❑ 77 Scratch-It .08 .25
❑ 78 Freakenstein .08 .25
❑ 79 Ocula .08 .25
❑ 80 Chip Hazard .08 .25
❑ 81 Nick Nitro .08 .25
❑ 82 Butch Meathook .08 .25
❑ 83 Brick Bazooka .08 .25
❑ 84 Kip Killigan .08 .25
❑ 85 Link Static .08 .25
❑ 86 Alan Abernathy .08 .25
❑ 87 Christy Fimple .08 .25
❑ 88 Tim Fimple .08 .25
❑ 89 The Investors .08 .25
❑ 90 Checklist .08 .25
❑ S1 The Gorgonites 2.00 5.00
The Commando Elite

1998 Small Soldiers Autographs
COMPLETE SET (4) 75.00 150.00
RANDOM INSERTS IN PACKS
❑ A1 Gregory Smith 6.00 15.00
❑ A2 Kirsten Dunst 70.00 120.00
❑ A3 Joe Dante 6.00 15.00
❑ A4 Stan Winston 10.00 25.00

1998 Small Soldiers Battle
COMPLETE SET (6) 6.00 15.00
STATED ODDS 1:27
❑ B1 The Power Assault Vehicle 1.25 3.00
❑ B2 Buzzsaw Tank 1.25 3.00
❑ B3 Helicopter 1.25 3.00
❑ B4 Toaster Tank 1.25 3.00
❑ B5 Flaming Tennis Ball Shooter 1.25 3.00
❑ B6 Skateboard Flame Thrower 1.25 3.00

1998 Small Soldiers Promos
COMPLETE SET (3) 2.00 5.00
❑ P1 If It Launches, Lacerates, Detonates I Want It .75 2.00
❑ P2 Gentlemen, We Got Us a War to Win .75 2.00
❑ P3 Our Mission: Destroy the Gorgonite .75 2.00
Enemy Defeat Him

1998 Small Soldiers Tattoos
COMPLETE SET (9) .75 2.00
STATED ODDS ONE PER PACK
❑ T1 Chip Hazard .08 .25
Brick Bazooka
❑ T2 Kip Killigan .08 .25
Link Static
❑ T3 Nick Nitro .08 .25
Butch Meathook
❑ T4 Archer .08 .25
Punch-It/Scratch-It
❑ T5 Slamfist .08 .25
Ocula
❑ T6 Insaniac .08 .25
Freakenstein
❑ T7 Archer vs. Chip Hazard .08 .25
❑ T8 The Gorgonites .08 .25
❑ T9 The Commando Elite .08 .25

1998 Spawn Toy Files
COMPLETE SET (88) 5.00 12.00
❑ 1 Title Card .15 .40
❑ 2 Spawn .15 .40
❑ 3 Medieval Spawn .15 .40
❑ 4 Tremor .15 .40
❑ 5 Violator .15 .40
❑ 6 Clown .15 .40
❑ 7 Overtkill .15 .40
❑ 8 Spawn Alley .15 .40
❑ 9 Spawn Mobile .15 .40
❑ 10 Violator Monster Rig .15 .40
❑ 11 Commando Spawn .15 .40
❑ 12 Angels .15 .40
❑ 13 Malebolgia .15 .40
❑ 14 Pilot's Spawn .15 .40
❑ 15 Spawn II .15 .40
❑ 16 Violator II .15 .40
❑ 17 Vertebreaker .15 .40
❑ 18 Redeemer .15 .40
❑ 19 The Curse .15 .40
❑ 20 Cosmic Angela .15 .40
❑ 21 Future Spawn .15 .40
❑ 22 Ninja Spawn .15 .40
❑ 23 Battle Horse .15 .40
❑ 24 Air Cycle & Violator Chopper .15 .40
❑ 25 Exo-Skeleton Spawn .15 .40
❑ 26 Sho-Spawn .15 .40
❑ 27 Cy-Gor .15 .40
❑ 28 Clown II .15 .40
❑ 29 The Maxx .15 .40
❑ 30 Shadowhawk .15 .40
❑ 31 Nuclear Spawn .15 .40
❑ 32 Viking Spawn .15 .40
❑ 33 Vandalizer .15 .40
❑ 34 Overtkill II .15 .40
❑ 35 Tremor II .15 .40
❑ 36 Widow Maker .15 .40
❑ 37 Battleclad Spawn .15 .40
❑ 38 Alien Spawn .15 .40
❑ 39 Mutant Spawn .15 .40
❑ 40 Tiffany the Amazon .15 .40
❑ 41 The Freak .15 .40
❑ 42 Sansker .15 .40
❑ 43 Superpatriot .15 .40
❑ 44 Spawn III .15 .40
❑ 45 Zombie Spawn .15 .40
❑ 46 The Mangler .15 .40
❑ 48 Crutch .15 .40
❑ 49 No-Body .15 .40
❑ 50 Sam and Twitch .15 .40
❑ 51 Curse of the Spawn .15 .40
❑ 52 Renegade .15 .40
❑ 53 Sabra .15 .40
❑ 54 Gate Keeper .15 .40
❑ 55 Grave Digger .15 .40
❑ 56 Rotarr .15 .40
❑ 57 Manga Spawn .15 .40
❑ 58 Manga Ninja Spawn .15 .40
❑ 59 Goddess .15 .40
❑ 60 Manga Clown .15 .40
❑ 61 Manga Violator .15 .40
❑ 62 Manga Curse .15 .40
❑ 63 Manga Cyber-Tooth .15 .40
❑ 64 Manga Freak .15 .40
❑ 65 Manga Overtkill .15 .40
❑ 66 Manga Samurai Spawn .15 .40
❑ 67 Manga Cyber-Violator .15 .40
❑ 68 Manga Dead Spawn .15 .40
❑ 69 The Spellcaster .15 .40
❑ 70 The Horrid .15 .40
❑ 71 The Ogre .15 .40
❑ 72 Spawn: The Black Knight .15 .40
❑ 73 The Raider .15 .40
❑ 74 The Skull Queen .15 .40
❑ 75 The Creech .15 .40
❑ 76 Spawn IV: Arsenal of Doom .15 .40
❑ 77 Top Gun .15 .40
❑ 78 Bottom Line .15 .40
❑ 79 The Heap .15 .40
❑ 80 Reanimated Spawn .15 .40
❑ 81 Cy-Gor 2 .15 .40
❑ 82 Spawn .15 .40
❑ 83 Al Simmons .15 .40
❑ 85 Jessica Priest .15 .40
❑ 86 Jason Wynn .15 .40
❑ 87 Clown .15 .40
❑ 88 Violation .15 .40
❑ 89 Attack Spawn .15 .40
❑ 90 Checklist .15 .40

1998 Star Trek Insurrection
COMPLETE SET (72) 5.00 12.00
❑ 1 Checklist .15 .40
❑ 2 Mission Log 1 .15 .40
❑ 3 Mission Log 2 .15 .40
❑ 4 Mission Log 3 .15 .40
❑ 5 Mission Log 4 .15 .40
❑ 6 Mission Log 5 .15 .40
❑ 7 Mission Log 6 .15 .40
❑ 8 Mission Log 7 .15 .40
❑ 9 Mission Log 8 .15 .40
❑ 10 Mission Log 9 .15 .40
❑ 11 Mission Log 10 .15 .40
❑ 12 Mission Log 11 .15 .40
❑ 13 Mission Log 12 .15 .40
❑ 14 Mission Log 13 .15 .40
❑ 15 Mission Log 14 .15 .40
❑ 16 Mission Log 15 .15 .40
❑ 17 Mission Log 16 .15 .40
❑ 18 Mission Log 17 .15 .40
❑ 19 Mission Log 18 .15 .40
❑ 20 Mission Log 19 .15 .40
❑ 21 Mission Log 20 .15 .40
❑ 22 Mission Log 21 .15 .40
❑ 23 Mission Log 22 .15 .40
❑ 24 Mission Log 23 .15 .40
❑ 25 Crusher and Picard .15 .40
❑ 26 Riker and Picard .15 .40
❑ 27 Librarian .15 .40
❑ 28 Riker and Troi .15 .40
❑ 29 Picard and Worf .15 .40
❑ 30 Ru'afo and Picard .15 .40
❑ 31 Picard and Worf .15 .40
❑ 32 Troi and Riker .15 .40
❑ 33 Picard and Data .15 .40
❑ 34 Data and Artim .15 .40
❑ 35 Anij .15 .40
❑ 36 Data .15 .40
❑ 37 Riker .15 .40
❑ 38 Riker .15 .40
❑ 39 Picard .15 .40
❑ 40 LaForge .15 .40
❑ 41 Picard and Dougherty .15 .40
❑ 42 Picard and Dougherty .15 .40
❑ 43 Data .15 .40
❑ 44 Ru'afo .15 .40
❑ 45 Artim and Data .15 .40
❑ 46 Worf .15 .40
❑ 47 Worf .15 .40
❑ 48 Riker and LaForge .15 .40
❑ 49 LaForge .15 .40
❑ 50 Ru'afo .15 .40
❑ 51 Artim .15 .40
❑ 52 Captain Picard .15 .40
❑ 53 Cmdr. Riker .15 .40
❑ 54 Lt. Cmdr. Data .15 .40
❑ 55 Counselor Troi .15 .40
❑ 56 Dr. Crusher .15 .40
❑ 57 Lt. Cmdr. LaForge .15 .40
❑ 58 Lt.Cmdr. Worf .15 .40
❑ 59 Adm. Dougherty .15 .40
❑ 60 Ru'afo .15 .40
❑ 61 Gallatin .15 .40
❑ 62 Anij .15 .40
❑ 63 Sojef .15 .40
❑ 64 Artim .15 .40
❑ 65 Son'a .15 .40
❑ 66 Ba'ku .15 .40
❑ 67 Ellorans .15 .40
❑ 68 Tarlac .15 .40
❑ 69 Cuzar .15 .40
❑ 70 Bolians .15 .40
❑ 71 Trill .15 .40
❑ 72 Vulcans .15 .40

1998 Star Trek Insurrection Autographs
COMPLETE SET (19) 400.00 750.00
STATED ODDS 1:36
❑ A1 Patrick Stewart 60.00 120.00
❑ A2 Jonathan Frakes 60.00 120.00
❑ A3 Brent Spiner 60.00 120.00
❑ A4 Marina Sirtis 60.00 120.00
❑ A5 Levar Burton 30.00 60.00
❑ A6 Gates McFadden 50.00 100.00
❑ A7 Michael Westmore 7.50 15.00
❑ A8 Jennifer Tung 7.50 15.00
❑ A9 Mark Deakins 7.50 15.00
❑ A10 Anthony Zerbe 7.50 15.00
❑ A11 Gregg Henry 7.50 15.00
❑ A12 John Hostetter 7.50 15.00
❑ A13 Stephanie Niznik 7.50 15.00
❑ A14 Breon Gorman 7.50 15.00
❑ A15 Lee Arnone 7.50 15.00
❑ A16 Michael Welch 7.50 15.00
❑ A17 Bruce French 7.50 15.00
❑ A18 Larry Anderson 7.50 15.00
❑ A19 Donna Murphy 7.50 15.00

1998 Star Trek Insurrection Gold
COMPLETE SET (7) 400.00 600.00
STATED PRINT RUN 400 SETS
❑ G1 Captain Picard 60.00 100.00
❑ G2 Commander Riker 60.00 100.00
❑ G3 Lt. Commander Data 60.00 100.00
❑ G4 Counselor Troi 60.00 100.00
❑ G5 Dr. Crusher 60.00 100.00
❑ G6 Lt. Commander LaForge 60.00 100.00
❑ G7 Lt. Commander Worf 60.00 100.00

1998 Star Trek Insurrection Okudagrams
COMPLETE SET (9) 6.00 15.00
STATED ODDS 1:8
❑ OK1 Son'a Tactical Display .75 2.00
❑ OK2 Son'a Tactical Table .75 2.00
❑ OK3 Son'a Bridge .75 2.00
❑ OK4 Son'a Ship's Systems Display .75 2.00
❑ OK5 Son'a Body Enhancement Display .75 2.00
❑ OK6 Son'a Body Enhancement Equipment .75 2.00
❑ OK7 USS Enterprise-E Bridge Display .75 2.00
❑ OK8 USS Enterprise-E Library Display .75 2.00
❑ OK9 USS Enterprise-E Padd Displays .75 2.00

1998 Star Trek Insurrection Relationships
COMPLETE SET (9) 7.50 20.00
STATED ODDS 1:8
❑ R1 Anij, Picard 1.25 3.00
❑ R2 Artim, Data 1.25 3.00
❑ R3 Dougherty, Ru'afo 1.25 3.00
❑ R4 Troi, Riker 1.25 3.00
❑ R5 Crusher, Picard 1.25 3.00
❑ R6 Data, LaForge 1.25 3.00
❑ R7 Picard, Riker 1.25 3.00
❑ R8 Data, Worf 1.25 3.00
❑ R9 Ru'afo, Picard 1.25 3.00

1998 Star Trek Insurrection Schematics
COMPLETE SET (9) 2.00 5.00
STATED ODDS 1:4
❑ S1 USS Enterprise-E .40 1.00
❑ S2 Core Dump .40 1.00
❑ S3 Federation Scout Ship .40 1.00
❑ S4 Enterprise-E Shuttle .40 1.00
❑ S5 Captain's Yacht .40 1.00
❑ S6 Son'a Collector Ship .40 1.00
❑ S7 Son'a Ship .40 1.00
❑ S8 Ru'afo's Ship .40 1.00
❑ S9 Holo-Ship .40 1.00

1998 Star Trek Insurrection Wardrobe
COMPLETE SET (9) 2.00 5.00
STATED ODDS 1:4
❑ W1 Picard .40 1.00
❑ W2 Data .40 1.00
❑ W3 Worf .40 1.00
❑ W4 Anij .40 1.00
❑ W5 Cuzar .40 1.00
❑ W6 Artim .40 1.00
❑ W7 Elloran Woman .40 1.00
❑ W8 Tarlac Man .40 1.00
❑ W9 Son'a Man .40 1.00

1998 Star Trek Voyager Profiles
COMPLETE SET (90) 6.00 15.00
❑ 1 Crew Manifest .15 .40
❑ 2 Admiral's Log .15 .40
❑ 3 Personal Log .15 .40
❑ 4 Personal Log .15 .40
❑ 5 Personal Log .15 .40
❑ 6 Reflections - Seven of Nine .15 .40
❑ 7 Reflections - Tuvok .15 .40
❑ 8 Reflections - Chakotay .15 .40
❑ 9 Alien Encounter - Q .15 .40
❑ 10 Crew Manifest .15 .40
❑ 11 Captain's Log .15 .40
❑ 12 Personal Log .15 .40
❑ 13 Personal Log .15 .40
❑ 14 Personal Log .15 .40
❑ 15 Reflections - Riley Frasier .15 .40
❑ 16 Reflections - Annorax .15 .40
❑ 17 Reflections - Neelix .15 .40
❑ 18 Alien Encounter - Sleeping Aliens .15 .40
❑ 19 Crew Manifest .15 .40
❑ 20 Captain's Log .15 .40
❑ 21 Personal Log .15 .40
❑ 22 Personal Log .15 .40
❑ 23 Personal Log .15 .40
❑ 24 Reflections - Rain Robinson .15 .40
❑ 25 Reflections - Tuvok .15 .40
❑ 26 Reflections - Seven of Nine .15 .40
❑ 27 Alien Encounter - Reptilian Humanoid .15 .40
❑ 28 Crew Manifest .15 .40
❑ 29 Captain's Log .15 .40
❑ 30 Personal Log .15 .40
❑ 31 Personal Log .15 .40
❑ 32 Personal Log .15 .40
❑ 33 Reflections - Suder .15 .40
❑ 34 Reflections - Kim .15 .40
❑ 35 Reflections - Neelix .15 .40
❑ 36 Alien Encounter - Maryana .15 .40
❑ 37 Crew Manifest .15 .40
❑ 38 Captain's Log .15 .40
❑ 39 Personal Log .15 .40
❑ 40 Personal Log .15 .40
❑ 41 Personal Log .15 .40
❑ 42 Reflections - the Doctor .15 .40
❑ 43 Reflections - Vorik .15 .40
❑ 44 Reflections - Paris .15 .40
❑ 45 Alien Encounter - Cardassians .15 .40
❑ 46 Crew Manifest .15 .40
❑ 47 Captain's Log .15 .40
❑ 48 Personal Log .15 .40
❑ 49 Personal Log .15 .40
❑ 50 Personal Log .15 .40
❑ 51 Reflections - Paris .15 .40
❑ 52 Reflections - Seven of Nine .15 .40
❑ 53 Reflections - Torres .15 .40
❑ 54 Alien Encounter - Hirogen .15 .40
❑ 55 Crew Manifest .15 .40
❑ 56 Captain's Log .15 .40
❑ 57 Personal Log .15 .40
❑ 58 Personal Log .15 .40
❑ 59 Personal Log .15 .40
❑ 60 Reflections - Ramen .15 .40
❑ 61 Reflections - Torres .15 .40
❑ 62 Reflections - Hirogen Hunter .15 .40
❑ 63 Alien Encounter - Hirogen .15 .40
❑ 64 Crew Manifest .15 .40
❑ 65 Captain's Log .15 .40
❑ 66 Personal Log .15 .40
❑ 67 Personal Log .15 .40
❑ 68 Personal Log .15 .40
❑ 69 Reflections - Kes .15 .40
❑ 70 Reflections - EMH Mark II .15 .40
❑ 71 Reflections - Seven of Nine .15 .40
❑ 72 Alien Encounter - Kazon .15 .40
❑ 73 Crew Manifest .15 .40
❑ 74 Captain's Log .15 .40
❑ 75 Personal Log .15 .40
❑ 76 Personal Log .15 .40
❑ 77 Personal Log .15 .40
❑ 78 Reflections - Paris .15 .40
❑ 79 Reflections - Tuvok .15 .40
❑ 80 Reflections - Kes .15 .40
❑ 81 Alien Encounter - Ferengi .15 .40
❑ 82 Crew Manifest .15 .40
❑ 83 Captain's Log .15 .40
❑ 84 Personal Log .15 .40
❑ 85 Personal Log .15 .40
❑ 86 Personal Log .15 .40
❑ 87 Reflections - Tanis .15 .40
❑ 88 Reflections - Zahir .15 .40
❑ 89 Alien Encounters - Ilari .15 .40
❑ 90 Checklist .15 .40
❑ C4 Captain Janeway/1200

1998 Star Trek Voyager Profiles Alien Technology
COMPLETE SET (9) 8.00 20.00
STATED ODDS 1:6
❑ AT1 The Swarm 1.50 4.00
❑ AT2 The Voth 1.50 4.00
❑ AT3 Borg 1.50 4.00
❑ AT4 Hirogen Ship 1.50 4.00
❑ AT5 Species 8472 1.50 4.00
❑ AT6 Annorax Ship 1.50 4.00
❑ AT7 Bomar Ships 1.50 4.00

❑ AT8 Ramorans Ship 1.50 4.00
❑ AT9 Arturis 1.50 4.00

1998 Star Trek Voyager Profiles Autograph Challenge
COMP.SET w/o SP (9) 2.50 6.00
❑ A Chakotay .40 1.00
❑ E Doctor .40 1.00
❑ G Cast .40 1.00
❑ K Torres .40 1.00
❑ O Kim .40 1.00
❑ R Paris .40 1.00
❑ S Janeway .40 1.00
❑ T Tuvok .40 1.00
❑ V Neelix .40 1.00
❑ Y Seven of Nine SP 40.00 80.00

1998 Star Trek Voyager Profiles Autographs
STATED ODDS 1:36
❑ A1 Kate Mulgrew 30.00 60.00
as Janeway
❑ A2 Robert Beltran 20.00 50.00
as Chakotay
❑ A3 Garrett Wang 30.00 60.00
as Harry Kim
❑ A4 Tim Russ 20.00 50.00
as Tuvok
❑ A5 Roxann Dawson 35.00 70.00
as B'Elanna Torres
❑ A6 Robert Duncan McNeill 30.00 60.00
as Tom Paris
❑ A7 Jeri Ryan 60.00 120.00
as Seven of Nine
❑ A8 Robert Picardo 30.00 60.00
as The Doctor
❑ A9 Ethan Phillips 20.00 50.00
as Neelix
❑ A10 Jennifer Lien 40.00 80.00
as Kes
❑ A11 John De Lancie 30.00 60.00
as Q
❑ A12 Dwight Schultz 20.00 50.00
as Reginald Barclay
❑ A13 Henry Darrow 20.00 50.00
as Kolopak
❑ A14 Alexander Enberg 15.00 40.00
as Vorik
❑ A15 Tony Todd 12.00 30.00
as Alpha-Hirogen Hunter
❑ A16 Leland Orser 10.00 25.00
as Dejarenj
❑ A17a Michael McKean 10.00 25.00
as The Clown (gold lettering on front)
❑ A17b Michael McKean 20.00 50.00
as The Clown (white lettering on front)
❑ A18 Josh Clark 15.00 40.00
as Lt. Carey
❑ A19 John Rhys-Davies 30.00 60.00
as Leonardo Da Vinci
❑ A20 George Takei 35.00 70.00
as Capt. Sulu

1998 Star Trek Voyager Profiles Makeup with Michael Westmore
COMPLETE SET (9) 5.00 12.00
STATED ODDS 1:4
❑ MW1 Man of Many Faces 1.00 2.50
❑ MW2 Spare Parts 1.00 2.50
❑ MW3 A Little Piece of Seven 1.00 2.50
❑ MW4 Beastly Boys 1.00 2.50
❑ MW5 Pin-Ups 1.00 2.50
❑ MW6 Head Games 1.00 2.50
❑ MW7 The Making of a Talaxian - I 1.00 2.50
❑ MW8 The Making of a Talaxian - II 1.00 2.50
❑ MW9 The Making of a Talaxian - III 1.00 2.50

1998 Star Trek Voyager Profiles Seven of Nine
COMPLETE SET (9) 12.00 30.00
COMP.SET w/o SP (8) 8.00 20.00
STATED ODDS 1:8
SP STATED ODDS 1:144
❑ 1 Physical I 2.00 5.00
❑ 2 Physical II 2.00 5.00
❑ 3 Physical III 2.00 5.00
❑ 4 Emotional I 2.00 5.00
❑ 5 Emotional II 2.00 5.00
❑ 6 Emotional III 2.00 5.00
❑ 7 Duty Assignment I SP 8.00 20.00
❑ 8 Duty Assignment II 2.00 5.00
❑ 9 Duty Assignment III 2.00 5.00

1998 TV's Coolest Classics
COMPLETE SET (90) 5.00 12.00
BH1 ISSUED IN COLLECTORS ALBUM
❑ 1 TV's Coolest Classics .15 .40
❑ 2 The Beverly Hillbillies .15 .40
❑ 3 The Andy Griffith Show .15 .40
❑ 4 Brady Bunch .15 .40
❑ 5 Get Smart .15 .40
❑ 6 Hogan's Heroes .15 .40
❑ 7 Get Smart .15 .40
❑ 8 The Beverly Hillbillies .15 .40
❑ 9 The Andy Griffith Show .15 .40
❑ 10 Brady Bunch .15 .40
❑ 11 The Beverly Hillbillies .15 .40
❑ 12 Get Smart .15 .40
❑ 13 The Andy Griffith Show .15 .40
❑ 14 Brady Bunch .15 .40
❑ 15 Hogan's Heroes .15 .40
❑ 16 Brady Bunch .15 .40
❑ 17 The Andy Griffith Show .15 .40
❑ 18 Hogan's Heroes .15 .40
❑ 19 The Andy Griffith Show .15 .40
❑ 20 The Andy Griffith Show .15 .40
❑ 21 The Andy Griffith Show .15 .40
❑ 22 The Andy Griffith Show .15 .40
❑ 23 Brady Bunch .15 .40
❑ 24 Brady Bunch .15 .40
❑ 25 Brady Bunch .15 .40
❑ 26 The Beverly Hillbillies .15 .40
❑ 27 Get Smart: Just Married .15 .40
❑ 28 The Andy Griffith Show .15 .40
❑ 29 Hogan's Heroes .15 .40
❑ 30 Get Smart .15 .40
❑ 31 Brady Bunch .15 .40
❑ 32 Get Smart .15 .40
❑ 33 Brady Bunch .15 .40
❑ 34 The Beverly Hillbillies .15 .40
❑ 35 The Andy Griffith Show .15 .40
❑ 36 Get Smart .15 .40
❑ 37 The Andy Griffith Show .15 .40
❑ 38 The Andy Griffith Show .15 .40
❑ 39 The Beverly Hillbillies .15 .40
❑ 40 Brady Bunch .15 .40
❑ 41 Brady Bunch .15 .40
❑ 42 The Beverly Hillbillies .15 .40
❑ 43 Get Smart .15 .40
❑ 44 The Andy Griffith Show .15 .40
❑ 45 Brady Bunch .15 .40
❑ 46 The Andy Griffith Show .15 .40
❑ 47 Brady Bunch .15 .40
❑ 48 The Beverly Hillbillies .15 .40
❑ 49 The Beverly Hillbillies .15 .40
❑ 50 The Andy Griffith Show .15 .40
❑ 51 The Beverly Hillbillies .15 .40
❑ 52 The Beverly Hillbillies .15 .40
❑ 53 The Andy Griffith Show .15 .40
❑ 54 Get Smart .15 .40
❑ 55 The Andy Griffith Show .15 .40
❑ 56 Brady Bunch .15 .40
❑ 57 Brady Bunch .15 .40
❑ 58 The Andy Griffith Show .15 .40
❑ 59 The Beverly Hillbillies .15 .40
❑ 60 Get Smart .15 .40
❑ 61 The Beverly Hillbillies .15 .40
❑ 62 The Beverly Hillbillies .15 .40
❑ 63 The Andy Griffith Show .15 .40
❑ 64 Get Smart .15 .40
❑ 65 Get Smart .15 .40
❑ 66 Get Smart .15 .40
❑ 67 Get Smart .15 .40
❑ 68 Get Smart .15 .40
❑ 69 Hogan's Heroes .15 .40
❑ 70 Hogan's Heroes .15 .40
❑ 71 Hogan's Heroes .15 .40
❑ 72 Hogan's Heroes .15 .40
❑ 73 The Andy Griffith Show .15 .40
❑ 74 Brady Bunch .15 .40
❑ 75 The Beverly Hillbillies .15 .40
❑ 76 Brady Bunch .15 .40
❑ 77 The Beverly Hillbillies .15 .40
❑ 78 The Andy Griffith Show .15 .40
❑ 79 Hogan's Heroes .15 .40
❑ 80 The Beverly Hillbillies .15 .40
❑ 81 The Andy Griffith Show .15 .40
❑ 82 The Andy Griffith Show .15 .40
❑ 83 The Andy Griffith Show .15 .40
❑ 84 The Andy Griffith Show .15 .40
❑ 85 Brady Bunch .15 .40
❑ 86 Brady Bunch .15 .40
❑ 87 Brady Bunch .15 .40
❑ 88 Brady Bunch .15 .40
❑ 89 The Andy Griffith Show .15 .40
❑ 90 Coolest Checklist .15 .40
❑ BH1 Beverly Hillbillies/ (issued in collectors album) 1.50 4.00

1998 TV's Coolest Classics Autographs
COMPLETE SET (7) 100.00 200.00
STATED ODDS 1:180
❑ A1 Barbara Feldon 25.00 50.00
❑ A2 Donna Douglas 25.00 50.00
❑ A3 Susan Olsen 7.50 20.00
❑ A4 Betty Lynn 7.50 20.00
❑ A5 Robert Clary 7.50 20.00
❑ A6 Barry Williams 25.00 50.00
❑ A7 Elinore Donahue 7.50 20.00

1998 TV's Coolest Classics Dream Girls
COMPLETE SET (6) 12.50 30.00
STATED ODDS 1:20
❑ D1 Thelma Lou 2.50 6.00
❑ D2 Marcia Brady 2.50 6.00
❑ D3 Elly May Clampett 2.50 6.00
❑ D4 Carol Brady 2.50 6.00
❑ D5 Agent 99 2.50 6.00
❑ D6 Ellie Mae Walker 2.50 6.00

1998 TV's Coolest Classics Memorable Moments
COMPLETE SET (9) 7.50 20.00
STATED ODDS 1:11
❑ M1 The Andy Griffith Show 1.25 3.00
❑ M2 Hogan's Heroes 1.25 3.00
❑ M3 The Beverly Hillbillies 1.25 3.00
❑ M4 The Beverly Hillbillies 1.25 3.00
❑ M5 Brady Bunch 1.25 3.00
❑ M6 Brady Bunch 1.25 3.00
❑ M7 The Andy Griffith Show 1.25 3.00
❑ M8 Brady Bunch 1.25 3.00
❑ M9 The Andy Griffith Show 1.25 3.00

1998 TV's Coolest Classics Promos
COMPLETE SET (3) 2.50 6.00
❑ P1 Greg Brady 1.00 2.50
❑ P2 Maxwell Smart 1.00 2.50
❑ P3 Sgt. Schultz 1.00 2.50

1998 TV's Coolest Classics Smell-o-Rama
COMPLETE SET (3) 10.00 25.00
STATED ODDS 1:30
❑ S1 Aunt Bea's Cherry Pie 4.00 10.00
❑ S2 Greg Brady's New Car 4.00 10.00
❑ S3 Maxwell Smart's Shoe Phone 4.00 10.00

1998 The Women of James Bond
COMPLETE SET (72) 15.00 30.00
M1 STATED ODDS 1:108
❑ 1 The Women of James Bond .40 1.00
❑ 2 Miss Taro .40 1.00
❑ 3 Rosa Klebb .40 1.00
❑ 4 Vida and Zora .40 1.00
❑ 5 Bonita .40 1.00
❑ 6 Fiona Volpe .40 1.00
❑ 7 Helga Brandt .40 1.00
❑ 8 Bambi and Thumper .40 1.00
❑ 9 Naomi .40 1.00
❑ 10 Melina Havelock .40 1.00
❑ 11 May Day .40 1.00
❑ 12 Xenia Onatopp .40 1.00
❑ 13 M .40 1.00
❑ 14 Miss Moneypenny .40 1.00
❑ 15 Tatiana Romanova .40 1.00
❑ 16 Paula Caplan .40 1.00
❑ 17 Kissy/Aki .40 1.00
❑ 18 Miss Caruso .40 1.00
❑ 19 Rosie Carver .40 1.00
❑ 20 Anya Amasova .40 1.00
❑ 21 Holly Goodhead .40 1.00
❑ 22 Log Cabin Girl .40 1.00
❑ 23 Pam Bouvier .40 1.00
❑ 24 Wai Lin .40 1.00
❑ 25 Sylvia Trench .40 1.00
❑ 26 Pussy Galore .40 1.00
❑ 27 Domino Derval .40 1.00
❑ 28 Patricia Fearing .40 1.00
❑ 29 Tracy di Vicenzo .40 1.00
❑ 30 Tiffany Case .40 1.00
❑ 31 Mary Goodnight .40 1.00
❑ 32 Octopussy .40 1.00
❑ 33 Stacey Sutton .40 1.00
❑ 34 Kara Milovy .40 1.00
❑ 35 Natalya Simonova .40 1.00
❑ 36 Paris Carver .40 1.00
❑ 37 Honey Ryder .40 1.00
❑ 38 Jill Masterson .40 1.00
❑ 39 Plenty O'Toole .40 1.00
❑ 40 Solitaire .40 1.00
❑ 41 Andrea Anders .40 1.00
❑ 42 Corinne Dufour .40 1.00
❑ 43 Manuela .40 1.00
❑ 44 Bibi Dahl .40 1.00
❑ 45 Magda .40 1.00
❑ 46 Lupe Lamora .40 1.00
❑ 47 Irina .40 1.00
❑ 48 Inga Bergstrom .40 1.00
❑ 49 Dr. No .40 1.00
❑ 50 From Russia with Love .40 1.00
❑ 51 Goldfinger .40 1.00
❑ 52 Thunderball .40 1.00
❑ 53 You Only Live Twice .40 1.00
❑ 54 On Her Majesty's Secret Service .40 1.00
❑ 55 Diamonds Are Forever .40 1.00
❑ 56 Live and Let Die .40 1.00
❑ 57 The Man with the Golden Gun .40 1.00
❑ 58 The Spy Who Loved Me .40 1.00
❑ 59 Moonraker .40 1.00
❑ 60 For Your Eyes Only .40 1.00
❑ 61 Octopussy .40 1.00
❑ 62 A View to a Kill .40 1.00
❑ 63 The Living Daylights .40 1.00
❑ 64 License to Kill .40 1.00
❑ 65 GoldenEye .40 1.00
❑ 66 Tomorrow Never Dies .40 1.00
❑ 67 The Women of Dr. No .40 1.00
❑ 68 Pussy Galore's Flying Circus .40 1.00
❑ 69 Beauties on the Beach .40 1.00
❑ 70 007 and the Girl Bombs .40 1.00
❑ 71 Circus Exotica .40 1.00
❑ 72 Checklist .40 1.00
❑ M1 Mystery Girl

1998 The Women of James Bond Autographs
❑ A1 Caroline Munro 20.00 40.00
❑ A2 Lois Maxwell 30.00 60.00
❑ A3 Lois Chiles 20.00 40.00
❑ A4 Shirley Eaton 20.00 40.00
❑ A5 Lana Wood 20.00 40.00

1998 The Women of James Bond Bond's Best
COMPLETE SET (3) 10.00 25.00
STATED ODDS 1:35
❑ B1 Tracy di Vicenzo 4.00 10.00
❑ B2 Anya Amasova 4.00 10.00
❑ B3 Wai Lin 4.00 10.00

1998 The Women of James Bond Early Encounters
COMPLETE SET (6) 8.00 20.00
STATED ODDS 1:17
❑ E1 Miss Taro 2.50 6.00
❑ E2 Honey Ryder 2.50 6.00
❑ E3 Flying Circus 2.50 6.00
❑ E4 Tatiana Romanova 2.50 6.00
❑ E5 Jill Masterson 2.50 6.00
❑ E6 Pussy Galore 2.50 6.00

1998 The Women of James Bond Promos
❑ P1 Pussy and the Flying Circus 1.25 3.00
❑ P2 Paris Carver/James Bond 2.00 5.00

1998 The X-Files Fight the Future
COMPLETE SET (72) 5.00 12.00
❑ 1 Title Card .15 .40
❑ 2 The X-Files .15 .40
❑ 3 Fox Mulder .15 .40
❑ 4 Dana Scully .15 .40
❑ 5 Walter Skinner .15 .40
❑ 6 The Lone Gunmen .15 .40
❑ 7 The Cigarette Smoking Man .15 .40
❑ 8 The Well Manicured Man .15 .40
❑ 9 The Syndicate .15 .40
❑ 10 The Black Oil .15 .40
❑ 11 The Vaccine .15 .40
❑ 12 The Bees .15 .40
❑ 13 Prehistoric Close Encounter .15 .40
❑ 14 Stevie .15 .40
❑ 15 The Haz-Mat Team .15 .40
❑ 16 Search for a Bomb .15 .40
❑ 17 Sac Darius Michaud .15 .40
❑ 18 The Explosion .15 .40
❑ 19 Mulder & Scully Questioned .15 .40
❑ 20 Skinner Offers His Support .15 .40
❑ 21 Distressing News .15 .40
❑ 22 Dr. Alvin Kurtzweil .15 .40
❑ 23 Kurtzweil warns Mulder .15 .40
❑ 24 Three A.M. .15 .40
❑ 25 Something to Show Me .15 .40
❑ 26 Dr. Ben Bronschweig .15 .40
❑ 27 The Dead Fireman .15 .40
❑ 28 Fema .15 .40
❑ 29 Fossil Remains .15 .40
❑ 30 Lethal Confrontation .15 .40
❑ 31 The Syndicate Meets .15 .40
❑ 32 Outvoted .15 .40
❑ 33 Conrad Strughold .15 .40
❑ 34 They Went That Way .15 .40
❑ 35 Desert Chase .15 .40
❑ 36 The Bee Dome .15 .40
❑ 37 Pursued by Helicopters .15 .40
❑ 38 Presenting New Evidence .15 .40
❑ 39 Mulder Updates Kurtzweil .15 .40
❑ 40 An Intimate Moment .15 .40
❑ 41 Scully Infected .15 .40
❑ 42 Mulder Shot .15 .40
❑ 43 Scully is Transported .15 .40
❑ 44 The Two Bugs .15 .40
❑ 45 Skinner's Update .15 .40
❑ 46 Taken For a Ride .15 .40
❑ 47 The Truth is Revealed .15 .40
❑ 48 The Limo Explodes .15 .40
❑ 49 Pole of Inaccessability .15 .40
❑ 50 A Discovery is Made .15 .40
❑ 51 The Cryopods .15 .40
❑ 52 Freeing Scully .15 .40
❑ 53 Finding a Way Out .15 .40
❑ 54 Breath of Life .15 .40
❑ 55 The Creatures Hatch .15 .40
❑ 56 The Ice Field .15 .40
❑ 57 The Craft .15 .40
❑ 58 OPR .15 .40
❑ 59 Reinvested .15 .40
❑ 60 The Telegram .15 .40
❑ 61 Carter & Duhovny .15 .40
❑ 62 Bowman & Carter .15 .40
❑ 63 Filming the Explosion .15 .40
❑ 64 In Front of the Green Screen .15 .40
❑ 65 Filming the Helicopter Chase .15 .40
❑ 66 Translucent Bodies .15 .40
❑ 67 The Alien Fetus .15 .40
❑ 68 The Alien .15 .40
❑ 69 Spacecraft Design .15 .40
❑ 70 The Cast .15 .40
❑ 71 Production Credits .15 .40
❑ 72 Checklist .15 .40

1998 The X-Files Fight the Future Autographs
COMPLETE SET (6) 150.00 300.00
STATED ODDS 1:72
❑ NNO William B. Davis 30.00 60.00
❑ NNO Dean Haglund 30.00 60.00
❑ NNO Bruce Harwood 30.00 60.00
❑ NNO Mitch Pileggi 30.00 60.00
❑ NNO Tom Braidwood 30.00 60.00
❑ NNO John Neville 30.00 60.00

1998 The X-Files Fight the Future Foil Mystery
COMPLETE SET (6) 10.00 25.00
STATED ODDS 1:12
❑ M1 Mulder and Scully 2.50 6.00
❑ M2 Mulder in Alien Space Craft 2.50 6.00
❑ M3 Mulder with Flashlight 2.50 6.00
❑ M4 Alien Space Craft 2.50 6.00
❑ M5 Human Host 2.50 6.00
❑ M6 Gestating Alien 2.50 6.00

1998 Xena Warrior Princess
COMPLETE SET (72) 7.50 20.00
❑ 1 Xena Warrior Princess .20 .50
❑ 2 Xena Allies .20 .50
❑ 3 Gabrielle .20 .50
❑ 4 Joxer .20 .50
❑ 5 Hercules .20 .50
❑ 6 Iolaus .20 .50
❑ 7 Draco .20 .50
❑ 8 Autolycus .20 .50
❑ 9 Duo for Danger .20 .50
❑ 10 Pledged to Fight Evil .20 .50
❑ 11 Stalked From on High .20 .50
❑ 12 Clashing with Callisto .20 .50
❑ 13 Night of the Bacchae .20 .50
❑ 14 Supreme Swordswoman .20 .50
❑ 15 In the Thick of Battle .20 .50
❑ 16 When You're Hot .20 .50
❑ 17 The Bigger They Are .20 .50
❑ 18 Of War and Orphans .20 .50
❑ 19 Up From the Depths .20 .50
❑ 20 Engulfed by the Fire Demon .20 .50
❑ 21 Fighting the Furies .20 .50
❑ 22 Staff of Justice .20 .50
❑ 23 Harpies Against Us .20 .50
❑ 24 Xena vs The Dryads .20 .50
❑ 25 Ares .20 .50
❑ 26 Callisto .20 .50
❑ 27 Julius Caesar .20 .50
❑ 28 Thersites .20 .50
❑ 29 Velasca .20 .50
❑ 30 Bacchus .20 .50
❑ 31 Storytelling Team .20 .50
❑ 32 Hold On, Gabrielle .20 .50
❑ 33 Filming Aboard Ship .20 .50
❑ 34 Photographing Callisto .20 .50
❑ 35 Cast and Crew .20 .50
❑ 36 Conferring with Michael Hurst .20 .50
❑ 37 Sins of the Past .20 .50
❑ 38 Chariots of War .20 .50
❑ 39 Death in Chains .20 .50
❑ 40 The Titans .20 .50
❑ 41 Dreamworker .20 .50
❑ 42 Cradle of Hope .20 .50
❑ 43 The Path Not Taken .20 .50
❑ 44 The Reckoning .20 .50
❑ 45 Prometheus .20 .50
❑ 46 Hooves and Harlots .20 .50
❑ 47 The Black Wolf .20 .50
❑ 48 Beware Greeks Bearing Gifts .20 .50
❑ 49 The Prodigal .20 .50
❑ 50 Athens City Academy of the Performing Bards .20 .50
❑ 51 Death Mask .20 .50
❑ 52 A Fistful of Dinars .20 .50
❑ 53 Mortal Beloved .20 .50
❑ 54 Callisto .20 .50
❑ 55 Warrior Princess .20 .50
❑ 56 The Royal Couple of Thieves .20 .50
❑ 57 Ties That Bind .20 .50
❑ 58 The Greater Good .20 .50
❑ 59 Is There A Doctor in the House? .20 .50
❑ 60 Altared States .20 .50
❑ 61 Dave Stevens .20 .50
❑ 62 Terese Nielsen .20 .50
❑ 63 Zina Saunders .20 .50
❑ 64 Aaron Lopresti .20 .50
❑ 65 Earl Norem .20 .50
❑ 66 Jim Silke .20 .50
❑ 67 Joe Smith .20 .50
❑ 68 Dave Devries .20 .50
❑ 69 The Battle For Mt. Olympus .20 .50
❑ 70 Battle On, Xena .20 .50
❑ 71 A Heroine's Destiny .20 .50
❑ 72 Checklist .20 .50

1999 Babylon 5 Profiles
COMPLETE SET (100) 4.00 10.00
HE1 STATED PRINT RUN 1000
❑ 1 Knock Knock .15 .40
❑ 2 Who's There .15 .40
❑ 3 Babylon 5: Profiles .15 .40
❑ 4 Some Gathered: Commander Jeffrey Sinclair .15 .40
❑ 5 Some Gathered: Lyta Alexander .15 .40
❑ 6 Some Gathered: Ambassador G'Kar .15 .40
❑ 7 Some Gathered: Ambassador Londo Mollari .15 .40
❑ 8 Some Gathered: Ambassador Delenn .15 .40
❑ 9 Some Gathered: Michael Garibaldi .15 .40
❑ 10 A Few Knew Bester .15 .40
❑ 11 A Few Knew What To Say .15 .40
❑ 12 A Few Knew They Were Stronger .15 .40
❑ 13 A Few Knew Change Was Eminent .15 .40
❑ 14 A Few Knew They Had No Control .15 .40
❑ 15 A Few Knew The End Was Near .15 .40
❑ 16 A Few Knew The Truth .15 .40
❑ 17 A Few Knew Their Part .15 .40
❑ 18 A Few Knew Who To Tell .15 .40
❑ 19 Some Sacrificed More than Time .15 .40
❑ 20 Some Sacrificed With Style .15 .40
❑ 21 Some Sacrificed Though Not In Silence .15 .40
❑ 22 Some Suffered For a Lifetime .15 .40
❑ 23 Some Suffered As a People .15 .40
❑ 24 Some Suffered With Vengeance .15 .40
❑ 25 One Pledged Service .15 .40
❑ 26 One Pledged Honor .15 .40
❑ 27 One Pledged Love .15 .40
❑ 28 Three Held Steady In the Face of Challenge .15 .40
❑ 29 Three Held Steady With Their Entire Being .15 .40
❑ 30 Three Held Steady In Spite of Themselves .15 .40
❑ 31 Three Held Steady In the Company .15 .40
❑ 32 Three Held Steady Through Change .15 .40
❑ 33 Three Held Steady In Times of Uncertainty .15 .40
❑ 34 Three Held Steady Beside the Enemy .15 .40
❑ 35 Three Held Steady Most of the Time .15 .40
❑ 36 Three Held Steady To the End .15 .40
❑ 37 A Voice of Mystery And Intention .15 .40
❑ 38 A Voice of Mystery Yet Amazing Clarity .15 .40
❑ 39 A Voice of Mystery And Comfort .15 .40
❑ 40 A Voice of Reason And Determination .15 .40
❑ 41 A Voice of Reason And Observation .15 .40
❑ 42 A Voice of Reason Amongst Controversy .15 .40
❑ 43 A Voice of the Future We Couldn't Change .15 .40
❑ 44 A Voice of the Future We Trusted .15 .40
❑ 45 A Voice of the Future We Hoped .15 .40
❑ 46 A Guide With Humor .15 .40
❑ 47 A Guide With Stamina .15 .40
❑ 48 A Guide Of Resource .15 .40
❑ 49 A Leader With Strength .15 .40
❑ 50 A Leader Not Without Struggle .15 .40
❑ 51 A Leader With a Past .15 .40
❑ 52 A Witness Of Terror .15 .40
❑ 53 A Witness Of Change .15 .40
❑ 54 A Witness Of Challenge .15 .40
❑ 55 A Few We Lost: Kosh .15 .40
❑ 56 A Few We Lost: Lady Adira Tyree .15 .40
❑ 57 A Few We Lost: Talia Winters .15 .40
❑ 58 A Few We Lost: Morden .15 .40
❑ 59 A Few We Lost: Centauri Regent .15 .40
❑ 60 A Few We Lost: Dodger .15 .40
❑ 61 A Few We Lost: Byron .15 .40
❑ 62 A Few We Lost: Marcus .15 .40
❑ 63 A Few We Lost: Sheridan .15 .40
❑ 64 A Friendship Gained Against Great Odds .15 .40
❑ 65 A Friendship Gained Despite Painful History .15 .40
❑ 66 A Friendship Gained: A Fight to the Death .15 .40
❑ 67 A Friendship Gained Without Compromise .15 .40
❑ 68 A Friendship Gained In Baby Steps .15 .40
❑ 69 A Friendship Gained Out of Caring .15 .40
❑ 70 A Friendship Gained Through Apology .15 .40
❑ 71 A Friendship Gained By Accepting .15 .40
❑ 72 A Friendship Gained By Forgiving .15 .40
❑ 73 The One Who Was There for the Beginning .15 .40
❑ 74 The One Who Was One Step Ahead .15 .40
❑ 75 The One Who Was More Than Expected .15 .40
❑ 76 The One Who Is Not Afraid .15 .40
❑ 77 The One Who Is Undaunted .15 .40
❑ 78 The One Who Is Always Aware .15 .40
❑ 79 The One Who Will Be Our Future .15 .40
❑ 80 The One Who Will Be Often Alone .15 .40
❑ 81 The One Who Will Be Never Forgotten .15 .40
❑ 82 Some Will Never Forget The Beginning .15 .40
❑ 83 Some Will Never Forget How News Traveled .15 .40
❑ 84 Some Will Never Forget Cats .15 .40
❑ 85 Some Will Never Forget The Madness .15 .40
❑ 86 Some Will Never Forget Emperor Vir .15 .40
❑ 87 Some Will Never Forget That Voice .15 .40
❑ 88 Some Will Never Forget Zack's Cough .15 .40
❑ 89 Some Will Never Forget The Elevator Scene .15 .40
❑ 90 Some Will Never Forget The Big Return .15 .40
❑ 91 Some Will Never Forget The View .15 .40
❑ 92 Some Will Never Forget Londo's Denial .15 .40
❑ 93 Some Will Never Forget Spellbinding Visitors .15 .40
❑ 94 Some Will Never Forget Z'Ha'Dum .15 .40
❑ 95 Some Will Never Forget A Hell of a Day .15 .40
❑ 96 Some Will Never Forget The Holobrothel .15 .40
❑ 97 Some Will Never Forget The Final Moments .15 .40
❑ 98 Some Will Never Forget Zathras .15 .40
❑ 99 Some Will Never Forget The Three .15 .40
❑ 100 Babylon 5: Profiles Checklist .15 .40
❑ HE1 Harlon Ellison/1000 25.00 50.00
❑ NNO Group of five PROMO 1.25 3.00

1999 Babylon 5 Profiles Autographs
OVERALL AUTO ODDS 1:36
❑ A1 Harlan Ellison 20.00 40.00
❑ A2 Martin Sheen 25.00 50.00
❑ A3 Peter Jurasik 20.00 40.00
❑ A4 Bill Mumy 20.00 40.00
❑ A5 Efrem Zimbalist, Jr. 12.00 25.00
❑ A6 Adrienne Barbeau 12.00 25.00
❑ A7 Michael York 12.00 25.00
❑ A8 Shari Belafonte 15.00 30.00

1999 Babylon 5 Profiles Director's Chair
COMPLETE SET (5) 6.00 15.00
STATED ODDS 1:16
❑ DC1 John Flinn III 2.00 5.00
❑ DC2 Tony Dow 2.00 5.00
❑ DC3 Stephen Furst 2.00 5.00
❑ DC4 John Copeland 2.00 5.00
❑ DC5 J. Michael Straczynski 2.00 5.00

1999 Babylon 5 Profiles Optic Nerve
COMPLETE SET (9) 10.00 25.00
STATED ODDS 1:12
❑ ON1 The First Ones 2.00 5.00
❑ ON2 Ralgan 2.00 5.00
❑ ON3 Soul Hunter 2.00 5.00
❑ ON4 Llort 2.00 5.00
❑ ON5 Pak'ma'ra 2.00 5.00
❑ ON6 Drakh 2.00 5.00
❑ ON7 Surgery Aliens 2.00 5.00
❑ ON8 Brakiri 2.00 5.00
❑ ON9 Narn 2.00 5.00

1999 Babylon 5 Profiles Prop Cage
COMPLETE SET (18) 8.00 20.00
STATED ODDS 1:4

❑ PC1 Pin Links 1.25 3.00
❑ PC2 PPG's 1.25 3.00
❑ PC3 Comp Pads 1.25 3.00
❑ PC4 G'Kar Statue 1.25 3.00
❑ PC5 Triluminary 1.25 3.00
❑ PC6 Letters & Time Stabilizer 1.25 3.00
❑ PC7 Ranger Pike and Pin 1.25 3.00
❑ PC8 Crystal Construct 1.25 3.00
❑ PC9 Soul Globe 1.25 3.00
❑ PC10 Londo Doll 1.25 3.00
❑ PC11 Green Man Dummy 1.25 3.00
❑ PC12 Tricks of the Trade 1.25 3.00
❑ PC13 Centauri Weaponry 1.25 3.00
❑ PC14 Remnants of Psi Corps 1.25 3.00
❑ PC15 Sebastian's Cane 1.25 3.00
❑ PC16 Starfury Trappings 1.25 3.00
❑ PC17 ISN Floating Camera 1.25 3.00
❑ PC18 Shadow Eggs 1.25 3.00

1999 Babylon 5 Profiles Sleeping in Light Autographs

OVERALL AUTO ODDS 1:36
❑ SA1 Bruce Boxleitner 30.00 60.00
❑ SA2 Claudia Christian 30.00 60.00
❑ SA3 Jerry Doyle 15.00 30.00
❑ SA4 Mira Furlan 30.00 60.00
❑ SA5 Richard Biggs 20.00 40.00
❑ SA6 Stephen Furst 20.00 40.00
❑ SA7 Jeff Conaway 40.00 80.00

1999 Babylon 5 Profiles Writer's Desk

COMPLETE SET (3) 4.00 10.00
STATED ODDS 1:16
❑ WD1 Lawrence G. Ditillio 2.00 5.00
❑ WD2 D.C. Fontana 2.00 5.00
❑ WD3 Neil Gaiman 2.00 5.00

1999 Buffy the Vampire Slayer Season Two

COMPLETE SET (90) 5.00 12.00
❑ 1 Buffy The Vampire Slayer .15 .40
❑ 2 She's Posessed! .15 .40
❑ 3 It's A Trap! .15 .40
❑ 4 If They Hurt Willow... .15 .40
❑ 5 Speaking Of Love .15 .40
❑ 6 The Science Project .15 .40
❑ 7 Dream Girl .15 .40
❑ 8 New In Town .15 .40
❑ 9 Studying .15 .40
❑ 10 On Target .15 .40
❑ 11 Just One More .15 .40
❑ 12 This Won't Hurt .15 .40
❑ 13 Some Party! .15 .40
❑ 14 True Believers .15 .40
❑ 15 Receive Our Offering .15 .40
❑ 16 On Patrol .15 .40
❑ 17 Showtime .15 .40
❑ 18 You Don't Know Me? .15 .40
❑ 19 An Old Acquaintance .15 .40
❑ 20 The Lonely Ones .15 .40
❑ 21 Let's Make A Deal .15 .40
❑ 22 Let's Stay In .15 .40
❑ 23 Was It Good For You? .15 .40
❑ 24 Winner & Still Champion .15 .40
❑ 25 Career Week .15 .40
❑ 26 Something's Coming .15 .40
❑ 27 The Order Of Taraka .15 .40
❑ 28 Flexibility Is Required .15 .40
❑ 29 Innocent Bystander .15 .40
❑ 30 Two Slayers No Waiting .15 .40
❑ 31 Beg To Differ .15 .40
❑ 32 Rules Are Rules .15 .40
❑ 33 Responsibility .15 .40
❑ 34 The Drones Are Coming .15 .40
❑ 35 It Wasn't Real .15 .40
❑ 36 It Explains A Lot .15 .40
❑ 37 Happy Birthday .15 .40
❑ 38 More Music .15 .40
❑ 39 Crashers .15 .40
❑ 40 Take Me Instead .15 .40
❑ 41 Heeee's Back! .15 .40
❑ 42 Was It Good? .15 .40
❑ 43 Give Me Time .15 .40
❑ 44 The Hunter .15 .40
❑ 45 The Hunted .15 .40
❑ 46 Angel Sends His Love .15 .40
❑ 47 A Disturbing Trend .15 .40
❑ 48 Is This Love? .15 .40
❑ 49 The Orb Of Thessulah .15 .40
❑ 50 Everything's Under Control .15 .40
❑ 51 Visiting Hours Are Over .15 .40
❑ 52 Can't Fight Death .15 .40
❑ 53 We're Not Finished .15 .40
❑ 54 Love Is Forever .15 .40
❑ 55 No More Tears .15 .40
❑ 56 Next! .15 .40
❑ 57 Undercover .15 .40
❑ 58 It's A Big Rock .15 .40
❑ 59 Someone Wasn't Worthy .15 .40
❑ 60 Freeze! .15 .40
❑ 61 I'm All You Got .15 .40
❑ 62 It's Just Fate .15 .40
❑ 63 Close Your Eyes .15 .40
❑ 64 Buffy Summers .15 .40
❑ 65 Rupert Giles .15 .40
❑ 66 Willow Rosenberg .15 .40
❑ 67 Xander Harris And Cordelia Chase .15 .40
❑ 68 Jenny Calendar .15 .40
❑ 69 Oz .15 .40
❑ 70 Kendra .15 .40
❑ 71 Joyce Summers .15 .40
❑ 72 Principal Snyder .15 .40
❑ 73 Angelus .15 .40
❑ 74 Spike .15 .40
❑ 75 Drusilla .15 .40
❑ 76 Ampata .15 .40
❑ 77 Machida .15 .40
❑ 78 Eyghon .15 .40
❑ 79 Ted .15 .40
❑ 80 Bezoar .15 .40
❑ 81 The Judge .15 .40
❑ 82 Werewolf .15 .40
❑ 83 Amy Madison .15 .40
❑ 84 The Kindestod .15 .40
❑ 85 James Stanley .15 .40
❑ 86 Gill Monsters .15 .40
❑ 87 Acathla .15 .40
❑ 88 Big Ugly .15 .40
❑ 89 The Spell Of Restoration .15 .40
❑ 90 Checklist .15 .40
❑ NNO How To Lose Your Soul 4.00 10.00

1999 Buffy the Vampire Slayer Season Two Autographs

COMPLETE SET (5) 600.00 1000.00
RANDOM INSERTS IN PACKS
❑ A5 Charisma Carpenter 200.00 400.00
❑ A6 Anthony Stewart Head 175.00 300.00
❑ A7 John Ritter 150.00 250.00
❑ A8 Robia Lamorte 75.00 150.00
❑ A9 Bianca Lawson 75.00 150.00

1999 Buffy the Vampire Slayer Season Two Dark Destiny

COMPLETE SET (9) 15.00 40.00
STATED ODDS 1:11
❑ D1 Dark Destiny 2.50 6.00
❑ D2 Dark Destiny 2.50 6.00
❑ D3 Dark Destiny 2.50 6.00
❑ D4 Dark Destiny 2.50 6.00
❑ D5 Dark Destiny 2.50 6.00
❑ D6 Dark Destiny 2.50 6.00
❑ D7 Dark Destiny 2.50 6.00
❑ D8 Dark Destiny 2.50 6.00
❑ D9 Dark Destiny 2.50 6.00

1999 Buffy the Vampire Slayer Season Two Love Bites

COMPLETE SET (6) 12.50 30.00
STATED ODDS 1:18
❑ B1 Buffy & Angel 3.00 8.00
❑ B2 Xander & Cordelia 3.00 8.00
❑ B3 Willow & Oz 3.00 8.00
❑ B4 Giles & Jenny 3.00 8.00
❑ B5 Joyce & Ted 3.00 8.00
❑ B6 Drusilla & Spike 3.00 8.00

1999 Buffy the Vampire Slayer Season Two Promos

COMPLETE SET (3) 5.00 12.00
❑ BP1 Buffy the Vampire Slayer 2.00 5.00
❑ BP2 Buffy the Vampire Slayer 2.00 5.00
❑ B2AL1 Buffy the Vampire Slayer 2.00 5.00

1999 Buffy the Vampire Slayer Season Three

COMPLETE SET (90) 5.00 12.00
❑ 1 Senior Year .15 .40
❑ 2 Pay At The Counter .15 .40
❑ 3 No One .15 .40
❑ 4 You Fought Back! .15 .40
❑ 5 Kicking Undead Booty .15 .40
❑ 6 Shindig Or Hootenanny? .15 .40
❑ 7 New Slayer In Town .15 .40
❑ 8 Get A Life .15 .40
❑ 9 Kissing Toast .15 .40
❑ 10 Call Of The Wild .15 .40
❑ 11 Super Mas Macho .15 .40
❑ 12 Beauty Tames The Beast .15 .40
❑ 13 Competition .15 .40
❑ 14 Slayerfest '98 .15 .40
❑ 15 Work It Out .15 .40
❑ 16 Milbars .15 .40
❑ 17 Fun City .15 .40
❑ 18 I Want Candy .15 .40
❑ 19 New Watcher .15 .40
❑ 20 Guiltfest .15 .40
❑ 21 Betrayal .15 .40
❑ 22 My Way .15 .40
❑ 23 Love Worm .15 .40
❑ 24 Love Hurts .15 .40
❑ 25 Make It So .15 .40
❑ 26 Dynamic Duo .15 .40
❑ 27 The Real World .15 .40
❑ 28 Deck The Halls .15 .40
❑ 29 Destiny .15 .40
❑ 30 Hope For The Holidays .15 .40
❑ 31 The Bad Thing .15 .40
❑ 32 Mob Rules .15 .40
❑ 33 Eighteen .15 .40
❑ 34 The Testing .15 .40
❑ 35 Uncool .15 .40
❑ 36 Zero To Hero .15 .40
❑ 37 It's A Slayer Thing .15 .40
❑ 38 No Limits .15 .40
❑ 39 Guilty .15 .40
❑ 40 Unrepentant .15 .40
❑ 41 Deja Voodoo .15 .40
❑ 42 Nothing Changes .15 .40
❑ 43 Tease .15 .40
❑ 44 For The Taking .15 .40
❑ 45 Fake .15 .40
❑ 46 I Hear You .15 .40
❑ 47 Mulligan Stew .15 .40
❑ 48 Proactive With Pep .15 .40
❑ 49 Tradeoff .15 .40
❑ 50 Last Dance .15 .40
❑ 51 Ladies Choice .15 .40
❑ 52 Wallflowers .15 .40
❑ 53 Shall We Dance .15 .40
❑ 54 Daddy's Girl .15 .40
❑ 55 Panic Time .15 .40
❑ 56 Avenging Angel .15 .40
❑ 57 Engagement .15 .40
❑ 58 Armament .15 .40
❑ 59 Battle .15 .40
❑ 60 Survivors .15 .40
❑ 61 Ruper Giles .15 .40
❑ 62 Quentin Travers .15 .40
❑ 63 Weslye Wyndham-Bryce .15 .40
❑ 64 The Right Ingredients .15 .40
❑ 65 The Right Attitude .15 .40
❑ 66 The Right Purpose .15 .40
❑ 67 Undying Love .15 .40
❑ 68 Love Is Hell .15 .40
❑ 69 Doomed Love .15 .40
❑ 70 Balthazar .15 .40
❑ 71 Gingerbread Demon .15 .40
❑ 72 Mr. Trick .15 .40
❑ 73 Anyanka .15 .40
❑ 74 Lagos .15 .40
❑ 75 Bringers .15 .40
❑ 76 Ovu Mobani .15 .40
❑ 77 The Mayor .15 .40
❑ 78 D'Hoffryn .15 .40
❑ 79 Hell Hound .15 .40
❑ 80 Kulak .15 .40
❑ 81 Candy And Lyle Gortch .15 .40
❑ 82 Buffy Summers .15 .40
❑ 83 Willow And Oz .15 .40
❑ 84 Xander Harris And Cordelia Chase .15 .40
❑ 85 Willow Rosenberg .15 .40
❑ 86 Principal Snyder .15 .40
❑ 87 Angel Preview 1 .15 .40
❑ 88 Angel Preview 2 .15 .40
❑ 89 Angel Preview 3 .15 .40
❑ 90 Checklist .15 .40

1999 Buffy the Vampire Slayer Season Three Autographs

COMPLETE SET (6) 300.00 600.00
RANDOM INSERTS IN PACKS
❑ A10 Julie Benz 40.00 80.00
❑ A11 Nicholas Brendon 60.00 120.00
❑ A12 James Marsters 150.00 250.00
❑ A13 Juliet Landau 25.00 50.00
❑ A14 Kristine Sutherland 25.00 50.00
❑ A15 Eliza Dushku 100.00 200.00

1999 Buffy the Vampire Slayer Season Three Graduation Day

COMPLETE SET (9) 12.50 30.00
STATED ODDS 1:11
❑ G1 Graduation Day 2.00 5.00
❑ G2 Graduation Day 2.00 5.00
❑ G3 Graduation Day 2.00 5.00
❑ G4 Graduation Day 2.00 5.00
❑ G5 Graduation Day 2.00 5.00
❑ G6 Graduation Day 2.00 5.00
❑ G7 Graduation Day 2.00 5.00
❑ G8 Graduation Day 2.00 5.00
❑ G9 Graduation Day 2.00 5.00

1999 Buffy the Vampire Slayer Season Three Promos

COMPLETE SET (9) 15.00 40.00
❑ B3-1 Angel & Buffy 2.00 5.00
❑ B3-2 Angel & Buffy 2.00 5.00
❑ B3-3 Angel & Buffy 2.00 5.00
❑ B3-4 Angel & Buffy 2.00 5.00
❑ B3-5 Angel, Buffy, & Xander 2.00 5.00
❑ B3SC Angel & Buffy 2.00 5.00
❑ SFX1 Buffy cast 2.00 5.00
❑ SD1999 Angel, Buffy, & Xander 2.00 5.00
❑ WC1999 Angel, Buffy, & Xander 2.00 5.00

1999 Buffy the Vampire Slayer Season Three The Future Is Ours

COMPLETE SET (6) 12.50 30.00
STATED ODDS 1:18
❑ Y1 Cordelia & Xander 3.00 8.00
❑ Y2 Willow & Oz 3.00 8.00
❑ Y3 Check it Out 3.00 8.00
❑ Y4 Bridge Over Troubled Water 3.00 8.00
❑ Y5 School Spirit 3.00 8.00
❑ Y6 Farewell 3.00 8.00

1999 Buffy the Vampire Slayer Photo-Cards

COMPLETE SET (54) 6.00 15.00
❑ 1 Cast .20 .50
❑ 2 Buffy .20 .50
❑ 3 Angel .20 .50
❑ 4 Cordelia .20 .50
❑ 5 Xander .20 .50
❑ 6 Willow .20 .50
❑ 7 Willow and Oz .20 .50
❑ 8 Buffy and Kendra .20 .50
❑ 9 Giles .20 .50
❑ 10 Angel .20 .50
❑ 11 Angel and Buffy .20 .50
❑ 12 Xander and Buffy .20 .50
❑ 13 Buffy .20 .50
❑ 14 Spike .20 .50
❑ 15 Angel .20 .50
❑ 16 Drusilla and Spike .20 .50
❑ 17 Buffy and Angel .20 .50
❑ 18 Cast .20 .50
❑ 19 Xander and Cordelia .20 .50
❑ 20 The Master and Buffy .20 .50
❑ 21 Angel .20 .50
❑ 22 Buffy and Xander .20 .50
❑ 23 Willow and Xander .20 .50
❑ 24 Giles .20 .50
❑ 25 Angel .20 .50
❑ 26 Cast .20 .50
❑ 27 Willow .20 .50
❑ 28 Drusilla and Spike .20 .50
❑ 29 Cordelia .20 .50
❑ 30 Ted and Buffy .20 .50
❑ 31 Buffy .20 .50
❑ 32 Angel .20 .50
❑ 33 Willow .20 .50
❑ 34 Drusilla .20 .50
❑ 35 Oz .20 .50
❑ 36 Xander, Buffy, and Angel .20 .50
❑ 37 Angel .20 .50
❑ 38 Buffy .20 .50
❑ 39 Giles .20 .50
❑ 40 Xander .20 .50
❑ 41 Angel .20 .50
❑ 42 Cordelia .20 .50
❑ 43 Faith .20 .50
❑ 44 Willow .20 .50
❑ 45 Xander .20 .50
❑ 46 Buffy .20 .50
❑ 47 Angel .20 .50
❑ 48 Giles and Buffy .20 .50
❑ 49 Willows .20 .50
❑ 50 Angel .20 .50
❑ 51 Xander and Willow .20 .50
❑ 52 Buffy .20 .50
❑ 53 Angel and Buffy .20 .50
❑ 54 Buffy .20 .50

1999 Buffy the Vampire Slayer PhotoCards Bonus Foil

COMPLETE SET (6) 20.00 50.00
STATED ODDS 1:17
❑ B1 Buffy 4.00 10.00
❑ B2 Buffy 4.00 10.00
❑ B3 Buffy 4.00 10.00
❑ B4 Buffy 4.00 10.00
❑ B5 Buffy 4.00 10.00
❑ B6 Angel, Buffy 4.00 10.00

1999 Elvis The Platinum Collection

COMPLETE SET (90) 5.00 12.00
SP1 STATED ODDS 1:108
G1 STATED ODDS 1:1411
❑ 1 Title Card .15 .40
❑ 2 The King of Rock & Roll .15 .40
❑ 3 Rise of A Legend .15 .40
❑ 4 Family Portrait .15 .40
❑ 5 What's in a Name .15 .40
❑ 6 Dreaming in Tupelo .15 .40
❑ 7 The Need for Song .15 .40
❑ 8 Just a Kid in the Courts .15 .40
❑ 9 Crossroads .15 .40
❑ 10 A New Sound .15 .40
❑ 11 Bring On Bill and Scotty .15 .40
❑ 12 Elvis is Ready .15 .40
❑ 13 Next Stop, Rock & Roll .15 .40
❑ 14 At the Piano .15 .40
❑ 15 Center of a Storm .15 .40
❑ 16 Style to Spare .15 .40
❑ 17 Time Out for a New Hit .15 .40
❑ 18 Back in the Studio .15 .40
❑ 19 Shake, Rattle and Rock .15 .40
❑ 20 Blue Moon Boys .15 .40
❑ 21 DJ Who Launched Elvis .15 .40
❑ 22 Atomic Singing Sensation .15 .40
❑ 23 So This is New York .15 .40
❑ 24 Elvis & the Jordanaires .15 .40
❑ 25 The Devil in Disguise? .15 .40
❑ 26 A New Frontier .15 .40
❑ 27 Viva Las Vegas, '56 .15 .40
❑ 28 Good Rockin' Tonight .15 .40
❑ 29 The Hillbilly Cat .15 .40
❑ 30 A Hit on the Hayride .15 .40
❑ 31 The Elvis Phenomenon .15 .40
❑ 32 Win One for the Nipper .15 .40
❑ 33 Rehearsing for Big Ed .15 .40
❑ 34 More Than a Music Man .15 .40
❑ 35 The Cat Can Sing .15 .40
❑ 36 Concert in Canada, '57 .15 .40
❑ 37 Ready, Teddy .15 .40
❑ 38 Girls, Girls, Girls .15 .40
❑ 39 The South Rises Again .15 .40
❑ 40 Always Time for His Fans .15 .40
❑ 41 Breaking All Barriers .15 .40
❑ 42 Autographs Unlimited .15 .40
❑ 43 Sincerely, Elvis .15 .40
❑ 44 Panting for Their Idol .15 .40
❑ 45 A Singer's Best Friend .15 .40
❑ 46 First Train to Memphis .15 .40
❑ 47 Heartbreak .15 .40
❑ 48 A Breather .15 .40
❑ 49 The King and His Chariot .15 .40
❑ 50 A New Cycle .15 .40
❑ 51 Honored In Louisiana .15 .40
❑ 52 The House of Presley .15 .40
❑ 53 The Graceland Gates .15 .40
❑ 54 Guitarathon .15 .40
❑ 55 Elvis Presley, Movie Star .15 .40
❑ 56 On the Reno Set .15 .40
❑ 57 Of Paramount Importance .15 .40
❑ 58 Deke Rivers on Guitar .15 .40
❑ 59 Hot Wheels .15 .40
❑ 60 Return to Sender, With Love .15 .40
❑ 61 Lights! Camera! Elvis! .15 .40
❑ 62 Go Directly to Jail .15 .40
❑ 63 King Creole Rocks .15 .40
❑ 64 A Brother Betrayed .15 .40
❑ 65 Young Man With A Song .15 .40
❑ 66 The Rage of Clint Reno .15 .40
❑ 67 Deke Rivers in Concert .15 .40
❑ 68 Rock 'em and Sock 'em .15 .40
❑ 69 On the Road to Stardom .15 .40
❑ 70 Enter Vince Everett .15 .40
❑ 71 Don't Be Cruel .15 .40
❑ 72 Promoting King Creole .15 .40
❑ 73 Hair Today... .15 .40
❑ 74 Operation Elvis .15 .40
❑ 75 The Passing of Gladys Presley .15 .40
❑ 76 Don't Stop the Music .15 .40
❑ 77 On the Road Again .15 .40
❑ 78 Welcoming Der Elvis .15 .40
❑ 79 Family Man .15 .40
❑ 80 Elvis Does Europe .15 .40
❑ 81 The Perfect Furlough .15 .40
❑ 82 A Man In Uniform .15 .40
❑ 83 Elvis...Dead or Alive? .15 .40
❑ 84 Mom and Me .15 .40
❑ 85 G.I. Blues, for Real .15 .40
❑ 86 Soldier Boy and Beyond .15 .40
❑ 87 Sure-Shot Hotshot .15 .40
❑ 88 Beautiful Dreamer .15 .40
❑ 89 The Evolution of Elvis .15 .40
❑ 90 Checklist .15 .40
❑ G1 Elvis Presley 12.00 30.00
❑ SP1 Elvis Presley 8.00 20.00

1999 Elvis The Platinum Collection Gold Records

COMPLETE SET (9) 12.50 30.00
STATED ODDS 1:11
❑ R1 Elvis Presley 2.00 5.00
❑ R2 Elvis 2.00 5.00
❑ R3 Loving You 2.00 5.00
❑ R4 Elvis' Christmas Album 2.00 5.00
❑ R5 Elvis' Golden Records 2.00 5.00
❑ R6 King Creole 2.00 5.00
❑ R7 For LP Fans Only 2.00 5.00
❑ R8 A Date With Elvis 2.00 5.00
❑ R9 Elvis' Gold Records Volume 2 2.00 5.00

1999 Elvis The Platinum Collection Return To Sender Postcards

COMPLETE SET (6) 10.00 25.00
STATED ODDS 1:17
❑ PC1 Tupelo, MS 2.00 5.00
❑ PC2 Graceland, Memphis, TN 2.00 5.00
❑ PC3 New York City, NY 2.00 5.00
❑ PC4 Las Vegas, NV 2.00 5.00
❑ PC5 Hollywood, CA 2.00 5.00
❑ PC6 West Germany 2.00 5.00

1999 Planet of the Apes Archives

COMPLETE SET (90) 5.00 12.00
L1 STATED ODDS 1:108
❑ 1 The Planet of the Apes .15 .40
❑ 2 Star Voyagers .15 .40
❑ 3 An Accident in Time .15 .40
❑ 4 Splashdown .15 .40
❑ 5 Scarecrows .15 .40
❑ 6 The Wild Hunt .15 .40
❑ 7 Human Harvest .15 .40
❑ 8 Day of the Hunter .15 .40
❑ 9 Caged .15 .40
❑ 10 Dodge's Fate .15 .40
❑ 11 Freak or Missing Link? .15 .40
❑ 12 Monkey Trial .15 .40
❑ 13 The Escape .15 .40
❑ 14 A Less Intelligent Look .15 .40
❑ 15 Key to the Past .15 .40
❑ 16 You're so Damned Ugly! .15 .40
❑ 17 Zaius' Secret .15 .40
❑ 18 The Terrible Truth .15 .40
❑ 19 Beneath the Planet of the Apes .15 .40
❑ 20 An Ill Fated Rescue .15 .40
❑ 21 The Gorilla War Machine .15 .40
❑ 22 Brent's Fight For Life .15 .40
❑ 23 A Plea for Peace .15 .40
❑ 24 Shocking Discovery .15 .40
❑ 25 The Mutant Humans .15 .40
❑ 26 Powers of the Mind .15 .40
❑ 27 Ursus on the March .15 .40
❑ 28 The Burning Idol .15 .40
❑ 29 Their True Selves Revealed .15 .40
❑ 30 Taylor, Alive! .15 .40
❑ 31 Invading the Mutant Stronghold .15 .40
❑ 32 The Death of Nova .15 .40
❑ 33 The Bomb under Seige .15 .40
❑ 34 Brent's Final Stand .15 .40
❑ 35 It's Doomsday! .15 .40
❑ 36 Death of a Planet .15 .40
❑ 37 Escape from the Planet of the Apes .15 .40
❑ 38 The Astrochimps .15 .40
❑ 39 Friend of Foe? .15 .40
❑ 40 The Inquisition .15 .40
❑ 41 Chimp about Town .15 .40
❑ 42 Zira's Blessed Event .15 .40
❑ 43 No Way Out .15 .40
❑ 44 End of a Love Story .15 .40
❑ 45 The Hope of Tomorrow .15 .40
❑ 46 Conquest of the Planet of the Apes .15 .40
❑ 47 Cruel New World .15 .40
❑ 48 A Race in Chains .15 .40
❑ 49 Simian Slavery .15 .40
❑ 50 Torture and Revolt .15 .40
❑ 51 City of Riots .15 .40
❑ 52 Confrontation .15 .40
❑ 53 The Capture of Breck .15 .40
❑ 54 King Caesar Speaks .15 .40
❑ 55 Battle of the Planet of the Apes .15 .40
❑ 56 Caesar's Dream .15 .40
❑ 57 The Mutants Strike Back .15 .40
❑ 58 Son of the Ape King .15 .40
❑ 59 Prisoners .15 .40
❑ 60 Can't we all get Along? .15 .40
❑ 61 Taylor's Flight .15 .40
❑ 62 Unseen Incarnations .15 .40
❑ 63 The Unkindest Cuts .15 .40
❑ 64 Zira .15 .40
❑ 65 Cornelius .15 .40
❑ 66 The Right Stuff .15 .40
❑ 67 Orangutan Elders .15 .40
❑ 68 Nova .15 .40
❑ 69 The Human Mutants .15 .40
❑ 70 Gorilla Warmongers .15 .40
❑ 71 Human Justice? .15 .40
❑ 72 Caesar's World .15 .40
❑ 73 Ape Conceptions .15 .40
❑ 74 Trek Across the Desert .15 .40
❑ 75 Scarecrow Encounter .15 .40
❑ 76 City of the Apes .15 .40
❑ 77 Mutant Conceptions .15 .40
❑ 78 Depicting a Revolution .15 .40
❑ 79 Make-up Wizard John Chambers .15 .40
❑ 80 Bringing Zira to Life .15 .40
❑ 81 Simian Transformation .15 .40
❑ 82 Shooting Taylor's Trial .15 .40
❑ 83 The Agony of Captivity .15 .40
❑ 84 Two for the Road .15 .40
❑ 85 Knowing the Score .15 .40
❑ 86 A Sequel Roars to Life .15 .40
❑ 87 Fun on the Set .15 .40
❑ 88 Supervising Movie Mayhem .15 .40
❑ 89 Caesar's Conflict .15 .40
❑ 90 Checklist .15 .40
❑ L1 Future of Liberty

1999 Planet of the Apes Archives Autographs

COMPLETE SET (5) 75.00 200.00
RANDOM INSERTS IN PACKS
❑ A1 Linda Harrison 40.00 80.00
❑ A2 Natalie Trundy 15.00 30.00
❑ A3 Jeff Corey 40.00 80.00
❑ A4 Pedro Colley 15.00 30.00
❑ A5 Buck Kartalia 15.00 30.00

1999 Planet of the Apes Archives Posters

COMPLETE SET (9) 15.00 40.00
❑ P1 Planet of the Apes 2.00 5.00
❑ P2 Planet of the Apes 2.00 5.00
❑ P3 Planet of the Apes 2.00 5.00
❑ P4 Planet of the Apes 2.00 5.00
❑ P5 Planet of the Apes 2.00 5.00
❑ P6 Planet of the Apes 2.00 5.00
❑ P7 Planet of the Apes 2.00 5.00
❑ P8 Planet of the Apes 2.00 5.00
❑ P9 Planet of the Apes 2.00 5.00

1999 Planet of the Apes Archives Roddy Revealed

COMPLETE SET (4) 5.00 12.00
❑ R1 Roddy McDowell 1.50 4.00
❑ R2 Roddy McDowell 1.50 4.00
❑ R3 Roddy McDowell 1.50 4.00
❑ R4 Roddy McDowell 1.50 4.00

1999 Sleepy Hollow

COMPLETE SET (90) 5.00 12.00
T1 STATED ODDS 1:108
❑ 1 Sleepy Hollow .10 .25
❑ 2 Ichabod Crane's New Mission .10 .25
❑ 3 The High Constable .10 .25
❑ 4 Arrival .10 .25
❑ 5 Love Is Blind .10 .25
❑ 6 Rivals .10 .25
❑ 7 The Sleepy Hollow Elite .10 .25
❑ 8 Legend of the Horseman .10 .25
❑ 9 The Hessian Warrior .10 .25
❑ 10 The Horseman Surrounded .10 .25
❑ 11 Death Struggle .10 .25
❑ 12 The Headless Corpse .10 .25
❑ 13 The Constable's New Methods .10 .25
❑ 14 Forming a Bond with Young Masbeth .10 .25
❑ 15 Digging Up the Past .10 .25
❑ 16 Startling Discovery .10 .25
❑ 17 A Ride on the Wild Side .10 .25
❑ 18 True or False Phantom .10 .25

❑ 19 Arrogant Trickster .10 .25
❑ 20 Memories of Mom .10 .25
❑ 21 The Lovely Katrina .10 .25
❑ 22 The Horseman Attacks .10 .25
❑ 23 The Fate of Philipse .10 .25
❑ 24 The Forbidden Arts .10 .25
❑ 25 Ichabod's Plan .10 .25
❑ 26 The Haunted Woods .10 .25
❑ 27 Approaching the Witch Cave .10 .25
❑ 28 Dwelling of the Damned .10 .25
❑ 29 Ritual of Evil .10 .25
❑ 30 A Message for Ichabod .10 .25
❑ 31 Approaching the Tree of the Dead .10 .25
❑ 32 The Horseman's Marker .10 .25
❑ 33 His Final Remains...But No Skull .10 .25
❑ 34 From within the Tree .10 .25
❑ 35 The Headless Horseman Appears .10 .25
❑ 36 Too Late To Save Her .10 .25
❑ 37 The Headless Witch .10 .25
❑ 38 A Family Marked for Doom .10 .25
❑ 39 Of Light and Shadow .10 .25
❑ 40 Dark Intruder .10 .25
❑ 41 Demon without a Head .10 .25
❑ 42 A Futile Fight .10 .25
❑ 43 Blood Trophies .10 .25
❑ 44 Death Reach .10 .25
❑ 45 Caught by the Hessian .10 .25
❑ 46 Facing a Fearsome Foe .10 .25
❑ 47 Battling Brom .10 .25
❑ 48 No Match for the Horseman .10 .25
❑ 49 Monstrous Memories .10 .25
❑ 50 In the Notary Office .10 .25
❑ 51 Unlikely Lovers .10 .25
❑ 52 Ghost Horse .10 .25
❑ 53 Attacking Sleepy Hollow .10 .25
❑ 54 Panic Inside the Church .10 .25
❑ 55 Outside God's Domain .10 .25
❑ 56 His Shameful Secrets Revealed .10 .25
❑ 57 Makeshift Weapon .10 .25
❑ 58 Impaled .10 .25
❑ 59 Pulled through the Window .10 .25
❑ 60 Lady van Tassel's Bloody Scheme .10 .25
❑ 61 The Witch Sisters .10 .25
❑ 62 Invading the Windmill .10 .25
❑ 63 Escape from Fiery Death .10 .25
❑ 64 The Final Card .10 .25
❑ 65 Retrieving the Skull .10 .25
❑ 66 Katrina Under Attack .10 .25
❑ 67 The High Constable .10 .25
❑ 68 Demonic Reunion .10 .25
❑ 69 The Hessian's Last Victim .10 .25
❑ 70 The Fate of Lady van Tassel .10 .25
❑ 71 Kiss of Death .10 .25
❑ 72 A Whole New World .10 .25
❑ 73 Ichabod Crane .10 .25
❑ 74 Katrina Van Tassel .10 .25
❑ 75 Baltus Van Tassel .10 .25
❑ 76 Lady Van Tassel .10 .25
❑ 77 Young Masbeth .10 .25
❑ 78 Clergyman Steenwyck .10 .25
❑ 79 Brom Van Brunt .10 .25
❑ 80 Lady Crane .10 .25
❑ 81 The Hessian Horseman .10 .25
❑ 82 Haunted Filmaker .10 .25
❑ 83 Of Witches and Goblins .10 .25
❑ 84 Monstrous Make-Up .10 .25
❑ 85 Setting the Proper Atmosphere .10 .25
❑ 86 Recreating Sleepy Hollow .10 .25
❑ 87 Fate of a Witch .10 .25
❑ 88 Fantastic Environment .10 .25
❑ 89 A Bloody Good Game .10 .25
❑ 90 Checklist .10 .25
❑ T1 Colonial Post newspaper 6.00 15.00

1999 Sleepy Hollow Autographs

RANDOM INSERTS IN PACKS
❑ A2 Lisa Marie 6.00 15.00
❑ A3 Jeffrey Jones 8.00 20.00
❑ A4 Casper van Dien 8.00 20.00
❑ A5 Danny Elfman 35.00 70.00
❑ R1 Redemption Card

1999 Sleepy Hollow Foil Lobby Cards

COMPLETE SET (6) 8.00 20.00
STATED ODDS 1:17
❑ LC1 A Warrior from Hell 2.50 6.00
❑ LC2 Battle to the Death 2.50 6.00
❑ LC3 The Mystery of Sleepy Hollow 2.50 6.00
❑ LC4 The Witching Ways 2.50 6.00
❑ LC5 Night of the Headless Horseman 2.50 6.00
❑ LC6 The Courage of Ichabod Crane 2.50 6.00

1999 Sleepy Hollow Heads Will Roll

COMPLETE SET (9) 5.00 12.00
STATED ODDS 1:11
❑ CC1 Getting A Head With Tim Burton 1.25 3.00
❑ CC2 Maven of the Macabre 1.25 3.00
❑ CC3 Disembodied Damsel 1.25 3.00
❑ CC4 Johnny Depp as Ichabod Crane 1.25 3.00
❑ CC5 Christina Ricci as Katrina 1.25 3.00
❑ CC6 Mark Pickering as Young Masbeth 1.25 3.00
❑ CC7 Miranda Richardson as Lady Van Tassel 1.25 3.00
❑ CC8 Jeffrey Jones as Clergyman Steenwyck 1.25 3.00
❑ CC9 Christopher Walken as The Hessian Horseman 1.25 3.00

1999 Sleepy Hollow Promos

❑ P1 Johnny Depp 1.25 3.00
❑ P2 The Headless Horseman 1.50 4.00
❑ P3 Christina Ricci 2.00 5.00
❑ R1 Redemption Card 1.25 3.00

1999 South Park

COMPLETE SET (70) 5.00 12.00
❑ 1 South Park .15 .40
❑ 2 Eric Cartman .15 .40
❑ 3 Stan Marsh .15 .40
❑ 4 Kyle Broslofski .15 .40
❑ 5 Kenny McCormick .15 .40
❑ 6 Ike .15 .40
❑ 7 Wendy Testaburger .15 .40
❑ 8 Chef .15 .40
❑ 9 Mr. Garrison Mr. Hat .15 .40
❑ 10 Officer Barbrady .15 .40
❑ 11 Mayor McDaniels .15 .40
❑ 12 Mrs. Cartman .15 .40
❑ 13 Ms. Crabtree .15 .40
❑ 14 Pip .15 .40
❑ 15 Jimbo Ned .15 .40
❑ 16 Alphonse Mephisto .15 .40
❑ 17 Mr. Mackie .15 .40
❑ 18 Jesus .15 .40
❑ 19 Cartman Gets an Anal Probe .15 .40
❑ 20 Cartman Gets an Anal Probe .15 .40
❑ 21 Cartman Gets an Anal Probe .15 .40
❑ 22 Weight Gain 4000 .15 .40
❑ 23 Weight Gain 4000 .15 .40
❑ 24 Weight Gain 4000 .15 .40
❑ 25 Volcano .15 .40
❑ 26 Vocano .15 .40
❑ 27 Vocano .15 .40
❑ 28 Big Gay Al's Big Gay Boat Ride .15 .40
❑ 29 Big Gay Al's Big Gay Boat Ride .15 .40
❑ 30 Big Gay Al's Big Gay Boat Ride .15 .40
❑ 31 An Elephant Makes Love to a Pig .15 .40
❑ 32 An Elephant Makes Love to a Pig .15 .40
❑ 33 An Elephant Makes Love to a Pig .15 .40
❑ 34 Death .15 .40
❑ 35 Death .15 .40
❑ 36 Death .15 .40
❑ 37 Pink Eye .15 .40
❑ 38 Pink Eye .15 .40
❑ 39 Pink Eye .15 .40
❑ 40 Damien .15 .40
❑ 41 Damien .15 .40
❑ 42 Damien .15 .40
❑ 43 Starvin' Marvin .15 .40
❑ 44 Starvin' Marvin .15 .40
❑ 45 Starvin' Marvin .15 .40
❑ 46 Mr. Hankey, the Christmas Poo .15 .40
❑ 47 Mr. Hankey, the Christmas Poo .15 .40
❑ 48 Mr. Hankey, the Christmas Poo .15 .40
❑ 49 Tom's Rhinoplasty .15 .40
❑ 50 Tom's Rhinoplasty .15 .40
❑ 51 Tom's Rhinoplasty .15 .40
❑ 52 Mecha-Streisand .15 .40
❑ 53 Mecha-Streisand .15 .40
❑ 54 Mecha-Streisand .15 .40
❑ 55 Cartman's Mom Is a Dirty Slut .15 .40
❑ 56 Cartman's Mom Is a Dirty Slut .15 .40
❑ 57 Cartman's Mom Is a Dirty Slut .15 .40
❑ 58 Terrence and Phillip's April Fool's Episode .15 .40
❑ 59 Terrence and Phillip's April Fool's Episode .15 .40
❑ 60 Terrence and Phillip's April Fool's Episode .15 .40
❑ 61 Cartman's Mom Is Still a Slut .15 .40
❑ 62 Cartman's Mom Is Still a Slut .15 .40
❑ 63 Cartman's Mom Is Still a Slut .15 .40
❑ 64 Weight Gain 4000 .15 .40
❑ 65 The Cows of South Park .15 .40
❑ 66 The South Park Cows .15 .40
❑ 67 Chef Song: Volcanoo .15 .40
❑ 68 Chef Song: Mr. Hankey, The Christmas Poo .15 .40
❑ 69 Yeah! Who doesn't love Cheesy Poofs .15 .40
❑ 70 Checklist .15 .40

1999 South Park Many Deaths of Kenny OmniChrome

COMPLETE SET (6) 6.00 15.00
STATED ODDS 1:20
❑ 1 Cartman Gets an Anal Probe 2.00 5.00
❑ 2 Weight Gain 4000 2.00 5.00
❑ 3 Volcano 2.00 5.00
❑ 4 Big Gay Al's Big Gay Boat Ride 2.00 5.00
❑ 5 An Elephant Makes Love to a Pig 2.00 5.00
❑ 6 Cartman's Mom Is Still a Slut 2.00 5.00

1999 South Park Promos

❑ P1 Eric Kyle/Stan/Kenny .75 2.00
❑ P2 South Park .75 2.00

1999 Star Trek DS9 Memories from the Future

COMPLETE SET (99) 5.00 12.00
❑ 1 Sisko The Emissary .15 .40
❑ 2 A Murderer? .15 .40
❑ 3 Q Hits The Deck .15 .40
❑ 4 Meet Grand Nagus Zek .15 .40
❑ 5 Kai Opakas Fate .15 .40
❑ 6 Bashir's Fantasy .15 .40
❑ 7 Odo Meet Lwaxana .15 .40
❑ 8 Kira's Duet .15 .40
❑ 9 Here Comes Trouble .15 .40
❑ 10 Bajoran Invasion .15 .40
❑ 11 Goodbye Melora .15 .40
❑ 12 Quark's Surprise .15 .40
❑ 13 Kira's Secret .15 .40
❑ 14 A Friendship Born .15 .40
❑ 15 O'Brien The Imposter .15 .40
❑ 16 Quarks Greatest Love .15 .40
❑ 17 Kingon Vengeance .15 .40
❑ 18 Phaser Blast .15 .40
❑ 19 Battling The Marquis .15 .40
❑ 20 Mirror, Mirror .15 .40
❑ 21 Bareil's Secret .15 .40
❑ 22 O'Brien's Trial .15 .40
❑ 23 The Jem Hader .15 .40
❑ 24 Odo's Origins .15 .40
❑ 25 Killer Quark .15 .40
❑ 26 Jadzia's Past .15 .40
❑ 27 Kira The Cardassian .15 .40
❑ 28 DS9 To Self-Destruct .15 .40
❑ 29 Tom Riker Returns .15 .40
❑ 30 Saving The Future .15 .40
❑ 31 The Death of Bareil .15 .40
❑ 32 Odo's Confession .15 .40
❑ 33 Nog Johns Starfleet .15 .40
❑ 34 New Rules of Acq. .15 .40
❑ 35 O'Briens Death .15 .40
❑ 36 Sisko Reunited .15 .40
❑ 37 Sailing Away .15 .40
❑ 38 Zhian Tara Ritual .15 .40
❑ 39 Together Forever? .15 .40
❑ 40 Captain Sisko .15 .40
❑ 41 Odo The Killer .15 .40
❑ 42 Worf Jones .15 .40
❑ 43 Father and Son .15 .40
❑ 44 Hippocratic Oath .15 .40
❑ 45 Teamwork .15 .40
❑ 46 A Kiss .15 .40
❑ 47 Little Green Men .15 .40
❑ 48 The Sword of Kahless .15 .40
❑ 49 Head of Security .15 .40
❑ 50 Thwarted Coup .15 .40
❑ 51 Sons of Mogh .15 .40
❑ 52 Strike! .15 .40
❑ 53 Prisoner O'Brien .15 .40
❑ 54 Wedding Bells .15 .40
❑ 55 Bashir's Gambit .15 .40
❑ 56 Quark for Sale .15 .40
❑ 57 Solid State .15 .40
❑ 58 D59 Goes Glingon .15 .40
❑ 59 The Happy Couple .15 .40
❑ 60 Romantic Liason .15 .40
❑ 61 Courage Under Fire .15 .40
❑ 62 Pah-Wrath Attack .15 .40
❑ 63 Sisko Saves Kirk .15 .40
❑ 64 Unlikely Allies .15 .40
❑ 65 Bajor Stay Out .15 .40
❑ 66 Shifting Back .15 .40
❑ 67 Sisko Triumphant .15 .40
❑ 68 Worf in the Ring .15 .40
❑ 69 Death of Tain .15 .40
❑ 70 Bashir's Secret .15 .40
❑ 71 First Itimacy .15 .40
❑ 72 Rom and Leeta .15 .40
❑ 73 Worf Reinstated .15 .40
❑ 74 Deadly Drink .15 .40
❑ 75 Dominion Takeover .15 .40
❑ 76 Reconciliation .15 .40
❑ 77 Odo and the Founder .15 .40
❑ 78 Gunned down .15 .40
❑ 79 Ziyal's Death .15 .40
❑ 80 Federation Payback .15 .40
❑ 81 Tying the Knot .15 .40
❑ 82 Geniuses? .15 .40
❑ 83 Saving Ishka .15 .40
❑ 84 Dukat's Escape .15 .40
❑ 85 Sisko the Sci-Fi Writer .15 .40
❑ 86 Personal Conflict .15 .40
❑ 87 Dukat's Lover .15 .40
❑ 88 Secret Section 31 .15 .40
❑ 89 Ethical Dilemma .15 .40
❑ 90 Together at Last .15 .40
❑ 91 The Shattered Tablet .15 .40
❑ 92 Rogue Warriors .15 .40
❑ 93 Quark's Transformation .15 .40
❑ 94 Jadzia's Death .15 .40
❑ 95 Return of Dax .15 .40
❑ 96 The Worm Hole .15 .40
❑ 97 Kira's Face-Off .15 .40
❑ 98 Bashir and Serena .15 .40
❑ 99 Weyoun Defects .15 .40

1999 Star Trek DS9 Memories from the Future Autographs

COMPLETE SET (20) 300.00 600.00
STATED ODDS ONE PER BOX
❑ 1 Alexander Siddig 20.00 50.00
❑ 2 Armin Shimerman 20.00 50.00
❑ 3 Cirroc Lofton 12.50 30.00
❑ 4 Nana Visitor 20.00 50.00
❑ 5 Rene Auberjonois 20.00 50.00
❑ 6 Terry Farrell 20.00 50.00
❑ 7 Nicole DeBoer 12.50 30.00
❑ 8 Andrew Robinson 12.50 30.00
❑ 9 Aron Eisenberg 12.50 30.00
❑ 10 William Campbell 12.50 30.00
❑ 11 Robert O'Reilly 20.00 50.00
❑ 12 Jennifer Hetrick 12.50 30.00
❑ 13 John Delancie 20.00 50.00
❑ 14 Louise Fletcher 12.50 30.00
❑ 15 Majel Barrett 20.00 50.00
❑ 16 Marc Alaimo 12.50 30.00
❑ 17 Max Grodenchik 12.50 30.00
❑ 18 Avery Brooks 12.50 30.00
❑ 19 Rick Berman 12.50 30.00
❑ 20 Chase Masterson 12.50 30.00

1999 Star Trek DS9 Memories from the Future Greatest Alien Races

COMPLETE SET (9) 4.00 10.00
❑ AR1 Cardassians .60 1.50
❑ AR2 Bajorans .60 1.50
❑ AR3 Ferengi .60 1.50
❑ AR4 Trill .60 1.50
❑ AR5 Klingons .60 1.50
❑ AR6 Founders .60 1.50
❑ AR7 Vorta .60 1.50
❑ AR8 Jem'Hadar .60 1.50
❑ AR9 Wormhole Aliens .60 1.50

1999 Star Trek DS9 Memories from the Future Greatest Legends

COMPLETE SET (9) 6.00 15.00
❑ L1 Capt. Benjamin Sisko 1.00 2.50
❑ L2 Colonel Kira Nerys 1.00 2.50
❑ L3 Security Chief Odo 1.00 2.50
❑ L4 Dr.Julian Bashir 1.00 2.50
❑ L5 Chief Miles O'Brien 1.00 2.50
❑ L6 Jadzia Dax-Ezri Dax 1.00 2.50
❑ L7 Lt. Comdr. Worf 1.00 2.50
❑ L8 Quark 1.00 2.50
❑ L9 Jake Sisko 1.00 2.50

1999 Star Trek DS9 Memories from the Future Greatest Space Battles

COMPLETE SET (6) 4.00 10.00
❑ B1 Wolf 1.00 2.50
❑ B2 Sisko vs Hudson 1.00 2.50
❑ B3 First Mission 1.00 2.50
❑ B4 Tain's Raid 1.00 2.50
❑ B5 Defending the Station 1.00 2.50
❑ B6 Friend or Foe 1.00 2.50

1999 Star Trek The Original Series In Motion

COMPLETE SET (24) 15.00 40.00
❑ 1 The Cage .75 2.00
❑ 2 The Cage .75 2.00
❑ 3 Where No Man Has Gone Before .75 2.00
❑ 4 Where No Man Has Gone Before .75 2.00
❑ 5 The Naked Time .75 2.00
❑ 6 The Naked Time .75 2.00
❑ 7 What Are Little Girls Made Of .75 2.00
❑ 8 What Are Little Girls Made Of .75 2.00
❑ 9 The Devil In The Dark .75 2.00
❑ 10 The Devil In The Dark .75 2.00
❑ 11 Amok Time .75 2.00
❑ 12 Amok Time .75 2.00
❑ 13 Mirror, Mirror .75 2.00
❑ 14 Mirror, Mirror .75 2.00
❑ 15 The Trouble With Tribbles .75 2.00
❑ 16 The Trouble With Tribbles .75 2.00
❑ 17 Journey To Babel .75 2.00
❑ 18 Journey To Babel .75 2.00
❑ 19 The Gamesters Of Triskelion .75 2.00
❑ 20 The Gamesters Of Triskelion .75 2.00
❑ 21 The Enterprise Incident .75 2.00
❑ 22 The Enterprise Incident .75 2.00
❑ 23 The Day Of The Dove .75 2.00
❑ 24 The Day Of The Dove .75 2.00

1999 Star Trek The Original Series In Motion DeForest Kelley Memoriam

COMPLETE SET (3) 100.00 200.00
STATED ODDS 1:120
❑ M1 DeForest Kelley 40.00 80.00
❑ M2 DeForest Kelley 40.00 80.00
❑ M3 DeForest Kelley 40.00 80.00

1999 Star Trek The Original Series In Motion Promos

COMPLETE SET (24) 30.00 60.00
❑ 1 The Cage 1.25 3.00
❑ 2 The Cage 1.25 3.00
❑ 3 Where No Man Has Gone Before 1.25 3.00
❑ 4 Where No Man Has Gone Before 1.25 3.00
❑ 5 The Naked Time 1.25 3.00
❑ 6 The Naked Time 1.25 3.00
❑ 7 What Are Little Girls Made Of 1.25 3.00
❑ 8 What Are Little Girls Made Of 1.25 3.00
❑ 9 The Devil In The Dark 1.25 3.00
❑ 10 The Devil In The Dark 1.25 3.00
❑ 11 Amok Time 1.25 3.00
❑ 12 Amok Time 1.25 3.00
❑ 13 Mirror, Mirror 1.25 3.00
❑ 14 Mirror, Mirror 1.25 3.00
❑ 15 The Trouble With Tribbles 1.25 3.00
❑ 16 The Trouble With Tribbles 1.25 3.00
❑ 17 Journey To Babel 1.25 3.00
❑ 18 Journey To Babel 1.25 3.00
❑ 19 The Gamesters Of Triskelion 1.25 3.00
❑ 20 The Gamesters Of Triskelion 1.25 3.00
❑ 21 The Enterprise Incident 1.25 3.00
❑ 22 The Enterprise Incident 1.25 3.00
❑ 23 The Day Of The Dove 1.25 3.00
❑ 24 The Day Of The Dove 1.25 3.00

1999 Star Trek The Original Series In Motion Sound in Motion

COMPLETE SET (6) 50.00 100.00
STATED ODDS ONE PER BOX
BS1 ISSUED IN COLLECTORS ALBUM
CS1 ISSUED AS CASE.TOPPER
❑ S1 The Cage 8.00 20.00
❑ S2 Amok Time 8.00 20.00
❑ S3 The Enterprise Incident 8.00 20.00
❑ S4 Mirror, Mirror 8.00 20.00
❑ S5 Journey To Babel 8.00 20.00
❑ S6 The Gamesters Of Triskelion 8.00 20.00
❑ BS1 The Devil In The Dark 8.00 20.00
❑ CS1 Amok Time 8.00 20.00

1999 Star Trek The Original Series Season 3

COMPLETE SET (75) 5.00 12.00
❑ 172 Spectre of the Gun .15 .40
❑ 173 Spectre of the Gun .15 .40
❑ 174 Spectre of the Gun .15 .40
❑ 175 Iaan of Troyius .15 .40
❑ 176 Elaan of Troyius .15 .40
❑ 177 Elaan of Troyius .15 .40
❑ 178 The Paradise Syndrome .15 .40
❑ 179 The Paradise Syndrome .15 .40
❑ 180 The Paradise Syndrome .15 .40
❑ 181 The Enterprise Incident .15 .40
❑ 182 The Enterprise Incident .15 .40
❑ 183 The Enterprise Incident .15 .40
❑ 184 And the Children .15 .40
❑ 185 And the Children .15 .40
❑ 186 And the Children .15 .40
❑ 187 Spock's Brain .15 .40
❑ 188 Spock's Brain .15 .40
❑ 189 Spock's Brain .15 .40
❑ 190 Is There No Truth .15 .40
❑ 191 Is There No Truth .15 .40
❑ 192 Is There No Truth .15 .40
❑ 193 The Empath .15 .40
❑ 194 The Empath .15 .40
❑ 195 The Empath .15 .40
❑ 196 The Tholian Web .15 .40
❑ 197 The Tholian Web .15 .40
❑ 198 The Tholian Web .15 .40
❑ 199 For The World Is .15 .40
❑ 200 For The World Is .15 .40
❑ 201 For The World Is .15 .40
❑ 202 Day of the Dove .15 .40
❑ 203 Day of the Dove .15 .40
❑ 204 Day of the Dove .15 .40
❑ 205 Plato's Stepchildren .15 .40
❑ 206 Plato's Stepchildren .15 .40
❑ 207 Plato's Stepchildren .15 .40
❑ 208 Wink of an Eye .15 .40
❑ 209 Wink of an Eye .15 .40
❑ 210 Wink of an Eye .15 .40
❑ 211 That Which Survives .15 .40
❑ 212 That Which Survives .15 .40
❑ 213 That Which Survives .15 .40
❑ 214 Let That Be Your .15 .40
❑ 215 Let That Be Your .15 .40
❑ 216 Let That Be Your .15 .40
❑ 217 Whom Gods .15 .40
❑ 218 Whom Gods .15 .40
❑ 219 Whom Gods .15 .40
❑ 220 The Mark of Gideon .15 .40
❑ 221 The Mark of Gideon .15 .40
❑ 222 The Mark of Gideon .15 .40
❑ 223 The Lights of Zetar .15 .40
❑ 224 The Lights of Zetar .15 .40
❑ 225 The Lights of Zetar .15 .40
❑ 226 The Cloudminders .15 .40
❑ 227 The Cloudminders .15 .40
❑ 228 The Cloudminders .15 .40
❑ 229 The Way to Eden .15 .40
❑ 230 The Way to Eden .15 .40
❑ 231 The Way to Eden .15 .40
❑ 232 Requiem for .15 .40
❑ 233 Requiem for .15 .40
❑ 234 Requien for .15 .40
❑ 235 The Savage Curtain .15 .40
❑ 236 The Savage Curtain .15 .40
❑ 237 The Savage Curtain .15 .40
❑ 238 All Our Yesterdays .15 .40
❑ 239 All Our Yesterdays .15 .40
❑ 240 All Our Yesterdays .15 .40
❑ 241 Turnabout Intruder .15 .40
❑ 242 Turnabout Intruder .15 .40
❑ 243 Turnabout Intruder .15 .40
❑ 244 Checklist .15 .40
❑ 245 Checklist .15 .40
❑ 246 Checklist .15 .40

1999 Star Trek The Original Series Season 3 Autographs

COMPLETE SET (27)
STATED ODDS 1:36
❑ A59 Leonard Nimoy 150.00 250.00
❑ A60 James Doohan 100.00 200.00
❑ A61 DeForest Kelly
❑ A62 Walter Koenig 30.00 60.00
❑ A63 John Winston 25.00 50.00
❑ A64 Herb Solow 15.00 30.00
❑ A65 Walter Jefferies
❑ A66 Ron Soble 15.00 30.00
❑ A67 Tony Young 12.00 25.00
❑ A68 Jay Robinson 20.00 40.00
❑ A69 Jack Donner 12.00 25.00
❑ A70 Diana Muldaur 15.00 30.00
❑ A71 Alan Bergmann 20.00 40.00
❑ A72 Michael Ansara 20.00 40.00
❑ A73 Susan Howard 25.00 50.00
❑ A74 Barbara Babcock 12.00 25.00
❑ A75 Jason Evers 12.00 25.00
❑ A76 Lee Meriwether 50.00 100.00
❑ A77 Frank Gorshin
❑ A78 Yvonne Craig 30.00 60.00
❑ A79 Sharon Acker 20.00 40.00
❑ A80 Gene Dynarski 15.00 30.00
❑ A81 Charles Napier 15.00 30.00
❑ A82 Victor Brandt 12.00 25.00
❑ A83 Phillip Pine 12.00 25.00
❑ A84 Nathan Jung 12.00 25.00
❑ A85 Mariette Hartley 20.00 40.00

1999 Star Trek The Original Series Season 3 Behind the Scenes

COMPLETE SET (48) 6.00 15.00
STATED ODDS 1:2
❑ 111 Spectre of the Gun .20 .50
❑ 112 Spectre of the Gun .20 .50
❑ 113 Elaan of Troyius .20 .50
❑ 114 Elaan of Troyius .20 .50
❑ 115 The Paradise .20 .50
❑ 116 The Paradise .20 .50
❑ 117 The Enterprise .20 .50
❑ 118 The Enterprise .20 .50
❑ 119 And the Children .20 .50
❑ 120 And the Children .20 .50
❑ 121 Spock's Brain .20 .50
❑ 122 Spock's Brain .20 .50
❑ 123 Is There No Truth .20 .50
❑ 124 Is There No Truth .20 .50
❑ 125 The Empath .20 .50
❑ 126 The Empath .20 .50
❑ 127 The Tholian Web .20 .50
❑ 128 The Tholian Web .20 .50
❑ 129 For The World Is .20 .50
❑ 130 For The World Is .20 .50
❑ 131 Day of the Dove .20 .50
❑ 132 Day of the Dove .20 .50
❑ 133 Plato's Stepchildren .20 .50
❑ 134 Plato's Stepchildren .20 .50
❑ 135 Wink of An Eye .20 .50
❑ 136 Wink of An Eye .20 .50
❑ 137 That Which Survives .20 .50
❑ 138 That Which Survives .20 .50
❑ 139 Let That Be Your .20 .50
❑ 140 Let That Be Your .20 .50
❑ 141 Whom Gods Destroy .20 .50
❑ 142 Whom Gods Destroy .20 .50
❑ 143 Whom Gods Destroy .20 .50
❑ 144 The Mark of Gideon .20 .50
❑ 145 The Lights of Zetar .20 .50
❑ 146 The Lights of Zetar .20 .50
❑ 147 The Cloudminders .20 .50
❑ 148 The Cloudminders .20 .50
❑ 149 The Way to Eden .20 .50
❑ 150 The Way to Eden .20 .50
❑ 151 Requiem for .20 .50
❑ 152 Requiem for .20 .50
❑ 153 The Savage Curtain .20 .50
❑ 154 The Savage Curtain .20 .50
❑ 155 All Our Yesterdays .20 .50
❑ 156 All Our Yesterdays .20 .50
❑ 157 Turnabout Intruder .20 .50
❑ 158 Turnabout Intruder .20 .50

1999 Star Trek The Original Series Season 3 Characters

COMPLETE SET (48) 6.00 15.00
STATED ODDS 2:1
❑ C111 Spectre of the Gun .20 .50
❑ C112 Spectre of the Gun .20 .50
❑ C113 Elaan of Troyius .20 .50
❑ C114 Elaan of Troyius .20 .50
❑ C115 The Paradise Syndrome .20 .50
❑ C116 The Paradise Syndrome .20 .50
❑ C117 The Enterprise Syndrome .20 .50
❑ C118 The Enterprise Incident .20 .50
❑ C119 And the Children Shall Lead .20 .50
❑ C120 And the Children Shall Lead .20 .50
❑ C121 Spock's Brain .20 .50
❑ C122 Spock's Brain .20 .50
❑ C123 Is There No Truth In Beauty? .20 .50
❑ C124 Is There No Truth In Beauty? .20 .50
❑ C125 The Empath .20 .50
❑ C126 The Empath .20 .50
❑ C127 The Tholian Web .20 .50
❑ C128 The Tholian Web .20 .50
❑ C129 For The World is Hollow .20 .50
❑ C130 For The World is Hollow .20 .50
❑ C131 Day of the Dove .20 .50
❑ C132 Day of the Dove .20 .50
❑ C133 Plato's Stepchildren .20 .50
❑ C134 Plato's Stepchildren .20 .50
❑ C135 Wink of An Eye .20 .50
❑ C136 Wink of An Eye .20 .50
❑ C137 That Which Survives .20 .50
❑ C138 That Which Survives .20 .50
❑ C139 Let That Be Your Last .20 .50
❑ C140 Let That Be Your Last .20 .50
❑ C141 Whom Gods Destroy .20 .50
❑ C142 Whom Gods Destroy .20 .50
❑ C143 The Mark of Gideon .20 .50
❑ C144 The Mark of Gideon .20 .50
❑ C145 The Lights of Zetar .20 .50

☐ C146 The Lights of Zetar .20 .50
☐ C147 The Cloudminders .20 .50
☐ C148 The Cloudminders .20 .50
☐ C149 The Way to Eden .20 .50
☐ C150 The Way to Eden .20 .50
☐ C151 Requiem for Methuselah .20 .50
☐ C152 Requiem for Methuselah .20 .50
☐ C153 Requiem for Methuselah .20 .50
☐ C154 The Savage Curtain .20 .50
☐ C155 The Savage Curtain .20 .50
☐ C156 All Our Yesterdays .20 .50
☐ C157 Turnabout Intruder .20 .50
☐ C158 Turnabout Intruder .20 .50

1999 Star Trek The Original Series Season 3 Gold Plaques

COMPLETE SET (24) 40.00 100.00
STATED ODDS 1:12

☐ 56 Spectre of the Gun 2.50 6.00
☐ 57 Elaan of Troyius 2.50 6.00
☐ 58 The Paradise Syndrome 2.50 6.00
☐ 59 The Enterprise Incident 2.50 6.00
☐ 60 And the Children Shall Lead 2.50 6.00
☐ 61 Spock's Brain 2.50 6.00
☐ 62 Is There No Truth In Beauty? 2.50 6.00
☐ 63 The Empath 2.50 6.00
☐ 64 The Tholian Web 2.50 6.00
☐ 65 For The World Is Hollow 2.50 6.00
☐ 66 Day of the Dove 2.50 6.00
☐ 67 Plato's Stepchildren 2.50 6.00
☐ 68 Wink of An Eye 2.50 6.00
☐ 69 That Which Survives 2.50 6.00
☐ 70 Let That Be Your Last 2.50 6.00
☐ 71 Whom Gods Destroy 2.50 6.00
☐ 72 The Mark of Gideon 2.50 6.00
☐ 73 The Lights of Zetar 2.50 6.00
☐ 74 The Cloudminders 2.50 6.00
☐ 75 The Way to Eden 2.50 6.00
☐ 76 Requiem for Methuselah 2.50 6.00
☐ 77 The Savage Curtain 2.50 6.00
☐ 78 All Our Yesterdays 2.50 6.00
☐ 79 Turnabout Intruder 2.50 6.00

1999 Star Trek The Original Series Season 3 Profiles

COMPLETE SET (24) 7.50 20.00
STATED ODDS 1:4

☐ 56 Spectre of the Gun .60 1.50
☐ 57 Elaan of Troyius .60 1.50
☐ 58 The Paradise .60 1.50
☐ 59 The Enterprise .60 1.50
☐ 60 And the Children .60 1.50
☐ 61 Spock's Brain .60 1.50
☐ 62 Is There No Truth .60 1.50
☐ 63 The Empath .60 1.50
☐ 64 The Tholian Web .60 1.50
☐ 65 For The World is Hollow .60 1.50
☐ 66 Day of the Dove .60 1.50
☐ 67 Plato's Stepchildren .60 1.50
☐ 68 Wink of An Eye .60 1.50
☐ 69 That Which Survives .60 1.50
☐ 70 Let That Be Your Last .60 1.50
☐ 71 Whom Gods Destroy .60 1.50
☐ 72 The Mark of Gideon .60 1.50
☐ 73 The Lights of .60 1.50
☐ 74 The Cloudminders .60 1.50
☐ 75 The Way to Eden .60 1.50
☐ 76 Requiem for Methuselah .60 1.50
☐ 77 The Savage Curtain .60 1.50
☐ 78 All Our Yesterdays .60 1.50
☐ 79 Turnabout Intruder .60 1.50

1999 Twilight Zone Premiere

COMPLETE SET (72) 5.00 12.00

☐ 1 Where Is Everybody .15 .40
☐ 2 Where Is Everybody .15 .40
☐ 3 Where Is Everybody .15 .40
☐ 4 Where Is Everybody .15 .40
☐ 5 Where Is Everybody .15 .40
☐ 6 Where Is Everybody .15 .40
☐ 7 Time Enough At Last .15 .40
☐ 8 Time Enough At Last .15 .40
☐ 9 Time Enough At Last .15 .40
☐ 10 Time Enough At Last .15 .40
☐ 11 Time Enough At Last .15 .40
☐ 12 Time Enough At Last .15 .40
☐ 13 And When The Sky Was Opened .15 .40
☐ 14 And When The Sky Was Opened .15 .40
☐ 15 And When The Sky Was Opened .15 .40
☐ 16 And When The Sky Was Opened .15 .40
☐ 17 And When The Sky Was Opened .15 .40
☐ 18 And When The Sky Was Opened .15 .40
☐ 19 Mirror Image .15 .40
☐ 20 Mirror Image .15 .40
☐ 21 Mirror Image .15 .40
☐ 22 Mirror Image .15 .40
☐ 23 Mirror Image .15 .40
☐ 24 Mirror Image .15 .40
☐ 25 Long Live Walter Jameson .15 .40
☐ 26 Long Live Walter Jameson .15 .40
☐ 27 Long Live Walter Jameson .15 .40
☐ 28 Long Live Walter Jameson .15 .40
☐ 29 Long Live Walter Jameson .15 .40
☐ 30 Long Live Walter Jameson .15 .40
☐ 31 The After Hours .15 .40
☐ 32 The After Hours .15 .40
☐ 33 The After Hours .15 .40
☐ 34 The After Hours .15 .40
☐ 35 The After Hours .15 .40
☐ 36 The After Hours .15 .40
☐ 37 The Eye Of The Beholder .15 .40
☐ 38 The Eye Of The Beholder .15 .40
☐ 39 The Eye Of The Beholder .15 .40
☐ 40 The Eye Of The Beholder .15 .40
☐ 41 The Eye Of The Beholder .15 .40
☐ 42 The Eye Of The Beholder .15 .40
☐ 43 The Obsolete Man .15 .40
☐ 44 The Obsolete Man .15 .40
☐ 45 The Obsolete Man .15 .40
☐ 46 The Obsolete Man .15 .40
☐ 47 The Obsolete Man .15 .40
☐ 48 The Obsolete Man .15 .40
☐ 49 It's A Good Life .15 .40
☐ 50 It's A Good Life .15 .40
☐ 51 It's A Good Life .15 .40
☐ 52 It's A Good Life .15 .40
☐ 53 It's A Good Life .15 .40
☐ 54 It's A Good Life .15 .40
☐ 55 To Serve Man .15 .40
☐ 56 To Serve Man .15 .40
☐ 57 To Serve Man .15 .40
☐ 58 To Serve Man .15 .40
☐ 59 To Serve Man .15 .40
☐ 60 To Serve Man .15 .40
☐ 61 Nightmare At 20,000 Feet .15 .40
☐ 62 Nightmare At 20,000 Feet .15 .40
☐ 63 Nightmare At 20,000 Feet .15 .40
☐ 64 Nightmare At 20,000 Feet .15 .40
☐ 65 Nightmare At 20,000 Feet .15 .40
☐ 66 Nightmare At 20,000 Feet .15 .40
☐ 67 Probe 7, Over And Out .15 .40
☐ 68 Probe 7, Over And Out .15 .40
☐ 69 Probe 7, Over And Out .15 .40
☐ 70 Probe 7, Over And Out .15 .40
☐ 71 Probe 7, Over And Out .15 .40
☐ 72 Probe 7, Over And Out .15 .40

1999 Twilight Zone Premiere Progressive Proofs Black

COMPLETE SET (81) 60.00 120.00
COMMON CARD .75 2.00
ANNOUNCED PRINT RUN 99

1999 Twilight Zone Premiere Progressive Proofs Cyan

COMPLETE SET (81) 60.00 120.00
COMMON CARD .75 2.00
ANNOUNCED PRINT RUN 99

1999 Twilight Zone Premiere Progressive Proofs Magenta

COMPLETE SET (81) 60.00 120.00
COMMON CARD .75 2.00
ANNOUNCED PRINT RUN 99

1999 Twilight Zone Premiere Progressive Proofs Yellow

COMPLETE SET (81) 60.00 120.00
COMMON CARD .75 2.00
ANNOUNCED PRINT RUN 99

1999 Twilight Zone Premiere Autograph Challenge

STATED ODDS ONE PER PACK

☐ E E=MC2
☐ G Glasses
☐ H Clock
☐ I Swirl
☐ L Twilight Zone Logo
☐ N Body
☐ O Eyeball
☐ T Thimble
☐ W Window Breaking
☐ Z Rod Serling SP

1999 Twilight Zone Premiere Autographs

COMPLETE SET (18) 500.00 800.00
STATED ODDS TWO PER BOX

☐ A1 William Shatner 300.00 500.00
☐ A2 Donna Douglas 15.00 40.00
☐ A3 Richard Kiel 15.00 40.00
☐ A4 Lloyd Bochner 8.00 20.00
☐ A5 Ann Blyth 8.00 20.00
☐ A6 Kevin McCarthy 15.00 40.00
☐ A7 Martin Milner 8.00 20.00
☐ A8 Vera Miles 8.00 20.00
☐ A9 Rod Taylor 15.00 40.00
☐ A10 William Windom 8.00 20.00
☐ A11 Antoinette Bower 8.00 20.00
☐ A12 Fritz Weaver 8.00 20.00
☐ A13 Earl Holliman 8.00 20.00
☐ A14 Anne Francis 15.00 40.00
☐ A16 Robert Sorrells 8.00 20.00
☐ A17 Cloris Leachman 8.00 20.00
☐ A18 Bill Mumy 15.00 40.00
☐ A19 Ruta Lee (issued in collectors album) 35.00 60.00

1999 Twilight Zone Premiere Commemorative

COMPLETE SET (2) 2.50 6.00
STATED ODDS 1:36

☐ C1 Rod Serling 1.50 4.00
☐ C2 Buck Houghton 1.50 4.00

1999 Twilight Zone Premiere Promos

☐ P1 To Serve Man 1.00 2.50
☐ P2 Nightmare at 20,000 Feet 1.00 2.50

1999 Twilight Zone Premiere Twilight Zone Stars

COMPLETE SET (9) 6.00 15.00
RANDOM INSERTS IN PACKS

☐ S1 William Shatner .75 2.00
☐ S2 Martin Milner .75 2.00
☐ S3 Rod Taylor .75 2.00
☐ S4 Earl Holliman .75 2.00
☐ S5 Anne Francis .75 2.00
☐ S6 Kevin McCarthy .75 2.00
☐ S7 Richard Basehart .75 2.00
☐ S8 Vera Miles .75 2.00
☐ S9 Bill Mumy .75 2.00

1999 Wild Wild West

COMPLETE SET (81) 5.00 12.00

☐ 1 Wild Wild West .15 .40
☐ 2 On the Prowl .15 .40
☐ 3 That Was No Lady .15 .40
☐ 4 The Better To hear You With .15 .40
☐ 5 Bringing the House Down .15 .40
☐ 6 The Ugly American .15 .40
☐ 7 You Must Be Over Eighteen .15 .40
☐ 8 Do You Come Here Often? .15 .40
☐ 9 Hot Soup! .15 .40
☐ 10 You're Not My Type .15 .40
☐ 11 Curtains For James T. West .15 .40
☐ 12 The Original Odd Couple .15 .40
☐ 13 Watch Out For Bumps! .15 .40
☐ 14 The Women Behind the Man .15 .40
☐ 15 Veto This, Mr. President! .15 .40
☐ 16 The Real McGrant .15 .40
☐ 17 Your Mission, Should You Decide To Accept It (Or Not) .15 .40
☐ 18 Unfriendly Allies .15 .40
☐ 19 A Wonderful Wanderer .15 .40
☐ 20 A Coal Man Named Coleman .15 .40
☐ 21 Taking Ad-Vise .15 .40
☐ 22 All the Comforts of Home .15 .40
☐ 23 An Unwanted Guest .15 .40
☐ 24 Strike Up the Band .15 .40
☐ 25 You Can't Be Too Careful .15 .40
☐ 26 The Spider In His Lair .15 .40
☐ 27 With Friends Like These... .15 .40
☐ 28 West Meets East .15 .40
☐ 29 I Don't Know Art, But I Know What I Hate! .15 .40
☐ 30 Alive and... Well? .15 .40
☐ 31 A Bird In a Gilded Cage .15 .40
☐ 32 Tanks A Lot .15 .40
☐ 33 Angels of Death .15 .40
☐ 34 Witnesses To Slaughter .15 .40
☐ 35 Taking Out the Trash .15 .40
☐ 36 What A Dish! .15 .40
☐ 37 Three's A Crowd .15 .40
☐ 38 Road Hog! .15 .40
☐ 39 Laying Down On the Job .15 .40
☐ 40 Partners To the End? .15 .40
☐ 41 A Little Off the Top .15 .40
☐ 42 Backseat Driver .15 .40
☐ 43 It Doesn't Do a Thing For Me .15 .40
☐ 44 Watch That First Step! .15 .40
☐ 45 Tastes Like Chicken .15 .40
☐ 46 Call the Exterminator! .15 .40
☐ 47 Two Heads Are Better Than One (I Think!) .15 .40
☐ 48 Railroaded .15 .40
☐ 49 Loveless the First -- and Last .15 .40
☐ 50 Now That's a Big Spider! .15 .40
☐ 51 President Gordon .15 .40
☐ 52 Loveless Triumphant! .15 .40
☐ 53 An Appreciative Audience .15 .40
☐ 54 Captive Audience .15 .40
☐ 55 A Target -- But No Practice .15 .40
☐ 56 Witnesses To History .15 .40
☐ 57 He's Not That Kind of Girl! .15 .40
☐ 58 The Worst Seats In the House .15 .40
☐ 59 Going Up In Smoke .15 .40
☐ 60 Party Crasher! .15 .40
☐ 61 Ladies First! .15 .40
☐ 62 If Man Were Meant To Fly... .15 .40
☐ 63 Up, Up and Away (We Hope) .15 .40
☐ 64 Any Landing You can Walk Away From... .15 .40
☐ 65 Grant Just Says No .15 .40
☐ 66 Painting the Town Dead .15 .40
☐ 67 Stooping To Conquer .15 .40
☐ 68 Her Business Is Death .15 .40
☐ 69 Delegged But Still Deadly .15 .40
☐ 70 Presidential Reception .15 .40
☐ 71 Broken Hearts and Happy Endings .15 .40
☐ 72 James T. West .15 .40
☐ 73 Artemus Gordon .15 .40
☐ 74 Rita Escobar .15 .40
☐ 75 Dr. Loveless .15 .40
☐ 76 McGrath .15 .40
☐ 77 Ms. Lippenreider .15 .40
☐ 78 Munitia .15 .40
☐ 79 Amazonia .15 .40
☐ 80 President Grant .15 .40
☐ 81 Checklist .15 .40
☐ NNO Wild Wild West PROMO 1.25 3.00

1999 Wild Wild West Autographs

STATED ODDS 1:36

☐ A1 Kevin Kline 100.00 200.00
☐ A2 Barry Sonnenfeld 4.00 10.00
☐ A3 Kenneth Branagh 8.00 20.00
☐ A4 Sofia Eng 4.00 10.00
☐ A5 Musetta Vander 8.00 20.00
☐ A6 Frederique Van Der Wal 8.00 20.00
☐ A7 Carlos Cervantes 4.00 10.00
☐ A8 M. Emmet Walsh 15.00 40.00
☐ A9 Ted Levine 4.00 10.00
☐ A10 Orestes Matacena 4.00 10.00
☐ A11 Christian Aubert 4.00 10.00
☐ A12 Ian Abercrombie 4.00 10.00
☐ A13 Rodney A. Grant 4.00 10.00
☐ A14 Jon Peters 4.00 10.00
☐ A15 Salma Hayek 150.00 250.00

1999 Wild Wild West Concept Sketches

COMPLETE SET (9) 5.00 12.00
STATED ODDS 1:4

☐ S1 Disc Launcher .75 2.00
☐ S2 Abe Lincoln Statue .75 2.00
☐ S3 Tarantula Vehicle .75 2.00
☐ S4 Magnetic Collars .75 2.00
☐ S5 Loveless Megaphone .75 2.00
☐ S6 Nitro-Cycle .75 2.00
☐ S7 Loveless Tank .75 2.00
☐ S8 Water Tower .75 2.00
☐ S9 Loveless Lair .75 2.00

1999 Wild Wild West Gordon's Gadgets

COMPLETE SET (9) 10.00 25.00
STATED ODDS 1:12

☐ G1 Pool Table 1.50 4.00
☐ G2 Escape Trolley 1.50 4.00
☐ G3 Perfume Bottle Gun 1.50 4.00
☐ G4 Belt Buckle Hypnotizer 1.50 4.00
☐ G5 Spring Loaded Corsage 1.50 4.00
☐ G6 Nitro-Cycle 1.50 4.00
☐ G7 Silver Buckle Gun 1.50 4.00
☐ G8 Flame Thrower Costume 1.50 4.00
☐ G9 Desert Wasp 1.50 4.00

1999 Wild Wild West Platinum Portraits

COMPLETE SET (3) 50.00 120.00
STATED PRINT RUN 750 SER.#'d SETS

☐ P1 James T. West 20.00 50.00
☐ P2 James T. West 20.00 50.00
☐ P3 James T. West 20.00 50.00

1999 The World Is Not Enough

COMPLETE SET (90) 5.00 12.00
S1 STATED ODDS 1:108

☐ 1 The World Is Not Enough .15 .40
☐ 2 A Cigar for Mr. Bond .15 .40
☐ 3 Reversal of Fortune .15 .40
☐ 4 Escaping with the Money .15 .40
☐ 5 A Job Well Done... But Unfinished .15 .40
☐ 6 Moneypenny's Fantasy .15 .40
☐ 7 MI-6 Blasted .15 .40
☐ 8 The Q-Boat in Action .15 .40
☐ 9 Bullets for Bond .15 .40
☐ 10 Chase Across the Thames .15 .40
☐ 11 Unscheduled Blast-Off .15 .40
☐ 12 Dinner Theatre .15 .40
☐ 13 Skyrider Over London .15 .40
☐ 14 Beautiful Assassin .15 .40
☐ 15 Close... But No Cigar Girl .15 .40
☐ 16 Mourning Sir Robert .15 .40
☐ 17 Inside Q's Workshop .15 .40
☐ 18 New Tools of the Trade .15 .40
☐ 19 Exploring the Painful Past .15 .40
☐ 20 Someone to Watch Over Her .15 .40
☐ 21 Elektra's Empire .15 .40
☐ 22 Ski Relief .15 .40
☐ 23 Trouble Up Ahead .15 .40
☐ 24 Parahawk Assault .15 .40
☐ 25 James Bombed .15 .40
☐ 26 When Parahawks Collide .15 .40
☐ 27 Spy with the X-Ray Eyes .15 .40
☐ 28 The Pain of No Pain .15 .40
☐ 29 Kindred Spirits .15 .40
☐ 30 Russian Flavoring .15 .40
☐ 31 Encounter with Renard .15 .40
☐ 32 You Can Catch the Devil .15 .40
☐ 33 But You Can't Hold Him Long .15
☐ 34 Last Chance to Escape .15 .40
☐ 35 Master of the Bomb .15 .40
☐ 36 Using the Q-Line .15 .40
☐ 37 High-Flying Exit .15 .40
☐ 38 Flight to Freedom .15 .40
☐ 39 Fire in the Hole .15 .40
☐ 40 Mission... Aborted .15 .40
☐ 41 The Entrapment of M .15 .40
☐ 42 Putting the Squeeze on Zukovsky .15 .40
☐ 43 Blades of Death .15 .40
☐ 44 A Spy's Best Friend .15 .40
☐ 45 One Agent Army .15 .40
☐ 46 Bond Means Business .15 .40
☐ 47 Caviar Quicksand .15 .40
☐ 48 Unfriendly Waters .15 .40
☐ 49 Strange Alliance .15 .40
☐ 50 Bull Gets the Drop .15 .40
☐ 51 The Torture Chair .15 .40
☐ 52 Elektra's Revenge .15 .40
☐ 53 Twisted Seduction .15 .40
☐ 54 A Man to His Task .15 .40
☐ 55 Zukovsky's Final Shot .15 .40
☐ 56 Bond in Control .15 .40
☐ 57 He Never Misses .15 .40
☐ 58 Spy Dive .15 .40
☐ 59 The World Holds Its Breath .15 .40
☐ 60 Clashing Titans .15 .40
☐ 61 Cylinder of Chaos .15 .40
☐ 62 Renard's Fate .15 .40
☐ 63 Christmas Present .15 .40
☐ 64 He Takes Pleasure... In Great Beauty .15 .40
☐ 65 Polar Opposites .15 .40
☐ 66 Sophie Marceau as Elektra King .15 .40
☐ 67 More than Meets the Eye .15 .40
☐ 68 Denise Richards as Christmas Jones .15 .40
☐ 69 Celebrating Christmas .15 .40
☐ 70 Maria Grazia Cucinotta as the Cigar Girl .15 .40
☐ 71 Serena Scott-Thomas as Dr. Warmflash .15 .40
☐ 72 The Bond Girl Legacy .15 .40
☐ 73 A new Kind of Bond .15 .40
☐ 74 Everybody Say Cheese .15 .40
☐ 75 Relationship Explored .15 .40
☐ 76 Hitting the Ice .15 .40
☐ 77 Fantastic Sets and Set-Pieces .15 .40
☐ 78 Fate of a Spy Car .15 .40
☐ 79 Boat Chase .15 .40
☐ 80 By Design .15 .40
☐ 81 Pit Stop .15 .40
☐ 82 James Bond .15 .40
☐ 83 Elektra King .15 .40
☐ 84 Dr. Christmas Jones .15 .40
☐ 85 Renard .15 .40
☐ 86 Valentin Zukovsky .15 .40
☐ 87 Mr. Bullion .15 .40
☐ 88 M .15 .40
☐ 89 MI-6 Headquarters .15 .40
☐ 90 Checklist .15 .40
☐ S1 Shaken Not Stirred SP 6.00 15.00

1999 The World Is Not Enough Autographs

☐ A1 Denise Richards 40.00 80.00
☐ A2 Judi Dench 25.00 50.00
☐ A3 Desmond Llewelyn 75.00 125.00
☐ A4 Serena Scott-Thomas 15.00 30.00
☐ A5 Samantha Bond 15.00 30.00
☐ A6 Goldie 8.00 20.00
☐ R1 Redemption Card

1999 The World Is Not Enough Bond Is Back

COMPLETE SET (9) 4.00 10.00
STATED ODDS 1:11

☐ B1 The Cigar Girl opens the briefcase .75 2.00
☐ B2 Bond produces the cigar .75 2.00
☐ B3 Dr. Warmflash's blouse drops .75 2.00
☐ B4 A Scot in a kilt plays the bagpipes .75 2.00
☐ B5 Bond slides to a halt .75 2.00
☐ B6 The Bull turns to Bond .75 2.00
☐ B7 Bond has just managed to heave .75 2.00
☐ B8 Christmas approaches .75 2.00
☐ B9 Bond and Christmas Jones .75 2.00

1999 The World Is Not Enough Poker Chips

COMPLETE SET (3) 25.00 50.00
STATED ODDS ONE PER BOX

☐ C1 James Bond 8.00 20.00
☐ C2 King 8.00 20.00
Bond/Jones
☐ C3 Christmas Jones 8.00 20.00
Elektra King

1999 The World Is Not Enough Q Branch

COMPLETE SET (6) 3.00 8.00
STATED ODDS 1:17

☐ Q1 The Hydroboat 1.00 2.50
☐ Q2 The Watch 1.00 2.50
☐ Q3 X-Ray Glasses 1.00 2.50
☐ Q4 BMW Z8 1.00 2.50
☐ Q5 Jacket 1.00 2.50
Airbag
☐ Q6 Tribute to Q 1.00 2.50

2000 Angel Season One

COMPLETE SET (90) 5.00 12.00

☐ 1 Angel .15 .40
☐ 2 On a Mission .15 .40
☐ 3 To the Slaughter .15 .40
☐ 4 Not So Innocent .15 .40
☐ 5 Meet Market .15 .40
☐ 6 On the Job .15 .40
☐ 7 Burning Love .15 .40
☐ 8 Message from Sunnydale .15 .40
☐ 9 King of Pain .15 .40
☐ 10 Walking on Sunshine .15 .40
☐ 11 Keen an Eye Out .15 .40
☐ 12 Some Nerve .15 .40
☐ 13 Boxed In .15 .40
☐ 14 Amenities Not Included .15 .40
☐ 15 Security Deposit .15 .40
☐ 16 Cozy, Charming 1 Bedroom .15 .40
☐ 17 On the Trail .15 .40
☐ 18 Touchy Feely .15 .40
☐ 19 Law and Disorder .15 .40
☐ 20 Insightful .15 .40
☐ 21 Honored Guest .15 .40
☐ 22 Party Crasher .15 .40
☐ 23 Same Old Stuff .15 .40
☐ 24 Everything Changes .15 .40
☐ 25 Just a Memory .15 .40
☐ 26 Faking It .15 .40
☐ 27 Passing .15 .40
☐ 28 Making the Grade .15 .40
☐ 29 Missing You .15 .40
☐ 30 Returned .15 .40
☐ 31 Gone But Not Forgotten .15 .40
☐ 32 Walking After Midnight .15 .40
☐ 33 Copycat .15 .40
☐ 34 The Devil You Know .15 .40
☐ 35 Unplanned .15 .40
☐ 36 Anticipation .15 .40
☐ 37 Delivery .15 .40
☐ 38 Boogie Nights .15 .40
☐ 39 Hot Stuff .15 .40
☐ 40 Fever .15 .40
☐ 41 Family Matters .15 .40
☐ 42 Exorcist .15 .40
☐ 43 The Bad Seed .15 .40
☐ 44 Daddy Dearest .15 .40
☐ 45 Daddy's Girl .15 .40
☐ 46 My Heart Belongs to Daddy .15 .40
☐ 47 Fight Club .15 .40
☐ 48 Blood Sport .15 .40
☐ 49 Gladiator .15 .40
☐ 50 Starstruck .15 .40
☐ 51 Forever Young .15 .40
☐ 52 Uninhibited .15 .40
☐ 53 The Girl for the Job .15 .40
☐ 54 I'll Be Watching You .15 .40
☐ 55 Over the Edge .15 .40
☐ 56 Powerless .15 .40
☐ 57 Into Action .15 .40
☐ 58 Surrender .15 .40
☐ 59 The Other Half .15 .40
☐ 60 Drive By .15 .40
☐ 61 Urban Renewal .15 .40
☐ 62 Justice Is Blind .15 .40
☐ 63 Blood Money .15 .40
☐ 64 Don't Fear the Reaper .15 .40
☐ 65 Welcome Back .15 .40
☐ 66 Angel .15 .40
☐ 67 Francis Doyle .15 .40
☐ 68 Cordelia Chase .15 .40
☐ 69 Wesley Wyndam .15 .40
☐ 70 Buffy Summers .15 .40
☐ 71 Kate Lockley .15 .40
☐ 72 Jheira of Oden Tal .15 .40
☐ 73 Lilah Morgan .15 .40
☐ 74 Lindsey McDonald .15 .40
☐ 75 Holland Manners .15 .40
☐ 76 Talamour .15 .40
☐ 77 Marcus .15 .40
☐ 78 Dr. Ronald Meltzer .15 .40
☐ 79 Maude Pearson .15 .40
☐ 80 Griff .15 .40
☐ 81 Ano .15 .40
☐ 82 Mohra Demon .15 .40
☐ 83 Brachen Demon .15 .40
☐ 84 Lister Demon .15 .40
☐ 85 The Scourge .15 .40
☐ 86 Barney .15 .40
☐ 87 Kungai Demon .15 .40
☐ 88 Haxil Demon .15 .40
☐ 89 Vocah .15 .40
☐ 90 Checklist .15 .40

2000 Angel Season One Autographs

COMPLETE SET (6) 250.00 500.00
RANDOM INSERTS IN PACKS

☐ A1 David Boreanaz 125.00 300.00
☐ A2 Alexis Denisof 15.00 40.00
☐ A3 Glenn Quinn 40.00 100.00
☐ A4 Elizabeth Rohm 20.00 50.00
☐ A5 James Marsters 20.00 50.00
☐ A6 Christian Kane 15.00 40.00

2000 Angel Season One Dark Avengers

COMPLETE SET (9) 15.00 40.00

☐ DA1 Angel 2.00 5.00
☐ DA2 Angel 2.00 5.00
☐ DA3 Angel 2.00 5.00
☐ DA4 Doyle 2.00 5.00
☐ DA5 Doyle 2.00 5.00
☐ DA6 Wesley 2.00 5.00
☐ DA7 Wesley 2.00 5.00
☐ DA8 Cordelia 2.00 5.00
☐ DA9 Cordelia 2.00 5.00

2000 Angel Season One I Love L.A.

COMPLETE SET (6) 15.00 40.00

☐ LA1 Cordelia 3.00 8.00
☐ LA2 Cordelia 3.00 8.00
☐ LA3 Cordelia 3.00 8.00
☐ LA4 Cordelia 3.00 8.00
☐ LA5 Cordelia 3.00 8.00
☐ LA6 Cordelia 3.00 8.00

2000 The Best of The Wild Wild West Season One

COMPLETE SET (100) 5.00 12.00

☐ 1 The Night of the Murderous Spring .15 .40
☐ 2 The Night of the Murderous Spring .15 .40
☐ 3 The Night of the Murderous Spring .15 .40
☐ 4 The Night of the Murderous Spring .15 .40
☐ 5 The Night of the Murderous Spring .15 .40
☐ 6 The Night of the Murderous Spring .15 .40
☐ 7 The Night of the Murderous Spring .15 .40
☐ 8 The Night of the Murderous Spring .15 .40
☐ 9 The Night of the Murderous Spring .15 .40
☐ 10 The Night of the Deadly Bed .15 .40
☐ 11 The Night of the Deadly Bed .15 .40
☐ 12 The Night of the Deadly Bed .15 .40
☐ 13 The Night of the Deadly Bed .15 .40
☐ 14 The Night of the Deadly Bed .15 .40
☐ 15 The Night of the Deadly Bed .15 .40
☐ 16 The Night of the Deadly Bed .15 .40
☐ 17 The Night of the Deadly Bed .15 .40
☐ 18 The Night of the Deadly Bed .15 .40
☐ 19 The Night of the Whirring Death .15 .40
☐ 20 The Night of the Whirring Death .15 .40
☐ 21 The Night of the Whirring Death .15 .40
☐ 22 The Night of the Whirring Death .15 .40
☐ 23 The Night of the Whirring Death .15 .40
☐ 24 The Night of the Whirring Death .15 .40
☐ 25 The Night of the Whirring Death .15 .40

❑ 26 The Night of the Whirring Death .15 .40
❑ 27 The Night of the Whirring Death .15 .40
❑ 28 The Night of the Steel Assassin .15 .40
❑ 29 The Night of the Steel Assassin .15 .40
❑ 30 The Night of the Steel Assassin .15 .40
❑ 31 The Night of the Steel Assassin .15 .40
❑ 32 The Night of the Steel Assassin .15 .40
❑ 33 The Night of the Steel Assassin .15 .40
❑ 34 The Night of the Steel Assassin .15 .40
❑ 35 The Night of the Steel Assassin .15 .40
❑ 36 The Night of the Steel Assassin .15 .40
❑ 37 The Night of the Torture Chamber .15 .40
❑ 38 The Night of the Torture Chamber .15 .40
❑ 39 The Night of the Torture Chamber .15 .40
❑ 40 The Night of the Torture Chamber .15 .40
❑ 41 The Night of the Torture Chamber .15 .40
❑ 42 The Night of the Torture Chamber .15 .40
❑ 43 The Night of the Torture Chamber .15 .40
❑ 44 The Night of the Torture Chamber .15 .40
❑ 45 The Night of the Torture Chamber .15 .40
❑ 46 The Night of the Freebooters .15 .40
❑ 47 The Night of the Freebooters .15 .40
❑ 48 The Night of the Freebooters .15 .40
❑ 49 The Night of the Freebooters .15 .40
❑ 50 The Night of the Freebooters .15 .40
❑ 51 The Night of the Freebooters .15 .40
❑ 52 The Night of the Freebooters .15 .40
❑ 53 The Night of the Freebooters .15 .40
❑ 54 The Night of the Freebooters .15 .40
❑ 55 The Night the Wizard Shook the Earth .15 .40
❑ 56 The Night the Wizard Shook the Earth .15 .40
❑ 57 The Night the Wizard Shook the Earth .15 .40
❑ 58 The Night the Wizard Shook the Earth .15 .40
❑ 59 The Night the Wizard Shook the Earth .15 .40
❑ 60 The Night the Wizard Shook the Earth .15 .40
❑ 61 The Night the Wizard Shook the Earth .15 .40
❑ 62 The Night the Wizard Shook the Earth .15 .40
❑ 63 The Night the Wizard Shook the Earth .15 .40
❑ 64 The Night of the Puppeteer .15 .40
❑ 65 The Night of the Puppeteer .15 .40
❑ 66 The Night of the Puppeteer .15 .40
❑ 67 The Night of the Puppeteer .15 .40
❑ 68 The Night of the Puppeteer .15 .40
❑ 69 The Night of the Puppeteer .15 .40
❑ 70 The Night of the Puppeteer .15 .40
❑ 71 The Night of the Puppeteer .15 .40
❑ 72 The Night of the Puppeteer .15 .40
❑ 73 The Night of the Druid's Blood .15 .40
❑ 74 The Night of the Druid's Blood .15 .40
❑ 75 The Night of the Druid's Blood .15 .40
❑ 76 The Night of the Druid's Blood .15 .40
❑ 77 The Night of the Druid's Blood .15 .40
❑ 78 The Night of the Druid's Blood .15 .40
❑ 79 The Night of the Druid's Blood .15 .40
❑ 80 The Night of the Druid's Blood .15 .40
❑ 81 The Night of the Druid's Blood .15 .40
❑ 82 The Night of the Grand Emir .15 .40
❑ 83 The Night of the Grand Emir .15 .40
❑ 84 The Night of the Grand Emir .15 .40
❑ 85 The Night of the Grand Emir .15 .40
❑ 86 The Night of the Grand Emir .15 .40
❑ 87 The Night of the Grand Emir .15 .40
❑ 88 The Night of the Grand Emir .15 .40
❑ 89 The Night of the Grand Emir .15 .40
❑ 90 The Night of the Grand Emir .15 .40
❑ 91 The Night the Terror Stalked the Town .15 .40
❑ 92 The Night the Terror Stalked the Town .15 .40
❑ 93 The Night the Terror Stalked the Town .15 .40
❑ 94 The Night the Terror Stalked the Town .15 .40
❑ 95 The Night the Terror Stalked the Town .15 .40
❑ 96 The Night the Terror Stalked the Town .15 .40
❑ 97 The Night the Terror Stalked the Town .15 .40
❑ 98 The Night the Terror Stalked the Town .15 .40
❑ 99 The Night the Terror Stalked the Town .15 .40
❑ 100 Checklist .15 .40

2000 The Best of The Wild Wild West Season One Autographs

COMPLETE SET (14) 150.00 300.00
RANDOM INSERTS IN PACKS

❑ A1 Robert Conrad 15.00 30.00
❑ A2 Yvonne Craig 15.00 30.00
❑ A3 Lloyd Bochner 10.00 25.00
❑ A4 Jean Hale 10.00 25.00
❑ A5 Richard Kiel 15.00 30.00
❑ A6 Phoebe Dorin 10.00 25.00
❑ A7 J.D. Cannon 10.00 25.00
❑ A8 BarBara Luna 15.00 30.00
❑ A9 Bob Herron 10.00 25.00
❑ A10 Sigrid Valdis 10.00 25.00
❑ A11 Henry Beckman 10.00 25.00
❑ A12 Sue Ane Langdon 10.00 25.00
❑ A13 William Campbell 10.00 25.00
❑ A14 Don Rickles 20.00 40.00

2000 The Best of The Wild Wild West Season One Case Toppers

COMPLETE SET (5) 10.00 25.00
STATED ODDS ONE PER CASE

❑ T1 Wild Wild West Opening 2.50 6.00
❑ T2 Wild Wild West Opening 2.50 6.00
❑ T3 Wild Wild West Opening 2.50 6.00
❑ T4 Wild Wild West Opening 2.50 6.00
❑ T5 Wild Wild West Opening 2.50 6.00

2000 The Best of The Wild Wild West Season One Commemorative

COMPLETE SET (2) 6.00 15.00
STATED ODDS 1:36

❑ C1 Ross Martin 4.00 10.00
❑ C2 Michael Dunn 4.00 10.00

2000 The Best of The Wild Wild West Season One Master of Disguise

COMPLETE SET (9) 7.50 20.00
STATED ODDS 1:6

❑ M1 Artemus Gordon 1.00 2.50
❑ M2 Artemus Gordon 1.00 2.50
❑ M3 Artemus Gordon 1.00 2.50
❑ M4 Artemus Gordon 1.00 2.50
❑ M5 Artemus Gordon 1.00 2.50
❑ M6 Artemus Gordon 1.00 2.50
❑ M7 Artemus Gordon 1.00 2.50
❑ M8 Artemus Gordon 1.00 2.50
❑ M9 Artemus Gordon 1.00 2.50

2000 The Best of The Wild Wild West Season One Promos

COMPLETE SET (2) 2.00 5.00

❑ P1 Wild Wild West 1.25 3.00
❑ P2 Wild Wild West 1.25 3.00

2000 The Best of The Wild Wild West Season One Vintage West

COMPLETE SET (9) 5.00 12.00
STATED ODDS 1:4

❑ W1 James T. West .75 2.00
❑ W2 James T. West .75 2.00
❑ W3 James T. West .75 2.00
❑ W4 James T. West .75 2.00
❑ W5 James T. West .75 2.00
❑ W6 James T. West .75 2.00
❑ W7 James T. West .75 2.00
❑ W8 James T. West .75 2.00
❑ W9 James T. West .75 2.00

2000 Buffy the Vampire Slayer Reflections

COMPLETE SET (72) 6.00 15.00

❑ 1 Reflections .15 .40
❑ 2 Destiny Free .15 .40
❑ 3 Not Again .15 .40
❑ 4 Beautiful Stranger .15 .40
❑ 5 A Little Death .15 .40
❑ 6 Lost Innocence .15 .40
❑ 7 Slayer's Duty .15 .40
❑ 8 Tested .15 .40
❑ 9 Protector .15 .40
❑ 10 Librarian .15 .40
❑ 11 Romantic .15 .40
❑ 12 Magician .15 .40
❑ 13 Wounded .15 .40
❑ 14 Ripper .15 .40
❑ 15 Devoted .15 .40
❑ 16 Fighter .15 .40
❑ 17 Dedicated .15 .40
❑ 18 Closing .15 .40
❑ 19 Shopper .15 .40
❑ 20 Digital Gal .15 .40
❑ 21 Xander's Pal .15 .40
❑ 22 Invisible Girl .15 .40
❑ 23 Disillusioned .15 .40
❑ 24 Wicked Willow .15 .40
❑ 25 Oz's Girlfriend .15 .40
❑ 26 Tough Cookie .15 .40
❑ 27 Worthy Wicca .15 .40
❑ 28 Doofus .15 .40
❑ 29 Savior .15 .40
❑ 30 G.I.Guy .15 .40
❑ 31 Jock .15 .40
❑ 32 Xander and Cordie .15 .40
❑ 33 Xander and Willow .15 .40
❑ 34 Xander and Faith .15 .40
❑ 35 Xander and Anya .15 .40
❑ 36 True .15 .40
❑ 37 Leader .15 .40
❑ 38 Spirited .15 .40
❑ 39 Lonely .15 .40
❑ 40 Loving .15 .40
❑ 41 Vicious .15 .40
❑ 42 Wounded .15 .40
❑ 43 Wronged .15 .40
❑ 44 Watching the Watcher .15 .40
❑ 45 Working Class .15 .40
❑ 46 Starcrossed .15 .40
❑ 47 Rescuer .15 .40
❑ 48 Ageless .15 .40
❑ 49 Killer .15 .40
❑ 50 To Hell .15 .40
❑ 51 And Back .15 .40
❑ 52 Redeemed .15 .40
❑ 53 Renewed .15 .40
❑ 54 Farewell .15 .40
❑ 55 The Master .15 .40
❑ 56 The Anointed One .15 .40
❑ 57 Spike .15 .40
❑ 58 Drusilla .15 .40
❑ 59 Ethan Rayne .15 .40
❑ 60 Acathla .15 .40
❑ 61 Kakistos .15 .40
❑ 62 Faith .15 .40
❑ 63 Mayor Wilkins .15 .40
❑ 64 Joyce, Her Mom .15 .40
❑ 65 Harmony, The Snob .15 .40
❑ 66 Jenny, The Gypsy .15 .40
❑ 67 Amy, The Witch .15 .40
❑ 68 Kendra, The Other Slayer .15 .40
❑ 69 Wesley, The Watcher .15 .40
❑ 70 Oz, The Guitarist .15 .40
❑ 71 Jonathan Levenson, Classmate .15 .40
❑ 72 Checklist .15 .40

2000 Buffy the Vampire Slayer Reflections Autographs

❑ A1 Anthony Stewart Head 50.00 100.00
❑ A2 Eliza Dushku 100.00 200.00
❑ A3 Armin Shimerman 25.00 50.00
❑ A4 Harry Groener 10.00 20.00
❑ A5 Serena Scott Thomas 10.00 20.00
❑ A6 Juliet Landau 25.00 50.00

2000 Buffy the Vampire Slayer Reflections Portrait of a Slayer

COMPLETE SET (9) 15.00 40.00
STATED ODDS 1:11

❑ S1 Portrait of a Slayer 2.50 6.00
❑ S2 Portrait of a Slayer 2.50 6.00
❑ S3 Portrait of a Slayer 2.50 6.00
❑ S4 Portrait of a Slayer 2.50 6.00
❑ S5 Portrait of a Slayer 2.50 6.00
❑ S6 Portrait of a Slayer 2.50 6.00
❑ S7 Portrait of a Slayer 2.50 6.00
❑ S8 Portrait of a Slayer 2.50 6.00
❑ S9 Portrait of a Slayer 2.50 6.00

2000 Buffy the Vampire Slayer Reflections Promos

COMPLETE SET (3) 4.00 10.00

❑ P1 Buffy 2.00 5.00
❑ P2 Buffy & Angel 2.00 5.00
❑ P3 Buffy 2.00 5.00

2000 Buffy the Vampire Slayer Reflections Slayer's Journal

COMPLETE SET (6) 10.00 25.00
STATED ODDS 1:17

❑ J1 First Look 2.50 6.00
❑ J2 First Kiss 2.50 6.00
❑ J3 Lost Innocence 2.50 6.00
❑ J4 Lost Hope 2.50 6.00
❑ J5 Big Choice 2.50 6.00
❑ J6 Graduation Day 2.50 6.00

2000 Buffy the Vampire Slayer Season Four

COMPLETE SET (90) 5.00 12.00

❑ 1 Freshman Year .15 .40
❑ 2 Disorientation .15 .40
❑ 3 Uprooted .15 .40
❑ 4 Settling In .15 .40
❑ 5 Roomies .15 .40
❑ 6 Uncompromising .15 .40
❑ 7 Unacceptable .15 .40
❑ 8 Relationship Issues .15 .40
❑ 9 Lack Of Commitment .15 .40
❑ 10 Aftermath .15 .40
❑ 11 Scary Stuff .15 .40
❑ 12 Convincing Illusion .15 .40
❑ 13 Unimposing .15 .40
❑ 14 Basic Instincts .15 .40
❑ 15 Hair Of The Dog .15 .40
❑ 16 Blunt Object .15 .40
❑ 17 Tracking The Scent .15 .40
❑ 18 Animal Magnetism .15 .40
❑ 19 Blood Will Tell .15 .40
❑ 20 Situation .15 .40
❑ 21 Strategy .15 .40
❑ 22 Containment .15 .40
❑ 23 Guardian Angel .15 .40
❑ 24 Huddled Masses .15 .40
❑ 25 Avenging Spirit .15 .40
❑ 26 Hello Heartbreak .15 .40
❑ 27 Topsy-Turvy .15 .40
❑ 28 Love Is Blind .15 .40
❑ 29 Talk, Talk .15 .40
❑ 30 Kind Of A Hush .15 .40
❑ 31 Say My Name .15 .40
❑ 32 I Feel The Earth Move .15 .40
❑ 33 End Of The World As We Know It .15 .40
❑ 34 Apocalype, Now .15 .40
❑ 35 Old And In The Way .15 .40
❑ 36 Testing Limits .15 .40
❑ 37 Caught In The Middle .15 .40
❑ 38 Team Player? .15 .40
❑ 39 Maggie's Team .15 .40
❑ 40 Endgame .15 .40
❑ 41 No Trust .15 .40
❑ 42 No Replace .15 .40
❑ 43 No Answers .15 .40
❑ 44 These Dreams .15 .40
❑ 45 She's Baaaack! .15 .40
❑ 46 Parting Gift .15 .40
❑ 47 Mirror, Mirror .15 .40
❑ 48 Walk This Way .15 .40
❑ 49 Goody Two Shoes .15 .40
❑ 50 Mr. Perfect .15 .40
❑ 51 The Dark Side .15 .40
❑ 52 Reality Check .15 .40
❑ 53 Fever .15 .40
❑ 54 Frenzy .15 .40
❑ 55 Phantoms .15 .40
❑ 56 Self-Control .15 .40
❑ 57 Prejudice .15 .40
❑ 58 Ironic .15 .40
❑ 59 Minor Details .15 .40
❑ 60 Insidious .15 .40
❑ 61 Discord .15 .40
❑ 62 Lonely .15 .40
❑ 63 Unity .15 .40
❑ 64 The One .15 .40
❑ 65 To Sleep .15 .40
❑ 66 Perchance To Dream .15 .40
❑ 67 Buffy Summers .15 .40
❑ 68 Willow Rosenberg .15 .40
❑ 69 Rupert Giles .15 .40
❑ 70 Xander Harris .15 .40
❑ 71 Anya .15 .40
❑ 72 Tara .15 .40
❑ 73 Slayer Engaged To Foe .15 .40
❑ 74 Lovelorn Wicca Seeks New Friend .15 .40
❑ 75 Jonathanapalooza .15 .40
❑ 76 Jonathan: Uncovered .15 .40
❑ 77 Fashion Emergency .15 .40
❑ 78 Ex-Watcher Goes Native .15 .40
❑ 79 Professor Maggie Walsh .15 .40
❑ 80 Riley Finn .15 .40
❑ 81 Col. Mcnamara .15 .40
❑ 82 Close To The Edge .15 .40
❑ 83 Dangerous Liaisons .15 .40
❑ 84 Identity Crisis .15 .40
❑ 85 Gachnar .15 .40
❑ 86 D'Hoffryn .15 .40
❑ 87 The Gentlemen .15 .40
❑ 88 Vahrall Demon .15 .40
❑ 89 Adam .15 .40
❑ 90 Checklist .15 .40

2000 Buffy the Vampire Slayer Season Four Autographs

COMPLETE SET (6) 150.00 250.00
RANDOM INSERTS IN PACKS

❑ A16 Emma Caulfield 25.00 50.00
❑ A17 Lindsay Crouse 25.00 50.00
❑ A18 Adam Kaufman 25.00 50.00
❑ A19 Danny Strong 25.00 50.00
❑ A20 Mercedes Mcnab 25.00 50.00
❑ A21 Marc Blucas 25.00 50.00

2000 Buffy the Vampire Slayer Season Four New Beginnings

COMPLETE SET (9) 15.00 40.00
STATED ODDS 1:11

❑ NB1 New Beginnings 2.50 6.00
❑ NB2 New Beginnings 2.50 6.00
❑ NB3 New Beginnings 2.50 6.00
❑ NB4 New Beginnings 2.50 6.00
❑ NB5 New Beginnings 2.50 6.00
❑ NB6 New Beginnings 2.50 6.00
❑ NB7 New Beginnings 2.50 6.00
❑ NB8 New Beginnings 2.50 6.00
❑ NB9 New Beginnings 2.50 6.00

2000 Buffy the Vampire Slayer Season Four Promos

COMPLETE SET (7) 6.00 15.00

❑ B4-0 Buffy 1.25 3.00
❑ B4-1 Buffy 1.25 3.00
❑ B4-2 Buffy 1.25 3.00
❑ B4-3 Buffy 1.25 3.00
❑ SFX2 Buffy 1.25 3.00
❑ SD2000 Cast 1.25 3.00
❑ WW2000 Cast 1.25 3.00

2000 Buffy the Vampire Slayer Season Four The Ritual of Enjoining

COMPLETE SET (6) 10.00 25.00
STATED ODDS 1:17

❑ R1 The Kuhlina Ritual 2.00 5.00
❑ R2 Animus 2.00 5.00
❑ R3 Sophus 2.00 5.00
❑ R4 Spiritus 2.00 5.00
❑ R5 Manus 2.00 5.00
❑ R6 Aftermath 2.00 5.00

2000 Charmed Season One

COMPLETE SET (72) 5.00 12.00

❑ 1 Title Card .15 .40
❑ 2 Spirited Sisters .15 .40
❑ 3 Why Be Normal? .15 .40
❑ 4 Captivating .15 .40
❑ 5 Forever Young .15 .40
❑ 6 Daddy Dearest .15 .40
❑ 7 Appearances Deceive .15 .40
❑ 8 Momma Told Me .15 .40
❑ 9 Bad Timing .15 .40
❑ 10 A Dream Walking .15 .40
❑ 11 No Rest .15 .40
❑ 12 Devil To Pay .15 .40
❑ 13 Wedding Bell Blues .15 .40
❑ 14 Hey Little Sister .15 .40
❑ 15 Divide And Conquer .15 .40
❑ 16 Nothing But .15 .40
❑ 17 The Whole Truth .15 .40
❑ 18 Blast From The Past .15 .40
❑ 19 To Thine Own Self .15 .40
❑ 20 Prime Suspect .15 .40
❑ 21 The Calvary Arrives .15 .40
❑ 22 Walk Like An Egyptian Urn .15 .40
❑ 23 Second Chances .15 .40
❑ 24 The Claws That Scratch .15 .40
❑ 25 Heart Of Ice .15 .40
❑ 26 Triskaidekaphobia .15 .40
❑ 27 Face Your Fear .15 .40
❑ 28 Conflict Of Interest .15 .40
❑ 29 Peace With The Past .15 .40
❑ 30 Who's Down There .15 .40
❑ 31 Blinded By The Light .15 .40
❑ 32 Knockout .15 .40
❑ 33 Triple Threat .15 .40
❑ 34 Generations .15 .40
❑ 35 Fighting Fate .15 .40
❑ 36 Mr. Wrong? .15 .40
❑ 37 Higher Authority .15 .40
❑ 38 Investigative Reporting .15 .40
❑ 39 Grimlocks .15 .40
❑ 40 On Their Own .15 .40
❑ 41 The Other Side .15 .40
❑ 42 Whitelighter, Darklighter .15 .40
❑ 43 The Power Of Love .15 .40
❑ 44 Love You Always .15 .40
❑ 45 Andy's Sacrifice .15 .40
❑ 46 Javna .15 .40
❑ 47 Hecate .15 .40
❑ 48 Yama .15 .40
❑ 49 Kali .15 .40
❑ 50 Wendigo .15 .40
❑ 51 Barbas .15 .40
❑ 52 Woogy .15 .40
❑ 53 Nicholas .15 .40
❑ 54 Gabriel, Lord Of War .15 .40
❑ 55 Soul Ferrying Demon .15 .40
❑ 56 Tempus .15 .40
❑ 57 Rex And Hannah .15 .40
❑ 58 Prudence Halliwell .15 .40
❑ 59 Piper Halliwell .15 .40
❑ 60 Phoebe Halliwell .15 .40
❑ 61 Inspector Andy Trudeau .15 .40
❑ 62 Inspector Darryl Morris .15 .40
❑ 63 Leo Wyatt .15 .40
❑ 64 Little Prudence .15 .40
❑ 65 Little Piper .15 .40
❑ 66 Little Phoebe .15 .40
❑ 67 Victor .15 .40
❑ 68 Patty Halliwell .15 .40
❑ 69 Penny Halliwell .15 .40
❑ 70 Kit .15 .40
❑ 71 Melinda Warren .15 .40
❑ 72 Checklist .15 .40
❑ S1 Spirit Board .15 .40

2000 Charmed Season One Autographs

COMPLETE SET (6) 200.00 400.00
RANDOM INSERTS IN PACKS

❑ A1 Shannen Doherty 60.00 120.00
❑ A2 Holly Marie Combs 100.00 200.00
❑ A4 T.W. King 12.50 30.00
❑ A5 Brian Krause 12.50 30.00
❑ A6 Dorian Gregory 12.50 30.00
❑ A7 David Carradine 12.50 30.00

2000 Charmed Season One Promos

COMPLETE SET (8) 10.00 25.00

❑ P1 Piper, Prue, & Phoebe 1.50 4.00
❑ P2 Piper, Prue, & Phoebe 1.50 4.00
❑ ML1 Phoebe, Prue, & Piper 1.50 4.00
❑ P0a Phoebe, Prue, & Piper no TM 1.50 4.00
❑ P0b Phoebe, Prue, & Piper w TM 1.50 4.00
❑ PB1 Phoebe, Prue, & Piper 1.50 4.00
❑ SF1 Piper, Prue, & Phoebe 1.50 4.00
❑ NSU1 Piper, Prue, & Phoebe FOIL 1.50 4.00

2000 Charmed Season One The Book of Shadows

COMPLETE SET (6) 15.00 40.00
STATED ODDS 1:18

❑ B1 Book of Shadows 4.00 10.00
❑ B2 Book of Shadows 4.00 10.00
❑ B3 Book of Shadows 4.00 10.00
❑ B4 Book of Shadows 4.00 10.00
❑ B5 Book of Shadows 4.00 10.00
❑ B6 Book of Shadows 4.00 10.00

2000 Charmed Season One The Charmed Ones

COMPLETE SET (9) 20.00 50.00
STATED ODDS 1:11

❑ P1 The Charmed Ones 3.00 8.00
❑ P2 The Charmed Ones 3.00 8.00
❑ P3 The Charmed Ones 3.00 8.00
❑ P4 The Charmed Ones 3.00 8.00
❑ P5 The Charmed Ones 3.00 8.00
❑ P6 The Charmed Ones 3.00 8.00
❑ P7 The Charmed Ones 3.00 8.00
❑ P8 The Charmed Ones 3.00 8.00
❑ P9 The Charmed Ones 3.00 8.00

2000 Farscape In Motion Lenticular Preview

COMPLETE SET (9) 7.50 20.00

❑ M1 An Obsession Begins 1.25 3.00
❑ M2 Prepare For Starburst 1.25 3.00
❑ M3 Pilot In Control 1.25 3.00
❑ M4 Sharing Moyas Pain 1.25 3.00
❑ M5 Marauder In Pursuit 1.25 3.00
❑ M6 The Qualta Unsheathed 1.25 3.00
❑ M7 Aeryn Sun 1.25 3.00
❑ M8 In The Spirit Of Rygel The First 1.25 3.00
❑ M9 Where Is Home? 1.25 3.00

2000 Farscape Season One

COMPLETE SET (72) 5.00 12.00
PM1 STATED ODDS 1:36

❑ 1 Farscape Cast Montage .15 .40
❑ 2 Farscape Cast Montage .15 .40
❑ 3 Farscape Cast Montage .15 .40
❑ 4 Premiere .15 .40
❑ 5 Premiere .15 .40
❑ 6 Premiere .15 .40
❑ 7 I, ET .15 .40
❑ 8 I, ET .15 .40
❑ 9 I, ET .15 .40
❑ 10 Exodus From Genesis .15 .40
❑ 11 Exodus From Genesis .15 .40
❑ 12 Exodus From Genesis .15 .40
❑ 13 Throne For A Loss .15 .40
❑ 14 Throne For A Loss .15 .40
❑ 15 Throne For A Loss .15 .40
❑ 16 Back And Back And Back To The Future .15 .40
❑ 17 Back And Back And Back To The Future .15 .40
❑ 18 Back And Back And Back To The Future .15 .40
❑ 19 Thank God Its Friday Again .15 .40
❑ 20 Thank God Its Friday Again .15 .40
❑ 21 Thank God Its Friday Again .15 .40
❑ 22 PK Tech Girl .15 .40
❑ 23 PK Tech Girl .15 .40
❑ 24 PK Tech Girl .15 .40
❑ 25 That Old Black Magic .15 .40
❑ 26 That Old Black Magic .15 .40
❑ 27 That Old Black Magic .15 .40
❑ 28 DNA Mad Scientist .15 .40
❑ 29 DNA Mad Scientist .15 .40
❑ 30 DNA Mad Scientist .15 .40
❑ 31 They've Got A Secret .15 .40
❑ 32 They've Got A Secret .15 .40
❑ 33 They've Got A Secret .15 .40
❑ 34 Til The Blood Runs Clear .15 .40
❑ 35 Til The Blood Runs Clear .15 .40
❑ 36 Til The Blood Runs Clear .15 .40
❑ 37 Rhapsody In Blue .15 .40
❑ 38 Rhapsody In Blue .15 .40
❑ 39 Rhapsody In Blue .15 .40
❑ 40 The Flax .15 .40
❑ 41 The Flax .15 .40
❑ 42 The Flax .15 .40
❑ 43 Jeremiah Crichton .15 .40
❑ 44 Jeremiah Crichton .15 .40
❑ 45 Jeremiah Crichton .15 .40
❑ 46 Durka Returns .15 .40
❑ 47 Durka Returns .15 .40
❑ 48 Durka Returns .15 .40
❑ 49 A Human Reaction .15 .40
❑ 50 A Human Reaction .15 .40
❑ 51 A Human Reaction .15 .40
❑ 52 Through The Looking Glass .15 .40
❑ 53 Through The Looking Glass .15 .40
❑ 54 Through The Looking Glass .15 .40
❑ 55 A Bug's Life .15 .40
❑ 56 A Bug's Life .15 .40
❑ 57 A Bug's Life .15 .40
❑ 58 Nerve .15 .40
❑ 59 Nerve .15 .40
❑ 60 Nerve .15 .40
❑ 61 A Hidden Memory .15 .40
❑ 62 A Hidden Memory .15 .40
❑ 63 A Hidden Memory .15 .40
❑ 64 Bone To Be Wild .15 .40
❑ 65 Bone To Be Wild .15 .40
❑ 66 Bone To Be Wild .15 .40
❑ 67 Family Ties .15 .40
❑ 68 Family Ties .15 .40
❑ 69 Family Ties .15 .40
❑ 70 Checklist 1 .15 .40
❑ 71 Checklist 2 .15 .40
❑ 72 Checklist 3 .15 .40
❑ PM1 Farscape in Motion PROMO 2.00 5.00

2000 Farscape Season One Autographs

COMPLETE SET (5) 100.00 200.00
STATED ODDS 1:72
A5 ISSUED IN COLLECTORS ALBUM

❑ A1 Ben Browder 30.00 60.00
❑ A2 Anthony Simcoe 30.00 60.00
❑ A3 Gigi Edgley 30.00 60.00
❑ A4 Brian Henson 10.00 25.00
❑ A5 Rockne S. O'Bannon/ (issued in collectors album) 10.00 25.00

2000 Farscape Season One Behind the Scenes

COMPLETE SET (9) 10.00 25.00
STATED ODDS 1:6

❑ BTS1 Rockne S. O'Bannon on The Genesis of Farscape 1.50 4.00
❑ BTS2 Rockne S. O'Bannon on Moya (Part 1) 1.50 4.00
❑ BTS3 Rockne S. O'Bannon on Moya (Part 2) 1.50 4.00
❑ BTS4 Rockne S. O'Bannon on Ben Browder 1.50 4.00
❑ BTS5 Rockne S. O'Bannon on Aeryn Sun 1.50 4.00
❑ BTS6 Rockne S. O'Bannon on Farscape's Animatronics 1.50 4.00
❑ BTS7 Rockne S. O'Bannon on Plot Development 1.50 4.00
❑ BTS8 Rockne S. O'Bannon on Scorpius and Chiana 1.50 4.00
❑ BTS9 Rockne S. O'Bannon on Crais 1.50 4.00

2000 Farscape Season One Farscape Stars
COMPLETE SET (9) 6.00 15.00
STATED ODDS 1:4
FS1 Commander John Crichton 1.00 2.50
FS2 Officer Aeryn Sun 1.00 2.50
FS3 General Ka D'Argo 1.00 2.50
FS4 Pa'u Zotoh Zhaan 1.00 2.50
FS5 Rygel The XVI 1.00 2.50
FS6 Chiana 1.00 2.50
FS7 Captain Crais 1.00 2.50
FS8 Scorpius 1.00 2.50
FS9 Pilot 1.00 2.50

2000 Farscape Season One From The Archives Costumes
COMPLETE SET (7) 100.00 250.00
STATED ODDS ONE PER BOX
C7 ISSUED AS CASE TOPPER
C1 John Crichton 20.00 50.00
C2 Aeryn Sun 20.00 50.00
C3 Pa'u Zotoh Zhaan 10.00 25.00
C4 D'Argo 10.00 25.00
C5 Rygel 10.00 25.00
C6 Crais 20.00 50.00
C7 Chiana/ (issued as case topper) 30.00 60.00

2000 Farscape Season One Promos
COMPLETE SET (4) 4.00 10.00
P1 Zhaan/ (Non-Sport Update) .75 2.50
P2 Aeryn Sun/ (Album Exclusive) .75 2.50
TV1 Zhaan/ (Action Figure) 1.50 4.00
DVD1 Group of seven/ (DVD Exclusive) 1.50 4.00

2000 Farscape Season One Season Two Preview
COMPLETE SET (9) 15.00 40.00
STATED ODDS 1:8
P1 John Crichton 2.00 5.00
P2 Aeryn Sun 2.00 5.00
P3 D'Argo 2.00 5.00
P4 Pa'u Zotoh Zhaan 2.00 5.00
P5 Chiana 2.00 5.00
P6 Rygel 2.00 5.00
P7 Pilot 2.00 5.00
P8 Crais 2.00 5.00
P9 Scorpius 2.00 5.00

2000 Lara Croft Tomb Raider
COMPLETE SET (90) 5.00 12.00
BL1 STATED ODDS ONE PER BOX
1 Title Card .15 .40
2 The Illuminati Convene .15 .40
3 Kill Lara Croft! .15 .40
4 Lara's Party Mix .15 .40
5 Bryce .15 .40
6 Hillary .15 .40
7 Never A Good Day .15 .40
8 Viewing The Heavens .15 .40
9 A Dream Journey .15 .40
10 Time Past .15 .40
11 Dream Quest .15 .40
12 No Rest For Bryce .15 .40
13 The Mystery Of The Old Clock .15 .40
14 All Seeing Eye .15 .40
15 The Illuminati .15 .40
16 Road Show .15 .40
17 A Familiar Rival .15 .40
18 Expert Advice .15 .40
19 Meet Mr. Pimms .15 .40
20 Not So Ignorant .15 .40
21 Back At Croft Manor .15 .40
22 Betrayal Upon Betrayal .15 .40
23 Aerial Ballet .15 .40
24 Home Invasion .15 .40
25 Under Siege .15 .40
26 Ripped Off .15 .40
27 Friendly Fire .15 .40
28 The Dust Settles .15 .40
29 Secrets Revealed .15 .40
30 On The Trail .15 .40
31 In The Ruins .15 .40
32 Calculating Approach .15 .40
33 Unexpected Advice .15 .40
34 At The Heart .15 .40
35 Turn Back .15 .40
36 Protectors Of The Tomb .15 .40
37 Countdown .15 .40
38 Believing A Lie .15 .40
39 Handoff .15 .40
40 Sure Shot .15 .40
41 Showdown .15 .40
42 Catch! .15 .40
43 On The Edge .15 .40
44 Up The River .15 .40
45 May I Make A Call? .15 .40
46 Making A Connection .15 .40
47 Speak Of The Devil .15 .40
48 Calculated Risk .15 .40
49 A Moment's Pause .15 .40
50 At The Temple .15 .40
51 Secrets Revealed .15 .40
52 A Challenge .15 .40
53 The Offer .15 .40
54 The Expedition .15 .40
55 Northernmost .15 .40
56 Another Warning .15 .40
57 Crossing The Ice .15 .40
58 The Trek Continues .15 .40
59 Tough Sledding .15 .40
60 Dashing Through The Snow .15 .40
61 The Moment Arrives .15 .40
62 Entering The Tomb .15 .40
63 The Orrery .15 .40
64 Getting Warmer .15 .40
65 Targeted .15 .40
66 Coup D'Etat .15 .40
67 Incomplete .15 .40
68 Heart-Rending .15 .40
69 In The Timestorm .15 .40
70 A Fix In Time .15 .40
71 A Rarity Indeed .15 .40
72 The Adventure Continues .15 .40
73 Cambodia S.U.V. .15 .40
74 Lara's Sports Car .15 .40
75 Lara's Motorcycle .15 .40
76 S.I.M.O.N. .15 .40
77 Lara's Headset .15 .40
78 Lara's Pistols .15 .40
79 Lara's Shades .15 .40
80 Jon Voight .15 .40
81 Angelina Jolie .15 .40
82 Bungee Ballet: Director's Vision .15 .40
83 Bungee Ballet: Preparation .15 .40
84 Bungee Ballet: All Aj .15 .40
85 In The Cambodian Tomb .15 .40
86 Surfing The Log .15 .40
87 Not So Simple .15 .40
88 Reservations .15 .40
89 On Location .15 .40
90 Checklist .15 .40
BL1 Lara Croft Tomb Raider

2000 Lara Croft Tomb Raider Autographs
COMPLETE SET (4) 300.00 600.00
RANDOM INSERTS IN PACKS
A1 Angelina Jolie 300.00 550.00
A2 Leslie Phillips 20.00 40.00
A3 Julian Rhind-Tutt 20.00 40.00
A4 Chris Barrie 20.00 40.00

2000 Lara Croft Tomb Raider Pieceworks
RANDOM INSERTS IN PACKS
P1 Angelina Jolie 50.00 100.00

2000 Lara Croft Tomb Raider Puzzle Cards
COMPLETE SET (9) 12.50 30.00
STATED ODDS 1:11
LC1 Lara Croft Tomb Raider 2.00 5.00
LC2 Lara Croft Tomb Raider 2.00 5.00
LC3 Lara Croft Tomb Raider 2.00 5.00
LC4 Lara Croft Tomb Raider 2.00 5.00
LC5 Lara Croft Tomb Raider 2.00 5.00
LC6 Lara Croft Tomb Raider 2.00 5.00
LC7 Lara Croft Tomb Raider 2.00 5.00
LC8 Lara Croft Tomb Raider 2.00 5.00
LC9 Lara Croft Tomb Raider 2.00 5.00

2000 Lara Croft Tomb Raider The Quest
COMPLETE SET (6) 10.00 25.00
STATED ODDS 1:17
Q1 The Idealist 2.50 6.00
Q2 The Schemer 2.50 6.00
Q3 The Flunky 2.50 6.00
Q4 The Weak Link 2.50 6.00
Q5 The Knave 2.50 6.00
Q6 The Adventurer 2.50 6.00

2000 Lara Croft Tomb Raider Promos
COMPLETE SET (5) 6.00 15.00
TR1 Lara Croft Tomb Raider 1.50 4.00
TR2 Lara Croft Tomb Raider 1.50 4.00
TR3 Lara Croft Tomb Raider 1.50 4.00
TR4 Lara Croft Tomb Raider 1.50 4.00
TRi Lara Croft Tomb Raider 1.50 4.00

2000 Roswell Season One
COMPLETE SET (90) 5.00 12.00
RL1 STATED ODDS ONE PER BOX
1 Roswell .15 .40
2 Liz Parker .15 .40
3 Max Evans .15 .40
4 Isabel Evans .15 .40
5 Maria De Luca .15 .40
6 Michael Guerin .15 .40
7 Alex Whitman .15 .40
8 Kyle Valenti .15 .40
9 Sheriff Jim Valenti .15 .40
10 Saved By An Alien .15 .40
11 The Truth About Max .15 .40
12 Pilot .15 .40
13 Spying On A Spy .15 .40
14 Key To The Past .15 .40
15 The Morning After .15 .40
16 Suspicion .15 .40
17 The Unearthly .15 .40
18 Monsters .15 .40
19 Ganging Up On Max .15 .40
20 A Final Farewell .15 .40
21 Leaving Norman .15 .40
22 Vision On Canvas .15 .40
23 Topolsky's Mission .15 .40
24 Missing .15 .40
25 The House .15 .40
26 Out Of The Darkness .15 .40
27 285 South .15 .40
28 A Symbol Of Home .15 .40
29 The Cave .15 .40
30 River Dog .15 .40
31 The Desperate Hours .15 .40
32 Alex Saves The Day .15 .40
33 Blood Brother .15 .40
34 The Dream Dance .15 .40
35 First Kiss .15 .40
36 Heat Wave .15 .40
37 Michael's Ordeal .15 .40
38 Flash Memories .15 .40
39 The Balance .15 .40
40 Peril In The Kitchen .15 .40
41 The Big Game .15 .40
42 Toy House .15 .40
43 The Human Connection .15 .40
44 Closer To The Truth .15 .40
45 Into The Woods .15 .40
46 Roswell's Special Guest .15 .40
47 A Hunter Obsessed .15 .40
48 The Convention .15 .40
49 Love Is Universal .15 .40
50 Responding To The Signal .15 .40
51 Blind Date .15 .40
52 Battered And Bitter .15 .40
53 Striking Back .15 .40
54 Independence Day .15 .40
55 Liz's Fantasy .15 .40
56 The Orb .15 .40
57 Sexual Healing .15 .40
58 The Return Of Topolsky .15 .40
59 The Shape-Shifter .15 .40
60 Crazy .15 .40
61 Alien Seduction .15 .40
62 Valenti's Gamble .15 .40
63 Tess, Lies And Videotape .15 .40
64 The Threat Of Tess .15 .40
65 The Book .15 .40
66 Four-Square .15 .40
67 Deadly Reflections .15 .40
68 Max -- Captured! .15 .40
69 Max To The Max .15 .40
70 Tortured By Agent Pierce .15 .40
71 Isabel's Psychic Link .15 .40
72 The White Room .15 .40
73 Ruthless Protector .15 .40
74 No Place For Liz .15 .40
75 Destiny .15 .40
76 Max And Liz .15 .40
77 Michael And Maria .15 .40
78 Isabel And Alex .15 .40
79 Destined For Each Other? .15 .40
80 Kyle And Liz .15 .40
81 The Sheriff And The Ex-Hippie .15 .40
82 Resurrection .15 .40
83 Not Of This Earth .15 .40
84 Clues To Their Origin .15 .40
85 Powers From Beyond .15 .40
86 The Hand Of Life And Death .15 .40
87 The Signal .15 .40
88 Cosmic Reunion .15 .40
89 A Message From Mother .15 .40
90 Checklist .15 .40
RL1 Season Two Promo .75 2.00

2000 Roswell Season One Alien Orbs
COMPLETE SET (2) 10.00 25.00
STATED ODDS 1:72
O1 Alien Orb 6.00 15.00
O2 Alien Orb 6.00 15.00

2000 Roswell Season One Aliens Among Us
COMPLETE SET (9) 7.50 20.00
STATED ODDS 1:11
A1 Liz's Journal 1.25 3.00
A2 The Wisdom Of Max 1.25 3.00
A3 Isabel's Fearful Questions 1.25 3.00
A4 Babbling With Maria 1.25 3.00
A5 The World According To Michael 1.25 3.00
A6 Kyle In Denial 1.25 3.00
A7 In Alex's Dreams 1.25 3.00
A8 The Sheriffs Report 1.25 3.00
A9 Topolsky's Warning 1.25 3.00

2000 Roswell Season One Autographs
COMPLETE SET (6) 100.00 200.00
STATED ODDS 1:108
A1 Jonathan Frakes 15.00 40.00
A2 Shiri Appleby 15.00 40.00
A3 Colin Hanks 12.50 30.00
A4 Nick Wechsler 15.00 40.00
A5 William Sadler 12.50 30.00
A6 Julie Benz 12.50 30.00
R1 Autograph Redemption Card

2000 Roswell Season One Not Of This Earth
COMPLETE SET (6) 6.00 15.00
STATED ODDS 1:17
N1 What Lies Beneath 1.25 3.00
N2 Listening To A CD 1.25 3.00
N3 Nasedo Transforming 1.25 3.00
N4 Emerging From His Pod 1.25 3.00
N5 Attacked By An Alien 1.25 3.00
N6 Michael Uses His Powers 1.25 3.00

2000 Roswell Season One Promos
COMPLETE SET (4) 5.00 12.00
PR1 Roswell cast 1.50 4.00
PR2 Roswell cast 1.50 4.00
PR3 Roswell cast 1.50 4.00
PRi Roswell cast 1.50 4.00

2000 Seven of Nine The Women of Star Trek Extension
COMPLETE SET (5) 25.00 50.00
S1 Seven of Nine 5.00 12.00
S2 Seven of Nine 5.00 12.00
S3 Seven of Nine 5.00 12.00
S4 Seven of Nine 5.00 12.00
S5 Seven of Nine 5.00 12.00

2000 Ships Of Farscape
COMPLETE SET (9) 8.00 20.00
ANNOUNCED PRINT RUN 2,500 SETS
FS1 Moya 1.25 3.00
FS2 Talyn 1.25 3.00
FS3 Farscape One 1.25 3.00
FS4 Peacekeeper Prowler 1.25 3.00
FS5 Peacekeeper Marauder 1.25 3.00
FS6 Crais' Command Carrier 1.25 3.00
FS7 The Zelbinion 1.25 3.00
FS8 Moya's Transport Pod 1.25 3.00
FS9 Stannz's Salvage Ship 1.25 3.00

2000 The Simpsons Anniversary Celebration
COMPLETE SET (81) 5.00 12.00
T1 STATED ODDS ONE PER PACK
SC1 STATED ODDS ONE PER CASE
1 The Simpsons .15 .40
2 Good Night .15 .40
3 Making Faces .15 .40
4 Shut Up Simpsons .15 .40
5 Simpsons Premieres .15 .40
6 First Emmy .15 .40
7 Bart Gets An F .15 .40
8 Do The Bartman .15 .40
9 Stark Raving Dad .15 .40
10 Kamp Krusty .15 .40
11 Homer's Barbershop Quartet .15 .40
12 Bart Of Darkness .15 .40
13 Who Shot Mr. Burns? (Part 2) .15 .40
14 Treehouse Of Horror VII .15 .40
15 The City Of New York vs. Homer Simpson .15 .40
16 Lard Of The Dance .15 .40
17 Beyond Blunderdome .15 .40
18 Global Fan Fest .15 .40
19 Marge .15 .40
20 Grampa .15 .40
21 Homer .15 .40
22 Maggie .15 .40
23 Bart .15 .40
24 Lisa .15 .40
25 Snowball II .15 .40
26 Selma & Patty .15 .40
27 Santa's Little Helper .15 .40
28 Mr. Burns .15 .40
29 Waylon Smithers .15 .40
30 Seymour Skinner .15 .40
31 Edna Krabappel .15 .40
32 Dr. Julius Hibbert .15 .40
33 Chief Wiggum .15 .40
34 Krusty The Clown .15 .40
35 Sideshow Bob & Sideshow Mel .15 .40
36 Itchy & Scratchy .15 .40
37 The Flanders .15 .40
38 Apu .15 .40
39 Otto .15 .40
40 Groundskeeper Willie .15 .40
41 Moe & Barney .15 .40
42 Lenny & Carl .15 .40
43 The Thugs .15 .40
44 Sissies .15 .40
45 Milhouse .15 .40
46 Dali .15 .40
47 Hopper .15 .40
48 Botticelli .15 .40
49 Roy Lichtenstein .15 .40
50 Munch .15 .40
51 Michelangelo .15 .40
52 Tips .15 .40
53 Know-How .15 .40
54 Trivia .15 .40
55 Pick Pocket .15 .40
56 Super Dad .15 .40
57 In The Groove .15 .40
58 Pie-Pi .15 .40
59 Mischief Maker .15 .40
60 Homework Helper .15 .40
61 Kiss The Cook .15 .40
62 Couch Potato .15 .40
63 At The Beach .15 .40
64 Patty And Selma .15 .40
65 Bart Demure .15 .40
66 Kiss My .15 .40
67 Low Rider .15 .40
68 Howdy Homer .15 .40
69 Sweet Homer .15 .40
70 M In Mr. Burns .15 .40
71 Marge Arises .15 .40
72 Forbidden Fruit .15 .40
73 Bongo Bart .15 .40
74 Saxy Lisa .15 .40
75 Cool Maggie .15 .40
76 Big Foot .15 .40
77 Wall Mount .15 .40
78 Family Skeletons .15 .40
79 Reverse Order .15 .40
80 Underwater .15 .40
81 Checklist .15 .40
T1 Decoder .40 1.00
SC1 Greetings From Springfield 10.00 25.00

2000 The Simpsons Anniversary Celebration Autographs
COMPLETE SET (5) 125.00 250.00
RANDOM INSERT IN PACKS
A1 Harry Shearer 25.00 60.00
A2 Dan Castellaneta 25.00 60.00
A3 Yeardley Smith 25.00 60.00
A4 Nancy Cartwright 25.00 60.00
A5 Marcia Wallace 25.00 60.00

2000 The Simpsons Anniversary Celebration Cut-Ups
COMPLETE SET (8) 15.00 40.00
STATED ODDS 1:11
C1 Homer Simpson (Duff) 2.50 6.00
C2 Lisa Simpson 2.50 6.00
C3 Bart Simpson 2.50 6.00
C4 Maggie Simpson 2.50 6.00
C5 Marge Simpson 2.50 6.00
C6 Homer Simpson (TV) 2.50 6.00
C7 Grampa 2.50 6.00
C8 Krusty The Clown 2.50 6.00

2000 The Simpsons Anniversary Celebration Diorama-Rama
COMPLETE SET (4) 10.00 25.00
STATED ODDS 1:27
D1 Backyard 3.00 8.00
Kitchen Backgrounds
D2 Bar 3.00 8.00
Nuclear Plant Backgrounds
D3 Bart Overlay 3.00 8.00
D4 Homer Overlay 3.00 8.00

2000 The Simpsons Anniversary Celebration Nuclear Neon
COMPLETE SET (6) 12.50 30.00
STATED ODDS 1:17
N1 Three-Eyed Fish 2.50 6.00
N2 Bart X-Ray 2.50 6.00
N3 Homer with Barrel of Waste 2.50 6.00
N4 Homer with Doughnut 2.50 6.00
N5 Bart Skateboarding 2.50 6.00
N6 Springfield Nuclear Power Plant 2.50 6.00

2000 The Simpsons Anniversary Celebration Promos
COMPLETE SET (3) 2.00 5.00
P1 Bart 1.25 3.00
P2 Homer 1.25 3.00
P3 Marge 1.25 3.00

2000 Stargate SG-1 Preview
COMPLETE SET (6) 8.00 20.00
P1 SG-1 Team 1.50 4.00
P2 Richard Dean Anderson 1.50 4.00
P3 Michael Shanks 1.50 4.00
P4 Amanda Tapping 1.50 4.00
P5 Christopher Judge 1.50 4.00
P6 Don Davis 1.50 4.00

2000 Twilight Zone The Next Dimension
COMPLETE SET (73) 5.00 12.00
H1 SERIAL #'d TO 777
73 The Last Rites Of Jeff Myrtlebank .15 .40
74 The Last Rites Of Jeff Myrtlebank .15 .40
75 The Last Rites Of Jeff Myrtlebank .15 .40
76 The Last Rites Of Jeff Myrtlebank .15 .40
77 The Last Rites Of Jeff Myrtlebank .15 .40
78 The Last Rites Of Jeff Myrtlebank .15 .40
79 The Self-Improvement Of Salvadore Rose .15 .40
80 The Self-Improvement Of Salvadore Rose .15 .40
81 The Self-Improvement Of Salvadore Rose .15 .40
82 The Self-Improvement Of Salvadore Rose .15 .40
83 The Self-Improvement Of Salvadore Rose .15 .40
84 The Self-Improvement Of Salvadore Rose .15 .40
85 The Mind And The Matter .15 .40
86 The Mind And The Matter .15 .40
87 The Mind And The Matter .15 .40
88 The Mind And The Matter .15 .40
89 The Mind And The Matter .15 .40
90 The Mind And The Matter .15 .40
91 The Fear .15 .40
92 The Fear .15 .40
93 The Fear .15 .40
94 The Fear .15 .40
95 The Fear .15 .40
96 The Fear .15 .40
97 The Prime Mover .15 .40
98 The Prime Mover .15 .40
99 The Prime Mover .15 .40
100 The Prime Mover .15 .40
101 The Prime Mover .15 .40
102 The Prime Mover .15 .40
103 In Praise Of Pip .15 .40
104 In Praise Of Pip .15 .40
105 In Praise Of Pip .15 .40
106 In Praise Of Pip .15 .40
107 In Praise Of Pip .15 .40
108 In Praise Of Pip .15 .40
109 Nick Of Time .15 .40
110 Nick Of Time .15 .40
111 Nick Of Time .15 .40
112 Nick Of Time .15 .40
113 Nick Of Time .15 .40
114 Nick Of Time .15 .40
115 Shadow Play .15 .40
116 Shadow Play .15 .40
117 Shadow Play .15 .40
118 Shadow Play .15 .40
119 Shadow Play .15 .40
120 Shadow Play .15 .40
121 Four O'Clock .15 .40
122 Four O'Clock .15 .40
123 Four O'Clock .15 .40
124 Four O'Clock .15 .40
125 Four O'Clock .15 .40
126 Four O'Clock .15 .40
127 The Jungle .15 .40
128 The Jungle .15 .40
129 The Jungle .15 .40
130 The Jungle .15 .40
131 The Jungle .15 .40
132 The Jungle .15 .40
133 A World Of His Own .15 .40
134 A World Of His Own .15 .40
135 A World Of His Own .15 .40
136 A World Of His Own .15 .40
137 A World Of His Own .15 .40
138 A World Of His Own .15 .40
139 The Man In The Bottle .15 .40
140 The Man In The Bottle .15 .40
141 The Man In The Bottle .15 .40
142 The Man In The Bottle .15 .40
143 The Man In The Bottle .15 .40
144 The Man In The Bottle .15 .40
Z2 Checklist .15 .40
H1 Rod Serling
Steve Charendoff autograph

2000 Twilight Zone The Next Dimension Progressive Proofs Black
COMPLETE SET (72) 75.00 150.00
*PROG.PROOF: 2.5X TO 6X BASE CARDS 1.00 2.50
ANNOUNCED PRINT RUN 50

2000 Twilight Zone The Next Dimension Progressive Proofs Cyan
COMPLETE SET (72) 75.00 150.00
PROG.PROOF: 2.5X TO 6X BASE CARDS 1.00 2.50
ANNOUNCED PRINT RUN 50

2000 Twilight Zone The Next Dimension Progressive Proofs Magenta
COMPLETE SET (72) 75.00 150.00
*PROG.PROOF: 2.5X TO 6X BASE CARDS 1.00 2.50
ANNOUNCED PRINT RUN 50

2000 Twilight Zone The Next Dimension Progressive Proofs Yellow
COMPLETE SET (72) 75.00 150.00
*PROG.PROOF: 2.5X TO 6X BASE CARDS 1.00 2.50
ANNOUNCED PRINT RUN 50

2000 Twilight Zone The Next Dimension Autographs
STATED ODDS TWO PER BOX
A15 Elizabeth Allen
(issued as Autograph Challenge winner)
A20 William Shatner 100.00 200.00
A21 Beverly Garland 15.00 30.00
A22 Burt Reynolds 30.00 60.00
A23 Don Gordon 15.00 30.00
A24 Gail Kobe 15.00 30.00
A25 Don Rickles 15.00 30.00
A26 Joseph Ruskin 15.00 30.00
A27 Jean Carson 15.00 30.00
A28 Don Keefer 15.00 30.00
A29 Jack Klugman 30.00 60.00
A30 Theodore Bikel 15.00 30.00
A31 Peter Mark Richman 15.00 30.00
A32 James Best 15.00 30.00
A33 Sherry Jackson 15.00 30.00
A34 Buddy Ebsen 30.00 60.00
A35 Shelley Berman 15.00 30.00
A36 Dennis Weaver 15.00 30.00
A37 Suzanne Lloyd 15.00 30.00
(issued as album exclusive)
A38 Pat Hingle 15.00 30.00
issued as case topper)

2000 Twilight Zone The Next Dimension Rod Serling
COMPLETE SET (3) 5.00 12.00
STATED ODDS 1:40
RS1 Rod Serling 2.00 5.00
RS2 Rod Serling 2.00 5.00
RS3 Rod Serling 2.00 5.00

2000 Twilight Zone The Next Dimension Twilight Zone Stars
COMPLETE SET (9) 6.00 15.00
STATED ODDS 1:6
S10 Don Rickles .75 2.00
S11 Dennis Weaver .75 2.00
S12 Shelley Berman .75 2.00
S13 Buddy Ebsen .75 2.00
S14 Beverly Garland .75 2.00
S15 Burt Reynolds .75 2.00
S16 Jack Klugman .75 2.00
S17 Theodore Bikel .75 2.00
S18 William Shatner .75 2.00

2000 The Women of Star Trek In Motion

COMPLETE SET (32) 12.50 30.00

- ❑ 1 Andrea .40 1.00
- ❑ 2 B'Elanna Torres .40 1.00
- ❑ 3 Borg Queen .40 1.00
- ❑ 4 Borg Queen .40 1.00
- ❑ 5 Captain Janeway .40 1.00
- ❑ 6 Counselor Troi .40 1.00
- ❑ 7 Dr. Crusher .40 1.00
- ❑ 8 Dr. Gillian Taylor .40 1.00
- ❑ 9 Edith Keeler .40 1.00
- ❑ 10 Ensign Ro .40 1.00
- ❑ 11 Ezri Dax .40 1.00
- ❑ 12 Vina .40 1.00
- ❑ 13 Ilia .40 1.00
- ❑ 14 Jadzia Dax .40 1.00
- ❑ 15 Kai Winn .40 1.00
- ❑ 16 K'Ehleyr .40 1.00
- ❑ 17 Kes .40 1.00
- ❑ 18 Colonel Kira Nerys .40 1.00
- ❑ 19 Lawaxanna Troi .40 1.00
- ❑ 20 Leeta .40 1.00
- ❑ 21 Lt. Tasha Yar .40 1.00
- ❑ 22 Lursa & Betor .40 1.00
- ❑ 23 Martia .40 1.00
- ❑ 24 Mirror Kira .40 1.00
- ❑ 25 Mirror Uhura .40 1.00
- ❑ 26 Nurse Chapel .40 1.00
- ❑ 27 Saavek .40 1.00
- ❑ 28 Seska .40 1.00
- ❑ 29 Seven Of Nine .40 1.00
- ❑ 30 T'Pring .40 1.00
- ❑ 31 Uhura .40 1.00
- ❑ 32 Yeoman Rand .40 1.00

2000 The Women of Star Trek In Motion Archive Collection

COMPLETE SET (16) 60.00 120.00
STATED ODDS THREE PER BOX

- ❑ AC1 B'Elanna Torres 4.00 10.00
- ❑ AC2 Borg Queen 4.00 10.00
- ❑ AC3 Captain Janeway 4.00 10.00
- ❑ AC4 Counselor Troi 4.00 10.00
- ❑ AC5 Dr. Crusher 4.00 10.00
- ❑ AC6 Ezri Dax 4.00 10.00
- ❑ AC7 Nurse Chapel 4.00 10.00
- ❑ AC8 Jadzia Dax 4.00 10.00
- ❑ AC9 Kes 4.00 10.00
- ❑ AC10 Major Kira Nerys 4.00 10.00
- ❑ AC11 Lawaxanna Troi 4.00 10.00
- ❑ AC12 Leeta 4.00 10.00
- ❑ AC13 Lt. Tasha Yar 4.00 10.00
- ❑ AC14 Seven Of Nine 4.00 10.00
- ❑ AC15 Uhura 4.00 10.00
- ❑ AC16 Yeoman Rand 4.00 10.00

2000 The Women of Star Trek In Motion Archive Collection Gold

COMPLETE SET (4) 75.00 125.00
STATED PRINT RUN 500 SER. #'d SETS

- ❑ 1 Jadzia Dax 20.00 40.00
- ❑ 2 Captain Janeway 20.00 40.00
- ❑ 3 Seven Of Nine 20.00 40.00
- ❑ 4 Uhura 20.00 40.00

2000 The Women of Star Trek In Motion Autographs

COMPLETE SET (5) 75.00 150.00
STATED ODDS ONE PER BOX

- ❑ A1 Denise Crosby 15.00 40.00
- ❑ A2 Sherry Jackson 15.00 40.00
- ❑ A3 Arlene Martel 15.00 40.00
- ❑ A4 Alice Krige 15.00 40.00
- ❑ A5 Terry Farrell 15.00 40.00

2000 The Women of Star Trek In Motion Heroines of Star Trek

COMPLETE SET (4) 4.00 10.00
STATED ODDS 1:8

- ❑ H1 Jadzia Dax 1.25 3.00
- ❑ H2 Captain Janeway 1.25 3.00
- ❑ H3 Seven Of Nine 1.25 3.00
- ❑ H4 Uhura 1.25 3.00

2000 The Women of Star Trek In Motion Promos

COMPLETE SET (40) 75.00 150.00
ANNOUNCED PRINT RUN 300

- ❑ 1 Andrea 2.00 5.00
- ❑ 2 B'Elanna Torres 2.00 5.00
- ❑ 3 Borg Queen 2.00 5.00
- ❑ 4 Borg Queen 2.00 5.00
- ❑ 5 Captain Janeway 2.00 5.00
- ❑ 6 Counselor Troi 2.00 5.00
- ❑ 7 Dr. Crusher 2.00 5.00
- ❑ 8 Dr. Gillian Taylor 2.00 5.00
- ❑ 9 Edith Keeler 2.00 5.00
- ❑ 10 Ensign Ro 2.00 5.00
- ❑ 11 Ezri Dax 2.00 5.00
- ❑ 12 Vina 2.00 5.00
- ❑ 13 Ilia 2.00 5.00
- ❑ 14 Jadzia Dax 2.00 5.00
- ❑ 15 Kai Winn 2.00 5.00
- ❑ 16 K'Ehleyr 2.00 5.00
- ❑ 17 Kes 2.00 5.00
- ❑ 18 Colonel Kira Nerys 2.00 5.00
- ❑ 19 Lawaxanna Troi 2.00 5.00
- ❑ 20 Leeta 2.00 5.00
- ❑ 21 Lt. Tasha Yar 2.00 5.00
- ❑ 22 Lursa & Betor 2.00 5.00
- ❑ 23 Martia 2.00 5.00
- ❑ 24 Mirror Kira 2.00 5.00
- ❑ 25 Mirror Uhura 2.00 5.00
- ❑ 26 Nurse Chapel 2.00 5.00
- ❑ 27 Saavek 2.00 5.00
- ❑ 28 Seska 2.00 5.00
- ❑ 29 Seven Of Nine 2.00 5.00
- ❑ 30 T'Pring 2.00 5.00
- ❑ 31 Uhura 2.00 5.00
- ❑ 32 Yeoman Rand 2.00 5.00
- ❑ H1 Jadzia Dax 2.00 5.00
- ❑ H2 Captain Janeway 2.00 5.00
- ❑ H3 Seven Of Nine 2.00 5.00
- ❑ H4 Uhura 2.00 5.00
- ❑ V1 Borg Queen 2.00 5.00
- ❑ V2 Mirror Kira 2.00 5.00
- ❑ V3 Lursa & Betor 2.00 5.00
- ❑ V4 Seven Of Nine Full Borg 2.00 5.00

2000 The Women of Star Trek In Motion Sound in Motion

COMPLETE SET (6) 40.00 100.00
STATED ODDS ONE PER BOX
BS1 ISSUED IN COLLECTORS ALBUM
CS1 ISSUED AS CASE TOPPER

- ❑ S1 Borg Queen 8.00 20.00
- ❑ S2 Jadzia Dax 8.00 20.00
- ❑ S3 Captain Janeway 8.00 20.00
- ❑ S4 Lt. Tasha Yar 8.00 20.00
- ❑ S5 Seven Of Nine 8.00 20.00
- ❑ S6 Uhura 8.00 20.00
- ❑ BS1 Captain Janeway 8.00 20.00
- ❑ CS1 Seven Of Nine 8.00 20.00

2000 The Women of Star Trek In Motion Villainesses of Star Trek

COMPLETE SET (4) 5.00 12.00
STATED ODDS 1:5

- ❑ V1 Borg Queen 1.50 4.00
- ❑ V2 Mirror Kira 1.50 4.00
- ❑ V3 Lursa & Betor 1.50 4.00
- ❑ V4 Seven Of Nine Full Borg 1.50 4.00

2000 The Women of Star Trek In Motion Extension

COMPLETE SET (5) 30.00 75.00
STATED PRINT RUN 999 SER. #'d SETS

- ❑ G1 Seven of Nine 8.00 20.00
- ❑ G2 Kathryn Janeway 8.00 20.00
- ❑ G3 B'Elanna Torres 8.00 20.00
- ❑ G4 Kathryn Janeway 8.00 20.00
- ❑ G5 Seven of Nine 8.00 20.00

2000 X-Men The Movie

COMPLETE SET (72) 5.00 12.00

- ❑ 1 X-Men The Movie .15 .40
- ❑ 2 Professor X .15 .40
- ❑ 3 Magneto .15 .40
- ❑ 4 Jean Grey .15 .40
- ❑ 5 Cyclops .15 .40
- ❑ 6 Wolverine .15 .40
- ❑ 7 Sabretooth .15 .40
- ❑ 8 Rogue .15 .40
- ❑ 9 Storm .15 .40
- ❑ 10 Mystique .15 .40
- ❑ 11 Senator Kelly .15 .40
- ❑ 12 Toad .15 .40
- ❑ 13 The Nazi Trauma .15 .40
- ❑ 14 Love Can Kill .15 .40
- ❑ 15 Are Mutants Dangerous .15 .40
- ❑ 16 Two Old Friends .15 .40
- ❑ 17 A Bout with Wolverine .15 .40
- ❑ 18 The Feral Fury .15 .40
- ❑ 19 A Gun against Wolverine .15 .40
- ❑ 20 Adamantium Attack! .15 .40
- ❑ 21 Two for the Road .15 .40
- ❑ 22 Sabretooth Terror .15 .40
- ❑ 23 Primal Combatants .15 .40
- ❑ 24 Snow Titans .15 .40
- ❑ 25 Unexpected Rescue .15 .40
- ❑ 26 Kelly's Crusade .15 .40
- ❑ 27 The Awakening .15 .40
- ❑ 28 Inside X Headquarters .15 .40
- ❑ 29 The World of X .15 .40
- ❑ 30 Xavier's Offer .15 .40
- ❑ 31 The Capture of Kelly .15 .40
- ❑ 32 Inside Story .15 .40
- ❑ 33 Facing Magneto .15 .40
- ❑ 34 Magneto's Mad Plan .15 .40
- ❑ 35 The Senator Transformed .15 .40
- ❑ 36 Logan's Dream .15 .40
- ❑ 37 Absorbing His Power .15 .40
- ❑ 38 Kelly's Escape .15 .40
- ❑ 39 Mutant Misjudgment .15 .40
- ❑ 40 What's Wrong with Kelly .15 .40
- ❑ 41 Kindred Spirits .15 .40
- ❑ 42 Surprised by a Monster .15 .40
- ❑ 43 Terminal Mayhem .15 .40
- ❑ 44 Thrashed by the Enemy .15 .40
- ❑ 45 Unscheduled Stop .15 .40
- ❑ 46 Invading a Train .15 .40
- ❑ 47 Three the Hard Way .15 .40
- ❑ 48 Saved by Psychic Power .15 .40
- ❑ 49 Death of a Mutant .15 .40
- ❑ 50 It's Up to Team X .15 .40
- ❑ 51 Assault on Liberty Island .15 .40
- ❑ 52 Dr. Grey's Gamble .15 .40
- ❑ 53 Heroes on the Scene .15 .40
- ❑ 54 Psychic Slugfest .15 .40
- ❑ 55 Burning It Off .15 .40
- ❑ 56 Deadly Deception .15 .40
- ❑ 57 Good vs. Evil .15 .40
- ❑ 58 The Tables Turned .15 .40
- ❑ 59 Power against Power .15 .40
- ❑ 60 Sacrificing Rogue .15 .40
- ❑ 61 The Final Struggle .15 .40
- ❑ 62 Destroying the Machine .15 .40
- ❑ 63 Toward Tomorrow .15 .40
- ❑ 64 Fantastic Epic .15 .40
- ❑ 65 Action and Drama .15 .40
- ❑ 66 Logan's Fun .15 .40
- ❑ 67 Set Pieces .15 .40
- ❑ 68 Mutant Perils .15 .40
- ❑ 69 Girl Power .15 .40
- ❑ 70 Mad Machinery .15 .40
- ❑ 71 The Challenge .15 .40
- ❑ 72 X-Men The Movie .15 .40

2000 X-Men The Movie Autographs

COMPLETE SET (13) 400.00 800.00
STATED ODDS 1:36 HOBBY

- ❑ 1 Anna Paquin 75.00 150.00
- ❑ 2 Bruce Davison 6.00 15.00
- ❑ 3 Bryan Singer 100.00 200.00
- ❑ 4 Famke Janssen 40.00 80.00
- ❑ 5 Hugh Jackman 40.00 80.00
- ❑ 6 James Marsden 6.00 15.00
- ❑ 7 John Myhre 4.00 10.00
- ❑ 8 Lauren Shuler Donner 4.00 10.00
- ❑ 9 Patrick Stewart 150.00 300.00
- ❑ 10 Ray Park 25.00 50.00
- ❑ 11 Rebecca Romijn-Stamos 50.00 100.00
- ❑ 12 Sir Ian McKellen 20.00 40.00
- ❑ 13 Tyler Mane 6.00 15.00

2000 X-Men The Movie Chromium

COMPLETE SET (10) 12.50 30.00
RANDOM INSERTS IN PACKS

- ❑ C1 Professor X 1.50 4.00
- ❑ C2 Cyclops 1.50 4.00
- ❑ C3 Jean Grey 1.50 4.00
- ❑ C4 Storm 1.50 4.00
- ❑ C5 Wolverine 1.50 4.00
- ❑ C6 Rogue 1.50 4.00
- ❑ C7 Magneto 1.50 4.00
- ❑ C8 Mystique 1.50 4.00
- ❑ C9 Sabretooth 1.50 4.00
- ❑ C10 Toad 1.50 4.00

2000 X-Men The Movie Clings

COMPLETE SET (12) 10.00 25.00
STATED ODDS 1:3 RETAIL

- ❑ CL1 Cyclops 1.25 3.00
- ❑ CL2 Jean Grey 1.25 3.00
- ❑ CL3 Storm 1.25 3.00
- ❑ CL4 Wolverine 1.25 3.00
- ❑ CL5 Cyclops 1.25 3.00
- ❑ CL6 Wolverine 1.25 3.00
- ❑ CL7 Magneto 1.25 3.00
- ❑ CL8 Mystique 1.25 3.00
- ❑ CL9 Sabretooth 1.25 3.00
- ❑ CL10 Toad 1.25 3.00
- ❑ CL11 Toad 1.25 3.00
- ❑ CL12 Magneto 1.25 3.00

2000 X-Men The Movie Memorabilia

COMPLETE SET (4) 25.00 60.00
STATED ODDS 1:36 HOBBY

- ❑ 1 Famke Janssen 8.00 20.00
- ❑ 2 Halle Berry 8.00 20.00
- ❑ 3 Hugh Jackman 8.00 20.00
- ❑ 4 James Marsden 8.00 20.00

2000 X-Men The Movie Promos

COMPLETE SET (5) 4.00 10.00

- ❑ 0 Mutants Among Us 1.25 3.00
- ❑ X1 Wolverine 1.25 3.00
- ❑ X2 Cyclops 1.25 3.00
- ❑ X3 Storm 1.25 3.00
- ❑ X4 Magneto 1.25 3.00

2000 X-Men The Movie X-Foil

COMPLETE SET (10) 12.50 30.00
STATED ODDS 1:6 RETAIL

- ❑ 1 Professor Xavier 1.50 4.00
- ❑ 2 Cyclops 1.50 4.00
- ❑ 3 Jean Grey 1.50 4.00
- ❑ 4 Storm 1.50 4.00
- ❑ 5 Wolverine 1.50 4.00
- ❑ 6 Rogue 1.50 4.00
- ❑ 7 Magneto 1.50 4.00
- ❑ 8 Mystique 1.50 4.00
- ❑ 9 Sabretooth 1.50 4.00
- ❑ 10 Toad 1.50 4.00

2001 Andromeda Season One

COMPLETE SET (90) 5.00 12.00

- ❑ 1 The Long Night .15 .40
- ❑ 2 Night Falls .15 .40
- ❑ 3 The Big Score .15 .40
- ❑ 4 They'll Take It From Here .15 .40
- ❑ 5 Hit And Run .15 .40
- ❑ 6 Flat Lux .15 .40
- ❑ 7 Welcome Aboard .15 .40
- ❑ 8 Hail The High Guard .15 .40
- ❑ 9 Day Of Lightning .15 .40
- ❑ 10 Ship Made Flesh .15 .40
- ❑ 11 A Deadly Relic .15 .40
- ❑ 12 The Crazy Ivan .15 .40
- ❑ 13 A Final Gambit .15 .40
- ❑ 14 Orca And Than .15 .40
- ❑ 15 A Modest Proposal .15 .40
- ❑ 16 Trusting Tyr To Be Tyr .15 .40
- ❑ 17 A Dangerous Lesson .15 .40
- ❑ 18 Choices .15 .40
- ❑ 19 Destroyer Of Worlds .15 .40
- ❑ 20 A New Leaf? .15 .40
- ❑ 21 Double-Crossed .15 .40
- ❑ 22 The Narwhal's Horn .15 .40
- ❑ 23 Back To Hephaistos .15 .40
- ❑ 24 A Rescue Across Time .15 .40
- ❑ 25 A Final Farewell .15 .40
- ❑ 26 The Wrong Planet .15 .40
- ❑ 27 Insiders And Outsiders .15 .40
- ❑ 28 Time For An Upgrade .15 .40
- ❑ 29 An Interrupted Party .15 .40
- ❑ 30 The Usual Suspect .15 .40
- ❑ 31 A Killer Unmasked .15 .40
- ❑ 32 A Late Message .15 .40
- ❑ 33 Who's Your Uncle? .15 .40
- ❑ 34 Into The Sun .15 .40
- ❑ 35 Ship Of Gold .15 .40
- ❑ 36 Well-Preserved .15 .40
- ❑ 37 To Tell The Truth .15 .40
- ❑ 38 His Name Is Nobody .15 .40
- ❑ 39 Meet The Locals .15 .40
- ❑ 40 A Birthright Restored .15 .40
- ❑ 41 The Big Download .15 .40
- ❑ 42 A Hungry Hunter .15 .40
- ❑ 43 Control Alt Delete .15 .40
- ❑ 44 The Great Compass .15 .40
- ❑ 45 Dinner For Two .15 .40
- ❑ 46 The Best Intentions .15 .40
- ❑ 47 I Come In Pieces .15 .40
- ❑ 48 An Offer Spurned .15 .40
- ❑ 49 Start The Revolution .15 .40
- ❑ 50 An Old Friend .15 .40
- ❑ 51 My Happy Thought .15 .40
- ❑ 52 The Sanctum Sanctorum .15 .40
- ❑ 53 Serendipity .15 .40
- ❑ 54 Fighting The Slavers .15 .40
- ❑ 55 Tiama's Sacrifice .15 .40
- ❑ 56 A Royal Pain .15 .40
- ❑ 57 Only Human .15 .40
- ❑ 58 Bride's Family To The Left .15 .40
- ❑ 59 Terror In The Star-Lanes .15 .40
- ❑ 60 Fatal Attraction .15 .40
- ❑ 61 Final Judgment .15 .40
- ❑ 62 Happy Birthday .15 .40
- ❑ 63 Scylla And Charybdis .15 .40
- ❑ 64 A Slip Too Far .15 .40
- ❑ 65 Runaway Ship .15 .40
- ❑ 66 The Chanting Stops .15 .40
- ❑ 67 Final Orders? .15 .40
- ❑ 68 Nietzscheans .15 .40
- ❑ 69 Magog .15 .40
- ❑ 70 Than-Thre-Kull .15 .40
- ❑ 71 Nightsiders .15 .40
- ❑ 72 Perseids .15 .40
- ❑ 73 Marshall Jeger .15 .40
- ❑ 74 Technical Director Hohne .15 .40
- ❑ 75 Elssbett Mossadim .15 .40
- ❑ 76 Cuchulain Nez Perce .15 .40
- ❑ 77 Gabriel .15 .40
- ❑ 78 Lt. Jill Pearce .15 .40
- ❑ 79 Commander Gaheris Rhade .15 .40
- ❑ 80 Gerentex .15 .40
- ❑ 81 Sid Barry .15 .40

Sam Profit

- ❑ 82 The Slipstream .15 .40
- ❑ 83 Captain Dylan Hunt .15 .40
- ❑ 84 Tyr Anasazi .15 .40
- ❑ 85 Beka Valentine .15 .40
- ❑ 86 Seamus Harper .15 .40
- ❑ 87 Trance Gemini .15 .40
- ❑ 88 Rev Bem .15 .40
- ❑ 89 Andromeda Ascendant .15 .40
- ❑ 90 Checklist .15 .40
- ❑ R1 The Three Faces Of Rommie

2001 Andromeda Season One Autographs

STATED ODDS 1:45

- ❑ A1 Kevin Sorbo 8.00 20.00
- ❑ A2 Lisa Ryder 6.00 15.00
- ❑ A3 Lexa Doig 8.00 20.00
- ❑ A4 Laura Bertram 8.00 20.00
- ❑ A5 Gordon Michael Woolvett 6.00 15.00
- ❑ A6 Brent Stait 8.00 20.00
- ❑ A7 Sam Sorbo 6.00 15.00

2001 Andromeda Season One Diaries of the Mad Perseid

COMPLETE SET (6) 5.00 12.00
STATED ODDS 1:17

- ❑ D1 The Mad Perseid 1.25 3.00
- ❑ D2 Hephaistos Black Hole 1.25 3.00
- ❑ D3 The Pax Magellanic 1.25 3.00
- ❑ D4 Intangible Human 1.25 3.00
- ❑ D5 Magog World-Ship 1.25 3.00
- ❑ D6 Enigma Wall Drawing 1.25 3.00

2001 Andromeda Season One Pieceworks

COMPLETE SET (4) 25.00 60.00
STATED ODDS 1:65

- ❑ PW1 Beka's Pants 8.00 20.00
- ❑ PW2 Rommie's Vest 8.00 20.00
- ❑ PW3 Tyr's Tank 8.00 20.00
- ❑ PW4 Trance's Top 8.00 20.00

2001 Andromeda Season One Promos

COMPLETE SET (4) 4.00 10.00

- ❑ P1 Dylan Hunt 1.25 3.00
- ❑ Pi Andromeda 1.25 3.00
- ❑ UKP Andromeda 1.25 3.00
- ❑ SD2001 Dylan Hunt 1.25 3.00

2001 Andromeda Season One The Crew of Andromeda

COMPLETE SET (9) 6.00 15.00
STATED ODDS 1:11

- ❑ C1 The Crew Of Andromeda 1.00 2.50
- ❑ C2 The Crew Of Andromeda 1.00 2.50
- ❑ C3 The Crew Of Andromeda 1.00 2.50
- ❑ C4 The Crew Of Andromeda 1.00 2.50
- ❑ C5 The Crew Of Andromeda 1.00 2.50
- ❑ C6 The Crew Of Andromeda 1.00 2.50
- ❑ C7 The Crew Of Andromeda 1.00 2.50
- ❑ C8 The Crew Of Andromeda 1.00 2.50
- ❑ C9 The Crew Of Andromeda 1.00 2.50

2001 Angel Season Two

COMPLETE SET (90) 5.00 12.00

- ❑ 1 Angel .15 .40
- ❑ 2 Uncertain .15 .40
- ❑ 3 Paladin .15 .40
- ❑ 4 It Ain't Easy .15 .40
- ❑ 5 Haunted .15 .40
- ❑ 6 On the Lam .15 .40
- ❑ 7 Parasite .15 .40
- ❑ 8 Sleeptime .15 .40
- ❑ 9 On the Trail .15 .40
- ❑ 10 Driven .15 .40
- ❑ 11 Not So Innocent .15 .40
- ❑ 12 Pawn .15 .40
- ❑ 13 Stronger .15 .40
- ❑ 14 These Dreams .15 .40
- ❑ 15 Another Life .15 .40
- ❑ 16 Come Closer .15 .40
- ❑ 17 Contemplation .15 .40
- ❑ 18 Deception .15 .40
- ❑ 19 Revelation .15 .40
- ❑ 20 Soulmates .15 .40
- ❑ 21 Too Close .15 .40
- ❑ 22 Last Resort .15 .40
- ❑ 23 Flashback .15 .40
- ❑ 24 Unusual Suspects .15 .40
- ❑ 25 Stuck in the Middle .15 .40
- ❑ 26 Plight .15 .40
- ❑ 27 Quest .15 .40
- ❑ 28 All in Vain .15 .40
- ❑ 29 The Big Event .15 .40
- ❑ 30 Back and Badder than Ever .15 .40
- ❑ 31 Bad to the Bone .15 .40
- ❑ 32 Sacked .15 .40
- ❑ 33 Whacked .15 .40
- ❑ 34 Cracked .15 .40
- ❑ 35 A.K.A. Anne .15 .40
- ❑ 36 Benefit Scam .15 .40
- ❑ 37 Honor Bound .15 .40
- ❑ 38 Way the World Ends .15 .40
- ❑ 39 Great Teamwork .15 .40
- ❑ 40 With a Whimper .15 .40
- ❑ 41 Wesley Shot .15 .40
- ❑ 42 Zombie Cops .15 .40
- ❑ 43 A Bite out of Crime .15 .40
- ❑ 44 Power Struggle .15 .40
- ❑ 45 Hitting Bottom .15 .40
- ❑ 46 Hell on Earth .15 .40
- ❑ 47 Did It Again .15 .40
- ❑ 48 Made Some Mistakes .15 .40
- ❑ 49 Some Amends .15 .40
- ❑ 50 Old Friends .15 .40
- ❑ 51 Change Sometimes .15 .40
- ❑ 52 Now and Forever .15 .40
- ❑ 53 Hand of Fate .15 .40
- ❑ 54 Hand Jive .15 .40
- ❑ 55 Wave Bye-Bye .15 .40
- ❑ 56 Discontent .15 .40
- ❑ 57 Family Feud .15 .40
- ❑ 58 Disappeared .15 .40
- ❑ 59 Not in Kansas .15 .40
- ❑ 60 Walking on Sunshine .15 .40
- ❑ 61 Off to See the Wizard .15 .40
- ❑ 62 Off with Their Heads .15 .40
- ❑ 63 In a Fix .15 .40
- ❑ 64 Inside Out .15 .40
- ❑ 65 Flipped Lid .15 .40
- ❑ 66 On the Road .15 .40
- ❑ 67 Ruby Slippers .15 .40
- ❑ 68 Home Again .15 .40
- ❑ 69 Angel .15 .40
- ❑ 70 Wesley Wyndam-Pryce .15 .40
- ❑ 71 Cordelia Chase .15 .40
- ❑ 72 Charles Gunn .15 .40
- ❑ 73 The Host .15 .40
- ❑ 74 Angel .15 .40
- ❑ 75 Cordy, Gunn & Wesley .15 .40
- ❑ 76 Darla .15 .40
- ❑ 77 Lindsey McDonald .15 .40
- ❑ 78 Harmony .15 .40
- ❑ 79 Darla .15 .40
- ❑ 80 The Old Gang .15 .40
- ❑ 81 Angelus .15 .40
- ❑ 82 Holland Manners .15 .40
- ❑ 83 Hunt Ackrey .15 .40
- ❑ 84 Lindsey McDonald .15 .40
- ❑ 85 Lilah Morgan .15 .40
- ❑ 86 Thesulac Demon .15 .40
- ❑ 87 Merl .15 .40
- ❑ 88 Boone .15 .40
- ❑ 89 Drokken .15 .40
- ❑ 90 Checklist .15 .40

2001 Angel Season Two Autographs

COMPLETE SET (9) 350.00 700.00
RANDOM INSERTS IN PACKS

- ❑ A7 Charisma Carpenter 75.00 150.00
- ❑ A8 J. August Richards 20.00 50.00
- ❑ A9 Julie Benz 40.00 80.00
- ❑ A10 Juliet Landau 60.00 120.00
- ❑ A11 Stephanie Romanov 20.00 50.00
- ❑ A12 Andy Hallett 20.00 50.00
- ❑ A13 Brigid Brannagh 20.00 50.00
- ❑ A14 Julia Lee 20.00 50.00
- ❑ DA1 Juliet Landau 75.00 150.00

2001 Angel Season Two City of Angel

COMPLETE SET (9) 10.00 25.00
STATED ODDS 1:11

- ❑ CA1 Denver 1.50 4.00
- ❑ CA2 Angel 1.50 4.00
- ❑ CA3 Angel 1.50 4.00
- ❑ CA4 Cordelia 1.50 4.00
- ❑ CA5 Cordelia 1.50 4.00
- ❑ CA6 Puzzle piece 1.50 4.00
- ❑ CA7 Puzzle piece 1.50 4.00
- ❑ CA8 Gunn 1.50 4.00
- ❑ CA9 Host 1.50 4.00

2001 Angel Season Two L.A. Women

COMPLETE SET (6) 7.50 20.00
STATED ODDS 1:17

- ❑ LA1 Cordelia 1.50 4.00
- ❑ LA2 Kate 1.50 4.00
- ❑ LA3 Virginia 1.50 4.00
- ❑ LA4 Lilah 1.50 4.00
- ❑ LA5 Darla 1.50 4.00
- ❑ LA6 Drusilla 1.50 4.00

2001 Buffy the Vampire Slayer Season Five

COMPLETE SET (90) 5.00 12.00
Slayer's Gift STATED ODDS 1:100

- ❑ 1 This Is Growing Up .15 .40
- ❑ 2 In This Corner .15 .40
- ❑ 3 First Blood .15 .40
- ❑ 4 Winner And Still Slayer .15 .40
- ❑ 5 Sibling Rivalry .15 .40
- ❑ 6 Gang Warfare .15 .40
- ❑ 7 Saving Dawn .15 .40
- ❑ 8 Misfire .15 .40
- ❑ 9 Torn .15 .40
- ❑ 10 Double Or Nothing .15 .40
- ❑ 11 Zany Brainy .15 .40
- ❑ 12 Joe Normal .15 .40
- ❑ 13 Fake Out .15 .40
- ❑ 14 Monkish Business .15 .40
- ❑ 15 Glory Most Peculiar .15 .40
- ❑ 16 Nothing But The Truth .15 .40
- ❑ 17 Secrets .15 .40
- ❑ 18 Lies .15 .40
- ❑ 19 Belonging .15 .40
- ❑ 20 Close Call .15 .40
- ❑ 21 Inspiration .15 .40
- ❑ 22 Beneath .15 .40
- ❑ 23 Bad News .15 .40
- ❑ 24 Damage Done .15 .40
- ❑ 25 On The Edge .15 .40
- ❑ 26 Going Home .15 .40
- ❑ 27 Enter Night .15 .40
- ❑ 28 Summoner .15 .40
- ❑ 29 So Low .15 .40
- ❑ 30 So Distant .15 .40
- ❑ 31 So Gone .15 .40
- ❑ 32 At Odds .15 .40
- ❑ 33 Trolling .15 .40
- ❑ 34 Old Flames .15 .40
- ❑ 35 Inside Job .15 .40
- ❑ 36 British Invasion .15 .40
- ❑ 37 Revolution .15 .40
- ❑ 38 Mad God .15 .40
- ❑ 39 Nothing But Truth .15 .40
- ❑ 40 Switcheroo .15 .40
- ❑ 41 Tainted Love .15 .40
- ❑ 42 Dangerous .15 .40
- ❑ 43 Never Ever .15 .40
- ❑ 44 Living Doll .15 .40
- ❑ 45 Dating Game .15 .40
- ❑ 46 Unwanted .15 .40
- ❑ 47 Unexpected .15 .40
- ❑ 48 Unimaginable .15 .40
- ❑ 49 Forever .15 .40
- ❑ 50 Final .15 .40
- ❑ 51 Comfort .15 .40
- ❑ 52 Reanimator .15 .40
- ❑ 53 Nookie .15 .40
- ❑ 54 The One .15 .40
- ❑ 55 My Way .15 .40
- ❑ 56 Relinquish .15 .40
- ❑ 57 Taken .15 .40
- ❑ 58 Payback .15 .40
- ❑ 59 Flight .15 .40

☐ 60 Pursuit .15 .40
☐ 61 Defeat .15 .40
☐ 62 Breakdown .15 .40
☐ 63 Inside .15 .40
☐ 64 Enemy .15 .40
☐ 65 Battle .15 .40
☐ 66 Blood .15 .40
☐ 67 Sacrifice .15 .40
☐ 68 Dracula .15 .40
☐ 69 Glory .15 .40
☐ 70 Glory'S Minions .15 .40
☐ 71 Harmony .15 .40
☐ 72 Drusilla .15 .40
☐ 73 The Knights Of Byzantium .15 .40
☐ 74 Ghora Demon .15 .40
☐ 75 Doc .15 .40
☐ 76 Willow .15 .40
☐ 77 Xander .15 .40
☐ 78 Anya .15 .40
☐ 79 Giles .15 .40
☐ 80 Tara .15 .40
☐ 81 Spike .15 .40
☐ 82 Willow .15 .40
☐ 83 Anya .15 .40
☐ 84 Xander .15 .40
☐ 85 Buffy .15 .40
☐ 86 Riley .15 .40
☐ 87 Joyce .15 .40
☐ 88 Willow & Tara .15 .40
☐ 89 The Slayer's Life .15 .40
☐ 90 Checklist .15 .40
☐ SG1 Slayer's Gift FOIL 7.50 20.00

2001 Buffy the Vampire Slayer Season Five Autographs

COMPLETE SET (7) 250.00 500.00
RANDOM INSERTS IN PACKS
☐ A22 Michelle Trachtenberg 100.00 200.00
☐ A23 Amber Benson 50.00 100.00
☐ A24 Kelly Donavan EXCH 25.00 50.00
☐ A25 Charlie Weber 25.00 50.00
☐ A26 Kevin Weisman 25.00 50.00
☐ A27 Bailey Chase 25.00 50.00
☐ A28 Joel Grey 25.00 50.00

2001 Buffy the Vampire Slayer Season Five Big Bad Crush

COMPLETE SET (6) 15.00 40.00
STATED ODDS 1:17
☐ B1 Big Bad Crush 3.00 8.00
☐ B2 Big Bad Crush 3.00 8.00
☐ B3 Big Bad Crush 3.00 8.00
☐ B4 Big Bad Crush 3.00 8.00
☐ B5 Big Bad Crush 3.00 8.00
☐ B6 Big Bad Crush 3.00 8.00

2001 Buffy the Vampire Slayer Season Five Box Loaders

COMPLETE SET (3) 5.00 12.00
☐ BL1 Buffy & Dawn 2.00 5.00
☐ BL2 Tara & Willow 2.00 5.00
☐ BL3 Anya 2.00 5.00

2001 Buffy the Vampire Slayer Season Five Promos

COMPLETE SET (6) 7.50 20.00
☐ B5i Buffy 1.25 3.00
☐ B5-0 Buffy 1.25 3.00
☐ B5-1 Buffy 1.25 3.00
☐ B5-2 Rupert & Buffy 4.00 8.00
☐ B5-3 Buffy 4.00 8.00
☐ B5SD2001 Buffy 1.25 3.00

2001 Buffy the Vampire Slayer Season Five Protectors of the Key

COMPLETE SET (9) 12.50 30.00
STATED ODDS 1:11
☐ K1 Protectors Of The Key 1.50 4.00
☐ K2 Protectors Of The Key 1.50 4.00
☐ K3 Protectors Of The Key 1.50 4.00
☐ K4 Protectors Of The Key 1.50 4.00
☐ K5 Protectors Of The Key 1.50 4.00
☐ K6 Protectors Of The Key 1.50 4.00
☐ K7 Protectors Of The Key 1.50 4.00
☐ K8 Protectors Of The Key 1.50 4.00
☐ K9 Protectors Of The Key 1.50 4.00

2001 Farscape In Motion

COMPLETE SET (60) 5.00 12.00
A6 ISSUED AS CASE TOPPER
☐ 1 John Crichton .15 .40
☐ 2 John Crichton .15 .40
☐ 3 John Crichton .15 .40
☐ 4 John Crichton .15 .40
☐ 5 John Crichton .15 .40
☐ 6 John Crichton .15 .40
☐ 7 John Crichton .15 .40
☐ 8 John Crichton .15 .40
☐ 9 John Crichton .15 .40
☐ 10 Aeryn Sun .15 .40
☐ 11 Aeryn Sun .15 .40
☐ 12 Aeryn Sun .15 .40
☐ 13 Aeryn Sun .15 .40
☐ 14 Aeryn Sun .15 .40
☐ 15 Aeryn Sun .15 .40
☐ 16 Aeryn Sun .15 .40
☐ 17 Aeryn Sun .15 .40
☐ 18 Aeryn Sun .15 .40
☐ 19 Ka D'Argo .15 .40
☐ 20 Ka D'Argo .15 .40
☐ 21 Ka D'Argo .15 .40
☐ 22 Ka D'Argo .15 .40
☐ 23 Ka D'Argo .15 .40
☐ 24 Ka D'Argo .15 .40
☐ 25 Ka D'Argo .15 .40
☐ 26 Ka D'Argo .15 .40
☐ 27 Ka D'Argo .15 .40
☐ 28 Pa'u Zotoh Zhaan .15 .40
☐ 29 Pa'u Zotoh Zhaan .15 .40
☐ 30 Pa'u Zotoh Zhaan .15 .40
☐ 31 Pa'u Zotoh Zhaan .15 .40
☐ 32 Pa'u Zotoh Zhaan .15 .40
☐ 33 Pa'u Zotoh Zhaan .15 .40
☐ 34 Pa'u Zotoh Zhaan .15 .40
☐ 35 Pa'u Zotoh Zhaan .15 .40
☐ 36 Pa'u Zotoh Zhaan .15 .40
☐ 37 Chiana .15 .40
☐ 38 Chiana .15 .40
☐ 39 Chiana .15 .40
☐ 40 Chiana .15 .40
☐ 41 Chiana .15 .40
☐ 42 Chiana .15 .40
☐ 43 Captain Crais .15 .40
☐ 44 Captain Crais .15 .40
☐ 45 Captain Crais .15 .40
☐ 46 Captain Crais .15 .40
☐ 47 Captain Crais .15 .40
☐ 48 Captain Crais .15 .40
☐ 49 Scorpius .15 .40
☐ 50 Scorpius .15 .40
☐ 51 Scorpius .15 .40
☐ 52 Scorpius .15 .40
☐ 53 Scorpius .15 .40
☐ 54 Scorpius .15 .40
☐ 55 Rygel The XVI .15 .40
☐ 56 Rygel The XVI .15 .40
☐ 57 Rygel The XVI .15 .40
☐ 58 Pilot .15 .40
☐ 59 Pilot .15 .40
☐ 60 Pilot .15 .40
☐ A6 Claudia Black/ (issued as case topper)
☐ P1 John Crichton PROMO

2001 Farscape In Motion Close Encounters

COMPLETE SET (9) 8.00 20.00
STATED ODDS 1:6
☐ C1 Crichton Gilina 1.25 3.00
☐ C2 Crichton Alex 1.25 3.00
☐ C3 Crichton Lishala 1.25 3.00
☐ C4 Crichton Aeryn 1.25 3.00
☐ C5 Crichton Chiana 1.25 3.00
☐ C6 Chiana D'Argo 1.25 3.00
☐ C7 Zhaan Chiana 1.25 3.00
☐ C8 Natira Scorpius 1.25 3.00
☐ C9 Crichton Aeryn 1.25 3.00

2001 Farscape In Motion Portraits In Motion

COMPLETE SET (9) 12.50 30.00
STATED ODDS 1:8
☐ P1 John Crichton 1.50 4.00
☐ P2 Aeryn Sun 1.50 4.00
☐ P3 Ka D'Argo 1.50 4.00
☐ P4 Pa'u Zotoh Zhaan 1.50 4.00
☐ P5 Chiana 1.50 4.00
☐ P6 Rygel 1.50 4.00
☐ P7 Pilot 1.50 4.00
☐ P8 Crais 1.50 4.00
☐ P9 Scorpius 1.50 4.00

2001 Farscape In Motion Ships Of Farscape

COMPLETE SET (9) 8.00 20.00
STATED ODDS 1:3
☐ S1 Moya 1.25 3.00
☐ S2 Moya 1.25 3.00
☐ S3 Moya 1.25 3.00
☐ S4 Rygel 1.25 3.00
☐ S5 Talyn 1.25 3.00
☐ S6 Talyn 1.25 3.00
☐ S7 Crais Command Carrier 1.25 3.00
☐ S8 Transport In Flax 1.25 3.00
☐ S9 Prowler 1.25 3.00

2001 Farscape In Motion Sound inMotion

COMPLETE SET (6) 30.00 75.00
STATED ODDS ONE PER BOX
☐ S1 Crichton Sun 6.00 15.00
☐ S2 John Crichton 6.00 15.00
☐ S3 Chiana Crichton 6.00 15.00
☐ S4 Rygel The XVI 6.00 15.00
☐ S5 Crichton D'Argo 6.00 15.00
☐ S6 John Crichton 6.00 15.00

2001 Farscape In Motion The Good, The Bad And The Ugly

COMPLETE SET (18) 10.00 25.00
STATED ODDS 1:2
☐ U1 Bekhesh .75 2.00
☐ U2 Durka .75 2.00
☐ U3 Gilina .75 2.00
☐ U4 Lorana .75 2.00
☐ U5 Maldis .75 2.00
☐ U6 Matala .75 2.00
☐ U7 M''Lee .75 2.00
☐ U8 Natira .75 2.00
☐ U9 Peacekeeper Barbie .75 2.00
☐ U10 Rorf .75 2.00
☐ U11 Scarron .75 2.00
☐ U12 Sheyang .75 2.00
☐ U13 Staanz .75 2.00
☐ U14 Stark .75 2.00
☐ U15 Tahleen .75 2.00
☐ U16 Traltixx .75 2.00
☐ U17 Varla .75 2.00
☐ U18 Volmae .75 2.00

2001 Farscape Season Two

COMPLETE SET (72) 5.00 12.00
☐ 73 Cast Montage 1 .15 .40
☐ 74 Cast Montage 2 .15 .40
☐ 75 Cast Montage 3 .15 .40
☐ 76 Mind The Baby .15 .40
☐ 77 Mind The Baby .15 .40
☐ 78 Mind The Baby .15 .40
☐ 79 Vitas Mortis .15 .40
☐ 80 Vitas Mortis .15 .40
☐ 81 Vitas Mortis .15 .40
☐ 82 Taking The Stone .15 .40
☐ 83 Taking The Stone .15 .40
☐ 84 Taking The Stone .15 .40
☐ 85 Crackers Don't Matter .15 .40
☐ 86 Crackers Don't Matter .15 .40
☐ 87 Crackers Don't Matter .15 .40
☐ 88 Picture If You Will .15 .40
☐ 89 Picture If You Will .15 .40
☐ 90 Picture If You Will .15 .40
☐ 91 The Way We Weren't .15 .40
☐ 92 The Way We Weren't .15 .40
☐ 93 The Way We Weren't .15 .40
☐ 94 Home On The Remains .15 .40
☐ 95 Home On The Remains .15 .40
☐ 96 Home On The Remains .15 .40
☐ 97 Dream A Little Dream .15 .40
☐ 98 Dream A Little Dream .15 .40
☐ 99 Dream A Little Dream .15 .40
☐ 100 Out Of Their Minds .15 .40
☐ 101 Out Of Their Minds .15 .40
☐ 102 Out Of Their Minds .15 .40
☐ 103 My Three Crichtons .15 .40
☐ 104 My Three Crichtons .15 .40
☐ 105 My Three Crichtons .15 .40
☐ 106 Look At The Princess Part I .15 .40
☐ 107 Look At The Princess Part I .15 .40
☐ 108 Look At The Princess Part I .15 .40
☐ 109 Look At The Princess Part II .15 .40
☐ 110 Look At The Princess Part II .15 .40
☐ 111 Look At The Princess Part II .15 .40
☐ 112 Look At The Princess Part III .15 .40
☐ 113 Look At The Princess Part III .15 .40
☐ 114 Look At The Princess Part III .15 .40
☐ 115 Beware Of Dog .15 .40
☐ 116 Beware Of Dog .15 .40
☐ 117 Beware Of Dog .15 .40
☐ 118 Won't Get Fooled Again .15 .40
☐ 119 Won't Get Fooled Again .15 .40
☐ 120 Won't Get Fooled Again .15 .40
☐ 121 The Locket .15 .40
☐ 122 The Locket .15 .40
☐ 123 The Locket .15 .40
☐ 124 The Ugly Truth .15 .40
☐ 125 The Ugly Truth .15 .40
☐ 126 The Ugly Truth .15 .40
☐ 127 A Clockwork Nebari .15 .40
☐ 128 A Clockwork Nebari .15 .40
☐ 129 A Clockwork Nebari .15 .40
☐ 130 Liars Guns And Money Part I .15 .40
☐ 131 Liars Guns And Money Part I .15 .40
☐ 132 Liars Guns And Money Part I .15 .40
☐ 133 Liars Guns And Money Part II .15 .40
☐ 134 Liars Guns And Money Part II .15 .40
☐ 135 Liars Guns And Money Part II .15 .40
☐ 136 Liars Guns And Money Part III .15 .40
☐ 137 Liars Guns And Money Part III .15 .40
☐ 138 Liars Guns And Money Part III .15 .40
☐ 139 Die Me Dichotomy .15 .40
☐ 140 Die Me Dichotomy .15 .40
☐ 141 Die Me Dichotomy .15 .40
☐ 142 Checklist 1 .15 .40
☐ 143 Checklist 2 .15 .40
☐ 144 Checklist 3 .15 .40

2001 Farscape Season Two Progressive Proofs Black

COMPLETE SET (82) 50.00 125.00
*PROOF: 3X TO 8X BASIC CARDS
ANNOUNCED PRINT RUN 50 SETS

2001 Farscape Season Two Progressive Proofs Cyan

COMPLETE SET (82) 50.00 125.00
*PROOF: 3X TO 8X BASIC CARDS
ANNOUNCED PRINT RUN 50 SETS

2001 Farscape Season Two Progressive Proofs Magenta

COMPLETE SET (82) 50.00 125.00
*PROOF: 3X TO 8X BASIC CARDS
ANNOUNCED PRINT RUN 50 SETS

2001 Farscape Season Two Progressive Proofs Yellow

COMPLETE SET (82) 50.00 125.00
*PROOF: 3X TO 8X BASIC CARDS
ANNOUNCED PRINT RUN 50 SETS

2001 Farscape Season Two Alien Life

COMPLETE SET (12) 10.00 25.00
STATED ODDS 1:10
☐ AL1 Delvians 1.25 3.00
☐ AL2 Luxans 1.25 3.00
☐ AL3 Hynerians 1.25 3.00
☐ AL4 Leviathans 1.25 3.00
☐ AL5 Nebari 1.25 3.00
☐ AL6 Scarrans 1.25 3.00
☐ AL7 Sebaceans 1.25 3.00
☐ AL8 Baniks 1.25 3.00
☐ AL9 Vocarian Blood Trackers 1.25 3.00
☐ AL10 Tavleks 1.25 3.00
☐ AL11 Sheyangs 1.25 3.00
☐ AL12 Plokavians 1.25 3.00

2001 Farscape Season Two Autographs

STATED ODDS 1:100
A11 ISSUED IN COLLECTORS ALBUM
A12 ISSUED AS CASE TOPPER
☐ A7 Virginia Hey 25.00 50.00
☐ A8 Lani Tupu 10.00 20.00
☐ A9 Wayne Pygram 20.00 40.00
☐ A10 David Kemper 20.00 40.00
☐ A11 Chris Haywood 20.00 40.00
(issued in collectors album)
☐ A12 David Wheeler 20.00 40.00
(issued as case topper)

2001 Farscape Season Two Behind the Scenes

COMPLETE SET (22) 10.00 25.00
STATED ODDS 1:5
☐ BK1 Mind The Baby .75 2.00
☐ BK2 Vitas Mortis .75 2.00
☐ BK3 Taking The Stone .75 2.00
☐ BK4 Crackers Don't Matter .75 2.00
☐ BK5 Picture If You Will .75 2.00
☐ BK6 The Way We Weren't .75 2.00
☐ BK7 Home On The Remains .75 2.00
☐ BK8 Dream A Little Dream .75 2.00
☐ BK9 Out Of Their Minds .75 2.00
☐ BK10 My Three Crichtons .75 2.00
☐ BK11 Look At The Princess Part I .75 2.00
☐ BK12 Look At The Princess Part II .75 2.00
☐ BK13 Look At The Princess Part III .75 2.00
☐ BK14 Beware Of Dog .75 2.00
☐ BK15 Won't Get Fooled Again .75 2.00
☐ BK16 The Locket .75 2.00
☐ BK17 The Ugly Truth .75 2.00
☐ BK18 A Clockwork Nebari .75 2.00
☐ BK19 Liars Guns And Money Part I .75 2.00
☐ BK20 Liars Guns And Money Part II .75 2.00
☐ BK21 Liars Guns And Money Part III .75 2.00
☐ BK22 Die Me Dichotomy .75 2.00

2001 Farscape Season Two From The Archives Costumes

STATED ODDS TWO PER BOX
☐ CC1 John Crichton 10.00 25.00
☐ CC2 John Crichton 15.00 40.00
☐ CC3 John Crichton 15.00 40.00
☐ CC4 Stark 6.00 15.00
☐ CC5 Rygel XVI 6.00 15.00
☐ CC6 Ka D'Argo 6.00 15.00
☐ CC7 Scorpius 6.00 15.00
☐ CC8 Captain Crais 40.00 100.00
☐ CC9 Chiana 6.00 15.00
☐ CC10 Chiana 60.00 150.00
☐ CC11 Chiana 6.00 15.00
☐ CC12 P'au Zotoh Zhaan 6.00 15.00
☐ CC13 P'au Zotoh Zhaan 6.00 15.00

2001 Farscape Season Two Promos

COMPLETE SET (2) 2.00 5.00
☐ BP1 Chiana/ (Binder Exclusive) 1.50 4.00
☐ NNO Scorpius 1.00 2.50

2001 Farscape Season Two The Quotable Farscape

COMPLETE SET (22) 10.00 25.00
STATED ODDS 1:5
☐ Q1 Mind The Baby .75 2.00
☐ Q2 Vitas Mortis .75 2.00
☐ Q3 Taking The Stone .75 2.00
☐ Q4 Crackers Don't Matter .75 2.00
☐ Q5 Picture If You Will .75 2.00
☐ Q6 The Way We Weren't .75 2.00
☐ Q7 Home On The Remains .75 2.00
☐ Q8 Dream A Little Dream .75 2.00
☐ Q9 Out Of Their Minds .75 2.00
☐ Q10 My Three Crichtons .75 2.00
☐ Q11 Look At The Princess Part I .75 2.00
☐ Q12 Look At The Princess Part II .75 2.00
☐ Q13 Look At The Princess Part III .75 2.00
☐ Q14 Beware Of Dog .75 2.00
☐ Q15 Won't Get Fooled Again .75 2.00
☐ Q16 The Locket .75 2.00
☐ Q17 The Ugly Truth .75 2.00
☐ Q18 A Clockwork Nebari .75 2.00
☐ Q19 Liars Guns And Money Part I .75 2.00
☐ Q20 Liars Guns And Money Part II .75 2.00
☐ Q21 Liars Guns And Money Part III .75 2.00
☐ Q22 Die Me Dichotomy .75 2.00

2001 Hercules The Complete Journeys

COMPLETE SET (120) 5.00 12.00
HC1 ODDS ONE PER CASE
☐ 1 Title Card .08 .25
☐ 2 Season One Overview .08 .25
☐ 3 The Wrong Path .08 .25
☐ 4 Eye Of The Beholder .08 .25
☐ 5 The Road To Calydon .08 .25
☐ 6 The Festival Of Dionysus .08 .25
☐ 7 Ares .08 .25
☐ 8 As Darkness Falls .08 .25
☐ 9 Pride Comes Before A Brawl .08 .25
☐ 10 The March To Freedom .08 .25
☐ 11 The Warrior Princess .08 .25
☐ 12 The Gladiator .08 .25
☐ 13 The Vanishing Dead .08 .25
☐ 14 The Gauntlet .08 .25
☐ 15 The Unchained Heart .08 .25
☐ 16 Season Two Overview .08 .25
☐ 17 King Of Thieves .08 .25
☐ 18 All That Glitters .08 .25
☐ 19 What's In A Name .08 .25
☐ 20 The Siege At Naxos .08 .25
☐ 21 Outcast .08 .25
☐ 22 Under The Broken Sky .08 .25
☐ 23 The Mother Of All Monsters .08 .25
☐ 24 The Other Side .08 .25
☐ 25 The Fire Down Below .08 .25
☐ 26 Cast A Giant Shadow .08 .25
☐ 27 Highway To Hades .08 .25
☐ 28 Sword Of Veracity .08 .25
☐ 29 The Enforcer .08 .25
☐ 30 Once A Hero .08 .25
☐ 31 Heedless Hearts .08 .25
☐ 32 Let The Games Begin .08 .25
☐ 33 The Apple .08 .25
☐ 34 Promises .08 .25
☐ 35 King For A Day .08 .25
☐ 36 Protean Challenge .08 .25
☐ 37 The Wedding Of Alcheme .08 .25
☐ 38 The Power .08 .25
☐ 39 Centaur Mentor Journey .08 .25
☐ 40 Cave Of Echoes .08 .25
☐ 41 Season Three Overview .08 .25
☐ 42 Mercenary .08 .25
☐ 43 Doomsday .08 .25
☐ 44 Love Takes A Holiday .08 .25
☐ 45 Mummy Dearest .08 .25
☐ 46 Not Fade Away .08 .25
☐ 47 Monster-Child In The Promised Land .08 .25
☐ 48 The Green Eyed Monster .08 .25
☐ 49 Prince Hercules .08 .25
☐ 50 A Star To Guide Them .08 .25
☐ 51 Lady And The Dragon .08 .25
☐ 52 Long Live The King .08 .25
☐ 53 Surprise .08 .25
☐ 54 Encounter .08 .25
☐ 55 When A Man Loves A Woman .08 .25
☐ 56 Judgement Day .08 .25
☐ 57 Lost City .08 .25
☐ 58 Les Contemptibles .08 .25
☐ 59 Reign Of Terror .08 .25
☐ 60 End Of The Beginning .08 .25
☐ 61 War Brides .08 .25
☐ 62 Rock And A Hard Place .08 .25
☐ 63 Atlantis .08 .25
☐ 64 Season Four Overview .08 .25
☐ 65 Beanstalks And Bad Eggs .08 .25
☐ 66 Hero's Heart .08 .25
☐ 67 Regrets... I've Had A Few .08 .25
☐ 68 Web Of Desire .08 .25
☐ 69 Stranger In A Strange World .08 .25
☐ 70 Two Men And A Baby .08 .25
☐ 71 Prodigal Sister .08 .25
☐ 72 And Fancy Free .08 .25
☐ 73 If I Had A Hammer .08 .25
☐ 74 Hercules On Trial .08 .25
☐ 75 Medea Culpa .08 .25
☐ 76 Men In Pink .08 .25
☐ 77 Armageddon Now I .08 .25
☐ 78 Armageddon Now II .08 .25
☐ 79 Yes, Virginia, There Is A Hercules .08 .25
☐ 80 Porkules .08 .25
☐ 81 One Fowl Day .08 .25
☐ 82 My Fair Cupcake .08 .25
☐ 83 War Wounds .08 .25
☐ 84 Twilight .08 .25
☐ 85 Top God .08 .25
☐ 86 Reunions .08 .25
☐ 87 Season Five Overview .08 .25
☐ 88 Faith .08 .25
☐ 89 Descent .08 .25
☐ 90 Resurrection .08 .25
☐ 91 Genies And Grecians And Geeks, Oh My .08 .25
☐ 92 Render Unto Caesar .08 .25
☐ 93 Norse By Norsevest .08 .25
☐ 94 Somewhere Over The Rainbow Bridge .08 .25
☐ 95 Darkness Rising .08 .25
☐ 96 For Those Of You Just Joining Us .08 .25
☐ 97 Let There Be Light .08 .25
☐ 98 Redemption .08 .25
☐ 99 Sky High .08 .25
☐ 100 Stranger And Stranger .08 .25
☐ 101 Just Passing Through .08 .25
☐ 102 Greece Is Burning .08 .25
☐ 103 We'll Always Have Cyprus .08 .25
☐ 104 The Academy .08 .25
☐ 105 Love On The Rocks .08 .25
☐ 106 Once Upon A Future King .08 .25
☐ 107 Fade Out .08 .25
☐ 108 My Best Girl's Wedding .08 .25
☐ 109 Revelations .08 .25
☐ 110 Season Six Overview .08 .25
☐ 111 Be Deviled .08 .25
☐ 112 Love, Amazon Style .08 .25
☐ 113 Rebel With A Cause .08 .25
☐ 114 Darkness Visible .08 .25
☐ 115 Hercules, Tramps And Thieves .08 .25
☐ 116 City Of The Dead .08 .25
☐ 117 Wicked Good Time .08 .25
☐ 118 Full Circle .08 .25
☐ 119 Checklist 1 .08 .25
☐ 120 Checklist 2 .08 .25
☐ HC1 Hercules MEM/ (issued as case topper) 15.00 30.00

2001 Hercules The Complete Journeys Autographs

STATED ODDS THREE PER BOX
A15 ISSUED IN COLLECTORS ALBUM
☐ HA1 Kevin Sorbo 35.00 60.00
☐ A2 Sam Sorbo 10.00 20.00
☐ A3 Martin Kove 10.00 20.00
☐ A4 Cory Everson 10.00 20.00
☐ A5 Kevin Smith 15.00 30.00
☐ A6 Tawny Kitaen 12.50 25.00
☐ A7 Ian Bohen 10.00 20.00
☐ A8 Robert Trebor 10.00 20.00
☐ A9 Liddy Holloway 10.00 20.00
☐ A10 Grant Bridger 10.00 20.00
☐ A11 Lisa Chappell 10.00 20.00
☐ A12 Josephine Davison 10.00 20.00
☐ A13 Joel Tobeck 10.00 20.00
☐ A14 Michael Hurst 10.00 20.00
☐ A15 Meighan Desmond 10.00 20.00
(issued in collectors album)
☐ A16 Gina Torres 15.00 30.00
☐ A17 Alexandra Tydings 10.00 20.00
☐ A18 Kerry Gallagher 10.00 20.00

2001 Hercules The Complete Journeys Heavenly Bodies

COMPLETE SET (9) 6.00 15.00
STATED ODDS 1:8
☐ HB1 Xena 1.00 2.50
☐ HB2 Gabrielle 1.00 2.50
☐ HB3 Aphrodite 1.00 2.50
☐ HB4 Serena 1.00 2.50
☐ HB5 Atalanta 1.00 2.50
☐ HB6 Deianeira 1.00 2.50
☐ HB7 Athena and Artemis 1.00 2.50
☐ HB8 Niobe 1.00 2.50
☐ HB9 The Enforcer 1.00 2.50

2001 Hercules The Complete Journeys Hercules HoloFEX

COMPLETE SET (6) 20.00 40.00
STATED ODDS 1:40
☐ H1 Hercules 4.00 10.00
☐ H2 Hercules 4.00 10.00
☐ H3 Hercules 4.00 10.00
☐ H4 Hercules 4.00 10.00
☐ H5 Hercules 4.00 10.00
☐ H6 Hercules 4.00 10.00

2001 Hercules The Complete Journeys Mythical Beasts

COMPLETE SET (9) 4.00 10.00
STATED ODDS 1:4
☐ M1 Hydra .60 1.50
☐ M2 Echidna .60 1.50
☐ M3 Golden Hind .60 1.50
☐ M4 Arachne .60 1.50
☐ M5 Typhon .60 1.50
☐ M6 Dahak .60 1.50
☐ M7 Primords .60 1.50
☐ M8 Baby Harpies .60 1.50
☐ M9 Centaur .60 1.50

2001 Hercules The Complete Journeys Promos

COMPLETE SET (2) 2.00 5.00
☐ BP1 Hercules/ (Binder Exclusive) 1.50 4.00
☐ NNO Hercules .75 2.00

2001 Hercules The Complete Journeys Xena Trilogy

COMPLETE SET (3) 6.00 15.00
STATED ODDS ONE PER BOX
☐ XT1 Warrior Princess 3.00 8.00
☐ XT2 The Gauntlet 3.00 8.00
☐ XT3 The Unchained Heart 3.00 8.00

2001 Jurassic Park III 3D

COMPLETE SET (72) 5.00 12.00
M1 STATED ODDS 1:107
CL1 ISSUED AS CASE TOPPER
DFX1 STATED ODDS 1:8
DFX2 STATED ODDS ONE PER HOBBY BOX
☐ 1 Title Card .15 .40
☐ 2 Forbidden Island .15 .40
☐ 3 Forever Friends .15 .40
☐ 4 Drumming Up Funds .15 .40

❑ 5 Billy, Idea Man .15 .40
❑ 6 A Tempting Offer .15 .40
❑ 7 The Nightmare Begins .15 .40
❑ 8 No Way Out .15 .40
❑ 9 Lost In The Jungle .15 .40
❑ 10 Clash Of Titans .15 .40
❑ 11 Drastic Discoveries .15 .40
❑ 12 Lab Of Horrors .15 .40
❑ 13 A Grinning Specimen .15 .40
❑ 14 Caught In The Open .15 .40
❑ 15 Hide And Seek .15 .40
❑ 16 Target Sighted .15 .40
❑ 17 A Joyous Reunion .15 .40
❑ 18 Billy's Foolish Gamble .15 .40
❑ 19 Ingen's Little Secret .15 .40
❑ 20 A Life For A Life .15 .40
❑ 21 Hope For Escape .15 .40
❑ 22 Go Get Mommy! .15 .40
❑ 23 Caged And Helpless .15 .40
❑ 24 Flames And Fury .15 .40
❑ 25 The Last Stand .15 .40
❑ 26 Deadly Mother Love .15 .40
❑ 27 The Nightmare Ends .15 .40
❑ 28 Dr. Alan Grant .15 .40
❑ 29 Eric Kirby .15 .40
❑ 30 Paul Kirby .15 .40
❑ 31 Amanda Kirby .15 .40
❑ 32 Billy Brennan .15 .40
❑ 33 Udesky .15 .40
❑ 34 Ellie Sattler .15 .40
❑ 35 Grant And Billy .15 .40
❑ 36 Grant And Eric .15 .40
❑ 37 Jaw 2 Claw – Spino-Skin .15 .40
❑ 38 Jaw 2 Claw – Spino-Eyes .15 .40
❑ 39 Jaw 2 Claw – Spino-Teeth .15 .40
❑ 40 Jaw 2 Claw – Raptor-View .15 .40
❑ 41 Jaw 2 Claw – Raptor-Camouflage .15 .40
❑ 42 Jaw 2 Claw – T-Rex Tint .15 .40
❑ 43 Jaw 2 Claw – T-Rex Feet .15 .40
❑ 44 Jaw 2 Claw – Pteranodon Eggs .15 .40
❑ 45 Jaw 2 Claw – Skyriders .15 .40
❑ 46 Pterror In The Sky .15 .40
❑ 47 Slash & Trash .15 .40
❑ 48 Raptor Rage .15 .40
❑ 49 Dive Bomber .15 .40
❑ 50 Stomp & Chomp .15 .40
❑ 51 Raptor Rumble .15 .40
❑ 52 Dinomania .15 .40
❑ 53 Pack Hunter .15 .40
❑ 54 Spinetingler .15 .40
❑ 55 Velociraptor .15 .40
❑ 56 Tyrannosaurus .15 .40
❑ 57 Spinosaurus .15 .40
❑ 58 Pteranodon .15 .40
❑ 59 Giant Pteranodon .15 .40
❑ 60 Dilophosaurus .15 .40
❑ 61 Brachiosaurus .15 .40
❑ 62 Anklosaurus .15 .40
❑ 63 Stegosaurus .15 .40
❑ 64 Compsognathus .15 .40
❑ 65 Corythosaurus .15 .40
❑ 66 Gallimimus .15 .40
❑ 67 Maiasaura .15 .40
❑ 68 Muttaburrasaurus .15 .40
❑ 69 Pachycephalosaurus .15 .40
❑ 70 Parasaurolophus .15 .40
❑ 71 Triceratops .15 .40
❑ 72 Checklist .15 .40
❑ M1 Mega Mayhem FOIL 6.00 15.00
❑ CL1 Reptile Rumble/case loader insert) 8.00 20.00
❑ DFX1 3-D Viewer .40 1.00
❑ DFX2 3-D Glasses .40 1.00

2001 Jurassic Park III 3D Extreme

COMPLETE SET (9) 12.50 30.00
STATED ODDS 1:11

❑ JE1 Die-Cut 1.50 4.00
❑ JE2 Die-Cut 1.50 4.00
❑ JE3 Die-Cut 1.50 4.00
❑ JE4 Die-Cut 1.50 4.00
❑ JE5 Die-Cut 1.50 4.00
❑ JE6 Die-Cut 1.50 4.00
❑ JE7 Die-Cut 1.50 4.00
❑ JE8 Die-Cut 1.50 4.00
❑ JE9 Die-Cut 1.50 4.00

2001 Jurassic Park III 3D Ragin' Refractors Blue

COMPLETE SET (6) 12.50 30.00
OVERALL REFRACTOR ODDS 1:17

❑ RR1 Prismatic Foil 2.50 6.00
❑ RR2 Prismatic Foil 2.50 6.00
❑ RR3 Prismatic Foil 2.50 6.00
❑ RR4 Prismatic Foil 2.50 6.00
❑ RR5 Prismatic Foil 2.50 6.00
❑ RR6 Prismatic Foil 2.50 6.00

2001 Lord of the Rings The Fellowship of the Ring

COMPLETE SET (90) 5.00 12.00

❑ 1 The Legend Comes to Life .15 .40
❑ 2 Gandalf .15 .40
❑ 3 Bilbo .15 .40
❑ 4 Frodo .15 .40
❑ 5 Sam .15 .40
❑ 6 Merry .15 .40
❑ 7 Pippin .15 .40
❑ 8 Aragorn .15 .40
❑ 9 Arwen .15 .40
❑ 10 Boromir .15 .40
❑ 11 Elrond .15 .40
❑ 12 Legolas .15 .40
❑ 13 Gimli .15 .40
❑ 14 Galadriel .15 .40
❑ 15 Celeborn .15 .40
❑ 16 Saruman .15 .40
❑ 17 Lurtz .15 .40
❑ 18 The Witch King .15 .40
❑ 19 Arriving in Hobbiton .15 .40
❑ 20 A Heartfelt Reunion .15 .40
❑ 21 Bag End .15 .40
❑ 22 Hobbit Celebration .15 .40
❑ 23 Bilbo's Big Night .15 .40
❑ 24 Trick or Treat .15 .40
❑ 25 Happy Birthday, Bilbo .15 .40
❑ 26 The Big Surprise .15 .40
❑ 27 Confronting Bilbo .15 .40
❑ 28 Secret of the Ring .15 .40
❑ 29 Dark Legacy .15 .40
❑ 30 The Quest Begins .15 .40
❑ 31 The Lord of Isengard .15 .40
❑ 32 Battle of the Wizards .15 .40
❑ 33 Hobbit Friends Reunited .15 .40
❑ 34 The Ringwraith .15 .40
❑ 35 The Hobbits Take Cover .15 .40
❑ 36 Escaping Death's Clutches .15 .40
❑ 37 Inn of the Prancing Pony .15 .40
❑ 38 Temptation .15 .40
❑ 39 Confronting Strider .15 .40
❑ 40 Death of the Gatekeeper .15 .40
❑ 41 Eluding the Ringwraiths .15 .40
❑ 42 A Treacherous Trek .15 .40
❑ 43 Facing the Dark Riders .15 .40
❑ 44 Caught by the Ringwraiths .15 .40
❑ 45 The Flame and the Sword .15 .40
❑ 46 Strider Attacks .15 .40
❑ 47 Vision of the Witch King .15 .40
❑ 48 Frodo Stricken .15 .40
❑ 49 Caverns of Horror .15 .40
❑ 50 Birthing of an Uruk-Hai .15 .40
❑ 51 Trollshaw Forest .15 .40
❑ 52 The Arrival of Arwen .15 .40
❑ 53 An Angel of Mercy .15 .40
❑ 54 Ringwraith Attack .15 .40
❑ 55 Reunited with Bilbo .15 .40
❑ 56 Elrond of Rivendell .15 .40
❑ 57 Dissent in the Council .15 .40
❑ 58 The Ringbearer's Move .15 .40
❑ 59 The Fellowship of Nine .15 .40
❑ 60 A Hobbit's Fate .15 .40
❑ 61 The Coming of Lurtz .15 .40
❑ 62 A New Breed of Orc .15 .40
❑ 63 The Pass of Caradhras .15 .40
❑ 64 Speak Friend and Enter .15 .40
❑ 65 Remembering the Way .15 .40
❑ 66 Inside Balin's Tomb .15 .40
❑ 67 Fool of a Took .15 .40
❑ 68 Drums of the Enemy .15 .40
❑ 69 The Fellowship Battles .15 .40
❑ 70 Frodo's Fight for Life .15 .40
❑ 71 The Balrog of Morgoth .15 .40
❑ 72 Escape to Lothlorien .15 .40
❑ 73 Toward New Adventure .15 .40
❑ 74 Pledged to the Cause .15 .40
❑ 75 The Uruk-Hai Attack .15 .40
❑ 76 The Might of a Dwarf .15 .40
❑ 77 The Battle of Amon-Hen .15 .40
❑ 78 The Horn of Gondor .15 .40
❑ 79 Army of the Damned .15 .40
❑ 80 Destiny of the Hobbits .15 .40
❑ 81 The Uruks Fall .15 .40
❑ 82 Of Magic and Make-up .15 .40
❑ 83 On the Dark Side .15 .40
❑ 84 Christopher Lee, Prince of Darkness .15 .40
❑ 85 Bringing Bad End to Life .15 .40
❑ 86 A Most Enchanting Subject .15 .40
❑ 87 Monsters, Monsters Everywhere .15 .40
❑ 88 A Rigorous Adventure .15 .40
❑ 89 The Director's Vision .15 .40
❑ 90 Checklist .15 .40

2001 Lord of the Rings The Fellowship of the Ring Autographs

HOBBY STATED ODDS 1:24
RETAIL STATED ODDS 1:72
SEAN BEAN AUTO UK HOBBY ONLY

❑ NNO Dominic Monaghan R
❑ NNO Liv Tyler H 100.00 200.00
❑ NNO Sir Ian Holm H 50.00 100.00
❑ NNO Billy Boyd H 50.00 100.00
❑ NNO Elijah Wood H 100.00 200.00
❑ NNO Orlando Bloom R 150.00 300.00
❑ NNO Sir Ian McKellen H 125.00 250.00
❑ NNO Christopher Lee R 150.00 300.00
❑ NNO John Rhys-Davies H 100.00 200.00
❑ NNO Sean Bean UK 125.00 250.00
❑ NNO Cate Blanchett H 60.00 120.00
❑ NNO Hugo Weaving R 150.00 300.00
❑ NNO Sean Astin H 50.00 100.00
❑ NNO Viggo Mortensen H 100.00 200.00

2001 Lord of the Rings The Fellowship of the Ring Box Loaders

COMPLETE SET (2) 5.00 12.00
STATED ODDS ONE PER BOX

❑ 1 Frodo 3.00 8.00
❑ 2 Frodo 3.00 8.00

2001 Lord of the Rings The Fellowship of the Ring Prismatics

COMPLETE SET (10) 7.50 20.00
STATED ODDS 1:6

❑ 1 Gimli 1.00 2.50
❑ 2 Saruman 1.00 2.50
❑ 3 Frodo 1.00 2.50
❑ 4 Lurtz 1.00 2.50
❑ 5 The Witch King 1.00 2.50
❑ 6 Boromir 1.00 2.50
❑ 7 Elrond 1.00 2.50
❑ 8 Lurtz 1.00 2.50
❑ 9 Ringwraiths 1.00 2.50
❑ 10 Orc Attack 1.00 2.50

2001 Lord of the Rings The Fellowship of the Ring Stickers

COMPLETE SET (10) 7.50 20.00
RANDOM INSERTS IN RETAIL PACKS

❑ 1 Bilbo 1.00 2.50
❑ 2 Boromir 1.00 2.50
❑ 3 Frodo 1.00 2.50
❑ 4 Gandalf 1.00 2.50
❑ 5 Gimli 1.00 2.50
❑ 6 Legolas 1.00 2.50
❑ 7 Aragorn 1.00 2.50
❑ 8 Gandalf 1.00 2.50
❑ 9 Arwen 1.00 2.50
❑ 10 Sam & Frodo 1.00 2.50

2001 The Mummy Returns

COMPLETE SET (81) 5.00 12.00

❑ 1 The Mummy Returns .15 .40
❑ 2 The Scorpion King .15 .40
❑ 3 Against The Sumerians .15 .40
❑ 4 The Undefeated .15 .40
❑ 5 The Curse .15 .40
❑ 6 Thebes Under Siege .15 .40
❑ 7 The O'Connells .15 .40
❑ 8 Evy's Quest .15 .40
❑ 9 Daunting Discovery .15 .40
❑ 10 Murder, Mummies And Mayhem .15 .40
❑ 11 Sling-Shot Attack! .15 .40
❑ 12 Chest Of Mystery .15 .40
❑ 13 Key To The Past .15 .40
❑ 14 Old Enemies .15 .40
❑ 15 Bay Watch .15 .40
❑ 16 Way To Go, Mom! .15 .40
❑ 17 The Past Comes Alive .15 .40
❑ 18 Out Of Harm's Way .15 .40
❑ 19 Imhotep Lives! .15 .40
❑ 20 The Rescue .15 .40
❑ 21 Fury Of The Mummy .15 .40
❑ 22 Lock-Nah's Mission .15 .40
❑ 23 Escape From The Museum .15 .40
❑ 24 The Mummy's Revenge .15 .40
❑ 25 The Soldier Mummies .15 .40
❑ 26 Bus Chase .15 .40
❑ 27 Alex…Kidnapped! .15 .40
❑ 28 The Mummy Lives .15 .40
❑ 29 Imhotep And Anck-Sunamun .15 .40
❑ 30 The Only Way To Travel? .15 .40
❑ 31 Captain Izzy .15 .40
❑ 32 Love To The Rescue .15 .40
❑ 33 Giving Lock-Nah Some Grief .15 .40
❑ 34 I Dream Of Nefertiri .15 .40
❑ 35 Alex Leaves A Clue .15 .40
❑ 36 Terror…And Sudden Death .15 .40
❑ 37 Going After The Big Guy .15 .40
❑ 38 The Final Battle Begins .15 .40
❑ 39 Within The Keyroom .15 .40
❑ 40 Threat Of The Ages .15 .40
❑ 41 The Curator's Fate .15 .40
❑ 42 An Eternity Of Evil .15 .40
❑ 43 Day Of The Medjai .15 .40
❑ 44 Army Of The Undead .15 .40
❑ 45 Ready For Action .15 .40
❑ 46 Hate Against Hate .15 .40
❑ 47 Battling To The Death .15 .40
❑ 48 Clash Of The Titans .15 .40
❑ 49 Medjai Vs. Anubis .15 .40
❑ 50 The Scorpion King Reborn .15 .40
❑ 51 Victors…Or Vanquished? .15 .40
❑ 52 O'Connell Triumphant .15 .40
❑ 53 No Way Out! .15 .40
❑ 54 Rescued! .15 .40
❑ 55 Evy's Mysterious Past .15 .40
❑ 56 Imhotep's Secret Love .15 .40
❑ 57 Love Eternal .15 .40
❑ 58 The Masked Fury .15 .40
❑ 59 Rage Of Anck-Sunamun .15 .40
❑ 60 Battle Royale .15 .40
❑ 61 Match And Rematch .15 .40
❑ 62 Scorpion King .15 .40
❑ 63 Imhotep Mummy .15 .40
❑ 64 Pygmy Mummies .15 .40
❑ 65 Anubis .15 .40
❑ 66 Rick O'Connell .15 .40
❑ 67 Evy O'Connell .15 .40
❑ 68 Alex O'Connell .15 .40
❑ 69 Imhotep .15 .40
❑ 70 Meela .15 .40
❑ 71 The Scorpion King .15 .40
❑ 72 Nefertiri .15 .40
❑ 73 Anck-Sunamun .15 .40
❑ 74 Ardeth Bay .15 .40
❑ 75 Lock-Nah .15 .40
❑ 76 Jonathan .15 .40
❑ 77 Izzy .15 .40
❑ 78 Red .15 .40
❑ 79 Jacques .15 .40
❑ 80 Spivey .15 .40
❑ 81 Checklist .15 .40
❑ MBL1 Scorpion King

2001 The Mummy Returns Autographs

COMPLETE SET (7) 300.00 500.00
RANDOM INSERTS IN PACKS

❑ A1 Brendan Fraser 50.00 100.00
❑ A2 Arnold Vosloo 30.00 60.00
❑ A3 Oded Fehr 30.00 60.00
❑ A4 John Hannah 30.00 60.00
❑ A5 Adewale Akinnuoye-Agbaje 30.00 60.00
❑ A6 Patricia Velasquez 30.00 60.00
❑ A7 The Rock 125.00 250.00

2001 The Mummy Returns Pieceworks

COMPLETE SET (3) 60.00 150.00
RANDOM INSERTS IN PACKS

❑ P1 Rachel Weisz 25.00 60.00
❑ P2 Rachel Weisz 25.00 60.00
❑ P3 Oded Fehr 25.00 60.00

2001 The Mummy Returns Promos

COMPLETE SET (5) 5.00 12.00

❑ MR1 The Mummy Returns 1.25 3.00
❑ MR2 The Mummy Returns 1.25 3.00
❑ MR3 The Mummy Returns 1.25 3.00
❑ MR4 The Mummy Returns 1.25 3.00
❑ MRi The Mummy Returns 1.25 3.00

2001 The Mummy Returns Sands of Time

COMPLETE SET (6) 10.00 25.00
STATED ODDS 1:17

❑ ST1 Sands of Time 2.00 5.00
❑ ST2 Sands of Time 2.00 5.00
❑ ST3 Sands of Time 2.00 5.00
❑ ST4 Sands of Time 2.00 5.00
❑ ST5 Sands of Time 2.00 5.00
❑ ST6 Sands of Time 2.00 5.00

2001 The Mummy Returns Scorpion King

COMPLETE SET (9) 15.00 40.00
STATED ODDS 1:11

❑ SK1 Scorpion King 2.00 5.00
❑ SK2 Scorpion King 2.00 5.00
❑ SK3 Scorpion King 2.00 5.00
❑ SK4 Scorpion King 2.00 5.00
❑ SK5 Scorpion King 2.00 5.00
❑ SK6 Scorpion King 2.00 5.00
❑ SK7 Scorpion King 2.00 5.00
❑ SK8 Scorpion King 2.00 5.00
❑ SK9 Scorpion King 2.00 5.00

2001 Simpson's Mania

COMPLETE SET (72) 5.00 12.00

❑ 1 Title Card .15 .40
❑ 2 Comic Book Guy .15 .40
❑ 3 Professor Frink .15 .40
❑ 4 Fat Tony .15 .40
❑ 5 Number One .15 .40
❑ 6 Gil .15 .40
❑ 7 Birch Barlow .15 .40
❑ 8 Disco Stu .15 .40
❑ 9 Dolph .15 .40
❑ 10 Wendell .15 .40
❑ 11 Uter .15 .40
❑ 12 Baby Gerald .15 .40
❑ 13 Helen Lovejoy .15 .40
❑ 14 Maude Flanders .15 .40
❑ 15 Lucius Sweet .15 .40
❑ 16 Drederick Tatum .15 .40
❑ 17 Cletus Del Roy .15 .40
❑ 18 Brandine Del Roy .15 .40
❑ 19 Luann vanHouten .15 .40
❑ 20 Kirk vanHouten .15 .40
❑ 21 Ucolin and Cesar .15 .40
❑ 22 Ernst and Gunter .15 .40
❑ 23 Jacques .15 .40
❑ 24 Chef Luigi .15 .40
❑ 25 Akira .15 .40
❑ 26 Sideshow Raheem .15 .40
❑ 27 Joey Jo Jo Jr. Shabbadoo .15 .40
❑ 28 McBabe .15 .40
❑ 29 Inanimate Carbon Rod .15 .40
❑ 30 Stuart The Duck .15 .40
❑ 31 Mr. Pinchy .15 .40
❑ 32 Homer '74 .15 .40
❑ 33 Marge '74 .15 .40
❑ 34 Principal Dondelinger '74 .15 .40
❑ 35 Barney '74 .15 .40
❑ 36 Artie Ziff '74 .15 .40
❑ 37 Flaming Willie .15 .40
❑ 38 Homer in the Box .15 .40
❑ 39 Witch Marge .15 .40
❑ 40 Dracula Burns .15 .40
❑ 41 The Simpsters .15 .40
❑ 42 Alien Maggie .15 .40
❑ 43 Brew 'n' Stew .15 .40
❑ 44 Donut Homer .15 .40
❑ 45 Werewolf Ned .15 .40
❑ 46 Barnacle Bill's Home Pregnancy Test .15 .40
❑ 47 Krusty O's .15 .40
❑ 48 Krusty Kologne .15 .40
❑ 49 Krusty Kough Syrup .15 .40
❑ 50 Jackie O's .15 .40
❑ 51 Cheezus H. Rice .15 .40
❑ 52 Uncle Jim's Country Fillin .15 .40
❑ 53 Much Ado About Stuffing .15 .40
❑ 54 Sulfuric Acid .15 .40
❑ 55 Duff Beer .15 .40
❑ 56 Buzz Cola .15 .40
❑ 57 Southern Cracker .15 .40
❑ 58 Strawberrito .15 .40
❑ 59 Lard Lad Donut Clumps .15 .40
❑ 60 Powersauce .15 .40
❑ 61 Soy Pop .15 .40
❑ 62 Squishee .15 .40
❑ 63 Heat Lamp Dogs .15 .40
❑ 64 Robbie Conal .15 .40
❑ 65 Chris Yambar .15 .40
❑ 66 Peter Kuper .15 .40
❑ 67 Sergio Aragones .15 .40
❑ 68 Dan Brereton .15 .40
❑ 69 Bill Morrison .15 .40
❑ 70 Craig Bartlett .15 .40
❑ 71 Tony Bennett .15 .40
❑ 72 Checklist .15 .40
❑ NNO Homer PROMO 1.25 3.00

2001 Simpson's Mania Autographs

COMPLETE SET (7) 150.00 300.00
STATED ODDS 1:72

❑ A1 Nancy Cartwright 25.00 50.00
❑ A2 Dan Castellaneta 25.00 50.00
❑ A3 Hank Azaria 30.00 60.00
❑ A4 Russi Taylor 25.00 50.00
❑ A5 Pamela Hayden 25.00 50.00
❑ A6 Tress MacNeille 25.00 50.00
❑ A7 Yeardley Smith 25.00 50.00

2001 Simpson's Mania SimpsaDelic

COMPLETE SET (9) 12.50 30.00
STATED ODDS 1:11

❑ S1 Larry Davis Experience 1.50 4.00
❑ S2 Bleeding Gums Murphy 1.50 4.00
❑ S3 Keep On Sucking 1.50 4.00
❑ S4 Let Your Spirit Soar 1.50 4.00
❑ S5 Springfied High Prom 1.50 4.00
❑ S6 The B Sharps 1.50 4.00
❑ S7 Marge 1.50 4.00
❑ S8 Scratch 1.50 4.00
❑ S9 Krusty 1.50 4.00

2001 Simpson's Mania Sketches

COMPLETE SET (9) 400.00 800.00
STATED ODDS 1:144

❑ SK1 Swinton Scott/237* 50.00 100.00
❑ SK2 Mark Kirkland/244* 50.00 100.00
❑ SK3 Phil Ortiz/240* 50.00 100.00
❑ SK4 Julius Priete/230* 50.00 100.00
❑ SK5 Wes Archer/233* 50.00 100.00
❑ SK6 Rich Moore/224* 50.00 100.00
❑ SK7 Mike Anderson/246* 50.00 100.00
❑ SK8 Jim Reardon/249* 50.00 100.00
❑ SK9 David Silverman/253* 50.00 100.00

2001 Star Trek 35th Anniversary HoloFEX

COMPLETE SET (72) 8.00 20.00

❑ 1 Captain Kirk .20 .50
❑ 2 Captain Kirk .20 .50
❑ 3 Captain Kirk .20 .50
❑ 4 Captain Kirk .20 .50
❑ 5 Captain Kirk .20 .50
❑ 6 Captain Kirk .20 .50
❑ 7 Captain Kirk .20 .50
❑ 8 Captain Kirk .20 .50
❑ 9 Captain Kirk .20 .50
❑ 10 Spock .20 .50
❑ 11 Spock .20 .50
❑ 12 Spock .20 .50
❑ 13 Spock .20 .50
❑ 14 Spock .20 .50
❑ 15 Spock .20 .50
❑ 16 Spock .20 .50
❑ 17 Spock .20 .50
❑ 18 Spock .20 .50
❑ 19 Dr. McCoy .20 .50
❑ 20 Dr. McCoy .20 .50
❑ 21 Dr. McCoy .20 .50
❑ 22 Dr. McCoy .20 .50
❑ 23 Dr. McCoy .20 .50
❑ 24 Dr. McCoy .20 .50
❑ 25 Mr. Scott .20 .50
❑ 26 Mr. Scott .20 .50
❑ 27 Mr. Scott .20 .50
❑ 28 Mr. Chekov .20 .50
❑ 29 Mr. Chekov .20 .50
❑ 30 Mr. Chekov .20 .50
❑ 31 Lt. Uhura .20 .50
❑ 32 Lt. Uhura .20 .50
❑ 33 Lt. Uhura .20 .50
❑ 34 Mr. Sulu .20 .50
❑ 35 Mr. Sulu .20 .50
❑ 36 Mr. Sulu .20 .50
❑ 37 Nurse Chapel .20 .50
❑ 38 Nurse Chapel .20 .50
❑ 39 Yeoman Rand .20 .50
❑ 40 Amanda .20 .50
❑ 41 Apollo .20 .50
❑ 42 Balok .20 .50
❑ 43 Captain Christopher .20 .50
❑ 44 Captain Merik .20 .50
❑ 45 Captain Pike .20 .50
❑ 46 Captain Ronald Tracey .20 .50
❑ 47 Commodore Decker .20 .50
❑ 48 Deela .20 .50
❑ 49 Dr. Daystrom .20 .50
❑ 50 Dr. Helen Noel .20 .50
❑ 51 Droxine .20 .50
❑ 52 Edith Keeler .20 .50
❑ 53 Flint .20 .50
❑ 54 Garth Of Izar .20 .50
❑ 55 Gary Seven .20 .50
❑ 56 Gem .20 .50
❑ 57 Khan .20 .50
❑ 58 Lenore Karidian .20 .50
❑ 59 Marlene Moreau .20 .50
❑ 60 Miramanee .20 .50
❑ 61 Miri .20 .50
❑ 62 Nancy Crater .20 .50
❑ 63 Nona .20 .50
❑ 64 Odona .20 .50
❑ 65 Sarek .20 .50
❑ 66 Shahna .20 .50
❑ 67 T'Pau .20 .50
❑ 68 The Gorn Captain .20 .50
❑ 69 Trelane .20 .50
❑ 70 Vina .20 .50
❑ 71 Zephram Cochran .20 .50
❑ 72 Checklist .20 .50

2001 Star Trek 35th Anniversary HoloFEX Autographs

STATED ODDS THREE PER BOX
A33 ISSUED AS CASE TOPPER
A34 ISSUED IN COLLECTORS ALBUM
DA1 STATED ODDS 1:480

❑ A1 Joanna Linville 25.00 50.00
❑ A2 Sean Kenney 6.00 15.00
❑ A3 Julie Newmar 15.00 30.00
❑ A4 Bob Herron 6.00 15.00
❑ A5 Sally Kellerman 15.00 30.00
❑ A6 Lawrence Montaigne 6.00 15.00
❑ A7 Jane Wyatt 15.00 30.00
❑ A8 Bobby Clark 6.00 15.00
❑ A9 Leslie Parrish 6.00 15.00
❑ A10 Paul Comi 6.00 15.00
❑ A11 Julie Parrish 6.00 15.00
❑ A12 Beverly Washburn 6.00 15.00
❑ A13 Michael Pataki 15.00 30.00
❑ A14 Emily Banks 12.00 25.00
❑ A15 Stewart Moss 6.00 15.00
❑ A16 Celeste Yarnall 6.00 15.00
❑ A17 Jeff Corey 6.00 15.00
❑ A18 Deborah Downey 12.00 25.00
❑ A19 David Ross 6.00 15.00
❑ A20 Marj Dusay 6.00 15.00
❑ A21 Michael Dante 6.00 15.00
❑ A22 Laurel Goodwin 6.00 15.00
❑ A23 Rhodes Reason 6.00 15.00
❑ A24 Elinor Donahue 12.00 25.00
❑ A25 Booker Bradshaw 6.00 15.00
❑ A26 Barbara Baldavin 12.00 25.00
❑ A27 William Smithers 12.00 25.00
❑ A28 Louise Sorel 12.00 25.00
❑ A29 Jan Shutan 12.00 25.00
❑ A30 Pamelyn Ferdin 12.00 25.00
❑ A31 Alexander Courage 12.00 25.00
❑ A32 Peter Duryea 6.00 15.00
❑ A33 Marianna Hill(issued as case topper) 20.00 40.00
❑ A34 Kate Woodville/(issued in collectors album)12.00 25.00
❑ DA1 William Shatner 250.00 400.00
Leonard Nimoy

2001 Star Trek 35th Anniversary HoloFEX Federation Foes

COMPLETE SET (6) 12.50 30.00
STATED ODDS 1:20

❑ FF1 Kor 2.50 6.00
❑ FF2 Koloth 2.50 6.00
❑ FF3 Kang 2.50 6.00
❑ FF4 Kahless 2.50 6.00
❑ FF5 Romulan Commander 2.50 6.00
❑ FF6 Romulan Commander 2.50 6.00

2001 Star Trek 35th Anniversary HoloFEX MorFEX

COMPLETE SET (9) 8.00 20.00
STATED ODDS 1:5

❑ M1 Captain Kirk 1.00 2.50
❑ M2 Captain Kirk 1.00 2.50
❑ M3 Kirk 1.00 2.50
Spock
❑ M4 Kirk 1.00 2.50
Spock
❑ M5 Kirk 1.00 2.50
Spock/Uhura/Chapel
❑ M6 Kirk 1.00 2.50
Uhura/Scotty/McCoy
❑ M7 Kirk 1.00 2.50
Spock/McCoy
❑ M8 Kirk 1.00 2.50
Spock/McCoy
❑ M9 Captain Pike 1.00 2.50

2001 Star Trek 35th Anniversary HoloFEX Progressive Proofs Black

COMPLETE SET (72) 75.00 150.00
COMMON CARD (1-72) 1.25 3.00
ANNOUNCED PRINT RUN 25

2001 Star Trek 35th Anniversary HoloFEX Progressive Proofs Cyan
COMPLETE SET (72) 75.00 150.00
COMMON CARD (1-72) 1.25 3.00
ANNOUNCED PRINT RUN 25

2001 Star Trek 35th Anniversary HoloFEX Progressive Proofs Magenta
COMPLETE SET (72) 75.00 150.00
COMMON CARD (1-72) 1.25 3.00
ANNOUNCED PRINT RUN 25

2001 Star Trek 35th Anniversary HoloFEX Progressive Proofs Yellow
COMPLETE SET (72) 75.00 150.00
COMMON CARD (1-72) 1.25 3.00
ANNOUNCED PRINT RUN 25

2001 Star Trek 35th Anniversary HoloFEX SketchaFEX
STATED ODDS 1:80

☐ 1 Cris Bolson/(USS Enterprise) 25.00 50.00
☐ 2 Cris Bolson/(Enterprise Shuttlecraft) 25.00 50.00
☐ 3 Cris Bolson/(Klingon Battle Cruiser) 25.00 50.00
☐ 4 John Czop/(Mugato) 30.00 60.00
☐ 5 John Czop/(Tellarite) 30.00 60.00
☐ 6 John Czop/(Balok's Puppet) 30.00 60.00
☐ 7 John Czop/(Mirror Spock) 30.00 60.00
☐ 8 Geoff Isherwood/(Uhura) 40.00 80.00
☐ 9 Warren Martineck/(Kor) 30.00 60.00
☐ 10 Warren Martineck/(Kahless) 30.00 60.00
☐ 11 Pablo Raimondi/(Capt. Kirk) 30.00 60.00
☐ 12 Pablo Raimondi/(Gorn captain) 25.00 50.00
☐ 13 Pablo Raimondi/(Salt Sucker) 25.00 50.00
☐ 14 Pablo Raimondi/(Talosian) 25.00 50.00
☐ 15 Pablo Raimondi/(Guardian of Forever) 25.00 50.00
☐ 16 Dan Schaefer/(Mister Spock) 30.00 60.00
☐ 17 Dan Schaefer/(Dr. McCoy) 30.00 60.00

2001 Star Trek 35th Anniversary HoloFEX The Best of Bones
COMPLETE SET (9) 8.00 20.00
STATED ODDS 1:10

☐ BB1 Moon Shuttle Conductor 1.25 3.00
☐ BB2 Bricklayer 1.25 3.00
☐ BB3 Mechanic 1.25 3.00
☐ BB4 Psychiatrist 1.25 3.00
☐ BB5 Escalator 1.25 3.00
☐ BB6 Engineer 1.25 3.00
☐ BB7 Magician 1.25 3.00
☐ BB8 Flesh Peddler 1.25 3.00
☐ BB9 Coal Miner 1.25 3.00

2001 Stargate SG-1
COMPLETE SET (72) 8.00 20.00

☐ 1 Season One Overview .20 .50
☐ 2 Children Of The Gods Part 1 .20 .50
☐ 3 Children Of The Gods Part 2 .20 .50
☐ 4 The Enemy Within .20 .50
☐ 5 Emancipation .20 .50
☐ 6 The Broca Divide .20 .50
☐ 7 The First Commandment .20 .50
☐ 8 Cold Lazarus .20 .50
☐ 9 The Nox .20 .50
☐ 10 Brief Candle .20 .50
☐ 11 Thors Hammer .20 .50
☐ 12 The Torment Of Tantalus .20 .50
☐ 13 Bloodlines .20 .50
☐ 14 Fire And Water .20 .50
☐ 15 Hathor .20 .50
☐ 16 Singularity .20 .50
☐ 17 Cor-ai .20 .50
☐ 18 Enigma .20 .50
☐ 19 Solitudes .20 .50
☐ 20 The Man .20 .50
☐ 21 There But For The Grace Of God .20 .50
☐ 22 Politics .20 .50
☐ 23 Within The Serpents Grasp .20 .50
☐ 24 Season Two Overview .20 .50
☐ 25 Serpents Lair .20 .50
☐ 26 In The Line Of Duty .20 .50
☐ 27 Prisoners .20 .50
☐ 28 The Gamekeeper .20 .50
☐ 29 Need .20 .50
☐ 30 Thors Chariot .20 .50
☐ 31 Message In A Bottle .20 .50
☐ 32 Family .20 .50
☐ 33 Secrets .20 .50
☐ 34 Bane .20 .50
☐ 35 The Tok'ra Part 1 .20 .50
☐ 36 The Tok'ra Part 2 .20 .50
☐ 37 Spirits .20 .50
☐ 38 Touchstone .20 .50
☐ 39 The Fifth Race .20 .50
☐ 40 A Matter Of Time .20 .50
☐ 41 Holiday .20 .50
☐ 42 Serpents Song .20 .50
☐ 43 One False Step .20 .50
☐ 44 Show And Tell .20 .50
☐ 45 1969 .20 .50
☐ 46 Out Of Mind .20 .50
☐ 47 Season Three Overview .20 .50
☐ 48 Into The Fire .20 .50
☐ 49 Seth .20 .50
☐ 50 Fair Game .20 .50
☐ 51 Legacy .20 .50
☐ 52 Learning Curve .20 .50
☐ 53 Point Of View .20 .50
☐ 54 Dead Man's Switch .20 .50
☐ 55 Demons .20 .50
☐ 56 Rules Of Engagement .20 .50
☐ 57 Forever In A Day .20 .50
☐ 58 Past And Present .20 .50
☐ 59 Jolinar's Memories .20 .50
☐ 60 The Devil You Know .20 .50
☐ 61 Foothold .20 .50
☐ 62 Pretense .20 .50
☐ 63 Urgo .20 .50
☐ 64 A Hundred Days .20 .50
☐ 65 Shades Of Gray .20 .50
☐ 66 New Ground .20 .50
☐ 67 Maternal Instinct .20 .50
☐ 68 Crystal Skull .20 .50
☐ 69 Nemesis .20 .50
☐ 70 Checklist 1 .20 .50
☐ 71 Checklist 2 .20 .50
☐ 72 Checklist 3 .20 .50

2001 Stargate SG-1 Progressive Proofs Black
COMPLETE SET (72) 75.00 150.00
COMMON CARD (1-72) 1.25 3.00
ANNOUNCED PRINT RUN 25 SETS

2001 Stargate SG-1 Progressive Proofs Cyan
COMPLETE SET (72) 75.00 150.00
COMMON CARD (1-72) 1.25 3.00
ANNOUNCED PRINT RUN 25 SETS

2001 Stargate SG-1 Progressive Proofs Magenta
COMPLETE SET (72) 75.00 150.00
COMMON CARD (1-72) 1.25 3.00
ANNOUNCED PRINT RUN 25 SETS

2001 Stargate SG-1 Progressive Proofs Yellow
COMPLETE SET (72) 75.00 150.00
COMMON CARD (1-72) 1.25 3.00
ANNOUNCED PRINT RUN 25 SETS

2001 Stargate SG-1 Autographs
STATED ODDS ONE PER BOX

☐ A1 Richard Dean Anderson 60.00 120.00
☐ A2 Don Davis 20.00 40.00
☐ A3 Teryl Rothery 10.00 25.00
☐ A4 Alexis Cruz 10.00 25.00
☐ A5 Vaitiare Bandera 10.00 25.00
☐ A6 Peter Williams 10.00 25.00
☐ A7 Vince Crestejo 10.00 25.00
☐ A8 Jay Acovone 10.00 25.00
☐ A9 Tony Amendola 10.00 25.00

2001 Stargate SG-1 From The Archives Costumes
COMPLETE SET (4) 100.00 250.00
STATED ODDS 1:80

☐ C1 Colonel Jack O'Neill 15.00 30.00
☐ C2 Dr. Daniel Jackson 15.00 30.00
☐ C3 Major Samantha Carter 60.00 120.00
☐ C4 Teal'c/ (issued as case topper) 50.00 100.00

2001 Stargate SG-1 Promos
COMPLETE SET (2) 2.00 5.00

☐ P1 Group shot (General Distribution) .75 2.00
☐ P2 Colonel Jack O'Neill (Binder Exclusive) 1.50 4.00

2001 Stargate SG-1 Stargate Aliens
COMPLETE SET (9) 2.00 5.00
STATED ODDS 1:3

☐ X1 The Asgards .40 1.00
☐ X2 The Spirits .40 1.00
☐ X3 The Oannes .40 1.00
☐ X4 The Aliens Of P3X-118 .40 1.00
☐ X5 The Tiermods .40 1.00
☐ X6 The Nox .40 1.00
☐ X7 The Unas .40 1.00
☐ X8 Aliens Of PJ2-455 .40 1.00
☐ X9 The Argosians .40 1.00

2001 Stargate SG-1 Stargate In Motion
COMPLETE SET (6) 8.00 20.00
STATED ODDS 1:27

☐ M1 Sha're Dr. Jackson 4.00 10.00
☐ M2 Dr. Daniel Jackson 4.00 10.00
☐ M3 Stargate 4.00 10.00
☐ M4 Teal'c 4.00 10.00
☐ M5 Colonel Jack O'Neill 4.00 10.00
☐ M6 Skaara 4.00 10.00

2001 Stargate SG-1 Stargate Stars
COMPLETE SET (5) 4.00 10.00
STATED ODDS 1:7

☐ S1 Colonel Jack O'Neill 1.00 2.50
☐ S2 Dr. Daniel Jackson 1.00 2.50
☐ S3 Major Samantha Carter 1.00 2.50
☐ S4 Teal'c 1.00 2.50
☐ S5 General George Hammond 1.00 2.50

2001 Tim Burton's The Nightmare Before Christmas
COMPLETE SET (72) 6.00 15.00
FILM FLIP CARD STATED ODDS 1:4

☐ 1 All the Ghosts, Goblins and Creatures .15 .40
☐ 2 While the Town Celebrates .15 .40
☐ 3 Secretly Watching Jack's Lament .15 .40
☐ 4 Jack's Walk Takes Him Deep .15 .40
☐ 5 Before He Knows It .15 .40
☐ 6 Back In Halloweentown .15 .40
☐ 7 Just When the Mayor .15 .40
☐ 8 At the Town Hall Jack Tells .15 .40
☐ 9 Back Home Jack Spends .15 .40
☐ 10 Sally Is Worried About Jack .15 .40
☐ 11 But Sally Is Not the Only One .15 .40
☐ 12 Then All of a Sudden .15 .40
☐ 13 Jack Gets Everyone In Town .15 .40
☐ 14 A Special Call Goes Out .15 .40
☐ 15 Lock, Shock and Barrel Head .15 .40
☐ 16 When Jack Asks Sally .15 .40
☐ 17 Dr. Finkelstein Is Also Given .15 .40
☐ 18 The Whole Town Is Busy .15 .40
☐ 19 In Christmastown, Santa Is Busy .15 .40
☐ 20 Lock, Shock and Barrel Bring .15 .40
☐ 21 Unfortunately For Santa .15 .40
☐ 22 Sally Sees Jack Is Almost Ready .15 .40
☐ 23 The Plan Almost Works .15 .40
☐ 24 At His First House .15 .40
☐ 25 When the Boy's Parents Come In .15 .40
☐ 26 All Over Town Jack Leaves .15 .40
☐ 27 Back In Halloweentown .15 .40
☐ 28 To Stop This Heinous Crime .15 .40
☐ 29 Meanwhile Sally Makes It .15 .40
☐ 30 In the Sky, the Fireworks Continue .15 .40
☐ 31 Back In Halloweentown .15 .40
☐ 32 But Actually Jack Landed .15 .40
☐ 33 But the More He Thinks About It .15 .40
☐ 34 So Off to Oogie Boogie's Lair .15 .40
☐ 35 And Just When It Looks Like .15 .40
☐ 36 Jack Apologizes to Santa .15 .40
☐ 37 While Santa Replaces All .15 .40
☐ 38 While the Town Celebrates .15 .40
☐ 39 Jack Skellington .15 .40
☐ 40 Sally .15 .40
☐ 41 Lock .15 .40
☐ 42 Shock .15 .40
☐ 43 Barrel .15 .40
☐ 44 Mayor .15 .40
☐ 45 Dr. Finklestein .15 .40
☐ 46 Oogie Boogie .15 .40
☐ 47 Zero .15 .40
☐ 48 Santa .15 .40
☐ 49 Art Department .15 .40
☐ 50 Sculpting Department .15 .40
☐ 51 Molding Department .15 .40
☐ 52 Armature Department .15 .40
☐ 53 Fabrication Department .15 .40
☐ 54 Jack Skellington (Chris Sarandon, Danny Elfman) .15 .40
☐ 55 Sally (Catherine O'Hara) .15 .40
☐ 56 Mayor (Glenn Shadix) .15 .40
☐ 57 Oogie Boogie (Ken Page) .15 .40
☐ 58 Lock, Shock and Barrel (Paul Reubens, Catherine O'Hara and Danny Elfman) .15 .40
☐ 59 Santa Claus (Ed Ivory) .15 .40
☐ 60 Evil Scientist (William Hickey) .15 .40
☐ 61 Zero .15 .40
☐ 62 Halloween Town .15 .40
☐ 63 The Producer - Tim Burton, Denise DiNovi .15 .40
☐ 64 The Director - Henry Selick .15 .40
☐ 65 The Composer/Lyricist - Danny Elfman .15 .40
☐ 66 The Screenwriter - Caroline Thompson .15 .40
☐ 67 The Storyboard Supervisor - Joe Ranft .15 .40
☐ 68 The Art Director - Deane Taylor .15 .40
☐ 69 The Set Designer - Gregg Olsson .15 .40
☐ 70 The Animation Supervisor - Eric Leighton .15 .40
☐ 71 Director of Photography - Pete Kozachik .15 .40
☐ 72 Checklist .15 .40
☐ FC Film Flip Card 6.00 15.00

2001 Tim Burton's The Nightmare Before Christmas Autographs
RANDOM INSERTS IN PACKS

☐ A1 Tim Burton
☐ A2 Danny Elfman 50.00 100.00
☐ A3 Chris Sarandon 20.00 40.00
☐ A4 Glenn Shadix 15.00 30.00

2001 The Women of Star Trek Voyager HoloFex
COMPLETE SET (72) 4.00 10.00

☐ 1 Captain Janeway .10 .30
☐ 2 Captain Janeway .10 .30
☐ 3 Captain Janeway .10 .30
☐ 4 Captain Janeway .10 .30
☐ 5 Captain Janeway .10 .30
☐ 6 Captain Janeway .10 .30
☐ 7 Captain Janeway .10 .30
☐ 8 Captain Janeway .10 .30
☐ 9 Captain Janeway .10 .30
☐ 10 Seven Of Nine .10 .30
☐ 11 Seven Of Nine .10 .30
☐ 12 Seven Of Nine .10 .30
☐ 13 Seven Of Nine .10 .30
☐ 14 Seven Of Nine .10 .30
☐ 15 Seven Of Nine .10 .30
☐ 16 Seven Of Nine .10 .30
☐ 17 Seven Of Nine .10 .30
☐ 18 Seven Of Nine .10 .30
☐ 19 B'Elanna Torres .10 .30
☐ 20 B'Elanna Torres .10 .30
☐ 21 B'Elanna Torres .10 .30
☐ 22 B'Elanna Torres .10 .30
☐ 23 B'Elanna Torres .10 .30
☐ 24 B'Elanna Torres .10 .30
☐ 25 B'Elanna Torres .10 .30
☐ 26 B'Elanna Torres .10 .30
☐ 27 B'Elanna Torres .10 .30
☐ 28 Kes .10 .30
☐ 29 Kes .10 .30
☐ 30 Kes .10 .30
☐ 31 Kes .10 .30
☐ 32 Kes .10 .30
☐ 33 Kes .10 .30
☐ 34 Borg Queen .10 .30
☐ 35 Borg Queen .10 .30
☐ 36 Borg Queen .10 .30
☐ 37 Seska .10 .30
☐ 38 Seska .10 .30
☐ 39 Seska .10 .30
☐ 40 Naomi Wildman .10 .30
☐ 41 Samantha Wildman .10 .30
☐ 42 Freya .10 .30
☐ 43 Amelia Earhart .10 .30
☐ 44 Libby .10 .30
☐ 45 Denara Pel .10 .30
☐ 46 Commander Rand .10 .30
☐ 47 Rain Robinson .10 .30
☐ 48 Female Q .10 .30
☐ 49 Marayna .10 .30
☐ 50 Riley Frazier .10 .30
☐ 51 Lyris .10 .30
☐ 52 Nimira .10 .30
☐ 53 Kellin .10 .30
☐ 54 Valerie .10 .30
☐ 55 Tessa Omund .10 .30
☐ 56 Noss .10 .30
☐ 57 Darren Tal .10 .30
☐ 58 3 of 9 .10 .30
☐ 59 Dayla .10 .30
☐ 60 Counselor Troi .10 .30
☐ 61 Maggie .10 .30
☐ 62 Tincoo .10 .30
☐ 63 Mezoti .10 .30
☐ 64 Lindsay Ballard .10 .30
☐ 65 Tal Celes .10 .30
☐ 66 Dala .10 .30
☐ 67 Leosa .10 .30
☐ 68 Kejal .10 .30
☐ 69 Jaryn .10 .30
☐ 70 Checklist .10 .30

2001 The Women of Star Trek Voyager HoloFex ArtiFex
COMPLETE SET (2)
STATED ODDS ONE PER CASE

☐ AR1 Seven Of Nine 10.00 25.00
☐ AR2 B'Elanna Torres 10.00 25.00

2001 The Women of Star Trek Voyager HoloFex Autographs
STATED ODDS TWO PER BOX
A2 ISSUED IN COLLECTORS ALBUM
A3 ISSUED AS CASE TOPPER

☐ A1 Martha Hackett 6.00 15.00
☐ A2 Nancy Hower/(issued in collectors album) 10.00 25.00
☐ A3 Vanessa Branch/(issued as case topper) 10.00 25.00
☐ A4 Sharon Lawrence 6.00 15.00
☐ A5 Virginia Madsen 6.00 15.00
☐ A6 Marjorie Monaghan 6.00 15.00
☐ A7 Tracey Ellis 6.00 15.00
☐ A8 Jessica Collins 6.00 15.00
☐ A9 Marley McLean 6.00 15.00
☐ A10 Carolyn Seymour 6.00 15.00
☐ A11 Gwynyth Walsh 6.00 15.00
☐ A12 Peggy Jo Jacobs 6.00 15.00
☐ A13 Kaitlin Hopkins 6.00 15.00
☐ A14 Kamala Lopez-Dawson 6.00 15.00
☐ A15 Lori Petty 6.00 15.00
☐ SA1 Jeri Ryan 50.00 80.00
☐ SA2 Katelin Peterson 6.00 15.00
☐ SA3 Erica Lynne Bryan 6.00 15.00
☐ SA4 Laura Stepp 6.00 15.00
☐ SA5 Nikki Tyler 6.00 15.00
☐ SA6 Kirk Baily 6.00 15.00
☐ SA7 J. Paul Boehmer 6.00 15.00

2001 The Women of Star Trek Voyager HoloFex From The Archives Costumes
COMPLETE SET (2) 40.00 80.00
STATED ODDS 1:120

☐ F1 Seven Of Nine 20.00 50.00
☐ F2 Captain Janeway 20.00 50.00

2001 The Women of Star Trek Voyager HoloFex MorFex
COMPLETE SET (9) 6.00 15.00
STATED ODDS 1:4

☐ M1 Captain Janeway .75 2.00
☐ M2 Captain Janeway .75 2.00
☐ M3 Captain Janeway .75 2.00
☐ M4 Seven Of Nine .75 2.00
☐ M5 Seven Of Nine .75 2.00
☐ M6 Seven Of Nine .75 2.00
☐ M7 B'Elanna Torres .75 2.00
☐ M8 B'Elanna Torres .75 2.00
☐ M9 B'Elanna Torres .75 2.00

2001 The Women of Star Trek Voyager HoloFex Printer's Proofs
COMPLETE SET (70) 30.00 60.00
COMMON CARD (1-70) .40 1.00
STATED ODDS 1:2

☐ 1 Captain Janeway .40 1.00
☐ 2 Captain Janeway .40 1.00
☐ 3 Captain Janeway .40 1.00
☐ 4 Captain Janeway .40 1.00
☐ 5 Captain Janeway .40 1.00
☐ 6 Captain Janeway .40 1.00
☐ 7 Captain Janeway .40 1.00
☐ 8 Captain Janeway .40 1.00
☐ 9 Captain Janeway .40 1.00
☐ 10 Seven Of Nine .40 1.00
☐ 11 Seven Of Nine .40 1.00
☐ 12 Seven Of Nine .40 1.00
☐ 13 Seven Of Nine .40 1.00
☐ 14 Seven Of Nine .40 1.00
☐ 15 Seven Of Nine .40 1.00
☐ 16 Seven Of Nine .40 1.00
☐ 17 Seven Of Nine .40 1.00
☐ 18 Seven Of Nine .40 1.00
☐ 19 B'Elanna Torres .40 1.00
☐ 20 B'Elanna Torres .40 1.00
☐ 21 B'Elanna Torres .40 1.00
☐ 22 B'Elanna Torres .40 1.00
☐ 23 B'Elanna Torres .40 1.00
☐ 24 B'Elanna Torres .40 1.00
☐ 25 B'Elanna Torres .40 1.00
☐ 26 B'Elanna Torres .40 1.00
☐ 27 B'Elanna Torres .40 1.00
☐ 28 Kes .40 1.00
☐ 29 Kes .40 1.00
☐ 30 Kes .40 1.00
☐ 31 Kes .40 1.00
☐ 32 Kes .40 1.00
☐ 33 Kes .40 1.00
☐ 34 Borg Queen .40 1.00
☐ 35 Borg Queen .40 1.00
☐ 36 Borg Queen .40 1.00
☐ 37 Seska .40 1.00
☐ 38 Seska .40 1.00
☐ 39 Seska .40 1.00
☐ 40 Naomi Wildman .40 1.00
☐ 41 Samantha Wildman .40 1.00
☐ 42 Freya .40 1.00
☐ 43 Amelia Earhart .40 1.00
☐ 44 Libby .40 1.00
☐ 45 Denara Pel .40 1.00
☐ 46 Commander Rand .40 1.00
☐ 47 Rain Robinson .40 1.00
☐ 48 Female Q .40 1.00
☐ 49 Marayna .40 1.00
☐ 50 Riley Frazier .40 1.00
☐ 51 Lyris .40 1.00
☐ 52 Nimira .40 1.00
☐ 53 Kellin .40 1.00
☐ 54 Valerie .40 1.00
☐ 55 Tessa Omund .40 1.00
☐ 56 Noss .40 1.00
☐ 57 Darren Tal .40 1.00
☐ 58 3 of 9 .40 1.00
☐ 59 Dayla .40 1.00
☐ 60 Counselor Troi .40 1.00
☐ 61 Maggie .40 1.00
☐ 62 Tincoo .40 1.00
☐ 63 Mezoti .40 1.00
☐ 64 Lindsay Ballard .40 1.00
☐ 65 Tal Celes .40 1.00
☐ 66 Dala .40 1.00
☐ 67 Leosa .40 1.00
☐ 68 Kejal .40 1.00
☐ 69 Jaryn .40 1.00
☐ 70 Checklist .40 1.00

2001 The Women of Star Trek Voyager HoloFex Progressive Proofs Black
COMPLETE SET (70) 75.00 150.00
COMMON CARD (1-70) 1.25 3.00
ANNOUNCED PRINT RUN 25

2001 The Women of Star Trek Voyager HoloFex Progressive Proofs Cyan
COMPLETE SET (70) 75.00 150.00
COMMON CARD (1-70) 1.25 3.00
ANNOUNCED PRINT RUN 25

2001 The Women of Star Trek Voyager HoloFex Progressive Proofs Magenta
COMPLETE SET (70) 75.00 150.00
COMMON CARD (1-70) 1.25 3.00
ANNOUNCED PRINT RUN 25

2001 The Women of Star Trek Voyager HoloFex Progressive Proofs Yellow
COMPLETE SET (70) 75.00 150.00
COMMON CARD (1-70) 1.25 3.00
ANNOUNCED PRINT RUN 25

2001 The Women of Star Trek Voyager HoloFex Promos
COMPLETE SET (3) 2.00 5.00

☐ 1 Seven Of Nine 1.00 2.50
☐ 2 Captain Janeway 1.00 2.50
☐ 3 Torres 1.00 2.50
Seven of Nine/Janeway

2001 The Women of Star Trek Voyager HoloFex ReflectFex
COMPLETE SET (9) 8.00 20.00
STATED ODDS 1:10

☐ R1 Captain Janeway 1.00 2.50
☐ R2 Captain Janeway 1.00 2.50
☐ R3 Captain Janeway 1.00 2.50
☐ R4 Seven Of Nine 1.00 2.50
☐ R5 Seven Of Nine 1.00 2.50
☐ R6 Seven Of Nine 1.00 2.50
☐ R7 B'Elanna Torres 1.00 2.50
☐ R8 B'Elanna Torres 1.00 2.50
☐ R9 B'Elanna Torres 1.00 2.50

2001 The Women of Star Trek Voyager HoloFex SketchaFex
STATED ODDS 1:120

☐ 1 Chris Bolson/(Voyager from above)
☐ 2 Chris Bolson/(Voyager from below)
☐ 3 John Czop/(B'Elanna)
☐ 4 John Czop/(Seven of Nine)
☐ 5 John Czop/(Kes)
☐ 6 Warren Martineck/(SS Raven)
☐ 7 Warren Martineck/(USS Voyager)
☐ 8 Warren Martineck/(Borg Tactical Cube)
☐ 9 Warren Martineck/(Borg Queen Ship)
☐ 10 Warren Martineck/(Voyager vs. Borg Queen)
☐ 11 Warren Martineck/(Voyager vs. Borg Cube)
☐ 12 Emir Ribeiro/(B'Elanna)
☐ 13 Emir Ribeiro/(Seven of Nine)

2001 The Women of Star Trek Voyager HoloFex SpaceFex
COMPLETE SET (6) 10.00 25.00
STATED ODDS 1:20

☐ SF1 Delta Flyer 2.50 6.00
☐ SF2 U.S.S. Excelsior 2.50 6.00
☐ SF3 Borg Sphere 2.50 6.00
☐ SF4 Hologram Ship 2.50 6.00
☐ SF5 Kazon Raider 2.50 6.00
☐ SF6 Caretaker's Array 2.50 6.00

2001 X-Files Seasons 4 and 5
COMPLETE SET (90) 5.00 12.00

☐ 1 The Truth Is Out There .15 .40
☐ 2 4X01: Herrenvolk .15 .40
☐ 3 4X02: Unruhe .15 .40
☐ 4 4X03: Home .15 .40
☐ 5 4X04: Teliko .15 .40
☐ 6 4X05: The Field Where I Died .15 .40
☐ 7 4X06: Sanguinarium .15 .40
☐ 8 4X07: Musings Of A Cigarette-Smoking Man .15 .40
☐ 9 4X08: Paper Hearts .15 .40
☐ 10 4X09: Tunguska .15 .40
☐ 11 4X10: Terma .15 .40
☐ 12 4X11: El Mundo Gira .15 .40
☐ 13 4X12: Kaddish .15 .40
☐ 14 4X13: Never Again .15 .40
☐ 15 4X14: Leonard Betts .15 .40
☐ 16 4X15: Memento Mori .15 .40
☐ 17 4X16: Unrequited .15 .40
☐ 18 4X17: Tempus Fugit .15 .40
☐ 19 4X18: Max .15 .40
☐ 20 4X19: Synchrony .15 .40
☐ 21 4X20: Small Potatoes .15 .40
☐ 22 4X21: Zero Sum .15 .40
☐ 23 4X22: Elegy .15 .40
☐ 24 4X23: Demons .15 .40
☐ 25 4X24: Gethsemane .15 .40
☐ 26 5X01: Unusual Suspects .15 .40
☐ 27 5X02: Redux .15 .40
☐ 28 5X03: Redux Ii .15 .40
☐ 29 5X04: Detour .15 .40
☐ 30 5X05: Christmas Carol .15 .40
☐ 31 5X06: Post-Modern Prometheus .15 .40
☐ 32 5X07: Emily .15 .40
☐ 33 5X08: Kitsunegari .15 .40
☐ 34 5X09: Schizogeny .15 .40
☐ 35 5X10: Chinga .15 .40
☐ 36 5X11: Kill Switch .15 .40
☐ 37 5X12: Bad Blood .15 .40
☐ 38 5X13: Patient X .15 .40
☐ 39 5X14: The Red And The Black .15 .40
☐ 40 5X15: Travelers .15 .40
☐ 41 5X16: Mind's Eye .15 .40
☐ 42 5X17: All Souls .15 .40
☐ 43 5X18: The Pine Bluff Variant .15 .40
☐ 44 5X19: Folie A Deux .15 .40
☐ 45 5X20: The End .15 .40
☐ 46 Special Agent Fox Mulder .15 .40
☐ 47 Special Agent Dana Scully .15 .40
☐ 48 Assistant Director Skinner .15 .40
☐ 49 John Fitzgerald Byers .15 .40
☐ 50 Melvin Frohike .15 .40
☐ 51 Ringo Langly .15 .40
☐ 52 Emily Sim .15 .40
☐ 53 Samantha Mulder .15 .40
☐ 54 Max Fenig .15 .40
☐ 55 The Cigarette-Smoking Man .15 .40
☐ 56 The Well-Manicured Man .15 .40
☐ 57 The First Elder .15 .40
☐ 58 Marita Covarrubias .15 .40
☐ 59 Alex Krycek .15 .40
☐ 60 Mrs. Mulder .15 .40
☐ 61 Agency Danny Pendrell .15 .40
☐ 62 Jeremiah Smith .15 .40
☐ 63 Alien Bounty Hunter .15 .40
☐ 64 Thoughtograph Terror .15 .40
☐ 65 The Melanin-Sucker .15 .40
☐ 66 The Face-Lifter .15 .40

- ❑ 67 A Picture Is Worth... .15 .40
- ❑ 68 All Bets Are Off .15 .40
- ❑ 69 Now You See Him... .15 .40
- ❑ 70 Frozen Stiff .15 .40
- ❑ 71 When Babies Had Tails .15 .40
- ❑ 72 Phantom Lady .15 .40
- ❑ 73 Don't Fool With Mother Nature .15 .40
- ❑ 74 Man-Made Monster .15 .40
- ❑ 75 Return Of The Pusher .15 .40
- ❑ 76 Mud Sucker .15 .40
- ❑ 77 The Doll From Hell .15 .40
- ❑ 78 Mulder The Vampire Slayer .15 .40
- ❑ 79 The Secret Invasion .15 .40
- ❑ 80 Guardian Angel .15 .40
- ❑ 81 Skinner...Bugged .15 .40
- ❑ 82 Pileggi Briefs .15 .40
- ❑ 83 Monster Maker .15 .40
- ❑ 84 To Bee Or Not To Bee .15 .40
- ❑ 85 Everywhere An E.T. .15 .40
- ❑ 86 Filming An Autopsy .15 .40
- ❑ 87 Fabricating A Forest Creature .15 .40
- ❑ 88 Munch-Ing On The Set .15 .40
- ❑ 89 Shining Directors .15 .40
- ❑ 90 Checklist .15 .40

2001 X-Files Seasons 4 and 5 Autographs

COMPLETE SET (5) 200.00 350.00
STATED ODDS 1:72

- ❑ A1 Chris Carter 100.00 200.00
- ❑ A2 Bruce Harwood 20.00 50.00
- ❑ A3 Jerry Hardin 20.00 50.00
- ❑ A4 Laurie Holden 20.00 50.00
- ❑ A5 Brendan Beiser 20.00 50.00

2001 X-Files Seasons 4 and 5 Black Oil

COMPLETE SET (6) 20.00 50.00
STATED ODDS 1:17

- ❑ B1 Black Oil 4.00 10.00
- ❑ B2 Black Oil 4.00 10.00
- ❑ B3 Black Oil 4.00 10.00
- ❑ B4 Black Oil 4.00 10.00
- ❑ B5 Black Oil 4.00 10.00
- ❑ B6 Black Oil 4.00 10.00

2001 X-Files Seasons 4 and 5 Box Loaders

COMPLETE SET (2) 2.00 5.00

- ❑ XBL1 Scully and Mulder 1.25 3.00
- ❑ XCL1 Scully 1.25 3.00

2001 X-Files Seasons 4 and 5 Death

COMPLETE SET (3) 25.00 60.00
STATED ODDS 1:48

- ❑ D1 Ace of Hearts 10.00 25.00
- ❑ D2 King of Hearts 10.00 25.00
- ❑ D3 Queen of Hearts 10.00 25.00

2001 X-Files Seasons 4 and 5 I Want To Believe

COMPLETE SET (3) 4.00 10.00
STATED ODDS 1:11

- ❑ P1 I Want To Believe 1.50 4.00
- ❑ P2 I Want To Believe 1.50 4.00
- ❑ P3 I Want To Believe 1.50 4.00

2001 X-Files Seasons 4 and 5 Pieceworks

STATED ODDS 1:115

- ❑ PW1 Mulder's Sweatshirt 40.00 80.00

2001 X-Files Seasons 4 and 5 Promos

COMPLETE SET (4) 4.00 10.00

- ❑ P1 Scully & Mulder 1.25 3.00
- ❑ P2 Lone Gunmen 1.25 3.00
- ❑ Pi Scully & Mulder 1.25 3.00
- ❑ XM1 Scully & Mulder 1.25 3.00

2001 X-Files Seasons 6 and 7

COMPLETE SET (90) 5.00 12.00

- ❑ 1 The Truth Is Out There .15 .40
- ❑ 2 6X01: The Beginning .15 .40
- ❑ 3 6X02: Drive .15 .40
- ❑ 4 6X03: Triangle .15 .40
- ❑ 5 6X04: Dreamland .15 .40
- ❑ 6 6X05: Dreamland II .15 .40
- ❑ 7 6X06: Terms Of Endearment .15 .40
- ❑ 8 6X07: The Rain King .15 .40
- ❑ 9 6X08: How The Ghosts Stole Christmas .15 .40
- ❑ 10 6X09: Tithonus .15 .40
- ❑ 11 6X10: S.R. 819 .15 .40
- ❑ 12 6X11: Two Fathers .15 .40
- ❑ 13 6X12: One Son .15 .40
- ❑ 14 6X13: Arcadia .15 .40
- ❑ 15 6X14: Agua Mala .15 .40
- ❑ 16 6X15: Monday .15 .40
- ❑ 17 6X16: Alpha .15 .40
- ❑ 18 6X17: Trevor .15 .40
- ❑ 19 6X18: Milagro .15 .40
- ❑ 20 6X19: Three Of A Kind .15 .40
- ❑ 21 6X20: The Unnatural .15 .40
- ❑ 22 6X21: Field Trip .15 .40
- ❑ 23 6X22: Biogenesis .15 .40
- ❑ 24 7X01: Hungry .15 .40
- ❑ 25 7X02: The Goldberg Variation .15 .40
- ❑ 26 7X03: The Sixth Extinction .15 .40
- ❑ 27 7X04: The Sixth Extinction II: Amor Fati .15 .40
- ❑ 28 7X05: Millennium .15 .40
- ❑ 29 7X06: Rush .15 .40
- ❑ 30 7X07: Orison .15 .40
- ❑ 31 7X08: The Amazing Maleeni .15 .40
- ❑ 32 7X09: Signs Of Wonders .15 .40
- ❑ 33 7X10: Sein Und Zeit .15 .40
- ❑ 34 7X11: Closure .15 .40
- ❑ 35 7X12: X-Cops .15 .40
- ❑ 36 7X13: First Person Shooter .15 .40
- ❑ 37 7X14: Theef .15 .40
- ❑ 38 7X15: En Ami .15 .40
- ❑ 39 7X16: Chimera .15 .40
- ❑ 40 7X17: All Things .15 .40
- ❑ 41 7X18: Hollywood A.D. .15 .40
- ❑ 42 7X19: Brand X .15 .40
- ❑ 43 7X20: Fight Club .15 .40
- ❑ 44 7X21: Je Souhaite .15 .40
- ❑ 45 7X22: Requiem .15 .40
- ❑ 46 Special Agent Fox Mulder .15 .40
- ❑ 47 Special Agent Dana Scully .15 .40
- ❑ 48 Assistant Director Skinner .15 .40
- ❑ 49 The Cigarette-Smoking Man .15 .40
- ❑ 50 Alex Krycek .15 .40
- ❑ 51 Special Agent Diana Fowley .15 .40
- ❑ 52 Special Agent Jeffrey Spender .15 .40
- ❑ 53 Cassandra Spender .15 .40
- ❑ 54 John Fitzgerald Byers .15 .40
- ❑ 55 Melvin Frohike .15 .40
- ❑ 56 Richard Ringo Langly .15 .40
- ❑ 57 Gibson Praise .15 .40
- ❑ 58 Mrs. Mulder .15 .40
- ❑ 59 Albert Hosteen .15 .40
- ❑ 60 Marita Covarrubias .15 .40
- ❑ 61 Michael Kritschgau .15 .40
- ❑ 62 Samantha Mulder .15 .40
- ❑ 63 Morris Fletcher .15 .40
- ❑ 64 I'm Him – He's Me .15 .40
- ❑ 65 White As A Ghost .15 .40
- ❑ 66 Veined Visage .15 .40
- ❑ 67 Scary Sewage .15 .40
- ❑ 68 Water Logged .15 .40
- ❑ 69 Chilly Dogs .15 .40
- ❑ 70 Dreamy Goo .15 .40
- ❑ 71 An Ordinary Monster .15 .40
- ❑ 72 Mind Games .15 .40
- ❑ 73 Waking The Dead .15 .40
- ❑ 74 Facing Demons .15 .40
- ❑ 75 Tricky Cards .15 .40
- ❑ 76 Rattle For Real .15 .40
- ❑ 77 Virtual Veracity .15 .40
- ❑ 78 Stinky's Good .15 .40
- ❑ 79 Raven Nevermore .15 .40
- ❑ 80 Mouth Infested .15 .40
- ❑ 81 Conspicuously Yellow .15 .40
- ❑ 82 Triple Threat .15 .40
- ❑ 83 Two Journeys .15 .40
- ❑ 84 Little Girld Gray .15 .40
- ❑ 85 Sleight Of Head? .15 .40
- ❑ 86 Giggling Gillian .15 .40
- ❑ 87 Famous Friends .15 .40
- ❑ 88 If The Armor Fits... .15 .40
- ❑ 89 Stand-In For Snakes .15 .40
- ❑ 90 Checklist .15 .40

2001 X-Files Seasons 6 and 7 Autographs

COMPLETE SET (6) 200.00 400.00
RANDOM INSERTS IN PACKS

- ❑ A6 Brian Thompson 15.00 40.00
- ❑ A7 Don S. Williams 15.00 40.00
- ❑ A8 John Neville 15.00 40.00
- ❑ A9 Gillian Anderson 200.00 300.00
- ❑ A10 Dean Haglund 15.00 40.00
- ❑ A11 Michael Mckean 15.00 40.00

2001 X-Files Seasons 6 and 7 Box Loaders

COMPLETE SET (3) 4.00 10.00

- ❑ BL1 Partners 1.50 4.00
- ❑ BL2 Friends 1.50 4.00
- ❑ BL3 Companions 1.50 4.00

2001 X-Files Seasons 6 and 7 Inside The Syndicate

COMPLETE SET (6) 6.00 15.00
STATED ODDS 1:17

- ❑ I1 Inside The Syndicate 1.25 3.00
- ❑ I2 Inside The Syndicate 1.25 3.00
- ❑ I3 Inside The Syndicate 1.25 3.00
- ❑ I4 Inside The Syndicate 1.25 3.00
- ❑ I5 Inside The Syndicate 1.25 3.00
- ❑ I6 Inside The Syndicate 1.25 3.00

2001 X-Files Seasons 6 and 7 Pieceworks

COMPLETE SET (2) 40.00 80.00
EXCH RANDOM INSERTS IN PACKS

- ❑ PW1 Mulder's T-Shirt 20.00 50.00
- ❑ PW2 Scully's Sweater 20.00 50.00

2001 X-Files Seasons 6 and 7 Promos

COMPLETE SET (4) 4.00 10.00

- ❑ X67I Mulder and Scully 1.25 3.00
- ❑ X67-0 Mulder and Scully 1.25 3.00
- ❑ X67-1 Mulder and Scully 1.25 3.00
- ❑ X67UK Mulder and Scully 1.25 3.00

2001 X-Files Seasons 6 and 7 The Truth Is Revealed

COMPLETE SET (3) 4.00 10.00
STATED ODDS 1:11

- ❑ P4 The Truth Is Revealed 2.00 5.00
- ❑ P5 The Truth Is Revealed 2.00 5.00
- ❑ P6 The Truth Is Revealed 2.00 5.00

2001 Xena Warrior Princess Preview

COMPLETE SET (9) 6.00 15.00
ANNOUNCED PRINT RUN 2,500 SETS

- ❑ P1 Xena .75 2.00
- ❑ P2 Gabrielle .75 2.00
- ❑ P3 Xena .75 2.00
- ❑ P4 Eli .75 2.00
- ❑ P5 Xena .75 2.00
- ❑ P6 Gabrielle .75 2.00
- ❑ P7 Xena .75 2.00
Gabrielle
- ❑ P8 Gabrielle .75 2.00
- ❑ P9 Xena .75 2.00

2001 Xena Warrior Princess Preview UK

COMPLETE SET (6) 10.00 25.00

- ❑ X1 Xena 2.50 6.00
- ❑ X2 Gabrielle 2.50 6.00
- ❑ X3 Autolycus and Joxer 2.50 6.00
- ❑ X4 Ares 2.50 6.00
- ❑ X5 Callisto 2.50 6.00
- ❑ X6 Aphrodite 2.50 6.00

2001 Xena Warrior Princess Season Six

COMPLETE SET (72) 5.00 12.00

- ❑ 1 Xena Montage 1 .15 .40
- ❑ 2 Xena Montage 2 .15 .40
- ❑ 3 Xena Montage 3 .15 .40
- ❑ 4 Coming Home .15 .40
- ❑ 5 Coming Home .15 .40
- ❑ 6 Coming Home .15 .40
- ❑ 7 The Haunting Of Amphipolis .15 .40
- ❑ 8 The Haunting Of Amphipolis .15 .40
- ❑ 9 The Haunting Of Amphipolis .15 .40
- ❑ 10 Heart Of Darkness .15 .40
- ❑ 11 Heart Of Darkness .15 .40
- ❑ 12 Heart Of Darkness .15 .40
- ❑ 13 Who's Gurkhan .15 .40
- ❑ 14 Who's Gurkhan .15 .40
- ❑ 15 Who's Gurkhan .15 .40
- ❑ 16 Legacy .15 .40
- ❑ 17 Legacy .15 .40
- ❑ 18 Legacy .15 .40
- ❑ 19 The Abyss .15 .40
- ❑ 20 The Abyss .15 .40
- ❑ 21 The Abyss .15 .40
- ❑ 22 The Rheingold .15 .40
- ❑ 23 The Rheingold .15 .40
- ❑ 24 The Rheingold .15 .40
- ❑ 25 The Ring .15 .40
- ❑ 26 The Ring .15 .40
- ❑ 27 The Ring .15 .40
- ❑ 28 Return Of The Valkyrie .15 .40
- ❑ 29 Return Of The Valkyrie .15 .40
- ❑ 30 Return Of The Valkyrie .15 .40
- ❑ 31 Old Ares Had A Farm .15 .40
- ❑ 32 Old Ares Had A Farm .15 .40
- ❑ 33 Old Ares Had A Farm .15 .40
- ❑ 34 Dangerous Prey .15 .40
- ❑ 35 Dangerous Prey .15 .40
- ❑ 36 Dangerous Prey .15 .40
- ❑ 37 The God You Know .15 .40
- ❑ 38 The God You Know .15 .40
- ❑ 39 The God You Know .15 .40
- ❑ 40 You Are There .15 .40
- ❑ 41 You Are There .15 .40
- ❑ 42 You Are There .15 .40
- ❑ 43 Path Of Vengeance .15 .40
- ❑ 44 Path Of Vengeance .15 .40
- ❑ 45 Path Of Vengeance .15 .40
- ❑ 46 To Helicon And Back .15 .40
- ❑ 47 To Helicon And Back .15 .40
- ❑ 48 To Helicon And Back .15 .40
- ❑ 49 Send In The Clones .15 .40
- ❑ 50 Send In The Clones .15 .40
- ❑ 51 Send In The Clones .15 .40
- ❑ 52 Last Of The Centaurs .15 .40
- ❑ 53 Last Of The Centaurs .15 .40
- ❑ 54 Last Of The Centaurs .15 .40
- ❑ 55 When Fates Collide .15 .40
- ❑ 56 When Fates Collide .15 .40
- ❑ 57 When Fates Collide .15 .40
- ❑ 58 Many Happy Returns .15 .40
- ❑ 59 Many Happy Returns .15 .40
- ❑ 60 Many Happy Returns .15 .40
- ❑ 61 Soul Possession .15 .40
- ❑ 62 Soul Possession .15 .40
- ❑ 63 Soul Possession .15 .40
- ❑ 64 A Friend In Need, Part I .15 .40
- ❑ 65 A Friend In Need, Part I .15 .40
- ❑ 66 A Friend In Need, Part I .15 .40
- ❑ 67 A Friend In Need, Part II .15 .40
- ❑ 68 A Friend In Need, Part II .15 .40
- ❑ 69 A Friend In Need, Part II .15 .40
- ❑ 70 Checklist 1 .15 .40
- ❑ 71 Checklist 2 .15 .40
- ❑ 72 Checklist 3 .15 .40

2001 Xena Warrior Princess Season Six Progressive Proofs Black

ANNOUNCED PRINT RUN 25 SETS

2001 Xena Warrior Princess Season Six Progressive Proofs Cyan

ANNOUNCED PRINT RUN 25 SETS

2001 Xena Warrior Princess Season Six Progressive Proofs Magenta

ANNOUNCED PRINT RUN 25 SETS

2001 Xena Warrior Princess Season Six Progressive Proofs Yellow

ANNOUNCED PRINT RUN 25 SETS

2001 Xena Warrior Princess Season Six Autographs

STATED ODDS ONE PER BOX

- ❑ A7 Hudson Leick 20.00 40.00
- ❑ A8 Adrienne Wilkinson 6.00 15.00
- ❑ A9 Kathryn Morris 6.00 15.00
- ❑ A10 Michael Hurst 6.00 15.00
- ❑ A11 Alexandra Tydings 20.00 40.00
- ❑ A12 Renee O'Connor 40.00 80.00
- ❑ A13 Ted Raimi 6.00 15.00
- ❑ A14 Lucy Lawless 40.00 80.00
- ❑ A15 Ebonie Smith 6.00 15.00
- ❑ A16 Paris Jefferson 6.00 15.00
- ❑ A17 Meighan Desmond 6.00 15.00
- ❑ A18 Jennifer Ward-Lealand 6.00 15.00
- ❑ A19 Danielle Cormack 6.00 15.00
- ❑ A20 Karl Urban 6.00 15.00
- ❑ A21 Willa O'Neill 6.00 15.00

2001 Xena Warrior Princess Season Six Busting Loose

COMPLETE SET (9) 5.00 12.00
STATED ODDS 1:8

- ❑ BL1 Xena .75 2.00
- ❑ BL2 Gabrielle .75 2.00
- ❑ BL3 Xena .75 2.00
- ❑ BL4 Gabrielle .75 2.00
- ❑ BL5 Xena .75 2.00
- ❑ BL6 Gabrielle .75 2.00
- ❑ BL7 Xena .75 2.00
- ❑ BL8 Gabrielle .75 2.00
- ❑ BL9 Xena .75 2.00

2001 Xena Warrior Princess Season Six Forever Gabrielle

COMPLETE SET (2) 25.00 50.00
STATED ODDS 1:480
STATED PRINT RUN 750 SER. #'d SETS

- ❑ G1 Gabrielle 12.50 30.00
- ❑ G2 Gabrielle 12.50 30.00

2001 Xena Warrior Princess Season Six From the Archives Costumes

STATED ODDS ONE PER BOX
R6 ISSUED IN COLLECTORS ALBUM
ANNOUNCED PRINT RUN 275-1575

- ❑ R3 Aphrodite/1490* 8.00 20.00
- ❑ R4 Xena/275* 50.00 100.00
- ❑ R5 Xena/1210* 15.00 30.00
- ❑ R6 Xena/ (issued in collectors album) 8.00 20.00
- ❑ R7 Alti/1125* 8.00 20.00
- ❑ R8 Borias/1175* 8.00 20.00
- ❑ R9 Callisto/1575* 8.00 20.00
- ❑ R10 Eli/1575* 8.00 20.00
- ❑ R11 Caesar/1575* 8.00 20.00

2001 Xena Warrior Princess Season Six God of War

COMPLETE SET (9) 4.00 10.00
STATED ODDS 1:4

- ❑ GW1 Ares .60 1.50
- ❑ GW2 Ares .60 1.50
- ❑ GW3 Ares .60 1.50
- ❑ GW4 Ares .60 1.50
- ❑ GW5 Ares .60 1.50
- ❑ GW6 Ares .60 1.50
- ❑ GW7 Ares .60 1.50
- ❑ GW8 Ares .60 1.50
- ❑ GW9 Ares .60 1.50

2001 Xena Warrior Princess Season Six Promos

COMPLETE SET (4)

- ❑ P1 Xena 1.00 2.50
- ❑ P2 Gabrielle 1.00 2.50
- ❑ BP1 Xena/ (Binder Exclusive)
- ❑ GUMMIE2001 Xena/ (Non-Sport Update Gummie)

2001 Xena Warrior Princess Season Six Wet Wicked and Wild

COMPLETE SET (9) 25.00 60.00
STATED ODDS 1:20

- ❑ WWW1 Xena 3.00 8.00
- ❑ WWW2 Gabrielle 3.00 8.00
- ❑ WWW3 Xena 3.00 8.00
- ❑ WWW4 Gabrielle 3.00 8.00
- ❑ WWW5 Xena 3.00 8.00
- ❑ WWW6 Gabrielle 3.00 8.00
- ❑ WWW7 Xena 3.00 8.00
- ❑ WWW8 Gabrielle 3.00 8.00
- ❑ WWW9 Xena 3.00 8.00

2001 Xena Warrior Princess Seasons Four and Five

COMPLETE SET (72) 5.00 12.00
R1 ISSUED AS CASE TOPPER
X1 STATED ODDS 1:480
X1 STATED PRINT RUN 999 SER. #'d SETS

- ❑ 1 Xena: Warrior Princess .15 .40
- ❑ 2 Adventures In The Sin Trade .15 .40
- ❑ 3 Adventures In The Sin Trade II .15 .40
- ❑ 4 A Family Affair .15 .40
- ❑ 5 In Sickness And In Hell .15 .40
- ❑ 6 A Good Day .15 .40
- ❑ 7 A Tale Of Two Muses .15 .40
- ❑ 8 Locked Up And Tied Down .15 .40
- ❑ 9 Crusader .15 .40
- ❑ 10 Past Imperfect .15 .40
- ❑ 11 Key To The Kingdom .15 .40
- ❑ 12 Daughter Of Pomira .15 .40
- ❑ 13 If The Shoe Fits .15 .40
- ❑ 14 Paradise Found .15 .40
- ❑ 15 Devi .15 .40
- ❑ 16 Between The Lines .15 .40
- ❑ 17 The Way .15 .40
- ❑ 18 The Plays The Thing .15 .40
- ❑ 19 The Convert .15 .40
- ❑ 20 Takes One To Know One .15 .40
- ❑ 21 Endgame .15 .40
- ❑ 22 Ides Of March .15 .40
- ❑ 23 Deja Vu All Over Again .15 .40
- ❑ 24 Fallen Angel .15 .40
- ❑ 25 Chakram .15 .40
- ❑ 26 Succession .15 .40
- ❑ 27 Animal Attraction .15 .40
- ❑ 28 Them Bones, Them Bones .15 .40
- ❑ 29 Purity .15 .40
- ❑ 30 Back In The Bottle .15 .40
- ❑ 31 Little Problems .15 .40
- ❑ 32 Seeds Of Faith .15 .40
- ❑ 33 Lyre, Lyre, Hearts On Fire .15 .40
- ❑ 34 Punch Lines .15 .40
- ❑ 35 God Fearing Child .15 .40
- ❑ 36 Eternal Bonds .15 .40
- ❑ 37 Amphipolis Under Seige .15 .40
- ❑ 38 Married With Fishsticks .15 .40
- ❑ 39 Lifeblood .15 .40
- ❑ 40 Kindred Spirits .15 .40
- ❑ 41 Anthony and Cleopatra .15 .40
- ❑ 42 Looking Death In The Eye .15 .40
- ❑ 43 Livia .15 .40
- ❑ 44 Eve .15 .40
- ❑ 45 Motherhood .15 .40
- ❑ 46 Warriors In Action .15 .40
- ❑ 47 Warriors In Action .15 .40
- ❑ 48 Warriors In Action .15 .40
- ❑ 49 Warriors In Action .15 .40
- ❑ 50 Warriors In Action .15 .40
- ❑ 51 Warriors In Action .15 .40
- ❑ 52 Warriors In Action .15 .40
- ❑ 53 Warriors In Action .15 .40
- ❑ 54 Warriors In Action .15 .40
- ❑ 55 Warriors In Action .15 .40
- ❑ 56 Warriors In Action .15 .40
- ❑ 57 Warriors In Action .15 .40
- ❑ 58 Warriors In Action .15 .40
- ❑ 59 Warriors In Action .15 .40
- ❑ 60 Warriors In Action .15 .40
- ❑ 61 Faithful Argo .15 .40
- ❑ 62 Faithful Argo .15 .40
- ❑ 63 Faithful Argo .15 .40
- ❑ 64 Sisters In Arms .15 .40
- ❑ 65 Sisters In Arms .15 .40
- ❑ 66 Sisters In Arms .15 .40
- ❑ 67 Sisters In Arms .15 .40
- ❑ 68 Sisters In Arms .15 .40
- ❑ 69 Sisters In Arms .15 .40
- ❑ 70 Sisters In Arms .15 .40
- ❑ 71 Sisters In Arms .15 .40
- ❑ 72 Sisters In Arms .15 .40
- ❑ R1 Lucy Lawless MEM/ (issued as case topper) 30.00 60.00
- ❑ X1 Xena 7.50 20.00
Argo/999

2001 Xena Warrior Princess Seasons Four and Five Autographs

STATED ODDS 1:80
A6 ISSUED IN COLLECTORS ALBUM
A6 ANNOUNCED PRINT RUN 2000

- ❑ A1 Lucy Lawless 50.00 100.00
- ❑ A2 Ted Raimi 10.00 25.00
- ❑ A3 Jennifer Sky 10.00 25.00
- ❑ A4 Kevin Smith 10.00 25.00
- ❑ A5 Claire Stansfield 12.50 30.00
- ❑ A6 Timothy Omundson/2000* 8.00 20.00
(issued in collectors album)

2001 Xena Warrior Princess Seasons Four and Five Face of a Warrior

COMPLETE SET (9) 15.00 40.00
STATED ODDS 1:40

- ❑ W1 Locked Up and Tied Down 3.00 8.00
- ❑ W2 Seeds of Faith 3.00 8.00
- ❑ W3 Animal Attraction 3.00 8.00
- ❑ W4 In Sickness and In Hell 3.00 8.00
- ❑ W5 The Way 3.00 8.00
- ❑ W6 Fallen Angel 3.00 8.00
- ❑ W7 Seeds of Faith 3.00 8.00
- ❑ W8 Crusader 3.00 8.00
- ❑ W9 A Good Day 3.00 8.00

2001 Xena Warrior Princess Seasons Four and Five Gabrielle the Battling Bard

COMPLETE SET (9) 12.50 30.00
STATED ODDS 1:10

- ❑ G1 Gabrielle 2.00 5.00
- ❑ G2 Gabrielle 2.00 5.00
- ❑ G3 Gabrielle 2.00 5.00
- ❑ G4 Gabrielle 2.00 5.00
- ❑ G5 Gabrielle 2.00 5.00
- ❑ G6 Gabrielle 2.00 5.00
- ❑ G7 Gabrielle 2.00 5.00
- ❑ G8 Gabrielle 2.00 5.00
- ❑ G9 Gabrielle 2.00 5.00

2001 Xena Warrior Princess Seasons Four and Five Xena Allies

COMPLETE SET (9) 4.00 10.00
STATED ODDS 1:4

- ❑ F1 Gabrielle .60 1.50
- ❑ F2 Joxer .60 1.50
- ❑ F3 Eli .60 1.50
- ❑ F4 Callisto .60 1.50
- ❑ F5 K'ao Hsin .60 1.50
- ❑ F6 Amarice .60 1.50
- ❑ F7 Argo .60 1.50
- ❑ F8 Borias .60 1.50
- ❑ F9 Phlanagus .60 1.50

2001 Xena Warrior Princess Seasons Four and Five Xena Enemies

COMPLETE SET (6) 7.50 20.00
STATED ODDS 1:9

- ❑ E1 Ares 1.50 4.00
- ❑ E2 The Destroyer 1.50 4.00
- ❑ E3 Demon Gabrielle 1.50 4.00
- ❑ E4 Aidan 1.50 4.00
- ❑ E5 Najara 1.50 4.00
- ❑ E6 Alti 1.50 4.00

2001 Xena Warrior Princess Seasons Four and Five Xena Undressed

COMPLETE SET (6) 50.00 100.00
STATED ODDS 1:80

- ❑ U1 Xena 8.00 20.00
- ❑ U2 Xena 8.00 20.00
- ❑ U3 Xena 8.00 20.00
- ❑ U4 Xena 8.00 20.00
- ❑ U5 Xena 8.00 20.00
- ❑ U6 Xena 8.00 20.00

2002 Alias Season One

COMPLETE SET (81) 5.00 12.00
CIA47 STATED ODDS 1:90

- ❑ 1 Title Card .15 .40
- ❑ 2 Secrets And Lies .15 .40
- ❑ 3 On The Run .15 .40
- ❑ 4 Maid Service .15 .40
- ❑ 5 Devil In A Blue Dress .15 .40
- ❑ 6 Casual Encounter .15 .40
- ❑ 7 An Intimate Moment .15 .40
- ❑ 8 Who's The Enemy? .15 .40
- ❑ 9 Hidden Weapon .15 .40
- ❑ 10 Sharing A Secret .15 .40
- ❑ 11 Watching And Waiting .15 .40
- ❑ 12 Full Circle .15 .40
- ❑ 13 Dead Men's Tales .15 .40
- ❑ 14 Cuckoo's Nest .15 .40
- ❑ 15 No More Lies .15 .40
- ❑ 16 Under Suspicion .15 .40
- ❑ 17 The Whole Truth .15 .40
- ❑ 18 Agent Down .15 .40
- ❑ 19 Someone'sListening .15 .40
- ❑ 20 Whodunit .15 .40
- ❑ 21 Twisted Web .15 .40
- ❑ 22 Who To Trust .15 .40
- ❑ 23 All In The Family .15 .40
- ❑ 24 Under Siege .15 .40
- ❑ 25 Working For The Man .15 .40
- ❑ 26 Teamwork .15 .40
- ❑ 27 Unyielding .15 .40
- ❑ 28 Deception .15 .40
- ❑ 29 Betrayal .15 .40
- ❑ 30 Dinner With Friends .15 .40
- ❑ 31 The Purloined Page .15 .40
- ❑ 32 Dilemma .15 .40
- ❑ 33 One Calm Moment .15 .40
- ❑ 34 Dear Old Dad .15 .40
- ❑ 35 Breakout .15 .40
- ❑ 36 Just Tourists .15 .40
- ❑ 37 Moving On .15 .40
- ❑ 38 Left Hanging .15 .40
- ❑ 39 Unmasked .15 .40
- ❑ 40 Disguised .15 .40
- ❑ 41 Face Of A Friend .15 .40
- ❑ 42 Enticing .15 .40
- ❑ 43 Exposed .15 .40
- ❑ 44 Losses .15 .40
- ❑ 45 Reunion .15 .40
- ❑ 46 Sloane, Arvin .15 .40
- ❑ 47 Bristow, Sydney .15 .40
- ❑ 48 Dixon, Marcus R. .15 .40
- ❑ 49 Flinkman, Marshall J. .15 .40
- ❑ 50 Bristow, Jonathan D. (Jack) .15 .40
- ❑ 51 Vaughn, Michael C. .15 .40
- ❑ 52 Weiss, Eric .15 .40
- ❑ 53 Barnett, Judy .15 .40
- ❑ 54 Cole, Mckenas .15 .40
- ❑ 55 Sark .15 .40
- ❑ 56 The Snowman (Aka Noah Hicks) .15 .40
- ❑ 57 Tippin, William D. (Will) .15 .40
- ❑ 58 Calfo, Francine D. (Francie) .15 .40
- ❑ 59 Psychic And Alchemist .15 .40
- ❑ 60 A Frozen Moment .15 .40
- ❑ 61 Wealth Of Knowledge .15 .40
- ❑ 62 The Prophecy Revealed .15 .40
- ❑ 63 The Heart Of The Matter .15 .40

64 Genius At Work .15 .40
65 Heartbeat .15 .40
66 Added Value .15 .40
67 A-Okay .15 .40
68 At His Best .15 .40
69 Cool And Undercover .15 .40
70 Token Of Affection .15 .40
71 Breaking Rules .15 .40
72 More Than Friends .15 .40
73 Remembering Mom .15 .40
74 Working With Dad .15 .40
75 Fondly Paternalistic .15 .40
76 From Almost Thirty Years .15 .40
77 Director On The Set .15 .40
78 Exterior Shot .15 .40
79 Can You Hear Me? .15 .40
80 Aka .15 .40
81 Checklist .15 .40
CIA47 CIA.net: Bristow Sydney 6.00 15.00

2002 Alias Season One Autographs

COMPLETE SET (7) 200.00 400.00
STATED ODDS 1:39
A1 Jennifer Garner 200.00 300.00
A2 J.J. Abrams 40.00 80.00
A3 Victor Garber 25.00 50.00
A4 Bradley Cooper 50.00 100.00
A5 Merrin Dungey 10.00 25.00
A6 Lindsay Crouse 10.00 25.00
A7 Ric Young 10.00 25.00

2002 Alias Season One Box Loaders

COMPLETE SET (4) 10.00 25.00
BL1 Taiwanese Torturer 1.50 4.00
BL2 Cole 1.50 4.00
BL3 Julian Sark 1.50 4.00
CL1 Sydney Bristow 7.50 20.00
CASE INSERT

2002 Alias Season One Double Agent Files

COMPLETE SET (6) 10.00 25.00
STATED ODDS 1:17
D1 Double Agent Files 2.00 5.00
D2 Double Agent Files 2.00 5.00
D3 Double Agent Files 2.00 5.00
D4 Double Agent Files 2.00 5.00
D5 Double Agent Files 2.00 5.00
D6 Double Agent Files 2.00 5.00

2002 Alias Season One Pieceworks

STATED ODDS 1:78
PW1 Jennifer Garner Blue Dress 30.00 60.00
PW2 Jennifer Garner Metal Dress 25.00 50.00
PW3 Jennifer Garner Bead Hat 125.00 200.00

2002 Alias Season One Secret Life

COMPLETE SET (9) 15.00 40.00
STATED ODDS 1:11
SL1 Sydney 2.00 5.00
SL2 Sydney 2.00 5.00
SL3 Sydney 2.00 5.00
SL4 Sydney 2.00 5.00
SL5 Will 2.00 5.00
SL6 Sydney 2.00 5.00
SL7 Sydney 2.00 5.00
SL8 Sydney 2.00 5.00
SL9 Dixon 2.00 5.00

2002 Angel Season Three

COMPLETE SET (90) 5.00 12.00
1 Angel .15 .40
2 Heartbroken .15 .40
3 Heartless .15 .40
4 Heavyhearted .15 .40
5 Violated .15 .40
6 Released .15 .40
7 Terminated .15 .40
8 Suspect .15 .40
9 Under Siege .15 .40
10 If You Please .15 .40
11 Body Snatcher .15 .40
12 Body Heat .15 .40
13 Body for Life .15 .40
14 Reunited .15 .40
15 Revealed .15 .40
16 Returned .15 .40
17 Mystery .15 .40
18 Madman .15 .40
19 Women's Work .15 .40
20 Papa Don't Preach .15 .40
21 Havin' My Baby .15 .40
22 We're in Trouble Deep .15 .40
23 Pilgrims .15 .40
24 Wise Men .15 .40
25 No Room .15 .40
26 Labor .15 .40
27 Contractions .15 .40
28 Delivery .15 .40
29 Chip .15 .40
30 Block .15 .40
31 Naming .15 .40
32 Your-Life .15 .40
33 No Longer .15 .40
34 An Option .15 .40
35 Highest Bidder .15 .40
36 False Promises .15 .40
37 Getting Paid .15 .40
38 At the Ballet .15 .40
39 Spellbound .15 .40
40 Tears of a Clown .15 .40
41 Smitten .15 .40
42 Replacement .15 .40
43 Unrequited .15 .40
44 Doting Dad .15 .40
45 Shifting Alliegences .15 .40
46 Signs and Portents .15 .40
47 Restless .15 .40
48 Sleepwalking .15 .40
49 Nightmare .15 .40
50 Bereaved .15 .40
51 Choosing Sides .15 .40
52 No Mercy .15 .40
53 Pay Up .15 .40
54 One Special Day .15 .40
55 Sucker Bet .15 .40
56 Infestation .15 .40
57 Entreaty .15 .40
58 Retribution .15 .40
59 Patricide .15 .40
60 Clean-Up Crew .15 .40
61 Reunited .15 .40
62 Purification .15 .40
63 Relinquished .15 .40
64 Sacrifice .15 .40
65 Ascent .15 .40
66 Descent .15 .40
67 Angel .15 .40
68 Wesley Wyndam-Pryce .15 .40
69 Cordelia Chase .15 .40
70 Charles Gunn .15 .40
71 Lorne .15 .40
72 Fred Burkle .15 .40
73 Lilah Morgan .15 .40
74 Linwood Morrow .15 .40
75 Gavin Park .15 .40
76 Cyril .15 .40
77 Files and Records .15 .40
78 Angel and Cordelia .15 .40
79 Cordelia and Groo .15 .40
80 Wesley and Fred .15 .40
81 Fred and Gunn .15 .40
82 Angelus .15 .40
83 James and Elizabeth .15 .40
84 Darla .15 .40
85 Holtz .15 .40
86 Sahjhan .15 .40
87 Holtz's Crew .15 .40
88 Justine .15 .40
89 Connor and Stephens .15 .40
90 Checklist .15 .40

2002 Angel Season Three Autographs

COMPLETE SET (9) 60.00 150.00
STATED ODDS 1:36
A15 Amy Acker 40.00 80.00
A16 Keith Szarabajka 6.00 15.00
A17 Daniel Dae Kim 6.00 15.00
A18 Jack Conley 6.00 15.00
A19 Mark Lutz 6.00 15.00
A20 Ron Melendez 6.00 15.00
A21 Jarrod Crawford 6.00 15.00
A22 Laurel Holloman 6.00 15.00
A23 John Rubinstein 6.00 15.00

2002 Angel Season Three Pieceworks

STATED ODDS 1:54
PW1 David Boreanaz 10.00 25.00
PW2 Charisma Carpenter 10.00 25.00

2002 Angel Season Three Prophesies Unfold

COMPLETE SET (9) 7.50 20.00
PR1 The Scrolls 1.25 3.00
PR2 The Tro-clon 1.25 3.00
PR3 Vampire Birth 1.25 3.00
PR4 A Bigger Picture 1.25 3.00
PR5 Miracle Child 1.25 3.00
PR6 No Birth, only Death 1.25 3.00
PR7 Father will Kill the Son 1.25 3.00
PR8 Fire and Earthquake 1.25 3.00
PR9 False Prophesy 1.25 3.00

2002 Angel Season Three Triangulation

COMPLETE SET (6) 10.00 25.00
TR1 Angel 2.00 5.00
TR2 Cordelia 2.00 5.00
TR3 Groo 2.00 5.00
TR4 Wesley 2.00 5.00
TR5 Fred 2.00 5.00
TR6 Gunn 2.00 5.00

2002 Buffy the Vampire Slayer Evolution

COMPLETE SET (50) 5.00 12.00
1 Evolution .15 .40
2 Buffy: Chosen .15 .40
3 Willow: Friend .15 .40
4 Xander: Devoted .15 .40
5 Cordelia: Rival .15 .40
6 Giles: The Watcher .15 .40
7 First Love: Angel .15 .40
8 First Challenge: The Master .15 .40
9 Rite of Passage: Meeting Her Destiny .15 .40
10 Emergence .15 .40
11 Buffy: Becoming .15 .40
12 Willow: Enchanting .15 .40
13 Xander: Warrior .15 .40
14 Oz: Feral .15 .40
15 Watcher: Avenging .15 .40
16 Lost Love: Angelus .15 .40
17 Challenge: Angelus, Dru and Spike .15 .40
18 Rite of Passage: Slaying Angel .15 .40
19 Rebellion .15 .40
20 Buffy: Alone .15 .40
21 Willow: Duality .15 .40
22 Xander: Reliable .15 .40
23 Cordelia: Survivor .15 .40
24 Giles and Wesley: Watchers .15 .40
25 Doomed Love: Angel .15 .40
26 Challenge: Renegade Slayer .15 .40
27 Rite of Passage: Graduation .15 .40
28 Transition .15 .40
29 Buffy: Doubting .15 .40
30 Willow: Exploring .15 .40
31 Xander: Searching .15 .40
32 Anya: Normal .15 .40
33 Giles: Watcher .15 .40
34 New Love: Riley .15 .40
35 Challenge: Adam .15 .40
36 Rite of Passage: Ritual of Enjoining .15 .40
37 Sacrifice .15 .40
38 Buffy: Losses .15 .40
39 Willow & Tara .15 .40
40 Xander & Anya .15 .40
41 Giles: Watcher & Proprietor .15 .40
42 Dawn: The Key .15 .40
43 Failed Love: Riley .15 .40
44 Challenge: Battling Glory .15 .40
45 Rite of Passage: Ultimate Sacrifice .15 .40
46 Aftermath .15 .40
47 Buffy: Resurrected .15 .40
48 Tainted Love: Spike .15 .40
49 Challenge: To Live Again .15 .40
50 Checklist .15 .40

2002 Buffy the Vampire Slayer Evolution Box Loaders

COMPLETE SET (4) 2.50 6.00
BL1 Buffy & Angel .75 2.00
BL2 Buffy & Riley .75 2.00
BL3 Buffy & Spike .75 2.00
BECL Season 6 Promo .75 2.00

2002 Buffy the Vampire Slayer Evolution Portraits

COMPLETE SET (9) 30.00 80.00
STATED ODDS 1:11
PT1 Buffy 4.00 10.00
PT2 Willow 4.00 10.00
PT3 Xander 4.00 10.00
PT4 Giles 4.00 10.00
PT5 Anya 4.00 10.00
PT6 Dawn 4.00 10.00
PT7 Cordelia 4.00 10.00
PT8 Angel 4.00 10.00
PT9 Spike 4.00 10.00

2002 Buffy the Vampire Slayer Evolution Refractors

COMPLETE SET (50) 15.00 40.00
COMMON CARD (1-50) .40 1.00
STATED ODDS ONE PER PACK
1 Evolution .40 1.00
2 Buffy: Chosen .40 1.00
3 Willow: Friend .40 1.00
4 Xander: Devoted .40 1.00
5 Cordelia: Rival .40 1.00
6 Giles: The Watcher .40 1.00
7 First Love: Angel .40 1.00
8 First Challenge: The Master .40 1.00
9 Rite of Passage: Meeting Her Destiny .40 1.00
10 Emergence .40 1.00
11 Buffy: Becoming .40 1.00
12 Willow: Enchanting .40 1.00
13 Xander: Warrior .40 1.00
14 Oz: Feral .40 1.00
15 Watcher: Avenging .40 1.00
16 Lost Love: Angelus .40 1.00
17 Challenge: Angelus, Dru and Spike .40 1.00
18 Rite of Passage: Slaying Angel .40 1.00
19 Rebellion .40 1.00
20 Buffy: Alone .40 1.00
21 Willow: Duality .40 1.00
22 Xander: Reliable .40 1.00
23 Cordelia: Survivor .40 1.00
24 Giles and Wesley: Watchers .40 1.00
25 Doomed Love: Angel .40 1.00
26 Challenge: Renegade Slayer .40 1.00
27 Rite of Passage: Graduation .40 1.00
28 Transition .40 1.00
29 Buffy: Doubting .40 1.00
30 Willow: Exploring .40 1.00
31 Xander: Searching .40 1.00
32 Anya: Normal .40 1.00
33 Giles: Watcher .40 1.00
34 New Love: Riley .40 1.00
35 Challenge: Adam .40 1.00
36 Rite of Passage: Ritual of Enjoining .40 1.00
37 Sacrifice .40 1.00
38 Buffy: Losses .40 1.00
39 Willow & Tara .40 1.00
40 Xander & Anya .40 1.00
41 Giles: Watcher & Proprietor .40 1.00
42 Dawn: The Key .40 1.00
43 Failed Love: Riley .40 1.00
44 Challenge: Battling Glory .40 1.00
45 Rite of Passage: Ultimate Sacrifice .40 1.00
46 Aftermath .40 1.00
47 Buffy: Resurrected .40 1.00
48 Tainted Love: Spike .40 1.00
49 Challenge: To Live Again .40 1.00
50 Checklist .40 1.00

2002 Buffy the Vampire Slayer Season Six

COMPLETE SET (90) 5.00 12.00
1 Title Card .15 .40
2 Keeping Up Appearances .15 .40
3 Goodbye, Hello .15 .40
4 Incomplete .15 .40
5 Underground .15 .40
6 On Instinct .15 .40
7 Reunited .15 .40
8 New Again .15 .40
9 The Price .15 .40
10 In Hell .15 .40
11 Held Up .15 .40
12 Homecoming .15 .40
13 Overwhelmed .15 .40
14 Tested .15 .40
15 Heavy Lifting .15 .40
16 Smoke And Mirrors .15 .40
17 Big Night .15 .40
18 Big Trouble .15 .40
19 Slayage .15 .40
20 Prelude .15 .40
21 Counterpoint .15 .40
22 Concerto .15 .40
23 Too Much Talk .15 .40
24 All Shook Up .15 .40
25 More Action .15 .40
26 Restored .15 .40
27 Defective .15 .40
28 Overboard .15 .40
29 Morning After .15 .40
30 Out Of Control .15 .40
31 Remorseful .15 .40
32 Vanished .15 .40
33 Outta Sight .15 .40
34 Fading Fast .15 .40
35 Happy Face .15 .40
36 Mystery Meat .15 .40
37 Surprise Inside .15 .40
38 Makin' It .15 .40
39 Fakin' It .15 .40
40 She's Gone .15 .40
41 Celebration .15 .40
42 Grounded .15 .40
43 Vengeance .15 .40
44 Signs Of Life .15 .40
45 Just Perfect .15 .40
46 Guilty As Charged .15 .40
47 Marry Me .15 .40
48 Deceived .15 .40
49 Unhappily Ever After .15 .40
50 Delusions .15 .40
51 Violent .15 .40
52 Paranoid .15 .40
53 Disenchanted .15 .40
54 Consolation .15 .40
55 Caught On Tape .15 .40
56 Hideout .15 .40
57 Big Bad .15 .40
58 Payback .15 .40
59 Critical .15 .40
60 Desperate .15 .40
61 Deadly .15 .40
62 Rampage .15 .40
63 Gauntlet .15 .40
64 Unstoppable .15 .40
65 The Calvary .15 .40
66 Knight Of Hearts .15 .40
67 Redeemed .15 .40
68 Dreadful Dresses .15 .40
69 Nervous Groom .15 .40
70 Beautiful Bride .15 .40
71 Friends And Family .15 .40
72 The Big Moment .15 .40
73 Buffy .15 .40
74 Xander .15 .40
75 Willow .15 .40
76 Tara .15 .40
77 Anya .15 .40
78 Dawn .15 .40
79 Giles .15 .40
80 Spike .15 .40
81 Clem .15 .40
82 Formidable .15 .40
83 Irresistible .15 .40
84 Indomitable .15 .40
85 Almost Ordinary .15 .40
86 In Too Deep .15 .40
87 Dark Willow .15 .40
88 Goodbyes Tara .15 .40
89 Goodbyes Giles .15 .40
90 Checklist .15 .40

2002 Buffy the Vampire Slayer Season Six Autographs

STATED ODDS 1:35
A29 Kali Rocha 10.00 25.00
A30 Dean Butler 10.00 25.00
A31 Elizabeth Anne Allen 10.00 25.00
A32 Adam Busch 10.00 25.00
A33 Tom Lenk 10.00 25.00
A34 James C. Leary 10.00 25.00
A35 Ivana Milicevic 10.00 25.00
A36 Jeff Kober 10.00 25.00
A37 Andy Umberger 10.00 25.00
A38 Amelinda Embry 10.00 25.00
A39 David Fury 10.00 25.00

2002 Buffy the Vampire Slayer Season Six Box Loaders

COMPLETE SET (4) 7.50 20.00
BL1 Rupert Giles .75 2.00
BL2 Xander Harris .75 2.00
BL3 Spike .75 2.00
B6CL Where Does She Go From Here? 7.50 20.00

2002 Buffy the Vampire Slayer Season Six Love Bites Back

COMPLETE SET (6) 12.50 30.00
STATED ODDS 1:17
LBB1 Love Bites Back 2.50 6.00
LBB2 Love Bites Back 2.50 6.00
LBB3 Love Bites Back 2.50 6.00
LBB4 Love Bites Back 2.50 6.00
LBB5 Love Bites Back 2.50 6.00
LBB6 Love Bites Back 2.50 6.00

2002 Buffy the Vampire Slayer Season Six Once More With Feeling

COMPLETE SET (9) 12.50 30.00
STATED ODDS 1:11
H1 Once More With Feeling 1.50 4.00
H2 Once More With Feeling 1.50 4.00
H3 Once More With Feeling 1.50 4.00
H4 Once More With Feeling 1.50 4.00
H5 Once More With Feeling 1.50 4.00
H6 Once More With Feeling 1.50 4.00
H7 Once More With Feeling 1.50 4.00
H8 Once More With Feeling 1.50 4.00
H9 Once More With Feeling 1.50 4.00

2002 Buffy the Vampire Slayer Season Six Pieceworks

COMPLETE SET (5) 75.00 200.00
STATED ODDS 1:64
PW1 Buffy's Blouse 20.00 50.00
PW2 Buffy's Jeans 20.00 50.00
PW3 Buffy's Uniform Top 20.00 50.00
PW4 Buffy's Uniform Slacks 20.00 50.00
PW5 Spike's T-Shirt 20.00 50.00

2002 Buffy the Vampire Slayer Season Six Promos

COMPLETE SET (9) 6.00 15.00
B6I Buffy .75 2.00
B6-1 Cast .75 2.00
B6GG Buffy .75 2.00
B6UK Buffy 2.00 5.00
B62A Cast .75 2.00
B62B Cast FOIL .75 2.00
NSUSD Buffy 2.00 5.00
B6SD2002 Cast .75 2.00
B6WW2002 Buffy .75 2.00

2002 The Complete Babylon 5

COMPLETE SET (120) 4.00 10.00
1 The Complete Babylon 5 .10 .30
2 The Gathering .10 .30
3 Season One Overview .10 .30
4 Midnight on the Firing Line .10 .30
5 Soul Hunter .10 .30
6 Born to the Purple .10 .30
7 Infection .10 .30
8 The Parliament of Dreams .10 .30
9 Mind War .10 .30
10 The War Prayer .10 .30
11 And The Sky Full Of Stars .10 .30
12 Deathwalker .10 .30
13 Believers .10 .30
14 Survivors .10 .30
15 By Any Means Necessary .10 .30
16 Signs and Portents .10 .30
17 TKO .10 .30
18 Grail .10 .30
19 Eyes .10 .30
20 Legacies .10 .30
21 A Voice in the Wilderness I .10 .30
22 A Voice in the Wilderness II .10 .30
23 Babylon Squared .10 .30
24 The Quality of Mercy .10 .30
25 Chrysalis .10 .30
26 Season Two Overview .10 .30
27 Points of Departure .10 .30
28 Revelations .10 .30
29 The Geometry of Shadows .10 .30
30 A Distant Star .10 .30
31 The Long Dark .10 .30
32 A Spider in the Web .10 .30
33 Soul Mates .10 .30
34 A Race Through Dark Places .10 .30
35 The Coming of Shadows .10 .30
36 GROPOS .10 .30
37 All Alone in the Night .10 .30
38 Acts of Sacrifice .10 .30
39 Hunter, Prey .10 .30
40 There All the Honor Lies .10 .30
41 And Now For a Word .10 .30
42 In the Shadow of Z'ha'dum .10 .30
43 Knives .10 .30
44 Confessions and Lamentations .10 .30
45 Divided Loyalties .10 .30
46 The Long, Twilight Struggle .10 .30
47 Comes the Inquisitor .10 .30
48 The Fall of Night .10 .30
49 Season Three Overview .10 .30
50 Matters of Honor .10 .30
51 Convictions .10 .30
52 A Day in the Strife .10 .30
53 Passing Through Gethsemane .10 .30
54 Voices of Authority .10 .30
55 Dust to Dust .10 .30
56 Exogenesis .10 .30
57 Messages from Earth .10 .30
58 Point of No Return .10 .30
59 Severed Dreams .10 .30
60 Ceremonies of Light and Dark .10 .30
61 Sic Transit Vir .10 .30
62 A Late Delivery from Avalon .10 .30
63 Ship of Tears .10 .30
64 Interludes and Examinations .10 .30
65 War Without End I .10 .30
66 War Without End II .10 .30
67 Walkabout .10 .30
68 Grey 17 Is Missing .10 .30
69 And the Rock Cried Out, No Hiding Place .10 .30
70 Shadow Dancing .10 .30
71 Z'ha'dum .10 .30
72 Season Four Overview .10 .30
73 The Hour of the Wolf .10 .30
74 Whatever Happened to Mr. Garibaldi .10 .30
75 The Summoning .10 .30
76 Falling Toward Apotheosis .10 .30
77 The Long Night .10 .30
78 Into the Fire .10 .30
79 Epiphanies .10 .30
80 The Illusion of Truth .10 .30
81 Atonement .10 .30
82 Racing Mars .10 .30
83 Lines of Communication .10 .30
84 Conflicts of Interest .10 .30
85 Rumors, Bargains and Lies .10 .30
86 Moments of Transition .10 .30
87 No Surrender, No Retreat .10 .30
88 The Exercise of Vital Powers .10 .30
89 The Face of the Enemy .10 .30
90 Intersections in Real Time .10 .30
91 Between the Darkness and the Light .10 .30
92 Endgame .10 .30
93 Rising Star .10 .30
94 The Deconstruction of Falling Stars .10 .30
95 Season Five Overview .10 .30
96 No Compromises .10 .30
97 The Very Long Night of Londo Mollari .10 .30
98 The Paragon of Animals .10 .30
99 A View from the Gallery .10 .30
100 Learning Curve .10 .30
101 Strange Relations .10 .30
102 Secrets of the Soul .10 .30
103 In the Kingdom of the Blind .10 .30
104 A Tragedy of Telepaths .10 .30
105 Phoenix Rising .10 .30
106 Day of the Dead .10 .30
107 The Ragged Edge .10 .30
108 The Corps is Mother, The Corps is Father .10 .30
109 Meditations on the Abyss .10 .30
110 Darkness Ascending .10 .30
111 And All My Dreams, Torn Asunder .10 .30
112 Movements of Fire and Shadow .10 .30
113 The Fall of Centauri Prime .10 .30
114 Wheel of Fire .10 .30
115 Objects in Motion .10 .30
116 Objects at Rest .10 .30
117 Sleeping in Light .10 .30
118 Checklist I .10 .30
119 Checklist II .10 .30
120 Checklist III .10 .30
P1 Collage PROMO .40 1.00

2002 The Complete Babylon 5 Autographs

STATED ODDS 1:20
A1a Michael O'Hare 15.00 40.00
as Jeffrey Sinclair
A1b J. Michael Straczynski 50.00 100.00
(issued as case topper)
A2 Andrea Thompson 6.00 15.00
as Talia Winters
A3 John Fleck 6.00 15.00
as Del Varner
A4 Tamlyn Tomita 8.00 20.00
as Laurel Takashima
A5 Blaire Baron 6.00 15.00
as Carolyn Sykes
A6 Julia Nickson 8.00 20.00
as Catherine Sakai
A7 Tim Choate 10.00 25.00
as Zathras
A8 Mary Kay Adams 6.00 15.00
as Na'Toth
A9 Robin Curtis 6.00 15.00
as Ambassador Kalika
A10 Jason Carter 8.00 20.00
as Marcus Cole
A11 Julie Caitlin-Brown 6.00 15.00
as Guinevere Corey
A12 Phil Morris 8.00 20.00
as Bill Trainor
A13 Sarah Douglas 6.00 15.00
as Jha'dur
DA1 Bruce Boxleitner/Melissa Gilbert 100.00 200.00
as Capt. Sheridan/Anna Sheridan

2002 The Complete Babylon 5 Classic Confrontations

COMPLETE SET (9) 2.00 5.00
STATED ODDS 1:4

❑ CC1 The Battle of the Line .50 1.25
❑ CC2 The Assault on Narn .50 1.25
❑ CC3 The Battle for Independence .50 1.25
❑ CC4 The Vorlon Engagement .50 1.25
❑ CC5 Confrontation in Sector 83 .50 1.25
❑ CC6 The Battle of Coriana 6 .50 1.25
❑ CC7 The Battle for Earth .50 1.25
❑ CC8 The Fall of Centauri Prime .50 1.25
❑ CC9 The Drakh Attack .50 1.25

2002 The Complete Babylon 5 Costumes

STATED ODDS 1:40

❑ C1 Capt. Sheridan/1275* 8.00 20.00
❑ C2 G'Kar/1275* 8.00 20.00
❑ C3 Londo Molari/900* 35.00 70.00
❑ C4 Garibaldi/1275* 8.00 20.00
❑ C5 Dr. Franklin/1275* 8.00 20.00
❑ C6 Susan Ivanova/1500* 10.00 25.00
(issued as binder exclusive)

2002 The Complete Babylon 5 Legend of the Rangers

COMPLETE SET (6) 8.00 20.00
STATED ODDS ONE PER BOX

❑ L1 David Martel 2.50 6.00
❑ L2 David Martel/Sarah Cantrell 2.50 6.00
❑ L3 David Martel/Sarah Cantrell 2.50 6.00
Citizen G'Kar/Dulann
❑ L4 Group of 8 2.50 6.00
❑ L5 David Martel/Citizen G'Kar 2.50 6.00
❑ L6 David Martel/Dulann 2.50 6.00
Sarah Cantrell/Malcolm Bridges

2002 The Complete Babylon 5 SketchaFEX

STATED ODDS 1:480

❑ 1 Chris Bolson "Babylon 5 Station"
❑ 2 Dan Schaler "Kosh"

2002 The Complete Babylon 5 The Movies

COMPLETE SET (12) 8.00 20.00
STATED ODDS 1:8

❑ M1 In the Beginning 1.25 3.00
❑ M2 In the Beginning 1.25 3.00
❑ M3 In the Beginning 1.25 3.00
❑ M4 Thirdspace 1.25 3.00
❑ M5 Thirdspace 1.25 3.00
❑ M6 Thirdspace 1.25 3.00
❑ M7 The River of Souls 1.25 3.00
❑ M8 The River of Souls 1.25 3.00
❑ M9 The River of Souls 1.25 3.00
❑ M10 A Call to Arms 1.25 3.00
❑ M11 A Call to Arms 1.25 3.00
❑ M12 A Call to Arms 1.25 3.00

2002 The Complete Babylon 5 The Women of Babylon 5 in Motion

COMPLETE SET (21) 25.00 50.00
STATED ODDS 1:10

❑ W1 Delenn 2.00 5.00
❑ W2 Delenn 2.00 5.00
❑ W3 Delenn 2.00 5.00
❑ W4 Delenn 2.00 5.00
❑ W5 Delenn 2.00 5.00
❑ W6 Delenn 2.00 5.00
❑ W7 Commander Susan Ivanova 2.00 5.00
❑ W8 Commander Susan Ivanova 2.00 5.00
❑ W9 Commander Susan Ivanova 2.00 5.00
❑ W10 Lyta Alexander 2.00 5.00
❑ W11 Lyta Alexander 2.00 5.00
❑ W12 Catherine Sakai 2.00 5.00
❑ W13 Captain Elizabeth Lochley 2.00 5.00
❑ W14 Captain Elizabeth Lochley 2.00 5.00
❑ W15 Number One 2.00 5.00
❑ W16 Adira Tyree 2.00 5.00
❑ W17 Adira Tyree 2.00 5.00
❑ W18 Anna Sheridan 2.00 5.00
❑ W19 Talia Winters 2.00 5.00
❑ W20 Talia Winters 2.00 5.00
❑ W21 Na'Toth 2.00 5.00

2002 Complete Star Trek Voyager

COMPLETE SET (180) 5.00 12.00

❑ 1 The Complete Star Trek Voyager .15 .40
❑ 2 SEASON ONE .15 .40
❑ 3 Caretaker Part I .15 .40
❑ 4 Caretaker Part II .15 .40
❑ 5 Parallax .15 .40
❑ 6 Time and Again .15 .40
❑ 7 Phage .15 .40
❑ 8 The Cloud .15 .40
❑ 9 Eye of the Needle .15 .40
❑ 10 Ex Post Facto .15 .40
❑ 11 Emanations .15 .40
❑ 12 Prime Factors .15 .40
❑ 13 State of Flux .15 .40
❑ 14 Heroes and Demons .15 .40
❑ 15 Cathexis .15 .40
❑ 16 Faces .15 .40
❑ 17 Jetrel .15 .40
❑ 18 Learning Curve .15 .40
❑ 19 SEASON TWO .15 .40
❑ 20 The 37's .15 .40
❑ 21 Initiations .15 .40
❑ 22 Projections .15 .40
❑ 23 Elogium .15 .40
❑ 24 Non Sequitur .15 .40
❑ 25 Twisted .15 .40
❑ 26 Parturition .15 .40
❑ 27 Persistence of Vision .15 .40
❑ 28 Tattoo .15 .40
❑ 29 Cold Fire .15 .40
❑ 30 Maneuvers .15 .40
❑ 31 Resistance .15 .40
❑ 32 Prototype .15 .40
❑ 33 Alliances .15 .40
❑ 34 Threshold .15 .40
❑ 35 Meld .15 .40
❑ 36 Dreadnought .15 .40
❑ 37 Death Wish .15 .40
❑ 38 Lifesigns .15 .40
❑ 39 Investigations .15 .40
❑ 40 Deadlock .15 .40
❑ 41 Innocence .15 .40
❑ 42 The Thaw .15 .40
❑ 43 Tuvix .15 .40
❑ 44 Resolutions .15 .40
❑ 45 Basics Part I .15 .40
❑ 46 SEASON THREE .15 .40
❑ 47 Basics Part II .15 .40
❑ 48 Flashback .15 .40
❑ 49 The Chute .15 .40
❑ 50 The Swarm .15 .40
❑ 51 False Profits .15 .40
❑ 52 Remember .15 .40
❑ 53 Sacred Ground .15 .40
❑ 54 Future's End Part I .15 .40
❑ 55 Future's End Part II .15 .40
❑ 56 Warlord .15 .40
❑ 57 The Q and the Grey .15 .40
❑ 58 Macrocosm .15 .40
❑ 59 Fair Trade .15 .40
❑ 60 Alter Ego .15 .40
❑ 61 Coda .15 .40
❑ 62 Blood Fever .15 .40
❑ 63 Unity .15 .40
❑ 64 Darkling .15 .40
❑ 65 Rise .15 .40
❑ 66 Favorite Son .15 .40
❑ 67 Before and After .15 .40
❑ 68 Real Life .15 .40
❑ 69 Distant Origin .15 .40
❑ 70 Worst Case Scenario .15 .40
❑ 71 Displaced .15 .40
❑ 72 Scorpion Part I .15 .40
❑ 73 SEASON FOUR .15 .40
❑ 74 Scorpion Part II .15 .40
❑ 75 The Gift .15 .40
❑ 76 Day of Honor .15 .40
❑ 77 Nemesis .15 .40
❑ 78 Revulsion .15 .40
❑ 79 The Raven .15 .40
❑ 80 Scientific Method .15 .40
❑ 81 Year of Hell Part I .15 .40
❑ 82 Year of Hell Part II .15 .40
❑ 83 Random Thoughts .15 .40
❑ 84 Concerning Flight .15 .40
❑ 85 Mortal Coil .15 .40
❑ 86 Waking Moments .15 .40
❑ 87 Message in a Bottle .15 .40
❑ 88 Hunters .15 .40
❑ 89 Prey .15 .40
❑ 90 Retrospect .15 .40
❑ 91 The Killing Game Part I .15 .40
❑ 92 The Killing Game Part II .15 .40
❑ 93 Vis a Vis .15 .40
❑ 94 The Omega Directive .15 .40
❑ 95 Unforgettable .15 .40
❑ 96 Living Witness .15 .40
❑ 97 Demon .15 .40
❑ 98 One .15 .40
❑ 99 Hope and Fear .15 .40
❑ 100 SEASON FIVE .15 .40
❑ 101 Night .15 .40
❑ 102 Drone .15 .40
❑ 103 Extreme Risk .15 .40
❑ 104 In the Flesh .15 .40
❑ 105 Once Upon a Time .15 .40
❑ 106 Timeless .15 .40
❑ 107 Infinite Regress .15 .40
❑ 108 Nothing Human .15 .40
❑ 109 Thirty Days .15 .40
❑ 110 Counterpoint .15 .40
❑ 111 Latent Image .15 .40
❑ 112 Bride of Chaotica! .15 .40
❑ 113 Gravity .15 .40
❑ 114 Bliss .15 .40
❑ 115 Dark Frontier Part I .15 .40
❑ 116 Dark Frontier Part II .15 .40
❑ 117 The Disease .15 .40
❑ 118 Course: Oblivion .15 .40
❑ 119 The Fight .15 .40
❑ 120 Think Tank .15 .40
❑ 121 Juggernaut .15 .40
❑ 122 Someone to Watch Over Me .15 .40
❑ 123 12/30/1899 11:59:00 AM .15 .40
❑ 124 Relativity .15 .40
❑ 125 Warhead .15 .40
❑ 126 Equinox Part I .15 .40
❑ 127 SEASON SIX .15 .40
❑ 128 Equinox Part II .15 .40
❑ 129 Survival Instinct .15 .40
❑ 130 Barge of the Dead .15 .40
❑ 131 Tinker, Tenor, Doctor, Spy .15 .40
❑ 132 Alice .15 .40
❑ 133 Riddles .15 .40
❑ 134 Dragon's Teeth .15 .40
❑ 135 One Small Step .15 .40
❑ 136 The Voyager Conspiracy .15 .40
❑ 137 Pathfinder .15 .40
❑ 138 Fair Haven .15 .40
❑ 139 Blink of an Eye .15 .40
❑ 140 Virtuoso .15 .40
❑ 141 Memorial .15 .40
❑ 142 Tsunkatse .15 .40
❑ 143 Collective .15 .40
❑ 144 Spirit Folk .15 .40
❑ 145 Ashes to Ashes .15 .40
❑ 146 Child's Play .15 .40
❑ 147 Good Shepherd .15 .40
❑ 148 Live Fast and Prosper .15 .40
❑ 149 Muse .15 .40
❑ 150 Fury .15 .40
❑ 151 Life Line .15 .40
❑ 152 The Haunting of Deck Twelve .15 .40
❑ 153 Unimatrix Zero Part I .15 .40
❑ 154 SEASON SEVEN .15 .40
❑ 155 Unimatrix Zero Part II .15 .40
❑ 156 Imperfection .15 .40
❑ 157 Drive .15 .40
❑ 158 Repression .15 .40
❑ 159 Critical Care .15 .40
❑ 160 Inside Man .15 .40
❑ 161 Body and Soul .15 .40
❑ 162 Nightingale .15 .40
❑ 163 Flesh and Blood Part I .15 .40
❑ 164 Flesh and Blood Part II .15 .40
❑ 165 Shattered .15 .40
❑ 166 Lineage .15 .40
❑ 167 Repentance .15 .40
❑ 168 Prophecy .15 .40
❑ 169 The Void .15 .40
❑ 170 Workforce Part I .15 .40
❑ 171 Workforce Part II .15 .40
❑ 172 Human Error .15 .40
❑ 173 Q2 .15 .40
❑ 174 Author, Author .15 .40
❑ 175 Friendship One .15 .40
❑ 176 Natural Law .15 .40
❑ 177 Homestead .15 .40
❑ 178 Renaissance Man .15 .40
❑ 179 Endgame Part I .15 .40
❑ 180 Endgame Part II .15 .40
❑ P1 The Complete Star Trek Voyager PROMO 1.00 2.50

2002 Complete Star Trek Voyager Adventures in the Holodeck

COMPLETE SET (9) 2.50 6.00
STATED ODDS 1:4

❑ H1 Beowulf .40 1.00
❑ H2 Polynesian Resort .40 1.00
❑ H3 Beta-Rho .40 1.00
❑ H4 Janeway Lambda-1 .40 1.00
❑ H5 French Resistance .40 1.00
❑ H6 The Adventures of Flotter .40 1.00
❑ H7 The Adventures of Captain Proton .40 1.00
❑ H8 Lessons In Dating .40 1.00
❑ H9 Fair Haven .40 1.00

2002 Complete Star Trek Voyager Autographs

STATED ODDS 1:20
CA1 ODDS ONE PER CASE

❑ A1 Manu Intiraymi 6.00 15.00
❑ A2 Richard Herd 6.00 15.00
❑ A3 Mark Harelik 6.00 15.00
❑ A4 Kurtwood Smith 8.00 20.00
❑ A5 Bruce McGill 6.00 15.00
❑ A6 Rob Labelle 6.00 15.00
❑ A7 Joseph Campanella 15.00 30.00
❑ A8 John Savage 6.00 15.00
❑ A9 Larry Drake 6.00 15.00
❑ A10 Tom Wright 6.00 15.00
❑ A11 Finton McKeown 6.00 15.00
❑ CA1 Jeri Ryan 40.00 80.00
❑ DA1 Robert McNeill 50.00 100.00
Roxann Dawson
❑ DA2 Ethan Phillips 40.00 80.00
Jennifer Lien
❑ DA3 Tim Russ 40.00 80.00
Marva Hicks
❑ PA1 Robert Duncan McNeill
❑ PA2 Martin Rayner 12.00 25.00
❑ PA3 Kate Mulgrew 30.00 60.00
❑ PA4 Garrett Wang 40.00 80.00
❑ PA5 Robert Picardo 30.00 60.00
❑ PA6 Nicholas Worth 12.00 25.00
❑ PA7 Jim Krestalude 8.00 20.00
❑ PA8 Heidi Kramer 8.00 20.00
❑ PA9 Alissa Kramer 8.00 20.00
❑ PA10 Tarik Ergin 6.00 15.00
❑ PA11 Kirsten Turner 8.00 20.00

2002 Complete Star Trek Voyager Costumes

STATED ODDS 1:480

❑ CC1 Seven of Nine 40.00 80.00
❑ CC2 B'Elanna Torres 20.00 40.00
❑ CC3 Chakotay 20.00 40.00

2002 Complete Star Trek Voyager Formidable Foes

COMPLETE SET (9) 5.00 12.00
STATED ODDS 1:8

❑ F1 The Kazon .75 2.00
❑ F2 Vidiians .75 2.00
❑ F3 Borg .75 2.00
❑ F4 Species 8472 .75 2.00
❑ F5 Hirogen .75 2.00
❑ F6 The Krenim .75 2.00
❑ F7 Devore .75 2.00
❑ F8 Voth .75 2.00
❑ F9 Think Tank .75 2.00

2002 Complete Star Trek Voyager Gallery Cels

COMPLETE SET (9) 30.00 75.00
STATED ODDS 1:40

❑ G1 Captain Janeway 4.00 10.00
❑ G2 Seven of Nine 4.00 10.00
❑ G3 Chakotay 4.00 10.00
❑ G4 Tom Paris 4.00 10.00
❑ G5 Harry Kim 4.00 10.00
❑ G6 B'Elanna Torres 4.00 10.00
❑ G7 Neelix 4.00 10.00
❑ G8 The Doctor 4.00 10.00
❑ G9 Tuvok 4.00 10.00

2002 Complete Star Trek Voyager SketchaFEX Sketches

STATED ODDS 1:165

❑ BOLS1 Chris Bolson
Delta Flyer
❑ BOLS2 Chris Bolson
Equinox
❑ CZOP1 John Czop
Dr. Chaotica
❑ CZOP2 John Czop
Seska
❑ CZOP3 John Czop
Satan's Robot
❑ CZOP4 John Czop
Kazon
❑ CZOP5 John Czop
Chakotay
❑ MART1 Warren Martineck
U.S.S. Relativity NCV-474439G
❑ MART2 Warren Martineck
Icheb
❑ MART3 Warren Martineck
Species 8472 BioShip
❑ RAIM1 Pablo Raimondi
Admiral Paris
❑ RAIM2 Pablo Raimondi
Tom Paris
❑ RAIM3 Pablo Raimondi
Tuvok
❑ SCHA1 Dan Schaefer
Harry Kim
❑ SCHA2 Dan Schaefer
Naomi Wildman
❑ SCHA3 Dan Schaefer
Seska

2002 The Crocodile Hunter

COMPLETE SET (72) 8.00 20.00

❑ 1 The Crocodile Hunter .25 .60
❑ 2 Who is Steve Irwin .25 .60
❑ 3 Terri (Raines) Irwin .25 .60
❑ 4 Australia Zoo .25 .60
❑ 5 DANGER-DANGER-DANGER .25 .60
❑ 6 Talk About a Dangerous job .25 .60
❑ 7 What a Ripper .25 .60
❑ 8 Check Out the Size of This Bloke .25 .60
❑ 9 Look at These Little Beauties .25 .60
❑ 10 Rhinoceros Iguana .25 .60
❑ 11 What a Cutie .25 .60
❑ 12 Scary Stuff .25 .60
❑ 13 Adorable Koalas .25 .60
❑ 14 Going our Way .25 .60
❑ 15 Eye to Eye With a Rusty Monitor .25 .60
❑ 16 Cassowary .25 .60
❑ 17 Isn't She Gorgeous .25 .60
❑ 18 You're Okay Mate .25 .60
❑ 19 Ayers Rock (Uluru) .25 .60
❑ 20 Tassie Devil .25 .60
❑ 21 G'day Mate .25 .60
❑ 22 Have a Look at These .25 .60
❑ 23 Crikey That's a Big One .25 .60
❑ 24 Crikey Sea Kraits .25 .60
❑ 25 Sui .25 .60
❑ 26 Check This Out .25 .60
❑ 27 Kookaburra .25 .60
❑ 28 No Worries .25 .60
❑ 29 Big Gray and Dangerous .25 .60
❑ 30 Look How Big, Look How Ferocious I Am .25 .60
❑ 31 Isn't She a Beauty .25 .60
❑ 32 What a Gorgeous Pair .25 .60
❑ 33 Hip Hop Pals .25 .60
❑ 34 Eastern Water Dragon .25 .60
❑ 35 Check this Out .25 .60
❑ 36 Ouch an Asian Porcupine .25 .60
❑ 37 Green Sea Turtle .25 .60
❑ 38 Charlie's Chompers .25 .60
❑ 39 Handle With Care .25 .60
❑ 40 More Than a Handful .25 .60
❑ 41 Don't Muck With it .25 .60
❑ 42 Have a Go at This .25 .60
❑ 43 Salt Water Crocs .25 .60
❑ 44 Steve Says .25 .60
❑ 45 Terri Says .25 .60
❑ 46 Charge .25 .60
❑ 47 Crocs Rule .25 .60
❑ 48 Great Stuff .25 .60
❑ 49 Careful Steve-o .25 .60
❑ 50 Little Beauties .25 .60
❑ 51 Looks Prehistoric .25 .60
❑ 52 Rattler .25 .60
❑ 53 Spotted Cuscus .25 .60
❑ 54 Sulphur Crested Cockatoo .25 .60
❑ 55 Poison Dart Frog .25 .60
❑ 56 Good Onya Mom .25 .60
❑ 57 Charlie the Champion .25 .60
❑ 58 Big Gnarly Boy .25 .60
❑ 59 Jungle in the Clouds .25 .60
❑ 60 Deadly Cobra .25 .60
❑ 61 Steve's Hit .25 .60
❑ 62 Cottonmouth .25 .60
❑ 63 What a Champion .25 .60
❑ 64 Look at This Lizard .25 .60
❑ 65 Tiger Sharks .25 .60
❑ 66 Angry Hippos .25 .60
❑ 67 Mouse Plague .25 .60
❑ 68 Fat Scorpion .25 .60
❑ 69 Steve Says .25 .60
❑ 70 Little Whipper .25 .60
❑ 71 Strike .25 .60
❑ 72 Checklist .25 .60
❑ B1 Steve Irwin (Box Bottom) 2.50 6.00
❑ CT1 Have a Look at These Dart Frogs 2.50 6.00
(issued as case topper)

2002 The Crocodile Hunter Authentic Danger-Ware

COMPLETE SET 5.00 12.00
OVERALL AUTO/MEM ODDS 1:36

❑ DW1 Steve Irwin 3.00 8.00
❑ DW2 Terri Irwin 3.00 8.00

2002 The Crocodile Hunter Most Dangerous Reptiles

COMPLETE SET (9) 6.00 15.00
OVERALL INSERT ODDS 1:7

❑ DR1 Boomslang 1.25 3.00
❑ DR2 Taipan 1.25 3.00
❑ DR3 Black Mamba 1.25 3.00
❑ DR4 Fierce Snake 1.25 3.00
❑ DR5 Russell's Viper 1.25 3.00
❑ DR6 Saltwater Crocodile 1.25 3.00
❑ DR7 Nile Crocodile 1.25 3.00
❑ DR8 Komodo Dragon 1.25 3.00
❑ DR9 Saw-Scaled Viper 1.25 3.00

2002 The Crocodile Hunter Most Lethal Insects

COMPLETE SET (6) 4.00 10.00
OVERALL INSERT ODDS 1:7

❑ LI1 Deadly Mosquito 1.25 3.00
❑ LI2 Sydney Funnel Web Spider 1.25 3.00
❑ LI3 Red Back Spider 1.25 3.00
❑ LI4 Bees 1.25 3.00
❑ LI5 White-Tailed Spider 1.25 3.00
❑ LI6 Mouse Spider 1.25 3.00

2002 The Crocodile Hunter Promos

❑ P1 Steve Irwin (General Distribution) .75 2.00
❑ NSU Steve Irwin (Non-Sport Update) .75 2.00
❑ SDCC Steve Irwin (San Diego Comic Con) .75 2.00

2002 Dark Angel

COMPLETE SET (72) 5.00 12.00

❑ 1 Dark Angel .15 .40
❑ 2 Max .15 .40
❑ 3 Logan .15 .40
❑ 4 Lydecker .15 .40
❑ 5 Original Cindy .15 .40
❑ 6 Sketchy .15 .40
❑ 7 Normal .15 .40
❑ 8 Kendra .15 .40
❑ 9 Herbal Thought .15 .40
❑ 10 Bling .15 .40
❑ 11 Renfro .15 .40
❑ 12 Zack .15 .40
❑ 13 Brin .15 .40
❑ 14 Tinga .15 .40
❑ 15 Det. Matt Sung .15 .40
❑ 16 Agent Sandoval .15 .40
❑ 17 PI Dan Vogelsang .15 .40
❑ 18 Sebastian .15 .40
❑ 19 Dark Angel Season One .15 .40
❑ 20 Pilot .15 .40
❑ 21 Escape From Manticore .15 .40
❑ 22 Encounter With Cale .15 .40
❑ 23 Max's Conscience .15 .40
❑ 24 Rescue And Redemption .15 .40
❑ 25 Heat .15 .40
❑ 26 Flushed .15 .40
❑ 27 CREAM .15 .40
❑ 28 411 On The DL .15 .40
❑ 29 Prodigy .15 .40
❑ 30 Cold Comfort .15 .40
❑ 31 Blah Blah Woof Woof .15 .40
❑ 32 Out .15 .40
❑ 33 Red .15 .40
❑ 34 Art Attack .15 .40
❑ 35 Rising .15 .40
❑ 36 The Kidz Are Aiight .15 .40
❑ 37 Female Trouble .15 .40
❑ 38 Haven .15 .40
❑ 39 Shorties In Love .15 .40
❑ 40 Pollo Loco .15 .40
❑ 41 I And I Am A Camera .15 .40
❑ 42 Hit A Sista Back .15 .40
❑ 43 Meow .15 .40
❑ 44 And Jesus Brought A Casserole .15 .40
❑ 45 Season One Wrap-Up .15 .40
❑ 46 Max On Top .15 .40
❑ 47 Swingers .15 .40
❑ 48 Girls Kick Butt .15 .40
❑ 49 Feline Power .15 .40
❑ 50 Crash And Burn .15 .40
❑ 51 Girl Vs. Machine .15 .40
❑ 52 Cameron's Way .15 .40
❑ 53 Catching The Action .15 .40
❑ 54 Love And War .15 .40
❑ 55 Woman Of Wonder .15 .40
❑ 56 Threesome .15 .40
❑ 57 Is It Me Or Manticore .15 .40
❑ 58 Second Season Sensation .15 .40
❑ 59 The Max Factor .15 .40
❑ 60 Angelic Beauty .15 .40
❑ 61 Xtreme Max .15 .40
❑ 62 Dynamic Duo .15 .40
❑ 63 Don't Mess With Max .15 .40
❑ 64 Alec .15 .40
❑ 65 Joshua .15 .40
❑ 66 Asha .15 .40
❑ 67 White .15 .40
❑ 68 New Allies New Dangers .15 .40
❑ 69 Creatures Featured .15 .40
❑ 70 Dressed To Thrill .15 .40
❑ 71 Teen Dream .15 .40
❑ 72 Checklist .15 .40
❑ P1 Built For Action .15 .40

2002 Dark Angel Autographs

STATED ODDS 1:33 HOBBY

❑ NNO Jessica Alba 400.00 700.00
❑ NNO Alimi Ballard 10.00 20.00
❑ NNO Peter Bryant 10.00 20.00
❑ NNO James Cameron 75.00 125.00
❑ NNO Richard Gunn 10.00 20.00
❑ NNO William Gregory 10.00 20.00
❑ NNO J.C. MacKenzie 10.00 20.00
❑ NNO Byron Mann 20.00 40.00

2002 Dark Angel Foil

COMPLETE SET (5) 4.00 10.00
STATED ODDS 1:6

❑ 1 Dark Angel 1.25 3.00
❑ 2 Dark Angel 1.25 3.00
❑ 3 Dark Angel 1.25 3.00
❑ 4 Dark Angel 1.25 3.00
❑ 5 Dark Angel 1.25 3.00

2002 Enterprise Preview

COMPLETE SET (9) 15.00 30.00
STATED PRINT RUN 2151 SER.#'d SETS

❑ 1 Enterprise Crew 1.50 4.00
❑ 2 Captain Jonathan Archer 1.50 4.00
❑ 3 Sub-Commander T'Pol 1.50 4.00
❑ 4 Chief Engineer Charles Trip Tucker III 1.50 4.00
❑ 5 Lieutenant Malcolm Reed 1.50 4.00
❑ 6 Ensign Travis Mayweather 1.50 4.00
❑ 7 Ensign Hoshi Sato 1.50 4.00
❑ 8 Doctor Phlox 1.50 4.00
❑ 9 Enterprise NX-01 1.50 4.00

2002 Enterprise Season One

COMPLETE SET (81) 4.00 10.00
BOLSON SKETCH ODDS ONE PER CASE
ZC1 STATED ODDS 1:480

❑ 1 Cast Photo .10 .30
Checklist 1
❑ 2 Cast Photo .10 .30
Checklist 2
❑ 3 Cast Photo .10 .30
Checklist 3
❑ 4 Broken Bow .10 .30
❑ 5 Broken Bow .10 .30
❑ 6 Broken Bow .10 .30
❑ 7 Broken Bow .10 .30
❑ 8 Broken Bow .10 .30
❑ 9 Broken Bow .10 .30
❑ 10 Fight Or Flight .10 .30
❑ 11 Fight Or Flight .10 .30
❑ 12 Fight Or Flight .10 .30
❑ 13 Strange New World .10 .30
❑ 14 Strange New World .10 .30
❑ 15 Strange New World .10 .30
❑ 16 Unexpected .10 .30
❑ 17 Unexpected .10 .30
❑ 18 Unexpected .10 .30
❑ 19 Terra Nova .10 .30
❑ 20 Terra Nova .10 .30
❑ 21 Terra Nova .10 .30
❑ 22 The Andorian Incident .10 .30
❑ 23 The Andorian Incident .10 .30
❑ 24 The Andorian Incident .10 .30
❑ 25 Breaking The Ice .10 .30
❑ 26 Breaking The Ice .10 .30
❑ 27 Breaking The Ice .10 .30
❑ 28 Civilization .10 .30
❑ 29 Civilization .10 .30
❑ 30 Civilization .10 .30
❑ 31 Fortunate Son .10 .30
❑ 32 Fortunate Son .10 .30
❑ 33 Fortunate Son .10 .30
❑ 34 Cold Front .10 .30
❑ 35 Cold Front .10 .30
❑ 36 Cold Front .10 .30

- ☐ 37 Silent Enemy .10 .30
- ☐ 38 Silent Enemy .10 .30
- ☐ 39 Silent Enemy .10 .30
- ☐ 40 Dear Doctor .10 .30
- ☐ 41 Dear Doctor .10 .30
- ☐ 42 Dear Doctor .10 .30
- ☐ 43 Sleeping Dogs .10 .30
- ☐ 44 Sleeping Dogs .10 .30
- ☐ 45 Sleeping Dogs .10 .30
- ☐ 46 Shadows Of P'Jem .10 .30
- ☐ 47 Shadows Of P'Jem .10 .30
- ☐ 48 Shadows Of P'Jem .10 .30
- ☐ 49 Shuttlepod One .10 .30
- ☐ 50 Shuttlepod One .10 .30
- ☐ 51 Shuttlepod One .10 .30
- ☐ 52 Fusion .10 .30
- ☐ 53 Fusion .10 .30
- ☐ 54 Fusion .10 .30
- ☐ 55 Rogue Planet .10 .30
- ☐ 56 Rogue Planet .10 .30
- ☐ 57 Rogue Planet .10 .30
- ☐ 58 Acquisition .10 .30
- ☐ 59 Acquisition .10 .30
- ☐ 60 Acquisition .10 .30
- ☐ 61 Oasis .10 .30
- ☐ 62 Oasis .10 .30
- ☐ 63 Oasis .10 .30
- ☐ 64 Detained .10 .30
- ☐ 65 Detained .10 .30
- ☐ 66 Detained .10 .30
- ☐ 67 Vox Sola .10 .30
- ☐ 68 Vox Sola .10 .30
- ☐ 69 Vox Sola .10 .30
- ☐ 70 Fallen Hero .10 .30
- ☐ 71 Fallen Hero .10 .30
- ☐ 72 Fallen Hero .10 .30
- ☐ 73 Desert Crossing .10 .30
- ☐ 74 Desert Crossing .10 .30
- ☐ 75 Desert Crossing .10 .30
- ☐ 76 Two Days And Two Nights .10 .30
- ☐ 77 Two Days And Two Nights .10 .30
- ☐ 78 Two Days And Two Nights .10 .30
- ☐ 79 Shockwave Part 1 .10 .30
- ☐ 80 Shockwave Part 1 .10 .30
- ☐ 81 Shockwave Part 1 .10 .30
- ☐ CB Cris Bolson 25.00 50.00
  Enterprise NX-01 SKETCH
- ☐ P1 Capt. Archer PROMO 1.00 2.50
- ☐ ZC1 Enterprise: To Boldy Go 20.00 40.00

2002 Enterprise Season One 22nd Century Technology

COMPLETE SET (9) 5.00 12.00
STATED ODDS 1:4

- ☐ T1 Enterprise NX-01 .75 2.00
- ☐ T2 Warp Engine .75 2.00
- ☐ T3 Transporter .75 2.00
- ☐ T4 Medical .75 2.00
- ☐ T5 Weaponry .75 2.00
- ☐ T6 Shuttle Pod .75 2.00
- ☐ T7 Grappler .75 2.00
- ☐ T8 Environmental Suits .75 2.00
- ☐ T9 Decontamination Chamber .75 2.00

2002 Enterprise Season One Aliens of Enterprise Autographs

OVERALL AUTO ODDS TWO PER BOX

- ☐ AA1 Clint Howard 10.00 25.00
  (issued in collectors album)
- ☐ AA2 Ethan Phillips 30.00 60.00
- ☐ AA3 Dean Stockwell 30.00 60.00
- ☐ AA4 Jeff Ricketts 6.00 15.00
- ☐ AA5 Randy Oglesby 6.00 15.00
- ☐ AA6 Bruce French 6.00 15.00
- ☐ AA7 Jeff Kober 6.00 15.00
- ☐ AA8 Vaughn Armstrong 6.00 15.00
- ☐ AA9 Keith Szarabajka 6.00 15.00
- ☐ AA10 William Utay 6.00 15.00
- ☐ AA11 Steven Dennis 6.00 15.00
- ☐ AA12 Eric Pierpoint 6.00 15.00
- ☐ AA13 Michelle C. Bonilla 6.00 15.00

2002 Enterprise Season One Autographs

OVERALL AUTO ODDS TWO PER BOX

- ☐ A1 Dominic Keating 30.00 60.00
- ☐ A2 John Billingsley 25.00 50.00
- ☐ A3 Erick Avari 15.00 30.00

2002 Enterprise Season One Broken Bow Autographs

OVERALL AUTO ODDS TWO PER BOX

- ☐ BBA1 John Fleck 6.00 15.00
- ☐ BBA2 Vaughn Armstrong 8.00 20.00
- ☐ BBA3 Joseph Ruskin 6.00 15.00
- ☐ BBA4 Diane Klimaszewski 6.00 15.00
- ☐ BBA5 Elaine Klimaszewski 6.00 15.00
- ☐ BBA6 Jim Beaver 6.00 15.00
- ☐ BBA7 Melinda Clarke 6.00 15.00
- ☐ BBA8 Tiny Lister 6.00 15.00
- ☐ BBA9 Thomas Kopache 6.00 15.00
- ☐ BBA10 Mark Moses 6.00 15.00
- ☐ BBA11 Gary Graham 6.00 15.00
- ☐ BBA12 John Fitzpatrick 6.00 15.00
- ☐ BBA13 Marty Davis 6.00 15.00

2002 Enterprise Season One First Contact

COMPLETE SET (12) 10.00 25.00
STATED ODDS 1:10

- ☐ F1 Andorians 1.25 3.00
- ☐ F2 Axanar 1.25 3.00
- ☐ F3 Kantare 1.25 3.00
- ☐ F4 Klingons 1.25 3.00
- ☐ F5 Mazarite 1.25 3.00
- ☐ F6 Menk 1.25 3.00
- ☐ F7 Risian 1.25 3.00
- ☐ F8 Suliban 1.25 3.00
- ☐ F9 Tandarans 1.25 3.00
- ☐ F10 Valakians 1.25 3.00
- ☐ F11 Wraiths 1.25 3.00
- ☐ F12 Xyrillians 1.25 3.00

2002 Farscape Season Three

COMPLETE SET (72) 5.00 12.00

- ☐ 145 Cast Montage .15 .40
- ☐ 146 Cast Montage .15 .40
- ☐ 147 Cast Montage .15 .40
- ☐ 148 Season Of Death .15 .40
- ☐ 149 Season Of Death .15 .40
- ☐ 150 Season Of Death .15 .40
- ☐ 151 Suns And Lovers .15 .40
- ☐ 152 Suns And Lovers .15 .40
- ☐ 153 Suns And Lovers .15 .40
- ☐ 154 Self-Inflicted Wounds Part 1 .15 .40
- ☐ 155 Self-Inflicted Wounds Part 1 .15 .40
- ☐ 156 Self-Inflicted Wounds Part 1 .15 .40
- ☐ 157 Self-Inflicted Wounds Part 2 .15 .40
- ☐ 158 Self-Inflicted Wounds Part 2 .15 .40
- ☐ 159 Self-Inflicted Wounds Part 2 .15 .40
- ☐ 160 Different Destinations .15 .40
- ☐ 161 Different Destinations .15 .40
- ☐ 162 Different Destinations .15 .40
- ☐ 163 Eat Me .15 .40
- ☐ 164 Eat Me .15 .40
- ☐ 165 Eat Me .15 .40
- ☐ 166 Thanks For Sharing .15 .40
- ☐ 167 Thanks For Sharing .15 .40
- ☐ 168 Thanks For Sharing .15 .40
- ☐ 169 Green-Eyed Monster .15 .40
- ☐ 170 Green-Eyed Monster .15 .40
- ☐ 171 Green-Eyed Monster .15 .40
- ☐ 172 Losing Time .15 .40
- ☐ 173 Losing Time .15 .40
- ☐ 174 Losing Time .15 .40
- ☐ 175 Relativity .15 .40
- ☐ 176 Relativity .15 .40
- ☐ 177 Relativity .15 .40
- ☐ 178 Incubator .15 .40
- ☐ 179 Incubator .15 .40
- ☐ 180 Incubator .15 .40
- ☐ 181 Meltdown .15 .40
- ☐ 182 Meltdown .15 .40
- ☐ 183 Meltdown .15 .40
- ☐ 184 Scratch N Sniff .15 .40
- ☐ 185 Scratch N Sniff .15 .40
- ☐ 186 Scratch N Sniff .15 .40
- ☐ 187 Infinite Possibilities Part 1 .15 .40
- ☐ 188 Infinite Possibilities Part 1 .15 .40
- ☐ 189 Infinite Possibilities Part 1 .15 .40
- ☐ 190 Infinite Possibilities Part 2 .15 .40
- ☐ 191 Infinite Possibilities Part 2 .15 .40
- ☐ 192 Infinite Possibilities Part 2 .15 .40
- ☐ 193 Revenging Angel .15 .40
- ☐ 194 Revenging Angel .15 .40
- ☐ 195 Revenging Angel .15 .40
- ☐ 196 The Choice .15 .40
- ☐ 197 The Choice .15 .40
- ☐ 198 The Choice .15 .40
- ☐ 199 Fractures .15 .40
- ☐ 200 Fractures .15 .40
- ☐ 201 Fractures .15 .40
- ☐ 202 I Yensch, You Yensch .15 .40
- ☐ 203 I Yensch, You Yensch .15 .40
- ☐ 204 I Yensch, You Yensch .15 .40
- ☐ 205 Into The Lions Den Part 1 .15 .40
- ☐ 206 Into The Lions Den Part 1 .15 .40
- ☐ 207 Into The Lions Den Part 1 .15 .40
- ☐ 208 Into The Lions Den Part 2 .15 .40
- ☐ 209 Into The Lions Den Part 2 .15 .40
- ☐ 210 Into The Lions Den Part 2 .15 .40
- ☐ 211 Dog With Two Bones .15 .40
- ☐ 212 Dog With Two Bones .15 .40
- ☐ 213 Dog With Two Bones .15 .40
- ☐ 214 Cast Montage .15 .40
- ☐ 215 Cast Montage .15 .40
- ☐ 216 Cast Montage .15 .40

2002 Farscape Season Three Progressive Proofs Black

COMPLETE SET (72) 40.00 100.00
COMMON CARD (145-216) 1.25 3.00
ANNOUNCED PRINT RUN 50 SETS

2002 Farscape Season Three Progressive Proofs Cyan

COMPLETE SET (72) 40.00 100.00
COMMON CARD (145-216) 1.25 3.00
ANNOUNCED PRINT RUN 50 SETS

2002 Farscape Season Three Progressive Proofs Magenta

COMPLETE SET (72) 40.00 100.00
COMMON CARD (145-216) 1.25 3.00
ANNOUNCED PRINT RUN 50 SETS

2002 Farscape Season Three Progressive Proofs Yellow

COMPLETE SET (72) 40.00 100.00
COMMON CARD (145-216) 1.25 3.00
ANNOUNCED PRINT RUN 50 SETS

2002 Farscape Season Three Autographs

STATED ODDS ONE PER BOX
A15 ISSUED IN COLLECTORS ALBUM
ZA1 ISSUED AS CASE TOPPER

- ☐ A13 Paul Goddard 8.00 20.00
- ☐ A14 Tammy MacIntosh 8.00 20.00
- ☐ A15 Jonathan Hardy/ (issued in collectors album)8.00 20.00
- ☐ A16 Matt Newton 8.00 20.00
- ☐ A17 Linda Cropper 8.00 20.00
- ☐ A18 Magda Szubanski 8.00 20.00
- ☐ A19 Evan Sheaves 8.00 20.00
- ☐ A20 Francesca Buller 8.00 20.00
- ☐ A21 Andrew Prowse 8.00 20.00
- ☐ ZA1 Virginia Hey/ (issued as case topper) 15.00 30.00

2002 Farscape Season Three Behind the Scenes

COMPLETE SET (22)
STATED ODDS 1:5

- ☐ BTS23 Season Of Death .75 2.00
- ☐ BTS24 Suns And Lovers .75 2.00
- ☐ BTS25 Self-Inflicted Wounds Part 1 .75 2.00
- ☐ BTS26 Self-Inflicted Wounds Part 2 .75 2.00
- ☐ BTS27 Different Destinations .75 2.00
- ☐ BTS28 Eat Me .75 2.00
- ☐ BTS29 Thanks For Sharing .75 2.00
- ☐ BTS30 Green-Eyed Monster .75 2.00
- ☐ BTS31 Losing Time .75 2.00
- ☐ BTS32 Relativity .75 2.00
- ☐ BTS33 Incubator .75 2.00
- ☐ BTS34 Meltdown .75 2.00
- ☐ BTS35 Scratch N Sniff .75 2.00
- ☐ BTS36 Infinite Possibilities Part 1 .75 2.00
- ☐ BTS37 Infinite Possibilities Part 2 .75 2.00
- ☐ BTS38 Revenging Angel .75 2.00
- ☐ BTS39 The Choice .75 2.00
- ☐ BTS40 Fractures .75 2.00
- ☐ BTS41 I Yensch, You Yensch .75 2.00
- ☐ BTS42 Into The Lions Den Part 1 .75 2.00
- ☐ BTS43 Into The Lions Den Part 2 .75 2.00
- ☐ BTS44 Dog With Two Bones .75 2.00

2002 Farscape Season Three Family Ties

COMPLETE SET (6) 6.00 15.00
STATED ODDS 1:20

- ☐ F1 John Crichton 1.25 3.00
- ☐ F2 Aeryn Sun 1.25 3.00
- ☐ F3 D'Argo 1.25 3.00
- ☐ F4 Chiana 1.25 3.00
- ☐ F5 Scorpius 1.25 3.00
- ☐ F6 Moya 1.25 3.00

2002 Farscape Season Three From The Archives Costumes

STATED ODDS 1:240

- ☐ CC14 Scorpius 20.00 40.00
  Harvey
- ☐ CC15 Xhalax Sun 15.00 30.00

2002 Farscape Season Three Promos

COMPLETE SET (2) 2.00 5.00

- ☐ P1 Group of seven/ (General Distribution) 1.00 2.50
- ☐ P2 Group of seven/ (Binder Exclusive) 1.50 4.00

2002 Farscape Season Three Revenging Angel Animation Cels

COMPLETE SET (18) 50.00 120.00
STATED ODDS 1:20

- ☐ R1 Revenging Angel 4.00 10.00
- ☐ R2 Revenging Angel 4.00 10.00
- ☐ R3 Revenging Angel 4.00 10.00
- ☐ R4 Revenging Angel 4.00 10.00
- ☐ R5 Revenging Angel 4.00 10.00
- ☐ R6 Revenging Angel 4.00 10.00
- ☐ R7 Revenging Angel 4.00 10.00
- ☐ R8 Revenging Angel 4.00 10.00
- ☐ R9 Revenging Angel 4.00 10.00
- ☐ R10 Revenging Angel 4.00 10.00
- ☐ R11 Revenging Angel 4.00 10.00
- ☐ R12 Revenging Angel 4.00 10.00
- ☐ R13 Revenging Angel 4.00 10.00
- ☐ R14 Revenging Angel 4.00 10.00
- ☐ R15 Revenging Angel 4.00 10.00
- ☐ R16 Revenging Angel 4.00 10.00
- ☐ R17 Revenging Angel 4.00 10.00
- ☐ R18 Revenging Angel 4.00 10.00

2002 Farscape Season Three SketchaFEX

STATED ODDS ONE PER BOX

- ☐ 1 Bridwell/ (Pilot)
- ☐ 2 Bridwell/ (Stark)
- ☐ 3 Carlsson/ (Stark)
- ☐ 4 Carlsson/ (Vocarian Blood Tracker)
- ☐ 5 Chris Prievo/ (Brainiac Crichton)
- ☐ 6 Chris Prievo/ (Pilot)
- ☐ 7 Chris Prievo/ (Stark)
- ☐ 8 Ed Herrera/ (Pilot)
- ☐ 9 Eric Strong/ (Pilot)
- ☐ 10 Eric Strong/ (Stark)
- ☐ 11 J. Davis/ (Pilot)
- ☐ 12 Joe Panico/ (Brainiac Crichton)
- ☐ 13 Joe Panico/ (Pilot)
- ☐ 14 Joe Panico/ (Scarran)
- ☐ 15 Joe Panico/ (Stark)
- ☐ 16 Joe Panico/ (Vocarian Blood Tracker)
- ☐ 17 John Czop/ (Chiana)
- ☐ 18 John Czop/ (DRD)
- ☐ 19 John Czop/ (Jool)
- ☐ 20 John Czop/ (Scorpius)
- ☐ 21 John Czop/ (Zhaan)
- ☐ 22 Jon Wheat/ (Brainiac Crichton)
- ☐ 23 Jon Wheat/ (Vocarian Blood Tracker)
- ☐ 24 Miscovic/ (Scarran)
- ☐ 25 Pablo Raimondi/ (D'Argo)
- ☐ 26 Pablo Raimondi/ (DRD)
- ☐ 27 Pablo Raimondi/ (Rygel)
- ☐ 28 Pablo Raimondi/ (Scorpius)
- ☐ 29 Rob Clark Jr./ (Stark)
- ☐ 30 Warren Martineck/ (Caveman Crichton)
- ☐ 31 Warren Martineck/ (Rygel)
- ☐ 32 Warren Martineck/ (Scarran)
- ☐ 33 Warren Martineck/ (Scorpius)

2002 Farscape Season Three The Quotable Farscape

COMPLETE SET (22) 10.00 25.00
STATED ODDS 1:5

- ☐ Q23 Season Of Death .75 2.00
- ☐ Q24 Suns And Lovers .75 2.00
- ☐ Q25 Self-Inflicted Wounds Part 3 .75 2.00
- ☐ Q26 Self-Inflicted Wounds Part 4 .75 2.00
- ☐ Q27 Different Destinations .75 2.00
- ☐ Q28 Eat Me .75 2.00
- ☐ Q29 Thanks For Sharing .75 2.00
- ☐ Q30 Green-Eyed Monster .75 2.00
- ☐ Q31 Losing Time .75 2.00
- ☐ Q32 Relativity .75 2.00
- ☐ Q33 Incubator .75 2.00
- ☐ Q34 Meltdown .75 2.00
- ☐ Q35 Scratch N Sniff .75 2.00
- ☐ Q36 Infinite Possibilities Part 3 .75 2.00
- ☐ Q37 Infinite Possibilities Part 4 .75 2.00
- ☐ Q38 Revenging Angel .75 2.00
- ☐ Q39 The Choice .75 2.00
- ☐ Q40 Fractures .75 2.00
- ☐ Q41 I Yensch, You Yensch .75 2.00
- ☐ Q42 Into The Lions Den Part 3 .75 2.00
- ☐ Q43 Into The Lions Den Part 4 .75 2.00
- ☐ Q44 Dog With Two Bones .75 2.00

2002 James Bond 40th Anniversary

COMPLETE SET (60) 5.00 12.00

- ☐ 1 40th Anniversary Montage .15 .40
- ☐ 2 40th Anniversary Montage .15 .40
- ☐ 3 40th Anniversary Montage .15 .40
- ☐ 4 Dr. No .15 .40
- ☐ 5 Dr. No .15 .40
- ☐ 6 Dr. No .15 .40
- ☐ 7 From Russia With Love .15 .40
- ☐ 8 From Russia With Love .15 .40
- ☐ 9 From Russia With Love .15 .40
- ☐ 10 Goldfinger .15 .40
- ☐ 11 Goldfinger .15 .40
- ☐ 12 Goldfinger .15 .40
- ☐ 13 Thunderball .15 .40
- ☐ 14 Thunderball .15 .40
- ☐ 15 Thunderball .15 .40
- ☐ 16 You Only Live Twice .15 .40
- ☐ 17 You Only Live Twice .15 .40
- ☐ 18 You Only Live Twice .15 .40
- ☐ 19 On Her Majesty's Secret Service .15 .40
- ☐ 20 On Her Majesty's Secret Service .15 .40
- ☐ 21 On Her Majesty's Secret Service .15 .40
- ☐ 22 Diamonds Are Forever .15 .40
- ☐ 23 Diamonds Are Forever .15 .40
- ☐ 24 Diamonds Are Forever .15 .40
- ☐ 25 Live and Let Die .15 .40
- ☐ 26 Live and Let Die .15 .40
- ☐ 27 Live and Let Die .15 .40
- ☐ 28 The Man with the Golden Gun .15 .40
- ☐ 29 The Man with the Golden Gun .15 .40
- ☐ 30 The Man with the Golden Gun .15 .40
- ☐ 31 The Spy Who Loved Me .15 .40
- ☐ 32 The Spy Who Loved Me .15 .40
- ☐ 33 The Spy Who Loved Me .15 .40
- ☐ 34 Moonraker .15 .40
- ☐ 35 Moonraker .15 .40
- ☐ 36 Moonraker .15 .40
- ☐ 37 For Your Eyes Only .15 .40
- ☐ 38 For Your Eyes Only .15 .40
- ☐ 39 For Your Eyes Only .15 .40
- ☐ 40 Octopussy .15 .40
- ☐ 41 Octopussy .15 .40
- ☐ 42 Octopussy .15 .40
- ☐ 43 A View to a Kill .15 .40
- ☐ 44 A View to a Kill .15 .40
- ☐ 45 A View to a Kill .15 .40
- ☐ 46 The Living Daylights .15 .40
- ☐ 47 The Living Daylights .15 .40
- ☐ 48 The Living Daylights .15 .40
- ☐ 49 Licence to Kill .15 .40
- ☐ 50 Licence to Kill .15 .40
- ☐ 51 Licence to Kill .15 .40
- ☐ 52 GoldenEye .15 .40
- ☐ 53 GoldenEye .15 .40
- ☐ 54 GoldenEye .15 .40
- ☐ 55 Tomorrow Never Dies .15 .40
- ☐ 56 Tomorrow Never Dies .15 .40
- ☐ 57 Tomorrow Never Dies .15 .40
- ☐ 58 The World is Not Enough .15 .40
- ☐ 59 The World is Not Enough .15 .40
- ☐ 60 The World is Not Enough .15 .40

2002 James Bond 40th Anniversary Autographs

STATED ODDS 1:10

- ☐ A1 Jonathan Pryce 10.00 25.00
- ☐ A2 Joe Don Baker 50.00 100.00
- ☐ A3 Shirley Eaton 25.00 50.00
- ☐ A5 Tsai Chin 10.00 25.00
- ☐ A6 George Lazenby 40.00 80.00
- ☐ A7 Trina Parks 10.00 25.00
- ☐ A8 Clifton James 30.00 60.00
- ☐ A9 Christopher Lee 60.00 120.00
- ☐ A10 Richard Kiel 25.00 50.00
- ☐ A11 Lois Chiles 25.00 50.00
- ☐ A12 Julian Glover 10.00 25.00
- ☐ A13 Vijay Amritraj 10.00 25.00
- ☐ A14 Tanya Roberts 12.00 30.00
- ☐ A15 Virginia Hey 10.00 25.00
- ☐ A16 David Hedison 20.00 40.00
- ☐ A17 Steven Berkoff 12.00 30.00
- ☐ A18 Robert Brown 10.00 25.00
- ☐ A19 Samantha Bond 12.00 30.00
- ☐ A20 Angela Scouler 10.00 25.00
- ☐ A21 Bernard Horsfall 10.00 25.00
- ☐ A22 Caroline Munro 10.00 25.00
- ☐ A23 Vincent Schiavelli 10.00 25.00
- ☐ A24 Patrick Macnee 25.00 50.00

2002 James Bond 40th Anniversary Bond Extras

COMPLETE SET (19) 6.00 15.00
STATED ODDS 1:1

- ☐ BE1 Dr. No .40 1.00
- ☐ BE2 From Russia With Love .40 1.00
- ☐ BE3 Goldfinger .40 1.00
- ☐ BE4 Thunderball .40 1.00
- ☐ BE5 You Only Live Twice .40 1.00
- ☐ BE6 On Her Majesty's Secret Service .40 1.00
- ☐ BE7 Diamonds Are Forever .40 1.00
- ☐ BE8 Live and Let Die .40 1.00
- ☐ BE9 The Man with the Golden Gun .40 1.00
- ☐ BE10 The Spy Who Loved Me .40 1.00
- ☐ BE11 Moonraker .40 1.00
- ☐ BE12 For Your Eyes Only .40 1.00
- ☐ BE13 Octopussy .40 1.00
- ☐ BE14 A View to a Kill .40 1.00
- ☐ BE15 The Living Daylights .40 1.00
- ☐ BE16 Licence to Kill .40 1.00
- ☐ BE17 GoldenEye .40 1.00
- ☐ BE18 Tomorrow Never Dies .40 1.00
- ☐ BE19 The World is Not Enough .40 1.00

2002 James Bond 40th Anniversary Bond Villians

COMPLETE SET (19) 6.00 15.00
STATED ODDS 1:2

- ☐ BV1 Dr. No .40 1.00
- ☐ BV2 Rosa Klebb .40 1.00
- ☐ BV3 Auric Goldfinger .40 1.00
- ☐ BV4 Emilio Largo .40 1.00
- ☐ BV5 Ernst Stavro Blofeld .40 1.00
- ☐ BV6 Ernst Stavro Blofeld .40 1.00
- ☐ BV7 Ernst Stavro Blofeld .40 1.00
- ☐ BV8 Kanaga .40 1.00
  Mr. Big
- ☐ BV9 Scaramanga .40 1.00
- ☐ BV10 Karl Stromberg .40 1.00
- ☐ BV11 Hugo Drax .40 1.00
- ☐ BV12 Aris Kristatos .40 1.00
- ☐ BV13 Kamal Khan .40 1.00
- ☐ BV14 Max Zorin .40 1.00
- ☐ BV15 Brad Whitaker .40 1.00
- ☐ BV16 Franz Sanchez .40 1.00
- ☐ BV17 Alec Trevelyan .40 1.00
- ☐ BV18 Elliot Carver .40 1.00
- ☐ BV19 Renard .40 1.00

2002 James Bond 40th Anniversary Bond Women

COMPLETE SET (19) 12.50 30.00
STATED ODDS 1:4

- ☐ BW1 Honey Ryder .75 2.00
- ☐ BW2 Tatiana Romanova .75 2.00
- ☐ BW3 Pussy Galore .75 2.00
- ☐ BW4 Domino Derval .75 2.00
- ☐ BW5 Kissy Suzuki .75 2.00
- ☐ BW6 Tracy DiVincenzo .75 2.00
- ☐ BW7 Tiffany Case .75 2.00
- ☐ BW8 Solitaire .75 2.00
- ☐ BW9 Mary Goodnight .75 2.00
- ☐ BW10 Major Anya Amasova .75 2.00
- ☐ BW11 Dr. Holly Goodhead .75 2.00
- ☐ BW12 Melina Havelock .75 2.00
- ☐ BW13 Octopussy .75 2.00
- ☐ BW14 Stacey Sutton .75 2.00
- ☐ BW15 Kara Milovy .75 2.00
- ☐ BW16 Pam Bouvier .75 2.00
- ☐ BW17 Natalya Simonova .75 2.00
- ☐ BW18 Wai Lin .75 2.00
- ☐ BW19 Dr. Christmas Jones .75 2.00

2002 James Bond 40th Anniversary Costumes

COMPLETE SET (3) 40.00 80.00
STATED ODDS 1:120

- ☐ CC1 James Bond 20.00 40.00
- ☐ CC2 Max Zorin 15.00 30.00
- ☐ CC3 Sir Godfrey Tibbett 15.00 30.00

2002 James Bond 40th Anniversary Game

STATED ODDS 1:1
SP ANNOUNCED PRINT RUN 40 SETS

- ☐ A Jack Wade .75 2.00
- ☐ B Valentin Zukovsky .75 2.00
- ☐ D James Bond SP
- ☐ E James Bond .75 2.00
- ☐ J James Bond .75 2.00
- ☐ M M .75 2.00
- ☐ N Miss Moneypenny .75 2.00
- ☐ O James Bond .75 2.00
- ☐ S Q .75 2.00

2002 James Bond 40th Anniversary Promos

COMPLETE SET (3) 1.50 4.00

- ☐ P1 Sean Connery .75 2.00
- ☐ P2 Roger Moore .75 2.00
- ☐ P3 Pierce Brosnan .75 2.00

2002 James Bond Die Another Day

COMPLETE SET (90) 5.00 12.00

- ☐ 1 Checklist 1 .15 .40
- ☐ 2 Checklist 2 .15 .40
- ☐ 3 Checklist 3 .15 .40
- ☐ 4 Bond Action .15 .40
- ☐ 5 Bond Action .15 .40
- ☐ 6 Bond Action .15 .40
- ☐ 7 Bond Action .15 .40
- ☐ 8 Bond Action .15 .40
- ☐ 9 Bond Action .15 .40
- ☐ 10 Bond Action .15 .40
- ☐ 11 Bond Action .15 .40
- ☐ 12 Bond Action .15 .40
- ☐ 13 Bond Action .15 .40
- ☐ 14 Bond Action .15 .40
- ☐ 15 Bond Action .15 .40
- ☐ 16 Bond Action .15 .40
- ☐ 17 Bond Action .15 .40
- ☐ 18 Bond Action .15 .40
- ☐ 19 Bond Action .15 .40
- ☐ 20 Bond Action .15 .40
- ☐ 21 Bond Action .15 .40
- ☐ 22 Bond Action .15 .40
- ☐ 23 Bond Action .15 .40
- ☐ 24 Bond Action .15 .40
- ☐ 25 Bond Action .15 .40
- ☐ 26 Bond Action .15 .40
- ☐ 27 Bond Action .15 .40
- ☐ 28 Bond Action .15 .40
- ☐ 29 Bond Action .15 .40
- ☐ 30 Bond Action .15 .40
- ☐ 31 Bond Action .15 .40
- ☐ 32 Bond Action .15 .40
- ☐ 33 Bond Action .15 .40
- ☐ 34 Bond Action .15 .40
- ☐ 35 Bond Action .15 .40
- ☐ 36 Bond Action .15 .40
- ☐ 37 Bond Action .15 .40
- ☐ 38 Bond Action .15 .40
- ☐ 39 Bond Action .15 .40
- ☐ 40 Bond Action .15 .40
- ☐ 41 Bond Action .15 .40
- ☐ 42 Bond Action .15 .40
- ☐ 43 Bond Action .15 .40
- ☐ 44 Bond Action .15 .40
- ☐ 45 Bond Action .15 .40
- ☐ 46 Bond Action .15 .40
- ☐ 47 Bond Action .15 .40
- ☐ 48 Bond Action .15 .40
- ☐ 49 Bond Action .15 .40
- ☐ 50 Bond Action .15 .40
- ☐ 51 Bond Action .15 .40
- ☐ 52 Bond Action .15 .40
- ☐ 53 Bond Action .15 .40
- ☐ 54 Bond Action .15 .40
- ☐ 55 Bond Action .15 .40
- ☐ 56 Bond Action .15 .40
- ☐ 57 Bond Action .15 .40
- ☐ 58 Bond Action .15 .40
- ☐ 59 Bond Action .15 .40
- ☐ 60 Bond Action .15 .40
- ☐ 61 The Quotable James Bond .15 .40
- ☐ 62 The Quotable James Bond .15 .40
- ☐ 63 The Quotable James Bond .15 .40
- ☐ 64 The Quotable James Bond .15 .40
- ☐ 65 The Quotable James Bond .15 .40
- ☐ 66 The Quotable James Bond .15 .40
- ☐ 67 The Quotable James Bond .15 .40
- ☐ 68 The Quotable James Bond .15 .40
- ☐ 69 The Quotable James Bond .15 .40
- ☐ 70 The Quotable James Bond .15 .40
- ☐ 71 The Quotable James Bond .15 .40
- ☐ 72 The Quotable James Bond .15 .40
- ☐ 73 The Quotable James Bond .15 .40
- ☐ 74 The Quotable James Bond .15 .40
- ☐ 75 The Quotable James Bond .15 .40
- ☐ 76 The Quotable James Bond .15 .40
- ☐ 77 The Quotable James Bond .15 .40
- ☐ 78 The Quotable James Bond .15 .40
- ☐ 79 The Quotable James Bond .15 .40
- ☐ 80 The Quotable James Bond .15 .40
- ☐ 81 The Quotable James Bond .15 .40
- ☐ 82 The Quotable James Bond .15 .40
- ☐ 83 The Quotable James Bond .15 .40
- ☐ 84 The Quotable James Bond .15 .40
- ☐ 85 The Quotable James Bond .15 .40
- ☐ 86 The Quotable James Bond .15 .40
- ☐ 87 The Quotable James Bond .15 .40
- ☐ 88 The Quotable James Bond .15 .40
- ☐ 89 The Quotable James Bond .15 .40
- ☐ 90 The Quotable James Bond .15 .40

2002 James Bond Die Another Day Autographs

COMPLETE SET (8) 150.00 300.00
STATED ODDS 1:40

❑ A1 John Cleese SP 75.00 125.00
❑ A2 Judi Dench 25.00 50.00
❑ A3 Michael Madsen 20.00 40.00
❑ A4 Samantha Bond 12.00 30.00
❑ A5 Rosamund Pike 20.00 40.00
❑ A6 Rick Yune 12.00 30.00
❑ A7 Colin Salmon 20.00 40.00
❑ A8 Kenneth Tsang 12.00 30.00

2002 James Bond Die Another Day Case Loaders

STATED ODDS ONE PER CASE

❑ AC1 From the Archives Costume 6.00 15.00
❑ MP1 Die Another Day Movie Poster 6.00 15.00

2002 James Bond Die Another Day Casting Call

COMPLETE SET (12) 4.00 10.00
STATED ODDS 1:4

❑ C1 Pierce Brosnan .40 1.00
James Bond
❑ C2 Halle Berry .40 1.00
Jinx
❑ C3 Toby Stephens .40 1.00
Gustav Graves
❑ C4 Rosamund Pike .40 1.00
Miranda Frost
❑ C5 Rick Yune .40 1.00
Zao
❑ C6 Judi Dench .40 1.00
M
❑ C7 John Cleese .40 1.00
Q
❑ C8 Michael Madsen .40 1.00
Falco
❑ C9 Wil Yun Lee .40 1.00
Colonel Moon
❑ C10 Kenneth Tsang .40 1.00
General Moon
❑ C11 Colin Salmon .40 1.00
Robinson
❑ C12 Samantha Bond .40 1.00
Miss Moneypenny

2002 James Bond Die Another Day Montage

COMPLETE SET (9) 4.00 10.00
STATED ODDS 1:4

❑ M1 Die Another Day Montage .60 1.50
❑ M2 Die Another Day Montage .60 1.50
❑ M3 Die Another Day Montage .60 1.50
❑ M4 Die Another Day Montage .60 1.50
❑ M5 Die Another Day Montage .60 1.50
❑ M6 Die Another Day Montage .60 1.50
❑ M7 Die Another Day Montage .60 1.50
❑ M8 Die Another Day Montage .60 1.50
❑ M9 Die Another Day Montage .60 1.50

2002 James Bond Die Another Day Promos

COMPLETE SET (2) 1.25 3.00

❑ P1 James Bond .75 2.00
❑ P2 James Bond and Jinx .75 2.00

2002 James Bond Die Another Day Star Cards

COMPLETE SET (6) 7.50 20.00
STATED ODDS 1:20

❑ S1 James Bond and Jinx 1.50 4.00
❑ S2 James Bond 1.50 4.00
❑ S3 Gustav Graves 1.50 4.00
❑ S4 Jinx 1.50 4.00
❑ S5 Miranda Frost 1.50 4.00
❑ S6 Zao 1.50 4.00

2002 James Bond Die Another Day The Women of Bond

COMPLETE SET (9) 10.00 25.00
STATED ODDS 1:10

❑ W1 Jinx 1.25 3.00
❑ W2 Jinx 1.25 3.00
❑ W3 Jinx 1.25 3.00
❑ W4 Jinx 1.25 3.00
❑ W5 Jinx 1.25 3.00
❑ W6 Jinx 1.25 3.00
❑ W7 Miranda Frost 1.25 3.00
❑ W8 Miranda Frost 1.25 3.00
❑ W9 Miranda Frost 1.25 3.00

2002 James Bond Dr. No Commemorative

COMP.FACT. SET (18) 10.00 25.00

❑ 1 Title Card .75 2.00
❑ 2 James Bond .75 2.00
❑ 3 James Bond .75 2.00
❑ 4 James Bond .75 2.00
❑ 5 Honey Ryder .75 2.00
❑ 6 Honey Ryder .75 2.00
❑ 7 Honey Ryder .75 2.00
❑ 8 Dr. No .75 2.00
❑ 9 Dr. No .75 2.00
❑ 10 Sylvia Trench .75 2.00
❑ 11 Sylvia Trench .75 2.00
❑ 12 Felix Leiter .75 2.00
❑ 13 Professor Dent .75 2.00
❑ 14 M .75 2.00
❑ 15 Quarrel .75 2.00
❑ 16 Miss Taro .75 2.00
❑ 17 Strangways .75 2.00
❑ 18 Miss Moneypenny .75 2.00

2002 Lord of the Rings The Fellowship of the Ring Update

COMPLETE SET (72) 5.00 12.00

❑ 91 Title Card .15 .40
❑ 92 Gift of the Rings .15 .40
❑ 93 The Dark Lord Sauron .15 .40
❑ 94 Forged in Fire .15 .40
❑ 95 Rallying Against Mordor .15 .40
❑ 96 The Clash of Steel .15 .40
❑ 97 The Invincible One .15 .40
❑ 98 Day of the Dark Lord .15 .40
❑ 99 The Defeat of Sauron .15 .40
❑ 100 Evil Never Dies .15 .40
❑ 101 Isildur's Prize .15 .40
❑ 102 Lure of the Ring .15 .40
❑ 103 Sauron's Stronghold .15 .40
❑ 104 In Search of the Truth .15 .40
❑ 105 The New Ringbearer .15 .40
❑ 106 Frodo's Mission .15 .40
❑ 107 Night of the Ringwraiths .15 .40
❑ 108 The Eye of Sauron .15 .40
❑ 109 Betrayed by Saruman .15 .40
❑ 110 Throttled by Evil Magic .15 .40
❑ 111 The Fall of Gandalf .15 .40
❑ 112 The Black Rider .15 .40
❑ 113 The Inn of the Prancing Pony .15 .40
❑ 114 In League with Evil .15 .40
❑ 115 In the Service of Saruman .15 .40
❑ 116 Assault on a Forest .15 .40
❑ 117 The Wraiths True Form .15 .40
❑ 118 The Witch King Attacks .15 .40
❑ 119 Encounter with Ghostly Terror .15 .40
❑ 120 Aragorn to the Rescue .15 .40
❑ 121 Help from a Flying Friend .15 .40
❑ 122 The Water Horses .15 .40
❑ 123 The Beauty of Rivendell .15 .40
❑ 124 Memories of the Epic Battle .15 .40
❑ 125 It Should Have Ended That Day .15 .40
❑ 126 Bilbo's Fond Farewell .15 .40
❑ 127 The Nine on Their Way .15 .40
❑ 128 The Watcher Attacks .15 .40
❑ 129 Seized by the Watcher .15 .40
❑ 130 Entering the Mines of Moria .15 .40
❑ 131 Bilbo's Life-Saving Gifts .15 .40
❑ 132 Bellow of the Cave Troll .15 .40
❑ 133 Monster in the Middle .15 .40
❑ 134 Hide and Seek .15 .40
❑ 135 The Cave Troll Battles On .15 .40
❑ 136 The Orc Swarm .15 .40
❑ 137 Surrounded! .15 .40
❑ 138 Leaping for Life .15 .40
❑ 139 A Bridge Too Far .15 .40
❑ 140 Fury of the Balrog .15 .40
❑ 141 Creature of Shadow and Flame .15 .40
❑ 142 His Final Stand .15 .40
❑ 143 The Fall of Gandalf .15 .40
❑ 144 The Splendor of Lothlorien .15 .40
❑ 145 Galadriel's Temptation .15 .40
❑ 146 The Fortress City .15 .40
❑ 147 The Coming of Lurtz .15 .40
❑ 148 Pillars of the Kings .15 .40
❑ 149 In the Twilight World .15 .40
❑ 150 United in Their Cause .15 .40
❑ 151 Against the Uruk-Hai .15 .40
❑ 152 Boromir's Funeral .15 .40
❑ 153 What Lies Beyond .15 .40
❑ 154 Against Sauron's Minions .15 .40
❑ 155 Conscience of the King .15 .40
❑ 156 The Battle of Helm's Deep .15 .40
❑ 157 The Courage of Aragorn .15 .40
❑ 158 Horrors and Heroes .15 .40
❑ 159 Eomer of Rohan .15 .40
❑ 160 A Woman of Wonder .15 .40
❑ 161 Fellowship Allies .15 .40
❑ 162 A Hobbit's Journey .15 .40

2002 Lord of the Rings The Fellowship of the Ring Update Memorabilia

COMPLETE SET (8) 700.00 1200.00
GROUP A STATED ODDS 1:45
GROUP B STATED ODDS 1:180

❑ NNO Arwen's Riding Outfit B 100.00 200.00
❑ NNO Frodo's Travel Jacket A 75.00 150.00
❑ NNO Frodo's Elven Nightshirt B 100.00 200.00
❑ NNO Sam's Travel Waistcoat A 75.00 150.00
❑ NNO Boromir's Cloak A 75.00 150.00
❑ NNO Pippin's Travel Cloak A 75.00 150.00
❑ NNO Bilbo's Rivendell Waistcoat B 100.00 200.00
❑ NNO Merry's Travel Cloak A 75.00 150.00

2002 Lord of the Rings The Two Towers

COMPLETE SET (90) 6.00 15.00

❑ 1 Frodo .15 .40
❑ 2 Gandalf The White .15 .40
❑ 3 Saruman .15 .40
❑ 4 Aragorn .15 .40
❑ 5 Legolas .15 .40
❑ 6 Gimli .15 .40
❑ 7 King Theoden .15 .40
❑ 8 Grima Wormtongue .15 .40
❑ 9 Lady Eowyn .15 .40
❑ 10 Eomer .15 .40
❑ 11 Faramir .15 .40
❑ 12 Treebeard .15 .40
❑ 13 Sam .15 .40
❑ 14 Merry .15 .40
❑ 15 Pippin .15 .40
❑ 16 Arwen .15 .40
❑ 17 Easterling .15 .40
❑ 18 Uruk-Hai .15 .40
❑ 19 Uruk-Hai On The March .15 .40
❑ 20 The Rescuers .15 .40
❑ 21 The Riders Of Rohan .15 .40
❑ 22 Eomer's Warning .15 .40
❑ 23 Off To Hunt Uruk-Hai .15 .40
❑ 24 Aftermath Of A Massacre .15 .40
❑ 25 A Lift From Treebeard .15 .40
❑ 26 Off To See A Wizard .15 .40
❑ 27 The Return Of Gandalf .15 .40
❑ 28 Visions Of Arwen .15 .40
❑ 29 The Dead Marshes .15 .40
❑ 30 Bog Of The Damned .15 .40
❑ 31 The Face Of Death .15 .40
❑ 32 Frodo's Benefactor .15 .40
❑ 33 Wormtongue's Ploy .15 .40
❑ 34 The Road To Edoras .15 .40
❑ 35 Guarding The Golden Hall .15 .40
❑ 36 The Exorcism .15 .40
❑ 37 Theoden's Return .15 .40
❑ 38 Begone, Wormtongue .15 .40
❑ 39 Stirring Up Hatred .15 .40
❑ 40 A Village Invaded .15 .40
❑ 41 The Pillagers .15 .40
❑ 42 Day Of The Evil Ones .15 .40
❑ 43 A King Once More .15 .40
❑ 44 March Of The Easterlings .15 .40
❑ 45 At The Black Gate .15 .40
❑ 46 The Master's Disciple .15 .40
❑ 47 Making Friends With Gimli .15 .40
❑ 48 Torn Between Worlds .15 .40
❑ 49 For The Love Of Aragorn .15 .40
❑ 50 Drawn To Each Other .15 .40
❑ 51 Battle Of The White Mountains .15 .40
❑ 52 Fury Of Theoden .15 .40
❑ 53 A Duel To The Death .15 .40
❑ 54 Orc Attack .15 .40
❑ 55 Crossing Paths With Faramir .15 .40
❑ 56 Faramir's Gamble .15 .40
❑ 57 The Possession Of Frodo .15 .40
❑ 58 Arriving At Helm's Deep .15 .40
❑ 59 Aragorn's Safe Return .15 .40
❑ 60 The Eve Of War .15 .40
❑ 61 The Courage To Fight .15 .40
❑ 62 To War .15 .40
❑ 63 The Hour Has Come .15 .40
❑ 64 Ready For The Onslaught .15 .40
❑ 65 Saruman's Army Attacks .15 .40
❑ 66 Night Of The Orcs .15 .40
❑ 67 Monster Against Warrior .15 .40
❑ 68 The Fury Of Aragorn .15 .40
❑ 69 Fierce Warfare .15 .40
❑ 70 The Inhuman Enemy .15 .40
❑ 71 The Vile And The Valiant .15 .40
❑ 72 Gandalf Returns .15 .40
❑ 73 Power Of The White Wizard .15 .40
❑ 74 Eomer To The Rescue .15 .40
❑ 75 No Escape From The Riders .15 .40
❑ 76 Warfare In The Courtyard .15 .40
❑ 77 Rohan Victorious .15 .40
❑ 78 In The Osgiliath Sewers .15 .40
❑ 79 Lord Of The Shoot .15 .40
❑ 80 Filming On Location .15 .40
❑ 81 Heroes New And Old .15 .40
❑ 82 My Life As A Hobbit .15 .40
❑ 83 Fine Tuning The Villains .15 .40
❑ 84 Making The Magical Real .15 .40
❑ 85 A Director's Dark Vision .15 .40
❑ 86 The Horror Of It All .15 .40
❑ 87 Filming A Savage Swordfight .15 .40
❑ 88 Painting With Light .15 .40
❑ 89 Making Up A Monster .15 .40
❑ 90 Checklist .15 .40

2002 Lord of the Rings The Two Towers Autographs

COMPLETE SET (14) 700.00 1200.00
GROUP A STATED ODDS 1:45 H, 1:158 R
GROUP B STATED ODDS 1:232 H, 1:804 R
GROUP C STATED ODDS 1:518 H, 1:1796 R
GROUP D STATED ODDS ONE PER CASE

❑ NNO Bernard Hill A 15.00 30.00
❑ NNO Craig Parker D 20.00 40.00
❑ NNO Karl Urban A 20.00 40.00
❑ NNO Peter Jackson A 15.00 30.00
❑ NNO Cate Blanchett A 60.00 120.00
❑ NNO Dominic Monaghan B 40.00 80.00
❑ NNO Miranda Otto C 150.00 250.00
❑ NNO Christopher Lee A 30.00 60.00
❑ NNO Elijah Wood A 150.00 250.00
❑ NNO Orlando Bloom B 150.00 250.00
❑ NNO Billy Boyd A 20.00 40.00
❑ NNO David Wenham A 20.00 40.00
❑ NNO Liv Tyler A 40.00 80.00
❑ NNO Sean Astin A 15.00 30.00

2002 Lord of the Rings The Two Towers Prismatics

COMPLETE SET (10) 8.00 20.00
STATED ODDS 1:6

❑ 1 Aragorn 1.25 3.00
❑ 2 Battle line 1.25 3.00
❑ 3 Line of archers 1.25 3.00
❑ 4 Eomer 1.25 3.00
❑ 5 Easterling Archers 1.25 3.00
❑ 6 Orc 1.25 3.00
❑ 7 Uruk-Hai on the March 1.25 3.00
❑ 8 Gimli 1.25 3.00
❑ 9 Eomer Enhorsed 1.25 3.00
❑ 10 Legolas 1.25 3.00

2002 Men In Black II

COMPLETE SET (81) 5.00 12.00

❑ 1 Men In Black II .15 .40
❑ 2 Bug In The System .15 .40
❑ 3 The New Scum .15 .40
❑ 4 Witness .15 .40
❑ 5 Howdy, Partner .15 .40
❑ 6 Something About Her .15 .40
❑ 7 25-Year-Old Mystery .15 .40
❑ 8 Hytuu Saee Habblimuu! .15 .40
❑ 9 The Truth Is Out There .15 .40
❑ 10 Coming Home .15 .40
❑ 11 Let's Save The World .15 .40
❑ 12 Flushed .15 .40
❑ 13 Revenge Of The Scum .15 .40
❑ 14 Give Me Jay .15 .40
❑ 15 Old Friends...Not .15 .40
❑ 16 Brain Fry .15 .40
❑ 17 Reboot .15 .40
❑ 18 Following Clues .15 .40
❑ 19 All Hail, Kay! .15 .40
❑ 20 Conspiracy Central .15 .40
❑ 21 Episode 27 .15 .40
❑ 22 No Deal .15 .40
❑ 23 Painful Memories .15 .40
❑ 24 Love Hurts .15 .40
❑ 25 Armed And Dangerous .15 .40
❑ 26 Gotcha Covered .15 .40
❑ 27 Showdown .15 .40
❑ 28 Victory Worms .15 .40
❑ 29 Just Like Old Times .15 .40
❑ 30 Little Red Button .15 .40
❑ 31 Taking Aim .15 .40
❑ 32 A Living Light .15 .40
❑ 33 Ultimate Sacrifice .15 .40
❑ 34 Saving The World .15 .40
❑ 35 Just Forget It .15 .40
❑ 36 A New Perspective .15 .40
❑ 37 Kay Quote .15 .40
❑ 38 Jay Quote .15 .40
❑ 39 Jay Quote .15 .40
❑ 40 Serleena Quote .15 .40
❑ 41 MIB Quote .15 .40
❑ 42 Serleena Quote .15 .40
❑ 43 The Work Guys Quote .15 .40
❑ 44 Frank Quote .15 .40
❑ 45 Jeebs Quote .15 .40
❑ 46 Hasmat Truck .15 .40
❑ 47 MIB Deneuralyzer .15 .40
❑ 48 MIB Standard-Issue Sunglasses .15 .40
❑ 49 Egg Display Board .15 .40
❑ 50 Alien Discuise Technology .15 .40
❑ 51 MIB Transportation .15 .40
❑ 52 MIB Customs Desk .15 .40
❑ 53 Light Of Zartha Bracelet .15 .40
❑ 54 Serleena's Getaway Ship .15 .40
❑ 55 Serleena Xath .15 .40
❑ 56 Scrad .15 .40
Charlie
❑ 57 Jack Jeebs .15 .40
❑ 58 The Worm Guys .15 .40
❑ 59 Jarra .15 .40
❑ 60 Laura Vasquez .15 .40
❑ 61 Ben .15 .40
❑ 62 Jeff .15 .40
❑ 63 I-C .15 .40
❑ 64 Lady Bird And Fire Bird .15 .40
❑ 65 Mosh Bulb .15 .40
❑ 66 Robot Squid .15 .40
❑ 67 Pineal Eye .15 .40
❑ 68 Splitz .15 .40
❑ 69 Corn Face .15 .40
❑ 70 Mosh Tendrils .15 .40
❑ 71 Stinkor .15 .40
❑ 72 Locker C-18 Aliens .15 .40
❑ 73 Lenny .15 .40
❑ 74 Spider Bunny .15 .40
❑ 75 Finnigan The Shark Mouth .15 .40
❑ 76 Jay .15 .40
❑ 77 Kay .15 .40
❑ 78 Zed .15 .40
❑ 79 Frank The Pug .15 .40
❑ 80 MIB Agents .15 .40
❑ 81 Checklist .15 .40

2002 Men In Black II Autographs

STATED ODDS 1:50

❑ A1 Tommy Lee Jones 250.00 500.00
❑ A2 Barry Sonnenfeld 50.00 100.00
❑ A3 Lara Flynn Boyle 50.00 100.00
❑ A4 Tony Shalhoub 10.00 25.00
❑ A5 Linda Kim 6.00 15.00
❑ A6 Mary Stein 6.00 15.00
❑ A7 Lowell Cunningham 6.00 15.00

2002 Men In Black II Box Loaders

COMPLETE SET (4) 7.50 20.00
STATED ODDS ONE PER BOX

❑ BL1 They're Back in Business 1.25 3.00
❑ BL2 They're Back in Action 1.25 3.00
❑ BL3 They're Back in Black 1.25 3.00
❑ CL1 Same Planet. New Scum. 6.00 15.00
CASE INSERT

2002 Men In Black II Neuralyzer

COMPLETE SET (2) 6.00 15.00
STATED ODDS 1:35 HOBBY ONLY

❑ N1 Neuralyzer Card 4.00 10.00
❑ N2 Neuralyzer Card 4.00 10.00

2002 Men In Black II Pieceworks

COMPLETE SET (3) 30.00 60.00
STATED ODDS 1:35

❑ PW1 MIB Agents 4.00 10.00
❑ PW2 Tommy Lee Jones 15.00 30.00
❑ PW3 Tommy Lee Jones 15.00 30.00

2002 Men In Black II Promos

COMPLETE SET (6) 4.00 10.00

❑ P1 Jones .75 2.00
Smith
❑ P2 Will Smith .75 2.00
❑ P3 Tommy Lee Jones .75 2.00
❑ P4 Jones .75 2.00
Smith
❑ Pi Lara Flynn Boyle 1.25 3.00
❑ PSD Jones .75 2.00
Smith

2002 Men In Black II Special

COMPLETE SET (3) 4.00 10.00
STATED ODDS 1:11 RETAIL ONLY

❑ R1 MIB Suitability Exam – Question #17 1.50 4.00
❑ R2 MIB Suitability Exam – Question #3 1.50 4.00
❑ R3 MIB Suitability Exam – Question #34 1.50 4.00

2002 Men In Black II Weapons Overview

COMPLETE SET (6) 7.50 20.00
STATED ODDS 1:17

❑ W1 Gun 77P 1.50 4.00
❑ W2 Noisy Cricket 1.50 4.00
❑ W3 The MIB Armory 1.50 4.00
❑ W4 Alien Identifier 1.50 4.00
❑ W5 MIB Trunk Weapons Rack 1.50 4.00
❑ W6 Kay's Secret Stash 1.50 4.00

2002 The Muppet Show 25th Anniversary

COMPLETE SET (25) 6.00 15.00

❑ MS1 Group Shot .40 1.00
❑ MS2 Group Shot .40 1.00
❑ MS3 Kermit .40 1.00
❑ MS4 Kermit .40 1.00
❑ MS5 Kermit .40 1.00
❑ MS6 Miss Piggy .40 1.00
❑ MS7 Miss Piggy .40 1.00
❑ MS8 Miss Piggy .40 1.00
❑ MS9 Fozzie Bear .40 1.00
❑ MS10 Gonzo .40 1.00
❑ MS11 Rowlf .40 1.00
❑ MS12 Statler And Waldorf .40 1.00
❑ MS13 The Swedish Chef .40 1.00
❑ MS14 Dr. Bunsen Honeydew .40 1.00
❑ MS15 Beaker .40 1.00
❑ MS16 Scooter .40 1.00
❑ MS17 Sam The Eagle .40 1.00
❑ MS18 Robin .40 1.00
❑ MS19 Sweetums .40 1.00
❑ MS20 Pigs In Space .40 1.00
❑ MS21 Animal .40 1.00
❑ MS22 Dr. Teeth .40 1.00
❑ MS23 Floyd Pepper .40 1.00
❑ MS24 Janice .40 1.00
❑ MS25 Zoot .40 1.00

2002 The Osbournes Season One

COMPLETE SET (72) 5.00 12.00

❑ 1 Crazy .15 .40
❑ 2 Kelly's Birthday .15 .40
❑ 3 Surprise For Ozzy .15 .40
❑ 4 Ozzy's Birthday .15 .40
❑ 5 Thanksgiving Day .15 .40
❑ 6 The Gravy Chef .15 .40
❑ 7 Christmas Dinner .15 .40
❑ 8 The Meaning Of Christmas .15 .40
❑ 9 Merry Christmas .15 .40
❑ 10 The Dad .15 .40
❑ 11 Family First .15 .40
❑ 12 Play By The Rules .15 .40
❑ 13 Be Unique .15 .40
❑ 14 Take Time For Yourself .15 .40
❑ 15 No Smoking .15 .40
❑ 16 Listen And Learn .15 .40
❑ 17 Care For Your Pets .15 .40
❑ 18 Fences Make Good Neighbors .15 .40
❑ 19 The Mom .15 .40
❑ 20 Inspirations .15 .40
❑ 21 Shopaholic .15 .40
❑ 22 No Martha Stewart .15 .40
❑ 23 Laugh Track .15 .40
❑ 24 Manager .15 .40
❑ 25 When Pigs Fly .15 .40
❑ 26 Sex, Drugs... .15 .40
❑ 27 Toilet Water .15 .40
❑ 28 The Daughter .15 .40
❑ 29 Heart Forever .15 .40
❑ 30 Daddy's Girl .15 .40
❑ 31 Lost And Found .15 .40
❑ 32 Curfews .15 .40
❑ 33 Different .15 .40
❑ 34 Fake Id .15 .40
❑ 35 That's The Ticket .15 .40
❑ 36 Rising Star .15 .40
❑ 37 The Son .15 .40
❑ 38 Fun & Games .15 .40
❑ 39 Hair Today .15 .40
❑ 40 Nanny Woes .15 .40
❑ 41 No Mall Rat .15 .40
❑ 42 Good Hair Day .15 .40
❑ 43 Empire Building .15 .40
❑ 44 Parents Say The Darndest Things .15 .40
❑ 45 Off To Camp .15 .40
❑ 46 Lola .15 .40
❑ 47 Minnie .15 .40
❑ 48 Crazy Baby .15 .40
❑ 49 Maggie .15 .40
❑ 50 Puss .15 .40
❑ 51 Lulu .15 .40
❑ 52 Martini .15 .40
❑ 53 Pipi .15 .40
❑ 54 Gus .15 .40
❑ 55 Maid Of The Mansion .15 .40
❑ 56 Star Treatment .15 .40
❑ 57 Room Service .15 .40
❑ 58 High Society .15 .40
❑ 59 Fine Dining .15 .40
❑ 60 Bearing Crosses .15 .40
❑ 61 Dirty Business .15 .40
❑ 62 On The Road Again .15 .40
❑ 63 Public Relations .15 .40
❑ 64 Tiny Bubbles .15 .40
❑ 65 The Remote .15 .40
❑ 66 Dog Toy .15 .40
❑ 67 Making A Living .15 .40
❑ 68 Non-Stop Rock 'n Roll .15 .40
❑ 69 Old Stand By .15 .40
❑ 70 The Smell Of Victory .15 .40
❑ 71 Falling For Ozzy .15 .40
❑ 72 Checklist .15 .40

2002 The Osbournes Season One Autographs

COMPLETE SET (4) 75.00 150.00
STATED ODDS 1:137

❑ A1 Ozzy 50.00 100.00
❑ A2 Sharon 15.00 30.00
❑ A3 Kelly 10.00 20.00
❑ A4 Jack 10.00 20.00

2002 The Osbournes Season One Box Loaders

COMPLETE SET (5) 7.50 20.00
STATED ODDS ONE PER BOX

❑ BL1 Ozzy 1.00 2.50
❑ BL2 Sharon 1.00 2.50
❑ BL3 Kelly 1.00 2.50
❑ BL4 Jack 1.00 2.50
❑ B6CL Lola 6.00 15.00
CASE INSERT

2002 The Osbournes Season One Family Portrait

COMPLETE SET (9) 7.50 20.00
STATED ODDS 1:11

❑ FP1 Family Portrait 1.25 3.00
❑ FP2 Family Portrait 1.25 3.00
❑ FP3 Family Portrait 1.25 3.00
❑ FP4 Family Portrait 1.25 3.00
❑ FP5 Family Portrait 1.25 3.00
❑ FP6 Family Portrait 1.25 3.00
❑ FP7 Family Portrait 1.25 3.00
❑ FP8 Family Portrait 1.25 3.00
❑ FP9 Family Portrait 1.25 3.00

2002 The Osbournes Season One Head Bangers

COMPLETE SET (5) 3.00 8.00
STATED ODDS 1:17

❑ H1 Ozzy .75 2.00
❑ H2 Sharon .75 2.00
❑ H3 Kelly .75 2.00
❑ H4 Jack .75 2.00
❑ H5 Lola .75 2.00

2002 The Osbournes Season One Pieceworks

COMPLETE SET (4) 20.00 40.00
STATED ODDS 1:36

❑ PW1 Ozzy 7.50 20.00
❑ PW2 Sharon 4.00 10.00
❑ PW3 Kelly 4.00 10.00
❑ PW4 Jack 4.00 10.00

2002 The Osbournes Season One Promos

COMPLETE SET (4) 2.00 5.00

❑ P0 The Osbournes .75 2.00
❑ P1 The Osbournes .75 2.00
❑ Pi Lola .75 2.00
❑ PUK The Osbournes .75 2.00

2002 The Outer Limits Premiere

COMPLETE SET (72) 4.00 10.00

❑ 1 Cold Hands, Warm Heart .10 .30
❑ 2 Cold Hands, Warm Heart .10 .30
❑ 3 Cold Hands, Warm Heart .10 .30
❑ 4 Cold Hands, Warm Heart .10 .30
❑ 5 Cold Hands, Warm Heart .10 .30
❑ 6 Cold Hands, Warm Heart .10 .30
❑ 7 Cold Hands, Warm Heart .10 .30
❑ 8 Cold Hands, Warm Heart .10 .30
❑ 9 Cold Hands, Warm Heart .10 .30
❑ 10 The Invisible Enemy .10 .30

MODERN ERA NON-SPORTS

- 11 The Invisible Enemy .10 .30
- 12 The Invisible Enemy .10 .30
- 13 The Invisible Enemy .10 .30
- 14 The Invisible Enemy .10 .30
- 15 The Invisible Enemy .10 .30
- 16 The Invisible Enemy .10 .30
- 17 The Invisible Enemy .10 .30
- 18 The Invisible Enemy .10 .30
- 19 The Galaxy Being .10 .30
- 20 The Galaxy Being .10 .30
- 21 The Galaxy Being .10 .30
- 22 The Galaxy Being .10 .30
- 23 The Galaxy Being .10 .30
- 24 The Galaxy Being .10 .30
- 25 The Galaxy Being .10 .30
- 26 The Galaxy Being .10 .30
- 27 The Galaxy Being .10 .30
- 28 The Sixth Finger .10 .30
- 29 The Sixth Finger .10 .30
- 30 The Sixth Finger .10 .30
- 31 The Sixth Finger .10 .30
- 32 The Sixth Finger .10 .30
- 33 The Sixth Finger .10 .30
- 34 The Sixth Finger .10 .30
- 35 The Sixth Finger .10 .30
- 36 The Sixth Finger .10 .30
- 37 It Crawled Out of the Woodwork .10 .30
- 38 It Crawled Out of the Woodwork .10 .30
- 39 It Crawled Out of the Woodwork .10 .30
- 40 It Crawled Out of the Woodwork .10 .30
- 41 It Crawled Out of the Woodwork .10 .30
- 42 It Crawled Out of the Woodwork .10 .30
- 43 It Crawled Out of the Woodwork .10 .30
- 44 It Crawled Out of the Woodwork .10 .30
- 45 It Crawled Out of the Woodwork .10 .30
- 46 Demon with a Glass Hand .10 .30
- 47 Demon with a Glass Hand .10 .30
- 48 Demon with a Glass Hand .10 .30
- 49 Demon with a Glass Hand .10 .30
- 50 Demon with a Glass Hand .10 .30
- 51 Demon with a Glass Hand .10 .30
- 52 Demon with a Glass Hand .10 .30
- 53 Demon with a Glass Hand .10 .30
- 54 Demon with a Glass Hand .10 .30
- 55 The Borderland .10 .30
- 56 The Borderland .10 .30
- 57 The Borderland .10 .30
- 58 The Borderland .10 .30
- 59 The Borderland .10 .30
- 60 The Borderland .10 .30
- 61 The Borderland .10 .30
- 62 The Borderland .10 .30
- 63 The Borderland .10 .30
- 64 I, Robot .10 .30
- 65 I, Robot .10 .30
- 66 I, Robot .10 .30
- 67 I, Robot .10 .30
- 68 I, Robot .10 .30
- 69 I, Robot .10 .30
- 70 I, Robot .10 .30
- 71 I, Robot .10 .30
- 72 I, Robot .10 .30
- C1 Checklist .40 1.00
- N1 Opening and Closing Narrations 6.00 15.00 (issued in collectors album)

2002 The Outer Limits Premiere Autographs

STATED ODDS THREE PER BOX

- A1 Adam West 40.00 80.00
- A2 Robert Culp 25.00 50.00
- A3 Leonard Nimoy 75.00 150.00
- A4 William Shatner 100.00 200.00
- A5 James B. Sikking 6.00 15.00
- A6 Lawrence Montaigne 6.00 15.00
- A7 Michael Constantine 6.00 15.00
- A8 Ed Asner 15.00 30.00
- A9 Michael Forest 6.00 15.00
- A10 Don Gordon 6.00 15.00
- A11 Cliff Robertson 15.00 30.00
- A12 Jacqueline Scott 6.00 15.00
- A13 Philip Pine 6.00 15.00
- A14 David McCallum 25.00 50.00
- A15 Jill Haworth 6.00 15.00
- A16 Peter Mark Richman 10.00 20.00
- A17 Joe Stefano 6.00 15.00
- A18 Harlan Ellison 20.00 40.00
- A19 BarBara Luna/ (issued as case topper)
- A20 Arlene Martel/ (issued in collectors album)

2002 The Outer Limits Premiere Beyond the Outer Limits

COMPLETE SET (9) 12.50 30.00
STATED ODDS 1:20

- B1 The Chameleon 2.00 5.00
- B2 The Mice 2.00 5.00
- B3 The Children of Spider County 2.00 5.00
- B4 Tourist Attraction 2.00 5.00
- B5 The Invisibles 2.00 5.00
- B6 The Sixth Finger 2.00 5.00
- B7 The Forms of Things Unknown 2.00 5.00
- B8 The Zanti Misfits 2.00 5.00
- B9 Wolf 359 2.00 5.00

2002 The Outer Limits Premiere Stars of the Outer Limits

COMPLETE SET (9) 5.00 12.00
STATED ODDS 1:4

- S1 William Shatner .75 2.00
- S2 Leonard Nimoy .75 2.00
- S3 Michael Constantine .75 2.00
- S4 David McCallum .75 2.00
- S5 Robert Culp .75 2.00
- S6 Edward Mulhare .75 2.00
- S7 Peter Mark Richman .75 2.00
- S8 Cliff Robertson .75 2.00
- S9 Adam West .75 2.00

2002 The Outer Limits Premiere Strange But True

COMPLETE SET (9) 8.00 20.00
STATED ODDS 1:8

- T1 The Sixth Finger 1.25 3.00
- T2 The Invisible Enemy 1.25 3.00
- T3 The Galaxy Being 1.25 3.00
- T4 Counterweight 1.25 3.00
- T5 Demon with a Glass Hand 1.25 3.00
- T6 I, Robot 1.25 3.00
- T7 Cold Hands, Warm Heart 1.25 3.00
- T8 The Duplicate Man 1.25 3.00
- T9 The Architects of Fear 1.25 3.00

2002 Red Dwarf

COMPLETE SET (64) 5.00 12.00
CC1 STATED ODDS ONE PER CASE
DC1 STATED PRINT RUN 50 SER. #'d SETS
GR1 STATED ODDS 1:1080
20 CREDIT BANKNOTE SER. #'D TO 250

- 1 The Crew .15 .40
- 2 Stasis .15 .40
- 3 Feline Groovy .15 .40
- 4 Resurrection .15 .40
- 5 Future Perfect .15 .40
- 6 Rimmer2 .15 .40
- 7 Admirable Kryten .15 .40
- 8 Holly Hop Drive .15 .40
- 9 Female Crew .15 .40
- 10 New Crew .15 .40
- 11 Caught with Your Pants Down .15 .40
- 12 Love Is .15 .40
- 13 We'll Always Have Parrots .15 .40
- 14 Double Polaroid .15 .40
- 15 Blind Justice .15 .40
- 16 What a Guy .15 .40
- 17 Mr Flibble's Very Cross .15 .40
- 18 The Real World .15 .40
- 19 Suicidal .15 .40
- 20 200 Years Later .15 .40
- 21 Hard Light .15 .40
- 22 Seconds Out .15 .40
- 23 Future Tense .15 .40
- 24 Bad Timing .15 .40
- 25 Smoke Me a Kipper .15 .40
- 26 Crossbow Climax .15 .40
- 27 No Cottage Cheese .15 .40
- 28 Tackle Tight .15 .40
- 29 Barely Able .15 .40
- 30 Mostly Armless .15 .40
- 31 Kicking Bottom .15 .40
- 32 Old Friends .15 .40
- 33 Smeghead Successor .15 .40
- 34 Cunning Captain .15 .40
- 35 Unusual Suspects .15 .40
- 36 Caged Canaries .15 .40
- 37 Viral Attack .15 .40
- 38 Mirror Mirror .15 .40
- 39 Dead Again .15 .40
- 40 Rimmer .15 .40
- 41 Lister .15 .40
- 42 The Cat .15 .40
- 43 Kryten .15 .40
- 44 Kochanski .15 .40
- 45 Holly .15 .40
- 46 Crash Landing .15 .40
- 47 Candid Camera .15 .40
- 48 Midget Moves .15 .40
- 49 Wild Things .15 .40
- 50 Downtown Dallas .15 .40
- 51 Future Echoes .15 .40
- 52 Queeg .15 .40
- 53 Polymorph .15 .40
- 54 Dimension Jump .15 .40
- 55 Back to Reality .15 .40
- 56 Gunmen of the Apocalypse .15 .40
- 57 Stoke Me a Kipper .15 .40
- 58 Cassandra .15 .40
- 59 Only the Good .15 .40
- 60 Only the Good .15 .40
- 61 Only the Good .15 .40
- 62 Only the Good .15 .40
- 63 Only the Good .15 .40
- 64 Checklist .15 .40
- CC1 Case Topper /562
- DC1 Dealer Card /50
- GR1 Gold Redemption Card /100
- NNO XL 20 Credit Banknote /250

2002 Red Dwarf Autographs

OVERALL AUTO/MEM ODDS 1:24

- 1 Danny John-Jules
- 2 Norman Lovett
- 3 Chloe Annett
- 4 Robert Llewellyn
- 5 Craig Charles
- 6 Chris Barrie
- 7 Sylvain Despretz
- AC1 Doug Naylor MEM

2002 Red Dwarf Chloe Annett Photoshoot

COMPLETE SET (6) 5.00 12.00
STATED ODDS 1:8

- CA1 Chloe Annett 1.25 3.00
- CA2 Chloe Annett 1.25 3.00
- CA3 Chloe Annett 1.25 3.00
- CA4 Chloe Annett 1.25 3.00
- CA5 Chloe Annett 1.25 3.00
- CA6 Chloe Annett 1.25 3.00

2002 Red Dwarf Chrome

COMPLETE SET (32) 10.00 25.00
STATED ODDS 1:2

- C1 Red Dwarf .40 1.00
- C2 Blue Midget .40 1.00
- C3 Starbug .40 1.00
- C4 Driving Under the Influence .40 1.00
- C5 Slippery When Wet .40 1.00
- C6 Lister of Smeg .40 1.00
- C7 Duct Surfing .40 1.00
- C8 Cow Curry .40 1.00
- C9 Archie Attacks .40 1.00
- C10 Chris Barrie .40 1.00
- C11 Craig Charles .40 1.00
- C12 Danny John-Jules .40 1.00
- C13 Robert Llewellyn .40 1.00
- C14 Chloë Annett .40 1.00
- C15 Norman Lovett .40 1.00
- C16 Ace Rimmer .40 1.00
- C17 Duane Dibbley .40 1.00
- C18 Jake Bullet .40 1.00
- C19 Low Lister .40 1.00
- C20 High Kryten .40 1.00
- C21 Future Crew .40 1.00
- C22 Mirror Kochanski .40 1.00
- C23 Sebastion Doyle .40 1.00
- C24 Curry Monster .40 1.00
- C25 Kinitawowi & Emohawk .40 1.00
- C26 Simulant .40 1.00
- C27 Polymorph .40 1.00
- C28 Inquisitor .40 1.00
- C29 Legion .40 1.00
- C30 Caroline Carmen .40 1.00
- C31 Hudzen 10 .40 1.00
- C32 Psiren .40 1.00

2002 Red Dwarf Memorabilia

OVERALL AUTO/MEM ODDS 1:24

- 1 Red Uniform
- 2 Holly Poloneck
- 3 Dibbley Wig
- 4 Kryten Head and Ear
- 5 Monster Lucky
- 6 JMC 5 Credit Note
- 7 Lister Cigarette Pack
- 8 JMC 10 Credit Note
- 9 Morris Dancer Monthly
- 10 RD Lucky Dip
- 11 Gold Uniform

2002 Red Dwarf Smeg

COMPLETE SET (6) 4.00 10.00
STATED ODDS 1:8

- SG1 Same Old Deep Space 1.00 2.50
- SG2 Bob and Madge 1.00 2.50
- SG3 Mr Flibble & Talkie Toaster 1.00 2.50
- SG4 Exterior Decorating 1.00 2.50
- SG5 Rat-Arsed 1.00 2.50
- SG6 Boyz from the Dwarf 1.00 2.50

2002 Red Dwarf Sylvain Despretz

COMPLETE SET (6) 5.00 12.00
STATED ODDS 1:8

- SD1 Sylvain Despretz 1.25 3.00
- SD2 Sylvain Despretz 1.25 3.00
- SD3 Sylvain Despretz 1.25 3.00
- SD4 Sylvain Despretz 1.25 3.00
- SD5 Sylvain Despretz 1.25 3.00
- SD6 Sylvain Despretz 1.25 3.00

2002 Scooby Doo The Movie

COMPLETE SET (72) 5.00 12.00

- 1 Title Card .15 .40
- 2 Another Mystery .15 .40
- 3 Daphne In Distress .15 .40
- 4 Behind You .15 .40
- 5 Ooops .15 .40
- 6 Two Years Later .15 .40
- 7 On To Spooky Island .15 .40
- 8 Chance Meeting .15 .40
- 9 Two Bags Only .15 .40
- 10 Helpless No More .15 .40
- 11 Shaggy's Grandma .15 .40
- 12 Distractions .15 .40
- 13 Tourist Class .15 .40
- 14 Recent Activity .15 .40
- 15 Welcome To Spooky Island .15 .40
- 16 The Mission .15 .40
- 17 Island Rituals .15 .40
- 18 Angry Demons .15 .40
- 19 Voodoo Hoodoo .15 .40
- 20 At Dead Mike's Bar .15 .40
- 21 At Spooky Castle .15 .40
- 22 In The Dining Room .15 .40
- 23 Outta Here .15 .40
- 24 Daphne Investigates .15 .40
- 25 In Danger .15 .40
- 26 Fred Finds A Secret .15 .40
- 27 Curious Artifact .15 .40
- 28 Henchmen .15 .40
- 29 Deciphering Clues .15 .40
- 30 Panic At Dead Mike's .15 .40
- 31 Gee, Thanks .15 .40
- 32 On Defense .15 .40
- 33 The Next Day .15 .40
- 34 Entertainment .15 .40
- 35 Suspicious Serenade .15 .40
- 36 Band On The Run .15 .40
- 37 Escape .15 .40
- 38 Woman Trouble .15 .40
- 39 Scooby Doo Snatched .15 .40
- 40 Soul Harvester .15 .40
- 41 Soul Man .15 .40
- 42 Topsy Turvy .15 .40
- 43 Point Of View .15 .40
- 44 Back Again .15 .40
- 45 Plan Of Action .15 .40
- 46 The Ritual Begins .15 .40
- 47 The Villian .15 .40
- 48 Willing Sacrifice .15 .40
- 49 Best Buddy .15 .40
- 50 Saved Soul .15 .40
- 51 Mortal Combat .15 .40
- 52 Triumphant .15 .40
- 53 Scooby Dooby Doo .15 .40
- 54 Fred Jones .15 .40
- 55 Daphne Blake .15 .40
- 56 Velma Dinkley .15 .40
- 57 Shaggy Rogers .15 .40
- 58 Scooby Doo .15 .40
- 59 Mystery Machine .15 .40
- 60 Barge Of The Damned .15 .40
- 61 Spooky Hotel .15 .40
- 62 Dead Mike's Bar .15 .40
- 63 Spooky Castle Ride .15 .40
- 64 Voodoo Maestro .15 .40
- 65 N'Goo .15 .40
- 66 Zarkos .15 .40
- 67 Mondavarious .15 .40
- 68 Scooby Doo Stand In .15 .40
- 69 Imaging Demons .15 .40
- 70 Demon Creation .15 .40
- 71 Collegial Case .15 .40
- 72 Checklist .15 .40

2002 Scooby Doo The Movie Sticker Parallel

COMPLETE SET (72) 15.00 40.00
*STICKER: .8X TO 2X BASE CARDS .30 .75
STATED ODDS ONE PER PACK

2002 Scooby Doo The Movie Box Loaders

COMPLETE SET (4) 6.00 15.00
STATED ODDS ONE PER BOX
CL1 STATED ODDS ONE PER CASE

- BL1 Fred .75 2.00
- BL2 Daphne .75 2.00
- BL3 Velma .75 2.00
- BL4 Shaggy Scooby .75 2.00
- CL1 Another Mystery Solved 4.00 10.00

2002 Scooby Doo The Movie Lenticular

COMPLETE SET (6) 7.50 20.00
STATED ODDS 1:11

- L1 Scooby-Doo 1.50 4.00
- L2 Scooby and the Gang 1.50 4.00
- L3 Fred 1.50 4.00
- L4 Daphne 1.50 4.00
- L5 Shaggy Scooby 1.50 4.00
- L6 Scooby Fred 1.50 4.00

2002 Scooby Doo The Movie Promos

COMPLETE SET (5) 4.00 10.00

- SD1 Scooby and the Gang General Distribution .75 2.00
- SD2 Scooby and the Gang Non Sport Update .75 2.00
- SD3 Scooby and the Gang UK Distribution .75 2.00
- SDI Scooby and the Gang Free Card Offer 1.25 3.00
- SDWW Scooby and the Gang Wizard World 1.25 3.00

2002 Scooby Doo The Movie Sparkly

COMPLETE SET (6) 10.00 25.00
STATED ODDS 1:11

- SP1 Fred 2.00 5.00
- SP2 Daphne 2.00 5.00
- SP3 Velma 2.00 5.00
- SP4 Scooby-Doo 2.00 5.00
- SP5 Shaggy 2.00 5.00
- SP6 Mystery Machine 2.00 5.00

2002 The Scorpion King

COMPLETE SET (72) 3.00 8.00
CL1 STATED ODDS ONE PER CASE

- 1 Title Card .08 .25
- 2 Mathayus .08 .25
- 3 Cassandra .08 .25
- 4 Balthazar .08 .25
- 5 Memnon .08 .25
- 6 Takmet .08 .25
- 7 Aprid .08 .25
- 8 Philos .08 .25
- 9 Isis .08 .25
- 10 The Reign Of Memnon .08 .25
- 11 The Tribes Strike Back .08 .25
- 12 Invading An Enemy Camp .08 .25
- 13 Asssassin... Or Hero .08 .25
- 14 Death To The King's Seer .08 .25
- 15 The Sorceress Revealed .08 .25
- 16 A Savage Struggle .08 .25
- 17 Evil Triumphs... For Now .08 .25
- 18 The Traitor Takmet .08 .25
- 19 An Unexpected Ally .08 .25
- 20 In The Throne Room .08 .25
- 21 Tommorrow The World .08 .25
- 22 The City Of Gomorrah .08 .25
- 23 A Ticket Into Town .08 .25
- 24 The Power Of Memnon .08 .25
- 25 Philos' Laboratory .08 .25
- 26 Science vs. Sorcery .08 .25
- 27 Hero In A Harem .08 .25
- 28 In Cassandra's Chamber .08 .25
- 29 The Kidnapped Sorceress .08 .25
- 30 Desert Trek .08 .25
- 31 Kindred Spirits .08 .25
- 32 Calm Before The Storm .08 .25
- 33 Against The Akkadian .08 .25
- 34 A Force Of Nature .08 .25
- 35 Poisoned! .08 .25
- 36 A Message For Memnon .08 .25
- 37 Fears Of A False King .08 .25
- 38 The Cure .08 .25
- 39 At The Oasis .08 .25
- 40 A Temporary Refuge .08 .25
- 41 Surprised By Bandits .08 .25
- 42 The Bandit Hideout .08 .25
- 43 Not The Warmest Welcome .08 .25
- 44 Mathayus And The Bandits .08 .25
- 45 An Uneasy Alliance .08 .25
- 46 Old Enemies Reunited .08 .25
- 47 Mathayus And Balthazar .08 .25
- 48 A Vision Of Death .08 .25
- 49 For The Love Of Mathayus .08 .25
- 50 Cassandra's Lover .08 .25
- 51 Return Of The Sorceress .08 .25
- 52 A Woman's Work .08 .25
- 53 In The Lower Halls .08 .25
- 54 The Test .08 .25
- 55 Choose .08 .25
- 56 Throne Room Invader .08 .25
- 57 The Battle Begins .08 .25
- 58 Fighting Fire With Fury .08 .25
- 59 The Flaming Swords .08 .25
- 60 Mighty Struggle .08 .25
- 61 His World In Flames .08 .25
- 62 Memnon's Savage Fury .08 .25
- 63 Tommorrow's King .08 .25
- 64 The Killing Of Takmet .08 .25
- 65 Making His Own Destiny .08 .25
- 66 Taking Aim At Evil .08 .25
- 67 Of Fire, Fury And Fate .08 .25
- 68 The Allies Victorious! .08 .25
- 69 Dawn Of A New Era .08 .25
- 70 The Magic Of Their Love .08 .25
- 71 The Scorpion King Forever .08 .25
- 72 Checklist .08 .25
- CL1 Cassandra Mathayus

2002 The Scorpion King Autographs

STATED ODDS 1:51

- A1 The Rock 125.00 250.00
- A2 Bernard Hill 4.00 10.00
- A3 Sherri Howard 4.00 10.00
- A4 Grant Heslov 4.00 10.00
- A5 Stephen Brand 4.00 10.00

2002 The Scorpion King Pieceworks

COMPLETE SET (4) 20.00 50.00
STATED ODDS 1:36

- PW1 Mathayus 6.00 15.00
- PW2 Cassandra 6.00 15.00
- PW3 Memnon 6.00 15.00
- PW4 The Warriors 6.00 15.00

2002 The Scorpion King Promos

COMPLETE SET (4) 2.00 5.00

- SKP1 General Distribution 1.00 2.50
- SKP2 Non Sport Update 1.00 2.50
- SKPi Free Card Offer 1.00 2.50
- SKPUK UK Distribution

2002 The Scorpion King The Future King Puzzle

COMPLETE SET (9) 8.00 20.00
STATED ODDS 1:11

- P1 The Adventure Continues 1.25 3.00
- P2 Evolution Of A Hero 1.25 3.00
- P3 All In The Family 1.25 3.00
- P4 Sands Of Fury 1.25 3.00
- P5 Power Packed Team 1.25 3.00
- P6 The Rock Of Ages 1.25 3.00
- P7 Women Of The Scorpion King 1.25 3.00
- P8 Glad To Be A Gladiator 1.25 3.00
- P9 The Dawn Of Science 1.25 3.00

2002 The Scorpion King The Rock

COMPLETE SET (3) 3.00 8.00
STATED ODDS ONE PER BOX

- BL1 Cassandra 1.25 3.00
- BL2 Isis 1.25 3.00
- BL3 Balthazar 1.25 3.00

2002 The Scorpion King Visions of the Sorceress

COMPLETE SET (6) 4.00 10.00
STATED ODDS 1:17

- S1 First Brush With Mathayus 1.00 2.50
- S2 Dark Days For Isis 1.00 2.50
- S3 The Coming Of Mathayus 1.00 2.50
- S4 The Fever Dream 1.00 2.50
- S5 Visions Of Death 1.00 2.50
- S6 The Killing Of Mathayus 1.00 2.50

2002 Smallville Season One

COMPLETE SET (90) 5.00 12.00

- 1 Smallville .15 .40
- 2 Clark Kent .15 .40
- 3 Lex Luthor .15 .40
- 4 Jonathan Kent .15 .40
- 5 Martha Kent .15 .40
- 6 Lana Lang .15 .40
- 7 Chloe Sullivan .15 .40
- 8 Pete Ross .15 .40
- 9 Whitney Fordman .15 .40
- 10 Lionel Luthor .15 .40
- 11 Nell Potter .15 .40
- 12 Roger Nixon .15 .40
- 13 Downtown Smallville .15 .40
- 14 Smallville High .15 .40
- 15 Fordman's .15 .40
- 16 The Kent Farm .15 .40
- 17 The Talon .15 .40
- 18 Luthorcorp .15 .40
- 19 King And Heir .15 .40
- 20 Fearless .15 .40
- 21 Love And War .15 .40
- 22 Home Turf .15 .40
- 23 The Stuff Of Legend .15 .40
- 24 Haunted Heritage .15 .40
- 25 Secrets .15 .40
- 26 Eye On The Prize .15 .40
- 27 King Of Doom? .15 .40
- 28 Stones From Space .15 .40
- 29 The Mad Scientist .15 .40
- 30 The Vibrating Man .15 .40
- 31 The Freezing Boy .15 .40
- 32 The Invisible Kid .15 .40
- 33 The Electric Boy .15 .40
- 34 The Phantom Burgers .15 .40
- 35 The Bug Boy .15 .40
- 36 The Queen Bee .15 .40
- 37 Ship From Space .15 .40
- 38 Super Strength .15 .40
- 39 Super Speed .15 .40
- 40 Invulnerability .15 .40
- 41 X-Ray Vision .15 .40
- 42 Fatal Weakness .15 .40
- 43 Picture Perfect .15 .40
- 44 Balancing Act .15 .40
- 45 Going Places .15 .40
- 46 Orphan From Space .15 .40
- 47 Accidental Meeting .15 .40
- 48 A Shocking End .15 .40
- 49 Going Buggy .15 .40
- 50 Friend Of The Devil .15 .40
- 51 Firing 'Em Up .15 .40
- 52 The Hot Story .15 .40
- 53 Scene Of The Crime .15 .40
- 54 Nick Of Time .15 .40
- 55 Dealing With The Devil .15 .40
- 56 Chillin' Out .15 .40
- 57 Second Sight .15 .40
- 58 A Close Save .15 .40
- 59 Meteor Men .15 .40
- 60 Midnight Snack .15 .40
- 61 All Shook Up .15 .40
- 62 Generation Gap .15 .40
- 63 Bus Stop .15 .40
- 64 Public Nuisance .15 .40
- 65 If Only... .15 .40
- 66 Bath Assaults .15 .40
- 67 Touchy Situation .15 .40
- 68 Filler 'Er Up? .15 .40
- 69 Pick Up Line .15 .40
- 70 Down And Out .15 .40
- 71 On The Edge .15 .40
- 72 Cruisin' For A Bruisin' .15 .40
- 73 Blast From The Past .15 .40
- 74 Poisoned Dreams .15 .40
- 75 Inner Demons .15 .40
- 76 Temptation .15 .40
- 77 Dream Team .15 .40
- 78 Like Father, Like Son? .15 .40
- 79 Touch Of Death .15 .40
- 80 Awkward Moments .15 .40
- 81 Campaign Issues .15 .40
- 82 Political Attacks .15 .40
- 83 Power Of A Kiss .15 .40
- 84 Haunted .15 .40
- 85 Intensive Care .15 .40
- 86 The Missing Piece .15 .40
- 87 Private Investigations .15 .40
- 88 Something In The Air .15 .40
- 89 Gathering Storm .15 .40
- 90 Checklist .15 .40

2002 Smallville Season One Autographs

COMPLETE SET (6) 100.00 200.00
STATED ODDS 1:59

- A1 John Schneider 30.00 60.00
- A2 Allison Mack 30.00 60.00
- A3 Eric Johnson 15.00 30.00

- A4 Kelly Brook 15.00 30.00
- A5 Hiro Kanagawa 10.00 25.00
- A6 Joe Morton 10.00 25.00

2002 Smallville Season One Box Loaders

COMPLETE SET (4) 7.50 20.00

- BL1 Secret Dreams - Clark 1.25 3.00
- BL2 Secret Dreams - Lex 1.25 3.00
- BL3 Secret Dreams - Lana 1.25 3.00
- B6CL Reign of Blood 6.00 15.00

CASE INSERT

2002 Smallville Season One Pieceworks

COMPLETE SET (4) 50.00 100.00
STATED ODDS 1:59

- PW1 Tom Welling 15.00 40.00
- PW2 Kristin Kreuk 15.00 40.00
- PW3 John Schneider 10.00 25.00
- PW4 Sam Jones III 10.00 25.00

2002 Smallville Season One Preview

COMPLETE SET (9) 7.50 20.00
STATED PRINT RUN 2500 SETS

- PR1 Smallville Cast 1.25 3.00
- PR2 Clark Kent 1.25 3.00
- PR3 Lana Lang 1.25 3.00
- PR4 Lex Luthor 1.25 3.00
- PR5 Pete Ross 1.25 3.00
- PR6 Chloe Sullivan 1.25 3.00
- PR7 Whitney Forman 1.25 3.00
- PR8 Jonathan Kent 1.25 3.00
- PR9 Martha Kent 1.25 3.00

2002 Smallville Season One Promos

COMPLETE SET (6) 6.00 15.00

- P1 Lana, Clark, & Lex 1.25 3.00
- P2 Clark Kent 1.25 3.00
- P3 Lex Luthor 1.25 3.00
- P4 Smallville 1.25 3.00
- Pi Lana Lang 1.25 3.00
- SM1SD Smallville 1.25 3.00

2002 Smallville Season One Smallville High

COMPLETE SET (9) 12.50 30.00
STATED ODDS 1:11

- SH1 Loser 1.50 4.00
- SH2 Do Your Best 1.50 4.00
- SH3 Football Tryouts 1.50 4.00
- SH4 School Politics 1.50 4.00
- SH5 Fantasy 1.50 4.00
- SH6 Geology 101 1.50 4.00
- SH7 Homework 1.50 4.00
- SH8 Class Projects 1.50 4.00
- SH9 Mr. Popular 1.50 4.00

2002 Smallville Season One Spring Formal

COMPLETE SET (6) 7.50 20.00
STATED ODDS 1:17

- LBB1 Clark 1.50 4.00
- LBB2 Pete 1.50 4.00
- LBB3 Lana & Whitney 1.50 4.00
- LBB4 Chloe 1.50 4.00
- LBB5 Clark & Chloe 1.50 4.00
- LBB6 Pete & Clark 1.50 4.00

2002 Star Trek Nemesis

COMPLETE SET (72) 5.00 12.00
RC1 STATED ODDS ONE PER CASE

- 1 Star Trek Nemesis .15 .40
- 2 Two Worlds .15 .40
- 3 The Romulan Senate .15 .40
- 4 Alaskan Wedding .15 .40
- 5 Data's Wedding Gift .15 .40
- 6 Best Man's Toast .15 .40
- 7 The Positronic Signal .15 .40
- 8 The Argo .15 .40
- 9 Finding B-4 .15 .40
- 10 Alien Pursuit .15 .40
- 11 Dr. Crusher, Meet B-4 .15 .40
- 12 Orders from Janeway .15 .40
- 13 Data's Briefing .15 .40
- 14 Memory Download .15 .40
- 15 Shadowy Nemesis .15 .40
- 16 B-4's Betrayal .15 .40
- 17 Dinner with Shinzon .15 .40
- 18 The Boy Who Would Be Praetor .15 .40
- 19 Troubling Images .15 .40
- 20 Mental Assault .15 .40
- 21 The Viceroy's Touch .15 .40
- 22 The Violation .15 .40
- 23 Incarceration .15 .40
- 24 Noble Picard Blood .15 .40
- 25 Picard's Escape .15 .40
- 26 Scorpion .15 .40
- 27 Shinzon's Plight .15 .40
- 28 Battle Plans .15 .40
- 29 Torpedo Blast .15 .40
- 30 Direct Hit! .15 .40
- 31 Enterprise Attacks .15 .40
- 32 Confident Shinzon .15 .40
- 33 Romulans Join the Fight .15 .40
- 34 Troi's Plan .15 .40
- 35 Enterprise Gains an Edge .15 .40
- 36 Reman Invaders .15 .40
- 37 Sucked into Space .15 .40
- 38 Riker vs. Viceroy .15 .40
- 39 Shinzon's Weapon .15 .40
- 40 Picard's Mission .15 .40
- 41 One Giant Leap .15 .40
- 42 The End of Shinzon .15 .40
- 43 Data's Sacrifice .15 .40
- 44 Farewell to Data .15 .40
- 45 Conversation with B-4 .15 .40
- 46 Checklist .15 .40
- 47 Checklist .15 .40
- 48 The Quotable Star Trek .15 .40
- 49 The Quotable Star Trek .15 .40
- 50 The Quotable Star Trek .15 .40
- 51 The Quotable Star Trek .15 .40
- 52 The Quotable Star Trek .15 .40
- 53 The Quotable Star Trek .15 .40
- 54 The Quotable Star Trek .15 .40
- 55 The Quotable Star Trek .15 .40
- 56 The Quotable Star Trek .15 .40
- 57 The Quotable Star Trek .15 .40
- 58 The Quotable Star Trek .15 .40
- 59 The Quotable Star Trek .15 .40
- 60 The Quotable Star Trek .15 .40
- 61 The Quotable Star Trek .15 .40
- 62 The Quotable Star Trek .15 .40
- 63 The Quotable Star Trek .15 .40
- 64 Behind-The-Scenes .15 .40
- 65 Behind-The-Scenes .15 .40
- 66 Behind-The-Scenes .15 .40
- 67 Behind-The-Scenes .15 .40
- 68 Behind-The-Scenes .15 .40
- 69 Behind-The-Scenes .15 .40
- 70 Behind-The-Scenes .15 .40
- 71 Behind-The-Scenes .15 .40
- 72 Behind-The-Scenes .15 .40
- RC1 Romulan Costume 12.50 30.00

2002 Star Trek Nemesis Autographs

COMPLETE SET (12) 300.00 600.00
STATED ODDS 1:20
NA11 ISSUED IN EXPANSION SET

- NA1 Michael Dorn SP 30.00 60.00
- NA2 Ron Perlman 10.00 25.00
- NA3 Tom Hardy 10.00 25.00
- NA4 Dina Meyer 10.00 25.00
- NA5 Kate Mulgrew 25.00 50.00
- NA6a Brent Spiner B-4 SP 75.00 150.00
- NA6b Brent Spiner Data SP 75.00 150.00
- NA7 Shannon Cochran 10.00 25.00
- NA8 Alan Dale 10.00 25.00
- NA9 Jude Ciccolella 10.00 25.00
- NA10 Marina Sirtis 20.00 40.00
- NA12 Patrick Stewart SP 50.00 100.00

2002 Star Trek Nemesis Casting Call

COMPLETE SET (7) 20.00 50.00
STATED ODDS 1:40

- CC1 Captain Jean-Luc Picard 3.00 8.00
- CC2 Lt. Commander Data 3.00 8.00
- CC3 Counselor Deanna Troi 3.00 8.00
- CC4 Lt. Commander Worf 3.00 8.00
- CC5 Commander William Riker 3.00 8.00
- CC6 Lt. Commander Geordi La Forge 3.00 8.00
- CC7 Dr. Beverly Crusher 3.00 8.00

2002 Star Trek Nemesis Promos

COMPLETE SET (9) 20.00 50.00

- P1 Data 1.25 3.00
  Worf/Picard/(General Distribution)
- P2 Reman/(NSU Magazine) 1.25 3.00
- P3 Riker 1.25 3.00
  Troi/(Album Exclusive)
- PT1 Picard 3.00 8.00
- PT2 Data 3.00 8.00
- PT3 Deanna Troi 3.00 8.00
- PT4 Worf 3.00 8.00
- PT5 Shinzon 3.00 8.00
- PT6 Viceroy 3.00 8.00

2002 Star Trek Nemesis Romulan History

COMPLETE SET (27) 7.50 20.00
STATED ODDS 1:3

- R1 Balance of Terror .40 1.00
- R2 The Enterprise Incident .40 1.00
- R3 The Neutral Zone .40 1.00
- R4 Contagion .40 1.00
- R5 The Enemy .40 1.00
- R6 The Defector .40 1.00
- R7 Future Imperfect .40 1.00
- R8 Data's Day .40 1.00
- R9 The Mind's Eye .40 1.00
- R10 Redemption .40 1.00
- R11 Unification .40 1.00
- R12 The Next Phase .40 1.00
- R13 Face of the Enemy .40 1.00
- R14 Birthright .40 1.00
- R15 The Chase .40 1.00
- R16 Gambit .40 1.00
- R17 The Pegasus .40 1.00
- R18 The Search .40 1.00
- R19 Visionary .40 1.00
- R20 Improbable Cause .40 1.00
- R21 The Die is Cast .40 1.00
- R22 In the Pale Moonlight .40 1.00
- R23 Image in the Sand .40 1.00
- R24 Inter Arma Enim Silent Leges .40 1.00
- R25 Eye of the Needle .40 1.00
- R26 Message In a Bottle .40 1.00
- R27 Star Trek VI: The Undiscovered Country .40 1.00

2002 Star Trek Nemesis Romulan History Autographs

COMPLETE SET (14) 150.00 300.00
STATED ODDS 1:20
RA4 STATED ODDS ONE PER COLLECTOR'S ALBUM

- RA1 Denise Crosby 10.00 25.00
- RA2 Martha Hackett 10.00 25.00
- RA3 Malachi Throne 10.00 25.00
- RA4 Lawrence Montaigne 15.00 30.00
- RA5 Alan Scarfe 10.00 25.00
- RA6 Jack Donner 10.00 25.00
- RA7 Carolyn Seymour 10.00 25.00
- RA8 Scott MacDonald 10.00 25.00
- RA9 Judson Scott 10.00 25.00
- RA10 Vaughn Armstrong 10.00 25.00
- RA11 Robin Curtis 10.00 25.00
- RA12 Andreas Katsulas SP 20.00 40.00
- RA13 Marc Alaimo 10.00 25.00
- RA14 Joanne Linville SP 20.00 40.00

2002 Star Trek Nemesis Technology

COMPLETE SET (8) 4.00 10.00
STATED ODDS 1:8

- T1 U.S.S. Enterprise-E .60 1.50
- T2 The Argo .60 1.50
- T3 24th Century 4x4 .60 1.50
- T4 B-4 .60 1.50
- T5 Scimitar .60 1.50
- T6 Cloning .60 1.50
- T7 Romulan Warbird .60 1.50
- T8 Scorpion Attack Flier .60 1.50

2002 Stargate SG-1 Season Four

COMPLETE SET (72) 4.00 10.00

- 1 Stargate SG-1 .10 .30
- 2 Stargate SG-1 .10 .30
- 3 Stargate SG-1 .10 .30
- 4 Small Victories .10 .30
- 5 Small Victories .10 .30
- 6 Small Victories .10 .30
- 7 The Other Side .10 .30
- 8 The Other Side .10 .30
- 9 The Other Side .10 .30
- 10 Upgrades .10 .30
- 11 Upgrades .10 .30
- 12 Upgrades .10 .30
- 13 Crossroads .10 .30
- 14 Crossroads .10 .30
- 15 Crossroads .10 .30
- 16 Divide And Conquer .10 .30
- 17 Divide And Conquer .10 .30
- 18 Divide And Conquer .10 .30
- 19 Window Of Opportunity .10 .30
- 20 Window Of Opportunity .10 .30
- 21 Window Of Opportunity .10 .30
- 22 Watergate .10 .30
- 23 Watergate .10 .30
- 24 Watergate .10 .30
- 25 The First Ones .10 .30
- 26 The First Ones .10 .30
- 27 The First Ones .10 .30
- 28 Scorched Earth .10 .30
- 29 Scorched Earth .10 .30
- 30 Scorched Earth .10 .30
- 31 Beneath The Surface .10 .30
- 32 Beneath The Surface .10 .30
- 33 Beneath The Surface .10 .30
- 34 Point Of No Return .10 .30
- 35 Point Of No Return .10 .30
- 36 Point Of No Return .10 .30
- 37 Tangent .10 .30
- 38 Tangent .10 .30
- 39 Tangent .10 .30
- 40 The Curse .10 .30
- 41 The Curse .10 .30
- 42 The Curse .10 .30
- 43 The Serpent's Venom .10 .30
- 44 The Serpent's Venom .10 .30
- 45 The Serpent's Venom .10 .30
- 46 Chain Reaction .10 .30
- 47 Chain Reaction .10 .30
- 48 Chain Reaction .10 .30
- 49 2010 .10 .30
- 50 2010 .10 .30
- 51 2010 .10 .30
- 52 Absolute Power .10 .30
- 53 Absolute Power .10 .30
- 54 Absolute Power .10 .30
- 55 The Light .10 .30
- 56 The Light .10 .30
- 57 The Light .10 .30
- 58 Prodigy .10 .30
- 59 Prodigy .10 .30
- 60 Prodigy .10 .30
- 61 Entity .10 .30
- 62 Entity .10 .30
- 63 Entity .10 .30
- 64 Double Jeopardy .10 .30
- 65 Double Jeopardy .10 .30
- 66 Double Jeopardy .10 .30
- 67 Exodus .10 .30
- 68 Exodus .10 .30
- 69 Exodus .10 .30
- 70 Checklist 1 .10 .30
- 71 Checklist 2 .10 .30
- 72 Checklist 3 .10 .30

2002 Stargate SG-1 Season Four Autographs

STATED ODDS ONE PER BOX
A19 ISSUED IN COLLECTORS ALBUM

- A10 Suanne Braun 6.00 15.00
- A11 Amanda Tapping 25.00 50.00
- A12 Carmen Argenziano 6.00 15.00
- A13 Michael Shanks 50.00 100.00
- A14 Peter Wingfield 6.00 15.00
- A15 Tom McBeath 6.00 15.00
- A16 Vanessa Angel 6.00 15.00
- A17 Colin Cunningham 6.00 15.00
- A18 J.R. Bourne 6.00 15.00
- A19 Erick Avari/ (issued in collectors album)10.00 20.00

2002 Stargate SG-1 Season Four Dial Us Home

COMPLETE SET (6) 2.50 6.00
STATED ODDS 1:6

- D1 Auriga .60 1.50
- D2 Cetus .60 1.50
- D3 Centaurus .60 1.50
- D4 Cancer .60 1.50
- D5 Scutum .60 1.50
- D6 Eridanus .60 1.50

2002 Stargate SG-1 Season Four From The Archives Costumes

STATED ODDS ONE PER BOX
C12 ISSUED AS CASE TOPPER
ANNOUNCED PRINT RUN 625-1450

- C5 Teal'c/1450* 6.00 15.00
- C6 General Hammond/1350* 6.00 15.00
- C7 Selmak/1350* 6.00 15.00
- C8 Colonel Maybourne/1300* 6.00 15.00
- C9 Anise 30.00 60.00
  Freya/625*
- C10 Mollem/1300* 6.00 15.00
- C11 Major Samantha Carter/625* 30.00 60.00
- C12 Major Samantha Carter DUAL/ (issued as case topper)
  40.00 80.00

2002 Stargate SG-1 Season Four Goa'uld Technology

COMPLETE SET (9) 6.00 15.00
STATED ODDS 1:8

- G1 AG-3 Defense System .75 2.00
- G2 Body Armor .75 2.00
- G3 Death Gliders .75 2.00
- G4 Ribbon Device .75 2.00
- G5 Rings .75 2.00
- G6 Sarcophagus .75 2.00
- G7 Staff Weapon .75 2.00
- G8 Teltac .75 2.00
- G9 Zat'n'ktel .75 2.00

2002 Stargate SG-1 Season Four Heroes In Action

COMPLETE SET (4) 8.00 20.00
STATED ODDS 1:40

- H1 Colonel Jack O'Neill 2.50 6.00
- H2 Teal'c 2.50 6.00
- H3 Major Samantha Carter 2.50 6.00
- H4 Daniel Jackson 2.50 6.00

2002 Stargate SG-1 Season Four Promos

COMPLETE SET (2) 2.00 5.00

- P1 Group of five/ (General Distribution) 1.00 2.50
- BP1 Group of four/ (Binder Exclusive) 1.50 4.00

2002 Stargate SG-1 Season Four SketchaFEX

STATED ODDS 1:480

- 1 John Czop (Teal'c) 40.00 80.00
  left side of puzzle
- 2 John Czop (Teal'c) 40.00 80.00
  right side of puzzle

2002 Twilight Zone Shadows and Substance

COMPLETE SET (72) 5.00 12.00

- 145 A Quality Of Mercy .15 .40
- 146 A Quality Of Mercy .15 .40
- 147 A Quality Of Mercy .15 .40
- 148 A Quality Of Mercy .15 .40
- 149 A Quality Of Mercy .15 .40
- 150 A Quality Of Mercy .15 .40
- 151 A Game Of Pool .15 .40
- 152 A Game Of Pool .15 .40
- 153 A Game Of Pool .15 .40
- 154 A Game Of Pool .15 .40
- 155 A Game Of Pool .15 .40
- 156 A Game Of Pool .15 .40
- 157 The Dummy .15 .40
- 158 The Dummy .15 .40
- 159 The Dummy .15 .40
- 160 The Dummy .15 .40
- 161 The Dummy .15 .40
- 162 The Dummy .15 .40
- 163 I Am The Night-Color Me Black .15 .40
- 164 I Am The Night-Color Me Black .15 .40
- 165 I Am The Night-Color Me Black .15 .40
- 166 I Am The Night-Color Me Black .15 .40
- 167 I Am The Night-Color Me Black .15 .40
- 168 I Am The Night-Color Me Black .15 .40
- 169 Execution .15 .40
- 170 Execution .15 .40
- 171 Execution .15 .40
- 172 Execution .15 .40
- 173 Execution .15 .40
- 174 Execution .15 .40
- 175 A Passage For Trumpet .15 .40
- 176 A Passage For Trumpet .15 .40
- 177 A Passage For Trumpet .15 .40
- 178 A Passage For Trumpet .15 .40
- 179 A Passage For Trumpet .15 .40
- 180 A Passage For Trumpet .15 .40
- 181 Of Late I Think Of Cliffordville .15 .40
- 182 Of Late I Think Of Cliffordville .15 .40
- 183 Of Late I Think Of Cliffordville .15 .40
- 184 Of Late I Think Of Cliffordville .15 .40
- 185 Of Late I Think Of Cliffordville .15 .40
- 186 Of Late I Think Of Cliffordville .15 .40
- 187 Of Late I Think Of Cliffordville .15 .40
- 188 Of Late I Think Of Cliffordville .15 .40
- 189 Of Late I Think Of Cliffordville .15 .40
- 190 Jess-Belle .15 .40
- 191 Jess-Belle .15 .40
- 192 Jess-Belle .15 .40
- 193 Jess-Belle .15 .40
- 194 Jess-Belle .15 .40
- 195 Jess-Belle .15 .40
- 196 Jess-Belle .15 .40
- 197 Jess-Belle .15 .40
- 198 Jess-Belle .15 .40
- 199 The Parallel .15 .40
- 200 The Parallel .15 .40
- 201 The Parallel .15 .40
- 202 The Parallel .15 .40
- 203 The Parallel .15 .40
- 204 The Parallel .15 .40
- 205 The Parallel .15 .40
- 206 The Parallel .15 .40
- 207 The Parallel .15 .40
- 208 The Incredible World Of Horace Ford .15 .40
- 209 The Incredible World Of Horace Ford .15 .40
- 210 The Incredible World Of Horace Ford .15 .40
- 211 The Incredible World Of Horace Ford .15 .40
- 212 The Incredible World Of Horace Ford .15 .40
- 213 The Incredible World Of Horace Ford .15 .40
- 214 The Incredible World Of Horace Ford .15 .40
- 215 The Incredible World Of Horace Ford .15 .40
- 216 The Incredible World Of Horace Ford .15 .40
- P1 Group Shot PROMO

2002 Twilight Zone Shadows and Substance Autographs

STATED ODDS FOUR PER BOX
CARDS A53, A54, A59, AND A60 WERE NOT ISSUED

- A39 Dean Stockwell
- A40 Patricia Breslin
- A41 Hazel Court
- A42 Jonathan Winters 25.00 50.00
- A43 Jack Klugman 25.00 50.00
- A44 Leonard Nimoy
- A45 Russell Johnson 20.00 40.00
- A46 Nan Martin 8.00 20.00
- A47 Philip Pine 8.00 20.00
- A48 Michael Constantine 8.00 20.00
- A49 Bill Mumy 15.00 30.00
- A50 Julie Newmar 30.00 60.00
- A51A George Takei/ (issued as case topper) 25.00 50.00
- A51B Wright King 6.00 15.00
- A52A George Murdock 6.00 15.00
- A52B H.M. Wynant 8.00 20.00
- A55A Bill Reynolds 8.00 20.00
- A55B Steve Forrest 15.00 30.00
- A56A Jonathan Harris 75.00 150.00
- A56B Paul Comi 6.00 15.00
- A57 Arlene Martel 15.00 30.00
- A58 Fredd Wayne 6.00 15.00
- A61 Jacqueline Scott 8.00 20.00
- A62 Gloria Pall 15.00 30.00
- A63 Asa Maynor 8.00 20.00
- A64 Frank Aletter 8.00 20.00
- A65 George Lindsey/ (issued in collectors album)15.00 30.00

2002 Twilight Zone Shadows and Substance SketchaFEX

STATED ODDS 1:480

- 1 Pablo Raimondi
  Fortune Telling Machine
- 2 Pablo Raimondi
  Kanamet

2002 Twilight Zone Shadows and Substance Twilight Zone Hall of Fame

COMPLETE SET (4) 100.00 200.00
STATED ODDS 1:100

- H1 William Shatner 30.00 60.00
- H2 Jack Klugman 30.00 60.00
- H3 Bill Mumy 30.00 60.00
- H4 James Best 30.00 60.00

2002 Twilight Zone Shadows and Substance Twilight Zone Stars

COMPLETE SET (9) 6.00 15.00
STATED ODDS 1:5

- S19 Leonard Nimoy 1.00 2.50
- S20 Cliff Robertson 1.00 2.50
- S21 Jonathan Winters 1.00 2.50
- S22 George Takei 1.00 2.50
- S23 Jonathan Harris 1.00 2.50
- S24 Julie Newmar 1.00 2.50
- S25 Dean Stockwell 1.00 2.50
- S26 Russell Johnson 1.00 2.50
- S27 Steve Forrest 1.00 2.50

2002 Witchblade Season One

COMPLETE SET (81) 4.00 10.00

- 1 Witchblade .10 .30
- 2 Sara Pezzini .10 .30
- 3 Jake McCartey .10 .30
- 4 Danny Woo .10 .30
- 5 Kenneth Irons .10 .30
- 6 Ian Nottingham .10 .30
- 7 Captain Bruno Dante .10 .30
- 8 Gabriel Bowman .10 .30
- 9 Conchobar .10 .30
- 10 Joe Siri .10 .30
- 11 Father Del Toro .10 .30
- 12 Dominique Boucher .10 .30
- 13 Witchblade Pilot: Credits .10 .30
- 14 The Death of Danny Woo .10 .30
- 15 Sara's Moment of Truth .10 .30
- 16 The Nottingham Factor .10 .30
- 17 Using the Blade .10 .30
- 18 A Warrior Reborn .10 .30
- 19 Joe Siro's Advice .10 .30
- 20 The Training of Joan .10 .30
- 21 Secrets of the Witchblade .10 .30
- 22 On the Trail of Gallo .10 .30
- 23 Ally or Enemy? .10 .30
- 24 Getting the Drop on Sara .10 .30
- 25 Terror in the Subway .10 .30
- 26 The Bladewielder .10 .30
- 27 No Escape from Justice .10 .30
- 28 Parallax: The Credits .10 .30
- 29 Parallax: The Story .10 .30
- 30 Parallax: The Mythology .10 .30
- 31 Conundrum: The Credits .10 .30
- 32 Conundrum: The Story .10 .30
- 33 Conundrum: The Mythology .10 .30
- 34 Diplopia: The Credits .10 .30
- 35 Diplopia: The Story .10 .30
- 36 Diplopia: The Mythology .10 .30
- 37 Sacrifice: The Credits .10 .30
- 38 Sacrifice: The Story .10 .30
- 39 Sacrifice: The Mythology .10 .30
- 40 Legion: The Credits .10 .30
- 41 Legion: The Story .10 .30
- 42 Legion: The Mythology .10 .30
- 43 Maelstrom: The Credits .10 .30
- 44 Maelstrom: The Story .10 .30
- 45 Maelstrom: The Mythology .10 .30
- 46 Periculum: The Credits .10 .30
- 47 Periculum: The Story .10 .30
- 48 Periculum: The Mythology .10 .30
- 49 Thanatopsis: The Credits .10 .30
- 50 Thanatopsis: The Story .10 .30
- 51 Thanatopsis: They Mythology .10 .30
- 52 Apprehension: The Credits .10 .30
- 53 Apprehension: The Story .10 .30
- 54 Apprehension: The Mythology .10 .30
- 55 Convergence: The Credits .10 .30
- 56 Convergence: The Story .10 .30
- 57 Convergence: The Mythology .10 .30
- 58 Transcendence: The Credits .10 .30
- 59 Transcendence: The Story .10 .30
- 60 Transcendence: The Mythology .10 .30
- 61 Saint Joan of Arc .10 .30
- 62 Warrior-Goddess Cathain .10 .30
- 63 Elizabeth Bronte .10 .30
- 64 Partners Forever .10 .30
- 65 Jake and Sara .10 .30
- 66 Of Good and Evil .10 .30
- 67 Power of the Ages .10 .30
- 68 The Master and Disciple .10 .30
- 69 Sara's Guardian Angel .10 .30
- 70 Dark Knight of the Witchblade .10 .30
- 71 Her Armored Alter-Ego .10 .30
- 72 The Wielder in Armor .10 .30
- 73 Setting Up a Stalk .10 .30
- 74 High Flying Heroics .10 .30
- 75 Woman of Steel .10 .30
- 76 Directing Danny Woo .10 .30
- 77 When Adversaries Meet .10 .30
- 78 Who's on Sara's Side? .10 .30
- 79 The Witchblade Prop .10 .30
- 80 The Blade Extended .10 .30
- 81 Checklist .10 .30

2002 Witchblade Season One Autographs

COMPLETE SET (6) 60.00 150.00
STATED ODDS 1:27

- A1 Yancy Butler 30.00 80.00
- A2 David Chokachi 10.00 25.00
- A3 Will Yun Lee 10.00 25.00
- A4 Anthony Cistaro 10.00 25.00
- A5 Eric Etebari 12.50 30.00
- A6 John Hensley 10.00 25.00

2002 Witchblade Season One Box Loaders

COMPLETE SET (5) 7.50 20.00

- 1 Witchblade .75 2.00
- 2 Witchblade .75 2.00
- 3 Witchblade .75 2.00
- 4 Witchblade .75 2.00
- CL1 Witchblade 6.00 15.00

2002 Witchblade Season One Legacy of the Witchblade

COMPLETE SET (6) 3.00 8.00
STATED ODDS 1:17

- L1 Legacy of the Witchblade .75 2.00
- L2 Legacy of the Witchblade .75 2.00
- L3 Legacy of the Witchblade .75 2.00
- L4 Legacy of the Witchblade .75 2.00
- L5 Legacy of the Witchblade .75 2.00
- L6 Legacy of the Witchblade .75 2.00

2002 Witchblade Season One Pieceworks

COMPLETE SET (2) 15.00 30.00
STATED ODDS 1:27

❑ PW1 Yancy Butler jacket 7.50 20.00
❑ PW2 Yancy Butler pants 7.50 20.00

2002 Witchblade Season One Promos
COMPLETE SET (4) 2.50 6.00
❑ P1 Witchblade .75 2.00
❑ Pi Witchblade .75 2.00
❑ UKP Witchblade .75 2.00
❑ DFP1 Witchblade .75 2.00

2002 Witchblade Season One Quest For Justice
COMPLETE SET (9) 6.00 15.00
STATED ODDS 1:11
❑ Q1 Quest For Justice .75 2.00
❑ Q2 Quest For Justice .75 2.00
❑ Q3 Quest For Justice .75 2.00
❑ Q4 Quest For Justice .75 2.00
❑ Q5 Quest For Justice .75 2.00
❑ Q6 Quest For Justice .75 2.00
❑ Q7 Quest For Justice .75 2.00
❑ Q8 Quest For Justice .75 2.00
❑ Q9 Quest For Justice .75 2.00

2002 X-Files Season 8
COMPLETE SET (90) 5.00 12.00
❑ 1 The Truth Is Out There .15 .40
❑ 2 8X01 Within .15 .40
❑ 3 8X01 Within .15 .40
❑ 4 8X01 Within .15 .40
❑ 5 8X02 Without .15 .40
❑ 6 8X02 Without .15 .40
❑ 7 8X02 Without .15 .40
❑ 8 8X03 Redrum .15 .40
❑ 9 8X03 Redrum .15 .40
❑ 10 8X03 Redrum .15 .40
❑ 11 8X04 Patience .15 .40
❑ 12 8X04 Patience .15 .40
❑ 13 8X05 Roadrunners .15 .40
❑ 14 8X05 Roadrunners .15 .40
❑ 15 8X05 Roadrunners .15 .40
❑ 16 8X06 Invocation .15 .40
❑ 17 8X06 Invocation .15 .40
❑ 18 8X06 Invocation .15 .40
❑ 19 8X07 Via Negativa .15 .40
❑ 20 8X07 Via Negativa .15 .40
❑ 21 8X07 Via Negativa .15 .40
❑ 22 8X08 Per Manum .15 .40
❑ 23 8X08 Per Manum .15 .40
❑ 24 8X08 Per Manum .15 .40
❑ 25 8X09 Surekill .15 .40
❑ 26 8X09 Surekill .15 .40
❑ 27 8X09 Surekill .15 .40
❑ 28 8X10 Salvage .15 .40
❑ 29 8X10 Salvage .15 .40
❑ 30 8X10 Salvage .15 .40
❑ 31 8X11 The Gift .15 .40
❑ 32 8X11 The Gift .15 .40
❑ 33 8X11 The Gift .15 .40
❑ 34 8X12 Badlaa .15 .40
❑ 35 8X12 Badlaa .15 .40
❑ 36 8X13 Medusa .15 .40
❑ 37 8X13 Medusa .15 .40
❑ 38 8X13 Medusa .15 .40
❑ 39 8X14 This Is Not Happening .15 .40
❑ 40 8X14 This Is Not Happening .15 .40
❑ 41 8X14 This Is Not Happening .15 .40
❑ 42 8X15 Deadalive .15 .40
❑ 43 8X15 Deadalive .15 .40
❑ 44 8X15 Deadalive .15 .40
❑ 45 8X16 Vienen .15 .40
❑ 46 8X16 Vienen .15 .40
❑ 47 8X16 Vienen .15 .40
❑ 48 8X17 Empedocles .15 .40
❑ 49 8X17 Empedocles .15 .40
❑ 50 8X17 Empedocles .15 .40
❑ 51 8X18 Three Words .15 .40
❑ 52 8X18 Three Words .15 .40
❑ 53 8X18 Three Words .15 .40
❑ 54 8X19 Alone .15 .40
❑ 55 8X19 Alone .15 .40
❑ 56 8X19 Alone .15 .40
❑ 57 8X20 Essence .15 .40
❑ 58 8X20 Essence .15 .40
❑ 59 8X20 Essence .15 .40
❑ 60 8X21 Existence .15 .40
❑ 61 8X21 Existence .15 .40
❑ 62 8X21 Existence .15 .40
❑ 63 8X21 Existence .15 .40
❑ 64 Special Agent Fox Mulder .15 .40
❑ 65 Special Agent Dana Scully .15 .40
❑ 66 Special Agent John Doggett .15 .40
❑ 67 Special Agent Monica Reyes .15 .40
❑ 68 Assistant Director Walter Skinner .15 .40
❑ 69 Alex Krycek .15 .40
❑ 70 Deputy Director Alvin Kersh .15 .40
❑ 71 The Lone Gunmen .15 .40
❑ 72 Gibson Praise .15 .40
❑ 73 Billy Miles .15 .40
❑ 74 Knowle Rohrer .15 .40
❑ 75 William .15 .40
❑ 76 Hangin' Out .15 .40
❑ 77 Holy Slug .15 .40
❑ 78 Metal Man .15 .40
❑ 79 Gross Visage .15 .40
❑ 80 Harmless Beggar .15 .40
❑ 81 Reptile .15 .40
❑ 82 Spitting Image .15 .40
❑ 83 Simulated Heat .15 .40
❑ 84 Phony Snowfall .15 .40
❑ 85 Creating Fire .15 .40
❑ 86 Low-Tech Future .15 .40
❑ 87 Tunnel Vision .15 .40
❑ 88 Color Spectrum .15 .40
❑ 89 Sleight Of Leg .15 .40
❑ 90 Checklist .15 .40

2002 X-Files Season 8 Autographs
COMPLETE SET (4) 75.00 150.00
STATED ODDS 1:48
❑ A12 Annabeth Gish 25.00 50.00
❑ A13 James Pickens Jr. 20.00 40.00
❑ A14 Adam Baldwin 20.00 40.00
❑ A15 Tom Braidwood 20.00 40.00

2002 X-Files Season 8 Believe To Understand
COMPLETE SET (3) 4.00 10.00
STATED ODDS 1:11
❑ P7 Believe To Understand 1.50 4.00
❑ P8 Believe To Understand 1.50 4.00
❑ P9 Believe To Understand 1.50 4.00

2002 X-Files Season 8 Box Loaders
COMPLETE SET (4) 7.50 20.00
❑ XBL1 Mulder & Scully 1.25 3.00
❑ XBL2 Doggett 1.25 3.00
❑ XBL3 Mulder & Scully 1.25 3.00
❑ X8CL1 X-Files 7.50 20.00

2002 X-Files Season 8 Pieceworks
COMPLETE SET (2) 40.00 80.00
STATED ODDS 1:115
❑ PW1 Mulder's T-Shirt 20.00 50.00
❑ PW2 Doggett's Tie 20.00 50.00

2002 X-Files Season 8 Promos
COMPLETE SET (4) 3.00 8.00
❑ XF8i Doggett, Scully, & Skinner 1.00 2.50
❑ XF8-1 Mulder, Scully, & Doggett 1.00 2.50
❑ XF8-2 Doggett, Scully, & Skinner 1.00 2.50
❑ XF8UK Doggett, Scully, & Reyes 1.00 2.50

2002 X-Files Season 8 The Search For Mulder
COMPLETE SET (6) 15.00 40.00
STATED ODDS 1:17
❑ B1 The Search For Mulder 3.00 8.00
❑ B2 The Search For Mulder 3.00 8.00
❑ B3 The Search For Mulder 3.00 8.00
❑ B4 The Search For Mulder 3.00 8.00
❑ B5 The Search For Mulder 3.00 8.00
❑ B6 The Search For Mulder 3.00 8.00

2002 Xena Beauty and Brawn
COMPLETE SET (72) 4.00 10.00
❑ 1 Xena .10 .30
❑ 2 Xena .10 .30
❑ 3 Xena .10 .30
❑ 4 Xena .10 .30
❑ 5 Xena .10 .30
❑ 6 Xena .10 .30
❑ 7 Xena .10 .30
❑ 8 Xena .10 .30
❑ 9 Xena .10 .30
❑ 10 Gabrielle .10 .30
❑ 11 Gabrielle .10 .30
❑ 12 Gabrielle .10 .30
❑ 13 Gabrielle .10 .30
❑ 14 Gabrielle .10 .30
❑ 15 Gabrielle .10 .30
❑ 16 Gabrielle .10 .30
❑ 17 Gabrielle .10 .30
❑ 18 Gabrielle .10 .30
❑ 19 Callisto .10 .30
❑ 20 Callisto .10 .30
❑ 21 Callisto .10 .30
❑ 22 Callisto .10 .30
❑ 23 Callisto .10 .30
❑ 24 Callisto .10 .30
❑ 25 Alti .10 .30
❑ 26 Alti .10 .30
❑ 27 Alti .10 .30
❑ 28 Ares .10 .30
❑ 29 Ares .10 .30
❑ 30 Ares .10 .30
❑ 31 Autolycus .10 .30
❑ 32 Autolycus .10 .30
❑ 33 Autolycus .10 .30
❑ 34 Joxer .10 .30
❑ 35 Joxer .10 .30
❑ 36 Joxer .10 .30
❑ 37 Amarice .10 .30
❑ 38 Aphrodite .10 .30
❑ 39 Argo .10 .30
❑ 40 Athena .10 .30
❑ 41 Boadicea .10 .30
❑ 42 Borias .10 .30
❑ 43 Caesar .10 .30
❑ 44 Cecrops .10 .30
❑ 45 Cleopatra .10 .30
❑ 46 Cupid .10 .30
❑ 47 Cyrene .10 .30
❑ 48 Diana .10 .30
❑ 49 Draco .10 .30
❑ 50 Eli .10 .30
❑ 51 Ephiny .10 .30
❑ 52 Eve .10 .30
❑ 53 Hera .10 .30
❑ 54 Hercules .10 .30
❑ 55 Hope .10 .30
❑ 56 Iolaus .10 .30
❑ 57 Jace .10 .30
❑ 58 Jett .10 .30
❑ 59 K'ao Hsin .10 .30
❑ 60 Leah .10 .30
❑ 61 Lila .10 .30
❑ 62 Livia .10 .30
❑ 63 Meg .10 .30
❑ 64 Meleager .10 .30
❑ 65 M'Lila .10 .30
❑ 66 Najara .10 .30
❑ 67 Palaemon .10 .30
❑ 68 Pompey .10 .30
❑ 69 Salmoneus .10 .30
❑ 71 Checklist 1 .10 .30
❑ 72 Checklist 2 .10 .30
❑ 73 Checklist 3 .10 .30

2002 Xena Beauty and Brawn Amazon Warriors
COMPLETE SET (9) 6.00 15.00
STATED ODDS 1:10
❑ AW1 Amazon Nation .75 2.00
❑ AW2 Amarice .75 2.00
❑ AW3 Cyane .75 2.00
❑ AW4 Ephiny .75 2.00
❑ AW5 Gabrielle .75 2.00
❑ AW6 Melosa .75 2.00
❑ AW7 Varia .75 2.00
❑ AW8 Velasca .75 2.00
❑ AW9 Xena .75 2.00

2002 Xena Beauty and Brawn Autographs
OVERALL AUTO ODDS ONE PER BOX
A30 ISSUED AS CASE TOPPER
A33 ISSUED IN COLLECTORS ALBUM
❑ A22 Victoria Pratt 6.00 15.00
❑ A23 Melinda Clarke 6.00 15.00
❑ A24 Alison Bruce 6.00 15.00
❑ A25 Jeremy Callaghan 6.00 15.00
❑ A26 Josephine Davison 6.00 15.00
❑ A27 Darien Takle 6.00 15.00
❑ A28 Kate Elliott 6.00 15.00
❑ A29 Erik Thomson 6.00 15.00
❑ A30 Meg Foster/ (issued as case topper) 10.00 25.00
❑ A31 Tim Thomerson 6.00 15.00
❑ A32A Marie Matiko as K'ao Hsin 6.00 15.00
❑ A32B Marie Matiko as Pao S'su 6.00 15.00
❑ A33 Brittney Powell/ (issued in collectors album) 7.50 20.00
❑ A34 Sheeri Rappaport 6.00 15.00

2002 Xena Beauty and Brawn Beauty and Brawn
COMPLETE SET (2)
STATED ODDS 1:480
❑ BB1 Draco 10.00 20.00
❑ BB2 Xena 10.00 20.00

2002 Xena Beauty and Brawn Dual Autographs
OVERALL AUTO ODDS ONE PER BOX
❑ DA1 Lucy Lawless 100.00 200.00
Renee O'Connor
❑ DA2 Hudson Leick 60.00 120.00
Renee O'Connor

2002 Xena Beauty and Brawn Footsteps of a Warrior
COMPLETE SET (9) 2.50 6.00
STATED ODDS 1:4
❑ FW1 India .40 1.00
❑ FW2 China .40 1.00
❑ FW3 Japan .40 1.00
❑ FW4 Egypt .40 1.00
❑ FW5 Macedonia .40 1.00
❑ FW6 North America .40 1.00
❑ FW7 North Africa .40 1.00
❑ FW8 Rome .40 1.00
❑ FW9 Netherlands .40 1.00

2002 Xena Beauty and Brawn From the Archives Autograph Costumes
OVERALL COSTUME ODDS TWO PER BOX
❑ AC1 Claire Stansfield 25.00 50.00
❑ AC2 Hudson Leick 25.00 50.00
❑ AC3 Meighan Desmond 25.00 50.00

2002 Xena Beauty and Brawn From the Archives Costumes
OVERALL COSTUME ODDS TWO PER BOX
❑ C1 Ares 6.00 15.00
❑ C2 Argo 6.00 15.00
❑ C3 Autolycus 8.00 20.00
❑ C4 Tyrella 8.00 20.00
❑ C5 Callisto 6.00 15.00
❑ C6 Xena 8.00 20.00
❑ C7 Xena 8.00 20.00
❑ C8 Leah 6.00 15.00
❑ C9 Xena 8.00 20.00
❑ C10 Borias 6.00 15.00
❑ C11 Hades 6.00 15.00
❑ C12 Amarice 6.00 15.00
❑ C13 Lucifer 6.00 15.00

2002 Xena Beauty and Brawn From the Archives Dual Costumes
OVERALL COSTUME ODDS TWO PER BOX
❑ DC1 Autolycus 8.00 20.00
❑ DC2 Cyane 8.00 20.00
❑ DC3 Gabrielle 75.00 150.00
❑ DC4 Xena 15.00 30.00
Gabrielle
❑ DC5 Amarice 8.00 20.00
❑ DC6 Gabrielle 15.00 30.00
Aphrodite
❑ DC7 Gabrielle 15.00 30.00
❑ DC8 Xena 15.00 30.00

2002 Xena Beauty and Brawn Kevin Smith Tribute
COMPLETE SET (9) 8.00 20.00
STATED ODDS 1:20
❑ KS1 Ares 1.25 3.00
❑ KS2 Iphicles 1.25 3.00
❑ KS3 Ares 1.25 3.00
❑ KS4 Ares 1.25 3.00
❑ KS5 Ares 1.25 3.00
❑ KS6 Ares God of Love 1.25 3.00
❑ KS7 Ares 1.25 3.00
❑ KS8 Ares 1.25 3.00
❑ KS9 Jerry Patrick Brown 1.25 3.00

2002 Xena Beauty and Brawn Promos
COMPLETE SET (3) 2.50 6.00
❑ P1 Xena/ (General Distribution) 1.00 2.50
❑ P2 Gabrielle/ (Non-Sport Update) 1.00 2.50
❑ P3 Ares/ (Binder Exclusive) 1.50 4.00

2002 Xena Beauty and Brawn Xena Scrolls
COMPLETE SET (6) 15.00 40.00
STATED ODDS 1:40
❑ XS1 Oh My 3.00 8.00
❑ XS2 Run Along Now Boys 3.00 8.00
❑ XS3 Now Dance 3.00 8.00
❑ XS4 The Scrolls 3.00 8.00
❑ XS5 I've Been Expecting You 3.00 8.00
❑ XS6 Think Again, Ares 3.00 8.00

2003 Alias Season Two
COMPLETE SET (81) 5.00 12.00
❑ 1 Alias Season Two .15 .40
❑ 2 The Man .15 .40
❑ 3 Walk In .15 .40
❑ 4 Reunion .15 .40
❑ 5 Countermission .15 .40
❑ 6 Meeting .15 .40
❑ 7 Concern .15 .40
❑ 8 Musing .15 .40
❑ 9 Officer .15 .40
❑ 10 Unwinding .15 .40
❑ 11 Uncovering .15 .40
❑ 12 Devoted .15 .40
❑ 13 Waiting .15 .40
❑ 14 Ordeal .15 .40
❑ 15 Deception .15 .40
❑ 16 Vacation .15 .40
❑ 17 Working .15 .40
❑ 18 Bonding .15 .40
❑ 19 Betrayal .15 .40
❑ 20 Stimulating .15 .40
❑ 21 Missing .15 .40
❑ 22 Access .15 .40
❑ 23 Rescue .15 .40
❑ 24 Punked .15 .40
❑ 25 Compromised .15 .40
❑ 26 Uncomfortable .15 .40
❑ 27 Ultimatum .15 .40
❑ 28 Survivor .15 .40
❑ 29 Duplicate .15 .40
❑ 30 Graduation .15 .40
❑ 31 Abducted .15 .40
❑ 32 Destroyer .15 .40
❑ 33 Partners .15 .40
❑ 34 Together .15 .40
❑ 35 Extracted .15 .40
❑ 36 Lovers .15 .40
❑ 37 Strikeforce .15 .40
❑ 38 Encoded .15 .40
❑ 39 Double Agents .15 .40
❑ 40 Enlightened .15 .40
❑ 41 Detonator .15 .40
❑ 42 Vengeance .15 .40
❑ 43 Dealmaker .15 .40
❑ 44 Chosen .15 .40
❑ 45 Showdown .15 .40
❑ 46 Bristow, Jack D. .15 .40
❑ 47 Bristow, Sydney A. .15 .40
❑ 48 Dixon, Marcus R. .15 .40
❑ 49 Flinkman, Marshall J. .15 .40
❑ 50 Tippin, William D. (Will) .15 .40
❑ 51 Kendall .15 .40
❑ 52 Vaughn, Michael C. .15 .40
❑ 53 Weiss, Eric .15 .40
❑ 54 Sloane, Emily .15 .40
❑ 55 Calfo, Francine D. (Francie) .15 .40
❑ 56 Derevko, Irina .15 .40
❑ 57 Sark .15 .40
❑ 58 Sloan, Arvin .15 .40
❑ 59 Geiger, Anthony .15 .40
❑ 60 Yeager, Mitchell .15 .40
❑ 61 Cute .15 .40
❑ 62 Conspiring .15 .40
❑ 63 Ambitious .15 .40
❑ 64 Quick .15 .40
❑ 65 Improved .15 .40
❑ 66 Research .15 .40
❑ 67 Enthusiasm .15 .40
❑ 68 Deep Cover .15 .40
❑ 69 Secret Agent Man .15 .40
❑ 70 Suave .15 .40
❑ 71 Adaptable .15 .40
❑ 72 Sensitive .15 .40
❑ 73 Haunted .15 .40
❑ 74 Blackmail .15 .40
❑ 75 Debugged .15 .40
❑ 76 Free .15 .40
❑ 77 Victory .15 .40
❑ 78 Completion .15 .40
❑ 79 Hidden Asset .15 .40
❑ 80 Responsible .15 .40
❑ 81 Checklist .15 .40

2003 Alias Season Two Autographs
COMPLETE SET (12) 200.00 400.00
STATED ODDS 1:24
❑ A8 Jennifer Garner 150.00 250.00
❑ A9 Michael Vartan 15.00 40.00
❑ A10 Carl Lumbly 7.50 20.00
❑ A11 Kevin Weisman 7.50 20.00
❑ A12 Ron Rifkin 7.50 20.00
❑ A13 Greg Grunberg 7.50 20.00
❑ A14 Amy Irving 7.50 20.00
❑ A15 Patricia Wettig 7.50 20.00
❑ A16 Rutger Hauer 25.00 50.00
❑ A17 Richard Lewis 7.50 20.00
❑ A18 Terry O'Quinn 7.50 20.00
❑ A19 David Anders 7.50 20.00

2003 Alias Season Two Box Loaders
COMPLETE SET (4) 8.00 20.00
❑ BL1 Jack Bristow 1.50 4.00
❑ BL2 Sydney Bristow 1.50 4.00
❑ BL3 Irina Derevko 1.50 4.00
❑ CL1 Sydney Bristow 6.00 15.00
CASE INSERT

2003 Alias Season Two Pieceworks
COMPLETE SET (10) 75.00 200.00
STATED ODDS 1:24
❑ PW1 Jennifer Garner Cowboy Hat 30.00 60.00
❑ PW2 Jennifer Garner Cowboy Shirt 10.00 25.00
❑ PW3 Jennifer Garner Cowboy Pants 10.00 25.00
❑ PW4 Jennifer Garner Geisha Outfit 10.00 25.00
❑ PW5 Lena Olin Jacket 6.00 15.00
❑ PW6 Lena Olin Pants 6.00 15.00
❑ PW7 Lena Olin Top 6.00 15.00
❑ PW8 Victor Garber Sportcoat 6.00 15.00
❑ PW9 Michael Vartan Camo Shirt 6.00 15.00
❑ PW10 Michael Vartan Camo Pants 6.00 15.00

2003 Alias Season Two Seeking Sydney
COMPLETE SET (6) 7.50 20.00
STATED ODDS 1:17
❑ SS1 Michael Vaughn 1.50 4.00
❑ SS2 Marcus Dixon 1.50 4.00
❑ SS3 Will Tippin 1.50 4.00
❑ SS4 Jack Bristow 1.50 4.00
❑ SS5 Arvin Sloane 1.50 4.00
❑ SS6 Marshall Flinkman 1.50 4.00

2003 Alias Season Two Undercover
COMPLETE SET (9) 6.00 15.00
COMMON CARD (1-9) 1.00 2.50
STATED ODDS 1:11
❑ U1 Sydney 1.00 2.50
❑ U2 Sydney 1.00 2.50
❑ U3 Sydney 1.00 2.50
❑ U4 Sydney 1.00 2.50
❑ U5 Sydney 1.00 2.50
❑ U6 Sydney 1.00 2.50
❑ U7 Marshall 1.00 2.50
❑ U8 Sydney 1.00 2.50
❑ U9 Vaughn 1.00 2.50

2003 Angel Season Four
COMPLETE SET (90) 5.00 12.00
❑ 1 Angel .15 .40
❑ 2 Carry On .15 .40
❑ 3 Daylight Again .15 .40
❑ 4 No Tears Left .15 .40
❑ 5 Unsolved Mysteries .15 .40
❑ 6 Shocking .15 .40
❑ 7 Resolution .15 .40
❑ 8 Viva Las Vegas .15 .40
❑ 9 High Stakes .15 .40
❑ 10 Cashing In .15 .40
❑ 11 Clean Slate .15 .40
❑ 12 Dangerous Intrigue .15 .40
❑ 13 Memento .15 .40
❑ 14 Singularity .15 .40
❑ 15 Causality .15 .40
❑ 16 Gravity .15 .40
❑ 17 Retrospective .15 .40
❑ 18 Flashback .15 .40
❑ 19 Hindsight .15 .40
❑ 20 Signs and Portents .15 .40
❑ 21 Seals and Signs .15 .40
❑ 22 Bad Mojo .15 .40
❑ 23 The Morning After .15 .40
❑ 24 Undead Law .15 .40
❑ 25 Destroyer .15 .40
❑ 26 Glimmer .15 .40
❑ 27 Dimming .15 .40
❑ 28 Blackout .15 .40
❑ 29 Unreliable .15 .40
❑ 30 Perfect .15 .40
❑ 31 Angel's Fantasy .15 .40
❑ 32 Manipulative .15 .40
❑ 33 Dangerous .15 .40
❑ 34 Scheming .15 .40
❑ 35 Missing .15 .40
❑ 36 Restored .15 .40
❑ 37 Deceived .15 .40
❑ 38 At Large .15 .40
❑ 39 Slayer .15 .40
❑ 40 Betrayal .15 .40
❑ 41 Menacing .15 .40
❑ 42 Seeking .15 .40
❑ 43 Capture .15 .40
❑ 44 Sacrifice .15 .40
❑ 45 Specialist .15 .40
❑ 46 Redemption .15 .40
❑ 47 Family Affair .15 .40
❑ 48 Secret Agent Gunn .15 .40
❑ 49 Evil Woman .15 .40
❑ 50 Herald .15 .40
❑ 51 Intercession .15 .40
❑ 52 Unholy Delivery .15 .40
❑ 53 Devoted .15 .40
❑ 54 Enlightened .15 .40
❑ 55 Deity .15 .40
❑ 56 On the Lam .15 .40
❑ 57 Desperate Act .15 .40
❑ 58 Vaccination .15 .40
❑ 59 Revelation .15 .40
❑ 60 Champion .15 .40
❑ 61 Final Battle .15 .40
❑ 62 The Word .15 .40
❑ 63 The Message .15 .40
❑ 64 Heartless .15 .40
❑ 65 An Offer .15 .40
❑ 66 The Deal .15 .40
❑ 67 Angel .15 .40
❑ 68 Wesley .15 .40
❑ 69 Cordelia .15 .40
❑ 70 Gunn .15 .40
❑ 71 Fred .15 .40
❑ 72 Lorne .15 .40
❑ 73 Fighting .15 .40
❑ 74 Loving .15 .40
❑ 75 Conflicted .15 .40
❑ 76 Star Power .15 .40
❑ 77 Spotlight .15 .40
❑ 78 Kooky .15 .40
❑ 79 Stylish .15 .40
❑ 80 Attitude .15 .40
❑ 81 Cordelia and Angel .15 .40
❑ 82 Cordelia and Connor .15 .40
❑ 83 Fred and Gunn .15 .40
❑ 84 Fred and Wesley .15 .40
❑ 85 Lilah and Wesley .15 .40
❑ 86 Gwen and gunn .15 .40
❑ 87 Lilah .15 .40
❑ 88 Connor .15 .40
❑ 89 Cordelia .15 .40
❑ 90 Checklist .15 .40

2003 Angel Season Four Autographs
COMPLETE SET (10) 100.00 200.00
STATED ODDS 1:36
❑ A24 Eliza Dushku 70.00 120.00
❑ A25 Gina Torres 6.00 15.00
❑ A26 David Denman 6.00 15.00
❑ A27 Vladimir Kulich 6.00 15.00
❑ A28 Randy Oglesby 6.00 15.00
❑ A29 Jack Kehler 6.00 15.00
❑ A30 Roger Yuan 6.00 15.00
❑ A31 David Monahan 6.00 15.00
❑ A32 Adrienne Wilkinson 6.00 15.00
❑ A33 Jeff Ricketts 6.00 15.00

2003 Angel Season Four Deceptions
COMPLETE SET (9) 10.00 25.00
STATED ODDS 1:11
❑ D1 Connor 1.50 4.00
❑ D2 Wesley 1.50 4.00
❑ D3 Cordelia 1.50 4.00
❑ D4 Jasmine 1.50 4.00
❑ D5 Fred 1.50 4.00
❑ D6 Lilah 1.50 4.00
❑ D7 Angelus 1.50 4.00
❑ D8 Gunn 1.50 4.00
❑ D9 Lorne 1.50 4.00

2003 Angel Season Four Redemption
COMPLETE SET (6) 12.50 30.00
STATED ODDS 1:17
❑ R1 Wesley 2.50 6.00
❑ R2 Faith 2.50 6.00
❑ R3 Darla 2.50 6.00
❑ R4 Connor 2.50 6.00
❑ R5 Angel 2.50 6.00
❑ R6 Angel 2.50 6.00

2003 Angel Season Four Impossible Dreams
COMPLETE SET (3) 4.00 10.00
❑ 1 A Devoted Son 1.50 4.00
❑ 2 A Peaceful Life 1.50 4.00
❑ 3 Perfect Happiness 1.50 4.00

2003 Angel Season Four Pieceworks
COMPLETE SET (4) 40.00 80.00
RANDOM INSERTS IN PACKS
❑ PW1 David Boreanaz 10.00 25.00
❑ PW2 Charisma Carpenter 10.00 25.00
❑ PW3 Vincent Kartheiser 10.00 25.00
❑ PW4 Gina Torres 10.00 25.00

2003 Buffy the Vampire Slayer Connections

COMPLETE SET (72) 5.00 12.00
❑ 1 Title Card .15 .40
❑ 2 Buffy & Dad - Early Connection .15 .40
❑ 3 Buffy & Angel - First Love Connection .15 .40
❑ 4 Buffy & Angelus - Dangerous Connection .15 .40
❑ 5 Buffy & Angel - Magical Connection .15 .40
❑ 6 Buffy & Riley - Tender Connection .15 .40
❑ 7 Buffy & Mom & Dawn - Family Connection .15 .40
❑ 8 Buffy & Giles - Fatherly Connection .15 .40
❑ 9 Buffy & Spike - Evil Connection .15 .40
❑ 10 Angel & Darla - Early Connection .15 .40
❑ 11 Angel & Darla - Lust Connection .15 .40
❑ 12 Angel & Drusilla - Passionate Connection .15 .40
❑ 13 Angel & Buffy - Fated Connection .15 .40
❑ 14 Angel & Buffy - Magical Connection .15 .40
❑ 15 Angel & Buffy - Redeeming Connection .15 .40
❑ 16 Angel & Buffy - Sundered Connection .15 .40
❑ 17 Angel & Buffy - Comforting Connection .15 .40
❑ 18 Angel & Faith - Dangerous Connection .15 .40
❑ 19 Spike & Drusilla - Early Connection .15 .40
❑ 20 Spike & Buffy - Unexpected Connection .15 .40
❑ 21 Spike & Joyce - Motherly Connection .15 .40
❑ 22 Spike & Willow - Unexpected Connection .15 .40
❑ 23 Spike & Buffy - Magical Connection .15 .40
❑ 24 Spike & Harmony - Lust Connection .15 .40
❑ 25 Spike & Buffy - Tender Connection .15 .40
❑ 26 Spike & Buffy - Passionate Connection .15 .40
❑ 27 Spike & The First - Evil Connection .15 .40
❑ 28 Willow & Xander - Early Connection .15 .40
❑ 29 Willow & Oz - First Love Connection .15 .40
❑ 30 Willow & Tara - Unexpected Connection .15 .40
❑ 31 Willow & Tara - Magical Connection .15 .40
❑ 32 Willow & Buffy - Central Connection .15 .40
❑ 33 Willow & Tara - Eternal Connection .15 .40
❑ 34 Willow & Xander - Enduring Connection .15 .40
❑ 35 Willow & Giles - Redeeming Connection .15 .40
❑ 36 Willow & Warren - Evil Connection .15 .40
❑ 37 Xander & Willow - Early Connection .15 .40
❑ 38 Xander & Cordelia - Lust Connection .15 .40
❑ 39 Xander & Faith - Dangerous Connection .15 .40
❑ 40 Xander & Xander - Magical Connection .15 .40
❑ 41 Xander & Buffy - Central Connection .15 .40
❑ 42 Xander & Anya - Passionate Connection .15 .40
❑ 43 Xander & Spike - Hate Connection .15 .40
❑ 44 Xander & Anya - Enduring Connection .15 .40
❑ 45 Xander & Willow - Evil Connection .15 .40
❑ 46 Giles & Buffy - Early Connection .15 .40
❑ 47 Giles & Jenny - First Love Connection .15 .40
❑ 48 Giles & Ethan Rayne - Hate Connection .15 .40
❑ 49 Giles & Jenny - Tragic Connection .15 .40
❑ 50 Giles & Buffy - Central Connection .15 .40
❑ 51 Giles & Joyce - Magical Connection .15 .40
❑ 52 Giles & Spike - Tentative Connection .15 .40
❑ 53 Giles & The Watchers' Council - Enduring Connection .15 .40
❑ 54 Giles & Glory Ben - Evil Connection .15 .40
❑ 55 Anya & Olaf - Early Connection .15 .40
❑ 56 Anya & Xander - Desperate Connection .15 .40
❑ 57 Anya & Capitalism - Unexpected Connection .15 .40
❑ 58 Anya & Giles - Magical Connection .15 .40
❑ 59 Anya & Buffy - Tentative Connection .15 .40
❑ 60 Anya & Xander - Passionate Connection .15 .40
❑ 61 Anya & Spike - Lust Connection .15 .40
❑ 62 Anya & Halfrek - Enduring Connection .15 .40
❑ 63 Anya & D'Hoffryn - Evil Connection .15 .40
❑ 64 Dawn & Mom - Early Connection .15 .40
❑ 65 Dawn & Xander - Crush Connection .15 .40
❑ 66 Dawn & Tara - Understanding Connection .15 .40
❑ 67 Dawn & Spike - Brotherly Connection .15 .40
❑ 68 Dawn & Buffy - Central Connection .15 .40
❑ 69 Dawn & Sweet - Magical Connection .15 .40
❑ 70 Dawn & Justin - First Kiss Connection .15 .40
❑ 71 Dawn & Ben Glory - Evil Connection .15 .40
❑ 72 Checklist .15 .40

2003 Buffy the Vampire Slayer Connections Box Loaders

COMPLETE SET (4) 20.00 50.00
❑ BL1 First Love 1.00 2.50
❑ BL2 Doomed Love 1.00 2.50
❑ BL3 Mad Love 1.00 2.50
❑ CL1 Coffin DIE CUT 20.00 50.00

2003 Buffy the Vampire Slayer Connections Heartbreaks

COMPLETE SET (6) 10.00 25.00
STATED ODDS 1:14
❑ HB1 Spike & Buffy 2.00 5.00
❑ HB2 Xander & Anya 2.00 5.00
❑ HB3 Willow & Tara 2.00 5.00
❑ HB4 Buffy & Angel 2.00 5.00
❑ HB5 Dawn, Buffy & Joyce 2.00 5.00
❑ HB6 Buffy 2.00 5.00

2003 Buffy the Vampire Slayer Connections Parallel

COMPLETE SET (72) 25.00 60.00
*PARALLEL: 1X TO 2.5X BASIC CARDS .40 1.00
STATED ODDS ONE PER PACK

2003 Buffy the Vampire Slayer Connections Pieceworks

COMPLETE SET (3) 40.00 100.00
STATED ODDS 1:24
❑ PWC1 Buffy & Spike 15.00 40.00
❑ PWC2 Anya & Xander 15.00 40.00
❑ PWC3 Willow & Tara 15.00 40.00

2003 Buffy the Vampire Slayer Connections Promos

COMPLETE SET (5) 7.50 20.00
❑ Pi Angel & Buffy 1.00 2.50
❑ P1 Dawn & Buffy 1.00 2.50
❑ P1P Dawn & Buffy 4.00 10.00
❑ PUK Rupert & Buffy 1.00 2.50
❑ PUKP Rupert & Buffy 4.00 10.00

2003 Buffy the Vampire Slayer Connections Slayer's Circle

COMPLETE SET (9) 12.50 30.00
STATED ODDS 1:11
❑ SC1 Slayer's Circle 1.50 4.00
❑ SC2 Slayer's Circle 1.50 4.00
❑ SC3 Slayer's Circle 1.50 4.00
❑ SC4 Slayer's Circle 1.50 4.00
❑ SC5 Slayer's Circle 1.50 4.00
❑ SC6 Slayer's Circle 1.50 4.00
❑ SC7 Slayer's Circle 1.50 4.00
❑ SC8 Slayer's Circle 1.50 4.00
❑ SC9 Slayer's Circle 1.50 4.00

2003 Buffy the Vampire Slayer Season Seven

COMPLETE SET (90) 5.00 12.00
❑ 1 The Slayer .15 .40
❑ 2 My Old School .15 .40
❑ 3 All Related .15 .40
❑ 4 Pretzel Logic .15 .40
❑ 5 Underground .15 .40
❑ 6 Entangled .15 .40
❑ 7 Tortured .15 .40
❑ 8 Missing .15 .40
❑ 9 Suspect .15 .40
❑ 10 Healed .15 .40
❑ 11 Doomed .15 .40
❑ 12 Intervention .15 .40
❑ 13 Inevitable .15 .40
❑ 14 Heartless .15 .40
❑ 15 Vengeance Personified .15 .40
❑ 16 Not Herself .15 .40
❑ 17 Boy Crazy .15 .40
❑ 18 Smitten .15 .40
❑ 19 Girls Gone Wild .15 .40
❑ 20 Returned .15 .40
❑ 21 Visions .15 .40
❑ 22 Deceiving .15 .40
❑ 23 Unconscious .15 .40
❑ 24 Suspicious .15 .40
❑ 25 Deadly .15 .40
❑ 26 Detox .15 .40
❑ 27 Interrogation .15 .40
❑ 28 Captive .15 .40
❑ 29 Overwhelmed .15 .40
❑ 30 Potentials .15 .40
❑ 31 Turok-Han .15 .40
❑ 32 Taunted .15 .40
❑ 33 Insight .15 .40
❑ 34 Victory .15 .40
❑ 35 Slayer Camp .15 .40
❑ 36 Revealed .15 .40
❑ 37 Surprising .15 .40
❑ 38 Chip Flips .15 .40
❑ 39 Sweet Kiss .15 .40
❑ 40 Dire Consequence .15 .40
❑ 41 Voodoo .15 .40
❑ 42 Jealousy .15 .40
❑ 43 Rescue .15 .40
❑ 44 Bag Of Tricks .15 .40
❑ 45 Days Of Old .15 .40
❑ 46 Conduit .15 .40
❑ 47 Flimmaker .15 .40
❑ 48 Afterglow .15 .40
❑ 49 Remorse .15 .40
❑ 50 Set Up .15 .40
❑ 51 Cornered .15 .40
❑ 52 Knocked Down .15 .40
❑ 53 Preacher Man .15 .40
❑ 54 Have Faith .15 .40
❑ 55 Touch Of Evil .15 .40
❑ 56 Loss Of Vision .15 .40
❑ 57 Lack Of Trust .15 .40
❑ 58 Sign Of Hope .15 .40
❑ 59 The New Boss .15 .40
❑ 60 Tender Moment .15 .40
❑ 61 Buffy's Back .15 .40
❑ 62 Recharged .15 .40
❑ 63 Guardian Angel .15 .40
❑ 64 Woman's Work .15 .40
❑ 65 Key To Victory .15 .40
❑ 66 Slayer In Battle .15 .40
❑ 67 His Finest Moment .15 .40
❑ 68 Buffy Summers .15 .40
❑ 69 Xander Harris .15 .40
❑ 70 Willow Rosenberg .15 .40
❑ 71 Rubert Giles .15 .40
❑ 72 Spike .15 .40
❑ 73 Dawn Summers .15 .40
❑ 74 Anya .15 .40
❑ 75 Robin Wood .15 .40
❑ 76 Faith .15 .40
❑ 77 The Master .15 .40
❑ 78 Jonathan .15 .40
❑ 79 The Mayor .15 .40
❑ 80 Buffy .15 .40
❑ 81 Hellmouth .15 .40
❑ 82 Ideal Slayer .15 .40
❑ 83 Living Like Gods .15 .40
❑ 84 Kennedy .15 .40
❑ 85 Amanda .15 .40
❑ 86 Rona .15 .40
❑ 87 Chloe .15 .40
❑ 88 Vi .15 .40
❑ 89 Molly .15 .40
❑ 90 Checklist .15 .40

2003 Buffy the Vampire Slayer Season Seven Autographs

COMPLETE SET (14) 150.00 300.00
STATED ODDS 1:36
❑ A40 DB Woodside 10.00 25.00
❑ A41 KD Aubert 10.00 25.00
❑ A42 Clare Kramer 12.50 30.00
❑ A43 Harris Yulin 10.00 25.00
❑ A44 Iyari Limon 12.50 30.00
❑ A45 Indigo 10.00 25.00
❑ A46 Sarah Hagan 10.00 25.00
❑ A47 Clara Bryant 10.00 25.00
❑ A48 Felicia Day 30.00 60.00
❑ A49 Kristy Wu 10.00 25.00
❑ A50 Lalaine 10.00 25.00
❑ A51 Amanda Fuller 10.00 25.00
❑ A52 Camden Toy 10.00 25.00
❑ A53 Nathan Fillion 40.00 80.00

2003 Buffy the Vampire Slayer Season Seven Box Loaders

COMPLETE SET (4) 75.00 150.00
❑ BL1 Warriors Reunite 1.00 2.50
❑ BL2 Warriors Reunite 1.00 2.50
❑ BL3 Warriors Reunite 1.00 2.50
❑ CL1 Final Farewell - Joss Whedon AU 75.00 150.00

2003 Buffy the Vampire Slayer Season Seven Pieceworks

COMPLETE SET (8) 75.00 200.00
STATED ODDS 1:36
❑ PW1 Andrew Toga 10.00 25.00
❑ PW2 Kennedy Sweater 10.00 25.00
❑ PW3 Kennedy T-Shirt 15.00 40.00
❑ PW4 Kennedy Pants 10.00 25.00
❑ PW5 Cassie T-Shirt 10.00 25.00
❑ PW6 Olaf Tunic 10.00 25.00
❑ PW7 Rachel Blouse 10.00 25.00
❑ PW8 Rachel Pants 10.00 25.00

2003 Buffy the Vampire Slayer Season Seven Slayer's Legacy

COMPLETE SET (6) 10.00 25.00
STATED ODDS 1:17
❑ SL1 The First Slayer 2.00 5.00
❑ SL2 The Guardian 2.00 5.00
❑ SL3 Nikki Wood 2.00 5.00
❑ SL4 Buffy Summers 2.00 5.00
❑ SL5 Faith 2.00 5.00
❑ SL6 Potentials & More 2.00 5.00

2003 Buffy the Vampire Slayer Season Seven The Final Battle

COMPLETE SET (9) 7.50 20.00
STATED ODDS 1:11
❑ FB1 The Final Battle 1.25 3.00
❑ FB2 The Final Battle 1.25 3.00
❑ FB3 The Final Battle 1.25 3.00
❑ FB4 The Final Battle 1.25 3.00
❑ FB5 The Final Battle 1.25 3.00
❑ FB6 The Final Battle 1.25 3.00
❑ FB7 The Final Battle 1.25 3.00
❑ FB8 The Final Battle 1.25 3.00
❑ FB9 The Final Battle 1.25 3.00

2003 Buffy the Vampire Slayer Season Seven The Final Battle Parallel

COMPLETE SET (9) 25.00 60.00
STATED ODDS 1:35
❑ FBP1 The Final Battle 3.00 8.00
❑ FBP2 The Final Battle 3.00 8.00
❑ FBP3 The Final Battle 3.00 8.00
❑ FBP4 The Final Battle 3.00 8.00
❑ FBP5 The Final Battle 3.00 8.00
❑ FBP6 The Final Battle 3.00 8.00
❑ FBP7 The Final Battle 3.00 8.00
❑ FBP8 The Final Battle 3.00 8.00
❑ FBP9 The Final Battle 3.00 8.00

2003 Charmed The Power of Three

COMPLETE SET (72) 5.00 12.00
❑ 1 Title Card .15 .40
❑ 2 Molecular Acceleration .15 .40
❑ 3 Molecular Inhibition .15 .40
❑ 4 Premonition .15 .40
❑ 5 Levitation .15 .40
❑ 6 Orbing .15 .40
❑ 7 Teleorbing .15 .40
❑ 8 White Lighter .15 .40
❑ 9 Demon .15 .40
❑ 10 Piper Halliwell .15 .40
❑ 11 Phoebe Halliwell .15 .40
❑ 12 Paige Matthews .15 .40
❑ 13 Patty Halliwell .15 .40
❑ 14 Victor Bennett .15 .40
❑ 15 Penny Halliwell .15 .40
❑ 16 Leo Wyatt .15 .40
❑ 17 Cole Turner .15 .40
❑ 18 Darryl Morris .15 .40
❑ 19 Evil Eye .15 .40
❑ 20 Once And Future Phoebe .15 .40
❑ 21 Vampire Sis .15 .40
❑ 22 Mer Phoebe .15 .40
❑ 23 Super Heroes .15 .40
❑ 24 Defender Of Innocents .15 .40
❑ 25 Jazz Age .15 .40
❑ 26 Egyption Temptress .15 .40
❑ 27 Labor Pains .15 .40
❑ 28 Summoning Paige .15 .40
❑ 29 To Enchant An Object .15 .40
❑ 30 To Hear Secret Thoughts .15 .40
❑ 31 To Vanquish The Source .15 .40
❑ 32 To Banish A Spirit .15 .40
❑ 33 To Track A Banshee .15 .40
❑ 34 Fearless Spell .15 .40
❑ 35 Revealing Evil .15 .40
❑ 36 A Spell For Invoking The Power Of Three .15 .40
❑ 37 Tempus: Master Of Time .15 .40
❑ 38 Seer: Demonic Adviser .15 .40
❑ 39 Lazarus Demon .15 .40
❑ 40 Belthazor: Mercenary .15 .40
❑ 41 Siren: Home Wrecker .15 .40
❑ 42 Gammill: Collector .15 .40
❑ 43 Barbas: Fear Demon .15 .40
❑ 44 Jeric: Egyptian Demon .15 .40
❑ 45 Avatar Of Power .15 .40
❑ 46 Not What He Seems .15 .40
❑ 47 Secret Face .15 .40
❑ 48 Another Life .15 .40
❑ 49 Dark Wedding .15 .40
❑ 50 Under The Influence .15 .40
❑ 51 Back Again .15 .40
❑ 52 Tainted Love .15 .40
❑ 53 Lost And Deluded .15 .40
❑ 54 Not Meant To Be .15 .40
❑ 55 Patty, Their Mom .15 .40
❑ 56 Andy, Prue's Sweetheart .15 .40
❑ 57 Remembering Prue .15 .40
❑ 58 Miles, Phoebe's Friend .15 .40
❑ 59 Sam, Paige's Dad .15 .40
❑ 60 Max, Paige's Boyfriend .15 .40
❑ 61 Elderly Phoebe .15 .40
❑ 62 Blessed Union .15 .40
❑ 63 Cole, Phoebe's Ex-Husband .15 .40
❑ 64 P3 .15 .40
❑ 65 Place To Be .15 .40
❑ 66 Changes .15 .40
❑ 67 Rendezvous .15 .40
❑ 68 Show Runner .15 .40
❑ 69 Costume Designer .15 .40
❑ 70 Co-Stars .15 .40
❑ 71 100th Episode .15 .40
❑ 72 Checklist .15 .40

2003 Charmed The Power of Three Autographs

COMPLETE SET (14) 300.00 600.00
STATED ODDS 1:24
❑ A3 Alyssa Milano 125.00 225.00
❑ A8 Rose McGowan 125.00 225.00
❑ A9 Julian McMahon 12.00 30.00
❑ A10 Robert Englund 15.00 40.00
❑ A11 Billy Drago 8.00 20.00
❑ A12 Dan Gauthier 8.00 20.00
❑ A13 Adrian Paul 8.00 20.00
❑ A14 Melinda Clarke 8.00 20.00
❑ A15 Emmanuelle Vaugier 8.00 20.00
❑ A16 James Read 8.00 20.00
❑ A17 Costas Mandylor 8.00 20.00
❑ A18 Louis Mandylor 8.00 20.00
❑ A19 Elizabeth Gracen 12.00 30.00
❑ A20 Michael Bailey Smith 8.00 20.00

2003 Charmed The Power of Three Box Loaders

COMPLETE SET (4) 7.50 20.00
❑ BL1 Leo Wyatt 1.00 2.50
❑ BL2 Cole Turner 1.00 2.50
❑ BL3 Darryl Morris 1.00 2.50
❑ CL1 Charmed 6.00 15.00
CASE INSERT

2003 Charmed The Power of Three Pieceworks

COMPLETE SET (5) 60.00 120.00
STATED ODDS 1:24
❑ PW1 Alyssa Milano 7.50 20.00
❑ PW2 Alyssa Milano 7.50 20.00
❑ PW3 Holly Marie Combs 7.50 20.00
❑ PW4 Rose McGowan 20.00 50.00
❑ PW5 Alyssa Milano 20.00 50.00

2003 Charmed The Power of Three Puzzle

COMPLETE SET (9) 7.50 20.00
STATED ODDS 1:11
❑ P1 The Power Of Three 1.25 3.00
❑ P2 The Power Of Three 1.25 3.00
❑ P3 The Power Of Three 1.25 3.00
❑ P4 The Power Of Three 1.25 3.00
❑ P5 The Power Of Three 1.25 3.00
❑ P6 The Power Of Three 1.25 3.00
❑ P7 The Power Of Three 1.25 3.00
❑ P8 The Power Of Three 1.25 3.00
❑ P9 The Power Of Three 1.25 3.00

2003 Charmed The Power of Three Spellbinders

COMPLETE SET (6) 4.00 10.00
STATED ODDS 1:11
❑ S1 Piper 1.00 2.50
❑ S2 Paige 1.00 2.50
❑ S3 Phoebe 1.00 2.50
❑ S4 Piper 1.00 2.50
❑ S5 Phoebe 1.00 2.50
❑ S6 Paige 1.00 2.50

2003 The Complete Highlander The Series

COMPLETE SET (126) 5.00 12.00
CC1 ISSUED IN COLLECTORS ALBUM
❑ 1 Title Card .08 .25
❑ 2 Season One Overview .08 .25
❑ 3 The Gathering .08 .25
❑ 4 Family Tree .08 .25
❑ 5 The Road Not Taken .08 .25
❑ 6 Innocent Man .08 .25
❑ 7 Free Fall .08 .25
❑ 8 Bad Day at Building A .08 .25
❑ 9 Mountain Men .08 .25
❑ 10 Deadly Medicine .08 .25
❑ 11 The Sea Witch .08 .25
❑ 12 Revenge is Sweet .08 .25
❑ 13 See No Evil .08 .25
❑ 14 Eyewitness .08 .25
❑ 15 Band of Brothers .08 .25
❑ 16 For Evil's Sake .08 .25
❑ 17 For Tomorrow We Die .08 .25
❑ 18 The Beast Below .08 .25
❑ 19 Saving Grace .08 .25
❑ 20 The Lady and the Tiger .08 .25
❑ 21 Eye of the Beholder .08 .25
❑ 22 Avenging Angel .08 .25
❑ 23 Nowhere to Run .08 .25
❑ 24 The Hunters .08 .25
❑ 25 Season Two Overview .08 .25
❑ 26 The Watchers .08 .25
❑ 27 Studies in Light .08 .25
❑ 28 Turnabout .08 .25
❑ 29 The Darkness .08 .25
❑ 30 An Eye for an Eye .08 .25
❑ 31 The Zone .08 .25
❑ 32 The Return of Amanda .08 .25
❑ 33 Revenge of the Sword .08 .25
❑ 34 Run For Your Life .08 .25
❑ 35 Epitaph for Tommy .08 .25
❑ 36 The Fighter .08 .25
❑ 37 Under Color of Authority .08 .25
❑ 38 Bless the Child .08 .25
❑ 39 Unholy Alliance, Part I .08 .25
❑ 40 Unholy Alliance, Part II .08 .25
❑ 41 The Vampire .08 .25
❑ 42 Warmonger .08 .25
❑ 43 Pharaoh's Daughter .08 .25
❑ 44 Legacy .08 .25
❑ 45 Prodigal Son .08 .25
❑ 46 Counterfeit, Part I .08 .25
❑ 47 Counterfeit, Part 2 .08 .25
❑ 48 Season Three Overview .08 .25
❑ 49 Samurai .08 .25
❑ 50 Line of Fire .08 .25
❑ 51 The Revolutionary .08 .25
❑ 52 The Cross of St. Antoine .08 .25
❑ 53 Rite of Passage .08 .25
❑ 54 Courage .08 .25
❑ 55 The Lamb .08 .25
❑ 56 Obsession .08 .25
❑ 57 Shadows .08 .25
❑ 58 Blackmail .08 .25
❑ 59 Vendetta .08 .25
❑ 60 They Also Serve .08 .25
❑ 61 Blind Faith .08 .25
❑ 62 Song of the Executioner .08 .25
❑ 63 Star Crossed .08 .25
❑ 64 Methos .08 .25
❑ 65 Take Back the Night .08 .25
❑ 66 Testimony .08 .25
❑ 67 Mortal Sins .08 .25
❑ 68 Reasonable Doubt .08 .25
❑ 69 Finale, Part I .08 .25
❑ 70 Finale, Part 2 .08 .25
❑ 71 Season Four Overview .08 .25
❑ 72 Homeland .08 .25
❑ 73 Brothers in Arm .08 .25
❑ 74 The Innocent .08 .25
❑ 75 Leader of the Pack .08 .25
❑ 76 Double Eagle .08 .25
❑ 77 Reunion .08 .25
❑ 78 The Colonel .08 .25
❑ 79 Reluctant Heroes .08 .25
❑ 80 The Wrath of Kali .08 .25
❑ 81 Chivalry .08 .25
❑ 82 Timeless .08 .25
❑ 83 The Blitz .08 .25
❑ 84 Something Wicked .08 .25
❑ 85 Deliverance .08 .25
❑ 86 Promise .08 .25
❑ 87 Methuselah's Gift .08 .25
❑ 88 The Immortal Cimoli .08 .25
❑ 89 Through a Glass, Darkly .08 .25
❑ 90 Double Jeopardy .08 .25
❑ 91 Til Death .08 .25
❑ 92 Judgment Day .08 .25
❑ 93 One Minute to Midnight .08 .25
❑ 94 Season Five Overview .08 .25
❑ 95 Prophecy .08 .25
❑ 96 The End of Innocence .08 .25
❑ 97 Manhunt .08 .25
❑ 98 Glory Days .08 .25
❑ 99 Dramatic License .08 .25
❑ 100 Money No Object .08 .25
❑ 101 The Haunted .08 .25
❑ 102 Little Tin God .08 .25
❑ 103 The Messenger .08 .25
❑ 104 The Valkyrie .08 .25
❑ 105 Comes a Horseman .08 .25
❑ 106 Revelation 6:8 .08 .25
❑ 107 Ransom of Richard Redstone .08 .25
❑ 108 Duende .08 .25
❑ 109 Forgive Us Our Trespasses .08 .25
❑ 110 The Stone of Scone .08 .25
❑ 111 The Modern Prometheus .08 .25
❑ 112 Archangel .08 .25
❑ 113 Season Six Overview .08 .25
❑ 114 Avatar .08 .25
❑ 115 Armageddon .08 .25
❑ 116 Sins of the Father .08 .25
❑ 117 Diplomatic Immunity .08 .25
❑ 118 Patient Number 7 .08 .25
❑ 119 Black Tower .08 .25
❑ 120 Unusual Suspect .08 .25
❑ 121 Justice .08 .25
❑ 122 Deadly Exposure .08 .25
❑ 123 Two of Hearts .08 .25
❑ 124 Indiscretions .08 .25
❑ 125 To Be .08 .25
❑ 126 Not To Be .08 .25
❑ CC1 Highlander: Endgame MEM (issued in binder) 8.00 20.00

2003 The Complete Highlander The Series Autographs

STATED ODDS THREE PER BOX
L (LIMITED): 300-500 COPIES
❑ A1 Adrian Paul L 6.00 15.00
❑ A2 Jim Byrnes 6.00 15.00
❑ A3 Stan Kirsch L 6.00 15.00
❑ A4 Elizabeth Gracen L 6.00 15.00
❑ A5 Traci Lords L 30.00 60.00
❑ A6 James Horan 6.00 15.00
❑ A7 Lisa Howard 6.00 15.00
❑ A8 Tom McBeath 6.00 15.00
❑ A9 Marcia Strassman 6.00 15.00
❑ A10 Sandra Bernhard 10.00 25.00
❑ A11 Claudia Christian 10.00 25.00
❑ A12 Michael Shanks 6.00 15.00
❑ A13 Ocean Hellman 6.00 15.00
❑ A14 Amanda Wyss 6.00 15.00
❑ A15 Anthony Head 6.00 15.00
❑ A16 Tamlyn Tomita 6.00 15.00
❑ A17 Matt Walker 6.00 15.00
❑ A18 Ron Perlman 10.00 25.00
❑ A19 Don S. Davis 6.00 15.00
❑ A20 Alan Scarfe 6.00 15.00

2003 The Complete Highlander The Series Lover

COMPLETE SET (9) 6.00 15.00
STATED ODDS 1:8
❑ L1 Amanda .75 2.00
❑ L2 Tessa .75 2.00
❑ L3 Debra Campbell .75 2.00
❑ L4 Carmen .75 2.00
❑ L5 Little Deer .75 2.00
❑ L6 Bess .75 2.00
❑ L7 Kristen Gilles .75 2.00
❑ L8 Sarah .75 2.00
❑ L9 Reagan Cole .75 2.00

2003 The Complete Highlander The Series Promos

COMPLETE SET (4) 3.00 8.00
❑ P1 General Distribution 1.00 2.50
❑ P2 Non-Sport Update Magazine 1.00 2.50
❑ P3 Binder Exclusive 1.00 2.50
❑ PCE2003 Promo Card Encyclopedia Exclusive 1.50 4.00

2003 The Complete Highlander The Series The Raven

COMPLETE SET (22) 6.00 15.00
STATED ODDS 1:3
❑ R1 Reborn .40 1.00
❑ R2 Full Disclosure .40 1.00
❑ R3 Bloodlines .40 1.00
❑ R4 Immunity .40 1.00
❑ R5 So Shall Ye Reap .40 1.00
❑ R6 Birthright .40 1.00
❑ R7 Crime and Punishment .40 1.00
❑ R8 The Unknown Soldier .40 1.00
❑ R9 Cloak and Dagger .40 1.00
❑ R10 Passion Play .40 1.00
❑ R11 The Devil You Know .40 1.00
❑ R12 A Matter of Time, Part 1 .40 1.00
❑ R13 The French Connection, Part 2 .40 1.00
❑ R14 The Rogue .40 1.00
❑ R15 Inferno .40 1.00
❑ R16 The Frame .40 1.00
❑ R17 Love and Death .40 1.00
❑ R18 thick as Thieves .40 1.00
❑ R19 The Manipulator .40 1.00
❑ R20 The Ex-Files .40 1.00

MODERN ERA NON-SPORTS

❑ R21 War and Peace .40 1.00
❑ R22 Dead on Arrival .40 1.00

2003 The Complete Highlander The Series Wanderer

COMPLETE SET (6) 12.00 30.00
STATED ODDS 1:40

❑ W1 1618 2.50 6.00
❑ W2 1635 2.50 6.00
❑ W3 1778 2.50 6.00
❑ W4 1815 2.50 6.00
❑ W5 1851 2.50 6.00
❑ W6 1864 2.50 6.00

2003 The Complete Highlander The Series Warrior

COMPLETE SET (9) 10.00 25.00
STATED ODDS 1:20

❑ Q1 Duncan 1.50 4.00
Otavio Consone
❑ Q2 Duncan 1.50 4.00
Martin Hyde
❑ Q3 Duncan 1.50 4.00
Hugh Fitzcairn
❑ Q4 Duncan 1.50 4.00
Paul Karros
❑ Q5 Duncan 1.50 4.00
Karros
❑ Q6 Duncan 1.50 4.00
Hideo Koto
❑ Q7 Duncan 1.50 4.00
Steven Keane
❑ Q8 Duncan 1.50 4.00
Nicholas War
❑ Q9 Duncan 1.50 4.00
Morgan D'Estaing

2003 The Complete Star Trek Animated Adventures

COMPLETE SET (198) 4.00 10.00
CHECKLIST STATED ODDS 1:20

❑ 1 Beyond the Farthest Star .08 .25
❑ 2 Beyond the Farthest Star .08 .25
❑ 3 Beyond the Farthest Star .08 .25
❑ 4 Beyond the Farthest Star .08 .25
❑ 5 Beyond the Farthest Star .08 .25
❑ 6 Beyond the Farthest Star .08 .25
❑ 7 Beyond the Farthest Star .08 .25
❑ 8 Beyond the Farthest Star .08 .25
❑ 9 Beyond the Farthest Star .08 .25
❑ 10 Yesteryear .08 .25
❑ 11 Yesteryear .08 .25
❑ 12 Yesteryear .08 .25
❑ 13 Yesteryear .08 .25
❑ 14 Yesteryear .08 .25
❑ 15 Yesteryear .08 .25
❑ 16 Yesteryear .08 .25
❑ 17 Yesteryear .08 .25
❑ 18 Yesteryear .08 .25
❑ 19 One of Our Planets is Missing .08 .25
❑ 20 One of Our Planets is Missing .08 .25
❑ 21 One of Our Planets is Missing .08 .25
❑ 22 One of Our Planets is Missing .08 .25
❑ 23 One of Our Planets is Missing .08 .25
❑ 24 One of Our Planets is Missing .08 .25
❑ 25 One of Our Planets is Missing .08 .25
❑ 26 One of Our Planets is Missing .08 .25
❑ 27 One of Our Planets is Missing .08 .25
❑ 28 The Lorelei Signal .08 .25
❑ 29 The Lorelei Signal .08 .25
❑ 30 The Lorelei Signal .08 .25
❑ 31 The Lorelei Signal .08 .25
❑ 32 The Lorelei Signal .08 .25
❑ 33 The Lorelei Signal .08 .25
❑ 34 The Lorelei Signal .08 .25
❑ 35 The Lorelei Signal .08 .25
❑ 36 The Lorelei Signal .08 .25
❑ 37 More Tribbles, More Troubles .08 .25
❑ 38 More Tribbles, More Troubles .08 .25
❑ 39 More Tribbles, More Troubles .08 .25
❑ 40 More Tribbles, More Troubles .08 .25
❑ 41 More Tribbles, More Troubles .08 .25
❑ 42 More Tribbles, More Troubles .08 .25
❑ 43 More Tribbles, More Troubles .08 .25
❑ 44 More Tribbles, More Troubles .08 .25
❑ 45 More Tribbles, More Troubles .08 .25
❑ 46 The Survivor .08 .25
❑ 47 The Survivor .08 .25
❑ 48 The Survivor .08 .25
❑ 49 The Survivor .08 .25
❑ 50 The Survivor .08 .25
❑ 51 The Survivor .08 .25
❑ 52 The Survivor .08 .25
❑ 53 The Survivor .08 .25
❑ 54 The Survivor .08 .25
❑ 55 The Infinite Vulcan .08 .25
❑ 56 The Infinite Vulcan .08 .25
❑ 57 The Infinite Vulcan .08 .25
❑ 58 The Infinite Vulcan .08 .25
❑ 59 The Infinite Vulcan .08 .25
❑ 60 The Infinite Vulcan .08 .25
❑ 61 The Infinite Vulcan .08 .25
❑ 62 The Infinite Vulcan .08 .25
❑ 63 The Infinite Vulcan .08 .25
❑ 64 The Magicks of Megas-Tu .08 .25
❑ 65 The Magicks of Megas-Tu .08 .25
❑ 66 The Magicks of Megas-Tu .08 .25
❑ 67 The Magicks of Megas-Tu .08 .25
❑ 68 The Magicks of Megas-Tu .08 .25
❑ 69 The Magicks of Megas-Tu .08 .25
❑ 70 The Magicks of Megas-Tu .08 .25
❑ 71 The Magicks of Megas-Tu .08 .25
❑ 72 The Magicks of Megas-Tu .08 .25
❑ 73 Once Upon A Planet .08 .25
❑ 74 Once Upon A Planet .08 .25
❑ 75 Once Upon A Planet .08 .25
❑ 76 Once Upon A Planet .08 .25
❑ 77 Once Upon A Planet .08 .25
❑ 78 Once Upon A Planet .08 .25
❑ 79 Once Upon A Planet .08 .25
❑ 80 Once Upon A Planet .08 .25
❑ 81 Once Upon A Planet .08 .25
❑ 82 Mudd's Passion .08 .25
❑ 83 Mudd's Passion .08 .25
❑ 84 Mudd's Passion .08 .25
❑ 85 Mudd's Passion .08 .25
❑ 86 Mudd's Passion .08 .25
❑ 87 Mudd's Passion .08 .25
❑ 88 Mudd's Passion .08 .25
❑ 89 Mudd's Passion .08 .25
❑ 90 Mudd's Passion .08 .25
❑ 91 The Terratin Incident .08 .25
❑ 92 The Terratin Incident .08 .25
❑ 93 The Terratin Incident .08 .25
❑ 94 The Terratin Incident .08 .25
❑ 95 The Terratin Incident .08 .25
❑ 96 The Terratin Incident .08 .25
❑ 97 The Terratin Incident .08 .25
❑ 98 The Terratin Incident .08 .25
❑ 99 The Terratin Incident .08 .25
❑ 100 The Time Trap .08 .25
❑ 101 The Time Trap .08 .25
❑ 102 The Time Trap .08 .25
❑ 103 The Time Trap .08 .25
❑ 104 The Time Trap .08 .25
❑ 105 The Time Trap .08 .25
❑ 106 The Time Trap .08 .25
❑ 107 The Time Trap .08 .25
❑ 108 The Time Trap .08 .25
❑ 109 The Ambergris Element .08 .25
❑ 110 The Ambergris Element .08 .25
❑ 111 The Ambergris Element .08 .25
❑ 112 The Ambergris Element .08 .25
❑ 113 The Ambergris Element .08 .25
❑ 114 The Ambergris Element .08 .25
❑ 115 The Ambergris Element .08 .25
❑ 116 The Ambergris Element .08 .25
❑ 117 The Ambergris Element .08 .25
❑ 118 Slaver Weapon .08 .25
❑ 119 Slaver Weapon .08 .25
❑ 120 Slaver Weapon .08 .25
❑ 121 Slaver Weapon .08 .25
❑ 122 Slaver Weapon .08 .25
❑ 123 Slaver Weapon .08 .25
❑ 124 Slaver Weapon .08 .25
❑ 125 Slaver Weapon .08 .25
❑ 126 Slaver Weapon .08 .25
❑ 127 The Eye of the Beholder .08 .25
❑ 128 The Eye of the Beholder .08 .25
❑ 129 The Eye of the Beholder .08 .25
❑ 130 The Eye of the Beholder .08 .25
❑ 131 The Eye of the Beholder .08 .25
❑ 132 The Eye of the Beholder .08 .25
❑ 133 The Eye of the Beholder .08 .25
❑ 134 The Eye of the Beholder .08 .25
❑ 135 The Eye of the Beholder .08 .25
❑ 136 The Jihad .08 .25
❑ 137 The Jihad .08 .25
❑ 138 The Jihad .08 .25
❑ 139 The Jihad .08 .25
❑ 140 The Jihad .08 .25
❑ 141 The Jihad .08 .25
❑ 142 The Jihad .08 .25
❑ 143 The Jihad .08 .25
❑ 144 The Jihad .08 .25
❑ 145 The Pirates of Orion .08 .25
❑ 146 The Pirates of Orion .08 .25
❑ 147 The Pirates of Orion .08 .25
❑ 148 The Pirates of Orion .08 .25
❑ 149 The Pirates of Orion .08 .25
❑ 150 The Pirates of Orion .08 .25
❑ 151 The Pirates of Orion .08 .25
❑ 152 The Pirates of Orion .08 .25
❑ 153 The Pirates of Orion .08 .25
❑ 154 Bem .08 .25
❑ 155 Bem .08 .25
❑ 156 Bem .08 .25
❑ 157 Bem .08 .25
❑ 158 Bem .08 .25
❑ 159 Bem .08 .25
❑ 160 Bem .08 .25
❑ 161 Bem .08 .25
❑ 162 Bem .08 .25
❑ 163 The Practical Joker .08 .25
❑ 164 The Practical Joker .08 .25
❑ 165 The Practical Joker .08 .25
❑ 166 The Practical Joker .08 .25
❑ 167 The Practical Joker .08 .25
❑ 168 The Practical Joker .08 .25
❑ 169 The Practical Joker .08 .25
❑ 170 The Practical Joker .08 .25
❑ 171 The Practical Joker .08 .25
❑ 172 Albatross .08 .25
❑ 173 Albatross .08 .25
❑ 174 Albatross .08 .25
❑ 175 Albatross .08 .25
❑ 176 Albatross .08 .25
❑ 177 Albatross .08 .25
❑ 178 Albatross .08 .25
❑ 179 Albatross .08 .25
❑ 180 Albatross .08 .25
❑ 181 How Sharper Than A Serpent's Tooth .08 .25
❑ 182 How Sharper Than A Serpent's Tooth .08 .25
❑ 183 How Sharper Than A Serpent's Tooth .08 .25
❑ 184 How Sharper Than A Serpent's Tooth .08 .25
❑ 185 How Sharper Than A Serpent's Tooth .08 .25
❑ 186 How Sharper Than A Serpent's Tooth .08 .25
❑ 187 How Sharper Than A Serpent's Tooth .08 .25
❑ 188 How Sharper Than A Serpent's Tooth .08 .25
❑ 189 How Sharper Than A Serpent's Tooth .08 .25
❑ 190 The Counter-Clock Incident .08 .25
❑ 191 The Counter-Clock Incident .08 .25
❑ 192 The Counter-Clock Incident .08 .25
❑ 193 The Counter-Clock Incident .08 .25
❑ 194 The Counter-Clock Incident .08 .25
❑ 195 The Counter-Clock Incident .08 .25
❑ 196 The Counter-Clock Incident .08 .25
❑ 197 The Counter-Clock Incident .08 .25
❑ 198 The Counter-Clock Incident .08 .25
❑ C1 Checklist .08 .25
❑ C2 Checklist .08 .25

2003 The Complete Star Trek Animated Adventures Autographs

COMPLETE SET (13) 100.00 200.00
STATED ODDS 1:40
A3 STATED ODDS ONE PER COLLECTOR'S ALBUM

❑ A1 William Shatner 60.00 100.00
❑ A2 Leonard Nimoy 75.00 125.00
❑ A3 George Takei 7.50 20.00
❑ A4 Nichelle Nichols 7.50 20.00
❑ A5a Majel Barrett Lt. M'Ress 12.50 30.00
❑ A5b Majel Barrett Nurse Chapel 12.50 30.00
❑ A6a James Doohan Lt. Commander Scott 12.50 30.00
❑ A6b James Doohan Lt. Arex 12.50 30.00
❑ A7 Dorothy Fontana 7.50 20.00
❑ A8 Hal Sutherland 7.50 20.00
❑ A9 Lou Scheimer 7.50 20.00
❑ A10 Norm Prescott 7.50 20.00
❑ A11 Walter Koenig 7.50 20.00

2003 The Complete Star Trek Animated Adventures Captain Kirk In Motion

COMPLETE SET (9) 12.50 30.00
STATED ODDS 1:20

❑ K1 Captain Kirk 1.50 4.00
❑ K2 Captain Kirk 1.50 4.00
❑ K3 Captain Kirk 1.50 4.00
❑ K4 Captain Kirk 1.50 4.00
❑ K5 Captain Kirk 1.50 4.00
❑ K6 Captain Kirk 1.50 4.00
❑ K7 Captain Kirk 1.50 4.00
❑ K8 Captain Kirk 1.50 4.00
❑ K9 Captain Kirk 1.50 4.00

2003 The Complete Star Trek Animated Adventures Die-Cut CD-ROMs

COMPLETE SET (5) 10.00 25.00
STATED ODDS ONE PER BOX

❑ NNO McCoy 2.50 6.00
❑ NNO Kirk 2.50 6.00
❑ NNO Sulu 2.50 6.00
❑ NNO Spock 2.50 6.00
❑ NNO Scotty 2.50 6.00

2003 The Complete Star Trek Animated Adventures James Doohan Tribute

COMPLETE SET (9) 2.50 6.00
STATED ODDS 1:4

❑ JD1 James Doohan .40 1.00
❑ JD2 James Doohan .40 1.00
❑ JD3 James Doohan .40 1.00
❑ JD4 James Doohan .40 1.00
❑ JD5 James Doohan .40 1.00
❑ JD6 James Doohan .40 1.00
❑ JD7 James Doohan .40 1.00
❑ JD8 James Doohan .40 1.00
❑ JD9 James Doohan .40 1.00

2003 The Complete Star Trek Animated Adventures Promos

❑ P1 Enterprise .75 2.00
(General Distribution)
❑ P2 McCoy/Kirk/Scott/Spock 3.00 8.00
(NSU Magazine)
❑ P3 McCoy/Kirk/Spock
(Album Exclusive)

2003 The Complete Star Trek Animated Adventures Star Trek Micro-Cels

COMPLETE SET (22) 40.00 100.00
STATED ODDS 1:20

❑ MC1 Beyond the Farthest Star 2.50 6.00
❑ MC2 Yesteryear 2.50 6.00
❑ MC3 One of Our Planets is Missing 2.50 6.00
❑ MC4 The Lorelei Signal 2.50 6.00
❑ MC5 More Tribbles, More Troubles 2.50 6.00
❑ MC6 The Survivor 2.50 6.00
❑ MC7 The Magicks of Megas-Tu 2.50 6.00
❑ MC8 The Infinite Vulcan 2.50 6.00
❑ MC9 Once Upon A Planet 2.50 6.00
❑ MC10 Mudd's Passion 2.50 6.00
❑ MC11 The Terratin Incident 2.50 6.00
❑ MC12 The Time Trap 2.50 6.00
❑ MC13 The Ambergris Element 2.50 6.00
❑ MC14 Slaver Weapon 2.50 6.00
❑ MC15 The Eye of the Beholder 2.50 6.00
❑ MC16 The Jihad 2.50 6.00
❑ MC17 The Pirates of Orion 2.50 6.00
❑ MC18 Bem 2.50 6.00
❑ MC19 The Practical Joker 2.50 6.00
❑ MC20 Albatross 2.50 6.00
❑ MC21 How Sharper Than A Serpent's Tooth 2.50 6.00
❑ MC22 The Counter-Clock Incident 2.50 6.00

2003 The Complete Star Trek Animated Adventures The Enterprise Bridge Crew

COMPLETE SET (9) 7.50 20.00
STATED ODDS 1:8

❑ BC1 Captain James Tiberius Kirk 1.25 3.00
❑ BC2 Commander Spock 1.25 3.00
❑ BC3 Doctor Leonard H. McCoy 1.25 3.00
❑ BC4 Lieutenant Commander Montgomery Scott1.25 3.00
❑ BC5 Lieutenant Hikaru Sulu 1.25 3.00
❑ BC6 Lieutenant Uhura 1.25 3.00
❑ BC7 Nurse Christine Chapel 1.25 3.00
❑ BC8 Lieutenant Arex 1.25 3.00
❑ BC9 Lieutenant M'Ress 1.25 3.00

2003 Complete Star Trek Deep Space Nine

COMPLETE SET (189) 4.00 10.00

❑ 1 Star Trek Deep Space Nine Montage .08 .25
❑ 2 Star Trek Deep Space Nine Montage .08 .25
❑ 3 Star Trek Deep Space Nine Montage .08 .25
❑ 4 SEASON ONE .08 .25
❑ 5 Emissary Part I .08 .25
❑ 6 Emissary Part II .08 .25
❑ 7 Past Prologue .08 .25
❑ 8 A Man Alone .08 .25
❑ 9 Babel .08 .25
❑ 10 Captive Pursuit .08 .25
❑ 11 Q-Less .08 .25
❑ 12 Dax .08 .25
❑ 13 The Passenger .08 .25
❑ 14 Move Along Home .08 .25
❑ 15 The Nagus .08 .25
❑ 16 Vortex .08 .25
❑ 17 Battle Lines .08 .25
❑ 18 The Storyteller .08 .25
❑ 19 Progress .08 .25
❑ 20 If Wishes Were Horses .08 .25
❑ 21 The Forsaken .08 .25
❑ 22 Dramatis Personae .08 .25
❑ 23 Duet .08 .25
❑ 24 In the Hands of the Prophets .08 .25
❑ 25 SEASON TWO .08 .25
❑ 26 The Homecoming .08 .25
❑ 27 The Circle .08 .25
❑ 28 The Siege .08 .25
❑ 29 Invasive Procedures .08 .25
❑ 30 Cardassians .08 .25
❑ 31 Melora .08 .25
❑ 32 Rules of Acquisition .08 .25
❑ 33 Necessary Evil .08 .25
❑ 34 Second Sight .08 .25
❑ 35 Sanctuary .08 .25
❑ 36 Rivals .08 .25
❑ 37 The Alternate .08 .25
❑ 38 Armageddon Game .08 .25
❑ 39 Whispers .08 .25
❑ 40 Paradise .08 .25
❑ 41 Shadowplay .08 .25
❑ 42 Playing God .08 .25
❑ 43 Profit and Loss .08 .25
❑ 44 Blood Oath .08 .25
❑ 45 The Maquis Part I .08 .25
❑ 46 The Maquis Part II .08 .25
❑ 47 The Wire .08 .25
❑ 48 Crossover .08 .25
❑ 49 The Collaborator .08 .25
❑ 50 Tribunal .08 .25
❑ 51 The Jem'Hadar .08 .25
❑ 52 SEASON THREE .08 .25
❑ 53 The Search Part I .08 .25
❑ 54 The Search Part II .08 .25
❑ 55 The House of Quark .08 .25
❑ 56 Equilibrium .08 .25
❑ 57 Second Skin .08 .25
❑ 58 The Abandoned n .08 .25
❑ 59 Civil Defense .08 .25
❑ 60 Meridian .08 .25
❑ 61 Defiant .08 .25
❑ 62 Fascination .08 .25
❑ 63 Past Tense Part I .08 .25
❑ 64 Past Tense Part II .08 .25
❑ 65 Life Support .08 .25
❑ 66 Heart of Stone .08 .25
❑ 67 Destiny .08 .25
❑ 68 Prophet Motive .08 .25
❑ 69 Visionary .08 .25
❑ 70 Distant Voices .08 .25
❑ 71 Through the Looking Glass .08 .25
❑ 72 Improbable Cause .08 .25
❑ 73 The Die Is Cast .08 .25
❑ 74 Explorers .08 .25
❑ 75 Family Business .08 .25
❑ 76 Shakaar .08 .25
❑ 77 Facets .08 .25
❑ 78 The Adversary .08 .25
❑ 79 SEASON FOUR .08 .25
❑ 80 The Way of the Warrior Part I .08 .25
❑ 81 The Way of the Warrior Part II .08 .25
❑ 82 The Visitor .08 .25
❑ 83 Hippocratic Oath .08 .25
❑ 84 Indiscretion .08 .25
❑ 85 Rejoined .08 .25
❑ 86 Starship Down .08 .25
❑ 87 Little Green Men .08 .25
❑ 88 The Sword of Kahless .08 .25
❑ 89 Our Man Bashir .08 .25
❑ 90 Homefront .08 .25
❑ 91 Paradise Lost .08 .25
❑ 92 Crossfire .08 .25
❑ 93 Return to Grace .08 .25
❑ 94 Sons of Mogh .08 .25
❑ 95 Bar Association .08 .25
❑ 96 Accession .08 .25
❑ 97 Rules of Engagement .08 .25
❑ 98 Hard Time .08 .25
❑ 99 Shattered Mirror .08 .25
❑ 100 The Muse .08 .25
❑ 101 For the Cause .08 .25
❑ 102 To the Death .08 .25
❑ 103 The Quickening .08 .25
❑ 104 Body Parts .08 .25
❑ 105 Broken Link .08 .25
❑ 106 SEASON FIVE .08 .25
❑ 107 Apocalypse Rising .08 .25
❑ 108 The Ship .08 .25
❑ 109 Looking for par'Mach .08 .25
❑ 110 Nor the Battle to the Strong .08 .25
❑ 111 The Assignment .08 .25
❑ 112 Trials and Tribble-ations .08 .25
❑ 113 Let He Who Is Without Sin .08 .25
❑ 114 Things Past .08 .25
❑ 115 The Ascent .08 .25
❑ 116 Rapture .08 .25
❑ 117 The Darkness and the Light .08 .25
❑ 118 The Begotten .08 .25
❑ 119 For the Uniform .08 .25
❑ 120 In Purgatory's Shadow .08 .25
❑ 121 By Inferno's Light .08 .25
❑ 122 Doctor Bashir, I Presume? .08 .25
❑ 123 A Simple Investigation .08 .25
❑ 124 Business as Usual .08 .25
❑ 125 Ties of Blood and Water .08 .25
❑ 126 Ferengi Love Songs .08 .25
❑ 127 Soldiers of the Empire .08 .25
❑ 128 Children of Time .08 .25
❑ 129 Blaze of Glory .08 .25
❑ 130 Empok Nor .08 .25
❑ 131 In the Cards .08 .25
❑ 132 Call to Arms .08 .25
❑ 133 SEASON SIX .08 .25
❑ 134 A Time to Stand .08 .25
❑ 135 Rocks and Shoals .08 .25
❑ 136 Sons and Daughters .08 .25
❑ 137 Behind the Lines .08 .25
❑ 138 Favor the Bold .08 .25
❑ 139 Sacrifice of Angels .08 .25
❑ 140 You Are Cordially Invited .08 .25
❑ 141 Resurrection .08 .25
❑ 142 Statistical Probabilities .08 .25
❑ 143 The Magnificent Ferengi .08 .25
❑ 144 Waltz .08 .25
❑ 145 Who Mourns for Morn? .08 .25
❑ 146 Far Beyond the Stars .08 .25
❑ 147 One Little Ship .08 .25
❑ 148 Honor Among Thieves .08 .25
❑ 149 Change of Heart .08 .25
❑ 150 Wrongs Darker than Death or Night .08 .25
❑ 151 Inquisition .08 .25
❑ 152 In the Pale Moonlight .08 .25
❑ 153 His Way .08 .25
❑ 154 The Reckoning .08 .25
❑ 155 Valiant .08 .25
❑ 156 Profit and Lace .08 .25
❑ 157 Time's Orphan .08 .25
❑ 158 The Sound of Her Voice .08 .25
❑ 159 Tears of the Prophets .08 .25
❑ 160 SEASON SEVEN .08 .25
❑ 161 Image in the Sand .08 .25
❑ 162 Shadows and Symbols .08 .25
❑ 163 Afterimage .08 .25
❑ 164 Take Me Out to the Holosuite .08 .25
❑ 165 Chrysalis .08 .25
❑ 166 Treachery, Faith, and the Great River .08 .25
❑ 167 Once More Unto the Breach .08 .25
❑ 168 The Siege of AR-558 .08 .25
❑ 169 Covenant .08 .25
❑ 170 It's Only a Paper Moon .08 .25
❑ 171 Prodigal Daughter .08 .25
❑ 172 The Emperor's New Cloak .08 .25
❑ 173 Field of Fire .08 .25
❑ 174 Chimera .08 .25
❑ 175 Badda-Bing Badda-Bang .08 .25
❑ 176 Inter Arma Enim Silent Leges .08 .25
❑ 177 Penumbra .08 .25
❑ 178 'Til Death Do Us Part .08 .25
❑ 179 Strange Bedfellows .08 .25
❑ 180 The Changing Face of Evil .08 .25
❑ 181 When It Rains .08 .25
❑ 182 Tacking Into the Wind .08 .25
❑ 183 Extreme Measures .08 .25
❑ 184 The Dogs of War .08 .25
❑ 185 What You Leave Behind Part I .08 .25
❑ 186 What You Leave Behind Part II .08 .25
❑ 187 Checklist .08 .25
❑ 188 Checklist .08 .25
❑ 189 Checklist .08 .25

2003 Complete Star Trek Deep Space Nine Allies and Enemies

COMPLETE SET (27) 8.00 20.00
STATED ODDS 1:3

❑ B1 Admiral Bill Ross .40 1.00
❑ B2 Locutus of Borg .40 1.00
❑ B3 Damar .40 1.00
❑ B4 Female Founder .40 1.00
❑ B5 Garak .40 1.00
❑ B6 General Martok .40 1.00
❑ B7 Gowron .40 1.00
❑ B8 Grand Nagus Zek .40 1.00
❑ B9 Gul Dukat .40 1.00
❑ B10 Ishka .40 1.00
❑ B11 Jake Sisko .40 1.00
❑ B12 Jennifer Sisko .40 1.00
❑ B13 Joseph Sisko .40 1.00
❑ B14 Kai Opaka .40 1.00
❑ B15 Kai Adami Winn .40 1.00
❑ B16 Kasidy Yates .40 1.00
❑ B17 Keiko O'Brien .40 1.00
❑ B18 Leeta .40 1.00
❑ B19 Michael Eddington .40 1.00
❑ B20 Molly O'Brien .40 1.00
❑ B21 Morn .40 1.00
❑ B22 Nog .40 1.00
❑ B23 Rom .40 1.00
❑ B24 Vedek Bareil .40 1.00
❑ B25 Vic Fontaine .40 1.00
❑ B26 Weyoun .40 1.00
❑ B27 Tora Ziyal .40 1.00

2003 Complete Star Trek Deep Space Nine Alternate Realities

COMPLETE SET (7) 30.00 80.00
STATED ODDS 1:80

❑ AR1 Benjamin Sisko 6.00 15.00
❑ AR2 Kira Nerys 6.00 15.00
❑ AR3 Miles O'Brien 6.00 15.00
❑ AR4 Julian Bashir 6.00 15.00
❑ AR5 Jennifer Sisko 6.00 15.00
❑ AR6 Worf 6.00 15.00
❑ AR7 Garak 6.00 15.00

2003 Complete Star Trek Deep Space Nine Autographs

STATED ODDS 1:20 10.00 25.00
DA2 ODDS ONE PER CASE
L (LIMITED): 300-500 CARDS

❑ A1 Avery Brooks L 60.00 120.00
❑ A2 Colm Meaney L 50.00 100.00
❑ A3 Michael Dorn L 50.00 100.00
❑ A4 Armin Shimerman 10.00 25.00
❑ A5 Nana Visitor L 10.00 25.00
❑ A6 Mary Kay Adams 10.00 25.00
❑ A7 Kitty Swink 10.00 25.00
❑ A8 William Sadler 10.00 25.00
❑ A9 Wallace Shawn 10.00 25.00
❑ A10 Rene Auberjonois L 10.00 25.00
❑ A11 Alexander Siddig L 10.00 25.00
❑ A12 Chase Masterson 10.00 25.00
❑ A13 Terry Farrell L 10.00 25.00
❑ A14 Jeffrey Combs L 10.00 25.00
❑ A15 Nicole DeBoer L 10.00 25.00
❑ A16 Casey Biggs 10.00 25.00
❑ A17 J.G. Hertzler 10.00 25.00
❑ A19 Cecily Adams 10.00 25.00
❑ A20 Lawrence Monoson 10.00 25.00
❑ A21 Tony Todd L 10.00 25.00
❑ A22 Felecia Bell Shafer 10.00 25.00
❑ A23 William Schallert 10.00 25.00
❑ A24 Brian Thompson 10.00 25.00
❑ A26 Barry Jenner 10.00 25.00
❑ DA1 Michael Dorn 50.00 100.00
Terry Farrell L
❑ DA2 Barbara March 30.00 60.00
Gwynyth Walsh

2003 Complete Star Trek Deep Space Nine From The Archives Costumes

STATED ODDS 1:100

❑ CC1a Quark 6.00 15.00
Yellow Green Shirt
❑ CC1b Quark 6.00 15.00
Plaid Pants
❑ CC2a Worf 6.00 15.00
Red
❑ CC2b Worf 6.00 15.00
Black
❑ CC3a Garak 6.00 15.00
Black and Green
❑ CC3b Garak 6.00 15.00
Green and Red
❑ CC3c Garak 6.00 15.00
Black and Green Pattern
❑ CC4a Kira 6.00 15.00
Shiny Silver and Black
❑ CC4b Kira 6.00 15.00
Dull Silver
❑ CC5 Odo 6.00 15.00

2003 Complete Star Trek Deep Space Nine Gallery

COMPLETE SET (10) 40.00 80.00
STATED ODDS 1:40

❑ G1 Captain Benjamin Sisko 5.00 12.00
❑ G2 Colonel Kira Nerys 5.00 12.00
❑ G3 Lt. Commander Worf 5.00 12.00
❑ G4 Chief Miles O'Brien 5.00 12.00
❑ G5 Lt. Commander Jadzia Dax 5.00 12.00

❑ G6 Dr. Julian Bashir 5.00 12.00
❑ G7 Jake Sisko 5.00 12.00
❑ G8 Constable Odo 5.00 12.00
❑ G9 Quark 5.00 12.00
❑ G10 Ensign Ezri Dax 5.00 12.00

2003 Complete Star Trek Deep Space Nine Ships of the Dominion War

COMPLETE SET (9) 2.50 6.00
STATED ODDS 1:8

❑ S1 Deep Space Nine .40 1.00
❑ S2 U.S.S. Defiant .40 1.00
❑ S3 Runabout .40 1.00
❑ S4 Jem'Hadar Attack Ship .40 1.00
❑ S5 Jem'Hadar Battleship .40 1.00
❑ S6 Cardassian Warship .40 1.00
❑ S7 Klingon Bird of Prey .40 1.00
❑ S8 Romulan Warbird .40 1.00
❑ S9 Federation Galaxy Class Starship .40 1.00

2003 Daredevil Movie

COMPLETE SET (72) 6.00 15.00
DD COSTUME STATED ODDS 1:72

❑ 1 Justice Is Blind .15 .40
❑ 2 Matt Murdock .15 .40
❑ 3 Daredevil .15 .40
❑ 4 Elecktra Natchios .15 .40
❑ 5 Wilson Fisk .15 .40
The Kingpin
❑ 6 Bullseye .15 .40
❑ 7 Franklin Foggy Nelson .15 .40
❑ 8 Ben Urich .15 .40
❑ 9 Nikolas Natchios .15 .40
❑ 10 Wesley Welch .15 .40
❑ 11 Jack The Devil Murdock .15 .40
❑ 12 Young Matt .15 .40
❑ 13 The Fallen Angel .15 .40
❑ 14 Night of Redemption .15 .40
❑ 15 Sins of the Father .15 .40
❑ 16 The Comeback Kids .15 .40
❑ 17 King of the Ring .15 .40
❑ 18 The Price of Glory .15 .40
❑ 19 Jack Murdock...Slain .15 .40
❑ 20 Justice for All? .15 .40
❑ 21 The Night Stalker .15 .40
❑ 22 Flight of the Avenger .15 .40
❑ 23 All in a Knight's Work .15 .40
❑ 24 Hell's Avenger .15 .40
❑ 25 Justice Finds Quesada .15 .40
❑ 26 Daredevil Rules! .15 .40
❑ 27 The Emperor of Crime .15 .40
❑ 28 Partners in Justice .15 .40
❑ 29 Meeting Their Match .15 .40
❑ 30 Kindred Combatants .15 .40
❑ 31 A Very Special Assassin .15 .40
❑ 32 Defending Jackson .15 .40
❑ 33 Two of a Kind .15 .40
❑ 34 In High Society .15 .40
❑ 35 Dancing with the Devil .15 .40
❑ 36 Fisk and His Flunkies .15 .40
❑ 37 A Skill To Die For .15 .40
❑ 38 Murder on Wheels .15 .40
❑ 39 Confronting Bullseye .15 .40
❑ 40 Mayhem in the Streets .15 .40
❑ 41 Race with the Devil .15 .40
❑ 42 Life, Death...and Revenge .15 .40
❑ 43 Wrongly Accused .15 .40
❑ 44 Alliance of Evil .15 .40
❑ 45 The Mourners .15 .40
❑ 46 Training for Battle .15 .40
❑ 47 Urich's Discovery .15 .40
❑ 48 Dressed to Kill .15 .40
❑ 49 Lovers and Other Killers .15 .40
❑ 50 Hell Hath No Fury .15 .40
❑ 51 The Devil to Pay .15 .40
❑ 52 Elektra...Assassin? .15 .40
❑ 53 Against a Female Fury .15 .40
❑ 54 Sympathy for the Devil .15 .40
❑ 55 Bullseye Reveals Himself .15 .40
❑ 56 You Killed My Father .15 .40
❑ 57 Bullseye Never Misses .15 .40
❑ 58 The Death of Elektra .15 .40
❑ 59 Dark Retribution .15 .40
❑ 60 Dealing with the Devil .15 .40
❑ 61 The Kingpin Toppled .15 .40
❑ 62 Elektra Eternal .15 .40
❑ 63 Heroes without Fear .15 .40
❑ 64 Bringing Daredevil to Life .15 .40
❑ 65 New York.. Marvel-Style .15 .40
❑ 66 Directing Urban Warriors .15 .40
❑ 67 The Devil's Next Move .15 .40
❑ 68 When Superheroes Collide .15 .40
❑ 69 The Marvel Age of Movies .15 .40
❑ 70 Action and Empathy .15 .40
❑ 71 The Devil's in the Details .15 .40
❑ 72 Checklist .15 .40
❑ NNO Daredevil Costume MEM 10.00 25.00

2003 Daredevil Movie Autographs

STATED ODDS 1:72
GARNER AUTO ISSUED AS DEALER CONTEST EXCLUSIVE

❑ 1 Ben Affleck 250.00 350.00
❑ 2 Coolio 8.00 20.00
❑ 3 Joe Pantoliano 8.00 20.00
❑ 4 Mark Steven Johnson 6.00 15.00
❑ 5 Scott Terra 8.00 20.00
❑ 6 Jennifer Garner/50* 300.00 500.00

2003 Enterprise Season Two

COMPLETE SET (81) 4.00 10.00
C1 ISSUED IN COLLECTORS ALBUM
T1 ISSUED AS MULTI-CASE INCENTIVE

❑ 82 Cast Photo .10 .30
(Checklist 1
❑ 83 Cast Photo .10 .30
(Checklist 2
❑ 84 Cast Photo .10 .30
(Checklist 3
❑ 85 Shockwave, Part 2 .10 .30
❑ 86 Shockwave, Part 2 .10 .30
❑ 87 Shockwave, Part 2 .10 .30
❑ 88 Carbon Creek .10 .30
❑ 89 Carbon Creek .10 .30
❑ 90 Carbon Creek .10 .30
❑ 91 Minefield .10 .30
❑ 92 Minefield .10 .30
❑ 93 Minefield .10 .30
❑ 94 Dead Stop .10 .30
❑ 95 Dead Stop .10 .30
❑ 96 Dead Stop .10 .30
❑ 97 A Night in Sickbay .10 .30
❑ 98 A Night in Sickbay .10 .30
❑ 99 A Night in Sickbay .10 .30
❑ 100 Marauders .10 .30
❑ 101 Marauders .10 .30
❑ 102 Marauders .10 .30
❑ 103 The Seventh .10 .30
❑ 104 The Seventh .10 .30
❑ 105 The Seventh .10 .30
❑ 106 The Communicator .10 .30
❑ 107 The Communicator .10 .30
❑ 108 The Communicator .10 .30
❑ 109 Singularity .10 .30
❑ 110 Singularity .10 .30
❑ 111 Singularity .10 .30
❑ 112 Vanishing Point .10 .30
❑ 113 Vanishing Point .10 .30
❑ 114 Vanishing Point .10 .30
❑ 115 Precious Cargo .10 .30
❑ 116 Precious Cargo .10 .30
❑ 117 Precious Cargo .10 .30
❑ 118 The Catwalk .10 .30
❑ 119 The Catwalk .10 .30
❑ 120 The Catwalk .10 .30
❑ 121 Dawn .10 .30
❑ 122 Dawn .10 .30
❑ 123 Dawn .10 .30
❑ 124 Stigma .10 .30
❑ 125 Stigma .10 .30
❑ 126 Stigma .10 .30
❑ 127 Cease Fire .10 .30
❑ 128 Cease Fire .10 .30
❑ 129 Cease Fire .10 .30
❑ 130 Future Tense .10 .30
❑ 131 Future Tense .10 .30
❑ 132 Future Tense .10 .30
❑ 133 Canamar .10 .30
❑ 134 Canamar .10 .30
❑ 135 Canamar .10 .30
❑ 136 The Crossing .10 .30
❑ 137 The Crossing .10 .30
❑ 138 The Crossing .10 .30
❑ 139 Judgement .10 .30
❑ 140 Judgement .10 .30
❑ 141 Judgement .10 .30
❑ 142 Horizon .10 .30
❑ 143 Horizon .10 .30
❑ 144 Horizon .10 .30
❑ 145 The Breach .10 .30
❑ 146 The Breach .10 .30
❑ 147 The Breach .10 .30
❑ 148 Cogenitor .10 .30
❑ 149 Cogenitor .10 .30
❑ 150 Cogenitor .10 .30
❑ 151 Regeneration .10 .30
❑ 152 Regeneration .10 .30
❑ 153 Regeneration .10 .30
❑ 154 First Flight .10 .30
❑ 155 First Flight .10 .30
❑ 156 First Flight .10 .30
❑ 157 Bounty .10 .30
❑ 158 Bounty .10 .30
❑ 159 Bounty .10 .30
❑ 160 The Expanse: Part 11 .10 .30
❑ 161 The Expanse: Part 11 .10 .30
❑ 162 The Expanse: Part 11 .10 .30
❑ C1 T'Pol MEM 15.00 30.00
(issued in collectors album)
❑ T1 T'Pol/333
(issued as multi-case incentive)

2003 Enterprise Season Two Silver

COMPLETE SET (81) 20.00 40.00
*SILVER: 1.5X TO 4X BASIC CARDS
STATED ODDS ONE PER PACK

2003 Enterprise Season Two 22nd Century Vessels

COMPLETE SET (12) 8.00 20.00
STATED ODDS 1:5

❑ V1 Tellarite Ship .75 2.00
❑ V2 Automated Space Station .75 2.00
❑ V3 Romulan Ship .75 2.00
❑ V4 Vissian Stratopod .75 2.00
❑ V5 Alien Probe .75 2.00
❑ V6 Whisp Alien Ship .75 2.00
❑ V7 NX Beta Test Ship .75 2.00
❑ V8 Borg Modified Transport .75 2.00
❑ V9 Arkonian Ship .75 2.00
❑ V10 Retellian Cargo ship .75 2.00
❑ V11 Enolian Prison Transport .75 2.00
❑ V12 Takret Warship .75 2.00

2003 Enterprise Season Two Autographs

STATED ODDS TWO PER BOX
L (LIMITED): 300-500 COPIES
VL (VERY LIMITED): 200-300 COPIES

❑ A4 Anthony Montgomery L 30.00 60.00
❑ A5 Linda Park L 30.00 60.00
❑ A6 Scott Bakula VL 100.00 200.00
❑ A8 J.G. Hertzler 6.00 15.00
❑ A9 D.C. Douglas 6.00 15.00
❑ A10 Zach Grenier 6.00 15.00
❑ A11 Robert O'Reilly 6.00 15.00
❑ A12 Gregg Henry 6.00 15.00
❑ A13 Daniel Riordan L 12.50 25.00
❑ A14 Brigid Brannagh 30.00 60.00
❑ A15 Ed O'Ross L 8.00 20.00
❑ A16 Suzie Plakson 6.00 15.00
❑ A17 Kellie Waymire 8.00 20.00
❑ A18 Matt Winston L 15.00 30.00
❑ A19 Keone Young 6.00 15.00
❑ A20 Bruce Davison L 15.00 30.00
❑ A21 Aaron Lusting 6.00 15.00
❑ A22 Padma Lakshmi 6.00 15.00
❑ AA14 Jeffrey Combs VL 40.00 80.00

2003 Enterprise Season Two Enterprise Gallery

COMPLETE SET (7) 30.00 60.00
STATED ODDS 1:40

❑ G1 Captain Archer 5.00 12.00
❑ G2 Sub-Commander T'Pol 5.00 12.00
❑ G3 Chief Engineer Tucker 5.00 12.00
❑ G4 Lieutenant Reed 5.00 12.00
❑ G5 Ensign Mayweather 5.00 12.00
❑ G6 Ensign Sato 5.00 12.00
❑ G7 Doctor Phlox 5.00 12.00

2003 Enterprise Season Two First Contact

COMPLETE SET (9) 10.00 25.00
STATED ODDS 1:10

❑ F13 Kreetassans 1.25 3.00
❑ F14 Quonset 1.25 3.00
❑ F15 Retellian 1.25 3.00
❑ F16 Takret 1.25 3.00
❑ F17 Arkonian 1.25 3.00
❑ F18 Enolian 1.25 3.00
❑ F19 Vissian 1.25 3.00
❑ F20 Borg 1.25 3.00
❑ F21 Tellarite 1.25 3.00

2003 Enterprise Season Two In Motion Case Toppers

COMPLETE SET (2) 10.00 25.00
STATED ODDS ONE SET PER CASE

❑ E1 Enterprise 6.00 15.00
❑ E2 T'Pol 6.00 15.00

2003 Enterprise Season Two Promos

COMPLETE SET (5) 4.00 10.00

❑ P1 Tucker 1.00 2.50
T'Pol/Archer/Reed/ (General Distribution)
❑ P2 Klingons/ (NSU Magazine) 1.00 2.50
❑ P3 T'Pol/ (Binder Exclusive) 1.00 2.50
❑ C2003 Borgs/ (Various Fall 2003 Conventions)1.50 4.00
❑ MNCE2003 Mayweather 1.50 4.00
Archer/ (Mid-West NonSport Card Expo)

2003 Fantasy Worlds of Irwin Allen

COMPLETE SET (100) 8.00 20.00

❑ 1 Title Card .20 .50
❑ 2 Land of the Giants .20 .50
❑ 3 Land of the Giants .20 .50
❑ 4 Land of the Giants .20 .50
❑ 5 Land of the Giants .20 .50
❑ 6 Land of the Giants .20 .50
❑ 7 Land of the Giants .20 .50
❑ 8 Land of the Giants .20 .50
❑ 9 Land of the Giants .20 .50
❑ 10 Land of the Giants .20 .50
❑ 11 Land of the Giants .20 .50
❑ 12 Land of the Giants .20 .50
❑ 13 Land of the Giants .20 .50
❑ 14 Land of the Giants .20 .50
❑ 15 Land of the Giants .20 .50
❑ 16 Land of the Giants .20 .50
❑ 17 Land of the Giants .20 .50
❑ 18 Land of the Giants .20 .50
❑ 19 Land of the Giants .20 .50
❑ 20 Land of the Giants .20 .50
❑ 21 Land of the Giants .20 .50
❑ 22 Land of the Giants .20 .50
❑ 23 Land of the Giants .20 .50
❑ 24 Land of the Giants .20 .50
❑ 25 Land of the Giants .20 .50
❑ 26 Lost In Space .20 .50
❑ 27 Lost In Space .20 .50
❑ 28 Lost In Space .20 .50
❑ 29 Lost In Space .20 .50
❑ 30 Lost In Space .20 .50
❑ 31 Lost In Space .20 .50
❑ 32 Lost In Space .20 .50
❑ 33 Lost In Space .20 .50
❑ 34 Lost In Space .20 .50
❑ 35 Lost In Space .20 .50
❑ 36 Lost In Space .20 .50
❑ 37 Lost In Space .20 .50
❑ 38 Lost In Space .20 .50
❑ 39 Lost In Space .20 .50
❑ 40 Lost In Space .20 .50
❑ 41 Lost In Space .20 .50
❑ 42 Lost In Space .20 .50
❑ 43 Lost In Space .20 .50
❑ 44 Lost In Space .20 .50
❑ 45 Lost In Space .20 .50
❑ 46 Lost In Space .20 .50
❑ 47 Lost In Space .20 .50
❑ 48 Lost In Space .20 .50
❑ 49 Lost In Space .20 .50
❑ 50 Time Tunnel .20 .50
❑ 51 Time Tunnel .20 .50
❑ 52 Time Tunnel .20 .50
❑ 53 Time Tunnel .20 .50
❑ 54 Time Tunnel .20 .50
❑ 55 Time Tunnel .20 .50
❑ 56 Time Tunnel .20 .50
❑ 57 Time Tunnel .20 .50
❑ 58 Time Tunnel .20 .50
❑ 59 Time Tunnel .20 .50
❑ 60 Time Tunnel .20 .50
❑ 61 Time Tunnel .20 .50
❑ 62 Time Tunnel .20 .50
❑ 63 Time Tunnel .20 .50
❑ 64 Time Tunnel .20 .50
❑ 65 Time Tunnel .20 .50
❑ 66 Time Tunnel .20 .50
❑ 67 Time Tunnel .20 .50
❑ 68 Time Tunnel .20 .50
❑ 69 Time Tunnel .20 .50
❑ 70 Time Tunnel .20 .50
❑ 71 Time Tunnel .20 .50
❑ 72 Time Tunnel .20 .50
❑ 73 Time Tunnel .20 .50
❑ 74 Voyage to the Bottom of the Sea .20 .50
❑ 75 Voyage to the Bottom of the Sea .20 .50
❑ 76 Voyage to the Bottom of the Sea .20 .50
❑ 77 Voyage to the Bottom of the Sea .20 .50
❑ 78 Voyage to the Bottom of the Sea .20 .50
❑ 79 Voyage to the Bottom of the Sea .20 .50
❑ 80 Voyage to the Bottom of the Sea .20 .50
❑ 81 Voyage to the Bottom of the Sea .20 .50
❑ 82 Voyage to the Bottom of the Sea .20 .50
❑ 83 Voyage to the Bottom of the Sea .20 .50
❑ 84 Voyage to the Bottom of the Sea .20 .50
❑ 85 Voyage to the Bottom of the Sea .20 .50
❑ 86 Voyage to the Bottom of the Sea .20 .50
❑ 87 Voyage to the Bottom of the Sea .20 .50
❑ 88 Voyage to the Bottom of the Sea .20 .50
❑ 89 Voyage to the Bottom of the Sea .20 .50
❑ 90 Voyage to the Bottom of the Sea .20 .50
❑ 91 Voyage to the Bottom of the Sea .20 .50
❑ 92 Voyage to the Bottom of the Sea .20 .50
❑ 93 Voyage to the Bottom of the Sea .20 .50
❑ 94 Voyage to the Bottom of the Sea .20 .50
❑ 95 Voyage to the Bottom of the Sea .20 .50
❑ 96 Voyage to the Bottom of the Sea .20 .50
❑ 97 Voyage to the Bottom of the Sea .20 .50
❑ 98 Checklist 1 .20 .50
❑ 99 Checklist 2 .20 .50
❑ 100 Checklist 3 .20 .50
❑ C1 Captain Lee Crane COSTUME 10.00 25.00
(issued as album exclusive)

2003 Fantasy Worlds of Irwin Allen Autographs

THREE AUTOS PER BOX

❑ A1 Bill Mumy 12.00 30.00
as Will Robinson L
❑ A2 Heather Young 12.00 30.00
as Betty Hamilton
❑ A3 Lee Meriwether 15.00 40.00
as Dr. Ann MacGregor
❑ A4 David Hedison 12.00 30.00
as Captain Lee Crane
❑ A5 Bob May 25.00 50.00
as The Robot (issued as case topper)
❑ A6 Don Marshall 12.00 30.00
as Dan Erickson
❑ A7 Marta Kristen 15.00 40.00
as Judy Robinson L
❑ A8 Robert Colbert 12.00 30.00
as Dr. Douglas Phillips
❑ A9 Deanna Lund 15.00 40.00
as Valerie Scott L
❑ A10 Angela Cartwright 25.00 50.00
as Penny Robinson
❑ A11 Don Matheson 12.00 30.00
as Mark Wilson
❑ A12 Mark Goddard 12.00 30.00
as Major Don West
❑ A13 Gary Conway 12.00 30.00
as Captain Steve Burton
❑ A14 Stefan Arngrim 12.00 30.00
as Barry Lockridge
❑ A15 Dick Tufeld 12.00 30.00
as The Voice of Robot B9
❑ A17 June Lockhart 25.00 50.00
as Maureen Robinson

2003 Fantasy Worlds of Irwin Allen Behind the Scenes

COMPLETE SET (9)
STATED ODDS 1:40

❑ B1 Behind-the-Scenes with Irwin Allen 3.00 8.00
❑ B2 Behind-the-Scenes with Irwin Allen 3.00 8.00
❑ B3 Behind-the-Scenes with Irwin Allen 3.00 8.00
❑ B4 Behind-the-Scenes with Irwin Allen 3.00 8.00
❑ B5 Behind-the-Scenes with Irwin Allen 3.00 8.00
❑ B6 Behind-the-Scenes with Irwin Allen 3.00 8.00
❑ B7 Behind-the-Scenes with Irwin Allen 3.00 8.00
❑ B8 Behind-the-Scenes with Irwin Allen 3.00 8.00
❑ B9 Behind-the-Scenes with Irwin Allen 3.00 8.00

2003 Fantasy Worlds of Irwin Allen Gallery

COMPLETE SET (4)
STATED ODDS 1:120

❑ G1 Voyage to the Bottom of the Sea 12.00 30.00
❑ G2 Lost In Space 12.00 30.00
❑ G3 Time Tunnel 12.00 30.00
❑ G4 Land of the Giants 12.00 30.00

2003 Fantasy Worlds of Irwin Allen Promos

❑ P1 Holiday 2003 .75 2.00
(General Distribution)
❑ P2 Holiday 2003 2.00 5.00
(NSU Magazine)
❑ P3 Album Exclusive 4.00 10.00

2003 Fantasy Worlds of Irwin Allen The Openings

COMPLETE SET (12) 8.00 20.00
STATED ODDS 1:8

❑ L1 Land of the Giants 1.25 3.00
❑ L2 Land of the Giants 1.25 3.00
❑ L3 Land of the Giants 1.25 3.00
❑ L4 Lost In Space 1.25 3.00
❑ L5 Lost In Space 1.25 3.00
❑ L6 Lost In Space 1.25 3.00
❑ L7 Time Tunnel 1.25 3.00
❑ L8 Time Tunnel 1.25 3.00
❑ L9 Time Tunnel 1.25 3.00
❑ L10 Voyage to the Bottom of the Sea 1.25 3.00
❑ L11 Voyage to the Bottom of the Sea 1.25 3.00
❑ L12 Voyage to the Bottom of the Sea 1.25 3.00

2003 Farscape Season Four

COMPLETE SET (72) 5.00 12.00
CZOP SKETCH ISSUED AS CASE TOPPER

❑ 217 Cast Montage .15 .40
❑ 218 Cast Montage .15 .40
❑ 219 Cast Montage .15 .40
❑ 220 Crichton Kicks .15 .40
❑ 221 Crichton Kicks .15 .40
❑ 222 Crichton Kicks .15 .40
❑ 223 What Was Lost Part 1: Sacrifice .15 .40
❑ 224 What Was Lost Part 1: Sacrifice .15 .40
❑ 225 What Was Lost Part 1: Sacrifice .15 .40
❑ 226 What Was Lost Part 2: Resurrection .15 .40
❑ 227 What Was Lost Part 2: Resurrection .15 .40
❑ 228 What Was Lost Part 2: Resurrection .15 .40
❑ 229 Lava's A Many Splendored Thing .15 .40
❑ 230 Lava's A Many Splendored Thing .15 .40
❑ 231 Lava's A Many Splendored Thing .15 .40
❑ 232 Promises .15 .40
❑ 233 Promises .15 .40
❑ 234 Promises .15 .40
❑ 235 Natural Election .15 .40
❑ 236 Natural Election .15 .40
❑ 237 Natural Election .15 .40
❑ 238 John Quixote .15 .40
❑ 239 John Quixote .15 .40
❑ 240 John Quixote .15 .40
❑ 241 I Shrink, Therefore I Am .15 .40
❑ 242 I Shrink, Therefore I Am .15 .40
❑ 243 I Shrink, Therefore I Am .15 .40
❑ 244 A Perfect Murder .15 .40
❑ 245 A Perfect Murder .15 .40
❑ 246 A Perfect Murder .15 .40
❑ 247 Coup By Clam .15 .40
❑ 248 Coup By Clam .15 .40
❑ 249 Coup By Clam .15 .40
❑ 250 Unrealized Reality .15 .40
❑ 251 Unrealized Reality .15 .40
❑ 252 Unrealized Reality .15 .40
❑ 253 Kansas .15 .40
❑ 254 Kansas .15 .40
❑ 255 Kansas .15 .40
❑ 256 Terra Firma .15 .40
❑ 257 Terra Firma .15 .40
❑ 258 Terra Firma .15 .40
❑ 259 Twice Shy .15 .40
❑ 260 Twice Shy .15 .40
❑ 261 Twice Shy .15 .40
❑ 262 Mental As Anything .15 .40
❑ 263 Mental As Anything .15 .40
❑ 264 Mental As Anything .15 .40
❑ 265 Bringing Home The Beacon .15 .40
❑ 266 Bringing Home The Beacon .15 .40
❑ 267 Bringing Home The Beacon .15 .40
❑ 268 A Constellation Of Doubt .15 .40
❑ 269 A Constellation Of Doubt .15 .40
❑ 270 A Constellation Of Doubt .15 .40
❑ 271 Prayer .15 .40
❑ 272 Prayer .15 .40
❑ 273 Prayer .15 .40
❑ 274 We're So Screwed Part 1: Fetal Attraction .15 .40
❑ 275 We're So Screwed Part 1: Fetal Attraction .15 .40
❑ 276 We're So Screwed Part 1: Fetal Attraction .15 .40
❑ 277 We're So Screwed Part 2: Hot To Katratz! .15 .40
❑ 278 We're So Screwed Part 2: Hot To Katratz! .15 .40
❑ 279 We're So Screwed Part 2: Hot To Katratz! .15 .40
❑ 280 We're So Screwed Part 3: La Bomba .15 .40
❑ 281 We're So Screwed Part 3: La Bomba .15 .40
❑ 282 We're So Screwed Part 3: La Bomba .15 .40
❑ 283 Bad Timing .15 .40
❑ 284 Bad Timing .15 .40
❑ 285 Bad Timing .15 .40
❑ 286 Checklist 1 .15 .40
❑ 287 Checklist 2 .15 .40
❑ 288 Checklist 3 .15 .40
❑ JC John Czop (Sikozu) SKETCH/ (issued as case topper)

2003 Farscape Season Four Behind the Scenes

COMPLETE SET (22) 6.00 15.00
STATED ODDS 1:5

❑ BTS45 Crichton Kicks .75 2.00
❑ BTS46 What Was Lost Part 1: Sacrifice .75 2.00
❑ BTS47 What Was Lost Part 2: Resurrection .75 2.00
❑ BTS48 Lava's A Many Splendored Thing .75 2.00
❑ BTS49 Promises .75 2.00
❑ BTS50 Natural Election .75 2.00
❑ BTS51 John Quixote .75 2.00
❑ BTS52 I Shrink, Therefore I Am .75 2.00
❑ BTS53 A Perfect Murder .75 2.00
❑ BTS54 Coup By Clam .75 2.00
❑ BTS55 Unrealized Reality .75 2.00
❑ BTS56 Kansas .75 2.00
❑ BTS57 Terra Firma .75 2.00
❑ BTS58 Twice Shy .75 2.00
❑ BTS59 Mental As Anything .75 2.00
❑ BTS60 Bringing Home The Beacon .75 2.00
❑ BTS61 A Constellation Of Doubt .75 2.00
❑ BTS62 Prayer .75 2.00
❑ BTS63 We're So Screwed Part 1: Fetal Attraction.75 2.00
❑ BTS64 We're So Screwed Part 2: Hot To Katratz!.75 2.00
❑ BTS65 We're So Screwed Part 3: La Bomba .75 2.00
❑ BTS66 Bad Timing .75 2.00

2003 Farscape Season Four Farscape ArtiFEX

COMPLETE SET (9) 7.50 20.00
STATED ODDS 1:10
HEY AUTO STATED ODDS 1:480

❑ X1 John Crichton 1.25 3.00
❑ X2 Aeryn Sun 1.25 3.00
❑ X3 D'Argo 1.25 3.00
❑ X4 Chiana 1.25 3.00
❑ X5 Captain Crais 1.25 3.00
❑ X6 Zhaan 1.25 3.00
❑ X7 Scorpius 1.25 3.00
❑ X8 Grayza 1.25 3.00
❑ X9 Sikozu 1.25 3.00
❑ XH6 Virginia Hey AU (Zhaan) 25.00 50.00

2003 Farscape Season Four Farscape Autographs

STATED ODDS TWO PER BOX

❑ A22 Raelee Hill 8.00 20.00
❑ A23 Melissa Jaffer 8.00 20.00
❑ A24 Rebecca Riggs 8.00 20.00
❑ A25 David Franklin 8.00 20.00
❑ A26 Lani Tupu 8.00 20.00
❑ A27 Rowan Woods 8.00 20.00
❑ A28 Elizabeth Alexander 8.00 20.00
❑ A29 Murray Bartlett 8.00 20.00
❑ A30 Bruce Spence 8.00 20.00
❑ A31 John Bach 8.00 20.00
❑ A32 Wayne Pygram 8.00 20.00
❑ A33 Gigi Edgley 15.00 30.00
❑ A34 Kent McCord 25.00 50.00

2003 Farscape Season Four Farscape Gallery

COMPLETE SET (8) 40.00 80.00
STATED ODDS 1:40

❑ G1 John Crichton 5.00 12.00
❑ G2 Aeryn Sun 5.00 12.00
❑ G3 D'Argo 5.00 12.00
❑ G4 Chiana 5.00 12.00
❑ G5 Captain Crais 5.00 12.00
❑ G6 Scorpius 5.00 12.00
❑ G7 Grayza 5.00 12.00
❑ G8 Sikozu 5.00 12.00

2003 Farscape Season Four From The Archives Costumes

STATED ODDS ONE PER BOX
C21 ISSUED IN COLLECTORS ALBUM

❑ C16 Jool 7.50 20.00
❑ C17 Jothee 7.50 20.00
❑ C18 Noranti 6.00 15.00
❑ C19 Lt. Braca 6.00 15.00
❑ C20 Grayza 6.00 15.00
❑ C21 Moya/ (issued in collectors album) 6.00 15.00

2003 Farscape Season Four Promos

COMPLETE SET (3) 2.00 5.00

❑ P1 Group shot/ (General Distribution) 1.00 2.50
❑ P2 Aeryn 1.00 2.50
Chiana/John/Sikozu/ (Non Sport Update)
❑ P3 Aeryn 1.50 4.00
John/ (Binder Exclusive)

2003 Farscape Season Four The Quotable Farscape

COMPLETE SET (22) 10.00 25.00
STATED ODDS 1:5

❑ Q45 Crichton Kicks .75 2.00
❑ Q46 What Was Lost Part 1: Sacrifice .75 2.00
❑ Q47 What Was Lost Part 2: Resurrection .75 2.00
❑ Q48 Lava's A Many Splendored Thing .75 2.00
❑ Q49 Promises .75 2.00
❑ Q50 Natural Election .75 2.00
❑ Q51 John Quixote .75 2.00

MODERN ERA NON-SPORTS

❑ Q52 I Shrink, Therefore I Am .75 2.00
❑ Q53 A Perfect Murder .75 2.00
❑ Q54 Coup By Clam .75 2.00
❑ Q55 Unrealized Reality .75 2.00
❑ Q56 Kansas .75 2.00
❑ Q57 Terra Firma .75 2.00
❑ Q58 Twice Shy .75 2.00
❑ Q59 Mental As Anything .75 2.00
❑ Q60 Bringing Home The Beacon .75 2.00
❑ Q61 A Constellation Of Doubt .75 2.00
❑ Q62 Prayer .75 2.00
❑ Q63 We're So Screwed Part 1: Fetal Attraction .75 2.00
❑ Q64 We're So Screwed Part 2: Hot To Katratzi .75 2.00
❑ Q65 We're So Screwed Part 3: La Bomba .75 2.00
❑ Q66 Bad Timing .75 2.00

2003 Garbage Pail Kids All New Series 1

COMPLETE SET (80) 6.00 15.00
❑ 1a Bone Head Ed .10 .25
❑ 1b Neanderthal Nathan .10 .25
❑ 2a1 On Fire Mariah (Small Sticker checklist) .10 .25
❑ 2a2 On Fire Mariah (Gold Sticker checklist) .10 .25
❑ 2b Abby Birthday .10 .25
❑ 3a Bustin' Justin .10 .25
❑ 3b Wesley Wormhole .10 .25
❑ 4a Cootie Cody .10 .25
❑ 4b Buggin' Brandon .10 .25
❑ 5a Crazy Casey .10 .25
❑ 5b1 Ridiculous Nicholas (Big Sticker checklist) .10 .25
❑ 5b2 Ridiculous Nicholas (Sticker checklist) .10 .25
❑ 6a Seth Pool .10 .25
❑ 6b Canned Kayla .10 .25
❑ 7a Forged George .10 .25
❑ 7b Shane Pain .10 .25
❑ 8a Derailed Derek .10 .25
❑ 8b Train Wreck Trevor .10 .25
❑ 9a Cheesy Charlie .10 .25
❑ 9b Pizza Face Chase .10 .25
❑ 10a Shovelin' Shannon .10 .25
❑ 10b Stuffin' Stephanie .10 .25
❑ 11a1 Jarred Jared (Small Sticker checklist) .10 .25
❑ 11a2 Jarred Jared (Gold Sticker checklist) .10 .25
❑ 11b Carly Cue .10 .25
❑ 12a Kyle Tile .10 .25
❑ 12b1 Bathroom Tyler (Big Sticker checklist) .10 .25
❑ 12b2 Bathroom Tyler (Sticker checklist) .10 .25
❑ 13a Leggy Lauren .10 .25
❑ 13b Victoria's Secret .10 .25
❑ 14a1 Little Barfin' Anna (Small Sticker checklist) .10 .25
❑ 14a2 Little Barfin' Anna (Gold Sticker checklist) .10 .25
❑ 14b Brittney Spews .10 .25
❑ 15a Bill Board .10 .25
❑ 15b Blinkin' Blake .10 .25
❑ 16a Photo Matt .10 .25
❑ 16b Vic Pic .10 .25
❑ 17a Monstrous Monica .10 .25
❑ 17b Colossal Cole .10 .25
❑ 18a Rodent Rob .10 .25
❑ 18b Pat Rat .10 .25
❑ 19a Shelled Michelle .10 .25
❑ 19b Lobster Shelby .10 .25
❑ 20a Sprayed Ray .10 .25
❑ 20b Alex Terminated .10 .25
❑ 21a Boardin' Jordan .10 .25
❑ 21b Rad Brad .10 .25
❑ 22a Gross Greg .10 .25
❑ 22b1 BMX Ben (Big Sticker checklist) .10 .25
❑ 22b2 BMX Ben (Sticker checklist) .10 .25
❑ 23a Sushi Susie .10 .25
❑ 23b Yuckie Tori .10 .25
❑ 24a Gutsy Gabriel .10 .25
❑ 24b Disgustin' Dustin .10 .25
❑ 25a Drew Tattoo .10 .25
❑ 25b Marked Mark .10 .25
❑ 26a Peein' Ian .10 .25
❑ 26b Jacob's Bladder .10 .25
❑ 27a Mini Vinnie .10 .25
❑ 27b Punchy Paul .10 .25
❑ 28a Duped David .10 .25
❑ 28b Twice Bryce .10 .25
❑ 29a Vendin' Brendan .10 .25
❑ 29b Cheap Chad .10 .25
❑ 30a Freewheelin' Frank .10 .25
❑ 30b Dashboard Dennis .10 .25
❑ 31a Fartin' Martin .10 .25
❑ 31b Rewin' Evan .10 .25
❑ 32a Zitty Whitney .10 .25
❑ 32b Juicy Jess .10 .25
❑ 33a Phat Phil .10 .25
❑ 33b Ill Will .10 .25
❑ 34a Metallic Alec .10 .25
❑ 34b Pierced Pete .10 .25
❑ 35a Rootin' Ruben .10 .25
❑ 35b1 Booger Brian (Big Sticker checklist) .10 .25
❑ 35b2 Booger Brian (Sticker checklist) .10 .25
❑ 36a Messy Jesse .10 .25
❑ 36b Rocky Ricardo .10 .25
❑ 37a Yecchie Becky .10 .25
❑ 37b Dizzy Lizzy .10 .25
❑ 38a Lethal Ethan .10 .25
❑ 38b Troy Destroy .10 .25
❑ 39a Colin 911 .10 .25
❑ 39b1 Andrew Spew (Small Sticker checklist) .10 .25
❑ 39b2 Andrew Spew (Gold Sticker checklist) .10 .25
❑ 40a Harry Potty .10 .25
❑ 40b Magic Max .10 .25

2003 Garbage Pail Kids All New Series 1 Foil Silver Glossy Back

COMPLETE SET (50) 40.00 80.00
STATED ODDS ONE PER FIRST PRINTING PACK
❑ 1a Adam Bomb 1.00 2.50
❑ 1b Blasted Billy 1.00 2.50
❑ 2a Bony Joanie 1.00 2.50
❑ 2b Thin Lynne 1.00 2.50
❑ 3a Bony Tony 1.00 2.50
❑ 3b Unzipped Zack 1.00 2.50
❑ 4a Brainy Janey 1.00 2.50
❑ 4b Jenny Genius 1.00 2.50
❑ 5a Corroded Carl 1.00 2.50
❑ 5b Crater Chris 1.00 2.50
❑ 6a Dead Ted 1.00 2.50
❑ 6b Jay Decay 1.00 2.50
❑ 7a Double Heather 1.00 2.50
❑ 7b Schizo Fran 1.00 2.50
❑ 8a Drippy Dan 1.00 2.50
❑ 8b Leaky Lou 1.00 2.50
❑ 9a Explorin' Norman 1.00 2.50
❑ 9b Drillin' Dylan 1.00 2.50
❑ 10a Ghastly Ashley 1.00 2.50
❑ 10b Acne Amy 1.00 2.50
❑ 11a Gore May 1.00 2.50
❑ 11b Connie Sewer 1.00 2.50
❑ 12a Jenny Jelly 1.00 2.50
❑ 12b Sarah Slime 1.00 2.50
❑ 13a Leaky Lindsay 1.00 2.50
❑ 13b Messy Tessie 1.00 2.50
❑ 14a Many Lenny 1.00 2.50
❑ 14b Lotta Carlotta 1.00 2.50
❑ 15a Michael Mutant 1.00 2.50
❑ 15b Zeke Freak 1.00 2.50
❑ 16a Patty Putty 1.00 2.50
❑ 16b Muggin' Megan 1.00 2.50
❑ 17a Potty Scotty 1.00 2.50
❑ 17b Jason Basin 1.00 2.50
❑ 18a Richie Retch 1.00 2.50
❑ 18b Luke Puke 1.00 2.50
❑ 19a Slimy Hymie 1.00 2.50
❑ 19b Crawlin' Rollin 1.00 2.50
❑ 20a Sy Clops 1.00 2.50
❑ 20b One-Eyed Jack 1.00 2.50
❑ 21a Toothie Ruthie 1.00 2.50
❑ 21b Dental Flossie 1.00 2.50
❑ 22a Trap Dora 1.00 2.50
❑ 22b Rear View Myra 1.00 2.50
❑ 23a Up Chuck 1.00 2.50
❑ 23b Heavin' Steven 1.00 2.50
❑ 24a Varicose Wayne 1.00 2.50
❑ 24b Elaine Vein 1.00 2.50
❑ 25a Windy Winston 1.00 2.50
❑ 25b Johnny One-Note 1.00 2.50

2003 Garbage Pail Kids All New Series 1 Foil Silver Matte Back

COMPLETE SET (50) 100.00 200.00
STATED ODDS ONE PER SECOND PRINTING PACK

2003 Garbage Pail Kids All New Series 1 Foil Gold

COMPLETE SET (50) 40.00 80.00
STATED ODDS ONE PER THIRD AND FOURTH PRINTING PACKS

2003 Garbage Pail Kids All New Series 1 Gum Wraps

COMPLETE SET (60) 5.00 12.00
STATED ODDS FOUR PER PACK
❑ 1a Adam Bomb .10 .25
❑ 1b Blasted Billy .10 .25
❑ 2a Bony Joanie .10 .25
❑ 2b Thin Lynne .10 .25
❑ 3a Bony Tony .10 .25
❑ 3b Unzipped Zack .10 .25
❑ 4a Brainy Janey .10 .25
❑ 4b Jenny Genius .10 .25
❑ 5a Corroded Carl .10 .25
❑ 5b Crater Chris .10 .25
❑ 6a Dead Ted .10 .25
❑ 6b Jay Decay .10 .25
❑ 7a Double Heather .10 .25
❑ 7b Schizo Fran .10 .25
❑ 8a Drippy Dan .10 .25
❑ 8b Leaky Lou .10 .25
❑ 9a Explorin' Norman .10 .25
❑ 9b Drillin' Dylan .10 .25
❑ 10a Ghastly Ashley .10 .25
❑ 10b Acne Amy .10 .25
❑ 11a Gore May .10 .25
❑ 11b Connie Sewer .10 .25
❑ 12a Jenny Jelly .10 .25
❑ 12b Sarah Slime .10 .25
❑ 13a Joe Blow .10 .25
❑ 13b Rod Wad .10 .25
❑ 14a Leaky Lindsay .10 .25
❑ 14b Messy Tessie .10 .25
❑ 15a Many Lenny .10 .25
❑ 15b Lotta Carlotta .10 .25
❑ 16a Michael Mutant .10 .25
❑ 16b Zeke Freak .10 .25
❑ 17a Over Flo .10 .25
❑ 17b Moist Joyce .10 .25
❑ 18a Patty Putty .10 .25
❑ 18b Muggin' Megan .10 .25
❑ 19a Potty Scotty .10 .25
❑ 19b Jason Basin .10 .25
❑ 20a Richie Retch .10 .25
❑ 20b Luke Puke .10 .25
❑ 21a Sally Suction .10 .25
❑ 21b Teethin' Trina .10 .25
❑ 22a Slimy Hymie .10 .25
❑ 22b Crawlin' Rollin .10 .25
❑ 23a Split Kit .10 .25
❑ 23b Mixed-Up Mitch .10 .25
❑ 24a Slarin' Darren .10 .25
❑ 24b Peepin' Tom .10 .25
❑ 25a Sy Clops .10 .25
❑ 25b One-Eyed Jack .10 .25
❑ 26a Toothie Ruthie .10 .25
❑ 26b Dental Flossie .10 .25
❑ 27a Trap Dora .10 .25
❑ 27b Rear View Myra .10 .25
❑ 28a Up Chuck .10 .25
❑ 28b Heavin' Steven .10 .25
❑ 29a Varicose Wayne .10 .25
❑ 29b Elaine Vein .10 .25
❑ 30a Windy Winston .10 .25
❑ 30b Johnny One-Note .10 .25

2003 James Bond Die Another Day Expansion

COMPLETE SET (19) 15.00 30.00
ANNOUNCED PRINT RUN 999 SETS
❑ 1 James Bond .75 2.00
❑ 2 James Bond .75 2.00
❑ 3 James Bond .75 2.00
❑ 4 Jinx .75 2.00
❑ 5 Jinx .75 2.00
❑ 6 Jinx .75 2.00
❑ 7 Zao .75 2.00
❑ 8 Zao .75 2.00
❑ 9 Miranda Frost .75 2.00
❑ 10 Miranda Frost .75 2.00
❑ 11 Gustav Graves .75 2.00
❑ 12 Gustav Graves .75 2.00
❑ 13 M .75 2.00
❑ 14 Q .75 2.00
❑ 15 Miss Moneypenny .75 2.00
❑ 16 Colonel Moon .75 2.00
❑ 17 Falco .75 2.00
❑ 18 Robinson .75 2.00
❑ AC2 Wetsuit

2003 Lara Croft Tomb Raider The Cradle of Life

COMPLETE SET (81) 5.00 12.00
❑ 1 Title Card .15 .40
❑ 2 Lara Croft .15 .40
❑ 3 Terry Sheridan .15 .40
❑ 4 Dr. Jonathan Reiss .15 .40
❑ 5 Hillary .15 .40
❑ 6 Bryce .15 .40
❑ 7 Sean .15 .40
❑ 8 Hosa Maasai .15 .40
❑ 9 Chen Lo .15 .40
❑ 10 Splashed! .15 .40
❑ 11 Lara On Board .15 .40
❑ 12 Salvaging The Past .15 .40
❑ 13 Diving Into Danger .15 .40
❑ 14 Toward The Sunken City .15 .40
❑ 15 Alexander's Great Prize .15 .40
❑ 16 Her Friends Massacred! .15 .40
❑ 17 Undersea Escape .15 .40
❑ 18 Rescuing Lara At Sea .15 .40
❑ 19 The Doctor's Mad Dream .15 .40
❑ 20 Conferring With Sean .15 .40
❑ 21 The Croft Workout .15 .40
❑ 22 Sticking It To Hillary .15 .40
❑ 23 A Call To Hosa .15 .40
❑ 24 Horsing Around .15 .40
❑ 25 A Mission For Mi6 .15 .40
❑ 26 One Man For The Job .15 .40
❑ 27 Kindred Spirits .15 .40
❑ 28 The Mission Begins .15 .40
❑ 29 Hot Wheels .15 .40
❑ 30 Taking The High Road .15 .40
❑ 31 The Trust Factor .15 .40
❑ 32 Nabbed By The Enemy .15 .40
❑ 33 Inside The Great Cave .15 .40
❑ 34 Hiding And Seeking .15 .40
❑ 35 Smashing Time .15 .40
❑ 36 Pinned And Pounded .15 .40
❑ 37 The Spoils Of Victory .15 .40
❑ 38 Hero Or Madman? .15 .40
❑ 39 On The Ropes .15 .40
❑ 40 Signing On For Trouble .15 .40
❑ 41 The Dragon Lady Strikes! .15 .40
❑ 42 Blasted By Lara .15 .40
❑ 43 Run, Lara, Run! .15 .40
❑ 44 In The Reiss Lab .15 .40
❑ 45 Lara In A Jam .15 .40
❑ 46 Shoot To Kill .15 .40
❑ 47 Scanning The Orb .15 .40
❑ 48 Terry's Counterattack .15 .40
❑ 49 Winging It .15 .40
❑ 50 From Lara With Love .15 .40
❑ 51 The Bryce Connection .15 .40
❑ 52 Help From On High .15 .40
❑ 53 Toward Cradle Country .15 .40
❑ 54 Wise Words Of Warning .15 .40
❑ 55 Quick Wits, Fast Guns .15 .40
❑ 56 Hands In The Air .15 .40
❑ 57 A Guild For Dr. Reiss .15 .40
❑ 58 The Hostages .15 .40
❑ 59 Lead On, Lara .15 .40
❑ 60 The Petrified Forest .15 .40
❑ 61 Of Cones And Cons .15 .40
❑ 62 Inside Pandora's Chamber .15 .40
❑ 63 Makeover Takeover .15 .40
❑ 64 The Bikini Blast .15 .40
❑ 65 Suited For The Sea .15 .40
❑ 66 Riding And Shooting .15 .40
❑ 67 All Bundled Up .15 .40
❑ 68 Outfitted For Action .15 .40
❑ 69 For Jungle Travel .15 .40
❑ 70 High-Tech Heroine .15 .40
❑ 71 Girl With A Gun .15 .40
❑ 72 Flying High .15 .40
❑ 73 Behind The Camera .15 .40
❑ 74 Bike Scene .15 .40
❑ 75 Going Underwater .15 .40
❑ 76 A Most Worthy Adversary .15 .40
❑ 77 Comes A Horsewoman .15 .40
❑ 78 Terracotta Warriors .15 .40
❑ 79 Which Way Is Up? .15 .40
❑ 80 Girl On A Motorcycle .15 .40
❑ 81 Checklist .15 .40

2003 Lara Croft Tomb Raider The Cradle of Life Autographs

STATED ODDS 1:36
❑ A1 Angelina Jolie 250.00 450.00
❑ A2 Chris Barry 7.50 20.00
❑ A3 Ciaran Hinds 7.50 20.00
❑ A4 Til Schweiger 7.50 20.00
❑ A5 Simon Yam 7.50 20.00
❑ A6 Jan De Bont 7.50 20.00

2003 Lara Croft Tomb Raider The Cradle of Life Box Loaders

COMPLETE SET (4) 7.50 20.00
BL1-BL3 STATED ODDS ONE PER BOX
CL1 STATED ODDS ONE PER CASE
❑ BL1 Brave and Beautiful 1.00 2.50
❑ BL2 Easy Rider Deadly Mission 1.00 2.50
❑ BL3 Statuesque 1.00 2.50
❑ CL1 Lara Croft Tomb Raider 6.00 15.00

2003 Lara Croft Tomb Raider The Cradle of Life Pieceworks

COMPLETE SET (2) 100.00 250.00
STATED ODDS 1:36
❑ PW1a Angelina Jolie Jacket 30.00 60.00
❑ PW1b Angelina Jolie Jacket Lining Red 40.00 80.00
❑ PW2 Angelina Jolie Wet Suit 30.00 60.00
❑ PW1c Angelina Jolie Jacket Patch 50.00 100.00

2003 Lara Croft Tomb Raider The Cradle of Life Puzzle Cards

COMPLETE SET (9) 7.50 20.00
STATED ODDS 1:11
❑ COL1 The Cradle Of Life 1.25 3.00
❑ COL2 The Cradle Of Life 1.25 3.00
❑ COL3 The Cradle Of Life 1.25 3.00
❑ COL4 The Cradle Of Life 1.25 3.00
❑ COL5 The Cradle Of Life 1.25 3.00
❑ COL6 The Cradle Of Life 1.25 3.00
❑ COL7 The Cradle Of Life 1.25 3.00
❑ COL8 The Cradle Of Life 1.25 3.00
❑ COL9 The Cradle Of Life 1.25 3.00

2003 Lara Croft Tomb Raider The Cradle of Life Secret of the Orb

COMPLETE SET (6) 7.50 20.00
STATED ODDS 1:17
❑ SO1 Orb of the Ages 1.50 4.00
❑ SO2 The Key to Armageddon 1.50 4.00
❑ SO3 Temptation Time 1.50 4.00
❑ SO4 What Makes It Tick 1.50 4.00
❑ SO5 The Root of All Evil 1.50 4.00
❑ SO6 Doomsday Doctor 1.50 4.00

2003 Lara Croft Tomb Raider The Cradle of Life Promos

COMPLETE SET (4) 3.00 8.00
❑ TR2i Lara Croft Tomb Raider 1.00 2.50
❑ TR2-1 Lara Croft Tomb Raider 1.00 2.50
❑ TR2UK Lara Croft Tomb Raider 1.00 2.50
❑ TR2SD2003 Lara Croft Tomb Raider 1.00 2.50

2003 Looney Tunes Back In Action

COMPLETE SET (72) 5.00 12.00
❑ 1 Title Card .15 .40
❑ 2 DJ Drake .15 .40
❑ 3 Kate Houghton .15 .40
❑ 4 Mr. Chairman .15 .40
❑ 5 Damian Drake .15 .40
❑ 6 Dusty Tails .15 .40
❑ 7 Mother .15 .40
❑ 8 Mr. Smith .15 .40
❑ 9 The Warner Brothers .15 .40
❑ 10 Bugs Bunny .15 .40
❑ 11 Daffy Duck .15 .40
❑ 12 Elmer Fudd .15 .40
❑ 13 Foghorn Leghorn .15 .40
Pepe Le Pew
❑ 14 Yosemite Sam And Thugs .15 .40
❑ 15 Wile E. Coyote .15 .40
Porky Pig/Speedy Gonzales
❑ 16 Granny .15 .40
Sylvester/Tweety
❑ 17 Tasmanian Devil .15 .40
❑ 18 Marvin The Martian .15 .40
❑ 19 Daffy Doomed .15 .40
❑ 20 Duck Amuck .15 .40
❑ 21 Assignment Blue Monkey .15 .40
❑ 22 Off To Save Dad .15 .40
❑ 23 Going Psycho .15 .40
❑ 24 Glitter And Greed .15 .40
❑ 25 Smooth Moves .15 .40
❑ 26 Spied A Poppin .15 .40
❑ 27 Cannon Fodder .15 .40
❑ 28 Capture The Card .15 .40
❑ 29 An Interesting Feature .15 .40
❑ 30 The Obligatory Car Chase .15 .40
❑ 31 Fun In The Sun .15 .40
❑ 32 Shhh! Restricted Area! .15 .40
❑ 33 About The Blue Monkey .15 .40
❑ 34 High-Tech Toys .15 .40
❑ 35 Calling All Monsters .15 .40
❑ 36 Rip Trip To Paris .15 .40
❑ 37 The Secret Revealed .15 .40
❑ 38 Evil Elmer Strikes .15 .40
❑ 39 Mr. Slap Yourself .15 .40
❑ 40 On To Africa .15 .40
❑ 41 Face-Off .15 .40
❑ 42 DJ's Dilemma .15 .40
❑ 43 Duck Dodgers To The Rescue .15 .40
❑ 44 Our Heroes Triumph .15 .40
❑ 45 That's All Folks .15 .40
❑ 46 Spy Car .15 .40
❑ 47 Spy Cell Phone .15 .40
❑ 48 Spy Supplies .15 .40
❑ 49 Spy Style .15 .40
❑ 50 Spy Disguises .15 .40
❑ 51 Spy Clues .15 .40
❑ 52 Spy Villians .15 .40
❑ 53 Spy Splats .15 .40
❑ 54 The Ultimate Spy Guy .15 .40
❑ 55 Yosemite Sam's Review .15 .40
❑ 56 Yosemite Sam's Review .15 .40
❑ 57 Yosemite Sam's Review .15 .40
❑ 58 Yosemite Sam's Review .15 .40
❑ 59 Yosemite Sam's Review .15 .40
❑ 60 Yosemite Sam's Review .15 .40
❑ 61 Welcome To Warner Brothers .15 .40
❑ 62 Be A Star At Warner Brothers .15 .40
❑ 63 Hello From Nowhere .15 .40
❑ 64 Howdy From Yosemite Sam .15 .40
Ya Goldarned Galoot
❑ 65 Welcome To The Best Kept .15 .40
Secret In The Universe
❑ 66 Fall In Love In Paris .15 .40
❑ 67 Go Kooky In Africa .15 .40
❑ 68 Jungle Greetings .15 .40
❑ 69 A Good Luck Rabbit Hint .15 .40
❑ 70 I Got, I Say, I Got A Hint For Ya .15 .40
❑ 71 Don't Just Sit There Hint .15 .40
❑ 72 Checklist .15 .40

2003 Looney Tunes Back In Action Acme Cards

COMPLETE SET (6) 6.00 15.00
STATED ODDS 1:17
❑ A1 Instant Piranha 1.25 3.00
❑ A2 Deluxe Defense Umbrella 1.25 3.00
❑ A3 Mobile Snack Chair 1.25 3.00
❑ A4 Monster In a Jar 1.25 3.00
❑ A5 Inflatable Giant Ruby 1.25 3.00
❑ A6 Heavy Duty Cook Pot 1.25 3.00

2003 Looney Tunes Back In Action Autographs

COMPLETE SET (8) 150.00 300.00
STATED ODDS 1:36
❑ A1 Brendan Fraser 25.00 50.00
❑ A2 Jenna Elfman 30.00 60.00
❑ A3 Steve Martin 35.00 70.00
❑ A4 Heather Locklear 40.00 80.00
❑ A5 Bill Goldberg 15.00 30.00
❑ A6 Don Stanton 7.50 20.00
❑ A7 Dan Stanton 7.50 20.00
❑ A8 Joe Dante 7.50 20.00

2003 Looney Tunes Back In Action Box Loaders

COMPLETE SET (3) 7.50 20.00
STATED ODDS ONE PER BOX
CL1 STATED ODDS ONE PER CASE
❑ BL1 You're a Coyote 1.00 2.50
❑ BL2 I've Been Shot 1.00 2.50
❑ BL3 I Once Caught a Sock-Eyed Salmon 1.00 2.50
❑ CL1 To the Duck Cave 6.00 15.00

2003 Looney Tunes Back In Action Official Looney Tunes Tours

COMPLETE SET (9) 6.00 15.00
STATED ODDS 1:11
❑ LTT1 Official Looney Tunes Tours .75 2.00
❑ LTT2 Official Looney Tunes Tours .75 2.00
❑ LTT3 Official Looney Tunes Tours .75 2.00
❑ LTT4 Official Looney Tunes Tours .75 2.00
❑ LTT5 Official Looney Tunes Tours .75 2.00
❑ LTT6 Official Looney Tunes Tours .75 2.00
❑ LTT7 Official Looney Tunes Tours .75 2.00
❑ LTT8 Official Looney Tunes Tours .75 2.00
❑ LTT9 Official Looney Tunes Tours .75 2.00

2003 Looney Tunes Back In Action Promos

COMPLETE SET (4) 3.00 8.00
❑ BIA1 Group Shot 1.00 2.50
General Distribution
❑ BIAI Group Shot 1.00 2.50
Free Card Offer
❑ LTSD Daffy 1.00 2.50
Taz/Bugs/San Diego Comic Con
❑ BIAUK Kate 1.00 2.50
DJ/Bugs/Daffy/UK Distribution

2003 Looney Tunes Back In Action Wooden Nickel Casino Chips

COMPLETE SET (4) 60.00 120.00
STATED ODDS ONE CHIP AND HOLDER PER CASE
❑ WN1G Gray Chip 25.00 50.00
❑ WN1O Orange Chip 25.00 50.00
❑ WN1Y Yellow Chip 25.00 50.00

2003 Lord of the Rings The Two Towers Update

COMPLETE SET (72) 5.00 12.00
❑ 91 Title Card .15 .40
❑ 92 Against the Balrog .15 .40
❑ 93 Battle to the Death .15 .40
❑ 94 Into the Abyss .15 .40
❑ 95 They Stole It From Us .15 .40
❑ 96 The Creature Called Gollum .15 .40
❑ 97 Hobbits Attacked .15 .40
❑ 98 Captured By the Hobbits .15 .40
❑ 99 Trusting Gollum .15 .40
❑ 100 Isengard's Evil Master .15 .40
❑ 101 Tower of Evil .15 .40
❑ 102 Awakening Treebeard .15 .40
❑ 103 Captured By Treebeard .15 .40
❑ 104 The Hobbits' New Guide .15 .40
❑ 105 Souls of the Damned .15 .40
❑ 106 Underwater Assault .15 .40
❑ 107 Fearing The Flying Nazgul .15 .40
❑ 108 Searching In Fangorn Forest .15 .40
❑ 109 Return of a Friend .15 .40
❑ 110 Pursued By the Wizard .15 .40
❑ 111 Gandalf Triumphant .15 .40
❑ 112 The Black Gates of Mordor .15 .40
❑ 113 Opening Mordor's Gates .15 .40
❑ 114 Another Way In .15 .40
❑ 115 Wormtongue's Betrayal .15 .40
❑ 116 Casting Out Evil .15 .40
❑ 117 Saruman's Grip Released .15 .40
❑ 118 Friend or Fiendish Foe .15 .40
❑ 119 Smeagol's Inner Torment .15 .40
❑ 120 A Tasty Treat .15 .40
❑ 121 Fat, Nasty Hobbit Ruins It .15 .40
❑ 122 Servants of Sauron .15 .40
❑ 123 March of the Oliphants .15 .40
❑ 124 Love Immortal .15 .40
❑ 125 The Wargs of Isengard .15 .40
❑ 126 Warg Attack .15 .40
❑ 127 Deadly Fangs .15 .40
❑ 128 Clash On The Plains .15 .40
❑ 129 Saruman's Evil Scheme .15 .40
❑ 130 The Uruk-Hai Army .15 .40
❑ 131 Aragorn Survives .15 .40
❑ 132 Arwen's Choice .15 .40
❑ 133 The Gathering .15 .40
❑ 134 The Forbidden Pool .15 .40
❑ 135 Gollum Betrayed .15 .40
❑ 136 The Battle of Helm's Deep .15 .40
❑ 137 Elven Allies .15 .40
❑ 138 Show Them No Mercy .15 .40
❑ 139 The Fortress Breached .15 .40
❑ 140 Against Impossible Odds .15 .40
❑ 141 The Ultimate Sacrifice .15 .40
❑ 142 A Wizard Should Know Better .15 .40
❑ 143 Ents March To War .15 .40
❑ 144 The Ents Strike Back .15 .40
❑ 145 Saruman's Army Stomped .15 .40
❑ 146 Vengeance Of The Ents .15 .40
❑ 147 The Fall Of Isengard .15 .40
❑ 148 The Wizard Returns .15 .40
❑ 149 Forces Of Light And Darkness .15 .40
❑ 150 Spell Of The Ring .15 .40
❑ 151 The Struggle Within .15 .40
❑ 152 Which Side Is He On .15 .40
❑ 153 Battle For Middle-Earth .15 .40
❑ 154 Terrors of Shelob .15 .40
❑ 155 Hobbits To The Rescue .15 .40
❑ 156 The Steward of Gondor .15 .40
❑ 157 United In Their Quest .15 .40
❑ 158 To Love A Mortal .15 .40
❑ 159 Heroes Against Evil .15 .40
❑ 160 Rohan's Finest .15 .40
❑ 161 A Royal Son Scorned .15 .40
❑ 162 Tomorrow's King .15 .40

2003 Lord of the Rings The Two Towers Update Autographs

COMPLETE SET (3) 100.00 200.00
STATED ODDS 1:113
❑ NNO Sean Bean 40.00 80.00
❑ NNO Viggo Mortensen 40.00 80.00
❑ NNO Andy Serkis 40.00 80.00

2003 Lord of the Rings The Two Towers Update Memorabilia

COMPLETE SET (9) 150.00 300.00
STATED ODDS 1:33
❑ NNO Arwen's Requiem Cloak 30.00 80.00
❑ NNO Gandalf's Silk Shirt 12.50 30.00
❑ NNO Eowyn's Underfrock 12.50 30.00
❑ NNO Sam's Travel Jacket 12.50 30.00
❑ NNO Aragorn's Travel Coat 12.50 30.00
❑ NNO Galadriel's Silk Chiffon 12.50 30.00

❑ NNO Wormtongue's Velvet Underfrock 12.50 30.00
❑ NNO Faramir's Ranger Outfit 12.50 30.00
❑ NNO Saruman's Overtunic 12.50 30.00

2003 Lord of the Rings The Return of the King

COMPLETE SET (90) 5.00 12.00
❑ 1 Gandalf .15 .40
❑ 2 Frodo .15 .40
❑ 3 Sam .15 .40
❑ 4 Aragorn .15 .40
❑ 5 Legolas .15 .40
❑ 6 Gimli .15 .40
❑ 7 Theoden .15 .40
❑ 8 Eowyn .15 .40
❑ 9 Eomer .15 .40
❑ 10 Denethor .15 .40
❑ 11 Faramir .15 .40
❑ 12 Arwen .15 .40
❑ 13 Pippin .15 .40
❑ 14 Merry .15 .40
❑ 15 The Witch-king .15 .40
❑ 16 Elrond .15 .40
❑ 17 Gollum .15 .40
❑ 18 Sauron .15 .40
❑ 19 Journey to Mount Doom .15 .40
❑ 20 Friend Against Friend .15 .40
❑ 21 Gollum's Scheme .15 .40
❑ 22 Victory Celebration .15 .40
❑ 23 Pippin's Folly .15 .40
❑ 24 Fool of a Took .15 .40
❑ 25 A New Danger .15 .40
❑ 26 In Aragorn's Care .15 .40
❑ 27 Under a Wizard's Wing .15 .40
❑ 28 A Farewell to Friends .15 .40
❑ 29 Escape From Osgiliath .15 .40
❑ 30 Deadly Fellbeast Attack .15 .40
❑ 31 Addressing King Denethor .15 .40
❑ 32 What The Wizard Sees .15 .40
❑ 33 Gandalf's Plan .15 .40
❑ 34 Lighting the Beacon .15 .40
❑ 35 The Signal At Last .15 .40
❑ 36 Leaving Edoras .15 .40
❑ 37 The Road to Gondor .15 .40
❑ 38 Return to Rivendell .15 .40
❑ 39 The Sword Reborn .15 .40
❑ 40 Faramir's Suicide Mission .15 .40
❑ 41 Monarch Or Madman .15 .40
❑ 42 Dunharrow Encampment .15 .40
❑ 43 A King's Counsel .15 .40
❑ 44 Anduril Bestowed .15 .40
❑ 45 The Trio United .15 .40
❑ 46 Fortress Of Evil .15 .40
❑ 47 A Dangerous Trek .15 .40
❑ 48 The Lord of Minas Morgul .15 .40
❑ 49 Kingdom Under Siege .15 .40
❑ 50 Rallying His Warriors .15 .40
❑ 51 Barbarians At The Gates .15 .40
❑ 52 Paths Of The Dead .15 .40
❑ 53 What Say You .15 .40
❑ 54 King Theoden's Crusade .15 .40
❑ 55 Battle of Pelennor Fields .15 .40
❑ 56 The Rohan Offensive .15 .40
❑ 57 An Army of Monsters .15 .40
❑ 58 Victory or Death .15 .40
❑ 59 Whither Minas Tirith .15 .40
❑ 60 A Premature Funeral .15 .40
❑ 61 Battling The Witch-king .15 .40
❑ 62 Rescuing Faramir .15 .40
❑ 63 Arwen Imperiled .15 .40
❑ 64 Lured Into Death's Domain .15 .40
❑ 65 A Gift Against Darkness .15 .40
❑ 66 The Threat of Shelob .15 .40
❑ 67 A Narrow Escape .15 .40
❑ 68 Captured By Orcs .15 .40
❑ 69 Gorbag's Prey .15 .40
❑ 70 The Wounds of War .15 .40
❑ 71 United Against Sauron .15 .40
❑ 72 Their Greatest Challenge .15 .40
❑ 73 March on the Black Gates .15 .40
❑ 74 Orcs Against Them .15 .40
❑ 75 Fury of the White Wizard .15 .40
❑ 76 The King Has Returned .15 .40
❑ 77 Decision at Mount Doom .15 .40
❑ 78 The Trilogy Concludes .15 .40
❑ 79 Movie Masterpiece .15 .40
❑ 80 The Truth About Gollum .15 .40
❑ 81 Making Up An Orc .15 .40
❑ 82 Filmmaker in the Field .15 .40
❑ 83 A Poet's Approach .15 .40
❑ 84 Making the Unreal Real .15 .40
❑ 85 The Magic of Blue Screen .15 .40
❑ 86 Filming Pippin's Perils .15 .40
❑ 87 A Fateful Friendship .15 .40
❑ 88 Master of Middle-earth .15 .40
❑ 89 Ghoulish Delights .15 .40
❑ 90 Checklist .15 .40

2003 Lord of the Rings The Return of the King Autographs

COMPLETE SET (16) 600.00 1000.00
STATED ODDS 1:36 H, 1:122 R
❑ NNO Andy Serkis 60.00 120.00
❑ NNO Bruce Hopkins 20.00 40.00
❑ NNO John Noble 30.00 60.00
❑ NNO Richard Taylor 20.00 40.00
❑ NNO Bret McKenzie 30.00 60.00
❑ NNO Ian Holm 30.00 60.00
❑ NNO Liv Tyler 60.00 120.00
❑ NNO Viggo Mortensen 40.00 80.00
❑ NNO Billy Boyd 30.00 60.00
❑ NNO David Wenham 20.00 40.00
❑ NNO Lawrence Makoare 30.00 60.00
❑ NNO Stephen Ure 20.00 40.00
❑ NNO Bernard Hill 20.00 40.00
❑ NNO Christopher Lee SP 60.00 120.00
❑ NNO Karl Urban 20.00 40.00
❑ NNO Sean Astin 20.00 40.00

2003 Lord of the Rings The Return of the King Box Loaders

COMPLETE SET (2) 1.50 4.00
STATED ODDS ONE PER BOX
❑ 1 Aragorn 1.00 2.50
❑ 2 Aragorn 1.00 2.50

2003 Lord of the Rings The Return of the King Prismatics

COMPLETE SET (10) 8.00 20.00
STATED ODDS 1:6
❑ 1 Aragorn 1.25 3.00
❑ 2 Denethor 1.25 3.00
❑ 3 Orc 1.25 3.00
❑ 4 Gandalf 1.25 3.00
❑ 5 3 ugly dudes 1.25 3.00
❑ 6 Legolas 1.25 3.00
❑ 7 Shagrat 1.25 3.00
❑ 8 Theoden 1.25 3.00
❑ 9 3 ugly dudes 1.25 3.00
❑ 10 Eomer 1.25 3.00

2003 The Outer Limits Sex Cyborgs and Science Fiction

COMPLETE SET (81) 4.00 10.00
❑ 1 Title Card .10 .30
❑ 2 Sandkings .10 .30
❑ 3 Sandkings .10 .30
❑ 4 Sandkings .10 .30
❑ 5 Sandkings .10 .30
❑ 6 Sandkings .10 .30
❑ 7 Sandkings .10 .30
❑ 8 Sandkings .10 .30
❑ 9 Sandkings .10 .30
❑ 10 Valerie 23 .10 .30
❑ 11 Valerie 23 .10 .30
❑ 12 Valerie 23 .10 .30
❑ 13 Valerie 23 .10 .30
❑ 14 Valerie 23 .10 .30
❑ 15 Valerie 23 .10 .30
❑ 16 Bits of Love .10 .30
❑ 17 Bits of Love .10 .30
❑ 18 Bits of Love .10 .30
❑ 19 Bits of Love .10 .30
❑ 20 Bits of Love .10 .30
❑ 21 Bits of Love .10 .30
❑ 22 A Special Edition .10 .30
❑ 23 A Special Edition .10 .30
❑ 24 A Special Edition .10 .30
❑ 25 A Special Edition .10 .30
❑ 26 A Special Edition .10 .30
❑ 27 A Special Edition .10 .30
❑ 28 Skin Deep .10 .30
❑ 29 Skin Deep .10 .30
❑ 30 Skin Deep .10 .30
❑ 31 Skin Deep .10 .30
❑ 32 Skin Deep .10 .30
❑ 33 Skin Deep .10 .30
❑ 34 Stasis .10 .30
❑ 35 Stasis .10 .30
❑ 36 Stasis .10 .30
❑ 37 Stasis .10 .30
❑ 38 Stasis .10 .30
❑ 39 Stasis .10 .30
❑ 40 Revival .10 .30
❑ 41 Revival .10 .30
❑ 42 Revival .10 .30
❑ 43 Revival .10 .30
❑ 44 Revival .10 .30
❑ 45 Revival .10 .30
❑ 46 Final Appeal .10 .30
❑ 47 Final Appeal .10 .30
❑ 48 Final Appeal .10 .30
❑ 49 Final Appeal .10 .30
❑ 50 Final Appeal .10 .30
❑ 51 Final Appeal .10 .30
❑ 52 Final Appeal .10 .30
❑ 53 Final Appeal .10 .30
❑ 54 Final Appeal .10 .30
❑ 55 Mona Lisa .10 .30
❑ 56 Mona Lisa .10 .30
❑ 57 Mona Lisa .10 .30
❑ 58 Mona Lisa .10 .30
❑ 59 Mona Lisa .10 .30
❑ 60 Mona Lisa .10 .30
❑ 61 Think Like a Dinosaur .10 .30
❑ 62 Think Like a Dinosaur .10 .30
❑ 63 Think Like a Dinosaur .10 .30
❑ 64 Think Like a Dinosaur .10 .30
❑ 65 Think Like a Dinosaur .10 .30
❑ 66 Think Like a Dinosaur .10 .30
❑ 67 Zig Zag .10 .30
❑ 68 Zig Zag .10 .30
❑ 69 Zig Zag .10 .30
❑ 70 Zig Zag .10 .30
❑ 71 Zig Zag .10 .30
❑ 72 Zig Zag .10 .30
❑ 73 Rule of Law .10 .30
❑ 74 Rule of Law .10 .30
❑ 75 Rule of Law .10 .30
❑ 76 Rule of Law .10 .30
❑ 77 Rule of Law .10 .30
❑ 78 Rule of Law .10 .30
❑ 79 Checklist 1 .10 .30
❑ 80 Checklist 2 .10 .30
❑ 81 Checklist 3 .10 .30

2003 The Outer Limits Sex Cyborgs and Science Fiction Autographs

STATED ODDS THREE PER BOX
L (LIMITED): 300-500 COPIES
CARD A15 WAS NOT ISSUED
❑ A1 Natasha Henstridge 20.00 40.00
❑ A2 Brent Spiner L 30.00 60.00
❑ A3 Margot Kidder 15.00 30.00
❑ A4 Michael Ironside 15.00 30.00
❑ A5 Nana Visitor L 25.00 50.00
❑ A6 Hal Holbrook L 25.00 50.00
❑ A7 Alan Thicke 10.00 20.00
❑ A8 Robert Picardo L 15.00 30.00
❑ A9 Burt Young 10.00 20.00
❑ A10 Beau Bridges 10.00 20.00
❑ A11 Dylan Bridges 7.50 15.00
❑ A12 Rebecca DeMornay
❑ A13 Sofia Shinas 10.00 20.00
❑ A14 William Sadler 10.00 20.00
❑ A16 William B. Davis 10.00 20.00
❑ A17 Alex Diakun 7.50 15.00

2003 The Outer Limits Sex Cyborgs and Science Fiction From the Archives Costumes

STATED ODDS 1:20
CC11 ISSUED AS CASE TOPPER
CC12 ISSUED IN COLLECTORS ALBUM
L (LIMITED): 300-500 COPIES
❑ CC1 Ezra Burnham L 8.00 20.00
❑ CC2 Peter Yastrzemski 6.00 15.00
❑ CC3 Dr. Simon Kress 6.00 15.00
❑ CC4 Eric L 8.00 20.00
❑ CC5 Kamala Shamstri 6.00 15.00
❑ CC6 Zig Fowler 6.00 15.00
❑ CC7 Sid Camden 6.00 15.00
❑ CC8 Frank Hellner 6.00 15.00
❑ CC9 Thomas L 8.00 20.00
❑ CC10 Mona 6.00 15.00
❑ CC11 Professor Davis/ (issued as case topper)15.00 30.00
❑ CC12 Emmet Harley/ (issued in collectors album)10.00 20.00

2003 The Outer Limits Sex Cyborgs and Science Fiction Opening Monologue

COMPLETE SET (9) 2.00 5.00
STATED ODDS 1:3
❑ M1 Opening Monologue .40 1.00
❑ M2 Opening Monologue .40 1.00
❑ M3 Opening Monologue .40 1.00
❑ M4 Opening Monologue .40 1.00
❑ M5 Opening Monologue .40 1.00
❑ M6 Opening Monologue .40 1.00
❑ M7 Opening Monologue .40 1.00
❑ M8 Opening Monologue .40 1.00
❑ M9 Opening Monologue .40 1.00

2003 The Outer Limits Sex Cyborgs and Science Fiction Stars of the Outer Limits

COMPLETE SET (18) 12.50 30.00
STATED ODDS 1:6
❑ S1 Natasha Henstridge 1.00 2.50
❑ S2 Brent Spiner 1.00 2.50
❑ S3 Margot Kidder 1.00 2.50
❑ S4 Michael Ironside 1.00 2.50
❑ S5 Nana Visitor 1.00 2.50
❑ S6 Robert Picardo 1.00 2.50
❑ S7 Charlton Heston 1.00 2.50
❑ S8 Sheena Easton 1.00 2.50
❑ S9 Jeremy Sisto 1.00 2.50
❑ S10 Hal Holbrook 1.00 2.50
❑ S11 Kelly McGillis 1.00 2.50
❑ S12 John Amos 1.00 2.50
❑ S13 Alan Thicke 1.00 2.50
❑ S14 Bruce Harwood 1.00 2.50
❑ S15 Sean Patrick Flanery 1.00 2.50
❑ S16 Beau Bridges 1.00 2.50
❑ S17 Gary Busey 1.00 2.50
❑ S18 William B. Davis 1.00 2.50

2003 The Quotable Xena Warrior Princess

COMPLETE SET (138) 5.00 12.00
C14 ISSUED IN COLLECTORS ALBUM
❑ 1 Title Card .08 .25
❑ 2 Sins Of The Past .08 .25
❑ 3 Chariots Of War .08 .25
❑ 4 Dreamworker .08 .25
❑ 5 Cradle Of Hope .08 .25
❑ 6 The Path Not Taken .08 .25
❑ 7 The Reckoning .08 .25
❑ 8 The Titans .08 .25
❑ 9 Prometheus .08 .25
❑ 10 Death In Chains .08 .25
❑ 11 Hooves And Harlots .08 .25
❑ 12 The Black Wolf .08 .25
❑ 13 Beware Greeks Bearing Gifts .08 .25
❑ 14 Athens City Academy Of The Performing Bards.08 .25
❑ 15 A Fistful Of Dinars .08 .25
❑ 16 Warrior…Princess .08 .25
❑ 17 Mortal Beloved .08 .25
❑ 18 The Royal Couple Of Thieves .08 .25
❑ 19 The Prodigal .08 .25
❑ 20 Altared States .08 .25
❑ 21 Ties That Bind .08 .25
❑ 22 The Greater Good .08 .25
❑ 23 Callisto .08 .25
❑ 24 Deathmask .08 .25
❑ 25 Is There A Doctor In The House…? .08 .25
❑ 26 Orphan Of War .08 .25
❑ 27 Remember Nothing .08 .25
❑ 28 Giant Killer .08 .25
❑ 29 Girls Just Wanna Have Fun .08 .25
❑ 30 Return Of Callisto .08 .25
❑ 31 Warrior…Princess…Tramp .08 .25
❑ 32 Intimate Stranger .08 .25
❑ 33 Ten Little Warlords .08 .25
❑ 34 A Solstice Carol .08 .25
❑ 35 The Xena Scrolls .08 .25
❑ 36 Here She Comes…Miss Amphipolis .08 .25
❑ 37 Destiny .08 .25
❑ 38 The Quest .08 .25
❑ 39 A Necessary Evil .08 .25
❑ 40 A Day In The Life .08 .25
❑ 41 For Him The Bell Tolls .08 .25
❑ 42 The Execution .08 .25
❑ 43 Blind Faith .08 .25
❑ 44 Ulysses .08 .25
❑ 45 The Price .08 .25
❑ 46 Lost Mariner .08 .25
❑ 47 A Comedy Of Eros .08 .25
❑ 48 The Furies .08 .25
❑ 49 Been There, Done That .08 .25
❑ 50 The Dirty Half Dozen .08 .25
❑ 51 The Deliverer .08 .25
❑ 52 Gabrielle's Hope .08 .25
❑ 53 The Debt I .08 .25
❑ 54 The Debt II .08 .25
❑ 55 The King Of Assassins .08 .25
❑ 56 Warrior…Princess…Tramp .08 .25
❑ 57 The Quill Is Mightier .08 .25
❑ 58 Maternal Instincts .08 .25
❑ 59 The Bitter Suite .08 .25
❑ 60 One Against An Army .08 .25
❑ 61 Forgiven .08 .25
❑ 62 King Con .08 .25
❑ 63 When In Rome .08 .25
❑ 64 Forget Me Not .08 .25
❑ 65 Fins, Femmes, And Gems .08 .25
❑ 66 Tsunami .08 .25
❑ 67 Vanishing Act .08 .25
❑ 68 Sacrifice I .08 .25
❑ 69 Sacrifice II .08 .25
❑ 70 Adventures In The Sin Trade I .08 .25
❑ 71 Adventures In The Sin Trade II .08 .25
❑ 72 A Family Affair .08 .25
❑ 73 In Sickness And In Hell .08 .25
❑ 74 A Good Day .08 .25
❑ 75 A Tale Of Two Muses .08 .25
❑ 76 Locked Up And Tied Down .08 .25
❑ 77 Crusader .08 .25
❑ 78 Past Imperfect .08 .25
❑ 79 Key To The Kingdom .08 .25
❑ 80 Daughter Of Pomira .08 .25
❑ 81 If The Shoe Fits .08 .25
❑ 82 Paradise Found .08 .25
❑ 83 Devi .08 .25
❑ 84 Between The Lines .08 .25
❑ 85 The Way .08 .25
❑ 86 The Play's The Thing .08 .25
❑ 87 The Convert .08 .25
❑ 88 Takes One To Know One .08 .25
❑ 89 Endgame .08 .25
❑ 90 Ides Of March .08 .25
❑ 91 Deja Vu All Over Again .08 .25
❑ 92 Fallen Angel .08 .25
❑ 93 Chakram .08 .25
❑ 94 Succession .08 .25
❑ 95 Animal Attraction .08 .25
❑ 96 Them Bones, Them Bones .08 .25
❑ 97 Purity .08 .25
❑ 98 Back In The Bottle .08 .25
❑ 99 Little Problems .08 .25
❑ 100 Seeds Of Faith .08 .25
❑ 101 Lyre Lyre, Hearts On Fire .08 .25
❑ 102 Punchlines .08 .25
❑ 103 God Fearing Child .08 .25
❑ 104 Eternal Bonds .08 .25
❑ 105 Amphipolis Under Seige .08 .25
❑ 106 Married With Fishsticks .08 .25
❑ 107 Lifeblood .08 .25
❑ 108 Kindred Spirits .08 .25
❑ 109 Anthony And Cleopatra .08 .25
❑ 110 Looking Death In The Eye .08 .25
❑ 111 Livia .08 .25
❑ 112 Eve .08 .25
❑ 113 Motherhood .08 .25
❑ 114 Coming Home .08 .25
❑ 115 The Haunting Of Amphipolis .08 .25
❑ 116 Heart Of Darkness .08 .25
❑ 117 Who's Gurkhan .08 .25
❑ 118 Legacy .08 .25
❑ 119 The Abyss .08 .25
❑ 120 The Rheingold .08 .25
❑ 121 The Ring .08 .25
❑ 122 Return Of The Valkyrie .08 .25
❑ 123 Old Ares Had A Farm .08 .25
❑ 124 Dangerous Prey .08 .25
❑ 125 The God You Know .08 .25
❑ 126 You Are There .08 .25
❑ 127 Path Of Vengeance .08 .25
❑ 128 To Helicon And Back .08 .25
❑ 129 Send In The Clones .08 .25
❑ 130 The Last Of The Centaurs .08 .25
❑ 131 When Fates Collide .08 .25
❑ 132 Many Happy Returns .08 .25
❑ 133 Soul Possession .08 .25
❑ 134 A Friend In Need 1 .08 .25
❑ 135 A Friend In Need 2 .08 .25
❑ C1 Checklist 1 .08 .25
❑ C2 Checklist 2 .08 .25
❑ C3 Checklist 3 .08 .25
❑ C14 Xena MEM/ (issued in collectors album)25.00 50.00

2003 The Quotable Xena Warrior Princess Foil

COMPLETE SET (138) 15.00 40.00
*FOIL: .6X TO 1.5X BASIC CARDS
STATED ODDS ONE PER PACK

2003 The Quotable Xena Warrior Princess Autograph Costumes

STATED ODDS 1:200
AC10 ISSUED AS MULTI-CASE INCENTIVE
❑ AC4 Lucy Lawless 40.00 80.00
❑ AC5 Erik Thomson 25.00 50.00
❑ AC6 Bruce Campbell 25.00 50.00
❑ AC7 Timothy Omundson 25.00 50.00
❑ AC8 Alexandra Tydings 25.00 50.00
❑ A09 Victoria Pratt 25.00 50.00
❑ AC10 Renee O'Connor/ (issued as multi-case incentive) 50.00 100.00

2003 The Quotable Xena Warrior Princess Autographs

OVERALL AUTO ODDS TWO PER BOX
L (LIMITED): 300-500 COPIES
❑ A35 Tsianina Joelson 6.00 15.00
❑ A36 Alex Mendoza 6.00 15.00
❑ A37 Jacqueline Kim 6.00 15.00
❑ A38 Bruce Campbell 6.00 15.00
❑ A39 David Franklin 6.00 15.00
❑ A40 Tony Todd 6.00 15.00
❑ A41 John D'Aquino 6.00 15.00
❑ A42 Colin Moy 6.00 15.00
❑ A43 Joel Tobeck 6.00 15.00
❑ A44 Jay Laga'aia 6.00 15.00
❑ A45 Dean O'Gorman 6.00 15.00
❑ A46 Jeffrey Thomas 6.00 15.00
❑ A47 Charles Mesure 6.00 15.00
❑ A48 Daniel Sing L 6.00 15.00
❑ A49 George Kee Cheung 6.00 15.00
❑ A50 William Gregory Lee 6.00 15.00
❑ A51 Gina Torres 6.00 15.00

2003 The Quotable Xena Warrior Princess Dual Autographs

OVERALL AUTO ODDS TWO PER BOX
L (LIMITED): 300-500 COPIES
❑ DA3 Alexandra Tydings 20.00 40.00
Meighan Desmond
❑ DA4 Karl Urban 20.00 40.00
Alexandra Tydings
❑ DA5 Karl Urban 20.00 40.00
David Franklin
❑ DA6 Daniel Sing 20.00 40.00
Marie Matiko
❑ DA8 Ted Raimi 30.00 60.00
Lucy Lawless

2003 The Quotable Xena Warrior Princess Eternal Friends

COMPLETE SET (9) 6.00 15.00
STATED ODDS 1:10
❑ E1 Eternal Friends .75 2.00
❑ E2 Eternal Friends .75 2.00
❑ E3 Eternal Friends .75 2.00
❑ E4 Eternal Friends .75 2.00
❑ E5 Eternal Friends .75 2.00
❑ E6 Eternal Friends .75 2.00
❑ E7 Eternal Friends .75 2.00
❑ E8 Eternal Friends .75 2.00
❑ E9 Eternal Friends .75 2.00

2003 The Quotable Xena Warrior Princess Forged in the Heat of Battle

COMPLETE SET (6) 12.50 30.00
STATED ODDS 1:40
❑ F1 Forged In The Heat Of Battle 2.50 6.00
❑ F2 Forged In The Heat Of Battle 2.50 6.00
❑ F3 Forged In The Heat Of Battle 2.50 6.00
❑ F4 Forged In The Heat Of Battle 2.50 6.00
❑ F5 Forged In The Heat Of Battle 2.50 6.00
❑ F6 Forged In The Heat Of Battle 2.50 6.00

2003 The Quotable Xena Warrior Princess Promos

COMPLETE SET (4) 3.00 8.00
❑ P1 Xena and Argo/ (General Distribution) 1.00 2.50
❑ P2 Xena/ (Non-Sport Update) 1.00 2.50
❑ P3 Gabrielle 1.50 4.00
Xena/Argo/ (Binder Exclusive)
❑ C2003 Xena/ (Convention Distribution) 1.50 4.00

2003 The Quotable Xena Warrior Princess Words From the Bard

COMPLETE SET (9) 2.50 6.00
STATED ODDS 1:4
❑ B1 Words From the Bard .40 1.00
❑ B2 Words From the Bard .40 1.00
❑ B3 Words From the Bard .40 1.00
❑ B4 Words From the Bard .40 1.00
❑ B5 Words From the Bard .40 1.00
❑ B6 Words From the Bard .40 1.00
❑ B7 Words From the Bard .40 1.00
❑ B8 Words From the Bard .40 1.00
❑ B9 Words From the Bard .40 1.00

2003 The Quotable Xena Warrior Princess Xena in Motion

COMPLETE SET (6) 10.00 25.00
STATED ODDS 1:40
CT1 ISSUED AS CASE TOPPER
❑ M1 Xena In Motion 2.50 6.00
❑ M2 Xena In Motion 2.50 6.00
❑ M3 Xena In Motion 2.50 6.00
❑ M4 Xena In Motion 2.50 6.00
❑ M5 Xena In Motion 2.50 6.00
❑ M6 Xena In Motion 2.50 6.00
❑ CT1 Xena In Motion/ (issued as case topper)15.00 40.00

2003 Scooby Doo Mysteries And Monsters

COMPLETE SET (72) 5.00 12.00
❑ 1 America's Favorite .15 .40
❑ 2 Scooby Doo .15 .40
❑ 3 Shaggy .15 .40
❑ 4 Fred .15 .40
❑ 5 Daphne .15 .40
❑ 6 Velma .15 .40
❑ 7 Scrappy Doo .15 .40
❑ 8 Scooby Doo And Scooby Dee .15 .40
❑ 9 The Mystery Machine .15 .40
❑ 10 Episode Stats .15 .40
❑ 11 Character Appearances .15 .40
❑ 12 Character Appearances .15 .40
❑ 13 Villian Appearances .15 .40
❑ 14 Villian Appearances .15 .40
❑ 15 Fast Food Facts .15 .40
❑ 16 Guest Stars: TV Stars And Comedians .15 .40
❑ 17 Guest Stars: Pop Stars And Cartoon Stars .15 .40
❑ 18 Guest Stars: Famous Ghosts And Monsters .15 .40
❑ 19 Charlie The Robot .15 .40
❑ 20 Ghost Clown .15 .40
❑ 21 Woltman .15 .40
❑ 22 Carlotta The Gypsy .15 .40
❑ 23 Frankenstein's Monster .15 .40
❑ 24 Dracula .15 .40
❑ 25 Zombie .15 .40
❑ 26 The Ghost Of Redbeard .15 .40
❑ 27 Neanderthal Caveman .15 .40
❑ 28 The Creeper .15 .40
❑ 29 The Phantom Puppeteer .15 .40
❑ 30 Miner 49er .15 .40
❑ 31 The Snow Ghost .15 .40
❑ 32 Ghost Of Zen Tuo .15 .40
❑ 33 Mummy .15 .40
❑ 34 The Black Knight .15 .40
❑ 35 Green Ghost .15 .40
❑ 36 Witch Doctor .15 .40
❑ 37 Scooby Doo Where Are You? .15 .40
❑ 38 The New Scooby Doo Movies .15 .40
❑ 39 Scooby Doo .15 .40
Dynomutt Show
❑ 40 Scooby Doo's All Star Laff A Lympics .15 .40
❑ 41 Scooby Doo .15 .40
Scrappy Doo Show Series
❑ 42 Scooby Doo .15 .40
Scrappy Doo Show Segment
❑ 43 Scooby Doo .15 .40
Scrappy Doo/Yabba Doo
❑ 44 The Scrappy Doo Show .15 .40
❑ 45 The 13 Ghosts Of Scooby Doo .15 .40
❑ 46 A Pup Named Scooby Doo .15 .40
❑ 47 Scooby Doo TV Movies 1 .15 .40
❑ 48 Scooby Doo TV Movies 2 .15 .40
❑ 49 Scooby Doo TV Movies 3 .15 .40
❑ 50 Scooby Doo Video TV Movies 1 .15 .40
❑ 51 Scooby Doo Video TV Movies 2 .15 .40
❑ 52 Scooby Doo Video TV Movies 3 .15 .40
❑ 53 Scooby Doo Remakes 1 .15 .40
❑ 54 Scooby Doo Remakes 2 .15 .40
❑ 55 Character Design .15 .40
❑ 56 Model Sheets .15 .40
❑ 57 Turnarounds .15 .40
❑ 58 Villians .15 .40
❑ 59 Backgrounds .15 .40
❑ 60 The Script .15 .40
❑ 61 Storyboards .15 .40
❑ 62 Color Palettes .15 .40
❑ 63 Title Card Design .15 .40
❑ 64 Another Mystery Solved .15 .40
❑ 65 Another Mystery Solved .15 .40
❑ 66 Another Mystery Solved .15 .40
❑ 67 Another Mystery Solved .15 .40
❑ 68 Another Mystery Solved .15 .40
❑ 69 Another Mystery Solved .15 .40
❑ 70 Another Mystery Solved .15 .40
❑ 71 Another Mystery Solved .15 .40
❑ 72 Checklist .15 .40

2003 Scooby Doo Mysteries And Monsters Autographs

COMPLETE SET (6) 60.00 120.00
STATED ODDS 1:62 HOBBY
❑ A1 Casey Kasem 25.00 50.00
❑ A2 Tim Conway 15.00 30.00
❑ A3 Susan Blu 7.50 20.00

MODERN ERA NON-SPORTS

❑ A4 Frank Weller 7.50 20.00
❑ A5 Nicole (Jaffe) David 7.50 20.00
❑ A6 Heather (Kenney) North 7.50 20.00

2003 Scooby Doo Mysteries And Monsters Box Loaders

COMPLETE SET (4) 7.50 20.00
STATED ODDS ONE PER BOX
CL1 STATED ODDS ONE PER CASE

❑ BL1 Velma 1.00 2.50
Scooby/Daphne
❑ BL2 Daphne 1.00 2.50
Scooby/Velma
❑ BL3 Daphne 1.00 2.50
Scooby/Velma
❑ BL4 Shaggy 1.00 2.50
Scooby
❑ CL1 We'd Have Put a Great Illustration 6.00 15.00

2003 Scooby Doo Mysteries And Monsters Promos

COMPLETE SET (3) 2.00 5.00

❑ SDMM1 Scooby and Shaggy 1.00 2.50
General Distribution
❑ SDMM2 Scooby and Fred 1.00 2.50
UK Distribution
❑ SDMMi Scooby and Daphne 1.00 2.50
Free Card Offer

2003 Scooby Doo Mysteries And Monsters Sketches

COMPLETE SET (9) 150.00 250.00
STATED ODDS 1:85 HOBBY

❑ SK1 Chynna Clugston-Major 30.00 60.00
❑ SK2 David Crosland 15.00 30.00
❑ SK3 Rod Deleon 15.00 30.00
❑ SK4 Dan Fraga 15.00 30.00
❑ SK5 Mario Gully 15.00 30.00
❑ SK6 Christine Norrie 15.00 30.00
❑ SK7 William O'Neill 15.00 30.00
❑ SK8 Tone Rodriguez 15.00 30.00
❑ SK9 John Strangeland 15.00 30.00

2003 Scooby Doo Mysteries And Monsters Sparkly

COMPLETE SET (6) 10.00 25.00
STATED ODDS 1:7 HOBBY

❑ SP1 Scooby Doo 2.00 5.00
❑ SP2 Shaggy 2.00 5.00
❑ SP3 Fred 2.00 5.00
❑ SP4 Daphne 2.00 5.00
❑ SP5 Velma 2.00 5.00
❑ SP6 The Mystery Machine 2.00 5.00

2003 Scooby Doo Mysteries And Monsters Stickers

COMPLETE SET (9) 1.50 4.00
STATED ODDS ONE PER PACK

❑ S1 Zoinks .20 .50
❑ S2 Relp .20 .50
❑ S3 Jinkies .20 .50
❑ S4 Like Wow .20 .50
❑ S5 Scooby Dooby Doo .20 .50
❑ S6 Oohhh Scooby .20 .50
❑ S7 I Guess That Wraps Up Another Mystery .20 .50
❑ S8 Scooby Snack .20 .50
❑ S9 The Mystery Machine .20 .50

2003 Smallville Season Two

COMPLETE SET (90) 5.00 12.00

❑ 1 Smallville .15 .40
❑ 2 Clark Kent .15 .40
❑ 3 Lex Luthor .15 .40
❑ 4 Lana Lang .15 .40
❑ 5 Chloe Sullivan .15 .40
❑ 6 Pete Ross .15 .40
❑ 7 Jonathan Kent .15 .40
❑ 8 Martha Kent .15 .40
❑ 9 Lionel Luthor .15 .40
❑ 10 New Doc In Town .15 .40
❑ 11 Dead Scientist .15 .40
❑ 12 The Newest Luthor .15 .40
❑ 13 Green Kryptonite .15 .40
❑ 14 Red Kryptonite .15 .40
❑ 15 Green Power .15 .40
❑ 16 The Kryptonite Way .15 .40
❑ 17 Kryptonite Kills .15 .40
❑ 18 Red Runaway .15 .40
❑ 19 The Kent Family .15 .40
❑ 20 Clark And Lana .15 .40
❑ 21 Clark And Chloe .15 .40
❑ 22 Clark And Lex .15 .40
❑ 23 Lex And Lionel .15 .40
❑ 24 Lex, Lionel And Lucas .15 .40
❑ 25 Lana And Henry Small .15 .40
❑ 26 Lana And Chloe .15 .40
❑ 27 Clark And Jor-El .15 .40
❑ 28 Dropping In .15 .40
❑ 29 Legend Of The Cave .15 .40
❑ 30 The Key To The Cave .15 .40
❑ 31 Rave In A Cave .15 .40
❑ 32 Language Lessons .15 .40
❑ 33 Shock Doc .15 .40
❑ 34 It's The Day .15 .40
❑ 35 Getting Down .15 .40
❑ 36 The Green Key .15 .40
❑ 37 Reprieve .15 .40
❑ 38 The Ship Speaks .15 .40
❑ 39 Rule Them! .15 .40
❑ 40 Ultimatum .15 .40
❑ 41 Killer Key .15 .40
❑ 42 Disaster .15 .40
❑ 43 Twister Fallout .15 .40
❑ 44 Buried Alive .15 .40
❑ 45 Hot Flashes .15 .40
❑ 46 Things Heat Up .15 .40
❑ 47 Pete's Spaceship .15 .40
❑ 48 Meteor Rock Menace .15 .40
❑ 49 Red Alert! .15 .40
❑ 50 Bad Boy Clark .15 .40
❑ 51 Graveyard Romance .15 .40
❑ 52 The Bwast Within .15 .40
❑ 53 A Fatal Kiss .15 .40
❑ 54 The Death-Defier .15 .40
❑ 55 Blood Relations .15 .40
❑ 56 Smother Love .15 .40
❑ 57 Cry For Help .15 .40
❑ 58 Reach For The Sky .15 .40
❑ 59 Double Trouble .15 .40
❑ 60 Doctor! Doctor! .15 .40
❑ 61 Hidden History .15 .40
❑ 62 Going Native .15 .40
❑ 63 Tina Re-Turner .15 .40
❑ 64 Morphing Menace .15 .40
❑ 65 Bugged! .15 .40
❑ 66 Hostage Crisis .15 .40
❑ 67 Suspect .15 .40
❑ 68 Chain Of Evidence .15 .40
❑ 69 Cave Rave .15 .40
❑ 70 Over The Edge .15 .40
❑ 71 Brother 2 Brother .15 .40
❑ 72 Sibling Rivalry .15 .40
❑ 73 Killer Flu .15 .40
❑ 74 Saved By The Ship .15 .40
❑ 75 Heritage Found .15 .40
❑ 76 Son Of Krypton .15 .40
❑ 77 A Fellow Alien .15 .40
❑ 78 Rescue .15 .40
❑ 79 Fighting Back .15 .40
❑ 80 Stalked .15 .40
❑ 81 Puff K Daddy .15 .40
❑ 82 Intimidation .15 .40
❑ 83 Little Girl Lost .15 .40
❑ 84 Drowning Sorrows .15 .40
❑ 85 The Day Is Coming .15 .40
❑ 86 Clark Must Die! .15 .40
❑ 87 The Day Dawns .15 .40
❑ 88 Fallout .15 .40
❑ 89 End Of The Line .15 .40
❑ 90 Checklist .15 .40

2003 Smallville Season Two Autographs

COMPLETE SET (10) 100.00 200.00
STATED ODDS 1:36

❑ A7 Annette O'Toole 20.00 40.00
❑ A8 Sam Jones III 8.00 20.00
❑ A9 Sarah-Jane Redmond 8.00 20.00
❑ A10 Tom O'Brien 8.00 20.00
❑ A11 John Glover 12.00 30.00
❑ A12 Emmanuelle Vaugier 10.00 25.00
❑ A13 Jason Connery 8.00 20.00
❑ A14 Patrick Cassidy 8.00 20.00
❑ A15 Richar Moll 8.00 20.00
❑ A16 Gwynyth Walsh 8.00 20.00

2003 Smallville Season Two Box Loaders

COMPLETE SET (4) 7.50 20.00

❑ BL1 Dr. Virgil Swann 1.00 2.50
❑ BL2 Krypton - The Lost Planet 1.00 2.50
❑ BL3 Hope 1.00 2.50
❑ CL1 The Mark Of Jor-El 6.00 15.00
CASE INSERT

2003 Smallville Season Two Pieceworks

COMPLETE SET (8) 60.00 120.00
STATED ODDS 1:36

❑ PW1 Tom Welling 12.00 30.00
❑ PW2 Kristin Kreuk 12.00 30.00
❑ PW3 Allison Mack 12.00 30.00
❑ PW4 Sam Jones III 8.00 20.00
❑ PW5 Annette O'Toole 8.00 20.00
❑ PW6 John Schneider 10.00 25.00
❑ PW7 John Glover 8.00 20.00
❑ PW8 Michael Rosenbaum 10.00 25.00

2003 Smallville Season Two Promos

COMPLETE SET (5) 3.00 8.00

❑ SM2i Lex & Lionel .75 2.00
❑ SM2-1 Smallville .75 2.00
❑ SM2-2 Smallville .75 2.00
❑ SM2SD Smallville .75 2.00
❑ SM2UK Clark & Lana .75 2.00

2003 Smallville Season Two The Day Is Coming

COMPLETE SET (9) 12.50 30.00
STATED ODDS 1:11

❑ DC1 The Day Is Coming 1.50 4.00
❑ DC2 The Day Is Coming 1.50 4.00
❑ DC3 The Day Is Coming 1.50 4.00
❑ DC4 The Day Is Coming 1.50 4.00
❑ DC5 The Day Is Coming 1.50 4.00
❑ DC6 The Day Is Coming 1.50 4.00
❑ DC7 The Day Is Coming 1.50 4.00
❑ DC8 The Day Is Coming 1.50 4.00
❑ DC9 The Day Is Coming 1.50 4.00

2003 Smallville Season Two Till Death Do Us Part

COMPLETE SET (6) 7.50 20.00
STATED ODDS 1:17

❑ DP1 The Proposal 1.50 4.00
❑ DP2 Bad Blood 1.50 4.00
❑ DP3 The Nervous Groom 1.50 4.00
❑ DP4 The Blushing Bride 1.50 4.00
❑ DP5 Mr. and Mrs. Luthor 1.50 4.00
❑ DP6 Till Death 1.50 4.00

2003 Star Trek Nemesis Expansion

COMPLETE SET (19) 10.00 25.00
STATED PRINT RUN 999 SER. #'d SETS
NA11 STATED ODDS ONE PER 5 SET PURCHASE

❑ NE1 The Enterprise NCC-1701-E .75 2.00
❑ NE2 The Argo Takes Flight .75 2.00
❑ NE3 Romulan Encounter .75 2.00
❑ NE4 Blasting Through .75 2.00
❑ NE5 Evasive Maneuvers .75 2.00
❑ NE6 On the Offensive .75 2.00
❑ NE7 An Unlikely Ally .75 2.00
❑ NE8 Battle Stations .75 2.00
❑ NE9 Romulans Under Attack .75 2.00
❑ NE10 Waiting for Shinzon .75 2.00
❑ NE11 Phaser Fire .75 2.00
❑ NE12 Face to Face .75 2.00
❑ NE13 Ramming Speed .75 2.00
❑ NE14 Weapon of Mass Destruction .75 2.00
❑ NE15 Transporting to the Scimitar .75 2.00
❑ NE16 The Scimitar's Ultimate Weapon .75 2.00
❑ NE17 Taking Out the Enemy .75 2.00
❑ NE18 Space Dock .75 2.00
❑ CC1 Commander William Riker MEM 15.00 30.00
❑ NA11 Bryan Singer AU 90.00 150.00

2003 Stargate SG-1 Season Five

COMPLETE SET (72) 4.00 10.00

❑ 1 Dual-Sided Montage .10 .30
❑ 2 Dual-Sided Montage .10 .30
❑ 3 Dual-Sided Montage .10 .30
❑ 4 Enemies .10 .30
❑ 5 Enemies .10 .30
❑ 6 Enemies .10 .30
❑ 7 Threshold .10 .30
❑ 8 Threshold .10 .30
❑ 9 Threshold .10 .30
❑ 10 Ascension .10 .30
❑ 11 Ascension .10 .30
❑ 12 Ascension .10 .30
❑ 13 The Fifth Man .10 .30
❑ 14 The Fifth Man .10 .30
❑ 15 The Fifth Man .10 .30
❑ 16 Red Sky .10 .30
❑ 17 Red Sky .10 .30
❑ 18 Red Sky .10 .30
❑ 19 Rite Of Passage .10 .30
❑ 20 Rite Of Passage .10 .30
❑ 21 Rite Of Passage .10 .30
❑ 22 Beast Of Burden .10 .30
❑ 23 Beast Of Burden .10 .30
❑ 24 Beast Of Burden .10 .30
❑ 25 The Tomb .10 .30
❑ 26 The Tomb .10 .30
❑ 27 The Tomb .10 .30
❑ 28 Between Two Fires .10 .30
❑ 29 Between Two Fires .10 .30
❑ 30 Between Two Fires .10 .30
❑ 31 2001 .10 .30
❑ 32 2001 .10 .30
❑ 33 2001 .10 .30
❑ 34 Desperate Measures .10 .30
❑ 35 Desperate Measures .10 .30
❑ 36 Desperate Measures .10 .30
❑ 37 Wormhole X-Treme! .10 .30
❑ 38 Wormhole X-Treme! .10 .30
❑ 39 Wormhole X-Treme! .10 .30
❑ 40 Proving Ground .10 .30
❑ 41 Proving Ground .10 .30
❑ 42 Proving Ground .10 .30
❑ 43 48 Hours .10 .30
❑ 44 48 Hours .10 .30
❑ 45 48 Hours .10 .30
❑ 46 Summit .10 .30
❑ 47 Summit .10 .30
❑ 48 Summit .10 .30
❑ 49 Last Stand .10 .30
❑ 50 Last Stand .10 .30
❑ 51 Last Stand .10 .30
❑ 52 Fail Safe .10 .30
❑ 53 Fail Safe .10 .30
❑ 54 Fail Safe .10 .30
❑ 55 The Warrior .10 .30
❑ 56 The Warrior .10 .30
❑ 57 The Warrior .10 .30
❑ 58 Menace .10 .30
❑ 59 Menace .10 .30
❑ 60 Menace .10 .30
❑ 61 The Sentinel .10 .30
❑ 62 The Sentinel .10 .30
❑ 63 The Sentinel .10 .30
❑ 64 Meridian .10 .30
❑ 65 Meridian .10 .30
❑ 66 Meridian .10 .30
❑ 67 Revelations .10 .30
❑ 68 Revelations .10 .30
❑ 69 Revelations .10 .30
❑ 70 Checklist 1 .10 .30
❑ 71 Checklist 2 .10 .30
❑ 72 Checklist 3 .10 .30

2003 Stargate SG-1 Season Five Autographs

OVERALL AUTO ODDS TWO PER BOX
A25 ISSUED AS CASE TOPPER

❑ A20 Gary Jones 6.00 15.00
❑ A21 Christopher Judge 6.00 15.00
❑ A22 Garwin Sanford 6.00 15.00
❑ A23 Elisabeth Rosen 6.00 15.00
❑ A24 Dan Shea 6.00 15.00
❑ A25 John De Lance/ (issued as case topper) 20.00 40.00

2003 Stargate SG-1 Season Five Dr. Daniel Jackson Tribute

COMPLETE SET (9) 2.50 6.00
STATED ODDS 1:4

❑ D1 Dr. Daniel Jackson .40 1.00
❑ D2 Dr. Daniel Jackson .40 1.00
❑ D3 Dr. Daniel Jackson .40 1.00
❑ D4 Dr. Daniel Jackson .40 1.00
❑ D5 Dr. Daniel Jackson .40 1.00
❑ D6 Dr. Daniel Jackson .40 1.00
❑ D7 Dr. Daniel Jackson .40 1.00
❑ D8 Dr. Daniel Jackson .40 1.00
❑ D9 Dr. Daniel Jackson .40 1.00

2003 Stargate SG-1 Season Five False Gods

COMPLETE SET (12) 10.00 25.00
STATED ODDS 1:12

❑ F1 Apophis 1.25 3.00
❑ F2 Baal 1.25 3.00
❑ F3 Bastet 1.25 3.00
❑ F4 Cronus 1.25 3.00
❑ F5 Hathor 1.25 3.00
❑ F6 Kali 1.25 3.00
❑ F7 Morrigan 1.25 3.00
❑ F8 Nurrit 1.25 3.00
❑ F9 Olokun 1.25 3.00
❑ F10 Osiris 1.25 3.00
❑ F11 Seth 1.25 3.00
❑ F12 Yu 1.25 3.00

2003 Stargate SG-1 Season Five From The Archives Costumes

STATED ODDS 1:160
C16 ISSUED IN COLLECTORS ALBUM

❑ C13 Colonel Jack O'Neill 6.00 15.00
❑ C14 Bra'tac 30.00 60.00
❑ C15 Sha're 6.00 15.00
❑ C16 Colonel Danning/ (issued in collectors album) 6.00 15.00

2003 Stargate SG-1 Season Five Promos

COMPLETE SET (3) 2.50 6.00

❑ P1 Teal'c/ (General Distribution) 1.00 2.50
❑ P2 Colonel Jack O'Neill/ (Convention Exclusive) 1.00 2.50
❑ P3 Dr. Daniel Jackson/ (Binder Exclusive) 1.50 4.00

2003 Stargate SG-1 Season Five SketchaFEX

STATED ODDS ONE PER BOX

❑ 1 John Czop (Crystal Skull)
❑ 2 John Czop (Hathor)
❑ 3 John Czop (Jaffa Warrior)
❑ 4 John Czop (Major Carter)
❑ 5 John Czop (The Nox)
❑ 6 John Czop (Osiris)
❑ 7 John Czop (Rings)
❑ 8 Michael Kraiger (Asgard)
❑ 9 Warren Martineck (Osiris)
❑ 10 Warren Martineck (Rings)
❑ 11 Warren Martineck (Sha're)
❑ 12 Warren Martineck (Stargate)
❑ 13 Pablo Raimondi (Asgard)
❑ 14 Pablo Raimondi (Jack O'Neill)
❑ 15 Pablo Raimondi (Jaffa Warrior)
❑ 16 Pablo Raimondi (Teal'c)
❑ 17 Dan Schaefer (Dannes)
❑ 18 Dan Schaefer (Sam Carter)
❑ 19 Dan Schaefer (Unas)

2003 Stargate SG-1 Season Five Wormhole X-Treme

COMPLETE SET (9) 6.00 15.00
STATED ODDS 1:8

❑ W1 Wormhole X-Treme! .75 2.00
❑ W2 Wormhole X-Treme! .75 2.00
❑ W3 Wormhole X-Treme! .75 2.00
❑ W4 Wormhole X-Treme! .75 2.00
❑ W5 Wormhole X-Treme! .75 2.00
❑ W6 Wormhole X-Treme! .75 2.00
❑ W7 Wormhole X-Treme! .75 2.00
❑ W8 Wormhole X-Treme! .75 2.00
❑ W9 Wormhole X-Treme! .75 2.00

2003 Stargate SG-1 Season Five Wormhole X-Treme Autographs

OVERALL AUTO ODDS TWO PER BOX

❑ WXA1 Michael DeLuise 6.00 15.00
❑ WXA2 Jill Teed 6.00 15.00
❑ WXA3 Christian Bocher 6.00 15.00
❑ WXA4 Herbert Duncanson 6.00 15.00
❑ WXA5 Kiara Hunter 6.00 15.00
❑ WXA6 Willie Garson 6.00 15.00

2003 Terminator 2 Judgement Day FilmCardz

COMPLETE SET (72) 5.00 12.00

❑ 1 The Terminator .15 .40
❑ 2 Endoskeleton .15 .40
❑ 3 John Connor .15 .40
❑ 4 T1000 .15 .40
❑ 5 Sarah Connor .15 .40
❑ 6 Miles Dyson .15 .40
❑ 7 T1000 .15 .40
❑ 8 Dr. Peter Silberman .15 .40
❑ 9 Enrique Salceda .15 .40
❑ 10 Cyberdyne Technology .15 .40
❑ 11 Heading to L.A. .15 .40
❑ 12 Time to Roll .15 .40
❑ 13 Assessing Sarah Connor .15 .40
❑ 14 I Am Much Better Now .15 .40
❑ 15 Sarah Pleads to See Her Son .15 .40
❑ 16 The Search for John Connor .15 .40
❑ 17 Awaiting His Adversary .15 .40
❑ 18 Tracking a Terminator .15 .40
❑ 19 John Connor at the Galleria .15 .40
❑ 20 Closing in on Its Prey .15 .40
❑ 21 A Frightened John Connor .15 .40
❑ 22 Encounter at the Mall .15 .40
❑ 23 Outpacing a Kenworth .15 .40
❑ 24 Entering the Flood Control Channel .15 .40
❑ 25 Hot Pursuit on a Harley .15 .40
❑ 26 Who Sent You .15 .40
❑ 27 Escaping the Inferno .15 .40
❑ 28 You Are a Terminator .15 .40
❑ 29 Interrogation .15 .40
❑ 30 Not Quite Seeing Eye to Eye .15 .40
❑ 31 Now Don't Move .15 .40
❑ 32 Squeezing through the Bars .15 .40
❑ 33 Dr. Silberman Watches in Disbelief .15 .40
❑ 34 Surviving a Point-Blank Blast .15 .40
❑ 35 Old Friends .15 .40
❑ 36 You Get Out Tonight, Too, Okay .15 .40
❑ 37 No Problemo .15 .40
❑ 38 Nuclear Nightmare .15 .40
❑ 39 Forseeing the Future .15 .40
❑ 40 No Fate .15 .40
❑ 41 Zeroing in on Dyson .15 .40
❑ 42 Sarah and John Connor .15 .40
❑ 43 Dyson's Future Revealed .15 .40
❑ 44 Gaining Entry .15 .40
❑ 45 Changing the Future .15 .40
❑ 46 Inside Cyberdyne's Vault .15 .40
❑ 47 Dyson Destroys Life's Work .15 .40
❑ 48 Everything Must Be Destroyed .15 .40
❑ 49 Buying Time outside Cyberdyne .15 .40
❑ 50 T1000 Arrives at the Scene .15 .40
❑ 51 Morphing into Position .15 .40
❑ 52 The Chase Is On .15 .40
❑ 53 T1000 in Helicopter .15 .40
❑ 54 A Narrow Escape .15 .40
❑ 55 A Dangerous Load .15 .40
❑ 56 Headed for a Showdown .15 .40
❑ 57 Unstoppable .15 .40
❑ 58 Frozen in Liquid Nitrogen .15 .40
❑ 59 Confronting the T1000 .15 .40
❑ 60 The Ever-Morphing T1000 .15 .40
❑ 61 Final Stand .15 .40
❑ 62 Locked and Loaded .15 .40
❑ 63 Surprise .15 .40
❑ 64 Hole in the Head .15 .40
❑ 65 Sneak Attack .15 .40
❑ 66 Bad Move .15 .40
❑ 67 Damage Inflicted by a M-79 .15 .40
❑ 68 I Need a Vacation .15 .40
❑ 69 Saying Goodbye .15 .40
❑ 70 A Fateful Decision .15 .40
❑ 71 It Must End Here .15 .40
❑ 72 John Gets a Final Thumbs Up .15 .40
❑ CL Checklist .15 .40
❑ T2 On the Inside (collector's tin exclusive) 1.50 4.00
❑ FX1 Liquid Metal from T1000 MEM

2003 Terminator 2 Judgement Day FilmCardz Autographs

STATED ODDS 1:24

❑ 1 Dan Stanton 6.00 15.00
❑ 2 Don Stanton 6.00 15.00
❑ 3 Earl Boen 6.00 15.00
❑ 4 Edward Fulong 20.00 40.00
❑ 5 Joe Morton 6.00 15.00
❑ 6 Linda Hamilton /275* 125.00 250.00
❑ 7 Robert Patrick /275* 125.00 200.00
❑ 8 Don Stanton 20.00 40.00
Dan Stanton/ (issued as case topper)

2003 Terminator 2 Judgement Day FilmCardz CyberEtch

COMPLETE SET (24) 5.00 12.00
STATED ODDS ONE PER PACK

❑ CE1 The Fate of Mankind .40 1.00
❑ CE2 Hunting Humans .40 1.00
❑ CE3 The T1000 Spots Its Target .40 1.00
❑ CE4 A Close Resemblance .40 1.00
❑ CE5 Trouble at the Mall .40 1.00
❑ CE6 Close Behind .40 1.00
❑ CE7 Creator of the Machines .40 1.00
❑ CE8 Stopping for Nothing .40 1.00
❑ CE9 Escaping the Insanity .40 1.00
❑ CE10 Protecting the Mission .40 1.00
❑ CE11 Liquid-Floor Effect .40 1.00
❑ CE12 You Broke My Arm .40 1.00
❑ CE13 Hunted by a Killing Machine .40 1.00
❑ CE14 A Clever Disguise .40 1.00
❑ CE15 The Terminator Stitches Sarah Connor .40 1.00
❑ CE16 A Welcome Greeting .40 1.00
❑ CE17 Observing the Terminator .40 1.00
❑ CE18 Why Do You Cry .40 1.00
❑ CE19 Destroy Cyberdyne .40 1.00
❑ CE20 Trading Places .40 1.00
❑ CE21 Chase on the Freeway .40 1.00
❑ CE22 Air Assault .40 1.00
❑ CE23 The T1000 Shatters into Pieces .40 1.00
❑ CE24 The T1000 Prepares to Destroy the Connors .40 1.00

2003 Terminator 2 Judgement Day FilmCardz FilmWear

STATED ODDS 1:24

❑ FW1 T800 Pants 12.00 25.00
❑ FW2 John Connor Jacket 5.00 10.00
❑ FW3 T1000 Pants 5.00 10.00
❑ FW4 Sarah Connor Shirt 6.00 15.00
❑ FW5 T800 Leather Jacket 15.00 30.00
❑ CT1 T800 Shirt CT 20.00 40.00

2003 Terminator 2 Judgement Day FilmCardz Preview

COMPLETE SET (5) 3.00 6.00
STATED PRINT RUN 1008 SER. #'d SETS

❑ PS1 The Terminator 1.00 2.50
❑ PS2 Endoskeleton 1.00 2.50
❑ PS3 Sarah Connor 1.00 2.50
❑ PS4 Model T1000 1.00 2.50
❑ PS5 John Connor 1.00 2.50

2003 Terminator 2 Judgement Day FilmCardz Preview Silver

COMPLETE SET (5) 3.00 6.00

❑ PS1 The Terminator 1.00 2.50
❑ PS2 Endoskeleton 1.00 2.50
❑ PS3 Sarah Connor 1.00 2.50
❑ PS4 Model T1000 1.00 2.50
❑ PS5 John Connor 1.00 2.50

2003 Terminator 2 Judgement Day FilmCardz Promos

COMPLETE SET (2) 1.50 3.00

❑ P1 I'll Be Back .75 2.00
❑ P2 Endoskeleton .75 2.00

2003 Terminator 2 Judgement Day FilmCardz Rare Metal

COMPLETE SET (6) 5.00 12.00
STATED ODDS 1:8

❑ R1 On the Hunt 1.50 4.00
❑ R2 Chasing John Connor 1.50 4.00
❑ R3 Shotgun Blasts to the Chest 1.50 4.00
❑ R4 In the Face of Death 1.50 4.00
❑ R5 Sarah Fights to Change the Future 1.50 4.00
❑ R6 Altering the Neural-Net Processor 1.50 4.00

2003 Terminator 2 Judgement Day FilmCardz Ultra Rare Metal

COMPLETE SET (3) 4.00 10.00
STATED ODDS 1:12

❑ UR1 Seek and Destroy 2.50 6.00
❑ UR2 Fight to the Death 2.50 6.00
❑ UR3 Get Out 2.50 6.00

2003 Terminator 2 Judgement Day FilmCardz Ultra Rare Metal Box Toppers

COMPLETE SET (3) 5.00 12.00
STATED ODDS ONE PER BOX

❑ BT1 The Face of the Future 3.00 8.00
❑ BT2 The Real Sarah Connor 3.00 8.00
❑ BT3 Come with Me If You Want To Live 3.00 8.00

2003 Terminator 3 Rise of the Machines

COMPLETE SET (72) 5.00 12.00

❑ 1 New Chapter .10 .30
❑ 2 The Terminator .10 .30
❑ 3 T-X .10 .30
❑ 4 John Connor .10 .30
❑ 5 Kate Brewster .10 .30
❑ 6 Gen. Robert Brewster .10 .30
❑ 7 Scott Peterson .10 .30
❑ 8 Dr. Peter Silberman .10 .30
❑ 9 Robot Warriors .10 .30
❑ 10 Judgment Day .10 .30
❑ 11 Still Running .10 .30
❑ 12 He's Back .10 .30
❑ 13 Now .10 .30
❑ 14 I Like This Car .10 .30
❑ 15 Caged .10 .30
❑ 16 Slam .10 .30
❑ 17 I Lied .10 .30
❑ 18 Fire .10 .30
❑ 19 Flaming Debris .10 .30
❑ 20 It Is Time .10 .30
❑ 21 Follow That Tundra .10 .30
❑ 22 He'll Drive .10 .30
❑ 23 Killer Caravan .10 .30
❑ 24 Behind the Wheel .10 .30
❑ 25 Hook-and-Ladder .10 .30
❑ 26 Road Rage .10 .30
❑ 27 Scott ... Terminated .10 .30
❑ 28 In Pursuit .10 .30
❑ 29 Cemetery Siege .10 .30
❑ 30 From the Grave .10 .30
❑ 31 Out of My Way .10 .30
❑ 32 Crash .10 .30
❑ 33 Jump .10 .30
❑ 34 New Wheels .10 .30
❑ 35 In Uniform .10 .30

MODERN ERA NON-SPORTS

❑ 36 CRS Command Center .10 .30
❑ 37 Morphing .10 .30
❑ 38 She'll Be Back .10 .30
❑ 39 The Enemy Is Us .10 .30
❑ 40 First Generation .10 .30
❑ 41 Return Fire .10 .30
❑ 42 Shut Down .10 .30
❑ 43 No Match .10 .30
❑ 44 Smoking Gun .10 .30
❑ 45 Blown Apart .10 .30
❑ 46 Carnage .10 .30
❑ 47 Full-Bore .10 .30
❑ 48 Swing .10 .30
❑ 49 Shattered .10 .30
❑ 50 180 .10 .30
❑ 51 Power Up .10 .30
❑ 52 Flame-Thrower .10 .30
❑ 53 Aftermath .10 .30
❑ 54 Desire Is Irrelevant .10 .30
❑ 55 Destiny .10 .30
❑ 56 Crystal Peak .10 .30
❑ 57 She's Back .10 .30
❑ 58 Closing In .10 .30
❑ 59 Juggernaut .10 .30
❑ 60 Half-Man, Half-Machine .10 .30
❑ 61 Pinned .10 .30
❑ 62 Until We Meet Again .10 .30
❑ 63 Action .10 .30
❑ 64 Winston's Wizardry .10 .30
❑ 65 On Location .10 .30
❑ 66 Attack .10 .30
❑ 67 Off Camera .10 .30
❑ 68 Playback .10 .30
❑ 69 Adversaries .10 .30
❑ 70 Fembot .10 .30
❑ 71 Close Up .10 .30
❑ 72 Checklist .10 .30

2003 Terminator 3 Rise of the Machines Autographs

STATED ODDS 1:96 HOBBY, 1:144 RETAIL
A1 AND A2 ONLY IN HOBBY PACKS
❑ A1 Arnold Schwarzenegger/300* 200.00 350.00
❑ A2 Kristanna Loken/300* 40.00 80.00
❑ A3 Stan Winston/600* 8.00 20.00
❑ A4 Jonathan Mostow/600* 8.00 20.00
❑ A5, Nick Stahl (issued as case incentive) 10.00 25.00

2003 Terminator 3 Rise of the Machines Promos

❑ P1 T-800 1.50 4.00
❑ P2 T-X 1.50 4.00
❑ P3 T-800 w fire (Non-Sport Update exclusive) 3.00 8.00

2003 Terminator 3 Rise of the Machines T-Worn Costumes

STATED ODDS 1:58
❑ T1 T-800 shirt /600* 10.00 25.00
❑ T2 Officer's battle jacket /1200* 8.00 20.00
❑ T3 Hearse upholstery /1200* 8.00 20.00
❑ R1 T1 Redemption
❑ R2 T2 Redemption
❑ R3 T3 Redemption

2003 Terminator 3 Rise of the Machines The Skynet War Machines

COMPLETE SET (6) 6.00 15.00
STATED ODDS 1:12
❑ C1 T-100 2.00 5.00
❑ C2 T-850 2.00 5.00
❑ C3 T-900 2.00 5.00
❑ C4 T-X (Skeletal) 2.00 5.00
❑ C5 T-X (Flesh) 2.00 5.00
❑ C6 Hunter-Killer 2.00 5.00

2003 Women of James Bond In Motion

COMPLETE SET (63) 5.00 12.00
❑ 1 Honey Ryder .15 .40
❑ 2 Honey Ryder .15 .40
❑ 3 Miss Taro .15 .40
❑ 4 Sylvia Trench .15 .40
❑ 5 Tatiana Romanova .15 .40
❑ 6 Tatiana Romanova .15 .40
❑ 7 Jill Masterson .15 .40
❑ 8 Tilly Masterson .15 .40
❑ 9 Pussy Galore .15 .40
❑ 10 Pussy Galore .15 .40
❑ 11 Patricia Fearing .15 .40
❑ 12 Domino Derval .15 .40
❑ 13 Domino Derval .15 .40
❑ 14 Fiona Volpe .15 .40
❑ 15 Aki .15 .40
❑ 16 Helga Brandt .15 .40
❑ 17 Kissy Suzuki .15 .40
❑ 18 Kissy Suzuki .15 .40
❑ 19 Traci De Vincenzo .15 .40
❑ 20 Traci De Vincenzo .15 .40
❑ 21 Ruby Bartlett .15 .40
❑ 22 Tiffany Case .15 .40
❑ 23 Tiffany Case .15 .40
❑ 24 Plenty O'Toole .15 .40
❑ 25 Miss Caruso .15 .40
❑ 26 Rosie Carver .15 .40
❑ 27 Solitaire .15 .40
❑ 28 Solitaire .15 .40
❑ 29 Andrea Anders .15 .40
❑ 30 Mary Goodnight .15 .40
❑ 31 Mary Goodnight .15 .40
❑ 32 Major Anya Amasova .15 .40
❑ 33 Major Anya Amasova .15 .40
❑ 34 Corinne Dufour .15 .40
❑ 35 Dr. Holly Goodhead .15 .40
❑ 36 Dr. Holly Goodhead .15 .40
❑ 37 Bibi .15 .40
❑ 38 Melina Havelock .15 .40
❑ 39 Melina Havelock .15 .40
❑ 40 Magda .15 .40
❑ 41 Octopussy .15 .40
❑ 42 Octopussy .15 .40
❑ 43 Mayday .15 .40
❑ 44 Stacey Sutton .15 .40
❑ 45 Stacey Sutton .15 .40
❑ 46 Pola Ivanova .15 .40
❑ 47 Kara Milovy .15 .40
❑ 48 Kara Milovy .15 .40
❑ 49 Pam Bouvier .15 .40
❑ 50 Pam Bouvier .15 .40
❑ 51 Lupe Lamora .15 .40
❑ 52 Natalya Simonova .15 .40
❑ 53 Natalya Simonova .15 .40
❑ 54 Xenia Onatopp .15 .40
❑ 55 Paris Carver .15 .40
❑ 56 Wai Lin .15 .40
❑ 57 Wai Lin .15 .40
❑ 58 Elektra King .15 .40
❑ 59 Dr. Christmas Jones .15 .40
❑ 60 Dr. Christmas Jones .15 .40
❑ 61 Miranda Frost .15 .40
❑ 62 Jinx .15 .40
❑ 63 Jinx .15 .40

2003 Women of James Bond In Motion Autographs

COMPLETE SET (15) 300.00 600.00
STATED ODDS 1:10
❑ WA1 Jill St. John 20.00 40.00
❑ WA2 Maryam d'Abo 20.00 40.00
❑ WA3 Barbara Bach 75.00 150.00
❑ WA4 Karin Dor 15.00 30.00
❑ WA5 Gloria Hendry 15.00 30.00
❑ WA6 Zena Marshall 20.00 40.00
❑ WA7 Kristina Wayborn 20.00 40.00
❑ WA8 Eunice Gayson 10.00 25.00
❑ WA9 Lynn-Holly Johnson 10.00 25.00
❑ WA10 Maud Adams 25.00 50.00
❑ WA11 Britt Ekland 20.00 40.00
❑ WA12 Luciana Paluzzi 15.00 30.00
❑ WA13 Mie Hama 60.00 120.00
❑ WA14 Jane Seymour 25.00 50.00
❑ WA15 Lois Chiles 60.00 120.00

2003 Women of James Bond In Motion Bond Girls Are Forever

COMPLETE SET (20) 25.00 60.00
STATED ODDS 1:5
❑ BG1 Honey Ryder 1.50 4.00
❑ BG2 Tatiana Romanova 1.50 4.00
❑ BG3 Pussy Galore 1.50 4.00
❑ BG4 Domino Derval 1.50 4.00
❑ BG5 Kissy Suzuki 1.50 4.00
❑ BG6 Tracy DiVincenzo 1.50 4.00
❑ BG7 Tiffany Case 1.50 4.00
❑ BG8 Solitaire 1.50 4.00
❑ BG9 Mary Goodnight 1.50 4.00
❑ BG10 Major Anya Amasova 1.50 4.00
❑ BG11 Dr. Holly Goodhead 1.50 4.00
❑ BG12 Melina Havlock 1.50 4.00
❑ BG13 Octopussy 1.50 4.00
❑ BG14 Stacey Sutton 1.50 4.00
❑ BG15 Kara Milovy 1.50 4.00
❑ BG16 Pam Bouvier 1.50 4.00
❑ BG17 Natalya Simonova 1.50 4.00
❑ BG18 Wai Lin 1.50 4.00
❑ BG19 Christmas Jones 1.50 4.00
❑ BG20 Jinx 1.50 4.00

2003 Women of James Bond In Motion Case Toppers

COMPLETE SET (3) 12.50 30.00
STATED ODDS ONE PER CASE
❑ CT1 Sean Connery 5.00 12.00
❑ CT2 Roger Moore 5.00 12.00
❑ CT3 Pierce Brosnan 5.00 12.00

2003 Women of James Bond In Motion Femmes Fatales

COMPLETE SET (9) 4.00 10.00
STATED ODDS 1:4
❑ F1 Jill Masterson .60 1.50
❑ F2 Fiona Volpe .60 1.50
❑ F3 Helga Brandt .60 1.50
❑ F4 Rosie Carver .60 1.50
❑ F5 Andrea Anders .60 1.50
❑ F6 May Day .60 1.50
❑ F7 Xenia Onatopp .60 1.50
❑ F8 Elektra King .60 1.50
❑ F9 Miranda Frost .60 1.50

2003 Women of James Bond In Motion Jinx

COMPLETE SET (9) 4.00 10.00
STATED ODDS 1:7
❑ J1 Jinx .60 1.50
❑ J2 Jinx .60 1.50
❑ J3 Jinx .60 1.50
❑ J4 Jinx .60 1.50
❑ J5 Jinx .60 1.50
❑ J6 Jinx .60 1.50
❑ J7 Jinx .60 1.50
❑ J8 Jinx .60 1.50
❑ J9 Jinx .60 1.50

2003 Women of James Bond In Motion Promos

COMPLETE SET (3) 4.00 10.00
❑ P1 Honey Ryder 2.00 5.00
❑ P2 Women of James Bond In Motion 1.00 2.50
❑ P3 Women of James Bond In Motion 2.00 5.00

2003 Women of James Bond In Motion Women of MI6

COMPLETE SET (6) 3.00 8.00
STATED ODDS 1:3.3
❑ M1 M .75 2.00
❑ M2 M .75 2.00
❑ M3 M .75 2.00
❑ M4 Moneypenny .75 2.00
❑ M5 Moneypenny .75 2.00
❑ M6 Moneypenny .75 2.00

2003 X-Files Season 9

COMPLETE SET (90) 5.00 12.00
❑ 1 The Truth Is Out There .15 .40
❑ 2 9X01: Nothing Important Happened Part 1 .15 .40
❑ 3 9X01: Nothing Important Happened Part 1 .15 .40
❑ 4 9X01: Nothing Important Happened Part 1 .15 .40
❑ 5 9X02: Nothing Important Happened Part 2 .15 .40
❑ 6 9X02: Nothing Important Happened Part 2 .15 .40
❑ 7 9X02: Nothing Important Happened Part 2 .15 .40
❑ 8 9X03: Daemonicus .15 .40
❑ 9 9X03: Daemonicus .15 .40
❑ 10 9X03: Daemonicus .15 .40
❑ 11 9X04: Hellbound .15 .40
❑ 12 9X04: Hellbound .15 .40
❑ 13 9X04: Hellbound .15 .40
❑ 14 9X05: 4-D .15 .40
❑ 15 9X05: 4-D .15 .40
❑ 16 9X05: 4-D .15 .40
❑ 17 9X06: Lord Of The Flies .15 .40
❑ 18 9X06: Lord Of The Flies .15 .40
❑ 19 9X06: Lord Of The Flies .15 .40
❑ 20 9X07: John Doe .15 .40
❑ 21 9X07: John Doe .15 .40
❑ 22 9X07: John Doe .15 .40
❑ 23 9X08: Trust No 1 .15 .40
❑ 24 9X08: Trust No 1 .15 .40
❑ 25 9X08: Trust No 1 .15 .40
❑ 26 9X09: Underneath .15 .40
❑ 27 9X09: Underneath .15 .40
❑ 28 9X09: Underneath .15 .40
❑ 29 9X10: Provenance .15 .40
❑ 30 9X10: Provenance .15 .40
❑ 31 9X10: Provenance .15 .40
❑ 32 9X11: Providence .15 .40
❑ 33 9X11: Providence .15 .40
❑ 34 9X11: Providence .15 .40
❑ 35 9X12: Scary Monsters .15 .40
❑ 36 9X12: Scary Monsters .15 .40
❑ 37 9X12: Scary Monsters .15 .40
❑ 38 9X13: Audrey Pauley .15 .40
❑ 39 9X13: Audrey Pauley .15 .40
❑ 40 9X13: Audrey Pauley .15 .40
❑ 41 9X14: Improbable .15 .40
❑ 42 9X14: Improbable .15 .40
❑ 43 9X14: Improbable .15 .40
❑ 44 9X15: Jump The Shark .15 .40
❑ 45 9X15: Jump The Shark .15 .40
❑ 46 9X15: Jump The Shark .15 .40
❑ 47 9X16: Release .15 .40
❑ 48 9X16: Release .15 .40
❑ 49 9X16: Release .15 .40
❑ 50 9X17: William .15 .40
❑ 51 9X17: William .15 .40
❑ 52 9X17: William .15 .40
❑ 53 9X18: Sunshine Days .15 .40
❑ 54 9X18: Sunshine Days .15 .40
❑ 55 9X18: Sunshine Days .15 .40
❑ 56 9X19: The Truth Pt 1 .15 .40
❑ 57 9X19: The Truth Pt 1 .15 .40
❑ 58 9X19: The Truth Pt 1 .15 .40
❑ 59 9X19: The Truth Pt 1 .15 .40
❑ 60 9X20: The Truth Pt 2 .15 .40
❑ 61 9X20: The Truth Pt 2 .15 .40
❑ 62 9X20: The Truth Pt 2 .15 .40
❑ 63 9X20: The Truth Pt 2 .15 .40
❑ 64 Special Agent Fox Mulder .15 .40
❑ 65 Special Agent Dana Scully .15 .40
❑ 66 Special Agent John Doggett .15 .40
❑ 67 Special Agent Monica Reyes .15 .40
❑ 68 Assistant Director Walter Skinner .15 .40
❑ 69 Deputy Director Alvin Kersh .15 .40
❑ 70 Assistant Director Brad Follmer .15 .40
❑ 71 The Lone Gunmen .15 .40
❑ 72 Jeffrey Spender .15 .40
❑ 73 Knowle Rohrer .15 .40
❑ 74 Shannon Mcmahon .15 .40
❑ 75 Shadow Man .15 .40
❑ 76 Psychic Plasma .15 .40
❑ 77 Skinned Alive .15 .40
❑ 78 Parallel Lines .15 .40
❑ 79 Car Cocoon .15 .40
❑ 80 In The Void .15 .40
❑ 81 New Perspective .15 .40
❑ 82 Celebration .15 .40
❑ 83 Up Close .15 .40
❑ 84 Taking Direction .15 .40
❑ 85 Between Shots .15 .40
❑ 86 Playback .15 .40
❑ 87 Old Friends .15 .40
❑ 88 Fun On Location .15 .40
❑ 89 Last Looks .15 .40
❑ 90 Checklist .15 .40

2003 X-Files Season 9 Autographs

COMPLETE SET (7) 300.00 600.00
STATED ODDS 1:41
❑ AF Gillian Anderson 200.00 350.00
❑ A16 Robert Patrick 60.00 120.00
❑ A16 Mitch Pileggi 60.00 120.00
❑ A17 William B. Davis 10.00 25.00
❑ A18 Chris Owens 10.00 25.00
❑ A19 Steven Williams 10.00 25.00
❑ A20 Burt Reynolds 25.00 50.00

2003 X-Files Season 9 Box Loaders

COMPLETE SET (4) 7.50 20.00
❑ BL1 Mulder & Scully 1.50 4.00
❑ BL2 Doggett & Reyes 1.50 4.00
❑ BL3 Skinner 1.50 4.00
❑ CL1 Smoking Man 6.00 15.00

2003 X-Files Season 9 Pieceworks

COMPLETE SET (5) 60.00 120.00
STATED ODDS 1:24
❑ PW1 Mr. Burt's Shirt 7.50 20.00
❑ PW2 Doggett's Shirt 7.50 20.00
❑ PW3 Skinner's Shirt 7.50 20.00
❑ PW4 Skinner's Tie 40.00 80.00
❑ PW5 Skinner's Pants 7.50 20.00

2003 X-Files Season 9 Promos

COMPLETE SET (3) 3.00 8.00
❑ P1 Mulder & Scully 1.00 2.50
❑ Pi Reyes & Doggett 1.00 2.50
❑ PUK Scully & Skinner 2.00 5.00

2003 X-Files Season 9 Reunion

COMPLETE SET (6) 7.50 20.00
STATED ODDS 1:17
❑ R1 Reunion 1.50 4.00
❑ R2 Reunion 1.50 4.00
❑ R3 Reunion 1.50 4.00
❑ R4 Reunion 1.50 4.00
❑ R5 Reunion 1.50 4.00
❑ R6 Reunion 1.50 4.00

2003 X-Files Season 9 The Truth On Trial

COMPLETE SET (9) 12.50 30.00
STATED ODDS 1:11
❑ T1 The Truth On Trial 1.50 4.00
❑ T2 The Truth On Trial 1.50 4.00
❑ T3 The Truth On Trial 1.50 4.00
❑ T4 The Truth On Trial 1.50 4.00
❑ T5 The Truth On Trial 1.50 4.00
❑ T6 The Truth On Trial 1.50 4.00
❑ T7 The Truth On Trial 1.50 4.00
❑ T8 The Truth On Trial 1.50 4.00
❑ T9 The Truth On Trial 1.50 4.00

2003 X2 X-Men United

COMPLETE SET (72) 5.00 12.00
❑ 1 Professor X .15 .40
❑ 2 Wolverine .15 .40
❑ 3 Jean Grey .15 .40
❑ 4 Cyclops .15 .40
❑ 5 Storm .15 .40
❑ 6 Magneto .15 .40
❑ 7 Mystique .15 .40
❑ 8 Colonel Stryker .15 .40
❑ 9 Lady Deathstrike .15 .40
❑ 10 Rogue .15 .40
❑ 11 Iceman .15 .40
❑ 12 Nightcrawler .15 .40
❑ 13 Pyro .15 .40
❑ 14 Colossus .15 .40
❑ 15 Mutant 143 .15 .40
❑ 16 Terror Is a Mutant .15 .40
❑ 17 The White House Invaded .15 .40
❑ 18 An Ominous Warning .15 .40
❑ 19 Of Power and Passion .15 .40
❑ 20 The X-Team Confers .15 .40
❑ 21 Stryker's Game .15 .40
❑ 22 Logan's Return .15 .40
❑ 23 Off on a Mission .15 .40
❑ 24 Where Demons Dwell .15 .40
❑ 25 Attacked by Nightcrawler .15 .40
❑ 26 The Teleporter Nabbed .15 .40
❑ 27 Birth of a Mutant .15 .40
❑ 28 Friends or Deadly Foes .15 .40
❑ 29 Heroes Under Siege .15 .40
❑ 30 Deadly Opponents .15 .40
❑ 31 The Defeat of Cyclops .15 .40
❑ 32 Night Raid on the X-Mansion .15 .40
❑ 33 Colossus The Rescuer .15 .40
❑ 34 Wolverine's Fury .15 .40
❑ 35 His Wrath Unleashed .15 .40
❑ 36 Escape and Survive .15 .40
❑ 37 The Prize .15 .40
❑ 38 Mutants on the Run .15 .40
❑ 39 Magneto Takes Control .15 .40
❑ 40 Logan Comes Quietly .15 .40
❑ 41 Pyro's Revenge .15 .40
❑ 42 Grand Illusion .15 .40
❑ 43 Fracas in the Sky .15 .40
❑ 44 An Unlikely Alliance .15 .40
❑ 45 What Nightcrawler Knows .15 .40
❑ 46 For the Love of Logan .15 .40
❑ 47 War Games .15 .40
❑ 48 Mission...Accomplished .15 .40
❑ 49 The Professor's Little-Girl .15 .40
❑ 50 Inside Dark Cerebro .15 .40
❑ 51 Mutants Invade the Base .15 .40
❑ 52 The Power of Cyclops .15 .40
❑ 53 Beam of Destruction .15 .40
❑ 54 Love Is Blind .15 .40
❑ 55 Rescues and Revelations .15 .40
❑ 56 Lady Deathstrike Attacks .15 .40
❑ 57 When Mutants Collide .15 .40
❑ 58 Magneto's Counterplan .15 .40
❑ 59 The Showdown .15 .40
❑ 60 Cool World .15 .40
❑ 61 Logan's Temptation .15 .40
❑ 62 Against the Flood .15 .40
❑ 63 Rescued by Rogue .15 .40
❑ 64 Escape from Armageddon .15 .40
❑ 65 By George, It's Nightcrawler! .15 .40
❑ 66 Here to Stay .15 .40
❑ 67 A Director's Challenge .15 .40
❑ 68 Filming Fantastic Femmes .15 .40
❑ 69 Checkmaters .15 .40
❑ 70 Kids with Something X-tra .15 .40
❑ 71 Just the Beast in Him .15 .40
❑ 72 Checklist .15 .40

2003 X2 X-Men United Autographs

COMPLETE SET (10) 150.00 300.00
STATED ODDS 1:36 HOBBY
❑ NNO Aaron Stanford 7.50 20.00
❑ NNO Alan Cumming 25.00 50.00
❑ NNO Bruce Davison 7.50 20.00
❑ NNO Bryan Singer 75.00 150.00
❑ NNO Daniel Cudmore 7.50 20.00
❑ NNO James Marsden 7.50 20.00
❑ NNO Katie Stuart 12.50 30.00
❑ NNO Kea Wong 7.50 20.00
❑ NNO Michael Reid Mackay 7.50 20.00
❑ NNO Shawn Ashmore 7.50 20.00

2003 X2 X-Men United Clear

COMPLETE SET (5) 6.00 15.00
STATED ODDS 1:12 RETAIL
❑ C1 Magneto 1.50 4.00
❑ C2 Nightcrawler 1.50 4.00
❑ C3 Storm 1.50 4.00
❑ C4 Wolverine 1.50 4.00
❑ C5 Lady Deathstrike 1.50 4.00

2003 X2 X-Men United Foil

COMPLETE SET (10) 12.50 30.00
STATED ODDS 1:6 RETAIL
❑ 1. Cyclops 1.50 4.00
❑ 2 Jean Grey 1.50 4.00
❑ 3 Magneto 1.50 4.00
❑ 4 Mystique 1.50 4.00
❑ 5 Nightcrawler 1.50 4.00
❑ 6 Professor Xavier 1.50 4.00
❑ 7 Rogue 1.50 4.00
❑ 8 Storm 1.50 4.00
❑ 9 Wolverine 1.50 4.00
❑ 10 Lady Deathstrike 1.50 4.00

2003 X2 X-Men United Memorabilia

COMPLETE SET (3) 30.00 60.00
STATED ODDS 1:64 HOBBY'
❑ NNO Halle Berry 15.00 30.00
❑ NNO Hugh Jackman 15.00 30.00
❑ NNO Kelly Hu 15.00 30.00

2003 X2 X-Men United Promos

COMPLETE SET (3) 2.00 5.00
❑ P1 Wolverine .75 2.00
❑ P2 Wolverine .75 2.00
❑ P3 Nightcrawler .75 2.00

2004 Alias Season Three

❑ 1 Title Card .15 .40
❑ 2 Restored .15 .40
❑ 3 Extortion .15 .40
❑ 4 Switch .15 .40
❑ 5 Unexpected .15 .40
❑ 6 Dressy .15 .40
❑ 7 Uniform .15 .40
❑ 8 Familiar .15 .40
❑ 9 Betrayed .15 .40
❑ 10 Mole .15 .40
❑ 11 Fold .15 .40
❑ 12 Phoenix .15 .40
❑ 13 Ghost .15 .40
❑ 14 Trust .15 .40
❑ 15 Interference .15 .40
❑ 16 Tortured .15 .40
❑ 17 Absolution .15 .40
❑ 18 Deal .15 .40
❑ 19 Memories .15 .40
❑ 20 Reunited .15 .40
❑ 21 Payback .15 .40
❑ 22 Revelation .15 .40
❑ 23 Traumatic .15 .40
❑ 24 Farewell .15 .40
❑ 25 Relative .15 .40
❑ 26 Playmakers .15 .40
❑ 27 Lucky .15 .40
❑ 28 Undercover .15 .40
❑ 29 Choices .15 .40
❑ 30 Deceit .15 .40
❑ 31 Reality .15 .40
❑ 32 Family .15 .40
❑ 33 Tradeoff .15 .40
❑ 34 Happiness .15 .40
❑ 35 Clues .15 .40
❑ 36 Suspicion .15 .40
❑ 37 Guilty .15 .40
❑ 38 Raid .15 .40
❑ 39 Condemned .15 .40
❑ 40 Captured .15 .40
❑ 41 Recovered .15 .40
❑ 42 Obsessed .15 .40
❑ 43 Desperate .15 .40
❑ 44 Ironic .15 .40
❑ 45 Showdown .15 .40
❑ 46 Bristow, Jack D. .15 .40
❑ 47 Bristow, Sydney A. .15 .40
❑ 48 Dixon, Marcus R. .15 .40
❑ 49 Flinkman, Marshall J. .15 .40
❑ 50 Vaughn, Michael C. .15 .40
❑ 51 Weiss, Eric .15 .40
❑ 52 Kendall .15 .40
❑ 53 Barnett, Judy .15 .40
❑ 54 Derevko, Yekaterina .15 .40
❑ 55 Reed, Lauren .15 .40
❑ 56 Sark, Julian .15 .40
❑ 57 Sloane, Arvin .15 .40
❑ 58 Santos, Nadia .15 .40
❑ 59 Cole, Mckenas .15 .40
❑ 60 Doren, Allison Georgia .15 .40
❑ 61 Arrogant .15 .40
❑ 62 Captured .15 .40
❑ 63 Battered .15 .40
❑ 64 Dad .15 .40
❑ 65 Inspired .15 .40
❑ 66 Distracted .15 .40
❑ 67 Curious .15 .40
❑ 68 Caffeinated .15 .40
❑ 69 Precise .15 .40
❑ 70 Wanted .15 .40
❑ 71 Observant .15 .40
❑ 72 Julia's Friend .15 .40
❑ 73 Serpent's Tooth .15 .40
❑ 74 In Laws .15 .40
❑ 75 Daddy's Girl .15 .40
❑ 76 The Senator .15 .40
❑ 77 His Wife .15 .40
❑ 78 Sisters .15 .40
❑ 79 Reunion .15 .40
❑ 80 Auntie .15 .40
❑ 81 Checklist .15 .40

2004 Alias Season Three Autographs

STATED ODDS 1:24
❑ A20 Melissa George 15.00 30.00
❑ A21 David Cronenberg 8.00 20.00
❑ A22 Mia Maestro 15.00 30.00
❑ A23 David Carradine 20.00 40.00
❑ A24 Vivica A. Fox 8.00 20.00
❑ A25 Amanda Foreman 8.00 20.00
❑ A26 Mark Bramhall 8.00 20.00
❑ A27 Justin Theroux 8.00 20.00
❑ A28 Raymond Barry 8.00 20.00
❑ A29 Kurt Fuller 8.00 20.00
❑ A30 Peggy Lipton 8.00 20.00
❑ A31 Ian Buchanan 8.00 20.00

2004 Alias Season Three Box Loaders

COMPLETE SET (4) 8.00 20.00
❑ BL1 Betrayal 1.50 4.00
❑ BL2 Betrayal 1.50 4.00
❑ BL3 Betrayal 1.50 4.00
❑ CL1 Julie Bell artwork AU CASE INSERT 6.00 15.00

2004 Alias Season Three Pieceworks

STATED ODDS 1:24
❑ PW1 Jennifer Garner Dress 15.00 30.00
❑ PW2 Michael Vartan Pants 6.00 15.00
❑ PW3 Melissa George Shirt 6.00 15.00
❑ PW4 David Anders Sweater 6.00 15.00
❑ PW5 Ron Rifkin Jacket 6.00 15.00
❑ PW6 Isabella Rossellini Blouse 6.00 15.00
❑ PW7 Victor Garber Sweater 6.00 15.00
❑ PW8 Carl Lumbly Shirt 6.00 15.00
❑ PW9 Kevin Weisman Shirt 6.00 15.00

2004 Alias Season Three The Lost Years

COMPLETE SET (9) 8.00 20.00
STATED ODDS 1:11
❑ L1 The Lost Years 1.25 3.00
❑ L2 The Lost Years 1.25 3.00
❑ L3 The Lost Years 1.25 3.00
❑ L4 The Lost Years 1.25 3.00
❑ L5 The Lost Years 1.25 3.00
❑ L6 The Lost Years 1.25 3.00
❑ L7 The Lost Years 1.25 3.00
❑ L8 The Lost Years 1.25 3.00
❑ L9 The Lost Years 1.25 3.00

2004 Alias Season Three Wicked Games

COMPLETE SET (6) 8.00 20.00
STATED ODDS 1:17
❑ WG1 Assassination 1.50 4.00
❑ WG2 Secrets 1.50 4.00
❑ WG3 Threats 1.50 4.00
❑ WG4 Back-Up 1.50 4.00

❑ WG5 Deception 1.50 4.00
❑ WG6 Masquerade 1.50 4.00

2004 Alien vs. Predator

COMPLETE SET (90) 4.00 10.00

❑ 1 Title Card .10 .30
❑ 2 Lex .10 .30
❑ 3 Weyland .10 .30
❑ 4 Sebastian .10 .30
❑ 5 Miller .10 .30
❑ 6 Max .10 .30
❑ 7 Thomas .10 .30
❑ 8 Verheiden .10 .30
❑ 9 Quinn .10 .30
❑ 10 Connors .10 .30
❑ 11 Rousseau .10 .30
❑ 12 Scar .10 .30
❑ 13 Weyland's Team .10 .30
❑ 14 A Perilous Mission .10 .30
❑ 15 Into The Unknown .10 .30
❑ 16 The Sacrificial Chamber .10 .30
❑ 17 An Unknown Species .10 .30
❑ 18 Heart Of The Pyramid .10 .30
❑ 19 Who Goes There .10 .30
❑ 20 Slaughter Station .10 .30
❑ 21 The Unstoppable One .10 .30
❑ 22 Furious Struggle .10 .30
❑ 23 Quinn's Final Stand .10 .30
❑ 24 The Queen's Stolen Eggs .10 .30
❑ 25 Birth Of A Face Hugger .10 .30
❑ 26 Trapped And Terrified .10 .30
❑ 27 Max Netted .10 .30
❑ 28 Facing The Predator .10 .30
❑ 29 Savage Stranglehold .10 .30
❑ 30 The Hunter Distracted .10 .30
❑ 31 Challenged By An Alien .10 .30
❑ 32 Hunted Or Hunter .10 .30
❑ 33 Unearthly Opponents .10 .30
❑ 34 The Terror Titans Clash .10 .30
❑ 35 A Predator Against Them .10 .30
❑ 36 Weyland's Plea .10 .30
❑ 37 As The Monster Advances .10 .30
❑ 38 Taking On The Terror .10 .30
❑ 39 Courageous... But Futile .10 .30
❑ 40 Don't Turn Your Back On Me .10 .30
❑ 41 Where There's Smoke .10 .30
❑ 42 Cocooned .10 .30
❑ 43 Death Of A Beaker .10 .30
❑ 44 The Abyss .10 .30
❑ 45 Behind You .10 .30
❑ 46 A Too Close Encounter .10 .30
❑ 47 Kindred Warriors .10 .30
❑ 48 Armed For Alien Battle .10 .30
❑ 49 Chamber Of Death .10 .30
❑ 50 An Act Of Mercy .10 .30
❑ 51 The Tragic Task .10 .30
❑ 52 Blowing Up The Pyramid .10 .30
❑ 53 Back To The Surface .10 .30
❑ 54 Escaping Armageddon .10 .30
❑ 55 Blown Into Oblivion .10 .30
❑ 56 Lex's Blooding .10 .30
❑ 57 A Weapon Well Deserved .10 .30
❑ 58 Return Of The Queen .10 .30
❑ 59 Mother Of All Monsters .10 .30
❑ 60 Armed Against The Alien .10 .30
❑ 61 The Whalebone Graveyard .10 .30
❑ 62 Teamed Against The Terror .10 .30
❑ 63 Vanquished .10 .30
❑ 64 In This Corner .10 .30
❑ 65 Suited For Mayhem .10 .30
❑ 66 Setting Up Scar .10 .30
❑ 67 A Soldier's Story .10 .30
❑ 68 All Hail The Queen .10 .30
❑ 69 The Monster's Makers .10 .30
❑ 70 Lights Camera Carnage .10 .30
❑ 71 All Fired Up .10 .30
❑ 72 Preparing A Predator .10 .30
❑ 73 The Young Filmmakers .10 .30
❑ 74 The Queen's Big Scene .10 .30
❑ 75 Shooting The Climax .10 .30
❑ 76 Graveyard Shift .10 .30
❑ 77 A Ledge Too Far .10 .30
❑ 78 Death In Slow Motion .10 .30
❑ 79 Directing Lex .10 .30
❑ 80 Filming Sebastian's Dig .10 .30
❑ 81 The Women Of AVP .10 .30
❑ 82 Art: The Hunter's Prize .10 .30
❑ 83 Art: When Creatures Clash .10 .30
❑ 84 Art: The Rite Of Passage .10 .30
❑ 85 Graphics: Predator .10 .30
❑ 86 Graphics: Alien .10 .30
❑ 87 Line Art: The Victors .10 .30
❑ 88 Line Art: Predator .10 .30
❑ 89 Line Art: Alien .10 .30
❑ 90 Checklist .10 .30

2004 Alien vs. Predator Autographs

STATED ODDS ONE PER BOX

❑ A1 Sanaa Lathan 6.00 15.00
❑ A2 Colin Salmon 6.00 15.00
❑ A3 Sam Troughton 6.00 15.00
❑ A4 Agathe De La Boulaye 6.00 15.00
❑ A5 Joseph Rye 6.00 15.00
❑ A6 Ian Whyte 6.00 15.00
❑ A7 Adrian Bouchet 6.00 15.00

2004 Alien vs. Predator Blood Hunters

COMPLETE SET (3) 5.00 12.00
STATED ODDS ONE PER BOX

❑ BL1 Predator 2.00 5.00
❑ BL2 Alien 2.00 5.00
❑ BL3 Queen 2.00 5.00

2004 Alien vs. Predator Pieceworks

STATED ODDS ONE PER BOX

❑ PW1 Lex 6.00 15.00
❑ PW2 Weyland 6.00 15.00
❑ PW3 Quinn 6.00 15.00
❑ PW4 Max 6.00 15.00
❑ PW5 Max 6.00 15.00
❑ PW6 Verheiden 6.00 15.00
❑ PW7 Connors 6.00 15.00

2004 Alien vs. Predator Sketches

STATED ODDS ONE PER CASE AND RANDOM IN PACKS

❑ CL1 William O'Neill/351 15.00 40.00
❑ CL2 Tone Rodriguez/352 15.00 40.00
❑ CL3 Joel Angel Gomez/301 15.00 40.00

2004 Alien vs. Predator Survival of the Fiercest Puzzle

COMPLETE SET (9) 10.00 25.00
STATED ODDS 1:11

❑ SF1 Ten Years in the Making 1.50 4.00
❑ SF2 A New Action Hero 1.50 4.00
❑ SF3 Bova and the Beasts 1.50 4.00
❑ SF4 A Dance Against Dragons 1.50 4.00
❑ SF5 Building a Better Monster 1.50 4.00
❑ SF6 A Regal Makeover 1.50 4.00
❑ SF7 Power Puppetry 1.50 4.00
❑ SF8 Inside the Chamber 1.50 4.00
❑ SF9 How It All Began 1.50 4.00

2004 Alien vs. Predator The Deadliest Game

COMPLETE SET (6) 6.00 15.00
STATED ODDS 1:17

❑ DG1 The Big the Bad and the Ugly 1.50 4.00
❑ DG2 Out of the Past 1.50 4.00
❑ DG3 Introducing Scar 1.50 4.00
❑ DG4 We Admire Its Purity 1.50 4.00
❑ DG5 Day of the Face Huggers 1.50 4.00
❑ DG6 Look Ma No Survivors 1.50 4.00

2004 American Chopper

COMPLETE SET (50) 5.00 12.00

❑ 1 Black Widow Bike .15 .40
❑ 2 Fire Bike .15 .40
❑ 3 Jet Bike .15 .40
❑ 4 Comanche Bike .15 .40
❑ 5 Mikey's Bike .15 .40
❑ 6 Old School Chopper .15 .40
❑ 7 Black Widow Bike .15 .40
❑ 8 Fire Bike .15 .40
❑ 9 Jet Bike .15 .40
❑ 10 Comanche Bike .15 .40
❑ 11 Mikey's Bike .15 .40
❑ 12 Old School Chopper .15 .40
❑ 13 Black Widow Bike .15 .40
❑ 14 Fire Bike .15 .40
❑ 15 Jet Bike .15 .40
❑ 16 Comanche Bike .15 .40
❑ 17 Mikey's Bike .15 .40
❑ 18 Old School Chopper .15 .40
❑ 19 Black Widow Bike .15 .40
❑ 20 Fire Bike .15 .40
❑ 21 Jet Bike .15 .40
❑ 22 Comanche Bike .15 .40
❑ 23 Mikey's Bike .15 .40
❑ 24 Old School Chopper .15 .40
❑ 25 Black Widow Bike .15 .40
❑ 26 Fire Bike .15 .40
❑ 27 Jet Bike .15 .40
❑ 28 Comanche Bike .15 .40
❑ 29 Mikey's Bike .15 .40
❑ 30 Old School Chopper .15 .40
❑ 31 Paul Teutel Jr. .15 .40
❑ 32 Paul Teutel Jr. .15 .40
❑ 33 Paul Teutel Jr. .15 .40
Paul Teutel Sr.
❑ 34 Paul Teutel Jr. .15 .40
Paul Teutel Sr.
❑ 35 Paul Teutel Jr. .15 .40
❑ 36 Paul Teutel Jr. .15 .40
Paul Teutel Sr.
❑ 37 Paul Teutel Jr. .15 .40
Paul Teutel Sr.
❑ 38 Paul Teutel Jr. .15 .40
❑ 39 Rolling Thunder .15 .40
❑ 40 Rolling Thunder .15 .40
❑ 41 Rolling Thunder .15 .40
❑ 42 Rolling Thunder .15 .40
❑ 43 Rolling Thunder .15 .40
❑ 44 Rolling Thunder .15 .40
❑ 45 Daytona .15 .40
❑ 46 Daytona .15 .40
❑ 47 Daytona .15 .40
❑ 48 Daytona .15 .40
❑ 49 Daytona .15 .40
❑ 50 Daytona .15 .40

2004 American Chopper Autographs

COMPLETE SET (5) 150.00 250.00

❑ NNO Cody 15.00 40.00
❑ NNO Vinny 40.00 80.00
❑ NNO Paul Teutel Jr. 40.00 80.00
❑ NNO Mikey 15.00 40.00
❑ NNO Paul Teutel Sr. 40.00 80.00

2004 American Idol Season Three

COMPLETE SET (89) 6.00 15.00

❑ 1 Tiara Purifoy .15 .40
❑ 2 John Stevens .15 .40
❑ 3 Noel Roman .15 .40
❑ 4 Jennifer Hudson .25 .60
❑ 5 Matthew Rogers .15 .40
❑ 6 Jasmine Trias .15 .40
❑ 7 Susan Vulaca .15 .40
❑ 8 Jesus Roman .15 .40
❑ 9 Lisa Leuschner .15 .40
❑ 10 Elizabeth LeTendre .15 .40
❑ 11 La Toya London .15 .40
❑ 12 Diana DeGarmo .15 .40
❑ 13 Katie Webber .15 .40
❑ 14 Charly Lowry .15 .40
❑ 15 Leah LaBelle .15 .40
❑ 16 George Huff .15 .40
❑ 17 Kara Master .15 .40
❑ 18 Camile Velasco .15 .40
❑ 19 John Preator .15 .40
❑ 20 Ashley Thomas .15 .40
❑ 21 Jon Peter Lewis .15 .40
❑ 22 Amy Adams .15 .40
❑ 23 Jonah Moananu .15 .40
❑ 24 Briana Ramirez-Rial .15 .40
❑ 25 Matthew Metzger .15 .40
❑ 26 Heather Piccinini .15 .40
❑ 27 Marisa Joy .15 .40
❑ 28 Erskine Walcott .15 .40
❑ 29 Lisa Wilson .15 .40
❑ 30 Eric Yoder .15 .40
❑ 31 Marque Lynche .15 .40
❑ 32 Fantasia Barrino .40 1.00
❑ 33 Alan Ritchson .15 .40
❑ 34 Sonny Kapu .15 .40
❑ 35 Michael Keown .15 .40
❑ 36 Cassie LaBeau .15 .40
❑ 37 Nicole Tieri .15 .40
❑ 38 Jasmine Arteaga .15 .40
❑ 39 Paula Abdul .40 1.00
❑ 40 Randy Jackson .25 .60
❑ 41 Ryan Seacrest .15 .40
❑ 42 William Hung .15 .40
❑ 43 Danny Parker .15 .40
❑ 44 Jonathan Rey .15 .40
❑ 45 Tiffany Ballard .15 .40
❑ 46 Jacqueline Roman .15 .40
❑ 47 Sergey Shor .15 .40
❑ 48 Tiara Purifoy .15 .40
❑ 49 Kara Master .15 .40
❑ 50 La Toya London .15 .40
❑ 51 Marisa Joy .15 .40
❑ 52 Jesus Roman .15 .40
❑ 53 Briana Ramirez-Rial .15 .40
❑ 54 John Stevens .15 .40
❑ 55 Camile Velasco .15 .40
❑ 56 Lisa Leuschner .15 .40
❑ 57 Matthew Metzger .15 .40
❑ 58 Noel Roman .15 .40
❑ 59 John Preator .15 .40
❑ 60 George Huff .15 .40
❑ 61 Fantasia Barrino .15 .40
❑ 62 Elizabeth LeTendre .15 .40
❑ 63 Heather Piccinini .15 .40
❑ 64 Katie Webber .15 .40
❑ 65 Lisa Wilson .15 .40
❑ 66 Susan Vulaca .15 .40
❑ 67 Jonah Moananu .15 .40
❑ 68 Jennifer Hudson .15 .40
❑ 69 Ashley Thomas .15 .40
❑ 70 Charly Lowry .15 .40
❑ 71 Eric Yoder .15 .40
❑ 72 Matthew Rogers .15 .40
❑ 73 Jon Peter Lewis .15 .40
❑ 74 Leah LaBelle .15 .40
❑ 75 Marque Lynche .15 .40
❑ 76 Diana DeGarmo .15 .40
❑ 77 Erskine Walcott .15 .40
❑ 78 Jasmine Trias .15 .40
❑ 79 Amy Adams .15 .40
❑ 80 American Idol Set .15 .40
❑ 81 The Judges Table .15 .40
❑ 82 The Red Room .15 .40
❑ 83 Monitoring the Action .15 .40
❑ 84 The Performance Stage .15 .40
❑ 85 Authorized Personnel Only .15 .40
❑ 86 The Control Room .15 .40
❑ 87 Stage Left .15 .40
❑ 88 Randy's Spot .15 .40
❑ 89 The Sign .15 .40

2004 American Idol Season Three Silver

COMPLETE SET (41) 8.00 20.00
STATED ODDS 1:4

2004 American Idol Season Three Gold

COMPLETE SET (41) 50.00 120.00
STATED ODDS 1:36

2004 American Idol Season Three Behind the Scenes

COMPLETE SET (15) 3.00 8.00
STATED ODDS 1:4

❑ BS1 Paula's Dressing Room .40 1.00
❑ BS2 Randy and Ryan in Hawaii .40 1.00
❑ BS3 Ryan in a Sea of Idol Fans .40 1.00
❑ BS4 Paula Enjoys the Hawaiian Sun .40 1.00
❑ BS5 Vocal Instruction from Debra Byrd .40 1.00
❑ BS6 Group One Watches Britney Spears .40 1.00
❑ BS7 The American Idol Band Warms Up .40 1.00
❑ BS8 Randy Greets the Studio Audience .40 1.00
❑ BS9 Tension Begins to Mount .40 1.00
❑ BS10 The American Idol Shuttle Van .40 1.00
❑ BS11 Pregame before Taping Begins .40 1.00
❑ BS12 Group One Castoffs Share .40 1.00
❑ BS13 Matthew Rogers Hammin' It Up .40 1.00
❑ BS14 Kara Master Applies Her Makeup .40 1.00
❑ BS15 Randy Consoles Briana .40 1.00

2004 American Idol Season Three Idol Chatter

COMPLETE SET (32) 6.00 15.00
STATED ODDS 1:6

❑ IC1 Tiara Purifoy .40 1.00
❑ IC2 John Stevens .40 1.00
❑ IC3 Noel Roman .40 1.00
❑ IC4 Jennifer Hudson .40 1.00
❑ IC5 Matthew Rogers .40 1.00
❑ IC6 Jasmine Trias .40 1.00
❑ IC7 Susan Vulaca .40 1.00
❑ IC8 Jesus Roman .40 1.00
❑ IC9 Lisa Leuschner .40 1.00
❑ IC10 Elizabeth LeTendre .40 1.00
❑ IC11 La Toya London .40 1.00
❑ IC12 Diana DeGarmo .40 1.00
❑ IC13 Katie Webber .40 1.00
❑ IC14 Charly Lowry .40 1.00
❑ IC15 Lean LaBelle .40 1.00
❑ IC16 George Huff .40 1.00
❑ IC17 Kara Master .40 1.00
❑ IC18 Camile Velasco .40 1.00
❑ IC19 John Preator .40 1.00
❑ IC20 Ashley Thomas .40 1.00
❑ IC21 Jon Peter Lewis .40 1.00
❑ IC22 Amy Adams .40 1.00
❑ IC23 Jonah Moananu .40 1.00
❑ IC24 Briana Ramirez-Rial .40 1.00
❑ IC25 Matthew Metzger .40 1.00
❑ IC26 Heather Piccinini .40 1.00
❑ IC27 Marisa Joy .40 1.00
❑ IC28 Erskine Walcott .40 1.00
❑ IC29 Lisa Wilson .40 1.00
❑ IC30 Eric Yoder .40 1.00
❑ IC31 Marque Lynche .40 1.00
❑ IC32 Fantasia Barrino .40 1.00

2004 Andromeda Reign of the Commonwealth

COMPLETE SET (90) 4.00 10.00

❑ 1 Title Card .10 .30
❑ 2 Dylan Hunt .10 .30
❑ 3 Beka Valentine .10 .30
❑ 4 Seamus Harper .10 .30
❑ 5 Andromeda .10 .30
❑ 6 Trance Gemini .10 .30
❑ 7 Tyr Anasazi .10 .30
❑ 8 Rev Bem .10 .30
❑ 9 Captain Metis .10 .30
❑ 10 Sid Barry .10 .30
❑ 11 Professor Logich .10 .30
❑ 12 Charlemagne Bolivar .10 .30
❑ 13 Telemachus Rhade .10 .30
❑ 14 Bobby Jensen .10 .30
❑ 15 Queen Of Ymir .10 .30
❑ 16 Tura .10 .30
❑ 17 Constantine Stark .10 .30
❑ 18 Remiel .10 .30
❑ 19 Toward Tomorrow .10 .30
❑ 20 Armed And Dangerous .10 .30
❑ 21 Beka's New Career .10 .30
❑ 22 Harper's Way .10 .30
❑ 23 Lighter Moments .10 .30
❑ 24 Command And Compassion .10 .30
❑ 25 Everyone's An Alien .10 .30
❑ 26 A Magog Among Us .10 .30
❑ 27 Where No Avatar Has Gone Before .10 .30
❑ 28 The Widening Gyre .10 .30
❑ 29 Exit Strategies .10 .30
❑ 30 Heart For Falsehood Framed .10 .30
❑ 31 Pitiless As The Sun .10 .30
❑ 32 Last Call At The Broken Hammer .10 .30
❑ 33 All Too Human .10 .30
❑ 34 Una Salus Victus .10 .30
❑ 35 Home Fires .10 .30
❑ 36 Into The Labyrinth .10 .30
❑ 37 The Prince .10 .30
❑ 38 Bunker Hill .10 .30
❑ 39 Ouroboros .10 .30
❑ 40 Lava And Rockets .10 .30
❑ 41 Be All My Sins Remembered .10 .30
❑ 42 Dance Of The Mayflies .10 .30
❑ 43 In Heaven Now Are Three .10 .30
❑ 44 The Things We Cannot Change .10 .30
❑ 45 Fair Unknown .10 .30
❑ 46 Belly Of The Beast .10 .30
❑ 47 Knight, Death And The Devil .10 .30
❑ 48 Immaculate Perception .10 .30
❑ 49 Tunnel At The End Of The Light .10 .30
❑ 50 If The Wheel Is Fixed .10 .30
❑ 51 The Shards Of Rimni .10 .30
❑ 52 Mad To Be Saved .10 .30
❑ 53 Cui Bono .10 .30
❑ 54 The Lone And Level Sands .10 .30
❑ 55 Slipfighter The Dogs Of War .10 .30
❑ 56 The Leper's Kiss .10 .30
❑ 57 For Whom The Bell Tolls .10 .30
❑ 58 And Your Heart Will Fly Away .10 .30
❑ 59 The Unconquerable Man .10 .30
❑ 60 Delenda Est .10 .30
❑ 61 The Dark Backward .10 .30
❑ 62 The Risk All Point .10 .30
❑ 63 The Right Horse .10 .30
❑ 64 What Happens To A Rev Deferred .10 .30
❑ 65 Point Of The Spear .10 .30
❑ 66 Vault Of The Heavens .10 .30
❑ 67 Deep Midnight's Voice .10 .30
❑ 68 The Illusion Of Majesty .10 .30
❑ 69 Twilight Of The Idos .10 .30
❑ 70 Day Of Judgment, Day Of Wrath .10 .30
❑ 71 Shadows Cast By A Final Salute .10 .30
❑ 72 Season Four .10 .30
❑ 73 Andromeda Ascendant .10 .30
❑ 74 Eureka Maru .10 .30
❑ 75 Slipfighters .10 .30
❑ 76 Spaceways .10 .30
❑ 77 The Magog Worldship .10 .30
❑ 78 Galatic Assault .10 .30
❑ 79 The Dimensional Tunnel .10 .30
❑ 80 At War With The Dragans .10 .30
❑ 81 A Universe Of Hope .10 .30
❑ 82 Harper's Dream Factory .10 .30
❑ 83 The Vtol Pod .10 .30
❑ 84 The Force Lance .10 .30
❑ 85 Dylan Takes A Break .10 .30
❑ 86 Serving The Captain .10 .30
❑ 87 Hot Head, Cool Jokes .10 .30
❑ 88 Laughs With Laura .10 .30
❑ 89 Space Shots .10 .30
❑ 90 Checklist .10 .30

2004 Andromeda Reign of the Commonwealth Autographs

STATED ODDS 1:36

❑ A1 Kevin Sorbo 8.00 20.00
❑ A2 Lisa Ryder 6.00 15.00
❑ A3 Lexa Doig 6.00 15.00
❑ A4 Gordon Michael Woolvett 6.00 15.00
❑ A5 Laura Bertram 6.00 15.00
❑ A6 Steve Bacic 6.00 15.00

2004 Andromeda Reign of the Commonwealth Battle for the Commonwealth

COMPLETE SET (9) 10.00 25.00
STATED ODDS 1:11

❑ BC1 Battle For The Commonwealth 1.50 4.00
❑ BC2 Battle For The Commonwealth 1.50 4.00
❑ BC3 Battle For The Commonwealth 1.50 4.00
❑ BC4 Battle For The Commonwealth 1.50 4.00
❑ BC5 Battle For The Commonwealth 1.50 4.00
❑ BC6 Battle For The Commonwealth 1.50 4.00
❑ BC7 Battle For The Commonwealth 1.50 4.00
❑ BC8 Battle For The Commonwealth 1.50 4.00
❑ BC9 Battle For The Commonwealth 1.50 4.00

2004 Andromeda Reign of the Commonwealth Box Loaders

COMPLETE SET (4) 8.00 20.00

❑ BL1 Rommie 1.50 4.00
❑ BL2 Beka Valentine 1.50 4.00
❑ BL3 Trance Gemini 1.50 4.00
❑ CL1 Andromeda Ascendant 6.00 15.00

2004 Andromeda Reign of the Commonwealth Fragile Allegiances

COMPLETE SET (6) 8.00 20.00
STATED ODDS 1:17

❑ FA1 Dylan Hunt 1.50 4.00
❑ FA2 Beka Valentine 1.50 4.00
❑ FA3 Tyr Anasazi 1.50 4.00
❑ FA4 Seamus Harper 1.50 4.00
❑ FA5 Trance Gemini 1.50 4.00
❑ FA6 Rev Bem 1.50 4.00

2004 Andromeda Reign of the Commonwealth Pieceworks

STATED ODDS 1:36

❑ PW5 Dylan's Jacket 6.00 15.00
❑ PW6 Beka's Top 20.00 40.00
❑ PW7 Harper's T-Shirt 6.00 15.00
❑ PW8 Trance's Outfit 6.00 15.00
❑ PW9 Rommie's Vest 20.00 40.00
❑ PW10 Beka's Top 20.00 40.00

2004 Andromeda Reign of the Commonwealth Promos

COMPLETE SET (4) 4.00 10.00

❑ ARC1 Andromeda 1.00 2.50
❑ ARCi Tyr, Dylan, & Beka 1.50 4.00
❑ ARCUK Harper, Rommie, & Trance 1.50 4.00
❑ PLVCC Andromeda 1.50 4.00

2004 Angel Season Five

COMPLETE SET (90) 5.00 12.00

❑ 1 Angel .15 .40
❑ 2 Corporate .15 .40
❑ 3 Gal Friday .15 .40
❑ 4 Enhanced .15 .40
❑ 5 Reconstituted .15 .40
❑ 6 Possessed .15 .40
❑ 7 Fading .15 .40
❑ 8 Wild Night .15 .40
❑ 9 Hunger .15 .40
❑ 10 Apparitions .15 .40
❑ 11 Reaper .15 .40
❑ 12 Sacrifice .15 .40
❑ 13 High Life .15 .40
❑ 14 Elite .15 .40
❑ 15 Unconscious .15 .40
❑ 16 Once a Hero .15 .40
❑ 17 Reunited .15 .40
❑ 18 Patriarch .15 .40
❑ 19 Untrustworthy .15 .40
❑ 20 Oedipal .15 .40
❑ 21 Allies .15 .40
❑ 22 Rivals .15 .40
❑ 23 Negotiation .15 .40
❑ 24 Girlfight .15 .40
❑ 25 Visionary .15 .40
❑ 26 Nightmare .15 .40
❑ 27 Traumatized .15 .40
❑ 28 Captive .15 .40
❑ 29 Intervention .15 .40
❑ 30 Awakening .15 .40
❑ 31 Interrogation .15 .40
❑ 32 Revelation .15 .40
❑ 33 Enemy .15 .40
❑ 34 Combatants .15 .40
❑ 35 Casuality .15 .40
❑ 36 Transformed .15 .40
❑ 37 Leader .15 .40
❑ 38 Stricken .15 .40
❑ 39 Powerless .15 .40
❑ 40 Farewell .15 .40
❑ 41 Abiding .15 .40
❑ 42 Fierce .15 .40
❑ 43 Exiled .15 .40
❑ 44 Enforcer .15 .40
❑ 45 In Hell .15 .40
❑ 46 Left Behind .15 .40
❑ 47 Normal .15 .40
❑ 48 Altered .15 .40
❑ 49 Restored .15 .40
❑ 50 Proactive .15 .40
❑ 51 Timeless .15 .40
❑ 52 Diminished .15 .40
❑ 53 Annoyed .15 .40
❑ 54 Obsessed .15 .40
❑ 55 Moving On .15 .40
❑ 56 Killer .15 .40
❑ 57 Distraction .15 .40
❑ 58 Illusion .15 .40
❑ 59 Scheming .15 .40
❑ 60 One Last Job .15 .40
❑ 61 Babysitting .15 .40
❑ 62 Misspoken .15 .40
❑ 63 Showdown .15 .40
❑ 64 Angel .15 .40
❑ 65 Wesley Wyndam-Pryce .15 .40
❑ 66 Spike .15 .40
❑ 67 Charles Gunn .15 .40
❑ 68 Winifred Burkle .15 .40
❑ 69 Lorne .15 .40
❑ 70 Harmony .15 .40
❑ 71 Eve .15 .40
❑ 72 Hamilton .15 .40
❑ 73 Angel and Eve .15 .40
❑ 74 Wesley and Fred .15 .40
❑ 75 Eve and Lindsey .15 .40
❑ 76 Harmony and Hamilton .15 .40
❑ 77 Archduke Sebassis .15 .40
❑ 78 Matthias Pavayne .15 .40
❑ 79 Cyrus Vail .15 .40
❑ 80 The Prince of Lies .15 .40
❑ 81 Senator Bruckner .15 .40
❑ 82 Wesley and Roger Wyndam-Pryce .15 .40
❑ 83 Fred, Trish and Roger Burkle .15 .40
❑ 84 Angel and Connor .15 .40
❑ 85 Cordelia .15 .40
❑ 86 Fred .15 .40
❑ 87 Drogyn .15 .40
❑ 88 Lindsey .15 .40
❑ 89 Wesley .15 .40
❑ 90 Checklist .15 .40

2004 Angel Season Five Autographs

COMPLETE SET (12) 60.00 150.00
STATED ODDS 1:36

❑ A34 Mercedes McNab 15.00 30.00
❑ A35 David Fury 6.00 15.00
❑ A36 Adam Baldwin 15.00 30.00
❑ A37 Vincent Kartheiser 6.00 15.00
❑ A38 Marc Vann 6.00 15.00
❑ A39 Jonathan Woodward 6.00 15.00
❑ A40 Alec Newman 6.00 15.00
❑ A41 Tom Lenk 6.00 15.00
❑ A42 Eyal Podell 6.00 15.00
❑ A43 Camden Toy 6.00 15.00
❑ A44 Jennifer Griffin 6.00 15.00
❑ A45 Gary Grubbs 6.00 15.00

2004 Angel Season Five Breaking the Circle

COMPLETE SET (9) 10.00 25.00
STATED ODDS 1:11

❑ BC1 Hamilton 1.50 4.00
❑ BC2 Hamilton 1.50 4.00
❑ BC3 Lorne 1.50 4.00
❑ BC4 Spike 1.50 4.00
❑ BC5 Angel 1.50 4.00
❑ BC6 Gunn 1.50 4.00
❑ BC7 Lorne 1.50 4.00
❑ BC8 Illyria 1.50 4.00
❑ BC9 Vail 1.50 4.00

2004 Angel Season Five Pieceworks

COMPLETE SET (7) 60.00 150.00

- ☐ PW1 Amy Acker 10.00 25.00
- ☐ PW2 Amy Acker 10.00 25.00
- ☐ PW3 David Boreanaz 12.50 30.00
- ☐ PW4 Alexis Denisof 10.00 25.00
- ☐ PW5 August Richards 10.00 25.00
- ☐ PW6 James Marsters 10.00 25.00
- ☐ PW7 Andy Hallett 10.00 25.00

2004 Angel Season Five The Last Days

COMPLETE SET (6) 8.00 20.00
STATED ODDS 1:17

- ☐ LD1 Angel 1.50 4.00
- ☐ LD2 Gunn 1.50 4.00
- ☐ LD3 Spike 1.50 4.00
- ☐ LD4 Wesley 1.50 4.00
- ☐ LD5 Lorne 1.50 4.00
- ☐ LD6 Lindsey and Eve 1.50 4.00

2004 Buffy the Vampire Slayer Big Bads

COMPLETE SET (72) 5.00 12.00

- ☐ 1 Big Bads .15 .40
- ☐ 2 The Master .15 .40
- ☐ 3 Angelus .15 .40
- ☐ 4 Faith .15 .40
- ☐ 5 The Mayor .15 .40
- ☐ 6 Adam .15 .40
- ☐ 7 Glory .15 .40
- ☐ 8 Dark Willow .15 .40
- ☐ 9 The First .15 .40
- ☐ 10 The Master .15 .40
- ☐ 11 Ethan Rayne .15 .40
- ☐ 12 Angelus .15 .40
- ☐ 13 Drusilla .15 .40
- ☐ 14 The Mayor .15 .40
- ☐ 15 The Initiative .15 .40
- ☐ 16 Glory .15 .40
- ☐ 17 Dark Willow .15 .40
- ☐ 18 The First .15 .40
- ☐ 19 She-Mantis .15 .40
- ☐ 20 The Master .15 .40
- ☐ 21 Angelus .15 .40
- ☐ 22 Zombie Guys .15 .40
- ☐ 23 Dracula .15 .40
- ☐ 24 Spike .15 .40
- ☐ 25 Dark Willow .15 .40
- ☐ 26 Lissa .15 .40
- ☐ 27 Caleb .15 .40
- ☐ 28 Moloch .15 .40
- ☐ 29 Faith .15 .40
- ☐ 30 The Mayor .15 .40
- ☐ 31 Veruca .15 .40
- ☐ 32 The Gentlemen .15 .40
- ☐ 33 Glory .15 .40
- ☐ 34 Evil Trio .15 .40
- ☐ 35 Dark Willow .15 .40
- ☐ 36 The First .15 .40
- ☐ 37 Darla .15 .40
- ☐ 38 The Master .15 .40
- ☐ 39 Drusilla And Spike .15 .40
- ☐ 40 Angelus .15 .40
- ☐ 41 Faith .15 .40
- ☐ 42 The Mayor .15 .40
- ☐ 43 Chumash Warrior .15 .40
- ☐ 44 Spike .15 .40
- ☐ 45 The First .15 .40
- ☐ 46 Glory .15 .40
- ☐ 47 Ben .15 .40
- ☐ 48 Glory'S Minions .15 .40
- ☐ 49 Doe .15 .40
- ☐ 50 Justin .15 .40
- ☐ 51 Sweet .15 .40
- ☐ 52 Halfrek .15 .40
- ☐ 53 Dark Willow .15 .40
- ☐ 54 The First .15 .40
- ☐ 55 The Anointed One .15 .40
- ☐ 56 Angelus .15 .40
- ☐ 57 Drusilla .15 .40
- ☐ 58 The Initiative .15 .40
- ☐ 59 Harmony .15 .40
- ☐ 60 Glory .15 .40
- ☐ 61 Loan Shark .15 .40
- ☐ 62 Soul Broker .15 .40
- ☐ 63 The First .15 .40
- ☐ 64 Giles .15 .40
- ☐ 65 Glory .15 .40
- ☐ 66 Olaf The Troll .15 .40
- ☐ 67 Bunnies .15 .40
- ☐ 68 Evil Trio .15 .40
- ☐ 69 Dark Willow .15 .40
- ☐ 70 D'Hoffryn .15 .40
- ☐ 71 The First .15 .40
- ☐ 72 Checklist .15 .40

2004 Buffy the Vampire Slayer Big Bads Box Loaders

COMPLETE SET (4) 6.00 15.00

- ☐ BL1 Triple Threat 1.25 3.00
- ☐ BL2 Triple Threat 1.25 3.00
- ☐ BL3 Triple Threat 1.25 3.00
- ☐ CL1 Bad Boys 4.00 10.00

2004 Buffy the Vampire Slayer Big Bads Pieceworks

STATED ODDS 1:24

- ☐ PW1 Spike's T-Shirt
- ☐ PW2 Dru's Top
- ☐ PW3 D'Hoffryn's Robe 8.00 20.00
- ☐ PW4 Adam's Pants 8.00 20.00
- ☐ PW5 Halfrek's Top 8.00 20.00
- ☐ PW6 Warren's Jacket 8.00 20.00
- ☐ PW7 Lissa's Outfit 8.00 20.00

2004 Buffy the Vampire Slayer Big Bads Promos

COMPLETE SET (5)

- ☐ P1 Buffy & The Master 1.00 2.50
- ☐ P2 Buffy & Angelus 1.00 2.50
- ☐ P3 Buffy & Dark Willow 1.50 4.00
- ☐ Pi Buffy & Spike 1.50 4.00
- ☐ PUK Buffy & Glory 4.00 10.00

2004 Buffy the Vampire Slayer Big Bads Seasons of Evil

COMPLETE SET (9) 10.00 25.00
STATED ODDS 1:11

- ☐ SE1 Seasons Of Evil 1.50 4.00
- ☐ SE2 Seasons Of Evil 1.50 4.00
- ☐ SE3 Seasons Of Evil 1.50 4.00
- ☐ SE4 Seasons Of Evil 1.50 4.00
- ☐ SE5 Seasons Of Evil 1.50 4.00
- ☐ SE6 Seasons Of Evil 1.50 4.00
- ☐ SE7 Seasons Of Evil 1.50 4.00
- ☐ SE8 Seasons Of Evil 1.50 4.00
- ☐ SE9 Seasons Of Evil 1.50 4.00

2004 Buffy the Vampire Slayer Big Bads The Other Side

COMPLETE SET (6) 8.00 20.00
STATED ODDS 1:17

- ☐ OS1 The Master 1.50 4.00
- ☐ OS2 Angelus 1.50 4.00
- ☐ OS3 The Mayor 1.50 4.00
- ☐ OS4 Glory 1.50 4.00
- ☐ OS5 Dark Willow 1.50 4.00
- ☐ OS6 Caleb 1.50 4.00

2004 Buffy the Vampire Slayer Women of Sunnydale

COMPLETE SET (90) 5.00 12.00

- ☐ 1 Women Of Sunnydale .10 .30
- ☐ 2 Old Fashioned .10 .30
- ☐ 3 Class Protector .10 .30
- ☐ 4 Uber Buffy .10 .30
- ☐ 5 Unselfish .10 .30
- ☐ 6 Feral .10 .30
- ☐ 7 Dreaming .10 .30
- ☐ 8 Imitation .10 .30
- ☐ 9 Slayer .10 .30
- ☐ 10 Nerdette .10 .30
- ☐ 11 Grunge .10 .30
- ☐ 12 Hip .10 .30
- ☐ 13 Goth .10 .30
- ☐ 14 Prom Night .10 .30
- ☐ 15 In Love .10 .30
- ☐ 16 Acting Out .10 .30
- ☐ 17 Big Bad Will .10 .30
- ☐ 18 Oh My Goddess .10 .30
- ☐ 19 May Queen .10 .30
- ☐ 20 Cheerleader .10 .30
- ☐ 21 Armed And Dangerous .10 .30
- ☐ 22 Made .10 .30
- ☐ 23 Tough .10 .30
- ☐ 24 Vengeful .10 .30
- ☐ 25 Working Girl .10 .30
- ☐ 26 Cinderella .10 .30
- ☐ 27 Graduation .10 .30
- ☐ 28 New Girl .10 .30
- ☐ 29 Trapped As Teen .10 .30
- ☐ 30 Inappropriate .10 .30
- ☐ 31 Merchant .10 .30
- ☐ 32 Marital Jitters .10 .30
- ☐ 33 Bride .10 .30
- ☐ 34 Demon Again .10 .30
- ☐ 35 Burglar .10 .30
- ☐ 36 Aud .10 .30
- ☐ 37 Conjuring .10 .30
- ☐ 38 Willow's Friend .10 .30
- ☐ 39 Glory's Victim .10 .30
- ☐ 40 Magic Girl .10 .30
- ☐ 41 Under Her Spell .10 .30
- ☐ 42 Dawn's Pal .10 .30
- ☐ 43 Reflective .10 .30
- ☐ 44 Together Again .10 .30
- ☐ 45 Final Moment .10 .30
- ☐ 46 Not Just A Girl .10 .30
- ☐ 47 Slayer's Sister .10 .30
- ☐ 48 Captive Of Glory .10 .30
- ☐ 49 Possessed .10 .30
- ☐ 50 Sweet's Plaything .10 .30
- ☐ 51 Bridesmaid .10 .30
- ☐ 52 Mini Slayer .10 .30
- ☐ 53 Hot Stuff .10 .30
- ☐ 54 Finding Her Role .10 .30
- ☐ 55 Joyce Summers .10 .30
- ☐ 56 Jenny Calendar .10 .30
- ☐ 57 Kendra The Slayer .10 .30
- ☐ 58 Faith .10 .30
- ☐ 59 Mrs. Sam Finn .10 .30
- ☐ 60 The Guardian .10 .30
- ☐ 61 First Slayer .10 .30
- ☐ 62 Slayers In Training .10 .30
- ☐ 63 Kennedy .10 .30
- ☐ 64 Darla .10 .30
- ☐ 65 Ampata .10 .30
- ☐ 66 Drusilla .10 .30
- ☐ 67 She-Mantis .10 .30
- ☐ 68 Faith .10 .30
- ☐ 69 Vamp Will .10 .30
- ☐ 70 Gwendolyn Post .10 .30
- ☐ 71 Cafeteria Lady .10 .30
- ☐ 72 Veruca .10 .30
- ☐ 73 Kathy, Buffy's Roommate .10 .30
- ☐ 74 Harmony .10 .30
- ☐ 75 Dr. Maggie Walsh .10 .30
- ☐ 76 Glory .10 .30
- ☐ 77 Amy The Witch .10 .30
- ☐ 78 Halfrek .10 .30
- ☐ 79 Dark Willow .10 .30
- ☐ 80 Lissa .10 .30
- ☐ 81 First Evil .10 .30
- ☐ 82 Willow Vs. Anya .10 .30
- ☐ 83 Vamp Will Vs. Willow .10 .30
- ☐ 84 Dawn Vs. Buffy .10 .30
- ☐ 85 Buffy Vs. Glory .10 .30
- ☐ 86 Buffy Vs. Faith .10 .30
- ☐ 87 Anya Vs. Buffy .10 .30
- ☐ 88 Darla Vs. Buffy .10 .30
- ☐ 89 Buffy Vs. Dark Willow .10 .30
- ☐ 90 Checklist .10 .30
- ☐ TFR1 Tara Figure Redemption

2004 Buffy the Vampire Slayer Women of Sunnydale Autographs

STATED ODDS 1:36

- ☐ A1 Emma Caulfield 30.00 60.00
- ☐ A2 Amber Benson 30.00 60.00
- ☐ A3 Juliet Landau 25.00 50.00
- ☐ A4 Kristine Sutherland 8.00 20.00
- ☐ A5 Clare Kramer 25.00 50.00
- ☐ A6 Kali Rocha 8.00 20.00
- ☐ A7 Bianca Lawson 20.00 40.00
- ☐ A8 Julie Benz 15.00 30.00
- ☐ A9 Sharon Ferguson 8.00 20.00
- ☐ A10 Musetta Vander 8.00 20.00
- ☐ A11 Paige Moss 8.00 20.00
- ☐ A12 Elizabeth Anne Allen 20.00 40.00
- ☐ A13 Robia La Morte 8.00 20.00
- ☐ A14 Marti Noxon 8.00 20.00
- ☐ A15 Iyari Limon 8.00 20.00

2004 Buffy the Vampire Slayer Women of Sunnydale Box Loaders

COMPLETE SET (4) 5.00 12.00

- ☐ BL1 Willow 1.25 3.00
- ☐ BL2 Buffy 1.25 3.00
- ☐ BL3 Faith 1.25 3.00
- ☐ CL1 Working Girl 4.00 10.00

2004 Buffy the Vampire Slayer Women of Sunnydale Fashion Emergency

COMPLETE SET (9) 10.00 25.00
STATED ODDS 1:11

- ☐ FE1 Fashion Emergency 1.50 4.00
- ☐ FE2 Fashion Emergency 1.50 4.00
- ☐ FE3 Fashion Emergency 1.50 4.00
- ☐ FE4 Fashion Emergency 1.50 4.00
- ☐ FE5 Fashion Emergency 1.50 4.00
- ☐ FE6 Fashion Emergency 1.50 4.00
- ☐ FE7 Fashion Emergency 1.50 4.00
- ☐ FE8 Fashion Emergency 1.50 4.00
- ☐ FE9 Fashion Emergency 1.50 4.00

2004 Buffy the Vampire Slayer Women of Sunnydale Ladies Choice

COMPLETE SET (6) 8.00 20.00
STATED ODDS 1:17

- ☐ LC1 Xander 1.50 4.00
- ☐ LC2 Angel 1.50 -4.00
- ☐ LC3 Riley 1.50 4.00
- ☐ LC4 Spike 1.50 4.00
- ☐ LC5 Oz 1.50 4.00
- ☐ LC6 Giles 1.50 4.00

2004 Buffy the Vampire Slayer Women of Sunnydale Pieceworks

COMPLETE SET (6) 40.00 100.00
STATED ODDS 1:36

- ☐ PW1 Buffy's Leather Pants 8.00 20.00
- ☐ PW2 Drusilla's Dress 8.00 20.00
- ☐ PW3 Anya's Dress 8.00 20.00
- ☐ PW4 Tara's Sweater 8.00 20.00
- ☐ PW5 Dawn's Jeans 8.00 20.00
- ☐ PW6 Buffy's Homecoming Dress 8.00 20.00

2004 Buffy the Vampire Slayer Women of Sunnydale Promos

COMPLETE SET (4) 4.00 10.00

- ☐ P1 Buffy 1.00 2.50
- ☐ Pi Dawn 1.50 4.00
- ☐ PUK Anya 1.50 4.00
- ☐ NSUSD Women of Sunnydale 1.50 4.00
- ☐ SD2004 Tara 1.00 2.50

2004 Catwoman

COMPLETE SET (72) 4.00 10.00

- ☐ 1 Title Card .10 .30
- ☐ 2 Patience Phillips .10 .30
- ☐ 3 Catwoman .10 .30
- ☐ 4 Detective Tom Lane .10 .30
- ☐ 5 Laurel Hedare .10 .30
- ☐ 6 George Hedare .10 .30
- ☐ 7 Sally .10 .30
- ☐ 8 Ophelia Powers .10 .30
- ☐ 9 Drina .10 .30
- ☐ 10 Armando .10 .30
- ☐ 11 Wesley .10 .30
- ☐ 12 Midnight .10 .30
- ☐ 13 Keeper Of Secrets .10 .30
- ☐ 14 Blessed And Cursed .10 .30
- ☐ 15 Finding The Center .10 .30
- ☐ 16 Two Become One .10 .30
- ☐ 17 Stalking A Different Prey .10 .30
- ☐ 18 Transformation Compete .10 .30
- ☐ 19 Here, Kitty Kitty! .10 .30
- ☐ 20 Cat-Astrophe At Work .10 .30
- ☐ 21 Mutual Humiliations .10 .30
- ☐ 22 Tom Cat .10 .30
- ☐ 23 On The Prowl .10 .30
- ☐ 24 Dead End .10 .30
- ☐ 25 Resurrection .10 .30
- ☐ 26 Alley Cat .10 .30
- ☐ 27 What The Cat Dragged In .10 .30
- ☐ 28 House Of Secrets .10 .30
- ☐ 29 Tea And Catnip .10 .30
- ☐ 30 Hissy Fits .10 .30
- ☐ 31 A Woman Scorned .10 .30
- ☐ 32 Shattered World .10 .30
- ☐ 33 Warning Sign .10 .30
- ☐ 34 Coffee For A Tom Cat .10 .30
- ☐ 35 A Purr-Fect Play .10 .30
- ☐ 36 Letting The Cat Out .10 .30
- ☐ 37 Prowlin' And Growlin' .10 .30
- ☐ 38 Kitty's First Heist .10 .30
- ☐ 39 Pushed Aside .10 .30
- ☐ 40 Kitty Pretties .10 .30
- ☐ 41 The Power Of Bast .10 .30
- ☐ 42 A Little Push .10 .30
- ☐ 43 Cool Cat Strut .10 .30
- ☐ 44 Cat Got Your Tongue? .10 .30
- ☐ 45 Cream And The Kill .10 .30
- ☐ 46 Paw Prints .10 .30
- ☐ 47 Wheel Of Misfortune .10 .30
- ☐ 48 Catty Conversation .10 .30
- ☐ 49 At The Big Top .10 .30
- ☐ 50 Catwalk Confrontation .10 .30
- ☐ 51 Edge Of Run .10 .30
- ☐ 52 Cats Napping .10 .30
- ☐ 53 Kitty Cornered .10 .30
- ☐ 54 The Hunter Is Hunted .10 .30
- ☐ 55 Cat Captured .10 .30
- ☐ 56 Kitty Caged .10 .30
- ☐ 57 New Queen Of Hedare .10 .30
- ☐ 58 Squeeze Play .10 .30
- ☐ 59 Playing Dirty .10 .30
- ☐ 60 Cat Fight .10 .30
- ☐ 61 The Claws Are Out .10 .30
- ☐ 62 Shattered Beauty .10 .30
- ☐ 63 From Foes To Friends .10 .30
- ☐ 64 Hiss Off .10 .30
- ☐ 65 Jumpin' Jack Cat .10 .30
- ☐ 66 Post-Dead Close-Up .10 .30
- ☐ 67 Lights! Camera! Pounce! .10 .30
- ☐ 68 Say Cheese! Or Not .10 .30
- ☐ 69 Wait For The Clap .10 .30
- ☐ 70 Proto Cat .10 .30
- ☐ 71 Happy Campers .10 .30
- ☐ 72 Checklist .10 .30

2004 Catwoman Autographs

STATED ODDS 1:36

- ☐ A1 Lambert Wilson 6.00 15.00
- ☐ A2 Alex Borstein 6.00 15.00
- ☐ A3 Michael Massee 6.00 15.00
- ☐ A4 Kim Smith 20.00 50.00
- ☐ A5 Byron Mann 6.00 15.00
- ☐ A7 Peter Wingfield 6.00 15.00

2004 Catwoman Box Loaders

STATED ODDS ONE PER BOX

- ☐ BL1 The Cat Came Back 1.25 3.00
- ☐ BL2 Staking Out Turf 1.25 3.00
- ☐ BL3 Cool Cat And Lone Wolf 1.25 3.00
- ☐ CL1 I Rule The Night 4.00 10.00

CASE INSERT

2004 Catwoman Cat Vision

COMPLETE SET (6) 8.00 20.00
STATED ODDS 1:17

- ☐ CV1 Cat Vision 1.50 4.00
- ☐ CV2 Cat Vision 1.50 4.00
- ☐ CV3 Cat Vision 1.50 4.00
- ☐ CV4 Cat Vision 1.50 4.00
- ☐ CV5 Cat Vision 1.50 4.00
- ☐ CV6 Cat Vision 1.50 4.00

2004 Catwoman Fearless

COMPLETE SET (9) 10.00 25.00
STATED ODDS 1:11

- ☐ F1 Fearless 1.50 4.00
- ☐ F2 Fearless 1.50 4.00
- ☐ F3 Fearless 1.50 4.00
- ☐ F4 Fearless 1.50 4.00
- ☐ F5 Fearless 1.50 4.00
- ☐ F6 Fearless 1.50 4.00
- ☐ F7 Fearless 1.50 4.00
- ☐ F8 Fearless 1.50 4.00
- ☐ F9 Fearless 1.50 4.00

2004 Catwoman Pieceworks

STATED ODDS 1:36

- ☐ PW1 Halle Berry 20.00 40.00
- ☐ PW2 Halle Berry 20.00 40.00
- ☐ PW3 Halle Berry 8.00 20.00
- ☐ PW4 Halle Berry 20.00 40.00
- ☐ PW5 Benjamin Bratt 8.00 20.00
- ☐ PW6 Sharon Stone 8.00 20.00
- ☐ PW7 Halle Berry 8.00 20.00
- ☐ PW8 Halle Berry 8.00 20.00
- ☐ PW9 Lambert Wilson 8.00 20.00
- ☐ PW10 Halle Berry 8.00 20.00
- ☐ PW11 Halle Berry 8.00 20.00
- ☐ PW12 Halle Berry 8.00 20.00
- ☐ PW13 Sharon Stone 8.00 20.00
- ☐ PW14 Benjamin Bratt 8.00 20.00

2004 Catwoman Promos

COMPLETE SET (5) 4.00 10.00

- ☐ P1 Catwoman 1.00 2.50
- ☐ P2 Catwoman 1.00 2.50
- ☐ Pi Catwoman 1.00 2.50
- ☐ PUK Catwoman 1.50 4.00
- ☐ FCBD1 Catwoman FOIL 1.50 4.00

2004 Charmed Connections

COMPLETE SET (72) 4.00 10.00

- ☐ 1 Title Card .10 .30
- ☐ 2 Piper Halliwell .10 .30
- ☐ 3 Piper+Powers: Power Connection .10 .30
- ☐ 4 Piper+Leo: Romantic Connection .10 .30
- ☐ 5 Piper+Career: Career Connection .10 .30
- ☐ 6 Piper+Leo: Romantic Connection .10 .30
- ☐ 7 Piper+Leo: Magical Connection .10 .30
- ☐ 8 Piper+Her Sisters Family Connection .10 .30
- ☐ 9 Piper+Leo: Romantic Connection .10 .30
- ☐ 10 Piper+Wyatt: Family Connection .10 .30
- ☐ 11 Piper+The Crone: Magical Connection .10 .30
- ☐ 12 Piper+Grams: Family Connection .10 .30
- ☐ 13 Piper The Goddess: Magical Connection .10 .30
- ☐ 14 Piper+Leo: Heartbreak Connection .10 .30
- ☐ 15 Piper+The Cleaners: Magical Connection .10 .30
- ☐ 16 Piper+Mordaunt: Magical Connection .10 .30
- ☐ 17 Piper+The Pretender: Evil Connection .10 .30
- ☐ 18 Piper+Her Sisters: Family Connection .10 .30
- ☐ 19 Phoebe Halliwell .10 .30
- ☐ 20 Phoebe+Powers: Power Connection .10 .30
- ☐ 21 Phoebe+Career: Career Connection .10 .30
- ☐ 22 Phoebe+Cole: Romantic Connection .10 .30
- ☐ 23 Phoebe+Prue: Tragic Connection .10 .30
- ☐ 24 Phoebe+Balthazar: Evil Connection .10 .30
- ☐ 25 Phoebe+Cole: Romantic Connection .10 .30
- ☐ 26 Phoebe+The Seer: Evil Connection .10 .30
- ☐ 27 Phoebe+Cole: Heartbreak Connection .10 .30
- ☐ 28 Phoebe+Cole: Tragic Connection .10 .30
- ☐ 29 Phoebe The Goddess: Magical Connection .10 .30
- ☐ 30 Phoebe+Powers: Power Connection .10 .30
- ☐ 31 Phoebe+Jason: Romantic Connection .10 .30
- ☐ 32 Phoebe+Powers: Magical Connection .10 .30
- ☐ 33 Phoebe+Paige: Family Connection .10 .30
- ☐ 34 Phoebe+The Book: Magical Connection .10 .30
- ☐ 35 Phoebe+Piper: Family Connection .10 .30
- ☐ 36 Phoebe+Her Sisters: Family Connection .10 .30
- ☐ 37 Paige Matthews .10 .30
- ☐ 38 Paige+Her Sisters: Family Connection .10 .30
- ☐ 39 Paige+Powers: Power Connection .10 .30
- ☐ 40 Paige+Leo: Family Connection .10 .30
- ☐ 41 Paige+Sam: Family Connection .10 .30
- ☐ 42 Paige+Barbas: Evil Connection .10 .30
- ☐ 43 Paige+Grams: Family Connection .10 .30
- ☐ 44 Paige The Chanteuse: Career Connection .10 .30
- ☐ 45 Paige+Nate: Heartbreak Connection .10 .30
- ☐ 46 Paige+Darryl: Magical Connection .10 .30
- ☐ 47 Paige+Career: Career Connection .10 .30
- ☐ 48 Paige+Richard: Romantic Connection .10 .30
- ☐ 49 Paige+The Cleaners: Magical Connection .10 .30
- ☐ 50 Paige+Magic: Magical Connection .10 .30
- ☐ 51 Paige+Phoebe: Family Connection .10 .30
- ☐ 52 Paige+Spider Demon: Evil Connection .10 .30
- ☐ 53 Paige+Phoebe: Family Connection .10 .30
- ☐ 54 Paige+Wyatt: Family Connection .10 .30
- ☐ 55 Leo Wyatt .10 .30
- ☐ 56 Leo+The Charmed Ones: Power Connection .10 .30
- ☐ 57 Leo+Cole: Family Connection .10 .30
- ☐ 58 Leo+Piper: Romantic Connection .10 .30
- ☐ 59 Leo+Wyatt: Family Connection .10 .30
- ☐ 60 Leo'S Nightmare: Magical Connection .10 .30
- ☐ 61 Leo+Chris: Mystery Connection .10 .30
- ☐ 62 Leo+ Valhalla : Dangerous Connection .10 .30
- ☐ 63 Leo+Chris: Magical Connection .10 .30
- ☐ 64 Chris Perry .10 .30
- ☐ 65 Chris' Secrets .10 .30
- ☐ 66 Chris+The Blondes: Magical Connection .10 .30
- ☐ 67 Chris+Spider Demon: Mystery Connection .10 .30
- ☐ 68 Chris+Bianca: Heartbreak Connection .10 .30
- ☐ 69 Chris+Wyatt: Power Connection .10 .30
- ☐ 70 Chris+Spider Demon: Evil Connection .10 .30
- ☐ 71 Chris+His Family: Family Connection .10 .30
- ☐ 72 Checklist .10 .30

2004 Charmed Connections Box Loaders

COMPLETE SET (4) 8.00 20.00

- ☐ BL1 Leo 1.25 3.00
- ☐ BL2 Piper 1.25 3.00
- ☐ BL3 Baby Wyatt 1.25 3.00
- ☐ CL1 P3 6.00 15.00

CASE INSERT

2004 Charmed Connections Foil

COMPLETE SET (72) 15.00 30.00
*FOIL: .8X TO 2X BASIC CARDS .25 .60
STATED ODDS ONE PER PACK

2004 Charmed Connections Pieceworks

STATED ODDS 1:24

- ☐ PWC1 Alyssa Milano 25.00 50.00
Rose McGowan
- ☐ PWC2 Holly Marie Combs 25.00 50.00
Rose McGown
- ☐ PWC3 Alyssa Milano 25.00 50.00
- ☐ PWC4 Brian Krause 20.00 40.00
- ☐ PWC5 Drew Fuller 20.00 40.00
- ☐ PWC6 Julian McMahon 20.00 40.00
- ☐ PWC7 Alyssa Milano 20.00 40.00
- ☐ PWC8 Holly Marie Combs 20.00 40.00
- ☐ PWC9 Rose McGowan 20.00 40.00

2004 Charmed Connections Under Their Spell

COMPLETE SET (9) 10.00 25.00
STATED ODDS 1:11

- ☐ SP1 Under Their Spell 1.50 4.00
- ☐ SP2 Under Their Spell 1.50 4.00
- ☐ SP3 Under Their Spell 1.50 4.00
- ☐ SP4 Under Their Spell 1.50 4.00
- ☐ SP5 Under Their Spell 1.50 4.00
- ☐ SP6 Under Their Spell 1.50 4.00
- ☐ SP7 Under Their Spell 1.50 4.00
- ☐ SP8 Under Their Spell 1.50 4.00
- ☐ SP9 Under Their Spell 1.50 4.00

2004 Charmed Connections Vanquishing Evil

COMPLETE SET (6) 8.00 20.00
STATED ODDS 1:14

- ☐ VE1 Paige 1.50 4.00
- ☐ VE2 Paige, Phoebe & Piper 1.50 4.00
- ☐ VE3 Phoebe & Paige 1.50 4.00
- ☐ VE4 Piper & Paige 1.50 4.00
- ☐ VE5 Phoebe, Piper & Paige 1.50 4.00
- ☐ VE6 Paige 1.50 4.00

2004 The Chronicles of Riddick

COMPLETE SET (72) 4.00 10.00

- ☐ 1 Title Card .10 .30
- ☐ 2 Iceman Cometh .10 .30
- ☐ 3 Relentless Pursuit .10 .30
- ☐ 4 Revelation .10 .30
- ☐ 5 Old Friends .10 .30
- ☐ 6 Unexpected Guest .10 .30
- ☐ 7 Ethereal Aereon .10 .30
- ☐ 8 Invasion .10 .30
- ☐ 9 Necromongers .10 .30
- ☐ 10 Riddick Attacks .10 .30
- ☐ 11 Next Move, .10 .30
- ☐ 12 Ship Quest .10 .30
- ☐ 13 A Way Out .10 .30
- ☐ 14 War Zone .10 .30
- ☐ 15 In Control .10 .30
- ☐ 16 Spiritual Leader .10 .30
- ☐ 17 Watching, Plotting .10 .30
- ☐ 18 Dangerous Beauty .10 .30
- ☐ 19 Animal Attraction .10 .30
- ☐ 20 Consorts .10 .30
- ☐ 21 Co-Conspirators .10 .30
- ☐ 22 Among Quasi-Deads .10 .30
- ☐ 23 Captured Again .10 .30
- ☐ 24 New Direction .10 .30
- ☐ 25 Lord Marshal .10 .30
- ☐ 26 Encouragement .10 .30
- ☐ 27 Another Captive .10 .30
- ☐ 28 In The Slam .10 .30
- ☐ 29 Reunion .10 .30
- ☐ 30 Meeting The Guv .10 .30
- ☐ 31 Tests of Loyalty .10 .30
- ☐ 32 At Home .10 .30
- ☐ 33 Valuable Commodity .10 .30
- ☐ 34 Escapees .10 .30
- ☐ 35 Blasting Through .10 .30
- ☐ 36 Experienced Con .10 .30
- ☐ 37 Taking The Lead .10 .30
- ☐ 38 Death Wish .10 .30
- ☐ 39 Through The Ashes .10 .30
- ☐ 40 Climbing To Freedom .10 .30
- ☐ 41 Lensing Necros .10 .30
- ☐ 42 Battle Station .10 .30
- ☐ 43 Fearless Warrior .10 .30
- ☐ 44 At War .10 .30
- ☐ 45 Necro Soldiers .10 .30
- ☐ 46 Surveying The Damage .10 .30
- ☐ 47 The Purifier .10 .30

Overseer

- ☐ 48 The Guv No More .10 .30
- ☐ 49 Carnage .10 .30
- ☐ 50 Furyans Alike .10 .30
- ☐ 51 Blade Of Revenge .10 .30
- ☐ 52 Back For More .10 .30
- ☐ 53 Confrontation .10 .30
- ☐ 54 Unlikely Convert .10 .30
- ☐ 55 Moment of Truth .10 .30
- ☐ 56 Battle Royal .10 .30
- ☐ 57 Stabbed In The Back .10 .30
- ☐ 58 Vaako's Time .10 .30
- ☐ 59 Rule Change .10 .30
- ☐ 60 Triumph And Tragedy .10 .30
- ☐ 61 Checklist 1-36 .10 .30
- ☐ 62 Checklist 37-72 .10 .30
- ☐ 63 Bonus Card Checklist .10 .30
- ☐ 64 Puzzle Card .10 .30
- ☐ 65 Puzzle Card .10 .30
- ☐ 66 Puzzle Card .10 .30
- ☐ 67 Puzzle Card .10 .30
- ☐ 68 Puzzle Card .10 .30
- ☐ 69 Puzzle Card .10 .30

❑ 70 Puzzle Card .10 .30
❑ 71 Puzzle Card .10 .30
❑ 72 Puzzle Card .10 .30

2004 The Chronicles of Riddick Autographs

STATED ODDS TWO PER BOX
L (LIMITED): 300-500 COPIES
VL (VERY LIMITED): 200-300 COPIES

❑ A1 Vin Diesel VL 75.00 125.00
❑ A2 Judi Dench 20.00 40.00
❑ A3 Karl Urban 10.00 25.00
❑ A4 Colm Feore 10.00 25.00
❑ A5 Alexa Davalos 20.00 40.00
❑ A6 Thandie Newton 20.00 40.00
❑ A10 Keith David L

2004 The Chronicles of Riddick Casting Call

COMPLETE SET (9) 7.50 20.00
STATED ODDS 1:10

❑ CC1 Vin Diesel 1.25 3.00
❑ CC2 Judi Dench 1.25 3.00
❑ CC3 Colm Feore 1.25 3.00
❑ CC4 Alexa Davalos 1.25 3.00
❑ CC5 Karl Urban 1.25 3.00
❑ CC6 Nick Chinlund 1.25 3.00
❑ CC7 Thandie Newton 1.25 3.00
❑ CC8 Linus Roache 1.25 3.00
❑ CC9 Yorick van Wageningen 1.25 3.00

2004 The Chronicles of Riddick Pitch Black

COMPLETE SET (18) 10.00 25.00
STATED ODDS 1:3

❑ PB1 Voyage Through Space .75 2.00
❑ PB2 Rough Landing .75 2.00
❑ PB3 Search For Riddick .75 2.00
❑ PB4 Watchful Eyes .75 2.00
❑ PB5 Alien Encounter .75 2.00
❑ PB6 Carolyn's Discovery .75 2.00
❑ PB7 Allies Or Enemies .75 2.00
❑ PB8 Night Visions .75 2.00
❑ PB9 Claws Of Terror .75 2.00
❑ PB10 Warrior Mode .75 2.00
❑ PB11 Close Encounter .75 2.00
❑ PB12 Final Approach .75 2.00
❑ PB13 Life Saver .75 2.00
❑ PB14 Turning Point .75 2.00
❑ PB15 Path To Safety .75 2.00
❑ PB16 Man vs. Beast .75 2.00
❑ PB17 Deadly Assault .75 2.00
❑ PB18 Liberation .75 2.00

2004 The Chronicles of Riddick Pitch Black Autographs

A7 ISSUED AS CASE TOPPER
A8 ISSUED IN COLLECTORS ALBUM
A9 ISSUED AS MULTI-CASE INCENTIVE

❑ A7 Keith David/ (issued as case topper)
❑ A8 Radha Mitchell/ (issued in collectors album)20.00 40.00
❑ A9 Claudia Black/ (issued as multi-case incentive)

2004 The Chronicles of Riddick Promos

COMPLETE SET (3) 2.50 6.00

❑ P1 Riddick/ (General Distribution) 1.00 2.50
❑ P2 Riddick/ (Non Sport Update) 1.00 2.50
❑ P3 Riddick/ (Collectors Album) 2.00 5.00

2004 The Complete Battlestar Galactica

COMPLETE SET (72) 4.00 10.00
CC1 ISSUED IN COLLECTORS ALBUM
CT1 ISSUED AS CASE TOPPER

❑ 1 Title Montage Checklist .10 .30
❑ 2 Title Montage Checklist .10 .30
❑ 3 Title Montage Checklist .10 .30
❑ 4 Saga of a Star World: Part I .10 .30
❑ 5 Saga of a Star World: Part I .10 .30
❑ 6 Saga of a Star World: Part II .10 .30
❑ 7 Saga of a Star World: Part II .10 .30
❑ 8 Saga of a Star World: Part III .10 .30
❑ 9 Saga of a Star World: Part III .10 .30
❑ 10 Lost Planet of the Gods: Part I .10 .30
❑ 11 Lost Planet of the Gods: Part I .10 .30
❑ 12 Lost Planet of the Gods: Part I .10 .30
❑ 13 Lost Planet of the Gods: Part II .10 .30
❑ 14 Lost Planet of the Gods: Part II .10 .30
❑ 15 Lost Planet of the Gods: Part II .10 .30
❑ 16 The Lost Warrior .10 .30
❑ 17 The Lost Warrior .10 .30
❑ 18 The Lost Warrior .10 .30
❑ 19 The Long Patrol .10 .30
❑ 20 The Long Patrol .10 .30
❑ 21 The Long Patrol .10 .30
❑ 22 Gun on Ice Planet Zero: Part I .10 .30
❑ 23 Gun on Ice Planet Zero: Part I .10 .30
❑ 24 Gun on Ice Planet Zero: Part I .10 .30
❑ 25 Gun on Ice Planet Zero: Part II .10 .30
❑ 26 Gun on Ice Planet Zero: Part II .10 .30
❑ 27 Gun on Ice Planet Zero: Part II .10 .30
❑ 28 The Magnificent Warriors .10 .30
❑ 29 The Magnificent Warriors .10 .30
❑ 30 The Magnificent Warriors .10 .30
❑ 31 The Young Lords .10 .30
❑ 32 The Young Lords .10 .30
❑ 33 The Young Lords .10 .30
❑ 34 The Living Legend: Part I .10 .30
❑ 35 The Living Legend: Part I .10 .30
❑ 36 The Living Legend: Part I .10 .30
❑ 37 The Living Legend: Part II .10 .30
❑ 38 The Living Legend: Part II .10 .30
❑ 39 The Living Legend: Part II .10 .30
❑ 40 Fire in Space .10 .30
❑ 41 Fire in Space .10 .30
❑ 42 Fire in Space .10 .30
❑ 43 War of the Gods: Part I .10 .30
❑ 44 War of the Gods: Part I .10 .30
❑ 45 War of the Gods: Part I .10 .30
❑ 46 War of the Gods: Part II .10 .30
❑ 47 War of the Gods: Part II .10 .30
❑ 48 War of the Gods: Part II .10 .30
❑ 49 The Man with Nine Lives .10 .30
❑ 50 The Man with Nine Lives .10 .30
❑ 51 The Man with Nine Lives .10 .30
❑ 52 Murder on the Rising Star .10 .30
❑ 53 Murder on the Rising Star .10 .30
❑ 54 Murder on the Rising Star .10 .30
❑ 55 Greetings from Earth: Part I .10 .30
❑ 56 Greetings from Earth: Part I .10 .30
❑ 57 Greetings from Earth: Part I .10 .30
❑ 58 Greetings from Earth: Part II .10 .30
❑ 59 Greetings from Earth: Part II .10 .30
❑ 60 Greetings from Earth: Part II .10 .30
❑ 61 Baltar's Escape .10 .30
❑ 62 Baltar's Escape .10 .30
❑ 63 Baltar's Escape .10 .30
❑ 64 Experiment in Terra .10 .30
❑ 65 Experiment in Terra .10 .30
❑ 66 Experiment in Terra .10 .30
❑ 67 Take the Celestra .10 .30
❑ 68 Take the Celestra .10 .30
❑ 69 Take the Celestra .10 .30
❑ 70 The Hand of God .10 .30
❑ 71 The Hand of God .10 .30
❑ 72 The Hand of God .10 .30
❑ CC1 Commander Adama Album 12.00 30.00
(issued as album exclusive)
❑ CT1 Opening Monologue/(issued as case topper)20.00 50.00

2004 The Complete Battlestar Galactica Autographs

STATED ODDS TWO PER BOX
L (LIMITED): 300-500 COPIES
VL (VERY LIMITED): 200-300 COPIES

❑ A1 Richard Hatch L 50.00 80.00
❑ A2 Dirk Benedict VL 60.00 120.00
❑ A3 Jack Stauffer 8.00 20.00
❑ A4 Noah Hathaway 8.00 20.00
❑ A5 Lloyd Bochner 8.00 20.00
❑ A6 Lance LeGault 8.00 20.00
❑ A7 Audrey Landers 8.00 20.00
❑ A9 Herbert Jefferson Jr. 8.00 20.00
❑ A10 Patrick Macnee L 25.00 50.00
❑ A11 John Dullaghan 8.00 20.00
❑ A13 Felix Silla 8.00 20.00
❑ A14 George Murdock 8.00 20.00
❑ A15 Laurette Spang 8.00 20.00
❑ A16 Terry Carter 8.00 20.00
❑ CIA Kent McCord/(issued as two-case incentive)30.00 60.00

2004 The Complete Battlestar Galactica Colonial Warriors

COMPLETE SET (9) 15.00 30.00
STATED ODDS 1:10

❑ CW1 Commander Adama 2.00 5.00
❑ CW2 Commander Caine 2.00 5.00
❑ CW3 Col. Tigh 2.00 5.00
❑ CW4 Capt. Apollo 2.00 5.00
❑ CW5 Lt. Starbuck 2.00 5.00
❑ CW6 Lt. Boomer 2.00 5.00
❑ CW7 Lt. Sheba 2.00 5.00
❑ CW8 Lt. Athena 2.00 5.00
❑ CW9 Lt. Bojay 2.00 5.00

2004 The Complete Battlestar Galactica Galactica 1980

COMPLETE SET (20) 6.00 15.00
STATED ODDS 1:3

❑ G1 Galactica Discovers Earth .40 1.00
❑ G2 Galactica Discovers Earth .40 1.00
❑ G3 Galactica Discovers Earth: Part II .40 1.00
❑ G4 Galactica Discovers Earth: Part II .40 1.00
❑ G5 Galactica Discovers Earth: Part III .40 1.00
❑ G6 Galactica Discovers Earth: Part III .40 1.00
❑ G7 The Super Scouts: Part I .40 1.00
❑ G8 The Super Scouts: Part I .40 1.00
❑ G9 The Super Scouts: Part II .40 1.00
❑ G10 The Super Scouts: Part II .40 1.00
❑ G11 Spaceball .40 1.00
❑ G12 Spaceball .40 1.00
❑ G13 The Night The Cylons Landed: Part I .40 1.00
❑ G14 The Night The Cylons Landed: Part I .40 1.00
❑ G15 The Night The Cylons Landed: Part II .40 1.00
❑ G16 The Night The Cylons Landed: Part II .40 1.00
❑ G17 Space Croppers .40 1.00
❑ G18 Space Croppers .40 1.00
❑ G19 The Return of Starbuck .40 1.00
❑ G20 The Return of Starbuck .40 1.00

2004 The Complete Battlestar Galactica Matt Busch ArtiFex

COMPLETE SET (6) 10.00 25.00
STATED ODDS 1:20

❑ N1 Apollo 2.50 6.00
❑ N2 Starbuck 2.50 6.00
❑ N3 Villians 2.50 6.00
❑ N4 Cylons 2.50 6.00
❑ N5 Raiders 2.50 6.00
❑ N6 Vipers 2.50 6.00

2004 The Complete Battlestar Galactica SketchaFex

STATED ODDS 1:120

❑ S1 John Czop
❑ S2 Warren Martineck
❑ S3 Michael Kraiger
❑ S4 Cris Bolson
❑ S5 Eduardo Pansica
❑ S6 Dan Schaefer
❑ S7 David Day
❑ S8 Dan Day
❑ S9 Sean Pence

2004 The Complete Six Million Dollar Man Seasons One and Two

COMPLETE SET (72) 4.00 10.00

❑ 1 Title Card Checklist .10 .30
❑ 2 Title Card Checklist .10 .30
❑ 3 Population: Zero .10 .30
❑ 4 Population: Zero .10 .30
❑ 5 Survival of the Fittest .10 .30
❑ 6 Survival of the Fittest .10 .30
❑ 7 Operation Firefly .10 .30
❑ 8 Operation Firefly .10 .30
❑ 9 Day of the Robot .10 .30
❑ 10 Day of the Robot .10 .30
❑ 11 Little Orphan Airplane .10 .30
❑ 12 Little Orphan Airplane .10 .30
❑ 13 Doomsday and Counting .10 .30
❑ 14 Doomsday and Counting .10 .30
❑ 15 Eyewitness to Murder .10 .30
❑ 16 Eyewitness to Murder .10 .30
❑ 17 The Rescue of Athena One .10 .30
❑ 18 The Rescue of Athena One .10 .30
❑ 19 Dr. Wells is Missing .10 .30
❑ 20 Dr. Wells is Missing .10 .30
❑ 21 The Last of the Fourth of Julys .10 .30
❑ 22 The Last of the Fourth of Julys .10 .30
❑ 23 Burning Bright .10 .30
❑ 24 Burning Bright .10 .30
❑ 25 The Coward .10 .30
❑ 26 The Coward .10 .30
❑ 27 Run, Steve, Run .10 .30
❑ 28 Run, Steve, Run .10 .30
❑ 29 Nuclear Alert .10 .30
❑ 30 Nuclear Alert .10 .30
❑ 31 The Pioneers .10 .30
❑ 32 The Pioneers .10 .30
❑ 33 Pilot Error .10 .30
❑ 34 Pilot Error .10 .30
❑ 35 The Pal-Mir Escort .10 .30
❑ 36 The Pal-Mir Escort .10 .30
❑ 37 The Seven Million Dollar Man .10 .30
❑ 38 The Seven Million Dollar Man .10 .30
❑ 39 Straight on 'till Morning .10 .30
❑ 40 Straight on 'till Morning .10 .30
❑ 41 The Midas Touch .10 .30
❑ 42 The Midas Touch .10 .30
❑ 43 The Deadly Replay .10 .30
❑ 44 The Deadly Replay .10 .30
❑ 45 Act of Piracy .10 .30
❑ 46 Act of Piracy .10 .30
❑ 47 Stranger in Broken Fork .10 .30
❑ 48 Stranger in Broken Fork .10 .30
❑ 49 The Peeping Blonde .10 .30
❑ 50 The Peeping Blonde .10 .30
❑ 51 Cross Country Kidnap .10 .30
❑ 52 Cross Country Kidnap .10 .30
❑ 53 Lost Love .10 .30
❑ 54 Lost Love .10 .30
❑ 55 The Last Kamikaze .10 .30
❑ 56 The Last Kamikaze .10 .30
❑ 57 Return of the Robot Maker .10 .30
❑ 58 Return of the Robot Maker .10 .30
❑ 59 Taneha .10 .30
❑ 60 Taneha .10 .30
❑ 61 Look Alike .10 .30
❑ 62 Look Alike .10 .30
❑ 63 The E.S.P. Spy .10 .30
❑ 64 The E.S.P. Spy .10 .30
❑ 65 The Bionic Woman, Part One .10 .30
❑ 66 The Bionic Woman, Part One .10 .30
❑ 67 The Bionic Woman, Part Two .10 .30
❑ 68 The Bionic Woman, Part Two .10 .30
❑ 69 Outrage In Balinderry .10 .30
❑ 70 Outrage In Balinderry .10 .30
❑ 71 Steve Austin, Fugitive .10 .30
❑ 72 Steve Austin, Fugitive .10 .30

2004 The Complete Six Million Dollar Man Seasons One and Two Autographs

STATED ODDS TWO PER BOX

❑ A1 Lee Majors VL 25.00 50.00
❑ A2 Richard Anderson 8.00 20.00
❑ A3 Alan Oppenheimer VL 15.00 30.00
❑ A4 Monte Markham 8.00 20.00
❑ A5 John Saxon 8.00 20.00
❑ A6 Malachi Throne 8.00 20.00
❑ A7 Arlene Martel 8.00 20.00
❑ A8 Meg Foster 8.00 20.00
❑ A9 William Schallert 8.00 20.00
❑ A10 Paul Carr 8.00 20.00
❑ A11 Jennifer Darling 8.00 20.00
(issued in collectors album)
❑ A12 Gary Lockwood/ (issued as case topper) 8.00 20.00
❑ A13 William Shatner/ (issued as multi-case incentive)

2004 The Complete Six Million Dollar Man Seasons One and Two Bionics

COMPLETE SET (3) 10.00 25.00
STATED ODDS 1:40

❑ B1 Eye 4.00 10.00
❑ B2 Arm 4.00 10.00
❑ B3 Legs 4.00 10.00

2004 The Complete Six Million Dollar Man Seasons One and Two Made for Each Other

COMPLETE SET (9) 8.00 20.00
STATED ODDS 1:10

❑ SJ1 Steve and Jaime 1.25 3.00
❑ SJ2 Steve and Jaime 1.25 3.00
❑ SJ3 Steve and Jaime 1.25 3.00
❑ SJ4 Steve and Jaime 1.25 3.00
❑ SJ5 Steve and Jaime 1.25 3.00
❑ SJ6 Steve and Jaime 1.25 3.00
❑ SJ7 Steve and Jaime 1.25 3.00
❑ SJ8 Steve and Jaime 1.25 3.00
❑ SJ9 Steve and Jaime 1.25 3.00

2004 The Complete Six Million Dollar Man Seasons One and Two OSI Files

COMPLETE SET (9) 15.00 40.00
STATED ODDS 1:20

❑ O1 Cryogenic Orbiter 2.50 6.00
❑ O2 Barney Miller 2.50 6.00
❑ O3 Josh Lang 2.50 6.00
❑ O4 Bionic Heart 2.50 6.00
❑ O5 HL-10 2.50 6.00
❑ O6 Portable Laser Projector 2.50 6.00
❑ O7 Robot of Oscar Goldman 2.50 6.00
❑ O8 Peregrine-I Bomb 2.50 6.00
❑ O9 Bionic Ear 2.50 6.00

2004 The Complete Six Million Dollar Man Seasons One and Two The Movies

COMPLETE SET (9) 5.00 12.00
STATED ODDS 1:6

❑ M1 The Moon and the Desert .75 2.00
❑ M2 The Moon and the Desert .75 2.00
❑ M3 The Moon and the Desert .75 2.00
❑ M4 Wine, Women and War .75 2.00
❑ M5 Wine, Women and War .75 2.00
❑ M6 Wine, Women and War .75 2.00
❑ M7 Solid Gold Kidnapping .75 2.00
❑ M8 Solid Gold Kidnapping .75 2.00
❑ M9 Solid Gold Kidnapping .75 2.00

2004 Conan Art of the Hyborian Age

COMPLETE SET (72) 4.00 10.00
LEE AUTO ISSUED AS CASE TOPPER

❑ 1 Title Card .10 .30
❑ 2 Title Card .10 .30
❑ 3 Title Card .10 .30
❑ 4 Pablo Marcos #9 .10 .30
❑ 5 Brunner #14 .10 .30
❑ 6 Thorne #16 .10 .30
❑ 7 Buscema #17 .10 .30
❑ 8 Conrad #18 .10 .30
❑ 9 Nasser #20 .10 .30
❑ 10 Alcazar #24 .10 .30
❑ 11 Buscema #26 .10 .30
❑ 12 Nebres #27 .10 .30
❑ 13 Buscema And Alcala #28 .10 .30
❑ 14 Kane #29 .10 .30
❑ 15 Jodloman #33 .10 .30
❑ 16 Wilson And Rubenstein #34 .10 .30
❑ 17 Maitz #35 .10 .30
❑ 18 Wenzel #36 .10 .30
❑ 19 Gammill #46 .10 .30
❑ 20 Redondo #51 .10 .30
❑ 21 Jusko #55 .10 .30
❑ 22 Nebres #57 .10 .30
❑ 23 Pollard #59 .10 .30
❑ 24 DeZuniga #60 .10 .30
❑ 25 Toth #64 .10 .30
❑ 26 Chiodo #65 .10 .30
❑ 27 Layton And McConnell #66 .10 .30
❑ 28 Kane #67 .10 .30
❑ 29 Potts #71 .10 .30
❑ 30 Marcos #72 .10 .30
❑ 31 Marcos #73 .10 .30
❑ 32 Potts #75 .10 .30
❑ 33 Marcos #84 .10 .30
❑ 34 Marcos #85 .10 .30
❑ 35 Buscema #87 .10 .30
❑ 36 Chan #89 .10 .30
❑ 37 Chan #92 .10 .30
❑ 38 Chan #110 .10 .30
❑ 39 Chan #113 .10 .30
❑ 40 Docherty #120 .10 .30
❑ 41 Nebres #122 .10 .30
❑ 42 Nebres #123 .10 .30
❑ 43 Nebres #126 .10 .30
❑ 44 Nebres #127 .10 .30
❑ 45 Garcia #130 .10 .30
❑ 46 Bator #137 .10 .30
❑ 47 Bator #138 .10 .30
❑ 48 Bator #141 .10 .30
❑ 49 Bator #142 .10 .30
❑ 50 Unknown #143 .10 .30
❑ 51 Gil #145 .10 .30
❑ 52 Docherty #150 .10 .30
❑ 53 Hondru #155 .10 .30
❑ 54 Simons #156 .10 .30
❑ 55 Smith #162 .10 .30
❑ 56 Simons #172 .10 .30
❑ 57 Carillo #173 .10 .30
❑ 58 Simons #175 .10 .30
❑ 59 Villagran #182 .10 .30
❑ 60 Adkins #185 .10 .30
❑ 61 DeCarlo #189 .10 .30
❑ 62 Hondru #195 .10 .30
❑ 63 Hoburg And Bryant #196 .10 .30
❑ 64 Cruz #198 .10 .30
❑ 65 Buscema And Chan #200 .10 .30
❑ 66 Abrams #201 .10 .30
❑ 67 Cooper And Sandu #204 .10 .30
❑ 68 Buscema #222 .10 .30
❑ 69 Garcia #225 .10 .30
❑ 70 Evans #227 .10 .30
❑ 71 Castro #231 .10 .30
❑ 72 Martineck #235 .10 .30
❑ A1 Stan Lee/ (autographed)

2004 Conan Art of the Hyborian Age Ode to the Cimmerian

COMPLETE SET (12) 3.00 8.00
STATED ODDS 1:4

❑ C1 Lion Of The Waves .40 1.00
❑ C2 Lion Of The Waves .40 1.00
❑ C3 Lion Of The Waves .40 1.00
❑ C4 Lion Of The Waves .40 1.00
❑ C5 Lion Of The Waves .40 1.00
❑ C6 Lion Of The Waves .40 1.00
❑ C7 Challenge .40 1.00
❑ C8 Challenge .40 1.00
❑ C9 Challenge .40 1.00
❑ C10 Challenge .40 1.00
❑ C11 Challenge .40 1.00
❑ C12 Challenge .40 1.00

2004 Conan Art of the Hyborian Age Promos

COMPLETE SET (3) 2.50 6.00

❑ P1 Conan in snow/ (General Distribution) 1.00 2.50
❑ P2 Conan w dead pterodactyl/ (Binder Exclusive) 1.50 4.00
❑ SD2004 Conan under full moon (San Diego Comic Con) 1.00 2.50

2004 Conan Art of the Hyborian Age Rise of the King

COMPLETE SET (6) 12.50 30.00
STATED ODDS 1:40

❑ R1 Conan Of Cimmeria 2.50 6.00
❑ R2 Conan The Thief 2.50 6.00
❑ R3 Conan The Gladiator 2.50 6.00
❑ R4 Conan The Renegade 2.50 6.00
❑ R5 Conan The Buccaneer 2.50 6.00
❑ R6 Conan The King 2.50 6.00

2004 Conan Art of the Hyborian Age Savage Sisterhood

COMPLETE SET (9) 6.00 15.00
STATED ODDS 1:8

❑ S1 Salome .75 2.00
❑ S2 Yasmina .75 2.00
❑ S3 Jondra .75 2.00
❑ S4 Princess Ayella .75 2.00
❑ S5 Belit .75 2.00
❑ S6 Frost Giant's Daughter .75 2.00
❑ S7 Lady Gorbek .75 2.00
❑ S8 Valeria .75 2.00
❑ S9 Jamilah .75 2.00

2004 Conan Art of the Hyborian Age SketchaFEX

STATED ODDS ONE PER BOX

❑ 1 Darren Auck
❑ 2 Darren Auck/ (issued in collectors album)
❑ 3 Dan Day
❑ 4 David Day
❑ 5 Geoff Isherwood
❑ 6 Michael Kraiger
❑ 7 Pablo Marcos
❑ 8 Warren Martineck
❑ 9 Warren Martineck COLOR/ (issued as multi-case incentive)
❑ 10 Mark Pennington

2004 The Dead Zone Seasons One and Two

COMPLETE SET (100) 4.00 10.00

❑ 1 Title Card .10 .30
❑ 2 Title Card .10 .30
❑ 3 Title Card .10 .30
❑ 4 Wheel of Fortune .10 .30
❑ 5 Wheel of Fortune .10 .30
❑ 6 Wheel of Fortune .10 .30
❑ 7 What It Seems .10 .30
❑ 8 What It Seems .10 .30
❑ 9 What It Seems .10 .30
❑ 10 Quality of Life .10 .30
❑ 11 Quality of Life .10 .30
❑ 12 Quality of Life .10 .30
❑ 13 Enigma .10 .30
❑ 14 Enigma .10 .30
❑ 15 Enigma .10 .30
❑ 16 Unreasonable Doubt .10 .30
❑ 17 Unreasonable Doubt .10 .30
❑ 18 Unreasonable Doubt .10 .30
❑ 19 The House .10 .30
❑ 20 The House .10 .30
❑ 21 The House .10 .30
❑ 22 Enemy Mind .10 .30
❑ 23 Enemy Mind .10 .30
❑ 24 Enemy Mind .10 .30
❑ 25 Netherworld .10 .30
❑ 26 Netherworld .10 .30
❑ 27 Netherworld .10 .30
❑ 28 The Siege .10 .30
❑ 29 The Siege .10 .30
❑ 30 The Siege .10 .30
❑ 31 Here There Be Monsters .10 .30
❑ 32 Here There Be Monsters .10 .30
❑ 33 Here There Be Monsters .10 .30
❑ 34 Dinner With Dana .10 .30
❑ 35 Dinner With Dana .10 .30
❑ 36 Dinner With Dana .10 .30
❑ 37 Shaman .10 .30
❑ 38 Shaman .10 .30
❑ 39 Shaman .10 .30
❑ 40 Destiny .10 .30
❑ 41 Destiny .10 .30
❑ 42 Destiny .10 .30
❑ 43 Valley of the Shadow .10 .30
❑ 44 Valley of the Shadow .10 .30
❑ 45 Valley of the Shadow .10 .30
❑ 46 Descent .10 .30
❑ 47 Descent .10 .30
❑ 48 Descent .10 .30
❑ 49 Ascent .10 .30
❑ 50 Ascent .10 .30
❑ 51 Ascent .10 .30
❑ 52 The Outsider .10 .30
❑ 53 The Outsider .10 .30
❑ 54 The Outsider .10 .30
❑ 55 Precipitate .10 .30
❑ 56 Precipitate .10 .30
❑ 57 Precipitate .10 .30
❑ 58 Scars .10 .30
❑ 59 Scars .10 .30
❑ 60 Scars .10 .30
❑ 61 Misbegotten .10 .30
❑ 62 Misbegotten .10 .30
❑ 63 Misbegotten .10 .30
❑ 64 Cabin Pressure .10 .30
❑ 65 Cabin Pressure .10 .30
❑ 66 Cabin Pressure .10 .30
❑ 67 The Man Who Never Was .10 .30
❑ 68 The Man Who Never Was .10 .30
❑ 69 The Man Who Never Was .10 .30
❑ 70 Dead Men Tell Tales .10 .30
❑ 71 Dead Men Tell Tales .10 .30
❑ 72 Dead Men Tell Tales .10 .30
❑ 73 Playing God .10 .30
❑ 74 Playing God .10 .30
❑ 75 Playing God .10 .30
❑ 76 Zion .10 .30
❑ 77 Zion .10 .30
❑ 78 Zion .10 .30
❑ 79 The Storm .10 .30
❑ 80 The Storm .10 .30
❑ 81 The Storm .10 .30
❑ 82 Plague .10 .30
❑ 83 Plague .10 .30
❑ 84 Plague .10 .30
❑ 85 Deja Voodoo .10 .30
❑ 86 Deja Voodoo .10 .30
❑ 87 Deja Voodoo .10 .30
❑ 88 The Hunt .10 .30
❑ 89 The Hunt .10 .30
❑ 90 The Hunt .10 .30
❑ 91 The Mountain .10 .30
❑ 92 The Mountain .10 .30
❑ 93 The Mountain .10 .30
❑ 94 The Combination .10 .30
❑ 95 The Combination .10 .30
❑ 96 The Combination .10 .30
❑ 97 Visions .10 .30
❑ 98 Visions .10 .30
❑ 99 Visions .10 .30
❑ 100 Checklist .10 .30

2004 The Dead Zone Seasons One and Two Autographs

STATED ODDS TWO PER BOX
L (LIMITED): 300-500 COPIES

❑ 1 Adam Beach 3.00 8.00
❑ 2 Alicia Coppola 3.00 8.00
❑ 3 Ally Sheedy L 40.00 80.00
❑ 4 Alvin Sanders 3.00 8.00
❑ 5 Anthony Michael Hall L 50.00 100.00
❑ 6 Blu Mankuma 3.00 8.00
❑ 7 David Julian Hirsh 3.00 8.00
❑ 8 Donnelly Rhodes 3.00 8.00
❑ 9 John L. Adams L 15.00 30.00
❑ 10 Julie Patzwald 5.00 12.00
❑ 11 Kristen Dalton L 20.00 40.00
❑ 12 Peter Wingfield 3.00 8.00
❑ 13 Rick Tae/ (issued in collectors album) 10.00 25.00
❑ 14 Robert Picardo 30.00 60.00
(issued as multi-case incentive)
❑ 15 Scott William Winters 3.00 8.00
❑ 16 Sean Patrick Flanery L
❑ 17 Stephen Tobolowsky 3.00 8.00

2004 The Dead Zone Seasons One and Two Behind the Scenes

COMPLETE SET (13) 5.00 12.00
STATED ODDS 1:5

❑ B1 Wheel of Fortune .60 1.50
❑ B2 What It Seems .60 1.50
❑ B3 Quality of Life .60 1.50
❑ B4 Enigma .60 1.50
❑ B5 Unreasonable Doubt .60 1.50
❑ B6 The House .60 1.50
❑ B7 Enemy Mind .60 1.50
❑ B8 Netherworld .60 1.50
❑ B9 The Siege .60 1.50
❑ B10 Here There Be Monsters .60 1.50
❑ B11 Dinner With Dana .60 1.50
❑ B12 Shaman .60 1.50
❑ B13 Destiny .60 1.50

2004 The Dead Zone Seasons One and Two Casting Call

COMPLETE SET (5) 30.00 75.00
STATED ODDS 1:160
DZ5 ISSUED AS CASE TOPPER

❑ DZ1 Johnny Smith 6.00 15.00
❑ DZ2 Sarah Bannerman 6.00 15.00
❑ DZ3 Walt Bannerman 6.00 15.00
❑ DZ4 Bruce Lewis 6.00 15.00
❑ DZ5 Cast/ (issued as case topper) 15.00 30.00

2004 The Dead Zone Seasons One and Two Stars of the Zone

COMPLETE SET (7) 10.00 25.00
STATED ODDS 1:20

❑ S1 Anthony Michael Hall 2.00 5.00
❑ S2 Nicole deBoer 2.00 5.00
❑ S3 Chris Bruno 2.00 5.00
❑ S4 John L. Adams 2.00 5.00
❑ S5 David Odgen Stiers 2.00 5.00
❑ S6 Kristen Dalton 2.00 5.00
❑ S7 Sean Patrick Flanery 2.00 5.00

2004 Enterprise Season Three

COMPLETE SET (72) 4.00 10.00
C2 ISSUED IN COLLECTORS ALBUM
LA1 ISSUED AS MULTI-CASE INCENTIVE

❑ 163 The Xindi .10 .30
❑ 164 The Xindi .10 .30
❑ 165 The Xindi .10 .30
❑ 166 Anomaly .10 .30
❑ 167 Anomaly .10 .30
❑ 168 Anomaly .10 .30
❑ 169 Extinction .10 .30
❑ 170 Extinction .10 .30
❑ 171 Extinction .10 .30
❑ 172 Raijin .10 .30
❑ 173 Raijin .10 .30
❑ 174 Raijin .10 .30
❑ 175 Impulse .10 .30
❑ 176 Impulse .10 .30
❑ 177 Impulse .10 .30
❑ 178 Exile .10 .30
❑ 179 Exile .10 .30
❑ 180 Exile .10 .30
❑ 181 The Shipment .10 .30
❑ 182 The Shipment .10 .30
❑ 183 The Shipment .10 .30
❑ 184 Twilight .10 .30
❑ 185 Twilight .10 .30
❑ 186 Twilight .10 .30
❑ 187 North Star .10 .30
❑ 188 North Star .10 .30
❑ 189 North Star .10 .30
❑ 190 Similitude .10 .30
❑ 191 Similitude .10 .30
❑ 192 Similitude .10 .30
❑ 193 Carpenter Street .10 .30
❑ 194 Carpenter Street .10 .30
❑ 195 Carpenter Street .10 .30
❑ 196 Chosen Realm .10 .30
❑ 197 Chosen Realm .10 .30
❑ 198 Chosen Realm .10 .30
❑ 199 Proving Ground .10 .30
❑ 200 Proving Ground .10 .30
❑ 201 Proving Ground .10 .30
❑ 202 Stratagem .10 .30
❑ 203 Stratagem .10 .30
❑ 204 Stratagem .10 .30
❑ 205 Harbinger .10 .30
❑ 206 Harbinger .10 .30
❑ 207 Harbinger .10 .30
❑ 208 Doctor's Orders .10 .30
❑ 209 Doctor's Orders .10 .30
❑ 210 Doctor's Orders .10 .30
❑ 211 Hatchery .10 .30
❑ 212 Hatchery .10 .30
❑ 213 Hatchery .10 .30
❑ 214 Azati Prime .10 .30
❑ 215 Azati Prime .10 .30
❑ 216 Azati Prime .10 .30
❑ 217 Damage .10 .30
❑ 218 Damage .10 .30
❑ 219 Damage .10 .30
❑ 220 The Forgotten .10 .30
❑ 221 The Forgotten .10 .30
❑ 222 The Forgotten .10 .30
❑ 223 E2 .10 .30
❑ 224 E2 .10 .30
❑ 225 E2 .10 .30
❑ 226 The Council .10 .30
❑ 227 The Council .10 .30
❑ 228 The Council .10 .30
❑ 229 Countdown .10 .30
❑ 230 Countdown .10 .30
❑ 231 Countdown .10 .30
❑ 232 Zero Hour .10 .30
❑ 233 Zero Hour .10 .30
❑ 234 Zero Hour .10 .30
❑ C2 Captain Archer MEM 25.00 50.00
(issued in collectors album)
❑ LA1 Scott Bakula AU 75.00 150.00
(issued as multi-case incentive)

2004 Enterprise Season Three Autographs

OVERALL AUTO ODDS TWO PER BOX
L (LIMITED): 300-500 COPIES
VL (VERY LIMITED): 200-300 COPIES

❑ A7 Connor Trinneer L 30.00 60.00
❑ A23 Jolene Blalock VL
❑ A24 Casey Biggs 6.00 15.00
❑ A25 Rick Worthy 6.00 15.00
❑ A26 Scott MacDonald 6.00 15.00
❑ A27 Tucker Smallwood 6.00 15.00
❑ A28 Randy Oglesby 6.00 15.00
❑ A29 Nikita Ager 6.00 15.00
❑ A30 Emily Bergl 6.00 15.00
❑ A31 Robert Rusler 6.00 15.00

2004 Enterprise Season Three Enterprise Crew

COMPLETE SET (7) 25.00 50.00
STATED ODDS 1:40

❑ CC1 Captain Jonathan Archer 4.00 10.00
❑ CC2 Sub-Commander T'Pol 4.00 10.00
❑ CC3 Chief Engineer Charles Trip Tucker III 4.00 10.00
❑ CC4 Lieutenant Malcolm Reed 4.00 10.00
❑ CC5 Ensign Hoshi Sato 4.00 10.00
❑ CC6 Ensign Travis Mayweather 4.00 10.00
❑ CC7 Doctor Phlox 4.00 10.00

2004 Enterprise Season Three First Contact

COMPLETE SET (9) 10.00 25.00
STATED ODDS 1:20

❑ F22 Xindi-Humanoid 1.50 4.00
❑ F23 Xindi-Reptilian 1.50 4.00
❑ F24 Xindi-Arboreal (Sloth) 1.50 4.00
❑ F25 Xindi-Insectiod 1.50 4.00
❑ F26 Xindi-Aquatic 1.50 4.00
❑ F27 Osaarian 1.50 4.00
❑ F28 Skagarans 1.50 4.00
❑ F29 Illyrian 1.50 4.00
❑ F30 Triannon 1.50 4.00

2004 Enterprise Season Three MACO Autographs

COMPLETE SET (7)
OVERALL AUTO ODDS TWO PER BOX

❑ MACO1 Steven Culp 6.00 15.00
❑ MACO2 Noa Tishby 6.00 15.00
❑ MACO3 Daniel Dae Kim 8.00 20.00
❑ MACO4 Julia Rose 6.00 15.00
❑ MACO5 Sean McGowan 6.00 15.00
❑ MACO6 Marco Sanchez 6.00 15.00
❑ MACO7 Nathan Anderson 6.00 15.00

2004 Enterprise Season Three MACOs in Action

COMPLETE SET (9) 6.00 15.00
STATED ODDS 1:10

❑ M1 MACO Soldiers 1.25 3.00
❑ M2 MACO Soldiers 1.25 3.00
❑ M3 MACO Soldiers 1.25 3.00
❑ M4 MACO Soldiers 1.25 3.00
❑ M5 MACO Soldiers 1.25 3.00
❑ M6 MACO Soldiers 1.25 3.00
❑ M7 MACO Soldiers 1.25 3.00
❑ M8 MACO Soldiers 1.25 3.00
❑ M9 MACO Soldiers 1.25 3.00

2004 Enterprise Season Three The Ultimate Jolene

COMPLETE SET (9) 30.00 75.00
STATED ODDS 1:40

❑ J1 Jolene Blalock as T'Pol 4.00 10.00
❑ J2 Jolene Blalock as T'Pol 4.00 10.00
❑ J3 Jolene Blalock as T'Pol 4.00 10.00
❑ J4 Jolene Blalock as T'Pol 4.00 10.00
❑ J5 Jolene Blalock as T'Pol 4.00 10.00
❑ J6 Jolene Blalock as T'Pol 4.00 10.00
❑ J7 Jolene Blalock as T'Pol 4.00 10.00
❑ J8 Jolene Blalock as T'Pol 4.00 10.00
❑ J9 Jolene Blalock as T'Pol 4.00 10.00

2004 Enterprise Season Three Women Of Enterprise SketchaFEX

STATED ODDS ONE PER CASE

❑ 1 John Czop
Hoshi
❑ 2 John Czop
T'Pol

2004 Farscape Through the Wormhole

COMPLETE SET (72) 4.00 10.00

❑ 1 John Crichton .10 .30
❑ 2 John Crichton .10 .30
❑ 3 John Crichton .10 .30
❑ 4 John Crichton .10 .30
❑ 5 John Crichton .10 .30
❑ 6 John Crichton .10 .30
❑ 7 John Crichton .10 .30
❑ 8 John Crichton .10 .30
❑ 9 John Crichton .10 .30
❑ 10 Aeryn Sun .10 .30
❑ 11 Aeryn Sun .10 .30
❑ 12 Aeryn Sun .10 .30
❑ 13 Aeryn Sun .10 .30
❑ 14 Aeryn Sun .10 .30
❑ 15 Aeryn Sun .10 .30
❑ 16 Aeryn Sun .10 .30
❑ 17 Aeryn Sun .10 .30
❑ 18 Aeryn Sun .10 .30
❑ 19 Ka D'Argo .10 .30
❑ 20 Ka D'Argo .10 .30
❑ 21 Ka D'Argo .10 .30
❑ 22 Ka D'Argo .10 .30
❑ 23 Ka D'Argo .10 .30
❑ 24 Ka D'Argo .10 .30
❑ 25 Ka D'Argo .10 .30
❑ 26 Ka D'Argo .10 .30
❑ 27 Ka D'Argo .10 .30
❑ 28 Chiana .10 .30
❑ 29 Chiana .10 .30
❑ 30 Chiana .10 .30
❑ 31 Chiana .10 .30
❑ 32 Chiana .10 .30
❑ 33 Chiana .10 .30
❑ 34 Chiana .10 .30
❑ 35 Chiana .10 .30
❑ 36 Chiana .10 .30
❑ 37 Scorpius .10 .30
❑ 38 Scorpius .10 .30
❑ 39 Scorpius .10 .30
❑ 40 Scorpius .10 .30
❑ 41 Scorpius .10 .30
❑ 42 Scorpius .10 .30
❑ 43 Harvey .10 .30
❑ 44 Harvey .10 .30
❑ 45 Harvey .10 .30
❑ 46 Zhaan .10 .30
❑ 47 Zhaan .10 .30
❑ 48 Zhaan .10 .30
❑ 49 Zhaan .10 .30
❑ 50 Zhaan .10 .30
❑ 51 Zhaan .10 .30
❑ 52 Rygel .10 .30
❑ 53 Rygel .10 .30
❑ 54 Rygel .10 .30
❑ 55 Pilot .10 .30
❑ 56 Pilot .10 .30
❑ 57 Stark .10 .30
❑ 58 Stark .10 .30
❑ 59 Crais .10 .30
❑ 60 Crais .10 .30
❑ 61 Sikozu .10 .30
❑ 62 Sikozu .10 .30
❑ 63 Jool .10 .30
❑ 64 Jool .10 .30
❑ 65 Braca .10 .30
❑ 66 Braca .10 .30
❑ 67 Grayza .10 .30
❑ 68 Jothee .10 .30
❑ 69 Noranti .10 .30
❑ 70 Checklist 1 .10 .30
❑ 71 Checklist 2 .10 .30
❑ 72 Checklist 3 .10 .30

2004 Farscape Through the Wormhole Autographs

OVERALL AUTO ODDS TWO PER BOX
A39 ISSUED IN COLLECTORS ALBUM
ALL AUTOS LIMITED (300-500 COPIES) UNLESS NOTED
VL (VERY LIMITED): 200-300 COPIES

❑ A35 Carmen Duncan 6.00 15.00
❑ A36 Justin Monjo 6.00 15.00
❑ A37 Alyssa-Jane Cook 15.00 30.00
❑ A38 Claudia Black VL
❑ A39 Bianca Chiminello 6.00 15.00
(issued in collectors album)
❑ A40 Rhys Muldoon 6.00 15.00
❑ A41 Nick Tate 6.00 15.00
❑ A42 Felix Williamson 6.00 15.00
❑ A43 Marta Dusseldorp 6.00 15.00
❑ A44 Rachel Gordon 6.00 15.00
❑ A45 Tina Bursil 6.00 15.00
❑ A46 Matt Day 6.00 15.00
❑ A47 Claudia Karvan
❑ A48 Natalie Mendoza 8.00 20.00
❑ A49 Imogen Annesley 12.00 25.00
❑ A50 Mark Mitchell 6.00 15.00
❑ A51 Victoria Longley 6.00 15.00
❑ A52 Barry Otto 6.00 15.00
❑ A53 Jeremy Sims 6.00 15.00
❑ A54 Angie Milliken 8.00 20.00
❑ A55 Jamie Croft 6.00 15.00
❑ A56 Darlene Vogel 6.00 15.00
❑ A57 Lisa Hensley 6.00 15.00
❑ A58 Susan Lyons 8.00 20.00
❑ A59 Anthony Hayes 6.00 15.00
❑ A60 Felicity Price 6.00 15.00
❑ A61 Alex Dimitriades 6.00 15.00
❑ A62 Alyson Standen 6.00 15.00
❑ A63 Chris Haywood 6.00 15.00
❑ A64 Anna Lise Phillips 6.00 15.00
❑ A65 David Franklin 12.00 25.00
❑ A66 Gigi Edgley 25.00 50.00
❑ A67 Anthony Simcoe 6.00 15.00
❑ A68 Wayne Pygram VL
❑ A69 Raelee Hill 12.00 25.00
❑ A70 Paul Goddard 6.00 15.00

2004 Farscape Through the Wormhole Crichton's Women

COMPLETE SET (9) 30.00 75.00

❑ W1 Aeryn Sun 4.00 10.00
❑ W2 Chiana 4.00 10.00
❑ W3 Gilina Renaez 4.00 10.00
❑ W4 Princess Katralla 4.00 10.00
❑ W5 Alex O'Connor 4.00 10.00
❑ W6 Zhaan 4.00 10.00
❑ W7 Grayza 4.00 10.00
❑ W8 Karen Shaw 4.00 10.00
❑ W9 Jenavian Charto 4.00 10.00

2004 Farscape Through the Wormhole Dual Autographs

OVERALL AUTO ODDS TWO PER BOX
DA2 ISSUED AS MULTI-CASE INCENTIVE
VL (VERY LIMITED): 200-300 COPIES

❑ DA1 Ben Browder
Claudia Black VL
❑ DA2 Ben Browder
Wayne Pygram/ (issued as multi-case incentive)
❑ DA3 Virginia Hey
Paul Goddard

2004 Farscape Through the Wormhole Farscape Peacekeeper Wars

COMPLETE SET (18) 7.50 20.00
STATED ODDS 1:5

❑ PW1 Farscape Peacekeeper Wars .75 2.00
❑ PW2 Farscape Peacekeeper Wars .75 2.00
❑ PW3 Farscape Peacekeeper Wars .75 2.00
❑ PW4 Farscape Peacekeeper Wars .75 2.00
❑ PW5 Farscape Peacekeeper Wars .75 2.00
❑ PW6 Farscape Peacekeeper Wars .75 2.00
❑ PW7 Farscape Peacekeeper Wars .75 2.00
❑ PW8 Farscape Peacekeeper Wars .75 2.00
❑ PW9 Farscape Peacekeeper Wars .75 2.00
❑ PW10 Farscape Peacekeeper Wars .75 2.00
❑ PW11 Farscape Peacekeeper Wars .75 2.00
❑ PW12 Farscape Peacekeeper Wars .75 2.00
❑ PW13 Farscape Peacekeeper Wars .75 2.00
❑ PW14 Farscape Peacekeeper Wars .75 2.00
❑ PW15 Farscape Peacekeeper Wars .75 2.00
❑ PW16 Farscape Peacekeeper Wars .75 2.00
❑ PW17 Farscape Peacekeeper Wars .75 2.00
❑ PW18 Farscape Peacekeeper Wars .75 2.00

2004 Farscape Through the Wormhole Sean Pence ArtiFEX

COMPLETE SET (9) 10.00 25.00
STATED ODDS 1:13

❑ SPA1 John Crichton 1.50 4.00
❑ SPA2 Aeryn Sun 1.50 4.00
❑ SPA3 Ka D'Argo 1.50 4.00
❑ SPA4 Chiana 1.50 4.00
❑ SPA5 Zhaan 1.50 4.00
❑ SPA6 Rygel 1.50 4.00
❑ SPA7 Pilot 1.50 4.00
❑ SPA8 Noranti 1.50 4.00
❑ SPA9 Sikozu 1.50 4.00

2004 Farscape Through the Wormhole The Quotable Farscape Season One

COMPLETE SET (22) 15.00 30.00
STATED ODDS 1:5

❑ Q1 Premiere 1.00 2.50
❑ Q2 I, ET 1.00 2.50
❑ Q3 Exodus From Genesis 1.00 2.50
❑ Q4 Throne For A Loss 1.00 2.50
❑ Q5 Back And Back And Back To The Future 1.00 2.50
❑ Q6 Thank God It's Friday Again 1.00 2.50
❑ Q7 PK Tech Girl 1.00 2.50
❑ Q8 That Old Black Magic 1.00 2.50
❑ Q9 DNA Mad Scientist 1.00 2.50
❑ Q10 They've Got A Secret 1.00 2.50
❑ Q11 Til The Blood Runs Clear 1.00 2.50
❑ Q12 Rhapsody In Blue 1.00 2.50
❑ Q13 The Flax 1.00 2.50
❑ Q14 Jeremiah Crichton 1.00 2.50
❑ Q15 Durka Returns 1.00 2.50
❑ Q16 A Human Reaction 1.00 2.50
❑ Q17 Through The Looking Glass 1.00 2.50
❑ Q18 A Bug's Life 1.00 2.50
❑ Q19 Nerve 1.00 2.50
❑ Q20 A Hidden Memory 1.00 2.50
❑ Q21 Bone To Be Wild 1.00 2.50
❑ Q22 Family Ties 1.00 2.50

2004 Garbage Pail Kids All New Series 2

COMPLETE SET (80) 6.00 15.00

❑ 1a Peg Leg Greg .10 .25
❑ 1b Justin Timber Leg .10 .25
❑ 2a Aerial Ariel .10 .25
❑ 2b Bubbly Brianna .10 .25
❑ 3a Eaten Ethan .10 .25
❑ 3b Jose Souffle .10 .25
❑ 4a Umbilical Corey .10 .25
❑ 4b Unraveled Rafael .10 .25
❑ 5a Lost In Austin .10 .25
❑ 5b Fat Chance .10 .25
❑ 6a Leakin' Lee .10 .25
❑ 6b Joustin' Josh .10 .25
❑ 7a Game Over Gary .10 .25
❑ 7b Germy Jeremy .10 .25
❑ 8a Sk8 Nate .10 .25
❑ 8b Flyin' Ryan .10 .25
❑ 9a Waxed Zack .10 .25
❑ 9b Max Wax .10 .25
❑ 10a Hooked Brooke .10 .25
❑ 10b Kate Bait .10 .25
❑ 11a Bobble Bob .10 .25
❑ 11b Will Wobble .10 .25
❑ 12a Bungee Benjy .10 .25
❑ 12b Xtreme Xavier .10 .25
❑ 13a Scuzzy Ozzy .10 .25
❑ 13b Rockin' Rick .10 .25
❑ 14a Scarin' Aaron .10 .25
❑ 14b Corny Cody .10 .25
❑ 15a Skid Mark .10 .25
❑ 15b Trackin' Travis .10 .25
❑ 16a Dandruff Dan .10 .25
❑ 16b Jake Flake .10 .25
❑ 17a Dish Grabe .10 .25
❑ 17b Amped Amanda .10 .25
❑ 18a Taylor Tubby .10 .25
❑ 18b Morgan Organ .10 .25
❑ 19a Spider Manny .10 .25
❑ 19b Webby Wesley .10 .25
❑ 20a Number Juan .10 .25
❑ 20b Tinklin' Tyler .10 .25
❑ 21a Nicole Mole .10 .25
❑ 21b Warty Courtney .10 .25
❑ 22a Handy Hannah .10 .25
❑ 22b Mary Mucous .10 .25
❑ 23a Downloadin' Logan .10 .25
❑ 23b Digital Devin .10 .25
❑ 24a Hairy Henry .10 .25
❑ 24b Wolfman Jack .10 .25
❑ 25a Cookie-Tosser Tessa .10 .25
❑ 25b Krummy Kim .10 .25
❑ 26a Piranha Conner .10 .25
❑ 26b Sean Gone .10 .25
❑ 27a Scabby Abby .10 .25
❑ 27b Crusty Chris .10 .25
❑ 28a Armed Arnie .10 .25
❑ 28b Oscar La Vista .10 .25
❑ 29a Gassy Garret .10 .25
❑ 29b Fizzy Francisco .10 .25
❑ 30a Lippy Laura .10 .25
❑ 30b Alyssa Kisser .10 .25
❑ 31a Linty Lindsey .10 .25
❑ 31b Bailey Button .10 .25
❑ 32a Hecklin' Hector .10 .25
❑ 32b Newsworthy Nick .10 .25
❑ 33a Car Sick Caroline .10 .25
❑ 33b Icky Vicky .10 .25
❑ 34a Toe Jam Sam .10 .25
❑ 34b Jammin' Amber .10 .25
❑ 35a Hayden Go Seek .10 .25
❑ 35b Timid Tim .10 .25
❑ 36a Pete Achoo .10 .25
❑ 36b Dorky Don .10 .25
❑ 37a Rest Stop Russ .10 .25
❑ 37b Wet Brett .10 .25
❑ 38a Torn Tori .10 .25
❑ 38b Tearin' Erin .10 .25
❑ 39a Deflated David .10 .25
❑ 39b Squirtin' Stephen .10 .25
❑ 40a Lisa Loser .10 .25
❑ 40b Marooned Marissa .10 .25

2004 Garbage Pail Kids All New Series 2 Bonus

COMPLETE SET (2)
STATED ODDS ONE PER RETAIL BONUS BOX

❑ B1 On Camera Cameron 30.00 60.00
❑ B2 Paintball Paul 10.00 20.00

2004 Garbage Pail Kids All New Series 2 Foil

COMPLETE SET (50) 15.00 40.00
STATED ODDS ONE PER PACK

❑ F1a Ailin' Al .40 1.00
❑ F1b Mauled Paul .40 1.00
❑ F2a Wacky Jacky .40 1.00
❑ F2b Loony Lenny .40 1.00
❑ F3a Cranky Frankie .40 1.00
❑ F3b Bad Brad .40 1.00
❑ F4a Junky Jeff .40 1.00
❑ F4b Stinky Stan .40 1.00
❑ F5a Slobby Robbie .40 1.00
❑ F5b Fat Matt .40 1.00
❑ F6a Run Down Rhoda .40 1.00
❑ F6b Flat Pat .40 1.00
❑ F7a Hot Scott .40 1.00
❑ F7b Luke Warm .40 1.00
❑ F8a Sewer Sue .40 1.00
❑ F8b Michelle Muck .40 1.00
❑ F9a Hurt Curt .40 1.00
❑ F9b Pat Splat .40 1.00
❑ F10a Drew Blood .40 1.00
❑ F10b Bustin' Dustin .40 1.00
❑ F11a Smelly Sally .40 1.00
❑ F11b Fishy Phyllis .40 1.00
❑ F12a Snooty Sam .40 1.00
❑ F12b U.S. Arnie .40 1.00
❑ F13a Second Hand .40 1.00
❑ F13b Trashed Tracy .40 1.00
❑ F14a Basket Casey .40 1.00
❑ F14b Dribblin' Derek .40 1.00
❑ F15a Yicchy Mickey .40 1.00
❑ F15b Barfin' Bart .40 1.00
❑ F16a Handy Randy .40 1.00
❑ F16b Jordan Nuts .40 1.00
❑ F17a Nat Nerd .40 1.00
❑ F17b Clark Can't .40 1.00
❑ F18a Jules Drools .40 1.00
❑ F18b Kit Spit .40 1.00
❑ F19a Barfin' Barbara .40 1.00
❑ F19b Valerie Vomit .40 1.00
❑ F20a Bratty Maddy .40 1.00
❑ F20b Dirty Birdie .40 1.00
❑ F21a Short Mort .40 1.00
❑ F21b Noah Body .40 1.00
❑ F22a Heartless Hal .40 1.00
❑ F22b Bowen Arrow .40 1.00
❑ F23a Lem Phlegm .40 1.00
❑ F23b Gezundt Heidi .40 1.00
❑ F24a Cute Tippi .40 1.00
❑ F24b Waxy Wendy .40 1.00
❑ F25a Scalped Ralph .40 1.00
❑ F25b Bone-Head Fred .40 1.00

2004 Garbage Pail Kids All New Series 2 Scratch 'n Stink

COMPLETE SET (12) 4.00 10.00
STATED ODDS 1:6

❑ S1a Stony Tony .75 2.00
❑ S1b Ol' Faith Phil .75 2.00
❑ S2a Cheese Luis .75 2.00
❑ S2b Eruptin' Eric .75 2.00
❑ S3a Moldy Molly .75 2.00
❑ S3b Stinkin' Stephanie .75 2.00
❑ S4a Careless Carlos .75 2.00
❑ S4b Klutzy Kevin .75 2.00
❑ S5a Topping Tom .75 2.00
❑ S5b Dom E. Nose .75 2.00
❑ S6a Gotta Go Joe .75 2.00
❑ S6b Ken Not Hold It .75 2.00

2004 Garbage Pail Kids All New Series 3

COMPLETE SET (80) 6.00 15.00
P1 ISSUED AS SDCC EXCLUSIVE

❑ 1a Christina Ugliera .10 .25
❑ 1b Diana Diva .10 .25
❑ 2a Jet Ski Jesse .10 .25
❑ 2b Flayed Jay .10 .25
❑ 3a Saucey Sarah .10 .25
❑ 3b Mary Nara .10 .25
❑ 4a Sweaty Betty .10 .25
❑ 4b Clammy Sammy .10 .25
❑ 5a Swampy Shaq .10 .25
❑ 5b Omar Ogre .10 .25
❑ 6a Tom Tongue .10 .25
❑ 6b Coated Cody .10 .25
❑ 7a Donald Dump .10 .25
❑ 7b Trumped Trevor .10 .25
❑ 8a Urine Nate .10 .25
❑ 8b Backwoods Brandon .10 .25
❑ 9a Bro Ken .10 .25
❑ 9b Jumbled Jim .10 .25
❑ 10a Astro Nat .10 .25
❑ 10b Yuck Roger .10 .25
❑ 11a Picky Ricky .10 .25
❑ 11b Stringy Steve .10 .25
❑ 12a Sprinklin' Spence .10 .25
❑ 12b Hosed Jose .10 .25
❑ 13a Jake Quake .10 .25
❑ 13b Sergio Regurgio .10 .25
❑ 14a Bob Gnarly .10 .25
❑ 14b Dread Ed .10 .25
❑ 15a Dartin' Dalton .10 .25
❑ 15b Mike Spike .10 .25
❑ 16a Cheesy Chelsea .10 .25
❑ 16b Flossin' Jordan .10 .25
❑ 17a Broken Crystal .10 .25
❑ 17b Summer Break .10 .25
❑ 18a Lava Levi .10 .25
❑ 18b Retro Pedro .10 .25
❑ 19a Jack Hammer .10 .25
❑ 19b Hammered Henry .10 .25
❑ 20a Birdbrain Brian .10 .25
❑ 20b Cuckoo Chris .10 .25
❑ 21a X Ray .10 .25
❑ 21b Tanner Scanner .10 .25
❑ 22a Cup O'Joe .10 .25
❑ 22b Maxwell Louse .10 .25
❑ 23a Snotty Scotty .10 .25
❑ 23b Bubble Juan .10 .25
❑ 24a Shredded Paige .10 .25
❑ 24b Heather Shredder .10 .25
❑ 25a Wranglin' Rachel .10 .25
❑ 25b Calamity Jane .10 .25
❑ 26a Taggin' Tyler .10 .25
❑ 26b Popped Paul .10 .25
❑ 27a Bigfoot Brittany .10 .25
❑ 27b Alicia Creature .10 .25
❑ 28a Laura Cough .10 .25
❑ 28b Hackin' Hannah .10 .25
❑ 29a Divin' Devin .10 .25
❑ 29b Nosedive Noah .10 .25
❑ 30a Chopper Chad .10 .25
❑ 30b Hurlin' Harley .10 .25
❑ 31a Poopdeck Pete .10 .25
❑ 31b Marco Polo .10 .25
❑ 32a Picked Nikki .10 .25
❑ 32b Antsy Nancy .10 .25
❑ 33a Troy Story .10 .25
❑ 33b Trojan Warren .10 .25
❑ 34a Vegan Ian .10 .25
❑ 34b Cesar Salad .10 .25

❑ 35a Malcolm Middle .10 .25
❑ 35b Messed Up Miguel .10 .25
❑ 36a Offensive Oscar .10 .25
❑ 36b Foul Fernando .10 .25
❑ 37a Field Goal Joel .10 .25
❑ 37b Kicked Mick .10 .25
❑ 38a Jerry Rigged .10 .25
❑ 38b Raul Model .10 .25
❑ 39a Davey Croquet .10 .25
❑ 39b Wacked Zack .10 .25
❑ 40a Janet Jackass .10 .25
❑ 40b Has-Been Jasmine .10 .25
❑ P1 Christina Ugliera 2.00 5.00

2004 Garbage Pail Kids All New Series 3 Bonus

COMPLETE SET (3)
B3 STATED ODDS ONE PER WALMART BONUS BOX
B4 STATED ODDS ONE PER TARGET BONUS BOX
B5 STATED ODDS ONE PER TOYS R US/KMART BONUS BOX

❑ B3 Gator Adrian 4.00 10.00
❑ B4 Hill Billy 30.00 60.00
❑ B5 Cole Gate 60.00 120.00

2004 Garbage Pail Kids All New Series 3 Foil

COMPLETE SET (50) 12.00 30.00
STATED ODDS ONE PER PACK

❑ 1a Ball 'N Shane .40 1.00
❑ 1b Hard Rocky .40 1.00
❑ 2a Half Price .40 1.00
❑ 2b Checked-Out Chet .40 1.00
❑ 3a Phooey To Hugh .40 1.00
❑ 3b Razzin' Ross .40 1.00
❑ 4a Upsy Daisys .40 1.00
❑ 4b Barfy Barbies .40 1.00
❑ 5a Seasick Cecil .40 1.00
❑ 5b Dinner At Eytan .40 1.00
❑ 6a Missing Marcia .40 1.00
❑ 6b Hidden Heidi .40 1.00
❑ 7a Quick Sandy .40 1.00
❑ 7b Abraham Sinkin' .40 1.00
❑ 8a Freestyle Kyle .40 1.00
❑ 8b Rad Rod .40 1.00
❑ 9a Louise Trapeze .40 1.00
❑ 9b 3-Ring Cyril .40 1.00
❑ 10a Heavy Meryl .40 1.00
❑ 10b One-Night Stan .40 1.00
❑ 11a Sole Food Sol .40 1.00
❑ 11b Gooey Stuey .40 1.00
❑ 12a Barf Band Ben .40 1.00
❑ 12b Off Key Lee .40 1.00
❑ 13a Target Prentice .40 1.00
❑ 13b Blow Hardy .40 1.00
❑ 14a Misfortune Cookie .40 1.00
❑ 14b Chow Maynard .40 1.00
❑ 15a Gulpin' Gabe .40 1.00
❑ 15b Over Eatin' Ethan .40 1.00
❑ 16a Robby Rubbish .40 1.00
❑ 16b Garbage Pail Kitty .40 1.00
❑ 17a Car-Stick Karla .40 1.00
❑ 17b Cruisin' Susan .40 1.00
❑ 18a Lickin' Leo .40 1.00
❑ 18b Lappin' Lenny .40 1.00
❑ 19a Tim Can .40 1.00
❑ 19b Rusty Bolts .40 1.00
❑ 20a Seymour Barf .40 1.00
❑ 20b Kent Stand It .40 1.00
❑ 21a Dead Letter Debbie .40 1.00
❑ 21b Maimed Mamie .40 1.00
❑ 22a Mitch Match .40 1.00
❑ 22b Hot Dot .40 1.00
❑ 23a Gloppy Glen .40 1.00
❑ 23b Slop Top Todd .40 1.00
❑ 24a Cat-Cradle Cathy .40 1.00
❑ 24b Gooey Gwen .40 1.00
❑ 25a Ill Windsor .40 1.00
❑ 25b Horatio Hornblower .40 1.00

2004 Garbage Pail Kids All New Series 3 Pop-Ups

COMPLETE SET (10) 4.00 10.00
STATED ODDS 1:6

❑ 1 Lethal Ethan .60 1.50
❑ 2 Gutsy Gabriel .60 1.50
❑ 3 Colin 911 .60 1.50
❑ 4 Phat Phil .60 1.50
❑ 5 Harry Potty .60 1.50
❑ 6 Aerial Ariel .60 1.50
❑ 7 Lost In Austin .60 1.50
❑ 8 Sk8 Nate .60 1.50
❑ 9 Waxed Zack .60 1.50
❑ 10 Downloadin' Logan .60 1.50

2004 Garbage Pail Kids All New Series 3 Scratch 'n Stink

COMPLETE SET (24) 10.00 25.00
STATED ODDS 1:6

❑ S1a Trashy Ashley .75 2.00
❑ S1b Garbage Pail Kim .75 2.00
❑ S2a Howard Burned .75 2.00
❑ S2b Shock Jacques .75 2.00
❑ S3a Stinkin' Sydney .75 2.00
❑ S3b Danielle Smell .75 2.00
❑ S4a Al Goredita .75 2.00
❑ S4b Wally Tamale .75 2.00
❑ S5a Brad Pit .75 2.00
❑ S5b Dakota Odor .75 2.00
❑ S6a Gaseous Clay .75 2.00
❑ S6b Hot Aaron .75 2.00
❑ S7a Eyeball Ivan .75 2.00
❑ S7b Eye-Candy Andy .75 2.00
❑ S8a Despicable Destiny .75 2.00
❑ S8b Nasty Natalie .75 2.00
❑ S9a Anna Innards .75 2.00
❑ S9b Emptied Emily .75 2.00
❑ S10a Rancid Randy .75 2.00
❑ S10b Dissin' Terry .75 2.00
❑ S11a Bryce-Sickle .75 2.00
❑ S11b Icy Isaac .75 2.00
❑ S12a Ashy Ashton .75 2.00
❑ S12b Combustin' Dustin .75 2.00

2004 Harry Potter and the Prisoner of Azkaban

COMPLETE SET (90) 5.00 12.00

❑ 1 Title Card .15 .40
❑ 2 Harry Potter .15 .40
❑ 3 Ron Weasley .15 .40
❑ 4 Hermione Granger .15 .40
❑ 5 Sirius Black .15 .40
❑ 6 Remus Lupin .15 .40
❑ 7 Peter Pettigrew .15 .40
❑ 8 Sibyll Trelawney .15 .40
❑ 9 Severus Snape .15 .40
❑ 10 Rubeus Hagrid .15 .40
❑ 11 Albus Dumbledore .15 .40
❑ 12 Minerva McGonagall .15 .40
❑ 13 Draco Malfoy .15 .40
❑ 14 Nevill Longbottom .15 .40
❑ 15 Cornelius Fudge .15 .40
❑ 16 Argus Filch .15 .40
❑ 17 Vincent Crabbe .15 .40
❑ 18 Gregory Goyle .15 .40
❑ 19 A Visit From Aunt Marge .15 .40
❑ 20 Harry Loses His Temper .15 .40
❑ 21 Aunt Marge Inflates .15 .40
❑ 22 Floating Into the Sky .15 .40
❑ 23 Leaving the Dursleys .15 .40
❑ 24 Something in the Shadows .15 .40
❑ 25 The Knight Bus Appears .15 .40
❑ 26 Boarding the Knight Bus .15 .40
❑ 27 Arriving at the Leaky Cauldron .15 .40
❑ 28 A Chat with Cornelius Fudge .15 .40
❑ 29 The Monster Book of Monsters .15 .40
❑ 30 Inside the Leaky Cauldron .15 .40
❑ 31 Greeted by Ron and Hermione .15 .40
❑ 32 Learning About Sirius Black .15 .40
❑ 33 A Dementor Appears .15 .40
❑ 34 Return to Hogwarts .15 .40
❑ 35 The Choir Sings Out .15 .40
❑ 36 Welcoming the Students .15 .40
❑ 37 Magical Creatures Class .15 .40
❑ 38 Hagrid's Class .15 .40
❑ 39 Draco Taunts Harry .15 .40
❑ 40 Introducing Buckbeak .15 .40
❑ 41 A Ride on Buckbeak's Back .15 .40
❑ 42 Clawed by Buckbeak .15 .40
❑ 43 Sirius Black Sighted! .15 .40
❑ 44 Professor Lupin's Class .15 .40
❑ 45 Teaching 'Riddikulus' .15 .40
❑ 46 Repelling a Boggart .15 .40
❑ 47 Signed Permission Forms .15 .40
❑ 48 Permission to Leave Refused .15 .40
❑ 49 A Goodbye to His Friends .15 .40
❑ 50 Discussing Harry's Boggart .15 .40
❑ 51 The Portrait Attacked! .15 .40
❑ 52 In the Great Hall .15 .40
❑ 53 Snape's Werewolf Lesson .15 .40
❑ 54 Draco's New Taunt .15 .40
❑ 55 The 'Moth' Parchment .15 .40
❑ 56 After the Quidditch Match .15 .40
❑ 57 Setting Hedwig Free .15 .40
❑ 58 Near the Shrieking Shack .15 .40
❑ 59 A Mysterious Attack .15 .40
❑ 60 The Invisibility Cloak .15 .40
❑ 61 Madam Rosmerta's Inquiry .15 .40
❑ 62 In the Three Broomsticks .15 .40
❑ 63 A Most Wanted Wizard .15 .40
❑ 64 Lupin's Conjuring Lesson .15 .40
❑ 65 Producing a Patronus .15 .40
❑ 66 Checking With Sir Cadogan .15 .40
❑ 67 The Three Friends Argue .15 .40
❑ 68 Peril of the Marauder's Map .15 .40
❑ 69 Threatening Draco .15 .40
❑ 70 Hagrid's Hut .15 .40
❑ 71 A Hasty Retreat .15 .40
❑ 72 Hiding Amongst the Pumpkins .15 .40
❑ 73 The Executioner's Task .15 .40
❑ 74 Sirius and Lupin .15 .40
❑ 75 The Truth Revealed .15 .40
❑ 76 Scabbers Transformed! .15 .40
❑ 77 Holding Pettigrew and Snape .15 .40
❑ 78 Pettigrew's Escape .15 .40
❑ 79 Night of the Werewolf .15 .40
❑ 80 Beast Against Beast .15 .40
❑ 81 Dementors at the Black Lake .15 .40
❑ 82 Watching Time Replayed .15 .40
❑ 83 Rescuing Buckbeak .15 .40
❑ 84 Dumbledore's Diversion .15 .40
❑ 85 Has Harry Seen His Dad? .15 .40
❑ 86 Saved From the Dementors .15 .40
❑ 87 Freeing Sirius Black .15 .40
❑ 88 A Farewell From Sirius .15 .40
❑ 89 Leaving the Map Behind .15 .40
❑ 90A Checklist - Hobby (w R1-R9) .15 .40
❑ 90B Checklist - Retail (w M1-M9) .15 .40

2004 Harry Potter and the Prisoner of Azkaban Autographs

STATED ODDS 1:48

❑ 1 Emma Watson 250.00 400.00
❑ 2 David Thewlis 50.00 100.00
❑ 3 James Phelps 25.00 50.00
❑ 4 Oliver Phelps 25.00 50.00
❑ 5 Matthew Lewis 30.00 60.00
❑ 6 Bonnie Wright 40.00 80.00
❑ 7 Michael Gambon 50.00 100.00
❑ 8 Robert Hardy 20.00 40.00
❑ 9 Gary Oldman 200.00 300.00
❑ 10 Julie Christie 20.00 40.00

2004 Harry Potter and the Prisoner of Azkaban Box Loaders

STATED ODDS ONE PER BOX

❑ BT1 Gryffindor 1.25 3.00
❑ BT2 Hufflepuff 1.25 3.00
❑ BT3 Slytherin 1.25 3.00
❑ BT4 Ravenclaw 1.25 3.00

2004 Harry Potter and the Prisoner of Azkaban Case Loaders

STATED ODDS ONE PER CASE

❑ 1 Title 20.00 40.00
❑ 2 Dementor 15.00 30.00
❑ 3 Sirius Black Wanted Poster 15.00 30.00

2004 Harry Potter and the Prisoner of Azkaban Chase Cards Hobby

COMPLETE SET (9) 6.00 15.00
STATED ODDS 1:5 HOBBY

❑ R1 Lupin's Wolf Form .75 2.00
❑ R2 Riding Buckbeak .75 2.00
❑ R3 Flying Through Dementors .75 2.00
❑ R4 Dementor .75 2.00
❑ R5 Shrieking Shack .75 2.00
❑ R6 Hogwarts .75 2.00
❑ R7 Harry The Seeker .75 2.00
❑ R8 Protecting From Dementor .75 2.00
❑ R9 Snowy Gate .75 2.00

2004 Harry Potter and the Prisoner of Azkaban Chase Cards Retail

❑ M1 Lupin's Wolf Form .75 2.00
❑ M2 Riding Buckbeak .75 2.00
❑ M3 Flying through Dementors .75 2.00
❑ M4 Dementor .75 2.00
❑ M5 Shrieking Shack .75 2.00
❑ M6 Hogwarts .75 2.00
❑ M7 Prongs Protects .75 2.00
❑ M8 Wand Against Dementor .75 2.00
❑ M9 Hedwig Delivery .75 2.00

2004 Harry Potter and the Prisoner of Azkaban Costumes

STATED ODDS 1:24

❑ C1 Danielle Radcliffe Robe/100 100.00 175.00
❑ C2 Rupert Grint Robe/100 100.00 175.00
❑ C3 Danielle Radcliffe Robe/750 25.00 50.00
❑ C4 Emma Watson Robe/900 25.00 50.00
❑ C5 Danielle Radcliffe Shirt/600 25.00 50.00
❑ C6 Emma Watson Jacket/450 30.00 60.00
❑ C7 Oliver Phelps Robe/1300 10.00 20.00

2004 Harry Potter and the Prisoner of Azkaban Dealer Incentive Props

❑ 1 Honeydukes Candy 200.00 350.00
❑ 2 Pear Tree Leaves

2004 Harry Potter and the Prisoner of Azkaban Props

STATED ODDS 1:24

❑ P1 Chocolate Frog/86 250.00 350.00
❑ P2 Zonko's Bag/300 30.00 60.00
❑ P3 Spindle's Lick 'O' Rish Spiders/70 250.00 350.00
❑ P4 Honeydukes Bag/434 25.00 50.00
❑ P5 Dervish and Banges Bag/484 25.00 50.00
❑ P6 Black Pepper Imps/90 200.00 300.00
❑ P7 Exploding Bop Bons/96 250.00 350.00
❑ P8 The Daily Prophet/200 25.00 50.00
❑ P9 Permission Form/160 175.00 300.00

2004 Harry Potter and the Prisoner of Azkaban Update

COMPLETE SET (90) 5.00 12.00

❑ 91 Let Me Tell You...! .15 .40
❑ 92 Dinner's Over .15 .40
❑ 93 I've Got You Marge .15 .40
❑ 94 The Stranded Wizard .15 .40
❑ 95 A Bumpy Ride .15 .40
❑ 96 Little Old Lady at Twelve O'Clock .15 .40
❑ 97 A Murderer .15 .40
❑ 98 Mind your Head .15 .40
❑ 99 The Train Rattled, the Rain Hammered, the Wind Roared... .15 .40
❑ 100 Something Out There .15 .40
❑ 101 A Long, Slow, Rattling Breath .15 .40
❑ 102 Repelling a Dementor .15 .40
❑ 103 A Welcome Home .15 .40
❑ 104 A Smashing Performance .15 .40
❑ 105 Cat Got Your Tongue? .15 .40
❑ 106 A Fiery Treat .15 .40
❑ 107 Look Beyond! .15 .40
❑ 108 An Omen of Death .15 .40
❑ 109 Don't Be Shy .15 .40
❑ 110 Nothing Like a Broomstick .15 .40
❑ 111 Easily Offended, Hippogriffs Are .15 .40
❑ 112 Laying It on Thick .15 .40
❑ 113 Like Trying to Catch Smoke .15 .40
❑ 114 What Do You Fear the Very Most? .15 .40
❑ 115 Think Neville, Think! .15 .40
❑ 116 On a Roll .15 .40
❑ 117 Ending the Lesson .15 .40
❑ 118 Let Him Sleep .15 .40
❑ 119 Page Three Hundred and Ninety-Four .15 .40
❑ 120 Passing Notes in Class .15 .40
❑ 121 Trifles Such as Thunderstorms .15 .40
❑ 122 The Best Seeker Gryffindor Has Ever Had .15 .40
❑ 123 Arresto Momento! .15 .40
❑ 124 There's Something Else You Should Know .15 .40
❑ 125 No Permission to Go .15 .40
❑ 126 Not Clever Enough .15 .40
❑ 127 The Secret to Success .15 .40
❑ 128 The Most Haunted Building in Britain .15 .40
❑ 129 Hurling Insults and Snowballs .15 .40
❑ 130 Teaching Draco Some Respect .15 .40
❑ 131 Best Friends .15 .40
❑ 132 What Permission Form? .15 .40
❑ 133 Sirius Balck? in Hogsmeade? .15 .40
❑ 134 Learning the Truth .15 .40
❑ 135 Betrayal .15 .40
❑ 136 Wand at the Ready! .15 .40
❑ 137 Enough for Today .15 .40
❑ 138 A Restless Night .15 .40
❑ 139 Searching for Pettigrew .15 .40
❑ 140 The Noble Art of Divination .15 .40
❑ 141 Visiting Hagrid .15 .40
❑ 142 He Bit Me! .15 .40
❑ 143 Dragged into the Whomping Willow .15 .40
❑ 144 Trying to Get to Ron .15 .40
❑ 145 An Animagus .15 .40
❑ 146 Expellarmus! .15 .40
❑ 147 The Right to Know Why .15 .40
❑ 148 Attacking a Teacher .15 .40
❑ 149 The Map Never Lies .15 .40
❑ 150 The Evidence Against Scabbers .15 .40
❑ 151 Admiring Hogwarts .15 .40
❑ 152 An Ominous Moon .15 .40
❑ 153 Pettigrew Transforms .15 .40
❑ 154 Nice Doggie .15 .40
❑ 155 Fully Transformed .15 .40
❑ 156 A Fierce Battle .15 .40
❑ 157 A Dangerous Distraction .15 .40
❑ 158 Dementors Swarm the Black Lake .15 .40
❑ 159 Trying to Protect Sirius .15 .40
❑ 160 The Dementors' Kiss .15 .40
❑ 161 A Valiant Effort .15 .40
❑ 162 A Child's Voice .15 .40
❑ 163 Curious Thing, Time .15 .40
❑ 164 Three Turns Should Do It .15 .40
❑ 165 Back in Time .15 .40
❑ 166 Hiding from Themselves .15 .40
❑ 167 Go Harry, Go! .15 .40
❑ 168 Appetizing Bait .15 .40
❑ 169 And Now We Wait .15 .40
❑ 170 Saving Harry's Life .15 .40
❑ 171 Waiting for his Father .15 .40
❑ 172 EXPECTO PATRONUM! .15 .40
❑ 173 The Demontors Falling Back .15 .40
❑ 174 Forever Grateful .15 .40
❑ 175 Time Is Running Out .15 .40
❑ 176 Just in Time .15 .40
❑ 177 I've Looked Worse .15 .40
❑ 178 The Fastest Broom in the World .15 .40
❑ 179 Zero to 150 Miles an Hour in Ten Seconds .15 .40
❑ 180 Checklist .15 .40

2004 Harry Potter and the Prisoner of Azkaban Update Autographs

STATED ODDS 1:110 HOBBY
CARD 14 UK TIN SET ONLY
CARD 18 DEALER INCENTIVE ONLY

❑ 1 Daniel Radcliffe 1000.00 1500.00
Emma Watson/Rupert Grint
❑ 2 James Phelps 30.00 60.00
Oliver Phelps
❑ 3 Daniel Radcliffe 400.00 800.00
❑ 4 Emma Watson 300.00 500.00
❑ 5 Rupert Grint 200.00 300.00
❑ 6 Jamie Waylett 25.00 50.00
❑ 7 Harry Melling 20.00 40.00
❑ 8 Chris Rankin 20.00 40.00
❑ 9 Dawn French 40.00 80.00
❑ 10 David Bradley 20.00 40.00
❑ 11 Genevieve Gaunt 25.00 50.00
❑ 12 Lee Ingleby 20.00 40.00
❑ 13 Warwick Davis 20.00 40.00
❑ 14 Warwick Davis/ (issued in U.K. collector's tin) 20.00 40.00
❑ 15 Jimmy Gardner 20.00 40.00
❑ 16 Pam Ferris 30.00 60.00
❑ 17 Richard Griffiths 30.00 60.00
❑ 18 Peter Best/ (issued as multi-case incentive) 20.00 40.00

2004 Harry Potter and the Prisoner of Azkaban Update Box Loaders

COMPLETE SET (4) 5.00 12.00
STATED ODDS ONE PER HOBBY BOX

❑ BT1 Drowning In Cold 1.25 3.00
❑ BT2 Disquieting Guests 1.25 3.00
❑ BT3 Too Weak To Move 1.25 3.00
❑ BT4 No One's Coming, Harry... 1.25 3.00

2004 Harry Potter and the Prisoner of Azkaban Update Case Loaders

STATED ODDS ONE PER CASE

❑ 1 Harry with Buckbeak 12.00 30.00
❑ 2 Confronting Draco 12.00 30.00
❑ 3 Sirius Black in Prison 12.00 30.00

2004 Harry Potter and the Prisoner of Azkaban Update Chase Cards Hobby

COMPLETE SET (9) 6.00 15.00
STATED ODDS 1:5 HOBBY

❑ R1 The Hogwarts Experess .75 2.00
❑ R2 Waiting for Siruis Black .75 2.00
❑ R3 Hogsmeade Blanketed in Snow .75 2.00
❑ R4 A Stormy Quiddith Match .75 2.00
❑ R5 Chasing the Golden Snitch .75 2.00
❑ R6 Surrounded by Dementors .75 2.00
❑ R7 The Grim .75 2.00
❑ R8 A Fully Grown Werewolf .75 2.00
❑ R9 A True Patronus .75 2.00

2004 Harry Potter and the Prisoner of Azkaban Update Chase Cards Retail

COMPLETE SET (9) 6.00 15.00
STATED ODDS 1:5 RETAIL

❑ M1 A Stormy Quidditch Match .75 2.00
❑ M2 Chasing the Golden Snitch .75 2.00
❑ M3 Surrounded by Dementors .75 2.00
❑ M4 The Grim .75 2.00
❑ M5 A Fully Grown Werewolf .75 2.00
❑ M6 A True Patronus .75 2.00
❑ M7 Hedwig .75 2.00
❑ M8 Quidditch .75 2.00
❑ M9 Buckbeak .75 2.00

2004 Harry Potter and the Prisoner of Azkaban Update Costumes

STATED ODDS C1-C19 1:36 HOBBY
STATED ODDS C20-C21 1:24 RETAIL

❑ C1 Rupert Grint Sweater
❑ C2 Emma Watson Sweater
❑ C3 Pam Ferris Jacket
❑ C4 Daniel Radcliffe Quidditch/ (w Stripe)
❑ C5 Daniel Radcliffe Quidditch/ (w o Stripe)
❑ C6 Robert Hardy Coat
❑ C7 Emma Thompson Dress
❑ C8 Tom Felton Robe
❑ C9 Mathew Lewis Cloak
❑ C10 Emma Watson Pants
❑ C11 David Thewlis Shirt
❑ C12 Harry Cedric Quidditch Robes
❑ C13 Cedric Diggory Quidditch Robe
❑ C14 Griffindor House Members Robe 40.00 80.00
❑ C15 Julie Christie Jacket 40.00 80.00
❑ C16 David Thewlis Jacket
❑ C17 Slytherin House Members Tie 40.00 80.00
❑ C18 Daniel Radcliffe Robe
❑ C19 Emma Watson Sweater
❑ C20 Daniel Radcliffe Cloak
❑ C21 Oliver Phelps Quidditch Robe

2004 Harry Potter and the Prisoner of Azkaban Update Dealer Incentive Memorabilia

❑ 1 Monster Book of Monsters/310 50.00 100.00
❑ 2 Whomping Willow Tree/172 100.00 150.00
❑ 3 Emma Watson Robe/830 40.00 80.00
❑ 4 Daniel Radcliffe Shirt/475 50.00 100.00

2004 Harry Potter and the Prisoner of Azkaban Update Film Cels

STATED ODDS 1:80 HOBBY
STATED PRINT RUN 900 SER. #'d SETS

❑ CFC1 Harry Potter 15.00 30.00
❑ CFC2 Emma's Punch 15.00 30.00
❑ CFC3 Werewolf 15.00 30.00
❑ CFC4 Professor Snape 15.00 30.00
❑ CFC5 Professor Lupin 15.00 30.00
❑ CFC6 Harry and Hedwig 15.00 30.00
❑ CFC7 Buckbeak 15.00 30.00
❑ CFC8 Harry and Arther Weasley 15.00 30.00
❑ CFC9 Knightbus 15.00 30.00

2004 Harry Potter and the Prisoner of Azkaban Update Props

STATED ODDS 1:80 HOBBY

❑ P1 Buckbeak Feather 50.00 100.00
❑ P2 Sleeping Bag 10.00 25.00
❑ P3 The Marauder's Map 40.00 80.00
❑ P4 Wanted Poster 30.00 60.00
❑ P5 Daily Prophet Newspaper 30.00 60.00
❑ P6 Fizzing Whizzbees 30.00 60.00
❑ P7 Unfogging the Future (Cover & Pages) 10.00 25.00
❑ P8 Devination Class Red 10.00 25.00
❑ P9 Devination Class Purple 10.00 25.00
❑ P10 Grim Fur 15.00 40.00

2004 Harry Potter and the Prisoner of Azkaban FilmCardz

COMPLETE SET (72) 6.00 15.00

❑ 1 A Visit From Aunt Marge .20 .50
❑ 2 Aunt Marge Starts On Harry .20 .50
❑ 3 Aunt Marge Inflates .20 .50
❑ 4 Floating Into The Sky .20 .50
❑ 5 Leaving The Dursleys .20 .50
❑ 6 Something In The Shadows .20 .50
❑ 7 The Knight Bus Appears .20 .50
❑ 8 Boarding The Knight Bus .20 .50
❑ 9 At The Leaky Cauldron .20 .50
❑ 10 A Chat With Cornelius Fudge .20 .50
❑ 11 The Monster Book Of Monsters .20 .50
❑ 12 Harry Greets His Friends .20 .50
❑ 13 Greeted By Ron and Hermione .20 .50
❑ 14 Learning About Sirius Black .20 .50
❑ 15 A Dementor Appears .20 .50
❑ 16 Confronting A Dementor .20 .50
❑ 17 Return To Hogwarts .20 .50
❑ 18 Welcoming The Students .20 .50
❑ 19 The Dementors Surround Hogwarts .20 .50
❑ 20 You, Boy! Is Your Grandmother Well? .20 .50
❑ 21 Magical Creatures Class .20 .50
❑ 22 Hagrid's Class .20 .50
❑ 23 Draco Taunts Harry .20 .50
❑ 24 Meeting Buckbeak .20 .50
❑ 25 A Ride On Buckbeak's Back .20 .50
❑ 26 Clawed By Buckbeak .20 .50
❑ 27 Sirius Black Sighted! .20 .50
❑ 28 Professor Lupin's Class .20 .50
❑ 29 Teaching 'Riddikulus' .20 .50
❑ 30 Neville Repels His Boggart .20 .50
❑ 31 Signed Permission Forms .20 .50
❑ 32 Permission To Leave Refused .20 .50
❑ 33 Discussing Harry's Boggart .20 .50
❑ 34 The Portrait Attacked! .20 .50
❑ 35 In The Great Hall .20 .50
❑ 36 Snapes's Werewolf Lesson .20 .50
❑ 37 Draco's New Taunt .20 .50
❑ 38 The Golden Snitch Within Reach .20 .50
❑ 39 After The Quidditch Match .20 .50
❑ 40 A Better Way To Get To Hogsmeade .20 .50
❑ 41 Near The Shrieking Shack .20 .50
❑ 42 A Mysterious Attack .20 .50
❑ 43 A Most Wanted Wizard .20 .50
❑ 44 Madam Rosmerta's Inquiry .20 .50
❑ 45 In The Three Broomsticks .20 .50
❑ 46 The Invisibility Cloak .20 .50
❑ 47 Lupin's Conjuring Lesson .20 .50
❑ 48 Producing A Patronus .20 .50
❑ 49 Peril Of The Marauder's Map .20 .50
❑ 50 Divination: A Very Wooly Discipline .20 .50
❑ 51 Come To See The Show? .20 .50
❑ 52 Threatening Draco .20 .50
❑ 53 A Hasty Retreat From Hagrid's Hut .20 .50
❑ 54 Hiding Amongst The Pumpkins .20 .50
❑ 55 The Executioner's Task .20 .50
❑ 56 Old Friends Sirius And Lupin Reunited .20 .50
❑ 57 The Truth Revealed .20 .50
❑ 58 Scabbers Transformed! .20 .50
❑ 59 How Dare You Speak To Harry! .20 .50
❑ 60 Pettigrew's Escape .20 .50
❑ 61 Night Of The Werewolf .20 .50
❑ 62 Attacked By A Werewolf .20 .50
❑ 63 Dementors At The Black Lake .20 .50
❑ 64 Hermoine Explains The Time-Turner .20 .50
❑ 65 Rescuing Buckbeak .20 .50
❑ 66 Dumbledore's Diversion .20 .50
❑ 67 Has Harry Seen His Dad? .20 .50
❑ 68 Harry Conjurs A True Patronus .20 .50
❑ 69 Freeing Sirius Black .20 .50
❑ 70 A Farewell From Sirius .20 .50
❑ 71 Leaving The Map Behind .20 .50
❑ 72 Harry Takes Flight On His New Broom .20 .50

2004 Harry Potter and the Prisoner of Azkaban FilmCardz Promos

❑ 1 Aunt Marge 1.50 4.00
❑ 2 Harry and Buckbeak 1.50 4.00

2004 Harry Potter and the Prisoner of Azkaban FilmCardz Rare Chase Cards

COMPLETE SET (9) 12.00 30.00
STATED ODDS 1:5

❑ R1 Divination Class 1.50 4.00
❑ R2 Do You Possess The Sight? 1.50 4.00
❑ R3 Professor Sybill Trelawney 1.50 4.00
❑ R4 Care Of Magical Creatures Class 1.50 4.00
❑ R5 Give 'Im A Pat 1.50 4.00
❑ R6 Professor Rubeus Hagrid 1.50 4.00
❑ R7 Defense Against The Dark Arts Class 1.50 4.00
❑ R8 Riddikulus! 1.50 4.00
❑ R9 Professor Remus Lupin 1.50 4.00

2004 Harry Potter and the Prisoner of Azkaban FilmCardz Ultra Rare Chase Cards

COMPLETE SET (9) 15.00 40.00
STATED ODDS 1:8

❑ UR1 Aunt Marge Swells With...Anger? 2.00 5.00
❑ UR2 A Monstrous Balloon 2.00 5.00
❑ UR3 Uncle Vernon Lets Go 2.00 5.00
❑ UR4 A Magnificent Creature 2.00 5.00
❑ UR5 Good Man, Harry! 2.00 5.00
❑ UR6 A Reckon He Migh' Let Yeh Ride Him 2.00 5.00
❑ UR7 Old Friends Tend To Unfinished Business 2.00 5.00
❑ UR8 Pettigrew's Alive 2.00 5.00
❑ UR9 Peter Pettigrew Begs For Mercy 2.00 5.00

2004 Hellboy

COMPLETE SET (72) 3.00 8.00

❑ 1 Title Card .08 .25
❑ 2 Hellboy .08 .25
❑ 3 Abe Sapien .08 .25
❑ 4 Liz Sherman .08 .25
❑ 5 Agent John Myers .08 .25

❑ 6 Professor Trevor Broom .08 .25
❑ 7 Karl Kroenen .08 .25
❑ 8 Ilsa Hupstein .08 .25
❑ 9 Grigori Rasputin .08 .25
❑ 10 War...Is Hell .08 .25
❑ 11 In The Abbey Ruins .08 .25
❑ 12 Seekers Of Dark Truth .08 .25
❑ 13 Using The Mechanical Glove .08 .25
❑ 14 The Cosmic Portal .08 .25
❑ 15 No Match For Kroenen .08 .25
❑ 16 Where Evil Slumbers .08 .25
❑ 17 Finding The Hellbaby .08 .25
❑ 18 Debunking Popular Myths .08 .25
❑ 19 Grigori's Resurrection .08 .25
❑ 20 Welcome To The B.P.R.D. .08 .25
❑ 21 The Professor's Domain .08 .25
❑ 22 Aquatic Enigma .08 .25
❑ 23 Top Secret Sentinels .08 .25
❑ 24 Paranormals On The Job .08 .25
❑ 25 Terror At The Machen Library .08 .25
❑ 26 Confronting A Hell Hound .08 .25
❑ 27 That's All For You Sammy .08 .25
❑ 28 Back Alley Beast Brawl .08 .25
❑ 29 Tongued By Sammael .08 .25
❑ 30 Attacked And Tracked .08 .25
❑ 31 Leaping Into Action .08 .25
❑ 32 Sensing The Enemy .08 .25
❑ 33 Panic In The Subway! .08 .25
❑ 34 A Third Rail Roasting .08 .25
❑ 35 Evil's Right Hand .08 .25
❑ 36 The Unstoppable One .08 .25
❑ 37 Slaymaster In Action .08 .25
❑ 38 Unearthly Empathy .08 .25
❑ 39 Burning With Desire .08 .25
❑ 40 Hellish Operations .08 .25
❑ 41 The Catalyst Of Chaos .08 .25
❑ 42 Help From A Saintly Bone .08 .25
❑ 43 A Riot At Rush Hour .08 .25
❑ 44 The Fury Of Sammael .08 .25
❑ 45 The Unlikeliest Heroes .08 .25
❑ 46 Man Down .08 .25
❑ 47 Love And Curses .08 .25
❑ 48 Boys In The 'Hood .08 .25
❑ 49 Grigori's Mad Plan .08 .25
❑ 50 Death Of Professor Broom .08 .25
❑ 51 Like Tears In Rain... .08 .25
❑ 52 Sparky To Big Red .08 .25
❑ 53 Waking The Dead .08 .25
❑ 54 Invading Kroenen's Lair .08 .25
❑ 55 You Killed My Father! .08 .25
❑ 56 The Trap Door Pit .08 .25
❑ 57 Facing A Hellswarm .08 .25
❑ 58 When Hell Creatures Collide .08 .25
❑ 59 Opening The Gateway .08 .25
❑ 60 His Hellish Power Unleashed .08 .25
❑ 61 A Demon's Destiny .08 .25
❑ 62 Rebelling Against Grigori .08 .25
❑ 63 A Love Beyond Reality .08 .25
❑ 64 Shooting In The City .08 .25
❑ 65 As Good (And Evil) As It Gets .08 .25
❑ 66 Tips For A Man-Monster .08 .25
❑ 67 Filming The Subway Attack .08 .25
❑ 68 Bringing Sammael To Life .08 .25
❑ 69 A Boy And His Corpse .08 .25
❑ 70 From Comics To Film .08 .25
❑ 71 Seeing Red...And Loving It .08 .25
❑ 72 Checklist .08 .25

2004 Hellboy Autographs

STATED ODDS 1:36

❑ A1 Ron Perlman 30.00 60.00
❑ A2 Doug Jones 10.00 25.00
❑ A3 Karel Roden 7.50 20.00
❑ A4 John William Johnson 7.50 20.00
❑ A5 Mike Mignola 25.00 50.00
❑ A6 Guillermo Del Toro 150.00 250.00
❑ A7 Rupert Evans 7.50 20.00

2004 Hellboy B.P.R.D.

COMPLETE SET (6) 6.00 15.00
STATED ODDS 1:17

❑ B1 Shedding Light On The Dark 1.50 4.00
❑ B2 The Beings Best Hidden 1.50 4.00
❑ B3 Saved By Super-Science 1.50 4.00
❑ B4 Food For Thought 1.50 4.00
❑ B5 Amazing Mastermind 1.50 4.00
❑ B6 Brave Are The Lonely 1.50 4.00

2004 Hellboy Box Loaders

COMPLETE SET (4) 7.50 20.00

❑ BL1 Hellboy 1.50 4.00
❑ BL2 Abe Sapien 1.50 4.00
❑ BL3 Elizabeth Sherman 1.50 4.00
❑ CL1 The Meaning Of Pain 6.00 15.00

2004 Hellboy Pieceworks

STATED ODDS 1:36

❑ PW1 Ron Perlman 7.50 20.00
❑ PW2 Ron Perlman 7.50 20.00
❑ PW3 Selma Blair 6.00 15.00
❑ PW4 Selma Blair 6.00 15.00
❑ PW5 Doug Jones 6.00 15.00
❑ PW6 Rupert Evans 5.00 15.00
❑ PW7 John Hurt 6.00 15.00
❑ PW8 John Hurt 6.00 15.00
❑ PW9 Karel Roden 6.00 15.00
❑ PW10 Biddy Hodson 6.00 15.00
❑ PW11 Biddy Hodson 6.00 15.00
❑ PW12 Ladislav Beran 6.00 15.00

2004 Hellboy Promos

COMPLETE SET (4) 3.00 8.00

❑ P1 Hellboy 1.00 2.50
❑ P2 Hellboy 1.00 2.50
❑ Pi Hellboy 1.00 2.50
❑ PUK Hellboy 1.50 4.00

2004 Hellboy To Hell And Back

COMPLETE SET (9) 7.50 20.00
STATED ODDS 1:11

❑ P1 Hellboy's Good Samaritan 1.25 3.00
❑ P2 The Hound Of Hell 1.25 3.00
❑ P3 More Than Human 1.25 3.00
❑ P4 Top Secret Superhero 1.25 3.00
❑ P5 Loss Of A Loved One 1.25 3.00
❑ P6 Life, Death, And All That Jazz 1.25 3.00
❑ P7 The Prophecy Fulfilled 1.25 3.00
❑ P8 Rebel With A Cause 1.25 3.00
❑ P9 Love's Eternal Embrace 1.25 3.00

2004 History of the United States

COMPLETE SET (300) 20.00 40.00

❑ BN1 The Constitution of the United States .10 .25
❑ BN2 Northwest Ordinance .10 .25
❑ BN3 The Legislative, Executive and Judicial Branches .10 .25
❑ BN4 John Hancock .10 .25
❑ BN5 Alexander Hamilton .10 .25
❑ BN6 James Madison .10 .25
❑ BN7 George Washington .10 .25
❑ BN8 John Adams .10 .25
❑ BN9 Bill of Rights .10 .25
❑ BN10 Census Act .10 .25
❑ BN11 The House of Representatives .10 .25
❑ BN12 The Senate .10 .25
❑ BN13 Alien & Sedition Acts .10 .25
❑ BN14 John Jay .10 .25
❑ BN15 Federalist Papers .10 .25
❑ CD1 Williamsburg (Virginia) .10 .25
❑ CD2 Plymouth (Massachusetts) .10 .25
❑ CD3 Sir Walter Raleigh .10 .25
❑ CD4 William Penn .10 .25
❑ CD5 Jamestown (Virginia) .10 .25
❑ CD6 St. Augustine (Florida) .10 .25
❑ CD7 Anne Hutchinson .10 .25
❑ CD8 John Smith .10 .25
❑ CD9 Pocahontas .10 .25
❑ CD10 King Philip's War .10 .25
❑ EA1 Hohokum .10 .25
❑ EA2 Hopewellians .10 .25
❑ EA3 Anasazi Indians .10 .25
❑ EA4 Christopher Columbus .10 .25
❑ EA5 John Cabot .10 .25
❑ EA6 Iroquois Indians .10 .25
❑ EA7 Cherokee Indians .10 .25
❑ EA8 Clovis Culture .10 .25
❑ EA9 Folsom Culture .10 .25
❑ EA10 Bering Land Bridge (Beringia) .10 .25
❑ EX1 Francisco Pizarro: Spanish Influence .10 .25
❑ EX2 John Colter: Into the Wilderness .10 .25
❑ EX3 Samuel de Champlain: Settler of Quebec .10 .25
❑ EX4 George Vancouver: Exploring the North .10 .25
❑ EX5 Ferdinand Magellan: Around the World .10 .25
❑ EX6 Sir Francis Drake: The Dragon .10 .25
❑ EX7 Amerigo Vespucci: It's All in a Name .10 .25
❑ EX8 Jacques Cartier: The French Connection .10 .25
❑ EX9 Leif Ericson: Eric the Red .10 .25
❑ EX10 Giovanni da Verrazano: East Coast Connection .10 .25
❑ EX11 John Smith: English Influence .10 .25
❑ EX12 Sir John Franklin: Northern Exposure .10 .25
❑ EX13 Henry Hudson: Northwest Route .10 .25
❑ EX14 Juan Batista de Anza: North of the Border .10 .25
❑ EX15 Sir John Hawkins: The Slave Trade .10 .25
❑ EX16 Henry Kelsey: Let's Make a Deal .10 .25
❑ EX17 Juan Cabrillo: California Dreamin' .10 .25
❑ EX18 Steven Long: Manifest Destiny .10 .25
❑ EX19 Richard Byrd: Polar Pioneer .10 .25
❑ EX20 Jim Bridger: Follow Me .10 .25
❑ EX21 Robert Gray: Around the World .10 .25
❑ EX22 Father Jacques Marquette: Spreading the Word .10 .25
❑ EX23 Joe Walker: Into the Valley .10 .25
❑ EX24 Robert LaSalle: Completing the Mission .10 .25
❑ EX25 Father Junipero Serra: Man on a Mission .10 .25
❑ EX26 John Cabot: Northern Adventure .10 .25
❑ EX27 Sacajawea: Tremendous Trio .10 .25
❑ EX28 Admiral Robert E. Peary: Pole Position .10 .25
❑ EX29 Hernan Cortes: Aztec Conquistador .10 .25
❑ EX30 Juan Ponce de Leon: Youthful Voyage .10 .25
❑ EX31 Vitus J. Bering: Major Mission .10 .25
❑ EX32 Antoine de Cadillac: Detroit's Founder .10 .25
❑ EX33 James Cook: Pacific Islander .10 .25
❑ EX34 Lewis & Clark: The New Frontier .10 .25
❑ EX35 Francisco Vasquez de Coronado: Golden Journey .10 .25
❑ EX36 John Fremont: Improving the West .10 .25
❑ EX37 Vasco Nunez de Balboa: The New Coast .10 .25
❑ EX38 Christopher Columbus: Coming to America .10 .25
❑ EX39 Jean Nicollet: Great Explorer .10 .25
❑ EX40 Louis Joliet: Discoverer of Mississippi River .10 .25
❑ EX41 Daniel Boone: Taming Kentucky .10 .25
❑ EX42 Jedediah Smith: Coast to Coast .10 .25
❑ EX43 Peter Minuit: Deal of a Lifetime .10 .25
❑ EX44 Alexander von Humboldt: Journey to the South .10 .25
❑ EX45 Hernando de Soto: Exploring the South .10 .25
❑ EX46 Kit Carson: Mountain Man .10 .25
❑ EX47 William Dampier: The New Continent .10 .25
❑ EX48 Christopher Newport: Next stop: Jamestown .10 .25
❑ EX49 Jean-Francois la Perouse: Alaska-bound .10 .25
❑ EX50 Lt. Zebulon Pike: The Highest Peak .10 .25
❑ II1 Samuel F.B. Morse: Morse Code .10 .25
❑ II2 Alexander Graham Bell: Telephone .10 .25
❑ II3 Thomas A. Edison: Incandescent lamp .10 .25
❑ II4 Thomas A. Edison: Phonograph .10 .25
❑ II5 George Eastman and Thomas Edison: Motion picture .10 .25
❑ II6 Cyrus McCormick: Reaper .10 .25
❑ II7 George Washington Carver: Uses for the peanut, sweet potato and soybean .10 .25
❑ II8 Albert Einstein: Theory of relativity .10 .25
❑ II9 Eli Whitney: Cotton Gin .10 .25
❑ II10 Orville and Wilbur Wright: First Powered Flight .10 .25
❑ II11 Glenn Curtiss: Flying boats .10 .25
❑ II12 John Pemberton: Coca-Cola .10 .25
❑ II13 RCA: Compact disc .10 .25
❑ II14 Steve Wozniak: Personal Computer .10 .25
❑ II15 Dr. Robert Jarvik: Permanent artificial heart implanted in a human .10 .25
❑ II16 Benjamin Franklin: Conservation of electric charge .10 .25
❑ II17 Benjamin Franklin: Bifocal lens .10 .25
❑ II18 John F. Enders and Thomas Peebles: Measles vaccine .10 .25
❑ II19 Edwin Armstrong: FM radio .10 .25
❑ II20 Henry Ford: Moving assembly line .10 .25
❑ II21 Lewis E. Waterman: Fountain pen .10 .25
❑ II22 Jonas E. Salk: Polio vaccine .10 .25
❑ II23 Willard F. Libby: Radiocarbon dating .10 .25
❑ II24 King Gillette: Successfully marketed safety razor .10 .25
❑ II25 Jacob Perkins: Refrigerator .10 .25
❑ II26 Samuel Colt: Revolver .10 .25
❑ II27 Charles F. Richter: Richter scale .10 .25
❑ II28 Robert Goddard: Liquid-fueled rocket .10 .25
❑ II29 Charles Goodyear: Rubber .10 .25
❑ II30 Elias Howe: Sewing machine .10 .25
❑ II31 John Ericsson: Solar energy .10 .25
❑ II32 Robert Fulton: First commercially successful steamship .10 .25
❑ II33 Vladimir Zworykin: Television .10 .25
❑ II34 Christopher Sholes and Carlos Glidden: Typewriter .10 .25
❑ II35 Chester Carlson: Xeography Photocopier .10 .25
❑ II36 David Bushnell: Submarine .10 .25
❑ II37 John Fitch: Steamboat .10 .25
❑ II38 Richard Gatling: Gatling gun .10 .25
❑ II39 Jacob Fussell: Ice cream .10 .25
❑ II40 Elisha Graves Otis: Lift Elevator .10 .25
❑ II41 Thomas Adams: Chewing gum .10 .25
❑ II42 Levi Strauss: Blue jeans .10 .25
❑ II43 Les Paul: Electric guitar .10 .25
❑ II44 Frank Zamboni: Zamboni .10 .25
❑ II45 Edwin Land: Polaroid .10 .25
❑ II46 Peter Carl Goldmark: Color television .10 .25
❑ II47 Richard James: Slinky .10 .25
❑ II48 Nolan Bushnell: Video games .10 .25
❑ II49 Clarence Birdseye: Frozen food .10 .25
❑ II50 Garrett Morgan: Gas mask and traffic signal .10 .25
❑ IW1 Wyatt Earp .10 .25
❑ IW2 Crazy Horse .10 .25
❑ IW3 Sitting Bull .10 .25
❑ IW4 Geronimo .10 .25
❑ IW5 William F. Buffalo Bill Cody .10 .25
❑ IW6 Frank and Jesse James .10 .25
❑ IW7 Davy Crockett .10 .25
❑ IW8 Daniel Boone .10 .25
❑ IW9 Billy the Kid .10 .25
❑ IW10 General George Armstrong Custer .10 .25
❑ RR1 14th Amendment .10 .25
❑ RR2 Reconstruction Act .10 .25
❑ RR3 15th Amendement .10 .25
❑ RR4 Military Reconstruction Act .10 .25
❑ RR5 Enforcement Act .10 .25
❑ RR6 Amnesty Act .10 .25
❑ RR7 Jim Crow Laws .10 .25
❑ RR8 Sherman Antitrust Act .10 .25
❑ RR9 Civil Rights Act of 1875 .10 .25
❑ RR10 Compromise of 1877 .10 .25
❑ SC1 Delaware .10 .25
❑ SC2 Pennsylvania .10 .25
❑ SC3 New Jersey .10 .25
❑ SC4 Georgia .10 .25
❑ SC5 Connecticut .10 .25
❑ SC6 Massachusetts .10 .25
❑ SC7 Maryland .10 .25
❑ SC8 South Carolina .10 .25
❑ SC9 New Hampshire .10 .25
❑ SC10 Virginia .10 .25
❑ SC11 New York .10 .25
❑ SC12 North Carolina .10 .25
❑ SC13 Rhode Island .10 .25
❑ SC14 Vermont .10 .25
❑ SC15 Kentucky .10 .25
❑ SC16 Tennessee .10 .25
❑ SC17 Ohio .10 .25
❑ SC18 Louisiana .10 .25
❑ SC19 Indiana .10 .25
❑ SC20 Mississippi .10 .25
❑ SC21 Illinois .10 .25
❑ SC22 Alabama .10 .25
❑ SC23 Maine .10 .25
❑ SC24 Missouri .10 .25
❑ SC25 Arkansas .10 .25
❑ SC26 Michigan .10 .25
❑ SC27 Florida .10 .25
❑ SC28 Texas .10 .25
❑ SC29 Iowa .10 .25
❑ SC30 Wisconsin .10 .25
❑ SC31 California .10 .25
❑ SC32 Minnesota .10 .25
❑ SC33 Oregon .10 .25
❑ SC34 Kansas .10 .25
❑ SC35 West Virginia .10 .25
❑ SC36 Nevada .10 .25
❑ SC37 Nebraska .10 .25
❑ SC38 Colorado .10 .25
❑ SC39 South Dakota .10 .25
❑ SC40 North Dakota .10 .25
❑ SC41 Montana .10 .25
❑ SC42 Washington .10 .25
❑ SC43 Idaho .10 .25
❑ SC44 Wyoming .10 .25
❑ SC45 Utah .10 .25
❑ SC46 Oklahoma .10 .25
❑ SC47 New Mexico .10 .25
❑ SC48 Arizona .10 .25
❑ SC49 Alaska .10 .25
❑ SC50 Hawaii .10 .25
❑ TP1 George Washington .10 .25
❑ TP2 John Adams .10 .25
❑ TP3 Thomas Jefferson .10 .25
❑ TP4 James Madison .10 .25
❑ TP5 James Monroe .10 .25
❑ TP6 John Quincy Adams .10 .25
❑ TP7 Andrew Jackson .10 .25
❑ TP8 Martin Van Buren .10 .25
❑ TP9 William Henry Harrison .10 .25
❑ TP10 John Tyler .10 .25
❑ TP11 James K. Polk .10 .25
❑ TP12 Zachary Taylor .10 .25
❑ TP13 Millard Fillmore .10 .25
❑ TP14 Franklin Pierce .10 .25
❑ TP15 James Buchanan .10 .25
❑ TP16 Abraham Lincoln .10 .25
❑ TP17 Andrew Johnson .10 .25
❑ TP18 Ulysses S. Grant .10 .25
❑ TP19 Rutherford B. Hayes .10 .25
❑ TP20 James A. Garfield .10 .25
❑ TP21 Chester A. Arthur .10 .25
❑ TP22 Grover Cleveland .10 .25
❑ TP23 Bejamin Harrison .10 .25
❑ TP24 Grover Cleveland .10 .25
❑ TP25 William McKinley .10 .25
❑ TP26 Theodore Roosevelt .10 .25
❑ TP27 William H. Taft .10 .25
❑ TP28 Woodrow Wilson .10 .25
❑ TP29 Warren G. Harding .10 .25
❑ TP30 Calvin Coolidge .10 .25
❑ TP31 Herbert C. Hoover .10 .25
❑ TP32 Franklin D. Roosevelt .10 .25
❑ TP33 Harry S Truman .10 .25
❑ TP34 Dwight D. Eisenhower .10 .25
❑ TP35 John F. Kennedy .10 .25
❑ TP36 Lyndon B. Johnson .10 .25
❑ TP37 Richard M. Nixon .10 .25
❑ TP38 Gerald Ford .10 .25
❑ TP39 Jimmy Carter .10 .25
❑ TP40 Ronald Reagan .10 .25
❑ TP41 George Bush .10 .25
❑ TP42 Bill Clinton .10 .25
❑ TP43 George W. Bush .10 .25
❑ TP44 The White House .10 .25
❑ TP45 The Oval Office .10 .25
❑ TP46 The West Wing .10 .25
❑ TP47 The Seal of the President of the United States .10 .25
❑ TP48 Air Force One .10 .25
❑ TP49 Commander-in-Chief of the Armed-Forces .10 .25
❑ TP50 State of the Union Address .10 .25
❑ TR1 Patrick Henry .10 .25
❑ TR2 Benjamin Franklin .10 .25
❑ TR3 John Adams .10 .25
❑ TR4 Boston Tea Party .10 .25
❑ TR5 Samuel Adams .10 .25
❑ TR6 Paul Revere .10 .25
❑ TR7 First Shots of War - Lexington and Concord .10 .25
❑ TR8 Battle of Bunker Hill .10 .25
❑ TR9 General George Washington .10 .25
❑ TR10 Signing of the Declaration of Independence .10 .25
❑ TR11 Thomas Jefferson .10 .25
❑ TR12 General Horatio Gates' Victory at Saratoga .10 .25
❑ TR13 The Winter at Valley Forge .10 .25
❑ TR14 Cornwallis Surrenders at Yorktown .10 .25
❑ TR15 The Treaty of Paris .10 .25
❑ WS1 President Abraham Lincoln .10 .25
❑ WS2 Jefferson Davis .10 .25
❑ WS3 General Ulysses S. Grant .10 .25
❑ WS4 General Robert E. Lee .10 .25
❑ WS5 General William T. Sherman .10 .25
❑ WS6 General Thomas J. Stonewall Jackson .10 .25
❑ WS7 General George B. McClellan .10 .25
❑ WS8 General P.G.T. Beauregard .10 .25
❑ WS9 Confederates Attack Fort Sumter .10 .25
❑ WS10 Confederates Repel Union at Bull Run .10 .25
❑ WS11 Grant Victory at Fort Donelson .10 .25
❑ WS12 Battle of Shiloh .10 .25
❑ WS13 Battle of Gettysburg .10 .25
❑ WS14 The Atlanta Campaign .10 .25
❑ WS15 Lee Surrenders .10 .25
❑ 20th1 Spanish-American War .10 .25
❑ 20th2 President McKinley Assassinated .10 .25
❑ 20th3 Gold Standard Act .10 .25
❑ 20th4 Theodore Roosevelt .10 .25
❑ 20th5 Henry Ford Introduces the Model T .10 .25
❑ 20th6 The Panama Canal .10 .25
❑ 20th7 Orville and Wilbur Wright .10 .25
❑ 20th8 Albert Einstein .10 .25
❑ 20th9 Mark Twain .10 .25
❑ 20th10 NAACP Founded .10 .25
❑ 20th11 Upton Sinclair's The Jungle .10 .25
❑ 20th12 Philippine-American War .10 .25
❑ 20th13 Booker T. Washington .10 .25
❑ 20th14 Klondike Gold Rush .10 .25
❑ 20th15 Pullman Strike .10 .25

2004 History of the United States Documents Monuments and Places

COMPLETE SET (15) 5.00 12.00
STATED ODDS 1:3

❑ DMP1 Declaration of Independence .60 1.50
❑ DMP2 The Articles of Confederation .60 1.50
❑ DMP3 The U.S. Constitution .60 1.50
❑ DMP4 Constitutional Amendments .60 1.50
❑ DMP5 The Bill of Rights .60 1.50
❑ DMP6 The White House .60 1.50
❑ DMP7 U.S. Capitol Building .60 1.50
❑ DMP8 The Supreme Court .60 1.50
❑ DMP9 The Washington Monument .60 1.50
❑ DMP10 The Lincoln Memorial .60 1.50
❑ DMP11 The Thomas Jefferson Memorial .60 1.50
❑ DMP12 Yosemite National Park .60 1.50
❑ DMP13 Vietnam Veterans Memorial .60 1.50
❑ DMP14 Korean War Veterans Memorial .60 1.50
❑ DMP15 Mount Rushmore .60 1.50

2004 History of the United States Etched in History Cut Signatures

STATED PRINT RUN 1 SER. SET
UNPRICED DUE TO SCARCITY

❑ 1 Admiral Chester A. Nimitz
❑ 2 Admiral Robert E. Peary
❑ 3 Benjamin Franklin
❑ 4 Eleanor Roosevelt
❑ 5 Elliot Ness
❑ 6 Frederick Douglass
❑ 7 General George C. Marshall
❑ 8 General George S. Patton
❑ 9 General John Pershing
❑ 10 General Robert E. Lee
❑ 11 General William T. Sherman
❑ 12 Helen Keller
❑ 13 Jefferson Davis
❑ 14 John Hancock
❑ 15 Norman Rockwell
❑ 16 Orville Wright
❑ 17 Robert F. Kennedy
❑ 18 Samuel Adams
❑ 19 Samuel Clemens
❑ 20 Thomas Edison

2004 History of the United States Famous Americans

COMPLETE SET (10) 5.00 12.00
STATED ODDS 1:5

❑ FA1 Neil Armstrong 1.00 2.50
❑ FA2 Ernest Hemingway 1.00 2.50
❑ FA3 Jesse Owens 1.00 2.50
❑ FA4 John Philip Sousa 1.00 2.50
❑ FA5 Charles Lindbergh 1.00 2.50
❑ FA6 General Douglas MacArthur 1.00 2.50
❑ FA7 John Steinbeck 1.00 2.50
❑ FA8 Mark Twain 1.00 2.50
❑ FA9 Norman Rockwell 1.00 2.50
❑ FA10 Clara Barton 1.00 2.50

2004 History of the United States Presidential Cut Signatures

STATED PRINT RUN 1 SER. #'d SET
UNPRICED DUE TO SCARCITY

❑ 1 Abraham Lincoln
❑ 2 Dwight Eisenhower
❑ 3 George Washington
❑ 4 Harry S Truman
❑ 5 Harry S Truman
❑ 6 John Adams
❑ 7 Thomas Jefferson
❑ 8 William H. Taft
❑ 9 Woodrow Wilson
❑ 10 Woodrow Wilson

2004 History of the United States State Quarters

STATED ODDS ONE PER BOX

❑ SQ1 Delaware 8.00 20.00
❑ SQ2 Pennsylvania 8.00 20.00
❑ SQ3 New Jersey 8.00 20.00
❑ SQ4 Georgia 8.00 20.00
❑ SQ5 Connecticut 8.00 20.00
❑ SQ6 Massachusetts 8.00 20.00
❑ SQ7 Maryland 8.00 20.00
❑ SQ8 South Carolina 8.00 20.00
❑ SQ9 New Hampshire 8.00 20.00
❑ SQ10 Virginia 8.00 20.00
❑ SQ11 New York 8.00 20.00
❑ SQ12 North Carolina 8.00 20.00
❑ SQ13 Rhode Island 8.00 20.00
❑ SQ14 Vermont 8.00 20.00
❑ SQ15 Kentucky 8.00 20.00
❑ SQ16 Tennessee 8.00 20.00
❑ SQ17 Ohio 8.00 20.00
❑ SQ18 Louisiana 8.00 20.00
❑ SQ19 Indiana 8.00 20.00
❑ SQ20 Mississippi 8.00 20.00
❑ SQ21 Illinois 8.00 20.00
❑ SQ22 Alabama 8.00 20.00

2004 History of the United States The Greatest Moments in American History

COMPLETE SET (25) 10.00 25.00
STATED ODDS 1:4

❑ GM1 The Boston Tea Party .75 2.00
❑ GM2 Signing of the Declaration of Independence .75 2.00
❑ GM3 The Battle of Saratoga .75 2.00
❑ GM4 British Surrender at Yorktown .75 2.00
❑ GM5 Ratification of the Articles of Confederation .75 2.00
❑ GM6 Signing of the U.S. Constitution .75 2.00
❑ GM7 Washington Takes Office .75 2.00
❑ GM8 The Louisiana Purchase .75 2.00
❑ GM9 MacDonough's Victory in the War of 1812 .75 2.00
❑ GM10 Major Armistead's Holding of Fort McHenry .75 2.00
❑ GM11 Signing of the Treaty of Ghent .75 2.00
❑ GM12 Jackson's Victory at New Orleans .75 2.00
❑ GM13 Monroe Doctrine Established .75 2.00
❑ GM14 The Battle of the Alamo .75 2.00
❑ GM15 Treaty of Guadalupe Hidalgo .75 2.00
❑ GM16 The Emancipation Proclamation .75 2.00
❑ GM17 The Gettysburg Address .75 2.00
❑ GM18 Lee Surrenders at Appomattox .75 2.00
❑ GM19 Graham Bell Tests the First Telephone .75 2.00
❑ GM20 Edison Invents the Light Bulb .75 2.00
❑ GM21 The Statue of Liberty .75 2.00
❑ GM22 Wright Brothers' First Airplane Flight .75 2.00
❑ GM23 Einstein Introduces Theory of Relativity .75 2.00
❑ GM24 Germany Surrenders to End WWI .75 2.00
❑ GM25 D-Day - Allies Land in Normandy .75 2.00

2004 History of the United States The Making of America

COMPLETE SET (15) 6.00 15.00
STATED ODDS 1:6

❑ MA1 George Washington 1.00 2.50
❑ MA2 Benjamin Franklin 1.00 2.50
❑ MA3 Thomas Jefferson 1.00 2.50
❑ MA4 Samuel Adams 1.00 2.50
❑ MA5 Abraham Lincoln 1.00 2.50
❑ MA6 Francis Scott Key 1.00 2.50
❑ MA7 Betsy Ross 1.00 2.50
❑ MA8 Thomas Edison 1.00 2.50
❑ MA9 Booker T. Washington 1.00 2.50
❑ MA10 Clara Barton 1.00 2.50
❑ MA11 Henry Ford 1.00 2.50
❑ MA12 William Randolph Hearst 1.00 2.50
❑ MA13 Andrew Carnegie 1.00 2.50
❑ MA14 John D. Rockefeller 1.00 2.50
❑ MA15 Cornelius Vanderbilt 1.00 2.50

2004 Legends of Star Trek Dr. McCoy

COMPLETE SET (9) 10.00 20.00

❑ L1 Dr. McCoy 1.00 2.50
❑ L2 Dr. McCoy 1.00 2.50
❑ L3 Dr. McCoy 1.00 2.50
❑ L4 Dr. McCoy 1.00 2.50
❑ L5 Dr. McCoy 1.00 2.50
❑ L6 Dr. McCoy 1.00 2.50
❑ L7 Dr. McCoy 1.00 2.50
❑ L8 Dr. McCoy 1.00 2.50
❑ L9 Dr. McCoy 1.00 2.50

2004 Legends of Star Trek Scotty Uhura Sulu

COMPLETE SET (9) 10.00 20.00

❑ L1 Scotty 1.00 2.50
❑ L2 Scotty 1.00 2.50
❑ L3 Scotty 1.00 2.50
❑ L4 Uhura 1.00 2.50
❑ L5 Uhura 1.00 2.50
❑ L6 Uhura 1.00 2.50
❑ L7 Sulu 1.00 2.50
❑ L8 Sulu 1.00 2.50
❑ L9 Sulu 1.00 2.50

2004 Legends of Star Trek Spock

COMPLETE SET (9) 10.00 20.00

❑ L1 Spock 1.00 2.50
❑ L2 Spock 1.00 2.50
❑ L3 Spock 1.00 2.50
❑ L4 Spock 1.00 2.50
❑ L5 Spock 1.00 2.50
❑ L6 Spock 1.00 2.50
❑ L7 Spock 1.00 2.50
❑ L8 Spock 1.00 2.50
❑ L9 Spock 1.00 2.50

2004 Lord of the Rings The Return of the King Update

COMPLETE SET (72) 5.00 12.00

❑ 91 Title Card .15 .40
❑ 92 Smeagol's Great Desire .15 .40
❑ 93 Uneasy Alliance .15 .40
❑ 94 Isengard's Fall .15 .40
❑ 95 In the Golden Hall .15 .40
❑ 96 A Soul in Torment .15 .40
❑ 97 Lure of the Palantir .15 .40
❑ 98 Arwen's Decision .15 .40
❑ 99 Toward Minas Tirith .15 .40

❑ 100 The Gates of Minas Morgul .15 .40
❑ 101 Sauron's Footsoldiers .15 .40
❑ 102 The Flaming Signal .15 .40
❑ 103 Terror From the Skies .15 .40
❑ 104 Nazgul Triumphant .15 .40
❑ 105 Day of the Nazgul .15 .40
❑ 106 Friend or Fiend .15 .40
❑ 107 Return of the Sword .15 .40
❑ 108 King of the Dead .15 .40
❑ 109 Regain Your Honor .15 .40
❑ 110 Massive Orc Army .15 .40
❑ 111 Attack of the Trolls .15 .40
❑ 112 Winged Horror .15 .40
❑ 113 A Wizard Among Them .15 .40
❑ 114 Leviathans Against Us .15 .40
❑ 115 Inside Shelob's Lair .15 .40
❑ 116 The Horror of Shelob .15 .40
❑ 117 Smashing Through .15 .40
❑ 118 Trolls on the Rampage .15 .40
❑ 119 Along Came a Spider .15 .40
❑ 120 Caught .15 .40
❑ 121 Cornering Her Prey .15 .40
❑ 122 Sam Battles Shelob .15 .40
❑ 123 Mumakil on the March .15 .40
❑ 124 A Deadly Advance .15 .40
❑ 125 Hero of Rohan .15 .40
❑ 126 Spectacular Battle .15 .40
❑ 127 Facing the Fellbeast .15 .40
❑ 128 Eowyn's Challenge .15 .40
❑ 129 Wrath of the Witch-king .15 .40
❑ 130 Aragorn's Phantom Army .15 .40
❑ 131 Army of the Dead .15 .40
❑ 132 Spectral Warriors .15 .40
❑ 133 Slaying the Witch-king .15 .40
❑ 134 Legolas's Bold Assault .15 .40
❑ 135 Depart and Be At Rest .15 .40
❑ 136 Rescued By Sam .15 .40
❑ 137 At the Black Gate .15 .40
❑ 138 Facing The Ultimate Evil .15 .40
❑ 139 Toward Mount Doom .15 .40
❑ 140 Monsters of Mordor .15 .40
❑ 141 This Day We Fight .15 .40
❑ 142 Gollum Returns .15 .40
❑ 143 Fury of the Fellbeasts .15 .40
❑ 144 Gandalf's Resolve .15 .40
❑ 145 Winged Fury .15 .40
❑ 146 Moment of Truth .15 .40
❑ 147 Gollum's Savage Attack .15 .40
❑ 148 Rampaging Trolls .15 .40
❑ 149 The Ring At Last .15 .40
❑ 150 My Precious .15 .40
❑ 151 The Ring Destroyed .15 .40
❑ 152 The Fall of Barad-Dûr .15 .40
❑ 153 Falling From the Skies .15 .40
❑ 154 The Great Eagles .15 .40
❑ 155 A Fellowship Reunited .15 .40
❑ 156 The Crown of Gondor .15 .40
❑ 157 Love and Valor .15 .40
❑ 158 Sam's Wedding Day .15 .40
❑ 159 Bilbo's Last Adventure .15 .40
❑ 160 It Is Time, Frodo .15 .40
❑ 161 The Sea Calls Them Home .15 .40
❑ 162 The Journey Ends .15 .40

2004 Lord of the Rings The Return of the King Update Autographs

AUTO/MEM COMBINED ODDS 1:36

❑ NNO Sala Baker 20.00 40.00
❑ NNO Peter Jackson 100.00 175.00
❑ NNO Mark Ordesky 25.00 50.00

2004 Lord of the Rings The Return of the King Update Memorabilia

AUTO/MEM COMBINED ODDS 1:36

❑ NNO Eowyn's Coronation Dress 10.00 25.00
❑ NNO Sam's Wedding Jacket 8.00 20.00
❑ NNO Arwen's Coronation Dress 15.00 40.00
❑ NNO Frodo's Grey Havens Vest 60.00 120.00
❑ NNO Elrond's Bronze Silk Robe 15.00 40.00
❑ NNO Merry's Rohan Cloak 8.00 20.00
❑ NNO Aragorn's Coronation Shirt 40.00 80.00
❑ NNO Eowyn's Golden Hall Party Dress 12.00 30.00
❑ NNO The Witch-King's Cloak 12.00 30.00

2004 Lord of the Rings Trilogy Chrome

COMPLETE SET (100) 8.00 20.00

❑ 1 The Rings Bestowed .20 .50
❑ 2 Sauron's Key to Power .20 .50
❑ 3 The Fall of Isildur .20 .50
❑ 4 Into a Hobbit's Hands .20 .50
❑ 5 Magic in the Shire .20 .50
❑ 6 The Epic Journey Begins .20 .50
❑ 7 Passing of the Elves .20 .50
❑ 8 Practitioners of Power .20 .50
❑ 9 A New Ally .20 .50
❑ 10 The Dark Riders .20 .50
❑ 11 Mountaintop Terror .20 .50
❑ 12 Stabbed by a Spectre .20 .50
❑ 13 Uruk-Hai Master .20 .50
❑ 14 Arwen's Escape .20 .50
❑ 15 Awakening in Rivendell .20 .50
❑ 16 Wizards in Conflict .20 .50
❑ 17 Once and Future Kings .20 .50
❑ 18 Challenge for Frodo .20 .50
❑ 19 The Fellowship Is Formed .20 .50
❑ 20 Avalanche .20 .50
❑ 21 The Watcher .20 .50
❑ 22 They Call It a Mine .20 .50
❑ 23 Terror of the Cave Troll .20 .50
❑ 24 Vanquished! .20 .50
❑ 25 Shadow and Flame .20 .50
❑ 26 Friends, Foes and Fiends .20 .50
❑ 27 Dark Vision .20 .50
❑ 28 Evil Queen .20 .50
❑ 29 Gifts from the Elves .20 .50
❑ 30 Troubled Companions .20 .50
❑ 31 Attacked by Uruk-Hai .20 .50
❑ 32 The Fate of Boromir .20 .50
❑ 33 Friends to the End .20 .50
❑ 34 Plunge into an Abyss .20 .50
❑ 35 Elven Rope .20 .50
❑ 36 The Taming of Gollum .20 .50
❑ 37 March to Isengard .20 .50
❑ 38 Poisoning Rohan .20 .50
❑ 39 The Three Hunters .20 .50
❑ 40 Way through the Marshes .20 .50
❑ 41 Spectral Terrors .20 .50
❑ 42 Treeherder .20 .50
❑ 43 The White Wizard .20 .50
❑ 44 The Black Gate .20 .50
❑ 45 Dark Times in Rohan .20 .50
❑ 46 The King's Release .20 .50
❑ 47 Make for Helm's Deep .20 .50
❑ 48 Culinary Delights .20 .50
❑ 49 Torn from Within .20 .50
❑ 50 Warg Ambush .20 .50
❑ 51 Clash on the Plains .20 .50
❑ 52 Isengard Unleashed .20 .50
❑ 53 Brothers of Gondor .20 .50
❑ 54 Master Betrayed Us .20 .50
❑ 55 The Eve of Battle .20 .50
❑ 56 Elves Join the Fight .20 .50
❑ 57 Helm's Deep Under Siege .20 .50
❑ 58 War Affects Us All .20 .50
❑ 59 Breaching the Deeping Wall .20 .50
❑ 60 Furious Fight to Survive .20 .50
❑ 61 Gandalf Turns the Tide .20 .50
❑ 62 Isengard Flooded .20 .50
❑ 63 Saved from the Nazgul .20 .50
❑ 64 The Final Tally .20 .50
❑ 65 The Spoils of War .20 .50
❑ 66 Choosing the Dark Path .20 .50
❑ 67 Smeagol and Deagol .20 .50
❑ 68 Seeing Stone of Power .20 .50
❑ 69 Saruman's Wrath .20 .50
❑ 70 Gollum's Deception .20 .50
❑ 71 Journey to the Grey Havens .20 .50
❑ 72 Deep Breath .20 .50
❑ 73 Minas Morgul .20 .50
❑ 74 A Beacon of Hope .20 .50
❑ 75 Pledge to Theoden .20 .50
❑ 76 Flight of the Fellbeasts .20 .50
❑ 77 Saved by the White Wizard .20 .50
❑ 78 Go Home Sam .20 .50
❑ 79 Retake Osgiliath .20 .50
❑ 80 Join Us .20 .50
❑ 81 Isildur's Heir .20 .50
❑ 82 Corsair Boson .20 .50
❑ 83 Orc Hordes .20 .50
❑ 84 Nazgul Terror .20 .50
❑ 85 Morgul Lord .20 .50
❑ 86 Caught in a Web .20 .50
❑ 87 Let Him Go .20 .50
❑ 88 Funeral Pyre .20 .50
❑ 89 Legion of Mumakil .20 .50
❑ 90 I Am No Man .20 .50
❑ 91 Oath Fulfilled .20 .50
❑ 92 The Mouth of Sauron .20 .50
❑ 93 Destroy It .20 .50
❑ 94 Precious .20 .50
❑ 95 Quest Fulfilled .20 .50
❑ 96 Coronation of the King .20 .50
❑ 97 Heroes of the Shire .20 .50
❑ 98 End of the Journey .20 .50
❑ 99 Into the West .20 .50
❑ 100 Checklist .20 .50

2004 Lord of the Rings Trilogy Chrome Autographs

STATED ODDS 1:18 H, 1:83 R 8.00 20.00

❑ NNO Bernard Hill 8.00 20.00
❑ NNO David Wenham SP 10.00 25.00
❑ NNO Liv Tyler 25.00 50.00
❑ NNO Viggo Mortensen 25.00 50.00
Aragorn
❑ NNO Bret McKenzie 8.00 20.00
❑ NNO John Noble 8.00 20.00
❑ NNO Sala Baker 8.00 20.00
❑ NNO Bruce Hopkins 8.00 20.00
❑ NNO Karl Urban 8.00 20.00
❑ NNO Stephen Ure 8.00 20.00
❑ NNO Billy Boyd 8.00 20.00
❑ NNO Ian Holm 8.00 20.00
❑ NNO Noel Appleby 8.00 20.00
❑ NNO Viggo Mortensen 25.00 50.00
King Elessar

2004 Lord of the Rings Trilogy Chrome Memorabilia

STATED ODDS 1:36 H, 1:55 R

❑ NNO Bilbo's Waistcoat 12.00 30.00
❑ NNO Frodo's Tunic 12.00 30.00
❑ NNO Eowyn's Edoras Stables Dress 12.00 30.00
❑ NNO Sam's Tunic 40.00 80.00
❑ NNO Aragorn's Shirt 12.00 30.00
❑ NNO Eowyn's Golden Hall Dress 20.00 50.00
❑ NNO The Witch-King's Robe 10.00 25.00
❑ NNO Elrond's Robe 10.00 25.00
❑ NNO Pippin's Tunic 40.00 80.00

2004 The Outer Limits Expansion

COMPLETE SET (4)
NIMOY AUTO ISSUED AS 5-SET INCENTIVE
MCCAMMON MEM ISSUED AS 5-SET INCENTIVE

❑ A18 Jon Tenney AU 8.00 20.00
❑ A19 Bruce Harwood AU 8.00 20.00
❑ A20 Leonard Nimoy AU/ (issued as 5-set incentive) 150.00 250.00
❑ A21 Gary Busey AU 20.00 40.00
❑ A22 Sheena Easton AU 40.00 80.00
❑ CC13 Melissa McCammon MEM/ (issued as 5-set incentive)

2004 The Quotable James Bond

COMPLETE SET (100) 4.00 10.00
CC5 STATED ODDS ONE PER COLLECTOR'S ALBUM

❑ 1 Quote Cards .10 .30
❑ 2 Quote Cards .10 .30
❑ 3 Quote Cards .10 .30
❑ 4 Quote Cards .10 .30
❑ 5 Quote Cards .10 .30
❑ 6 Quote Cards .10 .30
❑ 7 Quote Cards .10 .30
❑ 8 Quote Cards .10 .30
❑ 9 Quote Cards .10 .30
❑ 10 Quote Cards .10 .30
❑ 11 Quote Cards .10 .30
❑ 12 Quote Cards .10 .30
❑ 13 Quote Cards .10 .30
❑ 14 Quote Cards .10 .30
❑ 15 Quote Cards .10 .30
❑ 16 Quote Cards .10 .30
❑ 17 Quote Cards .10 .30
❑ 18 Quote Cards .10 .30
❑ 19 Quote Cards .10 .30
❑ 20 Quote Cards .10 .30
❑ 21 Quote Cards .10 .30
❑ 22 Quote Cards .10 .30
❑ 23 Quote Cards .10 .30
❑ 24 Quote Cards .10 .30
❑ 25 Quote Cards .10 .30
❑ 26 Quote Cards .10 .30
❑ 27 Quote Cards .10 .30
❑ 28 Quote Cards .10 .30
❑ 29 Quote Cards .10 .30
❑ 30 Quote Cards .10 .30
❑ 31 Quote Cards .10 .30
❑ 32 Quote Cards .10 .30
❑ 33 Quote Cards .10 .30
❑ 34 Quote Cards .10 .30
❑ 35 Quote Cards .10 .30
❑ 36 Quote Cards .10 .30
❑ 37 Quote Cards .10 .30
❑ 38 Quote Cards .10 .30
❑ 39 Quote Cards .10 .30
❑ 40 Quote Cards .10 .30
❑ 41 Quote Cards .10 .30
❑ 42 Quote Cards .10 .30
❑ 43 Quote Cards .10 .30
❑ 44 Quote Cards .10 .30
❑ 45 Quote Cards .10 .30
❑ 46 Quote Cards .10 .30
❑ 47 Quote Cards .10 .30
❑ 48 Quote Cards .10 .30
❑ 49 Quote Cards .10 .30
❑ 50 Quote Cards .10 .30
❑ 51 Quote Cards .10 .30
❑ 52 Quote Cards .10 .30
❑ 53 Quote Cards .10 .30
❑ 54 Quote Cards .10 .30
❑ 55 Quote Cards .10 .30
❑ 56 Quote Cards .10 .30
❑ 57 Quote Cards .10 .30
❑ 58 Quote Cards .10 .30
❑ 59 Quote Cards .10 .30
❑ 60 Quote Cards .10 .30
❑ 61 Quote Cards .10 .30
❑ 62 Quote Cards .10 .30
❑ 63 Quote Cards .10 .30
❑ 64 Quote Cards .10 .30
❑ 65 Quote Cards .10 .30
❑ 66 Quote Cards .10 .30
❑ 67 Quote Cards .10 .30
❑ 68 Quote Cards .10 .30
❑ 69 Quote Cards .10 .30
❑ 70 Quote Cards .10 .30
❑ 71 Quote Cards .10 .30
❑ 72 Quote Cards .10 .30
❑ 73 Quote Cards .10 .30
❑ 74 Quote Cards .10 .30
❑ 75 Quote Cards .10 .30
❑ 76 Quote Cards .10 .30
❑ 77 Quote Cards .10 .30
❑ 78 Quote Cards .10 .30
❑ 79 Quote Cards .10 .30
❑ 80 Quote Cards .10 .30
❑ 81 Quote Cards .10 .30
❑ 82 Quote Cards .10 .30
❑ 83 Quote Cards .10 .30
❑ 84 Quote Cards .10 .30
❑ 85 Quote Cards .10 .30
❑ 86 Quote Cards .10 .30
❑ 87 Quote Cards .10 .30
❑ 88 Quote Cards .10 .30
❑ 89 Quote Cards .10 .30
❑ 90 Quote Cards .10 .30
❑ 91 Quote Cards .10 .30
❑ 92 Quote Cards .10 .30
❑ 93 Quote Cards .10 .30
❑ 94 Quote Cards .10 .30
❑ 95 Quote Cards .10 .30
❑ 96 Quote Cards .10 .30
❑ 97 Quote Cards .10 .30
❑ 98 Quote Cards .10 .30
❑ 99 Quote Cards .10 .30
❑ 100 Quote Cards .10 .30
❑ CC5 Aristotle Kristatos Clothing

2004 The Quotable James Bond Autographs

STATED ODDS 1:20
d'ABO AUTO STATED ODDS ONE PER U.S. CASE
KIEL AUTO STATED ODDS ONE PER MULTI-CASE PURCHASE
EATON AUTO STATED ODDS ONE PER U.K. CASE
L (LIMITED): 300-500 COPIES
VL (VERY LIMITED): 200-300 COPIES

❑ A4 Serena Scott-Thomas L 15.00 30.00
❑ A28 Sophie Marceau L 60.00 120.00
❑ A29 Roger Moore VL 150.00 250.00
❑ A30 Michelle Yeoh L 75.00 150.00
❑ A31 Martine Beswick L 25.00 50.00
❑ A33 Mollie Peters L 30.00 60.00
❑ A34 Blanche Ravalec 8.00 20.00
❑ A35 Deborah Moore 15.00 30.00
❑ A36 Will Yun Lee L 15.00 30.00
❑ A37 Goldie 25.00 50.00
❑ A38 Lawrence Makoare 8.00 20.00
❑ A39 John Wyman 8.00 20.00
❑ A40 Jan Williams 8.00 20.00
❑ A41 Douglas Wilmer 8.00 20.00
❑ A42 John Moreno 8.00 20.00
❑ A43 Michael Billington 15.00 30.00
❑ A44 Shane Rimmer 8.00 20.00
❑ A45 Carey Lowell VL 150.00 250.00
❑ A46 Maria Grazia Cucinotta L 30.00 60.00
❑ A47 Burt Kwouk 20.00 40.00
❑ A48 Rachel Grant L 30.00 60.00
❑ A49 Madeline Smith VL 40.00 80.00
❑ WA16 Sophie Marceau L 60.00 120.00
❑ WA17 Michelle Yeoh L 75.00 150.00
❑ WA18 Serena Scott-Thomas L 20.00 40.00
❑ WA20 Mollie Peters L 30.00 60.00
❑ WA21 Carey Lowell VL 200.00 300.00
❑ WA22 Maria Grazia Cucinotta L 30.00 60.00
❑ WA23 Martine Beswick L 40.00 80.00
❑ WA24 Rachel Grant L 30.00 60.00
❑ WA25 Madeline Smith VL 40.00 80.00
❑ NNO Maryam d'Abo/ (issued as US case topper) 40.00 80.00
❑ NNO Richard Kiel/ (issued as multi-case incentive) 60.00 120.00
❑ NNO Shirley Eaton/ (issued as UK case topper) 75.00 150.00

2004 The Quotable James Bond Bond Girls Are Forever

COMPLETE SET (9) 40.00 80.00
STATED ODDS 1:40 U.S. PACKS

❑ BG21 Elektra King 6.00 15.00
❑ BG22 Fiona Volpe 6.00 15.00
❑ BG23 Jill Masterson 6.00 15.00
❑ BG24 Miranda Frost 6.00 15.00
❑ BG25 Paris Carver 6.00 15.00
❑ BG26 Sylvia Trench 6.00 15.00
❑ BG27 Xenia Onatopp 6.00 15.00
❑ BG28 Lupe Lamora 6.00 15.00
❑ BG29 Patricia Fearing 6.00 15.00

2004 The Quotable James Bond The Quotable Bond Villains

COMPLETE SET (20) 40.00 80.00
STATED ODDS 1:14

❑ F1 Dr. No 2.00 5.00
❑ F2 Rosa Klebb 2.00 5.00
❑ F3 Auric Goldfinger 2.00 5.00
❑ F4 Emilio Largo 2.00 5.00
❑ F5 Blofeld 2.00 5.00
❑ F6 Blofeld 2.00 5.00
❑ F7 Blofeld 2.00 5.00
❑ F8 Dr. Kananga 2.00 5.00
❑ F9 Francisco Scaramanga 2.00 5.00
❑ F10 Karl Stromberg 2.00 5.00
❑ F11 Hugo Drax 2.00 5.00
❑ F12 Aris Kristatos 2.00 5.00
❑ F13 Kamal Khan 2.00 5.00
❑ F14 Max Zorin 2.00 5.00
❑ F15 General Koskov 2.00 5.00
❑ F16 Franz Sanchez 2.00 5.00
❑ F17 Alec Trevelyan 2.00 5.00
❑ F18 Elliot Carver 2.00 5.00
❑ F19 Elektra King 2.00 5.00
❑ F20 Gustav Graves 2.00 5.00

2004 The Quotable James Bond The Quotable Theme Songs

COMPLETE SET (10) 8.00 20.00
STATED ODDS 1:10

❑ T1 The World Is Not Enough 1.00 2.50
Goldfinger
❑ T2 A View To A Kill 1.00 2.50
Diamonds Are Forever
❑ T3 The Living Daylights 1.00 2.50
Moonraker
❑ T4 The Man With The Golden Gun 1.00 2.50
For Your Eyes Only
❑ T5 GoldenEye 1.00 2.50
On Her Majesty's Secret Service
❑ T6 Live And Let Die 1.00 2.50
Thunderball
❑ T7 Octopussy 1.00 2.50
The Spy Who Loved Me
❑ T8 Licence to Kill 1.00 2.50
You Only Live Twice
❑ T9 Tomorrow Never Dies 1.00 2.50
Die Another Day
❑ T10 From Russia With Love 1.00 2.50
Dr. No

2004 The Quotable James Bond Villains & Vixens

COMPLETE SET (9)
STATED ODDS 1:40 U.K. PACKS

❑ UK1 Villains & Vixens
❑ UK2 Villains & Vixens
❑ UK3 Villains & Vixens
❑ UK4 Villains & Vixens
❑ UK5 Villains & Vixens
❑ UK6 Villains & Vixens
❑ UK7 Villains & Vixens
❑ UK8 Villains & Vixens
❑ UK9 Villains & Vixens

2004 The Quotable James Bond Vintage Bond

COMPLETE SET (5) 60.00 120.00
STATED ODDS 1:120
STATED PRINT RUN 700 SER. #'d SETS

❑ VB1 Sean Connery 12.50 25.00
❑ VB2 George Lazenby 12.50 25.00
❑ VB3 Roger Moore 12.50 25.00
❑ VB4 Timothy Dalton 12.50 25.00
❑ VB5 Pierce Brosnan 12.50 25.00

2004 The Quotable Star Trek Original Series

COMPLETE SET (110) 4.00 10.00

❑ 1 Captain Kirk .15 .40
❑ 2 Uhura .15 .40
❑ 3 Captain Kirk .15 .40
❑ 4 The Keeper .15 .40
❑ 5 Kara .15 .40
❑ 6 Dr. McCoy .15 .40
❑ 7 Mr. Spock .15 .40
❑ 8 Kirk .15 .40
Spock
❑ 9 Bela Oxmyx .15 .40
❑ 10 Kor .15 .40
❑ 11 Uhura .15 .40
Scotty
❑ 12 Scotty .15 .40
Tomar
❑ 13 Spock .15 .40
❑ 14 Patron .15 .40
❑ 15 Captain Kirk .15 .40
❑ 16 Kirk .15 .40
Kang
❑ 17 Captain Kirk .15 .40
❑ 18 Dr. McCoy .15 .40
❑ 19 Spock .15 .40
❑ 20 Chekov .15 .40
McCoy
❑ 21 Spock .15 .40
❑ 22 Spock .15 .40
❑ 23 McCoy .15 .40
Spock
❑ 24 Dr. McCoy .15 .40
❑ 25 Decker .15 .40
Spock
❑ 26 Dr. McCoy .15 .40
❑ 27 Sarek .15 .40
Amanda
❑ 28 Captain Kirk .15 .40
❑ 29 Dr. McCoy .15 .40
❑ 30 Chekov .15 .40
❑ 31 Captain Kirk .15 .40
❑ 32 Colonel Green .15 .40
❑ 33 Trelane .15 .40
❑ 34 Captain Kirk .15 .40
❑ 35 Scotty .15 .40
Chekov
❑ 36 Dr. McCoy .15 .40
❑ 37 Spock .15 .40
❑ 38 Kirk .15 .40
Spock
❑ 39 Spock .15 .40
McCoy
❑ 40 Sarek .15 .40
❑ 41 Kor .15 .40
❑ 42 McCoy .15 .40
Spock
❑ 43 Spock .15 .40
Kirk
❑ 44 Captain Kirk .15 .40
❑ 45 Kirk .15 .40
Spock
❑ 46 Kirk .15 .40
Spock
❑ 47 Sulu .15 .40
Kirk
❑ 48 Dr. Dehner .15 .40
❑ 49 Spock .15 .40
T'Pau
❑ 50 Spock .15 .40
❑ 51 Captain Kirk .15 .40
❑ 52 Mirror Marlena .15 .40
❑ 53 Captain Kirk .15 .40
❑ 54 Dr. McCoy .15 .40
❑ 55 Chekov .15 .40
Kirk
❑ 56 Captain Kirk .15 .40
❑ 57 Nomad .15 .40
Kirk
❑ 58 Captain Kirk .15 .40
❑ 59 Korax .15 .40
❑ 60 Spock .15 .40
❑ 61 Spock .15 .40
❑ 62 McCoy .15 .40
Spock
❑ 63 Scotty .15 .40
❑ 64 Sarek .15 .40
❑ 65 Captain Kirk .15 .40
❑ 66 Barris .15 .40
Kirk/Darvin
❑ 67 Kang .15 .40
❑ 68 Spock .15 .40
❑ 69 Captain Kirk .15 .40
❑ 70 The Keeper .15 .40
❑ 71 Gary Mitchell .15 .40
❑ 72 Captain Kirk .15 .40
❑ 73 Dr. McCoy .15 .40
❑ 74 Spock .15 .40
❑ 75 Walsh .15 .40
Kirk
❑ 76 Kirk .15 .40
Spock
❑ 77 Dr. McCoy .15 .40
❑ 78 Captain Kirk .15 .40
❑ 79 Abraham Lincoln .15 .40
❑ 80 Khan .15 .40
❑ 81 Kirk .15 .40
Spock
❑ 82 Captain Kirk .15 .40
❑ 83 Dr. McCoy .15 .40
❑ 84 Kirk .15 .40
Chekov/Spock
❑ 85 Captain Kirk .15 .40
❑ 86 Dr. McCoy .15 .40
❑ 87 Spock .15 .40
❑ 88 Captain Kirk .15 .40
❑ 89 Spock .15 .40
❑ 90 Mudd .15 .40
Kirk
❑ 91 Chekov .15 .40
❑ 92 Captain Kirk .15 .40
❑ 93 McCoy .15 .40
Spock
❑ 94 Captain Kirk .15 .40
❑ 95 Kirk .15 .40
Kor
❑ 96 Captain Kirk .15 .40
❑ 97 Romulan .15 .40
Spock
❑ 98 Captain Kirk .15 .40
❑ 99 Spock .15 .40
❑ 100 Spock .15 .40
McCoy
❑ 101 Captain Kirk .15 .40
❑ 102 Scotty .15 .40
❑ 103 Spock .15 .40
Kirk
❑ 104 Oxmyx .15 .40
Spock
❑ 105 Spock .15 .40
❑ 106 Captain Kirk .15 .40
❑ 107 McCoy .15 .40
Spock
❑ 108 Kirk .15 .40
Spock
❑ 109 Dr. McCoy .15 .40
❑ 110 Dr. McCoy .15 .40

2004 The Quotable Star Trek Original Series Animated Series

COMPLETE SET (18) 8.00 20.00
STATED ODDS 1:5

❑ Q1 Captain Kirk .50 1.25
❑ Q2 Spock .50 1.25
❑ Q3 Scotty .50 1.25
❑ Q4 Sulu .50 1.25
Kirk
❑ Q5 Kirk .50 1.25
Scotty
❑ Q6 McCoy .50 1.25
Spock
❑ Q7 Kirk .50 1.25
McCoy
❑ Q8 Dr. McCoy .50 1.25
❑ Q9 Spock .50 1.25
❑ Q10 Kirk .50 1.25
Spock/Chapel
❑ Q11 McCoy .50 1.25
Spock
❑ Q12 Spock .50 1.25
❑ Q13 Dr. McCoy .50 1.25
❑ Q14 Captain Kirk .50 1.25
❑ Q15 Commodore April .50 1.25
❑ Q16 Spock .50 1.25
Thelin
❑ Q17 Captain Kirk .50 1.25
❑ Q18 McCoy .50 1.25
Spock

2004 The Quotable Star Trek Original Series Autographs

STATED ODDS 1:20
L (LIMITED): 300-500 COPIES

❑ A86 Bruce Mars 12.00 25.00
❑ A87 Sally Kellerman L 60.00 120.00
❑ A88 Patrick Horgan 12.00 25.00

❑ A89 Morgan Woodward 15.00 30.00
❑ A90 Don Marshall 12.00 25.00
❑ A91 Sean Kenney 12.00 25.00
❑ A92 Harry Landers 12.00 25.00
❑ A93 Phyllis Douglas 15.00 30.00
❑ A94 Tanya Lemani 15.00 30.00
❑ A95 Sarah Marshall 12.00 25.00
❑ A96 Peter Marko 12.00 25.00
❑ A97 Mary-Linda Rapelye 12.00 25.00
❑ A98 Stephen Mines 12.00 25.00
❑ A99 Julie Newmar L 75.00 150.00
❑ A100 Lois Jewell 15.00 30.00
❑ A101 Eddie Paskey 12.00 25.00
❑ A102 Gary Walberg 12.00 25.00
❑ A103 Charles Dierkop 12.00 25.00
❑ A105 Lawrence Montaigne 12.00 25.00

2004 The Quotable Star Trek Original Series Comic Books

COMPLETE SET (9) 15.00 40.00
STATED ODDS 1:10

❑ GK1 Captain Kirk 2.00 5.00
The Planet of No Return
❑ GK2 Spock 2.00 5.00
Execution Asteroid
❑ GK3 Captain Kirk 2.00 5.00
Invasion of the City Builders
❑ GK4 Captain Kirk 2.00 5.00
The Peril of Planet Quick Change
❑ GK5 Spock 2.00 5.00
The Ghost Planet
❑ GK6 Captain Kirk 2.00 5.00
When Planets Collide
❑ GK7 Captain Kirk 2.00 5.00
The Voodoo Planet
❑ GK8 Captain Kirk 2.00 5.00
The Youth Trap
❑ GK9 Captain Kirk 2.00 5.00
The Legacy of Lazarus

2004 The Quotable Star Trek Original Series From The Archives Costumes

C1 STATED ODDS ONE PER U.S. CASE
C2 STATED ODDS ONE PER COLLECTOR'S ALBUM
C3 STATED ODDS ONE PER INTERNATIONAL CASE

❑ C1 Captain Kirk/ (issued as US case topper)
❑ C2 Scotty/ (issued in collectors album)
❑ C3 Yeoman Rand/ (issued as UK case topper)

2004 The Quotable Star Trek Original Series Quotable Autographs

STATED ODDS 1:20
DQA1 STATED ODDS ONE PER MULTI CASE PURCHASE
L (LIMITED): 300-500 COPIES
VL (VERY LIMITED): 200-300 COPIES

❑ QA1A William Shatner I'm a Soldier L 250.00 350.00
❑ QA1B William Shatner Only a Fool L 250.00 350.00
❑ QA1C William Shatner Space L 300.00 400.00
❑ QA2A Leonard Nimoy Fascinating VL 250.00 350.00
❑ QA2B Leonard Nimoy Live Long VL 250.00 350.00
❑ QA3A George Takei May the Great Bird L 40.00 80.00
❑ QA3B George Takei Phasers Locked L 40.00 80.00
❑ QA4A Walter Koenig Cossackel L 40.00 80.00
❑ QA4B Walter Koenig Invented By L 40.00 80.00
❑ QA5 Nichelle Nichols L 30.00 60.00
❑ QA6 Majel Barrett L 40.00 80.00
❑ QA7A James Doohan I Can't Change L 100.00 175.00
❑ QA7B James Doohan The Haggie L 100.00 175.00
❑ DQA1 Sally Kelleman 50.00 100.00
Gary Lockwood/ (issued as multi-case incentive)
❑ DQA2 Lawrence Montaigne 12.00 30.00
Arlene Martel

2004 The Quotable Star Trek Original Series Starfleet's Finest

COMPLETE SET (9) 200.00 400.00
STATED ODDS 1:120
STATED PRINT RUN 399 SER. #'d SETS

❑ F1 Captain Kirk 20.00 50.00
❑ F2 Spock 20.00 50.00
❑ F3 Dr. McCoy 20.00 50.00
❑ F4 Scotty 20.00 50.00
❑ F5 Sulu 20.00 50.00
❑ F6 Uhura 20.00 50.00
❑ F7 Chekov 20.00 50.00
❑ F8 Nurse Chapel 20.00 50.00
❑ F9 Yeoman Rand 20.00 50.00

2004 The Quotable Star Trek Original Series The Captain's Women

COMPLETE SET (6) 40.00 80.00
STATED ODDS 1:40 INTERNATIONAL PACKS

❑ W1 Yeoman Rand 6.00 15.00
❑ W2 Marlena Moreau 6.00 15.00
❑ W3 Lenore Karidian 6.00 15.00
❑ W4 Edith Keeler 6.00 15.00
❑ W5 Shahna 6.00 15.00
❑ W6 Andrea 6.00 15.00

2004 The Quotable Star Trek Original Series The Final Frontier

COMPLETE SET (9) 4.00 10.00
STATED ODDS 1:5

❑ ST1 The Final Frontier .50 1.25
❑ ST2 The Final Frontier .50 1.25
❑ ST3 The Final Frontier .50 1.25
❑ ST4 The Final Frontier .50 1.25
❑ ST5 The Final Frontier .50 1.25
❑ ST6 The Final Frontier .50 1.25
❑ ST7 The Final Frontier .50 1.25
❑ ST8 The Final Frontier .50 1.25
❑ ST9 The Final Frontier .50 1.25

2004 The Quotable Star Trek Original Series TV Guide Covers

COMPLETE SET (7) 30.00 60.00
STATED ODDS 1:40 U.S. PACKS

❑ TV1 Captain Kirk 4.00 10.00
❑ TV2 Spock 4.00 10.00
❑ TV3 Dr. McCoy 4.00 10.00
❑ TV4 Chekov 4.00 10.00
❑ TV5 Scotty 4.00 10.00
❑ TV6 Sulu 4.00 10.00
❑ TV7 Uhura 4.00 10.00

2004 Scooby Doo 2 Monsters Unleashed

COMPLETE SET (72) 3.00 8.00

❑ 1 Title Card .08 .25
❑ 2 Fred Jones .08 .25
❑ 3 Daphne Blake .08 .25
❑ 4 Velma Dinkley .08 .25
❑ 5 Shaggy Rogers .08 .25
❑ 6 Scooby Doo .08 .25
❑ 7 Patrick Wisely .08 .25
❑ 8 Heather Jasper-Howe .08 .25
❑ 9 Dr. Jonathan Jacobo .08 .25
❑ 10 Old Man Wickles .08 .25
❑ 11 Ned .08 .25
❑ 12 Big Brovaz .08 .25
❑ 13 Evil Masked Figure .08 .25
❑ 14 Captain Cutler .08 .25
❑ 15 Black Knight Ghost .08 .25
❑ 16 Pterodactyl Ghost .08 .25
❑ 17 Zombie .08 .25
❑ 18 Miner 49er .08 .25
❑ 19 The Ghost Clown .08 .25
❑ 20 Headless Horseman .08 .25
❑ 21 Giggling Green Ghost .08 .25
❑ 22 10000 Volt Ghost .08 .25
❑ 23 Cotton Candy Glob .08 .25
❑ 24 Skeleton Man .08 .25
❑ 25 The Creeper .08 .25
❑ 26 Chickenstein .08 .25
❑ 27 The Ghost Of Redbeard .08 .25
❑ 28 Coolsville Celebs .08 .25
❑ 29 The Stage Is Set .08 .25
❑ 30 Pterodactyl Attack .08 .25
❑ 31 Follow The Masters .08 .25
❑ 32 Jacobo's Evil Past .08 .25
❑ 33 Mysterious Mansion .08 .25
❑ 34 Monster Making 101 .08 .25
❑ 35 Knight Of The Roundtables .08 .25
❑ 36 A Randamonium Sample .08 .25
❑ 37 Hottie .08 .25
❑ 38 Who's The Fool .08 .25
❑ 39 Get The Pickleaculas .08 .25
❑ 40 Alley Oops .08 .25
❑ 41 The Wrong Guy .08 .25
❑ 42 It's Alive .08 .25
❑ 43 Time To Run .08 .25
❑ 44 Surrender Or Else .08 .25
❑ 45 The Good Ol Days .08 .25
❑ 46 Joust Plain Creepy .08 .25
❑ 47 Out Of The Frying Pan .08 .25
❑ 48 Velma's Heroes .08 .25
❑ 49 Flaws And Sensitivities .08 .25
❑ 50 Unexpected Meetings .08 .25
❑ 51 Ghosts Go Boom .08 .25
❑ 52 Surrounded .08 .25
❑ 53 Who Dunnit .08 .25
❑ 54 Victory Pah-Tay .08 .25
❑ 55 Creepy Cookbook .08 .25
❑ 56 Control (Panel) Freaks .08 .25
❑ 57 Scooby Clues .08 .25
❑ 58 Sign Of Danger .08 .25
❑ 59 Gesundheit .08 .25
❑ 60 Ahoy, Coolsville .08 .25
❑ 61 Picture This .08 .25
❑ 62 Blow By Blow .08 .25
❑ 63 Gadgets To Go .08 .25
❑ 64 Mystery, Inc. Headquarters .08 .25
❑ 65 Mystery, Inc. Clubhouse .08 .25
❑ 66 The Coolsonian Criminology Museum .08 .25
❑ 67 Wickles Mansion .08 .25
❑ 68 Jacobo's Lair .08 .25
❑ 69 The Silver Mines .08 .25
❑ 70 Jacobo Shrine .08 .25
❑ 71 The Faux Ghost .08 .25
❑ 72 Checklist .08 .25

2004 Scooby Doo 2 Monsters Unleashed Autographs

STATED ODDS 1:36
CARD A3 WAS NOT ISSUED

❑ A1 Matthew Lillard 15.00 30.00
❑ A2 Linda Cardellini 30.00 60.00
❑ A4 Alicia Silverstone 40.00 80.00
❑ A5 Pat O'Brien 4.00 10.00
❑ A6 Scott McNeil 4.00 10.00
❑ A7 C. Ernst Harth 4.00 10.00
❑ A8 Kevin Durand 4.00 10.00

2004 Scooby Doo 2 Monsters Unleashed Box Loaders

COMPLETE SET (3) 6.00 15.00
STATED ODDS ONE PER BOX
CL1 STATED ODDS ONE PER CASE

❑ BL1 Peek-A-Boo 1.50 4.00
❑ BL2 Buff-O-Rama 1.50 4.00
❑ BL3 Horrific Headlines 1.50 4.00
❑ CL1 Yo Bro 4.00 10.00

2004 Scooby Doo 2 Monsters Unleashed Mystery, Inc.

COMPLETE SET (6) 12.50 30.00
STATED ODDS 1:17

❑ MI1 Mystery, Inc. 3.00 8.00
❑ MI2 Mystery, Inc. 3.00 8.00
❑ MI3 Mystery, Inc. 3.00 8.00
❑ MI4 Mystery, Inc. 3.00 8.00
❑ MI5 Mystery, Inc. 3.00 8.00
❑ MI6 Mystery, Inc. 3.00 8.00

2004 Scooby Doo 2 Monsters Unleashed Pieceworks

STATED ODDS 1:36

❑ PW1 Fred's Jacket 5.00 12.00
❑ PW2 Fred's T-Shirt 5.00 12.00
❑ PW3 Fred's Jeans 5.00 12.00
❑ PW4 Shaggy's Pants 5.00 12.00
❑ PW5 Shaggy's Jacket 5.00 12.00
❑ PW6 Shaggy's Shirt 5.00 12.00
❑ PW7 Velma's Top 5.00 12.00
❑ PW8 Velma's Sweater 5.00 12.00
❑ PW9 Daphne's Jacket 7.50 20.00
❑ PW10 Daphne's Pants 7.50 20.00
❑ PW11 Daphne's Top 7.50 20.00
❑ PW12 Velma's Jumpsuit 5.00 12.00

2004 Scooby Doo 2 Monsters Unleashed Promos

COMPLETE SET (4) 3.00 8.00

❑ P1 Group Shot 1.00 2.50
Distributors
❑ P2 Group Shot 1.00 2.50
Non Sport Update
❑ P3 Group Shot 1.00 2.50
UK Distribution
❑ PI Group Shot 1.00 2.50
Free Card Offer

2004 Scooby Doo 2 Monsters Unleashed Puzzle

COMPLETE SET (9) 2.50 6.00
STATED ODDS 1:11

❑ MU1 Monsters Unleashed .40 1.00
❑ MU2 Monsters Unleashed .40 1.00
❑ MU3 Monsters Unleashed .40 1.00
❑ MU4 Monsters Unleashed .40 1.00
❑ MU5 Monsters Unleashed .40 1.00
❑ MU6 Monsters Unleashed .40 1.00
❑ MU7 Monsters Unleashed .40 1.00
❑ MU8 Monsters Unleashed .40 1.00
❑ MU9 Monsters Unleashed .40 1.00

2004 Six Feet Under Seasons One and Two

COMPLETE SET (81) 4.00 10.00

❑ 1 Six Feet Under Checklist .10 .30
❑ 2 Six Feet Under Checklist .10 .30
❑ 3 Six Feet Under Checklist .10 .30
❑ 4 Six Feet Under (Pilot) .10 .30
❑ 5 Six Feet Under (Pilot) .10 .30
❑ 6 Six Feet Under (Pilot) .10 .30
❑ 7 The Will .10 .30
❑ 8 The Will .10 .30
❑ 9 The Will .10 .30
❑ 10 The Foot .10 .30
❑ 11 The Foot .10 .30
❑ 12 The Foot .10 .30
❑ 13 Familia .10 .30
❑ 14 Familia .10 .30
❑ 15 Familia .10 .30
❑ 16 An Open Book .10 .30
❑ 17 An Open Book .10 .30
❑ 18 An Open Book .10 .30
❑ 19 The Room .10 .30
❑ 20 The Room .10 .30
❑ 21 The Room .10 .30
❑ 22 Brotherhood .10 .30
❑ 23 Brotherhood .10 .30
❑ 24 Brotherhood .10 .30
❑ 25 Crossroads .10 .30
❑ 26 Crossroads .10 .30
❑ 27 Crossroads .10 .30
❑ 28 Life's Too Short .10 .30
❑ 29 Life's Too Short .10 .30
❑ 30 Life's Too Short .10 .30
❑ 31 The New Person .10 .30
❑ 32 The New Person .10 .30
❑ 33 The New Person .10 .30
❑ 34 The Trip .10 .30
❑ 35 The Trip .10 .30
❑ 36 The Trip .10 .30
❑ 37 A Private Life .10 .30
❑ 38 A Private Life .10 .30
❑ 39 A Private Life .10 .30
❑ 40 Knock, Knock .10 .30
❑ 41 Knock, Knock .10 .30
❑ 42 Knock, Knock .10 .30
❑ 43 In The Game .10 .30
❑ 44 In The Game .10 .30
❑ 45 In The Game .10 .30
❑ 46 Out, Out Brief Candle .10 .30
❑ 47 Out, Out Brief Candle .10 .30
❑ 48 Out, Out Brief Candle .10 .30
❑ 49 The Plan .10 .30
❑ 50 The Plan .10 .30
❑ 51 The Plan .10 .30
❑ 52 Driving Mr. Mossback .10 .30
❑ 53 Driving Mr. Mossback .10 .30
❑ 54 Driving Mr. Mossback .10 .30
❑ 55 The Invisible Woman .10 .30
❑ 56 The Invisible Woman .10 .30
❑ 57 The Invisible Woman .10 .30
❑ 58 In Place of Anger .10 .30
❑ 59 In Place of Anger .10 .30
❑ 60 In Place of Anger .10 .30
❑ 61 Back to the Garden .10 .30
❑ 62 Back to the Garden .10 .30
❑ 63 Back to the Garden .10 .30
❑ 64 It's the Most Wonderful Time of the Year .10 .30
❑ 65 It's the Most Wonderful Time of the Year .10 .30
❑ 66 It's the Most Wonderful Time of the Year .10 .30
❑ 67 Someone Else's Eyes .10 .30
❑ 68 Someone Else's Eyes .10 .30
❑ 69 Someone Else's Eyes .10 .30
❑ 70 The Secret .10 .30
❑ 71 The Secret .10 .30
❑ 72 The Secret .10 .30
❑ 73 The Liar and the Whore .10 .30
❑ 74 The Liar and the Whore .10 .30
❑ 75 The Liar and the Whore .10 .30
❑ 76 I'll Take You .10 .30
❑ 77 I'll Take You .10 .30
❑ 78 I'll Take You .10 .30
❑ 79 The Last Time .10 .30
❑ 80 The Last Time .10 .30
❑ 81 The Last Time .10 .30

2004 Six Feet Under Seasons One and Two Autographs

STATED ODDS THREE PER BOX
BALL AUTO ISSUED AS CASE TOPPER
BLACK AUTO ISSUED IN COLLECTORS ALBUM
DOUGLAS AUTO ISSUED AS MULTI-CASE INCENTIVE
L (LIMITED): 300-500 COPIES

❑ 1 Alan Ball/(Series Creator 20.00 40.00
Producer)/issued as case topper)
❑ 2 Marina Black/(issued as album exclusive) 6.00 15.00
❑ 3 Joel Brooks 6.00 15.00
❑ 4 Joanna Cassidy L 20.00 40.00
❑ 5 Illeana Douglas/(issued as multi-case incentive) 15.00 30.00
❑ 6 Michael C. Hall L 60.00 120.00
❑ 7 Eddie Jemison L 6.00 15.00
❑ 8 Peter Krause L 40.00 80.00
❑ 9 Tim Maculan 6.00 15.00
❑ 10 Nicki Micheaux 6.00 15.00
❑ 11 David Norona 6.00 15.00
❑ 12 Ed O'Ross 6.00 15.00
❑ 13 Aysia Polk 6.00 15.00
❑ 14 Rusty Schwimmer 6.00 15.00
❑ 15 Jessica Stone 6.00 15.00
❑ 16 Beverly Todd 6.00 15.00
❑ 17 Julie White L 6.00 15.00

2004 Six Feet Under Seasons One and Two Promos

COMPLETE SET (3) 2.00 5.00

❑ P1 Summer 2004 1.00 2.50
❑ P2 The Room 1.00 2.50
❑ P3 Brotherhood 1.00 2.50

2004 Six Feet Under Seasons One and Two The Opening Montage

COMPLETE SET (9) 7.50 20.00
STATED ODDS 1:14

❑ M1 The Opening Montage 1.25 3.00
❑ M2 The Opening Montage 1.25 3.00
❑ M3 The Opening Montage 1.25 3.00
❑ M4 The Opening Montage 1.25 3.00
❑ M5 The Opening Montage 1.25 3.00
❑ M6 The Opening Montage 1.25 3.00
❑ M7 The Opening Montage 1.25 3.00
❑ M8 The Opening Montage 1.25 3.00
❑ M9 The Opening Montage 1.25 3.00

2004 Six Feet Under Seasons One and Two The Players

COMPLETE SET (9) 7.50 20.00
STATED ODDS (1:14)

❑ PL1 Nate Fisher 1.25 3.00
❑ PL2 David Fisher 1.25 3.00
❑ PL3 Claire Fisher 1.25 3.00
❑ PL4 Ruth Fisher 1.25 3.00
❑ PL5 Brenda Chenowith 1.25 3.00
❑ PL6 Federico Diaz 1.25 3.00
❑ PL7 Keith Charles 1.25 3.00
❑ PL8 Nathaniel Fisher 1.25 3.00
❑ PL9 Billy Chenowith 1.25 3.00

2004 Six Feet Under Seasons One and Two The Relationships

COMPLETE SET (27) 8.00 20.00
STATED ODDS 1:5

❑ R1 Nate Fisher .75 2.00
Brenda Chenowith
❑ R2 Nate Fisher .75 2.00
David Fisher
❑ R3 Nate Fisher .75 2.00
Lisa Kimmel
❑ R4 David Fisher .75 2.00
Keith Charles
❑ R5 David Fisher .75 2.00
Ruth Fisher
❑ R6 David Fisher .75 2.00
Mitzi-Dalton Huntley
❑ R7 Claire Fisher .75 2.00
Ruth Fisher
❑ R8 Claire Fisher .75 2.00
Billy Chenowith
❑ R9 Claire Fisher .75 2.00
Gabriel Dimas
❑ R10 Ruth Fisher .75 2.00
Nikolai
❑ R11 Ruth Fisher .75 2.00
Nathaniel Fisher
❑ R12 Ruth Fisher .75 2.00
Sarah O'Conner
❑ R13 Brenda Chenowith .75 2.00
Billy Chenowith
❑ R14 Brenda Chenowith .75 2.00
Margaret Chenowith
❑ R15 Brenda Chenowith .75 2.00
Melissa
❑ R16 Keith Charles .75 2.00
Taylor
❑ R17 Keith Charles .75 2.00
Karla
❑ R18 Keith Charles .75 2.00
Mr. Charles
❑ R19 Federico Diaz .75 2.00
Nathaniel Fisher
❑ R20 Federico Diaz .75 2.00
Vanessa Diaz
❑ R21 Federico Diaz .75 2.00
Nate Fisher
❑ R22 Billy Chenowith .75 2.00
Nate Fisher
❑ R23 Billy Chenowith .75 2.00
Margaret Chenowith
❑ R24 Billy Chenowith .75 2.00
Bernard Chenowith
❑ R25 Nathaniel Fisher .75 2.00
Nate Fisher
❑ R26 Nathaniel Fisher .75 2.00
David Fisher
❑ R27 Nathaniel Fisher .75 2.00
Claire Fisher

2004 Smallville Season Three

COMPLETE SET (90) 5.00 12.00

❑ 1 Title Card .15 .40
❑ 2 Clark Kent .15 .40
❑ 3 Lex Luthor .15 .40
❑ 4 Jonathan Kent .15 .40
❑ 5 Martha Kent .15 .40
❑ 6 Lana Lang .15 .40
❑ 7 Chloe Sullivan .15 .40
❑ 8 Pete Ross .15 .40
❑ 9 Lionel Luthor .15 .40
❑ 10 The Kowatche Caves .15 .40
❑ 11 Jor-El Gives .15 .40
❑ 12 Jor-El Takes .15 .40
❑ 13 The Heart Of Jor-El .15 .40
❑ 14 The Promise Of Jor-El .15 .40
❑ 15 Naman And Sageeth .15 .40
❑ 16 The Rival .15 .40
❑ 17 The Honey Trap .15 .40
❑ 18 Now You Shall Be Reborn .15 .40
❑ 19 The Hidden Face .15 .40
❑ 20 A Prodigal's Welcome .15 .40
❑ 21 ...Had A Great Fall .15 .40
❑ 22 Total Commitment .15 .40
❑ 23 Electroshock .15 .40
❑ 24 A Devilish Deal .15 .40
❑ 25 Flashbacks .15 .40
❑ 26 Smother Love .15 .40
❑ 27 The Burden Of Enlightenment .15 .40
❑ 28 Bloodlines .15 .40
❑ 29 Blood Price .15 .40
❑ 30 Super Serum .15 .40
❑ 31 Bad Blood .15 .40
❑ 32 In Need Of New Blood .15 .40
❑ 33 Spilled Blood .15 .40
❑ 34 The Bloody End .15 .40
❑ 35 Bloodless Love .15 .40
❑ 36 Red Blood, Gray Bars .15 .40
❑ 37 In Over My Head... .15 .40
❑ 38 Perry White (!!!) .15 .40
❑ 39 W.O.W Update .15 .40
❑ 40 Live On Tape! .15 .40
❑ 41 Taking A Stand .15 .40
❑ 42 Running Scared .15 .40
❑ 43 Big City Kal .15 .40
❑ 44 Imaginary Friend .15 .40
❑ 45 Rescuing Clark .15 .40
❑ 46 Fathers And Son .15 .40
❑ 47 Killer Newlywed .15 .40
❑ 48 Trail Of Blood .15 .40
❑ 49 Fatal Weakness .15 .40
❑ 50 Showdown .15 .40
❑ 51 Nightmare World .15 .40
❑ 52 Dream Escape .15 .40
❑ 53 Bottom Feeder .15 .40
❑ 54 Forcing The Issue .15 .40
❑ 55 A Father's Footsteps .15 .40
❑ 56 Ghost From The Past .15 .40
❑ 57 Mind Games .15 .40
❑ 58 Polar Opposites .15 .40
❑ 59 Don't Wake The Baby .15 .40
❑ 60 Descent Into Madness .15 .40
❑ 61 Blasts From The Past .15 .40
❑ 62 Shocking Ends .15 .40
❑ 63 Super Screamer .15 .40
❑ 64 Fighting Blind .15 .40
❑ 65 Death By E-Mail .15 .40
❑ 66 Fighting Mad .15 .40
❑ 67 Fatal Visions .15 .40
❑ 68 Flash Point .15 .40
❑ 69 Boss Ross .15 .40
❑ 70 Crash And Burn .15 .40
❑ 71 Falling In Love .15 .40
❑ 72 He Loves Me Not .15 .40
❑ 73 Reborn To Die .15 .40
❑ 74 Explosive Temper .15 .40
❑ 75 A Timely Call .15 .40
❑ 76 Last Call .15 .40
❑ 77 Turning The Key .15 .40
❑ 78 I Am Waiting .15 .40
❑ 79 The Truth Is Out There .15 .40
❑ 80 The Truth Hurts .15 .40
❑ 81 Down Memory Lane .15 .40
❑ 82 Repressed Truths .15 .40
❑ 83 Heroes And Villains .15 .40
❑ 84 Touched By Fate .15 .40
❑ 85 Lonely Girl .15 .40
❑ 86 A Loyal Friend .15 .40
❑ 87 Kin .15 .40
❑ 88 Multiple Division .15 .40
❑ 89 The Lion In Winter .15 .40
❑ 90 Checklist .15 .40

2004 Smallville Season Three Autographs

STATED ODDS 1:36

❑ A17 Camille Mitchell 8.00 20.00
❑ A18 Michael McKean 8.00 20.00
❑ A19 William B. Davis 8.00 20.00
❑ A20 Jesse Metcalfe 8.00 20.00
❑ A21 Jonathan Taylor Thomas 8.00 20.00
❑ A22 Felecia Bell-Schafer 8.00 20.00
❑ A23 Neil Flynn 8.00 20.00
❑ A24 Adrianne Palicki 15.00 40.00
❑ A25 Teryl Rothery 8.00 20.00

2004 Smallville Season Three Box Loaders

❑ BL1 Jor-El Calls 2.00 5.00
❑ BL2 The Ultimate Sacrifice 2.00 5.00
❑ BL3 Bad to the Bone 2.00 5.00
❑ CL1 The Last Son of Krypton 4.00 10.00
CASE INSERT

2004 Smallville Season Three Departures

COMPLETE SET (6) 8.00 20.00
STATED ODDS 1:17

❑ D1 A Sign of Change 1.50 4.00
❑ D2 Sting of the Viper 1.50 4.00
❑ D3 Adieu, Clark. Bonjour, Paris. 1.50 4.00
❑ D4 Breath of the Dragon 1.50 4.00
❑ D5 Opting Out 1.50 4.00
❑ D6 Bait 1.50 4.00

2004 Smallville Season Three Generations

COMPLETE SET (9) 10.00 25.00
STATED ODDS 1:11

❑ G1 Generations 1.25 3.00
❑ G2 Generations 1.25 3.00
❑ G3 Generations 1.25 3.00
❑ G4 Generations 1.25 3.00
❑ G5 Generations 1.25 3.00
❑ G6 Generations 1.25 3.00
❑ G7 Generations 1.25 3.00
❑ G8 Generations 1.25 3.00
❑ G9 Generations 1.25 3.00

2004 Smallville Season Three Pieceworks

STATED ODDS 1:36

❑ PW1 Tom Welling Shirt 12.00 30.00
❑ PW2 Kristin Kreuk Sweater 12.00 30.00
❑ PW3 Allison-Mack Dress 12.00 30.00
❑ PW4 Sam Jones III Shirt 8.00 20.00
❑ PW5 Annette O'Toole Blouse 8.00 20.00
❑ PW6 John Schneider Shirt 8.00 20.00
❑ PW7 Michael Rosenbaum Shirt 8.00 20.00

2004 Stargate SG-1 Season Six

COMPLETE SET (72) 4.00 10.00

❑ 1 Title Card .10 .30
❑ 2 Title Card .10 .30
❑ 3 Title Card .10 .30
❑ 4 Redemption Part 1 .10 .30
❑ 5 Redemption Part 1 .10 .30
❑ 6 Redemption Part 1 .10 .30
❑ 7 Redemption Part 2 .10 .30
❑ 8 Redemption Part 2 .10 .30
❑ 9 Redemption Part 2 .10 .30
❑ 10 Descent .10 .30
❑ 11 Descent .10 .30
❑ 12 Descent .10 .30
❑ 13 Frozen .10 .30
❑ 14 Frozen .10 .30
❑ 15 Frozen .10 .30
❑ 16 Nightwalkers .10 .30
❑ 17 Nightwalkers .10 .30
❑ 18 Nightwalkers .10 .30
❑ 19 Abyss .10 .30
❑ 20 Abyss .10 .30
❑ 21 Abyss .10 .30

22 Shadow Play .10 .30
23 Shadow Play .10 .30
24 Shadow Play .10 .30
25 The Other Guys .10 .30
26 The Other Guys .10 .30
27 The Other Guys .10 .30
28 Allegiance .10 .30
29 Allegiance .10 .30
30 Allegiance .10 .30
31 Cure .10 .30
32 Cure .10 .30
33 Cure .10 .30
34 Prometheus .10 .30
35 Prometheus .10 .30
36 Prometheus .10 .30
37 Unnatural Selection .10 .30
38 Unnatural Selection .10 .30
39 Unnatural Selection .10 .30
40 Sight Unseen .10 .30
41 Sight Unseen .10 .30
42 Sight Unseen .10 .30
43 Smoke And Mirrors .10 .30
44 Smoke And Mirrors .10 .30
45 Smoke And Mirrors .10 .30
46 Paradise Lost .10 .30
47 Paradise Lost .10 .30
48 Paradise Lost .10 .30
49 Metamorphosis .10 .30
50 Metamorphosis .10 .30
51 Metamorphosis .10 .30
52 Disclosure .10 .30
53 Disclosure .10 .30
54 Disclosure .10 .30
55 Forsaken .10 .30
56 Forsaken .10 .30
57 Forsaken .10 .30
58 The Changeling .10 .30
59 The Changeling .10 .30
60 The Changeling .10 .30
61 Memento .10 .30
62 Memento .10 .30
63 Memento .10 .30
64 Prophecy .10 .30
65 Prophecy .10 .30
66 Prophecy .10 .30
67 Full Circle .10 .30
68 Full Circle .10 .30
69 Full Circle .10 .30
70 Checklist 1 .10 .30
71 Checklist 2 .10 .30
72 Checklist 3 .10 .30

2004 Stargate SG-1 Season Six Autographs

STATED ODDS TWO PER BOX
A33 ISSUED AS CASE TOPPER
DA1 ISSUED AS MULTI-CASE INCENTIVE
L (LIMITED): 300-500 COPIES

A26 Corin Nemec 15.00 40.00
A27 Enid-Raye Adams 8.00 20.00
A28 Ronny Cox 8.00 20.00
A29 Garry Chalk 8.00 20.00
A30 Bruce Harwood 8.00 20.00
A31 John Billingsley 15.00 40.00
A32 Peter Stebbings 8.00 20.00
A33 Musetta Vander/ (issued as case topper) 12.00 30.00
A34 Cliff Simon 8.00 20.00
A35 Obi Ndefo 8.00 20.00
A36 Ian Buchanan 8.00 20.00
A37 Amanda Tapping L 40.00 80.00
A38 Michael Shanks L 40.00 80.00
A39 Jacqueline Samuda 8.00 20.00
A40 Brad Wright L 15.00 40.00
A41 Ona Grauer 8.00 20.00
DA1 Michael Shanks
Amanda Tapping/ (issued as multi-case incentive)

2004 Stargate SG-1 Season Six Behind The Scenes

COMPLETE SET (9) 8.00 20.00
STATED ODDS 1:5

B1 Children of the Gods 1.00 2.50
B2 Solitudes 1.00 2.50
B3 One False Step 1.00 2.50
B4 Window of Opportunity 1.00 2.50
B5 Wormhole X-Treme 1.00 2.50
B6 Prodigy 1.00 2.50
B7 Descent 1.00 2.50
B8 2010 1.00 2.50
B9 Urgo 1.00 2.50

2004 Stargate SG-1 Season Six Costumes

STATED ODDS 1:120
C21 ISSUED IN COLLECTORS ALBUM

C17 Major Samantha Carter 10.00 25.00
C18 Jonas Quinn 10.00 25.00
C19 Dr. Frasier 10.00 25.00
C20 General Hammond 10.00 25.00
C21 Colonel O'Neill/ (issued in collectors album) 10.00 25.00

2004 Stargate SG-1 Season Six In the Line of Duty Colonel O'Neill

COMPLETE SET (9) 15.00 40.00
STATED ODDS 1:10 US PACKS

CO1 Colonel Jack O'Neill 2.00 5.00
CO2 Colonel Jack O'Neill 2.00 5.00
CO3 Colonel Jack O'Neill 2.00 5.00
CO4 Colonel Jack O'Neill 2.00 5.00
CO5 Colonel Jack O'Neill 2.00 5.00
CO6 Colonel Jack O'Neill 2.00 5.00
CO7 Colonel Jack O'Neill 2.00 5.00
CO8 Colonel Jack O'Neill 2.00 5.00
CO9 Colonel Jack O'Neill 2.00 5.00

2004 Stargate SG-1 Season Six In the Line of Duty Major Carter

COMPLETE SET (9) 25.00 60.00
STATED ODDS 1:10 UK PACKS

MC1 Major Samantha Carter 3.00 8.00
MC2 Major Samantha Carter 3.00 8.00
MC3 Major Samantha Carter 3.00 8.00
MC4 Major Samantha Carter 3.00 8.00
MC5 Major Samantha Carter 3.00 8.00
MC6 Major Samantha Carter 3.00 8.00
MC7 Major Samantha Carter 3.00 8.00
MC8 Major Samantha Carter 3.00 8.00
MC9 Major Samantha Carter 3.00 8.00

2004 Stargate SG-1 Season Six Stargate Gallery

COMPLETE SET (6) 50.00 100.00
STATED ODDS 1:40

G1 Colonel Jack O'Neill 8.00 20.00
G2 Major Samantha Carter 8.00 20.00
G3 Dr. Daniel Jackson 8.00 20.00
G4 Teal'c 8.00 20.00
G5 Jonas Quinn 8.00 20.00
G6 General Hammond 8.00 20.00

2004 Xena Warrior Princess Art and Images

COMPLETE SET (63) 4.00 10.00

1 Xena .10 .30
2 Xena .10 .30
3 Xena .10 .30
4 Xena .10 .30
5 Xena .10 .30
6 Xena .10 .30
7 Xena .10 .30
8 Xena .10 .30
9 Xena .10 .30
10 Gabrielle .10 .30
11 Gabrielle .10 .30
12 Gabrielle .10 .30
13 Gabrielle .10 .30
14 Gabrielle .10 .30
15 Gabrielle .10 .30
16 Gabrielle .10 .30
17 Gabrielle .10 .30
18 Gabrielle .10 .30
19 Forever Friends .10 .30
20 Forever Friends .10 .30
21 Forever Friends .10 .30
22 Forever Friends .10 .30
23 Forever Friends .10 .30
24 Forever Friends .10 .30
25 Forever Friends .10 .30
26 Forever Friends .10 .30
27 Forever Friends .10 .30
28 Eve .10 .30
29 Valaria .10 .30
30 Ephiny .10 .30
31 Amarice .10 .30
32 Athena .10 .30
33 Callisto .10 .30
34 Waltraute .10 .30
35 Najara .10 .30
36 Hera .10 .30
37 Joxer .10 .30
38 Hercules .10 .30
39 Borias .10 .30
40 Ares .10 .30
41 Caesar .10 .30
42 Autolycus .10 .30
43 Virgil .10 .30
44 Ioalus .10 .30
45 Draco .10 .30
46 Battle On Xena .10 .30
47 Battle On Xena .10 .30
48 Battle On Xena .10 .30
49 Battle On Xena .10 .30
50 Battle On Xena .10 .30
51 Battle On Xena .10 .30
52 Battle On Xena .10 .30
53 Battle On Xena .10 .30
54 Battle On Xena .10 .30
55 Battle On Xena .10 .30
56 Battle On Xena .10 .30
57 Battle On Xena .10 .30
58 Battle On Xena .10 .30
59 Battle On Xena .10 .30
60 Battle On Xena .10 .30
61 Battle On Xena .10 .30
62 Battle On Xena .10 .30
63 Battle On Xena .10 .30

2004 Xena Warrior Princess Art and Images Autographs

A54 ISSUED IN COLLECTORS ALBUM
DA7 ISSUED AS MULTI-CASE INCENTIVE
XA1 ISSUED AS N.AMER. CASE TOPPER
XA2 ISSUED AS INT'L CASE TOPPER

A54 Alison Wall/ (issued in collectors album) 6.00 15.00
DA7 Ted Raimi 50.00 100.00
Renee O'Connor
XA1 Lucy Lawless/ (issued as North American case topper) 40.00 80.00
XA2 Renee O'Connor/ (issued as Int'l case topper) 30.00 60.00

2004 Xena Warrior Princess Art and Images Douglas Shuler ArtiFEX

COMPLETE SET (9) 6.00 15.00
STATED ODDS 1:10 INT'L PACKS

IA1 Salmoneus 1.25 3.00
IA2 Ares 1.25 3.00
IA3 Athena 1.25 3.00
IA4 Joxer 1.25 3.00
IA5 Xena 1.25 3.00
IA6 Gabrielle 1.25 3.00
IA7 Hercules 1.25 3.00
IA8 Callisto 1.25 3.00
IA9 Ioalus 1.25 3.00

2004 Xena Warrior Princess Art and Images Portraits of a Warrior

COMPLETE SET (18) 15.00 40.00
STATED ODDS 1:4

PP1 Adventures In The Sin Trade 1.00 2.50
PP2 The Debt 1.00 2.50
PP3 The Debt 1.00 2.50
PP4 Destiny 1.00 2.50
PP5 A Friend In Need 1.00 2.50
PP6 A Friend In Need 1.00 2.50
PP7 Legacy 1.00 2.50
PP8 Ares 1.00 2.50
PP9 Doctor Janice Covington 1.00 2.50
PP10 Gabrielle 1.00 2.50
PP11 When Fates Collide 1.00 2.50
PP12 When Fates Collide 1.00 2.50
PP13 Together 1.00 2.50
PP14 Many Happy Returns 1.00 2.50
PP15 Cleopatra 1.00 2.50
PP16 The Tempter 1.00 2.50
PP17 Sacrifice 1.00 2.50
PP18 One Against An Army 1.00 2.50

2004 Xena Warrior Princess Art and Images Rebekah Lynn ArtiFEX

COMPLETE SET (9) 40.00 80.00
STATED ODDS 1:10 N.AMER. PACKS

NA1 Xena 4.00 10.00
NA2 Gabrielle 4.00 10.00
NA3 Xena 4.00 10.00
NA4 Gabrielle 4.00 10.00
NA5 Xena 4.00 10.00
NA6 Xena 4.00 10.00
Argo
NA7 Gabrielle 4.00 10.00
Xena
NA8 Gabrielle 4.00 10.00
Xena/Argo
NA9 Callisto 4.00 10.00

2004 Xena Warrior Princess Art and Images Renee O'Connor ArtiFEX

COMPLETE SET (9) 40.00 80.00
STATED ODDS 1:20

R1 Gabrielle 6.00 15.00
R2 Alti 6.00 15.00
R3 Aphrodite 6.00 15.00
R4 Ares 6.00 15.00
R5 Autolycus 6.00 15.00
R6 Callisto 6.00 15.00
R7 Eli 6.00 15.00
R8 Joxer 6.00 15.00
R9 Xena 6.00 15.00

2004 Xena Warrior Princess Art and Images SketchaFEX

STATED ODDS ONE PER BOX

1 Cris Bolson
2 Joe Corroney
3 John Czop
4 Patrick Hamill
5 Warren Martineck
6 Steven Miller
7 Eduardo Pansica
8 Patricia Parker
9 Sean Pence
10 Emir Ribeiro
11 Scott Rosema

2004 Xena Warrior Princess Art and Images Women and Warriors

COMPLETE SET (5) 100.00 200.00
STATED ODDS 1:90
STATED PRINT RUN 500 SER. #'d SETS

WW1 Xena 15.00 40.00
Ares
WW2 Xena 15.00 40.00
Hercules
WW3 Xena 15.00 40.00
Borias
WW4 Gabrielle 15.00 40.00
Ioalus
WW5 Gabrielle 15.00 40.00
Joxer

2004 Xena Warrior Princess Art and Images Women of Xena

COMPLETE SET (9) 25.00 50.00
STATED ODDS 1:20

WX1 Xena 2.50 6.00
WX2 Gabrielle 2.50 6.00
WX3 Najara 2.50 6.00
WX4 Cyane 2.50 6.00
WX5 Athena 2.50 6.00
WX6 Livia 2.50 6.00
WX7 Callisto 2.50 6.00
WX8 Amarice 2.50 6.00
WX9 Ephiny 2.50 6.00

2004 Xena Warrior Princess Art and Images Xena Gallery

COMPLETE SET (6) 20.00 40.00
STATED ODDS 1:30

GX1 Xena 3.00 8.00
GX2 Xena 3.00 8.00
GX3 Xena 3.00 8.00
GX4 Xena 3.00 8.00
GX5 Xena 3.00 8.00
GX6 Xena 3.00 8.00

2005 American Idol Season Four

COMPLETE SET (80) 6.00 15.00

1 David Brown .15 .40
2 Jessica Sierra .15 .40
3 Nikko Smith .15 .40
4 Aloha Mischeaux .15 .40
5 Anthony Fedorov .15 .40
6 Mikalah Gordon .15 .40
7 Judd Harris .15 .40
8 Nadia Turner .15 .40
9 Joseph Murena .15 .40
10 Vonzell Solomon .15 .40
11 Anwar Robinson .15 .40
12 Carrie Underwood .40 1.00
13 Mario Vazquez .15 .40
14 Sarah Mather .15 .40
15 Bo Bice .15 .40
16 Celena Rae Batchelor .15 .40
17 Jared Yates .15 .40
18 Janay Castine .15 .40
19 Constantine Maroulis .15 .40
20 Lindsey Cardinale .15 .40
21 Scott Savol .15 .40
22 Melinda Lira .15 .40
23 Travis Tucker .15 .40
24 Amanda Avila .15 .40
25 David Brown .15 .40
26 Jessica Sierra .15 .40
27 Nikko Smith .15 .40
28 Aloha Mischeaux .15 .40
29 Anthony Fedorov .15 .40
30 Mikalah Gordon .15 .40
31 Judd Harris .15 .40
32 Nadia Turner .15 .40
33 Joseph Murena .15 .40
34 Vonzell Solomon .15 .40
35 Anwar Robinson .15 .40
36 Carrie Underwood .40 1.00
37 Mario Vazquez .15 .40
38 Sarah Mather .15 .40
39 Bo Bice .15 .40
40 Celena Rae Batchelor .15 .40
41 Jared Yates .15 .40
42 Janay Castine .15 .40
43 Constantine Maroulis .15 .40
44 Lindsey Cardinale .15 .40
45 Scott Savol .15 .40
46 Melinda Lira .15 .40
47 Travis Tucker .15 .40
48 Amanda Avila .15 .40
49 David Brown .15 .40
50 Jessica Sierra .15 .40
51 Nikko Smith .15 .40
52 Aloha Mischeaux .15 .40
53 Anthony Fedorov .15 .40
54 Mikalah Gordon .15 .40
55 Judd Harris .15 .40
56 Nadia Turner .15 .40
57 Joseph Murena .15 .40
58 Vonzell Solomon .15 .40
59 Anwar Robinson .15 .40
60 Carrie Underwood .40 1.00
61 Mario Vazquez .15 .40
62 Sarah Mather .15 .40
63 Bo Bice .15 .40
64 Celena Rae Batchelor .15 .40
65 Jared Yates .15 .40
66 Janay Castine .15 .40
67 Constantine Maroulis .15 .40
68 Lindsey Cardinale .15 .40
69 Scott Savol .15 .40
70 Melinda Lira .15 .40
71 Travis Tucker .15 .40
72 Amanda Avila .15 .40
73 The Orpheum Theatre .15 .40
74 Stage Right .15 .40
75 Boom .15 .40
76 Vocal Backup .15 .40
77 Watchful Eye .15 .40
78 Directions .15 .40
79 Emotions .15 .40
80 American Idol .15 .40
CL 2005 American Idol Checklist .15 .40

2005 American Idol Season Four Gold

*GOLD: 1.2X TO 3X BASE CARD
STATED ODDS 1:4

2005 American Idol Season Four Platinum

*PLATINUM: 4X TO 10X BASE CARD
STATED ODDS 1:24

2005 American Idol Season Four Behind the Scenes

COMPLETE SET (15) 6.00 15.00
STATED ODDS 1:4

BS1 Interview .50 1.25
BS2 On Stage .50 1.25
BS3 Tens of Thousands .50 1.25
BS4 First Step .50 1.25
BS5 The Wait .50 1.25
BS6 Practice .50 1.25
BS7 Sleep .50 1.25
BS8 Taking a Break .50 1.25
BS9 Seeing the Sights .50 1.25
BS10 Food .50 1.25
BS11 Keeping Them Straight .50 1.25
BS12 Relax .50 1.25
BS13 Hollywood, We Made It! .50 1.25
BS14 Morning Brief .50 1.25
BS15 In the Spotlight .50 1.25

2005 American Idol Season Four Idol Chatter

COMPLETE SET (24) 8.00 20.00
STATED ODDS 1:6

IC1 David Brown .40 1.00
IC2 Jessica Sierra .40 1.00
IC3 Nikko Smith .40 1.00
IC4 Aloha Mischeaux .40 1.00
IC5 Anthony Fedorov .40 1.00
IC6 Mikalah Gordon .40 1.00
IC7 Judd Harris .40 1.00
IC8 Nadia Turner .40 1.00
IC9 Joseph Murena .40 1.00
IC10 Vonzell Solomon .40 1.00
IC11 Anwar Robinson .40 1.00
IC12 Carrie Underwood .40 1.00
IC13 Mario Vazquez .40 1.00
IC14 Sarah Mather .40 1.00
IC15 Bo Bice .40 1.00
IC16 Celena Rae Batchelor .40 1.00
IC17 Jared Yates .40 1.00
IC18 Janay Castine .40 1.00
IC19 Constantine Maroulis .40 1.00
IC20 Lindsey Cardinale .40 1.00
IC21 Scott Savol .40 1.00
IC22 Melinda Lira .40 1.00
IC23 Travis Tucker .40 1.00
IC24 Amanda Avila .40 1.00

2005 American Idol Season Four Reality Bits

OVERALL AUTO/MEM ODDS 1:18

RBAF Anthony Fedorov 5.00 12.00
RBAR Anwar Robinson 5.00 12.00
RBBB Bo Bice 5.00 12.00
RBCM Constantine Maroulis 5.00 12.00
RBCU Carrie Underwood 15.00 30.00
RBJS Jessica Sierra 5.00 12.00
RBLC Lindsey Cardinale 5.00 12.00
RBMG Mikalah Gordon 5.00 12.00
RBNS Nikko Smith 5.00 12.00
RBNT Nadia Turner 5.00 12.00
RBSS Scott Savol 5.00 12.00
RBVS Vonzell Solomon 5.00 12.00

2005 American Idol Season Four Reality Bits Silver

*SILVER: .5X TO 1.2X BASE BITS
STATED PRINT RUN 100 SER. #'d SETS

2005 American Idol Season Four Reality Bits Gold

*GOLD: .8X TO 2X BASE BITS
STATED PRINT RUN 25 SER. #'d SETS

2005 American Idol Season Four Reality Bits Masterpiece

STATED PRINT RUN 1 SER. #'d SET
UNPRICED DUE TO SCARCITY

2005 American Idol Season Four Signed Sealed Delivered Autographs

OVERALL AUTO/MEM ODDS 1:18

SSCJS Jessica Sierra 6.00 15.00
SSDAF Anthony Fedorov 6.00 15.00
SSDAR Anwar Robinson 6.00 15.00
SSDBB Bo Bice 6.00 15.00
SSDCM Constantine Maroulis 6.00 15.00
SSDCU Carrie Underwood 60.00 120.00
SSDLC Lindsey Cardinale 6.00 15.00
SSDMG Mikalah Gordon 6.00 15.00
SSDNS Nikko Smith 6.00 15.00
SSDNT Nadia Turner 6.00 15.00
SSDSS Scott Savol 6.00 15.00
SSDVS Vonzell Solomon 6.00 15.00

2005 American Idol Season Four Signed Sealed Delivered Autographs Silver

*SILVER: .6X TO 1.5X BASE AUTO
STATED PRINT RUN 100 SER. #'d SETS

2005 American Idol Season Four Signed Sealed Delivered Autographs Gold

*GOLD: .8X TO 2X BASE AUTO
STATED PRINT RUN 25 SER. #'d SETS

2005 American Idol Season Four Signed Sealed Delivered Autographs Masterpiece

STATED PRINT RUN 1 SER. #'d SET
UNPRICED DUE TO SCARCITY

2005 Batman Begins Movie

COMPLETE SET (90) 5.00 12.00

1 Batman Begins .15 .40
2 Bruce Wayne .15 .40
3 Batman .15 .40
4 Rachel Dawes .15 .40
5 Alfred Pennyworth .15 .40
6 Lucius Fox .15 .40
7 Henri Ducard .15 .40
8 Dr. Jonathan Crane .15 .40
9 Scarecrow .15 .40
10 Ra's Al Ghul .15 .40
11 James Gordon .15 .40
12 Thomas Wayne .15 .40
13 Fun With Bruce and Rachel .15 .40
14 A Taste of Terror .15 .40
15 His Father's Son .15 .40
16 A StrangerIn Hell .15 .40
17 Survival of the Strongest .15 .40
18 First Brush With Ducard .15 .40
19 In Search of His Destiny .15 .40
20 The Flower Delivered .15 .40
21 Testing Wayne's Strength .15 .40
22 A Night at the Opera .15 .40
23 The Hold-Up .15 .40
24 He Watches Them Die .15 .40
25 Looking After Bruce .15 .40
26 Violence on Ice .15 .40
27 The Law vs. Joe Chill .15 .40
28 Slain in Plain Sight .15 .40
29 Facing the Crime Lord .15 .40
30 In Warrior Training .15 .40
31 Execution Order .15 .40
32 Duel With Ra's Al Ghul .15 .40
33 Rescuing Ducard .15 .40
34 Back in Crime City .15 .40
35 Beneath Wayne Manor .15 .40
36 The Prodigal Son .15 .40
37 Building the Batcave .15 .40
38 Weapons and Wardrobe .15 .40
39 Strength of a Cowl .15 .40
40 Knight Patrol .15 .40
41 Gordon's Visitor .15 .40
42 Batsuit and the Tumbler .15 .40
43 Batman's First Night .15 .40
44 No Escape from Batman .15 .40
45 Of Fear and Fury .15 .40
46 A Very Special Delivery .15 .40
47 Gotham's Most Wanted .15 .40
48 Flass's Confession .15 .40
49 Dark Knight on the Trail .15 .40
50 Invading Crane's Lair .15 .40
51 Batman's Discovery .15 .40
52 Poisoned By Fear Gas .15 .40
53 Batman Set Aflame! .15 .40
54 Escape from the Narrows .15 .40
55 Facing the Fear .15 .40
56 The Night Has Ears .15 .40
57 In Crane's Clutches .15 .40
58 Inside Arkham Asylum .15 .40
59 Rematch With Scarecrow .15 .40
60 Batman Turns the Tables .15 .40
61 Crane Gripped By Fear .15 .40
62 The Rescue of Rachel .15 .40
63 Trusting the Dark Knight .15 .40
64 Batman Takes Flight .15 .40
65 Chase Through the City .15 .40
66 Heading For the Batcave .15 .40
67 His Dark Domain .15 .40
68 Master of the Batcave .15 .40
69 Rachel and the Antidote .15 .40
70 To Save Gotham City .15 .40
71 A Birthday Surprise .15 .40
72 Wayne Manor Under Siege .15 .40
73 Fleeing the Inferno .15 .40
74 Madman in Custody .15 .40
75 The Microwave Emitter .15 .40
76 To Thwart Ghul's Evil .15 .40
77 Scarecrow's Revenge .15 .40
78 Escape from Arkham .15 .40
79 The Longest Night .15 .40
80 The Rescuers .15 .40
81 Batman and Gordon .15 .40
82 Descending into Danger .15 .40
83 Swinging to the Rescue .15 .40
84 The Final Battle .15 .40
85 The Defeat of Ra's Al Ghul .15 .40
86 A New Beginning .15 .40
87 Love and Destiny .15 .40
88 A Signal for Batman .15 .40
89 The Dark Knight Forever .15 .40
90 Checklist .15 .40

2005 Batman Begins Movie Autographs

STATED ODDS 1:120 HOBBY

1 Cillian Murphy 40.00 80.00
2 Gary Oldman
3 Katie Holmes 75.00 150.00
4 Liam Neeson
5 Michael Caine 60.00 120.00

2005 Batman Begins Movie Blister Bonus

COMPLETE SET (3) 1.25 3.00
STATED ODDS ONE PER BLISTER PACK

B1 He is the Dark Avenger .75 2.00
B2 What Does It Take .75 2.00
B3 To Challenge the Pervasive 75.00 2.00

2005 Batman Begins Movie Embossed Foil

COMPLETE SET (5) 3.00 6.00
STATED ODDS 1:8

MODERN ERA NON-SPORTS

❑ 1 Batman facing forward GREEN 1.00 2.50
❑ 2 Batman facing his right RED 1.00 2.50
❑ 3 Batman BLUE 1.00 2.50
❑ 4 Batman facing his left GREEN 1.00 2.50
❑ 5 Batman facing forward RED 1.00 2.50

2005 Batman Begins Movie Holograms

COMPLETE SET (5) 4.00 8.00
STATED ODDS 1:12

❑ 1 Batman swinging to his left 1.25 3.00
❑ 2 Batman ready to choke 1.25 3.00
❑ 3 Batman with curtain rod 1.25 3.00
❑ 4 Batman swinging and kicking 1.25 3.00
❑ 5 Batman swinging to his right 1.25 3.00

2005 Batman Begins Movie Memorabilia

STATED ODDS 1:24 HOBBY

❑ 1 Batman's Cape 10.00 25.00
❑ 2 Batman's Costume
❑ 3 Batmobile Tire 10.00 25.00

2005 Batman Begins Movie Stickers

COMPLETE SET (10) 1.50 4.00
STATED ODDS 1:2 RETAIL

❑ 1 Batman .40 1.00
❑ 2 What Do You Fear .40 1.00
❑ 3 Batman .40 1.00
❑ 4 Knight Warrior .40 1.00
❑ 5 One with the Night .40 1.00
❑ 6 Batman .40 1.00
❑ 7 sleeping on symbol .40 1.00
❑ 8 Face Your Fear .40 1.00
❑ 9 Gotham Guardian .40 1.00
❑ 10 Master of the Game .40 1.00

2005 Batman Begins Movie Tattoos

COMPLETE SET (10) 2.00 5.00
STATED ODDS 1:4 RETAIL

❑ 1 Batman .60 1.50
❑ 2 Batman .60 1.50
❑ 3 Batman .60 1.50
❑ 4 Batman .60 1.50
❑ 5 Batman .60 1.50
❑ 6 Batman .60 1.50
❑ 7 Batman .60 1.50
❑ 8 Batman .60 1.50
❑ 9 Batman .60 1.50
❑ 10 Batman .60 1.50

2005 Battlestar Galactica Premiere

COMPLETE SET (72) 4.00 10.00

❑ 1 Title Card .10 .30
❑ 2 Created By Man .10 .30
❑ 3 Remote Space Station .10 .30
❑ 4 It Has Begun .10 .30
❑ 5 The Last Battlestar .10 .30
❑ 6 End of an Era .10 .30
❑ 7 Classic Viper, Restored .10 .30
❑ 8 Impetuous Starbuck .10 .30
❑ 9 Bad News .10 .30
❑ 10 A Killer Among Us .10 .30
❑ 11 Gaius Baltar .10 .30
❑ 12 The Feel Like Us .10 .30
❑ 13 Apollo's Arrival .10 .30
❑ 14 Number Six .10 .30
❑ 15 Conflict of Wills .10 .30
❑ 16 Old Wounds .10 .30
❑ 17 Judgement Day .10 .30
❑ 18 Bitter Meeting .10 .30
❑ 19 A Revelation .10 .30
❑ 20 Humanity's Children .10 .30
❑ 21 Playing God .10 .30
❑ 22 The Fall of Caprica .10 .30
❑ 23 No Drill .10 .30
❑ 24 We Are at War .10 .30
❑ 25 Return of the Mark IIs .10 .30
❑ 26 Attack Squadron Destroyed .10 .30
❑ 27 Warheads Inbound .10 .30
❑ 28 Colonial Flight 798 .10 .30
❑ 29 Mourn the Dead Later .10 .30
❑ 30 Caprica Refugees .10 .30
❑ 31 Find the Survivors .10 .30
❑ 32 Brace for Impact .10 .30
❑ 33 The Battlestar Quakes .10 .30
❑ 34 Tough Decision .10 .30
❑ 35 Baltar's Escape .10 .30
❑ 36 Adama Takes Commands .10 .30
❑ 37 Case Orange .10 .30
❑ 38 Colonial One Destroyed? .10 .30
❑ 39 Fate Unknown .10 .30
❑ 40 War Game Tactic .10 .30
❑ 41 FTL Jump! .10 .30
❑ 42 Lone Gunman .10 .30
❑ 43 Ragnar Mishap .10 .30
❑ 44 The President's Plan .10 .30
❑ 45 Unshakable Companion .10 .30
❑ 46 Rag-Tag Fleet .10 .30
❑ 47 Ugly Numbers Game .10 .30
❑ 48 Terminal Condition .10 .30
❑ 49 Cylon in Disguise .10 .30
❑ 50 Colonial Ships Inbound .10 .30
❑ 51 Reunions .10 .30
❑ 52 Adama's Fight .10 .30
❑ 53 Misplaced Sympathy .10 .30
❑ 54 No Conscience, No Guilt .10 .30
❑ 55 Baltar's Dilemma .10 .30
❑ 56 Family Ties .10 .30
❑ 57 The Amazing Cylon Detector .10 .30
❑ 58 Starbuck's Revelation .10 .30
❑ 59 Fight or Flee? .10 .30
❑ 60 Beyond the Red Line .10 .30
❑ 61 Engaging the Enemy .10 .30
❑ 62 Risky Maneuver .10 .30
❑ 63 The Thirteenth Tribe .10 .30
❑ 64 So Say We All .10 .30
❑ 65 One-Sided Apology .10 .30
❑ 66 Tenuous Alliance .10 .30
❑ 67 Taking Sides .10 .30
❑ 68 Life Goes On .10 .30
❑ 69 Cylon Rendezvous .10 .30
❑ 70 Checklist .10 .30
❑ 71 Checklist .10 .30
❑ 72 Checklist .10 .30

2005 Battlestar Galactica Premiere Autographs

STATED ODDS 1:40
L (LIMITED): 300-500 CARDS
VL (VERY LIMITED): 200-300 CARDS

❑ AD Aaron Douglas L 8.00 20.00
❑ AJ Alessandro Juliani L 8.00 20.00
❑ BH Barclay Hope L 8.00 20.00
❑ CR Callum Keith Rennie 8.00 20.00
❑ CW Connor Widdows L 8.00 20.00
❑ KS Katee Sackhoff VL 60.00 100.00
❑ MB Matthew Bennett L 8.00 20.00
❑ MH Michael Hogan L 8.00 20.00
❑ NC Nicki Clyne L 8.00 20.00
❑ PC Paul Campbell L 8.00 20.00
❑ RR Ryan Robbins L 8.00 20.00
❑ TH Tricia Helfer VL 60.00 100.00
❑ TO Ty Olsson L 8.00 20.00
❑ JBKS Jamie Bamber 60.00 100.00
Katee Sackhoff

2005 Battlestar Galactica Premiere Costumes

STATED ODDS 1:40

❑ CC1 Number Six 10.00 25.00
❑ CC2 Lt. Kara Starbuck Thrace 10.00 25.00
❑ CC3 Lt. Sharon Boomer Valerii 25.00 50.00
❑ CC4 Lt. Kara Starbuck Thrace 15.00 30.00
❑ CC5 Captain Lee Apollo Adama 10.00 25.00
❑ CC6 Commander William Adama 10.00 25.00
❑ CC7 Captain Lee Apollo Adama 10.00 25.00
❑ CC8 Col. Saul Tigh 10.00 25.00

2005 Battlestar Galactica Premiere Cylon Threat

COMPLETE SET (9) 25.00 50.00
STATED ODDS 1:20

❑ CT1 Base Star 2.50 6.00
❑ CT2 Cylon Raider 2.50 6.00
❑ CT3 Cylon 2.50 6.00
❑ CT4 Number Six 2.50 6.00
❑ CT5 Aaron Doral 2.50 6.00
❑ CT6 Leoben Conroy 2.50 6.00
❑ CT7 Boomer 2.50 6.00
❑ CT8 Cylon Centurion 2.50 6.00
❑ CT9 Dr. Gaius Baltar 2.50 6.00

2005 Battlestar Galactica Premiere Promos

❑ P1 Group of Four .75 2.00
(General Distribution)
❑ P2 Group of Seven 1.25 3.00
(NSU Magazine)
❑ P3 Number 6/Baltar 4.00 10.00
(Album Exclusive)
❑ UK Commander Adama/Laura Roslin 4.00 10.00
(UK Exclusive)

2005 Battlestar Galactica Premiere Quotable Battlestar Galactica

COMPLETE SET (9) 60.00 120.00
STATED ODDS 1:40

❑ Q1 Baltar 6.00 15.00
Number Six
❑ Q2 Number Six 6.00 15.00
Baltar
❑ Q3 Commander Adama 6.00 15.00
❑ Q4 Number Six 6.00 15.00
Baltar
❑ Q5 Tyrol 6.00 15.00
❑ Q6 Leoben Conroy 6.00 15.00
Commander Adama
❑ Q7 Commander Adama 6.00 15.00
Colonel Tigh
❑ Q8 Starbuck 6.00 15.00
Viper
❑ Q9 Commander Adama 6.00 15.00

2005 Battlestar Galactica Premiere Roll Call

COMPLETE SET (9) 8.00 20.00
STATED ODDS 1:10

❑ R1 Commander William Adama 1.00 2.50
❑ R2 Captain Lee Apollo Adama 1.00 2.50
❑ R3 Lt. Kara Starbuck Thrace 1.00 2.50
❑ R4 Number 6 1.00 2.50
❑ R5 Dr. Gaius Baltar 1.00 2.50
❑ R6 Lt. Sharon Boomer Valerii 1.00 2.50
❑ R7 Laura Roslin 1.00 2.50
❑ R8 Colonel Saul Tigh 1.00 2.50
❑ R9 Chief Petty Office Tyrol 1.00 2.50

2005 Battlestar Galactica Premiere Sketches

HEND ODDS ONE PER CASE
MART ODDS ONE PER 2-CASE PURCHASE

❑ HEND Chris Henderson Sketch
❑ MART Warren Martineck Sketch

2005 Buffy the Vampire Slayer Men of Sunnydale

COMPLETE SET (81) 4.00 10.00

❑ 1 Men of Sunnydale .10 .30
❑ 2 Rupert Giles .10 .30
❑ 3 Ripper .10 .30
❑ 4 Confrontation .10 .30
❑ 5 Grief .10 .30
❑ 6 Slayer Returned .10 .30
❑ 7 To the Rescue .10 .30
❑ 8 Under Suspicion .10 .30
❑ 9 At the Hellmouth .10 .30
❑ 10 Xander Harris .10 .30
❑ 11 Ladies' Man .10 .30
❑ 12 Divided .10 .30
❑ 13 Proposal .10 .30
❑ 14 Reluctant .10 .30
❑ 15 Courageous .10 .30
❑ 16 Working Man .10 .30
❑ 17 Dreadful Date .10 .30
❑ 18 Wounded .10 .30
❑ 19 Angel .10 .30
❑ 20 Mysterious .10 .30
❑ 21 Doomed Romance .10 .30
❑ 22 Last Dance .10 .30
❑ 23 Leaving .10 .30
❑ 24 Clandestine Visit .10 .30
❑ 25 Apologetic .10 .30
❑ 26 Consoling .10 .30
❑ 27 Farewell .10 .30
❑ 28 Daniel Osbourne .10 .30
❑ 29 In Love .10 .30
❑ 30 Tempted .10 .30
❑ 31 On the Road .10 .30
❑ 32 Controlled .10 .30
❑ 33 The Other Woman .10 .30
❑ 34 Feral .10 .30
❑ 35 Caged .10 .30
❑ 36 Gone .10 .30
❑ 37 Riley Finn .10 .30
❑ 38 More .10 .30
❑ 39 Secret Agent Man .10 .30
❑ 40 Altered .10 .30
❑ 41 Slayer's Beau .10 .30
❑ 42 Bad Habits .10 .30
❑ 43 Busted .10 .30
❑ 44 Retreat .10 .30
❑ 45 Reunion .10 .30
❑ 46 Spike .10 .30
❑ 47 His Way .10 .30
❑ 48 Chipped .10 .30
❑ 49 Romancing .10 .30
❑ 50 Got Soul? .10 .30
❑ 51 Haunted .10 .30
❑ 52 Mum's Lad .10 .30
❑ 53 Tender Moment .10 .30
❑ 54 Hero .10 .30
❑ 55 Whistler .10 .30
❑ 56 Wesley Wyndham-Pryce .10 .30
❑ 57 Jonathan Levinson .10 .30
❑ 58 Classmates .10 .30
❑ 59 Riley's Pals .10 .30
❑ 60 Order of Dagon .10 .30
❑ 61 Clem .10 .30
❑ 62 Principal Wood .10 .30
❑ 63 Andrew Wells .10 .30
❑ 64 The Master .10 .30
❑ 65 Mayor Wilkins .10 .30
❑ 66 Ethan Rayne .10 .30
❑ 67 Olaf the Troll .10 .30
❑ 68 The Gentlemen .10 .30
❑ 69 Adam .10 .30
❑ 70 Dracula .10 .30
❑ 71 Angelus .10 .30
❑ 72 D'Hoffryn .10 .30
❑ 73 Doc .10 .30
❑ 74 Demon Sweet .10 .30
❑ 75 Jonathan and Andrew .10 .30
❑ 76 Warren Mears .10 .30
❑ 77 Gnarl .10 .30
❑ 78 Bringers .10 .30
❑ 79 Turok-Han .10 .30
❑ 80 Caleb .10 .30
❑ 81 Checklist .10 .30

2005 Buffy the Vampire Slayer Men of Sunnydale Autographs

STATED ODDS 1:36

❑ A1 Nicholas Brendan
❑ A2 Marc Blucas 8.00 20.00
❑ A3 Mark Metcalf 6.00 15.00
❑ A4 Robin Sachs 4.00 10.00
❑ A5 Harry Groener 4.00 10.00
❑ A6 Danny Strong 8.00 20.00
❑ A7 Tom Lenk 8.00 20.00
❑ A8 Adam Busch 8.00 20.00
❑ A9 Charlie Weber 6.00 15.00
❑ A10 Camden Toy 4.00 10.00
❑ A11 Danny Strong 50.00 100.00
Tom Lenk/Adam Busch

2005 Buffy the Vampire Slayer Men of Sunnydale Box Loaders

❑ BL1 Xander 2.00 5.00
❑ BL2 Giles 2.00 5.00
❑ BL3 Spike 2.00 5.00
❑ CL1 Angel, Riley, & Spike 6.00 15.00

2005 Buffy the Vampire Slayer Men of Sunnydale Dressed to Kill

COMPLETE SET (9) 6.00 15.00
STATED ODDS 1:11

❑ DK1 Dressed To Kill .75 2.00
❑ DK2 Dressed To Kill .75 2.00
❑ DK3 Dressed To Kill .75 2.00
❑ DK4 Dressed To Kill .75 2.00
❑ DK5 Dressed To Kill .75 2.00
❑ DK6 Dressed To Kill .75 2.00
❑ DK7 Dressed To Kill .75 2.00
❑ DK8 Dressed To Kill .75 2.00
❑ DK9 Dressed To Kill .75 2.00

2005 Buffy the Vampire Slayer Men of Sunnydale Pieceworks

STATED ODDS 1:36

❑ PW1 Xander's Jacket 6.00 15.00
❑ PW2 Xander's Trousers 6.00 15.00
❑ PW3 Giles' Shirt 6.00 15.00
❑ PW4 Andrew's T-Shirt 6.00 15.00
❑ PW5a Principal Wood's Shirt 5.00 12.00
❑ PW5b Principal Wood's Tie SP

2005 Buffy the Vampire Slayer Men of Sunnydale Women Men Adore

COMPLETE SET (6) 6.00 15.00
STATED ODDS 1:17

❑ WA1 Buffy 1.25 3.00
❑ WA2 Willow 1.25 3.00
❑ WA3 Cordelia 1.25 3.00
❑ WA4 Anya 1.25 3.00
❑ WA5 Faith 1.25 3.00
❑ WA6 Dawn 1.25 3.00

2005 Charlie and the Chocolate Factory

COMPLETE SET (90) 5.00 12.00
T1 STATED ODDS ONE PER TIN

❑ 1 Charlie and the Chocolate Factory .15 .40
❑ 2 Willy Wonka .15 .40
❑ 3 Charlie Bucket .15 .40
❑ 4 Grandpa Joe .15 .40
❑ 5 Augustus Gloop .15 .40
❑ 6 Mrs. Gloop .15 .40
❑ 7 Veruca Salt .15 .40
❑ 8 Mr. Salt .15 .40
❑ 9 Violet Beuregarde .15 .40
❑ 10 Mrs. Beauregarde .15 .40
❑ 11 Mike Teavee .15 .40
❑ 12 Mr. Teavee .15 .40
❑ 13 Mrs. Bucket .15 .40
❑ 14 Mr. Bucket .15 .40
❑ 15 Dr. Wilbur Wonka .15 .40
❑ 16 Oompa-Loompas .15 .40
❑ 17 Grandma Josephine .15 .40
❑ 18 Grandpa George & Grandma Georgina .15 .40
❑ 19 Every Corner Of The World .15 .40
❑ 20 A Horrible Empty Feeling .15 .40
❑ 21 Nothing Goes Better Than .15 .40
Cabbage With Cabbage
❑ 22 A Head For Willy Wonka! .15 .40
❑ 23 Working For Wonka .15 .40
❑ 24 That Man Was A Genius! .15 .40
❑ 25 Just The Beginning... .15 .40
❑ 26 One Hundred Rooms Of Chocolate .15 .40
❑ 27 The Largest Chocolate Factory In History .15 .40
❑ 28 Opening Day .15 .40
❑ 29 Don't Make It Gross .15 .40
❑ 30 I'm Closing My Factory Forever .15 .40
❑ 31 Nothing's Impossible .15 .40
❑ 32 The First Ticket .15 .40
❑ 33 What A Repulsive Boy .15 .40
❑ 34 Told You It'd Be A Porker! .15 .40
❑ 35 V-E-R-U-C-A .15 .40
❑ 36 Where's My Golden Ticket?! .15 .40
❑ 37 A Whipple-Scrumptious Birthday Present .15 .40
❑ 38 We'll Share It .15 .40
❑ 39 A Gumchewer, Mostly .15 .40
❑ 40 I Hate Chocolate .15 .40
❑ 41 A Secret Hoard .15 .40
❑ 42 One Wonka's Whipple-Scrumptious .15 .40
Fudgemallow Delight, Please
❑ 43 Take It Straight Home .15 .40
❑ 44 Yippeeeeeee! .15 .40
❑ 45 The First Of February .15 .40
❑ 46 Welcome To My Humble Factory .15 .40
❑ 47 Willy Wonka! .15 .40
❑ 48 Far Too Much To See .15 .40
❑ 49 An Important Room, This! .15 .40
❑ 50 Don't Lose Your Heads .15 .40
❑ 51 Enjoy! .15 .40
❑ 52 Just Delicious .15 .40
❑ 53 Better Than Cabbage Soup! .15 .40
❑ 54 It's a Little Person! .15 .40
❑ 55 They're Oompa-Loompas .15 .40
❑ 56 The Call Of His Enormous Stomach .15 .40
❑ 57 He's Gonna Stick .15 .40
❑ 58 What's So Funny? .15 .40
❑ 59 Wonka's Private Yacht .15 .40
❑ 60 Onward! .15 .40
❑ 61 Trick Or Treat! .15 .40
❑ 62 The Most Important Room .15 .40
In The Entire Factory
❑ 63 Hiss, Sizzle, Clank, Sputter! .15 .40
❑ 64 What's This? .15 .40
❑ 65 A Full Three-Course Dinner .15 .40
❑ 66 My Kind Of Gum .15 .40
❑ 67 A Blueberry As A Daughter .15 .40
❑ 68 A True Calling .15 .40
❑ 69 Squirrels! .15 .40
❑ 70 Not For Sale .15 .40
❑ 71 Is That Mink? .15 .40
❑ 72 Don't Touch... .15 .40
❑ 73 A Bad Nut .15 .40
❑ 74 The Television Room .15 .40
❑ 75 The Latest And Greatest Invention .15 .40
❑ 76 Mumbler! .15 .40
❑ 77 It's Gotta Be Real Big .15 .40
❑ 78 Watch The Screen .15 .40
❑ 79 What About People? .15 .40
❑ 80 All You Think About Is Chocolate! .15 .40
❑ 81 Try Every Channel! .15 .40
❑ 82 Smaller Than An Oompa-Loompa .15 .40
❑ 83 There's Someone At The Door .15 .40
❑ 84 P-p-p-p-p-... .15 .40
❑ 85 Open! .15 .40
❑ 86 I Haven't Seen Bicuspids Like These Since....15 .40
❑ 87 Brainstorming .15 .40
❑ 88 You Smell Like Peanuts! .15 .40
❑ 89 Raspberry Kites? .15 .40
❑ 90 Checklist .15 .40
❑ T1 Johnny Depp/ (issued in tins only)

2005 Charlie and the Chocolate Factory Autographs

STATED ODDS 1:72

❑ 1 Annasophia Robb 100.00 175.00
❑ 2 Christopher Lee 100.00 175.00
❑ 3 David Kelly 30.00 60.00
❑ 4 Deep Roy 10.00 25.00
❑ 5 Freddie Highmore 75.00 150.00
❑ 6 Helena Bonham Carter 50.00 100.00
❑ 7 James Fox 6.00 15.00
❑ 8 Johnny Depp 400.00 700.00
❑ 9 Jordan Fry 6.00 15.00
❑ 10 Julia Winter 30.00 60.00
❑ 11 Missi Pyle 30.00 60.00
❑ 12 Philip Wiegratz 6.00 15.00

2005 Charlie and the Chocolate Factory Costumes

OVERALL COSTUME/PROP ODDS ONE PER HOBBY BOX

❑ 1 Augustus Goop's striped top/430 8.00 20.00
❑ 2 Charlie Bucket's pants/330 8.00 20.00
❑ 3 Grandpa Joe's jacket/530 8.00 20.00
❑ 4 Mike Teavee's skull shirt/305 10.00 25.00
❑ 5 Mr. Salt's costume/265 8.00 20.00
❑ 6 Mr. Salt's tie/165 12.00 30.00
❑ 7 Mr. Teavee's pants/430 8.00 20.00
❑ 8 Mrs. Beauregarde's track halter/230 8.00 20.00
❑ 9 Mrs. Gloop's dress/480 8.00 20.00
❑ 10 Oompa Loompa's black outfit/240 8.00 20.00
❑ 11 Oompa Loompa's red outfit/240 8.00 20.00
❑ 12 Veruca Salt's costume/330 8.00 20.00
❑ 13 Violet Beauregarde's tracksuit top/330 8.00 20.00
❑ 14 Workers in the Candy Store/380 8.00 20.00
❑ 15 Wonka Factory Employees 6.00 15.00
(issued as case topper)
❑ 16 Oompa Loompa's white outfit 10.00 25.00
(issued as UK 2-case incentive)
❑ 17 Charlie Bucket's sweater 8.00 20.00
(issued as 10-case incentive)
❑ 18 Mrs. Beauregarde's pants 8.00 20.00
(issued in SDCC tins)

2005 Charlie and the Chocolate Factory Foil Hobby

COMPLETE SET (9) 4.00 10.00
STATED ODDS 1:5 HOBBY

❑ R1 The Best Kind Of Prize Is A Surprise! .75 2.00
❑ R2 There's No Knowing Where They're Going .75 2.00
❑ R3 I Eat More Candy! .75 2.00
❑ R4 I Want It Now! .75 2.00
❑ R5 Chewing Gum Is Really Gross, .75 2.00
Chewing Gum I Hate The Most
❑ R6 Once Again You Really Shouldn't Mumble .75 2.00
❑ R7 WW (Oompa-Loompa in red) .75 2.00
❑ R8 WW (Oompa-Loompa in orange) .75 2.00
❑ R9 WW (Oompa-Loompa in green) .75 2.00

2005 Charlie and the Chocolate Factory Foil Retail

COMPLETE SET (9) 4.00 10.00
STATED ODDS 1:5 RETAIL

❑ M1 The Best Kind Of Prize Is A Surprise! .75 2.00
❑ M2 There's No Knowing Where They're Going .75 2.00
❑ M3 I Eat More Candy! .75 2.00
❑ M4 I Want My Golden Ticket .75 2.00
❑ M5 Chewing Gum Is Really Gross, .75 2.00
Chewing Gum I Hate The Most
❑ M6 Once Again You Really Shouldn't Mumble .75 2.00
❑ M7 Red Oompa-Loompa .75 2.00
❑ M8 Green Oompa-Loompa .75 2.00
❑ M9 Yellow Oompa-Loompa .75 2.00

2005 Charlie and the Chocolate Factory Props Hobby

OVERALL COSTUME/PROP ODDS ONE PER HOBBY BOX

❑ 1 Burlap Nut Bag and Worker's Apron/324 8.00 20.00
❑ 2 Chilly Chocolate Creme Candy wrapper/3906.00 15.00
❑ 3 Chocolate Bar/490 10.00 25.00
❑ 4 Contest Announcement/490 10.00 25.00
❑ 5 Golden Ticket/18
❑ 6 Nutty Crunch Surprise Candy wrapper/290 6.00 15.00
❑ 7 Red Ribbon/340 10.00 25.00
❑ 8 Smilex Toothpaste Box/340 15.00 30.00
❑ 9 Tablecloth from the Bucket Household/543 6.00 15.00
❑ 10 Triple Dazzle Caramel Candy wrapper/29015.00 30.00
❑ 11 Whipple-Scrumptious Fudgemallow 8.00 20.00
Delight wrapper/190
❑ 12 Wonka Box of Chocolates/390 12.00 30.00
❑ 13 Wrapping Paper from Charlie's Birthday/72150.00 250.00
❑ 14 Wonka Display Box/ (issued as case topper)15.00 30.00
❑ 15 Short Grass from factory/ (issued as 25-case incentive)
❑ 16 Long Grass from factory 100.00 200.00
(issued as NY exclusive)

2005 Charlie and the Chocolate Factory Props Retail

STATED ODDS ONE PER RETAIL BOX

❑ 1 Chilly Chocolate Creme 5.00 12.00
Candy wrapper/2330
❑ 2 Nutty Crunch Surprise 5.00 12.00
Candy wrapper/2330
❑ 3 Triple Dazzle Caramel 5.00 12.00
Candy wrapper/2330
❑ 4 Whipple-Scrumptious Fudgemallow 5.00 12.00
Delight wrapper/1530

2005 Charlie and the Chocolate Factory Scratch and Sniff Box Toppers

COMPLETE SET (4) 8.00 20.00
STATED ODDS ONE PER BOX

❑ BT1 Bubblegum 3.00 8.00
❑ BT2 Marshmallow 3.00 8.00
❑ BT3 Peppermint 3.00 8.00
❑ BT4 Chocolate 3.00 8.00

2005 Charmed Conversations

COMPLETE SET (72) 4.00 10.00

❑ 1 Title Card .10 .30
❑ 2 Piper Halliwell .10 .30
❑ 3 Powers .10 .30
❑ 4 Motherhood .10 .30
❑ 5 Thoughtful .10 .30
❑ 6 Expecting Again .10 .30
❑ 7 Almost Normal .10 .30
❑ 8 At Work .10 .30
❑ 9 Questioning .10 .30
❑ 10 Phoebe Halliwell .10 .30
❑ 11 Alluring .10 .30
❑ 12 Teen Phoebe .10 .30
❑ 13 Powerless .10 .30
❑ 14 Professional .10 .30
❑ 15 At Work .10 .30
❑ 16 Premonition .10 .30
❑ 17 Blindsided .10 .30
❑ 18 Continetal .10 .30
❑ 19 Paige Matthews .10 .30
❑ 20 New Calling .10 .30
❑ 21 Younger Sisters .10 .30
❑ 22 Bad Paige .10 .30
❑ 23 Sister-In-Law .10 .30
❑ 24 Skilled At Magic .10 .30
❑ 25 Protective Aunt .10 .30
❑ 26 Persistence .10 .30
❑ 27 Researching Magic .10 .30
❑ 28 Leo Wyatt .10 .30
❑ 29 Father .10 .30
❑ 30 Meeting Destiny .10 .30
❑ 31 Evil Leo .10 .30
❑ 32 Leo & Grown Chris .10 .30
❑ 33 Masked Demon .10 .30
❑ 34 Demon Unmasked .10 .30
❑ 35 Choices .10 .30
❑ 36 Secrets .10 .30
❑ 37 Grams .10 .30
❑ 38 Patty Halliwell .10 .30
❑ 39 Victor Bennett .10 .30
❑ 40 Samuel Wilder .10 .30
❑ 41 Chris Perry .10 .30
❑ 42 Evil Chris .10 .30
❑ 43 Baby Wyatt .10 .30
❑ 44 Threatening .10 .30
❑ 45 Generations .10 .30
❑ 46 Leo .10 .30
❑ 47 Jason Dean .10 .30
❑ 48 Richard Montana .10 .30
❑ 49 Mr. Right .10 .30
❑ 50 Mr. Wrong (Vincent) .10 .30
❑ 51 Leslie St. Claire .10 .30
❑ 52 Brody .10 .30
❑ 53 Drake Robin .10 .30
❑ 54 Cole Turner .10 .30
❑ 55 The Cleaners .10 .30
❑ 56 Bianca .10 .30
❑ 57 Darryl Morris .10 .30
❑ 58 Elder Zola .10 .30
❑ 59 Inspector Sheridan .10 .30
❑ 60 Agent Kyle Brody .10 .30
❑ 61 Brody's Sacrifice .10 .30
❑ 62 Wild Ride .10 .30
❑ 63 Sophisticated Demon .10 .30
❑ 64 Gideon .10 .30
❑ 65 Lord Dyson .10 .30
❑ 66 Barbas .10 .30
❑ 67 Seer .10 .30
Kira
❑ 68 Sirk .10 .30
❑ 69 Avatar Alpha .10 .30
❑ 70 The Avatars .10 .30
❑ 71 Zankou .10 .30
❑ 72 Checklist .10 .30

2005 Charmed Conversations Autographs
STATED ODDS 1:36

A1 Alyssa Milano 75.00 150.00
A2 Dorian Gregory 3.00 8.00
A3 Drew Fuller 3.00 8.00
A4 Jennifer Rhodes 3.00 8.00
A5 Billy Drago 30.00 60.00
A6 Oded Fehr 3.00 8.00
A7 James Avery 3.00 8.00
A8 Patrice Fisher 3.00 8.00
A9 Zack Ward 3.00 8.00
A10 James Read 3.00 8.00

2005 Charmed Conversations Box Loaders
COMPLETE SET (4) 7.50 20.00

BL1 Leo & Piper 1.25 3.00
BL2 Leo & Chris 1.25 3.00
BL3 Wyatt & Piper 1.25 3.00
CL1 Sisters 6.00 15.00
CASE INSERT

2005 Charmed Conversations Charming Men
STATED ODDS 1:14

CM1 Leo 1.25 3.00
CM2 Cole 1.25 3.00
CM3 Darryl 1.25 3.00
CM4 Chris 1.25 3.00
CM5 Kyle 1.25 3.00
CM6 Les 1.25 3.00

2005 Charmed Conversations Pieceworks
STATED ODDS 1:36

PWCC1 Alyssa Milano 12.00 30.00
PWCC2 Holly Marie Combs 10.00 25.00
PWCC3 Rose McGowan 10.00 25.00
PWCC4 Drew Fuller 8.00 20.00
PWCC5 Brian Krause 8.00 20.00
PWCC6 James Avery 8.00 20.00
PWCC7 Alyssa Milano 10.00 25.00
PWCC8 Holly Marie Combs 10.00 25.00

2005 Charmed Conversations Transformations
STATED ODDS 1:11

T1 Genie 1.00 2.50
T2 Punked 1.00 2.50
T3 Goddess 1.00 2.50
T4 Lost Her Head 1.00 2.50
T5 Mermaid 1.00 2.50
T6 Super Heroes 1.00 2.50
T7 Back in Time 1.00 2.50
T8 Valkyries 1.00 2.50
T9 Gladiator 1.00 2.50

2005 The Complete Lost in Space
COMPLETE SET (90) 4.00 10.00
FS ODDS ONE PER COLLECTORS ALBUM

1 Lost In Space .10 .30
Title Card
2 Season 1 Overview .10 .30
3 The Reluctant Stowaway .10 .30
4 The Derelict .10 .30
5 Island in the Sky .10 .30
6 There Were Giants in the Earth .10 .30
7 The Hungry Sea .10 .30
8 Welcome Stranger .10 .30
9 My Friend, Mr. Nobody .10 .30
10 Invaders from the Fifth Dimension .10 .30
11 The Oasis .10 .30
12 The Sky Is Falling .10 .30
13 Wish Upon a Star .10 .30
14 The Raft .10 .30
15 One of Our Dogs Is Missing .10 .30
16 Attack of the Monster Plants .10 .30
17 Return from Outer Space .10 .30
18 The Keeper, Part 1 .10 .30
19 The Keeper, Part 2 .10 .30
20 The Sky Pirate .10 .30
21 Ghost in Space .10 .30
22 War of the Robots .10 .30
23 The Magic Mirror .10 .30
24 The Challenge .10 .30
25 The Space Trader .10 .30
26 His Majesty Smith .10 .30
27 The Space Croppers .10 .30
28 All That Glitters .10 .30
29 The Lost Civilization .10 .30
30 A Change of Space .10 .30
31 Follow the Leader .10 .30
32 Season 2 Overview .10 .30
33 Blast Off into Space .10 .30
34 Wild Adventure .10 .30
35 The Ghost Planet .10 .30
36 Forbidden World .10 .30
37 Space Circus .10 .30
38 The Prisoners of Space .10 .30
39 The Android Machine .10 .30
40 The Deadly Games of Gamma 6 .10 .30
41 The Thief from Outer Space .10 .30
42 The Curse of Cousin Smith .10 .30
43 West of Mars .10 .30
44 A Visit to Hades .10 .30
45 The Wreck of the Robot .10 .30
46 The Dream Monster .10 .30
47 The Golden Man .10 .30
48 The Girl From the Green Dimension .10 .30
49 The Questing Beast .10 .30
50 The Toymaker .10 .30
51 Mutiny in Space .10 .30
52 The Space Vikings .10 .30
53 Rocket to Earth .10 .30
54 The Cave of the Wizards .10 .30
55 Treasures of the Lost Planet .10 .30
56 Revolt of the Androids .10 .30
57 The Colonists .10 .30
58 Trip Through the Robot .10 .30
59 The Phantom Family .10 .30
60 The Mechanical Men .10 .30
61 The Astral Traveler .10 .30
62 The Galaxy Gift .10 .30
63 Season 3 Overview .10 .30
64 Condemned of Space .10 .30
65 Visit to a Hostile Planet .10 .30
66 Kidnapped in Space .10 .30
67 Hunter's Moon .10 .30
68 The Space Primevals .10 .30
69 The Space Destructors .10 .30
70 The Haunted Lighthouse .10 .30
71 Flight into the Future .10 .30
72 Collision of the Planets .10 .30
73 The Space Creature .10 .30
74 Deadliest of the Species .10 .30
75 A Day at the Zoo .10 .30
76 Two Weeks in Space .10 .30
77 Castles in Space .10 .30
78 The Anti-Matter Man .10 .30
79 Target: Earth .10 .30
80 Princess of Space .10 .30
81 The Time Merchant .10 .30
82 The Promised Planet .10 .30
83 Fugitives in Space .10 .30
84 Space Beauty .10 .30
85 The Flaming Planet .10 .30
86 The Great Vegetable Rebellion .10 .30
87 Junkyard of Space .10 .30
88 Checklist 1 .10 .30
89 Checklist 2 .10 .30
90 Checklist 3 .10 .30
FS Costume from Fugitives in Space 15.00 40.00
(issued as album exclusive)

2005 The Complete Lost in Space 1966 Expansion
COMPLETE SET (55) 12.00 30.00
STATED ODDS 1:8

R56 Prof. John Robinson .30 .75
R57 Maureen Robinson .30 .75
R58 Major Don West .30 .75
R59 Will Robinson .30 .75
R60 Pilot & Penny Robinson .30 .75
R61 Judy Robinson and Friend .30 .75
R62 Dr. Zachary Smith .30 .75
R63 Final Systems Check .30 .75
R64 An Optimistic Outlook .30 .75
R65 Robot In Magnetic Lock .30 .75
R66 Pre-Launch Admiration .30 .75
R67 Five and a Half Year Sleep .30 .75
R68 Awaiting The Countdown .30 .75
R69 Launch Plus Eight Hours...Destroy! .30 .75
R70 A State of Suspended Animation .30 .75
R71 Perilous Space-Walk .30 .75
R72 Hopelessly Lost In Space .30 .75
R73 Ready for Action .30 .75
R74 Frozen For The Crash .30 .75
R75 Now Who's The Dr.? You or Me? .30 .75
R76 Robot Reporting .30 .75
R77 Thoughts Of Home .30 .75
R78 Unessential Liquidations .30 .75
R79 Trapped! .30 .75
R80 A Boy and His B-9 .30 .75
R81 The Journey South Begins .30 .75
R82 Sentimental Departures .30 .75
R83 The Giant Cyclops .30 .75
R84 Attack On The Chariot .30 .75
R85 Exploring Ancient Ruins .30 .75
R86 Tomb Secrets Revealed .30 .75
R87 The Sun Shield .30 .75
R88 Waiting For Relief .30 .75
R89 Interplanetary Survivors .30 .75
R90 Devistation Diverted .30 .75
R91 Across The Hungry Sea .30 .75
R92 Seeking A Humaniod Brain .30 .75
R93 A Sinister Plan For The Doctor .30 .75
R94 Calling All Creatures .30 .75
R95 Unexpected Proposal .30 .75
R96 Monsterous Moment of Peril .30 .75
R97 The Jet Pack .30 .75
R98 The Thought Machine .30 .75
R99 I Said, You May Serve Me Now. .30 .75
R100 Facing The Robotoid .30 .75
R101 Lurking Evil .30 .75
R102 You Are The King? .30 .75
R103 Computerized Compuations .30 .75
R104 Possessed By An Alien Spirit .30 .75
R105 Rock 'n' Roll Robot .30 .75
R106 Joyful Moments .30 .75
R107 Boy Genius .30 .75
R108 That Move Does Not Compute! .30 .75
R109 A Hilarious Profile .30 .75
R110 Never Fear, Smith is Here! .30 .75

2005 The Complete Lost in Space 1966 Reprint
COMPLETE SET (55) 12.00 30.00
STATED ODDS 1:8

R1 The World Waits .30 .75
R2 Aliens are Listening .30 .75
R3 Ready For Take-Off .30 .75
R4 The Pilot Dreams .30 .75
R5 Good-Bye, Earth! .30 .75
R6 Destination - The Stars! .30 .75
R7 Ship Off Course .30 .75
R8 Silence From Earth .30 .75
R9 The Mystery Below .30 .75
R10 Who Goes There? .30 .75
R11 The Stowaway .30 .75
R12 Readying The Robot .30 .75
R13 Fear On Board .30 .75
R14 Terror Strikes .30 .75
R15 Trapped! .30 .75
R16 Two In Danger .30 .75
R17 Danger Ahead .30 .75
R18 A New Peril .30 .75
R19 No Escape .30 .75
R20 Last Chance .30 .75
R21 The Metal Menace .30 .75
R22 Shock Landing .30 .75
R23 Victim Of The Crash .30 .75
R24 Opening The Way .30 .75
R25 Robot Research .30 .75
R26 The Strange Planet .30 .75
R27 The Chariot .30 .75
R28 Robot Reporting .30 .75
R29 Alarming News .30 .75
R30 Urgent Warning .30 .75
R31 The Ground Trembles .30 .75
R32 The Deadly Sun .30 .75
R33 Safe From The Sun .30 .75
R34 The Robinsons Report .30 .75
R35 Penny's Pet .30 .75
R36 Where Is Penny? .30 .75
R37 The Plants of Peril .30 .75
R38 The Terrible Sight .30 .75
R39 The Plants' Prey .30 .75
R40 Lost In Darkness .30 .75
R41 The Mystery Ship .30 .75
R42 Running For Help .30 .75
R43 The Search .30 .75
R44 In The Lost City .30 .75
R45 The Stranger Helps .30 .75
R46 The Terrible Cold .30 .75
R47 What Was That? .30 .75
R48 One-Eyed Terror .30 .75
R49 The Giant Threatens .30 .75
R50 The Awesome Menace .30 .75
R51 Readying An Attack .30 .75
R52 The Flying Warrior .30 .75
R53 The Battle Begins .30 .75
R54 In Death's Grip .30 .75
R55 Facing The Future .30 .75

2005 The Complete Lost in Space Autographs
STATED ODDS TWO PER BOX
HARRIS AUTO ISSUED AS 6-CASE INCENTIVE

AC Angela Cartwright 60.00 120.00
AJ Arte Johnson 15.00 40.00
BM Bill Mumy 60.00 120.00
DH Dee Hartford 12.00 30.00
DT Daniel J. Travanti 12.00 30.00
FY Francine York 10.00 25.00
JH Jonathan Harris as Dr. Smith CUT/50
(issued as 6-case incentive)
JL June Lockhart 50.00 100.00
KH Kevin Hagen 10.00 25.00
LS Leonard Stone 12.00 30.00
MA Michael Ansara 10.00 25.00
MG Mark Goddard 40.00 80.00
MK Marta Kristen 50.00 100.00
MT Malachi Throne 10.00 25.00
SJ Sherry Jackson 15.00 40.00
VM Vitina Marcus 12.00 30.00
DM1 Don Matheson 30.00 60.00
Idak)
DM2 Don Matheson 30.00 60.00
Rethso)
LKC June Lockhart 100.00 175.00
Marta Kristen/Angela Cartwright
SA1 Sheila Allen 10.00 25.00
Aunt Gamma)
SA2 Sheila Allen 10.00 25.00
Brynhilde)
SA3 Sheila Allen 10.00 25.00
Ruth Templeton)
BMAC Bill Mumy 60.00 120.00
Angela Cartwright
BMDT Bob May 100.00 175.00
Dick Tufeld
MGMK Mark Goddard 60.00 120.00
Marta Kristen

2005 The Complete Lost in Space Characters
COMPLETE SET (7) 10.00 25.00
STATED ODDS 1:20

R1 Professor John Robinson 1.50 4.00
R2 Maureen Robinson 1.50 4.00
R3 Dr. Zachary Smith 1.50 4.00
R4 Will Robinson 1.50 4.00
R5 Major Don West 1.50 4.00
R6 Penny Robinson 1.50 4.00
R7 Judy Robinson 1.50 4.00

2005 The Complete Lost in Space Faces of Dr. Smith
COMPLETE SET (9) 10.00 25.00
STATED ODDS 1:16

F1 Montage of Dr. Smith 1.25 3.00
F2 Montage of Dr. Smith 1.25 3.00
F3 Montage of Dr. Smith 1.25 3.00
F4 Montage of Dr. Smith 1.25 3.00
F5 Montage of Dr. Smith 1.25 3.00
F6 Montage of Dr. Smith 1.25 3.00
F7 Montage of Dr. Smith 1.25 3.00
F8 Montage of Dr. Smith 1.25 3.00
F9 Montage of Dr. Smith 1.25 3.00

2005 The Complete Lost in Space SketchaFex
STATED ODDS 1:480
PANSICA CHARIOT SKETCH ISSUED AS CASE TOPPER
PANSICA ROBOT SKETCH ISSUED AS 2-CASE INCENTIVE

1 Cris Bolson/(Space Pos) 25.00 50.00
2 Cris Bolson/(Jupiter 2) 25.00 50.00
3 Eduardo Pansica 25.00 50.00
The Chariot/(issued as case topper)
4 Eduardo Pansica 25.00 50.00
Robot B9/(issued as 2-case incentive)

2005 The Complete Lost in Space The Good, The Bad, and the Ugly
COMPLETE SET (9) 6.00 15.00
STATED ODDS 1:8

S1 Montage of Aliens .75 2.00
Robots/Creatures
S2 Montage of Aliens .75 2.00
Robots/Creatures
S3 Montage of Aliens .75 2.00
Robots/Creatures
S4 Montage of Aliens .75 2.00
Robots/Creatures
S5 Montage of Aliens .75 2.00
Robots/Creatures
S6 Montage of Aliens .75 2.00
Robots/Creatures
S7 Montage of Aliens .75 2.00
Robots/Creatures
S8 Montage of Aliens .75 2.00
Robots/Creatures
S9 Montage of Aliens .75 2.00
Robots/Creatures

2005 Doom Movie
COMPLETE SET (72) 4.00 10.00

1 Title Card .10 .30
2 Sarge .10 .30
3 John Reaper Grimm .10 .30
4 Samantha Grimm .10 .30
5 Destroyer .10 .30
6 Portman .10 .30
7 The Kid .10 .30
8 Duke .10 .30
9 Goat .10 .30
10 Pinky .10 .30
11 Hell Knight .10 .30
12 Carmack Albino Imp .10 .30
13 Preparing for Leave .10 .30
14 Leave Is Cancelled .10 .30
15 Chopper Ride .10 .30
16 Reaper Arrives .10 .30
17 Distress Call .10 .30
18 Disembark .10 .30
19 Sarge Barks Orders .10 .30
20 The Ark .10 .30
21 Assignment on Mars .10 .30
22 Light It Up .10 .30
23 Animal Lab .10 .30
24 Shocking Discovery .10 .30
25 Weapons Lab .10 .30
26 Access Denied .10 .30
27 Rookie Mistake .10 .30
28 Sleeveless Fashion .10 .30
29 Retrieving Data .10 .30
30 Lucy .10 .30
31 Super Lucy .10 .30
32 First Contact .10 .30
33 Dr. Carmack .10 .30
34 The Doctor Is Insane .10 .30
35 Well Done .10 .30
36 Whacked Scientist .10 .30
37 Ventilated .10 .30
38 Hell at the Animal Lab .10 .30
39 Bad Blood .10 .30
40 Sewer-cide Mission .10 .30
41 Scientific Discovery .10 .30
42 Split Decision .10 .30
43 Afraid of the Dark .10 .30
44 Eyes in the Dark .10 .30
45 Man Down .10 .30
46 Emergency .10 .30
47 Looking for Answers .10 .30
48 Open Wide .10 .30
49 Airlock Inspections .10 .30
50 Decapitation .10 .30
51 Confrontation .10 .30
52 Run for Your Lives .10 .30
53 Entrapment .10 .30
54 Sarge Needs a Hand .10 .30
55 BFG .10 .30
56 Yanked into Darkness .10 .30
57 Electric Battle .10 .30
58 Human Discovery .10 .30
59 Born Again .10 .30
60 Regroup .10 .30
61 Curtis Stahle .10 .30
62 Back to the Ark .10 .30
63 Selective Evil .10 .30
64 The Other Side .10 .30
65 Don't Axe, Don't Tell .10 .30
66 Hell Knight Returns .10 .30
67 Desperate Measures .10 .30
68 Demons Abound .10 .30
69 A Knight to Remember .10 .30
70 Out of the Shadows .10 .30
71 End of the Line .10 .30
72 Checklist .10 .30

2005 Doom Movie Autographs
STATED ODDS 1:24

1 Dwayne Johnson 125.00 200.00
2 Rosamund Pike
3 Karl Urban
4 Deobia Oparei 6.00 15.00
5 Raz Adoti 6.00 15.00
6 Ben Daniels
7 Richard Brake
8 Dexter Fletcher
9 Al Weaver 6.00 15.00
10 Phil Adams 6.00 15.00
11 Doug Jones
12 Brian Steele

2005 Doom Movie Promos
P1 Group of Six
P2 Sarge

2005 Doom Movie Villains
COMPLETE SET (9) 3.00 8.00
STATED ODDS 5:24

R1 Curtis Stahle .60 1.50
R2 Hell Knight .60 1.50
R3 Infected Carmack .60 1.50
R4 Demon .60 1.50
R5 Sewer Imp .60 1.50
R6 Imp .60 1.50
R7 Carmack Albino Imp .60 1.50
R8 Imp in Nonowall .60 1.50
R9 Axe Zombie .60 1.50

2005 Enterprise Season Four
COMPLETE SET (72) 4.00 10.00

235 Title Card .10 .30
236 Title Card .10 .30
237 Title Card .10 .30
238 Storm Front, Part 1 .10 .30
239 Storm Front, Part 1 .10 .30
240 Storm Front, Part 1 .10 .30
241 Storm Front, Part 2 .10 .30
242 Storm Front, Part 2 .10 .30
243 Storm Front, Part 2 .10 .30
244 Home .10 .30
245 Home .10 .30
246 Home .10 .30
247 Borderland .10 .30
248 Borderland .10 .30
249 Borderland .10 .30
250 Cold Station 12 .10 .30
251 Cold Station 12 .10 .30
252 Cold Station 12 .10 .30
253 The Augments .10 .30
254 The Augments .10 .30
255 The Augments .10 .30
256 The Forge .10 .30
257 The Forge .10 .30
258 The Forge .10 .30
259 Awakening .10 .30
260 Awakening .10 .30
261 Awakening .10 .30
262 Kir'Shara .10 .30
263 Kir'Shara .10 .30
264 Kir'Shara .10 .30
265 Daedalus .10 .30
266 Daedalus .10 .30
267 Daedalus .10 .30
268 Observer Effect .10 .30
269 Observer Effect .10 .30
270 Observer Effect .10 .30
271 Babel One .10 .30
272 Babel One .10 .30
273 Babel One .10 .30
274 United .10 .30
275 United .10 .30
276 United .10 .30
277 The Aenar .10 .30
278 The Aenar .10 .30
279 The Aenar .10 .30
280 Affliction .10 .30
281 Affliction .10 .30
282 Affliction .10 .30
283 Divergence .10 .30
284 Divergence .10 .30
285 Divergence .10 .30
286 Bound .10 .30
287 Bound .10 .30
288 Bound .10 .30
289 In a Mirror, Darkly - Part 1 .10 .30
290 In a Mirror, Darkly - Part 1 .10 .30
291 In a Mirror, Darkly - Part 1 .10 .30
292 In a Mirror, Darkly - Part 2 .10 .30
293 In a Mirror, Darkly - Part 2 .10 .30
294 In a Mirror, Darkly - Part 2 .10 .30
295 Demons .10 .30
296 Demons .10 .30
297 Demons .10 .30
298 Terra Prime .10 .30
299 Terra Prime .10 .30
300 Terra Prime .10 .30
301 These Are the Voyages .10 .30
302 These Are the Voyages .10 .30
303 These Are the Voyages .10 .30
304 Checklist 1 .10 .30
305 Checklist 2 .10 .30
306 Checklist 3 .10 .30

2005 Enterprise Season Four Archer in Action
COMPLETE SET (9) 40.00 80.00

AIA1 Desert Crossing 5.00 12.00
AIA2 The Seventh 5.00 12.00
AIA3 Harbinger 5.00 12.00
AIA4 Cold Station 12 5.00 12.00
AIA5 The Forge 5.00 12.00
AIA6 Kir'Shara 5.00 12.00
AIA7 United 5.00 12.00
AIA8 Divergence 5.00 12.00
AIA9 In a Mirror, Darkly 5.00 12.00

2005 Enterprise Season Four Autographs
STATED ODDS TWO PER BOX
ARENBERG AUTO ISSUED IN COLLECTORS ALBUM
L (LIMITED): 300-500 COPIES
VL (VERY LIMITED): 200-300 COPIES

1 Abby Brammell 8.00 20.00
2 Alec Newman 8.00 20.00
3 Alexandra Lydon 8.00 20.00
4 Anthony Montgomery VL 20.00 40.00
5 Bill Cobbs VL 8.00 20.00
6 Bobbi Sue Luther 15.00 30.00
7 Brent Spiner L 75.00 150.00
8 Brian Thompson 8.00 20.00
9 Bruce Gray 8.00 20.00
10 Crystal Allen 15.00 30.00
11 Eric Pierpoint 8.00 20.00
12 Gary Graham L 10.00 25.00
13 J. Paul Boehmer 8.00 20.00
14 Jeffrey Combs 15.00 30.00
15 Johanna Watts 8.00 20.00
16 John Schuck 8.00 20.00
17 Jolene Blalock L
18 Kaj-Erik Eriksen 8.00 20.00
19 Kara Zediker 8.00 20.00
20 Lee Arenberg 8.00 20.00
(issued in collectors album)
21 Leslie Silva 8.00 20.00
22 Linda Park L
23 Menina Fortunato 10.00 25.00
24 Richard Riehle 10.00 25.00
25 Steve Schirripa VL 15.00 30.00
26 Vaughn Armstrong VL 10.00 25.00

2005 Enterprise Season Four Costume Autographs
PARK AUTO ISSUED AS 2-CASE INCENTIVE
BLALOCK AUTO ISSUED AS 6-CASE INCENTIVE

1 Linda Park 60.00 120.00
(issued as 2-case incentive)
2 Jolene Blalock
(issued as 6-case incentive)

2005 Enterprise Season Four From the Archives Costumes
STATED ODDS ONE PER BOX
DC1 ISSUED AS CASE TOPPER

C3 T'Pol 20.00 40.00
C4 T'Pol 20.00 40.00
C5 T'Pol (Mirror Universe) 20.00 40.00
C6 Travis Mayweather (Mirror Universe) 6.00 15.00
C7 Archer (Mirror Universe) 15.00 30.00
C8 Silik 6.00 15.00
C9 Degra 6.00 15.00
C10 Daniels 10.00 25.00
C11 Lieutenant Talas 6.00 15.00
C12 Lieutenant Talas 6.00 15.00
C13 Malik 6.00 15.00
C14 Persis 8.00 20.00
C15 Raakin 6.00 15.00
C16 Soval 8.00 20.00
DC1 Dr. Arik Soong DUAL 25.00 50.00
(issued as case topper)

2005 Enterprise Season Four Genesis
COMPLETE SET (9) 15.00 40.00
STATED ODDS 1:20

G1 Orions 2.00 5.00
G2 Ugenic Wars (Augments) 2.00 5.00
G3 Klingons 2.00 5.00
G4 Andorians 2.00 5.00
G5 Tellarites 2.00 5.00
G6 Surak 2.00 5.00
G7 Mirror Universe 2.00 5.00
G8 Gorn 2.00 5.00
G9 The Tholians 2.00 5.00

2005 Enterprise Season Four In a Mirror
COMPLETE SET (9) 10.00 25.00
STATED ODDS 1:10

M1 Commander Archer 1.25 3.00
M2 Captain Archer 1.25 3.00
M3 T'Pol 1.25 3.00
M4 Charles Trip Tucker III 1.25 3.00
M5 Major Reed 1.25 3.00
M6 Sergeant Mayweather 1.25 3.00
M7 Dr. Phlox 1.25 3.00
M8 Ensign Hoshi Sato 1.25 3.00
M9 Captain Maxwell Forrest 1.25 3.00

2005 Family Guy Season One

COMPLETE SET (72)	4.00	10.00
❑ 1 The Family Guy	.10	.30
❑ 2 Peter Griffin	.10	.30
❑ 3 Lois Griffin	.10	.30
❑ 4 Meg Griffin	.10	.30
❑ 5 Chris Griffin	.10	.30
❑ 6 Brian Griffin	.10	.30
❑ 7 Stewie Griffin	.10	.30
❑ 8 Old-Fashioned Values	.10	.30
❑ 9 Lucky Is A Family Guy	.10	.30
❑ 10 Glen Quagmire	.10	.30
❑ 11 Cleveland	.10	.30
❑ 12 Loretta	.10	.30
❑ 13 Joe Swanson	.10	.30
❑ 14 Bonnie Swanson	.10	.30
❑ 15 Kevin Swanson	.10	.30
❑ 16 Tom Tucker	.10	.30
❑ 17 Diane Simmons	.10	.30
❑ 18 Mr. Weed	.10	.30
❑ 19 Home Sweet Home	.10	.30
❑ 20 Happy-Go-Lucky Toys Inc.	.10	.30
❑ 21 Quahog Institute Of Cosmetic Surgery	.10	.30
❑ 22 Quahog Airport	.10	.30
❑ 23 James Woods Regional High School	.10	.30
❑ 24 Stop N Shop	.10	.30
❑ 25 Quahog DMV	.10	.30
❑ 26 Quahog Hospital	.10	.30
❑ 27 Quahog Jail	.10	.30
❑ 28 Raising The Bar	.10	.30
❑ 29 Rip-Off	.10	.30
❑ 30 Super Return	.10	.30
❑ 31 Cable's Out	.10	.30
❑ 32 Must See TV	.10	.30
❑ 33 Damned Broccoli	.10	.30
❑ 34 The Fight	.10	.30
❑ 35 Circus At The Griffins	.10	.30
❑ 36 Cult Buddies	.10	.30
❑ 37 Hitting A Girl	.10	.30
❑ 38 House Arrest	.10	.30
❑ 39 Time Machine	.10	.30
❑ 40 New Neighbors	.10	.30
❑ 41 A Crapple Wins The Game	.10	.30
❑ 42 Fake Hero	.10	.30
❑ 43 Scouts A Drag	.10	.30
❑ 44 Bets Are Off	.10	.30
❑ 45 Vision Quest	.10	.30
❑ 46 Dog Show	.10	.30
❑ 47 Going Solo	.10	.30
❑ 48 Dog Day In Court	.10	.30
❑ 49 Vile Woman	.10	.30
❑ 50 Gun Sandwich	.10	.30
❑ 51 Victory	.10	.30
❑ 52 Silence	.10	.30
❑ 53 Wax Idiotic	.10	.30
❑ 54 Between The Sheets	.10	.30
❑ 55 Observing Peter	.10	.30
❑ 56 Correcting Bad Behavior	.10	.30
❑ 57 Marital Advice	.10	.30
❑ 58 Supporting A Friend	.10	.30
❑ 59 Thoughts On New York	.10	.30
❑ 60 Thoughts On Stewie	.10	.30
❑ 61 Thoughts On Other Dogs	.10	.30
❑ 62 Brian And Peter	.10	.30
❑ 63 Mixin It Up	.10	.30
❑ 64 ...Tried To Give Up Candy?	.10	.30
❑ 65 ...Tried To Do The Laundry?	.10	.30
❑ 66 ...Tried To Change Stewie?	.10	.30
❑ 67 ...Hit That Deer?	.10	.30
❑ 68 ...Found You?	.10	.30
❑ 69 ...Got Drunk On The Communion Wine?	.10	.30
❑ 70 Soccer Moms	.10	.30
❑ 71 This Place Is Dead	.10	.30
❑ 72 Checklist	.10	.30

2005 Family Guy Season One Autographs

❑ A1 Seth Mcfarlane	350.00	600.00
❑ A2 Alex Borstein	10.00	20.00
❑ A3 Erik Estrada	10.00	20.00
❑ A4 Mike Henry	5.00	10.00
❑ A5 Lori Alan	5.00	10.00
❑ A6 Wally Wingert	5.00	10.00

2005 Family Guy Season One Bad Dog

STATED ODDS 1:17		
❑ BD1 Foul Mouth	1.00	2.50
❑ BD2 Bar Hound	1.00	2.50
❑ BD3 Horn-Dog	1.00	2.50
❑ BD4 Butt Head	1.00	2.50
❑ BD5 The Sauce	1.00	2.50
❑ BD6 Dirty Dawg	1.00	2.50

2005 Family Guy Season One Box Loaders

COMPLETE SET (4)	8.00	20.00
STATED ODDS ONE PER BOX		
❑ BL1 Soldier Magazine	1.50	4.00
❑ BL2 Machiavelli+D2 The Prince	1.50	4.00
❑ BL3 Sun Tsu & The Art Of War	1.50	4.00
❑ CL1 The Peter Principle	5.00	12.00
CASE INSERT		

2005 Family Guy Season One Griffin Family Photos

STATED ODDS 1:11		
❑ FP1 Disco Family	.75	2.00
❑ FP2 Family Sing Along	.75	2.00
❑ FP3 Watching TV With The Family	.75	2.00
❑ FP4 Family Bonding	.75	2.00
❑ FP5 TV Family	.75	2.00
❑ FP6 Family Origins	.75	2.00
❑ FP7 Lois Loves Her Family	.75	2.00
❑ FP8 Cheering For Family	.75	2.00
❑ FP9 Family Love	.75	2.00

2005 Family Guy Season One Sketches

STATED ODDS 1:24		
❑ SK1 Tone Rodriguez	20.00	40.00
❑ SK2 John Czop	30.00	60.00
❑ SK3 Andrew Meisner	20.00	40.00
❑ SK4 Chris Moreno	20.00	40.00
❑ SK5 Mark Dos Santos	30.00	60.00
❑ SK6 Jeff Zugale	20.00	40.00
❑ SK7 Joel Gomez	20.00	40.00
❑ SK8 Nar	100.00	200.00
❑ SK9 Billy Martinez	15.00	30.00
❑ SK10 Becky Grutzik	15.00	30.00
❑ SK11 Matt Wendt	20.00	40.00
❑ SK12 Rich Koslowski	20.00	40.00
❑ SK13 Roland Paris	30.00	60.00
❑ SK14 Greg Colton	75.00	150.00

2005 Fantastic Four Movie

COMPLETE SET (100)	6.00	15.00
❑ 1 Fantastic 4	.15	.40
❑ 2 Reed Richards - Mr. Fantastic	.15	.40
❑ 3 Sue Storm - The Invisible Woman	.15	.40
❑ 4 Johnny Storm - The Human Torch	.15	.40
❑ 5 Ben Grimm - The Thing	.15	.40
❑ 6 Victor Von Doom - Dr. Doom	.15	.40
❑ 7 Debbie - Ben's Fiancee	.15	.40
❑ 8 Alicia Masters	.15	.40
❑ 9 Leonardo - Dr. Doom's Assistant	.15	.40
❑ 10 Mission into Space	.15	.40
❑ 11 The Team Reunited	.15	.40
❑ 12 Until We Meet Again	.15	.40
❑ 13 Tomorrow's Heroes	.15	.40
❑ 14 On the Space Station	.15	.40
❑ 15 Suited for Danger	.15	.40
❑ 16 In the Airlock	.15	.40
❑ 17 Victor's Surprise	.15	.40
❑ 18 Close the Shields Now	.15	.40
❑ 19 Space Walk Peril	.15	.40
❑ 20 The Cosmic Storm	.15	.40
❑ 21 After Effects	.15	.40
❑ 22 Temperature Rising	.15	.40
❑ 23 Going Invisible	.15	.40
❑ 24 Bend and Stretch	.15	.40
❑ 25 Flame On	.15	.40
❑ 26 Breaking in on Ben	.15	.40
❑ 27 The Fifth Mutant	.15	.40
❑ 28 This Man... This Monster	.15	.40
❑ 29 A Tragic Farewell	.15	.40
❑ 30 One Way to Stop Traffic	.15	.40
❑ 31 A Little Help Here	.15	.40
❑ 32 Simply Fantastic	.15	.40
❑ 33 Makeshift Rescue	.15	.40
❑ 34 Invisible Beauty	.15	.40
❑ 35 Firetruck Peril!	.15	.40
❑ 36 Power of the Thing	.15	.40
❑ 37 Sudden Celebrities	.15	.40
❑ 38 Hero or Horror	.15	.40
❑ 39 Under Analysis	.15	.40
❑ 40 Inside the Thing	.15	.40
❑ 41 The Siblings Reborn	.15	.40
❑ 42 Perils of Supernova	.15	.40
❑ 43 A Specimen Strikes Back	.15	.40
❑ 44 The Doctor's Doom	.15	.40
❑ 45 A Way Back to Normal	.15	.40
❑ 46 Grimm's Lonely Nights	.15	.40
❑ 47 At the Pub	.15	.40
❑ 48 Kindred Spirits	.15	.40
❑ 49 Johnny Storm - Superstar	.15	.40
❑ 50 The Ladies Call Him Torch	.15	.40
❑ 51 Grimm's Grim Warning	.15	.40
❑ 52 Divided They Fall	.15	.40
❑ 53 Heroes in Conflict	.15	.40
❑ 54 The Torch Steamed Up	.15	.40
❑ 55 You Two Need a Time-Out	.15	.40
❑ 56 Crackle of Doom	.15	.40
❑ 57 The Killing of Ned Cecil	.15	.40
❑ 58 What Is That Thing	.15	.40
❑ 59 How Bad Could It Be	.15	.40
❑ 60 Some Thing About You	.15	.40
❑ 61 Kindness Is Blind	.15	.40
❑ 62 Under the Stars	.15	.40
❑ 63 Divide and Conquer	.15	.40
❑ 64 Friend against Friend	.15	.40
❑ 65 The Thing on a Rampage	.15	.40
❑ 66 Taking a Major Step	.15	.40
❑ 67 Ben Grimm Restored	.15	.40
❑ 68 Disaster at Fantastic 4 Central	.15	.40
❑ 69 The Fate of Two Mutants	.15	.40
❑ 70 Firing a Heat-Seeker	.15	.40
❑ 71 Target: The Human Torch	.15	.40
❑ 72 Monarch of Menace	.15	.40
❑ 73 To Save Reed's Life	.15	.40
❑ 74 Facing Doctor Doom	.15	.40
❑ 75 Against His Fiendish Fury	.15	.40
❑ 76 Grasp of a Madman	.15	.40
❑ 77 Return of the Thing	.15	.40
❑ 78 It's Clobberin' Time	.15	.40
❑ 79 A Punch Long Awaited	.15	.40
❑ 80 Super Streetfighter	.15	.40
❑ 81 Too Much for Grimm	.15	.40
❑ 82 Heroes on the Scene	.15	.40
❑ 83 And Johnny Makes Four	.15	.40
❑ 84 Fighting a Metallic Maniac	.15	.40
❑ 85 The Challenge of Doom	.15	.40
❑ 86 Their Powers Combined	.15	.40
❑ 87 Defeat of Dr. Doom	.15	.40
❑ 88 Metamorphosis	.15	.40
❑ 89 Doom's Dark Monument	.15	.40
❑ 90 A Team for All Time	.15	.40
❑ 91 Directing Outer Space	.15	.40
❑ 92 Building a Better Thing	.15	.40
❑ 93 The Quasimodo Effect	.15	.40
❑ 94 Preparing Dr. Doom	.15	.40
❑ 95 The Wildcard	.15	.40
❑ 96 Recreating the Locations	.15	.40
❑ 97 Lights! Camera! Super-Action	.15	.40
❑ 98 An Invisible Woman's Place	.15	.40
❑ 99 Fantastic Filmmaking	.15	.40
❑ 100 Fun with the Fantastic Founder	.15	.40

2005 Fantastic Four Movie Authentic Costumes

STATED ODDS 1:20		
❑ DD1 Victor Von Doom - Shirt ORANGE/1899	5.00	12.00
❑ DD2 Victor Von Doom - Suit ORANGE/999	6.00	15.00
❑ DD3 Dr. Doom - Cloak ORANGE /4999	4.00	10.00
❑ DD4 Dr. Doom - Cloak BLUE/499	8.00	20.00
❑ FF1 Human Torch - Suit ORANGE/969	12.00	30.00
❑ FF2 Human Torch - Suit BLUE/499	20.00	50.00
❑ FF3 Mr. Fantastic - Suit ORANGE/969	12.00	30.00
❑ FF4 Mr. Fantastic - Suit BLUE/499	20.00	50.00
❑ FF5 Invisible Woman - Suit ORANGE/349	40.00	80.00
❑ FF6 Invisible Woman - Suit BLUE/299	40.00	80.00
❑ FF7 The Thing - Suit ORANGE/399	20.00	50.00
❑ FF8 The Thing - Suit BLUE/299	20.00	50.00
❑ FF9 Invisible Woman - Suit BLUE/699	30.00	60.00

2005 Garbage Pail Kids All New Series 4

COMPLETE SET (80)	6.00	15.00
PROMO ISSUED AS SDCC EXCLUSIVE		
❑ 1a Green Cheese Chase	.10	.25
❑ 1b Phil Moon	.10	.25
❑ 2a Paris Embarrassed	.10	.25
❑ 2b Maris Wiltin'	.10	.25
❑ 3a Worked-Up Warren	.10	.25
❑ 3b Chin-Up Chandler	.10	.25
❑ 4a Jimmy Dean	.10	.25
❑ 4b Sausage Sam	.10	.25
❑ 5a Allie Oops	.10	.25
❑ 5b Swingin' Sierra	.10	.25
❑ 6a Paul Vault	.10	.25
❑ 6b Impaled Dale	.10	.25
❑ 7a Nin Jack	.10	.25
❑ 7b Marshall Artless	.10	.25
❑ 8a Anna Cornea	.10	.25
❑ 8b Monica Ails	.10	.25
❑ 9a Clay Achin'	.10	.25
❑ 9b Idol Ivan	.10	.25
❑ 10a Colin Bowel	.10	.25
❑ 10b Scoutin' Scott	.10	.25
❑ 11a Grunge Bob	.10	.25
❑ 11b Spongey Spencer	.10	.25
❑ 12a Brainwashed Brett	.10	.25
❑ 12b Ed N. Shoulders	.10	.25
❑ 13a Fallen Angel	.10	.25
❑ 13b Airsick Ariel	.10	.25
❑ 14a Headless Leslie	.10	.25
❑ 14b Madison Halved	.10	.25
❑ 15a Jumpin' Jen	.10	.25
❑ 15b Megan Trouble	.10	.25
❑ 16a Cole Slawed	.10	.25
❑ 16b Sal Salad	.10	.25
❑ 17a Walter Cooler	.10	.25
❑ 17b Wizzin' Will	.10	.25
❑ 18a Harry Who Didn't	.10	.25
❑ 18b Noel Escape	.10	.25
❑ 19a Tom Turkey	.10	.25
❑ 19b Thanks Gavin	.10	.25
❑ 20a Vomitin' Victor	.10	.25
❑ 20b Ralphin' Ryan	.10	.25
❑ 21a Blown Away Ray	.10	.25
❑ 21b Breezy Brady	.10	.25
❑ 22a Snakey Jake	.10	.25
❑ 22b Charming Charlie	.10	.25
❑ 23a Blastin' Sebastian	.10	.25
❑ 23b Explosive Xavier	.10	.25
❑ 24a Cleaved Steve	.10	.25
❑ 24b Tandem Randy	.10	.25
❑ 25a Totem Tim	.10	.25
❑ 25b High Man Dan	.10	.25
❑ 26a Wishful Wes	.10	.25
❑ 26b Al Addin' Fumes	.10	.25
❑ 27a Wolver-Ian	.10	.25
❑ 27b Pokin' Logan	.10	.25
❑ 28a Fuelin' Julian	.10	.25
❑ 28b Gassin' Grant	.10	.25
❑ 29a Scuba Doo Lou	.10	.25
❑ 29b Harpoonin' Hunter	.10	.25
❑ 30a Turd King Travis	.10	.25
❑ 30b Poo-A-Mid Parker	.10	.25
❑ 31a Snotty Sarah	.10	.25
❑ 31b Jessica Simpleton	.10	.25
❑ 32a Mulched Mitch	.10	.25
❑ 32b Cut Up Chris	.10	.25
❑ 33a Hollow Wayne	.10	.25
❑ 33b Jacqueline Lantern	.10	.25
❑ 34a Zitty Zak	.10	.25
❑ 34b Acne Andy	.10	.25
❑ 35a Floodgate Nate	.10	.25
❑ 35b Levee Levi	.10	.25
❑ 36a Noah's Barf	.10	.25
❑ 36b High-Water Mark	.10	.25
❑ 37a Log Roland	.10	.25
❑ 37b Roger Logger	.10	.25
❑ 38a Recycled Michael	.10	.25
❑ 38b Overflowin' Owen	.10	.25
❑ 39a Nasty Ashley	.10	.25
❑ 39b Mary-Kate Ate	.10	.25
❑ 40a Adam Bomb	.10	.25
❑ 40b Blasted Billy	.10	.25
❑ Promo Batty Brad	1.00	2.50

2005 Garbage Pail Kids All New Series 4 Bonus

COMPLETE SET (4)		
B6 STATED ODDS ONE PER WALMART BONUS BOX		
B7 STATED ODDS ONE PER TOYS R US/KMART BONUS BOX		
B8 STATED ODDS ONE PER TARGET BONUS BOX		
B9 STATED ODDS ONE PER TWO-PACK BLISTER		
❑ B6 Doug Sledding	6.00	15.00
❑ B7 Propelled Miguel	6.00	15.00
❑ B8 Swarmed Norm	4.00	10.00
❑ B9 Dancin' Dominic	1.25	3.00

2005 Garbage Pail Kids All New Series 4 Game

COMPLETE SET (36)	25.00	50.00
COMP.SET w/o SP's (33)	4.00	10.00
STATED ODDS ONE PER PACK		
SP STATED ODDS 1:72		
❑ GPK1 Barfin' Marvin	.15	.40
❑ GPK2 Bad Breath Seth	.15	.40
❑ GPK3 Basket Casey	.15	.40
❑ GPK4 BMX Ben	.15	.40
❑ GPK5 Blow Hardy	.15	.40
❑ GPK6 Beasty Boyd	.15	.40
❑ GPK7 Drippy Debbie	.15	.40
❑ GPK8 Dead Ted	.15	.40
❑ GPK9 Bony Joanie	.15	.40
❑ GPK10 Fartin' Martin FOIL SP	10.00	20.00
❑ GPK11 Bratty Maddy	.15	.40
❑ GPK12 Off Key Lee	.15	.40
❑ GPK13 Shel Game	.15	.40
❑ GPK14 Richie Retch FOIL SP	10.00	20.00
❑ GPK15 Explorin' Norman	.15	.40
❑ GPK16 Horatio Hornblower	.15	.40
❑ GPK17 Leaky Lou	.15	.40
❑ GPK18 Johnny One-Note	.15	.40
❑ GPK19 Seymour Barf	.15	.40
❑ GPK20 Lost In Austin	.15	.40
❑ GPK21 Snot-Ball Saul	.15	.40
❑ GPK22 Lethal Ethan	.15	.40
❑ GPK23 Snotwich Sandra	.15	.40
❑ GPK24 Over Flo	.15	.40
❑ GPK25 Up Chuck	.15	.40
❑ GPK26 Rear View Myra	.15	.40
❑ GPK27 Potty Scotty	.15	.40
❑ GPK28 Valerie Vomit	.15	.40
❑ GPK29 Sewer Sue	.15	.40
❑ GPK30 Sk8 Nate	.15	.40
❑ GPK31 Adam Bomb FOIL SP	10.00	20.00
❑ GPK32 Yicchy Mickey	.15	.40
❑ GPK33 Ronny Nose	.15	.40
❑ GPK34 Stinker Belle	.15	.40
❑ GPK35 Juicy Jules	.15	.40
❑ GPK36 Varicose Wayne	.15	.40

2005 Garbage Pail Kids All New Series 4 Scratch 'n Stink

COMPLETE SET (12)	6.00	15.00
STATED ODDS 1:6		
❑ S1a Frank N. Wiener	.75	2.00
❑ S1b Oscar Mire	.75	2.00
❑ S2a Mount St. Helen	.75	2.00
❑ S2b Volcanic Vanessa	.75	2.00
❑ S3a Intest-Tina	.75	2.00
❑ S3b Oblivious Olivia	.75	2.00
❑ S4a Forrest Sump	.75	2.00
❑ S4b Wastin' Jason	.75	2.00
❑ S5a Stink Biot Stephanie	.75	2.00
❑ S5b Rorschach Tessa	.75	2.00
❑ S6a Vinnie Vomit	.75	2.00
❑ S6b Bart Bag Brad	.75	2.00

2005 Garbage Pail Kids All New Series 4 Sketches

STATED ODDS ONE PER HOBBY BOX

- ❑ 1 Don Perlin
- ❑ 2 Jay Lynch
- ❑ 3 John Czop
- ❑ 4 John Pound
- ❑ 5 Justin Green
- ❑ 6 Stephon Taylor
- ❑ 7 Tom Bunk

2005 Garbage Pail Kids All New Series 4 Tattoos

COMPLETE SET (10)	2.50	6.00
STATED ODDS 1:4		
❑ 1 Snakey Jake	.30	.75
❑ 2 Harry Who Didn't	.30	.75
❑ 3 Turd King Travis	.30	.75
❑ 4 Nin Jack	.30	.75
❑ 5 Paul Vault	.30	.75
❑ 6 Jumpin' Jen	.30	.75
❑ 7 Wishful Wes	.30	.75
❑ 8 Fallen Angel	.30	.75
❑ 9 Adam Bomb	.30	.75
❑ 10 Worked-Up Warren	.30	.75

2005 Harry Potter and the Goblet of Fire

COMPLETE SET (90)	5.00	12.00
❑ 1 Title Card	.15	.40
❑ 2 Harry Potter	.15	.40
❑ 3 Ron Weasley	.15	.40
❑ 4 Hermione Granger	.15	.40
❑ 5 Viktor Krum	.15	.40
❑ 6 Cedric Diggory	.15	.40
❑ 7 Fleur Delacour	.15	.40
❑ 8 Cho Chang	.15	.40
❑ 9 Albus Dumbledore	.15	.40
❑ 10 Mad-Eye-Moody	.15	.40
❑ 11 Barty Crouch Jr.	.15	.40
❑ 12 Rita Skeeter	.15	.40
❑ 13 Madame Maxime	.15	.40
❑ 14 Minerva McGonagall	.15	.40
❑ 15 Neville Longbottom	.15	.40
❑ 16 Lucius Malfoy	.15	.40
❑ 17 Severus Snape	.15	.40
❑ 18 Igor Karkaroff	.15	.40
❑ 19 Interesting News	.15	.40
❑ 20 A Manky Old Boot	.15	.40
❑ 21 The Diggorys	.15	.40
❑ 22 I Love Magic	.15	.40
❑ 23 Death Eaters	.15	.40
❑ 24 Get Back To The Portkey!	.15	.40
❑ 25 The Dark Mark	.15	.40
❑ 26 Morsmordre!	.15	.40
❑ 27 A Legendary Event	.15	.40
❑ 28 The Lovely Ladies Of Beauxbatons	.15	.40
❑ 29 The Proud Sons Of Durmstrang	.15	.40
❑ 30 Three Very Dangerous Tasks	.15	.40
❑ 31 A Practical Approach	.15	.40
❑ 32 The Unforgivable Curses	.15	.40
❑ 33 Talented, Isn't She?	.15	.40
❑ 34 The Age Line	.15	.40
❑ 35 Bottoms Up!	.15	.40
❑ 36 A Durmstrang Entry	.15	.40
❑ 37 The Champions	.15	.40
❑ 38 The First Hogwarts Champion	.15	.40
❑ 39 A Fourth Champion	.15	.40
❑ 40 A Binding Magical Contract	.15	.40
❑ 41 I Don't Want Eternal Glory!	.15	.40
❑ 42 Shall We Start With The Youngest?	.15	.40
❑ 43 You Don't Have a Choice!	.15	.40
❑ 44 Amazing...	.15	.40
❑ 45 Ronald Would Like Me To Tell You...	.15	.40
❑ 46 Dragons	.15	.40
❑ 47 My Father And I Have A Bet	.15	.40
❑ 48 Oh No You Don't!	.15	.40
❑ 49 Is That A Student?!	.15	.40
❑ 50 Cheating's A Tradition	.15	.40
❑ 51 Taking Bets	.15	.40
❑ 52 Good Evening, Champions	.15	.40
❑ 53 Last, But Not Least	.15	.40
❑ 54 The First Task	.15	.40
❑ 55 Accio Firebolt!	.15	.40
❑ 56 The Hungarian Horntail	.15	.40
❑ 57 The Golden Egg	.15	.40
❑ 58 She's Done It Again!	.15	.40
❑ 59 Mum's Sent Me A Dress	.15	.40
❑ 60 A Babbling Bumbling Band Of Baboons	.15	.40
❑ 61 Why Do They Have To Travel In Packs?	.15	.40
❑ 62 Wanngoballwime?	.15	.40
❑ 63 The Champions Arrive	.15	.40
❑ 64 Is That Hermione Granger?	.15	.40
❑ 65 The Belle Of The Ball	.15	.40
❑ 66 Take My Waist	.15	.40
❑ 67 She Looks...Beautiful	.15	.40
❑ 68 Not A Bad Place For Bath	.15	.40
❑ 69 You Could Always Use Gillyweed	.15	.40
❑ 70 The Second Task	.15	.40
❑ 71 Outstanding Moral Fiber	.15	.40
❑ 72 The Pensieve	.15	.40
❑ 73 Karkaroff On Trial	.15	.40
❑ 74 I Have Names, Sir	.15	.40
❑ 75 Hello, Father	.15	.40
❑ 76 Your Memories?	.15	.40
❑ 77 People Change In The Maze	.15	.40
❑ 78 The Thrid Task	.15	.40
❑ 79 Potter! Duck!	.15	.40
❑ 80 Lost In The Maze	.15	.40
❑ 81 The Triwizard Cup	.15	.40
❑ 82 It's A Portkey	.15	.40
❑ 83 Kill The Spare	.15	.40
❑ 84 Blood Of The Enemy	.15	.40
❑ 85 He's Back	.15	.40
❑ 86 That's My Son!	.15	.40
❑ 87 Come, Potter	.15	.40
❑ 88 Priori Incantatem	.15	.40
❑ 89 A Fierce Friend	.15	.40
❑ 90 Checklist	.15	.40

2005 Harry Potter and the Goblet of Fire Autographs

STATED ODDS 1:48 HOBBY		
❑ 1 Gary Oldman	200.00	350.00
❑ 2 Predrag Bjelac	25.00	50.00
❑ 3 Robert Pattinson	250.00	500.00
❑ 4 Tiana Benjamin	40.00	80.00
❑ 5 Shirley Henderson	75.00	150.00
❑ 6 Warwick Davis	20.00	40.00
❑ 7 Brendan Gleeson	200.00	400.00
❑ 8 Henry Lloyd-Hughes	20.00	40.00
❑ 9 Angelica Mandy	75.00	150.00
❑ 10 Jeff Rawle	30.00	60.00
❑ 11 James Phelps	75.00	150.00
Oliver Phelps		
❑ 12 Rupert Grint	125.00	250.00
❑ 13 Stanislav Ianevski	75.00	150.00
❑ 14 Miranda Richardson	75.00	150.00

2005 Harry Potter and the Goblet of Fire Box Loaders

STATED ODDS ONE PER HOBBY BOX		
❑ BT1 Hungarian Horntail	1.50	4.00
❑ BT2 Grindylow	1.50	4.00
❑ BT3 Durmstrang Ship	1.50	4.00
❑ BT4 Dark Mark	1.50	4.00

2005 Harry Potter and the Goblet of Fire Case Loaders

STATED ODDS ONE PER HOBBY CASE		
❑ 1 Cemetery	8.00	20.00
❑ 2 First Task With Dragon	8.00	20.00
❑ 3 First Task With Dragon	8.00	20.00

2005 Harry Potter and the Goblet of Fire Costumes

STATED ODDS 1:24 HOBBY		
❑ C1 Daniel Radcliffe Outfit/400	25.00	50.00
❑ C2 Robert Pattinson Shirt/500	25.00	50.00
❑ C3 Clemence Poesy Outfit/250	25.00	50.00
❑ C4 Stanislav Ianevski Outfit/700	10.00	25.00
❑ C5 Stanislav Ianevski Shirt/400	12.00	30.00
❑ C6 Durmstrang Student Outfit/725	12.00	30.00
❑ C7 Beauxbatons Student Outfit/800	12.00	30.00
❑ C8 Emma Watson Pants/300	75.00	150.00
❑ C9 Matthew Lewis Pajamas/900	10.00	25.00
❑ C10 Clemence Poesy Sweater/275	25.00	50.00
❑ C11 David Tennant Shirt/800	12.00	30.00
❑ C12 Miranda Richardson Dress/300	30.00	60.00
❑ C13 Death Eater Robe/250	15.00	40.00
❑ C14 Predrag Bjelac Outfit/800	10.00	25.00

2005 Harry Potter and the Goblet of Fire Dealer Incentive Memorabilia

❑ Cla Daniel Radcliffe Outfit/374	25.00	50.00
❑ TF1 Michael Gambon Outfit/175		
❑ Cl3a Death Eater Robe/188	25.00	50.00
❑ ClP1 Quidditch Burnt Tent/205	20.00	40.00
❑ Pl0a Trial Chamber Paper/317		
❑ Pl3a Monolith Trophy/105		
❑ Pl4a Death Eater Wand/64		

2005 Harry Potter and the Goblet of Fire Film Cels

STATED ODDS 1:80 HOBBY		
❑ CFC1 Nagini and Barty Couch Jr.	20.00	40.00
❑ CFC2 Mermaid	20.00	40.00
❑ CFC3 Dragon	20.00	40.00
❑ CFC4 Goblet of Fire	20.00	40.00
❑ CFC5 Dumbledore	20.00	40.00
❑ CFC6 Maze	20.00	40.00
❑ CFC7 Harry	20.00	40.00
❑ CFC8 Dumbledore	20.00	40.00
❑ CFC9 Harry	20.00	40.00

2005 Harry Potter and the Goblet of Fire Foil Chase Cards

STATED ODDS 1:5 HOBBY		
❑ R1 Harry Potter	1.00	2.50
❑ R2 Harry Potter	1.00	2.50
❑ R3 Harry Potter	1.00	2.50
❑ R4 Harry Potter	1.00	2.50
❑ R5 Harry Potter	1.00	2.50
❑ R6 Harry Potter	1.00	2.50
❑ R7 Hungarian Horntail	1.00	2.50
❑ R8 Grindylow	1.00	2.50
❑ R9 Mermaid	1.00	2.50

2005 Harry Potter and the Goblet of Fire Props

STATED ODDS 1:80 HOBBY		
❑ P1 Yule Ball Drapes/275	20.00	40.00
❑ P2 Yule Ball Program/125	75.00	150.00
❑ P3 Yule Ball Poster/105	30.00	60.00
❑ P4 Bulgarian Flag/300	20.00	40.00
❑ P5 Quidditch Burnt Tent/290	20.00	40.00
❑ P6 Quidditch Program/205	40.00	80.00
❑ P7 First Task Tent/250	40.00	80.00
❑ P8 The Dark Forces Book/75		
❑ P9 First Task Sack/125	40.00	80.00
❑ P10 Trial Chamber Paper/95		
❑ P11 First Task Canopy/290	20.00	40.00
❑ P12 Gryffindor Banner/265	25.00	50.00

2005 Harry Potter and the Goblet of Fire Tin Bonus

STATED ODDS ONE PER RETAIL TIN		
❑ T1 Harry and Dragon	1.25	3.00
❑ T2 Harry and Dark Mark	1.25	3.00

2005 Harry Potter and the Sorcerer's Stone

COMPLETE SET (90)	5.00	12.00
❑ 1 Title Card	.15	.40
❑ 2 Harry Potter	.15	.40
❑ 3 Ron Weasley	.15	.40
❑ 4 Hermione Granger	.15	.40
❑ 5 Albus Dumbledore	.15	.40
❑ 6 Minerva McGonagall	.15	.40
❑ 7 Rubeus Hagrid	.15	.40
❑ 8 Severus Snape	.15	.40
❑ 9 Professor Quirrell	.15	.40

MODERN ERA NON-SPORTS

Card	Low	High
10 Draco Malfoy	.15	.40
11 Neville Longbottom	.15	.40
12 Seamus Finnigan	.15	.40
13 Madam Hooch	.15	.40
14 Argus Filch	.15	.40
15 Professor Flitwick	.15	.40
16 Vernon Dursley	.15	.40
17 Petunia Dursley	.15	.40
18 Dudley Dursley	.15	.40
19 The Rumors Are True	.15	.40
20 The Boy Who Lived	.15	.40
21 No Funny Business	.15	.40
22 Like Magic	.15	.40
23 A New Exhibit?	.15	.40
24 There's No Such Thing as Magic!	.15	.40
25 Harry's Letter	.15	.40
26 Going Mad	.15	.40
27 Make a Wish	.15	.40
28 Dry Up!	.15	.40
29 P-pleased to Meet You	.15	.40
30 No Safer Place	.15	.40
31 The Vaults of Gringotts	.15	.40
32 Curious	.15	.40
33 A Mother's Love	.15	.40
34 A Bit of a Run	.15	.40
35 Is it True?	.15	.40
36 Let's See Then	.15	.40
37 Firs' Years	.15	.40
38 Welcome to Hogwarts	.15	.40
39 Start of Term	.15	.40
40 A Sharp	.15	.40
41 Not Slytherin	.15	.40
42 Nearly Headless?	.15	.40
43 Caput Draconis	.15	.40
44 Transfiguration	.15	.40
45 Subtle Science and Exact Art	.15	.40
46 I Can't Remember...	.15	.40
47 Break-in at Gringotts	.15	.40
48 Up!	.15	.40
49 A Bit Beyond Your Reach?	.15	.40
50 It's in Your Blood	.15	.40
51 The Third-Floor Corridor	.15	.40
52 Three Heads Are Better Than One	.15	.40
53 Easy Enough	.15	.40
54 Troll in the Dungeon!	.15	.40
55 Do Something!	.15	.40
56 Explain Yourselves!	.15	.40
57 That's Not Just a Broomstick...	.15	.40
58 A Nice Clean Game	.15	.40
59 Eye Contact	.15	.40
60 Gryffindor Wins!	.15	.40
61 I Shouldn't 've Said That	.15	.40
62 Some Kind of Cloak	.15	.40
63 The Restricted Section	.15	.40
64 Erised stra ehru oyt ube cafru oyt on wohsi	.15	.40
65 Neither Knowledge Nor Truth	.15	.40
66 Nicolas Flamel	.15	.40
67 He Knows 'Is Mummy	.15	.40
68 Detention	.15	.40
69 Got to Have Your Wits About You	.15	.40
70 A Monstrous Deed	.15	.40
71 A Cursed Life	.15	.40
72 The Stranger in the Pub	.15	.40
73 Standing up to Your Friends	.15	.40
74 Does It Seem A Bit Quiet?	.15	.40
75 Sulk in the Sun	.15	.40
76 They're Not Birds	.15	.40
77 It's a Chessboard	.15	.40
78 Checkmate	.15	.40
79 P-poor St-stuttering Professor Quirrell	.15	.40
80 What Do You See?	.15	.40
81 We Can Bring Them Back	.15	.40
82 Kill Him!	.15	.40
83 What Is This Magic?	.15	.40
84 A Terrifying Apparition	.15	.40
85 Relax Dear Boy	.15	.40
86 Well Done Slytherin	.15	.40
87 A Few Last-Minute Points	.15	.40
88 A Goodbye Gift	.15	.40
89 Not Going Home ... Not Really	.15	.40
90 Checklist	.15	.40

2005 Harry Potter and the Sorcerer's Stone Autographs

STATED ODDS 1:48

Card	Low	High
1 Leslie Phillips	100.00	175.00
2 Matthew Lewis	20.00	40.00
3 Warwick Davis (as bank teller)	20.00	40.00
4 Adrian Rawlins	25.00	50.00
5 Ray Fearon	25.00	50.00
6 Ian Hart	25.00	50.00
7 Alfred Enoch	25.00	50.00
8 Devon Murray	20.00	40.00
9 Luke Youngblood	20.00	40.00
10 Geraldine Somerville	75.00	150.00
11 Warwick Davis (as Prof. Flitwick)	20.00	40.00
12 Joshua Herdman	25.00	50.00
13 John Cleese	100.00	200.00
14 John Hurt	250.00	450.00

2005 Harry Potter and the Sorcerer's Stone Box Loaders

STATED ODDS ONE PER BOX

Card	Low	High
BT1 Slytherin vs. Gryffindor	1.50	4.00
BT2 Ten Points for Gryffindor!	1.50	4.00
BT3 Neck and Neck	1.50	4.00
BT4 Nearly Swallowed It	1.50	4.00

2005 Harry Potter and the Sorcerer's Stone Case Loaders

STATED ODDS ONE PER CASE

Card	Low	High
1 Title	8.00	20.00
2 Neville's Flying Lesson	8.00	20.00
3 Minerva McGonagall Turning Into Cat	8.00	20.00

2005 Harry Potter and the Sorcerer's Stone Chase Cards

STATED ODDS 1:5

Card	Low	High
R1 Harry Potter	1.00	2.50
R2 Dear Mr. Potter	1.00	2.50
R3 Gringotts	1.00	2.50
R4 Platform 9 3/4	1.00	2.50
R5 The First Flying Lesson	1.00	2.50
R6 Wingardium Leviosa	1.00	2.50
R7 Quidditch	1.00	2.50
R8 Norbert the Norwegian Ridgeback	1.00	2.50
R9 The Sorcerer's Stone	1.00	2.50

2005 Harry Potter and the Sorcerer's Stone Costumes

STATED ODDS 1:48

Card	Low	High
C1 Mathew Lewis Teddy Bear Pajamas/520	10.00	25.00
C2 Griffindor Tie/360	20.00	40.00
C3 David Bradley Pants/360	15.00	30.00
C4 Robbie Coltrane Shirt/710	15.00	30.00
C5 Danielle Radcliffe Quiddich Sweater/410	20.00	40.00
C6 Danielle Radcliffe Quiddich Sweater/335	20.00	40.00
C7 Oliver Wood Sweater/300	25.00	50.00
C8 Hogwarts Pants/750	10.00	25.00
C9 Griffindor Sweater/460	10.00	25.00
C10 Danielle Radcliffe Pajamas/360	25.00	50.00
C11 Hogwarts Skirts/510	15.00	30.00
C12 Tom Felton Scarf/485	20.00	40.00

2005 Harry Potter and the Sorcerer's Stone Dealer Incentive Props

Card	Low	High
1 Wand		
2 Wizard Coin Silver		
3 Wizard Coin Bronze		
4 Wizard Coin Gold		

2005 Harry Potter and the Sorcerer's Stone Film Cels

STATED ODDS 1:80

Card	Low	High
CFC1 Diagon Alley	10.00	25.00
CFC2 Harry with Wand	10.00	25.00
CFC3 Harry with Sorting Hat	10.00	25.00
CFC4 Ron with Troll	10.00	25.00
CFC5 Nimbus 2000	10.00	25.00
CFC6 Quidditch	10.00	25.00
CFC7 Hagrid Pulling X'masTree	10.00	25.00
CFC8 Harry, Hermoine and Ron on Chess Board	10.00	25.00
CFC9 He Who Must Not be Named	10.00	25.00

2005 Harry Potter and the Sorcerer's Stone Hogwarts Ties

SAN DIEGO COMIC CON EXCLUSIVE

Card	Low	High
SDCC1 Gryffindor		
SDCC2 Hufflepuff		
SDCC3 Slytherin		
SDCC4 Ravenclaw		

2005 Harry Potter and the Sorcerer's Stone Props

P1-P13 STATED ODDS 1:48
NNO NY TOY FAIR EXCLUSIVE

Card	Low	High
P1 Wand Box/842	15.00	30.00
P2 The Sorcerer's Stone/265	75.00	150.00
P3 4 Pivet Drive/130	125.00	200.00
P4 Restricted Section Library Book/485	15.00	30.00
P5 Practice Broom/450	20.00	40.00
P6 Fluffy's Fur/700	25.00	50.00
P7 Chocolate Frog/127	200.00	300.00
P8 The Daily Prophet/733	15.00	3.00
P9 Gringotts Top Secret Letter/140	125.00	200.00
P10 Shopping List/130	125.00	200.00
P11 Cake Box/490	15.00	30.00
P12 Wizard Candy/538	50.00	100.00
P13 Devil's Snare/100	200.00	300.00
NNO Slytherin Sweater/165		

2005 King Kong Movie

Card	Low	High
COMPLETE SET (80)	5.00	12.00
1 King Kong	.15	.40
2 Ann Darrow	.15	.40
3 King Kong	.15	.40
4 Carl Denham	.15	.40
5 Jack Driscoll	.15	.40
6 Preston	.15	.40
7 Captain Englehorn	.15	.40
8 Hayes	.15	.40
9 Jimmy	.15	.40
10 Bruce Baxter	.15	.40
11 Choy	.15	.40
12 Lumpy the Cook	.15	.40
13 Is Vaudeville Dead	.15	.40
14 The Big Pitch	.15	.40
15 A Passion for Movies	.15	.40
16 Out of Work, Out of Luck	.15	.40
17 Denham's Offer	.15	.40
18 On a Tramp Steamer	.15	.40
19 A Script Too Short	.15	.40
20 Crew of the Venture	.15	.40
21 The Prettiest Passenger	.15	.40
22 An Inspired Screenplay	.15	.40
23 Finding the Old Map	.15	.40
24 Outside Shipping Lanes	.15	.40
25 Uncharted Waters	.15	.40
26 Approaching Skull Island	.15	.40
27 Love Finds Ann Darrow	.15	.40
28 The Landing	.15	.40
29 The Moviemakers	.15	.40
30 Island of Mystery	.15	.40
31 Courageous Captain	.15	.40
32 An Offering for Kong	.15	.40
33 Mighty Kong Appears	.15	.40
34 Kong's Captive	.15	.40
35 A Showman's Paradise	.15	.40
36 The Past Comes Alive	.15	.40
37 Dinosaur Island	.15	.40
38 Brontosaurus Stampede	.15	.40
39 Hero of Thunder Lizards	.15	.40
40 Strange Kinship	.15	.40
41 The Raft	.15	.40
42 Dinosaurs Attack	.15	.40
43 Menaced By Monsters	.15	.40
44 Here Comes V-Rex	.15	.40
45 The Earth Trembles	.15	.40
46 Battle of the Giants	.15	.40
47 Three Against One	.15	.40
48 Cliffhanger	.15	.40
49 Entangled Terrors	.15	.40
50 Clash of the Titans	.15	.40
51 Nature's Primal Fury	.15	.40
52 The King Triumphant	.15	.40
53 Is Ann Alive	.15	.40
54 Skull Island Horrors	.15	.40
55 The Log of Death	.15	.40
56 Lumpy's Fight for Life	.15	.40
57 Against Kong's Fury	.15	.40
58 A Long Way Down	.15	.40
59 Shock and Awe	.15	.40
60 Terrors Unending	.15	.40
61 Are Movies Worth It	.15	.40
62 In Kong's Lair	.15	.40
63 Rescued by a Writer	.15	.40
64 The Capture of Kong	.15	.40
65 Return to New York	.15	.40
66 The New Ann Darrow	.15	.40
67 Denham's Big Night	.15	.40
68 A King in New York	.15	.40
69 Darrow's Desperate Plea	.15	.40
70 Atop the Tallest Building	.15	.40
71 Beauty Killed the Beast	.15	.40
72 Making a Love Story	.15	.40
73 Mr. Jackson on Location	.15	.40
74 Filming Jack Black	.15	.40
75 One Director to Another	.15	.40
76 Of Romance and Discovery	.15	.40
77 A Filmmaker's Obsession	.15	.40
78 Fight to the Finish	.15	.40
79 When Behemoths Clash	.15	.40
80 Checklist	.15	.40

2005 King Kong Movie Autographs

STATED ODDS 1:24 HOBBY

Card	Low	High
1 Colin Hanks	8.00	20.00
2 Evan Parke	4.00	10.00
3 Jamie Bell	12.00	30.00
4 Kyle Chandler	12.00	30.00
5 Richard Taylor	4.00	10.00

2005 King Kong Movie Blister Bonus

STATED ODDS ONE PER BLISTER PACK

Card	Low	High
COMPLETE SET (3)	1.25	3.00
B1 The King Returns	.75	2.00
B2 Land of the Lost	.75	2.00
B3 A 21st Century Kong	.75	2.00

2005 King Kong Movie Embossed Foil

STATED ODDS 1:6 RETAIL

Card	Low	High
COMPLETE SET (10)	5.00	12.00
1 Kong	1.00	2.50
2 Kong	1.00	2.50
3 Kong	1.00	2.50
4 Kong	1.00	2.50
5 Kong	1.00	2.50
6 Kong	1.00	2.50
7 Kong	1.00	2.50
8 Kong	1.00	2.50
9 Kong	1.00	2.50
10 Kong	1.00	2.50

2005 King Kong Movie Flocked

STATED ODDS 1:8

Card	Low	High
COMPLETE SET (5)	3.00	8.00
1 Kong Holding Club	1.25	3.00
2 Rage	1.25	3.00
3 Kong	1.25	3.00
4 Fight to Survive	1.25	3.00
5 Kong On the Town	1.25	3.00

2005 King Kong Movie Memorabilia

STATED ODDS 1:24 HOBBY

Card	Low	High
1 Ann Darrow's Dressing Gown	25.00	50.00
2 Ann Darrow's Dressing Room Dress	20.00	40.00
3 Ann Darrow's Film Dress	20.00	40.00
4 Carl Denham's Sisal Suit	15.00	30.00
5 Carl Denham's Waistcoat	15.00	30.00
6 Jack Driscoll's Jacket	15.00	30.00
7 Jack Driscoll's Silk Shirt	15.00	30.00

2005 King Kong Movie Promos

Card	Low	High
P1 Kong (general distribution)	1.00	2.50
P2 Kong (Non-Sport Update exclusive)	1.50	4.00

2005 King Kong Movie Stickers

STATED ODDS 1:4 RETAIL

Card	Low	High
COMPLETE SET (10)	3.00	8.00
1 Kong fighting	.75	2.00
2 Fight to Survive	.75	2.00
3 Kong fighting	.75	2.00
4 Kong fighting	.75	2.00
5 Rampage	.75	2.00
6 Rage	.75	2.00
7 Kong	.75	2.00
8 Skull Island	.75	2.00
9 The Greatest Adventure	.75	2.00
10 Kong climbing building	.75	2.00

2005 King Kong Movie Video Game Creatures

STATED ODDS 1:4

Card	Low	High
COMPLETE SET (5)	2.00	5.00
C1 This Creature Can Attack	.75	2.00
C2 This Creature Attacks With	.75	2.00
C3 This Creature is Very Fast	.75	2.00
C4 This Creature is Slow	.75	2.00
C5 This Creature Looks Like	.75	2.00

2005 Legends of Star Trek Chekov Rand Chapel

Card	Low	High
COMPLETE SET (9)	8.00	20.00
L1 Chekov	1.00	2.50
L2 Chekov	1.00	2.50
L3 Chekov	1.00	2.50
L4 Rand	1.00	2.50
L5 Rand	1.00	2.50
L6 Rand	1.00	2.50
L7 Chapel	1.00	2.50
L8 Chapel	1.00	2.50
L9 Chapel	1.00	2.50

2005 Lost Season One

Card	Low	High
COMPLETE SET (90)	5.00	12.00
1 Lost	.15	.40
2 Hero	.15	.40
3 Courage	.15	.40
4 Count To Five	.15	.40
5 The Signal	.15	.40
6 Moving On	.15	.40
7 Miracle	.15	.40
8 Hunter	.15	.40
9 Memorial	.15	.40
10 Grief	.15	.40
11 Panic	.15	.40
12 Remembering	.15	.40
13 Amends	.15	.40
14 Rockstar	.15	.40
15 Decision	.15	.40
16 Walk Away	.15	.40
17 Truth	.15	.40
18 Interrogator	.15	.40
19 Captive	.15	.40
20 Prediction	.15	.40
21 Abduction	.15	.40
22 Illusion	.15	.40
23 Rescue	.15	.40
24 Heist	.15	.40
25 Beyond The Sea	.15	.40
26 Conned	.15	.40
27 Heartbroken	.15	.40
28 Alone	.15	.40
29 Reunited	.15	.40
30 Lure	.15	.40
31 Retribution	.15	.40
32 Witness	.15	.40
33 Target	.15	.40
34 Gangster	.15	.40
35 Jealous	.15	.40
36 Validated	.15	.40
37 Nursery	.15	.40
38 Accepted	.15	.40
39 Stricken	.15	.40
40 Commitment	.15	.40
41 Dedicated	.15	.40
42 Questioned	.15	.40
43 Mercy	.15	.40
44 Sweethearts	.15	.40
45 Unintended	.15	.40
46 French Woman	.15	.40
47 Departure	.15	.40
48 Kidnapped	.15	.40
49 Taken	.15	.40
50 Revealed	.15	.40
51 Jack: Heroic	.15	.40
52 Jack: Doctor	.15	.40
53 Kate: Practical	.15	.40
54 Kate: Fugitive	.15	.40
55 Sawyer: Entrepreneur	.15	.40
56 Sawyer: Con Man	.15	.40
57 Charlie: Addict	.15	.40
58 Charlie: Rocker	.15	.40
59 Hurley: Likeable	.15	.40
60 Hurley: Winner	.15	.40
61 Shannon: Emotional	.15	.40
62 Shannon: Petulant	.15	.40
63 Boone: Searching	.15	.40
64 Boone: Silver Spoon	.15	.40
65 Sayid: Resourceful	.15	.40
66 Sayid: Authority	.15	.40
67 Michael: Builder	.15	.40
68 Michael: Artist	.15	.40
69 Walt: Different	.15	.40
70 Walt: Willful	.15	.40
71 Locke: Mystic	.15	.40
72 Locke: Routine	.15	.40
73 Jin: Isolated	.15	.40
74 Jin: Devoted	.15	.40
75 Sun: Healer	.15	.40
76 Sun: Naïve	.15	.40
77 Claire: Tested	.15	.40
78 Claire: Innocent	.15	.40
79 Resilient	.15	.40
80 Restored	.15	.40
81 Revenge	.15	.40
82 Jack & Kate: Affection	.15	.40
83 Michael & Jin: Affiliation	.15	.40
84 Shannon & Sayid: Protection	.15	.40
85 Kate & Sawyer: Attraction	.15	.40
86 Boone & Locke: Illumination	.15	.40
87 Walt & Locke: Affirmation	.15	.40
88 Claire & Charlie: Devotion	.15	.40
89 Jack & Locke: Accomodation	.15	.40
90 Checklist	.15	.40

2005 Lost Season One Autographs

STATED ODDS 1:36

Card	Low	High
A1 Evangeline Lilly	75.00	150.00
A2 Josh Holloway	35.00	70.00
A3 Maggie Grace	50.00	100.00
A4 Malcolm David Kelley	8.00	20.00
A5 Mira Furlan	8.00	20.00
A6 William Mapother	6.00	15.00
A7 John Terry	8.00	20.00
A8 Nick Jameson	6.00	15.00
A9 Daniel Roebuck	8.00	20.00
A10 Fredric Lane	6.00	15.00
A11 Kevin Tighe	10.00	25.00
A12 Swoozie Kurtz	8.00	20.00

2005 Lost Season One Box Loaders

BL STATED ODDS ONE PER BOX
CL STATED ODDS ONE PER CASE

Card	Low	High
BL1 Jack & Kate	2.00	5.00
BL2 Sawyer & Jack	2.00	5.00
BL3 Sawyer & Kate	2.00	5.00
CL1 The Hatch	5.00	12.00

2005 Lost Season One Missing:Oceanic 815

STATED ODDS 1:11

Card	Low	High
M1 Missing: Oceanic 815	1.00	2.50
M2 Missing: Oceanic 815	1.00	2.50
M3 Missing: Oceanic 815	1.00	2.50
M4 Missing: Oceanic 815	1.00	2.50
M5 Missing: Oceanic 815	1.00	2.50
M6 Missing: Oceanic 815	1.00	2.50
M7 Missing: Oceanic 815	1.00	2.50
M8 Missing: Oceanic 815	1.00	2.50
M9 Missing: Oceanic 815	1.00	2.50

2005 Lost Season One Numbers

STATED ODDS 1:17

Card	Low	High
N4 Number 4	1.25	3.00
N8 Number 8	1.25	3.00
N15 Number 15	1.25	3.00
N16 Number 16	1.25	3.00
N23 Number 23	1.25	3.00
N42 Number 42	1.25	3.00

2005 Lost Season One Pieceworks

STATED ODDS 1:36

Card	Low	High
PW1 Evangeline Lilly	20.00	40.00
PW2 Josh Holloway	8.00	20.00
PW3 Maggie Grace		
PW4 Matthew Fox	10.00	25.00
PW5 Dominic Monaghan	8.00	20.00
PW6 Terry O'Quinn	10.00	25.00
PW7 Naveen Andrews	8.00	20.00
PW8 Jorge Garcia	8.00	20.00
PW9 Daniel Dae Kim	8.00	20.00
PW10 Yunjin Kim	10.00	25.00
PW11 Emilie De Ravin	10.00	25.00
PW12 Harold Perrineau	12.00	30.00
Malcolm David Kelley		
PWA1 Evangeline Lilly AU	75.00	150.00
PWA2 Josh Holloway AU	35.00	70.00
PWA3 Maggie Grace AU	50.00	100.00

2005 The Quotable Star Trek The Next Generation

Card	Low	High
COMPLETE SET (110)	5.00	12.00
1 Encounter at Farpoint, Part I	.15	.40
2 Encounter at Farpoint, Part I	.15	.40
3 Encounter at Farpoint, Part I	.15	.40
4 Deja Q	.15	.40
5 The Game	.15	.40
6 Encounter at Farpoint, Part I	.15	.40
7 Ethics	.15	.40
8 Where Silence Has Lease	.15	.40
9 Encounter at Farpoint, Part I	.15	.40
10 The Defector	.15	.40
11 The Child	.15	.40
12 The Emissary	.15	.40
13 Haven	.15	.40
14 Justice	.15	.40
15 Chain of Command, Part II	.15	.40
16 Encounter at Farpoint, Part I	.15	.40
17 New Ground	.15	.40
18 The Naked Now	.15	.40
19 Unification, Part II	.15	.40
20 The Birthright, Part II	.15	.40
21 The Naked Now	.15	.40
22 The Emissary	.15	.40
23 Peak Performance	.15	.40
24 Justice	.15	.40
25 Schisms	.15	.40
26 Sins of the Father	.15	.40
27 The Best of Both Worlds, Part I	.15	.40
28 Up the Long Ladder	.15	.40
29 The Perfect Mate	.15	.40
30 Manhunt	.15	.40
31 Up the Long Ladder	.15	.40
32 The Emissary	.15	.40
33 Yesterday's Enterprise	.15	.40
34 The Dauphin	.15	.40
35 Longly Among Us	.15	.40
36 Up the Long Ladder	.15	.40
37 Skin of Evil	.15	.40
38 Skin of Evil	.15	.40
39 Skin of Evil	.15	.40
40 Skin of Evil	.15	.40
41 Skin of Evil	.15	.40
42 The Measure of a Man	.15	.40
43 Q Who?	.15	.40
44 Angel One	.15	.40
45 The Drumhead	.15	.40
46 Justice	.15	.40
47 The Loss	.15	.40
48 The Bonding	.15	.40
49 The Battle	.15	.40
50 In Theory	.15	.40
51 Up the Long Ladder	.15	.40
52 Contagion	.15	.40
53 The Neutral Zone	.15	.40
54 Deja Q	.15	.40
55 The Dauphin	.15	.40
56 Q Who?	.15	.40
57 Unnatural Selection	.15	.40
58 Disaster	.15	.40
59 Disaster	.15	.40
60 The Naked Now	.15	.40
61 Relics	.15	.40
62 The Child	.15	.40
63 Peak Performance	.15	.40
64 Hide and Q	.15	.40
65 The Measure of a Man	.15	.40
66 The High Ground	.15	.40
67 Angel One	.15	.40
68 The Best of Both Worlds, Part II	.15	.40
69 Deja Q	.15	.40
70 Unnatural Selection	.15	.40
71 The Naked Now	.15	.40
72 Manhunt	.15	.40
73 Violations	.15	.40
74 Datalore	.15	.40
75 The Emissary	.15	.40
76 Parallels	.15	.40
77 Liaisons	.15	.40
78 The Ensigns of Command	.15	.40
79 The Emissary	.15	.40
80 Q Who?	.15	.40
81 Lessons	.15	.40
82 Hide and Q	.15	.40
83 Cost of Living	.15	.40
84 Unification, Part I	.15	.40
85 Heart of Glory	.15	.40
86 The Game	.15	.40
87 The Dauphin	.15	.40
88 Contagion	.15	.40
89 Peak Performance	.15	.40
90 The Measure of a Man	.15	.40
91 Liaisons	.15	.40
92 Rightful Heir	.15	.40
93 The Offspring	.15	.40
94 Power Play	.15	.40
95 Reunion	.15	.40
96 The Wounded	.15	.40
97 Deja Q	.15	.40
98 Heart of Glory	.15	.40
99 Hide and Q	.15	.40
100 The Icarus Factor	.15	.40
101 When the Bough Breaks	.15	.40
102 The Next Phase	.15	.40
103 Violations	.15	.40
104 The Drumhead	.15	.40
105 Haven	.15	.40
106 Heart of Glory	.15	.40
107 Yesterday's Enterprise	.15	.40
108 Conspiracy	.15	.40
109 The Battle	.15	.40
110 All Good Things, Part II	.15	.40

2005 The Quotable Star Trek The Next Generation Autographs

STATED ODDS ONE PER BOX
MD AUTO ONE PER COLLECTORS ALBUM
PSBS AUTO ONE PER SIX-CASE PURCHASE
L (LIMITED): 300-500 CARDS
VL (VERY LIMITED): 200-300 CARDS

Card	Low	High
BS Brent Spiner VL	50.00	100.00
CS Carel Struycken	10.00	25.00
DC Denise Crosby L	15.00	30.00
DM Diana Muldaur L	20.00	40.00
FJ Famke Janssen VL	60.00	120.00
JB Julie Caitlin Brown	8.00	20.00
JD John de Lancie L	20.00	40.00
JH Jennifer Hetrick	8.00	20.00
MB Majel Barrett VL	60.00	120.00
MD Marta DuBoise ALBUM		
MF Michelle Forbes	15.00	30.00
PS Patrick Stewart VL	75.00	150.00
PY Patti Yasutake	8.00	20.00
RC Rosalind Chao L	8.00	20.00
SP Suzie Plakson	10.00	25.00
WW Wil Wheaton L	25.00	50.00
QA1 Patrick Stewart VL	100.00	200.00

MODERN ERA NON-SPORTS

❑ QA2 Brent Spiner VL 50.00 100.00
❑ QA3 Jonathan Frakes VL 50.00 100.00
❑ QA4 Marina Sirtis VL 40.00 80.00
❑ QA5 Michael Dorn VL 40.00 80.00
❑ JFMS Jonathan Frakes 60.00 120.00
Marina Sirtis VL
❑ MBCS Majel Barrett 60.00 120.00
Carel Struycken VL
❑ MDSP Michael Dorn 60.00 120.00
Suzie Plakson VL
❑ MSMB Marina Sirtis 125.00 200.00
Majel Barrett VL
❑ PSBS Patrick Stewart
Brent Spiner

2005 The Quotable Star Trek The Next Generation Comic Book Covers

COMPLETE SET (6) 10.00 25.00
STATED ODDS 1:14
❑ CB1 Comic Book Cover 2.00 5.00
❑ CB2 Comic Book Cover 2.00 5.00
❑ CB3 Comic Book Cover 2.00 5.00
❑ CB4 Comic Book Cover 2.00 5.00
❑ CB5 Comic Book Cover 2.00 5.00
❑ CB6 Comic Book Cover 2.00 5.00

2005 The Quotable Star Trek The Next Generation From The Archives Costumes

STATED ODDS ONE PER BOX
❑ C1 Captain Jean-Luc Picard 30.00 60.00
❑ C2 Lt. Commander Data 20.00 40.00
❑ C3 Commander William Riker 20.00 40.00
❑ C4 Counselor Deanna Troi 20.00 40.00
❑ C5 Lt. Geordi LaForge 8.00 20.00
❑ C6 Dr. Beverly Crusher 15.00 30.00
❑ C7 Lt. Worf 8.00 20.00
❑ C8 Lt. Tasha Yar 8.00 20.00
❑ C9 Ensign Wesley Crusher 10.00 25.00

2005 The Quotable Star Trek The Next Generation SketchaFex

STATED ODDS 1:480
ROMULAN WARBIRD SKETCH ONE PER U.S. CASE
BORG CUBE SKETCH ONE PER INT'L CASE
❑ 1 Cris Bolson
U.S.S. Enterprise/(Saucer Section Separated)
❑ 2 Cris Bolson
U.S.S. Enterprise/(Orbiting Star)
❑ 3 Cris Bolson
U.S.S. Enterprise/(Bottom View Orbiting Planet)
❑ 4 Cris Bolson
U.S.S. Enterprise/(Pointing Right)
❑ 5 Cris Bolson
U.S.S. Enterprise/(Rear View Orbiting Planet)
❑ 6 Cris Bolson
U.S.S. Enterprise/(Entering Warp)
❑ 7 Cris Bolson
U.S.S. Enterprise/(Pointing Left)
❑ 8 Romulan Warbird
❑ 9 Borg Cube
U.S.S. Enterprise

2005 The Quotable Star Trek The Next Generation Starfleet's Finest

STATED ODDS 1:120
❑ F1 Captain Jean-Luc Picard 12.00 30.00
❑ F2 Lt. Commander Data 12.00 30.00
❑ F3 Commander William Riker 12.00 30.00
❑ F4 Counselor Deanna Troi 12.00 30.00
❑ F5 Lt. Geordi LaForge 12.00 30.00
❑ F6 Dr. Beverly Crusher 12.00 30.00
❑ F7 Lt. Worf 12.00 30.00
❑ F8 Lt. Tasha Yar 12.00 30.00
❑ F9 Ensign Wesley Crusher 12.00 30.00

2005 The Quotable Star Trek The Next Generation The Captain's Women

STATED ODDS 1:40 INT'L PACKS
❑ W1 Dr. Jenice Manheim 5.00 12.00
❑ W2 Vash 5.00 12.00
❑ W3 Kamala 5.00 12.00
❑ W4 Eline 5.00 12.00
❑ W5 Lt. Commander Neela Daren 5.00 12.00
❑ W6 Anna 5.00 12.00
❑ W7 Lwaxana Troi 5.00 12.00
❑ W8 Captain Phillipa Louvois 5.00 12.00
❑ W9 Madeline 5.00 12.00

2005 The Quotable Star Trek The Next Generation The Final Frontier

COMPLETE SET (9) 4.00 10.00
STATED ODDS 1:5
❑ ST1 Locutus .50 1.25
❑ ST2 Captain Jean-Luc Picard .50 1.25
❑ ST3 Q .50 1.25
❑ ST4 Commander William Riker .50 1.25
Counselor Deanna Troi
❑ ST5 U.S.S. Enterprise .50 1.25
❑ ST6 Aliens .50 1.25
❑ ST7 Commander Data .50 1.25
Lt. Geordi LaForge/Lt. Worf
❑ ST8 Lt. Tasha Yar .50 1.25
Ensign Wesley Crusher/Dr. Beverly Crusher
❑ ST9 Aliens .50 1.25

2005 The Quotable Star Trek The Next Generation TV Guide Covers

COMPLETE SET (9) 30.00 75.00
STATED ODDS 1:40 U.S. PACKS
SIRTIS AUTO ONE PER TWO-CASE PURCHASE
❑ TV1 Patrick Stewart 4.00 10.00
as Captain Jean-Luc Picard
❑ TV2 Brent Spiner 4.00 10.00
as Lt. Commander Data
❑ TV3 Jonathan Frakes 4.00 10.00
as Commander William
❑ TV4 LeVar Burton 4.00 10.00
as Lt. Geordi LaForge
❑ TV5 Wil Wheaton 4.00 10.00
as Ensign Wesley Crusher/Gates McFadden/as Dr. Beverly Crusher
❑ TV6 Denise Crosby 4.00 10.00
as Lt. Tasha Yar/Denise Crosby/as Commander Sela
❑ TV7 Marina Sirtis 4.00 10.00
as Counselor Deanna Troi
❑ TV8 Michael Dorn 4.00 10.00
as Lt. Worf
❑ TV9 John de Lancie 4.00 10.00
as Q
❑ MS Marina Sirtis
as Counselor Deanna Troi AUTO

2005 Robots

COMPLETE SET (90) 4.00 10.00
❑ 1 Title Card .10 .30
❑ 2 Rodney Copperbottom .10 .30
❑ 3 Wonderbot .10 .30
❑ 4 Cappy .10 .30
❑ 5 Mr. & Mrs. Copperbottom .10 .30
❑ 6 Bigweld .10 .30
❑ 7 Ratchet .10 .30
❑ 8 Madame Gasket .10 .30
❑ 9 Fender .10 .30
❑ 10 Piper Pinwheeler .10 .30
❑ 11 Crank Casey .10 .30
❑ 12 Lug .10 .30
❑ 13 Diesel Springer .10 .30
❑ 14 Aunt Fan .10 .30
❑ 15 Jackhammer .10 .30
❑ 16 Some Assembly Required .10 .30
❑ 17 Hand-Me-Downs .10 .30
❑ 18 Looking Into The Future .10 .30
❑ 19 Building A Baby .10 .30
❑ 20 Bot Meets World .10 .30
❑ 21 Creation! .10 .30
❑ 22 It Works! Sort Of .10 .30
❑ 23 Failure! .10 .30
❑ 24 A Life In Gear .10 .30
❑ 25 Bot In The Big City .10 .30
❑ 26 Directionally Snubbed .10 .30
❑ 27 Loose Screw .10 .30
❑ 28 Teaser Tim .10 .30
❑ 29 Sez You! .10 .30
❑ 30 Why Be You? .10 .30
❑ 31 Don't You Love It? .10 .30
❑ 32 Love At First Flop .10 .30
❑ 33 Hello, You Must Be Going .10 .30
❑ 34 Magnetic Melee .10 .30
❑ 35 Footjacked! .10 .30
❑ 36 A Head Behind .10 .30
❑ 37 Emergency Repairs .10 .30
❑ 38 We Have No Replacements .10 .30
❑ 39 I Can Fix You! .10 .30
❑ 40 Trouble Ahead .10 .30
❑ 41 Gasket & Son .10 .30
❑ 42 The Bot Hits The Fan .10 .30
❑ 43 Fenderbonding .10 .30
❑ 44 Hot And Greasy .10 .30
❑ 45 No Outrage Here .10 .30
❑ 46 Find Bigweld! .10 .30
❑ 47 Fix Me, Please! .10 .30
❑ 48 Crashing The Ball .10 .30
❑ 49 On The Scrap Belt .10 .30
❑ 50 Tracking Bigweld .10 .30
❑ 51 Pure Genius .10 .30
❑ 52 Down The Domino Trail .10 .30
❑ 53 A Big Shock .10 .30
❑ 54 Give Up! .10 .30
❑ 55 Rodney Blows Up .10 .30
❑ 56 Defeated .10 .30
❑ 57 Jeepers Sweepers! .10 .30
❑ 58 Heart Recharge .10 .30
❑ 59 The Return Of Bigweld .10 .30
❑ 60 Hauling Steel .10 .30
❑ 61 Outmodes On The March .10 .30
❑ 62 Cornered! .10 .30
❑ 63 To Victory! .10 .30
❑ 64 Dishrag Dad .10 .30
❑ 65 A Working Couple .10 .30
❑ 66 Creative Craftsman .10 .30
❑ 67 A Real Fixer-Upper .10 .30
❑ 68 Jack Of All Trades .10 .30
❑ 69 Magnet Truck .10 .30
❑ 70 I See You! .10 .30
❑ 71 Just Say No! .10 .30
❑ 72 Chairbot Of The Board .10 .30
❑ 73 Rodney Copperbottom .10 .30
❑ 74 Wonderbot .10 .30
❑ 75 Cappy .10 .30
❑ 76 Fender .10 .30
❑ 77 Piper .10 .30
❑ 78 Aunt Fan .10 .30
❑ 79 Bigweld .10 .30
❑ 80 Ratchet .10 .30
❑ 81 Madame Gasket .10 .30
❑ 82 Cityscape .10 .30
❑ 83 Happy Houses .10 .30
❑ 84 Aunt Fan's Boarding House .10 .30
❑ 85 Jackhammer's Store .10 .30
❑ 86 Rustie Alley .10 .30
❑ 87 Street Sweepers .10 .30
❑ 88 Minion Design .10 .30
❑ 89 An Evil Castle .10 .30
❑ 90 Checklist .10 .30

2005 Robots Box Loaders

COMPLETE SET (3)
STATED ODDS ONE PER HOBBY BOX
CL1 ISSUED AS HOBBY CASE TOPPER
❑ BL1 Piper Pinwheeler
❑ BL2 Fender
❑ BL3 Diesel Springer and Lug
❑ CL1 Bigweld CL

2005 Robots Fender Bender

COMPLETE SET (6)
STATED ODDS 1:11 HOBBY
❑ FB1 Smooth to the Last Drop
❑ FB2 Let's Dance
❑ FB3 Okay Time to Panic
❑ FB4 Friends in Need
❑ FB5 Spazz-o-Matic
❑ FB6 Mighty Warrior

2005 Robots Postcards From The Big City Film

COMPLETE SET (6)
STATED ODDS 1:17 HOBBY
❑ PC1 Gateway to Invention
❑ PC2 Pinnacle of Success
❑ PC3 Can You Shine?
❑ PC4 Crush Hour Traffic
❑ PC5 The Big City Revs
❑ PC6 I Made It I'm Here

2005 Robots Retail Foil

COMPLETE SET (4)
STATED ODDS 1:11 RETAIL
❑ RE1 Rodney Copperbottom
❑ RE2 Crank Casey
❑ RE3 Fender
❑ RE4 Bigweld

2005 Robots Rusties to the Rescue

COMPLETE SET (9)
STATED ODDS 1:11
❑ RR1 Friends to the End
❑ RR2 Living on Borrowed Time
❑ RR3 Rusties Headquarters
❑ RR4 Rusties Unite
❑ RR5 Rekindling the Dream
❑ RR6 Hidden Talents
❑ RR7 Teens in the Big City
❑ RR8 Aunt Fan the Minivan
❑ RR9 Surprise

2005 Robots Sketches

STATED ODDS 1:36 HOBBY
❑ SK1 Dave Dorman/149
❑ SK2 Tone Rodriguez/528
❑ SK3 John Czop/300
❑ SK4 Chris Moreno/524
❑ SK5 Chad Frye/515
❑ SK6 Mark Dos Santos/489
❑ SK7 Jeff Zugale/501
❑ SK8 Joel Gomez/511
❑ SK9 Nar/404
❑ SK10 Warren Martineck/300
❑ SK11 Michael Kraiger/355
❑ SK12 Darren Auck/500

2005 Serenity

COMPLETE SET (72) 5.00 12.00
CL1 STATED ODDS ONE PER CASE
❑ 1 Title Card .15 .40
❑ 2 Malcolm (Mal) Reynolds .15 .40
❑ 3 Zoe Alleyne-Washburne .15 .40
❑ 4 Hoban (Wash) Washburne .15 .40
❑ 5 Inara Serra .15 .40
❑ 6 Jayne Cobb .15 .40
❑ 7 Kaylee Frye .15 .40
❑ 8 Simon Tam .15 .40
❑ 9 River Tam .15 .40
❑ 10 Shepherd Meria Book .15 .40
❑ 11 The Operative .15 .40
❑ 12 Reavers .15 .40
❑ 13 Earth-That-Was .15 .40
❑ 14 Trouble In Utopia .15 .40
❑ 15 River's Ordeal .15 .40
❑ 16 Escaping The Alliance .15 .40
❑ 17 Aboard The Serenity .15 .40
❑ 18 Four Robbers And A Mule .15 .40
❑ 19 Inside The Train Station .15 .40
❑ 20 Entering The Vault .15 .40
❑ 21 A Monster Among Us .15 .40
❑ 22 The Big Heist .15 .40
❑ 23 Spotted By The Reavers .15 .40
❑ 24 The Great Chase .15 .40
❑ 25 Companions-In-Training .15 .40
❑ 26 Mingo And Fanty .15 .40
❑ 27 River's Rampage .15 .40
❑ 28 Meet Mr. Universe .15 .40
❑ 29 The Girl Most Wanted .15 .40
❑ 30 The Mining Camp .15 .40
❑ 31 The Shepherd's Flock .15 .40
❑ 32 Love... Or A Trap? .15 .40
❑ 33 Inara's World .15 .40
❑ 34 The Deadly Pursuer .15 .40
❑ 35 Visions Of Horror .15 .40
❑ 36 The Road To Miranda .15 .40
❑ 37 Fateful Decision .15 .40
❑ 38 Death Of A Friend .15 .40
❑ 39 Target: The Alliance .15 .40
❑ 40 Significant Others .15 .40
❑ 41 The Miranda Landing .15 .40
❑ 42 A Team Will-Suited .15 .40
❑ 43 City Of The Dead .15 .40
❑ 44 Armed Against Terror .15 .40
❑ 45 Ghosts Of Miranda .15 .40
❑ 46 The Operative's Ship .15 .40
❑ 47 Serenity Under Fire .15 .40
❑ 48 Within A Sea Of Ships .15 .40
❑ 49 Dodging Enemy Blasts .15 .40
❑ 50 A Leaf On The Wind... .15 .40
❑ 51 Taking A Stand .15 .40
❑ 52 A Robot's Best Friend .15 .40
❑ 53 The First Wave .15 .40
❑ 54 Attack Of The Reavers .15 .40
❑ 55 Mal's Vital Mission .15 .40
❑ 56 Team Serenity Strikes! .15 .40
❑ 57 More Than A Woman .15 .40
❑ 58 The Unstoppable One .15 .40
❑ 59 The Final Round .15 .40
❑ 60 The Dear Departed .15 .40
❑ 61 Repairing A Firefly .15 .40
❑ 62 Two For The Road .15 .40
❑ 63 A New Beginning .15 .40
❑ 64 One Man's Brainchild .15 .40
❑ 65 the Inara Connection .15 .40
❑ 66 Vehicles And Lovers .15 .40
❑ 67 A Galactic Western .15 .40
❑ 68 Space Vehicles .15 .40
❑ 69 The Mule Hovercraft .15 .40
❑ 70 Ships Of The Alliance .15 .40
❑ 71 River And The Town .15 .40
❑ 72 Checklist .15 .40
❑ CL1 Browncoats Unite 8.00 20.00

2005 Serenity Action Figure Inserts

COMPLETE SET (5)
❑ DSS1 Malcolm
❑ DSS2 Flight to the Finish
❑ DSS3 Reavers Attack
❑ DSS4 Soldier of Fortune
❑ DSS5 Jayne

2005 Serenity Autographs

STATED ODDS ONE PER BOX
❑ A1 Nathan Fillion 50.00 100.00
❑ A2 Gina Torres 20.00 40.00
❑ A3 Adam Baldwin 20.00 40.00
❑ A4 Alan Tudyk 20.00 40.00
❑ A5 Jewel Staite 25.00 50.00
❑ A6 Morena Baccarin 30.00 60.00
❑ A7 Summer Glau 100.00 150.00
❑ A8 Sean Maher 15.00 30.00
❑ A9 Ron Glass 15.00 30.00
❑ A10 Chiwetel Ejiofor 10.00 20.00
❑ AR1 Redemption card

2005 Serenity Pieceworks

STATED ODDS ONE PER BOX
❑ PW1 Mal 30.00 60.00
❑ PW2 Zoe 20.00 40.00
❑ PW3 Jayne 20.00 40.00
❑ PW4 Wash 15.00 30.00
❑ PW5 Kaylee 30.00 60.00
❑ PW6 Inara 8.00 20.00
❑ PW7 Simon 8.00 20.00
❑ PW8 The Operative 15.00 30.00

2005 Serenity Renegades Puzzle

COMPLETE SET (9) 10.00 25.00
STATED ODDS 1:11
❑ R1 Zoe's Better Half 1.50 4.00
❑ R2 Captain of the Ship 1.50 4.00
❑ R3 Armed and Dangerous 1.50 4.00
❑ R4 Serenity's Crew 1.50 4.00
❑ R5 A Firefly of His Own 1.50 4.00
❑ R6 Madness on Miranda 1.50 4.00
❑ R7 A Boy Named Jayne 1.50 4.00
❑ R8 Jayne the Hard Way 1.50 4.00
❑ R9 The Doctor Is In 1.50 4.00

2005 Serenity The Truth Within

COMPLETE SET (3) 6.00 15.00
STATED ODDS ONE PER BOX
❑ BL1 The Girl Who Knew Too Much 2.50 6.00
❑ BL2 A Child Shall Lead Them 2.50 6.00
❑ BL3 Beauty is the Beast 2.50 6.00

2005 Serenity Women of Serenity

COMPLETE SET (5) 10.00 25.00
STATED ODDS 1:17
❑ WS1 Zoe on the Job 2.50 6.00
❑ WS2 Inara the Companion 2.50 6.00
❑ WS3 A Mechanic Named Kaylee 2.50 6.00
❑ WS4 Girl on the Run 2.50 6.00
❑ WS5 Serenity's Angels 2.50 6.00

2005 Smallville Season Four

COMPLETE SET (90) 5.00 12.00
❑ 1 Smallville .15 .40
❑ 2 Clark Kent .15 .40
❑ 3 Lois Lane .15 .40
❑ 4 Lana Lang .15 .40
❑ 5 Jason Teague .15 .40
❑ 6 Lex Luthor .15 .40
❑ 7 Chloe Sullivan .15 .40
❑ 8 Jonathan & Martha Kent .15 .40
❑ 9 Lionel Luthor .15 .40
❑ 10 Buried Secrects .15 .40
❑ 11 The Second Stone .15 .40
❑ 12 Clark's Quest .15 .40
❑ 13 Witch Crafty .15 .40
❑ 14 The Guardian .15 .40
❑ 15 The Root Of Power .15 .40
❑ 16 The Final Stone .15 .40
❑ 17 Completion .15 .40
❑ 18 On To Higher Learning .15 .40
❑ 19 A Mystery Wrapped In An Enigma .15 .40
❑ 20 Witness .15 .40
❑ 21 Clean Slate .15 .40
❑ 22 Hidden Assests .15 .40
❑ 23 A Real Hottie .15 .40
❑ 24 To The Rescue .15 .40
❑ 25 Chloe R.I.P. .15 .40
❑ 26 The Boy Of Steel .15 .40
❑ 27 Bet Your Life .15 .40
❑ 28 The Sand Man Cometh .15 .40
❑ 29 Tempus Fugit .15 .40
❑ 30 Least Likely To Be... .15 .40
❑ 31 The Lion At Bay .15 .40
❑ 32 Switching Fates .15 .40
❑ 33 The Price Of Freedom .15 .40
❑ 34 The Tipping Point .15 .40
❑ 35 Soul Mates .15 .40
❑ 36 The Son You Always Wanted .15 .40
❑ 37 Lightning Strikes .15 .40
❑ 38 Hot Water .15 .40
❑ 39 On Guard .15 .40
❑ 40 A Witch In Time .15 .40
❑ 41 Ptomaine Course .15 .40
❑ 42 Tough Enough .15 .40
❑ 43 Three Months Later... .15 .40
❑ 44 Magic In Paris .15 .40
❑ 45 Krypton's Child Is Fleet In Flight .15 .40
❑ 46 Black K .15 .40
❑ 47 Grave Matters .15 .40
❑ 48 Chloe Lives! .15 .40
❑ 49 Skin Deep .15 .40
❑ 50 A Bad Face Day .15 .40
❑ 51 Commanding Attention .15 .40
❑ 52 Krypton-Ade .15 .40
❑ 53 Speed Thrills .15 .40
❑ 54 On The Run .15 .40
❑ 55 Foreign Exchange .15 .40
❑ 56 Power Unfettered .15 .40
❑ 57 Pushing Her Luck .15 .40
❑ 58 Skewing The Odds .15 .40
❑ 59 Mark Of The Switch .15 .40
❑ 60 Witches' Brew .15 .40
❑ 61 Killer Date .15 .40
❑ 62 A Woman Scorned .15 .40
❑ 63 Day-Mares .15 .40
❑ 64 Apolcalyptic Visions .15 .40
❑ 65 Rehabilitated? .15 .40
❑ 66 Red Love .15 .40
❑ 67 Scapegoat .15 .40
❑ 68 Sacrifice .15 .40
❑ 69 Killer In Bunny Slippers? .15 .40
❑ 70 Blood Ties .15 .40
❑ 71 Doggone .15 .40
❑ 72 Family Matters .15 .40
❑ 73 Legacy .15 .40
❑ 74 Crouching Tiger, Hidden Lana .15 .40
❑ 75 Wild Child .15 .40
❑ 76 A Merry Chase .15 .40
❑ 77 The Real Lex? .15 .40
❑ 78 I Am The Villian... .15 .40
❑ 79 Queen B .15 .40
❑ 80 Revenge Chic .15 .40
❑ 81 Tabula Rasa .15 .40
❑ 82 Pentimento .15 .40
❑ 83 Evan's Gift .15 .40
❑ 84 Vita Brevis .15 .40
❑ 85 High School High .15 .40
❑ 86 Hostages .15 .40
❑ 87 Graduation .15 .40
❑ 88 The Sentries .15 .40
❑ 89 Commencement .15 .40
❑ 90 Checklist .15 .40

2005 Smallville Season Four Autographs

STATED ODDS 1:36
❑ A26 Michael Rosenbaum 30.00 60.00
❑ A27 Erica Durance 30.00 60.00
❑ A28 Margot Kidder 12.00 30.00
❑ A29 Sarah Carter 8.00 20.00
❑ A30 Peyton List 8.00 20.00
❑ A31 Jonathan Bennett 8.00 20.00
❑ A32 Rob Freeman 8.00 20.00
❑ A33 Kyle Gallner 8.00 20.00
❑ A34 Trent Ford 8.00 20.00

2005 Smallville Season Four Box Loaders

BL STATED ODDS ONE PER BOX
CL STATED ODDS ONE PER CASE
❑ BL1 Fire - Passion 2.00 5.00
❑ BL2 Water - Emotion 2.00 5.00
❑ BL3 Air - Intellect 2.00 5.00
❑ CL1 Nemesis 4.00 10.00
CASE INSERT

2005 Smallville Season Four Lois & Clark

STATED ODDS 1:11
❑ LC1 Lois & Clark 1.25 3.00
❑ LC2 Lois & Clark 1.25 3.00
❑ LC3 Lois & Clark 1.25 3.00
❑ LC4 Lois & Clark 1.25 3.00
❑ LC5 Lois & Clark 1.25 3.00
❑ LC6 Lois & Clark 1.25 3.00
❑ LC7 Lois & Clark 1.25 3.00
❑ LC8 Lois & Clark 1.25 3.00
❑ LC9 Lois & Clark 1.25 3.00

2005 Smallville Season Four Pieceworks

STATED ODDS 1:36
❑ PW1 Michael Rosenbaum 8.00 20.00
❑ PW1A Michael Rosenbaum AU
❑ PW2 Tom Welling 12.00 30.00
❑ PW3 Kristin Kreuk 12.00 30.00
❑ PW4 Erica Durance 12.00 30.00
❑ PW5 Jensen Ackles 10.00 25.00
❑ PW6 Jane Seymour 8.00 20.00
❑ PW7 Margot Kidder 8.00 20.00

2005 Smallville Season Four Switchcraft

STATED ODDS 1:17
❑ SW1 The Dying Curse 1.50 4.00
❑ SW2 Sign of Change 1.50 4.00
❑ SW3 Belle, Book & Bloodstain 1.50 4.00
❑ SW4 Witch Switch 1.50 4.00
❑ SW5 Stone Killer 1.50 4.00
❑ SW6 Blood Price 1.50 4.00

2005 The Sopranos Season One

COMPLETE SET (72) 5.00 12.00
❑ 1 The Sopranos Season One .15 .40
❑ 2 Anthony Soprano .15 .40
❑ 3 Dr. Jennifer Melfi .15 .40
❑ 4 Carmela Soprano .15 .40
❑ 5 Christopher Moltisanti .15 .40
❑ 6 Livia Soprano .15 .40
❑ 7 Corrado Junior Soprano .15 .40
❑ 8 Silvio Dante .15 .40
❑ 9 Paulie Walnuts Gualtieri .15 .40
❑ 10 Big Pussy Bonpensiero .15 .40
❑ 11 Meadow Soprano .15 .40
❑ 12 A.J. Soprano .15 .40
❑ 13 Artie Bucco .15 .40
❑ 14 Charmaine Bucco .15 .40
❑ 15 Adrinana La Cerva .15 .40
❑ 16 Mikey Palmice .15 .40
❑ 17 Hesh Rabkin .15 .40
❑ 18 Detective Vin Makazian .15 .40
❑ 19 Brendan Filone .15 .40
❑ 20 Father Phil Intintola .15 .40
❑ 21 Johnny Sack Sacramoni .15 .40
❑ 22 An American Family .15 .40
❑ 23 Lethal Loyalty .15 .40
❑ 24 Passing the Torch .15 .40
❑ 25 Livia's Problems .15 .40
❑ 26 Running into Fanny .15 .40
❑ 27 At Green Grove .15 .40
❑ 28 Goyum or Golem .15 .40
❑ 29 A Taste of Bucco .15 .40
❑ 30 Special Delivery .15 .40
❑ 31 Make Peace or War .15 .40
❑ 32 Mikey Gets Stapled .15 .40
❑ 33 The Power of Pride .15 .40
❑ 34 Educating Meadow .15 .40
❑ 35 Death of a Rat .15 .40
❑ 36 Father Phil's Sleepover .15 .40
❑ 37 All Hail The Boss .15 .40
❑ 38 Over and Under .15 .40
❑ 39 In This Together .15 .40
❑ 40 Johnny Boy's Story .15 .40
❑ 41 AJ Spills the Beans .15 .40
❑ 42 Getting It Together .15 .40
❑ 43 Dr. Melfi's Ex .15 .40
❑ 44 A Visit from the Feds .15 .40
❑ 45 Trouble with Agent Grasso .15 .40
❑ 46 Daddies Little Athlete .15 .40
❑ 47 Winners Take All .15 .40
❑ 48 A Friendly Game of Golf .15 .40
❑ 49 Adriana's Possibilities .15 .40
❑ 50 Amusing the Neighbors .15 .40
❑ 51 Sit-Down with Hesh .15 .40
❑ 52 The Betrayal .15 .40
❑ 53 The Lowdown on Pussy .15 .40
❑ 54 Vin Takes a Dive .15 .40
❑ 55 Lunch with a Vision .15 .40
❑ 56 A Hit Gone to Hell .15 .40
❑ 57 The Split .15 .40
❑ 58 Truth and Consequences .15 .40
❑ 59 Taking Care of Business .15 .40
❑ 60 The Moments of Good .15 .40
❑ 61 Deleted Scene .15 .40
❑ 62 A Second Family .15 .40
❑ 63 Power Players .15 .40
❑ 64 Where Melfi Fits In .15 .40
❑ 65 Love and Choices .15 .40
❑ 66 The Lightning Rod .15 .40
❑ 67 Hesh in the Fold .15 .40
❑ 68 Honor Thy Uncle .15 .40
❑ 69 The Mayonnaisers .15 .40
❑ 70 Dr. Melfi's Office .15 .40
❑ 71 Satriale's Pork Store .15 .40
❑ 72 Checklist .02 .10

2005 The Sopranos Season One Autographs

COMPLETE SET (9) 75.00 150.00
❑ AAT Aida Turturro SP 7.50 20.00
❑ ADC Dominic Chianese 20.00 50.00
❑ AFP Frank Pellegrino 6.00 15.00
❑ AJA Jerry Adler 6.00 15.00
❑ AJD Jamie Lynn DiScala SP 15.00 40.00
❑ AKN Kathrine Narducci 6.00 15.00
❑ AMS Matt Servitto 6.00 15.00

MODERN ERA NON-SPORTS

Card	Low	High
❑ APS Paul Schulze	6.00	15.00
❑ ASA Sharon Angela	6.00	15.00

2005 The Sopranos Season One Box Toppers

Card	Low	High
COMPLETE SET (3)	4.00	10.00
❑ BL1 A Deal is a Deal	1.50	4.00
❑ BL2 Pulling Strings	1.50	4.00
❑ BL3 The Law Closing In	1.50	4.00

2005 The Sopranos Season One Family Matters

Card	Low	High
COMPLETE SET (9)	6.00	15.00
❑ FM1 The Gangs All Here	1.00	2.50
❑ FM2 Say Uncle	1.00	2.50
❑ FM3 A Boys Best Friend	1.00	2.50
❑ FM4 Doctor and Patient	1.00	2.50
❑ FM5 Boot in Black	1.00	2.50
❑ FM6 Tour with Meadow	1.00	2.50
❑ FM7 Meet the Sopranos	1.00	2.50
❑ FM8 Taking on AJ	1.00	2.50
❑ FM9 Future of the Family	1.00	2.50

2005 The Sopranos Season One La Belle Donne

Card	Low	High
COMPLETE SET (6)	4.00	10.00
❑ BD1 Carmella Soprano	1.00	2.50
❑ BD2 Meadow Soprano	1.00	2.50
❑ BD3 Dr. Melfi	1.00	2.50
❑ BD4 Isabella	1.00	2.50
❑ BD5 Jeannie Cusamano	1.00	2.50
❑ BD6 Adrianna La Cerva	1.00	2.50

2005 Spike The Complete Story

Card	Low	High
COMPLETE SET (72)	4.00	10.00
BV1 PTR1 STATED ODDS 1:432		
❑ 1 Spike: The Complete Story	.10	.30
❑ 2 Bloody Awful	.10	.30
❑ 3 Dru's Pet	.10	.30
❑ 4 Momma's Boy	.10	.30
❑ 5 Amigos	.10	.30
❑ 6 Betrayed	.10	.30
❑ 7 Hung Up	.10	.30
❑ 8 Slayer	.10	.30
❑ 9 Recruited	.10	.30
❑ 10 Passion	.10	.30
❑ 11 Trophy	.10	.30
❑ 12 Recuperation	.10	.30
❑ 13 New Slayer	.10	.30
❑ 14 Reversal of Fortune	.10	.30
❑ 15 Triangle	.10	.30
❑ 16 Dealing with the Enemy	.10	.30
❑ 17 My Way	.10	.30
❑ 18 Heartbreak	.10	.30
❑ 19 Drowning Sorrows	.10	.30
❑ 20 Captured	.10	.30
❑ 21 Manipulative	.10	.30
❑ 22 Quest	.10	.30
❑ 23 Ball and Chain	.10	.30
❑ 24 Defiant	.10	.30
❑ 25 Devastated	.10	.30
❑ 26 Empathy	.10	.30
❑ 27 Rough Stuff	.10	.30
❑ 28 Bargain	.10	.30
❑ 29 Lost	.10	.30
❑ 30 Taken	.10	.30
❑ 31 Rescued	.10	.30
❑ 32 Restored	.10	.30
❑ 33 Wild Ones	.10	.30
❑ 34 Sorting it Out	.10	.30
❑ 35 Hero at Last	.10	.30
❑ 36 Far From Over	.10	.30
❑ 37 To Hell	.10	.30
❑ 38 Reconstituted	.10	.30
❑ 39 Karma	.10	.30
❑ 40 Destiny	.10	.30
❑ 41 Mission	.10	.30
❑ 42 Bound	.10	.30
❑ 43 Courageous	.10	.30
❑ 44 Tough but Tender	.10	.30
❑ 45 Champion	.10	.30
❑ 46 The Master	.10	.30
❑ 47 Angel	.10	.30
❑ 48 Xander	.10	.30
❑ 49 Riley	.10	.30
❑ 50 Giles	.10	.30
❑ 51 Robin Wood	.10	.30
❑ 52 Glory	.10	.30
❑ 53 Pavayne	.10	.30
❑ 54 Lindsey	.10	.30
❑ 55 Effulgent	.10	.30
❑ 56 Shirty	.10	.30
❑ 57 Randy	.10	.30
❑ 58 Mate	.10	.30
❑ 59 Fancy	.10	.30
❑ 60 Nancy-Boy	.10	.30
❑ 61 Prat	.10	.30
❑ 62 Sod	.10	.30
❑ 63 Git	.10	.30
❑ 64 Drusilla	.10	.30
❑ 65 Harmony	.10	.30
❑ 66 Willow	.10	.30
❑ 67 Buffy Bot	.10	.30
❑ 68 Dawn	.10	.30
❑ 69 Buffy	.10	.30
❑ 70 Anya	.10	.30
❑ 71 Fred	.10	.30
❑ 72 Checklist	.10	.30
❑ BV1 Boris Vallejo AU	25.00	60.00

2005 Spike The Complete Story Autographs

Card	Low	High
STATED ODDS 1:36		
❑ A1 James Marsters	50.00	100.00
❑ A2 Juliet Landau	20.00	40.00
❑ A3 Julie Benz	12.00	30.00
❑ A4 Mercedes McNab	12.00	30.00
❑ A5 K.D. Aubert	10.00	25.00
❑ A6 Kali Rocha	10.00	25.00
❑ A7 George Hertzberg	10.00	25.00
❑ A8 Steven W. Bailey	10.00	25.00
❑ A9 James C. Leary	10.00	25.00
❑ A10 Simon Templeman	10.00	25.00

2005 Spike The Complete Story Box Loaders

Card	Low	High
❑ BL1 Soul	1.50	4.00
❑ BL2 Heart	1.50	4.00
❑ BL3 Destiny	1.50	4.00
❑ CL1 Bloodlines	7.50	20.00

2005 Spike The Complete Story Heart & Soul

Card	Low	High
STATED ODDS 1:11		
❑ HS1 Heart & Soul	1.25	3.00
❑ HS2 Heart & Soul	1.25	3.00
❑ HS3 Heart & Soul	1.25	3.00
❑ HS4 Heart & Soul	1.25	3.00
❑ HS5 Heart & Soul	1.25	3.00
❑ HS6 Heart & Soul	1.25	3.00
❑ HS7 Heart & Soul	1.25	3.00
❑ HS8 Heart & Soul	1.25	3.00
❑ HS9 Heart & Soul	1.25	3.00

2005 Spike The Complete Story Pieceworks

Card	Low	High
❑ PW1 James Marsters Leather Coat	10.00	25.00
❑ PW1A James Marsters Leather Coat AU	75.00	150.00
❑ PW2 James Marsters Leather Coat	10.00	25.00
❑ PW2A James Marsters Leather Coat AU	75.00	150.00

2005 Spike The Complete Story Promos

Card	Low	High
❑ P1 Spike	1.00	2.50
❑ Pi Spike	1.00	2.50
❑ PUK Spike	1.00	2.50
❑ PUKP Spike FOIL	1.50	4.00

2005 Spike The Complete Story Spike & Buffy

Card	Low	High
STATED ODDS 1:17		
❑ SB1 Menacing	2.00	5.00
❑ SB2 Uneasy Allies	2.00	5.00
❑ SB3 First Kiss	2.00	5.00
❑ SB4 Lust	2.00	5.00
❑ SB5 Intimacy	2.00	5.00
❑ SB6 Farewell	2.00	5.00

2005 Star Trek The Original Series Art & Images

Card	Low	High
COMPLETE SET (81)	4.00	10.00
❑ 1 The Cage	.10	.30
❑ 2 Where No Man Has Gone Before	.10	.30
❑ 3 The Corbomite Maneuver	.10	.30
❑ 4 Mudd's Women	.10	.30
❑ 5 The Enemy Within	.10	.30
❑ 6 The Man Trap	.10	.30
❑ 7 The Naked Time	.10	.30
❑ 8 Charlie X	.10	.30
❑ 9 Balance of Terror	.10	.30
❑ 10 What Are Little Girls Made Of	.10	.30
❑ 11 Dagger of the Mind	.10	.30
❑ 12 Miri	.10	.30
❑ 13 The Conscience of the King	.10	.30
❑ 14 The Galileo Seven	.10	.30
❑ 15 Court Martial	.10	.30
❑ 16 The Menagerie	.10	.30
❑ 17 Shore Leave	.10	.30
❑ 18 The Squire of Gothos	.10	.30
❑ 19 Arena	.10	.30
❑ 20 The Alternative Factor	.10	.30
❑ 21 Tomorrow is Yesterday	.10	.30
❑ 22 The Return of the Archons	.10	.30
❑ 23 A Taste of Armageddon	.10	.30
❑ 24 Space Seed	.10	.30
❑ 25 This Side of Paradise	.10	.30
❑ 26 The Devil in the Dark	.10	.30
❑ 27 Errand of Mercy	.10	.30
❑ 28 The City on the Edge of Forever	.10	.30
❑ 29 Operation -- Annihilate	.10	.30
❑ 30 Catspaw	.10	.30
❑ 31 Metamorphosis	.10	.30
❑ 32 Friday's Child	.10	.30
❑ 33 Who Mourns for Adonais	.10	.30
❑ 34 Amok Time	.10	.30
❑ 35 The Doomsday Machine	.10	.30
❑ 36 Wolf in The Fold	.10	.30
❑ 37 The Changeling	.10	.30
❑ 38 The Apple	.10	.30
❑ 39 Mirror, Mirror	.10	.30
❑ 40 The Deadly Years	.10	.30
❑ 41 I, Mudd	.10	.30
❑ 42 The Trouble With Tribbles	.10	.30
❑ 43 Bread and Circuses	.10	.30
❑ 44 Journey to Babel	.10	.30
❑ 45 A Private Little War	.10	.30
❑ 46 The Gamesters of Triskelion	.10	.30
❑ 47 Obsession	.10	.30
❑ 48 The Immunity Syndrome	.10	.30
❑ 49 A Piece of the Action	.10	.30
❑ 50 By Any Other Name	.10	.30
❑ 51 Return to Tomorrow	.10	.30
❑ 52 Patterns of Force	.10	.30
❑ 53 The Ultimate Computer	.10	.30
❑ 54 The Omega Glory	.10	.30
❑ 55 Assignment: Earth	.10	.30
❑ 56 Spectre of the Gun	.10	.30
❑ 57 Elaan of Troyius	.10	.30
❑ 58 The Paradise Syndrome	.10	.30
❑ 59 The Enterprise Incident	.10	.30
❑ 60 And the Children Shall Lead	.10	.30
❑ 61 Spock's Brain	.10	.30
❑ 62 Is There in Truth No Beauty	.10	.30
❑ 63 The Empath	.10	.30
❑ 64 The Tholian Web	.10	.30
❑ 65 For the World is Hollow	.10	.30
❑ 66 Day of the Dove	.10	.30
❑ 67 Plato's Stepchildren	.10	.30
❑ 68 Wink of an Eye	.10	.30
❑ 69 That Which Survives	.10	.30
❑ 70 Let That Be Your Last Battlefield	.10	.30
❑ 71 Whom Gods Destroy	.10	.30
❑ 72 The Mark of Gideon	.10	.30
❑ 73 The Lights of Zetar	.10	.30
❑ 74 The Cloudminders	.10	.30
❑ 75 The Way to Eden	.10	.30
❑ 76 Requiem for Methuselah	.10	.30
❑ 77 The Savage Curtain	.10	.30
❑ 78 All Our Yesterdays	.10	.30
❑ 79 Turnabout Intruder	.10	.30
❑ 80 Checklist	.10	.30
❑ 81 Checklist	.10	.30

2005 Star Trek The Original Series Art & Images Animated Series Expanded Universe

Card	Low	High
COMPLETE SET (39)	40.00	100.00
STATED ODDS 1:8		
❑ AS1 Adam	1.25	3.00
❑ AS2 Akuta	1.25	3.00
❑ AS3 Andrea	1.25	3.00
❑ AS4 Apollo	1.25	3.00
❑ AS5 Balok's Puppet	1.25	3.00
❑ AS6 Captain Pike	1.25	3.00
❑ AS7 Captain Pike (crippled)	1.25	3.00
❑ AS8 Charlie Evans	1.25	3.00
❑ AS9 Chekov	1.25	3.00
❑ AS10 Commissioner Bele	1.25	3.00
❑ AS11 Edith Keeler	1.25	3.00
❑ AS12 Elaan of Troyius	1.25	3.00
❑ AS13 Galt	1.25	3.00
❑ AS14 Gary Mitchell	1.25	3.00
❑ AS15 Gem	1.25	3.00
❑ AS16 Kang	1.25	3.00
❑ AS17 Khan	1.25	3.00
❑ AS18 Lal	1.25	3.00
❑ AS19 Lazarus	1.25	3.00
❑ AS20 Losira	1.25	3.00
❑ AS21 Maab	1.25	3.00
❑ AS22 Marta	1.25	3.00
❑ AS23 Mirror Kirk	1.25	3.00
❑ AS24 Mirror Marlena	1.25	3.00
❑ AS25 Mirror Spock	1.25	3.00
❑ AS26 Mirror Sulu	1.25	3.00
❑ AS27 Natira	1.25	3.00
❑ AS28 Ruk	1.25	3.00
❑ AS29 Shahna	1.25	3.00
❑ AS30 Subcommander Tal	1.25	3.00
❑ AS31 Sylvia	1.25	3.00
❑ AS32 The Gorn	1.25	3.00
❑ AS33 The Keeper	1.25	3.00
❑ AS34 The Mugato	1.25	3.00
❑ AS35 T'Pring	1.25	3.00
❑ AS36 Trelane	1.25	3.00
❑ AS37 Vina	1.25	3.00
❑ AS38 Yeoman Colt	1.25	3.00
❑ AS39 Yeoman Rand	1.25	3.00

2005 Star Trek The Original Series Art & Images ArtiFex

Card	Low	High
COMPLETE SET (9)	30.00	75.00
STATED ODDS 1:24		
❑ CZ1 Mirror, Mirror	4.00	10.00
❑ CZ2 The City on the Edge of Forever	4.00	10.00
❑ CZ3 Amok Time	4.00	10.00
❑ CZ4 The Trouble With Tribbles	4.00	10.00
❑ CZ5 The Squire of Gothos	4.00	10.00
❑ CZ6 All Our Yesterdays	4.00	10.00
❑ CZ7 What Are Little Girls Made Of	4.00	10.00
❑ CZ8 The Enterprise Incident	4.00	10.00
❑ CZ9 Journey To Babel	4.00	10.00

2005 Star Trek The Original Series Art & Images Autographs

STATED ODDS 1:12
A15 STATED ODDS ONE PER COLLECTOR'S ALBUM
LA3 STATED ODDS ONE PER 6 CASE PURCHASE
L (LIMITED): 300-500 COPIES
VL (VERY LIMITED): 200-300 COPIES

Card	Low	High
❑ A11 Walter Koenig L	15.00	30.00
❑ A12 Grace Lee Whitney L	20.00	40.00
❑ A13 Bobby Clark L	15.00	30.00
❑ A14 Joan Collins VL	50.00	100.00
❑ A15 Arlene Martel/ (issued in collectors album)	10.00	25.00
❑ A16 Ricardo Montalban VL	125.00	200.00
❑ A17 Leonard Nimoy VL	150.00	250.00
❑ A18 George Takei VL		
❑ A19 BarBara Luna	10.00	25.00
❑ A20 William Campbell	8.00	20.00
❑ A21 Gary Lockwood	8.00	20.00
❑ A22 Sherry Jackson	10.00	25.00
❑ A23 William Windom L	10.00	25.00
❑ A24 Joseph Ruskin	8.00	20.00
❑ A25 Jack Donner	8.00	20.00
❑ A26 Michael Ansara L	20.00	40.00
❑ A27 Lee Meriwether L	10.00	25.00
❑ A28 William O'Connell	8.00	20.00
❑ A29 Michael Forest	8.00	20.00
❑ A30 Laurel Goodwin VL	20.00	40.00
❑ A31 Sean Kenney	8.00	20.00
❑ A32 Majel Barrett VL	50.00	100.00
❑ A33 Antoinette Bower	8.00	20.00
❑ A34 Joanne Linville L	10.00	25.00
❑ A35 Lois Jewell	8.00	20.00
❑ A36 Kathryn Hays L	8.00	20.00
❑ A37 Kate Woodville L	8.00	20.00
❑ A38 Michael Dante	8.00	20.00
❑ A39 Yvonne Craig VL	25.00	50.00
❑ A41 Robert Brown	8.00	20.00
❑ A42 Charles Napier	10.00	25.00
❑ LA3 William Shatner/ (issued as 6-case incentive)	150.00	250.00

2005 Star Trek The Original Series Art & Images Comic Book Art

Card	Low	High
COMPLETE SET (61)	30.00	60.00
STATED ODDS 1:4		
❑ GK1 K-G, Planet of Death	.60	1.50
❑ GK2 Planet of the Condemned	.60	1.50
❑ GK3 Automated Destroyers	.60	1.50
❑ GK4 Strange Invader	.60	1.50
❑ GK5 Numero Uno	.60	1.50
❑ GK6 Galactic Disaster	.60	1.50
❑ GK7 Voodoo Magic	.60	1.50
❑ GK8 Doomed to Infancy	.60	1.50
❑ GK9 Heroes of the Past	.60	1.50
❑ GK10 Science vs. Sorcery	.60	1.50
❑ GK11 Vulcan Furies	.60	1.50
❑ GK12 Space Pirates	.60	1.50
❑ GK13 Battle for Paradise	.60	1.50
❑ GK14 Unfit for Command	.60	1.50
❑ GK15 The Land of Limbo	.60	1.50
❑ GK16 Planet of the Dark Ages	.60	1.50
❑ GK17 Unlikely Idol	.60	1.50
❑ GK18 Project Atlas	.60	1.50
❑ GK19 Haunted Asteroid	.60	1.50
❑ GK20 World Gone Mad	.60	1.50
❑ GK21 Mummy Attack	.60	1.50
❑ GK22 Siege in Superspace	.60	1.50
❑ GK23 Child's Play	.60	1.50
❑ GK24 The Trial of Captain Kirk	.60	1.50
❑ GK25 The Shrinking Society	.60	1.50
❑ GK26 Starship of Clones	.60	1.50
❑ GK27 Ice Journey	.60	1.50
❑ GK28 Parasitic Life Form	.60	1.50
❑ GK29 K-G, Planet of Death	.60	1.50
❑ GK30 A Star's Last Gasp	.60	1.50
❑ GK31 The Eye of Litn	.60	1.50
❑ GK32 The Animal People	.60	1.50
❑ GK33 Kirk vs. Kirk	.60	1.50
❑ GK34 PsychoCrystals	.60	1.50
❑ GK35 Strange Invader	.60	1.50
❑ GK36 Doomsday Bomb	.60	1.50
❑ GK37 Numero Uno	.60	1.50
❑ GK38 One of Our Captains Is Missing	.60	1.50
❑ GK39 The Peace Activist	.60	1.50
❑ GK40 Triangle of Peril	.60	1.50
❑ GK41 The Evictors	.60	1.50
❑ GK42 Age Reversal	.60	1.50
❑ GK43 Hostile Mutants	.60	1.50
❑ GK44 Red Raven's Revolt	.60	1.50
❑ GK45 Voodoo Magic	.60	1.50
❑ GK46 Spock to the Rescue	.60	1.50
❑ GK47 The Tree of Life	.60	1.50
❑ GK48 Murder Aboard the Enterprise!	.60	1.50
❑ GK49 The Return of the Companion	.60	1.50
❑ GK50 Induku's Return	.60	1.50
❑ GK51 False God	.60	1.50
❑ GK52 Child Hero	.60	1.50
❑ GK53 Odyssey of Peril	.60	1.50
❑ GK54 The Killer Birds	.60	1.50
❑ GK55 A World Against Itself	.60	1.50
❑ GK56 Back to the Guardian of Forever	.60	1.50
❑ GK57 The Great Vrunon	.60	1.50
❑ GK58 Brain-Damaged Planetoid	.60	1.50
❑ GK59 To Err Is Vulcan	.60	1.50
❑ GK60 Cyborg Savior	.60	1.50
❑ GK61 Operation Con Game	.60	1.50

2005 Star Trek The Original Series Art & Images SketchaFex

STATED ODDS 1:48
U.S.S. ENTERPRISE STATED ODDS ONE PER 2 CASE PURCHASE

❑ NNO The Cage
❑ NNO The Enemy Within
❑ NNO Balance of Terror
❑ NNO The Conscience of the King
❑ NNO Shore Leave
❑ NNO Tomorrow is Yesterday
❑ NNO This Side of Paradise
❑ NNO Operation -- Annihilate
❑ NNO U.S.S. Enterprise COLOR
❑ NNO The Corbomite Maneuver
❑ NNO The Naked Time
❑ NNO Dagger of the Mind
❑ NNO Court Martial
❑ NNO Arena
❑ NNO A Taste of Armageddon
❑ NNO Errand of Mercy
❑ NNO Tricorder
❑ NNO Where No Man Has Gone Before
❑ NNO The Man Trap
❑ NNO What Are Little Girls Made Of
❑ NNO The Galileo Seven
❑ NNO The Squire of Gothos
❑ NNO The Return of the Archons
❑ NNO The Devil in the Dark
❑ NNO Communicator
❑ NNO Mudd's Women
❑ NNO Charlie X
❑ NNO Miri
❑ NNO The Menagerie
❑ NNO The Alternative Factor
❑ NNO Space Seed
❑ NNO The City on the Edge of Forever
❑ NNO Phaser

2005 Star Trek The Original Series Art & Images SketchaFex Case Toppers

Card	Low	High
COMPLETE SET (3)	10.00	25.00
STATED ODDS ONE PER CASE		
❑ NNO Tricorder	4.00	10.00
❑ NNO Phaser	4.00	10.00
❑ NNO Communicator	4.00	10.00

2005 Stargate Atlantis Season One

Card	Low	High
COMPLETE SET (63)	4.00	10.00
❑ 1 Title Card Checklist 1	.10	.30
❑ 2 Title Card Checklist 2	.10	.30
❑ 3 Title Card Checklist 3	.10	.30
❑ 4 Rising, Part 1	.10	.30
❑ 5 Rising, Part 1	.10	.30
❑ 6 Rising, Part 1	.10	.30
❑ 7 Rising, Part 2	.10	.30
❑ 8 Rising, Part 2	.10	.30
❑ 9 Rising, Part 2	.10	.30
❑ 10 Hide and Seek	.10	.30
❑ 11 Hide and Seek	.10	.30
❑ 12 Hide and Seek	.10	.30
❑ 13 Thirty-Eight Minutes	.10	.30
❑ 14 Thirty-Eight Minutes	.10	.30
❑ 15 Thirty-Eight Minutes	.10	.30
❑ 16 Suspicion	.10	.30
❑ 17 Suspicion	.10	.30
❑ 18 Suspicion	.10	.30
❑ 19 Childhood's end	.10	.30
❑ 20 Childhood's end	.10	.30
❑ 21 Childhood's end	.10	.30
❑ 22 Poisoning The Well	.10	.30
❑ 23 Poisoning The Well	.10	.30
❑ 24 Poisoning The Well	.10	.30
❑ 25 Underground	.10	.30
❑ 26 Underground	.10	.30
❑ 27 Underground	.10	.30
❑ 28 Home	.10	.30
❑ 29 Home	.10	.30
❑ 30 Home	.10	.30
❑ 31 The Storm	.10	.30
❑ 32 The Storm	.10	.30
❑ 33 The Storm	.10	.30
❑ 34 The Eye	.10	.30
❑ 35 The Eye	.10	.30
❑ 36 The Eye	.10	.30
❑ 37 The Defiant One	.10	.30
❑ 38 The Defiant One	.10	.30
❑ 39 The Defiant One	.10	.30
❑ 40 Hot Zone	.10	.30
❑ 41 Hot Zone	.10	.30
❑ 42 Hot Zone	.10	.30
❑ 43 Sanctuary	.10	.30
❑ 44 Sanctuary	.10	.30
❑ 45 Sanctuary	.10	.30
❑ 46 Before I Sleep	.10	.30
❑ 47 Before I Sleep	.10	.30
❑ 48 Before I Sleep	.10	.30
❑ 49 The Brotherhood	.10	.30
❑ 50 The Brotherhood	.10	.30
❑ 51 The Brotherhood	.10	.30
❑ 52 Letter from Pegasus	.10	.30
❑ 53 Letter from Pegasus	.10	.30
❑ 54 Letter from Pegasus	.10	.30
❑ 55 The Gift	.10	.30
❑ 56 The Gift	.10	.30
❑ 57 The Gift	.10	.30
❑ 58 The Siege, Part 1	.10	.30
❑ 59 The Siege, Part 1	.10	.30
❑ 60 The Siege, Part 1	.10	.30
❑ 61 The Siege, Part 2	.10	.30
❑ 62 The Siege, Part 2	.10	.30
❑ 63 The Siege, Part 2	.10	.30

2005 Stargate Atlantis Season One Ancient Technology

Card	Low	High
COMPLETE SET (9)	25.00	60.00
STATED ODDS 1:20		
❑ AT1 Puddle Jumper	3.00	8.00
❑ AT2 Personal Shield	3.00	8.00
❑ AT3 Zero Point Modules	3.00	8.00
❑ AT4 Cryogenic Chamber Statis Unit	3.00	8.00
❑ AT5 Atlantis	3.00	8.00
❑ AT6 Defense Drones	3.00	8.00
❑ AT7 Lagrange Point Satellite	3.00	8.00
❑ AT8 Command Chair	3.00	8.00
❑ AT9 Repository of Knowledge	3.00	8.00

2005 Stargate Atlantis Season One Atlantis Crew

Card	Low	High
COMPLETE SET (9)	50.00	120.00
STATED ODDS 1:40		
❑ C1 Major John Sheppard	6.00	15.00
❑ C2 Dr. Elizabeth Weir	6.00	15.00
❑ C3 Teyla Emmagan	6.00	15.00
❑ C4 Lt. Aiden Ford	6.00	15.00
❑ C5 Dr. Rodney McKay	6.00	15.00
❑ C6 Dr. Carson Beckett	6.00	15.00
❑ C7 Major John Sheppard Dr. Elizabeth Weir	6.00	15.00
❑ C8 Dr. Rodney McKay Dr. Elizabeth Weir	6.00	15.00
❑ C9 Major John Sheppard Lt. Aiden Ford	6.00	15.00

2005 Stargate Atlantis Season One Autographs

STATED ODDS ONE PER BOX
CHAMBERS AUTO ISSUED AS CASE TOPPER
DAVI AUTO ISSUED AS 2-CASE INCENTIVE
SCARFE AUTO ISSUED IN COLLECTORS ALBUM
L (LIMITED): 300-500 COPIES
VL (VERY LIMITED): 200-300 COPIES

❑ 1 Erin Chambers issued as case topper)
❑ 2 Ari Cohen
❑ 3 Robert Davi/(issued as 2-case incentive)
❑ 4 Joe Flanigan VL
❑ 5 Christopher Heyerdahl
❑ 6 Gildart Jackson
❑ 7 Colm Meaney L
❑ 8 Laura Mennell
❑ 9 Melia McClure
❑ 10 Paul McGillion VL
❑ 11 Jana Mitsoula
❑ 12 David Nykl
❑ 13 Alan Scarfe/(issued in album)
❑ 14 Craig Veroni
❑ 15 Boyan Vukelic

2005 Stargate Atlantis Season One Costumes

STATED ODDS ONE PER BOX
AC1 ISSUED AS 6-CASE INCENTIVE

❑ 1 Acastus Kolya
❑ 2 Chaya Sar
❑ 3 Dr. Carson Beckett
❑ 4 Dr. Elizabeth Weir
❑ 5 Dr. Rodney McKay
❑ 6 Janus
❑ 7 Lt. Aiden Ford
❑ 8 Male Wraith
❑ 9 Melia
❑ 10 Sora
❑ 11 Teyla Emmagan
❑ AC1 Rachel Luttrell as Teyla Emmagan AUTO (issued as 6-case incentive)

2005 Stargate Atlantis Season One Fallen Hero

Card	Low	High
STATED ODDS 1:480		
❑ H1 Colonel Marshall Sumner	50.00	100.00
❑ H2 Colonel Marshall Sumner	50.00	100.00

2005 Stargate Atlantis Season One Quotable Stargate Atlantis

Card	Low	High
COMPLETE SET (20)	40.00	100.00
STATED ODDS 1:6		
❑ Q1 Rising, Part 1	2.50	6.00
❑ Q2 Rising, Part 2	2.50	6.00
❑ Q3 Hide and Seek	2.50	6.00
❑ Q4 Thirty-Eight Minutes	2.50	6.00
❑ Q5 Suspicion	2.50	6.00
❑ Q6 Childhood's end	2.50	6.00
❑ Q7 Poisoning The Well	2.50	6.00
❑ Q8 Underground	2.50	6.00
❑ Q9 Home	2.50	6.00
❑ Q10 The Storm	2.50	6.00
❑ Q11 The Eye	2.50	6.00
❑ Q12 The Defiant One	2.50	6.00
❑ Q13 Hot Zone	2.50	6.00
❑ Q14 Sanctuary	2.50	6.00
❑ Q15 Before I Sleep	2.50	6.00
❑ Q16 The Brotherhood	2.50	6.00
❑ Q17 Letter from Pegasus	2.50	6.00
❑ Q18 The Gift	2.50	6.00
❑ Q19 The Siege, Part 1	2.50	6.00
❑ Q20 The Siege, Part 2	2.50	6.00

2005 Stargate SG-1 Season Seven

Card	Low	High
COMPLETE SET (72)	4.00	10.00
❑ 1 Title Card	.10	.30
❑ 2 Title Card	.10	.30
❑ 3 Title Card	.10	.30
❑ 4 Fallen	.10	.30
❑ 5 Fallen	.10	.30
❑ 6 Fallen	.10	.30
❑ 7 Homecoming	.10	.30
❑ 8 Homecoming	.10	.30
❑ 9 Homecoming	.10	.30
❑ 10 Fragile Balance	.10	.30
❑ 11 Fragile Balance	.10	.30
❑ 12 Fragile Balance	.10	.30
❑ 13 Orpheus	.10	.30
❑ 14 Orpheus	.10	.30
❑ 15 Orpheus	.10	.30
❑ 16 Revisions	.10	.30
❑ 17 Revisions	.10	.30
❑ 18 Revisions	.10	.30
❑ 19 Lifeboat	.10	.30
❑ 20 Lifeboat	.10	.30
❑ 21 Lifeboat	.10	.30
❑ 22 Enemy Mine	.10	.30
❑ 23 Enemy Mine	.10	.30

☐ 24 Enemy Mine .10 .30
☐ 25 Space Race .10 .30
☐ 26 Space Race .10 .30
☐ 27 Space Race .10 .30
☐ 28 Avenger 2.0 .10 .30
☐ 29 Avenger 2.0 .10 .30
☐ 30 Avenger 2.0 .10 .30
☐ 31 Birthright .10 .30
☐ 32 Birthright .10 .30
☐ 33 Birthright .10 .30
☐ 34 Evolutions Part 1 .10 .30
☐ 35 Evolutions Part 1 .10 .30
☐ 36 Evolutions Part 1 .10 .30
☐ 37 Evolutions Part 2 .10 .30
☐ 38 Evolutions Part 2 .10 .30
☐ 39 Evolutions Part 2 .10 .30
☐ 40 Grace .10 .30
☐ 41 Grace .10 .30
☐ 42 Grace .10 .30
☐ 43 Fallout .10 .30
☐ 44 Fallout .10 .30
☐ 45 Fallout .10 .30
☐ 46 Chimera .10 .30
☐ 47 Chimera .10 .30
☐ 48 Chimera .10 .30
☐ 49 Death Knell .10 .30
☐ 50 Death Knell .10 .30
☐ 51 Death Knell .10 .30
☐ 52 Heroes Part 1 .10 .30
☐ 53 Heroes Part 1 .10 .30
☐ 54 Heroes Part 1 .10 .30
☐ 55 Heroes Part 2 .10 .30
☐ 56 Heroes Part 2 .10 .30
☐ 57 Heroes Part 2 .10 .30
☐ 58 Resurrection .10 .30
☐ 59 Resurrection .10 .30
☐ 60 Resurrection .10 .30
☐ 61 Inauguration .10 .30
☐ 62 Inauguration .10 .30
☐ 63 Inauguration .10 .30
☐ 64 Lost City Part 1 .10 .30
☐ 65 Lost City Part 1 .10 .30
☐ 66 Lost City Part 1 .10 .30
☐ 67 Lost City Part 2 .10 .30
☐ 68 Lost City Part 2 .10 .30
☐ 69 Lost City Part 2 .10 .30
☐ 70 Checklist .10 .30
☐ 71 Checklist .10 .30
☐ 72 Checklist .10 .30

2005 Stargate SG-1 Season Seven Autographs

STATED ODDS ONE PER BOX
A42 ISSUED AS 6-CASE INCENTIVE
A46 ISSUED AS 2-CASE INCENTIVE
L (LIMITED): 300-500 COPIES
VL (VERY LIMITED): 200-300 COPIES

☐ A42 Michael Shanks/ (issued as 6-case incentive)
☐ A43 Robert Picardo VL
☐ A44 Don Davis L
☐ A45 Teryl Rothery L
☐ A46 Jolene Blalock/ (issued as 2-case incentive)
☐ A47 Anna-Louise Plowman L
☐ A48 Jessica Steen L
☐ A49 Saul Rubinek L
☐ A50 Kristen Dalton L
☐ A51 David Palffy L
☐ A52 Michael Adamthwaite L
☐ A53 Christopher Cousins L
☐ A54 Rick Worthy L
☐ A55 David DeLuise L
☐ A56 Dion Johnstone L
☐ A57 Katie Smart L
☐ A58 George Wyner L
☐ A59 Dom DeLuise L
☐ A60 Tony Amendola L
☐ A61 Christopher Judge VL

2005 Stargate SG-1 Season Seven Behind The Scenes

COMPLETE SET (9) 15.00 40.00
STATED ODDS 1:10

☐ B10 Urgo 2.00 5.00
☐ B11 One False Step 2.00 5.00
☐ B12 Foothold 2.00 5.00
☐ B13 Broca Divide 2.00 5.00
☐ B14 Upgrades 2.00 5.00
☐ B15 Singularity 2.00 5.00
☐ B16 2010 2.00 5.00
☐ B17 Rite of Passage 2.00 5.00
☐ B18 Lifeboat 2.00 5.00

2005 Stargate SG-1 Season Seven Costumes

OVERALL COSTUME/RELIC ODDS ONE PER BOX
C26 ISSUED IN COLLECTORS ALBUM

☐ C22 Colonel Jack O'Neill
☐ C23 Teal'c
☐ C24 Major Samantha Carter
☐ C25 Jonas Quinn
☐ C26 Dr. Daniel Jackson/ (issued in collectors album)
☐ C27 Teal'c

2005 Stargate SG-1 Season Seven Dr. Frasier Tribute

STATED ODDS 1:480

☐ F1 Dr. Frasier Tribute 40.00 80.00
☐ F2 Dr. Frasier Tribute 40.00 80.00

2005 Stargate SG-1 Season Seven In The Line Of Duty Dr. Jackson

COMPLETE SET (9) 40.00 80.00
STATED ODDS 1:20 UK PACKS

☐ DJ1 Fire And Water 4.00 10.00
☐ DJ2 There But For The Grace Of God 4.00 10.00
☐ DJ3 Within The Serpents Grasp 4.00 10.00
☐ DJ4 The Serpent's Lair 4.00 10.00
☐ DJ5 Into The Fire 4.00 10.00
☐ DJ6 Need 4.00 10.00
☐ DJ7 The Curse 4.00 10.00
☐ DJ8 Beast Of Burden 4.00 10.00
☐ DJ9 Meridian 4.00 10.00

2005 Stargate SG-1 Season Seven In The Line Of Duty Teal'C

COMPLETE SET (9) 30.00 60.00
STATED ODDS 1:20 N.AMERICAN PACKS

☐ T1 Children Of The Gods 3.00 8.00
☐ T2 Cor'Ai 3.00 8.00
☐ T3 Bane 3.00 8.00
☐ T4 Warriors 3.00 8.00
☐ T5 Enemies 3.00 8.00
Threshold
☐ T6 Out Of Mind 3.00 8.00
Into The Fire
☐ T7 The Changeling 3.00 8.00
☐ T8 Orpheus 3.00 8.00
☐ T9 Birthright 3.00 8.00

2005 Stargate SG-1 Season Seven Relics

OVERALL COSTUME/RELIC ODDS ONE PER BOX
R8 ISSUED AS N.AMERICAN CASE TOPPER
R9 ISSUED AS UK CASE TOPPER
STATED PRINT RUN 240-481

☐ R1 Jonas' Journal/459
☐ R2 Alien Diary/457
☐ R3 Carter's Surveillance Map/481
☐ R4 Alien Ship Blueprint/473
☐ R5 NID Fax/461
☐ R6 Schematics/464
☐ R7 EDS Dossier/466
☐ R8 Capt. Brooks Health File/375/ (issued as US case topper)
☐ R9 60's Style Poster/240/ (issued as UK case topper)

2005 Stargate SG-1 Season Seven SG-1 Team

COMPLETE SET (4) 75.00 150.00
STATED ODDS 1:200
STATED PRINT RUN 600 SER. #'d SETS

☐ S1 Colonel Jack O'Neill 20.00 40.00
☐ S2 Major Samantha Carter 20.00 40.00
☐ S3 Dr. Daniel Jackson 20.00 40.00
☐ S4 Teal'c 20.00 40.00

2005 Stargate SG-1 Season Seven Stargate Casting Call

COMPLETE SET (4)
STATED ODDS 1:40

☐ CC1 Richard Dean Anderson
☐ CC2 Amanda Tapping
☐ CC3 Michael Shanks
☐ CC4 Christopher Judge

2005 The Three Stooges

COMPLETE SET (72) 6.00 15.00

☐ 1 1930 Soup to Nuts .20 .50
☐ 2 1934 Woman Haters .20 .50
☐ 3 1934 Men in Black .20 .50
☐ 4 1935 Horses' Collars .20 .50
☐ 5 1935 Uncivil Warriors .20 .50
☐ 6 1936 Ants in the Pantry .20 .50
☐ 7 1937 Goofs and Saddles .20 .50
☐ 8 1937 The Sitter Downers .20 .50
☐ 9 1938 Termites of 1938 .20 .50
☐ 10 1938 Three Missing Links .20 .50
☐ 11 1936 Disorder in the Court .20 .50
☐ 12 1939 Yes, We Have No Bonanza .20 .50
☐ 13 1939 Three Sappy People .20 .50
☐ 14 1940 A Plumbing We Will Go .20 .50
☐ 15 1940 No Census, No Feeling .20 .50
☐ 16 1941 So Long, Mr. Chumps .20 .50
☐ 17 1941 In the Sweet Pie and Pie .20 .50
☐ 18 1941 I'll Never Heil Again .20 .50
☐ 19 1942 Loco Boy Makes Good .20 .50
☐ 20 1942 Sock-A-Bye Baby .20 .50
☐ 21 1943 Phony Express .20 .50
☐ 22 1943 A Gem of a Jam .20 .50
☐ 23 1944 Idle Roomers .20 .50
☐ 24 1944 Gents Without Cents .20 .50
☐ 25 1945 Booby Dupes .20 .50
☐ 26 1945 If a Body Meets a Body .20 .50
☐ 27 1946 Three Loan Wolves .20 .50
☐ 28 1946 G.I. Wanna Home .20 .50
☐ 29 1946 Rhythm and Weep .20 .50
☐ 30 1946 Rhythm and Weep .20 .50
☐ 31 1946 Three Little Pirates .20 .50
☐ 32 1947 Half-Wit's Holiday .20 .50
☐ 33 1947 Fright Night .20 .50
☐ 34 1947 Out West .20 .50
☐ 35 1947 Brideless Groom .20 .50
☐ 36 1947 All Gummed Up .20 .50
☐ 37 1948 Fiddlers Three .20 .50
☐ 38 1949 Who Done It .20 .50
☐ 39 1949 Malice in the Palace .20 .50
☐ 40 1949 Dunked in the Deep .20 .50
☐ 41 1950 Studio Stoops .20 .50
☐ 42 1950 A Snitch in Time .20 .50
☐ 43 1951 Don't Throw That Knife .20 .50
☐ 44 1951 Scrambled Brains .20 .50
☐ 45 1951 Pest Man Wins .20 .50
☐ 46 1952 Three Dark Horses .20 .50
☐ 47 1952 Cuckoo On A Choo-Choo .20 .50
☐ 48 1953 Spooks .20 .50
☐ 49 1954 Income Tax Sappy .20 .50
☐ 50 1954 Shot in the Frontier .20 .50
☐ 51 1955 Of Cash and Hash .20 .50
☐ 52 1955 Bedlam in Paradise .20 .50
☐ 53 1955 Stone Age Romeos .20 .50
☐ 54 1956 Husbands Beware .20 .50
☐ 55 1956 Creeps .20 .50
☐ 56 1957 For Crimin' Out Loud .20 .50
☐ 57 1956 Commotion on the Ocean .20 .50
☐ 58 1957 Hoofs and Goofs .20 .50
☐ 59 1957 Muscle Up A Little Closer .20 .50
☐ 60 1957 A Merry Mix-Up .20 .50
☐ 61 1957 Rusty Romeos .20 .50
☐ 62 1958 Fifi Blows Her Top .20 .50
☐ 63 1958 Pies and Guys .20 .50
☐ 64 1958 Oil's Well That Ends Well .20 .50
☐ 65 1958 Sappy Bullfighters .20 .50
☐ 66 1960 The Three Stooges Scrapbook .20 .50
☐ 67 1965 The New Three Stooges .20 .50
☐ 68 1961 Snow White and The Three Stooges .20 .50
☐ 69 1962 The Three Stooges Meet Hercules .20 .50
☐ 70 1962 The Three Stooges in Orbit .20 .50
☐ 71 1963 The Three Stooges Go Around .20 .50
the World in a Daze
☐ 72 Checklist .20 .50

2005 The Three Stooges Printing Plates Black

ANNOUNCED PRINT RUN 1
UNPRICED DUE TO SCARCITY

2005 The Three Stooges Printing Plates Cyan

ANNOUNCED PRINT RUN 1
UNPRICED DUE TO SCARCITY

2005 The Three Stooges Printing Plates Magenta

ANNOUNCED PRINT RUN 1
UNPRICED DUE TO SCARCITY

2005 The Three Stooges Printing Plates Yellow

ANNOUNCED PRINT RUN 1
UNPRICED DUE TO SCARCITY

2005 The Three Stooges Costume Memorabilia

OVERALL COSTUME/PROP ODDS 1:80

☐ C1 Curly Joe DeRita pink shirt 6.00 15.00
☐ C2 Curly Joe DeRita striped shirt 6.00 15.00
☐ C3 Curly Joe DeRita short pants 6.00 15.00
☐ C4 Curly Joe DeRita pink shirt 6.00 15.00
☐ C5 Curly Joe DeRita striped shirt 6.00 15.00
☐ C6 Curly Joe DeRita short pants 6.00 15.00

2005 The Three Stooges Cut Signatures

☐ CS1 Moe Howard/9
☐ CS2 Joe DeRita/28

2005 The Three Stooges Film Cel Case Toppers

STATED ODDS ONE PER CASE

☐ F1 Dizzy Doctors 10.00 25.00
☐ F2 Yes, We Have No Bonanza 10.00 25.00

2005 The Three Stooges Oversize Box Toppers

ONE PER WOODEN BOX

☐ WB1 The Ear Pull
☐ WB2 Financial Planning
☐ WB3 The Boys

2005 The Three Stooges Promos

☐ NNO Noazark Shipbuilding 1.00 2.50
(NSU Magazine)
☐ NNO Seltzer 1.00 2.50
(Philly Non-Sports Exclusive)
☐ NNO Choking Curly 1.00 2.50
(SDCC Exclusive)
☐ PROMO1 Dewey, Cheatem, and Howe 1.25 3.00
☐ PROMO2 Flowers 1.25 3.00
☐ PROMO3 Doctors 1.25 3.00

2005 The Three Stooges Prop Memorabilia

OVERALL COSTUME/PROP ODDS 1:80

☐ DP Curly Joe Desk
(issued as 6-case incentive)
☐ RC Larry Fine Residual Check
☐ S1 Curly Joe Stationery/24
☐ SGJ Moe Howard Necklace/57

2005 The Three Stooges Shemp the Original Third Stooge

COMPLETE SET (12) 15.00 30.00
STATED ODDS 1:40

☐ SS1 Young Shemp 2.00 5.00
☐ SS2 Publicity Shot From Hold That Lion 2.00 5.00
☐ SS3 Later Gruff Shemp Publicity Shot 2.00 5.00
☐ SS4 Shemp in Brideless Groom 2.00 5.00
☐ SS5 Shemp in The Ghost Talks 2.00 5.00
☐ SS6 Shot from Dopey Dicks 2.00 5.00
☐ SS7 Shemp in Scrambled Brains 2.00 5.00
☐ SS8 Shemp in Spooks 2.00 5.00
☐ SS9 Shemp in Income Tax Sappy 2.00 5.00
☐ SS10 Shemp in Creeps 2.00 5.00
☐ SS11 Shemp in Out West 2.00 5.00
☐ SS12 Shemp Publicity Shot 2.00 5.00

2005 The Three Stooges Sketches

STATED ODDS 1:80

☐ 1 Chris Henderson 8.00 20.00
☐ 2 Cynthia Cummens
☐ 3 Darren Auck
☐ 4 Warren Martineck 15.00 30.00

2005 The Three Stooges Stooge Milestones

COMPLETE SET (4) 15.00 30.00
STATED ODDS 1:160

☐ SM1 Ted Healy and His Racketeers 6.00 15.00
☐ SM2 Hold That Lion 6.00 15.00
☐ SM3 The Ghost Talks 6.00 15.00
☐ SM4 A Merry Mix-Up 6.00 15.00

2005 The Three Stooges The Curly Years

COMPLETE SET (9) 20.00 40.00
STATED ODDS 1:40

☐ CY1 Hello Pop! 3.00 8.00
☐ CY2 Woman Haters 3.00 8.00
☐ CY3 Publicity shot 3.00 8.00
☐ CY4 Hoi Polloi 3.00 8.00
☐ CY5 Rhythm and Weep 3.00 8.00
☐ CY6 MLC and Joan 3.00 8.00
☐ CY7 A Gem of a Jam 3.00 8.00
☐ CY8 Dutiful But Dumb 3.00 8.00
☐ CY9 CML 3.00 8.00

2005 Twilight Zone Science and Superstition

COMPLETE SET (73) 4.00 10.00
UNPRICED SERLING AUTO PRINT RUN 5

☐ 217 The Last Night Of A Jockey .10 .30
☐ 218 The Last Night Of A Jockey .10 .30
☐ 219 The Last Night Of A Jockey .10 .30
☐ 220 The Last Night Of A Jockey .10 .30
☐ 221 The Last Night Of A Jockey .10 .30
☐ 222 The Last Night Of A Jockey .10 .30
☐ 223 Mr. Bevis .10 .30
☐ 224 Mr. Bevis .10 .30
☐ 225 Mr. Bevis .10 .30
☐ 226 Mr. Bevis .10 .30
☐ 227 Mr. Bevis .10 .30
☐ 228 Mr. Bevis .10 .30
☐ 229 The Bard .10 .30
☐ 230 The Bard .10 .30
☐ 231 The Bard .10 .30
☐ 232 The Bard .10 .30
☐ 233 The Bard .10 .30
☐ 234 The Bard .10 .30
☐ 235 The Passersby .10 .30
☐ 236 The Passersby .10 .30
☐ 237 The Passersby .10 .30
☐ 238 The Passersby .10 .30
☐ 239 The Passersby .10 .30
☐ 240 The Passersby .10 .30
☐ 241 Dead Man's Shoes .10 .30
☐ 242 Dead Man's Shoes .10 .30
☐ 243 Dead Man's Shoes .10 .30
☐ 244 Dead Man's Shoes .10 .30
☐ 245 Dead Man's Shoes .10 .30
☐ 246 Dead Man's Shoes .10 .30
☐ 247 Back There .10 .30
☐ 248 Back There .10 .30
☐ 249 Back There .10 .30
☐ 250 Back There .10 .30
☐ 251 Back There .10 .30
☐ 252 Back There .10 .30
☐ 253 The Purple Testament .10 .30
☐ 254 The Purple Testament .10 .30
☐ 255 The Purple Testament .10 .30
☐ 256 The Purple Testament .10 .30
☐ 257 The Purple Testament .10 .30
☐ 258 The Purple Testament .10 .30
☐ 259 Piano In The House .10 .30
☐ 260 Piano In The House .10 .30
☐ 261 Piano In The House .10 .30
☐ 262 Piano In The House .10 .30
☐ 263 Piano In The House .10 .30
☐ 264 Piano In The House .10 .30
☐ 265 Night Call .10 .30
☐ 266 Night Call .10 .30
☐ 267 Night Call .10 .30
☐ 268 Night Call .10 .30
☐ 269 Night Call .10 .30
☐ 270 Night Call .10 .30
☐ 271 A Hundred Yards Over The Rim .10 .30
☐ 272 A Hundred Yards Over The Rim .10 .30
☐ 273 A Hundred Yards Over The Rim .10 .30
☐ 274 A Hundred Yards Over The Rim .10 .30
☐ 275 A Hundred Yards Over The Rim .10 .30
☐ 276 A Hundred Yards Over The Rim .10 .30
☐ 277 Midnight Sun .10 .30
☐ 278 Midnight Sun .10 .30
☐ 279 Midnight Sun .10 .30
☐ 280 Midnight Sun .10 .30
☐ 281 Midnight Sun .10 .30
☐ 282 Midnight Sun .10 .30
☐ 283 The Fugitive .10 .30
☐ 284 The Fugitive .10 .30
☐ 285 The Fugitive .10 .30
☐ 286 The Fugitive .10 .30
☐ 287 The Fugitive .10 .30
☐ 288 The Fugitive .10 .30
☐ Z4 Checklist
☐ NNO Rod Serling HOF AU/5*

2005 Twilight Zone Science and Superstition Autographs

STATED ODDS FOUR PER BOX
A97 ISSUED IN COLLECTORS ALBUM
L (LIMITED): 300-500 COPIES
VL (VERY LIMITED): 200-300 COPIES

☐ A66 Barry Morse 10.00 25.00
☐ A67 Ron Howard VL 300.00 500.00
☐ A68 Joanne Linville 15.00 40.00
☐ A69 Collin Wilcox 8.00 20.00
☐ A70 Don Durant 8.00 20.00
☐ A71 Wright King 8.00 20.00
☐ A72 Mickey Rooney L 40.00 80.00
☐ A73 Sydney Pollack 15.00 40.00
☐ A74 Alan Sues 8.00 20.00
☐ A75 Lois Nettleton 10.00 25.00
☐ A76A Jason Wingreen 25.00 50.00
Mr. Schuster (w/hat) L
☐ A76B Jason Wingreen 25.00 50.00
The Bard (no hat) L
☐ A77 Veronica Cartwright 12.00 30.00
☐ A78 Dana Dillaway 8.00 20.00
☐ A79 Judy Strangis 8.00 20.00
☐ A80 Russell Johnson L 25.00 50.00
☐ A81 John Lasell 8.00 20.00
☐ A82 Orson Bean L 15.00 40.00
☐ A83 William Schallert 8.00 20.00
☐ A84 Ron Masak 8.00 20.00
☐ A85 Patricia Barry 10.00 25.00
☐ A86 Susan Gordon 8.00 20.00
☐ A87 Natalie Trundy 10.00 25.00
☐ A88 Nancy Malone 10.00 25.00
☐ A89 Bill Erwin 8.00 20.00
☐ A90 Arte Johnson L 25.00 50.00
☐ A91 Ben Cooper 8.00 20.00
☐ A92 Jeanne Cooper 8.00 20.00
☐ A93 Warren Stevens 8.00 20.00
☐ A94 Kevin Hagen 10.00 25.00
☐ A95 James Doohan L 250.00 350.00
☐ A96 Anne Francis L 50.00 100.00
☐ A97 Edson Stroll ALBUM 8.00 20.00

2005 Twilight Zone Science and Superstition SketchaFEX

GREMLIN SKETCH ISSUED AS 2-CASE INCENTIVE
ROBBIE SKETCH ISSUED AS CASE TOPPER

☐ 1 Chris Bolson
Gremlin/ (issued as 2-case incentive)
☐ 2 Chris Bolson
Robbie the Robot/ (issued as case topper)

2005 Twilight Zone Science and Superstition The Quotable Twilight Zone

COMPLETE SET (18) 20.00 50.00
STATED ODDS 1:7

☐ Q1 Nightmare at 20,000 Feet 1.25 3.00
☐ Q2 I Am the Night 1.25 3.00
☐ Q3 Where is Everybody 1.25 3.00
☐ Q4 Mirror Mirror 1.25 3.00
☐ Q5 The After Hours 1.25 3.00
☐ Q6 The Eye of the Beholder 1.25 3.00
☐ Q7 The Obsolete Man 1.25 3.00
☐ Q8 The Fear 1.25 3.00
☐ Q9 Perchance to Dream 1.25 3.00
☐ Q10 In Praise of Pip 1.25 3.00
☐ Q11 Shadow Play 1.25 3.00
☐ Q12 The Jungle 1.25 3.00
☐ Q13 The Prime Mover 1.25 3.00
☐ Q14 A Quality of Mercy 1.25 3.00
☐ Q15 A Game of Pool 1.25 3.00
☐ Q16 I Am the Night 1.25 3.00
☐ Q17 Of Late I Think of Cliffordville 1.25 3.00
☐ Q18 Jess-Belle 1.25 3.00

2005 Twilight Zone Science and Superstition Twilight Zone Hall of Fame

COMPLETE SET (8) 250.00 500.00
STATED ODDS 1:100
STATED PRINT RUN 333 SER. #'d SETS

☐ H5 Jonathan Harris 40.00 80.00
☐ H6 Jack Weston 40.00 80.00
☐ H7 Russell Johnson 40.00 80.00
☐ H8 Gladys Cooper 40.00 80.00
☐ H9 Cliff Robertson 40.00 80.00
☐ H10 Anne Francis 40.00 80.00
☐ H11 Mickey Rooney 40.00 80.00
☐ H12 Fritz Weaver 40.00 80.00

2005 Twilight Zone Science and Superstition Twilight Zone Stars

COMPLETE SET (9) 8.00 20.00
STATED ODDS 1:14

☐ S28 Mickey Rooney 1.00 2.50
☐ S29 Jack Weston 1.00 2.50
☐ S30 Barry Morse 1.00 2.50
☐ S31 Sydney Pollack 1.00 2.50
☐ S32 Ron Howard 1.00 2.50
☐ S33 Veronica Cartwright 1.00 2.50
☐ S34 Warren Stevens 1.00 2.50
☐ S35 Gladys Cooper 1.00 2.50
☐ S36 Patricia Barry 1.00 2.50

2005 X-Files Connections

COMPLETE SET (72) 5.00 12.00

☐ 1 Mulder & Scully: Supportive Connection .15 .40
☐ 2 Mulder & Samantha: Early Connection .15 .40
☐ 3 Mulder & Krycek: Hate Connection .15 .40
☐ 4 Mulder & The Smoking Man: .15 .40
Painful Connection
☐ 5 Mulder & Morris Fletcher: .15 .40
Unexpected Connection
☐ 6 Mulder & Jeffrey Spender: Family Connection .15 .40
☐ 7 Mulder & Diana Fowley: Past Love Connection .15 .40
☐ 8 Mulder & Doggett: Respectful Connection .15 .40
☐ 9 Mulder & Scully: Love Connection .15 .40
☐ 10 Scully & Mulder: Professional Connection .15 .40
☐ 11 Scully & William Scully: Spiritual Connection .15 .40
☐ 12 Scully & Duane Barry: Dangerous Connection .15 .40
☐ 13 Scully & Penny Northern: .15 .40
Accepting Connection
☐ 14 Scully & The Smoking Man: .15 .40
Perilous Connection
☐ 15 Scully & Doggett: Supportive Connection .15 .40
☐ 16 Scully & Reyes: Understanding Connection .15 .40
☐ 17 Scully & William: Maternal Connection .15 .40
☐ 18 Scully & Mulder: Tender Connection .15 .40
☐ 19 Skinner & Mulder: Confrontational Connection .15 .40
☐ 20 Skinner & Scully: Wary Connection .15 .40
☐ 21 Skinner & The Smoking Man: .15 .40
Servile Connection
☐ 22 Skinner & Krycek: Volatile Connection .15 .40
☐ 23 Skinner & Kersh: Uneasy Connection .15 .40
☐ 24 Skinner & Doggett: Tense Connection .15 .40
☐ 25 Skinner & Scully: Protective Connection .15 .40
☐ 26 Skinner & Mulder: Respectful Connection .15 .40
☐ 27 Skinner & The Syndicate: .15 .40
Dangerous Connection
☐ 28 Doggett & Scully: Early Connection .15 .40
☐ 29 Doggett & Mulder: Tentative Connection .15 .40
☐ 30 Doggett & Kersh: Distrustful Connection .15 .40
☐ 31 Doggett & Reyes: Professional Connection .15 .40
☐ 32 Doggett & Barbara Doggett: Grief Connection .15 .40
☐ 33 Doggett & Brad Follmer: Tense Connection .15 .40
☐ 34 Doggett & Knowle Rohrer: .15 .40
Dangerous Connection
☐ 35 Doggett & Skinner: Conspiratorial Connection .15 .40
☐ 36 Doggett & Reyes: Tender Connection .15 .40
☐ 37 Reyes & Doggett: Early Connection .15 .40
☐ 38 Reyes & The Occult: Natural Connection .15 .40
☐ 39 Reyes & Scully: Friendly Connection .15 .40
☐ 40 Reyes & Mulder: Understanding Connection .15 .40
☐ 41 Reyes & Brad Follmer: Past Love Connection .15 .40
☐ 42 Reyes & Audrey Pauley: Spiritual Connection .15 .40
☐ 43 Reyes & Doggett: Betrayal Connection .15 .40
☐ 44 Reyes & Scully: Sympathetic Connection .15 .40
☐ 45 Reyes & Doggett: Caring Connection .15 .40
☐ 46 Lone Gunmen & Mulder: Early Connection .15 .40
☐ 47 Lone Gunmen & Scully: Lust Connection .15 .40
☐ 48 Lone Gunmen & Hacking: Natural Connection .15 .40
☐ 49 Lone Gunmen & Scully: Caring Connection .15 .40
☐ 50 Lone Gunmen & Suzanne Modeski: .15 .40
Love Connection
☐ 51 Lone Gunmen & Reyes: .15 .40
Informative Connection
☐ 52 Lone Gunmen & William: .15 .40
Protective Connection
☐ 53 Lone Gunmen & Morris Fletcher: .15 .40
Adversarial Connection
☐ 54 Lone Gunmen & Mulder: Ghostly Connection .15 .40
☐ 55 Smoking Man & Skinner: .15 .40
Controlling Connection
☐ 56 Smoking Man & Mulder: Paternal Connection .15 .40
☐ 57 Smoking Man & Teena Mulder: .15 .40
Past Love Connection
☐ 58 Smoking Man & The Syndicate: .15 .40
Unstable Connection
☐ 59 Smoking Man & Krycek: Volatile Connection .15 .40
☐ 60 Smoking Man & Diana Fowley: .15 .40
Seductive Connection
☐ 61 Smoking Man & Spender: .15 .40
Murderous Connection
☐ 62 Smoking Man & Scully: Confusing Connection .15 .40
☐ 63 Smoking Man & Mulder: Prophetic Connection .15 .40
☐ 64 Krycek & Mulder: Hate Connection .15 .40
☐ 65 Krycek & The Syndicate: Servile Connection .15 .40
☐ 66 Krycek & The Black Oil: .15 .40
Possessing Connection
☐ 67 Krycek & Marita Covarrubias: Love Connection .15 .40
☐ 68 Krycek & The Smoking Man: .15 .40
Murderous Connection
☐ 69 Krycek & William: Treacherous Connection .15 .40
☐ 70 Krycek & Skinner: Deadly Connection .15 .40
☐ 71 Krycek & Mulder: Ghostly Connection .15 .40
☐ 72 Checklist .15 .40

2005 X-Files Connections Parallel

COMPLETE SET (72) 10.00 25.00
*PARALLEL: 1X TO 2.5X BASIC CARDS
STATED ODDS ONE PER PACK

2005 X-Files Connections Autographs

STATED ODDS 1:24

☐ A1 Gillian Anderson EXCH 100.00 200.00
☐ A2 Annabeth Gish 40.00 80.00
☐ A3 Mimi Rogers 12.00 30.00
☐ A4 William B. Davis 20.00 40.00
☐ A5 Chris Owens 8.00 20.00
☐ A6 Nicholas Lea 20.00 40.00
☐ A7 Tom Braidwood 12.00 30.00
☐ A8 Bruce Harwood 10.00 25.00
☐ A9 Dean Haglund 10.00 25.00
☐ A10 Nick Chinlund 8.00 20.00
☐ A11 Veronica Cartwright 8.00 20.00

2005 X-Files Connections Box Loaders

COMPLETE SET (4) 8.00 20.00
STATED ODDS ONE PER BOX

☐ BL1 Deep Throat 1.50 4.00
☐ BL2 X 1.50 4.00

- ❑ BL3 Marita Covarrubias 1.50 4.00
- ❑ CL1 The Truth Is Out There 5.00 12.00

2005 X-Files Connections Haunting Cases
STATED ODDS 1:14

- ❑ HC1 Flukeman 1.25 3.00
- ❑ HC2 Eugene Victor Tooms 1.25 3.00
- ❑ HC3 Donnie Pfaster 1.25 3.00
- ❑ HC4 Robert Pusher Modell 1.25 3.00
- ❑ HC5 Clyde Bruckman 1.25 3.00
- ❑ HC6 John Lee Roche 1.25 3.00

2005 X-Files Connections Mulder's Secret Files
STATED ODDS 1:11

- ❑ M1 Mulder's Secret Files 1.00 2.50
- ❑ M2 Mulder's Secret Files 1.00 2.50
- ❑ M3 Mulder's Secret Files 1.00 2.50
- ❑ M4 Mulder's Secret Files 1.00 2.50
- ❑ M5 Mulder's Secret Files 1.00 2.50
- ❑ M6 Mulder's Secret Files 1.00 2.50
- ❑ M7 Mulder's Secret Files 1.00 2.50
- ❑ M8 Mulder's Secret Files 1.00 2.50
- ❑ M9 Mulder's Secret Files 1.00 2.50

2005 X-Files Connections Pieceworks
- ❑ PW1 Scully's Shirt 25.00 50.00
- ❑ PW1A Scully's Shirt - Gillian Anderson AU 150.00 250.00
- ❑ PW2 Mulder's Shirt 8.00 20.00

2005 Xena and Hercules The Animated Series
COMPLETE SET (72) 4.00 10.00

- ❑ 1 The Battle For Mt. Olympus .10 .30
- ❑ 2 Hercules Shows His Might .10 .30
- ❑ 3 Victorious Hercules .10 .30
- ❑ 4 Xena and Gabrielle .10 .30
- ❑ 5 Xena Packs a Powerful Punch .10 .30
- ❑ 6 Xena and Ares .10 .30
- ❑ 7 Planning Next Moves .10 .30
- ❑ 8 Alcmene and Zeus .10 .30
- ❑ 9 Hercules Enraged .10 .30
- ❑ 10 Beautiful Aphrodite .10 .30
- ❑ 11 Hera's Gaze .10 .30
- ❑ 12 Zeus and Ares .10 .30
- ❑ 13 Artemis .10 .30
- ❑ 14 Hera Steals the Chronos Stone .10 .30
- ❑ 15 Hercules to the Rescue .10 .30
- ❑ 16 Xena Restores Order .10 .30
- ❑ 17 Porphyrion Confronts Hercules .10 .30
- ❑ 18 Gabrielle Spots the Titans .10 .30
- ❑ 19 Ares and Aphrodite .10 .30
- ❑ 20 Hera Plays It Cool .10 .30
- ❑ 21 Hercules Stands Firm .10 .30
- ❑ 22 Artemis .10 .30
- ❑ 23 Gabrielle .10 .30
- ❑ 24 Xena in Despair .10 .30
- ❑ 25 Tethys .10 .30
- ❑ 26 Fly Gabrielle Fly .10 .30
- ❑ 27 Xena and Artemis .10 .30
- ❑ 28 A Suspicious Xena .10 .30
- ❑ 29 Climbing Mt. Olympus .10 .30
- ❑ 30 Powerful Zeus .10 .30
- ❑ 31 The Awesome Titans .10 .30
- ❑ 32 Battling the Titans .10 .30
- ❑ 33 Aphrodite Tries to Escape .10 .30
- ❑ 34 Ares Battles Porphyrion .10 .30
- ❑ 35 Xena to the Rescue .10 .30
- ❑ 36 In Search of Alcmene .10 .30
- ❑ 37 Iolaus in Action .10 .30
- ❑ 38 Hercules Saves His Mother .10 .30
- ❑ 39 Iolaus Wields a Mighty Sword .10 .30
- ❑ 40 Xena Casts Her Deadly Chakram .10 .30
- ❑ 41 Hercules Carries Alcmene to Safety .10 .30
- ❑ 42 Iolaus Strikes a Blow .10 .30
- ❑ 43 Xena in Battle .10 .30
- ❑ 44 Iolaus and Xena .10 .30
- ❑ 45 A Skeptical Hercules .10 .30
- ❑ 46 A God or a Mouse .10 .30
- ❑ 47 Hercules Enjoys a Laugh .10 .30
- ❑ 48 Returning to Safety .10 .30
- ❑ 49 Xena Stuns Hercules .10 .30
- ❑ 50 Xena Confronts the Gods .10 .30
- ❑ 51 A Tortured Hercules .10 .30
- ❑ 52 Artemis the Bunny .10 .30
- ❑ 53 What Next .10 .30
- ❑ 54 Xena and Hercules .10 .30
- ❑ 55 Face of a Warrior .10 .30
- ❑ 56 Hercules Forms a Plan .10 .30
- ❑ 57 Hera in Charge .10 .30
- ❑ 58 Crius .10 .30
- ❑ 59 Hera Loses Control .10 .30
- ❑ 60 Hercules Leads the Attack .10 .30
- ❑ 61 Sizing Up the Titans .10 .30
- ❑ 62 Taking On the Titans .10 .30
- ❑ 63 Iolaus Battles Hard .10 .30
- ❑ 64 Looking for a Solution .10 .30
- ❑ 65 Hercules Breaks the Chronos Stone .10 .30
- ❑ 66 Xena Prevails .10 .30
- ❑ 67 Hercules Tested .10 .30
- ❑ 68 Hercules Shows His Strength .10 .30
- ❑ 69 Hercules Pushed to the Limit .10 .30
- ❑ 70 The Return of Gabrielle .10 .30
- ❑ 71 The Gods Restored to Power .10 .30
- ❑ 72 A Fearsome Foursome .10 .30

2005 Xena and Hercules The Animated Series Animated Casting Call
COMPLETE SET (14) 6.00 15.00
STATED ODDS 1:14

- ❑ C1 Xena .60 1.50
- ❑ C2 Hercules .60 1.50
- ❑ C3 Gabrielle .60 1.50
- ❑ C4 Iolaus .60 1.50
- ❑ C5 Ares .60 1.50
- ❑ C6 Aphrodite .60 1.50
- ❑ C7 Alcmene .60 1.50
- ❑ C8 Artemis .60 1.50
- ❑ C9 Hera .60 1.50
- ❑ C10 Zeus .60 1.50
- ❑ C11 Porphyrion .60 1.50
- ❑ C12 Tethys .60 1.50
- ❑ C13 Mnemosyne .60 1.50
- ❑ C14 Crius .60 1.50

2005 Xena and Hercules The Animated Series Animated Extras
COMPLETE SET (18) 12.50 30.00
STATED ODDS 1:20

- ❑ X1 Callisto 1.25 3.00
- ❑ X2 Autolycus 1.25 3.00
- ❑ X3 Joxer 1.25 3.00
- ❑ X4 Amarice 1.25 3.00
- ❑ X5 Morrigan 1.25 3.00
- ❑ X6 Livia 1.25 3.00
- ❑ X7 Ephiny 1.25 3.00
- ❑ X8 Salmoneus 1.25 3.00
- ❑ X9 Alti 1.25 3.00
- ❑ X10 Demetrius 1.25 3.00
- ❑ X11 Eli 1.25 3.00
- ❑ X12 Athena 1.25 3.00
- ❑ X13 Cyane 1.25 3.00
- ❑ X14 Varia 1.25 3.00
- ❑ X15 Nebula 1.25 3.00
- ❑ X16 Discord 1.25 3.00
- ❑ X17 Lao Ma 1.25 3.00
- ❑ X18 Enforcer 1.25 3.00

2005 Xena and Hercules The Animated Series Animated Mythical Beasts
COMPLETE SET (6) 15.00 40.00
STATED ODDS 1:60

- ❑ B1 Hydra 3.00 8.00
- ❑ B2 Echidna 3.00 8.00
- ❑ B3 Golden Hind 3.00 8.00
- ❑ B4 Arachne 3.00 8.00
- ❑ B5 Dahak 3.00 8.00
- ❑ B6 Centaur 3.00 8.00

2005 Xena and Hercules The Animated Series Autographs
STATED ODDS TWO PER BOX
TREBOR AUTO ISSUED IN COLLECTORS ALBUM
L (LIMITED): 300-500 COPIES
VL (VERY LIMITED): 200-300 COPIES

- ❑ 1 Bruce Campbell L
- ❑ 2 Danielle Cormack L
- ❑ 3 Josephine Davison as Alcmene L
- ❑ 4 Josephine Davison as Artemis L
- ❑ 5 Meighan Desmond L
- ❑ 6 Tamara Gorski L
- ❑ 7 Michael Hurst L
- ❑ 8 Paris Jefferson L
- ❑ 9 Tsianina Joelson L
- ❑ 10 Jacqueline Kim L
- ❑ 11 Lucy Lawless VL
- ❑ 12 Hudson Leick VL
- ❑ 13 David Mackie L
- ❑ 14 Renee O'Connor VL
- ❑ 15 Timothy Omundson L
- ❑ 16 Victoria Pratt L
- ❑ 17 Ted Raimi Crius L
- ❑ 18 Ted Raimi Joxer VL
- ❑ 19 Peter Rowley L
- ❑ 20 Karen Sheperd L
- ❑ 21 Kevin Sorbo VL
- ❑ 22 Claire Stansfield L
- ❑ 23 Robert Trebor/ (issued in collectors album)
- ❑ 24 Alexandra Tydings L
- ❑ 25 Alison Wall as Mnemosyne L
- ❑ 26 Alison Wall as Tethys VL
- ❑ 27 Joy Watson L
- ❑ 28 Adrienne Wilkinson as Eve L
- ❑ 29 Adrienne Wilkinson as Livia L

2005 Xena and Hercules The Animated Series Dual Autographs
LAWLESS/O'CONNOR AUTO ISSUED AS 2-CASE INCENTIVE
SORBO/LAWLESS AUTO ISSUED AS 6-CASE INCENTIVE

- ❑ 1 Lucy Lawless
Renee O'Connor
- ❑ 2 Kevin Sorbo
Lucy Lawless

2005 Xena and Hercules The Animated Series Limited Edition
COMPLETE SET (3)
STATED ODDS 1:240 UK PACKS

- ❑ CT1 Xena
Gabrielle
- ❑ CT2 Hercules
Iolaus
- ❑ XH1 Xena
Hercules

2005 Xena and Hercules The Animated Series SketchaFEX
ALTI SKETCH ISSUED AS UK CASE TOPPER
CALLISTO SKETCH ISSUED AS US CASE TOPPER

- ❑ 1 John Czop/ (Alti)
- ❑ 2 John Czop/ (Callisto)

2005 Xena and Hercules The Animated Series The Musical Xena and Hercules
COMPLETE SET (9) 8.00 20.00
STATED ODDS 1:14

- ❑ M1 Across The Sea Of Time 1.25 3.00
- ❑ M2 Across The Sea Of Time 1.25 3.00
- ❑ M3 Across The Sea Of Time 1.25 3.00
- ❑ M4 Titan's Song 1.25 3.00
- ❑ M5 Titan's Song 1.25 3.00
- ❑ M6 Titan's Song 1.25 3.00
- ❑ M7 Xena's Song 1.25 3.00
- ❑ M8 Xena's Song 1.25 3.00
- ❑ M9 Xena's Song 1.25 3.00

2005 Xena and Hercules The Animated Series Xena and Hercules in Action
COMPLETE SET (9) 8.00 20.00
STATED ODDS 1:14

- ❑ HX1 Xena 1.25 3.00
- ❑ HX2 Hercules 1.25 3.00
- ❑ HX3 Xena 1.25 3.00
- ❑ HX4 Hercules 1.25 3.00
- ❑ HX5 Xena 1.25 3.00
- ❑ HX6 Hercules 1.25 3.00
- ❑ HX7 Xena 1.25 3.00
- ❑ HX8 Hercules 1.25 3.00
- ❑ HX9 Xena 1.25 3.00
Hercules

2005 Xena and Hercules The Animated Series Xena Hercules ArtiFEX
COMPLETE SET (6)
STATED ODDS 1:40 US PACKS

- ❑ CZ1 Heroes
- ❑ CZ2 Heroes
- ❑ CZ3 Heroes
- ❑ CZ4 Villians
- ❑ CZ5 Villians
- ❑ CZ6 Villians

2006 Alias Season Four
COMPLETE SET (81) 5.00 12.00

- ❑ 1 Title Card .15 .40
- ❑ 2 Working For Sloane .15 .40
- ❑ 3 Meant To Be .15 .40
- ❑ 4 The Hit .15 .40
- ❑ 5 Mourning .15 .40
- ❑ 6 Undercover .15 .40
- ❑ 7 Revenge .15 .40
- ❑ 8 Peril .15 .40
- ❑ 9 Backup .15 .40
- ❑ 10 New Couple .15 .40
- ❑ 11 Neighbors .15 .40
- ❑ 12 Catching .15 .40
- ❑ 13 Webs .15 .40
- ❑ 14 Mission Planning .15 .40
- ❑ 15 Improvisation .15 .40
- ❑ 16 Hostage .15 .40
- ❑ 17 Sprung .15 .40
- ❑ 18 Deal .15 .40
- ❑ 19 Imposter .15 .40
- ❑ 20 Subterfuge .15 .40
- ❑ 21 Endgame .15 .40
- ❑ 22 Betrayal .15 .40
- ❑ 23 New Life .15 .40
- ❑ 24 Acquiring Plans .15 .40
- ❑ 25 The Past Returns .15 .40
- ❑ 26 Entombed .15 .40
- ❑ 27 Not Jack Bristow .15 .40
- ❑ 28 Vaughn's Quest .15 .40
- ❑ 29 Father's Duty .15 .40
- ❑ 30 Suspicious .15 .40
- ❑ 31 Truth .15 .40
- ❑ 32 Simulation .15 .40
- ❑ 33 Set Up .15 .40
- ❑ 34 Genuine .15 .40
- ❑ 35 Concerned .15 .40
- ❑ 36 Collateral .15 .40
- ❑ 37 Listening .15 .40
- ❑ 38 Fatal .15 .40
- ❑ 39 Another Alias .15 .40
- ❑ 40 Confrontation .15 .40
- ❑ 41 Fantasy .15 .40
- ❑ 42 Reality .15 .40
- ❑ 43 Bugged .15 .40
- ❑ 44 Secret Romance .15 .40
- ❑ 45 Waiting .15 .40
- ❑ 46 Mistaken .15 .40
- ❑ 47 Rescued .15 .40
- ❑ 48 Reunited .15 .40
- ❑ 49 Proposal .15 .40
- ❑ 50 Disaster .15 .40
- ❑ 51 Mastermind .15 .40
- ❑ 52 Infected .15 .40
- ❑ 53 Determined .15 .40
- ❑ 54 Doomed .15 .40
- ❑ 55 Sydney Bristow .15 .40
- ❑ 56 Jack Bristow .15 .40
- ❑ 57 Arvin Sloane .15 .40
- ❑ 58 Marcus Dixon .15 .40
- ❑ 59 Marshall Flinkman .15 .40
- ❑ 60 Michael Vaughn .15 .40
- ❑ 61 Nadia Santos .15 .40
- ❑ 62 Eric Weiss .15 .40
- ❑ 63 Hayden Chase .15 .40
- ❑ 64 Busted .15 .40
- ❑ 65 Recruited .15 .40
- ❑ 66 In The Lab .15 .40
- ❑ 67 Quality Control .15 .40
- ❑ 68 Mobbed Up .15 .40
- ❑ 69 Flinkman Sr. & Jr. .15 .40
- ❑ 70 Ingenious .15 .40
- ❑ 71 Innovating .15 .40
- ❑ 72 Bluffing .15 .40
- ❑ 73 Irina Derevko .15 .40
- ❑ 74 Katya Derevko .15 .40
- ❑ 75 Elena Derevko .15 .40
- ❑ 76 Sydney Bristow .15 .40
- ❑ 77 Nadia Santos .15 .40
- ❑ 78 Sloane .15 .40
- ❑ 79 Cloane .15 .40
- ❑ 80 Daughter .15 .40
- ❑ 81 Checklist .15 .40

2006 Alias Season Four Autographs
STATED ODDS 1:24

- ❑ A32 Joel Grey 6.00 15.00
- ❑ A33 Gina Torres 5.00 12.00
- ❑ A34 Sonia Braga 5.00 12.00
- ❑ A35 Michael McKean 5.00 12.00
- ❑ A36 Elya Baskin 5.00 12.00
- ❑ A37 Izabella Scorupco 8.00 20.00
- ❑ A38 Anthony Cistaro 5.00 12.00
- ❑ A39 Robin Sachs 5.00 12.00
- ❑ A40 Angus Scrimm 5.00 12.00
- ❑ ATS Ron Rifkin 20.00 40.00

2006 Alias Season Four Box Loaders
COMPLETE SET (4) 8.00 20.00
STATED ODDS ONE PER BOX

- ❑ BL1 Jack and Sydney 1.50 4.00
- ❑ BL2 Jack and Arvin 1.50 4.00
- ❑ BL3 Arvin and Nadia 1.50 4.00
- ❑ CL1 Realities Collide 4.00 10.00
CASE INSERT

2006 Alias Season Four Pieceworks
STATED ODDS 1:24

- ❑ PW1 Jennifer Garner Dress 8.00 20.00
- ❑ PW2 Jennifer Garner Top 8.00 20.00
- ❑ PW3 Mia Maestro T-Shirt 4.00 10.00
- ❑ PW4 Mia Maestro Dress 4.00 10.00
- ❑ PW5 Carl Lumbly Hospital Gown 4.00 10.00
- ❑ PW6 Carl Lumbly Jacket 4.00 10.00
- ❑ PW7 Michael Vartan Jacket 4.00 10.00
- ❑ PW8 Michael Vartan T-Shirt 4.00 10.00
- ❑ PW9 Victor Garber Jacket 4.00 10.00
- ❑ PW10 Victor Garber Shirt 4.00 10.00

2006 Alias Season Four Regrets
STATED ODDS 1:17

- ❑ R1 Irina Derevko 1.50 4.00
- ❑ R2 Arvin Sloane 1.50 4.00
- ❑ R3 Sydney Bristow 1.50 4.00
- ❑ R4 Michael Vaughn 1.50 4.00
- ❑ R5 Jack Bristow 1.50 4.00
- ❑ R6 Arvin Sloane 1.50 4.00

2006 Battlestar Galactica Colonial Warriors
COMPLETE SET (72) 4.00 10.00

- ❑ 1 Captain Apollo .10 .30
- ❑ 2 Captain Apollo .10 .30
- ❑ 3 Captain Apollo .10 .30
- ❑ 4 Captain Apollo .10 .30
- ❑ 5 Captain Apollo .10 .30
- ❑ 6 Captain Apollo .10 .30
- ❑ 7 Captain Apollo .10 .30
- ❑ 8 Captain Apollo .10 .30
- ❑ 9 Captain Apollo .10 .30
- ❑ 10 Lt. Starbuck .10 .30
- ❑ 11 Lt. Starbuck .10 .30
- ❑ 12 Lt. Starbuck .10 .30
- ❑ 13 Lt. Starbuck .10 .30
- ❑ 14 Lt. Starbuck .10 .30
- ❑ 15 Lt. Starbuck .10 .30
- ❑ 16 Lt. Starbuck .10 .30
- ❑ 17 Lt. Starbuck .10 .30
- ❑ 18 Lt. Starbuck .10 .30
- ❑ 19 Lt. Boomer .10 .30
- ❑ 20 Lt. Boomer .10 .30
- ❑ 21 Lt. Boomer .10 .30
- ❑ 22 Lt. Boomer .10 .30
- ❑ 23 Lt. Boomer .10 .30
- ❑ 24 Lt. Boomer .10 .30
- ❑ 25 Col. Tigh .10 .30
- ❑ 26 Col. Tigh .10 .30
- ❑ 27 Col. Tigh .10 .30
- ❑ 28 Lt. Sheba .10 .30
- ❑ 29 Lt. Sheba .10 .30
- ❑ 30 Lt. Sheba .10 .30
- ❑ 31 Lt. Sheba .10 .30
- ❑ 32 Lt. Sheba .10 .30
- ❑ 33 Lt. Sheba .10 .30
- ❑ 34 Serina .10 .30
- ❑ 35 Serina .10 .30
- ❑ 36 Serina .10 .30
- ❑ 37 Lt. Athena .10 .30
- ❑ 38 Lt. Athena .10 .30
- ❑ 39 Lt. Athena .10 .30
- ❑ 40 Lt. Athena .10 .30
- ❑ 41 Lt. Athena .10 .30
- ❑ 42 Lt. Athena .10 .30
- ❑ 43 Boxey .10 .30
- ❑ 44 Boxey .10 .30
- ❑ 45 Boxey .10 .30
- ❑ 46 Cassiopeia .10 .30
- ❑ 47 Cassiopeia .10 .30
- ❑ 48 Cassiopeia .10 .30
- ❑ 49 Cassiopeia .10 .30
- ❑ 50 Dr. Salik .10 .30
- ❑ 51 Dr. Salik .10 .30
- ❑ 52 Dr. Wilker .10 .30
- ❑ 53 Dr. Wilker .10 .30
- ❑ 54 Flight Cpl. Rigel .10 .30
- ❑ 55 Muffit .10 .30
- ❑ 56 Muffit .10 .30
- ❑ 57 Lt. Bojay .10 .30
- ❑ 58 Lt. Bojay .10 .30
- ❑ 59 Captain Troy .10 .30
- ❑ 60 Captain Troy .10 .30
- ❑ 61 Captain Troy .10 .30
- ❑ 62 Captain Troy .10 .30
- ❑ 63 Captain Troy .10 .30
- ❑ 64 Captain Troy .10 .30
- ❑ 65 Jamie Hamilton .10 .30
- ❑ 66 Jamie Hamilton .10 .30
- ❑ 67 Jamie Hamilton .10 .30
- ❑ 68 Dr. Zee .10 .30
- ❑ 69 Xavier .10 .30
- ❑ 70 Checklist .10 .30
- ❑ 71 Checklist .10 .30
- ❑ 72 Checklist .10 .30

2006 Battlestar Galactica Colonial Warriors 1978 Battlestar Galactica Expansion
COMPLETE SET (54) 30.00 60.00
STATED ODDS 1:8

- ❑ 133 Colonial Fleet .60 1.50
- ❑ 134 Winning Hand .60 1.50
- ❑ 135 A Boy and His Daggit .60 1.50
- ❑ 136 Ovion Queen .60 1.50
- ❑ 137 Horror! .60 1.50
- ❑ 138 Destruction of a Basestar .60 1.50
- ❑ 139 Vipers, Launch When Ready .60 1.50
- ❑ 140 Training New Pilots .60 1.50
- ❑ 141 Captured! .60 1.50
- ❑ 142 Attack Formation .60 1.50
- ❑ 143 A Full Pyramid .60 1.50
- ❑ 144 Red Eye .60 1.50
- ❑ 145 Father and Son .60 1.50
- ❑ 146 Prisoner Bootlegger 137 .60 1.50
- ❑ 147 Deep Freeze .60 1.50
- ❑ 148 Snowram .60 1.50
- ❑ 149 Final Attack .60 1.50
- ❑ 150 Seeing Triple .60 1.50
- ❑ 151 Tricked! .60 1.50
- ❑ 152 Constable Nogow .60 1.50
- ❑ 153 Crash Landing .60 1.50
- ❑ 154 Prisoner of the Cylons! .60 1.50
- ❑ 155 Cassiopeia and Starbuck .60 1.50
- ❑ 156 Weapons Ready .60 1.50
- ❑ 157 Wounded in Battle .60 1.50
- ❑ 158 Battlestar vs Basestar .60 1.50
- ❑ 159 Suicide Attack .60 1.50
- ❑ 160 Messanger Muffit .60 1.50
- ❑ 161 Count Iblis .60 1.50
- ❑ 162 Cassiopeia, Starbuck and Apollo .60 1.50
- ❑ 163 Fallen Warrior .60 1.50
- ❑ 164 Reunited! .60 1.50
- ❑ 165 Borellian Nomen .60 1.50
- ❑ 166 Warriors Three .60 1.50
- ❑ 167 Triad .60 1.50
- ❑ 168 On the Run .60 1.50
- ❑ 169 Viper on Patrol .60 1.50
- ❑ 170 Ship From Earth? .60 1.50
- ❑ 171 Directions from an Android .60 1.50
- ❑ 172 Grandfatherly Advise .60 1.50
- ❑ 173 Commadant Leiter .60 1.50
- ❑ 174 Another Round! .60 1.50
- ❑ 175 Ship of Light .60 1.50
- ❑ 176 Galactica Fires it Weapons .60 1.50
- ❑ 177 Colonial Warriors .60 1.50
- ❑ 178 Starbuck and Colonel Tigh .60 1.50
- ❑ 179 Battle Plans .60 1.50
- ❑ 180 A Kiss Goodbye .60 1.50
- ❑ 181 Cylon Basestar In Orbit .60 1.50
- ❑ 182 IL Series Cylon .60 1.50
- ❑ 183 Imperious Leader .60 1.50
- ❑ 184 Mechanical Menance .60 1.50
- ❑ 185 Threat from Above! .60 1.50
- ❑ 186 Cylon Raider .60 1.50

2006 Battlestar Galactica Colonial Warriors ArtiFEX
COMPLETE SET (9) 60.00 120.00
STATED ODDS 1:40

- ❑ S1 Chris Scalf art 6.00 15.00
- ❑ S2 Chris Scalf art 6.00 15.00
- ❑ S3 Chris Scalf art 6.00 15.00
- ❑ S4 Chris Scalf art 6.00 15.00
- ❑ S5 Chris Scalf art 6.00 15.00
- ❑ S6 Chris Scalf art 6.00 15.00
- ❑ S7 Chris Scalf art 6.00 15.00
- ❑ S8 Chris Scalf art 6.00 15.00
- ❑ S9 Chris Scalf art 6.00 15.00

2006 Battlestar Galactica Colonial Warriors Autograph Costumes
- ❑ DB Dirk Benedict
- ❑ HJ Herbert Jefferson Jr.
- ❑ RH Richard Hatch
- ❑ TC Terry Carter

2006 Battlestar Galactica Colonial Warriors Autographs
STATED ODDS ONE PER BOX
VL (VERY LIMITED): LESS THAN 300 CARDS
A8 ODDS ONE PER CASE
DA1 ODDS ONE PER 6-CASE PURCHASE

- ❑ A8 Alex Hyde-White
- ❑ A12 Jane Seymour VL
- ❑ A17 Anne Lockhart VL
- ❑ A18 Sarah Rush VL
- ❑ A19 Glen A. Larson VL
- ❑ A20 Ed Begley, Jr VL
- ❑ A21 Christine Belford VL
- ❑ A22 Arlene Martel VL
- ❑ A23 Britt Ekland VL
- ❑ A24 Richard Lynch VL
- ❑ A25 Melody Anderson VL
- ❑ A27 James Patrick Stuart VL
- ❑ A28 Randolph Mantooth VL
- ❑ DA1 Richard Hatch
Dirk Benedict

2006 Battlestar Galactica Colonial Warriors Casting Call
COMPLETE SET (9) 30.00 60.00
STATED ODDS 1:20

- ❑ W1 Lorne Greene 3.00 8.00
- ❑ W2 Richard Hatch 3.00 8.00
- ❑ W3 Dirk Benedict 3.00 8.00
- ❑ W4 Jane Seymour 3.00 8.00
- ❑ W5 Maren Jensen 3.00 8.00
- ❑ W6 Anne Lockhart 3.00 8.00
- ❑ W7 Laurette Spang 3.00 8.00
- ❑ W8 Terry Carter 3.00 8.00
- ❑ W9 Herbert Jefferson Jr. 3.00 8.00

2006 Battlestar Galactica Colonial Warriors Costumes
STATED ODDS ONE PER BOX
CC12 ODDS ONE PER COLLECTORS ALBUM
DC1 ODDS ONE PER 2-CASE PURCHASE

- ❑ CC2 Lt. Starbuck
- ❑ CC3 Commander Adama
- ❑ CC4 Lt. Boomer
- ❑ CC5 Spector
- ❑ CC6 Captain Apollo
- ❑ CC7 Lt. Boomer
- ❑ CC8 Lt. Starbuck
- ❑ CC9 Serina
- ❑ CC10 Col. Tigh
- ❑ CC11 Captain Apollo
- ❑ CC12 Lt. Athena
- ❑ DC1 Commander Adama
Captain Apollo

2006 Battlestar Galactica Colonial Warriors Promos
- ❑ P1 Lieutenant Starbuck .75 2.00
(General Distribution)
- ❑ P2 Captain Apollo .75 2.00
(NSU Magazine)
- ❑ P3 Ensign Greenbeam 6.00 15.00
(Album Exclusive)
- ❑ UK Lieutenant Boomer 3.00 8.00
(UK Exclusive)

2006 Battlestar Galactica Colonial Warriors Tribute
COMPLETE SET (2)
STATED ODDS 1:480

- ❑ T1 Lorne Greene
as Commander Adama
- ❑ T2 John Colicos
as Baltar

2006 Battlestar Galactica Season One
COMPLETE SET (81) 4.00 10.00
WBG ODDS 1:480
HEND SKETCH ODDS ONE PER 2-CASE PURCHASE

- ❑ 1 Title Card .10 .30
Checklist
- ❑ 2 Title Card .10 .30
Checklist
- ❑ 3 Title Card .10 .30
Checklist
- ❑ 4 33 .10 .30
- ❑ 5 33 .10 .30
- ❑ 6 33 .10 .30
- ❑ 7 33 .10 .30
- ❑ 8 33 .10 .30
- ❑ 9 33 .10 .30
- ❑ 10 Water .10 .30
- ❑ 11 Water .10 .30
- ❑ 12 Water .10 .30
- ❑ 13 Water .10 .30
- ❑ 14 Water .10 .30
- ❑ 15 Water .10 .30
- ❑ 16 Bastille Day .10 .30
- ❑ 17 Bastille Day .10 .30
- ❑ 18 Bastille Day .10 .30
- ❑ 19 Bastille Day .10 .30
- ❑ 20 Bastille Day .10 .30
- ❑ 21 Bastille Day .10 .30
- ❑ 22 Act of Contrition .10 .30
- ❑ 23 Act of Contrition .10 .30
- ❑ 24 Act of Contrition .10 .30
- ❑ 25 Act of Contrition .10 .30
- ❑ 26 Act of Contrition .10 .30
- ❑ 27 Act of Contrition .10 .30

❑ 28 You Can't Go Home Again .10 .30
❑ 29 You Can't Go Home Again .10 .30
❑ 30 You Can't Go Home Again .10 .30
❑ 31 You Can't Go Home Again .10 .30
❑ 32 You Can't Go Home Again .10 .30
❑ 33 You Can't Go Home Again .10 .30
❑ 34 Litmus .10 .30
❑ 35 Litmus .10 .30
❑ 36 Litmus .10 .30
❑ 37 Litmus .10 .30
❑ 38 Litmus .10 .30
❑ 39 Litmus .10 .30
❑ 40 Six Degrees of Separation .10 .30
❑ 41 Six Degrees of Separation .10 .30
❑ 42 Six Degrees of Separation .10 .30
❑ 43 Six Degrees of Separation .10 .30
❑ 44 Six Degrees of Separation .10 .30
❑ 45 Six Degrees of Separation .10 .30
❑ 46 Flesh and Bone .10 .30
❑ 47 Flesh and Bone .10 .30
❑ 48 Flesh and Bone .10 .30
❑ 49 Flesh and Bone .10 .30
❑ 50 Flesh and Bone .10 .30
❑ 51 Flesh and Bone .10 .30
❑ 52 Tigh Me Up, Tigh Me Down .10 .30
❑ 53 Tigh Me Up, Tigh Me Down .10 .30
❑ 54 Tigh Me Up, Tigh Me Down .10 .30
❑ 55 Tigh Me Up, Tigh Me Down .10 .30
❑ 56 Tigh Me Up, Tigh Me Down .10 .30
❑ 57 Tigh Me Up, Tigh Me Down .10 .30
❑ 58 The Hand of God .10 .30
❑ 59 The Hand of God .10 .30
❑ 60 The Hand of God .10 .30
❑ 61 The Hand of God .10 .30
❑ 62 The Hand of God .10 .30
❑ 63 The Hand of God .10 .30
❑ 64 Colonial Day .10 .30
❑ 65 Colonial Day .10 .30
❑ 66 Colonial Day .10 .30
❑ 67 Colonial Day .10 .30
❑ 68 Colonial Day .10 .30
❑ 69 Colonial Day .10 .30
❑ 70 Kobol's Last Gleaming, Part 1 .10 .30
❑ 71 Kobol's Last Gleaming, Part 1 .10 .30
❑ 72 Kobol's Last Gleaming, Part 1 .10 .30
❑ 73 Kobol's Last Gleaming, Part 1 .10 .30
❑ 74 Kobol's Last Gleaming, Part 1 .10 .30
❑ 75 Kobol's Last Gleaming, Part 1 .10 .30
❑ 76 Kobol's Last Gleaming, Part 2 .10 .30
❑ 77 Kobol's Last Gleaming, Part 2 .10 .30
❑ 78 Kobol's Last Gleaming, Part 2 .10 .30
❑ 79 Kobol's Last Gleaming, Part 2 .10 .30
❑ 80 Kobol's Last Gleaming, Part 2 .10 .30
❑ 81 Kobol's Last Gleaming, Part 2 .10 .30
❑ HEND Chris Henderson Sketch
❑ WBG Women of Battlestar Galactica

2006 Battlestar Galactica Season One ArtiFEX

COMPLETE SET (9)
STATED ODDS 1:20

❑ SPA1 Commander William Adama
❑ SPA2 President Laura Roslin
❑ SPA3 Captain Lee Apollo Adama
❑ SPA4 Lt. Kara Starbuck Thrace
❑ SPA5 Number Six
❑ SPA6 Dr. Gaius Baltar
❑ SPA7 Lt. Sharon Boomer Valerii
❑ SPA8 Lt. Karl C. Helo Agathon
❑ SPA9 Colonel Saul Tigh

2006 Battlestar Galactica Season One Autographs

STATED ODDS 1:40
THJC ODDS ONE PER 6-CASE PURCHASE
L (LIMITED): 300-500 CARDS
VL (VERY LIMITE): LESS THAN 300 CARDS

❑ AO Alonso Oyarzun L
❑ BG Biski Gugushe L
❑ GP Grace Park L
❑ JB Jamie Bamber VL
❑ JT Jill Teed L
❑ KM Kandyse McClure L
❑ LG Lorena Gale L
❑ MM Mary McDonnell VL
❑ RH Richard Hatch VL
❑ RW Robert Wisden L
❑ SW Sam Witwer L
❑ TM Tobias Mehler L
❑ TP Tahmoh Penikett L
❑ THJC Tricia Helfer
James Callis

2006 Battlestar Galactica Season One Costumes

STATED ODDS 1:40
CC9 ODDS ONE PER COLLECTORS ALBUM
LC ODDS ONE PER CASE

❑ CC9 Commander William Adama
❑ CC10 Lt. Kara Starbuck Thrace
❑ CC11 Chief Petty Officer Galen Tyrol
❑ CC12 Dr. Gaius Baltar
❑ CC13 President Laura Roslin
❑ CC14 Number Six
❑ CC15 Petty Officer Anastasia Dualla
❑ CC16 Number Six
❑ CC17 Tom Zarek
❑ CC18 Dr. Gaius Baltar
❑ CC19 Captain Lee Apollo Adama
❑ CC20 Dr. Gaius Baltar
❑ LC Leoben Conoy DUAL

2006 Battlestar Galactica Season One Crossroads

COMPLETE SET (9) 20.00 50.00
STATED ODDS 1:10

❑ CR1 Truth Revealed 2.50 6.00
❑ CR2 Love over Duty 2.50 6.00
❑ CR3 Painful Memories 2.50 6.00
❑ CR4 Strange Bed Fellows 2.50 6.00
❑ CR5 Yet Another Secret 2.50 6.00
❑ CR6 AWOL 2.50 6.00
❑ CR7 Breaking Ranks 2.50 6.00
❑ CR8 Choosing Sides 2.50 6.00
❑ CR9 Finding God! 2.50 6.00

2006 Battlestar Galactica Season One In Motion

COMPLETE SET (6) 40.00 100.00
STATED ODDS 1:80

❑ M1 In Motion 8.00 20.00
❑ M2 In Motion 8.00 20.00
❑ M3 In Motion 8.00 20.00
❑ M4 In Motion 8.00 20.00
❑ M5 In Motion 8.00 20.00
❑ M6 In Motion 8.00 20.00

2006 Battlestar Galactica Season One Number Six

COMPLETE SET (6) 40.00 100.00
STATED ODDS 1:80

❑ N1 Mother 8.00 20.00
❑ N2 Prophet 8.00 20.00
❑ N3 Seductress 8.00 20.00
❑ N4 Manipulator 8.00 20.00
❑ N5 Warrior 8.00 20.00
❑ N6 Lover 8.00 20.00

2006 Battlestar Galactica Season One Promos

❑ P1 Boomer .75 2.00
(General Distribution)
❑ P2 Viper .75 2.00
(NSU Magazine)
❑ P3 Number 6/Apollo 3.00 8.00
(Album Exclusive)
❑ UK Apollo 5.00 12.00
(UK Exclusive)
❑ CP1 Starbuck 4.00 10.00
(Convention Promo)

2006 Bench Warmer Holiday

COMPLETE SET (24) 6.00 15.00

❑ 1 Mary Riley .75 2.00
❑ 2 Carrie Stroup .40 1.00
❑ 3 Ericka Underwood .40 1.00
❑ 4 Jen Sibley .40 1.00
❑ 5 Yvette Lopez .40 1.00
❑ 6 Vilayna LaSalle .40 1.00
❑ 7 Shauna Walters .40 1.00
❑ 8 Yancey Todd .40 1.00
❑ 9 Lindsey Roeper .40 1.00
❑ 10 Candice Michelle .40 1.00
❑ 11 Alejandra Gutierrez .40 1.00
❑ 12 Krisi Ballentine .40 1.00
❑ 13 Rochelle Loewen .40 1.00
❑ 14 Star Noelle .40 1.00
❑ 15 Molly Shea .40 1.00
❑ 16 Holly Huddleston .40 1.00
❑ 17 Cecille Gahr .40 1.00
❑ 18 Lora-Lyn Peterson .40 1.00
❑ 19 CJ Gibson .40 1.00
❑ 20 Sarah Coggin .40 1.00
❑ 21 Shannon Roberts .40 1.00
❑ 22 Bonnie Conte .40 1.00
❑ 23 Heather Betts .40 1.00
❑ 24 Miki Black .40 1.00

2006 Bench Warmer Holiday Autographs

STATED ODDS ONE PER FACT. SET

❑ 1 Lisa Gleave 6.00 15.00
❑ 2 Candice Michelle 6.00 15.00
❑ 3 Tamara Witmer 6.00 15.00
❑ 4 Mary Riley 8.00 20.00
❑ 5 Aubrie Lemon 6.00 15.00
❑ 6 Holly Huddleston 6.00 15.00
❑ 7 Molly Shea 6.00 15.00
❑ 8 Miki Black 6.00 15.00
❑ 9 Lindsey Roeper 6.00 15.00
❑ 10 Holly Madison 6.00 15.00
❑ 11 Michelle Baena/ (issued in 2006 Bench Warmer Series Two)
6.00 15.00
❑ 12 Bridget Marquardt 6.00 15.00
❑ 13 Tina Jordan 6.00 15.00
❑ 14 Jaime Hammer 6.00 15.00
❑ 15 Cassandra Lynn 6.00 15.00
❑ 16 Krisi Ballentine 6.00 15.00
❑ NNO Tiffany Richardson 6.00 15.00

2006 Bench Warmer Holiday Hotties

COMPLETE SET (10)
STATED ODDS 1:3 FACT. SETS

❑ 1 Tamara Witmer 3.00 8.00
❑ 2 Mary Riley 4.00 10.00
❑ 3 Holly Madison 3.00 8.00
❑ 4 Aubrie Lemon 3.00 8.00
❑ 5 Bridget Marquardt 3.00 8.00
❑ 6 Alicia Arden 3.00 8.00
❑ 7 Tiffany Richardson 3.00 8.00
❑ 8 Candice Michelle 3.00 8.00
❑ 9 Holly Madison 3.00 8.00
Bridget Marquardt
❑ 10 Santa's Helpers 3.00 8.00
Nichole Jackson/Ericka Underwood/Taren Cassidy

2006 Bench Warmer Holiday Kiss

STATED ODDS 1:4 FACT. SETS

❑ 1 Mary Riley 15.00 30.00
❑ 2 Candice Michelle 8.00 20.00
❑ 3 Cassandra Lynn 8.00 20.00
❑ 4 Lana Kinnear 8.00 20.00
❑ 5 Krisi Ballentine 8.00 20.00
❑ 6 Tina Jordan 8.00 20.00
❑ 7 Yancey Todd 8.00 20.00
❑ 8 Cecille Gahr 8.00 20.00
❑ 9 Brooke Morales 8.00 20.00
❑ 10 Jaime Hammer 8.00 20.00

2006 Bench Warmer Holiday Super Rare Autographs

STATED ODDS 1:80 FACT. SETS
STATED PRINT RUN 25 SER. #'d SETS
UNPRICED DUE TO SCARCITY

❑ 1 Lisa Gleave
❑ 2 Candice Michelle
❑ 3 Holly Madison
Bridget Marquardt
❑ 4 Cecille Gahr

2006 Bench Warmer Holiday Super Rare Autographs Red Ink

STATED PRINT RUN 5 SER. #'d SETS
UNPRICED DUE TO SCARCITY

2006 Bench Warmer Holiday Swatches

STATED ODDS 1:10 FACT. SETS

❑ 1 Candice Michelle 25.00 50.00
❑ 2 Mary Riley 30.00 60.00
❑ 3 Lisa Gleave 25.00 50.00
❑ 4 Jaime Hammer 25.00 50.00
❑ 5 Carrie Stroup 25.00 50.00
❑ 6 Holly Madison 25.00 50.00
❑ 7 Bridget Marquardt 25.00 50.00
❑ 8 Tina Jordan 25.00 50.00
❑ 9 Cecille Gahr 25.00 50.00
❑ 10 Holly Madison 25.00 50.00
Bridget Marquardt

2006 Bench Warmer Holiday Swatches Autographs

STATED PRINT RUN 10 SER. #'d SETS

❑ 1 Candice Michelle
❑ 2 Mary Riley
❑ 3 Lisa Gleave
❑ 4 Jaime Hammer
❑ 5 Carrie Stroup
❑ 6 Holly Madison
❑ 7 Bridget Marquardt
❑ 8 Tina Jordan
❑ 9 Cecille Gahr
❑ 10 Holly Madison
Bridget Marquardt

2006 Bench Warmer Series One

COMPLETE SET (100)
COMP.SET w/o SP's (72) 6.00 15.00
SP STATED ODDS 1:4

❑ 1 Nikki Ziering .15 .40
❑ 2 Cindy Margolis .25 .60
❑ 3 Buffy Tyler .15 .40
❑ 4 Kimberly Page .15 .40
❑ 5 Cecille Louise Gahr .15 .40
❑ 6 Tiffany Selby .15 .40
❑ 7 Holly Weber .15 .40
❑ 8 Shay Lyn .15 .40
❑ 9 Lisa Lakatos .15 .40
❑ 10 Jacqueline Finnan .15 .40
❑ 11 Lisa Gleave .15 .40
❑ 12 Nikki Zeno .15 .40
❑ 13 Ashley Smith .15 .40
❑ 14 Tamara Witmer .15 .40
❑ 15 Paige Peterson .15 .40
❑ 16 Kasie Head .15 .40
❑ 17 Aiko Tanaka .15 .40
❑ 18 Brooke Banx .15 .40
❑ 19 Jaime Hammer .15 .40
❑ 20 Tanaya Nicole .15 .40
❑ 21 Amie Decker .15 .40
❑ 22 Nikki Gray .15 .40
❑ 23 Stephanie Foder .15 .40
❑ 24 Angela Picciolo .15 .40
❑ 25 Tabitha Taylor .15 .40
❑ 26 Laurie Milan .15 .40
❑ 27 Bonnie Conte .15 .40
❑ 28 Lauren Mary Kim .15 .40
❑ 29 Lisa Ligon .15 .40
❑ 30 Meriah Nelson .15 .40
❑ 31 Tammy Vallejos .15 .40
❑ 32 Jenny Anania .15 .40
❑ 33 Barbara Moore .15 .40
❑ 34 Heather Bryant .15 .40
❑ 35 Nadia Dawn .15 .40
❑ 36 Lana Kinnear .15 .40
❑ 37 Lindsey Roeper .15 .40
❑ 38 Vilayna LaSalle .15 .40
❑ 39 Kylah Kim .15 .40
❑ 40 Nicole Bennett .15 .40
❑ 41 Christina Morris .15 .40
❑ 42 Jenae Altschwager .15 .40
❑ 43 Paula LaRocca .15 .40
❑ 44 Christy Hemme .25 .60
❑ 45 Stacy Blosser .15 .40
❑ 46 Mary Riley .40 1.00
❑ 47 Jaime Bergman .15 .40
❑ 48 Kari Ann Peniche .15 .40
❑ 49 Heather Bryant AS .15 .40
❑ 50 Yvette Nelson AS .15 .40
❑ 51 Brooke Morales AS .15 .40
❑ 52 Holly Weber AS .15 .40
❑ 53 Tira Provost AS .15 .40
❑ 54 Cecille Gahr AS .15 .40
❑ 55 Tamara Witmer AS .15 .40
❑ 56 Nikki Zeno AS .15 .40
❑ 57 Tiffany Kyees AS .15 .40
❑ 58 Catherine Kluthe AS .15 .40
❑ 59 Katarina Van Derham AS .15 .40
❑ 60 Jen Sibley AS .15 .40
❑ 61 Amie Decker AS .15 .40
❑ 62 Alix Agar AS .15 .40
❑ 63 Tiffany Selby AS .15 .40
❑ 64 Ashley Smith AS .15 .40
❑ 65 Leslie Gomez AS .15 .40
❑ 66 Nikki Gray AS .15 .40
❑ 67 Renee Stone AS .15 .40
❑ 68 Kylah Kim AS .15 .40
❑ 69 Mary Riley AS .40 1.00
❑ 70 Nikki Zeno .15 .40
Alix Agar
❑ 71 Ashley Smith .15 .40
Kasie Head
❑ 72 Denise Tillery .15 .40
Victoria Fuller
❑ H73 Nikki Ziering 1.25 3.00
❑ H74 Mary Riley 2.00 5.00
❑ H75 Buffy Tyler 1.25 3.00
❑ H76 Cassandra Lynn LB SP 1.25 3.00
❑ H77 Leslie Gomez LB SP 1.25 3.00
❑ H78 Samantha Schacher LB SP 1.25 3.00
❑ H79 Cora Skinner LB SP 1.25 3.00
❑ H80 Angelina Zamora LB SP 1.25 3.00
❑ H81 Meriah Nelson LB SP 1.25 3.00
❑ H82 Paige Peterson LB SP 1.25 3.00
❑ H83 Vilayna LaSalle LB SP 1.25 3.00
❑ H84 Molly Shea LB SP 1.25 3.00
❑ H85 Holly Huddleston LB SP 1.25 3.00
❑ H86 Lindsey Roeper LB SP 1.25 3.00
❑ H87 Jen Johnson LB SP 1.25 3.00
❑ H88 Shay Lyn VT SP 1.25 3.00
❑ H89 Aubrie Lemon VT SP 1.25 3.00
❑ H90 Carrie Stroup VT SP 1.25 3.00
❑ H91 Miki Black VT SP 1.25 3.00
❑ H92 Sarah Coggin VT SP 1.25 3.00
❑ H93 Bonnie Conte VT SP 1.25 3.00
❑ H94 Shannon Roberts VT SP 1.25 3.00
❑ H95 CJ Gibson VT SP 1.25 3.00
❑ H96 Rady Ouzounova VT SP 1.25 3.00
❑ H97 Lana Kinnear VT SP 1.25 3.00
❑ H98 Lena Yada VT SP 1.25 3.00
❑ H99 Yvette Nelson VT SP 1.25 3.00
❑ H100 Mary Riley VT SP 2.00 5.00

2006 Bench Warmer Series One Authentic Swatches

STATED ODDS 1:288

❑ 1 Cindy Margolis
❑ 2 Nikki Ziering 15.00 30.00
❑ 3 Buffy Tyler 15.00 30.00
❑ 4 Kimberly Page 15.00 30.00
❑ 5 Cassandra Lynn 15.00 30.00
❑ 6 Cecille Gahr 15.00 30.00
❑ 7 Rebecca Mary 15.00 30.00
❑ 8 Tiffany Selby 15.00 30.00
❑ 9 Tiffany Granath 15.00 30.00
❑ 10 Jenna Morasca 15.00 30.00

2006 Bench Warmer Series One Authentic Swatches Autographs

STATED PRINT RUN 25 SER.#'d SETS
UNPRICED DUE TO SCARCITY

❑ 1 Cindy Margolis/10
❑ 2 Nikki Ziering
❑ 3 Buffy Tyler
❑ 4 Kimberly Page
❑ 5 Cassandra Lynn
❑ 6 Cecille Gahr
❑ 7 Rebecca Mary
❑ 8 Tiffany Selby
❑ 9 Tiffany Granath
❑ 10 Jenna Morasca

2006 Bench Warmer Series One Autographs Silver Foil

STATED ODDS 1:12

❑ 1 Cindy Margolis 8.00 20.00
❑ 2 Christy Hemme 8.00 20.00
❑ 3 Buffy Tyler 6.00 15.00
❑ 4 Nikki Ziering 6.00 15.00
❑ 5 Heather Bryant 6.00 15.00
❑ 6 Tanaya Nicole 6.00 15.00
❑ 7 Mary Riley 8.00 20.00
❑ 8 Aiko Tanaka 6.00 15.00
❑ 9 Leslie Gomez 6.00 15.00
❑ 10 Cora Skinner 6.00 15.00
❑ 11 Tiffany Selby 6.00 15.00
❑ 12 Kimberly Page 6.00 15.00
❑ 13 Jacqueline Finnan 6.00 15.00
❑ 14 Paige Peterson 6.00 15.00
❑ 15 Meriah Nelson 6.00 15.00
❑ 16 Holly Weber 6.00 15.00
❑ 17 Lindsey Roeper 6.00 15.00
❑ 18 Jaime Hammer 6.00 15.00
❑ 19 Bonnie Conte 6.00 15.00
❑ 20 Rebecca Mary 6.00 15.00

2006 Bench Warmer Series One Autographs Gold Foil

STATED PRINT RUN 100 SER. #'d SETS

2006 Bench Warmer Series One Case Toppers Autographs

STATED ODDS ONE PER CASE

❑ CT1 Shay Lyn 8.00 20.00
Bonnie Conte
❑ CT2 Lisa Lakatos 10.00 25.00
Jennifer Korbin/Rebecca Mary
❑ CT3 Buffy Tyler 8.00 20.00
Tiffany Selby/Cassandra Lynn/Jaime Hammer
❑ CT4 Cecille Gahr 8.00 20.00
Lindsey Roeper
❑ CT5 Carrie Stroup
Katarina Van Derham/Yvette Nelson
❑ CT6 Buffy Tyler
Tiffany Selby
❑ CT7 Cassandra Lynn 20.00 40.00
Cora Skinner/Meriah Nelson/Paige Peterson/Lindsey Roeper/Lana Kinnear/Leslie Gomez/Jennifer Cantrell
❑ CT8 Tanaya Nicole 30.00 60.00
Aiko Tanaka/Jacqueline Finnan/Holly Weber/Bonnie Conte/Rebecca Mary/Jaime Hammer/Shay Lyn

2006 Bench Warmer Series One Halloween Foil

COMPLETE SET (10) 8.00 20.00
STATED ODDS 1:6

❑ 1 Julianna Prada 1.50 4.00
❑ 2 Tishara Cousino 1.50 4.00
❑ 3 Kathie Smith 1.50 4.00
❑ 4 Crystal Colar 1.50 4.00
❑ 5 Cassandra Lynn 1.50 4.00
❑ 6 Holly Madison 1.50 4.00
❑ 7 Janis Kowalsky 1.50 4.00
❑ 8 Michelle Baena 1.50 4.00
❑ 9 Bridget Marquardt 1.50 4.00
❑ 10 Renee Stone 1.50 4.00

2006 Bench Warmer Series One Jumbo Box Toppers Silver Foil

COMPLETE SET (6) 8.00 20.00
OVERALL BOX TOPPER ODDS ONE PER BOX

❑ 1 Nikki Ziering 2.50 6.00
❑ 2 Kimberly Page 2.50 6.00
❑ 3 Tiffany Selby 2.50 6.00
❑ 4 Buffy Tyler 2.50 6.00
❑ 5 Heather Bryant 2.50 6.00
❑ 6 Bonnie Conte 2.50 6.00

2006 Bench Warmer Series One Jumbo Box Toppers Gold Foil

COMPLETE SET (6) 12.00 30.00
OVERALL BOX TOPPER ODDS ONE PER BOX

2006 Bench Warmer Series One Jumbo Box Toppers Autographs

OVERALL BOX TOPPER ODDS ONE PER BOX

❑ 1 Nikki Ziering 20.00 40.00
❑ 2 Kimberly Page 20.00 40.00
❑ 3 Tiffany Selby 20.00 40.00
❑ 4 Buffy Tyler 20.00 40.00
❑ 5 Heather Bryant 20.00 40.00
❑ 6 Bonnie Conte 20.00 40.00

2006 Bench Warmer Series One Jumbo Box Toppers Dual Kiss

STATED ODDS ONE PER CASE

❑ DK1 Jacqueline Finnan 20.00 40.00
Shay Lyn
❑ DK2 Buffy Tyler 20.00 40.00
Tiffany Selby

2006 Bench Warmer Series One Jumbo Box Toppers Dual Kiss Autographs

STATED PRINT RUN 20 SER. #'d SETS
UNPRICED DUE TO SCARCITY

❑ DK1 Jacqueline Finnan
Shay Lyn
❑ DK2 Buffy Tyler
Tiffany Selby

2006 Bench Warmer Series One Kiss

STATED ODDS 1:72

❑ 1 Cindy Margolis 8.00 20.00
❑ 2 Christy Hemme 8.00 20.00
❑ 3 Sandra Taylor 6.00 15.00
❑ 4 Jennifer Korbin 8.00 20.00
❑ 5 Heather Bryant 6.00 15.00
❑ 6 Bonnie Conte 6.00 15.00
❑ 7 Buffy Tyler 6.00 15.00
❑ 8 Tiffany Selby 6.00 15.00
❑ 9 Lindsey Roeper 6.00 15.00
❑ 10 Yvette Nelson 6.00 15.00
❑ 11 Jaime Hammer 6.00 15.00
❑ 12 Alejandra Gutierrez 6.00 15.00
❑ 13 Rebecca Mary 6.00 15.00
❑ 14 Kimberly Page 6.00 15.00
❑ 15 Tabitha Taylor 6.00 15.00
❑ 16 Nikki Ziering 6.00 15.00

2006 Bench Warmer Series One Kiss Autographs

STATED PRINT RUN 10 SER. #'d SETS
UNPRICED DUE TO SCARCITY

❑ 1 Cindy Margolis
❑ 2 Christy Hemme
❑ 3 Sandra Taylor
❑ 4 Jennifer Korbin
❑ 5 Heather Bryant
❑ 6 Bonnie Conte
❑ 7 Buffy Tyler
❑ 8 Tiffany Selby
❑ 9 Lindsey Roeper
❑ 10 Yvette Nelson
❑ 11 Jaime Hammer
❑ 12 Alejandra Gutierrez
❑ 13 Rebecca Mary
❑ 14 Kimberly Page
❑ 15 Tabitha Taylor
❑ 16 Nikki Ziering

2006 Bench Warmer Series One Lingerie Foil

COMPLETE SET (10) 10.00 25.00
STATED ODDS 1:12

❑ 1 Rochelle Loewen 2.00 5.00
❑ 2 Camille Anderson 2.00 5.00
❑ 3 Shannon Malone 2.00 5.00
❑ 4 Tiffany Selby 2.00 5.00
❑ 5 Sherry Goggin 2.00 5.00
❑ 6 Nicole Bennett 2.00 5.00
❑ 7 Victoria Fuller 2.00 5.00
❑ 8 Lena Yada 2.00 5.00
❑ 9 Jennifer England 2.00 5.00
❑ 10 Zoe Gregory 2.00 5.00

2006 Bench Warmer Series One School Girls Autographs

STATED ODDS 1:48

❑ 1 Mary Riley 15.00 30.00
❑ 2 Katie Lohmann 10.00 25.00
❑ 3 Denyce Lawton 10.00 25.00
❑ 4 Jennifer Korbin 15.00 30.00
❑ 5 Alejandra Gutierrez 10.00 25.00
❑ 6 Flo Jalin 10.00 25.00
❑ 7 Tira Provost 10.00 25.00
❑ 8 Katarina Van Derham 10.00 25.00

2006 Bench Warmer Series One Super Rare Autographs Silver Foil

STATED ODDS 1:2,400
STATED PRINT RUN 25 SER. #'d SETS
UNPRICED DUE TO SCARCITY

❑ 1 Mary Riley
❑ 2 Christy Hemme
❑ 3 Buffy Tyler
❑ 4 Nikki Ziering
❑ 5 Tiffany Selby
❑ 6 Kimberly Page

2006 Bench Warmer Series One Super Rare Autographs Gold Foil

STATED PRINT RUN 10 SER. #'d SETS
UNPRICED DUE TO SCARCITY

2006 Bench Warmer Series Two

COMPLETE SET (100)
COMP.SET w/o SP's (72) 6.00 15.00
SP STATED ODDS 1:4

❑ 1 Costello Twins .30 .75
❑ 2 Candice Michelle .15 .40
❑ 3 Trishelle Cannatella .15 .40
❑ 4 Cecille Gahr .15 .40
❑ 5 Tina Jordan .15 .40
❑ 6 Bridget Marquardt .15 .40
❑ 7 Holly Madison .15 .40
❑ 8 Michelle Baena .15 .40
❑ 9 Colleen Shannon .15 .40
❑ 10 Mary Riley .40 1.00
❑ 11 Tamie Sheffield .15 .40
❑ 12 Jen Sibley .15 .40
❑ 13 Miki Black .15 .40
❑ 14 Yvette Nelson .15 .40
❑ 15 Rebecca Mary .15 .40
❑ 16 Chanel Ryan .15 .40
❑ 17 Heather Betts .15 .40
❑ 18 Laurie Young .15 .40
❑ 19 Angelina Zamura .15 .40
❑ 20 Jessie Camacho .15 .40
❑ 21 Jessica Kramer .15 .40
❑ 22 Cora Skinner .15 .40
❑ 23 Aubrie Lemon .15 .40
❑ 24 Samantha Schacher .15 .40
❑ 25 Shannon Roberts .15 .40
❑ 26 Molly Shea .15 .40
❑ 27 Holly Huddleston .15 .40
❑ 28 The Olly Girls .15 .40
❑ 29 Rochelle Loewen .15 .40
❑ 30 Star Noelle .15 .40
❑ 31 Ericka Underwood .15 .40
❑ 32 Yvette Lopez .15 .40
❑ 33 Krisi Ballentine .15 .40
❑ 34 Brandy Grace .15 .40

- ❑ 35 Lora-Lyn Peterson .15 .40
- ❑ 36 Nichole Jackson .15 .40
- ❑ 37 Taren Cassidy .15 .40
- ❑ 38 Alicia Arden .15 .40
- ❑ 39 Jacqueline Miller .15 .40
- ❑ 40 Yancey Todd .15 .40
- ❑ 41 Leslie Gomez .15 .40
- ❑ 42 Galen Brown .15 .40
- ❑ 43 Shamron Moore .15 .40
- ❑ 44 Erika Seifred .15 .40
- ❑ 45 Katherine Thom .15 .40
- ❑ 46 Carolyn Bolin .15 .40
- ❑ 47 Shauna Walters .15 .40
- ❑ 48 Jamie Walsh .15 .40
- ❑ 49 Jen Johnson .15 .40
- ❑ 50 Sabrina Rose .15 .40
- ❑ 51 Tracy Paris .15 .40
- ❑ 52 Tamara Sky .15 .40
- ❑ 53 CJ Gibson .15 .40
- ❑ 54 Sarah Coggin .15 .40
- ❑ 55 Rady Ouzounova .15 .40
- ❑ 56 Danielle Strader .15 .40
- ❑ 57 Yvette Nelson .15 .40
- ❑ 58 Nadia Dawn .15 .40
- ❑ 59 Laurie Milan .15 .40
- ❑ 60 Jacqueline Finnan .15 .40
- ❑ 61 Meriah Nelson .15 .40
- ❑ 62 Brooke Morales .15 .40
- ❑ 63 Julianna Prada .15 .40
- ❑ 64 Sandra Taylor .15 .40
- ❑ 65 Michelle Perez .15 .40
- ❑ 66 Presley Rose .15 .40
- ❑ 67 Cassandra Lynn .15 .40
- ❑ 68 Vilayna Lasalle .15 .40
- ❑ 69 Jaime Hammer .15 .40
- ❑ 70 Holly Madison .15 .40
  Bridget Marquardt
- ❑ 71 Shay Lyn .15 .40
  Sarah Coggin
- ❑ 72 Chanel Ryan .15 .40
  Sandi Taylor
- ❑ H73 Trishelle Cannatella LB SP 1.25 3.00
- ❑ H74 Kylah Kim LB SP 1.25 3.00
- ❑ H75 Lana Kinnear LB SP 1.25 3.00
- ❑ H76 Rochelle Loewen LB SP 1.25 3.00
- ❑ H77 Jessie Camacho LB SP 1.25 3.00
- ❑ H78 Holly Madison LB SP 1.25 3.00
- ❑ H79 Laurie Young LB SP 1.25 3.00
- ❑ H80 Jamie Walsh LB SP 1.25 3.00
- ❑ H81 Sabrina Rose LB SP 1.25 3.00
- ❑ H82 Danielle Strader LB SP 1.25 3.00
- ❑ H83 Jackie Miller LB SP 1.25 3.00
- ❑ H84 Bridget Marquardt 1.25 3.00
  Holly Madison LB SP
- ❑ H85 Shauna Walters LEY SP 1.25 3.00
- ❑ H86 Katherine Thom LEY SP 1.25 3.00
- ❑ H87 Angie Valle LEY SP 1.25 3.00
- ❑ H88 Carolyn Bolin LEY SP 1.25 3.00
- ❑ H89 Anise Duran LEY SP 1.25 3.00
- ❑ H90 Lauren Marquez LEY SP 1.25 3.00
- ❑ H91 Buffy Tyler BC SP 1.25 3.00
- ❑ H92 Candice Michelle BC SP 1.25 3.00
- ❑ H93 Leslie Gomez BC SP 1.25 3.00
- ❑ H94 Chanel Ryan BC SP 1.25 3.00
- ❑ H95 Shawnie Costello BC SP 1.25 3.00
- ❑ H96 Amie Decker BC SP 1.25 3.00
- ❑ H97 Molly Shea BC SP 1.25 3.00
- ❑ H98 Holly Huddleston BC SP 1.25 3.00
- ❑ H99 Tabitha Taylor BC SP 1.25 3.00
- ❑ H100 Sandra Taylor BC SP 1.25 3.00

2006 Bench Warmer Series Two Authentic Swatches

STATED ODDS 1:288

- ❑ 1 Candice Michelle 15.00 30.00
- ❑ 2 Chanel Ryan 15.00 30.00
- ❑ 3 Christy Hemme
- ❑ 4 Costello Twins 15.00 30.00
- ❑ 5 Jenn Walcott
- ❑ 6 Mary Riley 20.00 40.00
- ❑ 7 Michelle Baena 15.00 30.00
- ❑ 8 Nikki Ziering 15.00 30.00
- ❑ 9 Shamron Moore 15.00 30.00
- ❑ 10 Trishelle 15.00 30.00

2006 Bench Warmer Series Two Authentic Swatches Autographs

STATED PRINT RUN 25 SER. #'d SETS
UNPRICED DUE TO SCARCITY

- ❑ 1 Candice Michelle
- ❑ 2 Chanel Ryan
- ❑ 3 Christy Hemme
- ❑ 4 Costello Twins
- ❑ 5 Jenn Walcott
- ❑ 6 Mary Riley
- ❑ 7 Michelle Baena
- ❑ 8 Nikki Ziering
- ❑ 9 Shamron Moore
- ❑ 10 Trishelle

2006 Bench Warmer Series Two Autographs Silver Foil

STATED ODDS 1:12

- ❑ 1 Costello Twins 8.00 20.00
- ❑ 2 Costello Twins 8.00 20.00
- ❑ 3 Candice Michelle 6.00 15.00
- ❑ 4 Trishelle Cannatella 6.00 15.00
- ❑ 5 Heather Betts 6.00 15.00
- ❑ 6 Lisa Lakatos 6.00 15.00
- ❑ 7 Tamie Sheffield 6.00 15.00
- ❑ 8 Heather Schirra 6.00 15.00
- ❑ 9 Laurie Milan 6.00 15.00
- ❑ 10 Sandi Taylor 6.00 15.00
- ❑ 11 Krisi Ballentine 6.00 15.00
- ❑ 12 Brandy Grace 6.00 15.00
- ❑ 13 Lora-Lyn Peterson 6.00 15.00
- ❑ 14 Shamron Moore 6.00 15.00
- ❑ 15 Alicia Arden 6.00 15.00
- ❑ 16 Tabitha Taylor 6.00 15.00
- ❑ 17 Michelle Baena 6.00 15.00
- ❑ 18 Kylah Kim 6.00 15.00
- ❑ 19 Chanel Ryan 6.00 15.00
- ❑ 20 Mary Riley 8.00 20.00

2006 Bench Warmer Series Two Autographs Gold Foil

STATED PRINT RUN 100 SER. #'d SETS

2006 Bench Warmer Series Two Bettie Page Autographs Gold Foil

STATED ODDS 1:3,000
PRINT RUN 15-50
UNPRICED DUE TO SCARCITY

- ❑ 1 Bettie Page/50
- ❑ 2 Bettie Page/25
- ❑ 3 Bettie Page/15

2006 Bench Warmer Series Two Bettie Page Autographs Holofoil

PRINT RUN 3-5
UNPRICED DUE TO SCARCITY

2006 Bench Warmer Series Two Bettie Page Silver Foil

COMPLETE SET (8) 15.00 30.00
STATED ODDS 1:24

- ❑ 1 Bettie Page 3.00 8.00
- ❑ 2 Bettie Page 3.00 8.00
- ❑ 3 Bettie Page 3.00 8.00
- ❑ 4 Bettie Page 3.00 8.00
- ❑ 5 Bettie Page 3.00 8.00
- ❑ 6 Bettie Page 3.00 8.00
- ❑ 7 Bettie Page 3.00 8.00
- ❑ 8 Bettie Page 3.00 8.00

2006 Bench Warmer Series Two Bettie Page Gold Foil

COMPLETE SET (8) 25.00 50.00
STATED ODDS ONE PER CASE

2006 Bench Warmer Series Two Bettie Page Red Foil

COMPLETE SET (8) 40.00 100.00
STATED ODDS 1:2 CASES

2006 Bench Warmer Series Two Jumbo Box Toppers

COMPLETE SET (5) 6.00 15.00
OVERALL BOX TOPPER ODDS ONE PER BOX

- ❑ 1 Cecille Gahr 2.50 6.00
- ❑ 2 Costello Twins 2.50 6.00
- ❑ 3 Trishelle Cannatella 2.50 6.00
- ❑ 4 Krisi Ballentine 2.50 6.00
- ❑ 5 Candice Michelle 2.50 6.00

2006 Bench Warmer Series Two Jumbo Box Toppers Autographs

OVERALL BOX TOPPER ODDS ONE PER BOX
STATED PRINT RUN 100 SER. #'d SETS

- ❑ 1 Cecille Gahr 15.00 30.00
- ❑ 2 Costello Twins 20.00 40.00
- ❑ 3 Trishelle Cannatella 15.00 30.00
- ❑ 4 Krisi Ballentine 15.00 30.00
- ❑ 5 Candice Michelle 15.00 30.00

2006 Bench Warmer Series Two Jumbo Box Toppers Dual Kiss

OVERALL BOX TOPPER ODDS ONE PER BOX

- ❑ DK3 The Costello Twins 20.00 40.00
- ❑ DK4 Mary Riley 20.00 40.00
  Amie Decker

2006 Bench Warmer Series Two Jumbo Box Toppers Dual Kiss Autographs

OVERALL BOX TOPPER ODDS ONE PER BOX
STATED PRINT RUN 20 SER. #'d SETS
UNPRICED DUE TO SCARCITY

- ❑ DK3 The Costello Twins
- ❑ DK4 Mary Riley
  Amie Decker

2006 Bench Warmer Series Two Kiss

STATED ODDS 1:144

- ❑ 1 Cindy Margolis 8.00 20.00
- ❑ 2 Christy Hemme 8.00 20.00
- ❑ 3 Shawnie Costello 6.00 15.00
- ❑ 4 Julie Costello 6.00 15.00
- ❑ 5 Trishelle Cannatella 6.00 15.00
- ❑ 6 Candice Michelle
- ❑ 7 Lisa Lakatos 6.00 15.00
- ❑ 8 Tamie Sheffield 6.00 15.00
- ❑ 9 Shamron Moore 6.00 15.00
- ❑ 10 Alicia Arden 6.00 15.00
- ❑ 11 Lora-Lyn Peterson 6.00 15.00
- ❑ 12 Michelle Baena 6.00 15.00
- ❑ 13 Amie Decker 6.00 15.00
- ❑ 14 Leslie Gomez 6.00 15.00
- ❑ 15 Brandy Grace 6.00 15.00
- ❑ 16 Candice Michelle

2006 Bench Warmer Series Two Kiss Autographs

UNPRICED DUE TO SCARCITY

- ❑ 1 Cindy Margolis
- ❑ 2 Christy Hemme
- ❑ 3 Shawnie Costello
- ❑ 4 Julie Costello
- ❑ 5 Trishelle Cannatella
- ❑ 6 Candice Michelle
- ❑ 7 Lisa Lakatos
- ❑ 8 Tamie Sheffield
- ❑ 9 Shamron Moore
- ❑ 10 Alicia Arden
- ❑ 11 Lora-Lyn Peterson
- ❑ 12 Michelle Baena
- ❑ 13 Amie Decker
- ❑ 14 Leslie Gomez
- ❑ 15 Brandy Grace
- ❑ 16 Candice Michelle

2006 Bench Warmer Series Two Lingerie Foil

COMPLETE SET (10)
STATED ODDS 1:8
CARDS 1-10 ISSUED IN SERIES ONE

- ❑ 11 Tina Jordan 2.00 5.00
- ❑ 12 Jessica Kramer 2.00 5.00
- ❑ 13 Mary Riley 2.50 6.00
- ❑ 14 Lisa Gleave 2.00 5.00
- ❑ 15 The Bentley Twins 2.00 5.00
- ❑ 16 Aiko Tanaka 2.00 5.00
- ❑ 17 Aubrie Lemon 2.00 5.00
- ❑ 18 Shannon Malone 2.00 5.00
- ❑ 19 Zoe Gregory 2.00 5.00
- ❑ 20 Presley Rose 2.00 5.00

2006 Bench Warmer Series Two School Girls Autographs

STATED ODDS 1:48
CARDS 1-8 ISSUED IN SERIES ONE

- ❑ 9 Miki Black 10.00 25.00
- ❑ 10 Tiffany Kyees 10.00 25.00
- ❑ 11 Catherine Kluthe 10.00 25.00
- ❑ 12 Jen Sibley 10.00 25.00
- ❑ 13 Brooke Morales 10.00 25.00
- ❑ 14 Yvette Nelson 10.00 25.00
- ❑ 15 Rebecca Mary 10.00 25.00
- ❑ 16 Tiffany Selby 10.00 25.00
- ❑ 17 Cecille Gahr 10.00 25.00
- ❑ 18 Molly Shea 10.00 25.00
- ❑ 19 Jaime Hammer 10.00 25.00
- ❑ 20 Candice Michelle 10.00 25.00
- ❑ 21 Renee Stone 10.00 25.00
- ❑ 22 Lora Lyn Peterson 10.00 25.00
- ❑ 23 Amie Decker 10.00 25.00
- ❑ 24 Carrie Stroup 10.00 25.00

2006 Bench Warmer Series Two Super Rare Autographs

STATED ODDS 1:2,400
STATED PRINT RUN 25 SER. #'d SETS
UNPRICED DUE TO SCARCITY
CARD 4 WAS NOT ISSUED

- ❑ 1 Carrie Stroup
- ❑ 2 Trishelle Cannatella
- ❑ 3 Michelle Baena
- ❑ 5 Costello Twins/10
- ❑ 6 Jaimie Hammer

2006 Bench Warmer World Cup Soccer

COMPLETE SET (90)
COMP.SET w/o SPs (72) 6.00 15.00
SP STATED ODDS 1:3

- ❑ 1 Christy Hemme .30 .75
- ❑ 2 Carrie Stroup .15 .40
- ❑ 3 Mary Riley .40 1.00
- ❑ 4 Nikki Zeno .15 .40
- ❑ 5 Shay Lyn .15 .40
- ❑ 6 Katarina Van Derham .15 .40
- ❑ 7 Yvette Nelson .15 .40
- ❑ 8 Alejandra Gutierrez .15 .40
- ❑ 9 Catherine Kluthe .15 .40
- ❑ 10 Flo Jalin .15 .40
- ❑ 11 Cecille Gahr .15 .40
- ❑ 12 Tamara Witmer .15 .40
- ❑ 13 Kasie Head .15 .40
- ❑ 14 Denyce Lawton .15 .40
- ❑ 15 Brooke Morales .15 .40
- ❑ 16 Katie Lohmann .15 .40
- ❑ 17 Nicole Bennett .15 .40
- ❑ 18 Lisa Lakatos .15 .40
- ❑ 19 Tira Provost .15 .40
- ❑ 20 Ashley Smith .15 .40
- ❑ 21 Jen Sibley .15 .40
- ❑ 22 Alix Agar .15 .40
- ❑ 23 Nikki Gray .15 .40
- ❑ 24 Tiffany Kyees .15 .40
- ❑ 25 Miki Twining .15 .40
- ❑ 26 Crystal Lett .15 .40
- ❑ 27 Alana Curry .15 .40
- ❑ 28 Jennifer Korbin .25 .60
- ❑ 29 Crystal Lett .15 .40
- ❑ 30 Allegra Wynne .15 .40
- ❑ 31 Denise Tillery .15 .40
- ❑ 32 Rochelle Loewen .15 .40
- ❑ 33 Lori Ann Valencia .15 .40
- ❑ 34 Melissa Mojo Hunter .15 .40
- ❑ 35 Stephanie Foder .15 .40
- ❑ 36 Lana Kinnear .15 .40
- ❑ 37 Catherine Kluthe .15 .40
- ❑ 38 Janice Kowalsky .15 .40
- ❑ 39 Jenny Oliver .15 .40
- ❑ 40 Kayla Paige .15 .40
- ❑ 41 Tiffany Selby .15 .40
- ❑ 42 Zoe Gregory .15 .40
- ❑ 43 Brandy Flores .15 .40
- ❑ 44 Victoria Fuller .15 .40
- ❑ 45 Destiny Davis .15 .40
- ❑ 46 Barbara Moore .15 .40
- ❑ 47 Emily Rose .15 .40
- ❑ 48 Kathie Smith .15 .40
- ❑ 49 Alana Curry .15 .40
- ❑ 50 Tira Provost .15 .40
- ❑ 51 Jaqueline Finnan .15 .40
- ❑ 52 Aiko Tanaka .15 .40
- ❑ 53 Laura Marie Buka .15 .40
- ❑ 54 Lena Yada .15 .40
- ❑ 55 Aubrie Lemon .15 .40
- ❑ 56 Lisa Gleave .15 .40
- ❑ 57 Jill Wagner .15 .40
- ❑ 58 Jessica Landon .15 .40
- ❑ 59 DJ Lady Tribe .15 .40
- ❑ 60 Angela Piccolo .15 .40
- ❑ 61 Tammy Vallejos .15 .40
- ❑ 62 Lauren Kim .15 .40
- ❑ 63 Tina Jordan .15 .40
- ❑ 64 Mishel Thorpe .15 .40
- ❑ 65 Carrie Stroup .15 .40
- ❑ 66 Jen Sibley .15 .40
- ❑ 67 Marla Esposito .15 .40
- ❑ 68 Julianna Prada .15 .40
- ❑ 69 Flo Jalin .15 .40
- ❑ 70 Shannon Malone .15 .40
- ❑ 71 Denyce Lawton .15 .40
- ❑ 72 Lisa Ligon .15 .40
- ❑ H73 Cindy Margolis SP 2.00 5.00
- ❑ H74 Nikki Ziering SP 1.25 3.00
- ❑ H75 Brande Roderick SP 1.25 3.00
- ❑ H76 Jaime Bergman SP 1.25 3.00
- ❑ H77 Christy Hemme SP 2.00 5.00
- ❑ H78 Jennifer Walcott SP 1.50 4.00
- ❑ H79 Katie Lohman 1.25 3.00
  Alana Curry SP
- ❑ H80 Katarina Van Derham SP 1.25 3.00
- ❑ H81 Cecille Gahr 1.25 3.00
  Nicole Bennett SP
- ❑ H82 Buffy Tyler SP 1.25 3.00
- ❑ H83 Costello Twins SP 1.25 3.00
- ❑ H84 Holly Madison SP 1.25 3.00
- ❑ H85 Katie Lohman SP 1.25 3.00
- ❑ H86 Nikki Zeno SP 1.25 3.00
- ❑ H87 Tiffany Kyees SP 1.25 3.00
- ❑ H88 Carrie Stroup SP 1.25 3.00
- ❑ H89 Shay Lyn SP 1.25 3.00
- ❑ H90 Mary Riley SP 2.00 5.00

2006 Bench Warmer World Cup Soccer Authentic Jersey Swatches

STATED ODDS 1:288
STATED PRINT RUN 100 SER. #'d SETS

- ❑ 1 Christy Hemme 25.00 50.00
- ❑ 2 Mary Riley 25.00 50.00
- ❑ 3 Jennifer Korbin 20.00 40.00
- ❑ 4 Carrie Stroup 15.00 30.00
- ❑ 5 Yvette Nelson 15.00 30.00
- ❑ 6 Brooke Morales 15.00 30.00
- ❑ 7 Nikki Zeno 15.00 30.00
- ❑ 8 Tamara Witmer 15.00 30.00
- ❑ 9 Katie Lohmann 15.00 30.00
- ❑ 10 Alana Curry 15.00 30.00
- ❑ 11 Alejandra Gutierrez 15.00 30.00
- ❑ 12 Flo Jalin 15.00 30.00

2006 Bench Warmer World Cup Soccer Authentic Jersey Swatches Autographs

STATED PRINT RUN 10 SER. #'d SETS
UNPRICED DUE TO SCARCITY

- ❑ 1 Christy Hemme
- ❑ 2 Mary Riley
- ❑ 3 Jennifer Korbin
- ❑ 4 Carrie Stroup
- ❑ 5 Yvette Nelson
- ❑ 6 Brooke Morales
- ❑ 7 Nikki Zeno
- ❑ 8 Tamara Witmer
- ❑ 9 Katie Lohmann
- ❑ 10 Alana Curry
- ❑ 11 Alejandra Gutierrez
- ❑ 12 Flo Jalin

2006 Bench Warmer World Cup Soccer Authentic Soccer Ball

STATED ODDS 1:2400
STATED PRINT RUN 25 SER. #'d SETS
UNPRICED DUE TO SCARCITY

- ❑ 1 Christy Hemme
- ❑ 2 Jennifer Korbin
- ❑ 3 Mary Riley
- ❑ 4 Nikki Zeno
- ❑ 5 Katarina Van Derham
- ❑ 6 Brooke Morales

2006 Bench Warmer World Cup Soccer Authentic Soccer Ball Autographs

STATED PRINT RUN 5 SER. #'d SETS

- ❑ 1 Christy Hemme
- ❑ 2 Jennifer Korbin
- ❑ 3 Mary Riley
- ❑ 4 Nikki Zeno
- ❑ 5 Katarina Van Derham
- ❑ 6 Brooke Morales

2006 Bench Warmer World Cup Soccer Autographs

STATED ODDS 1:24

- ❑ 1A Mary Riley 10.00 25.00
- ❑ 1B Brande Roderick SP
- ❑ 1C Christy Hemme SP
- ❑ 1D Nikki Ziering SP
- ❑ 2 Catherine Kluthe 6.00 15.00
- ❑ 3 Flo Jalin 6.00 15.00
- ❑ 4 Brooke Morales 6.00 15.00
- ❑ 5 Denyce Lawton 6.00 15.00
- ❑ 6 Yvette Nelson 6.00 15.00
- ❑ 7 Alana Curry 6.00 15.00
- ❑ 8 Crystal Lett 6.00 15.00
- ❑ 9 Shay Lyn 6.00 15.00
- ❑ 10 Alejandra Gutierrez 6.00 15.00
- ❑ 11A Katie Lohmann 6.00 15.00
- ❑ 11B Sandi Taylor SP
- ❑ 12 Miki Twining 6.00 15.00
- ❑ 13 Katarina Van Derham 6.00 15.00
- ❑ 14 Tira Provost 6.00 15.00
- ❑ 15 Tiffany Kyees 6.00 15.00
- ❑ 16 Jennifer Korbin 6.00 15.00
- ❑ 17A Cecille Gahr 6.00 15.00
- ❑ 17B Buffy Tyler SP 8.00 20.00
- ❑ 18 Tamara Whitmer 6.00 15.00
- ❑ 19 Jen Sibley 6.00 15.00
- ❑ 20 Nikki Gray 6.00 15.00
- ❑ 21 Alix Agar 6.00 15.00
- ❑ 22 Nikki Zeno 6.00 15.00
- ❑ 23 Kasie Head 6.00 15.00
- ❑ 24A Tabitha Taylor 6.00 15.00
- ❑ 24B Ashley Smith SP 6.00 15.00
- ❑ 25 Barbara Moore 6.00 15.00
- ❑ 26 Nicole Bennett 6.00 15.00
- ❑ 27 Lisa Lakatos 6.00 15.00
- ❑ 28 Melissa Mojo Hunter 6.00 15.00
- ❑ 29 Lana Kinnear 6.00 15.00
- ❑ 30 Carrie Stroup 6.00 15.00

2006 Bench Warmer World Cup Soccer Kiss

STATED ODDS 1:288

- ❑ 1A Christy Hemme
- ❑ 1B Nikki Ziering SP
- ❑ 2A Brooke Morales 6.00 15.00
- ❑ 2B Mary Riley SP
- ❑ 3A Catherine Kluthe 6.00 15.00
- ❑ 3B Jen Sibley SP 8.00 20.00
- ❑ 4A Yvette Nelson 6.00 15.00
- ❑ 4B Nikki Zeno SP
- ❑ 5A Jennifer Korbin - green top 8.00 20.00
- ❑ 5B Jennifer Korbin - orange top SP
- ❑ 6 Tamara Whitmer 6.00 15.00
- ❑ 7 Alejandra Gutierrez 6.00 15.00
- ❑ 8 Denyce Lawton 6.00 15.00
- ❑ 9 Flo Jalin 6.00 15.00
- ❑ 10 Katie Lohman
- ❑ 11 Lana Kinnear 6.00 15.00
- ❑ 12 Carrie Stroup

2006 Bench Warmer World Cup Soccer Kiss Autographs

STATED PRINT RUN 5 SER. #'d SETS

- ❑ 1A Christy Hemme
- ❑ 1B Nikki Ziering
- ❑ 2A Brooke Morales
- ❑ 2B Mary Riley
- ❑ 3A Catherine Kluthe
- ❑ 3B Jen Sibley
- ❑ 4A Yvette Nelson
- ❑ 4B Nikki Zeno
- ❑ 5A Jennifer Korbin
- ❑ 5B Jennifer Korbin
- ❑ 6 Tamara Whitmer
- ❑ 7 Alejandra Gutierrez
- ❑ 8 Denyce Lawton
- ❑ 9 Flo Jalin
- ❑ 10 Katie Lohman
- ❑ 11 Lana Kinnear
- ❑ 12 Carrie Stroup

2006 Bench Warmer World Cup Soccer Racer Girls

COMPLETE SET (12) 12.00 30.00
STATED ODDS 1:12

- ❑ 1 Lisa Ligon 2.50 6.00
- ❑ 2 Alicia Benham 2.50 6.00
- ❑ 3 Amy Currie 2.50 6.00
- ❑ 4 Mackenzie Mack 2.50 6.00
- ❑ 5 Annamarie Lytle 2.50 6.00
- ❑ 6 Shay Lyn SP 2.50 6.00
- ❑ 7 Tina Jordan 2.50 6.00
- ❑ 8 Kathie Smith 2.50 6.00
- ❑ 9 Masha Christensen 2.50 6.00
- ❑ 10 Kerri Kasem SP 2.50 6.00
- ❑ 11 Stacy Fuson SP 2.50 6.00
- ❑ 12 Nikki Zeno SP 2.50 6.00

2006 Buffy the Vampire Slayer Memories

COMPLETE SET (90) 5.00 12.00

- ❑ 1 Buffy Memories .15 .40
- ❑ 2 Arrival .15 .40
- ❑ 3 Kiss .15 .40
- ❑ 4 Angelus .15 .40
- ❑ 5 Friend Or Foe? .15 .40
- ❑ 6 Alive Again .15 .40
- ❑ 7 Killer Poker .15 .40
- ❑ 8 Drawn To Spike .15 .40
- ❑ 9 Final Battle .15 .40
- ❑ 10 New Blood .15 .40
- ❑ 11 Losing Jenny .15 .40
- ❑ 12 Working Retail .15 .40
- ❑ 13 Watcher's Nightmare .15 .40
- ❑ 14 Watcher Turned Slayer .15 .40
- ❑ 15 Buffy Lives .15 .40
- ❑ 16 Channel Of Power .15 .40
- ❑ 17 Last Watcher .15 .40
- ❑ 18 Leaving The Hellmouth .15 .40
- ❑ 19 Volunteer .15 .40
- ❑ 20 Fluke .15 .40
- ❑ 21 Doubled .15 .40
- ❑ 22 Anya .15 .40
- ❑ 23 Proposing .15 .40
- ❑ 24 Duped .15 .40
- ❑ 25 Jealous .15 .40
- ❑ 26 Facing Willow .15 .40
- ❑ 27 Wounded .15 .40
- ❑ 28 Befriending Buffy .15 .40
- ❑ 29 Doppelganger .15 .40
- ❑ 30 Oz .15 .40
- ❑ 31 Captive .15 .40
- ❑ 32 Raising Buffy .15 .40
- ❑ 33 Reunited .15 .40
- ❑ 34 Dark .15 .40
- ❑ 35 New Love .15 .40
- ❑ 36 Transcendent .15 .40
- ❑ 37 Popular .15 .40
- ❑ 38 Bound .15 .40
- ❑ 39 Xander .15 .40
- ❑ 40 Disrespected .15 .40
- ❑ 41 Discovered .15 .40
- ❑ 42 Together .15 .40
- ❑ 43 Broke .15 .40
- ❑ 44 Prom .15 .40
- ❑ 45 Graduation .15 .40
- ❑ 46 Liam .15 .40
- ❑ 47 Evil .15 .40
- ❑ 48 Slain .15 .40
- ❑ 49 Together .15 .40
- ❑ 50 Breaking Off .15 .40
- ❑ 51 Ideal .15 .40
- ❑ 52 Poor Apologies .15 .40
- ❑ 53 Forever .15 .40
- ❑ 54 Leaving .15 .40
- ❑ 55 Another Day .15 .40
- ❑ 56 Loss .15 .40
- ❑ 57 Returned .15 .40
- ❑ 58 Menaced .15 .40
- ❑ 59 Resolved .15 .40
- ❑ 60 Neglected .15 .40
- ❑ 61 Bride .15 .40
- ❑ 62 Clem .15 .40
- ❑ 63 Sister .15 .40
- ❑ 64 Aud .15 .40
- ❑ 65 Stuck .15 .40
- ❑ 66 Capitalist .15 .40
- ❑ 67 Singing Bride .15 .40
- ❑ 68 Demon .15 .40
- ❑ 69 Bunny Fear .15 .40
- ❑ 70 Slain .15 .40
- ❑ 71 Halfrek .15 .40
- ❑ 72 Gone .15 .40
- ❑ 73 Poet .15 .40
- ❑ 74 Drusilla .15 .40
- ❑ 75 Good Day .15 .40
- ❑ 76 Harmony .15 .40
- ❑ 77 Niblet .15 .40
- ❑ 78 Ensouled .15 .40
- ❑ 79 Mum .15 .40
- ❑ 80 Enchanted Evening .15 .40
- ❑ 81 Champion .15 .40
- ❑ 82 Willow .15 .40
- ❑ 83 Commitement .15 .40
- ❑ 84 Attacked .15 .40
- ❑ 85 Cared For .15 .40
- ❑ 86 Enchanted .15 .40
- ❑ 87 Dawn's Friend .15 .40
- ❑ 88 Leaving .15 .40
- ❑ 89 Cut Down .15 .40
- ❑ 90 Checklist .15 .40

2006 Buffy the Vampire Slayer Memories Inkplates Blue

STATED PRINT RUN 1 SER. #'d SET
UNPRICED DUE TO SCARCITY

2006 Buffy the Vampire Slayer Memories Inkplates Cyan

STATED PRINT RUN 1 SER. #'d SET
UNPRICED DUE TO SCARCITY

2006 Buffy the Vampire Slayer Memories Inkplates Magenta

STATED PRINT RUN 1 SER. #'d SET
UNPRICED DUE TO SCARCITY

2006 Buffy the Vampire Slayer Memories Inkplates Yellow

STATED PRINT RUN 1 SER. #'d SET
UNPRICED DUE TO SCARCITY

2006 Buffy the Vampire Slayer Memories Apocalypses

STATED ODDS 1:17

- AP1 The Master 1.25 3.00
- AP2 Acathla 1.25 3.00
- AP3 The Mayor 1.25 3.00
- AP4 Glory 1.25 3.00
- AP5 Dark Willow 1.25 3.00
- AP6 First Evil 1.25 3.00

2006 Buffy the Vampire Slayer Memories Box Loaders

COMPLETE SET (4) 10.00 25.00
STATED ODDS ONE PER BOX

- BL1 Buffy 2.00 5.00
- BL2 Kendra 2.00 5.00
- BL3 Faith 2.00 5.00
- CL1 Legacy 5.00 12.00

2006 Buffy the Vampire Slayer Memories Pieceworks

STATED ODDS 1:18

- PW1 Buffy's Pants 10.00 25.00
- PW2 Buffy's Sweater & Camisole 10.00 25.00
- PW3 Buffy's Leather Jacket
- PW4 Anya's Dress & Slip 4.00 10.00
- PW5 Giles' Shirt 4.00 10.00
- PW6 Dawn's Pajama Top 4.00 10.00
- PW7 Willow's Top 4.00 10.00
- PW8 Tara's Sweater 4.00 10.00
- PW9 Principal Wood's Suit Pants 4.00 10.00
- PW10 Xander's Jeans 4.00 10.00
- PW11 Kennedy's Pajama Top 4.00 10.00
- PW12 Molly's Pajama Bottoms 4.00 10.00
- PW13 Vi's T-Shirt 4.00 10.00
- PW14 Shadow Man's Tunic 4.00 10.00
- PW15 Rona's Overalls 4.00 10.00
- PW16a Andrew's Jacket
- PW16b Andrew's Jacket w Stripe
- PW17A Molly & Kennedy
- PW17B Rona, Vi, & Amanda
- PR1 Pieceworks Redemption

2006 Buffy the Vampire Slayer Memories Reinforcements

STATED ODDS 1:11

- R1 Reinforcements .75 2.00
- R2 Reinforcements .75 2.00
- R3 Reinforcements .75 2.00
- R4 Reinforcements .75 2.00
- R5 Reinforcements .75 2.00
- R6 Reinforcements .75 2.00
- R7 Reinforcements .75 2.00
- R8 Reinforcements .75 2.00
- R9 Reinforcements .75 2.00

2006 Charmed Destiny

COMPLETE SET (72) 4.00 10.00

- 1 Title Card .10 .30
- 2 Pru Halliwell .10 .30
- 3 The Painted World .10 .30
- 4 Ms. Hellfire .10 .30
- 5 P3 H2O .10 .30
- 6 They're Everywhere .10 .30
- 7 Aunt Prue? .10 .30
- 8 She's A Man, Baby, A Man .10 .30
- 9 Give Me A Sign .10 .30
- 10 Piper Halliwell .10 .30
- 11 Excalibur .10 .30
- 12 Magic School .10 .30
- 13 Chris-Crossed .10 .30
- 14 Love Conquers All .10 .30
- 15 Run, Piper, Run .10 .30
- 16 Out Of Focus .10 .30
- 17 Vaya Con Leos .10 .30
- 18 Magical Mothering .10 .30
- 19 Phoebe Halliwell .10 .30
- 20 Ask Phoebe .10 .30
- 21 Movie Magic .10 .30
- 22 Pick A Potion .10 .30
- 23 Love Or Magic? .10 .30
- 24 Baby Steps .10 .30
- 25 On Ice .10 .30
- 26 Kid Stuff .10 .30
- 27 Beauty And Grace .10 .30
- 28 Paige Matthews .10 .30
- 29 Once In A Blue Moon .10 .30
- 30 Witchness Protection .10 .30
- 31 Oh, Sister! .10 .30
- 32 The Power Of Three Unplugged .10 .30
- 33 Where's Wyatt .10 .30
- 34 Save Billie: Vol. 1 .10 .30
- 35 Cops And Kids .10 .30
- 36 A Beautiful Bride .10 .30
- 37 La Femme Billie .10 .30
- 38 By The Book .10 .30
- 39 Agent Murphy .10 .30
- 40 Paige And Sam .10 .30
- 41 Little Boys, Big Toys .10 .30
- 42 All Grown Up .10 .30
- 43 All Dressed Up .10 .30
- 44 Back From The Future .10 .30
- 45 Pinch Hitting .10 .30
- 46 Piper & Leo .10 .30
- 47 Leo Wyatt .10 .30
- 48 Phoebe & Dex .10 .30
- 49 Coop .10 .30
- 50 Paige & Henry .10 .30
- 51 Paige & Kyle .10 .30
- 52 Billie & J.D. .10 .30
- 53 Grams & The Necromancer .10 .30
- 54 Rebecca & Jim .10 .30
- 55 True Love .10 .30
- 56 Reality Bites .10 .30
- 57 Magical Mortal .10 .30
- 58 Cupid's Arrow .10 .30
- 59 Future Chris .10 .30
- 60 Drake .10 .30
- 61 Super Billie .10 .30
- 62 The Key .10 .30
- 63 Frozen Moment .10 .30
- 64 Gideon .10 .30
- 65 The Avatars .10 .30
- 66 Kira .10 .30
- 67 Zankou .10 .30
- 68 The Ultimate Power .10 .30
- 69 Angel Of Destiny .10 .30
- 70 Grams .10 .30
- 71 The Charmed Ones .10 .30
- 72 Checklist .10 .30

2006 Charmed Destiny Autographs

STATED ODDS 1:36

- A1 Holly Marie Combs 75.00 150.00
- A2 Holly Marie Combs 100.00 175.00
Brian Krause
- A3 Jennifer Rhodes 5.00 12.00
- A4 Scott Jaeck 5.00 12.00
- A5 Rebecca Balding 5.00 12.00
- A6 Eric Dane 5.00 12.00
- A7 Kerr Smith 5.00 12.00
- A8 Gildart Jackson 5.00 12.00
- A9 Billy Drago 20.00 40.00
- A10 Brandon Quinn 5.00 12.00
- A11 Marnette Patterson 6.00 15.00

2006 Charmed Destiny Bad Karma

STATED ODDS 1:17

- BK1 Imara 1.00 2.50
- BK2 Evil Wyatt 1.00 2.50
- BK3 Haas 1.00 2.50
- BK4 The Dogon 1.00 2.50
- BK5 Burke 1.00 2.50
- BK6 Reinhardt 1.00 2.50

2006 Charmed Destiny Box Loaders

COMPLETE SET (3) 3.00 8.00
STATED ODDS ONE PER BOX
CL1 STATED ODDS ONE PER CASE

- BL1 Power Shortage 1.25 3.00
- BL2 Powered by Possession 1.25 3.00
- BL3 The Power of Love 1.25 3.00
- CL1 Brad Kern AU
CASE INSERT

2006 Charmed Destiny Pieceworks

STATED ODDS 1:36

- PW1a Rose McGowan 15.00 30.00
- PW1b Rose McGowan 60.00 120.00
(Bead and Lace variant)
- PW2 Alyssa Milano 20.00 40.00
- PW3 Holly Marie Combs 15.00 30.00
- PW4 Brian Krause 4.00 10.00
- PW5 Kaley Cuoco 6.00 15.00
- PW6 Ivan Sergei 4.00 10.00
- PW7 Jason Lewis 4.00 10.00
- PW8 Alyssa Milano 20.00 40.00
- PW9 Holly Marie Combs 25.00 50.00
Alyssa Milano
- PWR1 Redemption Card

2006 Charmed Destiny Unforgettable

STATED ODDS 1:11

- U1 Magical Matrimony 1.00 2.50
- U2 Wedded Bliss 1.00 2.50
- U3 Beautiful Bridesmaids 1.00 2.50
- U4 Cupid's Arrow 1.00 2.50
- U5 Charmed Again 1.00 2.50
- U6 Farewell, Prue 1.00 2.50
- U7 Black Magic Bride 1.00 2.50
- U8 Lana & The Fed 1.00 2.50
- U9 Family History 1.00 2.50

2006 The Complete Avengers

COMPLETE SET (81) 4.00 10.00
ARCHIVE CUT ISSUED AS 2-CASE INCENTIVE

- 1 Title Card .10 .30
- 2 Issue 1, September 1963 .10 .30
- 3 Issue 4, March 1964 .10 .30
- 4 Issue 8, September 1964 .10 .30
- 5 Issue 9, October 1964 .10 .30
- 6 Issue 16, May 1965 .10 .30
- 7 Issue 19, August 1965 .10 .30
- 8 Issue 28, May 1966 .10 .30
- 9 Issue 32, September 1966 .10 .30
- 10 Issue 38, March 1967 .10 .30
- 11 Issue 52, May 1968 .10 .30
- 12 Issue 58, November 1968 .10 .30
- 13 Issue 60, January 1969 .10 .30
- 14 Issue 63, April 1969 .10 .30
- 15 Issue 69, October 1969 .10 .30
- 16 Issue 72, January 1970 .10 .30
- 17 Issue 89, June 1971 .10 .30
- 18 Issue 94, December 1971 .10 .30
- 19 Issue 96, February 1972 .10 .30
- 20 Issue 102, August 1972 .10 .30
- 21 Issue 114, August 1973 .10 .30
- 22 Issue 118, December 1973 .10 .30
- 23 Issue 120, February 1974 .10 .30
- 24 Issue 127, September 1974 .10 .30
- 25 Issue 131, January 1975 .10 .30
- 26 Issue 149, July 1976 .10 .30
- 27 Issue 153, November 1976 .10 .30
- 28 Issue 161, July 1977 .10 .30
- 29 Issue 165, November 1977 .10 .30
- 30 Issue 177, November 1978 .10 .30
- 31 Issue 171, May 1978 .10 .30
- 32 Issue 181, March 1979 .10 .30
- 33 Issue 187, September 1979 .10 .30
- 34 Issue 196, June 1980 .10 .30
- 35 Issue 213, November 1981 .10 .30
- 36 Issue 217, March 1982 .10 .30
- 37 Issue 221, July 1982 .10 .30
- 38 Issue 227, January 1983 .10 .30
- 39 Issue 230, April 1983 .10 .30
- 40 Issue 243, May 1984 .10 .30
- 41 Issue 255, May 1985 .10 .30
- 42 Issue 261, November 1985 .10 .30
- 43 Issue 269, July 1986 .10 .30
- 44 Issue 274, December 1986 .10 .30
- 45 Issue 276, February 1987 .10 .30
- 46 Issue 297, November 1988 .10 .30
- 47 Issue 300, February 1989 .10 .30
- 48 Issue 316, April 1990 .10 .30
- 49 Issue 318, June 1990 .10 .30
- 50 Issue 329, February 1991 .10 .30
- 51 Issue 333, June 1991 .10 .30
- 52 Issue 347, May 1992 .10 .30
- 53 Issue 355, October 1992 .10 .30
- 54 Issue 360, March 1993 .10 .30
- 55 Issue 362, May 1993 .10 .30
- 56 Issue 375, June 1994 .10 .30
- 57 Issue 387, June 1995 .10 .30
- 58 Issue 395, February 1996 .10 .30
- 59 Issue 1, November 1996 .10 .30
- 60 Issue 7, May 1997 .10 .30
- 61 Issue 10, August 1997 .10 .30
- 62 Issue 1, February 1998 .10 .30
- 63 Issue 3, April 1998 .10 .30
- 64 Issue 22, November 1999 .10 .30
- 65 Issue 34, November 2000 .10 .30
- 66 Issue 43, August 2001 .10 .30
- 67 Issue 45, October 2001 .10 .30
- 68 Issue 49, February 2002 .10 .30
- 69 Issue 54, July 2002 .10 .30
- 70 Issue 68, August 2003 .10 .30
- 71 Issue 70, October 2003 .10 .30
- 72 Issue 85, October 2004 .10 .30
- 73 Issue 88, December 2004 .10 .30
- 74 Issue 1, February 2005 .10 .30
- 75 Issue 6, June 2005 .10 .30
- 76 Annual 1, April 2006 .10 .30
- 77 Issue 20, August 2006 .10 .30
- 78 Issue 22, September 2006 .10 .30
- 79 Checklist 1 .10 .30
- 80 Checklist 2 .10 .30
- 81 Checklist 3 .10 .30
- NNO Archive Cut 25.00 60.00
(issued as 2-case incentive)

2006 The Complete Avengers Autographs

COLAN STATED ODDS ONE PER CASE
THOMAS STATED ODDS ONE PER BINDER

- 1 Gene Colan 10.00 25.00
- 2 Roy Thomas 10.00 25.00

2006 The Complete Avengers Earth's Mightiest Heroes

STATED ODDS 1:20

- MH1 Earth's Mightiest Heroes 1.50 4.00
- MH2 Earth's Mightiest Heroes 1.50 4.00
- MH3 Earth's Mightiest Heroes 1.50 4.00
- MH4 Earth's Mightiest Heroes 1.50 4.00
- MH5 Earth's Mightiest Heroes 1.50 4.00
- MH6 Earth's Mightiest Heroes 1.50 4.00
- MH7 Earth's Mightiest Heroes 1.50 4.00
- MH8 Earth's Mightiest Heroes 1.50 4.00
- MH9 Earth's Mightiest Heroes 1.50 4.00
- MH10 Earth's Mightiest Heroes 1.50 4.00
- MH11 Earth's Mightiest Heroes 1.50 4.00
- MH12 Earth's Mightiest Heroes 1.50 4.00
- MH13 Earth's Mightiest Heroes 1.50 4.00
- MH14 Earth's Mightiest Heroes 1.50 4.00
- MH15 Earth's Mightiest Heroes 1.50 4.00
- MH16 Earth's Mightiest Heroes 1.50 4.00
- MH17 Earth's Mightiest Heroes 1.50 4.00
- MH18 Earth's Mightiest Heroes 1.50 4.00

2006 The Complete Avengers Greatest Enemies

COMPLETE SET (9) 4.00 10.00
STATED ODDS 1:10

- GE1 Lords of Chaos 1.00 2.50
- GE2 Lords of Chaos 1.00 2.50
- GE3 Lords of Chaos 1.00 2.50
- GE4 Conquerors of the Cosmos 1.00 2.50
- GE5 Conquerors of the Cosmos 1.00 2.50
- GE6 Conquerors of the Cosmos 1.00 2.50
- GE7 Masters of Evil 1.00 2.50
- GE8 Masters of Evil 1.00 2.50
- GE9 Masters of Evil 1.00 2.50

2006 The Complete Avengers Legendary Heroes

STATED ODDS 1:40

- LH1 Captain America 3.00 8.00
- LH2 Thor 3.00 8.00
- LH3 Iron Man 3.00 8.00
- LH4 Giant Man 3.00 8.00
- LH5 The Wasp 3.00 8.00
- LH6 Hulk 3.00 8.00
- LH7 Sub-Mariner 3.00 8.00
- LH8 Scarlet Witch 3.00 8.00
- LH9 Hawkeye 3.00 8.00

2006 The Complete Avengers Sketch Cards

STATED ODDS 1:40

- 1 Mahmud A. Asrar/310*
- 2 Darren Auck/268*
- 3 James Bukauskas/117*
- 4 Jose Carlos/305*
- 5 Jeff Chandler/250*
- 6 Justin Chung/126*
- 7 Igor Cicarini/224*
- 8 Dan Day/300*
- 9 David Day/307*
- 10 Renae De Liz/399*
- 11 Ray Dillon/398*
- 12 Guy Dorian/132*
- 13 Ian Dorian/77*
- 14 Brent Engstrom/346*
- 15 Dave Fox/188*
- 16 Otis Frampton/100*
- 17 Matthew Goodmanson/275*
- 18 Grant Gould/251*
- 19 Don Hillsman/300*
- 20 Tom Hodges/265*
- 21 John Jackman/240*
- 22 Brian Kong/378*
- 23 Jim Kyle/296*
- 24 Stan Lee/100*
- 25 Mike Lilly/150*
- 26 Dave Lynch/250*
- 27 Warren Martineck/266*
- 28 Brandon McKinney/307*
- 29 Rich Molinelli/298*
- 30 Tom Nguyen/139*
- 31 Tony Perna/250*
- 32 Ricardo Ratton/266*
- 33 Tyler Richlen/257*
- 34 Tone Rodriguez/295*
- 35 Scott Rosema/121*
- 36 Joe Rubinstein/335*
- 37 Uko Smith/356*
- 38 Jason Sobol/228*
- 39 Mark Texeira/360*
- 40 Eddie Valdo/210*
- 41 Jeff Welborn/310*
- 42 Ron Wilson/170*
- 43 Cat Staggs SP

2006 The Dead Zone Autograph Expansion

DEBOER/BRUNO AUTO ISSUED AS 2-SET INCENTIVE

- 1 Anna Hagan
- 2 Anne Marie Loder
- 3 Anthony Michael Hall
- 4 Bill Mondy
- 5 Chris Bruno
- 6 Frank Whaley
- 7 Ione Skye
- 8 James Handy
- 9 Lochlyn Monro
- 10 Nicole deBoer
- 11 Nicole deBoer
Chris Bruno/ (issued as 2-set incentive)

2006 Elvis Lives

COMPLETE SET (90) 4.00 10.00

- 1 Sun Studios .10 .30
- 2 Louisiana Hayride .10 .30
- 3 RCA Studios .10 .30
- 4 Andy Griffith Show .10 .30
- 5 Overton Park Concert .10 .30
- 6 Tampa 1955 .10 .30
- 7 Cadillacs .10 .30
- 8 On the Road .10 .30
- 9 Backstage in Vegas .10 .30
- 10 New Frontier Hotel .10 .30
- 11 Motorcycles .10 .30
- 12 Hound Dog .10 .30
- 13 Ed Sullivan Show .10 .30
- 14 Love Me Tender .10 .30
- 15 Love Me Tender .10 .30
- 16 Tupelo Homecoming .10 .30
- 17 1957 Tupelo .10 .30
- 18 Graceland .10 .30
- 19 Graceland .10 .30
- 20 Hawaii .10 .30
- 21 Army Recording .10 .30
- 22 Loving You (Movie) .10 .30
- 22 Loving You (Record) .10 .30
- 24 Jailhouse Rock (Record) .10 .30
- 25 Jailhouse Rock (Movie) .10 .30
- 26 King Creole (Record) .10 .30
- 27 King Creole (Movie) .10 .30
- 28 GI Blues .10 .30
- 29 Flaming Star .10 .30
- 30 Blue Hawaii .10 .30
- 31 Follow that Dream .10 .30
- 32 Kid Gallahad .10 .30
- 33 Girls Girls Girls .10 .30
- 34 It Happened at the World's Fair .10 .30
- 35 Viva Las Vegas .10 .30
- 36 Roustabout .10 .30
- 37 Girl Happy .10 .30
- 38 Frankie & Johnny .10 .30
- 39 Spinout .10 .30
- 40 Easy Come, Easy Go .10 .30
- 41 Stay Away, Joe .10 .30
- 42 Speedway .10 .30
- 43 Charro .10 .30
- 44 The Trouble With Girls .10 .30
- 45 Elvis on the Big Screen .10 .30
- 46 Run-Throughs and Rehearsals .10 .30
- 47 Production .10 .30
- 48 Opening Number .10 .30
- 49 68 Special Portraits .10 .30
- 50 Gospel Taping .10 .30
- 51 The Sit Down .10 .30
- 52 Sit Down 2 .10 .30
- 53 The Stand Up .10 .30
- 54 Stand Up Rolling Stone Cover .10 .30
- 55 Black Leather .10 .30
- 56 Finale .10 .30
- 57 Finale .10 .30
- 58 That's the Way it Is .10 .30
- 59 MGM Studios .10 .30
- 60 Capes .10 .30
Jumpsuit
- 61 Las Vegas Summer Show .10 .30
- 62 Phoenix Show .10 .30
- 63 Las Vegas Winter Show .10 .30
- 64 Scarves .10 .30
- 65 Aloha from Hawaii .10 .30
- 66 Aloha from Hawaii .10 .30
- 67 Houston Show .10 .30
- 68 The Records .10 .30
- 69 Huntsville Alabama .10 .30
- 70 Concert Stats .10 .30
- 71 On the Road .10 .30
- 72 On Tour .10 .30
- 73 Dorsey Brothers Show .10 .30
- 74 On the Phone .10 .30
- 75 Steve Allen Show .10 .30
- 76 Recording Sessions .10 .30
- 77 Listening to Records .10 .30
- 78 Train Ride .10 .30
- 79 On a Date .10 .30
- 80 Elvis and Parents .10 .30
- 81 Audubon Drive .10 .30
- 82 Elvis on Motorcycle .10 .30
- 83 Russwood Stadium .10 .30
- 84 Army .10 .30
- 85 CC Rider .10 .30
- 86 Home for Christmas .10 .30
- 87 Comeback Sheet .10 .30
- 88 Glory Halleluiah .10 .30
- 89 Psychedelic Elvis .10 .30
- 90 Checklist .10 .30
US Male

2006 Elvis Lives Artist Proofs Autographs

- AW1 Alfred Wertheimer
On the Phone
- AW2 Alfred Wertheimer
Motorcycle
- JP1 Joe Petruccio
Home for X-Mas
- JP2 Joe Petruccio
CC Rider

2006 Elvis Lives Autographs

STATED ODDS 1:144
CARDS LISTED ALPHABETICALLY

- 1 James Burton
- 2 Yvonne Craig
- 3 DJ Fontana
- 4 Scotty Moore
- 5 Gordon Stoker
- 6 Ray Walker
- 7 DJ Fontana
Scotty Moore

2006 Elvis Lives Cut Signatures

UNPRICED DUE TO SCARCITY

- HC1 Elvis Presley Check/2
- HC2 Elvis Presley Photo/1

2006 Elvis Lives Elvis Worn Memorabilia

MEMORABILIA COMBINED ODDS 1:240

- EWS1 Blue Shirt with White Polka Dots
- EWS2 Red Shirt
- EWS3 Blue Scarf

2006 Elvis Lives Elvis Worn Memorabilia Gold

MEMORABILIA COMBINED ODDS 1:240
PRINT RUN 299 SERIAL #'d SETS

- EWS1 Blue Shirt with White Polka Dots
- EWS2 Red Shirt
- EWS3 Blue Scarf

2006 Elvis Lives Elvis Worn Memorabilia Platinum

MEMORABILIA COMBINED ODDS 1:240
PRINT RUN 99 SERIAL #'d SETS

- EWS1 Blue Shirt with White Polka Dots
- EWS2 Red Shirt
- EWS3 Blue Scarf

2006 Elvis Lives Fashions

STATED ODDS 1:6

- 1 Gold Lame Suit .50 1.25
- 2 68 Special-Finale .50 1.25
- 3 68 Special-Black Leather .50 1.25
- 4 Concho .50 1.25
- 5 Burning Love .50 1.25
- 6 Powder Blue Nailhead .50 1.25
- 7 White .50 1.25
Turquoise
- 8 Butterfly .50 1.25
- 9 Tiffany .50 1.25
- 10 American Eagle Suit .50 1.25
- 11 American Indian .50 1.25
- 12 Blue Phoenix .50 1.25

2006 Family Guy Season Two

COMPLETE SET (72) 4.00 10.00

- 1 Family Guy .10 .30
- 2 Kiss My Ass .10 .30
- 3 Jump Through Hoops .10 .30
- 4 Gas And Bullets .10 .30
- 5 Whoops! .10 .30
- 6 The Couch It Is .10 .30
- 7 One-Upmanship .10 .30
- 8 Boxcar Crooners .10 .30
- 9 Giddyap .10 .30
- 10 Home Sweet Home? .10 .30
- 11 The Fuzzy Clam .10 .30
- 12 Flappy Jacks .10 .30
- 13 Quahog Beautiful People'S Club .10 .30
- 14 Quahog City Hall .10 .30
- 15 The 13Th Step Liquor Store .10 .30
- 16 Health Care Center .10 .30
- 17 New Quahog City Hall .10 .30
- 18 Hugs And Kisses Day Care .10 .30
- 19 Money, Money...Money! .10 .30
- 20 Impossible Job .10 .30
- 21 Tyrant .10 .30
- 22 Freakin' Pope .10 .30
- 23 Y2K .10 .30
- 24 Better Late Than Never .10 .30
- 25 Outrages! .10 .30
- 26 Urine Love .10 .30
- 27 Who'S The Boss .10 .30
- 28 Crack & Pancakes .10 .30
- 29 Man Boob .10 .30
- 30 Death For Its Own Sake .10 .30
- 31 Talent Coming Out His Ass .10 .30
- 32 Song .10 .30
- 33 He'S So Sensitive .10 .30
- 34 Catfight! .10 .30
- 35 Tumor-Syphillis..Itis..O-Osis .10 .30
- 36 Dirty, Dirty, Dirty .10 .30
- 37 Mud Slinging .10 .30
- 38 This Is Man'S Work .10 .30
- 39 There's Only Christobel .10 .30
- 40 Baby'S Got Back .10 .30
- 41 Got Acrimony? .10 .30
- 42 Hot Meg? .10 .30
- 43 Biscuit In Stitches .10 .30
- 44 Caught Red Handed .10 .30
- 45 Give Up The Toad Now .10 .30
- 46 Coolest Kid In School .10 .30
- 47 Cookiedigger .10 .30
- 48 Coffee, Tea Or Milk? .10 .30
- 49 Badda Bing .10 .30
- 50 Always Valet .10 .30
- 51 No "Normies" Allowed .10 .30
- 52 Chunky Monkey .10 .30
- 53 Joe-Hio .10 .30
- 54 Glorious Surrender .10 .30
- 55 So Wrong .10 .30
- 56 The Real Scoop .10 .30
- 57 Peter'S Mecca .10 .30
- 58 B-Flat Loaded .10 .30
- 59 Fathers And Sons .10 .30
- 60 Mind Control .10 .30
- 61 Rooster? .10 .30
- 62 Yummy .10 .30
- 63 Tom Under Fire! .10 .30
- 64 Potty Training .10 .30
- 65 Sleepover Nightmare .10 .30
- 66 Ewwwww .10 .30
- 67 Be Honest .10 .30
- 68 Advice For Stewie .10 .30
- 69 The Colors, Man .10 .30
- 70 Banana .10 .30
- 71 U-G-L-Y .10 .30
- 72 Checklist .10 .30

2006 Family Guy Season Two Autographs

- A7 Alex Borstein 7.50 15.00
- A8 Adam Carolla 10.00 20.00
- A9 Michael Mckean 5.00 10.00
- A10 Faith Ford 5.00 10.00
- A11 Jennifer Tilly 10.00 20.00
- A12 Wally Wingert 5.00 10.00

2006 Family Guy Season Two Box Loaders

COMPLETE SET (4) 8.00 20.00
STATED ODDS ONE PER BOX
CL1 STATED ODDS ONE PER CASE

- BL1 Please Fasten Seatbelts 1.50 4.00
- BL2 The Real Stewie 1.50 4.00
- BL3 Stewie Loves Death 1.50 4.00
- CL1 The Real World 5.00 12.00
CASE INSERT

2006 Family Guy Season Two Griffin Family Tree

STATED ODDS 1:11

- FT1 Aunt Margarite Pewterschmidt .75 2.00
- FT2 Babs Pewterschmidt .75 2.00
- FT3 Great Great Uncle Angus Griffin .75 2.00

FT4 Grandma Griffin .75 2.00
FT5 Carter Pewterschmidt .75 2.00
FT6 Huck Finn Griffin .75 2.00
FT7 Jabba the Griffin .75 2.00
FT8 Grandpa Francis Griffin .75 2.00
FT9 Ulysses S. Griffin .75 2.00

2006 Family Guy Season Two Sketch Cards
STATED ODDS 1:24
S1 Tone Rodriguez 25.00 50.00
S2 Mark Dos Santos 25.00 50.00
S3 Nar 150.00 300.00
S4 John Czop 25.00 50.00
S5 Billy Martinez 12.50 25.00
S6 Chris Moreno 12.50 25.00
S7 Joel Gomez 15.00 30.00
S8 Rich Koslowski 15.00 30.00
S9 Cynthia Cummens 20.00 40.00
S10 James Rogovoy 12.50 25.00
S11 Rudy Vasquez 12.50 25.00
S12 Chance Raspberry 15.00 30.00
S13 William O'Neill 15.00 30.00

2006 Family Guy Season Two The Life Of Brian
STATED ODDS 1:17
LB1 Open Bar 1.00 2.50
LB2 Therapy 1.00 2.50
LB3 Gulp! 1.00 2.50
LB4 Good Try 1.00 2.50
LB5 Bar Fly 1.00 2.50
LB6 Always There For You 1.00 2.50

2006 Firefly The Complete Collection
COMPLETE SET (72) 5.00 12.00
1 Firefly .15 .40
2 Malcolm Reynolds .15 .40
3 Zoe Washburne .15 .40
4 Hoban Washburne .15 .40
5 Inara Serra .15 .40
6 Jayne Cobb .15 .40
7 Kaylee Frye .15 .40
8 Simon Tam .15 .40
9 River Tam .15 .40
10 Shepherd Book .15 .40
11 Saffron .15 .40
12 Jubal Early .15 .40
13 Betrayal At Serenity .15 .40
14 Mysterious Stowaway .15 .40
15 On The Run From The Reavers .15 .40
16 Heist From On High .15 .40
17 A Getaway Ship .15 .40
18 The Only Choice .15 .40
19 Ship Of Mystery .15 .40
20 Dark Survivor .15 .40
21 Eluding The Alliance .15 .40
22 An Affair To Remember .15 .40
23 Trouble On The Way .15 .40
24 A Duel For Her Honor .15 .40
25 Cattleman At Heart .15 .40
26 The Tams Captured .15 .40
27 Doctor Or Deliverer? .15 .40
28 Disguised Intentions .15 .40
29 The Truth About Saffron .15 .40
30 Blasting The Space Web .15 .40
31 Living Legend Jayne .15 .40
32 Fear Of The Unknown .15 .40
33 Stitch And The Statue .15 .40
34 A Birthday Gone Bad .15 .40
35 The Ship Under Siege .15 .40
36 Rescuers Or Marauders? .15 .40
37 Invading A Hospital .15 .40
38 Bringing River Back .15 .40
39 A Boat Divided .15 .40
40 Niska's Revenge .15 .40
41 Woman To Woman .15 .40
42 Mal's Fight For Life .15 .40
43 Back For More Mayhem .15 .40
44 A Gun Worth Stealing .15 .40
45 Go Naked In The World .15 .40
46 Fate Of A Comrade .15 .40
47 Tracey's Desperate Move .15 .40
48 Death Of A Soldier .15 .40
49 Sinners And Heroes .15 .40
50 For The Love Of Mal .15 .40
51 Defying Rance's Might .15 .40
52 The Bounty Hunter .15 .40
53 Armored Intruder .15 .40
54 Early To Bed...For Good .15 .40
55 A Firefly To The Rescue .15 .40
56 Precision Landing .15 .40
57 Narrow Escapes .15 .40
58 Inara's Shuttle .15 .40
59 A Universe In Conflict .15 .40
60 Reavers Pushing On .15 .40
61 Tracked By The Alliance .15 .40
62 Stations In Space .15 .40
63 Caught In A Web .15 .40
64 When Kaylee Met Shepherd .15 .40
65 His Name Is Jayne .15 .40
66 The Captain's Story .15 .40
67 Doctor, Brother, Lover .15 .40
68 Defining Serenity's Crew .15 .40
69 Small Screen Filmmaking .15 .40
70 An Early Departure .15 .40
71 Forging A Family .15 .40
72 Checklist .15 .40

2006 Firefly The Complete Collection Autographs
STATED ODDS 1:36
A1 Nathan Fillion 35.00 70.00
A2 Gina Torres 15.00 30.00
A3 Morena Baccarin 25.00 50.00
A4 Adam Baldwin 15.00 30.00
A5 Jewel Staite 25.00 50.00
A6 Sean Maher 8.00 20.00
A7 Ron Glass 8.00 20.00
A8 Michael Fairman 6.00 15.00
A9 Gregg Henry 6.00 15.00
A10 Christina Hendricks 40.00 80.00
A11 Jonathan M. Woodward 6.00 15.00

2006 Firefly The Complete Collection Box Loaders
STATED ODDS ONE PER BOX
BL1 Mal & Inara PAR 1.50 4.00
BL2 Zoe & Wash PAR 1.50 4.00
BL3 Kaylee & Simon PAR 1.50 4.00
CL1 Outlaws 4.00 10.00
CASE INSERT

2006 Firefly The Complete Collection Firefly Forever
STATED ODDS 1:11
F1 Firefly Forever 1.25 3.00
F2 Firefly Forever 1.25 3.00
F3 Firefly Forever 1.25 3.00
F4 Firefly Forever 1.25 3.00
F5 Firefly Forever 1.25 3.00
F6 Firefly Forever 1.25 3.00
F7 Firefly Forever 1.25 3.00
F8 Firefly Forever 1.25 3.00
F9 Firefly Forever 1.25 3.00

2006 Firefly The Complete Collection The Battle of Serenity
STATED ODDS 1:17
B1 The Battle Of Serenity 1.25 3.00
B2 The Battle Of Serenity 1.25 3.00
B3 The Battle Of Serenity 1.25 3.00
B4 The Battle Of Serenity 1.25 3.00
B5 The Battle Of Serenity 1.25 3.00
B6 The Battle Of Serenity 1.25 3.00

2006 The 4400 Season One
COMPLETE SET (72) 4.00 10.00
CL1 STATED ODDS ONE PER CASE
1 Title Card .10 .30
2 Tom Baldwin .10 .30
3 Diana Skouris .10 .30
4 Dennis Ryland .10 .30
5 Maia Rutledge .10 .30
6 Richard Tyler .10 .30
7 Lily Moore .10 .30
8 Shawn Farrell .10 .30
9 Jordan Collier .10 .30
10 Little Girl Lost .10 .30
11 M.I.A. .10 .30
12 Late For Dinner .10 .30
13 Boys' Night Out .10 .30
14 Mr. Anybody .10 .30
15 Killing Time .10 .30
16 Incoming .10 .30
17 Point Blank .10 .30
18 Touchdown .10 .30
19 Out Of The Mouths Of Babes .10 .30
20 Temper, Temper .10 .30
21 Vigilante .10 .30
22 Persuasion .10 .30
23 Touched .10 .30
24 Enigma .10 .30
25 Indefinite Conception .10 .30
26 Blood Line .10 .30
27 Custody Battle .10 .30
28 Departures .10 .30
29 Arrivals .10 .30
30 The Displaced .10 .30
31 The Rejected .10 .30
32 The Changed .10 .30
33 4400-Phobia .10 .30
34 Out Of Control .10 .30
35 Out Of The Ashes .10 .30
36 Hands That Heal .10 .30
37 Reality And Theory .10 .30
38 Carl,...Plus .10 .30
39 Sparks Of Life .10 .30
40 Nesting .10 .30
41 Coincidence Or Ripple .10 .30
42 Unsettling And Resettling .10 .30
43 Sibling Rivalry .10 .30
44 A Hero Fails Or Does He .10 .30
45 Oasis And Crisis .10 .30
46 Hiatus .10 .30
47 Kindred .10 .30
48 Family Affair .10 .30
49 Death By Proxy .10 .30
50 Mortem Ex Machina .10 .30
51 Welcomes And Warnings .10 .30
52 Flashback .10 .30
53 Bait And Trap .10 .30
54 Restoration .10 .30
55 Stranger In A Strange Land .10 .30
56 Prime Targets .10 .30
57 Breaking Up Is Hard To Do .10 .30
58 Prodigal Son .10 .30
59 Mass Revenge .10 .30
60 Ripples And Response .10 .30
61 Playing Hardball .10 .30
62 Bombs Away .10 .30
63 Outsider's Insight .10 .30
64 Black Knight's Gambit .10 .30
65 Confidentiality Breached .10 .30
66 Off The Reservation .10 .30
67 Fateful Detour .10 .30
68 Heat And Retreat .10 .30
69 Escape .10 .30
70 Revelation .10 .30
71 Mortality .10 .30
72 Checklist .10 .30
CL1 Emerging Power

2006 The 4400 Season One Autographs
STATED ODDS ONE PER BOX
A1 Jacqueline McKenzie 6.00 15.00
A2 Peter Coyote 6.00 15.00
A3 Billy Campbell 5.00 12.00
A4 Patrick Flueger 5.00 12.00
A5 Laura Allen 6.00 15.00
A6 Kaj-Erik Eriksen 5.00 12.00
A7 Brooke Nevin 6.00 15.00
A8 David Eigenberg 5.00 12.00
A9 Richard Kahan 5.00 12.00
AR1 Redemption card

2006 The 4400 Season One Changed Puzzle
COMPLETE SET (9) 10.00 25.00
STATED ODDS 1:11
C1 Changed 1 1.25 3.00
C2 Changed 2 1.25 3.00
C3 Changed 3 1.25 3.00
C4 Changed 4 1.25 3.00
C5 Changed 5 1.25 3.00
C6 Changed 6 1.25 3.00
C7 Changed 7 1.25 3.00
C8 Changed 8 1.25 3.00
C9 Changed 9 1.25 3.00

2006 The 4400 Season One Ripples
COMPLETE SET (6) 6.00 15.00
STATED ODDS 1:17
R1 Pebbles in a Lake 1.25 3.00
R2 Death Before Disaster 1.25 3.00
R3 The Catalyst 1.25 3.00
R4 Bad Company 1.25 3.00
R5 Benevolent Despot 1.25 3.00
R6 Future Tense 1.25 3.00

2006 The 4400 Season One Turf Wars
COMPLETE SET (3) 4.00 10.00
STATED ODDS ONE PER BOX
BL1 The A Team 1.50 4.00
BL2 Hijack 1.50 4.00
BL3 SNAFU 1.50 4.00

2006 Garbage Pail Kids All New Series 5
COMPLETE SET (80) 6.00 15.00
1a Meteor Mark .10 .25
1b Asteroid Anthony .10 .25
2a Sam Bidexterous .10 .25
2b Multi-Taskin' Ashton .10 .25
3a Internal Morgan .10 .25
3b Demonic Danielle .10 .25
4a Matt Mobile .10 .25
4b Batty Brad .10 .25
5a Marty Mucous .10 .25
5b Runny Ryan .10 .25
6a Matrix Miguel .10 .25
6b Skinned Jim .10 .25
7a Ann Urism .10 .25
7b Esther Basket .10 .25
8a Norman Notwell .10 .25
8b Vincent Van Gross .10 .25
9a Furious George .10 .25
9b King Kyle .10 .25
10a Headless Heather .10 .25
10b Head Alexis .10 .25
11a Slam-Dunk Dylan .10 .25
11b Jumpshot Josh .10 .25
12a Heavin' Hunter .10 .25
12b Rabbit Chase .10 .25
13a Inmate Nate .10 .25
13b Last-Leg Luke .10 .25
14a Regurgita-Ted .10 .25
14b Zack Snack .10 .25
15a Armless Aaron .10 .25
15b Unarmed Adrian .10 .25
16a Al Poe .10 .25
16b Gnawed Claude .10 .25
17a Red-Eye Rob .10 .25
17b Pink-Eye Guy .10 .25
18a Corey Cola .10 .25
18b Coca-Cole .10 .25
19a Samantha Swirl .10 .25
19b Decorating Deb .10 .25
20a Paul Package .10 .25
20b Tongue-Tied Toby .10 .25
21a Eric The Wreck .10 .25
21b Moto Carl .10 .25
22a Courtin' Cody .10 .25
22b Al Entine .10 .25
23a Claire Snare .10 .25
23b Lunchtime Lindsey .10 .25
24a Stormcloud Shawn .10 .25
24b Boltin' Colton .10 .25
25a Nick Pick .10 .25
25b Picky Dicky .10 .25
26a Milkin' Milt .10 .25
26b Diary Barry .10 .25
27a Hay Bailey .10 .25
27b Petey Wheatey .10 .25
28a Karate Kyle .10 .25
28b Ty Kwon Don't .10 .25
29a Yo-Yo Joe .10 .25
29b Tricky Nick .10 .25
30a Yoga Olga .10 .25
30b Mel Smell .10 .25
31a Turntable Tim .10 .25
31b Dee-Jay Jason .10 .25
32a Gamblin' Gabe .10 .25
32b Luis Vegas .10 .25
33a Tether Bill .10 .25
33b Sporty Spencer .10 .25
34a Eye-Candy Mandy .10 .25
34b Molly Pop .10 .25
35a Quick-Pick Rick .10 .25
35b Mega-Million Mike .10 .25
36a Christina Barfarina .10 .25
36b Spewin' Shannon .10 .25
37a Farrah Faucet .10 .25
37b Leakin' Lacey .10 .25
38a Railroaded Richard .10 .25
38b Choo-Choo Charlie .10 .25
39a Doomed Dwayne .10 .25
39b Toasted Todd .10 .25
40a Chopper-Chopped Chris .10 .25
40b Sliced Sammy .10 .25

2006 Garbage Pail Kids All New Series 5 Bonus
COMPLETE SET (5)
B10 STATED ODDS ONE PER WALMART BONUS BOX
B11 STATED ODDS ONE PER TARGET/KB BONUS BOX
B12, B13, B14 STATED ODDS ONE PER BLISTER PACK
B10 Bruce Brush 6.00 15.00
B11 Opera Ursula 6.00 15.00
B12 Patrick Pinata 1.25 3.00
B13 Blake Quake 1.25 3.00
B14 Pete Heat 1.25 3.00

2006 Garbage Pail Kids All New Series 5 Letters
COMPLETE SET (15) 2.00 5.00
STATED ODDS 1:2
1 A (K .15 .40
2 B (X .15 .40
3 E (O .15 .40
4 N (V .15 .40
5 F (O .15 .40
6 Y (U .15 .40
7 S (A .15 .40
8 M (E .15 .40
9 C (D .15 .40
10 R (H .15 .40
11 G (J .15 .40
12 Q (I .15 .40
13 I (P .15 .40
14 Z (T .15 .40
15 L (W .15 .40

2006 Garbage Pail Kids All New Series 5 Magnets
COMPLETE SET (9) 6.00 15.00
STATED ODDS 1:6
1 Varicose Wayne .75 2.00
2 Mason Mace .75 2.00
3 Magic Wanda .75 2.00
4 Over Eatin' Ethan .75 2.00
5 Seymour Barf .75 2.00
6 Rocco Socko .75 2.00
7 Slimy Hymie .75 2.00
8 Little Leak Len .75 2.00
9 William Won't Tell .75 2.00

2006 Harry Potter and the Goblet of Fire Update
COMPLETE SET (90) 5.00 12.00
91 The Riddle Tombstone .15 .40
92 Bloody Kids! .15 .40
93 Gather Our Old Comrades .15 .40
94 Heading To The Portkey .15 .40
95 I'll Bet That Cleared Your Sinuses! .15 .40
96 Stick Together! .15 .40
97 Clear The Runway! .15 .40
98 Not For the Faint-Hearted .15 .40
99 One Big Woman .15 .40
100 Friends From The North .15 .40
101 Eternal Glory .15 .40
102 The Goblet Of Fire .15 .40
103 Give Us A Curse .15 .40
104 The Imperius Curse .15 .40
105 Completely Harmless? .15 .40
106 What Should I Have Her Do Next? .15 .40
107 Here's The Rub... .15 .40
108 The Durmstrang Champion .15 .40
109 It's Not Going To Wo-ork .15 .40
110 The Hogwarts Champion? .15 .40
111 Champion Selection .15 .40
112 The Second Champion .15 .40
113 Vessel Of Victory .15 .40
114 Chalice Of Champions .15 .40
115 Mysterious Flames .15 .40
116 A Fourth Champion? .15 .40
117 No... No .15 .40
118 He's A Cheat .15 .40
119 In Shock .15 .40
120 This Can't Go On... .15 .40
121 Friends? .15 .40
122 They've Got One For Each Of Us .15 .40
123 Young Love .15 .40
124 How... Stirring .15 .40
125 This Tent Is For Champions .15 .40
126 Harry! Harry! .15 .40
127 Your Wand! .15 .40
128 Well, It Does Match Your Eyes .15 .40
129 Lordly Lions? .15 .40
130 Everybody Come Together .15 .40
131 A Dragon Or A Date? .15 .40
132 I Didn't Catch That? .15 .40
133 Beautiful .15 .40
134 Hermione And Viktor .15 .40
135 Preparing To Dance .15 .40
136 No. Absolutely Not. .15 .40
137 Now! .15 .40
138 Practice Makes Perfect .15 .40
139 A Subtle Invitation .15 .40
140 Ruddy Pumpkin Head .15 .40
141 Mulling Things Over .15 .40
142 One Good Turn .15 .40
143 Come Seek Us... .15 .40
144 I've Killed Harry Potter .15 .40
145 Eerie Voices .15 .40
146 She's My Friend Too! .15 .40
147 Ascendio! .15 .40
148 The Youngest Triwizard Champion? .15 .40
149 An Almighty Lurch .15 .40
150 Brought From Azkaban .15 .40
151 Rosier Is Dead .15 .40
152 A Spy? .15 .40
153 Head Of The Department Of International Magical Co-Operation .15 .40
154 I've Heard About One More .15 .40
155 Deep Within The Maze .15 .40
156 Tied For First .15 .40
157 Hearing Things .15 .40
158 A Tight Squeeze .15 .40
159 Not Himself .15 .40
160 Panicked .15 .40
161 Withdrawal From The Task .15 .40
162 Yes! .15 .40
163 Reducto! .15 .40
164 Together - One, Two, Three! .15 .40
165 Where Are We? .15 .40
166 Get Back To The Cup! .15 .40
167 What Do You Want? .15 .40
168 The Dark Lord Shall Rise Again .15 .40
169 Resurrection .15 .40
170 Welcome My Friends .15 .40
171 You Have Proved Yourself Useful .15 .40
172 How Lies Have Fed Your Legend! .15 .40
173 A Few Drops Of Blood .15 .40
174 The Dark Lord .15 .40
175 A Wand Meets Its Brother .15 .40
176 He's Mine To Finish .15 .40
177 The Reverse Spell Effect .15 .40
178 You Must Get To the Portkey .15 .40
179 What Was It Like? .15 .40
180 Checklist .15 .40

2006 Harry Potter and the Goblet of Fire Update Autographs
STATED ODDS 1:48 HOBBY
1 Daniel Radcliffe 400.00 600.00
2 Michael Gambon 30.00 60.00
3 David Tennant 75.00 150.00
4 Clemence Poesy 75.00 150.00
5 Katie Leung 30.00 60.00
6 Bonnie Wright 30.00 60.00
7 Afshan Azad 20.00 40.00
8 Shefali Chowdhury 25.00 50.00
9 Roger Lloyd-Pack 25.00 50.00
10 Frances de la Tour 20.00 40.00
11 Daniel Radcliffe 1200.00 1500.00
Stanislav Janevski/Clemence Poesy/Robert Pattinson
DE1 Ashley Artus MEM
DE2 Alex Palmer MEM

2006 Harry Potter and the Goblet of Fire Update Box Loaders
STATED ODDS ONE PER BOX
BT1 Graveyard 1.50 4.00
BT2 Harry and Dragon 1.50 4.00
BT3 Maze 1.50 4.00
BT4 Mermaid 1.50 4.00

2006 Harry Potter and the Goblet of Fire Update Case Loaders
STATED ODDS ONE PER CASE
1 Carriage Arriving 6.00 15.00
2 Harry's Second Task 6.00 15.00
3 Mad-Eye Moody 6.00 15.00

2006 Harry Potter and the Goblet of Fire Update Costumes
STATED ODDS 1:24 HOBBY
C1 Jason Isaacs Robe/475 10.00 25.00
C2 Katie Leung Dress/700 20.00 40.00
C3 Maggie Smith Dress/350 20.00 40.00
C4 Frances de la Tour Dress/825 10.00 25.00
C5 Daniel Radcliffe Outfit/275 25.00 50.00
C6 Clemence Poesy Dress/1050 10.00 25.00
C7 Emma Watson Dress/600 60.00 120.00
C8 Robert Pattinson Robe/700 25.00 50.00
C9 Predrag Bjelac Coat/850 10.00 25.00
C10 Clemence Poesy Outfit/1025 10.00 25.00
C11 Daniel Radcliffe Outfit/250 30.00 60.00
C12 Robert Pattinson Shirt/300 30.00 60.00
C13 Clemence Poesy Shirt/900 10.00 25.00
C14 Daniel Radcliffe Outfit/300 25.00 50.00
C15 Gryffindor Tie/400 20.00 40.00

2006 Harry Potter and the Goblet of Fire Update Dealer Incentive Memorabilia
BCI Slytherin Tie/114 35.00 70.00
Ci1 Clemence Poesy Dress/230 15.00 30.00
Ci2 Ralph Fiennes Cloak/155 50.00 100.00
Ci3 Daily Prophet/455 20.00 40.00
Ci4a Daniel Radcliffe Wand/28
Ci4b Robert Pattison Wand/28
Ci4c Clemence Poesy Wand/28
Ci4d Stanislav Ianevski Wand/28

2006 Harry Potter and the Goblet of Fire Update Film Cels
STATED ODDS 1:80 HOBBY
CFC1 Triwizard Cup 10.00 25.00
CFC2 Dragon 10.00 25.00
CFC3 Dumbledore 10.00 25.00
CFC4 Ron and Harry 10.00 25.00
CFC5 Durmstrang Student 10.00 25.00
CFC6 Mad-Eye Moody 10.00 25.00
CFC7 Harry 10.00 25.00
CFC8 Hermione and Harry 10.00 25.00
CFC9 Ron and Harry 10.00 25.00

2006 Harry Potter and the Goblet of Fire Update Foil Chase Cards
STATED ODDS 1:5
R1 Harry 1.25 2.50
R2 Grindylows 1.25 2.50
R3 Harry 1.25 2.50
R4 Mermaid 1.25 2.50
R5 Nagini 1.25 2.50
R6 Durmstrang Ship 1.25 2.50
R7 Harry 1.25 2.50
R8 Goblet of Fire 1.25 2.50
R9 Harry 1.25 2.50

2006 Harry Potter and the Goblet of Fire Update Jumbo Props
ONE PER SDCC BINDER
1 First Task Tent 50.00 100.00
2 Quidditch Burnt Tent 50.00 100.00

2006 Harry Potter and the Goblet of Fire Update Props
STATED ODDS 1:80 HOBBY
P1 Irish Flag 10.00 25.00
P2 Memorial Banner 15.00 30.00
P3 Books 25.00 50.00
P4 Weasley Tent 15.00 30.00
P5 Riddle House 15.00 30.00
P6 Chudley Cannons Poster 75.00 150.00
P7 Stadium Banner 10.00 25.00
P8 Ron's Yule Ball Dress Robe 15.00 30.00
Package Wrapping
P9 Rita Skeeter's Notepad 75.00 150.00
P10 Hermione's Book
P11 Harry's Letter to Sirius Black

2006 Harry Potter and the Chamber of Secrets
COMPLETE SET (90) 5.00 12.00
1 Harry Potter and the Chamber of Secrets .15 .40
2 Harry Potter .15 .40
3 Ron Weasley .15 .40
4 Hermione Granger .15 .40
5 Ginny Weasley .15 .40
6 Draco Malfoy .15 .40
7 Albus Dumbledore .15 .40
8 Professor McGonagall .15 .40
9 Rubeus Hagrid .15 .40
10 Professor Snape .15 .40
11 Professor Lockhart .15 .40
12 Lucius Malfoy .15 .40
13 Tom Riddle .15 .40
14 Dobby .15 .40
15 Professor Sprout .15 .40
16 Madam Pomfrey .15 .40
17 Argus Filch .15 .40
18 Fawkes .15 .40
19 The Biggest Deal Of My Career .15 .40
20 One Family Forever .15 .40
21 A Ruined Punch Line .15 .40
22 Dobby... Please... No .15 .40
23 C'mon Harry! Hurry up! .15 .40
24 A Lesson In Floo Powder .15 .40
25 Diagonally .15 .40

❑ 26 Reunion .15 .40
❑ 27 The Front Page .15 .40
❑ 28 Famous Harry Potter .15 .40
❑ 29 Why Can't We Get Through? .15 .40
❑ 30 Getting Close... .15 .40
❑ 31 Welcome Home .15 .40
❑ 32 We Are In Trouble .15 .40
❑ 33 Lucky To Be In Gryffindor .15 .40
❑ 34 Mandrake, Or Mandragora .15 .40
❑ 35 Weasley's Got Himself A Howler .15 .40
❑ 36 Freshly Caught .15 .40
❑ 37 Immobilus! .15 .40
❑ 38 Eat Slugs! .15 .40
❑ 39 Better Out Than In .15 .40
❑ 40 Enemies Of The Heir... Beware .15 .40
❑ 41 Fera Verto .15 .40
❑ 42 Brackium Emendo .15 .40
❑ 43 You're In For A Rough Night .15 .40
❑ 44 With Friends Like These... .15 .40
❑ 45 The Safety Of The Girls' Lavatory .15 .40
❑ 46 Scared, Potter? .15 .40
❑ 47 Back To The Common Room .15 .40
❑ 48 More Victims Of The Heir .15 .40
❑ 49 Sherbet Lemon .15 .40
❑ 50 He Just Caught Fire! .15 .40
❑ 51 Hermione's Plan .15 .40
❑ 52 Easy Targets .15 .40
❑ 53 Cheers .15 .40
❑ 54 Wandering The Dungeons .15 .40
❑ 55 S-s-car...! .15 .40
❑ 56 It's Awful .15 .40
❑ 57 Let Me Take You Back... .15 .40
❑ 58 Mad 'N' Hairy .15 .40
❑ 59 A Petrified Hermione .15 .40
❑ 60 Bad Business .15 .40
❑ 61 Why Couldn't It Be "Follow The Butterflies?" .15 .40
❑ 62 Go? I Think Not .15 .40
❑ 63 Pipes .15 .40
❑ 64 The Basilisk .15 .40
❑ 65 This Is It .15 .40
❑ 66 Heart Of A Lion... .15 .40
❑ 67 The Entrance .15 .40
❑ 68 How Did You Escape...? .15 .40
❑ 69 My Past, Present And Future .15 .40
❑ 70 The Heir Of Slytherin .15 .40
❑ 71 No Escape .15 .40
❑ 72 Fawkes To The Rescue .15 .40
❑ 73 Trapped? .15 .40
❑ 74 A Gleaming Silver Sword .15 .40
❑ 75 The Demise Of The Basilisk .15 .40
❑ 76 A Lethal Injury? .15 .40
❑ 77 A Silly Little Book .15 .40
❑ 78 What Are You Doing? .15 .40
❑ 79 Follow The Chamber .15 .40
❑ 80 You Were Brilliant, Fawkes .15 .40
❑ 81 You Have Broken Perhaps .15 .40
A Dozen School Rules
❑ 82 Proof You Belong In Gryffindor .15 .40
❑ 83 So This Is Your Master .15 .40
❑ 84 I Have Something Of Yours .15 .40
❑ 85 Open It .15 .40
❑ 86 Dobby Is Free! .15 .40
❑ 87 You Shall Not Harm Harry Potter! .15 .40
❑ 88 Welcome Back, Hermione .15 .40
❑ 89 I'd Just Like Ter Say Thanks .15 .40
❑ 90 Checklist .15 .40

2006 Harry Potter and the Chamber of Secrets Autographs

STATED ODDS 1:48
❑ 1 Richard Griffiths 20.00 40.00
❑ 2 Julian Glover 20.00 40.00
❑ 3 Fiona Shaw 30.00 60.00
❑ 4 Gemma Jones 25.00 50.00
❑ 5 Harry Melling 20.00 40.00
❑ 6 Shirley Henderson 60.00 120.00
❑ 7 Miriam Margoyles 25.00 50.00
❑ 8 Kenneth Branagh 35.00 70.00
❑ 9 Chris Rankin 20.00 40.00
❑ 10 Bonnie Wright 40.00 80.00

2006 Harry Potter and the Chamber of Secrets Box Loaders

STATED ODDS ONE PER BOX
❑ BT1 The Sorting Hat 1.50 4.00
❑ BT2 Mrs. Norris 1.50 4.00
❑ BT3 Platform 9 3/4 1.50 4.00
❑ BT4 Flourish and Blotts 1.50 4.00

2006 Harry Potter and the Chamber of Secrets Case Loaders

STATED ODDS ONE PER CASE
❑ 1 Basilisk 6.00 15.00
❑ 2 Floo Powder 6.00 15.00

2006 Harry Potter and the Chamber of Secrets Costumes

STATED ODDS 1:24
❑ C1 Daniel Radcliffe Shirt/190 25.00 50.00
❑ C2 Rupert Grint Sweater/290 15.00 30.00
❑ C3 Kenneth Branagh Jacket/640 8.00 20.00
❑ C4 Daniel Radcliffe Shirt/540 10.00 25.00
❑ C5 Rupert Grint Shirt/490 10.00 25.00
❑ C6 Christian Coulson Sweater/240 20.00 40.00
❑ C7 David Bradley Coat/665 8.00 20.00
❑ C8 Jason Isaacs Cloak/640 12.00 30.00
❑ C9 Bonnie Wright Sweater/190 25.00 50.00
❑ C10 Emma Watson Sweater/165 100.00 150.00
❑ C11 Daniel Radcliffe Blue Sweater/440 12.00 30.00
❑ C12 Daniel Radcliffe Red Sweater/540 12.00 30.00
❑ C13 Tom Felton Robe/165 30.00 60.00
❑ C14 Robbie Coltrane Shirt/515 12.00 30.00
❑ C15 Devon Murray Jacket/240 10.00 25.00
❑ C16 Bonnie Wright Pajamas/340 20.00 40.00
❑ C17 Richard Griffiths Suit/390 12.00 30.00

2006 Harry Potter and the Chamber of Secrets Dealer Incentive Memorabilia

❑ CI1 Daniel Radcliffe Pajamas/340 12.00 30.00
❑ CI2 Hermione's Cauldron/160 40.00 80.00
❑ CI3 Basilisk Fang/100
❑ CI4 Hogwarts Letter/64

2006 Harry Potter and the Chamber of Secrets Film Cels

STATED ODDS 1:80
❑ CFC1 Lockhart 10.00 25.00
❑ CFC2 Sorting Hat 10.00 25.00
❑ CFC3 Portraits 10.00 25.00
❑ CFC4 Sleigh 10.00 25.00
❑ CFC5 Draco 10.00 25.00
❑ CFC6 Acromantula 10.00 25.00
❑ CFC7 Harry 10.00 25.00
❑ CFC8 Draco 10.00 25.00
❑ CFC9 Harry 10.00 25.00

2006 Harry Potter and the Chamber of Secrets Foil Chase Cards

STATED ODDS 1:5
❑ R1 Harry 1.00 2.50
❑ R2 Hermione 1.00 2.50
❑ R3 Ron 1.00 2.50
❑ R4 Gilderoy 1.00 2.50
❑ R5 Draco 1.00 2.50
❑ R6 Dumbledore 1.00 2.50
❑ R7 Lucius 1.00 2.50
❑ R8 Ginny 1.00 2.50
❑ R9 Rubeus 1.00 2.50

2006 Harry Potter and the Chamber of Secrets Props

STATED ODDS 1:80
❑ P1 Floo Powder/290 25.00 50.00
❑ P2 Howler/190 60.00 120.00
❑ P3 Dumbledore's Books/290 30.00 60.00
❑ P4 Fawkes' Feathers/140 60.00 120.00
❑ P5 Mandrake/360 30.00 60.00
❑ P6 Dueling Club Cloth/80 200.00 300.00
❑ P7 Magical Me Book/280 25.00 50.00
❑ P8 Aragog's Legs/215 30.00 60.00
❑ P9 Potions Book/115 75.00 150.00
❑ P10 Christmas Crackers/240 25.00 50.00

2006 Harry Potter Memorable Moments

COMPLETE SET (72) 5.00 12.00
❑ 1 I'm Harry, Harry Potter .15 .40
❑ 2 Devil's Snare, Devil's Snare .15 .40
❑ 3 Ahh. Tokens. From your admirers? .15 .40
❑ 4 You're a wizard, Harry .15 .40
❑ 5 Harry P-p-p-otter. Can't tell you .15 .40
❑ 6 Your father left this in my possession .15 .40
❑ 7 But Hagrid, we're not allowed to do magic .15 .40
❑ 8 Good afternoon, Madam Hooch .15 .40
❑ 9 The wand chooses the wizard, Mr. Potter .15 .40
❑ 10 How is it I got the Stone, sir? .15 .40
❑ 11 You'll soon find out .15 .40
❑ 12 And then, if you please .15 .40
❑ 13 I demand that you leave at once, sir .15 .40
❑ 14 This boy will be famous .15 .40
❑ 15 This is no graveyard .15 .40
❑ 16 There is no good and evil .15 .40
❑ 17 The Forewst? .15 .40
❑ 18 Assuming that my calculations are correct .15 .40
❑ 19 Because of recent events .15 .40
❑ 20 Why are you wearing glasses? .15 .40
❑ 21 You'll pay for that one, Malfoy .15 .40
❑ 22 Harry Potter should have listed to Dobby .15 .40
❑ 23 What did you do to your glasses? .15 .40
❑ 24 I'm well aware of our bylaws, Severus .15 .40
❑ 25 Nice big smile, Harry .15 .40
❑ 26 RONALD WEASLEY! .15 .40
❑ 27 This is it .15 .40
❑ 28 Freshly caught Cornish pixies .15 .40
❑ 29 It was Hagrid .15 .40
❑ 30 Bee in your bonnet, Potter? .15 .40
❑ 31 Harry Potter! Such an honor it is .15 .40
❑ 32 Everyone will proceed .15 .40
❑ 33 Harry... First, I want to thank you, Harry .15 .40
❑ 34 Of course, Phoenix tears have healing powers .15 .40
❑ 35 But, Harry's never traveled by Floo .15 .40
❑ 36 Nothin' to do but wait 'til it stops .15 .40
❑ 37 You bring her back! .15 .40
❑ 38 No permission form signed .15 .40
❑ 39 Not a single professor inside this castle .15 .40
❑ 40 Your father, James, on the other hand .15 .40
❑ 41 Before, down by the lake .15 .40
❑ 42 You! You foul loathsome evil little cockroach .15 .40
❑ 43 You don't think that Grim .15 .40
❑ 44 I'm the teacher, I'll do it .15 .40
❑ 45 You know, your father never set much .15 .40
❑ 46 I found him! .15 .40
❑ 47 Headmaster, you've got to stop them .15 .40
❑ 48 Not so fast Harry .15 .40
❑ 49 Welcome, welcome .15 .40
❑ 50 It's beautiful, isn't it? .15 .40
❑ 51 Bless you, boy. Bless you .15 .40
❑ 52 I did my waiting .15 .40
❑ 53 Now open your books to page 49 .15 .40
❑ 54 Give me a reason. I beg you .15 .40
❑ 55 Hogwarts has been chosen to host .15 .40
❑ 56 This can't go on, Albus .15 .40
❑ 57 Give us a curse .15 .40
❑ 58 I haven't a clue .15 .40
❑ 59 So, who's feeling up to sharing? .15 .40
❑ 60 Hey, listen. About the badges .15 .40
❑ 61 Harry! Harry! .15 .40
❑ 62 My father will hear about this .15 .40
❑ 63 Sorry - I didn't catch that? .15 .40
❑ 64 a genius like Dumbledore .15 .40
❑ 65 Merlin's beard! .15 .40
❑ 66 What's got your wand in a knot? .15 .40
❑ 67 You're sure about this, Neville .15 .40
❑ 68 Sir, these dreams .15 .40
❑ 69 Go on, take it! You saved me! .15 .40
❑ 70 Harry! When the connection is broken .15 .40
❑ 71 people change in the maze .15 .40
❑ 72 Checklist .15 .40

2006 Harry Potter Memorable Moments Autographs

OVERALL AUTO ODDS 1:48
❑ 1 Emma Watson 400.00 600.00
❑ 2 David Bradley 30.00 60.00
❑ 3 Maggie Smith 60.00 120.00
❑ 4 Jason Isaacs 75.00 150.00
❑ 5 Eric Sykes 20.00 40.00

2006 Harry Potter Memorable Moments Coin Cards Gold

❑ CC1 Dobby
❑ CC2 Harry and Hedwig

2006 Harry Potter Memorable Moments Coin Cards Silver

COMPLETE SET (2) 15.00 30.00
STATED ODDS ONE SET PER BOX
❑ CC1 Dobby 8.00 20.00
❑ CC2 Harry and Hedwig 8.00 20.00

2006 Harry Potter Memorable Moments Costumes

STATED PRINT RUN 170-660
❑ C1 Jamie Waylett/660 6.00 15.00
❑ C2 Tom Felton/170 40.00 80.00
❑ C3 Farry Melling/660 6.00 15.00
❑ C4 Josh Herdman/535 6.00 15.00
❑ C5 Maggie Smith/360 25.00 50.00

2006 Harry Potter Memorable Moments Costume Autographs

OVERALL AUTO ODDS 1:48
❑ DE3 Philip Rham 50.00 100.00
❑ DE4 Paschal Friel 30.00 60.00
❑ DE5 Olivia Higginbottom 20.00 40.00
❑ DE6 Richard Rosson 30.00 60.00

2006 Harry Potter Memorable Moments Dealer Incentive Memorabilia

❑ CI1 Neville's Book
❑ CI2 Defense Against the Dark Arts Book
❑ CI3 Letter from Sirius

2006 Harry Potter Memorable Moments Dual Costumes

STATED PRINT RUN 210-460
❑ DC1 Rupert Grint/310 12.00 30.00
❑ DC2 James Phelps
Oliver Phelps/235
❑ DC3 Daniel Radcliffe/360 20.00 40.00
❑ DC4 Josh Herdman/460 10.00 25.00
❑ DC5 Stanislav Ianevski 25.00 50.00
Robert Pattinson/275
❑ DC6 Clemence Poesy 20.00 40.00
Angelica Mandy/235
❑ DC7 Clemence Poesy
Robert Pattinson/210

2006 Harry Potter Memorable Moments Foil Chase Cards

STATED ODDS 1:5
❑ R1 Aragog 1.00 2.50
❑ R2 Dementor 1.00 2.50
❑ R3 Nagini 1.00 2.50
❑ R4 Fang 1.00 2.50
❑ R5 Cornish Pixie 1.00 2.50
❑ R6 Chinese Fireball 1.00 2.50
❑ R7 Hungarian Horntail 1.00 2.50
❑ R8 Fawkes 1.00 2.50
❑ R9 Hedwig 1.00 2.50

2006 Harry Potter Memorable Moments Props

STATED ODDS 1:80
❑ P1 Practice Broom Bristles/235
❑ P2 Norbert's Egg/140
❑ P3 Basilisk Skin/160
❑ P4 Tom Riddle's Diary/180
❑ P5 Chudley Cannons Poster/150
❑ P6 Christmas Card/180
❑ P7 Moon and Star Christmas Ornaments/150
❑ P8 Student Wands and Quills/115
❑ PC1 Buckbeak's Feather
Tom Felton Robe/50
❑ PC2 Marauder's Map
David Thewlis Shirt/110
❑ PC3 Daniel Radcliffe Shirt
Grim Fur/105
❑ PC4 Daniel Radcliffe Pajamas/90

2006 James Bond Dangerous Liaisons

COMPLETE SET (110) 5.00 12.00
❑ 1 Dr. No .15 .40
❑ 2 Dr. No .15 .40
❑ 3 Dr. No .15 .40
❑ 4 Dr. No .15 .40
❑ 5 Dr. No .15 .40
❑ 6 Dr. No .15 .40
❑ 7 Dr. No .15 .40
❑ 8 Dr. No .15 .40
❑ 9 From Russia With Love .15 .40
❑ 10 From Russia With Love .15 .40
❑ 11 From Russia With Love .15 .40
❑ 12 From Russia With Love .15 .40
❑ 13 From Russia With Love .15 .40
❑ 14 From Russia With Love .15 .40
❑ 15 From Russia With Love .15 .40
❑ 16 Goldfinger .15 .40
❑ 17 Goldfinger .15 .40
❑ 18 Goldfinger .15 .40
❑ 19 Goldfinger .15 .40
❑ 20 Goldfinger .15 .40
❑ 21 Goldfinger .15 .40
❑ 22 Thunderball .15 .40
❑ 23 Thunderball .15 .40
❑ 24 Thunderball .15 .40
❑ 25 Thunderball .15 .40
❑ 26 Thunderball .15 .40
❑ 27 Thunderball .15 .40
❑ 28 Thunderball .15 .40
❑ 29 You Only Live Twice .15 .40
❑ 30 You Only Live Twice .15 .40
❑ 31 You Only Live Twice .15 .40
❑ 32 You Only Live Twice .15 .40
❑ 33 You Only Live Twice .15 .40
❑ 34 On Her Majesty's Secret Service .15 .40
❑ 35 On Her Majesty's Secret Service .15 .40
❑ 36 On Her Majesty's Secret Service .15 .40
❑ 37 On Her Majesty's Secret Service .15 .40
❑ 38 On Her Majesty's Secret Service .15 .40
❑ 39 Diamonds Are Forever .15 .40
❑ 40 Diamonds Are Forever .15 .40
❑ 41 Diamonds Are Forever .15 .40
❑ 42 Diamonds Are Forever .15 .40
❑ 43 Diamonds Are Forever .15 .40
❑ 44 Diamonds Are Forever .15 .40
❑ 45 Live And Let Die .15 .40
❑ 46 Live And Let Die .15 .40
❑ 47 Live And Let Die .15 .40
❑ 48 Live And Let Die .15 .40
❑ 49 Live And Let Die .15 .40
❑ 50 Live And Let Die .15 .40
❑ 51 Live And Let Die .15 .40
❑ 52 The Man With The Golden Gun .15 .40
❑ 53 The Man With The Golden Gun .15 .40
❑ 54 The Man With The Golden Gun .15 .40
❑ 55 The Man With The Golden Gun .15 .40
❑ 56 The Man With The Golden Gun .15 .40
❑ 57 The Man With The Golden Gun .15 .40
❑ 58 The Man With The Golden Gun .15 .40
❑ 59 The Spy Who Loved Me .15 .40
❑ 60 The Spy Who Loved Me .15 .40
❑ 61 The Spy Who Loved Me .15 .40
❑ 62 The Spy Who Loved Me .15 .40
❑ 63 The Spy Who Loved Me .15 .40
❑ 64 Moonraker .15 .40
❑ 65 Moonraker .15 .40
❑ 66 Moonraker .15 .40
❑ 67 Moonraker .15 .40
❑ 68 Moonraker .15 .40
❑ 69 For Your Eyes Only .15 .40
❑ 70 For Your Eyes Only .15 .40
❑ 71 For Your Eyes Only .15 .40
❑ 72 Octopussy .15 .40
❑ 73 Octopussy .15 .40
❑ 74 Octopussy .15 .40
❑ 75 Octopussy .15 .40
❑ 76 A View To A Kill .15 .40
❑ 77 A View To A Kill .15 .40
❑ 78 A View To A Kill .15 .40
❑ 79 A View To A Kill .15 .40
❑ 80 The Living Daylights .15 .40
❑ 81 The Living Daylights .15 .40
❑ 82 The Living Daylights .15 .40
❑ 83 Licence To Kill .15 .40
❑ 84 Licence To Kill .15 .40
❑ 85 GoldenEye .15 .40
❑ 86 GoldenEye .15 .40
❑ 87 GoldenEye .15 .40
❑ 88 GoldenEye .15 .40
❑ 89 GoldenEye .15 .40
❑ 90 GoldenEye .15 .40
❑ 91 GoldenEye .15 .40
❑ 92 Tomorrow Never Dies .15 .40
❑ 93 Tomorrow Never Dies .15 .40
❑ 94 Tomorrow Never Dies .15 .40
❑ 95 Tomorrow Never Dies .15 .40
❑ 96 Tomorrow Never Dies .15 .40
❑ 97 Tomorrow Never Dies .15 .40
❑ 98 The World Is Not Enough .15 .40
❑ 99 The World Is Not Enough .15 .40
❑ 100 The World Is Not Enough .15 .40
❑ 101 Die Another Day .15 .40
❑ 102 Die Another Day .15 .40
❑ 103 Die Another Day .15 .40
❑ 104 Die Another Day .15 .40
❑ 105 Die Another Day .15 .40
❑ 106 Die Another Day .15 .40
❑ 107 Die Another Day .15 .40
❑ 108 Checklist .15 .40
❑ 109 Checklist .15 .40
❑ 110 Checklist .15 .40

2006 James Bond Dangerous Liaisons Autographs

STATED ODDS 1:20
MOORE AUTO STATED ODDS ONE PER 6 CASE PURCHASE
L (LIMITED): 300-500 COPIES
VL (VERY LIMITED): 200-300 COPIES
❑ A37 Goldie 6.00 15.00
❑ A50 Jenny Hanley 12.00 30.00
❑ A59 Earl Cameron 6.00 15.00
❑ A60 Nadim Sawahla 6.00 15.00
❑ A61 Joe Robinson 8.00 20.00
❑ A62 Cary-Hiroyuki Tagawa 8.00 20.00
❑ A64 Don Stroud 8.00 20.00
❑ A66 Britt Ekland L 20.00 40.00
❑ A67 George Baker 30.00 60.00
❑ WA19 Ursula Andress VL 200.00 300.00
❑ WA26 Maud Adams VL 150.00 250.00
❑ WA28 Lana Wood L 30.00 60.00
❑ WA29 Tanya Roberts 20.00 40.00
❑ WA30 Denise Richards L
❑ NNO Alan Cumming VL 25.00 50.00
❑ NNO Famke Janssen VL 150.00 250.00
❑ NNO Jenny Hanley 20.00 40.00
❑ NNO John Bowe 6.00 15.00
❑ NNO Kristina Wayborn VL 60.00 120.00
❑ NNO Lana Wood SP 40.00 80.00
❑ NNO Lynn-Holly Johnson VL 30.00 60.00
❑ NNO Madeline Smith L 40.00 80.00
❑ NNO Maud Adams 150.00 250.00
Octopussy VL
❑ NNO Maud Adams 150.00 250.00
The Man With The Golden Gun VL
❑ NNO Robert Davi 30.00 60.00
❑ NNO Tania Mallet 25.00 50.00
❑ NNO Tanya Roberts 20.00 40.00
❑ NNO Timothy Moxon 12.00 30.00
❑ NNO Yaphet Kotto VL 100.00 175.00
❑ NNO Roger Moore 200.00 300.00

2006 James Bond Dangerous Liaisons Bond Allies

COMPLETE SET (18) 25.00 50.00
STATED ODDS 1:10
❑ BA1 Felix Leiter 1.50 4.00
❑ BA2 Quarrel 1.50 4.00
❑ BA3 Kerim Bey 1.50 4.00
❑ BA4 Paula Caplan 1.50 4.00
❑ BA5 Tiger Tanaka 1.50 4.00
❑ BA6 Henderson 1.50 4.00
❑ BA7 Willard Whyte 1.50 4.00
❑ BA8 Sheriff J.W. Pepper 1.50 4.00
❑ BA9 General Gogol 1.50 4.00
❑ BA10 Manuela 1.50 4.00
❑ BA11 Milos Columbo 1.50 4.00
❑ BA12 Vijay 1.50 4.00
❑ BA13 Sir Godfrey Tibbett 1.50 4.00
❑ BA14 General Leonid Pushkin 1.50 4.00
❑ BA15 Kamran Shah 1.50 4.00
❑ BA16 General Ourumov 1.50 4.00
❑ BA17 Jack Wade 1.50 4.00
❑ BA18 Valentin Zukovsky 1.50 4.00

2006 James Bond Dangerous Liaisons Bond Girls Are Forever

COMPLETE SET (17) 50.00 100.00
STATED ODDS 1:20
BG46 IS RITTENHOUSE REWARD EXCLUSIVE
❑ BG30 Miss Taro 3.00 8.00
❑ BG31 Kerith Bey's Woman 3.00 8.00
❑ BG32 Aki 3.00 8.00
❑ BG33 Helga Brandt 3.00 8.00
❑ BG34 Ruby Bartlett 3.00 8.00
❑ BG35 Plenty O'Toole 3.00 8.00
❑ BG36 Miss Caruso 3.00 8.00
❑ BG37 Rosie Carver 3.00 8.00
❑ BG38 Andrea Anders 3.00 8.00
❑ BG39 Corinne Dufour 3.00 8.00
❑ BG40 Bibi Dahl 3.00 8.00
❑ BG41 Magda 3.00 8.00
❑ BG42 May Day 3.00 8.00
❑ BG43 Pola Ivanova 3.00 8.00
❑ BG44 Professor Bergstrom 3.00 8.00
❑ BG45 Dr. Molly Warmflash 3.00 8.00
❑ BG46 Honey Rider 3.00 8.00

2006 James Bond Dangerous Liaisons Bond Villains

COMPLETE SET (20) 40.00 80.00
STATED ODDS 1:12
❑ F21 Professor Dent 2.00 5.00
❑ F22 Red Grant 2.00 5.00
❑ F23 Oddjob 2.00 5.00
❑ F24 Vargas 2.00 5.00
❑ F25 Mr. Osato 2.00 5.00
❑ F26 Irma Bunt 2.00 5.00
❑ F27 Mr. Wint-Mr. Kidd 2.00 5.00
❑ F28 Baron Samedi 2.00 5.00
❑ F29 Nick Nack 2.00 5.00
❑ F30 Naomi 2.00 5.00
❑ F31 Jaws 2.00 5.00
❑ F32 Emile Locque 2.00 5.00
❑ F33 Gobinda 2.00 5.00
❑ F34 General Orlov 2.00 5.00
❑ F35 Brad Whitaker 2.00 5.00
❑ F36 Dario 2.00 5.00
❑ F37 Boris Grishenko 2.00 5.00
❑ F38 Stamper 2.00 5.00
❑ F39 Renard 2.00 5.00
❑ F40 Cigar Girl 2.00 5.00

2006 James Bond Dangerous Liaisons Costumes

CC4 STATED ODDS ONE PER CASE
CC6 STATED ODDS ONE PER 2 CASE PURCHASE
❑ CC4 James Bond Ski Jacket 25.00 50.00
❑ CC6 Jinx Dress 30.00 60.00

2006 James Bond Dangerous Liaisons The Art & Images of 007

STATED ODDS 1:40
PRINT RUN 375 SER. #'d SETS
❑ AR1 Dr. Julius No 12.00 30.00
❑ AR2 Tatiana Romanova 12.00 30.00
❑ AR3 Pussy Galore 12.00 30.00
❑ AR4 Thunderball 12.00 30.00
❑ AR5 James Bond 12.00 30.00
❑ AR6 James Bond 12.00 30.00
Tracy Bivicenzo
❑ AR7 Tiffany Case 12.00 30.00
❑ AR8 Solitaire 12.00 30.00
❑ AR9 The Man With The Golden Gun 12.00 30.00
❑ AR10 Major Anya Amasova 12.00 30.00
❑ AR11 James Bond 12.00 30.00
❑ AR12 Milos Columbo 12.00 30.00
❑ AR13 Magda 12.00 30.00
❑ AR14 Max Zorin 12.00 30.00
❑ AR15 James Bond 12.00 30.00
❑ AR16 Lupe Lamora 12.00 30.00
❑ AR17 Xenia Onatopp 12.00 30.00
❑ AR18 James Bond 12.00 30.00
❑ AR19 Dr. Christmas Jones 12.00 30.00
❑ AR20 James Bond 12.00 30.00

2006 Legends of Star Trek Captain Picard

COMPLETE SET (9) 10.00 20.00
❑ L1 Captain Picard 1.00 2.50
❑ L2 Captain Picard 1.00 2.50
❑ L3 Captain Picard 1.00 2.50
❑ L4 Captain Picard 1.00 2.50
❑ L5 Captain Picard 1.00 2.50
❑ L6 Captain Picard 1.00 2.50
❑ L7 Captain Picard 1.00 2.50
❑ L8 Captain Picard 1.00 2.50
❑ L9 Captain Picard 1.00 2.50

2006 Legends of Star Trek Commander William T. Riker

COMPLETE SET (9) 10.00 20.00
❑ L1 Commander William T. Riker 1.00 2.50
❑ L2 Commander William T. Riker 1.00 2.50
❑ L3 Commander William T. Riker 1.00 2.50
❑ L4 Commander William T. Riker 1.00 2.50
❑ L5 Commander William T. Riker 1.00 2.50
❑ L6 Commander William T. Riker 1.00 2.50
❑ L7 Commander William T. Riker 1.00 2.50
❑ L8 Commander William T. Riker 1.00 2.50
❑ L9 Commander William T. Riker 1.00 2.50

2006 Legends of Star Trek Counselor Deanna Troi

COMPLETE SET (9) 10.00 20.00
❑ L1 Counselor Deanna Troi 1.00 2.50
❑ L2 Counselor Deanna Troi 1.00 2.50
❑ L3 Counselor Deanna Troi 1.00 2.50
❑ L4 Counselor Deanna Troi 1.00 2.50
❑ L5 Counselor Deanna Troi 1.00 2.50
❑ L6 Counselor Deanna Troi 1.00 2.50
❑ L7 Counselor Deanna Troi 1.00 2.50
❑ L8 Counselor Deanna Troi 1.00 2.50
❑ L9 Counselor Deanna Troi 1.00 2.50

2006 Legends of Star Trek Lt. Commander Data

COMPLETE SET (9) 10.00 20.00
❑ L1 Lt. Commander Data 1.00 2.50
❑ L2 Lt. Commander Data 1.00 2.50
❑ L3 Lt. Commander Data 1.00 2.50
❑ L4 Lt. Commander Data 1.00 2.50
❑ L5 Lt. Commander Data 1.00 2.50
❑ L6 Lt. Commander Data 1.00 2.50
❑ L7 Lt. Commander Data 1.00 2.50
❑ L8 Lt. Commander Data 1.00 2.50
❑ L9 Lt. Commander Data 1.00 2.50

2006 Lord of the Rings Evolution

COMPLETE SET (72) 5.00 12.00
❑ 1 Aragorn .15 .40
❑ 2 Arwen .15 .40
❑ 3 Bilbo .15 .40
❑ 4 Boromir .15 .40
❑ 5 Cave Troll .15 .40
❑ 6 Celeborn .15 .40
❑ 7 Deagol .15 .40
❑ 8 Denethor .15 .40
❑ 9 Elrond .15 .40
❑ 10 Eomer .15 .40
❑ 11 Eowyn .15 .40

❑ 12 Everard Proudfoot .15 .40
❑ 13 Faramir .15 .40
❑ 14 Figwit .15 .40
❑ 15 Frodo .15 .40
❑ 16 Galadriel .15 .40
❑ 17 Gamling .15 .40
❑ 18 Gandalf .15 .40
❑ 19 Gash-Face .15 .40
❑ 20 Gimli .15 .40
❑ 21 Gollum .15 .40
❑ 22 Gorbag .15 .40
❑ 23 Gothmog .15 .40
❑ 24 Grishnakh .15 .40
❑ 25 Haldir .15 .40
❑ 26 Hama .15 .40
❑ 27 Isildur .15 .40
❑ 28 King Elendil .15 .40
❑ 29 King of the Dead .15 .40
❑ 30 Legolas .15 .40
❑ 31 Lurtz .15 .40
❑ 32 Merry .15 .40
❑ 33 Mouth of Sauron .15 .40
❑ 34 Pippin .15 .40
❑ 35 Rosie Cotton .15 .40
❑ 36 Sam .15 .40
❑ 37 Saruman .15 .40
❑ 38 Sauron .15 .40
❑ 39 Sharku .15 .40
❑ 40 Smeagol .15 .40
❑ 41 Snaga .15 .40
❑ 42 The Bounder .15 .40
❑ 43 Theoden .15 .40
❑ 44 Treebeard .15 .40
❑ 45 Ugluk .15 .40
❑ 46 Witch-King .15 .40
❑ 47 Wormtongue .15 .40
❑ 48 Army of the Dead .15 .40
❑ 49 Corsairs .15 .40
❑ 50 Dwarves .15 .40
❑ 51 Easterlings .15 .40
❑ 52 Elves .15 .40
❑ 53 Ents .15 .40
❑ 54 Gondor .15 .40
❑ 55 Harad .15 .40
❑ 56 Hobbit .15 .40
❑ 57 Nazgul .15 .40
❑ 58 Orcs .15 .40
❑ 59 Rohan .15 .40
❑ 60 Trolls .15 .40
❑ 61 Uruk-hai .15 .40
❑ 62 Wildmen .15 .40
❑ 63 Wizard .15 .40
❑ 64 Balrog .15 .40
❑ 65 Fell Beasts .15 .40
❑ 66 Great Beasts .15 .40
❑ 67 Great Eagles .15 .40
❑ 68 Mumakil .15 .40
❑ 69 Shelob .15 .40
❑ 70 Wargs .15 .40
❑ 71 Watcher .15 .40
❑ 72 Checklist .15 .40

2006 Lord of the Rings Evolution A Uncommon

COMPLETE SET (20) 8.00 20.00
STATED ODDS 1:4

❑ 1A Aragorn .75 2.00
❑ 2A Arwen .75 2.00
❑ 3A Bilbo .75 2.00
❑ 4A Boromir .75 2.00
❑ 5A Elrond .75 2.00
❑ 6A Eomer .75 2.00
❑ 7A Eowyn .75 2.00
❑ 8A Faramir .75 2.00
❑ 9A Frodo .75 2.00
❑ 10A Galadriel .75 2.00
❑ 11A Gandalf .75 2.00
❑ 12A Haldir .75 2.00
❑ 13A Legolas .75 2.00
❑ 14A Lurtz .75 2.00
❑ 15A Merry .75 2.00
❑ 16A Pippin .75 2.00
❑ 17A Sam .75 2.00
❑ 18A Sauron .75 2.00
❑ 19A Theoden .75 2.00
❑ 20A Witch-King .75 2.00

2006 Lord of the Rings Evolution B Rare

COMPLETE SET (12) 20.00 40.00
STATED ODDS 1:12

❑ 1B Aragorn 2.50 6.00
❑ 2B Arwen 2.50 6.00
❑ 3B Bilbo 2.50 6.00
❑ 4B Elrond 2.50 6.00
❑ 5B Eomer 2.50 6.00
❑ 6B Eowyn 2.50 6.00
❑ 7B Faramir 2.50 6.00
❑ 8B Frodo 2.50 6.00
❑ 9B Galadriel 2.50 6.00
❑ 10B Gandalf 2.50 6.00
❑ 11B Sam 2.50 6.00
❑ 12B Theoden 2.50 6.00

2006 Lord of the Rings Evolution Memorabilia

STATED ODDS 1:24 RETAIL

❑ NNO Galadriel's Grey Havens Cloak 12.00 30.00
❑ NNO Gandalf the White's Cloak 20.00 40.00
❑ NNO Pippin's Travel Cloak 8.00 20.00
❑ NNO Arwen's Nightgown 25.00 50.00
❑ NNO Gandalf the White's Shirt 20.00 40.00
❑ NNO Frodo's Travel Cloak 8.00 20.00
❑ NNO Merry's Travel Cloak 8.00 20.00

2006 Lord of the Rings Evolution Sketches

OVERALL STATED ODDS 1:14 HOBBY
GROUP A STATED ODDS 1:32
GROUP B STATED ODDS 1:346
GROUP C STATED ODDS 1:70
GROUP D STATED ODDS 1:111
GROUP E STATED ODDS 1:93
GROUP F STATED ODDS 1:209

❑ NNO Allison Sohn E
❑ NNO Cat Staggs C
❑ NNO Dan Norton D
❑ NNO Davide Fabbri A
❑ NNO Howard Shum A
❑ NNO Jeff Chandler D
❑ NNO Joseph Booth D
❑ NNO Matt Busch F
❑ NNO Otis Frampton A
❑ NNO Ray Dillon D
❑ NNO Russ Walks E
❑ NNO Thomas Hodges A
❑ NNO Amy Pronovost C
❑ NNO Chris Eliopoulos F
❑ NNO Dan Parsons C
❑ NNO Dennis Budd E
❑ NNO Jake Myler C
❑ NNO Jeff Zapata F
❑ NNO Juan Carlos Ramos E
❑ NNO Michael Duron E
❑ NNO Paul Gutierrez A
❑ NNO Renae De Liz E
❑ NNO Ryan Benjamin F
❑ NNO Tom Mandrake C
❑ NNO Brent Woodside B
❑ NNO Christian Dalla Vecchia A
❑ NNO Dave Dorman E
❑ NNO Gabriel Hernandez F
❑ NNO James Hodgkins A
❑ NNO Joe Corroney F
❑ NNO Justin Chung F
❑ NNO Mike Lilly F
❑ NNO Rafael Kayanan E
❑ NNO Rich Molinelli F
❑ NNO Sarah Wilkinson D
❑ NNO William O'Neill E
❑ NNO Brian Rood C
❑ NNO Cynthia Cummens D
❑ NNO David Rabbitte E
❑ NNO Grant Gould E
❑ NNO Jan Duursema F
❑ NNO John McCrea D
❑ NNO Mary Mitchell E
❑ NNO Monte Moore F
❑ NNO Randy Martinez A
❑ NNO Robert Teranishi C
❑ NNO Scott Erwert E

2006 Lord of the Rings Evolution Stained Glass

COMPLETE SET (10) 8.00 20.00
STATED ODDS 1:6

❑ S1 Aragorn 1.25 3.00
❑ S2 Bilbo 1.25 3.00
❑ S3 Boromir 1.25 3.00
❑ S4 Frodo 1.25 3.00
❑ S5 Gandalf 1.25 3.00
❑ S6 Gimli 1.25 3.00
❑ S7 Legolas 1.25 3.00
❑ S8 Merry 1.25 3.00
❑ S9 Pippin 1.25 3.00
❑ S10 Sam 1.25 3.00

2006 Lord of the Rings Masterpieces

COMPLETE SET (90) 5.00 12.00

❑ 1 The Lord of the Rings Masterpieces .15 .40
❑ 2 Gandalf .15 .40
❑ 3 Frodo .15 .40
❑ 4 Gimli .15 .40
❑ 5 Legolas .15 .40
❑ 6 Aragorn .15 .40
❑ 7 Eowyn .15 .40
❑ 8 Sam .15 .40
❑ 9 Galadriel .15 .40
❑ 10 Bilbo .15 .40
❑ 11 Gollum .15 .40
❑ 12 Saruman .15 .40
❑ 13 Peace and Harmony .15 .40
❑ 14 Evil Never Sleeps .15 .40
❑ 15 The Dark Rider .15 .40
❑ 16 Gandalf's Ally .15 .40
❑ 17 Night of the Watcher .15 .40
❑ 18 Taking on the Terror .15 .40
❑ 19 Forest and the Fortress .15 .40
❑ 20 A Terrible Fate .15 .40
❑ 21 Concept Minas Morgul .15 .40
❑ 22 City Under Siege .15 .40
❑ 23 The Power of Grond .15 .40
❑ 24 Gandalf vs. the Nazgul .15 .40
❑ 25 Lair of the Spider Monster .15 .40
❑ 26 Of Flames and Fury .15 .40
❑ 27 Mammoths on the March .15 .40
❑ 28 Attack of the Mumakil .15 .40
❑ 29 Challenge of the Witch-King .15 .40
❑ 30 Allied with Aragorn .15 .40
❑ 31 A Light Upon Darkness .15 .40
❑ 32 Slopes of Mount Doom .15 .40
❑ 33 The Crack of Doom .15 .40
❑ 34 Flight of the Fell Beasts .15 .40
❑ 35 Gandalf Prevails .15 .40
❑ 36 The Grey Havens .15 .40
❑ 37 Gandalf .15 .40
❑ 38 Frodo .15 .40
❑ 39 Elrond .15 .40
❑ 40 Aragorn .15 .40
❑ 41 Legolas .15 .40
❑ 42 Gimli .15 .40
❑ 43 Galadriel .15 .40
❑ 44 Arwen .15 .40
❑ 45 Eowyn .15 .40
❑ 46 Arwen's Crusade .15 .40
❑ 47 Battlechant .15 .40
❑ 48 Dol Guldur .15 .40
❑ 49 Day of the Dragon .15 .40
❑ 50 Winged Fury .15 .40
❑ 51 Army of the Dwarves .15 .40
❑ 52 Dwarven Stronghold .15 .40
❑ 53 Elrond's Legions .15 .40
❑ 54 Heroic Elves and Dwarves .15 .40
❑ 55 Attack of the Giants .15 .40
❑ 56 The Goblin Camp .15 .40
❑ 57 The Goblin Spider .15 .40
❑ 58 Deadly Encounter .15 .40
❑ 59 Trolls of Moria .15 .40
❑ 60 March of the Inhumans .15 .40
❑ 61 Lair of the Orc Spider .15 .40
❑ 62 A New Dawn .15 .40
❑ 63 Troll Trouble .15 .40
❑ 64 The Witch-King Rises .15 .40
❑ 65 Gandalf .15 .40
❑ 66 Frodo & Sam .15 .40
❑ 67 Gimli .15 .40
❑ 68 Gollum .15 .40
❑ 69 Smeagol .15 .40
❑ 70 Arwen & Frodo .15 .40
❑ 71 Saruman & Wormtongue .15 .40
❑ 72 Treebeard .15 .40
❑ 73 You Shall Not Pass .15 .40
❑ 74 The Three Women .15 .40
❑ 75 Wormtongue & Theoden .15 .40
❑ 76 The Young Baggins .15 .40
❑ 77 A Hobbit Obsessed .15 .40
❑ 78 Merry and Pippin .15 .40
❑ 79 The Warrior Dwarf .15 .40
❑ 80 A Being Transformed .15 .40
❑ 81 Dark Sorcery .15 .40
❑ 82 The Ringbearer .15 .40
❑ 83 The Wizard .15 .40
❑ 84 The Betrayer .15 .40
❑ 85 Sauron's Ring .15 .40
❑ 86 The Wretched .15 .40
❑ 87 The Searchers .15 .40
❑ 88 Saruman's Champion .15 .40
❑ 89 The Future King .15 .40
❑ 90 Checklist .15 .40

2006 Lord of the Rings Masterpieces Etched Foil

COMPLETE SET (6) 6.00 15.00
STATED ODDS 1:6

❑ 1 Sam, Frodo, and Gollum 1.25 3.00
❑ 2 Saruman and Gandalf 1.25 3.00
❑ 3 Merry, Boromir, and Pippin 1.25 3.00
❑ 4 Gimli 1.25 3.00
❑ 5 Aragorn 1.25 3.00
❑ 6 Legolas 1.25 3.00

2006 Lord of the Rings Masterpieces Etched Foil Original Art

STATED ODDS 1:68,000 HOBBY
UNPRICED DUE TO SCARCITY

❑ 1 Sam, Frodo, and Gollum
❑ 2 Saruman and Gandalf
❑ 3 Merry, Boromir, and Pippin
❑ 4 Gimli
❑ 5 Aragorn
❑ 6 Legolas

2006 Lord of the Rings Masterpieces Foil

COMPLETE SET (9) 8.00 20.00
STATED ODDS 1:4

❑ 1 Aragorn 1.25 3.00
❑ 2 Legolas 1.25 3.00
❑ 3 Gimli 1.25 3.00
❑ 4 Gandalf 1.25 3.00
❑ 5 Frodo 1.25 3.00
❑ 6 Sam 1.25 3.00
❑ 7 Pippin 1.25 3.00
❑ 8 Merry 1.25 3.00
❑ 9 Boromir 1.25 3.00

2006 Lord of the Rings Masterpieces Foil Bronze

COMPLETE SET (9) 60.00 120.00
STATED ODDS 1:36 HOBBY

❑ 1 Aragorn 6.00 15.00
❑ 2 Legolas 6.00 15.00
❑ 3 Gimli 6.00 15.00
❑ 4 Gandalf 6.00 15.00
❑ 5 Frodo 6.00 15.00
❑ 6 Sam 6.00 15.00
❑ 7 Pippin 6.00 15.00
❑ 8 Merry 6.00 15.00
❑ 9 Boromir 6.00 15.00

2006 Lord of the Rings Masterpieces Foil Gold

STATED ODDS 1:484 HOBBY

❑ 1 Aragorn
❑ 2 Legolas
❑ 3 Gimli
❑ 4 Gandalf
❑ 5 Frodo
❑ 6 Sam
❑ 7 Pippin
❑ 8 Merry
❑ 9 Boromir

2006 Lord of the Rings Masterpieces Foil Refractor

STATED ODDS 1:45,000 HOBBY
UNPRICED DUE TO SCARCITY

2006 Lord of the Rings Masterpieces Sketches

OVERALL STATED ODDS 1:18 HOBBY
GROUP A STATED ODDS 1:1653
GROUP B STATED ODDS 1:146
GROUP C STATED ODDS 1:122
GROUP D STATED ODDS 1:163
GROUP E STATED ODDS 1:314
GROUP F STATED ODDS 1:265
GROUP G STATED ODDS 1:248
GROUP H STATED ODDS 1:89
GROUP I STATED ODDS 1:59

❑ NNO Brandon McKinney C
❑ NNO Christian Dalla Vecchia I
❑ NNO Darla Ecklund D
❑ NNO Davide Fabbri I
❑ NNO Howard Shum I
❑ NNO Josh Howard B
❑ NNO Jim Kyle C
❑ NNO John Watkins-Chow D
❑ NNO Justin Chung A
❑ NNO Kyle Babbitt B
❑ NNO Mary Huang B
❑ NNO Mike Deming B
❑ NNO Paul Gutierrez D
❑ NNO Robert Teranishi H
❑ NNO Sarah Wilkinson G
❑ NNO Tess Fowler C
❑ NNO William O'Neill E
❑ NNO Allison Sohn C
❑ NNO Brian Rood B
❑ NNO Colleen Doran D
❑ NNO Dave Fox B
❑ NNO Gabe Hernandez B
❑ NNO James Hodgkins A
❑ NNO Jerry Vanderstelt B
❑ NNO Joe Corroney B
❑ NNO Joseph Booth C
❑ NNO Keith Phillips D
❑ NNO Lee Kohse D
❑ NNO Michael Duron C
❑ NNO Otto Dieffenbach B
❑ NNO Renae De Liz B
❑ NNO Russ Walks A
❑ NNO Steve Oatney B
❑ NNO Tom Hodges E
❑ NNO Brent Engstrom C
❑ NNO Chuck Zsolnai B
❑ NNO Dave Dorman B
❑ NNO Dennis Budd B
❑ NNO Jake Myler D
❑ NNO Jeff Zapata A
❑ NNO Joanne Mutch B
❑ NNO Jon Ocampo C
❑ NNO Katie Cook H
❑ NNO Leah Mangue G
❑ NNO Matthew Goodmanson F
❑ NNO Otis Frampton B
❑ NNO Ray Dillon C
❑ NNO Roberto Flores F
❑ NNO Sean Pence C
❑ NNO Thomas Denmark B
❑ NNO Amy Pronovost C
❑ NNO Cat Staggs C
❑ NNO Connie Persampieri D
❑ NNO David Rabbitte B
❑ NNO Grant Gould H
❑ NNO Jeff Chandler B
❑ NNO Jessica Hickman F
❑ NNO John McCrea A
❑ NNO Juan Carlos Ramos B
❑ NNO Kevin Graham E
❑ NNO Len Bellinger B
❑ NNO Mike Lilly B
❑ NNO Patrick Hamill C
❑ NNO Rich Molinelli C
❑ NNO Ryan Waterhouse H
❑ NNO Steven Miller B
❑ NNO Walter Rice C

2006 Lost Revelations

COMPLETE SET (81) 5.00 12.00

❑ 1 Lost: Revelations .15 .40
❑ 2 Jack Shephard .15 .40
❑ 3 Kate Austen .15 .40
❑ 4 John Locke .15 .40
❑ 5 Michael Dawson .15 .40
❑ 6 Walt Lloyd .15 .40
❑ 7 James "Sawyer" Ford .15 .40
❑ 8 Sun Kwon .15 .40
❑ 9 Jin Kwon .15 .40
❑ 10 Sayid Jarrah .15 .40
❑ 11 Shannon Rutherford .15 .40
❑ 12 Boone Carlyle .15 .40
❑ 13 Claire Littleton .15 .40
❑ 14 Aaron Littleton .15 .40
❑ 15 Charlie Pace .15 .40
❑ 16 Hugo "Hurley" Reyes .15 .40
❑ 17 Rose Henderson .15 .40
❑ 18 Dr. Leslie Arzt .15 .40
❑ 19 Ana Lucia Cortez .15 .40
❑ 20 Bernard Nadler .15 .40
❑ 21 Libby .15 .40
❑ 22 Nathan .15 .40
❑ 23 Mr. Eko .15 .40
❑ 24 Cindy .15 .40
❑ 25 Emma & Zach .15 .40
❑ 26 First Contact .15 .40
❑ 27 Together .15 .40
❑ 28 Claire .15 .40
❑ 29 Walt .15 .40
❑ 30 Zach .15 .40
❑ 31 Emma .15 .40
❑ 32 Nathan .15 .40
❑ 33 Cindy .15 .40
❑ 34 Alex .15 .40
❑ 35 Kate .15 .40
❑ 36 Michael .15 .40
❑ 37 Ethan Rom .15 .40
❑ 38 Terrorized .15 .40
❑ 39 Goodwin .15 .40
❑ 40 Mr. Friendly .15 .40
❑ 41 Henry Gale .15 .40
❑ 42 Disguised .15 .40
❑ 43 Alex .15 .40
❑ 44 Medical Unit .15 .40
❑ 45 Deal .15 .40
❑ 46 Desmond .15 .40
❑ 47 The Film .15 .40
❑ 48 Food .15 .40
❑ 49 Shower .15 .40
❑ 50 Computer .15 .40
❑ 51 Timer .15 .40
❑ 52 Missing Footage .15 .40
❑ 53 Lockdown .15 .40
❑ 54 Food Drop .15 .40
❑ 55 4 Minutes To Enter Code .15 .40
❑ 56 Aaron Awake For 8 Hours .15 .40
❑ 57 Lock Tells Jack Vault Code R15 .15 .40
❑ 58 16 Virgin Mary Statues .15 .40
❑ 59 23 Tail Section Survivors .15 .40
❑ 60 Locke's Crossword Clue 42 Down .15 .40
❑ 61 Others Vaccine .15 .40
❑ 62 Numbers Needed For Computer Code .15 .40
❑ 63 Total = 108 .15 .40
❑ 64 Locke Obsessed With The Hatch .15 .40
❑ 65 Michael Must Find Walt .15 .40
❑ 66 Shannon Must Be Believed .15 .40
❑ 67 Charlie Fixated On Statue .15 .40
❑ 68 Claire Worried About Aaron .15 .40
❑ 69 Tree Frog .15 .40
❑ 70 Hurley's Friend .15 .40
❑ 71 Bernard's Rescue Plan .15 .40
❑ 72 Mr. Eko Builds Church .15 .40
❑ 73 Hatch Inhabitant .15 .40
❑ 74 Sawyer Injured .15 .40
❑ 75 Ana Lucia Kills Goodwin .15 .40
❑ 76 Mr. Eko And Jin See The Others .15 .40
❑ 77 Ana Lucia's Mistake .15 .40
❑ 78 Alex Helps Claire .15 .40
❑ 79 Sun Abducted .15 .40
❑ 80 Mr. Eko Faces The Smoke "Monster" .15 .40
❑ 81 Checklist .15 .40

2006 Lost Revelations Autographs

STATED ODDS 1:36

❑ A1 Yunjin Kim 25.00 50.00
❑ A2 Neil Hopkins 6.00 15.00
❑ A3 Julie Bowen 15.00 30.00
❑ A4 Veronica Hamel 6.00 15.00
❑ A5 Andrea Gabriel 6.00 15.00
❑ A6 Tamara Taylor 6.00 15.00
❑ A7 Katey Sagal 20.00 40.00
❑ A8 Adetokumboh M'Cormack 6.00 15.00
❑ A9 M.C. Gainey 6.00 15.00
❑ A10 Dustin Watchman 6.00 15.00
❑ A11 Byron Chung 6.00 15.00

2006 Lost Revelations Black & White

STATED ODDS 1:17

❑ BW1 Black & White 1.25 3.00
❑ BW2 Black & White 1.25 3.00
❑ BW3 Black & White 1.25 3.00
❑ BW4 Black & White 1.25 3.00
❑ BW5 Black & White 1.25 3.00
❑ BW6 Black & White 1.25 3.00

2006 Lost Revelations Box Loaders

BL1-BL3 STATED ODDS ONE PER BOX
CL1 STATED ODDS ONE PER CASE

❑ BL1 Box Loader 1 – Mission Survival
❑ BL2 Box Loader 2 – Mission Survival
❑ BL3 Box Loader 3 – Mission Survival
❑ CL1 Case Loader – Countdown

2006 Lost Revelations Inside The Island

STATED ODDS 1:11

❑ I1 Inside The Island 1.00 2.50
❑ I2 Inside The Island 1.00 2.50
❑ I3 Inside The Island 1.00 2.50
❑ I4 Inside The Island 1.00 2.50
❑ I5 Inside The Island 1.00 2.50
❑ I6 Inside The Island 1.00 2.50
❑ I7 Inside The Island 1.00 2.50
❑ I8 Inside The Island 1.00 2.50
❑ I9 Inside The Island 1.00 2.50

2006 Lost Revelations Pieceworks

STATED ODDS 1:36

❑ PW1 Matthew Fox 8.00 20.00
❑ PW2 Evangeline Lilly 12.00 30.00
❑ PW3 Josh Holloway 8.00 20.00
❑ PW4 Harold Perrineau 8.00 20.00
❑ PW5 Jorge Garcia 6.00 15.00
❑ PW6 Emilie De Ravin 10.00 25.00
❑ PW7 Cynthia Watros 8.00 20.00
❑ PW8 Matthew Fox Evangeline Lilly 125.00 200.00
❑ PW9 Josh Holloway Evangeline Lilly 50.00 100.00

2006 Lost Season Two

COMPLETE SET (90) 5.00 12.00

❑ 1 Lost .15 .40
❑ 2 Fixed .15 .40
❑ 3 Lift It Up .15 .40
❑ 4 Farewell .15 .40
❑ 5 Resolved .15 .40
❑ 6 Let Go .15 .40
❑ 7 Faith .15 .40
❑ 8 Unchanged .15 .40
❑ 9 Generous .15 .40
❑ 10 Orange .15 .40
❑ 11 Missed .15 .40
❑ 12 Left Behind .15 .40
❑ 13 Believed .15 .40
❑ 14 Enemy .15 .40
❑ 15 Mistake .15 .40
❑ 16 Trusting .15 .40
❑ 17 Despair .15 .40
❑ 18 Black Horse .15 .40
❑ 19 Not Good .15 .40
❑ 20 Warlord .15 .40
❑ 21 Transformed .15 .40
❑ 22 Tempted .15 .40
❑ 23 Taunted .15 .40
❑ 24 Desperate .15 .40
❑ 25 Determined .15 .40
❑ 26 Attacked .15 .40
❑ 27 Hooked .15 .40
❑ 28 Captured .15 .40
❑ 29 Interrogation .15 .40
❑ 30 Euphoric .15 .40
❑ 31 Searching .15 .40
❑ 32 Withheld .15 .40
❑ 33 Miracle .15 .40
❑ 34 Consequences .15 .40
❑ 35 Tested .15 .40
❑ 36 Friends .15 .40
❑ 37 On The Edge .15 .40
❑ 38 Beyond Help .15 .40
❑ 39 Truth .15 .40
❑ 40 Vengeful .15 .40
❑ 41 Victim .15 .40
❑ 42 Godly .15 .40
❑ 43 Discovery .15 .40
❑ 44 Orders .15 .40
❑ 45 Mission .15 .40
❑ 46 Returned .15 .40
❑ 47 Confronted .15 .40
❑ 48 Countdown .15 .40
❑ 49 Blown .15 .40
❑ 50 Captured .15 .40
❑ 51 Jack: Man Of Science .15 .40
❑ 52 Kate: Wanted .15 .40
❑ 53 Sawyer: Confidence .15 .40
❑ 54 Locke: Man Of Faith .15 .40
❑ 55 Sun: Privileged .15 .40
❑ 56 Jin: Loyal .15 .40
❑ 57 Charlie: Family Man .15 .40
❑ 58 Claire: Mother .15 .40
❑ 59 Hurley: Lucky .15 .40
❑ 60 Michael: Desperate .15 .40
❑ 61 Walt: Missing .15 .40
❑ 62 Sayid: Soldier .15 .40
❑ 63 Shannon: Spoiled .15 .40
❑ 64 Rose: Faithful .15 .40
❑ 65 Bernard: Protector .15 .40
❑ 66 Ana Lucia: Haunted .15 .40
❑ 67 Mr. Eko: Righteous .15 .40
❑ 68 Libby: Healing .15 .40
❑ 69 Desmond: On A Quest .15 .40
❑ 70 The Others: Ethan .15 .40
❑ 71 The Others: Goodwin .15 .40
❑ 72 The Others: Henry Gale .15 .40
❑ 73 The Others: Mr. Friendly .15 .40
❑ 74 The Others: Ms. Klugh .15 .40
❑ 75 The Others: Pickett .15 .40
❑ 76 The Others: Alex .15 .40
❑ 77 Rambina .15 .40
❑ 78 Muttonchops .15 .40
❑ 79 Cool Hand .15 .40
❑ 80 Pippi Longstocking .15 .40
❑ 81 Shaft .15 .40
❑ 82 Sayid + Shannon .15 .40
❑ 83 Hurley + Libby .15 .40
❑ 84 Desmond + Penny .15 .40
❑ 85 Sawyer + Ana Lucia .15 .40

□ 86 Ana Lucia .15 .40
Christian/Jack
□ 87 Richard Malkin .15 .40
Mr. Eko/Claire
□ 88 Desmond .15 .40
Libby
□ 89 Kate .15 .40
Sam Austen/Sayid
□ 90 Checklist .15 .40

2006 Lost Season Two Question Mark

STATED ODDS 1:11

□ 1 Question Mark 1.00 2.50
□ 2 Question Mark 1.00 2.50
□ 3 Question Mark 1.00 2.50
□ 4 Question Mark 1.00 2.50
□ 5 Question Mark 1.00 2.50
□ 6 Question Mark 1.00 2.50
□ 7 Question Mark 1.00 2.50
□ 8 Question Mark 1.00 2.50
□ 9 Question Mark 1.00 2.50

2006 Lost Season Two Autographs

STATED ODDS 1:36

□ A13 Emilie De Ravin 25.00 50.00
□ A14 Yunjin Kim 25.00 50.00
□ A15 L. Scott Caldwell 6.00 15.00
□ A16 Sam Anderson 5.00 12.00
□ A17 Michael Emerson 25.00 50.00
□ A18 Brett Cullen 5.00 12.00
□ A19 Tania Raymonde 8.00 20.00
□ A20 Kimberly Joseph 6.00 15.00
□ A21 Josh Randall 5.00 12.00
□ A22 Monica Dean 6.00 15.00
□ A23 Francois Chau 6.00 15.00
□ A24 Sonya Walger 8.00 20.00

2006 Lost Season Two Betrayal

STATED ODDS 1:17

□ B1 Betrayal 1.25 3.00
□ B2 Betrayal 1.25 3.00
□ B3 Betrayal 1.25 3.00
□ B4 Betrayal 1.25 3.00
□ B5 Betrayal 1.25 3.00
□ B6 Betrayal 1.25 3.00

2006 Lost Season Two Box Loaders

BL1-BL3 STATED ODDS ONE PER BOX
CL1 STATED ODDS ONE PER CASE

□ BL1 Jack CAP 2.00 5.00
□ BL2 Kate CAP 2.00 5.00
□ BL3 Sawyer CAP 2.00 5.00
□ CL1 Fail Safe 5.00 12.00

2006 Lost Season Two Pieceworks

STATED ODDS 1:36

□ PW1 Terry O'Quinn 8.00 20.00
□ PW2 Naveen Andrews 5.00 12.00
□ PW3 Yunjin Kim 10.00 25.00
□ PW4 Josh Holloway 8.00 20.00
□ PW5 Jorge Garcia 5.00 12.00
□ PW6 Evangeline Lilly 25.00 50.00
□ PW7 Dominic Monaghan 5.00 12.00
□ PW8 Adewale Akinnouye-Agbaje 5.00 12.00
□ PW9 Dominic Monaghan Sand 20.00 40.00
□ PW10 Jorge Garcia Sand 15.00 30.00
□ PW11 Josh Holloway Shirt/Sand 20.00 40.00
□ PW12A Harold Perrineau 15.00 30.00
□ PW12B Jack Shepard 15.00 30.00

2006 Razor Poker

COMPLETE SET (76) 10.00 25.00

□ 1 Daniel Negreanu .25 .60
□ 2 Josh Arieh .25 .60
□ 3 Hoyt Corkins .25 .60
□ 4 Juan Carlos Mortensen .25 .60
□ 5 Kathy Liebert .25 .60
□ 6 Phil Gordon .25 .60
□ 7 David Williams .25 .60
□ 8 Erick Lindgren .25 .60
□ 9 Erik Seidel .25 .60
□ 10 T.J. Cloutier .25 .60
□ 11 Phil Hellmuth .25 .60
□ 12 John Juanda .25 .60
□ 13 Antonio Esfandiari .25 .60
□ 14 Phil Laak .25 .60
□ 15 Amir Vahedi .25 .60
□ 16 Layne Flack .25 .60
□ 17 Ted Forrest .25 .60
□ 18 Chip Jett .25 .60
□ 19 Jennifer Harman .25 .60
□ 20 Michael Gracz .25 .60
□ 21 Michael Mizrachi .25 .60
□ 22 Evelyn Ng .25 .60
□ 23 Isabelle Mercier .25 .60
□ 24 Cyndy Violette .25 .60
□ 25 Jerry Buss .25 .60
□ 26 Gavin Smith .25 .60
□ 27 Jennifer Tilly .25 .60
□ 28 Greg Raymer .25 .60
□ 29 Chris Moneymaker .25 .60
□ 30 Joe Hachem .25 .60
□ 31 Scotty Nguyen .25 .60
□ 32 Todd Brunson .25 .60
□ 33 Sean Sheikhan .25 .60
□ 34 Mike Matusow .25 .60
□ 35 Kenna James .25 .60
□ 36 Sammy Farha .25 .60
□ 37 Men Nguyen .25 .60
□ 38 T.J. Cloutier .25 .60
□ 39 Men Nguyen .25 .60
□ 40 Scotty Nguyen .25 .60
□ 41 Ted Forrest .25 .60
□ 42 Phil Hellmuth .25 .60
□ 43 Phil Hellmuth .25 .60
Mike Matusow
□ 44 Greg Raymer .25 .60
David Williams
□ 45 Layne Flack .25 .60
Jerry Buss
□ 46 Phil Gordon .25 .60
Chris Moneymaker
□ 47 Phil Hellmuth .25 .60
T.J. Cloutier
□ 48 Daniel Negreanu .25 .60
David Williams
□ 49 Gavin Smith .25 .60
Ted Forrest
□ 50 Todd Brunson .25 .60
Sean Sheikhan
□ 51 Scotty Nguyen .25 .60
Michael Mizrachi
□ 52 Sammy Farha .25 .60
Chris Moneymaker
□ 53 Scotty Nguyen .25 .60
Phil Hellmuth
□ 54 Todd Brunson .25 .60
Men Nguyen
□ 55 Mike Matusow .25 .60
Hoyt Corkins
□ 56 John Juanda .25 .60
Men Nguyen
□ 57 Amir Vahedi .25 .60
Chip Jett
□ 58 Phil Hellmuth .25 .60
Daniel Negreanu
□ 59 Erik Seidel .25 .60
Cyndy Violette
□ 60 Greg Raymer .25 .60
Mike Matusow
□ 61 Greg Raymer .25 .60
□ 62 Chris Moneymaker .25 .60
□ 63 Phil Hellmuth .25 .60
□ 64 T.J. Cloutier .25 .60
□ 65 Erik Seidel .25 .60
□ 66 Layne Flack .25 .60
□ 67 Daniel Negreanu .25 .60
□ 68 Mike Matusow .25 .60
□ 69 Jennifer Harman .25 .60
□ 70 Todd Brunson .25 .60
□ 71 Hoyt Corkins .25 .60
□ 72 Joe Hachem .25 .60
□ 73 Kathy Liebert .25 .60
□ 74 Cyndy Violette .25 .60
□ 75 Ted Forrest .25 .60
□ 76 Checklist .25 .60

2006 Razor Poker Poker Paraphernalia Autographs

STATED ODDS 1:288
CARD PP1 WAS NOT ISSUED

□ PP2 Phil Hellmuth
□ PP3 Ted Forrest
□ PP4 Phil Laak
□ PP5 Antonio Esfandiari

2006 Razor Poker Showdown Signatures

STATED ODDS 1:12
A38 AVAILABLE THROUGH CASE PURCHASE ONLY

□ A1 Daniel Negreanu
□ A2 Josh Arieh
□ A3 Hoyt Corkins
□ A4 Juan Carlos Mortensen
□ A5 Kathy Liebert
□ A6 Phil Gordon
□ A7 David Williams
□ A8 Erick Lindgren SP
□ A9 Erik Seidel
□ A10 T.J. Cloutier
□ A11 Phil Hellmuth
□ A12 John Juanda SP
□ A13 Antonio Esfandiari
□ A14 Phil Laak
□ A15 Amir Vahedi
□ A16 Layne Flack
□ A17 Ted Forrest SP
□ A18 Chip Jett
□ A19 Jennifer Harman
□ A20 Michael Gracz
□ A21 Michael Mizrachi SP
□ A22 Evelyn Ng
□ A23 Isabelle Mercier
□ A24 Cyndy Violette
□ A25 Jerry Buss
□ A26 Gavin Smith
□ A27 Jennifer Tilly
□ A28 Greg Raymer SP
□ A29 Chris Moneymaker
□ A30 Joe Hachem SP
□ A31 Scotty Nguyen
□ A32 Todd Brunson
□ A33 Sean Sheikhan
□ A34 Mike Matusow
□ A35 Kenna James
□ A36 Sammy Farha SP
□ A37 Men Nguyen
□ A38 Cindy Margolis

2006 Smallville Season Five

COMPLETE SET (90) 5.00 12.00

□ 1 Title Card .15 .40
□ 2 Clark Kent .15 .40
□ 3 Lois Lane .15 .40
□ 4 Lana Lang .15 .40
□ 5 Lex Luthor .15 .40
□ 6 Chloe Sullivan .15 .40
□ 7 Jonathan Kent .15 .40
□ 8 Martha Kent .15 .40
□ 9 Lionel Luthor .15 .40
□ 10 Men Of Conscience .15 .40
□ 11 Put The Heart Back In The Heartland .15 .40
□ 12 Lois Lane – Campaign Manager? .15 .40
□ 13 Killer Appeal .15 .40
□ 14 Senator Kent – The Win .15 .40
□ 15 Senator Kent – The Loss .15 .40
□ 16 Taking Up The Task .15 .40
□ 17 Pressing The Issues .15 .40
□ 18 Sky's The Limit .15 .40
□ 19 Sparky & The Bubble Tent Twins .15 .40
□ 20 Nuclear Family – Smallville Style .15 .40
□ 21 Pledge Night Bites .15 .40
□ 22 Hostess With A Ghostess .15 .40
□ 23 Bad Vibrations .15 .40
□ 24 See No Evil .15 .40
□ 25 Aquaman .15 .40
□ 26 Vigilante .15 .40
□ 27 Cyborg .15 .40
□ 28 Mortal Mates .15 .40
□ 29 Back To Square One .15 .40
□ 30 Telling The Truth... .15 .40
□ 31 Alienation .15 .40
□ 32 Breakup Breakdown .15 .40
□ 33 Rebound .15 .40
□ 34 Chariot Of Zod .15 .40
□ 35 Brain Interactive Construct .15 .40
□ 36 Oracle .15 .40
□ 37 Silver K .15 .40
□ 38 Kill The Fortress! .15 .40
□ 39 As Many As It Takes .15 .40
□ 40 Preparing The Vessel .15 .40
□ 41 Killing The Wrong Bad Guy .15 .40
□ 42 Kneel Before Zod! .15 .40
□ 43 Fortress .15 .40
□ 44 Disciples Of Zod .15 .40
□ 45 Phantom Zone Exile .15 .40
□ 46 State Of Shock .15 .40
□ 47 Human Power .15 .40
□ 48 Merely Mortal .15 .40
□ 49 Rocket Man .15 .40
□ 50 Aqua-Terrorist .15 .40
□ 51 Water Torture .15 .40
□ 52 Sorority Vamps .15 .40
□ 53 One For The Heart .15 .40
□ 54 A Picture Of Concern .15 .40
□ 55 Pole Position .15 .40
□ 56 Paranoid Blues .15 .40
□ 57 Extracting Trust .15 .40
□ 58 Killer From Krypton .15 .40
□ 59 Kill The Messenger .15 .40
□ 60 It's A Wonderful Wife .15 .40
□ 61 Poor & Powerless .15 .40
□ 62 The Very Loyal Opposition .15 .40
□ 63 Assassin .15 .40
□ 64 Safe Tomb .15 .40
□ 65 Out Of The Fiery Furnace .15 .40
□ 66 If I Could Turn Back Time... .15 .40
□ 67 High Cost Of Loving .15 .40
□ 68 Over The Line .15 .40
□ 69 Avenging Angel .15 .40
□ 70 Edge Of Madness .15 .40
□ 71 K Is For Karma .15 .40
□ 72 Bleeding Edge Technology .15 .40
□ 73 Independence Not An Option .15 .40
□ 74 Stone Cold Simone .15 .40
□ 75 The Spell Shatters .15 .40
□ 76 To See Beyond .15 .40
□ 77 Grim Vision .15 .40
□ 78 Through A Glass Sharply .15 .40
□ 79 Jagged Relations .15 .40
□ 80 The Deadliest Game .15 .40
□ 81 Secrets Revealed .15 .40
□ 82 See No Evil .15 .40
□ 83 The End .15 .40
□ 84 The Deadliest Game .15 .40
□ 85 Bad Advice .15 .40
□ 86 Kill The Vessel! .15 .40
□ 87 End Of The World .15 .40
□ 88 Killer Of Worlds .15 .40
□ 89 After Me...The Dynasty .15 .40
□ 90 Checklist .15 .40

2006 Smallville Season Five Autographs

STATED ODDS 1:36

□ A35 James Marsters 8.00 20.00
□ A36 Tom Wopat 25.00 50.00
□ A37 Alan Ritchson 8.00 20.00
□ A38 Lee Thompson Young 8.00 20.00
□ A39 Denise Quinones 8.00 20.00
□ A40 Alisen Down 8.00 20.00
□ A41 Brooke Nevin 8.00 20.00
□ A42 Johnny Lewis 8.00 20.00
□ A43 Rekha Sharma 8.00 20.00
□ A44 Nichole Hiltz 8.00 20.00
□ A45 Jerry Wasserman 8.00 20.00

2006 Smallville Season Five Box Loaders

COMPLETE SET (4) 8.00 20.00
STATED ODDS ONE PER BOX
CL1 ISSUED AS CASE TOPPER

□ BL1 Nam-Ek & Aethyr 2.00 5.00
□ BL2 Brainiac 2.00 5.00
□ BL3 Zod 2.00 5.00
□ CL1 Banished 4.00 10.00
(issued as case topper)

2006 Smallville Season Five Pieceworks

STATED ODDS 1:36

□ PW1 Tom Welling 12.00 30.00
□ PW2 Michael Rosenbaum 10.00 25.00
□ PW3 Kristin Kreuk 12.00 30.00
□ PW4 Allison Mack 12.00 30.00
□ PW5 Erica Durance 12.00 30.00
□ PW6 John Schneider 10.00 25.00
□ PW7 Annette O'Toole 10.00 25.00
□ PW8 John Glover 10.00 25.00
□ PW9 James Marsters 10.00 25.00
□ PW10 Tom Wopat 10.00 25.00
□ PW11A Tom Wopat 30.00 60.00
(issued as multi-case incentive)
□ PW11B John Schneider 30.00 60.00
(issued as multi-case incentive)

2006 Smallville Season Five The Price of Life

STATED ODDS 1:17

□ PL1 Time of Death 1.50 4.00
□ PL2 Resurrection 1.50 4.00
□ PL3 Who Will It Be? 1.50 4.00
□ PL4 Debt Collection 1.50 4.00
□ PL5 Buying a Second Chance 1.50 4.00
□ PL6 Funerals Are For The Living 1.50 4.00

2006 Smallville Season Five Triangles

STATED ODDS 1:11

□ TR1 Bound for Life 1.25 3.00
□ TR2 Chloe to Conscience 1.25 3.00
□ TR3 Friendship Defined 1.25 3.00
□ TR4 Heartland Heartbreak 1.25 3.00
□ TR5 Secret is Out 1.25 3.00
□ TR6 Faithful Servant 1.25 3.00
□ TR7 Like Family 1.25 3.00
□ TR8 A Common Interest 1.25 3.00
□ TR9 Father Figure 1.25 3.00

2006 Star Trek 40th Anniversary

COMPLETE SET (90) 5.00 12.00
LA2 STATED ODDS ONE PER 6 CASE PURCHASE

□ 1 Where No Man Has Gone Before .15 .40
□ 2 The Corbomite Maneuver .15 .40
□ 3 Space Seed .15 .40
□ 4 Court-Martial .15 .40
□ 5 Balance of Terror .15 .40
□ 6 What Are Little Girls Made Of .15 .40
□ 7 Arena .15 .40
□ 8 The Changeling .15 .40
□ 9 The City on the Edge of Forever .15 .40
□ 10 The Doomsday Machine .15 .40
□ 11 Errand of Mercy .15 .40
□ 12 The Devil in the Dark .15 .40
□ 13 A Piece of the Action .15 .40
□ 14 Journey to Babel .15 .40
□ 15 The Gamesters of Triskelion .15 .40
□ 16 The Enterprise Incident .15 .40
□ 17 Mirror, Mirror .15 .40
□ 18 Conscience of the King .15 .40
□ 19 The Battle .15 .40
□ 20 The Big Goodbye .15 .40
□ 21 The Measure of a Man .15 .40
□ 22 Time Squared .15 .40
□ 23 Captain's Holiday .15 .40
□ 24 Best of Both Worlds .15 .40
□ 25 Family .15 .40
□ 26 Darmok .15 .40
□ 27 The Perfect Mate .15 .40
□ 28 The Inner Light .15 .40
□ 29 Chain of Command .15 .40
□ 30 Tapestry .15 .40
□ 31 Starship Mine .15 .40
□ 32 Lessons .15 .40
□ 33 Gambit .15 .40
□ 34 Attached .15 .40
□ 35 Bloodlines .15 .40
□ 36 All Good Things .15 .40
□ 37 Emissary .15 .40
□ 38 In the Hands of the Prophets .15 .40
□ 39 Second Sight .15 .40
□ 40 The Search .15 .40
□ 41 Past Tense .15 .40
□ 42 Through the Looking Glass .15 .40
□ 43 Explorers .15 .40
□ 44 The Adversary .15 .40
□ 45 Homefront .15 .40
□ 46 Shattered Mirror .15 .40
□ 47 Rapture .15 .40
□ 48 For the Uniform .15 .40
□ 49 Blaze of Glory .15 .40
□ 50 Rocks and Shoals .15 .40
□ 51 Far Beyond the Stars .15 .40
□ 52 In the Pale Moonlight .15 .40
□ 53 Shadows and Symbols .15 .40
□ 54 What You Leave Behind .15 .40
□ 55 Caretaker .15 .40
□ 56 Resistance .15 .40
□ 57 Alliances .15 .40
□ 58 Tuvix .15 .40
□ 59 Sacred Ground .15 .40
□ 60 The Q and the Grey .15 .40
□ 61 Coda .15 .40
□ 62 Concerning Flight .15 .40
□ 63 Scientific Method .15 .40
□ 64 Year of Hell .15 .40
□ 65 The Killing Game .15 .40
□ 66 Counterpoint .15 .40
□ 67 Bride of Chaotica .15 .40
□ 68 Dark Frontier .15 .40
□ 69 Equinox .15 .40
□ 70 Fair Haven .15 .40
□ 71 Good Shepherd .15 .40
□ 72 Endgame .15 .40
□ 73 The Andorian Incident .15 .40
□ 74 Cold Front .15 .40
□ 75 Rogue Planet .15 .40
□ 76 Desert Crossing .15 .40
□ 77 Shockwave .15 .40
□ 78 A Night in Sickbay .15 .40
□ 79 Judgment .15 .40
□ 80 First Flight .15 .40
□ 81 Stratagem .15 .40
□ 82 Hatchery .15 .40
□ 83 Azati Prime .15 .40
□ 84 Damage .15 .40
□ 85 Zero Hour .15 .40
□ 86 Storm Front .15 .40
□ 87 Awakening .15 .40
□ 88 Observer Effect .15 .40
□ 89 United .15 .40
□ 90 Bound .15 .40
□ LA2 Patrick Stewart AU 125.00 200.00

2006 Star Trek 40th Anniversary ArtiFEX Box Toppers

COMPLETE SET (5)
STATED ODDS ONE PER BOX

□ BT1 The Original Series Crew
□ BT2 The Next Generation Crew
□ BT3 Deep Space Nine Crew
□ BT4 Voyager Crew
□ BT5 Enterprise Crew

2006 Star Trek 40th Anniversary ArtiFEX Bridge Crew Portraits

COMPLETE SET (43) 50.00 120.00
STATED ODDS 1:10

□ FP1 Captain James T. Kirk 1.50 4.00
□ FP2 Lt. Commander Spock 1.50 4.00
□ FP3 Dr. Leonard McCoy 1.50 4.00
□ FP4 Lt. Commander Montgomery Scott 1.50 4.00
□ FP5 Ensign Pavel Chekov 1.50 4.00
□ FP6 Lt. Uhura 1.50 4.00
□ FP7 Lt. Hikaru Sulu 1.50 4.00
□ FP8 Nurse Christine Chapel 1.50 4.00
□ FP9 Yeoman Janice Rand 1.50 4.00
□ FP10 Captain Jean-Luc Picard 1.50 4.00
□ FP11 Commander William Riker 1.50 4.00
□ FP12 Lt. Commander Data 1.50 4.00
□ FP13 Lt. Geordi LaForge 1.50 4.00
□ FP14 Lt. Worf 1.50 4.00
□ FP15 Dr. Beverly Crusher 1.50 4.00
□ FP16 Lt. Commander Deanna Troi 1.50 4.00
□ FP17 Lt. Natasha Yar 1.50 4.00
□ FP18 Ensign Wesley Crusher 1.50 4.00
□ FP19 Captain Benjamin Sisko 1.50 4.00
□ FP20 Constable Odo 1.50 4.00
□ FP21 Lt. Ezri Dax 1.50 4.00
□ FP22 Lt. Commander Worf 1.50 4.00
□ FP23 Lt. Commander Jadzia Dax 1.50 4.00
□ FP24 Chief Petty Officer Miles O'Brien 1.50 4.00
□ FP25 Quark 1.50 4.00
□ FP26 Dr. Julian Bashir 1.50 4.00
□ FP27 Col. Kira Nerys 1.50 4.00
□ FP28 Captain Kathryn Janeway 1.50 4.00
□ FP29 Commander Chakotay 1.50 4.00
□ FP30 Lt. B'Elanna Torres 1.50 4.00
□ FP31 Lt. Tom Paris 1.50 4.00
□ FP32 Neelix 1.50 4.00
□ FP33 The Doctor 1.50 4.00
□ FP34 Lt. CommanderTuvok 1.50 4.00
□ FP35 Seven of Nine 1.50 4.00
□ FP36 Ensign Harry Kim 1.50 4.00
□ FP37 Captain Jonathan Archer 1.50 4.00
□ FP38 Subcommander T'Pol 1.50 4.00
□ FP39 Lt. Commander Charles Tucker III 1.50 4.00
□ FP40 Lt. Malcolm Reed 1.50 4.00
□ FP41 Ensign Hoshi Sato 1.50 4.00
□ FP42 Ensign Travis Mayweather 1.50 4.00
□ FP43 Dr. Phlox 1.50 4.00

2006 Star Trek 40th Anniversary ArtiFEX Villains Portraits

COMPLETE SET (9) 60.00 120.00
STATED ODDS 1:40 UK PACKS

□ VP1 Borg Queen 6.00 15.00
□ VP2 Q 6.00 15.00
□ VP3 Khan 6.00 15.00
□ VP4 Gul Dukat 6.00 15.00
□ VP5 Silik 6.00 15.00
□ VP6 Kor 6.00 15.00
□ VP7 Hirogen 6.00 15.00
□ VP8 Jem'Hadar 6.00 15.00
□ VP9 Romulans Sela 6.00 15.00

2006 Star Trek 40th Anniversary Autographed Costumes

STATED ODDS 1:240

□ C1 Jeri Ryan 125.00 200.00
□ NNO William Shatner
□ NNO Avery Brooks 75.00 150.00
□ NNO Scott Bakula 60.00 120.00
□ NNO Brent Spiner 75.00 150.00

2006 Star Trek 40th Anniversary First Officers

COMPLETE SET (6) 25.00 60.00
STATED ODDS 1:40

□ N1 Number One 5.00 12.00
□ N2 Commander Spock 5.00 12.00
□ N3 Commander William Riker 5.00 12.00
□ N4 Colonel Kira Nerys 5.00 12.00
□ N5 Commander Chakotay 5.00 12.00
□ N6 Commander T'Pol 5.00 12.00

2006 Star Trek 40th Anniversary From the Archives Costumes

STATED ODDS 1:20
DC1 STATED ODDS ONE PER 2 CASE PURCHASE

□ C4 Ensign Chekov
□ C5 Lenore Karidan
□ C6 Lt. Sulu DUAL
□ C7 Spock
□ C8 Ayelborne
□ C9 Commissioner Bele
□ C10 Mea 3
□ C11 Deanna Troi
□ C12 Seven of Nine
□ C13 Kes
□ C14 Seska
□ C15 Leeta
□ C16 Quark
□ C17 Neelix
□ C18 T'Pol
□ C19 Doctor Phlox
□ C20 Captain Jonathan Archer
□ C21 B4
□ C22 Tal Sh'air
□ C23 Female Shape Shifter
□ C24 Major Kira Nerys
□ C25 Seven of Nine
□ C26 Commander Dolim
□ C27 Major Hayes
□ C28 Captain Jonathan Archer
□ C29 Commander Charles Tucker
□ C30 Chief Miles O'Brien
□ C31 Sela
□ C32 Captain Solok
□ C33 Captain Jean-Luc Picard
□ C34 Seven of Nine
□ C35 T'Pol
□ C36 Doctor Phlox
□ C37 Commander Charles Tucker
□ C38 N'Vek
□ C39 DaiMon Goss
□ C40 Captain Benjamin Sisko
□ C41 Gul Danar
□ C42 Ezri Dax
□ C43 T'Pol
□ C44 Commander Charles Tucker
□ DC1 Captain Kirk
Captain Picard DUAL

2006 Star Trek 40th Anniversary In Motion

COMPLETE SET (5)
STATED ODDS 1:240

□ M1 Captain Kirk
Spock
□ M2 Captain Picard
□ M3 Captain Sisko
□ M4 Captain Janeway
□ M5 Captain Archer

2006 Star Trek 40th Anniversary James Doohan In Memoriam

COMPLETE SET (3) 12.00 30.00
STATED ODDS ONE PER CASE
CARDS MEASURE 5 X 7

□ M4 James Doohan 5.00 12.00
□ M5 James Doohan 5.00 12.00
□ M6 James Doohan 5.00 12.00

2006 Star Trek 40th Anniversary TV Guide Covers

COMPLETE SET (17) 25.00 60.00
STATED ODDS 1:20 US PACKS

□ TV1 Captain Benjamin Sisko 1.50 4.00
□ TV2 Constable Odo 1.50 4.00
□ TV3 Col. Kira Nerys 1.50 4.00
Dr. Julian Bashir
□ TV4 Lt. Com. Jadzia Dax 1.50 4.00
Lt. Ezri Dax
□ TV5 Quark 1.50 4.00
□ TV6 Chief Miles O'Brien 1.50 4.00
Jake Sisko
□ TV7 Captain Kathryn Janeway 1.50 4.00
□ TV8 Seven of Nine 1.50 4.00
□ TV9 Commander Chakotay 1.50 4.00
□ TV10 Kes 1.50 4.00
Neelix
□ TV11 The Doctor 1.50 4.00
□ TV12 Lt. Tom Paris 1.50 4.00
Lt. B'Elanna Torres
□ TV13 Lt. Tuvok 1.50 4.00
Ensign Harry Kim
□ TV14 Captain Jonathan Archer 1.50 4.00
□ TV15 Dr. Phlox 1.50 4.00
Ensign Hoshi Sato
□ TV16 Ens. Travis mayweather 1.50 4.00
Lt. Malcolm Reed
□ TV17 Subcom. T'Pol 1.50 4.00
Lt. Commander Tucker

2006 Star Trek The Original Series 40th Anniversary

COMPLETE SET (110) 6.00 15.00

☐ 1 Captain Kirk .15 .40
☐ 2 Science Officer Spock .15 .40
☐ 3 Dr. McCoy .15 .40
☐ 4 Scotty .15 .40
☐ 5 Uhura .15 .40
☐ 6 Yeoman Rand .15 .40
☐ 7 Sulu .15 .40
☐ 8 Nurse Chapel .15 .40
☐ 9 The U.S.S. Enterprise .15 .40
☐ 10 The Enterprise in Orbit .15 .40
☐ 11 Kirk Captured by the Archons .15 .40
☐ 12 Working the Ship's Computer .15 .40
☐ 13 The Romulan Bird of Prey .15 .40
☐ 14 The Eyes of Evil .15 .40
☐ 15 The Guardian of Forever .15 .40
☐ 16 The Enterprise Out of Control .15 .40
☐ 17 Kirk Battles Khan .15 .40
☐ 18 Transporter Operations .15 .40
☐ 19 Beauty and the Beast .15 .40
☐ 20 Phaser Danger .15 .40
☐ 21 The Vulcan Mind Meld .15 .40
☐ 22 Shipboard Communications .15 .40
☐ 23 Hailing Frequencies Open .15 .40
☐ 24 Capt. Kirk and Dr. McCoy .15 .40
☐ 25 Fire Phasers .15 .40
☐ 26 Landru .15 .40
☐ 27 Beautiful Janice .15 .40
☐ 28 Kirk and Spock Undercover .15 .40
☐ 29 The Shuttlecraft Galileo .15 .40
☐ 30 Scotty in the Jefferies Tube .15 .40
☐ 31 En Garde .15 .40
☐ 32 Entering Strange Space .15 .40
☐ 33 Femme Fatale .15 .40
☐ 34 Kirk in Disguise .15 .40
☐ 35 The Romulan Commander .15 .40
☐ 36 Chief Medical Officer .15 .40
☐ 37 Standing Trial .15 .40
☐ 38 Scotty in Command .15 .40
☐ 39 Battling the Gorn .15 .40
☐ 40 The Enterprise Attacks .15 .40
☐ 41 Yeoman's Plants .15 .40
☐ 42 Kirk Meets Kirk .15 .40
☐ 43 The Salt Creature .15 .40
☐ 44 Top Secret File .15 .40
☐ 45 Trouble on the Bridge .15 .40
☐ 46 Kirk Fires on the Enemy .15 .40
☐ 47 The Eyes of a God .15 .40
☐ 48 The Infection Spreads .15 .40
☐ 49 Vulcan Curiosity .15 .40
☐ 50 Lazarus .15 .40
☐ 51 Charlie Evans .15 .40
☐ 52 Entertaining the Enterprise Crew .15 .40
☐ 53 The Captain Deep in Thought .15 .40
☐ 54 Opening Shuttle Bay Doors .15 .40
☐ 55 Lovers Embrace .15 .40
☐ 56 In Search of a Cure .15 .40
☐ 57 Captain Kirk and Yeoman Rand .15 .40
☐ 58a Lovers Embrace ERR .15 .40
☐ 58b Searching for the Horta COR .15 .40
☐ 59 Ruk, the Last of His Kind .15 .40
☐ 60 Captain Pike .15 .40
☐ 61 Captain's Medical Exam .15 .40
☐ 62 Balok's True Appearance .15 .40
☐ 63 Fire Photon Torpedos! .15 .40
☐ 64 Tracking an Adversary .15 .40
☐ 65 Doctor... and Bricklayer .15 .40
☐ 66 Look of Determination .15 .40
☐ 67 Lt. Kevin Riley .15 .40
☐ 68 Bio-Scanner .15 .40
☐ 69 Receiving Deep Space Signals .15 .40
☐ 70 McCoy Tests an Alien Sample .15 .40
☐ 71 Finnegan, Kirk's Academy Nemesis .15 .40
☐ 72 Mischievous Eyes .15 .40
☐ 73 Dressed for the Occasion .15 .40
☐ 74 The S.S. Botany Bay .15 .40
☐ 75 Scotty and Uhura Take Charge .15 .40
☐ 76 Chasing an Alien Vessel .15 .40
☐ 77 Fearless Leader .15 .40
☐ 78 Close Encounter .15 .40
☐ 79 Attacking the Horta .15 .40
☐ 80 Staying in Shape .15 .40
☐ 81 Desperate Shuttlecraft .15 .40
☐ 82 In Search of a Stowaway .15 .40
☐ 83 Dr. Korby's Women .15 .40
☐ 84 The Secret of Talos IV .15 .40
☐ 85 Miri and Jahn .15 .40
☐ 86 Unrequited Love .15 .40
☐ 87 From Humans to Gods .15 .40
☐ 88 Mock Trial .15 .40
☐ 89 The Chief Engineer .15 .40
☐ 90 20th Century Interrogation .15 .40
☐ 91 Into the Unknown .15 .40
☐ 92 Beautiful Leila Kalomi .15 .40
☐ 93 Steering the Enterprise to Safety .15 .40
☐ 94 A Look of Concern .15 .40
☐ 95 McCoy Delivers a Needed Injection .15 .40
☐ 96 An Alien Deception .15 .40
☐ 97 Kirk Mentors Charlie .15 .40
☐ 98 Dr. Helen Noel .15 .40
☐ 99 Making an Android Kirk .15 .40
☐ 100 Captain Kirk and Edith Keeler .15 .40
☐ 101 In the Captain's Chair .15 .40
☐ 102 Tracking the Enterprise .15 .40
☐ 103 Discussing Strategy .15 .40
☐ 104 Dr. McCoy and Yeoman Barrows .15 .40
☐ 105 Beaming Up the Landing Party .15 .40
☐ 106 Swahili Beauty .15 .40
☐ 107 Captains Kirk and Pike .15 .40
☐ 108 Captain of the Enterprise .15 .40
☐ 109 Checklist .15 .40
☐ 110 Checklist .15 .40

2006 Star Trek The Original Series 40th Anniversary 1967 Expansion

COMPLETE SET (18) 60.00 120.00
STATED ODDS 1:40

☐ 73 Capt. Pike and Mr. Spock 3.00 8.00
☐ 74 Number One 3.00 8.00
☐ 75 Navigator Jose Tyler 3.00 8.00
☐ 76 Mysterious Alien 3.00 8.00
☐ 77 Beautiful Vina 3.00 8.00
☐ 78 The Search for Answers 3.00 8.00
☐ 79 Alien Abduction 3.00 8.00
☐ 80 Fire Phasers 3.00 8.00
☐ 81 The Caged Captain 3.00 8.00
☐ 82 Trapped in an Illusion 3.00 8.00
☐ 83 Falling in Love 3.00 8.00
☐ 84 Trapped in Hell 3.00 8.00
☐ 85 Searching for Reality 3.00 8.00
☐ 86 Sexy Slave Dancer 3.00 8.00
☐ 87 Yeoman Colt 3.00 8.00
☐ 88 Fighting the Alien 3.00 8.00
☐ 89 No More Illusions 3.00 8.00
☐ 90 The Real Vina 3.00 8.00

2006 Star Trek The Original Series 40th Anniversary Autographs

STATED ODDS 1:20
A126 STATED ODDS ONE PER COLLECTOR'S ALBUM
QA8 STATED ODDS ONE PER 2 CASE PURCHASE
E.RODDENBERRY AU #'D TO 225
G.RODDENBERRY AU #'D TO 25
NIMOY AU/MEM STATED ODDS ONE PER 6 CASE PURCHASE
L (LIMITED): 300-500 COPIES
VL (VERY LIMITED): 200-300 COPIES

☐ A104 Carl Held
☐ A106 Jason Wingreen
☐ A107 Lawrence Montaigne
☐ A108 Dick Durock
☐ A109 Robert Walker Jr. VL
☐ A110 Kathryn Hays L
☐ A111 France Nuyen VL
☐ A112 Joan Collins L
☐ A113 Brian Tochi
☐ A114 Sheldon Collins
☐ A115 David Soul
☐ A116 John Crawford L
☐ A117 Ned Romero
☐ A118 Peter Duryea
☐ A119 Leonard Nimoy VL
☐ A120 Majel Barrett VL
☐ A121 Laurel Goodwin
☐ A122 Bobby Clark L
☐ A123 Bruce Hyde
☐ A124 Beverly Washburn
☐ A125 Malachi Throne
☐ A126 Walter Koenig
☐ A127 Paul Comi
☐ A128 Marianne Hill
☐ A129 Emily Banks
☐ A130 Victor Lundin
☐ A131 Garrison True
☐ A133 Kate Woodville
☐ A134 Mary Rice
☐ A135 Richard Compton
☐ A136 George Takei L
☐ A137 Rhodes Reason
☐ QA8 Grace Lee Whitney
☐ NNO Leonard Nimoy/ (issued as 6-case incentive)
☐ NNO Gene Roddenberry/25
☐ NNO Eugene Roddenberry Jr./225

2006 Star Trek The Original Series 40th Anniversary Bridge Crew Delta Shield Patches

COMPLETE SET (7)
STATED ODDS 1:200

☐ DS1 Captain James T. Kirk
☐ DS2 Commander Spock
☐ DS3 Dr. Leonard McCoy
☐ DS4 Chief Engineer Scott
☐ DS5 Lieutenant Sulu
☐ DS6 Ensign Chekov
☐ DS7 Lieutenant Uhura

2006 Star Trek The Original Series 40th Anniversary Captain Pike

COMPLETE SET (9) 10.00 25.00
STATED ODDS 1:14

☐ CP1 Captain Pike 1.25 3.00
☐ CP2 Captain Pike 1.25 3.00
☐ CP3 Captain Pike 1.25 3.00
☐ CP4 Captain Pike 1.25 3.00
☐ CP5 Captain Pike 1.25 3.00
☐ CP6 Captain Pike 1.25 3.00
☐ CP7 Captain Pike 1.25 3.00
☐ CP8 Captain Pike 1.25 3.00
☐ CP9 Captain Pike 1.25 3.00

2006 Star Trek The Original Series 40th Anniversary Portraits

COMPLETE SET (18)
STATED ODDS 1:40

☐ PT1 Captain Kirk
☐ PT2 Spock
☐ PT3 Dr. McCoy
☐ PT4 Scotty
☐ PT5 Sulu
☐ PT6 Uhura
☐ PT7 Chekov
☐ PT8 Nurse Chapel
☐ PT9 Yeoman Rand
☐ PT10 Talosian
☐ PT11 Balok's Puppet
☐ PT12 The Salt Creature
☐ PT13 Romulan Commander
☐ PT14 Ruk
☐ PT15 The Gorn
☐ PT16 Khan
☐ PT17 Kor
☐ PT18 Edith Keeler

2006 Star Trek The Original Series 40th Anniversary The Faces of Vina

COMPLETE SET (6) 6.00 15.00
STATED ODDS 1:20

☐ FV1 Vina 1.25 3.00
☐ FV2 Vina 1.25 3.00
☐ FV3 Vina 1.25 3.00
☐ FV4 Vina 1.25 3.00
☐ FV5 Vina 1.25 3.00
☐ FV6 Vina 1.25 3.00

2006 Star Trek The Original Series 40th Anniversary The Quotable Star Trek Expansion

COMPLETE SET (18) 30.00 60.00
STATED ODDS 1:10

☐ 111 The Cage 1.50 4.00
☐ 112 The Cage 1.50 4.00
☐ 113 Where No Man Has Gone Before 1.50 4.00
☐ 114 The Corbomite Maneuver 1.50 4.00
☐ 115 The Corbomite Maneuver 1.50 4.00
☐ 116 Mudd's Women 1.50 4.00
☐ 117 The Naked Time 1.50 4.00
☐ 118 Balance of Terror 1.50 4.00
☐ 119 Miri 1.50 4.00
☐ 120 The Conscience of the King 1.50 4.00
☐ 121 Court-Martial 1.50 4.00
☐ 122 Shore Leave 1.50 4.00
☐ 123 The Alternative Factor 1.50 4.00
☐ 124 Tomorrow Is Yesterday 1.50 4.00
☐ 125 A Taste of Armageddon 1.50 4.00
☐ 126 Errand of Mercy 1.50 4.00
☐ 127 The Doomsday Machine 1.50 4.00
☐ 128 The City on the Edge of Forever 1.50 4.00

2006 Star Trek The Original Series 40th Anniversary TV Guide Covers

COMPLETE SET (2) 6.00 15.00
STATED ODDS ONE PER CASE

☐ TV8 Nurse Chapel 4.00 10.00
☐ TV9 Yeoman Rand 4.00 10.00

2006 Stargate Atlantis Season Two

COMPLETE SET (72) 4.00 10.00

☐ 1 Title Card .10 .30
☐ 2 Title Card .10 .30
☐ 3 Title Card .10 .30
☐ 4 The Siege, Part 3 .10 .30
☐ 5 The Siege, Part 3 .10 .30
☐ 6 The Siege, Part 3 .10 .30
☐ 7 The Intruder .10 .30
☐ 8 The Intruder .10 .30
☐ 9 The Intruder .10 .30
☐ 10 Runner .10 .30
☐ 11 Runner .10 .30
☐ 12 Runner .10 .30
☐ 13 Duet .10 .30
☐ 14 Duet .10 .30
☐ 15 Duet .10 .30
☐ 16 Condemned .10 .30
☐ 17 Condemned .10 .30
☐ 18 Condemned .10 .30
☐ 19 Trinity .10 .30
☐ 20 Trinity .10 .30
☐ 21 Trinity .10 .30
☐ 22 Instinct .10 .30
☐ 23 Instinct .10 .30
☐ 24 Instinct .10 .30
☐ 25 Conversion .10 .30
☐ 26 Conversion .10 .30
☐ 27 Conversion .10 .30
☐ 28 Aurora .10 .30
☐ 29 Aurora .10 .30
☐ 30 Aurora .10 .30
☐ 31 The Lost Boys .10 .30
☐ 32 The Lost Boys .10 .30
☐ 33 The Lost Boys .10 .30
☐ 34 The Hive .10 .30
☐ 35 The Hive .10 .30
☐ 36 The Hive .10 .30
☐ 37 Epiphany .10 .30
☐ 38 Epiphany .10 .30
☐ 39 Epiphany .10 .30
☐ 40 Critical Mass .10 .30
☐ 41 Critical Mass .10 .30
☐ 42 Critical Mass .10 .30
☐ 43 Grace Under Pressure .10 .30
☐ 44 Grace Under Pressure .10 .30
☐ 45 Grace Under Pressure .10 .30
☐ 46 The Tower .10 .30
☐ 47 The Tower .10 .30
☐ 48 The Tower .10 .30
☐ 49 The Long Goodbye .10 .30
☐ 50 The Long Goodbye .10 .30
☐ 51 The Long Goodbye .10 .30
☐ 52 Coup D'etat .10 .30
☐ 53 Coup D'etat .10 .30
☐ 54 Coup D'etat .10 .30
☐ 55 Michael .10 .30
☐ 56 Michael .10 .30
☐ 57 Michael .10 .30
☐ 58 Inferno .10 .30
☐ 59 Inferno .10 .30
☐ 60 Inferno .10 .30
☐ 61 Allies .10 .30
☐ 62 Allies .10 .30
☐ 63 Allies .10 .30
☐ 64 On the Set .10 .30
☐ 65 On the Set .10 .30
☐ 66 On the Set .10 .30
☐ 67 On the Set .10 .30
☐ 68 On the Set .10 .30
☐ 69 On the Set .10 .30
☐ 70 Checklist .10 .30
☐ 71 Checklist .10 .30
☐ 72 Checklist .10 .30

2006 Stargate Atlantis Season Two Atlantis Team

COMPLETE SET (7)
STATED ODDS 1:40

☐ P1 Lt. Colonel John Sheppard
☐ P2 Dr. Elizabeth Weir
☐ P3 Teyla Emmagan
☐ P4 Ronon Dex
☐ P5 Dr. Carson Beckett
☐ P6 Dr. Rodney McKay
☐ P7 Col. Steven Caldwell

2006 Stargate Atlantis Season Two Autographs

STATED ODDS TWO PER BOX

☐ 1 Andee Frizzell
☐ 2 Brandy Ledford
☐ 3 Chad Morgan
☐ 4 Christian Bocher
☐ 5 Claire Rankin
☐ 6 Clayton Landey
☐ 7 Connor Trinneer
☐ 8 Ellie Harvie
☐ 9 James Lafazanos
☐ 10 Kavan Smith
☐ 11 Pascale Hutton
☐ 12 Peter Woodward
☐ 13 Rachel Luttrell
☐ 14 Ryan Robbins
☐ 15 Torri Higginson
☐ 16 Garwin Sanford/ (issued in collectors album)
☐ 17 Amanda Tapping/ (issued as 2-case incentive)

2006 Stargate Atlantis Season Two Costumes

STATED ODDS 1:120

☐ 1 Dr. Rodney McKay
☐ 2 Halling
☐ 3 Major John Sheppard
☐ 4 Wraith Warrior

2006 Stargate Atlantis Season Two In Motion

COMPLETE SET (3)
STATED ODDS 1:240

☐ M1 Stargate Atlantis In Motion
☐ M2 Stargate Atlantis In Motion
☐ M3 Stargate Atlantis In Motion

2006 Stargate Atlantis Season Two Quotable Stargate Atlantis

COMPLETE SET (20)
STATED ODDS 1:8

☐ Q21 The Siege, Part 3
☐ Q22 The Intruder
☐ Q23 Runner
☐ Q24 Duet
☐ Q25 Condemned
☐ Q26 Trinity
☐ Q27 Instinct
☐ Q28 Conversion
☐ Q29 Aurora
☐ Q30 The Lost Boys
☐ Q31 The Hive
☐ Q32 Epiphany
☐ Q33 Critical Mass
☐ Q34 Grace Under Pressure
☐ Q35 The Tower
☐ Q36 The Long Goodbye
☐ Q37 Coup D'etat
☐ Q38 Michael
☐ Q39 Inferno
☐ Q40 Allies

2006 Stargate Atlantis Season Two Warriors in Action

COMPLETE SET (9)
STATED ODDS 1:20

☐ W1 Lt. Colonel John Sheppard
☐ W2 Lt. Colonel John Sheppard
☐ W3 Lt. Colonel John Sheppard
☐ W4 Teyla Emmagan
☐ W5 Teyla Emmagan
☐ W6 Teyla Emmagan
☐ W7 Ronon Dex
☐ W8 Ronon Dex
☐ W9 Ronon Dex

2006 Stargate SG-1 Season Eight

COMPLETE SET (72) 4.00 10.00

☐ 1 Title Card .10 .30
☐ 2 Title Card .10 .30
☐ 3 Title Card .10 .30
☐ 4 New Order Part 1 .10 .30
☐ 5 New Order Part 1 .10 .30
☐ 6 New Order Part 1 .10 .30
☐ 7 New Order Part 2 .10 .30
☐ 8 New Order Part 2 .10 .30
☐ 9 New Order Part 2 .10 .30
☐ 10 Lockdown .10 .30
☐ 11 Lockdown .10 .30
☐ 12 Lockdown .10 .30
☐ 13 Zero Hour .10 .30
☐ 14 Zero Hour .10 .30
☐ 15 Zero Hour .10 .30
☐ 16 Icon .10 .30
☐ 17 Icon (Misnumbered As Card #1) .10 .30
☐ 18 Icon .10 .30
☐ 19 Avatar .10 .30
☐ 20 Avatar .10 .30
☐ 21 Avatar .10 .30
☐ 22 Affinity .10 .30
☐ 23 Affinity .10 .30
☐ 24 Affinity .10 .30
☐ 25 Covenant .10 .30
☐ 26 Covenant .10 .30
☐ 27 Covenant .10 .30
☐ 28 Sacrifices .10 .30
☐ 29 Sacrifices .10 .30
☐ 30 Sacrifices .10 .30
☐ 31 Endgame .10 .30
☐ 32 Endgame .10 .30
☐ 33 Endgame .10 .30
☐ 34 Gemini .10 .30
☐ 35 Gemini .10 .30
☐ 36 Gemini .10 .30
☐ 37 Prometheus Unbound .10 .30
☐ 38 Prometheus Unbound .10 .30
☐ 39 Prometheus Unbound .10 .30
☐ 40 It's Good To Be King .10 .30
☐ 41 It's Good To Be King .10 .30
☐ 42 It's Good To Be King .10 .30
☐ 43 Full Alert .10 .30
☐ 44 Full Alert .10 .30
☐ 45 Full Alert .10 .30
☐ 46 Citizen Joe .10 .30
☐ 47 Citizen Joe .10 .30
☐ 48 Citizen Joe .10 .30
☐ 49 Reckoning Part 1 .10 .30
☐ 50 Reckoning Part 1 .10 .30
☐ 51 Reckoning Part 1 .10 .30
☐ 52 Reckoning Part 2 .10 .30
☐ 53 Reckoning Part 2 .10 .30
☐ 54 Reckoning Part 2 .10 .30
☐ 55 Threads .10 .30
☐ 56 Threads .10 .30
☐ 57 Threads .10 .30
☐ 58 Moebius Part 1 .10 .30
☐ 59 Moebius Part 1 .10 .30
☐ 60 Moebius Part 1 .10 .30
☐ 61 Moebius Part 2 .10 .30
☐ 62 Moebius Part 2 .10 .30
☐ 63 Moebius Part 2 .10 .30
☐ 64 Behind The Scenes .10 .30
☐ 65 Behind The Scenes .10 .30
☐ 66 Behind The Scenes .10 .30
☐ 67 Behind The Scenes .10 .30
☐ 68 Behind The Scenes .10 .30
☐ 69 Behind The Scenes .10 .30
☐ 70 Checklist 1 .10 .30
☐ 71 Checklist 2 .10 .30
☐ 72 Checklist 3 .10 .30

2006 Stargate SG-1 Season Eight Autographs

OVERALL AUTO ODDS ONE PER BOX
A68 ISSUED IN COLLECTORS ALBUM
L (LIMITED): 300-500 COPIES
VL (VERY LIMITED): 200-300 COPIES

☐ A62 Sam Jones 6.00 15.00
☐ A63 Cary-Hiroyuki Tagawa L 8.00 20.00
☐ A64 Kevin McNulty 8.00 20.00
☐ A65 Michael Welch 6.00 15.00
☐ A66 Alisen Down 6.00 15.00
☐ A67 Claudia Black VL
☐ A68 Erica Durance 15.00 40.00
(issued in collectors album)
☐ A69 Peter Williams L 6.00 15.00
☐ A71 William de Vry 6.00 15.00
☐ A72 Mel Harris 8.00 20.00
☐ A73 Isaac Hayes VL 50.00 100.00
☐ A75 Charles Shaughnessy 6.00 15.00
☐ A76 Dan Castelleneta VL 40.00 80.00
☐ A78 George Dzundza 8.00 20.00

2006 Stargate SG-1 Season Eight Costumes

COMP.SET w/o C35 25.00 50.00
OVERALL COSTUME/RELIC ODDS ONE PER BOX
C35 ISSUED AS CASE TOPPER

☐ C28 Jonas Quinn 4.00 10.00
☐ C29 Dr. Daniel Jackson 4.00 10.00
☐ C30 Colonel Jack O'Neill 4.00 10.00
☐ C31 Teal'c 4.00 10.00
☐ C32 Major Kawalsky 4.00 10.00
☐ C33 Urgo 4.00 10.00
☐ C34 Kasuf 4.00 10.00
☐ C35 Apophis DUAL 10.00 25.00
(issued as case topper)

2006 Stargate SG-1 Season Eight Dual Autographs

OVERALL AUTO ODDS ONE PER BOX
DA2 ISSUED AS 2-CASE INCENTIVE
DA3 ISSUED AS 6-CASE INCENTIVE

☐ DA2 Christopher Judge
Tony Amendola/ (issued as 2-case incentive)
☐ DA3 Claudia Black
Michael Shanks/ (issued as 6-case incentive)

2006 Stargate SG-1 Season Eight Kneel Before Your God

STATED ODDS 1:480
STATED PRINT RUN 375 SER. #'d SETS

☐ G1 Ra 40.00 80.00
☐ G2 Apophis 40.00 80.00

2006 Stargate SG-1 Season Eight Personnel Files

COMPLETE SET (9) 8.00 20.00
STATED ODDS 1:20

☐ PF1 General Jack O'Neill 1.50 4.00
☐ PF2 Lt. Colonel Samantha Carter 1.50 4.00
☐ PF3 Dr. Daniel Jackson 1.50 4.00
☐ PF4 Teal'c 1.50 4.00
☐ PF5 General George Hammond 1.50 4.00
☐ PF6 Dr. Frasier 1.50 4.00
☐ PF7 Lt. Colonel Cameron Mitchell 1.50 4.00
☐ PF8 General Hank Landry 1.50 4.00
☐ PF9 Dr. Carolyn Lam 1.50 4.00

2006 Stargate SG-1 Season Eight Promos

COMPLETE SET (4)

☐ P1 Vala/Dr. Jackson .75 2.00
(General Distribution)
☐ P2 Major Samantha Carter 1.50 4.00
(Non Sport Update)
☐ P3 Teal'c 6.00 15.00
(Album Exclusive)
☐ UK Dr. Daniel Jackson 2.00 5.00
(UK Exclusive)

2006 Stargate SG-1 Season Eight Relics

COMPLETE SET (5) 50.00 100.00
OVERALL COSTUME/RELIC ODDS ONE PER BOX
STATED PRINT RUN 403-434

☐ R10 Kelownan Files/434 12.00 30.00
☐ R11 Map/411 12.00 30.00
☐ R12 Alien Newspaper/407 12.00 30.00
☐ R13 Mission Report/403 12.00 30.00
☐ R14 Operations Manual/420 12.00 30.00

2006 Stargate SG-1 Season Eight Twisted

COMPLETE SET (9) 6.00 15.00
STATED ODDS 1:10

☐ TW1 Jack O'Neill 1.00 2.50
☐ TW2 Jack O'Neill 1.00 2.50
☐ TW3 Samantha Carter 1.00 2.50
☐ TW4 Samantha Carter 1.00 2.50
☐ TW5 Samantha Carter 1.00 2.50
☐ TW6 Daniel Jackson 1.00 2.50
☐ TW7 Daniel Jackson 1.00 2.50
☐ TW8 Teal'c 1.00 2.50
☐ TW9 Teal'c 1.00 2.50

2006 Superman Returns

COMPLETE SET (90) 5.00 12.00

☐ 1 Superman Returns .15 .40
☐ 2 Superman .15 .40
☐ 3 Clark Kent .15 .40
☐ 4 Lois Lane .15 .40
☐ 5 Richard White .15 .40
☐ 6 Lex Luthor .15 .40
☐ 7 Perry White .15 .40
☐ 8 Jimmy Olsen .15 .40
☐ 9 Kitty Kowalski .15 .40
☐ 10 Martha Kent .15 .40
☐ 11 Ben Hubbard .15 .40
☐ 12 Jason .15 .40
☐ 13 Stanford .15 .40
☐ 14 Grant .15 .40
☐ 15 Brutus .15 .40
☐ 16 Riley .15 .40
☐ 17 Bobbie Faye .15 .40
☐ 18 Bo the Bartender .15 .40
☐ 19 Where Is Superman? .15 .40
☐ 20 Voyage to Krypton .15 .40
☐ 21 Kal-El's Quest .15 .40
☐ 22 Emergency Escape! .15 .40
☐ 23 Landing in Smallville .15 .40
☐ 24 Toward the Crash Site .15 .40
☐ 25 To Save Her Son .15 .40
☐ 26 Back from Beyond .15 .40
☐ 27 The Groom of Doom .15 .40
☐ 28 Gertrude's Millions .15 .40
☐ 29 At the Kent Farm .15 .40
☐ 30 Powers of a Super-Teen .15 .40
☐ 31 An Unexpected Flight .15 .40
☐ 32 Young Clark's Discovery .15 .40
☐ 33 Legacy of the Cosmos .15 .40
☐ 34 The Kryptonian Crystal .15 .40
☐ 35 Burying the Spaceship .15 .40
☐ 36 Descending into the Past .15 .40
☐ 37 Mother Knows Best .15 .40
☐ 38 Meeting Ben Hubbard .15 .40
☐ 39 His Latest Mad Plan .15 .40

MODERN ERA NON-SPORTS

❑ 40 Approaching the Fortress .15 .40
❑ 41 The Secrets of Jor-El .15 .40
❑ 42 A Return to Metropolis .15 .40
❑ 43 The New Daily Planet .15 .40
❑ 44 Welcome Back, Mr. Kent! .15 .40
❑ 45 The More Things Change .15 .40
❑ 46 Lois on Assignment .15 .40
❑ 47 At the Bar with Bo .15 .40
❑ 48 Lex's Master Plan .15 .40
❑ 49 Luthor's Model City .15 .40
❑ 50 Unlimited Power? .15 .40
❑ 51 Old Times Interrupted .15 .40
❑ 52 Trouble in Outer Space .15 .40
❑ 53 Looks Like a Job For... .15 .40
❑ 54 Out of the Broom Closet .15 .40
❑ 55 Soaring to New Heights .15 .40
❑ 56 A Family Affair .15 .40
❑ 57 A Day at the Office .15 .40
❑ 58 No Fan of Superman .15 .40
❑ 59 Just Like Old Times? .15 .40
❑ 60 The Caped Wonder Is Back! .15 .40
❑ 61 A Happy Homemaker .15 .40
❑ 62 Spaceborn Hero .15 .40
❑ 63 The Museum Besieged .15 .40
❑ 64 A Grateful World .15 .40
❑ 65 A Superman Expert? .15 .40
❑ 66 All in the Family .15 .40
❑ 67 What's a Nice Girl Like Me...? .15 .40
❑ 68 On the Planet Roof .15 .40
❑ 69 Rooftop Rendezvous .15 .40
❑ 70 The Kiss That Wasn't .15 .40
❑ 71 An Enemy's Revenge .15 .40
❑ 72 On the Trail of Trouble .15 .40
❑ 73 Into a Lion's Den .15 .40
❑ 74 Luthor's Hairy Lair .15 .40
❑ 75 Lex Lets His Hair Down .15 .40
❑ 76 Lex vs. Lois .15 .40
❑ 77 A Fax in Time .15 .40
❑ 78 Escape from Luthor's Yacht .15 .40
❑ 79 A Challenge for Superman .15 .40
❑ 80 Maker of a New World .15 .40
❑ 81 Struck by an Earthquake .15 .40
❑ 82 The World in His Hands .15 .40
❑ 83 His City Imperiled .15 .40
❑ 84 Lex Luthor's Debacle .15 .40
❑ 85 Praying for His Life .15 .40
❑ 86 Superman's Loved Ones .15 .40
❑ 87 The Man of Steel Forever? .15 .40
❑ 88 A Starship for Superman .15 .40
❑ 89 Creating Mini-worlds .15 .40
❑ 90 Superman Returns Checklist .15 .40

2006 Superman Returns Autographs

STATED ODDS 1:58 HOBBY

❑ 1 Kevin Spacey
❑ 2 Brandon Routh
❑ 3 Kate Bosworth 40.00 80.00
❑ 4 Sam Huntington 8.00 20.00
❑ 5 James Marsden 15.00 30.00
❑ 6 Parker Posey 10.00 25.00

2006 Superman Returns Blister Bonus

COMPLETE SET (3) 3.00 8.00
STATED ODDS ONE PER BLISTER PACK

❑ B1 Superman 1.25 3.00
❑ B2 Lex Luthor 1.25 3.00
❑ B3 Kal-El 1.25 3.00

2006 Superman Returns Embossed

COMPLETE SET (5) 5.00 12.00
STATED ODDS 1:12

❑ 1 Superman 1.00 2.50
❑ 2 Superman 1.00 2.50
❑ 3 Superman 1.00 2.50
❑ 4 Superman 1.00 2.50
❑ 5 Superman 1.00 2.50

2006 Superman Returns Magnets

COMPLETE SET (9) 5.00 12.00
STATED ODDS 1:12 RETAIL

❑ 1 Superman 1.25 3.00
❑ 2 Superman 1.25 3.00
❑ 3 Superman 1.25 3.00
❑ 4 Superman 1.25 3.00
❑ 5 Superman 1.25 3.00
❑ 6 Superman 1.25 3.00
❑ 7 Superman 1.25 3.00
❑ 8 Superman 1.25 3.00
❑ 9 Superman 1.25 3.00

2006 Superman Returns Saved By Superman Memorabilia

STATED ODDS 1:12 HOBBY

❑ 1 Clark Kent's Coat 8.00 20.00
❑ 2 Clark Kent's Suit 8.00 20.00
❑ 3 Kitty's Flower Dress 6.00 15.00
❑ 4 Kitty's Zebra Dress 6.00 15.00
❑ 5 Lex Luthor's Coat 6.00 15.00
❑ 6 Lex Luthor's Suit 6.00 15.00
❑ 7 Lois Lane's Pants 20.00 40.00
❑ 8 Lois Lane's Skirt 20.00 40.00
❑ 9 Perry White's Coat 6.00 15.00
❑ 10 Perry White's Suit 6.00 15.00
❑ 11 Superman's Briefs 75.00 150.00
❑ 12 Superman's Cape 20.00 40.00
❑ 13 Superman's Suit 15.00 30.00

2006 Superman Returns Stickers

COMPLETE SET (10) 6.00 15.00
STATED ODDS 1:6 RETAIL

❑ 1 Superman .75 2.00
❑ 2 Superman .75 2.00
❑ 3 Superman .75 2.00
❑ 4 Superman .75 2.00
❑ 5 Superman .75 2.00
❑ 6 Superman .75 2.00
❑ 7 Superman .75 2.00
❑ 8 Superman .75 2.00
❑ 9 Superman .75 2.00
❑ 10 Superman .75 2.00

2006 Superman Returns Tin Lid

COMPLETE SET (6) 6.00 15.00
STATED ODDS ONE PER TIN

❑ A Superman 1.25 3.00
❑ B Superman 1.25 3.00
❑ C Superman 1.25 3.00
❑ D Superman 1.25 3.00
❑ E Superman 1.25 3.00
❑ F Superman 1.25 3.00

2006 Superman Returns Tin Story

COMPLETE SET (6) 6.00 15.00
STATED ODDS ONE PER TIN

❑ 1 Superman's Return 6.00 15.00
❑ 2 Lex's Main Squeeze 6.00 15.00
❑ 3 A Crystal Clear Goal 6.00 15.00
❑ 4 Superman's Return 6.00 15.00
❑ 5 Man a Woman Wants 6.00 15.00
❑ 6 To Save His Friends 6.00 15.00

2006 Supernatural Season One

COMPLETE SET (90) 4.00 10.00

❑ 1 Title .10 .30
❑ 2 Woman In White .10 .30
❑ 3 Not Again .10 .30
❑ 4 Missing Camper .10 .30
❑ 5 Hidden .10 .30
❑ 6 Torched .10 .30
❑ 7 Witness .10 .30
❑ 8 Tub Terror .10 .30
❑ 9 Saved .10 .30
❑ 10 Demon Message .10 .30
❑ 11 In-Flight Feature .10 .30
❑ 12 Grateful .10 .30
❑ 13 Vengeful .10 .30
❑ 14 Guilty .10 .30
❑ 15 Forgiven .10 .30
❑ 16 Killer .10 .30
❑ 17 Shapeshifter .10 .30
❑ 18 End Of The Line .10 .30
❑ 19 Dem Bones .10 .30
❑ 20 Gift .10 .30
❑ 21 Destroyed .10 .30
❑ 22 Overrun .10 .30
❑ 23 Skull .10 .30
❑ 24 Fired Up .10 .30
❑ 25 Aggressor .10 .30
❑ 26 Protector .10 .30
❑ 27 Ramblin' Man .10 .30
❑ 28 Brainwashed .10 .30
❑ 29 Sibling Rivalry .10 .30
❑ 30 Exit .10 .30
❑ 31 Expert .10 .30
❑ 32 Captives .10 .30
❑ 33 Bad To The Bone .10 .30
❑ 34 Blown Away .10 .30
❑ 35 Fear The Reaper .10 .30
❑ 36 Miracles .10 .30
❑ 37 Phantom Truck .10 .30
❑ 38 Cassie's Plea .10 .30
❑ 39 Hallowed Ground .10 .30
❑ 40 These Dreams .10 .30
❑ 41 Payback .10 .30
❑ 42 Finale .10 .30
❑ 43 Captured .10 .30
❑ 44 People .10 .30
❑ 45 Justice .10 .30
❑ 46 Meg's Doom .10 .30
❑ 47 Trap .10 .30
❑ 48 Farewell .10 .30
❑ 49 Ghost Hunters .10 .30
❑ 50 Axe Man .10 .30
❑ 51 Deleted .10 .30
❑ 52 Watch Out .10 .30
❑ 53 Old Business .10 .30
❑ 54 Innocence Lost .10 .30
❑ 55 Enduring .10 .30
❑ 56 Clues .10 .30
❑ 57 Dolly .10 .30
❑ 58 Teeth .10 .30
❑ 59 Friction .10 .30
❑ 60 One Less Bullet .10 .30
❑ 61 Halted .10 .30
❑ 62 Saved .10 .30
❑ 63 Lost .10 .30
❑ 64 Exorcism .10 .30
❑ 65 Possessed .10 .30
❑ 66 Sam's Choice .10 .30
❑ 67 Fire .10 .30
❑ 68 Holy Water .10 .30
❑ 69 Knives .10 .30
❑ 70 Crossbow .10 .30
❑ 71 Guns .10 .30
❑ 72 Classic Car .10 .30
❑ 73 U.S. Wildlife Agents .10 .30
❑ 74 Priests .10 .30
❑ 75 Alarm Technicians .10 .30
❑ 76 Mary Winchester .10 .30
❑ 77 Jessica Moore .10 .30
❑ 78 Haley Collins .10 .30
❑ 79 Meg Masters .10 .30
❑ 80 Cassie Robinson .10 .30
❑ 81 Sarah Blake .10 .30
❑ 82 Coordinates .10 .30
❑ 83 Wendigo .10 .30
❑ 84 Picture Of Home .10 .30
❑ 85 First Page .10 .30
❑ 86 Frequently Illegible .10 .30
❑ 87 Another Lead .10 .30
❑ 88 A Special Weapon .10 .30
❑ 89 Replica .10 .30
❑ 90 Checklist .10 .30

2006 Supernatural Season One Autographs

STATED ODDS 1:36

❑ A1 Jared Padalecki 50.00 100.00
❑ A2 Jensen Ackles 50.00 100.00
❑ A3 Amy Acker 20.00 40.00
❑ A4 Julie Benz 20.00 40.00
❑ A6 Marnette Patterson 10.00 25.00

2006 Supernatural Season One Box Loaders

STATED ODDS ONE PER BOX
CL1 STATE ODDS ONE PER CASE

❑ BL1 John Winchester 1.50 4.00
❑ BL2 Dean Winchester 1.50 4.00
❑ BL3 Sam Winchester 1.50 4.00
❑ CL1 Crash 5.00 12.00
CASE INSERT

2006 Supernatural Season One Dead End

STATED ODDS 1:17

❑ D1 Unexplained 1.25 3.00
❑ D2 Bad Company 1.25 3.00
❑ D3 Sandman 1.25 3.00
❑ D4 The Demon 1.25 3.00
❑ D5 Dean's Trial 1.25 3.00
❑ D6 Sam's Choice 1.25 3.00

2006 Supernatural Season One Pieceworks

STATED ODDS 1:36

❑ PW1 Jared Padalecki 50.00 100.00
❑ PW2 Jensen Ackles 100.00 150.00
❑ PW3 Jared Padalecki 35.00 70.00
❑ PW4 Jensen Ackles 50.00 100.00
❑ PW5 Jeffrey Dean Morgan 25.00 50.00
❑ PW6 Jeffrey Dean Morgan 25.00 50.00
❑ PW7 Jeffrey Dean Morgan 25.00 50.00
❑ PW8 Nicki Aycox 12.00 30.00
❑ PW9 Julie Benz 25.00 50.00
❑ PW10 Brooke Nevin 12.00 30.00
❑ PW11 Amy Acker 15.00 40.00
❑ PW12 Jeannie Epper 12.00 30.00
❑ PW13A Jensen Ackles
(issued as a multi-case incentive)
❑ PW13B Jared Padalecki
(issued as a multi-case incentive)
❑ PWA1 Julie Benz AU 25.00 50.00
❑ PWA2 Amy Acker AU 25.00 50.00

2006 Supernatural Season One Searching

STATED ODDS 1:11

❑ S1 Unavailable 1.00 2.50
❑ S2 Cursed 1.00 2.50
❑ S3 Raised Like Warriors 1.00 2.50
❑ S4 Fatal Weakness 1.00 2.50
❑ S5 Calling 1.00 2.50
❑ S6 Hiding 1.00 2.50
❑ S7 Together 1.00 2.50
❑ S8 Reunited 1.00 2.50
❑ S9 Responsibility 1.00 2.50

2006 Veronica Mars Season One

COMPLETE SET (72) 3.00 8.00

❑ 1 Title Card .08 .25
❑ 2 Seeking Justice .08 .25
❑ 3 Busted .08 .25
❑ 4 Surprising .08 .25
❑ 5 Cracked .08 .25
❑ 6 Unexpected .08 .25
❑ 7 Duped .08 .25
❑ 8 Promise .08 .25
❑ 9 Watched .08 .25
❑ 10 Revealed .08 .25
❑ 11 Unambitious .08 .25
❑ 12 Embarrassed .08 .25
❑ 13 The Couple .08 .25
❑ 14 Mistake .08 .25
❑ 15 Purity Test .08 .25
❑ 16 Buried Truth .08 .25
❑ 17 Deprogrammed .08 .25
❑ 18 Better Not Knowing .08 .25
❑ 19 Whodunit .08 .25
❑ 20 Seasons Greetings .08 .25
❑ 21 Don't Move .08 .25
❑ 22 Switched .08 .25
❑ 23 Blame Veronica .08 .25
❑ 24 Unmasked .08 .25
❑ 25 Starcrossed .08 .25
❑ 26 Desperate .08 .25
❑ 27 Punked .08 .25
❑ 28 Stunned .08 .25
❑ 29 Secret Crush .08 .25
❑ 30 Dance Night .08 .25
❑ 31 Polly Gone .08 .25
❑ 32 Investment .08 .25
❑ 33 One Up .08 .25
❑ 34 More Evidence .08 .25
❑ 35 Shocking .08 .25
❑ 36 Who Knew .08 .25
❑ 37 Same Spots .08 .25
❑ 38 Protective .08 .25
❑ 39 Revenge .08 .25
❑ 40 Waiting .08 .25
❑ 41 Drugged .08 .25
❑ 42 Outed .08 .25
❑ 43 Hidden .08 .25
❑ 44 Bravado .08 .25
❑ 45 Terrorized .08 .25
❑ 46 Logan Echolls And Duncan Kane .08 .25
❑ 47 Dick And Beaver Casablancas .08 .25
❑ 48 Madison Sinclair .08 .25
❑ 49 Meg Manning .08 .25
❑ 50 Wallance Fennel .08 .25
❑ 51 Eli "Weevil" Narvarro .08 .25
❑ 52 Cindy "Mac" Mackenzie .08 .25
❑ 53 Yolanda Hamilton .08 .25
❑ 54 Veronica Mars .08 .25
❑ 55 Jake And Celeste Kane .08 .25
❑ 56 Lianne Mars .08 .25
❑ 57 The Echolls Family .08 .25
❑ 58 Lynn Echolls .08 .25
❑ 59 Trina Echolls .08 .25
❑ 60 Alicia Fennel And Keith Mars .08 .25
❑ 61 Haunted .08 .25
❑ 62 Warning .08 .25
❑ 63 Remember Me .08 .25
❑ 64 Disguise .08 .25
❑ 65 Internet .08 .25
❑ 66 Location .08 .25
❑ 67 Surveillance .08 .25
❑ 68 Tools .08 .25
❑ 69 The Planner .08 .25
❑ 70 The Fall Guy .08 .25
❑ 71 The Beneficiary .08 .25
❑ 72 Checklist .08 .25

2006 Veronica Mars Season One Autographs

STATED ODDS 1:24

❑ A1 Kristen Bell 100.00 175.00
❑ A2 Francis Capra 5.00 12.00
❑ A3 Teddy Dunn 5.00 12.00
❑ A4 Jason Dohring 6.00 15.00
❑ A5 Corinne Bohrer 5.00 12.00
❑ A6 Amanda Seyfried 30.00 60.00
❑ A7 Tina Majorino 6.00 15.00
❑ A8 Anthony Anderson 6.00 15.00
❑ A9 Max Greenfield 6.00 15.00
❑ A10 Paula Marshall 6.00 15.00
❑ A11 Sydney Tamiia Poitier 5.00 12.00
❑ AR1 Autograph Redemption Card

2006 Veronica Mars Season One Box Loaders

❑ BL1 Veronica & Duncan
❑ BL2 Veronica & Logan
❑ BL3 Veronica Mars
❑ CL1 Veronica & Lilly

2006 Veronica Mars Season One Pieceworks

STATED ODDS 1:24

❑ PW1 Kristen Bell
❑ PW2 Jason Dohring
❑ PW3 Percy Daggs III
❑ PW4 Teddy Dunn
❑ PW5 Francis Capra
❑ PW6 Amanda Seyfried
❑ PW7 Harry Hamlin
❑ PW8 Lisa Rinna
❑ PW9 Alona Tal
❑ PW10 Ryan Hansen
❑ PW11 Kyle Secor
❑ PW12 Paris Hilton

2006 Veronica Mars Season One Revolving Around Mars

STATED ODDS 1:17

❑ R1 Logan Echolls 1.25 3.00
❑ R2 Duncan Kane 1.25 3.00
❑ R3 Keith Mars 1.25 3.00
❑ R4 Leo D'Amato 1.25 3.00
❑ R5 Wallace Fennel 1.25 3.00
❑ R6 Weevil Navarro 1.25 3.00

2006 Veronica Mars Season One Who Killed Lilly Kane

STATED ODDS 1:11

❑ W1 Who Killed Lilly Kane 1.00 2.50
❑ W2 Who Killed Lilly Kane 1.00 2.50
❑ W3 Who Killed Lilly Kane 1.00 2.50
❑ W4 Who Killed Lilly Kane 1.00 2.50
❑ W5 Who Killed Lilly Kane 1.00 2.50
❑ W6 Who Killed Lilly Kane 1.00 2.50
❑ W7 Who Killed Lilly Kane 1.00 2.50
❑ W8 Who Killed Lilly Kane 1.00 2.50
❑ W9 Who Killed Lilly Kane 1.00 2.50

2006 X-Men The Last Stand

COMPLETE SET (72) 5.00 12.00

❑ 1 Title Card .15 .40
Movie Poster
❑ 2 Professor Xavier .15 .40
❑ 3 Wolverine .15 .40
❑ 4 Jean Grey .15 .40
❑ 5 Storm .15 .40
❑ 6 Beast .15 .40
❑ 7 Rogue .15 .40
❑ 8 Iceman .15 .40
❑ 9 Kitty Pryde .15 .40
❑ 10 Angel .15 .40
❑ 11 Cyclops .15 .40
❑ 12 Colossus .15 .40
❑ 13 Magneto .15 .40
❑ 14 Mystique .15 .40
❑ 15 Pyro .15 .40
❑ 16 Callisto .15 .40
❑ 17 Juggernaut .15 .40
❑ 18 Multiple Man .15 .40
❑ 19 Movie Action .15 .40
❑ 20 Movie Action .15 .40
❑ 21 Movie Action .15 .40
❑ 22 Movie Action .15 .40
❑ 23 Movie Action .15 .40
❑ 24 Movie Action .15 .40
❑ 25 Movie Action .15 .40
❑ 26 Movie Action .15 .40
❑ 27 Movie Action .15 .40
❑ 28 Movie Action .15 .40
❑ 29 Movie Action .15 .40
❑ 30 Movie Action .15 .40
❑ 31 Movie Action .15 .40
❑ 32 Movie Action .15 .40
❑ 33 Movie Action .15 .40
❑ 34 Movie Action .15 .40
❑ 35 Movie Action .15 .40
❑ 36 Movie Action .15 .40
❑ 37 Movie Action .15 .40
❑ 38 Movie Action .15 .40
❑ 39 Movie Action .15 .40
❑ 40 Movie Action .15 .40
❑ 41 Movie Action .15 .40
❑ 42 Movie Action .15 .40
❑ 43 Movie Action .15 .40
❑ 44 Movie Action .15 .40
❑ 45 Movie Action .15 .40
❑ 46 Movie Action .15 .40
❑ 47 Movie Action .15 .40
❑ 48 Movie Action .15 .40
❑ 49 Movie Action .15 .40
❑ 50 Movie Action .15 .40
❑ 51 Movie Action .15 .40
❑ 52 Movie Action .15 .40
❑ 53 Movie Action .15 .40
❑ 54 Movie Action .15 .40
❑ 55 The Quotable X-Men: The Last Stand .15 .40
❑ 56 The Quotable X-Men: The Last Stand .15 .40
❑ 57 The Quotable X-Men: The Last Stand .15 .40
❑ 58 The Quotable X-Men: The Last Stand .15 .40
❑ 59 The Quotable X-Men: The Last Stand .15 .40
❑ 60 The Quotable X-Men: The Last Stand .15 .40
❑ 61 The Quotable X-Men: The Last Stand .15 .40
❑ 62 The Quotable X-Men: The Last Stand .15 .40
❑ 63 The Quotable X-Men: The Last Stand .15 .40
❑ 64 The Quotable X-Men: The Last Stand .15 .40
❑ 65 The Quotable X-Men: The Last Stand .15 .40
❑ 66 The Quotable X-Men: The Last Stand .15 .40
❑ 67 The Quotable X-Men: The Last Stand .15 .40
❑ 68 The Quotable X-Men: The Last Stand .15 .40
❑ 69 The Quotable X-Men: The Last Stand .15 .40
❑ 70 The Quotable X-Men: The Last Stand .15 .40
❑ 71 The Quotable X-Men: The Last Stand .15 .40
❑ 72 The Quotable X-Men: The Last Stand .15 .40

2006 X-Men The Last Stand Art & Images of the X-Men

COMPLETE SET (9) 40.00 80.00
STATED ODDS 1:20

❑ ART1 Professor Xavier 4.00 10.00
❑ ART2 Wolverine 4.00 10.00
❑ ART3 Jean Grey 4.00 10.00
❑ ART4 Cyclops 4.00 10.00
❑ ART5 Magneto 4.00 10.00
❑ ART6 Mystique 4.00 10.00
❑ ART7 Rogue 4.00 10.00
❑ ART8 Storm 4.00 10.00
❑ ART9 Beast 4.00 10.00
❑ ART10 Iceman (issued as a Rittenhouse Reward)10.00 25.00

2006 X-Men The Last Stand Autographs

STATED ODDS 1:40
RATNER AUTO ISSUED AS CASE TOPPER
AGHDASHLOO AUTO ISSUED IN COLLECTORS ALBUM
LEE AUTO ISSUED AS 2-CASE INCENTIVE
JACKMAN AUTO ISSUED AS 6-CASE INCENTIVE
L (LIMITED): 300-500 COPIES
VL (VERY LIMITED): 200-300 COPIES

❑ 1 Aaron Stanford 8.00 20.00
❑ 2 Anna Paquin VL 75.00 150.00
❑ 3 Bill Duke L 15.00 40.00
❑ 4 Bryce Hodgson 6.00 15.00
❑ 5 Cameron Bright 6.00 15.00
❑ 6 Cayden Boyd 6.00 15.00
❑ 7 Dania Ramirez 25.00 50.00
❑ 8 Daniel Cudmore L 10.00 25.00
❑ 9 Desiree Zurowski 8.00 20.00
❑ 10 Haley Ramm 8.00 20.00
❑ 11 James Marsden L 12.00 30.00
❑ 12 Kelsey Grammer VL 75.00 150.00
❑ 13 Michael Murphy 6.00 15.00
❑ 14 Olivia Williams 8.00 20.00
❑ 15 Omahyra Garcia 8.00 20.00
❑ 16 Patrick Stewart VL 75.00 150.00
❑ 17 Shawn Ashmore 8.00 20.00
❑ 18 Vinnie Jones L 25.00 50.00
❑ 19 Brett Ratner/ (issued as case topper) 8.00 20.00
❑ 20 Shohreh Aghdashloo 8.00 20.00
(issued in collectors album)
❑ 21 Stan Lee/ (issued as 2-case incentive) 50.00 100.00
❑ 22 Hugh Jackman/ (issued as 6-case incentive)200.00 300.00

2006 X-Men The Last Stand Casting Call

COMPLETE SET (16) 20.00 40.00
STATED ODDS 1:20
CARD CC3 WAS NOT ISSUED

❑ CC1 Patrick Stewart 1.50 4.00
Professor Xavier
❑ CC2 Hugh Jackman 1.50 4.00
Wolverine
❑ CC4b Halle Berry 1.50 4.00
Storm
❑ CC4a Ian McKellen 1.50 4.00
Magneto
❑ CC5 Famke Janssen 1.50 4.00
Phoenix
❑ CC6 Anna Paquin 1.50 4.00
Rogue
❑ CC7 Rebecca Romijn 1.50 4.00
Mystique
❑ CC8 Kelsey Grammer 1.50 4.00
Beast
❑ CC9 Shawn Ashmore 1.50 4.00
Iceman
❑ CC10 Ellen Page 1.50 4.00
Shadowcat
❑ CC11 Aaron Stanford 1.50 4.00
Pyro
❑ CC12 James Marsden 1.50 4.00
Cyclops
❑ CC13 Daniel Cudmore 1.50 4.00
Colossus
❑ CC14 Vinnie Jones 1.50 4.00
Juggernaut
❑ CC15 Dania Ramirez 1.50 4.00
Callisto
❑ CC16 Ben Foster 1.50 4.00
Angel

2006 X-Men The Last Stand SketchaFex

STATED ODDS 1:320

❑ NNO Cat Staggs
❑ NNO Sean Pence
❑ NNO Steven Miller
❑ NNO Scott Rosema

2006 X-Men The Last Stand Take A Stand

COMPLETE SET (6) 25.00 50.00
STATED ODDS 1:80

❑ T1 Wolverine 4.00 10.00
❑ T2 Storm 4.00 10.00
❑ T3 Phoenix 4.00 10.00
❑ T4 Rogue 4.00 10.00
❑ T5 Beast 4.00 10.00
❑ T6 Angel 4.00 10.00

2006 X-Men The Last Stand Wolverine Portraits of a Hero

COMPLETE SET (9) 8.00 20.00
STATED ODDS 1:13

❑ W1 Wolverine 1.00 2.50
❑ W2 Wolverine 1.00 2.50
❑ W3 Wolverine 1.00 2.50
❑ W4 Wolverine 1.00 2.50
❑ W5 Wolverine 1.00 2.50
❑ W6 Wolverine 1.00 2.50
❑ W7 Wolverine 1.00 2.50
❑ W8 Wolverine 1.00 2.50
❑ W9 Wolverine 1.00 2.50

2007 Alien vs. Predator Requiem

COMPLETE SET (81) 4.00 10.00
CL1 STATED ODDS ONE PER CASE

❑ 1 Title Card .10 .30
❑ 2 Sheriff Morales .10 .30
❑ 3 Dallas Howard .10 .30
❑ 4 Ricky Howard .10 .30
❑ 5 Kelly O'Brien .10 .30
❑ 6 Molly O'Brien .10 .30
❑ 7 The Alien .10 .30
❑ 8 The Predator .10 .30
❑ 9 The Predalien .10 .30
❑ 10 Day Of The Hunters .10 .30
❑ 11 Targeting A Face Hugger .10 .30
❑ 12 The Aliens' First Victims .10 .30
❑ 13 Dallas Comes Home .10 .30
❑ 14 The O'Briens Reunited .10 .30
❑ 15 Chest Buster Horror .10 .30
❑ 16 The Monster Inside Him .10 .30
❑ 17 Ricky's Special Delivery .10 .30
❑ 18 Battered By A Bully .10 .30
❑ 19 Attack On The Homeless .10 .30
❑ 20 Invading The Local Sewer .10 .30
❑ 21 Arrival .10 .30
❑ 22 Monster On A Mission .10 .30
❑ 23 His Fallen Comrades .10 .30
❑ 24 Behind The Mask .10 .30
❑ 25 A Clean Up Specialist .10 .30
❑ 26 What The Hell Is This .10 .30
❑ 27 What Lies Beneath .10 .30
❑ 28 Into The Woods .10 .30
❑ 29 Slaughtered And Skinned .10 .30
❑ 30 Even Science Is Stunned .10 .30
❑ 31 They Crawl By Night .10 .30
❑ 32 Skirmish With The Enemy .10 .30
❑ 33 Savage Struggle .10 .30

- ❑ 34 One Against Many .10 .30
- ❑ 35 Dark Pursuer .10 .30
- ❑ 36 Emergency Escape .10 .30
- ❑ 37 Disaster At The Diner .10 .30
- ❑ 38 Carrie's Final Moments .10 .30
- ❑ 39 Extreme Terror .10 .30
- ❑ 40 Death On The Menu .10 .30
- ❑ 41 Lovers And Haters .10 .30
- ❑ 42 Night Of The Pursued .10 .30
- ❑ 43 Hell And Heated Water .10 .30
- ❑ 44 Speared By The Predator .10 .30
- ❑ 45 Don't Let The Bedbugs Bite! .10 .30
- ❑ 46 Alien At The Window .10 .30
- ❑ 47 Dad Under Attack .10 .30
- ❑ 48 Alien In An Alien Land .10 .30
- ❑ 49 A Town Under Siege .10 .30
- ❑ 50 Saving Little Molly .10 .30
- ❑ 51 After Visiting Hours .10 .30
- ❑ 52 An Orderly Demise .10 .30
- ❑ 53 Is That You, Doctor .10 .30
- ❑ 54 Dying In Bed...The Hard Way .10 .30
- ❑ 55 The Predalien Was Here .10 .30
- ❑ 56 A Doctor Meets His Doom .10 .30
- ❑ 57 Horror In Store .10 .30
- ❑ 58 Monster Against Monster .10 .30
- ❑ 59 Dale's Gruesome Demise .10 .30
- ❑ 60 Horrors Of Acid Blood .10 .30
- ❑ 61 Hitching A Deadly Ride .10 .30
- ❑ 62 On The Road Again .10 .30
- ❑ 63 Monster Mashed .10 .30
- ❑ 64 There's No Stopping Him .10 .30
- ❑ 65 Losing His Horrid Head .10 .30
- ❑ 66 In The Alien Hive .10 .30
- ❑ 67 At Last...They Meet .10 .30
- ❑ 68 Deadly Confrontation .10 .30
- ❑ 69 When Worlds Collide .10 .30
- ❑ 70 Face-To-Face .10 .30
- ❑ 71 Whoever Wins...We Lose .10 .30
- ❑ 72 The Predator's End Game .10 .30
- ❑ 73 An Acid Bath .10 .30
- ❑ 74 Deformed Hybrid .10 .30
- ❑ 75 Ramming His Enemy .10 .30
- ❑ 76 Ground Zero .10 .30
- ❑ 77 Aftermath .10 .30
- ❑ 78 The World Isn't Ready .10 .30
- ❑ 79 Suited For Mayhem .10 .30
- ❑ 80 Helming The Horrors .10 .30
- ❑ 81 Checklist .10 .30
- ❑ CL1 AVP Unleashed

2007 Alien vs. Predator Requiem Autographs

STATED ODDS ONE PER BOX

- ❑ A1 Reiko Aylesworth 30.00 60.00
- ❑ A2 John Ortiz
- ❑ A3 Johnny Lewis 5.00 12.00
- ❑ A4 Kristen Hager 15.00 30.00
- ❑ A5 Ariel Gade 10.00 20.00
- ❑ A6 David Paetkau 5.00 12.00
- ❑ A7 Gina Holden 15.00 30.00
- ❑ A8 Kurt Max Runte 5.00 12.00
- ❑ A9 Robert Joy
- ❑ A10 Ian Whyte

2007 Alien vs. Predator Requiem Battlefield on Earth Puzzle

COMPLETE SET (9) 4.00 10.00
STATED ODDS 1:11

- ❑ B1 Birth Of The Predalien .75 2.00
- ❑ B2 Armed And Ruthless .75 2.00
- ❑ B3 The Legacy .75 2.00
- ❑ B4 When Monsters Clash .75 2.00
- ❑ B5 The Ultimate Predator Warrior vs. The Predator.75 2.00
- ❑ B6 Heritage Of Horror .75 2.00
- ❑ B7 What Chance Do They Have .75 2.00
- ❑ B8 The Perfect Killing Machine .75 2.00
- ❑ B9 An Awesome Battle .75 2.00

2007 Alien vs. Predator Requiem Deadly

COMPLETE SET (3) 4.00 10.00
STATED ODDS 1:24

- ❑ D1 The Arrival 2.00 5.00
- ❑ D2 Hitching A Ride 2.00 5.00
- ❑ D3 Monsters In Mortal Combat 2.00 5.00

2007 Alien vs. Predator Requiem Massacre on Main Street

COMPLETE SET (6) 4.00 10.00
STATED ODDS 1:17

- ❑ M1 Horror From In High 1.25 3.00
- ❑ M2 Monster In The Woods 1.25 3.00
- ❑ M3 Acid Blood And Beyond 1.25 3.00
- ❑ M4 Suited For The Task 1.25 3.00
- ❑ M5 Loose Upon Earth 1.25 3.00
- ❑ M6 Predator Technology 1.25 3.00

2007 Alien vs. Predator Requiem Pieceworks

STATED ODDS ONE PER BOX
PW12A, PW12B ISSUED AS MULTI-CASE INCENTIVES

- ❑ PW1 Kelly 8.00 20.00
- ❑ PW2 Dallas 4.00 10.00
- ❑ PW3A Sheriff Morales Jacket 4.00 10.00
- ❑ PW3B Sheriff Morales Fur
- ❑ PW4 Ricky 4.00 10.00
- ❑ PW5 Carrie 4.00 10.00
- ❑ PW6 Jesse 8.00 20.00
- ❑ PW7 Molly DUAL 10.00 25.00
- ❑ PW8 Dallas 4.00 10.00
- ❑ PW9 Ricky DUAL 8.00 20.00
- ❑ PW10 Darcy 6.00 15.00
- ❑ PW11 Curtis 4.00 10.00
- ❑ PW12A Dallas/ (issued as multi-case incentive)25.00 50.00
- ❑ PW12B Kelly/ (issued as multi-case incentive)25.00 50.00
- ❑ PWR1 Redemption card

2007 Alien vs. Predator Requiem Sketches

STATED ODDS ONE PER BOX

- ❑ SCC Cynthia Cummens/312
- ❑ SCM Chris Moreno/300
- ❑ SDC Daniel Cooney/300
- ❑ SDR David Rabbitte/299
- ❑ SIH Ingrid Hardy/193
- ❑ SJZ Jeff Zugale/300
- ❑ SKA Kristin Allen/299
- ❑ SKB Kate Red Bradley/278
- ❑ SKG Kevin Graham/302
- ❑ SLK Lee Kohse/323
- ❑ SMD Mark Dos Santos/294
- ❑ SMW Matt Wendt/299
- ❑ SRL Randi Leeann/317
- ❑ SRM Rich A. Molinelli/295
- ❑ SRN Rafael Navarro/300
- ❑ STR Tone Rodriguez/313

2007 American Idol Season Six

COMPLETE SET (72) 4.00 10.00

- ❑ 1 Consider it a cattle call .10 .25
- ❑ 2 Auditions can be a painful process .10 .25
- ❑ 3 Season 6 auditions took place .10 .25
- ❑ 4 Kelly Clarkson - 1 .10 .25
- ❑ 5 Ruben Studdard - 1 .10 .25
- ❑ 6 Fantasia - 1 .10 .25
- ❑ 7 Fantasia - 2 .10 .25
- ❑ 8 Carrie Underwood - 1 .20 .50
- ❑ 9 Carrie Underwood - 2 .20 .50
- ❑ 10 Taylor Hicks - 1 .10 .25
- ❑ 11 Taylor Hicks - 2 .10 .25
- ❑ 12 Randy Jackson - 1 .10 .25
- ❑ 13 Randy Jackson - 2 .10 .25
- ❑ 14 Paula Abdul - 1 .10 .25
- ❑ 15 Paula Abdul - 2 .10 .25
- ❑ 16 Ryan Seacrest - 1 .10 .25
- ❑ 17 Ryan Seacrest - 2 .10 .25
- ❑ 18 Forget a week of fun in the sun! .10 .25
- ❑ 19 Rest up! .10 .25
- ❑ 20 For contestants, adjusting to life in L.A. .10 .25
- ❑ 21 Rejection is never easy to handle .10 .25
- ❑ 22 Alaina Alexander .10 .25
- ❑ 23 Antonella Barba .10 .25
- ❑ 24 Rudy Cardenas .10 .25
- ❑ 25 Jared Cotter .10 .25
- ❑ 26 Melinda Doolittle .10 .25
- ❑ 27 Stephanie Edwards .10 .25
- ❑ 28 Gina Glocksen .10 .25
- ❑ 29 Sundance Head .10 .25
- ❑ 30 Leslie Hunt .10 .25
- ❑ 31 LaKisha Jones .10 .25
- ❑ 32 Paul Kim .10 .25
- ❑ 33 Amy Krebs .10 .25
- ❑ 34 Blake Lewis .10 .25
- ❑ 35 Sanjaya Malakar .10 .25
- ❑ 36 Nick Pedro .10 .25
- ❑ 37 Chris Richardson .10 .25
- ❑ 38 Brandon Rogers .10 .25
- ❑ 39 Haley Scarnato .10 .25
- ❑ 40 Chris Sligh .10 .25
- ❑ 41 Sabrina Sloan .10 .25
- ❑ 42 Jordin Sparks .10 .25
- ❑ 43 Phil Stacey .10 .25
- ❑ 44 A.J. Tabaldo .10 .25
- ❑ 45 Nicole Tranquillo .10 .25
- ❑ 46 Debra Byrd - Vocal Coach .10 .25
- ❑ 47 Michael Orland - Associate Musical Director and Pianist .10 .25
- ❑ 48 Dorian Holley - Vocal Coach .10 .25
- ❑ 49 From Day One, the male contestants .10 .25
- ❑ 50 Notable AI Statistics .10 .25
- ❑ 51 Rehearsals are a time to support .10 .25
- ❑ 52 The contestants lounge backstage .10 .25
- ❑ 53 AI6 contestants are divided up into pairs .10 .25
- ❑ 54 For AI6, stylists were available .10 .25
- ❑ 55 Elimination night is never easy .10 .25
- ❑ 56 Performing before all of America .10 .25
- ❑ 57 Results night each week .10 .25
- ❑ 58 Top 12 Introduction .10 .25
- ❑ 59 Melinda Doolittle .10 .25
- ❑ 60 Stephanie Edwards .10 .25
- ❑ 61 Gina Glocksen .10 .25
- ❑ 62 LaKisha Jones .10 .25
- ❑ 63 Blake Lewis .10 .25
- ❑ 64 Sanjaya Malakar .10 .25
- ❑ 65 Chris Richardson .10 .25
- ❑ 66 Brandon Rogers .10 .25
- ❑ 67 Haley Scarnato .10 .25
- ❑ 68 Chris Sligh .10 .25
- ❑ 69 Jordin Sparks .10 .25
- ❑ 70 Phil Stacey .10 .25
- ❑ 71 Checklist 1 .10 .25
- ❑ 72 Checklist 2 .10 .25

2007 American Idol Season Six Autographs

STATED ODDS 1:15

- ❑ 1 Blake Lewis 3.00 8.00
- ❑ 2 Brandon Rogers 3.00 8.00
- ❑ 3 Chris Richardson 3.00 8.00
- ❑ 4 Chris Sligh 3.00 8.00
- ❑ 5 Gina Glocksen 3.00 8.00
- ❑ 6 Haley Scarnato 3.00 8.00
- ❑ 7 Jordin Sparks 8.00 20.00
- ❑ 8 Lakisha Jones 3.00 8.00
- ❑ 9 Melinda Doolittle 3.00 8.00
- ❑ 10 Phil Stacey 3.00 8.00
- ❑ 11 Sanjaya Malakar 3.00 8.00
- ❑ 12 Stephanie Edwards 3.00 8.00

2007 Battlestar Galactica Season Two

COMPLETE SET (72) 4.00 10.00
KYLE SKETCH ODDS ONE PER 6-CASE PURCHASE

- ❑ 1 Title Card .10 .30
- ❑ 2 Title Card .10 .30
- ❑ 3 Title Card .10 .30
- ❑ 4 Scattered .10 .30
- ❑ 5 Scattered .10 .30
- ❑ 6 Scattered .10 .30
- ❑ 7 Valley of Darkness .10 .30
- ❑ 8 Valley of Darkness .10 .30
- ❑ 9 Valley of Darkness .10 .30
- ❑ 10 Fragged .10 .30
- ❑ 11 Fragged .10 .30
- ❑ 12 Fragged .10 .30
- ❑ 13 Resistance .10 .30
- ❑ 14 Resistance .10 .30
- ❑ 15 Resistance .10 .30
- ❑ 16 The Farm .10 .30
- ❑ 17 The Farm .10 .30
- ❑ 18 The Farm .10 .30
- ❑ 19 Home, Part 1 .10 .30
- ❑ 20 Home, Part 1 .10 .30
- ❑ 21 Home, Part 1 .10 .30
- ❑ 22 Home, Part 2 .10 .30
- ❑ 23 Home, Part 2 .10 .30
- ❑ 24 Home, Part 2 .10 .30
- ❑ 25 Final Cut .10 .30
- ❑ 26 Final Cut .10 .30
- ❑ 27 Final Cut .10 .30
- ❑ 28 Flight of the Phoenix .10 .30
- ❑ 29 Flight of the Phoenix .10 .30
- ❑ 30 Flight of the Phoenix .10 .30
- ❑ 31 Pegasus .10 .30
- ❑ 32 Pegasus .10 .30
- ❑ 33 Pegasus .10 .30
- ❑ 34 Resurrection Ship, Part 1 .10 .30
- ❑ 35 Resurrection Ship, Part 1 .10 .30
- ❑ 36 Resurrection Ship, Part 1 .10 .30
- ❑ 37 Resurrection Ship, Part 2 .10 .30
- ❑ 38 Resurrection Ship, Part 2 .10 .30
- ❑ 39 Resurrection Ship, Part 2 .10 .30
- ❑ 40 Epiphanies .10 .30
- ❑ 41 Epiphanies .10 .30
- ❑ 42 Epiphanies .10 .30
- ❑ 43 Black Market .10 .30
- ❑ 44 Black Market .10 .30
- ❑ 45 Black Market .10 .30
- ❑ 46 Scar .10 .30
- ❑ 47 Scar .10 .30
- ❑ 48 Scar .10 .30
- ❑ 49 Sacrifice .10 .30
- ❑ 50 Sacrifice .10 .30
- ❑ 51 Sacrifice .10 .30
- ❑ 52 The Captain's Hand .10 .30
- ❑ 53 The Captain's Hand .10 .30
- ❑ 54 The Captain's Hand .10 .30
- ❑ 55 Downloaded .10 .30
- ❑ 56 Downloaded .10 .30
- ❑ 57 Downloaded .10 .30
- ❑ 58 Lay Down Your Burdens, Part 1 .30
- ❑ 59 Lay Down Your Burdens, Part 1 .10 .30
- ❑ 60 Lay Down Your Burdens, Part 1 .10 .30
- ❑ 61 Lay Down Your Burdens, Part 2 .10 .30
- ❑ 62 Lay Down Your Burdens, Part 2 .10 .30
- ❑ 63 Lay Down Your Burdens, Part 2 .10 .30
- ❑ 64 New Caprica .10 .30
- ❑ 65 New Caprica .10 .30
- ❑ 66 New Caprica .10 .30
- ❑ 67 New Caprica .10 .30
- ❑ 68 New Caprica .10 .30
- ❑ 69 New Caprica .10 .30
- ❑ 70 Checklist .10 .30
- ❑ 71 Checklist .10 .30
- ❑ 72 Checklist .10 .30
- ❑ KYLE Jim Kyle Sketch

2007 Battlestar Galactica Season Two Alliances

COMPLETE SET (9) 6.00 15.00
STATED ODDS 1:20

- ❑ A1 Gaius Baltar / Gina 1.25 3.00
- ❑ A2 Kara Thrace / Samuel Anders 1.25 3.00
- ❑ A3 Lee Adama / Kara Thrace 1.25 3.00
- ❑ A4 Tom Zarek / Meier 1.25 3.00
- ❑ A5 Lee Adama / Anastasia Dualla 1.25 3.00
- ❑ A6 Galen Tyrol / Gaius Baltar 1.25 3.00
- ❑ A7 Caprica Six / Caprica Sharon 1.25 3.00
- ❑ A8 Sharon Valerii / Karl Agathon 1.25 3.00
- ❑ A9 Galen Tyrol / Karl Agathon 1.25 3.00

2007 Battlestar Galactica Season Two Autographs

STATED ODDS 1:40
L (LIMITED): 300-500 CARDS
VL (VERY LIMITED): LESS THAN 300 CARDS

- ❑ CF Colm Feore L 10.00 25.00
- ❑ CM Claudette Mink L 6.00 15.00
- ❑ CS Christina Schild L 6.00 15.00
- ❑ DR Donnelly Rhodes L 6.00 15.00
- ❑ EC Erica Cerra L 15.00 30.00
- ❑ JC James Callis VL
- ❑ JH John Heard L 8.00 20.00
- ❑ KV Kate Vernon L 6.00 15.00
- ❑ LC Leah Cairns L 15.00 30.00
- ❑ LL Lucy Lawless VL
- ❑ MT Michael Trucco L 10.00 25.00
- ❑ TH Tricia Helfer VL

2007 Battlestar Galactica Season Two Costumes

STATED ODDS 1:40
CC31 ODDS ONE PER COLLECTORS ALBUM
DC2 ODDS ONE PER CASE
KS ODDS ONE PER 2-CASE PURCHASE

- ❑ CC21 Number Six 10.00 25.00
- ❑ CC22 Galen Tyrol 6.00 15.00
- ❑ CC23 Gaius Baltar 5.00 12.00
- ❑ CC24 Samuel Anders 6.00 15.00
- ❑ CC25 Karl Agathon 5.00 12.00
- ❑ CC26 Billy Keikeya 5.00 12.00
- ❑ CC27 Sharon Valerii 6.00 15.00
- ❑ CC28 Saul Tigh 6.00 15.00
- ❑ CC29 William Adama 5.00 12.00
- ❑ CC30 Kara Thrace 8.00 20.00
- ❑ CC31 Number Six
- ❑ DC2 Priest Elosha 25.00 50.00
- ❑ KS Capt. Kara Thrace / Katie Sackoff AU

2007 Battlestar Galactica Season Two Crew

COMPLETE SET (9) 15.00 40.00
STATED ODDS 1:40

- ❑ T1 Admiral William Adama 3.00 8.00
- ❑ T2 Commander Lee Adama 3.00 8.00
- ❑ T3 Captain Kara Thrace 3.00 8.00
- ❑ T4 Number 6 3.00 8.00
- ❑ T5 Dr. Gaius Baltar 3.00 8.00
- ❑ T6 Lt. Sharon Valerii 3.00 8.00
- ❑ T7 President Laura Roslin 3.00 8.00
- ❑ T8 Colonel Saul Tigh 3.00 8.00
- ❑ T9 CPO Galen Tyrol 3.00 8.00

2007 Battlestar Galactica Season Two Promos

- ❑ P1 Lee Adama/Kara Thrace (General Distribution) .75 2.00
- ❑ P2 Lee Adama (NSU Magazine) 1.25 3.00
- ❑ P3 Lee Adama (Album Exclusive) 5.00 12.00

2007 Battlestar Galactica Season Two Rag Tag Fleet

COMPLETE SET (9) 4.00 10.00
STATED ODDS 1:13

- ❑ R1 Battlestar Galactica .75 2.00
- ❑ R2 Battlestar Pegasus .75 2.00
- ❑ R3 Colonial One .75 2.00
- ❑ R4 Cloud Nine .75 2.00
- ❑ R5 Astral Queen .75 2.00
- ❑ R6 Raptor .75 2.00
- ❑ R7 Viper Mark VII .75 2.00
- ❑ R8 Geminon Traveler .75 2.00
- ❑ R9 Ring Ship .75 2.00

2007 Battlestar Galactica Season Two Shelter Posters

COMPLETE SET (4)
STATED ODDS 1:240
STATED PRINT RUN 250 SER. #'d SETS

- ❑ S1 Destoyer / Creator
- ❑ S2 Betrayer / Betrayed
- ❑ S3 Defiant / Defied
- ❑ S4 Player / Pawn

2007 Battlestar Galactica Season Two Women of Battlestar Galactica

COMPLETE SET (6) 12.00 30.00
STATED ODDS 1:40

- ❑ W1 Captain Kara Thrace 4.00 10.00
- ❑ W2 Sharon Valerii 4.00 10.00
- ❑ W3 Number Six 4.00 10.00
- ❑ W4 Laura Roslin 4.00 10.00
- ❑ W5 D'anna Biers 4.00 10.00
- ❑ W6 Admiral Helena Cain 4.00 10.00

2007 Bench Warmer

COMP.SET w/o SPs (72) 6.00 15.00
SP STATED ODDS 1:4

- ❑ 1 April Scott .15 .40
- ❑ 2 Sara Underwood .15 .40
- ❑ 3 Jennifer Korbin .15 .40
- ❑ 4 Lindsey Roeper .15 .40
- ❑ 5 Miriam Gonzalez .25 .60
- ❑ 6 Amanda Mixon .15 .40
- ❑ 7 Leilene Stuecklin .15 .40
- ❑ 8 Paige Peterson .15 .40
- ❑ 9 Jessica Rockwell .15 .40
- ❑ 10 Kirsty Lingman .15 .40
- ❑ 11 Wrenna Monet .15 .40
- ❑ 12 Amber Hay .15 .40
- ❑ 13 Meagan Hauserman .15 .40
- ❑ 14 Simona Fusco .15 .40
- ❑ 15 Alice Bradley .15 .40
- ❑ 16 Amanda Carraway .15 .40
- ❑ 17 Jessica Burciaga .15 .40
- ❑ 18 Rachel Bernstein .15 .40
- ❑ 19 Bambi Lashell .15 .40
- ❑ 20 Lachelle Benet .15 .40
- ❑ 21 Amanda Carrier .15 .40
- ❑ 22 Shana Palmira .15 .40
- ❑ 23 Tiffany Toth .15 .40
- ❑ 24 Melissa Taylor .15 .40
- ❑ 25 Michelle Anderson .15 .40
- ❑ 26 Melissa Mojo Hunter .15 .40
- ❑ 27 Brandi MacLaren .15 .40
- ❑ 28 Leigh Ann Spence .15 .40
- ❑ 29 Jennifer England .15 .40
- ❑ 30 Brianne Blessing .15 .40
- ❑ 31 Sherry Goggin .15 .40
- ❑ 32 Jenae Alt .15 .40
- ❑ 33 Cristal Camden .15 .40
- ❑ 34 Brandi Michelle Bourgon .15 .40
- ❑ 35 Alix Agar .15 .40
- ❑ 36 Natalie Davidson .15 .40
- ❑ 37 Kristia Bonita .15 .40
- ❑ 38 Brandi Cunningham .15 .40
- ❑ 39 Erika Jordan .15 .40
- ❑ 40 Heather Tindell .15 .40
- ❑ 41 Kiearah Figueroa .15 .40
- ❑ 42 Carrie Minter .15 .40
- ❑ 43 Jaimarie .15 .40
- ❑ 44 Daniela Pane .15 .40
- ❑ 45 Alika Ray .15 .40
- ❑ 46 Kerrilee Kaski .15 .40
- ❑ 47 Catherine Kluthe .15 .40
- ❑ 48 Lindsay Dennis AS .15 .40
- ❑ 49 Katie Lohmann AS .15 .40
- ❑ 50 Melissa Taylor AS .15 .40
- ❑ 51 Shay Lyn AS .15 .40
- ❑ 52 Nicole Bennett AS .15 .40
- ❑ 53 Brandy Grace AS .15 .40
- ❑ 54 Tamara Witmer AS .15 .40
- ❑ 55 Jen Sibley AS .15 .40
- ❑ 56 Lisa Lakatos AS .15 .40
- ❑ 57 Michelle Baena AS .15 .40
- ❑ 58 Katarina Van Derham AS .15 .40
- ❑ 59 Tiffany Richardson AS .15 .40
- ❑ 60 Nikki Zeno AS .15 .40
- ❑ 61 Jennifer Korbin BC .15 .40
- ❑ 62 Laurie Milan BC .15 .40
- ❑ 63 Tamara Witmer BC .15 .40
- ❑ 64 Amanda Carrier BC .15 .40
- ❑ 65 Jen Sibley BC .15 .40
- ❑ 66 Wrenna Monet BC .15 .40
- ❑ 67 Alana Curry BC .15 .40
- ❑ 68 Amber Hay BC .15 .40
- ❑ 69 Shay Lyn BC .15 .40
- ❑ 70 Lora Peterson BC .15 .40
- ❑ 71 Dani Armstrong BC .15 .40
- ❑ 72 Kristina Rodrigues BC .15 .40
- ❑ H73 Mary Riley AA SP 2.00 5.00
- ❑ H74 Krisi Ballentine AA SP 1.25 3.00
- ❑ H75 Lisa Ligon AA SP 1.25 3.00
- ❑ H76 Amber Hay AA SP 1.25 3.00
- ❑ H77 Brianne Blessing AA SP 1.25 3.00
- ❑ H78 Amanda Mixon AA SP 1.25 3.00
- ❑ H79 Bambi Lashell AA SP 1.25 3.00
- ❑ H80 Brandi MacLaren AA SP 1.25 3.00
- ❑ H81 Amanda Carrier AA SP 1.25 3.00
- ❑ H82 Shana Palmira AA SP 1.25 3.00
- ❑ H83 Erin Tietsort ST SP 1.25 3.00
- ❑ H84 Dana Workman ST SP 1.25 3.00
- ❑ H85 Janelle Perry ST SP 1.25 3.00
- ❑ H86 Keely Williams ST SP 1.25 3.00
- ❑ H87 Ania Migdal ST SP 1.25 3.00
- ❑ H88 Holly Huddleston ST SP 1.25 3.00
- ❑ H89 Molly Shea ST SP 1.25 3.00
- ❑ H90 The Olly Girls ST SP 1.25 3.00
- ❑ H91 Lisa Ligon PA SP 1.25 3.00
- ❑ H92 Christy Hemme PA SP 2.00 5.00
- ❑ H93 Laurie Milan PA SP 1.25 3.00
- ❑ H94 Tanea Brooks PA SP 1.25 3.00
- ❑ H95 Renee Stone PA SP 1.25 3.00
- ❑ H96 Kerrilee Kaski PA SP 1.25 3.00
- ❑ H97 Kristina Rodrigues PA SP 1.25 3.00
- ❑ H98 Lindsay Dennis PA SP 1.25 3.00
- ❑ H99 Alika Ray PA SP 1.25 3.00
- ❑ H100 Dani Armstrong PA SP 1.25 3.00

2007 Bench Warmer Authentic Swatch

STATED ODDS 1:288

- ❑ 1 April Scott 10.00 25.00
- ❑ 2 Sara Underwood 15.00 30.00
- ❑ 3 Holly Huddleston 10.00 25.00
- ❑ 4 Molly Shea 10.00 25.00
- ❑ 5 The Olly girls 15.00 30.00
- ❑ 6 Miriam Gonzalez 15.00 30.00
- ❑ 7 Paige Peterson 10.00 25.00
- ❑ 8 Jennifer England 10.00 25.00
- ❑ 9 Lindsey Roeper 10.00 25.00
- ❑ 10 Michelle Baena 10.00 25.00
- ❑ 11 Simona Fusco 10.00 25.00
- ❑ 12 Jennifer Korbin 10.00 25.00

2007 Bench Warmer Authentic Swatch Autographs

STATED PRINT RUN 25 SER. #'d SETS

- ❑ 1 April Scott 100.00 175.00
- ❑ 2 Sara Underwood 125.00 200.00
- ❑ 3 Holly Huddleston 100.00 175.00
- ❑ 4 Molly Shea 100.00 175.00
- ❑ 5 The Olly girls 125.00 200.00
- ❑ 6 Miriam Gonzalez 125.00 200.00
- ❑ 7 Paige Peterson 100.00 175.00
- ❑ 8 Jennifer England 100.00 175.00
- ❑ 9 Lindsey Roeper 100.00 175.00
- ❑ 10 Michelle Baena 100.00 175.00
- ❑ 11 Simona Fusco 100.00 175.00
- ❑ 12 Jennifer Korbin 100.00 175.00

2007 Bench Warmer Autographs

STATED ODDS 1:12
CARD 11 NOT ISSUED

- ❑ 1 April Scott 5.00 12.00
- ❑ 2 Sara Underwood 8.00 20.00
- ❑ 3 Jennifer England 5.00 12.00
- ❑ 4 Miriam Gonzalez 6.00 15.00
- ❑ 5 Holly Huddleston 5.00 12.00
- ❑ 6 Molly Shea 5.00 12.00
- ❑ 7 Krisi Ballentine 5.00 12.00
- ❑ 8 Jessica Rockwell 5.00 12.00
- ❑ 9 Bambi Lashell 5.00 12.00
- ❑ 10 Jennifer Korbin 5.00 12.00
- ❑ 12 Shana Palmira 5.00 12.00
- ❑ 13 Heather Tindell 5.00 12.00
- ❑ 14 Leilene Stuecklin 5.00 12.00
- ❑ 15 Jessica Burciaga 5.00 12.00
- ❑ 16 Amber Hay 5.00 12.00
- ❑ 17 Wrenna Monet 5.00 12.00
- ❑ 18 Alice Bradley 5.00 12.00
- ❑ 19 Rachel Bernstein 5.00 12.00
- ❑ 20 Lindsey Roeper 5.00 12.00
- ❑ 21 Michelle Anderson 5.00 12.00
- ❑ 22 Paige Peterson 5.00 12.00
- ❑ 23 Jenae Alt 5.00 12.00
- ❑ 24 The Olly Girls 6.00 15.00

2007 Bench Warmer Autographs Gold Foil

STATED ODDS 1:144
STATED PRINT RUN 100 SER. #'d SETS

2007 Bench Warmer Autographs Red Foil

STATED ODDS 1:576
STATED PRINT RUN 25 SER. #'d SETS

2007 Bench Warmer Case Topper Autographs

STATED ODDS ONE PER CASE

- ❑ 1 Holiday/ Nicole Bennet Jessica Korbin/Katarina Van Derham/Catherine
- ❑ 2 Purrfect Angelz Lisa Ligon/Christy Hemme/Laurie Milan/Tanea Brooks#
- ❑ 3 School Girl
- ❑ 4 Sweet Sixteen

2007 Bench Warmer Holiday Autographs

STATED ODDS 1:48

- ❑ 1 April Scott 5.00 12.00
- ❑ 2 Nicole Bennett 5.00 12.00
- ❑ 3 Simona Fusco 5.00 12.00
- ❑ 4 Katarina Van Derham 5.00 12.00
- ❑ 5 Bambi Lashell 5.00 12.00
- ❑ 6 Brandi Bourgon 5.00 12.00
- ❑ 7 Paige Peterson 5.00 12.00
- ❑ 8 Catherine Kluthe 5.00 12.00
- ❑ 9 Alika Ray 5.00 12.00
- ❑ 10 Maggie Cash 5.00 12.00
- ❑ 11 Mary Riley 6.00 15.00
- ❑ 12 Jennifer Korbin 6.00 15.00

2007 Bench Warmer Holiday Autographs Gold Foil

STATED ODDS 1:576

2007 Bench Warmer Kiss

COMPLETE SET (16)
STATED ODDS 1:72

- ❑ 1 April Scott 5.00 12.00
- ❑ 2 Sara Underwood 6.00 15.00
- ❑ 3 Miriam Gonzalez 6.00 15.00
- ❑ 4 Jennifer England 5.00 12.00
- ❑ 5 Simona Fusco 5.00 12.00
- ❑ 6 Wrenna Monet 5.00 12.00
- ❑ 7 Jessica Rockwell 5.00 12.00
- ❑ 8 Krisi Ballentine 5.00 12.00
- ❑ 9 Lindsey Roeper 5.00 12.00
- ❑ 10 Christy Hemme 6.00 15.00
- ❑ 11 Paige Peterson 5.00 12.00
- ❑ 12 Leilene Stuecklin 5.00 12.00
- ❑ 13 Heather Tindell 5.00 12.00
- ❑ 14 Amber Hay 5.00 12.00
- ❑ 15 Tiffany Toth 5.00 12.00
- ❑ 16 Bambi Lashell 5.00 12.00

2007 Bench Warmer Gold Autographs

STATED ODDS 1:12

- ❑ 1 Cindy Margolis 6.00 15.00
- ❑ 2 Mary Riley 8.00 20.00
- ❑ 3 Candice Michelle 6.00 15.00
- ❑ 4 Christy Hemme 6.00 15.00
- ❑ 5 Nikki Ziering 5.00 12.00
- ❑ 6 Cecille Gahr 5.00 12.00
- ❑ 7 Megan Hauserman 5.00 12.00
- ❑ 8 Holly Madison 5.00 12.00
- ❑ 9 Molly Shea 5.00 12.00
- ❑ 10 Holly Huddleston 5.00 12.00
- ❑ 11 Shay Lyn 5.00 12.00
- ❑ 12 Krisi Ballentine 5.00 12.00
- ❑ 13 Nicole Bennett 5.00 12.00

❑ 14 Brande Roderick 5.00 12.00
❑ 15 Sandra Taylor 5.00 12.00
❑ 16 Michelle Baena 5.00 12.00
❑ 17 Carrie Stroup 5.00 12.00
❑ 18 Sarah Coggin 5.00 12.00
❑ 19 Leigh Ann Spence 5.00 12.00
❑ 20 Buffy Tyler 5.00 12.00
❑ 21 Trishelle Cannatella 5.00 12.00
❑ 22 Colleen Shannon 5.00 12.00
❑ 23 Aubrie Lemon 5.00 12.00
❑ 24 Yvette Nelson 5.00 12.00
❑ 25 Claudia Jordan 5.00 12.00
❑ 26 Jaime Hammer 5.00 12.00
❑ 27 Flo Jalin 5.00 12.00
❑ 28 Jennifer Korbin 5.00 12.00
❑ 29 Brandy Grace 5.00 12.00
❑ 30 Shauna Sand 5.00 12.00

2007 Buffy the Vampire Slayer 10th Anniversary

COMPLETE SET (90) 5.00 12.00
M1 STATED ODDS 1:145
CL1 STATED ODDS ONE PER CASE

❑ 1 Buffy: Enduring .15 .40
❑ 2 Buffy: Triumphant .15 .40
❑ 3 Giles: Protective .15 .40
❑ 4 Angel: Mysterious .15 .40
❑ 5 Xander: Devoted .15 .40
❑ 6 Willow: Resilient .15 .40
❑ 7 Joyce: Maternal .15 .40
❑ 8 Cordelia: Feisty .15 .40
❑ 9 Joss' Notes .15 .40
❑ 10 Buffy: Shattered .15 .40
❑ 11 Giles: Regrets .15 .40
❑ 12 Xander: Heroic .15 .40
❑ 13 Willow: Talented .15 .40
❑ 14 Cordelia: Heartbreaker .15 .40
❑ 15 Joyce: Defender .15 .40
❑ 16 Angel: Changed .15 .40
❑ 17 Oz: Transformed .15 .40
❑ 18 Joss' Notes .15 .40
❑ 19 Buffy: Recognized .15 .40
❑ 20 Giles: Confrontational .15 .40
❑ 21 Xander: Unrecognizable .15 .40
❑ 22 Willow: Captive .15 .40
❑ 23 Cordelia: Unlucky In Love .15 .40
❑ 24 Faith: Fighter .15 .40
❑ 25 Angel: Reflective .15 .40
❑ 26 Oz: Unexpected .15 .40
❑ 27 Joss' Notes .15 .40
❑ 28 Buffy: Ultimate .15 .40
❑ 29 Giles: Needed .15 .40
❑ 30 Xander: Unnoticed .15 .40
❑ 31 Willow: Magical .15 .40
❑ 32 Tara: Essential .15 .40
❑ 33 Oz: Untamed .15 .40
❑ 34 Riley: New Boyfriend .15 .40
❑ 35 Spike: Hiding .15 .40
❑ 36 Joss' Notes .15 .40
❑ 37 Buffy: Sacrificing .15 .40
❑ 38 Giles: Greiving .15 .40
❑ 39 Xander: Conflicted .15 .40
❑ 40 Willow: Powerful .15 .40
❑ 41 Tara: Taken .15 .40
❑ 42 Anya: Invented .15 .40
❑ 43 Dawn: Related .15 .40
❑ 44 Spike: Obsessed .15 .40
❑ 45 Joss' Notes .15 .40
❑ 46 Buffy: Reborn .15 .40
❑ 47 Giles: Intervening .15 .40
❑ 48 Xander: Certain .15 .40
❑ 49 Willow: Uncontrolled .15 .40
❑ 50 Tara: Extinguished .15 .40
❑ 51 Anya: Choosing .15 .40
❑ 52 Dawn: Out Of Place .15 .40
❑ 53 Spike: Twisted .15 .40
❑ 54 Joss' Notes .15 .40
❑ 55 Buffy: New Beginning .15 .40
❑ 56 Giles: Inquiring .15 .40
❑ 57 Xander: Loyal .15 .40
❑ 58 Willow: Conduit .15 .40
❑ 59 Anya: Fierce .15 .40
❑ 60 Dawn: Secure .15 .40
❑ 61 Spike: Heroic .15 .40
❑ 62 Faith Reformed .15 .40
❑ 63 Joss' Notes .15 .40
❑ 64 Faith Arrives .15 .40
❑ 65 Faith Lost .15 .40
❑ 66 Faith & The Mayor .15 .40
❑ 67 Faith & Angel .15 .40
❑ 68 Faith Returns .15 .40
❑ 69 Faith & Spike .15 .40
❑ 70 Faith Leads .15 .40
❑ 71 Faith & Love .15 .40
❑ 72 Battling Faith .15 .40
❑ 73 The Master .15 .40
❑ 74 Spike And Drusilla .15 .40
❑ 75 Glory .15 .40
❑ 76 Caleb And The First Evil .15 .40
❑ 77 Johathan .15 .40
❑ 78 Andrew .15 .40
❑ 79 Amy Madison .15 .40
❑ 80 Halfrek .15 .40
❑ 81 Robin Wood .15 .40
❑ 82 Buffy .15 .40
❑ 83 Xander .15 .40
❑ 84 Willow .15 .40
❑ 85 Dawn .15 .40
❑ 86 Faith .15 .40
❑ 87 Giles .15 .40
❑ 88 Ethan Rayne .15 .40
❑ 89 Amy & Warren .15 .40
❑ 90 Checklist .15 .40
❑ M1 Welcome To Sunnydale Map 6.00 15.00
❑ CL1 Buffy - Legendary 8.00 20.00
(issued as case loader)

2007 Buffy the Vampire Slayer 10th Anniversary Forever

STATED ODDS 1:11

❑ F1 Forever 2.00 5.00
❑ F2 Forever 2.00 5.00
❑ F3 Forever 2.00 5.00
❑ F4 Forever 2.00 5.00
❑ F5 Forever 2.00 5.00
❑ F6 Forever 2.00 5.00
❑ F7 Forever 2.00 5.00
❑ F8 Forever 2.00 5.00
❑ F9 Forever 2.00 5.00

2007 Buffy the Vampire Slayer 10th Anniversary Friends Forever Pieceworks

STATED ODDS 1:287

❑ FF1 Buffy's Coat 50.00 100.00
❑ FF2 Willow's Jacket 40.00 80.00
❑ FF3 Xander's Shirt 30.00 60.00
❑ FF4 Giles' Sweater 30.00 60.00

2007 Buffy the Vampire Slayer 10th Anniversary Leader of Slayers

STATED ODDS 1:23

❑ L1 Divided 2.50 6.00
❑ L2 Inspired 2.50 6.00
❑ L3 United 2.50 6.00

2007 Buffy the Vampire Slayer 10th Anniversary Pieceworks

STATED ODDS 1:24
SE1 STATED ODDS 1:2304

❑ PW1 Buffy's Coat 12.00 30.00
❑ PW2 Buffy's Pants 12.00 30.00
❑ PW3a Buffy's Jacket 12.00 30.00
❑ PW3b Buffy's Jacket
(with trim)
❑ PW4a Willow's Jacket 8.00 20.00
❑ PW4b Willow's Jacket
(with trim)
❑ PW5 Xander's T-Shirt & Jeans 8.00 20.00
❑ PW6 Xander's Shirt 8.00 20.00
❑ PW7 Giles' Sweater 8.00 20.00
❑ PW8 Anya's Dress 8.00 20.00
❑ PW9 Anya's Top & Pants 8.00 20.00
❑ PW10a Dawn's Pajama Pants 8.00 20.00
❑ PW10b Dawn's Pajama Pants 12.00 30.00
(lace variant)
❑ PW11 Kennedy's Top & Pants 8.00 20.00
❑ PW12 Vi's Knit Cap 8.00 20.00
❑ PW13 Lissa's Purse 8.00 20.00
❑ PW14 Double Meat Palace Shirt & Pants 8.00 20.00
❑ SE1 Slayer's Essential Stake Card 600.00 800.00

2007 Buffy the Vampire Slayer 10th Anniversary Promos

❑ P1 Buffy 1.25 3.00
(General Distribution)
❑ Pi Buffy 1.00 2.50
(inkworks.com exclusive)
❑ PK Buffy 1.25 3.00
(UK Distribution)
❑ NSU Buffy 5.00 10.00
(Non-Sport Update)
❑ SD2007 Buffy 1.00 2.50
(San Diego CC exclusive)

2007 Buffy the Vampire Slayer 10th Anniversary Recollections

STATED ODDS 1:17

❑ R1 Buffy 3.00 8.00
❑ R2 Willow 3.00 8.00
❑ R3 Giles 2.50 6.00
❑ R4 Xander 2.50 6.00
❑ R5 Cordelia 2.50 6.00
❑ R6 Oz 2.50 6.00
❑ R7 Anya 2.50 6.00
❑ R8 Dawn 2.50 6.00

2007 Charmed Forever

COMPLETE SET (72) 4.00 10.00
UNPRICED INKPLATES PRINT RUN 1

❑ 1 Title Card .10 .30
❑ 2 Freedom! .10 .30
❑ 3 Who Are You? .10 .30
❑ 4 Home Sweet Home .10 .30
❑ 5 Watch Out! .10 .30
❑ 6 Hulkus Pocus .10 .30
❑ 7 Getting A Do-Over .10 .30
❑ 8 Rewriting History .10 .30
❑ 9 Forever And Ever .10 .30
❑ 10 Magic-Free Phoebe .10 .30
❑ 11 Shaky Start .10 .30
❑ 12 Happily Never After .10 .30
❑ 13 Goodbye .10 .30
❑ 14 Looking For Trouble .10 .30
❑ 15 Crossed Up .10 .30
❑ 16 Lucy Milano .10 .30
❑ 17 Celebration .10 .30
❑ 18 Staring Down The Enemy .10 .30
❑ 19 Coffee Break .10 .30
❑ 20 Jo Bennett .10 .30
❑ 21 Desperate Aunt .10 .30
❑ 22 Getting The Picture .10 .30
❑ 23 Getting To Know You .10 .30
❑ 24 Bridging Two Worlds .10 .30
❑ 25 Here Comes The Bride .10 .30
❑ 26 Betrayed And Confused .10 .30
❑ 27 Forever Safe .10 .30
❑ 28 Billie Jenkins .10 .30
❑ 29 Billie's First Demon .10 .30
❑ 30 Taxi! .10 .30
❑ 31 Frozen Out .10 .30
❑ 32 Every Trick In The Book .10 .30
❑ 33 The Secret Garden .10 .30
❑ 34 Fire Power .10 .30
❑ 35 And Then There Was One .10 .30
❑ 36 The Ultimate Sacrifice .10 .30
❑ 37 Previously...On Charmed .10 .30
❑ 38 The Feds .10 .30
❑ 39 Charmed Undercover .10 .30
❑ 40 Paige-Ing Grams .10 .30
❑ 41 New Witch On The Block .10 .30
❑ 42 Magical Mentoring .10 .30
❑ 43 Best Intentions .10 .30
❑ 44 Mr. & Mrs. Dex Lawson .10 .30
❑ 45 Rewitched .10 .30
❑ 46 The Dogon .10 .30
❑ 47 Distupted Domesticity .10 .30
❑ 48 Meet The Parents .10 .30
❑ 49 Sign Of Things To Come .10 .30
❑ 50 Reunited .10 .30
❑ 51 The Nightmare Continues .10 .30
❑ 52 Christy's Lack Of Candor .10 .30
❑ 53 Desperate Measures .10 .30
❑ 54 The Ultimate Powers .10 .30
❑ 55 Dumain .10 .30
❑ 56 Thrown Face-Off .10 .30
❑ 57 Thrown For A Loop .10 .30
❑ 58 United In Spirit .10 .30
❑ 59 A Hollow Idea .10 .30
❑ 60 A Hollow Idea, Part Two .10 .30
❑ 61 Third Time's The Charm .10 .30
❑ 62 The Ultimate Battle .10 .30
❑ 63 The End? .10 .30
❑ 64 The Charmed One .10 .30
❑ 65 Coop's Ring .10 .30
❑ 66 Reinforcements .10 .30
❑ 67 Grams And Gramps? .10 .30
❑ 68 The Angel Of Destiny .10 .30
❑ 69 Christy's Last Stand .10 .30
❑ 70 Triumph .10 .30
❑ 71 A Perfect Ending .10 .30
❑ 72 Checklist .10 .30
❑ CL1 The Power Of 4 8.00 20.00

2007 Charmed Forever And They Lived Happily Ever After

STATED ODDS 1:35

❑ LH1 Piper and Leo 2.00 5.00
❑ LH2 Phoebe and Coop 2.00 5.00
❑ LH3 Paige and Henry 2.00 5.00

2007 Charmed Forever Family

COMPLETE SET (6) 4.00 10.00
STATED ODDS 1:17

❑ FF1 Brad Kern 1.25 3.00
❑ FF2 And Action 1.25 3.00
❑ FF3 Brian & Kaley 1.25 3.00
❑ FF4 Forever Friends 1.25 3.00
❑ FF5 That's a Wrap 1.25 3.00
❑ FF6 Forever Family 1.25 3.00

2007 Charmed Forever Legacy

COMPLETE SET (9) 4.00 10.00
STATED ODDS 1:11

❑ L1 Band of Brothers .75 2.00
❑ L2 The Gramswitch .75 2.00
❑ L3 Forever Charmed .75 2.00
❑ L4 Sam Wilder .75 2.00
❑ L5 Boys and Their Toys .75 2.00
❑ L6 Past, Present, & Future .75 2.00
❑ L7 Grams .75 2.00
❑ L8 Catching Up .75 2.00
❑ L9 Victor Bennett .75 2.00

2007 Charmed Forever Pieceworks

STATED ODDS 1:18

❑ PW1 Alyssa Milano 10.00 25.00
❑ PW2 Holly Marie Combs 8.00 20.00
❑ PW3 Rose McGowan 8.00 20.00
❑ PW4 Kaley Cuoco 6.00 15.00
❑ PW5 Drew Fuller 3.00 8.00
❑ PW6 Alyssa Milano 10.00 25.00
❑ PW7a Holly Marie Combs 8.00 20.00
❑ PW7b Holly Marie Combs
❑ PW8 Rose McGowan 8.00 20.00
❑ PW9 Alyssa Milano 10.00 25.00
❑ PW10 Rose McGowan 8.00 20.00
❑ PW11 Holly Marie Combs 15.00 30.00
❑ PW12 Rose McGowan 8.00 20.00
❑ PW13 Rose McGowan 8.00 20.00
❑ PW14 Alyssa Milano 30.00 60.00
Holly Marie Combs/Rose McGowan/ (issued as multi-case incentive)

2007 The Complete James Bond

COMPLETE SET (189) 8.00 20.00

❑ 1 Dr. No .15 .40
❑ 2 Dr. No .15 .40
❑ 3 Dr. No .15 .40
❑ 4 Dr. No .15 .40
❑ 5 Dr. No .15 .40
❑ 6 Dr. No .15 .40
❑ 7 Dr. No .15 .40
❑ 8 Dr. No .15 .40
❑ 9 Dr. No .15 .40
❑ 10 From Russia With Love .15 .40
❑ 11 From Russia With Love .15 .40
❑ 12 From Russia With Love .15 .40
❑ 13 From Russia With Love .15 .40
❑ 14 From Russia With Love .15 .40
❑ 15 From Russia With Love .15 .40
❑ 16 From Russia With Love .15 .40
❑ 17 From Russia With Love .15 .40
❑ 18 From Russia With Love .15 .40
❑ 19 Goldfinger .15 .40
❑ 20 Goldfinger .15 .40
❑ 21 Goldfinger .15 .40
❑ 22 Goldfinger .15 .40
❑ 23 Goldfinger .15 .40
❑ 24 Goldfinger .15 .40
❑ 25 Goldfinger .15 .40
❑ 26 Goldfinger .15 .40
❑ 27 Goldfinger .15 .40
❑ 28 Thunderball .15 .40
❑ 29 Thunderball .15 .40
❑ 30 Thunderball .15 .40
❑ 31 Thunderball .15 .40
❑ 32 Thunderball .15 .40
❑ 33 Thunderball .15 .40
❑ 34 Thunderball .15 .40
❑ 35 Thunderball .15 .40
❑ 36 Thunderball .15 .40
❑ 37 You Only Live Twice .15 .40
❑ 38 You Only Live Twice .15 .40
❑ 39 You Only Live Twice .15 .40
❑ 40 You Only Live Twice .15 .40
❑ 41 You Only Live Twice .15 .40
❑ 42 You Only Live Twice .15 .40
❑ 43 You Only Live Twice .15 .40
❑ 44 You Only Live Twice .15 .40
❑ 45 You Only Live Twice .15 .40
❑ 46 On Her Majesty's Secret Service .15 .40
❑ 47 On Her Majesty's Secret Service .15 .40
❑ 48 On Her Majesty's Secret Service .15 .40
❑ 49 On Her Majesty's Secret Service .15 .40
❑ 50 On Her Majesty's Secret Service .15 .40
❑ 51 On Her Majesty's Secret Service .15 .40
❑ 52 On Her Majesty's Secret Service .15 .40
❑ 53 On Her Majesty's Secret Service .15 .40
❑ 54 On Her Majesty's Secret Service .15 .40
❑ 55 Diamonds Are Forever .15 .40
❑ 56 Diamonds Are Forever .15 .40
❑ 57 Diamonds Are Forever .15 .40
❑ 58 Diamonds Are Forever .15 .40
❑ 59 Diamonds Are Forever .15 .40
❑ 60 Diamonds Are Forever .15 .40
❑ 61 Diamonds Are Forever .15 .40
❑ 62 Diamonds Are Forever .15 .40
❑ 63 Diampnds Are Forever .15 .40
❑ 64 Live And Let Die .15 .40
❑ 65 Live And Let Die .15 .40
❑ 66 Live And Let Die .15 .40
❑ 67 Live And Let Die .15 .40
❑ 68 Live And Let Die .15 .40
❑ 69 Live And Let Die .15 .40
❑ 70 Live And Let Die .15 .40
❑ 71 Live And Let Die .15 .40
❑ 72 Live And Let Die .15 .40
❑ 73 The Man With The Golden Gun .15 .40
❑ 74 The Man With The Golden Gun .15 .40
❑ 75 The Man With The Golden Gun .15 .40
❑ 76 The Man With The Golden Gun .15 .40
❑ 77 The Man With The Golden Gun .15 .40
❑ 78 The Man With The Golden Gun .15 .40
❑ 79 The Man With The Golden Gun .15 .40
❑ 80 The Man With The Golden Gun .15 .40
❑ 81 The Man With The Golden Gun .15 .40
❑ 82 The Spy Who Loved Me .15 .40
❑ 83 The Spy Who Loved Me .15 .40
❑ 84 The Spy Who Loved Me .15 .40
❑ 85 The Spy Who Loved Me .15 .40
❑ 86 The Spy Who Loved Me .15 .40
❑ 87 The Spy Who Loved Me .15 .40
❑ 88 The Spy Who Loved Me .15 .40
❑ 89 The Spy Who Loved Me .15 .40
❑ 90 The Spy Who Loved Me .15 .40
❑ 91 Moonraker .15 .40
❑ 92 Moonraker .15 .40
❑ 93 Moonraker .15 .40
❑ 94 Moonraker .15 .40
❑ 95 Moonraker .15 .40
❑ 96 Moonraker .15 .40
❑ 97 Moonraker .15 .40
❑ 98 Moonraker .15 .40
❑ 99 Moonraker .15 .40
❑ 100 For Your Eyes Only .15 .40
❑ 101 For Your Eyes Only .15 .40
❑ 102 For Your Eyes Only .15 .40
❑ 103 For Your Eyes Only .15 .40
❑ 104 For Your Eyes Only .15 .40
❑ 105 For Your Eyes Only .15 .40
❑ 106 For Your Eyes Only .15 .40
❑ 107 For Your Eyes Only .15 .40
❑ 108 For Your Eyes Only .15 .40
❑ 109 Octopussy .15 .40
❑ 110 Octopussy .15 .40
❑ 111 Octopussy .15 .40
❑ 112 Octopussy .15 .40
❑ 113 Octopussy .15 .40
❑ 114 Octopussy .15 .40
❑ 115 Octopussy .15 .40
❑ 116 Octopussy .15 .40
❑ 117 Octopussy .15 .40
❑ 118 A View To A Kill .15 .40
❑ 119 A View To A Kill .15 .40
❑ 120 A View To A Kill .15 .40
❑ 121 A View To A Kill .15 .40
❑ 122 A View To A Kill .15 .40
❑ 123 A View To A Kill .15 .40
❑ 124 A View To A Kill .15 .40
❑ 125 A View To A Kill .15 .40
❑ 126 A View To A Kill .15 .40
❑ 127 The Living Daylights .15 .40
❑ 128 The Living Daylights .15 .40
❑ 129 The Living Daylights .15 .40
❑ 130 The Living Daylights .15 .40
❑ 131 The Living Daylights .15 .40
❑ 132 The Living Daylights .15 .40
❑ 133 The Living Daylights .15 .40
❑ 134 The Living Daylights .15 .40
❑ 135 The Living Daylights .15 .40
❑ 136 Licence To Kill .15 .40
❑ 137 Licence To Kill .15 .40
❑ 138 Licence To Kill .15 .40
❑ 139 Licence To Kill .15 .40
❑ 140 Licence To Kill .15 .40
❑ 141 Licence To Kill .15 .40
❑ 142 Licence To Kill .15 .40
❑ 143 Licence To Kill .15 .40
❑ 144 Licence To Kill .15 .40
❑ 145 GoldenEye .15 .40
❑ 146 GoldenEye .15 .40
❑ 147 GoldenEye .15 .40
❑ 148 GoldenEye .15 .40
❑ 149 GoldenEye .15 .40
❑ 150 GoldenEye .15 .40
❑ 151 GoldenEye .15 .40
❑ 152 GoldenEye .15 .40
❑ 153 GoldenEye .15 .40
❑ 154 Tomorrow Never Dies .15 .40
❑ 155 Tomorrow Never Dies .15 .40
❑ 156 Tomorrow Never Dies .15 .40
❑ 157 Tomorrow Never Dies .15 .40
❑ 158 Tomorrow Never Dies .15 .40
❑ 159 Tomorrow Never Dies .15 .40
❑ 160 Tomorrow Never Dies .15 .40
❑ 161 Tomorrow Never Dies .15 .40
❑ 162 Tomorrow Never Dies .15 .40
❑ 163 The World Is Not Enough .15 .40
❑ 164 The World Is Not Enough .15 .40
❑ 165 The World Is Not Enough .15 .40
❑ 166 The World Is Not Enough .15 .40
❑ 167 The World Is Not Enough .15 .40
❑ 168 The World Is Not Enough .15 .40
❑ 169 The World Is Not Enough .15 .40
❑ 170 The World Is Not Enough .15 .40
❑ 171 The World Is Not Enough .15 .40
❑ 172 Die Another Day .15 .40
❑ 173 Die Another Day .15 .40
❑ 174 Die Another Day .15 .40
❑ 175 Die Another Day .15 .40
❑ 176 Die Another Day .15 .40
❑ 177 Die Another Day .15 .40
❑ 178 Die Another Day .15 .40
❑ 179 Die Another Day .15 .40
❑ 180 Die Another Day .15 .40
❑ 181 Casino Royale .15 .40
❑ 182 Casino Royale .15 .40
❑ 183 Casino Royale .15 .40
❑ 184 Casino Royale .15 .40
❑ 185 Casino Royale .15 .40
❑ 186 Casino Royale .15 .40
❑ 187 Casino Royale .15 .40
❑ 188 Casino Royale .15 .40
❑ 189 Casino Royale .15 .40

2007 The Complete James Bond Autographs

STATED ODDS 1:40
A90 STATED ODDS ONE PER COLLECTOR'S ALBUM
LAZENBY AUTO STATED ODDS ONE PER 2 CASE PURCHASE
RICHARDS AUTO STATED ODDS ONE PER 6 CASE PURCHASE
L (LIMITED): 300-500 COPIES
VL (VERY LIMITED): 200-300 COPIES

❑ A32 Ursula Andress VL 300.00 400.00
❑ A51 Yaphet Kotto VL 100.00 200.00
❑ A52 Lynn-Holly Johnson VL 20.00 40.00
❑ A53 Kristina Wayborn VL
❑ A54 Maud Adams VL 50.00 100.00
❑ A55 Maud Adams VL 50.00 100.00
❑ A56 Famke Janssen VL
❑ A57 Tania Mallet L 10.00 25.00
❑ A58 John Bowe L 8.00 20.00
❑ A63 Lana Wood VL 20.00 40.00
❑ A65 Timothy Moxon L 15.00 30.00
❑ A66 Britt Ekland L 30.00 60.00
❑ A68 Alan Cumming VL 60.00 120.00
❑ A70 Caroline Bliss VL 60.00 120.00
❑ A71 Izabella Scorupco VL 60.00 120.00
❑ A72 Honor Blackman VL 200.00 300.00
❑ A73 Marguerite Lewars VL 35.00 70.00
❑ A74 George Leech 6.00 15.00
❑ A75 Judi Dench VL 30.00 60.00
❑ A76 Simon Abkarian L 10.00 25.00
❑ A77 Mads Mikkelsen VL 30.00 60.00
❑ A78 Caterina Murino L 30.00 60.00
❑ A79 Giancarlo Giannini L 15.00 30.00
❑ A80 John Rhys-Davies VL 200.00 300.00
❑ A81 Sebastien Foucan L 8.00 20.00
❑ A90 Jeremy Bulloch 10.00 25.00
❑ NNO Denise Richards (Full Bleed)/ (issued as 6-case incentive)
❑ NNO George Lazenby (Full Bleed) 100.00 200.00
(issued as 2-case incentive)

2007 The Complete James Bond Casino Royale Dangerous Liaisons

COMPLETE SET (9)
STATED ODDS 1:14

❑ DL1 James Bond
Mollaka
❑ DL2 James Bond
M
❑ DL3 James Bond
Felix Leiter
❑ DL4 James Bond
Vesper Lynd
❑ DL5 Le Chiffre
Dimitrios
❑ DL6 James Bond
Le Chiffre
❑ DL7 James Bond
Vesper Lynd/Mathis
❑ DL8 James Bond
Vesper Lynd
❑ DL9 James Bond
Solange

2007 The Complete James Bond Casino Royale Expansion

COMPLETE SET (10)
STATED ODDS 1:20

❑ 64 Casino Royale
❑ 65 Casino Royale
❑ 66 Casino Royale
❑ G21 Vesper Lynd
❑ T21 Bond Tech Casino Royale
❑ V21 Le Chiffre
❑ BA19 Felix Leiter
❑ BG47 Vesper Lynd
❑ BG48 Solange
❑ BV41 Le Chiffre

2007 The Complete James Bond Relics

STATED ODDS 1:40
DC1 STATED ODDS ONE PER CASE
L (LIMITED): 300-500 COPIES
VL (VERY LIMITED): 200-300 COPIES

❑ RC1 Cayman Island Bank Check
❑ RC2 James Bond Medical Report VL
❑ RC3 Fontainebleau Letterhead VL
❑ RC4 San Monique Flag
❑ RC5 Circus Program
❑ RC6 Casino Chip VL
❑ RC7 Sir Robert King Bank Statement VL
❑ RC8 Parahawk Parachute VL
❑ RC9 Zorin Industries Patch
❑ RC10 Fontainebleau Score Sheet VL
❑ RC11 Jinx Jordan Medical File
❑ RC12 Tarot Card L
❑ RC13 Casino Chip VL
❑ RC14 Casino L'or Noir Check VL
❑ RC15 Bomb Grenade Sack
❑ RC16 Osato Stationary
❑ RC17 Playing Card
❑ RC18 Casino Chip VL
❑ DC1 James Bond Dual Shirt/ (issued as case topper)

2007 The Complete James Bond The Quotable Casino Royale

COMPLETE SET (6)
STATED ODDS 1:20

❑ Q1 The Quotable Casino Royale
❑ Q2 The Quotable Casino Royale
❑ Q3 The Quotable Casino Royale
❑ Q4 The Quotable Casino Royale
❑ Q5 The Quotable Casino Royale
❑ Q6 The Quotable Casino Royale

2007 Complete Star Trek Movies

COMPLETE SET (90) 5.00 12.00

❑ 1 Star Trek: The Motion Picture .15 .40
❑ 2 Star Trek: The Motion Picture .15 .40
❑ 3 Star Trek: The Motion Picture .15 .40
❑ 4 Star Trek: The Motion Picture .15 .40
❑ 5 Star Trek: The Motion Picture .15 .40
❑ 6 Star Trek: The Motion Picture .15 .40
❑ 7 Star Trek: The Motion Picture .15 .40
❑ 8 Star Trek: The Motion Picture .15 .40
❑ 9 Star Trek: The Motion Picture .15 .40
❑ 10 Star Trek II: The Wrath of Khan .15 .40
❑ 11 Star Trek II: The Wrath of Khan .15 .40
❑ 12 Star Trek II: The Wrath of Khan .15 .40
❑ 13 Star Trek II: The Wrath of Khan .15 .40
❑ 14 Star Trek II: The Wrath of Khan .15 .40
❑ 15 Star Trek II: The Wrath of Khan .15 .40
❑ 16 Star Trek II: The Wrath of Khan .15 .40
❑ 17 Star Trek II: The Wrath of Khan .15 .40
❑ 18 Star Trek II: The Wrath of Khan .15 .40
❑ 19 Star Trek III: The Search for Spock .15 .40
❑ 20 Star Trek III: The Search for Spock .15 .40
❑ 21 Star Trek III: The Search for Spock .15 .40
❑ 22 Star Trek III: The Search for Spock .15 .40
❑ 23 Star Trek III: The Search for Spock .15 .40
❑ 24 Star Trek III: The Search for Spock .15 .40
❑ 25 Star Trek III: The Search for Spock .15 .40

❑ 26 Star Trek III: The Search for Spock .15 .40
❑ 27 Star Trek III: The Search for Spock .15 .40
❑ 28 Star Trek IV: The Voyage Home .15 .40
❑ 29 Star Trek IV: The Voyage Home .15 .40
❑ 30 Star Trek IV: The Voyage Home .15 .40
❑ 31 Star Trek IV: The Voyage Home .15 .40
❑ 32 Star Trek IV: The Voyage Home .15 .40
❑ 33 Star Trek IV: The Voyage Home .15 .40
❑ 34 Star Trek IV: The Voyage Home .15 .40
❑ 35 Star Trek IV: The Voyage Home .15 .40
❑ 36 Star Trek IV: The Voyage Home .15 .40
❑ 37 Star Trek V: The Final Frontier .15 .40
❑ 38 Star Trek V: The Final Frontier .15 .40
❑ 39 Star Trek V: The Final Frontier .15 .40
❑ 40 Star Trek V: The Final Frontier .15 .40
❑ 41 Star Trek V: The Final Frontier .15 .40
❑ 42 Star Trek V: The Final Frontier .15 .40
❑ 43 Star Trek V: The Final Frontier .15 .40
❑ 44 Star Trek V: The Final Frontier .15 .40
❑ 45 Star Trek V: The Final Frontier .15 .40
❑ 46 Star Trek VI: The Undiscovered Country .15 .40
❑ 47 Star Trek VI: The Undiscovered Country .15 .40
❑ 48 Star Trek VI: The Undiscovered Country .15 .40
❑ 49 Star Trek VI: The Undiscovered Country .15 .40
❑ 50 Star Trek VI: The Undiscovered Country .15 .40
❑ 51 Star Trek VI: The Undiscovered Country .15 .40
❑ 52 Star Trek VI: The Undiscovered Country .15 .40
❑ 53 Star Trek VI: The Undiscovered Country .15 .40
❑ 54 Star Trek VI: The Undiscovered Country .15 .40
❑ 55 Star Trek Generations .15 .40
❑ 56 Star Trek Generations .15 .40
❑ 57 Star Trek Generations .15 .40
❑ 58 Star Trek Generations .15 .40
❑ 59 Star Trek Generations .15 .40
❑ 60 Star Trek Generations .15 .40
❑ 61 Star Trek Generations .15 .40
❑ 62 Star Trek Generations .15 .40
❑ 63 Star Trek Generations .15 .40
❑ 64 Star Trek: First Contact .15 .40
❑ 65 Star Trek: First Contact .15 .40
❑ 66 Star Trek: First Contact .15 .40
❑ 67 Star Trek: First Contact .15 .40
❑ 68 Star Trek: First Contact .15 .40
❑ 69 Star Trek: First Contact .15 .40
❑ 70 Star Trek: First Contact .15 .40
❑ 71 Star Trek: First Contact .15 .40
❑ 72 Star Trek: First Contact .15 .40
❑ 73 Star Trek: Insurrection .15 .40
❑ 74 Star Trek: Insurrection .15 .40
❑ 75 Star Trek: Insurrection .15 .40
❑ 76 Star Trek: Insurrection .15 .40
❑ 77 Star Trek: Insurrection .15 .40
❑ 78 Star Trek: Insurrection .15 .40
❑ 79 Star Trek: Insurrection .15 .40
❑ 80 Star Trek: Insurrection .15 .40
❑ 81 Star Trek: Insurrection .15 .40
❑ 82 Star Trek Nemesis .15 .40
❑ 83 Star Trek Nemesis .15 .40
❑ 84 Star Trek Nemesis .15 .40
❑ 85 Star Trek Nemesis .15 .40
❑ 86 Star Trek Nemesis .15 .40
❑ 87 Star Trek Nemesis .15 .40
❑ 88 Star Trek Nemesis .15 .40
❑ 89 Star Trek Nemesis .15 .40
❑ 90 Star Trek Nemesis .15 .40

2007 Complete Star Trek Movies Autographs

STATED ODDS 1:12
A20 ODDS ONE PER 2-CASE PURCHASE
A40 ODDS ONE PER COLLECTORS ALBUM
A50 ODDS ONE PER 6-CASE PURCHASE
L (LIMITED): 300-500 CARDS
VL (VERY LIMITED): 200-300 CARDS

❑ A1 Ricardo Montalban VL 200.00 300.00
❑ A2 Stephen Collins VL 60.00 120.00
❑ A3 Malcolm McDowell VL 100.00 200.00
❑ A4 Linda Fetters-Howard 6.00 15.00
❑ A5 Billy Van Zandt 6.00 15.00
❑ A6 Robin Curtis 10.00 25.00
❑ A7 George Murdock 8.00 20.00
❑ A8 John Schuck 6.00 15.00
❑ A9 Harve Bennett VL 75.00 150.00
❑ A10 Michele Ameen Billy 8.00 20.00
❑ A11 Phil Morris L 20.00 40.00
❑ A12 Ike Eisenmann 8.00 20.00
❑ A13 Cathie Shirriff 8.00 20.00
❑ A14 Christopher Lloyd VL 75.00 150.00
❑ A15 Todd Bryant 8.00 20.00
❑ A16 Charles Cooper 8.00 20.00
❑ A17 Spice Williams 8.00 20.00
❑ A18 Michael Berryman 6.00 15.00
❑ A19 Jenette Goldstein 8.00 20.00
❑ A20 George Takei/ (issued as 2-case incentive) 30.00 60.00
❑ A21 Leon Russom 6.00 15.00
❑ A22 Darryl Henriques 6.00 15.00
❑ A23 Scott McGinnis 6.00 15.00
❑ A24 David Gautreaux 6.00 15.00
❑ A25 Cynthia Gouw 8.00 20.00
❑ A26 Neal McDonough L 10.00 25.00
❑ A27 Kirk Thatcher 6.00 15.00
❑ A28 Robert Picardo VL 60.00 120.00
❑ A29 Tom Morga 6.00 15.00
❑ A30 Walter Koenig L 30.00 60.00
❑ A31 Scott Strozier 6.00 15.00
❑ A32 Robert Ellenstein 6.00 15.00
❑ A33 F. Murray Abraham L 10.00 25.00
❑ A34 W. Morgan Sheppard L 10.00 25.00
❑ A35 Cully Fredricksen 6.00 15.00
❑ A36 Michael Snyder 6.00 15.00
❑ A37 Stephen Manley 6.00 15.00
❑ A38 Rene Auberjonois VL 60.00 120.00
❑ A39 Judson Scott 8.00 20.00
❑ A40 Miguel Ferrer/ (issued in collectors album)
❑ A49 Catherine Hicks L 20.00 40.00
❑ A50 William Shatner/ (issued as 6-case incentive)

2007 Complete Star Trek Movies Behind-the-Scenes

COMPLETE SET (10) 12.00 30.00
STATED ODDS 1:24

❑ B1 Star Trek: The Motion Picture 2.50 6.00
❑ B2 Star Trek II: The Wrath of Khan 2.50 6.00
❑ B3 Star Trek III: The Search for Spock 2.50 6.00
❑ B4 Star Trek IV: The Voyage Home 2.50 6.00
❑ B5 Star Trek V: The Final Frontier 2.50 6.00
❑ B6 Star Trek VI: The Undiscovered Country 2.50 6.00
❑ B7 Star Trek Generations 2.50 6.00
❑ B8 Star Trek: First Contact 2.50 6.00
❑ B9 Star Trek: Insurrection 2.50 6.00
❑ B10 Star Trek Nemesis 2.50 6.00

2007 Complete Star Trek Movies Camp Khitomer Banners

COMPLETE SET (4) 75.00 150.00
STATED ODDS 1:120
STATED PRINT RUN 575 SER. #'d SETS

❑ KB1 Camp Khitomer United Federation of Planets Flag 25.00 50.00
❑ KB2 Camp Khitomer Vulcan Flag 25.00 50.00
❑ KB3 Camp Khitomer Romulan Flag 25.00 50.00
❑ KB4 Camp Khitomer Klingon Flag 25.00 50.00

2007 Complete Star Trek Movies Character Logs

COMPLETE SET (10) 15.00 40.00
STATED ODDS 1:24

❑ C1 Captain Kirk Star Trek 3.00 8.00
❑ C2 Captain Kirk Star Trek II 3.00 8.00
❑ C3 Captain Kirk Star Trek III 3.00 8.00
❑ C4 Captain Kirk Star Trek IV 3.00 8.00
❑ C5 Captain Kirk Star Trek V 3.00 8.00
❑ C6 Captain Kirk Star Trek VI 3.00 8.00
❑ C7 Captain Picard Generations 3.00 8.00
❑ C8 Captain Picard First Contact 3.00 8.00
❑ C9 Captain Picard Insurrection 3.00 8.00
❑ C10 Captain Picard Nemesis 3.00 8.00

2007 Complete Star Trek Movies Costumes

STATED ODDS 1:12

❑ MC1 Captain Kirk Star Trek 25.00 50.00
❑ MC2 Spock Star Trek 10.00 25.00
❑ MC3 Lt. Sulu Star Trek 8.00 20.00
❑ MC4 Lt. Chekov Star Trek 8.00 20.00
❑ MC5 Scotty Star Trek VI 8.00 20.00
❑ MC6 Lt. Uhura Star Trek 6.00 15.00
❑ MC7 CPO Janice Rand Star Trek 5.00 12.00
❑ MC8 Lt. Ilia Star Trek 5.00 12.00
❑ MC9 Lt. Uhura Star Trek 6.00 15.00
❑ MC10 Lt. Saavik Star Trek II 5.00 12.00
❑ MC11 Dr. McCoy Star Trek II 8.00 20.00
❑ MC12 Dr. Carol Marcus Star Trek II 5.00 12.00
❑ MC13 Lt. Chekov Star Trek III 6.00 15.00
❑ MC14 Dr. McCoy Star Trek V 8.00 20.00
❑ MC15 Data Nemesis 6.00 15.00
❑ MC16 Commander Riker Nemesis 6.00 15.00

2007 Complete Star Trek Movies Gold Plaque

COMPLETE SET (10) 15.00 40.00
STATED ODDS 1:24

❑ G1 Star Trek: The Motion Picture 3.00 8.00
❑ G2 Star Trek II: The Wrath of Khan 3.00 8.00
❑ G3 Star Trek III: The Search for Spock 3.00 8.00
❑ G4 Star Trek IV: The Voyage Home 3.00 8.00
❑ G5 Star Trek V: The Final Frontier 3.00 8.00
❑ G6 Star Trek VI: The Undiscovered Country 3.00 8.00
❑ G7 Star Trek Generations 3.00 8.00
❑ G8 Star Trek: First Contact 3.00 8.00
❑ G9 Star Trek: Insurrection 3.00 8.00
❑ G10 Star Trek Nemesis 3.00 8.00

2007 Complete Star Trek Movies In Motion

COMPLETE SET (10) 15.00 40.00
STATED ODDS 1:24

❑ L1 Star Trek: The Motion Picture 3.00 8.00
❑ L2 Star Trek II: The Wrath of Khan 3.00 8.00
❑ L3 Star Trek III: The Search for Spock 3.00 8.00
❑ L4 Star Trek IV: The Voyage Home 3.00 8.00
❑ L5 Star Trek V: The Final Frontier 3.00 8.00
❑ L6 Star Trek: First Contact 3.00 8.00
❑ L7 Star Trek VI: The Undiscovered Country 3.00 8.00
❑ L8 Star Trek Generations 3.00 8.00
❑ L9 Star Trek: Insurrection 3.00 8.00
❑ L10 Star Trek Nemesis 3.00 8.00

2007 Complete Star Trek Movies Movie Posters

COMPLETE SET (2)
STATED ODDS ONE PER CASE

❑ MP1 Star Trek Star Date 12.25.08
❑ MP2 2008

2007 Complete Star Trek Movies Plot Synopses

COMPLETE SET (30) 15.00 40.00
STATED ODDS 1:8

❑ S1 Star Trek: The Motion Picture .75 2.00
❑ S2 Star Trek: The Motion Picture .75 2.00
❑ S3 Star Trek: The Motion Picture .75 2.00
❑ S4 Star Trek II: The Wrath of Khan .75 2.00
❑ S5 Star Trek II: The Wrath of Khan .75 2.00
❑ S6 Star Trek II: The Wrath of Khan .75 2.00
❑ S7 Star Trek III: The Search for Spock .75 2.00
❑ S8 Star Trek III: The Search for Spock .75 2.00
❑ S9 Star Trek III: The Search for Spock .75 2.00
❑ S10 Star Trek IV: The Voyage Home .75 2.00
❑ S11 Star Trek IV: The Voyage Home .75 2.00
❑ S12 Star Trek IV: The Voyage Home .75 2.00
❑ S13 Star Trek V: The Final Frontier .75 2.00
❑ S14 Star Trek V: The Final Frontier .75 2.00
❑ S15 Star Trek V: The Final Frontier .75 2.00
❑ S16 Star Trek VI: The Undiscovered Country .75 2.00
❑ S17 Star Trek VI: The Undiscovered Country .75 2.00
❑ S18 Star Trek VI: The Undiscovered Country .75 2.00
❑ S19 Star Trek Generations .75 2.00
❑ S20 Star Trek Generations .75 2.00
❑ S21 Star Trek Generations .75 2.00
❑ S22 Star Trek: First Contact .75 2.00
❑ S23 Star Trek: First Contact .75 2.00
❑ S24 Star Trek: First Contact .75 2.00
❑ S25 Star Trek: Insurrection .75 2.00
❑ S26 Star Trek: Insurrection .75 2.00
❑ S27 Star Trek: Insurrection .75 2.00
❑ S28 Star Trek Nemesis .75 2.00
❑ S29 Star Trek Nemesis .75 2.00
❑ S30 Star Trek Nemesis .75 2.00

2007 Complete Star Trek Movies Profiles

COMPLETE SET (20) 15.00 40.00
STATED ODDS 1:12

❑ P1 Lt. Ilia 1.25 3.00
❑ P2 Captain Willard Decker 1.25 3.00
❑ P3 Khan Noonien Singh 1.25 3.00
❑ P4 Dr. Carol Marcus 1.25 3.00
❑ P5 Lt. Saavik 1.25 3.00
❑ P6 Commander Kruge 1.25 3.00
❑ P7 Dr. Gillian Taylor 1.25 3.00
❑ P8 Admiral Cartwright 1.25 3.00
❑ P9 Sybok 1.25 3.00
❑ P10 St. John Talbot 1.25 3.00
❑ P11 Lt. Valeris 1.25 3.00
❑ P12 General Chang 1.25 3.00
❑ P13 Dr. Tolian Soran 1.25 3.00
❑ P14 Captain Kirk 1.25 3.00
❑ P15 Zefram Cochrane 1.25 3.00
❑ P16 Borg Queen 1.25 3.00
❑ P17 Ru'afo 1.25 3.00
❑ P18 Anij 1.25 3.00
❑ P19 Shinzon 1.25 3.00
❑ P20 Viceroy 1.25 3.00

2007 DC Legacy

COMPLETE SET (50) 4.00 10.00

❑ 1 Title Card Checklist .10 .30
❑ 2 Aqualad .10 .30
❑ 3 Aquaman .10 .30
❑ 4 Atom .10 .30
❑ 5 Batgirl .10 .30
❑ 6 Batman .10 .30
❑ 7 Batwoman .10 .30
❑ 8 Black Canary .10 .30
❑ 9 Blue Beetle .10 .30
❑ 10 Captain Marvel Jr. .10 .30
❑ 11 Cyborg .10 .30
❑ 12 Doctor Fate .10 .30
❑ 13 Doctor Mid-Nite .10 .30
❑ 14 Firestorm .10 .30
❑ 15 Green Arrow .10 .30
❑ 16 Green Lantern .10 .30
❑ 17 Hawkgirl .10 .30
❑ 18 Hawkman .10 .30
❑ 19 Hourman .10 .30
❑ 20 Kid Flash .10 .30
❑ 21 Martian Manhunter .10 .30
❑ 22 Nightwing .10 .30
❑ 23 Plastic Man .10 .30
❑ 24 Raven .10 .30
❑ 25 Robin .10 .30
❑ 26 Shazam! .10 .30
❑ 27 The Spectre .10 .30
❑ 28 Speedy .10 .30
❑ 29 Starfire .10 .30
❑ 30 Supergirl .10 .30
❑ 31 Superman .10 .30
❑ 32 The Flash .10 .30
❑ 33 Wonder Girl .10 .30
❑ 34 Wonder Woman .10 .30
❑ 35 Zatanna .10 .30
❑ 36 Black Adam .10 .30
❑ 37 Brainiac .10 .30
❑ 38 Captain Cold .10 .30
❑ 39 Catwoman .10 .30
❑ 40 Cheetah .10 .30
❑ 41 Darkseid .10 .30
❑ 42 The Joker .10 .30
❑ 43 Lex Luthor .10 .30
❑ 44 Mr. Freeze .10 .30
❑ 45 Poison Ivy .10 .30
❑ 46 Reverse-Flash .10 .30
❑ 47 The Riddler .10 .30
❑ 48 Sinestro .10 .30
❑ 49 The Penguin .10 .30
❑ 50 Two-Face .10 .30

2007 DC Legacy Gold

*GOLD: 2X TO 5X BASIC CARDS
STATED ODDS 1:6

2007 DC Legacy Archive Exclusive Sketches

AVAILABLE ONLY IN ARCHIVE BOXES

❑ 1 Guy Dorian
❑ 2 Ian Dorian
❑ 3 Jessica Hickman
❑ 4 Bryan Hitchen
❑ 5 Mike Lilly

2007 DC Legacy Autographs

O'NEIL STATED ODDS ONE PER CASE
KUBERT STATED ODDS ONE PER BINDER

❑ NNO Joe Kubert/ (issued in collectors album) 15.00 30.00
❑ NNO Denny O'Neil/ (issued as case topper) 10.00 20.00

2007 DC Legacy DC Gallery

STATED ODDS 1:24

❑ AR1 Batman Flash/Green Lantern 2.00 5.00
❑ AR2 Martian Manhunter Aquaman/Wonder Woman/Superman 2.00 5.00
❑ AR3 Superman 2.00 5.00
❑ AR4 Batman Superman/Wonder Woman/Martian Manhunter/Flash 2.00 5.00
❑ AR5 Green Lantern Aquaman/Green Arrow/Hawkman/Black Canary 2.00 5.00
❑ AR6 Batman 2.00 5.00
❑ AR7 Batman Wonder Woman/Green Lantern/Flash 2.00 5.00
❑ AR8 Aquaman Superman/Martian Manhunter 2.00 5.00
❑ AR9 Wonder Woman 2.00 5.00

2007 DC Legacy Dealer Exclusive Sketches

CARDY/DOMINGUEZ 3-CASE INCENTIVE
SPEARS/STAGGS 9-CASE INCENTIVE

❑ 1 Nick Cardy/ (issued as 3-case incentive)
❑ 2 Luis Dominguez/ (issued as 3-case incentive)
❑ 3 Mark Spears PAINTED/ (issued as 9-case incentive)
❑ 4 Cat Staggs PAINTED/ (issued as 9-case incentive)

2007 DC Legacy First Title Covers

STATED ODDS 1:12

❑ FC1 Superman #1 .75 2.00
❑ FC2 Batman #1 .75 2.00
❑ FC3 Wonder Woman #1 .75 2.00
❑ FC4 The Flash #105 .75 2.00
❑ FC5 Shazam #1 .75 2.00
❑ FC6 Green Lantern #1 .75 2.00
❑ FC7 Aquaman #1 .75 2.00
❑ FC8 Green Arrow #1 .75 2.00
❑ FC9 Hawkman #1 .75 2.00

2007 DC Legacy Legendary Heroes

STATED ODDS 1:48

❑ L1 Superman 6.00 15.00
❑ L2 Batman 6.00 15.00
❑ L3 Wonder Woman 6.00 15.00
❑ L4 Flash 6.00 15.00
❑ L5 Green Lantern 6.00 15.00
❑ L6 Shazam 6.00 15.00

2007 DC Legacy Sketches

STATED ODDS 1:24

❑ 1 Di Amorin/250*
❑ 2 Lui Antonio/200*
❑ 3 Mahmud Anjum Asrar/274*
❑ 4 Darren Auck/347*
❑ 5 Darryl Banks/100*
❑ 6 Al Bigley/200*
❑ 7 Dan Borgonos/225*
❑ 8 Daniel Brandao/350*
❑ 9 James Bukauskas/300*
❑ 10 Jeff Chandler/100*
❑ 11 Justin Chung/125*
❑ 12 Katie Cook/132*
❑ 13 John Czop/425*
❑ 14 Dan Day/466*
❑ 15 David Day/450*
❑ 16 Renae De Liz/300*
❑ 17 Ray Dillon/500*
❑ 18 Mark Dos Santos/501*
❑ 19 Brent Engstrom/300*
❑ 20 Dave Fox/100*
❑ 21 Otis T. Frampton IV/100*
❑ 22 Sean Galloway/100*
❑ 23 Matthew Goodmanson/300*
❑ 24 Grant Gould/300*
❑ 25 Don Hillsman II/200*
❑ 26 Thomas Hodges/550*
❑ 27 Brian Kong/450*
❑ 28 Jim Kyle/250*
❑ 29 Cully Long/150*
❑ 30 Dave Lynch/150*
❑ 31 Warren Martineck/200*
❑ 32 Mark McHaley/300*
❑ 33 Bob Mcleod/250*
❑ 34 Steven Miller/225*
❑ 35 Rich Molinelli/324*
❑ 36 Tom Nguyen/200*
❑ 37 Tony Perna/275*
❑ 38 Andy Price/498*
❑ 39 Cezar Razek/499*
❑ 40 Ted Rechlin/200*
❑ 41 Tyler Richlen/300*
❑ 42 Tone Rodriguez/350*
❑ 43 Louis Small/150*
❑ 44 Uko Smith/750*
❑ 45 Jason Sobol/200*
❑ 46 Allison Sohn/100*
❑ 47 Mark Spears/600*
❑ 48 Eddie Wagner/250*
❑ 49 Jeff Wellborn/275*
❑ 50 Ron Wilson/250*

2007 Elvis Is

COMPLETE SET (100) 4.00 10.00
UNPRICED PRINT PLATE PRINT RUN 1

❑ 1 Elvis is born .10 .30
❑ 2 Gladys and Vernon .10 .30
❑ 3 Grade School .10 .30
❑ 4 Elvis at 10 .10 .30
❑ 5 First Guitar .10 .30
❑ 6 Junior High .10 .30
❑ 7 High School .10 .30
❑ 8 Teenager .10 .30
❑ 9 Prom .10 .30
❑ 10 ROTC Cadet .10 .30
❑ 11 Image .10 .30
❑ 12 Blue Collar Blues .10 .30
❑ 13 Football .10 .30
❑ 14 Cars .10 .30
❑ 15 Motorcycles .10 .30
❑ 16 Karate .10 .30
❑ 17 Water Skiing .10 .30
❑ 18 Singing .10 .30
❑ 19 Music & Instruments .10 .30
❑ 20 Baseball .10 .30
❑ 21 Guns .10 .30
❑ 22 Law Enforcement .10 .30
❑ 23 Fashion .10 .30
❑ 24 Food .10 .30
❑ 25 Amusement Parks .10 .30
❑ 26 Horses .10 .30
❑ 27 Golf Carts .10 .30
❑ 28 Drafted .10 .30
❑ 29 Haircut .10 .30
❑ 30 Fort Hood, TX .10 .30
❑ 31 Tragedy Strikes .10 .30
❑ 32 On Leave .10 .30
❑ 33 1st Battalion, 32nd Armored Division .10 .30
❑ 34 Setting Sail .10 .30
❑ 35 Germany .10 .30
❑ 36 Maneuvers .10 .30
❑ 37 Paris .10 .30
❑ 38 Private Presley .10 .30
❑ 39 Fan Mail .10 .30
❑ 40 Discharge .10 .30
❑ 41 Music .10 .30
❑ 42 The Girl Left Behind .10 .30
❑ 43 Jaycee Award .10 .30
❑ 44 Elvis Presley Youth Recreation Center .10 .30
❑ 45 March of Dimes .10 .30
❑ 46 Signing Autographs .10 .30
❑ 47 Polio Vaccine .10 .30
❑ 48 Service to Country .10 .30
❑ 49 USS Arizona benefit .10 .30
❑ 50 Narcotics Bureau Member .10 .30
❑ 51 Memphis Charities .10 .30
❑ 52 Band List .10 .30
❑ 53 Duffle Bags .10 .30
❑ 54 Bank Card .10 .30
❑ 55 Briefcase Phone .10 .30
❑ 56 Hawaii Schedule .10 .30
❑ 57 Mailbox .10 .30
❑ 58 Social Security Card .10 .30
❑ 59 Karate Movie Proposal .10 .30
❑ 60 How Great Thou Art .10 .30
❑ 61 Suspicious Minds .10 .30
❑ 62 Devil in Disguise .10 .30
❑ 63 Guitar Man .10 .30
❑ 64 Don't Cry Daddy .10 .30
❑ 65 If I Can Dream .10 .30
❑ 66 Burning Love .10 .30
❑ 67 Yvonne Craig .10 .30
❑ 68 James Burton .10 .30
❑ 69 DJ Fontana .10 .30
❑ 70 Barbara Eden .10 .30
❑ 71 Gordon Stoker .10 .30
❑ 72 Ray Walker .10 .30
❑ 73 Heartbreak Hotel .10 .30
❑ 74 I Want You, I Need You, I Love You .10 .30
❑ 75 Don't Be Cruel .10 .30
❑ 76 Hound Dog .10 .30
❑ 77 Love Me Tender .10 .30
❑ 78 Too Much .10 .30
❑ 79 All Shook Up .10 .30
❑ 80 Teddy Bear .10 .30
❑ 81 Jailhouse Rock .10 .30
❑ 82 Don't .10 .30
❑ 83 Hard Headed Woman .10 .30
❑ 84 A Big Hunk O' Love .10 .30
❑ 85 Stuck on You .10 .30
❑ 86 It's Now or Never .10 .30
❑ 87 Are You Lonesome Tonight? .10 .30
❑ 88 Surrender .10 .30
❑ 89 Good Luck Charm .10 .30
❑ 90 Suspicious Minds .10 .30
❑ 91 Elvis on a Train .10 .30
❑ 92 Elvis in a Hat .10 .30
❑ 93 Elvis and the Hound Dog .10 .30
❑ 94 Elvis Sleeping .10 .30
❑ 95 Elvis Signing Autographs .10 .30
❑ 96 Elvis Styling Hair .10 .30
❑ 97 Fan Mail .10 .30
❑ 98 Elvis Shaving .10 .30
❑ 99 The Kiss .10 .30
❑ 100 Checklist .10 .30
❑ NNO Contest Entry Card

2007 Elvis Is Al Wertheimer Artist Proofs Autographs

OVERALL AUTO ODDS 1:96

❑ AW3 The Kiss/100
❑ AW4 Fan Mail/400

2007 Elvis Is Autographs

STATED ODDS 1:96

❑ 1 Barbara Eden 30.00 60.00
❑ 2 Chris Noel 20.00 40.00
❑ 3 Cynthia Pepper 25.00 50.00
❑ 4 Nancy Sinatra 75.00 150.00
❑ NNO Elvis Presley/4

2007 Elvis Is Autographs Gold

PRINT RUN 50 SERIAL #'d SETS

❑ 1 Barbara Eden
❑ 2 Chris Noel
❑ 3a Cynthia Pepper/99
❑ 3b Cynthia Pepper
❑ 4 Nancy Sinatra

2007 Elvis Is Elvis Worn Memorabilia

MEMORABILIA COMBINED ODDS 1:84

❑ EWKU Karate Warm-up Suit
❑ EWPJ Monogrammed Pajamas
❑ EWSJ Red Smoking Jacket

2007 Elvis Is Elvis Worn Memorabilia Gold

PRINT RUN 299 SERIAL #'d SETS

❑ EWKU Karate Warm-Up Suit
❑ EWPJ Monogrammed Pajamas
❑ EWPS Polka-Dot Shirt
❑ EWRS Red Shirt
❑ EWSC Scarf/99
❑ EWSJ Red Smoking Jacket
❑ EWKUb Karate Warm-Up Suit Tag/6

2007 Elvis Is Elvis Worn Memorabilia Platinum

PRINT RUN 99 SERIAL #'d SETS

❑ EWPJ Monogrammed Pajamas
❑ EWSC Scarf/25
❑ EWSJ Red Smoking Jacket

2007 Elvis Is Foil Inserts

COMPLETE SET (6) 2.50 6.00
STATED ODDS 1:12

❑ EI1 A Friend .75 2.00
❑ EI2 An Actor .75 2.00
❑ EI3 A Singer .75 2.00
❑ EI4 A Humanitarian .75 2.00
❑ EI5 An Icon .75 2.00
❑ EI6 A Performer .75 2.00

2007 Elvis Is On The Record

COMPLETE SET (9) 3.00 8.00
STATED ODDS 1:8

❑ OR1 Perfectionist .60 1.50
❑ OR2 Acting Ambitions .60 1.50
❑ OR3 Sideburns .60 1.50
❑ OR4 God .60 1.50
❑ OR5 Music .60 1.50
❑ OR6 Happiness .60 1.50
❑ OR7 Mom .60 1.50
❑ OR8 Memphis .60 1.50
❑ OR9 Dreamer (Jaycee Award Speech) .60 1.50

2007 Elvis Is Timelines

COMPLETE SET (4) 2.00 5.00
STATED ODDS ONE PER BLASTER BOX

❑ 1 1935-1957 1.00 2.50
❑ 2 1958-1965 1.00 2.50
❑ 3 1966-1969 1.00 2.50
❑ 4 1970-1977 1.00 2.50

2007 Elvis The Music

COMPLETE SET (81) 4.00 10.00
UNPRICED PRINT PLATE PRINT RUN 1

❑ 1 Heartbreak Hotel .10 .30
❑ 2 Don't Be Cruel .10 .30
❑ 3 Hound Dog .10 .30
❑ 4 Love Me Tender .10 .30
❑ 5 Too Much .10 .30

❑ 6 All Shook Up .10 .30
❑ 7 Teddy Bear .10 .30
❑ 8 Jailhouse Rock .10 .30
❑ 9 Don't .10 .30
❑ 10 Hard Headed Woman .10 .30
❑ 11 One Night .10 .30
❑ 12 A Fool Such As I .10 .30
❑ 13 A Big Hunk o' Love .10 .30
❑ 14 Stuck On You .10 .30
❑ 15 It's Now or Never .10 .30
❑ 16 Are You Lonesome Tonight? .10 .30
❑ 17 Wooden Heart .10 .30
❑ 18 Surrender .10 .30
❑ 19 His Latest Flame .10 .30
❑ 20 Can't Help Falling in Love .10 .30
❑ 21 Good Luck Charm .10 .30
❑ 22 She's Not You .10 .30
❑ 23 Return to Sender .10 .30
❑ 24 Devil in Disguise .10 .30
❑ 25 Crying in the Chapel .10 .30
❑ 26 In the Ghetto .10 .30
❑ 27 Suspicious Minds .10 .30
❑ 28 The Wonder of You .10 .30
❑ 29 Burning Love .10 .30
❑ 30 Way Down .10 .30
❑ 31 That's All Right .10 .30
❑ 32 I Forgot to Remember to Forget .10 .30
❑ 33 Blue Suede Shoes .10 .30
❑ 34 I Want You, I Need You, I Love You .10 .30
❑ 35 Love Me .10 .30
❑ 36 Loving You .10 .30
❑ 37 King Creole .10 .30
❑ 38 I Need Your Love Tonight .10 .30
❑ 39 Little Sister .10 .30
❑ 40 Viva Las Vegas .10 .30
❑ 41 If I Can Dream .10 .30
❑ 42 Don't Cry Daddy .10 .30
❑ 43 Kentucky Rain .10 .30
❑ 44 Always on My Mind .10 .30
❑ 45 Moody Blue .10 .30
❑ 46 Las Vegas 1956 .10 .30
❑ 47 Canada 1957 .10 .30
❑ 48 Tupelo 1957 .10 .30
❑ 49 USS General Randall 1958 .10 .30
❑ 50 Las Vegas 1970 .10 .30
❑ 51 Philadelphia June '71 .10 .30
❑ 52 Madison Square Garden June '72 .10 .30
❑ 53 Hawaii November '72 .10 .30
❑ 54 Seattle April '73 .10 .30
❑ 55 Houston '74 .10 .30
❑ 56 Niagara Falls, NY June '74 .10 .30
❑ 57 Huntsville May '75 .10 .30
❑ 58 Milton Berle .10 .30
❑ 59 Stage Show .10 .30
❑ 60 Stage Show .10 .30
❑ 61 Steve Allen Show .10 .30
❑ 62 Ed Sullivan .10 .30
❑ 63 Ed Sullivan .10 .30
❑ 64 Frank Sinatra Timex .10 .30
❑ 65 Elvis 1968 Special .10 .30
❑ 66 Elvis 1968 Special .10 .30
❑ 67 Elvis 1968 Special .10 .30
❑ 68 Elvis 1968 Special .10 .30
❑ 69 Elvis 1968 Special .10 .30
❑ 70 Elvis 1968 Special .10 .30
❑ 71 Aloha From Hawaii .10 .30
❑ 72 Aloha From Hawaii .10 .30
❑ 73 Let the Show Begin .10 .30
❑ 74 Karate Moves .10 .30
❑ 75 Telling Jokes .10 .30
❑ 76 Reaching Out to Fans .10 .30
❑ 77 Raw Emotion .10 .30
❑ 78 Getting Personal .10 .30
❑ 79 Gifts From Fans .10 .30
❑ 80 Finale .10 .30
❑ 81 Checklist .10 .30

2007 Elvis The Music TCB

COMPLETE SET (81) 12.00 30.00
*TCB: 1.2X TO 3X BASIC CARDS
STATED ODDS ONE PER PACK

2007 Elvis The Music Celebrity Signatures

ONE RELIC OR AUTO PER BOX

❑ CSCN Chris Noel 20.00 40.00
❑ CSCP Cynthia Pepper 25.00 50.00
❑ CSDF DJ Fontana 25.00 50.00
❑ CSGS Gordon Stoker 15.00 30.00
❑ CSJB James Burton 15.00 30.00
❑ CSMM Mary Ann Mobley 20.00 40.00
❑ CSNS Nancy Sinatra 75.00 150.00
❑ CSRW Ray Walker 30.00 60.00
❑ CSSM Scotty Moore 30.00 60.00
❑ CSYC Yvonne Craig 20.00 40.00
❑ NNO Elvis Presley

2007 Elvis The Music Celebrity Signatures Blue

PRINT RUN 30 SERIAL #'d SETS

❑ CSCN Chris Noel
❑ CSCP Cynthia Pepper
❑ CSDF DJ Fontana
❑ CSGS Gordon Stoker
❑ CSJB James Burton
❑ CSMM Mary Ann Mobley
❑ CSNS Nancy Sinatra
❑ CSRW Ray Walker
❑ CSSM Scotty Moore
❑ CSYC Yvonne Craig

2007 Elvis The Music Celebrity Signatures Red

PRINT RUN 30 SERIAL #'d SETS

❑ CSCN Chris Noel
❑ CSCP Cynthia Pepper
❑ CSDF DJ Fontana
❑ CSGS Gordon Stoker
❑ CSJB James Burton
❑ CSMM Mary Ann Mobley
❑ CSNS Nancy Sinatra/25
❑ CSRW Ray Walker
❑ CSSM Scotty Moore
❑ CSYC Yvonne Craig/25

2007 Elvis The Music Celebrity Signatures Silver

PRINT RUN 50 SERIAL #'d SETS
ONE RELIC OR AUTO PER BOX

❑ CSCN Chris Noel 25.00 50.00
❑ CSCP Cynthia Pepper 30.00 60.00
❑ CSDF DJ Fontana 30.00 60.00
❑ CSGS Gordon Stoker 20.00 40.00
❑ CSJB James Burton 20.00 40.00
❑ CSMM Mary Ann Mobley 25.00 50.00
❑ CSNS Nancy Sinatra 100.00 175.00
❑ CSRW Ray Walker 40.00 80.00
❑ CSSM Scotty Moore 40.00 80.00
❑ CSYC Yvonne Craig 25.00 50.00

2007 Elvis The Music Rock 'n' Roll Relics

ONE RELIC OR AUTO PER BOX

❑ RRKW Karate Warm-Up Suit 15.00 30.00
❑ RRPJ Purple Silk Pajamas 15.00 30.00
❑ RRPP Plaid Pajamas 15.00 30.00
❑ RRSJ Red Smoking Jacket 15.00 30.00
❑ RRWU Mint Green Warm-Up Suit 15.00 30.00

2007 Elvis The Music Rock 'n' Roll Relics Gold

PRINT RUN 299 SERIAL #'d SETS
ONE RELIC OR AUTO PER BOX

❑ RRDS Blue-White Polka Dot Shirt/150
❑ RRKW Karate Warm-Up Suit 20.00 40.00
❑ RRPJ Purple Silk Pajamas 20.00 40.00
❑ RRPP Plaid Pajamas 20.00 40.00
❑ RRSJ Red Smoking Jacket 20.00 40.00
❑ RRWS Red Western Shirt/150
❑ RRWU Mint Green Warm-Up Suit 20.00 40.00

2007 Elvis The Music Rock 'n' Roll Relics Platinum

PRINT RUN 99 SERIAL #'d SETS
ONE RELIC OR AUTO PER BOX

❑ RRCS Blue-White Concert Scarf/25
❑ RRKW Karate Warm-Up Suit 25.00 50.00
❑ RRPJ Purple Silk Pajamas 25.00 50.00
❑ RRPP Plaid Pajamas 25.00 50.00
❑ RRSJ Red Smoking Jacket 25.00 50.00
❑ RRWU Mint Green Warm-Up Suit 25.00 50.00

2007 Elvis The Music Wertheimer Negatives

STATED ODDS 1:14

❑ WN1 Signing Autographs 1.25 3.00
❑ WN2 Hound Dog 1.25 3.00
❑ WN3 On The Train To Memphis 1.25 3.00
❑ WN4 Listening To His Music 1.25 3.00
❑ WN4b Listening To His Music AU/199
❑ WN4c Listening To His Music AU/56
❑ WN5 Making Friends 1.25 3.00
❑ WN6 Adoring Fans 1.25 3.00
❑ WN7 Prepping For The Show 1.25 3.00

2007 eTopps Allen and Ginter Presidents

COMPLETE SET (6)
STATED PRINT RUN 999 SER. #'d SETS

❑ 1 Dwight D. Eisenhower 2.00 5.00
❑ 2 John F. Kennedy 8.00 20.00
❑ 3 Gerald Ford 2.00 5.00
❑ 4 Ronald Reagan 10.00 25.00
❑ 5 Bill Clinton 5.00 12.00
❑ 6 George W. Bush 3.00 8.00

2007 The 4400 Season Two

COMPLETE SET (81) 4.00 10.00
CL1 STATED ODDS ONE PER CASE

❑ 1 Title Card .10 .30
❑ 2 Tom Baldwin .10 .30
❑ 3 Diana Skouris .10 .30
❑ 4 Nina Jarvis .10 .30
❑ 5 Marco Pacella .10 .30
❑ 6 Dennis Ryland .10 .30
❑ 7 Maia Skouris .10 .30
❑ 8 Shawn Farrell .10 .30
❑ 9 Jordan Collier .10 .30
❑ 10 Richard Tyler And Lily Moore Tyler .10 .30
❑ 11 Isabelle Tyler .10 .30
❑ 12 Kyle Baldwin .10 .30
❑ 13 Kevin Burkhoff .10 .30
❑ 14 Gary Navarro .10 .30
❑ 15 Trent Appelbaum .10 .30
❑ 16 Heather Tobey .10 .30
❑ 17 Alana Mareva .10 .30
❑ 18 Edwin Mayuya .10 .30
❑ 19 The 4400 Center .10 .30
❑ 20 Second In Command .10 .30
❑ 21 Funding And Partnerships .10 .30
❑ 22 The Key System .10 .30
❑ 23 Fact Or Fiction .10 .30
❑ 24 If I Should Die .10 .30
❑ 25 The Past Sees Tomorrow .10 .30
❑ 26 The Present Molds Today .10 .30
❑ 27 The Future Comes Back .10 .30
❑ 28 Tom And Diana .10 .30
❑ 29 Lily, Richard, And Isabelle .10 .30
❑ 30 Diana, Maia, And April .10 .30
❑ 31 Tom And Alana .10 .30
❑ 32 Kyle And Shawn .10 .30
❑ 33 Lily, Brian, And Heidi .10 .30
❑ 34 Shawn And Liu .10 .30
❑ 35 Collier And Isabelle .10 .30
❑ 36 Diana And Marco .10 .30
❑ 37 Six Months Later .10 .30
❑ 38 Desk Jockey Blues .10 .30
❑ 39 Mysterious Tower .10 .30
❑ 40 An Orderly Death .10 .30
❑ 41 Isabelle's Touch .10 .30
❑ 42 The Ant Theory .10 .30
❑ 43 Doorway To Hell .10 .30
❑ 44 Things I See .10 .30
❑ 45 The Future Unfolds .10 .30
❑ 46 Too Many Voices .10 .30
❑ 47 Nobody's Happy .10 .30
❑ 48 Busted Deals .10 .30
❑ 49 I Am The Product .10 .30
❑ 50 Changes In Fortune .10 .30
❑ 51 More Than Weight Loss .10 .30
❑ 52 Fanning The Spark .10 .30
❑ 53 Helping Hands .10 .30
❑ 54 Can't Heal Everyone .10 .30
❑ 55 Of Mothers And Murders .10 .30
❑ 56 Threats And Promises .10 .30
❑ 57 Nightmares Come True .10 .30
❑ 58 Change Of Venue .10 .30
❑ 59 Playing Along .10 .30
❑ 60 Beyond The Door .10 .30
❑ 61 Walking Plague .10 .30
❑ 62 Winners And Losers .10 .30
❑ 63 The Time Is At Hand .10 .30
❑ 64 Miracle Worker .10 .30
❑ 65 Love And War .10 .30
❑ 66 Coming To Terms .10 .30
❑ 67 Following Clues .10 .30
❑ 68 Keeping Cool .10 .30
❑ 69 Revealed .10 .30
❑ 70 Birthday Surprise .10 .30
❑ 71 Infant Studies .10 .30
❑ 72 Flashpoint .10 .30
❑ 73 Outbreak .10 .30
❑ 74 Mutual Warnings .10 .30
❑ 75 Lethal Side Effects .10 .30
❑ 76 Failed Inhibitions .10 .30
❑ 77 Nowhere Safe .10 .30
❑ 78 Clashing Motives .10 .30
❑ 79 Cleansings .10 .30
❑ 80 The End... And Beginning .10 .30
❑ 81 Checklist .10 .30
❑ CL1 Unlock Your Mind

2007 The 4400 Season Two 4400 And Counting Puzzle

COMPLETE SET (9)
STATED ODDS 1:11

❑ AC1 4400 And Counting 1
❑ AC2 4401 And Counting 1
❑ AC3 4402 And Counting 1
❑ AC4 4403 And Counting 1
❑ AC5 4404 And Counting 1
❑ AC6 4405 And Counting 1
❑ AC7 4406 And Counting 1
❑ AC8 4407 And Counting 1
❑ AC9 4408 And Counting 1

2007 The 4400 Season Two Autographs

STATED ODDS 1:36

❑ A10 Chad Faust
❑ A11 Conchita Campbell
❑ A12 Joel Gretsch
❑ A13 Mahershalalhashbaz Ali
❑ A14 Samantha Ferris
❑ A15 Natasha Gregson Wagner
❑ A16 Robert Picardo
❑ A17 Jeffrey Combs
❑ A18 Kavan Smith
❑ AR1 Redemption card

2007 The 4400 Season Two Life Interrupted

COMPLETE SET (6)
STATED ODDS 1:17

❑ L1 On The Run
❑ L2 Virtual Enhancement
❑ L3 Erased
❑ L4 The Darkness Returns
❑ L5 Healing A Family
❑ L6 Genius Interrupted

2007 The 4400 Season Two Pieceworks

STATED ODDS ONE PER BOX
PW10 ISSUED AS MULTI-CASE INCENTIVE

❑ PW1 Jordan Collier
❑ PW2 Jordan Collier
❑ PW3 Richard Tyler
❑ PW4 Richard Tyler
❑ PW5 Nina Jarvis
❑ PW6 Andrew Arlie
❑ PW7 Gabriel
❑ PW8 Owen DUAL
❑ PW9 Major Culp
❑ PW10 Jordan Collier
Richard Tyler/ (issued as multi-case incentive)

2007 The 4400 Season Two States of Being

COMPLETE SET (3)
STATED ODDS ONE PER BOX

❑ BL1 Alive
❑ BL2 Dead
❑ BL3 Reborn

2007 Garbage Pail Kids All New Series 6

COMPLETE SET (80) 6.00 15.00
P2 ISSUED AS SDCC EXCLUSIVE

❑ 1a Orange Julius .10 .25
❑ 1b Peeled Neal .10 .25
❑ 2a Showerin' Howard .10 .25
❑ 2b Rinsin' Vincent .10 .25
❑ 3a Me Too Lou .10 .25
❑ 3b Mirror Max .10 .25
❑ 4a Jess Married .10 .25
❑ 4b Married Mia .10 .25
❑ 5a Canned Carl .10 .25
❑ 5b Dogged Doug .10 .25
❑ 6a Carter Farter .10 .25
❑ 6b Curtis Blow .10 .25
❑ 7a Hangin' Hayden .10 .25
❑ 7b Hung Hunter .10 .25
❑ 8a Rod N' Reel .10 .25
❑ 8b Fisher Manny .10 .25
❑ 9a Carol-Sel .10 .25
❑ 9b Mary Go Round .10 .25
❑ 10a Nested Ernesto .10 .25
❑ 10b Elliot Nest .10 .25
❑ 11a Snakes In Dwayne .10 .25
❑ 11b Tapeworm Tanner .10 .25
❑ 12a Blown Away Ray .10 .25
❑ 12b Over Blown Ramon .10 .25
❑ 13a Tara Too .10 .25
❑ 13b Naughty Natalie .10 .25
❑ 14a Deli Connor .10 .25
❑ 14b Cole Cut .10 .25
❑ 15a Axe In Jackson .10 .25
❑ 15b Stumped Steve .10 .25
❑ 16a Hacked Hogan .10 .25
❑ 16b Russel Mania .10 .25
❑ 17a Scott Pocket .10 .25
❑ 17b Cal Zoned .10 .25
❑ 18a Enter Net Nate .10 .25
❑ 18b Sliced Bryce .10 .25
❑ 19a Poop Head Paul .10 .25
❑ 19b Turd Face Trace .10 .25
❑ 20a Brady Back Ribs .10 .25
❑ 20b Spare Rob .10 .25
❑ 21a Stuffy Stephanie .10 .25
❑ 21b Congested Jessica .10 .25
❑ 22a Tailored Tyler .10 .25
❑ 22b Mitch Stitched .10 .25
❑ 23a Poker Face Chase .10 .25
❑ 23b Card Shark Mark .10 .25
❑ 24a Bunk Ben .10 .25
❑ 24b Tom Bunk .10 .25
❑ 25a Socked Brock .10 .25
❑ 25b Refer-Reed .10 .25
❑ 26a Mike Strike .10 .25
❑ 26b Bowling For Dallas .10 .25
❑ 27a Lemon Ned .10 .25
❑ 27b Puckered Parker .10 .25
❑ 28a Sam Castle .10 .25
❑ 28b Crushed Kayla .10 .25
❑ 29a Rasta Roni Tony .10 .25
❑ 29b Spaghetti Eddy .10 .25
❑ 30a Clawed Claude .10 .25
❑ 30b Roy Toy .10 .25
❑ 31a Booger Ken .10 .25
❑ 31b Whopper Wyatt .10 .25
❑ 32a Thomas The Train Wreck .10 .25
❑ 32b Off The Rails Gail .10 .25
❑ 33a Stabbed Sabrina .10 .25
❑ 33b Targeted Taylor .10 .25
❑ 34a Bobby Q .10 .25
❑ 34b Barbecue Stu .10 .25
❑ 35a Webbed Whitney .10 .25
❑ 35b Digestin' Jasmine .10 .25
❑ 36a Tusky Tiffany .10 .25
❑ 36b Buck Toothed Brenda .10 .25
❑ 37a Cat Sup .10 .25
❑ 37b Bottled Bailey .10 .25
❑ 38a I-Clod Todd .10 .25
❑ 38b MP Trey .10 .25
❑ 39a Shot Scott .10 .25
❑ 39b Fired Fred .10 .25
❑ 40a Leonard Nimrod .10 .25
❑ 40b Trekkie Trevor .10 .25
❑ P2 Alien Alan 1.00 2.50

2007 Garbage Pail Kids All New Series 6 Action Punch-Outs

COMPLETE SET (12) 2.00 5.00
STATED ODDS 1:3

❑ 1 Metallic Alec Pencil Pal .20 .50
❑ 2 Change The Baby's Diaper .20 .50
❑ 3 Marty Mucous' Botched Nose Job .20 .50
❑ 4 Spit-Kickers .20 .50
❑ 5 Sleaze Up Your Soft Drink .20 .50
❑ 6 Tastefully Moon Your Friends .20 .50
❑ 7 Photo Matt's Enchanted Photograph .20 .50
❑ 8 Over Eatin' Ethan's Dinner Plan .20 .50
❑ 9 Reanimate Internal Morgan .20 .50
❑ 10 Show-And-Tell Vomit .20 .50
❑ 11 Practice Your Ventriloquism .20 .50
❑ 12 Pop-Out Puzzle .20 .50

2007 Garbage Pail Kids All New Series 6 Bonus

COMPLETE SET (5)
B15, B16, B17 STATED ODDS ONE PER BLISTER PACK
B18 STATED ODDS ONE PER WALMART BONUS BOX
B19 STATED ODDS ONE PER TARGET/KB BONUS BOX

❑ B15 Barfs Of Holly
❑ B16 Watery Eyes Walter
❑ B17 Levitating Levi
❑ B18 Seth-Shimi
❑ B19 Scrapped Brooke

2007 Garbage Pail Kids All New Series 6 Magnets

COMPLETE SET (9) 5.00 12.00
STATED ODDS 1:6

❑ 1 Twinny Vinnie .75 2.00
❑ 2 Ann Chovie .75 2.00
❑ 3 Cracked Sheldon .75 2.00
❑ 4 Upset Tommy .75 2.00
❑ 5 Barfin' Marvin .75 2.00
❑ 6 Fun Gus .75 2.00
❑ 7 Mothy Martha .75 2.00
❑ 8 Dim-Bulb Bob .75 2.00
❑ 9 Hungry Ivan .75 2.00

2007 Garbage Pail Kids All New Series 7

COMPLETE SET (110) 8.00 20.00
P1 ISSUED AS SDCC EXCLUSIVE

❑ 1a Ty Dee Knot .10 .25
❑ 1b Ty Dee Knot .10 .25
❑ 2a Lindsay Lo-Life .10 .25
❑ 2b Snotty Sara .10 .25
❑ 3a Offense Spence .10 .25
❑ 3b Rebound Roy .10 .25
❑ 4a Knifin' Ivan .10 .25
❑ 4b Gin Sue .10 .25
❑ 5a Space Chase .10 .25
❑ 5b Cosmic Ray .10 .25
❑ 6a Morgan Donor .10 .25
❑ 6b Di Sect .10 .25
❑ 7a Drew Drool .10 .25
❑ 7b Flood Ted .10 .25
❑ 8a Big Top Tony .10 .25
❑ 8b Ol' Faith Phil .10 .25
❑ 9a Deodor Brent .10 .25
❑ 9b Roll On Rob .10 .25
❑ 10a Spartan Martin .10 .25
❑ 10b Warrior Warren .10 .25
❑ 11a Stormy Heather .10 .25
❑ 11b Gail Force Wind .10 .25
❑ 12a Vinny Son .10 .25
❑ 12b Deer Hunter .10 .25
❑ 13a Pee-On Leon .10 .25
❑ 13b Ski Cliff .10 .25
❑ 14a Coral Carson .10 .25
❑ 14b Cora Reef .10 .25
❑ 15a Prime Nate .10 .25
❑ 15b Sim Ian .10 .25
❑ 16a Ceiling Fran .10 .25
❑ 16b Head Les .10 .25
❑ 17a O.J. Jose .10 .25
❑ 17b Juiced Jayden .10 .25
❑ 18a Cooper Pooper .10 .25
❑ 18b Dung Beetle Bailey .10 .25
❑ 19a Ice Cole .10 .25
❑ 19b Stuck Buck .10 .25
❑ 20a Peter Puker .10 .25
❑ 20b Web Head Ne .10 .25
❑ 21a Bryce Iced .10 .25
❑ 21b Scraped Jake .10 .25
❑ 22a David Choppin' Squeal .10 .25
❑ 22b Todd Da! .10 .25
❑ 23a Gator Abe .10 .25
❑ 23b We Winnie .10 .25
❑ 24a Killer Wally .10 .25
❑ 24b Chum Charlie .10 .25
❑ 25a Britney Shears .10 .25
❑ 25b Claire Cut .10 .25
❑ 26a Waft Wyatt .10 .25
❑ 26b Windy Wendell .10 .25
❑ 27a Dog Troy .10 .25
❑ 27b Michael Victim .10 .25
❑ 28a Glass Blow Joe .10 .25
❑ 28b Gas-Blowin' Owen .10 .25
❑ 29a Eye Scream Lee .10 .25
❑ 29b Scooped Shannon .10 .25
❑ 30a Foamy Phil .10 .25
❑ 30b Shave Dave .10 .25
❑ 31a Lyin' Ryan .10 .25
❑ 31b Tall Tale Tim .10 .25
❑ 32a Abandoned Andy .10 .25
❑ 32b Cast Away Jay .10 .25
❑ 33a Wash Josh .10 .25
❑ 33b Hans Soap .10 .25
❑ 34a Willie Of Fortune .10 .25
❑ 34b Nicholas Caged .10 .25
❑ 35a Ghost Tory .10 .25
❑ 35b Spectre Hector .10 .25
❑ 36a Car Jack .10 .25
❑ 36b Scrap Heath .10 .25
❑ 37a Extra Christie .10 .25
❑ 37b Chick Ken .10 .25
❑ 38a Drum Kit .10 .25
❑ 38b Tom Tom .10 .25
❑ 39a Sub Maureen .10 .25
❑ 39b Diver Don .10 .25
❑ 40a Hollow Hal .10 .25
❑ 40b Goal Noel .10 .25
❑ 41a Sculpted Scott .10 .25
❑ 41b Molded Miguel .10 .25
❑ 42a Braided Brook .10 .25
❑ 42b Tyra Eyes .10 .25
❑ 43a Walked-On Walker .10 .25
❑ 43b Dennis Shoe .10 .25
❑ 44a Breakin' Brandon .10 .25
❑ 44b Buster Move .10 .25
❑ 45a Manuel Labor .10 .25
❑ 45b Landon Scaping .10 .25
❑ 46a Flamin' Damon .10 .25
❑ 46b Dryin' Bryan .10 .25
❑ 47a On The Mark .10 .25
❑ 47b Snot Rocket Ricky .10 .25
❑ 48a Del Icious .10 .25
❑ 48b Licked Vic .10 .25
❑ 49a Tyler Tilt .10 .25
❑ 49b Pinball Willard .10 .25
❑ 50a Desiree Disarray .10 .25
❑ 50b Yard Sally .10 .25
❑ 51a Billy Bling .10 .25
❑ 51b Gil Grill .10 .25
❑ 52a Winter Jill .10 .25
❑ 52b Kindle Lynne .10 .25
❑ 53a Trish Washer .10 .25
❑ 53b Reese Cycle .10 .25
❑ 54a Molly Pop .10 .25
❑ 54b Sophie Sucker .10 .25
❑ 55a Dough Boyd .10 .25
❑ 55b Pills Barry .10 .25
❑ P1 Dough Boyd 1.00 2.50

2007 Garbage Pail Kids All New Series 7 Action Punch-Outs

COMPLETE SET (10) 5.00 12.00
STATED ODDS 1:4

❑ 1 Hacked Hogan's Let 'Er Rip .60 1.50
❑ 2 A Real Rib Tickler .60 1.50
❑ 3 Sickening Poop For The Soul .60 1.50
❑ 4 Common Horse Sense .60 1.50
❑ 5 Throw Your Voice To Make Him Talk .60 1.50
❑ 6 Shot Scott's Big Bang .60 1.50
❑ 7 Which Spinner's The Winner .60 1.50
❑ 8 Pickin' An' Grinnin' .60 1.50
❑ 9 Let 'Em Eat Snake .60 1.50
❑ 10 Hide 'N Geek .60 1.50

2007 Garbage Pail Kids All New Series 7 Bonus

COMPLETE SET (6)
B1 STATED ODDS ONE PER WALMART/KB BONUS BOX
B2 STATED ODDS ONE PER TARGET BONUS BOX
B3, B4, B5 STATED ODDS ONE PER BLISTER PACK
B6 STATED ODDS ONE PER KMART/TOYS R US BONUS BOX

❑ B1 Leaky Leslie
❑ B2 Carl Wreck
❑ B3 Lock Mess Rex
❑ B4 Snack Attack Zack
❑ B5 Tongue Tied Tara
❑ B6 George Clowny

2007 Garbage Pail Kids All New Series 7 Loco-Motion

COMPLETE SET (5) 8.00 20.00
STATED ODDS 1:8

❑ 1 Sliced Brad 2.00 5.00
❑ 2 Split Cord 2.00 5.00
❑ 3 Rocco Socko 2.00 5.00
❑ 4 Burnt-Out Brett 2.00 5.00
❑ 5 Ecch Benedict 2.00 5.00

2007 Garbage Pail Kids All New Series 7 Pop-Ups

COMPLETE SET (10) 4.00 10.00
STATED ODDS 1:6

❑ 1 Crazy Casey .60 1.50
❑ 2 Boardin' Jordan .60 1.50
❑ 3 Umbilical Corey .60 1.50
❑ 4 Tom Tongue .60 1.50
❑ 5 Astro Nat .60 1.50
❑ 6 Broken Crystal .60 1.50
❑ 7 Birdbrain Brian .60 1.50
❑ 8 Wranglin' Rachel .60 1.50
❑ 9 Bigfoot Brittany .60 1.50
❑ 10 Malcolm Middle .60 1.50

2007 Garbage Pail Kids All New Series 7 Puzzle

COMPLETE SET (10) 3.00 8.00
STATED ODDS 1:6

❑ 1 Spider Manny .50 1.25
❑ 2 Cookie-Tosser Tessa .50 1.25
❑ 3 Car Sick Caroline .50 1.25
❑ 4 Toe Jam Sam .50 1.25
❑ 5 Jet Ski Jesse .50 1.25
❑ 6 Lava Levi .50 1.25
❑ 7 Troy Story .50 1.25
❑ 8 Field Goal Joel .50 1.25
❑ 9 Hollow Wayne .50 1.25
❑ 10 Noah's Barf .50 1.25

2007 The Golden Compass

COMPLETE SET (72) 4.00 10.00

- 1 The Golden Compass .10 .30
- 2 Lyra Belacqua .10 .30
- 3 Roger Parslow .10 .30
- 4 Mrs. Coulter .10 .30
- 5 Lord Asriel .10 .30
- 6 Master Of Jordan College .10 .30
- 7 Fra Pavel .10 .30
- 8 The Gyptians .10 .30
- 9 Ma Costa .10 .30
- 10 John Faa .10 .30
- 11 Farder Coram .10 .30
- 12 Billy Costa .10 .30
- 13 Lee Scoresby .10 .30
- 14 Iorek Byrnison .10 .30
- 15 Serafina Pekkala .10 .30
- 16 Witches' Words .10 .30
- 17 Off-Limits .10 .30
- 18 Scheming .10 .30
- 19 Stop! .10 .30
- 20 Discovery .10 .30
- 21 Reprimand .10 .30
- 22 Kidnappers .10 .30
- 23 Caught! .10 .30
- 24 Opportunity .10 .30
- 25 Secrets .10 .30
- 26 The Alethiometer .10 .30
- 27 Departure .10 .30
- 28 Seeing London .10 .30
- 29 Compass Secrets .10 .30
- 30 A New Threat .10 .30
- 31 Danger .10 .30
- 32 New Friends .10 .30
- 33 Evil Work .10 .30
- 34 Gyption King .10 .30
- 35 Captured .10 .30
- 36 Queen Of The Witches .10 .30
- 37 Help For Hire .10 .30
- 38 Fearsome Friend .10 .30
- 39 Armor-Clad .10 .30
- 40 In A Fix .10 .30
- 41 Journey .10 .30
- 42 Ghostly Cabin .10 .30
- 43 Rescued .10 .30
- 44 Attack .10 .30
- 45 Kidnapped .10 .30
- 46 Icy Reception .10 .30
- 47 Rightful King .10 .30
- 48 Bear Ride .10 .30
- 49 Farewell .10 .30
- 50 Arrival .10 .30
- 51 Reunited .10 .30
- 52 Trapped .10 .30
- 53 Clinical Captive .10 .30
- 54 The Truth .10 .30
- 55 A Way Out .10 .30
- 56 Foiled? .10 .30
- 57 Saviors .10 .30
- 58 Reinforcements .10 .30
- 59 Up And Away .10 .30
- 60 Future Fights .10 .30
- 61 At Work .10 .30
- 62 Magesterial Police .10 .30
- 63 Magesterial Spies .10 .30
- 64 A Ghastly Truth .10 .30
- 65 The Magisterial Seat .10 .30
- 66 Non-Believers .10 .30
- 67 Mrs. Coulter And Lyra .10 .30
- 68 The Magisterium And Lord Asriel .10 .30
- 69 Iorek Byrinson And King Ragnar Sturlusson .10 .30
- 70 The Gyptians And The Gobblers .10 .30
- 71 The Witches And The Tartars .10 .30
- 72 Checklist .10 .30
- CL1 Other Worlds 3.00 8.00

2007 The Golden Compass Daemon Forms

STATED ODDS 1:23

- DF1 Lyra & Pantalaimon
- DF2 Lord Asriel & Stelmaria
- DF3 Mrs. Coulter & The Golden Monkey

2007 The Golden Compass Fight to the Death

STATED ODDS 1:7

- FD1 Quick Thinking
- FD2 Uneven Fight
- FD3 Face To Face
- FD4 In Control
- FD5 A Last Blow
- FD6 The Rightful King

2007 The Golden Compass Lyra's World

STATED ODDS 1:9

- LW1 Oxford
- LW2 London
- LW3 Trollesund
- LW4 Bolvangar
- LW5 Svalbard
- LW6 North Pole

2007 The Golden Compass Pieceworks

STATED ODDS 1:24

- PW1 Lord Asriel's Suit
- PW2 Mrs. Coulter's Dinner Dress
- PW3 Lyra's Blue Dress
- PW4 Serafina's Dress
- PW5 Mrs. Coulter's Cocktail Dress
- PW6 Mrs. Coulter's Capelet
- PW7 Lord Asriel's Tweed Jacket
- PW8 Lyra's Artic Coat
- PW9 Lyra's Best Dress
- PW10 Farder Coram's Coat
- PW11 Fra Pavel's Coat

2007 The Golden Compass Truth Teller

STATED ODDS 1:9

- TT1 Learning Curve
- TT2 Lost Art
- TT3 Rightful Owner
- TT4 Ghost Hunt
- TT5 Face-Off
- TT6 Royal Request

2007 Harry Potter and the Order of the Phoenix

COMPLETE SET (90) 5.00 12.00

- 1 Harry Potter and the Order of the Phoenix .15 .40
- 2 Harry Potter .15 .40
- 3 Ron Weasley .15 .40
- 4 Hermione Granger .15 .40
- 5 Neville Longbottom .15 .40
- 6 Ginny Weasley .15 .40
- 7 Luna Lovegood .15 .40
- 8 Cho Chang .15 .40
- 9 Remus Lupin .15 .40
- 10 Draco Malfoy .15 .40
- 11 Dolores Umbridge .15 .40
- 12 Severus Snape .15 .40
- 13 Albus Dumbledore .15 .40
- 14 Sirius Black .15 .40
- 15 Alastor Mad-Eye Moody .15 .40
- 16 Argus Filch .15 .40
- 17 Minerva McGonagall .15 .40
- 18 Rubeus Hagrid .15 .40
- 19 Intruders? .15 .40
- 20 Rescuing You, Of Course .15 .40
- 21 The Advance Guard .15 .40
- 22 First Door On The Left .15 .40
- 23 We Wanted To Write .15 .40
- 24 Discussion in The Order .15 .40
- 25 The Real Mad-Eye Moody .15 .40
- 26 Show Him .15 .40
- 27 Lies in The Prophet .15 .40
- 28 Traveling Through London .15 .40
- 29 The Visitors' Entrance .15 .40
- 30 A Trip To The Ministry .15 .40
- 31 Morning, Arthur .15 .40
- 32 The Hearing .15 .40
- 33 A Witness .15 .40
- 34 Senior Undersecretary To The Minister .15 .40
- 35 Encountering Draco .15 .40
- 36 The Quibbler .15 .40
- 37 The Newest Professor .15 .40
- 38 An Empty Chair .15 .40
- 39 Progress For Progress' Sake .15 .40
  Must Be Discouraged
- 40 Good Morning, Children! .15 .40
- 41 Risk-Free? .15 .40
- 42 Theoretical Knowledge .15 .40
- 43 Detention .15 .40
- 44 Umbridge's Special Quill .15 .40
- 45 Trying To Understand .15 .40
- 46 Saving Sybill .15 .40
- 47 The Umbridge Effect .15 .40
- 48 Hall Monitor .15 .40
- 49 That loul, Evil Old Gargoyle! .15 .40
- 50 The Mysterious Barman .15 .40
- 51 Forming An Army .15 .40
- 52 The First Meeting .15 .40
- 53 Ravenclaw DA Members .15 .40
- 54 I'm Hopeless .15 .40
- 55 Stupefy! .15 .40
- 56 Budding Romance? .15 .40
- 57 Stupefy! Levicorpus! Expelliarmus! .15 .40
- 58 I-I Did It .15 .40
- 59 The Kiss .15 .40
- 60 Sir -? .15 .40
- 61 Occlumency .15 .40
- 62 You're Not A Bad Person .15 .40
- 63 Harry And Cho .15 .40
- 64 Giant Injuries .15 .40
- 65 A Storm Comin' .15 .40
- 66 Bombarda Maxima! .15 .40
- 67 Loony? .15 .40
- 68 Proof! .15 .40
- 69 Not Potter's Army .15 .40
- 70 Hagrid's Half-Brother .15 .40
- 71 Snivellus .15 .40
- 72 Your Lessons Are At An End .15 .40
- 73 We Won't Be Seeing You! .15 .40
- 74 A Dramatic Exit .15 .40
- 75 Cruc- .15 .40
- 76 No Secret Weapon .15 .40
- 77 Battling Death Eaters .15 .40
- 78 Protecting The Prophecy .15 .40
- 79 Luna, Trapped .15 .40
- 80 Ron Struggles .15 .40
- 81 Watching The Battle .15 .40
- 82 You Should Have Stayed In Hiding .15 .40
- 83 Good One, James! .15 .40
- 84 An Evil Cousin .15 .40
- 85 Revenge .15 .40
- 86 A Great Wizard .15 .40
- 87 The Fault Is Mine .15 .40
- 88 Feat's About To Start .15 .40
- 89 An Unexpected Friend .15 .40
- 90 Checklist .15 .40

2007 Harry Potter and the Order of the Phoenix Retail

COMPLETE SET (90) 5.00 12.00

- 1 Harry Potter and the Order of the Phoenix .15 .40
- 2 Harry Potter .15 .40
- 3 Ron Weasley .15 .40
- 4 Hermione Granger .15 .40
- 5 Neville Longbottom .15 .40
- 6 Ginny Weasley .15 .40
- 7 Luna Lovegood .15 .40
- 8 Cho Chang .15 .40
- 9 Remus Lupin .15 .40
- 10 Draco Malfoy .15 .40
- 11 Dolores Umbridge .15 .40
- 12 Severus Snape .15 .40
- 13 Albus Dumbledore .15 .40
- 14 Sirius Black .15 .40
- 15 Alastor Mad-Eye Moody .15 .40
- 16 Argus Filch .15 .40
- 17 Minerva McGonagall .15 .40
- 18 Rubeus Hagrid .15 .40
- 19 Intruders? .15 .40
- 20 Rescuing You, Of Course .15 .40
- 21 The Advance Guard .15 .40
- 22 First Door On The Left .15 .40
- 23 We Wanted To Write .15 .40
- 24 Discussion in The Order .15 .40
- 25 The Real Mad-Eye Moody .15 .40
- 26 Show Him .15 .40
- 27 Lies in The Prophet .15 .40
- 28 Traveling Through London .15 .40
- 29 The Visitors' Entrance .15 .40
- 30 A Trip To The Ministry .15 .40
- 31 Morning, Arthur .15 .40
- 32 The Hearing .15 .40
- 33 A Witness .15 .40
- 34 Senior Undersecretary To The Minister .15 .40
- 35 Encountering Draco .15 .40
- 36 The Quibbler .15 .40
- 37 The Newest Professor .15 .40
- 38 An Empty Chair .15 .40
- 39 Progress For Progress' Sake .15 .40
  Must Be Discouraged
- 40 Good Morning, Children! .15 .40
- 41 Risk-Free? .15 .40
- 42 Theoretical Knowledge .15 .40
- 43 Detention .15 .40
- 44 Umbridge's Special Quill .15 .40
- 45 Trying To Understand .15 .40
- 46 Saving Sybill .15 .40
- 47 The Umbridge Effect .15 .40
- 48 Hall Monitor .15 .40
- 49 That loul, Evil Old Gargoyle! .15 .40
- 50 The Mysterious Barman .15 .40
- 51 Forming An Army .15 .40
- 52 The First Meeting .15 .40
- 53 Ravenclaw DA Members .15 .40
- 54 I'm Hopeless .15 .40
- 55 Stupefy! .15 .40
- 56 Budding Romance? .15 .40
- 57 Stupefy! Levicorpus! Expelliarmus! .15 .40
- 58 I-I Did It .15 .40
- 59 The Kiss .15 .40
- 60 Sir -? .15 .40
- 61 Occlumency .15 .40
- 62 You're Not A Bad Person .15 .40
- 63 Harry And Cho .15 .40
- 64 Giant Injuries .15 .40
- 65 A Storm Comin' .15 .40
- 66 Bombarda Maxima! .15 .40
- 67 Loony? .15 .40
- 68 Proof! .15 .40
- 69 Not Potter's Army .15 .40
- 70 Hagrid's Half-Brother .15 .40
- 71 Snivellus .15 .40
- 72 Your Lessons Are At An End .15 .40
- 73 We Won't Be Seeing You! .15 .40
- 74 A Dramatic Exit .15 .40
- 75 Cruc- .15 .40
- 76 No Secret Weapon .15 .40
- 77 Battling Death Eaters .15 .40
- 78 Protecting The Prophecy .15 .40
- 79 Luna, Trapped .15 .40
- 80 Ron Struggles .15 .40
- 81 Watching The Battle .15 .40
- 82 You Should Have Stayed In Hiding .15 .40
- 83 Good One, James! .15 .40
- 84 An Evil Cousin .15 .40
- 85 Revenge .15 .40
- 86 A Great Wizard .15 .40
- 87 The Fault Is Mine .15 .40
- 88 Feat's About To Start .15 .40
- 89 An Unexpected Friend .15 .40
- 90 Checklist .15 .40

2007 Harry Potter and the Order of the Phoenix Autographs

STATED ODDS 1:48

- 1 Daniel Radcliffe 400.00 650.00
- 2 Emma Watson 400.00 650.00
- 3 Rupert Grint 150.00 300.00
- 4 Tony Maudsley 20.00 40.00
- 5 Jason Isaacs 60.00 120.00
- 6 Evanna Lynch 75.00 150.00
- 7 George Harris 25.00 50.00
- 8 Bonnie Wright 40.00 80.00
- 9 Jim McManus 20.00 40.00
- 10 Warwick Davis 15.00 30.00
- 11 Katie Leung 30.00 60.00
- 12 Michael Gambon 50.00 100.00
- 13 Matthew Lewis 25.00 50.00

2007 Harry Potter and the Order of the Phoenix Box Loaders

COMPLETE SET (4) 5.00 12.00
STATED ODDS ONE PER BOX

- BT1 Thestral 1.50 4.00
- BT2 Centaur 1.50 4.00
- BT3 Thestral 1.50 4.00
- BT4 Centaur 1.50 4.00

2007 Harry Potter and the Order of the Phoenix Case Loaders

COMPLETE SET (2) 15.00 30.00
STATED ODDS ONE PER CASE

- CT1 Aurors 10.00 20.00
- CT2 Dumbledore's Army 10.00 20.00

2007 Harry Potter and the Order of the Phoenix Costumes

STATED ODDS 1:24

- C1 Daniel Radcliffe Shirt 20.00 40.00
- C2 Rupert Grint Shirt 8.00 20.00
- C3 Emma Watson Sweater 30.00 60.00
- C4 Oliver Phelps Shirt 12.00 30.00
- C5 Bonnie Wright Sweater 12.00 30.00
- C6 Katie Leung Robe 12.00 30.00
- C7 Katie Leung Tie 40.00 80.00
- C8 Evanna Lynch Shirt 25.00 50.00
- C9 Daniel Radcliffe Sweater 8.00 20.00
- C10 Imelda Staunton Outfit 8.00 20.00
- C11 George Harris Outfit 6.00 15.00
- C12 Michael Gambon Outfit 20.00 40.00
- C13 Slytherin Robe 6.00 15.00
- C14 Ravenclaw Robe 8.00 20.00
- C15 Gryffindor Robe 6.00 15.00
- C16 Death Eater Robe 12.00 30.00
- C17 Death Eater Robe 12.00 30.00
- C18 Death Eater Robe 12.00 30.00

2007 Harry Potter and the Order of the Phoenix Dealer Incentive Memorabilia

- CI1 Emma Watson Sweater/410 40.00 80.00
- CI2 Ralph Fiennes Outfit/200 40.00 80.00
- CI3 Death Eater Mask/130 50.00 100.00
- CI4 Hog's Head Hair/88 75.00 150.00

2007 Harry Potter and the Order of the Phoenix Death Eater Puzzle

COMPLETE SET (9) 4.00 10.00
STATED ODDS 1:5 RETAIL

- R1 Death Eater .75 2.00
- R2 Death Eater .75 2.00
- R3 Death Eater .75 2.00
- R4 Death Eater .75 2.00
- R5 Death Eater .75 2.00
- R6 Death Eater .75 2.00
- R7 Death Eater .75 2.00
- R8 Death Eater .75 2.00
- R9 Death Eater .75 2.00

2007 Harry Potter and the Order of the Phoenix Film Cels

COMPLETE SET (9) 100.00 175.00
STATED ODDS 1:80

- CFC1 Harry 12.00 30.00
- CFC2 Hermione 12.00 30.00
- CFC3 Dudley, Harry, and Mrs. Figg 12.00 30.00
- CFC4 Neville 12.00 30.00
- CFC5 Ron 12.00 30.00
- CFC6 Filch 12.00 30.00
- CFC7 Fred and George 12.00 30.00
- CFC8 Harry and Advance Guard 12.00 30.00
- CFC9 Hogwarts Express 12.00 30.00

2007 Harry Potter and the Order of the Phoenix Foil Chase Cards

COMPLETE SET (9) 5.00 12.00
STATED ODDS 1:5 HOBBY

- R1 Death Eater .75 2.00
- R2 Voldemort and Harry .75 2.00
- R3 Harry Potter's Stag Patronus .75 2.00
- R4 Dumbledore's Army .75 2.00
- R5 Ministry of Magic .75 2.00
- R6 The Forbidden Forest .75 2.00
- R7 The Dark Arts .75 2.00
- R8 Harry Potter and the Thestrals .75 2.00
- R9 Harry and Friends .75 2.00

2007 Harry Potter and the Order of the Phoenix Props

STATED ODDS 1:80

- P1 Dumbledore's Army Parchment 60.00 120.00
- P2 Death Eater Mask 75.00 150.00
- P3 Daily Prophet 20.00 40.00
- P4 O.W.L. 20.00 40.00
- P5 Dolores Umbridge Doily 30.00 60.00
- P6 Dolores Umbridge Progress Report 20.00 40.00
- P7 Death Eater Mask 75.00 150.00
- P8 Quibbler 40.00 80.00
- P9 Ministry Munchies Sack 20.00 40.00
- P10 Daily Prophet 20.00 40.00
- P11 Dolores Umbridge Curtains 20.00 40.00
- P12 Death Eater Mask 75.00 150.00

2007 Harry Potter and the Order of the Phoenix Update

COMPLETE SET (90) 5.00 12.00

- 91 Title Card .15 .40
- 92 Lord Voldemort .15 .40
- 93 Lucius Malfoy .15 .40
- 94 Fred Weasley .15 .40
- 95 George Weasley .15 .40
- 96 Seamus Finnegan .15 .40
- 97 Bellatrix Lestrange .15 .40
- 98 Nymphadora Tonks .15 .40
- 99 Nigel .15 .40
- 100 Who's Cedric - Your Boyfriend? .15 .40
- 101 A Change in The Weather .15 .40
- 102 A Chill In The Air .15 .40
- 103 The Dementor's Kiss .15 .40
- 104 The Patronus Charm .15 .40
- 105 Expecto Patronum! .15 .40
- 106 They Might Come Back! .15 .40
- 107 Keeping An Eye On Harry .15 .40
- 108 Diddykins! .15 .40
- 109 The Rescue .15 .40
- 110 Away From Privet Drive .15 .40
- 111 Let It Out! .15 .40
- 112 He'll Find Out Soon Enough .15 .40
- 113 He's Been Recruiting .15 .40
- 114 He's After Something .15 .40
- 115 The Red Telephone Box .15 .40
- 116 Heading To Trial .15 .40
- 117 Witness For The Defense .15 .40
- 118 Dreaming? .15 .40
- 119 The Castle .15 .40
- 120 Cho And Her Friends .15 .40
- 121 What's What? .15 .40
- 122 Lies in The Prophet .15 .40
- 123 You Won't Need Ink .15 .40
- 124 How He Wants You To Feel .15 .40
- 125 Medieval Methods .15 .40
- 126 A Shocking Announcement .15 .40
- 127 An Unwelcome Guest .15 .40
- 128 Hogwarts Is My Home! .15 .40
- 129 Educational Decree Number Twenty-Three .15 .40
- 130 Lack Of Authority .15 .40
- 131 The Barman At The Hog's Head .15 .40
- 132 Some Sort Of Freak .15 .40
- 133 Just Being Modest .15 .40
- 134 Real Need .15 .40
- 135 Levicorpus .15 .40
- 136 Magical Mind Defense .15 .40
- 137 Discipline Your Mind .15 .40
- 138 The Inquisitorial Squad .15 .40
- 139 A Nightmare? .15 .40
- 140 The Tapestry Room .15 .40
- 141 Always Saying Goodbye .15 .40
- 142 Sirius's Cousins .15 .40
- 143 Bit O' Fresh Air .15 .40
- 144 Jus' Like Last Time .15 .40
- 145 Mass Breakout .15 .40
- 146 Tracking The D.A. .15 .40
- 147 Proud To Be Their Son .15 .40
- 148 Luna's Patronus .15 .40
- 149 Trapped in The Room Of Requirement .15 .40
- 150 Caught .15 .40
- 151 In This Together .15 .40
- 152 No Idea .15 .40
- 153 A Young Snape .15 .40
- 154 The Calm Before The Storm .15 .40
- 155 A Special Kind Of Detention .15 .40
- 156 Interrupting The O.W.L.s .15 .40
- 157 Quite An Exit .15 .40
- 158 We Fly, Of Course .15 .40
- 159 The Hall Of Prophecy .15 .40
- 160 Preparing To Fight .15 .40
- 161 Shielding The Prophecy .15 .40
- 162 A Serious Threat .15 .40
- 163 An Even Exchange? .15 .40
- 164 Ron, Trapped .15 .40
- 165 The Exchange .15 .40
- 166 Help Arrives .15 .40
- 167 Ruthless .15 .40
- 168 Battle in The Atrium .15 .40
- 169 An Epic Battle .15 .40
- 170 Powerful Spells .15 .40
- 171 A Serpent Of Flame .15 .40
- 172 Trapped in The Fountain .15 .40
- 173 Raining Glass .15 .40
- 174 You've Been Lied To .15 .40
- 175 Glass into Sand .15 .40
- 176 Not Himself .15 .40
- 177 Possessed? .15 .40
- 178 After The Battle .15 .40
- 179 Things We Lose .15 .40
- 180 Checklist .15 .40

2007 Harry Potter and the Order of the Phoenix Update Autographs

STATED ODDS 1:48

- 1 Daniel Radcliffe 250.00 400.00
  Katie Leung
- 2 Tav MacDougall 50.00 100.00
- 3 Richard Cubison 40.00 80.00
- 4 Richard Trinder 30.00 60.00
- 5 Tom Felton 75.00 150.00
- 6 Helena Bonham Carter 75.00 150.00
- 7 Sian Thomas 20.00 40.00
- 8 Brendan Gleeson
- 9 Kathryn Hunter 20.00 40.00
- 10 Harry Melling 15.00 30.00
- 11 Timothy Bateson 25.00 50.00
- 12 Jason Piper 20.00 40.00
- 13 David Thewlis 20.00 40.00
- 14 Robert Hardy 15.00 30.00
- 15 Natalia Tena 30.00 60.00
- 16 Michael Gambon 50.00 100.00

2007 Harry Potter and the Order of the Phoenix Update Box Toppers

STATED ODDS ONE PER BOX

- BT1 Bane 1.50 4.00
- BT2 Centaur 1.50 4.00
- BT3 Centaurs 1.50 4.00
- BT4 Harry, Hermione, and Ron 1.50 4.00

2007 Harry Potter and the Order of the Phoenix Update Case Toppers

COMPLETE SET 50.00 100.00
BLUE/YELLOW VARIATIONS
STATED ODDS ONE PER CASE

- 1b Harry and Dumbledore's Army - Blue 10.00 25.00
- 1y Harry and Dumbledore's Army - Yellow 10.00 25.00
- 2b Hermione - Blue 10.00 25.00
- 2y Hermione -Yellow 10.00 25.00
- 3b Voldemort - Blue 10.00 25.00
- 3y Voldemort - Yellow 10.00 25.00

2007 Harry Potter and the Order of the Phoenix Update Costumes

STATED ODDS 1:24

- C1 Daniel Radcliffe Shirt/375 10.00 25.00
- C2 Emma Watson Sweater/400 20.00 40.00
- C3 Evanna Lynch Sweater/475 15.00 30.00
- C4 Katie Leung Sweater/680 15.00 30.00
- C5 Daniel Radcliffe Sweater/275 10.00 25.00
- C6 Rupert Grint Tie/120 50.00 100.00
- C7 Bonnie Wright Jacket/625 10.00 25.00
- C8 Evanna Lynch Pants/570 20.00 40.00
- C9 Bonnie Wright Pants/600 10.00 25.00
- C10 Rupert Grint Pants/600 15.00 30.00
- C11 Jason Isaacs Outfit/625 10.00 25.00
- C12 Oliver Phelps Shirt/600 10.00 25.00
- C13 James Phelps 15.00 30.00
  Oliver Phelps Shirt/475
- C14 Ralph Fiennes 60.00 120.00
  Michael Gambon Outfit/185
- C15 Gryffindor 15.00 30.00
  Slytherin Outfit/295

2007 Harry Potter and the Order of the Phoenix Update Dealer Incentive Memorabilia

- CI1 Grimmauld Place Material/360 15.00 30.00
- CI2 Defense Against the Dark Arts Book/180 50.00 100.00
- CI3 Death Eater Costume/120 40.00 80.00
- CI4 Dumbledore/Umbridge Outfits/84 60.00 120.00

2007 Harry Potter and the Order of the Phoenix Update Film Cels

STATED ODDS 1:80

- CFC1 Luna and Thestral 12.00 30.00
- CFC2 Voldemort 12.00 30.00
- CFC3 Neville 12.00 30.00
- CFC4 Dolores Umbridge 12.00 30.00
- CFC5 Peter Pettigrew 12.00 30.00
- CFC6 Dolores Umbridge and Hermione 12.00 30.00
- CFC7 Neville 12.00 30.00
- CFC8 Dumbledore 12.00 30.00
- CFC9 Goyle 12.00 30.00

2007 Harry Potter and the Order of the Phoenix Update Foil Chase Cards

STATED ODDS 1:5

- R1 The Prophecy .75 2.00
- R2 The Trial Chamber .75 2.00
- R3 Order of the Phoenix .75 2.00
- R4 Voldemort and the Death Eaters .75 2.00
- R5 Harry Potter .75 2.00
  [Sirius Black
- R6 Ministry of Magic .75 2.00
- R7 Dumbledore's Army .75 2.00
- R8 The Weasleys .75 2.00
- R9 Educational Decree No. 98 .75 2.00

2007 Harry Potter and the Order of the Phoenix Update Props

STATED ODDS 1:80

- P1 Cauldron/150 75.00 150.00
- P2 Flying Memos/435 20.00 40.00
- P3 The Daily Prophet/505 15.00 30.00
- P4 Defense Against the Dark Arts Book/100 75.00 150.00
- P5 The Daily Prophet/280 15.00 30.00
- P6 Dolores Umbridge Stationary/450 10.00 25.00
- P7 Ravenclaw Outfit 75.00 150.00
  O.W.L. Exam Papers/100
- P8 Death Eater Mask/Robe/100 60.00 120.00
- P9 Death Eater Mask/Robe/95 60.00 120.00
- P10 Death Eater Mask/Robe/90 60.00 120.00
- P11 Dolores Umbridge Doily/Curtains/115 60.00 120.00
- P12 Severus Snape Test Tube/Stand/100 100.00 200.00

2007 Jericho Season One

COMPLETE SET (72) 4.00 10.00

- 1 Title Card .10 .30
- 2 Jake Green .10 .30
- 3 Emily Sullivan .10 .30
- 4 Heather Lisinski .10 .30
- 5 Eric Green .10 .30
- 6 Robert Hawkins .10 .30
- 7 Gray Anderson .10 .30

- 8 Johnston Green .10 .30
- 9 Gail Green .10 .30
- 10 Dale Turner .10 .30
- 11 Skylar Stevens .10 .30
- 12 Gracie Leigh .10 .30
- 13 Stanley Richmond .10 .30
- 14 Mimi Clark .10 .30
- 15 Bonnie Richmond .10 .30
- 16 Darcy Hawkins .10 .30
- 17 April Green .10 .30
- 18 Mary Bailey .10 .30
- 19 Roger Hammond .10 .30
- 20 Jonah Prowse .10 .30
- 21 Sarah Mason .10 .30
- 22 The First 17 Hours (Pilot) .10 .30
- 23 Panic In Year Zero .10 .30
- 24 Fallout .10 .30
- 25 Criminal Intent .10 .30
- 26 Four Horsemen .10 .30
- 27 Out There .10 .30
- 28 Walls Of Jericho .10 .30
- 29 He Knows Hawkins .10 .30
- 30 Federal Response .10 .30
- 31 Terror Strikes Home .10 .30
- 32 9:02 .10 .30
- 33 No Good, No Bad .10 .30
- 34 Long Live The Mayor .10 .30
- 35 Family Ties .10 .30
- 36 Rogue River .10 .30
- 37 Beware Of Ravenwood .10 .30
- 38 Crossroads .10 .30
- 39 A Bridge Too Near .10 .30
- 40 Red Flag .10 .30
- 41 Dance With The Devil .10 .30
- 42 Vox Populi .10 .30
- 43 Changing Of The Guard .10 .30
- 44 The Day Before .10 .30
- 45 Countdown To Doomsday .10 .30
- 46 Black Jack .10 .30
- 47 Pieces Of The Puzzle .10 .30
- 48 Heart Of Winter .10 .30
- 49 Change Of Heart .10 .30
- 50 Semper Fidelis .10 .30
- 51 When Hope Is A Lie .10 .30
- 52 Winter's End .10 .30
- 53 Life And Death .10 .30
- 54 One Man's Terrorist .10 .30
- 55 Roger Sees The Light .10 .30
- 56 A.K.A .10 .30
- 57 Project Red Bell .10 .30
- 58 Casus Belli .10 .30
- 59 Kill Thy Neighbor .10 .30
- 60 One If By Land .10 .30
- 61 Adversaries .10 .30
- 62 Coalition Of The Willing .10 .30
- 63 No Way Back .10 .30
- 64 Why We Fight .10 .30
- 65 Who Will Survive? .10 .30
- 66 Bombed Cities .10 .30
- 67 Allies Or Enemies? .10 .30
- 68 Night Of The Emp .10 .30
- 69 Hawkin's Package .10 .30
- 70 Who's In Charge .10 .30
- 71 Brave New Town .10 .30
- 72 Checklist .10 .30

2007 Jericho Season One Autographs

STATED ODDS 1:36

- A1 Skeet Ulrich 15.00 40.00
- A2 Ashley Scott 12.00 30.00
- A3 Sprague Grayden 8.00 20.00
- A4 Kenneth Mitchell 6.00 15.00
- A5 Michael Gaston 4.00 10.00
- A6 Brad Beyer 4.00 10.00
- A7 Shoshannah Stern 6.00 15.00
- A8 Erik Knudsen 4.00 10.00

2007 Jericho Season One Box Loaders

- CH1 The Return Of Jake Green 2.00 5.00
- CH2 The Greens Of Jericho 2.00 5.00
- CH3 Love And Survival 2.00 5.00
- CL1 Welcome To Jericho 4.00 10.00

2007 Jericho Season One Fallout

STATED ODDS 1:11

- F1 Day of the Bombs .75 2.00
- F2 Dark Homecoming .75 2.00
- F3 Divorce in Year Zero .75 2.00
- F4 Thicker Than Water .75 2.00
- F5 Suspicion .75 2.00
- F6 Kindred Spirits .75 2.00
- F7 Set This Town on Fire .75 2.00
- F8 For the Love of Jake .75 2.00
- F9 Family Matters .75 2.00

2007 Jericho Season One Pieceworks

STATED ODDS 1:36

- PW1 Skeet Ulrich 6.00 15.00
- PW2 Skeet Ulrich 8.00 20.00
- PW3 Lennie James 6.00 15.00
- PW4 Lennie James 8.00 20.00
- PW5 Lennie James 8.00 20.00
- PW6 Kenneth Mitchell 8.00 20.00
- PW7 Kenneth Mitchell 6.00 15.00
- PW8 Ashley Scott 8.00 20.00
- PW9 Ashley Scott 8.00 20.00
- PW10 Brad Beyer 6.00 15.00
- PW11 Brad Beyer 6.00 15.00
- PW12 Alicia Coppola 8.00 20.00
- PW13 Alicia Coppola 8.00 20.00
- PWA1 Skeet Ulrich AU 15.00 40.00
- PWA2 Ashley Scott AU 15.00 40.00
- PWA3 Kenneth Mitchell AU 8.00 20.00

2007 Jericho Season One Survivors

STATED ODDS 1:17

- S1 Jake Green 1.00 2.50
- S2 Emily Sullivan 1.00 2.50
- S3 Dale Turner/Gracie Leigh 1.00 2.50
- S4 Robert Hawkins 1.00 2.50
- S5 Eric Green 1.00 2.50
- S6 Johnston/Gail Green 1.00 2.50

2007 Legends of Star Trek Dr. Beverly Crusher

COMPLETE SET (9) 1.50 4.00
STATED PRINT RUN 1,701 SER. #'d SETS 10.00 20.00

- L1 Dr. Beverly Crusher 1.50 4.00
- L2 Dr. Beverly Crusher 1.50 4.00
- L3 Dr. Beverly Crusher 1.50 4.00
- L4 Dr. Beverly Crusher 1.50 4.00
- L5 Dr. Beverly Crusher 1.50 4.00
- L6 Dr. Beverly Crusher 1.50 4.00
- L7 Dr. Beverly Crusher 1.50 4.00
- L8 Dr. Beverly Crusher 1.50 4.00
- L9 Dr. Beverly Crusher 1.50 4.00

2007 Legends of Star Trek LaForge Yar Will Crusher

COMPLETE SET (9) 1.50 4.00
STATED PRINT RUN 1,701 SER. #'d SETS 10.00 20.00

- L1 LaForge 1.50 4.00
- L2 LaForge 1.50 4.00
- L3 LaForge 1.50 4.00
- L4 Yar 1.50 4.00
- L5 Yar 1.50 4.00
- L6 Yar 1.50 4.00
- L7 Will Crusher 1.50 4.00
- L8 Will Crusher 1.50 4.00
- L9 Will Crusher 1.50 4.00

2007 Legends of Star Trek Lt. Commander Worf

COMPLETE SET (9) 10.00 20.00
STATED PRINT RUN 1,701 SER. #'d SETS

- L1 Lt. Commander Worf 1.50 4.00
- L2 Lt. Commander Worf 1.50 4.00
- L3 Lt. Commander Worf 1.50 4.00
- L4 Lt. Commander Worf 1.50 4.00
- L5 Lt. Commander Worf 1.50 4.00
- L6 Lt. Commander Worf 1.50 4.00
- L7 Lt. Commander Worf 1.50 4.00
- L8 Lt. Commander Worf 1.50 4.00
- L9 Lt. Commander Worf 1.50 4.00

2007 Lost Season Three

COMPLETE SET (90) 5.00 12.00
CL1 STATED ODDS ONE PER CASE

- 1 Lost .15 .40
- 2 Obsessed .15 .40
- 3 Stubborn .15 .40
- 4 Joiner .15 .40
- 5 Cleaning .15 .40
- 6 Betrayal .15 .40
- 7 Committed .15 .40
- 8 Con Man .15 .40
- 9 No Escape .15 .40
- 10 Protector .15 .40
- 11 Warning .15 .40
- 12 Bridal Blues .15 .40
- 13 Caged .15 .40
- 14 Impossible .15 .40
- 15 Three Minutes .15 .40
- 16 Failed .15 .40
- 17 Doomed .15 .40
- 18 Taboo .15 .40
- 19 Among Us .15 .40
- 20 Cursed .15 .40
- 21 Lucky .15 .40
- 22 Secrets .15 .40
- 23 Lies .15 .40
- 24 Guilt .15 .40
- 25 Hope .15 .40
- 26 Betrayal .15 .40
- 27 Surprise .15 .40
- 28 Means .15 .40
- 29 Motive .15 .40
- 30 Partners .15 .40
- 31 Rivals .15 .40
- 32 Stuck .15 .40
- 33 Planted .15 .40
- 34 Tested .15 .40
- 35 Sacrifice .15 .40
- 36 Shame .15 .40
- 37 Good News .15 .40
- 38 Delegation .15 .40
- 39 Had It Coming .15 .40
- 40 Newcomer .15 .40
- 41 No Turning Back .15 .40
- 42 Accomplished .15 .40
- 43 Welcome Party .15 .40
- 44 On The Brink .15 .40
- 45 Left For Dead .15 .40
- 46 Long March .15 .40
- 47 Signal To Noise .15 .40
- 48 Last Chance .15 .40
- 49 Get Back .15 .40
- 50 Jack .15 .40
- 51 Kate .15 .40
- 52 Sawyer .15 .40
- 53 Locke .15 .40
- 54 Sun .15 .40
- 55 Jin .15 .40
- 56 Charlie .15 .40
- 57 Claire .15 .40
- 58 Hurley .15 .40
- 59 Sayid .15 .40
- 60 Desmond .15 .40
- 61 Mr. Eko .15 .40
- 62 Ben .15 .40
- 63 Juliet .15 .40
- 64 Pickett .15 .40
- 65 Mr. Friendly .15 .40
- 66 Alex .15 .40
- 67 Karl .15 .40
- 68 Isabel .15 .40
- 69 Mikhail .15 .40
- 70 Richard .15 .40
- 71 Black Smoke Monster .15 .40
- 72 Cooper On The Island .15 .40
- 73 Walt Appears .15 .40
- 74 Naomi Dorrit .15 .40
- 75 Juliet'S Loyalty .15 .40
- 76 Jacob .15 .40
- 77 Jack Christian/Claire .15 .40
- 78 Kate Cassidy/Sawyer .15 .40
- 79 Charlie Nadia/Sayid .15 .40
- 80 Ben Alex/Rousseau .15 .40
- 81 Sawyer Cooper/Locke .15 .40
- 82 Mr. Eko .15 .40
- 83 Nikki & Paulo .15 .40
- 84 Charlie .15 .40
- 85 Kate + Sawyer .15 .40
- 86 Sawyer + Kate .15 .40
- 87 Kate + Jack .15 .40
- 88 Jack + Juliet .15 .40
- 89 Call For Help .15 .40
- 90 Checklist .15 .40
- CL1 Rescue Or Ruin

2007 Lost Season Three Autographs

STATED ODDS 1:36

- A25 Michael Emerson 15.00 40.00
- A26 Elizabeth Mitchell 15.00 40.00
- A27 April Grace 5.00 12.00
- A28 Michael Bowen 5.00 12.00
- A29 Marsha Thomason 5.00 12.00
- A30 Nestor Carbonell 6.00 15.00
- A31 Tracy Middendorf 5.00 12.00
- A32 Blake Bashoff 5.00 12.00
- A33 Ian Somerhalder 12.00 30.00
- A34 Andrew Divoff 8.00 20.00

2007 Lost Season Three Through the Looking Glass

COMPLETE SET (3) 4.00 10.00
STATED ODDS 1:36

- LG1 Frequent Flyer 2.00 5.00
- LG2 Memorial 2.00 5.00
- LG3 Differences 2.00 5.00

2007 Lost Season Three Fighting Back

COMPLETE SET (9) 4.00 10.00
STATED ODDS 1:11

- FB1 Fighting Back .75 2.00
- FB2 Fighting Back .75 2.00
- FB3 Fighting Back .75 2.00
- FB4 Fighting Back .75 2.00
- FB5 Fighting Back .75 2.00
- FB6 Fighting Back .75 2.00
- FB7 Fighting Back .75 2.00
- FB8 Fighting Back .75 2.00
- FB9 Fighting Back .75 2.00

2007 Lost Season Three Pieceworks

PW1-PW11 STATED ODDS 1:36
PW12A AND PW12B DEALER EXCLUSIVE
PWA1 AND PWA2 RANDOM INSERTS IN PACKS

- PW1 Evangeline Lilly 12.00 30.00
- PW2 Marsha Thomason 6.00 15.00
- PW3 Yunjin Kim 8.00 20.00
- PW4 Elizabeth Mitchell 12.00 30.00
- PW5 Matthew Fox 6.00 15.00
- PW6 Adewale Akinnuoye-Agbaje 5.00 12.00
- PW7 Daniel Dae Kim 5.00 12.00
- PW8 Andrew Divoff 5.00 12.00
- PW9 Rodrigo Santoro 5.00 12.00
- PW10 Josh Holloway 5.00 12.00
- PW11 Matthew Fox Elizabeth Mitchell 12.00 30.00
- PW12A Rodrigo Santoro 10.00 25.00
- PW12B Kiele Sanchez 10.00 25.00
- PWA1 Andrew Divoff AU 15.00 40.00
- PWA2 Marsha Thomason AU 20.00 50.00

2007 Lost Season Three Propworks

- PPW1 Exploding airplane 35.00 70.00
- PPWA1 Greg Grunberg Airplane AU 40.00 80.00

2007 Lost Season Three Ties to the Island

COMPLETE SET (6) 4.00 10.00
STATED ODDS 1:17

- TI1 Arrival 1.00 2.50
- TI2 Always Together 1.00 2.50
- TI3 Chance Meeting 1.00 2.50
- TI4 Patience 1.00 2.50
- TI5 Talks To Jacob 1.00 2.50
- TI6 Not Exactly True 1.00 2.50

2007 Marvel Masterpieces

COMPLETE SET (90) 4.00 10.00

- 1 Title Card .10 .25
- 2 The Abomination .10 .25
- 3 Adam Warlock .10 .25
- 4 Apocalypse .10 .25
- 5 Archangel .10 .25
- 6 Baron Zemo .10 .25
- 7 The Beast .10 .25
- 8 Bishop .10 .25
- 9 Black Cat .10 .25
- 10 Black Panther .10 .25
- 11 Black Widow .10 .25
- 12 Blade .10 .25
- 13 Blob .10 .25
- 14 Bullseye .10 .25
- 15 Cable .10 .25
- 16 Captain America .10 .25
- 17 Carnage .10 .25
- 18 The Chameleon .10 .25
- 19 Colossus .10 .25
- 20 Cyclops .10 .25
- 21 Dagger .10 .25
- 22 Daredevil .10 .25
- 23 Dr. Doom .10 .25
- 24 Dr. Octopus .10 .25
- 25 Dr. Strange .10 .25
- 26 Dormammu .10 .25
- 27 Dracula .10 .25
- 28 Elektra .10 .25
- 29 The Falcon .10 .25
- 30 Galactus .10 .25
- 31 Gambit .10 .25
- 32 Ghost Rider .10 .25
- 33 Giant-Man .10 .25
- 34 Green Goblin .10 .25
- 35 Hawkeye .10 .25
- 36 Hobgoblin .10 .25
- 37 The Hulk .10 .25
- 38 The Human Torch .10 .25
- 39 Hyperion .10 .25
- 40 Iceman .10 .25
- 41 The Invisible Woman .10 .25
- 42 Iron Fist .10 .25
- 43 Iron Man .10 .25
- 44 Juggernaut .10 .25
- 45 Kang .10 .25
- 46 Kingpin .10 .25
- 47 Kitty Pryde .10 .25
- 48 Kraven the Hunter .10 .25
- 49 Lady Deathstrike .10 .25
- 50 The Lizard .10 .25
- 51 Loki .10 .25
- 52 Luke Cage .10 .25
- 53 Mach-IV .10 .25
- 54 Magneto .10 .25
- 55 Man-Thing .10 .25
- 56 Mephisto .10 .25
- 57 Mr. Fantastic .10 .25
- 58 Moon Knight .10 .25
- 59 Ms. Marvel .10 .25
- 60 Mysterio .10 .25
- 61 Mystique .10 .25
- 62 Nick Fury .10 .25
- 63 Nightcrawler .10 .25
- 64 Phoenix .10 .25
- 65 Professor X .10 .25
- 66 Punisher .10 .25
- 67 Pyro .10 .25
- 68 Rhino .10 .25
- 69 Rogue .10 .25
- 70 Sabretooth .10 .25
- 71 Sandman .10 .25
- 72 Scarlet Witch .10 .25
- 73 The Scorpion .10 .25
- 74 Sentry .10 .25
- 75 The She-Hulk .10 .25
- 76 Silver Sable .10 .25
- 77 The Silver Surfer .10 .25
- 78 Spider-Girl .10 .25
- 79 Spider-Man .10 .25
- 80 Spider-Woman .10 .25
- 81 Storm .10 .25
- 82 Sub-Mariner .10 .25
- 83 Super-Skrull .10 .25
- 84 Thanos .10 .25
- 85 The Thing .10 .25
- 86 Thor .10 .25
- 87 Toad .10 .25
- 88 Venom .10 .25
- 89 The Wasp .10 .25
- 90 Wolverine .10 .25

2007 Marvel Masterpieces Foil

COMPLETE SET (90) 30.00 60.00
*FOIL: 2X TO 5X BASIC CARDS
STATED ODDS 5:6

2007 Marvel Masterpieces Gold

COMPLETE SET (90) 50.00 120.00
*GOLD: 5X TO 12X BASIC CARDS
STATED ODDS 1:6

2007 Marvel Masterpieces Sketches

STATED ODDS 1:36

- 1 Aaron Lopresti
- 2 Aaron Sowd
- 3 Adam Cleveland
- 4 Adam Cline
- 5 Adam Rex
- 6 Alex Saviuk
- 7 Allison Sohn
- 8 Andrew Robinson
- 9 Anjin Anhut
- 10 Anthony Winn
- 11 Ariel Padilla
- 12 Arthur Adams
- 13 Ben Herrera
- 14 Ben Thompson
- 15 Benjamin Glendenning
- 16 Bill Meiggs
- 17 Bill Reinhold
- 18 Bill Sienkiewicz
- 19 Bill Thompson
- 20 Blair Shedd
- 21 Bo Hampton
- 22 Brad Vancata
- 23 Brent Engstrom
- 24 Brent Schoonover
- 25 Brian Denham
- 26 Brian Hagan
- 27 Brian Kong
- 28 Brian Shearer
- 29 Carlo Barberi
- 30 Cat Staggs
- 31 Cedric Nocon
- 32 Chachi Hernandez
- 33 Chad Hurd
- 34 Chris Bachalo
- 35 Chris Brunner
- 36 Chris Copeland
- 37 Chris Marrinan
- 38 Chris Moreno
- 39 Chris Ortega
- 40 Chris Warner
- 41 Christian Meesey (Meesimo)
- 42 Claude Bordeleau
- 43 Colleen Doran
- 44 Conan Momchilov
- 45 Cory Walker
- 46 Craig Rousseau
- 47 Dan Brereton
- 48 Dan Norton
- 49 Dan Panosian
- 50 Dan Quiles
- 51 Daniel Cooney
- 52 Darla Ecklund
- 53 Dave Johnson
- 54 David Esbri
- 55 David Mack
- 56 David Williams
- 57 Dennis Calero
- 58 Dennis Crisostomo (9Tails)
- 59 Dietrich Smith
- 60 Doodlestan
- 61 Drew Tucker
- 62 Dusty Abell
- 63 Emily Warren
- 64 Eric Canete
- 65 Ethan Slayton
- 66 Franz Garcia
- 67 Gian Moreno
- 68 Gil Garcia
- 69 Glen Llorin
- 70 Grant Gould
- 71 Hamilton Cline
- 72 Harvey Tolibao (9Tails Studio)
- 73 Henry Liao
- 74 Humberto Ramos
- 75 James Zhang
- 76 Jason Keith Phillips
- 77 Jason LaTour
- 78 Jason Pearson
- 79 Jay Jiminez
- 80 Jeff Chandler
- 81 Jeff Poulin
- 82 Jerome Moore
- 83 Jessica Hickman
- 84 Jim Cheung
- 85 Jim Jiminez
- 86 Jim Kyle
- 87 Jim Nelson
- 88 Joaquim Dos Santos
- 89 Joe Jusko
- 90 Joe Phillips
- 91 Joey Masori
- 92 John Paul Leon
- 93 John Wycough
- 94 Jon Mills
- 95 Jonboy Meyers
- 96 Joyce Chin
- 97 Julio Naranjo (Nar)
- 98 Kate 'Red' Bradley
- 99 Ken Steacy
- 100 Kerry Gammill
- 101 Kevin McGuire
- 102 Kieron Dwyer
- 103 Leinil Yu
- 104 Louis Small Jr.
- 105 Lui Antonio (9Tails Studio)
- 106 Mark Brooks
- 107 Mark Irwin
- 108 Mark Romanoski
- 109 Mat Broome
- 110 Matt Smith
- 111 Michael Jason Paz (9Tails)
- 112 Mike Christian
- 113 Mike Miller
- 114 Nicole Goff
- 115 Noah Salonga (9Tails Studio)
- 116 Pat Carlucci
- 117 Patrick Scherberger
- 118 Paul Gutierrez
- 119 Peter Nguyen
- 120 Polo Jasso
- 121 Pop Mhan
- 122 Ragan de la Rosa
- 123 Randy Monces (9Tails Studio)
- 124 Ray Dillon
- 125 Renae De Liz
- 126 Rich Molinelli
- 127 Richard Pace
- 128 Robin Mitchell
- 129 Romulo Fajardo (9Tails Studio)
- 130 Ron Garney
- 131 Ron Spencer
- 132 Ruben Martinez
- 133 Ryan Orosco (9Tails Studio)
- 134 Ryan Ottley
- 135 Sarah Wilkinson
- 136 Scot Terry
- 137 Sean O'Reilly (Arcana Studios)
- 138 Sergio Cariello
- 139 Stan Brown
- 140 Stephen Segovia (9Tails Studio)
- 141 Steve Ellis
- 142 Steven Miller
- 143 Taki Soma
- 144 Tariq Hassan
- 145 Thomas Murphy
- 146 Thomas Wu
- 147 Tim Kane
- 148 Tim Townsend
- 149 Tom Feister
- 150 Tom Nguyen
- 151 Tom Palmer
- 152 Tony Harris
- 153 Tony Perna
- 154 Tony Shasteen
- 155 Travis Charest
- 156 Uko Smith
- 157 William Neff
- 158 Zak Plucinski

2007 Marvel Masterpieces Spider-Man

COMPLETE SET (9) 8.00 20.00
STATED ODDS 1:4

- S1 Spider-Man 1.50 4.00
- S2 Peter Parker 1.50 4.00
- S3 Venom 1.50 4.00
- S4 M.J. 1.50 4.00
- S5 The Green Goblin 1.50 4.00
- S6 Dr. Octopus 1.50 4.00
- S7 J. Jonah Jameson 1.50 4.00
- S8 The Sandman 1.50 4.00
- S9 The Lizard 1.50 4.00

2007 Marvel Masterpieces Spider-Man Foil

COMPLETE SET (9) 12.00 30.00
*FOIL: .6X TO 1.5X BASIC CARD
STATED ODDS 1:18

2007 Marvel Masterpieces Splash Page Alex Ross

COMPLETE SET (3) 3.00 8.00
STATED ODDS 1:6

- 1 History of Marvel Comics Part One 1.50 4.00
- 2 History of Marvel Comics Part Two 1.50 4.00
- 3 Alex Ross 1.50 4.00

2007 Marvel Masterpieces Splash Page Alex Ross Ash Can Box Toppers

COMPLETE SET (3) 5.00 12.00
*ASH CAN: .6X TO 1.5X BASIC CARD 2.50 6.00
STATED ODDS ONE PER BOX

2007 Marvel Masterpieces Splash Page Art Adams

COMPLETE SET (3) 3.00 8.00
STATED ODDS 1:6

- 1 Galactus Part One 1.50 4.00
- 2 Galactus Part Two 1.50 4.00
- 3 Art Adams 1.50 4.00

2007 Marvel Masterpieces Splash Page Art Adams Ash Can Case Toppers

COMPLETE SET (3)
STATED ODDS ONE PER CASE

- 1 Galactus Part One
- 2 Galactus Part Two
- 3 Art Adams

2007 Marvel Masterpieces Splash Page Drew Struzan

COMPLETE SET (3) 3.00 8.00
STATED ODDS 1:6

- 1 Marvel on Television 1.50 4.00
- 2 Marvel at the Movies 1.50 4.00
- 3 Drew Struzan 1.50 4.00

2007 Marvel Masterpieces Subcasts

COMPLETE SET (5) .75 2.00
STATED ODDS ONE PER PACK

❑ 1 Spider-Man .25 .60
❑ 2 Iron Man .25 .60
❑ 3 Ghost Rider .25 .60
❑ 4 Wolverine .25 .60
❑ 5 Captain America .25 .60

2007 Marvel Masterpieces X-Men

COMPLETE SET (9) 3.00 8.00
STATED ODDS 1:4

❑ X1 Professor X .60 1.50
❑ X2 Wolverine 1.00 2.50
❑ X3 Jean Grey .60 1.50
❑ X4 Cyclops .60 1.50
❑ X5 Storm .60 1.50
❑ X6 Iceman .60 1.50
❑ X7 Rogue .60 1.50
❑ X8 Nightcrawler .60 1.50
❑ X9 The Beast .60 1.50

2007 Marvel Masterpieces X-Men Foil

COMPLETE SET (9) 4.00 10.00
*FOIL: .5X TO 1.2X BASIC CARD
STATED ODDS 1:18

2007 The Quotable Star Trek Deep Space Nine

COMPLETE SET (108) 6.00 15.00
DST07 STATED ODDS 1:40

❑ 1 Emissary, Part I .15 .40
❑ 2 Emissary, Part I .15 .40
❑ 3 Emissary, Part I .15 .40
❑ 4 Emissary, Part I .15 .40
Emissary, Part II
❑ 5 Emissary, Part II .15 .40
❑ 6 Past Prologue .15 .40
Babel
❑ 7 Babel .15 .40
Q-Less
❑ 8 Q-Less .15 .40
❑ 9 The Passenger .15 .40
❑ 10 The Passenger .15 .40
Move Along Home
❑ 11 The Nagus .15 .40
❑ 12 The Nagus .15 .40
❑ 13 The Nagus .15 .40
The Storyteller
❑ 14 If Wishes Were Horses .15 .40
The Forsaken
❑ 15 The Forsaken .15 .40
❑ 16 In the Hands of the Prophets .15 .40
Duet
❑ 17 The Homecoming .15 .40
❑ 18 The Siege .15 .40
Cardassians
❑ 19 Melora .15 .40
Rules of Acquisition
❑ 20 Rules of Acquisition .15 .40
❑ 21 Rules of Acquisition .15 .40
❑ 22 Rules of Acquisition .15 .40
❑ 23 Necessary Evil .15 .40
Second Sight
❑ 24 The Alternate .15 .40
❑ 25 Rivals .15 .40
❑ 26 Armageddon Game .15 .40
Whispers
❑ 27 Paradise .15 .40
Shadow Play
❑ 28 Playing God .15 .40
Profit and Loss
❑ 29 Profit and Loss .15 .40
❑ 30 Blood Oath .15 .40
❑ 31 The Maquis, Part I .15 .40
❑ 32 The Maquis, Part II .15 .40
The Wire
❑ 33 The Wire .15 .40
❑ 34 Crossover .15 .40
The Collaborator
❑ 35 The Collaborator .15 .40
The Jem'Hadar
❑ 36 The Jem'Hadar .15 .40
❑ 37 The Jem'Hadar .15 .40
The Search, Part II
❑ 38 The Search, Part II .15 .40
The House of Quark
❑ 39 The House of Quark .15 .40
❑ 40 Equilibrium .15 .40
❑ 41 The Abandoned .15 .40
Civil Defense
❑ 42 Civil Defense .15 .40
Fascination
❑ 43 Past Tense, Part I .15 .40
❑ 44 Life Support .15 .40
Heart of Stone
❑ 45 Heart of Stone .15 .40
❑ 46 Destiny .15 .40
Prophet Motive
❑ 47 Improbable Cause .15 .40
❑ 48 Facets .15 .40
The Die Is Cast
❑ 49 The Adversary .15 .40
The Way of the Warrior, Part I
❑ 50 The Way of the Warrior, Part II .15 .40
❑ 51 Indiscretion .15 .40
Rejoined
❑ 52 The Sword of Kahless .15 .40
Little Green Men
❑ 53 Little Green Men .15 .40
❑ 54 Little Green Men .15 .40
Starship Down
❑ 55 Homefront .15 .40
❑ 56 Homefront .15 .40
❑ 57 Homefront .15 .40
❑ 58 Paradise Lost .15 .40
❑ 59 Crossfire .15 .40
Sons of Mogh
❑ 60 Bar Association .15 .40
❑ 61 Bar Association .15 .40
❑ 62 Bar Association .15 .40
Accession
❑ 63 Accession .15 .40
Rules of Engagement
❑ 64 Rules of Engagement .15 .40
❑ 65 Rules of Engagement .15 .40
The Muse
❑ 66 The Quickening .15 .40
To the Death
❑ 67 To the Death .15 .40
❑ 68 To the Death .15 .40
❑ 69 To the Death .15 .40
Body Parts
❑ 70 Body Parts .15 .40
❑ 71 Body Parts .15 .40
❑ 72 Body Parts .15 .40
The Ship
❑ 73 Looking for Par'Mach in All the Wrong Places .15 .40
❑ 74 Trials and Tribble-ations .15 .40
❑ 75 Trials and Tribble-ations .15 .40
❑ 76 Things Past .15 .40
The Ascent
❑ 77 The Ascent .15 .40
The Darkness and the Light
❑ 78 The Darkness and the Light .15 .40
For the Uniform
❑ 79 In Purgatory's Shadow .15 .40
By Inferno's Light
❑ 80 By Inferno's Light .15 .40
❑ 81 Doctor Bashir, I Presume .15 .40
❑ 82 Doctor Bashir, I Presume .15 .40
Ferengi Love Song
❑ 83 Ferengi Love Song .15 .40
❑ 84 Ferengi Love Song .15 .40
Children of Time
❑ 85 Empok Nor .15 .40
❑ 86 A Call to Arms .15 .40
❑ 87 A Time to Stand .15 .40
❑ 88 Sons and Daughters .15 .40
Behind the Lines
❑ 89 Favor the Bold .15 .40
The Sacrifice of Angels
❑ 90 The Sacrifice of Angels .15 .40
❑ 91 You Are Cordially Invited .15 .40
❑ 92 You Are Cordially Invited .15 .40
❑ 93 You Are Cordially Invited .15 .40
❑ 94 You Are Cordially Invited .15 .40
Resurrection
❑ 95 Resurrection .15 .40
❑ 96 Statistical Probabilities .15 .40
The Magnificent Ferengi
❑ 97 The Magnificent Ferengi .15 .40
❑ 98 Waltz .15 .40
Change of Heart
❑ 99 In the Pale Moonlight .15 .40
❑ 100 His Way .15 .40
Valiant
❑ 101 Time's Orphan .15 .40
The Sound of Her Voice
❑ 102 Tears of the Prophets .15 .40
❑ 103 Afterimage .15 .40
❑ 104 Afterimage .15 .40
❑ 105 Inter Arma Enim Silent Leges .15 .40
The Siege of AR-558
❑ 106 The Dogs of War .15 .40
What You Leave Behind
❑ 107 What You Leave Behind .15 .40
❑ 108 What You Leave Behind .15 .40
❑ DST07 DS9 Action Figure Promo

2007 The Quotable Star Trek Deep Space Nine Autographs

STATED ODDS ONE PER BOX
RB ODDS ONE PER 3-CASE PURCHASE
L (LIMITED): 300-500 CARDS
VL (VERY LIMITED): 200-300 CARDS

❑ AE Aron Eisenberg L
❑ AK Andrew Koenig
❑ AS Armin Shimerman L
❑ CL Cirroc Lofton L
❑ JH Jennifer Hetrick VL
❑ KC K.Callan
❑ LV Lark Voorhies
❑ MG Max Grodenchik L
❑ NV Nana Visitor L
❑ RA Rene Auberjonois L
❑ RB Rick Berman 3CI
❑ TF Terry Farrell VL
❑ AB1 Adrienne Barbeau
❑ AB2 Avery Brooks VL
❑ JD1 James Darren L
❑ JD2 John De Lancie VL

2007 The Quotable Star Trek Deep Space Nine Comic Books

COMPLETE SET (9)
STATED ODDS 1:35

❑ CB1 Nov '96 Cover
❑ CB2 Dec '96 Cover
❑ CB3 Jan '97 Cover
❑ CB4 Feb '97 Cover
❑ CB5 Mar '97 Cover
❑ CB6 Apr '97 Cover
❑ CB7 May '97 Cover
❑ CB8 Aug '97 Cover
❑ CB9 Sept '97 Cover

2007 The Quotable Star Trek Deep Space Nine Costumes

STATED ODDS TWO PER BOX
C22 ODDS ONE PER COLLECTORS ALBUM
AC1 ODDS ONE PER 6-CASE PURCHASE

❑ C1 Capt. Benjamin Sisko
❑ C2 Col. Kira Nerys
❑ C3 Security Chief Odo
❑ C4 Lt. Comm. Jadzia Dax
❑ C5 Lt. Commander Worf
❑ C6 CPO Miles O'Brien
❑ C7 Dr. Julian Bashir
❑ C8 Lt. Ezri Dax
❑ C9 Capt. Benjamin Sisko
❑ C10 Dr. Noah
❑ C11 Capt. Benjamin Sisko
❑ C12 Lt. Comm. Jadzia Dax
❑ C13 Lt. Comm. Jadzia Dax
❑ C14 Dulmer
❑ C15 Lt. Comm. Worf
❑ C16 Security Chief Odo
❑ C17 Waitress
❑ C18 Waitress
❑ C19 Quark
❑ C20 Promenade Banner
❑ C21 Promenade Banner
❑ C22 Grand Nagus Zek ALBUM
❑ AC1 Terry Farrell AU
as Lt. Comm. Jadzia Dax/ (issued as 6-case incentive)

2007 The Quotable Star Trek Deep Space Nine SketchaFEX Sketches

STATED ODDS ONE PER CASE

❑ 1 Dan Day
Runabout
❑ 2 Dan Day
U.S.S. Defiant
❑ 3 David Day
Deep Space Nine
❑ 4 David Day
DS9 and Runabout

2007 The Quotable Star Trek Deep Space Nine Starfleets Finest

COMPLETE SET
STATED ODDS 1:120
STATED PRINT RUN 399 SER. #'d SETS

❑ F1 Captain Benjamin Sisko
❑ F2 Colonel Kira Nerys
❑ F3 Lt. Commander Jadzia Dax
❑ F4 Lt. Commander Worf
❑ F5 Security Chief Odo
❑ F6 Chief Petty Officer Miles O'Brien
❑ F7 Dr. Julian Bashir
❑ F8 Quark
❑ F9 Lt. Ezri Dax
❑ F10 Jake Sisko
(issued as Rittenhouse Reward)

2007 The Quotable Star Trek Deep Space Nine The Final Frontier

COMPLETE SET (9)
STATED ODDS 1:8

❑ DSN1 Founder Leader
Weyoun
❑ DSN2 Ben Sisko
Jake Sisko
❑ DSN3 Worf
Jadzia Dax
❑ DSN4 Gowron
Jem'Hadar Soldier
❑ DSN5 Defiant
❑ DSN6 Kira Nerys
Julian Bashir
❑ DSN7 Jem'Hadar Soldier
Tal'Aura
❑ DSN8 Garak
Quark
❑ DSN9 Odo
Miles O'Brien

2007 The Quotable Star Trek Deep Space Nine TV Guide Covers

COMPLETE SET (9)
STATED ODDS 1:20

❑ TV1 Sisko
Picard/January 2-8, 1993
❑ TV2 Quark
July 24-30, 1993
❑ TV3 Commander Benjamin Sisko
January 15-21, 1994
❑ TV4 Sisko
Worf/October 7-13, 1995
❑ TV5 Lt. Commander Jadzia Dax
November 8-14, 1997
❑ TV6 Kira
Odo/May 29-June 4, 1999
❑ TV7 Captain Benjamin Sisko
May 29-June 4, 1999
❑ TV8 Worf
Ezra/Quark/May 29-June 4, 1999
❑ TV9 Bashir
O'Brien/Jake/May 29-June 4, 1999

2007 The Seeker The Dark is Rising

COMPLETE SET (72) 4.00 10.00
CL1 ISSUED AS CASE TOPPER

❑ 1 The Seeker The Dark is Rising .10 .30
❑ 2 Will Stanton .10 .30
❑ 3 Merriman Lyon and Miss Greythorne .10 .30
❑ 4 Dawson and Old George .10 .30
❑ 5 The Walker .10 .30
❑ 6 Gwen, Robin and Paul Stanton .10 .30
❑ 7 James Stanton .10 .30
❑ 8 Max Stanton .10 .30
❑ 9 John and Mary Stanton .10 .30
❑ 10 The Rider .10 .30
❑ 11 Maggie Barnes .10 .30
❑ 12 The Doctor .10 .30
❑ 13 Sign of Stone .10 .30
❑ 14 Sign of Bronze .10 .30
❑ 15 Sign of Iron .10 .30
❑ 16 Sign of Wood .10 .30
❑ 17 Sign of Fire .10 .30
❑ 18 Sign of Water .10 .30
❑ 19 Family of Light .10 .30
❑ 20 Missing Twin .10 .30
❑ 21 Prison of Snow .10 .30
❑ 22 Maker of Signs .10 .30
❑ 23 Thesis .10 .30
❑ 24 The Stantons Return .10 .30
❑ 25 Ancient Foe .10 .30
❑ 26 Souls and Signs .10 .30
❑ 27 Eternal Guardians .10 .30
❑ 28 Meet the Stantons .10 .30
❑ 29 The Invitation .10 .30
❑ 30 Guess Who! .10 .30
❑ 31 Family Secrets .10 .30
❑ 32 Birthday Boy .10 .30
❑ 33 Busted .10 .30
❑ 34 Horror in Uniform .10 .30
❑ 35 Nowhere to Turn .10 .30
❑ 36 Crush .10 .30
❑ 37 Enter the Dark .10 .30
❑ 38 Surprise Rescue .10 .30
❑ 39 You Are the Seeker .10 .30
❑ 40 The Book of Signs .10 .30
❑ 41 Visions of Dark .10 .30
❑ 42 The Physics of Doom .10 .30
❑ 43 Doctor Darkness .10 .30
❑ 44 Lost Twin .10 .30
❑ 45 Finding the First Sign .10 .30
❑ 46 New Powers .10 .30
❑ 47 Mysterious Thief .10 .30
❑ 48 Face-Off in 1290 .10 .30
❑ 49 Power of Light! .10 .30
❑ 50 Hissing Death .10 .30
❑ 51 Another Thomas .10 .30
❑ 52 Maker of the Signs .10 .30
❑ 53 Maggie's Little Secret .10 .30
❑ 54 Not a Superhero .10 .30
❑ 55 Loosing It .10 .30
❑ 56 Help from Gwen .10 .30
❑ 57 Tell No One .10 .30
❑ 58 Merriman's Lecture .10 .30
❑ 59 Dark Max .10 .30
❑ 60 Brother vs. Brother .10 .30
❑ 61 Sign of the Champion .10 .30
❑ 62 The Dark Attacks .10 .30
❑ 63 Professor Stanton's Guilt .10 .30
❑ 64 Lost Soul .10 .30
❑ 65 Deadly Cold .10 .30
❑ 66 The Battle Begins .10 .30
❑ 67 Temptress and Victim .10 .30
❑ 68 Whole at Last .10 .30
❑ 69 Darkness Rushes In .10 .30
❑ 70 I Am the Light .10 .30
❑ 71 The Light Prevails .10 .30
❑ 72 Checklist .10 .30
❑ CL1 Unlikely Warrior/(issued as case topper) 3.00 8.00

2007 The Seeker The Dark is Rising Autographs

STATED ODDS ONE PER BOX

❑ AAL Alexander Ludwig
❑ AAW Amelia Warner
❑ ADB Drew Tyler Bell
❑ AEE Edmund Entin
❑ AEL Emma Lockhart
❑ AFC Frances Conroy
❑ AGE Gary Entin
❑ AGS Gregory Smith
❑ AIM Ian McShane
❑ AJH John Benjamin Hickey
❑ AWC Wendy Crewson

2007 The Seeker The Dark is Rising Eternal Enemies

COMPLETE SET (6)
STATED ODDS 1:17

❑ E1 Sign Seeker
❑ E2 Dark Rider
❑ E3 Guardians of Light
❑ E4 Minions of Dark
❑ E5 Unwilling Sacrifice
❑ E6 Betrayer of Light

2007 The Seeker The Dark is Rising Hidden

COMPLETE SET (3)
STATED ODDS 1:23

❑ H1 Symbols
❑ H2 Identity
❑ H3 Family Tree

2007 The Seeker The Dark is Rising Pieceworks

STATED ODDS ONE PER BOX

❑ PW1 Will Stanton Sweater
❑ PW2 The Rider Cloak
❑ PW3 Max Stanton Jacket
❑ PW4 Maggie Barnes Scarf
❑ PW5 Miss Greythorne Jacket
❑ PW6 The Walker Scarf

2007 The Seeker The Dark is Rising Signs of Light Puzzle

COMPLETE SET (9)
STATED ODDS 1:1

❑ S1 Signs of Light
❑ S2 Signs of Light
❑ S3 Signs of Light
❑ S4 Signs of Light
❑ S5 Signs of Light
❑ S6 Signs of Light
❑ S7 Signs of Light
❑ S8 Signs of Light
❑ S9 Signs of Light

2007 Shrek the Third

COMPLETE SET (72) 4.00 10.00
CL1 STATED ODDS ONE PER HOBBY CASE

❑ 1 Title Card .10 .30
❑ 2 Shrek .10 .30
❑ 3 Fiona .10 .30
❑ 4 Donkey .10 .30
❑ 5 Puss In Boots .10 .30
❑ 6 Artie .10 .30
❑ 7 Merlin .10 .30
❑ 8 Queen Lillian .10 .30
❑ 9 King Harold .10 .30
❑ 10 Prince Charming .10 .30
❑ 11 Lancelot .10 .30
❑ 12 Evil Cohorts .10 .30
❑ 13 The Nightly Brawl .10 .30
❑ 14 Sleeping Beauty .10 .30
❑ 15 Snow White .10 .30
❑ 16 Cinderella .10 .30
❑ 17 Rapunzel .10 .30
❑ 18 Fiona .10 .30
❑ 19 Romance .10 .30
❑ 20 Food .10 .30
❑ 21 Antics .10 .30
❑ 22 Welcome! .10 .30
❑ 23 Athletics .10 .30
❑ 24 School Spirit .10 .30
❑ 25 Popular... Or Not .10 .30
❑ 26 Safety First .10 .30
❑ 27 To Drive .10 .30
❑ 28 Consider The Cookie .10 .30
❑ 29 Dough .10 .30
❑ 30 Good Times .10 .30
❑ 31 Welcome To The Swamp .10 .30
❑ 32 Worchester High .10 .30
❑ 33 Far Far Away .10 .30
❑ 34 Royal Courtyard .10 .30
❑ 35 Gotta Love Them Wide Open Spaces .10 .30
❑ 36 Find Your Happily Ever After .10 .30
❑ 37 Not So Charming .10 .30
❑ 38 Mommy's Little Angel .10 .30
❑ 39 Executive Morning .10 .30
❑ 40 Official Disasters .10 .30
❑ 41 Royal Makeover .10 .30
❑ 42 Grand Entrance .10 .30
❑ 43 Party Pandemonium .10 .30
❑ 44 The King Is Gone .10 .30
❑ 45 Final Farewell .10 .30
❑ 46 The Poison Apple .10 .30
❑ 47 Charming Army .10 .30
❑ 48 The Big Goodbyes .10 .30
❑ 49 Breaking The News .10 .30
❑ 50 Wait, Fiona's What .10 .30
❑ 51 High School Headaches .10 .30
❑ 52 Where's This Artie Guy .10 .30
❑ 53 Artie's Sword Trick .10 .30
❑ 54 Baby Shower Fun .10 .30
❑ 55 Broom Troops .10 .30
❑ 56 Nope, No Princess Here .10 .30
❑ 57 Not King Material .10 .30
❑ 58 Right Up Word On .10 .30
❑ 59 Something In Common .10 .30
❑ 60 In The Catacombs .10 .30
❑ 61 Cruel Betrayal .10 .30
❑ 62 A Zoomy Zoom Zoom .10 .30
❑ 63 Go Go Away .10 .30
❑ 64 It Was A Lie .10 .30
❑ 65 Everybody Behind Bars .10 .30
❑ 66 Royalty To The Rescue .10 .30
❑ 67 Artie Reconsiders .10 .30
❑ 68 Let's Split Up .10 .30
❑ 69 Operation: Break In .10 .30
❑ 70 Is This The End .10 .30
❑ 71 Artie Saves The Day .10 .30
❑ 72 Checklist .10 .30
❑ CL1 Ogre Love 3.00 8.00

2007 Shrek the Third Fiona's Fairytale Five

COMPLETE SET (5)
STATED ODDS 1:17

❑ F1 Fiona
❑ F2 Cinderella
❑ F3 Snow White
❑ F4 Sleeping Beauty
❑ F5 Rapunzel

2007 Shrek the Third Raul's Make-Up Tips

COMPLETE SET (3)
STATED ODDS ONE PER HOBBY BOX

❑ BL1 Green Canvas
❑ BL2 Femininity
❑ BL3 Ready to Party Hearty

2007 Shrek the Third Scratch and Stink Gold

COMPLETE SET (6)
STATED ODDS 1:5 HOBBY

❑ SH1 Shrek
❑ SH2 Fiona
❑ SH3 Puss In Boots
❑ SH4 Donkey
❑ SH5 Gingy
❑ SH6 Pinocchio

2007 Shrek the Third Scratch and Stink Green

COMPLETE SET (6)
STATED ODDS 1:1 RETAIL

❑ S1 Shrek
❑ S2 Fiona
❑ S3 Puss In Boots
❑ S4 Donkey
❑ S5 Gingy
❑ S6 Pinocchio

2007 Shrek the Third Sketches

STATED ODDS ONE PER HOBBY BOX

❑ SCC Cynthia Cummens/288
❑ SCF Chad Frye/133
❑ SCM Chris Moreno/156
❑ SCS Cat Staggs/195
❑ SLK Lee Kohse/338
❑ SMD Mark Dos Santos/272
❑ SMW Matt Wendt/316
❑ SRD Ray Dillon/261
❑ SRL Renae De Liz/331
❑ STB Taylor Bills/323
❑ STF Tess Fowler/318
❑ STR Tone Rodriguez/328

2007 Shrek the Third Tattoos

COMPLETE SET (6)
STATED ODDS 1:2 RETAIL

❑ T1 Shrek
❑ T2 I'm All Ears
❑ T3 Happily Ever After
❑ T4 Holy Guaca-Moly
❑ T5 I'm Into Mythical Creatures
❑ T6 Ogres Rock

2007 Six Million Dollar Man Color Autograph Expansion

MAJORS/WAGNER AUTO ISSUED AS 2-SET INCENTIVE

❑ A14 Lee Majors
❑ A15 Richard Anderson
❑ A16 Lindsay Wagner
❑ A21 Alan Oppenheimer
❑ DA1 Lee Majors
Richard Anderson
❑ DA2 Lee Majors
Lindsay Wagner/ (issued as 2-set incentive)

2007 Smallville Season Six

COMPLETE SET (90) 5.00 12.00

❑ 1 Title Card .15 .40
❑ 2 Clark Kent .15 .40
❑ 3 Lana Lang .15 .40
❑ 4 Lex Luthor .15 .40
❑ 5 Lois Lane .15 .40
❑ 6 Chloe Sullivan .15 .40
❑ 7 Martha Kent .15 .40
❑ 8 Jimmy Olsen .15 .40
❑ 9 Lionel Luthor .15 .40
❑ 10 Oliver Queen .15 .40
Green Arrow
❑ 11 John Jones .15 .40
Martian Manhunter
❑ 12 Arthur Curry .15 .40
Aquaman
❑ 13 Bart Allen .15 .40
Impulse
❑ 14 Victor Stone .15 .40
Cyborg
❑ 15 Clark Kent .15 .40
The Man Of Steel
❑ 16 Lois And Oliver .15 .40
❑ 17 Lois And Green Arrow .15 .40
❑ 18 Lois And Clark .15 .40
❑ 19 Lana And Lex .15 .40
❑ 20 Lana's Pregnant .15 .40
❑ 21 The Proposal .15 .40
❑ 22 The Ex .15 .40
❑ 23 Rehearsal Dinner .15 .40
❑ 24 The Wedding Day .15 .40
❑ 25 Lionel's Threat .15 .40

MODERN ERA NON-SPORTS

- 26 The Marriage .15 .40
- 27 Lies .15 .40
- 28 Chloe Sullivan: Reporter .15 .40
- 29 Planet's Best .15 .40
- 30 Front Page News .15 .40
- 31 Lois Lane: Reporter .15 .40
- 32 Anything To Get The Story .15 .40
- 33 First Big Expose .15 .40
- 34 Jimmy Olsen: Photographer .15 .40
- 35 His Pics: Her Words .15 .40
- 36 First Assignment .15 .40
- 37 Clark Kent Learns To Breathe .15 .40
- 38 Chloe Sullivan On The Wall Of Weird .15 .40
- 39 Martha Kent Goes To Washington .15 .40
- 40 Lex's Obsession .15 .40
- 41 Meteor Freaks .15 .40
- 42 Phantoms .15 .40
- 43 Experimentation .15 .40
- 44 Oliver Vs Lex .15 .40
- 45 A Private Army .15 .40
- 46 All In The Family .15 .40
- 47 Kneel Before Zod .15 .40
- 48 Bless You! .15 .40
- 49 Return To Normalcy .15 .40
- 50 Flower Power .15 .40
- 51 Boyfriend In A Bind .15 .40
- 52 First Meeting .15 .40
- 53 Wanted: The Green Arrow .15 .40
- 54 It's All Fun And Games... .15 .40
- 55 ...Until Someone Gets Hurt .15 .40
- 56 Bad Game .15 .40
- 57 Battle For The Fortress .15 .40
- 58 Green Arrow – Dead?!? .15 .40
- 59 A Dangerous Habit .15 .40
- 60 Can You See Me Now? .15 .40
- 61 Help From Above .15 .40
- 62 Dangerous Escape .15 .40
- 63 Freak Farm .15 .40
- 64 Juicy Gossip .15 .40
- 65 Washed Away .15 .40
- 66 Run For Your Life .15 .40
- 67 Saving The World .15 .40
- 68 Have You Lost Your Mind? .15 .40
- 69 Mental Prison Break .15 .40
- 70 Revelations? .15 .40
- 71 Scorned Lover .15 .40
- 72 The Feeling Of Bing Watched .15 .40
- 73 Like Old Times .15 .40
- 74 Seeing Without Eyes .15 .40
- 75 Freak Tracking .15 .40
- 76 Wedding Day Jitters .15 .40
- 77 A Loveless Marriage .15 .40
- 78 Getting The Dirt .15 .40
- 79 Fight Of His Life .15 .40
- 80 Mother Knows Best .15 .40
- 81 Favorite Daughter .15 .40
- 82 Trapped Underground .15 .40
- 83 With Friends Like These... .15 .40
- 84 Movie-Like Mystery .15 .40
- 85 Dreaming Of Reality .15 .40
- 86 A New Generation Of Soldier .15 .40
- 87 Stopping A One-Man Army .15 .40
- 88 The Dam Breaks .15 .40
- 89 Bizzaro .15 .40
- 90 Checklist .15 .40
- CL1 Wrath of Zod/ (issued as case topper) 8.00 20.00

2007 Smallville Season Six Archer's Quest

COMPLETE SET (3) 4.00 10.00
STATED ODDS 1:35

- AQ1 No Man's An Island 2.50 6.00
- AQ2 Billion Dollar Hero 2.50 6.00
- AQ3 Fighting For Justice 2.50 6.00

2007 Smallville Season Six Autographs

STATED ODDS 1:36

- A46 Justin Hartley 30.00 60.00
- A47 Aaron Ashmore 8.00 20.00
- A48 Lucas Grabeel 8.00 20.00
- A49 Tori Spelling 12.00 30.00
- A50 Tahmoh Penikett 8.00 20.00
- A51 Greyston Holt 8.00 20.00
- A52 John Novak 8.00 20.00
- A53 Amber McDonald 8.00 20.00
- A54 Tyler Posey 8.00 20.00
- AJA Justin Hartley 40.00 80.00
  Kyle Gallner
- AJB Alan Ritchson 30.00 60.00
  Lee Thompson Young

2007 Smallville Season Six Justice

COMPLETE SET (9) 5.00 12.00
STATED ODDS 1:11

- J1 Justice 1.50 4.00
- J2 Justice 1.50 4.00
- J3 Justice 1.50 4.00
- J4 Justice 1.50 4.00
- J5 Justice 1.50 4.00
- J6 Justice 1.50 4.00
- J7 Justice 1.50 4.00
- J8 Justice 1.50 4.00
- J9 Justice 1.50 4.00

2007 Smallville Season Six Pieceworks

STATED ODDS 1:36

- PW1 Tom Welling 12.00 30.00
- PW2 Kristin Kreuk 12.00 30.00
- PW3 Michael Rosenbaum 10.00 25.00
- PW4 Allison Mack 12.00 30.00
- PW5 Erica Durance 20.00 40.00
- PW6 Justin Hartley 12.00 30.00
- PW7 Aaron Ashmore 8.00 20.00
- PW8 Kyle Gallner 8.00 20.00
- PW9 Lynda Carter 12.00 30.00
- PW10 Tori Spelling 8.00 20.00
- PW11 Phil Morris 8.00 20.00

2007 Smallville Season Six The Powers That Be

COMPLETE SET (6) 6.00 15.00
STATED ODDS 1:17

- PB1 Strength 2.00 5.00
- PB2 Speed 2.00 5.00
- PB3 Heat Vision 2.00 5.00
- PB4 X-Ray Vision 2.00 5.00
- PB5 Breath 2.00 5.00
- PB6 Hearing 2.00 5.00

2007 Spider-Man 3

COMPLETE SET (79) 4.00 10.00

- 1 Title Card .10 .30
- 2 Movie Plot Card .10 .30
- 3 Movie Plot Card .10 .30
- 4 Movie Plot Card .10 .30
- 5 Movie Plot Card .10 .30
- 6 Movie Plot Card .10 .30
- 7 Movie Plot Card .10 .30
- 8 Movie Plot Card .10 .30
- 9 Movie Plot Card .10 .30
- 10 Movie Plot Card .10 .30
- 11 Movie Plot Card .10 .30
- 12 Movie Plot Card .10 .30
- 13 Movie Plot Card .10 .30
- 14 Movie Plot Card .10 .30
- 15 Movie Plot Card .10 .30
- 16 Movie Plot Card .10 .30
- 17 Movie Plot Card .10 .30
- 18 Movie Plot Card .10 .30
- 19 Movie Plot Card .10 .30
- 20 Movie Plot Card .10 .30
- 21 Movie Plot Card .10 .30
- 22 Movie Plot Card .10 .30
- 23 Movie Plot Card .10 .30
- 24 Movie Plot Card .10 .30
- 25 Movie Plot Card .10 .30
- 26 Movie Plot Card .10 .30
- 27 Movie Plot Card .10 .30
- 28 Movie Plot Card .10 .30
- 29 Movie Plot Card .10 .30
- 30 Movie Plot Card .10 .30
- 31 Movie Plot Card .10 .30
- 32 Movie Plot Card .10 .30
- 33 Movie Plot Card .10 .30
- 34 Movie Plot Card .10 .30
- 35 Movie Plot Card .10 .30
- 36 Movie Plot Card .10 .30
- 37 Movie Plot Card .10 .30
- 38 Movie Plot Card .10 .30
- 39 Movie Plot Card .10 .30
- 40 Movie Plot Card .10 .30
- 41 Movie Plot Card .10 .30
- 42 Movie Plot Card .10 .30
- 43 Movie Plot Card .10 .30
- 44 Movie Plot Card .10 .30
- 45 Movie Plot Card .10 .30
- 46 Movie Plot Card .10 .30
- 47 Movie Plot Card .10 .30
- 48 Movie Plot Card .10 .30
- 49 Movie Plot Card .10 .30
- 50 Movie Plot Card .10 .30
- 51 Movie Plot Card .10 .30
- 52 Movie Plot Card .10 .30
- 53 Movie Plot Card .10 .30
- 54 Movie Plot Card .10 .30
- 55 Movie Plot Card .10 .30
- 56 Movie Plot Card .10 .30
- 57 Movie Plot Card .10 .30
- 58 Movie Plot Card .10 .30
- 59 Movie Plot Card .10 .30
- 60 Movie Plot Card .10 .30
- 61 Movie Plot Card .10 .30
- 62 Movie Plot Card .10 .30
- 63 Movie Plot Card .10 .30
- 64 Movie Plot Card .10 .30
- 65 Movie Plot Card .10 .30
- 66 Movie Plot Card .10 .30
- 67 Movie Plot Card .10 .30
- 68 Movie Plot Card .10 .30
- 69 Movie Plot Card .10 .30
- 70 Movie Plot Card .10 .30
- BTS1 Behind The Scenes .10 .30
- BTS2 Behind The Scenes .10 .30
- BTS3 Behind The Scenes .10 .30
- BTS4 Behind The Scenes .10 .30
- BTS5 Behind The Scenes .10 .30
- BTS6 Behind The Scenes .10 .30
- BTS7 Behind The Scenes .10 .30
- BTS8 Behind The Scenes .10 .30
- C1 Checklist .10 .30

2007 Spider-Man 3 Autographs

STATED ODDS 1:20
L (LIMITED): 300-500 COPIES
VL (VERY LIMITED): 200-300 COPIES

- 1 Aasif Madvi 6.00 15.00
- 2 Avi Arad VL 25.00 50.00
- 3 Bill Nunn 6.00 15.00
- 4 Brent Briscoe 6.00 15.00
- 5 Bruce Campbell L
- 6 Dylan Baker 12.00 25.00
- 7 Elizabeth Banks L
- 8 Elyse Dinh 6.00 15.00
- 9 Hal Sparks 12.00 25.00
- 10 J.K. Simmons 12.00 25.00
- 11 Jack Betts 6.00 15.00
- 12 James Franco L 50.00 100.00
- 13 Jayce Bartok 6.00 15.00
- 14 Joe Manganiello 6.00 15.00
- 15 Larry Joshua 6.00 15.00
- 16 Lucy Lawless VL 50.00 100.00
- 17 Mageina Tovah 25.00 50.00
- 18 Stan Lee 40.00 80.00
- 19 Tobey Maguire VL 125.00 200.00
- 20 Willem Dafoe L 40.00 80.00

2007 Spider-Man 3 Black Costume

COMPLETE SET (6) 8.00 20.00
STATED ODDS 1:40

- B1 Spider-Man 2.50 6.00
- B2 Spider-Man 2.50 6.00
- B3 Spider-Man 2.50 6.00
- B4 Spider-Man 2.50 6.00
- B5 Spider-Man 2.50 6.00
- B6 Spider-Man 2.50 6.00

2007 Spider-Man 3 Memorabilia

STATED ODDS ONE PER CASE
AU: TWO CASE DEALER INCENTIVE

- NNO J.K. Simmons Tie AU 30.00 60.00
- NNO J. Jonah Jameson Shirt 20.00 40.00
- NNO J. Jonah Jameson Tie 20.00 40.00

2007 Spider-Man 3 Red/Blue

COMPLETE SET (6) 8.00 20.00
STATED ODDS 1:40

- R1 Spider-Man 2.50 6.00
- R2 Spider-Man 2.50 6.00
- R3 Spider-Man 2.50 6.00
- R4 Spider-Man 2.50 6.00
- R5 Spider-Man 2.50 6.00
- R6 Spider-Man 2.50 6.00

2007 Spider-Man 3 Sketches

SKETCHES: THREE CASE DEALER INCENTIVE

- NNO Steven Miller
- NNO Jim Kyle
- NNO Brian Kong
- NNO Sarah Wilkinson
- NNO Jonathan D. Gordon
- NNO Cat Staggs

2007 Spider-Man 3 The Goblin

COMPLETE SET (5) 6.00 15.00
STATED ODDS 1:40

- G1 Goblin 2.50 6.00
- G2 Goblin 2.50 6.00
- G3 Goblin 2.50 6.00
- G4 Goblin 2.50 6.00
- G5 Goblin 2.50 6.00

2007 Spider-Man 3 The Sandman

COMPLETE SET (5) 6.00 15.00
STATED ODDS 1:40

- S1 Sandman 2.50 6.00
- S2 Sandman 2.50 6.00
- S3 Sandman 2.50 6.00
- S4 Sandman 2.50 6.00
- S5 Sandman 2.50 6.00

2007 Spider-Man 3 Venom

COMPLETE SET (5) 6.00 15.00
STATED ODDS 1:40

- V1 Venom 2.50 6.00
- V2 Venom 2.50 6.00
- V3 Venom 2.50 6.00
- V4 Venom 2.50 6.00
- V5 Venom 2.50 6.00

2007 Sports Illustrated Swimsuit

COMPLETE SET (100) 8.00 20.00

- 1 Aline Nakashima .15 .40
- 2 Aline Nakashima .15 .40
- 3 Aline Nakashima .15 .40
- 4 Ana Beatriz Barros .15 .40
- 5 Ana Beatriz Barros .15 .40
- 6 Ana Beatriz Barros .15 .40
- 7 Ana Paula Araujo .15 .40
- 8 Ana Paula Araujo .15 .40
- 9 Ana Paula Araujo .15 .40
- 10 Ana Paula Araujo .15 .40
- 11 Anne V .15 .40
- 12 Anne V .15 .40
- 13 Anne V .15 .40
- 14 Anne V .15 .40
- 15 Anne V .15 .40
- 16 Anne V .15 .40
- 17 Anne V .15 .40
- 18 Anne V .15 .40
- 19 Anne V .15 .40
- 20 Anne V .15 .40
- 21 Bar Refaeli .40 1.00
- 22 Bar Refaeli .40 1.00
- 23 Bar Refaeli .40 1.00
- 24 Bar Refaeli .40 1.00
- 25 Bar Refaeli .40 1.00
- 26 Bar Refaeli .40 1.00
- 27 Bar Refaeli .40 1.00
- 28 Bar Refaeli .40 1.00
- 29 Bar Refaeli .40 1.00
- 30 Bar Refaeli .40 1.00
- 31 Brooklyn Decker .60 1.50
- 32 Brooklyn Decker .60 1.50
- 33 Brooklyn Decker .60 1.50
- 34 Brooklyn Decker .60 1.50
- 35 Brooklyn Decker .60 1.50
- 36 Daniella Sarahyba .15 .40
- 37 Daniella Sarahyba .15 .40
- 38 Daniella Sarahyba .15 .40
- 39 Fernanda Motta .15 .40
- 40 Fernanda Motta .15 .40
- 41 Fernanda Motta .15 .40
- 42 Fernanda Tavares .15 .40
- 43 Fernanda Tavares .15 .40
- 44 Irina Shayk .15 .40
- 45 Irina Shayk .15 .40
- 46 Irina Shayk .15 .40
- 47 Julie Henderson .15 .40
- 48 Julie Henderson .15 .40
- 49 Julie Henderson .15 .40
- 50 Julie Henderson .15 .40
- 51 Julie Henderson .15 .40
- 52 Julie Henderson .15 .40
- 53 Julie Henderson .15 .40
- 54 Marisa Miller .60 1.50
- 55 Marisa Miller .60 1.50
- 56 Marisa Miller .60 1.50
- 57 Marisa Miller .60 1.50
- 58 Marisa Miller .60 1.50
- 59 Marisa Miller .60 1.50
- 60 Marisa Miller .60 1.50
- 61 Marisa Miller .60 1.50
- 62 Marisa Miller .60 1.50
- 63 Marisa Miller .60 1.50
- 64 Marisa Miller .60 1.50
- 65 Oluchi Onweagba .15 .40
- 66 Oluchi Onweagba .15 .40
- 67 Oluchi Onweagba .15 .40
- 68 Oluchi Onweagba .15 .40
- 69 Oluchi Onweagba .15 .40
- 70 Oluchi Onweagba .15 .40
- 71 Oluchi Onweagba .15 .40
- 72 Raica Oliveira .15 .40
- 73 Raica Oliveira .15 .40
- 74 Selita Ebanks .15 .40
- 75 Selita Ebanks .15 .40
- 76 Selita Ebanks .15 .40
- 77 Selita Ebanks .15 .40
- 78 Selita Ebanks .15 .40
- 79 Selita Ebanks .15 .40
- 80 Selita Ebanks .15 .40
- 81 Selita Ebanks .15 .40
- 82 Tori Praver .15 .40
- 83 Tori Praver .15 .40
- 84 Tori Praver .15 .40
- 85 Tori Praver .15 .40
- 86 Tori Praver .15 .40
- 87 Tori Praver .15 .40
- 88 Yesica Toscanini .15 .40
- 89 Yesica Toscanini .15 .40
- 90 Jessica White .15 .40
- 91 Jessica White .15 .40
- 92 Jessica White .15 .40
- 93 Jessica White .15 .40
- 94 Jessica White .15 .40
- 95 Jessica White .15 .40
- 96 Jessica White .15 .40
- 97 Preview .15 .40
- 98 Preview .15 .40
- 99 Checklist .15 .40
- 100 Checklist .15 .40

2007 Sports Illustrated Swimsuit Printing Plates Black

STATED PRINT RUN 1 SER. #'d SET
UNPRICED DUE TO SCARCITY

2007 Sports Illustrated Swimsuit Printing Plates Cyan

STATED PRINT RUN 1 SER. #'d SET
UNPRICED DUE TO SCARCITY

2007 Sports Illustrated Swimsuit Printing Plates Magenta

STATED PRINT RUN 1 SER. #'d SET
UNPRICED DUE TO SCARCITY

2007 Sports Illustrated Swimsuit Printing Plates Yellow

STATED PRINT RUN 1 SER. #'d SET
UNPRICED DUE TO SCARCITY

2007 Sports Illustrated Swimsuit Autographs

STATED ODDS 1:18

- 1 Ana Paula Araujo 15.00 30.00
- 2 Anne V 15.00 30.00
- 3 Bar Refaeli
- 4 Brooklyn Decker
- 5 Daniella Sarahyba 15.00 30.00
- 6 Fernanda Motta 15.00 30.00
- 7 Irina Shayk 30.00 60.00
- 8 Julie Henderson 15.00 30.00
- 9 Tori Praver 20.00 40.00
- 10 Yamila Diaz-Rahi 20.00 40.00

2007 Sports Illustrated Swimsuit Beyonce

COMPLETE SET (10) 15.00 30.00
STATED ODDS 1:4

- 1 Beyonce Knowles 2.50 8.00
- 2 Beyonce Knowles 2.50 6.00
- 3 Beyonce Knowles 2.50 6.00
- 4 Beyonce Knowles 2.50 6.00
- 5 Beyonce Knowles 2.50 6.00
- 6 Beyonce Knowles 2.50 6.00
- 7 Beyonce Knowles 2.50 6.00
- 8 Beyonce Knowles 2.50 6.00
- 9 Beyonce Knowles 2.50 6.00
- 10 Beyonce Knowles 2.50 6.00

2007 Sports Illustrated Swimsuit Rookies

COMPLETE SET (10) 8.00 20.00
STATED ODDS 1:4

- 1 Ana Paula Araujo 1.25 3.00
- 2 Bar Refaeli 2.00 5.00
- 3 Irina Shayk 1.25 3.00
- 4 Julie Henderson 1.25 3.00
- 5 Raica Oliveira 1.25 3.00
- 6 Selita Ebanks 1.25 3.00
- 7 Tori Praver 1.25 3.00
- 8 Heidi Klum 2.00 5.00
- 9 Kathy Ireland 2.00 5.00
- 10 Stacy Williams 1.25 3.00

2007 Sports Illustrated Swimsuit Rookies Printing Plates Black

STATED PRINT RUN 1 SER. #'d SET
UNPRICED DUE TO SCARCITY

2007 Sports Illustrated Swimsuit Rookies Printing Plates Cyan

STATED PRINT RUN 1 SER. #'d SET
UNPRICED DUE TO SCARCITY

2007 Sports Illustrated Swimsuit Rookies Printing Plates Magenta

STATED PRINT RUN 1 SER. #'d SET
UNPRICED DUE TO SCARCITY

2007 Sports Illustrated Swimsuit Rookies Printing Plates Yellow

STATED PRINT RUN 1 SER. #'d SET
UNPRICED DUE TO SCARCITY

2007 Stargate SG-1 Season Nine

COMPLETE SET (72) 4.00 10.00

- 1 Title Card .10 .30
- 2 Title Card .10 .30
- 3 Title Card .10 .30
- 4 Avalon Part 1 .10 .30
- 5 Avalon Part 1 .10 .30
- 6 Avalon Part 1 .10 .30
- 7 Avalon Part 2 .10 .30
- 8 Avalon Part 2 .10 .30
- 9 Avalon Part 2 .10 .30
- 10 Origin .10 .30
- 11 Origin .10 .30
- 12 Origin .10 .30
- 13 The Ties That Bind .10 .30
- 14 The Ties That Bind .10 .30
- 15 The Ties That Bind .10 .30
- 16 The Powers That Be .10 .30
- 17 The Powers That Be .10 .30
- 18 The Powers That Be .10 .30
- 19 Beachhead .10 .30
- 20 Beachhead .10 .30
- 21 Beachhead .10 .30
- 22 Ex Deus Machina .10 .30
- 23 Ex Deus Machina .10 .30
- 24 Ex Deus Machina .10 .30
- 25 Babylon .10 .30
- 26 Babylon .10 .30
- 27 Babylon .10 .30
- 28 Prototype .10 .30
- 29 Prototype .10 .30
- 30 Prototype .10 .30
- 31 The Fourth Horseman Part 1 .10 .30
- 32 The Fourth Horseman Part 1 .10 .30
- 33 The Fourth Horseman Part 1 .10 .30
- 34 The Fourth Horseman Part 2 .10 .30
- 35 The Fourth Horseman Part 2 .10 .30
- 36 The Fourth Horseman Part 2 .10 .30
- 37 Collateral Damage .10 .30
- 38 Collateral Damage .10 .30
- 39 Collateral Damage .10 .30
- 40 Ripple Effect .10 .30
- 41 Ripple Effect .10 .30
- 42 Ripple Effect .10 .30
- 43 Stronghold .10 .30
- 44 Stronghold .10 .30
- 45 Stronghold .10 .30
- 46 Ethon .10 .30
- 47 Ethon .10 .30
- 48 Ethon .10 .30
- 49 Off The Grid .10 .30
- 50 Off The Grid .10 .30
- 51 Off The Grid .10 .30
- 52 The Scourge .10 .30
- 53 The Scourge .10 .30
- 54 The Scourge .10 .30
- 55 Arthur's Mantle .10 .30
- 56 Arthur's Mantle .10 .30
- 57 Arthur's Mantle .10 .30
- 58 Crusade .10 .30
- 59 Crusade .10 .30
- 60 Crusade .10 .30
- 61 Camelot .10 .30
- 62 Camelot .10 .30
- 63 Camelot .10 .30
- 64 Behind The Scenes .10 .30
- 65 Behind The Scenes .10 .30
- 66 Behind The Scenes .10 .30
- 67 Behind The Scenes .10 .30
- 68 Behind The Scenes .10 .30
- 69 Behind The Scenes .10 .30
- 70 Checklist .10 .30
- 71 Checklist .10 .30
- 72 Checklist .10 .30

2007 Stargate SG-1 Season Nine Autographs

STATED ODDS TWO PER BOX
DA4 ISSUED AS MULTI-CASE INCENTIVE
VL (VERY LIMITED): 200-300 COPIES

- A74 William B. Davis
- A79 Steve Bacic
- A80 Kira Clavell
- A81 Matthew Bennett
- A82 Amy Sloan
- A83 Alessandro Juliani
- A84 Michael Ironside
- A85 Ben Browder VL
- A87 Lexa Doig
- A88 Ernie Hudson
- A89 Greg Anderson
- A90 Tony Todd
- A91 Matthew Walker
- A92 Cameron Bright
- A93 Peter Flemming
- A94 Kendall Cross
- DA4 Michael Shanks/Ben Browder
  (issued as multi-case incentive)

2007 Stargate SG-1 Season Nine Cast Posters

COMPLETE SET (7)
STATED ODDS 1:40

- CP1 Jack O'Neill
- CP2 Samantha Carter
- CP3 Teal'c
- CP4 Daniel Jackson
- CP5 Cameron Mitchell
- CP6 Hank Landry
- CP7 Vala

2007 Stargate SG-1 Season Nine Costumes

OVERALL COSTUME/RELIC ODDS ONE PER BOX

- C35 Daniel Jackson
- C36 Daniel Jackson
- C37 Daniel Jackson
- C38 Fourth
- C39 Unas
- C40 General Jack O'Neill
- C41 Lt. Col. Cameron Mitchell
- C42 General Hammond
- C43 Rya'c

2007 Stargate SG-1 Season Nine Dual Costumes

C13 ISSUED IN COLLECTORS ALBUM
C14 ISSUED AS CASE TOPPER

- C13 Cronus
  (issued in collectors album)
- C14 Kali
  (issued as case topper)

2007 Stargate SG-1 Season Nine Production Sketches

COMPLETE SET (18)
STATED ODDS 1:10

- S1 Children of the Gods
- S2 The Enemy Within
- S3 The Broca Divide
- S4 The First Commandment
- S5 The First Commandment
- S6 Brief Candle
- S7 Brief Candle
- S8 Thor's Hammer
- S9 Thor's Hammer
- S10 Thor's Hammer
- S11 Bloodlines
- S12 Bloodlines
- S13 Fire and Water
- S14 Fire and Water
- S15 Hathor
- S16 Singularity
- S17 The Cor-ai
- S18 The Cor-ai

2007 Stargate SG-1 Season Nine Relics

OVERALL COSTUME/RELIC ODDS ONE PER BOX
R75 ISSUED AS MULTI-CASE INCENTIVE

- R15 Alien Newspaper/500
- R16 Roses/378
- R17 Alien Documents/454
- R75 R75 Bug/120/ (issued as multi-case incentive)

2007 Stargate SG-1 Season Nine The Book Of Origin

COMPLETE SET (9)

- BO1 He Spoke to the Sky
- BO2 As He Lay There
- BO3 Guide Us on the Path
- BO4 And Those Who Are Prideful
- BO5 Fear Not the Ori
- BO6 Pity Not the Blind Man
- BO7 Let Not the Words
- BO8 Blessed Are the True
- BO9 Life and Death

2007 Supernatural Season Two
COMPLETE SET (90) 4.00 10.00

- ❑ 1 Title .10 .30
- ❑ 2 Out Of Body .10 .30
- ❑ 3 Don't Fear .10 .30
- ❑ 4 Too Soon .10 .30
- ❑ 5 Carnival .10 .30
- ❑ 6 Grieving .10 .30
- ❑ 7 Hunter .10 .30
- ❑ 8 No Good .10 .30
- ❑ 9 Resisting .10 .30
- ❑ 10 No Angel .10 .30
- ❑ 11 At Rest .10 .30
- ❑ 12 Introspective .10 .30
- ❑ 13 Visions .10 .30
- ❑ 14 Bad Twin .10 .30
- ❑ 15 No Secrets .10 .30
- ❑ 16 In The Walls .10 .30
- ❑ 17 Bad Touch .10 .30
- ❑ 18 Interred .10 .30
- ❑ 19 Captured .10 .30
- ❑ 20 Silent Clues .10 .30
- ❑ 21 Scapegoat .10 .30
- ❑ 22 Hellhound .10 .30
- ❑ 23 Hoodoo .10 .30
- ❑ 24 Devil's Trap .10 .30
- ❑ 25 Attacked .10 .30
- ❑ 26 Vanished .10 .30
- ❑ 27 Summoned .10 .30
- ❑ 28 Warning .10 .30
- ❑ 29 Targets .10 .30
- ❑ 30 Apprehended .10 .30
- ❑ 31 Real .10 .30
- ❑ 32 Repeat .10 .30
- ❑ 33 Thanks .10 .30
- ❑ 34 Interview .10 .30
- ❑ 35 Contained .10 .30
- ❑ 36 Cornered .10 .30
- ❑ 37 Touched .10 .30
- ❑ 38 Mistaken .10 .30
- ❑ 39 Close Call .10 .30
- ❑ 40 Proof .10 .30
- ❑ 41 Aided .10 .30
- ❑ 42 Possessed .10 .30
- ❑ 43 Feuding .10 .30
- ❑ 44 Staked .10 .30
- ❑ 45 Illusion .10 .30
- ❑ 46 Ghost .10 .30
- ❑ 47 Explanation .10 .30
- ❑ 48 Free .10 .30
- ❑ 49 Fierce .10 .30
- ❑ 50 Tender .10 .30
- ❑ 51 Brave .10 .30
- ❑ 52 Action .10 .30
- ❑ 53 Payback .10 .30
- ❑ 54 Sunset .10 .30
- ❑ 55 Jailbirds .10 .30
- ❑ 56 Grave .10 .30
- ❑ 57 Wrong Place .10 .30
- ❑ 58 Dream .10 .30
- ❑ 59 Dead People .10 .30
- ❑ 60 Rescued .10 .30
- ❑ 61 Disaster .10 .30
- ❑ 62 One Winner .10 .30
- ❑ 63 Taken Out .10 .30
- ❑ 64 The Plan .10 .30
- ❑ 65 Freed .10 .30
- ❑ 66 Final .10 .30
- ❑ 67 Mom .10 .30
- ❑ 68 Player .10 .30
- ❑ 69 Engaged .10 .30
- ❑ 70 Domesticated .10 .30
- ❑ 71 Still Brothers .10 .30
- ❑ 72 Hunting .10 .30
- ❑ 73 John Winchester .10 .30
- ❑ 74 Madison .10 .30
- ❑ 75 Ash .10 .30
- ❑ 76 Harvelle's Roadhouse .10 .30
- ❑ 77 Moyamensing Prison, Pennsylvania .10 .30
- ❑ 78 Lloyd's Bar, Greenwood, Mississippi .10 .30
- ❑ 79 Winchester Home, Lawrence, Kansas .10 .30
- ❑ 80 Cold Oak, South Dakota .10 .30
- ❑ 81 Fossil Butte Cemetery .10 .30
- ❑ 82 John's Life For Dean .10 .30
- ❑ 83 No Deal .10 .30
- ❑ 84 Sam Possessed .10 .30
- ❑ 85 Bad Deal .10 .30
- ❑ 86 Wanted .10 .30
- ❑ 87 Revealed .10 .30
- ❑ 88 The Key .10 .30
- ❑ 89 One More Shot .10 .30
- ❑ 90 Checklist .10 .30

2007 Supernatural Season Two Autographs
STATED ODDS 1:36

- ❑ A9 Jared Padalecki 50.00 100.00
- ❑ A10 Jensen Ackles 75.00 150.00
- ❑ A11 Samantha Ferris
- ❑ A12 Alona Tal
- ❑ A13 Chad Lindbergh
- ❑ A14 Amber Benson
- ❑ A15 Jason Gedrick
- ❑ A16 Samantha Smith
- ❑ A17 Aldis Hodge

2007 Supernatural Season Two Box Loaders
STATED ODDS ONE PER BOX

- ❑ FM1 John Winchester FM
- ❑ FM2 Dean Winchester FM
- ❑ FM3 Sam Winchester FM
- ❑ CL1 Intervention
CASE INSERT

2007 Supernatural Season Two Hunters
STATED ODDS 1:17

- ❑ H1 Ellen Harvelle
- ❑ H2 Ash
- ❑ H3 Jo Harvelle
- ❑ H4 Gordon Walker
- ❑ H5 Bobby Singer
- ❑ H6 Winchesters

2007 Supernatural Season Two Pieceworks
STATED ODDS 1:36

- ❑ PW1A Jared Padalecki 35.00 70.00
- ❑ PW1B Jensen Ackles 35.00 70.00
- ❑ PW2 Jensen Ackles 100.00 150.00
- ❑ PW3 Jared Padalecki 15.00 40.00
- ❑ PW4 Jeffrey Dean Morgan 15.00 40.00
- ❑ PW5 Alona Tal
Jensen Ackles
- ❑ PW6 Alona Tal
- ❑ PW7 Samantha Ferris
- ❑ PW8 Amber Benson
- ❑ PW9 Emmanuelle Vaugier
- ❑ PW10 Tricia Helfer
- ❑ PW11 Tricia Helfer
- ❑ PW12 Samantha Smith
- ❑ PW13 Fredric Lehne
- ❑ PW14 Linda Blair
- ❑ PW15 Linda Blair
Jared Padalecki
- ❑ PW16 Jason Gedrick
- ❑ PW17A Jensen Ackles
- ❑ PW17B Jared Padalecki
- ❑ PWYA Jensen Ackles
- ❑ PWYB Jared Padalecki

2007 Supernatural Season Two The Devil's Due
STATED ODDS 1:11

- ❑ DD1 The Truth About Sam
- ❑ DD2 Special Kids
- ❑ DD3 Chosen Ones
- ❑ DD4 Disqualified
- ❑ DD5 Favorite
- ❑ DD6 Demon Blood
- ❑ DD7 Bad Timing
- ❑ DD8 Second Choice
- ❑ DD9 Payback

2007 Transformers
COMPLETE SET (90) 6.00 15.00
FOX AUTO STATED ODDS 1:396 HOBBY

- ❑ 1 Optimus Prime .15 .40
- ❑ 2 Optimus Prime .15 .40
- ❑ 3 Bumblebee .15 .40
- ❑ 4 Bumblebee .15 .40
- ❑ 5 Megatron .15 .40
- ❑ 6 Megatron .15 .40
- ❑ 7 Barricade .15 .40
- ❑ 8 Ironhide .15 .40
- ❑ 9 Jazz .15 .40
- ❑ 10 Starscream .15 .40
- ❑ 11 Ratchet .15 .40
- ❑ 12 Ratchet .15 .40
- ❑ 13 Blackout .15 .40
- ❑ 14 Blackout .15 .40
- ❑ 15 Frenzy .15 .40
- ❑ 16 Frenzy .15 .40
- ❑ 17 Optimus Prime .15 .40
- ❑ 18 Bumblebee .15 .40
- ❑ 19 Sam Witwicky .15 .40
- ❑ 20 Mikaela Banes .15 .40
- ❑ 21 John Keller .15 .40
- ❑ 22 Capt. Lennox .15 .40
- ❑ 23 Maggie Marconi .15 .40
- ❑ 24 Glen Whitmann .15 .40
- ❑ 25 Staff Sgt. Epps .15 .40
- ❑ 26 Agent Simmons .15 .40
- ❑ 27 Ron and Judy Witwicky .15 .40
- ❑ 28 A Chilling Discovery .15 .40
- ❑ 29 More Than meets the Eye .15 .40
- ❑ 30 Incident at SOCCENT .15 .40
- ❑ 31 Attacked by Blackout .15 .40
- ❑ 32 Cut the Hard Lines .15 .40
- ❑ 33 Just a Teen Named Sam .15 .40
- ❑ 34 A Global Emergency .15 .40
- ❑ 35 Desert Trek .15 .40
- ❑ 36 Mega-Hot Grease Monkey .15 .40
- ❑ 37 Assault on Qatar .15 .40
- ❑ 38 Robot on the Rampage .15 .40
- ❑ 39 It Won't Go Down .15 .40
- ❑ 40 Rescued .15 .40
- ❑ 41 A Bot, a Girl and a Robot .15 .40
- ❑ 42 In Barricade's Clutches .15 .40
- ❑ 43 Terror from the Stars .15 .40
- ❑ 44 Transformers on Earth .15 .40
- ❑ 45 Not the Tooth Fairy .15 .40
- ❑ 46 Heavy Metal Allies .15 .40
- ❑ 47 Metal Morphosis .15 .40
- ❑ 48 On the Road Again .15 .40
- ❑ 49 A Conference with Keller .15 .40
- ❑ 50 Destination: Hoover Dam .15 .40
- ❑ 51 Inside Hoover Dam .15 .40
- ❑ 52 Alien Metamorphosis .15 .40
- ❑ 53 Battle of the Giants .15 .40
- ❑ 54 Against the Decepticons .15 .40
- ❑ 55 Fearsome Adversary .15 .40
- ❑ 56 Airborne Menace .15 .40
- ❑ 57 Our World Under Siege .15 .40
- ❑ 58 To Defend the Earth .15 .40
- ❑ 59 Has Sam the Right Stuff .15 .40
- ❑ 60 Earth's Final Stand .15 .40
- ❑ 61 Protecting the Allspark .15 .40
- ❑ 62 Aftermath .15 .40
- ❑ 63 Tomorrow's Conflict .15 .40
- ❑ 64 Filming Frenzy .15 .40
- ❑ 65 Blood and Sand .15 .40
- ❑ 66 Hero with a Heart .15 .40
- ❑ 67 On Location .15 .40
- ❑ 68 Behemoth on Ice .15 .40
- ❑ 69 The Weirdest Props Ever .15 .40
- ❑ 70 Filming a Secret World .15 .40
- ❑ 71 A Canvas of Conflict .15 .40
- ❑ 72 The Witwicky Legacy .15 .40
- ❑ 73 From Above and Behind .15 .40
- ❑ 74 Titans Unleashed .15 .40
- ❑ 75 Cybernetic Life-Form .15 .40
- ❑ 76 Programmed to Kill .15 .40
- ❑ 77 Robotic Defenders .15 .40
- ❑ 78 Megatron Transforms .15 .40
- ❑ 79 Invading the Skies .15 .40
- ❑ 80 Terror from On High .15 .40
- ❑ 81 Above the Stricken City .15 .40
- ❑ 82 Passing the Allspark .15 .40
- ❑ 83 The Dream of Optimus Prime .15 .40
- ❑ 84 Behold Cybertron .15 .40
- ❑ 85 Prequel Cover .15 .40
- ❑ 86 Robot World .15 .40
- ❑ 87 Somewhere in Space .15 .40
- ❑ 88 Killer Instinct .15 .40
- ❑ 89 Ba-Doom .15 .40
- ❑ 90 Checklist .15 .40
- ❑ NNO Megan Fox AU 350.00 500.00

2007 Transformers Authentic Movie Memorabilia
STATED ODDS 1:39 HOBBY

- ❑ NNO SOCCENT Soldiers Jacket 6.00 15.00
- ❑ NNO SOCCENT Soldiers Pants 6.00 15.00

2007 Transformers Embossed Foil
COMPLETE SET (10) 5.00 12.00
STATED ODDS 1:6

- ❑ 1 Blackout .75 2.00
- ❑ 2 Bumblebee .75 2.00
- ❑ 3 Barricade .75 2.00
- ❑ 4 Frenzy .75 2.00
- ❑ 5 Ironhide .75 2.00
- ❑ 6 Jazz .75 2.00
- ❑ 7 Megatron .75 2.00
- ❑ 8 Optimus Prime .75 2.00
- ❑ 9 Ratchet .75 2.00
- ❑ 10 Starscream .75 2.00

2007 Transformers Flix-Pix
COMPLETE SET (5) 4.00 10.00
STATED ODDS 1:12 RETAIL

- ❑ 1 Optimus Prime 1.25 3.00
- ❑ 2 Megatron 1.25 3.00
- ❑ 3 Bumblebee 1.25 3.00
- ❑ 4 Barricade 1.25 3.00
- ❑ 5 Ratchet 1.25 3.00

2007 Transformers Foil
COMPLETE SET (10) 5.00 12.00
STATED ODDS 1:6

- ❑ 1 Bumblebee .75 2.00
- ❑ 2 Optimus Prime .75 2.00
- ❑ 3 Ratchet .75 2.00
- ❑ 4 Jazz .75 2.00
- ❑ 5 Ironhide .75 2.00
- ❑ 6 Blackout .75 2.00
- ❑ 7 Barricade .75 2.00
- ❑ 8 Megatron .75 2.00
- ❑ 9 Frenzy .75 2.00
- ❑ 10 Starscream .75 2.00

2007 Transformers Sketches
STATED ODDS 1:72 HOBBY

- ❑ 1 Alex Milne
- ❑ 2 Guido Guidi
- ❑ 3 James Bukshot Bukauskas
- ❑ 4 James Orfalo
- ❑ 5 Josh Burcham
- ❑ 6 Juan Carlos Ramos
- ❑ 7 Marcel Matere
- ❑ 8 Nick Roche
- ❑ 9 Pablo Hidalgo
- ❑ 10 Rob Ruffalo
- ❑ 11 Robby Musso
- ❑ 12 Tom Hodges

2007 Veronica Mars Season Two
COMPLETE SET (81) 3.00 8.00
UNPRICED INKPLATE PRINT RUN 1

- ❑ 1 Veronica Mars .08 .25
- ❑ 2 Decked .08 .25
- ❑ 3 Wrecked .08 .25
- ❑ 4 No Regrets .08 .25
- ❑ 5 Silent Witness .08 .25
- ❑ 6 Tawdriness .08 .25
- ❑ 7 Man On The Run .08 .25
- ❑ 8 Devoted .08 .25
- ❑ 9 Inside Tip .08 .25
- ❑ 10 Claws .08 .25
- ❑ 11 Exit .08 .25
- ❑ 12 Inquiry .08 .25
- ❑ 13 Promises .08 .25
- ❑ 14 Confined .08 .25
- ❑ 15 Sympathetic .08 .25
- ❑ 16 Hero .08 .25
- ❑ 17 Pirate .08 .25
- ❑ 18 Revealed .08 .25
- ❑ 19 Awake .08 .25
- ❑ 20 Returned .08 .25
- ❑ 21 Dejected .08 .25
- ❑ 22 Protected .08 .25
- ❑ 23 Spied .08 .25
- ❑ 24 Lied .08 .25
- ❑ 25 Found .08 .25
- ❑ 26 Faked .08 .25
- ❑ 27 Outed .08 .25
- ❑ 28 Discovered .08 .25
- ❑ 29 Sideline .08 .25
- ❑ 30 Undone .08 .25
- ❑ 31 Keeping Score .08 .25
- ❑ 32 Not Guilty .08 .25
- ❑ 33 Doomed .08 .25
- ❑ 34 Contrition .08 .25
- ❑ 35 Remembered .08 .25
- ❑ 36 No Excuses .08 .25
- ❑ 37 Last Stand .08 .25
- ❑ 38 Mercy .08 .25
- ❑ 39 Lucky's Secret .08 .25
- ❑ 40 Dirty Shame .08 .25
- ❑ 41 Snapped .08 .25
- ❑ 42 No Justice .08 .25
- ❑ 43 Loser .08 .25
- ❑ 44 Winner .08 .25
- ❑ 45 Graduate .08 .25
- ❑ 46 Veronica Mars .08 .25
- ❑ 47 Wallace Fennel .08 .25
- ❑ 48 Duncan Kane .08 .25
- ❑ 49 Logan Echolls .08 .25
- ❑ 50 Cindy "Mac" Mackenzie .08 .25
- ❑ 51 Meg Manning .08 .25
- ❑ 52 Jackie Cook .08 .25
- ❑ 53 Dick Casablancas .08 .25
- ❑ 54 Cassidy "Beaver" Casablancas .08 .25
- ❑ 55 Hannah Griffith .08 .25
- ❑ 56 Eli "Weevil" Navarro .08 .25
- ❑ 57 Eduardo "Thumper" Orozco .08 .25
- ❑ 58 Gia Goodman .08 .25
- ❑ 59 Douglas Aka "Corny" .08 .25
- ❑ 60 Principal Van Clemmons .08 .25
- ❑ 61 Ms. Debora Hauser .08 .25
- ❑ 62 Rebecca James .08 .25
- ❑ 63 Keith Mars .08 .25
- ❑ 64 Alicia Fennel, Nathan Woods .08 .25
- ❑ 65 Terrence Cook .08 .25
- ❑ 66 Kendall Casablancas .08 .25
- ❑ 67 Woody Goodman .08 .25
- ❑ 68 Dr. Tom Griffith .08 .25
- ❑ 69 Sheriff Don Lamb .08 .25
- ❑ 70 Cliff Mccormack .08 .25
- ❑ 71 Deputy Leo D'Amato .08 .25
- ❑ 72 Deputy Sacks .08 .25
- ❑ 73 Molly Fitzpatrick .08 .25
- ❑ 74 Fitzpatricks .08 .25
- ❑ 75 Basketball Star .08 .25
- ❑ 76 Ladies' Man .08 .25
- ❑ 77 Void Of Mars .08 .25
- ❑ 78 Misleading .08 .25
- ❑ 79 Recurring .08 .25
- ❑ 80 Thumper .08 .25
- ❑ 81 Checklist .08 .25

2007 Veronica Mars Season Two Autographs
STATED ODDS 1:24

- ❑ A12 Kristen Bell 75.00 150.00
- ❑ A13 Enrico Colantoni 8.00 20.00
- ❑ A14 Percy Daggs III 6.00 15.00
- ❑ A15 Kyle Gallner 8.00 20.00
- ❑ A16 Kristin Cavallari 10.00 20.00
- ❑ A17 Krysten Ritter 15.00 30.00
- ❑ A18 Alona Tal 6.00 15.00
- ❑ A19 Charisma Carpenter 30.00 60.00
- ❑ A20 Lucas Grabeel 6.00 15.00
- ❑ A21 Christine Estarook 6.00 15.00

2007 The World of Harry Potter 3-D
COMPLETE SET (72) 5.00 12.00

- ❑ 1 Norbert after hatching .15 .40
- ❑ 2 Troll with wand in nose .15 .40
- ❑ 3 Harry levitates broom .15 .40
- ❑ 4 Fluffy over trap door .15 .40
- ❑ 5 Shattering chess piece .15 .40
- ❑ 6 Trio with broom at locked door .15 .40
- ❑ 7 Snitch in hand .15 .40
- ❑ 8 Flying keys .15 .40
- ❑ 9 Quirrell at Mirror .15 .40
- ❑ 10 The quaffle is released .15 .40
- ❑ 11 Trio among chess pieces .15 .40
- ❑ 12 Red Wizard Chess pieces .15 .40
- ❑ 13 Hogwarts Express .15 .40
- ❑ 14 Harry flying at Quidditch .15 .40
- ❑ 15 McGonagall as cat leads class .15 .40
- ❑ 16 Harry in the Cupboard Under the Stairs .15 .40
- ❑ 17 Trio in Common Room after Forest .15 .40
- ❑ 18 Harry descending stairs for confrontation .15 .40
- ❑ 19 Trio brewing Polyjuice Potion .15 .40
- ❑ 20 Dobby .15 .40
- ❑ 21 Harry in Chamber .15 .40
- ❑ 22 Harry with Gryffindor's Sword .15 .40
- ❑ 23 Anglia over Hogwart's Express .15 .40
- ❑ 24 Freezing pixies .15 .40
- ❑ 25 Harry & Draco seeking Snitch .15 .40
- ❑ 26 Ron's Howler .15 .40
- ❑ 27 Lockhart tries to charm snake .15 .40
- ❑ 28 Class repotting Mandrakes .15 .40
- ❑ 29 Defense Against Dark Arts class .15 .40
- ❑ 30 Platform 9-3/4 .15 .40
- ❑ 31 Harry casting for Lockhart .15 .40
- ❑ 32 Harry & Ron with Scabbers .15 .40
- ❑ 33 Cedric flying .15 .40
- ❑ 34 Harry with Riddle's Diary .15 .40
- ❑ 35 Draco smirking .15 .40
- ❑ 36 Susan Bones and trio in Lockhart's class .15 .40
- ❑ 37 Buckbeak .15 .40
- ❑ 38 Marauder's Map .15 .40
- ❑ 39 Vernon & Petunia post-Marge fly-off .15 .40
- ❑ 40 Harry gleeful down stairs .15 .40
- ❑ 41 Hermione & Ron in Diagon Alley .15 .40
- ❑ 42 Hagrid's hut with pumpkins .15 .40
- ❑ 43 Harry looking under bed at Monster Book .15 .40
- ❑ 44 Hermione & Harry freeing Buckbeak .15 .40
- ❑ 45 Harry gazing .15 .40
- ❑ 46 Tom the Innkeeper (Jim Tavare) .15 .40
- ❑ 47 Draco taunts Harry .15 .40
- ❑ 48 Trio behind pumpkins .15 .40
- ❑ 49 Descending hill to Hagrid's .15 .40
- ❑ 50 Parvati's clown boggart .15 .40
- ❑ 51 Lupin as werewolf .15 .40
- ❑ 52 McGonagall and Harry .15 .40
- ❑ 53 Stag Patronus .15 .40
- ❑ 54 Lupin reaches for boggart .15 .40
- ❑ 55 Fleur de bleu .15 .40
- ❑ 56 Harry quizzed after Goblet selection .15 .40
- ❑ 57 Hermione and Viktor dance .15 .40
- ❑ 58 In canoe after Second Task .15 .40
- ❑ 59 Barty Jr. at Quidditch campsite .15 .40
- ❑ 60 Wormtail cradles Voldemort .15 .40
- ❑ 61 Fred & George put names in Goblet .15 .40
- ❑ 62 Statue at Riddle graveyard .15 .40
- ❑ 63 Beauxbatons students .15 .40
- ❑ 64 Triwizard Cup .15 .40
- ❑ 65 Dumbledore with Harry's name from Goblet .15 .40
- ❑ 66 Harry with Fawkes .15 .40
- ❑ 67 Dumbledore to crowd for Third Task .15 .40
- ❑ 68 Dumbledore address in Banquet Hall .15 .40
- ❑ 69 Harry in Owlery .15 .40
- ❑ 70 Harry & Ron in class .15 .40
- ❑ 71 Arena for Third Task .15 .40
- ❑ 72 The World of Harry Potter Checklist .15 .40

2007 The World of Harry Potter 3-D Autographs
1-12 STATED ODDS 1:48
CARDS 13 AND 14 SDCC EXCLUSIVE

- ❑ 1 Daniel Radcliffe 300.00 500.00
- ❑ 2 David Bradley 15.00 30.00
- ❑ 3 Richard Bremmer 50.00 100.00
- ❑ 4 Robert Pattinson 150.00 300.00
Stanislav Ianevski
- ❑ 5 Joshua Herdman 50.00 100.00
Jamie Waylett
- ❑ 6 Harry Taylor 40.00 80.00
- ❑ 7 David Thewlis 35.00 70.00
- ❑ 8 Oliver Phelps 25.00 50.00
- ❑ 9 James Phelps 25.00 50.00
- ❑ 10 Warwick Davis 15.00 30.00
- ❑ 11 Robert Hardy 15.00 30.00
- ❑ 12 Richard Griffiths 50.00 100.00
Harry Melling
- ❑ 13 Bonnie Wright/100 75.00 150.00
- ❑ 14 David Tennant/250 75.00 150.00

2008 24 Season Five
COMPLETE SET (90) 6.00 15.00

- ❑ 1 Day Five .15 .40
- ❑ 2 Jack Bauer .15 .40
- ❑ 3 Audrey Raines .15 .40
- ❑ 4 Chloe O'Brian .15 .40
- ❑ 5 Curtis Manning .15 .40
- ❑ 6 Edgar Stiles .15 .40
- ❑ 7 Bill Buchanan .15 .40
- ❑ 8 Lynn McGill .15 .40
- ❑ 9 Karen Hayes .15 .40
- ❑ 10 Tony Almeida .15 .40
- ❑ 11 Mike Novick .15 .40
- ❑ 12 Aaron Pierce .15 .40
- ❑ 13 Wayne Palmer .15 .40
- ❑ 14 Walt Cummings .15 .40
- ❑ 15 Vladimir Bierko .15 .40
- ❑ 16 Christopher Henderson .15 .40
- ❑ 17 President Charles Logan .15 .40
- ❑ 18 Martha Logan .15 .40
- ❑ 19 Presidential Legacy .15 .40
- ❑ 20 More Attacks .15 .40
- ❑ 21 A Pattern Emerges .15 .40
- ❑ 22 Surprise Passenger .15 .40
- ❑ 23 First Lady and the President .15 .40
- ❑ 24 Chloe and Jack .15 .40
- ❑ 25 Short Reunion .15 .40
- ❑ 26 Hostage Situation Options .15 .40
- ❑ 27 The President's Call .15 .40
- ❑ 28 Held Hostage .15 .40
- ❑ 29 Lynn Catches a Code .15 .40
- ❑ 30 Jack Returns to CTU .15 .40
- ❑ 31 Secret Meeting .15 .40
- ❑ 32 Jack Surrenders .15 .40
- ❑ 33 Stressed First Couple .15 .40
- ❑ 34 On the Trail .15 .40
- ❑ 35 Capturing Rossler .15 .40
- ❑ 36 Chloe and Spenser .15 .40
- ❑ 37 Cummings Is Dead .15 .40
- ❑ 38 More Bad Choices .15 .40
- ❑ 39 CTU Monitors .15 .40
- ❑ 40 An Important Lead .15 .40
- ❑ 41 Jack on the Run .15 .40
- ❑ 42 Old Friends .15 .40
- ❑ 43 Covering the Bases .15 .40
- ❑ 44 Tony Awakens .15 .40
- ❑ 45 Michelle Is Dead .15 .40
- ❑ 46 Under the Gun .15 .40
- ❑ 47 Henderson Arrives .15 .40
- ❑ 48 Harsh Gamble .15 .40
- ❑ 49 Henderson Interrogated .15 .40
- ❑ 50 Kim Back at CTU .15 .40
- ❑ 51 Edgar Investigates .15 .40
- ❑ 52 Biohazard Alert .15 .40
- ❑ 53 Edgar's Demise .15 .40
- ❑ 54 Attack and Response .15 .40
- ❑ 55 Consequences at CTU .15 .40
- ❑ 56 Martial Law .15 .40
- ❑ 57 Audrey Arrested .15 .40
- ❑ 58 Pumping Station .15 .40
- ❑ 59 Unnatural Gas .15 .40
- ❑ 60 After the Explosion .15 .40
- ❑ 61 Kidnapped Daughter .15 .40
- ❑ 62 Wayne and Jack .15 .40
- ❑ 63 Horrible Confirmation .15 .40
- ❑ 64 Kill Jack Bauer .15 .40
- ❑ 65 Heller's Visit .15 .40
- ❑ 66 Jack Restrained .15 .40
- ❑ 67 Audrey Wounded .15 .40
- ❑ 68 Henderson's Gamble .15 .40
- ❑ 69 Heller vs. Logan .15 .40
- ❑ 70 Working from Home .15 .40
- ❑ 71 Henderson Targets Heller .15 .40
- ❑ 72 Goodbye for Now .15 .40
- ❑ 73 Under the Gun .15 .40
- ❑ 74 Airborne .15 .40
- ❑ 75 Hijacked .15 .40
- ❑ 76 Shoot It Down .15 .40
- ❑ 77 Berko To Be Moved .15 .40
- ❑ 78 Aaron Held Captive .15 .40
- ❑ 79 Henderson in Holding .15 .40
- ❑ 80 Henderson Names Contact .15 .40
- ❑ 81 Jack and Aaron .15 .40
- ❑ 82 CTU Coordinating .15 .40
- ❑ 83 Taking Off .15 .40
- ❑ 84 Logan Held Prisoner .15 .40
- ❑ 85 Jack Stands Down .15 .40
- ❑ 86 Threatening Martha .15 .40
- ❑ 87 David Palmer's Casket .15 .40
- ❑ 88 Logan's Farewell .15 .40
- ❑ 89 Jack Is Grabbed .15 .40
- ❑ 90 Checklist .15 .40

2008 24 Season Five Autographs
STATED ODDS 1:36

- ❑ 1 Carlo Rota 10.00 20.00
- ❑ 2 Connie Britton 15.00 30.00
- ❑ 3 Gregory Itzin 10.00 20.00
- ❑ 4 James Morrison 20.00 40.00
- ❑ 5 Jayne Atkinson 15.00 30.00
- ❑ 6 Jean Smart 20.00 40.00
- ❑ 7 Jeff Kober 6.00 15.00
- ❑ 8 Mark Sheppard 10.00 20.00
- ❑ 9 Mary Lynn Rajskub 75.00 150.00
- ❑ 10 Paul McCrane 6.00 15.00
- ❑ 11 Ray Wise 15.00 30.00
- ❑ 12 Sean Astin 25.00 50.00

2008 24 Season Five Case Incentive Costumes

- ❑ CI1 President Logan - shirt and tie/153 25.00 50.00
(issued as 2-case incentive)
- ❑ CI2 Chloe O'Brian - shirt/85 40.00 80.00
(issued as 5-case incentive)
- ❑ CI3 Kim Bauer - blouse/63 60.00 120.00
(issued as 10-case incentive)

2008 24 Season Five Case Topper Costumes
STATED ODDS ONE PER CASE

- ❑ CT1 Tony Almeida - t-shirt 12.00 30.00
- ❑ CT2 Michelle Dessler - blouse 12.00 30.00

2008 24 Season Five Costumes
STATED ODDS 1:36
PRINT RUN 90-265

- ❑ C1 Jack Bauer - jacket/115 30.00 60.00
- ❑ C2 President Palmer - shirt/105 8.00 20.00
- ❑ C3 Haas - jacket/200 6.00 15.00
- ❑ C4 Tony Almeida - pants/200
- ❑ C5 Michelle Dessler - pants/175
- ❑ C6 Chloe O'Brian - sweater/115
- ❑ C7 Bill Buchanan - tie/115 20.00 40.00
- ❑ C8 Walt Cummings - tie/90 40.00 80.00
- ❑ C9 Anton Beresch - sweater/265 5.00 12.00
- ❑ C10 Curtis Manning - shirt/115 8.00 20.00
- ❑ C11 Derek Huxley - shirt/210 5.00 12.00
- ❑ C12 Edgar Stiles - pants/215 5.00 12.00
- ❑ C13 Shari Rothenberg - blouse/200 5.00 12.00
- ❑ C14 Wayne Palmer - sweater/165 6.00 15.00
- ❑ C15 Anton Beresch - mask/115 8.00 20.00

2008 24 Season Five Promos

- ❑ P1 Jack Bauer 1.00 2.50
- ❑ P2 Curtis Manning 1.00 2.50
- ❑ P3 Jack Bauer 2.00 5.00
(Album Exclusive)

2008 24 Season Five Props
STATED PRINT RUN 60-190
❑ P1 Terrorist's Bomb Vest/190 6.00 15.00
❑ P2 CTU Folder/165 10.00 25.00
❑ P3 Arms Treaty/190 6.00 15.00
❑ P4 Bloody Bandages/115 30.00 60.00
❑ P5 CTU ID Card/60
❑ P6 Timing Mechanism/90
❑ P7 Mall Bag/150 35.00 70.00
❑ P8 Terrorist's Bomb Vest/110 35.00 70.00
❑ S6P1 Explosion Debris - stool/100 40.00 80.00
❑ S6P2 Explosion Debris - lectern/90 40.00 80.00
❑ S6P3 Explosion Debris - body/80 40.00 80.00

2008 24 Season Five Puzzle
COMPLETE SET (9) 4.00 10.00
STATED ODDS 1:9
❑ PZ1 Puzzle 1 .75 2.00
❑ PZ2 Puzzle 2 .75 2.00
❑ PZ3 Puzzle 3 .75 2.00
❑ PZ4 Puzzle 4 .75 2.00
❑ PZ5 Puzzle 5 .75 2.00
❑ PZ6 Puzzle 6 .75 2.00
❑ PZ7 Puzzle 7 .75 2.00
❑ PZ8 Puzzle 8 .75 2.00
❑ PZ9 Puzzle 9 .75 2.00

2008 24 Season Five Rare Foil
COMPLETE SET (6) 4.00 10.00
STATED ODDS 1:12
❑ R1 Jack Bauer 1.00 2.50
Curtis Manning
❑ R2 Chloe O'Brian 1.00 2.50
Bill Buchanan
❑ R3 Miriam Henderson 1.00 2.50
Bill Buchanan
❑ R4 Mike Novick 1.00 2.50
Aaron Pierce
❑ R5 Vladimir Bierko 1.00 2.50
Christopher Henderson
❑ R6 Martha Logan 1.00 2.50
President Logan

2008 24 Season Five Ultra Rare Foil
COMPLETE SET (3) 5.00 12.00
STATED ODDS 1:36
❑ UR1 Audrey Raines 2.50 6.00
Jack Bauer
❑ UR2 Kim Bauer 2.50 6.00
Jack Bauer
❑ UR3 Mike Novick 2.50 6.00
President Logan

2008 Batman Archives
ROBINSON AU STATED ODDS ONE PER CASE
❑ 1 Issue #1 .15 .40
❑ 2 Issue #11 .15 .40
❑ 3 Issue #16 .15 .40
❑ 4 Issue #20 .15 .40
❑ 5 Issue #25 .15 .40
❑ 6 Issue #37 .15 .40
❑ 7 Issue #42 .15 .40
❑ 8 Issue #49 .15 .40
❑ 9 Issue #50 .15 .40
❑ 10 Issue #59 .15 .40
❑ 11 Issue #63 .15 .40
❑ 12 Issue #72 .15 .40
❑ 13 Issue #81 .15 .40
❑ 14 Issue #92 .15 .40
❑ 15 Issue #100 .15 .40
❑ 16 Issue #104 .15 .40
❑ 17 Issue #121 .15 .40
❑ 18 Issue #128 .15 .40
❑ 19 Issue #133 .15 .40
❑ 20 Issue #139 .15 .40
❑ 21 Issue #156 .15 .40
❑ 22 Issue #166 .15 .40
❑ 23 Issue #181 .15 .40
❑ 24 Issue #183 .15 .40
❑ 25 Issue #197 .15 .40
❑ 26 Issue #200 .15 .40
❑ 27 Issue #207 .15 .40
❑ 28 Issue #227 .15 .40
❑ 29 Issue #232 .15 .40
❑ 30 Issue #244 .15 .40
❑ 31 Issue #251 .15 .40
❑ 32 Issue #263 .15 .40
❑ 33 Issue #269 .15 .40
❑ 34 Issue #292 .15 .40
❑ 35 Issue #300 .15 .40
❑ 36 Issue #308 .15 .40
❑ 37 Issue #320 .15 .40
❑ 38 Issue #324 .15 .40
❑ 39 Issue #343 .15 .40
❑ 40 Issue #357 .15 .40
❑ 41 Issue #400 .15 .40
❑ 42 Issue #404 .15 .40
❑ 43 Issue #414 .15 .40
❑ 44 Issue #428 .15 .40
❑ 45 Issue #442 .15 .40
❑ 46 Issue #451 .15 .40
❑ 47 Issue #461 .15 .40
❑ 48 Issue #465 .15 .40
❑ 49 Issue #493 .15 .40
❑ 50 Issue #497 .15 .40
❑ 51 Issue #500 .15 .40
❑ 52 Issue #512 .15 .40
❑ 53 Issue #558 .15 .40
❑ 54 Issue #567 .15 .40
❑ 55 Issue #586 .15 .40
❑ 56 Issue #598 .15 .40
❑ 57 Issue #600 .15 .40
❑ 58 Issue #609 .15 .40
❑ 59 Issue #612 .15 .40
❑ 60 Issue #629 .15 .40
❑ 61 Issue #650 .15 .40
❑ 62 Issue #660 .15 .40
❑ 63 Issue #670 .15 .40
❑ NNO Jerry Robinson AU

2008 Batman Archives 1940 Batman Gum
STATED ODDS 1:8
❑ 1 Batman 1.25 3.00
❑ 2 Robin 1.25 3.00
❑ 3 The Bat Signal 1.25 3.00
❑ 4 Crimefighting Costumes 1.25 3.00
❑ 5 The Bat Mobile 1.25 3.00
❑ 6 The Joker 1.25 3.00
❑ 7 The Penguin 1.25 3.00
❑ 8 Two-Face 1.25 3.00
❑ 9 Batman, Robin and Alfred 1.25 3.00

2008 Batman Archives Dark Victory
STATED ODDS 1:12
❑ DV1 Riddler 2.00 5.00
❑ DV2 Scarecrow 2.00 5.00
❑ DV3 Catwoman 2.00 5.00
❑ DV4 Penguin 2.00 5.00
❑ DV5 Batman 2.00 5.00
❑ DV6 Joker 2.00 5.00
❑ DV7 Mr. Freeze 2.00 5.00
❑ DV8 Poison Ivy 2.00 5.00
❑ DV9 Two-Face 2.00 5.00

2008 Batman Archives Motion Cards
STATED ODDS 1:24
❑ L1 Batman 4.00 10.00
❑ L2 Riddler 4.00 10.00
❑ L3 Robin 4.00 10.00
❑ L4 Catwoman 4.00 10.00
❑ L5 Joker 4.00 10.00
❑ L6 Killer Croc 4.00 10.00
❑ L7 Ra's al Ghul 4.00 10.00
❑ L8 Scarecrow 4.00 10.00
❑ L9 Two-Face 4.00 10.00

2008 Batman Archives Promos
❑ P1 Batman standing on rooftop 1.00 2.50
(General Distribution)
❑ P2 Batman and Robin 1.25 3.00
(NSU Magazine)
❑ P3 Batgirl 1.25 3.00
(Binder Exclusive)
❑ CP1 Batman behind castle
(Convention Distribution)
❑ SD08 Batman throwing batarangs 3.00 8.00
(2008 SDCC Exclusive)

2008 Batman Archives Sketches
STATED ODDS ONE PER BOX
MCHALEY CARD IS 3 CASE INCENTIVE
GIORDANO CARD IS 9 CASE INCENTIVE
❑ 1 Eddy Barrows 20.00 50.00
❑ 2 Al Bigley 20.00 50.00
❑ 3 Chris Bolson
❑ 4 Jose Carlos 20.00 50.00
❑ 5 Cassaro 20.00 50.00
❑ 6 Marcelo di Chiara 20.00 50.00
❑ 7 James Cordeiro 20.00 50.00
❑ 8 Jorge Correa 20.00 50.00
❑ 9 Carlos Ferreira 20.00 50.00
❑ 10 Marcelo Ferreira 20.00 50.00
❑ 11 Renato Guedes 20.00 50.00
❑ 12 Sam Hart 20.00 50.00
❑ 13 Jack Jadson 20.00 50.00
❑ 14 Jeff 20.00 50.00
❑ 15 Magno 20.00 50.00
❑ 16 Merlo 20.00 50.00
❑ 17 Dio Neves 20.00 50.00
❑ 18 Nonato 20.00 50.00
❑ 19 Oak 20.00 50.00
❑ 20 Bruno Oliveira 20.00 50.00
❑ 21 Amilcar Pinna 20.00 50.00
❑ 22 Andy Price 40.00 100.00
❑ 23 Raapack 20.00 50.00
❑ 24 Rod Reis 20.00 50.00
❑ 25 Tone Rodriguez 20.00 50.00
❑ 26 Steve Russell 20.00 50.00
❑ 27 Samicler 20.00 50.00
❑ 28 Amilton Santos 20.00 50.00
❑ 29 Sict 20.00 50.00
❑ 30 Uko Smith 20.00 50.00
❑ 31 Rick Stasi
❑ 32 Joe Staton
❑ 33 Tamura 20.00 50.00
❑ 34 Mark McHaley 75.00 150.00
❑ 35 Dick Giordano

2008 Battlestar Galactica Season Three
COMPLETE SET (63) 4.00 10.00
❑ 1 Title Card .10 .30
Checklist
❑ 2 Title Card .10 .30
Checklist
❑ 3 Title Card .10 .30
Checklist
❑ 4 Occupation .10 .30
❑ 5 Occupation .10 .30
❑ 6 Occupation .10 .30
❑ 7 Precipice .10 .30
❑ 8 Precipice .10 .30
❑ 9 Precipice .10 .30
❑ 10 Exodus: Part 1 .10 .30
❑ 11 Exodus: Part 1 .10 .30
❑ 12 Exodus: Part 1 .10 .30
❑ 13 Exodus: Part 2 .10 .30
❑ 14 Exodus: Part 2 .10 .30
❑ 15 Exodus: Part 2 .10 .30
❑ 16 Collaborators .10 .30
❑ 17 Collaborators .10 .30
❑ 18 Collaborators .10 .30
❑ 19 Torn .10 .30
❑ 20 Torn .10 .30
❑ 21 Torn .10 .30
❑ 22 A Measure of Salvation .10 .30
❑ 23 A Measure of Salvation .10 .30
❑ 24 A Measure of Salvation .10 .30
❑ 25 Hero .10 .30
❑ 26 Hero .10 .30
❑ 27 Hero .10 .30
❑ 28 Unfinished Business .10 .30
❑ 29 Unfinished Business .10 .30
❑ 30 Unfinished Business .10 .30
❑ 31 The Passage .10 .30
❑ 32 The Passage .10 .30
❑ 33 The Passage .10 .30
❑ 34 The Eye of Jupiter .10 .30
❑ 35 The Eye of Jupiter .10 .30
❑ 36 The Eye of Jupiter .10 .30
❑ 37 Rapture .10 .30
❑ 38 Rapture .10 .30
❑ 39 Rapture .10 .30
❑ 40 Taking a Break from All Your Worries .10 .30
❑ 41 Taking a Break from All Your Worries .10 .30
❑ 42 Taking a Break from All Your Worries .10 .30
❑ 43 The Woman King .10 .30
❑ 44 The Woman King .10 .30
❑ 45 The Woman King .10 .30
❑ 46 A Day in the Life .10 .30
❑ 47 A Day in the Life .10 .30
❑ 48 A Day in the Life .10 .30
❑ 49 Dirty Hands .10 .30
❑ 50 Dirty Hands .10 .30
❑ 51 Dirty Hands .10 .30
❑ 52 Maelstrom .10 .30
❑ 53 Maelstrom .10 .30
❑ 54 Maelstrom .10 .30
❑ 55 The Son Also Rises .10 .30
❑ 56 The Son Also Rises .10 .30
❑ 57 The Son Also Rises .10 .30
❑ 58 Crossroads: Part 1 .10 .30
❑ 59 Crossroads: Part 1 .10 .30
❑ 60 Crossroads: Part 1 .10 .30
❑ 61 Crossroads: Part 2 .10 .30
❑ 62 Crossroads: Part 2 .10 .30
❑ 63 Crossroads: Part 2 .10 .30

2008 Battlestar Galactica Season Three Autographs
STATED ODDS 1:12
EO ODDS ONE PER 6-CASE PURCHASE
L (LIMITED): 300-500 CARDS
❑ AD Alisen Down 5.00 12.00
❑ AP Amanda Plummer 6.00 15.00
❑ BD1 Bruce Davison 6.00 15.00
❑ BD2 Bill Duke L 6.00 15.00
❑ CT Christian Tessier 5.00 12.00
❑ EO Edward James Olmos
❑ FC Fulvio Cecere 5.00 12.00
❑ GP Grace Park 75.00 150.00
❑ GR Gabrielle Rose 5.00 12.00
❑ JB Jamie Bamber L
❑ JC James Callis L 8.00 20.00
❑ JH Jennifer Halley 5.00 12.00
❑ KS Katee Sackhoff
❑ LC Luciana Carro 10.00 25.00
❑ MF Michelle Forbes L 25.00 50.00
❑ MH Michael Hogan 8.00 20.00
❑ MM Mary McDonnell L
❑ MS Mark Sheppard L 8.00 20.00
❑ RM Ronald D. Moore 10.00 25.00
❑ RW Rick Worthy 8.00 20.00
❑ SH Susan Hogan 5.00 12.00
❑ TL Tiffany Lyndall-Knight 6.00 15.00
❑ TP Tahmoh Penikett 10.00 25.00

2008 Battlestar Galactica Season Three Costumes
STATED ODDS 1:24
TH ODDS ONE PER 2-CASE PURCHASE
L (LIMITED): 300-500 CARDS
❑ CC32 William Adama 5.00 12.00
❑ CC33 Karl Agathon 4.00 10.00
❑ CC34 D'anna Biers 5.00 12.00
❑ CC35 Number Six 6.00 15.00
❑ CC36 Sharon Valerii 10.00 25.00
❑ CC37 Sharon Valerii 10.00 25.00
❑ CC38 Samuel Anders 4.00 10.00
❑ CC39 Number Six 6.00 15.00
❑ CC40 Simon 4.00 10.00
❑ DC3 Gaius Baltar 12.00 30.00
Number Six L
❑ DC4 Gaius Baltar 12.00 30.00
Sharon Valerii
❑ DC5 Gaius Baltar 12.00 30.00
Number Six L
❑ TH Number 6 50.00 100.00
Tricia Helfer AU

2008 Battlestar Galactica Season Three Film Clip Gallery
COMPLETE SET (9)
STATED ODDS 1:24
❑ F1 William Adama 4.00 10.00
❑ F2 Saul Tigh 4.00 10.00
❑ F3 Karl Agathon 4.00 10.00
❑ F4 Lee Adama 4.00 10.00
❑ F5 Kara Thrace 4.00 10.00
Sam Anders
❑ F6 Sharon Agathon 4.00 10.00
❑ F7 Number Six 4.00 10.00
❑ F8 Gaius Baltar 4.00 10.00
❑ F9 Laura Roslin 4.00 10.00

2008 Battlestar Galactica Season Three Love in War
COMPLETE SET (9)
STATED ODDS 1:12
❑ L1 Lee 1.50 4.00
Dualla
❑ L2 Kara 1.50 4.00
Sam
❑ L3 Kara 1.50 4.00
Lee
❑ L4 William 1.50 4.00
Carolanne
❑ L5 Gaius 1.50 4.00
Number Six
❑ L6 Leoben 1.50 4.00
Kara
❑ L7 Sharon 1.50 4.00
Karl
❑ L8 Dualla 1.50 4.00
Billy
❑ L9 Gaius 1.50 4.00
Gina

2008 Battlestar Galactica Season Three Promos
❑ P1 Group of Four .75 2.00
(General Distribution)
❑ P2 Kara Thrace/Lee Adama .75 2.00
(NSU Magazine)
❑ P3 Apollo/Number 6 4.00 10.00
(Album Exclusive)

2008 Battlestar Galactica Season Three Shelter Posters
COMPLETE SET (3)
STATED ODDS 1:144
❑ S5 Lee Adama 15.00 30.00
William Adama/Kara Thrace
❑ S6 Laura Roslin 15.00 30.00
William Adama/Gaius Baltar
❑ S7 Gaius Baltar 15.00 30.00
Number Six/Sharon Valerii

2008 Battlestar Galactica Season Three Significant Seven
COMPLETE SET (7)
STATED ODDS 1:8
❑ SS1 Brother Cavil 1.25 3.00
❑ SS2 Leoben Conoy 1.25 3.00
❑ SS3 D'anna Biers 1.25 3.00
❑ SS4 Simon 1.25 3.00
❑ SS5 Aaron Doral 1.25 3.00
❑ SS6 Number Six 1.25 3.00
❑ SS7 Sharon Valerii 1.25 3.00

2008 Bench Warmer Limited
COMPLETE SET (90)
COMP.SET w/o SP's (72) 5.00 12.00
❑ 1 Traci Bingham .15 .40
❑ 2 Nikki Ziering .15 .40
❑ 3 Gail Kim .15 .40
❑ 4 Kitana Baker .15 .40
❑ 5 Lisa Gleave .15 .40
❑ 6 Buffy Tyler .15 .40
❑ 7 Spencer Scott R .15 .40
❑ 8 Claudia Jordan .15 .40
❑ 9 Carrie Stroup .15 .40
❑ 10 Jennifer Korbin .15 .40
❑ 11 Camille Anderson .15 .40
❑ 12 Candace Kita .15 .40
❑ 13 Christy Hemme .40 1.00
❑ 14 Traci Brooks .15 .40
❑ 15 Martina Andrews .15 .40
❑ 16 Cat Miller .15 .40
❑ 17 Kayla Collins .15 .40
❑ 18 Enya Flack .15 .40
❑ 19 Jenae Alt .15 .40
❑ 20 Lana Kinnear .15 .40
❑ 21 Rachel Bernstein .15 .40
❑ 22 Michelle McLaughlin .15 .40
❑ 23 Melissa Paz .15 .40
❑ 24 Holley Ann Dorrough .15 .40
❑ 25 Vanessa Cervantes .15 .40
❑ 26 Jessica Hall .15 .40
❑ 27 Mia St. John .15 .40
❑ 28 Charity Hodges .15 .40
❑ 29 Laurena Lacey .15 .40
❑ 30 Raven Lexy .15 .40
❑ 31 Eurydice Davis .15 .40
❑ 32 Xi Xi Yang .15 .40
❑ 33 Anna Chudoba .15 .40
❑ 34 Jessica Michaels .15 .40
❑ 35 Masumi Max .15 .40
❑ 36 Michelle Lei .15 .40
❑ 37 Brittany McGraw .15 .40
❑ 38 Denyce Lawton .15 .40
❑ 39 Amanda Paige .15 .40
❑ 40 Teresa Noreen .15 .40
❑ 41 Tiffany Selby .15 .40
❑ 42 Robyn Watkins .15 .40
❑ 43 Bobbi Billard .15 .40
❑ 44 Angela Shih .15 .40
❑ 45 Katy Johnson .15 .40
❑ 46 Jenn Grace .15 .40
❑ 47 Amie Nicole .15 .40
❑ 48 Louise Glover .15 .40
❑ 49 Brandie Moses .15 .40
❑ 50 Camille Cardinale .15 .40
❑ 51 Traci Bingham AS .15 .40
❑ 52 Mary Riley AS .40 1.00
❑ 53 April Scott AS .15 .40
❑ 54 Shay Lyn AS .15 .40
❑ 55 Jennifer England AS .15 .40
❑ 56 Jessica Rockwell AS .15 .40
❑ 57 Melissa Mojo Hunter AS .15 .40
❑ 58 Molly Shea AS .15 .40
❑ 59 Holly Huddleston AS .15 .40
❑ 60 Lindsey Roeper AS .15 .40
❑ 61 Charity Hodges AS .15 .40
❑ 62 Camille Anderson AS .15 .40
❑ 63 Spencer Scott AS .15 .40
❑ 64 Holley Ann Dorrough AS .15 .40
❑ 65 Mia St. John AS .15 .40
❑ 66 Jennifer Korbin AS .15 .40
❑ 67 Brittany McGraw AS .15 .40
❑ 68 Kitana Baker AS .15 .40
❑ 69 The Olly Girls .15 .40
❑ 70 Carrie Stroup .15 .40
Rachel Bernstein
❑ 71 Lindsey Roeper .15 .40
Angela Shih
❑ 72 G.Kim .15 .40
C.Hemme/T.Brooks
❑ H73 Traci Bingham AA 2.00 5.00
❑ H74 Camille Anderson AA 2.00 5.00
❑ H75 Brandie Moses AA 2.00 5.00
❑ H76 Kitana Baker AA 2.00 5.00
❑ H77 Seanna Mitchell AA 2.00 5.00
❑ H78 Jessica Michaels AA 2.00 5.00
❑ H79 Samantha Werbow AA 2.00 5.00
❑ H80 Camille Cardinale AA 2.00 5.00
❑ H81 Nikki Ziering BC 2.00 5.00
❑ H82 Buffy Tyler BC 2.00 5.00
❑ H83 Claudia Jordan BC 2.00 5.00
❑ H84 Vanessa Cervantes BC 2.00 5.00
❑ H85 Amie Decker BC 2.00 5.00
❑ H86 April Scott BC 2.00 5.00
❑ H87 Charity Hodges BC 2.00 5.00
❑ H88 Lena Yada BC 2.00 5.00
❑ H89 Raven Lexy BC 2.00 5.00
❑ H90 Denyce Lawton BC 2.00 5.00

2008 Bench Warmer Limited Autographs Gold Foil
STATED ODDS 1:12
❑ 1 Traci Bingham 5.00 12.00
❑ 2 April Scott 5.00 12.00
❑ 3 Kitana Baker 5.00 12.00
❑ 4 Lena Yada 5.00 12.00
❑ 5 Brittany McGraw 5.00 12.00
❑ 6 Jessica Michaels 5.00 12.00
❑ 7 Holley Ann Dorrough 5.00 12.00
❑ 8 Candace Kita 5.00 12.00
❑ 9 Cat Miller 5.00 12.00
❑ 10 Katy Johnson 5.00 12.00
❑ 11 Masumi Max 5.00 12.00
❑ 12 Shay Lyn 5.00 12.00
❑ 13 Amie Decker 5.00 12.00
❑ 14 Brandie Moses 5.00 12.00
❑ 15 Amanda Paige 5.00 12.00
❑ 16 Michelle Lei 5.00 12.00
❑ 17 Melissa Paz 5.00 12.00
❑ 18 Gail Kim 5.00 12.00
❑ 19 Tracy Brooks 5.00 12.00
❑ 20 Mary Riley 6.00 15.00

2008 Bench Warmer Limited Autographs Pink Foil
STATED PRINT RUN 25 SER. #'d SETS

2008 Bench Warmer Limited Autographs Blue Foil
STATED PRINT RUN 10 SER. #'d SETS

2008 Bench Warmer Limited Decision 2008
COMPLETE SET (5) 10.00 25.00
STATED ODDS 1:24
❑ 1 Hillary Clinton 3.00 8.00
❑ 2 Cindy McCain 3.00 8.00
❑ 3 Michelle Obama 3.00 8.00
❑ 4 Sarah Palin 3.00 8.00
❑ 5 Bill Clinton 3.00 8.00

2008 Bench Warmer Limited Halloween Foil
COMPLETE SET (11)
COMP.SET w/o SP (10)
STATED ODDS 1:8
❑ 1 Jennifer Korbin 2.50 6.00
❑ 2 Mary Riley 3.00 8.00
❑ 3 Molly Shea 2.50 6.00
❑ 4 Lana Kinnear 2.50 6.00
❑ 5 Cora Skinner 2.50 6.00
❑ 6 Heather Bryant 2.50 6.00
❑ 7 April Scott 2.50 6.00
❑ 8 Lindsey Roeper 2.50 6.00
❑ 9 Cecille Gahr 2.50 6.00
❑ 10A Aiko Tanaka - Maid 2.50 6.00
❑ 10B Aiko Tanaka - Devil SP

2008 Bench Warmer Limited Kiss
STATED ODDS 1:72
❑ 1 Traci Bingham 10.00 25.00
❑ 2 Mary Riley 12.00 30.00
❑ 3 April Scott 10.00 25.00
❑ 4 Brandi Moses 10.00 25.00
❑ 5 Jennifer Korbin 10.00 25.00
❑ 6 Lena Yada 10.00 25.00
❑ 7 Mellissa Taylor 10.00 25.00
❑ 8 Kayla Collins 10.00 25.00
❑ 9 Rachel Bernstein 10.00 25.00
❑ 10 Lisa Gleave 10.00 25.00
❑ 11 Martina Andrews 10.00 25.00
❑ 12 Masumi Max 10.00 25.00

2008 Bench Warmer Limited Kiss Autographs Pink Foil
STATED PRINT RUN 10 SER. #'d SETS
❑ 1 Traci Bingham
❑ 2 Mary Riley
❑ 3 April Scott
❑ 4 Brandi Moses
❑ 5 Jennifer Korbin
❑ 6 Lena Yada
❑ 7 Mellissa Taylor
❑ 8 Kayla Collins
❑ 9 Rachel Bernstein
❑ 10 Lisa Gleave
❑ 11 Martina Andrews
❑ 12 Masumi Max

2008 Bench Warmer Limited Kiss Autographs Blue Foil
STATED PRINT RUN 5 SER. #'d SETS

2008 Bench Warmer Limited School Girls Autographs Gold Foil
STATED ODDS 1:48
❑ 1 Lisa Gleave 6.00 15.00
❑ 2 Kitana Baker 6.00 15.00
❑ 3 Nikki Ziering 6.00 15.00
❑ 4 Spencer Scott 6.00 15.00
❑ 5 Jennifer Korbin 6.00 15.00
❑ 6 Bobbi Billard 6.00 15.00
❑ 7 Lindsey Roeper 6.00 15.00
❑ 8 Enya Flack 6.00 15.00
❑ 9 April Scott 6.00 15.00

2008 Bench Warmer Limited School Girls Autographs Pink Foil
STATED PRINT RUN 25 SER. #'d SETS

2008 Bench Warmer Limited School Girls Autographs Blue Foil
STATED PRINT RUN 10 SER. #'d SETS

2008 Bench Warmer Limited Schoolgirl Swatch Autographs
STATED PRINT RUN 10 SER. #'d SETS
❑ 1 Nikki Ziering
❑ 2 Kitana Baker
❑ 3 Jennifer Korbin
❑ 4 Buffy Tyler
❑ 5 Spencer Scott
❑ 6 Tiffany Selby
❑ 7 April Scott
❑ 8 Lindsey Roeper
❑ 9 Bobbi Billard
❑ 10 Gail Kim
❑ 11 Lisa Gleave
❑ 12 Mary Riley

2008 Bench Warmer Limited Super Rare Autographs Pink Foil
STATED PRINT RUN 10 SER. #'d SETS

2008 Bench Warmer Limited Super Rare Autographs Blue Foil
STATED PRINT RUN 5 SER. #'d SETS

2008 Bench Warmer Limited International Autographs Gold Foil
STATED PRINT RUN 60 SER. #'d SETS
❑ 1 Lisa Gleave
❑ 2 Gail Kim
❑ 3 Jennifer Korbin
❑ 4 Lena Yada
❑ 5 Traci Brooks
❑ 6 Lindsey Roeper
❑ 7 Nikki Ziering
❑ 8 Carrie Stroup
❑ 9 Louise Glover
❑ 10 April Scott

2008 Bench Warmer Limited International Autographs Pink Foil
STATED PRINT RUN 10 SER. #'d SETS
UNPRICED DUE TO SCARCITY

2008 Bench Warmer Limited International Autographs Blue Foil
UNPRICED DUE TO SCARCITY

2008 Bench Warmer Limited International Bikini Swatches

STATED PRINT RUN 10 SER. #'d SETS
UNPRICED DUE TO SCARCITY

- ❑ 1 Lisa Gleave
- ❑ 2 Kitana Baker
- ❑ 3 Nikki Ziering
- ❑ 4 April Scott
- ❑ 5 Jennifer Korbin
- ❑ 6 Martina Andrews
- ❑ 7 Melissa Taylor

2008 Bench Warmer Limited International Bikini Swatches Autographs

STATED PRINT RUN 1 SER. #'d SETS
UNPRICED DUE TO SCARCITY

- ❑ 1 Lisa Gleave
- ❑ 2 Kitana Baker
- ❑ 3 Nikki Ziering
- ❑ 4 April Scott
- ❑ 5 Jennifer Korbin
- ❑ 6 Martina Andrews
- ❑ 7 Melissa Taylor

2008 Bench Warmer Limited International Kiss Gold Foil

STATED PRINT RUN 50 SER. #'d SETS

- ❑ 1 Nikki Ziering
- ❑ 2 Buffy Tyler
- ❑ 3 Cat Miller
- ❑ 4 Lisa Gleave
- ❑ 5 Spencer Scott

2008 Bench Warmer Limited International Kiss Autographs Pink Foil

STATED PRINT RUN 5 SER. #'d SETS
UNPRICED DUE TO SCARCITY

- ❑ 1 Nikki Ziering
- ❑ 2 Buffy Tyler
- ❑ 3 Cat Miller
- ❑ 4 Lisa Gleave
- ❑ 5 Spencer Scott

2008 Bench Warmer Limited International Kiss Autographs Blue Foil

STATED PRINT RUN 1 SER. #'d SET
UNPRICED DUE TO SCARCITY

2008 Bench Warmer Signature Series

COMPLETE SET (60) 5.00 12.00

- ❑ 1 The Olly Girls .15 .40
- ❑ 2 Sara Jean Underwood .15 .40
- ❑ 3 Cindy Margolis .15 .40
- ❑ 4 Nikki Ziering .15 .40
- ❑ 5 Lisa Gleave .15 .40
- ❑ 6 Buffy Tyler .15 .40
- ❑ 7 Christy Hemme .15 .40
- ❑ 8 Mary Riley .15 .40
- ❑ 9 Kitana Baker .15 .40
- ❑ 10 Claudia Jordan .15 .40
- ❑ 11 Camille Anderson .15 .40
- ❑ 12 Spencer Scott .15 .40
- ❑ 13 Jessica Rockwell .15 .40
- ❑ 14 Kayla Collins .15 .40
- ❑ 15 Martina Andrews .15 .40
- ❑ 16 Enya Flack .15 .40
- ❑ 17 Michelle Mclaughlin .15 .40
- ❑ 18 Gail Kim .15 .40
- ❑ 19 Jenae Alt .15 .40
- ❑ 20 Jessica Hall .15 .40
- ❑ 21 Robyn Watkins .15 .40
- ❑ 22 Michelle Baena .15 .40
- ❑ 23 Katarina Van Derham .15 .40
- ❑ 24 Shay Lyn .15 .40
- ❑ 25 Melissa Taylor .15 .40
- ❑ 26 Erin Tietsort .15 .40
- ❑ 27 Traci Brooks .15 .40
- ❑ 28 Jennifer Korbin .15 .40
- ❑ 29 Keely Williams .15 .40
- ❑ 30 Tamara Witmer .15 .40
- ❑ 31 Catherine Kluthe .15 .40
- ❑ 32 Miriam Gonzalez .15 .40
- ❑ 33 Lisa Lakatos .15 .40
- ❑ 34 Sherry Goggin .15 .40
- ❑ 35 Jen Sibley .15 .40
- ❑ 36 Tamie Sheffield .15 .40
- ❑ 37 Renee Stone .15 .40
- ❑ 38 Jessica Burciaga .15 .40
- ❑ 39 Paige Peterson .15 .40
- ❑ 40 Krisi Ballentine .15 .40
- ❑ 41 Leigh Ann Spence .15 .40
- ❑ 42 Rachel Bernstein .15 .40
- ❑ 43 Carrie Stroup .15 .40
- ❑ 44 Tiffany Selby .15 .40
- ❑ 45 Candice Michelle .15 .40
- ❑ 46 Amber Hay .15 .40
- ❑ 47 Jennifer England .15 .40
- ❑ 48 Lisa Ligon .15 .40
- ❑ 49 Sandra Taylor .15 .40
- ❑ 50 Brande Roderick .15 .40
- ❑ 51 Jaime Bergman .15 .40
- ❑ 52 Colleen Shannon .15 .40
- ❑ 53 Brandy Grace .15 .40
- ❑ 54 Simona Fusco .15 .40
- ❑ 55 Charity Hodges .15 .40
- ❑ 56 Bobbi Billard .15 .40
- ❑ 57 Holly Huddleston .15 .40
- ❑ 58 Molly Shea .15 .40
- ❑ 59 Mia St. John .15 .40
- ❑ 60 Flo Jalin .15 .40

2008 Bench Warmer Signature Series Printing Plates Front Black

STATED PRINT RUN 1 SER. #'d SET
UNPRICED DUE TO SCARCITY

2008 Bench Warmer Signature Series Printing Plates Front Cyan

STATED PRINT RUN 1 SER. #'d SET
UNPRICED DUE TO SCARCITY

2008 Bench Warmer Signature Series Printing Plates Front Magenta

STATED PRINT RUN 1 SER. #'d SET
UNPRICED DUE TO SCARCITY

2008 Bench Warmer Signature Series Printing Plates Front Yellow

STATED PRINT RUN 1 SER. #'d SET
UNPRICED DUE TO SCARCITY

2008 Bench Warmer Signature Series Autographs Blue Foil

STATED PRINT RUN 5 SER. #'d SETS
UNPRICED DUE TO SCARCITY

2008 Bench Warmer Signature Series Autographs Gold Foil

STATED PRINT RUN 125 SER. #'d SETS

2008 Bench Warmer Signature Series Autographs Green Foil

STATED PRINT RUN 10 SER. #'d SETS
UNPRICED DUE TO SCARCITY

2008 Bench Warmer Signature Series Autographs Pink Foil

STATED PRINT RUN 50 SER. #'d SETS

2008 Bench Warmer Signature Series Autographs Purple Foil

STATED PRINT RUN 25 SER. #'d SETS

2008 Bench Warmer Signature Series Autographs Red Foil

STATED PRINT RUN 1 SER. #'d SET
UNPRICED DUE TO SCARCITY

2008 Bench Warmer Signature Series Autographs Silver Foil

OVERALL AUTO ODDS ONE PER PACK

- ❑ 1 The Olly Girls 6.00 15.00
- ❑ 2 Sara Jean Underwood 6.00 15.00
- ❑ 3 Cindy Margolis 6.00 15.00
- ❑ 4 Nikki Ziering 5.00 12.00
- ❑ 5 Lisa Gleave 5.00 12.00
- ❑ 6 Buffy Tyler 5.00 12.00
- ❑ 7 Christy Hemme 8.00 20.00
- ❑ 8 Mary Riley 6.00 15.00
- ❑ 9 Kitana Baker 5.00 12.00
- ❑ 10 Claudia Jordan 5.00 12.00
- ❑ 11 Camille Anderson 5.00 12.00
- ❑ 12 Spencer Scott 5.00 12.00
- ❑ 13 Jessica Rockwell 5.00 12.00
- ❑ 14 Kayla Collins 5.00 12.00
- ❑ 15 Martina Andrews 5.00 12.00
- ❑ 16 Enya Flack 5.00 12.00
- ❑ 17 Michelle Mclaughlin 5.00 12.00
- ❑ 18 Gail Kim 5.00 12.00
- ❑ 19 Jenae Alt 5.00 12.00
- ❑ 20 Jessica Hall 5.00 12.00
- ❑ 21 Robyn Watkins 5.00 12.00
- ❑ 22 Michelle Baena 5.00 12.00
- ❑ 23 Katarina Van Derham 5.00 12.00
- ❑ 24 Shay Lyn 5.00 12.00
- ❑ 25 Melissa Taylor 5.00 12.00
- ❑ 26 Erin Tietsort 5.00 12.00
- ❑ 27 Traci Brooks 5.00 12.00
- ❑ 28 Jennifer Korbin 5.00 12.00
- ❑ 29 Keely Williams 5.00 12.00
- ❑ 30 Tamara Witmer 5.00 12.00
- ❑ 31 Catherine Kluthe 5.00 12.00
- ❑ 32 Miriam Gonzalez 5.00 12.00
- ❑ 33 Lisa Lakatos 5.00 12.00
- ❑ 34 Sherry Goggin 5.00 12.00
- ❑ 35 Jen Sibley 5.00 12.00
- ❑ 36 Tamie Sheffield 5.00 12.00
- ❑ 37 Renee Stone 5.00 12.00
- ❑ 38 Jessica Burciaga 5.00 12.00
- ❑ 39 Paige Peterson 5.00 12.00
- ❑ 40 Krisi Ballentine 5.00 12.00
- ❑ 41 Leigh Ann Spence 5.00 12.00
- ❑ 42 Rachel Bernstein 5.00 12.00
- ❑ 43 Carrie Stroup 5.00 12.00
- ❑ 44 Tiffany Selby 5.00 12.00
- ❑ 45 Candice Michelle 5.00 12.00
- ❑ 46 Amber Hay 5.00 12.00
- ❑ 47 Jennifer England 5.00 12.00
- ❑ 48 Lisa Ligon 5.00 12.00
- ❑ 49 Sandra Taylor 5.00 12.00
- ❑ 50 Brande Roderick 5.00 12.00
- ❑ 51 Jaime Bergman 5.00 12.00
- ❑ 52 Colleen Shannon 5.00 12.00
- ❑ 53 Brandy Grace 5.00 12.00
- ❑ 54 Simona Fusco 5.00 12.00
- ❑ 55 Charity Hodges 5.00 12.00
- ❑ 56 Bobbi Billard 5.00 12.00
- ❑ 57 Holly Huddleston 5.00 12.00
- ❑ 58 Molly Shea 5.00 12.00
- ❑ 59 Mia St. John 5.00 12.00
- ❑ 60 Flo Jalin 5.00 12.00

2008 Bench Warmer Signature Series Autographs Printing Plates Back Black

STATED PRINT RUN 1 SER. #'d SET
UNPRICED DUE TO SCARCITY

2008 Bench Warmer Signature Series Autographs Printing Plates Back Cyan

STATED PRINT RUN 1 SER. #'d SET
UNPRICED DUE TO SCARCITY

2008 Bench Warmer Signature Series Autographs Printing Plates Back Magenta

STATED PRINT RUN 1 SER. #'d SET
UNPRICED DUE TO SCARCITY

2008 Bench Warmer Signature Series Autographs Printing Plates Back Yellow

STATED PRINT RUN 1 SER. #'d SET
UNPRICED DUE TO SCARCITY

2008 Bench Warmer Signature Series Autographs Printing Plates Front Black

STATED PRINT RUN 1 SER. #'d SET
UNPRICED DUE TO SCARCITY

2008 Bench Warmer Signature Series Autographs Printing Plates Front Cyan

STATED PRINT RUN 1 SER. #'d SET
UNPRICED DUE TO SCARCITY

2008 Bench Warmer Signature Series Autographs Printing Plates Front Magenta

STATED PRINT RUN 1 SER. #'d SET
UNPRICED DUE TO SCARCITY

2008 Bench Warmer Signature Series Autographs Printing Plates Front Yellow

STATED PRINT RUN 1 SER. #'d SET
UNPRICED DUE TO SCARCITY

2008 Bench Warmer Signature Series Bikini Swatches Autographs

UNPRICED DUE TO SCARCITY

- ❑ 1 The Olly Girls
- ❑ 2 Nikki Ziering
- ❑ 3 Buffy Tyler
- ❑ 4 Lisa Gleave
- ❑ 5 Mary Riley
- ❑ 6 Kitana Baker
- ❑ 7 Christy Hemme
- ❑ 8 Tiffany Selby
- ❑ 9 Claudia Jordan
- ❑ 10 The Costello Twins
- ❑ 11 Bobbi Billard
- ❑ 12 The Bentley Twins

2008 Bench Warmer Signature Series Kiss Gold Foil

STATED PRINT RUN 50-100

2008 Bench Warmer Signature Series Kiss Silver Foil

COMPLETE SET (16)
STATED ODDS 1:30

- ❑ 1 Holly Huddleston 8.00 20.00
- ❑ 2 Molly Shea 8.00 20.00
- ❑ 3 Nikki Ziering 8.00 20.00
- ❑ 4 Spencer Scott 8.00 20.00
- ❑ 5 Jenae Alt 8.00 20.00
- ❑ 6 Lisa Gleave 8.00 20.00
- ❑ 7 Kitana Baker 8.00 20.00
- ❑ 8 Buffy Tyler 8.00 20.00
- ❑ 9 Claudia Jordan 8.00 20.00
- ❑ 10 Mary Riley 10.00 25.00
- ❑ 11 Christy Hemme 10.00 25.00
- ❑ 12 Jennifer England 8.00 20.00
- ❑ 13 Carrie Stroup 8.00 20.00
- ❑ 14 Candice Michelle 8.00 20.00
- ❑ 15 Bobbi Billard 8.00 20.00
- ❑ 16 Sara Underwood 8.00 20.00

2008 Bench Warmer Signature Series Kiss Purple Foil

STATED PRINT RUN 25 SER. #'d SETS

2008 Bench Warmer Signature Series Kiss Printing Plates Back Black

STATED PRINT RUN 1 SER. #'d SET
UNPRICED DUE TO SCARCITY

2008 Bench Warmer Signature Series Kiss Printing Plates Back Cyan

STATED PRINT RUN 1 SER. #'d SET
UNPRICED DUE TO SCARCITY

2008 Bench Warmer Signature Series Kiss Printing Plates Back Magenta

STATED PRINT RUN 1 SER. #'d SET
UNPRICED DUE TO SCARCITY

2008 Bench Warmer Signature Series Kiss Printing Plates Back Yellow

STATED PRINT RUN 1 SER. #'d SET
UNPRICED DUE TO SCARCITY

2008 Bench Warmer Signature Series Kiss Printing Plates Front Black

STATED PRINT RUN 1 SER. #'d SET
UNPRICED DUE TO SCARCITY

2008 Bench Warmer Signature Series Kiss Printing Plates Front Cyan

STATED PRINT RUN 1 SER. #'d SET
UNPRICED DUE TO SCARCITY

2008 Bench Warmer Signature Series Kiss Printing Plates Front Magenta

STATED PRINT RUN 1 SER. #'d SET
UNPRICED DUE TO SCARCITY

2008 Bench Warmer Signature Series Kiss Printing Plates Front Yellow

STATED PRINT RUN 1 SER. #'d SET
UNPRICED DUE TO SCARCITY

2008 Bench Warmer Signature Series Lingerie

COMPLETE SET 6.00 15.00
STATED ODDS 1:5

- ❑ 1 Jennifer Korbin 1.25 3.00
- ❑ 2 Camille Anderson 1.25 3.00
- ❑ 3 Claudia Jordan 1.25 3.00
- ❑ 4 Nikki Ziering 1.25 3.00
- ❑ 5 Lisa Gleave 1.25 3.00
- ❑ 6 Gail Kim 1.25 3.00
- ❑ 7 Buffy Tyler 1.25 3.00
- ❑ 8 Kitana Baker 1.25 3.00
- ❑ 9 Jessica Rockwell 1.25 3.00
- ❑ 10 Christy Hemme 1.50 4.00
- ❑ 11 Spencer Scott 1.25 3.00
- ❑ 12 Mary Riley 1.50 4.00

2008 Bench Warmer Signature Series Props

STATED ODDS 1:60

- ❑ 1 Mary Riley (Baseball Helmet 10.00 25.00
- ❑ 2 Lisa Gleave (Baseball Bat 8.00 20.00
- ❑ 3 Buffy Tyler (Pink Soccer Ball 8.00 20.00
- ❑ 4 Christy Hemme (Hockey Stick 10.00 25.00
- ❑ 5 Jennifer Korbin (Football 8.00 20.00
- ❑ 6 Spencer Scott (Softball
- ❑ 7 Kitana Baker (Pink Basketball 8.00 20.00
- ❑ 8 Rachel Bernstein (Pink Soccer Ball 8.00 20.00
- ❑ 9 Claudia Jordan (Baseball Glove 8.00 20.00
- ❑ 10A Jessica Hall (Blue Soccer Ball 8.00 20.00
- ❑ 10B Miriam Gonzalez (Basketball 10.00 25.00
- ❑ 11 Camille Anderson (Basketball 8.00 20.00
- ❑ 12 Bobbi Billard (Volleyball 8.00 20.00
- ❑ 13 Mia St. John (Pink Boxing Gloves 8.00 20.00
- ❑ 14 Charity Hodges (Football 8.00 20.00
- ❑ 15A Jenae Alt (Baseball Bat 8.00 20.00
- ❑ 15B Nikki Ziering (Hockey Stick 8.00 20.00

2008 Bench Warmer Signature Series Props Autographs

STATED ODDS

2008 Bench Warmer Signature Series Sketches

STATED ODDS TWO PER CASE

- ❑ 1 Molly Shea 10.00 20.00
- ❑ 2 Holly Huddleston 10.00 20.00
- ❑ 3 Jennifer England 10.00 20.00
- ❑ 4 Aubrie Lemon 10.00 20.00
- ❑ 5 Mary Riley 10.00 20.00
- ❑ 6 Kitana Baker 10.00 20.00
- ❑ 7 Sara Underwood 10.00 20.00
- ❑ 8 Brande Roderick 10.00 20.00
- ❑ 9 Miriam Gonzalez 10.00 20.00
- ❑ 10 Bobbi Billard 10.00 20.00
- ❑ 11 Nikki Ziering 10.00 20.00
- ❑ 12 Buffy Tyler 10.00 20.00
- ❑ 13 Sandra Taylor 10.00 20.00
- ❑ 14 Jaime Hammer 10.00 20.00
- ❑ 15 Lisa Gleave 10.00 20.00
- ❑ 16 Suzanne Stokes 10.00 20.00
- ❑ 17 Lisa Latakos 10.00 20.00
- ❑ 18 Jessica Rockwell 10.00 20.00
- ❑ 19 Katarina Van Derham 10.00 20.00
- ❑ 20 Jennifer Korbin 10.00 20.00
- ❑ 21 The Olly Girls 10.00 20.00

2008 Camp Rock

COMPLETE SET (71) 4.00 10.00

- ❑ 1 Mitchie Torres .10 .30
- ❑ 2 Shane Gray .10 .30
- ❑ 3 Nate, Shane, and Jason .10 .30
- ❑ 4 Mitchie and Shane .10 .30
- ❑ 5 Mitchie and the Band .10 .30
- ❑ 6 You're Dreamin'! .10 .30
- ❑ 7 Who Will I Be? .10 .30
- ❑ 8 Dress For School - Act Cool! .10 .30
- ❑ 9 Passion For Fashion .10 .30
- ❑ 10 Who's That Rock Star? .10 .30
- ❑ 11 Mirror, Mirror .10 .30
- ❑ 12 Rock 'n' Roll Girl .10 .30
- ❑ 13 The Write Stuff .10 .30
- ❑ 14 This Is Who? .10 .30
- ❑ 15 Uh... Hello? .10 .30
- ❑ 16 Jammin' Cabin .10 .30
- ❑ 17 Displaced? .10 .30
- ❑ 18 Tess Tests Mitchie .10 .30
- ❑ 19 Tess Impressed .10 .30
- ❑ 20 Keepin' The Beat .10 .30
- ❑ 21 Who Starts? .10 .30
- ❑ 22 Let 'er Rip! .10 .30
- ❑ 23 Take A Bow .10 .30
- ❑ 24 Kitchen Duty .10 .30
- ❑ 25 Pop Star Phantom .10 .30
- ❑ 26 Shane, Unplugged & Unhinged .10 .30
- ❑ 27 What's The Haps? .10 .30
- ❑ 28 Hit The Groove .10 .30
- ❑ 29 Wannabe? .10 .30
- ❑ 30 Too Cool .10 .30
- ❑ 31 Moody Superstar .10 .30
- ❑ 32 A Fan Is Born .10 .30
- ❑ 33 Food Fight! .10 .30
- ❑ 34 Busted! .10 .30
- ❑ 35 Who Started It? .10 .30
- ❑ 36 The Voice Inside My Head .10 .30
- ❑ 37 Mitchie Unplugged .10 .30
- ❑ 38 Kitchen Confidential .10 .30
- ❑ 39 Hey, Mom, How Ya Doing? .10 .30
- ❑ 40 Splish Splash! .10 .30
- ❑ 41 Drowning In Lies .10 .30
- ❑ 42 Caitlyn's Confession .10 .30
- ❑ 43 Beach Jam .10 .30
- ❑ 44 Play My Music .10 .30
- ❑ 45 A Secret Spilled .10 .30
- ❑ 46 I Thought You Were Different .10 .30
- ❑ 47 Strummin' His Pain .10 .30
- ❑ 48 Independent Me .10 .30
- ❑ 49 Something To Talk About .10 .30
- ❑ 50 Tess Eavesdrops .10 .30
- ❑ 51 Sneaky Girl .10 .30
- ❑ 52 Confession Session .10 .30
- ❑ 53 Mitchie Mortified .10 .30
- ❑ 54 Outcast .10 .30
- ❑ 55 Shane's Pride .10 .30
- ❑ 56 Shane's Message To Mitchie .10 .30
- ❑ 57 Bracelet Brouhaha .10 .30
- ❑ 58 Lost & Found .10 .30
- ❑ 59 Tess Triumphant .10 .30
- ❑ 60 Not For Amateurs .10 .30
- ❑ 61 Nobody's Back-Up .10 .30
- ❑ 62 Follow Your Dream .10 .30
- ❑ 63 Caitlyn Gets Her Shine On .10 .30
- ❑ 64 The Girl With The Voice .10 .30
- ❑ 65 Two Stars Are Brighter Than One .10 .30
- ❑ 66 Where You Are Is Where I Wanna Be .10 .30
- ❑ 67 The Suspense Builds! .10 .30
- ❑ 68 And The Winner Is .10 .30
- ❑ 69 Camp Of What's Happenin' Now! .10 .30
- ❑ 70 We Rock Final Jam! .10 .30
- ❑ 71 Checklist .10 .30
- ❑ P1 Reach for the Stars .40 1.00

2008 Camp Rock Foil

STATED ODDS TWO PER BLISTER PACK

- ❑ F1 Mitchie Torres
- ❑ F2 Shane Gray
- ❑ F3 Nate, Shane, and Jason
- ❑ F4 Mitchie and Shane
- ❑ F5 Mitchie and the Band
- ❑ F6 Moody Superstar
- ❑ F7 A Fan is Born
- ❑ F8 Play My Music

2008 Camp Rock Foil Stickers

STATED ODDS 1:2

- ❑ F1 Mitchie
- ❑ F2 Follow Your Dream
- ❑ F3 Shane
- ❑ F4 Shane and Mitchie
- ❑ F5 Mitchie
- ❑ F6 Moody Superstar
- ❑ F7 Nate, Shane, and Jason
- ❑ F8 Final Jam
- ❑ F9 Mitchie and the Band
- ❑ F10 Shane

2008 Camp Rock Stickers

STATED ODDS 1:2

- ❑ 1 Mitchie
- ❑ 2 Shane
- ❑ 3 Shane and Mitchie
- ❑ 4 Mitchie
- ❑ 5 Shane and Mitchie
- ❑ 6 Nate, Shane, and Jason
- ❑ 7 Mitchie
- ❑ 8 Mitchie and Shane
- ❑ 9 Shane
- ❑ 10 Mitchie

2008 Elvis By The Numbers

COMPLETE SET (80) 5.00 12.00

- ❑ 1 0 .15 .40
- ❑ 2 2:22 .15 .40
- ❑ 3 4:35 .15 .40
- ❑ 4 7:00 .15 .40
- ❑ 5 9:15 .15 .40
- ❑ 6 1 .15 .40
- ❑ 7 $1.00 .15 .40
- ❑ 8 2 .15 .40
- ❑ 9 3 .15 .40
- ❑ 10 3.5 .15 .40
- ❑ 11 $5 .15 .40
- ❑ 12 6 .15 .40
- ❑ 13 11 .15 .40
- ❑ 14 12.95 .15 .40
- ❑ 15 3/8/1961 .15 .40
- ❑ 16 20 .15 .40
- ❑ 17 31 .15 .40
- ❑ 18 33 .15 .40
- ❑ 19 35 .15 .40
- ❑ 20 36.58 .15 .40
- ❑ 21 50 .15 .40
- ❑ 22 51 .15 .40
- ❑ 23 52 .15 .40
- ❑ 24 60 .15 .40
- ❑ 25 72 .15 .40
- ❑ 26 92 .15 .40
- ❑ 27 109 .15 .40
- ❑ 28 111 .15 .40
- ❑ 29 2,681 .15 .40
- ❑ 30 625 .15 .40
- ❑ 31 1,100 .15 .40
- ❑ 32 1954 .15 .40
- ❑ 33 17,552 .15 .40
- ❑ 34 18,000 .15 .40
- ❑ 35 11/15/1956 .15 .40
- ❑ 36 50000 .15 .40
- ❑ 37 65,000 .15 .40
- ❑ 38 102500 .15 .40
- ❑ 39 $22,000,000 .15 .40
- ❑ 40 53310761 .15 .40
- ❑ 41 1,000,000,000+ .15 .40
- ❑ 42 409-52-2002 .15 .40
- ❑ 43 $49,000,000 .15 .40
- ❑ 44 1,000 .15 .40
- ❑ 45 8 .15 .40
- ❑ 46 Kalinsky Gallery .15 .40
- ❑ 47 Kalinsky Gallery .15 .40
- ❑ 48 Kalinsky Gallery .15 .40
- ❑ 49 Kalinsky Gallery .15 .40
- ❑ 50 Kalinsky Gallery .15 .40
- ❑ 51 Kalinsky Gallery .15 .40
- ❑ 52 Kalinsky Gallery .15 .40
- ❑ 53 Kalinsky Gallery .15 .40
- ❑ 54 Kalinsky Gallery .15 .40
- ❑ 55 Kalinsky Gallery .15 .40
- ❑ 56 Kalinsky Gallery .15 .40
- ❑ 57 Kalinsky Gallery .15 .40
- ❑ 58 Kalinsky Gallery .15 .40
- ❑ 59 Kalinsky Gallery .15 .40
- ❑ 60 Kalinsky Gallery .15 .40
- ❑ 61 Kalinsky Gallery .15 .40
- ❑ 62 Kalinsky Gallery .15 .40
- ❑ 63 Kalinsky Gallery .15 .40
- ❑ 64 50 Years Ago (1958-2008) .15 .40
- ❑ 65 50 Years Ago (1958-2008) .15 .40
- ❑ 66 50 Years Ago (1958-2008) .15 .40
- ❑ 67 Wertheimer Army Collection .15 .40
- ❑ 68 Wertheimer Army Collection .15 .40
- ❑ 69 Wertheimer Army Collection .15 .40
- ❑ 70 Wertheimer Army Collection .15 .40
- ❑ 71 Wertheimer Army Collection .15 .40
- ❑ 72 Wertheimer Army Collection .15 .40
- ❑ 73 Wertheimer Army Collection .15 .40
- ❑ 74 Wertheimer Army Collection .15 .40
- ❑ 75 Wertheimer Army Collection .15 .40
- ❑ 76 Wertheimer Army Collection .15 .40
- ❑ 77 Wertheimer Army Collection .15 .40
- ❑ 78 Wertheimer Army Collection .15 .40
- ❑ 79 Wertheimer Army Collection .15 .40
- ❑ 80 Checklist .15 .40
- ❑ ST1 Showtime '56 Concert Ticket/56

2008 Elvis By The Numbers Canvas

COMPLETE SET
STATED ODDS ONE PER PACK

2008 Family Guy Episode IV A New Hope

COMPLETE SET (50) 5.00 12.00
CL1 STATED ODDS ONE PER CASE

- ❑ 1 Epic Story .15 .40
- ❑ 2 Peter Griffin as Han Solo .15 .40
- ❑ 3 Lois Griffin as Princess Leia .15 .40
- ❑ 4 Cleveland as R2-D2 .15 .40
  Quagmire as C-3PO
- ❑ 5 Chris Griffin as Luke .15 .40
- ❑ 6 Herbert as Obi-Wan Kenobi .15 .40
- ❑ 7 Stewie Griffin as Darth Vader .15 .40
- ❑ 8 Brian Griffin as Chewbacca .15 .40
- ❑ 9 Mayor West as Grand Moff Tarkin .15 .40
- ❑ 10 The Story Begins .15 .40
- ❑ 11 Recording a Message .15 .40
- ❑ 12 Narrow Escape .15 .40
- ❑ 13 Interrogation .15 .40
- ❑ 14 In the Desert .15 .40
- ❑ 15 Rebels .15 .40
- ❑ 16 Life on Tatooine .15 .40
- ❑ 17 Empire .15 .40
- ❑ 18 Call for Help .15 .40
- ❑ 19 He's Gone .15 .40
- ❑ 20 Reunited .15 .40
- ❑ 21 Stranger .15 .40
- ❑ 22 Message Is Delivered .15 .40

❑ 23 Training Begins .15 .40
❑ 24 Too Late .15 .40
❑ 25 To Mos Eisley .15 .40
❑ 26 Familiar Song .15 .40
❑ 27 Pilot Found .15 .40
❑ 28 Visitor .15 .40
❑ 29 The Ship .15 .40
❑ 30 Experienced Maneuvers .15 .40
❑ 31 Proven Power .15 .40
❑ 32 The Force .15 .40
❑ 33 Asteroids! .15 .40
❑ 34 The Time of My Life .15 .40
❑ 35 The Rescue .15 .40
❑ 36 Into the Garbage Chute .15 .40
❑ 37 Walls Closing .15 .40
❑ 38 Saved by the Button .15 .40
❑ 39 Lightsabers Drawn .15 .40
❑ 40 Save the Couch .15 .40
❑ 41 Thai Fighters .15 .40
❑ 42 Too Fast! .15 .40
❑ 43 Planning the Attack .15 .40
❑ 44 Reward .15 .40
❑ 45 Battle Begins .15 .40
❑ 46 Going In .15 .40
❑ 47 Use the Force .15 .40
❑ 48 Closing In .15 .40
❑ 49 Target Hit .15 .40
❑ 50 Checklist .15 .40
❑ CL1 Evil Empire/ (issued as case loader) 12.00 25.00

2008 Family Guy Episode IV A New Hope Droid Chat

COMPLETE SET (3) 4.00 10.00
STATED ODDS 1:23

❑ DC1 Bag 'Em 2.00 5.00
❑ DC2 Matrix Love 2.00 5.00
❑ DC3 R2-PAC 2.00 5.00

2008 Family Guy Episode IV A New Hope Puzzle

COMPLETE SET (9) 4.00 10.00
STATED ODDS 1:7

❑ NH1 A New Hope .75 2.00
❑ NH2 A New Hope .75 2.00
❑ NH3 A New Hope .75 2.00
❑ NH4 A New Hope .75 2.00
❑ NH5 A New Hope .75 2.00
❑ NH6 A New Hope .75 2.00
❑ NH7 A New Hope .75 2.00
❑ NH8 A New Hope .75 2.00
❑ NH9 A New Hope .75 2.00

2008 Family Guy Episode IV A New Hope Scenes From Space

COMPLETE SET (6) 4.00 10.00
STATED ODDS 1:11

❑ S1 Scenes From Space 1.25 3.00
❑ S2 Scenes From Space 1.25 3.00
❑ S3 Scenes From Space 1.25 3.00
❑ S4 Scenes From Space 1.25 3.00
❑ S5 Scenes From Space 1.25 3.00
❑ S6 Scenes From Space 1.25 3.00

2008 Family Guy Episode IV A New Hope Spaceships and Transports

COMPLETE SET (9) 4.00 10.00
STATED ODDS 1:9

❑ ST1 Millennium Falcon 1.00 2.50
❑ ST2 TIE Fighter 1.00 2.50
❑ ST3 X-Wing Starfighter 1.00 2.50
❑ ST4 Y-Wing Starfighter 1.00 2.50
❑ ST5 Imperial Cruiser 1.00 2.50
❑ ST6 Blockade Runner 1.00 2.50
❑ ST7 Sandcrawler 1.00 2.50
❑ ST8 Death Star 1.00 2.50
❑ ST9 Landspeeder 1.00 2.50

2008 Family Guy Episode IV A New Hope What Happens Next

COMPLETE SET (6) 4.00 10.00
STATED ODDS 1:11

❑ WN1 You Thought It 1.25 3.00
❑ WN2 Why'd They Separate? 1.25 3.00
❑ WN3 Lost and Found 1.25 3.00
❑ WN4 Missing Railing 1.25 3.00
❑ WN5 Another Drill 1.25 3.00
❑ WN6 Some Maneuvers! 1.25 3.00

2008 Fantastic Four Archives

COMPLETE SET (72)

❑ 1 Issue #1 - November 1961 .15 .40
❑ 2 Issue #4 - May 1962 .15 .40
❑ 3 Issue #10 - January 1963 .15 .40
❑ 4 Annual #1 - 1963 .15 .40
❑ 5 Issue #25 - April 1964 .15 .40
❑ 6 Issue #28 - July 1964 .15 .40
❑ 7 Issue #36 - March 1965 .15 .40
❑ 8 Issue #40 - July 1965 .15 .40
❑ 9 Issue #46 - January 1966 .15 .40
❑ 10 Issue #48 - March 1966 .15 .40
❑ 11 Issue #56 - November 1966 .15 .40
❑ 12 Annual #4 - 1966 .15 .40
❑ 13 Issue #59 - February 1967 .15 .40
❑ 14 Issue #73 - April 1968 .15 .40
❑ 15 Issue #79 - October 1968 .15 .40
❑ 16 Annual #6 - November 1968 .15 .40
❑ 17 Issue #81 - December 1968 .15 .40
❑ 18 Issue #88 - June 1969 .15 .40
❑ 19 Issue #99 - June 1970 .15 .40
❑ 20 Issue #103 - October 1970 .15 .40
❑ 21 Issue #105 - December 1970 .15 .40
❑ 22 Issue #115 - October 1971 .15 .40
❑ 23 Issue #117 - December 1971 .15 .40
❑ 24 Issue #120 - March 1972 .15 .40
❑ 25 Issue #133 - April 1973 .15 .40
❑ 26 Issue #144 - February 1974 .15 .40
❑ 27 Issue #147 - June 1974 .15 .40
❑ 28 Issue #149 - August 1974 .15 .40
❑ 29 Issue #150 - September 1974 .15 .40
❑ 30 Issue #153 - December 1974 .15 .40
❑ 31 Issue #166 - January 1976 .15 .40
❑ 32 Issue #170 - May 1976 .15 .40
❑ 33 Issue #186 - September 1977 .15 .40
❑ 34 Issue #197 - August 1978 .15 .40
❑ 35 Issue #213 - December 1979 .15 .40
❑ 36 Issue #218 - May 1980 .15 .40
❑ 37 Issue #230 - May 1981 .15 .40
❑ 38 Issue #235 - October 1981 .15 .40
❑ 39 Issue #247 - October 1982 .15 .40
❑ 40 Issue #250 - January 1983 .15 .40
❑ 41 Issue #265 - April 1984 .15 .40
❑ 42 Issue #270 - September 1984 .15 .40
❑ 43 Issue #281 - August 1985 .15 .40
❑ 44 Issue #299 - February 1987 .15 .40
❑ 45 Issue #306 - September 1987 .15 .40
❑ 46 Issue #310 - January 1988 .15 .40
❑ 47 Issue #324 - March 1989 .15 .40
❑ 48 Issue #336 - January 1990 .15 .40
❑ 49 Issue #347 - December 1990 .15 .40
❑ 50 Issue #357 - October 1991 .15 .40
❑ 51 Issue #362 - April 1992 .15 .40
❑ 52 Issue #375 - April 1993 .15 .40
❑ 53 Issue #381 - October 1993 .15 .40
❑ 54 Issue #391 - August 1994 .15 .40
❑ 55 Issue #406 - November 1995 .15 .40
❑ 56 Issue #416 - September 1996 .15 .40
❑ 57 Vol 2, Issue #3 - January 1997 .15 .40
❑ 58 Vol 2, Issue #12 - October 1997 .15 .40
❑ 59 Vol 3, Issue #1 - January 1998 .15 .40
❑ 60 Vol 3, Issue #11 - November 1988 .15 .40
❑ 61 Vol 3, Issue #22 - October 1999 .15 .40
❑ 62 Vol 3, Issue #27 - March 2000 .15 .40
❑ 63 Vol 3, Issue #37 - January 2001 .15 .40
❑ 64 Vol 3, Issue #49 - January 2002 .15 .40
❑ 65 Vol 3, Issue #60 - October 2002 .15 .40
❑ 66 Issue #504 - December 2003 .15 .40
❑ 67 Issue #519 - December 2004 .15 .40
❑ 68 Issue #532 - December 2005 .15 .40
❑ 69 Issue #537 - June 2006 .15 .40
❑ 70 Issue #543 - March 2007 .15 .40
❑ 71 Issue #552 - February 2008 .15 .40
❑ 72 Checklist .15 .40

2008 Fantastic Four Archives Color Sketches

STATED ODDS ONE PER BOX

❑ 1 Adam Cleveland 10.00 25.00
❑ 2 Al Bigley
❑ 3 Al Stefano 10.00 25.00
❑ 4 Alexandre Benhossi
❑ 5 Alexandre Magno 12.00 30.00
❑ 6 Andre Toma 12.00 30.00
❑ 7 Andy Price 50.00 100.00
❑ 8 Anthony Castrillo
❑ 9 Anthony Wheeler 10.00 25.00
❑ 10 Blair Shedd 8.00 20.00
❑ 11 Brian Kong 10.00 25.00
❑ 12 Brian Postman 10.00 25.00
❑ 13 Cezar Razek
❑ 14 Chris Wilson
❑ 15 Claude St. Aubin 10.00 25.00
❑ 16 Daniel Brandao 15.00 40.00
❑ 17 Daniel Campos
❑ 18 Daniel Cooney 8.00 20.00
❑ 19 Daryl Banks 12.00 30.00
❑ 20 Dave Fox
❑ 21 Dave Simons 15.00 40.00
❑ 22 Dennis Crisostomo 25.00 50.00
❑ 23 Edde Wagner 10.00 25.00
❑ 24 Eduardo Ferrara 10.00 25.00
❑ 25 Felipe Massafera 15.00 40.00
❑ 26 Gabriel Hernandez
❑ 27 Gabriella Starling 8.00 20.00
❑ 28 Gerry Acerno 12.00 30.00
❑ 29 Jason Sobol 12.00 30.00
❑ 30 Jim Kyle
❑ 31 Joe Rubinstein 15.00 40.00
❑ 32 Joe Sinnott
❑ 33 John Watkins-Chow
❑ 34 Jose Marzan Jr 10.00 25.00
❑ 35 Justin Chung
❑ 36 Justin Vandemark
❑ 37 Kate Bradley 30.00 60.00
❑ 38 Katie Cook 50.00 100.00
❑ 39 Kristin Allen 12.00 30.00
❑ 40 Leeahd Goldberg 8.00 20.00
❑ 41 Lui Antonio 10.00 25.00
❑ 42 Mahmud Asrar
❑ 43 Marcelo Ferreira 12.00 30.00
❑ 44 Mark Dos Santos 15.00 40.00
❑ 45 Mark Spears 15.00 40.00
❑ 46 Nicole Goff
❑ 47 Oak 10.00 25.00
❑ 48 Ray Dillon
❑ 49 Rich Molinelli 15.00 40.00
❑ 50 Ron Wilson 10.00 25.00
❑ 51 Ryan Orosco
❑ 52 Scott Jones
❑ 53 Tess Fowler 20.00 50.00
❑ 54 Thony Silas 12.00 30.00
❑ 55 Tone Rodriguez 10.00 25.00
❑ 56 Tony Perna
❑ 57 Uko Smith 10.00 25.00
❑ 58 Warren Martineck
❑ 59 Yildiray Cinar
❑ 60 Bard
(issued as four-case incentive)
❑ 61 Nar
(issued as ten-case incentive)

2008 Fantastic Four Archives Legendary Heroes

COMPLETE SET (9) 25.00 50.00
STATED ODDS 1:24

❑ LH1 Mr. Fantastic 3.00 8.00
❑ LH2 Invisible Woman 3.00 8.00
❑ LH3 Human Torch 3.00 8.00
❑ LH4 Thing 3.00 8.00
❑ LH5 Crystal 3.00 8.00
❑ LH6 Medusa 3.00 8.00
❑ LH7 Power Man 3.00 8.00
❑ LH8 She-Hulk 3.00 8.00
❑ LH9 Black Panther 3.00 8.00

2008 Fantastic Four Archives Nemesis

COMPLETE SET (9) 5.00 10.00
STATED ODDS 1:8

❑ N1 Annihilus 1.00 2.50
❑ N2 Diablo 1.00 2.50
❑ N3 Dr. Doom 1.00 2.50
❑ N4 Ego The Living Planet 1.00 2.50
❑ N5 Galactus 1.00 2.50
❑ N6 Mole Man 1.00 2.50
❑ N7 Red Ghost 1.00 2.50
❑ N8 Ronan The Accuser 1.00 2.50
❑ N9 Super-Skrull 1.00 2.50

2008 Fantastic Four Archives Ready For Action

COMPLETE SET (18) 12.00 30.00
STATED ODDS 1:12

❑ A1 Marvel Knights 4 #1 1.25 3.00
❑ A2 Marvel Knights 4 #9 1.25 3.00
❑ A3 Marvel Knights 4 #11 1.25 3.00
❑ A4 Marvel Knights 4 #14 1.25 3.00
❑ A5 Marvel Knights 4 #20 1.25 3.00
❑ A6 Fantastic Four Foes #1 1.25 3.00
❑ A7 Fantastic Four Foes #509 1.25 3.00
❑ A8 Fantastic Four Foes #510 1.25 3.00
❑ A9 Fantastic Four Foes #514 1.25 3.00
❑ A10 Fantastic Four Foes #515 1.25 3.00
❑ A11 Fantastic Four Foes #516 1.25 3.00
❑ A12 Fantastic Four Foes #517 1.25 3.00
❑ A13 Fantastic Four Foes #523 1.25 3.00
❑ A14 Fantastic Four Foes #527 1.25 3.00
❑ A15 Fantastic Four Foes #534 1.25 3.00
❑ A16 Fantastic Four Foes #535 1.25 3.00
❑ A17 Fantastic Four Special #1 1.25 3.00
❑ A18 Marvel Adventures Fantastic Four #0 1.25 3.00

2008 Heroes Series One

COMPLETE SET (90) 5.00 12.00

❑ 1 Heroes: The Beginning .15 .40
❑ 2 Peter Petrelli .15 .40
❑ 3 Claire Bennet .15 .40
❑ 4 Hiro Nakamura .15 .40
❑ 5 Nathan Petrelli .15 .40
❑ 6 Isaac Mendez .15 .40
❑ 7 Mohinder Suresh .15 .40
❑ 8 Gabriel Sylar .15 .40
❑ 9 Matt Parkman .15 .40
❑ 10 Niki Sanders .15 .40
❑ 11 D.L. Hawkins .15 .40
❑ 12 Micah Sanders .15 .40
❑ 13 Noah Bennet .15 .40
❑ 14 The Haitian .15 .40
❑ 15 Angela Petrelli .15 .40
❑ 16 Claude Raines .15 .40
❑ 17 Ted Sprague .15 .40
❑ 18 Simone Deveaux .15 .40
❑ 19 Ando Masahashi .15 .40
❑ 20 Eden McCain .15 .40
❑ 21 Mr. Linderman .15 .40
❑ 22 Candice Wilmer .15 .40
❑ 23 Mr. Thompson .15 .40
❑ 24 Kaito Nakamura .15 .40
❑ 25 The Original Pilot .15 .40
❑ 26 Genesis .15 .40
❑ 27 Power of Flight Revealed .15 .40
❑ 28 Don't Look Back .15 .40
❑ 29 Agents of Our Destiny .15 .40
❑ 30 One Giant Leap .15 .40
❑ 31 Claire's Awakening .15 .40
❑ 32 Collision .15 .40
❑ 33 Painting the Answers .15 .40
❑ 34 Hiro's .15 .40
❑ 35 Zugunruhe .15 .40
❑ 36 Better Halves .15 .40
❑ 37 Healing the Burns .15 .40
❑ 38 Nothing to Hide .15 .40
❑ 39 The Petrelli Brothers .15 .40
❑ 40 Seven Minutes to Midnight .15 .40
❑ 41 No Place to Hide .15 .40
❑ 42 Homecoming .15 .40
❑ 43 The Sum of Our Fears .15 .40
❑ 44 Six Months Ago .15 .40
❑ 45 Eden's Journey Begins .15 .40
❑ 46 Fallout .15 .40
❑ 47 Searching for the Truth .15 .40
❑ 48 Godsend .15 .40
❑ 49 Peter's Frightening Fate .15 .40
❑ 50 The Fix .15 .40
❑ 51 Micah's Hidden Talent .15 .40
❑ 52 Distractions .15 .40
❑ 53 All in the Family .15 .40
❑ 54 Run .15 .40
❑ 55 Jessica Caught Off Guard .15 .40
❑ 56 Unexpected .15 .40
❑ 57 A New Direction .15 .40
❑ 58 Company Man .15 .40
❑ 59 He Chose a Family .15 .40
❑ 60 Parasite .15 .40
❑ 61 The Fate of New York .15 .40
❑ 62 0.7 percent .15 .40
❑ 63 The Passage of Precognition .15 .40
❑ 64 Five Years Ago .15 .40
❑ 65 Future Shock .15 .40
❑ 66 The Hard Part .15 .40
❑ 67 A Failed First Attempt .15 .40
❑ 68 Landslide .15 .40
❑ 69 Sylar's New Trick .15 .40
❑ 70 How to Stop an Exploding Man .15 .40
❑ 71 Changing the Future .15 .40
❑ 72 What's Next for Heroes .15 .40
❑ 73 The Art of Flight .15 .40
❑ 74 Death of a Cheerleader .15 .40
❑ 75 Bloody Homecoming .15 .40
❑ 76 Shadows and Fear .15 .40
❑ 77 Adventures of Super-Hiro .15 .40
❑ 78 Up, Up and Away .15 .40
❑ 79 Marked by Destiny .15 .40
❑ 80 Out of the Flames .15 .40
❑ 81 Superhuman Powers .15 .40
❑ 82 Come Fly with Me .15 .40
❑ 83 Radiation Rampage .15 .40
❑ 84 The Transparent Man .15 .40
❑ 85 Charred Cheerleader .15 .40
❑ 86 The Sylar Slayings .15 .40
❑ 87 Showdown at Kirby Plaza .15 .40
❑ 88 The Coming of Heroes .15 .40
❑ 89 The Future of Heroes .15 .40
❑ 90 Checklist .15 .40

2008 Heroes Series One Authentic Worn Costumes

STATED ODDS 1:44 HOBBY

❑ 1 Claire Bennet Cheerleading Uniform (facing left) 25.00 50.00
❑ 2 Claire Bennet Cheerleading Patch (facing right) 125.00 200.00
❑ 3 Hiro Nakamura Jacket 8.00 20.00
Shirt
❑ 4 Isaac Mendez Shirt 6.00 15.00
❑ 5 Matt Parkman Uniform 6.00 15.00

2008 Heroes Series One Autographs

STATED ODDS 1:135 HOBBY

❑ 1 Adrian Pasdar 20.00 40.00
❑ 2 Greg Grunberg 8.00 20.00
❑ 3 Hayden Panettiere 150.00 250.00
❑ 4 Jack Coleman 8.00 20.00
❑ 5 Jason Kyson Lee 15.00 30.00
❑ 6 Masi Oka 25.00 50.00
❑ 7 Milo Ventimiglia 25.00 50.00
❑ 8 Noah Gray-Cabey 8.00 20.00
❑ 9 Sendhil Ramamurthy 10.00 25.00
❑ 10 Zachary Quinto 40.00 80.00

2008 Heroes Series One Foil

COMPLETE SET (10) 4.00 10.00
STATED ODDS 1:3

❑ 1 Claire Bennet 1.00 2.50
❑ 2 Peter Petrelli 1.00 2.50
❑ 3 Hiro Nakmura 1.00 2.50
❑ 4 Nathan Petrelli 1.00 2.50
❑ 5 Matt Parkman 1.00 2.50
❑ 6 Mohinder Suresh 1.00 2.50
❑ 7 Niki Sanders 1.00 2.50
❑ 8 Micah Sanders 1.00 2.50
❑ 9 D.L. Hawkins 1.00 2.50
❑ 10 Issac Mendez 1.00 2.50

2008 Heroes Series One Sketches

STATED ODDS 1:86 HOBBY

❑ 1 Alex Buechel
❑ 2 Allison Sohn
❑ 3 Amy Pronovost
❑ 4 Brian Ashmore
❑ 5 Brian Kong
❑ 6 Cat Staggs
❑ 7 Craig Rousseau
❑ 8 Cynthia Cummens
❑ 9 Dan Cooney
❑ 10 Edward Mize
❑ 11 Edward Pun
❑ 12 Gabe Hernandez
❑ 13 Grant Gould
❑ 14 Howard Shum
❑ 15 Ingrid Hardy
❑ 16 Jake Minor
❑ 17 Jason Palmer
❑ 18 Jeff Chandler
❑ 19 Joe Corroney
❑ 20 John Watkins-Chow
❑ 21 Jon Ocampo
❑ 22 Joseph Booth
❑ 23 Katie Cook
❑ 24 Kevin Doyle
❑ 25 Leah Mangue
❑ 26 Lord Mesa
❑ 27 Mark McHaley
❑ 28 Matt Busch
❑ 29 Matthew Goodmanson
❑ 30 Michael Duron
❑ 31 Noah Albrecht
❑ 32 Otis Frampton
❑ 33 Otto Dieffenbach
❑ 34 Paul Allen Ballard
❑ 35 Paul Gutierrez
❑ 36 Randy Martinez
❑ 37 Rich Molinelli
❑ 38 Russ Walks
❑ 39 Sean Pence
❑ 40 Steve Oatney
❑ 41 Taki Soma
❑ 42 Tim Sale
❑ 43 Tom Hodges
❑ 44 Tony Shasteen
❑ 45 William O'Neill

2008 Heroes Series Two

COMPLETE SET (90) 5.00 12.00

❑ 1 Generations .15 .40
❑ 2 Hiro Nakamura .15 .40
❑ 3 Adam Monroe .15 .40
Takezo Kensei
❑ 4 Peter Petrelli .15 .40
❑ 5 Nathan Petrelli .15 .40
❑ 6 Angela Petrelli .15 .40
❑ 7 Noah Bennet .15 .40
❑ 8 Clair Bennet .15 .40
❑ 9 West Rosen .15 .40
❑ 10 Mohinder Suresh .15 .40
❑ 11 Molly Walker .15 .40
❑ 12 Matt Parkman .15 .40
❑ 13 Bob Bishop .15 .40
❑ 14 Elle Bishop .15 .40
❑ 15 Sylar .15 .40
❑ 16 Niki Sanders .15 .40
❑ 17 Micah Sanders .15 .40
❑ 18 Monica Dawson .15 .40
❑ 19 Maya Herrera .15 .40
❑ 20 Kaito Nakamura .15 .40
❑ 21 Ando Masahashi .15 .40
❑ 22 Four Month's Later .15 .40
❑ 23 An Unlikely Hero .15 .40
❑ 24 A Whole New Life .15 .40
❑ 25 Challenges and Choices .15 .40
❑ 26 The Fate of Nakamura .15 .40
❑ 27 More than Mortal Men .15 .40
❑ 28 Lizards .15 .40
❑ 29 Cure for a Curse .15 .40
❑ 30 A Hero for All Time .15 .40
❑ 31 The Terror Within .15 .40
❑ 32 Bleed for Me .15 .40
❑ 33 The Regenerators .15 .40
❑ 34 Kindred .15 .40
❑ 35 A Challenge for Kensei .15 .40
❑ 36 Come Fly with Me .15 .40
❑ 37 Real and Imagined .15 .40
❑ 38 The Blood of Others .15 .40
❑ 39 Time to Love, Time to Die .15 .40
❑ 40 The Kindness of Strangers .15 .40
❑ 41 Night Flight .15 .40
❑ 42 A New Hero? .15 .40
❑ 43 Is Molly the Key? .15 .40
❑ 44 Slaughtered for Silence .15 .40
❑ 45 Inside the Company .15 .40
❑ 46 Fight or Flight .15 .40
❑ 47 Nathan's Apocalypse .15 .40
❑ 48 Niki on the Rampage .15 .40
❑ 49 Woman of Power .15 .40
❑ 50 Precognitive Peter .15 .40
❑ 51 Death and Life .15 .40
❑ 52 The Line .15 .40
❑ 53 Madness in Any Language .15 .40
❑ 54 Victims of a Night Flyer? .15 .40
❑ 55 A Jam in Japan .15 .40
❑ 56 A Kiss of Consequence .15 .40
❑ 57 Walk on the Dark Side .15 .40
❑ 58 Out of Time .15 .40
❑ 59 The Nightmare Is Real .15 .40
❑ 60 Confrontation with Kensei .15 .40
❑ 61 Blissful Love, Raging Fury .15 .40
❑ 62 Fathers and Sons .15 .40
❑ 63 The Man Who Couldn't Die .15 .40
❑ 64 Four Months Ago .15 .40
❑ 65 How the Horror Began .15 .40
❑ 66 Hot Spot .15 .40
❑ 67 The Fate of Hawkins .15 .40
❑ 68 An Unlikely Alliance .15 .40
❑ 69 Two Against Two .15 .40
❑ 70 Cautionary Tales .15 .40
❑ 71 Of Pain and Loss .15 .40
❑ 72 Nakamura's Killer .15 .40
❑ 73 Swapping Prisoners .15 .40
❑ 74 Noah Bennet Is Shot .15 .40
❑ 75 There Is No Death .15 .40
❑ 76 Truth & Consequences .15 .40
❑ 77 Killing Victoria Pratt .15 .40
❑ 78 Siding with Sylar .15 .40
❑ 79 Hero or Hostage? .15 .40
❑ 80 Girl Power .15 .40
❑ 81 Hiro Vows Revenge! .15 .40
❑ 82 Powerless .15 .40
❑ 83 Suspended .15 .40
❑ 84 Enemies or Allies? .15 .40
❑ 85 Evil Takes a Beating .15 .40
❑ 86 Death... and Far Worse .15 .40
❑ 87 The Terror Returns .15 .40
❑ 88 The Fate of Noah Bennet .15 .40
❑ 89 The Dead Zone .15 .40
❑ 90 Checklist .15 .40

2008 Heroes Series Two Autograph Costumes

STATED ODDS 1:3,760

❑ 1 Adrian Pasdar
❑ 2 Dana Davis
❑ 3 Milo Ventimiglia
❑ 4 Nicholas D'Agosto

2008 Heroes Series Two Autographs

STATED ODDS 1:72

❑ 1 Adair Tishler 15.00 40.00
❑ 2 Adrian Pasdar 8.00 20.00
❑ 3 Alan Blumenfield 4.00 10.00
❑ 4 Ali Larter 75.00 125.00
❑ 5 Ashley Crow 4.00 10.00
❑ 6 Cristine Rose 5.00 12.00
❑ 7 Dana Davis 4.00 10.00
❑ 8 David Anders 5.00 12.00
❑ 9 James Kyson Lee 4.00 10.00
❑ 10 Jimmy Jean-Louis 4.00 10.00
❑ 11 Milo Ventimiglia
❑ 12 Nicholas D'Agosto 4.00 10.00
❑ 13 Sendhil Ramamurthy 6.00 15.00
❑ 14 Stephen Tobolowsky 4.00 10.00

2008 Heroes Series Two Costumes

STATED ODDS 1:72

❑ 1 Claire Bennet Uniform 15.00 40.00
❑ 2 Elle Bishop Shirt 10.00 25.00
❑ 3 Hiro Nakumura Sweater 3.00 8.00
❑ 4 Maya Herrera Shirt 4.00 10.00
❑ 5 Monica Dawson Uniform 8.00 20.00
❑ 6 Nathan Petrelli Shirt 5.00 12.00
❑ 7 Noah Bennet Shirt 5.00 12.00
❑ 8 Peter Petrelli Shirt 5.00 12.00
❑ 9 Sylar Jacket 10.00 25.00
❑ 10 West Rosen Sweater 3.00 8.00

2008 Heroes Series Two Sketches

STATED ODDS 1:72

❑ 1 Alex Buechel
❑ 2 Brent Engstrom
❑ 3 Brent Woodside
❑ 4 Brian Kong
❑ 5 Bryan Morton
❑ 6 Chris Henderson
❑ 7 Cynthia Cummens
❑ 8 Dan Cooney
❑ 9 Edward Pun
❑ 10 Eric Wolfe Hansen (Wolfe)
❑ 11 Howard Shum
❑ 12 Ingrid Hardy
❑ 13 Jake Minor (JM)
❑ 14 James Bukauskas (Bukshot)
❑ 15 Jamie Snell
❑ 16 Jason Hughes
❑ 17 Jeff Chandler
❑ 18 Jeremy Treece
❑ 19 Jim Kyle
❑ 20 John Watkins-Chow
❑ 21 Juan Carlos Ramos
❑ 22 Katie Cook
❑ 23 Ken Branch
❑ 24 Kevin Graham
❑ 25 Kyle Babbitt
❑ 26 Leah Mangue
❑ 27 Marlin Shoop
❑ 28 Matthew Goodmanson
❑ 29 Matthew Minor (MSM)
❑ 30 Michael Duron
❑ 31 Nathan Watson
❑ 32 Noah Albrecht
❑ 33 Otto Dieffenbach
❑ 34 Paul Gutierrez
❑ 35 Randy Siplon
❑ 36 Sean Pence
❑ 37 Shelli Paroline
❑ 38 Stephanie Yue
❑ 39 Steve Oatney
❑ 40 Steven Miller
❑ 41 Zack Giallongo

2008 Incredible Hulk Movie Expansion

❑ CC1 Bruce Banner MEM 4.00 10.00
❑ CC2 Betty Ross MEM 10.00 25.00
❑ CC3 Emil Blonsky MEM 4.00 10.00
❑ CC4 Samuel Sterns MEM 3.00 8.00
❑ CC5 Leonard MEM 3.00 8.00
❑ CC6 General Ross MEM 3.00 8.00
❑ EN1 Edward Norton AU 60.00 120.00
❑ EN2 Edward Norton AU/ (issued as 3-set incentive) 108.00 175.00
❑ LF1 Lou Ferrigno AU 25.00 50.00
❑ LF2 Lou Ferrigno AU/ (issued as 3-set incentive) 50.00 100.00

2008 Indiana Jones and the Kingdom of the Crystal Skull

COMPLETE SET (90) 5.00 12.00

❑ 1 The Return of Dr. Jones .15 .40
❑ 2 Indiana Jones .15 .40
❑ 3 Mutt Williams .15 .40
❑ 4 Marion Ravenwood .15 .40
❑ 5 Dr. Irina Spalko .15 .40
❑ 6 George Mac McHale .15 .40
❑ 7 Harold Ox Oxley .15 .40

❑ 8 Colonel Dovchenko .15 .40
❑ 9 Dean Charles Stanforth .15 .40
❑ 10 General Ross .15 .40
❑ 11 Agent Smith .15 .40
❑ 12 Agent Taylor .15 .40
❑ 13 Desert Troopers .15 .40
❑ 14 Base under Siege! .15 .40
❑ 15 Prisoner of the Reds .15 .40
❑ 16 Two Battered Buddies .15 .40
❑ 17 Invading Hangar 51 .15 .40
❑ 18 Mysterious Artifact .15 .40
❑ 19 Jones Unleashed .15 .40
❑ 20 Aiming for Action .15 .40
❑ 21 The Truth about Mac .15 .40
❑ 22 Score One for Indy! .15 .40
❑ 23 The Rocket Sled .15 .40
❑ 24 A Rocket Built for Two! .15 .40
❑ 25 Welcome to Doom Town .15 .40
❑ 26 Only One Way Out .15 .40
❑ 27 Howdy, Stranger! .15 .40
❑ 28 The Destroyer of Worlds .15 .40
❑ 29 At Marshall College .15 .40
❑ 30 Is Indy a Commie? .15 .40
❑ 31 In Search of ... Himself .15 .40
❑ 32 A Shout for Help .15 .40
❑ 33 A Guy Called Mutt .15 .40
❑ 34 Indy Takes a Spin .15 .40
❑ 35 The Sedan Chase .15 .40
❑ 36 Nailing Mac .15 .40
❑ 37 Landing in the Library .15 .40
❑ 38 Heroes on the Run .15 .40
❑ 39 A new Adventure Begins .15 .40
❑ 40 So This Is Peru .15 .40
❑ 41 Within Chauchilla Cemetery .15 .40
❑ 42 Into a Dark Domain .15 .40
❑ 43 Indy's Discovery .15 .40
❑ 44 Of Glory and Terror .15 .40
❑ 45 Protector of the Past .15 .40
❑ 46 Blow-Dart Attack .15 .40
❑ 47 The Interrogation .15 .40
❑ 48 Ox Holds the Key .15 .40
❑ 49 Mutt and Marion .15 .40
❑ 50 Trapped in the Sand Pit .15 .40
❑ 51 The Unsinkable Dr. Jones? .15 .40
❑ 52 Jungle Raiders .15 .40
❑ 53 Dr. Jones and Company .15 .40
❑ 54 Nailing Mac... Again! .15 .40
❑ 55 Against a One-Man Army .15 .40
❑ 56 Target: Marion! .15 .40
❑ 57 From Switchblade to Sword .15 .40
❑ 58 The Duel with Spalko .15 .40
❑ 59 Keeping Up with the Caravan .15 .40
❑ 60 Dovchenko vs. Indy .15 .40
❑ 61 Triple Peril Escape! .15 .40
❑ 62 Behold: Akator Temple .15 .40
❑ 63 The Walls Come Alive! .15 .40
❑ 64 The City of Doom .15 .40
❑ 65 Terror of the Ughas .15 .40
❑ 66 Saved by the Skull .15 .40
❑ 67 Secret of the Temple .15 .40
❑ 68 The Sands of Time .15 .40
❑ 69 Spalko's Wish Fulfilled .15 .40
❑ 70 The Demise of an Old Friend .15 .40
❑ 71 A Promotion for Dr. Jones .15 .40
❑ 72 Indy Forever! .15 .40
❑ 73 Secrets of Akator .15 .40
❑ 74 Crashing Down .15 .40
❑ 75 Dealing with Danger .15 .40
❑ 76 Art of the Temple .15 .40
❑ 77 Running Out of Time .15 .40
❑ 78 The Hypnotic Skull .15 .40
❑ 79 Two Lost Worlds .15 .40
❑ 80 Up and Onward .15 .40
❑ 81 Deadliest of Dangers .15 .40
❑ 82 Examining the Crystal Skull .15 .40
❑ 83 Temples and Raiders .15 .40
❑ 84 A Lost City Found .15 .40
❑ 85 Adventure Has a Name .15 .40
❑ 86 Trouble in Hangar 51 .15 .40
❑ 87 Challenge of Dovchenko .15 .40
❑ 88 Saved by the Fridge .15 .40
❑ 89 Atom-Age Adventurer .15 .40
❑ 90 Checklist .02 .10

2008 Indiana Jones and the Kingdom of the Crystal Skull Holofoil

COMPLETE SET (90) 100.00 250.00
*HOLOFOIL: 3X TO 8X BASIC CARDS
STATED PRINT RUN 350 SER. #'d SETS

2008 Indiana Jones and the Kingdom of the Crystal Skull Autographs

HOBBY STATED ODDS 1:78
RETAIL STATED ODDS 1:100

❑ NNO David Koepp 4.00 10.00
❑ NNO Jim Broadbent 4.00 10.00
❑ NNO Ray Winstone 7.50 20.00
❑ NNO Harrison Ford
George Lucas/Steven Spielberg
❑ NNO Andrew Divoff 4.00 10.00
❑ NNO Igor Jijikine H 4.00 10.00
❑ NNO Pasha Lychnikoff 4.00 10.00
❑ NNO Shia LaBeouf
Karen Allen
❑ NNO Karen Allen H 10.00 25.00
❑ NNO Steven Spielberg 700.00 1200.00
❑ NNO Karen Allen R 10.00 25.00
❑ NNO Alan Dale 4.00 10.00
❑ NNO Harrison Ford 1800.00 3000.00
❑ NNO George Lucas 400.00 800.00
❑ NNO John Hurt 20.00 40.00
❑ NNO Shia LaBeouf 40.00 80.00
❑ NNO Igor Jijikine R 4.00 10.00

2008 Indiana Jones and the Kingdom of the Crystal Skull Foil Inserts

COMPLETE SET (10) 5.00 12.00
STATED ODDS 1:6

❑ 1 Indy and Mutt .60 1.50
❑ 2 Crystal Skull .60 1.50
❑ 3 Indy and Mutt .60 1.50
❑ 4 Indy and Mutt .60 1.50
❑ 5 Mutt .60 1.50
❑ 6 Indy and Mutt .60 1.50
❑ 7 Mutt .60 1.50
❑ 8 Indy and Mutt .60 1.50
❑ 9 Indy and Mutt .60 1.50
❑ 10 Indiana Jones .60 1.50

2008 Indiana Jones and the Kingdom of the Crystal Skull Sketches

STATED ODDS 1:35

❑ NNO Don Pedicini Jr. 7.50 20.00
❑ NNO Jason Potratz
Jack Hai
❑ NNO David Rabbitte 15.00 40.00
❑ NNO Brent Schoonover 15.00 40.00
❑ NNO Jamie Snell 4.00 10.00
❑ NNO Ryan Waterhouse 2.00 5.00
❑ NNO Rich Woodall 4.00 10.00
❑ NNO Paul Allan Ballard 25.00 60.00
❑ NNO Alex Buechel 7.50 20.00
❑ NNO Jeff Chandler 30.00 80.00
❑ NNO Joe Corroney 50.00 125.00
❑ NNO Ted Dastick Jr. 12.50 30.00
❑ NNO Michael Duron 15.00 40.00
❑ NNO Dave Fox 7.50 20.00
❑ NNO Grant Gould 2.00 5.00
❑ NNO Paul Gutierrez 12.50 30.00
❑ NNO Tom Hodges 12.50 30.00
❑ NNO Brian Kong 12.50 30.00
❑ NNO Erik Maell 20.00 50.00
❑ NNO Mark McHaley 30.00 80.00
❑ NNO Nick Neocleous 20.00 50.00
❑ NNO Shelli Paroline 7.50 20.00
❑ NNO Jason Potratz 30.00 80.00
❑ NNO Mark Raats 30.00 80.00
❑ NNO Brian Rood 12.50 30.00
❑ NNO Uko Smith 7.50 20.00
❑ NNO Jerry Vanderstelt 50.00 125.00
❑ NNO Marc Wolfe
❑ NNO Kate Bradley 7.50 20.00
❑ NNO James Bukauskas 12.50 30.00
❑ NNO Hamilton Cline 7.50 20.00
❑ NNO Doug Cowan 12.50 30.00
❑ NNO Brian Denham 2.00 5.00
❑ NNO Chris Eliopoulos 6.00 15.00
❑ NNO Zach Giallongo 4.00 10.00
❑ NNO Art Grafunkel 12.50 30.00
❑ NNO Ingrid Hardy 12.50 30.00
❑ NNO Adam Hughes 40.00 100.00
❑ NNO Karen Krajenbrink 3.00 8.00
❑ NNO Leah Mangue 30.00 80.00
❑ NNO Peter McKinstry 12.50 30.00
❑ NNO William O'Neill 15.00 40.00
❑ NNO Noah Albrecht 4.00 10.00
❑ NNO Spencer Brinkerhoff III 4.00 10.00
❑ NNO Matt Busch 12.50 30.00
❑ NNO Katie Cook-Wilcox 15.00 40.00
❑ NNO Cynthia Cummens 12.50 30.00
❑ NNO Otto Dieffenbach 4.00 10.00
❑ NNO Brent Engstrom 12.50 30.00
❑ NNO Kate Glasheen 4.00 10.00
❑ NNO Kevin Graham 6.00 15.00
❑ NNO Chris Henderson 12.50 30.00
❑ NNO Jason Hughes 2.00 5.00
❑ NNO Jim Kyle 12.50 30.00
❑ NNO Randy Martinez
❑ NNO Lord Mesa 4.00 10.00
❑ NNO Steve Oatney 7.50 20.00
❑ NNO Sean Pence 30.00 80.00
❑ NNO Amy Pronovost 12.50 30.00
❑ NNO Juan Carlos Ramos 4.00 10.00
❑ NNO Howard Shum 2.00 5.00
❑ NNO Jason Sobol 4.00 10.00
❑ NNO John Watkins-Chow 7.50 20.00
❑ NNO Brent Woodside 2.00 5.00
❑ NNO Kyle Babbitt 12.50 30.00
❑ NNO Dennis Budd 4.00 10.00
❑ NNO Jeff Carlisle 12.50 30.00
❑ NNO Dan Cooney 4.00 10.00
❑ NNO Christian Dalla Vecchia
❑ NNO Kevin Doyle 4.00 10.00
❑ NNO Tess Fowler 12.50 30.00
❑ NNO Matthew Goodmanson 4.00 10.00
❑ NNO Trevor Grove
❑ NNO Jessica Hickman 6.00 15.00
❑ NNO Ben Curtis Jones
❑ NNO Wayne Lo
❑ NNO Clay McCormack 20.00 50.00
❑ NNO Rich Molinelli 4.00 10.00
❑ NNO Jon Ocampo 12.50 30.00
❑ NNO Jason Keith Phillips 2.00 5.00
❑ NNO Edward Pun 7.50 20.00
❑ NNO Patrick Richardson 20.00 50.00
❑ NNO Randy Siplon 12.50 30.00
❑ NNO Cat Staggs 40.00 100.00
❑ NNO Sarah Wilkinson 6.00 15.00
❑ NNO Stephanie Yue 7.50 20.00

2008 Indiana Jones Heritage

COMPLETE SET (90) 5.00 12.00

❑ 1 The Quest of Indiana Jones .15 .40
❑ 2 Danger Everywhere! .15 .40
❑ 3 A Game of Chance .15 .40
❑ 4 The Trap Is Sprung! .15 .40
❑ 5 In the hands of Belloq! .15 .40
❑ 6 Recruiting Dr. Jones .15 .40
❑ 7 Marion's Victory .15 .40
❑ 8 The Wicked Persuasion of Toht .15 .40
❑ 9 Escaping the Fire .15 .40
❑ 10 Business in Cairo .15 .40
❑ 11 A New Friend? .15 .40
❑ 12 Defending the Fair Marion .15 .40
❑ 13 Behold... The Swordsman! .15 .40
❑ 14 The Taunts of Rene Belloq .15 .40
❑ 15 The Great Map Room .15 .40
❑ 16 A Drink with Belloq? .15 .40
❑ 17 Digging for the Ark .15 .40
❑ 18 Surrounded by Snakes .15 .40
❑ 19 The Ark of the Covenant .15 .40
❑ 20 Trapped Beneath the Desert .15 .40
❑ 21 Fist Fight on the Tarmac .15 .40
❑ 22 Rest on the Bantu Wind .15 .40
❑ 23 Hidden in Plain Sight .15 .40
❑ 24 Belloq's Challenge to Indy .15 .40
❑ 25 Close Your Eyes Marion .15 .40
❑ 26 The Ritual's Gruesome End .15 .40
❑ 27 The Hands of... Top Men? .15 .40
❑ 28 An Evening at Club Obi Wan .15 .40
❑ 29 Searching for the Antidote .15 .40
❑ 30 Driving By Short Round .15 .40
❑ 31 The Futile Escape .15 .40
❑ 32 Napping to Their Doom .15 .40
❑ 33 The Problem with Flying Lao Che .15 .40
❑ 34 The Village Beseeches .15 .40
❑ 35 A Crooked Card Game .15 .40
❑ 36 Journey through the Jungle .15 .40
❑ 37 The Magnificent Pankot Palace .15 .40
❑ 38 The Great Banquet .15 .40
❑ 39 Five Minutes! .15 .40
❑ 40 A Deadly Intrusion .15 .40
❑ 41 Another Gruesome Trap .15 .40
❑ 42 Covered by Creatures .15 .40
❑ 43 A Sacrifice to kali .15 .40
❑ 44 Possessed by the Priest .15 .40
❑ 45 Short Round Breaks the Spell .15 .40
❑ 46 Indy's Grueling Fight .15 .40
❑ 47 Freeing the Young Prince .15 .40
❑ 48 Mine Car to Freedom .15 .40
❑ 49 Indy Hangs On for Life .15 .40
❑ 50 Short Round's Peril .15 .40
❑ 51 Trapped on the Bridge .15 .40
❑ 52 The Only Escape .15 .40
❑ 53 In the Nick of Time .15 .40
❑ 54 A Village Rejoices .15 .40
❑ 55 Straying from the Path .15 .40
❑ 56 The Cross of Coronado .15 .40
❑ 57 Origin of a Snake Fear .15 .40
❑ 58 The Rightful Owners Return .15 .40
❑ 59 The Cross Lost... Again! .15 .40
❑ 60 Summoned by Donovan .15 .40
❑ 61 Passage to the Tombs .15 .40
❑ 62 Face to Face with Sir Richard .15 .40
❑ 63 A Lunchtime Surprise .15 .40
❑ 64 The Pursuit's Violent End .15 .40
❑ 65 Swinging to the Rescue .15 .40
❑ 66 Capture of the Jones Boys .15 .40
❑ 67 The Treachery of Elsa .15 .40
❑ 68 A Burning Prison .15 .40
❑ 69 Detour to Berlin .15 .40
❑ 70 Indy Faces the Fuhrer .15 .40
❑ 71 Escaping the Enemy .15 .40
❑ 72 Across the Countryside .15 .40
❑ 73 A Most Handsome Exchange .15 .40
❑ 74 Race to the Grail .15 .40
❑ 75 Indiana Jones Versus the Tank .15 .40
❑ 76 An Unfair Advantage .15 .40
❑ 77 Indy's Most Important Mission .15 .40
❑ 78 The Surviving Grail Guardian .15 .40
❑ 79 Donovan Chooses... Poorly .15 .40
❑ 80 The Greatest Temptation .15 .40
❑ 81 Headed into the Sunset .15 .40
❑ 82 Desert Raiders .15 .40
❑ 83 The Truck Chase .15 .40
❑ 84 Slugfest on the Runway .15 .40
❑ 85 The Man Who Hated Snakes .15 .40
❑ 86 The Richard Amsel Touch .15 .40
❑ 87 World of the Lost Ark .15 .40
❑ 88 Inside the Temple of Doom .15 .40
❑ 89 Family Affair .15 .40
❑ 90 Checklist .02 .10

2008 Indiana Jones Heritage Gold

COMPLETE SET (90) 75.00 200.00
*GOLD: 2.5X TO 6X BASIC CARDS
STATED PRINT RUN 500 SER. #'d SETS

2008 Indiana Jones Heritage Autographs

STATED ODDS 1:42
CUT SIGNATURES PRINT RUN 1 SER. #'d SET

❑ NNO Michael Byrne 4.00 10.00
❑ NNO Paul Freeman 60.00 120.00
❑ NNO Wolf Kahler 4.00 10.00
❑ NNO Kevork Malikyan 6.00 15.00
❑ NNO John Rhys-Davies 75.00 150.00
❑ NNO Philip Tan 4.00 10.00
❑ NNO Pat Roach
❑ NNO Vernon Dobtcheff 4.00 10.00
❑ NNO George Harris 4.00 10.00
❑ NNO Kathleen Kennedy 100.00 200.00
❑ NNO Alfred Molina 75.00 150.00
❑ NNO Steven Spielberg 900.00 1500.00
❑ NNO Ric Young 4.00 10.00
❑ NNO Isla Blair 4.00 10.00
❑ NNO Harrison Ford 3000.00 4500.00
❑ NNO Anthony Higgins 4.00 10.00
❑ NNO George Lucas 500.00 1000.00
❑ NNO Ke Huy Quan 15.00 30.00
❑ NNO Vic Tablian 4.00 10.00
❑ NNO Denholm Elliot
❑ NNO Karen Allen 25.00 50.00
❑ NNO Kate Capshaw 125.00 250.00
❑ NNO Julian Glover 4.00 10.00
❑ NNO Lawrence Kasdan 100.00 200.00
❑ NNO Frank Marshall
❑ NNO Roshan Seth 4.00 10.00
❑ NNO David Yip 4.00 10.00

2008 Indiana Jones Heritage Box Loader Promos

COMPLETE SET (3) 4.00 10.00
STATED ODDS ONE PER BOX

❑ P1 Continuing the Adventure 1.50 4.00
❑ P2 The Great Discovery 1.50 4.00
❑ P3 Indiana Jones 1.50 4.00

2008 Indiana Jones Heritage Sketches

STATED ODDS 1:54

❑ NNO Shelli Paroline
❑ NNO Killian Plunkett 30.00 80.00
❑ NNO Mark Raats
❑ NNO Ronald Salas
❑ NNO Uko Smith
❑ NNO Chris Trevas 30.00 80.00
❑ NNO John Watkins-Chow
❑ NNO Len Bellinger
❑ NNO Mark Brooks
❑ NNO Joseph E. Cappabianco
❑ NNO Katie Cook 30.00 80.00
❑ NNO Cynthia Cummens
❑ NNO Kevin Doyle 7.50 20.00
❑ NNO Tom Feister 12.50 30.00
❑ NNO Matthew Goodmanson 6.00 15.00
❑ NNO Paul Gutierrez 6.00 15.00
❑ NNO Tom Hodges 20.00 50.00
❑ NNO Lee Kohse 4.00 10.00
❑ NNO Leah Mangue 30.00 80.00
❑ NNO Jake Minor
❑ NNO Jason Palmer
❑ NNO Sean Pence 40.00 100.00
❑ NNO Mark Propst
❑ NNO Sarah Wilkinson
❑ NNO Joseph Booth
❑ NNO Dennis Budd 4.00 10.00
❑ NNO Kody Chamberlain
❑ NNO Daniel Cooney
❑ NNO Ted Dastick Jr.
❑ NNO Michael Duron 20.00 50.00
❑ NNO Tess Fowler
❑ NNO Grant Gould 4.00 10.00
❑ NNO Ingrid Hardy 15.00 40.00
❑ NNO Josh Howard
❑ NNO Brian Kong 30.00 80.00
❑ NNO Randy Martinez 10.00 25.00
❑ NNO Rich Molinelli 4.00 10.00
❑ NNO Ron Boyd
❑ NNO Alex Buechel
❑ NNO Jeff Chandler 30.00 80.00
❑ NNO Joe Corroney 75.00 200.00
❑ NNO Otto Dieffenbach
❑ NNO Jan Duursema
❑ NNO Zack Giallongo
❑ NNO Kevin Graham 4.00 10.00
❑ NNO Chris Henderson
❑ NNO Adam Hughes
❑ NNO Karen Krajenbrink
❑ NNO Clay McCormack
❑ NNO William O'Neill
❑ NNO Dan Parsons 20.00 50.00
❑ NNO Jason Potratz
Jack Hai
❑ NNO David Rabbitte
❑ NNO Patrick Schoenmaker
❑ NNO Jason Sobol
❑ NNO Jerry Vanderstelt
❑ NNO Craig Rousseau 6.00 15.00
❑ NNO Howard Shum 5.00
❑ NNO Cat Staggs 30.00 80.00
❑ NNO Ryan Waterhouse
❑ NNO Kyle Babbitt
❑ NNO Spencer Brinkerhoff III
❑ NNO Matt Busch 20.00 50.00
❑ NNO Justin Chung
❑ NNO Doug Cowan 30.00 80.00
❑ NNO Colleen Doran 4.00 10.00
❑ NNO Tommy Lee Edwards 12.50 30.00
❑ NNO Kate Glasheen
❑ NNO Trevor Grove
❑ NNO Jessica Hickman 7.50 20.00
❑ NNO Ben Curtis Jones
❑ NNO Erik Maell
❑ NNO Mark McHaley 30.00 80.00
❑ NNO Steve Oatney
❑ NNO Don Pedicini Jr.
❑ NNO Amy Pronovost 12.50 30.00
❑ NNO Jon Roscetti
❑ NNO Brent Schoonover 20.00 50.00
❑ NNO Allison Sohn 60.00 150.00
❑ NNO Russ Walks 40.00 100.00
❑ NNO Stephanie Yue

2008 Iron Man The Movie

COMPLETE SET (70) 4.00 10.00

❑ 1 Title Card .10 .30
Checklist
❑ 2 Tony Stark .10 .30
❑ 3 Col. Rhodes .10 .30
❑ 4 Stane .10 .30
Rhodes
❑ 5 Col. Rhodes .10 .30
❑ 6 Stark .10 .30
Everhart
❑ 7 Christine Everhart .10 .30
❑ 8 Potts .10 .30
Stark
❑ 9 Tony Stark .10 .30
❑ 10 Tony Stark .10 .30
❑ 11 Stark .10 .30
Yinsen
❑ 12 Stark .10 .30
Yinsen
❑ 13 Raza .10 .30
Yinsen/Stark
❑ 14 Tony Stark .10 .30
❑ 15 Tony Stark .10 .30
❑ 16 Yinsen .10 .30
Stark
❑ 17 Stark .10 .30
Yinsen
❑ 18 Iron Man .10 .30
❑ 19 Col. Rhodes .10 .30
❑ 20 Rhodes .10 .30
Potts
❑ 21 Stark .10 .30
Stane
❑ 22 Raza .10 .30
❑ 23 Potts .10 .30
Stark
❑ 24 Tony Stark .10 .30
❑ 25 Stark .10 .30
Rhodes
❑ 26 Tony Stark .10 .30
❑ 27 Potts .10 .30
Stark
❑ 28 Stark .10 .30
Stane
❑ 29 Raza .10 .30
❑ 30 Iron Man .10 .30
❑ 31 Iron Man .10 .30
❑ 32 Iron Man .10 .30
❑ 33 Stark .10 .30
Stane
❑ 34 Pepper Potts .10 .30
❑ 35 Stark .10 .30
Potts
❑ 36 Christine Everhart .10 .30
❑ 37 Stark .10 .30
Stane
❑ 38 Iron Man .10 .30
❑ 39 Iron Man .10 .30
❑ 40 Iron Man .10 .30
❑ 41 Iron Man .10 .30
❑ 42 Oliver Stane .10 .30
❑ 43 Oliver Stane .10 .30
❑ 44 Oliver Stane .10 .30
❑ 45 Tony Stark .10 .30
❑ 46 Stane .10 .30
Potts
❑ 47 Iron Man .10 .30
❑ 48 Stark .10 .30
Rhodes
❑ 49 Pepper Potts .10 .30
❑ 50 Iron Man .10 .30
❑ 51 Iron Man .10 .30
❑ 52 Potts .10 .30
Stark
❑ 53 Favreau .10 .30
Downey Jr.
❑ 54 Bridges .10 .30
Favreau/Tahir
❑ 55 Feige .10 .30
Favreau/Paltrow
❑ 56 Paltrow .10 .30
Downey Jr.
❑ 57 Downey Jr. .10 .30
Favreau
❑ 58 Robert Downey Jr. .10 .30
❑ 59 Paltrow .10 .30
Feige/Howard
❑ 60 Downey Jr. .10 .30
Favreau
❑ 61 Robert Downey Jr. .10 .30
❑ 62 Downey Jr. .10 .30
Favreau
❑ 63 Favreau .10 .30
Downey Jr.
❑ 64 Bridges .10 .30
Favreau
❑ 65 Howard .10 .30
Favreau/Downey Jr.
❑ 66 Jon Favreau .10 .30
❑ 67 Downey Jr. .10 .30
Favreau
❑ 68 Jon Favreau .10 .30
❑ 69 Favreau .10 .30
Downey Jr.
❑ 70 Robert Downey Jr. .10 .30

2008 Iron Man The Movie Armored Hero

COMPLETE SET (9) 6.00 15.00
STATED ODDS 1:24

❑ H1 Armored Hero 1.25 3.00
❑ H2 Armored Hero 1.25 3.00
❑ H3 Armored Hero 1.25 3.00
❑ H4 Armored Hero 1.25 3.00
❑ H5 Armored Hero 1.25 3.00
❑ H6 Armored Hero 1.25 3.00
❑ H7 Armored Hero 1.25 3.00
❑ H8 Armored Hero 1.25 3.00
❑ H9 Armored Hero 1.25 3.00

2008 Iron Man The Movie Autographs

OVERALL AUTO/MEM/SKETCH ODDS 1:12
LEIBER AUTO ONE PER CASE

❑ NNO Jeff Bridges VL
❑ NNO Robert Downey Jr. VL 250.00 400.00
❑ NNO Shaun Toub 6.00 15.00
❑ NNO Clark Gregg 25.00 50.00
❑ NNO Terrence Howard 25.00 50.00
❑ NNO Jon Favreau 30.00 60.00
❑ NNO Faran Tahir 8.00 20.00
❑ NNO Larry Lieberman/ (issued as case topper)

2008 Iron Man The Movie Casting Call

COMPLETE SET (9) 4.00 10.00
STATED ODDS 1:12

❑ CC1 Robert Downey Jr. .75 2.00
❑ CC2 Terrence Howard .75 2.00
❑ CC3 Jeff Bridges .75 2.00
❑ CC4 Gwyneth Paltrow .75 2.00
❑ CC5 Faran Tahir .75 2.00
❑ CC6 Shaun Toub .75 2.00
❑ CC7 Leslie Bibb .75 2.00
❑ CC8 Clark Gregg .75 2.00
❑ CC9 Jon Favreau .75 2.00

2008 Iron Man The Movie Costumes

OVERALL AUTO/MEM/SKETCH ODDS 1:12
ARMOR PROP CARDS: TWO CASE DEALER INCENTIVE
L (LIMITED): 300-500 COPIES
VL (VERY LIMITED): 200-300 COPIES

❑ 3 Tony Stark Jacket 8.00 20.00
❑ 7 Obadiah Stane Shirt 3.00 8.00
❑ 11 Pepper Potts Skirt 10.00 25.00
❑ 15 Yinsen Vest 3.00 8.00
❑ 19 Iron Man Mark III/ (issued as 2-case incentive) 75.00 150.00
❑ 2 Tony Stark Pants 8.00 20.00
❑ 6 Jim Rhodes Pants 3.00 8.00
❑ 10 Pepper Potts Bustier L 12.00 30.00
❑ 14 Raza Jacket 3.00 8.00
❑ 18 Iron Man Mark I/ (issued as 2-case incentive) 75.00 150.00
❑ 4 Jim Rhodes Shirt 3.00 8.00
❑ 8 Obadiah Stane Shirt 3.00 8.00
❑ 12 Pepper Potts Jacket 10.00 25.00
❑ 16 Yinsen Jacket 3.00 8.00
❑ 20 Iron Monger/ (issued as 2-case incentive)
❑ 1 Tony Stark Shirt 8.00 20.00
❑ 5 Jim Rhodes Shirt 3.00 8.00
❑ 9 Obadiah Stane Tie VL 30.00 60.00
❑ 13 Raza Jacket 3.00 8.00
❑ 17 Christine Everhart Skirt 6.00 15.00

2008 Iron Man The Movie Iron Man Archives

COMPLETE SET (9) 3.00 8.00
STATED ODDS 1:8

❑ AR1 Tales of Suspense #39 .60 1.50
❑ AR2 Tales of Suspense #40 .60 1.50
❑ AR3 Tales of Suspense #46 .60 1.50
❑ AR4 Tales of Suspense #48 .60 1.50
❑ AR5 Tales of Suspense #50 .60 1.50
❑ AR6 Tales of Suspense #52 .60 1.50
❑ AR7 Tales of Suspense #57 .60 1.50
❑ AR8 Tales of Suspense #58 .60 1.50
❑ AR9 Tales of Suspense #65 .60 1.50

2008 Iron Man The Movie Sketches

OVERALL AUTO/MEM/SKETCH ODDS 1:12
LAYTON SKETCH: FOUR CASE DEALER INCENTIVE

❑ NNO Brent Schoonover
❑ NNO Chris Wilson
❑ NNO Harvey Tolibao
❑ NNO Justin Chung
❑ NNO Sarah Wilkinson
❑ NNO Bob Layton/ (issued as 4-case incentive)
❑ NNO Brian Denham
❑ NNO Dan Cooney
❑ NNO James Bukauskas
❑ NNO Kevin Graham
❑ NNO Sean Pence
❑ NNO Brian Kong
❑ NNO Gabriel Hernandez
❑ NNO Jason Sobol
❑ NNO Matthew Goodmanson
❑ NNO Steven Miller
❑ NNO Cat Staggs
❑ NNO Grant Gould
❑ NNO Jim Kyle
❑ NNO Rich Mollineli
❑ NNO Tom Hodges

2008 James Bond In Motion

COMPLETE SET (63) 5.00 12.00

❑ 1 Dr. No .15 .40
❑ 2 Dr. No .15 .40

❑ 3 Dr. No .15 .40
❑ 4 From Russia With Love .15 .40
❑ 5 From Russia With Love .15 .40
❑ 6 From Russia With Love .15 .40
❑ 7 Goldfinger .15 .40
❑ 8 Goldfinger .15 .40
❑ 9 Goldfinger .15 .40
❑ 10 Thunderball .15 .40
❑ 11 Thunderball .15 .40
❑ 12 Thunderball .15 .40
❑ 13 You Only Live Twice .15 .40
❑ 14 You Only Live Twice .15 .40
❑ 15 You Only Live Twice .15 .40
❑ 16 On Her Majesty's Secret Service .15 .40
❑ 17 On Her Majesty's Secret Service .15 .40
❑ 18 On Her Majesty's Secret Service .15 .40
❑ 19 Diamonds Are Forever .15 .40
❑ 20 Diamonds Are Forever .15 .40
❑ 21 Diamonds Are Forever .15 .40
❑ 22 Live And Let Die .15 .40
❑ 23 Live And Let Die .15 .40
❑ 24 Live And Let Die .15 .40
❑ 25 The Man With The Golden Gun .15 .40
❑ 26 The Man With The Golden Gun .15 .40
❑ 27 The Man With The Golden Gun .15 .40
❑ 28 The Spy Who Loved Me .15 .40
❑ 29 The Spy Who Loved Me .15 .40
❑ 30 The Spy Who Loved Me .15 .40
❑ 31 Moonraker .15 .40
❑ 32 Moonraker .15 .40
❑ 33 Moonraker .15 .40
❑ 34 For Your Eyes Only .15 .40
❑ 35 For Your Eyes Only .15 .40
❑ 36 For Your Eyes Only .15 .40
❑ 37 Octopussy .15 .40
❑ 38 Octopussy .15 .40
❑ 39 Octopussy .15 .40
❑ 40 A View To A Kill .15 .40
❑ 41 A View To A Kill .15 .40
❑ 42 A View To A Kill .15 .40
❑ 43 The Living Daylights .15 .40
❑ 44 The Living Daylights .15 .40
❑ 45 The Living Daylights .15 .40
❑ 46 Licence To Kill .15 .40
❑ 47 Licence To Kill .15 .40
❑ 48 Licence To Kill .15 .40
❑ 49 GoldenEye .15 .40
❑ 50 GoldenEye .15 .40
❑ 51 GoldenEye .15 .40
❑ 52 Tomorrow Never Dies .15 .40
❑ 53 Tomorrow Never Dies .15 .40
❑ 54 Tomorrow Never Dies .15 .40
❑ 55 The World Is Not Enough .15 .40
❑ 56 The World Is Not Enough .15 .40
❑ 57 The World Is Not Enough .15 .40
❑ 58 Die Another Day .15 .40
❑ 59 Die Another Day .15 .40
❑ 60 Die Another Day .15 .40
❑ 61 Casino Royale .15 .40
❑ 62 Casino Royale .15 .40
❑ 63 Casino Royale .15 .40

2008 James Bond In Motion Autographs

OVERALL AUTO ODDS 1:12
A113 STATED ODDS ONE PER COLLECTOR'S ALBUM
HAMILTON AU STATED ODDS ONE PER 3 CASE PURCHASE
MOORE AU STATED ODDS ONE PER 6 CASE PURCHASE
L (LIMITED): 300-500 COPIES
VL (VERY LIMITED): 200-300 COPIES

❑ A69 Denise Richards VL 100.00 200.00
❑ A82 Albert Moses L 6.00 15.00
❑ A83 Thomas Wheatley VL 30.00 60.00
❑ A84 Terence Mountain L 8.00 20.00
❑ A85 David Meyer L 6.00 15.00
❑ A86 Tony Meyer L 6.00 15.00
❑ A87 Kate Gayson L 10.00 25.00
❑ A88 Alkis Kritikos 6.00 15.00
❑ A89 Ivana Milicevic 8.00 20.00
❑ A92 Isaach De Bankole L 8.00 20.00
❑ A93 Patrick Bauchau 6.00 15.00
❑ A94 Sid Haig L 10.00 25.00
❑ A95 Priscilla Barnes L 12.00 30.00
❑ A96 Daniel Andreas 6.00 15.00
❑ A97 Richard Sammel L 6.00 15.00
❑ A98 Joe Don Baker VL 200.00 300.00
❑ A100 Ludger Pistor L 6.00 15.00
❑ A101 Daud Shah L 10.00 25.00
❑ A102 Malcolm Sinclair L 6.00 15.00
❑ A103 Clemens Schick 6.00 15.00
❑ A104 Joseph Millson L 12.00 30.00
❑ A105 Tsai Chin L 8.00 20.00
❑ A106 Urbano Barberini L 8.00 20.00
❑ A107 Jesper Christensen L 8.00 20.00
❑ A108 Margaret Nolan L 25.00 50.00
❑ A112 Serena Gordon 12.00 30.00
❑ A113 Anthony Starke/ (issued in collectors album)12.00 30.00
❑ A114 Grand L. Bush 6.00 15.00
❑ A115 Wayne Newton VL 60.00 120.00
❑ A116 John Terry VL 30.00 60.00
❑ A117 David Calder 8.00 20.00
❑ A118 Robert Carlyle VL 30.00 60.00
❑ A120 Carmen Du Sautoy L 20.00 40.00
❑ A121 Vernon Dobtcheff 6.00 15.00
❑ WA31 Honor Blackman VL 150.00 250.00
❑ NNO Guy Hamilton/ (issued as 3-case incentive)30.00 60.00
❑ NNO Roger Moore/ (issued as 6-case incentive)100.00 200.00

2008 James Bond In Motion Full Bleed Autographs

OVERALL AUTO ODDS 1:12
L (LIMITED): 300-500 COPIES
VL (VERY LIMITED): 200-300 COPIES

❑ NNO Isaach De Bankole L 8.00 20.00
❑ NNO Richard Sammel L 8.00 20.00
❑ NNO Virginia Hey 8.00 20.00
❑ NNO Giancarlo Giannini 12.00 30.00
❑ NNO Joseph Millson L 12.00 30.00
❑ NNO Simon Abkarian 8.00 20.00
❑ NNO Thomas Wheatley VL 30.00 60.00
❑ NNO Malcolm Sinclair 6.00 15.00
❑ NNO Anthony Starke 12.00 30.00
❑ NNO Ivana Milicevic L 10.00 25.00
❑ NNO Sebastien Foucan 10.00 25.00
❑ NNO Tsai Chin L 8.00 20.00
❑ NNO David Calder L 8.00 20.00

2008 James Bond In Motion Bond Allies

COMPLETE SET (17) 20.00 40.00
STATED ODDS 1:12

❑ BA20 M 1.50 4.00
❑ BA21 Rene Mathis 1.50 4.00
❑ BA22 Q 1.50 4.00
❑ BA23 Sharkey 1.50 4.00
❑ BA24 Saunders 1.50 4.00
❑ BA25 Luigi Ferrara 1.50 4.00
❑ BA26 Felix Leiter 1.50 4.00
❑ BA27 Lt. Hip 1.50 4.00
❑ BA28 Marc Ange Draco 1.50 4.00
❑ BA29 Felix Leiter 1.50 4.00
❑ BA30 Felix Leiter 1.50 4.00
❑ BA31 Q 1.50 4.00
❑ BA32 Raoul 1.50 4.00
❑ BA33 M 1.50 4.00
❑ BA34 Rosika Miklos 1.50 4.00
❑ BA35 Felix Leiter 1.50 4.00
❑ BA36 M 1.50 4.00

2008 James Bond In Motion Bond Girls Are Forever

COMPLETE SET (24) 20.00 40.00
STATED ODDS 1:8

❑ BG49 Camille 1.25 3.00
❑ BG50 Agent Fields 1.25 3.00
❑ BG51 Peaceful Fountains of Desire 1.25 3.00
❑ BG52 Caroline 1.25 3.00
❑ BG53 Linda 1.25 3.00
❑ BG54 Jenny Flex 1.25 3.00
❑ BG55 Countess Lisl 1.25 3.00
❑ BG56 Manuela 1.25 3.00
❑ BG57 Girl 1.25 3.00
❑ BG58 Felicca 1.25 3.00
❑ BG59 Saida 1.25 3.00
❑ BG60 Nancy 1.25 3.00
❑ BG61 Ling 1.25 3.00
❑ BG62 Paula Caplan 1.25 3.00
❑ BG63 Dink 1.25 3.00
❑ BG64 Tilly Masterson 1.25 3.00
❑ BG65 Vida & Zora 1.25 3.00
❑ BG66 Mei-Lei 1.25 3.00
❑ BG67 Gypsy Belly Dancer 1.25 3.00
❑ BG68 Bonita 1.25 3.00
❑ BG69 Chew Mee 1.25 3.00
❑ BG70 Photographer 1.25 3.00
❑ BG71 Miss Moneypenny 1.25 3.00
❑ BG72 Miss Moneypenny 1.25 3.00

2008 James Bond In Motion Bond Villains

COMPLETE SET (22) 10.00 25.00
STATED ODDS 1:9

❑ F42 Mr. White 1.00 2.50
❑ F43 Dominic Greene 1.00 2.50
❑ F44 Elvis 1.00 2.50
❑ F45 Dryden 1.00 2.50
❑ F46 Steven Obanno 1.00 2.50
❑ F47 Valenka 1.00 2.50
❑ F48 Mollaka 1.00 2.50
❑ F49 Gettler 1.00 2.50
❑ F50 Zao 1.00 2.50
❑ F51 Colonel Moon 1.00 2.50
❑ F52 Miranda Frost 1.00 2.50
❑ F53 Xenia Onatopp 1.00 2.50
❑ F54 Milton Krest 1.00 2.50
❑ F55 Necros 1.00 2.50
❑ F56 Dr. Carl Mortner 1.00 2.50
❑ F57 Hai Fat 1.00 2.50
❑ F58 Erich Kriegler 1.00 2.50
❑ F59 Whisper 1.00 2.50
❑ F60 Mr. Big 1.00 2.50
❑ F61 Helga Brandt 1.00 2.50
❑ F62 Count Lippe 1.00 2.50
❑ F63 Kirilencu 1.00 2.50

2008 James Bond In Motion Costumes

OVERALL COSTUME/RELIC ODDS 1:12
L (LIMITED): 300-500 COPIES

❑ SC1 James Bond Shirt 12.00 30.00
❑ SC2 M Shirt L 20.00 50.00
❑ SC3 James Bond Pants 12.00 30.00
❑ SC4 Gettler Suit 6.00 15.00
❑ SC5 Carlos Shirt 6.00 15.00

2008 James Bond In Motion Dual Costumes

OVERALL COSTUME/RELIC ODDS 1:12
DC2 STATED ODDS ONE PER CASE
VL (VERY LIMITED): 200-300 COPIES

❑ DC2 Vesper Lynd Dress 20.00 50.00
Cardigan/ (issued as case topper)
❑ DC3 James Bond Shirt 8.00 20.00
Pants
❑ DC4 Felix Leiter Shirt 4.00 10.00
Jacket
❑ DC5 Mr. White Shirt 4.00 10.00
Pants
❑ DC6 Solange Bathing Suit 50.00 100.00
Sarong VL
❑ DC7 Steven Obanno Shirt 4.00 10.00
Jacket

2008 James Bond In Motion Triple Costumes

OVERALL COSTUME/RELIC ODDS 1:12
VL (VERY LIMITED): 200-300 COPIES

❑ TC1 James Bond Shirt 8.00 20.00
Jacket/Pants
❑ TC2 Mollaka Shirt 5.00 12.00
Jacket/Pants
❑ TC3 James Bond Shirt 8.00 20.00
Shirt/Pants
❑ TC4 Rene Mathis Shirt 5.00 12.00
Jacket/Pants
❑ TC5 James Bond Shirt 20.00 50.00
Shirt/Pants
❑ TC6 James Bond Shirt 8.00 20.00
Jacket/Pants
❑ TC7 James Bond Shirt 8.00 20.00
Jacket/Pants
❑ TC8 James Bond Shirt 8.00 20.00
Jacket/Pants
❑ QC1 Le Chiffre Shirt 50.00 100.00
Vest/Jacket/Pants VL

2008 James Bond In Motion James Bond Lenticular

COMPLETE SET (6) 3.00 6.00
STATED ODDS 1:4

❑ JB1 Sean Connery .60 1.50
❑ JB2 Roger Moore .60 1.50
❑ JB3 George Lazeby .60 1.50
❑ JB4 Timothy Dalton .60 1.50
❑ JB5 Pierce Brosnan .60 1.50
❑ JB6 Daniel Craig .60 1.50

2008 James Bond In Motion Relics

OVERALL COSTUME/RELIC ODDS 1:12
L (LIMITED): 300-500 COPIES
VL (VERY LIMITED): 200-300 COPIES

❑ RC19 Casino Table Felt L 30.00 60.00
❑ RC20 Diamond Bed Sheet L 35.00 70.00
❑ RC21 Vesper Lynd's Business Card VL
❑ RC22 Gustav Graves' Parachute 10.00 25.00
❑ RC23 Miranda Frost Bed Cover L 20.00 50.00

2008 Journey to the Center of the Earth 3D

COMPLETE SET (50) 4.00 10.00

❑ 1 The Ultimate Journey .15 .40
❑ 2 Prof. Trevor Anderson .15 .40
❑ 3 Hanna Asgeirsson .15 .40
❑ 4 Sean Anderson .15 .40
❑ 5 Dean Alan Kitzens .15 .40
❑ 6 Lab Assistant Leonard .15 .40
❑ 7 Max's Destiny .15 .40
❑ 8 In the Classroom .15 .40
❑ 9 You and me, Kid .15 .40
❑ 10 Can It Be Real .15 .40
❑ 11 Struck by Lightning .15 .40
❑ 12 Hannah's Way .15 .40
❑ 13 A Long Way Down .15 .40
❑ 14 Descent into History .15 .40
❑ 15 The Old Mine .15 .40
❑ 16 Treacherous Tunnel .15 .40
❑ 17 A Wild Ride Begins .15 .40
❑ 18 Interrupted Journey .15 .40
❑ 19 Free Fall .15 .40
❑ 20 The World Below .15 .40
❑ 21 Glowbirds .15 .40
❑ 22 The Glowing Guide .15 .40
❑ 23 Giant Mushrooms .15 .40
❑ 24 Wonder beyond Belief .15 .40
❑ 25 Key to the Past .15 .40
❑ 26 The Raft .15 .40
❑ 27 Underground Ocean .15 .40
❑ 28 Storm at Sea .15 .40
❑ 29 Attack of the Sea Monsters .15 .40
❑ 30 Savage Sea Serpent .15 .40
❑ 31 Killer Fish Attack .15 .40
❑ 32 Terrors of the Deep .15 .40
❑ 33 Deadly Plants .15 .40
❑ 34 Nature's Savage Way .15 .40
❑ 35 Sean's Salvation .15 .40
❑ 36 The Challenge Ahead .15 .40
❑ 37 A Rocky Start .15 .40
❑ 38 Magnetic Surfing .15 .40
❑ 39 The Search for Sean .15 .40
❑ 40 Ancient Graveyard .15 .40
❑ 41 Terror on Their Tails .15 .40
❑ 42 Furious Jaws .15 .40
❑ 43 No Place To Run .15 .40
❑ 44 Inside a Volcano .15 .40
❑ 45 Salvation on a Skull .15 .40
❑ 46 Brace Yourself .15 .40
❑ 47 Breaking Through .15 .40
❑ 48 Airborne Explorers .15 .40
❑ 49 The Landing .15 .40
❑ 50 Checklist .15 .40
❑ CL1 Underworld Adventure 3.00 8.00
(issued as case loader)

2008 Journey to the Center of the Earth 3D Challenging the Unknown

COMPLETE SET (6) 5.00 12.00
STATED ODDS 1:17

❑ CU1 Trevor's Journey 1.50 4.00
❑ CU2 Experienced Guide 1.50 4.00
❑ CU3 Not Exactly Kid Stuff 1.50 4.00
❑ CU4 Unusual Creatures 1.50 4.00
❑ CU5 A Whole New World 1.50 4.00
❑ CU6 More than Just Science 1.50 4.00

2008 Journey to the Center of the Earth 3D Forgotten World Puzzle

COMPLETE SET (9) 4.00 10.00
STATED ODDS 1:11

❑ FW1 The World Below 1.00 2.50
❑ FW2 Escape Raft 1.00 2.50
❑ FW3 Giant Mushrooms 1.00 2.50
❑ FW4 Waterlogged Explorers 1.00 2.50
❑ FW5 Inner Space 1.00 2.50
❑ FW6 Heroes in a Jam 1.00 2.50
❑ FW7 Skull of Salvation 1.00 2.50
❑ FW8 Sean's Stepping Stones 1.00 2.50
❑ FW9 Dinosaur Graveyard 1.00 2.50

2008 Journey to the Center of the Earth 3D Pieceworks

STATED ODDS 1:24

❑ PW1 Trevor shirt 6.00 15.00
❑ PW2 Sean T-shirt 6.00 15.00
❑ PW3 Hannah T-shirt 6.00 15.00
❑ PW4 Hannah Shirt 6.00 15.00
❑ PW5 Trevor shirt 6.00 15.00
❑ PW6 Hannah headband 6.00 15.00
❑ PW7 Hannah shirt 6.00 15.00
❑ PW8 Hannah shorts 6.00 15.00
❑ PW9 Sean T-shirt 6.00 15.00
❑ PW10 Trevor T-shirt 6.00 15.00
❑ PW11 Sean backpack 6.00 15.00
❑ PW12A Sean T-shirt 8.00 20.00
(issued as dealer incentive)
❑ PW12B Trevor Shirt 8.00 20.00
(issued as dealer incentive)
❑ PW12C Hannah T-shirt 8.00 20.00
(issued as dealer incentive)

2008 Journey to the Center of the Earth 3D Prehistoric Peril

COMPLETE SET (3) 4.00 10.00
STATED ODDS 1:24

❑ PR1 Giant from the Unknown 2.50 6.00
❑ PR2 Amphibious Assault 2.50 6.00
❑ PR3 Sea Monsters Attack 2.50 6.00

2008 Journey to the Center of the Earth 3D Promos

❑ P1 Trevor/Sean/Hannah .60 1.50
(General Distribution)
❑ Pi Trevor/Sean/Hannah .75 2.00
(inkworks.com Exclusive)

2008 Lord of the Rings Masterpieces II

COMPLETE SET (72) 5.00 12.00

❑ 1 Table of Contents .15 .40
❑ 2 The Great Gandalf .15 .40
❑ 3 Wizard of Evil .15 .40
❑ 4 Gollum's Fury .15 .40
❑ 5 Master Archer .15 .40
❑ 6 Queen of Elves .15 .40
❑ 7 A Ring Restored .15 .40
❑ 8 Eomer .15 .40
❑ 9 Burden of the Ring .15 .40
❑ 10 Wrath of Gandalf .15 .40
❑ 11 A Kiss for Frodo .15 .40
❑ 12 Their Love Undenied .15 .40
❑ 13 A Hobbit's Challenge .15 .40
❑ 14 Courage of Legolas .15 .40
❑ 15 Gandalf Everlasting .15 .40
❑ 16 Portrait of Galadriel .15 .40
❑ 17 Portrait of Arwen .15 .40
❑ 18 Portrait of Eowyn .15 .40
❑ 19 Gandalf the White .15 .40
❑ 20 The Eye of Sauron .15 .40
❑ 21 Nazgul Terror .15 .40
❑ 22 The King of the Dead .15 .40
❑ 23 Behold the Balrog .15 .40
❑ 24 Battle beneath the Earth .15 .40
❑ 25 Power of Gandalf .15 .40
❑ 26 Frodo and the One Ring .15 .40
❑ 27 Gollum's Torment .15 .40
❑ 28 Isildur's Temptation .15 .40
❑ 29 Lord of Rivendell .15 .40
❑ 30 A Ring for Galadriel .15 .40
❑ 31 Fury of Gandalf .15 .40
❑ 32 Orcs Out for Blood .15 .40
❑ 33 Army of Monsters .15 .40
❑ 34 Bilbo's Metamorphosis .15 .40
❑ 35 Mouth of Sauron .15 .40
❑ 36 Elven Ally .15 .40
❑ 37 Gandalf in Rivendell .15 .40
❑ 38 Demon of Demons .15 .40
❑ 39 Aragorn vs. the Ringwraiths .15 .40
❑ 40 Legolas in Lothlorien .15 .40
❑ 41 Return of the King .15 .40
❑ 42 Legolas of Mirkwood .15 .40
❑ 43 The Man Called Boromir .15 .40
❑ 44 Rohan's Royalty .15 .40
❑ 45 Death in the Night .15 .40
❑ 46 The Gorgoroth Plains .15 .40
❑ 47 Fate of the Rings .15 .40
❑ 48 Within Mount Doom .15 .40
❑ 49 A Hobbit's Home .15 .40
❑ 50 Against Sauron's Might .15 .40
❑ 51 Splendor of Rivendell .15 .40
❑ 52 Spectral Corpse .15 .40
❑ 53 Home of the Ents .15 .40
❑ 54 Helm's Deep Under Siege .15 .40
❑ 55 Battle of Helm's Deep .15 .40
❑ 56 The Morgul River .15 .40
❑ 57 Minas Morgul .15 .40
❑ 58 The Court of Kings .15 .40
❑ 59 Hands of the Dead .15 .40
❑ 60 The Grey Havens .15 .40
❑ 61 Forces for Good .15 .40
❑ 62 Challengers of the Ring .15 .40
❑ 63 Wonder of Treebeard .15 .40
❑ 64 Twisted Followers .15 .40
❑ 65 A Gnome Named Gollum .15 .40
❑ 66 Guardians of Fangorn .15 .40
❑ 67 Orcs on the Rampage .15 .40
❑ 68 Deadly Phantoms .15 .40
❑ 69 Balrog and the Troll .15 .40
❑ 70 When the Watcher Strikes .15 .40
❑ 71 Horror of the Black Riders .15 .40
❑ 72 Checklist .15 .40

2008 Lord of the Rings Masterpieces II Etched Foil

COMPLETE SET (6) 3.00 6.00
STATED ODDS 1:6

❑ 1 Boromir and Gimli .60 1.50
❑ 2 Frodo .60 1.50
❑ 3 Legolas and Galadriel .60 1.50
❑ 4 Gandalf,Merry,Pippin and Sam .60 1.50
❑ 5 Aragorn and Arwen .60 1.50
❑ 6 Saruman and Gollum .60 1.50

2008 Lord of the Rings Masterpieces II Etched Foil Original Art

STATED ODDS 1:108,000 HOBBY
UNPRICED DUE TO SCARCITY

❑ 1 Boromir and Gimli
❑ 2 Frodo
❑ 3 Legolas and Galadriel
❑ 4 Gandalf,Merry,Pippin and Sam
❑ 5 Aragorn and Arwen
❑ 6 Saruman and Gollum

2008 Lord of the Rings Masterpieces II Foil Silver

COMPLETE SET (9) 3.00 6.00
STATED ODDS 1:4

❑ 1 Arwen .40 1.00
❑ 2 Galadriel .40 1.00
❑ 3 Theoden .40 1.00
❑ 4 Elrond .40 1.00
❑ 5 Eowyn .40 1.00
❑ 6 Faramir .40 1.00
❑ 7 Eomer .40 1.00
❑ 8 Gollum .40 1.00
❑ 9 Bilbo .40 1.00

2008 Lord of the Rings Masterpieces II Foil Bronze

COMPLETE SET (9) 15.00 30.00
*BRONZE: 2X TO 5X SILVER
STATED ODDS 1:36 HOBBY

❑ 1 Arwen 2.00 5.00
❑ 2 Galadriel 2.00 5.00
❑ 3 Theoden 2.00 5.00
❑ 4 Elrond 2.00 5.00
❑ 5 Eowyn 2.00 5.00
❑ 6 Faramir 2.00 5.00
❑ 7 Eomer 2.00 5.00
❑ 8 Gollum 2.00 5.00
❑ 9 Bilbo 2.00 5.00

2008 Lord of the Rings Masterpieces II Foil Gold

STATED ODDS 1:836 HOBBY
STATED PRINT RUN 90 SER. #'d SETS

❑ 1 Arwen
❑ 2 Galadriel
❑ 3 Theoden
❑ 4 Elrond
❑ 5 Eowyn
❑ 6 Faramir
❑ 7 Eomer
❑ 8 Gollum
❑ 9 Bilbo

2008 Lord of the Rings Masterpieces II Foil Refractor

STATED ODDS 1:72,000 HOBBY

❑ 1 Arwen
❑ 2 Galadriel
❑ 3 Theoden
❑ 4 Elrond
❑ 5 Eowyn
❑ 6 Faramir
❑ 7 Eomer
❑ 8 Gollum
❑ 9 Bilbo

2008 Lord of the Rings Masterpieces II Sketches

STATED ODDS 1:18 HOBBY

❑ NNO Alex Buechel
❑ NNO Brent Woodside
❑ NNO Carly Monardo
❑ NNO Chris Henderson
❑ NNO Cynthia Cummens
❑ NNO Dave Bryant
❑ NNO Dennis Budd
❑ NNO Ed Tadem
❑ NNO Hamilton Cline
❑ NNO Jake Minor
❑ NNO Jason Keith Phillips
❑ NNO Jason Sobol
❑ NNO Joanne Ellen Mutch
❑ NNO Jon Morris
❑ NNO Steve Oatney
❑ NNO Tom Hodges
❑ NNO Zach Giallongo
❑ NNO Brent Engstrom
❑ NNO Bruce Gerlach
❑ NNO Chad Hurd
❑ NNO Colleen Doran
❑ NNO Darla Ecklund
❑ NNO Davide Fabbri
❑ NNO Dustin Weaver
❑ NNO Grant Gould
❑ NNO Irma Ahmed
❑ NNO Jan Duursema
❑ NNO Jason Potratz
Jack Hai
❑ NNO Jim Kyle
❑ NNO John Watkins-Chow
❑ NNO Karen Krajenbrink
❑ NNO Kevin Doyle
❑ NNO Leah Mangue
❑ NNO Mark Propst
❑ NNO Megan Correnti
❑ NNO Nick Neocleous
❑ NNO Otto Dieffenbach
❑ NNO Paul Gutierrez
❑ NNO Ray Lago
❑ NNO Ronald Salas
❑ NNO Shell Paroline
❑ NNO Kate Bradley
❑ NNO Kevin Graham
❑ NNO Lee Kohse
❑ NNO Mary Huang
❑ NNO Michael Duron
❑ NNO Nicole Falk
❑ NNO Patrick Hamill
❑ NNO Peter Lazarski
❑ NNO Renae DeLiz
❑ NNO Ryan Waterhouse
❑ NNO Soni Alcorn-Hender
❑ NNO Steven Miller
❑ NNO Tony Perna
❑ NNO Amy Pronovost
❑ NNO Brian Kong
❑ NNO Cat Staggs
❑ NNO Clay McCormack
❑ NNO Dan Cooney
❑ NNO David Rabbitte
❑ NNO Doug Cowan
❑ NNO Evan Bryce
❑ NNO Ingrid Hardy
❑ NNO Jamie Snell
❑ NNO Jason Potratz
❑ NNO Jess Hickman
❑ NNO John Jackman
❑ NNO Josh Howard
❑ NNO Katie Cook
❑ NNO Kyle Babbitt
❑ NNO Mark McHaley
❑ NNO Matthew Goodmanson
❑ NNO Monte Moore
❑ NNO Noah Albrecht
❑ NNO Paul Ballard
❑ NNO Randy Siplon
❑ NNO Rich Woodall
❑ NNO Sean Pence
❑ NNO Stephanie Yue
❑ NNO Tess Fowler
❑ NNO Wayne Lo
❑ NNO Allison Sohn
❑ NNO Brian Ashmore
❑ NNO Cassandra Seimons
❑ NNO Christian Dalla Vecchia
❑ NNO Dan Beswick
❑ NNO Dave Fox
❑ NNO Don Pedicini Jr.
❑ NNO Edward Pun
❑ NNO Howard Shum
❑ NNO James Bukauskas
❑ NNO Jason Martin
❑ NNO Jeff Carlisle
❑ NNO Joe Corroney
❑ NNO Jon Ocampo
❑ NNO Kate Glasheen
❑ NNO Killian Plunkett
❑ NNO Len Bellinger
❑ NNO Matt Busch
❑ NNO Michael Segawa
❑ NNO Nina Edlund
❑ NNO Patrick Richardson
❑ NNO Ramsey Sibaja
❑ NNO Rich Molinelli
❑ NNO Sarah Wilkinson
❑ NNO Spencer Brinkerhoff III
❑ NNO Taki Soma
❑ NNO Tristan Henry-Wilson

2008 Marvel Masterpieces 2

Card	Low	High
COMPLETE SET (90)	4.00	10.00
☐ 1 Marvel Masterpieces 2	.10	.25
☐ 2 Archangel	.10	.25
☐ 3 The Beast	.10	.25
☐ 4 The Beetle	.10	.25
☐ 5 Black Queen	.10	.25
☐ 6 Bullseye	.10	.25
☐ 7 Cannonball	.10	.25
☐ 8 Captain America	.10	.25
☐ 9 Captain Marvel	.10	.25
☐ 10 Cloak	.10	.25
☐ 11 Colossus	.10	.25
☐ 12 Crimson Commando	.10	.25
☐ 13 Cyclops	.10	.25
☐ 14 Daredevil	.10	.25
☐ 15 Dazzler	.10	.25
☐ 16 Dead Girl	.10	.25
☐ 17 Destiny	.10	.25
☐ 18 Dr. Doom	.10	.25
☐ 19 Dr. Octopus	.10	.25
☐ 20 Dr. Spectrum	.10	.25
☐ 21 Dr. Strange	.10	.25
☐ 22 Egghead	.10	.25
☐ 23 Elektra	.10	.25
☐ 24 Emma Frost	.10	.25
☐ 25 Enchantress	.10	.25
☐ 26 Firestar	.10	.25
☐ 27 Galactus	.10	.25
☐ 28 Ghost Rider	.10	.25
☐ 29 Green Goblin	.10	.25
☐ 30 Hammerhead	.10	.25
☐ 31 Hellcat	.10	.25
☐ 32 Hellstorm	.10	.25
☐ 33 Howard the Duck	.10	.25
☐ 34 The Hulk	.10	.25
☐ 35 Human Torch	.10	.25
☐ 36 Iceman	.10	.25
☐ 37 Invisible Woman	.10	.25
☐ 38 Iron Man	.10	.25
☐ 39 J. Jonah Jameson	.10	.25
☐ 40 Jean Grey	.10	.25
☐ 41 Jubilee	.10	.25
☐ 42 Kang	.10	.25
☐ 43 Ka-Zar	.10	.25
☐ 44 Kingpin	.10	.25
☐ 45 Kraven the Hunter	.10	.25
☐ 46 Lady Deathstrike	.10	.25
☐ 47 Machine Man	.10	.25
☐ 48 Magneto	.10	.25
☐ 49 Medusa	.10	.25
☐ 50 Mimic	.10	.25
☐ 51 Mr. Fantastic	.10	.25
☐ 52 Mole Man	.10	.25
☐ 53 Moondragon	.10	.25
☐ 54 Morbius	.10	.25
☐ 55 Mystique	.10	.25
☐ 56 Nick Fury	.10	.25
☐ 57 Nightcrawler	.10	.25
☐ 58 Northstar	.10	.25
☐ 59 Nova	.10	.25
☐ 60 Professor X	.10	.25
☐ 61 Psylocke	.10	.25
☐ 62 The Punisher	.10	.25
☐ 63 Pyro	.10	.25
☐ 64 Quasar	.10	.25
☐ 65 Quicksilver	.10	.25
☐ 66 Red Queen	.10	.25
☐ 67 Red Skull	.10	.25
☐ 68 Rocket Racer	.10	.25
☐ 69 Rogue	.10	.25
☐ 70 Sabretooth	.10	.25
☐ 71 Sandman	.10	.25
☐ 72 Scarlet Witch	.10	.25
☐ 73 The Scorpion	.10	.25
☐ 74 Sebastian Shaw	.10	.25
☐ 75 The Sentinel	.10	.25
☐ 76 Shadowcat	.10	.25
☐ 77 Shanna	.10	.25
☐ 78 Shocker	.10	.25
☐ 79 Silver Surfer	.10	.25
☐ 80 Spider-Man	.10	.25
☐ 81 Spider-Woman	.10	.25
☐ 82 Storm	.10	.25
☐ 83 Sub-Mariner	.10	.25
☐ 84 The Thing	.10	.25
☐ 85 Thor	.10	.25
☐ 86 Valkyrie	.10	.25
☐ 87 Venom	.10	.25
☐ 88 The Vulture	.10	.25
☐ 89 The Watcher	.10	.25
☐ 90 Wolverine	.10	.25

2008 Marvel Masterpieces 2 Avengers

Card	Low	High
COMPLETE SET (9)	5.00	12.00
STATED ODDS 2:9		
☐ A1 Ant-Man	1.00	2.50
☐ A2 Captain America	1.00	2.50
☐ A3 Hawkeye	1.00	2.50
☐ A4 The Hulk	1.00	2.50
☐ A5 Iron Man	1.00	2.50
☐ A6 Scarlet Witch	1.00	2.50
☐ A7 Thor	1.00	2.50
☐ A8 The Vision	1.00	2.50
☐ A9 The Wasp	1.00	2.50

2008 Marvel Masterpieces 2 Fantastic Four Memorabilia

Card	Low	High
STATED ODDS 1:36		
☐ FF1 Mr. Fantastic	5.00	12.00
☐ FF2 Invisible Woman	25.00	50.00
☐ FF3 Human Torch	4.00	10.00
☐ FF4 The Thing	4.00	10.00
☐ FF5 Dr. Doom	4.00	10.00

2008 Marvel Masterpieces 2 Hulk Die-Cut

Card	Low	High
COMPLETE SET (3)		
CARD A STATED ODDS 1:18 HOBBY		
CARDS B AND C RANDOM INSERT IN RETAIL PACKS		
☐ A Hulk H	1.50	4.00
☐ B Hulk R		
☐ C Hulk R		

2008 Marvel Masterpieces 2 Iron Man Die-Cut

Card	Low	High
COMPLETE SET (3)		
CARD A STATED ODDS 1:18 HOBBY		
CARDS B AND C RANDOM INSERT IN RETAIL PACKS		
☐ A Iron Man H	1.50	4.00
☐ B Iron Man R		
☐ C Iron Man R		

2008 Marvel Masterpieces 2 Jumbo Box Toppers

Card	Low	High
COMPLETE SET (5)	12.00	30.00
STATED ODDS ONE PER BOX		
☐ 1 Dr. Strange	4.00	10.00
☐ 2 Scarlet Witch	4.00	10.00
☐ 3 Spider-Woman	4.00	10.00
☐ 4 The X-Men	4.00	10.00
☐ 5 X-Men Villains	4.00	10.00

2008 Marvel Masterpieces 2 Marvel Heroines

Card	Low	High
COMPLETE SET (9)	5.00	12.00
STATED ODDS 2:9		
☐ MH1 Elektra	1.00	2.50
☐ MH2 Invisible Woman	1.00	2.50
☐ MH3 Jean Grey	1.00	2.50
☐ MH4 Ms. Marvel	1.00	2.50
☐ MH5 Mystique	1.00	2.50
☐ MH6 She-Hulk	1.00	2.50
☐ MH7 She-Thing	1.00	2.50
☐ MH8 Spider-Woman	1.00	2.50
☐ MH9 Storm	1.00	2.50

2008 Marvel Masterpieces 2 Sketches

STATED ODDS 1:36

☐ 1 (Edwards)
☐ 2 Aaron Sowd
☐ 3 Adam Cleveland
☐ 4 Adam Cline
☐ 5 Adam DeKraker
☐ 6 Adam Hicks
☐ 7 Adelso Corona
☐ 8 Alex Maleev
☐ 9 Alex Saviuk
☐ 10 Andre Moore
☐ 11 Andrew Robinson
☐ 12 Anjin Anhut
☐ 13 Anthony Winn
☐ 14 Arthur Adams
☐ 15 Beau Scheмery
☐ 16 Ben Curtis Jones
☐ 17 Ben Herrera
☐ 18 Benjamin Glendenning
☐ 19 Bill Meiggs
☐ 20 Bill Reinhold
☐ 21 Bill Thompson
☐ 22 Blair Shedd
☐ 23 Bob Budiansky
☐ 24 Brent Engstrom
☐ 25 Brent McKee
☐ 26 Brent Schoonover
☐ 27 Brian Kong
☐ 28 Brian Pierce
☐ 29 Brian Shearer
☐ 30 Brian Walker
☐ 31 Bryan Turner
☐ 32 Bryce Gunkel
☐ 33 Carlo Soriano
☐ 34 Casey Jones
☐ 35 Chad Hardin
☐ 36 Chad LaForce
☐ 37 Chadd Keim
☐ 38 Charles Holbert
☐ 39 Chris Bachalo
☐ 40 Chris Brunner
☐ 41 Chris Marrinan
☐ 42 Chris Ortega
☐ 43 Chris Peterson
☐ 44 Chris Warner
☐ 45 Christopher Higginson
☐ 46 Chuk Wojtkiewicz
☐ 47 Colleen Doran
☐ 48 Conan Momchilov
☐ 49 Corbett Vanoni
☐ 50 Cory Walker
☐ 51 Cully Hamner
☐ 52 D. T. Amos
☐ 53 Dan Cooney
☐ 54 Dan Panosian
☐ 55 Dan Quiles
☐ 56 Dan Schoening (Dapper Dan)
☐ 57 Dane Ault
☐ 58 Daniel Duncan
☐ 59 Darla Ecklund
☐ 60 Dave Bullock
☐ 61 David Mack
☐ 62 David Williams
☐ 63 Dean Trippe
☐ 64 Dennis Calero
☐ 65 Dennis Culver
☐ 66 Dexter Vines
☐ 67 Dietrich Smith
☐ 68 Don Pedicini Jr
☐ 69 Eric Canete
☐ 70 Ethan Beavers
☐ 71 Frank Cho
☐ 72 Frank Rapoza
☐ 73 Gary McKee
☐ 74 Georges Jeanty
☐ 75 Greg Paulsen
☐ 76 Guile
☐ 77 Gus Vazquez
☐ 78 Hamilton Cline
☐ 79 Howard Shum
☐ 80 Ive Sorocuk (Sirive)
☐ 81 Jake Minor
☐ 82 Jason Martin
☐ 83 Jeff Johnson
☐ 84 Jenn Lee
☐ 85 Jeremy Haun
☐ 86 Jerome Moore
☐ 87 Jesse Labbe
☐ 88 Jessica Hickman
☐ 89 Jim Kyle
☐ 90 Jim Mahfood
☐ 91 Joe Jusko
☐ 92 Joe Manzella
☐ 93 Joel Carroll
☐ 94 John Beatty
☐ 95 John Watkins-Chow
☐ 96 John Wycough
☐ 97 Jon Sommariva
☐ 98 Jonboy Meyers
☐ 99 Josh Alves
☐ 100 Joyce Chin
☐ 101 Justin Chung
☐ 102 Justin Vandemark
☐ 103 Karen Krajenbrink
☐ 104 Kate Bradley (Red)
☐ 105 Katie Cook
☐ 106 Keith O'Malley
☐ 107 Ken Steacy
☐ 108 Kerry Gammill
☐ 109 Kevin Gentilcore
☐ 110 Kevin Graham
☐ 111 Kristin Allen
☐ 112 Lisa Redfern
☐ 113 Lyn Lau
☐ 114 Marat Mychaels
☐ 115 Mark Irwin
☐ 116 Mark Romanoski
☐ 117 Mark Tannacore
☐ 118 Mat Broome
☐ 119 Matthew Humphreys
☐ 120 Michael Dooney
☐ 121 Michael Duron
☐ 122 Michael Kasinger (MEK)
☐ 123 Michael O'Hare
☐ 124 Mike Deodato Jr
☐ 125 Mike Kunkel
☐ 126 Mike Manley
☐ 127 Mike Mayhew
☐ 128 Mike Torrance
☐ 129 MOthbot
☐ 130 Nar
☐ 131 Nelson DeCastro
☐ 132 Nicholas Alexander Johnson
☐ 133 Olivier Coipel
☐ 134 Otis Frampton
☐ 135 Pat Carlucci
☐ 136 Patrick Gerrity
☐ 137 Patrick Scherberger
☐ 138 Paul Gutierrez
☐ 139 Penelope Gaylord (Peng Peng)
☐ 140 Pop Mhan
☐ 141 Ramsey Sibaja (Raz)
☐ 142 Randy Green
☐ 143 Remy Mokhtar (Eisu)
☐ 144 Rich Molinelli
☐ 145 Rich Woodall
☐ 146 Richard Barkman (Virge)
☐ 147 Richard Case
☐ 148 Richard Pace
☐ 149 Robin Mitchell
☐ 150 Robin Riggs
☐ 151 Ron Garney
☐ 152 Ruben Martinez
☐ 153 Russell Platt
☐ 154 Ryan Benjamin
☐ 155 Ryan Odagawa
☐ 156 Ryan Orosco
☐ 157 Ryan Ottley
☐ 158 Sean Galloway
☐ 159 Sean Moore
☐ 160 Sean Phillips
☐ 161 Sergio Cariello
☐ 162 Shawn Crystal
☐ 163 Skottie Young
☐ 164 Soul
☐ 165 Spencer Brinkerhoff
☐ 166 Steven Miller
☐ 167 Taki Soma
☐ 168 Tariq Hassan
☐ 169 Ted Dastick Jr.
☐ 170 Tod Allen Smith
☐ 171 Tom Feister
☐ 172 Tom Hodges
☐ 173 Tom Nguyen
☐ 174 Tom Palmer
☐ 175 Tommy Smith
☐ 176 Tony Dennison (Aden)
☐ 177 Tony Harris
☐ 178 Tony Miello
☐ 179 Tony Parker
☐ 180 Tony Perna
☐ 181 Trevor Hairsine
☐ 182 Vince Smith
☐ 183 Wendy Lewis
☐ 184 Will Caligan
☐ 185 William Tucci
☐ 186 Zak Plucinski

2008 Marvel Masterpieces 3

Card	Low	High
COMPLETE SET (90)	4.00	10.00
☐ 1 Ahab	.10	.25
☐ 2 Annihilus	.10	.25
☐ 3 Baron Zemo	.10	.25
☐ 4 Black Tom	.10	.25
☐ 5 Blastaar	.10	.25
☐ 6 The Blob	.10	.25
☐ 7 Dark Phoenix	.10	.25
☐ 8 Death-Stalker	.10	.25
☐ 9 Dormammu and Umar	.10	.25
☐ 10 Dr. Doom	.10	.25
☐ 11 Egghead	.10	.25
☐ 12 Elektra	.10	.25
☐ 13 Enchantress	.10	.25
☐ 14 Fin Fang Foom	.10	.25
☐ 15 Green Goblin	.10	.25
☐ 16 Grey Gargoyle	.10	.25
☐ 17 Hobgoblin	.10	.25
☐ 18 Jack O'Lantern	.10	.25
☐ 19 Juggernaut	.10	.25
☐ 20 Kang	.10	.25
☐ 21 The Kingpin	.10	.25
☐ 22 Klaw	.10	.25
☐ 23 Kraven The Hunter	.10	.25
☐ 24 Magneto	.10	.25
☐ 25 Master Mold	.10	.25
☐ 26 Maximus	.10	.25
☐ 27 Mephisto	.10	.25
☐ 28 Mister Hyde	.10	.25
☐ 29 Mister Sinister	.10	.25
☐ 30 Nightmare	.10	.25
☐ 31 Nimrod	.10	.25
☐ 32 Onslaught	.10	.25
☐ 33 Quagmire	.10	.25
☐ 34 Radioactive Man	.10	.25
☐ 35 Sabretooth	.10	.25
☐ 36 Sentinels	.10	.25
☐ 37 Skrull	.10	.25
☐ 38 Spiral	.10	.25
☐ 39 Super-Skrull	.10	.25
☐ 40 Terrax The Tamer	.10	.25
☐ 41 The Tinkerer	.10	.25
☐ 42 Titania	.10	.25
☐ 43 Typhoid Mary	.10	.25
☐ 44 Venom	.10	.25
☐ 45 The Wrecking Crew	.10	.25
☐ 46 Adamantium Extraction	.10	.25
☐ 47 Archenemies	.10	.25
☐ 48 Bloody Battle	.10	.25
☐ 49 Caught	.10	.25
☐ 50 Caught in a Whirlwind	.10	.25
☐ 51 Combat for a Kingdom	.10	.25
☐ 52 Cosmic Chess Game	.10	.25
☐ 53 Death of Elektra	.10	.25
☐ 54 Defeated by The Kingpin	.10	.25
☐ 55 Destroy All Vampires	.10	.25
☐ 56 Fight for Freedom	.10	.25
☐ 57 For the Power Cosmic	.10	.25
☐ 58 Invasion of Avengers Mansion	.10	.25
☐ 59 Life, Liberty, and Justice	.10	.25
☐ 60 Magneto Strikes	.10	.25
☐ 61 The Mandarin Strikes	.10	.25
☐ 62 Metal on Metal	.10	.25
☐ 63 Namor Takes His Bride	.10	.25
☐ 64 Rise of The Sinister Six	.10	.25
☐ 65 Sound and Fury	.10	.25
☐ 66 Spider-Man vs. The Green Goblin	.10	.25
☐ 67 Stop the War	.10	.25
☐ 68 To Court Death	.10	.25
☐ 69 To Rule the Morlocks	.10	.25
☐ 70 To Save the Earth	.10	.25
☐ 71 Ultimate Battle	.10	.25
☐ 72 Under Ultron's Control	.10	.25
☐ 73 Doc Ock Captured	.10	.25
☐ 74 Doc Ock Mug Shot 1	.10	.25
☐ 75 Doc Ock Mug Shot 2	.10	.25
☐ 76 Electro Captured	.10	.25
☐ 77 Electro Mug Shot 1	.10	.25
☐ 78 Electro Mug Shot 2	.10	.25
☐ 79 Kraven Captured	.10	.25
☐ 80 Kraven Mug Shot 1	.10	.25
☐ 81 Kraven Mug Shot 2	.10	.25
☐ 82 Mysterio Captured	.10	.25
☐ 83 Mysterio Mug Shot 1	.10	.25
☐ 84 Mysterio Mug Shot 2	.10	.25
☐ 85 Sandman Captured	.10	.25
☐ 86 Sandman Mug Shot 1	.10	.25
☐ 87 Sandman Mug Shot 2	.10	.25
☐ 88 Vulture Captured	.10	.25
☐ 89 Vulture Mug Shot 1	.10	.25
☐ 90 Vulture Mug Shot 2	.10	.25

2008 Marvel Masterpieces 3 Marvel Knights

Card	Low	High
COMPLETE SET (9)	4.00	10.00
☐ MK1 Blade	.75	2.00
☐ MK2 Brother Voodoo	.75	2.00
☐ MK3 Cloak	.75	2.00
☐ MK4 Dagger	.75	2.00
☐ MK5 Dr. Strange	.75	2.00
☐ MK6 Iron Fist	.75	2.00
☐ MK7 Moon Knight	.75	2.00
☐ MK8 Power Man	.75	2.00
☐ MK9 The Punisher	.75	2.00

2008 Marvel Masterpieces 3 Marvel Moments

Card	Low	High
COMPLETE SET (9)	6.00	15.00
☐ MM1 Atlantis Attacks	1.00	2.50
☐ MM2 Birth of the Surfer	1.00	2.50
☐ MM3 Black Bolt Speaks	1.00	2.50
☐ MM4 Bucky's Back	1.00	2.50
☐ MM5 I Hunger	1.00	2.50
☐ MM6 The Mole Man Cometh	1.00	2.50
☐ MM7 My Name Is Peter Parker	1.00	2.50
☐ MM8 To Threaten Cape Citadel	1.00	2.50
☐ MM9 What's a Little Hot Foot Between Friends	1.00	2.50

2008 Marvel Masterpieces 3 Sketches

STATED ODDS 1:36

☐ 1 Aaron Sowd
☐ 2 Adam Cline
☐ 3 Adam DeKraker
☐ 4 Adam Hicks
☐ 5 Adelso Corona
☐ 6 Andre Moore
☐ 7 Andrew Robinson
☐ 8 Andy Genen
☐ 9 Anjin Anhut
☐ 10 Arie Monroe
☐ 11 Armando Durruthy
☐ 12 Autumn Turkel
☐ 13 Ben Herrera
☐ 14 Benjamin Glendenning
☐ 15 Bill Thompson
☐ 16 Billy Martin
☐ 17 Blair Shedd
☐ 18 Bob Wiacek
☐ 19 Brent Schoonover
☐ 20 Brian Shearer
☐ 21 Brian Walker
☐ 22 Bruce Gerlach
☐ 23 Bryan Turner
☐ 24 Bryce Lee
☐ 25 Buddy Prince
☐ 26 Butch Mapa
☐ 27 Carlo Soriano
☐ 28 Chad Hardin
☐ 29 Charles Hall
☐ 30 Chris Bachalo
☐ 31 Chris Butler
☐ 32 Chris Ortega
☐ 33 Chris Warner
☐ 34 Christian Meesey
☐ 35 Chuck George
☐ 36 Cynthia Cummens
☐ 37 Dan Borganos
☐ 38 Dan Cooney
☐ 39 Dan Duncan
☐ 40 Dan Panosian
☐ 41 Dan Quiles
☐ 42 Dan Schaefer
☐ 43 Dane Ault
☐ 44 Daniel Campos
☐ 45 Danny Kuang
☐ 46 Dapper Dan Schoening
☐ 47 Dave Pops Tata
☐ 48 Dave Strong
☐ 49 David Hahn
☐ 50 David Mack
☐ 51 David Rabbitte
☐ 52 Dennis Crisostomo
☐ 53 Dennis Culver
☐ 54 Dennis jimmymcwicked Miller
☐ 55 Edwin David
☐ 56 Eric Merced
☐ 57 Erica Hesse
☐ 58 Eugene Commodore
☐ 59 Felicia Cano
☐ 60 Frank Rapoza
☐ 61 George (Geo) Davis
☐ 62 Gilbert Monsanto
☐ 63 Gilbert Mothbot Leiker
☐ 64 Graham Nolan
☐ 65 Guile
☐ 66 Hakjoon x-raykid Kang
☐ 67 Hanie Mohd
☐ 68 Harwinder Singh
☐ 69 Howard Shum
☐ 70 Irma Ahmed
☐ 71 Jake Minor
☐ 72 James Bukshot Bukauskas
☐ 73 James James Q Nguyen
☐ 74 Jason Keith Phillips
☐ 75 Jason Martin
☐ 76 Jason Reeves
☐ 77 Jason Sobol
☐ 78 Jeff Johnson
☐ 79 Jeff Victor
☐ 80 Jeff Wamester
☐ 81 Jenn Lee
☐ 82 Jeremy Treece
☐ 83 Jerry The Franchize Gaylord
☐ 84 Jessica Hickman
☐ 85 Jim Cheung
☐ 86 Jim Hanna
☐ 87 Joe Dodd
☐ 88 Joe Manzella
☐ 89 Joe Mulvey
☐ 90 Joe Pekar
☐ 91 Joel Carroll
☐ 92 Jon Riggle
☐ 93 Jon Sommariva
☐ 94 Jonboy Meyers
☐ 95 Josh Alves
☐ 96 Joyce Chin
☐ 97 Julian Lytle
☐ 98 Justin Barrett
☐ 99 Justin Chung
☐ 100 Justin Peterson
☐ 101 Justin Vandemark
☐ 102 Karen Krajenbrink
☐ 103 Kat Laurange
☐ 104 Kate Red Bradley
☐ 105 Kathryn Layno Lewis
☐ 106 Kelly Yates
☐ 107 Kent Clark
☐ 108 Kevin Gentilcore
☐ 109 Kevin Graham
☐ 110 Kristin Allen
☐ 111 Kyle Bice
☐ 112 Lak Lim
☐ 113 Lance Sawyer
☐ 114 Leigh Dragoon
☐ 115 Lisa Redfern
☐ 116 Lord Mesa
☐ 117 Marcus A. Smith (MAS)
☐ 118 Mark Irwin
☐ 119 Mark Tannacore
☐ 120 Martheux Wade
☐ 121 Mary Bellamy
☐ 122 Matthew Warlick
☐ 123 Megan Hetrick
☐ 124 Mel Celestial
☐ 125 Melissa Erickson
☐ 126 Michael Kasinger
☐ 127 Michael Locoduck Duron
☐ 128 Mike Maihack
☐ 129 Mike S. Miller
☐ 130 Mike Van Orden
☐ 131 Nate Lovett
☐ 132 Nate Snareser
☐ 133 Nathan Ohlendorf
☐ 134 Pablo Praino
☐ 135 Patrick Gerrity
☐ 136 Penelope Peng-Peng Gaylord
☐ 137 Peter Nguyen
☐ 138 Randy Green
☐ 139 Randy Siplon
☐ 140 Ray Anthony Height
☐ 141 Remy Eisu Mokhtar
☐ 142 Rian Hughes
☐ 143 Rich A. Molinelli
☐ 144 Rich Woodall
☐ 145 Richard Pace
☐ 146 Rob Granito
☐ 147 Ron Salas
☐ 148 Ryan Kinnaird
☐ 149 Ryan Wong
☐ 150 Sal Abbinanti
☐ 151 Sanna U
☐ 152 Scot Terry
☐ 153 Scott Koblish
☐ 154 Sean Galloway
☐ 155 Sean Moore
☐ 156 Shawn Henderson
☐ 157 Sherry Leak
☐ 158 Siya Oum
☐ 159 Soul (Soul-the-Awkward)
☐ 160 Spencer Brinkerhoff
☐ 161 Stephen Arthur Schaffer
☐ 162 Stephen Reid
☐ 163 Steven Miller
☐ 164 Tanya Roberts
☐ 165 Tim Kane
☐ 166 Tod Allen Smith
☐ 167 Tom Fiester
☐ 168 Tom Palmer
☐ 169 Tony Miello
☐ 170 Tony Perna
☐ 171 Travis Moore
☐ 172 Wesley Gunn
☐ 173 William Neff
☐ 174 Zak Plucinski
☐ 175 Zane DeGaine

2008 Marvel Masterpieces 3 Writer Autographs

STATED ODDS 1:108

☐ AL Andy Lanning
☐ BR Ben Raab
☐ DA Dan Abnett
☐ GP Greg Pak
☐ HM Howard Mackie
☐ JL Jeph Loeb
☐ JS Jim Salicrup
☐ LH Larry Hama
☐ MB Mike Baron
☐ MO Mike Avon Oeming
☐ PJ Paul Jenkins

- PT Paul Tobin
- RS Roger Stern
- RT Roy Thomas
- SE Steve Englehart
- WS Walt Simonson
- BKV Brian K. Vaughan
- CBC C. B. Cebulski
- DM1 David Mack
- DM2 Dwayne McDuffie
- FVL Fred Van Lente
- JP1 Jeff Parker
- JP2 Jimmy Palmiotti
- TD1 Todd Dezago
- TD2 Tom DeFalco

2008 Marvel Masterpieces 3 X-Men Secret Identities

COMPLETE SET (9) 6.00 15.00

- XM1 Days of Future Present 1.25 3.00
- XM2 Fastball Special 1.25 3.00
- XM3 Legacy of Violence 1.25 3.00
- XM4 No Ruby Quartz 1.25 3.00
- XM5 Professor X's Dream Team 1.25 3.00
- XM6 Rise of Krakoa 1.25 3.00
- XM7 Weapon X 1.25 3.00
- XM8 The White Queen 1.25 3.00
- XM9 X-citing Trio 1.25 3.00

2008 The Spirit

COMPLETE SET (72) 4.00 10.00
CL1 STATED ODDS ONE PER CASE

- 1 Title Card .10 .30
- 2 The Spirit .10 .30
- 3 The Octopus .10 .30
- 4 Sand Saref .10 .30
- 5 Commissioner Dolan .10 .30
- 6 Ellen Dolan .10 .30
- 7 Silken Floss .10 .30
- 8 Officer Morgenstern .10 .30
- 9 Lorelei .10 .30
- 10 Wildwood's Sentinel .10 .30
- 11 Night And The City .10 .30
- 12 The Rescue .10 .30
- 13 The Spirit's Beat .10 .30
- 14 Mad Advesary .10 .30
- 15 Up From The Depths .10 .30
- 16 Looking For Trouble .10 .30
- 17 Enter Silken Floss .10 .30
- 18 A Clash Of Titans .10 .30
- 19 Mud Sluggers .10 .30
- 20 Send In The Clones .10 .30
- 21 Spirit's Deadliest Foe .10 .30
- 22 A Dirty Cop .10 .30
- 23 An Elusive Ally .10 .30
- 24 Hero At Large .10 .30
- 25 The Way We Were .10 .30
- 26 Eyes On The Prize .10 .30
- 27 Urban Playground .10 .30
- 28 A Tragic Twist .10 .30
- 29 Octopus, Eastern-Style .10 .30
- 30 Sand's Nasty Plan .10 .30
- 31 Love And Bandages .10 .30
- 32 New Kid In Town .10 .30
- 33 Minions Of The Law .10 .30
- 34 Public Hero Number One .10 .30
- 35 Just Part Of The Plan .10 .30
- 36 High Roller Heist .10 .30
- 37 Something's A Foot .10 .30
- 38 The Doctor Is In…Sane .10 .30
- 39 A Special Call .10 .30
- 40 The Girl Has Changed .10 .30
- 41 The Challenge .10 .30
- 42 The Goon Throttler .10 .30
- 43 Pinning A Pinhead .10 .30
- 44 Captured! .10 .30
- 45 Plaster Of Paris .10 .30
- 46 Getting The Spirit .10 .30
- 47 The Fate Of Denny Colt .10 .30
- 48 The Body Of His Work .10 .30
- 49 Back From The Dead .10 .30
- 50 A Hero Born Again .10 .30
- 51 Song Of The Lorelei .10 .30
- 52 Nabbing An Octopus .10 .30
- 53 Sand In The Middle .10 .30
- 54 Which Way, Ms. Floss .10 .30
- 55 Armed And Demented .10 .30
- 56 Aiming For Mayhem .10 .30
- 57 The Big Blaster .10 .30
- 58 Cops On The Scene .10 .30
- 59 Open Fire Now .10 .30
- 60 The Prize In His Grasp .10 .30
- 61 An Unexpected Twist .10 .30
- 62 Blown Apart .10 .30
- 63 Someone To Watch Over Us .10 .30
- 64 Will Eisner Classic-The Prom .10 .30
- 65 Will Eisner Classic-River Of Crime (AKA Slippery Eel) .10 .30
- 66 Will Eisner Classic-The Name Is Powder .10 .30
- 67 Will Eisner Classic-Lorelei Rox .10 .30
- 68 Will Eisner Classic-Plaster Of Paris .10 .30
- 69 Will Eisner Classic-Death Of Autumn Mews .10 .30
- 70 Will Eisner Classic-Bring In Sand Saref .10 .30
- 71 Will Eisner Classic-The Jewel Of Gizen .10 .30
- 72 Checklist .10 .30
- CL1 The Key To The City

2008 The Spirit Autographs

STATED ODDS 1:48

- A1 Gabriel Macht 8.00 20.00
- A2 Jaime King 8.00 20.00
- A3 Sarah Paulson 6.00 15.00
- A4 Paz Vega 10.00 25.00
- A5 Stana Katic 12.00 30.00
- A6 Dan Lauria 6.00 15.00
- A7 Samuel L. Jackson 300.00 400.00

2008 The Spirit Good Guys Bad Guys

COMPLETE SET (6)
STATED ODDS 1:17

- GB1 Boss Or Blowhard 1.25 3.00
- GB2 Evil With A Twist 1.25 3.00
- GB3 Dolan's Packin' 1.25 3.00
- GB4 Captured…For Now 1.25 3.00
- GB5 The Guy With The Tie 1.25 3.00
- GB6 Partners In Peril 1.25 3.00

2008 The Spirit My City Screams

COMPLETE SET (3)
STATED ODDS 1:24

- MC1 Dedicated Dean Man 2.00 5.00
- MC2 Crime For Crime's Sake 2.00 5.00
- MC3 Someone To Watch Over Me 2.00 5.00

2008 The Spirit Pieceworks

STATED ODDS 1:36
PW12A, PW12B ISSUED AS MULTI-CASE INCENTIVES

- PW1 The Spirit 5.00 12.00
- PW2 Plaster of Paris 10.00 25.00
- PW3 The Octopus 5.00 12.00
- PW4 Sand Saref 20.00 40.00
- PW5 The Octopus 5.00 12.00
- PW6 The Octopus 5.00 12.00
- PW7 Ellen 5.00 12.00
- PW8 The Octopus 5.00 12.00
- PW9 Silken Floss 20.00 40.00
- PW10 Silken Floss 20.00 40.00
- PW11 The Octopus 10.00 25.00
  Silken Floss DUAL
- PW12A The Spirit 8.00 20.00
  (issued as multi-case incentive)
- PW12B The Spirit 8.00 20.00
  (issued as multi-case incentive)

2008 The Spirit Promos

COMPLETE SET (6)

- P1 The Spirit .60 1.50
  (General Distribution)
- P2 Ellen Dolan .60 1.50
  (Non Sport Update)
- Pi Silken Floss 2.00 5.00
  (Free Card Offer)
- PMS I'm Gonna Kill You All Kinds of Dead 1.50 4.00
  (Memorabilia Show)
- PPS Sand Seref 1.50 4.00
  (Philly Non Sport Show)
- PUK Lorelei 2.00 5.00
  (UK Distribution)
- H2008 The Spirit
  (Holiday Promo)

2008 The Spirit Sketches

STATED ODDS 1:28

- SK1 Tone Rodriguez/102*
- SK2 Chris Moreno/246* 6.00 15.00
- SK3 Jeff Zugale/244* 4.00 10.00
- SK4 William O'Neill/238* 8.00 20.00
- SK5 Kevin Graham/203*
- SK6 Daniel Cooney/180* 5.00 12.00
- SK7 Tess Fowler/164* 8.00 20.00
- SK8 Chris Henderson/197* 4.00 10.00
- SK9 Bryan Morton/191* 4.00 10.00
- SK10 Nick (Nik) Neocleous/193* 6.00 15.00
- SK11 Steve Oatney/194* 8.00 20.00
- SK12 Sean Pence/196*
- SK13 Michael T. Sandborn/190* 5.00 12.00
- SK14 Jamie Snell/203* 8.00 20.00
- SK15 Kyle Babbitt/179* 4.00 10.00
- SK16 Benjamin Glendenning/207* 8.00 20.00
- SK17 Leah Mangue/161*
- SK18 Brian C. Kong/198* 6.00 15.00
- SK19 Otto Dieffenbach/198* 4.00 10.00
- SK20 Steven Miller/198*
- SK21 Corbett Vanoni/190* 6.00 15.00
- SK22 John Watkins-Chow/105*
- SK23 Leeahd Goldberg/93*
- SK24 Randy Martinez/128*

2008 The Spirit Spirit of the City Puzzle

COMPLETE SET (9)
STATED ODDS 1:11

- SC1 Married To The City 1.00 2.50
- SC2 Sea And Sand 1.00 2.50
- SC3 Cop On The Rise 1.00 2.50
- SC4 An Uneasy Alliance 1.00 2.50
- SC5 Madness On Parade 1.00 2.50
- SC6 Calling The Spirit 1.00 2.50
- SC7 Farewell To Innocence 1.00 2.50
- SC8 Public Menace Number One 1.00 2.50
- SC9 Phantom Of Wildwood 1.00 2.50

2008 Sports Illustrated Swimsuit

COMPLETE SET (75) 6.00 15.00

- 1 Ana Beatriz Barros .15 .40
- 2 Ana Beatriz Barros .15 .40
- 3 Ana Beatriz Barros .15 .40
- 4 Ana Beatriz Barros .15 .40
- 5 Ana Beatriz Barros .15 .40
- 6 Ana Beatriz Barros .15 .40
- 7 Anne V .15 .40
- 8 Anne V .15 .40
- 9 Anne V .15 .40
- 10 Anne V .15 .40
- 11 Anne V .15 .40
- 12 Anne V .15 .40
- 13 Bar Refaeli .40 1.00
- 14 Bar Refaeli .40 1.00
- 15 Bar Refaeli .40 1.00
- 16 Bar Refaeli .40 1.00
- 17 Bar Refaeli .40 1.00
- 18 Bar Refaeli .40 1.00
- 19 Brooklyn Decker .60 1.50
- 20 Brooklyn Decker .60 1.50
- 21 Brooklyn Decker .60 1.50
- 22 Brooklyn Decker .60 1.50
- 23 Brooklyn Decker .60 1.50
- 24 Brooklyn Decker .60 1.50
- 25 Daniella Sarahyba .15 .40
- 26 Daniella Sarahyba .15 .40
- 27 Daniella Sarahyba .15 .40
- 28 Daniella Sarahyba .15 .40
- 29 Daniella Sarahyba .15 .40
- 30 Daniella Sarahyba .15 .40
- 31 Irina Shayk .15 .40
- 32 Irina Shayk .15 .40
- 33 Irina Shayk .15 .40
- 34 Irina Shayk .15 .40
- 35 Irina Shayk .15 .40
- 36 Irina Shayk .15 .40
- 37 Jessica White .15 .40
- 38 Jessica White .15 .40
- 39 Jessica White .15 .40
- 40 Jessica White .15 .40
- 41 Jessica White .15 .40
- 42 Jessica White .15 .40
- 43 Julie Henderson .15 .40
- 44 Julie Henderson .15 .40
- 45 Julie Henderson .15 .40
- 46 Julie Henderson .15 .40
- 47 Julie Henderson .15 .40
- 48 Julie Henderson .15 .40
- 49 Marisa Miller .60 1.50
- 50 Marisa Miller .60 1.50
- 51 Marisa Miller .60 1.50
- 52 Marisa Miller .60 1.50
- 53 Marisa Miller .60 1.50
- 54 Marisa Miller .60 1.50
- 55 Oluchi Onweagba .15 .40
- 56 Oluchi Onweagba .15 .40
- 57 Oluchi Onweagba .15 .40
- 58 Oluchi Onweagba .15 .40
- 59 Oluchi Onweagba .15 .40
- 60 Oluchi Onweagba .15 .40
- 61 Selita Ebanks .15 .40
- 62 Selita Ebanks .15 .40
- 63 Selita Ebanks .15 .40
- 64 Selita Ebanks .15 .40
- 65 Selita Ebanks .15 .40
- 66 Selita Ebanks .15 .40
- 67 Tori Praver .15 .40
- 68 Tori Praver .15 .40
- 69 Tori Praver .15 .40
- 70 Tori Praver .15 .40
- 71 Tori Praver .15 .40
- 72 Tori Praver .15 .40
- 73 Preview .15 .40
- 74 Preview .15 .40
- 75 Checklist .15 .40

2008 Sports Illustrated Swimsuit Autographs

STATED ODDS 1:16

- AV1 Anne V - leaning on glass 10.00 25.00
- AV2 Anne V - standing in boat 10.00 25.00
- DS1 Daniella Sarahyba - striped bikini 10.00 25.00
- DS2 Daniella Sarahyba - solid bikini 10.00 25.00
- JC1 Jeisa Chiminazzo - ruffled top 20.00 40.00
- JC2 Jeisa Chiminazzo - striped top 20.00 40.00
- JG1 Jessica Gomes - blue and white bikini 25.00 50.00
- JG2 Jessica Gomes - brown and red bikini 25.00 50.00
- JH1 Julie Henderson - gold one-piece 10.00 25.00
- JH2 Julie Henderson - yellow bikini 10.00 25.00
- JM1 Jarah Mariano 10.00 25.00
- JM2 Jarah Mariano 10.00 25.00
- QG1 Quiana Grant - no top 10.00 25.00
- QG2 Quiana Grant - black one-piece 10.00 25.00

2008 Sports Illustrated Swimsuit Danica Patrick

COMPLETE SET (10) 75.00 150.00
STATED ODDS 1:4

- DP1 Danica Patrick 8.00 20.00
- DP2 Danica Patrick 8.00 20.00
- DP3 Danica Patrick 8.00 20.00
- DP4 Danica Patrick 8.00 20.00
- DP5 Danica Patrick 8.00 20.00
- DP6 Danica Patrick 8.00 20.00
- DP7 Danica Patrick 8.00 20.00
- DP8 Danica Patrick 8.00 20.00
- DP9 Danica Patrick 8.00 20.00
- DP10 Danica Patrick 8.00 20.00

2008 Sports Illustrated Swimsuit Editors Choice

- EC1 Ana Beatriz Barros 15.00 30.00
- EC2 Brooklyn Decker 20.00 40.00
- EC3 Daniella Sarahyba
- EC4 Marisa Miller 30.00 60.00
- EC5 Danica Patrick

2008 Sports Illustrated Swimsuit Material

STATED ODDS 1:16
PRAVER JEWEL ODDS 1:6 CASES

- BDM Brooklyn Decker 20.00 40.00
- BRM Bar Refaeli 20.00 40.00
- DPM Danica Patrick 75.00 125.00
- ISM Irina Shayk 15.00 30.00
- JMM Jarah Mariano 15.00 30.00
- MMM Marisa Miller 30.00 60.00
- TPM Tori Praver 15.00 30.00
- TPMJ Tori Praver JEWEL/20*

2008 Sports Illustrated Swimsuit Rookies

COMPLETE SET (10) 8.00 20.00
STATED ODDS 1:4

- R1 Quiana Grant 1.25 3.00
- R2 Jessica Gomes 1.50 4.00
- R3 Melissa Haro 1.25 3.00
- R4 Yasmin Brunet 1.25 3.00
- R5 Melissa Baker 1.25 3.00
- R6 Jeisa Chiminazzo 1.25 3.00
- R7 Jarah Mariano 1.50 4.00
- R8 Christie Brinkley 2.00 5.00
- R9 Elle Macpherson 2.50 6.00
- R10 Elsa Benitez 1.25 3.00

2008 Star Trek Movies In Motion

COMPLETE SET (60) 6.00 15.00

- 1 Star Trek: The Motion Picture .20 .50
- 2 Star Trek: The Motion Picture .20 .50
- 3 Star Trek: The Motion Picture .20 .50
- 4 Star Trek: The Motion Picture .20 .50
- 5 Star Trek: The Motion Picture .20 .50
- 6 Star Trek: The Motion Picture .20 .50
- 7 Star Trek II: The Wrath of Khan .20 .50
- 8 Star Trek II: The Wrath of Khan .20 .50
- 9 Star Trek II: The Wrath of Khan .20 .50
- 10 Star Trek II: The Wrath of Khan .20 .50
- 11 Star Trek II: The Wrath of Khan .20 .50
- 12 Star Trek II: The Wrath of Khan .20 .50
- 13 Star Trek III: The Search for Spock .20 .50
- 14 Star Trek III: The Search for Spock .20 .50
- 15 Star Trek III: The Search for Spock .20 .50
- 16 Star Trek III: The Search for Spock .20 .50
- 17 Star Trek III: The Search for Spock .20 .50
- 18 Star Trek III: The Search for Spock .20 .50
- 19 Star Trek IV: The Voyage Home .20 .50
- 20 Star Trek IV: The Voyage Home .20 .50
- 21 Star Trek IV: The Voyage Home .20 .50
- 22 Star Trek IV: The Voyage Home .20 .50
- 23 Star Trek IV: The Voyage Home .20 .50
- 24 Star Trek IV: The Voyage Home .20 .50
- 25 Star Trek V: The Final Frontier .20 .50
- 26 Star Trek V: The Final Frontier .20 .50
- 27 Star Trek V: The Final Frontier .20 .50
- 28 Star Trek V: The Final Frontier .20 .50
- 29 Star Trek V: The Final Frontier .20 .50
- 30 Star Trek V: The Final Frontier .20 .50
- 31 Star Trek VI: The Undiscovered Country .20 .50
- 32 Star Trek VI: The Undiscovered Country .20 .50
- 33 Star Trek VI: The Undiscovered Country .20 .50
- 34 Star Trek VI: The Undiscovered Country .20 .50
- 35 Star Trek VI: The Undiscovered Country .20 .50
- 36 Star Trek VI: The Undiscovered Country .20 .50
- 37 Star Trek: Generations .20 .50
- 38 Star Trek: Generations .20 .50
- 39 Star Trek: Generations .20 .50
- 40 Star Trek: Generations .20 .50
- 41 Star Trek: Generations .20 .50
- 42 Star Trek: Generations .20 .50
- 43 Star Trek: First Contact .20 .50
- 44 Star Trek: First Contact .20 .50
- 45 Star Trek: First Contact .20 .50
- 46 Star Trek: First Contact .20 .50
- 47 Star Trek: First Contact .20 .50
- 48 Star Trek: First Contact .20 .50
- 49 Star Trek: Insurrection .20 .50
- 50 Star Trek: Insurrection .20 .50
- 51 Star Trek: Insurrection .20 .50
- 52 Star Trek: Insurrection .20 .50
- 53 Star Trek: Insurrection .20 .50
- 54 Star Trek: Insurrection .20 .50
- 55 Star Trek: Nemesis .20 .50
- 56 Star Trek: Nemesis .20 .50
- 57 Star Trek: Nemesis .20 .50
- 58 Star Trek: Nemesis .20 .50
- 59 Star Trek: Nemesis .20 .50
- 60 Star Trek: Nemesis .20 .50

2008 Star Trek Movies In Motion Autographs

STATED ODDS 1:8
L (LIMITED): 300-500 COPIES
VL (VERY LIMITED): 200-300 COPIES

- A41 James Cromwell L 25.00 60.00
- A42 James B. Sikking 20.00 50.00
- A43 Majel Barrett VL 50.00 100.00
- A44 Patrick Stewart VL 150.00 250.00
- A45 David Warner L 12.00 30.00
- A46 Kirstie Alley L 50.00 100.00
- A47 Alice Krige L 10.00 25.00
- A48 Laurence Luckinbill L 15.00 40.00
- A51 Grace Lee Whitney
- A52 Eric Steinberg 5.00 12.00
- A53 Ronald D. Moore L 5.00 12.00
- A54 Nick Guest 5.00 12.00
- A55 Alex Henteloff 5.00 12.00
- A57 Robert Easton 8.00 20.00
- A57 Christopher Plummer 40.00 80.00
- A58 Rosana DeSoto 5.00 12.00
- A60 Nichelle Nichols VL 30.00 60.00
- A61 Jeremy Roberts 5.00 12.00
- A62 Stephen Liska 6.00 15.00
- A63 Leonard Nimoy 150.00 250.00
- A64 Michael Welch 5.00 12.00
- A65 Roger Aaron Brown 5.00 12.00
- A66 Marina Sirtis VL 40.00 80.00
- A67 Thomas Kopache 5.00 12.00
- A68 Don Stark 5.00 12.00
- A69 Barbara March 5.00 12.00
- A70 Gwyneth Walsh 6.00 15.00
- A71 Stephanie Niznik 6.00 15.00
- A72 Jacqueline Kim 5.00 12.00
- A73 Tim Russ VL 25.00 50.00
- A74 Alfre Woodard 20.00 40.00
- A75 Rif Hutton L 6.00 15.00
- A76 Dendrie Taylor 5.00 12.00

2008 Twilight

COMPLETE SET (72) 15.00 30.00

- 1 Twilight .40 1.00
- 2 Bella Swan .40 1.00
- 3 Edward Cullen .40 1.00
- 4 Jacob Black .40 1.00
- 5 Dr. Carlisle Cullen .40 1.00
- 6 Esme Cullen .40 1.00
- 7 Rosalie Hale .40 1.00
- 8 Jasper Hale .40 1.00
- 9 Alice Cullen .40 1.00
- 10 Emmett Cullen .40 1.00
- 11 Charlie Swan .40 1.00
- 12 James .40 1.00
- 13 Victoria .40 1.00
- 14 Laurent .40 1.00
- 15 Billy Black .40 1.00
- 16 Mike Newton .40 1.00
- 17 Mr. Molina .40 1.00
- 18 Waylon Forge .40 1.00
- 19 A New Beginning .40 1.00
- 20 Welcome Home Present .40 1.00
- 21 Not Daddy's Little Girl .40 1.00
- 22 The Black Family .40 1.00
- 23 First Day of School .40 1.00
- 24 Lunchtime Gossip .40 1.00
- 25 The Cullen Family .40 1.00
- 26 Biology Class .40 1.00
- 27 Mysterious Lab Partner .40 1.00
- 28 Dinner with Charlie .40 1.00
- 29 The People of Forks .40 1.00
- 30 Forman Introduction .40 1.00
- 31 Dealing with Biology .40 1.00
- 32 A Chance to Talk .40 1.00
- 33 Saved .40 1.00
- 34 A Family's Concern .40 1.00
- 35 Field Trip .40 1.00
- 36 Making Up .40 1.00
- 37 La Push Beach .40 1.00
- 38 Legends .40 1.00
- 39 Drawing First Blood .40 1.00
- 40 Prom Shopping .40 1.00
- 41 Closer to the Truth .40 1.00
- 42 Haunted .40 1.00
- 43 Answers .40 1.00
- 44 Transformation .40 1.00
- 45 The Real Me .40 1.00
- 46 In Love with Him .40 1.00
- 47 Since 1918 .40 1.00
- 48 Stick With Me .40 1.00
- 49 The Cullen Home .40 1.00
- 50 Meeting the Parents .40 1.00
- 51 Rosalie's Fears .40 1.00
- 52 Flying through the Trees .40 1.00
- 53 What Alice Sees .40 1.00
- 54 Hunter becomes the Prey .40 1.00
- 55 Forks in Fear .40 1.00
- 56 Midnight Visitor .40 1.00
- 57 Baseball with the Cullens .40 1.00
- 58 Evil Arrives .40 1.00
- 59 Going into Hiding .40 1.00
- 60 An Enemy's Warning .40 1.00
- 61 Preparing for a Fight .40 1.00
- 62 Alice's Nightmarish Vision .40 1.00
- 63 Home Invasion .40 1.00
- 64 Captured .40 1.00
- 65 Stopping James .40 1.00
- 66 Venom .40 1.00
- 67 The Battle for Bella .40 1.00
- 68 Saving Bella's Life .40 1.00
- 69 Repairing Relationships .40 1.00
- 70 Prom Night .40 1.00
- 71 Forever .40 1.00
- 72 Checklist .40 1.00
- CL1 Protector 25.00 50.00
  (issued as case topper)
- HT1 Who Is Bella 5.00 12.00
  (Hot Topic exclusive)

2008 Twilight Always Puzzle

COMPLETE SET (9) 60.00 120.00
STATED ODDS 1:11

- AL1 Always - Top Left 8.00 20.00
- AL2 Always - Top Middle 8.00 20.00
- AL3 Always - Top Right 8.00 20.00
- AL4 Always - Center Left 8.00 20.00
- AL5 Always - Center Middle 8.00 20.00
- AL6 Always - Center Right 8.00 20.00
- AL7 Always - Bottom Left 8.00 20.00
- AL8 Always - Bottom Middle 8.00 20.00
- AL9 Always - Bottom Right 8.00 20.00

2008 Twilight Different

COMPLETE SET (6) 20.00 40.00
STATED ODDS 1:17

- D1 The Cullens 4.00 10.00
- D2 Bella Alone 4.00 10.00
- D3 Edward Alone 4.00 10.00
- D4 Friends 4.00 10.00
- D5 Bella's Boys 4.00 10.00
- D6 No One More Different 4.00 10.00

2008 Twilight In Pursuit

COMPLETE SET (3)
STATED ODDS 1:23

- IP1 The Hunter 5.00 12.00
- IP2 Hunters and Lovers 5.00 12.00
- IP3 Hunter and Prey 5.00 12.00

2008 Twilight Pieceworks

STATED ODDS 1:24

- PW1 Bella Swan - Jacket 150.00 250.00
- PW2 Edward Cullen - Shirt 250.00 400.00
- PW3 Alice Cullen - Jacket 60.00 120.00
- PW4 Jasper Cullen - Jacket 75.00 150.00
- PW5 Emmett Cullen - Jacket 75.00 150.00
- PW6 Rosalie Hale - Vest 60.00 120.00
- PW7 Jacob Black - Jeans 100.00 175.00
- PW8 Esme Cullen - Jacket 60.00 120.00
- PW9 Carlisle Cullen - Shirt 60.00 120.00
- PW10 Victoria - Shirt 50.00 100.00
- PW11 Laurent - Pants 50.00 100.00
- PW12 James - Jeans 50.00 100.00

2008 Twilight Promos

- P1 Bella/Edward 1.50 4.00
  (General Distribution)
- Pi Bella/Billy/Charlie 40.00 80.00
  (inkworks.com Exclusive)
- PMS Bella/Edward 8.00 20.00
  (Convention Exclusive)
- PPS Bella/Edward 10.00 25.00
  (Philly Non-Sport Exclusive)
- PUK Bella 10.00 25.00
  (UK Exclusive)

2008 Women of Marvel

COMPLETE SET (81) 5.00 12.00
HUGHES AUTO ISSUED AS CASE TOPPER

- 1 Title Card .15 .40
  Checklist
- 2 Arachne .15 .40
- 3 Arsenic .15 .40
- 4 Aurora .15 .40
- 5 Black Cat .15 .40
- 6 Black Widow .15 .40
- 7 Blink .15 .40
- 8 Bruiser .15 .40
- 9 Callisto .15 .40
- 10 Crystal .15 .40
- 11 Dark Phoenix .15 .40
- 12 Dazzler .15 .40
- 13 Doctor Octopus .15 .40
- 14 Domino .15 .40
- 15 Echo .15 .40
- 16 Elektra .15 .40
- 17 Emma Frost .15 .40
- 18 Enchantress .15 .40
- 19 Gwen Stacy .15 .40
- 20 Hawkeye (Kate Bishop) .15 .40
- 21 Hela .15 .40
- 22 Hepzibah .15 .40
- 23 Hollow .15 .40
- 24 Husk .15 .40
- 25 Invisible Woman .15 .40
- 26 Jean Grey .15 .40
- 27 Jessica Jones Cage .15 .40
- 28 Jolt .15 .40
- 29 Joystick .15 .40
- 30 Layla Miller .15 .40
- 31 Lilandra Neramani .15 .40
- 32 Lilith .15 .40
- 33 Lucy In the Sky .15 .40
- 34 Madame Masque .15 .40
- 35 Madame Web .15 .40
- 36 Madelyne Pryor .15 .40
- 37 Magik .15 .40
- 38 Magma .15 .40
- 39 Marrow .15 .40
- 40 Marvel Girl .15 .40
- 41 Mary Jane Watson-Parker .15 .40
- 42 Moonstone .15 .40
- 43 Ms. Marvel .15 .40
- 44 Mystique .15 .40
- 45 Nahrees .15 .40
- 46 Namora .15 .40
- 47 Noctrune .15 .40
- 48 Nova .15 .40
- 49 Polaris .15 .40
- 50 Power Princess .15 .40
- 51 Psylocke .15 .40
- 52 Quasar .15 .40
- 53 Rogue .15 .40
- 54 Satana .15 .40
- 55 Scarlet Witch .15 .40
- 56 Scorpion .15 .40
- 57 Sersi .15 .40
- 58 Shadow Cat .15 .40
- 59 Shanna .15 .40
- 60 She-Hulk .15 .40
- 61 Sif .15 .40
- 62 Siryn .15 .40
- 63 Sister Grimm .15 .40

❑ 64 Songbird .15 .40
❑ 65 Spider Woman .15 .40
❑ 66 Spider-Girl .15 .40
❑ 67 Spiral .15 .40
❑ 68 Stepford Cuckoos .15 .40
❑ 69 Storm 1 .15 .40
❑ 70 Sunpyre .15 .40
❑ 71 Surge .15 .40
❑ 72 Talisman .15 .40
❑ 73 Tigra .15 .40
❑ 74 Titania .15 .40
❑ 75 Typhoid Mary .15 .40
❑ 76 Ultron .15 .40
❑ 77 Viper .15 .40
❑ 78 White Tiger .15 .40
❑ 79 Wicked .15 .40
❑ 80 Wolfsbane .15 .40
❑ 81 X-23 .15 .40
❑ NNO Adam Hughes AU/ (issued as case topper)10.00 25.00

2008 Women of Marvel Embossed

STATED ODDS 1:12

❑ T1 Black Cat 3.00 8.00
❑ T2 Black Widow 3.00 8.00
❑ T3 Elektra 3.00 8.00
❑ T4 Ms. Marvel 3.00 8.00
❑ T5 Mystique 3.00 8.00
❑ T6 Rogue 3.00 8.00
❑ T7 Shanna 3.00 8.00
❑ T8 She-Hulk 3.00 8.00
❑ T9 Spider Woman 3.00 8.00
❑ T10 Ms. Marvel/Spider-Woman SP
(issued as Rittenhouse Reward)

2008 Women of Marvel Embrace

STATED ODDS 1:24

❑ E1 Rogue and Gambit 6.00 15.00
❑ E2 Captain America and Scarlet Witch 6.00 15.00
❑ E3 Colossus and Shadowcat 6.00 15.00
❑ E4 Daredevil and Elektra 6.00 15.00
❑ E5 Cyclops and Emma Frost 6.00 15.00
❑ E6 Phoenix and Wolverine 6.00 15.00
❑ E7 Mr. Fantastic and Invisible Woman 6.00 15.00
❑ E8 Wolverine and Rogue 6.00 15.00
❑ E9 Bishop and Aliyah 6.00 15.00

2008 Women of Marvel Promos

❑ P1 Rogue 1.50 4.00
(General Distribution)
❑ P2 Elektra 2.00 5.00
(NSU Magazine)
❑ P3 Ms. Marvel 2.00 5.00
(Album Exclusive)
❑ CP1 Black Widow 6.00 15.00
(WonderCon Exclusive)
❑ CP2 She-Hulk 2.00 5.00
Philly Non-Sport Exclusive)

2008 Women of Marvel Sketches

STATED ODDS 1:24

❑ 1 Kristin Allen
❑ 2 Lui Antonio
❑ 3 Mahmud Asrar
❑ 4 Bruno Auriema
❑ 5 Kate Red Bradley
❑ 6 Daniel Campos
❑ 7 Anthony Castrillo
❑ 8 Yildiray Cinar
❑ 9 Katie Cook
❑ 10 Daniel Cooney
❑ 11 Dennis Crisostomo
❑ 12 John Czop
❑ 13 Dan Day
❑ 14 Mark Dos Santos
❑ 15 Eduardo Ferrara
❑ 16 Tess Fowler
❑ 17 Dave Fox
❑ 18 Matthew Goodmanson
❑ 19 Gabe Hernandez
❑ 20 Brian Kong
❑ 21 Jim Kyle
❑ 22 Alex Magno
❑ 23 Mark McHaley
❑ 24 Bob Mcleod
❑ 25 Steven Miller
❑ 26 Rich Molinelli
❑ 27 Nar
❑ 28 William O'Neill
❑ 29 Ryan Orosco
❑ 30 Eduardo Pansica
❑ 31 Michael Jason Paz
❑ 32 Tony Perna
❑ 33 Andy Price
❑ 34 Ricardo Ratton
❑ 35 Cezar Razek
❑ 36 Joe Rubinstein
❑ 37 Dave Simons
❑ 38 Uko Smith
❑ 39 Mark Spears
❑ 40 Cat Staggs
❑ 41 Alexandre Starling
❑ 42 Andre Toma
❑ 43 Justin Vandemark
❑ 44 Eddie Vieira
❑ 45 Edde Wagner
❑ 46 Ron Wilson
❑ NNO Allison Sohn 5 x 7
❑ NNO Warren Martineck

2008 Women of Marvel Swimsuit

STATED ODDS 1:6

❑ S1 Black Cat 2.50 6.00
❑ S2 Black Widow 2.50 6.00
❑ S3 Domino and Val Cooper 2.50 6.00
❑ S4 Elektra 2.50 6.00
❑ S5 Emma Frost 2.50 6.00
❑ S6 Jean Grey 2.50 6.00
❑ S7 Mary Jane Watson-Parker 2.50 6.00
❑ S8 Namorita 2.50 6.00
❑ S9 Phoenix 2.50 6.00
❑ S10 Polaris 2.50 6.00
❑ S11 Psylocke 2.50 6.00
❑ S12 Rogue 2.50 6.00
❑ S13 Sersi 2.50 6.00
❑ S14 She Hulk 2.50 6.00
❑ S15 Silver Sable 2.50 6.00
❑ S16 Spider-Woman 2.50 6.00
❑ S17 Storm 2.50 6.00
❑ S18 Wasp 2.50 6.00

2008 The World of Harry Potter 3-D Series Two

COMPLETE SET (72)

❑ 1 Tower .20 .50
❑ 2 Chesspiece .20 .50
❑ 3 Troll .20 .50
❑ 4 Norbert .20 .50
❑ 5 Harry Swooping for Snitch .20 .50
❑ 6 Professor Quirrell .20 .50
❑ 7 Young Ron's First Attempts .20 .50
❑ 8 Hedwig .20 .50
❑ 9 Mirror of Erised .20 .50
❑ 10 Harry Releases Chocolate Frog .20 .50
❑ 11 Dursley's Beach House .20 .50
❑ 12 Slytherin Beater .20 .50
❑ 13 Dementor at Lake .20 .50
❑ 14 Broom Practice .20 .50
❑ 15 Young Hermione Mixes .20 .50
❑ 16 Dobby Cringes .20 .50
❑ 17 Basilisk .20 .50
❑ 18 Scabbers on Books .20 .50
❑ 19 Harry Zooms Left .20 .50
❑ 20 Cornish Pixie .20 .50
❑ 21 Horse-drawn Sleighs .20 .50
❑ 22 Fawkes .20 .50
❑ 23 Polyjuice Potion Takes Effect .20 .50
❑ 24 Chamber of Secrets .20 .50
❑ 25 Hermione in Diagon Pet Shop .20 .50
❑ 26 Professor Lockhart .20 .50
❑ 27 Healing Harry's Arm .20 .50
❑ 28 Buckbeak .20 .50
❑ 29 Padfoot Protects .20 .50
❑ 30 Practicing a Patronus .20 .50
❑ 31 Trio in Snow .20 .50
❑ 32 Patronus Protection at Lake .20 .50
❑ 33 Ron Protects Scabbers .20 .50
❑ 34 Professor Lupin .20 .50
❑ 35 Malfoy Passing Notes .20 .50
❑ 36 Hagrid Applauding .20 .50
❑ 37 Neville Learns Riddiculus .20 .50
❑ 38 Down the Steps to Hagrid's .20 .50
❑ 39 Aunt Marge Floats Off .20 .50
❑ 40 Dementor Boggart .20 .50
❑ 41 Goblet of Fire .20 .50
❑ 42 Beauxbatons Flying Carriage .20 .50
❑ 43 Voldemort Reanimated .20 .50
❑ 44 Hungarian Horntail .20 .50
❑ 45 Harry Battles Voldemort .20 .50
❑ 46 Moody's Insect .20 .50
❑ 47 Death Eater .20 .50
❑ 48 Merpeople .20 .50
❑ 49 Wormtail Mixes Kettle .20 .50
❑ 50 Two Death Eaters .20 .50
❑ 51 Hogwarts Orchestra .20 .50
❑ 52 Professor Moody .20 .50
❑ 53 Dumbledore at Lectern .20 .50
❑ 54 Caged Dragon .20 .50
❑ 55 Grindylows .20 .50
❑ 56 Wormtail and Voldemort .20 .50
❑ 57 Harry's Dementor on Train .20 .50
❑ 58 Lord Voldemort .20 .50
❑ 59 Professor Umbridge .20 .50
❑ 60 Thestral .20 .50
❑ 61 Azkaban Tower .20 .50
❑ 62 Dumbledore Battles .20 .50
❑ 63 D.A. Professor Harry .20 .50
❑ 64 Bellatrix Attacks .20 .50
❑ 65 Kreacher .20 .50
❑ 66 Hogwarts Express .20 .50
❑ 67 Moody and Tonks .20 .50
❑ 68 Levitating Nigel .20 .50
Dennis
❑ 69 Sirius Black .20 .50
❑ 70 Dumbledore at Ministry .20 .50
❑ 71 Voldemort's Fireball .20 .50
❑ 72 Checklist .20 .50

2008 The World of Harry Potter 3-D Series Two Autographs

STATED ODDS 1:48
R = RARE
UR = ULTRA RARE

❑ 1 Alfred Enoch 10.00 25.00
❑ 2 Charles Hughes R 10.00 25.00
❑ 3 Christian Coulson R 25.00 50.00
❑ 4 Daniel Radcliffe UR 300.00 500.00
❑ 5 Emma Watson UR 350.00 600.00
❑ 6 Hugh Mitchell 10.00 25.00
❑ 7 James Walters R 10.00 25.00
❑ 8 Nick Shirm 10.00 25.00
❑ 9 Robert Wilfort 10.00 25.00
❑ 10 Rupert Grint UR 150.00 250.00
❑ 11 William Melling 10.00 25.00

2008 The World of Harry Potter 3-D Series Two Case Loaders

COMPLETE SET (3)
STATED ODDS ONE PER CASE

❑ CT1 Lord Voldemort 8.00 20.00
❑ CT2 Ron and Death Eater 8.00 20.00
❑ CT3 Bellatrix 8.00 20.00

2008 The World of Harry Potter 3-D Series Two Costumes

STATED ODDS 1:80

❑ C1 Harry Potter Quidditch sweater/360 15.00 40.00
❑ C2 Gryffindor Students' costume/560 6.00 15.00
❑ C3 Hermione Granger pants/260 15.00 40.00
❑ C4 Slytherin students/260 DUAL 12.00 30.00
❑ C5 Gryffindor students/210 DUAL 12.00 30.00
❑ C6 Harry Potter jacket/210 6.00 15.00

2008 The World of Harry Potter 3-D Series Two Dealer Incentive Memorabilia

❑ Ci1 Pixie Cage/310/ (issued as 2-case incentive)15.00 40.00
❑ Ci2 Proclamations/160/ (issued as 5-case incentive) 15.00
40.00
❑ Ci3 Umbridge's Special Quill/110/ (issued as 10-case incentive)
35.00 70.00
❑ Ci4 Professor Lupin's Wand/80/ (issued as 25-case incentive)
50.00 100.00

2008 The World of Harry Potter 3-D Series Two Promos

COMPLETE SET

❑ P1 Magical Creatures 2.50 6.00
❑ P2 Harry Potter 3.00 8.00
❑ P3 Charms and Spells 3.00 8.00
❑ P4 The Dark Arts 2.50 6.00
❑ P5 Dumbledore's Army 3.00 8.00

2008 The World of Harry Potter 3-D Series Two Props

STATED ODDS 1:40

❑ P1 Lantern/240 25.00 50.00
❑ P2 Cage/260 25.00 50.00
❑ P3 Quidditch Bat/180 25.00 50.00
❑ P4 Quiddith Quaffle and Bludgers/270 15.00 40.00
❑ P5 McGonagall's Class Books/310 15.00 40.00
❑ P6 Bone/120
❑ P7 Lockhart's Class Books/360 10.00 25.00
❑ P8 Chain/310 15.00 40.00
❑ P9 Exam Paper/390 10.00 25.00
❑ P10 Hospital Wing Sheets/560 8.00 20.00
❑ P11 Durmstrang Staff/360 10.00 25.00
❑ P12 Dagger/100
❑ P13 Quidditch Programs and Flags/320 15.00 40.00

2008 The World of Harry Potter 3-D Series Two Puzzle

COMPLETE SET (9)
STATED ODDS 5:24

❑ PZ1 Puzzle Card 1 .75 2.00
❑ PZ2 Puzzle Card 2 .75 2.00
❑ PZ3 Puzzle Card 3 .75 2.00
❑ PZ4 Puzzle Card 4 .75 2.00
❑ PZ5 Puzzle Card 5 .75 2.00
❑ PZ6 Puzzle Card 6 .75 2.00
❑ PZ7 Puzzle Card 7 .75 2.00
❑ PZ8 Puzzle Card 8 .75 2.00
❑ PZ9 Puzzle Card 9 .75 2.00

2008 X-Files I Want to Believe

COMPLETE SET (72) 5.00 12.00
CL1 STATED ODDS ONE PER BOX

❑ 1 Title Card .15 .40
❑ 2 Fox Mulder .15 .40
❑ 3 Dana Scully .15 .40
❑ 4 Assistant Director Skinner .15 .40
❑ 5 ASAC Dakota Whitney .15 .40
❑ 6 Special Agent Drummy .15 .40
❑ 7 Father Joe .15 .40
❑ 8 Cheryl Cunningham .15 .40
❑ 9 Father Ybarra .15 .40
❑ 10 Pursuits .15 .40
❑ 11 Seeking .15 .40
❑ 12 The Offer .15 .40
❑ 13 Mulder's Condition .15 .40
❑ 14 Best Chance .15 .40
❑ 15 The Psychic .15 .40
❑ 16 Passing The Test .15 .40
❑ 17 A New Victim .15 .40
❑ 18 Making Connections .15 .40
❑ 19 A New Lead .15 .40
❑ 20 Halted Progress .15 .40
❑ 21 Fixation .15 .40
❑ 22 Dirty Glass .15 .40
❑ 23 Trapped .15 .40
❑ 24 New Evidence .15 .40
❑ 25 Taking A Risk .15 .40
❑ 26 Rejecting The Darkness .15 .40
❑ 27 Seeing Answers .15 .40
❑ 28 Father Joe's Link .15 .40
❑ 29 Disappointment .15 .40
❑ 30 Whitney's Sacrifice .15 .40
❑ 31 Confrontation .15 .40
❑ 32 Defending Truth .15 .40
❑ 33 Parting Ways .15 .40
❑ 34 Returning To The Scene .15 .40
❑ 35 A Dangerous Turn .15 .40
❑ 36 An Old Friend .15 .40
❑ 37 Tracks In The Snow .15 .40
❑ 38 A New Body .15 .40
❑ 39 Barking Dogs .15 .40
❑ 40 Gruesome Discovery .15 .40
❑ 41 Rescued .15 .40
❑ 42 Cleaning Up .15 .40
❑ 43 Out Of The Cold .15 .40
❑ 44 The Accomplice .15 .40
❑ 45 A New Life .15 .40
❑ 46 Beginnings .15 .40
❑ 47 Abduction Theories .15 .40
❑ 48 Cover-Up .15 .40
❑ 49 Allies .15 .40
❑ 50 Visitations .15 .40
❑ 51 Bargaining .15 .40
❑ 52 Letting Go .15 .40
❑ 53 Beneath The Surface .15 .40
❑ 54 Strange Discoveries .15 .40
❑ 55 Regenerations .15 .40
❑ 56 Predictions .15 .40
❑ 57 Reluctant Psychic .15 .40
❑ 58 Immortality .15 .40
❑ 59 Facing Death .15 .40
❑ 60 Devastating Prognosis .15 .40
❑ 61 Seeking The Truth .15 .40
❑ 62 Holding On .15 .40
❑ 63 Mysterious Attacks .15 .40
❑ 64 The Doctor's Wife .15 .40
❑ 65 Confronting Monsters .15 .40
❑ 66 She Said… .15 .40
❑ 67 He Said… .15 .40
❑ 68 Uncertain Truths .15 .40
❑ 69 The Perfect Murder .15 .40
❑ 70 Burning Hearts .15 .40
❑ 71 Brought To Life .15 .40
❑ 72 Checklist .15 .40
❑ CL1 Out of Darkness

2008 X-Files I Want to Believe Autographs

STATED ODDS ONE PER BOX
AD1 ISSUED AS 10-CASE INCENTIVE

❑ A1 David Duchovny 125.00 200.00
❑ A2 Gillian Anderson 125.00 200.00
❑ A3 Chris Carter 25.00 50.00
❑ A4 Frank Spotnitz 6.00 15.00
❑ A5 Xzibit 6.00 15.00
❑ A6 Adam Godley 6.00 15.00
❑ A7 Chris Owens 6.00 15.00
❑ A8 Sheila Larken 6.00 15.00
❑ A9 Nestor Serrano 6.00 15.00
❑ AD1 David Duchovny 350.00 500.00
Gillian Anderson/ (issued as 10-case incentive)

2008 X-Files I Want to Believe Back to Basics

COMPLETE SET (3) 4.00 10.00
STATED ODDS 1:24

❑ BB1 Mulder 2.50 6.00
❑ BB2 Scully 2.50 6.00
❑ BB3 Skinner 2.50 6.00

2008 X-Files I Want to Believe In Search Of Puzzle

COMPLETE SET (9) 5.00 12.00
STATED ODDS 1:11

❑ S1 In Search Of 1 1.25 3.00
❑ S2 In Search Of 2 1.25 3.00
❑ S3 In Search Of 3 1.25 3.00
❑ S4 In Search Of 4 1.25 3.00
❑ S5 In Search Of 5 1.25 3.00
❑ S6 In Search Of 6 1.25 3.00
❑ S7 In Search Of 7 1.25 3.00
❑ S8 In Search Of 8 1.25 3.00
❑ S9 In Search Of 9 1.25 3.00

2008 X-Files I Want to Believe Pieceworks

STATED ODDS ONE PER BOX
PW14A, PW14B ISSUED AS 3-CASE INCENTIVES

❑ PW1A Mulder Jacket 15.00 30.00
❑ PW1B Mulder Fur 40.00 80.00
❑ PW2 Scully 15.00 30.00
❑ PW3 Scully 15.00 30.00
❑ PW4 Agent Drummy 4.00 10.00
❑ PW5 Father Joe 4.00 10.00
❑ PW6 Father Joe 4.00 10.00
❑ PW7 Skinner 6.00 15.00
❑ PW8 Scully DUAL 25.00 50.00
❑ PW9 Scully 15.00 30.00
❑ PW10 Mulder DUAL 25.00 50.00
❑ PW11 Agent Whitney 6.00 15.00
❑ PW12 Agent Whitney 6.00 15.00
❑ PW13 Agent Whitney 6.00 15.00
❑ PW14A David Duchovny
(issued as 3-case incentive)
❑ PW14B Gillian Anderson
(issued as 3-case incentive)
❑ PWR1 Redemption card

2008 X-Files I Want to Believe Wanting to Believe

COMPLETE SET (6) 5.00 12.00
STATED ODDS 1:17

❑ WB1 Wanting To Believe 1 1.50 4.00
❑ WB2 Wanting To Believe 2 1.50 4.00
❑ WB3 Wanting To Believe 3 1.50 4.00
❑ WB4 Wanting To Believe 4 1.50 4.00
❑ WB5 Wanting To Believe 5 1.50 4.00
❑ WB6 Wanting To Believe 6 1.50 4.00

2009 American Idol Season Eight

COMPLETE SET (97)
31-61 ARE SWEEPSTAKES ENTRIES
62-97 ARE LENTICULAR
SWEEPSTAKES STATED ODDS 1:1
LENTICULAR STATED ODDS 1:8
SP: RANDOM INSERT IN PACKS

❑ 1 Ryan Seacrest .15 .40
❑ 2 Paula Abdul .15 .40
❑ 3 Randy Jackson .15 .40
❑ 4 Kara DioGuardi .15 .40
❑ 5 Paula Abdul .15 .40
Randy Jackson
❑ 6 Paula Abdul .15 .40
Kara DioGuardi
❑ 7 David Cook .15 .40
❑ 8 David Archuleta .15 .40
❑ 9 Jordin Sparks .15 .40
❑ 10 Blake Lewis .15 .40
❑ 11 Taylor Hicks .15 .40
❑ 12 Katherine McPhee .15 .40
❑ 13 Carrie Underwood .40 1.00
❑ 14 Bo Bice .15 .40
❑ 15 Fantasia Barrino .15 .40
❑ 16 Diana DeGarmo .15 .40
❑ 17 Ruben Studdard .15 .40
❑ 18 Clay Aiken .30 .75
❑ 19 Kelly Clarkson .30 .75
❑ 20 Justin Guarini .15 .40
❑ 21 Chris Daughtry .15 .40
❑ 22 Jennifer Hudson .15 .40
❑ 23 Al Stage .15 .40
❑ 24 Al Stage .15 .40
❑ 25 Michael Johns .15 .40
Carly Smithson
❑ 26 Al Stage .15 .40
❑ 27 Bikini Girl .30 .75
❑ 28 Al Stage .15 .40
❑ 29 Randy Jackson .15 .40
Paula Abdul/Kara DioGuardi
❑ 30 Paula Abdul .15 .40
Kara DioGuardi/Randy Jackson
❑ 31 Almost Idols .20 .50
❑ 32 Almost Idols .20 .50
❑ 33 Almost Idols .20 .50
❑ 34 Almost Idols .20 .50
❑ 35 Almost Idols .20 .50
❑ 36 Almost Idols .20 .50
❑ 37 Almost Idols .20 .50
❑ 38 Almost Idols .20 .50
❑ 39 Almost Idols .20 .50
❑ 40 Fantasia Barrino .20 .50
❑ 41 Judges .20 .50
❑ 42 Al Stage .20 .50
❑ 43 David Archuleta .20 .50
David Cook
❑ 44 David Cook .30 .75
❑ 45 David Cook .30 .75
❑ 46 William Hung .30 .75
❑ 47 Paula Abdul .20 .50
❑ 48 David Cook .20 .50
❑ 49 David Archuleta .20 .50
❑ 50 Jordin Sparks .20 .50
❑ 51 Blake Lewis .20 .50
❑ 52 Taylor Hicks .20 .50
❑ 53 Katherine McPhee .20 .50
❑ 54 Carrie Underwood .50 1.25
❑ 55 Bo Bice .20 .50
❑ 56 Fantasia Barrino .20 .50
❑ 57 Diana DeGarmo .20 .50
❑ 58 Ruben Studdard .20 .50
❑ 59 Clay Aiken .40 1.00
❑ 60 Kelly Clarkson .40 1.00
❑ 61 Justin Guarini .20 .50
❑ 62 Arianna Atsar 1.50 4.00
❑ 63 Kris Allen 4.00 10.00
❑ 64 Felicia Barton 1.50 4.00
❑ 65 Kendall Beard 1.50 4.00
❑ 66 Ann Marie Boskovich 1.50 4.00
❑ 67 Ricky Braddy 1.50 4.00
❑ 68 Matt Breitzke 1.50 4.00
❑ 69 Casey Carlson 1.50 4.00
❑ 70 Megan Corkrey 3.00 8.00
❑ 71 Tatiana Del Toro 1.50 4.00
❑ 72 Anoop Desai 2.50 6.00
❑ 73 Stephen Fowler 1.50 4.00
❑ 74 Matt Giraud 1.50 4.00
❑ 75 Danny Gokey 6.00 15.00
❑ 76 Alexis Grace 3.00 8.00
❑ 77 Mishavonna Henson 1.50 4.00
❑ 78 Allison Iraheta 1.50 4.00
❑ 79 Ju' Not Joyner 1.50 4.00
❑ 80 Kai Kalama 1.50 4.00
❑ 81 Brent Keith 1.50 4.00
❑ 82 Adam Lambert 20.00 40.00
❑ 83 Jesse Langseth 1.50 4.00
❑ 84 Scott MacIntyre 1.50 4.00
❑ 85 Nathaniel Marshall 1.50 4.00
❑ 86 Kristen McNamara 1.50 4.00
❑ 87 Nick Mitchell 1.50 4.00
❑ 88 Jasmine Murray 1.50 4.00
❑ 89 Jorge Nunez-Mendez 1.50 4.00
❑ 90 Lil Rounds 3.00 8.00
❑ 91 Michael Sarver 1.50 4.00
❑ 92 Von Smith 1.50 4.00
❑ 93 Jackie Tohn 1.50 4.00
❑ 94 Taylor Vaifanua 1.50 4.00
❑ 95 Jeanine Vailes 1.50 4.00
❑ 96 Alex Wagner-Trugman 1.50 4.00
❑ 97 Stevie Wright 1.50 4.00
❑ NNO Bruce Springsteen
Diddy
❑ NNO Beyonce
Madonna

2009 American Idol Season Eight Autographs

STATED ODDS 1:12 HOBBY, 1:65 RETAIL

❑ AA Arianna Afsar 6.00 15.00
❑ AB Ann Marie Boskovich 6.00 15.00
❑ AD Anoop Desai 10.00 25.00
❑ AG Alexis Grace 25.00 50.00
❑ AI Allison Iraheta 40.00 80.00
❑ AL Adam Lambert 125.00 200.00
❑ AR David Archuleta 60.00 100.00
❑ AW Alex Wagner-Trugman 5.00 12.00
❑ BA Fantasia Barrino 15.00 30.00
❑ BK Brent Keith 6.00 15.00
❑ CC Casey Carlson 6.00 15.00
❑ CS Carly Smithson 20.00 40.00
❑ DA David Archuleta 60.00 100.00
❑ DG Danny Gokey 50.00 100.00
❑ EY Elliot Yamin 15.00 30.00
❑ FB Felicia Barton 6.00 15.00
❑ JJ Ju' Not Joyner 6.00 15.00
❑ JL Jesse Langseth 6.00 15.00
❑ JM Jasmine Murray 7.50 20.00
❑ JN Jorge Nunez-Mendez 6.00 15.00
❑ JS Jordin Sparks 40.00 80.00
❑ JT Jackie Tohn 6.00 15.00
❑ JV Jeanine Vailes 6.00 15.00
❑ KA Kris Allen 90.00 150.00
❑ KB Kendall Beard 6.00 15.00
❑ KK Kai Kalama 5.00 12.00
❑ KM Kristen McNamara 6.00 15.00
❑ LR Lil Rounds 10.00 25.00
❑ MB Matt Breitzke 6.00 15.00
❑ MC Megan Corkrey 30.00 60.00
❑ MG Matt Giraud 25.00 50.00
❑ MH Mishavonna Henson 5.00 12.00
❑ MI Nick Mitchell 6.00 15.00
❑ MJ Michael Johns 15.00 30.00
❑ MS Michael Sarver 6.00 15.00
❑ NM Nathaniel Marshall 5.00 12.00
❑ RB Ricky Braddy 5.00 12.00
❑ SF Stephen Fowler 5.00 12.00
❑ SM Scott MacIntyre 15.00 30.00
❑ SW Stevie Wright 7.50 20.00
❑ TD Tatiana Del Toro 12.50 25.00
❑ TV Taylor Vaifanua 5.00 12.00
❑ VS Von Smith 5.00 12.00

2009 Battlestar Galactica Season Four

COMPLETE SET (63) 6.00 15.00

❑ 1 Title Card .15 .40
Checklist
❑ 2 Title Card .15 .40
Checklist
❑ 3 Title Card .15 .40
Checklist
❑ 4 He That Believeth in Me .15 .40
❑ 5 He That Believeth in Me .15 .40
❑ 6 He That Believeth in Me .15 .40
❑ 7 Six of One .15 .40
❑ 8 Six of One .15 .40
❑ 9 Six of One .15 .40
❑ 10 The Ties That Bind .15 .40
❑ 11 The Ties That Bind .15 .40
❑ 12 The Ties That Bind .15 .40
❑ 13 Escape Velocity .15 .40
❑ 14 Escape Velocity .15 .40
❑ 15 Escape Velocity .15 .40
❑ 16 The Road Less Traveled .15 .40
❑ 17 The Road Less Traveled .15 .40
❑ 18 The Road Less Traveled .15 .40
❑ 19 Faith .15 .40
❑ 20 Faith .15 .40
❑ 21 Faith .15 .40
❑ 22 Guess What's Coming to Dinner .15 .40
❑ 23 Guess What's Coming to Dinner .15 .40
❑ 24 Guess What's Coming to Dinner .15 .40
❑ 25 Sine Qua Non .15 .40
❑ 26 Sine Qua Non .15 .40
❑ 27 Sine Qua Non .15 .40
❑ 28 The Hub .15 .40
❑ 29 The Hub .15 .40
❑ 30 The Hub .15 .40
❑ 31 Revelations .15 .40
❑ 32 Revelations .15 .40
❑ 33 Revelations .15 .40
❑ 34 Sometimes a Great Notion .15 .40
❑ 35 Sometimes a Great Notion .15 .40
❑ 36 Sometimes a Great Notion .15 .40
❑ 37 A Disquiet Follows My Soul .15 .40
❑ 38 A Disquiet Follows My Soul .15 .40
❑ 39 A Disquiet Follows My Soul .15 .40
❑ 40 The Oath .15 .40
❑ 41 The Oath .15 .40
❑ 42 The Oath .15 .40
❑ 43 Blood on the Scales .15 .40
❑ 44 Blood on the Scales .15 .40
❑ 45 Blood on the Scales .15 .40
❑ 46 No Exit .15 .40
❑ 47 No Exit .15 .40

MODERN ERA NON-SPORTS

❑ 48 No Exit .15 .40
❑ 49 Deadlock .15 .40
❑ 50 Deadlock .15 .40
❑ 51 Deadlock .15 .40
❑ 52 Someone to Watch Over Me .15 .40
❑ 53 Someone to Watch Over Me .15 .40
❑ 54 Someone to Watch Over Me .15 .40
❑ 55 Islanded In a Stream of Stars .15 .40
❑ 56 Islanded In a Stream of Stars .15 .40
❑ 57 Islanded In a Stream of Stars .15 .40
❑ 58 Daybreak Part 1 .15 .40
❑ 59 Daybreak Part 1 .15 .40
❑ 60 Daybreak Part 1 .15 .40
❑ 61 Daybreak Part 2 .15 .40
❑ 62 Daybreak Part 2 .15 .40
❑ 63 Daybreak Part 2 .15 .40

2009 Battlestar Galactica Season Four Autograph Costumes

CALLIS STATED ODDS ONE PER 4 CASE PURCHASE
❑ 1 Jamie Bamber 30.00 60.00
❑ 2 Leah Cairns 30.00 60.00
❑ 3 Matthew Bennett 25.00 50.00
❑ 4 Nicki Clyne 25.00 50.00
❑ 5 Rekha Sharma 25.00 50.00
❑ 6 Rick Worthy 25.00 50.00
❑ 7 James Callis SP 75.00 150.00

2009 Battlestar Galactica Season Four Autographs

STATED ODDS 1:12
EICK STATED ODDS ONE PER CASE
HOGAN/VERNON STATED ODDS ONE PER 2 CASE PURCHASE
❑ 1 Aleks Paunovic 5.00 10.00
❑ 2 Andrew McIlroy 5.00 10.00
❑ 3 Bodie Olmos 5.00 10.00
❑ 4 Colby Johannson 5.00 10.00
❑ 5 Colin Corrigan 5.00 10.00
❑ 6 Colin Lawrence 5.00 10.00
❑ 7 Dominic Zamprogna 5.00 10.00
❑ 8 Edward James Olmos 250.00 450.00
❑ 9 James Callis 15.00 30.00
❑ 10 Jamie Bamber 20.00 40.00
❑ 11 Kate Vernon 12.00 25.00
❑ 12 Katee Sackhoff 25.00 50.00
❑ 13 Keegan Connor Tracy 7.50 15.00
❑ 14 Leah Cairns 12.00 25.00
❑ 15 Leela Savasta 10.00 20.00
❑ 16 Matthew Bennett 10.00 20.00
❑ 17 Michael Hogan 35.00 70.00
❑ 18 Nicki Clyne 12.00 25.00
❑ 19 Rekha Sharma 12.00 25.00
❑ 20 Rick Worthy 10.00 20.00
❑ 21 Stephanie Jacobsen 20.00 40.00
❑ 22 David Eick 10.00 20.00
❑ 23 Michael Hogan 35.00 70.00
Kate Vernon

2009 Battlestar Galactica Season Four Costumes

COSTUME/RELIC COMBINED ODDS 1:12
❑ C41 William Adama 4.00 10.00
❑ C42 Lee Adama 5.00 12.00
❑ C43 Cally Tyrol 4.00 10.00
❑ C44 Elosha 5.00 12.00
❑ C45 Tory Foster 5.00 12.00
❑ C46 Doral 4.00 10.00
❑ C47 Simon 4.00 10.00
❑ C48 Carolanne Adama 4.00 10.00
❑ C49 Racetrack 4.00 10.00
❑ C50 Jean Barolay 4.00 10.00
❑ C51 Tory Foster 4.00 10.00

2009 Battlestar Galactica Season Four Dual Costumes

COSTUME/RELIC COMBINED ODDS 1:12
❑ DC6 Carolanne 6.00 15.00
William Adama
❑ DC7 Shevon 8.00 20.00
❑ DC8 Phelan 6.00 15.00
❑ DC9 Lee Adama 10.00 25.00
❑ DC10 Cally Tyrol 8.00 20.00
❑ DC11 Racetrack 8.00 20.00
❑ DC12 Laura Roslin 8.00 20.00
❑ DC13 Elosha 6.00 15.00
❑ DC14 Tory Foster 6.00 15.00
❑ DC15 Doral 6.00 15.00
❑ DC16 Doctor Simon 6.00 15.00
❑ DC17 Emily Kowalski 6.00 15.00
❑ DC18 Cavil 6.00 15.00
❑ DC19 Enzo 6.00 15.00
❑ DC20 Jean Barolay 6.00 15.00

2009 Battlestar Galactica Season Four Final Five

COMPLETE SET (5) 4.00 10.00
STATED ODDS 1:12
❑ FF1 Galen Tyrol 1.50 4.00
❑ FF2 Samuel Anders 1.50 4.00
❑ FF3 Saul Tigh 1.50 4.00
❑ FF4 Tory Foster 1.50 4.00
❑ FF5 Ellen Tigh 1.50 4.00

2009 Battlestar Galactica Season Four Gallery

COMPLETE SET (10)
COMP.SET w/o SP (9) 20.00 40.00
STATED ODDS 1:24
G10 AVAILABLE AS REDEMPTION ONLY
❑ G1 Karl Agathon 3.00 8.00
Sharon Agathon
❑ G2 Tory Foster 3.00 8.00
Gaius Baltar
❑ G3 Number Six 3.00 8.00
Sharon Valerii
❑ G4 Gaius Baltar 3.00 8.00
Number Six
❑ G5 William Adama 3.00 8.00
Kara Thrace
❑ G6 William Adama 3.00 8.00
Lee Adama
❑ G7 Kara Thrace 3.00 8.00
Sam Anders
❑ G8 Lee Adama 3.00 8.00
Kara Thrace
❑ G9 Lee Adama 3.00 8.00
Laura Roslin
❑ G10 Kara Thrace 35.00 70.00
Laura Roslin SP

2009 Battlestar Galactica Season Four Razor

COMPLETE SET (9) 4.00 10.00
STATED ODDS 1:8
❑ R1 Razor 1.00 2.50
❑ R2 Razor 1.00 2.50
❑ R3 Razor 1.00 2.50
❑ R4 Razor 1.00 2.50
❑ R5 Razor 1.00 2.50
❑ R6 Razor 1.00 2.50
❑ R7 Razor 1.00 2.50
❑ R8 Razor 1.00 2.50
❑ R9 Razor 1.00 2.50

2009 Battlestar Galactica Season Four Relics

PRINT RUN B/WN 200-350
❑ RC1 BSG Pegasus Systems Upgrade Folder 25.00 50.00
❑ RC2 Quorum Agenda Cylon FTL Integration Question 40.00 80.00
❑ RC3 Flight Status Documents 25.00 50.00
❑ RC4 New Caprica Documents 40.00 80.00
❑ RC5 Election Documents 50.00 100.00

2009 Battlestar Galactica Season Four Shelter Posters

COMPLETE SET (3) 35.00 70.00
STATED ODDS 1:144
PRINT RUN 375 SER. #'d SETS
❑ S8 Lee Adama 15.00 30.00
William Adama/Kara Thrace
❑ S9 Gaius Baltar 15.00 30.00
Lee Adama/Laura Roslin
❑ S10 Williama Adama 15.00 30.00
Galen Tyrol/Saul Tigh

2009 Bench Warmer Limited

COMPLETE SET (90)
COMP.SET w/o SP's (72) 5.00 12.00
SP STATED ODDS 1:4
❑ 1 Lisa Gleave .15 .40
❑ 2 Torrie Wilson .40 1.00
❑ 3 Jennifer Walcott .40 1.00
❑ 4 Gail Kim .15 .40
❑ 5 Katie Lohmann .15 .40
❑ 6 Alison Waite .15 .40
❑ 7 Cecille Gahr .15 .40
❑ 8 Miriam Gonzalez .15 .40
❑ 9 Carrie Stroup .15 .40
❑ 10 Athena Lundberg .15 .40
❑ 11 Jana Z .15 .40
❑ 12 Alexis Lopez .15 .40
❑ 13 Mandy Lynn .15 .40
❑ 14 Renee Stone .15 .40
❑ 15 Brooke Morales .15 .40
❑ 16 Yvette Nelson .15 .40
❑ 17 Jo Garcia .15 .40
❑ 18 Sarah Coggin .15 .40
❑ 19 Flo Jalin .15 .40
❑ 20 Brittany Herrera .15 .40
❑ 21 Megan Hauserman .15 .40
❑ 22 Talor Marion .15 .40
❑ 23 Mary Riley .40 1.00
❑ 24 Lena Yada .15 .40
❑ 25 Aubrie Lemon .15 .40
❑ 26 Shay Lyn .15 .40
❑ 27 Melinda Myers .15 .40
❑ 28 Gina Gianni .15 .40
❑ 29 Audrey DalSoglio .15 .40
❑ 30 Buffy Tyler .15 .40
❑ 31 Jennifer Korbin .15 .40
Replay
❑ 32 Traci Brooks .15 .40
Replay
❑ 33 Buffy Tyler .15 .40
Replay
❑ 34 Jessica Michaels .15 .40
Replay
❑ 35 Shana Palmira .15 .40
Replay
❑ 36 Katarina Van Derham .15 .40
Replay
❑ 37 Melissa Taylor .15 .40
Replay
❑ 38 April Scott .15 .40
Replay
❑ 39 Jessica Burciaga .15 .40
Replay
❑ 40 Brandy Grace .15 .40
Replay
❑ 41 Traci Bingham .15 .40
Replay
❑ 42 Spencer Scott .15 .40
Replay
❑ 43 Brandie Moses .15 .40
Replay
❑ 44 Katy Johnson .15 .40
All Star
❑ 45 Amanda Paige .15 .40
All Star
❑ 46 Angela Shih .15 .40
All Star
❑ 47 Amanda Paige .15 .40
All Star
❑ 48 Jennifer England .15 .40
All Star
❑ 49 Xi Xi Yang .15 .40
All Star
❑ 50 Martina Andrews .15 .40
All Star
❑ 51 Teresa Noreen .15 .40
All Star
❑ 52 Camille Anderson .15 .40
All Star
❑ 53 Cat Miller .15 .40
All Star
❑ 54 Kayla Collins .15 .40
All Star
❑ 55 Enya Flack .15 .40
All Star
❑ 56 Lana Kinnear .15 .40
All Star
❑ 57 Lindsey Roeper .15 .40
All Star
❑ 58 Jennifer England .15 .40
All Star
❑ 59 Louise Glover .15 .40
All Star
❑ 60 Candi Kita .15 .40
All Star
❑ 61 Rachel Bernstein .15 .40
All Star
❑ 62 Holley Ann Dorrough .15 .40
All Star
❑ 63 Ania Migdal .15 .40
All Star
❑ 64 Brittany McGraw .15 .40
All Star
❑ 65 Vanessa Cervantes .15 .40
All Star
❑ 66 Denyce Lawton .15 .40
All Star
❑ 67 Michelle Mclaughlin .15 .40
All Star
❑ 68 Michelle Lei .15 .40
All Star
❑ 69 Jaimarie .15 .40
All Star
❑ 70 Robyn Watkins .15 .40
All Star
❑ 71 Charity Hodges .15 .40
All Star
❑ 72 Cecille .15 .40
Megan
❑ 73 Traci Bingham 2.00 5.00
Boot Camp SP
❑ 74 Brooke Morales 2.00 5.00
Boot Camp SP
❑ 75 Jana Z 2.00 5.00
Boot Camp SP
❑ 76 Lisa Gleave 2.00 5.00
Boot Camp SP
❑ 77 Allison Waite 2.00 5.00
Boot Camp SP
❑ 78 Mandy Lynn 2.00 5.00
Boot Camp SP
❑ 79 Michelle Lei 2.00 5.00
Boot Camp SP
❑ 80 Flo Jalin 2.00 5.00
Boot Camp SP
❑ 81 Jennifer Korbin 2.00 5.00
All American SP
❑ 82 Katie Lohmann 2.00 5.00
All American SP
❑ 83 Lisa Gleave 2.00 5.00
All American SP
❑ 84 Sarah Coggin 2.00 5.00
All American SP
❑ 85 Renee Stone 2.00 5.00
All American SP
❑ 86 Dana Workman 2.00 5.00
All American SP
❑ 87 Jennifer Walcott 5.00 12.00
All American SP
❑ 88 Talor Marion 2.00 5.00
All American SP
❑ 89 Spencer Scott 2.00 5.00
All American SP
❑ 90 Lisa Ligon 2.00 5.00
All American SP

2009 Bench Warmer Limited As Seen on TV

COMPLETE SET (10) 10.00 25.00
STATED ODDS 1:10
❑ 1 Jennifer Korbin 2.50 6.00
❑ 2 Traci Bingham 2.50 6.00
❑ 3 Lisa Gleave 2.50 6.00
❑ 4 Claudia Jordan 2.50 6.00
❑ 5 Megan Hauserman 2.50 6.00
❑ 6 Christy Hemme 3.00 8.00
❑ 7 Brandi Cunningham 2.50 6.00
❑ 8 Aubrie Lemon 2.50 6.00
❑ 9 Lena Yada 2.50 6.00
❑ 10 Torrie Wilson 3.00 8.00

2009 Bench Warmer Limited Autographs Blue Foil

STATED PRINT RUN 5 SER. #'d SETS
UNPRICED DUE TO SCARCITY
❑ 1 Torrie Wilson
❑ 2 Jennifer Walcott
❑ 3 Lisa Gleave
❑ 4 Aubrie Lemon
❑ 5 Brooke Morales
❑ 6 Alison Waite
❑ 7 Katie Lohmann
❑ 8 Miriam Gonzalez
❑ 9 Flo Jalin
❑ 10 Kerrilee Kaski
❑ 11 Buffy Tyler
❑ 12 Spencer Scott
❑ 13 Cecille Gahr
❑ 14 Megan Hauserman
❑ 15 Brittany Herrera
❑ 16 Talor Marion
❑ 17 Brandi Cunningham
❑ 18 Renee Stone
❑ 19 Jessica Hall
❑ 20 Sarah Coggin
❑ 21 Athena Lundberg
❑ 22 Yvette Nelson
❑ 23 Jo Garcia
❑ 24 Jana Z

2009 Bench Warmer Limited Autographs Gold Foil

STATED ODDS 1:12
❑ 1 Torrie Wilson 8.00 20.00
❑ 2 Jennifer Walcott 8.00 20.00
❑ 3 Lisa Gleave 5.00 12.00
❑ 4 Aubrie Lemon 5.00 12.00
❑ 5 Brooke Morales 5.00 12.00
❑ 6 Alison Waite 5.00 12.00
❑ 7 Katie Lohmann 5.00 12.00
❑ 8 Miriam Gonzalez 6.00 15.00
❑ 9 Flo Jalin 5.00 12.00
❑ 10 Kerrilee Kaski 5.00 12.00
❑ 11 Buffy Tyler 5.00 12.00
❑ 12 Spencer Scott 5.00 12.00
❑ 13 Cecille Gahr 5.00 12.00
❑ 14 Megan Hauserman 5.00 12.00
❑ 15 Brittany Herrera 5.00 12.00
❑ 16 Talor Marion 5.00 12.00
❑ 17 Brandi Cunningham 5.00 12.00
❑ 18 Renee Stone 5.00 12.00
❑ 19 Jessica Hall 5.00 12.00
❑ 20 Sarah Coggin 5.00 12.00
❑ 21 Athena Lundberg 5.00 12.00
❑ 22 Yvette Nelson 5.00 12.00
❑ 23 Jo Garcia 5.00 12.00
❑ 24 Jana Z 5.00 12.00

2009 Bench Warmer Limited Autographs Green Foil

STATED PRINT RUN 10 SER. #'d SETS
UNPRICED DUE TO SCARCITY
❑ 1 Torrie Wilson
❑ 2 Jennifer Walcott
❑ 3 Lisa Gleave
❑ 4 Aubrie Lemon
❑ 5 Brooke Morales
❑ 6 Alison Waite
❑ 7 Katie Lohmann
❑ 8 Miriam Gonzalez
❑ 9 Flo Jalin
❑ 10 Kerrilee Kaski
❑ 11 Buffy Tyler
❑ 12 Spencer Scott
❑ 13 Cecille Gahr
❑ 14 Megan Hauserman
❑ 15 Brittany Herrera
❑ 16 Talor Marion
❑ 17 Brandi Cunningham
❑ 18 Renee Stone
❑ 19 Jessica Hall
❑ 20 Sarah Coggin
❑ 21 Athena Lundberg
❑ 22 Yvette Nelson
❑ 23 Jo Garcia
❑ 24 Jana Z

2009 Bench Warmer Limited Autographs Pink Foil

*PINK: .8X TO 2X GOLD
STATED PRINT RUN 25 SER. #'d SETS
❑ 1 Torrie Wilson 15.00 40.00
❑ 2 Jennifer Walcott 15.00 40.00
❑ 3 Lisa Gleave 10.00 25.00
❑ 4 Aubrie Lemon 10.00 25.00
❑ 5 Brooke Morales 10.00 25.00
❑ 6 Alison Waite 10.00 25.00
❑ 7 Katie Lohmann 10.00 25.00
❑ 8 Miriam Gonzalez 12.00 30.00
❑ 9 Flo Jalin 10.00 25.00
❑ 10 Kerrilee Kaski 10.00 25.00
❑ 11 Buffy Tyler 10.00 25.00
❑ 12 Spencer Scott 10.00 25.00
❑ 13 Cecille Gahr 10.00 25.00
❑ 14 Megan Hauserman 10.00 25.00
❑ 15 Brittany Herrera 10.00 25.00
❑ 16 Talor Marion 10.00 25.00
❑ 17 Brandi Cunningham 10.00 25.00
❑ 18 Renee Stone 10.00 25.00
❑ 19 Jessica Hall 10.00 25.00
❑ 20 Sarah Coggin 10.00 25.00
❑ 21 Athena Lundberg 10.00 25.00
❑ 22 Yvette Nelson 10.00 25.00
❑ 23 Jo Garcia 10.00 25.00
❑ 24 Jana Z 10.00 25.00

2009 Bench Warmer Limited Autographs Red Foil

STATED PRINT RUN 1 SER. #'d SET
UNPRICED DUE TO SCARCITY
❑ 1 Torrie Wilson
❑ 2 Jennifer Walcott
❑ 3 Lisa Gleave
❑ 4 Aubrie Lemon
❑ 5 Brooke Morales
❑ 6 Alison Waite
❑ 7 Katie Lohmann
❑ 8 Miriam Gonzalez
❑ 9 Flo Jalin
❑ 10 Kerrilee Kaski
❑ 11 Buffy Tyler
❑ 12 Spencer Scott
❑ 13 Cecille Gahr
❑ 14 Megan Hauserman
❑ 15 Brittany Herrera
❑ 16 Talor Marion
❑ 17 Brandi Cunningham
❑ 18 Renee Stone
❑ 19 Jessica Hall
❑ 20 Sarah Coggin
❑ 21 Athena Lundberg
❑ 22 Yvette Nelson
❑ 23 Jo Garcia
❑ 24 Jana Z

2009 Bench Warmer Limited Head of the Class

COMPLETE SET (8) 15.00 30.00
STATED ODDS 1:24
❑ 1 Mary Riley 4.00 10.00
❑ 2 Bobbi Billard 3.00 8.00
❑ 3 April Scott 3.00 8.00
❑ 4 Brooke Morales 3.00 8.00
❑ 5 Katie Lohmann 3.00 8.00
❑ 6 Megan Hauserman 3.00 8.00
❑ 7 Spencer Scott 3.00 8.00
❑ 8 Jennifer Korbin 3.00 8.00

2009 Bench Warmer Limited Kiss Blue Foil Autographs

UNPRICED DUE TO SCARCITY
❑ 1 Jennifer Walcott
❑ 2 Torrie Wilson
❑ 3 Lisa Gleave
❑ 4 Jessica Michaels
❑ 5 Brittany Herrera
❑ 6 Brooke Morales
❑ 7 Katie Lohmann
❑ 8 Miriam Gonzalez
❑ 9 Buffy Tyler
❑ 10 Flo Jalin
❑ 11 Megan Hauserman
❑ 12 Sarah Coggin
❑ 13 Brandi Cunningham
❑ 14 Jo Garcia
❑ 15 Athena Lundberg

2009 Bench Warmer Limited Kiss Gold Foil

STATED PRINT RUN 50 SER. #'d SETS
❑ 1 Jennifer Walcott 12.00 30.00
❑ 2 Torrie Wilson 12.00 30.00
❑ 3 Lisa Gleave 10.00 25.00
❑ 4 Jessica Michaels 10.00 25.00
❑ 5 Brittany Herrera 10.00 25.00
❑ 6 Brooke Morales 10.00 25.00
❑ 7 Katie Lohmann 10.00 25.00
❑ 8 Miriam Gonzalez 12.00 30.00
❑ 9 Buffy Tyler 10.00 25.00
❑ 10 Flo Jalin 10.00 25.00
❑ 11 Megan Hauserman 10.00 25.00
❑ 12 Sarah Coggin 10.00 25.00
❑ 13 Brandi Cunningham 10.00 25.00
❑ 14 Jo Garcia 10.00 25.00
❑ 15 Athena Lundberg 10.00 25.00

2009 Bench Warmer Limited Kiss Green Foil Autographs

STATED PRINT RUN 10 SER. #'d SETS
UNPRICED DUE TO SCARCITY
❑ 1 Jennifer Walcott
❑ 2 Torrie Wilson
❑ 3 Lisa Gleave
❑ 4 Jessica Michaels
❑ 5 Brittany Herrera
❑ 6 Brooke Morales
❑ 7 Katie Lohmann
❑ 8 Miriam Gonzalez
❑ 9 Buffy Tyler
❑ 10 Flo Jalin
❑ 11 Megan Hauserman
❑ 12 Sarah Coggin
❑ 13 Brandi Cunningham
❑ 14 Jo Garcia
❑ 15 Athena Lundberg

2009 Bench Warmer Limited Kiss Pink Foil

*PINK: .5X TO 1.2X GOLD
STATED PRINT RUN 25 SER. #'d SETS
❑ 1 Jennifer Walcott 15.00 40.00
❑ 2 Torrie Wilson 15.00 40.00
❑ 3 Lisa Gleave 12.00 30.00
❑ 4 Jessica Michaels 12.00 30.00
❑ 5 Brittany Herrera 12.00 30.00
❑ 6 Brooke Morales 12.00 30.00
❑ 7 Katie Lohmann 12.00 30.00
❑ 8 Miriam Gonzalez 15.00 40.00
❑ 9 Buffy Tyler 12.00 30.00
❑ 10 Flo Jalin 12.00 30.00
❑ 11 Megan Hauserman 12.00 30.00
❑ 12 Sarah Coggin 12.00 30.00
❑ 13 Brandi Cunningham 12.00 30.00
❑ 14 Jo Garcia 12.00 30.00
❑ 15 Athena Lundberg 12.00 30.00

2009 Bench Warmer Limited Kiss Red Foil Autographs

STATED PRINT RUN 1 SER. #'d SET
UNPRICED DUE TO SCARCITY
❑ 1 Jennifer Walcott
❑ 2 Torrie Wilson
❑ 3 Lisa Gleave
❑ 4 Jessica Michaels
❑ 5 Brittany Herrera
❑ 6 Brooke Morales
❑ 7 Katie Lohmann
❑ 8 Miriam Gonzalez
❑ 9 Buffy Tyler
❑ 10 Flo Jalin
❑ 11 Megan Hauserman
❑ 12 Sarah Coggin
❑ 13 Brandi Cunningham
❑ 14 Jo Garcia
❑ 15 Athena Lundberg

2009 Bench Warmer Limited School Girl Autographs Blue Foil

STATED PRINT RUN 5 SER. #'d SETS
UNPRICED DUE TO SCARCITY
❑ 1 Traci Bingham
❑ 2 Jana Z
❑ 3 Jennifer Walcott
❑ 4 Jennifer England
❑ 5 Megan Hauserman
Cecille Gahr
❑ 6 Athena Lundberg
❑ 7 Lena Yada
❑ 8 Amanda Paige

2009 Bench Warmer Limited School Girl Autographs Gold Foil

STATED ODDS 1:48
❑ 1 Traci Bingham 6.00 15.00
❑ 2 Jana Z 6.00 15.00
❑ 3 Jennifer Walcott 10.00 25.00
❑ 4 Jennifer England 6.00 15.00
❑ 5 Megan Hauserman 8.00 20.00
Cecille Gahr
❑ 6 Athena Lundberg 6.00 15.00
❑ 7 Lena Yada 6.00 15.00
❑ 8 Amanda Paige 6.00 15.00

2009 Bench Warmer Limited School Girl Autographs Green Foil

STATED PRINT RUN 10 SER. #'d SETS
UNPRICED DUE TO SCARCITY
❑ 1 Traci Bingham
❑ 2 Jana Z
❑ 3 Jennifer Walcott
❑ 4 Jennifer England
❑ 5 Megan Hauserman
Cecille Gahr
❑ 6 Athena Lundberg
❑ 7 Lena Yada
❑ 8 Amanda Paige

2009 Bench Warmer Limited School Girl Autographs Pink Foil

*PINK: .8X TO 2X GOLD
STATED PRINT RUN 25 SER. #'d SETS
❑ 1 Traci Bingham 12.00 30.00
❑ 2 Jana Z 12.00 30.00
❑ 3 Jennifer Walcott 20.00 50.00
❑ 4 Jennifer England 12.00 30.00
❑ 5 Megan Hauserman 15.00 40.00
Cecille Gahr
❑ 6 Athena Lundberg 12.00 30.00
❑ 7 Lena Yada 12.00 30.00
❑ 8 Amanda Paige 12.00 30.00

2009 Bench Warmer Limited School Girl Autographs Red Foil

STATED PRINT RUN 1 SER. #'d SET
UNPRICED DUE TO SCARCITY
❑ 1 Traci Bingham
❑ 2 Jana Z
❑ 3 Jennifer Walcott
❑ 4 Jennifer England
❑ 5 Megan Hauserman

Cecille Gahr
❑ 6 Athena Lundberg
❑ 7 Lena Yada
❑ 8 Amanda Paige

2009 Bench Warmer Limited School Girl Swatches

STATED ODDS 1:144
STATED PRINT RUN 50 SER. #'d SETS

❑ 1 Traci Bingham 20.00 40.00
❑ 2 Amanda Paige 20.00 40.00
❑ 3 Brooke Morales 20.00 40.00
❑ 4 Flo Jalin 20.00 40.00
❑ 5 Megan Hauserman 20.00 40.00
❑ 6 Cecille Gahr 20.00 40.00
❑ 7 Christy Hemme 25.00 50.00
❑ 8 Lena Yada 20.00 40.00
❑ 9 Athena Lundberg 20.00 40.00
❑ 10 Katie Lohmann 20.00 40.00
❑ 11 Jennifer England 20.00 40.00
❑ 12A Claudia Jordan 20.00 40.00
❑ 12B Jennifer Walcott 25.00 50.00

2009 Bench Warmer Limited School Girl Swatches Autographs

STATED PRINT RUN 10 SER. #'d SETS
UNPRICED DUE TO SCARCITY

❑ 1 Traci Bingham
❑ 2 Amanda Paige
❑ 3 Brooke Morales
❑ 4 Flo Jalin
❑ 5 Megan Hauserman
❑ 6 Cecille Gahr
❑ 7 Christy Hemme
❑ 8 Lena Yada
❑ 9 Athena Lundberg
❑ 10 Katie Lohmann
❑ 11 Jennifer England
❑ 12A Claudia Jordan
❑ 12B Jennifer Walcott

2009 Bench Warmer Limited Super Rare Autographs Blue Foil

STATED PRINT RUN 5 SER. #'d SETS
UNPRICED DUE TO SCARCITY

❑ 1 Jennifer Walcott
❑ 2 Torrie Wilson
❑ 3 Flo Jalin
❑ 4 Megan Hauserman
❑ 5 Lisa Gleave

2009 Bench Warmer Limited Super Rare Autographs Green Foil

STATED PRINT RUN 10 SER. #'d SETS
UNPRICED DUE TO SCARCITY

❑ 1 Jennifer Walcott
❑ 2 Torrie Wilson
❑ 3 Flo Jalin
❑ 4 Megan Hauserman
❑ 5 Lisa Gleave

2009 Bench Warmer Limited Super Rare Autographs Red Foil

STATED PRINT RUN 1 SER. #'d SET
UNPRICED DUE TO SCARCITY

❑ 1 Jennifer Walcott
❑ 2 Torrie Wilson
❑ 3 Flo Jalin
❑ 4 Megan Hauserman
❑ 5 Lisa Gleave

2009 Bench Warmer Limited Swatches

STATED PRINT RUN 25 SER. #'d SETS

❑ 1 Torrie Wilson
❑ 2 Jennifer Walcott
❑ 3 Buffy Tyler
❑ 4 Lisa Gleave
❑ 5 Miriam Gonzalez
❑ 6 Flo Jalin
❑ 7 April Scott
❑ 8 Aubrie Lemon
❑ 9 Brittany Herrera
❑ 10 Katie Lohmann
❑ 11 Megan Hauserman
❑ 12 Tailor Marion

2009 Bench Warmer Limited Swatches Autographs

STATED PRINT RUN 5 SER. #'d SETS
UNPRICED DUE TO SCARCITY

❑ 1 Torrie Wilson
❑ 2 Jennifer Walcott
❑ 3 Buffy Tyler
❑ 4 Lisa Gleave
❑ 5 Miriam Gonzalez
❑ 6 Flo Jalin
❑ 7 April Scott
❑ 8 Aubrie Lemon
❑ 9 Brittany Herrera
❑ 10 Katie Lohmann
❑ 11 Megan Hauserman
❑ 12 Tailor Marion

2009 Bench Warmer Ultimate Autographs Blue Foil

STATED PRINT RUN 5 SER. #'d SETS
UNPRICED DUE TO SCARCITY

2009 Bench Warmer Ultimate Autographs Gold Foil

STATED PRINT RUN 100 SER. #'d SETS

2009 Bench Warmer Ultimate Autographs Green Foil

STATED PRINT RUN 10 SER. #'d SETS
UNPRICED DUE TO SCARCITY

2009 Bench Warmer Ultimate Autographs Pink Foil

*PINK: .6X TO 1.5X GOLD
STATED PRINT RUN 25 SER. #'d SETS

2009 Bench Warmer Ultimate Autographs Red Foil

STATED PRINT RUN 1 SER. #'d SET
UNPRICED DUE TO SCARCITY

2009 Bench Warmer Ultimate Bikini Swatches Blue Foil Autographs

STATED PRINT RUN 5 SER. #'d SETS
UNPRICED DUE TO SCARCITY

2009 Bench Warmer Ultimate Bikini Swatches Gold Foil

STATED PRINT RUN 50 SER. #'d SETS

❑ 1 Torrie Wilson 20.00 40.00
❑ 2 Traci Bingham 15.00 30.00
❑ 3 Mary Riley 15.00 30.00
❑ 4 Lisa Gleave 15.00 30.00
❑ 5 Brooke Morales 15.00 30.00
❑ 6 Jennifer Walcott 20.00 40.00
❑ 7 April Scott 15.00 30.00
❑ 8 Claudia Jordan 15.00 30.00
❑ 9 Christy Hemme 20.00 40.00
❑ 10 Aubrie Lemon 15.00 30.00
❑ 11 Katie Lohmann 15.00 30.00
❑ 12 Jennifer England 15.00 30.00

2009 Bench Warmer Ultimate Bikini Swatches Green Foil Autographs

STATED PRINT RUN 10 SER. #'d SETS
UNPRICED DUE TO SCARCITY

❑ 1 Torrie Wilson
❑ 2 Traci Bingham
❑ 3 Mary Riley
❑ 4 Lisa Gleave
❑ 5 Brooke Morales
❑ 6 Jennifer Walcott
❑ 7 April Scott
❑ 8 Claudia Jordan
❑ 9 Christy Hemme
❑ 10 Aubrie Lemon
❑ 11 Katie Lohmann
❑ 12 Jennifer England

2009 Bench Warmer Ultimate Bikini Swatches Pink Foil

*PINK: .5X TO 1.2X GOLD
STATED PRINT RUN 25 SER. #'d SETS

2009 Bench Warmer Ultimate Bikini Swatches Red Foil Autographs

STATED PRINT RUN 1 SER. #'d SET
UNPRICED DUE TO SCARCITY

2009 Bench Warmer Ultimate Kiss Blue Foil Autographs

STATED PRINT RUN 5 SER. #'d SETS
UNPRICED DUE TO SCARCITY

2009 Bench Warmer Ultimate Kiss Gold Foil

STATED PRINT RUN 50 SER. #'d SETS

2009 Bench Warmer Ultimate Kiss Green Foil Autographs

STATED PRINT RUN 10 SER. #'d SETS
UNPRICED DUE TO SCARCITY

2009 Bench Warmer Ultimate Kiss Pink Foil

STATED PRINT RUN 25 SER. #'d SETS

2009 Bench Warmer Ultimate Lingerie Swatches Blue Foil Autographs

STATED PRINT RUN 5 SER. #'d SETS
UNPRICED DUE TO SCARCITY

2009 Bench Warmer Ultimate Lingerie Swatches Gold Foil

STATED PRINT RUN 50 SER. #'d SETS

2009 Bench Warmer Ultimate Lingerie Swatches Green Foil Autographs

STATED PRINT RUN 10 SER. #'d SETS
UNPRICED DUE TO SCARCITY

❑ 1 Jennifer Walcott
❑ 2 Jennifer England
❑ 3 Jennifer Korbin
❑ 4 Mary Riley
❑ 5 Flo Jalin
❑ 6 Traci Bingham
❑ 7 Amanda Paige
❑ 8 Jessica Hall
❑ 9 Lena Yada
❑ 10 Torrie Wilson
❑ 11 Shay Lynn
❑ 12 April Scott
❑ 13 Athena Lundberg
❑ 14 Claudia Jordan
❑ 15 Lisa Gleave
❑ 16 Brooke Morales

2009 Bench Warmer Ultimate Lingerie Swatches Pink Foil

*PINK: .5X TO 1.2X GOLD
STATED PRINT RUN 25 SER. #'d SETS

2009 Bench Warmer Ultimate Lingerie Swatches Red Foil Autographs

STATED PRINT RUN 1 SER. #'d SET
UNPRICED DUE TO SCARCITY

2009 Bench Warmer Ultimate Props Blue Foil Autographs

STATED PRINT RUN 5 SER. #'d SETS
UNPRICED DUE TO SCARCITY

2009 Bench Warmer Ultimate Props Gold Foil

PRINT RUN 75-175

❑ 1 Jennifer Walcott/175 8.00 20.00
❑ 2 Torrie Wilson/175 8.00 20.00
❑ 3 Katie Lohmann/150 6.00 15.00
❑ 4 Spencer Scott/125 6.00 15.00
❑ 5 Sarah Coggin/75 6.00 15.00
❑ 6 Mary Riley/150 6.00 15.00
❑ 7 Carrie Stroup/100 6.00 15.00
❑ 8 Aubrie Lemon/175 6.00 15.00
❑ 9 Brittany Herrera/150 6.00 15.00
❑ 10 Jennifer Korbin/150 6.00 15.00
❑ 11 Lena Yada/175 6.00 15.00
❑ 12 Flo Jalin/165 6.00 15.00
❑ 13 Brooke Morales/150 6.00 15.00
❑ 14 Sara Underwood/165 8.00 20.00
❑ 15 Lisa Gleave/175 6.00 15.00

2009 Bench Warmer Ultimate Props Green Foil Autographs

STATED PRINT RUN 10 SER. #'d SETS
UNPRICED DUE TO SCARCITY

2009 Bench Warmer Ultimate Props Pink Foil Autographs

STATED PRINT RUN 25 SER. #'d SETS

❑ 1 Jennifer Walcott
❑ 2 Torrie Wilson
❑ 3 Katie Lohmann
❑ 4 Spencer Scott
❑ 5 Sarah Coggin
❑ 6 Mary Riley
❑ 7 Carrie Stroup
❑ 8 Aubrie Lemon
❑ 9 Brittany Herrera
❑ 10 Jennifer Korbin
❑ 11 Lena Yada
❑ 12 Flo Jalin
❑ 13 Brooke Morales
❑ 14 Sara Underwood
❑ 15 Lisa Gleave

2009 Bench Warmer Ultimate Props Red Foil Autographs

STATED PRINT RUN 1 SER. #'d SET
UNPRICED DUE TO SCARCITY

2009 Bench Warmer Ultimate Shoes Blue Foil Autographs

STATED PRINT RUN 5 SER. #'d SETS
UNPRICED DUE TO SCARCITY

2009 Bench Warmer Ultimate Shoes Gold Foil

STATED PRINT RUN 50 SER. #'d SETS

2009 Bench Warmer Ultimate Shoes Green Foil Autographs

STATED PRINT RUN 10 SER. #'d SETS
UNPRICED DUE TO SCARCITY

❑ 1 Jennifer Walcott
❑ 2 Mary Riley
❑ 3 Torrie Wilson
❑ 4 Gail Kim
❑ 5 Jessica Rockwell
❑ 6 Brooke Morales
❑ 7 Flo Jalin
❑ 8 Miriam Gonzalez
❑ 9 Athena Lundberg
❑ 10 Kitana Baker
❑ 11 Shay Lynn
❑ 12 Spencer Scott
❑ 13 April Scott
❑ 14 Lisa Gleave
❑ 15 Traci Bingham
❑ 16 Jennifer England
❑ 17 Holly Huddleston
❑ 18 Lena Yada
❑ 19 Buffy Tyler
❑ 20 Jennifer Korbin

2009 Bench Warmer Ultimate Shoes Pink Foil

*PINK: .6X TO 1.2X GOLD
STATED PRINT RUN 25 SER. #'d SETS

2009 Bench Warmer Ultimate Shoes Red Foil Autographs

STATED PRINT RUN 1 SER. #'d SET
UNPRICED DUE TO SCARCITY

2009 Complete Twilight Zone

COMPLETE SET (79) 5.00 12.00

❑ 1 The Twilight Zone .15 .40
And When The Sky Was Opened
❑ 2 Where Is Everybody? .15 .40
Judgment Night
❑ 3 One For The Angels .15 .40
Perchance To Dream
❑ 4 Mr. Denton on Doomsday .15 .40
Third From The Sun
❑ 5 The Sixteen Millimeter Shrine .15 .40
The Four Of Us Are Dying
❑ 6 Walking Distance .15 .40
What You Need
❑ 7 Escape Clause .15 .40
The Fever
❑ 8 The Lonely .15 .40
The Hitch-Hiker
❑ 9 Time Enough At Last .15 .40
I Shot An Arrow Into The Air
❑ 10 The Last Flight .15 .40
Nightmare As A Child
❑ 11 The Purple Testament .15 .40
A Nice Place To Visit
❑ 12 Elegy .15 .40
The Big Tall Wish
❑ 13 Mirror Image .15 .40
A Passage For Trumpet
❑ 14 The Monsters Are Due On Maple Street .15 .40
The Chaser
❑ 15 A World Of Difference .15 .40
A Stop At Willoughby
❑ 16 Long Live Walter Jameson .15 .40
The Mighty Casey
❑ 17 People Are Alike All Over .15 .40
The After Hours
❑ 18 Execution .15 .40
Mr. Bevis
❑ 19 A World Of His Own .15 .40
The Night of the Meek
❑ 20 King Nine Will Not Return .15 .40
A Most Unusual Camera
❑ 21 The Man In The Bottle .15 .40
The Trouble With Templeton
❑ 22 Nervous Man In A Four Dollar Room .15 .40
The Whole Truth
❑ 23 A Thing About Machines .15 .40
Back There
❑ 24 The Howling Man .15 .40
Dust
❑ 25 Eye Of The Beholder .15 .40
Twenty Two
❑ 26 Nick of Time .15 .40
A Penny For Your Thoughts
❑ 27 The Lateness Of The Hour .15 .40
The Invaders
❑ 28 The Odyssey Of Flight 33 .15 .40
The Obsolete Man
❑ 29 Mr. Dingle, The Strong .15 .40
Will The Real Martian Please Stand Up?
❑ 30 Static .15 .40
The Mind And The Matter
❑ 31 The Prime Mover .15 .40
The Shelter
❑ 32 Long Distance Call .15 .40
The Arrival
❑ 33 A Hundred Yards Over The Rim .15 .40
Two
❑ 34 The Rip Van Winkle Caper .15 .40
The Mirror
❑ 35 The Silence .15 .40
A Game Of Pool
❑ 36 Shadow Play .15 .40
The Passerby
❑ 37 The Grave .15 .40
Dead Man's Shoes
❑ 38 It's A Good Life .15 .40
One More Pallbearer
❑ 39 Deaths-Head Revisited .15 .40
Nothing In The Dark
❑ 40 The Midnight Sun .15 .40
Kick The Can
❑ 41 Still Valley .15 .40
Showdown With Rance McGrew
❑ 42 The Jungle .15 .40
The Hunt
❑ 43 Once Upon A Time .15 .40
To Serve Man
❑ 44 Five Characters In Search Of An Exit .15 .40
The Last Rites Of Jeff Myrtlebank
❑ 45 A Quality Of Mercy .15 .40
A Piano In The House
❑ 46 The Fugitive .15 .40
Cavender Is Coming
❑ 47 Little Girl Lost .15 .40
I Sing The Body Electric
❑ 48 Person Or Persons Unknown .15 .40
Young Man's Fancy
❑ 49 The Little People .15 .40
The Thirty-Fathom Grave
❑ 50 Four O'Clock .15 .40
In His Image
❑ 51 Hocus-Pocus .15 .40
Frisby/The Changing Of The Guard
❑ 52 The Trade-Ins .15 .40
Mute
❑ 53 The Gift .15 .40
He's Alive
❑ 54 The Dummy .15 .40
Valley of the Shadow
❑ 55 Death Ship .15 .40
Passage On The Lady Anne
❑ 56 Jess-Belle .15 .40
On Thursday We Leave For Home
❑ 57 Miniature .15 .40
The Incredible World Of Horace Ford
❑ 58 Printer's Devil .15 .40
Steel
❑ 59 No Time Like The Past .15 .40
In Praise Of Pip
❑ 60 The Parallel .15 .40
The Bard
❑ 61 I Dream Of Genie .15 .40
The Last Night Of A Jockey
❑ 62 The New Exhibit .15 .40
A Kind Of Stopwatch
❑ 63 Of Late I Think Of Cliffordville .15 .40
Nightmare At 20,000 Feet
❑ 64 Living Doll .15 .40
Number 12 Looks Just Like You
❑ 65 The Old Man In The Cave .15 .40
The Self-Improvement Of Salvadore Ross
❑ 66 Uncle Simon .15 .40
The Long Morrow
❑ 67 Probe 7, Over And Out .15 .40
From Agnes - With Love
❑ 68 The 7th Is Made Up Of Phantoms .15 .40
Night Call
❑ 69 A Short Drink From A Certain Fountain .15 .40
Black Leather Jackets
❑ 70 Ninety Years Without Slumbering .15 .40
Queen Of The Nile
❑ 71 Ring-A-Ding Girl .15 .40
An Occurrence At Owl Creek Bridge
❑ 72 You Drive .15 .40
Spur Of The Moment
❑ 73 What's In The Box .15 .40
The Brain Center At Whipple's
❑ 74 The Masks .15 .40
Mr. Garrity And The Graves
❑ 75 I Am The Night - Color Me Black .15 .40
The Encounter
❑ 76 Sounds And Silences .15 .40
The Bewitchin' Pool
❑ 77 Caesar And Me .15 .40
The Fear
❑ 78 The Jeopardy Room .15 .40
Come Wander With Me
❑ 79 Stopover In A Quiet Town .15 .40
Twilight Zone

2009 Complete Twilight Zone Autographs

STATED ODDS 1:6
A126 STATED ODDS ONE PER CASE
A136 STATED ODDS ONE PER 3 CASE PURCHASE
A149 STATED ODDS ONE PER 6 CASE PURCHASE
ALL AUTOS LIMITED (300-500 COPIES) UNLESS NOTED
VL (VERY LIMITED): 200-300 COPIES

❑ A098 Morgan Brittany 100.00 175.00
Susanne Cupito VL
❑ A099 Mariette Hartley 20.00 40.00
❑ A100 Tom Reese 10.00 20.00
❑ A101 Jack Grinnage 10.00 20.00
❑ A102 Michael Forest 10.00 20.00
❑ A103 Brooke Hayward 10.00 20.00
❑ A104 William Sargent 10.00 20.00
❑ A105 June Foray 12.00 25.00
❑ A106 Dee Hartford 10.00 20.00
❑ A107 Patrick Macnee 25.00 50.00
❑ A108 Bonnie Beecher 10.00 20.00
❑ A109 Richard Erdman 10.00 20.00
❑ A110 Read Morgan 10.00 20.00
❑ A111 Cliff Osmond VL 50.00 100.00
❑ A112 Larrian Gillespie 10.00 20.00
❑ A113 Sarah Marshall 10.00 20.00
❑ A114 Phyllis Love 10.00 20.00
❑ A115 Terry Becker 10.00 20.00
❑ A116 Mary Badham 10.00 20.00
❑ A117 Jean Marsh 12.00 25.00
❑ A118 Doris Singleton 10.00 20.00
❑ A119 Arlene Martel (Arline Sax) 10.00 20.00
❑ A120 Earl Holliman 10.00 20.00
❑ A121 Barbara Perry 10.00 20.00
❑ A122 David Macklin 10.00 20.00
❑ A123 Linden Chiles 10.00 20.00
❑ A124 Susan Harrison 10.00 20.00
❑ A125 Paul Comi 10.00 20.00
❑ A126 Dana Dillaway/ (issued as case topper) 15.00 30.00
❑ A127 Tom Lowell 10.00 20.00
❑ A128 Tim Stafford (Jeffrey Byron) VL 50.00 100.00
❑ A129 Tim O'Connor 10.00 20.00
❑ A130 Jack Ging 10.00 20.00
❑ A131 Doug Heyes Jr. 10.00 20.00
❑ A132 Robert Sampson 10.00 20.00
❑ A133 Lea Waggner 10.00 20.00
❑ A134 Randy Boone 10.00 20.00
❑ A135 Cliff Robertson 100.00 175.00
The Dummy VL
❑ A136 Cliff Robertson 100.00 175.00
A Hundred Yards/ (issued as 3-case incentive)
❑ A137 Louie Elias 10.00 20.00
❑ A138 Anthony Call 10.00 20.00
❑ A139 Chuck Hicks 10.00 20.00
❑ A140 Mary Gregory 10.00 20.00
❑ A141 John Astin 25.00 50.00
❑ A142 Camille Franklin 10.00 20.00
❑ A143 Margarita Cordova 10.00 20.00
❑ A144 Charles Herbert 10.00 20.00
❑ A145 Denise Alexander 10.00 20.00
❑ A146 Noah Keen 10.00 20.00
❑ A147 Edson Stroll 10.00 20.00
❑ A148 Joyce Van Patten 10.00 20.00
❑ A149 George Clayton Johnson 200.00 300.00
(Writer)/ (issued as 6-case incentive)

2009 Complete Twilight Zone In Motion

COMPLETE SET (18) 20.00 40.00
STATED ODDS 1:12

❑ L1 Twilight Zone (logo 1) 1.50 4.00
❑ L2 Where Is Everybody? 1.50 4.00
❑ L3 Nightmare At 20,000 Feet 1.50 4.00
❑ L4 It's A Good Life 1.50 4.00
❑ L5 A Game Of Pool 1.50 4.00
❑ L6 Twilight Zone (logo 2) 1.50 4.00
❑ L7 Perchance To Dream 1.50 4.00
❑ L8 The After Hours 1.50 4.00
❑ L9 Living Doll 1.50 4.00
❑ L10 Twilight Zone (logo 3) 1.50 4.00
❑ L11 A Passage For Trumpet 1.50 4.00
❑ L12 The Dummy 1.50 4.00
❑ L13 The Fugitive 1.50 4.00
❑ L14 The Mind And The Matter 1.50 4.00
❑ L15 Nick Of Time 1.50 4.00
❑ L16 Eye Of The Beholder 1.50 4.00
❑ L17 And When The Sky Was Opened 1.50 4.00
❑ L18 Twilight Zone (logo 4) 1.50 4.00

2009 Complete Twilight Zone Life of It's Own

COMPLETE SET (9) 10.00 25.00
STATED ODDS 1:12

❑ Z1 Mystic Seer from Nick of Time 1.50 4.00
❑ Z2 Talky Tina from Living Doll 1.50 4.00
❑ Z3 Willie from The Dummy 1.50 4.00
❑ Z4 Jack The Ripper from The New Exhibit 1.50 4.00
❑ Z5 Camera from A Most Unusual Camera 1.50 4.00
❑ Z6 Mannequin from The After Hours 1.50 4.00
❑ Z7 Toy Phone from Long Distance Call 1.50 4.00
❑ Z8 Genie's Bottle from The Man In The Bottle 1.50 4.00
❑ Z9 Shoes from Dead Man's Shoes 1.50 4.00

2009 Complete Twilight Zone Portraits

COMPLETE SET (9) 10.00 25.00
STATED ODDS 1:12

❑ POR1 William Shatner 1.50 4.00
❑ POR2 Burgess Meredith 1.50 4.00
❑ POR3 Jack Klugman 1.50 4.00
❑ POR4 Anne Francis 1.50 4.00
❑ POR5 Russell Johnson 1.50 4.00
❑ POR6 Ed Wynn 1.50 4.00
❑ POR7 Gladys Cooper 1.50 4.00
❑ POR8 Fritz Weaver 1.50 4.00
❑ POR9 Cliff Robertson 1.50 4.00

2009 Conan Movies Autograph Extension

COMPLETE SET (9)
COMP.SET w/o INCENTIVE (8)
ANNOUNCED PRINT RUN 333 SETS

❑ AS Arnold Schwarzenegger/ (issued as 10-set incentive)
❑ BD Ben Davidson AU
❑ CG Cassandra Gava AU
❑ JJ James Earl Jones AU
❑ MA Mako AU
❑ SD Sarah Douglas AU
❑ CC1 Conan
❑ CC2 Conan
❑ CC3 Conan

2009 Dexter

COMPLETE SET (72) 6.00 15.00

❑ 1 Dexter .15 .40
❑ 2 Dexter Morgan .15 .40
❑ 3 Rita Bennett .15 .40
❑ 4 Debra Morgan .15 .40
❑ 5 Lt. Maria LaGuerta .15 .40
❑ 6 Sgt. James Doakes .15 .40
❑ 7 Angel Batista .15 .40
❑ 8 Harry Morgan .15 .40
❑ 9 Vince Masuka .15 .40
❑ 10 Clean living .15 .40
❑ 11 Miami is a great town .15 .40
❑ 12 Blood spatter is his business .15 .40
❑ 13 Getting down to work .15 .40
❑ 14 Prized possessions .15 .40
❑ 15 This is unique .15 .40
❑ 16 Hunting for The Code .15 .40
❑ 17 The Slice of Life .15 .40
❑ 18 What's in the fridge .15 .40
❑ 19 Getting to know you .15 .40
❑ 20 A career move .15 .40
❑ 21 Hockey is a brutal sport .15 .40
❑ 22 Look Ma, no fingers .15 .40
❑ 23 Rita and the kids .15 .40
❑ 24 Paul Bennett .15 .40
❑ 25 Something's a foot .15 .40
❑ 26 Couple counseling .15 .40
❑ 27 Trailer trash .15 .40
❑ 28 Déjà vu .15 .40
❑ 29 Like old times .15 .40
❑ 30 That hits the spot .15 .40
❑ 31 Seeking treasure .15 .40
❑ 32 Every picture tells a story .15 .40
❑ 33 A good fit .15 .40
❑ 34 Digging deeper .15 .40
❑ 35 And how does that make you feel .15 .40
❑ 36 Are you my Dad .15 .40
❑ 37 Can't breathe .15 .40
❑ 38 Angel almost becomes one .15 .40
❑ 39 Here's to us .15 .40
❑ 40 Sleep tight Sis .15 .40
❑ 41 Dexter chooses .15 .40

MODERN ERA NON-SPORTS

❑ 42 Mourning Brian's loss .15 .40
❑ 43 The vacant stare .15 .40
❑ 44 Doakes' watch .15 .40
❑ 45 Dexter's got game .15 .40
❑ 46 Dexter speaks .15 .40
❑ 47 Lila's Rules .15 .40
❑ 48 The Bay Harbor Butcher victims .15 .40
❑ 49 Rock Star Agent Frank Lundy .15 .40
❑ 50 Don't lie to me .15 .40
❑ 51 Stay clean .15 .40
❑ 52 To know some body .15 .40
❑ 53 The Dark Defender .15 .40
❑ 54 Confronting your demons .15 .40
❑ 55 The Copy Cat .15 .40
❑ 56 Come for dinner .15 .40
❑ 57 Dexter makes a complaint .15 .40
❑ 58 If you were the Bay Harbor Butcher .15 .40
❑ 59 Doakes attacks Dexter .15 .40
❑ 60 Lila paints a picture .15 .40
❑ 61 Dreaming in color .15 .40
❑ 62 How did Harry die .15 .40
❑ 63 Reamed out .15 .40
❑ 64 Do the right thing .15 .40
❑ 65 Doomed .15 .40
❑ 66 A clear view .15 .40
❑ 67 Fire prevention .15 .40
❑ 68 Time To Bid Adieu .15 .40
❑ 69 Devastated .15 .40
❑ 70 The low down on Lila .15 .40
❑ 71 Case closed .15 .40
❑ 72 Checklist .15 .40

2009 Dexter Autographs

STATED ODDS 1:48

❑ DA1 Michael C. Hall 60.00 120.00
❑ DA2 Julie Benz 40.00 80.00
❑ DA3 Jennifer Carpenter 40.00 80.00
❑ DA4 Lauren Velez 15.00 30.00
❑ DA5 David Zayas 15.00 30.00
❑ DA6 James Remar 15.00 30.00
❑ DA7 C.S. Lee 15.00 30.00
❑ DA8 Erik King 15.00 30.00
❑ DA9 Margo Martindale 10.00 20.00
❑ DA10 Mark L. Young 10.00 20.00
❑ DA11 Mark Pellegrino 10.00 20.00

2009 Dexter Behind the Scenes

COMPLETE SET (5) 4.00 10.00
STATED ODDS 1:24

❑ DB1 Dexter In the bath 1.25 3.00
❑ DB2 Dexter Jogging 1.25 3.00
❑ DB3 Dexter Bloody floor 1.25 3.00
❑ DB4 Dexter Strangling 1.25 3.00
❑ DB5 Dexter Leaning on podium 1.25 3.00

2009 Dexter Case Incentive Memorabilia

DCI1 STATED ODDS ONE PER 3 CASE PURCHASE
DCI2 STATED ODDS ONE PER 10 CASE PURCHASE

❑ DCI1 Dexter Morgan 30.00 75.00
❑ DCI2 Blood Slide 250.00 350.00

2009 Dexter Costumes

STATED ODDS 1:13

❑ DC1 Astor 6.00 15.00
❑ DC2 Astor 6.00 15.00
❑ DC3 Angel Batista 8.00 20.00
❑ DC4 Angel Batista 8.00 20.00
❑ DC5 Cody 8.00 20.00
❑ DC6 Cody 8.00 20.00
❑ DC7 Debra Morgan 10.00 25.00
❑ DC8a Debra Morgan 10.00 25.00
Uniform Shirt
❑ DC8b Debra Morgan
Patch
❑ DC9 Dexter Morgan 10.00 25.00
❑ DC10 Sgt. Doakes 6.00 15.00
❑ DC11 Frank Lundy 8.00 20.00
❑ DC12 Frank Lundy 10.00 25.00
❑ DC13 Harry Morgan 6.00 15.00
❑ DC14 Lila 8.00 20.00
❑ DC15 Lt. Maria LaGuerta 6.00 15.00
❑ DC16 Lt. Maria LaGuerta 6.00 15.00
❑ DC17 Lt. Maria LaGuerta 8.00 20.00
❑ DC18 Rita Bennett 10.00 25.00
❑ DC19 Rudy Cooper 8.00 20.00
❑ DC20 Vince Masuka 6.00 15.00
❑ DC21 Vince Masuka 6.00 15.00

2009 Dexter Dexter's Relationships

COMPLETE SET (4) 4.00 10.00
STATED ODDS 1:24

❑ DR1 Dexter and Rita 1.50 4.00
❑ DR2 Debra and Dexter 1.50 4.00
❑ DR3 Dexter and Harry 1.50 4.00
❑ DR4 Lila 1.50 4.00

2009 Dexter Dream Scenes

COMPLETE SET (2) 3.00 8.00
STATED ODDS 1:24

❑ DS1 Not a Drag to Dexter 2.50 6.00
❑ DS2 Hey 2.50 6.00

2009 Dexter Group

COMPLETE SET (2) 2.50 6.00
STATED ODDS 1:24

❑ DG1 Slice of Life 1.50 4.00
❑ DG2 Friends and Colleagues 1.50 4.00

2009 Dexter Portraits

COMPLETE SET (4) 4.00 10.00
STATED ODDS 1:24

❑ DT1 Shhhh 1.50 4.00
❑ DT2 Handsome 1.50 4.00
❑ DT3 Blood Spatter 1.50 4.00
❑ DT4 Dexter the Killer 1.50 4.00

2009 Dexter Props

STATED ODDS 1:96

❑ DPC1 Foot 100.00 200.00
❑ DPC2 Hand 100.00 200.00
❑ DPC3 Crime Scene Tape 8.00 20.00
❑ DPC4 Evidence Flag 15.00 40.00
❑ DPC5 Evidence Bag 12.50 30.00

2009 Dexter Sketches

STATED ODDS 1:288
PENCE STATED ODDS ONE PER 6 CASE PURCHASE
MILLER STATED ODDS ONE PER 8 CASE PURCHASE

❑ NNO Jason Carrier 20.00 50.00
❑ NNO Brian Kong 20.00 50.00
❑ NNO Steven Miller/ (issued as 8-case incentive)75.00 150.00
❑ NNO Sean Pence/ (issued as 6-case incentive)75.00 150.00

2009 Dexter The Dark Defender

COMPLETE SET (4) 4.00 10.00
STATED ODDS 1:24

❑ DD1 The Dark Defender 1.50 4.00
Dexter
❑ DD2 The Dark Defender 1.50 4.00
❑ DD3 Dexter close-up 1.50 4.00
❑ DD4 Dexter with victim 1.50 4.00

2009 Dexter The Killer

COMPLETE SET (6) 6.00 15.00
STATED ODDS 1:24

❑ DK1 Dexter Has a Drink 1.50 4.00
❑ DK2 Dexter Ties One On 1.50 4.00
❑ DK3 Dexter is Sharp 1.50 4.00
❑ DK4 No Blood On My Hands 1.50 4.00
❑ DK5 Dexter Knows All the Moves 1.50 4.00
❑ DK6 According to Dexter 1.50 4.00

2009 eTopps Allen and Ginter Moments

STATED PRINT RUN 999 SER. #'d SETS

❑ EMK Ted Kennedy 2.00 5.00

2009 eTopps Allen and Ginter Presidents

COMPLETE SET (5)
STATED PRINT RUN 999 SER. #'d SETS

❑ 7 George H.W. Bush 2.00 5.00
❑ 8 Harry S Truman 2.00 5.00
❑ 9 Franklin D. Roosevelt 2.00 5.00
❑ 10 Woodrow Wilson 2.00 5.00
❑ 11 William Howard Taft 2.00 5.00

2009 Ghost Whisperer Seasons One and Two

COMPLETE SET (72) 6.00 15.00
SN1 STATED ODDS 1 PER CASE

❑ 1 The Ghost Whisperer .15 .40
❑ 2 Melinda Gordon .15 .40
❑ 3 Jim Clancy .15 .40
❑ 4 Andrea Moreno .15 .40
❑ 5 Delia Banks .15 .40
❑ 6 Ned Banks .15 .40
❑ 7 Professor Rick Payne .15 .40
❑ 8 Young Melinda .15 .40
❑ 9 Homer .15 .40
❑ 10 Dead Man Walking .15 .40
❑ 11 Tragic Loss .15 .40
❑ 12 Good Twin, Ghost Twin .15 .40
❑ 13 To Life .15 .40
❑ 14 Old Friends .15 .40
❑ 15 Restless Spirit .15 .40
❑ 16 Errand of Mercy .15 .40
❑ 17 When Doves Cry .15 .40
❑ 18 Interference .15 .40
❑ 19 A Veiled Threat .15 .40
❑ 20 Family Reunion .15 .40
❑ 21 Open Mic Night .15 .40
❑ 22 Neighborhood Watch .15 .40
❑ 23 Final Thoughts .15 .40
❑ 24 Generations .15 .40
❑ 25 A Shoulder to Lean On .15 .40
❑ 26 Big Brother Is Watching .15 .40
❑ 27 A Read on the Situation .15 .40
❑ 28 Anger Management .15 .40
❑ 29 Comforting Arms .15 .40
❑ 30 Chilling Announcement .15 .40
❑ 31 Dark Visitor .15 .40
❑ 32 The Aftermath .15 .40
❑ 33 The Sad Truth .15 .40
❑ 34 Funeral for a Friend .15 .40
❑ 35 Unexpected Interruption .15 .40
❑ 36 The Melinda Triangle .15 .40
❑ 37 Watery Grave .15 .40
❑ 38 Inner Glow .15 .40
❑ 39 Model Behavior .15 .40
❑ 40 Burning Issues .15 .40
❑ 41 The Umbrella Room .15 .40
❑ 42 Silenced Symphony .15 .40
❑ 43 Take Us Out to the Ballgame .15 .40
❑ 44 Uncaria Tormentosa .15 .40
❑ 45 Silence Speaks .15 .40
❑ 46 Multiple Personalities in Disorder .15 .40
❑ 47 Skull Fragments .15 .40
❑ 48 Who's Got Spirit .15 .40
❑ 49 Hostage Situation .15 .40
❑ 50 Two Ghosts in One .15 .40
❑ 51 I'll Be Watching You .15 .40
❑ 52 Dark Angel, Gabriel .15 .40
❑ 53 Payneful Message .15 .40
❑ 54 Past and Future Collide .15 .40
❑ 55 Art Imitates Life .15 .40
❑ 56 Life Imitates Art .15 .40
❑ 57 The Light .15 .40
❑ 58 The Ghost Whisperer .15 .40
❑ 59 The Guardian .15 .40
❑ 60 The Prophet .15 .40
❑ 61 Benevolent Spirits .15 .40
❑ 62 Lost Souls .15 .40
❑ 63 Sensitives .15 .40
❑ 64 Loved Ones .15 .40
❑ 65 The Collector .15 .40
❑ 66 Romano .15 .40
❑ 67 The Laughing Man .15 .40
❑ 68 Malevolent Spirits .15 .40
❑ 69 Lost Souls .15 .40
❑ 70 Innocent Victims .15 .40
❑ 71 The Battle .15 .40
❑ 72 Checklist .15 .40
❑ SN1 Same As It Never Was 12.50 30.00

2009 Ghost Whisperer Seasons One and Two Autograph Costumes

❑ GA1 Jennifer Love Hewitt 100.00 175.00
❑ GAC2 David Conrad 25.00 50.00
❑ GAC3 Camryn Manheim 20.00 40.00

2009 Ghost Whisperer Seasons One and Two Autographs

STATED ODDS 1:48
GCI1 STATED ODDS ONE PER 6 CASE PURCHASE
GCI2 STATED ODDS ONE PER 10 CASE PURCHASE

❑ GA1 Jennifer Love Hewitt 100.00 175.00
❑ GA2 David Conrad 25.00 50.00
❑ GA3 Camryn Manheim 20.00 40.00
❑ GA4 Christoph Sanders 8.00 20.00
❑ GA5 Jamie Kennedy 10.00 25.00
❑ GA6 Jamie Kennedy 30.00 60.00
Christoph Sanders
❑ GA7 Ian Sander 8.00 20.00
❑ GA8 John Gray 10.00 25.00
❑ GA9 Kim Moses 10.00 25.00
❑ GCI1 J.L. Hewitt 100.00 175.00
D.Conrad/ (issued as 6-case incentive)
❑ GCI2 J.L. Hewitt 150.00 250.00
D.Conrad/C.Manheim/ (issued as 10-case incentive)

2009 Ghost Whisperer Seasons One and Two Costumes

STATED ODDS 1:12
GCI3 STATED ODDS ONE PER 3 CASE PURCHASE

❑ GC1 Melinda Gordon Jacket 10.00 25.00
❑ GC2 Melinda Gordon Dress 8.00 20.00
❑ GC3 Melinda Gordon Teddy 8.00 20.00
❑ GC4 Melinda Gordon Nightgown 20.00 50.00
❑ GC5 Melinda Gordon Robe 8.00 20.00
❑ GC6 Melinda Gordon Dress 10.00 25.00
❑ GC7 Melinda Gordon Sweater 8.00 20.00
❑ GC8 Melinda Gordon Shirt 15.00 40.00
❑ GC9 Melinda Gordon Dress 8.00 20.00
❑ GC10 Melinda Gordon Nightgown 8.00 20.00
❑ GC11 Melinda Gordon Dress 8.00 20.00
❑ GC12 Melinda Gordon Dress 8.00 20.00
❑ GC13 Melinda Gordon Dress 8.00 20.00
❑ GC14 Melinda Gordon Jacket 10.00 25.00
Scarf
❑ GC15 Melinda Gordon Robe 10.00 25.00
Robe
❑ GC16 Melinda Gordon PJs 10.00 25.00
PJs
❑ GC17 Delia Banks Sweater 6.00 15.00
❑ GC18 Delia Banks Dress 6.00 15.00
❑ GC19 Rick Payne Jacket 6.00 15.00
❑ GC20 Sarah Applewhite Nightgown 8.00 20.00
❑ GCI3 Melinda Gordon Dress 30.00 60.00
Dress/ (issued as 3-case incentive)

2009 Ghost Whisperer Seasons One and Two Crossing Over

COMPLETE SET (3) 4.00 10.00
RANDOM INSERTS IN PACKS

❑ C1 Crossing Over 1.50 4.00
❑ C2 Crossing Over 1.50 4.00
❑ C3 Crossing Over 1.50 4.00

2009 Ghost Whisperer Seasons One and Two Kindred Spirits

COMPLETE SET (9) 6.00 15.00
RANDOM INSERTS IN PACKS

❑ K1 Puzzle Card 1.00 2.50
❑ K2 Puzzle Card 1.00 2.50
❑ K3 Puzzle Card 1.00 2.50
❑ K4 Puzzle Card 1.00 2.50
❑ K5 Puzzle Card 1.00 2.50
❑ K6 Puzzle Card 1.00 2.50
❑ K7 Puzzle Card 1.00 2.50
❑ K8 Puzzle Card 1.00 2.50
❑ K9 Puzzle Card 1.00 2.50

2009 Ghost Whisperer Seasons One and Two Signs

COMPLETE SET (6) 6.00 15.00
RANDOM INSERTS IN PACKS

❑ S1 Five Signs 1.50 4.00
❑ S2 Death Will Come 1.50 4.00
❑ S3 Mors Dilecti 1.50 4.00
❑ S4 The Dead Will Rise 1.50 4.00
❑ S5 When the Forgotten Return 1.50 4.00
❑ S6 Death Will Be Twice Closer 1.50 4.00

2009 Ghost Whisperer Seasons One and Two Trivia

COMPLETE SET (9) 6.00 15.00
RANDOM INSERTS IN PACKS

❑ T1 Careful Consideration 1.00 2.50
❑ T2 The Menacing Laugh 1.00 2.50
❑ T3 Lost Boys' Storytime 1.00 2.50
❑ T4 Newborn Spirits 1.00 2.50
❑ T5 Melinda's Best Friend Andrea Moreno 1.00 2.50
❑ T6 Melinda's Husband Jim Clancy 1.00 2.50
❑ T7 Melinda Consults with Professor Payne 1.00 2.50
❑ T8 Delia and Ned Banks 1.00 2.50
❑ T9 Melinda in Downtown Grandview 1.00 2.50

2009 Harry Potter and the Half-Blood Prince

COMPLETE SET (90) 6.00 15.00

❑ 1 Harry Potter and the Half-Blood Prince .15 .40
❑ 2 Harry Potter .15 .40
❑ 3 Ron Weasley .15 .40
❑ 4 Hermione Granger .15 .40
❑ 5 Horace Slughorn .15 .40
❑ 6 Luna Lovegood .15 .40
❑ 7 Albus Dumbledore .15 .40
❑ 8 Nymphadora Tonks .15 .40
❑ 9 Remus Lupin .15 .40
❑ 10 Lavender Brown .15 .40
❑ 11 Draco Malfoy .15 .40
❑ 12 Arthur Weasley .15 .40
❑ 13 Molly Weasley .15 .40
❑ 14 Severus Snape .15 .40
❑ 15 Rubeus Hagrid .15 .40
❑ 16 Young Tom Riddle .15 .40
❑ 17 Ginny Weasley .15 .40
❑ 18 Minerva McGonagall .15 .40
❑ 19 Eleven. That's When I Get Off .15 .40
❑ 20 What Is It, Ginny? .15 .40
❑ 21 Wondering About Draco .15 .40
❑ 22 The New Potions Professor .15 .40
❑ 23 Announcing the Newest Defense .15 .40
❑ 24 Their Greatest Weapon .15 .40
❑ 25 Flitwick Listens .15 .40
❑ 26 Looks Like It's His Own .15 .40
❑ 27 Lavender and Won-Won .15 .40
❑ 28 Testing .15 .40
❑ 29 Fixing the Vanishing Cabinet .15 .40
❑ 30 Good Evening, Harry .15 .40
❑ 31 He's a Funny Boy - Tom .15 .40
❑ 32 No Guarantees .15 .40
❑ 33 The Future Gryffindor Keeper .15 .40
❑ 34 Argus Filch and Mrs. Norris .15 .40
❑ 35 Reminiscing .15 .40
❑ 36 Looking at Lavender .15 .40
❑ 37 Ever Heard of this Spell? .15 .40
❑ 38 Katie Bell - Cursed .15 .40
❑ 39 The Slug Club .15 .40
❑ 40 To Hogwarts' Best and Brightest .15 .40
❑ 41 Leader of the Club .15 .40
❑ 42 Cormac McLaggen Tries to Impress Slughorn.15 .40
❑ 43 Blaise Zabini - Slug Club Member .15 .40
❑ 44 The Slytherin Twins .15 .40
❑ 45 Did Voldemort Ever Make the Shelf .15 .40
❑ 46 He Killed my Parents .15 .40
❑ 47 I'm Resigning .15 .40
❑ 48 Confronted by Cormac .15 .40
❑ 49 The Competition .15 .40
❑ 50 Before the Big Match .15 .40
❑ 51 I Know You'll Be Brilliant .15 .40
❑ 52 A True Fan .15 .40
❑ 53 Is It a Tonic? .15 .40
❑ 54 King Weasley .15 .40
❑ 55 She Thinks You're the Chosen One .15 .40
❑ 56 Planning his Move .15 .40
❑ 57 Snape Monitors the Party .15 .40
❑ 58 Luna Holds Court .15 .40
❑ 59 The Gate-Crasher .15 .40
❑ 60 An Uninvited Guest .15 .40
❑ 61 Ginny Enters the Room .15 .40
❑ 62 Discussing Things .15 .40
❑ 63 Let Me Assist You .15 .40
❑ 64 Sworn to Protect .15 .40
❑ 65 Snape Was Offering to Help .15 .40
❑ 66 Don't Trust Me? .15 .40
❑ 67 In the Workshop .15 .40
❑ 68 We're Being Followed .15 .40
❑ 69 There's Someone Out There .15 .40
❑ 70 Harry, No! .15 .40
❑ 71 Attack on The Burrow .15 .40
❑ 72 The Map is Never Wrong .15 .40
❑ 73 Can You Introduce Me? .15 .40
❑ 74 A Bit Put Out .15 .40
❑ 75 Broken-Hearted Lavender .15 .40
❑ 76 Spotting Katie .15 .40
❑ 77 The Gryffindor Table .15 .40
❑ 78 Suspect .15 .40
❑ 79 I Don't Know Who Cursed Me .15 .40
❑ 80 Listening to the Story .15 .40
❑ 81 Amusing Friends .15 .40
❑ 82 Haunted by a Memory .15 .40
❑ 83 Memories in the Pensieve .15 .40
❑ 84 Memories About Riddle .15 .40
❑ 85 On a Mission .15 .40
❑ 86 Beyond Imagination .15 .40
❑ 87 The Final Piece of the Puzzle .15 .40
❑ 88 Overhearing Snape .15 .40
❑ 89 Too Quiet .15 .40
❑ 90 Checklist .15 .40

2009 Harry Potter and the Half-Blood Prince Autographs

STATED ODDS 1:120
UNNUMBERED CARDS LISTED ALPHABETICALLY

❑ 1 Daniel Radcliffe 300.00 450.00
Tom Felton
❑ 2 David Thewlis 40.00 80.00
❑ 3 Emma Watson 300.00 400.00
❑ 4 Evanna Lynch 40.00 80.00
❑ 5 Helena Bonham Carter 50.00 100.00
❑ 6 Jessie Cave 25.00 50.00
❑ 7 Maggie Smith 60.00 120.00
❑ 8 Michael Gambon 40.00 80.00
❑ 9 Natalia Tena 25.00 50.00
❑ 10 Ralph Ineson 10.00 20.00
❑ 11 Rupert Grint 150.00 250.00
❑ 12 Suzanne Toase 10.00 20.00

2009 Harry Potter and the Half-Blood Prince Case Incentive Memorabilia

CI1 STATED ODDS ONE PER TWO CASE PURCHASE
CI2 STATED ODDS ONE PER FIVE CASE PURCHASE
CI3 STATED ODDS ONE PER TEN CASE PURCHASE
CI4 STATED ODDS ONE PER 25 CASE PURCHASE

❑ CI1 Gryffindor Students 15.00 30.00
❑ CI2 Boxing Telescope Boxes 50.00 100.00
❑ CI3 Beater's Bats 75.00 150.00
❑ CI4 Chicken Foot Goblets 125.00 225.00

2009 Harry Potter and the Half-Blood Prince Costumes

COMPLETE SET (14) 250.00 300.00
STATED ODDS 1:30

❑ C1 Bellatrix Lestrange 15.00 40.00
❑ C2 Horace Slughorn 20.00 50.00
❑ C3 Ron Weasley 15.00 40.00
❑ C4 Rubeus Hagrid 12.00 30.00
❑ C5 Gryffindor Students 10.00 25.00
❑ C6 Horace Slughorn 12.00 30.00
❑ C7 Albus Dumbledore 12.00 30.00
❑ C8 Gryffindor Students 12.00 30.00
❑ C9 Professor McGonagall 12.00 30.00
❑ C10 Horace Slughorn 10.00 25.00
❑ C11 Ravenclaw Students 35.00 70.00
❑ C12 Slytherin Students 10.00 25.00
❑ C13 Fenrir Greyback 12.00 30.00
❑ C14 Nymphadora Tonks 15.00 40.00

2009 Harry Potter and the Half-Blood Prince Crystal Case Toppers

COMPLETE SET (6)
STATED ODDS ONE PER CASE

❑ 1 Dumbledore CLEAR 50.00 100.00
❑ 2 Dumbledore PURPLE 50.00 100.00
❑ 3 Remus Lupin 50.00 100.00
Nymphadora Tonks CLEAR
❑ 4 Remus Lupin 50.00 100.00
Nymphadora Tonks PURPLE
❑ 5 Ron Weasley 50.00 100.00
Harry Potter CLEAR
❑ 6 Ron Weasley 50.00 100.00
Harry Potter PURPLE

2009 Harry Potter and the Half-Blood Prince FilmCards

COMPLETE SET (9) 100.00 150.00
STATED ODDS 1:80

❑ CFC1 Ginny and Harry 10.00 25.00
❑ CFC2 Harry 10.00 25.00
❑ CFC3 Filch 10.00 25.00
❑ CFC4 Luna 10.00 25.00
❑ CFC5 Harry and Nymphadora 10.00 25.00
❑ CFC6 Harry and Luna 10.00 25.00
❑ CFC7 Quidditch 10.00 25.00
❑ CFC8 Slughorn 10.00 25.00
❑ CFC9 King Weasley 10.00 25.00

2009 Harry Potter and the Half-Blood Prince Metal Box Toppers

COMPLETE SET (4) 10.00 25.00
STATED ODDS ONE PER CASE

❑ BT1 Draco Malfoy 3.00 8.00
❑ BT2 Snape 3.00 8.00
❑ BT3 Bellatrix 3.00 8.00
❑ BT4 Death Eater 3.00 8.00

2009 Harry Potter and the Half-Blood Prince Props

COMPLETE SET (12) 300.00 400.00
STATED ODDS 1:60

❑ P1 Slughorn's Christmas Party Lanterns 20.00 50.00
❑ P2 Advanced Potion-Making Book Pages 25.00 60.00
❑ P3 Cushions from The Burrow 20.00 50.00
❑ P4 Quidditch Quaffle Ball 60.00 120.00
❑ P5 Slughorn's Office Wall Covering 15.00 40.00
❑ P6 Slughorn's Christmas Party Drapes 15.00 40.00
❑ P7 Just Like That Hat Boxes 20.00 50.00
❑ P8 Records from Slughorn's House 25.00 60.00
❑ P9 Slughorn's Office Curtains 15.00 40.00
❑ P10 Skiving Snackbox Boxes 20.00 50.00
❑ P11 Advanced Potion-Making Book Covers 30.00 75.00
❑ P12 Nose Biting Tea Cup Boxes 30.00 75.00

2009 Harry Potter and the Half-Blood Prince Puzzle

COMPLETE SET (9) 6.00 15.00
STATED ODDS 5:24

❑ R1 Death Eaters Attack 1.00 2.50
❑ R2 The Burrow 1.00 2.50
❑ R3 Draco 1.00 2.50
❑ R4 Dumbledore 1.00 2.50
❑ R5 Greyback 1.00 2.50
❑ R6 Hedwig 1.00 2.50
❑ R7 Hermione 1.00 2.50
❑ R8 Ginny 1.00 2.50
❑ R9 Potions 1.00 2.50

2009 Harry Potter and the Half-Blood Prince Update

COMPLETE SET (90) 6.00 15.00

❑ 91 Attack at Ollivanders .15 .40
❑ 92 Dumbledore Waits .15 .40
❑ 93 Spinner's End .15 .40
❑ 94 Visiting Knockturn Alley .15 .40
❑ 95 The Hogwarts Express .15 .40
❑ 96 Peruvian Instant Darkness Powder .15 .40
❑ 97 A Thinning Mist of Darkness .15 .40
❑ 98 Leaving the Scene .15 .40
❑ 99 Seeing Wrackspurts .15 .40
❑ 100 Friends .15 .40
❑ 101 The Slytherin Table .15 .40
❑ 102 Another Seamus Finnigan Explosion .15 .40
❑ 103 Viewing a Memory .15 .40
❑ 104 You Can Do Things, Can't You, Tom? .15 .40
❑ 105 Something Trying to Get Out .15 .40
❑ 106 The Box in the Wardrobe .15 .40
❑ 107 Nothing Personal .15 .40
❑ 108 A Nervous Wreck .15 .40
❑ 109 A Confident Keeper .15 .40
❑ 110 A Little Unsteady .15 .40
❑ 111 Hanging in There .15 .40
❑ 112 On the Way Home .15 .40
❑ 113 An Argument Between Friends .15 .40
❑ 114 Lucky to Be Alive .15 .40
❑ 115 A Most Intriguing Object .15 .40
❑ 116 Pre-Match Support .15 .40
❑ 117 How Does It Feel? .15 .40
❑ 118 But I Am The Chosen One .15 .40
❑ 119 A Secret Mission .15 .40
❑ 120 One of a Pair .15 .40
❑ 121 A Sign of Romance .15 .40
❑ 122 A Magical Christmas Cake .15 .40
❑ 123 Lestrange Attacks .15 .40
❑ 124 Racing for the Reeds .15 .40
❑ 125 Going After Harry .15 .40
❑ 126 A Trap .15 .40
❑ 127 A Battle in the Darkness .15 .40
❑ 128 Trapped in the Reeds .15 .40
❑ 129 Defending The Burrow .15 .40
❑ 130 Covering All Angles .15 .40
❑ 131 Star Student .15 .40
❑ 132 A Bit of Rare Magic .15 .40
❑ 133 Not a True Memory .15 .40
❑ 134 This Memory Is Everything .15 .40
❑ 135 I Happen To Be His... Friend .15 .40
❑ 136 A Mysterious Connection .15 .40
❑ 137 Draco, Devastated .15 .40
❑ 138 Battle with Draco .15 .40
❑ 139 Sectumsempra .15 .40
❑ 140 Felix .15 .40
❑ 141 Aragog's Burial .15 .40
❑ 142 Farewell... Aragog .15 .40
❑ 143 Enjoying the Moment .15 .40
❑ 144 Odo the Hero .15 .40
❑ 145 I Am The Chosen One .15 .40
❑ 146 Don't Think Too Badly of Me .15 .40
❑ 147 The True Memory .15 .40
❑ 148 At Last .15 .40
❑ 149 Preparing to Learn the Truth .15 .40
❑ 150 Known Horcruxes .15 .40
❑ 151 Precious Blood .15 .40
❑ 152 Searching for Horcruxes .15 .40
❑ 153 Raising the Boat .15 .40
❑ 154 The Location of the Horcrux .15 .40
❑ 155 It Has To Be Drunk .15 .40
❑ 156 Preparing for the Worst .15 .40
❑ 157 The Third Horcrux? .15 .40
❑ 158 The Bottom of the Basin .15 .40
❑ 159 Something in the Water .15 .40
❑ 160 Inferi .15 .40
❑ 161 Battling the Inferi .15 .40
❑ 162 Inferi Attack .15 .40
❑ 163 Reaching for His Wand .15 .40
❑ 164 Trapped Under Water .15 .40
❑ 165 Pulled into the Depths .15 .40
❑ 166 Screaming in Agony .15 .40
❑ 167 An Inferno .15 .40
❑ 168 Rising to the Challenge .15 .40
❑ 169 Overwhelmed by Heat .15 .40
❑ 170 A Path to Safety .15 .40
❑ 171 Finalizing the Plan .15 .40
❑ 172 Darkness on the Horizon .15 .40
❑ 173 I've Done Things that Would Shock You .15 .40
❑ 174 Keeping Quiet .15 .40
❑ 175 The Dark Mark .15 .40
❑ 176 Leaving Hogwarts .15 .40
❑ 177 Fire at Hagrid's Hut .15 .40
❑ 178 Mourning the Headmaster .15 .40
❑ 179 The Dark Mark .15 .40
❑ 180 Checklist .15 .40

2009 Harry Potter and the Half-Blood Prince Update Autographs
STATED ODDS 1:48
GALLACHER AUTO ONE PER 3 CASE PURCHASE
❑ AB Amelda Brown SP 10.00 25.00
❑ AS Anna Shaffer 12.00 30.00
❑ DL Dave Legeno 12.00 30.00
❑ EG Elarica Gallacher 25.00 50.00
(issued as 3-case incentive)
❑ FD Frank Dillane SP 25.00 50.00
❑ FS Freddie Stroma 10.00 25.00
❑ GL Georgina Leonidas SP 15.00 30.00
❑ HM Helen McCrory SP 40.00 80.00
❑ IL Isabella Laughland 12.00 30.00
❑ JW Julie Walters SP 50.00 100.00
❑ LC Louis Cordice 10.00 25.00
❑ AERE Amber Evans 50.00 100.00
Ruby Evans SP
❑ RGJC Rupert Grint 125.00 250.00
Jessie Cave SP

2009 Harry Potter and the Half-Blood Prince Update Case Incentive Memorabilia
CI1 STATED ODDS ONE PER 2 CASE PURCHASE
CI2 STATED ODDS ONE PER 5 CASE PURCHASE
CI3 STATED ODDS ONE PER 10 CASE PURCHASE
CI4 STATED ODDS ONE PER 25 CASE PURCHASE
❑ CI1 Hermione Granger Shirt 12.00 30.00
❑ CI2 Slytherin Dishes 15.00 40.00
❑ CI3 Luna Lovegood's Glasses 50.00 100.00
❑ CI4 Memory Vial 75.00 150.00

2009 Harry Potter and the Half-Blood Prince Update Case Toppers
COMPLETE SET (3) 20.00 50.00
STATED ODDS ONE PER CASE
❑ CT1 Bellatrix 10.00 25.00
❑ CT2 Ocean 10.00 25.00
❑ CT3 Seamus 10.00 25.00

2009 Harry Potter and the Half-Blood Prince Update Costumes
STATED ODDS 1:24
❑ C1 Harry Potter 10.00 25.00
❑ C2 Ron Weasley 8.00 20.00
❑ C3 Hermione Granger 15.00 40.00
❑ C4 Draco Malfoy 6.00 15.00
❑ C5 Ginny Weasley 8.00 20.00
❑ C6 Harry Potter 10.00 25.00
❑ C7 Luna Lovegood 8.00 20.00
❑ C8 the waitress 8.00 20.00
❑ C9 Harry Potter 10.00 25.00
❑ C10 Hermione Granger 15.00 40.00
❑ C11 Leanne 6.00 15.00
❑ C12 Katie Bell 6.00 15.00
❑ C13 Luna Lovegood 8.00 20.00
❑ C14 Cormac McLaggen 6.00 15.00

2009 Harry Potter and the Half-Blood Prince Update FilmCards
COMPLETE SET (9) 40.00 100.00
STATED ODDS 1:80
❑ CFC1 Seamus 8.00 20.00
❑ CFC2 Quidditch 8.00 20.00
❑ CFC3 Draco 8.00 20.00
❑ CFC4 Aragog 8.00 20.00
❑ CFC5 Harry Potter 8.00 20.00
❑ CFC6 Luna Lovegood 8.00 20.00
❑ CFC7 Hermione,Ron, and Harry 10.00 25.00
❑ CFC8 Harry Potter 8.00 20.00
❑ CFC9 Slughorn 8.00 20.00

2009 Harry Potter and the Half-Blood Prince Update Props
STATED ODDS 1:80
❑ P1 Weasley Wizard Wheezes Hand 10.00 25.00
❑ P2 Slughorn Christmas Party Bottles 25.00 60.00
❑ P3 Ron Weasley Hospital Bed Sheets 20.00 50.00
❑ P4 Slughorn Classroom Bottles 25.00 60.00
❑ P5 Quidditch Flags and Poles 10.00 25.00
❑ P6 Slughorn Christmas Party Table Cloth 10.00 25.00
❑ P7 Slughorn House Pictures 25.00 60.00
❑ P8 Seamus Finnegan Cauldron 20.00 50.00
❑ P9 Potion Mixing Sticks 25.00 60.00
❑ P10 Bellatrix Lestrange Wanted Poster 12.00 30.00
❑ P11 Amycus Carrow Wanted Poster 12.00 30.00
❑ P12 Alecto Carrow Wanted Poster 12.00 30.00

2009 Harry Potter and the Half-Blood Prince Update Puzzle
COMPLETE SET (9) 6.00 15.00
STATED ODDS 5:24
❑ R1 Severus Snape 1.50 4.00
❑ R2 Top Score 1.50 4.00
❑ R3 Harry & Ginny 1.50 4.00
❑ R4 Hogwarts 1.50 4.00
❑ R5 Memories 1.50 4.00
❑ R6 Bezoars 1.50 4.00
❑ R7 Danger at The Burrow 1.50 4.00
❑ R8 Dumbledore 1.50 4.00
❑ R9 Amortentia 1.50 4.00

2009 Harry Potter and the Half-Blood Prince Update Wood Box Toppers
COMPLETE SET (4) 8.00 20.00
STATED ODDS ONE PER BOX
❑ BT1 Severus Snape 3.00 8.00
❑ BT2 Albus Dumbledore 3.00 8.00
❑ BT3 Rubeus Hagrid 3.00 8.00
❑ BT4 Minerva McGonagall 3.00 8.00

2009 Harry Potter Memorable Moments 2
COMPLETE SET (72) 5.00 12.00
❑ 1 Isn't he beautiful .15 .40
❑ 2 Jump .15 .40
❑ 3 Hermione, move .15 .40
❑ 4 Clear as they come, goblins .15 .40
❑ 5 The little tyke fell fer sleep .15 .40
❑ 6 Lucky this plant thing's here, really .15 .40
❑ 7 If I didn't know better, Draco .15 .40
❑ 8 Give me that letter .15 .40
❑ 9 Think you're bein' funny, do ya .15 .40
❑ 10 It is curious that you should be destined .15 .40
❑ 11 Who'd be writing to you .15 .40
❑ 12 Now, when I call your name .15 .40
❑ 13 Troll in the dungeon .15 .40
❑ 14 What do I do with it .15 .40
❑ 15 Is this yours .15 .40
❑ 16 My name is Harry Potter .15 .40
❑ 17 Let me introduce you .15 .40
❑ 18 Not today, Mr. Weasley .15 .40
❑ 19 Five times winner of Witch Weekly's .15 .40
❑ 20 You wish .15 .40
❑ 21 Let's go .15 .40
❑ 22 I strongly recommend caution .15 .40
❑ 23 You'll still have your Potions Master .15 .40
❑ 24 Fera Verto .15 .40
❑ 25 She was found near the library .15 .40
❑ 26 What the devil are you doing up here .15 .40
❑ 27 Rescuing you, of course .15 .40
❑ 28 Fascinating creatures, phoenixes .15 .40
❑ 29 Harry .15 .40
❑ 30 You two shopping for your new dream home.15 .40
❑ 31 Vernon, do something .15 .40
❑ 32 That's the rule, Potter .15 .40
❑ 33 Is it true you fainted .15 .40
❑ 34 Show me .15 .40
❑ 35 Think Neville, think .15 .40
❑ 36 Sirius Black was - and remains to this day .15 .40
❑ 37 Is that my little neph-e-kins .15 .40
❑ 38 You'd have to be in two classes at once .15 .40
❑ 39 My name is Stan Shunpike .15 .40
❑ 40 But what's he got to do with me .15 .40
❑ 41 A remarkable feat, don't you think .15 .40
❑ 42 He bit me .15 .40
❑ 43 Amazing... Amazing .15 .40
❑ 44 Any bets .15 .40
❑ 45 The lovely ladies of the Beauxbatons Academy.15 .40
❑ 46 Uh... Uhm .15 .40
❑ 47 Place your right hand on my waist .15 .40
❑ 48 Blood of the enemy .15 .40
❑ 49 Hogwarts has been chosen .15 .40
❑ 50 Is that a threat .15 .40
❑ 51 Mum sent me a dress .15 .40
❑ 52 C'mon, Potter. What are your strengths .15 .40
❑ 53 Barty Crouch .15 .40
❑ 54 No! No! .15 .40
❑ 55 Ah, but that's why it's so brilliant .15 .40
❑ 56 Hmmmm, hmmmm .15 .40
❑ 57 Rescuing you, of course .15 .40
❑ 58 Hello, Harry Potter .15 .40
❑ 59 To question my practices .15 .40
❑ 60 You're right Harry .15 .40
❑ 61 Those wishing to join the Inquisitorial Squad.15 .40
❑ 62 There's a storm comin', Harry .15 .40
❑ 63 I'm quite proud to be their son .15 .40
❑ 64 Get away from my godson .15 .40
❑ 65 Good - I want to join .15 .40
❑ 66 Reducto .15 .40
❑ 67 Harry - it isn't how you are alike .15 .40
❑ 68 What are you doing .15 .40
❑ 69 Whoaaa .15 .40
❑ 70 I've never used the visitors' entrance before .15 .40
❑ 71 I've gone all summer without a scrap of news.15 .40
❑ 72 Checklist .15 .40

2009 Harry Potter Memorable Moments 2 3-D Case Toppers
COMPLETE SET (3) 30.00 60.00
STATED ODDS ONE PER CASE
❑ CT1 Harry Potter 15.00 30.00
Hedwig
❑ CT2 Draco Malfoy 15.00 30.00
Dark Mark
❑ CT3 Dragon 15.00 30.00
Harry Potter

2009 Harry Potter Memorable Moments 2 Autographs
OVERALL AUTO ODDS 1:48
❑ 1 Apple Brook 8.00 20.00
❑ 2 Richard Leaf R 8.00 20.00
❑ 3 Robert Jarvis 15.00 30.00
❑ 4 Ryan Nelson 8.00 20.00
❑ 5 Tolga Safer 8.00 20.00
❑ 6 Verne Troyer R 20.00 50.00

2009 Harry Potter Memorable Moments 2 Autographs Dual
OVERALL AUTO ODDS 1:48
❑ 1 Daniel Radcliffe 350.00 500.00
Gary Oldman UR
❑ 2 Henry Lloyd-Hughes 40.00 80.00
Clemence Poesy UR
❑ 3 Jason Isaacs 100.00 200.00
Tom Felton UR
❑ 4 Pedja Bjelac 30.00 60.00
Stanislav Ianevski R

2009 Harry Potter Memorable Moments 2 Case Incentive Memorabilia
❑ CI1 Sleeping Bags 20.00 40.00
Hospital Wing Sheets/380/(issued as 2-case incentive)
❑ CI2 Harry Potter 30.00 60.00
Lord Voldemort/200/(issued as 5-case incentive)
❑ CI3 Ron Weasley 40.00 80.00
Neville Longbottom/140/(issued as 10-case incentive)
❑ CI4 Hermione Granger 50.00 100.00
Professor Remus/104/(issued as 25-case incentive)

2009 Harry Potter Memorable Moments 2 Costumes
STATED ODDS 1:30
❑ C1 Ginny Weasley/670 10.00 25.00
❑ C2 Professor Gilderoy Lockhart/570 8.00 20.00
❑ C3 Ron Weasley/500 10.00 25.00
❑ C4 Uncle Vernon Dursley/600 8.00 20.00
❑ C5 Aunt Petunia/700 8.00 20.00
❑ C6 Dudley Dursley/590 10.00 25.00
❑ C7 Harry Potter 20.00 40.00
Oliver Wood/430
❑ C8 Hermione Granger 25.00 50.00
Harry Potter/350
❑ C9 Hermione Granger 25.00 50.00
Cho Chang/290
❑ C10 Fleur Delacour/470 10.00 25.00
❑ C11 Ron Weasley 20.00 40.00
Ginny Weasley/300
❑ C12 Hermione Granger 30.00 60.00
Ginny Weasley/250

2009 Harry Potter Memorable Moments 2 Dumbledore's Army Box Toppers
COMPLETE SET (5) 10.00 25.00
STATED ODDS ONE PER BOX
❑ BT1 Harry Potter 3.00 8.00
❑ BT2 Harry Potter 3.00 8.00
❑ BT3 Harry Potter 3.00 8.00
❑ BT4 Harry Potter 3.00 8.00
❑ BT5 Dumbledore's Army 3.00 8.00

2009 Harry Potter Memorable Moments 2 Etched Binder Case Incentive
COMPLETE SET (2) 12.00 30.00
❑ BC1 Fluffy 8.00 20.00
❑ BC2 Aragog 8.00 20.00

2009 Harry Potter Memorable Moments 2 Foil Puzzle
COMPLETE SET (9) 6.00 15.00
STATED ODDS 5:24
❑ PZ1 Dumbledore's Army 1.25 3.00
❑ PZ2 Harry Potter 1.25 3.00
❑ PZ3 Harry Potter 1.25 3.00
❑ PZ4 Hermione Granger 1.25 3.00
❑ PZ5 Hermione Granger 1.25 3.00
❑ PZ6 Ron Weasley 1.25 3.00
❑ PZ7 Luna Lovegood 1.25 3.00
❑ PZ8 Ginny Weasley 1.25 3.00
❑ PZ9 Neville Longbottom 1.25 3.00

2009 Harry Potter Memorable Moments 2 Promos
❑ P1 The Golden Snitch 1.00 2.50
❑ P2 Duelling Club 1.00 2.50
❑ P3 The Monster Book of Monsters 1.00 2.50
❑ P4 Riddle Graveyard (Binder Exclusive) 1.50 4.00
❑ P5 Walkway (Binder Exclusive) 1.50 4.00

2009 Harry Potter Memorable Moments 2 Props
STATED ODDS 1:80
❑ P1 Hedwig's Perch/100
❑ P2 Ron's Compass/90
❑ P3 Devil's Snare and Fluffy's Fur/260
❑ P4 Mandrake and Fawkes's Feather/260
❑ P5 Buckbeak's Feathers and Chain/150
❑ P6 Honeydukes Candy Wrappers and Bags/100
❑ P7 Quidditch World Cup Irish and Bulgarian Flags/150
❑ P8 Yule Ball Drapes and Programs/400
❑ P9 Defense Against the Dark Arts Books/190
❑ P10 Dolores Umbridge's Reports and Stationery/280
❑ P11 Proclamation Frame Wood and Glass/270
❑ P12 First Task Tent and Canopy Material/410

2009 James Bond Archives
COMPLETE SET (66) 6.00 15.00
HOBBY BOX (24) 40.00 80.00
❑ 1 James Bond .15 .40
❑ 2 Honey Ryder .15 .40
❑ 3 Dr. No .15 .40
❑ 4 Tatiana Romanova .15 .40
❑ 5 James Bond .15 .40
❑ 6 Kerim Bey .15 .40
❑ 7 James Bond .15 .40
❑ 8 Jill Masterson .15 .40
❑ 9 Pussy Galore .15 .40
❑ 10 Emilio Largo .15 .40
❑ 11 Domino Derval .15 .40
❑ 12 Fiona Volpe .15 .40
❑ 13 James Bond .15 .40
❑ 14 Ernst Stavro Blofeld .15 .40
❑ 15 Kissy Suzuki .15 .40
❑ 16 Tracy Di Vicenzo .15 .40
❑ 17 Ersnt Stavro Blofeld .15 .40
❑ 18 James Bond .15 .40
❑ 19 Ernst Stavro Blofeld .15 .40
❑ 20 James Bond .15 .40
❑ 21 Tiffany Case .15 .40
❑ 22 James Bond .15 .40
❑ 23 Solitaire .15 .40
❑ 24 Sheriff J.W. Pepper .15 .40
❑ 25 Francisco Scaramanga .15 .40
❑ 26 Mary Goodnight .15 .40
❑ 27 James Bond .15 .40
❑ 28 Anya Amasova .15 .40
❑ 29 Jaws .15 .40
❑ 30 James Bond .15 .40
❑ 31 Jaws .15 .40
❑ 32 Holly Goodhead .15 .40
❑ 33 James Bond .15 .40
❑ 34 Melina Havelock .15 .40
❑ 35 James Bond .15 .40
❑ 36 Emile Locque .15 .40
❑ 37 Kamal Khan .15 .40
❑ 38 Octopussy .15 .40
❑ 39 James Bond .15 .40
❑ 40 James Bond .15 .40
❑ 41 May Day .15 .40
❑ 42 Max Zorin .15 .40
❑ 43 James Bond .15 .40
❑ 44 General Koskov .15 .40
❑ 45 Kara Milovy .15 .40
❑ 46 James Bond .15 .40
❑ 47 Pam Bouvier .15 .40
❑ 48 Franz Sanchez .15 .40
❑ 49 Alec Trevelyan .15 .40
❑ 50 James Bond .15 .40
❑ 51 Xenia Onatopp .15 .40
❑ 52 Elliot Carver .15 .40
❑ 53 James Bond .15 .40
❑ 54 Wai Lin .15 .40
❑ 55 Christmas Jones .15 .40
❑ 56 Elektra King .15 .40
❑ 57 James Bond .15 .40
❑ 58 Miranda Frost .15 .40
❑ 59 Jinx .15 .40
❑ 60 James Bond .15 .40
❑ 61 James Bond .15 .40
❑ 62 Le Chiffre .15 .40
❑ 63 Vesper Lynd .15 .40
❑ 64 Camille .15 .40
❑ 65 James Bond .15 .40
❑ 66 Mr. Greene .15 .40

2009 James Bond Archives Autographs
STATED ODDS 1:12
DENCH AUTO STATED ODDS ONE PER 3 CASE PURCHASE
JANSSEN WOJB AUTO STATED ODDS ONE PER 6 CASE PURCHASE
RHYS-DAVIES AUTO STATED ODDS ONE PER 15 CASE PURCHASE
❑ A91 Stefan Kalipha 6.00 15.00
❑ A109 Tom Chadbon 6.00 15.00
❑ A122 Neil Jackson 6.00 15.00
❑ A126 Paul Brooke 6.00 15.00
❑ A128 Tobias Menzies 6.00 15.00
❑ A129 Christina Cole 12.00 30.00
❑ CB Caroline Bliss 40.00 80.00
❑ CC Christina Cole 12.00 30.00
❑ FJ1 Famke Janssen 100.00 200.00
❑ HB Honor Blackman 100.00 200.00
❑ JT John Terry 25.00 50.00
❑ NJ Neil Jackson 8.00 20.00
❑ PB2 Priscilla Barnes 15.00 40.00
❑ SB Samantha Bond 10.00 25.00
❑ JD Judi Dench (Full Bleed) 50.00 100.00
❑ CD Carmen Du Sautoy 25.00 50.00
❑ CT2 Chaim Topol 50.00 100.00
❑ EG Eunice Gayson 12.00 30.00
❑ GF Glenn Foster 8.00 20.00
❑ JC John Cleese 75.00 150.00
❑ ML Marguerite Lewars 25.00 50.00
❑ PR Paul Ritter 6.00 15.00
❑ RK Rory Kinnear 6.00 15.00
❑ WN Wayne Newton 50.00 100.00
❑ BA Belle Avery 30.00 60.00
❑ CT1 Cecilie Thomsen 30.00 60.00
❑ DH David Hedison 10.00 25.00
❑ GL George Lazenby 60.00 120.00
❑ JB Joe Don Baker 75.00 150.00
❑ MN Margaret Nolan 25.00 50.00
❑ PB1 Paul Brooke 6.00 15.00
❑ RM Roger Moore 125.00 225.00
❑ TM Tobias Menzies 8.00 20.00
❑ JR John Rhys-Davies
❑ CM Caterina Murino 30.00 60.00
❑ CB Crispin Bonham-Carter 6.00 15.00
❑ GH Geoffrey Holder 50.00 100.00
❑ IS Izabella Scorupco 50.00 100.00
❑ MM Mads Mikkelsen 75.00 150.00
❑ OK Olga Kurylenko 125.00 200.00
❑ RC Robert Carlyle 30.00 60.00
❑ SK Stefan Kalipha 6.00 15.00
❑ FJ2 Famke Janssen (Women of James Bond)200.00 300.00

2009 James Bond Archives Promos
COMPLETE SET (3) 10.00 25.00
❑ P1 James Bond 2.00 5.00
General Distribution
❑ P2 Camille 10.00 25.00
Non-Sport Update Magazine
❑ P3 Strawberry Fields 2.00 5.00
Album Exclusive

2009 James Bond Archives Quantum of Solace Dangerous Liaisons
COMPLETE SET (9) 8.00 20.00
STATED ODDS 1:12
❑ DL10 Camille 2.00 5.00
James Bond
❑ DL11 M 2.00 5.00
Mr. White/James Bond
❑ DL12 Mr. Greene 2.00 5.00
Elvis
❑ DL13 Medrano 2.00 5.00
Camille
❑ DL14 James Bond 2.00 5.00
Mathis
❑ DL15 Medrano 2.00 5.00
Mr. Greene
❑ DL16 James Bond 2.00 5.00
Agent Fields
❑ DL17 James Bond 2.00 5.00
Camille
❑ DL18 Felix Leiter 2.00 5.00
James Bond

2009 James Bond Archives Quantum of Solace Expansion
COMPLETE SET (9) 8.00 20.00
STATED ODDS 1:12
❑ 67 Quantum of Solace 2.00 5.00
❑ 68 Quantum of Solace 2.00 5.00
❑ 69 Quantum of Solace 2.00 5.00
❑ F64 General Medrano 2.00 5.00
❑ F65 Mitchell 2.00 5.00
❑ F66 Guy Haines 2.00 5.00
❑ F67 Yusef 2.00 5.00
❑ BA34 Tanner 2.00 5.00
❑ BE22 Bond Extras 2.00 5.00

2009 James Bond Archives Relics
COMPLETE SET (27) 200.00 300.00
STATED ODDS 1:12
AMR1 STATED ODDS ONE PER CASE
❑ QC1 Camille Camisole 15.00 40.00
Skirt
❑ QC2 James Bond & Camille Jacket 10.00 25.00
Dress
❑ QC3 James Bond Jacket 20.00 40.00
Tie
❑ QC4 Camille Dress 8.00 20.00
❑ QC5 Camille Tank Top 20.00 40.00
Blouse/Pants
❑ QC6 General Medrano Jacket 6.00 15.00
❑ QC7 Mr. Greene Shirt 6.00 15.00
Pants
❑ QC8 General Medrano & Mr. Greene Jacket 6.00 15.00
Shirt
❑ QC9 Mathis Shirt 8.00 20.00
Jacket/Pants
❑ QC10 Mathis & James Bond Jacket 6.00 15.00
Jacket
❑ QC11 Mr. White Shirt 6.00 15.00
Jacket/Pants
❑ QC12 James Bond Shirt 8.00 20.00
Jacket/Pants
❑ QC13 Mr. White & James Bond Jacket 6.00 15.00
Pants
❑ QC14 Mitchell Shirt 10.00 25.00
Tie
❑ QC15 James Bond & Mitchell Pants 6.00 15.00
Jacket
❑ QC16 Elvis Shirt 6.00 15.00
Jacket/Pants
❑ QC17 James Bond Jacket 6.00 15.00
Pants
❑ QC18 James Bond Shirt 6.00 15.00
Jacket
❑ QC19 James Bond Pants 8.00 20.00
❑ QC20 James Bond Jacket 6.00 15.00
❑ QC21 James Bond Shirt 8.00 20.00
Jeans
❑ QC22 James Bond Shirt 8.00 20.00
Pants
❑ QC23 James Bond Jacket 6.00 15.00
❑ QC24 James Bond Shirt 10.00 25.00
❑ QC25 James Bond Tie 50.00 100.00
❑ QC26 Greene's Driver Jacket 6.00 15.00
❑ QC27 James Bond & Camille Jkt 30.00 60.00
Pnts/Cmsl/Skrt
❑ AMR1 Aston Martin Windshield 30.00 60.00

2009 James Bond Archives The Complete James Bond 007 Expansion
COMPLETE SET (9) 8.00 20.00
STATED ODDS 1:12
❑ 190 Quantum of Solace - James Bond 2.00 5.00
❑ 191 Quantum of Solace - James Bond 2.00 5.00
❑ 192 Quantum of Solace - James Bond 2.00 5.00
❑ 193 Quantum of Solace - Mr. Greene 2.00 5.00
❑ 194 Quantum of Solace - Quantum 2.00 5.00
of Solace Movie Poster
❑ 195 Quantum of Solace - General Madrano 2.00 5.00
❑ 196 Quantum of Solace - Agent Fields 2.00 5.00
❑ 197 Quantum of Solace - Camille 2.00 5.00
❑ 198 Quantum of Solace - Camille 2.00 5.00

2009 James Bond Archives The Quotable Quantum of Solace
COMPLETE SET (8) 8.00 20.00
STATED ODDS 1:14
❑ Q7 M 2.00 5.00
Mr. White/James Bond
❑ Q8 M 2.00 5.00
James Bond
❑ Q9 M 2.00 5.00
❑ Q10 Mathis 2.00 5.00
❑ Q11 James Bond 2.00 5.00
Agent Fields
❑ Q12 James Bond 2.00 5.00
Agent Fields
❑ Q13 James Bond 2.00 5.00
Camille
❑ Q14 James Bond 2.00 5.00

2009 Justice League of America Archives
COMPLETE SET (72) 5.00 12.00
ANDERSON AUTO INSERTED ONE PER CASE
❑ 1 Brave and The Bold #28 .15 .40
❑ 2 Brave and The Bold #29 .15 .40
❑ 3 Brave and The Bold #30 .15 .40
❑ 4 Justice League of America #1 .15 .40
❑ 5 Justice League of America #2 .15 .40
❑ 6 Justice League of America #3 .15 .40
❑ 7 Justice League of America #4 .15 .40
❑ 8 Justice League of America #5 .15 .40
❑ 9 Justice League of America #6 .15 .40
❑ 10 Justice League of America #7 .15 .40
❑ 11 Justice League of America #8 .15 .40
❑ 12 Justice League of America #9 .15 .40
❑ 13 Justice League of America #10 .15 .40
❑ 14 Justice League of America #11 .15 .40
❑ 15 Justice League of America #12 .15 .40
❑ 16 Justice League of America #13 .15 .40
❑ 17 Justice League of America #14 .15 .40
❑ 18 Justice League of America #15 .15 .40
❑ 19 Justice League of America #16 .15 .40
❑ 20 Justice League of America #17 .15 .40
❑ 21 Justice League of America #18 .15 .40
❑ 22 Justice League of America #19 .15 .40
❑ 23 Justice League of America #20 .15 .40
❑ 24 Justice League of America #21 .15 .40
❑ 25 Justice League of America #22 .15 .40
❑ 26 Justice League of America #23 .15 .40
❑ 27 Justice League of America #24 .15 .40
❑ 28 Justice League of America #25 .15 .40
❑ 29 Justice League of America #26 .15 .40
❑ 30 Justice League of America #27 .15 .40
❑ 31 Justice League of America #28 .15 .40
❑ 32 Justice League of America #29 .15 .40
❑ 33 Justice League of America #30 .15 .40
❑ 34 Justice League of America #31 .15 .40
❑ 35 Justice League of America #32 .15 .40
❑ 36 Justice League of America #33 .15 .40
❑ 37 Justice League of America #34 .15 .40
❑ 38 Justice League of America #35 .15 .40
❑ 39 Justice League of America #36 .15 .40
❑ 40 Justice League of America #37 .15 .40
❑ 41 Justice League of America #38 .15 .40
❑ 42 Justice League of America #40 .15 .40
❑ 43 Justice League of America #41 .15 .40
❑ 44 Justice League of America #42 .15 .40
❑ 45 Justice League of America #43 .15 .40
❑ 46 Justice League of America #44 .15 .40
❑ 47 Justice League of America #45 .15 .40
❑ 48 Justice League of America #46 .15 .40
❑ 49 Justice League of America #47 .15 .40
❑ 50 Justice League of America #49 .15 .40
❑ 51 Justice League of America #50 .15 .40
❑ 52 Justice League of America #51 .15 .40
❑ 53 Justice League of America #52 .15 .40
❑ 54 Justice League of America #53 .15 .40
❑ 55 Justice League of America #54 .15 .40
❑ 56 Justice League of America #55 .15 .40
❑ 57 Justice League of America #56 .15 .40
❑ 58 Justice League of America #57 .15 .40
❑ 59 Justice League of America #59 .15 .40
❑ 60 Justice League of America #60 .15 .40
❑ 61 Justice League of America #61 .15 .40
❑ 62 Justice League of America #62 .15 .40
❑ 63 Justice League of America #63 .15 .40
❑ 64 Justice League of America #64 .15 .40
❑ 65 Justice League of America #65 .15 .40
❑ 66 Justice League of America #66 .15 .40
❑ 67 Justice League of America #68 .15 .40
❑ 68 Justice League of America #69 .15 .40
❑ 69 Justice League of America #70 .15 .40
❑ 70 Justice League of America #71 .15 .40
❑ 71 Justice League of America #72 .15 .40
❑ 72 Justice League of America #73 .15 .40
❑ MA Murphy Anderson AU 15.00 30.00
❑ P1 Green Lantern/Flash .75 2.00
Aquaman/Wonder Woman PROMO

2009 Justice League of America Archives Founding Members
COMPLETE SET (7) 15.00 40.00
STATED ODDS 1:24
❑ FM1 Superman 3.00 8.00
❑ FM2 Batman 3.00 8.00
❑ FM3 Wonder Woman 3.00 8.00
❑ FM4 Flash 3.00 8.00
❑ FM5 Green Lantern 3.00 8.00
❑ FM6 Aquaman 3.00 8.00
❑ FM7 Martian Manhunter 3.00 8.00

2009 Justice League of America Archives Other Earths

COMPLETE SET (6) 4.00 10.00
STATED ODDS 1:12

❑ OE1 Ultraman 1.25 3.00
❑ OE2 Owlman 1.25 3.00
❑ OE3 Super Woman 1.25 3.00
❑ OE4 Johnny Quick 1.25 3.00
❑ OE5 Power Ring 1.25 3.00
❑ OE6 Adult Robin 1.25 3.00

2009 Justice League of America Archives Super Friends

COMPLETE SET (18) 12.50 30.00
STATED ODDS 1:8

❑ SF1 Superman 1.00 2.50
❑ SF2 Batman 1.00 2.50
❑ SF3 Robin 1.00 2.50
❑ SF4 Wonder Woman 1.00 2.50
❑ SF5 Aquaman 1.00 2.50
❑ SF6 Wonder Twins 1.00 2.50
❑ SF7 Gleek 1.00 2.50
❑ SF8 Green Lantern 1.00 2.50
❑ SF9 Hawkman 1.00 2.50
❑ SF10 The Flash 1.00 2.50
❑ SF11 Apache Chief 1.00 2.50
❑ SF12 Black Vulcan 1.00 2.50
❑ SF13 Samurai 1.00 2.50
❑ SF14 Lex Luthor 1.00 2.50
❑ SF15 Bizarro 1.00 2.50
❑ SF16 Cheetah, Giganta and Gorilla Grodd 1.00 2.50
❑ SF17 The Riddler, The Scarecrow and Toyman 1.00 2.50
❑ SF18 Captain Cold, Manta and Sinestro 1.00 2.50

2009 KISS 360

COMPLETE SET (90) 12.00 30.00

❑ 1 Lick It Up .15 .40
❑ 2 Heaven's On Fire .15 .40
❑ 3 Tears Are Falling .15 .40
❑ 4 Crazy Crazy Nights .15 .40
❑ 5 Unholy .15 .40
❑ 6 Take It Off .15 .40
❑ 7 Spit .15 .40
❑ 8 God Gave Rock And Roll To You II .15 .40
❑ 9 Domino .15 .40
❑ 10 Legacy .15 .40
❑ 11 Here And Now .15 .40
❑ 12 Fan-Routed Tour .15 .40
❑ 13 The Fans .15 .40
❑ 14 Chemistry .15 .40
❑ 15 The Band .15 .40
❑ 16 New Album .15 .40
❑ 17 Roots .15 .40
❑ 18 Songwriting .15 .40
❑ 19 Soundchecks .15 .40
❑ 20 The Venue .15 .40
❑ 21 Superman .15 .40
❑ 22 Calm Before the Storm .15 .40
❑ 23 Quiet Time .15 .40
❑ 24 Warm Up .15 .40
❑ 25 Makeup .15 .40
❑ 26 Space Ace .15 .40
❑ 27 God of Thunder .15 .40
❑ 28 Strapped In .15 .40
❑ 29 In the Dressing Room .15 .40
❑ 30 The Quiet One .15 .40
❑ 31 Amped Up .15 .40
❑ 32 Routine .15 .40
❑ 33 Fan Connection .15 .40
❑ 34 Meet and Greet .15 .40
❑ 35 Daily Grind .15 .40
❑ 36 Down Time .15 .40
❑ 37 Fan Appreciation .15 .40
❑ 38 Substance .15 .40
❑ 39 Stubbornness .15 .40
❑ 40 Four-Wheel Drive .15 .40
❑ 41 That's a KISS Song .15 .40
❑ 42 Listen to No One .15 .40
❑ 43 Blood Spitting .15 .40
❑ 44 Home .15 .40
❑ 45 Failure Is Not An Option .15 .40
❑ 46 No Doubt .15 .40
❑ 47 Melody .15 .40
❑ 48 Merry Christmas .15 .40
❑ 49 KISS Is Life .15 .40
❑ 50 Obstacles .15 .40
❑ 51 Playing Live .15 .40
❑ 52 110 Percent .15 .40
❑ 53 Be Proud .15 .40
❑ 54 Priceless .15 .40
❑ 55 Hotel Fishing .15 .40
❑ 56 Locked Up .15 .40
❑ 57 Shocker .15 .40
❑ 58 Drag Queens .15 .40
❑ 59 Bow Hunting .15 .40
❑ 60 Scrambled Eggs .15 .40
❑ 61 Road Warriors .15 .40
❑ 62 Under the Covers .15 .40
❑ 63 Wrecking Crew .15 .40
❑ 64 Pants on Fire .15 .40
❑ 65 Shrimp Toss .15 .40
❑ 66 Crazy Cats .15 .40
❑ 67 Star Struck .15 .40
❑ 68 A New Generation .15 .40
❑ 69 Dream Come True .15 .40
❑ 70 Move Music .15 .40
❑ 71 Fan Mail .15 .40
❑ 72 Worldwide Phenomenon .15 .40
❑ 73 KISS .15 .40
❑ 74 Hotter Than Hell .15 .40
❑ 75 Dressed to Kill .15 .40
❑ 76 Alive .15 .40
❑ 77 Destroyer .15 .40
❑ 78 Rock and Roll Over .15 .40
❑ 79 Love Gun .15 .40
❑ 80 Alive II .15 .40
❑ 81 Dynasty .15 .40
❑ 82 Unmasked .15 .40
❑ 83 Creatures of the Night .15 .40
❑ 84 Lick It Up .15 .40
❑ 85 Animalize .15 .40
❑ 86 Asylum .15 .40
❑ 87 Crazy Nights .15 .40
❑ 88 Hot in the Shade .15 .40
❑ 89 Revenge .15 .40
❑ 90 Psycho Circus .15 .40

2009 KISS 360 Blood-Spitting

COMPLETE SET (90) 150.00 300.00
*BLOOD-SPITTING: 8X TO 20X BASIC CARDS
STATED ODDS 1:4

2009 KISS 360 Blue KISS

COMPLETE SET (90) 5.00 12.00
COMP.BOX SET 20.00 30.00
*BLUE: .3X TO .8X BASIC CARDS

2009 KISS 360 $

*$/50: 30X TO 80X BASIC CARDS
STATED ODDS 1:24 HOBBY
PRINT RUN 50 SER. #'d SETS

2009 KISS 360 Dr Love

*DR.LOVE: 20X TO 50X BASIC CARDS
STATED PRINT RUN 50 SER. #'d SETS
ONLY AVAILABLE IN WALMART PACKS

2009 KISS 360 Kissed

COMPLETE SET (90)
*KISSED/25: 50X TO 120X BASIC CARDS
STATED PRINT RUN 25 SER. #'d SETS
ONLY AVAILABLE IN TARGET PACKS

2009 KISS 360 Printing Plates Black Back

STATED PRINT RUN 1 SER. #'d SET
NO PRICING DUE TO SCARCITY

2009 KISS 360 Printing Plates Black Front

STATED PRINT RUN 1 SER. #'d SET
NO PRICING DUE TO SCARCITY

2009 KISS 360 Printing Plates Cyan Back

STATED PRINT RUN 1 SER. #'d SET
NO PRICING DUE TO SCARCITY

2009 KISS 360 Printing Plates Cyan Front

STATED PRINT RUN 1 SER. #'d SET
NO PRICING DUE TO SCARCITY

2009 KISS 360 Printing Plates Magenta Back

STATED PRINT RUN 1 SER. #'d SET
NO PRICING DUE TO SCARCITY

2009 KISS 360 Printing Plates Magenta Front

STATED PRINT RUN 1 SER. #'d SET
NO PRICING DUE TO SCARCITY

2009 KISS 360 Printing Plates Yellow Back

STATED PRINT RUN 1 SER. #'d SET
NO PRICING DUE TO SCARCITY

2009 KISS 360 Printing Plates Yellow Front

STATED PRINT RUN 1 SER. #'d SET
NO PRICING DUE TO SCARCITY

2009 KISS 360 KISSignatures

STATED PRINT RUN 99 SER. #'d SETS
QUAD AUTO STATED PRINT RUN 5 SER. #'d SETS
QUAD AUTO UNPRICED DUE TO SCARCITY

❑ AF Ace Frehley 150.00 250.00
❑ GS Gene Simmons 200.00 300.00
❑ PC Peter Criss 150.00 250.00
❑ PS Paul Stanley 175.00 300.00
❑ KISS Paul Stanley
Gene Simmons/Ace Frehley/Peter Criss/5

2009 KISS 360 Rock Star Relics

STATED ODDS 1:90

❑ EC Eric Carr Drumheads 50.00 120.00
❑ GS1 Gene Simmons Pants 20.00 50.00
❑ PS1 Paul Stanley Vest 25.00 60.00
❑ PS2 Paul Stanley Vest 25.00 60.00
❑ PS3 Paul Stanley Jumpsuit 25.00 60.00
❑ GSPS Gene Simmons Pants 50.00 120.00
Paul Stanley Jumpsuit

2009 KISS 360 Rock Star Relics Silver Foil

STATED PRINT RUN 99 SER. #'d SETS

❑ EC Eric Carr Drumheads/50 60.00 150.00
❑ GS1 Gene Simmons Pants 25.00 60.00
❑ PS1 Paul Stanley Vest 30.00 75.00
❑ PS2 Paul Stanley Vest 30.00 75.00
❑ PS3 Paul Stanley Jumpsuit 30.00 75.00
❑ GSPS Gene Simmons Pants 60.00 150.00
Paul Stanley Jumpsuit

2009 KISS 360 Rock Star Relics Red Foil

STATED PRINT RUN 5-25 SER. #'d SETS
SERIAL #'d UNDER 25 NOT PRICED

❑ EC Eric Carr Drumheads/5
❑ GS1 Gene Simmons Pants 60.00 150.00
❑ PS1 Paul Stanley Vest 75.00 175.00
❑ PS2 Paul Stanley Vest 75.00 175.00
❑ PS3 Paul Stanley Jumpsuit 75.00 175.00
❑ GSPS Gene Simmons Pants/10
Paul Stanley Jumpsuit

2009 KISS 360 Snapshots

COMPLETE SET (12) 12.00 30.00
STATED ODDS 1:6

❑ SS1 London, 1976 1.25 3.00
❑ SS2 Calgary, Alberta, CA 1977 1.25 3.00
❑ SS3 Hempstead, NY, 1975 1.25 3.00
❑ SS4 San Francisco, CA 1975 1.25 3.00
❑ SS5 MSG, NY, 1979 1.25 3.00
❑ SS6 Cadillac, MI, 1975 1.25 3.00
❑ SS7 Terre Haute, IN, 1975 1.25 3.00
❑ SS8 Texas, 1976 1.25 3.00
❑ SS9 Miami, FL, 1999 1.25 3.00
❑ SS10 Gene & Nick, 1988 1.25 3.00
❑ SS11 Hartford, CT, 1977 1.25 3.00
❑ SS12 American Idol, 2009 1.25 3.00

2009 KISS 360 Transformations

COMPLETE SET (6) 12.00 30.00
STATED ODDS 1:12

❑ TF1 Gene Simmons 2.50 6.00
Demon
❑ TF2 Paul Stanley 2.50 6.00
Starchild
❑ TF3 Ace Frehley 2.50 6.00
Spaceman
❑ TF4 Peter Criss 2.50 6.00
Catman
❑ TF5 Tommy Thayer 2.50 6.00
Spaceman
❑ TF6 Eric Singer 2.50 6.00
Catman

2009 KISS Ikons

COMPLETE SET (90) 8.00 20.00
INSTANT WIN CARDS TOTAL PRINT RUN OF 100
UNPRICED PRINT PLATE PRINT RUN 1

❑ 1 23rd Street Loft .15 .40
❑ 2 Ace Joins KISS .15 .40
❑ 3 Coining the Name .15 .40
❑ 4 Ikons .15 .40
❑ 5 Early Image .15 .40
❑ 6 Ambition .15 .40
❑ 7 Motivation .15 .40
❑ 8 Breathing Fire .15 .40
❑ 9 Getting Signed .15 .40
❑ 10 First KISS Album .15 .40
❑ 11 First KISS Album .15 .40
❑ 12 Strutter .15 .40
❑ 13 Nothin' to Lose .15 .40
❑ 14 Firehouse .15 .40
❑ 15 Cold Gin .15 .40
❑ 16 Let Me Know .15 .40
❑ 17 Deuce .15 .40
❑ 18 Love Theme From KISS .15 .40
❑ 19 100,000 Years .15 .40
❑ 20 Black Diamond .15 .40
❑ 21 Kissin' Time .15 .40
❑ 22 Dressed to Kill (Gene) .15 .40
❑ 23 Rock and Roll Over (Paul) .15 .40
❑ 24 Alive! .15 .40
❑ 25 Destroyer .15 .40
❑ 26 Rock and Roll Over (Gene) .15 .40
❑ 27 Love Gun .15 .40
❑ 28 Alive II (Ace and Paul) .15 .40
❑ 29 Dynasty .15 .40
❑ 30 Unmasked .15 .40
❑ 31 The Elder (Gene) .15 .40
❑ 32 Alive II (Paul) .15 .40
❑ 33 The Elder (Paul) .15 .40
❑ 34 Hotter Than Hell .15 .40
❑ 35 Watchin' You .15 .40
❑ 36 Strange Ways .15 .40
❑ 37 C'mon and Love Me .15 .40
❑ 38 Rock and Roll All Nite .15 .40
❑ 39 Detroit Rock City .15 .40
❑ 40 King of the Night Time World .15 .40
❑ 41 God of Thunder .15 .40
❑ 42 Shout It Out Loud .15 .40
❑ 43 Do You Love Me? .15 .40
❑ 44 I Want You .15 .40
❑ 45 Love 'Em and Leave 'Em .15 .40
❑ 46 Hard Luck Woman .15 .40
❑ 47 Christine Sixteen .15 .40
❑ 48 I Stole Your Love .15 .40
❑ 49 Shock Me .15 .40
❑ 50 Plaster Caster .15 .40
❑ 51 Love Gun .15 .40
❑ 52 Rocket Ride .15 .40
❑ 53 I Was Made For Lovin' You .15 .40
❑ 54 Sure Know Something .15 .40
❑ 55 A World Without Heroes .15 .40
❑ 56 I .15 .40
❑ 57 Creatures of the Night .15 .40
❑ 58 I Love It Loud .15 .40
❑ 59 Makin' Love .15 .40
❑ 60 Psycho Circus .15 .40
❑ 61 Academy of Music Show NYE 1973-74 .15 .40
❑ 62 Japan Tour 1977 .15 .40
❑ 63 Marvel Comics 1977 .15 .40
❑ 64 Cadillac, Michigan 1975 .15 .40
❑ 65 MTV Unplugged 1995 .15 .40
❑ 66 KISS With the Melbourne Symphony 2003 .15 .40
❑ 67 Keeping It Real .15 .40
❑ 68 Playing Live .15 .40
❑ 69 Putting It on the Line .15 .40
❑ 70 Performing .15 .40
❑ 71 KISS Motto .15 .40
❑ 72 Fans .15 .40
❑ 73 Timeless .15 .40
❑ 74 Chemistry .15 .40
❑ 75 Dreams .15 .40
❑ 76 Rite of Passage .15 .40
❑ 77 Attitude .15 .40
❑ 78 Legacy .15 .40
❑ 79 Roger Daltrey .15 .40
❑ 80 John Entwistle .15 .40
❑ 81 Bob Seger .15 .40
❑ 82 Paul Rodgers .15 .40
❑ 83 Joe Perry .15 .40
❑ 84 Lenny Kravitz .15 .40
❑ 85 Nikki Sixx .15 .40
❑ 86 Ted Nugent .15 .40
❑ 87 Peter Frampton .15 .40
❑ 88 Rick Nielsen .15 .40
❑ 89 James Young .15 .40
❑ 90 Kevin Bacon .15 .40
❑ NNO Instant Winner Autograph Paul EXCH 150.00 250.00
❑ NNO Instant Winner Autograph Gene EXCH 150.00 250.00

2009 KISS Ikons Blood-Spitting

COMPLETE SET (90) 150.00 300.00
*BLOOD-SPITTING: 8X TO 20X BASE
STATED ODDS 1:4

2009 KISS Ikons Blue KISS

COMPLETE SET (90) 5.00 12.00

2009 KISS Ikons Fire-Breathing

*FIRE-BREATHING: 40X TO 100X BASE
STATED ODDS 1:20 HOBBY
STATED PRINT RUN 50 SER. #'d SETS

2009 KISS Ikons Kissed

*KISSED: 40X TO 100X BASE
PRINT RUN 50 SER. #'d SETS
ONLY AVAILABLE IN TARGET PACKS

2009 KISS Ikons Klothes

STATED ODDS 1:96

❑ KK1 Gene Simmons Pants 20.00 40.00
❑ KK2 Gene Simmons Jumpsuit 20.00 40.00

2009 KISS Ikons Klothes Die Cut

K STATED PRINT RUN 249 SER. #'d SETS
I STATED PRINT RUN 149 SER. #'d SETS
S STATED PRINT RUN 99 SER. #'d SETS

❑ KK1i Gene Simmons Pants - I 50.00 100.00
❑ KK1k Gene Simmons Pants - K 40.00 80.00
❑ KK1s Gene Simmons Pants - S 75.00 150.00
❑ KK2i Gene Simmons Jumpsuit - I 50.00 100.00
❑ KK2k Gene Simmons Jumpsuit - K 40.00 80.00
❑ KK2s Gene Simmons Jumpsuit - S 75.00 150.00

2009 KISS Ikons Stickers

COMPLETE SET (12) 3.00 8.00
STATED ODDS 1:2

❑ 1 Head Shots .40 1.00
❑ 2 Standing .40 1.00
❑ 3 Picture Logo .40 1.00
❑ 4 Army Flag Through Planet .40 1.00
❑ 5 Red Background .40 1.00
❑ 6 Dressed To Kill .40 1.00
❑ 7 In Flames .40 1.00
❑ 8 Black and White Portraits .40 1.00
❑ 9 Army Patch .40 1.00
❑ 10 Live in Concert .40 1.00
❑ 11 Concert Poster .40 1.00
❑ 12 Explosion .40 1.00

2009 KISS Ikons Tattoos

COMPLETE SET (18) 5.00 12.00
STATED ODDS 1:4 H, 1:2 R

❑ 1 Love Guns 77 .40 1.00
❑ 2 Hotter Than Hell 74 .40 1.00
❑ 3 Orange KISS Logo .40 1.00
❑ 4 KISS with Individual Logos .40 1.00
❑ 5 KISS Army Coat of Arms .40 1.00
❑ 6 Sunburst .40 1.00
❑ 7 KISS Army Patch .40 1.00
❑ 8 Individual Logos .40 1.00
❑ 9 Sawblade Logo .40 1.00
❑ 10 Silver KISS Logo .40 1.00
❑ 11 Paul Bear .40 1.00
❑ 12 Gene Bear .40 1.00
❑ 13 Ace Bear .40 1.00
❑ 14 Peter Bear .40 1.00
❑ 15 Heart with Banner .40 1.00
❑ 16 Bird with Star .40 1.00
❑ 17 Catfish .40 1.00
❑ 18 Skull .40 1.00

2009 KISS Komplete

❑ KK1 The Demon
❑ KK2 The Starchild
❑ KK3 Spaceman
❑ KK4 The Catman
❑ KK5 The Band

2009 Legends of Star Trek Captain Benjamin Sisko

COMPLETE SET (9) 7.50 20.00

❑ L1 Captain Benjamin Sisko 1.25 3.00
❑ L2 Captain Benjamin Sisko 1.25 3.00
❑ L3 Captain Benjamin Sisko 1.25 3.00
❑ L4 Captain Benjamin Sisko 1.25 3.00
❑ L5 Captain Benjamin Sisko 1.25 3.00
❑ L6 Captain Benjamin Sisko 1.25 3.00
❑ L7 Captain Benjamin Sisko 1.25 3.00
❑ L8 Captain Benjamin Sisko 1.25 3.00
❑ L9 Captain Benjamin Sisko 1.25 3.00

2009 Legends of Star Trek Captain Jonathan Archer

COMPLETE SET (9) 7.50 20.00

❑ L1 Captain Jonathan Archer 1.25 3.00
❑ L2 Captain Jonathan Archer 1.25 3.00
❑ L3 Captain Jonathan Archer 1.25 3.00
❑ L4 Captain Jonathan Archer 1.25 3.00
❑ L5 Captain Jonathan Archer 1.25 3.00
❑ L6 Captain Jonathan Archer 1.25 3.00
❑ L7 Captain Jonathan Archer 1.25 3.00
❑ L8 Captain Jonathan Archer 1.25 3.00
❑ L9 Captain Jonathan Archer 1.25 3.00

2009 Legends of Star Trek Captain Kathryn Janeway

COMPLETE SET (L1-L9) 7.50 20.00

❑ L1 Captain Kathryn Janeway 1.25 3.00
❑ L2 Captain Kathryn Janeway 1.25 3.00
❑ L3 Captain Kathryn Janeway 1.25 3.00
❑ L4 Captain Kathryn Janeway 1.25 3.00
❑ L5 Captain Kathryn Janeway 1.25 3.00
❑ L6 Captain Kathryn Janeway 1.25 3.00
❑ L7 Captain Kathryn Janeway 1.25 3.00
❑ L8 Captain Kathryn Janeway 1.25 3.00
❑ L9 Captain Kathryn Janeway 1.25 3.00

2009 Legends of Star Trek Lt. B'Elaana Torres

COMPLETE SET (9) 7.50 20.00

❑ L1 Lt. B'Elaana Torres 1.25 3.00
❑ L2 Lt. B'Elaana Torres 1.25 3.00
❑ L3 Lt. B'Elaana Torres 1.25 3.00
❑ L4 Lt. B'Elaana Torres 1.25 3.00
❑ L5 Lt. B'Elaana Torres 1.25 3.00
❑ L6 Lt. B'Elaana Torres 1.25 3.00
❑ L7 Lt. B'Elaana Torres 1.25 3.00
❑ L8 Lt. B'Elaana Torres 1.25 3.00
❑ L9 Lt. B'Elaana Torres 1.25 3.00

2009 Legends of Star Trek Lt. Hoshi Sato

COMPLETE SET (9) 7.50 20.00

❑ L1 Lt. Hoshi Sato 1.25 3.00
❑ L2 Lt. Hoshi Sato 1.25 3.00
❑ L3 Lt. Hoshi Sato 1.25 3.00
❑ L4 Lt. Hoshi Sato 1.25 3.00
❑ L5 Lt. Hoshi Sato 1.25 3.00
❑ L6 Lt. Hoshi Sato 1.25 3.00
❑ L7 Lt. Hoshi Sato 1.25 3.00
❑ L8 Lt. Hoshi Sato 1.25 3.00
❑ L9 Lt. Hoshi Sato 1.25 3.00

2009 Legends of Star Trek Quark

COMPLETE SET (9) 7.50 20.00

❑ L1 Quark 1.25 3.00
❑ L2 Quark 1.25 3.00
❑ L3 Quark 1.25 3.00
❑ L4 Quark 1.25 3.00
❑ L5 Quark 1.25 3.00
❑ L6 Quark 1.25 3.00
❑ L7 Quark 1.25 3.00
❑ L8 Quark 1.25 3.00
❑ L9 Quark 1.25 3.00

2009 Politicians

❑ AK1R Don Young .20 .50
❑ AK1S Mark Begich .20 .50
❑ AL1R Jo Bonner .20 .50
❑ AL2R Bobby Bright .20 .50
❑ AL3R Mike Rogers .20 .50
❑ AL1S Jeff Sessions .20 .50
❑ AL4R Robert B. Aderholt .20 .50
❑ AR1R Marion Berry .20 .50
❑ AR2R Vic Snyder .20 .50
❑ AR1S Mark Pryor .20 .50
❑ AZ2R Trent Franks .20 .50
❑ AZ3R John Shadegg .20 .50
❑ AZ4R Ed Pastor .20 .50
❑ AZ1S Jon Kyl .20 .50
❑ AZ2S John McCain 3.00 8.00
❑ CA1R Mike Thompson .20 .50
❑ CA2R Wally Herger .20 .50
❑ CA3R Dan Lungren .20 .50
❑ CA4R Tom McClintock .20 .50
❑ CA5R Doris Matsui .20 .50
❑ CA6R Lynn Woolsey .20 .50
❑ CA7R George Miller .20 .50
❑ CA8R Nancy Pelosi 2.00 5.00
❑ CA9R Barbara Lee .20 .50
❑ CA10R Ellen Tauscher .20 .50
❑ CA11R Jerry McNerney .20 .50
❑ CA12R Jackie Speier .20 .50
❑ CA13R Pete Stark .20 .50
❑ CA14R Anna G. Eshoo .20 .50
❑ CA15R Mike Honda .20 .50
❑ CA16R Zoe Lofgren .20 .50
❑ CA17R Sam Farr .20 .50
❑ CA18R Dennis Cardoza .20 .50
❑ CA19R George P. Radanovich .20 .50
❑ CA20R Jim Costa .20 .50
❑ CA21R Devin Nunes .20 .50
❑ CA22R Kevin McCarthy .20 .50
❑ CA23R Lois Capps .20 .50
❑ CA24R Elton Gallegly .20 .50
❑ CA25R Buck McKeon .20 .50
❑ CA26R David Dreier .20 .50
❑ CA27R Brad Sherman .20 .50
❑ CA1S Dianne Feinstein .20 .50
❑ CO1R Diana DeGette .20 .50
❑ CO2R Jared Polis .20 .50
❑ CO3R John T. Salazar .20 .50
❑ CO1S Mark Udall .20 .50
❑ CT1R John B. Larson .20 .50
❑ CT2R Joe Courtney .20 .50
❑ CT3R Rosa L. DeLauro .20 .50
❑ CT1S Joe Lieberman .40 1.00
❑ DC1R Eleanor Holmes Norton .20 .50
❑ DE1R Mike Castle .20 .50
❑ DE1S Tom Carper .20 .50
❑ FL1R Jeff Miller .20 .50
❑ FL2R Allen Boyd .20 .50
❑ FL3R Corrine Brown .20 .50
❑ FL4R Ander Crenshaw .20 .50
❑ FL5R Ginny Brown-Waite .20 .50
❑ FL6R Cliff Stems .20 .50
❑ FL7R John L. Mica .20 .50
❑ FL8R Alan Grayson .20 .50
❑ FL9R Gus Bilirakis .20 .50
❑ FL10R C. W. Bill Young .20 .50
❑ FL11R Kathy Castor .20 .50
❑ FL12R Adam H. Putnam .20 .50
❑ FL1S Bill Nelson .20 .50
❑ GA1R Jack Kingston .20 .50
❑ GA2R Stanford D. Bishop, Jr. .20 .50
❑ GA3R Lynn A. Westmoreland .20 .50
❑ GA4R Hank Johnson .20 .50
❑ GA5R John Lewis .20 .50
❑ GA6R Tom Price .20 .50
❑ GA1S Saxby Chambliss .20 .50
❑ GU1R Madeleine Z. Bordallo .20 .50
❑ HI1R Neil Abercrombie .20 .50
❑ HI1S Daniel Kahikina Akaka .20 .50
❑ IA1R Bruce Braley .20 .50
❑ IA2R Dave Loebsack .20 .50
❑ IA1S Tom Harkin .20 .50
❑ ID1R Walt Minnick .20 .50
❑ ID1S James E. Risch .20 .50
❑ IL1R Bobby L. Rush .20 .50
❑ IL2R Jesse L. Jackson, Jr. .20 .50
❑ IL3R Daniel Lipinski .20 .50
❑ IL4R Luis V. Gutierrez .20 .50
❑ IL5R Mike Quigley .20 .50
❑ IL6R Peter Roskam .20 .50
❑ IL7R Danny K. Davis .20 .50
❑ IL8R Melissa Bean .20 .50
❑ IL9R Jan Schakowsky .20 .50
❑ IL10R Mark Steven Kirk .20 .50
❑ IL1S Dick Durbin .20 .50
❑ IN1R Pete Visclosky .20 .50
❑ IN2R Joe Donnelly .20 .50
❑ IN3R Mark Souder .20 .50
❑ IN4R Steve Buyer .20 .50
❑ IN5R Dan Burton .20 .50
❑ IN1S Richard G. Lugar .20 .50
❑ KS1R Jerry Moran .20 .50
❑ KS2R Lynn Jenkins .20 .50
❑ KS1S Pat Roberts .20 .50
❑ KY1R Ed Whitfield .20 .50
❑ KY2R Brett Guthrie .20 .50
❑ KY3R John Yarmuth .20 .50
❑ KY2S Jim Bunning .20 .50
❑ LA1R Steve Scalise .20 .50
❑ LA2R Joseph Cao .20 .50
❑ LA3R Charlie Melancon .20 .50
❑ LA1S Mary Landrieu .20 .50
❑ MA1R John W. Olver .20 .50
❑ MA2R Richard E. Neal .20 .50
❑ MA3R Jim McGovern .20 .50
❑ MA4R Barney Frank .20 .50
❑ MA5R Niki Tsongas .20 .50
❑ MA1S Edward M. Kennedy 3.00 8.00
❑ MD1R Frank M. Kratovil, Jr. .20 .50
❑ MD2R Dutch Ruppersberger .20 .50
❑ MD3R John Sarbanes .20 .50
❑ MD4R Donna F. Edwards .20 .50
❑ MD1S Benjamin L. Cardin .20 .50
❑ ME1R Chellie Pingree .20 .50
❑ ME1S Olympia J. Snowe .20 .50
❑ MI1R Bart Stupak .20 .50
❑ MI2R Pete Hoekstra .20 .50
❑ MI3R Vern Ehlers .20 .50
❑ MI4R Dave Camp .20 .50
❑ MI5R Dale E. Kildee .20 .50
❑ MI6R Fred Upton .20 .50
❑ MI7R Mark Schauer .20 .50
❑ MI8R Mike Rogers .20 .50
❑ MI1S Debbie Stabenow .20 .50
❑ MN1R Tim Walz .20 .50
❑ MN2R John Kline .20 .50
❑ MN3R Erik Paulsen .20 .50
❑ MN4R Betty McCollum .20 .50
❑ MN1S Amy Klobuchar .20 .50
❑ MO1R Wm. Lacy Clay .20 .50
❑ MO2R Todd Akin .20 .50
❑ MO3R Russ Carnahan .20 .50
❑ MO4R Ike Skelton .20 .50
❑ MO5R Emanuel Cleaver, II .20 .50
❑ MO1S Claire McCaskill .20 .50
❑ MS1R Travis W. Childers .20 .50
❑ MS2R Bennie Thompson .20 .50
❑ MS1S Roger Wicker .20 .50
❑ MT1R Denny Rehberg .20 .50
❑ MT1S Jon Tester .20 .50
❑ NC1R G.K. Butterfield .20 .50

❑ NC2R Bob Etheridge .20 .50
❑ NC3R Walter B. Jones .20 .50
❑ NC4R David Price .20 .50
❑ NC5R Virginia Foxx .20 .50
❑ NC6R Howard Coble .20 .50
❑ NC1S Kay Hagan .20 .50
❑ ND1S Kent Conrad .20 .50
❑ NE1R Jeff Fortenberry .20 .50
❑ NE2R Lee Terry .20 .50
❑ NE1S Ben Nelson .20 .50
❑ NH1R Carol Shea-Porter .20 .50
❑ NH1S Jeanne Shaheen .20 .50
❑ NJ1R Robert E. Andrews .20 .50
❑ NJ2R Frank A. LoBiondo .20 .50
❑ NJ3R John Adler .20 .50
❑ NJ4R Chris Smith .20 .50
❑ NJ5R Scott Garrett .20 .50
❑ NJ6R Frank Pallone, Jr. .20 .50
❑ NJ1S Robert Menendez .20 .50
❑ NM1R Martin T. Heinrich .20 .50
❑ NM1S Jeff Bingaman .20 .50
❑ NV1R Shelley Berkley .20 .50
❑ NV1S John Ensign .20 .50
❑ NY1R Tim Bishop .20 .50
❑ NY2R Steve Israel .20 .50
❑ NY3R Pete King .20 .50
❑ NY4R Carolyn McCarthy .20 .50
❑ NY5R Gary Ackerman .20 .50
❑ NY6R Gregory W. Meeks .20 .50
❑ NY7R Joseph Crowley .20 .50
❑ NY8R Jerrold Nadler .20 .50
❑ NY9R Anthony Weiner .20 .50
❑ NY10R Edolphus Towns .20 .50
❑ NY11R Yvette D. Clarke .20 .50
❑ NY12R Nydia M. Velázquez .20 .50
❑ NY13R Michael E. McMahon .20 .50
❑ NY14R Carolyn B. Maloney .20 .50
❑ NY15R Charles B. Rangel .20 .50
❑ NY1S Kirsten Gillibrand .20 .50
❑ OH1R Steve Driehaus .20 .50
❑ OH2R Jean Schmidt .20 .50
❑ OH3R Michael Turner .20 .50
❑ OH4R Jim Jordan .20 .50
❑ OH5R Bob Latta .20 .50
❑ OH6R Charlie Wilson .20 .50
❑ OH7R Steve Austria .20 .50
❑ OH8R John Boehner .20 .50
❑ OH9R Marcy Kaptur .20 .50
❑ OH1S Sherrod Brown .20 .50
❑ OK1R John Sullivan .20 .50
❑ OK2R Dan Boren .20 .50
❑ OK3R Frank Lucas .20 .50
❑ OK1S James M. Inhofe .20 .50
❑ OR1R David Wu .20 .50
❑ OR2R Greg Walden .20 .50
❑ OR1S Jeff Merkley .20 .50
❑ PA1R Robert Brady .20 .50
❑ PA2R Chaka Fattah .20 .50
❑ PA3R Kathy Dahlkemper .20 .50
❑ PA4R Jason Altmire .20 .50
❑ PA5R Glenn Thompson .20 .50
❑ PA6R Jim Gerlach .20 .50
❑ PA7R Joe Sestak .20 .50
❑ PA8R Patrick J. Murphy .20 .50
❑ PA9R Bill Schuster .20 .50
❑ PA10R Christopher P. Carney .20 .50
❑ PA1S Robert P. Casey, Jr. .20 .50
❑ RI1R Patrick J. Kennedy .20 .50
❑ RI1S Sheldon Whitehouse .20 .50
❑ SC1R Henry E. Brown, Jr. .20 .50
❑ SC2R Joe Wilson .20 .50
❑ SC3R J. Gresham Barrett .20 .50
❑ SC1S Lindsey Graham .20 .50
❑ SD1S Tim Johnson .20 .50
❑ TN1R Phil Roe .20 .50
❑ TN2R John J. Duncan, Jr. .20 .50
❑ TN3R Zach Wamp .20 .50
❑ TN4R Lincoln Davis .20 .50
❑ TN1S Bob Corker .20 .50
❑ TX1R Louie Gohmert .20 .50
❑ TX2R Ted Poe .20 .50
❑ TX3R Sam Johnson .20 .50
❑ TX4R Ralph M. Hall .20 .50
❑ TX5R Jeb Hensarling .20 .50
❑ TX6R Joe Barton .20 .50
❑ TX7R John Culberson .20 .50
❑ TX8R Kevin Brady .20 .50
❑ TX9R Al Green .20 .50
❑ TX10R Michael McCaul .20 .50
❑ TX11R Mike Conaway .20 .50
❑ TX12R Kay Granger .20 .50
❑ TX13R Mac Thornberry .20 .50
❑ TX14R Ron Paul 2.00 5.00
❑ TX15R Rubén Hinojosa .20 .50
❑ TX1S Kay Bailey Hutchison .20 .50
❑ UT1R Rob Bishop .20 .50
❑ UT2R Jim Matheson .20 .50
❑ UT1S Orrin Hatch .20 .50
❑ VA1R Rob Wittman .20 .50
❑ VA2R Glenn Nye .20 .50
❑ VA3R Bobby Scott .20 .50
❑ VA4R J. Randy Forbes .20 .50
❑ VA5R Tom Perriello .20 .50
❑ VA1S Jim Webb .20 .50
❑ VT1S Bernard Sanders .20 .50
❑ WA1R Jay Inslee .20 .50
❑ WA2R Rick Larsen .20 .50
❑ WA3R Brian Baird .20 .50
❑ WA4R Doc Hastings .20 .50
❑ WA1S Maria Cantwell .20 .50
❑ WI1R Paul Ryan 2.00 5.00
❑ WI2R Tammy Baldwin .20 .50
❑ WI3R Ron Kind .20 .50
❑ WI4R Gwen Moore .20 .50
❑ WI1S Herb Kohl .20 .50
❑ WV1R Alan B. Mollohan .20 .50
❑ WV2R Shelley Moore Capito .20 .50
❑ WV1S Robert C. Byrd .20 .50
❑ WY1R Cynthia Lummis .20 .50
❑ WY1S John Barrasso .20 .50
❑ EX1 Barack Hussein Obama 10.00 25.00
❑ EX3 Hillary Rodham Clinton 6.00 15.00
❑ EX5 Robert M. Gates .20 .50
❑ EX7 Ken Salazar .20 .50
❑ EX9 Gary Locke .20 .50
❑ EX11 Kathleen Sebelius .20 .50
❑ EX13 Ray LaHood .20 .50
❑ EX15 Arne Duncan .20 .50
❑ EX17 Janet Napolitano .20 .50
❑ EX19 Lisa Jackson .20 .50
❑ EX21 Ron Kirk .20 .50
❑ EX23 Rahm Emanuel .20 .50
❑ EXG Barack Obama Gold SP 150.00 300.00
❑ JU1 John Roberts 2.00 5.00
❑ JU3 Stephen Breyer .20 .50
❑ JU5 Anthony Kennedy .20 .50
❑ JU8 John Paul Stevens .20 .50
❑ JU9 Clarence Thomas .20 .50
❑ WH1 Michelle Obama 1.00 2.50
❑ WH2 Bo .40 1.00
❑ WH3 Air Force One .40 1.00
❑ WH4 Marine One .40 1.00

2009 Spider-Man Archives

COMPLETE SET (72) 4.00 10.00
❑ 1 Spider-Man .10 .30
❑ 2 Spider Bite .10 .30
❑ 3 Wall-Crawling .10 .30
❑ 4 Web-Shooters .10 .30
❑ 5 Webbing .10 .30
❑ 6 Web-Swinging .10 .30
❑ 7 Spider-Sense .10 .30
❑ 8 Hero No More .10 .30
❑ 9 Friendly Neighborhood Spider-Man .10 .30
❑ 10 Enemies and Allies .10 .30
❑ 11 Man-Spider .10 .30
❑ 12 Black Costume .10 .30
❑ 13 House of M .10 .30
❑ 14 Iron Spider Armor .10 .30
❑ 15 Photographer .10 .30
❑ 16 Daily Bugle .10 .30
❑ 17 Secret Indentity: Peter Parker .10 .30
❑ 18 Family .10 .30
❑ 19 Bullseye .10 .30
❑ 20 Carnage .10 .30
❑ 21 Doctor Octopus .10 .30
❑ 22 Electro .10 .30
❑ 23 Green Goblin .10 .30
❑ 24 Hobgoblin .10 .30
❑ 25 Kingpin .10 .30
❑ 26 Kraven .10 .30
❑ 27 Lizard .10 .30
❑ 28 Morbius .10 .30
❑ 29 Mysterio .10 .30
❑ 30 Jack O'Lantern .10 .30
❑ 31 Rhino .10 .30
❑ 32 Scorpion .10 .30
❑ 33 Shocker .10 .30
❑ 34 Swarm .10 .30
❑ 35 Venom .10 .30
❑ 36 Vulture .10 .30
❑ 37 Spider-Man vs. Doctor Octopus .10 .30
❑ 38 Spider-Man vs. Green Goblin .10 .30
❑ 39 Spider-Man vs. Vulture .10 .30
❑ 40 Spider-Man vs. Rhino .10 .30
❑ 41 Spider-Man vs. Scorpion .10 .30
❑ 42 Spider-Man vs. Lizard .10 .30
❑ 43 Spider-Man vs. Kraven .10 .30
❑ 44 Spider-Man vs. Sandman .10 .30
❑ 45 Spider-Man vs. Shocker .10 .30
❑ 46 Spider-Man vs. Hydro-Man .10 .30
❑ 47 Spider-Man vs. Mysterio .10 .30
❑ 48 Spider-Man vs. Swarm .10 .30
❑ 49 Spider-Man vs. Molten Man .10 .30
❑ 50 Spider-Man vs. Freak .10 .30
❑ 51 Spider-Man vs. Morlun .10 .30
❑ 52 Spider-Man vs. Menace .10 .30
❑ 53 Spider-Man vs. Electro .10 .30
❑ 54 Spider-Man vs. Jack O'Lantern .10 .30
❑ 55 Captain America .10 .30
❑ 56 Thor .10 .30
❑ 57 Iron Man .10 .30
❑ 58 Storm .10 .30
❑ 59 Shadow Cat .10 .30
❑ 60 Daredevil .10 .30
❑ 61 Ms. Marvel .10 .30
❑ 62 Silver Surfer .10 .30
❑ 63 She-Hulk .10 .30
❑ 64 Moon Knight .10 .30
❑ 65 X-Men .10 .30
❑ 66 Fantastic Four .10 .30
❑ 67 Avengers .10 .30
❑ 68 New Avengers .10 .30
❑ 69 Black Cat .10 .30
❑ 70 Punisher .10 .30
❑ 71 Man-Thing .10 .30
❑ 72 Checklist .10 .30

2009 Spider-Man Archives Foil

COMPLETE SET (72) 25.00 60.00
*FOIL: 2X TO 5X BASIC CARDS
STATED ODDS 1:3

2009 Spider-Man Archives Allies

COMPLETE SET (9) 4.00 10.00
STATED ODDS 1:8
❑ A1 Black Cat .75 2.00
❑ A2 Cloak & Dagger .75 2.00
❑ A3 Daredevil .75 2.00
❑ A4 Ghost Rider .75 2.00
❑ A5 Iron Fist .75 2.00
❑ A6 Madame Web .75 2.00
❑ A7 Moon Knight .75 2.00
❑ A8 Punisher .75 2.00
❑ A9 Spider-Woman .75 2.00

2009 Spider-Man Archives Case Toppers

COMPLETE SET (3)
STATED ODDS ONE PER CASE
❑ CT1 Spider-Man
❑ CT2 Spider-Man
❑ CT3 Spider-Man

2009 Spider-Man Archives Rogues Gallery

COMPLETE SET (9) 6.00 15.00
STATED ODDS 1:12
❑ R1 Doctor Octopus 1.00 2.50
❑ R2 Electro 1.00 2.50
❑ R3 Green Goblin 1.00 2.50
❑ R4 Kraven The Hunter 1.00 2.50
❑ R5 Lizard 1.00 2.50
❑ R6 Rhino 1.00 2.50
❑ R7 Sandman 1.00 2.50
❑ R8 Scorpion 1.00 2.50
❑ R9 Shocker 1.00 2.50

2009 Spider-Man Archives Swinging Into Action

COMPLETE SET (9) 12.50 30.00
STATED ODDS 1:24
❑ E1 Spider-Man 2.00 5.00
❑ E2 Spider-Man 2.00 5.00
❑ E3 Spider-Man 2.00 5.00
❑ E4 Spider-Man 2.00 5.00
❑ E5 Spider-Man 2.00 5.00
❑ E6 Spider-Man 2.00 5.00
❑ E7 Spider-Man 2.00 5.00
❑ E8 Spider-Man 2.00 5.00
❑ E9 Spider-Man 2.00 5.00
❑ E10 Spider-Man SP 10.00 25.00
(issued as Rittenhouse Reward)

2009 Sports Illustrated Swimsuit

COMPLETE SET (80) 6.00 15.00
❑ 1 Anne V .15 .40
❑ 2 Anne V .15 .40
❑ 3 Anne V .15 .40
❑ 4 Anne V .15 .40
❑ 5 Anne V .15 .40
❑ 6 Ariel Meredith .15 .40
❑ 7 Ariel Meredith .15 .40
❑ 8 Ariel Meredith .15 .40
❑ 9 Bar Refaeli .40 1.00
❑ 10 Bar Refaeli .40 1.00
❑ 11 Bar Refaeli .40 1.00
❑ 12 Bar Refaeli .40 1.00
❑ 13 Bar Refaeli .40 1.00
❑ 14 Brooklyn Decker .60 1.50
❑ 15 Brooklyn Decker .60 1.50
❑ 16 Brooklyn Decker .60 1.50
❑ 17 Brooklyn Decker .60 1.50
❑ 18 Brooklyn Decker .60 1.50
❑ 19 Cintia Dicker .30 .75
❑ 20 Cintia Dicker .30 .75
❑ 21 Cintia Dicker .30 .75
❑ 22 Damaris Lewis .15 .40
❑ 23 Damaris Lewis .15 .40
❑ 24 Damaris Lewis .15 .40
❑ 25 Daniella Sarahyba .15 .40
❑ 26 Daniella Sarahyba .15 .40
❑ 27 Daniella Sarahyba .15 .40
❑ 28 Daniella Sarahyba .15 .40
❑ 29 Daniella Sarahyba .15 .40
❑ 30 Esti Ginzburg .15 .40
❑ 31 Esti Ginzburg .15 .40
❑ 32 Esti Ginzburg .15 .40
❑ 33 Hillary Rhoda .30 .75
❑ 34 Hillary Rhoda .30 .75
❑ 35 Hillary Rhoda .30 .75
❑ 36 Irina Shayk .15 .40
❑ 37 Irina Shayk .15 .40
❑ 38 Irina Shayk .15 .40
❑ 39 Irina Shayk .15 .40
❑ 40 Irina Shayk .15 .40
❑ 41 Jarah Mariano .30 .75
❑ 42 Jarah Mariano .30 .75
❑ 43 Jarah Mariano .30 .75
❑ 44 Jarah Mariano .30 .75
❑ 45 Jarah Mariano .30 .75
❑ 46 Jessica Gomes .30 .75
❑ 47 Jessica Gomes .30 .75
❑ 48 Jessica Gomes .30 .75
❑ 49 Jessica Gomes .30 .75
❑ 50 Jessica Gomes .30 .75
❑ 51 Jessica Hart .15 .40
❑ 52 Jessica Hart .15 .40
❑ 53 Jessica Hart .15 .40
❑ 54 Jessica White .15 .40
❑ 55 Jessica White .15 .40
❑ 56 Jessica White .15 .40
❑ 57 Jessica White .15 .40
❑ 58 Jessica White .15 .40
❑ 59 Julie Henderson .15 .40
❑ 60 Julie Henderson .15 .40
❑ 61 Julie Henderson .15 .40
❑ 62 Julie Henderson .15 .40
❑ 63 Julie Henderson .15 .40
❑ 64 Kim Cloutier .15 .40
❑ 65 Kim Cloutier .15 .40
❑ 66 Kim Cloutier .15 .40
❑ 67 Lucia Dvorska .15 .40
❑ 68 Lucia Dvorska .15 .40
❑ 69 Lucia Dvorska .15 .40
❑ 70 Melissa Haro .15 .40
❑ 71 Melissa Haro .15 .40
❑ 72 Melissa Haro .15 .40
❑ 73 Melissa Haro .15 .40
❑ 74 Melissa Haro .15 .40
❑ 75 Tori Praver .15 .40
❑ 76 Tori Praver .15 .40
❑ 77 Tori Praver .15 .40
❑ 78 Tori Praver .15 .40
❑ 79 Tori Praver .15 .40
❑ 80 Checklist .15 .40

2009 Sports Illustrated Swimsuit Body Paint

COMPLETE SET (10) 8.00 20.00
STATED ODDS 1:4
❑ B1 Brooklyn Decker 2.50 6.00
❑ B2 Brooklyn Decker 2.50 6.00
❑ B3 Heidi Klum 2.00 5.00
❑ B4 Heidi Klum 2.00 5.00
❑ B5 Irina Shayk 1.25 3.00
❑ B6 Irina Shayk 1.25 3.00
❑ B7 Jessica White 1.25 3.00
❑ B8 Jessica White 1.25 3.00
❑ B9 Julie Henderson 1.25 3.00
❑ B10 Julie Henderson 1.25 3.00

2009 Sports Illustrated Swimsuit Danica Patrick

COMPLETE SET (10) 50.00 100.00
STATED ODDS 1:4
❑ D1 Danica Patrick 6.00 15.00
❑ D2 Danica Patrick 6.00 15.00
❑ D3 Danica Patrick 6.00 15.00
❑ D4 Danica Patrick 6.00 15.00
❑ D5 Danica Patrick 6.00 15.00
❑ D6 Danica Patrick 6.00 15.00
❑ D7 Danica Patrick 6.00 15.00
❑ D8 Danica Patrick 6.00 15.00
❑ D9 Danica Patrick 6.00 15.00
❑ D10 Danica Patrick 6.00 15.00

2009 Sports Illustrated Swimsuit Material

STATED ODDS 1:8
❑ BHM Bridget Hall 6.00 15.00
❑ BRM Bar Refaeli 25.00 50.00
❑ CDM Cintia Dicker 8.00 20.00
❑ DCM Deleah Caro 6.00 15.00
❑ DSM Daniella Sarahyba 6.00 15.00
❑ EMM Elle Macpherson/ (issued as case topper)20.00 40.00
❑ HKM Heidi Klum 20.00 40.00
❑ HRM Hillary Rhoda 8.00 20.00
❑ JGM Jessica Gomes 8.00 20.00
❑ JWM Jessica White 6.00 15.00
❑ MAM Michelle Alves 6.00 15.00
❑ MHM Melissa Haro 6.00 15.00
❑ MKM Maria Kirilenko 20.00 40.00
❑ MMM Marisa Miller 25.00 50.00
❑ MSM Maria Sharapova 40.00 80.00
❑ NLM Noemie Lenoir 6.00 15.00
❑ PRM Pania Rose 8.00 20.00
❑ TBM Tracy Burns 6.00 15.00
❑ ZDM Zoe Duchesne 6.00 15.00
❑ DP1M Danica Patrick 75.00 150.00
❑ DP2M Danica Patrick 75.00 150.00

2009 Star Trek Movie

COMPLETE SET (81) 8.00 20.00
❑ 1 Movie Plot Card .15 .40
❑ 2 Movie Plot Card .15 .40
❑ 3 Movie Plot Card .15 .40
❑ 4 Movie Plot Card .15 .40
❑ 5 Movie Plot Card .15 .40
❑ 6 Movie Plot Card .15 .40
❑ 7 Movie Plot Card .15 .40
❑ 8 Movie Plot Card .15 .40
❑ 9 Movie Plot Card .15 .40
❑ 10 Movie Plot Card .15 .40
❑ 11 Movie Plot Card .15 .40
❑ 12 Movie Plot Card .15 .40
❑ 13 Movie Plot Card .15 .40
❑ 14 Movie Plot Card .15 .40
❑ 15 Movie Plot Card .15 .40
❑ 16 Movie Plot Card .15 .40
❑ 17 Movie Plot Card .15 .40
❑ 18 Movie Plot Card .15 .40
❑ 19 Movie Plot Card .15 .40
❑ 20 Movie Plot Card .15 .40
❑ 21 Movie Plot Card .15 .40
❑ 22 Movie Plot Card .15 .40
❑ 23 Movie Plot Card .15 .40
❑ 24 Movie Plot Card .15 .40
❑ 25 Movie Plot Card .15 .40
❑ 26 Movie Plot Card .15 .40
❑ 27 Movie Plot Card .15 .40
❑ 28 Movie Plot Card .15 .40
❑ 29 Movie Plot Card .15 .40
❑ 30 Movie Plot Card .15 .40
❑ 31 Movie Plot Card .15 .40
❑ 32 Movie Plot Card .15 .40
❑ 33 Movie Plot Card .15 .40
❑ 34 Movie Plot Card .15 .40
❑ 35 Movie Plot Card .15 .40
❑ 36 Movie Plot Card .15 .40
❑ 37 Movie Plot Card .15 .40
❑ 38 Movie Plot Card .15 .40
❑ 39 Movie Plot Card .15 .40
❑ 40 Movie Plot Card .15 .40
❑ 41 Movie Plot Card .15 .40
❑ 42 Movie Plot Card .15 .40
❑ 43 Movie Plot Card .15 .40
❑ 44 Movie Plot Card .15 .40
❑ 45 Movie Plot Card .15 .40
❑ 46 Movie Plot Card .15 .40
❑ 47 Movie Plot Card .15 .40
❑ 48 Movie Plot Card .15 .40
❑ 49 Movie Plot Card .15 .40
❑ 50 Movie Plot Card .15 .40
❑ 51 Movie Plot Card .15 .40
❑ 52 Movie Plot Card .15 .40
❑ 53 Movie Plot Card .15 .40
❑ 54 Movie Plot Card .15 .40
❑ 55 Movie Plot Card .15 .40
❑ 56 Movie Plot Card .15 .40
❑ 57 Movie Plot Card .15 .40
❑ 58 Movie Plot Card .15 .40
❑ 59 Movie Plot Card .15 .40
❑ 60 Movie Plot Card .15 .40
❑ 61 Movie Plot Card .15 .40
❑ 62 Movie Plot Card .15 .40
❑ 63 Movie Plot Card .15 .40
❑ 64 Movie Plot Card .15 .40
❑ 65 Movie Plot Card .15 .40
❑ 66 Movie Plot Card .15 .40
❑ 67 Movie Plot Card .15 .40
❑ 68 Movie Plot Card .15 .40
❑ 69 Movie Plot Card .15 .40
❑ 70 Movie Plot Card .15 .40
❑ 71 Movie Plot Card .15 .40
❑ 72 Movie Plot Card .15 .40
❑ 73 Movie Plot Card .15 .40
❑ 74 Movie Plot Card .15 .40
❑ 75 Movie Plot Card .15 .40
❑ 76 Movie Plot Card .15 .40
❑ 77 Movie Plot Card .15 .40
❑ 78 Movie Plot Card .15 .40
❑ 79 Movie Plot Card .15 .40
❑ 80 Movie Plot Card .15 .40
❑ 81 Movie Plot Card .15 .40

2009 Star Trek Movie Autographs

AUTO/MEM COMBINED ODDS TWO PER BOX
❑ 1 Alex Kurtzman 75.00 150.00
❑ 2 Anton Yelchin 40.00 80.00
❑ 3 Bruce Greenwood 25.00 50.00
❑ 4 Chris Hemsworth 50.00 100.00
❑ 5 Chris Pine 300.00 450.00
❑ 6 Eric Bana 60.00 120.00
❑ 7 Faran Tahir 10.00 20.00
❑ 8 J.J. Abrams 125.00 225.00
❑ 9 Jacob Kogan 15.00 30.00
❑ 10 John Cho 50.00 100.00
❑ 11 Karl Urban 50.00 100.00
❑ 12 Roberto Orci 75.00 150.00
❑ 13 Simon Pegg 60.00 120.00
❑ 14 Zachary Quinto 75.00 150.00
❑ 15 Zoe Saldana 60.00 120.00

2009 Star Trek Movie Behind the Scenes

COMPLETE SET (6) 5.00 12.00
STATED ODDS 1:9
❑ B1 J.J. Abrams with crew 1.00 2.50
❑ B2 Anton Yelchin 1.00 2.50
J.J. Abrams
❑ B3 Eric Bana 1.00 2.50
J.J. Abrams
❑ B4 Bruce Greenwood 1.00 2.50
J.J. Abrams/John Cho
❑ B5 J.J. Abrams 1.00 2.50
Chris Pine
❑ B6 Zachary Quinto 1.00 2.50
J.J. Abrams

2009 Star Trek Movie Case Topper Posters

STATED ODDS ONE PER CASE
❑ 1 Kirk 15.00 30.00
❑ 2 Spock 15.00 30.00

2009 Star Trek Movie Costumes

AUTO/MEM COMBINED ODDS TWO PER BOX
❑ CC1 Kirk 15.00 40.00
❑ CC2 Spock 15.00 40.00
❑ CC3 Uhura 12.00 30.00
❑ CC4 Sulu 12.00 30.00
❑ CC5 Chekov 12.00 30.00
❑ CC6 Spock 15.00 40.00
❑ CC7 Bones 15.00 40.00
❑ CC8 Captain Pike 12.00 30.00
❑ CC9 Nero 15.00 40.00
❑ CC10 Male Cadet 8.00 20.00
❑ CC11 Female Cadet 10.00 25.00

2009 Star Trek Movie Relics

RC1 STATED ODDS ONE PER 3 CASE PURCHASE
RC2,RC3 STATED ODDS ONE PER 6 CASE PURCHASE
❑ RC1 Secure Order Attache 60.00 120.00
❑ RC2 Starfleet Cadet Badge
❑ RC3 Starfleet Badge

2009 Star Trek Movie Stars

COMPLETE SET w/o SP's (9) 5.00 12.00
STATED ODDS 1:6
SP10 ISSUED AS RITTENHOUSE REWARD
❑ S1 Kirk .75 2.00
❑ S2 Spock .75 2.00
❑ S3 Bones .75 2.00
❑ S4 Scotty .75 2.00
❑ S5 Sulu .75 2.00
❑ S6 Uhura .75 2.00
❑ S7 Chekov .75 2.00
❑ S8 Captain Pike .75 2.00
❑ S9 Nero .75 2.00
❑ S10 Spock SP 10.00 25.00

2009 Star Trek Movie U.S.S. Enterprise

COMPLETE SET (6) 5.00 12.00
STATED ODDS 1:9
❑ E1 U.S.S. Enterprise NCC-1701 1.00 2.50
❑ E2 U.S.S. Enterprise NCC-1701 1.00 2.50
❑ E3 U.S.S. Enterprise NCC-1701 1.00 2.50
❑ E4 U.S.S. Enterprise NCC-1701 1.00 2.50
❑ E5 U.S.S. Enterprise NCC-1701 1.00 2.50
❑ E6 U.S.S. Enterprise NCC-1701 1.00 2.50

2009 Star Trek The Original Series

COMPLETE SET (110) 6.00 15.00
❑ 221 Captain James T. Kirk .15 .40
❑ 222 Spock .15 .40
❑ 223 Dr. McCoy .15 .40
❑ 224 Scotty .15 .40
❑ 225 Uhura .15 .40
❑ 226 Sulu .15 .40
❑ 227 Checkov .15 .40
❑ 228 Nurse Chapel .15 .40
❑ 229 U.S.S. Enterprise .15 .40
❑ 230 Live Long and Prosper .15 .40
❑ 231 Black and White Foes .15 .40
❑ 232 Bridge Conference .15 .40
❑ 233 Learning Annex .15 .40
❑ 234 Phasers on Stun .15 .40
❑ 235 The Evil Gorgon .15 .40
❑ 236 Kirk and Scotty .15 .40
❑ 237 Surrounded .15 .40
❑ 238 Full House .15 .40
❑ 239 Federation Formal .15 .40
❑ 240 Spock's IDIC Pin .15 .40
❑ 241 Savage Rock Creature .15 .40
❑ 242 Chekov Goes Mad .15 .40
❑ 243 The Klingon Kang .15 .40
❑ 244 Self-Destruct Mode .15 .40
❑ 245 Peace, Herbert .15 .40
❑ 246 City in the Clouds .15 .40
❑ 247 The Enterprise Captured .15 .40
❑ 248 Scotty in Charge .15 .40
❑ 249 Alexander the Great .15 .40
❑ 250 The Tholian Web .15 .40
❑ 251 Youthful Commander .15 .40
❑ 252 Brain Drain .15 .40
❑ 253 Klingon Attack .15 .40
❑ 254 Kurok the God .15 .40
❑ 255 All Rise .15 .40
❑ 256 McCoy and Chapel .15 .40
❑ 257 Unwilling Lovers .15 .40
❑ 258 Elaan of Troyius .15 .40
❑ 259 Spock the Musician .15 .40
❑ 260 The Real Rayna .15 .40
❑ 261 Computer or God? .15 .40
❑ 262 Deadly Fruit .15 .40
❑ 263 Eternal Enemies .15 .40
❑ 264 Nightmare Vision .15 .40
❑ 265 Spock at Work .15 .40
❑ 266 Prepared for Battle .15 .40
❑ 267 Orphans Aboard the Enterprise .15 .40
❑ 268 Kurok and Miramanee .15 .40
❑ 269 Lawmen .15 .40
❑ 270 Vulcan Eyes .15 .40
❑ 271 Deadly Enemies .15 .40
❑ 272 Kirk in Trouble .15 .40
❑ 273 Vulcan Legend Surak .15 .40
❑ 274 Marta, Orion Slave Woman .15 .40
❑ 275 Kirk Takes Control .15 .40
❑ 276 Nefarious Aliens .15 .40
❑ 277 Red Alert .15 .40
❑ 278 Top Medical Team .15 .40
❑ 279 Vulcan Death Grip .15 .40
❑ 280 An Unwilling Captive .15 .40
❑ 281 Scotty Saves the Day .15 .40
❑ 282 Deadly to the Touch .15 .40
❑ 283 Beam Me Up, Scotty .15 .40
❑ 284 Brainless Vulcan .15 .40
❑ 285 Alien Torture Chamber .15 .40
❑ 286 Ghost Ship .15 .40
❑ 287 McCoy and Natira .15 .40
❑ 288 Gran Theft Cloaking Device .15 .40
❑ 289 Deela's Power .15 .40
❑ 290 Heroic Helmsman .15 .40
❑ 291 Jim's Dead .15 .40
❑ 292 Falling in Love .15 .40
❑ 293 McCoy at Work .15 .40
❑ 294 Spock and Droxine .15 .40
❑ 295 Deadly Force .15 .40
❑ 296 Heroic Trio .15 .40
❑ 297 Enterprise to the Rescue .15 .40
❑ 298 Alluring Orion .15 .40

❑ 299 Trading Places .15 .40
❑ 300 In Search of Brain .15 .40
❑ 301 Captured Captain .15 .40
❑ 302 Romulan Imposter .15 .40
❑ 303 The Empath .15 .40
❑ 304 Trapped in Another Body .15 .40
❑ 305 Vulcan Mind Meld .15 .40
❑ 306 Repository of Knowledge .15 .40
❑ 307 Brainwashed .15 .40
❑ 308 Landing Party .15 .40
❑ 309 Lt. Mira Romaine .15 .40
❑ 310 Trouble in Engineering .15 .40
❑ 311 Transporting Dignitaries .15 .40
❑ 312 Kirk and Odona .15 .40
❑ 313 Spirited Connection .15 .40
❑ 314 Toga Party .15 .40
❑ 315 Lights of Zetar .15 .40
❑ 316 Showdown Coming .15 .40
❑ 317 Investigating a Mystery .15 .40
❑ 318 Medal of Honor .15 .40
❑ 319 Kirk Battles Kirk .15 .40
❑ 320 Spock's Analysis .15 .40
❑ 321 Like the Devil Himself .15 .40
❑ 322 Fearsome Foursome .15 .40
❑ 323 Kirk Plays the Part .15 .40
❑ 324 Marta and Lord Garth .15 .40
❑ 325 Concerned Scotty .15 .40
❑ 326 A Dirty Trick .15 .40
❑ 327 Kirk behind Bars .15 .40
❑ 328 Dodge City Doctor .15 .40
❑ 329 Champions of Justice .15 .40
(Checklist
❑ 330 The Enterprise NCC-1701 .15 .40
(Checklist

2009 Star Trek The Original Series Autographs

STATED ODDS 1:8
KOENIG AUTO ONE PER 3 CASE PURCHASE
SHATNER/NICHOLS AUTO ONE PER 6 CASE PURCHASE

❑ A140 Leslie Shatner 40.00 80.00
❑ A160 Lisabeth Shatner
❑ A168 Leslie Parrish 40.00 80.00
❑ A191 Paul Baxley 6.00 15.00
❑ A192 Paul Baxley 6.00 15.00
❑ A193 Leonard Nimoy 150.00 250.00
❑ A194 David Gerrold 6.00 15.00
❑ A195 Rex Holman 6.00 15.00
❑ A196 Skip Homeier 6.00 15.00
❑ A197 Barbara Babcock 6.00
❑ A198 Elinor Donahue 6.00 15.00
❑ A199 William Shatner 150.00 250.00
❑ A201 Hagan Beggs 6.00 15.00
❑ A203 Sandra Smith 8.00 20.00
❑ A204 Harry Landers 6.00 15.00
❑ A205 William Wintersole 40.00 80.00
❑ A206 Lee Meriwether 15.00 30.00
❑ A207 Sabrina Scharf 8.00 20.00
❑ A208 Mariette Hartley 25.00 50.00
❑ A209 Mark Robert Brown 6.00 15.00
❑ A210 Carol Daniels 6.00 15.00
❑ A211 Harry Basch 6.00 15.00
❑ A212 Eddie Paskey 6.00 15.00
❑ A213 Garland Lee Thompson 6.00 15.00
❑ A214 John Winston 40.00 80.00
❑ A215 William O'Connell 6.00 15.00
❑ A216 William Sargent 6.00 15.00
❑ A217 Janet MacLachlan 6.00 15.00
❑ A218 David Frankham 6.00 15.00
❑ A219 Roger Perry 8.00 20.00
❑ A220 Kim Darby 8.00 20.00
❑ A221 Marc Adams 6.00 15.00
❑ A222 Venita Wolf 6.00 15.00
❑ A223 Miko Mayama 6.00 15.00
❑ A224 Shari Nims 6.00 15.00
❑ A225 Susanne Wasson 6.00 15.00
❑ A226 Tom Troupe 6.00 15.00
❑ A227 Louie Elias 6.00 15.00
❑ A228 Gary Combs 8.00 20.00
❑ A229 Gary Combs 8.00 20.00
❑ A231 Shirley Bonne 10.00 25.00
❑ A232 Barbara Bouchet 50.00 100.00
❑ A233 Lezlie Dalton 6.00 15.00
❑ A234 Bob Bralver 6.00 15.00
❑ A235 Phyllis Douglas 6.00 15.00
❑ A237 Naomi Pollack 6.00 15.00
❑ A238 Marlys Burdette 6.00 15.00
❑ A241 William Smithers 6.00 15.00
❑ NNO William Shatner 200.00 300.00
Nichelle Nichols
❑ NNO Walter Koenig MEM 50.00 100.00

2009 Star Trek The Original Series Case Toppers

ONE PER CASE

❑ M7 Majel Barrett as Nurse Chapel
❑ M8 Majel Barrett as Number One

2009 Star Trek The Original Series In Motion

COMPLETE SET (18) 8.00 20.00
STATED ODDS 1:6

❑ L1 The Cage 1.00 2.50
❑ L2 The Cage 1.00 2.50
❑ L3 The Cage 1.00 2.50
❑ L4 The Cage 1.00 2.50
❑ L5 The Cage 1.00 2.50
❑ L6 The Cage 1.00 2.50
❑ L7 The Cage 1.00 2.50
❑ L8 The Cage 1.00 2.50
❑ L9 The Cage 1.00 2.50
❑ L10 The Cage 1.00 2.50
❑ L11 The Cage 1.00 2.50
❑ L12 The Cage 1.00 2.50
❑ L13 The Cage 1.00 2.50
❑ L14 The Cage 1.00 2.50
❑ L15 The Cage 1.00 2.50
❑ L16 The Cage 1.00 2.50
❑ L17 The Cage 1.00 2.50
❑ L18 The Cage 1.00 2.50

2009 Star Trek The Original Series Portraits

COMPLETE SET (18) 10.00 25.00
STATED ODDS 1:8

❑ M46 Kara 1.25 3.00
❑ M47 Romulan Commander 1.25 3.00
❑ M48 Miramanee 1.25 3.00
❑ M49 Dr. Miranda Jones 1.25 3.00
❑ M50 Kang 1.25 3.00
❑ M51 Natira 1.25 3.00
❑ M52 Alexander 1.25 3.00
❑ M53 Deela 1.25 3.00
❑ M54 Gem 1.25 3.00
❑ M55 Garth 1.25 3.00
❑ M56 Bele 1.25 3.00
❑ M57 Odona 1.25 3.00
❑ M58 Losira 1.25 3.00
❑ M59 Rayna Kapec 1.25 3.00
❑ M60 Dr. Sevrin 1.25 3.00
❑ M61 Droxine 1.25 3.00
❑ M62 Zarabeth 1.25 3.00
❑ M63 Janice Lester 1.25 3.00

2009 Star Trek The Original Series Tribute

COMPLETE SET (18) 30.00 60.00
STATED ODDS 1:12

❑ T1 Captain Christopher Pike 2.00 5.00
❑ T2 Vina 2.00 5.00
❑ T3 Eve McHuron 2.00 5.00
❑ T4 Nancy Crater 2.00 5.00
❑ T5 Romulan Commander 2.00 5.00
❑ T6 Ruk 2.00 5.00
❑ T7 Dr. Roger Korby 2.00 5.00
❑ T8 Dr. Tristan Adams 2.00 5.00
❑ T9 Anton Karidian 2.00 5.00
❑ T10 Lt. Areel Shaw 2.00 5.00
❑ T11 Commodore Stone 2.00 5.00
❑ T12 Cogley 2.00 5.00
❑ T13 Caretaker 2.00 5.00
❑ T14 Anan 7 2.00 5.00
❑ T15 Ambassador Robert Fox 2.00 5.00
❑ T16 Leila Kalomi 2.00 5.00
❑ T17 Kor 2.00 5.00
❑ T18 Ayelborne 2.00 5.00

2009 Stargate Heroes

COMPLETE SET (90) 4.00 10.00

❑ 1 Jack O'Neill .10 .30
❑ 2 Jack O'Neill .10 .30
❑ 3 Jack O'Neill .10 .30
❑ 4 Jack O'Neill .10 .30
❑ 5 Jack O'Neill .10 .30
❑ 6 Jack O'Neill .10 .30
❑ 7 Jack O'Neill .10 .30
❑ 8 Jack O'Neill .10 .30
❑ 9 Jack O'Neill .10 .30
❑ 10 Samantha Carter .10 .30
❑ 11 Samantha Carter .10 .30
❑ 12 Samantha Carter .10 .30
❑ 13 Samantha Carter .10 .30
❑ 14 Samantha Carter .10 .30
❑ 15 Samantha Carter .10 .30
❑ 16 Samantha Carter .10 .30
❑ 17 Samantha Carter .10 .30
❑ 18 Samantha Carter .10 .30
❑ 19 Daniel Jackson .10 .30
❑ 20 Daniel Jackson .10 .30
❑ 21 Daniel Jackson .10 .30
❑ 22 Daniel Jackson .10 .30
❑ 23 Daniel Jackson .10 .30
❑ 24 Daniel Jackson .10 .30
❑ 25 Daniel Jackson .10 .30
❑ 26 Daniel Jackson .10 .30
❑ 27 Daniel Jackson .10 .30
❑ 28 Teal'c .10 .30
❑ 29 Teal'c .10 .30
❑ 30 Teal'c .10 .30
❑ 31 Teal'c .10 .30
❑ 32 Teal'c .10 .30
❑ 33 Teal'c .10 .30
❑ 34 Teal'c .10 .30
❑ 35 Teal'c .10 .30
❑ 36 Teal'c .10 .30
❑ 37 Cameron Mitchell .10 .30
❑ 38 Cameron Mitchell .10 .30
❑ 39 Cameron Mitchell .10 .30
❑ 40 Cameron Mitchell .10 .30
❑ 41 Cameron Mitchell .10 .30
❑ 42 Cameron Mitchell .10 .30
❑ 43 Cameron Mitchell .10 .30
❑ 44 Cameron Mitchell .10 .30
❑ 45 Cameron Mitchell .10 .30
❑ 46 John Sheppard .10 .30
❑ 47 John Sheppard .10 .30
❑ 48 John Sheppard .10 .30
❑ 49 John Sheppard .10 .30
❑ 50 John Sheppard .10 .30
❑ 51 John Sheppard .10 .30
❑ 52 John Sheppard .10 .30
❑ 53 John Sheppard .10 .30
❑ 54 John Sheppard .10 .30
❑ 55 Rodney McKay .10 .30
❑ 56 Rodney McKay .10 .30
❑ 57 Rodney McKay .10 .30
❑ 58 Rodney McKay .10 .30
❑ 59 Rodney McKay .10 .30
❑ 60 Rodney McKay .10 .30
❑ 61 Rodney McKay .10 .30
❑ 62 Rodney McKay .10 .30
❑ 63 Rodney McKay .10 .30
❑ 64 Teyla Emmagan .10 .30
❑ 65 Teyla Emmagan .10 .30
❑ 66 Teyla Emmagan .10 .30
❑ 67 Teyla Emmagan .10 .30
❑ 68 Teyla Emmagan .10 .30
❑ 69 Teyla Emmagan .10 .30
❑ 70 Teyla Emmagan .10 .30
❑ 71 Teyla Emmagan .10 .30
❑ 72 Teyla Emmagan .10 .30
❑ 73 Ronon Dex .10 .30
❑ 74 Ronon Dex .10 .30
❑ 75 Ronon Dex .10 .30
❑ 76 Ronon Dex .10 .30
❑ 77 Ronon Dex .10 .30
❑ 78 Ronon Dex .10 .30
❑ 79 Ronon Dex .10 .30
❑ 80 Ronon Dex .10 .30
❑ 81 Ronon Dex .10 .30
❑ 82 Vala Mal Doran .10 .30
❑ 83 Vala Mal Doran .10 .30
❑ 84 Vala Mal Doran .10 .30
❑ 85 Dr. Beckett .10 .30
❑ 86 Dr. Beckett .10 .30
❑ 87 Dr. Weir .10 .30
❑ 88 Dr. Weir .10 .30
❑ 89 Dr. Keller .10 .30
❑ 90 General Hank Landry .10 .30
❑ 91 Hammond SP 10.00 25.00
(issued as Rittenhouse Reward)

2009 Stargate Heroes Continuum

COMPLETE SET (18) 15.00 40.00
STATED ODDS 1:8

❑ SC1 Stargate Continuum 1.25 3.00
❑ SC2 Stargate Continuum 1.25 3.00
❑ SC3 Stargate Continuum 1.25 3.00
❑ SC4 Stargate Continuum 1.25 3.00
❑ SC5 Stargate Continuum 1.25 3.00
❑ SC6 Stargate Continuum 1.25 3.00
❑ SC7 Stargate Continuum 1.25 3.00
❑ SC8 Stargate Continuum 1.25 3.00
❑ SC9 Stargate Continuum 1.25 3.00
❑ SC10 Stargate Continuum 1.25 3.00
❑ SC11 Stargate Continuum 1.25 3.00
❑ SC12 Stargate Continuum 1.25 3.00
❑ SC13 Stargate Continuum 1.25 3.00
❑ SC14 Stargate Continuum 1.25 3.00
❑ SC15 Stargate Continuum 1.25 3.00
❑ SC16 Stargate Continuum 1.25 3.00
❑ SC17 Stargate Continuum 1.25 3.00
❑ SC18 Stargate Continuum 1.25 3.00

2009 Stargate Heroes In Motion

COMPLETE SET (9) 10.00 25.00
STATED ODDS 1:12

❑ M1 Stargate in Motion 1.50 4.00
❑ M2 Stargate in Motion 1.50 4.00
❑ M3 Stargate in Motion 1.50 4.00
❑ M4 Stargate in Motion 1.50 4.00
❑ M5 Stargate in Motion 1.50 4.00
❑ M6 Stargate in Motion 1.50 4.00
❑ M7 Stargate in Motion 1.50 4.00
❑ M8 Stargate in Motion 1.50 4.00
❑ M9 Stargate in Motion 1.50 4.00

2009 Stargate Heroes Stargate Atlantis Autographs

OVERALL AUTOGRAPH ODDS 1:8
VL (VERY LIMITED): 200-300 COPIES

❑ AH Adrian Hein 4.00 10.00
❑ AT Amanda Tapping VL 60.00 120.00
❑ BN Bill Nye 6.00 15.00
❑ CC Chuck Campbell 4.00 10.00
❑ DA Daneilla Alonso 4.00 10.00
❑ DH1 David Hewlett VL 30.00 60.00
❑ DH2 David Hewlett VL 30.00 60.00
❑ DN Dylan Neal 4.00 10.00
❑ DO Dawn Olivieri 4.00 10.00
❑ JM Jason Momoa VL 60.00 120.00
❑ JN Jaime Ray Newman 10.00 20.00
❑ KM Kirby Morrow 4.00 10.00
❑ KZ Kyra Zagorsky 4.00 10.00
❑ LS Leela Savasta 4.00 10.00
❑ ML Megan Leitch 4.00 10.00
❑ MM Michelle Morgan 6.00 15.00
❑ PS Patrick Sabongui 6.00 15.00
❑ RF1 Rainbow Francks VL 30.00 60.00
❑ RF2 Rainbow Francks VL 30.00 60.00
❑ RP Robert Picardo VL 60.00 120.00
❑ ST Sharon Taylor 4.00 10.00
❑ TM Tyler McClendon 4.00 10.00

2009 Stargate Heroes Stargate Atlantis Relics

OVERALL RELIC ODDS 1:12

❑ FO Ford
❑ RO Ronon
❑ SH1 Sheppard
❑ SH2 Sheppard
❑ TE1 Teyla
❑ TE2 Teyla
❑ TE3 Teyla DUAL

2009 Stargate Heroes Stargate Atlantis Season Five

COMPLETE SET (20) 4.00 10.00
STATED ODDS 1:4

❑ 1 Search and Rescue .30 .75
❑ 2 The Seed .30 .75
❑ 3 Broken Ties .30 .75
❑ 4 The Daedalus Variations .30 .75
❑ 5 Ghost In the Machine .30 .75
❑ 6 The Shrine .30 .75
❑ 7 Whispers .30 .75
❑ 8 The Queen .30 .75
❑ 9 Tracker .30 .75
❑ 10 First Contact .30 .75
❑ 11 The Lost Tribe .30 .75
❑ 12 Outsiders .30 .75
❑ 13 Inquisition .30 .75
❑ 14 The Prodigal .30 .75
❑ 15 Remnants .30 .75
❑ 16 Brain Storm .30 .75
❑ 17 Infection .30 .75
❑ 18 Identity .30 .75
❑ 19 Vegas .30 .75
❑ 20 Enemy At the Gate .30 .75

2009 Stargate Heroes Stargate SG-1 Autograph Relics

OVERALL AUTOGRAPH ODDS 1:8
VL (VERY LIMITED): 200-300 COPIES

❑ AC2 Beau Bridges VL 25.00 50.00
❑ AC3 Amanda Tapping VL 25.00 50.00

2009 Stargate Heroes Stargate SG-1 Autographs

OVERALL AUTOGRAPH ODDS 1:8
SHANKS AUTO STATED ODDS ONE PER 3-CASE PURCHASE
L (LIMITED): 300-500 COPIES

❑ A77 Patrick Currie 6.00 15.00
❑ A86 Beau Bridges 40.00 80.00
❑ A109 Adrian Holmes 6.00 15.00
❑ A110 Don Stark L 6.00 15.00
❑ A111 John Novak 6.00 15.00
❑ A112 Joshua Malina 6.00 15.00
❑ A113 Sarah Douglas 6.00 15.00
❑ A114 John Nobel 6.00 15.00
❑ A115 Tobin Bell 6.00 15.00
❑ MS Michael Shanks/ (issued as 3-case incentive)30.00 60.00

2009 Stargate Heroes Stargate SG-1 Dual Relics

OVERALL RELIC ODDS 1:12

❑ BA Baal
❑ SC Samantha Carter
❑ TE Teal'c
❑ VMD Vala Mal Doran

2009 Stargate Heroes Stargate SG-1 Relics

OVERALL RELIC ODDS 1:12

❑ C59 Samantha Carter 7.50 20.00
❑ C60 Samantha Carter 7.50 20.00
❑ C61 Samantha Carter 7.50 20.00
❑ C62 Samantha Carter 7.50 20.00
❑ C63 Vala Mal Doran 6.00 15.00
❑ C64 Vala Mal Doran 6.00 15.00
❑ C65 Vala Mal Doran 6.00 15.00
❑ C66 Cameron Mitchell 6.00 15.00
❑ C67 Baal 4.00 10.00
❑ C68 Teal'c 4.00 10.00
❑ C69 Teal'c 4.00 10.00
❑ C70 Parey 4.00 10.00
❑ C71 Teal'c 4.00 10.00
❑ C72 Zombie Pilot 4.00 10.00

2009 Stargate Heroes Stargate Universe Preview

COMPLETE SET (9) 8.00 20.00
STATED ODDS 1:24

❑ SU1 Eli Wallace 2.00 5.00
❑ SU2 Dr. Nicholas Rush 2.00 5.00
❑ SU3 1st Lt Tamara Johansen 2.00 5.00
❑ SU4 Chloe Armstrong 2.00 5.00
❑ SU5 1st Lt. Matthew Scott 2.00 5.00
❑ SU6 MSgt. Ronald Greer 2.00 5.00
❑ SU7 Colonel Telford 2.00 5.00
❑ SU8 Col. Everett Young 2.00 5.00
❑ SU9 Camille Wray 2.00 5.00
❑ SU10 5 Cast Members SP 10.00 25.00
(issued as Rittenhouse Reward)

2009 Terminator Salvation

COMPLETE SET (90) 4.00 10.00

❑ 1 Terminator Salvation .08 .25
❑ 2 John Connor .08 .25
❑ 3 Marcus Wright .08 .25
❑ 4 Kyle Reese .08 .25
❑ 5 Kate Connor .08 .25
❑ 6 Blair Williams .08 .25
❑ 7 Barnes .08 .25
❑ 8 Star .08 .25
❑ 9 Virginia .08 .25
❑ 10 The Execution of Marcus .08 .25
❑ 11 Target: Skynet .08 .25
❑ 12 Man Against Machine .08 .25
❑ 13 An Inside Operation .08 .25
❑ 14 To Save Human Lives .08 .25
❑ 15 Connor's Narrow Escape .08 .25
❑ 16 Of Death and Rebirth .08 .25
❑ 17 The Last of the Finest .08 .25
❑ 18 Man Behind the Warrior .08 .25
❑ 19 The Dead Zone .08 .25
❑ 20 Terror and a Teammate .08 .25
❑ 21 The Daylight Stalker .08 .25
❑ 22 Blasting All Humans .08 .25
❑ 23 Surviving to Fight .08 .25
❑ 24 Fear and Trust .08 .25
❑ 25 A Captured Hydrobot .08 .25
❑ 26 Inspired to Action .08 .25
❑ 27 Aerostat Attack .08 .25
❑ 28 Ravaged by the Robots .08 .25
❑ 29 Their Greatest Challenge .08 .25
❑ 30 Road Warriors .08 .25
❑ 31 Terminators on Wheels .08 .25
❑ 32 Kyle's Road Rage .08 .25
❑ 33 Blast Off .08 .25
❑ 34 Blair: All Hung Up .08 .25
❑ 35 A Most Welcome Rescue .08 .25
❑ 36 The Freedom Seekers .08 .25
❑ 37 A Little Local Trouble .08 .25
❑ 38 High-Risk Experiment .08 .25
❑ 39 A Date with Death .08 .25
❑ 40 Night of Terror .08 .25
❑ 41 Skynet Processing .08 .25
❑ 42 No Escape from Skynet .08 .25
❑ 43 Resistance to the Rescue .08 .25
❑ 44 Man or Terminator .08 .25
❑ 45 Escape from the Outpost .08 .25
❑ 46 Cycling to Freedom .08 .25
❑ 47 Fury of the Hydrobot .08 .25
❑ 48 A Matter of Death and Life .08 .25
❑ 49 The Resistance Strikes Back .08 .25
❑ 50 Kate's Warning .08 .25
❑ 51 A Way In for Connor .08 .25
❑ 52 Entering Skynet .08 .25
❑ 53 Terminator On Patrol .08 .25
❑ 54 Connor's Bold Plan .08 .25
❑ 55 Facing John Connor .08 .25
❑ 56 The Terminator Factory .08 .25
❑ 57 Terror in Mass Production .08 .25
❑ 58 Humanity's Last Chance .08 .25
❑ 59 We Who Survive .08 .25
❑ 60 In Memory of Marcus .08 .25
❑ 61 T-1 .08 .25
❑ 62 T-600 .08 .25
❑ 63 Aerostat .08 .25
❑ 64 Hunter-Killer .08 .25
❑ 65 Hydrobot .08 .25
❑ 66 Moto-Terminator .08 .25
❑ 67 Transporter .08 .25
❑ 68 Harvester .08 .25
❑ 69 Filming an Aquatic Attack .08 .25
❑ 70 Hatching a Hydrobot .08 .25
❑ 71 Before a Blue Screen .08 .25
❑ 72 Terror of the T-600 .08 .25
❑ 73 Designing a Dark Future .08 .25
❑ 74 The New Terminator .08 .25
❑ 75 Marcus Maimed and Mangled .08 .25
❑ 76 Face of the Enemy .08 .25
❑ 77 An Enemy Within .08 .25
❑ 78 Inside the Missile Silo .08 .25
❑ 79 Freedom's Outpost .08 .25
❑ 80 Under Skynet's Thumb .08 .25
❑ 81 Power Tower Dangling .08 .25
❑ 82 Our Ravaged World .08 .25
❑ 83 Crumbled California .08 .25
❑ 84 Tarnished Gateway of Hope .08 .25
❑ 85 At Death's Gleaming Door .08 .25
❑ 86 Death has Red Eyes .08 .25
❑ 87 Child's Play .08 .25
❑ 88 Mission: Destroy Humanity .08 .25
❑ 89 Checklist .08 .25
❑ 90 Checklist .08 .25

2009 Terminator Salvation Autographs

STATED ODDS 1:24 HOBBY

❑ 1 Chris Ashworth 4.00 10.00
❑ 2 Dylan Kenin 4.00 10.00
❑ 3 Jadagrace 4.00 10.00
❑ 4 Jane Alexander 4.00 10.00
❑ 5 Michael Ironside 6.00 15.00
❑ 6 Michael Papajohn 4.00 10.00

2009 Terminator Salvation Battle Pop-Ups

COMPLETE SET (9) 2.00 5.00
STATED ODDS 1:4 RETAIL

❑ 1 T-1 .30 .75
❑ 2 T-600 .30 .75
❑ 3 T-700 .30 .75
❑ 4 Moto-Terminator .30 .75
❑ 5 Aerostat .30 .75
❑ 6 Hunter-Killer .30 .75
❑ 7 Transporter .30 .75
❑ 8 Harvester .30 .75
❑ 9 Hydrobot .30 .75

2009 Terminator Salvation Embossed Foil

COMPLETE SET (9) 2.50 6.00
STATED ODDS 1:6

❑ 1 T-1 .40 1.00
❑ 2 T-600 .40 1.00
❑ 3 T-700 .40 1.00
❑ 4 Transporter .40 1.00
❑ 5 Aerostat .40 1.00
❑ 6 Hunter-Killer .40 1.00
❑ 7 Moto-Terminator .40 1.00
❑ 8 Harvester .40 1.00
❑ 9 T-600 .40 1.00

2009 Terminator Salvation Memorabilia

STATED ODDS 1:48 HOBBY

❑ 1 John Connor 6.00 15.00
Fatigues
❑ 2 John Connor 6.00 15.00
Jacket
❑ 3 Kyle Reece 6.00 15.00
Jacket
❑ 4 Kyle Reece 6.00 15.00
Vest
❑ 5 Marcus Wright 6.00 15.00
Coat
❑ 6 Marcus Wright 6.00 15.00
Shirt

2009 Terminator Salvation Sketches

STATED ODDS 1:48 HOBBY

❑ 1 Bob Larkin
❑ 2 Brent Engstrom
❑ 3 Brian Kong
❑ 4 Bruce Gerlach
❑ 5 Denise Vasquez
❑ 6 Don Pedicini Jr.
❑ 7 Don Perlin
❑ 8 Greg Moutafis
❑ 9 Hayden Davis
❑ 10 Jake Minor
❑ 11 Jake Myler
❑ 12 Jamie Snell
❑ 13 Jason Davies
❑ 14 Jeremy Treece
❑ 15 Jonathan D. Gordon
❑ 16 Kate Glasheen (Katie Crimespree)
❑ 17 Ken Branch
❑ 18 Kevin Graham
❑ 19 Lance Sawyer
❑ 20 Layron Dejarnette
❑ 21 Luis Diaz
❑ 22 Mathew Minor
❑ 23 Michael Zapata
❑ 24 Peter Pachoumis
❑ 25 Randy Martinez
❑ 26 Richard Clark
❑ 27 Robert Teranishi
❑ 28 Scott Barnett

2009 Topps President Obama Inaugural

COMP.SET w/o 44B AND PUP (90) 20.00 50.00
BK ALL STAR #44B ODDS 1:192 PACKS
PRESIDENTIAL PUP ODDS 1:384 PACKS
ONE POSTER PER BOX
PUP EXCHANGE DEADLINE 1/20/2011

❑ 1 U.S. President Barack Obama .15 .40
❑ 2 Obama: Just the Facts .15 .40
❑ 3 From Hawaii to Washington .15 .40
❑ 4 The Long Journey Begins .15 .40
❑ 5 Dreams from My Father .15 .40
❑ 6 Little Man on the Go .15 .40
❑ 7 Loving, Nurturing Grandparents .15 .40
❑ 8 Fun with Gramps and Toot .15 .40
❑ 9 Next Stop: Indonesia .15 .40
❑ 10 Hawaii Hoops Star .15 .40
❑ 11 Gone But Not Forgotten .15 .40
❑ 12 The Newlyweds .15 .40
❑ 13 First Lady Michelle Obama .15 .40
❑ 14 America's Newest First Family .15 .40
❑ 15 From Pineapples to The Big Apple .15 .40
❑ 16 Welcome to the Windy City .15 .40
❑ 17 Pioneer at Harvard Law .15 .40
❑ 18 Welcome Back Obama .15 .40
❑ 19 Get Out the Vote .15 .40
❑ 20 A Political Star Is Born .15 .40
❑ 21 Run, Barack, Run! .15 .40
❑ 22 The Speech .15 .40
❑ 23 Victory! .15 .40
❑ 24 Mr. Obama Goes to Washington .15 .40
❑ 25 Playing Political Hardball .15 .40
❑ 26 Building International Cred .15 .40
❑ 27 Best-Selling Author…Again .15 .40
❑ 28 I'm Running for President .15 .40
❑ 29 Stumping in the Heartland .15 .40
❑ 30 Change Is Coming! .15 .40
❑ 31 The Democratic Debates .15 .40
❑ 32 Victory's Within Reach .15 .40
❑ 33 I Will Be the Nominee .15 .40
❑ 34 A Family Time-Out .15 .40
❑ 35 Rousing Warm-Up Act .15 .40
❑ 36 Rocky Mountain Highlight .15 .40
❑ 37 Greek Theater, Denver-Style .15 .40
❑ 38 O Picks Joe .15 .40
❑ 39 Cool Running Mates .15 .40
❑ 40 Hello, Michigan! .15 .40
❑ 41 Issue No. 1: The Economy .15 .40
❑ 42 Cheering for Change .15 .40
❑ 43 Please Pass the Syrup .15 .40
❑ 44a Good Morning, Baghdad! .15 .40
❑ 44b Barack Obama All Star SP 20.00 40.00
❑ 45 Thank You for Your Service .15 .40
❑ 46 Ready for Prime Time .15 .40
❑ 47 Middle East Peacemaker? .15 .40
❑ 48 Round 1 in Oxford .15 .40
❑ 49 Veep Candidates Face Off .15 .40
❑ 50 Hall of a Debate .15 .40
❑ 51 The Final Showdown .15 .40

MODERN ERA NON-SPORTS

❑ 52 Michelle Speaks Out .15 .40
❑ 53 Former Rivals Unite .15 .40
❑ 54 Bill Lends a Hand .15 .40
❑ 55 Future First Family Frolic .15 .40
❑ 56 The (Really Big) Crowd-Pleaser .15 .40
❑ 57 Team Obama All-Stars .15 .40
❑ 58 The Power of Oprah .15 .40
❑ 59 The O Street Band .15 .40
❑ 60 Don't Forget to Laugh .15 .40
❑ 61 Kennedys for Obama .15 .40
❑ 62 Sad Farewell to Toot .15 .40
❑ 63 Not-So-Secret Ballots .15 .40
❑ 64 Obama Wins! .15 .40
❑ 65 Not Your Typical Family Anymore .15 .40
❑ 66 Hello, Chicago! .15 .40
❑ 67 Sharing a Historic Moment .15 .40
❑ 68 Grant Park Celebrates .15 .40
❑ 69 Joe the Vice President-Elect .15 .40
❑ 70 Washington's New Dynamic Duo .15 .40
❑ 71 McCain Graciously Concedes .15 .40
❑ 72 I Like It Here! .15 .40
❑ 73 One President at a Time, but .15 .40
❑ 74 Hail to the Chief of Staff .15 .40
❑ 75 The Magnificent 17 .15 .40
❑ 76 Meet the Press(ure) .15 .40
❑ 77 The First Spokesman .15 .40
❑ 78 Yes They Did! .15 .40
❑ 79 Economic Team Takes the Field .15 .40
❑ 80 Burying the Hatchet .15 .40
❑ 81 The First Granny .15 .40
❑ 82 American Dream Come True .15 .40
❑ 83 Life, Liberty, Happiness .15 .40
❑ 84 Land of Opportunity .15 .40
❑ 85 I Love This Country .15 .40
❑ 86 Healing Racial Divisions .15 .40
❑ 87 All Hands on Deck .15 .40
❑ 88 The Power of Our Democracy .15 .40
❑ 89 Yes, We Will! .15 .40
❑ 90 Checklist .15 .40
❑ NNO Barack Obama Poster 4.00 10.00
❑ NNO Presidential Pup 20.00 40.00

2009 Topps President Obama Inaugural Silver Foil

*SILVER: 2X TO 5X BASIC
STATED ODDS 1:3 PACKS

2009 Topps President Obama Inaugural Stickers

COMPLETE SET (18) 6.00 15.00
COMMON STICKER (1-18) .60 1.50
STATED ODDS ONE PER PACK

❑ 1 Yes We Can .60 1.50
❑ 2 Hope .60 1.50
❑ 3 Change .60 1.50
❑ 4 Obama .60 1.50
❑ 5 We Are The Ones We've Been Waiting For .60 1.50
❑ 6 Progress .60 1.50
❑ 7 I Heart Obama .60 1.50
❑ 8 A More Perfect Union .60 1.50
❑ 9 Dream Come True .60 1.50
❑ 10 America .60 1.50
❑ 11 We Are The Change That We Seek .60 1.50
❑ 12 Unity .60 1.50
❑ 13 Believe .60 1.50
❑ 14 History .60 1.50
❑ 15 Obama Biden 2012 Button .60 1.50
❑ 16 Our Time .60 1.50
❑ 17 Change Has Come .60 1.50
❑ 18 Yes We Did .60 1.50

2009 Topps President Obama Inaugural Stickers Foil

COMPLETE SET (18) 10.00 25.00
*FOIL: .6X TO 1.5X BASIC STICKER
STATED ODDS 1:4 PACKS

2009 SpongeBob Squarepants Series 1

COMPLETE SET (90) 15.00 25.00
UNOPENED BOX (24 packs) 38.00 45.00
Sticker Set (15) 5.00 10.00
Sticker Cards (1-15) .75 1.00
Sponge Set (5) 50.00 65.00
Sponge Cards (1-5) 10.00 15.00
Create-A-Scene Set (10) 10.00 20.00
Create-A-Scene Cards (1-10) 1.00 2.00
Paul Tibbitt Sketch Card 35.00 60.00

❑ 1 Spongebob .50 1.00
❑ 2 Patrick .50 1.00
❑ 3 Squidward .50 1.00
❑ 4 Mr. Krabs .50 1.00
❑ 5 Gary .50 1.00
❑ 6 Sandy Cheeks .50 1.00
❑ 7 Plankton .50 1.00
❑ 8 Mrs. Puff .20 .50
❑ 9 Mermaidman .20 .50
❑ 10 Barnacleboy .20 .50
❑ 11 Pearl .20 .50
❑ 12 Snellie .20 .50
❑ 13 Karen .20 .50
❑ 14 Flying Dutchman .20 .50
❑ 15 Mayor .20 .50
❑ 16 The Big Day .20 .50
❑ 17 Sponge Quest .20 .50
❑ 18 Anchovies by the Busload .20 .50
❑ 19 Return of the Sponge .20 .50
❑ 20 Saving Sandy .20 .50
❑ 21 Over for Tea & Cookies .20 .50
❑ 22 Waterless World .20 .50
❑ 23 Drink Up! .20 .50
❑ 24 Wannabes .20 .50
❑ 25 Super Zeros .20 .50
❑ 26 Grumpy Old Heroes .20 .50
❑ 27 Back in Action .20 .50
❑ 28 Sales Gimmick .20 .50
❑ 29 The Big Night .20 .50
❑ 30 A Disaster .20 .50
❑ 31 A Sponge Is Born .20 .50
❑ 32 Hi-Yah! .20 .50
❑ 33 Hi-Nah! .20 .50
❑ 34 No More Karate .20 .50
❑ 35 Sponge-Chop .20 .50
❑ 36 Switching Lives .20 .50
❑ 37 Mr. Plankton .20 .50
❑ 38 Red Alert .20 .50
❑ 39 So Long! .20 .50
❑ 40 Never Tasted One .20 .50
❑ 41 Try It .20 .50
❑ 42 Squidward's Secret .20 .50
❑ 43 More! .20 .50
❑ 44 Santa Who? .20 .50
❑ 45 Bah, Squidbug! .20 .50
❑ 46 The Giving Spirit .20 .50
❑ 47 Squidward Claus .20 .50
❑ 48 24 Hours? .20 .50
❑ 49 Hash-Slinging Whaaat? .20 .50
❑ 50 The Three Signs .20 .50
❑ 51 The Slasher? .20 .50
❑ 52 The Tough Guy Line .20 .50
❑ 53 Not a Weenie! .20 .50
❑ 54 Weenie Hut Jr.'s .20 .50
❑ 55 Tough Enough .20 .50
❑ 56 Caveman .20 .50
❑ 57 Viking .20 .50
❑ 58 Knight .20 .50
❑ 59 Pirate .20 .50
❑ 60 Cowboy .20 .50
❑ 61 Aviator .20 .50
❑ 62 Ready Ride! .20 .50
(Goo Lagoon
❑ 63 Spongebob Meets the Guru .20 .50
❑ 64 The Long Board .20 .50
(The Big One
❑ 65 Training for The Big One .20 .50
❑ 66 Jack Kahuna .20 .50
❑ 67 Jack's Surf School .20 .50
❑ 68 Catch a Wave .20 .50
Did You Know...
❑ 69 Let's Go Surfin' .20 .50
Did You Know...
❑ 70 Get Totally Stoked .20 .50
SpongeBob Beach
❑ 71 Can you tell which of these are real .20 .50
❑ 72 Zen and the Art of Surfing .20 .50
❑ 73 Surfin' Safari .20 .50
❑ 74 She Came from Texas! .20 .50
❑ 75 The Spatula .20 .50
❑ 76 Patrick's Secret Box .20 .50
❑ 77 Rock Bottom .20 .50
❑ 78 I Was a Teenage Gary .20 .50
❑ 79 The Chaperone .20 .50
❑ 80 Beware the Hooks .20 .50
❑ 81 The Chum Bucket of Dr. P! .20 .50
❑ 82 The Ghostly Curse of the Flying Dutch .20 .50
❑ 83 Creature with Six Tentacles .20 .50
❑ 84 Robot Chef .20 .50
❑ 85 I Touched My Braion .20 .50
❑ 86 Fear the Bat-Sponge of Bikini Bottom .20 .50
❑ 87 Orb of Confusion .20 .50
❑ 88 They Came from Planet Goofball! .20 .50
❑ 89 The Hash-Slinging Slasher .20 .50
❑ 90 Checklist .20 .50

2009 SpongeBob Squarepants Series 2

COMPLETE SET (90) 10.00 18.00
UNOPENED BOX (24 packs) 38.00 45.00
Magnet Set (9) 12.00 20.00
Magnet Cards (1-9) 2.00 3.00
Make Your Own Set (10) 7.00 15.00
Make Your Own Cards (1-10) 1.00 2.00
Pop-Ups Set (10) 8.00 15.00
Pop-Ups Cards (1-10) 1.00 2.00
Tattoo Set (9) 4.00 8.00
Tattoo Cards (1-9) .50 1.00
Sticker Puzzle Set (9) 4.00 8.00
Sticker Puzzle Cards (1-9) .50 1.00

❑ 1 Jolly Jelly-Fisherman .50 1.00
❑ 2 Starfish Stinky Breath .20 .50
❑ 3 Master of Misery .20 .50
❑ 4 Texas Transplant .20 .50
❑ 5 Money Loving Miser .20 .50
❑ 6 Conniving Copepod .20 .50
❑ 7 Super Sea Snail .20 .30
❑ 8 Teenage Whale .20 .30
❑ 9 Karen .20 .30
❑ 10 Pertistence of SpongeBob .20 .30
❑ 11 SpongeBob Nouveau .20 .30
❑ 12 Bikini Bottom Gothic .20 .30
❑ 13 Composition in Red, Blue and Sponge .20 .30
❑ 14 Self Portrait of SpongeBrandt .20 .30
❑ 15 The Son of Sponge .20 .30
❑ 16 Self Portrait with Bandaged Ear .20 .30
❑ 17 The Birth of SpongeBob .20 .30
❑ 18 Sunday Afternoon in Jellyfish Fields .20 .30
❑ 19 Sponge Rind .20 .30
❑ 20 Sponge with Spatula .20 .30
❑ 21 Spongeiosseur .20 .30
❑ 22 Bikini Bottom's Greatest Hero .20 .30
❑ 23 The Legend of the Sponge .20 .30
❑ 24 Escape from the Vortex .20 .30
❑ 25 SandBob Squidpants .20 .30
❑ 26 Oops! I Ripped My Pants! .20 .30
❑ 27 Surfin' Split Pants .20 .30
❑ 28 The Snail Plasma Takes Effect .20 .30
❑ 29 Squidward Meets SnailBob .20 .30
❑ 30 Singing Snail Party! .20 .30
❑ 31 Magic Pencil Mischief .20 .30
❑ 32 The Ol' Magic Doodle Money Trick! .20 .30
❑ 33 Revenge of DoodleBob .20 .30
❑ 34 Octo-mom Earplugs .20 .30
❑ 35 Wiping the Fancy Away .20 .30
❑ 36 Tattle Tails .20 .30
❑ 37 SpongBob the...Disguise? .20 .30
❑ 38 The Great Skill Crane Challenge .20 .30
❑ 39 Secret of the Skill Crane .20 .30
❑ 40 Wig Wearin' Fry Cook .20 .30
❑ 41 Bug Struck .20 .30
❑ 42 Cool and Fashionable? .20 .30
❑ 43 The Mark Has Been Left .20 .30
❑ 44 Plantkons's Buying a Stamp, Over. .20 .30
❑ 45 Unscathed .20 .30
❑ 46 SpongeBob: Liberated .20 .30
❑ 47 Squidward to Launch .20 .30
❑ 48 Vikings Need...Security Blankets? .20 .30
❑ 49 Nothing to Play With .20 .30
❑ 50 After Hours at the Toy Barrel .20 .30
❑ 51 Toy Store Soldiers .20 .30
❑ 52 Lost in Time .20 .30
❑ 53 Where's Gary? .20 .30
❑ 54 Friend or Foe .20 .30
❑ 55 Atlantis Squarepants .20 .30
❑ 56 Best Day Ever .20 .30
❑ 57 Christams Who? .20 .30
❑ 58 Pest of the West .20 .30
❑ 59 WhoBob Whatpants .20 .30
❑ 60 SpongeSLAM .20 .30
❑ 61 Pirate Party .20 .30
❑ 62 Sponge in Space .20 .30
❑ 63 SpongeBob Squarepunt .20 .30
❑ 64 Bikini Kart Circuit .20 .30
❑ 65 CubicleBob .20 .30
❑ 66 FireSponge .20 .30
❑ 67 Sponge-Guards .20 .30
❑ 68 Sk8, Don't Hate .20 .30
❑ 69 SpongeRider .20 .30
❑ 70 Sponge Cup .20 .30
❑ 71 Super-Buddies .20 .30
❑ 72 The Smallest Evil in the Sea .20 .30
❑ 73 A Plankton in the hand... .20 .30
❑ 74 Watch Your Step .20 .30
❑ 75 The Conquest of Plankton .20 .30
❑ 76 Pelagic Relaxation .20 .30
❑ 77 Ripped Archaea .20 .30
❑ 78 Secret Plan # 042261432 .20 .30
❑ 79 Giant Red Crab .20 .30
❑ 80 Chum Burger Chariot .20 .30
❑ 81 To Squarepants or Not to... .20 .30
❑ 82 SpongeBob Pointypants .20 .30
❑ 83 Pant Knees Please .20 .30
❑ 84 Showing off the Roundpants .20 .30
❑ 85 Gary Roundpants .20 .30
❑ 86 Hugepant Long Legs .20 .30
❑ 87 Tiny Pants, Underpants! .20 .30
❑ 88 SpongeBob's Tubular New Look .20 .30
❑ 89 The Sharpest Sponge! .20 .30
❑ 90 Checklist .20 .30

2009 Transformers Revenge of the Fallen

COMPLETE SET (45) 3.00 8.00

❑ 1 Optimus Prime .15 .40
❑ 2 Bumblebee .15 .40
❑ 3 Ratchet .15 .40
❑ 4 Ironhide .15 .40
❑ 5 Skids and Mudflap .15 .40
❑ 6 Megatron .15 .40
❑ 7 Starscream .15 .40
❑ 8 The Fallen .15 .40
❑ 9 Devastator .15 .40
❑ 10 Sideswipe .15 .40
❑ 11 Ravage .15 .40
❑ 12 Optimus Prime .15 .40
❑ 13 Bumblebee .15 .40
❑ 14 Ratchet .15 .40
❑ 15 Ironhide .15 .40
❑ 16 Skids and Mudflap .15 .40
❑ 17 Megatron .15 .40
❑ 18 Starscream .15 .40
❑ 19 The Fallen .15 .40
❑ 20 Devastator .15 .40
❑ 21 Sideswipe .15 .40
❑ 22 Optimus Prime .15 .40
❑ 23 Megatron .15 .40
❑ 24 Starscream .15 .40
❑ 25 Decepticons .15 .40
❑ 26 Autobots .15 .40
❑ 27 Autobots .15 .40
❑ 28 Autobots .15 .40
❑ 29 Decepticons .15 .40
❑ 30 Autobots .15 .40
❑ 31 Decepticons .15 .40
❑ 32 Optimus Prime .15 .40
❑ 33 Optimus Prime .15 .40
❑ 34 Bumblebee .15 .40
❑ 35 Bumblebee .15 .40
❑ 36 Ratchet .15 .40
❑ 37 Ironhide .15 .40
❑ 38 Skids & Mudflap .15 .40
❑ 39 Skids & Mudflap .15 .40
❑ 40 Megatron .15 .40
❑ 41 Starscream .15 .40
❑ 42 Ravage .15 .40
❑ 43 Ironhide .15 .40
❑ 44 The Fallen .15 .40
❑ 45 Sideswipe .15 .40

2009 Transformers Revenge of the Fallen Autographs

STATED ODDS 1:91

❑ 1 Shia LeBeouf 100.00 150.00
❑ 2 Charles Adler 20.00 40.00
❑ 3 Peter Cullen 40.00 80.00
❑ 4 Robert Foxworth 20.00 40.00
❑ 5 Jess Harnel 20.00 40.00
❑ 6 Mark Ryan 25.00 50.00

2009 Transformers Revenge of the Fallen Comic Art

COMPLETE SET (12) 2.00 5.00
COMIC ART/MOVIE RECAP/PREVIEW COMBINED ODDS 2:1

❑ 1 Alliance .25 .60
❑ 2 Alliance .25 .60
❑ 3 Alliance .25 .60
❑ 4 Alliance .25 .60
❑ 5 Defiance .25 .60
❑ 6 Defiance .25 .60
❑ 7 Defiance .25 .60
❑ 8 Defiance .25 .60
❑ 9 ROTF .25 .60
❑ 10 ROTF .25 .60
❑ 11 ROTF .25 .60
❑ 12 ROTF .25 .60

2009 Transformers Revenge of the Fallen Movie Recap

COMPLETE SET (9) 1.25 3.00
COMIC ART/MOVIE RECAP/PREVIEW COMBINED ODDS 2:1

❑ 1 Meeting the Autobots .25 .60
❑ 2 Key to the AllSpark .25 .60
❑ 3 Sector 7's Living Relic .25 .60
❑ 4 Ironhide Engaged .25 .60
❑ 5 Primed and Ready .25 .60
❑ 6 Megatron's Assault .25 .60
❑ 7 Decepticons on Wilshire .25 .60
❑ 8 Sam's Desperate Plan .25 .60
❑ 9 Bumblebee's Decision .25 .60

2009 Transformers Revenge of the Fallen Popups

COMPLETE SET (9) 2.00 5.00
STATED ODDS 1:2

❑ 1 Optimus Prime .40 1.00
❑ 2 Bumblebee .40 1.00
❑ 3 Megatron .40 1.00
❑ 4 Ironhide .40 1.00
❑ 5 Ratchet .40 1.00
❑ 6 Starscream .40 1.00
❑ 7 Skids & Mudflap .40 1.00
❑ 8 The Fallen .40 1.00
❑ 9 Sideswipe .40 1.00

2009 Transformers Revenge of the Fallen Preview

COMPLETE SET (3) .40 1.00
COMIC ART/MOVIE RECAP/PREVIEW COMBINED ODDS 2:1

❑ 1 The Stealth of Ravage .25 .60
❑ 2 Sam's Interrogation .25 .60
❑ 3 Starscream Is Back .25 .60

2009 Transformers Revenge of the Fallen Tattoos

COMPLETE SET (10) 2.00 5.00
STATED ODDS 1:2

❑ 1 Autobot logo .30 .75
❑ 2 Decepticon logo .30 .75
❑ 3 Transformers Revenge of the Fallen .30 .75
❑ 4 Bumblebee .30 .75
❑ 5 Ironhide .30 .75
❑ 6 Megatron .30 .75
❑ 7 Ravage .30 .75
❑ 8 Starscream .30 .75
❑ 9 The Fallen .30 .75
❑ 10 Decepticon .30 .75

2009 Twilight New Moon

COMPLETE SET (84) 10.00 25.00
CL1 STATED ODDS 1:104
HT1 STATED ODDS 1:24 HOT TOPIC PACKS
T1 STATED ODDS 1:15 TARGET PACKS

❑ 1 New Moon .25 .60
❑ 2 Bella .25 .60
❑ 3 Edward .25 .60
❑ 4 Jacob .25 .60
❑ 5 Alice .25 .60
❑ 6 Jasper .25 .60
❑ 7 Rosalie .25 .60
❑ 8 Emmett .25 .60
❑ 9 Carlisle .25 .60
❑ 10 Esme .25 .60
❑ 11 Victoria .25 .60
❑ 12 Laurent .25 .60
❑ 13 Sam .25 .60
❑ 14 Paul .25 .60
❑ 15 Jared .25 .60
❑ 16 Embry .25 .60
❑ 17 Jane .25 .60
❑ 18 Aro .25 .60
❑ 19 Caius .25 .60
❑ 20 Marcus .25 .60
❑ 21 Alec .25 .60
❑ 22 Charlie .25 .60
❑ 23 Billy .25 .60
❑ 24 Mike .25 .60
❑ 25 Jessica .25 .60
❑ 26 Angela .25 .60
❑ 27 Eric .25 .60
❑ 28 The Dream .25 .60
❑ 29 Happy Birthday, Bells .25 .60
❑ 30 Something to Celebrate .25 .60
❑ 31 Party Plans .25 .60
❑ 32 Plotting Revenge .25 .60
❑ 33 Cullens Celebrate .25 .60
❑ 34 Jasper's Weakness .25 .60
❑ 35 Get Jasper Out .25 .60
❑ 36 Mending .25 .60
❑ 37 Who Wants Normal .25 .60
❑ 38 The Promise .25 .60
❑ 39 Rescue Party .25 .60
❑ 40 Found .25 .60
❑ 41 Despair .25 .60
❑ 42 Charlie Intervenes .25 .60
❑ 43 Finding Danger .25 .60
❑ 44 Visiting Jacob .25 .60
❑ 45 Jacob's Garage .25 .60
❑ 46 On the Cliffs .25 .60
❑ 47 Jacob Concerned .25 .60
❑ 48 Lessons .25 .60
❑ 49 Speeding to Edward .25 .60
❑ 50 Movie Night .25 .60
❑ 51 Jacob's Different .25 .60
❑ 52a Breaking Up .25 .60
(back reads It's Not You)
❑ 52b Breaking Up
(back reads It's Not You...It's Me)
❑ 53 Unexpected Reunion .25 .60
❑ 54a Breaking Up .25 .60
❑ 54b Who's Afraid
❑ 55 Secret Withheld .25 .60
❑ 56 Secret Revealed .25 .60
❑ 57 You're a Werewolf .25 .60
❑ 58 Hunting Party .25 .60
❑ 59 The Jump .25 .60
❑ 60 You Won't Lose Yourself .25 .60
❑ 61 Alice Comes Back .25 .60
❑ 62 Edward in Italy .25 .60
❑ 63 Racing against Time .25 .60
❑ 64 Just in Time .25 .60
❑ 65 The Volturi .25 .60
❑ 66 Unreadable .25 .60
❑ 67 Edward in Trouble .25 .60
❑ 68 One of Us .25 .60
❑ 69 Back Together .25 .60
❑ 70 The Vote .25 .60
❑ 71 With Conditions .25 .60
❑ 72 Checklist .25 .60
❑ 73 A Disturbing Dream .25 .60
❑ 74 High School Friends .25 .60
❑ 75 Jacob Is There .25 .60
❑ 76 Alice Insists .25 .60
❑ 77 Edward Leaves .25 .60
❑ 78 Dream Catcher .25 .60
❑ 79 Rescued .25 .60
❑ 80 Can't Live without Bella .25 .60
❑ 81 Volturi To Judge .25 .60
❑ 82 Bella Swan .25 .60
❑ 83 Edward Cullen .25 .60
❑ 84 Jacob Black .25 .60
❑ CL1 Reckless 6.00 15.00
❑ HT1 Temptations 25.00 50.00
(Hot Topic exclusive)
❑ T1 Goodbye 4.00 10.00
(Target exclusive)

2009 Twilight New Moon Autographs

STATED ODDS 1:24 UPDATE PACKS

❑ 1 Ashley Green 15.00 30.00
❑ 2 Peter Facinelli 6.00 15.00

2009 Twilight New Moon Puzzle

COMPLETE SET (9) 10.00 25.00
STATED ODDS 1:7

❑ T1 New Moon - Top Left 2.00 5.00
❑ T2 New Moon - Top Center 2.00 5.00
❑ T3 New Moon - Top Right 2.00 5.00
❑ T4 New Moon - Middle Left 2.00 5.00
❑ T5 New Moon - Middle Center 2.00 5.00
❑ T6 New Moon - Middle Right 2.00 5.00
❑ T7 New Moon - Bottom Left 2.00 5.00
❑ T8 New Moon - Bottom Center 2.00 5.00
❑ T9 New Moon - Bottom Right 2.00 5.00

2009 Twilight New Moon Seeing Alice

COMPLETE SET (3) 8.00 20.00
STATED ODDS 1:23

❑ SE1 Alice and Jasper 4.00 10.00
❑ SE2 Alice and Bella 4.00 10.00
❑ SE3 Alice Will Change Her 4.00 10.00

2009 Twilight New Moon The Wolfpack Puzzle

COMPLETE SET (6) 8.00 20.00
STATED ODDS 1:11

❑ WP1 The Wolfpack - Top Left 2.50 6.00
❑ WP2 The Wolfpack - Top Center 2.50 6.00
❑ WP3 The Wolfpack - Top Right 2.50 6.00
❑ WP4 The Wolfpack - Bottom Left 2.50 6.00
❑ WP5 The Wolfpack - Bottom Center 2.50 6.00
❑ WP6 The Wolfpack - Bottom Right 2.50 6.00

2009 Twilight New Moon Volturi Coven

COMPLETE SET (6) 8.00 20.00
STATED ODDS 1:11

❑ VO1 The Volturi Coven 2.50 6.00
❑ VO2 Carlisle 2.50 6.00
❑ VO3 Aro 2.50 6.00
❑ VO4 Caius 2.50 6.00
❑ VO5 Marcus 2.50 6.00
❑ VO6 The Law 2.50 6.00

2009 X-Men Archives

COMPLETE SET (72) 5.00 12.00

❑ 1 Title Card .15 .40
❑ 2 Angel .15 .40
❑ 3 Armor .15 .40
❑ 4 Beast .15 .40
❑ 5 Bishop .15 .40
❑ 6 Blink .15 .40
❑ 7 Cable .15 .40
❑ 8 Caliban .15 .40
❑ 9 Callisto .15 .40
❑ 10 Cannonball .15 .40
❑ 11 Captain Britain .15 .40
❑ 12 Chamber .15 .40
❑ 13 Colossus .15 .40
❑ 14 Cyclops .15 .40
❑ 15 Dazzler .15 .40
❑ 16 Deadpool .15 .40
❑ 17 Domino .15 .40
❑ 18 Dust .15 .40
❑ 19 Elixir .15 .40
❑ 20 Emma Frost .15 .40
White Queen
❑ 21 Forge .15 .40
❑ 22 Gambit .15 .40
❑ 23 Guardian .15 .40
❑ 24 Havok .15 .40
❑ 25 Hellion .15 .40
❑ 26 Icarus .15 .40
❑ 27 Iceman .15 .40
❑ 28 Ink .15 .40
❑ 29 Jean Grey .15 .40
❑ 30 Jubilee .15 .40
❑ 31 Karma .15 .40
❑ 32 Kuan-Yin Xorn .15 .40
❑ 33 Lilandra .15 .40
❑ 34 Longshot .15 .40
❑ 35 M .15 .40
❑ 36 Magik .15 .40
❑ 37 Magma .15 .40
❑ 38 Marvel Girl .15 .40
❑ 39 Mercury .15 .40
❑ 40 Mimic .15 .40
❑ 41 Mirage .15 .40
❑ 42 Morph .15 .40
❑ 43 Multiple Man .15 .40
❑ 44 Nightcrawler .15 .40
❑ 45 Northstar .15 .40
❑ 46 Omega Sentinel .15 .40
❑ 47 Pixie .15 .40
❑ 48 Polaris .15 .40
❑ 49 Prodigy .15 .40
❑ 50 Professor Xavier .15 .40
❑ 51 Psylocke .15 .40
❑ 52 Quicksilver .15 .40
❑ 53 Rockslide .15 .40
❑ 54 Rogue .15 .40
❑ 55 Sage .15 .40
❑ 56 Shadowcat .15 .40
❑ 57 Shatterstar .15 .40
❑ 58 Shola Inkosi .15 .40
❑ 59 Siryn .15 .40
❑ 60 Starjammers .15 .40
❑ 61 Storm .15 .40
❑ 62 Strong Guy .15 .40
❑ 63 Sunfire .15 .40
❑ 64 Sunspot .15 .40
❑ 65 Surge .15 .40
❑ 66 Wallflower .15 .40
❑ 67 Warpath .15 .40
❑ 68 Wicked .15 .40
❑ 69 Wind Dancer .15 .40
❑ 70 Wolfsbane .15 .40
❑ 71 Wolverine .15 .40
❑ 72 X-23 .15 .40

2009 X-Men Archives Case Toppers

COMPLETE SET (3) 40.00 100.00
STATED ODDS ONE PER CASE

❑ CT1 Juggernaut 15.00 40.00
Rogue/Psylocke
❑ CT2 Beast 15.00 40.00
Cable/Wolverine
❑ CT3 Storm 15.00 40.00
Phoenix/Nightcrawler/Colossus

2009 X-Men Archives Cover Gallery

COMPLETE SET (9) 8.00 20.00
STATED ODDS 1:12

❑ CA1 Astonishing X-Men #1 1.50 4.00
❑ CA2 Astonishing X-Men #7 1.50 4.00
❑ CA3 Giant-Size X-Men #4 1.50 4.00
❑ CA4 Uncanny X-Men #488 1.50 4.00
❑ CA5 Uncanny X-Men #494 1.50 4.00

❑ CA6 Uncanny X-Men #495 1.50 4.00
❑ CA7 X-Men First Class #15 1.50 4.00
❑ CA8 X-Men Legacy #208 1.50 4.00
❑ CA9 X-Men #175 1.50 4.00

2009 X-Men Archives Legendary Heroes

COMPLETE SET (9) 20.00 50.00
STATED ODDS 1:24

❑ LH1 Angel 4.00 10.00
❑ LH2 Beast 4.00 10.00
❑ LH3 Colossus 4.00 10.00
❑ LH4 Cyclops 4.00
❑ LH5 Iceman 4.00
❑ LH6 Jean Grey 4.00 10.00
❑ LH7 Professor X 4.00 10.00
❑ LH8 Storm 4.00 10.00
❑ LH9 Wolverine 4.00 10.00
❑ LH10 Shadowcat SP 12.00 30.00
(issued as Rittenhouse Reward)

2009 X-Men Archives Nemesis

COMPLETE SET (9) 6.00 15.00
STATED ODDS 1:8

❑ N1 Mr. Sinister 1.25 3.00
❑ N2 Magneto 1.25 3.00
❑ N3 Mystique 1.25 3.00
❑ N4 Sabretooth 1.25 3.00
❑ N5 Mojo 1.25 3.00
❑ N6 Apocalypse 1.25 3.00
❑ N7 Juggernaut 1.25 3.00
❑ N8 Sentinels 1.25 3.00
❑ N9 Brotherhood of Evil Mutants 1.25 3.00

2009 X-Men Archives Sketches

STATED ODDS ONE PER BOX
PRICE SKETCH ONE PER 3 CASE PURCHASE
PALMER, DELIZ SKETCH ONE PER 6 CASE PURCHASE
UNNUMBERED CARDS LISTED ALPHABETICALLY

❑ 1 Adam Cleveland
❑ 2 Allison Sohn
❑ 3 Adriano Carreon
❑ 4 Anthony Castrillo
❑ 5 Anthony Tan
❑ 6 Anthony Wheeler
❑ 7 Arie Monroe
❑ 8 Benjamin Glendenning
❑ 9 Blair Shedd
❑ 10 Brandon Kenney
❑ 11 Brian Kong
❑ 12 Brian Postman
❑ 13 Buddy Prince
❑ 14 Butch Mapa
❑ 15 Carlo Sinfuengo Soriano
❑ 16 Cat Staggs
❑ 17 Charles George
❑ 18 Chris Wilson
❑ 19 Chris Gutierrez
❑ 20 Craig Yeung
❑ 21 Daniel Bradao
❑ 22 Daniel Campos
❑ 23 Daniel Cooney
❑ 24 Daniel HDR
❑ 25 Darren Chandler
❑ 26 Dave Fox
❑ 27 Dave Simons
❑ 28 Dennis Crisostomo
❑ 29 Doug Cowan
❑ 30 Edde Wagner
❑ 31 Erik Maell
❑ 32 Felipe Massafera
❑ 33 Fernando Merlo
❑ 34 Gabriel Hernandez
❑ 35 George Calloway
❑ 36 James McNeil
❑ 37 Jason Davies
❑ 38 Jason Sobol
❑ 39 Javier Gonzalez
❑ 40 Jeff Zugale
❑ 41 Jennifer Mercer
❑ 42 Jim Kyle
❑ 43 Joe Rubinstein
❑ 44 John Haun
❑ 45 John Watkins-Chow
❑ 46 Justin Chung
❑ 47 Justin Vandemark
❑ 48 Kate Bradley
❑ 49 Kathryn Layno
❑ 50 Katie Cook
❑ 51 Keith O'Malley
❑ 52 Ken Landgraf
❑ 53 Kevin West
❑ 54 Kristin Allen
❑ 55 Leeahd Goldberg
❑ 56 Lui Antonio
❑ 57 Mahmud Asrar
❑ 58 Marcelo Ferreira
❑ 59 Mark Dos Santos
❑ 60 Mark Spears
❑ 61 Megan McCausland
❑ 62 Michael Clark
❑ 63 Michael Axebone Potter
❑ 64 Newton Barbosa
❑ 65 Nick Neocleous
❑ 66 Nick Yakimovich
❑ 67 Nicole Goff
❑ 68 Oak
❑ 69 Randy Martinez
❑ 70 Randy Monces
❑ 71 Rhiannon Ownes
❑ 72 Rich Molinelli
❑ 73 Rodjer Goulart
❑ 74 Roger Medeiros
❑ 75 Ryan Orosco
❑ 76 Sanna Umemoto
❑ 77 Scott Barnett
❑ 78 Sonny Strait
❑ 79 Tess Fowler
❑ 80 Thony Sillas
❑ 81 Tom Kelly
❑ 82 Tone Rodriguez
❑ 83 Tony Perna
❑ 84 Uko Smith
❑ 85 Warren Martineck
❑ 86 Yildiray Cinar
❑ 87 Andy Price/ (issued as 3-case incentive)
❑ 88 Tom Palmer/ (issued as 6-case incentive)
❑ 89 Renae DeLiz/ (issued as 6-case incentive)

2009 X-Men Origins Wolverine

COMPLETE SET (72) 6.00 15.00
MOVIE POSTER CARD INSERTED ONE PER CASE
MOVIE POSTER CARD SER. #'d TO 600

❑ 1 Group Shot .15 .40
❑ 2 James Howlett .15 .40
John Howlett
❑ 3 James Howlett .15 .40
❑ 4 Victor Creed .15 .40
❑ 5 Thomas Logan .15 .40
❑ 6 James Howlett .15 .40
John Howlett
❑ 7 James Howlett .15 .40
❑ 8 Thomas Logan .15 .40
James Howlett
❑ 9 Victor Creed .15 .40
James Howlett
❑ 10 Victor Creed .15 .40
James Howlett
❑ 11 Logan's Home .15 .40
❑ 12 Bradley .15 .40
❑ 13 Bradley .15 .40
Victor Creed
❑ 14 William Stryker .15 .40
Agent Zero
❑ 15 Logan .15 .40
❑ 16 Zero .15 .40
Logan/Stryker
❑ 17 Victor Creed .15 .40
Logan
❑ 18 Creed .15 .40
Logan/Stryker
❑ 19 Kayla .15 .40
Logan
❑ 20 Kayla .15 .40
Logan
❑ 21 Logan .15 .40
❑ 22 Victor Creed .15 .40
❑ 23 Logan .15 .40
Kayla
❑ 24 Victor Creed .15 .40
❑ 25 Victor Creed .15 .40
❑ 26 Logan's Claws .15 .40
❑ 27 Victor Creed .15 .40
Logan
❑ 28 Victor Creed .15 .40
❑ 29 Victor Creed .15 .40
Logan
❑ 30 Logan .15 .40
❑ 31 Logan .15 .40
❑ 32 Logan .15 .40
❑ 33 General Munson .15 .40
❑ 34 Logan .15 .40
❑ 35 Logan .15 .40
❑ 36 Agent Zero .15 .40
❑ 37 Fred J. Dukes .15 .40
❑ 38 William Stryker .15 .40
❑ 39 Victor Creed .15 .40
❑ 40 Logan .15 .40
❑ 41 Travis Hudson .15 .40
❑ 42 Logan .15 .40
❑ 43 Travis Hudson .15 .40
Logan
❑ 44 Logan .15 .40
❑ 45 Logan .15 .40
Agent Zero
❑ 46 Logan .15 .40
❑ 47 John Wraith .15 .40
❑ 48 John Wraith .15 .40
Logan
❑ 49 Logan .15 .40
Fred J. Dukes
❑ 50 Fred J. Dukes .15 .40
❑ 51 Fred J. Dukes .15 .40
Logan
❑ 52 Scott .15 .40
❑ 53 Scott .15 .40
Victor Creed
❑ 54 Fred J. Dukes .15 .40
Victor Creed
❑ 55 Logan .15 .40
John Wraith
❑ 56 Remy LeBeau .15 .40
❑ 57 Remy LeBeau .15 .40
❑ 58 Victor Creed .15 .40
John Wraith
❑ 59 Logan .15 .40
Victor Creed
❑ 60 Logan .15 .40
Remy LeBeau
❑ 61 Logan .15 .40
Remy LeBeau
❑ 62 Remy LeBeau .15 .40
❑ 63 Victor Creed .15 .40
Logan
❑ 64 Taylor Kitsch .15 .40
❑ 65 Gavin Hood .15 .40
will.i.am
❑ 66 Kevin Durand .15 .40
❑ 67 Kevin Durand .15 .40
❑ 68 will.i.am .15 .40
Hood/Jackman
❑ 69 Gavin Hood .15 .40
❑ 70 Airplane .15 .40
❑ 71 Danny Huston .15 .40
Gavin Hood
❑ 72 Gavin Hood .15 .40
Hugh Jackman
❑ NNO Movie Poster 10.00 25.00

2009 X-Men Origins Wolverine Archives

COMPLETE SET (9) 4.00 10.00
STATED ODDS 1:8

❑ A1 Wolverine .75 2.00
❑ A2 Wolverine .75 2.00
❑ A3 Wolverine .75 2.00
❑ A4 Wolverine .75 2.00
❑ A5 Wolverine .75 2.00
❑ A6 Wolverine .75 2.00
❑ A7 Wolverine .75 2.00
❑ A8 Wolverine .75 2.00
❑ A9 Wolverine .75 2.00

2009 X-Men Origins Wolverine Autographs

STATED AUTO/SKETCH ODDS 1:12
will.i.am AUTO STATED ODDS ONE PER 2 CASE PURCHASE

❑ AJ Aaron Jeffery 6.00 15.00
❑ DH1 Daniel Henney 6.00 15.00
❑ DH2 Danny Huston 6.00 15.00
❑ GH Gavin Hood 6.00 15.00
❑ HJ Hugh Jackman 100.00 200.00
❑ JB Julia Blake 6.00 15.00
❑ KD Kevin Durand 10.00 25.00
❑ LS Liev Schrieber 40.00 100.00
❑ LC Lynn Collins 20.00 50.00
❑ MO Michael-James Olsen 6.00 15.00
❑ RR Ryan Reynolds 50.00 120.00
❑ SL Stephen Leeder 6.00 15.00
❑ TK Taylor Kitsch 20.00 50.00
❑ TP Tim Pocock 6.00 15.00
❑ TS Troye Sivan 6.00 15.00
❑ WIA will.i.am 25.00 60.00

2009 X-Men Origins Wolverine Casting Call

COMPLETE SET (9) 4.00 10.00
STATED ODDS 1:8

❑ C1 Hugh Jackman as Logan 1.25 3.00
❑ C2 Ryan Reynolds as Wade Wilson .75 2.00
❑ C3 Danny Huston as William Stryker .75 2.00
❑ C4 Liev Schrieber as Victor Creed .75 2.00
❑ C5 Lynn Collins as Silver Fox 1.25 3.00
❑ C6 Taylor Kitsch as Remy LeBeau .75 2.00
❑ C7 will.i.am as John Wraith .75 2.00
❑ C8 Daniel Henney as Agent Zero .75 2.00
❑ C9 Kevin Durand as Frederick J. Dukes .75 2.00

2009 X-Men Origins Wolverine Classic Confrontations

COMPLETE SET (6) 5.00 12.00
STATED ODDS 1:12

❑ G1 Wolverine vs Lady Deathstrike 1.25 3.00
❑ G2 Wolverine vs Sabertooth 1.25 3.00
❑ G3 Wolverine vs Sauron 1.25 3.00
❑ G4 Wolverine vs Cyber and Daken 1.25 3.00
❑ G5 Wolverine vs Wendigo 1.25 3.00
❑ G6 Wolverine vs Deadpool 1.25 3.00

2009 X-Men Origins Wolverine Sketches

STATED AUTO/SKETCH ODDS 1:12
McHALEY SKETCH STATED ODDS ONE PER 4 CASE PURCHASE

❑ 1 Adam Cleveland 25.00 60.00
❑ 2 Andrei Bressan 25.00 60.00
❑ 3 Anthony Castrillo 25.00 60.00
❑ 4 Anthony Tan 40.00 100.00
❑ 5 Benjamin Glendenning 60.00 150.00
❑ 6 Brandon Kenney 20.00 50.00
❑ 7 Brian Kong 20.00 50.00
❑ 8 Brian Postman
❑ 9 Buddy Prince 30.00 80.00
❑ 10 Carlo Sinfuego Soriano 60.00 150.00
❑ 11 Cezar Razek 60.00 150.00
❑ 12 Chris Bradberry (Cabbie) 40.00 100.00
❑ 13 Chris Foulkes 20.00 50.00
❑ 14 Chris Gutierrez 20.00 50.00
❑ 15 Chris Wilson 15.00 40.00
❑ 16 Chuck George 20.00 50.00
❑ 17 Craig Yeung 20.00 50.00
❑ 18 Daniel Brandão 15.00 40.00
❑ 19 Darren Chandler 25.00 60.00
❑ 20 Dennis Crisostomo 40.00 100.00
❑ 21 Don Hillsman II 25.00 60.00
❑ 22 Edde Wagner 15.00 40.00
❑ 23 Javier Gonzalez 20.00 50.00
❑ 24 Jim Kyle 60.00 150.00
❑ 25 John Haun 20.00 50.00
❑ 26 John Watkins Chow 25.00 60.00
❑ 27 Justin Vandemark
❑ 28 Katie Cook
❑ 29 Keith O'Malley
❑ 30 Ken Branch 20.00 50.00
❑ 31 Ken Landgraf 20.00 50.00
❑ 32 Kevin West 30.00 80.00
❑ 33 Lui Antonio
❑ 34 Mahmud Asrar 30.00 80.00
❑ 35 Marc Ferreira 30.00 80.00
❑ 36 Marcelo Di Chiara 20.00 50.00
❑ 37 Mark Dos Santos 30.00 80.00
❑ 38 Mark Spears 15.00 40.00
❑ 39 Nicole Goff 50.00 120.00
❑ 40 Oak 20.00 50.00
❑ 41 Rhiannon Owens 40.00 100.00
❑ 42 Rich Molinelli 20.00 50.00
❑ 43 Ryan Orosco 50.00 120.00
❑ 44 Steven Miller 20.00 50.00
❑ 45 Tone Rodriguez 30.00 80.00
❑ 46 Tony Perna
❑ 47 Tony Silas 20.00 50.00
❑ 48 Uko Smith 30.00 80.00
❑ 49 Warren Martineck
❑ 50 Yildiray Cinar 30.00 80.00
❑ 4CI Mark McHaley PAINTED

2010 Bench Warmer Signature Series

COMPLETE SET (100) 6.00 15.00

❑ 1 Jennifer Korbin .15 .40
❑ 2 Torrie Wilson .40 1.00
❑ 3 Jennifer Walcott .40 1.00
❑ 4 Mary Riley .40 1.00
❑ 5 Lisa Gleave .15 .40
❑ 6 Katie Lohmann .15 .40
❑ 7 Traci Bingham .15 .40
❑ 8 Miriam Gonzalez .15 .40
❑ 9 Athena Lundberg .15 .40
❑ 10 Christy Hemme .40 1.00
❑ 11 Carrie Stroup .15 .40
❑ 12 Brandy Grace .15 .40
❑ 13 Brittany Herrera .15 .40
❑ 14 April Scott .15 .40
❑ 15 Sara Underwood .40 1.00
❑ 16 Camille Anderson .15 .40
❑ 17 Nikki Zeno .15 .40
❑ 18 Jessica Rockwell .15 .40
❑ 19 Brandie Moses .15 .40
❑ 20 Jessica Hall .15 .40
❑ 21 Yvette Nelson .15 .40
❑ 22 Michelle Baena .15 .40
❑ 23 Tiffany Toth .15 .40
❑ 24 Jennifer England .15 .40
❑ 25 Kitana Baker .15 .40
❑ 26 Enya Flack .15 .40
❑ 27 Kayla Collins .15 .40
❑ 28 Shay Lyn .15 .40
❑ 29 Lana Kinnear .15 .40
❑ 30 Amie Nicole .15 .40
❑ 31 Jessica Michaels .15 .40
❑ 32 Rachel Bernstein .15 .40
❑ 33 Brittany McGraw .15 .40
❑ 34 Megan Hauserman .15 .40
❑ 35 Catherine Kluthe .15 .40
❑ 36 Sherry Goggin .15 .40
❑ 37 Jaimarie .15 .40
❑ 38 Tamara Witmer .15 .40
❑ 39 Brooke Morales .15 .40
❑ 40 Lindsey Roeper .15 .40
❑ 41 Sarah Coggin .15 .40
❑ 42 Talor Marion .15 .40
❑ 43 Flo Jalin .15 .40
❑ 44 Melissa Hunter .15 .40
❑ 45 Alika Ray .15 .40
❑ 46 Jenae Alt .15 .40
❑ 47 Wrenna Monet .15 .40
❑ 48 Lena Yada .15 .40
❑ 49 Nicole Bennett .15 .40
❑ 50 Michelle Anderson .15 .40
❑ 51 Paige Peterson .15 .40
❑ 52 Bobbi Billard .15 .40
❑ 53 Nikki Ziering .15 .40
❑ 54 Kerrilee Kaski .15 .40
❑ 55 Amber Strauser .15 .40
❑ 56 Candace Kita .15 .40
❑ 57 Renee Stone .15 .40
❑ 58 Tiffany Selby .15 .40
❑ 59 Kristina Rodrigues .15 .40
❑ 60 Raven Lexy .15 .40
❑ 61 Charity Hodges .15 .40
❑ 62 Jo Garcia .15 .40
❑ 63 Leigh Ann Spence .15 .40
❑ 64 Sandra Taylor .15 .40
❑ 65 Brandi Maclaren .15 .40
❑ 66 Miki Black .15 .40
❑ 67 Shana Palmira .15 .40
❑ 68 Jessica Burciaga .15 .40
❑ 69 Lisa Ligon .15 .40
❑ 70 Lauren Kim .15 .40
❑ 71 Kirsten Lingman .15 .40
❑ 72 Crystal Colar .15 .40
❑ 73 Denyce Lawton .15 .40
❑ 74 Buffy Tyler .15 .40
❑ 75 Chanel Ryan .15 .40
❑ 76 Amber Hay .15 .40
❑ 77 Leilene Joy .15 .40
❑ 78 Katarina Van Derham .15 .40
❑ 79 Alison Waite .15 .40
❑ 80 Martina Andrews .15 .40
❑ 81 Xi Xi Yang .15 .40
❑ 82 Tina Jordan .15 .40
❑ 83 Suzanne Le .15 .40
❑ 84 Michelle Lei .15 .40
❑ 85 Tabitha Taylor .15 .40
❑ 86 Alana Curry .15 .40
❑ 87 Aiko Tanaka .15 .40
❑ 88 Alicia Kozlowski .15 .40
❑ 89 Julianna Prada .15 .40
❑ 90 Mia St John .15 .40
❑ 91 Kiearah Figueroa .15 .40
❑ 92 Holly Huddleston .15 .40
❑ 93 Cecille Gahr .15 .40
❑ 94 Molly Shea .15 .40
❑ 95 Zoe Gregory .15 .40
❑ 96 Laurie Milan .15 .40
❑ 97 Alix Agar .15 .40
❑ 98 Nikki Gray .15 .40
❑ 99 Bambi Lashell .15 .40
❑ 100 Candice Michelle .15 .40

2010 Bench Warmer Signature Series Autographs Gold Foil

STATED ODDS ONE PER PACK
SP AUTOS WRAPPER EXCHANGE EXCLUSIVE

❑ 1 Jennifer Korbin 4.00 10.00
❑ 2 Torrie Wilson 6.00 15.00
❑ 3 Jennifer Walcott 6.00 15.00
❑ 4 Mary Riley 5.00 12.00
❑ 5 Lisa Gleave 4.00 10.00
❑ 6 Katie Lohmann 4.00 10.00
❑ 7 Traci Bingham 4.00 10.00
❑ 8 Miriam Gonzalez 4.00 10.00
❑ 9 Athena Lundberg 4.00 10.00
❑ 10 Christy Hemme 6.00 15.00
❑ 11 Carrie Stroup 4.00 10.00
❑ 12 Brandy Grace 4.00 10.00
❑ 13 Brittany Herrera 4.00 10.00
❑ 14 April Scott 4.00 10.00
❑ 15 Sara Underwood 10.00 20.00
❑ 16 Camille Anderson 4.00 10.00
❑ 17 Nikki Zeno 4.00 10.00
❑ 18 Jessica Rockwell 4.00 10.00
❑ 19 Brandie Moses 4.00 10.00
❑ 20 Jessica Hall 4.00 10.00
❑ 21 Yvette Nelson 4.00 10.00
❑ 22 Michelle Baena 4.00 10.00
❑ 23 Tiffany Toth 4.00 10.00
❑ 24 Jennifer England 5.00 12.00
❑ 25 Kitana Baker 4.00 10.00
❑ 26 Enya Flack 4.00 10.00
❑ 27 Kayla Collins 4.00 10.00
❑ 28 Shay Lyn 4.00 10.00
❑ 29 Lana Kinnear 4.00 10.00
❑ 30 Amie Nicole 4.00 10.00
❑ 31 Jessica Michaels 4.00 10.00
❑ 32 Rachel Bernstein 4.00 10.00
❑ 33 Brittany McGraw 4.00 10.00
❑ 34 Megan Hauserman 4.00 10.00
❑ 35 Catherine Kluthe 4.00 10.00
❑ 36 Sherry Goggin 4.00 10.00
❑ 37 Jaimarie 4.00 10.00
❑ 38 Tamara Witmer 4.00 10.00
❑ 39 Brooke Morales 4.00 10.00
❑ 40 Lindsey Roeper 4.00 10.00
❑ 41 Sarah Coggin 4.00 10.00
❑ 42 Talor Marion 4.00 10.00
❑ 43 Flo Jalin 4.00 10.00
❑ 44 Melissa Hunter 4.00 10.00
❑ 45 Alika Ray 4.00 10.00
❑ 46 Jenae Alt 4.00 10.00
❑ 47 Wrenna Monet 4.00 10.00
❑ 48 Lena Yada 4.00 10.00
❑ 49 Nicole Bennett 4.00 10.00
❑ 50 Michelle Anderson 4.00 10.00
❑ 51 Paige Peterson 4.00 10.00
❑ 52 Bobbi Billard 4.00 10.00
❑ 53 Nikki Ziering 4.00 10.00
❑ 54 Kerrilee Kaski 4.00 10.00
❑ 55 Amber Strauser 4.00 10.00
❑ 56 Candace Kita 4.00 10.00
❑ 57 Renee Stone 4.00 10.00
❑ 58 Tiffany Selby 4.00 10.00
❑ 59 Kristina Rodrigues 4.00 10.00
❑ 60 Raven Lexy 4.00 10.00
❑ 61 Charity Hodges 4.00 10.00
❑ 62 Jo Garcia 4.00 10.00
❑ 63 Leigh Ann Spence 4.00 10.00
❑ 64 Sandra Taylor 4.00 10.00
❑ 65 Brandi Maclaren 4.00 10.00
❑ 66 Miki Black 4.00 10.00
❑ 67 Shana Palmira 4.00 10.00
❑ 68 Jessica Burciaga SP 10.00 20.00
❑ 69 Lisa Ligon 4.00 10.00
❑ 70 Lauren Kim 4.00 10.00
❑ 71 Kirsten Lingman 4.00 10.00
❑ 72 Crystal Colar 4.00 10.00
❑ 73 Denyce Lawton 4.00 10.00
❑ 74 Buffy Tyler 4.00 10.00
❑ 75 Chanel Ryan 4.00 10.00
❑ 76 Amber Hay 4.00 10.00
❑ 77 Leilene Joy 4.00 10.00
❑ 78 Katarina Van Derham 4.00 10.00
❑ 79 Alison Waite SP 5.00 12.00
❑ 80 Martina Andrews 4.00 10.00
❑ 81 Xi Xi Yang 4.00 10.00
❑ 82 Tina Jordan 4.00 10.00
❑ 83 Suzanne Le 4.00 10.00
❑ 84 Michelle Lei 4.00 10.00
❑ 85 Tabitha Taylor 4.00 10.00
❑ 86 Alana Curry 4.00 10.00
❑ 87 Aiko Tanaka 4.00 10.00
❑ 88 Alicia Kozlowski 4.00 10.00
❑ 89 Julianna Prada 4.00 10.00
❑ 90 Mia St John 4.00 10.00
❑ 91 Kiearah Figueroa 4.00 10.00
❑ 92 Holly Huddleston 4.00 10.00
❑ 93 Cecille Gahr 4.00 10.00
❑ 94 Molly Shea 4.00 10.00
❑ 95 Zoe Gregory 4.00 10.00
❑ 96 Laurie Milan 4.00 10.00
❑ 97 Alix Agar 4.00 10.00
❑ 98 Nikki Gray 4.00 10.00
❑ 99 Bambi Lashell 4.00 10.00
❑ 100 Candice Michelle 5.00 12.00

2010 Bench Warmer Signature Series Autographs Blue Foil

STATED PRINT RUN 5 SER. #'d SETS
UNPRICED DUE TO SCARCITY

2010 Bench Warmer Signature Series Autographs Green Foil

STATED PRINT RUN 10 SER. #'d SETS
UNPRICED DUE TO SCARCITY

2010 Bench Warmer Signature Series Autographs Pink Foil

STATED PRINT RUN 25 SER. #'d SETS

2010 Bench Warmer Signature Series Autographs Purple Foil

STATED PRINT RUN 50 SER. #'d SETS

2010 Bench Warmer Signature Series Autographs Red Foil

STATED PRINT RUN 1 SER. #'d SET
UNPRICED DUE TO SCARCITY

2010 Bench Warmer Signature Series Bikini Swatches Blue Foil Autographs

STATED PRINT RUN 5 SER. #'d SETS
UNPRICED DUE TO SCARCITY

2010 Bench Warmer Signature Series Bikini Swatches Gold Foil

OVERALL BIKINI SWATCH ODDS 1:120

2010 Bench Warmer Signature Series Bikini Swatches Green Foil Autographs

STATED PRINT RUN 10 SER. #'d SETS
UNPRICED DUE TO SCARCITY

❑ 1 Jennifer Korbin
❑ 2 Mary Riley
❑ 3 Jennifer Walcott
❑ 4 Torrie Wilson
❑ 5 Carrie Stroup
❑ 6 Lisa Gleave
❑ 7 Christy Hemme
❑ 8 Amanda Paige
❑ 9 Jessica Burciaga
❑ 10 Chanel Ryan
❑ 11 Shay Lyn
❑ 12 Lindsey Roeper

2010 Bench Warmer Signature Series Bikini Swatches Red Foil Autographs

STATED PRINT RUN 1 SER. #'d SET
UNPRICED DUE TO SCARCITY

2010 Bench Warmer Signature Series Hair Cuts Blue Foil Autographs

STATED PRINT RUN 5 SER. #'d SETS
UNPRICED DUE TO SCARCITY

❑ 1 Mary Riley
❑ 2 Jennifer Korbin
❑ 3 Lisa Gleave
❑ 4 Buffy Tyler
❑ 5 Katie Lohmann
❑ 6 Shay Lyn

2010 Bench Warmer Signature Series Hair Cuts Gold Foil

STATED PRINT RUN 15 SER. #'d SETS

❑ 1 Mary Riley 150.00 200.00
❑ 2 Jennifer Korbin 125.00 175.00
❑ 3 Lisa Gleave 125.00 175.00
❑ 4 Buffy Tyler 125.00 175.00
❑ 5 Katie Lohmann 125.00 175.00
❑ 6 Shay Lyn 125.00 175.00

2010 Bench Warmer Signature Series Hair Cuts Red Foil Autographs

STATED PRINT RUN 1 SER. #'d SET
UNPRICED DUE TO SCARCITY

❑ 1 Mary Riley

2010 Bench Warmer Signature Series Lingerie Gold Foil

COMPLETE SET (17) 20.00 40.00
COMP.SET w/o SP (16) 20.00 40.00
OVERALL LINGERIE ODDS 1:5

❑ 1 Jennifer Korbin 2.00 5.00
❑ 2 Mary Riley 2.00 5.00
❑ 3A Bobbi Billard SP 3.00 8.00
❑ 3B Traci Brooks 2.00 5.00
❑ 4 Lisa Ligon 2.00 5.00
❑ 5 Xi Xi Yang 2.00 5.00
❑ 6 Spencer Scott 2.00 5.00
❑ 7 Charity Hodges 2.00 5.00
❑ 8 Lana Kinnear 2.00 5.00
❑ 9 Jessica Burciaga 2.00 5.00
❑ 10 Brittany Herrera 2.00 5.00
❑ 11 Sarah Coggin 2.00 5.00

- ❑ 12 Talor Marion 2.00 5.00
- ❑ 13 Rachel Bernstein 2.00 5.00
- ❑ 14 Michelle McLaughlin 2.00 5.00
- ❑ 15 Kayla Collins 2.00 5.00
- ❑ 16 Robyn Watkins 2.00 5.00

2010 Bench Warmer Signature Series Lingerie Blue Foil

STATED PRINT RUN 5 SER. #'d SETS

UNPRICED DUE TO SCARCITY

2010 Bench Warmer Signature Series Lingerie Green Foil

STATED PRINT RUN 10 SER. #'d SETS

UNPRICED DUE TO SCARCITY

2010 Bench Warmer Signature Series Lingerie Pink Foil

COMPLETE SET

STATED PRINT RUN 25 SER. #'d SETS

2010 Bench Warmer Signature Series Lingerie Red Foil

STATED PRINT RUN 1 SER. #'d SET

UNPRICED DUE TO SCARCITY

2010 Bench Warmer Signature Series Props Blue Foil Autographs

STATED PRINT RUN 5 SER. #'d SETS

UNPRICED DUE TO SCARCITY

2010 Bench Warmer Signature Series Props Gold Foil

STATED PRINT RUN 50 SER. #'d SETS

- ❑ 1 Jennifer Walcott 10.00 25.00
- ❑ 2 Torrie Wilson 10.00 25.00
- ❑ 3 Carrie Stroup 8.00 20.00
- ❑ 4 Jo Garcia 8.00 20.00
- ❑ 5 Tiffany Selby 8.00 20.00
- ❑ 6 Traci Brooks 8.00 20.00
- ❑ 7 Nicole Bennett 8.00 20.00
- ❑ 8 Lindsey Roeper 8.00 20.00
- ❑ 9 Candace Kita 8.00 20.00
- ❑ 10 Jennifer England 8.00 20.00
- ❑ 11 April Scott 8.00 20.00
- ❑ 12 Gail Kim 8.00 20.00

2010 Bench Warmer Signature Series Props Green Foil Autographs

STATED PRINT RUN 10 SER. #'d SETS

UNPRICED DUE TO SCARCITY

- ❑ 1 Jennifer Walcott
- ❑ 2 Torrie Wilson
- ❑ 3 Carrie Stroup
- ❑ 4 Jo Garcia
- ❑ 5 Tiffany Selby
- ❑ 6 Traci Brooks
- ❑ 7 Nicole Bennett
- ❑ 8 Lindsey Roeper
- ❑ 9 Candace Kita
- ❑ 10 Jennifer England
- ❑ 11 April Scott
- ❑ 12 Gail Kim

2010 Bench Warmer Signature Series Props Pink Foil

COMPLETE SET (12)

*PINK: .5X TO 1.2X GOLD

STATED PRINT RUN 25 SER. #'d SETS

2010 Bench Warmer Signature Series Props Red Foil Autographs

STATED PRINT RUN 1 SER. #'d SET

UNPRICED DUE TO SCARCITY

2010 Bench Warmer Signature Series Red Back Autographs Gold Foil

STATED ODDS 1:30

- ❑ 1 Jennifer Korbin 5.00 12.00
- ❑ 2 Christy Hemme 6.00 15.00
- ❑ 3 Traci Brooks 5.00 12.00
- ❑ 4 Lisa Gleave 5.00 12.00
- ❑ 5 Mary Riley 6.00 15.00
- ❑ 6 Carrie Stroup 5.00 12.00
- ❑ 7 Nikki Ziering 5.00 12.00
- ❑ 8 Buffy Tyler 5.00 12.00

2010 Bench Warmer Signature Series Red Back Autographs Blue Foil

STATED PRINT RUN 5 SER. #'d SETS

UNPRICED DUE TO SCARCITY

2010 Bench Warmer Signature Series Red Back Autographs Green Foil

STATED PRINT RUN 10 SER. #'d SETS

UNPRICED DUE TO SCARCITY

2010 Bench Warmer Signature Series Red Back Autographs Pink Foil

STATED PRINT RUN 25 SER. #'d SETS

2010 Bench Warmer Signature Series Red Back Autographs Red Foil

STATED PRINT RUN 1 SER. #'d SET

UNPRICED DUE TO SCARCITY

2010 Bench Warmer Signature Series International Autographs Gold Foil

STATED ODDS 1:10

- ❑ 1 Gail Kim 8.00 20.00
- ❑ 2 Lisa Gleave 8.00 20.00
- ❑ 3 Jennifer Walcott 10.00 25.00
- ❑ 4 Sara Underwood 10.00 25.00
- ❑ 5 Aubrie Lemon 8.00 20.00
- ❑ 6 Torrie Wilson 10.00 25.00
- ❑ 7 April Scott 8.00 20.00
- ❑ 8 Jennifer England 8.00 20.00
- ❑ 9 Lisa Lakatos 8.00 20.00

2010 Bench Warmer Signature Series International Autographs Pink Foil

*PINK: .5X TO 1.2X GOLD

STATED PRINT RUN 25 SER. #'d SETS

2010 Bench Warmer Signature Series International Autographs Green Foil

STATED PRINT RUN 10 SER. #'d SETS

UNPRICED DUE TO SCARCITY

2010 Bench Warmer Signature Series International Autographs Blue Foil

STATED PRINT RUN 5 SER. #'d SETS

UNPRICED DUE TO SCARCITY

2010 Bench Warmer Signature Series International Autographs Red Foil

STATED PRINT RUN 1 SER. #'d SET

UNPRICED DUE TO SCARCITY

2010 Bench Warmer Signature Series International Props Gold Foil

STATED PRINT RUN 25 SER. #'d SETS

- ❑ 1 Mary Riley
- ❑ 2 Carrie Stroup
- ❑ 3 Shay Lyn
- ❑ 4 Denyce Lawton
- ❑ 5 Cecille Gahr
- ❑ 6 Flo Jalin

2010 Bench Warmer Signature Series International Props Green Foil Autographs

STATED PRINT RUN 10 SER. #'d SETS

UNPRICED DUE TO SCARCITY

- ❑ 1 Mary Riley
- ❑ 2 Carrie Stroup
- ❑ 3 Shay Lyn
- ❑ 4 Denyce Lawton
- ❑ 5 Cecille Gahr
- ❑ 6 Flo Jalin

2010 Bench Warmer Signature Series International Props Blue Foil Autographs

STATED PRINT RUN 5 SER. #'d SETS

UNPRICED DUE TO SCARCITY

2010 Bench Warmer Signature Series International Props Red Foil Autographs

STATED PRINT RUN 1 SER. #'d SET

UNPRICED DUE TO SCARCITY

2010 Bench Warmer Signature Series International Swatches Gold Foil

STATED PRINT RUN 25 SER. #'d SETS

- ❑ 1 Mary Riley
- ❑ 2 Jessica Rockwell
- ❑ 3 Jennifer Korbin
- ❑ 4 Amanda Paige
- ❑ 5 Enya Flack
- ❑ 6 Flo Jalin

2010 Bench Warmer Signature Series International Swatches Green Foil Autographs

STATED PRINT RUN 10 SER. #'d SETS

UNPRICED DUE TO SCARCITY

- ❑ 1 Mary Riley
- ❑ 2 Jessica Rockwell
- ❑ 3 Jennifer Korbin
- ❑ 4 Amanda Paige
- ❑ 5 Enya Flack
- ❑ 6 Flo Jalin

2010 Bench Warmer Signature Series International Swatches Blue Foil Autographs

STATED PRINT RUN 5 SER. #'d SETS

UNPRICED DUE TO SCARCITY

2010 Bench Warmer Signature Series International Swatches Red Foil Autographs

STATED PRINT RUN 1 SER. #'d SET

UNPRICED DUE TO SCARCITY

2010 Bench Warmer Vault Autographs Gold Foil

COMPLETE SET (18)

OVERALL AUTOGRAPH ODDS ONE PER BOX

- ❑ 1 Cindy Margolis 6.00 15.00
- ❑ 2 Candice Michelle 8.00 20.00
- ❑ 3 Colleen Shannon 5.00 12.00
- ❑ 4 The Costello Twins 6.00 15.00
- ❑ 5 Mary Riley 6.00 15.00
- ❑ 6 Katie Lohmann 5.00 12.00
- ❑ 7 Darcy Donavan 5.00 12.00
- ❑ 8 Lisa Gleave 5.00 12.00
- ❑ 9 Marla Esposito 5.00 12.00
- ❑ 10 Jennifer Korbin 5.00 12.00
- ❑ 11 Suzanne Stokes 5.00 12.00
- ❑ 12 Claudia Jordan 5.00 12.00
- ❑ 13 Flo Jalin 5.00 12.00
- ❑ 14 Miriam Gonzalez 5.00 12.00
- ❑ 15 Buffy Tyler 5.00 12.00
- ❑ 16 April Scott 5.00 12.00
- ❑ 17 Aubrie Lemon 5.00 12.00
- ❑ 18 Jennifer Walcott 8.00 20.00

2010 Bench Warmer Vault Autographs Blue Foil

STATED PRINT RUN 5 SER. #'d SETS

UNPRICED DUE TO SCARCITY

2010 Bench Warmer Vault Autographs Green Foil

STATED PRINT RUN 10 SER. #'d SETS

UNPRICED DUE TO SCARCITY

2010 Bench Warmer Vault Autographs Pink Foil

*PINK: 1X TO 2.5X GOLD

STATED PRINT RUN 25 SER. #'d SETS

2010 Bench Warmer Vault Autographs Red Foil

STATED PRINT RUN 1 SER. #'d SET

UNPRICED DUE TO SCARCITY

2010 Bench Warmer Vault Boy Beater Swatches Blue Foil Autographs

STATED PRINT RUN 5 SER. #'d SETS

UNPRICED DUE TO SCARCITY

2010 Bench Warmer Vault Boy Beater Swatches Gold Foil

STATED PRINT RUN 50 SER. #'d SETS

- ❑ 1 Jessica Burciaga 20.00 50.00
- ❑ 2 Claudia Jordan 15.00 40.00
- ❑ 3 Carrie Stroup 15.00 40.00
- ❑ 4 Flo Jalin 15.00 40.00
- ❑ 5 Jennifer Walcott 20.00 50.00
- ❑ 6 Tiffany Selby 15.00 40.00
- ❑ 7 Zoe Gregory 15.00 40.00
- ❑ 8 Brandie Moses 15.00 40.00
- ❑ 9 Jessica Hall 15.00 40.00
- ❑ 10 Athena Lundberg 15.00 40.00
- ❑ 11 Jennifer England 15.00 40.00
- ❑ 12 Amanda Paige 15.00 40.00

2010 Bench Warmer Vault Boy Beater Swatches Green Foil Autographs

STATED PRINT RUN 10 SER. #'d SETS

UNPRICED DUE TO SCARCITY

2010 Bench Warmer Vault Boy Beater Swatches Red Foil Autographs

STATED PRINT RUN 1 SER. #'d SET

UNPRICED DUE TO SCARCITY

2010 Bench Warmer Vault Halloween Autographs Gold Foil

OVERALL HALLOWEEN ODDS ONE PER BOX

- ❑ 1 Jennifer Korbin 4.00 10.00
- ❑ 2 April Scott 4.00 10.00
- ❑ 3 Miriam Gonzalez 5.00 12.00
- ❑ 4 Chanel Ryan 4.00 10.00
- ❑ 5 Mary Riley 5.00 12.00
- ❑ 6 Bambi Lashell 4.00 10.00
- ❑ 7 Jessica Rockwell 4.00 10.00
- ❑ 8 Julianna Prada 4.00 10.00
- ❑ 9 Tiffany Toth 4.00 10.00
- ❑ 10 Alicia Arden 4.00 10.00
- ❑ 11 Camille Anderson 4.00 10.00
- ❑ 12 Crystal Colar 4.00 10.00
- ❑ 13 Renee Stone 4.00 10.00
- ❑ 14 Audrey Dalsoglio 4.00 10.00
- ❑ 15 Nikki Zeno 4.00 10.00
- ❑ 16 Tiffany Selby 4.00 10.00

2010 Bench Warmer Vault Halloween Autographs Blue Foil

STATED PRINT RUN 5 SER. #'d SETS

UNPRICED DUE TO SCARCITY

2010 Bench Warmer Vault Halloween Autographs Green Foil

STATED PRINT RUN 10 SER. #'d SETS

UNPRICED DUE TO SCARCITY

2010 Bench Warmer Vault Halloween Autographs Pink Foil

*PINK: .8X TO 2X GOLD

STATED PRINT RUN 25 SER. #'d SETS

2010 Bench Warmer Vault Halloween Autographs Red Foil

STATED PRINT RUN 1 SER. #'d SET

UNPRICED DUE TO SCARCITY

2010 Cartoon Sketch Art

COMPLETE SET (14)

- ❑ 1 Betty Boop
Adam Cleveland
- ❑ 2 Mighty Mouse
David Beaty
- ❑ 3 Mighty Mouse
David Harrigan
- ❑ 4 Mighty Mouse
Gilbert YoungRoland
- ❑ 5 Betty Boop
Jay P. Fosgitt
- ❑ 6 Betty
Casper/Felix/Lynne Anderson
- ❑ 7 Betty Boop
Mayumi Seto
- ❑ 8 Casper
Mayumi Seto
- ❑ 9 Felix
Sean Pence
- ❑ 10 Felix
Sean Pence
- ❑ 11 Felix
Shane McCormack
- ❑ 12 Casper
Steven Miller
- ❑ 13 Heckle and Jeckle
Vincent Fourneuf
- ❑ 14 Felix
Checklist/Andy Broome

2010 Cartoon Sketch Art Artist Proof Sketches

- ❑ 1 Maz Adams
- ❑ 2 Lynne Anderson
- ❑ 3 Robert Aragon
- ❑ 4 Jean Marcel Azevedo
- ❑ 5 David Beaty
- ❑ 6 Dan Bergren
- ❑ 7 Dan Borgonos
- ❑ 8 Andy Broome
- ❑ 9 Chris Chuckry
- ❑ 10 Mickey Clausen
- ❑ 11 Dennis Crisostomo
- ❑ 12 David Day
- ❑ 13 Otto Dieffenbach
- ❑ 14 Guy Dorian
- ❑ 15 Ben Dunn
- ❑ 16 Eman
- ❑ 17 Gabe Farber
- ❑ 18 Marc Ferreira
- ❑ 19 Juan Fontanez
- ❑ 20 Jay Fosgitt
- ❑ 21 Vincent Fourneuf
- ❑ 22 Tina Francisco
- ❑ 23 David Gacey
- ❑ 24 Bruce Gerlach
- ❑ 25 David Girdley
- ❑ 26 Stacey Girdley
- ❑ 27 Kevin Graham
- ❑ 28 David Harrigan
- ❑ 29 Chris Henderson
- ❑ 30 Ryan Heying
- ❑ 31 Jason Hughes
- ❑ 32 Laura Inglis
- ❑ 33 Kazuhiro Ito
- ❑ 34 Chadd Keim
- ❑ 35 Ryan M Kincaid
- ❑ 36 Brian Kong
- ❑ 37 Beck Kramer
- ❑ 38 Jayson Kretzer
- ❑ 39 Jim Kyle
- ❑ 40 Mark LeMieux
- ❑ 41 Daniel Lopez (Pez)
- ❑ 42 Josh Lyman
- ❑ 43 Gemma Magno
- ❑ 44 CC Martin
- ❑ 45 Shane McCormack
- ❑ 46 James McNeil
- ❑ 47 Manny Mederos II
- ❑ 48 Tony Miello
- ❑ 49 Steven Miller
- ❑ 50 Nur Hanie Mohd
- ❑ 51 Rich Molinelli
- ❑ 52 Trev Murphy
- ❑ 53 Rhiannon Owens
- ❑ 54 Don Pedicini Jr.
- ❑ 55 Sean Pence
- ❑ 56 Jason Potratz
Jack Hai
- ❑ 57 Buddy Prince
- ❑ 58 Bill Pulkovski
- ❑ 59 Walter Rice
- ❑ 60 Jezreel Rojales
- ❑ 61 Adam Schickling
- ❑ 62 Mayumi Seto
- ❑ 63 Brian Shearer
- ❑ 64 Amber Shelton
- ❑ 65 Kaori Shima
- ❑ 66 Jay Shimko
- ❑ 67 Scott D M Simmons
- ❑ 68 Louis Small Jr.
- ❑ 69 Danielle Soloud
- ❑ 70 Jay T
- ❑ 71 Anthony Tan
- ❑ 72 Ian Walker
- ❑ 73 Travis Walton
- ❑ 74 Jeremiah Witkowski
- ❑ 75 Asuka Yamamoto
- ❑ 76 The Yellow Maple
- ❑ 77 Gilbert YoungRoland
- ❑ 78 Chuck Zsolnai
- ❑ 79 Matthew Zucker

2010 Cartoon Sketch Art Sketches

STATED ODDS ONE PER PACK

- ❑ 1 Maz Adams
- ❑ 2 Lynne Anderson
- ❑ 3 Robert Aragon
- ❑ 4 Jean Marcel Azevedo
- ❑ 5 David Beaty
- ❑ 6 Dan Bergren
- ❑ 7 Dan Borgonos
- ❑ 8 Andy Broome
- ❑ 9 Chris Chuckry
- ❑ 10 Mickey Clausen
- ❑ 11 Dennis Crisostomo
- ❑ 12 David Day
- ❑ 13 Otto Dieffenbach
- ❑ 14 Guy Dorian
- ❑ 15 Ben Dunn
- ❑ 16 Eman
- ❑ 17 Gabe Farber
- ❑ 18 Marc Ferreira
- ❑ 19 Juan Fontanez
- ❑ 20 Jay Fosgitt
- ❑ 21 Vincent Fourneuf
- ❑ 22 Tina Francisco
- ❑ 23 David Gacey
- ❑ 24 Bruce Gerlach
- ❑ 25 David Girdley
- ❑ 26 Stacey Girdley
- ❑ 27 Kevin Graham
- ❑ 28 David Harrigan
- ❑ 29 Chris Henderson
- ❑ 30 Ryan Heying
- ❑ 31 Jason Hughes
- ❑ 32 Laura Inglis
- ❑ 33 Kazuhiro Ito
- ❑ 34 Chadd Keim
- ❑ 35 Ryan M Kincaid
- ❑ 36 Brian Kong
- ❑ 37 Beck Kramer
- ❑ 38 Jayson Kretzer
- ❑ 39 Jim Kyle
- ❑ 40 Mark LeMieux
- ❑ 41 Daniel Lopez (Pez)
- ❑ 42 Josh Lyman
- ❑ 43 Gemma Magno
- ❑ 44 CC Martin
- ❑ 45 Shane McCormack
- ❑ 46 James McNeil
- ❑ 47 Manny Mederos II
- ❑ 48 Tony Miello
- ❑ 49 Steven Miller
- ❑ 50 Nur Hanie Mohd
- ❑ 51 Rich Molinelli
- ❑ 52 Trev Murphy
- ❑ 53 Rhiannon Owens
- ❑ 54 Don Pedicini Jr.
- ❑ 55 Sean Pence
- ❑ 56 Jason Potratz
Jack Hai
- ❑ 57 Buddy Prince
- ❑ 58 Bill Pulkovski
- ❑ 59 Walter Rice
- ❑ 60 Jezreel Rojales
- ❑ 61 Adam Schickling
- ❑ 62 Mayumi Seto
- ❑ 63 Brian Shearer
- ❑ 64 Amber Shelton
- ❑ 65 Kaori Shima
- ❑ 66 Jay Shimko
- ❑ 67 Scott D M Simmons
- ❑ 68 Louis Small Jr.
- ❑ 69 Danielle Soloud
- ❑ 70 Jay T
- ❑ 71 Anthony Tan
- ❑ 72 Ian Walker
- ❑ 73 Travis Walton
- ❑ 74 Jeremiah Witkowski
- ❑ 75 Asuka Yamamoto
- ❑ 76 The Yellow Maple
- ❑ 77 Gilbert YoungRoland
- ❑ 78 Chuck Zsolnai
- ❑ 79 Matthew Zucker

2010 Dexter Season Three

COMPLETE SET (72) 6.00 15.00

- ❑ 1 Dexter finally seems to have .15 .40
- ❑ 2 Rita is madly in love .15 .40
- ❑ 3 Dexter poses as a crack addict .15 .40
- ❑ 4 Dexter worries .15 .40
- ❑ 5 Miguel Prado addresses .15 .40
- ❑ 6 Angel wants Dexter .15 .40
- ❑ 7 Miguel, who was just consoled .15 .40
- ❑ 8 Dexter tells Angel .15 .40
- ❑ 9 Ramon Prado joins Miguel .15 .40
- ❑ 10 While grocery shopping with Rita .15 .40
- ❑ 11 Dexter is wary .15 .40
- ❑ 12 Dexter researches pedophile .15 .40
- ❑ 13 Dexter explains to Miguel .15 .40
- ❑ 14 Dexter knows Nathan Marten .15 .40
- ❑ 15 Dexter and Rita try to explain .15 .40
- ❑ 16 Ramon Prado is upset .15 .40
- ❑ 17 Fiona Kemp, covered in blood .15 .40
- ❑ 18 Maria talks to Miguel .15 .40
- ❑ 19 Anton talks to Debra .15 .40
- ❑ 20 Ramon confronts Maria and Angel .15 .40
- ❑ 21 Dexter realizes the murderer .15 .40
- ❑ 22 Dexter pays Miguel a visit .15 .40
- ❑ 23 Dexter thinks back .15 .40
- ❑ 24 Dexter is in awe .15 .40
- ❑ 25 Dexter relaxes at his home .15 .40
- ❑ 26 Vince Masuka annoys Angel .15 .40
- ❑ 27 Rita and Sylvia are out .15 .40
- ❑ 28 Miguel and Dexter share a brewski .15 .40
- ❑ 29 Debra wonders if the Skinner .15 .40
- ❑ 30 Angel calls up Detective Gianna .15 .40
- ❑ 31 Yuki meets Debra .15 .40
- ❑ 32 Dexter fakes being a pal .15 .40
- ❑ 33 Dexter has a bizarre nightmare .15 .40
- ❑ 34 Debra and Quinn visit .15 .40
- ❑ 35 Dexter visits an ailing Camilla .15 .40
- ❑ 36 Debra requests more blood .15 .40
- ❑ 37 Yuki calls on Debra .15 .40
- ❑ 38 Debra spends an entire night .15 .40
- ❑ 39 Dexter considers the butterfly .15 .40
- ❑ 40 Debra interviews poker-face George .15 .40
- ❑ 41 Dexter and Miguel wear latex .15 .40
- ❑ 42 Ellen and Maria meet at a bar .15 .40
- ❑ 43 Dexter insists Miguel call off .15 .40
- ❑ 44 Debra spots trimmed trees .15 .40
- ❑ 45 Sylvia Prado visits Debra .15 .40
- ❑ 46 Debra wants to bring George .15 .40
- ❑ 47 Maria tells Dexter she is worried .15 .40
- ❑ 48 Quinn gets Debra to relax .15 .40
- ❑ 49 Dexter decides to teach .15 .40
- ❑ 50 Dexter samples some bits .15 .40
- ❑ 51 King shows up .15 .40
- ❑ 52 Sylvia, Miguel, Rita, and Dexter .15 .40
- ❑ 53 Debra sleeps in .15 .40
- ❑ 54 Quinn warns Debra .15 .40
- ❑ 55 Angel's girlfriend, Detective Gianna .15 .40
- ❑ 56 Maria Laguerta interviews Toby .15 .40
- ❑ 57 Rita tries on her wedding dress .15 .40
- ❑ 58 Quinn meets Anton at work .15 .40
- ❑ 59 The next day Miguel meets Dexter .15 .40
- ❑ 60 Dexter hands Angel the key file .15 .40
- ❑ 61 Dexter meets Miguel on top .15 .40
- ❑ 62 The vehicle races along .15 .40
- ❑ 63 Later Dexter tries to nap .15 .40
- ❑ 64 Harry shows Dexter .15 .40
- ❑ 65 Following Miguel's new routine .15 .40
- ❑ 66 The next day Maria asks Dexter .15 .40
- ❑ 67 Maria calls Dexter into her office .15 .40
- ❑ 68 Debra goes downstairs .15 .40
- ❑ 69 A jogger finds Miguel's corpse .15 .40
- ❑ 70 Dexter checks on Ramon .15 .40
- ❑ 71 Ramon is jailed for pulling .15 .40
- ❑ 72 Checklist .15 .40

2010 Dexter Season Three Autograph Costumes

OVERALL AUTO ODDS 1:48

- ❑ DH Desmond Harrington 20.00 40.00
- ❑ JB Julie Benz 50.00 100.00
- ❑ JC Jennifer Carpenter 35.00 70.00
- ❑ LV Lauren Velez 20.00 40.00
- ❑ CSL C.S. Lee 20.00 40.00
- ❑ MCH Michael C Hall 50.00 100.00

2010 Dexter Season Three Autographs

OVERALL AUTO ODDS 1:48

- ❑ JR James Remar 20.00 40.00
- ❑ JS Jimmy Smits 20.00 40.00
- ❑ MCHS Michael C Hall 40.00 80.00
- ❑ MCHJB Michael C Hall 60.00 120.00
Julie Benz
- ❑ MCHJS Michael C Hall 50.00 100.00
Jimmy Smits

2010 Dexter Season Three Costumes

OVERALL COSTUME/PROP CARD ODDS 1:10

CI STATED ODDS ONE PER CASE

- ❑ C1 Dexter Morgan 10.00 25.00
- ❑ C2 Dexter Morgan 10.00 25.00
- ❑ C3 Dexter Morgan 10.00 25.00
- ❑ C4 Dexter Morgan 10.00 25.00
- ❑ C5 Dexter Morgan 10.00 25.00
- ❑ C6 Rita Bennett 10.00 25.00
- ❑ C7 Rita Bennett 10.00 25.00
- ❑ C8 Rita Bennett 10.00 25.00
- ❑ C9 Rita Bennett 10.00 25.00
- ❑ C10 Maria Laguerta 6.00 15.00
- ❑ C11 Maria Laguerta 6.00 15.00
- ❑ C12 Maria Laguerta 6.00 15.00
- ❑ C13 Angel Batista 6.00 15.00
- ❑ C14 Angel Batista 6.00 15.00
- ❑ C15 Debra Morgan 8.00 20.00
- ❑ C16 Debra Morgan 8.00 20.00
- ❑ C17 Debra Morgan 8.00 20.00
- ❑ C18 Debra Morgan 8.00 20.00
- ❑ C19 Debra Morgan 8.00 20.00
- ❑ C20 Debra Morgan 8.00 20.00
- ❑ C21 Vince Masuka 6.00 15.00
- ❑ C22 Vince Masuka 6.00 15.00
- ❑ C23 Joey Quinn 6.00 15.00
- ❑ C24 Dexter Morgan 8.00 20.00
Miguel Prado
- ❑ C25 Rita Bennett 15.00 40.00
Dexter Morgan
- ❑ C26 Maria Laguerta 10.00 25.00
Miguel Prado
- ❑ C27 Debra Morgan 8.00 20.00
Joey Quinn
- ❑ C28 Dexter Morgan 15.00 40.00
Angel Batista/Debra Morgan/Vince Masuka
- ❑ C29 Dexter Morgan 15.00 40.00
Rita Bennett/Miguel Prado/Angel Batista/Debra Morgan/Joey Quinn/Maria Laguerta/Vince Masuka
- ❑ CI Dexter Morgan 15.00 40.00
Rita Bennett/Angel Batista/Maria Laguerta/Debra Morgan/Joey Quinn/Vince Masuka/ (issued as case incentive)

2010 Dexter Season Three Dexter's Victims

COMPLETE SET (9) 10.00 25.00

STATED ODDS 1:12

- ❑ V1 Victims 1 2.00 5.00
- ❑ V2 Victims 2 2.00 5.00
- ❑ V3 Victims 3 2.00 5.00
- ❑ V4 Victims 4 2.00 5.00
- ❑ V5 Victims 5 2.00 5.00
- ❑ V6 Victims 6 2.00 5.00

❑ V7 Victims 7 2.00 5.00
❑ V8 Victims 8 2.00 5.00
❑ V9 Victims 9 2.00 5.00

2010 Dexter Season Three Metallogloss Case Toppers

COMPLETE SET (2) 20.00 40.00
STATED ODDS ONE PER CASE

❑ 1 Len Bellinger 12.00 25.00
❑ 2 Trev Murphy 15.00 30.00

2010 Dexter Season Three Promos

COMPLETE SET (7)

❑ P1 Dexter
❑ P2 Dexter
❑ P3 Dexter
❑ P4 Dexter
❑ P5 Dexter
❑ AP1 Dexter
❑ AP2 Dexter

2010 Dexter Season Three Props

OVERALL COSTUME/PROP CARD ODDS 1:10

❑ P1 Target Paper 12.00 30.00
❑ P2 Evidence Bag 12.00 30.00
❑ P3 Bloody Framed Photograph 12.00 30.00
❑ P4 Trajectory String 12.00 30.00
❑ P5 Wedding Invitation 15.00 40.00
❑ P6 Tool Bag 12.00 30.00
❑ P7 Milk Carton 60.00 120.00
❑ P8 Police File Folder 12.00 30.00
❑ P9 Science Lab Folder 12.00 30.00
❑ P10 Forensics Quarterly 25.00 50.00
❑ P11 Dry Cleaner Tag 30.00 60.00

2010 Dexter Season Three Puzzle

COMPLETE SET (9) 10.00 25.00
STATED ODDS 1:12

❑ CP1 Puzzle 1 2.00 5.00
❑ CP2 Puzzle 2 2.00 5.00
❑ CP3 Puzzle 3 2.00 5.00
❑ CP4 Puzzle 4 2.00 5.00
❑ CP5 Puzzle 5 2.00 5.00
❑ CP6 Puzzle 6 2.00 5.00
❑ CP7 Puzzle 7 2.00 5.00
❑ CP8 Puzzle 8 2.00 5.00
❑ CP9 Puzzle 9 2.00 5.00

2010 Dexter Season Three Quotes

COMPLETE SET (10) 10.00 25.00
STATED ODDS 1:12

❑ Q1 Quotes 1 2.00 5.00
❑ Q2 Quotes 2 2.00 5.00
❑ Q3 Quotes 3 2.00 5.00
❑ Q4 Quotes 4 2.00 5.00
❑ Q5 Quotes 5 2.00 5.00
❑ Q6 Quotes 6 2.00 5.00
❑ Q7 Quotes 7 2.00 5.00
❑ Q8 Quotes 8 2.00 5.00
❑ Q9 Quotes 9 2.00 5.00
❑ Q10 Quotes 10 2.00 5.00

2010 Dexter Season Three Sketches

STATED ODDS 1:288

❑ 1 Brian Kong 20.00 40.00
❑ 2 David Desbois 75.00 150.00
❑ 3 Jason Carrier 30.00 60.00
❑ 4 Kevin Graham 30.00 60.00
❑ 5 Len Bellinger 30.00 60.00
❑ 6 Steven Miller 25.00 50.00
❑ 7 Tim Shay 40.00 80.00
❑ 8 Trev Murphy 50.00 100.00

2010 Elvis Milestones

COMPLETE SET (75) 4.00 10.00

❑ 1 Elvis is Born .10 .30
❑ 2 Elvis get his first guitar .10 .30
❑ 3 Family moves to Memphis .10 .30
❑ 4 Elvis records an acetate .10 .30
❑ 5 Elvis records That's All Right .10 .30
❑ 6 That's All Right hits the airwaves .10 .30
❑ 7 Elvis performs at Overton Park Shell .10 .30
❑ 8 Elvis performs at Louisiana Hayride .10 .30
❑ 9 Elvis signs first contract w .10 .30
RCA
❑ 10 Elvis arrives at RCA's Nashville studio .10 .30
❑ 11 Elvis' first network tv appearance .10 .30
❑ 12 RCA ships Elvis Presley .10 .30
❑ 13 Elvis and manager Colonel Parker .10 .30
❑ 14 Elvis screen tests at Paramount .10 .30
❑ 15 Elvis receives gold record .10 .30
❑ 16 Elvis performs Hound Dog .10 .30
❑ 17 Elvis on The Steve Allen Show .10 .30
❑ 18 Elvis on The Ed Sullivan Show .10 .30
❑ 19 Elvis performs two shows .10 .30
❑ 20 Elvis on The Ed Sullivan Show .10 .30
❑ 21 Elvis' Love Me Tender premieres .10 .30
❑ 22 Elvis makes final appearance .10 .30
❑ 23 Elvis buys Graceland mansion .10 .30
❑ 24 Jailhouse Rock opens nationally .10 .30
❑ 25 Elvis picks up his draft notice .10 .30
❑ 26 Elvis is inducted into the U.S. Army .10 .30
❑ 27 King Creole opens nationally .10 .30
❑ 28 Elvis ships out on USS Randall .10 .30
❑ 29 Priscilla Beaulieu and Elvis meet .10 .30
❑ 30 Elvis is released from active duty .10 .30
❑ 31 Elvis holds 1st post-Army recording session.10 .30
❑ 32 Elvis receives first degree black belt .10 .30
❑ 33 GI Blues soundtrack album releases .10 .30
❑ 34 Elvis performs 2 shows .10 .30
❑ 35 Elvis arrives in Hawaii .10 .30
❑ 36 Blue Hawaii soundtrack hits the chart .10 .30
❑ 37 Viva Las Vegas opens nationally .10 .30
❑ 38 The Beatles visit Elvis at his home .10 .30
❑ 39 Elvis and Priscilla wed in Las Vegas .10 .30
❑ 40 Priscilla gives birth to Lisa Marie .10 .30
❑ 41 Elvis rehearses for the '68 Special .10 .30
❑ 42 Elvis airs on NBC .10 .30
❑ 43 Elvis records at American Sound Studio .10 .30
❑ 44 Elvis films Change of Habit .10 .30
❑ 45 Elvis opens 4 week engagement .10 .30
❑ 46 Suspicious Minds ships .10 .30
❑ 47 Elvis performs at the Texas Livestock Show .10 .30
❑ 48 The Elvis Presley Summer Festival .10 .30
❑ 49 Elvis performs in Phoenix .10 .30
❑ 50 Elvis buys his first Stutz Blackhawk .10 .30
❑ 51 That's the Way It Is opens in theaters .10 .30
❑ 52 Elvis meets President Nixon .10 .30
❑ 53 Elvis receives award .10 .30
❑ 54 Elvis receives Lifetime Achievement Award .10 .30
❑ 55 Elvis performs sold out shows .10 .30
❑ 56 Concert documentary Elvis on Tour opens .10 .30
❑ 57 Elvis makes televison history .10 .30
❑ 58 Elvis records at Stax Studio .10 .30
❑ 59 Elvis wins Grammy .10 .30
❑ 60 Elvis purchases a 1958 Convair 880 jet .10 .30
❑ 61 New year's show grosses over $800,000 .10 .30
❑ 62 Elvis begins recording session .10 .30
❑ 63 Elvis begins his last concert tour .10 .30
❑ 64 Elvis gives his last performance .10 .30
❑ 65 Elvis passes away at Graceland .10 .30
❑ 66 Graceland opens for public tours .10 .30
❑ 67 Elvis is inducted into Rock 'n Roll HOF .10 .30
❑ 68 Elvis receives the Award of Merit by AMAs .10 .30
❑ 69 Elvis stamp is released by USPS .10 .30
❑ 70 Elvis stars in a concert production .10 .30
❑ 71 Remix of Elvis' song A Little Less Conversation.10 .30
❑ 72 ELVIS 30 #1 HITS debuts at #1 .10 .30
❑ 73 Graceland is named a Historic Landmark .10 .30
❑ 74 Cirque de Soleil announces new show .10 .30
❑ 75 Fans celebrate Elvis' 75th birthday .10 .30

2010 Elvis Milestones 75th Birthday

COMPLETE SET (75) 20.00 50.00
*75TH: 1.5X TO 4X BASIC CARDS
STATED ODDS ONE PER PACK

2010 Elvis Milestones Diamond

*DIAMOND: 15X TO 40X BASIC CARDS
STATED PRINT RUN 75 SER. #'d SETS

2010 Elvis Milestones Celebrity Signatures Blue

OVERALL AUTO/MEM ODDS ONE PER BOX

❑ CSCN Chris Noel 15.00 30.00
❑ CSCP Cynthia Pepper 15.00 30.00
❑ CSDJ DJ Fontana 20.00 40.00
❑ CSJB James Burton 15.00 30.00
❑ CSNS Nancy Sinatra 50.00 100.00
❑ CSPP Pat Priest 20.00 40.00
❑ CSYC Yvonne Craig 20.00 40.00
❑ CSMAM Mary Ann Mobley 15.00 30.00

2010 Elvis Milestones Celebrity Signatures Red

*RED: .8X TO 2X BASIC AUTO
OVERALL AUTO/MEM ODDS ONE PER BOX
STATED PRINT RUN 50 SER. #'d SETS

2010 Elvis Milestones Celebrity Signatures Green

*GREEN: 1.2X TO 3X BASIC CARDS
OVERALL AUTO/MEM ODDS ONE PER BOX
STATED PRINT RUN 25 SER. #'d SETS

2010 Elvis Milestones Historic Cut Autographs

UNPRICED DUE TO SCARCITY

❑ HC1 Elvis Presley
❑ HC2 Elvis Presley
❑ HC3 Elvis Presley
Vernon Presley

2010 Elvis Milestones Joe Petruccio Mini Masterpieces

UNPRICED DUE TO SCARCITY

❑ 1 Blue Scarf
❑ 2 Gold Scarf
❑ 3 Gold Sunglasses
❑ 4 Jailhouse Rock
❑ 5 Pink Jacket
❑ 6 Red Scarf
❑ 7 Silver Sunglasses

2010 Elvis Milestones King Size Swatches

COMPLETE SET (3)
OVERALL AUTO/MEM ODDS ONE PER BOX
STATED PRINT RUN 25 SER. #'d SETS

❑ KS1 Elvis Tweed Jacket
❑ KS2 Elvis Swim Trunks
❑ KS3 Elvis Kimono

2010 Elvis Milestones The King of Hollywood Pop-Ups

COMPLETE SET (6) 5.00 12.00
STATED ODDS 1:8

❑ PU1 Love Me Tender 1.50 4.00
❑ PU2 Loving You 1.50 4.00
❑ PU3 Jailhouse Rock 1.50 4.00
❑ PU4 Blue Hawaii 1.50 4.00
❑ PU5 Clambake 1.50 4.00
❑ PU6 Speedway 1.50 4.00

2010 Elvis Milestones The King's Things Memorabilia

OVERALL AUTO/MEM ODDS ONE PER BOX

❑ KT1 Elvis Smoking Jacket 15.00 30.00
❑ KT2 Elvis Warm-Up Suit 15.00 30.00
❑ KT3 Elvis Pajamas 15.00 30.00
❑ KT4 Elvis Kimono 15.00 30.00
❑ KT5 Elvis Swim Trunks 20.00 40.00
❑ KT6 Elvis Tweed Jacket 20.00 40.00

2010 Elvis Milestones The King's Things Memorabilia Holofoil

*HOLOFOIL: .6X TO 1.2X BASIC CARDS
OVERALL AUTO/MEM ODDS ONE PER BOX
STATED PRINT RUN 99 SER. #'d SETS

2010 Elvis Milestones The King's Things Memorabilia Red

OVERALL AUTO/MEM ODDS ONE PER BOX
STATED PRINT RUN 25 SER. #'d SETS

2010 Elvis Milestones Under the Lights

COMPLETE SET (12) 12.00 30.00
STATED ODDS 1:6

❑ UTL1 Elvis' '68 Comeback Special 1.50 4.00
❑ UTL2 International Hotel in Las Vegas 1.50 4.00
❑ UTL3 Elvis performs TX Livestock Show 1.50 4.00
❑ UTL4 1st Elvis Presley Summer Festival 1.50 4.00
❑ UTL5 2nd Elvis Presley Summer Festival 1.50 4.00
❑ UTL6 Elvis on Tour 1.50 4.00
❑ UTL7 Aloha from Hawaii 1.50 4.00
❑ UTL8 Elvis in Concert 1.50 4.00
❑ UTL9 T-R-O-U-B-L-E 1.50 4.00
❑ UTL10 7th Tour of the Year 1.50 4.00
❑ UTL11 Elvis' Last Tour 1.50 4.00
❑ UTL12 Elvis' Last Show 1.50 4.00

2010 Garbage Pail Kids Flashback

COMPLETE SET (160) 20.00 40.00
UNPRICED PRINT PLATE PRINT RUN 1

❑ 1a Nasty Nick .40 1.00
❑ 1b Evil Eddie .40 1.00
❑ 2a Dead Ted .20 .50
❑ 2b Jay Decay .20 .50
❑ 3a Adam Bomb .75 2.00
❑ 3b Blasted Billy .40 1.00
❑ 4a Tee-Vee Stevie .20 .50
❑ 4b Geeky Gary .20 .50
❑ 5a Potty Scotty .20 .50
❑ 5b Jason Basin .20 .50
❑ 6a Corroded Carl .20 .50
❑ 6b Crater Chris .20 .50
❑ 7a Bony Joanie .20 .50
❑ 7b Thin Lynn .20 .50
❑ 8a New Wave Dave .20 .50
❑ 8b Graffiti Petey .20 .50
❑ 9a Sy Clops .20 .50
❑ 9b One-Eyed Jack .20 .50
❑ 10a Rappin' Ron .20 .50
❑ 10b Ray Gun .20 .50
❑ 11a Double Heather .20 .50
❑ 11b Fran Fran .20 .50
❑ 12a Russell Muscle .20 .50
❑ 12b Brett Sweat .20 .50
❑ 13a Spacey Stacy .20 .50
❑ 13b Janet Planet .20 .50
❑ 14a Shrunken Ed .20 .50
❑ 14b Cheeky Charles .20 .50
❑ 15a Ghastly Ashley .20 .50
❑ 15b Acne Amy .20 .50
❑ 16a Split Kit .20 .50
❑ 16b Mixed-Up Mitch .20 .50
❑ 17a Joe Blow .20 .50
❑ 17b Rod Wad .20 .50
❑ 18a Hot Head Harvey .20 .50
❑ 18b Roy Bot .20 .50
❑ 19a Dinah Saur .20 .50
❑ 19b Farrah Fossil .20 .50
❑ 20a Blake Flake .20 .50
❑ 20b Hippie Skippy .20 .50
❑ 21a Ali Gator .20 .50
❑ 21b Marshy Marshall .20 .50
❑ 22a Silent Sandy .20 .50
❑ 22b Barren Aaron .20 .50
❑ 23a Starin' Darren .20 .50
❑ 23b Peepin' Tom .20 .50
❑ 24a Half-Nelson .20 .50
❑ 24b Glandular Angela .20 .50
❑ 25a Armpit Britt .20 .50
❑ 25b Shaggy Aggie .20 .50
❑ 26a Sloshed Josh .20 .50
❑ 26b Low Cal .20 .50
❑ 27a Stuffed Stephen .20 .50
❑ 27b Rutherford B. Hay .20 .50
❑ 28a Swollen Sue Ellen .20 .50
❑ 28b Bloated Blair .20 .50
❑ 29a Max Axe .20 .50
❑ 29b Deadly Dudley .20 .50
❑ 30a Alien Ian .20 .50
❑ 30b Outerspace Chase .20 .50
❑ 31a Baked Jake .20 .50
❑ 31b Dry Guy .20 .50
❑ 32a Losing Faith .20 .50
❑ 32b Dyin' Dinah .20 .50
❑ 33a Handy Randy .20 .50
❑ 33b Jordan Nuts .20 .50
❑ 34a Nat Nerd .20 .50
❑ 34b Clark Can't .20 .50
❑ 35a Meltin' Milton .20 .50
❑ 35b Lazy Louie .20 .50
❑ 36a Moe Skeeto .20 .50
❑ 36b Sting Ray .20 .50
❑ 37a Fran Furter .20 .50
❑ 37b Hot Doug .20 .50
❑ 38a Dangling Dolly .20 .50
❑ 38b Surreal Neal .20 .50
❑ 39a Fluoride Floyd .20 .50
❑ 39b Dental Daniel .20 .50
❑ 40a Toothie Ruthie .20 .50
❑ 40b Dental Flossie .20 .50
❑ 41a Over Flo .20 .50
❑ 41b Moist Joyce .20 .50
❑ 42a Joel Hole .20 .50
❑ 42b Teed-Off Tom .20 .50
❑ 43a Upliftin' Clifton .20 .50
❑ 43b Air-Head Jed .20 .50
❑ 44a Tiny Tim .20 .50
❑ 44b Small Saul .20 .50
❑ 45a Bea Sting .20 .50
❑ 45b Screaming Mimi .20 .50
❑ 46a Claire Stare .20 .50
❑ 46b Bloodshot Scott .20 .50
❑ 47a Harry Canary .20 .50
❑ 47b Burt Cage .20 .50
❑ 48a Marc Spark .20 .50
❑ 48b Cherry Bomb .20 .50
❑ 49a Milky Wayne .20 .50
❑ 49b Dairy Cari .20 .50
❑ 50a On The Mark .20 .50
❑ 50b Bull's Ira .20 .50
❑ 51a Cut-Up Carmen .20 .50
❑ 51b Dotted Lionel .20 .50
❑ 52a Curly Shirley .20 .50
❑ 52b Blown Joan .20 .50
❑ 53a Have A Nice Dave .20 .50
❑ 53b Miles Smiles .20 .50
❑ 54a Soured Howard .20 .50
❑ 54b Paul Bunion .20 .50
❑ 55a Manny Heads .20 .50
❑ 55b Max Stacks .20 .50
❑ 56a Grant Ant .20 .50
❑ 56b Sticky Nikki .20 .50
❑ 57a Bowling Elaine .20 .50
❑ 57b Mike Strike .20 .50
❑ 58a Heartless Hal .20 .50
❑ 58b Bowen Arrow .20 .50
❑ 59a Moe Bile .20 .50
❑ 59b Dang Len .20 .50
❑ 60a Haley's Vomit .20 .50
❑ 60b Inter Stella .20 .50
❑ 61a K.O.'d Karl .20 .50
❑ 61b Sparrin' Warren .20 .50
❑ 62a Waffle Ira .20 .50
❑ 62b Griddled Greta .20 .50
❑ 63a Leather Heather .20 .50
❑ 63b Chained Shane .20 .50
❑ 64a Glowing Amber .20 .50
❑ 64b Bright Dwight .20 .50
❑ 65a Pickled Pete .20 .50
❑ 65b Formaldehyde Fred .20 .50
❑ 66a Baby Abie .20 .50
❑ 66b Lincoln Park .20 .50
❑ 67a Global Warren .20 .50
❑ 67b Al Pocalypse .20 .50
❑ 68a Stitched Stella .20 .50
❑ 68b Patchwork Paula .20 .50
❑ 69a Raisin' Ella .20 .50
❑ 69b Grape Vi .20 .50
❑ 70a Finger-Paintin' Fifi .20 .50
❑ 70b Libby Stick .20 .50
❑ 71a Nasty Nick .30 .75
❑ 71b Evil Eddie .30 .75
❑ 72a Adam Bomb .30 .75
❑ 72b Blasted Billy .30 .75
❑ 73a Boozin' Bruce .20 .50
❑ 73b Drunk Ken .20 .50
❑ 74a Tee-Vee Stevie .20 .50
❑ 74b Geeky Gary .20 .50
❑ 75a Cranky Frankie .20 .50
❑ 75b Bad Brad .20 .50
❑ 76a Bony Joanie .20 .50
❑ 76b Thin Lynn .20 .50
❑ 77a Split Kit .20 .50
❑ 77b Mixed-Up Mitch .20 .50
❑ 78a Hot Head Harvey .20 .50
❑ 78b Roy Bot .20 .50
❑ 79a Babbling Brooke .20 .50
❑ 79b Jelly Kelly .20 .50
❑ 80a Nat Nerd .20 .50
❑ 80b Clark Can't .20 .50

2010 Garbage Pail Kids Flashback Green

*GREEN: 2X TO 5X BASIC CARD
STATED ODDS 1:2

2010 Garbage Pail Kids Flashback Pink

*PINK: 3X TO 8X BASIC CARD
STATED ODDS 1:3

2010 Garbage Pail Kids Flashback Silver

*SILVER: 6X TO 15X BASIC CARD
STATED ODDS 1:6

2010 Garbage Pail Kids Flashback Gold

*GOLD: 30X TO 80X
STATED ODDS 1:42

2010 Garbage Pail Kids Flashback Printing Plates Black

STATED ODDS 1:1,790
STATED PRINT RUN 1 SER. #'d SET

2010 Garbage Pail Kids Flashback Loco Motion

COMPLETE SET (10) 20.00 40.00
STATED ODDS 1:8

❑ 1 Up Chuck 2.50 6.00
❑ 2 Wacky Jackie 2.50 6.00
❑ 3 Drippy Dan 2.50 6.00
❑ 4 Cracked Jack 2.50 6.00
❑ 5 Boney Tony 2.50 6.00
❑ 6 Adam Boom 2.50 6.00
❑ 7 Gooey Huey 2.50 6.00
❑ 8 Reuben Cube 2.50 6.00
❑ 9 Explorin' Norman 2.50 6.00
❑ 10 Squashed Josh 2.50 6.00

2010 Garbage Pail Kids Flashback Sketches

STATED ODDS 1:229

❑ 1 Brent Engstrom 100.00 200.00
❑ 2 Colin Walton 150.00 300.00
❑ 3 David Gross 100.00 200.00
❑ 4 Fred Wheaton 150.00 300.00
❑ 5 Jay Lynch 50.00 100.00
❑ 6 Jeff Zapata 150.00 300.00
❑ 7 Joe Simko 50.00 100.00
❑ 8 Layron DeJarnette 100.00 200.00
❑ 9 Mark Pingatore 100.00 200.00
❑ 10 Tom Bunk 100.00 200.00

2010 Ghost Whisperer Seasons Three and Four

COMPLETE SET (72) 6.00 15.00

❑ 1 The Underneath .15 .40
❑ 2 Jennifer's Haunted Past .15 .40
❑ 3 Beth's Dark Secrets .15 .40
❑ 4 The Curse of Bloody Mary .15 .40
❑ 5 More Than a Hero's Welcome .15 .40
❑ 6 Melinda's in Peril .15 .40
❑ 7 The Dark Beneath Grandview .15 .40
❑ 8 More Than a Missing Image .15 .40
❑ 9 A Haunting Affair .15 .40
❑ 10 Spirit in the Woods .15 .40
❑ 11 A Ghostly Game .15 .40
❑ 12 Meeting of Ghost Whisperers .15 .40
❑ 13 Becca's Ghostly Encounters .15 .40
❑ 14 Santa's Coming to Grandview .15 .40
❑ 15 A Website's Menacing Messages .15 .40
❑ 16 An Ominous Rescue .15 .40
❑ 17 Guilt Over Ghosts .15 .40
❑ 18 Psychic Disturbances .15 .40
❑ 19 Ghostly Graffiti .15 .40
❑ 20 Melinda Unravels the Past .15 .40
❑ 21 Kylie is Swarmed By Ghostly Bees .15 .40
❑ 22 A Grim Reminder of Horrors Past .15 .40
❑ 23 Horror Film Finale .15 .40
❑ 24 Prof. Payne a Father .15 .40
❑ 25 Prof. Payne Pulls Through .15 .40
❑ 26 All is Forgiven .15 .40
❑ 27 Melinda's Father Returns .15 .40
❑ 28 Melinda Unravels the Mystery .15 .40
❑ 29 Tom Gordon in Danger .15 .40
❑ 30 Ghostly Warnings From Beyond .15 .40
❑ 31 Hospital Haunts .15 .40
❑ 32 Eli Hears the Truth .15 .40
❑ 33 Too Many Ghosts .15 .40
❑ 34 High School Haunts .15 .40
❑ 35 Melinda's Gamer-Ghost World .15 .40
❑ 36 Ship of Lost Souls .15 .40
❑ 37 Best Friends Forever .15 .40
❑ 38 Switched at Birth .15 .40
❑ 39 Not Just an Imaginary Friend .15 .40
❑ 40 Case of the Youthful Ghost .15 .40
❑ 41 Tragedy By the Lake .15 .40
❑ 42 The Late Jim Clancy .15 .40
❑ 43 Carl's Ghostly Dilemma .15 .40
❑ 44 Unexpected Soul Transferal .15 .40
❑ 45 Enter Sam Lucas .15 .40
❑ 46 Melinda's Living Nightmare .15 .40
❑ 47 Make a Wish .15 .40
❑ 48 Some Telltale Signs .15 .40
❑ 49 Unwanted Emergency Calls .15 .40
❑ 50 A Spirited Hitch-Hiker .15 .40
❑ 51 Delia Lays Down the Law .15 .40
❑ 52 The Unwanted Dead .15 .40
❑ 53 Dancing With the Dead .15 .40
❑ 54 Deborah Reveals Her Past .15 .40
❑ 55 Sorority Spirit Mishap .15 .40
❑ 56 Ghostly Cooperation .15 .40
❑ 57 A Gathering of Ghost Hunters .15 .40
❑ 58 Believing the Supernatural .15 .40
❑ 59 Beware the Haunted Hospital Patient .15 .40
❑ 60 Passage to a Ghostly World .15 .40
❑ 61 Poltergeist Moves on Morgan .15 .40
❑ 62 Melinda Reasons With Rick .15 .40
❑ 63 A Ghostly Soap Opera .15 .40
❑ 64 Miles Watches Over Cally .15 .40
❑ 65 The Haunted Dollhouse .15 .40
❑ 66 The Spirit Reaches Out .15 .40
❑ 67 Melinda and Delia Seek the Truth .15 .40
❑ 68 The Vampire Ghost .15 .40
❑ 69 Premonitions Over Grandview .15 .40
❑ 70 Encountering the Dark-Side .15 .40
❑ 71 Turning the Pages of Psychic Content .15 .40
❑ 72 Checklist .15 .40

2010 Ghost Whisperer Seasons Three and Four Autographs

STATED ODDS 1:48

❑ ACM Camryn Manheim 15.00 30.00
❑ ACS Christoph Sanders 10.00 20.00
❑ ADC David Conrad 15.00 30.00
❑ AHD Hillary Duff 40.00 80.00
❑ AJK Jamie Kennedy 10.00 20.00
❑ AJLH Jennifer Love Hewitt 50.00 100.00
❑ AJLHCM Jennifer Love Hewitt 40.00 80.00
Camryn Manheim DUAL
❑ AJLHJK Jennifer Love Hewitt 40.00 80.00
Jamie Kennedy DUAL

2010 Ghost Whisperer Seasons Three and Four Costumes

OVERALL COSTUME/PROP ODDS 1:10
CI1 SHOE ISSUED AS CASE INCENTIVE

❑ C1 Melinda Gordon pants 15.00 40.00
shirt DUAL
❑ C2 Melinda Gordon shirt 15.00 40.00
shirt DUAL
❑ C3 Melinda Gordon dress 15.00 40.00
dress DUAL
❑ C4 Melinda Gordon dress 15.00 40.00
dress DUAL
❑ C5 Melinda Gordon jacket 15.00 40.00
jacket DUAL
❑ C6 Melinda Gordon jacket 15.00 40.00
jacket DUAL
❑ C7 Melinda Gordon dress 15.00 40.00
dress DUAL
❑ C8 Melinda Gordon pjs 15.00 40.00
pjs DUAL
❑ C9 Melinda Gordon shirt 15.00 40.00
shirt DUAL
❑ C10 Melinda Gordon dress 15.00 40.00
sweater DUAL
❑ C11 Morgan Jeffries sweater 12.00 30.00
❑ C12A Jim Clancy shirt 12.00 30.00
❑ C12B Jim Clancy patch SP 30.00 60.00
❑ C13 Delia Banks shirt 12.00 30.00
❑ C14 Prof. Rick Payne jacket 12.00 30.00
❑ C15 Eli James sweater 12.00 30.00
❑ C16 Ned Banks jacket 12.00 30.00
❑ C17 Morgan Jeffries shirt 12.00 30.00
❑ C18 Jim Clancy shirt 12.00 30.00
❑ C19 Delia Banks shirt 12.00 30.00
❑ C20 Ned Banks tie 15.00 40.00
❑ C21 Morgan Jeffries pants 12.00 30.00
❑ C22 Jim Clancy shirt 12.00 30.00
❑ C23 Delia Banks shirt 12.00 30.00
❑ C24 Ned Banks vest 12.00 30.00
❑ C25 Justin Yates shirt 12.00 30.00
❑ C26 Justin Yates jacket 12.00 30.00
❑ C27 Det. Carl Neely shirt 12.00 30.00
❑ C28 Melinda Gordon 20.00 50.00
Jim Clancy/Justin Yates/Rick Payne/Delia Banks/Eli James/Carl Neely/Ned Banks/Morgan Jeffries
❑ C29 Melinda Gordon 20.00 50.00
Rick Payne/Delia Banks/Jim Clancy/Ned Banks/Eli James
❑ CI1 Melinda Gordon shoe 100.00 200.00
(issued as case incentive)

2010 Ghost Whisperer Seasons Three and Four Promos

❑ 1A Melinda Gordon
❑ 1B Melinda Gordon FOIL
❑ 2A Melinda Gordon
❑ 2B Melinda Gordon FOIL
❑ NSU Melinda Gordon/ (issued in Non-Sport Update)
❑ NSUF Melinda Gordon FOIL/ (issued in Non-Sport Update)
❑ SDCC Melinda Gordon/ (issued at San Diego Comic Con)
❑ SDCCF Melinda Gordon FOIL/ (issued at San Diego Comic Con)
❑ CECE1 Melinda Gordon (black dress)/ (issued at Chicagoland Entertainment Collectors Expo)
❑ CECE2 Melinda Gordon (white dress)/ (issued at Chicagoland Entertainment Collectors Expo)
❑ CECEF Melinda Gordon FOIL/ (issued at Chicagoland Entertainment Collectors Expo)
❑ PNSCS Melinda Gordon/ (issued at Philly Non-Sport Card Show)

2010 Ghost Whisperer Seasons Three and Four Props

OVERALL COSTUME/PROP ODDS 1:10
TOOTH ISSUED AS CASE TOPPER

❑ P1 Wooden Pentagram 15.00 40.00
❑ P2 Doll 15.00 40.00
❑ P3 Door Sign
❑ P4 Map 15.00 40.00
❑ P5 Vine 15.00 40.00
❑ P6 Mask 15.00 40.00
❑ CT Tooth (issued as case topper) 15.00 40.00

2010 Ghost Whisperer Seasons Three and Four Puzzle

COMPLETE SET (9) 6.00 15.00
STATED ODDS 1:12

❑ CP1 Puzzle 1 (upper left) 1.00 2.50
❑ CP2 Puzzle 2 (upper center) 1.00 2.50
❑ CP3 Puzzle 3 (upper right) 1.00 2.50
❑ CP4 Puzzle 4 (middle left) 1.00 2.50
❑ CP5 Puzzle 5 (middle center) 1.00 2.50
❑ CP6 Puzzle 6 (middle right) 1.00 2.50
❑ CP7 Puzzle 7 (lower left) 1.00 2.50
❑ CP8 Puzzle 8 (lower center) 1.00 2.50
❑ CP9 Puzzle 9 (lower right) 1.00 2.50

2010 Ghost Whisperer Seasons Three and Four Quotes

COMPLETE SET (9) 6.00 15.00
STATED ODDS 1:12

❑ Q1 B.Gordon 1.00 2.50
M.Gordon/J.Clancy
❑ Q2 Jim Clancy 1.00 2.50
❑ Q3 Melinda Gordon 1.00 2.50
❑ Q4 Tops of heads 1.00 2.50
❑ Q5 Beth Gordon 1.00 2.50
Melinda Gordon
❑ Q6 Melinda Gordon 1.00 2.50
Rick Payne
❑ Q7 Jim Clancy 1.00 2.50
❑ Q8 Melinda Gordon 1.00 2.50
❑ Q9 Eli James 1.00 2.50

2010 Ghost Whisperer Seasons Three and Four Trivia

COMPLETE SET (9) 6.00 15.00
STATED ODDS 1:12

❑ T1 Christmas Scene 1.00 2.50
❑ T2 Melinda Gordon 1.00 2.50
❑ T3 Computer Screen 1.00 2.50
❑ T4 Turning the Dial 1.00 2.50
❑ T5 Potter's House 1.00 2.50
❑ T6 Melinda Gordon 1.00 2.50
❑ T7 Prof. Rick Payne 1.00 2.50
❑ T8 Ghosts Among Us 1.00 2.50
❑ T9 Ghost Whisperer Spirit Guide 1.00 2.50

2010 Golden Age of Comics Heroes and Villians

COMPLETE SET (40) 20.00 50.00

❑ 1 Dr. Macabre .75 2.00
Adam Cleveland
❑ 2 Lady Serpent .75 2.00
Adam Schickling
❑ 3 Black Cat .75 2.00
Bennett Pisek
❑ 4 Madame Satan .75 2.00
Bill Pulkovski
❑ 5 Phantom Lady .75 2.00
Carolyn Edwards
❑ 6 Bob Phantom .75 2.00
Chuck Zsolnai
❑ 7 The Face .75 2.00
Darren Auck
❑ 8 Spider Queen .75 2.00
Darren Chandler
❑ 9 Black Terror .75 2.00
David Beaty
❑ 10 Queen of Evil .75 2.00
David Girdley
❑ 11 Frankenstein .75 2.00
David Harrigan
❑ 12 Rocketman .75 2.00
Gary Ochiltree
❑ 13 Cat-Man .75 2.00
George Deep
❑ 14 Torchy .75 2.00
Gilbert Young Roland
❑ 15 Atoman .75 2.00
Jason Carrier
❑ 16 Black Phantom .75 2.00
Jason Potratz/Jack Hai
❑ 17 V-Man .75 2.00
Jim Kyle
❑ 18 Captain Red Cross .75 2.00
Jon Hughes
❑ 19 Dr. Macabre .75 2.00
Kevin E Meinert
❑ 20 The Flame .75 2.00
Kevin Leen
❑ 21 Rex Dexter of Mars .75 2.00
Laura Inglis
❑ 22 Black Owl .75 2.00
Marc Ferreira
❑ 23 Frankenstein .75 2.00
Nick Neocleous
❑ 24 Dr. Nemesis .75 2.00
Robert Aragon
❑ 25 The Clown .75 2.00
Rupam Gupta
❑ 26 Purple Tigress .75 2.00
Ryan M Kincaid
❑ 27 Rulah Jungle Goddess .75 2.00
Soni Alcorn-Hender
❑ 28 Microface .75 2.00
Tim Levandoski
❑ 29 The Flame .75 2.00
Tim Shay
❑ 30 Bronze Terror .75 2.00
Tony Scott
❑ 31 Dr. Plasma .75 2.00
Trev Murphy
❑ 32 Tygra .75 2.00
Veronica O'Connell
❑ 33 Frankenstein .75 2.00
William Kenney
❑ 34 Black Cat .75 2.00
Elaine Perna
❑ 35 Tara the Pirate Queen .75 2.00
David Day
❑ 36 Princess Pantha .75 2.00
Tygra/Steven Miller
❑ 37 Rulah .75 2.00
Cave Girl/Steven Miller
❑ 38 Jun-Gal .75 2.00
Steven Miller
❑ 39 G-2 .75 2.00
Dan Borgonos
❑ 40 Checklist .75 2.00
❑ NNO Princess Pantha 12.00 30.00
Tygra/Rulah/Cave Girl/Jun-Gal/Steven Miller 3-Card Panel

2010 Golden Age of Comics Heroes and Villians Promos

COMP. SET w/o SP (7) 4.00 10.00
COMPLETE SET (8) 8.00 20.00
STATED ODDS ONE PER PACK
SP ONLY AVAILABLE FROM 2010 PHILLY NONSPORT EXPO

❑ 1 Miss Masque .75 2.00
❑ 2 Frankenstein .75 2.00
❑ 3 The Black Terror .75 2.00
❑ 4 Tygra .75 2.00
❑ 5 Moon Girl .75 2.00
❑ 6 Mr. Monster .75 2.00
❑ 7 Black Terror .75 2.00
❑ NNO Green Lama SP/2010 Philly 4.00 10.00
Non-Sport Exclusive

2010 Golden Age of Comics Heroes and Villians Sketches

STATED ODDS ONE PER PACK

❑ ALCO Soni Alcorn-Hender/20*
❑ ARAG Robert Aragon/100* 12.00 30.00
❑ AUCK Darren Auck/202* 10.00 25.00
❑ AUST Don Austin/25* 10.00 25.00
❑ AZEV Jean Marcel Azevedo/30* 8.00 20.00
❑ BAUT Eden Bautista/31* 8.00 20.00
❑ BEAT David Beaty/100* 10.00 25.00
❑ BORG Dan Borgonos/111* 10.00 25.00
❑ CARR Jason Carrier/25* 20.00 50.00
❑ CHAN Darren Chandler/56* 12.00 30.00
❑ CHUC Chris Chuckry/25* 10.00 25.00
❑ CLAU Mickey Clausen/50* 8.00 20.00
❑ CLEV Adam Cleveland/206* 12.00 30.00
❑ CRIS Dennis Crisostomo/50* 10.00 25.00
❑ DAY David Day/29*
❑ DEEP George Deep/60*
❑ DIEF Otto Dieffenbach/83*
❑ DIOS Gerald de Dios/22*
❑ DORI Guy Dorian/48* 10.00 25.00
❑ DUNA Kimberly Dunaway/30* 12.00 30.00
❑ DUNN Ben Dunn/42* 20.00 50.00
❑ EDWA Carolyn Edwards/43* 10.00 25.00
❑ EMAN Eman/111* 8.00 20.00
❑ EVAN Arvin C. Evangelista (John Ace)/90* 12.00 30.00
❑ FERR Marc Ferreira/54*
❑ GACE David Gacey/30* 8.00 20.00
❑ GEOR Charles George/20*
❑ GERL Bruce Gerlach/30* 10.00 25.00
❑ GIRD David Girdley/27*
❑ GRAN Danielle Soloud/20*
❑ GREE Diana Greenhalgh/20*
❑ GUPT Rupam Gupta/40* 20.00 50.00
❑ HALL Charles Hall/25* 30.00 80.00
❑ HARR David Harrigan/25* 12.00 30.00
❑ HEFN Hal Hefner/26*
❑ HEND Chris Henderson/28* 15.00 40.00
❑ HUDD Terry Huddleston/42* 8.00 20.00
❑ HUST Jeremy Hustad/25*
❑ INGL Laura Inglis/25*
❑ JACZ Veronica Jaczkowski/25*
❑ JAHU Jason Hughes/65* 8.00 20.00
❑ JAYT Jay T/30*
❑ JOHU Jon Hughes/93* 8.00 20.00
❑ JPJH Jason Potratz 20.00 60.00
Jack Hai/100*
❑ JROD James Rodriguez/50*
❑ KAIS Rachel Kaiser/27*
❑ KEIM Chadd Keim/25*
❑ KENN William Kenney/25* 12.00 30.00
❑ KINC Ryan M Kincaid/25* 25.00 60.00
❑ KOHS Lee Kohse/45*
❑ KONG Brian Kong/199* 8.00 20.00
❑ KRET Jayson Kretzer/50* 15.00 40.00
❑ KYLE Jim Kyle/100*
❑ LAMB Randi Lamb/60* 8.00 20.00
❑ LEEN Kevin Leen/34*
❑ LEVA Tim Levandoski/27*
❑ LIM Lak Lim/28* 10.00 25.00
❑ LOPE Alfredo Lopez Jr./100* 12.00 30.00
❑ LYMA Josh Lyman/54* 8.00 20.00
❑ MANR Esteban Manriquez/26*
❑ MARI Michael Santa Maria/105* 8.00 20.00
❑ MART CC Martin/29*
❑ MCCA Megan McCausland/30*
❑ MCNE James McNeil/25* 8.00 20.00
❑ MEDE Manny Mederos II/64* 8.00 20.00
❑ MEIN Kevin E Meinert/25*
❑ MIEL Tony Miello/60*
❑ MILL Steven Miller/75* 12.00 30.00
❑ MOHD Nur Hanie Mohd/25* 15.00 40.00
❑ MOLI Rich Molinelli/25* 12.00 30.00
❑ MURP Trev Murphy/28* 30.00 80.00
❑ NEOC Nick Neocleous/25*
❑ NGUY Vo Nguyen/44*
❑ NORT Alain Norte/15*
❑ OCHI Gary Ochiltree/25*
❑ OCON Veronica O'Connell/28* 125.00 250.00
❑ OHYA Satoru Ohya/20* 20.00 50.00
❑ OLSO Matt Olson/21*
❑ OROS Ryan Orosco/22* 25.00 60.00
❑ OWEN Rhiannon Owens/30* 25.00 60.00
❑ PANG Jay Pangan III/104* 12.00 30.00
❑ PENC Sean Pence/25*
❑ PERN Elaine Perna/24*
❑ PEZ Daniel Lopez (PEZ)/35* 12.00 30.00
❑ PIER Joe St Pierre/20* 20.00 50.00
❑ PISE Bennett Pisek/25* 12.00 30.00
❑ POPP Ashleigh Popplewell/65*
❑ POST Brian Postman/105* 12.00 30.00
❑ PRIN Buddy Prince/26* 12.00 30.00
❑ PULK Bill Pulkovski/40* 10.00 25.00
❑ RICE Walter Rice/65*
❑ ROBE Ian Roberts/28*
❑ ROLA Gilbert Young Roland/102* 15.00 40.00.
❑ ROSE Scott Rosema/35*
❑ ROUS Jason Roussel/25*
❑ SAWY Lance Sawyer/50*
❑ SCHI Adam Schickling/25* 30.00 80.00
❑ SCOT Tony Scott/25*
❑ SHAY Tim Shay/25* 12.00 30.00
❑ SHEA Brian Shearer/50* 8.00 20.00
❑ SIMM Scott D M Simmons/101*
❑ SLAT Mark Slater/20*
❑ SMAL Louis Small Jr/26* 15.00 40.00
❑ SORI Carlo Soriano/30*
❑ TAN Anthony Tan/111* 25.00 60.00
❑ TREE Jeremy Treece/50* 15.00 40.00
❑ VROD Victor Rodriguez/65* 8.00 20.00
❑ WALK Ian Walker/50*
❑ WALT Travis Walton/65* 8.00 20.00
❑ WASH Frankie B Washington/30* 12.00 30.00
❑ WHEE Anthony Wheeler/27*
❑ YAMA Ms Yamamoto/20*
❑ YOSH Mr Yoshihara/15*
❑ ZSOL Chuck Zsolnai/30*

2010 Green Hornet Movie Series One

COMPLETE SET (17) 75.00 125.00
STATED PRINT RUN 500 SER. #'d SETS

❑ C1 Green Hornet .75 2.00
❑ C2 Green Hornet .75 2.00
❑ C3 Green Hornet .75 2.00
❑ C4 Green Hornet .75 2.00
❑ C5 Green Hornet .75 2.00
❑ C6 Green Hornet .75 2.00
❑ C7 Green Hornet .75 2.00
❑ C8 Kato .75 2.00
❑ C9 Kato .75 2.00
❑ C10 Kato .75 2.00
❑ C11 Kato .75 2.00
❑ C12 Kato .75 2.00
❑ C13 Kato .75 2.00
❑ C14 Kato .75 2.00
❑ GH Green Hornet trench coat MEM 6.00 15.00
❑ KATO Kato jacket MEM 6.00 15.00
❑ JC Jay Chou AU 40.00 80.00
❑ CP1 Green Hornet 1.50 4.00
Kato PROMO

2010 Green Hornet Movie Series Two

COMPLETE SET (6) 125.00 200.00
COMP.SET w/o ROGEN AU (5) 30.00 60.00
ROGEN AUTO ISSUED AS 3-SET INCENTIVE

❑ 1 Britt Reid trench coat MEM 8.00 20.00
❑ 2 Chudnofsky trench coat MEM 8.00 20.00
❑ 3 Green Hornet suit MEM 8.00 20.00
❑ 4 Michael Axford shirt MEM 8.00 20.00
❑ 5 Scanlon suit MEM 8.00 20.00
❑ SR Seth Rogan AU/ (issued as 3-set incentive)100.00 150.00

2010 Harry Potter and the Deathly Hallows Part One

COMPLETE SET (90) 8.00 20.00

❑ 1 Title Card .15 .40
❑ 2 Harry Potter .15 .40
❑ 3 Hermione Granger .15 .40
❑ 4 Ron Weasley .15 .40
❑ 5 Severus Snape .15 .40
❑ 6 Lord Voldemort .15 .40
❑ 7 Draco Malfoy .15 .40
❑ 8 Lucius Malfoy .15 .40
❑ 9 Fenrir Greyback .15 .40
❑ 10 Scabior .15 .40
❑ 11 Bellatrix Lestrange .15 .40
❑ 12 Peter Pettigrew .15 .40
❑ 13 Rufus Scrimgeour .15 .40
❑ 14 Gregorovitch .15 .40
❑ 15 Xenophilius Lovegood .15 .40
❑ 16 Bathilda Bagshot .15 .40
❑ 17 Rubeus Hagrid .15 .40
❑ 18 Remus Lupin .15 .40
❑ 19 A Ghostly Apparition .15 .40
❑ 20 A Place to Hide .15 .40
❑ 21 Exploring the Hideout .15 .40
❑ 22 Lily's Letter .15 .40
❑ 23 Being Watched .15 .40
❑ 24 On His Own .15 .40
❑ 25 Sharing a Moment .15 .40
❑ 26 Regulus Arcturus Black .15 .40
❑ 27 Life on the Run .15 .40
❑ 28 Guard Duty .15 .40
❑ 29 The Mirror Shard .15 .40
❑ 30 Everything All Right .15 .40
❑ 31 A Peace Offering .15 .40
❑ 32 You Complete Arse .15 .40
❑ 33 Not the Most Expected Welcome .15 .40
❑ 34 Hermione .15 .40
❑ 35 A Little Light Reading .15 .40
❑ 36 Saying Goodbye .15 .40
❑ 37 The Life and Lies of Albus Dumbledore .15 .40
❑ 38 Ron Recovers .15 .40
❑ 39 It's Taboo .15 .40
❑ 40 Questioning the Mission .15 .40
❑ 41 Bathilda Bagshot .15 .40
❑ 42 Lumos .15 .40
❑ 43 Something's Not Right .15 .40
❑ 44 A Disturbing Discovery .15 .40
❑ 45 Nagini Attacks .15 .40
❑ 46 Devising a Plan .15 .40
❑ 47 Splinched .15 .40
❑ 48 The Middle of Nowhere .15 .40
❑ 49 An Encampment .15 .40
❑ 50 Looking For Help .15 .40
❑ 51 Reflection .15 .40
❑ 52 Not a Workman .15 .40
❑ 53 The Lovegood House .15 .40
❑ 54 Mr. Lovegood .15 .40
❑ 55 The Home of the Quibbler .15 .40
❑ 56 The Erumpent Horn .15 .40
❑ 57 Battle at the Lovegood House .15 .40
❑ 58 Ignotus Peverell .15 .40
❑ 59 A Solemn Moment .15 .40
❑ 60 Someone's Watching Us .15 .40
❑ 61 The Potters .15 .40
❑ 62 Conjuring Flames .15 .40
❑ 63 Snatchers .15 .40
❑ 64 What's That? That Smell? .15 .40
❑ 65 The Horcrux Locket .15 .40
❑ 66 Running From the Snatchers .15 .40
❑ 67 Attacked in the Forest .15 .40
❑ 68 In Hot Pursuit .15 .40
❑ 69 A Dangerous Pursuer .15 .40
❑ 70 Making an Escape .15 .40
❑ 71 Not Stan Shunpike .15 .40
❑ 72 You Smell Like Vanilla, Penelope .15 .40
❑ 73 What Happened to You, Ugly .15 .40
❑ 74 Runcorn and Cattermole .15 .40
❑ 75 For the Order .15 .40
❑ 76 Dumbledore's Oldest Friend .15 .40
❑ 77 A Happy Occasion .15 .40
❑ 78 They Are Coming .15 .40
❑ 79 Celebrating a Family Wedding .15 .40
❑ 80 Harry Go Go .15 .40
❑ 81 What Creature .15 .40
❑ 82 Waiting For the Others .15 .40
❑ 83 Zip Me Up .15 .40
❑ 84 Truly Identical .15 .40
❑ 85 The Real Harry .15 .40
❑ 86 A Meeting at Malfoy Manor .15 .40
❑ 87 Pius Thicknesse .15 .40
❑ 88 Loyal Death Eater .15 .40
❑ 89 Arriving at the Manor .15 .40
❑ 90 Checklist .15 .40

2010 Harry Potter and the Deathly Hallows Part One Autographs

STATED ODDS 1:48
R = RARE
UR = ULTRA RARE
EXCH EXPIRATION: 12/01/2011

❑ 1 Andy Linden R 12.00 30.00
❑ 2 Bonnie Wright 30.00 60.00
❑ 3 Clemence Poesy UR 30.00 60.00
❑ 4 Dave Legeno UR 12.00 30.00
❑ 5 David O'Hara 12.00 30.00
❑ 6 David Thewlis R 25.00 50.00
❑ 7 Evanna Lynch UR 50.00 100.00
❑ 8 Guy Henry 12.00 30.00
❑ 9 Helen McCrory R 30.00 60.00
❑ 10 Natalia Tena 30.00 60.00
❑ 11 Nick Moran UR 30.00 60.00
❑ 12 Rade Serbedzija R 20.00 40.00
❑ 13 Rhys Ifans R 50.00 100.00
❑ 14 Rupert Grint UR 125.00 200.00
❑ 15 Simon McBurney 20.00 40.00

2010 Harry Potter and the Deathly Hallows Part One Case Incentive Memorabilia

Ci1 ISSUED AS 2-CASE INCENTIVE
Ci2 ISSUED AS 5-CASE INCENTIVE
Ci3 ISSUED AS 10-CASE INCENTIVE
Ci4 ISSUED AS 25-CASE INCENTIVE
GOLD,SILVER, AND BRONZE VAR. EXIST FOR Ci4

❑ Ci1 Ron Weasley jacket 15.00 40.00
(issued as 2-case incentive)
❑ Ci2 Arthur Weasley jacket 30.00 60.00
(issued as 5-case incentive)
❑ Ci3 Harry Potter jacket 60.00 120.00
(issued as 10-case incentive)
❑ Ci4 Gringotts coins/ (issued as 25-case incentive)150.00250.00

2010 Harry Potter and the Deathly Hallows Part One Clear Box Toppers

COMPLETE SET (4) 8.00 20.00
STATED ODDS ONE PER BOX

❑ BT1 Harry Potter 3.00 8.00
❑ BT2 Ron Weasley 3.00 8.00
❑ BT3 Hermione Granger 3.00 8.00
❑ BT4 Ron Weasley 3.00 8.00

2010 Harry Potter and the Deathly Hallows Part One Costumes

STATED ODDS 1:24
PRINT RUN 240-580

❑ C1 Hermione Granger shirt/310 20.00 50.00
❑ C2 Bill Weasley vest/530 10.00 25.00
❑ C3 Draco Malfoy shirt/460 10.00 25.00
❑ C4 Hermione Granger shirt/280 25.00 60.00
❑ C5 Lucius Malfoy coat/500 10.00 25.00
❑ C6 Ron Weasley shirt/450 12.00 30.00
❑ C7 Harry Potter shirt/310 15.00 40.00
❑ C8 George Weasley shirt/580 10.00 25.00
❑ C9 Wormtail shirt/380 10.00 25.00
❑ C10 Luna Lovegood dress/240 25.00 60.00
❑ C11 Severus Snape robe/280 20.00 50.00
❑ C12 Ron Weasley jacket/380 10.00 25.00
❑ C13 Fred Weasley shirt/530 10.00 25.00
❑ C14 Bellatrix Lestrange dress/510 10.00 25.00
❑ C15 Ron Weasley shirt/460 10.00 25.00

2010 Harry Potter and the Deathly Hallows Part One Crystal Case Toppers

COMPLETE SET (3) 30.00 75.00
STATED ODDS ONE PER CASE

❑ CT1 Death Eater 12.00 30.00
❑ CT2 Bellatrix Lestrange 12.00 30.00
❑ CT3 Death Eater 12.00 30.00

2010 Harry Potter and the Deathly Hallows Part One FilmCards

COMPLETE SET (9) 100.00 200.00
STATED PRINT RUN 247 SER. #'d SETS

❑ CFC1 Harry 12.00 30.00
Ron/Hermione
❑ CFC2 Harry 12.00 30.00
❑ CFC3 Poster 12.00 30.00
❑ CFC4 Harry 12.00 30.00
❑ CFC5 Harry 12.00 30.00
❑ CFC6 Hermione 12.00 30.00
Harry
❑ CFC7 Hermione 12.00 30.00
❑ CFC8 Harry 12.00 30.00
❑ CFC9 Hermione 12.00 30.00

2010 Harry Potter and the Deathly Hallows Part One Foil

COMPLETE SET (9) 6.00 15.00
STATED ODDS 1:4

❑ R1 Harry Potter 1.00 2.50
❑ R2 Harry Potter 1.00 2.50
❑ R3 Harry Potter 1.00 2.50
❑ R4 Harry Potter 1.00 2.50
❑ R5 Hermione Granger 1.00 2.50
❑ R6 Hermione Granger 1.00 2.50
❑ R7 Hermione Granger 1.00 2.50
❑ R8 Ron Weasley 1.00 2.50
❑ R9 Ron Weasley 1.00 2.50

2010 Harry Potter and the Deathly Hallows Part One Promos

COMPLETE SET (5) 8.00 20.00

❑ 1 Ron Weasley 2.00 5.00
❑ 2 Harry Potter 2.00 5.00
Hermione Granger
❑ 3 Harry Potter 2.00 5.00
❑ 4 Ron Weasley 2.50 6.00
❑ 5 Hermione Granger 2.50 6.00

2010 Harry Potter and the Deathly Hallows Part One Props

STATED ODDS 1:80
PRINT RUN 110-330

❑ P1 The Daily Prophet/260 15.00 40.00
❑ P2 Tent Blanket/330 15.00 40.00
❑ P3 Saucers and Candles/110 40.00 80.00
❑ P4 Harry's Rucksack/140 25.00 50.00
❑ P5 Undesirable Poster/220 15.00 40.00
❑ P6 Magic Wand/140 50.00 100.00
❑ P7 Lovegood Drawings/200 40.00 80.00
❑ P8 Ron's Rucksack/160 25.00 50.00
❑ P9 The Daily Prophet/260 15.00 40.00
❑ P10 Courtroom Paperwork/290 15.00 40.00
❑ P11 Dumbledore Book/180 50.00 100.00
❑ P12 Tent Clothes Peg/110 50.00 100.00

2010 Harry Potter Heroes and Villains

COMPLETE SET (72) 8.00 20.00
55-72 STATED ODDS 1:2

❑ 1 Harry Potter .15 .40
❑ 2 Hermione Granger .15 .40
❑ 3 Ron Weasley .15 .40
❑ 4 Albus Dumbledore .15 .40
❑ 5 Rubeus Hagrid .15 .40
❑ 6 Minerva McGonagall .15 .40
❑ 7 Severus Snape .15 .40
❑ 8 Fred and George Weasley .15 .40
❑ 9 Ginny Weasley .15 .40
❑ 10 Neville Longbottom .15 .40
❑ 11 Luna Lovegood .15 .40
❑ 12 Sirius Black .15 .40
❑ 13 Remus Lupin .15 .40
❑ 14 Alastor Mad-Eye Moody .15 .40
❑ 15 Kingsley Shacklebolt .15 .40
❑ 16 Nymphadora Tonks .15 .40
❑ 17 Arthur Weasley .15 .40
❑ 18 Molly Weasley .15 .40
❑ 19 Dobby .15 .40
❑ 20 Dementors .15 .40
❑ 21 Argus Filch .15 .40
❑ 22 Quirinus Quirrell .15 .40
❑ 23 Gregory Goyle .15 .40
❑ 24 Draco Malfoy .15 .40
❑ 25 Vincent Crabbe .15 .40
❑ 26 Fenrir Greyback .15 .40
❑ 27 Bellatrix Lestrange .15 .40
❑ 28 Lucius Malfoy .15 .40
❑ 29 Peter Pettigrew .15 .40
❑ 30 Lord Voldemort .15 .40
❑ 31 Young Tom Riddle .15 .40
❑ 32 Barty Crouch Jr. .15 .40
❑ 33 Dolores Umbridge .15 .40
❑ 34 Dudley Dursley .15 .40
❑ 35 Vernon Dursley .15 .40
❑ 36 Igor Karkaroff .15 .40
❑ 37 Battle in the Chamber .15 .40
❑ 38 Scaling Slytherin .15 .40
❑ 39 The Dementor's Kiss .15 .40
❑ 40 Lupin's Transformation .15 .40
❑ 41 Guarding the Castle .15 .40
❑ 42 The Mysterious Patronus .15 .40
❑ 43 Reluctant Witness .15 .40
❑ 44 The Dark Lord Does Battle .15 .40
❑ 45 Taking Cover .15 .40
❑ 46 The Dark Lord Attacks .15 .40
❑ 47 Dumbledore Strikes .15 .40
❑ 48 Weasley's Revenge .15 .40
❑ 49 The Horcrux Cave .15 .40
❑ 50 Drinking the Potion .15 .40
❑ 51 A Deadly Fall .15 .40
❑ 52 An Unwilling Accomplice .15 .40
❑ 53 A Coward .15 .40
❑ 54 Checklist .15 .40
❑ 55 Bellatrix .30 .75
❑ 56 Lucius Malfoy .30 .75
❑ 57 Death Eaters .30 .75
❑ 58 Avada Kedavra .30 .75
❑ 59 Draco .30 .75
❑ 60 Lucius Malfoy .30 .75
❑ 61 Dumbledore .30 .75
❑ 62 Sirius Black .30 .75
❑ 63 Harry Potter .30 .75
❑ 64 Hermione Granger .30 .75
❑ 65 Ron Weasley .30 .75
❑ 66 Draco Malfoy .30 .75
❑ 67 Lucius Malfoy .30 .75
❑ 68 Harry Potter .30 .75
❑ 69 Dumbledore .30 .75
❑ 70 Dumbledore and Harry .30 .75
❑ 71 Hermione Granger .30 .75
❑ 72 Ron Weasley .30 .75

2010 Harry Potter Heroes and Villains Autographs

STATED ODDS 1:240

❑ 1 Rupert Grint 125.00 200.00
❑ 2 Ian Hart 20.00 40.00
❑ 3 Toby Jones 75.00 150.00
❑ 4 Matthew Lewis 20.00 40.00
❑ 5 Evanna Lynch 40.00 80.00
❑ 6 Jim Tavare 15.00 30.00
❑ 7 David Thewlis 25.00 50.00
❑ 8 Emma Watson 300.00 500.00
❑ 9 Bonnie Wright 30.00 60.00
❑ 10 Jamie Yeates 15.00 30.00
❑ 11 Natalia Tena 30.00 60.00
George Harris

2010 Harry Potter Heroes and Villains Box Toppers

COMPLETE SET (4) 8.00 20.00
STATED ODDS ONE PER BOX

❑ BT1 Harry Potter 4.00 10.00
❑ BT2 Ron Weasley 3.00 8.00
❑ BT3 Dumbledore 3.00 8.00
❑ BT4 Draco Malfoy 3.00 8.00

2010 Harry Potter Heroes and Villains Case Incentive Memorabilia

CI1 ISSUED AS 2-CASE INCENTIVE
CI2 ISSUED AS 5-CASE INCENTIVE
CI3 ISSUED AS 10-CASE INCENTIVE
CI4 ISSUED AS 25-CASE INCENTIVE
STATED PRINT RUN 92-230

❑ CI1 Hermione Granger/230 30.00 60.00
(issued as 2-case incentive)
❑ CI2 Harry Potter 35.00 70.00
Ginny Weasley/140/ (issued as 5-case incentive)
❑ CI3 Lucius Malfoy 60.00 120.00
Death Eater/110/ (issued as 10-case incentive)
❑ CI4 Slughorn Goblet/92 100.00 150.00
(issued as 25-case incentive)

2010 Harry Potter Heroes and Villains Costumes

OVERALL SINGLE/DUAL COSTUME ODDS 1:24
STATED PRINT RUN 130-480

❑ C1 Fred Weasley/380 10.00 25.00
❑ C2 Hermione Granger/130 30.00 80.00
❑ C3 Kingsley Shacklebolt/460 10.00 25.00
❑ C4 Narcissa Malfoy/430 12.00 30.00
❑ C5 Tom Riddle/230 12.00 30.00
❑ C6 Alecto Carrow/480 10.00 25.00
❑ C7 Hermione Granger/160 30.00 80.00
❑ C8 Dumbledore/280 10.00 25.00
❑ C9 Slytherin Quidditch/480 10.00 25.00
❑ C10 Bellatrix Lestrange/230 15.00 40.00
❑ C11 Cedric Diggory/380 15.00 40.00

2010 Harry Potter Heroes and Villains Dual Costumes

OVERALL SINGLE/DUAL COSTUME ODDS 1:24
STATED PRINT RUN 140-180

❑ DC1 Sirius Black 30.00 80.00
Harry Potter
❑ DC2 Barty Crouch Jr. 30.00 80.00
Igor Karkaroff
❑ DC3 Death Eater 25.00 60.00
Azkaban Prisoner

2010 Harry Potter Heroes and Villains Dual Props
OVERALL SINGLE/DUAL PROP ODDS 1:60
❑ DP1 Quidditch Quaffle 30.00 80.00
Broom Bristles/190
❑ PC1 Death Eater Mask and Costume/110 50.00 100.00

2010 Harry Potter Heroes and Villains Foil
COMPLETE SET (9) 6.00 15.00
STATED ODDS 1:6
❑ R1 Harry Potter 1.00 2.50
❑ R2 Harry Potter 1.00 2.50
❑ R3 Harry Potter 1.00 2.50
❑ R4 Hermione Granger 1.00 2.50
❑ R5 Hermione Granger 1.00 2.50
❑ R6 Hermione Granger 1.00 2.50
❑ R7 Ron Weasley 1.00 2.50
❑ R8 Ron Weasley 1.00 2.50
❑ R9 Ron Weasley 1.00 2.50

2010 Harry Potter Heroes and Villains Metal Case Toppers
COMPLETE SET (3) 25.00 60.00
STATED ODDS ONE PER CASE
❑ CT1 Hogwarts 10.00 25.00
❑ CT2 Gryffindor 10.00 25.00
❑ CT3 Slytherin 10.00 25.00

2010 Harry Potter Heroes and Villains Promos
COMPLETE SET (3) 3.00 8.00
❑ P1 Harry Potter 1.50 4.00
❑ P2 Rubeus Hagrid 1.50 4.00
❑ P3 Albus Dumbledore 1.50 4.00

2010 Harry Potter Heroes and Villains Props
COMPLETE SET (11) 300.00 500.00
OVERALL SINGLE/DUAL PROP ODDS 1:60
STATED PRINT RUN 120-250
❑ P1 Harry's Test Tube/140 30.00 80.00
❑ P2 Hagrid's Candle/230 20.00 50.00
❑ P3 Defence Test/200 25.00 60.00
❑ P4 Weasley House Papers/250 20.00 50.00
❑ P5 Burrow Picture/120 30.00 80.00
❑ P6 Mortar and Pestle/150 25.00 60.00
❑ P7 Hedwig's Cage/130 25.00 60.00
❑ P8 Pixie Cage Base/180 20.00 50.00
❑ P9 Hagrid's Bottle/210 20.00 50.00
❑ P10 Ministry Coffee Cups/160 30.00 80.00
❑ P11 Hagrid's Slughorn Cup/170 25.00 60.00

2010 Heroes Archives
COMPLETE SET (72) 5.00 12.00
❑ 1 Claire Bennet .15 .40
❑ 2 Noah Bennet .15 .40
❑ 3 Peter Petrelli .15 .40
❑ 4 Nathan Petrelli .15 .40
❑ 5 Angela Petrelli .15 .40
❑ 6 Hiro Nakamura .15 .40
❑ 7 Ando Masahashi .15 .40
❑ 8 Mohinder Suresh .15 .40
❑ 9 Matt Parkman .15 .40
❑ 10 Sylar .15 .40
❑ 11 Niki Sanders .15 .40
❑ 12 Rene (The Haitian) .15 .40
❑ 13 Sandra Bennet .15 .40
❑ 14 Micah Sanders .15 .40
❑ 15 Lyle Bennet .15 .40
❑ 16 Janice Parkman .15 .40
❑ 17 Robert Knepper .15 .40
❑ 18 Isaac Mendez .15 .40
❑ 19 D.L. Hawkins .15 .40
❑ 20 Daphne Millbrook .15 .40
❑ 21 Lydia .15 .40
❑ 22 Edgar .15 .40
❑ 23 Molly Walker .15 .40
❑ 24 Adam Monroe (Takezo Kensei) .15 .40
❑ 25 Maya Herrera .15 .40
❑ 26 Alejandro Herrera .15 .40
❑ 27 Simone Deveaux .15 .40
❑ 28 Charles Deveaux .15 .40
❑ 29 Emile Danko .15 .40
❑ 30 Elle Bishop .15 .40
❑ 31 Bob Bishop .15 .40
❑ 32 Zach .15 .40
❑ 33 Kaito Nakamura .15 .40
❑ 34 Eric Doyle .15 .40
❑ 35 Usutu .15 .40
❑ 36 Meredith Gordon .15 .40
❑ 37 Benjamin Knox Washington .15 .40
❑ 38 Flint Gordon .15 .40
❑ 39 Gretchen Berg .15 .40
❑ 40 West Rosen .15 .40
❑ 41 Eden McCain .15 .40
❑ 42 Arthur Petrelli .15 .40
❑ 43 Daniel Linderman .15 .40
❑ 44 Ted Sprague .15 .40
❑ 45 Jackie Wilcox .15 .40
❑ 46 Emma Coolidge .15 .40
❑ 47 FBI Agent Audrey Hansen .15 .40
❑ 48 Monica Dawson .15 .40
❑ 49 Thompson .15 .40
❑ 50 Lauren Gilmore .15 .40
❑ 51 Candice Wilmer .15 .40
❑ 52 Yaeko .15 .40
❑ 53 Maury Parkman .15 .40
❑ 54 Caitlin .15 .40
❑ 55 Lynette .15 .40
❑ 56 Saemi Nakamura .15 .40
❑ 57 Claude .15 .40
❑ 58 Tracy Strauss .15 .40
❑ 59 Heidi Petrelli .15 .40
❑ 60 Charlie Andrews .15 .40
❑ 61 Eli .15 .40
❑ 62 Rebecca Taylor .15 .40
❑ 63 Virginia Grey .15 .40
❑ 64 Dr. Chandra Suresh .15 .40
❑ 65 Venessa Wheeler .15 .40
❑ 66 Ishi Nakamura .15 .40
❑ 67 Jessica Sanders .15 .40
❑ 68 Gabriel Gray .15 .40
❑ 69 Takezo Kensi .15 .40
❑ 70 Future Peter Petrelli .15 .40
❑ 71 Future Claire Bennet .15 .40
❑ 72 Future Hiro Nakamura .15 .40

2010 Heroes Archives Autographs
STATED ODDS SIX PER BOX
CARDS 1A,19A,21A,24A, AND 37A ONLY IN ARCHIVE BOX
L (LIMITED): 300-500
VL (VERY LIMITED): 200-300
❑ 1A Adrian Pasdar (wearing suit) 25.00 50.00
(issued in archive box)
❑ 1B Adrian Pasdar (wearing t-shirt) VL 20.00 40.00
(issued in archive box)
❑ 2 Akihiro Kitamura L 8.00 20.00
❑ 3 Alan Blumenfeld 5.00 12.00
❑ 4A Ashley Crow (with dog) L 6.00 15.00
❑ 4B Ashley Crow (no dog) L 6.00 15.00
❑ 5 Blake Shields 5.00 12.00
❑ 6 Bruce Boxleitner 6.00 15.00
❑ 7 Cristine Rose L 8.00 20.00
❑ 8 Danielle Savre 5.00 12.00
❑ 9A David Anders (as Adam Monroe) L 8.00 20.00
❑ 9B David Anders (as Takezo Kensei) L 8.00 20.00
❑ 10A David H. Lawrence (hand showing) VL 8.00 20.00
❑ 10B David H. Lawrence (no hand showing) VL8.00 20.00
❑ 11A Dawn Oliveri/ (issued as case topper) 12.00 30.00
❑ 11B Dawn Oliveri (no hair clip) 10.00 25.00
❑ 12 Deanne Bray 6.00 15.00
❑ 13A Eric Roberts (looking forward) 100.00 150.00
(issued as 6-case incentive)
❑ 13B Eric Roberts (looking up) 40.00 80.00
(issued as Rittenhouse Reward)
❑ 14 Ernie Hudson 8.00 20.00
❑ 15 Francis Capra 5.00 12.00
❑ 16 Gabriel Olds 5.00 12.00
❑ 17 George Takei 40.00 80.00
(issued as 3-case incentive)
❑ 18 Greg Grunberg L 10.00 25.00
❑ 19A Hayden Panettiere 125.00 200.00
(wearing cheerleading outfit)
(issued in archive box)
❑ 19B Hayden Panettiere (wearing shirt) VL 100.00 175.00
❑ 20 Jack Coleman L 10.00 25.00
❑ 21A James Kyson Lee (wearing white shirt) 25.00 50.00
(issued in archive box)
❑ 21B James Kyson Lee (wearing red shirt) VL 15.00 40.00
❑ 22 Jamie Hector 5.00 12.00
❑ 23 Jessalyn Gilsig 6.00 15.00
❑ 24A Jimmy Jean-Louis (wearing striped shirt)25.00 50.00
(issued in archive box)
❑ 24B Jimmy Jean-Louis (wearing white shirt) VL12.00 30.00
❑ 25 Katherine Boecher 6.00 15.00
❑ 26 Katie Carr 5.00 12.00
❑ 27 Kavi Ladnier 5.00 12.00
❑ 28 Kristen Bell VL 75.00 150.00
❑ 29 Lisa Lackey 5.00 12.00
❑ 30 Madeline Zima 6.00 15.00
❑ 31 Malcolm McDowell VL 30.00 60.00
❑ 32 Matthew John Armstrong 5.00 12.00
❑ 33 Nicholas D'Agosto 5.00 12.00
❑ 34 Richard Roundtree 8.00 20.00
❑ 35 Rick Worthy 5.00 12.00
❑ 36 Sally Champlin L 5.00 12.00
❑ 37A Sendhil Ramamurthy (facing forward) 20.00 50.00
(issued in archive box)
❑ 37B Sendhil Ramamurthy (facing left) VL 12.00 30.00
❑ 38 Shalim Ortiz 5.00 12.00
❑ 39 Swoosie Kurtz VL 12.00 30.00
❑ 40 Tamlyn Tomita 5.00 12.00
❑ 41 Tessa Thompson 5.00 12.00
❑ 42A Todd Stashwick (green light in background) L5.00 12.00
❑ 42B Todd Stashwick (no light in background) L5.00 12.00
❑ 43 Zeljko Ivanek 5.00 12.00

2010 Heroes Archives Generations
COMPLETE SET (8) 6.00 15.00
STATED ODDS 1:12
❑ G1 Claire Bennet 1.50 4.00
❑ G2 Peter Petrelli 1.50 4.00
❑ G3 Nathan Petrelli 1.50 4.00
❑ G4 Hiro Nakamura 1.50 4.00
❑ G5 Micah Sanders 1.50 4.00
❑ G6 Sylar 1.50 4.00
❑ G7 Matt Parkman 1.50 4.00
❑ G8 Elle Bishop 1.50 4.00

2010 Heroes Archives Promos
❑ P1 Sylar/ (General Distribution)
❑ P2 Hiro Nakamura/ (Binder Exclusive) 4.00 10.00
❑ CP1 Claire Bennet/ (San Diego Comic Con 2010)3.00 8.00

2010 Heroes Archives Quotable Heroes
COMPLETE SET (9) 6.00 15.00
STATED ODDS 1:8
❑ Q1 Yatta 1.50 4.00
❑ Q2 Haven't I killed you before 1.50 4.00
❑ Q3 You don't understand 1.50 4.00
❑ Q4 You can skydive 1.50 4.00
❑ Q5 Save the cheerleader 1.50 4.00
❑ Q6 I'll keep trying to kill you 1.50 4.00
❑ Q7 I heal 1.50 4.00
❑ Q8 Cake 1.50 4.00
❑ Q9 One of us 1.50 4.00
❑ Q10 Are you going to eat it SP 12.00 30.00
(issued as Rittenhouse Reward)

2010 Heroes Archives Relics
STATED ODDS ONE PER BOX
❑ 1 Ando Masahashi 6.00 15.00
❑ 2 Angela Petrelli 6.00 15.00
❑ 3 Claire Bennet 20.00 50.00
❑ 4 Doyle 6.00 15.00
❑ 5 Hiro Nakamura 6.00 15.00
❑ 6 Hiro Nakamura Missing Poster/165 50.00 100.00
❑ 7 Lydia 12.00 30.00
❑ 8 Mohinder Suresh 6.00 15.00
❑ 9 Nathan Petrelli 6.00 15.00
❑ 10 Nathan Petrelli Campaign Poster/375 30.00 60.00
❑ 11 Noah Bennet 6.00 15.00
❑ 12 Peter Petrelli 8.00 20.00
❑ 13 Samuel Sullivan 8.00 20.00
❑ 14 Sylar 6.00 15.00
❑ 15 Wanted Posters/250 25.00 60.00

2010 Iron Man 2
COMPLETE SET (75) 8.00 20.00
❑ 1 Checklist .15 .40
❑ 2 Dropping In .15 .40
❑ 3 American Hero .15 .40
❑ 4 Welcome to the Stark Expo .15 .40
❑ 5 Ladies' Man .15 .40
❑ 6 Defendant Stark .15 .40
❑ 7 Tony and Pepper .15 .40
❑ 8 Order in the Court .15 .40
❑ 9 Jim Rhodey Rhodes .15 .40
❑ 10 The Hall of Armor .15 .40
❑ 11 The Mark I .15 .40
❑ 12 The Mark IV .15 .40
❑ 13 New Face at Stark Industries .15 .40
❑ 14 Natalie's Promotion .15 .40
❑ 15 Chief Executive Potts .15 .40
❑ 16 Ivan Vanko .15 .40
❑ 17 Another Arc Reactor .15 .40
❑ 18 Party in Monaco .15 .40
❑ 19 Something to Talk About .15 .40
❑ 20 Dirty Competition .15 .40
❑ 21 Race Day .15 .40
❑ 22 Whiplash Attacks .15 .40
❑ 23 Hustle, Hogan! .15 .40
❑ 24 Iron Man in a Box .15 .40
❑ 25 Aftermath .15 .40
❑ 26 Hammer Hatches a Plan .15 .40
❑ 27 Slow Poison .15 .40
❑ 28 Fun or Foolish? .15 .40
❑ 29 Concern for Tony .15 .40
❑ 30 Double Agent .15 .40
❑ 31 Greedy Ambition .15 .40
❑ 32 Evil Alliance .15 .40
❑ 33 The Drone Plan .15 .40
❑ 34 Toying Around .15 .40
❑ 35 Rhodey's Had Enough .15 .40
❑ 36 Fight Between Friends .15 .40
❑ 37 Ride in Style .15 .40
❑ 38 A Visit from Nick Fury .15 .40
❑ 39 I Am the Black Widow .15 .40
❑ 40 The Vanko Legacy .15 .40
❑ 41 Fatherly Advice .15 .40
❑ 42 Time for an Upgrade .15 .40
❑ 43 The Secrets of the Armor .15 .40
❑ 44 All of Them .15 .40
❑ 45 It's a War Machine .15 .40
❑ 46 Buried Treasure .15 .40
❑ 47 Give a Hand, DUM-E! .15 .40
❑ 48 New Power .15 .40
❑ 49 I'm in Control Now .15 .40
❑ 50 Hogan Steps Up .15 .40
❑ 51 Widow's Walk .15 .40
❑ 52 Smooth Moves .15 .40
❑ 53 Ominous Halls .15 .40
❑ 54 Grim Findings .15 .40
❑ 55 Iron Man and War Machine .15 .40
❑ 56 Behind the Scenes .15 .40
❑ 57 Behind the Scenes .15 .40
❑ 58 Behind the Scenes .15 .40
❑ 59 Behind the Scenes .15 .40
❑ 60 Behind the Scenes .15 .40
❑ 61 Behind the Scenes .15 .40
❑ 62 Behind the Scenes .15 .40
❑ 63 Behind the Scenes .15 .40
❑ 64 Behind the Scenes .15 .40
❑ 65 Behind the Scenes .15 .40
❑ 66 Behind the Scenes .15 .40
❑ 67 Mark VI Concept 1 .15 .40
❑ 68 Mark VI Concept 2 .15 .40
❑ 69 Mark VI Concept 3 .15 .40
❑ 70 Mark VI Concept 4 .15 .40
❑ 71 Mark VI Concept 5 .15 .40
❑ 72 Dossier: Drone 1 .15 .40
❑ 73 Dossier: Drone 2 .15 .40
❑ 74 Dossier: Drone 3 .15 .40
❑ 75 Dossier: Drone 4 .15 .40

2010 Iron Man 2 Actor Gallery Die Cuts
COMPLETE SET (9) 10.00 25.00
❑ AH1 Tony Stark 2.00 5.00
❑ AH2 Pepper Potts 2.50 6.00
❑ AH3 Jim Rhodey Rhodes 1.50 4.00
❑ AH4 Natasha Romanoff 2.50 6.00
❑ AH5 Ivan Whiplash Vanko 1.50 4.00
❑ AH6 Justin Hammer 1.50 4.00
❑ AH7 Nick Fury 1.50 4.00
❑ AH8 Happy Hogan 1.50 4.00
❑ AH9 Jon Favreau 1.50 4.00

2010 Iron Man 2 Armored Cards
COMPLETE SET (9) 8.00 20.00
❑ AC1 Iron Man Mark IV 1.50 4.00
❑ AC2 Iron Man Mark V 1.50 4.00
❑ AC3 Iron Man Mark VI 1.50 4.00
❑ AC4 War Machine 1.50 4.00
❑ AC5 War Machine 1.50 4.00
❑ AC6 War Machine 1.50 4.00
❑ AC7 Black Widow 1.50 4.00
❑ AC8 Nick Fury 1.50 4.00
❑ AC9 Whiplash 1.50 4.00

2010 Iron Man 2 Autographs
AUTO/MEM/SKETCH ODDS 3 PER BOX
❑ A1 Jon Favreau 20.00 40.00
❑ A2 Mickey Rourke 60.00 120.00
❑ A3 Leslie Bibb 25.00 50.00
❑ A4 Don Cheadle 40.00 80.00

2010 Iron Man 2 Classic Covers
COMPLETE SET (9) 5.00 12.00
❑ CC1 Tales of Suspense #39 .75 2.00
❑ CC2 Tales of Suspense #52 .75 2.00
❑ CC3 Tales of Suspense #57 .75 2.00
❑ CC4 Iron Man #1 .75 2.00
❑ CC5 Iron Man #47 .75 2.00
❑ CC6 Iron Man #80 .75 2.00
❑ CC7 Iron Man #118 .75 2.00
❑ CC8 Iron Man #126 .75 2.00
❑ CC9 Iron Man #152 .75 2.00

2010 Iron Man 2 Memorabilia
AUTO/MEM/SKETCH ODDS 3 PER BOX
❑ IMC1 Tony Stark 10.00 25.00
❑ IMC2 Nick Fury 8.00 20.00
❑ IMC3 Natasha Romanoff 15.00 40.00
❑ IMC4 Natasha Romanoff 15.00 40.00
❑ IMC5 Pepper Potts 12.00 30.00
❑ IMC6 Whiplash 12.00 30.00
❑ IMC7 Jim Rhodey Rhodes 6.00 15.00
❑ IMC8 Justin Hammer 6.00 15.00
❑ IMC9 Tony Stark 10.00 25.00
❑ IMC10 Jim Rhodey Rhodes 6.00 15.00
❑ IMC11 Justin Hammer 6.00 15.00
❑ IMC12 Armored Card SP 300.00 400.00

2010 Iron Man 2 Sketches
AUTO/MEM/SKETCH ODDS 3 PER BOX
❑ ACLI Adam Cline 75.00 150.00
❑ AHME Irma Ahmed
❑ ALVE Josh Alves 25.00 60.00
❑ ANDE Lynne Anderson 40.00 100.00
❑ BANN Matt Banning
❑ BARD BARD 30.00 80.00
❑ BELA Charles Belak
❑ BMAR Billy Martin
❑ BRAD Kate Red Bradley 40.00 100.00
❑ BSCH Brent Schoonover 12.00 30.00
❑ BUKA James Bukauskas 10.00 25.00
❑ BUTL Chris Butler
❑ BWAL Brian Walker
❑ CARR Joel Carroll
❑ CHEU Jim Cheung
❑ CHIN Joyce Chin
❑ CHRI John Christopher
❑ COON Daniel Cooney 8.00 20.00
❑ COPE Chris Copeland
❑ CORO Adelso Corona
❑ CRIS Dennis Crisostomo 12.00 30.00
❑ CRYS Shawn Crystal
❑ CULV Dennis Culver
❑ DAVI George Davis 30.00 80.00
❑ DEKR Adam DeKraker 20.00 50.00
❑ DMIL Dennis Miller (Jimmy McWicked) 12.00 30.00
❑ DODD Joe Dodd
❑ DOUS Remi Dousset
❑ DSCH Dan Schoening
❑ DSMI Dietrich Smith 8.00 20.00
❑ DURO Michael Locoduck Duron 12.00 30.00
❑ DURR Armando Durruthy 10.00 25.00
❑ EDWA Casey Edwards
❑ EMER Eric Merced 15.00 40.00
❑ EPER Elaine Perna 40.00 100.00
❑ FEIS Tom Feister
❑ FERG Lee Ferguson 8.00 20.00
❑ GALL Sean Galloway (Cheeks) 12.00 30.00
❑ GAYL Jerry Gaylord (The Franchize) 8.00 20.00
❑ GENT Kevin Gentilcore 12.00 30.00
❑ GERL Bruce Gerlach
❑ GERR Patrick Gerrity 10.00 25.00
❑ GLEN Benjamin Glendenning 40.00 100.00
❑ GMCK Garry McKee
❑ GONZ Gene Gonzales 15.00 40.00
❑ GRAH Kevin Graham 10.00 25.00
❑ GRAN Rob Granito 10.00 25.00
❑ HALL Charles Hall 75.00 150.00
❑ HANN Jim Hanna 12.00 30.00
❑ HARD Chad Hardin
❑ HASS Tariq Hassan
❑ HAYS Cutter Hays
❑ HCLI Hamilton Cline 12.00 30.00
❑ HEIG Ray-Anthony Height
❑ HENR Mark Henry (Profesone) 12.00 30.00
❑ HERR Ben Herrera
❑ HICK Jessica Hickman
❑ HOWA Zach Howard
❑ JARO Jose Jaro 20.00 50.00
❑ JMER Jennifer Mercer 25.00 60.00
❑ JMIN Jake Minor 10.00 25.00
❑ JOHN Jeff Johnson
❑ JWAL Jason Walker 15.00 40.00
❑ KASI Michael Kasinger
❑ KINN Ryan Kinnaird
❑ KRAJ Karen Krajenbrink 8.00 20.00
❑ LAFO Chad LaForce 10.00 25.00
❑ LATO Jason Latour
❑ LAYT Bob Layton 75.00 150.00
❑ LIM Lak Lim 20.00 50.00
❑ LUMI Rose Lumibao 15.00 40.00
❑ MACD Andy MacDonald 10.00 25.00
❑ MACK David Mack 20.00 50.00
❑ MAIH Mike Maihack
❑ MALI Jon Malin 20.00 50.00
❑ MANL Mike Manley 25.00 60.00
❑ MANZ Joe Manzella 10.00 25.00
❑ MAPA Butch Mapa 15.00 40.00
❑ MATS Jeff Matsuda
❑ MEIG Bill Meiggs
❑ MEND Robard Jason Mendoza
❑ MESA Lord Mesa 12.00 30.00
❑ MEYE JonBoy Meyers 25.00 60.00
❑ MIEL Tony Miello 10.00 25.00
❑ MMCK Mark McKenna
❑ MMIL Mike Miller 15.00 40.00
❑ MMIN Matthew Minor 20.00 50.00
❑ MOHD Hanie Mohd 25.00 60.00
❑ MOKH Remy Eisu Mokhtar 20.00 50.00
❑ MOLI Rich Molinelli 10.00 25.00
❑ MONS Gilbert Monsanto 20.00 50.00
❑ MSMI Marcus Smith
❑ MYCH Marat Mychaels 10.00 25.00
❑ NEFF Bill Neff 20.00 50.00
❑ NGUY Tom Nguyen 15.00 40.00
❑ NOLA Graham Nolan
❑ OHAR Michael O'Hare
❑ OMAL Keith O'Malley
❑ ONEI Shaun O'Neil 8.00 20.00
❑ OROS Ryan Orosco
❑ OUM Siya Oum 8.00 20.00
❑ PACE Richard Pace
❑ PANO Dan Panosian
❑ PAZ Jason Paz 30.00 80.00
❑ PEKA Joe Pekar 30.00 80.00
❑ PENN Mark Pennington 8.00 20.00
❑ PHIL Jason Keith Phillips 10.00 25.00
❑ PIER Brian Pierce
❑ PLUC Zak Plucinski
❑ PRAI Pablo Praino 15.00 40.00
❑ QUIL Dan Quiles 8.00 20.00
❑ RABB David Rabbitte
❑ RAPO Frank Rapoza 15.00 40.00
❑ REDF Lisa Redfern
❑ REYN Lawrence Reynolds 40.00 100.00
❑ RIVE Penelope Rivera
❑ ROBI Andrew Robinson 12.00 30.00
❑ RYAN Dave Ryan 75.00 150.00
❑ SALA Ron Salas 20.00 50.00
❑ SCHA Dan Schaefer 8.00 20.00
❑ SHEA Brian Shearer 15.00 40.00
❑ SHED Blair Shedd
❑ SHOO Marlin Shoop 12.00 30.00
❑ SIPL Randy Siplon
❑ SMAR Shawn Martinbrough
❑ SNEL Lawrence Snelly 10.00 25.00
❑ SOMM Jon Sommariva 25.00 60.00
❑ SORI Carlo Soriano 12.00 30.00
❑ SOWD Aaron Sowd 40.00 100.00
❑ STAG Cat Staggs 75.00 150.00
❑ STEA Ken Steacy 12.00 30.00
❑ STRO Dave Strong 8.00 20.00
❑ TATA Dave Pops Tata 8.00 20.00
❑ TCHI Ghislain Tchissafou (Spider Guile)
❑ THOM Bill Thompson 8.00 20.00
❑ TORR Mike Torrance 10.00 25.00
❑ TPER Tony Perna
❑ TREE Jeremy Treece 15.00 40.00
❑ TSMI Tod Smith
❑ TURK Autumn Rain Turkel 15.00 40.00
❑ TURN Bryan Turner 10.00 25.00
❑ UMEM Sanna Umemoto
❑ VAND Justin Vandemark 12.00 30.00
❑ VANO Michael Van Orden
❑ VASQ Gus Vasquez 10.00 25.00
❑ VICT Jeff Victor
❑ VOKE Neil Vokes
❑ WALT Travis Walton 12.00 30.00
❑ WILK Sarah Wilkinson
❑ WILL Erik Williams 10.00 25.00
❑ WONG Ryan Wong 25.00 60.00
❑ YATE Kelly Yates

2010 James Bond Heroes and Villians
COMPLETE SET (81) 6.00 15.00
❑ 1 James Bond .15 .40
in Dr. No
❑ 2 Dr. No .15 .40
in Dr. No
❑ 3 Miss Taro .15 .40
in Dr. No
❑ 4 Honey Ryder .15 .40
in Dr. No
❑ 5 Tatiana Romanova .15 .40
in From Russia With Love
❑ 6 Kerim Bey .15 .40
in From Russia With Love
❑ 7 Red Grant .15 .40
in From Russia With Love
❑ 8 Rosa Klebb .15 .40
in From Russia With Love
❑ 9 Pussy Galore .15 .40
in Goldfinger
❑ 10 Auric Goldfinger .15 .40
in Goldfinger
❑ 11 Oddjob .15 .40
in Goldfinger
❑ 12 Domino Derval .15 .40
in Thunderball
❑ 13 Fiona Volpe .15 .40
in Thunderball
❑ 14 Emilio Largo .15 .40
in Thunderball
❑ 15 Ernst Stavro Blofeld .15 .40
in You Only Live Twice
❑ 16 Helga Brandt .15 .40
in You Only Live Twice
❑ 17 Kissy Suzuki .15 .40
in You Only Live Twice
❑ 18 Aki .15 .40
in You Only Live Twice
❑ 19 Tiger Tanaka .15 .40
in You Only Live Twice
❑ 20 James Bond .15 .40
in On Her Majesty's Secret Service
❑ 21 Tracy Di Vicenzo .15 .40
in On Her Majesty's Secret Service
❑ 22 Ernst Stavro Blofeld .15 .40
in On Her Majesty's Secret Service
❑ 23 Marc Ange Draco .15 .40
in On Her Majesty's Secret Service
❑ 24 Irma Bunt .15 .40
in On Her Majesty's Secret Service
❑ 25 Tiffany Case .15 .40
in Diamonds Are Forever
❑ 26 Ernst Stavro Blofeld .15 .40
in Diamonds Are Forever
❑ 27 Wint & Kidd .15 .40
in Diamonds Are Forever
❑ 28 James Bond .15 .40
in Live And Let Die
❑ 29 Dr. Kananga .15 .40
Mr. Big/in Live And Let Die
❑ 30 Solitaire .15 .40
in Live And Let Die
❑ 31 Baron Samedi .15 .40
in Live And Let Die
❑ 32 Tee Hee .15 .40
in Live And Let Die
❑ 33 Sheriff J.W. Pepper .15 .40
in Live And Let Die
❑ 34 Rosie Carver .15 .40
in Live And Let Die
❑ 35 Francisco Scaramanga .15 .40
in The Man With The Golden Gun
❑ 36 Mary Goodnight .15 .40
in The Man With The Golden Gun
❑ 37 Nick Nack .15 .40
in The Man With The Golden Gun
❑ 38 Major Anya Amasova .15 .40
in The Spy Who Loved Me
❑ 39 Karl Stromberg .15 .40
in The Spy Who Loved Me
❑ 40 Jaws .15 .40
in The Spy Who Loved Me
❑ 41 Holly Goodhead .15 .40
in Moonraker
❑ 42 Corinne Dufour .15 .40
in Moonraker
❑ 43 Hugo Drax .15 .40
in Moonraker
❑ 44 Melina Havelock .15 .40
in For Your Eyes Only
❑ 45 Milos Columbo .15 .40
in For Your Eyes Only
❑ 46 Aris Kristatos .15 .40
in For Your Eyes Only
❑ 47 Emile Lacque .15 .40
in For Your Eyes Only
❑ 48 Octopussy .15 .40
in Octopussy
❑ 49 Kamal Khan .15 .40
in Octopussy
❑ 50 Magda .15 .40
in Octopussy
❑ 51 Max Zorin .15 .40
in A View To A Kill
❑ 52 Stacey Sutton .15 .40
in A View To A Kill
❑ 53 May Day .15 .40
in A View To A Kill
❑ 54 Sir Godfrey Tibbett .15 .40
in A View To A Kill
❑ 55 James Bond .15 .40
in The Living Daylights
❑ 56 Kara Milovy .15 .40
in The Living Daylights
❑ 57 General Georgi Koskov .15 .40
in The Living Daylights
❑ 58 Brad Whitaker .15 .40
in The Living Daylights
❑ 59 Pam Bouvier .15 .40
in Licence To Kill

❑ 60 Lupe Lamora .15 .40
in Licence To Kill
❑ 61 Franz Sanchez .15 .40
in Licence To Kill
❑ 62 James Bond .15 .40
in GoldenEye
❑ 63 Natalya Simonova .15 .40
in GoldenEye
❑ 64 Alec Trevelyan .15 .40
in GoldenEye
❑ 65 Xenia Onatopp .15 .40
in GoldenEye
❑ 66 Wai Lin .15 .40
in Tomorrow Never Dies
❑ 67 Elliot Carver .15 .40
in Tomorrow Never Dies
❑ 68 Dr. Kaufman .15 .40
in Tomorrow Never Dies
❑ 69 Renard .15 .40
in The World Is Not Enough
❑ 70 Elektra King .15 .40
in The World Is Not Enough
❑ 71 Dr. Christmas Jones .15 .40
in The World Is Not Enough
❑ 72 Gustav Graves .15 .40
in Die Another Day
❑ 73 Miranda Frost .15 .40
in Die Another Day
❑ 74 Jinx .15 .40
in Die Another Day
❑ 75 Zao .15 .40
in Die Another Day
❑ 76 James Bond .15 .40
in Casino Royale
❑ 77 Le Chiffre .15 .40
in Casino Royale
❑ 78 Vesper Lynd .15 .40
in Casino Royale
❑ 79 Dominic Greene .15 .40
in Quantum of Solace
❑ 80 General Medrano .15 .40
in Quantum of Solace
❑ 81 Camille .15 .40
in Quantum of Solace

2010 James Bond Heroes and Villains Autographs

STATED ODDS 3 PER BOX
L (LIMITED): 300-500 CARDS
VL (VERY LIMITED): LESS THAN 300 CARDS
RMGL ODDS ONE PER 6-CASE PURCHASE

❑ AS Angela Scoular 6.00 15.00
❑ BH Bernard Horsfall 6.00 15.00
❑ BL Bettine LeBeau L 8.00 20.00
❑ BR Blanche Ravalec L 8.00 20.00
❑ CA Carole Ashby L 8.00 20.00
❑ CM Caroline Munro VL 30.00 60.00
❑ CS Claudio Santamaria L 6.00 15.00
❑ DC Daniel Craig VL 250.00 450.00
❑ FW Frederick Warder L 6.00 15.00
❑ GA Gemma Arterton VL 125.00 200.00
❑ GH Gloria Hendry 6.00 15.00
❑ GJ Gottfried John L 6.00 15.00
❑ JC Joaquin Cosio L 6.00 15.00
❑ JG Julian Glover 6.00 15.00
❑ JP Jonathan Pryce L 10.00 25.00
❑ JS Jill St. John L 25.00 50.00
❑ KB Kabir Bedi L 8.00 20.00
❑ MK Michael Kitchen L 8.00 20.00
❑ OB Olga Bisera L 10.00 25.00
❑ PM Patrick Macnee VL 30.00 60.00
❑ PS Papillon Soo Soo L 8.00 20.00
❑ SB Sean Bean L 25.00 50.00
❑ SK Simon Kassianides L 6.00 15.00
❑ ST Serena Scott Thomas L 8.00 20.00
❑ TC Tsai Chin 6.00 15.00
❑ TP Tim Pigott-Smith L 6.00 15.00
❑ TP Trina Parks 6.00 15.00
❑ WL Will Yun Lee VL 20.00 40.00
❑ A119 Cecilie Thomsen VL 25.00 50.00
❑ A123 Belle Avery VL 20.00 40.00
❑ A124 Geoffrey Holder VL 40.00 80.00
❑ A125 John Cleese VL 60.00 120.00
❑ A127 Samantha Bond L 10.00 25.00
❑ A130 David Hedison L 10.00 25.00
❑ A131 Chaim Topol VL 40.00 80.00
❑ A132 Crispin Bonham-Carter L 6.00 15.00
❑ A133 Rory Kinnear L 6.00 15.00
❑ A134 Simon Kassianides L 6.00 15.00
❑ A135 Glenn Foster L 6.00 15.00
❑ A136 Olga Kurylenko L 75.00 150.00
❑ A137 Paul Ritter L 6.00 15.00
❑ A139 Tim Pigott-Smith L 6.00 15.00
❑ A140 Gottfried John L 6.00 15.00
❑ A141 Kabir Bedi L 8.00 20.00
❑ A142 Will Yun Lee VL 30.00 60.00
❑ A143 Joanna Lumley L 15.00 30.00
❑ A144 Michael Kitchen L 8.00 20.00
❑ A146 Joaquin Cosio L 6.00 15.00
❑ A147 Claudio Santamaria L 8.00 20.00
❑ A149 Papillon Soo Soo L 8.00 20.00
❑ A150 Olga Bisera L 15.00 30.00
❑ A152 Carole Ashby L 8.00 20.00
❑ A153 Corinne Clery L 20.00 40.00
❑ A154 Frederick Warder L 6.00 15.00
❑ A156 Bettine LeBeau L 8.00 20.00
❑ A161 Gabriele Ferzetti L 8.00 20.00
❑ DMTM David Meyer 15.00 30.00
Tony Meyer L
❑ EGKG Eunice Gayson 20.00 40.00
Kate Gayson L
❑ RMGL Roger Moore 150.00 250.00
George Lazenby/ (issued as 6-case incentive)
❑ WA32 Caroline Munro VL 40.00 80.00
❑ WA33 Izabella Scorupco L 20.00 40.00
❑ WA34 Corinne Clery VL 40.00 80.00
❑ WA35 Tsai Chin 8.00 20.00
❑ WA36 Angela Scoular 6.00 15.00

2010 James Bond Heroes and Villains James Bond Expansion

STATED ODDS 1:24

❑ F68 Bond Villains 2.50 6.00
Bert Saxby/Diamonds Are Forever
❑ F69 Bond Villains: Thumper from 2.50 6.00
Diamonds Are Forever
❑ F70 Bond Villains: Bambi from 2.50 6.00
Diamonds Are Forever
❑ T11 The Quotable Theme Songs 2.50 6.00
Casino Royale/Quantum of Solace
❑ AI21 Art & Images of 007 20.00 50.00
James Bond/Casino Royale
❑ AI22 Art & Images of 007 20.00 50.00
James Bond/Quantum of Solace
❑ BG73 Bond Girls Are Forever 2.50 6.00
Mlle. La Porte/Thunderball
❑ BV0022 Bond Villains 2.50 6.00
Dominic Greene/Quantum of Solace
❑ BW0022 Bond Girls 2.50 6.00
Camille/Casino Royale

2010 James Bond Heroes and Villains Lenticular Expansion

COMPLETE SET (9) 8.00 20.00
STATED ODDS 1:18

❑ 64 James Bond In Motion: James Bond 1.50 4.00
Quantum of Solace
❑ 64 Women of James Bond In Motion 1.50 4.00
Vesper Lynd/Casino Royale
❑ 65 James Bond In Motion 1.50 4.00
Dominic Greene/Quantum of Solace
❑ 65 Women of James Bond In Motion 1.50 4.00
Vesper Lynd/Casino Royale
❑ 66 James Bond In Motion 1.50 4.00
James Bond/Quantum of Solace
❑ 66 Women of James Bond In Motion 1.50 4.00
Camille/Quantum of Solace
❑ 67 Women of James Bond In Motion 1.50 4.00
Camille/Quantum of Solace
❑ 68 Women of James Bond In Motion 1.50 4.00
Agent Fields/Quantum of Solace
❑ 69 Women of James Bond In Motion 1.50 4.00
Agent Fields/Quantum of Solace

2010 James Bond Heroes and Villains Men of James Bond

COMPLETE SET (6) 4.00 10.00
STATED ODDS 1:18

❑ B1 Sean Connery 1.25 3.00
❑ B2 Roger Moore 1.25 3.00
❑ B3 George Lazenby 1.25 3.00
❑ B4 Timothy Dalton 1.25 3.00
❑ B5 Pierce Brosnan 1.25 3.00
❑ B6 Daniel Craig 1.25 3.00

2010 James Bond Heroes and Villains Promos

COMPLETE SET (4)

❑ P1 Daniel Craig/(General Distribution)
❑ P2 Pierce Brosnan/(Non-Sport Update Magainze)
❑ P3 Roger Moore/(Album Exclusive)
❑ CP1 Daniel Craig/(Convention Exclusive)

2010 James Bond Heroes and Villains Relics

STATED ODDS 1:120
JBR8 ODDS ONE PER CASE
JBR12 ODDS ONE PER 3-CASE PURCHASE

❑ JBR1 King Industries Canister /400 30.00 80.00
❑ JBR2 King Industries Dossier /175 200.00 400.00
❑ JBR3 IDA Emblem /150 200.00 400.00
❑ JBR4 Parahawk Parachute Bag /600 15.00 40.00
❑ JBR5 Jaguar XKR Leather Interior /333 40.00 100.00
❑ JBR7 Chase Boat Interior Leather /444 20.00 50.00
❑ JBR8 Speed Boat Interior Leather /777 15.00 40.00
❑ JBR9 Bomb Detonator Box /444 25.00 60.00
❑ JBR10 Renault Taxi Cloth Interior /200 100.00 175.00
❑ JBR12 Italian Carabinieri Windshield /333 40.00 100.00

2010 Legend of KISS

COMPLETE SET (100) 8.00 20.00

❑ 1 Formation Of KISS (1972) .15 .40
❑ 2 Formation Of KISS (1972) .15 .40
❑ 3 Formation of KISS-Paul Stanley .15 .40
❑ 4 Formation of KISS-Gene Simmons .15 .40
❑ 5 Peter Joins KISS (1972)-Gene Simmons .15 .40
❑ 6 Peter Joins KISS (1972)-Gene Simmons .15 .40
❑ 7 Ace Joins KISS (1972)-Gene Simmons .15 .40
❑ 8 Ace Joins KISS (1972)-Gene Simmons .15 .40
❑ 9 Ace Joins KISS (1972) .15 .40
❑ 10 Ace Joins KISS (1972)-Gene Simmons .15 .40
❑ 11 Ace Joins KISS (1972)-Gene Simmons .15 .40
❑ 12 Ace Joins KISS (1972)-Ace Frehley .15 .40
❑ 13 Putting the K-in KISS .15 .40
❑ 14 Putting the K-in KISS .15 .40
❑ 15 Coining the Name-Gene Simmons .15 .40
❑ 16 The Look-Gene Simmons .15 .40
❑ 17 The Look-Gene Simmons .15 .40
❑ 18 The Look-Paul Stanley .15 .40
❑ 19 The Look-KISS .15 .40
❑ 20 The Look-KISS .15 .40
❑ 21 The Look-KISS .15 .40
❑ 22 The Look-KISS .15 .40
❑ 23 The Look-KISS .15 .40
❑ 24 The Look-KISS .15 .40
❑ 25 The Look-KISS .15 .40
❑ 26 The Look-KISS .15 .40
❑ 27 The Look-KISS .15 .40
❑ 28 On the Road .15 .40
❑ 29 On the Road .15 .40
❑ 30 On the Road-Paul Stanley .15 .40
❑ 31 On the Road-Bill Aucoin .15 .40
❑ 32 On the Road-Bill Aucoin .15 .40
❑ 33 On the Road-Bill Aucoin .15 .40
❑ 34 On the Road .15 .40
❑ 35 Rock and Roll All Nite-Gene Simmons .15 .40
❑ 36 Rock and Roll All Nite-Gene Simmons .15 .40
❑ 37 Alive! (1975) .15 .40
❑ 38 Alive! (1975)-Paul Stanley .15 .40
❑ 39 Alive! (1975)-Gene Simmons .15 .40
❑ 40 Alive! (1975)-Gene Simmons .15 .40
❑ 41 Destroyer (1976)-Gene Simmons .15 .40
❑ 42 Destroyer (1976)-Gene Simmons .15 .40
❑ 43 Paul Lynde Halloween Special-Bill Aucoin .15 .40
❑ 44 Paul Lynde Halloween Special-Paul Stanley .15 .40
❑ 45 Paul Lynde Halloween Special .15 .40
❑ 46 Japan 1977 Tour-Gene Simmons .15 .40
❑ 47 Japan 1977 Tour-Gene Simmons .15 .40
❑ 48 Japan 1977 Tour-Gene Simmons .15 .40
❑ 49 Japan 1977 Tour-Paul Stanley .15 .40
❑ 50 Solo Albums-Bill Aucoin .15 .40
❑ 51 Solo Albums-Ace Frehley .15 .40
❑ 52 Creatures of the Night .15 .40
❑ 53 Creatures of the Night-Paul Stanley .15 .40
❑ 54 Creatures of the Night-Paul Stanley .15 .40
❑ 55 KISS Finally Unmasks (1983) .15 .40
❑ 56 KISS Finally Unmasks (1983) .15 .40
❑ 57 KISS Finally Unmasks (1983)-Paul Stanley .15 .40
❑ 58 KISS Finally Unmasks (1983)-Gene Simmons .15 .40
❑ 59 KISS Finally Unmasks (1983)-Eric Carr .15 .40
❑ 60 KISS Post-Makeup Years .15 .40
(1984-1985)-Gene Simmons
❑ 61 KISS Post-Makeup Years .15 .40
(1984-1985)-Gene Simmons
❑ 62 KISS Post-Makeup Years (1984-1985) .15 .40
❑ 63 KISS Post-Makeup Years (1984-1985) .15 .40
❑ 64 Reunion Tour (1996)-Ace Frehley .15 .40
❑ 65 Reunion Tour (1996)-Paul Stanley .15 .40
❑ 66 Reunion Tour (1996)-Paul Stanley .15 .40
❑ 67 Reunion Tour (1996)-Paul Stanley .15 .40
❑ 68 Reunion Tour (1996)-Paul Stanley .15 .40
❑ 69 Psycho Circus (1998)-Paul Stanley .15 .40
❑ 70 Psycho Circus (1998)-Paul Stanley .15 .40
❑ 71 Psycho Circus (1998)-Paul Stanley .15 .40
❑ 72 Psycho Circus (1998) .15 .40
❑ 73 Moving On With New Lineup .15 .40
❑ 74 Moving On .15 .40
❑ 75 Moving On-Paul Stanley .15 .40
❑ 76 Moving On-Paul Stanley .15 .40
❑ 77 Moving On-Tommy Thayer .15 .40
❑ 78 Moving On .15 .40
❑ 79 Moving On-Tommy Thayer .15 .40
❑ 80 Moving On-Tommy Thayer .15 .40
❑ 81 Moving On-Paul Stanley .15 .40
❑ 82 Moving On-KISS .15 .40
❑ 83 Moving On-KISS .15 .40
❑ 84 Moving On-KISS .15 .40
❑ 85 Moving On-KISS .15 .40
❑ 86 Moving On-KISS .15 .40
❑ 87 Moving On-KISS .15 .40
❑ 88 Moving On-KISS .15 .40
❑ 89 Moving On-KISS .15 .40
❑ 90 Moving On-KISS .15 .40
❑ 91 Sonic Boom (2009)- Paul Stanley .15 .40
❑ 92 Sonic Boom (2009)- Paul Stanley .15 .40
❑ 93 Alive 35 Tour (2009)-Gene Simmons .15 .40
❑ 94 Alive 35 Tour (2009)-Paul Stanley .15 .40
❑ 95 Alive 35 Tour (2009)-Eric Singer .15 .40
❑ 96 Alive 35 Tour (2009)-Gene Simmons .15 .40
❑ 97 Alive 35 Tour (2009)-Paul Stanley .15 .40
❑ 98 Legacy-Tommy Thayer .15 .40
❑ 99 Legacy .15 .40
❑ 100 Sonic Boom (2009)- Paul Stanley .15 .40

2010 Legend of KISS Black

COMPLETE SET (100) 100.00 250.00
*BLACK: 4X TO 10X BASIC CARDS
COMBINED BLACK/BLUE ODDS 1:4

2010 Legend of KISS Blue

*BLUE: 20X TO 50X BASIC CARDS
COMBINED BLACK/BLUE ODDS 1:4
STATED PRINT RUN 25 SER. #'d SETS

2010 Legend of KISS First Edition

*FIRST EDITION: 15X TO 40X BASIC CARS
STATED PRINT RUN 33 SER. #'d SETS

2010 Legend of KISS KISS Kuts

STATED PRINT RUN 10 SER. #'d SETS
UNPRICED DUE TO SCARCITY

❑ KKGS Gene Simmons
❑ KKPS Paul Stanley

2010 Legend of KISS KISSignatures

RANDOM INSERT IN PACKS
PRINT RUN 30-35

❑ KSAF Ace Frehley/30 200.00 300.00
❑ KSGS Gene Simmons/30 250.00 350.00
❑ KSPC Peter Criss/35 200.00 300.00
❑ KSPS Paul Stanley/30 200.00 300.00

2010 Legend of KISS Pop-Ups

COMPLETE SET (6) 5.00 12.00
STATED ODDS 1:6

❑ PU1 Gene Simmons 2.00 5.00
❑ PU2 Paul Stanley 1.50 4.00
❑ PU3 Peter Criss 1.50 4.00
❑ PU4 Ace Frehley 1.50 4.00
❑ PU5 Tommy Thayer 1.00 2.50
❑ PU6 Eric Singer 1.00 2.50

2010 Legend of KISS Rockstar Relics

OVERALL RELICS ODDS 1:90
PRINT RUN B/WN 122-425

❑ RREC Eric Carr Drum Head/122 30.00 60.00
❑ RRGS Gene Simmons Costume/160 30.00 60.00
❑ RRTT Tommy Thayer Costume/425 25.00 50.00
❑ RRPS1 Paul Stanley Vest/360 25.00 50.00
❑ RRPS2 Paul Stanley Vest/360 25.00 50.00
❑ RRPS3 Paul Stanley Vest/425 25.00 50.00

2010 Legend of KISS Rockstar Relics Holofoil

*HOLOFOIL: .6X TO 1.2X BASIC RELICS
OVERALL RELICS ODDS 1:90
STATED PRINT RUN 99 SER. #'d SETS

2010 Legend of KISS Rockstar Relics Gold

*GOLD: .8X TO 2X BASE INS/360-425
*GOLD: .6X TO 1.5X BASE INS/122-160
OVERALL RELICS ODDS 1:90
STATED PRINT RUN 25 SER. #'d SETS

2010 Lost Archives

COMPLETE SET (72) 5.00 12.00

❑ 1 Jack Shephard .15 .40
❑ 2 Christian Shephard .15 .40
❑ 3 Marshal Edward Mars .15 .40
❑ 4 Kate Austin .15 .40
❑ 5 Diane Janssen .15 .40
❑ 6 Bernard Nadler .15 .40
❑ 7 Rose Nadler .15 .40
❑ 8 Jin Kwon .15 .40
❑ 9 Sun Kwon .15 .40
❑ 10 Ben Linus .15 .40
❑ 11 Young Ben Linus .15 .40
❑ 12 Roger Linus .15 .40
❑ 13 Martin Keamy .15 .40
❑ 14 Alex Rousseau .15 .40
❑ 15 Danielle Rouseau .15 .40
❑ 16 Karl Martin .15 .40
❑ 17 Leslie Arzt .15 .40
❑ 18 Ana Lucia Cortez .15 .40
❑ 19 Charlie Pace .15 .40
❑ 20 Claire Littleton .15 .40
❑ 21 Aaron .15 .40
❑ 22 Ethan Rom .15 .40
❑ 23 Zoe .15 .40
❑ 24 Charles Widmore .15 .40
❑ 25 Desmond Hume .15 .40
❑ 26 Penelope Widmore .15 .40
❑ 27 Kelvin Inman .15 .40
❑ 28 Hugo Hurley Reyes .15 .40
❑ 29 Carmen Reyes .15 .40
❑ 30 David Reyes .15 .40
❑ 31 Libby Smith .15 .40
❑ 32 Dave .15 .40
❑ 33 Dr. Douglas Brooks .15 .40
❑ 34 Ilana Verdansky .15 .40
❑ 35 Frank Lapidus .15 .40
❑ 36 Mikhail Bakunin .15 .40
❑ 37 John Locke .15 .40
❑ 38 Helen Norwood .15 .40
❑ 39 Anthony Cooper .15 .40
❑ 40 Richard Alpert .15 .40
❑ 41 Jacob .15 .40
❑ 42 Man in Black .15 .40
❑ 43 Young Jacob .15 .40
❑ 44 Horace Goodspeed .15 .40
❑ 45 Phil .15 .40
❑ 46 James Sawyer Ford .15 .40
❑ 47 Cassidy Phillips .15 .40
❑ 48 Juliet Burke .15 .40
❑ 49 Harper Stanhope .15 .40
❑ 50 Goodwin Stanhope .15 .40
❑ 51 Tom Friendly .15 .40
❑ 52 Nikki Fernandez .15 .40
❑ 53 Paulo .15 .40
❑ 54 Cindy Chandler .15 .40
❑ 55 Sayid Jarrah .15 .40
❑ 56 Nadia .15 .40
❑ 57 Shannon Rutherford .15 .40
❑ 58 Boone Carlyle .15 .40
❑ 59 Yemi .15 .40
❑ 60 Mr. Eko .15 .40
❑ 61 Dogen .15 .40
❑ 62 Lennon .15 .40
❑ 63 Michael Dawson .15 .40
❑ 64 Walt Lloyd .15 .40
❑ 65 Vincent the Dog .15 .40
❑ 66 Young Eloise Hawking .15 .40
❑ 67 Eloise Hawking .15 .40
❑ 68 Daniel Faraday .15 .40
❑ 69 Naomi Dorrit .15 .40
❑ 70 Charlotte Lewis .15 .40
❑ 71 Miles Straume .15 .40
❑ 72 Dr. Pierre Chang .15 .40
❑ BT Banyan Tree/ (issued as 3-case incentive)30.00 60.00

2010 Lost Archives Artifex Expansion

COMPLETE SET (9) 12.00 30.00
STATED ODDS 1:12

❑ A27 Ilana Verdansky 2.50 6.00
❑ A28 Frank Lapidus 2.50 6.00
❑ A29 Bernard Nadler 2.50 6.00
❑ A30 Rose Nadler 2.50 6.00
❑ A31 Jacob 2.50 6.00
❑ A32 Penny Widmore 2.50 6.00
❑ A33 Dogen 2.50 6.00
❑ A34 Lennon 2.50 6.00
❑ A35 Ethan Rom 2.50 6.00
❑ A36 The Man in Black SP 10.00 25.00
(issued as Rittenhouse Reward)

2010 Lost Archives Autographs

STATED ODDS FOUR PER BOX
L (LIMITED): 300-500 COPIES
VL (VERY LIMITED): 200-300 COPIES

❑ 1 Sam Anderson L 10.00 25.00
❑ 2 Blake Bashoff 6.00 15.00
❑ 3 Sterling Beaumon 8.00 20.00
❑ 4 Grant Bowler 6.00 15.00
❑ 5 Beth Broderick 6.00 15.00
❑ 6 L. Scott Caldwell L 10.00 25.00
❑ 7 Nestor Carbonell VL 25.00 50.00
❑ 8 Francois Chau L 10.00 25.00
❑ 9 George Kee Cheung 6.00 15.00
❑ 10 Brett Cullen 6.00 15.00
❑ 11 Henry Ian Cusick VL 30.00 60.00
❑ 12 Bruce Davison 6.00 15.00
❑ 13 Kim Dickens 8.00 20.00
❑ 14 Andrew Divoff L 10.00 25.00
❑ 15 Michael Emerson VL 40.00 80.00
❑ 16 Gabrielle Fitzpatrick 6.00 15.00
❑ 17 Andrea Gabriel 6.00 15.00
❑ 18 M.C. Gainey 6.00 15.00
❑ 19 Jon Gries L 10.00 25.00
❑ 20 Neil Hopkins 6.00 15.00
❑ 21 James Horan 6.00 15.00
❑ 22 Malcolm David Kelley VL 25.00 50.00
❑ 23 Daniel Dae Kim L 25.00 50.00
❑ 24 Yunjin Kim VL 50.00 100.00
❑ 25 Swoosie Kurtz VL 25.00 50.00
❑ 26 Fredric Lehne 6.00 15.00
❑ 27 Ken Leung L 20.00 40.00
❑ 28 Bai Ling VL 40.00 80.00
❑ 29 William Mapother L 10.00 25.00
❑ 30 Navid Negahban 6.00 15.00
❑ 31 Harold Perrineau VL 40.00 80.00
❑ 32 Wayne Pygram 6.00 15.00
❑ 33 Tania Raymonde L 12.00 30.00
❑ 34 Zuleikha Robinson 12.00 30.00
❑ 35 Daniel Roebuck 6.00 15.00
❑ 36 Ian Somerhalder L 20.00 40.00
❑ 37 Sally Strecker 6.00 15.00
❑ 38 John Terry VL 25.00 50.00
❑ 39 Marc Vann 6.00 15.00
❑ 40 Sonya Walger L 10.00 25.00
❑ 41 Cynthia Watros 10.00 25.00
❑ 42 Cheech Marin/ (issued as 6-case incentive)100.00 200.00

2010 Lost Archives Costumes

STATED ODDS 1:96
STATED PRINT RUN 375 SER. #'d SETS

❑ 1 Ben Linus 25.00 50.00
❑ 2 Hugo Hurley Reyes 25.00 50.00
❑ 3 Jack Shephard 30.00 60.00
❑ 4 James Sawyer Ford 25.00 50.00
❑ 5 John Locke 25.00 50.00
❑ 6 Kate Austin 30.00 60.00
❑ 7 Sayid Jarrah/ (issued as case topper) 15.00 30.00

2010 Lost Archives Darma Patch

STATED ODDS 1:144
STATED PRINT RUN 250 SER. #'d SETS

❑ DP1 Jack Shephard 35.00 70.00
❑ DP2 James Sawyer Ford 35.00 70.00
❑ DP3 Kate Austin 35.00 70.00
❑ DP4 Hugo Hurley Reyes 35.00 70.00
❑ DP5 Juliet Burke 35.00 70.00
❑ DP6 Miles Straume 35.00 70.00
❑ DP7 Desmond Hume 35.00 70.00
❑ DP8 Jim Kwon 35.00 70.00
❑ DP9 Daniel Faraday 35.00 70.00

2010 Lost Archives Promos

COMPLETE SET (3)

❑ P1 Claire Littleton/ (General Distribution)
❑ P2 Richard Alpert/ (Non-Sport Update)
❑ CP1 Binder Exclusive

2010 Lost Archives Season Six

COMPLETE SET (18) 12.00 30.00
STATED ODDS 1:6

❑ 109 Season Six (Title Card) 1.50 4.00
❑ 110 LAX 1.50 4.00
❑ 111 What Kate Does 1.50 4.00
❑ 112 The Substitute 1.50 4.00
❑ 113 Lighthouse 1.50 4.00
❑ 114 Sundown 1.50 4.00
❑ 115 Dr. Linus 1.50 4.00
❑ 116 Recon 1.50 4.00
❑ 117 Ab Aeterno 1.50 4.00
❑ 118 The Package 1.50 4.00
❑ 119 Happily Ever After 1.50 4.00
❑ 120 Everybody Loves Hugo 1.50 4.00
❑ 121 The Last Recruit 1.50 4.00
❑ 122 The Candidate 1.50 4.00
❑ 123 Across the Sea 1.50 4.00
❑ 124 What They Died For 1.50 4.00
❑ 125 The End, Part 1 1.50 4.00
❑ 126 The End, Part 2 1.50 4.00

2010 Lost Seasons One Through Five

COMPLETE SET (108) 7.50 15.00
E. LILLY COSTUME CARD ONE PER 6-CASE PURCHASE

❑ 1 LOST .15 .40
❑ 2 Season One .15 .40
❑ 3 Pilot, Part 1 .15 .40
❑ 4 Pilot, Part 2 .15 .40
❑ 5 Tabula Rasa .15 .40
❑ 6 Walkabout .15 .40
❑ 7 White Rabbit .15 .40
❑ 8 House of the Rising Sun .15 .40
❑ 9 The Moth .15 .40
❑ 10 Confidence Man .15 .40
❑ 11 Solitary .15 .40
❑ 12 Raised By Another .15 .40
❑ 13 All the Best Cowboys Have Daddy Issues .15 .40
❑ 14 Whatever The Case May Be .15 .40
❑ 15 Hearts and Minds .15 .40
❑ 16 Special .15 .40
❑ 17 Homecoming .15 .40
❑ 18 Outlaws .15 .40
❑ 19 In Translation .15 .40
❑ 20 Numbers .15 .40
❑ 21 Deus Ex Machina .15 .40
❑ 22 Do No Harm .15 .40
❑ 23 The Greater Good .15 .40
❑ 24 Born To Run .15 .40
❑ 25 Exodus, Part 1 .15 .40
❑ 26 Exodus, Part 2 .15 .40
❑ 27 Season Two .15 .40
❑ 28 Man of Science, Man of Faith .15 .40
❑ 29 Adrift .15 .40
❑ 30 Orientation .15 .40
❑ 31 Everybody Hates Hugo .15 .40
❑ 32 And Found .15 .40
❑ 33 Abandoned .15 .40
❑ 34 The Other 48 Days .15 .40
❑ 35 Collision .15 .40
❑ 36 What Kate Did .15 .40
❑ 37 The 23rd Psalm .15 .40
❑ 38 The Hunting Party .15 .40
❑ 39 Fire + Water .15 .40
❑ 40 The Long Con .15 .40
❑ 41 One of Them .15 .40
❑ 42 Maternity Leave .15 .40
❑ 43 The Whole Truth .15 .40
❑ 44 Lockdown .15 .40
❑ 45 Dave .15 .40
❑ 46 S.O.S. .15 .40
❑ 47 Two for the Road .15 .40
❑ 48 Question Mark .15 .40
❑ 49 Three Minutes .15 .40
❑ 50 Live Together, Die Alone, Part 1 .15 .40
❑ 51 Live Together, Die Alone, Part 2 .15 .40
❑ 52 Season Three .15 .40
❑ 53 A Tale of Two Cities .15 .40
❑ 54 The Glass Ballerina .15 .40
❑ 55 Further Instructions .15 .40
❑ 56 Every Man For Himself .15 .40
❑ 57 The Cost of Living .15 .40
❑ 58 I Do .15 .40
❑ 59 Not in Portland .15 .40
❑ 60 Flashes Before Your Eyes .15 .40
❑ 61 Stranger in a Strange Land .15 .40
❑ 62 Tricia Tanaka is Dead .15 .40
❑ 63 Enter 77 .15 .40
❑ 64 Par Avion .15 .40
❑ 65 The Man from Tallahassee .15 .40
❑ 66 Exposé .15 .40
❑ 67 Left Behind .15 .40
❑ 68 One of Us .15 .40
❑ 69 Catch-22 .15 .40
❑ 70 D.O.C. .15 .40
❑ 71 The Brig .15 .40
❑ 72 The Man Behind the Curtain .15 .40
❑ 73 Greatest Hits .15 .40
❑ 74 Through the Looking Glass, Part 1 .15 .40
❑ 75 Through the Looking Glass, Part 2 .15 .40
❑ 76 Season Four .15 .40
❑ 77 The Beginning of the End .15 .40
❑ 78 Confirmed Dead .15 .40
❑ 79 The Economist .15 .40
❑ 80 Eggtown .15 .40
❑ 81 The Constant .15 .40
❑ 82 The Other Woman .15 .40
❑ 83 Ji Yeon .15 .40
❑ 84 Meet Kevin Johnson .15 .40
❑ 85 The Shape of Things to Come .15 .40
❑ 86 Something Nice Back Home .15 .40
❑ 87 Cabin Fever .15 .40
❑ 88 There's No Place Like Home, Part 1 .15 .40
❑ 89 There's No Place Like Home, Part 2 .15 .40
❑ 90 Season Five .15 .40
❑ 91 Because You Left .15 .40
❑ 92 The Lie .15 .40
❑ 93 Jughead .15 .40
❑ 94 The Little Prince .15 .40
❑ 95 This Place is Death .15 .40
❑ 96 316 .15 .40
❑ 97 The Life and Death of Jeremy Bentham .15 .40
❑ 98 LaFleur .15 .40
❑ 99 Namaste .15 .40
❑ 100 He's Our You .15 .40

❑ 101 Whatever Happened, Happened .15 .40
❑ 102 Dead is Dead .15 .40
❑ 103 Some Like It Hoth .15 .40
❑ 104 The Variable .15 .40
❑ 105 Follow The Leader .15 .40
❑ 106 The Incident, Part 1 .15 .40
❑ 107 The Incident, Part 2 .15 .40
❑ 108 Checklist .15 .40
❑ EL Evangeline Lilly MEM 150.00 250.00

2010 Lost Seasons One Through Five ArtiFex

COMPLETE SET (25) 15.00 30.00
STATED ODDS 1:6

❑ A1 Jack Shephard .75 2.00
❑ A2 Kate Austen .75 2.00
❑ A3 John Locke .75 2.00
❑ A4 Sayid Jarrah .75 2.00
❑ A5 James Sawyer Ford .75 2.00
❑ A6 Claire Littleton .75 2.00
❑ A7 Boone Carlyle .75 2.00
❑ A8 Sun-Hwa Kwon .75 2.00
❑ A9 Jin-Soo Kwon .75 2.00
❑ A10 Hugo Hurley Reyes .75 2.00
❑ A11 Shannon Rutherford .75 2.00
❑ A12 Charlie Pace .75 2.00
❑ A13 Michael Dawson .75 2.00
❑ A14 Walt Lloyd .75 2.00
❑ A15 Mr. Eko .75 2.00
❑ A16 Ana Lucia Cortez .75 2.00
❑ A17 Libby .75 2.00
❑ A18 Benjamin Linus .75 2.00
❑ A19 Desmond Hume .75 2.00
❑ A20 Juliet Burke .75 2.00
❑ A21 Nikki Fernandez .75 2.00
❑ A22 Paulo .75 2.00
❑ A23 Daniel Faraday .75 2.00
❑ A24 Charlotte Lewis .75 2.00
❑ A25 Miles Straume .75 2.00
❑ A26 Richard Alpert SP 10.00 25.00
(issued as Rittenhouse Reward)

2010 Lost Seasons One Through Five Autographs

STATED ODDS 1:8
LC STATED ODDS ONE PER CASE
HP STATED ODDS ONE PER 3-CASE PURCHASE
SB IS D23 EXPO EXCLUSIVE
L (LIMITED): 300-500 COPIES
VL (VERY LIMITED): 200-300 COPIES

❑ AB Anne Bedian 8.00 20.00
❑ AD1 Alan Dale 8.00 20.00
❑ AD2 Andrew Divoff 8.00 20.00
❑ AE Alice Evans 8.00 20.00
❑ AR Andrea Roth 8.00 20.00
❑ BG Billy Ray Gallion 8.00 20.00
❑ DH Doug Hutchison 8.00 20.00
❑ EH Evan Handler 8.00 20.00
❑ EL Eric Lange 8.00 20.00
❑ FC Francois Chau L 10.00 25.00
❑ HC Henry Ian Cusick L 35.00 70.00
❑ HP Harold Perrineau/ (issued as 3-case incentive)40.00 80.00
❑ IS Ian Somerhalder L 20.00 40.00
❑ JG Jon Gries L 10.00 25.00
❑ JT John Terry L 10.00 25.00
❑ KL Ken Leung VL 50.00 100.00
❑ KS Kiele Sanchez L 15.00 40.00
❑ LC L. Scott Caldwell/ (issued as case topper)15.00 40.00
❑ MC Monica Dean 8.00 20.00
❑ ME Michael Emerson VL 60.00 120.00
❑ MF Mira Furlan L 12.00 30.00
❑ MK Malcolm David Kelley L 12.00 30.00
❑ MP Mark Pellegrino 10.00 25.00
❑ MR Michelle Rodriguez VL 75.00 150.00
❑ NC Nestor Carbonell L 15.00 40.00
❑ PF Patrick Fischler 8.00 20.00
❑ SA Sam Anderson 8.00 20.00
❑ SB Sterling Beaumon 60.00 120.00
(Disney D23 Expo Exclusive)
❑ SL Sung Hi Lee 8.00 20.00
❑ SW Sonya Walger 10.00 25.00
❑ TC Tom Connolly 8.00 20.00
❑ TO Terry O'Quinn 35.00 70.00
❑ TR Tania Raymonde 10.00 25.00
❑ TW Titus Welliver 8.00 20.00
❑ WM William Mapother L 12.00 30.00
❑ WS William Sanderson 8.00 20.00
❑ YK Yunjin Kim VL 60.00 120.00

2010 Lost Seasons One Through Five Flash Forward

COMPLETE SET (4) 4.00 10.00
STATED ODDS 1:6

❑ FF1 Group Photo 1.25 3.00
❑ FF2 Mark Benford 1.25 3.00
❑ FF3 Demetri Noh 1.25 3.00
❑ FF4 Simon Campos 1.25 3.00

2010 Lost Seasons One Through Five In Motion

COMPLETE SET (9) 12.50 25.00
STATED ODDS 1:12

❑ L1 LOST Opening Sequence 1.50 4.00
❑ L2 Oceanic 815 Fuselage Break 1.50 4.00
❑ L3 Oceanic 815 Tail Crash 1.50 4.00
❑ L4 Charlie's Fate 1.50 4.00
❑ L5 Resetting the Clock 1.50 4.00
❑ L6 Mr. Cluck's Chicken Shack Hit by Meteor 1.50 4.00
❑ L7 Black Smoke Monster 1.50 4.00
❑ L8 Moving the Island 1.50 4.00
❑ L9 Freighter Explosion 1.50 4.00

2010 Lost Seasons One Through Five Oceanic Six

COMPLETE SET (6) 12.50 25.00
STATED ODDS 1:24

❑ S1 Jack Shephard 2.50 6.00
❑ S2 Kate Austen 2.50 6.00
❑ S3 Hugo Hurley Reyes 2.50 6.00
❑ S4 Sayid Jarrah 2.50 6.00
❑ S5 Sun-Hwa Kwon 2.50 6.00
❑ S6 Aaron Littleton 2.50 6.00

2010 Marvel 70th Anniversary

COMPLETE SET (72) 5.00 12.00

❑ 1 Checklist .15 .40
❑ 2 1939 .15 .40
❑ 3 1940 .15 .40
❑ 4 1941 .15 .40
❑ 5 1942 .15 .40
❑ 6 1943 .15 .40
❑ 7 1944 .15 .40
❑ 8 1945 .15 .40
❑ 9 1946 .15 .40
❑ 10 1947 .15 .40
❑ 11 1948 .15 .40
❑ 12 1949 .15 .40
❑ 13 1950 .15 .40
❑ 14 1951 .15 .40
❑ 15 1952 .15 .40
❑ 16 1953 .15 .40
❑ 17 1954 .15 .40
❑ 18 1955 .15 .40
❑ 19 1956 .15 .40
❑ 20 1957 .15 .40
❑ 21 1958 .15 .40
❑ 22 1959 .15 .40
❑ 23 1960 .15 .40
❑ 24 1961 .15 .40
❑ 25 1962 .15 .40
❑ 26 1963 .15 .40
❑ 27 1964 .15 .40
❑ 28 1965 .15 .40
❑ 29 1966 .15 .40
❑ 30 1967 .15 .40
❑ 31 1968 .15 .40
❑ 32 1969 .15 .40
❑ 33 1970 .15 .40
❑ 34 1971 .15 .40
❑ 35 1972 .15 .40
❑ 36 1973 .15 .40
❑ 37 1974 .15 .40
❑ 38 1975 .15 .40
❑ 39 1976 .15 .40
❑ 40 1977 .15 .40
❑ 41 1978 .15 .40
❑ 42 1979 .15 .40
❑ 43 1980 .15 .40
❑ 44 1981 .15 .40
❑ 45 1982 .15 .40
❑ 46 1983 .15 .40
❑ 47 1984 .15 .40
❑ 48 1985 .15 .40
❑ 49 1986 .15 .40
❑ 50 1987 .15 .40
❑ 51 1988 .15 .40
❑ 52 1989 .15 .40
❑ 53 1990 .15 .40
❑ 54 1991 .15 .40
❑ 55 1992 .15 .40
❑ 56 1993 .15 .40
❑ 57 1994 .15 .40
❑ 58 1995 .15 .40
❑ 59 1996 .15 .40
❑ 60 1997 .15 .40
❑ 61 1998 .15 .40
❑ 62 1999 .15 .40
❑ 63 2000 .15 .40
❑ 64 2001 .15 .40
❑ 65 2002 .15 .40
❑ 66 2003 .15 .40
❑ 67 2004 .15 .40
❑ 68 2005 .15 .40
❑ 69 2006 .15 .40
❑ 70 2007 .15 .40
❑ 71 2008 .15 .40
❑ 72 2009 .15 .40

2010 Marvel 70th Anniversary Foil

COMPLETE SET (72) 25.00 60.00
*FOIL: 2X TO 5X BASIC CARDS
STATED ODDS 1:3

2010 Marvel 70th Anniversary Case Toppers

COMPLETE SET (3) 50.00 100.00
STATED ODDS ONE PER CASE
STATED PRINT RUN 333 SER. #'d SETS

❑ CT1 Beast 20.00 40.00
Daredevil
❑ CT2 Group shot 20.00 40.00
❑ CT3 Group shot 20.00 40.00

2010 Marvel 70th Anniversary Characters

COMPLETE SET (9) 6.00 15.00
STATED ODDS 1:12

❑ C1 Captain America 1.25 3.00
❑ C2 Cyclops 1.25 3.00
❑ C3 Hulk 1.25 3.00
❑ C4 Iron Man 1.25 3.00
❑ C5 Silver Surfer 1.25 3.00
❑ C6 Spider-Man 1.25 3.00
❑ C7 Thing 1.25 3.00
❑ C8 Thor 1.25 3.00
❑ C9 Wolverine 1.25 3.00
❑ ALT Power Man SP 12.00 30.00
(issued as Rittenhouse Reward)

2010 Marvel 70th Anniversary Clearly Heroic

COMPLETE SET (6) 15.00 30.00
STATED ODDS 1:24

❑ PC1 Captain America 3.00 8.00
❑ PC2 Hulk 3.00 8.00
❑ PC3 Iron Man 3.00 8.00
❑ PC4 Spider-Man 3.00 8.00
❑ PC5 Thing 3.00 8.00
❑ PC6 Wolverine 3.00 8.00

2010 Marvel 70th Anniversary Sketches

STATED ODDS ONE PER BOX
L (LIMITED): OVER 250 MADE
VL (VERY LIMITED): 151-250 MADE
EL (EXTREMELY LIMITED): 50-150 MADE
S (SCARCE): LESS THAN 50 MADE
MARTINECK SKETCH ONE PER 6 CASE PURCHASE
LAYTON SKETCH ONE PER 9 CASE PURCHASE

❑ AM Alexandre Magno VL 40.00 100.00
❑ AP Andy Price
❑ AW Anthony Wheeler EL 25.00 60.00
❑ BG Benjamin Glendenning EL 50.00 125.00
❑ BM Butch Mapa VL 30.00 80.00
❑ BS Brian Shearer EL 25.00 60.00
❑ BT Bryan Turner VL 15.00 40.00
❑ CB Chris Bradberry EL 25.00 60.00
❑ CH Charles Hall EL 200.00 400.00
❑ CR Cezar Razek EL 60.00 150.00
❑ CS Cat Staggs EL 60.00 150.00
❑ CY Craig Yeung VL 30.00 80.00
❑ DB Darryl Banks EL 30.00 80.00
❑ DH Don Hillsman II EL 30.00 80.00
❑ DQ Dan Quiles VL 25.00 60.00
❑ EC Eugene Commodore VL 15.00 40.00
❑ EF Eduardo Ferrara VL 25.00 60.00
❑ EM Erik Maell EL 30.00 80.00
❑ EW Edde Wagner EL 20.00 50.00
❑ GC George Calloway VL 50.00 125.00
❑ GD Guy Dorian EL 20.00 50.00
❑ GT Gooney Toons EL 60.00 150.00
❑ IA Irma Ahmed EL 60.00 150.00
❑ ID Ian Dorian EL 25.00 60.00
❑ JH John Haun EL 50.00 125.00
❑ JK Jim Kyle L 20.00 50.00
❑ JP Joe Pekar L 30.00 80.00
❑ JS Jason Sobol EL 40.00 100.00
❑ JZ Jeff Zugale VL 30.00 80.00
❑ KA Kristin Allen EL 40.00 100.00
❑ KC Katie Cook EL 125.00 250.00
❑ KL Kat Laurange EL 50.00 125.00
❑ KW Kevin West EL 30.00 80.00
❑ LA Lui Antonio L 40.00 100.00
❑ LK Lee Kohse EL 30.00 80.00
❑ LL Lak Lim EL 30.00 80.00
❑ MF Marcelo Ferreira L 30.00 80.00
❑ MG Michael Glover EL 30.00 80.00
❑ MM Monte Moore EL 15.00 40.00
❑ MP Michael Axebone Potter EL 125.00 250.00
❑ NB Newton Barbosa VL 40.00 100.00
❑ NC Nestor Celario Jr EL 30.00 80.00
❑ NN Nick Neocleous EL 40.00 100.00
❑ PL Patrick Larcada S
❑ RC Richard Cox EL 60.00 150.00
❑ SB Scott Barnett EL 40.00 100.00
❑ SM Steven Miller EL 20.00 50.00
❑ SS Sonny Strait EL 50.00 125.00
❑ SU Sanna Umemoto S
❑ TB Thanh Bui EL 30.00 80.00
❑ TR Tone Rodriguez VL 20.00 50.00
❑ TS Tim Shay EL 25.00 60.00
❑ YC Yildiray Cinar EL 40.00 100.00
❑ AC1 Adriano Carreon EL 25.00 60.00
❑ AC2 Anthony Castrillo EL 25.00 60.00
❑ AC3 Adam Cleveland L 30.00 80.00
❑ ADS Alcione da Silva VL 20.00 50.00
❑ ARC Aston Roy Cover EL 60.00 150.00
❑ AT1 Anthony Tan EL 200.00 400.00
❑ AT2 Andre Toma EL 20.00 50.00
❑ BK1 Brandon Kenney EL 25.00 60.00
❑ BK2 Brian Kong EL 25.00 60.00
❑ BP1 Brian Postman L 20.00 50.00
❑ BP2 Buddy Prince L 40.00 100.00
❑ CG1 Charles George EL 25.00 60.00
❑ CG2 Chris Gutierrez EL 30.00 80.00
❑ DC1 Daniel Campos VL 30.00 80.00
❑ DC2 Darren Chandler VL 30.00 80.00
❑ DC3 Dan Cooney VL 15.00 40.00
❑ DC4 Dennis Crisostomo EL 30.00 80.00
❑ GEO George Geo Davis EL 30.00 80.00
❑ HDR Daniel HDR VL 25.00 60.00
❑ JAX John JAX Jackman S
❑ JC1 Justin Chung S 75.00 200.00
❑ JC2 Jeff Confer EL 30.00 80.00
❑ JC3 John Czop EL 50.00 125.00
❑ JG1 Jerry Gaylord VL 20.00 50.00
❑ JG2 Javier Gonzalez EL 25.00 60.00
❑ JM1 Jason McLellan EL 30.00 80.00
❑ JM2 Jake Minor EL 30.00 80.00
❑ JR1 Jack Redd EL 175.00 300.00
❑ JR2 Joe Rubinstein L 15.00 40.00
❑ JSP Joe St.Pierre EL 100.00 200.00
❑ JWC John Watkins-Chow EL 40.00 100.00
❑ KAL Kathryn A. Layno VL 30.00 80.00
❑ MDS Mark Dos Santos EL 30.00 80.00
❑ NHM Nur Hanie Mohd S 100.00 200.00
❑ RM1 Randy Martinez VL 20.00 50.00
❑ RM2 Rich Molinelli VL 15.00 40.00
❑ RM3 Randy Monces VL 20.00 50.00
❑ RO1 Ryan Orosco EL 60.00 150.00
❑ RO2 Rhiannon Owens VL 75.00 200.00
❑ SR1 Scott Rorie EL 40.00 100.00
❑ SR2 Scott Rosema VL 20.00 50.00
❑ TF1 Tony Fleecs EL 25.00 60.00
❑ TF2 Tess Fowler EL 25.00 60.00
❑ BL Bob Layton 125.00 250.00
❑ WM Warren Martineck 150.00 250.00

2010 Marvel 70th Anniversary Stickers

COMPLETE SET (18) 12.00 30.00
STATED ODDS 1:8

❑ S1 Spider-Man 1.25 3.00
❑ S2 Captain America 1.25 3.00
❑ S3 Hulk 1.25 3.00
❑ S4 Iron Man 1.25 3.00
❑ S5 Thor 1.25 3.00
❑ S6 Submariner 1.25 3.00
❑ S7 Mr. Fantastic 1.25 3.00
❑ S8 Thing 1.25 3.00
❑ S9 Human Torch 1.25 3.00
❑ S10 She-Hulk 1.25 3.00
❑ S11 Silver Surfer 1.25 3.00
❑ S12 Power Man 1.25 3.00
❑ S13 Spider-Woman 1.25 3.00
❑ S14 Daredevil 1.25 3.00
❑ S15 Marvel Girl 1.25 3.00
❑ S16 Angel 1.25 3.00
❑ S17 Beast 1.25 3.00
❑ S18 Wolverine 1.25 3.00

2010 Marvel 70th Anniversary Tribute

COMPLETE SET (9) 2.00 5.00

❑ T1 Captain America .40 1.00
❑ T2 Captain America .40 1.00
❑ T3 Captain America .40 1.00
❑ T4 Submariner .40 1.00
❑ T5 Submariner .40 1.00
❑ T6 Submariner .40 1.00
❑ T7 Human Torch .40 1.00
❑ T8 Human Torch .40 1.00
❑ T9 Human Torch .40 1.00

2010 Marvel 70th Anniversary Tribute Foil

COMPLETE SET
*FOIL: 1.2X TO 3X BASIC CARDS
RANDOM INSERT IN PACKS

2010 Marvel Heroes and Villains

COMPLETE SET (81) 6.00 15.00

❑ 1 War Machine vs. Iron Patriot .15 .40
❑ 2 Thor vs. Loki .15 .40
❑ 3 Skaar vs. Jugernaut .15 .40
❑ 4 Spider-Man vs. Kaine .15 .40
❑ 5 Ghost Rider vs. Scarecrow .15 .40
❑ 6 Nova vs. Penance .15 .40
❑ 7 Wolverine vs. Stryfe .15 .40
❑ 8 Nick Fury vs. Ares .15 .40
❑ 9 Hawkeye vs. Bullseye .15 .40
❑ 10 USAgent vs. The Unspoken .15 .40
❑ 11 Ms. Marvel vs. Skrull .15 .40
❑ 12 Wonder-Man vs. Penance .15 .40
❑ 13 Deadpool vs. Skrull .15 .40
❑ 14 Wolverine vs. Omega Red .15 .40
❑ 15 Punisher vs. Kraven The Hunter .15 .40
❑ 16 Gorilla-Man vs. Scourge .15 .40
❑ 17 Iron Man vs. Whiplash .15 .40
❑ 18 Thing vs. Dr. Doom .15 .40
❑ 19 Sasquatch vs. Sabretooth .15 .40
❑ 20 Nova vs. Super-Skrull .15 .40
❑ 21 Skaar vs. Tyrannus .15 .40
❑ 22 Iron Fist vs. Quan Yaozu .15 .40
❑ 23 Nova vs. Sphinx .15 .40
❑ 24 Miss America vs. Unknown .15 .40
❑ 25 X-Force vs. Stryfe .15 .40
❑ 26 Dr. Strange vs. Dormammu .15 .40
❑ 27 War Machine vs. Ares .15 .40
❑ 28 Wolverine and Armor vs. Brood .15 .40
❑ 29 Daredevil vs. Lady Bullseye .15 .40
❑ 30 Ms. Marvel vs. Ms. Marvel .15 .40
❑ 31 Thing vs. Clay Golem .15 .40
❑ 32 Ghost Rider vs. Blackout .15 .40
❑ 33 Thor vs. Gauntlet .15 .40
❑ 34 Rogue vs. Emplate .15 .40
❑ 35 Wolverine vs. Magneto .15 .40
❑ 36 Spider-Man vs. Mister Negative .15 .40
❑ 37 ArchAngel .15 .40
Vanisher vs. Pyro
❑ 38 Spider-Girl vs. Green Goblin .15 .40
❑ 39 Wolverine vs. Daken .15 .40
Cyber
❑ 40 Moon Knight vs. Venom .15 .40
❑ 41 Hulk vs. Fin Fang Foom .15 .40
❑ 42 Cable .15 .40
Bishop vs. Brood
❑ 43 Iron Man vs. Titanium Man .15 .40
❑ 44 Hercules vs. Ares .15 .40
❑ 45 Nova vs. Monark Starstalker .15 .40
❑ 46 Punisher vs. Bullseye .15 .40
❑ 47 Havok vs. Vulcan .15 .40
❑ 48 X-23 vs. Lady Deathstrike .15 .40
❑ 49 Rocket Raccoon vs. Blastaar .15 .40
❑ 50 Captain America vs. Red Skull .15 .40
❑ 51 Storm vs. Sabretooth .15 .40
❑ 52 Night Thrasher vs. Midnights Fire .15 .40
❑ 53 Wolverine vs. Mystique .15 .40
❑ 54 Elektra vs. Skrull Daredevil .15 .40
❑ 55 Major Victory vs. Starhawk .15 .40
❑ 56 Black Panther vs. Wakandan Tribesman .15 .40
❑ 57 Thing .15 .40
Human Torch vs. Rhino/Abomination
❑ 58 Spider-Man vs. Red Hulk .15 .40
❑ 59 Ronin vs. The Hand .15 .40
❑ 60 She-Hulk vs. Ursa Major .15 .40
❑ 61 Thor vs. Skrull .15 .40
❑ 62 Sage vs. Purge .15 .40
❑ 63 Wolverine vs. Daken .15 .40
❑ 64 Hulk vs. Red Hulk .15 .40
❑ 65 Wolverine vs. Sabretooth .15 .40
❑ 66 Moon Knight vs. Midnight .15 .40
❑ 67 Ghost Rider vs. Hoss .15 .40
❑ 68 Ms. Marvel vs. Moonstone .15 .40
❑ 69 Punisher vs. Skrull .15 .40
❑ 70 Captain America vs. Loki .15 .40
❑ 71 Thor vs. Frost Giant .15 .40
❑ 72 Iron Man vs. Winter Soldier .15 .40
❑ 73 Thor vs. Absorbing Man .15 .40
❑ 74 Spider-Man vs. Electro .15 .40
❑ 75 U.S. Agent vs. Nuke .15 .40
❑ 76 Nick Fury vs. Norman Osborn .15 .40
❑ 77 Daredevil vs. Bullseye .15 .40
❑ 78 Spider-Man vs. Morbius .15 .40
❑ 79 Moon Knight vs. Scarecrow .15 .40
❑ 80. Captain America vs. Baron Zemo .15 .40
❑ 81 Wolverine vs. Ruby Red .15 .40

2010 Marvel Heroes and Villains Alliances

COMPLETE SET (18) 10.00 25.00
STATED ODDS 1:12

❑ A1 New Mutants 1.25 3.00
❑ A2 Dark Avengers 1.25 3.00
❑ A3 Mighty Avengers 1.25 3.00
❑ A4 S.H.I.E.L.D. 1.25 3.00
❑ A5 Fantastic Four 1.25 3.00
❑ A6 Guardians of the Galaxy 1.25 3.00
❑ A7 Powerpack 1.25 3.00
❑ A8 The Runaways 1.25 3.00
❑ A9 Agents of Atlas 1.25 3.00
❑ A10 Marvel Knights 1.25 3.00
❑ A11 Immortal Weapons 1.25 3.00
❑ A12 Inhumans 1.25 3.00
❑ A13 The Cabal 1.25 3.00
❑ A14 Squadron Supreme 1.25 3.00
❑ A15 X-Men 1.25 3.00
❑ A16 Winter Guard 1.25 3.00
❑ A17 Secret Avengers 1.25 3.00
❑ A18 Masters of Evil 1.25 3.00

2010 Marvel Heroes and Villains Case Toppers

COMPLETE SET (5) 60.00 125.00
STATED ODDS ONE PER CASE

❑ CT1 Spider-Man 12.00 30.00
❑ CT2 Thor 12.00 30.00
❑ CT3 Captain America 12.00 30.00
❑ CT4 Fantastic Four 12.00 30.00
❑ CT5 Black Pather 12.00 30.00

2010 Marvel Heroes and Villains Foil

COMPLETE SET (81) 20.00 50.00
STATED ODDS 1:3

2010 Marvel Heroes and Villains Lenticular Flip

COMPLETE SET (6) 12.00 30.00
STATED ODDS 1:48

❑ L1 Hulk 4.00 10.00
Red Hulk
❑ L2 Thor 4.00 10.00
Destroyer
❑ L3 Captain America 4.00 10.00
Red Skull
❑ L4 Nova 4.00 10.00
Ronan
❑ L5 Punisher 4.00 10.00
Bullseye
❑ L6 Ms. Marvel 4.00 10.00
Ms. Marvel

2010 Marvel Heroes and Villains Marvels Most Wanted

COMPLETE SET (10) 25.00 60.00
COMP.SET w/o SP (9) 5.00 12.00
STATED ODDS 1:8
M10 ISSUED AS RITTENHOUSE REDEMPTION

❑ M1 The Hood 1.00 2.50
❑ M2 Red Hulk 1.00 2.50
❑ M3 The Leader 1.00 2.50
❑ M4 M.O.D.O.K 1.00 2.50
❑ M5 Deathlock 1.00 2.50
❑ M6 Sphinx 1.00 2.50
❑ M7 Red Skull 1.00 2.50
❑ M8 Viper 1.00 2.50
❑ M9 Mystique 1.00 2.50
❑ M10 Magneto SP 20.00 50.00
(issued as Rittenhouse redemption)

2010 Marvel Heroes and Villains Posters

COMPLETE SET (6) 12.00 30.00
STATED ODDS 1:48

❑ PC1 Poster 1 3.00 8.00
❑ PC2 Poster 2 3.00 8.00
❑ PC3 Poster 3 3.00 8.00
❑ PC4 Poster 4 3.00 8.00
❑ PC5 Poster 5 3.00 8.00
❑ PC6 Poster 6 3.00 8.00

2010 Marvel Heroes and Villains Promos

❑ P1 MODOK 1.50 4.00
Ms. Marvel/ (General Distribution)
❑ P2 Wolverine 3.00 8.00
Sabretooth/ (NSU Magazine)
❑ P3 Hulk 6.00 15.00
Abomination/ (Marvel 70th Anniversary Binder)
❑ CP1 Black Panther 3.00 8.00
Sabretooth/ (San Diego Comic Con 2010)
❑ PNSCS1 Capt.America 6.00 15.00
Red Skull/ (Philadelphia Non-Sport Show Fall 2010)
❑ PNSCS2 Green Hulk 6.00 15.00
Red Hulk/ (Philadelphia Non-Sport Show Fall 2010)

2010 Marvel Heroes and Villains Sketches

STATED ODDS ONE PER BOX
LIM SKETCH ISSUED AS 6-CASE INCENTIVE
TAN SKETCH ISSUED AS 9-CASE INCENTIVE
L (LIMITED): 251 OR MORE MADE
VL (VERY LIMITED): 151-250 MADE
EL (EXTREMELY LIMITED): 50-150 MADE
S (SCARCE): LESS THAN 50 MADE
PRICE/HERNANDEZ/DORIAN ARCHIVE ONLY

❑ 1 Adam Cleveland L 20.00 50.00
❑ 2 Alberto Silva S 40.00 80.00
❑ 3 Alexandre Magno L 30.00 80.00
❑ 4 Andre Toma VL 20.00 50.00
❑ 5 Anthony Fleecs VL 25.00 60.00
❑ 6 Anthony Wheeler EL 20.00 50.00
❑ 7 Arie Monroe VL 30.00 80.00
❑ 8 Brandon Kenney EL 15.00 40.00
❑ 9 Brian Kong L 15.00 40.00
❑ 10 Brian Postman L 12.00 30.00
❑ 11 Brian Shearer L 15.00 40.00
❑ 12 Buddy Prince VL 30.00 80.00
❑ 13 Butch Mapa VL 30.00 80.00
❑ 14 Cat Staggs S
❑ 15 Charles Hall S
❑ 16 Chris Gutierrez EL 20.00 50.00
❑ 17 Chris Moreno VL 20.00 50.00
❑ 18 Craig Yeung EL 50.00 100.00
❑ 19 Dan Quiles VL 15.00 40.00
❑ 20 Daniel HDR
❑ 21 Darren Chandler EL
❑ 22 Darryl Banks EL 25.00 60.00
❑ 23 Dennis Crisostomo VL 25.00 60.00
❑ 24 Don Hillsman EL 25.00 60.00
❑ 25 Edde Wagner VL 12.00 30.00
❑ 26 Eduardo Ferrara L 12.00 30.00
❑ 27 Eli Rutten EL
❑ 28 Erik Maell EL 15.00 40.00
❑ 29 Frank Kadar EL
❑ 30 George Calloway EL
❑ 31 George Davis EL
❑ 32 Irma Ahmed EL 25.00 60.00
❑ 33 Jack Redd EL 150.00 200.00
❑ 34 Jake Minor EL 15.00 40.00
❑ 35 Jason Potratz 50.00 100.00
Jack Hai S
❑ 36 Jason Sobol EL 15.00 40.00
❑ 37 Javier Gonzalez S
❑ 38 Jeff Confer EL 25.00 60.00
❑ 39 Jeff Zugale EL 12.00 30.00
❑ 40 Jeremy Treece EL
❑ 41 Jerry Gaylord EL 15.00 40.00
❑ 42 Jim Kyle S
❑ 43 Joe Pekar VL 30.00 80.00
❑ 44 Joe Rubinstein VL 15.00 40.00
❑ 45 Joe St.Pierre S
❑ 46 John Czop EL 50.00 100.00
❑ 47 John Haun EL 25.00 60.00
❑ 48 John Jackman VL 30.00 80.00
❑ 49 Jomar Bulda EL 30.00 80.00
❑ 50 Jon Hughes EL 20.00 50.00
❑ 51 Jose David Lee L 15.00 40.00
❑ 52 Juan Fontanez EL 20.00 50.00
❑ 53 Kat Laurange EL
❑ 54 Katie Cook EL 75.00 150.00
❑ 55 Kevin West S
❑ 56 Kristin Allen EL 20.00 50.00
❑ 57 Lee Kohse L 15.00 40.00
❑ 58 Lui Antonio VL 25.00 60.00
❑ 59 Marcello Ferreira L 20.00 50.00
❑ 60 Mark Dos Santos VL 20.00 50.00
❑ 61 Marlo Lodrigueza S
❑ 62 Mauro Fodra L 30.00 80.00
❑ 63 Melike Sevim Acar S
❑ 64 Michael Glover EL 20.00 50.00
❑ 65 Nestor Celario Jr EL 30.00 80.00
❑ 66 Nick Yakimovich EL 12.00 30.00
❑ 67 Nur Hanie Mohd EL 40.00 100.00
❑ 68 Patrick Larcada S
❑ 69 Raimundo Nonato L 12.00 30.00
❑ 70 Randy Martinez EL 15.00 40.00
❑ 71 Randy Monces VL 25.00 60.00
❑ 72 Remy Eisu Mokhtar EL 40.00 100.00
❑ 73 Rhiannon Owens VL 40.00 100.00
❑ 74 Richard Cox EL 75.00 150.00
❑ 75 Rodrigo Martins EL 12.00 30.00
❑ 76 Roy Cover EL
❑ 77 Scott Barnett EL 30.00 80.00
❑ 78 Scott Rorie EL 25.00 60.00
❑ 79 Steven Miller S

❑ 80 Thanh Bui L 25.00 60.00
❑ 81 Tim Shay EL 20.00 50.00
❑ 82 Tone Rodriguez EL 15.00 40.00
❑ 83 Wendell Rubio Silva EL 20.00 50.00
❑ 84 Zane Donnellan EL
❑ 85 Lak Lim/ (issued as 6-case incentive) 60.00 150.00
❑ 86 Anthony Tan/ (issued as 9-case incentive) 250.00 450.00
❑ 87 Andy Price 75.00 150.00
issued as hot box exclusive)
❑ 88 Chachi Hernandez
Gabe Hernandez/ (issued as hot box exclusive)
❑ 89 Guy Dorian/ (issued as hot box exclusive)
❑ 90 Ian Dorian/ (issued as hot box exclusive)

2010 Paranormal Activity

COMPLETE SET (50) 4.00 10.00
❑ 1 A Perfect Life .10 .30
❑ 2 Micah Sloat .10 .30
❑ 3 Katie Featherston .10 .30
❑ 4 Are You Happy .10 .30
❑ 5 Night 1 .10 .30
❑ 6 The First Event .10 .30
❑ 7 The Psychic - Dr. Fredrichs .10 .30
❑ 8 I Couldn't Even Move .10 .30
❑ 9 You Cannot Run From This .10 .30
❑ 10 Night 3 .10 .30
❑ 11 Micah and the Demon .10 .30
❑ 12 Night 5 .10 .30
❑ 13 Girl Time with Amber .10 .30
❑ 14 Communicating With Evil .10 .30
❑ 15 Night 13 .10 .30
❑ 16 EVP Experiment Number One .10 .30
❑ 17 Night 15 .10 .30
❑ 18 Katie Loses Control .10 .30
❑ 19 Katie's Trance .10 .30
❑ 20 Katie is Shocked .10 .30
❑ 21 Don't Open That Door .10 .30
❑ 22 The Doorway to Evil .10 .30
❑ 23 Deciphering the Message .10 .30
❑ 24 A Question Not to Be Asked .10 .30
❑ 25 Micah's Experiment .10 .30
❑ 26 Night 17 .10 .30
❑ 27 Demonic Traces .10 .30
❑ 28 Don't Go In There .10 .30
❑ 29 Poor Little Katie .10 .30
❑ 30 Night 18 .10 .30
❑ 31 Katie Pleads With Micah .10 .30
❑ 32 Broken Dreams .10 .30
❑ 33 A Plea For Help .10 .30
❑ 34 Night 19 .10 .30
❑ 35 The Unimaginable .10 .30
❑ 36 Unfortunately, You're Not Alone .10 .30
❑ 37 The Tragedy of Diane .10 .30
❑ 38 Overwhelming Stress .10 .30
❑ 39 A Bloodcurdling Night .10 .30
❑ 40 The Mark of Evil .10 .30
❑ 41 Please Save Me .10 .30
❑ 42 Everything is Gonna Be Alright .10 .30
❑ 43 Night 21 .10 .30
❑ 44 Katie is Possessed .10 .30
❑ 45 Katie Shrieks .10 .30
❑ 46 Micah is Attacked .10 .30
❑ 47 The Katie We Knew is Gone .10 .30
❑ 48 Micah is Gone .10 .30
❑ 49 Evil Has Triumphed .10 .30
❑ 50 Checklist .10 .30

2010 Paranormal Activity Autographs

OVERALL AUTO/MEM/FILM ODDS TWO PER PACK
❑ 1 Oren Peli 8.00 20.00
❑ 2 Katie Featherston 20.00 40.00
❑ 3 Micah Sloat 8.00 20.00
❑ 4 Katie Featherston 25.00 50.00
Micah Sloat

2010 Paranormal Activity Costumes

OVERALL AUTO/MEM/FILM ODDS TWO PER BOX
❑ C1 Micah Sloat 8.00 20.00
❑ C2 Katie Featherston 10.00 25.00
❑ C3 Micah Sloat 8.00 20.00
❑ C4 Katie Featherston 10.00 25.00

2010 Paranormal Activity Costumes Autographs

OVERALL AUTO/MEM/FILM ODDS TWO PER BOX
❑ CI1 Katie Featherston 20.00 40.00
❑ CI2 Micah Sloat 8.00 20.00

2010 Paranormal Activity Film Frames

OVERALL AUTO/MEM/FILM ODDS TWO PER BOX
❑ 1 Slippers 8.00 20.00
❑ 2 Micah and Katie 8.00 20.00
❑ 3 TV 8.00 20.00

2010 Paranormal Activity Portents of Evil

COMPLETE SET (9) 4.00 10.00
STATED ODDS ONE PER PACK

2010 Paranormal Activity Puzzle

COMPLETE SET (9) 4.00 10.00
STATED ODDS ONE PER PACK

2010 Pop Century

COMPLETE SET (99)
❑ AB1 Amber Benson AU 8.00 20.00
❑ AC1 Adrianne Curry AU 8.00 20.00
❑ AD1 Annie Duke AU 8.00 20.00
❑ AJ1 Ashley Judd AU 40.00 80.00
❑ AO1 Aubrey O'Day AU 10.00 25.00
❑ AP1 Adrian Pasdar AU 8.00 20.00
❑ AP2 Audrina Patridge AU 8.00 20.00
❑ AT1 Andrea Thompson AU 8.00 20.00
❑ AW1 Amy Weber AU 8.00 20.00
❑ BB1 Beau Bridges AU 8.00 20.00
❑ BC1 Bruce Campbell AU 12.00 30.00
❑ BD1 Bo Derek AU
❑ BF1 Bethenny-Frankel AU 10.00 25.00
❑ BJ1 Bruce Jenner AU 8.00 20.00
❑ BP1 Butch Patrick AU 10.00 25.00
❑ BW1 Barry Williams AU 6.00 15.00
❑ CA1 Christian Audigier AU 6.00 15.00
❑ CB1 Corbin Bernsen AU 10.00 25.00
❑ CC1 Charisma Carpenter AU 20.00 50.00
❑ CJ1 Christopher Judge AU 12.00 30.00
❑ CK1 Christopher Knight AU 10.00 25.00
❑ CL1 Christopher Lloyd AU 35.00 70.00
❑ DB1 Debby Boone AU 8.00 20.00
❑ DD1 Donna D'Errico AU 10.00 25.00
❑ DD2 Donna Douglas AU 10.00 25.00
❑ DJ1 Davy Jones AU 50.00 100.00
❑ DW1 Dawn Wells AU 20.00 50.00
❑ E1 Elvira AU 60.00 120.00
❑ EB1 Ernest Borgnine AU 20.00 50.00
❑ EE1 Erika Eleniak AU 10.00 25.00
❑ EG1 Erin Gray AU 12.00 30.00
❑ GG1 Gil Gerard AU 10.00 25.00
❑ HF1 Harrison Ford AU 400.00 600.00
❑ HP1 Hayden Panettiere AU 75.00 150.00
❑ HS1 Helen Slater AU 12.00 30.00
❑ HW1 Henry Winkler AU 35.00 70.00
❑ IT1 Ice-T AU 10.00 25.00
❑ JC1 Jeff Conaway AU 6.00 15.00
❑ JC2 Jennifer Coolidge AU 10.00 25.00
❑ JD1 Joyce DeWitt AU 15.00 40.00
❑ JG1 Justin Guarini AU 6.00 15.00
❑ JG2 Jennie Garth AU 15.00 40.00
❑ JK1 Jennifer Korbin AU 10.00 25.00
❑ JKL James Kyson Lee AU 6.00 15.00
❑ JM1 Jason Momoa AU 8.00 20.00
❑ JRD John Rhys-Davies AU
❑ JS1 Jewel Staite AU 15.00 40.00
❑ JS2 John Schneider AU 10.00 25.00
❑ JT1 Jeffrey Tambor AU 8.00 20.00
❑ JW1 Jimmie Walker AU 10.00 25.00
❑ KK1 Khloe Kardashian AU 15.00 40.00
❑ KK2 Kim Kardashian AU 75.00 150.00
❑ KK3 Kourtney Kardashian AU 20.00 50.00
❑ KL1 Kristanna Loken AU 15.00 40.00
❑ KP1 Kirsten Prout AU 15.00 40.00
❑ KS1 Kevin Sorbo AU 6.00 15.00
❑ KW1 Kendra Wilkinson AU 15.00 40.00
❑ LB1 Levar Burton AU 10.00 25.00
❑ LB2 Linda Blair AU 15.00 40.00
❑ LH1 Lauren Holly AU 35.00 70.00
❑ LH2 Larry Hagman AU 20.00 60.00
❑ LH3 Linda Hamilton AU
❑ LT1 Lea Thompson AU 15.00 40.00
❑ MF1 Mira Furlan AU 8.00 20.00
❑ MH1 Mark Hamill AU 75.00 150.00
❑ MK1 Margot Kidder AU 8.00 20.00
❑ MR1 Mickey Rooney AU 20.00 50.00
❑ MSJ Mia St. John AU 6.00 15.00
❑ NE1 Nicole Eggert AU 25.00 60.00
❑ NN1 Nichelle Nichols AU 12.00 30.00
❑ PA1 Pamela Anderson AU 75.00 150.00
❑ PF1 Peter Fonda AU 30.00 80.00
❑ PM1 Peter Mayhew AU 6.00 15.00
❑ PR1 Paul Rodriguez AU 6.00 15.00
❑ RC1 Richard Chamberlain AU 20.00 50.00
❑ RD1 Richard Dreyfuss AU 15.00 40.00
❑ RH1 Ron Howard AU 40.00 80.00
❑ RK1 Richard Kiel AU 10.00 25.00
❑ RM1 Rita Moreno AU 12.00 30.00
❑ SA1 Sean Astin AU 8.00 20.00
❑ SD1 Sarah Douglas AU 8.00 20.00
❑ SF1 Steve-O AU 10.00 25.00
❑ SL1 Shayne Lamas AU 8.00 20.00
❑ SL2 Stan Lee AU 50.00 100.00
❑ SO1 Stephen Furst AU 8.00 20.00
❑ SP1 Stephanie Pratt AU 10.00 25.00
❑ T1 Tiffany AU 15.00 40.00
❑ TB1 Todd Bridges AU 6.00 15.00
❑ TC1 Tia Carrere AU 15.00 40.00
❑ TD1 Taylor Dayne AU 10.00 25.00
❑ TD2 Thomas Dekker AU 8.00 20.00
❑ TM1 Taryn Manning AU 8.00 20.00
❑ TR1 Tanya Roberts AU 10.00 25.00
❑ TS1 Tori Spelling AU 8.00 20.00
❑ TUC The Unknown Comic AU 10.00 25.00
(Murray Langston)
❑ VT1 Verne Troyer AU 12.00 30.00
❑ WAY Weird Al Yankovic AU 20.00 50.00
❑ WJ1 Wynonna Judd AU 20.00 50.00
❑ WS1 William Shatner AU 50.00 100.00

2010 Pop Century Silver

UNPRICED SILVER PRINT RUN 5-25

2010 Pop Century Gold

UNPRICED GOLD PRINT RUN 1-5

2010 Pop Century Authentic Costumes Blue

OVERALL COSTUME ODDS 3 PER PACK
❑ SW1 50 Cent 5.00 12.00
❑ SW2 Adam Sandler 5.00 12.00
❑ SW3 Ali Larter 6.00 15.00
❑ SW4 Amy Adams 5.00 12.00
❑ SW5 Anne Hathaway 6.00 15.00
❑ SW6 Anthony Hopkins 5.00 12.00
❑ SW7 Arnold Schwarzenegger 8.00 20.00
❑ SW8 Ashley Judd 8.00 20.00
❑ SW9 Bill Murray 5.00 12.00
❑ SW10 Jon Bon Jovi 10.00 25.00
❑ SW11 Brad Pitt 6.00 15.00
❑ SW12 Brenda Song 6.00 15.00
❑ SW13 Britney Spears 15.00 40.00
❑ SW14 Brittany Murphy 8.00 20.00
❑ SW15 Cameron Diaz 10.00 25.00
❑ SW16 Charlie Sheen 6.00 15.00
❑ SW17 Colin Ferrell 5.00 12.00
❑ SW18 Corey Haim 8.00 20.00
❑ SW19 Courteney Cox 5.00 12.00
❑ SW20 Denzel Washington 5.00 12.00
❑ SW21 Drew Barrymore 6.00 15.00
❑ SW22 Dustin Hoffman 8.00 20.00
❑ SW23 Ed Norton Jr. 5.00 12.00
❑ SW24 Elisha Cuthbert 6.00 15.00
❑ SW25 Eliza Dushku 8.00 20.00
❑ SW26 Forest Whitaker 5.00 12.00
❑ SW27 Gwyneth Paltrow 6.00 15.00
❑ SW28 Harrison Ford 6.00 15.00
❑ SW29 Hilary Duff 8.00 20.00
❑ SW30 Jack Black 5.00 12.00
❑ SW31 Jack Nicholson 6.00 15.00
❑ SW32 Jaime Pressly 6.00 15.00
❑ SW33 Jeremy Piven 5.00 12.00
❑ SW34 John Wayne 12.00 30.00
❑ SW35 Jude Law 5.00 12.00
❑ SW36 Cate Blanchett 6.00 15.00
❑ SW37 Katherine Heigl 6.00 15.00
❑ SW38 Keri Russell 5.00 12.00
❑ SW39 Kevin Spacey 5.00 12.00
❑ SW40 Madonna 25.00 50.00
❑ SW41 Michelle Williams 5.00 12.00
❑ SW42 Mira Sorvino 5.00 12.00
❑ SW43 Morgan Freeman 5.00 12.00
❑ SW44 Richard Gere 5.00 12.00
❑ SW45 Russell Crow UER 5.00 12.00
❑ SW46 Sacha Baron Cohen 5.00 12.00
❑ SW47 Teri Hatcher 6.00 15.00
❑ SW48 Tom Hanks 5.00 12.00
❑ SW49 Uma Thurman 6.00 15.00
❑ SW50 Vince Vaughn 5.00 12.00

2010 Pop Century Authentic Costumes Red

STATED PRINT RUN 20 SER. #'d SETS
UNPRICED DUE TO SCARCITY

2010 Pop Century Authentic Costumes Gold

STATED PRINT RUN 5 SER. #'d SETS
UNPRICED DUE TO SCARCITY

2010 Pop Century Authentic Cut Signatures

STATED PRINT RUN 1 SER. #'d SET
UNPRICED DUE TO SCARCITY
❑ 1 Al Jolson
❑ 2 Andy Kaufman
❑ 3 Arthur Conan Doyle
❑ 4 Bettie Page
❑ 5 Boss Tweed
❑ 6 Charles Dickens
❑ 7 Charles Lindbergh
❑ 8 Charlie Chaplin
❑ 9 Clarence Darrow
❑ 10 Fidel Castro
❑ 11 Frank Sinatra
❑ 12 Fred Astaire
❑ 13 George Bush Sr.
❑ 14 Groucho Marx
❑ 15 Grover Cleveland
❑ 16 Harry Truman
❑ 17 J.C. Penny
❑ 18 Janis Joplin
❑ 19 Jimmy Hoffa
❑ 20 Joe DiMaggio
❑ 21 Joe Louis
❑ 22 John F. Kennedy
❑ 23 John Phillip Sousa
❑ 24 John Quincy Adams
❑ 25 King George VI
❑ 26 Lyndon Baines Johnson
❑ 27 Madonna
❑ 28 Mark Twain
❑ 29 Michael Jordan
❑ 30 Muhammad Ali
❑ 31 Oliver Wendell Holmes
❑ 32 P.T. Barnum
❑ 33 Pope Benedict XV
❑ 34 Pope Gregory XVI
❑ 35 Pope Pius XI
❑ 36 Pope Pius XII
❑ 37 Queen Elizabeth II
❑ 38 Red Auerbach
❑ 39 Richard Nixon
❑ 40 Ringo Starr
❑ 41 Robert Kennedy
❑ 42 Roger Maris
❑ 43 Ronald Reagan
❑ 44 Roy Orbison
❑ 45 Ted Kennedy
❑ 46 W.C. Fields
❑ 47 William Jennings Bryan
❑ 48 William McKinley
❑ 49 William Taft
❑ 50 Woodrow Wilson
❑ 51 Buddy Holly

2010 Pop Century Award Winners Autographs Blue

STATED PRINT RUN 10-100
❑ AWAD1 Annie Duke/50 10.00 25.00
❑ AWBB1 Beau Bridges/100 8.00 20.00
❑ AWBJ1 Bruce Jenner/100 8.00 20.00
❑ AWCL1 Christopher Lloyd50 35.00 70.00
❑ AWEB1 Ernest Borgnine/20
❑ AWEF1 Edward Furlong/50 12.00 30.00
❑ AWHP1 Hayden Panettiere/20 75.00 150.00
❑ AWHW1 Henry Winkler/50 25.00 50.00
❑ AWLB1 Linda Blair/50 15.00 40.00
❑ AWLH1 Lauren Holly/50 35.00 70.00
❑ AWLH3 Linda Hamilton/50 25.00 50.00
❑ AWLT1 Lea Thompson/50 15.00 40.00
❑ AWLW1 Lindsay Wagner/50 25.00 50.00
❑ AWMR1 Mickey Rooney/50 30.00 60.00
❑ AWPF1 Peter Fonda/10
❑ AWRC1 Richard Chamberlain/50 15.00 40.00
❑ AWRD1 Richard Dreyfuss/20 15.00 40.00
❑ AWRH1 Ron Howard/10
❑ AWRM1 Rita Moreno/50 15.00 40.00
❑ AWSA1 Sean Astin/100 8.00 20.00
❑ AWVT1 Verne Troyer/100 10.00 25.00
❑ AWWAY Weird Al Yankovic/100 20.00 50.00
❑ AWWJ1 Wynonna Judd/50 20.00 50.00
❑ AWWS1 William Shatner/20 50.00 100.00

2010 Pop Century Award Winners Autographs Red

UNPRICED RED PRINT RUN 5-25

2010 Pop Century Award Winners Autographs Silver

STATED PRINT RUN 5 SER. #'d SETS
UNPRICED DUE TO SCARCITY

2010 Pop Century Co-Stars Autographs Silver

STATED PRINT RUN 25 SER. #'d SETS
❑ CSACCK Adrianne Curry
Christopher Knight
❑ CSAJWJ Ashley Judd
Wynonna Judd
❑ CSAPCB Adrian Pasdar
Corbin Bernsen
❑ CSAPSD Adrian Pasdar
Sarah Douglas
❑ CSAPSP Audrina Patridge
Stephanie Pratt
❑ CSBBCJ Beau Bridges 25.00 50.00
Christopher Judge
❑ CSBBJS Beau Bridges
John Schneider
❑ CSBCCB Bruce Campbell
Corbin Bernsen
❑ CSBWCK Barry Williams
Christopher Knight
❑ CSBWT Barry Williams
Tiffany
❑ CSCBCA Corbin Bernsen
Christopher Atkins
❑ CSCSKP Christian Serrates
Kirsten Prout
❑ CSDJBP Davy Jones
Butch Patrick
❑ CSECAB Emma Caulfield
Amber Benson
❑ CSEEDE Erika Eleniak
Donna D'Errico
❑ CSEENE Erika Eleniak
Nicole Eggert
❑ CSEJC Elvira
Jeff Conaway
❑ CSGGEG Gil Gerard 35.00 70.00
Erin Gray
❑ CSHPAP Hayden Panettiere
Adrian Pasdar
❑ CSITEE Ice-T
Erika Eleniak
❑ CSJCCL Jeff Conaway
Christopher Lloyd
❑ CSJMCJ Jason Momoa
Christopher Judge
❑ CSJSBB Jewel Staite
Beau Bridges
❑ CSJSCJ Jewel Staite 20.00 40.00
Christopher Judge
❑ CSJSHS John Schneider
Helen Slater
❑ CSJTCB Jeffrey Tambor
Corbin Bernsen
❑ CSJTCL Jeffrey Tambor 30.00 60.00
Christopher Lloyd
❑ CSJTHS Jeffrey Tambor
Helen Slater
❑ CSKLIT Kristanna Loken 20.00 40.00
Ice-T
❑ CSKSIT Kevin Sorbo
Ice-T
❑ CSLBEB Linda Blair
Ernest Borgnine
❑ CSLHEF Linda Hamilton
Edward Furlong
❑ CSLTBP Larry Thomas
Butch Patrick
❑ CSLTCL Lea Thompson
Christopher Lloyd
❑ CSLTFW Larry Thomas
Fred Williamson
❑ CSLTJT Larry Thomas
Jeffrey Tambor
❑ CSLWEB Lindsay Wagner 25.00 50.00
Ernest Borgnine
❑ CSMBLH Michael Biehn 50.00 100.00
Linda Hamilton
❑ CSNEDE Nicole Eggert
Donna D'Errico
❑ CSNEEG Nicole Eggert
Erin Gray
❑ CSPADE Pamela Anderson
Donna D'Errico
❑ CSPAEE Pamela Anderson
Erika Eleniak
❑ CSPAJM Pamela Anderson
Jason Momoa
❑ CSPANE Pamela Anderson
Nicole Eggert
❑ CSPMMH Peter Mayhew
Mark Hamill
❑ CSPRJC Paul Rodriguez
Jennifer Coolidge
❑ CSPSCL Patrick Stewart
Christopher Lloyd
❑ CSPSMH Patrick Stewart
Mark Hamill
❑ CSPSSL Patrick Stewart
Stan Lee
❑ CSPSWS Patrick Stewart
William Shatner
❑ CSRHHW Ron Howard
Henry Winkler
❑ CSRHRD Ron Howard
Richard Dreyfuss
❑ CSRKDJ Richard Kiel
Davy Jones
❑ CSRKMR Richard Kiel
Mickey Rooney
❑ CSSDCJ Sarah Douglas
Christopher Judge
❑ CSSDMF Sarah Douglas
Mira Furlan
❑ CSSDMK Sarah Douglas
Margot Kidder
❑ CSSDNE Sarah Douglas
Nicole Eggert
❑ CSSFMF Stephen Furst
Mira Furlan
❑ CSTBLT Todd Bridges
Lea Thompson
❑ CSTCKS Tia Carrere
Kevin Sorbo
❑ CSTRJC Tanya Roberts
Jeff Conaway
❑ CSTRMB Tanya Roberts
Michael Biehn
❑ CSTSJG Tori Spelling 30.00 60.00
Jennie Garth
❑ CSWSNN William Shatner
Nichelle Nichols
❑ CSAPJKL Adrian Pasdar
James Kyson Lee
❑ CSHPJKL Hayden Panettiere
James Kyson Lee
❑ CSJRDJT John Rhys-Davies 25.00 50.00
Jeffrey Tambor
❑ CSKKKK1 Kim Kardashian
Khloe Kardashian
❑ CSKKKK2 Kim Kardashian
Kourtney Kardashian
❑ CSKKKK3 Kourtney Kardashian
Khloe Kardashian
❑ CSNNJKL Nichelle Nichols
James Kyson Lee
❑ CSPSJRD Patrick Stewart
John Rhys-Davies
❑ CSRCJRD Richard Chamberlain
John Rhys-Davies
❑ CSSAJRD Sean Astin 25.00 50.00
John Rhys-Davies
❑ CSTCJRD Tia Carrere
John Rhys-Davies

2010 Pop Century Co-Stars Autographs Gold

STATED PRINT RUN 5 SER. #'d SETS
UNPRICED DUE TO SCARCITY

2010 Pop Century Signatures Preview

❑ 1 Christopher Kid Reid/ (2010 Ink Vault) 5.00 10.00
❑ 2 Audrina Patridge/ (2010 Ink Vault) 10.00 20.00
❑ 3 Annie Duke/ (2010 Razor Poker) 12.00 25.00

2010 The Quotable Star Trek Movies

COMPLETE SET (90) 5.00 12.00
❑ 1 Star Trek: The Motion Picture .15 .40
❑ 2 Star Trek: The Motion Picture .15 .40
❑ 3 Star Trek: The Motion Picture .15 .40
❑ 4 Star Trek: The Motion Picture .15 .40
❑ 5 Star Trek: The Motion Picture .15 .40
❑ 6 Star Trek: The Motion Picture .15 .40
❑ 7 Star Trek: The Motion Picture .15 .40
❑ 8 Star Trek: The Motion Picture .15 .40
❑ 9 Star Trek: The Motion Picture .15 .40
❑ 10 Star Trek II: The Wrath of Khan .15 .40
❑ 11 Star Trek II: The Wrath of Khan .15 .40
❑ 12 Star Trek II: The Wrath of Khan .15 .40
❑ 13 Star Trek II: The Wrath of Khan .15 .40
❑ 14 Star Trek II: The Wrath of Khan .15 .40
❑ 15 Star Trek II: The Wrath of Khan .15 .40
❑ 16 Star Trek II: The Wrath of Khan .15 .40
❑ 17 Star Trek II: The Wrath of Khan .15 .40
❑ 18 Star Trek II: The Wrath of Khan .15 .40
❑ 19 Star Trek III: The Search for Spock .15 .40
❑ 20 Star Trek III: The Search for Spock .15 .40
❑ 21 Star Trek III: The Search for Spock .15 .40
❑ 22 Star Trek III: The Search for Spock .15 .40
❑ 23 Star Trek III: The Search for Spock .15 .40
❑ 24 Star Trek III: The Search for Spock .15 .40
❑ 25 Star Trek III: The Search for Spock .15 .40
❑ 26 Star Trek III: The Search for Spock .15 .40
❑ 27 Star Trek III: The Search for Spock .15 .40
❑ 28 Star Trek IV: The Voyage Home .15 .40
❑ 29 Star Trek IV: The Voyage Home .15 .40
❑ 30 Star Trek IV: The Voyage Home .15 .40
❑ 31 Star Trek IV: The Voyage Home .15 .40
❑ 32 Star Trek IV: The Voyage Home .15 .40
❑ 33 Star Trek IV: The Voyage Home .15 .40
❑ 34 Star Trek IV: The Voyage Home .15 .40
❑ 35 Star Trek IV: The Voyage Home .15 .40
❑ 36 Star Trek IV: The Voyage Home .15 .40
❑ 37 Star Trek V: The Final Frontier .15 .40
❑ 38 Star Trek V: The Final Frontier .15 .40
❑ 39 Star Trek V: The Final Frontier .15 .40
❑ 40 Star Trek V: The Final Frontier .15 .40
❑ 41 Star Trek V: The Final Frontier .15 .40
❑ 42 Star Trek V: The Final Frontier .15 .40
❑ 43 Star Trek V: The Final Frontier .15 .40
❑ 44 Star Trek V: The Final Frontier .15 .40
❑ 45 Star Trek V: The Final Frontier .15 .40
❑ 46 Star Trek VI: The Undiscovered Country .15 .40
❑ 47 Star Trek VI: The Undiscovered Country .15 .40
❑ 48 Star Trek VI: The Undiscovered Country .15 .40
❑ 49 Star Trek VI: The Undiscovered Country .15 .40
❑ 50 Star Trek VI: The Undiscovered Country .15 .40
❑ 51 Star Trek VI: The Undiscovered Country .15 .40
❑ 52 Star Trek VI: The Undiscovered Country .15 .40
❑ 53 Star Trek VI: The Undiscovered Country .15 .40
❑ 54 Star Trek VI: The Undiscovered Country .15 .40
❑ 55 Star Trek: Generations .15 .40
❑ 56 Star Trek: Generations .15 .40
❑ 57 Star Trek: Generations .15 .40
❑ 58 Star Trek: Generations .15 .40
❑ 59 Star Trek: Generations .15 .40
❑ 60 Star Trek: Generations .15 .40
❑ 61 Star Trek: Generations .15 .40
❑ 62 Star Trek: Generations .15 .40
❑ 63 Star Trek: Generations .15 .40
❑ 64 Star Trek: First Contact .15 .40
❑ 65 Star Trek: First Contact .15 .40
❑ 66 Star Trek: First Contact .15 .40
❑ 67 Star Trek: First Contact .15 .40
❑ 68 Star Trek: First Contact .15 .40
❑ 69 Star Trek: First Contact .15 .40
❑ 70 Star Trek: First Contact .15 .40
❑ 71 Star Trek: First Contact .15 .40
❑ 72 Star Trek: First Contact .15 .40
❑ 73 Star Trek: Insurrection .15 .40
❑ 74 Star Trek: Insurrection .15 .40
❑ 75 Star Trek: Insurrection .15 .40
❑ 76 Star Trek: Insurrection .15 .40
❑ 77 Star Trek: Insurrection .15 .40
❑ 78 Star Trek: Insurrection .15 .40
❑ 79 Star Trek: Insurrection .15 .40
❑ 80 Star Trek: Insurrection .15 .40
❑ 81 Star Trek: Insurrection .15 .40
❑ 82 Star Trek Nemesis .15 .40
❑ 83 Star Trek Nemesis .15 .40
❑ 84 Star Trek Nemesis .15 .40
❑ 85 Star Trek Nemesis .15 .40
❑ 86 Star Trek Nemesis .15 .40
❑ 87 Star Trek Nemesis .15 .40
❑ 88 Star Trek Nemesis .15 .40
❑ 89 Star Trek Nemesis .15 .40
❑ 90 Star Trek Nemesis .15 .40

2010 The Quotable Star Trek Movies Autographs

STATED ODDS THREE PER BOX
A96 ISSUED AS 3-CASE INCENTIVE
L (LIMITED): 300-500 COPIES
VL (VERY LIMITED): 200-300 COPIES
❑ A56 Kurtwood Smith/(Federation President) L 10.00 25.00
❑ A59 Kim Cattrall/(Lt. Valeris) L 30.00 60.00
❑ A77 Glenn Morshower/(Enterprise-B Navigations Officer) 6.00 15.00
❑ A78 Brian Thompson/(Klingon Helmsman) 6.00 15.00
❑ A79 Marnie McPhail/(Eiger) 6.00 15.00
❑ A80 Marcy Lafferty/(Chief DiFalco) 6.00 15.00
❑ A81 Gates McFadden/(Dr. Beverly Crusher) VL 40.00 80.00
❑ A82 Shannon Cochran/(Senator Tal'aura) 6.00 15.00
❑ A83b Alan Ruck/(Capt. John Harriman) 8.00 20.00
❑ A83a Paul Kent/(Lt. Cmdr. Beach) 6.00 15.00
❑ A84 John Vargas/(Jedda) 6.00 15.00
❑ A85 Bruce French/(Son'a Officer) 6.00 15.00
❑ A86 Larry Anderson/(Tarlac Officer) 6.00 15.00
❑ A87 Paul Rossilli/(Brig. General Kerla) 6.00 15.00
❑ A88 John Larroquette/(Maltz) L 20.00 40.00
❑ A89 Tommy Hinkley/(Journalist) 6.00 15.00
❑ A90 Jon Kamal Rashad/(Commander Sonak) 6.00 15.00
❑ A91 Rex Holman/(J'onn) VL 50.00 100.00
❑ A92 Jeff Lester/(FBI Agent) 6.00 15.00
❑ A93 Levar Burton/(Lt. Commander Geordi LaForge) VL 60.00 120.00
❑ A94 John Winston/(Commander Kyle) L 12.00 30.00
❑ A95 Michael Dorn/(Worf) VL 50.00 100.00
❑ A96 Michael Dorn/(Colonel Worf)/(issued as three-case incentive) 60.00 120.00
❑ A97 Jonathan Frakes/(Will Riker) VL 60.00 120.00
❑ A98 Michael Horton/(Lt. Daniels) L 10.00 25.00
❑ A99 Breon Gorman/(Lt. Curtis) 6.00 15.00
❑ A100 Brent Spiner/(Data) VL 50.00 100.00
❑ A101 Daniel Hugh Kelly/(Sojef) L 10.00 25.00
❑ A102 Mark Deakins/(Tournel) 6.00 15.00

❑ A103 Peggy Miley/(Regent Cuzar) 6.00 15.00
❑ A104 Dina Meyer/(Commander Donatra) 8.00 20.00
❑ A105 Dwight Schultz/(Lt. Reginald Barclay) VL50.00 100.00
❑ A106 Alan Dale/(Praetor Hiren) 6.00 15.00
❑ A108 Olivia Hack/(Olivia Picard) 6.00 15.00
❑ A109 Gregg Henry/(Gallatin) 6.00 15.00
❑ A110 Rick Worthy/(Elloran Officer) 6.00 15.00
❑ A112 Jude Ciccolella/(Commander Suran) 6.00 15.00

2010 The Quotable Star Trek Movies Bridge Crew Patches

COMPLETE SET (9) 350.00 650.00
STATED ODDS 1:110
STATED PRINT RUN 250 SER. #'d SETS

❑ PC1 Admiral Kirk 50.00 100.00
❑ PC2 Spock 50.00 100.00
❑ PC3 Dr. McCoy 50.00 100.00
❑ PC4 Commander Scott 40.00 80.00
❑ PC5 Lt. Commander Uhura 50.00 100.00
❑ PC6 Lt. Commander Sulu 40.00 80.00
❑ PC7 Lt. Chekov 40.00 80.00
❑ PC8 Dr. Chapel 40.00 80.00
❑ PC9 CPO Rand 40.00 80.00

2010 The Quotable Star Trek Movies Costumes

BS ISSUED AS 6-CASE INCENTIVE
MC17 ISSUED AS CASE TOPPER

❑ BS Brent Spiner AU/(issued as six-case incentive)150.00300.00
❑ MC17 Data Invisibility Suit/(issued as case topper) 15.00 40.00

2010 The Quotable Star Trek Movies Movie Posters

COMPLETE SET (10) 12.00 30.00
STATED ODDS 1:12

❑ MP1 Star Trek: The Motion Picture 2.00 5.00
❑ MP2 Star Trek II: The Wrath of Khan 2.00 5.00
❑ MP3 Star Trek III: The Search for Spock 2.00 5.00
❑ MP4 Star Trek IV: The Voyage Home 2.00 5.00
❑ MP5 Star Trek V: The Final Frontier 2.00 5.00
❑ MP6 Star Trek VI: The Undiscovered Country 2.00 5.00
❑ MP7 Star Trek: Generations 2.00 5.00
❑ MP8 Star Trek: First Contact 2.00 5.00
❑ MP9 Star Trek: Insurrection 2.00 5.00
❑ MP10 Star Trek Nemesis 2.00 5.00

2010 The Quotable Star Trek Movies Promos

❑ P1 Worf
❑ P2 Kirk
❑ P3 Enterprise/(issued in collectors album)

2010 The Quotable Star Trek Movies Transitions

COMPLETE SET (9) 12.00 30.00
STATED ODDS 1:12

❑ T1 Kirk 2.50 6.00
❑ T2 Spock 2.50 6.00
❑ T3 McCoy 2.00 5.00
❑ T4 Scotty 2.00 5.00
❑ T5 Uhura 2.00 5.00
❑ T6 Sulu 2.00 5.00
❑ T7 Chekov 2.00 5.00
❑ T8 Chapel 2.00 5.00
❑ T9 Rand 2.00 5.00
❑ T10 USS Enterprise NCC-1701 SP 10.00 25.00
(issued as Rittenhouse Reward)

2010 The Quotable Star Trek Movies Women of Star Trek Expansion

COMPLETE SET (9) 5.00 12.00
STATED ODDS 1:6

❑ 82 Lt. Ilya from Star Trek: The Motion Picture .75 2.00
❑ 83 Dr. Carol Marcus from Star Trek II: The Wrath of Khan .75 2.00
❑ 84 Lt. Saavik from Star Trek III: The Search for Spock .75 2.00
❑ 85 Dr. Gillian Taylor from Star Trek IV: The Voyage Home .75 2.00
❑ 86 Lt. Valeris from Star Trek VI: The Undiscovered Country .75 2.00
❑ 87 Lursa & B'Etor from Star Trek: Generations .75 2.00
❑ 88 Borg Queen from Star Trek: First Contact .75 2.00
❑ 89 Lily Sloane from Star Trek: First Contact .75 2.00
❑ 90 Anij from Star Trek: Insurrection .75 2.00

2010 Razor Poker

❑ 1 Antonio Esfandiari 6.00 15.00
❑ 2 Bill Edler 6.00 15.00
❑ 3 Chad Brown 6.00 15.00
❑ 4 Chris Moneymaker 6.00 15.00
❑ 5 Cindy Margolis 10.00 25.00
❑ 6 Cyndy Violette 8.00 20.00
❑ 7 Daniel Negreanu 12.00 30.00
❑ 8 David Chiu 6.00 15.00
❑ 9 David Pham
❑ 10 David Williams 6.00 15.00
❑ 11 Erica Schoenberg 8.00 20.00
❑ 12 Erick Lindgren 6.00 15.00
❑ 13 Evelyn Ng 8.00 20.00
❑ 14 Gavin Smith 6.00 15.00
❑ 15 Hoyt Corkins 6.00 15.00
❑ 16 Humberto Brenes 6.00 15.00
❑ 17 Isabelle Mercier 8.00 20.00
❑ 18 Ivan Demidov 6.00 15.00
❑ 19 Jamie Gold 6.00 15.00
❑ 20 Jean-Robert Bellande 6.00 15.00
❑ 21 Jennifer Harman 8.00 20.00
❑ 22 Jerry Buss 8.00 20.00
❑ 23 Joe Hachem 6.00 15.00
❑ 24 Josh Arieh 6.00 15.00
❑ 25 Kenny Tran 6.00 15.00
❑ 26 Lacey Jones UER/ (name spelled Lacy on back)8.00 20.00
❑ 27 Layne Flack 6.00 15.00
❑ 28 Marco Traniello 6.00 15.00
❑ 29 Men Nguyen 6.00 15.00
❑ 30 Michael Mizrachi 6.00 15.00
❑ 31 Mike Matusow 8.00 20.00
❑ 32 Nam Le 6.00 15.00
❑ 33 Patrik Antonius 6.00 15.00
❑ 34 Paul Wasicka 6.00 15.00
❑ 35 Phil Gordon 6.00 15.00
❑ 36 Phil Hellmuth 35.00 70.00
❑ 37 Scott Fischman
❑ 38 Scott Montgomery 6.00 15.00
❑ 39 Scotty Nguyen 6.00 15.00
❑ 40 TJ Cloutier 6.00 15.00
❑ 41 Todd Brunson 6.00 15.00
❑ 42 Tom Dwan 10.00 25.00
❑ 43 Vanessa Rousso 12.00 30.00
❑ SU1 Stu Ungar MEM 25.00 60.00

2010 Razor Poker Gold

*GOLD: 5X TO 1.2X BASIC CARDS
STATED PRINT RUN 25 SER. #'d SETS

2010 Razor Poker Red

STATED PRINT RUN 1 SER. #'d SET
UNPRICED DUE TO SCARCITY

2010 Razor Poker Bracelet Winners

❑ BH1 Doyle Brunson
❑ BH2 Greg Raymer
❑ BH3 Howard Lederer
❑ BH4 Johnny Chan
❑ BH5 Daniel Negreanu 12.00 30.00
❑ BH6 Jamie Gold 6.00 15.00
❑ BH7 Joe Hachem 6.00 15.00
❑ BH8 Phil Hellmuth 12.00 30.00
❑ BH9 Antonio Esfandiari 6.00 15.00
❑ BH10 Bill Edler 6.00 15.00
❑ BH11 Chris Moneymaker 6.00 15.00
❑ BH12 Cyndy Violette 8.00 20.00
❑ BH13 David Chiu 6.00 15.00
❑ BH14 David Pham
❑ BH15 Erick Lindgren 6.00 15.00
❑ BH16 Hoyt Corkins 6.00 15.00
❑ BH17 Humberto Brenes 6.00 15.00
❑ BH18 Jennifer Harman 8.00 20.00
❑ BH19 Josh Arieh 6.00 15.00
❑ BH20 Kenny Tran 6.00 15.00
❑ BH21 Layne Flack 6.00 15.00
❑ BH22 Men Nguyen 6.00 15.00
❑ BH23 Mike Matusow 8.00 20.00
❑ BH24 Scott Fischman 6.00 15.00
❑ BH25 Scotty Nguyen 6.00 15.00
❑ BH26 TJ Cloutier 6.00 15.00
❑ BH27 Todd Brunson 6.00 15.00

2010 Razor Poker Bracelet Winners Parallel

STATED PRINT RUN 1-10
UNPRICED DUE TO SCARCITY

2010 Razor Poker Bracelet Winners Printing Plates

UNPRICED DUE TO SCARCITY

2010 Razor Poker Dual Autographs

STATED PRINT RUN 50 SER. #'d SETS

❑ DS2 Vanessa Rousso 20.00 50.00
Chad Brown
❑ DS3 Phil Hellmuth 30.00 80.00
Daniel Negreanu
❑ DS4 Joe Hachem 20.00 50.00
Chris Moneymaker
❑ DS5 Jennifer Harman 20.00 50.00
Marco Traniello
❑ DS6 Jennifer Schoenberg 25.00 60.00
Evelyn Ng
❑ DS7 Lacey Jones 25.00 60.00
Cindy Margolis
❑ DS8 Cindy Violette 25.00 60.00
Jason Mercier
❑ DS9 Scotty Nguyen 20.00 50.00
Nam Lee
❑ DS11 Mike The Mouth Matusow
Phil Hellmuth
❑ DS13 Scott Montgomery 20.00 50.00
Ivan Demidov
❑ DS14 David Chiu 20.00 50.00
Men 'The Master' Nguyen
❑ DS15 Jamie Gold 25.00 60.00
Chris Moneymaker
❑ ELAE Erick Lindgren
Antonio Esfandiari
❑ JADW Josh Arieh
David Williams
❑ MMTD Michael Mizrachi
Tom Duuurrr Dwan
❑ PATD Patrick Antonius
Tom Duuurrr Dwan

2010 Razor Poker Favorite Hands Autographs

STATED PRINT RUN 10-50

❑ FHS1 Antonio Esfandiari 10.00 25.00
❑ FHS2 Bill Edler 10.00 25.00
❑ FHS3 Chad Brown 10.00 25.00
❑ FHS4 Chris Moneymaker 10.00 25.00
❑ FHS5 Cindy Margolis 15.00 40.00
❑ FHS6 Cyndy Violette 12.00 30.00
❑ FHS7 Daniel Negreanu
❑ FHS8 David Chiu 10.00 25.00
❑ FHS9 David Pham
❑ FHS10 David Williams 10.00 25.00
❑ FHS11 Doyle Brunson
❑ FHS12 Erica Schoenberg 12.00 30.00
❑ FHS13 Erick Lindgren 10.00 25.00
❑ FHS14 Evelyn Ng 12.00 30.00
❑ FHS15 Gavin Smith 10.00 25.00
❑ FHS16 Greg Raymer
❑ FHS17 Howard Lederer
❑ FHS18 Hoyt Corkins 10.00 25.00
❑ FHS19 Humberto Brenes 12.00 30.00
❑ FHS20 Isabelle Mercier 12.00 30.00
❑ FHS21 Ivan Demidov 10.00 25.00
❑ FHS22 Jamie Gold 10.00 25.00
❑ FHS23 Jean-Robert Bellande 10.00 25.00
❑ FHS24 Jennifer Harman 12.00 30.00
❑ FHS25 Jerry Buss 12.00 30.00
❑ FHS26 Joe Hachem 10.00 25.00
❑ FHS27 Johnny Chan
❑ FHS28 Josh Arieh 10.00 25.00
❑ FHS29 Kenny Tran 10.00 25.00
❑ FHS30 Lacey Jones 15.00 40.00
❑ FHS31 Layne Flack 10.00 25.00
❑ FHS32 Marco Traniello 10.00 25.00
❑ FHS33 Men Nguyen 10.00 25.00
❑ FHS34 Michael Mizrachi 10.00 25.00
❑ FHS35 Mike Matusow 12.00 30.00
❑ FHS36 Nam Le 10.00 25.00
❑ FHS37 Orel Hershiser
❑ FHS38 Patrik Antonius 10.00 25.00
❑ FHS39 Paul Wasicka 10.00 25.00
❑ FHS40 Phil Gordon 12.00 30.00
❑ FHS41 Phil Hellmuth 50.00 100.00
❑ FHS42 Scott Fischman 10.00 25.00
❑ FHS43 Scott Montgomery 10.00 25.00
❑ FHS44 Scotty Nguyen 10.00 25.00
❑ FHS45 Shannon Elizabeth
❑ FHS46 TJ Cloutier 10.00 25.00
❑ FHS47 Todd Brunson 10.00 25.00
❑ FHS48 Tom Dwan 25.00 60.00
❑ FHS49 Vanessa Rousso 20.00 50.00

2010 Razor Poker Favorite Hands Autographs 5

STATED PRINT RUN 5 SER. #'d SETS
UNPRICED DUE TO SCARCITY

2010 Razor Poker Favorite Hands Autographs 1

STATED PRINT RUN 1 SER. #'d SET
UNPRICED DUE TO SCARCITY

2010 Razor Poker Final Table Signatures

STATED PRINT RUN 25 SER. #'d SETS

❑ FTS1 Chris Moneymaker
❑ FTS2 Daniel Negreanu 50.00 100.00
❑ FTS3 Erick Lindgren 20.00 40.00
❑ FTS4 Jamie Gold 20.00 40.00
❑ FTS5 Joe Hachem 20.00 40.00
❑ FTS6 Men Nguyen 20.00 40.00
❑ FTS7 Mike Matusow
❑ FTS8 Phil Hellmuth 60.00 120.00
❑ FTS9 Scotty Nguyen 20.00 40.00
❑ FTS10 TJ Cloutier 20.00 40.00

2010 Razor Poker Final Table Signatures Parallel

STATED PRINT RUN 1 SER. #'d SET
UNPRICED DUE TO SCARCITY

2010 Razor Poker Las Vegas Summit Signatures Promo

❑ CM Chris Moneymaker 5.00 12.00
❑ EL Erick Lindgren 5.00 12.00
❑ MM Michael Mizrachi 5.00 12.00
❑ SE Shannon Elizabeth 40.00 80.00
❑ TF Ted Forrest 5.00 12.00

2010 Razor Poker Super Rare Signatures

STATED PRINT RUN 10 SER. #'d SETS
UNPRICED DUE TO SCARCITY

❑ SRS1 Doyle Brunson
❑ SRS2 Greg Raymer
❑ SRS3 Howard Lederer
❑ SRS4 Johnny Chan
❑ SRS5 Orel Hershiser
❑ SRS6 Shannon Elizabeth

2010 Razor Poker Super Rare Signatures Red

STATED PRINT RUN 1 SER. #'d SET
UNPRICED DUE TO SCARCITY

2010 Razor Poker Tournament Fabrics and Signatures

STATED PRINT RUN 99 SER. #'d SETS

❑ AE Antonio Esfandiari 12.00 30.00
❑ CM Cindy Margolis 15.00 40.00
❑ HC Hoyt Corkins 12.00 30.00
❑ JA Josh Arieh 12.00 30.00
❑ LF Layne Flack 12.00 30.00
❑ PG Phil Gordon 12.00 30.00
❑ PH Phil Hellmuth 25.00 60.00
❑ TC TJ Cloutier 12.00 30.00

2010 Razor Poker Tournament Fabrics and Signatures 10

STATED PRINT RUN 10 SER. #'d SETS
UNPRICED DUE TO SCARCITY

2010 Razor Poker Tournament Fabrics and Signatures 1

STATED PRINT RUN 1 SER. #'d SET
UNPRICED DUE TO SCARCITY

2010 Star Trek Remastered Original Series

COMPLETE SET (81) 4.00 10.00

❑ 1 The Cage .12 .30
❑ 2 Where No Man Has Gone Before .12 .30
❑ 3 The Corbomite Maneuver .12 .30
❑ 4 Mudd's Women .12 .30
❑ 5 The Enemy Within .12 .30
❑ 6 The Man Trap .12 .30
❑ 7 The Naked Time .12 .30
❑ 8 Charlie X .12 .30
❑ 9 Balance of Terror .12 .30
❑ 10 What Are Little Girls Made Of .12 .30
❑ 11 Dagger of the Mind .12 .30
❑ 12 Miri .12 .30
❑ 13 The Conscience of the King .12 .30
❑ 14 The Galileo Seven .12 .30
❑ 15 Court Martial .12 .30
❑ 16 The Menagerie .12 .30
❑ 17 Shore Leave .12 .30
❑ 18 The Squire of Gothos .12 .30
❑ 19 Arena .12 .30
❑ 20 The Alternative Factor .12 .30
❑ 21 Tomorrow is Yesterday .12 .30
❑ 22 The Return of the Archons .12 .30
❑ 23 A Taste of Armageddon .12 .30
❑ 24 Space Seed .12 .30
❑ 25 This Side of Paradise .12 .30
❑ 26 The Devil in the Dark .12 .30
❑ 27 Errand of Mercy .12 .30
❑ 28 The City on the Edge of Forever .12 .30
❑ 29 Operation Annihilate .12 .30
❑ 30 Catspaw .12 .30
❑ 31 Metamorphosis .12 .30
❑ 32 Friday's Child .12 .30
❑ 33 Who Mourns for Adonais .12 .30
❑ 34 Amok Time .12 .30
❑ 35 The Doomsday Machine .12 .30
❑ 36 Wolf in the Fold .12 .30
❑ 37 The Changeling .12 .30
❑ 38 The Apple .12 .30
❑ 39 Mirror, Mirror .12 .30
❑ 40 The Deadly Years .12 .30
❑ 41 I, Mudd .12 .30
❑ 42 The Trouble With Tribbles .12 .30
❑ 43 Bread and Circuses .12 .30
❑ 44 Journey to Babel .12 .30
❑ 45 A Private Little War .12 .30
❑ 46 The Gamesters of Triskelion .12 .30
❑ 47 Obsession .12 .30
❑ 48 The Immunity Syndrome .12 .30
❑ 49 A Piece of the Action .12 .30
❑ 50 By Any Other Name .12 .30
❑ 51 Return to Tomorrow .12 .30
❑ 52 Patterns of Force .12 .30
❑ 53 The Ultimate Computer .12 .30
❑ 54 The Omega Glory .12 .30
❑ 55 Assignment: Earth .12 .30
❑ 56 Spectre of the Gun .12 .30
❑ 57 Elaan of Troyius .12 .30
❑ 58 The Paradise Syndrome .12 .30
❑ 59 The Enterprise Incident .12 .30
❑ 60 And the Children Shall Lead .12 .30
❑ 61 Spock's Brain .12 .30
❑ 62 Is There in Truth No Beauty .12 .30
❑ 63 The Empath .12 .30
❑ 64 The Tholian Web .12 .30
❑ 65 For the World is Hollow .12 .30
❑ 66 Day of the Dove .12 .30
❑ 67 Plato's Stepchildren .12 .30
❑ 68 Wink of an Eye .12 .30
❑ 69 That Which Survives .12 .30
❑ 70 Let That Be Your Last Battlefield .12 .30
❑ 71 Whom Gods Destroy .12 .30
❑ 72 The Mark of Gideon .12 .30
❑ 73 The Lights of Zetar .12 .30
❑ 74 The Cloudminders .12 .30
❑ 75 The Way to Eden .12 .30
❑ 76 Requiem for Methuselah .12 .30
❑ 77 The Savage Curtain .12 .30
❑ 78 All Our Yesterdays .12 .30
❑ 79 Turnabout Intruder .12 .30
❑ 80 Checklist 1 .12 .30
❑ 81 Checklist 2 .12 .30

2010 Star Trek Remastered Original Series Gold

COMPLETE SET (81) 25.00 60.00
STATED ODDS

2010 Star Trek Remastered Original Series Autographs

STATED ODDS ONE PER BOX
L (LIMITED): 300-500 COPIES
VL (VERY LIMITED): 200-300 COPIES
NICHOLS AUTO ISSUED AS 3-CASE INCENTIVE
NIMOY AUTO ISSUED AS 6-CASE INCENTIVE

❑ A200 Leonard Nimoy/ (issued as 6-case incentive) 200.00 350.00
❑ A202 Maggie Threttt L 20.00 40.00
❑ A214 John Winston VL 35.00 70.00
❑ A230 George Takei VL 60.00 120.00
❑ A239 Sheila Leighton 8.00 20.00
❑ A240 Robert Sampson 8.00 20.00
❑ A243 Judith McConnell 8.00 20.00
❑ A244 Carole Shelyne 8.00 20.00
❑ A245 Seamon Glass 8.00 20.00
❑ A246 Jerry Ayres 8.00 20.00
❑ A247 Max Kleven 8.00 20.00
❑ A248 Nichelle Nichols/ (issued as 3-case incentive) 75.00 150.00
❑ A252 Tom LeGarde VL 15.00 30.00

2010 Star Trek Remastered Original Series Dual Autographs

STATED ODDS ONE PER BOX
L (LIMITED): 300-500 COPIES
VL (VERY LIMITED): 200-300 COPIES

❑ DA1 William Shatner 250.00 400.00
BarBara Luna VL
❑ DA2 Craig Huxley 30.00 60.00
Pamelyn Ferdin VL
❑ DA3 William Campbell 50.00 100.00
Michael Pataki VL
❑ DA6 Leonard Nimoy 250.00 400.00
Majel Barrett VL
❑ DA9 Malachi Throne 12.00 30.00
Sean Kenny
❑ DA10 Sandra Smith 15.00 40.00
Harry Landers L
❑ DA11 Richard Evans 12.00 30.00
William Wintersole L
❑ DA12 Stephen Mines 12.00 25.00
Barbara Baldavin L
❑ DA13 George Takei 75.00 125.00
Walter Koenig VL
❑ DA15 Gary Lockwood 12.00 30.00
Andrea Dromm
❑ DA16 William Schallert 12.00 30.00
Charlie Brill
❑ DA17 Joanne Linville 12.00 30.00
Jack Donner
❑ DA18 Mark Robert Brown 12.00 30.00
Pamelyn Ferdin L
❑ DA19 Brian Tochi 12.00 25.00
Melvni Caesar Belli
❑ DA23 Warren Stevens 15.00 40.00
Stewart Moss VL

2010 Star Trek Remastered Original Series Creatures

COMPLETE SET (9) 6.00 15.00
STATED ODDS 1:12

❑ AE1 Anthropoid Ape 1.00 2.50
❑ AE2 Balok's Puppet 1.00 2.50
❑ AE3 M-113 Creature 1.00 2.50
❑ AE4 Ruk 1.00 2.50
❑ AE5 Taurus II Anthropoid 1.00 2.50
❑ AE6 The Gorn 1.00 2.50
❑ AE7 The Horta 1.00 2.50
❑ AE8 The Mugato 1.00 2.50
❑ AE9 Yarnek 1.00 2.50

2010 Star Trek Remastered Original Series Elaan of Troyius Revised

COMPLETE SET (9) 20.00 50.00
STATED ODDS 1:24

❑ 175 Plot Synopses 3.00 8.00
❑ 176 Plot Synopses 3.00 8.00
❑ 177 Plot Synopses 3.00 8.00
❑ G57 Gold Plaque 3.00 8.00
❑ P57 Profile 3.00 8.00
❑ B113 Behind-the-Scenes 3.00 8.00
❑ B114 Behind-the-Scenes 3.00 8.00
❑ C113 Character Log 3.00 8.00
❑ C114 Character Log 3.00 8.00

2010 Star Trek Remastered Original Series Promos

COMPLETE SET (4)

❑ P1 General Distribution
❑ P2 Non-Sport Update
❑ P3 Album Exclusive
❑ P4 Fall 2010 Philly Non-Sport Show Exclusive

2010 Star Trek Remastered Original Series Ships In Motion

COMPLETE SET (11) 30.00 75.00
COMP.SET w/o SPs (9) 20.00 50.00
STATED ODDS 1:24

❑ RL1 U.S.S. Enterprise 3.00 8.00
❑ RL2 Galileo Seven Shuttlecraft 3.00 8.00
❑ RL3 U.S.S. Enterprise 3.00 8.00
❑ RL4 U.S.S. Enterprise 3.00 8.00
❑ RL5 U.S.S. Enterprise 3.00 8.00
❑ RL6 U.S.S. Enterprise 3.00 8.00
❑ RL7 U.S.S. Enterprise 3.00 8.00
❑ RL8 U.S.S. Enterprise 3.00 8.00
❑ RL9 U.S.S. Enterprise 3.00 8.00
❑ RL10 Doomsday Machine SP 10.00 25.00
(issued as case topper)
❑ RL11 U.S.S. Enterprise SP 12.00 30.00
(issued as Rittenhouse Reward)

2010 Star Trek Remastered Original Series Tribute

COMPLETE SET (18) 8.00 20.00
STATED ODDS 1:6

❑ T19 Korob .75 2.00
❑ T20 Zefram Cochrane .75 2.00
❑ T21 T'Pau .75 2.00
❑ T22 Sybo .75 2.00
❑ T23 Tharn .75 2.00
❑ T24 Commodore Stocker .75 2.00
❑ T25 Cyrano Jones .75 2.00
❑ T26 Mr. Lurry .75 2.00
❑ T27 Claudius Marcus .75 2.00
❑ T28 Sarek .75 2.00
❑ T29 Amanda .75 2.00
❑ T30 Tyree .75 2.00
❑ T31 Shahna .75 2.00
❑ T32 Norman .75 2.00
❑ T33 Stella Mudd .75 2.00
❑ T34 Jojo Krako .75 2.00
❑ T35 John Gill .75 2.00
❑ T36 Gary Seven .75 2.00
❑ T37 Trelane SP 12.00 30.00
(issued as Rittenhouse Reward)

2010 Stargate Universe Season One

COMPLETE SET (72) 5.00 12.00

❑ 1 Air, Part 1 .15 .40
❑ 2 Air, Part 1 .15 .40
❑ 3 Air, Part 1 .15 .40
❑ 4 Air, Part 2 .15 .40
❑ 5 Air, Part 2 .15 .40
❑ 6 Air, Part 2 .15 .40
❑ 7 Air, Part 3 .15 .40
❑ 8 Air, Part 3 .15 .40
❑ 9 Air, Part 3 .15 .40
❑ 10 Darkness .15 .40
❑ 11 Darkness .15 .40
❑ 12 Darkness .15 .40
❑ 13 Light .15 .40
❑ 14 Light .15 .40
❑ 15 Light .15 .40
❑ 16 Water .15 .40
❑ 17 Water .15 .40
❑ 18 Water .15 .40
❑ 19 Earth .15 .40
❑ 20 Earth .15 .40
❑ 21 Earth .15 .40
❑ 22 Time .15 .40
❑ 23 Time .15 .40
❑ 24 Time .15 .40
❑ 25 Life .15 .40
❑ 26 Life .15 .40
❑ 27 Life .15 .40
❑ 28 Justice .15 .40
❑ 29 Justice .15 .40
❑ 30 Justice .15 .40
❑ 31 Space .15 .40
❑ 32 Space .15 .40
❑ 33 Space .15 .40
❑ 34 Divided .15 .40
❑ 35 Divided .15 .40
❑ 36 Divided .15 .40
❑ 37 Faith .15 .40
❑ 38 Faith .15 .40
❑ 39 Faith .15 .40
❑ 40 Human .15 .40
❑ 41 Human .15 .40
❑ 42 Human .15 .40
❑ 43 Lost .15 .40
❑ 44 Lost .15 .40
❑ 45 Lost .15 .40
❑ 46 Sabotage .15 .40
❑ 47 Sabotage .15 .40
❑ 48 Sabotage .15 .40
❑ 49 Pain .15 .40
❑ 50 Pain .15 .40
❑ 51 Pain .15 .40
❑ 52 Subversion .15 .40
❑ 53 Subversion .15 .40
❑ 54 Subversion .15 .40
❑ 55 Incursion, Part 1 .15 .40
❑ 56 Incursion, Part 1 .15 .40
❑ 57 Incursion, Part 1 .15 .40
❑ 58 Incursion, Part 2 .15 .40
❑ 59 Incursion, Part 2 .15 .40
❑ 60 Incursion, Part 2 .15 .40
❑ 61 Behind the Scenes .15 .40
❑ 62 Behind the Scenes .15 .40
❑ 63 Behind the Scenes .15 .40
❑ 64 Behind the Scenes .15 .40
❑ 65 Behind the Scenes .15 .40
❑ 66 Behind the Scenes .15 .40
❑ 67 Behind the Scenes .15 .40
❑ 68 Behind the Scenes .15 .40
❑ 69 Behind the Scenes .15 .40
❑ 70 Checklist 1 .15 .40
❑ 71 Checklist 2 .15 .40
❑ 72 Checklist 3 .15 .40

2010 Stargate Universe Season One Autographs

STATED ODDS THREE PER BOX
PHILLIPS AUTO ISSUED AS 3-CASE INCENTIVE
VL (VERY LIMITED): 200-300 COPIES

❑ 1 Alaina Huffman VL 45.00 90.00
❑ 2 Brian J. Smith VL 25.00 50.00
❑ 3 Christina Schild 5.00 12.00
❑ 4 Christopher McDonald 8.00 20.00
❑ 5 David Blue VL 40.00 80.00
❑ 6 Elyse Levesque VL 50.00 100.00
❑ 7 Haig Sutherland 5.00 12.00
❑ 8 Jamil Walker Smith VL 30.00 60.00
❑ 9 Jennifer Spence 8.00 20.00
❑ 10 Josh Blacker 5.00 12.00
❑ 11 Julia Benson 8.00 20.00

❑ 12 Louis Ferreira VL 40.00 80.00
❑ 13 Mark Burgess 5.00 12.00
❑ 14 Ona Grauer 8.00 20.00
❑ 15 Patrick Gilmore VL 8.00 20.00
❑ 16 Peter Kelamis 5.00 12.00
❑ 17 Reiko Aylesworth 8.00 20.00
❑ 18 Tygh Runyan 5.00 12.00
❑ 19 Lou Diamond Phillips 75.00 150.00
(issued as 3-case incentive)

2010 Stargate Universe Season One Costumes

STATED ODDS TWO PER BOX
DUAL COSTUME CARD ISSUED AS CASE TOPPER

❑ R1 Eli Wallace shirt 5.00 12.00
❑ R2 Dr. Nicholas Rush white shirt 5.00 12.00
❑ R3 Dr. Nicholas Rush brown shirt 5.00 12.00
❑ R4 Ronald Greer camo jacket 5.00 12.00
❑ R5 Tamara Johansen pants 6.00 15.00
❑ R6 Matthew Scott pnts 5.00 12.00
❑ R7 Chloe Armstrong dress 8.00 20.00
❑ R8 Sen. Alan Armstrong grey suit 5.00 12.00
❑ R9 Sen. Alan Armstrong white shirt 5.00 12.00
❑ NNO Chloe Armstrong 30.00 60.00
Alan Armstrong/ (issued as case topper)

2010 Stargate Universe Season One Crew

COMPLETE SET (9) 20.00 50.00
STATED ODDS 1:24

❑ PL1 Dr. Nicholas Rush 4.00 10.00
❑ PL2 Camille Wray 4.00 10.00
❑ PL3 Everett Young 4.00 10.00
❑ PL4 David Telford 4.00 10.00
❑ PL5 Ronald Greer 4.00 10.00
❑ PL6 Matthew Scott 4.00 10.00
❑ PL7 Tamara Johansen 4.00 10.00
❑ PL8 Eli Wallace 4.00 10.00
❑ PL9 Chloe Armstrong 4.00 10.00

2010 Stargate Universe Season One Lenticular

COMPLETE SET (9) 15.00 40.00
STATED ODDS 1:12

❑ L1 Lenticular 1 3.00 8.00
❑ L2 Lenticular 2 3.00 8.00
❑ L3 Lenticular 3 3.00 8.00
❑ L4 Lenticular 4 3.00 8.00
❑ L5 Lenticular 5 3.00 8.00
❑ L6 Lenticular 6 3.00 8.00
❑ L7 Lenticular 7 3.00 8.00
❑ L8 Lenticular 8 3.00 8.00
❑ L9 Lenticular 9 3.00 8.00

2010 Stargate Universe Season One Promos

❑ CE Eli Wallace/ (Chicago Land Expo 2010)
❑ P1 Everett Young
Dr. Nicholas Rush/Camille Wray/ (General Distribution)
❑ P2 Eli Wallace
Dr.Nicholas Rush/ (Non-Sport Update)
❑ P3 Stargate Universe (Album Exclusive)
❑ CP1 Group of five/ (San Diego Comic Con 2010)
❑ CP2 Camille Wray
Eli Wallace/David Telford/ (Fall 2010 Philly Non-Sport Show)

2010 Stargate Universe Season One Quotable Eli

COMPLETE SET (9) 8.00 20.00
STATED ODDS 1:8

❑ Q1 I Assure You 1.50 4.00
❑ Q2 Just For Posterity's Sake 1.50 4.00
❑ Q3 Looks Like We've Entered the Hoth System1.50 4.00
❑ Q4 We Have Aliens on the Ship 1.50 4.00
❑ Q5 She's Not Gonna Understand 1.50 4.00
❑ Q6 OK I'll Go First 1.50 4.00
❑ Q7 Eli, Do Me a Favor 1.50 4.00
❑ Q8 In My Experience 1.50 4.00
❑ Q9 Once I Climbed the Redridge Mountains 1.50 4.00

2010 Stargate Universe Season One Sketches

STATED ODDS ONE PER 6-CASE PURCHASE

❑ 1 David Desbois 250.00 400.00
❑ 2 Sean Pence 250.00 400.00

2010 Twilight Eclipse

COMPLETE SET (160) 25.00 50.00
COMP.SER. 1 SET (80) 15.00 30.00
COMP.SER. 2 SET (80) 15.00 30.00
B1 STATED ODDS 1:104 SER. 1 PACKS
H1 STATED ODDS 1:104 SER. 2 PACKS

❑ 1 The Twilight Saga: Eclipse .25 .60
❑ 2 Bella .25 .60
❑ 3 Edward .25 .60
❑ 4 Jacob .25 .60
❑ 5 Alice .25 .60
❑ 6 Jasper .25 .60
❑ 7 Rosalie .25 .60
❑ 8 Emmett .25 .60
❑ 9 Carlisle .25 .60
❑ 10 Esme .25 .60
❑ 11 Jane .25 .60
❑ 12 Alec .25 .60
❑ 13 Felix .25 .60
❑ 14 Demitri .25 .60
❑ 15 Victoria .25 .60
❑ 16 Riley .25 .60
❑ 17 Bree .25 .60
❑ 18 Sam .25 .60
❑ 19 Paul .25 .60
❑ 20 Jared .25 .60
❑ 21 Embry .25 .60
❑ 22 Quil .25 .60
❑ 23 Leah .25 .60
❑ 24 Emily .25 .60
❑ 25 Run .25 .60
❑ 26 Grounded .25 .60
❑ 27 Graduate .25 .60
❑ 28 Another Party .25 .60
❑ 29 Police Chief .25 .60
❑ 30 A Gift .25 .60
❑ 31 The Forest Night .25 .60
❑ 32 Territory .25 .60
❑ 33 Wolf Territory .25 .60
❑ 34 Dangerous .25 .60
❑ 35 A Fight .25 .60
❑ 36 Hold on Tight .25 .60
❑ 37 Vampire Girl .25 .60
❑ 38 Say Goodbye .25 .60
❑ 39 A Vampire .25 .60
❑ 40 Charlie Asleep .25 .60
❑ 41 Newest Member .25 .60
❑ 42 Spirit Warriors .25 .60
❑ 43 A Snack .25 .60
❑ 44 Someone to Drink .25 .60
❑ 45 La Push Beach .25 .60
❑ 46 Flesh and Blood .25 .60
❑ 47 In the Sun .25 .60
❑ 48 Missing .25 .60
❑ 49 Proud .25 .60
❑ 50 Father and Daughter .25 .60
❑ 51 The Vision .25 .60
❑ 52 Young Major .25 .60
❑ 53 Three Women .25 .60
❑ 54 Kept Me Waiting .25 .60
❑ 55 Second in Command .25 .60
❑ 56 Newborn .25 .60
❑ 57 Marry Me .25 .60
❑ 58 Dark Embrace .25 .60
❑ 59 Carrying Bella .25 .60
❑ 60 Kiss Me .25 .60
❑ 61 Battle .25 .60
❑ 62 Unnecessary .25 .60
❑ 63 The Volturi Appear .25 .60
❑ 64 Torture .25 .60
❑ 65 He'll Be Alright .25 .60
❑ 66 I'm Sorry .25 .60
❑ 67 Magic Hour .25 .60
❑ 68 Marry Me .25 .60
❑ 69 Another Party .25 .60
❑ 70 Second in Command .25 .60
❑ 71 Edward .25 .60
❑ 72 Dangerous .25 .60
❑ 73 Hold on Tight .25 .60
❑ 74 A Fight .25 .60
❑ 75 He'll Be Alright .25 .60
❑ 76 Unnecessary .25 .60
❑ 77 Bella Swan .25 .60
❑ 78 Edward Cullen .25 .60
❑ 79 Jacob Black .25 .60
❑ 80 Checklist .25 .60
❑ 81 Eclipse .25 .60
❑ 82 Bella .25 .60
❑ 83 Edward .25 .60
❑ 84 Jacob .25 .60
❑ 85 Alice .25 .60
❑ 86 Jasper .25 .60
❑ 87 Rosalie .25 .60
❑ 88 Emmett .25 .60
❑ 89 Carlisle .25 .60
❑ 90 Esme .25 .60
❑ 91 Jane .25 .60
❑ 92 Alec .25 .60
❑ 93 Felix .25 .60
❑ 94 Demitri .25 .60
❑ 95 Victoria .25 .60
❑ 96 Riley .25 .60
❑ 97 Bree .25 .60
❑ 98 Sam .25 .60
❑ 99 Paul .25 .60
❑ 100 Jared .25 .60
❑ 101 Embry .25 .60
❑ 102 Quil .25 .60
❑ 103 Leah .25 .60
❑ 104 Emily .25 .60
❑ 105 Who's There .25 .60
❑ 106 Gotta Focus .25 .60
❑ 107 Concern .25 .60
❑ 108 Leave a Message .25 .60
❑ 109 The Shore .25 .60
❑ 110 Enraged .25 .60
❑ 111 Trust .25 .60
❑ 112 Wolf Pack .25 .60
❑ 113 His Case File .25 .60
❑ 114 Protection Detail .25 .60
❑ 115 'Bout Time .25 .60
❑ 116 Seth Clearwater .25 .60
❑ 117 The Cold Woman .25 .60
❑ 118 Problem Solved .25 .60
❑ 119 Pick Me .25 .60
❑ 120 Punched a Werewolf .25 .60
❑ 121 I Envy You .25 .60
❑ 122 You're Drunk .25 .60
❑ 123 Control Yourselves .25 .60
❑ 124 Indiscreet .25 .60
❑ 125 Uninvited .25 .60
❑ 126 Wolf Charm .25 .60
❑ 127 A Blood Bath .25 .60
❑ 128 Esme and Carlisle .25 .60
❑ 129 They're Here .25 .60
❑ 130 No Trust .25 .60
❑ 131 Welcome .25 .60
❑ 132 Don't Hold Back .25 .60
❑ 133 Them .25 .60
❑ 134 Training Newborns .25 .60
❑ 135 Bella's Nightmare .25 .60
❑ 136 Don't You Care .25 .60
❑ 137 Charlie and Alice .25 .60
❑ 138 One Condition .25 .60
❑ 139 Last Minute Decision .25 .60
❑ 140 A Drop of Blood .25 .60
❑ 141 Mountain Top .25 .60
❑ 142 The Fight Begins .25 .60
❑ 143 Seth Wolf .25 .60
❑ 144 How Long .25 .60
❑ 145 Leah Wolf .25 .60
❑ 146 Loose Ends .25 .60
❑ 147 Tie You to Me .25 .60
❑ 148 I Envy You .25 .60
❑ 149 Tie You to Me .25 .60
❑ 150 Don't You Care .25 .60
❑ 151 They're Here .25 .60
❑ 152 Enraged .25 .60
❑ 153 No Trust .25 .60
❑ 154 Trust .25 .60
❑ 155 The Shore .25 .60
❑ 156 Who's There .25 .60
❑ 157 Edward .25 .60
❑ 158 Bella .25 .60
❑ 159 Jacob .25 .60
❑ 160 Checklist .25 .60
❑ B1 Marry Me 15.00 30.00
❑ H1 Welcome to the Army 30.00 60.00

2010 Twilight Eclipse Protagonists

COMPLETE SET (3) 10.00 25.00
STATED ODDS 1:23 SERIES 1 PACKS

❑ F1 Bella Swan 5.00 12.00
❑ F2 Edward Cullen 5.00 12.00
❑ F3 Jacob Black 5.00 12.00

2010 Twilight Eclipse Puzzle

COMPLETE SET (9) 20.00 40.00
STATED ODDS 1:7

❑ A1 Eclipse - Top Left 3.00 8.00
❑ A2 Eclipse - Top Center 3.00 8.00
❑ A3 Eclipse - Top Right 3.00 8.00
❑ A4 Eclipse - Middle Left 3.00 8.00
❑ A5 Eclipse - Middle Center 3.00 8.00
❑ A6 Eclipse - Middle Right 3.00 8.00
❑ A7 Eclipse - Bottom Left 3.00 8.00
❑ A8 Eclipse - Bottom Center 3.00 8.00
❑ A9 Eclipse - Bottom Right 3.00 8.00

2010 Twilight Eclipse The Wolfpack Puzzle

COMPLETE SET (6) 15.00 30.00
STATED ODDS 1:11

❑ WP1 The Wolfpack - Top Left 3.00 8.00
❑ WP2 The Wolfpack - Top Center 3.00 8.00
❑ WP3 The Wolfpack - Top Right 3.00 8.00
❑ WP4 The Wolfpack - Bottom Left 3.00 8.00
❑ WP5 The Wolfpack - Bottom Center 3.00 8.00
❑ WP6 The Wolfpack - Bottom Right 3.00 8.00

2010 Twilight Eclipse Volturi Coven

COMPLETE SET (12) 25.00 50.00
COMP.SER. 1 SET (6) 15.00 30.00
COMP.SER. 2 SET (6) 15.00 30.00
VO1-VO6 STATED ODDS 1:11 SER. 1 PACKS
VO7-VO12 STATED ODDS 1:11 SER. 2 PACKS

❑ VO1 Demitri - Emblem 3.00 8.00
❑ VO2 Jane 3.00 8.00
❑ VO3 Alec 3.00 8.00
❑ VO4 Felix 3.00 8.00
❑ VO5 Demitri 3.00 8.00
❑ VO6 The Volturi Coven 3.00 8.00
❑ VO7 The Volturi Coven - Emblem 3.00 8.00
❑ VO8 Jane 3.00 8.00
❑ VO9 Alec 3.00 8.00
❑ VO10 Felix 3.00 8.00
❑ VO11 Demitri 3.00 8.00
❑ VO12 The Volturi Coven 3.00 8.00

2010 Wacky Packages Series 7

COMPLETE SET (55) 6.00 15.00
NNO POLIGRIPE ISSUED IN COLLECTORS ALBUM

❑ 1 Ghoul Scouts .15 .40
❑ 2 Play-Doze .15 .40
❑ 3 Just for Wolfman .15 .40
❑ 4 Dorkitos .15 .40
❑ 5 Chickless .15 .40
❑ 6 Hungry-Mantis .15 .40
❑ 7 Bumpkin Dimwits .15 .40
❑ 8 V6 .15 .40
❑ 9 Burnt Bees .15 .40
❑ 10 Seagerm's .15 .40
❑ 11 Cutz .15 .40
❑ 12 Bruise's .15 .40
❑ 13 Twitley .15 .40
❑ 14 Boredom .15 .40
❑ 15 Death Savers .15 .40
❑ 16 Stupid Pretzel .15 .40
❑ 17 Kreepy Kreme .15 .40
❑ 18 Mtn Dude .15 .40
❑ 19 Ditz .15 .40
❑ 20 Flabreze .15 .40
❑ 21 Smuggler's .15 .40
❑ 22 Air Sick .15 .40
❑ 23 Pinkies .15 .40
❑ 24 Honey Tomb .15 .40
❑ 25 Biteamanwater .15 .40
❑ 26 Bunyuns .15 .40
❑ 27 Fraid .15 .40
❑ 28 Grape-Newts .15 .40
❑ 29 Molten Salt .15 .40
❑ 30 Iris Stings .15 .40
❑ 31 County Time .15 .40
❑ 32 Mrs. Blabber Mouth's .15 .40
❑ 33 Raven Bran .15 .40
❑ 34 Simian Toes Crunch .15 .40
❑ 35 Hunks .15 .40
❑ 36 Ruffled .15 .40
❑ 37 Tiny Cats .15 .40
❑ 38 Baby Battle Pop .15 .40
❑ 39 Head and Smolders .15 .40
❑ 40 Vampire .15 .40
❑ 41 Stuffer's .15 .40
❑ 42 Armor Maul .15 .40
❑ 43 Log Coffin .15 .40
❑ 44 Old Slice .15 .40
❑ 45 Jowl-O .15 .40
❑ 46 Clunky .15 .40
❑ 47 Toupe Ramen .15 .40
❑ 48 Crutch .15 .40
❑ 49 Snoresages .15 .40
❑ 50 Sushi-Q's .15 .40
❑ 51 Raglue .15 .40
❑ 52 Rat Guard .15 .40
❑ 53 Sno Saps .15 .40
❑ 54 Beyond Pollution .15 .40
❑ 55 Kiss Kat .15 .40
❑ NNO Poligripe/ (issued in collectors album) 8.00 20.00

2010 Wacky Packages Series 7 Blister Bonus

COMPLETE SET (4) 8.00 20.00
STATED ODDS ONE PER BLISTER PACK

❑ B1 Hawaiian Tragic 3.00 8.00
❑ B2 Wite Out 3.00 8.00
❑ B3 Meowsporin 3.00 8.00
❑ B4 Baaabasol 3.00 8.00

2010 Wacky Packages Series 7 Cereal Box Bonus

COMPLETE SET (6) 8.00 20.00
STATED ODDS THREE PER 3-BOX CEREAL PACKAGE

❑ C1 Triks 2.00 5.00
❑ C2 Crookie Crisp 2.00 5.00
❑ C3 Cap'N Crud 2.00 5.00
❑ C4 Weakies 2.00 5.00
❑ C5 Awful Bits 2.00 5.00
❑ C6 All-Brain 2.00 5.00

2010 Wacky Packages Series 7 Classic Foil

COMPLETE SET (10) 12.00 30.00
STATED ODDS 1:4

❑ F1 Shrunken Donuts 2.00 5.00
❑ F2 Lox 2.00 5.00
❑ F3 Pupsi-Cola 2.00 5.00
❑ F4 Delinquent 2.00 5.00
❑ F5 Ruden's 2.00 5.00
❑ F6 Scream Sicle 2.00 5.00
❑ F7 Icicle 2.00 5.00
❑ F8 3 Mosquitoes 2.00 5.00
❑ F9 Flunk 2.00 5.00
❑ F10 Schnozmopolitan 2.00 5.00

2010 Wacky Packages Series 7 Classic Foil Jay Lynch Autographs

STATED ODDS 1:701

❑ F1 Shrunken Donuts 75.00 150.00
❑ F2 Lox 75.00 150.00
❑ F3 Pupsi-Cola 75.00 150.00
❑ F4 Delinquent 75.00 150.00
❑ F5 Ruden's 75.00 150.00
❑ F6 Scream Sicle 75.00 150.00
❑ F7 Icicle 75.00 150.00
❑ F8 3 Mosquitoes 75.00 150.00
❑ F9 Flunk 75.00 150.00
❑ F10 Schnozmopolitan 75.00 150.00

2010 Wacky Packages Series 7 Sketches

STATED ODDS 1:2,340

❑ 1 Brent Engstrom B&W 20.00 40.00
❑ 2 Brent Engstrom Color
❑ 3 Fred Wheaton B&W 30.00 60.00
❑ 4 Fred Wheaton Color
❑ 5 Jay Lynch B&W 10.00 20.00
❑ 6 Jay Lynch Color

2010 Wacky Packages Series 7 Wack-O-Mercials

COMPLETE SET (20) 8.00 20.00
STATED ODDS ONE PER PACK

❑ 1 Special Pre K .60 1.50
❑ 2 Blubber King .60 1.50
❑ 3 Mouse Mix .60 1.50
❑ 4 Ogre-Eaters .60 1.50
❑ 5 Octivia .60 1.50
❑ 6 Crimetapp .60 1.50
❑ 7 Stealthy Choice .60 1.50
❑ 8 Sweet 'N Slow .60 1.50
❑ 9 Crispux .60 1.50
❑ 10 MOB .60 1.50
❑ 11 Choppertone .60 1.50
❑ 12 Hide .60 1.50
❑ 13 Wiiz .60 1.50
❑ 14 Guitar Zero .60 1.50
❑ 15 Pounds .60 1.50
❑ 16 Yubang .60 1.50
❑ 17 Spread Bull .60 1.50
❑ 18 Wobblers .60 1.50
❑ 19 Maggoty Ann .60 1.50
❑ 20 Wetflix .60 1.50

2010 Wacky Packages Series 7 Wack-O-Mercials Red

COMPLETE SET (20) 25.00 60.00
*RED: 1.2X TO 3X BASIC CARD
STATED ODDS 1:4

2010 Wacky Packages Series 7 Wack-O-Mercials Flash Foil

COMPLETE SET (20) 80.00 200.00
*FLASH FOIL: 4X TO 10X BASIC CARD 6.00 15.00
STATED ODDS 1:12

2010 Wacky Packages Series 7 Wack-O-Mercials Gold Flash Foil

*GOLD: 60X TO 120X BASIC CARD
STATED ODDS 1:701

2010 Wacky Packages Series 7 Web Bonus

COMPLETE SET (3) 3.00 8.00
STATED ODDS THREE PER 3-BOX CEREAL PACKAGE

❑ 1 Fishbook 1.50 4.00
❑ 2 Crude Tube 1.50 4.00
❑ 3 Qwitter 1.50 4.00

2010 Warehouse 13 Season One

COMPLETE SET (72) 5.00 12.00

❑ 1 Pilot .15 .40
❑ 2 Pilot .15 .40
❑ 3 Pilot .15 .40
❑ 4 Pilot .15 .40
❑ 5 Pilot .15 .40
❑ 6 Pilot .15 .40
❑ 7 Resonance .15 .40
❑ 8 Resonance .15 .40
❑ 9 Resonance .15 .40
❑ 10 Resonance .15 .40
❑ 11 Resonance .15 .40
❑ 12 Resonance .15 .40
❑ 13 Magnetism .15 .40
❑ 14 Magnetism .15 .40
❑ 15 Magnetism .15 .40
❑ 16 Magnetism .15 .40
❑ 17 Magnetism .15 .40
❑ 18 Magnetism .15 .40
❑ 19 Claudia .15 .40
❑ 20 Claudia .15 .40
❑ 21 Claudia .15 .40
❑ 22 Claudia .15 .40
❑ 23 Claudia .15 .40
❑ 24 Claudia .15 .40
❑ 25 Elements .15 .40
❑ 26 Elements .15 .40
❑ 27 Elements .15 .40
❑ 28 Elements .15 .40
❑ 29 Elements .15 .40
❑ 30 Elements .15 .40
❑ 31 Burnout .15 .40
❑ 32 Burnout .15 .40
❑ 33 Burnout .15 .40
❑ 34 Burnout .15 .40
❑ 35 Burnout .15 .40
❑ 36 Burnout .15 .40
❑ 37 Implosion .15 .40
❑ 38 Implosion .15 .40
❑ 39 Implosion .15 .40
❑ 40 Implosion .15 .40
❑ 41 Implosion .15 .40
❑ 42 Implosion .15 .40
❑ 43 Duped .15 .40
❑ 44 Duped .15 .40
❑ 45 Duped .15 .40
❑ 46 Duped .15 .40
❑ 47 Duped .15 .40
❑ 48 Duped .15 .40
❑ 49 Regrets .15 .40
❑ 50 Regrets .15 .40
❑ 51 Regrets .15 .40
❑ 52 Regrets .15 .40
❑ 53 Regrets .15 .40
❑ 54 Regrets .15 .40
❑ 55 Breakdown .15 .40
❑ 56 Breakdown .15 .40
❑ 57 Breakdown .15 .40
❑ 58 Breakdown .15 .40
❑ 59 Breakdown .15 .40
❑ 60 Breakdown .15 .40
❑ 61 Nevermore .15 .40
❑ 62 Nevermore .15 .40
❑ 63 Nevermore .15 .40
❑ 64 Nevermore .15 .40
❑ 65 Nevermore .15 .40
❑ 66 Nevermore .15 .40
❑ 67 MacPherson .15 .40
❑ 68 MacPherson .15 .40
❑ 69 MacPherson .15 .40
❑ 70 MacPherson .15 .40
❑ 71 MacPherson .15 .40
❑ 72 MacPherson .15 .40

2010 Warehouse 13 Season One Autographs

STATED ODDS TWO PER BOX
L (LIMITED): 300-500 COPIES
VL (VERY LIMITED): 200-300 COPIES

❑ 1 Alec Medlock L 6.00 15.00
❑ 2 Eddie McClintock VL 40.00 80.00
❑ 3 Erica Cerra L 15.00 30.00
❑ 4 Genelle Williams VL 30.00 60.00
❑ 5 Joanne Kelly VL 75.00 150.00
❑ 6 Joe Morton L 8.00 20.00
❑ 7 Mark Sheppard L 10.00 25.00
❑ 8 Michael Boatman L 6.00 15.00
❑ 9 Michael Hogan L 8.00 20.00
❑ 10 Niall Matter L 8.00 20.00
❑ 11 Saul Rubinek VL 60.00 120.00
❑ 12 Simon Reynolds L 6.00 15.00
❑ 13 Susan Hogan L 6.00 15.00
❑ 14 Tricia Helfer L 30.00 60.00

2010 Warehouse 13 Season One Gallery

COMPLETE SET (6) 15.00 40.00
STATED ODDS 1:24

❑ G1 Peter Lattimer 4.00 10.00
❑ G2 Myka Bering 4.00 10.00
❑ G3 Arthur Nielsen 4.00 10.00
❑ G4 Leena 4.00 10.00
❑ G5 Mrs. Irene Frederic 4.00 10.00
❑ G6 Claudia Donovan 4.00 10.00

2010 Warehouse 13 Season One Promos

❑ P1 Pete Lattimer
Myka Bering/ (General Distribution)
❑ P2 Pete Lattimer 6.00 15.00
Myka Bering/ (Non-Sport Update)
❑ P3 Artie Nielsen
Claudia Donovan/ (Binder Exclusive)
❑ CP1 Myka Bering 2.00 5.00
Pete Lattimer/ (San Diego Comic Con)

2010 Warehouse 13 Season One Relics

STATED ODDS TWO PER BOX
VOLTA RELIC ISSUED AS CASE TOPPER
MCLINTOCK AUTO ISSUED AS 3-CASE INCENTIVE

❑ R1 Peter Lattimer 6.00 20.00
❑ R2 Peter Lattimer 6.00 15.00
❑ R3 Myka Bering 8.00 20.00
❑ R4 Myka Bering 8.00 20.00
❑ R5 Artie Nielsen 6.00 15.00
❑ R6 Claudia Donovan 8.00 20.00
❑ R7 Leena 6.00 15.00
❑ R8 Alice 6.00 15.00
❑ NNO Peter Lattimer 75.00 125.00
Eddie McClintock AU/ (issued as 3-case incentive)
❑ NNO Volta/ (issued as case topper) 15.00 30.00

2010 Warehouse 13 Season One Snag It Bag It Tag It

COMPLETE SET (18) 20.00 50.00
STATED ODDS 1:8

❑ A1 Aztec Bloodstone 2.00 5.00
❑ A2 Tesla Gun 2.00 5.00
❑ A3 Harry Houdini's Wallet 2.00 5.00
❑ A4 Lucretia Borgia's Comb 2.00 5.00
❑ A5 The Farnsworth 2.00 5.00
❑ A6 Jubilee Grand Poker Chip 2.00 5.00
❑ A7 Phoenix Charm 2.00 5.00
❑ A8 Slyvia Plath's Typewriter 2.00 5.00
❑ A9 Rheticus's Compass 2.00 5.00
❑ A10 Edgar Allan Poe's Quill Pen and Notebook2.00 5.00
❑ A11 Hanjo Masamune 2.00 5.00
❑ A12 Studio 54 Disco Ball 2.00 5.00
❑ A13 Alessandro Volta's Lab Coat 2.00 5.00
❑ A14 Baylor Dodgeball 2.00 5.00
❑ A15 Lenape Tribe's Cloak 2.00 5.00
❑ A16 Easter Island Conch 2.00 5.00
❑ A17 Clark Gable's Grooming Kit 2.00 5.00
❑ A18 Harriet Tubman's Thimble 2.00 5.00
❑ A19 Moon Rock 10.00 25.00
(issued as Rittenhouse Reward)

2010 Women of Star Trek

COMPLETE SET (81) 5.00 12.00

❑ 1 Lt. Uhura .15 .40
❑ 2 Nurse Chapel .15 .40
❑ 3 Yeoman Rand .15 .40
❑ 4 Vina .15 .40
❑ 5 Number One .15 .40
❑ 6 Dr. Elizabeth Dehner .15 .40
❑ 7 Sister Edith Keeler .15 .40
❑ 8 Andrea .15 .40
❑ 9 T'Pring .15 .40
❑ 10 T'Pau .15 .40
❑ 11 Lt. Palamas .15 .40
❑ 12 Miramanee .15 .40
❑ 13 Romulan Commander .15 .40
❑ 14 Dr. Janice Lester .15 .40
❑ 15 Dr. Helen Noel .15 .40
❑ 16 Yeoman Tonia Barrows .15 .40
❑ 17 Droxine .15 .40
❑ 18 Zarabeth .15 .40
❑ 19 Amanda .15 .40
❑ 20 Gem .15 .40
❑ 21 Nancy Crater .15 .40
❑ 22 Elaan .15 .40
❑ 23 Shahna .15 .40
❑ 24 Eleen .15 .40
❑ 25 Leila Kalomi .15 .40
❑ 26 Natira .15 .40
❑ 27 Eve McHuron .15 .40
❑ 28 Counselor Deanna Troi .15 .40
❑ 29 Dr. Beverly Crusher .15 .40
❑ 30 Guinan .15 .40
❑ 31 Ensign Ro Laren .15 .40
❑ 32 Dr. Kate Pulaski .15 .40
❑ 33 Lwaxana Troi .15 .40
❑ 34 Lt. Natasha Yar .15 .40

❑ 35 Nurse Alyssa Ogawa .15 .40
❑ 36 Captain Phillipa Louvois .15 .40
❑ 37 K'Ehleyr .15 .40
❑ 38 Dr. Leah Brahms .15 .40
❑ 39 Lal .15 .40
❑ 40 Lt. Commander Shelby .15 .40
❑ 41 Ensign Robin Lefler .15 .40
❑ 42 Admiral Alynna Nechayev .15 .40
❑ 43 Lt. Commander Neela Daren .15 .40
❑ 44 Vash .15 .40
❑ 45 Salia .15 .40
❑ 46 Ishara Yar .15 .40
❑ 47 Ardra .15 .40
❑ 48 Kamala .15 .40
❑ 49 Madeline .15 .40
❑ 50 Amanda Rogers .15 .40
❑ 51 Countess Regina Barthalomew .15 .40
❑ 52 Commander Sela .15 .40
❑ 53 Ensign Sonya Gomez .15 .40
❑ 54 Eline .15 .40
❑ 55 Jadzia Dax .15 .40
❑ 56 Kira Nerys .15 .40
❑ 57 Ezri Dax .15 .40
❑ 58 Keiko O'Brien .15 .40
❑ 59 Kasidy Yates .15 .40
❑ 60 Kai Winn .15 .40
❑ 61 Leeta .15 .40
❑ 62 Jennifer Sisko .15 .40
❑ 63 Ishka .15 .40
❑ 64 Captain Kathryn Janeway .15 .40
❑ 65 Lt. B'Elanna Torres .15 .40
❑ 66 Kes .15 .40
❑ 67 Seven of Nine .15 .40
❑ 68 Seska .15 .40
❑ 69 Borg Queen .15 .40
❑ 70 Tal Celes .15 .40
❑ 71 Female Q .15 .40
❑ 72 Naomi Wildman .15 .40
❑ 73 Hoshi Sato .15 .40
❑ 74 T'Pol .15 .40
❑ 75 Elizabeth Cutler .15 .40
❑ 76 Sarin .15 .40
❑ 77 Captain Erika Hernandez .15 .40
❑ 78 Talas .15 .40
❑ 79 Kaitaama .15 .40
❑ 80 Navaar .15 .40
❑ 81 T'Pau .15 .40

2010 Women of Star Trek ArtiFex

COMPLETE SET (10) 8.00 20.00
STATED ODDS 1:8
❑ 1 B'Elanna Torres 1.25 3.00
❑ 2 Captain Janeway 1.25 3.00
❑ 3 Jadzia Dax 1.25 3.00
❑ 4 Kira Nerys 1.25 3.00
❑ 5 Lt. Hoshi Sato 1.25 3.00
❑ 6 Lt. Uhura 1.25 3.00
❑ 7 Nurse Chapel 1.25 3.00
❑ 8 Seven of Nine 1.25 3.00
❑ 9 T'Pol 1.25 3.00
❑ 10 Yeoman Rand 1.25 3.00

2010 Women of Star Trek Autographs

STATED ODDS 1:8
L (LIMITED): 300-500 COPIES
VL (VERY LIMITED): 200-300 COPIES
❑ AB Antoinette Bower 6.00 15.00
❑ BL BarBara Luna 6.00 15.00
❑ BM Barbara March 6.00 15.00
❑ BW Barbara Williams 6.00 15.00
❑ CM Chase Masterson 8.00 20.00
❑ CR Claire Rankin 6.00 15.00
❑ CS Carolyn Seymour 6.00 15.00
❑ DC Denise Crosby 8.00 20.00
❑ EB Emily Banks 6.00 15.00
❑ ED Elizabeth Dennehy VL 30.00 60.00
❑ FJ Famke Janssen VL 100.00 175.00
❑ FN France Nuyen VL 45.00 90.00
❑ FS Felecia Bell Schafer 6.00 15.00
❑ GM Gates McFadden VL 45.00 90.00
❑ HT Hallie Todd 6.00 15.00
❑ JB Julie Caitlin Brown 6.00 15.00
❑ JC Joan Collins VL 60.00 120.00
❑ JL Jennifer Lien VL 40.00 80.00
❑ JR Jeri Ryan VL 75.00 125.00
❑ KM Kate Mulgrew VL 50.00 100.00
❑ KV Kate Vernon 6.00 15.00
❑ LF Louise Fletcher 6.00 15.00
❑ LM Lee Meriwether L 20.00 40.00
❑ LN Lycia Naff 6.00 15.00
❑ LW Lisa Wilcox 6.00 15.00
❑ MB Majel Barrett/ (issued as 6-case incentive) 150.00 250.00
❑ MF Michelle Forbes L 15.00 30.00
❑ MG Megan Gallagher 6.00 15.00
❑ MH Mariette Hartley L 30.00 60.00
❑ MV Musetta Vander 6.00 15.00
❑ NV Nana Visitor VL 40.00 80.00
❑ PJ Penny Johnson Jerald 6.00 15.00
❑ RA Rhonda Aldrich L 10.00 25.00
❑ RC Robin Curtis 6.00 15.00
❑ SG Susan Gibney 6.00 15.00
❑ SJ Sherry Jackson 8.00 20.00
❑ SK Sally Kellerman 10.00 25.00
❑ SP Suzie Plakson 6.00 15.00
❑ SS Sabrina Scharf 12.00 30.00
❑ TF Terry Farrell VL 50.00 100.00
❑ TL Tina Lifford 6.00 15.00
❑ AM1 Andrea Martin VL 25.00 50.00
❑ AM2 Amanda McBroom 6.00 15.00
❑ GW1 Gwynyth Walsh 6.00 15.00
❑ GW2 Grace Lee Whitney L 15.00 30.00
❑ KS1 Kathryn Leigh Scott 6.00 15.00
❑ KS2 Kitty Swink 6.00 15.00
❑ MS1 Michele Scarabelli 6.00 15.00
❑ MS2 Marina Sirtis VL 60.00 120.00
❑ NN1 Nichelle Nichols VL 75.00 150.00
❑ NN2 Natalija Nogulich L 10.00 25.00
❑ NVTF Nana Visitor 75.00 150.00
Terry Farrell

2010 Women of Star Trek Costumes

STATED ODDS 1:12
❑ WCC1 Kathryn Janeway 10.00 25.00
❑ WCC2 Kathryn Janeway 8.00 20.00
❑ WCC3 Kathryn Janeway 10.00 25.00
❑ WCC4 Beverly Crusher 8.00 20.00
❑ WCC5 Beverly Crusher 15.00 40.00
❑ WCC6 Beverly Crusher 8.00 20.00
❑ WCC7 Seven of Nine 10.00 25.00
❑ WCC8 Seven of Nine 10.00 25.00
❑ WCC9 T'Pol 12.00 30.00
❑ WCC10 T'Pol 10.00 25.00
❑ WCC11 T'Pol 10.00 25.00
❑ WCC12 Jadzia Dax 8.00 20.00
❑ WCC13 Kira Nerys 8.00 20.00
❑ WCC14 Ezri Dax 8.00 20.00
❑ WCC15 Deanna Troi SP 125.00 200.00
❑ WCC17 Kes 10.00 25.00
❑ WCC18 Beverly Crusher 8.00 20.00
❑ WCC19 Beverly Crusher 8.00 20.00
❑ WCC20 Kathryn Janeway 8.00 20.00
❑ WCC21 Kathryn Janeway 8.00 20.00
❑ WCC22 Seven of Nine SP 25.00 50.00
❑ WCC23 Seven of Nine 12.00 30.00
❑ WCC24 Seska 8.00 15.00
❑ WCC25 E'Tyshra 8.00 20.00
❑ WCC26 Lt. Jaryn 8.00 15.00

2010 Women of Star Trek Leading Ladies

COMPLETE SET (9) 15.00 40.00
STATED ODDS 1:24
❑ LL1 Lt. Uhura 3.00 8.00
❑ LL2 Counselor Troi 3.00 8.00
❑ LL3 Dr. Crusher 3.00 8.00
❑ LL4 Jadzia Dax 3.00 8.00
❑ LL5 Kira Nerys 3.00 8.00
❑ LL6 Captain Janeway 3.00 8.00
❑ LL7 Seven of Nine 3.00 8.00
❑ LL8 T'Pol 3.00 8.00
❑ LL9 Lt. Hoshi Sato 3.00 8.00

2010 Women of Star Trek Romantic Relationships

COMPLETE SET (9) 15.00 40.00
STATED ODDS 1:24
❑ RR1 Will Riker 3.00 8.00
Deanna Troi
❑ RR2 Worf 3.00 8.00
Jadzia Dax
❑ RR3 Captain Picard 3.00 8.00
Beverly Crusher
❑ RR4 Kes 3.00 8.00
Neelix
❑ RR5 Leeta 3.00 8.00
Rom
❑ RR6 Captain Sisko 3.00 8.00
Cassidy Yates
❑ RR7 Captain Kirk 3.00 8.00
Edith Keeler
❑ RR8 Spock 3.00 8.00
Nurse Chapel
❑ RR9 B'Elanna Torres 3.00 8.00
Tom Paris

2010 Woodstock Generation Rock Posters

COMPLETE SET (49)
❑ 1 Rock and Roll's Infancy
❑ 2 Rock 'n' Roll on the Marquis
❑ 3 A Mid-Summer's Night of Soul
❑ 4 A Raging Fire
❑ 5 A Detroit Success Story
❑ 6 Musical Pioneers
❑ 7 The Temptation of Rhythm and Blues
❑ 8 The Reverend Sings
❑ 9 A Jamaican Visionary
❑ 10 Fighting for Survival
❑ 11 Positive Vibrations
❑ 12 The Banner is Star Spangled
❑ 13 An Enduring Experience
❑ 14 A Magical Castle
❑ 15 The Relentless Pursuit of Peace
❑ 16 Daring to Imagine
❑ 17 People Are Strange
❑ 18 The Fire of a Poet
❑ 19 Love Life and Music
❑ 20 Who Knew How it Grew
❑ 21 A Lineup Never to be Repeated
❑ 22 A Legacy for Generations
❑ 23 The Woodstock Sound
❑ 24 A Legendary Film Documentary
❑ 25 A Music and Art Fair on a Dairy Farm
❑ 26 An Aquarian Exposition
❑ 27 The Summers of Love
❑ 28 The Hippie Bus
❑ 29 Any Regrets for Missing Out
❑ 30 Eight Arms to Hold You
❑ 31 An Overwhelming Success
❑ 32 A Most Magical Tour
❑ 33 A Ballad for Julian
❑ 34 Blisters on His Fingers
❑ 35 A More Personal Release
❑ 36 A Little Story of Liverpool
❑ 37 An Innocent Reference
❑ 38 What a Bash
❑ 39 Folk Rock at the Top
❑ 40 A Group of Musical Monkees
❑ 41 Born for a Wild Ride
❑ 42 Sexy, Sultry and Supernatural
❑ 43 Heavy Metal Hitters
❑ 44 The Cream Rises to the Top
❑ 45 Clearly Unique
❑ 46 A Grateful Following
❑ 47 A Melting Pot of Sweat and Style
❑ 48 Big Brother and His Sister Janis
❑ 49 Checklist

2010 Woodstock Generation Rock Posters Cut Signatures

❑ CS1 John Lennon
❑ CS2 Bob Marley
❑ CS3 Jim Morrison

2010 Woodstock Generation Rock Posters Metallogloss

COMPLETE SET (12)
STATED ODDS ONE PER PACK
❑ 1 The Doors of Perception
❑ 2 Break on Through
❑ 3 The Poet's Legend Lives On
❑ 4 Back in the Day
❑ 5 A Beautiful Day
❑ 6 Survival and Uprising
❑ 7 The Formidable Foursome
❑ 8 A Vision of Peace
❑ 9 Only the Good Die Young
❑ 10 A Guitar God is Born
❑ 11 Hey Joe
❑ 12 The Mastermind

2010 Woodstock Generation Rock Posters Sketches

STATED ODDS ONE PER PACK
❑ 1 Adam Cleveland/51*
❑ 2 Adam Schickling/25*
❑ 3 Amber Shelton/25*
❑ 4 Anthony Hochrein/35*
❑ 5 Ashleigh Popplewell/35*
❑ 6 Bill Pulkovski/20*
❑ 7 Brian Kong/176*
❑ 8 Bruce Gerlach/40*
❑ 9 Chris Bradberry/21*
❑ 10 Chris Henderson/43*
❑ 11 David Desbois/21*
❑ 12 David Girdley/25*
❑ 13 Denae Frazier/25*
❑ 14 Denise Vasquez/25
❑ 15 Eman/100*
❑ 16 Erik Maell/205*
❑ 17 Esteban Manriquez/100*
❑ 18 Gabe Farber/25*
❑ 19 Gemma Magno/38*
❑ 20 Gilbert Young Roland/100*
❑ 21 Guus Floor/27*
❑ 22 Ian Roberts/60*
❑ 23 Ingrid Hardy/25*
❑ 24 James McNeil/22*
❑ 25 Jason Hughes/134*
❑ 26 Jay Pangan III/108*
❑ 27 Jay Shimko/25*
❑ 28 Jean Marcel Azevedo/30*
❑ 29 Jennifer Mercer/30*
❑ 30 Jeremy Treece/35*
❑ 31 Joe Pekar/50*
❑ 32 Jon Hughes/104*
❑ 33 Kazuhiru Ito/19*
❑ 34 Kevin Graham/50*
❑ 35 Kimberly Dunaway/30*
❑ 36 Laura Inglis/25*
❑ 37 Leah Mangue/59*
❑ 38 Lynne Anderson/25*
❑ 39 Manny Mederos II/65*
❑ 40 MelJoy San Juan/12*
❑ 41 Michael Kraiger/69*
❑ 42 Mickey Clausen/48*
❑ 43 Nur Hanie Mohd/25*
❑ 44 Otto Dieffenbach/60*
❑ 45 Rainier Lagunsad/20*
❑ 46 Randy Martinez/35*
❑ 47 Ryan Heyling/2*
❑ 48 Samson Martinez/10*
❑ 49 Sarah Silva/27*
❑ 50 Sata M/12*
❑ 51 Scott DM Simmons/65*
❑ 52 Scott Rorie/50*
❑ 53 Scott Zambelli/47*
❑ 54 Soni Alcorn-Hender/20*
❑ 55 Stacey Girdley/48*
❑ 56 Steven Miller/35*
❑ 57 Ted Dastick Jr./30*
❑ 58 Tina Francisco/50*
❑ 59 Veronica Jaczkowski/24*
❑ 60 William Kenney/25*

2011 American Pie

COMPLETE SET (200) 10.00 25.00
❑ 1 World War II Ends .15 .40
❑ 2 Bob Hope .15 .40
❑ 3 Bud Abbott & Lou Costello .15 .40
❑ 4 The Bikini .15 .40
❑ 5 Dean Martin & Jerry Lewis .15 .40
❑ 6 Jimmy Stewart .15 .40
❑ 7 The Volkswagen Beetle Comes to the U.S. .15 .40
❑ 8 Robinson Breaks Color Barrier .15 .40
❑ 9 Aliens in Our Midst .15 .40
❑ 10 Marlon Brando .15 .40
❑ 11 The Doomsday Clock Is Set .15 .40
❑ 12 Bing Crosby .15 .40
❑ 13 Hells Angels Founded .15 .40
❑ 14 First Instant Camera .15 .40
❑ 15 The Kinsey Reports .15 .40
❑ 16 The Emmy Awards .15 .40
❑ 17 Death of a Salesman .15 .40
❑ 18 Grady the Cow .15 .40
❑ 19 Joe Louis Retires .15 .40
❑ 20 1984 .15 .40
❑ 21 First NASCAR Race Held .15 .40
❑ 22 Hopalong Cassidy Premieres on Television .15 .40
❑ 23 Diners Club Is First Credit Card .15 .40
❑ 24 Peanuts Debuts .15 .40
❑ 25 Groucho Marx .15 .40
❑ 26 First Pager Introduced .15 .40
❑ 27 World's First Remote Control .15 .40
❑ 28 Spencer Tracy .15 .40
❑ 29 Dennis the Menace Debuts .15 .40
❑ 30 Humphrey Bogart .15 .40
❑ 31 The Catcher in the Rye .15 .40
❑ 32 Lucille Ball & Desi Arnaz .15 .40
❑ 33 The Today Show Debuts .15 .40
❑ 34 Frank Sinatra .15 .40
❑ 35 First Corvette Released .15 .40
❑ 36 First Playboy Published .15 .40
❑ 37 Gary Cooper .15 .40
❑ 38 Hank Williams .15 .40
❑ 39 Vincent Price .15 .40
❑ 40 The First Color TV .15 .40
❑ 41 Iwo Jima Memorial .15 .40
❑ 42 Rock Around the Clock .15 .40
❑ 43 4/11/54 - Most Boring Day .15 .40
❑ 44 First Sports Illustrated .15 .40
❑ 45 The First Transistor Radio .15 .40
❑ 46 Burger King .15 .40
❑ 47 TV Dinners .15 .40
❑ 48 Scrabble .15 .40
❑ 49 Kroc Opens First McDonald's .15 .40
❑ 50 Disneyland Opens .15 .40
❑ 51 Jackie Gleason .15 .40
❑ 52 The Guinness Book of Records .15 .40
❑ 53 James Dean Dies .15 .40
❑ 54 Duke Ellington .15 .40
❑ 55 Grace Kelly .15 .40
❑ 56 Marciano Retires Undefeated .15 .40
❑ 57 Nat King Cole .15 .40
❑ 58 The Frisbee .15 .40
❑ 59 Dr. Seuss .15 .40
❑ 60 American Bandstand .15 .40
❑ 61 The Edsel Flops .15 .40
❑ 62 On the Road .15 .40
❑ 63 Leave it to Beaver .15 .40
❑ 64 The Peace Symbol .15 .40
❑ 65 The Jim Henson Company .15 .40
❑ 66 Orson Welles .15 .40
❑ 67 Donna Reed .15 .40
❑ 68 Motown Records Founded .15 .40
❑ 69 Barbie Debuts .15 .40
❑ 70 Miles Davis .15 .40
❑ 71 Pantyhose Invented .15 .40
❑ 72 Rod Serling .15 .40
❑ 73 Alfred Hitchcock .15 .40
❑ 74 Elizabeth Taylor .15 .40
❑ 75 The Fantasticks Begins .15 .40
❑ 76 Birth Control Pill in U.S. .15 .40
❑ 77 To Kill a Mockingbird .15 .40
❑ 78 The Fantastic Four Debuts .15 .40
❑ 79 Catch-22 .15 .40
❑ 80 Walmart Founded .15 .40
❑ 81 Warhol's Soup Cans .15 .40
❑ 82 Carson Takes Over The Tonight Show .15 .40
❑ 83 ZIP Codes Introduced .15 .40
❑ 84 First Push-Button Phone .15 .40
❑ 85 Instant Replay's First Use .15 .40
❑ 86 Ball Invents Smiley Face .15 .40
❑ 87 Jeopardy! .15 .40
❑ 88 Rudolph the Red-Nosed Reindeer .15 .40
❑ 89 Lenny Bruce .15 .40
❑ 90 Beatles Play Shea Stadium .15 .40
❑ 91 A Charlie Brown Christmas .15 .40
❑ 92 Gene Rodenberry .15 .40
❑ 93 Cary Grant .15 .40
❑ 94 How the Grinch Stole Christmas! .15 .40
❑ 95 Hot Wheels .15 .40
❑ 96 60 Minutes .15 .40
❑ 97 Louis Armstrong .15 .40
❑ 98 The Saturday Evening Post .15 .40
❑ 99 The Godfather Published .15 .40
❑ 100 Jimi Hendrix .40 1.00
❑ 101 The First ATM .15 .40
❑ 102 The Brady Bunch .15 .40
❑ 103 Sesame Street .15 .40
❑ 104 John Wayne .25 .60
❑ 105 American Top 40 Debuts .15 .40
❑ 106 Johnny Cash .25 .60
❑ 107 All in the Family .15 .40
❑ 108 John Lennon .25 .60
❑ 109 George Carlin .15 .40
❑ 110 The Price is Right .15 .40
❑ 111 Pong .15 .40
❑ 112 First Handheld Cell Phone .15 .40
❑ 113 World Trade Center Opens .15 .40
❑ 114 Secretariat's Triple Crown .15 .40
❑ 115 The Battle of the Sexes .15 .40
❑ 116 I am not a crook. .15 .40
❑ 117 Wire Walk Between WTC Towers .15 .40
❑ 118 First UPC Scanned .15 .40
❑ 119 Rubik's Cube .15 .40
❑ 120 Wheel of Fortune .15 .40
❑ 121 John Belushi .15 .40
❑ 122 Apple Founded .15 .40
❑ 123 Ramones Release Debut .15 .40
❑ 124 America's Bicentennial .15 .40
❑ 125 The Muppet Show .15 .40
❑ 126 Roots .15 .40
❑ 127 Commodore PET Released .15 .40
❑ 128 Atari 2600 Is Released .15 .40
❑ 129 Saturday Night Fever .15 .40
❑ 130 Christopher Reeve .15 .40
❑ 131 Atlantic City .15 .40
❑ 132 Garfield Debuts .15 .40
❑ 133 ESPN Launches .15 .40
❑ 134 Richard Pryor .15 .40
❑ 135 The Walkman Is Released .15 .40
❑ 136 The First Happy Meal .15 .40
❑ 137 The Miracle on Ice .15 .40
❑ 138 Pac-Man .15 .40
❑ 139 CNN Launches .15 .40
❑ 140 Who shot J.R.? .15 .40
❑ 141 MTV Means Music All Day .15 .40
❑ 142 Luke & Laura marry on GH .15 .40
❑ 143 CDs Revolutionize Music .15 .40
❑ 144 Michael Jackson's Thriller .15 .40
❑ 145 Final Episode of M*A*S*H .15 .40
❑ 146 Apple Macintosh Released .15 .40
❑ 147 Court Allows Home Recording .15 .40
❑ 148 We Are the World .15 .40
❑ 149 New Coke .15 .40
❑ 150 Route 66 Decommissioned .15 .40
❑ 151 Live Aid .15 .40
❑ 152 Nintendo's NES Released .15 .40
❑ 153 Calvin and Hobbes .15 .40
❑ 154 Fred Mister Rogers Rogers .15 .40
❑ 155 Windows 1.0 .15 .40
❑ 156 Tetris .15 .40
❑ 157 Opening Capone's Vault .15 .40
❑ 158 Hands Across America .15 .40
❑ 159 The Oprah Winfrey Show .15 .40
❑ 160 Tear down this wall! .15 .40
❑ 161 Baby Jessica .15 .40
❑ 162 Seinfeld Premieres .15 .40
❑ 163 The Simpsons Premieres .15 .40
❑ 164 Pale Blue Dot .15 .40
❑ 165 World Wide Web Launched .15 .40
❑ 166 Freddie Mercury Tribute .15 .40
❑ 167 The Real World Premieres .15 .40
❑ 168 Doom Is Released .15 .40
❑ 169 Nancy Kerrigan Attacked .15 .40
❑ 170 Kurt Cobain Suicide .40 1.00
❑ 171 DVD Introduced .15 .40
❑ 172 O.J. Simpson Found Not Guilty .15 .40
❑ 173 Unabomber Arrested .15 .40
❑ 174 Titanic .15 .40
❑ 175 Google Founded .15 .40
❑ 176 Napster Debuts .15 .40
❑ 177 U.S. Wins Women's World Cup .15 .40
❑ 178 Armstrong Wins 1st Tour .15 .40
❑ 179 Y2K Dud - New Millennium .15 .40
❑ 180 Survivor Premieres .15 .40
❑ 181 September 11th .15 .40
❑ 182 Enron Bankruptcy .15 .40
❑ 183 First iPod Released .15 .40
❑ 184 Martha Stewart Indicted .15 .40
❑ 185 Human Genome Project .15 .40
❑ 186 Saddam Hussein Captured .15 .40
❑ 187 Facebook Founded .15 .40
❑ 188 Blogging Takes Its Place .15 .40
❑ 189 YouTube Launches .15 .40
❑ 190 Twitter Launches .15 .40
❑ 191 Last Harry Potter Released .15 .40
❑ 192 Phelps Wins 8 Golds .15 .40
❑ 193 Obama Elected President .15 .40
❑ 194 Bernie Madoff Arrested .15 .40
❑ 195 Michael Jackson Dies .15 .40
❑ 196 Kanye Interrupts Swift .15 .40
❑ 197 Jersey Shore Premieres .15 .40
❑ 198 Osama bin Laden Killed .15 .40
❑ 199 Steve Jobs 1955-2011 .15 .40
❑ 200 Hurricane Irene .15 .40

2011 American Pie Foil

*FOIL: 1X TO 2.5X BASIC CARDS
OVERALL PARALLEL ODDS 1:4

2011 American Pie Spotlight Foil

*SPOTLIGHT FOIL: 5X TO 12X BASIC CARDS
STATED PRINT RUN 76 SER. #'d SETS

2011 American Pie American Pieces Relics

STATED ODDS 1:176
❑ APCRGB Gettysburg 20.00 40.00
❑ APCRGK Grassy Knoll 15.00 40.00
❑ APCRSL Statue of Liberty 15.00 40.00
❑ APCRLCT Lewis and Clark Trail 12.00 30.00

2011 American Pie Autographs

STATED ODDS 1:61
EXCHANGE DEADLINE 11/30/2014
❑ APA1 Mickey Rooney 20.00 40.00
❑ APA2 A.J. Hammer 3.00 8.00
❑ APA3 Maksim Chmerkovskiy 8.00 20.00
❑ APA4 Shanna Moakler 10.00 25.00
❑ APA5 Trista Sutter 8.00 20.00
❑ APA6 Kato Kaelin 8.00 20.00
❑ APA7 Joe Gannascoli 6.00 15.00
❑ APA8 Jimmie Walker 3.00 8.00
❑ APA9 Andrew Zimmern 8.00 20.00
❑ APA10 John O'Hurley 6.00 15.00
❑ APA11 Tia Carrere 15.00 30.00
❑ APA12 Tom Arnold 10.00 25.00
❑ APA13 Paul Teutul, Sr. 15.00 30.00
❑ APA14 Joey Fatone 8.00 20.00
❑ APA15 Gilbert Gottfried 10.00 25.00
❑ APA16 Dean Cain 15.00 30.00
❑ APA17 Justin Willman 3.00 8.00
❑ APA18 Sean Astin 6.00 15.00
❑ APA19 Buddy Valastro 15.00 30.00
❑ APA20 Carmen Electra 20.00 40.00
❑ APA21 Jack Hanna 10.00 25.00
❑ APA23 Naomi Judd 15.00 30.00
❑ APA24 Susan Lucci 25.00 50.00
❑ APA25 Butch Patrick 6.00 15.00
❑ APA26 John Ratzenberger 15.00 30.00
❑ APA27 Larry Thomas 3.00 8.00
❑ APA28 Bret Michaels EXCH 20.00 40.00
❑ APA29 Don McLean 20.00 40.00
❑ APA30 Wilmer Valderrama 10.00 25.00
❑ APA31 Henry Winkler 20.00 40.00
❑ APA33 Vincent Pastore 10.00 25.00
❑ APA35 Carrot Top 15.00 30.00
❑ APA36 Enrique Iglesias EXCH 15.00 30.00
❑ APA37 Louie Anderson 6.00 15.00
❑ APA38 Bob Costas 20.00 40.00
❑ APA39 Jamie Foxx 30.00 60.00
❑ ACSH Charlie Sheen 175.00 250.00

2011 American Pie Autographs Relics

STATED ODDS 1:250
EXCHANGE DEADLINE 11/30/2014
❑ APAR1 Mickey Rooney 25.00 50.00
❑ APAR2 A.J. Hammer 4.00 10.00
❑ APAR3 Maksim Chmerkovskiy 10.00 25.00
❑ APAR4 Shanna Moakler EXCH 12.00 30.00
❑ APAR5 Trista Sutter 10.00 25.00
❑ APAR6 Kato Kaelin 10.00 25.00
❑ APAR7 Joe Gannascoli 8.00 20.00
❑ APAR8 Jimmie Walker 4.00 10.00
❑ APAR9 Andrew Zimmern EXCH 10.00 25.00
❑ APAR10 John O'Hurley EXCH 8.00 20.00
❑ APAR11 Tia Carrere 20.00 40.00
❑ APAR12 Tom Arnold EXCH 12.00 30.00
❑ APAR13 Paul Teutul, Sr. 20.00 40.00
❑ APAR14 Joey Fatone EXCH 10.00 25.00
❑ APAR15 Gilbert Gottfried 12.00 30.00
❑ APAR16 Dean Cain 20.00 40.00
❑ APAR17 Justin Willman 4.00 10.00
❑ APAR18 Sean Astin 8.00 20.00
❑ APAR19 Buddy Valastro 20.00 40.00
❑ APAR20 Carmen Electra 25.00 50.00
❑ APAR21 Jack Hanna EXCH 12.00 30.00
❑ APAR23 Naomi Judd 25.00 50.00
❑ APAR24 Susan Lucci 30.00 60.00
❑ APAR25 Butch Patrick 8.00 20.00
❑ APAR26 John Ratzenberger 20.00 40.00
❑ APAR27 Larry Thomas 4.00 10.00
❑ APAR28 Bret Michaels EXCH 30.00 60.00
❑ APAR29 Don McLean 25.00 50.00
❑ APAR30 Wilmer Valderrama 12.00 30.00
❑ APAR31 Henry Winkler 25.00 50.00
❑ APAR33 Vincent Pastore 12.00 30.00
❑ APAR35 Carrot Top 20.00 40.00
❑ APAR36 Enrique Iglesias EXCH 20.00 40.00
❑ APAR37 Louie Anderson 8.00 20.00
❑ APAR38 Jamie Foxx EXCH 40.00 80.00

2011 American Pie Coin Collection Dime

STATED PRINT RUN 25 SER. #'d SETS
❑ APCC1 Buster Keaton 12.00 30.00
❑ APCC2 John Wayne 25.00 60.00
❑ APCC3 Marilyn Monroe 60.00 120.00
❑ APCC4 Groucho Marx 15.00 40.00
❑ APCC5 Humphrey Bogart 15.00 40.00
❑ APCC6 Spencer Tracy 12.00 30.00
❑ APCC7 Clark Gable 25.00 60.00
❑ APCC8 Gary Cooper 20.00 50.00
❑ APCC9 Christopher Reeve EXCH 20.00 50.00
❑ APCC10 Duke Ellington 12.00 30.00
❑ APCC11 Jimi Hendrix 25.00 60.00
❑ APCC12 Louis Armstrong 12.00 30.00
❑ APCC13 Bing Crosby 12.00 30.00
❑ APCC14 Rod Serling 12.00 30.00
❑ APCC15 Walt Disney 25.00 60.00

2011 American Pie Coin Collection Half-Dollar

STATED PRINT RUN 25 SER. #'d SETS
❑ APCC1 Buster Keaton 12.00 30.00
❑ APCC2 John Wayne 25.00 60.00
❑ APCC3 Marilyn Monroe 60.00 120.00
❑ APCC4 Groucho Marx 15.00 40.00
❑ APCC5 Humphrey Bogart 15.00 40.00
❑ APCC6 Spencer Tracy 12.00 30.00
❑ APCC7 Clark Gable 25.00 60.00
❑ APCC8 Gary Cooper 20.00 50.00
❑ APCC9 Christopher Reeve EXCH 20.00 50.00
❑ APCC10 Duke Ellington 12.00 30.00
❑ APCC11 Jimi Hendrix 25.00 60.00

❑ APCC12 Louis Armstrong 12.00 30.00
❑ APCC13 Bing Crosby 12.00 30.00
❑ APCC14 Rod Serling 12.00 30.00
❑ APCC15 Walt Disney 25.00 60.00

2011 American Pie Coin Collection Nickel

STATED PRINT RUN 25 SER. #'d SETS

❑ APCC1 Buster Keaton 12.00 30.00
❑ APCC2 John Wayne 25.00 60.00
❑ APCC3 Marilyn Monroe 60.00 120.00
❑ APCC4 Groucho Marx 15.00 40.00
❑ APCC5 Humphrey Bogart 15.00 40.00
❑ APCC6 Spencer Tracy 12.00 30.00
❑ APCC7 Clark Gable 25.00 60.00
❑ APCC8 Gary Cooper 20.00 50.00
❑ APCC9 Christopher Reeve EXCH 20.00 50.00
❑ APCC10 Duke Ellington 12.00 30.00
❑ APCC11 Jimi Hendrix 25.00 60.00
❑ APCC12 Louis Armstrong 12.00 30.00
❑ APCC13 Bing Crosby 12.00 30.00
❑ APCC14 Rod Serling 12.00 30.00
❑ APCC15 Walt Disney 25.00 60.00

2011 American Pie Coin Collection Penny

STATED PRINT RUN 25 SER. #'d SETS

❑ APCC1 Buster Keaton 12.00 30.00
❑ APCC2 John Wayne 25.00 60.00
❑ APCC3 Marilyn Monroe 60.00 120.00
❑ APCC4 Groucho Marx 15.00 40.00
❑ APCC5 Humphrey Bogart 15.00 40.00
❑ APCC6 Spencer Tracy 12.00 30.00
❑ APCC7 Clark Gable 25.00 60.00
❑ APCC8 Gary Cooper 20.00 50.00
❑ APCC9 Christopher Reeve EXCH 20.00 50.00
❑ APCC10 Duke Ellington 12.00 30.00
❑ APCC11 Jimi Hendrix 25.00 60.00
❑ APCC12 Louis Armstrong 12.00 30.00
❑ APCC13 Bing Crosby 12.00 30.00
❑ APCC14 Rod Serling 12.00 30.00
❑ APCC15 Walt Disney 25.00 60.00

2011 American Pie Coin Collection Quarter

STATED PRINT RUN 25 SER. #'d SETS

❑ APCC1 Buster Keaton 12.00 30.00
❑ APCC2 John Wayne 25.00 60.00
❑ APCC3 Marilyn Monroe 60.00 120.00
❑ APCC4 Groucho Marx 15.00 40.00
❑ APCC5 Humphrey Bogart 15.00 40.00
❑ APCC6 Spencer Tracy 12.00 30.00
❑ APCC7 Clark Gable 25.00 60.00
❑ APCC8 Gary Cooper 20.00 50.00
❑ APCC9 Christopher Reeve EXCH 20.00 50.00
❑ APCC10 Duke Ellington 12.00 30.00
❑ APCC11 Jimi Hendrix 25.00 60.00
❑ APCC12 Louis Armstrong 12.00 30.00
❑ APCC13 Bing Crosby 12.00 30.00
❑ APCC14 Rod Serling 12.00 30.00
❑ APCC15 Walt Disney 25.00 60.00

2011 American Pie Cut Signatures

STATED PRINT RUN 1 SER. #'d SET
UNPRICED DUE TO SCARCITY

❑ APCSAB Ann Blyth
❑ APCSAD Angie Dickinson
❑ APCSBB Brigitte Bardot
❑ APCSBF Barbara Feldon
❑ APCSBN Bob Newhart
❑ APCSCC Carol Coombs
❑ APCSCD Charlie Daniels
❑ APCSCL Cheryl Ladd
❑ APCSDA Danny Aiello
❑ APCSDB Debby Boone
❑ APCSDD Dana Delany
❑ APCSDK Dean Koontz
❑ APCSDR Debbie Reynolds
❑ APCSDS David Shire
❑ APCSEA Edward Albee
❑ APCSEG Elliott Gould
❑ APCSEH Earl Hamner
❑ APCSFS Felix Silla
❑ APCSGB Gary Busey
❑ APCSGL George Lindsey
❑ APCSHD Hugh Downs
❑ APCSJB Jacqueline Bissett
❑ APCSJG John Grisham
❑ APCSJL Judith Light
❑ APCSJP Jon Provost
❑ APCSJR John Romita
❑ APCSJV Jon Voight
❑ APCSKL Kenny Loggins
❑ APCSLB Lauren Bacall
❑ APCSLE Linda Evans
❑ APCSMH Monty Hall
❑ APCSMS Martin Sheen
❑ APCSNS Neil Simon
❑ APCSPB Pete Best
❑ APCSPH Paul Hogan
❑ APCSRD Robert Duvall
❑ APCSSJ Shirley Jones
❑ APCSSM Sarah McLachlan
❑ APCSTH Tippi Hedren
❑ APCSTK Ted Koppel
❑ APCSTR Tim Reid
❑ APCSTT Ted Turner
❑ APCSWC Wes Craven
❑ APCSBBU Bobby Burgess
❑ APCSDBR Dave Brubeck
❑ APCSDCL Dick Clark
❑ APCSEAS Ed Asner
❑ APCSJLA John Landis
❑ APCSMHA Marvin Hamlisch
❑ APCSWPB William Peter Blatty

2011 American Pie Cut Signatures Relics

STATED PRINT RUN 1 SER. #'d SET
UNPRICED DUE TO SCARCITY

❑ APCSR1 George H.W. Bush
❑ APCSR2 Gerald Ford
❑ APCSR3 Jimmy Carter
❑ APCSR4 Richard Nixon
❑ APCSR5 Calvin Coolidge

2011 American Pie Dual Cut Signatures

STATED PRINT RUN 1 SER. #'d SET
UNPRICED DUE TO SCARCITY

❑ APDCS1 Tony Randall
Jack Klugman
❑ APDCS2 Florence Henderson
Ann B. Davis
❑ APDCS3 David Prowse
James Earl Jones
❑ APDCS4 Carl Reiner
Rob Reiner
❑ APDCS5 Larry Flynt
Milos Forman
❑ APDCS6 Mike Farrell
Wayne Rogers
❑ APDCS7 Tyne Daly
Sharon Gless
❑ APDCS8 Paul Simon
Art Garfunkel
❑ APDCS9 Alex Trebek
Ken Jennings
❑ APDCS10 Cheech Marin
Tommy Chong

2011 American Pie Quad Cut Signatures

STATED PRINT RUN 1 SER. #'d SET
UNPRICED DUE TO SCARCITY

❑ APQCS1 Jim Davis
Stan Goldberg/Marcus Hamilton/Mort Walker
❑ APQCS2 Ron Howard
Tom Bosley/Marion Ross/Don Most
❑ APQCS3 Russell Johnson
Alan Hale Jr./Tina Louise/Jim Backus

2011 American Pie Entertainment Buybacks

STATED ODDS 1:24 HOBBY

❑ 1 Addams Family 1991
❑ 2 Alf 1988
❑ 3 Alien 1979
❑ 4 A-Team 1983
❑ 5 Baby 1985
❑ 6 Back to the Future 2 1989
❑ 7 Batman Movie 1989
❑ 8 Batman Returns 1992
❑ 9 Battlestar Galactica 1978
❑ 10 Beatles Black and White 1964
❑ 11 Beatles Color 1964
❑ 12 Black Hole 1979
❑ 13 Buck Rogers in the 25th Century 1979
❑ 14 Close Encounters of the Third Kind 1978
❑ 15 Dick Tracy 1990
❑ 16 E.T. 1982
❑ 17 Evel Knievel 1974
❑ 18 Fabian 1959
❑ 19 Funny Valentines 1959
❑ 20 Garbage Pail Kids 1986
❑ 21 Ghostbusters 2 1989
❑ 22 Goonies 1985
❑ 23 Grease 1978
❑ 24 Happy Days 1976
❑ 25 Harry and the Hendersons 1987
❑ 26 Hook 1991
❑ 27 Jaws 2 1978
❑ 28 Jaws 3-D 1983
❑ 29 John F. Kennedy 1964
❑ 30 Kiss 1978
❑ 31 Maya 1967
❑ 32 Monster Laffs 1966
❑ 33 Moonraker 1979
❑ 34 Mork and Mindy 1978
❑ 35 New Kids on the Block 1989
❑ 36 NSYNC 2000
❑ 37 Partridge Family 1971
❑ 38 Planet of the Apes 1967
❑ 39 Pokemon: Mewto Strikes Back
❑ 40 Raiders of the Lost Ark 1981
❑ 41 Rat Patrol 1966
❑ 42 Robin Hood Prince of Thieves 1991
❑ 43 Rocketeer 1991
❑ 44 Rocky II 1979
❑ 45 Rocky IV 1985
❑ 46 Star Trek the Motion Picture 1979
❑ 47 Star Wars 1977
❑ 48 Star Wars Chrome Archives 1999
❑ 49 Star Wars Empire Strikes Back 1980
❑ 50 Star Wars Return of the Jedi 1983
❑ 51 Superman 1978
❑ 52 Superman II 1980
❑ 53 Superman III 1983
❑ 54 Teenage Mutant Ninja Turtles 1989
❑ 55 Three's Company 1978
❑ 56 U.S. Presidents 1972
❑ 57 X-Files Fight the Future 1998
❑ 58 You'll Die Laughing 1973
❑ 59 You'll Die Laughing Creature Feature 1980

2011 American Pie Entertainment Buybacks Autographs

❑ 1 Adam West 1966 Batman/500
❑ 2 Jimmie Walker 1975 Good Times/25
❑ 3 Joey Fatone 2000 NSYNC/25
❑ 4 Lou Ferrigno 1979 Incredible Hulk/500

2011 American Pie Fads and Fashions

COMPLETE SET (30) 12.00 30.00
STATED ODDS 1:4

❑ FF1 Pogs .75 2.00
❑ FF2 Pet Rocks .75 2.00
❑ FF3 Slap Bracelets .75 2.00
❑ FF4 Trucker Hats .75 2.00
❑ FF5 Hula Hoops .75 2.00
❑ FF6 Coonskin Caps .75 2.00
❑ FF7 Poodle Skirts .75 2.00
❑ FF8 3D Movies .75 2.00
❑ FF9 Rickie Tickie Stickers .75 2.00
❑ FF10 Troll Dolls .75 2.00
❑ FF11 Lava Lamps .75 2.00
❑ FF12 Go-Go Boots .75 2.00
❑ FF13 Mood Rings .75 2.00
❑ FF14 Hypercolor Shirts .75 2.00
❑ FF15 Big Hair .75 2.00
❑ FF16 Baby on Board .75 2.00
❑ FF17 Friendship Bracelets .75 2.00
❑ FF18 The Macarena .75 2.00
❑ FF19 Bleached Hair .75 2.00
❑ FF20 Beanie Babies .75 2.00
❑ FF21 Tickle Me Elmo .75 2.00
❑ FF22 Texas Hold 'Em .75 2.00
❑ FF23 The Atkins Diet .75 2.00
❑ FF24 LiveStrong Wristbands .75 2.00
❑ FF25 Flagpole Sitting .75 2.00
❑ FF26 Goldfish Swallowing .75 2.00
❑ FF27 Kilroy Was Here .75 2.00
❑ FF28 SuperBalls .75 2.00
❑ FF29 Telephone-Booth Stuffing .75 2.00
❑ FF30 Zoot Suits .75 2.00

2011 American Pie Hirsute History

COMPLETE SET (20) 10.00 25.00
STATED ODDS 1:6

❑ HH1 Horseshoe Mustache 1.00 2.50
❑ HH2 The Mullet 1.00 2.50
❑ HH3 Muttonchops 1.00 2.50
❑ HH4 Chinstrap Beard 1.00 2.50
❑ HH5 Soul Patch 1.00 2.50
❑ HH6 Goatee 1.00 2.50
❑ HH7 Pompadour 1.00 2.50
❑ HH8 Beehive 1.00 2.50
❑ HH9 The Rachel 1.00 2.50
❑ HH10 Caesar 1.00 2.50
❑ HH11 Bob 1.00 2.50
❑ HH12 Handlebar Moustache 1.00 2.50
❑ HH13 Sideburns 1.00 2.50
❑ HH14 Fauxhawk 1.00 2.50
❑ HH15 Mohawk 1.00 2.50
❑ HH16 Blowout 1.00 2.50
❑ HH17 70s Feathered Hair 1.00 2.50
❑ HH18 The Afro 1.00 2.50
❑ HH19 Dreadlocks 1.00 2.50
❑ HH20 Cornrows 1.00 2.50

2011 American Pie Hollywood Sign Letter Patches

STATED ODDS 1:93
STATED PRINT RUN 25 SER. #'d SETS

❑ HSLP1 Alfred Hitchcock 5.00 12.00
❑ HSLP2 Bob Hope 6.00 15.00
❑ HSLP3 Buster Keaton 6.00 15.00
❑ HSLP4 Cary Grant 6.00 15.00
❑ HSLP5 Cecil B. DeMille 5.00 12.00
❑ HSLP6 Charlie Chaplin 8.00 20.00
❑ HSLP7 Clark Gable 8.00 20.00
❑ HSLP8 Douglas Fairbanks Sr. 5.00 12.00
❑ HSLP9 Elizabeth Taylor 8.00 20.00
❑ HSLP10 Errol Flynn 5.00 12.00
❑ HSLP11 Frank Sinatra 8.00 20.00
❑ HSLP12 Fred Astaire 5.00 12.00
❑ HSLP13 Gary Cooper 5.00 12.00
❑ HSLP14 Grace Kelly 5.00 12.00
❑ HSLP15 Groucho Marx 8.00 20.00
❑ HSLP16 Humphrey Bogart 6.00 15.00
❑ HSLP17 James Cagney 5.00 12.00
❑ HSLP18 James Stewart 5.00 12.00
❑ HSLP19 John Wayne 10.00 25.00
❑ HSLP20 Marilyn Monroe 15.00 40.00
❑ HSLP21 Marlon Brando 5.00 12.00
❑ HSLP22 Mickey Rooney 5.00 12.00
❑ HSLP23 Orson Welles 5.00 12.00
❑ HSLP24 Sean Astin 5.00 12.00
❑ HSLP25 Spencer Tracy 5.00 12.00

2011 American Pie Hollywood Sign Letter Patches Fold-Outs

STATED PRINT RUN 1 SER. #'d SET
UNPRICED DUE TO SCARCITY

❑ HSLP1 Alfred Hitchcock
❑ HSLP2 Bob Hope
❑ HSLP3 Buster Keaton
❑ HSLP4 Cary Grant
❑ HSLP5 Cecil B. DeMille
❑ HSLP6 Charlie Chaplin
❑ HSLP7 Clark Gable
❑ HSLP8 Douglas Fairbanks Sr.
❑ HSLP9 Elizabeth Taylor
❑ HSLP10 Errol Flynn
❑ HSLP11 Frank Sinatra
❑ HSLP12 Fred Astaire
❑ HSLP13 Gary Cooper
❑ HSLP14 Grace Kelly
❑ HSLP15 Groucho Marx
❑ HSLP16 Humphrey Bogart
❑ HSLP17 James Cagney
❑ HSLP18 James Stewart
❑ HSLP19 John Wayne
❑ HSLP20 Marilyn Monroe
❑ HSLP21 Marlon Brando
❑ HSLP22 Mickey Rooney
❑ HSLP23 Orson Welles
❑ HSLP24 Sean Astin
❑ HSLP25 Spencer Tracy

2011 American Pie Hollywood Walk of Fame

COMPLETE SET (50) 15.00 40.00
STATED ODDS 1:3

❑ HWF1 Alfred Hitchcock .75 2.00
❑ HWF2 Bing Crosby .75 2.00
❑ HWF3 Bob Hope .75 2.00
❑ HWF4 Cary Grant .75 2.00
❑ HWF5 Christopher Reeve .75 2.00
❑ HWF6 Chuck Berry .75 2.00
❑ HWF7 Dean Martin .75 2.00
❑ HWF8 Duke Ellington .75 2.00
❑ HWF9 Elizabeth Taylor .75 2.00
❑ HWF10 Frank Sinatra .75 2.00
❑ HWF11 Fred Mister Rogers .75 2.00
❑ HWF12 Gary Cooper .75 2.00
❑ HWF13 Gene Roddenberry .75 2.00
❑ HWF14 George Carlin .75 2.00
❑ HWF15 Hank Williams .75 2.00
❑ HWF16 Humphrey Bogart .75 2.00
❑ HWF17 James Stewart .75 2.00
❑ HWF18 Jimi Hendrix 1.25 3.00
❑ HWF19 John Belushi .75 2.00
❑ HWF20 John Lennon 1.00 2.50
❑ HWF21 John Wayne 1.00 2.50
❑ HWF22 Johnny Cash 1.00 2.50
❑ HWF23 Louis Armstrong .75 2.00
❑ HWF24 Lucille Ball .75 2.00
❑ HWF25 Marilyn Monroe 1.50 4.00
❑ HWF26 Marlon Brando .75 2.00
❑ HWF27 Miles Davis .75 2.00
❑ HWF28 Richard Pryor .75 2.00
❑ HWF29 Rod Serling .75 2.00
❑ HWF30 Walt Disney .75 2.00
❑ HWF31 Grace Kelly .75 2.00
❑ HWF32 Groucho Marx .75 2.00
❑ HWF33 Orson Welles .75 2.00
❑ HWF34 Spencer Tracy .75 2.00
❑ HWF35 Vincent Price .75 2.00
❑ HWF36 Buster Keaton .75 2.00
❑ HWF37 Cecil B. DeMille .75 2.00
❑ HWF38 Charlie Chaplin .75 2.00
❑ HWF39 Clark Gable .75 2.00
❑ HWF40 Douglas Fairbanks, Sr. .75 2.00
❑ HWF41 Errol Flynn .75 2.00
❑ HWF42 Fred Astaire .75 2.00
❑ HWF43 George Burns .75 2.00
❑ HWF44 Harry Houdini .75 2.00
❑ HWF45 James Cagney .75 2.00
❑ HWF46 Joanne Woodward .75 2.00
❑ HWF47 Leslie Nielsen .75 2.00
❑ HWF48 Mickey Rooney .75 2.00
❑ HWF49 Rodney Dangerfield .75 2.00
❑ HWF50 Sammy Davis, Jr. .75 2.00

2011 American Pie Hollywood Walk of Fame Patches

STATED PRINT RUN 50 SER. #'d SETS

❑ HWF1 Alfred Hitchcock 6.00 15.00
❑ HWF2 Bing Crosby 6.00 15.00
❑ HWF3 Bob Hope 6.00 15.00
❑ HWF4 Cary Grant 8.00 20.00
❑ HWF5 Christopher Reeve 8.00 20.00
❑ HWF6 Chuck Berry 8.00 20.00
❑ HWF7 Dean Martin 8.00 20.00
❑ HWF8 Duke Ellington 6.00 15.00
❑ HWF9 Elizabeth Taylor 10.00 25.00
❑ HWF10 Frank Sinatra 8.00 20.00
❑ HWF11 Fred Mister Rogers 6.00 15.00
❑ HWF12 Gary Cooper 6.00 15.00
❑ HWF13 Gene Roddenberry 8.00 20.00
❑ HWF14 George Carlin 8.00 20.00
❑ HWF15 Hank Williams 6.00 15.00
❑ HWF16 Humphrey Bogart 6.00 15.00
❑ HWF17 James Stewart 6.00 15.00
❑ HWF18 Jimi Hendrix 10.00 25.00
❑ HWF19 John Belushi 8.00 20.00
❑ HWF20 John Lennon 8.00 20.00
❑ HWF21 John Wayne 15.00 40.00
❑ HWF22 Johnny Cash 8.00 20.00
❑ HWF23 Louis Armstrong 6.00 15.00
❑ HWF24 Lucille Ball 6.00 15.00
❑ HWF25 Marilyn Monroe 15.00 40.00
❑ HWF26 Marlon Brando 6.00 15.00
❑ HWF27 Miles Davis 6.00 15.00
❑ HWF28 Richard Pryor 8.00 20.00
❑ HWF29 Rod Serling 6.00 15.00
❑ HWF30 Walt Disney 8.00 20.00
❑ HWF31 Grace Kelly 6.00 15.00
❑ HWF32 Groucho Marx 8.00 20.00
❑ HWF33 Orson Welles 6.00 15.00
❑ HWF34 Spencer Tracy 6.00 15.00
❑ HWF35 Vincent Price 6.00 15.00
❑ HWF36 Buster Keaton 6.00 15.00
❑ HWF37 Cecil B. DeMille 6.00 15.00
❑ HWF38 Charlie Chaplin 6.00 15.00
❑ HWF39 Clark Gable 6.00 15.00
❑ HWF40 Douglas Fairbanks, Sr. 6.00 15.00
❑ HWF41 Errol Flynn 6.00 15.00
❑ HWF42 Fred Astaire 6.00 15.00
❑ HWF43 George Burns 6.00 15.00
❑ HWF44 Harry Houdini 8.00 20.00
❑ HWF45 James Cagney 6.00 15.00
❑ HWF46 Joanne Woodward 6.00 15.00
❑ HWF47 Leslie Nielsen 6.00 15.00
❑ HWF48 Mickey Rooney 6.00 15.00
❑ HWF49 Rodney Dangerfield 6.00 15.00
❑ HWF50 Sammy Davis, Jr. 6.00 15.00

2011 American Pie Relics

STATED ODDS 1:13

❑ APR1 Mickey Rooney 2.50 6.00
❑ APR2 A.J. Hammer 2.50 6.00
❑ APR3 Maksim Chmerkovskiy 3.00 8.00
❑ APR4 Shanna Moakler EXCH 4.00 10.00
❑ APR5 Trista Sutter 2.50 6.00
❑ APR6 Kato Kaelin 2.50 6.00
❑ APR7 Joe Gannascoli 2.50 6.00
❑ APR8 Jimmie Walker 2.50 6.00
❑ APR9 Andrew Zimmern EXCH 3.00 8.00
❑ APR10 John O'Hurley 2.50 6.00
❑ APR11 Tia Carrere 4.00 10.00
❑ APR12 Tom Arnold EXCH 2.50 6.00
❑ APR13 Paul Teutul, Sr. 4.00 10.00
❑ APR14 Joey Fatone 3.00 8.00
❑ APR15 Gilbert Gottfried 2.50 6.00
❑ APR16 Dean Cain 3.00 8.00
❑ APR17 Justin Willman 2.50 6.00
❑ APR18 Sean Astin 2.50 6.00
❑ APR19 Buddy Valastro 2.50 6.00
❑ APR20 Carmen Electra 5.00 12.00
❑ APR21 Jack Hanna EXCH 6.00 15.00
❑ APR23 Naomi Judd 4.00 10.00
❑ APR24 Susan Lucci 5.00 12.00
❑ APR25 Butch Patrick 2.50 6.00
❑ APR26 John Ratzenberger 2.50 6.00
❑ APR27 Larry Thomas 2.50 6.00
❑ APR28 Bret Michaels EXCH 8.00 20.00
❑ APR29 Don McLean 2.50 6.00
❑ APR30 Wilmer Valderrama 2.50 6.00
❑ APR31 Henry Winkler 3.00 8.00
❑ APR33 Vincent Pastore 2.50 6.00
❑ APR34 Jimi Hendrix EXCH 125.00 200.00
❑ APR35 Carrot Top 2.50 6.00
❑ APR36 Enrique Iglesias EXCH 8.00 20.00
❑ APR37 Louie Anderson 2.50 6.00
❑ APR38 Jamie Foxx EXCH 6.00 15.00

2011 American Pie Stamp Collection

STATED PRINT RUN 76 SER. #'d SETS

❑ APSC1 Johnny Cash 25.00 50.00
❑ APSC2 James Cagney 15.00 30.00
❑ APSC3 Fred Astaire 15.00 30.00
❑ APSC4 Bob Hope 15.00 30.00
❑ APSC5 John Wayne 40.00 80.00
❑ APSC6 James Stewart 20.00 40.00
❑ APSC7 Orson Welles 15.00 30.00
❑ APSC8 Frank Sinatra 20.00 40.00
❑ APSC9 Mickey Rooney 20.00 40.00
❑ APSC10 Marlon Brando 30.00 60.00
❑ APSC11 Marilyn Monroe 40.00 80.00
❑ APSC12 Grace Kelly 25.00 50.00
❑ APSC13 Elizabeth Taylor 25.00 50.00
❑ APSC14 Miles Davis 15.00 30.00
❑ APSC15 Lucille Ball 20.00 40.00

2011 Americana

COMPLETE SET (100) 12.00 25.00

❑ 1 Pamela Anderson 1.00 2.50
❑ 2 Chris Noth .40 1.00
❑ 3 Burt Reynolds .40 1.00
❑ 4 Linda Hamilton .40 1.00
❑ 5 Justin Bieber .75 2.00
❑ 6 Ric Flair .75 2.00
❑ 7 Milo Ventimiglia .40 1.00
❑ 8 Linda Evans .40 1.00
❑ 9 Selma Blair .40 1.00
❑ 10 John Schneider .40 1.00
❑ 11 Marc McClure .40 1.00
❑ 12 Gloria Stuart .40 1.00
❑ 13 Josie Davis .40 1.00
❑ 14 Kenny Baker .40 1.00
❑ 15 Lawrence Hilton-Jacobs .40 1.00
❑ 16 Luke Goss .40 1.00
❑ 17 Bo Hopkins .40 1.00
❑ 18 Michael Madsen .40 1.00
❑ 19 Daniel Logan .40 1.00
❑ 20 Paul Le Mat .40 1.00
❑ 21 Charlene Tilton .40 1.00
❑ 22 Piper Laurie .40 1.00
❑ 23 Daniel Roebuck .40 1.00
❑ 24 Randal Kleiser .40 1.00
❑ 25 Eric Roberts .40 1.00
❑ 26 Robert Vaughn .40 1.00
❑ 27 Grayson Boucher .40 1.00
❑ 28 Sofia Milos .40 1.00
❑ 29 Tori Spelling .40 1.00
❑ 30 Willie Aames .40 1.00
❑ 31 David Carradine .40 1.00
❑ 32 Tony Todd .40 1.00
❑ 33 Christina Applegate .40 1.00
❑ 34 Tab Hunter .40 1.00
❑ 35 Stephen Baldwin .40 1.00
❑ 36 John Hurt .40 1.00
❑ 37 Scott Schwartz .40 1.00
❑ 38 Erin Moran .40 1.00
❑ 39 Johnny Yong Bosch .40 1.00
❑ 40 Alan Ruck .40 1.00
❑ 41 Barry Bostwick .40 1.00
❑ 42 Electra Avellan .40 1.00
❑ 43 Elise Avellan .40 1.00
❑ 44 Eileen Dietz .40 1.00
❑ 45 Erin Gray .40 1.00
❑ 46 Noel Neill .40 1.00
❑ 47 Jamie Donnelly .40 1.00
❑ 48 Patty Duke .40 1.00
❑ 49 Noureen DeWulf .40 1.00
❑ 50 Emmanuelle Chriqui .40 1.00
❑ 51 Barry Pearl .40 1.00
❑ 52 Corey Haim .40 1.00
❑ 53 Daniel Baldwin .40 1.00
❑ 54 David Ladd .40 1.00
❑ 55 Elena Verdugo .40 1.00
❑ 56 Erika Eleniak .40 1.00
❑ 57 George A. Romero .40 1.00
❑ 58 James Duval .40 1.00
❑ 59 Jill-Michele Melean .40 1.00
❑ 60 Annette Charles .40 1.00
❑ 61 Meredith Salenger .40 1.00
❑ 62 Anson Williams .40 1.00
❑ 63 Micky Dolenz .40 1.00
❑ 64 Edd Byrnes .40 1.00
❑ 65 Mitzi Gaynor .40 1.00
❑ 66 Noah Gray-Cabey .40 1.00
❑ 67 George Kennedy .40 1.00
❑ 68 Pash Lychnikoff .40 1.00
❑ 69 Joey Lawrence .40 1.00
❑ 70 Brigitte Nielsen .40 1.00
❑ 71 Peter Tork .40 1.00
❑ 72 Barry Williams .40 1.00
❑ 73 Ralph Macchio .40 1.00
❑ 74 Donna Pescow .40 1.00
❑ 75 Rhonda Fleming .40 1.00
❑ 76 Jeffrey Tambor .40 1.00
❑ 77 Katie Hoff .40 1.00
❑ 78 Lorna Luft .40 1.00
❑ 79 Barbara Morgan .40 1.00
❑ 80 Kirsty Coventry .40 1.00
❑ 81 Peter Vanderkaay .40 1.00
❑ 82 Bill Pogue .40 1.00
❑ 83 Dean McDermott .40 1.00
❑ 84 Kathryn Thornton .40 1.00
❑ 85 Heidi Androl .40 1.00
❑ 86 Lenny Krayzelburg .40 1.00
❑ 87 Leslie Nielsen .40 1.00
❑ 88 Dick Gordon .40 1.00
❑ 89 Jon Provost .40 1.00
❑ 90 Deborah Van Valkenburgh .40 1.00
❑ 91 Michelle Beadle .40 1.00
❑ 92 John Buccigross .40 1.00
❑ 93 Walt Cunningham .40 1.00
❑ 94 Fred Gregory .40 1.00
❑ 95 Ed Gibson .40 1.00
❑ 96 Tommy Chong .40 1.00
❑ 97 Robert Carradine .40 1.00
❑ 98 Willa Ford .40 1.00
❑ 99 John Kerr .40 1.00
❑ 100 Ami Dolenz .40 1.00

2011 Americana Retail

*RETAIL: .3X TO .75X HOBBY

2011 Americana Silver Proofs

COMPLETE SET (100) 50.00 100.00
*SILVER PROOFS: 1.5X TO 4X BASIC CARDS
STATED PRINT RUN 100 SER. #'d SETS

2011 Americana Silver Proofs Retail

*SILVER PROOF: 1.5X TO 4X BASIC CARDS
STATED PRINT RUN 100 SER. #'d SETS

2011 Americana Gold Proofs

*GOLD PROOFS: 2.5X TO 6X BASIC CARDS
STATED PRINT RUN 50 SER. #'d SETS

2011 Americana Gold Proofs Retail

*GOLD PROOF: 2X TO 5X BASIC CARDS
STATED PRINT RUN 50 SER. #'d SETS

2011 Americana Platinum Proofs

STATED PRINT RUN 10 SER. #'d SETS
UNPRICED DUE TO SCARCITY

2011 Americana Platinum Proofs Retail

STATED PRINT RUN 10 SER. #'d SETS
UNPRICED DUE TO SCARCITY

2011 Americana Casting Call Triple Autographs

STATED PRINT RUN 5-25

❑ 1 Leslie Nielsen 100.00 150.00
Ernest Borgnine/Stella Stevens /17
❑ 2 Goldie Hawn
David Carradine/Stephen Tobolowsky /5
❑ 3 Robert Hegyes 30.00 60.00
Ron Palillo/Lawrence Hilton-Jacobs /25
❑ 4 Josie Davis
Scott Baio/Willie Aames
❑ 5 Mark McClure
Robert Vaughn/Margot Kidder /6

2011 Americana Casting Call Quad Autographs

STATED PRINT RUN 10-25

❑ 1 Corey Feldman
Piper Laurie/Corey Haim/Meredith Salenger
❑ 2 Burt Reynolds

MODERN ERA NON-SPORTS

Catherine Bach/Dom DeLuise/Richard Kiel
❑ 3 Doug Jones
John Hurt/Luke Goss/Selma Blair
❑ 4 Annette Charles 30.00 60.00
Barry Pearl/Eddie Deezen/Jamie Donnelly /25
❑ 5 Burt Reynolds
Electra Avellan/James Duval/Michael Madsen

2011 Americana Celebrity Cut Autographs

STATED PRINT RUN 5-99
❑ 1A Josie Davis - Beverly Hills 90210 /20 10.00 20.00
❑ 2A Peter Mayhew - Chewbacca /20 20.00 40.00
❑ 2B Peter Mayhew - Empire Strikes Back /20 20.00 40.00
❑ 2C Peter Mayhew - Ret of Jedi /20 20.00 40.00
❑ 3 Bonnie Piesse - Star Wars /50 12.00 25.00
❑ 4A Tony Todd - Candyman /20 12.00 25.00
❑ 4B Tony Todd - Star Trek /20 12.00 25.00
❑ 4C Tony Todd - The Rock /20 12.00 25.00
❑ 5 Daniel Logan - Star Wars II /99 10.00 20.00
❑ 6 Linda Evans - Krystle Carrington /20 15.00 30.00
❑ 7 Jane Russell - Gentlemen Prefer Blondes /8
❑ 8 Christina Applegate - Anchorman /20 30.00 60.00
❑ 9 Joey Lawrence - Master of Dance /20 10.00 20.00
❑ 10A Brigitte Nielsen - Bev. Hills Cop II /20 20.00 40.00
❑ 10B Brigitte Nielsen - Cobra /20 20.00 40.00
❑ 10C Brigitte Nielsen - Red Sonja /20 20.00 40.00
❑ 10D Brigitte Nielsen - Rocky IV /40 20.00 40.00
❑ 11 Ron Howard
❑ 12A Dom DeLuise - History of the World /1520.00 40.00
❑ 12B Dom DeLuise - Cannonball Run /25 20.00 40.00
❑ 13 Doug Jones - BTVS /20 10.00 20.00
❑ 14 Hugh O'Brian - Wyatt Earp /40 20.00 40.00
❑ 15 Josh Duhamel - Las Vegas /20 30.00 60.00
❑ 16A Larry Hagman - Fail Safe /20 20.00 40.00
❑ 16B Larry Hagman - J.R. /10 25.00 50.00
❑ 16C Larry Hagman - Maj. Nelson /20 20.00 40.00
❑ 17 Margaret O'Brien - Meet Me in St. Louis /9
❑ 18A Michael Pare - Eddie and the Cruisers /5020.00 40.00
❑ 18B Michael Pare - Streets of Fire /25 20.00 40.00
❑ 19 Richard Anderson - Oscar Goldman /30 20.00 40.00
❑ 1B Josie Davis - Sonny /10 10.00 20.00
❑ 20 Richard Kiel - Jaws /50 20.00 40.00
❑ 21A Stella Stevens - Flamingo Road /30 12.00 25.00
❑ 21B Stella Stevens - Girls Girls Girls /30 12.00 25.00
❑ 21C Stella Stevens - The Poseidon Adv. /30 12.00 25.00
❑ 22A Warwick Davis - Harry Potter /20 20.00 40.00
❑ 22B Warwick Davis - Return of the Jedi /20 20.00 40.00
❑ 22C Warwick Davis - Wicket /20 20.00 40.00
❑ 23A Daniel Roebuck - Agent Cody Banks /20 7.50 15.00
❑ 23B Daniel Roebuck - U.S. Marshals /20 7.50 15.00
❑ 24A Randal Kleiser - Grease /35 7.50 15.00
❑ 24B Randal Kleiser - White Fang /20 7.50 15.00
❑ 25 Michael Madsen - Sin City /10
❑ 26A Bo Hopkins - Dynasty /10
❑ 26B Bo Hopkins - The Wild Bunch /40 7.50 15.00
❑ 27 Corey Feldman - Lost Boys /10 30.00 60.00
❑ 28 John Hurt - Alien /20 25.00 50.00
❑ 29A Pasha Lychnikoff - Deadwood /20 10.00 20.00
❑ 29B Pasha Lychnikoff - Star Trek /20 10.00 20.00
❑ 30A Alan Ruck - Bad Boys /20 10.00 20.00
❑ 30B Alan Ruck - Ferris Bueller /20 10.00 20.00
❑ 31 Michael Boatman - Spin City /30 7.50 15.00
❑ 32A Jeffrey Tambor - Arrested Development /2012.00 25.00
❑ 32B Jeffrey Tambor - Larry Sanders Show /2012.00 25.00
❑ 32C Jeffrey Tambor - Spongebob /10 15.00 30.00
❑ 33 Deborah Van Valkenburgh - The Warriors /15
❑ 34 Erin Moran - Joanie /10
❑ 35A Clint Howard - Waterboy /10 20.00 40.00
❑ 35B Clint Howard - Apollo 13 /5 20.00 40.00
❑ 36A Noah Gray-Cabey - Heroes /15 7.50 15.00
❑ 36B Noah Gray-Cabey - Micah /20 7.50 15.00
❑ 36C Noah Gray-Cabey - My Wife and Kids /407.50 15.00
❑ 37 Willie Aames - Charles in Charge /5
❑ 38A Kenny Baker - R2-D2 /30 20.00 40.00
❑ 38B Kenny Baker - Ret of the Jedi /30 20.00 40.00
❑ 39 Lawrence Hilton-Jacobs - Boom Boom /4010.00 20.00
❑ 40A Robert Hegyes - Epstein /40 10.00 20.00
❑ 40B Robert Hegyes - WB Kotter /10 10.00 20.00
❑ 41 Ron Palillo /40 7.50 15.00
❑ 42A Michael Beck - Houston Knights /20 7.50 15.00
❑ 42B Michael Beck - The Warriors /15 25.00 50.00
❑ 42C Michael Beck - Xanadu /40 12.00 25.00
❑ 43 George A. Romero /75 30.00 60.00
❑ 44 Tom Savini
❑ 45A Donna Pescow - Angie /40 10.00 20.00
❑ 45B Donna Pescow - Sat. Night Fever /40 10.00 20.00
❑ 46A Paul Le Mat - Melvin & Howard /40 10.00 20.00
❑ 46B Paul Le Mat - American Graffiti /35 10.00 20.00
❑ 47B Jamie Donnelly - Jan /40 7.50 15.00
❑ 47A Jamie Donnelly - Grease /35 7.50 15.00
❑ 48A Barry Pearl - Doody /20 10.00 20.00
❑ 48B Barry Pearl - T-Birds /40 10.00 20.00
❑ 48C Barry Pearl - Grease /15 10.00 20.00
❑ 49A Annette Charles - Cha Cha /40 12.00 25.00
❑ 49B Annette Charles - Grease /35 12.00 25.00
❑ 50 Edd Byrnes - Grease /60 10.00 20.00
❑ 51 Eddie Deezen - Grease /60 12.00 25.00
❑ 52A Barry Bostwick - Brad Majors /20 10.00 20.00
❑ 52B Barry Bostwick - Megaforce /20 10.00 20.00
❑ 52C Barry Bostwick - Rocky Horror /40 10.00 20.00
❑ 52D Barry Bostwick - Spin City /10 12.00 25.00
❑ 53A Electra Avellan 20.00 40.00
Elise Avellan /20
❑ 53B Electra Avellan - Grindhouse /30 15.00 30.00
❑ 53C Electra Avellan - Planet Terror /15 15.00 30.00
❑ 54 Elise Avellan - Grindhouse /30 15.00 30.00
❑ 55A Ed Asner - Elf /40 12.00 25.00
❑ 55B Ed Asner - Lou Grant /40 12.00 25.00
❑ 56A Steve Kanaly - Ray Krebbs /40 7.50 15.00
❑ 56B Steve Kanaly - The Wind & The Lion /20 7.50 15.00
❑ 56C Steve Kanaly - Dallas /20 7.50 15.00
❑ 57A Anson Williams - Potsie /20 12.00 25.00
❑ 57B Anson Williams - Happy Days /25 12.00 25.00
❑ 58 Tab Hunter
❑ 59A Dina Meyer - Johnny Mnemonic /20 20.00 40.00
❑ 59B Dina Meyer - Saw /50 20.00 40.00
❑ 59C Dina Meyer - Starship Troopers /40 15.00 30.00
❑ 60A Gina Phillips - Ally McBeal /30 7.50 15.00
❑ 60B Gina Phillips - Jeepers Creepers /40 7.50 15.00
❑ 60C Gina Phillips - Monk /40 7.50 15.00
❑ 61A Keiko Agena - Gilmore Girls /39 7.50 15.00
❑ 61B Keiko Agena - Major Movie Star /40 7.50 15.00
❑ 61C Keiko Agena - ??? /40 7.50 15.00
❑ 62 Catherine Hicks /15
❑ 63A Shawnee Smith - Becker /20 20.00 40.00
❑ 63B Shawnee Smith - The Blob /20 20.00 40.00
❑ 63C Shawnee Smith - Who's Harry Crumb /2020.00 40.00
❑ 63D Shawnee Smith - Saw /40 20.00 40.00
❑ 64A Lisa Marie - Ed Wood /40 10.00 20.00
❑ 64B Lisa Marie - Nova /19 10.00 20.00
❑ 65A Martin Kove - Rambo II /20
❑ 65B Martin Kove - Sensei /10
❑ 66A Louis Mandylor - Down the Shore /20 7.50 15.00
❑ 66B Louis Mandylor - Martial Law /30 7.50 15.00
❑ 66C Louis Mandylor - My Big Fat 7.50 15.00
Greek Wedding /50
❑ 66D Louis Mandylor - Necessary Roughness /207.50 15.00
❑ 67A Daniel Baldwin - Homicide /20 12.00 25.00
❑ 67B Daniel Baldwin - Vampires /80 12.00 25.00
❑ 68A Eileen Dietz - General Hospital /30 7.50 15.00
❑ 68B Eileen Dietz - Sibling Rivalry /20 7.50 15.00
❑ 68C Eileen Dietz - The Exorcist /20 7.50 15.00
❑ 68D Eileen Dietz - The Queen of Screams /30 7.50 15.00
❑ 69A Bruce Davison - Voyager /20 12.00 25.00
❑ 69B Bruce Davison - X-Men /30 12.00 25.00
❑ 70A John Saxon - Nightmare on Elm Street /4012.00 25.00
❑ 70B John Saxon - Black Christmas /20 12.00 25.00

2011 Americana Co-Stars Material

STATED PRINT RUN 25-249
❑ 1 James Dean
Natalie Wood
❑ 2 James Dean
Rock Hudson
❑ 3 Ernest Borgnine 5.00 12.00
Rock Hudson/199
❑ 4 Lee Meriwether 6.00 15.00
Rock Hudson/189
❑ 6 Ingrid Bergman 6.00 15.00
Rhonda Fleming/249
❑ 7 Bette Davis 8.00 20.00
Natalie Wood/99
❑ 8 Ava Gardner 8.00 20.00
Leslie Nielsen/89
❑ 9 Ava Gardner 6.00 15.00
Tab Hunter/49
❑ 10 Ava Gardner 6.00 15.00
George Raft/25

2011 Americana Co-Stars Material Silver Screen

STATED PRINT RUN 3-99

2011 Americana Co-Stars Material Golden Era

STATED PRINT RUN 3-49
NO PRICING ON CARDS #'d 20 OR LESS

2011 Americana Co-Stars Signatures

STATED PRINT RUN 5-49
NO PRICING ON CARDS #'d 20 OR LESS
❑ 1 Lee Majors
Linda Evans
❑ 2 Margot Kidder 25.00 50.00
Noel Neill /49
❑ 3 Corey Feldman
Corey Haim
❑ 4 George Kennedy 35.00 70.00
Leslie Nielsen /49
❑ 5 Erika Eleniak
Pamela Anderson /13
❑ 6 Linda Hamilton 30.00 60.00
Robert Carradine /49
❑ 7 Barbara Eden
George Kennedy /29
❑ 8 Christina Applegate
Selma Blair /15
❑ 9 Catherine Bach
John Schneider
❑ 10 Luke Goss 20.00 40.00
Val Kilmer /20
❑ 11 Mickey Dolenz 25.00 50.00
Peter Tork /29
❑ 12 Corey Haim
Piper Laurie /19
❑ 13 Burt Reynolds
Dom DeLuise
❑ 14 Goldie Hawn
Kurt Russell /8
❑ 15 Dolores Hart 15.00 30.00
Hugh O'Brian /30
❑ 16 Burt Reynolds
Richard Kiel
❑ 17 David Carradine
Michael Madsen /5
❑ 18 George Kennedy 20.00 40.00
William Forsythe /25
❑ 19 Ernest Borgnine
George Kennedy
❑ 20 Brigitte Nielsen 25.00 50.00
Corey Haim /49

2011 Americana Combo Cuts Autographs

STATED PRINT RUN 10-25
NO PRICING ON CARDS #'d 15 OR LESS
❑ 1 Milo Ventimiglia 10.00 20.00
Noah Gray-Cabey /25
❑ 2 Selma Blair
John Hurt /15
❑ 3 Bo Hopkins
Linda Evans /10
❑ 4 Josie Davis 15.00 30.00
Willie Aames /25
❑ 5 Malcolm McDowell 40.00 80.00
Corey Feldman /20
❑ 6 Peter Mayhew 35.00 70.00
Kenny Baker /25
❑ 7 Lawrence Hilton-Jacobs
Robert Hegyes
❑ 8 Lawrence Hilton-Jacobs 15.00 30.00
Ron Palillo /25
❑ 9 Robert Hegyes 15.00 30.00
Ron Palillo /25
❑ 10 Michael Pare 10.00 20.00
Deborah Van Valkenburgh /25
❑ 11 Deborah Van Valkenburgh
Michael Beck /25
❑ 12 George A. Romero
Tom Savini
❑ 13 Tony Todd 25.00 50.00
Tom Savini /20
❑ 14 Bo Hopkins 20.00 40.00
Paul Le Mat /25
❑ 15 Randal Kleiser 10.00 20.00
Jamie Donnelly /25
❑ 16 Annette Charles 15.00 30.00
Barry Pearl /25
❑ 17 Edd Byrnes 10.00 20.00
Eddie Deezen /25
❑ 18 Anson Williams
Erin Moran /20
❑ 19 Alan Ruck
Barry Bostwick /10
❑ 20 Electra Avellan 25.00 50.00
Elise Avellan /25
❑ 21 Corey Feldman 75.00 125.00
Corey Haim /22
❑ 22 John Hurt
Pasha Lychnikoff /15
❑ 23 Jeffrey Tambor
Luke Goss /15
❑ 24 Jeffrey Tambor
Doug Jones /10
❑ 25 Doug Jones
Selma Blair /10
❑ 26 Alan Ruck
Michael Boatman /10
❑ 27 Ed Asner 15.00 30.00
Michael Boatman /20
❑ 28 Clint Howard
Ron Howard
❑ 29 Steve Kanaly
Larry Hagman /19
❑ 30 Clint Howard
Jeffrey Tambor

2011 Americana Matinee Legends

COMPLETE SET (20) 10.00 20.00
❑ 1 James Dean 1.50 3.00
❑ 2 Bettie Page 1.50 3.00
❑ 3 Rock Hudson .75 2.00
❑ 4 Ingrid Bergman .75 2.00
❑ 5 Bette Davis .75 2.00
❑ 6 Ava Gardner .75 2.00
❑ 7 Ginger Rogers .75 2.00
❑ 8 Lillian Gish .75 2.00
❑ 9 Tyrone Power .75 2.00
❑ 10 Natalie Wood .75 2.00
❑ 11 Dorothy Lamour .75 2.00
❑ 12 Peter Sellers .75 2.00
❑ 13 Jayne Mansfield .75 2.00
❑ 14 Lana Turner .75 2.00
❑ 15 Telly Savalas .75 2.00
❑ 16 Hedy Lamarr .75 2.00
❑ 17 Jean Harlow .75 2.00
❑ 18 Gene Tierney .75 2.00
❑ 19 Leslie Howard .75 2.00
❑ 20 Carole Lombard .75 2.00

2011 Americana Matinee Legends Material

COMMON CARD 5.00 12.00
STATED PRINT RUN 499 SER. #'d SETS
❑ 1 James Dean/5
❑ 2 Bettie Page 20.00 40.00
❑ 3 Rock Hudson/299 5.00 12.00
❑ 4 Ingrid Bergman 6.00 15.00
❑ 5 Bette Davis 6.00 15.00
❑ 6 Ava Gardner 6.00 15.00
❑ 7 Ginger Rogers 5.00 12.00
❑ 8 Lillian Gish 5.00 12.00
❑ 9 Tyrone Power/199 5.00 12.00
❑ 10 Natalie Wood 8.00 20.00
❑ 11 Dorothy Lamour 5.00 12.00
❑ 12 Peter Sellers/99 6.00 15.00
❑ 13 Jayne Mansfield 8.00 20.00
❑ 14 Lana Turner 5.00 12.00
❑ 15 Telly Savalas 5.00 12.00
❑ 16 Hedy Lamarr 6.00 15.00
❑ 17 Jean Harlow 6.00 15.00
❑ 18 Gene Tierney 5.00 12.00
❑ 19 Leslie Howard/59 6.00 15.00
❑ 20 Carole Lombard 5.00 12.00

2011 Americana Matinee Legends Material Silver Screen

STATED PRINT RUN 99 SER. #'d SETS

2011 Americana Matinee Legends Material Golden Era

*GOLDEN/49: .6X TO 1.5X BASIC/499
STATED PRINT RUN 49 SER. #'d SETS

2011 Americana Matinee Legends Material Super Stars

*SUPER/25: 1.5X TO 3X BASIC/499
STATED PRINT RUN 25 SER. #'d SETS

2011 Americana Movie Posters Material

STATED PRINT RUN 499 SER. #'d SETS
❑ 1 Lillian Gish 8.00 20.00
❑ 2 Rita Hayworth 10.00 25.00
❑ 3 Joan Crawford 8.00 20.00
❑ 4 Jean Harlow 15.00 30.00
❑ 5 Bette Davis 8.00 20.00
❑ 6 Steve McQueen 20.00 40.00
❑ 7 Jerry Lewis 8.00 20.00
❑ 8 Bob Hope 8.00 20.00
❑ 9 John Wayne 8.00 20.00
❑ 10 John Wayne 8.00 20.00
❑ 11 Mae West 15.00 30.00
❑ 12 Mae West 15.00 30.00
❑ 13 Cary Grant 8.00 20.00
❑ 14 Humphrey Bogart/250 10.00 25.00
❑ 15 Shirley Temple 15.00 30.00
❑ 16 Liza Minelli 15.00 30.00
❑ 17 Charlie Chaplin 8.00 20.00
❑ 18 Jane Russell 8.00 20.00
❑ 19 Gary Cooper 8.00 20.00
❑ 20 Cary Grant 8.00 20.00
❑ 21 Charlie Chaplin 8.00 20.00
❑ 22 Elizabeth Taylor 8.00 20.00
❑ 23 Cary Grant 8.00 20.00
❑ 24 Leslie Howard/99 10.00 25.00
❑ 25 Cary Grant 8.00 20.00
❑ 26 Elizabeth Taylor/250 10.00 25.00
❑ 27 Vivien Leigh 8.00 20.00
❑ 28 Gloria Swanson 8.00 20.00
❑ 29 Ginger Rogers 8.00 20.00
❑ 30 James Cagney 8.00 20.00
❑ 31 Clark Gable/99 15.00 30.00
❑ 32 Vivien Leigh/250 10.00 25.00
❑ 33 Clark Gable/99 15.00 30.00
❑ 34 Vivien Leigh/250 10.00 25.00
❑ 35 Claudette Colbert 8.00 20.00
❑ 36 Marilyn Monroe/350 20.00 40.00
❑ 37 Grace Kelly 10.00 25.00
❑ 38 Natalie Wood 10.00 25.00
❑ 39 Greer Garson 8.00 20.00
❑ 40 Katharine Hepburn/300 10.00 25.00
❑ 41 Marilyn Monroe 15.00 30.00
❑ 42 Carolyn Jones 10.00 25.00
❑ 43 Deborah Kerr 8.00 20.00
❑ 44 Liza Minelli 15.00 30.00
❑ 45 Charlie Chaplin 8.00 20.00
❑ 46 Agnes Moorehead 8.00 20.00
❑ 47 Gary Cooper 8.00 20.00
❑ 48 Marlene Dietrich 8.00 20.00
❑ 49 Audrey Hepburn 15.00 30.00
❑ 50 Gregory Peck 8.00 20.00
❑ 51 Mary Astor 8.00 20.00
❑ 52 John Wayne 8.00 20.00
❑ 53 Anthony Quinn 8.00 20.00
❑ 54 Bing Crosby/99 10.00 25.00

2011 Americana Movie Posters Dual Material

STATED PRINT RUN 499 SER. #'d SETS
❑ 2 Rita Hayworth 10.00 25.00
Victor Mature
❑ 4 Jean Harlow 10.00 25.00
Clark Gable
❑ 6 Steve McQueen 15.00 30.00
Robert Wagner
❑ 7 Jerry Lewis 15.00 30.00
Donna Reed
❑ 8 Bob Hope 8.00 20.00
Dorothy Lamour
❑ 9 John Wayne 8.00 20.00
Joan Crawford
❑ 12 Mae West 8.00 20.00
Cary Grant
❑ 13 Cary Grant 15.00 30.00
Grace Kelly
❑ 14 Humphrey Bogart 10.00 25.00
Katharine Hepburn
❑ 18 Jane Russell 20.00 40.00
Marilyn Monroe
❑ 19 Gary Cooper 10.00 25.00
Grace Kelly
❑ 20 Cary Grant 8.00 20.00
Rosalind Russell
❑ 22 Elizabeth Taylor 8.00 20.00
Mickey Rooney
❑ 26 Elizabeth Taylor 8.00 20.00
Montgomery Clift
❑ 27 Vivien Leigh 8.00 20.00
Marlon Brando
❑ 31 Clark Gable 15.00 30.00
Vivien Leigh
❑ 32 Vivien Leigh 15.00 30.00
Clark Gable
❑ 33 Clark Gable 15.00 30.00
Vivien Leigh
❑ 34 Vivien Leigh 15.00 30.00
Clark Gable
❑ 35 Claudette Colbert 10.00 25.00
Clark Gable /150
❑ 36 Marilyn Monroe 20.00 40.00
Jane Russell
❑ 38 Natalie Wood 10.00 25.00
Sal Mineo
❑ 39 Greer Garson 8.00 20.00
Teresa Wright
❑ 40 Katharine Hepburn 10.00 25.00
Cary Grant
❑ 41 Marilyn Monroe 20.00 40.00
Carolyn Jones
❑ 42 Carolyn Jones 20.00 40.00
Marilyn Monroe
❑ 43 Deborah Kerr 10.00 25.00
Donna Reed
❑ 48 Marlene Dietrich 8.00 20.00
Gary Cooper
❑ 49 Audrey Hepburn 15.00 30.00
Humphrey Bogart
❑ 50 Gregory Peck 15.00 30.00
Audrey Hepburn
❑ 51 Mary Astor 10.00 25.00
Humphrey Bogart
❑ 53 Anthony Quinn 8.00 20.00
Dorothy Lamour
❑ 54 Bing Crosby 8.00 20.00
Dorothy Lamour

2011 Americana Movie Posters Triple Material

STATED PRINT RUN 20-499
❑ 6 Steve McQueen 40.00 80.00
Robert Wagner/Robert Vaughn /50
❑ 8 Bob Hope 10.00 25.00
Dorothy Lamour/Bing Crosby /499
❑ 24 Leslie Howard 75.00 125.00
Bette Davis/Humphrey Bogart /20
❑ 26 Elizabeth Taylor 15.00 30.00
Montgomery Clift/Shelley Winters /150
❑ 38 Natalie Wood 75.00 125.00
Sal Mineo/James Dean /50
❑ 49 Audrey Hepburn 40.00 80.00
Humphrey Bogart/William Holden /25
❑ 53 Anthony Quinn 10.00 25.00
Dorothy Lamour/Bing Crosby /499
❑ 54 Bing Crosby 10.00 25.00
Dorothy Lamour/Bob Hope /499

2011 Americana Movie Posters Quad Material

❑ 6 Steve McQueen
Robert Wagner/Robert Vaughn/William Holden
❑ 53 Anthony Quinn 20.00 40.00
Dorothy Lamour/Bing Crosby/Bob Hope

2011 Americana Prime Time Stars

COMPLETE SET (20) 6.00 15.00
❑ 1 Linda Evans .60 1.50
❑ 2 Erika Eleniak .60 1.50
❑ 3 Noel Neill .60 1.50
❑ 4 Milo Ventimiglia .60 1.50
❑ 5 Leslie Nielsen .60 1.50
❑ 6 Peter Tork .60 1.50
❑ 7 John Schneider .60 1.50
❑ 8 Erin Gray .60 1.50
❑ 9 Pam Anderson 1.25 3.00
❑ 10 Josie Davis .60 1.50
❑ 11 Linda Hamilton .60 1.50
❑ 12 Selma Blair .75 2.00
❑ 13 Piper Laurie .60 1.50
❑ 14 Luke Goss .60 1.50
❑ 15 Willie Aames .60 1.50
❑ 16 Chris Noth .60 1.50
❑ 17 Lee Majors .60 1.50
❑ 18 Erin Moran .60 1.50
❑ 19 Emmanuelle Chriqui .75 2.00
❑ 20 Michael Ontkean .60 1.50

2011 Americana Prime Time Stars Directors Cut Signatures

STATED PRINT RUN 10-75
❑ 1A Linda Evans - Big Valley /20 15.00 30.00
❑ 1B Linda Evans - Dynasty /10
❑ 2 Erika Eleniak - Baywatch /40 12.00 25.00
❑ 3A Noel Neill - Lois Lane /40 20.00 40.00
❑ 3B Noel Neill - Superman /60 20.00 40.00
❑ 4A Milo Ventimiglia - As Peter Petrelli /20
❑ 4B Milo Ventimiglia - Heroes /15
❑ 5 Leslie Nielsen /40 30.00 60.00
❑ 6 Peter Tork - The Monkees /75 20.00 40.00
❑ 7A John Schneider - Bo /60 10.00 20.00
❑ 7B John Schneider - J. Kent /20 10.00 20.00
❑ 8A Erin Gray - Buck Rogers /40 15.00 30.00
❑ 8B Erin Gray - Col. Wilma Deering /20 15.00 30.00
❑ 8C Erin Gray - Silver Spoons /40 15.00 30.00
❑ 9 Pam Anderson
❑ 10 Josie Davis
❑ 11 Linda Hamilton - Beauty and the Beast /2040.00 80.00
❑ 12 Selma Blair - Kath + Kim /20 20.00 40.00
❑ 13 Piper Laurie - Twin Peaks /20
❑ 14 Luke Goss - Frankenstein /20
❑ 15A Willie Aames - Charles in Charge /15
❑ 15B Willie Aames - 8 is Enough /20
❑ 16 Chris Noth
❑ 17 Lee Majors
❑ 18 Erin Moran - Daktari /20
❑ 19A Emmanuelle Chriqui - Entourage /10
❑ 19B Emmanuelle Chriqui - Sloan /10
❑ 20 Michael Ontkean

2011 Americana Prime Time Stars Material Small Screen

STATED PRINT RUN 125
❑ 5 Leslie Nielsen
❑ 9 Pam Anderson/125 20.00 40.00
❑ 13 Piper Laurie/125 5.00 12.00
❑ 17 Lee Majors/125 5.00 12.00

2011 Americana Prime Time Stars Material Big Screen

STATED PRINT RUN 10-49
❑ 1 Linda Evans
❑ 2 Erika Eleniak
❑ 3 Noel Neill
❑ 4 Milo Ventimiglia
❑ 5 Leslie Nielsen/29 12.00 25.00
❑ 6 Peter Tork/49 7.50 15.00
❑ 7 John Schneider/10
❑ 8 Erin Gray
❑ 9 Pam Anderson/19
❑ 10 Josie Davis
❑ 11 Linda Hamilton
❑ 12 Selma Blair
❑ 13 Piper Laurie/49
❑ 14 Luke Goss
❑ 15 Willie Aames
❑ 16 Chris Noth
❑ 17 Lee Majors/49 12.00 25.00
❑ 18 Erin Moran
❑ 19 Emmanuelle Chriqui
❑ 20 Michael Ontkean

2011 Americana Prime Time Stars Signature

STATED PRINT RUN 29-99
❑ 1 Linda Evans/29 15.00 30.00
❑ 2 Erika Eleniak/99 12.00 25.00
❑ 3 Noel Neill/29 15.00 30.00
❑ 4 Milo Ventimiglia/99 4.00 10.00
❑ 5 Leslie Nielsen/49 20.00 40.00
❑ 6 Peter Tork/49 12.00 25.00
❑ 7 John Schneider/39 10.00 20.00
❑ 8 Erin Gray/99 10.00 20.00
❑ 9 Pam Anderson/29 50.00 100.00
❑ 10 Josie Davis
❑ 11 Linda Hamilton/99 20.00 40.00
❑ 12 Selma Blair/49 20.00 40.00
❑ 13 Piper Laurie
❑ 14 Luke Goss/49
❑ 15 Willie Aames/99 7.50 15.00
❑ 16 Chris Noth
❑ 17 Lee Majors
❑ 18 Erin Moran/29 10.00 20.00
❑ 19 Emmanuelle Chriqui/95 40.00 80.00
❑ 20 Michael Ontkean

2011 Americana Prime Time Stars Signature Material

STATED PRINT RUN 29-49
❑ 1 Linda Evans
❑ 2 Erika Eleniak
❑ 3 Noel Neill
❑ 4 Milo Ventimiglia/39 7.50 15.00
❑ 5 Leslie Nielsen
❑ 6 Peter Tork/49 10.00 20.00
❑ 7 John Schneider/29 10.00 20.00
❑ 8 Erin Gray
❑ 9 Pam Anderson/29 50.00 100.00
❑ 10 Josie Davis
❑ 11 Linda Hamilton
❑ 12 Selma Blair
❑ 13 Piper Laurie
❑ 14 Luke Goss
❑ 15 Willie Aames
❑ 16 Chris Noth
❑ 17 Lee Majors
❑ 18 Erin Moran
❑ 19 Emmanuelle Chriqui
❑ 20 Michael Ontkean

2011 Americana Private Signings

STATED PRINT RUN 6-799
❑ 1 Pamela Anderson/29 50.00 100.00
❑ 2 Chris Noth/49 20.00 40.00
❑ 3 Burt Reynolds
❑ 4 Linda Hamilton/99 20.00 40.00
❑ 5 Justin Bieber/299 60.00 120.00
❑ 6 Ric Flair/99 50.00 100.00
❑ 7 Milo Ventimiglia/99 4.00 10.00
❑ 8 Linda Evans/99 20.00 40.00
❑ 9 Selma Blair/99 25.00 50.00
❑ 10 John Schneider/99 10.00 20.00
❑ 11 Marc McClure/59 4.00 10.00
❑ 12 Gloria Stuart
❑ 13 Josie Davis/49 10.00 20.00
❑ 14 Kenny Baker/49 15.00 30.00
❑ 15 Lawrence Hilton-Jacobs
❑ 16 Luke Goss/49 4.00 10.00
❑ 17 Bo Hopkins/49

- 18 Michael Madsen/20 10.00 20.00
- 19 Daniel Logan/19
- 20 Paul Le Mat/49 4.00 10.00
- 21 Charlene Tilton/25
- 22 Piper Laurie
- 23 Daniel Roebuck/49 4.00 10.00
- 24 Randal Kleiser/49 4.00 10.00
- 25 Eric Roberts/49 6.00 15.00
- 26 Robert Vaughn/49 15.00 30.00
- 27 Grayson Boucher/799 4.00 10.00
- 28 Sofia Milos/49 6.00 15.00
- 29 Tori Spelling/15
- 30 Willie Aames/49 6.00 15.00
- 31 David Carradine/49
- 32 Tony Todd/29 12.00 25.00
- 33 Christina Applegate
- 34 Tab Hunter
- 35 Stephen Baldwin/29 4.00 10.00
- 36 John Hurt/99 10.00 20.00
- 37 Scott Schwartz/199 6.00 15.00
- 38 Erin Moran/49 12.00 25.00
- 39 Johnny Yong Bosch/699 4.00 10.00
- 40 Alan Ruck/49 6.00 15.00
- 41 Barry Bostwick/49 10.00 20.00
- 42 Electra Avellan/99 10.00 25.00
- 43 Elise Avellan/99 10.00 20.00
- 44 Eileen Dietz/49 6.00 15.00
- 45 Erin Gray/49 10.00 20.00
- 46 Noel Neill/99 15.00 30.00
- 47 Jamie Donnelly/49 4.00 10.00
- 48 Patty Duke/49 15.00 30.00
- 49 Noureen DeWulf/99 10.00 20.00
- 50 Emmanuelle Chriqui/99 30.00 60.00
- 51 Barry Pearl/25 10.00 20.00
- 52 Corey Haim/149 30.00 60.00
- 53 Daniel Baldwin/29 10.00 20.00
- 54 David Ladd/49 4.00 10.00
- 55 Elena Verdugo/49 4.00 10.00
- 56 Erika Eleniak/49 12.00 25.00
- 57 George A. Romero
- 58 James Duval/29 10.00 20.00
- 59 Jill-Michele Melean/19
- 60 Annette Charles/49 12.00 25.00
- 61 Meredith Salenger/39 10.00 20.00
- 62 Anson Williams/49 10.00 20.00
- 63 Micky Dolenz/19 15.00 30.00
- 64 Edd Byrnes/49 6.00 15.00
- 65 Mitzi Gaynor/29
- 66 Noah Gray-Cabey/49 4.00 10.00
- 67 George Kennedy/49 20.00 40.00
- 68 Pasha Lychnikoff/49 4.00 10.00
- 69 Joey Lawrence/49 6.00 15.00
- 70 Brigitte Nielsen/6
- 71 Peter Tork/39 15.00 30.00
- 72 Barry Williams/49 6.00 15.00
- 73 Ralph Macchio/49 15.00 30.00
- 74 Donna Pescow/49 4.00 10.00
- 75 Rhonda Fleming
- 76 Jeffrey Tambor
- 77 Katie Hoff/199 10.00 20.00
- 78 Lorna Luft/49 6.00 15.00
- 79 Barbara Morgan/49 20.00 40.00
- 80 Kirsty Coventry/199 4.00 10.00
- 81 Peter Vanderkaay/199 4.00 10.00
- 82 Bill Pogue/25 30.00 60.00
- 83 Dean McDermott/15 20.00 40.00
- 84 Kathryn Thornton/59 20.00 40.00
- 85 Heidi Androl/59 15.00 30.00
- 86 Lenny Krayzelburg/199 4.00 10.00
- 87 Leslie Nielsen
- 88 Dick Gordon/15
- 89 Jon Provost/49 4.00 10.00
- 90 Deborah Van Valkenburgh/199 10.00 20.00
- 91 Michelle Beadle/59 25.00 50.00
- 92 John Buccigross
- 93 Walt Cunningham/59 20.00 40.00
- 94 Fred Gregory/25 20.00 40.00
- 95 Ed Gibson/29 25.00 50.00
- 96 Tommy Chong/59 20.00 40.00
- 97 Robert Carradine/99 4.00 10.00
- 98 Willa Ford
- 99 John Kerr/49 12.00 25.00
- 100 Ami Dolenz/49 6.00 15.00

2011 Americana Private Stars Material Gold Proofs

STATED PRINT RUN 25 SER. #'d SETS

- 1 Pamela Anderson
- 2 Chris Noth
- 3 Burt Reynolds
- 4 Linda Hamilton
- 5 Justin Bieber
- 6 Ric Flair
- 7 Milo Ventimiglia
- 8 Linda Evans
- 9 Selma Blair
- 10 John Schneider
- 11 Marc McClure
- 12 Gloria Stuart
- 13 Josie Davis
- 14 Kenny Baker
- 15 Lawrence Hilton-Jacobs
- 16 Luke Goss
- 17 Bo Hopkins
- 18 Michael Madsen
- 19 Daniel Logan
- 20 Paul Le Mat
- 21 Charlene Tilton
- 22 Piper Laurie
- 23 Daniel Roebuck
- 24 Randal Kleiser
- 25 Eric Roberts
- 26 Robert Vaughn
- 27 Grayson Boucher
- 28 Sofia Milos
- 29 Tori Spelling
- 30 Willie Aames
- 31 David Carradine
- 32 Tony Todd
- 33 Christina Applegate
- 34 Tab Hunter
- 35 Stephen Baldwin
- 36 John Hurt
- 37 Scott Schwartz
- 38 Erin Moran
- 39 Johnny Yong Bosch
- 40 Alan Ruck
- 41 Barry Bostwick
- 42 Electra Avellan
- 43 Elise Avellan
- 44 Eileen Dietz
- 45 Erin Gray
- 46 Noel Neill
- 47 Jamie Donnelly
- 48 Patty Duke
- 49 Noureen DeWulf
- 50 Emmanuelle Chriqui
- 51 Barry Pearl
- 52 Corey Haim
- 53 Daniel Baldwin
- 54 David Ladd
- 55 Elena Verdugo
- 56 Erika Eleniak
- 57 George A. Romero
- 58 James Duval
- 59 Jill-Michele Melean
- 60 Annette Charles
- 61 Meredith Salenger
- 62 Anson Williams
- 63 Micky Dolenz
- 64 Edd Byrnes
- 65 Mitzi Gaynor
- 66 Noah Gray-Cabey
- 67 George Kennedy
- 68 Pash Lychnikoff
- 69 Joey Lawrence
- 70 Brigitte Nielsen
- 71 Peter Tork
- 72 Barry Williams
- 73 Ralph Macchio
- 74 Donna Pescow
- 75 Rhonda Fleming
- 76 Jeffrey Tambor
- 77 Katie Hoff
- 78 Lorna Luft
- 79 Barbara Morgan
- 80 Kirsty Coventry
- 81 Peter Vanderkaay
- 82 Bill Pogue
- 83 Dean McDermott
- 84 Kathryn Thornton
- 85 Heidi Androl
- 86 Lenny Krayzelburg
- 87 Leslie Nielsen
- 88 Dick Gordon
- 89 Jon Provost
- 90 Deborah Van Valkenburgh
- 91 Michelle Beadle
- 92 John Buccigross
- 93 Walt Cunningham
- 94 Fred Gregory
- 95 Ed Gibson
- 96 Tommy Chong
- 97 Robert Carradine
- 98 Willa Ford
- 99 John Kerr
- 100 Ami Dolenz

2011 Americana Private Stars Signature Material

STATED PRINT RUN 10-249
NO PRICING ON CARDS #'d 20 OR LESS

- 1 Pamela Anderson/49 75.00 125.00
- 2 Chris Noth
- 3 Burt Reynolds
- 4 Linda Hamilton
- 5 Justin Bieber
- 6 Ric Flair/69 50.00 100.00
- 7 Milo Ventimiglia/99 4.00 10.00
- 8 Linda Evans
- 9 Selma Blair
- 10 John Schneider/99 10.00 20.00
- 11 Marc McClure
- 12 Gloria Stuart/15
- 13 Josie Davis/49 12.00 25.00
- 14 Kenny Baker
- 15 Lawrence Hilton-Jacobs/25
- 16 Luke Goss
- 17 Bo Hopkins/49 4.00 10.00
- 18 Michael Madsen
- 19 Daniel Logan/49 4.00 10.00
- 20 Paul Le Mat/49 4.00 10.00
- 21 Charlene Tilton/25
- 22 Piper Laurie/18
- 23 Daniel Roebuck/149 4.00 10.00
- 24 Randal Kleiser
- 25 Eric Roberts/10
- 26 Robert Vaughn
- 27 Grayson Boucher
- 28 Sofia Milos/49 4.00 10.00
- 29 Tori Spelling/10
- 30 Willie Aames
- 31 David Carradine
- 32 Tony Todd/49 7.50 15.00
- 33 Christina Applegate/79 30.00 60.00
- 34 Tab Hunter/20 7.50 15.00
- 35 Stephen Baldwin/99 4.00 10.00
- 36 John Hurt/25 12.00 25.00
- 37 Scott Schwartz/249 7.50 15.00
- 38 Erin Moran
- 39 Johnny Yong Bosch/249 4.00 10.00
- 40 Alan Ruck
- 41 Barry Bostwick
- 42 Electra Avellan
- 43 Elise Avellan
- 44 Eileen Dietz
- 45 Erin Gray
- 46 Noel Neill
- 47 Jamie Donnelly
- 48 Patty Duke
- 49 Noureen DeWulf
- 50 Emmanuelle Chriqui
- 51 Barry Pearl/149 4.00 10.00
- 52 Corey Haim
- 53 Daniel Baldwin/99 4.00 10.00
- 54 David Ladd/99 4.00 10.00
- 55 Elena Verdugo/99 4.00 10.00
- 56 Erika Eleniak
- 57 George A. Romero/99 20.00 40.00
- 58 James Duval/75 4.00 10.00
- 59 Jill-Michele Melean/49 4.00 10.00
- 60 Annette Charles
- 61 Meredith Salenger/99 10.00 20.00
- 62 Anson Williams/99 10.00 20.00
- 63 Micky Dolenz/24 12.00 25.00
- 64 Edd Byrnes
- 65 Mitzi Gaynor/99 7.50 15.00
- 66 Noah Gray-Cabey/249 4.00 10.00
- 67 George Kennedy
- 68 Pash Lychnikoff
- 69 Joey Lawrence/99 4.00 10.00
- 70 Brigitte Nielsen
- 71 Peter Tork/149 12.00 25.00
- 72 Barry Williams/99 4.00 10.00
- 73 Ralph Macchio
- 74 Donna Pescow/149 4.00 10.00
- 75 Rhonda Fleming/99 20.00 40.00
- 76 Jeffrey Tambor
- 77 Katie Hoff
- 78 Lorna Luft
- 79 Barbara Morgan/49
- 80 Kirsty Coventry/249 4.00 10.00
- 81 Peter Vanderkaay
- 82 Bill Pogue/99 15.00 30.00
- 83 Dean McDermott/10
- 84 Kathryn Thornton/189 12.00 25.00
- 85 Heidi Androl
- 86 Lenny Krayzelburg
- 87 Leslie Nielsen/119 30.00 60.00
- 88 Dick Gordon/99 25.00 50.00
- 89 Jon Provost/89 4.00 10.00
- 90 Deborah Van Valkenburgh
- 91 Michelle Beadle
- 92 John Buccigross
- 93 Walt Cunningham/99 20.00 40.00
- 94 Fred Gregory/109 12.00 25.00
- 95 Ed Gibson/99 20.00 40.00
- 96 Tommy Chong
- 97 Robert Carradine
- 98 Willa Ford
- 99 John Kerr/99 4.00 10.00
- 100 Ami Dolenz/99 4.00 10.00

2011 Americana ReCollection Buyback Signatures

- 1 Cindy Morgan/20 25.00 50.00
- 2 Karen Lynn Gorney/40 12.00 25.00
- 3 Micky Dolenz/33 25.00 50.00
- 4 Tatu/90 4.00 10.00
- 5 Peter Tork/38 20.00 40.00
- 6 John Schneider/55 20.00 40.00

2011 Americana Screen Gems

COMPLETE SET (20) 6.00 15.00

- 1 Linda Hamilton .60 1.50
- 2 Selma Blair .75 2.00
- 3 Corey Haim .60 1.50
- 4 Leslie Nielsen .60 1.50
- 5 George Kennedy .60 1.50
- 6 Robert Carradine .60 1.50
- 7 Piper Laurie .60 1.50
- 8 Gloria Stuart .60 1.50
- 9 Meredith Salenger .60 1.50
- 10 Luke Goss .60 1.50
- 11 Willa Ford .60 1.50
- 12 Noureen DeWulf .60 1.50
- 13 Milo Ventimiglia .60 1.50
- 14 Linda Evans .60 1.50
- 15 John Schneider .60 1.50
- 16 Erika Eleniak .60 1.50
- 17 Willie Aames .60 1.50
- 18 Justin Bieber 1.25 3.00
- 19 Josie Davis .60 1.50
- 20 John Hurt .60 1.50

2011 Americana Screen Gems Directors Cut Autographs

PRINT RUN 4-99

- 1A Linda Hamilton - The Terminator /20 30.00 60.00
- 1B Linda Hamilton - T2 /20 30.00 60.00
- 1C Linda Hamilton - Sarah Connor /20 30.00 60.00
- 1D Linda Hamilton - Dante's Peak /20 30.00 60.00
- 2A Selma Blair - Legally Blonde /20 20.00 40.00
- 2B Selma Blair - Storytelling /20 20.00 40.00
- 2C Selma Blair - Cruel Intentions /10 25.00 50.00
- 2D Selma Blair - Hellboy II /4
- 3A Corey Haim - Lost Boys /20 40.00 80.00
- 3B Corey Haim - Lucas /41 30.00 60.00
- 4A Leslie Nielsen - Naked Gun /60 30.00 60.00
- 4B Leslie Nielsen - Leslie Nielsen /20
- 4C Leslie Nielsen - Airplane /40 30.00 60.00
- 4D Leslie Nielsen - Frank Drebin /20
- 5 George Kennedy /99 20.00 40.00
- 6 Robert Carradine
- 7A Piper Laurie - Ain't Misbehavin' /19 7.50 15.00
- 7B Piper Laurie - The Hustler /40 7.50 15.00
- 7C Piper Laurie - Carrie /20 7.50 15.00
- 7D Piper Laurie - Other People's Money /20 7.50 15.00
- 8A Gloria Stuart - Titanic /40 20.00 40.00
- 8B Gloria Stuart - Old Rose /40 20.00 40.00
- 8C Gloria Stuart - The Invisible Man /20 20.00 40.00
- 9A Meredith Salenger - Harvard '92 /20 10.00 20.00
- 9B Meredith Salenger - Lake Placid /20 10.00 20.00
- 9C Meredith Salenger - Dream a Little Dream /20 10.00 20.00
- 10A Luke Goss - The Man /20 7.50 15.00
- 10B Luke Goss - One Night With the King /20 7.50 15.00
- 10C Luke Goss - Bone Dry /20 7.50 15.00
- 10D Luke Goss - Blade 2 /20 7.50 15.00
- 11 Willa Ford
- 12 Noureen DeWulf
- 13 Milo Ventimiglia - Pathology /20 7.50 15.00
- 14 Linda Evans - Tom Horn /20 15.00 30.00
- 15 John Schneider - Eddie Macon /20 10.00 20.00
- 16A Erika Eleniak - Under Siege /19 12.00 25.00
- 16B Erika Eleniak - Elly May /20 12.00 25.00
- 16C Erika Eleniak - ET /20 12.00 25.00
- 17 Willie Aames - Zapped /20 10.00 20.00
- 18 Justin Bieber
- 19A Josie Davis - Sonny /10
- 19B Josie Davis - Tranced /10
- 20A John Hurt - The Elephant Man /20 25.00 50.00
- 20B John Hurt - V for Vendetta /20 25.00 50.00

2011 Americana Screen Gems Material

PRINT RUN 99-249

- 4 Leslie Nielsen/199 3.00 8.00
- 7 Piper Laurie/249 3.00 8.00
- 8 Gloria Stuart/149 3.00 8.00
- 9 Meredith Salenger/249 3.00 8.00
- 13 Milo Ventimiglia/199 3.00 8.00
- 15 John Schneider/99 3.00 8.00
- 20 John Hurt

2011 Americana Screen Gems Material Silver Screen

PRINT RUN 5-99

2011 Americana Screen Gems Material Golden Era

*GOLDEN ERA: .6X TO 1.5X BASIC CARDS
PRINT RUN 49

2011 Americana Screen Gems Material Super Stars

PRINT RUN 25

2011 Americana Screen Gems Signature

PRINT RUN 29-99

- 1 Linda Hamilton
- 2 Selma Blair/99 25.00 50.00
- 3 Corey Haim/99 30.00 60.00
- 4 Leslie Nielsen
- 5 George Kennedy/79 15.00 30.00
- 6 Robert Carradine/49
- 7 Piper Laurie
- 8 Gloria Stuart
- 9 Meredith Salenger/49 8.00 20.00
- 10 Luke Goss/99 8.00 20.00
- 11 Willa Ford/99 8.00 20.00
- 12 Noureen DeWulf
- 13 Milo Ventimiglia/29
- 14 Linda Evans
- 15 John Schneider/29
- 16 Erika Eleniak
- 17 Willie Aames
- 18 Justin Bieber/99 100.00 150.00
- 19 Josie Davis/79 8.00 20.00
- 20 John Hurt/39 8.00 20.00

2011 Americana Screen Gems Signature Material

PRINT RUN 20-79

- 1 Linda Hamilton
- 2 Selma Blair
- 3 Corey Haim
- 4 Leslie Nielsen/39 30.00 60.00
- 5 George Kennedy
- 6 Robert Carradine
- 7 Piper Laurie/49
- 8 Gloria Stuart/35 20.00 40.00
- 9 Meredith Salenger/29 10.00 20.00
- 10 Luke Goss
- 11 Willa Ford
- 12 Noureen DeWulf
- 13 Milo Ventimiglia/69 10.00 20.00
- 14 Linda Evans
- 15 John Schneider/79 10.00 20.00
- 16 Erika Eleniak
- 17 Willie Aames
- 18 Justin Bieber
- 19 Josie Davis/69 12.00 25.00
- 20 John Hurt/20 25.00 50.00

2011 Avengers Kree Skrull War

COMPLETE SET (90) 5.00 12.00

- 1-01 Sacrifice .15 .40
- 1-02 Sacrifice .15 .40
- 1-03 Sacrifice .15 .40
- 1-04 Sacrifice .15 .40
- 1-05 Sacrifice .15 .40
- 1-06 Sacrifice .15 .40
- 1-07 Sacrifice .15 .40
- 1-08 Sacrifice .15 .40
- 1-09 Sacrifice .15 .40
- 1-10 Sacrifice .15 .40
- 1-11 Sacrifice .15 .40
- 1-12 Sacrifice .15 .40
- 1-13 Sacrifice .15 .40
- 1-14 Sacrifice .15 .40
- 1-15 Sacrifice .15 .40
- 1-16 Sacrifice .15 .40
- 1-17 Sacrifice .15 .40
- 1-18 Sacrifice .15 .40
- 1-19 Sacrifice .15 .40
- 1-20 Sacrifice .15 .40
- 1-21 Sacrifice .15 .40
- 1-22 Sacrifice .15 .40
- 1-23 Sacrifice .15 .40
- 1-24 Sacrifice .15 .40
- 1-25 Sacrifice .15 .40
- 1-26 Sacrifice .15 .40
- 1-27 Sacrifice .15 .40
- 1-28 Sacrifice .15 .40
- 1-29 Sacrifice .15 .40
- 1-30 Sacrifice .15 .40
- 1-31 Sacrifice .15 .40
- 1-32 Sacrifice .15 .40
- 1-33 Sacrifice .15 .40
- 1-34 Sacrifice .15 .40
- 1-35 Sacrifice .15 .40
- 1-36 Sacrifice .15 .40
- 1-37 Sacrifice .15 .40
- 1-38 Sacrifice .15 .40
- 1-39 Sacrifice .15 .40
- 1-40 Sacrifice .15 .40
- 1-41 Sacrifice .15 .40
- 1-42 Sacrifice .15 .40
- 1-43 Sacrifice .15 .40
- 1-44 Sacrifice .15 .40
- 1-45 Sacrifice .15 .40
- 1-46 Sacrifice .15 .40
- 1-47 Sacrifice .15 .40
- 1-48 Sacrifice .15 .40
- 1-49 Sacrifice .15 .40
- 1-50 Sacrifice .15 .40
- 1-51 Sacrifice .15 .40
- 1-52 Sacrifice .15 .40
- 1-53 Sacrifice .15 .40
- 1-54 Sacrifice .15 .40
- 1-55 Sacrifice .15 .40
- 1-56 Sacrifice .15 .40
- 1-57 Sacrifice .15 .40
- 1-58 Sacrifice .15 .40
- 1-59 Sacrifice .15 .40
- 1-60 Sacrifice .15 .40
- 1-61 Sacrifice .15 .40
- 1-62 Sacrifice .15 .40
- 1-63 Sacrifice .15 .40
- 1-64 Sacrifice .15 .40
- 1-65 Sacrifice .15 .40
- 1-66 Sacrifice .15 .40
- 1-67 Sacrifice .15 .40
- 1-68 Sacrifice .15 .40
- 1-69 Sacrifice .15 .40
- 1-70 Sacrifice .15 .40
- 1-71 Sacrifice .15 .40
- 1-72 Sacrifice .15 .40
- 1-73 Sacrifice .15 .40
- 1-74 Sacrifice .15 .40
- 1-75 Sacrifice .15 .40
- 1-76 Sacrifice .15 .40
- 1-77 Sacrifice .15 .40
- 1-78 Sacrifice .15 .40
- 1-79 Sacrifice .15 .40
- 1-80 Sacrifice .15 .40
- 1-81 Sacrifice .15 .40
- 1-82 Sacrifice .15 .40
- 1-83 Sacrifice .15 .40
- 1-84 Sacrifice .15 .40
- 1-85 Sacrifice .15 .40
- 1-86 Sacrifice .15 .40
- 1-87 Sacrifice .15 .40
- 1-88 Sacrifice .15 .40
- 1-89 Sacrifice .15 .40
- 1-90 Sacrifice .15 .40

2011 Avengers Kree Skrull War Characters

COMPLETE SET (9) 1.50 4.00
OVERALL CHARACTER ODDS 2.33:1

- 1 Captain America .30 .75
- 2 Captain Marvel .30 .75
- 3 Iron Man .30 .75
- 4 Nick Fury .30 .75
- 5 Quicksilver .30 .75
- 6 Scarlet Witch .30 .75
- 7 Super Skrull .30 .75
- 8 Thor .30 .75
- 9 Vision .30 .75

2011 Avengers Kree Skrull War Covers

COMPLETE SET (9) 1.50 4.00
OVERALL COVER ODDS 1:1

- C1 Cover - Top Left .30 .75
- C2 Cover - Top Center .30 .75
- C3 Cover - Top Right .30 .75
- C4 Cover - Middle Left .30 .75
- C5 Cover - Middle Center .30 .75
- C6 Cover - Middle Right .30 .75
- C7 Cover - Bottom Left .30 .75
- C8 Cover - Bottom Center .30 .75
- C9 Cover - Bottom Right .30 .75

2011 Avengers Kree Skrull War Covers Black and White

COMPLETE SET (9) 8.00 20.00
OVERALL COVER ODDS 1:1

- B1 Cover - Top Left 1.50 4.00
- B2 Cover - Top Center 1.50 4.00
- B3 Cover - Top Right 1.50 4.00
- B4 Cover - Middle Left 1.50 4.00
- B5 Cover - Middle Center 1.50 4.00
- B6 Cover - Middle Right 1.50 4.00
- B7 Cover - Bottom Left 1.50 4.00
- B8 Cover - Bottom Center 1.50 4.00
- B9 Cover - Bottom Right 1.50 4.00

2011 Avengers Kree Skrull War Covers Variant Art

COMPLETE SET (9) 3.00 8.00
OVERALL COVER ODDS 1:1

- V1 Cover - Top Left .60 1.50
- V2 Cover - Top Center .60 1.50
- V3 Cover - Top Right .60 1.50
- V4 Cover - Middle Left .60 1.50
- V5 Cover - Middle Center .60 1.50
- V6 Cover - Middle Right .60 1.50
- V7 Cover - Bottom Left .60 1.50
- V8 Cover - Bottom Center .60 1.50
- V9 Cover - Bottom Right .60 1.50

2011 Avengers Kree Skrull War Power

COMPLETE SET (18) 3.00 8.00
OVERALL MINI STORY ODDS 1.67:1

- 4-01 Power .40 1.00
- 4-02 Power .40 1.00
- 4-03 Power .40 1.00
- 4-04 Power .40 1.00
- 4-05 Power .40 1.00
- 4-06 Power .40 1.00
- 4-07 Power .40 1.00
- 4-08 Power .40 1.00
- 4-09 Power .40 1.00
- 4-10 Power .40 1.00
- 4-11 Power .40 1.00
- 4-12 Power .40 1.00
- 4-13 Power .40 1.00
- 4-14 Power .40 1.00
- 4-15 Power .40 1.00
- 4-16 Power .40 1.00
- 4-17 Power .40 1.00
- 4-18 Power .40 1.00

2011 Avengers Kree Skrull War Retro Characters

COMPLETE SET (27) 4.00 10.00
OVERALL CHARACTER ODDS 2.33:1

- R1 Annihilus SP .40 1.00
- R2 Ant-Man .30 .75
- R3 Black Bolt .30 .75
- R4 Captain America .30 .75
- R5 Captain Marvel .30 .75
- R6 Carol Danvers SP .40 1.00
- R7 Goliath .30 .75
- R8 H.W. Craddock SP .40 1.00
- R9 Iron Man .30 .75
- R10 Jarvis SP .40 1.00
- R11 Kree SP .40 1.00
- R12 Mandroids SP .40 1.00
- R13 Maximus SP .40 1.00
- R14 Nick Fury .30 .75
- R15 Quicksilver .30 .75
- R16 Rick Jones .30 .75
- R17 Ronan .30 .75
- R18 Scarlet Witch .30 .75
- R19 Skrull SP .40 1.00
- R20 Skrull Emperor .30 .75
- R21 Super Skrull .30 .75
- R22 Supreme Intelligence .30 .75
- R23 The Sentry .30 .75
- R24 Thor .30 .75
- R25 Triton SP .40 1.00
- R26 Vision .30 .75
- R27 Wasp .30 .75

2011 Avengers Kree Skrull War Soldiers' Honor

COMPLETE SET (18) 3.00 8.00
OVERALL MINI STORY ODDS 1.67:1

- 5-01 Soldiers' Honor .40 1.00
- 5-02 Soldiers' Honor .40 1.00
- 5-03 Soldiers' Honor .40 1.00
- 5-04 Soldiers' Honor .40 1.00
- 5-05 Soldiers' Honor .40 1.00
- 5-06 Soldiers' Honor .40 1.00

❑ 5-07 Soldiers' Honor .40 1.00
❑ 5-08 Soldiers' Honor .40 1.00
❑ 5-09 Soldiers' Honor .40 1.00
❑ 5-10 Soldiers' Honor .40 1.00
❑ 5-11 Soldiers' Honor .40 1.00
❑ 5-12 Soldiers' Honor .40 1.00
❑ 5-13 Soldiers' Honor .40 1.00
❑ 5-14 Soldiers' Honor .40 1.00
❑ 5-15 Soldiers' Honor .40 1.00
❑ 5-16 Soldiers' Honor .40 1.00
❑ 5-17 Soldiers' Honor .40 1.00
❑ 5-18 Soldiers' Honor .40 1.00

2011 Avengers Kree Skrull War The Debt

COMPLETE SET (36) 5.00 12.00
OVERALL MINI STORY ODDS 1.67:1

❑ 2-01 The Debt .40 1.00
❑ 2-02 The Debt .40 1.00
❑ 2-03 The Debt .40 1.00
❑ 2-04 The Debt .40 1.00
❑ 2-05 The Debt .40 1.00
❑ 2-06 The Debt .40 1.00
❑ 2-07 The Debt .40 1.00
❑ 2-08 The Debt .40 1.00
❑ 2-09 The Debt .40 1.00
❑ 2-10 The Debt .40 1.00
❑ 2-11 The Debt .40 1.00
❑ 2-12 The Debt .40 1.00
❑ 2-13 The Debt .40 1.00
❑ 2-14 The Debt .40 1.00
❑ 2-15 The Debt .40 1.00
❑ 2-16 The Debt .40 1.00
❑ 2-17 The Debt .40 1.00
❑ 2-18 The Debt .40 1.00
❑ 2-19 The Debt .40 1.00
❑ 2-20 The Debt .40 1.00
❑ 2-21 The Debt .40 1.00
❑ 2-22 The Debt .40 1.00
❑ 2-23 The Debt .40 1.00
❑ 2-24 The Debt .40 1.00
❑ 2-25 The Debt .40 1.00
❑ 2-26 The Debt .40 1.00
❑ 2-27 The Debt .40 1.00
❑ 2-28 The Debt .40 1.00
❑ 2-29 The Debt .40 1.00
❑ 2-30 The Debt .40 1.00
❑ 2-31 The Debt .40 1.00
❑ 2-32 The Debt .40 1.00
❑ 2-33 The Debt .40 1.00
❑ 2-34 The Debt .40 1.00
❑ 2-35 The Debt .40 1.00
❑ 2-36 The Debt .40 1.00

2011 Avengers Kree Skrull War The Fall

COMPLETE SET (27) 4.00 10.00
OVERALL MINI STORY ODDS 1.67:1

❑ 3-01 The Fall .40 1.00
❑ 3-02 The Fall .40 1.00
❑ 3-03 The Fall .40 1.00
❑ 3-04 The Fall .40 1.00
❑ 3-05 The Fall .40 1.00
❑ 3-06 The Fall .40 1.00
❑ 3-07 The Fall .40 1.00
❑ 3-08 The Fall .40 1.00
❑ 3-09 The Fall .40 1.00
❑ 3-10 The Fall .40 1.00
❑ 3-11 The Fall .40 1.00
❑ 3-12 The Fall .40 1.00
❑ 3-13 The Fall .40 1.00
❑ 3-14 The Fall .40 1.00
❑ 3-15 The Fall .40 1.00
❑ 3-16 The Fall .40 1.00
❑ 3-17 The Fall .40 1.00
❑ 3-18 The Fall .40 1.00
❑ 3-19 The Fall .40 1.00
❑ 3-20 The Fall .40 1.00
❑ 3-21 The Fall .40 1.00
❑ 3-22 The Fall .40 1.00
❑ 3-23 The Fall .40 1.00
❑ 3-24 The Fall .40 1.00
❑ 3-25 The Fall .40 1.00
❑ 3-26 The Fall .40 1.00
❑ 3-27 The Fall .40 1.00

2011 Bench Warmer Bubblegum

COMPLETE SET (100) 8.00 20.00

❑ 1 Jennifer Walcott .40 1.00
❑ 2 Lisa Gleave .20 .50
❑ 3 April Scott .20 .50
❑ 4 Mary Riley .40 1.00
❑ 5 Carrie Stroup .20 .50
❑ 6 Jessica Burciaga .20 .50
❑ 7 Cassandra Lynn .20 .50
❑ 8 Sara Underwood .40 1.00
❑ 9 Sandra Taylor .20 .50
❑ 10 Rachel Bernstein .20 .50
❑ 11 Bambi Lashell .20 .50
❑ 12 Jessica Hall .20 .50
❑ 13 Charity Hodges .20 .50
❑ 14 Alison Waite .20 .50
❑ 15 Athena Lundberg .20 .50
❑ 16 Brandy Grace .20 .50
❑ 17 Torrie Wilson .30 .75
❑ 18 Shay Lyn Veasy .20 .50
❑ 19 Victoria Fuller .20 .50
❑ 20 Miriam Gonzalez .30 .75
❑ 21 Michelle Baena .20 .50
❑ 22 Nicole Bennett .20 .50
❑ 23 Leigh Ann Spence .20 .50
❑ 24 Jaime Bergman .20 .50
❑ 25 Brooke Morales .20 .50
❑ 26 Jaimarie Cherie .20 .50
❑ 27 Krisi Ballentine .20 .50
❑ 28 Alana Curry .20 .50
❑ 29 Buffy Tyler .20 .50
❑ 30 Traci Bingham .20 .50
❑ 31 Wrenna Monet .20 .50
❑ 32 Melissa Hunter .20 .50
❑ 33 Yvette Lopez .20 .50
❑ 34 Brande Roderick .20 .50
❑ 35 Enya Flack .20 .50
❑ 36 Nikki Ziering .20 .50
❑ 37 Sarah Coggin .20 .50
❑ 38 Tamara Witmer .20 .50
❑ 39 Tiffany Granath .20 .50
❑ 40 Lindsey Roeper .20 .50
❑ 41 Alika Ray .20 .50
❑ 42 Jennifer England .20 .50
❑ 43 Katie Lohmann .20 .50
❑ 44 Amber Hay .20 .50
❑ 45 Brittany Herrera .20 .50
❑ 46 Brandie Moses .20 .50
❑ 47 Holley Dorrough .20 .50
❑ 48 Alice Bradley .20 .50
❑ 49 Colleen Shannon .20 .50
❑ 50 Simona Fusco .20 .50
❑ 51 Tiffany Selby .20 .50
❑ 52 Paige Peterson .20 .50
❑ 53 Tiffany Toth .20 .50
❑ 54 Megan Hauserman .20 .50
❑ 55 Lena Yada .20 .50
❑ 56 Kitana Baker .20 .50
❑ 57 Jo Garcia .20 .50
❑ 58 Cecille Gahr .20 .50
❑ 59 Bobbi Billard .20 .50
❑ 60 Denyce Lawton .20 .50
❑ 61 Lisa Lakatos .20 .50
❑ 62 Melissa Taylor .20 .50
❑ 63 Nikki Zeno .20 .50
❑ 64 Renee Stone .20 .50
❑ 65 Spencer Scott .20 .50
❑ 66 Xi Xi Yang .20 .50
❑ 67 Bridget Marquardt .20 .50
❑ 68 Kayla Collins .20 .50
❑ 69 Jennifer Korbin .30 .75
❑ 70 Flo Jalin .20 .50
❑ 71 Claudia Jordan .20 .50
❑ 72 Jessica Rockwell .20 .50
❑ 73 Martina Andrews .20 .50
❑ 74 Traci Brooks .20 .50
❑ 75 Mia St. John .20 .50
❑ 76 Louise Glover .20 .50
❑ 77 Holly Madison .20 .50
❑ 78 Gail Kim .20 .50
❑ 79 Cat Miller .20 .50
❑ 80 Catherine Kluthe .20 .50
❑ 81 Brittany McGraw .20 .50
❑ 82 Aubrie Lemon .20 .50
❑ 83 Alix Agar .20 .50
❑ 84 Alejandra Gutierrez .20 .50
❑ 85 Katarina Van Derham .20 .50
❑ 86 Candace Kita .20 .50
❑ 87 Holly Huddleston .20 .50
❑ 88 Molly Shea .20 .50
❑ 89 Camille Anderson .20 .50
❑ 90 Masumi Max .20 .50
❑ 91 Amanda Paige .20 .50
❑ 92 Leilene Joy .20 .50
❑ 93 Jenae Alt .20 .50
❑ 94 Kendra Wilkinson .30 .75
❑ 95 Aiko Tanaka .20 .50
❑ 96 Candice Michelle .30 .75
❑ 97 Christy Hemme .30 .75
❑ 98 Lisa Ligon .20 .50
❑ 99 Talor Marion .20 .50
❑ 100 Yvette Nelson .20 .50

2011 Bench Warmer Bubblegum Authentic Swatches

STATED ODDS 1:288

❑ 1 Christy Hemme 25.00 50.00
❑ 2 Jennifer Walcott 25.00 50.00
❑ 3 Torrie Wilson 25.00 50.00
❑ 4 Spencer Scott 20.00 40.00
❑ 5 TBD
❑ 6 Mary Riley 30.00 60.00
❑ 7 Aubrie Lemon 20.00 40.00
❑ 8 Claudia Jordan 20.00 40.00
❑ 9 Jessica Burciaga 20.00 40.00
❑ 10 Lisa Gleave 25.00 50.00
❑ 11 Brandie Moses 20.00 40.00
❑ 12 Jessica Hall 25.00 50.00
❑ 13 Traci Bingham 20.00 40.00
❑ 14 Sara Underwood 30.00 60.00
❑ 15 Kitana Baker 20.00 40.00
❑ 16 Michelle McLaughlin 20.00 40.00

2011 Bench Warmer Bubblegum Autographs

STATED ODDS 1:12

❑ A1 Mary Riley 8.00 20.00
❑ A2 Lisa Gleave 6.00 15.00
❑ A3 Miriam Gonzalez 5.00 12.00
❑ A4 Carrie Stroup 5.00 12.00
❑ A5 Katarina Van Derham 5.00 12.00
❑ A6 Kyara Tyler 5.00 12.00
❑ A7 Ryan Shamrock 5.00 12.00
❑ A8 Shay Lyn Veasy 5.00 12.00
❑ A9 Kara Monaco 5.00 12.00
❑ A10 Syd Wilder 5.00 12.00
❑ A11 Bambi Lashell 5.00 12.00
❑ A12 Patrice Hollis 5.00 12.00
❑ A13 Katie Lohmann 5.00 12.00
❑ A14 Jessica Hall 6.00 15.00
❑ A15 Cassandra Lynn 5.00 12.00
❑ A16 Rachel Bernstein 5.00 12.00
❑ A17 Jennifer Korbin 6.00 15.00
❑ A18 Sandi Taylor 5.00 12.00
❑ A19 Tiffany Selby 5.00 12.00
❑ A20 Caitlin O'Connor 5.00 12.00
❑ A21 Buffy Tyler 5.00 12.00
❑ A22 April Scott 5.00 12.00
❑ A23 Holley Dorrough 5.00 12.00
❑ A24 Brittany Herrera 5.00 12.00
❑ A25 Heather Rae Young
❑ A26 Heather Rene Smith 5.00 12.00
❑ A27 Nikki Ziering 5.00 12.00
❑ A28 Ramona Michelle 5.00 12.00
❑ A29 Jennifer Walcott 6.00 15.00
❑ A30 Sara Underwood 8.00 20.00
❑ A31 Torrie Wilson 5.00 12.00
❑ A32 Maria Kanellis 8.00 20.00
❑ A33 Andrea Lowell 5.00 12.00
❑ A34 Deanna Brooks 5.00 12.00
❑ A35 Jasmine Dustin 5.00 12.00
❑ A36 Brandy Grace 5.00 12.00

2011 Bench Warmer Holiday Factory Set

COMPLETE SET (22)
ANNOUNCED PRINT RUN 750 SETS

❑ 1 Brandy Grace 4.00 10.00
❑ 2 Mary Riley 6.00 15.00
❑ 3 Candace Kita 4.00 10.00
❑ 4 Carrie Minter 4.00 10.00
❑ 5 Sandra Taylor 5.00 12.00
❑ 6 Talor Marion 4.00 10.00
❑ 7 Cassandra Lynn 4.00 10.00
❑ 8 Katie Lohmann 4.00 10.00
❑ 9 Lisa Gleave 4.00 10.00
❑ 10 Shay Lyn Veasy 4.00 10.00
❑ 11 Jennifer Korbin 5.00 12.00
❑ 12 Michelle Baena 4.00 10.00
❑ 13 Syd Wilder 4.00 10.00
❑ 14 Maria Kanellis 6.00 15.00
❑ 15 Brande Roderick 4.00 10.00
❑ 16 Tiffany Toth 4.00 10.00
❑ 17 Crystal Harris 8.00 20.00
❑ 18 Katarina Van Derham 4.00 10.00
❑ 19 Miki Black 4.00 10.00
❑ 20 Torrie Wilson 8.00 20.00
❑ 21 Krisi Ballentine 4.00 10.00
❑ 22 Billie Jo Powers/750 4.00 10.00

2011 Bench Warmer Holiday Factory Set Pink Foil

COMPLETE SET (21)
STATED PRINT RUN 25 SER. #'d SETS

2011 Bench Warmer Holiday Factory Set Green Foil

STATED PRINT RUN 10 SER. #'d SETS
UNPRICED DUE TO SCARCITY

2011 Bench Warmer Holiday Factory Set Blue Foil

STATED PRINT RUN 5 SER. #'d SETS
UNPRICED DUE TO SCARCITY

2011 Bench Warmer Holiday Factory Set Red Foil

STATED PRINT RUN 1 SER. #'d SET
UNPRICED DUE TO SCARCITY

2011 Bench Warmer Hot For Teacher

COMPLETE SET
STATED PRINT RUN 50 SER. #'d SETS

❑ 1 Sara Underwood 20.00 40.00
❑ 2 Kara Monaco 8.00 20.00
❑ 3A Katie Lohmann 8.00 20.00
❑ 3B Jennifer Walcott 10.00 25.00
❑ 4 Maria Kanellis 10.00 25.00
❑ 5 Jessica Hall 10.00 25.00
❑ 6 Deanna Brooks 8.00 20.00
❑ 7 Mary Riley 12.00 30.00
❑ 8 Miriam Gonzalez 10.00 25.00
❑ 9 Stacie Hall 8.00 20.00
❑ 10 Torrie Wilson 10.00 25.00
❑ 11 Heather Rae Young 8.00 20.00
❑ 12 Cassandra Lynn 8.00 20.00
❑ 13 Holley Dorrough 8.00 20.00
❑ 14 Lisa Gleave 8.00 20.00
❑ 15 Jasmine Dustin 8.00 20.00
❑ 16 Brandy Grace 8.00 20.00
❑ 17 Buffy Tyler 8.00 20.00
❑ 18 Patrice Hollis 8.00 20.00
❑ 19 Sandra Taylor 12.00 30.00
❑ 20 Nikki Ziering 8.00 20.00
❑ 21 Carrie Stroup 8.00 20.00
❑ 22 Heather Rene Smith 8.00 20.00
❑ 23 Andrea Lowell 8.00 20.00
❑ 24 Ryan Shamrock 8.00 20.00
❑ 25 Kyara Tyler 8.00 20.00
❑ 26 Shay Lyn Veasy 8.00 20.00
❑ 27 Katarina Van Derham 8.00 20.00
❑ 28A Britany Lauren 8.00 20.00
❑ 28B Jennifer Korbin 10.00 25.00
❑ 29 Syd Wilder 8.00 20.00
❑ 30 Rachel Bernstein 8.00 20.00
❑ NNO Jessica Hall 12.00 30.00
Stacie Hall

2011 Bench Warmer Hot For Teacher Pink Foil

*PINK: .5X TO 1.25X BASIC CARDS
STATED PRINT RUN 25 SER. #'d SETS

2011 Bench Warmer Hot For Teacher Green Foil

STATED PRINT RUN 10 SER. #'d SETS
UNPRICED DUE TO SCARCITY

2011 Bench Warmer Hot For Teacher Blue Foil

STATED PRINT RUN 5 SER. #'d SETS
UNPRICED DUE TO SCARCITY

2011 Bench Warmer Hot For Teacher Red Foil

STATED PRINT RUN 1 SER. #'d SET
UNPRICED DUE TO SCARCITY

2011 Bench Warmer Hot For Teacher Printing Plates Black

STATED PRINT RUN 1 SER. #'d SET
UNPRICED DUE TO SCARCITY

2011 Bench Warmer Hot For Teacher Printing Plates Cyan

STATED PRINT RUN 1 SER. #'d SET
UNPRICED DUE TO SCARCITY

2011 Bench Warmer Hot For Teacher Printing Plates Magenta

STATED PRINT RUN 1 SER. #'d SET
UNPRICED DUE TO SCARCITY

2011 Bench Warmer Hot For Teacher Printing Plates Yellow

STATED PRINT RUN 1 SER. #'d SET
UNPRICED DUE TO SCARCITY

2011 Bench Warmer Hot For Teacher Class Cuts Hair Gold Foil

STATED PRINT RUN 15 SER. #'d SETS

❑ 1 Andrea Lowell
❑ 2 Nikki Ziering
❑ 3 Jessica Hall
❑ 4 Cassandra Lynn
❑ 5 Holley Dorrough
❑ 6 Traci Bingham
❑ 7 Heather Rae Young
❑ 8 Ryan Shamrock
❑ 9 Sandra Taylor
❑ 10 Kara Monaco
❑ 11 Patrice Hollis
❑ 12 Tiffany Selby
❑ 13 Rachel Bernstein
❑ 14 Stacie Hall
❑ 15 Katarina Van Derham

2011 Bench Warmer Hot For Teacher Class Cuts Hair Pink Foil

STATED PRINT RUN 5 SER. #'d SETS
UNPRICED DUE TO SCARCITY

2011 Bench Warmer Hot For Teacher Class Cuts Hair Autographs Green Foil

STATED PRINT RUN 3 SER. #'d SETS
UNPRICED DUE TO SCARCITY

❑ 1 Andrea Lowell
❑ 2 Nikki Ziering
❑ 3 Jessica Hall
❑ 4 Cassandra Lynn
❑ 5 Holley Dorrough
❑ 6 Traci Bingham
❑ 7 Heather Rae Young
❑ 8 Ryan Shamrock
❑ 9 Sandra Taylor
❑ 10 Kara Monaco
❑ 11 Patrice Hollis
❑ 12 Tiffany Selby
❑ 13 Rachel Bernstein
❑ 14 Stacie Hall
❑ 15 Katarina Van Derham

2011 Bench Warmer Hot For Teacher Class Cuts Hair Autographs Blue Foil

STATED PRINT RUN 2 SER. #'d SETS
UNPRICED DUE TO SCARCITY

2011 Bench Warmer Hot For Teacher Class Cuts Hair Autographs Red Foil

STATED PRINT RUN 1 SER. #'d SET
UNPRICED DUE TO SCARCITY

2011 Bench Warmer Hot For Teacher Hall Pass Autographs Gold Foil

STATED PRINT RUN 50 SER. #'d SETS

❑ 1 Sara Underwood 20.00 40.00
❑ 2 Deanna Brooks 8.00 20.00
❑ 3 Stacie Hall 8.00 20.00
❑ 4 Heather Rae Young 8.00 20.00
❑ 5 Patrice Hollis 8.00 20.00
❑ 6 Andrea Lowell 8.00 20.00
❑ 7 Shay Lyn Veasy 8.00 20.00
❑ 8 Jasmine Dustin 8.00 20.00
❑ 9 Katarina Van Derham 8.00 20.00
❑ 10 Jessica Kinni 8.00 20.00
❑ 11 Tiffany Selby 8.00 20.00
❑ 12 Kara Monaco 8.00 20.00

2011 Bench Warmer Hot For Teacher Hall Pass Autographs Pink Foil

STATED PRINT RUN 25 SER. #'d SETS

2011 Bench Warmer Hot For Teacher Hall Pass Autographs Green Foil

STATED PRINT RUN 10 SER. #'d SETS
UNPRICED DUE TO SCARCITY

2011 Bench Warmer Hot For Teacher Hall Pass Autographs Blue Foil

STATED PRINT RUN 5 SER. #'d SETS
UNPRICED DUE TO SCARCITY

2011 Bench Warmer Hot For Teacher Hall Pass Autographs Red Foil

STATED PRINT RUN 1 SER. #'d SET
UNPRICED DUE TO SCARCITY

2011 Bench Warmer Hot For Teacher Hall Pass Autographs Printing Plates Black

STATED PRINT RUN 1 SER. #'d SET
UNPRICED DUE TO SCARCITY

2011 Bench Warmer Hot For Teacher Hall Pass Autographs Printing Plates Cyan

STATED PRINT RUN 1 SER. #'d SET
UNPRICED DUE TO SCARCITY

2011 Bench Warmer Hot For Teacher Hall Pass Autographs Printing Plates Magenta

STATED PRINT RUN 1 SER. #'d SET
UNPRICED DUE TO SCARCITY

2011 Bench Warmer Hot For Teacher Hall Pass Autographs Printing Plates Yellow

STATED PRINT RUN 1 SER. #'d SET
UNPRICED DUE TO SCARCITY

2011 Bench Warmer Hot For Teacher High Heels Gold Foil

STATED PRINT RUN 25 SER. #'d SETS

❑ 1 Maria Kanellis 20.00 40.00
❑ 2 Sara Underwood 30.00 60.00
❑ 3 Jennifer Walcott 20.00 40.00
❑ 4 Nikki Ziering 15.00 30.00
❑ 5 Sandra Taylor 20.00 40.00
❑ 6 Shay Lyn Veasy 15.00 30.00
❑ 7 Heather Rae Young 15.00 30.00
❑ 8 Ryan Shamrock 15.00 30.00
❑ 9 Rachel Bernstein 15.00 30.00

2011 Bench Warmer Hot For Teacher High Heels Pink Foil

STATED PRINT RUN 15 SER. #'d SETS

2011 Bench Warmer Hot For Teacher High Heels Autographs Green Foil

STATED PRINT RUN 10 SER. #'d SETS
UNPRICED DUE TO SCARCITY

❑ 1 Maria Kanellis
❑ 2 Sara Underwood
❑ 3 Jennifer Walcott
❑ 4 Nikki Ziering
❑ 5 Sandra Taylor
❑ 6 Shay Lyn Veasy
❑ 7 Heather Rae Young
❑ 8 Ryan Shamrock
❑ 9 Rachel Bernstein

2011 Bench Warmer Hot For Teacher High Heels Autographs Blue Foil

STATED PRINT RUN 5 SER. #'d SETS
UNPRICED DUE TO SCARCITY

2011 Bench Warmer Hot For Teacher High Heels Autographs Red Foil

STATED PRINT RUN 1 SER. #'d SET
UNPRICED DUE TO SCARCITY

2011 Bench Warmer Hot For Teacher Inscriptions

STATED PRINT RUN 25 SER. #'d SETS

❑ 1 Mary Riley 40.00 80.00
❑ 2 Sara Underwood 60.00 120.00
❑ 3 Rachel Bernstein 20.00 40.00
❑ 4 Maria Kanellis 40.00 80.00
❑ 5 Jessica Hall 25.00 50.00
❑ 6 Deanna Brooks 20.00 40.00
❑ 7 Sandra Taylor 40.00 80.00
❑ 8 Miriam Gonzalez 30.00 60.00
❑ 9 Tiffany Selby 20.00 40.00
❑ 10 Torrie Wilson 30.00 60.00
❑ 11 Heather Rae Young
❑ 12 Cassandra Lynn 25.00 50.00
❑ 13 Holley Dorrough 25.00 50.00
❑ 14 Lisa Gleave 30.00 60.00
❑ 15 Andrea Lowell 20.00 40.00
❑ 16 Ryan Shamrock 25.00 50.00
❑ 17 Buffy Tyler 30.00 60.00
❑ 18 Patrice Hollis
❑ 19 Nikki Ziering
❑ 20 Shay Lyn Veasy

2011 Bench Warmer Hot For Teacher Kiss Gold Foil

STATED PRINT RUN 25 SER. #'d SETS

❑ 1 Kara Monaco 12.00 25.00
❑ 2 Sandra Taylor 20.00 40.00
❑ 3 Deanna Brooks 12.00 25.00
❑ 4 Sara Underwood 30.00 60.00
❑ 5 Jessica Hall 15.00 30.00
❑ 6 Maria Kanellis 15.00 30.00
❑ 7 Ryan Shamrock 12.00 25.00
❑ 8 Miriam Gonzalez 15.00 30.00
❑ 9 Heather Rae Young 12.00 25.00

2011 Bench Warmer Hot For Teacher Kiss Pink Foil

STATED PRINT RUN 15 SER. #'d SETS

2011 Bench Warmer Hot For Teacher Kiss Autographs Green Foil

STATED PRINT RUN 10 SER. #'d SETS
UNPRICED DUE TO SCARCITY

❑ 1 Kara Monaco
❑ 2 Sandra Taylor
❑ 3 Deanna Brooks
❑ 4 Sara Underwood
❑ 5 Jessica Hall
❑ 6 Maria Kanellis
❑ 7 Ryan Shamrock
❑ 8 Miriam Gonzalez
❑ 9 Heather Rae Young

2011 Bench Warmer Hot For Teacher Kiss Autographs Blue Foil

STATED PRINT RUN 5 SER. #'d SETS
UNPRICED DUE TO SCARCITY

2011 Bench Warmer Hot For Teacher Kiss Autographs Red Foil

STATED PRINT RUN 1 SER. #'d SET
UNPRICED DUE TO SCARCITY

2011 Bench Warmer Hot For Teacher Knee High Swatches Gold Foil

STATED PRINT RUN 50 SER. #'d SETS

❑ 1 Kara Monaco 15.00 30.00
❑ 2 Katarina Van Derham 15.00 30.00
❑ 3 Sara Underwood 30.00 60.00
❑ 4 Jessica Hall 15.00 30.00
❑ 5 Mary Riley 25.00 50.00
❑ 6 Stacie Hall 15.00 30.00
❑ 7 Nikki Ziering 15.00 30.00
❑ 8 Sandra Taylor 15.00 30.00
❑ 9 Andrea Lowell 15.00 30.00
❑ 10 Deanna Brooks 15.00 30.00
❑ 11 Jasmine Dustin 15.00 30.00
❑ 12 Heather Rae Young 15.00 30.00
❑ 13 Shay Lyn Veasy 15.00 30.00
❑ 14 Ryan Shamrock 15.00 30.00
❑ 15 Jennifer Korbin 20.00 40.00

2011 Bench Warmer Hot For Teacher Knee High Swatches Pink Foil

STATED PRINT RUN 25 SER. #'d SETS

2011 Bench Warmer Hot For Teacher Knee High Swatches Autographs Green Foil

STATED PRINT RUN 10 SER. #'d SETS
UNPRICED DUE TO SCARCITY

❑ 1 Kara Monaco
❑ 2 Katarina Van Derham
❑ 3 Sara Underwood
❑ 4 Jessica Hall
❑ 5 Mary Riley
❑ 6 Stacie Hall
❑ 7 Nikki Ziering
❑ 8 Sandra Taylor
❑ 9 Andrea Lowell
❑ 10 Deanna Brooks
❑ 11 Jasmine Dustin
❑ 12 Heather Rae Young
❑ 13 Shay Lyn Veasy
❑ 14 Ryan Shamrock
❑ 15 Jennifer Korbin

2011 Bench Warmer Hot For Teacher Knee High Swatches Autographs Blue Foil

STATED PRINT RUN 5 SER. #'d SETS
UNPRICED DUE TO SCARCITY

2011 Bench Warmer Hot For Teacher Knee High Swatches Autographs Red Foil

STATED PRINT RUN 1 SER. #'d SET
UNPRICED DUE TO SCARCITY

2011 Bench Warmer Hot For Teacher Knee High Swatches Autographs Printing Plates Black

STATED PRINT RUN 1 SER. #'d SET
UNPRICED DUE TO SCARCITY

2011 Bench Warmer Hot For Teacher Knee High Swatches Autographs Printing Plates Cyan

STATED PRINT RUN 1 SER. #'d SET
UNPRICED DUE TO SCARCITY

2011 Bench Warmer Hot For Teacher Knee High Swatches Autographs Printing Plates Magenta

STATED PRINT RUN 1 SER. #'d SET
UNPRICED DUE TO SCARCITY

2011 Bench Warmer Hot For Teacher Knee High Swatches Autographs Printing Plates Yellow
STATED PRINT RUN 1 SER. #'d SET
UNPRICED DUE TO SCARCITY

2011 Bench Warmer Hot For Teacher School Girl Swatches Gold Foil
STATED PRINT RUN 50 SER. #'d SETS

❑ 1 Torrie Wilson 20.00 40.00
❑ 2 Maria Kanellis 15.00 30.00
❑ 3 Sara Underwood 40.00 80.00
❑ 4 Kara Monaco 15.00 30.00
❑ 5 Jessica Hall 15.00 30.00
❑ 6 Cassandra Lynn 15.00 30.00
❑ 7 Buffy Tyler 15.00 30.00
❑ 8 Miriam Gonzalez 20.00 40.00
❑ 9 Jessica Burciaga 15.00 30.00
❑ 10 Sandra Taylor 15.00 30.00
❑ 11 Nikki Ziering 15.00 30.00
❑ 12 Ryan Shamrock 15.00 30.00
❑ 13 Heather Rae Young 15.00 30.00
❑ 14 Patrice Hollis 15.00 30.00
❑ 15 Katarina Van Derham 15.00 30.00
❑ 16 Heather Rene Smith 15.00 30.00
❑ 17 Holley Dorrough 15.00 30.00
❑ 18 Deanna Brooks 15.00 30.00
❑ 19 Lisa Gleave 15.00 30.00
❑ 20 Carrie Stroup 15.00 30.00
❑ 21 Charity Hodges 15.00 30.00
❑ 22 Stacie Hall 15.00 30.00
❑ 23 Shay Lyn Veasy 15.00 30.00
❑ 24 Andrea Lowell 15.00 30.00
❑ 25 Rachel Bernstein 15.00 30.00
❑ 26 Syd Wilder 15.00 30.00
❑ 27 Jennifer Walcott 20.00 40.00
❑ 28 Renee Stone 15.00 30.00
❑ 29 Caitlin O'Connor 15.00 30.00
❑ 30 Mary Riley 25.00 50.00

2011 Bench Warmer Hot For Teacher School Girl Swatches Pink Foil
STATED PRINT RUN 25 SER. #'d SETS

2011 Bench Warmer Hot For Teacher School Girl Swatches Autographs Green Foil
STATED PRINT RUN 10 SER. #'d SETS
UNPRICED DUE TO SCARCITY

❑ 1 Torrie Wilson
❑ 2 Maria Kanellis
❑ 3 Sara Underwood
❑ 4 Kara Monaco
❑ 5 Jessica Hall
❑ 6 Cassandra Lynn
❑ 7 Buffy Tyler
❑ 8 Miriam Gonzalez
❑ 9 Jessica Burciaga
❑ 10 Sandra Taylor
❑ 11 Nikki Ziering
❑ 12 Ryan Shamrock
❑ 13 Heather Rae Young
❑ 14 Patrice Hollis
❑ 15 Katarina Van Derham
❑ 16 Heather Rene Smith
❑ 17 Holley Dorrough
❑ 18 Deanna Brooks
❑ 19 Lisa Gleave
❑ 20 Carrie Stroup
❑ 21 Charity Hodges
❑ 22 Stacie Hall
❑ 23 Shay Lyn Veasy
❑ 24 Andrea Lowell
❑ 25 Rachel Bernstein
❑ 26 Syd Wilder
❑ 27 Jennifer Walcott
❑ 28 Renee Stone
❑ 29 Caitlin O'Connor
❑ 30 Mary Riley

2011 Bench Warmer Hot For Teacher School Girl Swatches Autographs Blue Foil
STATED PRINT RUN 5 SER. #'d SETS
UNPRICED DUE TO SCARCITY

2011 Bench Warmer Hot For Teacher School Girl Swatches Autographs Red Foil
STATED PRINT RUN 1 SER. #'d SET
UNPRICED DUE TO SCARCITY

2011 Bench Warmer Hot For Teacher School Girl Swatches Autographs Printing Plates Black
STATED PRINT RUN 1 SER. #'d SET
UNPRICED DUE TO SCARCITY

2011 Bench Warmer Hot For Teacher School Girl Swatches Autographs Printing Plates Cyan
STATED PRINT RUN 1 SER. #'d SET
UNPRICED DUE TO SCARCITY

2011 Bench Warmer Hot For Teacher School Girl Swatches Autographs Printing Plates Magenta
STATED PRINT RUN 1 SER. #'d SET
UNPRICED DUE TO SCARCITY

2011 Bench Warmer Hot For Teacher School Girl Swatches Autographs Printing Plates Yellow
STATED PRINT RUN 1 SER. #'d SET
UNPRICED DUE TO SCARCITY

2011 Bench Warmer Hot For Teacher School Props Gold Foil
STATED PRINT RUN 15 SER. #'d SETS

❑ 1 Cassandra Lynn red apple 20.00 40.00
❑ 2 Jessica Hall green apple 25.00 50.00
❑ 3 Maria Kanellis chalkboard 20.00 40.00
❑ 4 Kara Monaco notebook 20.00 40.00
❑ 5 Sara Underwood ruler 40.00 80.00
❑ 6 Jessica Hall 25.00 50.00
Stacie Hall hall pass
❑ 7 Ryan Shamrock ruler 20.00 40.00
❑ 8 Miriam Gonzalez chalkboard 25.00 50.00

2011 Bench Warmer Hot For Teacher School Props Pink Foil
STATED PRINT RUN 5 SER. #'d SETS
UNPRICED DUE TO SCARCITY

2011 Bench Warmer Hot For Teacher School Props Autographs Green Foil
STATED PRINT RUN 3 SER. #'d SETS
UNPRICED DUE TO SCARCITY

❑ 1 Cassandra Lynn red apple
❑ 2 Jessica Hall green apple
❑ 3 Maria Kanellis chalkboard
❑ 4 Kara Monaco notebook
❑ 5 Sara Underwood ruler
❑ 6 Jessica Hall
Stacie Hall hall pass
❑ 7 Ryan Shamrock ruler
❑ 8 Miriam Gonzalez chalkboard

2011 Bench Warmer Hot For Teacher School Props Autographs Blue Foil
STATED PRINT RUN 2 SER. #'d SETS
UNPRICED DUE TO SCARCITY

2011 Bench Warmer Hot For Teacher School Props Autographs Red Foil
STATED PRINT RUN 1 SER. #'d SET
UNPRICED DUE TO SCARCITY

2011 Bench Warmer Hot For Teacher Teacher's Pet Dual Swatches Gold Foil
STATED PRINT RUN 50 SER. #'d SETS

❑ 1 Kara Monaco 25.00 50.00
Sara Underwood
❑ 2 Jessica Hall 20.00 40.00
Shay Veasy
❑ 3 Jessica Hall 20.00 40.00
Stacie Hall
❑ 4 Cassandra Lynn 20.00 40.00
Holley Dorrough
❑ 5 Nikki Ziering 20.00 40.00
Sandra Taylor
❑ 6 Heather Rae Young 20.00 40.00
Heather Rene Smith
❑ 7 Ryan Shamrock 25.00 50.00
Torrie Wilson
❑ 8 Kyrah Tyler 20.00 40.00
Brittany Lauren
❑ 9 Katarina Van Derham 20.00 40.00
Carrie Stroup
❑ 10 Kara Monaco 20.00 40.00
Tiffany Selby

2011 Bench Warmer Hot For Teacher Teacher's Pet Dual Swatches Pink Foil
*PINK: .6X TO 1.25X BASIC CARDS
STATED PRINT RUN 25 SER. #'d SETS

2011 Bench Warmer Hot For Teacher Teacher's Pet Dual Swatches Autographs Green Foil
STATED PRINT RUN 10 SER. #'d SETS
UNPRICED DUE TO SCARCITY

❑ 1 Kara Monaco
Sara Underwood
❑ 2 Jessica Hall
Shay Veasy
❑ 3 Jessica Hall
Stacie Hall
❑ 4 Cassandra Lynn
Holley Dorrough
❑ 5 Nikki Ziering
Sandra Taylor
❑ 6 Heather Rae Young
Heather Rene Smith
❑ 7 Ryan Shamrock
Torrie Wilson
❑ 8 Kyrah Tyler
Brittany Lauren
❑ 9 Katarina Van Derham
Carrie Stroup
❑ 10 Kara Monaco
Tiffany Selby

2011 Bench Warmer Hot For Teacher Teacher's Pet Dual Swatches Autographs Blue Foil
STATED PRINT RUN 5 SER. #'d SETS
UNPRICED DUE TO SCARCITY

2011 Bench Warmer Hot For Teacher Teacher's Pet Dual Swatches Autographs Red Foil
STATED PRINT RUN 1 SER. #'d SET
UNPRICED DUE TO SCARCITY

2011 Bench Warmer Hot For Teacher Teacher's Pet Dual Swatches Autographs Printing Plates Black
STATED PRINT RUN 1 SER. #'d SET
UNPRICED DUE TO SCARCITY

2011 Bench Warmer Hot For Teacher Teacher's Pet Dual Swatches Autographs Printing Plates Cyan
STATED PRINT RUN 1 SER. #'d SET
UNPRICED DUE TO SCARCITY

2011 Bench Warmer Hot For Teacher Teacher's Pet Dual Swatches Autographs Printing Plates Magenta
STATED PRINT RUN 1 SER. #'d SET
UNPRICED DUE TO SCARCITY

2011 Bench Warmer Hot For Teacher Teacher's Pet Dual Swatches Autographs Printing Plates Yellow
STATED PRINT RUN 1 SER. #'d SET
UNPRICED DUE TO SCARCITY

2011 Bench Warmer Limited
COMPLETE SET (100) 6.00 15.00

❑ 1 Jennifer Walcott .40 1.00
❑ 2 Lisa Gleave .15 .40
❑ 3 April Scott .15 .40
❑ 4 Mary Riley .60 1.50
❑ 5 Carrie Stroup .15 .40
❑ 6 Jessica Burciaga .15 .40
❑ 7 Cassandra Lynn .15 .40
❑ 8 Sara Underwood .75 2.00
❑ 9 Sandra Taylor .40 1.00
❑ 10 Rachel Bernstein .15 .40
❑ 11 Bambi Lashell .15 .40
❑ 12 Jessica Hall .15 .40
❑ 13 Charity Hodges .15 .40
❑ 14 Alison Waite .15 .40
❑ 15 Athena Lundberg .15 .40
❑ 16 Brandy Grace .15 .40
❑ 17 Torrie Wilson .40 1.00
❑ 18 Shay Lyn Veasy .15 .40
❑ 19 Victoria Fuller .15 .40
❑ 20 Miriam Gonzalez .15 .40
❑ 21 Michelle Baena .15 .40
❑ 22 Nicole Bennett .15 .40
❑ 23 Leigh Ann Spence .15 .40
❑ 24 Jaime Bergman .15 .40
❑ 25 Brooke Morales .15 .40
❑ 26 Jaimarie Cherie .15 .40
❑ 27 Krisi Ballentine .15 .40
❑ 28 Alana Curry .15 .40
❑ 29 Buffy Tyler .15 .40
❑ 30 Traci Bingham .15 .40
❑ 31 Wrenna Monet .15 .40
❑ 32 Melissa Hunter .15 .40
❑ 33 Yvette Lopez .15 .40
❑ 34 Brande Roderick .15 .40
❑ 35 Enya Flack .15 .40
❑ 36 Nikki Ziering .15 .40
❑ 37 Sarah Coggin .15 .40
❑ 38 Tamara Witmer .15 .40
❑ 39 Tiffany Granath .15 .40
❑ 40 Lindsey Roeper .15 .40
❑ 41 Alika Ray .15 .40
❑ 42 Jennifer England .15 .40
❑ 43 Katie Lohmann .15 .40
❑ 44 Amber Hay .15 .40
❑ 45 Brittany Herrera .15 .40
❑ 46 Brandie Moses .15 .40
❑ 47 Holley Dorrough .15 .40
❑ 48 Alice Bradley .15 .40
❑ 49 Colleen Shannon .15 .40
❑ 50 Simona Fusco .15 .40
❑ 51 Tiffany Selby .15 .40
❑ 52 Paige Peterson .15 .40
❑ 53 Tiffany Toth .15 .40
❑ 54 Megan Hauserman .15 .40
❑ 55 Lena Yada .15 .40
❑ 56 Kitana Baker .15 .40
❑ 57 Jo Garcia .15 .40
❑ 58 Cecille Gahr .15 .40
❑ 59 Bobbi Billard .15 .40
❑ 60 Denyce Lawton .15 .40
❑ 61 Lisa Lakatos .15 .40
❑ 62 Melissa Taylor .15 .40
❑ 63 Nikki Zeno .15 .40
❑ 64 Renee Stone .15 .40
❑ 65 Spencer Scott .15 .40
❑ 66 Xi Xi Yang .15 .40
❑ 67 Bridget Marquardt .15 .40
❑ 68 Kayla Collins .15 .40
❑ 69 Jennifer Korbin .15 .40
❑ 70 Flo Jalin .15 .40
❑ 71 Claudia Jordan .15 .40
❑ 72 Jessica Rockwell .15 .40
❑ 73 Martina Andrews .15 .40
❑ 74 Traci Brooks .15 .40
❑ 75 Mia St. John .15 .40
❑ 76 Louise Glover .15 .40
❑ 77 Holly Madison .15 .40
❑ 78 Gail Kim .15 .40
❑ 79 Cat Miller .15 .40
❑ 80 Catherine Kluthe .15 .40
❑ 81 Brittany McGraw .15 .40
❑ 82 Aubrie Lemon .15 .40
❑ 83 Alix Agar .15 .40
❑ 84 Alejandra Gutierrez .15 .40
❑ 85 Katarina Van Derham .15 .40
❑ 86 Candace Kita .15 .40
❑ 87 Holly Huddleston .15 .40
❑ 88 Molly Shea .15 .40
❑ 89 Camille Anderson .15 .40
❑ 90 Masumi Max .15 .40
❑ 91 Amanda Paige .15 .40
❑ 92 Leilene Joy .15 .40
❑ 93 Jenae Alt .15 .40
❑ 94 Kendra Wilkinson .15 .40
❑ 95 Aiko Tanaka .15 .40
❑ 96 Candice Michelle .15 .40
❑ 97 Christy Hemme .40 1.00
❑ 98 Lisa Ligon .15 .40
❑ 99 Talor Marion .15 .40
❑ 100 Yvette Nelson .15 .40

2011 Bench Warmer Limited Gold Foil
COMPLETE SET (100) 8.00 20.00
STATED ODDS ONE PER PACK

2011 Bench Warmer Limited Purple Foil
COMPLETE SET (100)
STATED PRINT RUN 25 SER. #'d SETS

2011 Bench Warmer Limited Blue Foil
STATED PRINT RUN 5 SER. #'d SETS
UNPRICED DUE TO SCARCITY

2011 Bench Warmer Limited Red Foil
STATED PRINT RUN 1 SER. #'d SET
UNPRICED DUE TO SCARCITY

2011 Bench Warmer Limited All American Gold Foil
COMPLETE SET (8) 8.00 20.00
STATED ODDS 1:12

❑ 1 Alison Waite 2.00 5.00
❑ 2 Torrie Wilson 2.50 6.00
❑ 3 Shay Lyn Veasy 2.00 5.00
❑ 4 Jasmine Dustin 2.00 5.00
❑ 5 Rachel Bernstein 2.00 5.00
❑ 6 Heidi Freeman 2.00 5.00
❑ 7 Katarina Van Derham 2.00 5.00
❑ 8 Mary Riley 3.00 8.00

2011 Bench Warmer Limited All American Pink Foil
COMPLETE SET (8)
STATED PRINT RUN 25 SER. #'d SETS

2011 Bench Warmer Limited All American Green Foil
STATED PRINT RUN 10 SER. #'d SETS
UNPRICED DUE TO SCARCITY

2011 Bench Warmer Limited All American Red Foil
STATED PRINT RUN 1 SER. #'d SET
UNPRICED DUE TO SCARCITY

2011 Bench Warmer Limited Autographs Gold Foil
STATED ODDS 1:8

❑ 1 Bambi Lashell 4.00 10.00
❑ 2 Jessica Burciaga 4.00 10.00
❑ 3 Billie Jo Powers 4.00 10.00
❑ 4 Miriam Gonzalez 4.00 10.00
❑ 5 Shay Lyn Veasy 4.00 10.00
❑ 6 Patrice Hollis 4.00 10.00
❑ 7 Sara Underwood 10.00 25.00
❑ 8 Jessica Hall 4.00 10.00
❑ 9 Enya Flack 4.00 10.00
❑ 10 Sandra Taylor 8.00 20.00
❑ 11 Ramona Michelle 4.00 10.00
❑ 12 Tra'shell Thompson 4.00 10.00
❑ 13 Andrea Lowell 4.00 10.00
❑ 14 Syd Wilder 4.00 10.00
❑ 15 Cassandra Lynn 4.00 10.00
❑ 16 Janet Layug 4.00 10.00
❑ 17 Paige Peterson 4.00 10.00
❑ 18 Tiffany Toth 4.00 10.00
❑ 19 Maria Kanellis 6.00 15.00
❑ 20 Miki Black 4.00 10.00
❑ 21 Ryan Shamrock 4.00 10.00
❑ 22 Mary Riley 6.00 15.00
❑ 23 Holley Dorrough 4.00 10.00
❑ 24 Heather Rae Young 4.00 10.00
❑ 25 Stacie Hall 4.00 10.00
❑ 26 Deanna Brooks 4.00 10.00

2011 Bench Warmer Limited Autographs Pink Foil
STATED PRINT RUN 25 SER. #'d SETS

2011 Bench Warmer Limited Autographs Green Foil
STATED PRINT RUN 10 SER. #'d SETS
UNPRICED DUE TO SCARCITY

2011 Bench Warmer Limited Autographs Blue Foil
STATED PRINT RUN 5 SER. #'d SETS
UNPRICED DUE TO SCARCITY

2011 Bench Warmer Limited Autographs Red Foil
STATED PRINT RUN 1 SER. #'d SET
UNPRICED DUE TO SCARCITY

2011 Bench Warmer Limited Bikini Swatches Gold Foil
STATED ODDS 1:288
STATED PRINT RUN 25 SER. #'d SETS

❑ 1 Jessica Hall 30.00 60.00
❑ 2 Kara Monaco 30.00 60.00
❑ 3 Sandra Taylor 40.00 80.00
❑ 4 Heather Rae Young 30.00 60.00
❑ 5 Cassandra Lynn 30.00 60.00
❑ 6 Maria Kanellis 40.00 80.00

2011 Bench Warmer Limited Bikini Swatches Pink Foil
STATED PRINT RUN 15 SER. #'d SETS

2011 Bench Warmer Limited Bikini Swatches Autographs Green Foil
UNPRICED DUE TO SCARCITY

❑ 1 Jessica Hall
❑ 2 Kara Monaco
❑ 3 Sandra Taylor
❑ 4 Heather Rae Young
❑ 5 Cassandra Lynn
❑ 6 Maria Kanellis

2011 Bench Warmer Limited Bikini Swatches Autographs Blue Foil
STATED PRINT RUN 5 SER. #'d SETS
UNPRICED DUE TO SCARCITY

2011 Bench Warmer Limited Bikini Swatches Autographs Red Foil
STATED PRINT RUN 1 SER. #'d SET
UNPRICED DUE TO SCARCITY

2011 Bench Warmer Limited Boot Camp Gold Foil
COMPLETE SET (10) 6.00 15.00
STATED ODDS 1:8

❑ 1 Cassandra Lynn 1.25 3.00
❑ 2 Ryan Shamrock 1.25 3.00
❑ 3 Holley Ann Dorrough 1.25 3.00
❑ 4 Ramona Michelle 1.25 3.00
❑ 5 Heather Rene Smith 1.25 3.00
❑ 6 Jessica Kinni 1.25 3.00
❑ 7 Syd Wilder 1.25 3.00
❑ 8 Miriam Gonzalez 1.25 3.00
❑ 9 Deanna Brooks 1.25 3.00
❑ 10 Britany Lauren 1.25 3.00

2011 Bench Warmer Limited Boot Camp Pink Foil
COMPLETE SET (10)
STATED PRINT RUN 25 SER. #'d SETS

2011 Bench Warmer Limited Boot Camp Green Foil
STATED PRINT RUN 10 SER. #'d SETS
UNPRICED DUE TO SCARCITY

2011 Bench Warmer Limited Boot Camp Blue Foil
STATED PRINT RUN 5 SER. #'d SETS
UNPRICED DUE TO SCARCITY

2011 Bench Warmer Limited Boot Camp Red Foil
STATED PRINT RUN 1 SER. #'d SET
UNPRICED DUE TO SCARCITY

2011 Bench Warmer Limited Kiss Gold Foil
STATED ODDS 1:48

❑ 1 Andrea Lowell 8.00 20.00
❑ 2 Bambi Lashell 8.00 20.00
❑ 3 Cassandra Lynn 8.00 20.00
❑ 4 Holley Dorrough 8.00 20.00
❑ 5 Jessica Hall 8.00 20.00
❑ 6 Maria Kanellis 10.00 25.00
❑ 7 Ryan Shamrock 8.00 20.00
❑ 8 Sandra Taylor 10.00 25.00
❑ 9 Tiffany Toth 8.00 20.00

2011 Bench Warmer Limited Kiss Pink Foil
STATED PRINT RUN 25 SER. #'d SETS

2011 Bench Warmer Limited Kiss Autographs Green Foil
STATED PRINT RUN 10 SER. #'d SETS
UNPRICED DUE TO SCARCITY

❑ 1 Andrea Lowell
❑ 2 Bambi Lashell
❑ 3 Cassandra Lynn
❑ 4 Holley Dorrough
❑ 5 Jessica Hall
❑ 6 Maria Kanellis
❑ 7 Ryan Shamrock
❑ 8 Sandra Taylor
❑ 9 Tiffany Toth

2011 Bench Warmer Limited Kiss Autographs Blue Foil
STATED PRINT RUN 5 SER. #'d SETS
UNPRICED DUE TO SCARCITY

2011 Bench Warmer Limited Kiss Autographs Red Foil
STATED PRINT RUN 1 SER. #'d SET
UNPRICED DUE TO SCARCITY

2011 Bench Warmer Limited Lingerie Swatches Gold Foil
STATED ODDS 1:144
STATED PRINT RUN 25 SER. #'d SETS

❑ 1 Sara Underwood 50.00 100.00
❑ 2 Mary Riley 40.00 80.00
❑ 3 Kara Monaco 30.00 60.00
❑ 4 Andrea Lowell 30.00 60.00
❑ 5 Maria Kanellis 40.00 80.00
❑ 6 Heather Rae Young 30.00 60.00
❑ 7 Sandra Taylor 40.00 80.00
❑ 8 Miriam Gonzalez 40.00 80.00
❑ 9 Cassandra Lynn 30.00 60.00

2011 Bench Warmer Limited Lingerie Swatches Pink Foil
STATED PRINT RUN 15 SER. #'d SETS

2011 Bench Warmer Limited Lingerie Swatches Autographs Green Foil
STATED PRINT RUN 10 SER. #'d SETS
UNPRICED DUE TO SCARCITY

❑ 1 Sara Underwood
❑ 2 Mary Riley
❑ 3 Kara Monaco
❑ 4 Andrea Lowell
❑ 5 Maria Kanellis
❑ 6 Heather Rae Young
❑ 7 Sandra Taylor
❑ 8 Miriam Gonzalez
❑ 9 Cassandra Lynn

2011 Bench Warmer Limited Lingerie Swatches Autographs Blue Foil
STATED PRINT RUN 5 SER. #'d SETS
UNPRICED DUE TO SCARCITY

2011 Bench Warmer Limited Lingerie Swatches Autographs Red Foil
STATED PRINT RUN 1 SER. #'d SET
UNPRICED DUE TO SCARCITY

2011 Bench Warmer Limited School Girl Autographs Gold Foil
STATED ODDS 1:24

❑ 1 Caitlin O'Connor 4.00 10.00
❑ 2 Teresa Brown 4.00 10.00
❑ 3 Natalie Clarke 4.00 10.00
❑ 4 Tra'shell Thompson 4.00 10.00
❑ 5 Janet Layug 4.00 10.00
❑ 6 Alicia Johnson 4.00 10.00
❑ 7 Miriam Gonzalez 5.00 12.00
❑ 8 Dessie Mitcheson 4.00 10.00
❑ 9 Tara Ashley 4.00 10.00
❑ 10 Jessica Pribanic 4.00 10.00
❑ 11 Linsey Toole 4.00 10.00
❑ 12 Stevie Lynn Leow 4.00 10.00

2011 Bench Warmer Limited School Girl Autographs Pink Foil
STATED PRINT RUN 25 SER. #'d SETS

2011 Bench Warmer Limited School Girl Autographs Green Foil
STATED PRINT RUN 10 SER. #'d SETS
UNPRICED DUE TO SCARCITY

2011 Bench Warmer Limited School Girl Autographs Blue Foil
STATED PRINT RUN 5 SER. #'d SETS
UNPRICED DUE TO SCARCITY

2011 Bench Warmer Limited School Girl Autographs Red Foil
STATED PRINT RUN 1 SER. #'d SET
UNPRICED DUE TO SCARCITY

2011 Bench Warmer Vault Autographs Gold Foil

❑ 1 Sandra Taylor 6.00 15.00
❑ 2 Sara Underwood 10.00 20.00
❑ 3 Cassandra Lynn 5.00 12.00
❑ 4 Jessica Burciaga 6.00 15.00
❑ 5 Mary Riley 6.00 15.00
❑ 6 Nicole Bennett 5.00 12.00
❑ 7 Tamara Witmer 5.00 12.00
❑ 8 Buffy Tyler 5.00 12.00
❑ 9 Paige Peterson 5.00 12.00
❑ 10 Lisa Gleave 5.00 12.00
❑ 11 Brooke Morales 5.00 12.00
❑ 12 Candace Kita 5.00 12.00
❑ 13 Nikki Ziering 5.00 12.00
❑ 14 Miki Black 5.00 12.00
❑ 15 Tiffany Selby 5.00 12.00
❑ 16 Brande Roderick 5.00 12.00
❑ 17 Lisa Lakatos 5.00 12.00
❑ 18 Jennifer Walcott 5.00 12.00
❑ 19 Michelle Baena 5.00 12.00
❑ 20 Tiffany Toth 5.00 12.00

2011 Bench Warmer Vault Autographs Pink Foil
STATED PRINT RUN 25 SER. #'d SETS

2011 Bench Warmer Vault Autographs Green Foil

STATED PRINT RUN 10 SER. #'d SETS
UNPRICED DUE TO SCARCITY

2011 Bench Warmer Vault Autographs Blue Foil

STATED PRINT RUN 5 SER. #'d SETS
UNPRICED DUE TO SCARCITY

2011 Bench Warmer Vault Autographs Red Foil

STATED PRINT RUN 1 SER. #'d SET
UNPRICED DUE TO SCARCITY

2011 Bench Warmer Vault Daisy Duke Swatches Gold Foil

STATED PRINT RUN 25 SER. #'d SETS

❑ 1 April Scott 25.00 50.00
❑ 2 Sara Underwood 40.00 80.00
❑ 3 Cassandra Lynn 25.00 50.00
❑ 4 Jessica Hall 25.00 50.00
❑ 5 Maria Kanellis 25.00 50.00
❑ 6 Shay Lyn Vessy 25.00 50.00
❑ 7 Nikki Ziering 25.00 50.00
❑ 8 Kara Monaco 25.00 50.00
❑ 9 Deanna Brooks 25.00 50.00
❑ 10 Bambi Lashell 25.00 50.00
❑ 11 Heather Rae Young 25.00 50.00
❑ 12 Mary Riley 30.00 60.00

2011 Bench Warmer Vault Daisy Duke Swatches Pink Foil

STATED PRINT RUN 15 SER. #'d SETS

2011 Bench Warmer Vault Daisy Duke Swatches Autographs Green Foil

STATED PRINT RUN 10 SER. #'d SETS
UNPRICED DUE TO SCARCITY

❑ 1 April Scott
❑ 2 Sara Underwood
❑ 3 Cassandra Lynn
❑ 4 Jessica Hall
❑ 5 Maria Kanellis
❑ 6 Shay Lyn Veasy
❑ 7 Nikki Ziering
❑ 8 Kara Monaco
❑ 9 Deanna Brooks
❑ 10 Bambi Lashell
❑ 11 Heather Rae Young
❑ 12 Mary Riley

2011 Bench Warmer Vault Daisy Duke Swatches Autographs Blue Foil

STATED PRINT RUN 5 SER. #'d SETS
UNPRICED DUE TO SCARCITY

2011 Bench Warmer Vault Daisy Duke Swatches Autographs Red Foil

STATED PRINT RUN 1 SER. #'d SET
UNPRICED DUE TO SCARCITY

2011 Bench Warmer Vault Kiss Gold Foil

❑ 1 Jennifer Korbin 8.00 20.00
❑ 2 Candi Kita 6.00 15.00
❑ 3 Buffy Tyler 6.00 15.00
❑ 4 Michelle Baena 6.00 15.00
❑ 5 Miki Black 6.00 15.00
❑ 6 Sandra Taylor 10.00 25.00
❑ 7 Lisa Gleave 6.00 15.00
❑ 8 Holly Huddleston 6.00 15.00
❑ 9 Paige Peterson 6.00 15.00

2011 Bench Warmer Vault Kiss Pink Foil

STATED PRINT RUN 25 SER. #'d SETS

2011 Bench Warmer Vault Kiss Autographs Green Foil

STATED PRINT RUN 10 SER. #'d SETS
UNPRICED DUE TO SCARCITY

❑ 1 Jennifer Korbin
❑ 2 Candi Kita
❑ 3 Buffy Tyler
❑ 4 Michelle Baena
❑ 5 Miki Black
❑ 6 Sandra Taylor
❑ 7 Lisa Gleave
❑ 8 Holly Huddleston
❑ 9 Paige Peterson

2011 Bench Warmer Vault Kiss Autographs Blue Foil

STATED PRINT RUN 5 SER. #'d SETS
UNPRICED DUE TO SCARCITY

2011 Bench Warmer Vault Kiss Autographs Red Foil

STATED PRINT RUN 1 SER. #'d SET
UNPRICED DUE TO SCARCITY

2011 Bench Warmer Vault Racer Girl Autographs Gold Foil

❑ 1 Syd Wilder 5.00 12.00
❑ 2 Jasmine Dustin 5.00 12.00
❑ 3 Maria Kanellis 6.00 15.00
❑ 4 April Scott 5.00 12.00
❑ 5 Jessica Hall 6.00 15.00
❑ 6 Enya Flack 5.00 12.00
❑ 7 Holly Huddleston 5.00 12.00
❑ 8 Michelle Baena 5.00 12.00
❑ 9 Nikki Ziering 5.00 12.00
❑ 10 Krisi Ballentine 5.00 12.00
❑ 11 Ryan Shamrock 5.00 12.00
❑ 12 Bambi Lashell 5.00 12.00
❑ 13 Caitlin O'Connor 5.00 12.00
❑ 14 Lisa Ligon 5.00 12.00
❑ 15 Cecille Gahr 5.00 12.00
❑ 16 Miki Black 5.00 12.00
❑ 17 Julianna Prada 5.00 12.00
❑ 18 Candice Michelle 6.00 15.00
❑ 19 Mary Riley 6.00 15.00
❑ 20 Kara Monaco 5.00 12.00

2011 Bench Warmer Vault Racer Girl Autographs Pink Foil

*PINK: .5X TO 1.25X BASIC CARDS
STATED PRINT RUN 25 SER. #'d SETS

2011 Bench Warmer Vault Racer Girl Autographs Green Foil

STATED PRINT RUN 10 SER. #'d SETS
UNPRICED DUE TO SCARCITY

2011 Bench Warmer Vault Racer Girl Autographs Blue Foil

STATED PRINT RUN 5 SER. #'d SETS
UNPRICED DUE TO SCARCITY

2011 Bench Warmer Vault Racer Girl Autographs Red Foil

STATED PRINT RUN 1 SER. #'d SET
UNPRICED DUE TO SCARCITY

2011 Captain America Movie

COMPLETE SET (99) 6.00 15.00
UM14 STATED PRINT RUN 78

❑ 1 Movie scene .10 .30
❑ 2 Movie scene .10 .30
❑ 3 Movie scene .10 .30
❑ 4 Movie scene .10 .30
❑ 5 Movie scene .10 .30
❑ 6 Movie scene .10 .30
❑ 7 Movie scene .10 .30
❑ 8 Movie scene .10 .30
❑ 9 Movie scene .10 .30
❑ 10 Movie scene .10 .30
❑ 11 Movie scene .10 .30
❑ 12 Movie scene .10 .30
❑ 13 Movie scene .10 .30
❑ 14 Movie scene .10 .30
❑ 15 Movie scene .10 .30
❑ 16 Movie scene .10 .30
❑ 17 Movie scene .10 .30
❑ 18 Movie scene .10 .30
❑ 19 Movie scene .10 .30
❑ 20 Movie scene .10 .30
❑ 21 Movie scene .10 .30
❑ 22 Movie scene .10 .30
❑ 23 Movie scene .10 .30
❑ 24 Movie scene .10 .30
❑ 25 Movie scene .10 .30
❑ 26 Movie scene .10 .30
❑ 27 Movie scene .10 .30
❑ 28 Movie scene .10 .30
❑ 29 Movie scene .10 .30
❑ 30 Movie scene .10 .30
❑ 31 Movie scene .10 .30
❑ 32 Movie scene .10 .30
❑ 33 Movie scene .10 .30
❑ 34 Movie scene .10 .30
❑ 35 Movie scene .10 .30
❑ 36 Movie scene .10 .30
❑ 37 Movie scene .10 .30
❑ 38 Movie scene .10 .30
❑ 39 Movie scene .10 .30
❑ 40 Movie scene .10 .30
❑ 41 Movie scene .10 .30
❑ 42 Movie scene .10 .30
❑ 43 Movie scene .10 .30
❑ 44 Movie scene .10 .30
❑ 45 Movie scene .10 .30
❑ 46 Movie scene .10 .30
❑ 47 Movie scene .10 .30
❑ 48 Movie scene .10 .30
❑ 49 Movie scene .10 .30
❑ 50 Movie scene .10 .30
❑ 51 Movie scene .10 .30
❑ 52 Movie scene .10 .30
❑ 53 Movie scene .10 .30
❑ 54 Movie scene .10 .30
❑ 55 Movie scene .10 .30
❑ 56 Movie scene .10 .30
❑ 57 Movie scene .10 .30
❑ 58 Movie scene .10 .30
❑ 59 Movie scene .10 .30
❑ 60 Movie scene .10 .30
❑ 61 Movie scene .10 .30
❑ 62 Movie scene .10 .30
❑ 63 Movie scene .10 .30
❑ 64 Movie scene .10 .30
❑ 65 Movie scene .10 .30
❑ 66 Movie scene .10 .30
❑ 67 Movie scene .10 .30
❑ 68 Movie scene .10 .30
❑ 69 Movie scene .10 .30
❑ 70 Movie scene .10 .30
❑ 71 Movie scene .10 .30
❑ 72 Movie scene .10 .30
❑ 73 Movie scene .10 .30
❑ 74 Movie scene .10 .30
❑ 75 Movie scene .10 .30
❑ 76 Movie scene .10 .30
❑ 77 Movie scene .10 .30
❑ 78 Movie scene .10 .30
❑ 79 Movie scene .10 .30
❑ 80 Movie scene .10 .30
❑ 81 Movie scene .10 .30
❑ 82 Movie scene .10 .30
❑ 83 Movie scene .10 .30
❑ 84 Movie scene .10 .30
❑ 85 Movie scene .10 .30
❑ 86 Movie scene .10 .30
❑ 87 Steve Rogers .10 .30
❑ 88 Chester Phillips .10 .30
❑ 89 Johann Schmidt .10 .30
❑ 90 Peggy Carter .10 .30
❑ 91 James Bucky Barnes .10 .30
❑ 92 Abraham Erskine .10 .30
❑ 93 Howard Stark .10 .30
❑ 94 Arnim Zola .10 .30
❑ 95 Dum Dum Dugan .10 .30
❑ 96 Gabe Jones .10 .30
❑ 97 Jacques Dernier .10 .30
❑ 98 Montgomery Falsworth .10 .30
❑ 99 Jim Morita .10 .30
❑ UM14 The Avengers #4/78/ (Comic Book Panel)50.00 100.00

2011 Captain America Movie Printing Plates Black

STATED PRINT RUN 1 SER. #'d SET
UNPRICED DUE TO SCARCITY

2011 Captain America Movie Printing Plates Cyan

STATED PRINT RUN 1 SER. #'d SET
UNPRICED DUE TO SCARCITY

2011 Captain America Movie Printing Plates Magenta

STATED PRINT RUN 1 SER. #'d SET
UNPRICED DUE TO SCARCITY

2011 Captain America Movie Printing Plates Yellow

STATED PRINT RUN 1 SER. #'d SET
UNPRICED DUE TO SCARCITY

2011 Captain America Movie Autographs

STATED ODDS 1:288 HOBBY, 1:2,500 RETAIL

❑ BR Bruno Ricci 30.00 60.00
❑ JO Toby Jones 30.00 60.00
❑ KC Kenneth Choi 20.00 40.00
❑ NM Neal McDonough 30.00 60.00
❑ ST Stanley Tucci 60.00 120.00

2011 Captain America Movie Costumes

STATED ODDS 1:12 HOBBY, 1:36 RETAIL

❑ M1 Golden Age Capt. America 50.00 100.00
❑ M2 Bucky Barnes 75.00 150.00
❑ M3 Peggy Carter 12.00 30.00
❑ M4 Dr. Erskine 35.00 70.00
❑ M5 Howard Stark 12.00 30.00
❑ M6 Red Skull 20.00 40.00
❑ M7 Dr. Zola 12.00 30.00
❑ M8 Heinz Kruger 50.00 100.00
❑ M9 Dum Dum Dugan 20.00 40.00
❑ M10 Gabe Jones
❑ M11 Jacques Dernier 12.00 30.00
❑ M12 Steve Rogers 50.00 100.00
❑ M13 Captain America 75.00 150.00

2011 Captain America Movie Covers

COMPLETE SET (13) 4.00 10.00
STATED ODDS

❑ C1 Capt. America Issue 1 .60 1.50
❑ C2 Tales of Suspense Issue 59 .60 1.50
❑ C3 Capt. America Issue 100 .60 1.50
❑ C4 Capt. America Issue 110 .60 1.50
❑ C5 Capt. America Issue 111 .60 1.50
❑ C6 Capt. America Issue 193 .60 1.50
❑ C7 Capt. America Issue 321 .60 1.50
❑ C8 Capt. America Annual Issue 8 .60 1.50
❑ C9 Capt. America Issue 332 .60 1.50
❑ C10 Capt. America Issue 405 .60 1.50
❑ C11 Capt. America Issue 445 .60 1.50
❑ C12 Capt. America Issue 1 .60 1.50
❑ C13 Capt. America Issue 25 .60 1.50

2011 Captain America Movie Covers Printing Plates Black

STATED PRINT RUN 1 SER. #'d SET
UNPRICED DUE TO SCARCITY

2011 Captain America Movie Covers Printing Plates Cyan

STATED PRINT RUN 1 SER. #'d SET
UNPRICED DUE TO SCARCITY

2011 Captain America Movie Covers Printing Plates Magenta

STATED PRINT RUN 1 SER. #'d SET
UNPRICED DUE TO SCARCITY

2011 Captain America Movie Covers Printing Plates Yellow

STATED PRINT RUN 1 SER. #'d SET
UNPRICED DUE TO SCARCITY

2011 Captain America Movie Insignia Patches

COMPLETE SET (6) 40.00 80.00
STATED ODDS 1:16 HOBBY, 1:96 RETAIL

❑ I1 Johann Schmidt 8.00 20.00
❑ I2 Captain America 8.00 20.00
❑ I3 Red Skull 8.00 20.00
❑ I4 Captain America 8.00 20.00
❑ I5 Steve Rogers 8.00 20.00
❑ I6 Golden Age Capt. America 8.00 20.00

2011 Captain America Movie Posters

COMPLETE SET (12) 4.00 10.00
STATED ODDS

❑ P1 Victory .75 2.00
❑ P2 The First Avenger .75 2.00
❑ P3 Super Soldier .75 2.00
❑ P4 Super Soldier .75 2.00
❑ P5 Fighting Friend of Freedom .75 2.00
❑ P6 Sock Evil in the Jaw .75 2.00
❑ P7 Sock Evil in the Jaw .75 2.00
❑ P8 Sentinel of Liberty .75 2.00
❑ P9 Fighting Friend of Freedom .75 2.00
❑ P10 Captain A .75 2.00
❑ P11 Capt. America The First Avenger .75 2.00
❑ P12 Captain America .75 2.00

2011 Captain America Movie Posters Printing Plates Black

STATED PRINT RUN 1 SER. #'d SET
UNPRICED DUE TO SCARCITY

2011 Captain America Movie Posters Printing Plates Cyan

STATED PRINT RUN 1 SER. #'d SET
UNPRICED DUE TO SCARCITY

2011 Captain America Movie Posters Printing Plates Magenta

STATED PRINT RUN 1 SER. #'d SET
UNPRICED DUE TO SCARCITY

2011 Captain America Movie Posters Printing Plates Yellow

STATED PRINT RUN 1 SER. #'d SET
UNPRICED DUE TO SCARCITY

2011 Captain America Movie Sketches

STATED ODDS 1:48 HOBBY

❑ 1 Andy MacDonald
❑ 2 Aston Cover
❑ 3 Ben Herrera
❑ 4 Bill Pulkovski
❑ 5 Billy Martin
❑ 6 Brian Kong
❑ 7 Bruce Gerlach
❑ 8 Bryan Turner
❑ 9 Butch Mapa
❑ 10 Cal Slayton
❑ 11 Charles Hall
❑ 12 Daniel Gorman
❑ 13 Danielle Soloud
❑ 14 Eric Ninaltowski
❑ 15 Eugene Commodore
❑ 16 Frank Kadar
❑ 17 Frankie B Washington
❑ 18 George Davis
❑ 19 Gilbert Monsanto
❑ 20 Hanie Mohd
❑ 21 Irma Ahmed
❑ 22 Jake Minor
❑ 23 Jason Adams
❑ 24 Jason Keith Phillips
❑ 25 Jerry Gaylord
❑ 26 Joe Pekar
❑ 27 Joel Carroll
❑ 28 John Ace
❑ 29 John Haun
❑ 30 Johnboy Meyers
❑ 31 Jon Hughes
❑ 32 Joyce Chin
❑ 33 Ken Sleacy
❑ 34 Kevin Gentilcore
❑ 35 Kevin Graham
❑ 36 Lak Lim
❑ 37 Lawrence Reynolds
❑ 38 Lord Mesa
❑ 39 Mark DeCastro
❑ 40 Mason Schau
❑ 41 Matt Minor
❑ 42 Michael Duron
❑ 43 Mike Miller
❑ 44 Remi Dousset
❑ 45 Remy Mokhtar
❑ 46 Rich Molinelli
❑ 47 Ryan Kincaid
❑ 48 Tod Allen Smith
❑ 49 Travis Walton
❑ 50 Zane Donnellan
❑ 51 Cal Staggs
❑ 52 Chris Foreman
❑ 53 Dave Mack
❑ 54 Dave Ryan
❑ 55 Hamilton Cline
❑ 56 Jim Cheung
❑ 57 Katie Cook
❑ 58 Mark Henry
❑ 59 Mark McKenna
❑ 60 Matt Grigsby
❑ 61 Melike Acar
❑ 62 Sarah Wilkinson
❑ 63 Sebastian Mazuera

2011 Comic Book Legal Defense Fund Liberty

COMPLETE SET (72) 8.00 20.00

❑ 1 The Comic Book Legal Defense Fund .20 .50
❑ 2 The First Amendment .20 .50
❑ 3 Why We Fight .20 .50
❑ 4 Comics Under Fire .20 .50
❑ 5 Four-Color Worlds .20 .50
❑ 6 A Failed Attempt .20 .50
❑ 7 Fredric Wertham .20 .50
❑ 8 Comics on Trial .20 .50
❑ 9 Code of Silence .20 .50
❑ 10 Up from Underground .20 .50
❑ 11 Under Attack .20 .50
❑ 12 The Mainstream Fights the Code .20 .50
❑ 13 The Obscenity Test .20 .50
❑ 14 The End of an Era .20 .50
❑ 15 Fandom Carries the Torch .20 .50
❑ 16 Comics Grow Up .20 .50
❑ 17 A Novel Development .20 .50
❑ 18 86'd .20 .50
❑ 19 The First Arrest .20 .50
❑ 20 Kitchen Feels the Heat .20 .50
❑ 21 Artists to the Rescue .20 .50
❑ 22 Justice Is Served .20 .50
❑ 23 The CBLDF Is Born .20 .50
❑ 24 The Cases You Don't See .20 .50
❑ 25 CA v. Mavrides 1 .20 .50
❑ 26 CA v. Mavrides 2 .20 .50
❑ 27 CA v. Mavrides 3 .20 .50
❑ 28 FL v. Diana .20 .50
❑ 29 Underground's Underground .20 .50
❑ 30 The Switch and Bait .20 .50
❑ 31 Knee-Jerk Justice .20 .50
❑ 32 Cruel and Unusual .20 .50
❑ 33 Juris-Imprudence .20 .50
❑ 34 OK v. Planet Comics 1 .20 .50
❑ 35 OK v. Planet Comics 2 .20 .50
❑ 36 OK v. Planet Comics 3 .20 .50
❑ 37 Winter v. DC 1 .20 .50
❑ 38 Winter v. DC 2 .20 .50
❑ 39 Winter v. DC 3 .20 .50
❑ 40 From Hell's Heart .20 .50
❑ 41 The Siren Sounds .20 .50
❑ 42 The Right to Remain Silent .20 .50
❑ 43 TX v. Castillo 1 .20 .50
❑ 44 TX v. Castillo 2 .20 .50
❑ 45 TX v. Castillo 3 .20 .50
❑ 46 Kraft v. Helm 1 .20 .50
❑ 47 Kraft v. Helm 2 .20 .50
❑ 48 Kraft v. Helm 3 .20 .50
❑ 49 Strange Customs .20 .50
❑ 50 GA v. Lee 1 .20 .50
❑ 51 GA v. Lee 2 .20 .50
❑ 52 GA v. Lee 3 .20 .50
❑ 53 US v. Handley .20 .50
❑ 54 Schwarzenegger v. EMA .20 .50
❑ 55 Defenders of Liberty .20 .50
❑ 56 Lady Liberty and Blind Justice .20 .50
❑ 57 Lady Liberty and Blind Justice .20 .50
❑ 58 Martha Washington: The Battle Begins .20 .50
❑ 59 There's a Reason It Comes First .20 .50
❑ 60 I Read Banned Comics .20 .50
❑ 61 Hellboy Fights Censorship .20 .50
❑ 62 Cross the Border - Go Directly to Jail .20 .50
❑ 63 Always On Guard .20 .50
❑ 64 Volunteers Save the Day .20 .50
❑ 65 Conventions Connect .20 .50
❑ 66 Main Events .20 .50
❑ 67 Join Our Ranks .20 .50
❑ 68 The Bidder Way .20 .50
❑ 69 Stay Connected .20 .50
❑ 70 Creators Make a Difference .20 .50
❑ 71 Lending Hands .20 .50
❑ 72 Checklist .20 .50

2011 Comic Book Legal Defense Fund Liberty Autographs

STATED ODDS ONE PER BOX

❑ 1 Amanda Conner 10.00 20.00
❑ 2 Ben McCool 10.00 20.00
❑ 3 Bill Morrison 6.00 15.00
❑ 4 Brad Meltzer 6.00 15.00
❑ 5 Brian Azzarello 6.00 15.00
❑ 6 Charlie Adlard 6.00 15.00
❑ 7 Dan Panosian 6.00 15.00
❑ 8 Darick Robertson 10.00 20.00
❑ 9 Darwyn Cooke 10.00 20.00
❑ 10 Denny O'Neil 10.00 20.00
❑ 11 Eric Powell 6.00 15.00
❑ 12 Erik Larsen 10.00 20.00
❑ 13 Frank Quitely 6.00 15.00
❑ 14 Gail Simone 10.00 20.00
❑ 15 James Kochalka 6.00 15.00
❑ 16 Jeff Smith 10.00 20.00
❑ 17 Jim Valentino 6.00 15.00
❑ 18 Jimmy Palmiotti 6.00 15.00
❑ 19 John Layman 6.00 15.00
❑ 20 Judd Winick 10.00 20.00
❑ 21 Kurt Busiek 6.00 15.00
❑ 22 Larry Marder 6.00 15.00
❑ 23 Mark Waid 10.00 20.00
❑ 24 Marv Wolfman 6.00 15.00
❑ 25 Mike Richardson 6.00 15.00
❑ 26 Neil Gaiman 15.00 30.00
❑ 27 Paul Levitz 6.00 15.00
❑ 28 Peter David 6.00 15.00
❑ 29 Peter Kuper 6.00 15.00
❑ 30 Phil Hester 6.00 15.00
❑ 31 Rick Veitch 6.00 15.00
❑ 32 Rob Liefeld 10.00 20.00
❑ 33 Robert Kirkman 20.00 40.00
❑ 34 Ryan Ottley 6.00 15.00
❑ 35 Scott McCloud 6.00 15.00
❑ 36 Steve Bissette 6.00 15.00
❑ 37 Steve Lieber 6.00 15.00

2011 Comic Book Legal Defense Fund Liberty Promos

COMPLETE SET (3) 2.00 5.00

❑ P1 CBLDF T-Shirt/ (General Distribution) 1.50 4.00
❑ P2 Flag Raising/ (NSU Magazine) .60 1.50
❑ P3 Censored Girl/1000/ (Philly Non-Sport Show)1.50 4.00

2011 Comic Book Legal Defense Fund Liberty Puzzle Stickers

COMPLETE SET (9) 5.00 12.00
RANDOM INSERT IN PACKS

❑ 1 The Cases You Don't See .75 2.00
❑ 2 I Read Banned Comics .75 2.00
❑ 3 The Bidder Way .75 2.00
❑ 4 Fandom Carries the Torch .75 2.00
❑ 5 US v. Handley .75 2.00
❑ 6 Always On Guard .75 2.00
❑ 7 Code of Silence .75 2.00
❑ 8 GA v. Lee 2 .75 2.00
❑ 9 Hellboy Fights Censorship .75 2.00

2011 Comic Book Legal Defense Fund Liberty Sketches

STATED ODDS ONE PER BOX

❑ 1 Adam Talley
❑ 2 Alayna Lemmer
❑ 3 Alexis E. Fajardo (Kid Beowulf)
❑ 4 Ashleigh Popplewell
❑ 5 Aston Roy Cover
❑ 6 Austin Janowsky
❑ 7 Benjamin Mora
❑ 8 Bianca Thompson
❑ 9 Bill Morrison
❑ 10 Bobby Timony
❑ 11 Brian Germain
❑ 12 Brian Koln
❑ 13 Brian Lee
❑ 14 Browne
❑ 15 Chad Cicconi
❑ 16 Chip Skelton
❑ 17 Chris Cabbie Bradberry
❑ 18 Chris Foreman
❑ 19 Chris Giarrusso
❑ 20 Chris Metzen
❑ 21 Chris Thorne
❑ 22 Christian James Thomas
❑ 23 Cory Jones
❑ 24 Dan Smith
❑ 25 Daniel Abarca
❑ 26 Daniel P. Gorman
❑ 27 Danielle Soloud
❑ 28 Darrick Robertson
❑ 29 Dave Losso
❑ 30 David Castro
❑ 31 David Day
❑ 32 David Ryan
❑ 33 Diana Nock
❑ 34 Don Pedicini Jr
❑ 35 Don Simpson
❑ 36 Elliot Fernandez
❑ 37 Eric White
❑ 38 Erik Larsen
❑ 39 Evan Dorkin
❑ 40 Frank Quitely
❑ 41 Gary Kezele
❑ 42 Gene Espy
❑ 43 George Deep
❑ 44 George Webber
❑ 45 Henry Martinez
❑ 46 Ian Yoshio Roberts
❑ 47 Indigo Kelleigh
❑ 48 Ingrid Hardy
❑ 49 James Kolchalka
❑ 50 Jason Adams
❑ 51 Jason Durden
❑ 52 Jason Gonzalez
❑ 53 Jason Roussel
❑ 54 Jeff Smith
❑ 55 Jerry Fleming
❑ 56 Jesse Toves
❑ 57 Jin Han
❑ 58 Joe Keatinge
❑ 59 Joel Carroll
❑ 60 Joey Dangerous
❑ 61 John Haun
❑ 62 Josh Blaylock
❑ 63 Juan Antonio Fontanez Jr.
❑ 64 Kate Glasheen
❑ 65 Kokkinakis Axilleas
❑ 66 Kourtis Charalabos
❑ 67 Lak Lim
❑ 68 Lara Hudson
❑ 69 Larry Slickaway Schlekewy
❑ 70 Marat Mychels
❑ 71 Mark Tannacore
❑ 72 Mat Mastos
❑ 73 Matt Slay
❑ 74 Max Clotfelter
❑ 75 Mickey Clausen
❑ 76 Mike Richardson
❑ 77 Mike Rooth
❑ 78 Mike White
❑ 79 Neil Gaiman

MODERN ERA NON-SPORTS

❑ 80 Nikki Cook		
❑ 81 Ozzy Longoria		
❑ 82 Pablo Diaz		
❑ 83 Paul Fricke		
❑ 84 Paul Hoppe		
❑ 85 Peter Kuper		
❑ 86 Philip Tan		
❑ 87 Randy Emberlin		
❑ 88 Rantz Hosely		
❑ 89 Remy Eisu Mokhtar		
❑ 90 Rich Molinelli		
❑ 91 Richard Clark		
❑ 92 Rick Veitch		
❑ 93 Rob Liefeld		
❑ 94 Ross Leach		
❑ 95 Rusty Gilligan		
❑ 96 Ryan Ottley		
❑ 97 Scott McCloud		
❑ 98 Sean Dove		
❑ 99 Shannon Wheeler		
❑ 100 Simon Fraser		
❑ 101 Steve Ellis		
❑ 102 Tim Levandoski		
❑ 103 Tone Rodriguez		
❑ 104 Tyler Jeffers		
❑ 105 Victor Julio Rodriguez		
❑ 106 Vince Sunico		
❑ 107 Whilce Portacio		
❑ 108 Wilson Ramos		

2011 The Complete Brady Bunch

COMPLETE SET (59)	20.00	50.00
COMPLETE SET w/5 AUTO	100.00	175.00
PRINT RUN 500 SETS		
❑ 1 Here's the Story of a Lovely Lady	.60	1.50
❑ 2 The Honeymoon	.60	1.50
❑ 3 Dear Libby	.60	1.50
❑ 4 Eenie, Meenie, Mommy, Daddy	.60	1.50
❑ 5 Alice Doesn't Live Here Anymore	.60	1.50
❑ 6 Katchoo	.60	1.50
❑ 7 A Clubhouse is Not a Home	.60	1.50
❑ 8 Kitty Karry-All is Missing	.60	1.50
❑ 9 A-Camping We Will Go	.60	1.50
❑ 10 Tiger Tiger	.60	1.50
❑ 11 The Big Sprain	.60	1.50
❑ 12 Brace Yourself	.60	1.50
❑ 13 The Hero	.60	1.50
❑ 14 The Possible Dream	.60	1.50
❑ 15 To Move or Not to Move	.60	1.50
❑ 16 The Grass is Always Greener	.60	1.50
❑ 17 Lost Locket, Found Locket	.60	1.50
❑ 18 The Dropout	.60	1.50
❑ 19 What Goes Up	.60	1.50
❑ 20 Confessions, Confessions	.60	1.50
❑ 21 The Impractical Joker	.60	1.50
❑ 22 Where There's Smoke	.60	1.50
❑ 23 Will the Real Jan Brady Please Stand Up	.60	1.50
❑ 24 The Drummer Boy	.60	1.50
❑ 25 Coming-Out Party	.60	1.50
❑ 26 Our Son, the Man	.60	1.50
❑ 27 The Liberation of Marcia Brady	.60	1.50
❑ 28 My Sister, Benedict Arnold	.60	1.50
❑ 29 The Personality Kid	.60	1.50
❑ 30 Juliet is the Sun	.60	1.50
❑ 31 And Now, a Word From Our Sponsor	.60	1.50
❑ 32 The Private Ear	.60	1.50
❑ 33 Her Sister's Shadow	.60	1.50
❑ 34 Click	.60	1.50
❑ 35 Getting Davy Jones	.60	1.50
❑ 36 The Not-So-Rose Colored Glasses	.60	1.50
❑ 37 The Fender Benders	.60	1.50
❑ 38 Hawaii Bound	.60	1.50
❑ 39 Pass the Tuba	.60	1.50
❑ 40 The Tiki Caves	.60	1.50
❑ 41 Today, I am a Freshman	.60	1.50
❑ 42 Cyrano de Brady	.60	1.50
❑ 43 Fright Night	.60	1.50
❑ 44 The Show Must Go On	.60	1.50
❑ 45 Jan, the Only Child	.60	1.50
❑ 46 The Subject Was Noses	.60	1.50
❑ 47 How to Succeed in Business	.60	1.50
❑ 48 The Great Earring Caper	.60	1.50
❑ 49 You're Never Too Old	.60	1.50
❑ 50 You Can't Win 'em All	.60	1.50
❑ 51 Room at the Top	.60	1.50
❑ 52 Adios, Johnny Bravo	.60	1.50
❑ 53 Mail Order Hero	.60	1.50
❑ 54 Snow White and the Seven Bradys	.60	1.50
❑ 55 Miss Popularity	.60	1.50
❑ 56 Kelly's Kids	.60	1.50
❑ 57 The Driver's Seat	.60	1.50
❑ 58 Out of This World	.60	1.50
❑ 59 Welcome Aboard	.60	1.50

2011 The Complete Brady Bunch Autographs

COMPLETE SET (6)	125.00	200.00
COMP.SET w/o DAVIS AUTO (5)	75.00	150.00
5 AUTOS PER FACTORY SET		
DAVIS AUTO ISSUED AS 2-SET INCENTIVE		
❑ 1 Barry Williams	20.00	40.00
❑ 2 Christopher Knight	20.00	40.00
❑ 3 Eve Plumb	20.00	40.00
❑ 4 Mike Lookinland	20.00	40.00
❑ 5 Susan Olsen	20.00	40.00
❑ 6 Ann B. Davis (issued as 2-set incentive)	35.00	70.00

2011 The Complete Brady Bunch Promos

COMPLETE SET (2)	5.00	12.00
❑ P1 Marcia Brady/ (General Distribution)	1.50	4.00
❑ P2 Greg Brady/ (Non-Sport Update)	4.00	10.00

2011 The Complete Star Trek The Next Generation

COMPLETE SET (180)	12.00	30.00
COMP. SER. 1 SET (90)	6.00	15.00
COMP. SER. 2 SET (90)	6.00	15.00
❑ 1 Encounter at Farpoint	.15	.40
❑ 2 The Naked Now	.15	.40
❑ 3 Code of Honor	.15	.40
❑ 4 The Last Outpost	.15	.40
❑ 5 Where No One Has Gone Before	.15	.40
❑ 6 Lonely Among Us	.15	.40
❑ 7 Justice	.15	.40
❑ 8 The Battle	.15	.40
❑ 9 Hide and Q	.15	.40
❑ 10 Haven	.15	.40
❑ 11 The Big Goodbye	.15	.40
❑ 12 Datalore	.15	.40
❑ 13 Angel One	.15	.40
❑ 14 11001001	.15	.40
❑ 15 Too Short a Season	.15	.40
❑ 16 When the Bough Breaks	.15	.40
❑ 17 Home Soil	.15	.40
❑ 18 Coming of Age	.15	.40
❑ 19 Heart of Glory	.15	.40
❑ 20 The Arsenal of Freedom	.15	.40
❑ 21 Symbiosis	.15	.40
❑ 22 Skin of Evil	.15	.40
❑ 23 We'll Always Have Paris	.15	.40
❑ 24 Conspiracy	.15	.40
❑ 25 The Neutral Zone	.15	.40
❑ 26 The Child	.15	.40
❑ 27 Where Silence Has Lease	.15	.40
❑ 28 Elementary, Dear Data	.15	.40
❑ 29 The Outrageous Okona	.15	.40
❑ 30 Loud as a Whisper	.15	.40
❑ 31 The Schizoid Man	.15	.40
❑ 32 Unnatural Selection	.15	.40
❑ 33 A Matter of Honor	.15	.40
❑ 34 The Measure of a Man	.15	.40
❑ 35 The Dauphin	.15	.40
❑ 36 Contagion	.15	.40
❑ 37 The Royale	.15	.40
❑ 38 Time Squared	.15	.40
❑ 39 The Icarus Factor	.15	.40
❑ 40 Pen Pals	.15	.40
❑ 41 Q Who	.15	.40
❑ 42 Samaritan Snare	.15	.40
❑ 43 Up the Long Ladder	.15	.40
❑ 44 Manhunt	.15	.40
❑ 45 The Emissary	.15	.40
❑ 46 Peak Performance	.15	.40
❑ 47 Shades of Gray	.15	.40
❑ 48 Evolution	.15	.40
❑ 49 The Ensigns of Command	.15	.40
❑ 50 The Survivors	.15	.40
❑ 51 Who Watches the Watchers	.15	.40
❑ 52 The Bonding	.15	.40
❑ 53 Booby Trap	.15	.40
❑ 54 The Enemy	.15	.40
❑ 55 The Price	.15	.40
❑ 56 The Vengeance Factor	.15	.40
❑ 57 The Defector	.15	.40
❑ 58 The Hunted	.15	.40
❑ 59 The High Ground	.15	.40
❑ 60 Deja Q	.15	.40
❑ 61 A Matter of Perspective	.15	.40
❑ 62 Yesterday's Enterprise	.15	.40
❑ 63 The Offspring	.15	.40
❑ 64 Sins of the Father	.15	.40
❑ 65 Allegiance	.15	.40
❑ 66 Captain's Holiday	.15	.40
❑ 67 Tin Man	.15	.40
❑ 68 Hollow Pursuits	.15	.40
❑ 69 The Most Toys	.15	.40
❑ 70 Sarek	.15	.40
❑ 71 Menage a Troi	.15	.40
❑ 72 Transfigurations	.15	.40
❑ 73 The Best of Both Worlds, Part 1	.15	.40
❑ 74 The Best of Both Worlds, Part 2	.15	.40
❑ 75 Family	.15	.40
❑ 76 Brothers	.15	.40
❑ 77 Suddenly Human	.15	.40
❑ 78 Remember Me	.15	.40
❑ 79 Legacy	.15	.40
❑ 80 Reunion	.15	.40
❑ 81 Future Imperfect	.15	.40
❑ 82 Final Mission	.15	.40
❑ 83 The Loss	.15	.40
❑ 84 Data's Day	.15	.40
❑ 85 The Wounded	.15	.40
❑ 86 Devil's Due	.15	.40
❑ 87 Clues	.15	.40
❑ 88 First Contact	.15	.40
❑ 89 Galaxy's Child	.15	.40
❑ 90 Night Terrors	.15	.40
❑ 91 Identity Crisis	.15	.40
❑ 92 The Nth Degree	.15	.40
❑ 93 Qpid	.15	.40
❑ 94 The Drumhead	.15	.40
❑ 95 Half a Life	.15	.40
❑ 96 The Host	.15	.40
❑ 97 The Mind's Eye	.15	.40
❑ 98 In Theory	.15	.40
❑ 99 Redemption, Part 1	.15	.40
❑ 100 Redemption, Part 2	.15	.40
❑ 101 Darmok	.15	.40
❑ 102 Ensign Ro	.15	.40
❑ 103 Silicon Avatar	.15	.40
❑ 104 Disaster	.15	.40
❑ 105 The Game	.15	.40
❑ 106 Unification, Part 1	.15	.40
❑ 107 Unification, Part 2	.15	.40
❑ 108 A Matter of Time	.15	.40
❑ 109 New Ground	.15	.40
❑ 110 Hero Worship	.15	.40
❑ 111 Violations	.15	.40
❑ 112 The Masterpiece Society	.15	.40
❑ 113 Conundrum	.15	.40
❑ 114 Power Play	.15	.40
❑ 115 Ethics	.15	.40
❑ 116 The Outcast	.15	.40
❑ 117 Cause and Effect	.15	.40
❑ 118 The First Duty	.15	.40
❑ 119 Cost of Living	.15	.40
❑ 120 The Perfect Mate	.15	.40
❑ 121 Imaginary Friend	.15	.40
❑ 122 I, Borg	.15	.40
❑ 123 The Next Phase	.15	.40
❑ 124 The Inner Light	.15	.40
❑ 125 Time's Arrow, Part 1	.15	.40
❑ 126 Time's Arrow, Part 2	.15	.40
❑ 127 Realm of Fear	.15	.40
❑ 128 Man of the People	.15	.40
❑ 129 Relics	.15	.40
❑ 130 Schisms	.15	.40
❑ 131 True Q	.15	.40
❑ 132 Rascals	.15	.40
❑ 133 A Fistful of Datas	.15	.40
❑ 134 The Quality of Life	.15	.40
❑ 135 Chain of Command, Part 1	.15	.40
❑ 136 Chain of Command, Part 2	.15	.40
❑ 137 Ship in a Bottle	.15	.40
❑ 138 Aquiel	.15	.40
❑ 139 Face of the Enemy	.15	.40
❑ 140 Tapestry	.15	.40
❑ 141 Birthright, Part 1	.15	.40
❑ 142 Birthright, Part 2	.15	.40
❑ 143 Starship Mine	.15	.40
❑ 144 Lessons	.15	.40
❑ 145 The Chase	.15	.40
❑ 146 Frame of Mind	.15	.40
❑ 147 Suspicions	.15	.40
❑ 148 Rightful Heir	.15	.40
❑ 149 Second Chances	.15	.40
❑ 150 Timescape	.15	.40
❑ 151 Descent, Part 1	.15	.40
❑ 152 Descent, Part 2	.15	.40
❑ 153 Liaisons	.15	.40
❑ 154 Interface	.15	.40
❑ 155 Gambit, Part 1	.15	.40
❑ 156 Gambit, Part 2	.15	.40
❑ 157 Phantasms	.15	.40
❑ 158 Dark Page	.15	.40
❑ 159 Attached	.15	.40
❑ 160 Force of Nature	.15	.40
❑ 161 Inheritance	.15	.40
❑ 162 Parallels	.15	.40
❑ 163 The Pegasus	.15	.40
❑ 164 Homeward	.15	.40
❑ 165 Sub Rosa	.15	.40
❑ 166 Lower Decks	.15	.40
❑ 167 Thine Own Self	.15	.40
❑ 168 Masks	.15	.40
❑ 169 Eye of the Beholder	.15	.40
❑ 170 Genesis	.15	.40
❑ 171 Journey's End	.15	.40
❑ 172 Firstborn	.15	.40
❑ 173 Bloodlines	.15	.40
❑ 174 Emergence	.15	.40
❑ 175 Preemptive Strike	.15	.40
❑ 176 All Good Things	.15	.40
❑ 177 Series 1 Base checklist	.15	.40
❑ 178 Series 2 Bonus checklist	.15	.40
❑ 179 Series 2 Base checklist	.15	.40
❑ 180 Series 2 Bonus checklist	.15	.40
❑ GR Gene Roddenberry Business Card/350/ (issued as 3-case incentive)	75.00	125.00

2011 The Complete Star Trek The Next Generation Silver Foil

COMPLETE SET (180)	60.00	120.00
COMP. SER. 1 SET (90)	30.00	60.00
COMP. SER. 2 SET (90)	30.00	60.00
STATED ODDS 1:3		

2011 The Complete Star Trek The Next Generation Aliens

COMPLETE SET (13)	8.00	20.00
STATED ODDS 1:8		
❑ A1 Acamarian Aldean/Algolian	1.25	3.00
❑ A2 Antican Armus/Bandi	1.25	3.00
❑ A3 Betazoid Borg/Bre-Ellian	1.25	3.00
❑ A4 Cairn Caldonian/Chalnoth	1.25	3.00
❑ A5 Delbian Devidian/Dopterian	1.25	3.00
❑ A6 El-Aurian Ferengi/Gomtuu	1.25	3.00
❑ A7 Kaelonian Kesprytt/Klingon	1.25	3.00
❑ A8 Ligonian Lumerian/Lyan	1.25	3.00
❑ A9 Mintakan Mizarian/Nagilum	1.25	3.00
❑ A10 Pelian Q/Ramatisian	1.25	3.00
❑ A11 Sheliak Solari/Takaran	1.25	3.00
❑ A12 Tarchannen Tarellian/Traveler	1.25	3.00
❑ A13 Vorgon Vulcan/Yridian	1.25	3.00

2011 The Complete Star Trek The Next Generation Autographs

STATED ODDS 1:6
L (LIMITED): 300-500 COPIES
VL (VERY LIMITED): 200-300 COPIES
EL (EXTREMELY LIMITED): 200 OR FEWER COPIES

❑ 1 Alan Shearman	5.00	12.00
❑ 2 Amanda McBroom	5.00	12.00
❑ 3 Armin Shimerman L	8.00	20.00
❑ 4 Biff Yeager/ (issued as case topper)	10.00	25.00
❑ 5 Brenda Bakke	5.00	12.00
❑ 6 Brent Spiner as Lore VL	75.00	125.00
❑ 7 Brian Bonsall	6.00	15.00
❑ 8 Carolyn McCormick	6.00	15.00
❑ 9 Clayton Rohner	5.00	12.00
❑ 10 Clyde Kusatsu	5.00	12.00
❑ 11 Corbin Bernsen L	6.00	15.00
❑ 12 Dana Sparks	5.00	12.00
❑ 13 Daniel Benzali VL	30.00	60.00
❑ 14 Danitza Kingsley	5.00	12.00
❑ 15 Darryl Henriques	5.00	12.00
❑ 16 Dwight Schultz VL	25.00	50.00
❑ 17 Elizabeth Dennehy VL	20.00	40.00
❑ 18 Erik Menyuk L	6.00	15.00
❑ 19 Gates McFadden QUOTABLE ST:NG VL	40.00	80.00
❑ 20 Jeff McCarthy	5.00	12.00
❑ 21 Jessie Lawrence Ferguson	5.00	12.00
❑ 22 Joe Piscopo L	15.00	30.00
❑ 23 John Putch	5.00	12.00
❑ 24 John Tesh L	12.00	25.00
❑ 25 Judson Scott	5.00	12.00
❑ 26 Julia Nickson	5.00	12.00
❑ 27 Lance LeGault	5.00	12.00
❑ 28 LeVar Burton QUOTABLE ST:NG VL	60.00	120.00
❑ 29 Marco Rodriguez	5.00	12.00
❑ 30 Mark La Mura	5.00	12.00
❑ 31 Mark Margolis	5.00	12.00
❑ 32 Matt McCoy L	10.00	25.00
❑ 33 Michael Berryman	5.00	12.00
❑ 34 Michelle Phillips L	12.00	30.00
❑ 35 Nehemiah Persoff L	6.00	15.00
❑ 36 Nikki Cox	6.00	15.00
❑ 37 Patrick Stewart/ (issued as 6-case incentive)	250.00	350.00
❑ 38 Peter Mark Richman	5.00	12.00
❑ 39 R.J. Williams L	6.00	15.00
❑ 40 Ray Wise L	6.00	15.00
❑ 41 Rhonda Aldrich L	6.00	15.00
❑ 42 Richard Lineback	5.00	12.00
❑ 43 Sam Hennings	5.00	12.00
❑ 44 Saul Rubinek L	6.00	15.00
❑ 45 Scott Thomson	5.00	12.00
❑ 46 Suzie Plakson L	6.00	15.00
❑ 47 Vaughn Armstrong	5.00	12.00
❑ 48 W. Morgan Sheppard	5.00	12.00
❑ 49 Whitney Rydbeck	5.00	12.00
❑ 50 William Denis	5.00	12.00
❑ 51 William O. Campbell	5.00	12.00
❑ 52 Gene Rodenberry/30 CUT		
❑ 53 Albie Selznik L	6.00	15.00
❑ 54 Ashley Judd VL	75.00	150.00
❑ 55 Barbara Alyn Woods	5.00	12.00
❑ 56 Barbara Tarbuck	5.00	12.00
❑ 57 Barbara Williams	5.00	12.00
❑ 58 Ben Lemon L	6.00	15.00
❑ 59 Brent Spiner/ (issued as 3-case incentive)	60.00	120.00
❑ 60 Bruce French	5.00	12.00
❑ 61 Castulo Guerra	5.00	12.00
❑ 62 Chad Allen	6.00	15.00
❑ 63 Colm Meaney VL	40.00	80.00
❑ 64 David Ogden Stiers EL	75.00	150.00
❑ 65 Denise Crosby EL	40.00	80.00
❑ 66 Dey Young	5.00	12.00
❑ 67 Earl Boen/ (issued as case topper)	10.00	25.00
❑ 68 Ellen Geer L	6.00	15.00
❑ 69 Eve Brenner L	6.00	15.00
❑ 70 Fran Bennett L	6.00	15.00
❑ 71 Frank Collison L	6.00	15.00
❑ 72 Gabriel Damon	5.00	12.00
❑ 73 Gene Dynarski	5.00	12.00
❑ 74 Guy Vardaman	5.00	12.00
❑ 75 Hallie Todd	5.00	12.00
❑ 76 Jane Daly	5.00	12.00
❑ 77 JD Cullum L	6.00	15.00
❑ 78 Jeffrey Hayenga L	6.00	15.00
❑ 79 Jim Norton	5.00	12.00
❑ 80 John Delancie EL	60.00	120.00
❑ 81 John Fleck	5.00	12.00
❑ 82 Jonathan Del Arco L	8.00	20.00
❑ 83 Jonathan Frakes EL	60.00	120.00
❑ 84 Joshua Harris	5.00	12.00
❑ 85 Kelsey Grammer VL	50.00	100.00
❑ 86 Leonard Nimoy/ (issued as 6-case incentive)	200.00	300.00
❑ 87 Malachi Throne	5.00	12.00
❑ 88 Marina Sirtis EL	50.00	100.00
❑ 89 Mark L. Taylor	5.00	12.00
❑ 90 Matt Frewer EL	35.00	70.00
❑ 91 Megan Cole L	6.00	15.00
❑ 92 Michael Snyder L	6.00	15.00
❑ 93 Natalija Nogulich L	6.00	15.00
❑ 94 Nicholas Kepros L	6.00	15.00
❑ 95 Nicole Orth-Pallavicini L	8.00	20.00
❑ 96 Patti Yasutake L	6.00	15.00
❑ 97 Richard Fancy	5.00	12.00
❑ 98 Robert O'Reilly VL	25.00	50.00
❑ 99 Ron Canada L	6.00	15.00
❑ 100 Stephen Lee L	6.00	15.00
❑ 101 Steven Anderson	5.00	12.00
❑ 102 Susan Diol VL	25.00	50.00
❑ 103 Tony Todd EL	40.00	80.00
❑ 104 Vyto Ruginis L	6.00	15.00
❑ 105 William Lithgow L	6.00	15.00
❑ 106 James Doohan CUT/50	500.00	1000.00

2011 The Complete Star Trek The Next Generation Best of the Holodeck

COMPLETE SET (9)	6.00	15.00
STATED ODDS 1:8		
❑ H1 The Big Goodbye	1.25	3.00
❑ H2 11001001	1.25	3.00
❑ H3 Elementary, Dear Data	1.25	3.00
❑ H4 A Fistful of Datas	1.25	3.00
❑ H5 Manhunt	1.25	3.00
❑ H6 Hollow Pursuits	1.25	3.00
❑ H7 Cost of Living	1.25	3.00
❑ H8 Ship in a Bottle	1.25	3.00
❑ H9 Emergence	1.25	3.00
❑ H10 Relics SP (issued as Rittenhouse Reward)	20.00	50.00

2011 The Complete Star Trek The Next Generation Communicator Pins

COMPLETE SET (10)	200.00	400.00
STATED ODDS 1:200		
STATED PRINT RUN 300 SER. #'d SETS		
❑ CP1 Captain Jean-Luc Picard	30.00	60.00
❑ CP2 Lt. Commander Data	30.00	60.00
❑ CP3 Commander William Riker	30.00	60.00
❑ CP4 Counselor Deanna Troi	30.00	60.00
❑ CP5 Dr. Beverly Crusher	30.00	60.00
❑ CP6 Lt. Geordi LaForge	30.00	60.00
❑ CP7 Lt. Worf	30.00	60.00
❑ CP8 Lt. Tasha Yar	30.00	60.00
❑ CP9 Ensign Wesley Crusher	30.00	60.00
❑ CP10 Dr. Kate Pulaski	30.00	60.00

2011 The Complete Star Trek The Next Generation Promos

COMPLETE SET	10.00	20.00
❑ P1 Picard Worf/ (General Distribution)	.75	2.00
❑ P2 Locutus Worf/Yar/ (NSU Magaine)	2.00	5.00
❑ P3 Data Picard/Riker/ (Collectors Album)	10.00	20.00
❑ P4 Picard Riker/ (Spring 2011 Philly Non-Sport Show)	2.00	5.00

2011 The Complete Star Trek The Next Generation Tribute

COMPLETE SET (36)	20.00	40.00
STATED ODDS 1:6		
❑ T1 Majel Barrett	1.00	2.50
❑ T2 Andreas Katsulas	1.00	2.50
❑ T3 DeForest Kelley	1.00	2.50
❑ T4 Frank Corsentino	1.00	2.50
❑ T5 Lawrence Tierney	1.00	2.50
❑ T6 William Boyett	1.00	2.50
❑ T7 Walter Gotell	1.00	2.50
❑ T8 Vincent Shiavelli	1.00	2.50
❑ T9 Merritt Butrick	1.00	2.50
❑ T10 Noble Willingham	1.00	2.50
❑ T11 Christopher Collins	1.00	2.50
❑ T12 Roy Brocksmith	1.00	2.50
❑ T13 John Anderson	1.00	2.50
Anne Haney		
❑ T14 Kevin Peter Hall	1.00	2.50
❑ T15 Nancy Parsons	1.00	2.50
❑ T16 Mark Lenard	1.00	2.50
❑ T17 Georgia Brown	1.00	2.50
❑ T18 Bill Erwin	1.00	2.50
❑ T19 Kay E. Kuter as Cytherian in The Nth Degree	1.00	2.50
❑ T20 Jean Simmons as Admiral Norah Satie in The Drumhead	1.00	2.50
❑ T21 Larry Dobkin as Ambassador Kell in The Mind's Eye	1.00	2.50
❑ T22 Ben Slack as K'Tal in Redemption	1.00	2.50
❑ T23 Paul Winfield as Captain Dathon in Darmok	1.00	2.50
❑ T24 Scott Marlowe as Keeve Falor in Ensign Ro	1.00	2.50
❑ T25 Graham Jarvis as Klim Dokachin in Unification	1.00	2.50
❑ T26 Harriet Leider as Amarie in Unification	1.00	2.50
❑ T27 Jack Murdock as Beggar in Time's Arrow	1.00	2.50
❑ T28 Ray Walston as Boothby in The First Duty	1.00	2.50
❑ T29 Tony Jay as Third Minister Campio in Cost of Living	1.00	2.50
❑ T30 Susan French as Sev Maylor in Man of the People	1.00	2.50
❑ T31 James Doohan as Captain Montgomery Scott in Relics	1.00	2.50
❑ T32 Joy Garrett as Annie Meyers in A Fistful of Datas	1.00	2.50
❑ T33 Madge Sinclair as Captain Silva La Forge in Interface	1.00	2.50
❑ T34 Bernard Kates as Dr. Sigmund Freud in Phantasms	1.00	2.50
❑ T35 Shay Duffin as Ned Quint in Sub Rosa	1.00	2.50
❑ T36 John Franklyn-Robbins as Macias in Preemptive Strike	1.00	2.50

2011 The Complete Star Trek The Next Generation USS Enterprise

COMPLETE SET (18)	10.00	25.00
STATED ODDS 1:12		
❑ E1 U.S.S. Enterprise NC-1701-D	1.50	4.00
❑ E2 U.S.S. Enterprise NC-1701-D	1.50	4.00
❑ E3 U.S.S. Enterprise NC-1701-D	1.50	4.00
❑ E4 U.S.S. Enterprise NC-1701-D	1.50	4.00
❑ E5 U.S.S. Enterprise NC-1701-D	1.50	4.00
❑ E6 U.S.S. Enterprise NC-1701-D	1.50	4.00
❑ E7 U.S.S. Enterprise NC-1701-D	1.50	4.00
❑ E8 U.S.S. Enterprise NC-1701-D	1.50	4.00
❑ E9 U.S.S. Enterprise NC-1701-D	1.50	4.00
❑ E10 U.S.S. Enterprise NC-1701-D	1.50	4.00
❑ E11 U.S.S. Enterprise NC-1701-D	1.50	4.00
❑ E12 U.S.S. Enterprise NC-1701-D	1.50	4.00
❑ E13 U.S.S. Enterprise NC-1701-D	1.50	4.00
❑ E14 U.S.S. Enterprise NC-1701-D	1.50	4.00
❑ E15 U.S.S. Enterprise NC-1701-D	1.50	4.00
❑ E16 U.S.S. Enterprise NC-1701-D	1.50	4.00
❑ E17 U.S.S. Enterprise NC-1701-D	1.50	4.00
❑ E18 U.S.S. Enterprise NC-1701-D	1.50	4.00

2011 Dangerous Divas

COMPLETE SET (72)	5.00	12.00
❑ 1 Black Panther	.15	.40
❑ 2 Black Panther	.15	.40
❑ 3 Black Panther	.15	.40
❑ 4 Psylocke	.15	.40
❑ 5 Psylocke	.15	.40
❑ 6 Psylocke	.15	.40
❑ 7 Ms. Marvel	.15	.40
❑ 8 Ms. Marvel	.15	.40
❑ 9 Ms. Marvel	.15	.40
❑ 10 Lady Bullseye	.15	.40
❑ 11 Lady Bullseye	.15	.40
❑ 12 Lady Bullseye	.15	.40
❑ 13 Black Widow	.15	.40
❑ 14 Black Widow	.15	.40
❑ 15 Black Widow	.15	.40
❑ 16 She-Hulk	.15	.40
❑ 17 She-Hulk	.15	.40
❑ 18 She-Hulk	.15	.40
❑ 19 Red She-Hulk	.15	.40
❑ 20 Red She-Hulk	.15	.40
❑ 21 Red She-Hulk	.15	.40
❑ 22 Spider-Woman	.15	.40
❑ 23 Spider-Woman	.15	.40
❑ 24 Spider-Woman	.15	.40
❑ 25 Rogue	.15	.40
❑ 26 Rogue	.15	.40
❑ 27 Rogue	.15	.40
❑ 28 Songbird	.15	.40
❑ 29 Songbird	.15	.40
❑ 30 Songbird	.15	.40
❑ 31 Elektra	.15	.40
❑ 32 Elektra	.15	.40
❑ 33 Elektra	.15	.40
❑ 34 Storm	.15	.40
❑ 35 Storm	.15	.40
❑ 36 Storm	.15	.40
❑ 37 Black Cat	.15	.40
❑ 38 Black Cat	.15	.40
❑ 39 Black Cat	.15	.40
❑ 40 Armor	.15	.40
❑ 41 Armor	.15	.40
❑ 42 Armor	.15	.40
❑ 43 Lyra	.15	.40
❑ 44 Lyra	.15	.40
❑ 45 Lyra	.15	.40
❑ 46 Sister Grimm	.15	.40
❑ 47 Sister Grimm	.15	.40
❑ 48 Sister Grimm	.15	.40
❑ 49 Mystique	.15	.40
❑ 50 Mystique	.15	.40
❑ 51 Mystique	.15	.40
❑ 52 Rescue	.15	.40
❑ 53 Rescue	.15	.40
❑ 54 Rescue	.15	.40
❑ 55 Tigra	.15	.40
❑ 56 Tigra	.15	.40
❑ 57 Tigra	.15	.40
❑ 58 Invisible Woman	.15	.40
❑ 59 Invisible Woman	.15	.40
❑ 60 Invisible Woman	.15	.40
❑ 61 Hope Summers	.15	.40
❑ 62 Hope Summers	.15	.40
❑ 63 Hope Summers	.15	.40
❑ 64 Scarlet Witch	.15	.40
❑ 65 Scarlet Witch	.15	.40
❑ 66 Scarlet Witch	.15	.40
❑ 67 Spider-Girl	.15	.40
❑ 68 Spider-Girl	.15	.40
❑ 69 Spider-Girl	.15	.40
❑ 70 Mocking Bird	.15	.40
❑ 71 Mocking Bird	.15	.40
❑ 72 Mocking Bird	.15	.40

2011 Dangerous Divas Foil
COMPLETE SET (72) 25.00 60.00
STATED ODDS 1:3

2011 Dangerous Divas Case Toppers
COMPLETE SET (3) 40.00 80.00
STATED ODDS ONE PER CASE
STATED PRINT RUN 350 SER. #'d SETS
❑ CT1 Black Panther and friends 20.00 40.00
❑ CT2 Iron Man and friends 20.00 40.00
❑ CT3 Wolverine and friends 20.00 40.00

2011 Dangerous Divas Embrace
COMPLETE SET (9) 20.00 40.00
STATED ODDS 1:24
❑ E10 Mockingbird 3.00 8.00
Ronin
❑ E11 Medusa 3.00 8.00
BlackBolt
❑ E12 Spider-Woman 3.00 8.00
IronMan
❑ E13 Mary Jane 3.00 8.00
Spider-Man
❑ E14 Emma Frost 3.00 8.00
Namor
❑ E15 Ms. Marvel (Moonstone) 3.00 8.00
Wolverine (Draken)
❑ E16 Domino 3.00 8.00
Wolverine
❑ E17 Rogue 3.00 8.00
Magneto
❑ E18 Enchantress 3.00 8.00
Wiccan
❑ E19 She-Hulk 15.00 40.00
Starfox SP (issued as Rittenhouse Reward)

2011 Dangerous Divas Sketches
STATED ODDS ONE PER BOX
L (LIMITED): 251+ MADE
VL (VERY LIMITED): 151-250 MADE
EL (EXTREMELY LIMITED): 51-150 MADE
S (SCARCE): LESS THAN 50 MADE
❑ 1 Adam Cleveland L 20.00 50.00
❑ 2 Alberto Silva EL 25.00 60.00
❑ 3 Alexandre Magno L 20.00 50.00
❑ 4 Allen Geneta EL 25.00 60.00
❑ 5 Andre Toma EL 35.00 80.00
❑ 6 Apriyadi Kusbiantoro EL 25.00 60.00
❑ 7 Arie Monroe EL 35.00 80.00
❑ 8 Aston Cover EL 30.00 75.00
❑ 9 Bill Pulkovski EL 20.00 50.00
❑ 10 Buddy Prince VL 30.00 75.00
❑ 11 Budi Setiawan EL 30.00 75.00
❑ 12 Butch Mapa EL 25.00 60.00
❑ 13 Charles Hall S
❑ 14 Chris Bradberry EL 30.00 75.00
❑ 15 Chris Foreman EL 20.00 50.00
❑ 16 Craig Yeung EL 25.00 60.00
❑ 17 Daniel Cooney S 20.00 50.00
❑ 18 Danielle Gransaull S 40.00 100.00
❑ 19 Darren Chandler EL 30.00 75.00
❑ 20 Darryl Banks EL 30.00 75.00
❑ 21 Dave Beaty EL 25.00 60.00
❑ 22 David Lee L 15.00 40.00
❑ 23 Dennis Crisostomo EL 20.00 50.00
❑ 24 Don Hillsman S 15.00 40.00
❑ 25 Edde Wagner EL 20.00 50.00
❑ 26 Eduardo Ferrara L 12.00 30.00
❑ 27 Eli Rutten EL 50.00 100.00
❑ 28 Elliot Fernandez VL 40.00 100.00
❑ 29 Eman EL 125.00 200.00
❑ 30 Frank Kadar S
❑ 31 George Calloway S
❑ 32 George Davis S
❑ 33 Ghislain SpiderGuile Tchissafou EL 25.00 60.00
❑ 34 Irma Suriani Ahmed EL 30.00 75.00
❑ 35 Iwan Nazif EL 25.00 60.00
❑ 36 Jake Minor EL 15.00 40.00
❑ 37 Jason Davies EL 35.00 80.00
❑ 38 Jason Potratz and Jack Hai 35.00 80.00
Raven Ngo EL
❑ 39 Jason Sobol S 25.00 60.00
❑ 40 Jay Fosgitt EL 20.00 50.00
❑ 41 JC Fabul VL 30.00 75.00
❑ 42 Jeff Confer EL 50.00 100.00
❑ 43 Jeremy Treece EL 30.00 75.00
❑ 44 Jerry The Franchize Gaylord EL 15.00 40.00
❑ 45 Jim Kyle S
❑ 46 Joe Pekar EL
❑ 47 Joe Rubinstein L 12.00 30.00
❑ 48 Joe St.Pierre S
❑ 49 John Czop S
❑ 50 John Haun EL
❑ 51 John Jackman EL 35.00 80.00
❑ 52 Jomar Bulda VL 25.00 60.00
❑ 53 Jon Hughes VL 25.00 60.00
❑ 54 Joshua Flower EL 25.00 60.00
❑ 55 Juan Fontanez EL 25.00 60.00
❑ 56 Justin Chung S
❑ 57 Kathryn Layno EL 30.00 75.00
❑ 58 Katie Cook S 150.00 250.00
❑ 59 Kevin West S 100.00 200.00
❑ 60 Kristin Allen VL 25.00 60.00
❑ 61 Lak Lim EL 30.00 75.00
❑ 62 Larry Schlekewy EL 100.00 175.00
❑ 63 Lawrence Reynolds EL 40.00 100.00
❑ 64 Lee Kohse EL 20.00 50.00
❑ 65 Leeahd Goldberg EL 25.00 60.00
❑ 66 Lui Antonio VL 30.00 75.00
❑ 67 Luiz Fernando Scheidt EL
❑ 68 Marcelo Ferreira L 35.00 80.00
❑ 69 Mark Dos Santos EL 20.00 50.00
❑ 70 Mark Spears EL 15.00 40.00
❑ 71 Mark Tannacore EL 25.00 60.00
❑ 72 Marlo Lodrigueza EL
❑ 73 Mary Bellamy VL 15.00 40.00
❑ 74 Mauro Fodra L 20.00 50.00
❑ 75 Meghan Hetrick EL 150.00 250.00
❑ 76 Melike Acar EL
❑ 77 Michael Axebone Potter S 150.00 250.00
❑ 78 Mike Glover EL 30.00 75.00
❑ 79 Mike Lilly S
❑ 80 Nestor Celario Jr. EL 25.00 60.00
❑ 81 Newton Barbosa EL 60.00 120.00
❑ 82 Nick Yakimovich EL 12.00 30.00
❑ 83 Nicole Goff S
❑ 84 Noval Hernawan EL 20.00 50.00
❑ 85 Nur Hanie Mohd EL
❑ 86 Patrick Lacarda S
❑ 87 Pot
Gulf S
❑ 88 Raimundo Nonato L 12.00 30.00
❑ 89 Rainier Lagunsad EL 25.00 60.00
❑ 90 Randy Martinez EL 20.00 50.00
❑ 91 Randy Monces EL 30.00 75.00
❑ 92 Remy Eisu Mokhtar EL 35.00 80.00
❑ 93 Rich Molinelli EL 20.00 50.00
❑ 94 Richard Cox EL 75.00 150.00
❑ 95 Rodrigo Martins L 20.00 50.00
❑ 96 Sanna Umemoto S
❑ 97 Sara Richard EL 40.00 100.00
❑ 98 Sarah Wilkinson EL 40.00 100.00
❑ 99 Scott Barnett EL
❑ 100 Scott Rorie EL 50.00 125.00
❑ 101 Sonny Strait EL 50.00 125.00
❑ 102 Steven Miller EL 30.00 75.00
❑ 103 Thanh Bui VL 15.00 40.00
❑ 104 Tim Shay S
❑ 105 Tom Kelly VL 15.00 40.00
❑ 106 Tony Fleecs EL 20.00 50.00
❑ 107 Wendell Rubio Silva EL 25.00 60.00
❑ 108 Yesim Gazioglu Asrar EL 50.00 125.00
❑ 109 Rhiannon Owens 100.00 200.00
(issued as 6-case incentive)
❑ 110 Tony Perna/ (issued as 9-case incentive)200.00 400.00
❑ 111 Warren Martineck/ (issued as 18-case incentive)
❑ 112 Renae De Liz/ (issued as 18-case incentive)250.00 450.00
❑ 113 Gabe Hernandez/ (issued as 18-case incentive)

2011 Dangerous Divas Sultry Seductresses
COMPLETE SET (9) 10.00 25.00
STATED ODDS 1:12
❑ S1 Black Cat 2.00 5.00
❑ S2 Black Queen 2.00 5.00
❑ S3 Brunhilde 2.00 5.00
❑ S4 Emma Frost 2.00 5.00
❑ S5 Goblin Queen 2.00 5.00
❑ S6 Kitty Pryde 2.00 5.00
❑ S7 Mary Jane Watson 2.00 5.00
❑ S8 Psylocke 2.00 5.00
❑ S9 Tigra 2.00 5.00

2011 Dangerous Divas Women of Marvel
COMPLETE SET (12) 10.00 25.00
STATED ODDS 1:8
❑ W1 Mary Jane Watson 1.50 4.00
Black Cat
❑ W2 Aquaria Nautica Neptunia 1.50 4.00
❑ W3 Scarlet Witch 1.50 4.00
❑ W4 Natasha Romanoff 1.50 4.00
❑ W5 Storm 1.50 4.00
❑ W6 Invisible Woman 1.50 4.00
❑ W7 Savage She-Hulk 1.50 4.00
❑ W8 Hope Summers 1.50 4.00
❑ W9 Mockingbird 1.50 4.00
❑ W10 Valkyrie 1.50 4.00
❑ W11 Anya Corazon 1.50 4.00
❑ W12 Laura Kinney 1.50 4.00

2011 Eureka Seasons One and Two
COMPLETE SET (25) 30.00 60.00
STATED PRINT RUN 250 SER. #'d SETS
❑ 1 Pilot 2.00 5.00
❑ 2 Many Happy Returns 2.00 5.00
❑ 3 Before I Forgot 2.00 5.00
❑ 4 Alienated 2.00 5.00
❑ 5 Invincible 2.00 5.00
❑ 6 Dr. Nobel 2.00 5.00
❑ 7 Blink 2.00 5.00
❑ 8 Right as Raynes 2.00 5.00
❑ 9 Primal 2.00 5.00
❑ 10 Purple Haze 2.00 5.00
❑ 11 H.O.U.S.E. Rules 2.00 5.00
❑ 12 Once in a Lifetime 2.00 5.00
❑ 13 Phoenix Rising 2.00 5.00
❑ 14 Try Try Again 2.00 5.00
❑ 15 Unpredictable 2.00 5.00
❑ 16 The Games People Play 2.00 5.00
❑ 17 Duck Duck Goose 2.00 5.00
❑ 18 Noche de Suenos 2.00 5.00
❑ 19 Family Reunion 2.00 5.00
❑ 20 E=MC? 2.00 5.00
❑ 21 Sight Unseen 2.00 5.00
❑ 22 God is in the Details 2.00 5.00
❑ 23 Maneater 2.00 5.00
❑ 24 All The Glitters 2.00 5.00
❑ 25 A Night in Global Dynamics 2.00 5.00

2011 Eureka Seasons One and Two Artifacts
STATED ODDS ONE PER PACK
STATED PRINT RUN 350 SER. #'d SETS
❑ AF1 White Global Dynamics Lab Coat 8.00 20.00
❑ AF2 Global Dynamics Scrubs 8.00 20.00
❑ AF3 Eureka Red Bowling T-Shirt 8.00 20.00
❑ AF4 Tesla School Graduation Gown 8.00 20.00
❑ AF5 White Global Dynamics Coveralls 8.00 20.00
❑ AF6 Tesla School Warm-Ups 8.00 20.00
❑ AF7 Yellow Global Dynamics Coveralls 8.00 20.00
❑ AF8 Area 51 Blue Bowling T-Shirt 8.00 20.00
❑ AF9 Yellow Global Dynamics Lab Coat 8.00 20.00

2011 Eureka Seasons One and Two Autographs
STATED ODDS TWO PER PACK
❑ 1 Barclay Hope 6.00 12.00
❑ 2 Chris Gauthier 10.00 20.00
❑ 3 Christopher Jacot 7.50 15.00
❑ 4 Colin Ferguson 40.00 80.00
❑ 5 Ed Quinn 10.00 20.00
❑ 6 Erica Cerra 15.00 30.00
❑ 7 Joe Morton 10.00 20.00
❑ 8 Matt Frewer 10.00 20.00
❑ 9 Meshach Peters 6.00 12.00
❑ 10 Neil Grayson 20.00 40.00
❑ 11 Niall Matter 7.50 15.00
❑ 12 Rob LaBelle 6.00 12.00
❑ 13 Shayn Solberg 6.00 12.00
❑ 14 Tamlyn Tomita 7.50 15.00

2011 Eureka Seasons One and Two Casting Call
COMPLETE SET (11) 20.00 40.00
STATED ODDS ONE PER PACK
STATED PRINT RUN 350 SER. #'d SETS
❑ C1 Sheriff Jack Carter 2.50 6.00
❑ C2 Allison Blake 2.50 6.00
❑ C3 Henry Deacon 2.50 6.00
❑ C4 Nathan Stark 2.50 6.00
❑ C5 Deputy Jo Lupo 2.50 6.00
❑ C6 Douglas Fargo 2.50 6.00
❑ C7 Zoe Carter 2.50 6.00
❑ C8 Vincent 2.50 6.00
❑ C9 Jim Taggart 2.50 6.00
❑ C10 Zane Donovan 2.50 6.00
❑ C11 Beverly Barlow 2.50 6.00
❑ C12 Sheriff Jack Carter/350 10.00 25.00
(issued as Rittenhouse Reward)

2011 Eureka Seasons One and Two Promos
COMPLETE SET (3) 2.50 6.00
❑ P1 Sheriff Carter and company .75 2.00
❑ P2 Allison Blake 1.50 4.00
Jack Carter/ (NSU Magazine)
❑ P3 Jo Lupo 1.50 4.00
Jack Carter/ (2011 SDCC or binder)

2011 Family Guy Seasons Three Through Five
COMPLETE SET (50) 8.00 20.00
❑ 1 Family Guy .30 .75
❑ 2 Family Guy .30 .75
❑ 3 Family Guy .30 .75
❑ 4 Family Guy .30 .75
❑ 5 Family Guy .30 .75
❑ 6 Family Guy .30 .75
❑ 7 Family Guy .30 .75
❑ 8 Family Guy .30 .75
❑ 9 Family Guy .30 .75
❑ 10 Family Guy .30 .75
❑ 11 Family Guy .30 .75
❑ 12 Family Guy .30 .75
❑ 13 Family Guy .30 .75
❑ 14 Family Guy .30 .75
❑ 15 Family Guy .30 .75
❑ 16 Family Guy .30 .75
❑ 17 Family Guy .30 .75
❑ 18 Family Guy .30 .75
❑ 19 Family Guy .30 .75
❑ 20 Family Guy .30 .75
❑ 21 Family Guy .30 .75
❑ 22 Family Guy .30 .75
❑ 23 Family Guy .30 .75
❑ 24 Family Guy .30 .75
❑ 25 Family Guy .30 .75
❑ 26 Family Guy .30 .75
❑ 27 Family Guy .30 .75
❑ 28 Family Guy .30 .75
❑ 29 Family Guy .30 .75
❑ 30 Family Guy .30 .75
❑ 31 Family Guy .30 .75
❑ 32 Family Guy .30 .75
❑ 33 Family Guy .30 .75
❑ 34 Family Guy .30 .75
❑ 35 Family Guy .30 .75
❑ 36 Family Guy .30 .75
❑ 37 Family Guy .30 .75
❑ 38 Family Guy .30 .75
❑ 39 Family Guy .30 .75
❑ 40 Family Guy .30 .75
❑ 41 Family Guy .30 .75
❑ 42 Family Guy .30 .75
❑ 43 Family Guy .30 .75
❑ 44 Family Guy .30 .75
❑ 45 Family Guy .30 .75
❑ 46 Family Guy .30 .75
❑ 47 Family Guy .30 .75
❑ 48 Family Guy .30 .75
❑ 49 Family Guy .30 .75
❑ 50 Family Guy .30 .75

2011 Family Guy Seasons Three Through Five Autographs
STATED ODDS ONE PER BOX
❑ AR1 Alfonso Ribeiro 8.00 20.00
❑ BT1 Brian Tochi 8.00 20.00
❑ CA1 Carlos Alazraqui 8.00 20.00
❑ CF1 Carrie Fisher 125.00 250.00
❑ DW1 Debra Wilson 8.00 20.00
❑ EA1 Ed Asner 10.00 25.00
❑ GG1 Gina Gershon 20.00 40.00
❑ JG1 Jennie Garth 20.00 40.00
❑ LB1 Levar Burton 10.00 25.00
❑ LG1 Leif Garrett 20.00 40.00
❑ MH1 Mark Hamill 100.00 200.00
❑ PD1 Patrick Duffy 10.00 25.00
❑ PS1 Patrick Stewart 40.00 80.00
❑ PW1 Patrick Warburton 20.00 40.00
❑ TD1 Thomas Dekker 8.00 20.00
❑ TS1 Tori Spelling 15.00 30.00
❑ LGJ1 Lou Gossett Jr. 8.00 20.00

2011 Family Guy Seasons Three Through Five Meet the Characters
❑ 1 Peter Griffin 2.00 5.00
❑ 2 Stewie Griffin 2.00 5.00
❑ 3 Lois Griffin 2.00 5.00
❑ 4 Meg Griffin 2.00 5.00
❑ 5 Chris Griffin 2.00 5.00
❑ 6 Brian Griffin 2.00 5.00
❑ 7 Glen Quagmire 2.00 5.00
❑ 8 Cleveland Brown 2.00 5.00
❑ 9 Joe Swanson 2.00 5.00
❑ 10 Evil Monkey

2011 Family Guy Seasons Three Through Five Meet the Characters Printing Plates Black
STATED PRINT RUN 1 SER. #'d SET
UNPRICED DUE TO SCARCITY

2011 Family Guy Seasons Three Through Five Meet the Characters Printing Plates Cyan
STATED PRINT RUN 1 SER. #'d SET
UNPRICED DUE TO SCARCITY

2011 Family Guy Seasons Three Through Five Meet the Characters Printing Plates Magenta
STATED PRINT RUN 1 SER. #'d SET
UNPRICED DUE TO SCARCITY

2011 Family Guy Seasons Three Through Five Meet the Characters Printing Plates Yellow
STATED PRINT RUN 1 SER. #'d SET
UNPRICED DUE TO SCARCITY

2011 Family Guy Seasons Three Through Five Quotables
COMPLETE SET (24) 20.00 40.00
❑ Q1 Mr. Griffin Goes To Washington 1.25 3.00
❑ Q2 One If By Clam, Two If By Sea 1.25 3.00
❑ Q3 Lethal Weapons 1.25 3.00
❑ Q4 Lethal Weapons 1.25 3.00
❑ Q5 Fish Out of Water 1.25 3.00
❑ Q6 Emission Impossible 1.25 3.00
❑ Q7 Emission Impossible 1.25 3.00
❑ Q8 A Very Special Family Guy Freakin' Christmas1.25 3.00
❑ Q9 When You Wish Upon a Weinstein 1.25 3.00
❑ Q10 Fast Times At Buddy Cianci Jr. High 1.25 3.00
❑ Q11 Don't Make Me Over 1.25 3.00
❑ Q12 The Cleveland-Loretta Quagmire 1.25 3.00
❑ Q13 Brian the Bachelor 1.25 3.00
❑ Q14 8 Simple Rules For Buying 1.25 3.00
My Teenage Daughter
❑ Q15 You May Now Kiss 1.25 3.00
The...Uh...Guy Who Receives
❑ Q16 The Father, The Son and the Holy Fonz 1.25 3.00
❑ Q17 You May Now Kiss 1.25 3.00
The...Uh...Guy Who Receives
❑ Q18 Stewie Loves Lois 1.25 3.00
❑ Q19 Barely Legal 1.25 3.00
❑ Q20 Prick Up Your Ears 1.25 3.00
❑ Q21 Airport '07 1.25 3.00
❑ Q22 Prick Up Your Ears 1.25 3.00
❑ Q23 No Meals On Wheels 1.25 3.00
❑ Q24 Mother Tucker 1.25 3.00

2011 Family Guy Seasons Three Through Five Quotables Prismatic
STATED PRINT RUN 70 SER. #'d SETS

2011 Family Guy Seasons Three Through Five Quotables Prismatic Black
STATED PRINT RUN 25 SER. #'d SETS

2011 Family Guy Seasons Three Through Five Quotables Prismatic Gold
STATED PRINT RUN 1 SER. #'d SET
UNPRICED DUE TO SCARCITY

2011 Family Guy Seasons Three Through Five Quotables Printing Plates Black
STATED PRINT RUN 1 SER. #'d SET
UNPRICED DUE TO SCARCITY

2011 Family Guy Seasons Three Through Five Quotables Printing Plates Cyan
STATED PRINT RUN 1 SER. #'d SET
UNPRICED DUE TO SCARCITY

2011 Family Guy Seasons Three Through Five Quotables Printing Plates Magenta
STATED PRINT RUN 1 SER. #'d SET
UNPRICED DUE TO SCARCITY

2011 Family Guy Seasons Three Through Five Quotables Printing Plates Yellow
STATED PRINT RUN 1 SER. #'d SET
UNPRICED DUE TO SCARCITY

2011 Family Guy Seasons Three Through Five Sketches
STATED ODDS
❑ 1 Bao Nguyen
❑ 2 Dante Leandado
❑ 3 Helen Kim
❑ 4 Ken Hayashi
❑ 5 Kristina Bustamante
❑ 6 Mark Covell
❑ 7 Mark Garcia
❑ 8 Raul Guerra
❑ 9 Ron Smith

2011 Garbage Pail Kids Flashback Series Two
COMPLETE SET (160) 12.00 30.00
❑ 1a Junkfood John .15 .40
❑ 1b Ray Decay .15 .40
❑ 2a Stormy Heather .15 .40
❑ 2b April Showers .15 .40
❑ 3a Weird Wendy .15 .40
❑ 3b Haggy Maggie .15 .40
❑ 4a Cranky Frankie .15 .40
❑ 4b Bad Brad .15 .40
❑ 5a Creepy Carol .15 .40
❑ 5b Scary Carrie .15 .40
❑ 6a Kim Kong .15 .40
❑ 6b Anna Banana .15 .40
❑ 7a Wrappin' Ruth .15 .40
❑ 7b Tommy Tomb .15 .40
❑ 8a Patty Putty .15 .40
❑ 8b Muggin' Megan .15 .40
❑ 9a Smelly Kelly .15 .40
❑ 9b Doug Plug .15 .40
❑ 10a Leaky Lindsay .15 .40
❑ 10b Messy Tessie .15 .40
❑ 11a Mad Donna .15 .40
❑ 11b Nutty Nicole .15 .40
❑ 12a Jolted Joel .15 .40
❑ 12b Live Mike .15 .40
❑ 13a Jolly Roger .15 .40
❑ 13b Pegleg Peter .15 .40
❑ 14a Sewer Sue .15 .40
❑ 14b Michelle Muck .15 .40
❑ 15a Hurt Curt .15 .40
❑ 15b Pat Splat .15 .40
❑ 16a Drew Blood .15 .40
❑ 16b Bustin' Dustin .15 .40
❑ 17a Bruised Lee .15 .40
❑ 17b Karate Kate .15 .40
❑ 18a Beaky Becky .15 .40
❑ 18b Picky Mickey .15 .40
❑ 19a Eerie Eric .15 .40
❑ 19b Berserk Kirk .15 .40
❑ 20a Babbling Brooke .15 .40
❑ 20b Jelly Kelly .15 .40
❑ 21a Apply Cory .15 .40
❑ 21b Dwight Bite .15 .40
❑ 22a Second Hand Rose .15 .40
❑ 22b Trashed Tracy .15 .40
❑ 23a Bony Tony .15 .40
❑ 23b Unzipped Zack .15 .40
❑ 24a Amazin' Grace .15 .40
❑ 24b Muscular Molly .15 .40
❑ 25a Hairy Harriet .15 .40
❑ 25b Bushy Bernice .15 .40
❑ 26a Warrin' Warren .15 .40
❑ 26b Brett Vet .15 .40
❑ 27a Yicchy Mickey .15 .40
❑ 27b Barfin' Bart .15 .40
❑ 28a Gored Gordon .15 .40
❑ 28b No Way Jose .15 .40
❑ 29a Dee Faced .15 .40
❑ 29b Terri Cloth .15 .40
❑ 30a Sprayed Wade .15 .40
❑ 30b Tagged Tad .15 .40
❑ 31a Diaper Dan .15 .40
❑ 31b Pinned Penny .15 .40
❑ 32a Lucas Mucus .15 .40
❑ 32b Dotty Dribble .15 .40
❑ 33a Dangling Dolly .15 .40
❑ 33b Surreal Neal .15 .40
❑ 34a Michael Mutant .15 .40
❑ 34b Zeke Freak .15 .40
❑ 35a Deaf Geoff .15 .40
❑ 35b Audio Augie .15 .40
❑ 36a Intense Payne .15 .40
❑ 36b First Ada .15 .40
❑ 37a Tom Thumb .15 .40
❑ 37b Bridget Digit .15 .40
❑ 38a Joan Clone .15 .40
❑ 38b Warty Ward .15 .40
❑ 39a Ugly Hans .15 .40
❑ 39b Jan Hand .15 .40
❑ 40a John John .15 .40
❑ 40b Flushing Floyd .15 .40
❑ 41a Hector Collector .15 .40
❑ 41b G.P. Kay .15 .40
❑ 42a Many Lenny .15 .40
❑ 42b Lotta Carlotta .15 .40
❑ 43a Mickey Mouths .15 .40
❑ 43b Oral Laurel .15 .40
❑ 44a Adam Boom .40 1.00
❑ 44b Blasted Billy II .30 .75
❑ 45a Pete Seat .15 .40
❑ 45b Noel Bowl .15 .40
❑ 46a Elastic Elwood .15 .40
❑ 46b Fletcher Stretcher .15 .40
❑ 47a Shut-Up Sherwin .15 .40
❑ 47b Filled Up Phillip .15 .40
❑ 48a Allen Alien .15 .40
❑ 48b Martian Marcia .15 .40
❑ 49a Haley Comet .15 .40
❑ 49b June Moon .15 .40
❑ 50a Explorin' Norman .15 .40
❑ 50b Drillin' Dylan .15 .40
❑ 51a Divin' Ivan .15 .40
❑ 51b Walter Sport .15 .40
❑ 52a Fritz Spritz .15 .40
❑ 52b Ella P. Record .15 .40
❑ 53a Messy Bessie .15 .40
❑ 53b Unclean Helene .15 .40
❑ 54a Lem Phlegm .15 .40
❑ 54b Gezundt Heidi .15 .40
❑ 55a Page Cage .15 .40
❑ 55b Tommy Ache .15 .40
❑ 56a Ortho Donny .15 .40
❑ 56b Ruth Canal .15 .40
❑ 57a Cute Tippi .15 .40
❑ 57b Waxy Wendy .15 .40
❑ 58a Early Bert .15 .40
❑ 58b Rotten Robin .15 .40
❑ 59a Snot Rope Hope .15 .40
❑ 59b Drippy Debbie .15 .40
❑ 60a Con Vic .15 .40
❑ 60b Al Catraz .15 .40
❑ 61a Clark Shark .15 .40
❑ 61b Manny Eater .15 .40
❑ 62a Beasty Boyd .15 .40
❑ 62b Semi Colin .15 .40
❑ 63a 3-Dee .15 .40
❑ 63b Blurry Blair .15 .40
❑ 64a Dent Al .15 .40
❑ 64b Fluoride Ida .15 .40
❑ 65a Scalped Ralph .15 .40
❑ 65b Bone-Head Fred .15 .40
❑ 66a Slammed Sloan .15 .40
❑ 66b Keith Out .15 .40
❑ 67a Scrawled Saul .15 .40
❑ 67b Bad Art .15 .40
❑ 68a Noah Parking .15 .40
❑ 68b Peter Meter .15 .40
❑ 69a Dead Flora .15 .40
❑ 69b Fetid Fern .15 .40
❑ 70a Idol Ira .15 .40
❑ 70b Ken Tiki .15 .40
❑ 71a Potty Scotty .15 .40
❑ 71b Jason Basin .15 .40
❑ 72a Ghastly Ashley .15 .40
❑ 72b Acne Amy .15 .40
❑ 73a Jolly Roger .15 .40
❑ 73b Pegleg Peter .15 .40
❑ 74a Greaser Greg .15 .40
❑ 74b Chris Hiss .15 .40
❑ 75a Smelly Sally .15 .40
❑ 75b Fishy Phyllis .15 .40
❑ 76a New Wave Dave .15 .40
❑ 76b Graffiti Petey .15 .40
❑ 77a Ultra Violet .15 .40
❑ 77b Tanya Hide .15 .40
❑ 78a Barfin' Barbara .15 .40
❑ 78b Valerie Vomit .15 .40
❑ 79a Wacky Jackie .15 .40
❑ 79b Loony Lenny .15 .40
❑ 80a Half-Nelson .15 .40
❑ 80b Glandular Angela .15 .40

2011 Garbage Pail Kids Flashback Series Two Green
COMPLETE SET (160) 40.00 80.00
*GREEN: .8X TO 2X BASIC CARDS
STATED ODDS 1:2
❑ 1a Junkfood John .30 .75
❑ 1b Ray Decay .30 .75
❑ 2a Stormy Heather .30 .75
❑ 2b April Showers .30 .75
❑ 3a Weird Wendy .30 .75
❑ 3b Haggy Maggie .30 .75
❑ 4a Cranky Frankie .30 .75
❑ 4b Bad Brad .30 .75
❑ 5a Creepy Carol .30 .75
❑ 5b Scary Carrie .30 .75
❑ 6a Kim Kong .30 .75
❑ 6b Anna Banana .30 .75
❑ 7a Wrappin' Ruth .30 .75
❑ 7b Tommy Tomb .30 .75
❑ 8a Patty Putty .30 .75
❑ 8b Muggin' Megan .30 .75
❑ 9a Smelly Kelly .30 .75
❑ 9b Doug Plug .30 .75
❑ 10a Leaky Lindsay .30 .75
❑ 10b Messy Tessie .30 .75
❑ 11a Mad Donna .30 .75

❑ 11b Nutty Nicole .30 .75
❑ 12a Jolted Joel .30 .75
❑ 12b Live Mike .30 .75
❑ 13a Jolly Roger .30 .75
❑ 13b Pegleg Peter .30 .75
❑ 14a Sewer Sue .30 .75
❑ 14b Michelle Muck .30 .75
❑ 15a Hurt Curt .30 .75
❑ 15b Pat Splat .30 .75
❑ 16a Drew Blood .30 .75
❑ 16b Bustin' Dustin .30 .75
❑ 17a Bruised Lee .30 .75
❑ 17b Karate Kate .30 .75
❑ 18a Beaky Becky .30 .75
❑ 18b Picky Mickey .30 .75
❑ 19a Eerie Eric .30 .75
❑ 19b Berserk Kirk .30 .75
❑ 20a Babbling Brooke .30 .75
❑ 20b Jelly Kelly .30 .75
❑ 21a Apply Cory .30 .75
❑ 21b Dwight Bite .30 .75
❑ 22a Second Hand Rose .30 .75
❑ 22b Trashed Tracy .30 .75
❑ 23a Bony Tony .30 .75
❑ 23b Unzipped Zack .30 .75
❑ 24a Amazin' Grace .30 .75
❑ 24b Muscular Molly .30 .75
❑ 25a Hairy Harriet .30 .75
❑ 25b Bushy Bernice .30 .75
❑ 26a Warrin' Warren .30 .75
❑ 26b Brett Vet .30 .75
❑ 27a Yicchy Mickey .30 .75
❑ 27b Barfin' Bart .30 .75
❑ 28a Gored Gordon .30 .75
❑ 28b No Way Jose .30 .75
❑ 29a Dee Faced .30 .75
❑ 29b Terri Cloth .30 .75
❑ 30a Sprayed Wade .30 .75
❑ 30b Tagged Tad .30 .75
❑ 31a Diaper Dan .30 .75
❑ 31b Pinned Penny .30 .75
❑ 32a Lucas Mucus .30 .75
❑ 32b Dotty Dribble .30 .75
❑ 33a Dangling Dolly .30 .75
❑ 33b Surreal Neal .30 .75
❑ 34a Michael Mutant .30 .75
❑ 34b Zeke Freak .30 .75
❑ 35a Deaf Geoff .30 .75
❑ 35b Audio Augie .30 .75
❑ 36a Intense Payne .30 .75
❑ 36b First Ada .30 .75
❑ 37a Tom Thumb .30 .75
❑ 37b Bridget Digit .30 .75
❑ 38a Joan Clone .30 .75
❑ 38b Warty Ward .30 .75
❑ 39a Ugly Hans .30 .75
❑ 39b Jan Hand .30 .75
❑ 40a John John .30 .75
❑ 40b Flushing Floyd .30 .75
❑ 41a Hector Collector .30 .75
❑ 41b G.P. Kay .30 .75
❑ 42a Many Lenny .30 .75
❑ 42b Lotta Carlotta .30 .75
❑ 43a Mickey Mouths .30 .75
❑ 43b Oral Laurel .30 .75
❑ 44a Adam Boom .75 2.00
❑ 44b Blasted Billy II .60 1.50
❑ 45a Pete Seat .30 .75
❑ 45b Noel Bowl .30 .75
❑ 46a Elastic Elwood .30 .75
❑ 46b Fletcher Stretcher .30 .75
❑ 47a Shut-Up Sherwin .30 .75
❑ 47b Filled Up Philip .30 .75
❑ 48a Alien Alan .30 .75
❑ 48b Martian Marcia .30 .75
❑ 49a Haley Comet .30 .75
❑ 49b June Moon .30 .75
❑ 50a Explorin' Norman .30 .75
❑ 50b Drillin' Dylan .30 .75
❑ 51a Divin' Ivan .30 .75
❑ 51b Walter Sport .30 .75
❑ 52a Fritz Spritz .30 .75
❑ 52b Ella P. Record .30 .75
❑ 53a Messy Bessie .30 .75
❑ 53b Unclean Helene .30 .75
❑ 54a Lem Phlegm .30 .75
❑ 54b Gezundt Heidi .30 .75
❑ 55a Page Cage .30 .75
❑ 55b Tommy Ache .30 .75
❑ 56a Ortho Donny .30 .75
❑ 56b Ruth Canal .30 .75
❑ 57a Cute Tippi .30 .75
❑ 57b Waxy Wendy .30 .75
❑ 58a Early Bert .30 .75
❑ 58b Rotten Robin .30 .75
❑ 59a Snot Rope Hope .30 .75
❑ 59b Drippy Debbie .30 .75
❑ 60a Con Vic .30 .75
❑ 60b Al Catraz .30 .75
❑ 61a Clark Shark .30 .75
❑ 61b Manny Eater .30 .75
❑ 62a Beasty Boyd .30 .75
❑ 62b Semi Colin .30 .75
❑ 63a 3-Dee .30 .75
❑ 63b Blurry Blair .30 .75
❑ 64a Dent Al .30 .75
❑ 64b Fluoride Ida .30 .75
❑ 65a Scalped Ralph .30 .75
❑ 65b Bone-Head Fred .30 .75
❑ 66a Slammed Sloan .30 .75
❑ 66b Keith Out .30 .75
❑ 67a Scrawled Saul .30 .75
❑ 67b Bad Art .30 .75
❑ 68a Noah Parking .30 .75
❑ 68b Peter Meter .30 .75
❑ 69a Dead Flora .30 .75
❑ 69b Fetid Fern .30 .75
❑ 70a Idol Ira .30 .75
❑ 70b Ken Tiki .30 .75
❑ 71a Potty Scotty .30 .75
❑ 71b Jason Basin .30 .75
❑ 72a Ghastly Ashley .30 .75
❑ 72b Acne Amy .30 .75
❑ 73a Jolly Roger .30 .75
❑ 73b Pegleg Peter .30 .75
❑ 74a Greaser Greg .30 .75
❑ 74b Chris Hiss .30 .75
❑ 75a Smelly Sally .30 .75
❑ 75b Fishy Phyllis .30 .75
❑ 76a New Wave Dave .30 .75
❑ 76b Graffiti Petey .30 .75
❑ 77a Ultra Violet .30 .75
❑ 77b Tanya Hide .30 .75
❑ 78a Barfin' Barbara .30 .75
❑ 78b Valerie Vomit .30 .75
❑ 79a Wacky Jackie .30 .75
❑ 79b Loony Lenny .30 .75
❑ 80a Half-Nelson .30 .75
❑ 80b Glandular Angela .30 .75

2011 Garbage Pail Kids Flashback Series Two Pink

COMPLETE SET (160) 75.00 150.00
STATED ODDS 1:3

❑ 1a Junkfood John .60 1.50
❑ 1b Ray Decay .60 1.50
❑ 2a Stormy Heather .60 1.50
❑ 2b April Showers .60 1.50
❑ 3a Weird Wendy .60 1.50
❑ 3b Haggy Maggie .60 1.50
❑ 4a Cranky Frankie .60 1.50
❑ 4b Bad Brad .60 1.50
❑ 5a Creepy Carol .60 1.50
❑ 5b Scary Carrie .60 1.50
❑ 6a Kim Kong .60 1.50
❑ 6b Anna Banana .60 1.50
❑ 7a Wrappin' Ruth .60 1.50
❑ 7b Tommy Tomb .60 1.50
❑ 8a Patty Putty .60 1.50
❑ 8b Muggin' Megan .60 1.50
❑ 9a Smelly Kelly .60 1.50
❑ 9b Doug Plug .60 1.50
❑ 10a Leaky Lindsay .60 1.50
❑ 10b Messy Tessie .60 1.50
❑ 11a Mad Donna .60 1.50
❑ 11b Nutty Nicole .60 1.50
❑ 12a Jolted Joel .60 1.50
❑ 12b Live Mike .60 1.50
❑ 13a Jolly Roger .60 1.50
❑ 13b Pegleg Peter .60 1.50
❑ 14a Sewer Sue .60 1.50
❑ 14b Michelle Muck .60 1.50
❑ 15a Hurt Curt .60 1.50
❑ 15b Pat Splat .60 1.50
❑ 16a Drew Blood .60 1.50
❑ 16b Bustin' Dustin .60 1.50
❑ 17a Bruised Lee .60 1.50
❑ 17b Karate Kate .60 1.50
❑ 18a Beaky Becky .60 1.50
❑ 18b Picky Mickey .60 1.50
❑ 19a Eerie Eric .60 1.50
❑ 19b Berserk Kirk .60 1.50
❑ 20a Babbling Brooke .60 1.50
❑ 20b Jelly Kelly .60 1.50
❑ 21a Apply Cory .60 1.50
❑ 21b Dwight Bite .60 1.50
❑ 22a Second Hand Rose .60 1.50
❑ 22b Trashed Tracy .60 1.50
❑ 23a Bony Tony .60 1.50
❑ 23b Unzipped Zack .60 1.50
❑ 24a Amazin' Grace .60 1.50
❑ 24b Muscular Molly .60 1.50
❑ 25a Hairy Harriet .60 1.50
❑ 25b Bushy Bernice .60 1.50
❑ 26a Warrin' Warren .60 1.50
❑ 26b Brett Vet .60 1.50
❑ 27a Yicchy Mickey .60 1.50
❑ 27b Barfin' Bart .60 1.50
❑ 28a Gored Gordon .60 1.50
❑ 28b No Way Jose .60 1.50
❑ 29a Dee Faced .60 1.50
❑ 29b Terri Cloth .60 1.50
❑ 30a Sprayed Wade .60 1.50
❑ 30b Tagged Tad .60 1.50
❑ 31a Diaper Dan .60 1.50
❑ 31b Pinned Penny .60 1.50
❑ 32a Lucas Mucus .60 1.50
❑ 32b Dotty Dribble .60 1.50
❑ 33a Dangling Dolly .60 1.50
❑ 33b Surreal Neal .60 1.50
❑ 34a Michael Mutant .60 1.50
❑ 34b Zeke Freak .60 1.50
❑ 35a Deaf Geoff .60 1.50
❑ 35b Audio Augie .60 1.50
❑ 36a Intense Payne .60 1.50
❑ 36b First Ada .60 1.50
❑ 37a Tom Thumb .60 1.50
❑ 37b Bridget Digit .60 1.50
❑ 38a Joan Clone .60 1.50
❑ 38b Warty Ward .60 1.50
❑ 39a Ugly Hans .60 1.50
❑ 39b Jan Hand .60 1.50
❑ 40a John John .60 1.50
❑ 40b Flushing Floyd .60 1.50
❑ 41a Hector Collector .60 1.50
❑ 41b G.P. Kay .60 1.50
❑ 42a Many Lenny .60 1.50
❑ 42b Lotta Carlotta .60 1.50
❑ 43a Mickey Mouths .60 1.50
❑ 43b Oral Laurel .60 1.50
❑ 44a Adam Boom 1.50 4.00
❑ 44b Blasted Billy II 1.25 3.00
❑ 45a Pete Seat .60 1.50
❑ 45b Noel Bowl .60 1.50
❑ 46a Elastic Elwood .60 1.50
❑ 46b Fletcher Stretcher .60 1.50
❑ 47a Shut-Up Sherwin .60 1.50
❑ 47b Filled Up Philip .60 1.50
❑ 48a Alien Alan .60 1.50
❑ 48b Martian Marcia .60 1.50
❑ 49a Haley Comet .60 1.50
❑ 49b June Moon .60 1.50
❑ 50a Explorin' Norman .60 1.50
❑ 50b Drillin' Dylan .60 1.50
❑ 51a Divin' Ivan .60 1.50
❑ 51b Walter Sport .60 1.50
❑ 52a Fritz Spritz .60 1.50
❑ 52b Ella P. Record .60 1.50
❑ 53a Messy Bessie .60 1.50
❑ 53b Unclean Helene .60 1.50
❑ 54a Lem Phlegm .60 1.50
❑ 54b Gezundt Heidi .60 1.50
❑ 55a Page Cage .60 1.50
❑ 55b Tommy Ache .60 1.50
❑ 56a Ortho Donny .60 1.50
❑ 56b Ruth Canal .60 1.50
❑ 57a Cute Tippi .60 1.50
❑ 57b Waxy Wendy .60 1.50
❑ 58a Early Bert .60 1.50
❑ 58b Rotten Robin .60 1.50
❑ 59a Snot Rope Hope .60 1.50
❑ 59b Drippy Debbie .60 1.50
❑ 60a Con Vic .60 1.50
❑ 60b Al Catraz .60 1.50
❑ 61a Clark Shark .60 1.50
❑ 61b Manny Eater .60 1.50
❑ 62a Beasty Boyd .60 1.50
❑ 62b Semi Colin .60 1.50
❑ 63a 3-Dee .60 1.50
❑ 63b Blurry Blair .60 1.50
❑ 64a Dent Al .60 1.50
❑ 64b Fluoride Ida .60 1.50
❑ 65a Scalped Ralph .60 1.50
❑ 65b Bone-Head Fred .60 1.50
❑ 66a Slammed Sloan .60 1.50
❑ 66b Keith Out .60 1.50
❑ 67a Scrawled Saul .60 1.50
❑ 67b Bad Art .60 1.50
❑ 68a Noah Parking .60 1.50
❑ 68b Peter Meter .60 1.50
❑ 69a Dead Flora .60 1.50
❑ 69b Fetid Fern .60 1.50
❑ 70a Idol Ira .60 1.50
❑ 70b Ken Tiki .60 1.50
❑ 71a Potty Scotty .60 1.50
❑ 71b Jason Basin .60 1.50
❑ 72a Ghastly Ashley .60 1.50
❑ 72b Acne Amy .60 1.50
❑ 73a Jolly Roger .60 1.50
❑ 73b Pegleg Peter .60 1.50
❑ 74a Greaser Greg .60 1.50
❑ 74b Chris Hiss .60 1.50
❑ 75a Smelly Sally .60 1.50
❑ 75b Fishy Phyllis .60 1.50
❑ 76a New Wave Dave .60 1.50
❑ 76b Graffiti Petey .60 1.50
❑ 77a Ultra Violet .60 1.50
❑ 77b Tanya Hide .60 1.50
❑ 78a Barfin' Barbara .60 1.50
❑ 78b Valerie Vomit .60 1.50
❑ 79a Wacky Jackie .60 1.50
❑ 79b Loony Lenny .60 1.50
❑ 80a Half-Nelson .60 1.50
❑ 80b Glandular Angela .60 1.50

2011 Garbage Pail Kids Flashback Series Two Silver

COMPLETE SET (160)
STATED ODDS 1:6

❑ 1a Junkfood John 2.50 6.00
❑ 1b Ray Decay 2.50 6.00
❑ 2a Stormy Heather 2.50 6.00
❑ 2b April Showers 2.50 6.00
❑ 3a Weird Wendy 2.50 6.00
❑ 3b Haggy Maggie 2.50 6.00
❑ 4a Cranky Frankie 2.50 6.00
❑ 4b Bad Brad 2.50 6.00
❑ 5a Creepy Carol 2.50 6.00
❑ 5b Scary Carrie 2.50 6.00
❑ 6a Kim Kong 2.50 6.00
❑ 6b Anna Banana 2.50 6.00
❑ 7a Wrappin' Ruth 2.50 6.00
❑ 7b Tommy Tomb 2.50 6.00
❑ 8a Patty Putty 2.50 6.00
❑ 8b Muggin' Megan 2.50 6.00
❑ 9a Smelly Kelly 2.50 6.00
❑ 9b Doug Plug 2.50 6.00
❑ 10a Leaky Lindsay 2.50 6.00
❑ 10b Messy Tessie 2.50 6.00
❑ 11a Mad Donna 2.50 6.00
❑ 11b Nutty Nicole 2.50 6.00
❑ 12a Jolted Joel 2.50 6.00
❑ 12b Live Mike 2.50 6.00
❑ 13a Jolly Roger 2.50 6.00
❑ 13b Pegleg Peter 2.50 6.00
❑ 14a Sewer Sue 2.50 6.00
❑ 14b Michelle Muck 2.50 6.00
❑ 15a Hurt Curt 2.50 6.00
❑ 15b Pat Splat 2.50 6.00
❑ 16a Drew Blood 2.50 6.00
❑ 16b Bustin' Dustin 2.50 6.00
❑ 17a Bruised Lee 2.50 6.00
❑ 17b Karate Kate 2.50 6.00
❑ 18a Beaky Becky 2.50 6.00
❑ 18b Picky Mickey 2.50 6.00
❑ 19a Eerie Eric 2.50 6.00
❑ 19b Berserk Kirk 2.50 6.00
❑ 20a Babbling Brooke 2.50 6.00
❑ 20b Jelly Kelly 2.50 6.00
❑ 21a Apply Cory 2.50 6.00
❑ 21b Dwight Bite 2.50 6.00
❑ 22a Second Hand Rose 2.50 6.00
❑ 22b Trashed Tracy 2.50 6.00
❑ 23a Bony Tony 2.50 6.00
❑ 23b Unzipped Zack 2.50 6.00
❑ 24a Amazin' Grace 2.50 6.00
❑ 24b Muscular Molly 2.50 6.00
❑ 25a Hairy Harriet 2.50 6.00
❑ 25b Bushy Bernice 2.50 6.00
❑ 26a Warrin' Warren 2.50 6.00
❑ 26b Brett Vet 2.50 6.00
❑ 27a Yicchy Mickey 2.50 6.00
❑ 27b Barfin' Bart 2.50 6.00
❑ 28a Gored Gordon 2.50 6.00
❑ 28b No Way Jose 2.50 6.00
❑ 29a Dee Faced 2.50 6.00
❑ 29b Terri Cloth 2.50 6.00
❑ 30a Sprayed Wade 2.50 6.00
❑ 30b Tagged Tad 2.50 6.00
❑ 31a Diaper Dan 2.50 6.00
❑ 31b Pinned Penny 2.50 6.00
❑ 32a Lucas Mucus 2.50 6.00
❑ 32b Dotty Dribble 2.50 6.00
❑ 33a Dangling Dolly 2.50 6.00
❑ 33b Surreal Neal 2.50 6.00
❑ 34a Michael Mutant 2.50 6.00
❑ 34b Zeke Freak 2.50 6.00
❑ 35a Deaf Geoff 2.50 6.00
❑ 35b Audio Augie 2.50 6.00
❑ 36a Intense Payne 2.50 6.00
❑ 36b First Ada 2.50 6.00
❑ 37a Tom Thumb 2.50 6.00
❑ 37b Bridget Digit 2.50 6.00
❑ 38a Joan Clone 2.50 6.00
❑ 38b Warty Ward 2.50 6.00
❑ 39a Ugly Hans 2.50 6.00
❑ 39b Jan Hand 2.50 6.00
❑ 40a John John 2.50 6.00
❑ 40b Flushing Floyd 2.50 6.00
❑ 41a Hector Collector 2.50 6.00
❑ 41b G.P. Kay 2.50 6.00
❑ 42a Many Lenny 2.50 6.00
❑ 42b Lotta Carlotta 2.50 6.00
❑ 43a Mickey Mouths 2.50 6.00
❑ 43b Oral Laurel 2.50 6.00
❑ 44a Adam Boom 20.00 40.00
❑ 44b Blasted Billy II 10.00 20.00
❑ 45a Pete Seat 2.50 6.00
❑ 45b Noel Bowl 2.50 6.00
❑ 46a Elastic Elwood 2.50 6.00
❑ 46b Fletcher Stretcher 2.50 6.00
❑ 47a Shut-Up Sherwin 2.50 6.00
❑ 47b Filled Up Philip 2.50 6.00
❑ 48a Alien Alan 2.50 6.00
❑ 48b Martian Marcia 2.50 6.00
❑ 49a Haley Comet 2.50 6.00
❑ 49b June Moon 2.50 6.00
❑ 50a Explorin' Norman 2.50 6.00
❑ 50b Drillin' Dylan 2.50 6.00
❑ 51a Divin' Ivan 2.50 6.00
❑ 51b Walter Sport 2.50 6.00
❑ 52a Fritz Spritz 2.50 6.00
❑ 52b Ella P. Record 2.50 6.00
❑ 53a Messy Bessie 2.50 6.00
❑ 53b Unclean Helene 2.50 6.00
❑ 54a Lem Phlegm 2.50 6.00
❑ 54b Gezundt Heidi 2.50 6.00
❑ 55a Page Cage 2.50 6.00
❑ 55b Tommy Ache 2.50 6.00
❑ 56a Ortho Donny 2.50 6.00
❑ 56b Ruth Canal 2.50 6.00
❑ 57a Cute Tippi 2.50 6.00
❑ 57b Waxy Wendy 2.50 6.00
❑ 58a Early Bert 2.50 6.00
❑ 58b Rotten Robin 2.50 6.00
❑ 59a Snot Rope Hope 2.50 6.00
❑ 59b Drippy Debbie 2.50 6.00
❑ 60a Con Vic 2.50 6.00
❑ 60b Al Catraz 2.50 6.00
❑ 61a Clark Shark 2.50 6.00
❑ 61b Manny Eater 2.50 6.00
❑ 62a Beasty Boyd 2.50 6.00
❑ 62b Semi Colin 2.50 6.00
❑ 63a 3-Dee 2.50 6.00
❑ 63b Blurry Blair 2.50 6.00
❑ 64a Dent Al 2.50 6.00
❑ 64b Fluoride Ida 2.50 6.00
❑ 65a Scalped Ralph 2.50 6.00
❑ 65b Bone-Head Fred. 2.50 6.00
❑ 66a Slammed Sloan 2.50 6.00
❑ 66b Keith Out 2.50 6.00
❑ 67a Scrawled Saul 2.50 6.00
❑ 67b Bad Art 2.50 6.00
❑ 68a Noah Parking 2.50 6.00
❑ 68b Peter Meter 2.50 6.00
❑ 69a Dead Flora 2.50 6.00
❑ 69b Fetid Fern 2.50 6.00
❑ 70a Idol Ira 2.50 6.00
❑ 70b Ken Tiki 2.50 6.00
❑ 71a Potty Scotty 2.50 6.00
❑ 71b Jason Basin 2.50 6.00
❑ 72a Ghastly Ashley 2.50 6.00
❑ 72b Acne Amy 2.50 6.00
❑ 73a Jolly Roger 2.50 6.00
❑ 73b Pegleg Peter 2.50 6.00
❑ 74a Greaser Greg 2.50 6.00
❑ 74b Chris Hiss 2.50 6.00
❑ 75a Smelly Sally 2.50 6.00
❑ 75b Fishy Phyllis 2.50 6.00
❑ 76a New Wave Dave 2.50 6.00
❑ 76b Graffiti Petey 2.50 6.00
❑ 77a Ultra Violet 2.50 6.00
❑ 77b Tanya Hide 2.50 6.00
❑ 78a Barfin' Barbara 2.50 6.00
❑ 78b Valerie Vomit 2.50 6.00
❑ 79a Wacky Jackie 2.50 6.00
❑ 79b Loony Lenny 2.50 6.00
❑ 80a Half-Nelson 2.50 6.00
❑ 80b Glandular Angela 2.50 6.00

2011 Garbage Pail Kids Flashback Series Two Gold

COMPLETE SET (160)
*GOLD: 40X TO 100X BASIC CARDS
STATED ODDS 1:62

❑ 1a Junkfood John 15.00 40.00
❑ 1b Ray Decay 15.00 40.00
❑ 2a Stormy Heather 15.00 40.00
❑ 2b April Showers 15.00 40.00
❑ 3a Weird Wendy 15.00 40.00
❑ 3b Haggy Maggie 15.00 40.00
❑ 4a Cranky Frankie 15.00 40.00
❑ 4b Bad Brad 15.00 40.00
❑ 5a Creepy Carol 15.00 40.00
❑ 5b Scary Carrie 15.00 40.00
❑ 6a Kim Kong 15.00 40.00
❑ 6b Anna Banana 15.00 40.00
❑ 7a Wrappin' Ruth 15.00 40.00
❑ 7b Tommy Tomb 15.00 40.00
❑ 8a Patty Putty 15.00 40.00
❑ 8b Muggin' Megan 15.00 40.00
❑ 9a Smelly Kelly 15.00 40.00
❑ 9b Doug Plug 15.00 40.00
❑ 10a Leaky Lindsay 15.00 40.00
❑ 10b Messy Tessie 15.00 40.00
❑ 11a Mad Donna 15.00 40.00
❑ 11b Nutty Nicole 15.00 40.00
❑ 12a Jolted Joel 15.00 40.00
❑ 12b Live Mike 15.00 40.00
❑ 13a Jolly Roger 15.00 40.00
❑ 13b Pegleg Peter 15.00 40.00
❑ 14a Sewer Sue 15.00 40.00
❑ 14b Michelle Muck 15.00 40.00
❑ 15a Hurt Curt 15.00 40.00
❑ 15b Pat Splat 15.00 40.00
❑ 16a Drew Blood 15.00 40.00
❑ 16b Bustin' Dustin 15.00 40.00
❑ 17a Bruised Lee 15.00 40.00
❑ 17b Karate Kate 15.00 40.00
❑ 18a Beaky Becky 15.00 40.00
❑ 18b Picky Mickey 15.00 40.00
❑ 19a Eerie Eric 15.00 40.00
❑ 19b Berserk Kirk 15.00 40.00
❑ 20a Babbling Brooke 15.00 40.00
❑ 20b Jelly Kelly 15.00 40.00
❑ 21a Apply Cory 15.00 40.00
❑ 21b Dwight Bite 15.00 40.00
❑ 22a Second Hand Rose 15.00 40.00
❑ 22b Trashed Tracy 15.00 40.00
❑ 23a Bony Tony 15.00 40.00
❑ 23b Unzipped Zack 15.00 40.00
❑ 24a Amazin' Grace 15.00 40.00
❑ 24b Muscular Molly 15.00 40.00
❑ 25a Hairy Harriet 15.00 40.00
❑ 25b Bushy Bernice 15.00 40.00
❑ 26a Warrin' Warren 15.00 40.00
❑ 26b Brett Vet 15.00 40.00
❑ 27a Yicchy Mickey 15.00 40.00
❑ 27b Barfin' Bart 15.00 40.00
❑ 28a Gored Gordon 15.00 40.00
❑ 28b No Way Jose 15.00 40.00
❑ 29a Dee Faced 15.00 40.00
❑ 29b Terri Cloth 15.00 40.00
❑ 30a Sprayed Wade 15.00 40.00
❑ 30b Tagged Tad 15.00 40.00
❑ 31a Diaper Dan 15.00 40.00
❑ 31b Pinned Penny 15.00 40.00
❑ 32a Lucas Mucus 15.00 40.00
❑ 32b Dotty Dribble 15.00 40.00
❑ 33a Dangling Dolly 15.00 40.00
❑ 33b Surreal Neal 15.00 40.00
❑ 34a Michael Mutant 15.00 40.00
❑ 34b Zeke Freak 15.00 40.00
❑ 35a Deaf Geoff 15.00 40.00
❑ 35b Audio Augie 15.00 40.00
❑ 36a Intense Payne 15.00 40.00
❑ 36b First Ada 15.00 40.00
❑ 37a Tom Thumb 15.00 40.00
❑ 37b Bridget Digit 15.00 40.00
❑ 38a Joan Clone 15.00 40.00
❑ 38b Warty Ward 15.00 40.00
❑ 39a Ugly Hans 15.00 40.00
❑ 39b Jan Hand 15.00 40.00
❑ 40a John John 15.00 40.00
❑ 40b Flushing Floyd 15.00 40.00
❑ 41a Hector Collector 15.00 40.00
❑ 41b G.P. Kay 15.00 40.00
❑ 42a Many Lenny 15.00 40.00
❑ 42b Lotta Carlotta 15.00 40.00
❑ 43a Mickey Mouths 15.00 40.00
❑ 43b Oral Laurel 15.00 40.00
❑ 44a Adam Boom 100.00 150.00
❑ 44b Blasted Billy II 30.00 60.00
❑ 45a Pete Seat 15.00 40.00
❑ 45b Noel Bowl 15.00 40.00
❑ 46a Elastic Elwood 15.00 40.00
❑ 46b Fletcher Stretcher 15.00 40.00
❑ 47a Shut-Up Sherwin 15.00 40.00
❑ 47b Filled Up Philip 15.00 40.00
❑ 48a Alien Alan 15.00 40.00
❑ 48b Martian Marcia 15.00 40.00
❑ 49a Haley Comet 15.00 40.00
❑ 49b June Moon 15.00 40.00
❑ 50a Explorin' Norman 15.00 40.00
❑ 50b Drillin' Dylan 15.00 40.00
❑ 51a Divin' Ivan 15.00 40.00
❑ 51b Walter Sport 15.00 40.00
❑ 52a Fritz Spritz 15.00 40.00
❑ 52b Ella P. Record 15.00 40.00
❑ 53a Messy Bessie 15.00 40.00
❑ 53b Unclean Helene 15.00 40.00
❑ 54a Lem Phlegm 15.00 40.00
❑ 54b Gezundt Heidi 15.00 40.00
❑ 55a Page Cage 15.00 40.00
❑ 55b Tommy Ache 15.00 40.00
❑ 56a Ortho Donny 15.00 40.00
❑ 56b Ruth Canal 15.00 40.00
❑ 57a Cute Tippi 15.00 40.00
❑ 57b Waxy Wendy 15.00 40.00
❑ 58a Early Bert 15.00 40.00
❑ 58b Rotten Robin 15.00 40.00
❑ 59a Snot Rope Hope 15.00 40.00
❑ 59b Drippy Debbie 15.00 40.00
❑ 60a Con Vic 15.00 40.00
❑ 60b Al Catraz 15.00 40.00
❑ 61a Clark Shark 15.00 40.00
❑ 61b Manny Eater 15.00 40.00
❑ 62a Beasty Boyd 15.00 40.00
❑ 62b Semi Colin 15.00 40.00
❑ 63a 3-Dee 15.00 40.00
❑ 63b Blurry Blair 15.00 40.00
❑ 64a Dent Al 15.00 40.00
❑ 64b Fluoride Ida 15.00 40.00
❑ 65a Scalped Ralph 15.00 40.00
❑ 65b Bone-Head Fred 15.00 40.00
❑ 66a Slammed Sloan 15.00 40.00
❑ 66b Keith Out 15.00 40.00
❑ 67a Scrawled Saul 15.00 40.00
❑ 67b Bad Art 15.00 40.00
❑ 68a Noah Parking 15.00 40.00
❑ 68b Peter Meter 15.00 40.00
❑ 69a Dead Flora 15.00 40.00
❑ 69b Fetid Fern 15.00 40.00
❑ 70a Idol Ira 15.00 40.00
❑ 70b Ken Tiki 15.00 40.00
❑ 71a Potty Scotty 15.00 40.00
❑ 71b Jason Basin 15.00 40.00
❑ 72a Ghastly Ashley 15.00 40.00
❑ 72b Acne Amy 15.00 40.00
❑ 73a Jolly Roger 15.00 40.00
❑ 73b Pegleg Peter 15.00 40.00
❑ 74a Greaser Greg 15.00 40.00
❑ 74b Chris Hiss 15.00 40.00
❑ 75a Smelly Sally 15.00 40.00
❑ 75b Fishy Phyllis 15.00 40.00
❑ 76a New Wave Dave 15.00 40.00
❑ 76b Graffiti Petey 15.00 40.00
❑ 77a Ultra Violet 15.00 40.00
❑ 77b Tanya Hide 15.00 40.00
❑ 78a Barfin' Barbara 15.00 40.00
❑ 78b Valerie Vomit 15.00 40.00
❑ 79a Wacky Jackie 15.00 40.00
❑ 79b Loony Lenny 15.00 40.00
❑ 80a Half-Nelson 15.00 40.00
❑ 80b Glandular Angela 15.00 40.00

2011 Garbage Pail Kids Flashback Series Two 3D

COMPLETE SET (5) 10.00 25.00
STATED ODDS 1:12
SP STATED ODDS 1:85

❑ 3D1 Dead Ted 3.00 8.00
❑ 3D2 Snotty Dotty 3.00 8.00
❑ 3D3 Impaled Gail 3.00 8.00
❑ 3D4 Alien Ian 3.00 8.00
❑ 3D5 Adam Bomb SP 6.00 15.00

2011 Garbage Pail Kids Flashback Series Two Adam Mania

COMPLETE SET (10) 12.00 30.00
STATED ODDS 1:8

❑ 1 Adam Bomb - Oil 2.50 6.00
❑ 2 Adam Bomb - Milk 2.50 6.00
❑ 3 Adam Bomb - Bubblegum 2.50 6.00
❑ 4 Adam Bomb - Texting 2.50 6.00

- 5 Adam Bomb - Bats 2.50 6.00
- 6 Adam Bomb - Coffee 2.50 6.00
- 7 Adam Bomb - Bed Bugs 2.50 6.00
- 8 Adam Bomb - Zombies 2.50 6.00
- 9 Adam Bomb - Mentos and Cola 2.50 6.00
- 10 Adam Bomb - GPK Cards 2.50 6.00

2011 Garbage Pail Kids Flashback Series Two Adam Mania Green

COMPLETE SET (10) 20.00 40.00
*GREEN: .5X TO 1.2X BASIC CARDS
STATED ODDS 1:24

- 1 Adam Bomb - Oil 3.00 8.00
- 2 Adam Bomb - Milk 3.00 8.00
- 3 Adam Bomb - Bubblegum 3.00 8.00
- 4 Adam Bomb - Texting 3.00 8.00
- 5 Adam Bomb - Bats 3.00 8.00
- 6 Adam Bomb - Coffee 3.00 8.00
- 7 Adam Bomb - Bed Bugs 3.00 8.00
- 8 Adam Bomb - Zombies 3.00 8.00
- 9 Adam Bomb - Mentos and Cola 3.00 8.00
- 10 Adam Bomb - GPK Cards 3.00 8.00

2011 Garbage Pail Kids Flashback Series Two Adam Mania Pink

COMPLETE SET (10) 30.00 60.00
*PINK: .8X TO 2X BASIC CARDS
STATED ODDS 1:48

- 1 Adam Bomb - Oil 5.00 12.00
- 2 Adam Bomb - Milk 5.00 12.00
- 3 Adam Bomb - Bubblegum 5.00 12.00
- 4 Adam Bomb - Texting 5.00 12.00
- 5 Adam Bomb - Bats 5.00 12.00
- 6 Adam Bomb - Coffee 5.00 12.00
- 7 Adam Bomb - Bed Bugs 5.00 12.00
- 8 Adam Bomb - Zombies 5.00 12.00
- 9 Adam Bomb - Mentos and Cola 5.00 12.00
- 10 Adam Bomb - GPK Cards 5.00 12.00

2011 Garbage Pail Kids Flashback Series Two Adam Mania Silver

*SILVER: 1.5X TO 4X BASIC CARDS
STATED ODDS 1:96

- 1 Adam Bomb - Oil 10.00 25.00
- 2 Adam Bomb - Milk 10.00 25.00
- 3 Adam Bomb - Bubblegum 10.00 25.00
- 4 Adam Bomb - Texting 10.00 25.00
- 5 Adam Bomb - Bats 10.00 25.00
- 6 Adam Bomb - Coffee 10.00 25.00
- 7 Adam Bomb - Bed Bugs 10.00 25.00
- 8 Adam Bomb - Zombies 10.00 25.00
- 9 Adam Bomb - Mentos and Cola 10.00 25.00
- 10 Adam Bomb - GPK Cards 10.00 25.00

2011 Garbage Pail Kids Flashback Series Two Adam Mania Gold

STATED ODDS 1:993

- 1 Adam Bomb - Oil 100.00 200.00
- 2 Adam Bomb - Milk 100.00 200.00
- 3 Adam Bomb - Bubblegum 100.00 200.00
- 4 Adam Bomb - Texting 100.00 200.00
- 5 Adam Bomb - Bats 100.00 200.00
- 6 Adam Bomb - Coffee 100.00 200.00
- 7 Adam Bomb - Bed Bugs 100.00 200.00
- 8 Adam Bomb - Zombies 100.00 200.00
- 9 Adam Bomb - Mentos and Cola 100.00 200.00
- 10 Adam Bomb - GPK Cards 100.00 200.00

2011 Garbage Pail Kids Flashback Series Two Die-Cut Sketches

OVERALL SKETCH ODDS 1:469

- S1 Tom Haubrick 50.00 100.00
- S2 Ken Garduno
- S3 Misha 40.00 80.00
- S4 Keith Noordzy 25.00 50.00
- S5 Irma Rivera

2011 Garbage Pail Kids Flashback Series Two Posters

COMPLETE SET (5) 10.00 25.00
STATED ODDS ONE PER RACK PACK

- 1 Adam Bomb 4.00 10.00
- 2 Bony Tony 3.00 8.00
- 3 Explorin Norman 3.00 8.00
- 4 Leaky Lindsay 3.00 8.00
- 5 Michael Mutant 3.00 8.00

2011 Garbage Pail Kids Flashback Series Two Retail Bonus

COMPLETE SET (4) 8.00 20.00
B1-B3 STATED ODDS ONE PER BLISTER PACK
B4 STATED ODDS ONE PER BLASTER BOX

- B1 Locked Dorian 3.00 8.00
- B2 Vermin Herman 3.00 8.00
- B3 Facey Tracie 3.00 8.00
- B4 Cleaned Up Clint 4.00 10.00

2011 Garbage Pail Kids Flashback Series Two Sketches

OVERALL SKETCH ODDS 1:469

- A1 Tom Bunk 60.00 120.00
- A2 Neil Camera 75.00 150.00
- A3 Layron DeJarnette 50.00 100.00
- A4 Brent Engstrom 100.00 200.00
- A5 Mark Pingitore 50.00 100.00
- A6 Joe Simko 60.00 120.00
- A7 Colin Walton 60.00 120.00
- A8 Fred Wheaton 50.00 100.00
- A9 Jeff Zapata 60.00 120.00

2011 Garbage Pail Kids Flashback Series Three

COMPLETE SET (160) 12.00 30.00
S1 STATED ODDS 1:7,700

- 1a Up Chuck .15 .40
- 1b Heavin' Steven .15 .40
- 2a Fryin' Brian .15 .40
- 2b Electric Bill .15 .40
- 3a Boozin' Bruce .15 .40
- 3b Drunk Ken .15 .40
- 4a Wacky Jackie .15 .40
- 4b Loony Lenny .15 .40
- 5a Buggy Betty .15 .40
- 5b Green Jean .15 .40
- 6a Mean Gene .15 .40
- 6b Joltin' Joe .15 .40
- 7a Disgustin' Justin .15 .40
- 7b Vile Kyle .15 .40
- 8a Fryin' Ryan .15 .40
- 8b Charred Chad .15 .40
- 9a Tommy Gun .15 .40
- 9b Dead Fred .15 .40
- 10a Clogged Duane .15 .40
- 10b Bye Bye Bobby .15 .40
- 11a Greaser Greg .15 .40
- 11b Chris Hiss .15 .40
- 12a Gorgeous George .15 .40
- 12b Dollar Bill .15 .40
- 13a Juicy Jessica .15 .40
- 13b Green Dean .15 .40
- 14a Smelly Sally .15 .40
- 14b Fishy Phyllis .15 .40
- 15a Snooty Sam .15 .40
- 15b U.S. Arnie .15 .40
- 16a Alice Island .15 .40
- 16b Liberty Libby .15 .40
- 17a Broad Maud .15 .40
- 17b Large Marge .15 .40
- 18a Hugh Mungous .15 .40
- 18b King-Size Kevin .15 .40
- 19a Ashley Can .15 .40
- 19b Greta Garbage .15 .40
- 20a Dale Snail .15 .40
- 20b Crushed Shelly .15 .40
- 21a Whisperin' Woody .15 .40
- 21b Van Triloquist .15 .40
- 22a Shorned Sean .15 .40
- 22b Hy Gene .15 .40
- 23a Richie Retch .15 .40
- 23b Luke Puke .15 .40
- 24a Willie Wipe-Out .15 .40
- 24b Spencer Dispenser .15 .40
- 25a Doughy Joey .15 .40
- 25b Starchy Archie .15 .40
- 26a Ultra Violet .15 .40
- 26b Tanya Hide .15 .40
- 27a See More Seymour .15 .40
- 27b Coy Roy .15 .40
- 28a Otto Whack .15 .40
- 28b Elliot Mess .15 .40
- 29a Monte Zuma .15 .40
- 29b Pagan Megan .15 .40
- 30a Newly-Dead Ed .15 .40
- 30b Dyna Mike .15 .40
- 31a Barfin' Barbara .15 .40
- 31b Valerie Vomit .15 .40
- 32a Gooey Huey .15 .40
- 32b Bobbi Booger .15 .40
- 33a Vincent Van Gone .15 .40
- 33b Modern Art .15 .40
- 34a Short Mort .15 .40
- 34b Noah Body .15 .40
- 35a Bloody Mary .15 .40
- 35b Donna Donor .15 .40
- 36a Buck Puck .15 .40
- 36b Lowell Goal .15 .40
- 37a Pumping Aaron .15 .40
- 37b Will Explode .15 .40
- 38a Squashed Josh .15 .40
- 38b Squoze Rose .15 .40
- 39a Cyril Bowl .15 .40
- 39b Soggy Oggie .15 .40
- 40a Misty Suds .15 .40
- 40b Amelia Airhead .15 .40
- 41a Bazooka Joanne .15 .40
- 41b Bubbly Babs .15 .40
- 42a Trap Dora .15 .40
- 42b Rear View Myra .15 .40
- 43a Ground Chuck .15 .40
- 43b Lean Jean .15 .40
- 44a Cracked Sheldon .15 .40
- 44b Wally Walnut .15 .40
- 45a Barnyard Barney .15 .40
- 45b Dick Hick .15 .40
- 46a Shootin' Newton .15 .40
- 46b Sherman Tank .15 .40
- 47a Ripped Fletch .15 .40
- 47b Taped Tate .15 .40
- 48a Ike Spike .15 .40
- 48b Mason Mace .15 .40
- 49a Impaled Gail .15 .40
- 49b Magic Wanda .15 .40
- 50a Sally Suction .15 .40
- 50b Teethin' Trina .15 .40
- 51a Ball 'n Shane .15 .40
- 51b Hard Rocky .15 .40
- 52a Upset Tommy .15 .40
- 52b Tub o' Lars .15 .40
- 53a Chiseler Chad .15 .40
- 53b Julius Sneezer .15 .40
- 54a Dead Letter Debbie .15 .40
- 54b Maimed Mamie .15 .40
- 55a Seymour Barf .15 .40
- 55b Kent Stand It .15 .40
- 56a Barfin' Marvin .15 .40
- 56b Over Elan .15 .40
- 57a Fun Gus .15 .40
- 57b Warty Morty .15 .40
- 58a Howie Hanging .15 .40
- 58b Rush Hour Russ .15 .40
- 59a Rocco Socko .15 .40
- 59b Destroyed Boyd .15 .40
- 60a Doomsday Dom .15 .40
- 60b A-Bomb Tom .15 .40
- 61a Dial-a-Twyla .15 .40
- 61b Phone Bella .15 .40
- 62a Burnt-Out Brett .15 .40
- 62b Burne Toast .15 .40
- 63a Take-Out Dinah .15 .40
- 63b Chow Mame .15 .40
- 64a Slimy Hymie .15 .40
- 64b Crawlin' Rollin .15 .40
- 65a Picky Nick .15 .40
- 65b Beulah Ghoul .15 .40
- 66a Claude Flesh .15 .40
- 66b Slasher Asher .15 .40
- 67a Prickly Pete .15 .40
- 67b Thorny Barb .15 .40
- 68a Arach Ned .15 .40
- 68b Web Jeb .15 .40
- 69a Shadowy Sheila .15 .40
- 69b Vaporized Val .15 .40
- 70a Dunkin' Duncan .15 .40
- 70b Will Hung .15 .40
- 71a Stormy Heather .15 .40
- 71b April Showers .15 .40
- 72a Jolted Joel .15 .40
- 72b Live Mike .15 .40
- 73a Phony Lisa .15 .40
- 73b Mona Loser .15 .40
- 74a Bony Tony .15 .40
- 74b Unzipped Zack .15 .40
- 75a Alien Ian .15 .40
- 75b Outerspace Chase .15 .40
- 76a Jack O. Lantern .15 .40
- 76b Duncan Pumpkin .15 .40
- 77a Toothie Ruthie .15 .40
- 77b Dental Flossie .15 .40
- 78a Chris Mess .15 .40
- 78b Sandy Clod .15 .40
- 79a Scalped Ralph .15 .40
- 79b Bone-Head Fred .15 .40
- 80a Bern-Out .15 .40
- 80b Dim-Bulb Bob .15 .40
- S1 Adam Bomb - John Pound AUTO 350.00 700.00

2011 Garbage Pail Kids Flashback Series Three Green

COMPLETE SET (160) 25.00 60.00
*GREEN: .8X TO 2X BASIC CARDS
STATED ODDS 1:2

2011 Garbage Pail Kids Flashback Series Three Pink

COMPLETE SET (160) 60.00 120.00
*PINK: 1.5X TO 4X BASIC CARDS
STATED ODDS 1:3

2011 Garbage Pail Kids Flashback Series Three Silver

*SILVER: 6X TO 15X BASIC CARDS
STATED ODDS 1:6

2011 Garbage Pail Kids Flashback Series Three Gold

*GOLD: 40X TO 100X BASIC CARDS
STATED ODDS 1:62

2011 Garbage Pail Kids Flashback Series Three 3D

COMPLETE SET (5) 10.00 25.00
STATED ODDS 1:12
SP STATED ODDS 1:85

- 3D1 Sy Clops 3.00 8.00
- 3D2 Gored Gordon 3.00 8.00
- 3D3 Tiny Tim 3.00 8.00
- 3D4 Con Vic 3.00 8.00
- 3D5 Adam Boom SP 6.00 15.00

2011 Garbage Pail Kids Flashback Series Three Adam Mania

COMPLETE SET (10) 12.00 30.00
STATED ODDS 1:8

- 1 Adam Bomb - Space Shuttle 2.50 6.00
- 2 Adam Bomb - Singer 2.50 6.00
- 3 Adam Bomb - Jackpot 2.50 6.00
- 4 Adam Bomb - Mushroom 2.50 6.00
- 5 Adam Bomb - Fireworks 2.50 6.00
- 6 Adam Bomb - Bubbles 2.50 6.00
- 7 Adam Bomb - Tornado 2.50 6.00
- 8 Adam Bomb - Hobos 2.50 6.00
- 9 Adam Bomb - Muscular System 2.50 6.00
- 10 Adam Bomb - Rainbows 2.50 6.00

2011 Garbage Pail Kids Flashback Series Three Adam Mania Green

COMPLETE SET (10) 15.00 40.00
*GREEN: .5X TO 1.2X BASIC CARDS
STATED ODDS 1:24

2011 Garbage Pail Kids Flashback Series Three Adam Mania Pink

COMPLETE SET (10) 30.00 60.00
*PINK: .8X TO 2X BASIC CARDS
STATED ODDS 1:48

2011 Garbage Pail Kids Flashback Series Three Adam Mania Silver

COMPLETE SET (10)
*SILVER: 1.5X TO 4X BASIC CARDS
STATED ODDS 1:96

2011 Garbage Pail Kids Flashback Series Three Adam Mania Gold

*GOLD: 15X TO 30X BASIC CARDS
STATED ODDS 1:990

2011 Garbage Pail Kids Flashback Series Three Retail Bonus

COMPLETE SET (5)
B1-B3 STATED ODDS ONE PER BLISTER PACK

- B1 Phony Lisa 3.00 8.00
- B2 Jack O. Lantern 3.00 8.00
- B3 Toothie Ruthie 3.00 8.00
- B4 Chris Mess
- B5 Bern-Out

2011 Garbage Pail Kids Flashback Series Three Sketches

STATED ODDS 1:467

- A1 Tom Bunk 50.00 100.00
- A2 Neil Camera 60.00 120.00
- A3 Layron DeJarnett 50.00 100.00
- A4 Brent Engstrom 50.00 100.00
- A5 Mark Pingitore 50.00 100.00
- A6 Joe Simko 75.00 150.00
- A7 Colin Walton 50.00 100.00
- A8 Fred Wheaton 75.00 150.00
- A9 Jeff Zapata 50.00 100.00

2011 Harry Potter and the Deathly Hallows Part Two

COMPLETE SET (54) 6.00 15.00

- 1 Harry Potter and the Deathly Hallows - Part 2 .15 .40
- 2 Harry Potter .15 .40
- 3 Hermione Granger .15 .40
- 4 Ron Weasley .15 .40
- 5 Lord Voldemort .15 .40
- 6 Neville Longbottom .15 .40
- 7 Griphook .15 .40
- 8 Aberforth Dumbledore .15 .40
- 9 Bill Weasley .15 .40
- 10 Be Exceptionally Careful .15 .40
- 11 A Free Elf .15 .40
- 12 A Proper Burial .15 .40
- 13 Looking for Someone .15 .40
- 14 The Sky Has Lost a Star .15 .40
- 15 A Shocking Disguise .15 .40
- 16 I Missed a Spot .15 .40
- 17 Hold Still .15 .40
- 18 That Bit in the Back .15 .40
- 19 Waiting for Griphook .15 .40
- 20 Griphook's Distrust .15 .40
- 21 Dragomir Dispard .15 .40
- 22 Too Cheery for Bellatrix .15 .40
- 23 Entering Gringotts .15 .40
- 24 Staying in Character .15 .40
- 25 Hufflepuff's Cup .15 .40
- 26 Undesirable No. 1 .15 .40
- 27 Setting Off the Caterwauling Charm .15 .40
- 28 Dementors in Hogsmeade .15 .40
- 29 Inside the Hog's Head .15 .40
- 30 Examining the Mirror Shard .15 .40
- 31 The Matching Mirror .15 .40
- 32 Meeting Aberforth .15 .40
- 33 Neville .15 .40
- 34 Seamus is Worse .15 .40
- 35 Like Punishment, the Carrows .15 .40
- 36 A Surprise .15 .40
- 37 A Bit of a Security Problem .15 .40
- 38 Coward .15 .40
- 39 Searching for Harry .15 .40
- 40 The Place Where Everything is Hidden .15 .40
- 41 The Lost Diadem .15 .40
- 42 You Have Something of Mine .15 .40
- 43 Learning the Truth .15 .40
- 44 Snape's True Love .15 .40
- 45 Is He Dead .15 .40
- 46 Leaving the Great Hall .15 .40
- 47 Defending the Castle .15 .40
- 48 Evading Voldemort .15 .40
- 49 Harry in Battle .15 .40
- 50 Arthur, Ginny and George .15 .40
- 51 Not My Daughter .15 .40
- 52 Come on, Granny .15 .40
- 53 Destroying the Last Horcrux .15 .40
- 54 Checklist .15 .40

2011 Harry Potter and the Deathly Hallows Part Two Autographs

OVERALL AUTO ODDS ONE PER BOX

- 1 Arben Bajraktaraj 12.00 30.00
- 2 Bonnie Wright 30.00 60.00
- 3 Chris Rankin 12.00 30.00
- 4 Ciaran Hinds 250.00 400.00 (issued as 25-case incentive)
- 5 Dave Legeno 12.00 30.00 (issued as 2-case incentive)
- 6 David Bradley 15.00 40.00
- 7 Emma Watson 300.00 450.00
- 8 Georgina Leonidas 20.00 40.00
- 9 Graham Duff 25.00 50.00 (issued as 5-case incentive)
- 10 John Hurt 40.00 80.00
- 11 Maggie Smith 75.00 125.00
- 12 Matthew Lewis 15.00 40.00
- 13 Michael Gambon 40.00 80.00
- 14 Oliver Phelps 50.00 100.00 (issued as 10-case incentive)
- 15 Warwick Davis 20.00 40.00

2011 Harry Potter and the Deathly Hallows Part Two Box Toppers

COMPLETE SET (4) 10.00 25.00
STATED ODDS ONE PER BOX

- BT1 Harry Potter 4.00 10.00
- BT2 Hermione Granger 4.00 10.00
- BT3 Ron Weasley 4.00 10.00
- BT4 Narcissa Malfoy 4.00 10.00

2011 Harry Potter and the Deathly Hallows Part Two Clear

COMPLETE SET (9) 5.00 12.00

- BC1 Aberforth Dumbledore 1.00 2.50
- BC2 Harry Potter 1.00 2.50
- BC3 Mask 1.00 2.50 Bellatrix
- BC4 Neville Longbottom 1.00 2.50
- BC5 Harry Potter 1.00 2.50
- BC6 Harry Potter 1.00 2.50
- BC7 Harry 1.00 2.50 Voldemort
- BC8 Harry Potter Horcrux 1.00 2.50
- BC9 Harry 1.00 2.50 Hermione/Ron

2011 Harry Potter and the Deathly Hallows Part Two Crystal Case Toppers

COMPLETE SET (3) 40.00 80.00
STATED ODDS ONE PER CASE

- CT1 Dementor 20.00 40.00
- CT2 Dragon 20.00 40.00
- CT3 Death Eater 20.00 40.00

2011 Harry Potter and the Deathly Hallows Part Two FilmCards

STATED PRINT RUN 213-214

- CFC1 Ron 15.00 30.00 Hermione
- CFC2 Hermione 15.00 30.00 Ron
- CFC3 Harry Potter 15.00 30.00
- CFC4 Hermione 15.00 30.00 Death Eather/Ron
- CFC5 Aberforth Dumbledore 15.00 30.00
- CFC6 Narcissa Malfoy 15.00 30.00
- CFC7 Bellatrix Lestrange 15.00 30.00
- CFC8 Harry Potter 15.00 30.00
- CFC9 Harry Potter 15.00 30.00
- CFC10 Castle Guard 15.00 30.00
- CFC11 Soldiers 15.00 30.00
- CFC12 Severus Snape 15.00 30.00
- CFC13 Lord Voldemort 15.00 30.00
- CFC14 Draco Malfoy 15.00 30.00
- CFC15 Harry Potter 15.00 30.00
- CFC16 Ginny Weasley 15.00 30.00
- CFC17 Ron Weasley 15.00 30.00
- CFC18 Narcissa Malfoy 15.00 30.00

2011 Harry Potter and the Deathly Hallows Part Two Foil

COMPLETE SET (9) 3.00 8.00

- R1 Dobby .75 2.00
- R2 Hogwarts Express .75 2.00
- R3 Remus .75 2.00 Nymphadora
- R4 Bellatrix Lestrange .75 2.00
- R5 Draco Malfoy .75 2.00
- R6 Severus Snape .75 2.00
- R7 Lord Voldemort .75 2.00
- R8 Harry Potter .75 2.00
- R9 Ron Weasley .75 2.00

2011 Harry Potter and the Deathly Hallows Part Two Puzzle

COMPLETE SET (9) 3.00 8.00

- BP1 Top Right .75 2.00
- BP2 Top Center .75 2.00
- BP3 Top Left .75 2.00
- BP4 Middle Right .75 2.00
- BP5 Middle Center .75 2.00
- BP6 Middle Left .75 2.00
- BP7 Bottom Right .75 2.00
- BP8 Bottom Center .75 2.00
- BP9 Bottom Left .75 2.00

2011 Harry Potter and the Deathly Hallows Part Two Puzzle Autographs

OVERALL AUTO ODDS ONE PER BOX

- PA1 Jon Key 15.00 30.00
- PA2 Jon Campling 15.00 30.00
- PA3 Jamie Campbell 20.00 40.00
- PA4 Toby Regbo 20.00 40.00
- PA5 Rusty Goffe 15.00 30.00
- PA6 Luke Newberry 20.00 40.00
- PA7 Pauline Stone 15.00 30.00
- PA8 Adrian Rawlins 15.00 30.00
- PA9 Michelle Fairley 15.00 30.00

2011 Horrors of War

COMPLETE SET (48)
ANNOUNCED PRINT RUN 40

- 1 The Third Reich
- 2 Hitler Visits Mussolini
- 3 Auschwitz
- 4 France Surrenders
- 5 London Bombed
- 6 Rommel, The Desert Fox
- 7 Pearl Harbor
- 8 Tuskegee Airmen
- 9 Bataan Death March
- 10 Doolittle's Raid on Tokyo
- 11 Mountbatten
- 12 Dieppe
- 13 PT-109
- 14 Beach at Buna
- 15 First Raids on Japan
- 16 Normandy
- 17 D-Day
- 18 Battle of the Bulge
- 19 Iwo Jima
- 20 Russian Flag over the Reichstag
- 21 Germany Surrenders
- 22 Celebration in Times Square
- 23 Potsdam Conference
- 24 Crew of the Enola Gay
- 25 Atomic Bomb
- 26 38th Parallel
- 27 American Casualty
- 28 Battle of Inchon
- 29 Flamethrowers
- 30 Buddhist Monk burning in Vietnam
- 31 LBJ Visits Vietnam
- 32 Execution of a Viet Cong Guerilla
- 33 My Lai Massacre
- 34 Hamburger Hill
- 35 Burning Fields
- 36 Kent State Massacre
- 37 Kim Phuc
- 38 Multinational Coalition
- 39 Burning Oil Fields
- 40 Highway of Death
- 41 Prisoners of the Iraq War
- 42 Hussein's Statue Falls
- 43 Saddam Hussein Captured
- 44 Osama Bin Laden
- 45 World Trade Center
- 46 New Yorkers in the Streets
- 47 The Pentagon
- 48 Obama Announces Bin Laden's Death

2011 Horrors of War Cut Signatures

ANNOUNCED PRINT RUN 1
UNPRICED DUE TO SCARCITY

- 1 A.J. Tony Denman (World War II)
- 2 Abie Abraham (World War II)
- 3 Abner Doubleday (Civil War)
- 4 Abner M. Aust (World War II)
- 5 Ace Parker (World War II)
- 6 Achim Wunderlich (World War II)
- 7 Adna Chaffee (Civil War)
- 8 Adolf Hitler (World War II)
- 9 Adolfo Celaya (World War II)
- 10 Adolphe Menjou (World War II)
- 11 Aeneas Ranald MacDonnell (World War II)
- 12 Agapito Silva (World War II)
- 13 Aharon Remez (World War II)
- 14 Ahrend Hoper (World War II)
- 15 Alan Charles Rawlinson (World War II)
- 16 Alan Deere (World War II)
- 17 Alan Peart (World War II)
- 18 Alan S. Boyd (World War II)
- 19 Albert C. Wedemeyer (World War II)
- 20 Albert Kerscher (World War II)
- 21 Albert S. Berry (Civil War)
- 22 Albert S. Crossfield (World War II)
- 23 Albert Wells (World War II)
- 24 Albert Witte (World War II)

❑ 25 Alberto Martin-Artajo (Spanish Civil War)
❑ 26 Alden Rigby (World War II)
❑ 27 Alex Vraciu (World War II)
❑ 28 Alexander Macomb (War of 1812)
❑ 29 Alexander McCook (Civil War)
❑ 30 Alexander Raab (World War II)
❑ 31 Alexander Stewart (Civil War)
❑ 32 Alf Larson (World War II)
❑ 33 Alfred Ambs (World War II)
❑ 34 Alfred Bjornstad (World War I)
❑ 35 Alfred Eick (World War II)
❑ 36 Alfred Gruenther (World War II)
❑ 37 Alfred Hille (World War II)
❑ 38 Alfred Rascon (Vietnam)
❑ 39 Alfred Rubbel (World War II)
❑ 40 Alfredo Sanchez Bella (Spanish Civil War)
❑ 41 Allan Kellogg (Vietnam)
❑ 42 Allan Scott (World War II)
❑ 43 Allan Smith (World War II)
❑ 44 Allen Gullion (World War I)
❑ 45 Allen Lynch (Vietnam)
❑ 46 Allen Visscher Reed (Civil War)
❑ 47 Alleta Sullivan (World War II)
❑ 48 Alois Schnaubelt (World War II)
❑ 49 Alton Knappenberger (World War II)
❑ 50 Alvan Cullem Gillem (Civil War)
❑ 51 Alvaro Rodrigues de Vasconcellos (World War II)
❑ 52 Amedee Passmard (World War II)
❑ 53 Anatoly Kozlov (World War II)
❑ 54 Andrew Goodpaster (World War II)
❑ 55 Andrew Weir, 1st Baron Inverforth (World War I)
❑ 56 Ann E. Dunwoody (Gulf War)
❑ 57 Anthony McAuliffe (World War II)
❑ 58 Anthony Zinni (Vietnam)
❑ 59 Anton Heinemann (World War II)
❑ 60 Anton Müller (World War II)
❑ 61 Anton Wehinger (World War II)
❑ 62 Archibald Philip Hope (World War II)
❑ 63 Archie Donahue (World War II)
❑ 64 Arleigh A. Burke (World War II)
❑ 65 Armistead B. Chick Smith (World War II)
❑ 66 Arnold Doring (World War II)
❑ 67 Art Hedstrom (World War II)
❑ 68 Artemus L. Gates (World War I)
❑ 69 Arthur C. Fiedler (Vietnam)
❑ 70 Arthur C. Fiedler (World War II)
❑ 71 Arthur E. Percival (World War II)
❑ 72 Arthur Hall (World War II)
❑ 73 Arthur Jackson (World War II)
❑ 74 Arthur Jeffrey (World War II)
❑ 75 Arthur Johnson (World War II)
❑ 76 Arthur Leenerman (World War II)
❑ 77 Arthur Saunders (World War II)
❑ 78 Arthur Spurgin (World War II)
❑ 79 Arthur Szyk (World War I)
❑ 80 Arthur Tedder (World War I)
❑ 81 Arthur Treacher (World War I)
❑ 82 Artur Becker (World War II)
❑ 83 Artur Pipan (World War II)
❑ 84 Asa Bird Gardiner (Civil War)
❑ 85 Asa P. Blunt (Civil War)
❑ 86 Audie Murphy (World War II)
❑ 87 B. Everett Jordan (World War I)
❑ 88 B.R. Cowen (Civil War)
❑ 89 Barney Hajiro (World War II)
❑ 90 Barney Ross (World War II)
❑ 91 Baron Auckland Geddes (World War I)
❑ 92 Baron John Jacques (World War I)
❑ 93 Baron Rennell Rodd (World War I)
❑ 94 Baron Sir George May (World War I)
❑ 95 Barrie Davis (World War II)
❑ 96 Basil Plumley (Vietnam)
❑ 97 Ben F. Jensen (World War I)
❑ 98 Ben King (World War II)
❑ 99 Ben Kuroki (World War II)
❑ 100 Benedict Crowell (World War I)
❑ 101 Benito Mussolini (World War II)
❑ 102 Benjamin Alvord (Civil War)
❑ 103 Benjamin Amsden (World War II)
❑ 104 Benjamin O. Davis Jr (World War II)
❑ 105 Berhard Imminger (World War II)
❑ 106 Bernard A. Clarey (World War II)
❑ 107 Bernard Fisher (Vietnam)
❑ 108 Bernard Law Montgomery (World War II)
❑ 109 Bernard Rogers (Korean War)
❑ 110 Bernd Schazle (World War II)
❑ 111 Bernice Falk Haydu (World War II)
❑ 112 Bertram T. Clayton (Spanish-American War)
❑ 113 Beryl Newman (World War II)
❑ 114 Bill Carpenter (Vietnam)
❑ 115 Bill Crawford Compton (World War II)
❑ 116 Bill Cullerton (World War II)
❑ 117 Bill Dickey (World War II)
❑ 118 Bill Overstreet (World War II)
❑ 119 Billy Edens (World War II)
❑ 120 Billy Johnson (World War II)
❑ 121 Bird Wilson (World War II)
❑ 122 Bob Dole (World War II)
❑ 123 Bob Dornan (Vietnam)
❑ 124 Bob Foster (World War II)
❑ 125 Bob Hanson (World War II)
❑ 126 Bob Hoover (World War II)
❑ 127 Bob Keeton (World War II)
❑ 128 Bob Kerrey (Vietnam)
❑ 129 Bob Layher (World War II)
❑ 130 Bob Lemon (World War II)
❑ 131 Bob Maxwell (World War II)
❑ 132 Bob Novogratz (Vietnam)
❑ 133 Bob Slaughter (World War II)
❑ 134 Bob Welden (World War II)
❑ 135 Bobby Doerr (World War II)
❑ 136 Boleslaw H. Drobinski (World War II)
❑ 137 Bradford Freeman (World War II)
❑ 138 Brent Scowcroft (Vietnam)
❑ 139 Brian P. Coote (World War II)
❑ 140 Brian Robertson (World War II)
❑ 141 Brock Strom (Vietnam)
❑ 142 Broderick Crawford (World War II)
❑ 143 Brooks Liles (World War II)
❑ 144 Bruce Barackman (World War II)
❑ 145 Bruce Bretherton (World War II)
❑ 146 Bruce DeMars (Vietnam)
❑ 147 Bruce Jaques (World War II)
❑ 148 Bruce Matheson (World War II)
❑ 149 Bruce Robinson (War on Terror)
❑ 150 Bruno Schmelzinger (World War II)
❑ 151 Buck Feldman (World War II)
❑ 152 Bud Alley (Vietnam)
❑ 153 Bud Anderson (World War II)
❑ 154 Bud Poile (World War II)
❑ 155 Buford Johnson (World War II)
❑ 156 Burgess Meredith (World War II)
❑ 157 C.J.S. Craig (Gulf War)
❑ 158 C.L. Keighley-Peach (World War II)
❑ 159 Carl Dodd (Korean War)
❑ 160 Carl Hayden (World War I)
❑ 161 Carl Muscarello (World War II)
❑ 162 Carl Spaatz (World War II)
❑ 163 Carlisle A.H. Trost (Gulf War)
❑ 164 Carlos Ogden (World War II)
❑ 165 Carmen Gisi (World War II)
❑ 166 Carroll Powell (World War II)
❑ 167 Carroll Smith (World War II)
❑ 168 Casimer Nastal (World War II)
❑ 169 Caspar Weinberger (World War II)
❑ 170 Cato D. Glover Jr. (World War II)
❑ 171 Cecil Calavan (World War II)
❑ 172 Cecil Foster (Korean War)
❑ 173 Charles Abbot (Gulf War)
❑ 174 Charles B. Morris (Vietnam)
❑ 175 Charles Bock Jr. (Korean War)
❑ 176 Charles Bolte (World War II)
❑ 177 Charles Bond Jr. (World War II)
❑ 178 Charles Coolidge (World War II)
❑ 179 Charles de Gaulle (World War II)
❑ 180 Charles DeBellevue (Vietnam)
❑ 181 Charles Donald Albury (World War II)
❑ 182 Charles Donald Griffin (World War II)
❑ 183 Charles Dragich (World War II)
❑ 184 Charles E. Gurney (Vietnam)
❑ 185 Charles E. Watts (World War II)
❑ 186 Charles Fischette (World War II)
❑ 187 Charles Griffin (Civil War)
❑ 188 Charles Hagemeister (Vietnam)
❑ 189 Charles Hauver (World War II)
❑ 190 Charles Haverland (World War II)
❑ 191 Charles Hays (Civil War)
❑ 192 Charles Horner (Gulf War)
❑ 193 Charles K. Duncan (World War II)
❑ 194 Charles Kunz (World War II)
❑ 195 Charles Lindberg (World War II)
❑ 196 Charles Mallory (World War II)
❑ 197 Charles McClure (World War II)
❑ 198 Charles McGee (World War II)
❑ 199 Charles Murray (World War II)
❑ 200 Charles O'Neil (Civil War)
❑ 201 Charles Ozuk (World War II)
❑ 202 Charles P. O'Sullivan (World War II)
❑ 203 Charles Percy (World War II)
❑ 204 Charles R. Larson (Cold War)
❑ 205 Charles S. Abbot (Vietnam)
❑ 206 Charles Sandy McCorkle (World War II)
❑ 207 Charles Shea (World War II)
❑ 208 Charles Sumner (Civil War)
❑ 209 Charles Sweeney (World War II)
❑ 210 Charles Tucker (World War II)
❑ 211 Charles W. Hill (Civil War)
❑ 212 Charlie Thone (World War II)
❑ 213 Charlton Heston (World War II)
❑ 214 Chase Nielsen (World War II)
❑ 215 Chauncey McKeever (Civil War)
❑ 216 Chester Nimitz (World War I)
❑ 217 Chester Nimitz (World War II)
❑ 218 Chiang Kai-Shek (World War II)
❑ 219 Christoph Kramer (World War II)
❑ 220 Christopher C. Augur (Civil War)
❑ 221 Christopher Navarre (World War II)
❑ 222 Chuck Baisden (World War II)
❑ 223 Chuck Older (World War II)
❑ 224 Clancy Lyall (World War II)
❑ 225 Clarence Borley (World War II)
❑ 226 Clarence Craft (World War II)
❑ 227 Clarence Sasser (Vietnam)
❑ 228 Clark Simmons (World War II)
❑ 229 Claude Kinsey (World War II)
❑ 230 Claude Platte (World War II)
❑ 231 Claus Peter Carlson (World War II)
❑ 232 Clayo Rice (World War II)
❑ 233 Clayton Campbell (World War II)
❑ 234 Clayton Gross (World War II)
❑ 235 Cleatus Lebow (World War II)
❑ 236 Clement Craig (World War II)
❑ 237 Clement Woodnutt Miller (World War II)
❑ 238 Clinton Burdick (World War II)
❑ 239 Clive Caldwell (World War II)
❑ 240 Clyde Curtin (Korean War)
❑ 241 Clyde East (World War II)
❑ 242 Colin Powell (Korean War)
❑ 243 Constantino Petrosellini (World War II)
❑ 244 Cortlandt V.R. Schuyler (World War II)
❑ 245 Count Johan Albert Ehrensvard (World War I)
❑ 246 Curtis LeMay (World War II)
❑ 247 Cuvier Grover (Civil War)
❑ 248 Cyriaque Gillain (World War I)
❑ 249 Dale Karger (World War II)
❑ 250 Dale Spencer (World War II)
❑ 251 Dan Carmichael (World War II)
❑ 252 Dan Keenan (Korean War)
❑ 253 Daniel Clymer (American Revolution)
❑ 254 Daniel Cunningham (World War II)
❑ 255 Daniel Inouye (World War II)
❑ 256 Daniel Noonan (World War II)
❑ 257 Danny McKnight (War on Terror)
❑ 258 Darrell Welch (World War II)
❑ 259 Dave Severance (World War II)
❑ 260 Davey Jones (World War II)
❑ 261 David B. Henderson (Civil War)
❑ 262 David Boren (Vietnam)
❑ 263 David C. Dolby (Vietnam)
❑ 264 David E. Jeremiah (Vietnam)
❑ 265 David G.S.R. Cox (World War II)
❑ 266 David H. Bagley (World War II)
❑ 267 David Hunter (Mexican-American War)
❑ 268 David Kindleberger (Civil War)
❑ 269 David L. McDonald (Vietnam)
❑ 270 David McNerney (Korean War)
❑ 271 David McNerney (Vietnam)
❑ 272 David Niven (World War II)
❑ 273 David Thatcher (World War II)
❑ 274 David Thwaites (World War II)
❑ 275 David Wilhelm (World War II)
❑ 276 Dawn Seymour (World War II)
❑ 277 Dean Davenport (World War II)
❑ 278 Denis Crowley-Milling (World War II)
❑ 279 Dennis Benchoff (Vietnam)
❑ 280 Dennis J. Roberts (World War II)
❑ 281 Denys Edgar Gillam (World War II)
❑ 282 Desmond Doss (World War II)
❑ 283 Dick Couch (Vietnam)
❑ 284 Dick Rossi (World War II)
❑ 285 Dieter Oster (World War II)
❑ 286 Dietrich Ascher (World War II)
❑ 287 Dirk Vlug (World War II)
❑ 288 Dolph Overton (Korean War)
❑ 289 Don Bond (World War II)
❑ 290 Don Bryan (World War II)
❑ 291 Don Carlos Buell (Mexican-American War)
❑ 292 Don Jenkins (Vietnam)
❑ 293 Don Lopez (World War II)
❑ 294 Don Malarkey (World War II)
❑ 295 Don McPherson (World War II)
❑ 296 Don Rickles (World War II)
❑ 297 Donald Aldridge (Vietnam)
❑ 298 Donald Baccus (World War II)
❑ 299 Donald Beaty (World War II)
❑ 300 Donald Blum (World War II)
❑ 301 Donald Bryan (World War II)
❑ 302 Donald Burgett (World War II)
❑ 303 Donald C. Davis (World War II)
❑ 304 Donald Cronin (World War II)
❑ 305 Donald Cummings (World War II)
❑ 306 Donald Gordon (World War II)
❑ 307 Donald Hillman (World War II)
❑ 308 Donald Marr Nelson (World War II)
❑ 309 Donald McGee (World War II)
❑ 310 Donald Ray Matthews (World War II)
❑ 311 Donald Rudolph (World War II)
❑ 312 Donald Rumsfeld (War in Iraq)
❑ 313 Donald Strait (World War II)
❑ 314 Donald Stratton (World War II)
❑ 315 Doug Canning (World War II)
❑ 316 Doug Kenna (World War II)
❑ 317 Douglas Fairbanks Jr. (World War II)
❑ 318 Douglas MacArthur (Korean War)
❑ 319 Douglas MacArthur (World War I)
❑ 320 Douglas MacArthur (World War II)
❑ 321 Dr Joseph D. Charles (World War II)
❑ 322 Dr. Alfred Regeniter (World War II)
❑ 323 Dr. Christopher B. Howard (War on Terror)
❑ 324 Dr. Josef-Georg Mulzer (World War II)
❑ 325 Dr. Karl Carstens (World War II)
❑ 326 Drew Dix (Vietnam)
❑ 327 Duane Dewey (Korean War)
❑ 328 Dudley Aman, 1st Baron Marley (World War I)
❑ 329 Duke Snider (World War II)
❑ 330 E. Gordon Lapp (World War II)
❑ 331 E. Ross Adair (World War II)
❑ 332 Earl McClung (World War II)
❑ 333 Earling Zaeske (World War II)
❑ 334 Eberhard Heder (World War II)
❑ 335 Eckart Afheldt (World War II)
❑ 336 Ed Figueroa (Vietnam)
❑ 337 Ed Freeman (Vietnam)
❑ 338 Ed Harper (World War II)
❑ 339 Ed Harrell (World War II)
❑ 340 Ed Horton (World War II)
❑ 341 Ed Johann (World War II)
❑ 342 Ed Koch (World War II)
❑ 343 Ed Mauser (World War II)
❑ 344 Ed McKellar (Korean War)
❑ 345 Ed Meyer (Vietnam)
❑ 346 Ed Olander (World War II)
❑ 347 Ed Ramsey (World War II)
❑ 348 Ed Schowalter Jr. (Korean War)
❑ 349 Ed Tillman (World War II)
❑ 350 Ed Wendy (World War II)
❑ 351 Eddie Albert (World War II)

❑ 352 Eddie Rickenbacker (World War I)
❑ 353 Edgar McElroy (World War II)
❑ 354 Edmond Moran (World War II)
❑ 355 Eduard Isken (World War II)
❑ 356 Edward Beach (World War II)
❑ 357 Edward Brown (World War II)
❑ 358 Edward Canby (Civil War)
❑ 359 Edward Flanagan (World War II)
❑ 360 Edward Gaulrapp (World War II)
❑ 361 Edward Giller (World War II)
❑ 362 Edward Joint (World War II)
❑ 363 Edward Kenna (World War II)
❑ 364 Edward Robinson (Vietnam)
❑ 365 Edward Saylor (World War II)
❑ 366 Edward Shames (World War II)
❑ 367 Edward Tipper (World War II)
❑ 368 Edward Townsend (Civil War)
❑ 369 Edward Wendorf (World War II)
❑ 370 Edwin Fobes (World War II)
❑ 371 Einar H. Ingman Jr. (Korean War)
❑ 372 Elaine Harmon (World War II)
❑ 373 Eldridge Williams (World War II)
❑ 374 Elias Kuehlein (World War II)
❑ 375 Elie Wiesel (World War II)
❑ 376 Elizabeth Strohfus (World War II)
❑ 377 Elliott Roosevelt (World War II)
❑ 378 Elmer Jones (World War II)
❑ 379 Elmo R. Zumwalt Jr. (World War II)
❑ 380 Elmo Zumwalt (Korean War)
❑ 381 Elmo Zumwalt (Vietnam)
❑ 382 Elvin Homan (World War II)
❑ 383 Elvin Lin Lindsay (World War II)
❑ 384 Emil R. Bedard (War on Terror)
❑ 385 Engelbert Bockhoff (World War II)
❑ 386 Enos Slaughter (World War II)
❑ 387 Ephraim P. Holmes (World War II)
❑ 388 Erhard Bauer (World War II)
❑ 389 Erhard Nippa (World War II)
❑ 390 Eric Evenson (World War II)
❑ 391 Erich Axthammer (World War II)
❑ 392 Erich Rudorffer (World War II)
❑ 393 Ernest Bankey (World War II)
❑ 394 Ernest Borgnine (World War II)
❑ 395 Ernest Childers (World War II)
❑ 396 Ernest West (Korean War)
❑ 397 Ernst Biehler (World War II)
❑ 398 Ernst Orzegowski (World War II)
❑ 399 Ernst Scheufele (World War II)
❑ 400 Erwin Diekwisch (World War II)
❑ 401 Erwin Fischer (World War II)
❑ 402 Erwin Hensch (World War II)
❑ 403 Erwin Prossl (World War II)
❑ 404 Erwin Rommel (World War II)
❑ 405 Ethel Finley (World War II)
❑ 406 Eugene B. Fluckey (World War II)
❑ 407 Eugene Derricotte (World War II)
❑ 408 Eugene Hanks (World War II)
❑ 409 Eugene Jensen (World War II)
❑ 410 Everett Alvarez (Vietnam)
❑ 411 Everett Holstrom (World War II)
❑ 412 Everett Miller (World War II)
❑ 413 Everett Pope (World War II)
❑ 414 Everett W. Holstrom (Cold War)
❑ 415 Felix K. Zollicoffer (Civil War)
❑ 416 Felix von Luckner (World War I)
❑ 417 Felix von Luckner (World War II)
❑ 418 Felton Outland (World War II)
❑ 419 Fidel Castro (Cold War)
❑ 420 Fleming Begaye (World War II)
❑ 421 Florian Stamm (World War II)
❑ 422 Floyd Kirkpatrick (World War II)
❑ 423 Forrest Guth (World War II)
❑ 424 Frances H. Griswold (World War II)
❑ 425 Francis A. Cook (Spanish-American War)
❑ 426 Francis Buckles (World War I)
❑ 427 Francis Case (World War I)
❑ 428 Francis Currey (World War II)
❑ 429 Francis D.S. Scott-Malden (World War II)
❑ 430 Francis Gerard (World War II)
❑ 431 Francis M. Cockrell (Civil War)
❑ 432 Francis P. Matthews (World War II)
❑ 433 Francis Sanza (World War II)
❑ 434 Francis Skinner Fiske (Civil War)
❑ 435 Frank A. Barrett (World War I)
❑ 436 Frank B. Kelso (Gulf War)
❑ 437 Frank Carey (World War II)
❑ 438 Frank Carlucci (Cold War)
❑ 439 Frank Everest (World War II)
❑ 440 Frank Gailer (World War II)
❑ 441 Frank Guidone (World War II)
❑ 442 Frank Hearrell (World War II)
❑ 443 Frank Hunter (World War I)
❑ 444 Frank Hurlbut (World War II)
❑ 445 Frank Kappeler (World War II)
❑ 446 Frank Klibbe (Korean War)
❑ 447 Frank Losonsky (World War II)
❑ 448 Frank Mathers (World War II)
❑ 449 Frank McCauley (World War II)
❑ 450 Frank Nash (Korean War)
❑ 451 Frank Neubert (World War II)
❑ 452 Frank O'Connor (World War II)
❑ 453 Frank Perconte (World War II)
❑ 454 Frank Soboleski (World War II)
❑ 455 Franklin E. Sigler (World War II)
❑ 456 Franklin Hagenbeck (War on Terror)
❑ 457 Franklin Lincoln Jr. (World War II)
❑ 458 Franklin Miller (Vietnam)
❑ 459 Franklin Rose (World War II)
❑ 460 Franklin Troup (World War II)
❑ 461 Franz Gapp (World War II)
❑ 462 Franz Kieslich (World War II)
❑ 463 Franz Lochman (World War II)
❑ 464 Franz Weber (World War II)
❑ 465 Fred Dungan (World War II)
❑ 466 Fred Johnson (World War II)
❑ 467 Fred Losch (World War II)
❑ 468 Fred Ohr (World War II)
❑ 469 Fred Olivi (World War II)
❑ 470 Frederick Anthony Gaze (World War II)
❑ 471 Frederick Bellenger (World War I)
❑ 472 Frederick Blesse (Korean War)
❑ 473 Frederick Blesse (Vietnam)
❑ 474 Frederick Desmond Hughes (World War II)
❑ 475 Frederick Dick (World War II)
❑ 476 Frederick Ferguson (Vietnam)
❑ 477 Frederick Gutt (World War II)
❑ 478 Frederick H. Michaelis (World War II)
❑ 479 Frederick Hauck (Vietnam)
❑ 480 Frederick Montague (World War II)
❑ 481 Frederick Payne (World War II)
❑ 482 French E. Chadwick (Spanish-American War)
❑ 483 Friedrich Carl (World War II)
❑ 484 Friedrich Hahl (World War II)
❑ 485 Friedrich Müller-Rochholz (World War II)
❑ 486 Friedrich Ruge (World War II)
❑ 487 Fritz Langanke (World War II)
❑ 488 Fritz Seyffardt (World War II)
❑ 489 Fritz Wiener (World War II)
❑ 490 Gail Halvorsen (World War II)
❑ 491 Gareth Nowell (World War II)
❑ 492 Gary Beikirch (Vietnam)
❑ 493 Gary Littrell (Vietnam)
❑ 494 Gary Wetzel (Vietnam)
❑ 495 Geoffrey Howitt (World War II)
❑ 496 Georg Bleher (World War II)
❑ 497 Georg Bose (World War II)
❑ 498 George Bud Day (Vietnam)
❑ 499 George Bud Day (World War II)
❑ 500 George Andrews (World War II)
❑ 501 George Bennions (World War II)
❑ 502 George Bomford (Civil War)
❑ 503 George Brown (World War II)
❑ 504 George C. Axtell (World War II)
❑ 505 George C. Wallace (World War II)
❑ 506 George Cadwalader (Civil War)
❑ 507 George Caron (World War II)
❑ 508 George Ceuleers (World War II)
❑ 509 George Chandler (World War II)
❑ 510 George Douglas-Hamilton, Earl of Selkirk (World War II)
❑ 511 George Gay (World War II)
❑ 512 George Getty (Civil War)
❑ 513 George Grunert (World War I)
❑ 514 George H. O'Brien Jr. (Korean War)
❑ 515 George Hollowell (World War II)
❑ 516 George Horvath (World War II)
❑ 517 George Hutchinson (World War I)
❑ 518 George Joulwan (Vietnam)
❑ 519 George Kirk (World War II)
❑ 520 George L. Andrews (Civil War)
❑ 521 George L. Mabry (World War II)
❑ 522 George Lang (Vietnam)
❑ 523 George Lininger (World War II)
❑ 524 George Loving (World War II)
❑ 525 George Luck (World War II)
❑ 526 George Marshal (World War II)
❑ 527 George McGovern (World War II)
❑ 528 George Mills Boyd (World War II)
❑ 529 George Novotny (World War II)
❑ 530 George P. Shultz (Cold War)
❑ 531 George P. Shultz (World War II)
❑ 532 George Robeson (Civil War)
❑ 533 George S. Vest (World War II)
❑ 534 George Sakato (World War II)
❑ 535 George Steenberg (Civil War)
❑ 536 George Vaughn (World War I)
❑ 537 George W. Anderson Jr. (World War II)
❑ 538 George Wahlen (World War II)
❑ 539 George Whiting (World War II)
❑ 540 Georgy Zhukov (World War II)
❑ 541 Gerald Ford (World War II)
❑ 542 Gerald Gibbs (World War I)
❑ 543 Gerald Poor (World War II)
❑ 544 Gerald W. Johnson (World War II)
❑ 545 Gerd Schmuckle (World War II)
❑ 546 Gerhard Beier (World War II)
❑ 547 Gerhard Fischer (World War II)
❑ 548 Gerhard Hein (World War II)
❑ 549 Gerhard Krems (World War II)
❑ 550 Gerhard Schopfel (World War II)
❑ 551 Gerhard Zoppoth (World War II)
❑ 552 Gino Merli (World War II)
❑ 553 Glendon Davis (World War II)
❑ 554 Glenn Bowers (World War II)
❑ 555 Glenn Frazier (World War II)
❑ 556 Gordon Batdorf (World War II)
❑ 557 Gordon Graham (World War II)
❑ 558 Gordon Roberts (Vietnam)
❑ 559 Gottfried Dulias (World War II)
❑ 560 Gottlieb Benz (World War II)
❑ 561 Grant McDonald (World War II)
❑ 562 Gray Davis (Vietnam)
❑ 563 Gregory Pappy Boyington (World War II)
❑ 564 Griffith Williams (World War II)
❑ 565 Gunter Braake (World War II)
❑ 566 Gunter Carsten/Chrzonsz (World War II)
❑ 567 Gunter Frenzel (World War II)
❑ 568 Gunter Glasner (World War II)
❑ 569 Gunter Seeger (World War II)
❑ 570 Gunther Bierbrauer (World War II)
❑ 571 Günther Marreck (World War II)
❑ 572 Gunther Rall (World War II)
❑ 573 Gunther Sinnecker (World War II)
❑ 574 Guy Bordelon (Korean War)
❑ 575 Guy Hamilton Burrage (World War I)
❑ 576 H.J. Ziegemeier (World War I)
❑ 577 Hajo Herrmann (World War II)
❑ 578 Hal Moore (Vietnam)
❑ 579 Hal Moore (World War II)
❑ 580 Hamilton McWhorter (World War II)
❑ 581 Hamish Mahaddie (World War II)
❑ 582 Hank Bauer (World War II)
❑ 583 Hank Potter (World War II)
❑ 584 Hanns Scharff (World War II)
❑ 585 Hans Busch (World War II)
❑ 586 Hans Elkmeier (World War II)
❑ 587 Hans Georg Borck (World War II)
❑ 588 Hans Goebeler (World War II)
❑ 589 Hans Iffland (World War II)
❑ 590 Hans Joachim Dierks (World War II)
❑ 591 Hans Joachim Heinrici (World War II)
❑ 592 Hans Krohn (World War II)
❑ 593 Hans Lange (World War II)
❑ 594 Hans Sturm (World War II)
❑ 595 Hans Uhde (World War II)
❑ 596 Hans-Ekkehard Bob (World War II)
❑ 597 Hansford Johnson (Vietnam)
❑ 598 Hans-Georg Hess (World War II)
❑ 599 Hanz Kurz (World War II)
❑ 600 Harald Nugiseks (World War II)
❑ 601 Harlan Twible (World War II)
❑ 602 Harold Bird-Wilson (World War II)
❑ 603 Harold Bray (World War II)
❑ 604 Harold Comstock (World War II)
❑ 605 Harold E. Shear (World War II)
❑ 606 Harold Fritz (Vietnam)
❑ 607 Harold Loch (World War II)
❑ 608 Harold Page Smith (World War II)
❑ 609 Harold Poole (World War II)
❑ 610 Harold W. Blot (Gulf War)
❑ 611 Harold W. Gehman Jr. (Vietnam)
❑ 612 Harold Walmsley (World War II)
❑ 613 Harris Mitchell (World War II)
❑ 614 Harrison Tordoff (World War II)
❑ 615 Harry Broadhurst (World War II)
❑ 616 Harry Brown (World War II)
❑ 617 Harry C. McCool (World War II)
❑ 618 Harry Cain (World War II)
❑ 619 Harry Clark (World War II)
❑ 620 Harry D. Felt (World War II)
❑ 621 Harry D. Train (Korean War)
❑ 622 Harry E. Hill (World War II)
❑ 623 Harry Ferrier (World War II)
❑ 624 Harry Pecorelli (Civil War)
❑ 625 Harry Stewart (World War II)
❑ 626 Harry Truman (World War I)
❑ 627 Harry Watson (World War II)
❑ 628 Harvey Alexander (World War II)
❑ 629 Harvey Barnum Jr. (Vietnam)
❑ 630 Harvey Burwell (World War II)
❑ 631 Hayden Gregory (World War II)
❑ 632 Heinrich Engel (World War II)
❑ 633 Heinrich Hellendoorn (World War II)
❑ 634 Heinrich Himmler (World War II)
❑ 635 Heinrich Kohler (World War II)
❑ 636 Heinrich Ruhl (World War II)
❑ 637 Heinrich Sonne (World War II)
❑ 638 Heinrich Sudel (World War II)
❑ 639 Heinrich Timpe (World War II)
❑ 640 Heinz Angelmaier (World War II)
❑ 641 Heinz Laebe (World War II)
❑ 642 Heinz Raforth (World War II)
❑ 643 Heinz Rokker (World War II)
❑ 644 Heinz Rothhardt (World War II)
❑ 645 Helen Wyatt Snapp (World War II)
❑ 646 Hellmut von Leipzig (World War II)
❑ 647 Helmut Eberspächer (World War II)
❑ 648 Helmut Groß (World War II)
❑ 649 Helmut Neumann (World War II)
❑ 650 Helmut Schmidt (World War II)
❑ 651 Henry A. Wiley (Spanish-American War)
❑ 652 Henry B. Sayler (World War II)
❑ 653 Henry Buttelmann (Korean War)
❑ 654 Henry Buttelmann (Vietnam)
❑ 655 Henry Dundas (Great French War)
❑ 656 Henry Dworshak (World War I)
❑ 657 Henry Erwin (World War II)
❑ 658 Henry G. Chiles Jr. (Cold War)
❑ 659 Henry H. Mauz Jr. (Vietnam)
❑ 660 Henry Hogan (World War II)
❑ 661 Henry Jackson Hunt (Civil War)
❑ 662 Henry Kissinger (World War II)
❑ 663 Henry Meigs (World War II)
❑ 664 Henry Moore (World War II)
❑ 665 Henry R. Gibson (Civil War)
❑ 666 Henry Schauer (World War II)
❑ 667 Henry White (World War I)
❑ 668 Henry Zimmerman (World War II)
❑ 669 Herbert Holden (World War II)
❑ 670 Herbert Isachsen (World War II)
❑ 671 Herbert Ross (World War II)
❑ 672 Herbert Suerth (World War II)
❑ 673 Herbert Weatherwax (World War II)
❑ 674 Herbert Winslow (Spanish-American War)
❑ 675 Heribert Koller (World War II)
❑ 676 Herman T. Schneebeli (World War II)
❑ 677 Hermann Eckardt (World War II)
❑ 678 Hermann Goering (World War II)
❑ 679 Hermann Kunz

(World War II)
❑ 680 Hermann Schleinhege (World War II)
❑ 681 Hermann Wehking (World War II)
❑ 682 Herndon Cummings (World War II)
❑ 683 Herschel Green (World War II)
❑ 684 Hershel Williams (World War II)
❑ 685 Hinrich Ahrens (World War II)
❑ 686 Hiram Mann (World War II)
❑ 687 Hiroshi Miyamura (Korean War)
❑ 688 Homer Sanders (World War II)
❑ 689 Horace Sally Crouch (World War II)
❑ 690 Horace B. Moranville (World War II)
❑ 691 Horace Reeves (World War II)
❑ 692 Horacio Rivero Jr. (World War II)
❑ 693 Horst Petzschler (World War II)
❑ 694 Horst Rippert (World War II)
❑ 695 Howard A. Sessler (World War II)
❑ 696 Howard V. Lee (Vietnam)
❑ 697 Howard W. Attarian (Vietnam)
❑ 698 Howie Meeker (World War II)
❑ 699 Hoyt Wilhelm (World War II)
❑ 700 Hubert Boitelet (World War II)
❑ 701 Hubert Humphrey (Vietnam)
❑ 702 Hubert Spadiut (World War II)
❑ 703 Hugh Dundas (World War II)
❑ 704 Hugh Nash Batten (World War II)
❑ 705 Hugo Broch (World War II)
❑ 706 Huntington Hardisty (Vietnam)
❑ 707 Huston Riley (World War II)
❑ 708 I.B. Donaldson (World War II)
❑ 709 Ian Edward Fraser (World War II)
❑ 710 Ian Freeland (World War II)
❑ 711 Ignatius J. Galantin (World War II)
❑ 712 Ira Allen Hayes (World War I)
❑ 713 Iris Cummings Critchell (World War II)
❑ 714 Isaac C. Kidd Jr. (World War II)
❑ 715 Isidor S. Ravdin (World War II)
❑ 716 Ivan Hasek (World War II)
❑ 717 Ivor H. Cosby (World War II)
❑ 718 J. James Exon (World War II)
❑ 719 J. Mike Wolf (World War II)
❑ 720 J. Paul Reason (Vietnam)
❑ 721 J. Ted Crosby (World War II)
❑ 722 J.D. Collinsworth (World War II)
❑ 723 J.M. Wainwright (World War II)
❑ 724 J.R. Stork (World War II)
❑ 725 J.S. McCain (World War II)
❑ 726 Jack Bryant (World War II)
❑ 727 Jack C. Montgomery (World War II)
❑ 728 Jack Foley (World War II)
❑ 729 Jack Hildebrandt (World War II)
❑ 730 Jack Ilfrey (World War II)
❑ 731 Jack Jacobs (Vietnam)
❑ 732 Jack Lemmon (World War II)
❑ 733 Jack Lenox (World War II)
❑ 734 Jack Lucas (World War II)
❑ 735 Jack McNiece (World War II)
❑ 736 Jack Rose (World War II)
❑ 737 Jack Watson (World War II)
❑ 738 Jacob Beser (World War II)
❑ 739 Jacob DeShazer (World War II)
❑ 740 James Anton (War of 1812)
❑ 741 James B. Busey (Vietnam)
❑ 742 James B. Tapp (World War II)
❑ 743 James Bare (World War II)
❑ 744 James Barnet Fry (Mexican-American War)
❑ 745 James Billo (World War II)
❑ 746 James Bounds (World War II)
❑ 747 James Brian Tait (World War II)
❑ 748 James Burt (World War II)
❑ 749 James Cain (World War II)
❑ 750 James Carter (World War II)
❑ 751 James Conway (War in Iraq)
❑ 752 James Coward (World War II)
❑ 753 James D. Watkins (World War II)
❑ 754 James Donald Hardman (World War I)
❑ 755 James Doug Lindsay (World War II)
❑ 756 James Duffy (World War II)
❑ 757 James Eikner (World War II)
❑ 758 James Empey (World War II)
❑ 759 James Fleming (Vietnam)
❑ 760 James Forrestal (World War I)
❑ 761 James G. Harbord (World War I)
❑ 762 James Goodson (World War II)
❑ 763 James Jarvis (World War II)
❑ 764 James Jim Cupp (World War II)
❑ 765 James Kasler (Korean War)
❑ 766 James L. Buckley (World War II)
❑ 767 James L. Dozier (Vietnam)
❑ 768 James L. Holloway (Korean War)
❑ 769 James L. Holloway (Vietnam)
❑ 770 James L. Holloway (World War II)
❑ 771 James L. Pearce (World War II)
❑ 772 James L. Stone (Korean War)
❑ 773 James Leathart (World War II)
❑ 774 James Livingston (Vietnam)
❑ 775 James Luma (World War II)
❑ 776 James Lynn Brooks (World War II)
❑ 777 James M. Comly (Civil War)
❑ 778 James Macia (World War II)
❑ 779 James Marshall-Cornwall (World War I)
❑ 780 James Morehead (World War II)
❑ 781 James Norton (Civil War)
❑ 782 James O. Ellis (Vietnam)
❑ 783 James O'Donnell (World War II)
❑ 784 James P. Kem (World War I)
❑ 785 James Pierce (World War II)
❑ 786 James R. Hendrix (World War II)
❑ 787 James Redpath (Civil War)
❑ 788 James Riggs (World War II)
❑ 789 James Sargent Russell (World War II)
❑ 790 James Schlesinger (Cold War)
❑ 791 James Sheddan (World War II)
❑ 792 James Starnes (World War II)
❑ 793 James Stewart (World War II)
❑ 794 James Storrar (World War II)
❑ 795 James Tallmadge Jr. (War of 1812)
❑ 796 James Taylor (Vietnam)
❑ 797 James Van Allen (World War II)
❑ 798 James Van Fleet (World War II)
❑ 799 James Verinis (World War II)
❑ 800 James Vote Bomford (Civil War)
❑ 801 James W. Nichols (Civil War)
❑ 802 Jan Preihs (World War II)
❑ 803 Janet Simpson (World War II)
❑ 804 Janusz Zurakowski (World War II)
❑ 805 Jay Vargas (Vietnam)
❑ 806 Jay Zeamer (World War II)
❑ 807 Jeanne Holm (World War II)
❑ 808 Jeff Fowler (War on Terror)
❑ 809 Jefferson Dorroh (World War II)
❑ 810 Jefferson J. DeBlanc (World War II)
❑ 811 Jennings C. Wise (World War I)
❑ 812 Jerauld Wright (World War I)
❑ 813 Jeremy M. Boorda (Vietnam)
❑ 814 Jerome L. Johnson (Vietnam)
❑ 815 Jerry Coleman (World War II)
❑ 816 Jerry Collinsworth (World War II)
❑ 817 Jerry O'Keefe (World War II)
❑ 818 Jessica Lynch (War on Terror)
❑ 819 Jim Hill (World War II)
❑ 820 Jim Nicholson (Vietnam)
❑ 821 Jim Swett (World War II)
❑ 822 Jimmy Carter (Cold War)
❑ 823 Jimmy Doolittle (World War II)
❑ 824 Joachim Melo (World War II)
❑ 825 Joe Cotton (Cold War)
❑ 826 Joe Forster (World War II)
❑ 827 Joe Foss (World War II)
❑ 828 Joe Jackson (Vietnam)
❑ 829 Joe Louis (World War II)
❑ 830 Joe Patient (World War II)
❑ 831 Joe Poshefko (World War II)
❑ 832 Joe Rosbert (Korean War)
❑ 833 Joe Rosbert (World War II)
❑ 834 Joe Sleffy (Korean War)
❑ 835 Johann Boos (World War II)
❑ 836 Johann Condne (World War II)
❑ 837 Johann Klaus (World War II)
❑ 838 Johann Pichler (World War II)
❑ 839 Johann Trummer (World War II)
❑ 840 Johannes Naumann (World War II)
❑ 841 Johannes Oesterhelt (World War II)
❑ 842 John Bud Hawk (World War II)
❑ 843 John A. Tilley (World War II)
❑ 844 John Abizaid (War in Iraq)
❑ 845 John Agar (World War II)
❑ 846 John Alexander McClernand (Civil War)
❑ 847 John Armstrong Jr. (American Revolution)
❑ 848 John Armstrong (American Revolution)
❑ 849 John B. Gordon (Civil War)
❑ 850 John Babcock (World War I)
❑ 851 John Baca (Vietnam)
❑ 852 John Baker (World War II)
❑ 853 John Barry Lawler (World War II)
❑ 854 John Bell Hood (Civil War)
❑ 855 John Bolt (World War II)
❑ 856 John Bolyard (World War II)
❑ 857 John Chafee (World War II)
❑ 858 John Crews (World War II)
❑ 859 John Cudahy (World War I)
❑ 860 John Cunningham (World War II)
❑ 861 John D. Long (Spanish-American War)
❑ 862 John D. Stokes (World War II)
❑ 863 John Dale (World War II)
❑ 864 John Eisenhower (World War II)
❑ 865 John Ellacombe (World War II)
❑ 866 John F. Kennedy (Cold War)
❑ 867 John F. Thornell (World War II)
❑ 868 John Fabian (Vietnam)
❑ 869 John Finn (World War II)
❑ 870 John Fremont (Civil War)
❑ 871 John G. Williams Jr. (World War II)
❑ 872 John Gorton (World War II)
❑ 873 John Griffith (World War II)
❑ 874 John Hall (World War II)
❑ 875 John Heller (World War II)
❑ 876 John Henry Bisley (World War II)
❑ 877 John Hobler (World War II)
❑ 878 John J. Hyland (Vietnam)
❑ 879 John J. McCloy (World War II)
❑ 880 John J. Pershing (World War I)
❑ 881 John Jestyn Llewellin (World War I)
❑ 882 John Kirla (World War II)
❑ 883 John L. McLucas (World War II)
❑ 884 John L. Mitchell (Civil War)
❑ 885 John Leahr (World War II)
❑ 886 John Loder (World War II)
❑ 887 John Loisel (World War II)
❑ 888 John Maas (World War II)
❑ 889 John Marlow Thompson (World War II)
❑ 890 John McCain (Vietnam)
❑ 891 John McClellan (World War I)
❑ 892 John McGoran (World War II)
❑ 893 John Mihalowski (World War II)
❑ 894 John Newman (World War II)
❑ 895 John P. Quinlan (World War II)
❑ 896 John P. Weinel (World War II)
❑ 897 John Parker Boyd (War of 1812)
❑ 898 John Payne (World War II)
❑ 899 John Philip Du Cane (World War I)
❑ 900 John Pratt, 1st Marquess Camden (Great French War)
❑ 901 John Purdy (World War II)
❑ 902 John Quitman (Mexican-American War)
❑ 903 John R. Alison (World War II)
❑ 904 John R. Bostick (Vietnam)
❑ 905 John S. Phelps (Civil War)
❑ 906 John Shalikashvili (Vietnam)
❑ 907 John Singlaub (World War II)
❑ 908 John Sloane (War of 1812)
❑ 909 John Stafford (World War II)
❑ 910 John Stewart (World War II)
❑ 911 John Tominac (World War II)
❑ 912 John Totushek (War on Terror)
❑ 913 John W. Philip (Civil War)
❑ 914 John Watson Barr (Civil War)
❑ 915 John Woolston (World War II)
❑ 916 John Zink (World War II)
❑ 917 Johnathan O. Seaman (World War II)
❑ 918 Johnny Bower (World War II)
❑ 919 Johnny Mize (World War II)
❑ 920 Jon Wallenius (Vietnam)
❑ 921 Jonathan M. Wainwright (World War II)
❑ 922 Jorg Czypionka (World War II)
❑ 923 Jorge Dodsworth Martins (World War II)
❑ 924 Jose Lopez (World War II)
❑ 925 Josef Mulzer (World War II)
❑ 926 Josef Pries (World War II)
❑ 927 Josef Schmauz (World War II)
❑ 928 Josef-Emile Clade (World War II)
❑ 929 Joseph A. Engelhard (Civil War)
❑ 930 Joseph Aucoin (War on Terror)
❑ 931 Joseph Finfrock (World War II)
❑ 932 Joseph Goebbels (World War II)
❑ 933 Joseph Griffin (World War II)
❑ 934 Joseph Hooker (Mexican-American War)
❑ 935 Joseph J. Clark (World War I)
❑ 936 Joseph Kerrey (Vietnam)
❑ 937 Joseph Manske (World War II)
❑ 938 Joseph Matte (World War II)
❑ 939 Joseph McGraw (World War II)
❑ 940 Joseph Poshefko (World War II)
❑ 941 Joseph Ralston (Vietnam)
❑ 942 Joseph Rodriguez (Korean War)
❑ 943 Joseph W. Prueher (Vietnam)
❑ 944 Judge Joseph Wapner (World War II)
❑ 945 Julius Finnern (World War II)
❑ 946 Julius Ireland (World War II)
❑ 947 Julius Jacobson (World War II)
❑ 948 Jurgen Oesten (World War II)
❑ 949 Karl Glatzer (World War II)
❑ 950 Karl Hollidt (World War II)
❑ 951 Karl Johannssen (World War II)
❑ 952 Karl Nicolussi-Leck (World War II)
❑ 953 Karl Radermacher (World War II)
❑ 954 Karl Schlossstein (World War II)
❑ 955 Karl-Heinz Boska (World War II)
❑ 956 Karl-Heinz Zillies (World War II)
❑ 957 Kee Pon (World War II)
❑ 958 Keith Bruce Chisholm (World War II)
❑ 959 Keith Payne (Vietnam)
❑ 960 Ken Chilstrom (World War II)
❑ 961 Ken Dahlberg (World War II)
❑ 962 Ken Hippe (World War II)
❑ 963 Ken Jernstedt (World War II)
❑ 964 Ken Reardon (World War II)
❑ 965 Ken Rees (World War II)
❑ 966 Kenneth Lake (World War II)
❑ 967 Kenneth Lee (World War I)
❑ 968 Kenneth M. Bruce (World War I)
❑ 969 Kenneth McNeel (World War II)
❑ 970 Kenneth R. Martin (World War II)
❑ 971 Kenneth Royall (World War I)
❑ 972 Kenneth Walsh (World War II)
❑ 973 Kenneth Wilkinson (World War II)
❑ 974 Kermit Tyler (World War II)
❑ 975 Kirk Douglas (World War II)
❑ 976 Kirk Fordice (Vietnam)
❑ 977 Klaus Feldt (World War II)
❑ 978 Klaus Scheer (World War II)
❑ 979 Klaus Voss (World War II)
❑ 980 Kohei Hanami (World War II)
❑ 981 Konrad Zecherle/Rittmeyer (World War II)
❑ 982 Kurt Dahlmann (World War II)
❑ 983 Kurt Dix (World War II)
❑ 984 Kurt Prinz (World War II)
❑ 985 Kurt Schulze (World War II)
❑ 986 Kurt Sochatzy (World War II)
❑ 987 Kurt Waldheim (World War II)
❑ 988 L. Peter Wren (World War II)
❑ 989 L.B. Peck (Civil War)
❑ 990 L.S. Kuter (World War II)
❑ 991 Larry O'Neill (World War II)
❑ 992 Lauris Norstad (World War II)
❑ 993 Lawrence Clark (World War II)
❑ 994 Lawrence Powell (World War II)
❑ 995 Lawrence Stellmon (Vietnam)
❑ 996 Lawrence Wackett (World War II)
❑ 997 Lee Baggett Jr. (Vietnam)
❑ 998 Lee P. Mankin (World War II)
❑ 999 Leighton W. Smith Jr. (Vietnam)
❑ 1000 Leighton Willhite (World War II)
❑ 1001 Len Keller (Vietnam)
❑ 1002 Len Lomell (World War II)
❑ 1003 Len Reid (World War II)
❑ 1004 Leo J. Powers (World War II)
❑ 1005 Leo Thorsness (Vietnam)
❑ 1006 Leon A. Edney (Vietnam)

❑ 1007 Leonard Cheshire (World War II)
❑ 1008 Leonard Reeves (World War II)
❑ 1009 Leonard Rochford (World War I)
❑ 1010 Leonard Trent (World War II)
❑ 1011 LeRoy Grosshuesch (World War II)
❑ 1012 Leslie Smith (World War II)
❑ 1013 Lester Arasmith (World War II)
❑ 1014 Lew Ayers (World War II)
❑ 1015 Lewis A. Horton (Civil War)
❑ 1016 Lewis Cass (War of 1812)
❑ 1017 Lewis Chick (World War II)
❑ 1018 Lewis Hershey (World War I)
❑ 1019 Lewis Sayre Van Duzer (Spanish-American War)
❑ 1020 Lewis Williams Douglas (World War I)
❑ 1021 Lila Davy (World War II)
❑ 1022 Lillian Yonally (World War II)
❑ 1023 Lloyd Brown (World War I)
❑ 1024 Lloyd McKeethen (World War II)
❑ 1025 Lord John Boyd Orr (World War I)
❑ 1026 Loris Baldi (World War II)
❑ 1027 Lothar Hofer (World War II)
❑ 1028 Lothar Kmitta (World War II)
❑ 1029 Louis E. Curdes (World War II)
❑ 1030 Louis Erwin (World War II)
❑ 1031 Louis Menard (World War II)
❑ 1032 Louis Wilson (World War II)
❑ 1033 Lowell Brueland (World War II)
❑ 1034 Lucian Adams (World War II)
❑ 1035 Lucien Fenton (Civil War)
❑ 1036 Lucius Clay (World War II)
❑ 1037 Ludwig Bauer (World War II)
❑ 1038 Ludwig Lang (World War II)
❑ 1039 Ludwig Laubmeier (World War II)
❑ 1040 Lyle Pasket (World War II)
❑ 1041 Lyle Umenhoffer (World War II)
❑ 1042 Lyman L. Lemnitzer (World War II)
❑ 1043 Lyman Middleditch Jr. (World War II)
❑ 1044 Lyndon Marshall (World War II)
❑ 1045 Lyndon Spencer (World War II)
❑ 1046 Lynn Buck Compton (World War II)
❑ 1047 M.J. Mansfield (World War II)
❑ 1048 Manfried Leisebein (World War II)
❑ 1049 Marcus Robinson (World War II)
❑ 1050 Margaret Ringenberg (World War II)
❑ 1051 Margaret Thatcher (Cold War)
❑ 1052 Marion Stegeman Hodgson (World War II)
❑ 1053 Mark Clark (World War II)
❑ 1054 Mark W. Clark (Korean War)
❑ 1055 Marlow Leikness (World War II)
❑ 1056 Martin B. McKneally (World War II)
❑ 1057 Martin Drewes (World War II)
❑ 1058 Martin Mitschke (World War II)
❑ 1059 Matthew C. Butler (Civil War)
❑ 1060 Matthew Ridgway (World War II)
❑ 1061 Maurice Britt (World War II)
❑ 1062 Maurice De Barescut (World War I)
❑ 1063 Maurice Long (World War II)
❑ 1064 Max Heimorehbein (World War II)
❑ 1065 Max Thompson (World War II)
❑ 1066 Max Zastrow (World War II)
❑ 1067 Maxwell Taylor (World War II)
❑ 1068 Means Johnston Jr. (World War II)
❑ 1069 Melvin Biddle (World War II)
❑ 1070 Melvin Laird (World War II)
❑ 1071 Melvin Shearer (World War II)
❑ 1072 Merle Coons (World War II)
❑ 1073 Merrill McPeak (Korean War)
❑ 1074 Michael Dikovitsky (World War II)
❑ 1075 Michael Durant (Gulf War)
❑ 1076 Michael J. Daly (World War II)
❑ 1077 Michael Jackson (World War II)
❑ 1078 Michael John Fitzmaurice (Vietnam)
❑ 1079 Michael L. Dodson (Vietnam)
❑ 1080 Michael Novosel (Vietnam)
❑ 1081 Michael Quirk (World War II)
❑ 1082 Michael T. Russo (World War II)
❑ 1083 Mickey Bright (World War II)
❑ 1084 Mike Colalillo (World War II)
❑ 1085 Mike Kawato (World War II)
❑ 1086 Mikhail N. Gerasimov (World War II)
❑ 1087 Miles J. Saunders (Civil War)
❑ 1088 Miles M. Dawson (World War II)
❑ 1089 Milt Schmidt (World War II)
❑ 1090 Mitchell Paige (World War II)
❑ 1091 Monte Irvin (World War II)
❑ 1092 Morgan Mosley (World War II)
❑ 1093 Morgan Vaux (World War II)
❑ 1094 Morris Jeppson (World War II)
❑ 1095 Morton Magoffin (World War II)
❑ 1096 Mountbatten of Burma (World War I)
❑ 1097 Mountbatten of Burma (World War II)
❑ 1098 Murphy J. Foster Jr. (Korean War)
❑ 1099 Nail K. Castle (World War II)
❑ 1100 Nathan Gordon (World War II)
❑ 1101 Neville Duke (World War II)
❑ 1102 Nicholas Oresko (World War II)
❑ 1103 Nick Bacon (Vietnam)
❑ 1104 Nikita Khrushchev (World War II)
❑ 1105 Nikolai Vashugin (World War II)
❑ 1106 Nikolai Vatutin (World War II)
❑ 1107 Nobile Giacomo de Martino (World War II)
❑ 1108 Noel A.M. Gayler (World War II)
❑ 1109 Noel Harris (World War II)
❑ 1110 Nolan Herndon (World War II)
❑ 1111 Norbert Hannig (World War II)
❑ 1112 Norbert Kujacinski (World War II)
❑ 1113 Norman Berree (World War II)
❑ 1114 Norman Fortier (World War II)
❑ 1115 Norman McDonald (World War II)
❑ 1116 Norman Neitzke (World War II)
❑ 1117 Norman Schwarzkopf (Gulf War)
❑ 1118 Norwald Quiel (World War II)
❑ 1119 Odysseus Angelis (World War II)
❑ 1120 Ola Lee Mize (Korean War)
❑ 1121 Oliver Lawrence Philpot (World War II)
❑ 1122 Oliver Lyttelton (World War I)
❑ 1123 Oliver North (Vietnam)
❑ 1124 Omar Bradley (World War II)
❑ 1125 Oscar Boesch (World War II)
❑ 1126 Oscar Coen (World War II)
❑ 1127 Othmar Hermes (World War II)
❑ 1128 Otto Ballasko (World War II)
❑ 1129 Otto Braun (World War II)
❑ 1130 Otto Carius (World War II)
❑ 1131 Otto Fries (World War II)
❑ 1132 Otto Kleinert (World War II)
❑ 1133 Paddy Dunn (World War II)
❑ 1134 Pat Brady (Vietnam)
❑ 1135 Paul Albert Kausch (World War II)
❑ 1136 Paul B. Huff (World War II)
❑ 1137 Paul Bechtel (World War II)
❑ 1138 Paul Brasack (World War II)
❑ 1139 Paul Bucha (Vietnam)
❑ 1140 Paul C. Murphey Jr. (World War II)
❑ 1141 Paul Clifford Webb (World War II)
❑ 1142 Paul Clouthier (World War II)
❑ 1143 Paul Goodyear (World War II)
❑ 1144 Paul Greene (World War II)
❑ 1145 Paul Kerchum (World War II)
❑ 1146 Paul Olson (World War II)
❑ 1147 Paul R. Ignatius (World War II)
❑ 1148 Paul Rogers (World War II)
❑ 1149 Paul Thayer (World War II)
❑ 1150 Paul Tibbets (World War II)
❑ 1151 Paul Wiedorfer (World War II)
❑ 1152 Paul Zorner (World War II)
❑ 1153 Paul-Georg Kleffel (World War II)
❑ 1154 Paul-Vincenz Jansky (World War II)
❑ 1155 Percy Lucas (World War II)
❑ 1156 Perkins Bass (World War II)
❑ 1157 Perry Dahl (World War II)
❑ 1158 Peter Brothers (World War II)
❑ 1159 Peter C. Lemon (Vietnam)
❑ 1160 Peter Gansevoort (American Revolution)
❑ 1161 Peter Goutiere (World War II)
❑ 1162 Peter H. Dominick (World War II)
❑ 1163 Peter Hearne (World War II)
❑ 1164 Peter Lemon (World War II)
❑ 1165 Peter M. Gosse (World War II)
❑ 1166 Peter Olver (World War II)
❑ 1167 Peter Spoden (World War II)
❑ 1168 Peter Townsend (World War II)
❑ 1169 Peter Wykeham (Korean War)
❑ 1170 Peter Wykeham (World War II)
❑ 1171 Phil DeLong (Korean War)
❑ 1172 Phil DeLong (World War II)
❑ 1173 Phil Rizzuto (World War II)
❑ 1174 Philip Brain Jr. (World War II)
❑ 1175 Philip Colman (World War II)
❑ 1176 Philip Kirkwood (World War II)
❑ 1177 Philip Perugini (World War II)
❑ 1178 Pierre Clostermann (World War II)
❑ 1179 Pierre G.T. Beauregard (Civil War)
❑ 1180 Powell F. Carter Jr. (Korean War)
❑ 1181 Prince Gelasio Caetani (World War I)
❑ 1182 Quintin Hogg Baron Hailsham (World War II)
❑ 1183 R.A. Kings (World War II)
❑ 1184 R.E. Galer (World War II)
❑ 1185 Ralph Barnaby (World War I)
❑ 1186 Ralph E. Foltz (World War II)
❑ 1187 Ralph Gibson (World War II)
❑ 1188 Ralph Goranson (World War II)
❑ 1189 Ralph H. Wandrey (World War II)
❑ 1190 Ralph Hanks (World War II)
❑ 1191 Ralph Kiner (World War II)
❑ 1192 Ralph Parr Jr. (Korean War)
❑ 1193 Ralph W. Cousins (World War II)
❑ 1194 Ralston Pound (World War II)
❑ 1195 Ranald Adams Jr. (Korean War)
❑ 1196 Randall Duke Cunningham (Vietnam)
❑ 1197 Randolph Churchill (World War II)
❑ 1198 Ray Davis (Korean War)
❑ 1199 Ray Davis (World War II)
❑ 1200 Ray Mabus (War on Terror)
❑ 1201 Ray Nitschke (Vietnam)
❑ 1202 Raymond Baldwin (World War I)
❑ 1203 Raymond Bank (World War II)
❑ 1204 Raymond F. Toliver (World War II)
❑ 1205 Raymond Jacobs (World War II)
❑ 1206 Raymond Murphy (Korean War)
❑ 1207 Rayne Dennis Schultz (World War II)
❑ 1208 Reade Tilley (World War II)
❑ 1209 Reuben Denoff (World War II)
❑ 1210 Rex Barber (World War II)
❑ 1211 Rex Harrison (World War II)
❑ 1212 Rich Wheeler (World War II)
❑ 1213 Richard Dick Cole (World War II)
❑ 1214 Richard Alexander (World War II)
❑ 1215 Richard Annand (World War II)
❑ 1216 Richard Asbury (World War II)
❑ 1217 Richard Bertelson (World War II)
❑ 1218 Richard Bolling (World War II)
❑ 1219 Richard D. Cowger (World War II)
❑ 1220 Richard DeLauer (World War II)
❑ 1221 Richard Devine (World War II)
❑ 1222 Richard E. Bush (World War II)
❑ 1223 Richard E. Fleming (World War II)
❑ 1224 Richard E. Stambook (World War II)
❑ 1225 Richard Fleischer (World War II)
❑ 1226 Richard Franchot (Civil War)
❑ 1227 Richard Franz (World War II)
❑ 1228 Richard Greene (World War II)
❑ 1229 Richard Hobson (Spanish-American War)
❑ 1230 Richard Joyce (World War II)
❑ 1231 Richard Knowles (World War II)
❑ 1232 Richard Lauren Bertelson (World War II)
❑ 1233 Richard Mangrum (World War II)
❑ 1234 Richard May (World War II)
❑ 1235 Richard McCool (World War II)
❑ 1236 Richard Milne (World War II)
❑ 1237 Richard Nixon (Vietnam)
❑ 1238 Richard O'Kane (World War II)
❑ 1239 Richard Rutledge (World War II)
❑ 1240 Richard S. Becker (Korean War)
❑ 1241 Richard Smith (World War II)
❑ 1242 Richard Sorenson (World War II)
❑ 1243 Richard Suehr (World War II)
❑ 1244 Richard Thelen (World War II)
❑ 1245 Richard Thill (World War II)
❑ 1246 Richard Todd (World War II)
❑ 1247 Richard W. Dunkin (World War II)
❑ 1248 Robert Anderson (Civil War)
❑ 1249 Robert Aschenbrener (World War II)
❑ 1250 Robert B. Carney (World War I)
❑ 1251 Robert B. Porter (World War II)
❑ 1252 Robert Bacon (World War I)
❑ 1253 Robert Baird (World War II)
❑ 1254 Robert Booth (World War II)
❑ 1255 Robert Bunai (World War II)
❑ 1256 Robert C. Coats (World War II)
❑ 1257 Robert C. Hendrickson (World War I)
❑ 1258 Robert Cardenas (World War II)
❑ 1259 Robert Cowper (World War II)
❑ 1260 Robert Curtis (World War II)
❑ 1261 Robert DeHaven (World War II)
❑ 1262 Robert Duncan (World War II)
❑ 1263 Robert Dunlap (World War II)
❑ 1264 Robert E. Wood (World War I)
❑ 1265 Robert Eugene Bush (World War II)
❑ 1266 Robert Foley (Vietnam)
❑ 1267 Robert Freiherr von Prochazka (World War II)
❑ 1268 Robert Gilliland (Korean War)
❑ 1269 Robert Goebel (World War II)
❑ 1270 Robert Higginbotham (World War II)
❑ 1271 Robert Hite (World War II)
❑ 1272 Robert Howard (Vietnam)
❑ 1273 Robert Ingram (Vietnam)
❑ 1274 Robert J. Baer (World War II)
❑ 1275 Robert J. Kelly (Vietnam)
❑ 1276 Robert J. Natter (Vietnam)
❑ 1277 Robert Justice (World War II)
❑ 1278 Robert L. Scott (World War II)
❑ 1279 Robert L. Stewart (Vietnam)
❑ 1280 Robert L.J. Long (World War II)
❑ 1281 Robert Liles (World War II)
❑ 1282 Robert Mason (Vietnam)
❑ 1283 Robert McClurg (World War II)
❑ 1284 Robert Milton (World War II)
❑ 1285 Robert Modrzejewski (Vietnam)
❑ 1286 Robert Morgan (World War II)
❑ 1287 Robert Murray (World War II)
❑ 1288 Robert Nett (World War II)
❑ 1289 Robert O'Malley (Vietnam)
❑ 1290 Robert P. Fash (World War II)
❑ 1291 Robert P. Patterson Sr. (World War I)
❑ 1292 Robert Rankin (World War I)
❑ 1293 Robert Rosenthal (World War II)
❑ 1294 Robert S. Johnson (World War II)
❑ 1295 Robert S. Scott (World War II)
❑ 1296 Robert Simanek (Korean War)
❑ 1297 Robert Sutcliffe (World War II)
❑ 1298 Robert T. Stafford (World War II)
❑ 1299 Robert Thomas (World War II)
❑ 1300 Robert While (World War II)
❑ 1301 Robert Willias Foster (World War II)
❑ 1302 Robert Winks (World War II)
❑ 1303 Robert Yaeger (World War II)
❑ 1304 Robert York (World War II)
❑ 1305 Robill Roberts (World War II)
❑ 1306 Robin Olds (World War II)
❑ 1307 Robinson Risner (Korean War)
❑ 1308 Robley Rex (World War I)
❑ 1309 Rod Steiger (World War II)
❑ 1310 Rod Strohl (World War II)
❑ 1311 Roderick Bain (World War II)
❑ 1312 Roderick Chisholm (World War II)
❑ 1313 Rodolfo Hernandez (Korean War)
❑ 1314 Roger Conant (World War II)
❑ 1315 Roger Donlon (Vietnam)
❑ 1316 Roger Hedrick (World War II)
❑ 1317 Roger Jones (War of 1812)
❑ 1318 Rolf Ebhardt (World War II)
❑ 1319 Rolland Richardson (World War II)
❑ 1320 Ronald E. Ray (Vietnam)
❑ 1321 Ronald Hamlyn (World War II)
❑ 1322 Ronald J. Hays (Vietnam)
❑ 1323 Ronald J. Zlatoper (Vietnam)
❑ 1324 Ronald Rosser (Korean War)
❑ 1325 Roswell P. Bishop (Civil War)
❑ 1326 Roy Evans (World War II)
❑ 1327 Roy Hawthorne (World War II)
❑ 1328 Roy L. Johnson (World War II)
❑ 1329 Roy Redgrave (World War II)
❑ 1330 Royce Priest (World War II)
❑ 1331 Rudolf Falkowski (World War II)
❑ 1332 Rudolf Hess (World War II)
❑ 1333 Rudolf Kendler (World War II)
❑ 1334 Rudolf Sauerbrei

(World War II)
❑ 1335 Rudolf von Ribbentrop
(World War II)
❑ 1336 Russell Dunham
(World War II)
❑ 1337 Russell Haworth
(World War II)
❑ 1338 Rusty March
(World War II)
❑ 1339 Saddam Hussein
(Gulf War)
❑ 1340 Sam Lopez
(World War II)
❑ 1341 Sammy Davis Jr.
(World War II)
❑ 1342 Samuel B. Smith
(Civil War)
❑ 1343 Samuel Fallows
(Civil War)
❑ 1344 Samuel Holiday
(World War II)
❑ 1345 Samuel Russell Thomas
(Civil War)
❑ 1346 Sanford Moats
(World War II)
❑ 1347 Sepp Brandner
(World War II)
❑ 1348 Seth W. Brown
(Civil War)
❑ 1349 Sheldon Hall
(World War II)
❑ 1350 Shizuya Hayashi
(World War II)
❑ 1351 Shorty Powers
(World War II)
❑ 1352 Sidney Woods
(World War II)
❑ 1353 Siegfried Fischer
(World War II)
❑ 1354 Siegfried Freyer
(World War II)
❑ 1355 Siegmund Matheja
(World War II)
❑ 1356 Sighart Dinkel
(World War II)
❑ 1357 Silas Casey
(Civil War)
❑ 1358 Silas Stringham
(War of 1812)
❑ 1359 Silvestre Herrera
(World War II)
❑ 1360 Simeon Thayer
(American Revolution)
❑ 1361 Simon Wiesenthal
(World War II)
❑ 1362 Sir Brian Urquhart
(World War II)
❑ 1363 Sir Christopher Addison
(World War I)
❑ 1364 Sir Colin Scragg
(World War II)
❑ 1365 Sir Denis Smallwood
(World War II)
❑ 1366 Sir Frederick Rosier
(World War II)
❑ 1367 Sir Frederick Sowrey
(World War I)
❑ 1368 Sir Geoffrey Tuttle
(World War II)
❑ 1369 Sir George Askwith
(World War I)
❑ 1370 Sir George Warrender, 7th Baronet
(World War I)
❑ 1371 Sir Gordon Macready
(World War II)
❑ 1372 Sir Harry Broadhurst
(World War II)
❑ 1373 Sir Herbert Taylor
(Great French War)
❑ 1374 Sir John Lapsley
(World War II)
❑ 1375 Sir John R. Whitley
(World War II)
❑ 1376 Sir Michael Beetham
(World War II)
❑ 1377 Sir Michael Wilford
(World War II)
❑ 1378 Sir Paul Holder
(World War II)
❑ 1379 Sir Robert Grainger Thompson
(World War II)
❑ 1380 Sir Roderick McGrigor
(World War II)
❑ 1381 Sir Thomas Kelly-Kenny
(Boer War)
❑ 1382 Sir Wallace Kyle
(World War II)
❑ 1383 Sir William Wratten
(Gulf War)
❑ 1384 Slade Gorton
(War on Terror)
❑ 1385 Soeren Kam
(World War II)
❑ 1386 Sol Smith Russell
(Civil War)
❑ 1387 Stan Musial
(World War II)
❑ 1388 Stanley Andrews
(World War II)
❑ 1389 Stanley Bernard Grant
(World War II)
❑ 1390 Stanley Butchart
(World War II)
❑ 1391 Stanley Jozefiak
(World War II)
❑ 1392 Stanley R. Arthur
(Vietnam)
❑ 1393 Stanley Vejtasa
(World War II)
❑ 1394 Stansfield Turner
(Korean War)
❑ 1395 Stephen Bonner
(World War II)
❑ 1396 Stephen Carr Lyford
(Civil War)
❑ 1397 Stephen Gregg
(World War II)
❑ 1398 Stephen Miles Bouton
(World War I)
❑ 1399 Sterling Cale
(Korean War)
❑ 1400 Sterling Cale
(World War II)
❑ 1401 Steve Gerick
(World War II)
❑ 1402 Steve Kellman
(World War II)
❑ 1403 Steve Pisanos
(Vietnam)
❑ 1404 Steve Pisanos
(World War II)
❑ 1405 Steve Souchock
(World War II)
❑ 1406 Stewart L. Woodford
(Civil War)
❑ 1407 Stuart Symington
(Cold War)
❑ 1408 Tadeusz Majewski
(World War II)
❑ 1409 Tadeusz Skowronek
(World War II)
❑ 1410 Ted King
(World War II)
❑ 1411 Ted Lyons
(World War II)
❑ 1412 Ted Williams
(World War II)
❑ 1413 Teddy Allen
(Vietnam)
❑ 1414 Teller Ammons
(World War I)
❑ 1415 Tex Hill
(World War II)
❑ 1416 Thad Allen
(War on Terror)
❑ 1417 Theo Kroj
(World War II)
❑ 1418 Theo Nau
(World War II)
❑ 1419 Theodore Dutch Van Kirk
(World War II)
❑ 1420 Theodore Hugh Winters
(World War II)
❑ 1421 Theodorus Bailey
(Civil War)
❑ 1422 Thomas Atkins
(World War II)
❑ 1423 Thomas B. Hayward
(Korean War)
❑ 1424 Thomas B. Richey
(World War I)
❑ 1425 Thomas Claiborne
(Civil War)
❑ 1426 Thomas E. Maloney
(World War II)
❑ 1427 Thomas F. Miller
(World War II)
❑ 1428 Thomas Ferebee
(World War II)
❑ 1429 Thomas Geoffrey Pike
(World War II)
❑ 1430 Thomas H. Moorer
(World War II)
❑ 1431 Thomas Hudner Jr.
(Korean War)
❑ 1432 Thomas J. Lopez
(Vietnam)
❑ 1433 Thomas Kinsman
(Vietnam)
❑ 1434 Thomas Neil
(World War II)
❑ 1435 Thomas Nelson Page
(World War I)
❑ 1436 Thomas Pinckney
(American Revolution)
❑ 1437 Thomas S. Bocock
(Civil War)
❑ 1438 Thomas Tomlinson
(World War II)
❑ 1439 Thornton Miller
(World War II)
❑ 1440 Tibor Rubin
(Korean War)
❑ 1441 Timothy J. Keating
(Gulf War)
❑ 1442 Tom Emrich
(World War II)
❑ 1443 Tom Griffin
(World War II)
❑ 1444 Tom Harris
(World War II)
❑ 1445 Tom Kelley
(Vietnam)
❑ 1446 Tom Ridge
(War on Terror)
❑ 1447 Tommy Byrne
(World War II)
❑ 1448 Tommy Franks
(Cold War)
❑ 1449 Tony Curtis
(World War II)
❑ 1450 Tova Petersen Wiley
(World War II)
❑ 1451 Tracy Sugarman
(World War II)
❑ 1452 Travis Hoover
(World War II)
❑ 1453 Trevor Howard
(World War II)
❑ 1454 Truman Barnes
(World War II)
❑ 1455 Ulysses S. Grant 3rd.
(World War II)
❑ 1456 Ulysses S.G. Sharp Jr.
(Korean War)
❑ 1457 Utha Knox
(World War II)
❑ 1458 Val Peterson
(World War II)
❑ 1459 Van Barfoot
(World War II)
❑ 1460 Verlin Fortin
(World War II)
❑ 1461 Vernon Baker
(World War II)
❑ 1462 Vernon E. Clark
(Gulf War)
❑ 1463 Vernon Hopson
(World War II)
❑ 1464 Vernon McGarity
(World War II)
❑ 1465 Victor Blue
(Spanish-American War)
❑ 1466 Viktor Vitali
(World War II)
❑ 1467 Vincent Rieger
(World War II)
❑ 1468 Violet Cowden
(World War II)
❑ 1469 Virgil Banning
(World War II)
❑ 1470 Vivien Crea
(War on Terror)
❑ 1471 W. Jim Benz
(World War II)
❑ 1472 W. Robert Maxwell
(World War II)
❑ 1473 Waldemar F.A. Wendt
(World War II)
❑ 1474 Walker Mahurin
(World War II)
❑ 1475 Wallace Johnson
(World War II)
❑ 1476 Walter Bohm
(World War II)
❑ 1477 Walter Boomer
(Vietnam)
❑ 1478 Walter Briegleb
(World War II)
❑ 1479 Walter Carl Beckham
(World War II)
❑ 1480 Walter E. Boomer
(Gulf War)
❑ 1481 Walter Ehlers
(World War II)
❑ 1482 Walter F. Boone
(World War I)
❑ 1483 Walter Fasel
(World War II)
❑ 1484 Walter Harriman
(Civil War)
❑ 1485 Walter Heinlein
(World War II)
❑ 1486 Walter Lee Hopkins
(World War I)
❑ 1487 Walter Lundin
(World War II)
❑ 1488 Walter Marm
(Vietnam)
❑ 1489 Walter Matthau
(World War II)
❑ 1490 Walter Pidgeon
(World War I)
❑ 1491 Walter Starck
(World War II)
❑ 1492 Walter Stewart
(World War II)
❑ 1493 Walter Wolfrum
(World War II)
❑ 1494 Walther Hagenah
(World War II)
❑ 1495 Walton H. Walker
(World War I)
❑ 1496 Warren Lewis
(World War II)
❑ 1497 Warren Magnuson
(World War II)
❑ 1498 Warren Spahn
(World War II)
❑ 1499 Wayne Blickenstaff
(World War II)
❑ 1500 Wayne Morris
(World War II)
❑ 1501 Webster Anderson
(Vietnam)
❑ 1502 Wendell Freeland
(World War II)
❑ 1503 Werner Hoffman
(World War II)
❑ 1504 Werner Molge
(World War II)
❑ 1505 Werner Roell
(World War II)
❑ 1506 Werner Schroer
(World War II)
❑ 1507 Wesley Clark
(Vietnam)
❑ 1508 Wesley Fox
(Vietnam)
❑ 1509 Wesley L. McDonald
(Vietnam)
❑ 1510 Whiley Ford
(Korean War)
❑ 1511 Wilber Brucker
(World War I)
❑ 1512 Wilbur B. Webb
(World War II)
❑ 1513 Wilburn Ross
(World War II)
❑ 1514 Wilfred Billey
(World War II)
❑ 1515 Wilfred DeFour
(World War II)
❑ 1516 Wilfred Dulton
(World War II)
❑ 1517 Wilhelm Bertram
(World War II)
❑ 1518 Wilhelm Kriessmann
(World War II)
❑ 1519 Wilhelm Noller
(World War II)
❑ 1520 Will Rogers Jr.
(World War II)
❑ 1521 Willard Eder
(World War II)
❑ 1522 Willi Dipberger
(World War II)
❑ 1523 Willi Reschke
(World War II)
❑ 1524 William A. Owens
(Vietnam)
❑ 1525 William Allen
(World War II)
❑ 1526 William Anderson
(World War II)
❑ 1527 William Atkins
(World War II)
❑ 1528 William Atterbury
(World War I)
❑ 1529 William B. Freeman
(World War II)
❑ 1530 William B. King
(World War II)
❑ 1531 William Babcock Hazen
(Civil War)
❑ 1532 William Beyer
(World War II)
❑ 1533 William Birch
(World War II)
❑ 1534 William Bower
(World War II)
❑ 1535 William Braye
(World War II)
❑ 1536 William C. Edwards
(World War II)
❑ 1537 William Charette
(Korean War)
❑ 1538 William Copeland
(World War II)
❑ 1539 William Dennis David
(World War II)
❑ 1540 William Driscoll
(Vietnam)
❑ 1541 William E. Hall
(World War II)
❑ 1542 William E. Lamoreaux
(World War II)
❑ 1543 William E. Riley
(World War II)
❑ 1544 William F. Bringle
(Vietnam)
❑ 1545 William F. Morris
(Spanish-American War)
❑ 1546 William Flood
(World War II)
❑ 1547 William G. Sheen
(Civil War)
❑ 1548 William H. Emory
(Civil War)
❑ 1549 William H. Ludlow
(Civil War)
❑ 1550 William Heier
(World War II)
❑ 1551 William J. Crowe
(Vietnam)
❑ 1552 William J. Fallon
(Vietnam)
❑ 1553 William J. Flanagan
(Vietnam)
❑ 1554 William J. Hardee
(Civil War)
❑ 1555 William J. Schildt
(World War II)
❑ 1556 William Knowland
(World War II)
❑ 1557 William Leahy
(World War II)
❑ 1558 William Leonard
(World War II)
❑ 1559 William Liebenow
(World War II)
❑ 1560 William Manchester
(World War II)
❑ 1561 William Mannerback
(American Revolution)
❑ 1562 William Marquat
(World War I)
❑ 1563 William Mathis
(World War II)
❑ 1564 William Mulvey
(World War II)
❑ 1565 William Pratt
(World War I)
❑ 1566 William R. O'Brien
(World War II)
❑ 1567 William R. Poage
(World War I)
❑ 1568 William Reid
(World War II)
❑ 1569 William S. Cowles
(Spanish-American War)
❑ 1570 William Shaffer
(World War II)
❑ 1571 William Southerland
(Spanish-American War)
❑ 1572 William Sprague
(Civil War)
❑ 1573 William T. Sherman
(Civil War)
❑ 1574 William Wescott
(Korean War)
❑ 1575 William Wescott
(World War II)
❑ 1576 William Westmoreland
(Korean War)
❑ 1577 William Westmoreland
(Vietnam)
❑ 1578 William Westmoreland
(World War II)
❑ 1579 William Whistler
(Mexican-American War)
❑ 1580 William Windham
(Great French War)
❑ 1581 William Wingett
(World War II)
❑ 1582 Willis Hardy
(World War II)
❑ 1583 Willy Coppens de Houthulst
(World War I)
❑ 1584 Willy Tscherning
(World War II)
❑ 1585 Willy Unger
(World War II)
❑ 1586 Wilson Eagleson
(World War II)
❑ 1587 Wiltz P. Segura
(World War II)
❑ 1588 Winfield Scott Schley
(Spanish-American War)
❑ 1589 Winrich Behr
(World War II)
❑ 1590 Winston Churchill
(World War II)
❑ 1591 Winton W. Marshall
(Korean War)
❑ 1592 Wolff-Rudiger Guercke
(World War II)
❑ 1593 Wolfgang Altenberg
(World War II)
❑ 1594 Wolfgang Falck
(World War II)
❑ 1595 Wolfgang Kaupisch
(World War II)
❑ 1596 Wolfram Eisenlohr
(World War I)
❑ 1597 Worth H. Bagley
(Vietnam)
❑ 1598 Yenwith Whitney
(World War II)
❑ 1599 Ynez Mendoza
(World War II)
❑ 1600 Yogi Berra
(World War II)

2011 James Bond Mission Logs

COMPLETE SET (66)	5.00	12.00
❑ 1 Dr. No	.15	.40
❑ 2 Dr. No	.15	.40
❑ 3 Dr. No	.15	.40
❑ 4 From Russia With Love	.15	.40
❑ 5 From Russia With Love	.15	.40
❑ 6 From Russia With Love	.15	.40
❑ 7 Goldfinger	.15	.40
❑ 8 Goldfinger	.15	.40
❑ 9 Goldfinger	.15	.40
❑ 10 Thunderball	.15	.40
❑ 11 Thunderball	.15	.40
❑ 12 Thunderball	.15	.40
❑ 13 You Only Live Twice	.15	.40
❑ 14 You Only Live Twice	.15	.40
❑ 15 You Only Live Twice	.15	.40
❑ 16 On Her Majesty's Secret Service	.15	.40
❑ 17 On Her Majesty's Secret Service	.15	.40
❑ 18 On Her Majesty's Secret Service	.15	.40
❑ 19 Diamonds Are Forever	.15	.40
❑ 20 Diamonds Are Forever	.15	.40
❑ 21 Diamonds Are Forever	.15	.40
❑ 22 Live And Let Die	.15	.40
❑ 23 Live And Let Die	.15	.40
❑ 24 Live And Let Die	.15	.40
❑ 25 The Man With The Golden Gun	.15	.40
❑ 26 The Man With The Golden Gun	.15	.40
❑ 27 The Man With The Golden Gun	.15	.40
❑ 28 The Spy Who Loved Me	.15	.40
❑ 29 The Spy Who Loved Me	.15	.40
❑ 30 The Spy Who Loved Me	.15	.40
❑ 31 Moonraker	.15	.40
❑ 32 Moonraker	.15	.40
❑ 33 Moonraker	.15	.40
❑ 34 For Your Eyes Only	.15	.40
❑ 35 For Your Eyes Only	.15	.40
❑ 36 For Your Eyes Only	.15	.40
❑ 37 Octopussy	.15	.40
❑ 38 Octopussy	.15	.40
❑ 39 Octopussy	.15	.40
❑ 40 A View To A Kill	.15	.40
❑ 41 A View To A Kill	.15	.40
❑ 42 A View To A Kill	.15	.40
❑ 43 The Living Daylights	.15	.40
❑ 44 The Living Daylights	.15	.40
❑ 45 The Living Daylights	.15	.40
❑ 46 Licence To Kill	.15	.40
❑ 47 Licence To Kill	.15	.40
❑ 48 Licence To Kill	.15	.40
❑ 49 GoldenEye	.15	.40
❑ 50 GoldenEye	.15	.40
❑ 51 GoldenEye	.15	.40
❑ 52 Tomorrow Never Dies	.15	.40
❑ 53 Tomorrow Never Dies	.15	.40
❑ 54 Tomorrow Never Dies	.15	.40
❑ 55 The World Is Not Enough	.15	.40
❑ 56 The World Is Not Enough	.15	.40
❑ 57 The World Is Not Enough	.15	.40
❑ 58 Die Another Day	.15	.40
❑ 59 Die Another Day	.15	.40
❑ 60 Die Another Day	.15	.40
❑ 61 Casino Royale	.15	.40
❑ 62 Casino Royale	.15	.40
❑ 63 Casino Royale	.15	.40
❑ 64 Quantum of Solace	.15	.40
❑ 65 Quantum of Solace	.15	.40
❑ 66 Quantum of Solace	.15	.40
❑ VB6 Daniel Craig VINTAGE BOND/700	10.00	25.00

(issued as case topper)

2011 James Bond Mission Logs Autographs

OVERALL AUTO ODDS TWO PER BOX
L (LIMITED): 300-500 COPIES
VL (VERY LIMITED): 200-300 COPIES

❑ A148 Anatole Taubman L	6.00	15.00
❑ A157 Geoffrey Palmer L	10.00	25.00
❑ A158 Ulrich Thomsen VL	20.00	40.00
❑ A160 Eunice Gayson VL	20.00	40.00
❑ A163 Marilyn Galsworthy L	6.00	15.00
❑ A164 Bogdan Kominowski L	6.00	15.00
❑ A165 Anne Lonnberg L	8.00	20.00
❑ A169 Tricia Muller	6.00	15.00
❑ A174 Colin Salmon L	8.00	20.00
❑ A175 Aleta Morrison L	10.00	25.00
❑ A178 Fernando Guillen Cuervo L	6.00	15.00
❑ A179 Catherina von Schell VL	30.00	60.00
❑ A182 Kenneth Tsang L	6.00	15.00
❑ A185 Fiona Fullerton VL	25.00	50.00
❑ A187 Ricky Jay L	10.00	25.00
❑ A190 Daniel Benzali VL	20.00	40.00
❑ A191 Valerie Leon L	10.00	25.00
❑ A193 Andreas Wisniewski L	6.00	15.00
❑ A197 Burt Kwouk VL	25.00	50.00

2011 James Bond Mission Logs Bond Allies

COMPLETE SET (11)	8.00	20.00
STATED ODDS 1:12		
❑ BA35 M	1.50	4.00
❑ BA36 Jill Masterson	1.50	4.00
❑ BA37 Aki	1.50	4.00
❑ BA38 Sir Hilary Bray	1.50	4.00
❑ BA39 Felix Leiter	1.50	4.00
❑ BA40 Strutter	1.50	4.00
❑ BA41 Mary Goodnight	1.50	4.00
❑ BA42 Felicca	1.50	4.00
❑ BA43 Corinne Dufour	1.50	4.00
❑ BA44 Dolly	1.50	4.00
❑ BA45 Bianca	1.50	4.00

2011 James Bond Mission Logs Bond Villains

COMPLETE SET (11)	8.00	20.00
STATED ODDS 1:12		
❑ F71 Photographer	1.50	4.00
❑ F72 Ernst Stavro Blofeld	1.50	4.00
❑ F73 Pussy Galore	1.50	4.00
❑ F74 Fiona Volpe	1.50	4.00
❑ F75 Grunther	1.50	4.00
❑ F76 Dr. Metz	1.50	4.00
❑ F77 Tee Hee	1.50	4.00
❑ F78 Chula	1.50	4.00
❑ F79 Log Cabin Girl	1.50	4.00

MODERN ERA NON-SPORTS

- F80 Chang 1.50 4.00
- F81 Mischka and Grischka 1.50 4.00

2011 James Bond Mission Logs Bond...James Bond

COMPLETE SET (11) 8.00 20.00
STATED ODDS 1:12

- B1 Sean Connery in Dr. No 1.50 4.00
- B2 Sean Connery in From Russia With Love 1.50 4.00
- B3 Sean Connery in Goldfinger 1.50 4.00
- B4 Sean Connery in Thunderball 1.50 4.00
- B5 Sean Connery in You Only Live Twice 1.50 4.00
- B6 George Lazenby in On Her Majesty's Secret Service 1.50 4.00
- B7 Sean Connery in Diamonds Are Forever 1.50 4.00
- B8 Roger Moore in Live And Let Die 1.50 4.00
- B9 Roger Moore in The Man With The Golden Gun 1.50 4.00
- B10 Roger Moore in The Spy Who Loved Me 1.50 4.00
- B11 Roger Moore in Moonraker 1.50 4.00

2011 James Bond Mission Logs Femme Fatales

COMPLETE SET (9) 15.00 30.00
STATED ODDS 1:12

- F10 Paris Carver 2.00 5.00
- F11 Pussy Galore 2.00 5.00
- F12 Tiffany Case 2.00 5.00
- F13 Solitaire 2.00 5.00
- F14 Lupe Lamora 2.00 5.00
- F15 Jinx 2.00 5.00
- F16 Vesper Lynd 2.00 5.00
- F17 Camille 2.00 5.00
- F18 Miss Taro 2.00 5.00

2011 James Bond Mission Logs Full Bleed Autographs

OVERALL AUTO ODDS TWO PER BOX
L (LIMITED): 300-500 COPIES
VL (VERY LIMITED): 200-300 COPIES
EL (EXTREMELY LIMITED): 200 OR FEWER COPIES

- 1 Albert Moses L 6.00 15.00
- 2 Anthony Zerbe VL 30.00 60.00
- 3 Carlos Leal L 8.00 20.00
- 4 Daniel Craig EL 300.00 500.00
- 5 Earl Cameron L 6.00 15.00
- 6 Gabriele Ferzetti L 6.00 15.00
- 7 Joanna Lumley L 20.00 40.00
- 8 John Moreno L 6.00 15.00
- 9 John Wyman L 6.00 15.00
- 10 Lana Wood L 20.00 40.00
- 11 Lesley Langley L 8.00 20.00
- 12 Luciana Paluzzi L 20.00 40.00
- 13A Michael Madsen (red ink) VL 40.00 80.00
- 13B Michael Madsen (blue ink) 60.00 120.00 (issued as Rittenhouse Reward)
- 14 Pierce Brosnan EL 300.00 500.00
- 15 Shane Rimmer 6.00 15.00
- 16 Toby Stephens L 8.00 20.00
- 17 Blanche Ravalec 20.00 40.00

Richard Kiel L

2011 James Bond Mission Logs Promos

- P1 Daniel Craig/ (General Distribution) 1.50 4.00
- P2 Pierce Brosnan/ (Non-Sport Update) 1.50 4.00
- P3 Roger Moore/ (Binder Exclusive) 6.00 15.00
- P4 Sean Connery/ (Philly Convention) 2.00 5.00
- ISP1 Pierce Brosnan/ (Industry Summit) 10.00 20.00

2011 James Bond Mission Logs Relics

STATED ODDS ONE PER BOX
JBR6 ISSUED AS 3-CASE INCENTIVE
CRAIG AUTO ISSUED AS 9-CASE INCENTIVE

- JBR6 007 Jump Boat Carpeting/199/ (issued as 3-case incentive)75.00 150.00
- JBR14 Honda ATV Seat Leather/400 35.00 70.00
- JBR15 Tosca Opera Program/350 40.00 80.00
- JBR16 James Bond's Parachute Pack/700 10.00 25.00
- JBR17 Tosca Gift Bag/250 100.00 200.00
- JBR18 Karl Stromberg's Submarine Crew Uniform/800 8.00 20.00
- JBR19 Renard's Nuclear Bunker Suit/800 8.00 20.00
- JBR20 Drax Industries Jumpsuit/900 8.00 20.00
- JBR21 James Bond's Motorcycle Gloves/200150.00 250.00
- JBR22 James Bond's Tactical Vest/600 20.00 40.00
- JBR23 Renard's Submarine Shirt/775 8.00 20.00
- JBR24 James Bond's Ski Suit/900 8.00 20.00
- JBR25 Russian Camouflage Uniform/875 8.00 20.00
- JBR26 Russian Nuclear Bunker Suit/875 8.00 20.00
- NNO Tuxedo Shirt 300.00 450.00

Daniel Craig AU/150/ (issued as 9-case incentive)

2011 James Bond Mission Logs Women of James Bond Autographs

OVERALL AUTO ODDS TWO PER BOX
L (LIMITED): 300-500 COPIES
VL (VERY LIMITED): 200-300 COPIES

- WA38 Samantha Bond L 10.00 25.00
- WA47 Martine Beswicke VL 40.00 80.00

2011 Justin Bieber 2.0

COMPLETE SET (131) 25.00 50.00
COMP.SET w/o SP's (100) 15.00 30.00

- 1 Puzzle - top left FOIL SP .75 2.00
- 2 Puzzle - top center FOIL SP .75 2.00
- 3 Puzzle - top right FOIL SP .75 2.00
- 4 Puzzle - middle left FOIL SP .75 2.00
- 5 Puzzle - middle center FOIL SP .75 2.00
- 6 Puzzle - middle right FOIL SP .75 2.00
- 7 Puzzle - bottom left FOIL SP .75 2.00
- 8 Puzzle - bottom center FOIL SP .75 2.00
- 9 Puzzle - bottom right FOIL SP .75 2.00
- 10 Justin got to show .20 .50
- 11 Justin's fans can pop .20 .50
- 12 The 2010 AMA Artist of the Year .20 .50
- 13 Justin's talents go beyond singing .20 .50
- 14 A self-professed Belieber .20 .50
- 15 Justin showcased a different kind .20 .50
- 16 Justin's fragrance Someday .20 .50
- 17 Few entertainers have utilized .20 .50
- 18 While most fans won't get .20 .50
- 19 Puzzle - top left .20 .50
- 20 Puzzle - top center .20 .50
- 21 Puzzle - top right .20 .50
- 22 Puzzle - middle left .20 .50
- 23 Puzzle - middle center .20 .50
- 24 Puzzle - middle right .20 .50
- 25 Puzzle - bottom left .20 .50
- 26 Puzzle - bottom center .20 .50
- 27 Puzzle - bottom right .20 .50
- 28 Having been a driver .20 .50
- 29 Justin's music is so popular .20 .50
- 30 In a hilarious comedy bit .20 .50
- 31 In the first of several appearances .20 .50
- 32 Red Hot Chili Peppers frontman .20 .50
- 33 It was surprising to Justin .20 .50
- 34 To say Justin was shocked .20 .50
- 35 The Canadian superstar was named .20 .50
- 36 Justin and rapper Eminem .20 .50
- 37 Puzzle - top left .20 .50
- 38 Puzzle - top center .20 .50
- 39 Puzzle - top right .20 .50
- 40 Puzzle - middle left .20 .50
- 41 Puzzle - middle center .20 .50
- 42 Puzzle - middle right .20 .50
- 43 Puzzle - bottom left .20 .50
- 44 Puzzle - bottom center .20 .50
- 45 Puzzle - bottom right .20 .50
- 46 Stars of the action-comedy film .20 .50
- 47 The Canadian star was honored .20 .50
- 48 Showing his philanthropic side .20 .50
- 49 Clearly a crowd favorite .20 .50
- 50 In yet another awards cameo .20 .50
- 51 Justin added four more trophies .20 .50
- 52 Not even old enough to .20 .50
- 53 Scott Scooter Braun .20 .50
- 54 Justin along with father Jeremy .20 .50
- 55 Puzzle - top left .20 .50
- 56 Puzzle - top center .20 .50
- 57 Puzzle - top right .20 .50
- 58 Puzzle - middle left .20 .50
- 59 Puzzle - middle center .20 .50
- 60 Puzzle - middle right .20 .50
- 61 Puzzle - bottom left .20 .50
- 62 Puzzle - bottom center .20 .50
- 63 Puzzle - bottom right .20 .50
- 64 In a unique way to honor .20 .50
- 65 Having heard of the Brown .20 .50
- 66 Justin released an autobiography .20 .50
- 67 The teenage superstar released .20 .50
- 68 The Canadian superstar walked .20 .50
- 69 The teen sensation helped .20 .50
- 70 Justin kept the holiday party .20 .50
- 71 Justin was honored at Variety .20 .50
- 72 Justin, a big L.A. Lakers fan .20 .50
- 73 The Canadian singer joined .20 .50
- 74 Justin won the People's Voice .20 .50
- 75 Born with natural rhythm .20 .50
- 76 With talent versatile enough .20 .50
- 77 On May 19, 2011 .20 .50
- 78 Blessed with immense musical .20 .50
- 79 Music and a powerful singing .20 .50
- 80 While Justin takes his music .20 .50
- 81 He may be a teenager .20 .50
- 82 Success came quick .20 .50
- 83 What would you do .20 .50
- 84 True Blood and The Ides of March .20 .50
- 85 Will.i.am of the immensely popular .20 .50
- 86 A leading fashion trendsetter .20 .50
- 87 Charity causes and hoops .20 .50
- 88 Inspired by Justin's new fragrance .20 .50
- 89 There are many artists who inspire .20 .50
- 90 For Justin, style is important .20 .50
- 91 The monthly American culture .20 .50
- 92 Justin is a noted fan and friend .20 .50
- 93 The teenage superstar's award .20 .50
- 94 Justin showed his keen sense .20 .50
- 95 As with any young entertainer .20 .50
- 96 A worldwide tour means being .20 .50
- 97 While Justin will admit he's .20 .50
- 98 You know you have a bona .20 .50
- 99 Justin took the stage .20 .50
- 100 On Forbes annual list .20 .50
- 101 After Justin's February 2011 haircut .20 .50
- 102 Justin's 2011 documentary Never .20 .50
- 103 It was merely a matter of time .20 .50
- 104 Justin and Usher honored .20 .50
- 105 Justin made an appearance .20 .50
- 106 If there was any doubt about .20 .50
- 107 Justin helps promote the Pencils .20 .50
- 108 Justin charmed the hostesses .20 .50
- 109 The superstar singer has become .20 .50
- 110 My World Tour SP .75 2.00
- 111 MWT .75 2.00
- 112 MWT - New York City, USA SP .75 2.00
- 113 MWT .75 2.00
- 114 MWT .75 2.00
- 115 MWT - Oberhausen, Germany SP .75 2.00
- 116 MWT - Rotterdam, Netherlands SP .75 2.00
- 117 MWT - Paris, France SP .75 2.00
- 118 MWT - Antwerp, Belgium SP .75 2.00
- 119 MWT - Herning, Denmark SP .75 2.00
- 120 MWT - Madrid, Spain SP .75 2.00
- 121 MWT .75 2.00
- 122 MWT - Milan, Itayl SP .75 2.00
- 123 MWT - Tel Aviv, Israel SP .75 2.00
- 124 MWT - Singapore, Singapore SP .75 2.00
- 125 MWT - Kuala Lumpur, Malaysia SP .75 2.00
- 126 MWT - Bogor, Indonesia SP .75 2.00
- 127 MWT - Brisbane, Australia SP .75 2.00
- 128 MWT - Manila, Philippines SP .75 2.00
- 129 MWT - Hong Kong, Hong Kong SP .75 2.00
- 130 MWT .75 2.00
- 131 MWT - Osaka, Japan SP .75 2.00

2011 Justin Bieber 2.0 Holokote

*HOLOKOTE: 1.5X TO 4X BASIC CARDS

2011 Justin Bieber 2.0 Autographs

- 1 Justin Bieber

2011 Justin Bieber 2.0 Relics

- I1 Justin Bieber - Pants 15.00 40.00
- I2 Justin Bieber - Sweater 15.00 40.00
- I3 Justin Bieber - Pants 15.00 40.00

2011 Justin Bieber 2.0 Stickers

COMPLETE SET (30) 7.50 15.00

- 1 pink cardigan .40 1.00
- 2 black cap .40 1.00
- 3 white vest .40 1.00
- 4 hand over heart .40 1.00
- 5 hands on sunglasses .40 1.00
- 6 hand to ear .40 1.00
- 7 racing suit .40 1.00
- 8 hands in the air .40 1.00
- 9 pointing at chest .40 1.00
- 10 hands together .40 1.00
- 11 singing to hand .40 1.00
- 12 blue denim vest .40 1.00
- 13 Justin Bieber .40 1.00
- 14 Justin Bieber .40 1.00
- 15 Justin Bieber .40 1.00
- 16 All I See is You .40 1.00
- 17 Holding Your Hand .40 1.00
- 18 I Can See a Better Day .40 1.00
- 19 Make My Heart Pound .40 1.00
- 20 Somebody To Love .40 1.00
- 21 The 1 That Makes Me Crazy .40 1.00
- 22 Knock Knock .40 1.00
- 23 We Will Never Be Apart .40 1.00
- 24 That Should Be Me .40 1.00
- 25 Making You Laugh .40 1.00
- 26 Acoustic .40 1.00
- 27 I Close My Eyes .40 1.00
- 28 Justin Bieber .40 1.00
- 29 Justin Bieber .40 1.00
- 30 Justin Bieber .40 1.00

2011 Justin Bieber 2.0 Wide Scream

COMPLETE SET (16) 12.00 25.00

- 1L 4/2/2011 1.25 3.00
- 1R 4/2/2011 1.25 3.00
- 2L 11/23/2010 1.25 3.00
- 2R 11/23/2010 1.25 3.00
- 3L 12/10/2010 1.25 3.00
- 3R 12/10/2010 1.25 3.00
- 4L 6/18/2011 1.25 3.00
- 4R 6/18/2011 1.25 3.00
- 5L 6/8/2011 1.25 3.00
- 5R 6/8/2011 1.25 3.00
- 6L 5/13/2011 1.25 3.00
- 6R 5/13/2011 1.25 3.00
- 7L 4/19/2011 1.25 3.00
- 7R 4/19/2011 1.25 3.00
- 8L 3/29/2011 1.25 3.00
- 8R 3/29/2011 1.25 3.00

2011 Lost Relics

COMPLETE SET (36)
COMP.SET w/o RC2 (35)
STATED PRINT RUN 350 SER. #'d SETS

- CC1 Jack Shephard 10.00 25.00
- CC2 Juliet Burke 10.00 25.00
- CC3 Charlie Pace 10.00 25.00
- CC4 Claire Littleton 8.00 20.00
- CC5 Hugo Hurley Reyes 6.00 15.00
- CC6 Ana Lucia Cortez 15.00 40.00
- CC7 Libby Smith 6.00 15.00
- CC8 Jin Kwon 6.00 15.00
- CC9 Sun Kwon 12.00 30.00
- CC10 Sayid Jarrah 8.00 20.00
- CC11 Shannon Rutherford 10.00 25.00
- CC12 John Locke 8.00 20.00
- CC13 Ben Linus 8.00 20.00
- CC14 Charles Widmore 6.00 15.00
- CC15 Penny Widmore 10.00 25.00
- CC16 Liam Pace 6.00 15.00
- CC17 Michael Dawson 6.00 15.00
- CC18 Walt Lloyd 6.00 15.00
- CC19 Bernard Nadler 6.00 15.00
- CC20 Rose Nadler 6.00 15.00
- CC21 James Sawyer Ford 10.00 25.00
- CC22 Goodwin Stanhope 8.00 20.00
- CC23 Miles Straume 8.00 20.00
- CC24 Ilana Verdansky 8.00 20.00
- CC25 Young Ben Linus 6.00 15.00
- CC26 Yemi 6.00 15.00
- CC27 Naomi Dorrit 8.00 20.00
- CC28 Edward Mars 6.00 15.00
- CC29 Tom Friendly 6.00 15.00
- CC30 Christian Shephard 6.00 15.00
- CC31 Sun Kwon 12.00 30.00
- CC32 Jin Kwon 6.00 15.00
- CC33 Shannon Rutherford 10.00 25.00
- CC34 Charlie Pace 12.00 30.00
- RC1 Mr. Cluck's Chicken Shack Sign 25.00 50.00
- RC2 Oceanic Airlines 815 Airplane/ (issued as box topper)50.00 100.00
- P1 Group of Twelve PROMO .75 2.00

2011 Lost Relics Autographs

STATED ODDS ONE PER PACK

- 1 Adetokumboh McCormack 6.00 15.00
- 2 Bai Ling 25.00 50.00
- 3 Carlton Cuse - Producer 50.00 100.00
- 4 Damon Lindelof - Producer 50.00 100.00
- 5 John Hawkes 6.00 15.00
- 6 Kenton Duty 6.00 15.00
- 7 Kimberly Joseph 6.00 15.00
- 8 Naveen Andrews w hat 25.00 50.00
- 9 Naveen Andrews w o hat 25.00 50.00

2011 Marvel Beginnings

COMPLETE SET (180) 20.00 40.00

- 1 Thor .15 .40
- 2 Doctor Doom .15 .40
- 3 Hawkeye .15 .40
- 4 Super Skrull .15 .40
- 5 Moondragon .15 .40
- 6 Mastermind .15 .40
- 7 Shatterstar .15 .40
- 8 Hulkling .15 .40
- 9 Black Bolt .15 .40
- 10 Fabian Cortez .15 .40
- 11 Phoenix .15 .40
- 12 Madame Masque .15 .40
- 13 Spider-Girl .15 .40
- 14 Radioactive Man .15 .40
- 15 Devil Dinosaur and Moon Boy .15 .40
- 16 Maelstrom .15 .40
- 17 Domino .15 .40
- 18 Snarks .15 .40
- 19 Warstar .15 .40
- 20 Mimic .15 .40
- 21 Spider-Man 2099 .15 .40
- 22 Nighthawk .15 .40
- 23 Jamie Braddock .15 .40
- 24 Starbolt .15 .40
- 25 Korvac .15 .40
- 26 Scarlet Spider .15 .40
- 27 Queen .15 .40
- 28 Zarathos .15 .40
- 29 Destiny .15 .40
- 30 Beyonder .15 .40
- 31 Invisible Woman .15 .40
- 32 Loki .15 .40
- 33 Box .15 .40
- 34 Red Hulk .15 .40
- 35 Hellcat .15 .40
- 36 Attuma .15 .40
- 37 Dusk .15 .40
- 38 Ego .15 .40
- 39 Hank Pym .15 .40
- 40 Kurse .15 .40
- 41 Jessica Jones .15 .40
- 42 Chameleon .15 .40
- 43 Changling .15 .40
- 44 Polaris .15 .40
- 45 Morlun .15 .40
- 46 Synch .15 .40
- 47 Baron Blood .15 .40
- 48 Thunderbird .15 .40
- 49 Cybele .15 .40
- 50 Bushwacker .15 .40
- 51 Doctor Strange .15 .40
- 52 Carnage .15 .40
- 53 Iceman .15 .40
- 54 Shatterax .15 .40
- 55 Doc Samson .15 .40
- 56 Sebastian Shaw .15 .40
- 57 Cannonball .15 .40
- 58 Swarm .15 .40
- 59 Electro .15 .40
- 60 Wiz Kid .15 .40
- 61 Nick Fury .15 .40
- 62 Sabretooth .15 .40
- 63 Magma .15 .40
- 64 Spider-Slayers .15 .40
- 65 Legion .15 .40
- 66 Gwen Stacey .15 .40
- 67 Belasco .15 .40
- 68 Stilt-Man .15 .40
- 69 Crimson Dynamo .15 .40
- 70 Wolfsbane .15 .40
- 71 Daredevil Noir .15 .40
- 72 Blackheart .15 .40
- 73 Quake .15 .40
- 74 Brood .15 .40
- 75 Lockheed .15 .40
- 76 Red Guardian .15 .40
- 77 Lilith .15 .40
- 78 D'Spayre .15 .40
- 79 Arsenic and Old Lace .15 .40
- 80 Sharon Carter .15 .40
- 81 Quicksilver .15 .40
- 82 Tarantula .15 .40
- 83 Titania .15 .40
- 84 Whizzer .15 .40
- 85 Madelyne Pryor .15 .40
- 86 Firebird .15 .40
- 87 Pyro .15 .40
- 88 J. Jonah Jameson .15 .40
- 89 Prodigy .15 .40
- 90 Phoenix Force .15 .40
- 91 Colossus .15 .40
- 92 Galactus .15 .40
- 93 Guardian .15 .40
- 94 Crystal .15 .40
- 95 Dragon Man .15 .40
- 96 Absorbing Man .15 .40
- 97 Shuma-Gorath .15 .40
- 98 Namorita .15 .40
- 99 Prowler .15 .40
- 100 Adversary .15 .40
- 101 Ghost Rider .15 .40
- 102 Firestar .15 .40
- 103 Winter Soldier .15 .40
- 104 Doppelganger .15 .40
- 105 Gorgon .15 .40
- 106 Justin Hammer .15 .40
- 107 Sister Grimm .15 .40
- 108 Stature .15 .40
- 109 Harry Osborn .15 .40
- 110 Alistair Smythe .15 .40
- 111 War Machine .15 .40
- 112 Blink .15 .40
- 113 Tiger Shark .15 .40
- 114 Jack Frost .15 .40
- 115 Mr. Fear .15 .40
- 116 Bucky Barnes .15 .40
- 117 Krang .15 .40
- 118 Ravage .15 .40
- 119 Shocker .15 .40
- 120 Amadeus Cho .15 .40
- 121 She-Hulk .15 .40
- 122 Elektra .15 .40
- 123 Turbo .15 .40
- 124 Morbius .15 .40
- 125 Clea .15 .40
- 126 Baron Mordo .15 .40
- 127 Machine Man .15 .40
- 128 Trevor Fitzroy .15 .40
- 129 Black Cat .15 .40
- 130 Graviton .15 .40
- 131 Gambit .15 .40
- 132 Bullseye .15 .40
- 133 Butterfly .15 .40
- 134 Hercules .15 .40
- 135 Hammerhead .15 .40
- 136 American Eagle .15 .40
- 137 Beetle .15 .40
- 138 Moonstar .15 .40
- 139 Venom .15 .40
- 140 Pip the Troll .15 .40
- 141 Ultimate Wolverine .15 .40
- 142 Jigsaw .15 .40
- 143 Strong Guy .15 .40
- 144 Spiral .15 .40
- 145 Yukio .15 .40
- 146 Deathbird .15 .40
- 147 Multiple Man .15 .40
- 148 Leader .15 .40
- 149 Night Thrasher .15 .40
- 150 Cameron Hodge .15 .40
- 151 Storm .15 .40
- 152 Kingpin .15 .40
- 153 Impossible Man .15 .40
- 154 Arcade .15 .40
- 155 Speedball .15 .40
- 156 Wonder Man .15 .40
- 157 Steel Serpent .15 .40
- 158 Joseph .15 .40
- 159 Vulture .15 .40
- 160 Wiccan .15 .40
- 161 Archangel .15 .40
- 162 N'astirh .15 .40
- 163 Eternity .15 .40
- 164 Obadiah Stane .15 .40
- 165 Cloak and Dagger .15 .40
- 166 William Stryker .15 .40
- 167 Stryfe .15 .40
- 168 Phantom Rider .15 .40
- 169 Supreme Intelligence .15 .40
- 170 Arachne .15 .40
- 171 Iron Man Noir .15 .40
- 172 Sunspot .15 .40
- 173 Onslaught .15 .40
- 174 Typhoid Mary .15 .40
- 175 Forgotten One .15 .40
- 176 Awesome Android .15 .40
- 177 Dr. Arnim Zola .15 .40
- 178 Karnak .15 .40
- 179 Avalanche .15 .40
- 180 Frankenstein's Monster .15 .40

2011 Marvel Beginnings Printing Plates Black

STATED PRINT RUN 1 SER. #'d SET
UNPRICED DUE TO SCARCITY

2011 Marvel Beginnings Printing Plates Cyan

STATED PRINT RUN 1 SER. #'d SET
UNPRICED DUE TO SCARCITY

2011 Marvel Beginnings Printing Plates Magenta

STATED PRINT RUN 1 SER. #'d SET
UNPRICED DUE TO SCARCITY

2011 Marvel Beginnings Printing Plates Yellow

STATED PRINT RUN 1 SER. #'d SET
UNPRICED DUE TO SCARCITY

2011 Marvel Beginnings Breakthrough Issues

COMPLETE SET (45) 15.00 30.00
STATED ODDS 1:1

- B1 Amazing Fantasy #15 .50 1.25
- B2 Giant-Size X-Men #1 .50 1.25
- B3 Avengers #4 .50 1.25
- B4 Wolverine #75 .50 1.25
- B5 Incredible Hulk #1 .50 1.25
- B6 X-Men #25 .50 1.25
- B7 Amazing Spider-Man #122 .50 1.25
- B8 Daredevil #181 .50 1.25
- B9 Uncanny X-Men #141 .50 1.25
- B10 Fantastic Four #5 .50 1.25
- B11 Journey Into Mystery #83 .50 1.25
- B12 Silver Surfer #1 .50 1.25
- B13 Wolverine Mini-Series #4 .50 1.25
- B14 Wolverine #145 .50 1.25
- B15 Amazing Spider-Man #6 .50 1.25
- B16 Avengers #1 .50 1.25
- B17 Uncanny X-Men #171 .50 1.25
- B18 Amazing Spider-Man #2 .50 1.25
- B19 Iron Man #225 .50 1.25
- B20 Fantastic Four #100 .50 1.25
- B21 Uncanny X-Men #100 .50 1.25
- B22 Uncanny X-Men #256 .50 1.25
- B23 Amazing Spider-Man #13 .50 1.25
- B24 Uncanny X-Men #14 .50 1.25
- B25 Iron Man #55 .50 1.25
- B26 X-Force #1 .50 1.25
- B27 Tales of Suspense #57 .50 1.25
- B28 Amazing Spider-Man #90 .50 1.25
- B29 Amazing Spider-Man #238 .50 1.25
- B30 Uncanny X-Men #248 .50 1.25
- B31 Uncanny X-Men #121 .50 1.25
- B32 Fantastic Four #18 .50 1.25
- B33 X-Factor #87 .50 1.25
- B34 Generation X #1 .50 1.25
- B35 Fantastic Four #60 .50 1.25
- B36 Ultimates #1 .50 1.25
- B37 Captain America #1 .50 1.25
- B38 Civil War #2 .50 1.25
- B39 Amazing Spider-Man #583 .50 1.25
- B40 Annihilation #1 .50 1.25
- B41 Daredevil #1 .50 1.25
- B42 Daredevil Noir #1 .50 1.25
- B43 X-Men Noir #1 .50 1.25
- B44 Invincible Iron Man #1 .50 1.25
- B45 Spider-Woman #1 .50 1.25

2011 Marvel Beginnings Breakthrough Issues Printing Plates Black

STATED PRINT RUN 1 SER. #'d SET
UNPRICED DUE TO SCARCITY

2011 Marvel Beginnings Breakthrough Issues Printing Plates Cyan

STATED PRINT RUN 1 SER. #'d SET
UNPRICED DUE TO SCARCITY

2011 Marvel Beginnings Breakthrough Issues Printing Plates Magenta

STATED PRINT RUN 1 SER. #'d SET
UNPRICED DUE TO SCARCITY

2011 Marvel Beginnings Breakthrough Issues Printing Plates Yellow

STATED PRINT RUN 1 SER. #'d SET
UNPRICED DUE TO SCARCITY

2011 Marvel Beginnings Breakthrough Issues Autographs

OVERALL AUTO ODDS 1:72

- B1 Stan Lee 200.00 300.00
- B2 Len Wein 15.00 30.00
- B3 Stan Lee
- B4A Adam Kubert 15.00 30.00
- B4B Dan Green 15.00 30.00
- B4C Larry Hama 15.00 30.00
- B5 Stan Lee 200.00 300.00
- B6A Fabian Nicieza 15.00 30.00
- B6B Matthew Ryan 15.00 30.00
- B7 Gerry Conway 15.00 30.00
- B9 Terry Austin 15.00 30.00
- B10A Joe Sinnott 30.00 60.00
- B10B Stan Lee
- B11A Joe Sinnott 30.00 60.00
- B11B Larry Lieber 20.00 40.00
- B11C Stan Lee 200.00 300.00
- B12A Joe Sinnott 30.00 60.00
- B12B Stan Lee
- B13 Tom Orzechowski 20.00 40.00
- B15 Stan Lee 200.00 300.00
- B16A George Perez 20.00 40.00
- B16B Kurt Busiek 15.00 30.00
- B16C Tom Smith 15.00 30.00
- B17A Bob Wiacek 15.00 30.00
- B17B Ron Zalme 15.00 30.00
- B18 Stan Lee 200.00 300.00

❑ B19A David Michelinie 15.00 30.00
❑ B19B Mark D. Bright 20.00 40.00
❑ B20A Joe Sinnott
❑ B20B Stan Lee
❑ B22 Tom Orzechowski 20.00 40.00
❑ B23 Stan Lee
❑ B24 Stan Lee
❑ B25 Joe Sinnott 30.00 60.00
❑ B26 Fabian Nicieza 15.00 30.00
❑ B27 Stan Lee
❑ B28 Stan Lee
❑ B29 Roger Stern 15.00 30.00
❑ B30 Dan Green 15.00 30.00
❑ B31 Terry Austin 15.00 30.00
❑ B32 Stan Lee
❑ B33A Joe Quesada 20.00 40.00
❑ B33B Peter David 15.00 30.00
❑ B35 Mark Waid 15.00 30.00
❑ B36 Bryan Hitch
❑ B38 Steve McNiven 15.00 30.00
❑ B39 Mark Waid 15.00 30.00
❑ B40 Gabriele Dell'otto 15.00 30.00
❑ B41 Stan Lee 200.00 300.00
❑ B42A Alex Irvine 15.00 30.00
❑ B42B Tomm Coker 20.00 40.00
❑ B43A Dennis Calero 15.00 30.00
❑ B43B Fred Van Lente 15.00 30.00
❑ B44 Salvador Larroca 20.00 40.00
❑ B45A Alex Maleev 20.00 40.00
❑ B45B Brian Michael Bendis 15.00 30.00

2011 Marvel Beginnings Breakthrough Issues Autographs Dual

OVERALL AUTO ODDS 1:72

❑ B4 Larry Hama
Adam Kubert
❑ B6 Fabian Nicieza
Matthew Ryan
❑ B9 Terry Austin
Tom Orzechowski
❑ B10 Joe Sinnott
Stan Lee
❑ B11 Stan Lee
Larry Lieber
❑ B12 Joe Sinnott
Stan Lee
❑ B16 George Perez
Tom Smith
❑ B17A Ron Zalme
Bob Wiacek
❑ B17B Tom Orzehowski
Bob Wiacek
❑ B19 Mark D. Bright
David Michelinie
❑ B20 Joe Sinnott
Stan Lee
❑ B30 Tom Orzechowski
Dan Green
❑ B33 Peter David
Joe Quesada
❑ B42 Tomm Coker
Alex Irvine
❑ B43 Fred Van Lente
Dennis Calero
❑ B45 Brian Michael Bendis
Alex Maleev

2011 Marvel Beginnings Breakthrough Issues Autographs Triple

OVERALL AUTO ODDS 1:72

❑ B4 Adam Kubert
Dan Green/Larry Hama
❑ B11 Joe Sinnott
Larry Lieber/Stan Lee
❑ B16 George Perez
Kurt Busiek/Tom Smith
❑ B17 Bob Wiacek
Ron Zalme/Tom Orzechowski

2011 Marvel Beginnings Comic Book Panels

STATED ODDS

❑ UM1 The Amazing Spider-Man #2 /66 50.00 100.00
❑ UM2 The Amazing Spider-Man #4 /53 50.00 100.00
❑ UM3 The Amazing Spider-Man #6 /61 50.00 100.00
❑ UM4 The Amazing Spider-Man #9 /68 50.00 100.00
❑ UM5 The Amazing Spider-Man #14 /66 50.00 100.00
❑ UM6 The Amazing Spider-Man #18 /51 50.00 100.00
❑ UM7 The Amazing Spider-Man #25 /45 50.00 100.00
❑ UM8 The Amazing Spider-Man #50 /39 50.00 100.00
❑ UM12 The Avengers #57 /50 50.00 100.00
❑ UM13 Daredevil #181 /55 50.00 100.00

2011 Marvel Beginnings Marvel Prime

COMPLETE SET (60) 40.00 80.00
STATED ODDS 1:2

❑ M1 Adam Warlock .75 2.00
❑ M2 Angel .75 2.00
❑ M3 Apocalypse .75 2.00
❑ M4 Beast .75 2.00
❑ M5 Black Panther .75 2.00
❑ M6 Black Widow .75 2.00
❑ M7 Captain America .75 2.00
❑ M8 Colossus .75 2.00
❑ M9 Cyclops .75 2.00
❑ M10 Daredevil .75 2.00
❑ M11 Deadpool .75 2.00
❑ M12 Doctor Doom .75 2.00
❑ M13 Doctor Octopus .75 2.00
❑ M14 Doctor Strange .75 2.00
❑ M15 Elektra .75 2.00
❑ M16 Emma Frost .75 2.00
❑ M17 Galactus .75 2.00
❑ M18 Gambit .75 2.00
❑ M19 Ghost Rider .75 2.00
❑ M20 Green Goblin .75 2.00
❑ M21 Hawkeye .75 2.00
❑ M22 Hulk .75 2.00
❑ M23 Human Torch .75 2.00
❑ M24 Iceman .75 2.00
❑ M25 Invisible Woman .75 2.00
❑ M26 Iron Fist .75 2.00
❑ M27 Iron Man .75 2.00
❑ M28 Jean Grey .75 2.00
❑ M29 Juggernaut .75 2.00
❑ M30 Kitty Pryde .75 2.00
❑ M31 Kraven .75 2.00
❑ M32 Loki .75 2.00
❑ M33 Luke Cage .75 2.00
❑ M34 Magneto .75 2.00
❑ M35 Marvel Girl .75 2.00
❑ M36 Mister Sinister .75 2.00
❑ M37 Mr. Fantastic .75 2.00
❑ M38 Ms. Marvel .75 2.00
❑ M39 Mystique .75 2.00
❑ M40 Nightcrawler .75 2.00
❑ M41 Professor X .75 2.00
❑ M42 Psylocke .75 2.00
❑ M43 Punisher .75 2.00
❑ M44 Red Skull .75 2.00
❑ M45 Rogue .75 2.00
❑ M46 Sabretooth .75 2.00
❑ M47 Scarlet Witch .75 2.00
❑ M48 She-Hulk .75 2.00
❑ M49 Silver Surfer .75 2.00
❑ M50 Spider-Man .75 2.00
❑ M51 Spider-Woman .75 2.00
❑ M52 Storm .75 2.00
❑ M53 Thanos .75 2.00
❑ M54 Thing .75 2.00
❑ M55 Thor .75 2.00
❑ M56 Venom .75 2.00
❑ M57 Vision .75 2.00
❑ M58 War Machine .75 2.00
❑ M59 Wasp .75 2.00
❑ M60 Wolverine .75 2.00

2011 Marvel Beginnings Sketches

STATED ODDS 1:72

❑ 1 Aaron Sowd
❑ 2 Andy MacDonald
❑ 3 Arvin John ACE Evangelista
❑ 4 Ben Herrera
❑ 5 Ben Young
❑ 6 Bill Pulkovski
❑ 7 Billy Martin
❑ 8 Brandon Singleton
❑ 9 Brian Kong
❑ 10 Bruce Gerlach
❑ 11 Bryan Turner
❑ 12 Cal Slayton
❑ 13 Cat Staggs
❑ 14 Charles Hall
❑ 15 Chris Forman
❑ 16 Dan Gorman
❑ 17 Dan Panosian
❑ 18 Dave Ryan
❑ 19 David Mack
❑ 20 Eric Ninaltowski
❑ 21 Frank Kadar
❑ 22 Frankie B. Washington
❑ 23 George Calloway
❑ 24 George Deep
❑ 25 George GEO Davis
❑ 26 Gilbert Monsanto
❑ 27 Hamilton Cline
❑ 28 Hanie Mohd
❑ 29 Irma Ahmed
❑ 30 Jake Minor
❑ 31 Jason Adams
❑ 32 Jason Keith Phillips
❑ 33 Jerry Fleming
❑ 34 Jerry Gaylord
❑ 35 Jim Cheung
❑ 36 Joe Pekar
❑ 37 Joel Carroll
❑ 38 Johnboy Meyers
❑ 39 Jon Hughes
❑ 40 Jose Jaro
❑ 41 Joyce Chin
❑ 42 Kate Bradley
❑ 43 Katie Cook
❑ 44 Ken Steacy
❑ 45 Kevin Gentilcore
❑ 46 Kevin Graham
❑ 47 Lak Lim
❑ 48 Lawrence Reynolds
❑ 49 Lord Mesa
❑ 50 Mark de Castro
❑ 51 Mark Henry
❑ 52 Mark McKenna
❑ 53 Matt Grigsby
❑ 54 Matthew Minor
❑ 55 Michael Duron
❑ 56 Mike Miller
❑ 57 Remi Dousset
❑ 58 Remy Eisu Mokhtar
❑ 59 Renato Butch Mapa
❑ 60 Richard Molinelli
❑ 61 Richard Pace
❑ 62 Rose Lumibao
❑ 63 Roy Cover
❑ 64 Rusty Gilligan
❑ 65 Ryan Kincaid
❑ 66 Ryan Orosco
❑ 67 Sarah Wilkinson
❑ 68 Sebastian Mazuera
❑ 69 Travis Walton
❑ 70 Wendy Chew

2011 Marvel Beginnings Villain Hologram

STATED ODDS 1:72

❑ H1 Apocalypse 20.00 40.00
❑ H2 Baron Zemo 20.00 40.00
❑ H3 Bullseye 20.00 40.00
❑ H4 Carnage 20.00 40.00
❑ H5 Dark Phoenix 20.00 40.00
❑ H6 Deadpool 20.00 40.00
❑ H7 Doctor Doom 20.00 40.00
❑ H8 Doctor Octopus 20.00 40.00
❑ H9 Dormammu 20.00 40.00
❑ H10 Dracula 20.00 40.00
❑ H11 Electro 20.00 40.00
❑ H12 Elektra 20.00 40.00
❑ H13 Enchantress 20.00 40.00
❑ H14 Fin Fang Foom 20.00 40.00
❑ H15 Galactus 20.00 40.00
❑ H16 Green Goblin 20.00 40.00
❑ H17 Hobgoblin 20.00 40.00
❑ H18 Hood 20.00 40.00
❑ H19 Juggernaut 20.00 40.00
❑ H20 Kang the Conquerer 20.00 40.00
❑ H21 Kingpin 20.00 40.00
❑ H22 Kraven 20.00 40.00
❑ H23 Lady Deathstrike 20.00 40.00
❑ H24 Lizard 20.00 40.00
❑ H25 Loki 20.00 40.00
❑ H26 Magneto 20.00 40.00
❑ H27 Mephisto 20.00 40.00
❑ H28 Mister Sinister 20.00 40.00
❑ H29 MODOK 20.00 40.00
❑ H30 Mysterio 20.00 40.00
❑ H31 Mystique 20.00 40.00
❑ H32 Red Skull 20.00 40.00
❑ H33 Sabretooth 20.00 40.00
❑ H34 Sandman 20.00 40.00
❑ H35 Satana 20.00 40.00
❑ H36 Scorpion 20.00 40.00
❑ H37 Sentinels 20.00 40.00
❑ H38 Stryfe 20.00 40.00
❑ H39 Super Skrull 20.00 40.00
❑ H40 Thanos 20.00 40.00
❑ H41 Ultron 20.00 40.00
❑ H42 Venom 20.00 40.00

2011 Marvel Beginnings X-Men Die-Cut

COMPLETE SET (45) 25.00 50.00
STATED ODDS 1:2

❑ X1 Angel .75 2.00
❑ X2 Armor .75 2.00
❑ X3 Banshee .75 2.00
❑ X4 Beast .75 2.00
❑ X5 Bishop .75 2.00
❑ X6 Boom-Boom .75 2.00
❑ X7 Cable .75 2.00
❑ X8 Cannonball .75 2.00
❑ X9 Chamber .75 2.00
❑ X10 Cloak .75 2.00
❑ X11 Colossus .75 2.00
❑ X12 Cyclops .75 2.00
❑ X13 Dagger .75 2.00
❑ X14 Darwin .75 2.00
❑ X15 Dazzler .75 2.00
❑ X16 Domino .75 2.00
❑ X17 Emma Frost .75 2.00
❑ X18 Forge .75 2.00
❑ X19 Gambit .75 2.00
❑ X20 Havok .75 2.00
❑ X21 Hepzibah .75 2.00
❑ X22 Husk .75 2.00
❑ X23 Iceman .75 2.00
❑ X24 Jean Grey .75 2.00
❑ X25 Jubilee .75 2.00
❑ X26 Karma .75 2.00
❑ X27 Kitty Pryde .75 2.00
❑ X28 Longshot .75 2.00
❑ X29 Marrow .75 2.00
❑ X30 Marvel Girl .75 2.00
❑ X31 Namor .75 2.00
❑ X32 Nightcrawler .75 2.00
❑ X33 Northstar .75 2.00
❑ X34 Pixie .75 2.00
❑ X35 Polaris .75 2.00
❑ X36 Professor X .75 2.00
❑ X37 Psylocke .75 2.00
❑ X38 Rogue .75 2.00
❑ X39 Storm .75 2.00
❑ X40 Sunfire .75 2.00
❑ X41 Thunderbird .75 2.00
❑ X42 Warpath .75 2.00
❑ X43 Wolverine .75 2.00
❑ X44 X-23 .75 2.00
❑ X45 Xorn .75 2.00

2011 Marvel Universe

COMPLETE SET (90) 6.00 15.00

❑ 1 The Korvac Saga .15 .40
❑ 2 The Korvac Saga .15 .40
❑ 3 The Korvac Saga .15 .40
❑ 4 The Korvac Saga .15 .40
❑ 5 The Korvac Saga .15 .40
❑ 6 The Korvac Saga .15 .40
❑ 7 The Korvac Saga .15 .40
❑ 8 The Korvac Saga .15 .40
❑ 9 The Korvac Saga .15 .40
❑ 10 Secret Wars I .15 .40
❑ 11 Secret Wars I .15 .40
❑ 12 Secret Wars I .15 .40
❑ 13 Secret Wars I .15 .40
❑ 14 Secret Wars I .15 .40
❑ 15 Secret Wars I .15 .40
❑ 16 Secret Wars I .15 .40
❑ 17 Secret Wars I .15 .40
❑ 18 Secret Wars I .15 .40
❑ 19 Fall of the Mutants .15 .40
❑ 20 Fall of the Mutants .15 .40
❑ 21 Fall of the Mutants .15 .40
❑ 22 Fall of the Mutants .15 .40
❑ 23 Fall of the Mutants .15 .40
❑ 24 Fall of the Mutants .15 .40
❑ 25 Fall of the Mutants .15 .40
❑ 26 Fall of the Mutants .15 .40
❑ 27 Fall of the Mutants .15 .40
❑ 28 Age of Apocalypse .15 .40
❑ 29 Age of Apocalypse .15 .40
❑ 30 Age of Apocalypse .15 .40
❑ 31 Age of Apocalypse .15 .40
❑ 32 Age of Apocalypse .15 .40
❑ 33 Age of Apocalypse .15 .40
❑ 34 Age of Apocalypse .15 .40
❑ 35 Age of Apocalypse .15 .40
❑ 36 Age of Apocalypse .15 .40
❑ 37 Heroes Reborn .15 .40
❑ 38 Heroes Reborn .15 .40
❑ 39 Heroes Reborn .15 .40
❑ 40 Heroes Reborn .15 .40
❑ 41 Heroes Reborn .15 .40
❑ 42 Heroes Reborn .15 .40
❑ 43 Heroes Reborn .15 .40
❑ 44 Heroes Reborn .15 .40
❑ 45 Heroes Reborn .15 .40
❑ 46 Civil War .15 .40
❑ 47 Civil War .15 .40
❑ 48 Civil War .15 .40
❑ 49 Civil War .15 .40
❑ 50 Civil War .15 .40
❑ 51 Civil War .15 .40
❑ 52 Civil War .15 .40
❑ 53 Civil War .15 .40
❑ 54 Civil War .15 .40
❑ 55 World War Hulk .15 .40
❑ 56 World War Hulk .15 .40
❑ 57 World War Hulk .15 .40
❑ 58 World War Hulk .15 .40
❑ 59 World War Hulk .15 .40
❑ 60 World War Hulk .15 .40
❑ 61 World War Hulk .15 .40
❑ 62 World War Hulk .15 .40
❑ 63 World War Hulk .15 .40
❑ 64 Secret Invasion .15 .40
❑ 65 Secret Invasion .15 .40
❑ 66 Secret Invasion .15 .40
❑ 67 Secret Invasion .15 .40
❑ 68 Secret Invasion .15 .40
❑ 69 Secret Invasion .15 .40
❑ 70 Secret Invasion .15 .40
❑ 71 Secret Invasion .15 .40
❑ 72 Secret Invasion .15 .40
❑ 73 Shadowland .15 .40
❑ 74 Shadowland .15 .40
❑ 75 Shadowland .15 .40
❑ 76 Shadowland .15 .40
❑ 77 Shadowland .15 .40
❑ 78 Shadowland .15 .40
❑ 79 Shadowland .15 .40
❑ 80 Shadowland .15 .40
❑ 81 Shadowland .15 .40
❑ 82 Fear Itself .15 .40
❑ 83 Fear Itself .15 .40
❑ 84 Fear Itself .15 .40
❑ 85 Fear Itself .15 .40
❑ 86 Fear Itself .15 .40
❑ 87 Fear Itself .15 .40
❑ 88 Fear Itself .15 .40
❑ 89 Fear Itself .15 .40
❑ 90 Fear Itself .15 .40

2011 Marvel Universe Clear Parallel

COMPLETE SET (90) 25.00 50.00
STATED ODDS 1:3

2011 Marvel Universe Artist Draft

COMPLETE SET (9) 4.00 10.00
STATED ODDS 1:8

❑ AD1 Civil War 1.00 2.50
❑ AD2 Civil War 1.00 2.50
❑ AD3 Civil War 1.00 2.50
❑ AD4 World War Hulk 1.00 2.50
❑ AD5 Fear Itself 1.00 2.50
❑ AD6 Fear Itself 1.00 2.50
❑ AD7 Fear Itself 1.00 2.50
❑ AD8 Secret Invasion 1.00 2.50
❑ AD9 Secret Invasion 1.00 2.50

2011 Marvel Universe Case Toppers

COMPLETE SET (3) 30.00 60.00
STATED ODDS ONE PER CASE

❑ CT1 Thor 10.00 25.00
Spider-Man/Capt. America
❑ CT2 Wolverine 10.00 25.00
Quicksilver/Blob
❑ CT3 Sabretooth 10.00 25.00
Magneto/Venom

2011 Marvel Universe Marvel Originals

COMPLETE SET (9) 6.00 15.00
STATED ODDS 1:12

❑ MO1 Marvel Universe 1.50 4.00
❑ MO2 Captain America 1.50 4.00
❑ MO3 Spider-Man 1.50 4.00
❑ MO4 Incredible Hulk 1.50 4.00
❑ MO5 Iron Man 1.50 4.00
❑ MO6 Wolverine 1.50 4.00
Psylocke
❑ MO7 Wolverine 1.50 4.00
Sabretooth
❑ MO8 Fantastic Four 1.50 4.00
❑ MO9 Fantastic Four 1.50 4.00

2011 Marvel Universe Promos

COMPLETE SET 10.00 25.00

❑ P1 Thor .75 2.00
Thing/Hulk/ (General Distribution)
❑ P2 Thing 2.00 5.00
Thor/Elektra/ (Non-Sport Update Magazine)
❑ P3 Capt. America 10.00 25.00
Hulk/Medusa/ (Binder Exclusive)
❑ P4 Daredevil 2.00 5.00
Hulk/Capt. America/ (Philly Non-Sport Show Fall 2011)

2011 Marvel Universe San Diego Comic Convention Promos

COMPLETE SET (9) 20.00 40.00

❑ SD1 Iron Man 3.00 8.00
❑ SD2 Capt. America 3.00 8.00
❑ SD3 Burning Building 3.00 8.00
❑ SD4 Odin 3.00 8.00
❑ SD5 Hulk 3.00 8.00
❑ SD6 Thor 3.00 8.00
❑ SD7 Juggernaut 3.00 8.00
❑ SD8 Watcher 3.00 8.00
❑ SD9 Red Skull 3.00 8.00

2011 Marvel Universe Sketches

STATED ODDS ONE PER BOX

❑ 1 Adam Cleveland 20.00 50.00
❑ 2 Adriano Carreon 20.00 50.00
❑ 3 Al Stefano 20.00 50.00
❑ 4 Alberto J. Silva 25.00 60.00
❑ 5 Alcione Silva 25.00 60.00
❑ 6 Alexandre Magno 20.00 50.00
❑ 7 Allen Geneta 20.00 50.00
❑ 8 Andre Toma 25.00 60.00
❑ 9 Andy Price 60.00 150.00
❑ 10 Apriyadi Kusbiantoro 15.00 40.00
❑ 11 Aston Cover 40.00 100.00
❑ 12 Axebone 150.00 250.00
❑ 13 Benjamin Glendenning 100.00 175.00
❑ 14 Bill Pulkovski 20.00 50.00
❑ 15 Brian Postman 10.00 25.00
❑ 16 Brian Shearer 10.00 25.00
❑ 17 Bryan Turner 20.00 50.00
❑ 18 Buddy Prince 30.00 80.00
❑ 19 Budi Setiawan 25.00 60.00
❑ 20 Caio Majado 25.00 60.00
❑ 21 Cal Slayton 30.00 80.00
❑ 22 Charles Hall 100.00 200.00
❑ 23 Chris Bradberry 30.00 80.00
❑ 24 Chris Foreman 25.00 60.00
❑ 25 Chris Moreno 20.00 50.00
❑ 26 Craig Yeung 25.00 60.00
❑ 27 Dan Borgonos 40.00 100.00
❑ 28 Daniel Horn DaRosa 25.00 60.00
❑ 29 Danielle Gransaull 25.00 60.00
❑ 30 Darren Chandler 25.00 60.00
❑ 31 Darryl Banks 25.00 60.00
❑ 32 David Lee 20.00 50.00
❑ 33 Denae Frazier 75.00 150.00
❑ 34 Dennis Crisostomo 20.00 50.00
❑ 35 Denver Brubaker 15.00 40.00
❑ 36 Don Hillsman 20.00 50.00
❑ 37 Edde Wagner 15.00 40.00
❑ 38 Eduardo Ferrara 12.00 30.00
❑ 39 Elaine Perna 60.00 150.00
❑ 40 Eli Rutten 75.00 150.00
❑ 41 Elvis Moura 15.00 40.00
❑ 42 Eman Casallos 200.00 350.00
❑ 43 Eric Ninaltowski 40.00 100.00
❑ 44 Erik Maell 25.00 60.00
❑ 45 Eugene Commodore 15.00 40.00
❑ 46 Fernando Gil 15.00 40.00
❑ 47 Fernando Scheidt 30.00 80.00
❑ 48 Frank A. Kadar 50.00 125.00
❑ 49 George Davis 40.00 100.00
❑ 50 Hanie Mohd 30.00 80.00
❑ 51 Irma Ahmed 20.00 50.00
❑ 52 Jake Minor 25.00 60.00
❑ 53 Jason McLellan 15.00 40.00
❑ 54 Jason Sobol 25.00 60.00
❑ 55 Jay Fosgitt 20.00 50.00
❑ 56 Jayson Kretzer 20.00 50.00
❑ 57 JC Fabul 40.00 100.00
❑ 58 Jeanette Swift 25.00 60.00
❑ 59 Jeff Confer 40.00 100.00
❑ 60 Jeff Zugale 20.00 50.00
❑ 61 Jennifer Mercer 50.00 125.00
❑ 62 Jerry Gaylord 15.00 40.00
❑ 63 Joe Rubenstein 12.00 30.00
❑ 64 Joe St. Pierre 50.00 125.00
❑ 65 Joey O'Brien 20.00 50.00
❑ 66 John Jackman 25.00 60.00
❑ 67 John Watkins-Chow 25.00 60.00
❑ 68 Jomar A. Bulda 25.00 60.00
❑ 69 Jon Hughes 15.00 40.00
❑ 70 Joshua Flower 30.00 80.00
❑ 71 Juan Fontanez 20.00 50.00
❑ 72 Justin Chung 30.00 80.00
❑ 73 Kat Laurange 20.00 50.00
❑ 74 Kathryn A. Layno 25.00 60.00
❑ 75 Kevin West 75.00 150.00
❑ 76 Kristin Allen 40.00 100.00
❑ 77 Lak Lim 25.00 60.00
❑ 78 Larry (Slickaway) Schlekewy 100.00 200.00
❑ 79 Lawrence Reynolds 25.00 60.00
❑ 80 Lee Kohse 20.00 50.00
❑ 81 Leeahd Goldberg 15.00 40.00
❑ 82 Lui Antonio 25.00 60.00
❑ 83 Luke Smarto 20.00 50.00
❑ 84 Lynne Anderson 30.00 80.00
❑ 85 Mahmud Asrar 50.00 125.00
❑ 86 Marcelo Ferreira 25.00 60.00
❑ 87 Mark Dos Santos 15.00 40.00
❑ 88 Mark J. Tannacore 25.00 60.00
❑ 89 Marlo Lodrigueza 60.00 150.00
❑ 90 Mary Bellamy 15.00 40.00
❑ 91 Matias Streb 75.00 175.00
❑ 92 Matt Glebe 150.00 300.00
❑ 93 Mauro Fodra 15.00 40.00
❑ 94 Meghan Hetrick-Murante 150.00 300.00
❑ 95 Melike Acar
❑ 96 Michael Glover 20.00 50.00
❑ 97 Michael Sta.Maria 30.00 80.00
❑ 98 Mick Glebe 150.00 300.00
❑ 99 Mike Rooth 25.00 60.00
❑ 100 MJ San Juan 25.00 60.00
❑ 101 Nestor Celario Jr. 20.00 50.00
❑ 102 Newton Barbosa 50.00 125.00
❑ 103 Noah Salonga 25.00 60.00
❑ 104 Noval Hernawan 25.00 60.00
❑ 105 Raimundo Nonato 12.00 30.00
❑ 106 Rainier Lagunsad 30.00 80.00
❑ 107 Randy Martinez 15.00 40.00
❑ 108 Randy Monces 20.00 50.00
❑ 109 Renato Mapa Jr. 30.00 80.00
❑ 110 Rhiannon Owens 60.00 150.00
❑ 111 Rich Molinelli 12.00 30.00
❑ 112 Richard Cox 30.00 80.00
❑ 113 Rodrigo Martins 25.00 60.00
❑ 114 Ryan M Kincaid 20.00 50.00
❑ 115 Saiful Remy Mokhtar 30.00 80.00
❑ 116 Sanna Umemoto 200.00 300.00
❑ 117 Sara Richard 75.00 150.00
❑ 118 Sarah Wilkinson 15.00 40.00
❑ 119 Scott Barnett
❑ 120 Scott Rorie 50.00 125.00
❑ 121 Sean Moore 12.00 30.00
❑ 122 Stacey Kardash 20.00 50.00
❑ 123 Stefanie Battalene 25.00 60.00
❑ 124 Steven Miller 15.00 40.00
❑ 125 Thanh Bui 20.00 50.00
❑ 126 Tim Shay 60.00 150.00
❑ 127 Tom Kelly 20.00 50.00
❑ 128 Tone Rodriguez 15.00 40.00
❑ 129 Tony Fleecs 15.00 40.00
❑ 130 Tony Scott 20.00 50.00
❑ 131 Wendell Rubio Silva 15.00 40.00
❑ 132 Yesim Asrar 100.00 175.00
❑ 133 Tony Perna
❑ 134 Anthony Tan 125.00 250.00

2011 Marvel Universe Ultimate Heroes

COMPLETE SET (9) 12.00 25.00
STATED ODDS 1:24

❑ UH1 Wolverine 2.50 6.00
❑ UH2 Colossus 2.50 6.00
❑ UH3 Storm 2.50 6.00
❑ UH4 Cyclops 2.50 6.00
❑ UH5 Beast 2.50 6.00
❑ UH6 Iceman 2.50 6.00
❑ UH7 Angel 2.50 6.00
❑ UH8 Gambit 2.50 6.00
❑ UH9 Jean Grey 2.50 6.00
❑ UH10 Polaris SP 12.00 30.00
(issued as Rittenhouse Reward)

2011 Michael Jackson

COMPLETE SET (190) 60.00 120.00

❑ 1 Michael's first solo world tour .30 .75
❑ 2 There were three .30 .75
❑ 3 This photo was taken .30 .75
❑ 4 As of the end of 2009 .30 .75
❑ 5 Michael Jackson's No. 1 single .30 .75
❑ 6 Michael always knew how .30 .75
❑ 7 Michael's Dangerous album .30 .75
❑ 8 Michael's pet python, Muscles .30 .75
❑ 9 In September 1986 .30 .75
❑ 10 At the 1995 MTV Video Music Awards .30 .75
❑ 11 Following the release of Thriller .30 .75
❑ 12 Michael holds 13 .30 .75
❑ 13 In 2001, Michael performed twice .30 .75
❑ 14 Michael has received .30 .75
❑ 15 Michael recorded two songs .30 .75
❑ 16 In September 1999 .30 .75
❑ 17 This is a snapshot .30 .75
❑ 18 The 1990s was a busy decade .30 .75
❑ 19 Most artists never make it .30 .75
❑ 20 In 1997, Michael released Blood .30 .75

☐ 21 It comes as no surprise .30 .75
☐ 22 One of seven Top 40 singles .30 .75
☐ 23 The highly anticipated .30 .75
☐ 24 In 2002, Michael appeared as Agent M .30 .75
☐ 25 During the 2006 World Music Awards .30 .75
☐ 26 With a career spanning .30 .75
☐ 27 Michael receives well-deserved credit .30 .75
☐ 28 The first solo concert performance .30 .75
☐ 29 Enjoying one of the longest .30 .75
☐ 30 Some of the directors .30 .75
☐ 31 Michael pioneered many techniques .30 .75
☐ 32 Here's a list of Michael's gold singles .30 .75
☐ 33 One of the best things .30 .75
☐ 34 The black band .30 .75
☐ 35 Earth Song was the third single .30 .75
☐ 36 Michael guest-starred on The Simpsons .30 .75
☐ 37 Nobody dances like Michael .30 .75
☐ 38 Michael has received 26 .30 .75
☐ 39 The magnitude of Michael's fame .30 .75
☐ 40 In 1993, Michael performed .30 .75
☐ 41 After release of Michael's Thriller album .30 .75
☐ 42 Michael was a big fan .30 .75
☐ 43 Michael's hairstyle changed quite a bit .30 .75
☐ 44 Every one of Michael's albums .30 .75
☐ 45 Michael walked away .30 .75
☐ 46 The world watched Michael Jackson .30 .75
☐ 47 Michael is one of the few artists .30 .75
☐ 48 In addition to Michael's own 13 .30 .75
☐ 49 In 1988, Doubleday published Moonwalk .30 .75
☐ 50 Among the thousands of honors .30 .75
☐ 51 What do Francis Ford Coppola .30 .75
☐ 52 Michael's HIStory World Tour .30 .75
☐ 53 Michael is shown here .30 .75
☐ 54 The only American Music Awards .30 .75
☐ 55 Michael did not embark .30 .75
☐ 56 Another Part of Me was used .30 .75
☐ 57 Early in his career, Michael was inspired .30 .75
☐ 58 Michael's career, by the numbers .30 .75
☐ 59 Michael's music has been featured .30 .75
☐ 60 Moonwalker the Storybook .30 .75
☐ 61 On March 21, 2001, Michael appeared .30 .75
☐ 62 In 1978, Michael co-starred .30 .75
☐ 63 Michael was the first entertainer .30 .75
☐ 64 The term King of Pop was not coined .30 .75
☐ 65 Thriller was released in 1982 .30 .75
☐ 66 Michael was asked to write music .30 .75
☐ 67 Michael was truly one of the great .30 .75
☐ 68 Artists who influenced Michael .30 .75
☐ 69 In 1990, Sega released the Moonwalker .30 .75
☐ 70 Michael is seen here .30 .75
☐ 71 Michael's Man in the Mirror video .30 .75
☐ 72 Two of the biggest names in pop music .30 .75
☐ 73 Michael's outfit for the Billie Jean music .30 .75
☐ 74 The cast for the music video .30 .75
☐ 75 Michael Jackson wrote many of his .30 .75
☐ 76 The short film for Black or White .30 .75
☐ 77 Fifty million people tuned in .30 .75
☐ 78 Michael revolutionized the art .30 .75
☐ 79 On May 14, 1984, Michael appeared .30 .75
☐ 80 The artwork featured on the bass drum .30 .75
☐ 81 Of all of Michael's No. 1 hits .30 .75
☐ 82 The short film for Michael's hit .30 .75
☐ 83 In March 2001, Michael went to Oxford .30 .75
☐ 84 The HIStory Tour, Michael's last .30 .75
☐ 85 Michael is the only artist in history .30 .75
☐ 86 With the album Off the Wall .30 .75
☐ 87 Michael's performance at Super Bowl XXVII .30 .75
☐ 88 After the Sept. 11, 2001 terrorist attacks .30 .75
☐ 89 Michael was a child prodigy .30 .75
☐ 90 The budgets for many of Michael's music .30 .75
☐ 91 In 1958, the year Michael was born .30 .75
☐ 92 The wind-tunnel effect produced .30 .75
☐ 93 Michael's album Bad was released .30 .75
☐ 94 Michael worked with many designers .30 .75
☐ 95 Michael's first overseas performance .30 .75
☐ 96 Beat It was the third single .30 .75
☐ 97 Michael's endorsement deal with Pepsi .30 .75
☐ 98 The shortest of Michael's solo world tours .30 .75
☐ 99 Released along with the Thriller .30 .75
☐ 100 During the 1980s, Michael released .30 .75
☐ 101 Michael Jackson .30 .75
☐ 102 Michael won a total of 26 .30 .75
☐ 103 In the Moonwalker arcade game .30 .75
☐ 104 In 1983, Michael set a Guinness .30 .75
☐ 105 Michael's crystal-studded white glove .30 .75
☐ 106 Michael Jackson .30 .75
☐ 107 When Michael teamed up with horror .30 .75
☐ 108 Those aren't Band-Aids on his fingers .30 .75
☐ 109 In 1988, Michael starred in a movie .30 .75
☐ 110 For younger fans and others .30 .75
☐ 111 Michael received multiple .30 .75
☐ 112 After Michael's unexpected death .30 .75
☐ 113 Best Recording for Children ACH .30 .75
☐ 114 Record of the Year ACH .30 .75
☐ 115 Album of the Year ACH .30 .75
☐ 116 Michael Jackson ACH .30 .75
☐ 117 Best Pop Vocal Performance ACH .30 .75
☐ 118 Producer of the Year ACH .30 .75
☐ 119 Best R and B Vocal ACH .30 .75
☐ 120 Michael Jackson ACH .30 .75
☐ 121 Best R and B Song ACH .30 .75
☐ 122 Best Rock Vocal Performance ACH .30 .75
☐ 123 Living Legend ACH .30 .75
☐ 124 Most Expensive Video ACH .30 .75
☐ 125 Biggest-Selling Album ACH .30 .75
☐ 126 First Song to Debut at No. 1 ACH .30 .75
☐ 127 Michael Jackson ACH .30 .75
☐ 128 Most Successful Concert Series ACH .30 .75
☐ 129 Most Grammys Won in a Year ACH .30 .75
☐ 130 Most No. 1 Hits in the '80s ACH .30 .75
☐ 131 No. 1 on Both Rock and R and B Charts ACH .30 .75
☐ 132 Greatest Audience ACH .30 .75
☐ 133 This photo was taken at Gardner Street DEC .30 .75
☐ 134 After the 1984 American Music Awards DEC .30 .75
☐ 135 In a time when music videos consisted DEC .30 .75
☐ 136 Michael Jackson DEC .30 .75
☐ 137 In 1983, Michael Jackson became DEC .30 .75
☐ 138 Fresh from producing the most successful DEC .30 .75
☐ 139 Michael's Bad World Tour DEC .30 .75
☐ 140 In 1984, Michael set a record DEC .30 .75
☐ 141 In 1984, President Ronald Reagan DEC .30 .75
☐ 142 Michael's first solo world tour sold out DEC .30 .75
☐ 143 During Michael's Dangerous tour DEC .30 .75
☐ 144 Michael met a few presidents DEC .30 .75
☐ 145 Michael's performance at the 1993 Super Bowl DEC .30 .75
☐ 146 At the 35th Annual Grammy Awards DEC .30 .75
☐ 147 Michael's gold costume DEC .30 .75
☐ 148 Michael Jackson DEC .30 .75
☐ 149 Many of the HIStory concerts DEC .30 .75
☐ 150 On Dec. 30, 1992, during a concert DEC .30 .75
☐ 151 Michael Jackson DEC .30 .75
☐ 152 At the opening of each concert DEC .30 .75
☐ 153 Michael was nominated DEC .30 .75
☐ 154 Michael's album Invincible was released DEC .30 .75
☐ 155 Michael was scheduled to perform DEC .30 .75
☐ 156 Michael's single You Rock My World DEC .30 .75
☐ 157 In 2008, Michael released a special DEC .30 .75
☐ 158 In September of 2001, there were two DEC .30 .75
☐ 159 Michael's greatest-hits album Number Ones DEC .30 .75
☐ 160 On May 27, 2006, Michael received DEC .30 .75
☐ 161 In March 2007, Michael Jackson visited DEC .30 .75
☐ 162 Butterflies is the lesser known of the two DEC .30 .75
☐ 163 Got To Be There T10 .30 .75
☐ 164 Off the Wall T10 .30 .75
☐ 165 She's Out of My Life T10 .30 .75
☐ 166 The Girl is Mine T10 .30 .75
☐ 167 Wanna Be Startin' Somethin' T10 .30 .75
☐ 168 Human Nature T10 .30 .75
☐ 169 P.Y.T. (Pretty Young Thing) T10 .30 .75
☐ 170 Thriller T10 .30 .75
☐ 171 Smooth Criminal T10 .30 .75
☐ 172 Michael Jackson T10 .30 .75
☐ 173 In the Closet T10 .30 .75
☐ 174 Heal the World T10 .30 .75
☐ 175 Will You Be There T10 .30 .75
☐ 176 Scream T10 .30 .75
☐ 177 You Rock My World T10 .30 .75
☐ 178 Ben NO1 .75 2.00
☐ 179 Don't Stop 'Til You Get Enough NO1 .75 2.00
☐ 180 Rock With You NO1 .75 2.00
☐ 181 Billie Jean NO1 .75 2.00
☐ 182 Beat It NO1 .75 2.00
☐ 183 Say Say Say NO1 .75 2.00
☐ 184 I Just Can't Stop Loving You NO1 .75 2.00
☐ 185 Bad NO1 .75 2.00
☐ 186 The Way You Make Me Feel NO1 .75 2.00
☐ 187 Man In the Mirror NO1 .75 2.00
☐ 188 Dirty Diana NO1 .75 2.00
☐ 189 Black or White NO1 .75 2.00
☐ 190 You Are Not Alone NO1 .75 2.00

2011 Michael Jackson Gold

*GOLD: X TO X BASIC CARDS

☐ 1 Michael's first solo world tour 4.00 12.00
☐ 2 There were three 4.00 12.00
☐ 3 This photo was taken 4.00 12.00
☐ 4 As of the end of 2009 4.00 12.00
☐ 5 Michael Jackson's No. 1 single 4.00 12.00
☐ 6 Michael always knew how 4.00 12.00
☐ 7 Michael's Dangerous album 4.00 12.00
☐ 8 Michael's pet python, Muscles 4.00 12.00
☐ 9 In September 1986 4.00 12.00
☐ 10 At the 1995 MTV Video Music Awards 4.00 12.00
☐ 11 Following the release of Thriller 4.00 12.00
☐ 12 Michael holds 13 4.00 12.00
☐ 13 In 2001, Michael performed twice 4.00 12.00
☐ 14 Michael has received 4.00 12.00
☐ 15 Michael recorded two songs 4.00 12.00
☐ 16 In September 1999 4.00 12.00
☐ 17 This is a snapshot 4.00 12.00
☐ 18 The 1990s was a busy decade 4.00 12.00
☐ 19 Most artists never make it 4.00 12.00
☐ 20 In 1997, Michael released Blood 4.00 12.00
☐ 21 It comes as no surprise 4.00 12.00
☐ 22 One of seven Top 40 singles 4.00 12.00
☐ 23 The highly anticipated 4.00 12.00
☐ 24 In 2002, Michael appeared as Agent M 4.00 12.00
☐ 25 During the 2006 World Music Awards 4.00 12.00
☐ 26 With a career spanning 4.00 12.00
☐ 27 Michael receives well-deserved credit 4.00 12.00
☐ 28 The first solo concert performance 4.00 12.00
☐ 29 Enjoying one of the longest 4.00 12.00
☐ 30 Some of the directors 4.00 12.00
☐ 31 Michael pioneered many techniques 4.00 12.00
☐ 32 Here's a list of Michael's gold singles 4.00 12.00
☐ 33 One of the best things 4.00 12.00
☐ 34 The black band 4.00 12.00
☐ 35 Earth Song was the third single 4.00 12.00
☐ 36 Michael guest-starred on The Simpsons 4.00 12.00
☐ 37 Nobody dances like Michael 4.00 12.00
☐ 38 Michael has received 26 4.00 12.00
☐ 39 The magnitude of Michael's fame 4.00 12.00
☐ 40 In 1993, Michael performed 4.00 12.00
☐ 41 After release of Michael's Thriller album 4.00 12.00
☐ 42 Michael was a big fan 4.00 12.00
☐ 43 Michael's hairstyle changed quite a bit 4.00 12.00
☐ 44 Every one of Michael's albums 4.00 12.00
☐ 45 Michael walked away 4.00 12.00
☐ 46 The world watched Michael Jackson 4.00 12.00
☐ 47 Michael is one of the few artists 4.00 12.00
☐ 48 In addition to Michael's own 13 4.00 12.00
☐ 49 In 1988, Doubleday published Moonwalk 4.00 12.00
☐ 50 Among the thousands of honors 4.00 12.00
☐ 51 What do Francis Ford Coppola 4.00 12.00
☐ 52 Michael's HIStory World Tour 4.00 12.00
☐ 53 Michael is shown here 4.00 12.00
☐ 54 The only American Music Awards 4.00 12.00
☐ 55 Michael did not embark 4.00 12.00
☐ 56 Another Part of Me was used 4.00 12.00
☐ 57 Early in his career, Michael was inspired 4.00 12.00
☐ 58 Michael's career, by the numbers 4.00 12.00
☐ 59 Michael's music has been featured 4.00 12.00
☐ 60 Moonwalker the Storybook 4.00 12.00
☐ 61 On March 21, 2001, Michael appeared 4.00 12.00
☐ 62 In 1978, Michael co-starred 4.00 12.00
☐ 63 Michael was the first entertainer 4.00 12.00
☐ 64 The term King of Pop was not coined 4.00 12.00
☐ 65 Thriller was released in 1982 4.00 12.00
☐ 66 Michael was asked to write music 4.00 12.00
☐ 67 Michael was truly one of the great 4.00 12.00
☐ 68 Artists who influenced Michael 4.00 12.00
☐ 69 In 1990, Sega released the Moonwalker 4.00 12.00
☐ 70 Michael is seen here 4.00 12.00
☐ 71 Michael's Man in the Mirror video 4.00 12.00
☐ 72 Two of the biggest names in pop music 4.00 12.00
☐ 73 Michael's outfit for the Billie Jean music 4.00 12.00
☐ 74 The cast for the music video 4.00 12.00
☐ 75 Michael Jackson wrote many of his 4.00 12.00
☐ 76 The short film for Black or White 4.00 12.00
☐ 77 Fifty million people tuned in 4.00 12.00
☐ 78 Michael revolutionized the art 4.00 12.00
☐ 79 On May 14, 1984, Michael appeared 4.00 12.00
☐ 80 The artwork featured on the bass drum 4.00 12.00
☐ 81 Of all of Michael's No. 1 hits 4.00 12.00
☐ 82 The short film for Michael's hit 4.00 12.00
☐ 83 In March 2001, Michael went to Oxford 4.00 12.00
☐ 84 The HIStory Tour, Michael's last 4.00 12.00
☐ 85 Michael is the only artist in history 4.00 12.00
☐ 86 With the album Off the Wall 4.00 12.00
☐ 87 Michael's performance at Super Bowl XXVII 4.00 12.00
☐ 88 After the Sept. 11, 2001 terrorist attacks 4.00 12.00
☐ 89 Michael was a child prodigy 4.00 12.00
☐ 90 The budgets for many of Michael's music 4.00 12.00
☐ 91 In 1958, the year Michael was born 4.00 12.00
☐ 92 The wind-tunnel effect produced 4.00 12.00
☐ 93 Michael's album Bad was released 4.00 12.00
☐ 94 Michael worked with many designers 4.00 12.00
☐ 95 Michael's first overseas performance 4.00 12.00
☐ 96 Beat It was the third single 4.00 12.00
☐ 97 Michael's endorsement deal with Pepsi 4.00 12.00
☐ 98 The shortest of Michael's solo world tours 4.00 12.00
☐ 99 Released along with the Thriller 4.00 12.00
☐ 100 During the 1980s, Michael released 4.00 12.00
☐ 101 Michael Jackson 4.00 12.00
☐ 102 Michael won a total of 26 4.00 12.00
☐ 103 In the Moonwalker arcade game 4.00 12.00
☐ 104 In 1983, Michael set a Guinness 4.00 12.00
☐ 105 Michael's crystal-studded white glove 4.00 12.00
☐ 106 Michael Jackson 4.00 12.00
☐ 107 When Michael teamed up with horror 4.00 12.00
☐ 108 Those aren't Band-Aids on his fingers 4.00 12.00
☐ 109 In 1988, Michael starred in a movie 4.00 12.00
☐ 110 For younger fans and others 4.00 12.00
☐ 111 Michael received multiple 4.00 12.00
☐ 112 After Michael's unexpected death 4.00 12.00
☐ 113 Best Recording for Children 4.00 12.00
☐ 114 Record of the Year 4.00 12.00
☐ 115 Album of the Year 4.00 12.00
☐ 116 Michael Jackson 4.00 12.00
☐ 117 Best Pop Vocal Performance 4.00 12.00
☐ 118 Producer of the Year 4.00 12.00
☐ 119 Best R and B Vocal 4.00 12.00
☐ 120 Michael Jackson 4.00 12.00
☐ 121 Best R and B Song 4.00 12.00
☐ 122 Best Rock Vocal Performance 4.00 12.00
☐ 123 Living Legend 4.00 12.00
☐ 124 Most Expensive Video 4.00 12.00
☐ 125 Biggest-Selling Album 4.00 12.00
☐ 126 First Song to Debut at No. 1 4.00 12.00
☐ 127 Michael Jackson 4.00 12.00
☐ 128 Most Successful Concert Series 4.00 12.00
☐ 129 Most Grammys Won in a Year 4.00 12.00
☐ 130 Most No. 1 Hits in the '80s 4.00 12.00
☐ 131 No. 1 on Both Rock and R and B Charts 4.00 12.00
☐ 132 Greatest Audience 4.00 12.00
☐ 133 This photo was taken at Gardner Street 4.00 12.00
☐ 134 After the 1984 American Music Awards 4.00 12.00
☐ 135 In a time when music videos consisted 4.00 12.00
☐ 136 Michael Jackson 4.00 12.00
☐ 137 In 1983, Michael Jackson became 4.00 12.00
☐ 138 Fresh from producing the most successful 4.00 12.00
☐ 139 Michael's Bad World Tour 4.00 12.00
☐ 140 In 1984, Michael set a record 4.00 12.00
☐ 141 In 1984, President Ronald Reagan 4.00 12.00
☐ 142 Michael's first solo world tour sold out 4.00 12.00
☐ 143 During Michael's Dangerous tour 4.00 12.00
☐ 144 Michael met a few presidents 4.00 12.00
☐ 145 Michael's performance at the 1993 Super Bowl 4.00 12.00
☐ 146 At the 35th Annual Grammy Awards 4.00 12.00
☐ 147 Michael's gold costume 4.00 12.00
☐ 148 Michael Jackson 4.00 12.00
☐ 149 Many of the HIStory concerts 4.00 12.00
☐ 150 On Dec. 30, 1992, during a concert 4.00 12.00
☐ 151 Michael Jackson 4.00 12.00
☐ 152 At the opening of each concert 4.00 12.00
☐ 153 Michael was nominated 4.00 12.00
☐ 154 Michael's album Invincible was released 4.00 12.00
☐ 155 Michael was scheduled to perform 4.00 12.00
☐ 156 Michael's single You Rock My World 4.00 12.00
☐ 157 In 2008, Michael released a special 4.00 12.00
☐ 158 In September of 2001, there were two 4.00 12.00
☐ 159 Michael's greatest-hits album Number Ones 4.00 12.00
☐ 160 On May 27, 2006, Michael received 4.00 12.00
☐ 161 In March 2007, Michael Jackson visited 4.00 12.00
☐ 162 Butterflies is the lesser known of the two 4.00 12.00
☐ 163 Got To Be There T10 4.00 12.00
☐ 164 Off the Wall T10 4.00 12.00
☐ 165 She's Out of My Life T10 4.00 12.00
☐ 166 The Girl is Mine T10 4.00 12.00
☐ 167 Wanna Be Startin' Somethin' T10 4.00 12.00
☐ 168 Human Nature T10 4.00 12.00
☐ 169 P.Y.T. (Pretty Young Thing) T10 4.00 12.00
☐ 170 Thriller T10 4.00 12.00
☐ 171 Smooth Criminal T10 4.00 12.00
☐ 172 Michael Jackson T10 4.00 12.00
☐ 173 In the Closet T10 4.00 12.00
☐ 174 Heal the World T10 4.00 12.00
☐ 175 Will You Be There T10 4.00 12.00
☐ 176 Scream T10 4.00 12.00
☐ 177 You Rock My World T10 4.00 12.00
☐ 178 Ben NO1 4.00 12.00
☐ 179 Don't Stop 'Til You Get Enough NO1 4.00 12.00
☐ 180 Rock With You NO1 4.00 12.00
☐ 181 Billie Jean NO1 4.00 12.00
☐ 182 Beat It NO1 4.00 12.00
☐ 183 Say Say Say NO1 4.00 12.00
☐ 184 I Just Can't Stop Loving You NO1 4.00 12.00
☐ 185 Bad NO1 4.00 12.00
☐ 186 The Way You Make Me Feel NO1 4.00 12.00
☐ 187 Man In the Mirror NO1 4.00 12.00
☐ 188 Dirty Diana NO1 4.00 12.00
☐ 189 Black or White NO1 4.00 12.00
☐ 190 You Are Not Alone NO1 4.00 12.00

2011 Michael Jackson Platinum

*PLATINUM: X TO X BASIC CARDS

☐ 1 Michael's first solo world tour 10.00 25.00
☐ 2 There were three 10.00 25.00
☐ 3 This photo was taken 10.00 25.00
☐ 4 As of the end of 2009 10.00 25.00
☐ 5 Michael Jackson's No. 1 single 10.00 25.00
☐ 6 Michael always knew how 10.00 25.00
☐ 7 Michael's Dangerous album 10.00 25.00
☐ 8 Michael's pet python, Muscles 10.00 25.00
☐ 9 In September 1986 10.00 25.00
☐ 10 At the 1995 MTV Video Music Awards 10.00 25.00
☐ 11 Following the release of Thriller 10.00 25.00
☐ 12 Michael holds 13 10.00 25.00
☐ 13 In 2001, Michael performed twice 10.00 25.00
☐ 14 Michael has received 10.00 25.00
☐ 15 Michael recorded two songs 10.00 25.00
☐ 16 In September 1999 10.00 25.00
☐ 17 This is a snapshot 10.00 25.00
☐ 18 The 1990s was a busy decade 10.00 25.00
☐ 19 Most artists never make it 10.00 25.00
☐ 20 In 1997, Michael released Blood 10.00 25.00
☐ 21 It comes as no surprise 10.00 25.00
☐ 22 One of seven Top 40 singles 10.00 25.00
☐ 23 The highly anticipated 10.00 25.00
☐ 24 In 2002, Michael appeared as Agent M 10.00 25.00
☐ 25 During the 2006 World Music Awards 10.00 25.00
☐ 26 With a career spanning 10.00 25.00
☐ 27 Michael receives well-deserved credit 10.00 25.00
☐ 28 The first solo concert performance 10.00 25.00
☐ 29 Enjoying one of the longest 10.00 25.00
☐ 30 Some of the directors 10.00 25.00
☐ 31 Michael pioneered many techniques 10.00 25.00
☐ 32 Here's a list of Michael's gold singles 10.00 25.00
☐ 33 One of the best things 10.00 25.00
☐ 34 The black band 10.00 25.00
☐ 35 Earth Song was the third single 10.00 25.00
☐ 36 Michael guest-starred on The Simpsons 10.00 25.00
☐ 37 Nobody dances like Michael 10.00 25.00
☐ 38 Michael has received 26 10.00 25.00
☐ 39 The magnitude of Michael's fame 10.00 25.00
☐ 40 In 1993, Michael performed 10.00 25.00
☐ 41 After release of Michael's Thriller album 10.00 25.00
☐ 42 Michael was a big fan 10.00 25.00
☐ 43 Michael's hairstyle changed quite a bit 10.00 25.00
☐ 44 Every one of Michael's albums 10.00 25.00
☐ 45 Michael walked away 10.00 25.00
☐ 46 The world watched Michael Jackson 10.00 25.00
☐ 47 Michael is one of the few artists 10.00 25.00
☐ 48 In addition to Michael's own 13 10.00 25.00
☐ 49 In 1988, Doubleday published Moonwalk 10.00 25.00
☐ 50 Among the thousands of honors 10.00 25.00
☐ 51 What do Francis Ford Coppola 10.00 25.00
☐ 52 Michael's HIStory World Tour 10.00 25.00
☐ 53 Michael is shown here 10.00 25.00
☐ 54 The only American Music Awards 10.00 25.00
☐ 55 Michael did not embark 10.00 25.00
☐ 56 Another Part of Me was used 10.00 25.00
☐ 57 Early in his career, Michael was inspired 10.00 25.00
☐ 58 Michael's career, by the numbers 10.00 25.00
☐ 59 Michael's music has been featured 10.00 25.00
☐ 60 Moonwalker the Storybook 10.00 25.00
☐ 61 On March 21, 2001, Michael appeared 10.00 25.00
☐ 62 In 1978, Michael co-starred 10.00 25.00
☐ 63 Michael was the first entertainer 10.00 25.00
☐ 64 The term King of Pop was not coined 10.00 25.00
☐ 65 Thriller was released in 1982 10.00 25.00
☐ 66 Michael was asked to write music 10.00 25.00
☐ 67 Michael was truly one of the great 10.00 25.00
☐ 68 Artists who influenced Michael 10.00 25.00
☐ 69 In 1990, Sega released the Moonwalker 10.00 25.00
☐ 70 Michael is seen here 10.00 25.00
☐ 71 Michael's Man in the Mirror video 10.00 25.00
☐ 72 Two of the biggest names in pop music 10.00 25.00
☐ 73 Michael's outfit for the Billie Jean music 10.00 25.00
☐ 74 The cast for the music video 10.00 25.00
☐ 75 Michael Jackson wrote many of his 10.00 25.00
☐ 76 The short film for Black or White 10.00 25.00
☐ 77 Fifty million people tuned in 10.00 25.00
☐ 78 Michael revolutionized the art 10.00 25.00
☐ 79 On May 14, 1984, Michael appeared 10.00 25.00
☐ 80 The artwork featured on the bass drum 10.00 25.00
☐ 81 Of all of Michael's No. 1 hits 10.00 25.00
☐ 82 The short film for Michael's hit 10.00 25.00
☐ 83 In March 2001, Michael went to Oxford 10.00 25.00
☐ 84 The HIStory Tour, Michael's last 10.00 25.00
☐ 85 Michael is the only artist in history 10.00 25.00
☐ 86 With the album Off the Wall 10.00 25.00
☐ 87 Michael's performance at Super Bowl XXVII 10.00 25.00
☐ 88 After the Sept. 11, 2001 terrorist attacks 10.00 25.00
☐ 89 Michael was a child prodigy 10.00 25.00
☐ 90 The budgets for many of Michael's music 10.00 25.00
☐ 91 In 1958, the year Michael was born 10.00 25.00
☐ 92 The wind-tunnel effect produced 10.00 25.00
☐ 93 Michael's album Bad was released 10.00 25.00
☐ 94 Michael worked with many designers 10.00 25.00
☐ 95 Michael's first overseas performance 10.00 25.00
☐ 96 Beat It was the third single 10.00 25.00
☐ 97 Michael's endorsement deal with Pepsi 10.00 25.00
☐ 98 The shortest of Michael's solo world tours 10.00 25.00
☐ 99 Released along with the Thriller 10.00 25.00
☐ 100 During the 1980s, Michael released 10.00 25.00
☐ 101 Michael Jackson 10.00 25.00
☐ 102 Michael won a total of 26 10.00 25.00
☐ 103 In the Moonwalker arcade game 10.00 25.00
☐ 104 In 1983, Michael set a Guinness 10.00 25.00
☐ 105 Michael's crystal-studded white glove 10.00 25.00
☐ 106 Michael Jackson 10.00 25.00
☐ 107 When Michael teamed up with horror 10.00 25.00
☐ 108 Those aren't Band-Aids on his fingers 10.00 25.00
☐ 109 In 1988, Michael starred in a movie 10.00 25.00
☐ 110 For younger fans and others 10.00 25.00
☐ 111 Michael received multiple 10.00 25.00
☐ 112 After Michael's unexpected death 10.00 25.00
☐ 113 Best Recording for Children 10.00 25.00
☐ 114 Record of the Year 10.00 25.00
☐ 115 Album of the Year 10.00 25.00
☐ 116 Michael Jackson 10.00 25.00
☐ 117 Best Pop Vocal Performance 10.00 25.00
☐ 118 Producer of the Year 10.00 25.00
☐ 119 Best R and B Vocal 10.00 25.00
☐ 120 Michael Jackson 10.00 25.00
☐ 121 Best R and B Song 10.00 25.00
☐ 122 Best Rock Vocal Performance 10.00 25.00
☐ 123 Living Legend 10.00 25.00
☐ 124 Most Expensive Video 10.00 25.00
☐ 125 Biggest-Selling Album 10.00 25.00
☐ 126 First Song to Debut at No. 1 10.00 25.00
☐ 127 Michael Jackson 10.00 25.00
☐ 128 Most Successful Concert Series 10.00 25.00
☐ 129 Most Grammys Won in a Year 10.00 25.00
☐ 130 Most No. 1 Hits in the '80s 10.00 25.00
☐ 131 No. 1 on Both Rock and R and B Charts 10.00 25.00
☐ 132 Greatest Audience 10.00 25.00
☐ 133 This photo was taken at Gardner Street 10.00 25.00
☐ 134 After the 1984 American Music Awards 10.00 25.00
☐ 135 In a time when music videos consisted 10.00 25.00
☐ 136 Michael Jackson 10.00 25.00
☐ 137 In 1983, Michael Jackson became 10.00 25.00
☐ 138 Fresh from producing the most successful 10.00 25.00
☐ 139 Michael's Bad World Tour 10.00 25.00
☐ 140 In 1984, Michael set a record 10.00 25.00
☐ 141 In 1984, President Ronald Reagan 10.00 25.00
☐ 142 Michael's first solo world tour sold out 10.00 25.00
☐ 143 During Michael's Dangerous tour 10.00 25.00
☐ 144 Michael met a few presidents 10.00 25.00
☐ 145 Michael's performance at the 1993 Super Bowl 10.00 25.00
☐ 146 At the 35th Annual Grammy Awards 10.00 25.00
☐ 147 Michael's gold costume 10.00 25.00
☐ 148 Michael Jackson 10.00 25.00
☐ 149 Many of the HIStory concerts 10.00 25.00
☐ 150 On Dec. 30, 1992, during a concert 10.00 25.00
☐ 151 Michael Jackson 10.00 25.00
☐ 152 At the opening of each concert 10.00 25.00
☐ 153 Michael was nominated 10.00 25.00
☐ 154 Michael's album Invincible was released 10.00 25.00
☐ 155 Michael was scheduled to perform 10.00 25.00
☐ 156 Michael's single You Rock My World 10.00 25.00
☐ 157 In 2008, Michael released a special 10.00 25.00
☐ 158 In September of 2001, there were two 10.00 25.00
☐ 159 Michael's greatest-hits album Number Ones 10.00 25.00
☐ 160 On May 27, 2006, Michael received 10.00 25.00
☐ 161 In March 2007, Michael Jackson visited 10.00 25.00
☐ 162 Butterflies is the lesser known of the two 10.00 25.00
☐ 163 Got To Be There T10 10.00 25.00
☐ 164 Off the Wall T10 10.00 25.00
☐ 165 She's Out of My Life T10 10.00 25.00
☐ 166 The Girl is Mine T10 10.00 25.00
☐ 167 Wanna Be Startin' Somethin' T10 10.00 25.00
☐ 168 Human Nature T10 10.00 25.00
☐ 169 P.Y.T. (Pretty Young Thing) T10 10.00 25.00
☐ 170 Thriller T10 10.00 25.00
☐ 171 Smooth Criminal T10 10.00 25.00
☐ 172 Michael Jackson T10 10.00 25.00
☐ 173 In the Closet T10 10.00 25.00
☐ 174 Heal the World T10 10.00 25.00
☐ 175 Will You Be There T10 10.00 25.00
☐ 176 Scream T10 10.00 25.00
☐ 177 You Rock My World T10 10.00 25.00
☐ 178 Ben NO1 10.00 25.00
☐ 179 Don't Stop 'Til You Get Enough NO1 10.00 25.00
☐ 180 Rock With You NO1 10.00 25.00
☐ 181 Billie Jean NO1 10.00 25.00
☐ 182 Beat It NO1 10.00 25.00
☐ 183 Say Say Say NO1 10.00 25.00
☐ 184 I Just Can't Stop Loving You NO1 10.00 25.00
☐ 185 Bad NO1 10.00 25.00
☐ 186 The Way You Make Me Feel NO1 10.00 25.00
☐ 187 Man In the Mirror NO1 10.00 25.00
☐ 188 Dirty Diana NO1 10.00 25.00
☐ 189 Black or White NO1 10.00 25.00
☐ 190 You Are Not Alone NO1 10.00 25.00

2011 Michael Jackson Diamond

*DIAMOND: X TO X BASIC CARDS

☐ 1 Michael's first solo world tour 50.00 100.00
☐ 2 There were three 50.00 100.00
☐ 3 This photo was taken 50.00 100.00
☐ 4 As of the end of 2009 50.00 100.00
☐ 5 Michael Jackson's No. 1 single 50.00 100.00
☐ 6 Michael always knew how 50.00 100.00
☐ 7 Michael's Dangerous album 50.00 100.00
☐ 8 Michael's pet python, Muscles 50.00 100.00
☐ 9 In September 1986 50.00 100.00
☐ 10 At the 1995 MTV Video Music Awards 50.00 100.00
☐ 11 Following the release of Thriller 50.00 100.00
☐ 12 Michael holds 13 50.00 100.00
☐ 13 In 2001, Michael performed twice 50.00 100.00
☐ 14 Michael has received 50.00 100.00
☐ 15 Michael recorded two songs 50.00 100.00
☐ 16 In September 1999 50.00 100.00
☐ 17 This is a snapshot 50.00 100.00
☐ 18 The 1990s was a busy decade 50.00 100.00
☐ 19 Most artists never make it 50.00 100.00
☐ 20 In 1997, Michael released Blood 50.00 100.00
☐ 21 It comes as no surprise 50.00 100.00
☐ 22 One of seven Top 40 singles 50.00 100.00
☐ 23 The highly anticipated 50.00 100.00
☐ 24 In 2002, Michael appeared as Agent M 50.00 100.00
☐ 25 During the 2006 World Music Awards 50.00 100.00
☐ 26 With a career spanning 50.00 100.00
☐ 27 Michael receives well-deserved credit 50.00 100.00
☐ 28 The first solo concert performance 50.00 100.00
☐ 29 Enjoying one of the longest 50.00 100.00
☐ 30 Some of the directors 50.00 100.00
☐ 31 Michael pioneered many techniques 50.00 100.00
☐ 32 Here's a list of Michael's gold singles 50.00 100.00
☐ 33 One of the best things 50.00 100.00
☐ 34 The black band 50.00 100.00
☐ 35 Earth Song was the third single 50.00 100.00
☐ 36 Michael guest-starred on The Simpsons 50.00 100.00
☐ 37 Nobody dances like Michael 50.00 100.00
☐ 38 Michael has received 26 50.00 100.00
☐ 39 The magnitude of Michael's fame 50.00 100.00
☐ 40 In 1993, Michael performed 50.00 100.00
☐ 41 After release of Michael's Thriller album 50.00 100.00
☐ 42 Michael was a big fan 50.00 100.00
☐ 43 Michael's hairstyle changed quite a bit 50.00 100.00
☐ 44 Every one of Michael's albums 50.00 100.00
☐ 45 Michael walked away 50.00 100.00
☐ 46 The world watched Michael Jackson 50.00 100.00
☐ 47 Michael is one of the few artists 50.00 100.00
☐ 48 In addition to Michael's own 13 50.00 100.00
☐ 49 In 1988, Doubleday published Moonwalk 50.00 100.00
☐ 50 Among the thousands of honors 50.00 100.00
☐ 51 What do Francis Ford Coppola 50.00 100.00
☐ 52 Michael's HIStory World Tour 50.00 100.00
☐ 53 Michael is shown here 50.00 100.00
☐ 54 The only American Music Awards 50.00 100.00
☐ 55 Michael did not embark 50.00 100.00
☐ 56 Another Part of Me was used 50.00 100.00
☐ 57 Early in his career, Michael was inspired 50.00 100.00
☐ 58 Michael's career, by the numbers 50.00 100.00
☐ 59 Michael's music has been featured 50.00 100.00
☐ 60 Moonwalker the Storybook 50.00 100.00
☐ 61 On March 21, 2001, Michael appeared 50.00 100.00
☐ 62 In 1978, Michael co-starred 50.00 100.00
☐ 63 Michael was the first entertainer 50.00 100.00
☐ 64 The term King of Pop was not coined 50.00 100.00
☐ 65 Thriller was released in 1982 50.00 100.00
☐ 66 Michael was asked to write music 50.00 100.00
☐ 67 Michael was truly one of the great 50.00 100.00
☐ 68 Artists who influenced Michael 50.00 100.00
☐ 69 In 1990, Sega released the Moonwalker 50.00 100.00
☐ 70 Michael is seen here 50.00 100.00
☐ 71 Michael's Man in the Mirror video 50.00 100.00
☐ 72 Two of the biggest names in pop music 50.00 100.00
☐ 73 Michael's outfit for the Billie Jean music 50.00 100.00
☐ 74 The cast for the music video 50.00 100.00
☐ 75 Michael Jackson wrote many of his 50.00 100.00
☐ 76 The short film for Black or White 50.00 100.00
☐ 77 Fifty million people tuned in 50.00 100.00
☐ 78 Michael revolutionized the art 50.00 100.00
☐ 79 On May 14, 1984, Michael appeared 50.00 100.00
☐ 80 The artwork featured on the bass drum 50.00 100.00
☐ 81 Of all of Michael's No. 1 hits 50.00 100.00
☐ 82 The short film for Michael's hit 50.00 100.00
☐ 83 In March 2001, Michaelwent to Oxford 50.00 100.00
☐ 84 The HIStory Tour, Michael's last 50.00 100.00
☐ 85 Michael is the only artist in history 50.00 100.00
☐ 86 With the album Off the Wall 50.00 100.00
☐ 87 Michael's performance at Super Bowl XXVII 50.00 100.00
☐ 88 After the Sept. 11, 2001 terrorist attacks 50.00 100.00
☐ 89 Michael was a child prodigy 50.00 100.00
☐ 90 The budgets for many of Michael's music 50.00 100.00
☐ 91 In 1958, the year Michael was born 50.00 100.00

Card	Low	High
☐ 92 The wind-tunnel effect produced	50.00	100.00
☐ 93 Michael's album Bad was released	50.00	100.00
☐ 94 Michael worked with many designers	50.00	100.00
☐ 95 Michael's first overseas performance	50.00	100.00
☐ 96 Beat It was the third single	50.00	100.00
☐ 97 Michael's endorsement deal with Pepsi	50.00	100.00
☐ 98 The shortest of Michael's solo world tours	50.00	100.00
☐ 99 Released along with the Thriller	50.00	100.00
☐ 100 During the 1980s, Michael released	50.00	100.00
☐ 101 Michael Jackson	50.00	100.00
☐ 102 Michael won a total of 26	50.00	100.00
☐ 103 In the Moonwalker arcade game	50.00	100.00
☐ 104 In 1983, Michael set a Guinness	50.00	100.00
☐ 105 Michael's crystal-studded white glove	50.00	100.00
☐ 106 Michael Jackson	50.00	100.00
☐ 107 When Michael teamed up with horror	50.00	100.00
☐ 108 Those aren't Band-Aids on his fingers	50.00	100.00
☐ 109 In 1988, Michael starred in a movie	50.00	100.00
☐ 110 For younger fans and others	50.00	100.00
☐ 111 Michael received multiple	50.00	100.00
☐ 112 After Michael's unexpected death	50.00	100.00
☐ 113 Best Recording for Children	50.00	100.00
☐ 114 Record of the Year	50.00	100.00
☐ 115 Album of the Year	50.00	100.00
☐ 116 Michael Jackson	50.00	100.00
☐ 117 Best Pop Vocal Performance	50.00	100.00
☐ 118 Producer of the Year	50.00	100.00
☐ 119 Best R and B Vocal	50.00	100.00
☐ 120 Michael Jackson	50.00	100.00
☐ 121 Best R and B Song	50.00	100.00
☐ 122 Best Rock Vocal Performance	50.00	100.00
☐ 123 Living Legend	50.00	100.00
☐ 124 Most Expensive Video	50.00	100.00
☐ 125 Biggest-Selling Album	50.00	100.00
☐ 126 First Song to Debut at No. 1	50.00	100.00
☐ 127 Michael Jackson	50.00	100.00
☐ 128 Most Successful Concert Series	50.00	100.00
☐ 129 Most Grammys Won in a Year	50.00	100.00
☐ 130 Most No. 1 Hits in the '80s	50.00	100.00
☐ 131 No. 1 on Both Rock and R and B Charts	50.00	100.00
☐ 132 Greatest Audience	50.00	100.00
☐ 133 This photo was taken at Gardner Street	50.00	100.00
☐ 134 After the 1984 American Music Awards	50.00	100.00
☐ 135 In a time when music videos consisted	50.00	100.00
☐ 136 Michael Jackson	50.00	100.00
☐ 137 In 1983, Michael Jackson became	50.00	100.00
☐ 138 Fresh from producing the most successful	50.00	100.00
☐ 139 Michael's Bad World Tour	50.00	100.00
☐ 140 In 1984, Michael set a record	50.00	100.00
☐ 141 In 1984, President Ronald Reagan	50.00	100.00
☐ 142 Michael's first solo world tour sold out	50.00	100.00
☐ 143 During Michael's Dangerous tour	50.00	100.00
☐ 144 Michael met a few presidents	50.00	100.00
☐ 145 Michael's performance at the 1993 Super Bowl	50.00	100.00
☐ 146 At the 35th Annual Grammy Awards	50.00	100.00
☐ 147 Michael's gold costume	50.00	100.00
☐ 148 Michael Jackson	50.00	100.00
☐ 149 Many of the HIStory concerts	50.00	100.00
☐ 150 On Dec. 30, 1992, during a concert	50.00	100.00
☐ 151 Michael Jackson	50.00	100.00
☐ 152 At the opening of each concert	50.00	100.00
☐ 153 Michael was nominated	50.00	100.00
☐ 154 Michael's album Invincible was released	50.00	100.00
☐ 155 Michael was scheduled to perform	50.00	100.00
☐ 156 Michael's single You Rock My World	50.00	100.00
☐ 157 In 2008, Michael released a special	50.00	100.00
☐ 158 In September of 2001, there were two	50.00	100.00
☐ 159 Michael's greatest-hits album Number Ones	50.00	100.00
☐ 160 On May 27, 2006, Michael received	50.00	100.00
☐ 161 In March 2007, Michael Jackson visited	50.00	100.00
☐ 162 Butterflies is the lesser known of the two	50.00	100.00
☐ 163 Got To Be There T10	50.00	100.00
☐ 164 Off the Wall T10	50.00	100.00
☐ 165 She's Out of My Life T10	50.00	100.00
☐ 166 The Girl is Mine T10	50.00	100.00
☐ 167 Wanna Be Startin' Somethin' T10	50.00	100.00
☐ 168 Human Nature T10	50.00	100.00
☐ 169 P.Y.T. (Pretty Young Thing) T10	50.00	100.00
☐ 170 Thriller T10	50.00	100.00
☐ 171 Smooth Criminal T10	50.00	100.00
☐ 172 Michael Jackson T10	50.00	100.00
☐ 173 In the Closet T10	50.00	100.00
☐ 174 Heal the World T10	50.00	100.00
☐ 175 Will You Be There T10	50.00	100.00
☐ 176 Scream T10	50.00	100.00
☐ 177 You Rock My World T10	50.00	100.00
☐ 178 Ben NO1	50.00	100.00
☐ 179 Don't Stop 'Til You Get Enough NO1	50.00	100.00
☐ 180 Rock With You NO1	50.00	100.00
☐ 181 Billie Jean NO1	50.00	100.00
☐ 182 Beat It NO1	50.00	100.00
☐ 183 Say Say Say NO1	50.00	100.00
☐ 184 I Just Can't Stop Loving You NO1	50.00	100.00
☐ 185 Bad NO1	50.00	100.00
☐ 186 The Way You Make Me Feel NO1	50.00	100.00
☐ 187 Man In the Mirror NO1	50.00	100.00
☐ 188 Dirty Diana NO1	50.00	100.00
☐ 189 Black or White NO1	50.00	100.00
☐ 190 You Are Not Alone NO1	50.00	100.00

2011 Michael Jackson Charted Albums Gold

COMPLETE SET (10)

Card	Low	High
☐ CA1 Off the Wall	40.00	80.00
☐ CA2 Thriller	40.00	80.00
☐ CA3 Bad	40.00	80.00
☐ CA4 Dangerous	40.00	80.00
☐ CA5 HIStory	40.00	80.00
☐ CA6 Blood on the Dance Floor	40.00	80.00
☐ CA7 Invincible	40.00	80.00
☐ CA8 Number Ones	40.00	80.00
☐ CA9 Essential Michael Jackson	40.00	80.00
☐ CA10 This Is It	40.00	80.00

2011 Michael Jackson Charted Albums Platinum

*PLATINUM: .6X TO 1.2X BASIC CARDS

2011 Michael Jackson Eclectic Threads

STATED ODDS

Card	Low	High
☐ ET1 Michael Jackson	100.00	175.00
☐ ET2 Michael Jackson	100.00	175.00
☐ ET3 Michael Jackson DUAL	125.00	225.00

2011 Michael Jackson Jackson Live

STATED ODDS

Card	Low	High
☐ JL1 Michael Jackson	100.00	175.00
☐ JL2 Michael Jackson	100.00	175.00
☐ JL3 Michael Jackson DUAL	125.00	225.00

2011 Michael Jackson Sequins

COMPLETE SET (4)
ANNCD PRINT RUN 50 SETS

Card	Low	High
☐ 1 MO	150.00	250.00
☐ 2 ON	150.00	250.00
☐ 3 WA	150.00	250.00
☐ 4 LK	150.00	250.00

2011 Michael Jackson Televised Fashions

STATED ODDS

Card	Low	High
☐ TV1 Michael Jackson	100.00	175.00
☐ TV2 Michael Jackson	100.00	175.00
☐ TV3 Michael Jackson	100.00	175.00
☐ TV4 Michael Jackson	100.00	175.00
☐ TV5 Michael Jackson	100.00	175.00
☐ 1 Michael Jackson 5 MEM	750.00	1250.00

2011 Pop Century

Card	Low	High
☐ BAAB1 Amber Benson	6.00	15.00
☐ BAAJ1 Ashley Judd	40.00	80.00
☐ BAAP2 Audrina Patridge	8.00	20.00
☐ BAAT1 Alan Thicke	4.00	10.00
☐ BAAT2 Andrea Thompson	4.00	10.00
☐ BAAW1 Amy Weber	6.00	15.00
☐ BABB2 Brett Butler	4.00	10.00
☐ BABE1 Barbara Eden SP	25.00	50.00
☐ BABF1 Bethenny Frankel	4.00	10.00
☐ BABJ1 Bruce Jenner SP		
☐ BABL1 Bai Ling	10.00	25.00
☐ BABM1 Bill Mumy	8.00	20.00
☐ BABS1 Boo Boo Stewart	4.00	10.00
☐ BABS2 Britney Spears SP	250.00	500.00
☐ BABW1 Barry Williams	4.00	10.00
☐ BACA1 Christian Audigier	4.00	10.00
☐ BACA2 Christina Applegate SP	30.00	60.00
☐ BACA3 Christopher Atkins	4.00	10.00
☐ BACA4 Curtis Armstrong	4.00	10.00
☐ BACB1 Corbin Bernsen SP	4.00	10.00
☐ BACE1 Carmen Electra	25.00	50.00
☐ BACL1 Christopher Lloyd SP		
☐ BACN1 Cam Newton	50.00	100.00
☐ BACS1A Charlie Sheen (wearing suit) SP	75.00	150.00
☐ BACS1B Charlie Sheen (Tiger Blood shirt) SP	75.00	150.00
☐ BACS1C Charlie Sheen (Winning shirt) SP	75.00	150.00
☐ BACT1 Cheryl Tiegs SP		
☐ BACZ1 Chuck Zito	4.00	10.00
☐ BADB1 Debby Boone	8.00	20.00
☐ BADD2 Donna Douglas	10.00	25.00
☐ BADR1 Della Reese	6.00	15.00
☐ BADR2 Dennis Rodman	20.00	40.00
☐ BADW1 Dawn Wells	10.00	25.00
☐ BAEC1 Emma Caulfield	4.00	10.00
☐ BAECP Elvira	30.00	60.00
☐ BAEM1 Erin Moran	8.00	20.00
☐ BAER1 Elisabeth Rohm	8.00	20.00
☐ BAER2 Eric Roberts	6.00	15.00
☐ BAFD1 Fred Dryer	4.00	10.00
☐ BAFW1 Fred Williamson	6.00	15.00
☐ BAGG1 Gil Gerard	8.00	20.00
☐ BAGH1 George Hamilton	8.00	20.00
☐ BAGLN Gena Lee Nolin	10.00	25.00
☐ BAHA1 Harry Anderson	8.00	20.00
☐ BAHF1 Harrison Ford SP	400.00	600.00
☐ BAHH1 Henry Hill	4.00	10.00
☐ BAHP1 Hayden Panettiere	40.00	80.00
☐ BAIZ1 Ian Ziering	4.00	10.00
☐ BAJA1 Jason Alexander SP	30.00	60.00
☐ BAJC1 Jeff Conaway	20.00	40.00
☐ BAJC2 Jennifer Coolidge	4.00	10.00
☐ BAJC3 Jose Canseco	20.00	40.00
☐ BAJD1 Joyce Dewitt SP	8.00	20.00
☐ BAJG2 Justin Guarini	4.00	10.00
☐ BAJK1 Jennifer Korbin	6.00	15.00
☐ BAJKL James Kyson Lee	4.00	10.00
☐ BAJM1 Jackie Martling	4.00	10.00
☐ BAJM2 Jason Momoa	10.00	25.00
☐ BAJS1 Jewel Staite	10.00	25.00
☐ BAJS2 John Schneider	8.00	20.00
☐ BAJT1 Jeffrey Tambor SP	6.00	15.00
☐ BAJW1 Jimmy Walker	6.00	15.00
☐ BAKB1 Kate Beckinsale SP	150.00	250.00
☐ BAKD1 Kara DioGuardi	6.00	15.00
☐ BAKK1 Khloe Kardashian	8.00	20.00
☐ BAKK2 Kim Kardashian SP	40.00	80.00
☐ BAKK3 Kourtney Kardashian	15.00	30.00
☐ BAKL1 Kelly LeBrock	15.00	30.00
☐ BAKP1 Kirsten Prout	6.00	15.00
☐ BAKW1 Kendra Wilkinson	15.00	30.00
☐ BALA1 Loni Anderson	20.00	40.00
☐ BALF1 Lita Ford	10.00	25.00
☐ BALH1 Larry Hagman	20.00	40.00
☐ BALH2 Lauren Holly	15.00	30.00
☐ BALL1 Lindsay Lohan SP	150.00	250.00
☐ BALT1 Larry Thomas	4.00	10.00
☐ BAMC1 Mike Connors	8.00	20.00
☐ BAMD1 Mickey Dolenz	10.00	25.00
☐ BAMF1 Mira Furlan	4.00	10.00
☐ BAMI1 Michael Imperioli	10.00	25.00
☐ BAMI2 Mark Ingram	20.00	40.00
☐ BAMK1 Margot Kidder	8.00	20.00
☐ BAML1 The Unknown Comic (Murray Langston)	4.00	10.00
☐ BAMR2 Mickey Rourke SP	20.00	40.00
☐ BAMVD Mamie Van Doren	10.00	25.00
☐ BAMW1 Mary Wilson SP	15.00	30.00
☐ BANE1 Nicole Eggert SP	20.00	40.00
☐ BANR1 Nolan Ryan SP	40.00	80.00
☐ BAODA Olivia D'Abo	10.00	25.00
☐ BAPA1 Pamela Anderson SP	75.00	150.00
☐ BAPF1 Peter Fonda SP	20.00	40.00
☐ BAPG1 Pam Grier	15.00	30.00
☐ BAPP1 Pat Priest	8.00	20.00
☐ BAPT1 Peter Tork	15.00	30.00
☐ BARC2 Robert Carradine	4.00	10.00
☐ BARD1 Richard Dreyfuss SP	30.00	60.00
☐ BARK1 Richard Kiel	6.00	15.00
☐ BARM1 Ralph Macchio	10.00	25.00
☐ BARM2 Rose Marie	6.00	15.00
☐ BARON Ryan O'Neal	10.00	25.00
☐ BARR1 Richard Roundtree	6.00	15.00
☐ BASA1 Sean Astin	6.00	15.00
☐ BASA2 Steven Adler	10.00	25.00
☐ BASD1 Sarah Douglas	6.00	15.00
☐ BASE1 Shannon Elizabeth		
☐ BASF1 Sherilyn Fenn	15.00	30.00
☐ BASF2 Stephen Furst	4.00	10.00
☐ BASL1 Shayne Lamas	4.00	10.00
☐ BASL2 Stan Lee	40.00	80.00
☐ BASO2 Susan Olsen	8.00	20.00
☐ BAST1 Stephen Tobolowsky	4.00	10.00
☐ BASY1 Sean Young	15.00	30.00
☐ BATC1 Tia Carrere	15.00	30.00
☐ BATL1 Traci Lords	40.00	80.00
☐ BATM1 Taryn Manning	4.00	10.00
☐ BATR1 Tanya Roberts	10.00	25.00
☐ BATW1 Tahnee Welch	6.00	15.00
☐ BAVAF Vivica A. Fox	8.00	20.00
☐ BAVN1 Vince Neil	10.00	25.00
☐ BAWK1 Walter Koenig	10.00	25.00
☐ BAWS1 William Shatner SP	60.00	120.00

2011 Pop Century Silver

PRINT RUN 3-25

Card	Low	High
☐ BAAB1 Amber Benson	8.00	20.00
☐ BAAJ1 Ashley Judd/10		
☐ BAAP2 Audrina Patridge/10		
☐ BAAT1 Alan Thicke	5.00	12.00
☐ BAAT2 Andrea Thompson	5.00	12.00
☐ BAAW1 Amy Weber	8.00	20.00
☐ BABB2 Brett Butler	5.00	12.00
☐ BABE1 Barbara Eden		
☐ BABF1 Bethenny Frankel	5.00	12.00
☐ BABJ1 Bruce Jenner/3		
☐ BABL1 Bai Ling	12.00	30.00
☐ BABM1 Bill Mumy	10.00	25.00
☐ BABS1 Boo Boo Stewart	5.00	12.00
☐ BABS2 Britney Spears/5		
☐ BABW1 Barry Williams	5.00	12.00
☐ BACA1 Christian Audigier	5.00	12.00
☐ BACA2 Christina Applegate/10		
☐ BACA3 Christopher Atkins	5.00	12.00
☐ BACA4 Curtis Armstrong	5.00	12.00
☐ BACB1 Corbin Bernsen	5.00	12.00
☐ BACE1 Carmen Electra	30.00	60.00
☐ BACL1 Christopher Lloyd/3		
☐ BACN1 Cam Newton	50.00	120.00
☐ BACS1A Charlie Sheen/3		
☐ BACS1B Charlie Sheen/3		
☐ BACS1C Charlie Sheen/3		
☐ BACT1 Cheryl Tiegs		
☐ BACZ1 Chuck Zito	5.00	12.00
☐ BADB1 Debby Boone	10.00	25.00
☐ BADD2 Donna Douglas	12.00	30.00
☐ BADR1 Della Reese	8.00	20.00
☐ BADR2 Dennis Rodman	25.00	50.00
☐ BADW1 Dawn Wells	12.00	30.00
☐ BAEC1 Emma Caulfield	10.00	25.00
☐ BAECP Elvira	40.00	80.00
☐ BAEM1 Erin Moran	10.00	25.00
☐ BAER1 Elisabeth Rohm	10.00	25.00
☐ BAER2 Eric Roberts	8.00	20.00
☐ BAFD1 Fred Dryer	5.00	12.00
☐ BAFW1 Fred Williamson	8.00	20.00
☐ BAGG1 Gil Gerard	10.00	25.00
☐ BAGH1 George Hamilton	10.00	25.00
☐ BAGLN Gena Lee Nolin	12.00	30.00
☐ BAHA1 Harry Anderson	10.00	25.00
☐ BAHF1 Harrison Ford		
☐ BAHH1 Henry Hill	5.00	12.00
☐ BAHP1 Hayden Panettiere/10		
☐ BAIZ1 Ian Ziering	5.00	12.00
☐ BAJA1 Jason Alexander/5		
☐ BAJC1 Jeff Conaway	25.00	50.00
☐ BAJC2 Jennifer Coolidge	5.00	12.00
☐ BAJC3 Jose Canseco	25.00	50.00
☐ BAJD1 Joyce Dewitt/10		
☐ BAJG2 Justin Guarini	5.00	12.00
☐ BAJK1 Jennifer Korbin	8.00	20.00
☐ BAJKL James Kyson Lee	5.00	12.00
☐ BAJM1 Jackie Martling	5.00	12.00
☐ BAJM2 Jason Momoa	12.00	30.00
☐ BAJS1 Jewel Staite	12.00	30.00
☐ BAJS2 John Schneider/10		
☐ BAJT1 Jeffrey Tambor	8.00	20.00
☐ BAJW1 Jimmy Walker	8.00	20.00
☐ BAKB1 Kate Beckinsale/5		
☐ BAKD1 Kara DioGuardi	8.00	20.00
☐ BAKK1 Khloe Kardashian	10.00	25.00
☐ BAKK2 Kim Kardashian/10		
☐ BAKK3 Kourtney Kardashian	20.00	40.00
☐ BAKL1 Kelly LeBrock	20.00	40.00
☐ BAKP1 Kirsten Prout	8.00	20.00
☐ BAKW1 Kendra Wilkinson	20.00	40.00
☐ BALA1 Loni Anderson	25.00	50.00
☐ BALF1 Lita Ford	12.00	30.00
☐ BALH1 Larry Hagman	25.00	50.00
☐ BALH2 Lauren Holly	20.00	40.00
☐ BALL1 Lindsay Lohan		
☐ BALT1 Larry Thomas	5.00	12.00
☐ BAMC1 Mike Connors	10.00	25.00
☐ BAMD1 Mickey Dolenz	12.00	30.00
☐ BAMF1 Mira Furlan	5.00	12.00
☐ BAMI1 Michael Imperioli	12.00	30.00
☐ BAMI2 Mark Ingram	25.00	50.00
☐ BAMK1 Margot Kidder	10.00	25.00
☐ BAML1 The Unknown Comic (Murray Langston)	5.00	12.00
☐ BAMR2 Mickey Rourke	25.00	50.00
☐ BAMVD Mamie Van Doren	12.00	30.00
☐ BAMW1 Mary Wilson/10		
☐ BANE1 Nicole Eggert	25.00	50.00
☐ BANR1 Nolan Ryan/10		
☐ BAODA Olivia D'Abo	12.00	30.00
☐ BAPA1 Pamela Anderson/5		
☐ BAPF1 Peter Fonda	25.00	50.00
☐ BAPG1 Pam Grier	20.00	40.00
☐ BAPP1 Pat Priest	10.00	25.00
☐ BAPT1 Peter Tork	20.00	40.00
☐ BARC2 Robert Carradine	5.00	12.00
☐ BARD1 Richard Dreyfuss		
☐ BARK1 Richard Kiel	8.00	20.00
☐ BARM1 Ralph Macchio	12.00	30.00
☐ BARM2 Rose Marie	8.00	20.00
☐ BARON Ryan O'Neal	12.00	30.00
☐ BARR1 Richard Roundtree	8.00	20.00
☐ BASA1 Sean Astin	8.00	20.00
☐ BASA2 Steven Adler	12.00	30.00
☐ BASD1 Sarah Douglas	8.00	20.00
☐ BASE1 Shannon Elizabeth		
☐ BASF1 Sherilyn Fenn	20.00	40.00
☐ BASF2 Stephen Furst	5.00	12.00
☐ BASL1 Shayne Lamas	5.00	12.00
☐ BASL2 Stan Lee	50.00	100.00
☐ BASO2 Susan Olsen	10.00	25.00
☐ BAST1 Stephen Tobolowsky	5.00	12.00
☐ BASY1 Sean Young	20.00	40.00
☐ BATC1 Tia Carrere	20.00	40.00
☐ BATL1 Traci Lords	50.00	100.00
☐ BATM1 Taryn Manning	5.00	12.00
☐ BATR1 Tanya Roberts	12.00	30.00
☐ BATW1 Tahnee Welch	8.00	20.00
☐ BAVAF Vivica A. Fox	10.00	25.00
☐ BAVN1 Vince Neil/10		
☐ BAWK1 Walter Koenig	20.00	40.00
☐ BAWS1 William Shatner/10		

2011 Pop Century Gold

STATED PRINT RUN 5 SER. #'d SETS
UNPRICED DUE TO SCARCITY

2011 Pop Century Award Winners Autographs

RANDOM INSERT IN PACKS

Card	Low	High
☐ AWBB2 Brett Butler	4.00	10.00
☐ AWBS2 Britney Spears SP		
☐ AWBW1 Barry Williams	4.00	10.00
☐ AWCA2 Christina Applegate SP	25.00	50.00
☐ AWCE1 Carmen Electra	25.00	50.00
☐ AWCN1 Cam Newton	50.00	100.00
☐ AWDB1 Debby Boone	8.00	20.00
☐ AWDD2 Donna Douglas	10.00	25.00
☐ AWDR1 Della Reese	6.00	15.00
☐ AWDR2 Dennis Rodman	20.00	40.00
☐ AWDW1 Dawn Wells	10.00	25.00
☐ AWEM1 Erin Moran	8.00	20.00
☐ AWGH1 George Hamilton	8.00	20.00
☐ AWJA1 Jason Alexander SP	30.00	60.00
☐ AWJC2 Jennifer Coolidge	4.00	10.00
☐ AWJRD John Rhys-Davies	10.00	25.00
☐ AWJS2 John Schneider SP	8.00	20.00
☐ AWKK1 Khloe Kardashian	8.00	20.00
☐ AWKK2 Kim Kardashian SP	40.00	80.00
☐ AWKK3 Kourtney Kardashian	15.00	30.00
☐ AWLL1 Lindsay Lohan SP	150.00	250.00
☐ AWMB1 Michael Biehn	20.00	40.00
☐ AWMC1 Mike Connors	8.00	20.00
☐ AWMI1 Michael Imperioli	10.00	25.00
☐ AWMI2 Mark Ingram	20.00	40.00
☐ AWMK1 Margot Kidder	8.00	20.00
☐ AWMR2 Mickey Rourke SP	20.00	40.00
☐ AWMSJ Mia St. John	6.00	15.00
☐ AWNR1 Nolan Ryan SP	40.00	80.00
☐ AWRR1 Richard Roundtree	6.00	15.00
☐ AWSL2 Stan Lee SP	40.00	80.00
☐ AWSO2 Susan Olsen	8.00	20.00
☐ AWTB1 Todd Bridges	4.00	10.00
☐ AWTL1 Traci Lords	40.00	80.00
☐ AWVAF Vivica A. Fox	8.00	20.00
☐ AWVN1 Vince Neil SP	10.00	25.00

2011 Pop Century Award Winners Autographs Silver

STATED PRINT RUN 10 SER. #'d SETS
UNPRICED DUE TO SCARCITY

2011 Pop Century Award Winners Autographs Gold

STATED PRINT RUN 5 SER. #'d SETS
UNPRICED DUE TO SCARCITY

2011 Pop Century Bettie Page Cut Signatures

STATED PRINT RUN 10 SER. #'d SETS

Card	Low	High
☐ BP1 Bettie Page	250.00	350.00
☐ BP2 Bettie Page	250.00	350.00
☐ BP3 Bettie Page	250.00	350.00
☐ BP4 Bettie Page	250.00	350.00

2011 Pop Century Co-Stars Dual Autographs

RANDOM INSERT IN PACKS

☐ APER Adrian Pasdar / Eric Roberts
☐ APOD Adrian Pasdar / Olivia D'Abo
☐ APSF Adrian Pasdar / Sherilyn Fenn
☐ ATBM Andrea Thompson / Bill Mumy
☐ ATCA Alan Thicke / Christina Applegate
☐ ATRR Alan Thicke / Richard Roundtree
☐ ATSY Andrea Thompson / Sean Young
☐ BBSA Beau Bridges / Sean Astin
☐ BCPF Bruce Campbell / Peter Fonda
☐ BCSL Bruce Campbell / Stan Lee
☐ BLMI Bai Ling / Michael Imperioli
☐ BLRR Bai Ling / Richard Roundtree
☐ BMSA Bill Mumy / Sean Astin
☐ BMSD Bill Mumy / Sarah Douglas
☐ BMST Bill Mumy / Stephen Tobolowsky
☐ BSKD Britney Spears / Kara DioGuardi
☐ BSKP Boo Boo Stewart / Kirsten Prout
☐ BSLL Britney Spears / Lindsay Lohan
☐ BWSO Barry Williams / Susan Olsen
☐ CAJT Curtis Armstrong / Jeffrey Tambor
☐ CARC Curtis Armstrong / Robert Carradine
☐ CASA Christina Applegate / Sean Astin
☐ CBAT Corbin Bernsen / Alan Thicke
☐ CBCA Corbin Bernsen / Christopher Atkins
☐ CBER Corbin Bernsen / Eric Roberts
☐ CBJR Corbin Bernsen / John Rhys-Davies
☐ CEFW Carmen Electra / Fred Williamson
☐ CEGL Carmen Electra / Gena Lee Nolin
☐ CEJT Carmen Electra / Jeffrey Tambor
☐ CNMI Cam Newton / Mark Ingram
☐ CZER Chuck Zito / Eric Roberts
☐ CZJM Chuck Zito / Jackie Martling
☐ CZMR Chuck Zito / Mickey Rourke
☐ DRCE Dennis Rodman / Carmen Electra
☐ DRPG Della Reese / Pam Grier
☐ EGGG Erin Gray / Gil Gerard
☐ EMHW Erin Moran / Henry Winkler
☐ ERHP Elisabeth Rohm / Hayden Panettiere
☐ ERMI Elisabeth Rohm / Michael Imperioli
☐ GHCA George Hamilton / Christopher Atkins
☐ ITFW Ice-T / Fred Williamson
☐ ITLW Ice-T / Lindsay Wagner
☐ JALT Jason Alexander / Larry Thomas
☐ JCST Jennifer Coolidge / Stephen Tobolowsky
☐ JGIZ Jennie Garth / Ian Ziering
☐ JGST Jennie Garth / Stephen Tobolowsky
☐ JKST James Kyson Lee / Stephen Tobolowsky
☐ JMMR Jason Momoa / Mickey Rourke
☐ JRKL John Rhys-Davies / Kristanna Loken
☐ JRMC John Rhys-Davies / Mike Connors
☐ JTBD Jeffrey Tambor / Bo Derek
☐ JTRK Jeffrey Tambor / Richard Kiel
☐ JWML Jimmy Walker / The Unknown Comic
☐ KDJG Kara DioGuardi / Justin Guarini
☐ LARM Loni Anderson / Rose Marie
☐ LFVN Lita Ford / Vince Neil
☐ LHBE Larry Hagman / Barbara Eden
☐ LWBM Lindsay Wagner / Bill Mumy
☐ MBJC Michael Biehn / Jeff Conaway
☐ MKBB Margot Kidder / Beau Bridges
☐ MKPF Margot Kidder / Peter Fonda
☐ MRIZ Mickey Rourke / Ian Ziering
☐ MRMV Mickey Rooney / Mamie Van Doren
☐ NEGL Nicole Eggert / Gena Lee Nolin
☐ NNWK Nichelle Nichols / Walter Koenig
☐ PGFW Pam Grier / Fred Williamson
☐ PGJC Pam Grier / Jeff Conaway
☐ PGKL Pam Grier / Kristanna Loken
☐ SDST Sarah Douglas / Stephen Tobolowsky
☐ SPAP Stephanie Pratt / Audrina Patridge
☐ SYJC Sean Young / Jeff Conaway
☐ SYSF Sean Young / Sherilyn Fenn
☐ VNSA Vince Neil / Steven Adler
☐ WJAJ Wynonna Judd / Ashley Judd
☐ WKWS Walter Koenig / William Shatner
☐ KKKK1 Kim Kardashian / Kourtney Kardashian
☐ KKKK2 Kim Kardashian / Khloe Kardashian
☐ KKKK3 Kourtney Kardashian / Khloe Kardashian

2011 Pop Century Co-Stars Dual Autographs Silver

UNPRICED DUE TO SCARCITY

2011 Pop Century Co-Stars Dual Autographs Gold

STATED PRINT RUN 1 SER. #'d SETS
UNPRICED DUE TO SCARCITY

2011 Pop Century Co-Stars Triple Autographs

RANDOM INSERT IN PACKS

☐ APHPST Adrian Pasdar / Hayden Panettiere/Stephen Tobolowsky
☐ ATBMSF Andrea Thompson / Bill Mumy/Stephen Furst
☐ CAEREC Christopher Atkins / Eric Roberts/Elvira
☐ CLCBST Christopher Lloyd / Corbin Bernsen/Stephen Tobolowsky
☐ EFGHKL Edward Furlong / George Hamilton/Kristanna Loken
☐ FWJRPF Fred Williamson / John Rhys-Davies/Peter Fonda
☐ GLNEDD Gena Lee Nolin / Nicole Eggert/Donna D'Errico
☐ KKKKKK Kim Kardashian / Khloe Kardashian/Kourtney Kardashian
☐ MDDJPT Mickey Dolenz / Davy Jones/Peter Tork
☐ MFBMSF Mira Furlan / Bill Mumy/Stephen Furst
☐ MFWKAT Mira Furlan / Walter Koenig/Andrea Thompson
☐ MRCCER Mickey Rourke / Charisma Carpenter/Eric Roberts
☐ RCROBD Robert Carradine / Ryan O'Neal/Bo Derek

2011 Pop Century Co-Stars Triple Autographs Silver

STATED PRINT RUN 5 SER. #'d SETS
UNPRICED DUE TO SCARCITY

2011 Pop Century Co-Stars Triple Autographs Gold

STATED PRINT RUN 1 SER. #'d SETS
UNPRICED DUE TO SCARCITY

2011 Pop Century Dressing Room Autograph Memorabilia

PRINT RUN 3-73

❑ DRBC1 Bruce Campbell/73 20.00 40.00
❑ DRBS2 Britney Spears
❑ DRDD1 Donna D'Errico/25 20.00 40.00
❑ DRJK1 Jennifer Korbin/36 20.00 40.00
❑ DRKK2 Kim Kardashian/24 100.00 200.00
❑ DRKK3 Kourtney Kardashian/51 25.00 50.00
❑ DRNE1 Nicole Eggert/25 25.00 50.00
❑ DRPA1 Pamela Anderson/19 100.00 200.00
❑ DRRD1 Richard Dreyfuss/3
❑ DRWS1 William Shatner/29 75.00 150.00

2011 Pop Century Dressing Room Autograph Memorabilia Silver

STATED PRINT RUN 10 SER. #'d SETS
UNPRICED DUE TO SCARCITY

2011 Pop Century Dressing Room Autograph Memorabilia Gold

STATED PRINT RUN 5 SER. #'d SETS
UNPRICED DUE TO SCARCITY

2011 Pop Century Keeping It Real Autographs

RANDOM INSERT IN PACKS

❑ KRAO2 Aubrey O'Day 4.00 10.00
❑ KRAP2 Audrina Patridge 8.00 20.00
❑ KRAT1 Alan Thicke 4.00 10.00
❑ KRBF1 Bethenny Frankel 4.00 10.00
❑ KRBL1 Bai Ling 10.00 25.00
❑ KRIZ1 Ian Ziering 4.00 10.00
❑ KRJC1 Jeff Conaway 20.00 40.00
❑ KRJC3 Jose Canseco 20.00 40.00
❑ KRJG2 Justin Guarini 4.00 10.00
❑ KRKD1 Kara DioGuardi 6.00 15.00
❑ KRKK2 Kim Kardashian SP 40.00 80.00
❑ KRKK3 Kourtney Kardashian 15.00 30.00
❑ KRKW1 Kendra Wilkinson 15.00 30.00
❑ KRPA1 Pamela Anderson SP 75.00 150.00
❑ KRSL1 Shayne Lamas 4.00 10.00
❑ KRSO1 Steve-O 10.00 25.00
❑ KRSP1 Stephanie Pratt 6.00 15.00
❑ KRSY1 Sean Young 15.00 30.00
❑ KRTC1 Tia Carrere 15.00 30.00
❑ KRVN1 Vince Neil SP 10.00 25.00

2011 Pop Century Keeping It Real Autographs Silver

STATED PRINT RUN 10 SER. #'d SETS
UNPRICED DUE TO SCARCITY

2011 Pop Century Keeping It Real Autographs Gold

STATED PRINT RUN 5 SER. #'d SETS
UNPRICED DUE TO SCARCITY

2011 Pop Century Sci-Fi Autographs

RANDOM INSERT IN PACKS

❑ SFAB1 Amber Benson 6.00 15.00
❑ SFAP1 Adrian Pasdar 4.00 10.00
❑ SFAT2 Andrea Thompson 4.00 10.00
❑ SFBB1 Beau Bridges 6.00 15.00
❑ SFBC1 Bruce Campbell 15.00 30.00
❑ SFBM1 Bill Mumy 8.00 20.00
❑ SFCC1 Charisma Carpenter 15.00 30.00
❑ SFCJ1 Christopher Judge SP
❑ SFEC1 Emma Caulfield 8.00 20.00
❑ SFEF1 Edward Furlong 8.00 20.00
❑ SFEG1 Erin Gray 15.00 30.00
❑ SFER2 Eric Roberts 6.00 15.00
❑ SFGG1 Gil Gerard 8.00 20.00
❑ SFHP1 Hayden Panettiere 40.00 80.00
❑ SFJKL James Kyson Lee 4.00 10.00
❑ SFJM2 Jason Momoa 10.00 25.00
❑ SFJS1 Jewel Staite 10.00 25.00
❑ SFKL2 Kristanna Loken 20.00 40.00
❑ SFLH3 Linda Hamilton SP 25.00 50.00
❑ SFLT2 Lea Thompson 10.00 25.00
❑ SFLW1 Lindsay Wagner 15.00 30.00
❑ SFMB1 Michael Biehn 20.00 40.00
❑ SFMF1 Mira Furlan 4.00 10.00
❑ SFNN1 Nichelle Nichols 20.00 40.00
❑ SFPM1 Peter Mayhew 6.00 15.00
❑ SFRD1 Richard Dreyfuss SP 30.00 60.00
❑ SFSF2 Stephen Furst 4.00 10.00
❑ SFST1 Stephen Tobolowsky 4.00 10.00
❑ SFVAF Vivica A. Fox 8.00 20.00
❑ SFWK1 Walter Koenig 10.00 25.00
❑ SFWS1 William Shatner SP 60.00 120.00

2011 Pop Century Sci-Fi Autographs Silver

STATED PRINT RUN 10 SER. #'d SETS
UNPRICED DUE TO SCARCITY

2011 Pop Century Sci-Fi Autographs Gold

STATED PRINT RUN 5 SER. #'d SETS
UNPRICED DUE TO SCARCITY

2011 Pop Century Smash Hit Autographs

PRINT RUN 3-78

❑ SHBS2 Britney Spears/3
❑ SHDB1 Debby Boone/36 8.00 20.00
❑ SHDJ1 Davy Jones/28 40.00 80.00
❑ SHIT1 Ice-T/20
❑ SHJG2 Justin Guarini/36 4.00 10.00
❑ SHKD1 Kara DioGuardi/36 8.00 20.00
❑ SHLF1 Lita Ford/60 10.00 25.00
❑ SHMD1 Mickey Dolenz/56 20.00 40.00
❑ SHMW1 Mary Wilson/26 15.00 30.00
❑ SHPT1 Peter Tork/56 20.00 40.00
❑ SHSA2 Steven Adler/40 10.00 25.00
❑ SHTD1 Taylor Dayne/48 6.00 15.00
❑ SHTIF Tiffany/48 10.00 25.00
❑ SHVN1 Vince Neil/19
❑ SHWJ1 Wynonna Judd/78 15.00 30.00

2011 Pop Century Smash Hit Autographs Silver

STATED PRINT RUN 10 SER. #'d SETS
UNPRICED DUE TO SCARCITY

2011 Pop Century Smash Hit Autographs Gold

STATED PRINT RUN 5 SER. #'d SETS
UNPRICED DUE TO SCARCITY

2011 Pop Century Stunning Starlets Autographs

RANDOM INSERT IN PACKS

❑ SSAJ1 Ashley Judd 50.00 100.00
❑ SSAO2 Aubrey O'Day 6.00 15.00
❑ SSAP2 Audrina Patridge 8.00 20.00
❑ SSAW1 Amy Weber 6.00 15.00
❑ SSBD1 Bo Derek 30.00 60.00
❑ SSBL1 Bai Ling 10.00 25.00
❑ SSBS2 Britney Spears SP 150.00 250.00
❑ SSCA2 Christina Applegate SP 25.00 50.00
❑ SSCC1 Charisma Carpenter 15.00 30.00
❑ SSCE1 Carmen Electra 25.00 50.00
❑ SSCT1 Cheryl Tiegs SP
❑ SSDD1 Donna D'Errico SP 8.00 20.00
❑ SSGLN Gena Lee Nolin 10.00 25.00
❑ SSHP1 Hayden Panettiere 40.00 80.00
❑ SSJG1 Jennie Garth SP
❑ SSJK1 Jennifer Korbin 6.00 15.00
❑ SSKB1 Kate Beckinsale SP 150.00 250.00
❑ SSKK1 Khloe Kardashian 8.00 20.00
❑ SSKK2 Kim Kardashian SP 40.00 80.00
❑ SSKK3 Kourtney Kardashian 15.00 30.00
❑ SSKL1 Kelly LeBrock 15.00 30.00
❑ SSKL2 Kristanna Loken 20.00 40.00
❑ SSKW1 Kendra Wilkinson 15.00 30.00
❑ SSLA1 Loni Anderson 20.00 40.00
❑ SSLL1 Lindsay Lohan SP 150.00 250.00
❑ SSMVD Mamie Van Doren 10.00 25.00
❑ SSNE1 Nicole Eggert 20.00 40.00
❑ SSPA1 Pamela Anderson SP 75.00 150.00
❑ SSSE1 Shannon Elizabeth
❑ SSSF1 Sherilyn Fenn 15.00 30.00
❑ SSSL1 Shayne Lamas 6.00 15.00
❑ SSSP1 Stephanie Pratt 6.00 15.00
❑ SSTC1 Tia Carrere 15.00 30.00
❑ SSTR1 Tanya Roberts 10.00 25.00
❑ SSTW1 Tahnee Welch 6.00 15.00
❑ SSVAF Vivica A. Fox 8.00 20.00

2011 Pop Century Stunning Starlets Autographs Silver

STATED PRINT RUN 10 SER. #'d SETS
UNPRICED DUE TO SCARCITY

2011 Pop Century Stunning Starlets Autographs Gold

STATED PRINT RUN 5 SER. #'d SETS
UNPRICED DUE TO SCARCITY

2011 Pop Century Walk of Fame Autographs

RANDOM INSERT IN PACKS

❑ WFBB1 Beau Bridges 6.00 15.00
❑ WFBE1 Barbara Eden SP 25.00 50.00
❑ WFBS2 Britney Spears SP 250.00 400.00
❑ WFDJ1 Davy Jones 40.00 80.00
❑ WFGH1 George Hamilton 8.00 20.00
❑ WFHW1 Henry Winkler 20.00 40.00
❑ WFLH1 Larry Hagman SP 20.00 40.00
❑ WFLW1 Lindsay Wagner 15.00 30.00
❑ WFMD1 Mickey Dolenz 10.00 25.00
❑ WFMR1 Mickey Rooney 20.00 40.00
❑ WFMVD Mamie Van Doren 10.00 25.00
❑ WFMW1 Mary Wilson 15.00 30.00
❑ WFNN1 Nichelle Nichols 20.00 40.00
❑ WFPF1 Peter Fonda 20.00 40.00
❑ WFPT1 Peter Tork 15.00 30.00
❑ WFRC1 Richard Chamberlain 15.00 30.00
❑ WFRD1 Richard Dreyfuss SP 30.00 60.00
❑ WFRH1 Ron Howard 30.00 60.00
❑ WFRM2 Rose Marie 6.00 15.00
❑ WFSL2 Stan Lee SP 40.00 80.00
❑ WFVN1 Vince Neil SP 10.00 25.00
❑ WFWS1 William Shatner SP 60.00 120.00

2011 Pop Century Walk of Fame Autographs Silver

STATED PRINT RUN 10 SER. #'d SETS
UNPRICED DUE TO SCARCITY

2011 Pop Century Walk of Fame Autographs Gold

STATED PRINT RUN 5 SER. #'d SETS
UNPRICED DUE TO SCARCITY

2011 Project Superpowers

COMPLETE SET (72) 6.00 15.00

❑ 1 It Begins .15 .40
❑ 2 Inside the Urn .15 .40
❑ 3 Heroes Front and Center .15 .40
❑ 4 The Call to Adventure .15 .40
❑ 5 This Hero's Journey .15 .40
❑ 6 Battle Plan .15 .40
❑ 7 Charge of the Golden Age .15 .40
❑ 8 The Urn of Pandora .15 .40
❑ 9 From the Urn .15 .40
❑ 10 Portrait of a Patriot .15 .40
❑ 11 The Black Terror .15 .40
❑ 12 Threshold Guardians .15 .40
❑ 13 The Truth Revealed .15 .40
❑ 14 More Heroes Return .15 .40
❑ 15 Death-Defying 'Devil .15 .40
❑ 16 The Mighty Samson .15 .40
❑ 17 A New Kind of Foe .15 .40
❑ 18 The Team Forms .15 .40
❑ 19 Fall of the Mighty .15 .40
❑ 20 Forever Changed .15 .40
❑ 21 His Own Worst Nightmare .15 .40
❑ 22 Heroes Emerge .15 .40
❑ 23 Victory .15 .40
❑ 24 Taking Aim at Evil .15 .40
❑ 25 Teamwork .15 .40
❑ 26 Death or Rebirth .15 .40
❑ 27 A New Kind of Hero .15 .40
❑ 28 Journey's End .15 .40
❑ 29 At Last The Claw .15 .40
❑ 30 The Dynamic Family .15 .40
❑ 31 Black Terror Goes Solo .15 .40
❑ 32 Trio of Superpowers .15 .40
❑ 33 A True Classic .15 .40
❑ 34 In the Darkness…Terror .15 .40
❑ 35 Mystery Courage Strength .15 .40
❑ 36 Masterpiece in Pencil .15 .40
❑ 37 A Golden Age Rendition .15 .40
❑ 38 Welcome to the White House .15 .40
❑ 39 Fighting for the Truth .15 .40
❑ 40 A Fine Art Flashback .15 .40
❑ 41 No Way Out .15 .40
❑ 42 Captured .15 .40
❑ 43 Separation Anxiety .15 .40
❑ 44 Meeting the Challenge .15 .40
❑ 45 A Hero Redefined .15 .40
❑ 46 The Golden Age Revisited .15 .40
❑ 47 Meet the 'Devil .15 .40
❑ 48 An Amazing Work of Art .15 .40
❑ 49 Now That's Death-Defying .15 .40
❑ 50 Silver Streak .15 .40
❑ 51 Smashing Through .15 .40
❑ 52 Weapons of Choice .15 .40
❑ 53 A Golden Age Great .15 .40
❑ 54 Team-Up With the Ghost .15 .40
❑ 55 Look Out The Claw .15 .40
❑ 56 Silent But Daring .15 .40
❑ 57 The Deadly Dreaded Dragon .15 .40
❑ 58 The Death-Defying 'Devil .15 .40
❑ 59 A Friend of the 'Devil's .15 .40
❑ 60 Battle Royal .15 .40
❑ 61 Evil Awakens .15 .40
❑ 62 Masquerade .15 .40
❑ 63 A Damsel Not in Distress .15 .40
❑ 64 Scourge of the Underworld .15 .40
❑ 65 The Truth Revealed .15 .40
❑ 66 Golden Age Greatness .15 .40
❑ 67 A Fan-Fave Effect .15 .40
❑ 68 Golden Age Portrait .15 .40
❑ 69 Moonlight Crime Fight .15 .40
❑ 70 Masquerade Unmasked .15 .40
❑ 71 The Quest is Over .15 .40
❑ 72 Checklist .15 .40

2011 Project Superpowers Alex Ross Autographs

COMPLETE SET (2) 15.00 30.00

❑ PSAAR1 Masquerade 10.00 20.00
❑ PSAAR2 The Team Forms 10.00 20.00

2011 Project Superpowers Chrome Inserts

COMPLETE SET (9) 5.00 12.00
STATED ODDS TWO PER BOX

❑ 1 Welcome to the White House 1.00 2.50
❑ 2 From the Urn 1.00 2.50
❑ 3 The Team Forms 1.00 2.50
❑ 4 Heroes Emerge 1.00 2.50
❑ 5 Taking Aim at Evil 1.00 2.50
❑ 6 A New Kind of Hero 1.00 2.50
❑ 7 Journey's End 1.00 2.50
❑ 8 At Last The Claw 1.00 2.50
❑ 9 Trio of Superpowers 1.00 2.50

2011 Project Superpowers Chrome Puzzle

COMPLETE SET (9) 4.00 10.00
STATED ODDS TWO PER BOX

❑ 1 Puzzle - Top Right .75 2.00
❑ 2 Puzzle - Middle Right .75 2.00
❑ 3 Puzzle - Bottom Right .75 2.00
❑ 4 Puzzle - Top Center .75 2.00
❑ 5 Puzzle - Middle Center .75 2.00
❑ 6 Puzzle - Bottom Center .75 2.00
❑ 7 Puzzle - Top Left .75 2.00
❑ 8 Puzzle - Middle Left .75 2.00
❑ 9 Puzzle - Bottom Left .75 2.00

2011 Project Superpowers Fighting Yank's War Journal

COMPLETE SET (18) 6.00 15.00
STATED ODDS FIVE PER BOX

❑ 1 The Green Lama .75 2.00
❑ 2 The American Spirit .75 2.00
❑ 3 The Black Terror .75 2.00
❑ 4 The Death-Defying 'Devil .75 2.00
❑ 5 Dynamic Man and the Dynamic Family .75 2.00
❑ 6 The Mighty Samson .75 2.00
❑ 7 Masquerade .75 2.00
❑ 8 Pyroman .75 2.00
❑ 9 The Flame .75 2.00
❑ 10 Police Corp .75 2.00
❑ 11 The Arrow .75 2.00
❑ 12 The Crusaders .75 2.00
❑ 13 Scarab .75 2.00
❑ 14 The Owl .75 2.00
❑ 15 Mr. Face .75 2.00
❑ 16 Hydro .75 2.00
❑ 17 The Target .75 2.00
❑ 18 F-Troop .75 2.00

2011 Project Superpowers Sketches

STATED ODDS TWO PER BOX

❑ 1 Adam Archer
❑ 2 Adam Cleveland
❑ 3 Anthony Tan 3CI
❑ 4 Clint Hilinski
❑ 5 Colton Worley
❑ 6 Dan Borgonos
❑ 7 Emmanuel Casallos
❑ 8 Gordon Purcell
❑ 9 Jay Liesten
❑ 10 John Czop
❑ 11 John Watson
❑ 12 Johnny Dangerous
❑ 13 Jonathan Lau
❑ 14 Ken Haeser
❑ 15 Kevin West
❑ 16 Mark Pennington
❑ 17 Mel Jay San Juan
❑ 18 Mel Rubi
❑ 19 Rich Molinelli
❑ 20 Sara Richard 3CI
❑ 21 Trev Murphy
❑ 22 Veronica O'Connell

2011 Spartacus Blood and Sand

COMPLETE SET (26) 50.00 100.00
STATED PRINT RUN 250 SER. #'d SETS
1B AVAILABLE VIA REDEMPTION

❑ 1A The Red Serpent/ (Incorrect synopsis on back) 3.00 8.00
❑ 1B The Red Serpent 3.00 8.00
(Corrected synopsis on back)
❑ 2 The Red Serpent 3.00 8.00
❑ 3 Sacramentum Gladiatorum 3.00 8.00
❑ 4 Sacramentum Gladiatorum 3.00 8.00
❑ 5 Legends 3.00 8.00
❑ 6 Legends 3.00 8.00
❑ 7 The Thing In The Pit 3.00 8.00
❑ 8 The Thing In The Pit 3.00 8.00
❑ 9 Shadow Games 3.00 8.00
❑ 10 Shadow Games 3.00 8.00
❑ 11 Delicate Things 3.00 8.00
❑ 12 Delicate Things 3.00 8.00
❑ 13 Great and Unfortunate Things 3.00 8.00
❑ 14 Great and Unfortunate Things 3.00 8.00
❑ 15 Mark of the Brotherhood 3.00 8.00
❑ 16 Mark of the Brotherhood 3.00 8.00
❑ 17 Whore 3.00 8.00
❑ 18 Whore 3.00 8.00
❑ 19 Party Favors 3.00 8.00
❑ 20 Party Favors 3.00 8.00
❑ 21 Old Wounds 3.00 8.00
❑ 22 Old Wounds 3.00 8.00
❑ 23 Revelations 3.00 8.00
❑ 24 Revelations 3.00 8.00
❑ 25 Kill Them All 3.00 8.00
❑ 26 Kill Them All 3.00 8.00

2011 Spartacus Blood and Sand Autographs

OVERALL AUTO ODDS TWO PER PACK

❑ 1 Manu Bennett 10.00 25.00
❑ 2 Viva Bianca 20.00 40.00
❑ 3 Lesley-Ann Brandt 20.00 40.00
❑ 4 Jai Courtney 10.00 25.00
❑ 5 Erin Cummings 15.00 30.00
❑ 6 John Hannah 30.00 60.00
❑ 7 Katrina Law 15.00 30.00
❑ 8 Lucy Lawless 75.00 150.00
❑ 9 Nick Tarabay 10.00 25.00
❑ 10 Antonio Te Maioha 12.00 25.00
❑ 11 Andy Whitfield 300.00 450.00

2011 Spartacus Blood and Sand Gods of the Arena Autographs

OVERALL AUTO ODDS TWO PER PACK

❑ 1 Antonio Te Maioha 12.00 25.00
❑ 2 Lesley-Ann Brandt 20.00 40.00

2011 Spartacus Blood and Sand Savage

COMPLETE SET (9) 20.00 40.00
STATED ODDS ONE PER PACK
STATED PRINT RUN 350 SER. #'d SETS

❑ SA1 Spartacus 2.50 6.00
❑ SA2 Two-Face 2.50 6.00
❑ SA3 Spartacus 2.50 6.00
❑ SA4 Spartacus 2.50 6.00
❑ SA5 Arena 2.50 6.00
❑ SA6 Spartacus 2.50 6.00
❑ SA7 Spartacus 2.50 6.00
❑ SA8 Spartacus 2.50 6.00
❑ SA9 Chest Wound Charlie 2.50 6.00

2011 Spartacus Blood and Sand Seductive

COMPLETE SET (9) 25.00 50.00
STATED ODDS ONE PER PACK
STATED PRINT RUN 350 SER. #'d SETS

❑ SE1 Spartacus 3.00 8.00
Sura
❑ SE2 Lucretia 3.00 8.00
❑ SE3 Spartacus 3.00 8.00
❑ SE4 Ilithyia 3.00 8.00
❑ SE5 Lucretia 3.00 8.00
❑ SE6 Naevia 3.00 8.00
❑ SE7 Ilithyia 3.00 8.00
❑ SE8 Batiatus 3.00 8.00
Lucretia
❑ SE9 Mira 3.00 8.00

2011 Star Trek Movies Heroes and Villains

COMP.SET w/o SP (54) 25.00 60.00
COMPLETE SET (55) 40.00 80.00
STATED PRINT RUN 550 SER. #'d SETS

❑ 1 Commander Decker 1.25 3.00
in Star Trek: The Motion Picture
❑ 2 V'Ger 1.25 3.00
Lt. Ilia/in Star Trek: The Motion Picture
❑ 3 Dr. Carol Marcus 1.25 3.00
in Star Trek II: The Wrath of Khan
❑ 4 Khan Noonien Singh 1.25 3.00
in Star Trek II: The Wrath of Khan
❑ 5 Lt. Saavik 1.25 3.00
in Star Trek II: The Wrath of Khan
❑ 6 Captain Terrell 1.25 3.00
in Star Trek II: The Wrath of Khan
❑ 7 Dr. David Marcus 1.25 3.00
in Star Trek III: The Search for Spock
❑ 8 Kruge 1.25 3.00
in Star Trek III: The Search for Spock
❑ 9 Lt. Saavik 1.25 3.00
in Star Trek III: The Search for Spock
❑ 10 Torg 1.25 3.00
in Star Trek III: The Search for Spock
❑ 11 Sarek 1.25 3.00
in Star Trek III: The Search for Spock
❑ 12 Maltz 1.25 3.00
in Star Trek III: The Search for Spock
❑ 13 Dr. Gillian Taylor 1.25 3.00
in Star Trek IV: The Voyage Home
❑ 14 Klingon Ambassador 1.25 3.00
in Star Trek IV: The Voyage Home
❑ 15 Amanda 1.25 3.00
in Star Trek IV: The Voyage Home
❑ 16 Space Probe 1.25 3.00
in Star Trek IV: The Voyage Home
❑ 17 Spock 1.25 3.00
in Star Trek V: The Final Frontier
❑ 18 Sybok 1.25 3.00
in Star Trek V: The Final Frontier
❑ 19 Dr. McCoy 1.25 3.00
in Star Trek V: The Final Frontier
❑ 20 God 1.25 3.00
Alien/in Star Trek V: The Final Frontier
❑ 21 Commander Scott 1.25 3.00
in Star Trek V: The Final Frontier
❑ 22 Captain Klaa 1.25 3.00
in Star Trek V: The Final Frontier
❑ 23 Captain James T. Kirk 1.25 3.00
in Star Trek VI: The Undiscovered Country
❑ 24 Martia 1.25 3.00
in Star Trek VI: The Undiscovered Country
❑ 25 Lt. Commander Uhura 1.25 3.00
in Star Trek VI: The Undiscovered Country
❑ 26 Klingon Prison Commander 1.25 3.00
in Star Trek VI: The Undiscovered Country
❑ 27 Lt. Commander Sulu 1.25 3.00
in Star Trek VI: The Undiscovered Country
❑ 28 Azetbur 1.25 3.00
in Star Trek VI: The Undiscovered Country
❑ 29 Chancellor Gorkon 1.25 3.00
in Star Trek VI: The Undiscovered Country
❑ 30 General Chang 1.25 3.00
in Star Trek VI: The Undiscovered Country
❑ 31 Rand 1.25 3.00
in Star Trek VI: The Undiscovered Country
❑ 32 Admiral Cartwright 1.25 3.00
in Star Trek VI: The Undiscovered Country
❑ 33 Lt. Chekov 1.25 3.00
in Star Trek VI: The Undiscovered Country
❑ 34 Lt. Valeris 1.25 3.00
in Star Trek VI: The Undiscovered Country
❑ 35 Dr. Crusher 1.25 3.00
in Star Trek Generations
❑ 36 Dr. Tolian Soran 1.25 3.00
in Star Trek Generations
❑ 37 Picard 1.25 3.00
in Star Trek Generations
❑ 38 Lursa 1.25 3.00
in Star Trek Generations
❑ 39 La Forge 1.25 3.00
in Star Trek Generations
❑ 40 B'Etor 1.25 3.00
in Star Trek Generations
❑ 41 Lily Sloane 1.25 3.00
in Star Trek First Contact
❑ 42 Lt. Hawk 1.25 3.00
Borg/in Star Trek First Contact
❑ 43 Zephram Cochrane 1.25 3.00
in Star Trek First Contact
❑ 44 Borg Queen 1.25 3.00
in Star Trek First Contact
❑ 45 Anij 1.25 3.00
in Star Trek Insurrection
❑ 46 Ru'afo 1.25 3.00
in Star Trek Insurrection
❑ 47 Worf 1.25 3.00
in Star Trek Insurrection
❑ 48 Gallatin 1.25 3.00
in Star Trek Insurrection
❑ 49 Riker 1.25 3.00
in Star Trek Insurrection
❑ 50 Admiral Dougherty 1.25 3.00
in Star Trek Insurrection
❑ 51 Data 1.25 3.00
in Star Trek Nemesis
❑ 52 Shinzon 1.25 3.00
in Star Trek Nemesis
❑ 53 Troi 1.25 3.00
in Star Trek Nemesis
❑ 54 Viceroy 1.25 3.00
in Star Trek Nemesis
❑ 55 Capt. James T. Kirk 12.00 30.00
in Star Trek: The Motino Picture SP/(issued as Rittenhouse Reward)

2011 Star Trek Movies Heroes and Villains Autographs

STATED ODDS TWO PER PACK
L (LIMITED): 300-500 COPIES
VL (VERY LIMITED): 200-300 COPIES
EL (EXTREMELY LTD): UNDER 200 COPIES

❑ A107 Donna Murphy as Anij L 10.00 20.00
❑ A111 Patti Yasutake as Nurse Alyssa Ogawa VL 12.00 25.00
❑ A113 Anthony Zerbe as Admiral Dougherty VL 20.00 40.00
❑ A114 John Hostetter as Boolian Officer 5.00 10.00
❑ A115 Hilary Hayes as Ruby 5.00 10.00
❑ A116 Allan Miller as Alien 5.00 10.00
❑ A117 Robert Hooks as Admiral Morrow 5.00 10.00
❑ A118 Scott De Venney as Bob Briggs 5.00 10.00
❑ A119 Brent Spiner as B4 VL 75.00 125.00
❑ A120 William Shatner as Captain 200.00 300.00
James T. Kirk VL
❑ A121 Christian Slater as U.S.S. 30.00 60.00
Excelsior Officer L
❑ A122 Nichelle Nichols as Uhura EL 125.00 175.00
(issued as 4-box incentive)
❑ A123 Michael Owen as Lt. Branson 5.00 10.00
❑ A124 Joseph Ruskin as Son'a Officer EL 75.00 125.00
❑ A125 Jonathan Simpson as Young Sarek 5.00 10.00
❑ A126 Leonard Nimoy as Spock VL 175.00 250.00
❑ A127 David Orange as Sleepy Klingon L 7.50 15.00
❑ A128 Vijay Amritraj as Captain Randolph 5.00 10.00
❑ A129 Conroy Gedeon as Civilian Agent 5.00 10.00
❑ A130 John Putch as Journalist 5.00 10.00
❑ A131 D. Elliot Woods as Starfleet Officer 5.00 10.00
❑ A132 Gary Faga as Transporter Technician 5.00 10.00

2011 Star Trek Movies Heroes and Villains Bridge Crew Patches

COMPLETE SET (2) 50.00 100.00
STATED ODDS ONE PER CASE
STATED PRINT RUN 250 SER. #'d SETS

❑ PC10 Decker in Star Trek: The Motion Picture 25.00 50.00
❑ PC11 Ilia in Star Trek: The Motion Picture 25.00 50.00

2011 Star Trek Movies Heroes and Villains Die-Cut Gold Plaques

COMPLETE SET (14) 25.00 60.00
STATED ODDS ONE PER PACK
STATED PRINT RUN 425 SER. #'d SETS

❑ H1 Kirk 5.00 12.00
❑ H2 Spock 4.00 10.00
❑ H3 McCoy 3.00 8.00
❑ H4 Scotty 3.00 8.00
❑ H5 Uhura 3.00 8.00
❑ H6 Sulu 3.00 8.00
❑ H7 Chekov 3.00 8.00
❑ H8 Picard 3.00 8.00
❑ H9 Riker 3.00 8.00
❑ H10 Data 3.00 8.00
❑ H11 Troi 3.00 8.00
❑ H12 Worf 3.00 8.00
❑ H13 La Forge 3.00 8.00
❑ H14 Crusher 3.00 8.00

2011 Star Trek Movies Heroes and Villains Promos

COMPLETE SET (4)

❑ P1 Khan
Kirk/ (General Distribution)
❑ P2 Spock
Valeris/ (NSU Magazine)
❑ P3 Data/ (Binder Exclusive)
❑ P4 Data/ (Fall 2011 Philly Non-Sport Show)

2011 Star Trek Movies Heroes and Villains Tribute

COMPLETE SET (12) 15.00 40.00
STATED ODDS ONE PER PACK
STATED PRINT RUN 475 SER. #'d SETS

❑ T1 DeForest Kelley as Dr. McCoy 3.00 8.00
❑ T2 James Doohan as Commander Scott 3.00 8.00
❑ T3 Persis Khambatta as Lieutenant Ilia 3.00 8.00
❑ T4 Ricardo Montalban as Khan Soonien Singh 3.00 8.00
❑ T5 Bebe Besch as Dr. Carol Marcus 3.00 8.00
❑ T6 Merritt Butrick as Dr. David Marcus 3.00 8.00
❑ T7 Paul Winfield as Captain Terrell 3.00 8.00
❑ T8 Vulcan High Priestess as Dame 3.00 8.00
Judith Anderson
❑ T9 Mark Lenard as Sarek 3.00 8.00
❑ T10 Jane Wyatt as Amanda 3.00 8.00
❑ T11 Brock Peters as Admiral Cartwright 3.00 8.00
❑ T12 Robert Ellenstein as Federation President 3.00 8.00

2011 Stargate Universe Season Two
COMPLETE SET (20) 30.00 60.00
STATED PRINT RUN 400 SER. #'d SETS

❑ 1 Intervention 2.00 5.00
❑ 2 Aftermath 2.00 5.00
❑ 3 Awakening 2.00 5.00
❑ 4 Pathogen 2.00 5.00
❑ 5 Cloverdale 2.00 5.00
❑ 6 Trial and Error 2.00 5.00
❑ 7 The Greater Good 2.00 5.00
❑ 8 Malice 2.00 5.00
❑ 9 Visitation 2.00 5.00
❑ 10 Resurgence 2.00 5.00
❑ 11 Deliverance 2.00 5.00
❑ 12 Twin Destinies 2.00 5.00
❑ 13 Alliances 2.00 5.00
❑ 14 Hope 2.00 5.00
❑ 15 Seizure 2.00 5.00
❑ 16 The Hunt 2.00 5.00
❑ 17 Common Descent 2.00 5.00
❑ 18 Epilogue 2.00 5.00
❑ 19 Blockade 2.00 5.00
❑ 20 Gauntlet 2.00 5.00

2011 Stargate Universe Season Two Autographs
STATED ODDS TWO PER PACK
L (LIMITED): 300-500 COPIES
VL (VERY LIMITED): 200-300 COPIES
EL (EXTREMELY LIMITED): LESS THAN 200 COPIES

❑ 1 Alaina Huffman VL 25.00 50.00
❑ 2 Brian J. Smith VL 15.00 30.00
❑ 3 David Blue VL 15.00 40.00
❑ 4 Elyse Levesque VL 30.00 60.00
❑ 5 Glynis Davies L 6.00 15.00
❑ 6 Jamil Walker Smith VL 10.00 25.00
❑ 7 Julie McNiven L 10.00 25.00
❑ 8 Lou Diamond Phillips VL 25.00 50.00
❑ 9 Louis Ferreira VL 15.00 40.00
❑ 10 Mike Dopud L 6.00 15.00
❑ 11A Ming-Na (full bleed) VL 30.00 60.00
❑ 11B Ming-Na (bordered) VL 20.00 40.00
❑ 12A Richard Dean Anderson (SG1) EL 150.00 250.00
❑ 12B Richard Dean Anderson (SGU) EL 200.00 300.00
❑ 13 Ryan Kennedy L 4.00 10.00
❑ 14 Sarah Mutch L 6.00 15.00
❑ 15 Zak Santiago L 4.00 10.00
❑ 16 Patrick Gilmore 6.00 15.00

2011 Stargate Universe Season Two Destiny
COMPLETE SET (9) 15.00 30.00
STATED ODDS ONE PER PACK
STATED PRINT RUN 444 SER. #'d SETS

❑ D1 Destiny 2.50 6.00
Shuttle
❑ D2 Bridge 2.50 6.00
❑ D3 Gateroom 2.50 6.00
❑ D4 Corridor 2.50 6.00
❑ D5 Control Interface Panel 2.50 6.00
Overhead Display
❑ D6 Observation Deck 2.50 6.00
Messhall
❑ D7 Medical Scanner 2.50 6.00
Air Scrubber
❑ D8 Rush's blackboard 2.50 6.00
Apple Core
❑ D9 Interface Chair 2.50 6.00
Defense Turrets

2011 Stargate Universe Season Two Promos
❑ P1 Johansen 1.25 3.00
Wray/Armstrong
❑ P2 Greer 2.00 5.00
Telford/Young

2011 Stargate Universe Season Two Secrets
COMPLETE SET (9) 15.00 30.00
STATED ODDS ONE PER PACK
STATED PRINT RUN 444 SER. #'d SETS

❑ S1 Murder 2.50 6.00
❑ S2 Adultery 2.50 6.00
❑ S3 Infatuation 2.50 6.00
❑ S4 Deceit 2.50 6.00
❑ S5 Subterfuge 2.50 6.00
❑ S6 Subversion 2.50 6.00
❑ S7 Despair 2.50 6.00
❑ S8 Forsaken 2.50 6.00
❑ S9 Hopefulness 2.50 6.00

2011 Thor Movie
COMPLETE SET (81) 6.00 15.00

❑ 1 Thor Movie .20 .50
❑ 2 Asgard, a planet .20 .50
❑ 3 Fandral, whose swordsmanship .20 .50
❑ 4 Odin's eldest son Thor .20 .50
❑ 5 Thor's father, Odin .20 .50
❑ 6 Thor listens patiently .20 .50
❑ 7 All of Asgard attends .20 .50
❑ 8 The Warriors Three .20 .50
❑ 9 Hogun is the level headed voice .20 .50
❑ 10 Thor's mother, Frigga .20 .50
❑ 11 Thor's brother Loki .20 .50
❑ 12 The Casket of Ancient Winters .20 .50
❑ 13 Loki knows that Laufey .20 .50
❑ 14 Thor's lifelong friend Sif .20 .50
❑ 15 After the Frost Giants .20 .50
❑ 16 Laufey considers the Asgardian .20 .50
❑ 17 Appalled by his son's actions .20 .50
❑ 18 Odin decides that Thor's actions .20 .50
❑ 19 Odin scolds his son .20 .50
❑ 20 The Warriors Three watch .20 .50
❑ 21 Thor's reckless behavior .20 .50
❑ 22 Heimdall is the guardian .20 .50
❑ 23 Frigga questions her husband .20 .50
❑ 24 Odin enters his chambers .20 .50
❑ 25 The extravagance of Asgard .20 .50
❑ 26 Thor's coronation .20 .50
❑ 27 With Odin in the Odinsleep .20 .50
❑ 28 Volstagg is the largest .20 .50
❑ 29 The first meeting .20 .50
❑ 30 Jane, along with Dr. Erik Selvig .20 .50
❑ 31 Thor wakes up .20 .50
❑ 32 Even though Darcy believes .20 .50
❑ 33 Dr. Erik Selvig .20 .50
❑ 34 Odin sends not only Thor .20 .50
❑ 35 S.H.I.E.L.D. Agent Phil Coulson .20 .50
❑ 36 As word spreads .20 .50
❑ 37 Unable to lift the hammer .20 .50
❑ 38 Dr. Selvig is very mistrusting .20 .50
❑ 39 Thor went from the most powerful .20 .50
❑ 40 Jane Foster is an astrophysicist .20 .50
❑ 41 Thor thinks it's time to tell Jane .20 .50
❑ 42 Even as Jane's scientific mind .20 .50
❑ 43 Tracking down the location .20 .50
❑ 44 S.H.I.E.L.D. has erected a base .20 .50
❑ 45 Agent Coulson has been busy .20 .50
❑ 46 Thor must navigate a maze .20 .50
❑ 47 Agent Coulson watches intently .20 .50
❑ 48 Only those deemed worthy .20 .50
❑ 49 Finding the hammer .20 .50
❑ 50 Unable to lift Mjolnir .20 .50
❑ 51 Disheartened by his defeat .20 .50
❑ 52 Agent Coulson is convinced .20 .50
❑ 53 Now the temporary ruler .20 .50
❑ 54 Sif and the Warriors Three .20 .50
❑ 55 Thor's friends have no choice .20 .50
❑ 56 Loki looks all too comfortable .20 .50
❑ 57 Going against Loki's wishes .20 .50
❑ 58 The Destroyer is an animated suit .20 .50
❑ 59 Outside of town .20 .50
❑ 60 Even though Fandral .20 .50
❑ 61 Thor tries desperately .20 .50
❑ 62 Thor knows that the Destroyer .20 .50
❑ 63 Following the battle .20 .50
❑ 64 Jane looks on .20 .50
❑ 65 Frigga .20 .50
❑ 66 In order to continue his reign .20 .50
❑ 67 Frigga greets Thor warmly .20 .50
❑ 68 Brother faces brother .20 .50
❑ 69 Although Sif would rather trade .20 .50
❑ 70 Dr. Selvig, Jane and Darcy .20 .50
❑ 71 Thor .20 .50
❑ 72 Loki .20 .50
❑ 73 Odin .20 .50
❑ 74 Jane Foster .20 .50
❑ 75 Dr. Erik Selvig .20 .50
❑ 76 Darcy Lewis .20 .50
❑ 77 Volstagg .20 .50
❑ 78 Fandral .20 .50
❑ 79 Hogun .20 .50
❑ 80 Sif .20 .50
❑ 81 Frigga .20 .50

2011 Thor Movie Printing Plates Black
STATED PRINT RUN 1 SER. #'d SETS
UNPRICED DUE TO SCARCITY

2011 Thor Movie Printing Plates Cyan
STATED PRINT RUN 1 SER. #'d SET
UNPRICED DUE TO SCARCITY

2011 Thor Movie Printing Plates Magenta
STATED PRINT RUN 1 SER. #'d SET
UNPRICED DUE TO SCARCITY

2011 Thor Movie Printing Plates Yellow
STATED PRINT RUN 1 SER. #'d SET
UNPRICED DUE TO SCARCITY

2011 Thor Movie Autographs
STATED ODDS 1:288 H, 1:2,500 R

❑ CF Colm Feore 100.00 200.00
(issued in 2012 Avengers Assemble)
❑ CG Clark Gregg 40.00 80.00
❑ CH Chris Hemsworth 200.00 400.00
❑ IE Idris Elba 175.00 250.00
(issued in 2012 Avengers Assemble)
❑ JA Jaimie Alexander 250.00 400.00
❑ JD Joshua Dallas 60.00 120.00
❑ KB Kenneth Branagh 40.00 80.00
❑ KD Kat Dennings 200.00 300.00
(issued in 2012 Avengers Assemble)
❑ TH Tom Hiddleston 250.00 400.00

2011 Thor Movie Classic Covers
COMPLETE SET (12) 3.00 8.00
RANDOM INSERT IN PACKS

❑ T1 Journey Into Mystery #83 .60 1.50
❑ T2 Journey Into Mystery #85 .60 1.50
❑ T3 Journey Into Mystery #119 .60 1.50
❑ T4 Journey Into Mystery King-Size Annual #1 .60 1.50
❑ T5 Thor #126 .60 1.50
❑ T6 Thor #337 .60 1.50
❑ T7 Thor #362 .60 1.50
❑ T8 Thor #366 .60 1.50
❑ T9 Thor #380 .60 1.50
❑ T10 Thor Volume 2 #85 .60 1.50
❑ T11 Thor Volume 3 #3 .60 1.50
❑ T12 Thor #600 .60 1.50

2011 Thor Movie Classic Covers Printing Plates Black
STATED PRINT RUN 1 SER. #'d SET
UNPRICED DUE TO SCARCITY

2011 Thor Movie Classic Covers Printing Plates Cyan
STATED PRINT RUN 1 SER. #'d SET
UNPRICED DUE TO SCARCITY

2011 Thor Movie Classic Covers Printing Plates Magenta
STATED PRINT RUN 1 SER. #'d SET
UNPRICED DUE TO SCARCITY

2011 Thor Movie Classic Covers Printing Plates Yellow
STATED PRINT RUN 1 SER. #'d SET
UNPRICED DUE TO SCARCITY

2011 Thor Movie Concept Art
COMPLETE SET (13) 3.00 8.00
RANDOM INSERT IN PACKS

❑ C1 Thor .50 1.25
❑ C2 Thor .50 1.25
❑ C3 Thor .50 1.25
❑ C4 Thor .50 1.25
❑ C5 Thor .50 1.25
❑ C6 Thor .50 1.25
❑ C7 Thor .50 1.25
❑ C8 Thor .50 1.25
❑ C9 Thor .50 1.25
❑ C10 Thor .50 1.25
❑ C11 Thor .50 1.25
❑ C12 Thor .50 1.25
❑ C13 Thor .50 1.25

2011 Thor Movie Concept Art Printing Plates Black
STATED PRINT RUN 1 SER. #'d SET
UNPRICED DUE TO SCARCITY

2011 Thor Movie Concept Art Printing Plates Cyan
STATED PRINT RUN 1 SER. #'d SET
UNPRICED DUE TO SCARCITY

2011 Thor Movie Concept Art Printing Plates Magenta
STATED PRINT RUN 1 SER. #'d SET
UNPRICED DUE TO SCARCITY

2011 Thor Movie Concept Art Printing Plates Yellow
STATED PRINT RUN 1 SER. #'d SET
UNPRICED DUE TO SCARCITY

2011 Thor Movie Film Cels
COMPLETE SET (41)
STATED ODDS 1:16

❑ M1 Asgard 3.00 8.00
❑ M2 Thor 3.00 8.00
❑ M3 Odin 3.00 8.00
❑ M4 Thor 3.00 8.00
❑ M5 Loki 3.00 8.00
❑ M6 Loki 3.00 8.00
❑ M7 Hogun 3.00 8.00
❑ M8 Sif 3.00 8.00
❑ M9 Loki 3.00 8.00
Thor
❑ M10 Laufrey 3.00 8.00
❑ M11 Sif 3.00 8.00
❑ M12 Odin 3.00 8.00
❑ M13 Loki 3.00 8.00
❑ M14 Volstagg 3.00 8.00
Sif/Fandral/Hogun
❑ M15 Odin 3.00 8.00
❑ M16 Bedroom 3.00 8.00
❑ M17 Volstagg 3.00 8.00
❑ M18 Thor 3.00 8.00
❑ M19 Thor 3.00 8.00
❑ M20 Darcy 3.00 8.00
❑ M21 Crater 3.00 8.00
❑ M22 Phil Coulson 3.00 8.00
❑ M23 Thor 3.00 8.00
❑ M24 Professor Andrews 3.00 8.00
❑ M25 Jane Foster 3.00 8.00
❑ M26 Jane Foster 3.00 8.00
❑ M27 Jane Foster 3.00 8.00
Thor
❑ M28 Jane Foster 3.00 8.00
❑ M29 Phil Coulson 3.00 8.00
❑ M30 Thor's Hammer 3.00 8.00
❑ M31 Thor 3.00 8.00
❑ M32 Loki 3.00 8.00
❑ M33 Sif 3.00 8.00
Loki/Warriors
❑ M34 Volstagg 3.00 8.00
❑ M35 Funnel Cloud 3.00 8.00
❑ M36 Fandral 3.00 8.00
❑ M37 Destroyer 3.00 8.00
❑ M38 Sif 3.00 8.00
❑ M39 Frigga 3.00 8.00
❑ M40 Loki 3.00 8.00
❑ M41 Loki 3.00 8.00

2011 Thor Movie Memorabilia
STATED ODDS 1:12 H, 1:48 R

❑ F1 Thor 10.00 25.00
❑ F2 Jane Foster 20.00 50.00
❑ F3 Odin 6.00 15.00
❑ F4 Loki 6.00 15.00
❑ F5 Heimdall 6.00 15.00
❑ F6 Sif 6.00 15.00
❑ F7 Hogun 6.00 15.00
❑ F8 Fandral 6.00 15.00
❑ F9 Figga 6.00 15.00
❑ F10 Volstagg 6.00 15.00
❑ F11 Odin 6.00 15.00
❑ F12 Jane Foster 15.00 40.00
❑ F13 Thor 10.00 25.00

2011 Thor Movie Sketches
STATED ODDS 1:48

❑ 1 Aaron Sowd
❑ 2 Andy MacDonald
❑ 3 Arvin John ACE Evangelista
❑ 4 Ben Young
❑ 5 Billy Martin
❑ 6 Brandon Singleton
❑ 7 Bryan Turner
❑ 8 Cal Slayton
❑ 9 Cat Staggs
❑ 10 Dan Gorman
❑ 11 Dan Panosian
❑ 12 Dave Ryan
❑ 13 David Mack
❑ 14 Frankie B. Washington
❑ 15 George Deep
❑ 16 George GEO Davis
❑ 17 Gilbert Monsanto
❑ 18 Graham Nolan
❑ 19 Hanie Mohd
❑ 20 Irma Ahmed
❑ 21 Jake Minor
❑ 22 Jason Adams
❑ 23 Jason Keith Phillips
❑ 24 Jerry The Franchize Gaylord
❑ 25 Jim Cheung
❑ 26 Joe Pekar
❑ 27 Joel Carroll
❑ 28 Johnboy Meyers
❑ 29 Jose Jaro
❑ 30 Joyce Chin
❑ 31 Kale Bradley
❑ 32 Ken Steacy
❑ 33 Kevin Genfilcore
❑ 34 Lawrence Reynolds
❑ 35 Lord Mesa
❑ 36 Mark de Castro
❑ 37 Mark Henry
❑ 38 Mark McKenna
❑ 39 Matt Grigsby
❑ 40 Michael Duran
❑ 41 Mike Miller
❑ 42 Remy Eisu Mokhtar
❑ 43 Renato Butch Mapa
❑ 44 Richard Molinelli
❑ 45 Richard Pace
❑ 46 Ryan Kincaid
❑ 47 Sarah Wilkinson
❑ 48 Sebastian Mazuera
❑ 49 Travis Walton
❑ 50 Wendy Chew
❑ 51 Wilson Ramos, Jr.

2011 The Tudors Seasons One Two and Three
COMPLETE SET (72) 6.00 15.00

❑ 1 King Henry VIII (Season One) .15 .40
❑ 2 King Henry VIII (Season Two) .15 .40
❑ 3 King Henry VIII (Season Three) .15 .40
❑ 4 Queen Katherine of Aragon .15 .40
❑ 5 Anne Boleyn .15 .40
❑ 6 Cardinal Wolsey .15 .40
❑ 7 Sir Thomas More .15 .40
❑ 8 Charles Brandon .15 .40
❑ 9 Thomas Howard .15 .40
❑ 10 Thomas Boleyn .15 .40
❑ 11 Thomas Cromwell .15 .40
❑ 12 Thomas Cranmer .15 .40
❑ 13 Pope Paul III .15 .40
❑ 14 Thomas Wyatt .15 .40
❑ 15 Jane Seymour .15 .40
❑ 16 Sir Francis Bryan .15 .40
❑ 17 Anne of Cleves .15 .40
❑ 18 The King of England .15 .40
❑ 19 Field of Cloth and Gold .15 .40
❑ 20 Masque With Anne .15 .40
❑ 21 Goodbye Margaret .15 .40
❑ 22 Official Mistress .15 .40
❑ 23 Arm Wrestling With Brandon .15 .40
❑ 24 Anne's Growing Influence .15 .40
❑ 25 The Sweat .15 .40
❑ 26 Reunion With Anne .15 .40
❑ 27 Henry Accuses Wolsey .15 .40
❑ 28 Queen Katherine Implores Henry .15 .40
❑ 29 Wolsey's Downfall .15 .40
❑ 30 Wolsey's End .15 .40
❑ 31 Henry and Anne's Frustration .15 .40
❑ 32 Reformation Begins .15 .40
❑ 33 Queen's Departure .15 .40
❑ 34 To France .15 .40
❑ 35 Anne's Coronation .15 .40
❑ 36 Elizabeth .15 .40
❑ 37 Elizabeth Baptized .15 .40
❑ 38 More Prays .15 .40
❑ 39 The Pope .15 .40
❑ 40 Anne's Nightmare .15 .40
❑ 41 Henry Injured .15 .40
❑ 42 Henry and Jane .15 .40
❑ 43 Anne to the Tower .15 .40
❑ 44 The Swan .15 .40
❑ 45 Henry and Jane Marry .15 .40
❑ 46 Pilgrimage of Grace .15 .40
❑ 47 Brandon Makes Promises .15 .40
❑ 48 With Child .15 .40
❑ 49 Heads on Sticks .15 .40
❑ 50 End of Revolt .15 .40
❑ 51 The Death of Jane .15 .40
❑ 52 Henry's Seclusion .15 .40
❑ 53 Choosing a New Wife .15 .40
❑ 54 Henry's Bad Leg .15 .40
❑ 55 The Beacon .15 .40
❑ 56 Henry Marries Anne of Cleves .15 .40
❑ 57 Anne and Mary .15 .40
❑ 58 Cromwell's End .15 .40
❑ 59 You Think You Know a Story .15 .40
❑ 60 Some People Think .15 .40
❑ 61 What Would a Silly Girl .15 .40
❑ 62 He Will See You .15 .40
❑ 63 I Ask You to Bear Witness .15 .40
❑ 64 Lastly I Make This Vow .15 .40
❑ 65 You and I are Both Young .15 .40
❑ 66 I Have a Little Neck .15 .40
❑ 67 My Own Darling .15 .40
❑ 68 If I Cannot Please the King .15 .40
❑ 69 Because In His Heart .15 .40
❑ 70 Majesty I Know What It Is .15 .40
❑ 71 Now My Love .15 .40
❑ 72 Checklist .15 .40

2011 The Tudors Seasons One Two and Three Autographs
OVERALL AUTO ODDS ONE PER BOX

❑ TAAV Alan Van Sprang 10.00 25.00
❑ TAGA Gabrielle Anwar 35.00 70.00
❑ TAHC Henry Czerny 10.00 25.00
❑ TAJF James Frain 10.00 25.00
❑ TAJK Joanne King 12.00 30.00
❑ TAJM Jonathan Rhys Meyers 40.00 80.00
❑ TAJT Jamie Thomas King 10.00 25.00
❑ TAMK Maria Doyle Kennedy 15.00 40.00
❑ TAND Natalie Dormer 30.00 60.00
❑ TASB Sarah Bolger 25.00 50.00
❑ TATM Tamzin Merchant 25.00 50.00

2011 The Tudors Seasons One Two and Three Costumes
OVERALL COSTUME/PROP ODDS ONE PER BOX
STATED PRINT RUN 200 SER. #'d SETS

❑ ABBD Anne Boleyn 15.00 40.00
❑ ABGD Anne Boleyn 15.00 40.00
❑ ABWG Anne Boleyn 15.00 40.00
❑ ACBD Anne of Cleves 12.00 30.00
❑ ACGD Anne of Cleves 12.00 30.00
❑ JSGD Jane Seymour 15.00 40.00
❑ JSPD Jane Seymour 15.00 40.00
❑ KHBC King Henry VIII 15.00 40.00
❑ KHCS King Henry VIII 15.00 40.00
❑ KHGL King Henry VIII 15.00 40.00
❑ KHNC King Henry VIII 15.00 40.00
❑ KHST King Henry VIII 15.00 40.00
❑ MTBD Mary Tudor 12.00 30.00
❑ HJD Jane Seymour 15.00 40.00
King Henry VIII

2011 The Tudors Seasons One Two and Three Heads Will Roll
COMPLETE SET (9) 15.00 30.00
OVERALL INSERT ODDS 9 PER BOX

❑ HWR1 Edward Stafford 2.50 6.00
❑ HWR2 John Fisher 2.50 6.00
❑ HWR3 Sir Thomas More 2.50 6.00
❑ HWR4 Henry Norris 2.50 6.00
❑ HWR5 William Brereton 2.50 6.00
❑ HWR6 Mark Smeaton 2.50 6.00
❑ HWR7 George Boleyn 2.50 6.00
❑ HWR8 Queen Anne Boleyn 2.50 6.00
❑ HWR9 Thomas Cromwell 2.50 6.00

2011 The Tudors Seasons One Two and Three Henry's Legacy
COMPLETE SET (3) 5.00 12.00
OVERALL INSERT ODDS 9 PER BOX

❑ HL1 Prince Edward 2.50 6.00
❑ HL2 Princess Mary 2.50 6.00
❑ HL3 Princess Elizabeth 2.50 6.00

2011 The Tudors Seasons One Two and Three Location
COMPLETE SET (9) 10.00 20.00
OVERALL INSERT ODDS 9 PER BOX

❑ L1 White Hall 2.00 5.00
❑ L2 Hampton Court Palace 2.00 5.00
❑ L3 Hever House 2.00 5.00
❑ L4 Hatfield House 2.00 5.00
❑ L5 Tower of London 2.00 5.00
❑ L6 Westminster Abbey 2.00 5.00
❑ L7 Wolf Hall 2.00 5.00
❑ L8 Nonsuch Palace 2.00 5.00
❑ L9 Vatican City 2.00 5.00

2011 The Tudors Seasons One Two and Three Props
OVERALL COSTUME/PROP ODDS ONE PER BOX
STATED PRINT RUN 200 SER. #'d SETS

❑ TQ Quills 20.00 40.00
❑ TAT Archery Targets 15.00 30.00
❑ TKM The King's Mirror/100 20.00 40.00
❑ TKS The King's Scribbles 15.00 30.00
❑ TMP Lady Ursula's Painting 20.00 40.00
❑ TWP Five Wounds Poster 20.00 40.00

2011 The Tudors Seasons One Two and Three Sketches
RANDOM INSERT IN BOXES

❑ 1 Charles Hall
❑ 2 David Desbois
❑ 3 Denae Frazier
❑ 4 Jason Potratz
❑ 5 Scott Rorie
❑ 6 Trev Murphy

2011 The Tudors Seasons One Two and Three The Leisurely King
COMPLETE SET (6) 5.00 12.00
OVERALL INSERT ODDS 9 PER BOX

❑ LK1 Tennis 2.00 5.00
❑ LK2 Joust 2.00 5.00
❑ LK3 Masques 2.00 5.00
❑ LK4 Archery 2.00 5.00
❑ LK5 Dance 2.00 5.00
❑ LK6 Wrestling 2.00 5.00

2011 The Vampire Diaries Season One
COMPLETE SET (63) 5.00 12.00

❑ 1 The Vampire Diaries .15 .40
❑ 2 Checklist 1 .15 .40
❑ 3 Checklist 2 .15 .40
❑ 4 Checklist 3 .15 .40
❑ 5 Introductions .15 .40
❑ 6 Meet at Mystic Grill .15 .40
❑ 7 Elena Meets Damon .15 .40
❑ 8 Doomed to Repeat the Past .15 .40
❑ 9 The Start of Something Epic .15 .40
❑ 10 Tormenting Vicki .15 .40
❑ 11 Tough Choice .15 .40
❑ 12 Single Life .15 .40
❑ 13 Jealousy .15 .40
❑ 14 Girl Talk .15 .40
❑ 15 Protection .15 .40
❑ 16 Pep Rally .15 .40
❑ 17 Varsity .15 .40
❑ 18 Protection from the Sun .15 .40
❑ 19 Founder's Party .15 .40
❑ 20 A Surprise Escort .15 .40
❑ 21 First Dance .15 .40
❑ 22 The Plan .15 .40
❑ 23 Night Terrors .15 .40
❑ 24 No Secrets .15 .40
❑ 25 Checkin In .15 .40
❑ 26 Whoops .15 .40
❑ 27 In the Way .15 .40
❑ 28 Just a Taste .15 .40
❑ 29 Casualty .15 .40
❑ 30 Into the Fire .15 .40
❑ 31 Brotherly Bonding .15 .40
❑ 32 A New Discovery .15 .40
❑ 33 Hot for Teacher .15 .40
❑ 34 Seance .15 .40
❑ 35 Protecting the Town .15 .40
❑ 36 Not so Fast .15 .40
❑ 37 Rescued .15 .40
❑ 38 We'll Find Him .15 .40
❑ 39 Wanna Dance .15 .40
❑ 40 The Grimoire .15 .40
❑ 41 Awkward .15 .40
❑ 42 New Relationship .15 .40
❑ 43 Unsealing the Tomb .15 .40
❑ 44 Big Reversal .15 .40
❑ 45 Auction .15 .40
❑ 46 Confrontation .15 .40
❑ 47 Double Date .15 .40
❑ 48 Pointed Talk .15 .40
❑ 49 Assurance .15 .40
❑ 50 Escape .15 .40
❑ 51 Craving .15 .40
❑ 52 Nerves .15 .40
❑ 53 Tension .15 .40
❑ 54 Control .15 .40
❑ 55 There's More .15 .40
❑ 56 Unlikely Allies .15 .40
❑ 57 Exchange .15 .40
❑ 58 Friendly Support .15 .40
❑ 59 Miss Mystic Falls .15 .40
❑ 60 Trying to Make Amends .15 .40
❑ 61 Battle of Willow Creek .15 .40
❑ 62 Miss Mystic Falls Court .15 .40
❑ 63 Just in Time .15 .40

2011 The Vampire Diaries Season One Autographs
OVERALL AUTO/MEM ODDS ONE PER BOX

❑ A1 Nina Dobrev 200.00 400.00
❑ A2 Paul Wesley 75.00 150.00
❑ A3 Ian Somerhalder 100.00 200.00
❑ A4 Steven R. McQueen 40.00 80.00
❑ A5 Katerina Graham 30.00 60.00
❑ A6 Candice Accola 40.00 80.00
❑ A7 Zach Roerig 20.00 40.00
❑ A8 Michael Trevino 35.00 70.00
❑ A9 Sara Canning 25.00 50.00
❑ A10 Matt Davis 25.00 50.00
❑ A11 Julie Plec 20.00 40.00
❑ A12 Kevin Williamson 10.00 25.00
❑ A13 David Anders 10.00 25.00
❑ A14 Arielle Kebbel 20.00 40.00
❑ A15 Kelly Hu 30.00 60.00

❑ A16 Kayla Ewell 10.00 25.00
❑ A17 Susan Walters 10.00 25.00
❑ A18 Chris William Martin 10.00 25.00
❑ A19 Malese Jow 25.00 50.00
❑ A20 Bianca Lawson 10.00 25.00

2011 The Vampire Diaries Season One Die-Cuts

COMPLETE SET (9) 15.00 40.00
OVERALL CHASE ODDS SIX PER BOX
❑ D1 The Vampire Diaries 3.00 8.00
❑ D2 Elena Gilbert 3.00 8.00
❑ D3 Caroline Forbes 3.00 8.00
❑ D4 Bonnie Bennett 3.00 8.00
❑ D5 Jeremy Gilbert 3.00 8.00
❑ D6 Jenna Sommers 3.00 8.00
❑ D7 Damon Salvatore 3.00 8.00
❑ D8 Stefan Salvatore 3.00 8.00
❑ D9 Alaric Saltzman 3.00 8.00

2011 The Vampire Diaries Season One Foil

COMPLETE SET (9) 10.00 25.00
OVERALL CHASE ODDS SIX PER BOX
❑ F1 Stefan Salvatore 2.00 5.00
❑ F2 Damon Salvatore 2.00 5.00
❑ F3 Katherine Pierce 2.00 5.00
❑ F4 Friendly Competition 2.00 5.00
❑ F5 Bewitched 2.00 5.00
❑ F6 Enslaved 2.00 5.00
❑ F7 Cruel 2.00 5.00
❑ F8 Soldier in Love 2.00 5.00
❑ F9 The Beginning of Forever 2.00 5.00

2011 The Vampire Diaries Season One Promos

❑ P1 Elena Gilbert/ (NSU Magazine) .75 2.00
❑ P2 Stefan Salvatore/ (general distribution) 2.00 5.00
❑ P3 Damon Salvatore/ (SDCC 2011) 3.00 8.00
❑ P4 Damon .75 2.00
Elena/Stefan/ (Philly Non-Sport)

2011 The Vampire Diaries Season One Wardrobe Memorabilia

OVERALL AUTO/MEM ODDS ONE PER BOX
❑ M1 Stefan Salvatore 12.00 30.00
❑ M2 Stefan Salvatore 12.00 30.00
❑ M3 Elena Gilbert 15.00 40.00
❑ M4 Elena Gilbert 100.00 200.00
❑ M5 Elena Gilbert 100.00 200.00
❑ M6 Bonnie Bennet 12.00 30.00
❑ M7 Bonnie Bennet 20.00 50.00
❑ M8 Jeremy Gilbert 10.00 25.00
❑ M9 Caroline Forbes 15.00 40.00
❑ M10 Caroline Forbes 15.00 40.00
❑ M11 Caroline Forbes 15.00 40.00
❑ M12 Damon Salvatore 15.00 40.00
❑ M13 Damon Salvatore 15.00 40.00
❑ M14 Damon Salvatore 20.00 50.00
❑ M15 Matt Donovan 10.00 25.00
❑ M16 John Gilbert 10.00 25.00
❑ M17 Vicki Donovan 15.00 40.00
❑ M18 Alaric Saltzman 10.00 25.00
❑ M19 Tyler Lockwood 10.00 25.00
❑ M20 Katherine Pierce 100.00 200.00
❑ M21 Elena Gilbert 20.00 50.00
(binder exclusive)

2011 Vampirella

COMPLETE SET (72) 6.00 15.00
❑ 1 Jose Pepe Gonzalez
❑ 2 Jim Silke
❑ 3 Matt Clark
❑ 4 Tom Fleming
❑ 5 Mark Texeira
❑ 6 Joe Quesada
❑ 7 Matt Busch
❑ 8 Joe Jusko
❑ 9 John Czop
❑ 10 Joe Chiodo
❑ 11 Jae Lee
❑ 12 Dan Brereton
❑ 13 Adam Hughes
❑ 14 Joe Linsner
❑ 15 Amanda Conner
Jimmy Palmiotti
❑ 16 Brian Rood
❑ 17 Arthur Adams
❑ 18 Mike Mayhew
❑ 19 Stephen Segovia
❑ 20 Rafael Kayanan
❑ 21 Eric Ebas Basaldua
❑ 22 Kim McCarthy
❑ 23 Mike Mayhew
❑ 24 Jose Gonzalez
❑ 25 JH Williams
❑ 26 Stephen Segovia
❑ 27 Simone Gabrielli
❑ 28 Ray Lago
❑ 29 Amanda Conner
❑ 30 Dan Parsons
❑ 31 Tim Sale
❑ 32 Joe Quesada
❑ 33 Ryan Stegman
❑ 34 Mike Mayhew
❑ 35 Mark Texeira
❑ 36 Joyce Chin
❑ 37 Al Rio
❑ 38 J. Scott Campbell
❑ 39 Jason Pearson
❑ 40 Mike Mayhew
❑ 41 Gordon Purcell
❑ 42 Bill Sienkiewicz
❑ 43 Alan Davis
❑ 44 Mike Mayhew
❑ 45 Joe Quesada
❑ 46 Jenny Frison
❑ 47 Dan Brereton
❑ 48 Lan Medina
❑ 49 Joe Chiodo
❑ 50 Gary Frank
❑ 51 Dan Day
❑ 52 Amanda Conner
❑ 53 David Mack
❑ 54 Franchesco
❑ 55 Mike Mayhew
❑ 56 Fiona Staples
❑ 57 Arthur Suydam
❑ 58 Rudy Nebres
❑ 59 Ray Lago
❑ 60 Brian Stelfreeze
❑ 61 Mike Mayhew
❑ 62 Dawn Brown
❑ 63 David Mack
❑ 64 Bruce Timm
❑ 65 J. Scott Campbell
❑ 66 Jason Alexander
❑ 67 Arthur Suydam
❑ 68 Jay Anacletto
❑ 69 Mike Choi
❑ 70 Joe Quesada
❑ 71 J. Scott Campbell
❑ 72 Checklist

2011 Vampirella Autographs

❑ VAAO Arban Ornelas 8.00 20.00
❑ VAGH Greg Hildebrandt 8.00 20.00
❑ VAJJ Joe Jusko 10.00 25.00
❑ VALC Leslie Culton 10.00 25.00
❑ VAMD Maria Di Angelis 8.00 20.00
❑ VASK Sascha Knopf 10.00 25.00

2011 Vampirella Best of Joe Jusko

COMPLETE SET (3) 6.00 15.00
STATED ODDS ONE PER BOX
❑ VJ1 One of the true masters 3.00 8.00
❑ VJ2 Joe Jusko has been working 3.00 8.00
❑ VJ3 When Joe Jusko and James Robinson 3.00 8.00

2011 Vampirella Lenticular

COMPLETE SET (15) 15.00 30.00
STATED ODDS FOUR PER BOX
❑ VL1 Joe Jusko's latest image 1.50 4.00
❑ VL2 In the clutches 1.50 4.00
❑ VL3 Vampirella welcomes you 1.50 4.00
❑ VL4 Another one of Amanda Conner 1.50 4.00
❑ VL5 Captive beauty 1.50 4.00
❑ VL6 Not even the undead can escape 1.50 4.00
❑ VL7 Cornered by all sorts 1.50 4.00
❑ VL8 Vampirella's baptism by fire 1.50 4.00
❑ VL9 Vampirella is the queen of the jungle 1.50 4.00
❑ VL10 Vampirella visits Mars 1.50 4.00
❑ VL11 David Finch 1.50 4.00
❑ VL12 Vampirella and her lavish weapons 1.50 4.00
❑ VL13 Getting ready to attack 1.50 4.00
❑ VL14 Joe Jusko's iconic cover 1.50 4.00
❑ VL15 Vampirella and her favorite pets 1.50 4.00

2011 Vampirella Puzzle

COMPLETE SET (9) 7.50 15.00
STATED ODDS FOUR PER BOX
❑ VP1 Vampirella's costume was designed 1.25 3.00
❑ VP2 Actress Barbara Leigh 1.25 3.00
❑ VP3 Legendary production company 1.25 3.00
❑ VP4 Frank Frazetta wasn't the original choice 1.25 3.00
❑ VP5 Before she got the name Vampirella 1.25 3.00
❑ VP6 The primary colors for Vampirella 1.25 3.00
❑ VP7 Vampirella had two 1.25 3.00
❑ VP8 Vampirella began a brief stint 1.25 3.00
❑ VP9 Vampirella's arch nemesis 1.25 3.00

2011 Vampirella Sketches

STATED ODDS 1-2 PER BOX
❑ 1 Adam Cleveland
❑ 2 Adam Schickling
❑ 3 Alex Buechel
❑ 4 Alex Riegel
❑ 5 Amber Shelton
❑ 6 Anthony Tan
❑ 7 Arie Monroe
❑ 8 Ashleigh Popplewell
❑ 9 Aston R Cover
❑ 10 Austin Janowsky
❑ 11 Axebone
❑ 12 Bennett Pisek
❑ 13 Bianca Thompson
❑ 14 Bill Maus
❑ 15 Bill Pulkovski
❑ 16 Bob Stevlic
❑ 17 Brian Kong
❑ 18 Bruce Gerlach
❑ 19 Buddy Prince
❑ 20 Caanan White
❑ 21 Carolyn Edwards
❑ 22 Charles Carvalho
❑ 23 Charles Hall
❑ 24 Chip Skelton
❑ 25 Chris Caniano
❑ 26 Chris Hoffman
❑ 27 Christopher Foulkes
❑ 28 Craig Yeung
❑ 29 Dan Bergren
❑ 30 Dan Borgonos
❑ 31 Daniel P. Gorman
❑ 32 Danielle Gransaull Soloud
❑ 33 Darren Auck
❑ 34 Darren Chandler
❑ 35 Dave Beaty
❑ 36 David Day
❑ 37 David Harrigan
❑ 38 Denae Frazier
❑ 39 Denise Parrish
❑ 40 Dennis M. Crisostomo
❑ 41 Diana Greenhalgh
❑ 42 Edward Chemiga
❑ 43 Elaine Perna
❑ 44 Elliot Fernandez
❑ 45 Eman Casallos
❑ 46 Erik Maell
❑ 47 Gabe Farber
❑ 48 Gary Kezele
❑ 49 George Deep
❑ 50 Gordon Purcell
❑ 51 Hanie Mohd
❑ 52 Heather Cromwell
❑ 53 J.C. Fabul
❑ 54 J.D. Seeber
❑ 55 Jack Redd
❑ 56 Jae Lee
❑ 57 Jason Hughes
❑ 58 Jason Keith Phillips
❑ 59 Jason Potratz
Jack Hai
❑ 60 Tom Nguyen
❑ 61 Jerome DABOS
❑ 62 Jez Rojales
❑ 63 Joe Jusko
❑ 64 John Czop
❑ 65 John Haun
❑ 66 Jon Hughes
❑ 67 Joseph Michael Linsner
❑ 68 Joseph O'Brien (Joey Dangerous)
❑ 69 Juan A. Fontanez Jr.
❑ 70 Katie Cook
❑ 71 Kevin Graham
❑ 72 Kevin Meinert
❑ 73 Kimberly Dunaway
❑ 74 Kimiko Tanaka
❑ 75 Lak Lim
❑ 76 Larry L. Schlekewy, Jr.
❑ 77 Louis Small Jr.
❑ 78 Lynne Anderson
❑ 79 M. Jason Reed
❑ 80 Mark McKenna
❑ 81 Mark Slater
❑ 82 Max Reynolds (MAX!)
❑ 83 Melike Sevim Acar
❑ 84 Michael Duron
❑ 85 Mike Lilly
❑ 86 MJ San Juan
❑ 87 Nick Neocleous
❑ 88 Pablo Diaz
❑ 89 Rainier Lagunsad
❑ 90 Renato Butch Mapa Jr.
❑ 91 Rhiannon Owens
❑ 92 Rich Molinelli
❑ 93 Richard Pace
❑ 94 Robert Hack
❑ 95 Rusty Gilligan
❑ 96 Ryan M Kincaid
❑ 97 Sam Agro
❑ 98 Sanna Umemoto
❑ 99 Sara Richard
❑ 100 Sarah Silva
❑ 101 Scott Barnett
❑ 102 Scott Blair
❑ 103 Scott Rorie
❑ 104 Scott Zambelli
❑ 105 Sean Pence
❑ 106 Shane McCormack
❑ 107 Steven Miller
❑ 108 Ted Dastick, Jr.
❑ 109 Terry Beatty
❑ 110 Tim Levandoski
❑ 111 Tim Shay
❑ 112 Tony Miello
❑ 113 Tony Perna
❑ 114 Trev Murphy
❑ 115 Vanessa Banky Farano
❑ 116 Veronica O'Connell
❑ 117 Warren Martineck
❑ 118 William Neff
❑ 119 Wu Wei

2011 Wacky Packages Series 8

COMPLETE SET (55) 5.00 12.00
❑ 1 Frite Loops .15 .40
❑ 2 Hawaiian Pants .15 .40
❑ 3 Mr. Picasso Head .15 .40
❑ 4 Dr. Pester .15 .40
❑ 5 Franken Bury .15 .40
❑ 6 Skittish Fish .15 .40
❑ 7 Eelio's .15 .40
❑ 8 Grenades and Ham .15 .40
❑ 9 6UP .15 .40
❑ 10 Can That's Dry .15 .40
❑ 11 ChapStink .15 .40
❑ 12 Hop Pockets .15 .40
❑ 13 Pop-Aparts .15 .40
❑ 14 RainyD .15 .40
❑ 15 Punkin' Donuts .15 .40
❑ 16 Showerade .15 .40
❑ 17 Tripicana .15 .40
❑ 18 Ghoulfish .15 .40
❑ 19 Jawson's Rabies .15 .40
❑ 20 Tutino's Pizza Wraps .15 .40
❑ 21 Trivial Lawsuit .15 .40
❑ 22 Frisk Me .15 .40
❑ 23 Crooker Jack .15 .40
❑ 24 Milk Dudes .15 .40
❑ 25 Buzzerfinger .15 .40
❑ 26 Chops Ahoy! .15 .40
❑ 27 Plunder Bread .15 .40
❑ 28 Peepsi .15 .40
❑ 29 Dumpin' Donuts .15 .40
❑ 30 Frothing Flakes .15 .40
❑ 31 Rice Kreepies .15 .40
❑ 32 WebSkinz .15 .40
❑ 33 Ball Point Franks .15 .40
❑ 34 Sling Pop .15 .40
❑ 35 Flunkables .15 .40
❑ 36 Snob Balls .15 .40
❑ 37 Haggies .15 .40
❑ 38 Call of Doody .15 .40
❑ 39 SkunkAroos .15 .40
❑ 40 Almond Jerk .15 .40
❑ 41 Troll House .15 .40
❑ 42 Livid-Plumbr .15 .40
❑ 43 Silly Bangz .15 .40
❑ 44 Squinties .15 .40
❑ 45 Buff .15 .40
❑ 46 Mentoads .15 .40
❑ 47 Puu Puu Pets .15 .40
❑ 48 Rice-A-Groani .15 .40
❑ 49 Aquafish .15 .40
❑ 50 Curst .15 .40
❑ 51 Coca-Collar .15 .40
❑ 52 Chef Boy U R Dumb .15 .40
❑ 53 Con Flakes .15 .40
❑ 54 Greed Giant .15 .40
❑ 55 Clucky Charms .15 .40

2011 Wacky Packages Series 8 Pink

COMPLETE SET (55) 12.00 30.00
STATED ODDS

2011 Wacky Packages Series 8 Flash Foil

COMPLETE SET (55) 200.00 300.00
STATED ODDS 1:6

2011 Wacky Packages Series 8 Gold Flash Foil

STATED ODDS 1:353

2011 Wacky Packages Series 8 Bonus

COMPLETE SET (5) 12.00 25.00
B1-B3 ODDS ONE PER BLISTER PACK
B4,B5 ODDS ONE PER BLASTER BOX
❑ B1 Cream of Tweet 2.00 5.00
❑ B2 deLays 2.00 5.00
❑ B3 Demonos 2.00 5.00
❑ B4 Maximum 6.00 15.00
❑ B5 Oct 5.00 12.00

2011 Wacky Packages Series 8 Go to the Movies

COMPLETE SET (8) 5.00 12.00
STATED ODDS 1:3
❑ 1 Kon Fused Panda 1.25 3.00
❑ 2 The Dork Knight 1.25 3.00
❑ 3 Harry Popper 1.25 3.00
❑ 4 Night at the Mausoleum 1.25 3.00
❑ 5 Shriek 1.25 3.00
❑ 6 Twilice 1.25 3.00
❑ 7 Transfarmers 1.25 3.00
❑ 8 Diary of a Wacky Kid 1.25 3.00

2011 Wacky Packages Series 8 Magnets

COMPLETE SET (10) 15.00 30.00
STATED ODDS 1:6
❑ 1 Milk Foam 2.50 6.00
❑ 2 Slayskool 2.50 6.00
❑ 3 Pupsi Cola 2.50 6.00
❑ 4 Blunder 2.50 6.00
❑ 5 Ditch Boy 2.50 6.00
❑ 6 Screech 2.50 6.00
❑ 7 Band Ache 2.50 6.00
❑ 8 Gyppy Pop 2.50 6.00
❑ 9 Crust 2.50 6.00
❑ 10 Drowny 2.50 6.00

2011 Wacky Packages Series 8 Motion Luggage Tags

COMPLETE SET (10) 10.00 25.00
STATED ODDS 1:6
❑ 1 Burn Ems 2.00 5.00
❑ 2 Frosted Snakes 2.00 5.00
❑ 3 Glutton 2.00 5.00
❑ 4 Cap'n Crud 2.00 5.00
❑ 5 Jolly Mean Giant 2.00 5.00
❑ 6 Quit 2.00 5.00
❑ 7 Spaz 2.00 5.00
❑ 8 Beanball 2.00 5.00
❑ 9 Cannibals 2.00 5.00
❑ 10 Grape News 2.00 5.00

2011 Wacky Packages Series 8 Pack to the Future

COMPLETE SET (10) 6.00 15.00
STATED ODDS 1:3
❑ 1 You Too 1.25 3.00
❑ 2 Borgresso 1.25 3.00
❑ 3 D.N.Animals 1.25 3.00
❑ 4 Polar Spring 1.25 3.00
❑ 5 Jupiter Mints 1.25 3.00
❑ 6 Aquafunda 1.25 3.00
❑ 7 I Can't Believe It's Big Brother 1.25 3.00
❑ 8 iimMobil 1.25 3.00
❑ 9 Like Cereal 1.25 3.00
❑ 10 Sewer Patch Kids 1.25 3.00

2011 Wacky Packages Series 8 Sketches

STATED ODDS 1:973
❑ 1 Brent Engstrom 100.00 200.00
❑ 2 Colin Walton 100.00 200.00
❑ 3 Fred Wheaton 100.00 200.00
❑ 4 Jeff Zapata 100.00 200.00
❑ 5 Joe Simko 100.00 200.00
❑ 6 Mark Parisi 150.00 250.00
❑ 7 Neil Camera 150.00 250.00
❑ 8 Tom Bunk 100.00 200.00

2011 The Walking Dead

COMPLETE SET (81) 12.00 30.00
❑ 1 Checklist .20 .50
❑ 2 Rick Grimes .20 .50
❑ 3 Lori Grimes .20 .50
❑ 4 Carl Grimes .20 .50
❑ 5 Shane Walsh .20 .50
❑ 6 Andrea .20 .50
❑ 7 Dale .20 .50
❑ 8 Glenn .20 .50
❑ 9 Frustrated Lawman .20 .50
❑ 10 Dedicated Lawman .20 .50
❑ 11 Fateful Decision .20 .50
❑ 12 Rude Awakening .20 .50
❑ 13 What Happened .20 .50
❑ 14 Don't Open .20 .50
❑ 15 Carnage .20 .50
❑ 16 Finally Home .20 .50
❑ 17 Friendly Survivors .20 .50
❑ 18 Batter Up .20 .50
❑ 19 Morgan, Protective Father .20 .50
❑ 20 Friendly Advice .20 .50
❑ 21 Scrounging for Weapons .20 .50
❑ 22 Back in Uniform .20 .50
❑ 23 Out of Gas .20 .50
❑ 24 God Forgive Us .20 .50
❑ 25 No Gas Required .20 .50
❑ 26 Unfettered Lawman .20 .50
❑ 27 Welcome to Atlanta .20 .50
❑ 28 Not a Good Sign .20 .50
❑ 29 Rookie Mistake .20 .50
❑ 30 Glenn to the Rescue .20 .50
❑ 31 Narrow Escape .20 .50
❑ 32 Trapped .20 .50
❑ 33 Drastic Measures .20 .50
❑ 34 Disguised as Walkers .20 .50
❑ 35 Diversion .20 .50
❑ 36 Someone's at the Door .20 .50
❑ 37 Stranded .20 .50
❑ 38 Base Camp .20 .50
❑ 39 Joyride .20 .50
❑ 40 Reunited .20 .50
❑ 41 That's My Deer .20 .50
❑ 42 Can't Let a Man Die .20 .50
❑ 43 Nothing's Killed Him Yet .20 .50
❑ 44 Plan of Attack .20 .50
❑ 45 Done Talking .20 .50
❑ 46 Clear a Path .20 .50
❑ 47 Merle's Gone .20 .50
❑ 48 WTF .20 .50
❑ 49 Follow the Corpses .20 .50
❑ 50 Get the Guns .20 .50
❑ 51 Don't Bring the Geeks .20 .50
❑ 52 We Need Glenn .20 .50
❑ 53 Where's the Van .20 .50
❑ 54 The Calm .20 .50
❑ 55 Invasion .20 .50
❑ 56 Happy Birthday .20 .50
❑ 57 Protect the Camp .20 .50
❑ 58 Close Call .20 .50
❑ 59 If You're Out There .20 .50
❑ 60 Cracks in the Friendship .20 .50
❑ 61 Laying Amy to Rest .20 .50
❑ 62 Green Eyed Monster .20 .50
❑ 63 United Front .20 .50
❑ 64 Vulnerable .20 .50
❑ 65 Is It Safe .20 .50
❑ 66 Keep Moving .20 .50
❑ 67 This is Hope .20 .50
❑ 68 Sanctuary .20 .50
❑ 69 Enhanced Internal View .20 .50
❑ 70 Out of Juice .20 .50
❑ 71 I Thought There'd Be More Time .20 .50
❑ 72 The Last Hope .20 .50
❑ 73 We're Out of Here .20 .50
❑ 74 Well Enough Alone .20 .50
❑ 75 We're All Done Now .20 .50
❑ 76 His Motivation .20 .50
❑ 77 An Open Door .20 .50
❑ 78 Secrets .20 .50
❑ 79 Andrea Loses Hope .20 .50
❑ 80 Make a Run for It .20 .50
❑ 81 We Choose Hope .20 .50

2011 The Walking Dead Autographs

STATED ODDS 1:24
❑ A1 Jon Bernthal 100.00 175.00
❑ A2 Jon Bernthal 100.00 175.00
❑ A5 Steven Yeun 25.00 50.00
❑ A6 Steven Yeun 25.00 50.00
❑ A7 Chandler Riggs 25.00 50.00
❑ A8 Chandler Riggs 25.00 50.00
❑ A9 Emma Bell 25.00 50.00
❑ A10 Emma Bell 25.00 50.00
❑ A11 Lennie James 25.00 50.00
❑ A12 Lennie James 25.00 50.00
❑ A13 Michael Rooker 75.00 150.00
❑ A14 Michael Rooker 75.00 150.00
❑ A15 IronE Singleton 25.00 50.00
❑ A16 IronE Singleton 25.00 50.00
❑ A17 Norman Reedus 200.00 350.00
❑ A18 Norman Reedus 200.00 350.00

2011 The Walking Dead Behind the Scenes

COMPLETE SET (9) 20.00 40.00
STATED ODDS
❑ C1 Behind the Scenes 3.00 8.00
❑ C2 Behind the Scenes 3.00 8.00
❑ C3 Behind the Scenes 3.00 8.00
❑ C4 Behind the Scenes 3.00 8.00
❑ C5 Behind the Scenes 3.00 8.00
❑ C6 Behind the Scenes 3.00 8.00
❑ C7 Behind the Scenes 3.00 8.00
❑ C8 Behind the Scenes 3.00 8.00
❑ C9 Behind the Scenes 3.00 8.00

2011 The Walking Dead Foil Walkers

COMPLETE SET (9) 12.00 30.00
STATED ODDS
❑ W1 Deceptive 2.50 6.00
❑ W2 Shelf Life 2.50 6.00
❑ W3 Careful With That Gun 2.50 6.00
❑ W4 Take Aim 2.50 6.00
❑ W5 Always Carriers 2.50 6.00
❑ W6 On the Move 2.50 6.00
❑ W7 Vicious 2.50 6.00
❑ W8 Dead and Buried 2.50 6.00
❑ W9 Omniumal 2.50 6.00

2011 The Walking Dead Promos

❑ P1 Deer Eating Zombie 1.25 3.00
(NSU Magazine)
❑ P2 8 cast members 2.00 5.00
(Philly Non-Sport)
❑ P3 Rick Grimes and friend 3.00 8.00
(general distribution)
❑ P4 Rick and mini walker 5.00 12.00
(Season 1 DVD)
❑ NNO Rick Grimes 4.00 10.00
(SDCC 2011)

2011 The Walking Dead Redemption Memorabilia

STATED PRINT RUN 1 SER. #'d SET
UNPRICED DUE TO SCARCITY
❑ R1 Rick Grimes JUMBO
❑ R2 Shane Walsh JUMBO
❑ R3 Rick Grimes
❑ R4 Rick Grimes
❑ R5 Rick Grimes
❑ R6 Rick Grimes
❑ R7 Rick Grimes
❑ R8 Rick Grimes
❑ R9 Rick Grimes
❑ R10 Rick Grimes
❑ R11 Rick Grimes
❑ R12 Rick Grimes
❑ R13 Rick Grimes
❑ R14 Rick Grimes
❑ R15 Rick Grimes
❑ R16 Rick Grimes
❑ R17 Rick Grimes
❑ R18 Rick Grimes
❑ R19 Rick Grimes
❑ R20 Rick Grimes

2011 The Walking Dead Sketches

STATED ODDS 1:288
❑ 1 Bianca Thompson
❑ 2 Bob Stevlic
❑ 3 Brian Kong
❑ 4 Chad Haverland
❑ 5 Chris Henderson
❑ 6 Chris Hoffman
❑ 7 Chris Thorne
❑ 8 Daniel Gorman
❑ 9 David Day
❑ 10 Edward Cherniga
❑ 11 Gabby Untermayerova
❑ 12 Gary Kezele
❑ 13 George Deep
❑ 14 Heather Cromwell
❑ 15 Ingrid Hardy
❑ 16 Jim Seeber
❑ 17 John Haun
❑ 18 Lak Lim
❑ 19 Patrick Hamill
❑ 20 Rich Molinelli
❑ 21 Scott Rorie
❑ 22 Tim Shay
❑ 23 Victor Rodriguez
❑ 24 Vince Sunico
❑ 25 Wu Wei

2011 The Walking Dead Wardrobe Memorabilia

STATED ODDS 1:12
M18 ANNOUNCED PRINT RUN 500
❑ M1 Rick Grimes 40.00 80.00

❑ M2 Lori Grimes 75.00 150.00
❑ M3 Lori Grimes 25.00 50.00
❑ M4 Carl Grimes 30.00 60.00
❑ M5 Shane Walsh 12.00 30.00
❑ M6 Shane Walsh 15.00 40.00
❑ M7 Glenn 20.00 40.00
❑ M8 Andrea 20.00 40.00
❑ M9 Amy 35.00 70.00
❑ M10 Dale 25.00 50.00
❑ M11 Daryl 60.00 120.00
❑ M12 Military Walker 8.00 20.00
❑ M13 Deer Eating Zombie 10.00 25.00
❑ M14 Walker 8.00 20.00
❑ M15 Walker 8.00 20.00
❑ M16 Walker 8.00 20.00
❑ M17 Walker 8.00 20.00
❑ M18 Rick's First Kill 40.00 80.00
(binder exclusive)

2011 Warehouse 13 Season Two

COMPLETE SET (26) 30.00 60.00
STATED PRINT RUN 250 SER. #'d SETS

❑ 1 Time Will Tell 2.00 5.00
❑ 2 Time Will Tell 2.00 5.00
❑ 3 Mild Mannered 2.00 5.00
❑ 4 Mild Mannered 2.00 5.00
❑ 5 Beyond our Control 2.00 5.00
❑ 6 Beyond our Control 2.00 5.00
❑ 7 Age Before Beauty 2.00 5.00
❑ 8 Age Before Beauty 2.00 5.00
❑ 9 13.1 2.00 5.00
❑ 10 13.1 2.00 5.00
❑ 11 Around the Ben 2.00 5.00
❑ 12 Around the Ben 2.00 5.00
❑ 13 For the Team 2.00 5.00
❑ 14 For the Team 2.00 5.00
❑ 15 Merge with Caution 2.00 5.00
❑ 16 Merge with Caution 2.00 5.00
❑ 17 Vendetta 2.00 5.00
❑ 18 Vendetta 2.00 5.00
❑ 19 Where and When 2.00 5.00
❑ 20 Where and When 2.00 5.00
❑ 21 Buried 2.00 5.00
❑ 22 Buried 2.00 5.00
❑ 23 Reset 2.00 5.00
❑ 24 Reset 2.00 5.00
❑ 25 Secret Santa 2.00 5.00
❑ 26 Secret Santa 2.00 5.00

2011 Warehouse 13 Season Two Artifacts

COMPLETE SET (9) 20.00 40.00
STATED PRINT RUN 350 SER. #'d SETS

❑ A20 Godfrid's Spoon 3.00 8.00
❑ A21 Man Ray's Camera 3.00 8.00
❑ A22 Mata Hari's Stockings 3.00 8.00
❑ A23 Pearl of Wisdom 3.00 8.00
❑ A24 Telegraph Island Telegraph 3.00 8.00
❑ A25 Max Wertheimer's Zoetrope 3.00 8.00
❑ A26 Norse Hammer 3.00 8.00
❑ A27 Lizzie Borden's Compact 3.00 8.00
❑ A28 Cinderella's Glass Knife 3.00 8.00

2011 Warehouse 13 Season Two Autographs

STATED ODDS TWO PER PACK

❑ 1 Allison Scagliotti 50.00 100.00
❑ 2 Armin Shimerman 6.00 15.00
❑ 3 CCH Pounder 20.00 40.00
❑ 4 Dillon Casey 6.00 15.00
❑ 5 Eddie McClintock 35.00 70.00
❑ 6 Faran Tahir 6.00 15.00
❑ 7 Genelle Williams 20.00 40.00
❑ 8 Jaime Murray 35.00 70.00
❑ 9 Joanne Kelly 40.00 80.00
❑ 10 Jun Yul-Kim 6.00 15.00
❑ 11 Neil Grayston 12.00 25.00
❑ 12 Nolan Gerard Funk 6.00 15.00
❑ 13 Roberta Maxwell 6.00 15.00
❑ 14 Sarah Allen 10.00 20.00
❑ 15 Saul Rubinek 25.00 50.00
❑ 16 Sherry Miller 6.00 15.00
❑ 17 Tia Carrere 12.00 25.00
❑ 18 Tyler Hynes 6.00 15.00

2011 Warehouse 13 Season Two Promos

COMPLETE SET 2.50 6.00

❑ P1 Pete Lattimer .75 2.00
Myka Bering/ (General Distribution)
❑ P2 Pete Lattimer 1.50 4.00
Myka Bering/ (NSU Magazine)
❑ P3 Artie Nielsen 2.00 5.00
Claudia Donovan/ (2011 SDCC and binder)

2011 Warehouse 13 Season Two Relics

STATED PRINT RUN 350 SER. #'d SETS

❑ 1 Artie Nielsen 8.00 20.00
(from Reset
❑ 2 Claudia Donovan 8.00 20.00
(from Burnout
❑ 3 Leena 8.00 20.00
(from Time Will Tell
❑ 4 Myka Bering 8.00 20.00
(from Around the Bend
❑ 5 Myka Bering 8.00 20.00
(from Pilot
❑ 6 Myka Bering 8.00 20.00
(from Pilot
❑ 7 Myka Bering 10.00 25.00
(from When and Where
❑ 8 Pete Lattimer 8.00 20.00
(from Claudia
❑ 9 Pete Lattimer 8.00 20.00
(from Mild Mannered

2012 Amazing Spider-Man Movie

COMPLETE SET 175.00 250.00
ONE AUTO WITH EVERY SET PURCHASED
AUR1 ISSUED AS 4 SET INCENTIVE

❑ C1 Spider-Man 1.50 4.00
❑ C2 Peter Parker 1.50 4.00
❑ C3 Gwen Stacy 1.50 4.00
❑ C4 Dr. Curt Connors 1.50 4.00
❑ C5 George Stacy 1.50 4.00
❑ C6 Dr. Ratha 1.50 4.00
❑ C7 Flash Thompson 1.50 4.00
❑ C8 Ben Parker 1.50 4.00
❑ C9 Young Peter Parker 1.50 4.00
❑ CC1 Spider-Man MEM 30.00 60.00
❑ CC2 Peter Parker MEM 8.00 20.00
❑ CC3 Gwen Stacy MEM 12.00 30.00
❑ CC4 Dr. Connors MEM 8.00 20.00
❑ CC5 Gwen Stacy MEM 12.00 30.00
❑ CC6 Peter Parker MEM 8.00 20.00
❑ CC7 Peter Parker MEM 8.00 20.00
❑ AU1 Andrew Garfield/222* 100.00 175.00
❑ AU2 Andrew Garfield/222* 100.00 175.00
(as Spider-Man) AU (full bleed)
❑ AUR1 Andrew Garfield AU MEM/111* 150.00 300.00

2012 Avengers Assemble

COMPLETE SET (176) 20.00 40.00
UM23 STATED PRINT RUN 84

❑ 1 Iron Man .20 .50
❑ 2 Iron Man .20 .50
❑ 3 Iron Man .20 .50
❑ 4 Iron Man .20 .50
❑ 5 Iron Man .20 .50
❑ 6 Iron Man .20 .50
❑ 7 Iron Man .20 .50
❑ 8 Iron Man .20 .50
❑ 9 Iron Man .20 .50
❑ 10 Iron Man .20 .50
❑ 11 Iron Man .20 .50
❑ 12 Iron Man .20 .50
❑ 13 Iron Man .20 .50
❑ 14 Iron Man .20 .50
❑ 15 Iron Man .20 .50
❑ 16 Iron Man .20 .50
❑ 17 Iron Man .20 .50
❑ 18 Iron Man .20 .50
❑ 19 Iron Man .20 .50
❑ 20 Incredible Hulk .20 .50
❑ 21 Incredible Hulk .20 .50
❑ 22 Incredible Hulk .20 .50
❑ 23 Incredible Hulk .20 .50
❑ 24 Incredible Hulk .20 .50
❑ 25 Incredible Hulk .20 .50
❑ 26 Incredible Hulk .20 .50
❑ 27 Iron Man 2 .20 .50
❑ 28 Iron Man 2 .20 .50
❑ 29 Iron Man 2 .20 .50
❑ 30 Iron Man 2 .20 .50
❑ 31 Iron Man 2 .20 .50
❑ 32 Iron Man 2 .20 .50
❑ 33 Iron Man 2 .20 .50
❑ 34 Iron Man 2 .20 .50
❑ 35 Iron Man 2 .20 .50
❑ 36 Iron Man 2 .20 .50
❑ 37 Iron Man 2 .20 .50
❑ 38 Iron Man 2 .20 .50
❑ 39 Iron Man 2 .20 .50
❑ 40 Iron Man 2 .20 .50
❑ 41 Iron Man 2 .20 .50
❑ 42 Iron Man 2 .20 .50
❑ 43 Iron Man 2 .20 .50
❑ 44 Iron Man 2 .20 .50
❑ 45 Iron Man 2 .20 .50
❑ 46 Thor .20 .50
❑ 47 Thor .20 .50
❑ 48 Thor .20 .50
❑ 49 Thor .20 .50
❑ 50 Thor .20 .50
❑ 51 Thor .20 .50
❑ 52 Thor .20 .50
❑ 53 Thor .20 .50
❑ 54 Thor .20 .50
❑ 55 Thor .20 .50
❑ 56 Thor .20 .50
❑ 57 Thor .20 .50
❑ 58 Thor .20 .50
❑ 59 Thor .20 .50
❑ 60 Thor .20 .50
❑ 61 Thor .20 .50
❑ 62 Thor .20 .50
❑ 63 Thor .20 .50
❑ 64 Thor .20 .50
❑ 65 Thor .20 .50
❑ 66 Thor .20 .50
❑ 67 Captain America .20 .50
❑ 68 Captain America .20 .50
❑ 69 Captain America .20 .50
❑ 70 Captain America .20 .50
❑ 71 Captain America .20 .50
❑ 72 Captain America .20 .50
❑ 73 Captain America .20 .50
❑ 74 Captain America .20 .50
❑ 75 Captain America .20 .50
❑ 76 Captain America .20 .50
❑ 77 Captain America .20 .50
❑ 78 Captain America .20 .50
❑ 79 Captain America .20 .50
❑ 80 Captain America .20 .50
❑ 81 Captain America .20 .50
❑ 82 Captain America .20 .50
❑ 83 Captain America .20 .50
❑ 84 Captain America .20 .50
❑ 85 Captain America .20 .50
❑ 86 Captain America .20 .50
❑ 87 Captain America .20 .50
❑ 88 Captain America .20 .50
❑ 89 Captain America .20 .50
❑ 90 Captain America .20 .50
❑ 91 Avengers .20 .50
❑ 92 Avengers .20 .50
❑ 93 Avengers .20 .50
❑ 94 Avengers .20 .50
❑ 95 Avengers .20 .50
❑ 96 Avengers .20 .50
❑ 97 Avengers .20 .50
❑ 98 Avengers .20 .50
❑ 99 Avengers .20 .50
❑ 100 Avengers .20 .50
❑ 101 Avengers .20 .50
❑ 102 Avengers .20 .50
❑ 103 Avengers .20 .50
❑ 104 Avengers .20 .50
❑ 105 Avengers .20 .50
❑ 106 Avengers .20 .50
❑ 107 Avengers .20 .50
❑ 108 Avengers .20 .50
❑ 109 Avengers .20 .50
❑ 110 Avengers .20 .50
❑ 111 Avengers .20 .50
❑ 112 Avengers .20 .50
❑ 113 Avengers .20 .50
❑ 114 Avengers .20 .50
❑ 115 Avengers .20 .50
❑ 116 Avengers .20 .50
❑ 117 Avengers .20 .50
❑ 118 Avengers .20 .50
❑ 119 Avengers .20 .50
❑ 120 Avengers .20 .50
❑ 121 Avengers .20 .50
❑ 122 Avengers .20 .50
❑ 123 Avengers .20 .50
❑ 124 Avengers .20 .50
❑ 125 Avengers .20 .50
❑ 126 Avengers .20 .50
❑ 127 Avengers .20 .50
❑ 128 Avengers .20 .50
❑ 129 Avengers .20 .50
❑ 130 Avengers .20 .50
❑ 131 Avengers .20 .50
❑ 132 Avengers .20 .50
❑ 133 Avengers .20 .50
❑ 134 Avengers .20 .50
❑ 135 Avengers .20 .50
❑ 136 Avengers .20 .50
❑ 137 Avengers .20 .50
❑ 138 Avengers .20 .50
❑ 139 Avengers .20 .50
❑ 140 Avengers .20 .50
❑ 141 Avengers .20 .50
❑ 142 Avengers .20 .50
❑ 143 Avengers .20 .50
❑ 144 Avengers .20 .50
❑ 145 Avengers .20 .50
❑ 146 Avengers .20 .50
❑ 147 Avengers .20 .50
❑ 148 Avengers .20 .50
❑ 149 Avengers .20 .50
❑ 150 Avengers .20 .50
❑ 151 Avengers .20 .50
❑ 152 Avengers .20 .50
❑ 153 Avengers .20 .50
❑ 154 Avengers .20 .50
❑ 155 Avengers .20 .50
❑ 156 Avengers .20 .50
❑ 157 Avengers .20 .50
❑ 158 Avengers .20 .50
❑ 159 Avengers .20 .50
❑ 160 Avengers .20 .50
❑ 161 Avengers .20 .50
❑ 162 Avengers .20 .50
❑ 163 Avengers .20 .50
❑ 164 Avengers .20 .50
❑ 165 Avengers .20 .50
❑ 166 Avengers .20 .50
❑ 167 Captain America .20 .50
❑ 168 Thor .20 .50
❑ 169 Bruce Banner .20 .50
❑ 170 Tony Stark .20 .50
❑ 171 Black Widow .20 .50
❑ 172 Hawkeye .20 .50
❑ 173 Nick Fury .20 .50
❑ 174 Maria Hill .20 .50
❑ 175 Agent Coulson .20 .50
❑ 176 Loki .20 .50
❑ UM23 Avengers Vol.1 No.1/84 60.00 120.00

2012 Avengers Assemble Printing Plates Black

STATED PRINT RUN 1 SER. #'d SET
UNPRICED DUE TO SCARCITY

2012 Avengers Assemble Printing Plates Cyan

STATED PRINT RUN 1 SER. #'d SET
UNPRICED DUE TO SCARCITY

2012 Avengers Assemble Printing Plates Magenta

STATED PRINT RUN 1 SER. #'d SET
UNPRICED DUE TO SCARCITY

2012 Avengers Assemble Printing Plates Yel-low

STATED PRINT RUN 1 SER. #'d SET
UNPRICED DUE TO SCARCITY

2012 Avengers Assemble Autographs

❑ CH Chris Hemsworth 200.00 300.00
❑ CS Cobie Smulders 200.00 300.00
❑ JR Jeremy Renner 200.00 300.00

2012 Avengers Assemble Classic Covers

COMPLETE SET (36) 10.00 20.00
STATED ODDS 1:2.5

❑ A1 The Avengers #1 .60 1.50
❑ A2 New Avengers #4 .60 1.50
❑ A3 The Avengers (vol. 2) #1 .60 1.50
❑ A4 The Avengers (vol. 3) #1 .60 1.50
❑ A5 The Avengers (vol. 3) #22 .60 1.50
❑ A6 The Avengers #221 .60 1.50
❑ A7 The Avengers #200 .60 1.50
❑ A8 The Avengers #162 .60 1.50
❑ A9 Avengers Annual #10 .60 1.50
❑ A10 The Avengers #93 .60 1.50
❑ A11 Avengers Annual #2 .60 1.50
❑ A12 West Coast Avengers (vol. 2) #23 .60 1.50
❑ A13 The Avengers #4 .60 1.50
❑ A14 The Avengers #8 .60 1.50
❑ A15 New Avengers (vol. 1) #1 .60 1.50
❑ A16 The Avengers (vol. 4) #1 .60 1.50
❑ A17 New Avengers (vol. 2) #1 .60 1.50
❑ A18 New Avengers (vol. 2) #10 .60 1.50
❑ A19 The Avengers #229 .60 1.50
❑ A20 The Avengers #195 .60 1.50
❑ A21 The Avengers (vol. 3) #75 .60 1.50
❑ A22 The Avengers #262 .60 1.50
❑ A23 The Avengers #500 .60 1.50
❑ A24 The Avengers #100 .60 1.50
❑ A25 The Avengers #300 .60 1.50
❑ A26 The Avengers #400 .60 1.50
❑ A27 The Avengers #395 .60 1.50
❑ A28 Secret Avengers #1 .60 1.50
❑ A29 Ultimate Comics Avengers #3 .60 1.50
❑ A30 Young Avengers #1 .60 1.50
❑ A31 West Coast Avengers (vol. 1) #1 .60 1.50
❑ A32 The Avengers #57 .60 1.50
❑ A33 The Avengers #177 .60 1.50
❑ A34 The Avengers (vol. 3) #2 .60 1.50
❑ A35 The Avengers (vol. 3) #25 .60 1.50
❑ A36 The Avengers #502 .60 1.50

2012 Avengers Assemble Classic Covers Printing Plates Black

STATED PRINT RUN 1 SER. #'d SET
UNPRICED DUE TO SCARCITY

2012 Avengers Assemble Classic Covers Printing Plates Cyan

STATED PRINT RUN 1 SER. #'d SET
UNPRICED DUE TO SCARCITY

2012 Avengers Assemble Classic Covers Printing Plates Magenta

STATED PRINT RUN 1 SER. #'d SET
UNPRICED DUE TO SCARCITY

2012 Avengers Assemble Classic Covers Printing Plates Yellow

STATED PRINT RUN 1 SER. #'d SET
UNPRICED DUE TO SCARCITY

2012 Avengers Assemble Concept Series

COMPLETE SET (9) 15.00 30.00
STATED ODDS 1:10

❑ CS1 Black Widow 2.50 6.00
❑ CS2 Incredible Hulk 2.50 6.00
❑ CS3 SHIELD Jet 2.50 6.00
❑ CS4 The Avengers 2.50 6.00
❑ CS5 Loki 2.50 6.00
❑ CS6 The Avengers 2.50 6.00
❑ CS7 Captain America Uniform 2.50 6.00
❑ CS8 SHIELD Conference Room 2.50 6.00
❑ CS9 Iron Man 2.50 6.00
Thor

2012 Avengers Assemble Concept Series Printing Plates Black

STATED PRINT RUN 1 SER. #'d SET
UNPRICED DUE TO SCARCITY

2012 Avengers Assemble Concept Series Printing Plates Cyan

STATED PRINT RUN 1 SER. #'d SET
UNPRICED DUE TO SCARCITY

2012 Avengers Assemble Concept Series Printing Plates Magenta

STATED PRINT RUN 1 SER. #'d SET
UNPRICED DUE TO SCARCITY

2012 Avengers Assemble Concept Series Printing Plates Yellow

STATED PRINT RUN 1 SER. #'d SET
UNPRICED DUE TO SCARCITY

2012 Avengers Assemble Heroes/Villains Evolve

COMPLETE SET (60) 20.00 40.00
STATED ODDS 1:2

❑ E1 Iron Man .60 1.50
❑ E2 Iron Man .60 1.50
❑ E3 Iron Man .60 1.50
❑ E4 Iron Man .60 1.50
❑ E5 Iron Man .60 1.50
❑ E6 Iron Man .60 1.50
❑ E7 Hulk .60 1.50
❑ E8 Hulk .60 1.50
❑ E9 Hulk .60 1.50
❑ E10 Hulk .60 1.50
❑ E11 Hulk .60 1.50
❑ E12 Hulk .60 1.50
❑ E13 Thor .60 1.50
❑ E14 Thor .60 1.50
❑ E15 Thor .60 1.50
❑ E16 Thor .60 1.50
❑ E17 Thor .60 1.50
❑ E18 Thor .60 1.50
❑ E19 Captain America .60 1.50
❑ E20 Captain America .60 1.50
❑ E21 Captain America .60 1.50
❑ E22 Captain America .60 1.50
❑ E23 Captain America .60 1.50
❑ E24 Captain America .60 1.50
❑ E25 Hawkeye .60 1.50
❑ E26 Hawkeye .60 1.50
❑ E27 Hawkeye .60 1.50
❑ E28 Hawkeye .60 1.50
❑ E29 Hawkeye .60 1.50
❑ E30 Hawkeye .60 1.50
❑ E31 Black Widow .60 1.50
❑ E32 Black Widow .60 1.50
❑ E33 Black Widow .60 1.50
❑ E34 Black Widow .60 1.50
❑ E35 Black Widow .60 1.50
❑ E36 Black Widow .60 1.50
❑ E37 Nick Fury .60 1.50
❑ E38 Nick Fury .60 1.50
❑ E39 Nick Fury .60 1.50
❑ E40 Nick Fury .60 1.50
❑ E41 Nick Fury .60 1.50
❑ E42 Nick Fury .60 1.50
❑ E43 Maria Hill .60 1.50
❑ E44 Maria Hill .60 1.50
❑ E45 Maria Hill .60 1.50
❑ E46 Maria Hill .60 1.50
❑ E47 Maria Hill .60 1.50
❑ E48 Maria Hill .60 1.50
❑ E49 Bruce Banner .60 1.50
❑ E50 Bruce Banner .60 1.50
❑ E51 Bruce Banner .60 1.50
❑ E52 Bruce Banner .60 1.50
❑ E53 Bruce Banner .60 1.50
❑ E54 Bruce Banner .60 1.50
❑ E55 Loki .60 1.50
❑ E56 Loki .60 1.50
❑ E57 Loki .60 1.50
❑ E58 Loki .60 1.50
❑ E59 Loki .60 1.50
❑ E60 Loki .60 1.50

2012 Avengers Assemble Memorabilia

RANDOM INSERTS IN PACKS

❑ AS1 Thor 10.00 25.00
❑ AS2 Captain America 20.00 50.00
❑ AS3 Tony Stark 10.00 25.00
❑ AS4 Bruce Banner 12.00 30.00
❑ AS5 Steve Rogers 12.00 30.00
❑ AS6 Loki 12.00 30.00
❑ AS7 Nick Fury
❑ AS8 Agent Coulson 6.00 15.00
❑ AS9 Black Widow 50.00 100.00
❑ AS10 Hawkeye 10.00 25.00
❑ AS11 Maria Hill 20.00 50.00

2012 Avengers Assemble Dual Memorabilia

RANDOM INSERTS IN PACKS

❑ AD1 Black Widow 60.00 120.00
❑ AD2 Justin Hammer 10.00 25.00
Tony Stark
❑ AD3 Ivan Vanko 10.00 25.00
Justin Hammer
❑ AD4 Ivan Vanko 12.00 30.00
Tony Stark
❑ AD5 Rhodey Rhodes 8.00 20.00
Justin Hammer
❑ AD6 Black Widow
Nick Fury
❑ AD7 Thor 12.00 30.00
Loki
❑ AD8 Thor 8.00 20.00
Heimdall
❑ AD9 Jane Foster 15.00 40.00
Thor
❑ AD10 Thor 10.00 25.00
Frigga
❑ AD11 Captain America 12.00 30.00
Nick Fury
❑ AD12 Captain America 15.00 40.00
Tony Stark
❑ AD13 Bruce Banner 8.00 20.00
Thor
❑ AD14 Nick Fury 8.00 20.00
Agent Coulson
❑ AD15 Nick Fury 8.00 20.00
Thor
❑ AD16 Hawkeye 10.00 25.00
Thor
❑ AD17 Thor 10.00 25.00
Tony Stark
❑ AD18 Bruce Banner 8.00 20.00
Steve Rogers
❑ AD19 Nick Fury 12.00 30.00
Maria Hill
❑ AD20 Hawkeye 10.00 25.00
Agent Coulson
❑ AD21 Thor 8.00 20.00
Nick Fury
❑ AD22 Thor 15.00 40.00
Loki
❑ AD23 Loki 15.00 40.00
Captain America
❑ AD24 Captain America 12.00 30.00
Hawkeye
❑ AD25 Hawkeye 10.00 25.00
Loki

2012 Avengers Assemble Triple Memorabilia

RANDOM INSERTS IN PACKS

❑ AT1 Justin Hammer 12.00 30.00
Tony Stark/Ivan Vanko
❑ AT2 Hogun 12.00 30.00
Fandral /Volstagg
❑ AT3 Thor 15.00 40.00
Jane Foster/Loki
❑ AT4 Loki 12.00 30.00
Thor/Frigga
❑ AT5 Captain America
Captain America/Captain America
❑ AT6 Captain America 12.00 30.00
Thor/Bruce Banner
❑ AT7 Agent Coulson 8.00 20.00
Tony Stark/Nick Fury
❑ AT8 Nick Fury 12.00 30.00
Thor/Loki
❑ AT9 Thor 15.00 40.00
Captain America/Tony Stark
❑ AT10 Bruce Banner 15.00 40.00
Steve Rogers/Maria Hill
❑ AT11 Maria Hill 12.00 30.00
Hawkeye/Nick Fury
❑ AT12 Nick Fury
Black Widow/Maria Hill
❑ AT13 Black Widow 15.00 40.00
Hawkeye/Nick Fury
❑ AT14 Nick Fury 15.00 40.00
Captain America/Hawkeye

2012 Avengers Assemble Quad Memorabilia

RANDOM INSERTS IN PACKS

❑ AQ1 Volstagg 20.00 50.00
Thor/ Fandral/ Hogun
❑ AQ2 Thor 35.00 70.00
❑ AQ3 Tony Stark 25.00 60.00
Hawkeye/ Black Widow/ Nick Fury
❑ AQ4 Nick Fury 25.00 60.00
Black Widow/ Maria Hill/Agent Coulson
❑ AQ5 Tony Stark 25.00 60.00
Black Widow/ Bruce Banner/ Steve Rogers
❑ AQ6 Nick Fury 35.00 70.00
❑ AQ7 Bruce Banner 40.00 80.00

2012 Avengers Assemble Sketches

STATED ODDS 1:24

❑ 1 Adam Talley
❑ 2 Adriana Melo
❑ 3 Ashleigh Popplewell
❑ 4 Aston Roy Cover
❑ 5 Bianca Thompson
❑ 6 Bill Pulkovski
❑ 7 Bo Hampton
❑ 8 Bob Stevlic
❑ 9 Boo
❑ 10 Bryan Tillman
❑ 11 Cal Slayton
❑ 12 Chadwick Haverland
❑ 13 Charles Hall
❑ 14 Charles Holbert
❑ 15 Chris Foreman
❑ 16 Cruddie Torian
❑ 17 Dan Smith
❑ 18 Daniel Gorman
❑ 19 Daniel Vest
❑ 20 Danielle Gransaull
Soloud
❑ 21 Daren Douglass
❑ 22 Dawn Wolf
❑ 23 Dennis Calero
❑ 24 Diana Greenhalgh
❑ 25 Dominike Stanton
❑ 26 Edward Chernica
❑ 27 Elaine Perna
❑ 28 Elfie Lebouleux
❑ 29 Elliot Fernandez
❑ 30 Elvin Hernandez
❑ 31 Eric Ninaltowski
❑ 32 Erik Reeves
❑ 33 Eugene Commodore
❑ 34 Frank Kadar
❑ 35 Frankie Washington
❑ 36 George Deep
❑ 37 Gilbert Monsanto
❑ 38 Guile Sharp
❑ 39 Ian Roberts
❑ 40 Isaiah Mcallister
❑ 41 j(ay)

- ❑ 42 James Riot Godfrey
- ❑ 43 Jason Adams
- ❑ 44 Jason Durden
- ❑ 45 Jason Keith Phillips
- ❑ 46 Jason Metcalf
- ❑ 47 Jayson Kretzer
- ❑ 48 Jerry Ma
- ❑ 49 Jim Cheung
- ❑ 50 Joe Hogan
- ❑ 51 Joe Rubenstein
- ❑ 52 Joel Gomez
- ❑ 53 John Beatty
- ❑ 54 Jonathan Gordon
- ❑ 55 Jonathan Racimo
- ❑ 56 Jose Jaro
- ❑ 57 Kate Bradley
- ❑ 58 Kevin Sharpe
- ❑ 59 Kimberley Dunaway
- ❑ 60 Lak Lim
- ❑ 61 Lawrence Reynolds
- ❑ 62 Layron DeJarnette
- ❑ 63 Livio Ramondelli
- ❑ 64 Marat Mychaels
- ❑ 65 Mark Henry
- ❑ 66 Mark Morales
- ❑ 67 Matt Slay
- ❑ 68 Matt Triano
- ❑ 69 Michael Duron
- ❑ 70 Michael Watkins
- ❑ 71 Mick Glebe
  Matt Glebe
- ❑ 72 Mike Mayhew
- ❑ 73 Penelope Gaylord
- ❑ 74 Randy Martinez
- ❑ 75 Ray-Anthony Height
- ❑ 76 Remi Dousset
- ❑ 77 Remy Eisu Mokhtar
- ❑ 78 Rhiannon Owens
- ❑ 79 Rodney Ramos
- ❑ 80 Rusty Gilligan
- ❑ 81 Ryan Kincaid
- ❑ 82 Sanford Greene
- ❑ 83 Sara Richard
- ❑ 84 Scott Cohn
- ❑ 85 Steve Scott
- ❑ 86 Terry Huddleston
- ❑ 87 TheOpticNerve
- ❑ 88 Tom Hodges
- ❑ 89 Tony Perna
- ❑ 90 Uko Smith
- ❑ 91 Vo Nguyen
- ❑ 92 Wendy Chew
- ❑ 93 Wes Huffer
- ❑ 94 Wesley Bernick

2012 Bench Warmer Daizy Dukez Autographs Gold Foil

- ❑ 1 Sara Underwood 10.00 25.00
- ❑ 2 Stacie Hall 4.00 10.00
- ❑ 3 Kara Monaco 6.00 15.00
- ❑ 4 April Scott 5.00 12.00
- ❑ 5 Stevie Lynn Leow 5.00 12.00
- ❑ 6 Trashell Thompson 4.00 10.00
- ❑ 7 Billie Jo Powers 4.00 10.00
- ❑ 8 Linsey Toole 4.00 10.00
- ❑ 9 Britanny Martin 4.00 10.00
- ❑ 10 Janet Layug 4.00 10.00
- ❑ 11 Natalie Clarke 4.00 10.00
- ❑ 12 Jile Cai 4.00 10.00
- ❑ 13 Jennifer Johnson 4.00 10.00
- ❑ 14 Lucy Clarke 4.00 10.00
- ❑ 15 Jessica Burciaga 8.00 20.00
- ❑ 16 Michelle Baena 5.00 12.00
- ❑ 17 Mary Riley 6.00 15.00
- ❑ 18 Kyara Tyler 4.00 10.00
- ❑ 19 Bambi Lashell 5.00 12.00
- ❑ 20 Syd Wilder 4.00 10.00
- ❑ 21 Heather Rae Young 4.00 10.00
- ❑ 22 Maria Kanellis 6.00 15.00
- ❑ 23 Jessica Hall 5.00 12.00
- ❑ 24 Shay Lyn Veasy 4.00 10.00
- ❑ 25 Deanna Brooks 4.00 10.00
- ❑ 26 Nikki Ziering 5.00 12.00
- ❑ 27 Caitlin O'Connor 4.00 10.00
- ❑ 28 Jenae Alt 4.00 10.00
- ❑ 29 Patrice Hollis 4.00 10.00
- ❑ 30 Holley Dorrough 4.00 10.00
- ❑ 31 Andrea Lowell 5.00 12.00
- ❑ 32 Jasmine Dustin 4.00 10.00
- ❑ 33 Ryan Shamrock 4.00 10.00
- ❑ 34 Miriam Gonzalez 5.00 12.00
- ❑ 35 Heather Rene Smith 4.00 10.00
- ❑ 36 Rachel Bernstein 4.00 10.00
- ❑ 37 Cassandra Lynn 5.00 12.00
- ❑ 38 Tiffany Selby 4.00 10.00
- ❑ 39 Tiffany Toth 5.00 12.00
- ❑ 40 Claudia Jordan 4.00 10.00
- ❑ 41 Tamara Witmer 5.00 12.00
- ❑ 42 Suzanne Stokes 6.00 15.00
- ❑ 43 Buffy Tyler 6.00 15.00
- ❑ 44 Candi Kita 5.00 12.00
- ❑ 45 Melissa Riso 5.00 12.00
- ❑ 46 Lisa Ligon 4.00 10.00
- ❑ 47 Miki Black 5.00 12.00
- ❑ 48 Jennifer Korbin 8.00 20.00
- ❑ 49 Brande Roderick 6.00 15.00
- ❑ 50 Crystal Harris 4.00 10.00
- ❑ 51 Torrie Wilson 8.00 20.00
- ❑ 52 Paige Peterson 4.00 10.00
- ❑ 53 Tanea Brooks 4.00 10.00
- ❑ 54 Brittany Herrera 4.00 10.00
- ❑ 55 Carrie Minter 4.00 10.00
- ❑ 56 Jessica Kinni 4.00 10.00
- ❑ 57 Lisa Gleave 5.00 12.00
- ❑ 58 Katie Lohmann 4.00 10.00
- ❑ 59 Casey Durkin 4.00 10.00
- ❑ 60 Brandie Moses 4.00 10.00
- ❑ 61 Cecille Gahr 4.00 10.00
- ❑ 62 Nicole Bennett 4.00 10.00
- ❑ 63 Brandy Grace 4.00 10.00
- ❑ 64 Talor Marion 4.00 10.00
- ❑ 65 Kirsty Lingman 4.00 10.00
- ❑ 66 Yancey Taylor 4.00 10.00
- ❑ 67 Yvette Nelson 4.00 10.00
- ❑ 68 Jaime Hammer 5.00 12.00
- ❑ 69 Carolyn Martin 4.00 10.00
- ❑ 70 Sandra Taylor 6.00 15.00
- ❑ 71 Britany Lauren 4.00 10.00
- ❑ 72 Kirsty Lingman 5.00 12.00
- ❑ 73 Kristine May 4.00 10.00
- ❑ 74 Kristina Rodrigues 4.00 10.00
- ❑ 75 Lindsay Dennis 5.00 12.00
- ❑ CB Catherine Bach 25.00 50.00
- ❑ CE Carmen Electra 20.00 50.00

2012 Bench Warmer Daizy Dukez Autographs Pink Foil

STATED PRINT RUN 25 SER. #'d SETS

2012 Bench Warmer Daizy Dukez Autographs Green Foil

STATED PRINT RUN 10 SER. #'d SETS
UNPRICED DUE TO SCARCITY

2012 Bench Warmer Daizy Dukez Autographs Blue Foil

STATED PRINT RUN 5 SER. #'d SETS
UNPRICED DUE TO SCARCITY

2012 Bench Warmer Daizy Dukez Autographs Red Foil

STATED PRINT RUN 1 SER. #'d SET
UNPRICED DUE TO SCARCITY

2012 Bench Warmer Daizy Dukez Dixie CJ-7 Autographs Gold Foil

STATED PRINT RUN 7 SER. #'d SETS
UNPRICED DUE TO SCARCITY

- ❑ 1 Alicia Johnson
- ❑ 2 Andrea Lowell
- ❑ 3 April Scott
- ❑ 4 Bambi Lashell
- ❑ 5 Billie Jo Powers
- ❑ 6 Brande Roderick
- ❑ 7 Brandie Moses
- ❑ 8 Brandy Grace
- ❑ 9 Buffy Tyler
- ❑ 10 Candi Kita
- ❑ 11 Carmen Electra
- ❑ 12 Cassandra Lynn
- ❑ 13 Cecille Gahr
- ❑ 14 Claudia Jordan
- ❑ 15 Crystal Harris
- ❑ 16 Deanna Brooks
- ❑ 17 Heather Rae Young
- ❑ 18 Heather Rene Smith
- ❑ 19 Holley Dorrough
- ❑ 20 Jennifer Korbin
- ❑ 21 Jessica Burciaga
- ❑ 22 Jessica Hall
- ❑ 23 Kara Monaco
- ❑ 24 Katie Lohmann
- ❑ 25 Kirsty Lingman
- ❑ 26 Lisa Gleave
- ❑ 27 Maria Kanellis
- ❑ 28 Mary Riley
- ❑ 29 Melissa Riso
- ❑ 30 Miki Black
- ❑ 31 Miriam Gonzalez
- ❑ 32 Nicole Bennett
- ❑ 33 Nikki Ziering
- ❑ 34 Paige Peterson
- ❑ 35 Patrice Hollis
- ❑ 36 Ryan Shamrock
- ❑ 37 Sara Underwood
- ❑ 38 Shay Lyn Veasy
- ❑ 39 Syd Wilder
- ❑ 40 Tamara Witmer
- ❑ 41 Tiffany Selby
- ❑ 42 Tiffany Toth
- ❑ 43 Torrie Wilson
- ❑ 44 Yancey Taylor
- ❑ 45 Yvette Nelson
- ❑ 46 Catherine Bach

2012 Bench Warmer Daizy Dukez Dixie CJ-7 Autographs Pink Foil

STATED PRINT RUN 5 SER. #'d SETS
UNPRICED DUE TO SCARCITY

2012 Bench Warmer Daizy Dukez Dixie CJ-7 Autographs Green Foil

STATED PRINT RUN 3 SER. #'d SETS
UNPRICED DUE TO SCARCITY

2012 Bench Warmer Daizy Dukez Dixie CJ-7 Autographs Blue Foil

STATED PRINT RUN 2 SER. #'d SETS
UNPRICED DUE TO SCARCITY

2012 Bench Warmer Daizy Dukez Dixie CJ-7 Autographs Red Foil

STATED PRINT RUN 1 SER. #'d SET
UNPRICED DUE TO SCARCITY

2012 Bench Warmer Daizy Dukez Farm Girl Jumbo Swatches

NO PRICING ON CARDS #'d TO 10 OR LESS

- ❑ 1 Carmen Electra Gold 15.00 40.00
- ❑ 2 Carmen Electra Pink/25 20.00 50.00
- ❑ 3 Carmen Electra Green AU/10
- ❑ 4 Carmen Electra Blue AU/5
- ❑ 5 Carmen Electra Red AU/1

2012 Bench Warmer Daizy Dukez General Lee 01 Autographs

STATED PRINT RUN 1 SER. #'d SET
UNPRICED DUE TO SCARCITY

- ❑ 1 Andrea Lowell
- ❑ 2 April Scott
- ❑ 3 Brande Roderick
- ❑ 4 Brandie Moses
- ❑ 5 Buffy Tyler
- ❑ 6 Candi Kita
- ❑ 7 Carmen Electra
- ❑ 8 Cassandra Lynn
- ❑ 9 Claudia Jordan
- ❑ 10 Crystal Harris
- ❑ 11 Deanna Brooks
- ❑ 12 Heather Rae Young
- ❑ 13 Jaime Hammer
- ❑ 14 Jennifer Korbin
- ❑ 15 Jessica Burciaga
- ❑ 16 Jessica Hall
- ❑ 17 Kara Monaco
- ❑ 18 Katie Lohmann
- ❑ 19 Lisa Gleave
- ❑ 20 Maria Kanellis
- ❑ 21 Mary Riley
- ❑ 22 Melissa Riso
- ❑ 23 Michelle Baena
- ❑ 24 Miki Black
- ❑ 25 Miriam Gonzalez
- ❑ 26 Nikki Ziering
- ❑ 27 Paige Peterson
- ❑ 28 Ryan Shamrock
- ❑ 29 Sara Underwood
- ❑ 30 Shay Lyn Veasy
- ❑ 31 Stacie Hall
- ❑ 32 Suzanne Stokes
- ❑ 33 Tamara Witmer
- ❑ 34 Tiffany Selby
- ❑ 35 Tiffany Toth
- ❑ 36 Torrie Wilson

2012 Bench Warmer Daizy Dukez Hair Cut Autographs Gold Foil

COMMON CARD 40.00 80.00
STATED PRINT RUN 15 SER. #'d SETS

- ❑ 1 Brandie Moses 40.00 80.00
- ❑ 2 Buffy Tyler 40.00 80.00
- ❑ 3 Cassandra Lynn 40.00 80.00
- ❑ 4 Jaime Hammer 40.00 80.00
- ❑ 5 Jennifer Korbin 60.00 120.00
- ❑ 6 Jessica Burciaga 60.00 120.00
- ❑ 7 Katie Lohmann 40.00 80.00
- ❑ 8 Lisa Gleave 50.00 100.00
- ❑ 9 Mary Riley 60.00 120.00
- ❑ 10 Michelle Baena 40.00 80.00
- ❑ 11 Miki Black 40.00 80.00
- ❑ 12 Nikki Ziering 40.00 80.00
- ❑ 13 Ryan Shamrock 40.00 80.00
- ❑ 14 Sandra Taylor 40.00 80.00
- ❑ 15 Shay Lyn Veasy 50.00 100.00
- ❑ 16 Stacie Hall
- ❑ 17 Tiffany Toth 40.00 80.00
- ❑ 18 Torrie Wilson 60.00 120.00

2012 Bench Warmer Daizy Dukez Hair Cut Autographs Pink Foil

STATED PRINT RUN 5 SER. #'d SETS
UNPRICED DUE TO SCARCITY

2012 Bench Warmer Daizy Dukez Hair Cut Autographs Green Foil

STATED PRINT RUN 3 SER. #'d SETS
UNPRICED DUE TO SCARCITY

2012 Bench Warmer Daizy Dukez Hair Cut Autographs Blue Foil

STATED PRINT RUN 2 SER. #'d SETS
UNPRICED DUE TO SCARCITY

2012 Bench Warmer Daizy Dukez Hair Cut Autographs Red Foil

STATED PRINT RUN 1 SER. #'d SET
UNPRICED DUE TO SCARCITY

2012 Bench Warmer Daizy Dukez High Heels Gold Foil

STATED PRINT RUN 25 SER. #'d SETS

- ❑ 1 Brande Roderick 12.00 30.00
- ❑ 2 Brandie Moses 12.00 30.00
- ❑ 3 Buffy Tyler 12.00 30.00
- ❑ 4 Carmen Electra 20.00 50.00
- ❑ 5 Cassandra Lynn 12.00 30.00
- ❑ 6 Crystal Harris 12.00 30.00
- ❑ 7 Jessica Burciaga 15.00 40.00
- ❑ 8 Jessica Hall 12.00 30.00
- ❑ 9 Katie Lohmann 12.00 30.00
- ❑ 10 Maria Kanellis 15.00 40.00
- ❑ 11 Mary Riley 20.00 50.00
- ❑ 12 Ryan Shamrock 12.00 30.00
- ❑ 13 Sara Underwood 20.00 50.00
- ❑ 14 Stacie Hall 12.00 30.00
- ❑ 15 Tamara Witmer 12.00 30.00
- ❑ 16 Tiffany Selby 12.00 30.00
- ❑ 17 Tiffany Toth 12.00 30.00
- ❑ 18 Torrie Wilson 12.00 30.00

2012 Bench Warmer Daizy Dukez High Heels Pink Foil

*PINK/15: .5X TO 1.2X GOLD
STATED PRINT RUN 15 SER. #'d SETS

2012 Bench Warmer Daizy Dukez High Heels Autographs Green Foil

STATED PRINT RUN 10 SER. #'d SETS
UNPRICED DUE TO SCARCITY

- ❑ 1 Brande Roderick
- ❑ 2 Brandie Moses
- ❑ 3 Buffy Tyler
- ❑ 4 Carmen Electra
- ❑ 5 Cassandra Lynn
- ❑ 6 Crystal Harris
- ❑ 7 Jessica Burciaga
- ❑ 8 Jessica Hall
- ❑ 9 Katie Lohmann
- ❑ 10 Maria Kanellis
- ❑ 11 Mary Riley
- ❑ 12 Ryan Shamrock
- ❑ 13 Sara Underwood
- ❑ 14 Stacie Hall
- ❑ 15 Tamara Witmer
- ❑ 16 Tiffany Selby
- ❑ 17 Tiffany Toth
- ❑ 18 Torrie Wilson

2012 Bench Warmer Daizy Dukez High Heels Autographs Blue Foil

STATED PRINT RUN 5 SER. #'d SETS
UNPRICED DUE TO SCARCITY

2012 Bench Warmer Daizy Dukez High Heels Autographs Red Foil

STATED PRINT RUN 1 SER. #'d SET
UNPRICED DUE TO SCARCITY

2012 Bench Warmer Daizy Dukez Inscriptions Gold Foil

STATED PRINT RUN 25 SER. #'d SETS

- ❑ 1 Andrea Lowell 20.00 40.00
- ❑ 2 April Scott 20.00 40.00
- ❑ 3 Bambi Lashell 20.00 40.00
- ❑ 4 Billie Jo Powers 20.00 40.00
- ❑ 5 Brande Roderick 25.00 50.00
- ❑ 6 Brandie Moses 25.00 50.00
- ❑ 7 Brandy Grace 20.00 40.00
- ❑ 8 Buffy Tyler 25.00 50.00
- ❑ 9 Candi Kita 20.00 40.00
- ❑ 10 Carmen Electra
- ❑ 11 Cassandra Lynn 25.00 50.00
- ❑ 12 Cecille Gahr 20.00 40.00
- ❑ 13 Deanna Brooks 20.00 40.00
- ❑ 14 Heather Rene Smith 20.00 40.00
- ❑ 15 Jennifer Korbin 25.00 50.00
- ❑ 16 Jessica Burciaga 30.00 60.00
- ❑ 17 Jessica Hall 25.00 50.00
- ❑ 18 Jessica Kinni 20.00 40.00
- ❑ 19 Kirsty Lingman 20.00 40.00
- ❑ 20 Lisa Gleave 25.00 50.00
- ❑ 21 Maria Kanellis 25.00 50.00
- ❑ 22 Mary Riley 25.00 50.00
- ❑ 23 Michelle Baena 20.00 40.00
- ❑ 24 Miki Black 20.00 40.00
- ❑ 25 Miriam Gonzalez 20.00 40.00
- ❑ 26 Nikki Ziering 20.00 40.00
- ❑ 27 Paige Peterson 20.00 40.00
- ❑ 28 Ryan Shamrock 20.00 40.00
- ❑ 29 Sandra Taylor 25.00 50.00
- ❑ 30 Sara Underwood 30.00 60.00
- ❑ 31 Shay Lyn Veasy 20.00 40.00
- ❑ 32 Stacie Hall 20.00 40.00
- ❑ 33 Syd Wilder 20.00 40.00
- ❑ 34 Tiffany Selby 20.00 40.00
- ❑ 35 Tiffany Toth 20.00 40.00
- ❑ 36 Yancey Taylor 20.00 40.00

2012 Bench Warmer Daizy Dukez Inscriptions Red Foil

STATED PRINT RUN 1 SER. #'d SET
UNPRICED DUE TO SCARCITY

2012 Bench Warmer Daizy Dukez Jean Shorts Swatches Gold Foil

STATED PRINT RUN 25 SER. #'d SETS

- ❑ 1 Andrea Lowell 10.00 25.00
- ❑ 2 Brande Roderick 12.00 30.00
- ❑ 3 Brandie Moses 12.00 30.00
- ❑ 4 Buffy Tyler 12.00 30.00
- ❑ 5 Candi Kita 12.00 30.00
- ❑ 6 Carmen Electra 20.00 50.00
- ❑ 7 Crystal Harris 10.00 25.00
- ❑ 8 Heather Rene Smith 10.00 25.00
- ❑ 9 Holley Dorrough 10.00 25.00
- ❑ 10 Jennifer Korbin 12.00 30.00
- ❑ 11 Jessica Burciaga 15.00 40.00
- ❑ 12 Lisa Gleave 12.00 30.00
- ❑ 13 Mary Riley 15.00 40.00
- ❑ 14 Miki Black 10.00 25.00
- ❑ 15 Miriam Gonzalez 12.00 30.00
- ❑ 16 Paige Peterson 10.00 25.00
- ❑ 17 Patrice Hollis 10.00 25.00
- ❑ 18 Ryan Shamrock 10.00 25.00
- ❑ 19 Stacie Hall 10.00 25.00
- ❑ 20 Suzanne Stokes 12.00 30.00
- ❑ 21 Tamara Witmer 10.00 25.00
- ❑ 22 Tiffany Selby 10.00 25.00
- ❑ 23 Tiffany Toth 10.00 25.00
- ❑ 24 Torrie Wilson 15.00 40.00

2012 Bench Warmer Daizy Dukez Jean Shorts Swatches Pink Foil

*PINK/15: .5X TO 1.2X GOLD
STATED PRINT RUN 15 SER. #'d SETS

2012 Bench Warmer Daizy Dukez Jean Shorts Swatches Autographs Green Foil

STATED PRINT RUN 10 SER. #'d SETS
UNPRICED DUE TO SCARCITY

- ❑ 1 Andrea Lowell
- ❑ 2 Brande Roderick
- ❑ 3 Brandie Moses
- ❑ 4 Buffy Tyler
- ❑ 5 Candi Kita
- ❑ 6 Carmen Electra
- ❑ 7 Crystal Harris
- ❑ 8 Heather Rene Smith
- ❑ 9 Holley Dorrough
- ❑ 10 Jennifer Korbin
- ❑ 11 Jessica Burciaga
- ❑ 12 Lisa Gleave
- ❑ 13 Mary Riley
- ❑ 14 Miki Black
- ❑ 15 Miriam Gonzalez
- ❑ 16 Paige Peterson
- ❑ 17 Patrice Hollis
- ❑ 18 Ryan Shamrock
- ❑ 19 Stacie Hall
- ❑ 20 Suzanne Stokes
- ❑ 21 Tamara Witmer
- ❑ 22 Tiffany Selby
- ❑ 23 Tiffany Toth
- ❑ 24 Torrie Wilson

2012 Bench Warmer Daizy Dukez Jean Shorts Swatches Autographs Blue Foil

STATED PRINT RUN 5 SER. #'d SETS
UNPRICED DUE TO SCARCITY

2012 Bench Warmer Daizy Dukez Jean Shorts Swatches Autographs Red Foil

STATED PRINT RUN 1 SER. #'d SET
UNPRICED DUE TO SCARCITY

2012 Bench Warmer Daizy Dukez Jean Shorts Dual Swatches Pink Foil

*PINK/15: .5X TO 1.2X GOLD
STATED PRINT RUN 15 SER. #'d SETS

2012 Bench Warmer Daizy Dukez Jean Shorts Dual Swatches Autographs Green Foil

STATED PRINT RUN 10 SER. #'d SETS
UNPRICED DUE TO SCARCITY

- ❑ 1 Brande Roderick
  Brandie Moses
- ❑ 2 Buffy Tyler
  Suzanne Stokes
- ❑ 3 Cassandra Lynn
  Holley Dorrough
- ❑ 4 Jessica Hall
  Stacie Hall
- ❑ 5 Mary Riley
  Shay Lyn Veasy
- ❑ 6 Sara Underwood
  Kara Monaco
- ❑ 7 Tiffany Selby
  Tiffany Toth

2012 Bench Warmer Daizy Dukez Jean Shorts Dual Swatches Autographs Blue Foil

STATED PRINT RUN 5 SER. #'d SETS
UNPRICED DUE TO SCARCITY

2012 Bench Warmer Daizy Dukez Jean Shorts Dual Swatches Autographs Red Foil

STATED PRINT RUN 1 SER. #'d SET
UNPRICED DUE TO SCARCITY

2012 Bench Warmer Daizy Dukez Jean Shorts Triple Swatches Gold Foil

STATED PRINT RUN 25 SER. #'d SETS

- ❑ 1 Deanna Brooks 12.00 30.00
  Heather Rae Young/Katie Lohmann
- ❑ 2 Jessica Burciaga 12.00 30.00
  Tamara Witmer/Cassandra Lynn
- ❑ 3 Jessica Hall 15.00 40.00
  Sara Underwood/Stacie Hall
- ❑ 4 Maria Kanellis 15.00 40.00
  Torrie Wilson/Ryan Shamrock

2012 Bench Warmer Daizy Dukez Jean Shorts Triple Swatches Pink Foil

*PINK/15: .5X TO 1.2X GOLD
STATED PRINT RUN 15 SER. #'d SETS

2012 Bench Warmer Daizy Dukez Jean Shorts Triple Swatches Autographs Green Foil

STATED PRINT RUN 10 SER. #'d SETS
UNPRICED DUE TO SCARCITY

- ❑ 1 Deanna Brooks
  Heather Rae Young/Katie Lohmann
- ❑ 2 Jessica Burciaga
  Tamara Witmer/Cassandra Lynn
- ❑ 3 Jessica Hall
  Sara Underwood/Stacie Hall
- ❑ 4 Maria Kanellis
  Torrie Wilson/Ryan Shamrock

2012 Bench Warmer Daizy Dukez Jean Shorts Triple Swatches Autographs Blue Foil

STATED PRINT RUN 5 SER. #'d SETS
UNPRICED DUE TO SCARCITY

2012 Bench Warmer Daizy Dukez Jean Shorts Triple Swatches Autographs Red Foil

STATED PRINT RUN 1 SER. #'d SET
UNPRICED DUE TO SCARCITY

2012 Bench Warmer Daizy Dukez Kiss Gold Foil

STATED PRINT RUN 25 SER. #'d SETS

- ❑ 1 Andrea Lowell 10.00 25.00
- ❑ 2 April Scott 10.00 25.00
- ❑ 3 Brande Roderick 12.00 30.00
- ❑ 4 Cassandra Lynn 10.00 25.00
- ❑ 5 Deanna Brooks 10.00 25.00
- ❑ 6 Heather Rene Smith 10.00 25.00
- ❑ 7 Jessica Burciaga 15.00 40.00
- ❑ 8 Jessica Kinni 10.00 25.00
- ❑ 9 Kyara Tyler 10.00 25.00
- ❑ 10 Maria Kanellis 15.00 40.00
- ❑ 11 Mary Riley 12.00 30.00
- ❑ 12 Melissa Riso 12.00 30.00
- ❑ 13 Nikki Ziering 10.00 25.00
- ❑ 14 Ryan Shamrock 10.00 25.00
- ❑ 15 Sandra Taylor 12.00 30.00
- ❑ 16 Sara Underwood 15.00 40.00
- ❑ 17 Stacie Hall 10.00 25.00
- ❑ 18 Syd Wilder 12.00 30.00
- ❑ 19 Catherine Bach 35.00 70.00

2012 Bench Warmer Daizy Dukez Kiss Pink Foil

*PINK/15: .5X TO 1.2X GOLD
STATED PRINT RUN 15 SER. #'d SETS

2012 Bench Warmer Daizy Dukez Kiss Autographs Green Foil

STATED PRINT RUN 10 SER. #'d SETS
UNPRICED DUE TO SCARCITY

- ❑ 1 Andrea Lowell
- ❑ 2 April Scott
- ❑ 3 Brande Roderick
- ❑ 4 Cassandra Lynn
- ❑ 5 Deanna Brooks
- ❑ 6 Heather Rene Smith
- ❑ 7 Jessica Burciaga
- ❑ 8 Jessica Kinni
- ❑ 9 Kyara Tyler
- ❑ 10 Maria Kanellis
- ❑ 11 Mary Riley
- ❑ 12 Melissa Riso
- ❑ 13 Nikki Ziering
- ❑ 14 Ryan Shamrock
- ❑ 15 Sandra Taylor
- ❑ 16 Sara Underwood
- ❑ 17 Stacie Hall
- ❑ 18 Syd Wilder
- ❑ 19 Catherine Bach

2012 Bench Warmer Daizy Dukez Kiss Autographs Blue Foil

STATED PRINT RUN 5 SER. #'d SETS
UNPRICED DUE TO SCARCITY

2012 Bench Warmer Daizy Dukez Kiss Autographs Red Foil

STATED PRINT RUN 1 SER. #'d SET
UNPRICED DUE TO SCARCITY

2012 Bench Warmer Daizy Dukez The Original Daisy Duke Autographs

STATED PRINT RUN 1-69
NO PRICING ON CARDS #'d TO 10 OR LESS

- ❑ 1 Catherine Bach Gold/69 20.00 50.00
- ❑ 2 Catherine Bach Pink/25 25.00 60.00
- ❑ 3 Catherine Bach Green/10
- ❑ 4 Catherine Bach Blue/5
- ❑ 5 Catherine Bach Red/1

2012 Bench Warmer 4th of July Autographs

COMPLETE SET (10) 40.00 80.00

- ❑ 1 Kyara Tyler 6.00 15.00
- ❑ 2 Stacie Hall 6.00 15.00
- ❑ 3 Crystal Harris 8.00 20.00
- ❑ 4 Jennifer Walcott 8.00 20.00
- ❑ 5 Jessica Burciaga 6.00 15.00
- ❑ 6 Lisa Gleave 6.00 15.00
- ❑ 7 Michelle Baena 6.00 15.00
- ❑ 8 Britany Lauren 8.00 20.00
- ❑ 9 Mary Riley 8.00 20.00
- ❑ 10 Jessica Kinni 6.00 15.00
- ❑ 11 Amanda Carrier 8.00 20.00
- ❑ 12 Flo Jalin 15.00 40.00
- ❑ 13 Julianna Prada 6.00 15.00
- ❑ 14 Kara Monaco 15.00 40.00
- ❑ 15 Maria Kanellis 8.00 20.00
- ❑ 16 Melissa Riso 6.00 15.00

2012 Bench Warmer Happy Easter Autographs

COMPLETE SET (5) 20.00 40.00

❑ 1 April Scott 6.00 15.00
❑ 2 Caitlin O'Connor 4.00 10.00
❑ 3 Kara Monaco 8.00 20.00
❑ 4 Lisa Gleave 12.00 30.00
❑ 5 Lisa Ligon 10.00 25.00

2012 Bench Warmer Happy Father's Day Autographs

COMPLETE SET (10) 50.00 100.00

❑ 1 Alicia Johnson 6.00 15.00
❑ 2 Billie Jo Powers 5.00 12.00
❑ 3 Brandie Moses 8.00 20.00
❑ 4 Jessica Hall 8.00 20.00
❑ 5 Jessica Kinni 6.00 15.00
❑ 6 Kara Monaco 5.00 12.00
❑ 7 Maria Kanellis 8.00 20.00
❑ 8 Melissa Riso 5.00 12.00
❑ 9 Sandra Taylor 8.00 20.00
❑ 10 Stacie Hall 5.00 12.00

2012 Bench Warmer Happy Mother's Day Autographs

COMPLETE SET (3) 15.00 30.00

❑ 1 Cassandra Lynn 6.00 15.00
❑ 2 Michelle Baena 6.00 15.00
❑ 3 Nikki Ziering 6.00 15.00

2012 Bench Warmer Happy New Year Autographs Green Foil

STATED PRINT RUN 10 SER. #'d SETS
UNPRICED DUE TO SCARCITY

2012 Bench Warmer Happy New Year Autographs Blue Foil

STATED PRINT RUN 5 SER. #'d SETS
UNPRICED DUE TO SCARCITY

2012 Bench Warmer Happy New Year Autographs Red Foil

STATED PRINT RUN 1 SER. #'d SET
UNPRICED DUE TO SCARCITY

2012 Bench Warmer Happy New Year Happy Holidays Autographs Pink Foil

*PINK/25: X TO X BASIC CARDS

2012 Bench Warmer Happy New Year Happy Holidays Autographs Green Foil

STATED PRINT RUN 10 SER. #'d SETS
UNPRICED DUE TO SCARCITY

2012 Bench Warmer Happy New Year Happy Holidays Autographs Blue Foil

STATED PRINT RUN 5 SER. #'d SETS
UNPRICED DUE TO SCARCITY

2012 Bench Warmer Happy New Year Happy Holidays Autographs Red Foil

STATED PRINT RUN 1 SER. #'d SET.
UNPRICED DUE TO SCARCITY

2012 Bench Warmer Holiday Autographs Blue Gold Foil

❑ 1 Andrea Lowell
❑ 2 April Scott
❑ 3 Athena Lundberg
❑ 4 Billie Jo Powers
❑ 5 Brande Roderick
❑ 6 Brandie Moses
❑ 7 Brandy Grace
❑ 8 Brittany Herrera
❑ 9 Brooke Morales
❑ 10 Caitlin O'Connor
❑ 11 Candace Kita
❑ 12 Carrie Minter Lagree
❑ 13 Casey Durkin
❑ 14 Cassandra Lynn
❑ 15 Cecille Gahr
❑ 16 Claudia Jordan
❑ 17 Cristal Camden
❑ 18 Crystal Colar
❑ 19 Crystal Harris
❑ 20 Deanna Brooks
❑ 21 Enya Flack
❑ 22 Flo Jalin
❑ 23 Heather Rae Young
❑ 24 Holley Dorrough
❑ 25 Jaime Hammer
❑ 26 Jenae Alt
❑ 27 Jennifer England
❑ 28 Jennifer Korbin
❑ 29 Jessica Burciaga
❑ 30 Jessica Rockwell
❑ 31 Julianna Prada
❑ 32 Kara Monaco
❑ 33 Kathryn Smith
❑ 34 Katie Lohmann
❑ 35 Lana Kinnear
❑ 36 Lisa Gleave
❑ 37 Lisa Ligon
❑ 38 Lora Peterson
❑ 39 Maria Kanellis
❑ 40 Mary Riley
❑ 41 Megan Hauserman
❑ 42 Michelle Baena
❑ 43 Miki Black
❑ 44 Miriam Gonzalez
❑ 45 Molly Shea
❑ 46 Nicole Bennett
❑ 47 Nikki Ziering
❑ 48 Sandra Taylor
❑ 49 Shannon Malone
❑ 50 Shay Lyn Veasy
❑ 51 Syd Wilder
❑ 52 Talor Marion
❑ 53 Tamara Witmer
❑ 54 Tanea Brooks
❑ 55 Tiffany Selby
❑ 56 Tiffany Toth
❑ 57 Tina Jordan
❑ 58 Tishara Cousino
❑ 59 Torrie Wilson
❑ 60 Traci Bingham

2012 Bench Warmer Holiday Autographs Blue Purple Foil

*PURPLE/25: X TO X BASIC CARDS

2012 Bench Warmer Holiday Autographs Blue Pink Foil

UNPRICED PINK PRINT RUN 15 SER. #'d SETS

2012 Bench Warmer Holiday Autographs Blue Green Foil

UNPRICED GREEN PRINT RUN 10 SER. #'d SETS

2012 Bench Warmer Holiday Autographs Blue Blue Foil

UNPRICED BLUE PRINT RUN 5 SER. #'d SETS

2012 Bench Warmer Holiday Autographs Blue Red Foil

UNPRICED RED PRINT RUN 1 SER. #'d SET

2012 Bench Warmer Holiday Autographs Green Gold Foil

STATED ODDS ONE PER BOX

2012 Bench Warmer Holiday Autographs Red Air Mail Gold Foil

*RED GOLD/25: X TO X BLUE GOLD

2012 Bench Warmer Holiday Autographs Red Air Mail Green Foil

UNPRICED GREEN PRINT RUN 10 SER. #'d SETS

2012 Bench Warmer Holiday Autographs Red Air Mail Blue Foil

UNPRICED BLUE PRINT RUN 5 SER. #'d SETS

2012 Bench Warmer Holiday Autographs Red Air Mail Red Foil

UNPRICED RED PRINT RUN 1 SER. #'d SET

2012 Bench Warmer Holiday Dec 25th Autographs Gold Foil

UNPRICED GOLD PRINT RUN 12 SER. #'d SETS

❑ 1 April Scott
❑ 2 Brande Roderick
❑ 3 Brandie Moses
❑ 4 Carmen Electra
❑ 5 Cassandra Lynn
❑ 6 Crystal Harris
❑ 7 Jennifer Korbin
❑ 8 Jessica Burciaga
❑ 9 Lisa Gleave
❑ 10 Mary Riley
❑ 11 Ryan Shamrock
❑ 12 Sara Underwood

2012 Bench Warmer Holiday Dec 25th Autographs Green Foil

UNPRICED GREEN PRINT RUN 5 SER. #'d SETS

2012 Bench Warmer Holiday Dec 25th Autographs Blue Foil

UNPRICED BLUE PRINT RUN 2 SER. #'d SETS

2012 Bench Warmer Holiday Dec 25th Autographs Red Foil

UNPRICED RED PRINT RUN 1 SER. #'d SET

2012 Bench Warmer Holiday Letter Patch Autographs Green Foil

ANNOUNCED PRINT RUN 20-45

❑ 1 Carmen Electra/30*
❑ 2 Cassandra Lynn/45*
❑ 3 Jaime Hammer/25*
❑ 4 Jennifer Korbin/40*
❑ 5 Jessica Burciaga/35*
❑ 6 Jessica Hall/35*
❑ 7 Julianna Prada/40*
❑ 8 Kara Monaco/20*
❑ 9 Lisa Gleave/20*
❑ 10 Maria Kanellis/25*
❑ 11 Mary Riley/20*
❑ 12 Miriam Gonzalez/30*
❑ 13 Nicole Bennett/30*
❑ 14 Nikki Ziering/25*
❑ 15 Sandra Taylor/30*
❑ 16 Sara Underwood/20*
❑ 17 Tamara Witmer/30*

2012 Bench Warmer Holiday Letter Patch Autographs Red Foil

UNPRICED RED ANNC'D PRINT RUN 4-9

2012 Bench Warmer Holiday Mistletoe Kiss Gold Foil

STATED PRINT RUN 15 SER. #'d SETS

❑ 1 Brande Roderick
❑ 2 Brandie Moses
❑ 3 Brandy Grace
❑ 4 Casey Durkin
❑ 5 Jennifer England
❑ 6 Jennifer Korbin
❑ 7 Jessica Burciaga
❑ 8 Jessica Hall
❑ 9 Katie Lohmann
❑ 10 Lisa Gleave AUTO
❑ 11 Mary Riley
❑ 12 Michelle Baena
❑ 13 Miriam Gonzalez
❑ 14 Ryan Shamrock
❑ 15 Sandra Taylor
❑ 16 Sara Underwood
❑ 17 Tamara Witmer
❑ 18 Tiffany Toth

2012 Bench Warmer Holiday Mistletoe Kiss Autographs Green Foil

UNPRICED GREEN PRINT RUN 10 SER. #'d SETS

❑ 1 Brande Roderick
❑ 2 Brandie Moses
❑ 3 Brandy Grace
❑ 4 Casey Durkin
❑ 5 Jennifer England
❑ 6 Jennifer Korbin
❑ 7 Jessica Burciaga
❑ 8 Jessica Hall
❑ 9 Katie Lohmann
❑ 10 Lisa Gleave
❑ 11 Mary Riley
❑ 12 Michelle Baena
❑ 13 Miriam Gonzalez
❑ 14 Ryan Shamrock
❑ 15 Sandra Taylor
❑ 16 Sara Underwood
❑ 17 Tamara Witmer
❑ 18 Tiffany Toth

2012 Bench Warmer Holiday Mistletoe Kiss Autographs Blue Foil

UNPRICED BLUE PRINT RUN 5 SER. #'d SETS

2012 Bench Warmer Holiday Mistletoe Kiss Autographs Red Foil

UNPRICED RED PRINT RUN 1 SER. #'d SET

2012 Bench Warmer Holiday Naughty or Nice Dual Autographs Gold Foil

STATED PRINT RUN 15 SER. #'d SETS

❑ 1 Carmen Electra
❑ 2 Cecille Gahr
Nicole Bennett
❑ 3 Cristal Camden
Kara Monaco
❑ 4 Jennifer England
Lisa Gleave
❑ 5 Jessica Hall
Sara Underwood
❑ 6 Mary Riley
Julianna Prada
❑ 7 Michelle Baena
Cassandra Lynn
❑ 8 Sandra Taylor
Nikki Ziering

2012 Bench Warmer Holiday Naughty or Nice Dual Autographs Green Foil

UNPRICED GREEN PRINT RUN 10 SER. #'d SETS

2012 Bench Warmer Holiday Naughty or Nice Dual Autographs Blue Foil

UNPRICED BLUE PRINT RUN 5 SER. #'d SETS

2012 Bench Warmer Holiday Naughty or Nice Dual Autographs Red Foil

UNPRICED RED PRINT RUN 1 SER. #'d SET

2012 Bench Warmer Holiday Presents Autographs Red Foil

STATED PRINT RUN 1 SER. #'d SET
UNPRICED DUE TO SCARCITY

❑ 1 Candace Kita
❑ 2 Lisa Ligon

2012 Bench Warmer Holiday Shoes Gold Foil

STATED PRINT RUN 50 SER. #'d SETS

❑ 1 Brandie Moses
❑ 2 Carmen Electra
❑ 3 Jennifer Korbin
❑ 4 Jessica Burciaga
❑ 5 Lisa Gleave
❑ 6 Maria Kanellis
❑ 7 Miriam Gonzalez
❑ 8 Suzanne Stokes

2012 Bench Warmer Holiday Shoes Pink Foil

*PINK/25: X TO X GOLD

2012 Bench Warmer Holiday Shoes Autographs Green Foil

UNPRICED GREEN PRINT RUN 10 SER. #'d SETS

❑ 1 Brandie Moses
❑ 2 Carmen Electra
❑ 3 Jennifer Korbin
❑ 4 Jessica Burciaga
❑ 5 Lisa Gleave
❑ 6 Maria Kanellis
❑ 7 Miriam Gonzalez
❑ 8 Suzanne Stokes

2012 Bench Warmer Holiday Shoes Autographs Blue Foil

UNPRICED BLUE PRINT RUN 5 SER. #'d SETS

2012 Bench Warmer Holiday Shoes Autographs Red Foil

UNPRICED RED PRINT RUN 1 SER. #'d SET

2012 Bench Warmer Holiday Swatches Gold Foil

STATED PRINT RUN 50 SER. #'d SETS

❑ 1 Billie Jo Powers
❑ 2 Brande Roderick
❑ 3 Brandie Moses
❑ 4 Brandy Grace
❑ 5 Candace Kita
❑ 6 Carmen Electra
❑ 7 Cassandra Lynn
❑ 8 Crystal Harris
❑ 9 Jennifer Korbin
❑ 10 Jessica Burciaga
❑ 11 Katie Lohmann
❑ 12 Lisa Gleave
❑ 13 Maria Kanellis
❑ 14 Mary Riley
❑ 15 Nicole Bennett
❑ 16 Nikki Ziering
❑ 17 Ryan Shamrock
❑ 18 Sandra Taylor
❑ 19 Sara Underwood
❑ 20 Shay Lyn Veasy
❑ 21 Tiffany Toth
❑ 22 Tishara Cousino

2012 Bench Warmer Holiday Swatches Pink Foil

*PINK/25: X TO X GOLD

2012 Bench Warmer Holiday Wish List Inscriptions Autographs Gold Foil

STATED PRINT RUN 25 SER. #'d SETS

❑ 1 Andrea Lowell
❑ 2 Brande Roderick
❑ 3 Brandie Moses
❑ 4 Brandy Grace
❑ 5 Brittany Herrera
❑ 6 Carrie Minter Lagree
❑ 7 Cassandra Lynn
❑ 8 Cristal Camden
❑ 9 Flo Jalin
❑ 10 Jaime Hammer
❑ 11 Jennifer England
❑ 12 Jennifer Korbin
❑ 13 Jessica Burciaga
❑ 14 Jessica Hall
❑ 15 Lisa Gleave
❑ 16 Mary Riley
❑ 17 Miriam Gonzalez
❑ 18 Nikki Ziering
❑ 19 Sandra Taylor
❑ 20 Tiffany Selby
❑ NNO Mystery Exchange

2012 Bench Warmer Hot For Teacher

STATED PRINT RUN 25 SER. #'d SETS

❑ 1 Angela Fong 8.00 20.00
❑ 2 April Scott 8.00 20.00
❑ 3 Athena Lundberg
❑ 4 Billie Jo Powers 8.00 20.00
❑ 5 Brande Roderick 8.00 20.00
❑ 6 Brandie Moses
❑ 7 Brandy Grace 8.00 20.00
❑ 8 Brittany Herrera 8.00 20.00
❑ 9 Brooke Morales 8.00 20.00
❑ 10 Buffy Tyler 8.00 20.00
❑ 11 Candace Kita 8.00 20.00
❑ 12 Carrie Minter 8.00 20.00
❑ 13 Cassandra Lynn 8.00 20.00
❑ 14 Cecille Gahr 8.00 20.00
❑ 15 Claudia Jordan
❑ 16 Cristal Camden 8.00 20.00
❑ 17 Crystal Harris 8.00 20.00
❑ 18 Enya Flack 8.00 20.00
❑ 19 Flo Jalin 8.00 20.00
❑ 20 Jaime Hammer 8.00 20.00
❑ 21 Jenae Alt 8.00 20.00
❑ 22 Jennifer England 8.00 20.00
❑ 23 Jennifer Korbin 10.00 25.00
❑ 24 Jennifer Lyons 8.00 20.00
❑ 25 Jessica Burciaga 12.00 30.00
❑ 26 Kara Monaco 8.00 20.00
❑ 27 Katarina Van Derham 8.00 20.00
❑ 28 Katie Lohmann 8.00 20.00
❑ 29 Kirsty Lingman 8.00 20.00
❑ 30 Lisa Gleave 8.00 20.00
❑ 31 Lisa Ligon 8.00 20.00
❑ 32 Maria Kanellis 10.00 25.00
❑ 33 Mary Riley 10.00 25.00
❑ 34 Megan Hauserman 8.00 20.00
❑ 35 Michelle Baena 8.00 20.00
❑ 36 Miki Black 8.00 20.00
❑ 37 Miriam Gonzalez 10.00 25.00
❑ 38 Nicole Bennett 8.00 20.00
❑ 39 Nikki Ziering 8.00 20.00
❑ 40 Paige Peterson 8.00 20.00
❑ 41 Sandra Taylor 8.00 20.00
❑ 42 Shay Lyn Veasy 8.00 20.00
❑ 43 Suzanne Stokes
❑ 44 Tamara Witmer 8.00 20.00
❑ 45 Tiffany Selby 8.00 20.00
❑ 46 Tiffany Toth 8.00 20.00
❑ 47 Tishara Cousino 8.00 20.00
❑ 48 Torrie Wilson 10.00 25.00
❑ 49 Traci Bingham 8.00 20.00
❑ 50 Trudi Pallas 8.00 20.00
❑ 51 Yancey Todd
❑ 52 Yvette Nelson 8.00 20.00
❑ 53 Sara Underwood
❑ BE Benchie 8.00 20.00
❑ BW Brian Wallos 8.00 20.00

2012 Bench Warmer Hot For Teacher Pink Foil

STATED PRINT RUN 15 SER. #'d SETS

2012 Bench Warmer Hot For Teacher Purple Foil

STATED PRINT RUN 20 SER. #'d SETS

2012 Bench Warmer Hot For Teacher Green Foil

STATED PRINT RUN 10 SER. #'d SETS
UNPRICED DUE TO SCARCITY

2012 Bench Warmer Hot For Teacher Blue Foil

STATED PRINT RUN 5 SER. #'d SETS
UNPRICED DUE TO SCARCITY

2012 Bench Warmer Hot For Teacher Red Foil

STATED PRINT RUN 1 SER. #'d SET
UNPRICED DUE TO SCARCITY

2012 Bench Warmer Hot For Teacher A+ Autographs Green Foil

STATED PRINT RUN 3 SER. #'d SETS
UNPRICED DUE TO SCARCITY

❑ 1 Andrea Lowell
❑ 2 April Scott
❑ 3 Athena Lundberg
❑ 4 Billie Jo Powers
❑ 5 Brande Roderick
❑ 6 Brandie Moses
❑ 7 Brooke Morales
❑ 8 Buffy Tyler
❑ 9 Carmen Electra
❑ 10 Cassandra Lynn
❑ 11 Cecille Gahr
❑ 12 Claudia Jordan
❑ 13 Crystal Harris
❑ 14 Flo Jalin
❑ 15 Jennifer England
❑ 16 Jennifer Korbin
❑ 17 Jennifer Walcott
❑ 18 Jessica Burciaga
❑ 19 Jessica Hall
❑ 20 Kara Monaco
❑ 21 Katarina Van Derham
❑ 22 Katie Lohmann
❑ 23 Kirsty Lingman
❑ 24 Lisa Gleave
❑ 25 Lisa Ligon
❑ 26 Maria Kanellis
❑ 27 Mary Riley
❑ 28 Megan Hauserman
❑ 29 Miki Black
❑ 30 Miriam Gonzalez
❑ 31 Nicole Bennett
❑ 32 Nikki Ziering
❑ 33 Rachel Bernstein
❑ 34 Ryan Shamrock
❑ 35 Sandra Taylor
❑ 36 Sara Underwood
❑ 37 Shay Lyn Veasy
❑ 38 Spencer Scott
❑ 39 Stacie Hall
❑ 40 Suzanne Stokes
❑ 41 Tamara Witmer
❑ 42 Tiffany Selby
❑ 43 Tiffany Toth
❑ 44 Torrie Wilson
❑ 45 Traci Bingham

2012 Bench Warmer Hot For Teacher A+ Autographs Blue Foil

STATED PRINT RUN 2 SER. #'d SETS
UNPRICED DUE TO SCARCITY

2012 Bench Warmer Hot For Teacher A+ Autographs Red Foil

STATED PRINT RUN 1 SER. #'d SET
UNPRICED DUE TO SCARCITY

2012 Bench Warmer Hot For Teacher Classic Cuts Hair Autographs Gold Foil

STATED PRINT RUN 15 SER. #'d SETS
UNPRICED DUE TO SCARCITY

❑ 1 Brande Roderick
❑ 2 Brandie Moses
❑ 3 Cecille Gahr
❑ 4 Jennifer Korbin
❑ 5 Jessica Burciaga
❑ 6 Lisa Gleave
❑ 7 Michelle Baena
❑ 8 Cassandra Lynn
❑ 9 Tamara Witmer
❑ 10 Nicole Bennett
❑ 11 Nikki Ziering
❑ 12 Sandra Taylor
❑ 13 Jaime Hammer
❑ 14 Kara Monaco
❑ 15 Tiffany Selby
❑ 16 Buffy Tyler
❑ 17 Crystal Harris
❑ 18 Tiffany Toth
❑ 19 Suzanne Stokes
❑ 20 Maria Kanellis
❑ 21 Brooke Morales
❑ 22 Jessica Hall
❑ 23 Katie Lohmann
❑ 24 Candace Kita
❑ 25 Mary Riley
❑ 26 Jennifer England
❑ 27 Flo Jalin

2012 Bench Warmer Hot For Teacher Classic Cuts Hair Autographs Green Foil

STATED PRINT RUN 5 SER. #'d SETS
UNPRICED DUE TO SCARCITY

2012 Bench Warmer Hot For Teacher Classic Cuts Hair Autographs Blue Foil

STATED PRINT RUN 3 SER. #'d SETS
UNPRICED DUE TO SCARCITY

2012 Bench Warmer Hot For Teacher Classic Cuts Hair Autographs Red Foil

STATED PRINT RUN 1 SER. #'d SET
UNPRICED DUE TO SCARCITY

2012 Bench Warmer Hot For Teacher Freshman Class Autographs Green Foil

STATED PRINT RUN 10 SER. #'d SETS
UNPRICED DUE TO SCARCITY

❑ 1 Carmen Electra
❑ 2 Melissa Riso
❑ 3 Casey Durkin
❑ 4 Caitlin O'Connor
❑ 5 Billie Jo Powers
❑ 6 Carolyn Martin
❑ 7 Alicia Johnson
❑ 8 Crystal Harris
❑ 9 Angela Fong
❑ 10 Trudi Pallas
❑ 11 Jennifer Lyons

2012 Bench Warmer Hot For Teacher Freshman Class Autographs Blue Foil

STATED PRINT RUN 5 SER. #'d SETS
UNPRICED DUE TO SCARCITY

2012 Bench Warmer Hot For Teacher Freshman Class Autographs Red Foil

STATED PRINT RUN 1 SER. #'d SET
UNPRICED DUE TO SCARCITY

2012 Bench Warmer Hot For Teacher Hall Pass Autographs Gold Foil

STATED PRINT RUN 15 SER. #'d SETS
UNPRICED DUE TO SCARCITY

❑ HP1 Sara Underwood
❑ HP2 Katarina Van Derham
❑ HP3 Deanna Brooks
❑ HP4 Shay Lyn Veasy
❑ HP5 Kara Monaco
❑ HP6 Athena Lundberg
❑ HP7 Andrea Lowell
❑ HP8 Stacie Hall
❑ HP9 Heather Rae Young
❑ HP10 Miriam Gonzalez
❑ HP11 Brandie Moses
❑ HP12 Talor Marion

2012 Bench Warmer Hot For Teacher Hall Pass Autographs Green Foil

STATED PRINT RUN 10 SER. #'d SETS
UNPRICED DUE TO SCARCITY

2012 Bench Warmer Hot For Teacher Hall Pass Autographs Blue Foil

STATED PRINT RUN 5 SER. #'d SETS
UNPRICED DUE TO SCARCITY

2012 Bench Warmer Hot For Teacher Hall Pass Autographs Red Foil

STATED PRINT RUN 1 SER. #'d SET
UNPRICED DUE TO SCARCITY

2012 Bench Warmer Hot For Teacher High Heels Gold Foil

STATED PRINT RUN 50 SER. #'d SETS

❑ 1 Carmen Electra 12.00 30.00
❑ 2 Mary Riley 12.00 30.00
❑ 3 Brande Roderick 8.00 20.00
❑ 4 Torrie Wilson 10.00 25.00
❑ 5 Michelle Baena 10.00 25.00
❑ 6 Brandy Grace 8.00 20.00
❑ 7 Nikki Ziering 8.00 20.00
❑ 8 Kara Monaco 10.00 25.00
❑ 9 Crystal Harris 8.00 20.00
❑ 10 Miki Black 8.00 20.00
❑ 11 Jessica Burciaga 12.00 30.00

❑ 12 Tishara Cousino 8.00 20.00
❑ 13 Suzanne Stokes 8.00 20.00
❑ 14 Cassandra Lynn 8.00 20.00
❑ 15 Claudia Jordan 8.00 20.00

2012 Bench Warmer Hot For Teacher High Heels Pink Foil

STATED PRINT RUN 25 SER. #'d SETS

2012 Bench Warmer Hot For Teacher High Heels Autographs Green Foil

STATED PRINT RUN 10 SER. #'d SETS
UNPRICED DUE TO SCARCITY

❑ 1 Carmen Electra
❑ 2 Mary Riley
❑ 3 Brande Roderick
❑ 4 Torrie Wilson
❑ 5 Michelle Baena
❑ 6 Brandy Grace
❑ 7 Nikki Ziering
❑ 8 Kara Monaco
❑ 9 Crystal Harris
❑ 10 Miki Black
❑ 11 Jessica Burciaga
❑ 12 Tishara Cousino
❑ 13 Suzanne Stokes
❑ 14 Cassandra Lynn
❑ 15 Claudia Jordan

2012 Bench Warmer Hot For Teacher High Heels Autographs Blue Foil

STATED PRINT RUN 5 SER. #'d SETS
UNPRICED DUE TO SCARCITY

2012 Bench Warmer Hot For Teacher High Heels Autographs Red Foil

STATED PRINT RUN 1 SER. #'d SET
UNPRICED DUE TO SCARCITY

2012 Bench Warmer Hot For Teacher Inscriptions Gold Foil

STATED PRINT RUN 25 SER. #'d SETS

❑ 1 Mary Riley 25.00 50.00
❑ 2 Kara Monaco 20.00 40.00
❑ 3 Lisa Gleave 20.00 40.00
❑ 4 Jessica Burciaga 25.00 50.00
❑ 5 Brande Roderick 20.00 40.00
❑ 6 Tiffany Toth 15.00 30.00
❑ 7 Jennifer Korbin 20.00 40.00
❑ 8 Miriam Gonzalez 20.00 40.00
❑ 9 Michelle Baena
❑ 10 Tamara Witmer 15.00 30.00
❑ 11 Nikki Ziering 15.00 30.00
❑ 12 Shay Lyn Veasy 15.00 30.00
❑ 13 Melissa Riso 15.00 30.00
❑ 14 Brandie Moses 15.00 30.00
❑ 15 Tiffany Selby 15.00 30.00
❑ 16 Cecille Gahr 15.00 30.00
❑ 17 Nicole Bennett 15.00 30.00
❑ 18 Buffy Tyler 15.00 30.00
❑ 19 Kirsty Lingman 15.00 30.00
❑ 20 Cristal Camden 15.00 30.00
❑ 21 Cassandra Lynn 15.00 30.00
❑ 22 Lisa Ligon 15.00 30.00
❑ 23 Brandy Grace 15.00 30.00
❑ 24 Miki Black 15.00 30.00
❑ 25 Sara Underwood 30.00 60.00
❑ 26 Maria Kanellis 20.00 40.00
❑ 27 Sandra Taylor 20.00 40.00
❑ 28 Candace Kita 15.00 30.00
❑ 29 Billie Jo Powers 15.00 30.00
❑ 30 Stacie Hall
❑ 31 Jennifer England 15.00 30.00
❑ 32 Jaime Hammer 15.00 30.00
❑ 33 Flo Jalin 15.00 30.00
❑ 34 Athena Lundberg 15.00 30.00
❑ 35 Claudia Jordan 15.00 30.00
❑ 36 Crystal Harris
❑ 37 Brooke Morales 15.00 30.00
❑ 38 Paige Peterson 15.00 30.00
❑ 39 Spencer Scott

2012 Bench Warmer Hot For Teacher Inscriptions Red Foil

STATED PRINT RUN 1 SER. #'d SET
UNPRICED DUE TO SCARCITY

2012 Bench Warmer Hot For Teacher Kiss Gold Foil

STATED PRINT RUN 15 SER. #'d SETS

❑ 1 Mary Riley 25.00 50.00
❑ 2 Jessica Burciaga 20.00 40.00
❑ 3 Tiffany Toth 10.00 25.00
❑ 4 Jennifer Korbin 12.00 30.00
❑ 5 Miriam Gonzalez 12.00 30.00
❑ 6 Michelle Baena 10.00 25.00
❑ 7 Brande Roderick 12.00 30.00
❑ 8 Nikki Ziering 10.00 25.00
❑ 9 Brandy Grace 10.00 25.00
❑ 10 Enya Flack 10.00 25.00
❑ 11 Lisa Gleave 10.00 25.00
❑ 12 Tiffany Selby 10.00 25.00
❑ 13 Cecille Gahr 10.00 25.00
❑ 14 Nicole Bennett 10.00 25.00
❑ 15 Buffy Tyler 10.00 25.00
❑ 16 Brandie Moses 10.00 25.00
❑ 17 Cristal Camden 10.00 25.00
❑ 18 Tamara Witmer 10.00 25.00
❑ 19 Jaime Hammer 10.00 25.00
❑ 20 Caitlin O'Connor 10.00 25.00
❑ 21 Miki Black 10.00 25.00
❑ 22 Carrie Minter 10.00 25.00
❑ 23 Talor Marion 10.00 25.00
❑ 24 Athena Lundberg 10.00 25.00
❑ 25 April Scott 10.00 25.00
❑ 26 Jennifer Walcott
❑ 27 Sara Underwood 25.00 50.00
❑ 28 Angela Fong 10.00 25.00
❑ 29 Jenae Alt 10.00 25.00
❑ 30 Sandra Taylor

2012 Bench Warmer Hot For Teacher Kiss Autographs Green Foil

STATED PRINT RUN 10 SER. #'d SETS
UNPRICED DUE TO SCARCITY

❑ 1 Mary Riley
❑ 2 Jessica Burciaga
❑ 3 Tiffany Toth
❑ 4 Jennifer Korbin
❑ 5 Miriam Gonzalez
❑ 6 Michelle Baena
❑ 7 Brande Roderick
❑ 8 Nikki Ziering
❑ 9 Brandy Grace
❑ 10 Enya Flack
❑ 11 Lisa Gleave
❑ 12 Tiffany Selby
❑ 13 Cecille Gahr
❑ 14 Nicole Bennett
❑ 15 Buffy Tyler
❑ 16 Brandie Moses
❑ 17 Cristal Camden
❑ 18 Tamara Witmer
❑ 19 Jaime Hammer
❑ 20 Caitlin O'Connor
❑ 21 Miki Black
❑ 22 Carrie Minter
❑ 23 Talor Marion
❑ 24 Athena Lundberg
❑ 25 April Scott
❑ 26 Jennifer Walcott
❑ 27 Sara Underwood
❑ 28 Angela Fong
❑ 29 Jenae Alt
❑ 30 Sandra Taylor

2012 Bench Warmer Hot For Teacher Kiss Autographs Blue Foil

STATED PRINT RUN 5 SER. #'d SETS
UNPRICED DUE TO SCARCITY

2012 Bench Warmer Hot For Teacher Kiss Autographs Red Foil

STATED PRINT RUN 1 SER. #'d SET
UNPRICED DUE TO SCARCITY

2012 Bench Warmer Hot For Teacher Knee High Swatches Gold Foil

STATED PRINT RUN 50 SER. #'d SETS

❑ 1 Carmen Electra 20.00 40.00
❑ 2 Mary Riley 20.00 40.00
❑ 3 Brande Roderick 10.00 25.00
❑ 4 Kara Monaco 10.00 25.00
❑ 5 Torrie Wilson 12.00 30.00
❑ 6 Tiffany Toth 10.00 25.00
❑ 7 Jessica Burciaga 12.00 30.00
❑ 8 Lisa Gleave 10.00 25.00
❑ 9 Katie Lohmann 10.00 25.00
❑ 10 Tiffany Selby 10.00 25.00
❑ 11 Nikki Ziering 10.00 25.00
❑ 12 Buffy Tyler 10.00 25.00
❑ 13 Jennifer Korbin 12.00 30.00
❑ 14 Cassandra Lynn 10.00 25.00
❑ 15 Brandie Moses 10.00 25.00
❑ 16 Crystal Harris 10.00 25.00
❑ 17 Nicole Bennett 10.00 25.00
❑ 18 Shay Lyn Veasy 10.00 25.00

2012 Bench Warmer Hot For Teacher Knee High Swatches Pink Foil

STATED PRINT RUN 25 SER. #'d SETS

2012 Bench Warmer Hot For Teacher Knee High Swatches Autographs Green Foil

STATED PRINT RUN 10 SER. #'d SETS
UNPRICED DUE TO SCARCITY

❑ 1 Carmen Electra
❑ 2 Mary Riley
❑ 3 Brande Roderick
❑ 4 Kara Monaco
❑ 5 Torrie Wilson
❑ 6 Tiffany Toth
❑ 7 Jessica Burciaga
❑ 8 Lisa Gleave
❑ 9 Katie Lohmann
❑ 10 Tiffany Selby
❑ 11 Nikki Ziering
❑ 12 Buffy Tyler
❑ 13 Jennifer Korbin
❑ 14 Cassandra Lynn
❑ 15 Brandie Moses
❑ 16 Crystal Harris
❑ 17 Nicole Bennett
❑ 18 Shay Lyn Veasy

2012 Bench Warmer Hot For Teacher Knee High Swatches Autographs Blue Foil

STATED PRINT RUN 5 SER. #'d SETS
UNPRICED DUE TO SCARCITY

2012 Bench Warmer Hot For Teacher Knee High Swatches Autographs Red Foil

STATED PRINT RUN 1 SER. #'d SET
UNPRICED DUE TO SCARCITY

2012 Bench Warmer Hot For Teacher Schoolgirl Swatches Gold Foil

STATED PRINT RUN 50 SER. #'d SETS

❑ 1 Carmen Electra 20.00 40.00
❑ 2 Mary Riley 20.00 40.00
❑ 3 Maria Kanellis 12.00 30.00
❑ 4 Kara Monaco 10.00 25.00
❑ 5 Torrie Wilson 12.00 30.00
❑ 6 Tiffany Toth 10.00 25.00
❑ 7 Jessica Burciaga 20.00 40.00
❑ 8 Miriam Gonzalez 12.00 30.00
❑ 9 Michelle Baena 12.00 30.00
❑ 10 Brande Roderick 12.00 30.00
❑ 11 Nikki Ziering 10.00 25.00
❑ 12 Katie Lohmann 10.00 25.00
❑ 13 Candace Kita 10.00 25.00
❑ 14 Lisa Gleave 10.00 25.00
❑ 15 Tiffany Selby 10.00 25.00
❑ 16 Cecille Gahr 10.00 25.00
❑ 17 Nicole Bennett 10.00 25.00
❑ 18 Buffy Tyler 10.00 25.00
❑ 19 Claudia Jordan 10.00 25.00
❑ 20 Shay Lyn Veasy 10.00 25.00
❑ 21 Suzanne Stokes 10.00 25.00
❑ 22 Brandie Moses 10.00 25.00
❑ 23 Brandy Grace 10.00 25.00
❑ 24 Crystal Harris 10.00 25.00
❑ 25 Melissa Riso 10.00 25.00
❑ 26 Billie Jo Powers 10.00 25.00
❑ 27 Tamara Witmer 10.00 25.00
❑ 28 Jennifer Korbin 12.00 30.00
❑ 29 Enya Flack 10.00 25.00
❑ 30 Cassandra Lynn 10.00 25.00
❑ 31 Miki Black 10.00 25.00
❑ 32 Kirsty Lingman 10.00 25.00
❑ 33 Cristal Camden 10.00 25.00
❑ 34 Tishara Cousino 10.00 25.00
❑ 35 Caitlin O'Connor 10.00 25.00
❑ 36 Katarina Van Derham 10.00 25.00

2012 Bench Warmer Hot For Teacher Schoolgirl Swatches Pink Foil

STATED PRINT RUN 25 SER. #'d SETS

2012 Bench Warmer Hot For Teacher Schoolgirl Swatches Autographs Green Foil

STATED PRINT RUN 10 SER. #'d SETS
UNPRICED DUE TO SCARCITY

❑ 1 Carmen Electra
❑ 2 Mary Riley
❑ 3 Maria Kanellis
❑ 4 Kara Monaco
❑ 5 Torrie Wilson
❑ 6 Tiffany Toth
❑ 7 Jessica Burciaga
❑ 8 Miriam Gonzalez
❑ 9 Michelle Baena
❑ 10 Brande Roderick
❑ 11 Nikki Ziering
❑ 12 Katie Lohmann
❑ 13 Candace Kita
❑ 14 Lisa Gleave
❑ 15 Tiffany Selby
❑ 16 Cecille Gahr
❑ 17 Nicole Bennett
❑ 18 Buffy Tyler
❑ 19 Claudia Jordan
❑ 20 Shay Lyn Veasy
❑ 21 Suzanne Stokes
❑ 22 Brandie Moses
❑ 23 Brandy Grace
❑ 24 Crystal Harris
❑ 25 Melissa Riso
❑ 26 Billie Jo Powers
❑ 27 Tamara Witmer
❑ 28 Jennifer Korbin
❑ 29 Enya Flack
❑ 30 Cassandra Lynn
❑ 31 Miki Black
❑ 32 Kirsty Lingman
❑ 33 Cristal Camden
❑ 34 Tishara Cousino
❑ 35 Caitlin O'Connor
❑ 36 Katarina Van Derham

2012 Bench Warmer Hot For Teacher Schoolgirl Swatches Autographs Blue Foil

STATED PRINT RUN 5 SER. #'d SETS
UNPRICED DUE TO SCARCITY

2012 Bench Warmer Hot For Teacher Schoolgirl Swatches Autographs Red Foil

STATED PRINT RUN 1 SER. #'d SET
UNPRICED DUE TO SCARCITY

2012 Bench Warmer Hot For Teacher Teacher's Pet Autographs Green Foil

STATED PRINT RUN 10 SER. #'d SETS
UNPRICED DUE TO SCARCITY

❑ 1 Brandy Grace
❑ 2 Brittany Herrera
❑ 3 Carrie Minter
❑ 4 Casey Durkin
❑ 5 Cassandra Lynn
❑ 6 Cecille Gahr
❑ 7 Jennifer Korbin
❑ 8 Lisa Gleave
❑ 9 Melissa Riso
❑ 10 Michelle Baena
❑ 11 Paige Peterson
❑ 12 Tamara Witmer
❑ 13 Yancey Todd

2012 Bench Warmer Hot For Teacher Teacher's Pet Autographs Blue Foil

STATED PRINT RUN 5 SER. #'d SETS
UNPRICED DUE TO SCARCITY

2012 Bench Warmer Hot For Teacher Teacher's Pet Autographs Red Foil

STATED PRINT RUN 1 SER. #'d SET
UNPRICED DUE TO SCARCITY

2012 Bench Warmer Long Beach Grand Prix

COMPLETE SET (8) 15.00 30.00

❑ 1 Syd Wilder 2.00 5.00
❑ 2 April Scott 2.00 5.00
❑ 3 Holly Huddleston 2.00 5.00
❑ 4 Michelle Baena 3.00 8.00
❑ 5 Nikki Ziering 2.00 5.00
❑ 6 Enya Flack 2.00 5.00
❑ 7 Krisi Ballentine 2.00 5.00
❑ 8 Lisa Ligon 2.00 5.00

2012 Bench Warmer National Convention Gold Foil

COMPLETE SET (56)

❑ 1 Andrea Lowell 4.00 10.00
❑ 2 April Scott 4.00 10.00
❑ 3 Bambi Lashell 4.00 10.00
❑ 4 Billie Jo Powers 4.00 10.00
❑ 5 Brande Roderick 4.00 10.00
❑ 6 Brandie Moses 4.00 10.00
❑ 7 Brandy Grace
❑ 8 Brooke Morales 4.00 10.00
❑ 9 Buffy Tyler 4.00 10.00
❑ 10 Caitlin O'Connor 4.00 10.00
❑ 11 Candi Kita 4.00 10.00
❑ 12 Carmen Electra 15.00 40.00
❑ 13 Carolyn Martin 4.00 10.00
❑ 14 Cassandra Lynn 5.00 12.00
❑ 15 Cecille Gahr 4.00 10.00
❑ 16 Claudia Jordan 4.00 10.00
❑ 17 Crystal Harris 4.00 10.00
❑ 18 Deanna Brooks 4.00 10.00
❑ 19 Heather Rae Young 4.00 10.00
❑ 20 Holley Dorrough 4.00 10.00
❑ 21 Jennifer Korbin 4.00 10.00
❑ 22 Jennifer Walcott 5.00 12.00
❑ 23 Jessica Burciaga 5.00 12.00
❑ 24 Jessica Hall 4.00 10.00
❑ 25 Jessica Kinni 4.00 10.00
❑ 26 Kara Monaco 4.00 10.00
❑ 27 Katarina Van Derham 4.00 10.00
❑ 28 Katie Lohmann 4.00 10.00
❑ 29 Kayla Collins 4.00 10.00
❑ 30 Kirsty Lingman Santos 4.00 10.00
❑ 31 Kyara Tyler 4.00 10.00
❑ 32 Lisa Gleave 5.00 12.00
❑ 33 Maria Kanellis 5.00 12.00
❑ 34 Mary Riley 6.00 15.00
❑ 35 Melissa Riso 4.00 10.00
❑ 36 Michelle Baena 4.00 10.00
❑ 37 Miki Black 4.00 10.00
❑ 38 Miriam Gonzalez 4.00 10.00
❑ 39 Nicole Bennett 4.00 10.00
❑ 40 Nikki Ziering 4.00 10.00
❑ 41 Patrice Hollis 4.00 10.00
❑ 42 Ryan Shamrock 4.00 10.00
❑ 43 Sandra Taylor 4.00 10.00
❑ 44 Sara Underwood 8.00 20.00
❑ 45 Shay Lyn Veasy 4.00 10.00
❑ 46 Stacie Hall 4.00 10.00
❑ 47 Suzanne Stokes 4.00 10.00
❑ 48 Syd Wilder 4.00 10.00
❑ 49 Tamara Witmer 4.00 10.00
❑ 50 Tanea Brooks 4.00 10.00
❑ 51 Tiffany Selby 4.00 10.00
❑ 52 Tiffany Toth 4.00 10.00
❑ 53 Tishara Cousino 4.00 10.00
❑ 54 Torrie Wilson 6.00 15.00
❑ 55 Tra'shell Thompson 4.00 10.00
❑ 56 Yancey Todd 4.00 10.00

2012 Bench Warmer National Convention Pink Foil

STATED PRINT RUN 25 SER. #'d SETS

2012 Bench Warmer National Convention Green Foil

STATED PRINT RUN 10 SER. #'d SETS
UNPRICED DUE TO SCARCITY

2012 Bench Warmer National Convention Blue Foil

STATED PRINT RUN 5 SER. #'d SETS
UNPRICED DUE TO SCARCITY

2012 Bench Warmer National Convention Red Foil

STATED PRINT RUN 1 SER. #'d SET
UNPRICED DUE TO SCARCITY

2012 Bench Warmer National Convention 1st and 10 Autographs Gold Foil

STATED PRINT RUN 10 SER. #'d SETS
UNPRICED DUE TO SCARCITY

❑ 1 Brande Roderick
❑ 2 Tamara Witmer
❑ 3 Lisa Gleave
❑ 4A Jennifer Walcott
❑ 4B Maria Kanellis
❑ 5 Miriam Gonzalez
❑ 6 Sandra Taylor
❑ 7 Jessica Burciaga
❑ 8 Michelle Baena
❑ 9 Torrie Wilson
❑ 10 Sara Underwood

2012 Bench Warmer National Convention 1st and 10 Autographs Pink Foil

STATED PRINT RUN 5 SER. #'d SETS
UNPRICED DUE TO SCARCITY

2012 Bench Warmer National Convention 1st and 10 Autographs Green Foil

STATED PRINT RUN 3 SER. #'d SETS
UNPRICED DUE TO SCARCITY

2012 Bench Warmer National Convention 1st and 10 Autographs Blue Foil

STATED PRINT RUN 2 SER. #'d SETS
UNPRICED DUE TO SCARCITY

2012 Bench Warmer National Convention 1st and 10 Autographs Red Foil

STATED PRINT RUN 1 SER. #'d SET
UNPRICED DUE TO SCARCITY

2012 Bench Warmer National Convention 7th Inning Stretch Autographs Gold Foil

STATED PRINT RUN 7 SER. #'d SETS
UNPRICED DUE TO SCARCITY

❑ 1 Carmen Electra
❑ 2 Jennifer Korbin
❑ 3 Ryan Shamrock
❑ 4 April Scott
❑ 5 Shay Lyn Veasy
❑ 6 Jessica Hall
❑ 7 Cassandra Lynn
❑ 8 Stacie Hall
❑ 9A Lisa Gleave
❑ 9B Suzanne Stokes
❑ 10A Heather Rae Young
❑ 10B Nikki Ziering

2012 Bench Warmer National Convention 7th Inning Stretch Autographs Pink Foil

STATED PRINT RUN 5 SER. #'d SETS
UNPRICED DUE TO SCARCITY

2012 Bench Warmer National Convention 7th Inning Stretch Autographs Green Foil

STATED PRINT RUN 3 SER. #'d SETS
UNPRICED DUE TO SCARCITY

2012 Bench Warmer National Convention 7th Inning Stretch Autographs Blue Foil

STATED PRINT RUN 2 SER. #'d SETS
UNPRICED DUE TO SCARCITY

2012 Bench Warmer National Convention 7th Inning Stretch Autographs Red Foil

STATED PRINT RUN 1 SER. #'d SET
UNPRICED DUE TO SCARCITY

2012 Bench Warmer National Convention Charm City Autographs Gold Foil

STATED PRINT RUN 25 SER. #'d SETS

❑ 1 Sara Underwood 15.00 40.00
❑ 2 Maria Kanellis 10.00 25.00
❑ 3 Brande Roderick 8.00 20.00
❑ 4 April Scott 8.00 20.00
❑ 5 Tishara Cousino 8.00 20.00
❑ 6 Nikki Ziering 8.00 20.00
❑ 7 Stacie Hall 8.00 20.00
❑ 8 Jessica Burciaga 10.00 25.00
❑ 9 Crystal Harris 8.00 20.00
❑ 10 Buffy Tyler 8.00 20.00
❑ 11 Torrie Wilson 12.00 30.00
❑ 12 Miriam Gonzalez 8.00 20.00

2012 Bench Warmer National Convention Charm City Autographs Pink Foil

STATED PRINT RUN 15 SER. #'d SETS

2012 Bench Warmer National Convention Charm City Autographs Green Foil

STATED PRINT RUN 10 SER. #'d SETS
UNPRICED DUE TO SCARCITY

2012 Bench Warmer National Convention Charm City Autographs Blue Foil

STATED PRINT RUN 5 SER. #'d SETS
UNPRICED DUE TO SCARCITY

2012 Bench Warmer National Convention Charm City Autographs Red Foil

STATED PRINT RUN 1 SER. #'d SET
UNPRICED DUE TO SCARCITY

2012 Bench Warmer National Convention Letters Autographs

STATED PRINT RUN 5 SER. #'d SETS

❑ ALA Andrea Lowell A/10
❑ ALD Andrea Lowell D/5
❑ ALE Andrea Lowell E/5
❑ ALN Andrea Lowell N/5
❑ ALR Andrea Lowell R/5
❑ ASA April Scott A/5
❑ ASI April Scott I/5
❑ ASL April Scott L/5
❑ ASP April Scott P/5
❑ ASR April Scott R/5
❑ BLA Bambi Lashell A/5
❑ BLB Bambi Lashell B/10
❑ BLI Bambi Lashell I/5
❑ BLM Bambi Lashell M/5
❑ BPB Billie Jo Powers B/5
❑ BPE Billie Jo Powers E/5
❑ BPI Billie Jo Powers I/10
❑ BPL Billie Jo Powers L/10
❑ BRA Brande Roderick A/5
❑ BRB Brande Roderick B/5
❑ BRD Brande Roderick D/5
❑ BRE Brande Roderick E/5
❑ BRN Brande Roderick N/5
❑ BRR Brande Roderick R/5
❑ BTB Buffy Tyler B/5
❑ BTF Buffy Tyler F/10
❑ BTU Buffy Tyler U/5
❑ BTY Buffy Tyler Y/5
❑ CEA Carmen Electra A/5
❑ CEC Carmen Electra C/5
❑ CEE Carmen Electra E/5
❑ CEM Carmen Electra M/5
❑ CEN Carmen Electra N/5
❑ CER Carmen Electra R/5
❑ CGC Cecille Gahr C/10
❑ CGE Cecille Gahr E/10
❑ CGI Cecille Gahr I/5
❑ CGL Cecille Gahr L/10
❑ CHA Crystal Harris A/5
❑ CHC Crystal Harris C/5
❑ CHL Crystal Harris L/5
❑ CHR Crystal Harris R/5
❑ CHS Crystal Harris S/5
❑ CHT Crystal Harris T/5
❑ CHY Crystal Harris Y/5
❑ CKA Candi Kita A/5
❑ CKC Candi Kita C/5
❑ CKD Candi Kita D/5
❑ CKI Candi Kita I/5
❑ CKN Candi Kita N/5
❑ CLA Cassandra Lynn A/15
❑ CLC Cassandra Lynn C/5
❑ CLD Cassandra Lynn D/5
❑ CLN Cassandra Lynn N/5
❑ CLR Cassandra Lynn R/5
❑ CLS Cassandra Lynn S/10
❑ DBA Deanna Brooks A/10
❑ DBD Deanna Brooks D/5
❑ DBE Deanna Brooks E/5
❑ DBN Deanna Brooks N/10
❑ JBA Jessica Burciaga A/5
❑ JBC Jessica Burciaga C/5
❑ JBE Jessica Burciaga E/5
❑ JBI Jessica Burciaga I/5
❑ JBJ Jessica Burciaga J/5
❑ JBS Jessica Burciaga S/10
❑ JHA Jessica Hall A/5
❑ JHC Jessica Hall C/5
❑ JHE Jessica Hall E/5
❑ JHI Jessica Hall I/5
❑ JHJ Jessica Hall J/5
❑ JHS Jessica Hall S/10
❑ JKIA Jessica Kinni A/5
❑ JKIC Jessica Kinni C/5
❑ JKIE Jessica Kinni E/5
❑ JKII Jessica Kinni I/5
❑ JKIJ Jessica Kinni J/5
❑ JKIS Jessica Kinni S/10
❑ JKOE Jennifer Korbin E/10
❑ JKOF Jennifer Korbin F/5
❑ JKOI Jennifer Korbin I/5
❑ JKOJ Jennifer Korbin J/5
❑ JKON Jennifer Korbin N/10
❑ JKOR Jennifer Korbin R/5
❑ JWE Jennifer Walcott E/10
❑ JWF Jennifer Walcott F/5
❑ JWI Jennifer Walcott I/5
❑ JWJ Jennifer Walcott J/5
❑ JWN Jennifer Walcott N/10
❑ JWR Jennifer Walcott R/5
❑ KLA Katie Lohmann A/5
❑ KLE Katie Lohmann E/5
❑ KLI Katie Lohmann I/5
❑ KLK Katie Lohmann K/5
❑ KLT Katie Lohmann T/5
❑ KVA Katarina Van Derham A/15
❑ KVI Katarina Van Derham I/5
❑ KVK Katarina Van Derham K/5
❑ KVN Katarina Van Derham N/5
❑ KVR Katarina Van Derham R/5
❑ KVT Katarina Van Derham T/5
❑ LGA Lisa Gleave A/5
❑ LGI Lisa Gleave I/5
❑ LGL Lisa Gleave L/5
❑ LGS Lisa Gleave S/5
❑ MARA Mary Riley A/5
❑ MARM Mary Riley M/5

❑ MARR Mary Riley R/5
❑ MARY Mary Riley Y/5
❑ MBAC Michelle Baena C/5
❑ MBAE Michelle Baena E/10
❑ MBAH Michelle Baena H/5
❑ MBAI Michelle Baena I/5
❑ MBAL Michelle Baena L/10
❑ MBAM Michelle Baena M/5
❑ MBLI Miki Black I/10
❑ MBLK Miki Black K/5
❑ MBLM Miki Black M/5
❑ MERA Melissa Riso A/5
❑ MERE Melissa Riso E/5
❑ MERI Melissa Riso I/5
❑ MERL Melissa Riso L/5
❑ MERM Melissa Riso M/5
❑ MERS Melissa Riso S/10
❑ MGA Miriam Gonzalez A/5
❑ MGI Miriam Gonzalez I/10
❑ MGM Miriam Gonzalez M/10
❑ MGR Miriam Gonzalez R/5
❑ MKA Maria Kanellis A/10
❑ MKI Maria Kanellis I/5
❑ MKM Maria Kanellis M/5
❑ MKR Maria Kanellis R/5
❑ NZI Nikki Ziering I/10
❑ NZK Nikki Ziering K/10
❑ NZN Nikki Ziering N/5
❑ RSA Ryan Shamrock A/5
❑ RSN Ryan Shamrock N/5
❑ RSR Ryan Shamrock R/5
❑ RSY Ryan Shamrock Y/5
❑ SHA Stacie Hall A/5
❑ SHC Stacie Hall C/5
❑ SHE Stacie Hall E/5
❑ SHI Stacie Hall I/5
❑ SHS Stacie Hall S/5
❑ SHT Stacie Hall T/5
❑ SSA Suzanne Stokes A/5
❑ SSE Suzanne Stokes E/5
❑ SSN Suzanne Stokes N/10
❑ SSS Suzanne Stokes S/5
❑ SSU Suzanne Stokes U/5
❑ SSZ Suzanne Stokes Z/5
❑ STA Sandra Taylor A/10
❑ STD Sandra Taylor D/5
❑ STN Sandra Taylor N/5
❑ STR Sandra Taylor R/5
❑ STS Sandra Taylor S/5
❑ SUA Sara Underwood A/10
❑ SUR Sara Underwood R/5
❑ SUS Sara Underwood S/5
❑ TSA Tiffany Selby A/5
❑ TSF Tiffany Selby F/10
❑ TSI Tiffany Selby I/5
❑ TSN Tiffany Selby N/5
❑ TST Tiffany Selby T/5
❑ TSY Tiffany Selby Y/5
❑ TTA Tiffany Toth A/5
❑ TTF Tiffany Toth F/10
❑ TTI Tiffany Toth I/5
❑ TTN Tiffany Toth N/5
❑ TTT Tiffany Toth T/5
❑ TTY Tiffany Toth Y/5
❑ TWE Torrie Wilson E/5
❑ TWI Torrie Wilson I/5
❑ TWO Torrie Wilson O/5
❑ TWR Torrie Wilson R/10
❑ TWT Torrie Wilson T/5

2012 Bench Warmer National Convention Maryland Mary Riley Autographs Gold Foil
STATED PRINT RUN 25 SER. #'d SETS

❑ 1 Mary Riley light blue top 12.00 30.00
❑ 2 Mary Riley polka dot top 12.00 30.00
❑ 3 Mary Riley white w/black stitch 12.00 30.00
❑ 4 Mary Riley black top 12.00 30.00
❑ 5 Mary Riley striped top 12.00 30.00
❑ 6 Mary Riley red top 12.00 30.00

2012 Bench Warmer National Convention Maryland Mary Riley Autographs Pink Foil
STATED PRINT RUN 15 SER. #'d SETS

2012 Bench Warmer National Convention Maryland Mary Riley Autographs Green Foil
STATED PRINT RUN 10 SER. #'d SETS
UNPRICED DUE TO SCARCITY

2012 Bench Warmer National Convention Maryland Mary Riley Autographs Blue Foil
STATED PRINT RUN 5 SER. #'d SETS
UNPRICED DUE TO SCARCITY

2012 Bench Warmer National Convention Maryland Mary Riley Autographs Red Foil
STATED PRINT RUN 1 SER. #'d SET
UNPRICED DUE TO SCARCITY

2012 Bench Warmer National Convention Props Gold Foil
STATED PRINT RUN 25 SER. #'d SETS

❑ 1 Carmen Electra - Football 20.00 40.00
❑ 2 Sara Underwood - Basketball 10.00 25.00
❑ 3 Brande Roderick - Basketball 8.00 20.00
❑ 4 Jessica Hall - Baseball Cap 8.00 20.00
❑ 5 Mary Riley - Football 10.00 25.00
❑ 6 Cassandra Lynn - BB Glove 8.00 20.00

2012 Bench Warmer National Convention Props Pink Foil
STATED PRINT RUN 15 SER. #'d SETS

2012 Bench Warmer National Convention Props Autographs Green Foil
STATED PRINT RUN 10 SER. #'d SETS
UNPRICED DUE TO SCARCITY

❑ 1 Carmen Electra
❑ 2 Sara Underwood
❑ 3 Brande Roderick
❑ 4 Jessica Hall
❑ 5 Mary Riley
❑ 6 Cassandra Lynn

2012 Bench Warmer National Convention Props Autographs Blue Foil
STATED PRINT RUN 5 SER. #'d SETS
UNPRICED DUE TO SCARCITY

2012 Bench Warmer National Convention Props Autographs Red Foil
STATED PRINT RUN 1 SER. #'d SET
UNPRICED DUE TO SCARCITY

2012 Bench Warmer National Convention Q and A Autographs
STATED PRINT RUN 20 SER. #'d SETS

❑ 1 Andrea Lowell 10.00 25.00
❑ 2 April Scott 10.00 25.00
❑ 3 Brande Roderick 10.00 25.00
❑ 4 Buffy Tyler 10.00 25.00
❑ 5 Candi Kita 10.00 25.00
❑ 6 Carmen Electra 20.00 40.00
❑ 7 Cassandra Lynn 10.00 25.00
❑ 8 Deanna Brooks 10.00 25.00
❑ 9 Jennifer Korbin 10.00 25.00
❑ 10 Jessica Burciaga 10.00 25.00
❑ 11 Jessica Hall 10.00 25.00
❑ 12 Jessica Kinni 10.00 25.00
❑ 13 Katie Lohmann 10.00 25.00
❑ 14 Lisa Gleave 10.00 25.00
❑ 15 Maria Kanellis
❑ 16 Mary Riley
❑ 17 Melissa Riso 10.00 25.00
❑ 18 Michelle Baena
❑ 19 Miriam Gonzalez 10.00 25.00
❑ 20 Nikki Ziering 10.00 25.00
❑ 21 Ryan Shamrock 10.00 25.00
❑ 22 Sandra Taylor 10.00 25.00
❑ 23 Sara Underwood 12.00 30.00
❑ 24 Stacie Hall 10.00 25.00
❑ 25 Tiffany Selby 10.00 25.00
❑ 26 Tiffany Toth 10.00 25.00
❑ 27 Torrie Wilson

2012 Bench Warmer National Convention Swatches Gold Foil
STATED PRINT RUN 25 SER. #'d SETS

❑ 1 Brande Roderick 12.00 30.00
❑ 2 Carmen Electra 25.00 50.00
❑ 3 Cassandra Lynn 12.00 30.00
❑ 4 Crystal Harris 12.00 30.00
❑ 5 Jessica Burciaga 20.00 40.00
❑ 6 Katie Lohmann 12.00 30.00
❑ 7 Lisa Gleave 12.00 30.00
❑ 8 Maria Kanellis 12.00 30.00
❑ 9 Mary Riley 15.00 40.00
❑ 10 Michelle Baena 12.00 30.00
❑ 11 Ryan Shamrock 12.00 30.00
❑ 12 Stacie Hall 12.00 30.00
❑ 13 Tiffany Toth 12.00 30.00
❑ 14 Torrie Wilson 15.00 40.00

2012 Bench Warmer National Convention Swatches Pink Foil
STATED PRINT RUN 15 SER. #'d SETS

2012 Bench Warmer National Convention Swatches Autographs Green Foil
STATED PRINT RUN 10 SER. #'d SETS
UNPRICED DUE TO SCARCITY

❑ 1 Brande Roderick
❑ 2 Carmen Electra
❑ 3 Cassandra Lynn
❑ 4 Crystal Harris
❑ 5 Jessica Burciaga
❑ 6 Katie Lohmann
❑ 7 Lisa Gleave
❑ 8 Maria Kanellis
❑ 9 Mary Riley
❑ 10 Michelle Baena
❑ 11 Ryan Shamrock
❑ 12 Stacie Hall
❑ 13 Tiffany Toth
❑ 14 Torrie Wilson

2012 Bench Warmer National Convention Swatches Autographs Blue Foil
STATED PRINT RUN 5 SER. #'d SETS
UNPRICED DUE TO SCARCITY

2012 Bench Warmer National Convention Swatches Autographs Red Foil
STATED PRINT RUN 1 SER. #'d SET
UNPRICED DUE TO SCARCITY

2012 Bench Warmer Soccer Premium Autographs Gold Foil
STATED PRINT RUN 50 SER. #'d SETS

❑ 1 Andrea Lowell 10.00 25.00
❑ 2 Bambi Lashell 8.00 20.00
❑ 3 Brande Roderick 12.00 30.00
❑ 4 Brandy Grace 8.00 20.00
❑ 5 Brooke Morales 8.00 20.00
❑ 6 Buffy Tyler 8.00 20.00
❑ 7 Candace Kita 8.00 20.00
❑ 8 Cassandra Lynn 8.00 20.00
❑ 9 Catherine Kluthe 8.00 20.00
❑ 10 Claudia Jordan 8.00 20.00
❑ 11 Crystal Harris 12.00 30.00
❑ 12 Deanna Brooks 8.00 20.00
❑ 13 Heather Rae Young 8.00 20.00
❑ 14 Heather Rene Smith
❑ 15 Holley Dorrough 8.00 20.00
❑ 16 Jasmine Dustin 8.00 20.00
❑ 17 Jenae Alt 8.00 20.00
❑ 18 Jennifer Korbin 10.00 25.00
❑ 19 Jessica Burciaga 12.00 30.00
❑ 20 Jessica Hall 8.00 20.00
❑ 21 Jessica Kinni 8.00 20.00
❑ 22 Kara Monaco 10.00 25.00
❑ 23 Lisa Gleave 10.00 25.00
❑ 24 Lisa Ligon 8.00 20.00
❑ 25 Maria Kanellis 12.00 30.00
❑ 26 Mary Riley 12.00 30.00
❑ 27 Michelle Baena 10.00 25.00
❑ 28 Miki Black 8.00 20.00
❑ 29 Miriam Gonzalez 15.00 40.00
❑ 30 Nikki Ziering 8.00 20.00
❑ 31 Paige Peterson 8.00 20.00
❑ 32 Patrice Hollis 8.00 20.00
❑ 33 Rachel Bernstein 8.00 20.00
❑ 34 Ryan Shamrock 8.00 20.00
❑ 35 Sandra Taylor 12.00 30.00
❑ 36 Sara Underwood 20.00 50.00
❑ 37 Shay Lyn Veasy 8.00 20.00
❑ 38 Stacie Hall
❑ 39 Suzanne Stokes 10.00 25.00
❑ 40 Syd Wilder 8.00 20.00
❑ 41 Tamara Witmer 8.00 20.00
❑ 42 Tiffany Selby 8.00 20.00
❑ 43 Tiffany Toth 8.00 20.00
❑ 44 Torrie Wilson 12.00 30.00
❑ 45 Yvette Nelson 8.00 20.00

2012 Bench Warmer Soccer Premium Autographs Pink Foil
COMPLETE SET
STATED PRINT RUN 25 SER. #'d SETS

2012 Bench Warmer Soccer Premium Autographs Green Foil
STATED PRINT RUN 10 SER. #'d SETS
UNPRICED DUE TO SCARCITY

2012 Bench Warmer Soccer Premium Autographs Blue Foil
STATED PRINT RUN 5 SER. #'d SETS
UNPRICED DUE TO SCARCITY

2012 Bench Warmer Soccer Premium Autographs Red Foil
STATED PRINT RUN 1 SER. #'d SET
UNPRICED DUE TO SCARCITY

2012 Bench Warmer Soccer Premium Autographs Printing Plates Black Back
STATED PRINT RUN 1 SER. #'d SET
UNPRICED DUE TO SCARCITY

2012 Bench Warmer Soccer Premium Autographs Printing Plates Black Front
STATED PRINT RUN 1 SER. #'d SET
UNPRICED DUE TO SCARCITY

2012 Bench Warmer Soccer Premium Autographs Printing Plates Cyan Back
STATED PRINT RUN 1 SER. #'d SET
UNPRICED DUE TO SCARCITY

2012 Bench Warmer Soccer Premium Autographs Printing Plates Cyan Front
STATED PRINT RUN 1 SER. #'d SET
UNPRICED DUE TO SCARCITY

2012 Bench Warmer Soccer Premium Autographs Printing Plates Magenta Back
STATED PRINT RUN 1 SER. #'d SET
UNPRICED DUE TO SCARCITY

2012 Bench Warmer Soccer Premium Autographs Printing Plates Magenta Front
STATED PRINT RUN 1 SER. #'d SET
UNPRICED DUE TO SCARCITY

2012 Bench Warmer Soccer Premium Autographs Printing Plates Yellow Back
STATED PRINT RUN 1 SER. #'d SET
UNPRICED DUE TO SCARCITY

2012 Bench Warmer Soccer Premium Autographs Printing Plates Yellow Front
STATED PRINT RUN 1 SER. #'d SET
UNPRICED DUE TO SCARCITY

2012 Bench Warmer Soccer Premium Authentic Hair Cut Gold Foil
STATED PRINT RUN 15 SER. #'d SETS

❑ 1 Brande Roderick 60.00 120.00
❑ 2 Crystal Harris 60.00 120.00
❑ 3 Jennifer Korbin 60.00 120.00
❑ 4 Jessica Burciaga 100.00 175.00
❑ 5 Maria Kanellis 60.00 120.00
❑ 6 Michelle Baena 50.00 100.00
❑ 7 Miki Black 50.00 100.00
❑ 8 Suzanne Stokes 50.00 100.00
❑ 9 Torrie Wilson 60.00 120.00

2012 Bench Warmer Soccer Premium Authentic Hair Cut Pink Foil
STATED PRINT RUN 5 SER. #'d SETS
UNPRICED DUE TO SCARCITY

2012 Bench Warmer Soccer Premium Authentic Hair Cut Autographs Green Foil
STATED PRINT RUN 5 SER. #'d SETS
UNPRICED DUE TO SCARCITY

❑ 1 Brande Roderick
❑ 2 Crystal Harris
❑ 3 Jennifer Korbin
❑ 4 Jessica Burciaga
❑ 5 Maria Kanellis
❑ 6 Michelle Baena
❑ 7 Miki Black
❑ 8 Suzanne Stokes
❑ 9 Torrie Wilson

2012 Bench Warmer Soccer Premium Authentic Hair Cut Autographs Blue Foil
STATED PRINT RUN 3 SER. #'d SETS
UNPRICED DUE TO SCARCITY

2012 Bench Warmer Soccer Premium Authentic Hair Cut Autographs Red Foil
STATED PRINT RUN 1 SER. #'d SET
UNPRICED DUE TO SCARCITY

2012 Bench Warmer Soccer Premium Dual Jersey Swatches Gold Foil
STATED PRINT RUN 50 SER. #'d SETS

❑ 1 Jessica Hall 12.00 30.00
Stacie Hall
❑ 2 Lisa Ligon 12.00 30.00
Paige Peterson
❑ 3 Suzanne Stokes 12.00 30.00
Buffy Tyler
❑ 4 Tiffany Selby 12.00 30.00
Tiffany Toth

2012 Bench Warmer Soccer Premium Dual Jersey Swatches Pink Foil
COMPLETE SET
STATED PRINT RUN 25 SER. #'d SETS

2012 Bench Warmer Soccer Premium Dual Jersey Swatches Autographs Green Foil
STATED PRINT RUN 10 SER. #'d SETS
UNPRICED DUE TO SCARCITY

❑ 1 Jessica Hall
Stacie Hall
❑ 2 Lisa Ligon
Paige Peterson
❑ 3 Suzanne Stokes
Buffy Tyler
❑ 4 Tiffany Selby
Tiffany Toth

2012 Bench Warmer Soccer Premium Dual Jersey Swatches Autographs Blue Foil
STATED PRINT RUN 5 SER. #'d SETS
UNPRICED DUE TO SCARCITY

2012 Bench Warmer Soccer Premium Dual Jersey Swatches Autographs Red Foil
STATED PRINT RUN 1 SER. #'d SET
UNPRICED DUE TO SCARCITY

2012 Bench Warmer Soccer Premium Dual Jersey Swatches Autographs Printing Plates Black Back
STATED PRINT RUN 1 SER. #'d SET
UNPRICED DUE TO SCARCITY

2012 Bench Warmer Soccer Premium Dual Jersey Swatches Autographs Printing Plates Black Front
STATED PRINT RUN 1 SER. #'d SET
UNPRICED DUE TO SCARCITY

2012 Bench Warmer Soccer Premium Dual Jersey Swatches Autographs Printing Plates Cyan Back
STATED PRINT RUN 1 SER. #'d SET
UNPRICED DUE TO SCARCITY

2012 Bench Warmer Soccer Premium Dual Jersey Swatches Autographs Printing Plates Cyan Front
STATED PRINT RUN 1 SER. #'d SET
UNPRICED DUE TO SCARCITY

2012 Bench Warmer Soccer Premium Dual Jersey Swatches Autographs Printing Plates Magenta Back
STATED PRINT RUN 1 SER. #'d SET
UNPRICED DUE TO SCARCITY

2012 Bench Warmer Soccer Premium Dual Jersey Swatches Autographs Printing Plates Magenta Front
STATED PRINT RUN 1 SER. #'d SET
UNPRICED DUE TO SCARCITY

2012 Bench Warmer Soccer Premium Dual Jersey Swatches Autographs Printing Plates Yellow Back
STATED PRINT RUN 1 SER. #'d SET
UNPRICED DUE TO SCARCITY

2012 Bench Warmer Soccer Premium Dual Jersey Swatches Autographs Printing Plates Yellow Front
STATED PRINT RUN 1 SER. #'d SET
UNPRICED DUE TO SCARCITY

2012 Bench Warmer Soccer Premium Inscriptions
STATED PRINT RUN 25 SER. #'d SETS

❑ 1 Bambi Lashell 35.00 70.00
❑ 2 Brande Roderick 40.00 80.00
❑ 3 Candace Kita 30.00 60.00
❑ 4 Cassandra Lynn 25.00 50.00
❑ 5 Crystal Harris 35.00 70.00
❑ 6 Jessica Burciaga 50.00 100.00
❑ 7 Lisa Gleave 30.00 60.00
❑ 8 Maria Kanellis 35.00 70.00
❑ 9 Mary Riley 45.00 90.00
❑ 10 Michelle Baena 25.00 50.00
❑ 11 Miki Black 25.00 50.00
❑ 12 Miriam Gonzalez 40.00 80.00
❑ 13 Paige Peterson 25.00 50.00
❑ 14 Sandra Taylor 45.00 90.00
❑ 15 Sara Underwood 100.00 200.00
❑ 16 Tiffany Selby 25.00 50.00
❑ 17 Tiffany Toth 30.00 60.00
❑ 18 Torrie Wilson 35.00 70.00

2012 Bench Warmer Soccer Premium Jersey Swatches Gold Foil
STATED PRINT RUN 50 SER. #'d SETS

❑ 1 Andrea Lowell 12.00 30.00
❑ 2 Brande Roderick 12.00 30.00
❑ 3 Candace Kita 12.00 30.00
❑ 4 Cassandra Lynn 12.00 30.00
❑ 5 Claudia Jordan 12.00 30.00
❑ 6 Crystal Harris 12.00 30.00
❑ 7 Deanna Brooks 12.00 30.00
❑ 8 Holley Dorrough 12.00 30.00
❑ 9 Jessica Burciaga 15.00 40.00
❑ 10 Kara Monaco 12.00 30.00
❑ 11 Lisa Gleave 12.00 30.00
❑ 12 Maria Kanellis 15.00 40.00
❑ 13 Mary Riley 15.00 40.00
❑ 14 Miki Black 12.00 30.00
❑ 15 Miriam Gonzalez 30.00 60.00
❑ 16 Sandra Taylor 15.00 40.00
❑ 17 Sara Underwood 25.00 50.00
❑ 18 Shay Lyn Veasy 12.00 30.00
❑ 19 Suzanne Stokes 12.00 30.00
❑ 20 Torrie Wilson 15.00 40.00

2012 Bench Warmer Soccer Premium Jersey Swatches Pink Foil
COMPLETE SET
STATED PRINT RUN 25 SER. #'d SETS

2012 Bench Warmer Soccer Premium Jersey Swatches Autographs Green Foil
STATED PRINT RUN 10 SER. #'d SETS
UNPRICED DUE TO SCARCITY

❑ 1 Andrea Lowell
❑ 2 Brande Roderick
❑ 3 Candace Kita
❑ 4 Cassandra Lynn
❑ 5 Claudia Jordan
❑ 6 Crystal Harris
❑ 7 Deanna Brooks
❑ 8 Holley Dorrough
❑ 9 Jessica Burciaga
❑ 10 Kara Monaco
❑ 11 Lisa Gleave
❑ 12 Maria Kanellis
❑ 13 Mary Riley
❑ 14 Miki Black
❑ 15 Miriam Gonzalez
❑ 16 Sandra Taylor
❑ 17 Sara Underwood
❑ 18 Shay Lyn Veasy
❑ 19 Suzanne Stokes
❑ 20 Torrie Wilson

2012 Bench Warmer Soccer Premium Jersey Swatches Autographs Blue Foil
STATED PRINT RUN 5 SER. #'d SETS
UNPRICED DUE TO SCARCITY

2012 Bench Warmer Soccer Premium Jersey Swatches Autographs Red Foil
STATED PRINT RUN 1 SER. #'d SET
UNPRICED DUE TO SCARCITY

2012 Bench Warmer Soccer Premium Jersey Swatches Autographs Printing Plates Black Back
STATED PRINT RUN 1 SER. #'d SET
UNPRICED DUE TO SCARCITY

2012 Bench Warmer Soccer Premium Jersey Swatches Autographs Printing Plates Black Front
STATED PRINT RUN 1 SER. #'d SET
UNPRICED DUE TO SCARCITY

2012 Bench Warmer Soccer Premium Jersey Swatches Autographs Printing Plates Cyan Back
STATED PRINT RUN 1 SER. #'d SET
UNPRICED DUE TO SCARCITY

2012 Bench Warmer Soccer Premium Jersey Swatches Autographs Printing Plates Cyan Front
STATED PRINT RUN 1 SER. #'d SET
UNPRICED DUE TO SCARCITY

2012 Bench Warmer Soccer Premium Jersey Swatches Autographs Printing Plates Magenta Back
STATED PRINT RUN 1 SER. #'d SET
UNPRICED DUE TO SCARCITY

2012 Bench Warmer Soccer Premium Jersey Swatches Autographs Printing Plates Magenta Front
STATED PRINT RUN 1 SER. #'d SET
UNPRICED DUE TO SCARCITY

2012 Bench Warmer Soccer Premium Jersey Swatches Autographs Printing Plates Yellow Back
STATED PRINT RUN 1 SER. #'d SET
UNPRICED DUE TO SCARCITY

2012 Bench Warmer Soccer Premium Jersey Swatches Autographs Printing Plates Yellow Front
STATED PRINT RUN 1 SER. #'d SET
UNPRICED DUE TO SCARCITY

2012 Bench Warmer Soccer Premium Kiss Gold Foil
STATED PRINT RUN 25 SER. #'d SETS

❑ 1 Brande Roderick 15.00 40.00
❑ 2 Crystal Harris 15.00 40.00
❑ 3 Jessica Burciaga 15.00 40.00
❑ 4 Kara Monaco 12.00 30.00
❑ 5 Michelle Baena 12.00 30.00
❑ 6 Suzanne Stokes 12.00 30.00
❑ 7 Tiffany Selby 12.00 30.00
❑ 8 Tiffany Toth 12.00 30.00
❑ 9 Torrie Wilson 15.00 40.00

2012 Bench Warmer Soccer Premium Kiss Pink Foil
COMPLETE SET
STATED PRINT RUN 15 SER. #'d SETS

2012 Bench Warmer Soccer Premium Kiss Autographs Green Foil
STATED PRINT RUN 10 SER. #'d SETS
UNPRICED DUE TO SCARCITY

❑ 1 Brande Roderick
❑ 2 Crystal Harris
❑ 3 Jessica Burciaga
❑ 4 Kara Monaco
❑ 5 Michelle Baena
❑ 6 Suzanne Stokes
❑ 7 Tiffany Selby
❑ 8 Tiffany Toth
❑ 9 Torrie Wilson

2012 Bench Warmer Soccer Premium Kiss Autographs Blue Foil
STATED PRINT RUN 5 SER. #'d SETS
UNPRICED DUE TO SCARCITY

2012 Bench Warmer Soccer Premium Kiss Autographs Red Foil
STATED PRINT RUN 1 SER. #'d SET
UNPRICED DUE TO SCARCITY

2012 Bench Warmer Soccer Premium Quad Jersey Swatches Gold Foil
STATED PRINT RUN 50 SER. #'d SETS

❑ 1 Jennifer Korbin 25.00 50.00
Michelle Baena/ Brandy Grace/ Nikki Ziering
❑ 2 Heather Rae Young 20.00 40.00
Buffy Tyler/ Tamara Witmer/ Patrice Hollis

2012 Bench Warmer Soccer Premium Quad Jersey Swatches Pink Foil
COMPLETE SET
STATED PRINT RUN 25 SER. #'d SETS

2012 Bench Warmer Soccer Premium Quad Jersey Swatches Autographs Green Foil
STATED PRINT RUN 10 SER. #'d SETS
UNPRICED DUE TO SCARCITY

❑ 1 Jennifer Korbin
Michelle Baena/ Brandy Grace/ Nikki Ziering
❑ 2 Heather Rae Young
Buffy Tyler/ Tamara Witmer/ Patrice Hollis

2012 Bench Warmer Soccer Premium Quad Jersey Swatches Autographs Blue Foil
STATED PRINT RUN 5 SER. #'d SETS
UNPRICED DUE TO SCARCITY

2012 Bench Warmer Soccer Premium Quad Jersey Swatches Autographs Red Foil
STATED PRINT RUN 1 SER. #'d SET
UNPRICED DUE TO SCARCITY

2012 Bench Warmer Soccer Premium Quad Jersey Swatches Autographs Printing Plates Black Back
STATED PRINT RUN 1 SER. #'d SET
UNPRICED DUE TO SCARCITY

2012 Bench Warmer Soccer Premium Quad Jersey Swatches Autographs Printing Plates Black Front
STATED PRINT RUN 1 SER. #'d SET
UNPRICED DUE TO SCARCITY

2012 Bench Warmer Soccer Premium Quad Jersey Swatches Autographs Printing Plates Cyan Back
STATED PRINT RUN 1 SER. #'d SET
UNPRICED DUE TO SCARCITY

2012 Bench Warmer Soccer Premium Quad Jersey Swatches Autographs Printing Plates Cyan Front
STATED PRINT RUN 1 SER. #'d SET
UNPRICED DUE TO SCARCITY

2012 Bench Warmer Soccer Premium Quad Jersey Swatches Autographs Printing Plates Magenta Back
STATED PRINT RUN 1 SER. #'d SET
UNPRICED DUE TO SCARCITY

2012 Bench Warmer Soccer Premium Quad Jersey Swatches Autographs Printing Plates Magenta Front
STATED PRINT RUN 1 SER. #'d SET
UNPRICED DUE TO SCARCITY

2012 Bench Warmer Soccer Premium Quad Jersey Swatches Autographs Printing Plates Yellow Back
STATED PRINT RUN 1 SER. #'d SET
UNPRICED DUE TO SCARCITY

2012 Bench Warmer Soccer Premium Quad Jersey Swatches Autographs Printing Plates Yellow Front
STATED PRINT RUN 1 SER. #'d SET
UNPRICED DUE TO SCARCITY

2012 Bench Warmer Soccer Premium Soccer Balls Gold Foil
STATED PRINT RUN 25 SER. #'d SETS

□ 1 Bambi Lashell 15.00 30.00
□ 2 Brande Roderick 15.00 30.00
□ 3 Brooke Morales 15.00 30.00
□ 4 Buffy Tyler 15.00 30.00
□ 5 Cassandra Lynn 20.00 40.00
□ 6 Crystal Harris 15.00 30.00
□ 7 Jenae Alt 15.00 30.00
□ 8 Jessica Burciaga 20.00 40.00
□ 9 Lisa Gleave 20.00 40.00
□ 10 Maria Kanellis 15.00 30.00
□ 11 Mary Riley 20.00 40.00
□ 12 Michelle Baena 15.00 30.00
□ 13 Miriam Gonzalez 20.00 40.00
□ 14 Ryan Shamrock 15.00 30.00
□ 15 Sara Underwood 30.00 60.00
□ 16 Shay Lyn Veasy 15.00 30.00
□ 17 Suzanne Stokes 15.00 30.00
□ 18 Tiffany Selby 15.00 30.00

2012 Bench Warmer Soccer Premium Soccer Balls Pink Foil
STATED PRINT RUN 15 SER. #'d SETS

2012 Bench Warmer Soccer Premium Soccer Balls Autographs Green Foil
STATED PRINT RUN 10 SER. #'d SETS
UNPRICED DUE TO SCARCITY

□ 1 Bambi Lashell
□ 2 Brande Roderick
□ 3 Brooke Morales
□ 4 Buffy Tyler
□ 5 Cassandra Lynn
□ 6 Crystal Harris
□ 7 Jenae Alt
□ 8 Jessica Burciaga
□ 9 Lisa Gleave
□ 10 Maria Kanellis
□ 11 Mary Riley
□ 12 Michelle Baena
□ 13 Miriam Gonzalez
□ 14 Ryan Shamrock
□ 15 Sara Jean Underwood
□ 16 Shay Lyn Veasy
□ 17 Suzanne Stokes
□ 18 Tiffany Selby

2012 Bench Warmer Soccer Premium Soccer Balls Autographs Blue Foil
STATED PRINT RUN 5 SER. #'d SETS
UNPRICED DUE TO SCARCITY

2012 Bench Warmer Soccer Premium Soccer Balls Autographs Red Foil
STATED PRINT RUN 1 SER. #'d SET
UNPRICED DUE TO SCARCITY

2012 Bench Warmer Soccer Premium Soccer Gloves Gold Foil
STATED PRINT RUN 25 SER. #'d SETS

□ 1 Brande Roderick 20.00 40.00
□ 2 Holley Ann Dorrough 20.00 40.00
□ 3 Jennifer Korbin 20.00 40.00
□ 4 Jessica Hall 25.00 50.00
□ 5 Lisa Gleave 20.00 40.00
□ 6 Mary Riley 25.00 50.00
□ 7 Miki Black 20.00 40.00
□ 8 Nikki Ziering 20.00 40.00
□ 9 Sandra Taylor 20.00 40.00

2012 Bench Warmer Soccer Premium Soccer Gloves Pink Foil
STATED PRINT RUN 5 SER. #'d SETS
UNPRICED DUE TO SCARCITY

2012 Bench Warmer Soccer Premium Soccer Gloves Autographs Green Foil
STATED PRINT RUN 3 SER. #'d SETS
UNPRICED DUE TO SCARCITY

□ 1 Brande Roderick
□ 2 Holley Ann Dorrough
□ 3 Jennifer Korbin
□ 4 Jessica Hall
□ 5 Lisa Gleave
□ 6 Mary Riley
□ 7 Miki Black
□ 8 Nikki Ziering
□ 9 Sandra Taylor

2012 Bench Warmer Soccer Premium Soccer Gloves Autographs Blue Foil
STATED PRINT RUN 2 SER. #'d SETS
UNPRICED DUE TO SCARCITY

2012 Bench Warmer Soccer Premium Soccer Gloves Autographs Red Foil
STATED PRINT RUN 1 SER. #'d SET
UNPRICED DUE TO SCARCITY

2012 Bench Warmer Soccer Premium Soccer Shorts Gold Foil
STATED PRINT RUN 50 SER. #'d SETS

□ 1 Cassandra Lynn 20.00 40.00
□ 2 Crystal Harris 15.00 30.00
□ 3 Heather Rae Young 15.00 30.00
□ 4 Jennifer Korbin 20.00 40.00
□ 5 Jessica Burciaga 25.00 50.00
□ 6 Kara Monaco 20.00 40.00
□ 7 Lisa Gleave 15.00 30.00
□ 8 Maria Kanellis 15.00 30.00
□ 9 Michelle Baena 15.00 30.00
□ 10 Patrice Hollis 15.00 30.00
□ 11 Sara Underwood 30.00 60.00
□ 12 Shay Lyn Veasy 15.00 30.00
□ 13 Tiffany Selby 15.00 30.00
□ 14 Tiffany Toth 15.00 30.00
□ 15 Torrie Wilson 25.00 50.00

2012 Bench Warmer Soccer Premium Soccer Shorts Pink Foil
COMPLETE SET
STATED PRINT RUN 25 SER. #'d SETS

2012 Bench Warmer Soccer Premium Soccer Shorts Autographs Green Foil
STATED PRINT RUN 10 SER. #'d SETS
UNPRICED DUE TO SCARCITY

□ 1 Cassandra Lynn
□ 2 Crystal Harris
□ 3 Heather Rae Young
□ 4 Jennifer Korbin
□ 5 Jessica Burciaga
□ 6 Kara Monaco
□ 7 Lisa Gleave
□ 8 Maria Kanellis
□ 9 Michelle Baena
□ 10 Patrice Hollis
□ 11 Sara Jean Underwood
□ 12 Shay Lyn Veasy
□ 13 Tiffany Selby
□ 14 Tiffany Toth
□ 15 Torrie Wilson

2012 Bench Warmer Soccer Premium Soccer Shorts Autographs Blue Foil
STATED PRINT RUN 5 SER. #'d SETS
UNPRICED DUE TO SCARCITY

2012 Bench Warmer Soccer Premium Soccer Shorts Autographs Red Foil
STATED PRINT RUN 1 SER. #'d SET
UNPRICED DUE TO SCARCITY

2012 Bench Warmer Soccer Premium Soccer Shorts Autographs Printing Plates Black Back
STATED PRINT RUN 1 SER. #'d SET
UNPRICED DUE TO SCARCITY

2012 Bench Warmer Soccer Premium Soccer Shorts Autographs Printing Plates Black Front
STATED PRINT RUN 1 SER. #'d SET
UNPRICED DUE TO SCARCITY

2012 Bench Warmer Soccer Premium Soccer Shorts Autographs Printing Plates Cyan Back
STATED PRINT RUN 1 SER. #'d SET
UNPRICED DUE TO SCARCITY

2012 Bench Warmer Soccer Premium Soccer Shorts Autographs Printing Plates Cyan Front
STATED PRINT RUN 1 SER. #'d SET
UNPRICED DUE TO SCARCITY

2012 Bench Warmer Soccer Premium Soccer Shorts Autographs Printing Plates Magenta Back
STATED PRINT RUN 1 SER. #'d SET
UNPRICED DUE TO SCARCITY

2012 Bench Warmer Soccer Premium Soccer Shorts Autographs Printing Plates Magenta Front
STATED PRINT RUN 1 SER. #'d SET
UNPRICED DUE TO SCARCITY

2012 Bench Warmer Soccer Premium Soccer Shorts Autographs Printing Plates Yellow Back
STATED PRINT RUN 1 SER. #'d SET
UNPRICED DUE TO SCARCITY

2012 Bench Warmer Soccer Premium Soccer Shorts Autographs Printing Plates Yellow Front
STATED PRINT RUN 1 SER. #'d SET
UNPRICED DUE TO SCARCITY

2012 Bench Warmer Soccer Premium Soccer Sox Gold Foil
STATED PRINT RUN 50 SER. #'d SETS

□ 1 Brande Roderick 15.00 30.00
□ 2 Brandy Grace 15.00 30.00
□ 3 Buffy Tyler 15.00 30.00
□ 4 Claudia Jordan 15.00 30.00
□ 5 Crystal Harris 15.00 30.00
□ 6 Jennifer Korbin 15.00 30.00
□ 7 Jessica Burciaga 20.00 40.00
□ 8 Mary Riley 20.00 40.00
□ 9 Nikki Ziering 15.00 30.00
□ 10 Tiffany Selby 15.00 30.00
□ 11 Tiffany Toth 15.00 30.00
□ 12 Torrie Wilson 20.00 40.00

2012 Bench Warmer Soccer Premium Soccer Sox Pink Foil
COMPLETE SET
STATED PRINT RUN 25 SER. #'d SETS

2012 Bench Warmer Soccer Premium Soccer Sox Autographs Green Foil
STATED PRINT RUN 10 SER. #'d SETS
UNPRICED DUE TO SCARCITY

□ 1 Brande Roderick
□ 2 Brandy Grace
□ 3 Buffy Tyler
□ 4 Claudia Jordan
□ 5 Crystal Harris
□ 6 Jennifer Korbin
□ 7 Jessica Burciaga
□ 8 Mary Riley
□ 9 Nikki Ziering
□ 10 Tiffany Selby
□ 11 Tiffany Toth
□ 12 Torrie Wilson

2012 Bench Warmer Soccer Premium Soccer Sox Autographs Blue Foil
STATED PRINT RUN 5 SER. #'d SETS
UNPRICED DUE TO SCARCITY

2012 Bench Warmer Soccer Premium Soccer Sox Autographs Red Foil
STATED PRINT RUN 1 SER. #'d SET
UNPRICED DUE TO SCARCITY

2012 Bench Warmer Soccer Premium Soccer Sox Autographs Printing Plates Black Back
STATED PRINT RUN 1 SER. #'d SET
UNPRICED DUE TO SCARCITY

2012 Bench Warmer Soccer Premium Soccer Sox Autographs Printing Plates Black Front
STATED PRINT RUN 1 SER. #'d SET
UNPRICED DUE TO SCARCITY

2012 Bench Warmer Soccer Premium Soccer Sox Autographs Printing Plates Cyan Back
STATED PRINT RUN 1 SER. #'d SET
UNPRICED DUE TO SCARCITY

2012 Bench Warmer Soccer Premium Soccer Sox Autographs Printing Plates Cyan Front
STATED PRINT RUN 1 SER. #'d SET
UNPRICED DUE TO SCARCITY

2012 Bench Warmer Soccer Premium Soccer Sox Autographs Printing Plates Magenta Back
STATED PRINT RUN 1 SER. #'d SET
UNPRICED DUE TO SCARCITY

2012 Bench Warmer Soccer Premium Soccer Sox Autographs Printing Plates Magenta Front
STATED PRINT RUN 1 SER. #'d SET
UNPRICED DUE TO SCARCITY

2012 Bench Warmer Soccer Premium Soccer Sox Autographs Printing Plates Yellow Back
STATED PRINT RUN 1 SER. #'d SET
UNPRICED DUE TO SCARCITY

2012 Bench Warmer Soccer Premium Soccer Sox Autographs Printing Plates Yellow Front
STATED PRINT RUN 1 SER. #'d SET
UNPRICED DUE TO SCARCITY

2012 Bench Warmer Soccer Premium Triple Jersey Swatches Gold Foil
STATED PRINT RUN 50 SER. #'d SETS

□ 1 Brande Roderick 25.00 50.00
Kara Monaco/ Sara Underwood
□ 2 Torrie Wilson 20.00 40.00
Maria Kanellis/ Ryan Shamrock

2012 Bench Warmer Soccer Premium Triple Jersey Swatches Pink Foil
*PINK: .5X TO 1.2X GOLD
STATED PRINT RUN 25 SER. #'d SETS

2012 Bench Warmer Soccer Premium Triple Jersey Swatches Autographs Green Foil
STATED PRINT RUN 10 SER. #'d SETS
UNPRICED DUE TO SCARCITY

□ 1 Brande Roderick
Kara Monaco/ Sara Underwood
□ 2 Torrie Wilson
Maria Kanellis/ Ryan Shamrock

2012 Bench Warmer Soccer Premium Triple Jersey Swatches Autographs Blue Foil
STATED PRINT RUN 5 SER. #'d SETS
UNPRICED DUE TO SCARCITY

2012 Bench Warmer Soccer Premium Triple Jersey Swatches Autographs Red Foil
STATED PRINT RUN 1 SER. #'d SETS
UNPRICED DUE TO SCARCITY

2012 Bench Warmer Soccer Premium Triple Jersey Swatches Autographs Printing Plates Black Back
STATED PRINT RUN 1 SER. #'d SET
UNPRICED DUE TO SCARCITY

2012 Bench Warmer Soccer Premium Triple Jersey Swatches Autographs Printing Plates Black Front
STATED PRINT RUN 1 SER. #'d SET
UNPRICED DUE TO SCARCITY

2012 Bench Warmer Soccer Premium Triple Jersey Swatches Autographs Printing Plates Cyan Back
STATED PRINT RUN 1 SER. #'d SET
UNPRICED DUE TO SCARCITY

2012 Bench Warmer Soccer Premium Triple Jersey Swatches Autographs Printing Plates Cyan Front
STATED PRINT RUN 1 SER. #'d SET
UNPRICED DUE TO SCARCITY

2012 Bench Warmer Soccer Premium Triple Jersey Swatches Autographs Printing Plates Magenta Back
STATED PRINT RUN 1 SER. #'d SET
UNPRICED DUE TO SCARCITY

2012 Bench Warmer Soccer Premium Triple Jersey Swatches Autographs Printing Plates Magenta Front
STATED PRINT RUN 1 SER. #'d SET
UNPRICED DUE TO SCARCITY

2012 Bench Warmer Soccer Premium Triple Jersey Swatches Autographs Printing Plates Yellow Back
STATED PRINT RUN 1 SER. #'d SET
UNPRICED DUE TO SCARCITY

2012 Bench Warmer Soccer Premium Triple Jersey Swatches Autographs Printing Plates Yellow Front
STATED PRINT RUN 1 SER. #'d SET
UNPRICED DUE TO SCARCITY

2012 Bench Warmer Vault Autographs Gold Foil

□ 1 Sara Underwood 10.00 25.00
□ 2 Yvette Nelson 8.00 20.00
□ 3 Amie Nicole 4.00 10.00
□ 4 Catherine Kluthe 4.00 10.00
□ 5 Julianna Prada 4.00 10.00
□ 6 Brooke Morales 4.00 10.00
□ 7 Lana Kinnear 5.00 12.00
□ 8 Katie Lohmann 5.00 12.00
□ 9 Candace Kita 4.00 10.00
□ 10 Kathie Smith 4.00 10.00
□ 11 Tamara Witmer 5.00 12.00
□ 12 Rebecca Mary 4.00 10.00
□ 13 Devin Devasquez 5.00 12.00
□ 14 Destiny Davis 4.00 10.00
□ 15 Victoria Fuller 4.00 10.00
□ 16 Carrie Stroup 5.00 12.00
□ 17 Nikki Ziering 6.00 15.00
□ 18 Flo Jalin 5.00 12.00
□ 19 Camille Anderson 4.00 10.00
□ 20 Shay Lyn Veasy 4.00 10.00
□ 21 Mary Riley 8.00 20.00
□ 22 Jaime Hammer 6.00 15.00
□ 23 Spencer Scott
□ 24 Shannon Malone 5.00 12.00
□ 25 Sherry Goggin 5.00 12.00
□ 26 Mishel Thorpe 4.00 10.00
□ 27 Tabitha Taylor 4.00 10.00
□ 28 Tina Jordan 5.00 12.00
□ 29 Alana Curry 5.00 12.00
□ 30 Buffy Tyler 5.00 12.00
□ 31 Teal Druda 4.00 10.00
□ 32 Cecille Gahr 4.00 10.00
□ 33 Brande Roderick
□ 34 Bobbi Billard 6.00 15.00
□ 35 Lisa Gleave 5.00 12.00
□ 36 Rochelle Loewen 6.00 15.00
□ 37 Sandra Taylor 5.00 12.00
□ 38 Amber Goetz 5.00 12.00
□ 39 Michelle Baena 4.00 10.00
□ 40 Jessica Hall 6.00 15.00
□ 41 Miki Black 4.00 10.00
□ 42 Brandie Moses 5.00 12.00
□ 43 Holley Dorrough 8.00 20.00
□ 44 Kayla Collins 6.00 15.00
□ 45 Jennifer England 5.00 12.00
□ 46 Lora Peterson 4.00 10.00
□ 47 Cassandra Lynn 4.00 10.00
□ 48 Nicole Bennett 4.00 10.00
□ 49 Molly Shea 5.00 12.00
□ 50 Zoe Gregory 4.00 10.00
□ 51 Tiffany Kyees 4.00 10.00
□ 52 Tiffany Selby 4.00 10.00
□ 53 Kerri Kasem 4.00 10.00
□ 54 Tiffany Granath 4.00 10.00
□ 55 Amanda Carrier 4.00 10.00
□ 56 Carolyn Martin 5.00 12.00
□ 57 Jennifer Korbin 10.00 25.00
□ 58 Torrie Wilson 12.00 30.00
□ 59 Cassandra Lynn Nurse 8.00 20.00
□ 60 Lana Kinnear Nurse 10.00 25.00
□ 61 Melissa Riso 6.00 15.00

2012 Bench Warmer Vault Autographs Pink Foil
*PINK/25: .5X TO 1.2X BASIC CARDS

2012 Bench Warmer Vault Autographs Green Foil
STATED PRINT RUN 10 SER. #'d SETS
UNPRICED DUE TO SCARCITY

2012 Bench Warmer Vault Autographs Blue Foil
STATED PRINT RUN 5 SER. #'d SETS
UNPRICED DUE TO SCARCITY

2012 Bench Warmer Vault Autographs Red Foil
STATED PRINT RUN 1 SER. #'d SET
UNPRICED DUE TO SCARCITY

2012 Bench Warmer Vault Authentic Swatches
ONE SWATCH OR KISS CARD PER BOX

□ 1 Spencer Scott 15.00 40.00
□ 2 Gail Kim 12.00 30.00
□ 3 Camille Anderson 10.00 25.00
□ 4 Bobbi Billard 10.00 25.00
□ 5 Nikki Ziering 12.00 30.00
□ 6 Torrie Wilson 15.00 40.00
□ 7 Flo Jalin 15.00 40.00
□ 8 Traci Brooks 10.00 25.00
□ 9 Candace Kita 15.00 40.00
□ 10 Kayla Collins 12.00 30.00
□ 11 Louise Glover 12.00 30.00
□ 12 Christy Hemme 15.00 40.00
□ 13 Brandie Moses 12.00 30.00
□ 14 April Scott 15.00 40.00
□ 15 Molly Shea 12.00 30.00
□ 16 Bambi Lashell 12.00 30.00
□ 17 Nikki Zeno 12.00 30.00
□ 18 Holly Madison 15.00 40.00

2012 Bench Warmer Vault Boy Beater Swatches
ONE SWATCH OR KISS CARD PER BOX

□ 1 Carmen Electra 25.00 50.00
□ 2 Brande Roderick 12.00 30.00
□ 3 Jennifer Korbin 20.00 50.00
□ 4 Crystal Harris 12.00 30.00
□ 5 Torrie Wilson 15.00 40.00
□ 6 Sara Underwood 30.00 60.00
□ 7 Tiffany Toth 12.00 30.00
□ 8 Maria Kanellis 20.00 50.00
□ 9 Mary Riley 20.00 50.00
□ 10 Suzanne Stokes 15.00 40.00
□ 11 Kara Monaco 12.00 30.00
□ 12 Miriam Gonzalez 15.00 40.00

2012 Bench Warmer Vault Kiss Gold Foil
ONE SWATCH OR KISS CARD PER BOX

□ 1 Mary Riley 10.00 25.00
□ 2 Nikki Ziering 8.00 20.00
□ 3 Zoe Gregory 6.00 15.00
□ 4 Nicole Bennett 6.00 15.00
□ 5 Jaime Hammer 8.00 20.00
□ 6 Jessica Burciaga
□ 7 Brandy Grace 8.00 20.00
□ 8 Katie Lohmann 10.00 25.00
□ 9 Mishel Thorpe 8.00 20.00
□ 10 Jennifer England 8.00 20.00
□ 11 Flo Jalin 10.00 25.00
□ 12 Miriam Gonzalez 8.00 20.00
□ 13 Victoria Fuller 8.00 20.00
□ 14 Tina Jordan 6.00 15.00
□ 15 Tiffany Selby 8.00 20.00
□ 16 Tamara Witmer 10.00 25.00
□ 17 Julianna Prada 8.00 20.00
□ 18 Sherry Goggin 6.00 15.00
□ 19 Catherine Kluthe 8.00 20.00
□ 20 Sara Underwood 15.00 40.00

2012 Bench Warmer Vault Kiss Autographs Purple Foil
ONE SWATCH OR KISS CARD PER BOX

□ 1 Mary Riley 15.00 40.00
□ 2 Nikki Ziering 12.00 30.00
□ 3 Zoe Gregory 10.00 25.00
□ 4 Nicole Bennett 10.00 25.00
□ 5 Jaime Hammer 12.00 30.00
□ 6 Jessica Burciaga
□ 7 Brandy Grace 12.00 30.00
□ 8 Katie Lohmann 15.00 40.00
□ 9 Mishel Thorpe 12.00 30.00
□ 10 Jennifer England 12.00 30.00
□ 11 Flo Jalin 15.00 40.00
□ 12 Miriam Gonzalez 12.00 30.00
□ 13 Victoria Fuller 12.00 30.00
□ 14 Tina Jordan 10.00 25.00
□ 15 Tiffany Selby 12.00 30.00
□ 16 Tamara Witmer 15.00 40.00
□ 17 Julianna Prada 12.00 30.00
□ 18 Sherry Goggin 10.00 25.00
□ 19 Catherine Kluthe 12.00 30.00
□ 20 Sara Underwood 30.00 60.00

2012 Bench Warmer Vault Kiss Autographs Pink Foil
STATED PRINT RUN 15 SER. #'d SETS
UNPRICED DUE TO SCARCITY

2012 Bench Warmer Vault Kiss Autographs Green Foil
STATED PRINT RUN 10 SER. #'d SETS
UNPRICED DUE TO SCARCITY

2012 Bench Warmer Vault Kiss Autographs Blue Foil
UNPRICED DUE TO SCARCITY

2012 Bench Warmer Vault Kiss Autographs Red Foil
STATED PRINT RUN 1 SER. #'d SET
UNPRICED DUE TO SCARCITY

2012 Bench Warmer Vegas Baby Autographs Gold Foil
RANDOM INSERT IN PACKS

□ 1 Alicia Johnson 5.00 12.00
□ 2 Bambi Lashell 5.00 12.00
□ 3 Billie Jo Powers 5.00 12.00
□ 4 Brande Roderick 5.00 12.00
□ 5 Brandie Moses 5.00 12.00
□ 6 Brandy Grace 5.00 12.00
□ 7 Brittany Herrera 5.00 12.00
□ 8 Buffy Tyler 5.00 12.00
□ 9 Candace Kita 5.00 12.00
□ 10 Carolyn Martin 5.00 12.00
□ 11 Carrie Minter 5.00 12.00
□ 12 Casey Durkin 5.00 12.00
□ 13 Cassandra Lynn 5.00 12.00
□ 14 Cecille Gahr 5.00 12.00
□ 15 Claudia Jordan 5.00 12.00
□ 16 Crystal Harris 6.00 15.00
□ 17 Deanna Brooks 5.00 12.00
□ 18 Heather Rae Young 5.00 12.00
□ 19 Holley Dorrough 5.00 12.00
□ 20 Jaime Hammer 5.00 12.00
□ 21 Jasmine Dustin 5.00 12.00
□ 22 Jenae Alt 5.00 12.00
□ 23 Jennifer Korbin 8.00 20.00
□ 24 Jessica Burciaga 8.00 20.00
□ 25 Jessica Kinni 5.00 12.00
□ 26 Kara Monaco 5.00 12.00
□ 27 Katie Lohmann 5.00 12.00
□ 28 Kirsty Lingman 5.00 12.00
□ 29 Lisa Gleave 5.00 12.00
□ 30 Lisa Ligon 5.00 12.00
□ 31 Maria Kanellis 6.00 15.00
□ 32 Mary Riley 8.00 20.00
□ 33 Melissa Riso 5.00 12.00
□ 34 Michelle Baena 5.00 12.00
□ 35 Miki Black 5.00 12.00

- ❑ 36 Nicole Bennett 5.00 12.00
- ❑ 37 Nikki Ziering 5.00 12.00
- ❑ 38 Paige Peterson 5.00 12.00
- ❑ 39 Rachel Bernstein 5.00 12.00
- ❑ 40 Ryan Shamrock 5.00 12.00
- ❑ 41 Sandra Taylor 8.00 20.00
- ❑ 42 Shay Lyn Veasy 5.00 12.00
- ❑ 43 Suzanne Stokes 5.00 12.00
- ❑ 44 Syd Wilder 5.00 12.00
- ❑ 45 Tabitha Taylor 5.00 12.00
- ❑ 46 Talor Marion 5.00 12.00
- ❑ 47 Tamara Witmer 5.00 12.00
- ❑ 48 Tanea Brooks 5.00 12.00
- ❑ 49 Tiffany Selby 5.00 12.00
- ❑ 50 Tiffany Toth 5.00 12.00
- ❑ 51 Torrie Wilson 8.00 20.00
- ❑ 52 Yancey Taylor 5.00 12.00
- ❑ 53 Yvette Lopez 5.00 12.00
- ❑ 54 Yvette Nelson 5.00 12.00
- ❑ CE1 Carmen Electra 40.00 80.00

2012 Bench Warmer Vegas Baby Autographs Pink Foil

COMPLETE SET
STATED PRINT RUN 21 SER. #'d SETS

2012 Bench Warmer Vegas Baby Kiss Gold Foil

STATED PRINT RUN 25 SER. #'d SETS

- ❑ 1 Buffy Tyler 12.00 30.00
- ❑ 2 Cassandra Lynn 12.00 30.00
- ❑ 3 Jennifer Korbin 15.00 40.00
- ❑ 4 Jessica Hall 12.00 30.00
- ❑ 5 Katie Lohmann 12.00 30.00
- ❑ 6 Kirsty Lingman 12.00 30.00
- ❑ 7 Lisa Gleave 12.00 30.00
- ❑ 8 Miriam Gonzalez 20.00 50.00
- ❑ 9 Sara Underwood 40.00 80.00

2012 Bench Warmer Vegas Baby Kiss Pink Foil

STATED PRINT RUN 15 SER. #'d SETS

2012 Bench Warmer Vegas Baby Sin City Swatches Gold Foil

STATED PRINT RUN 21 SER. #'d SETS

- ❑ 1 Brande Roderick 25.00 50.00
- ❑ 2 Cassandra Lynn 25.00 50.00
- ❑ 3 Crystal Harris 30.00 60.00
- ❑ 4 Jennifer Korbin 25.00 50.00
- ❑ 5 Jessica Burciaga 30.00 60.00
- ❑ 6 Maria Kanellis 25.00 50.00
- ❑ 7 Mary Riley 30.00 60.00
- ❑ 8 Sara Underwood 40.00 80.00
- ❑ 9 Torrie Wilson 30.00 60.00

2012 Bench Warmer Vegas Baby Sin City Swatches Pink Foil

STATED PRINT RUN 15 SER. #'d SETS

2012 Bench Warmer Vegas Baby Sportsbook Autographs Gold Foil

STATED PRINT RUN 25 SER. #'d SETS

- ❑ 1 Brande Roderick 12.00 30.00
- ❑ 2 Crystal Harris 12.00 30.00
- ❑ 3 Jessica Burciaga 15.00 40.00
- ❑ 4 Jessica Hall 12.00 30.00
- ❑ 5 Katie Lohmann 12.00 30.00
- ❑ 6 Lisa Gleave 12.00 30.00
- ❑ 7 Mary Riley 15.00 40.00
- ❑ 8 Ryan Shamrock 12.00 30.00
- ❑ 9 Sandra Taylor 20.00 50.00
- ❑ 10 Sara Underwood 30.00 60.00
- ❑ 11 Tiffany Selby 12.00 30.00
- ❑ 12 Torrie Wilson 15.00 40.00

2012 Bench Warmer Vegas Baby Sportsbook Autographs Pink Foil

STATED PRINT RUN 15 SER. #'d SETS

2012 The Big Bang Theory Seasons One and Two

COMPLETE SET (72) 8.00 20.00

- ❑ 1 Checklist .20 .50
- ❑ 2 Genetic Fraud .20 .50
- ❑ 3 String Theory Doodling .20 .50
- ❑ 4 Bon Douche .20 .50
- ❑ 5 Biological Impossibility .20 .50
- ❑ 6 Buttons .20 .50
- ❑ 7 Exactly Half .20 .50
- ❑ 8 Swirling Vortex of Entropy .20 .50
- ❑ 9 In an Apartment Not So Far Away .20 .50
- ❑ 10 Sarcasm Sign .20 .50
- ❑ 11 We're Okay .20 .50
- ❑ 12 Some Assembly Required .20 .50
- ❑ 13 Easy Fix .20 .50
- ❑ 14 The Gates of Elzebub .20 .50
- ❑ 15 Sounds Yummy .20 .50
- ❑ 16 Advantages of Bulk .20 .50
- ❑ 17 Last Resort .20 .50
- ❑ 18 Semiotics .20 .50
- ❑ 19 Something to Mull About .20 .50
- ❑ 20 Apathetic .20 .50
- ❑ 21 Party Faux Pas .20 .50
- ❑ 22 Diversity .20 .50
- ❑ 23 Always Prepared .20 .50
- ❑ 24 There, There .20 .50
- ❑ 25 Mock the Flog Technology .20 .50
- ❑ 26 A Sucky Notion .20 .50
- ❑ 27 Grasshopper .20 .50
- ❑ 28 L'Chai-im, L'Chai-im, to Life .20 .50
- ❑ 29 No Universal Remote Required .20 .50
- ❑ 30 Splash Zone .20 .50
- ❑ 31 Symposium .20 .50
- ❑ 32 Typhoid Penny .20 .50
- ❑ 33 Code Milky Green .20 .50
- ❑ 34 Radiation Suit .20 .50
- ❑ 35 Downy Feline .20 .50
- ❑ 36 Go Away .20 .50
- ❑ 37 The Needs of the Many .20 .50
- ❑ 38 Metaphors .20 .50
- ❑ 39 AA .20 .50
- ❑ 40 Smooth Escape .20 .50
- ❑ 41 Loin Guarder .20 .50
- ❑ 42 Juvenile Squabbling .20 .50
- ❑ 43 Non-Optional Social Convention .20 .50
- ❑ 44 r=d .20 .50
- ❑ 45 Homemade Jokes .20 .50
- ❑ 46 Don't Tell Leonard .20 .50
- ❑ 47 Salutations .20 .50
- ❑ 48 Deal Breaker .20 .50
- ❑ 49 Inspirational .20 .50
- ❑ 50 Viewing Area .20 .50
- ❑ 51 Desperate Measures .20 .50
- ❑ 52 Simple Children's Game .20 .50
- ❑ 53 Pick-Up Artist .20 .50
- ❑ 54 Defcon 1 . . . Or 5 .20 .50
- ❑ 55 Bromance .20 .50
- ❑ 56 Cacophonous Assault .20 .50
- ❑ 57 Eggnog + 1/5 of Rum .20 .50
- ❑ 58 MONTE .20 .50
- ❑ 59 Die, Toaster Die .20 .50
- ❑ 60 Stu the Cockatoo Theorem .20 .50
- ❑ 61 Invasive Medical Procedure .20 .50
- ❑ 62 Salt, Shot, Lime .20 .50
- ❑ 63 Wackadoodle .20 .50
- ❑ 64 Moonpie .20 .50
- ❑ 65 Penny Blossoms .20 .50
- ❑ 66 Problematic Glitter .20 .50
- ❑ 67 Market Expansion .20 .50
- ❑ 68 Homesick .20 .50
- ❑ 69 AKA Fan .20 .50
- ❑ 70 All the Perks .20 .50
- ❑ 71 Long Hug Goodbye .20 .50
- ❑ 72 90 Days and Nights .20 .50
- ❑ P1 Big Bang Theory PROMO 3.00 8.00

2012 The Big Bang Theory Seasons One and Two Authentic Wardrobe Costumes

STATED ODDS 1:24

- ❑ M1 Sheldon's Bathrobe 20.00 40.00
- ❑ M2 Sheldon's Purple Undershirt 20.00 40.00
- ❑ M3 Sheldon's Blue Undershirt 20.00 40.00
- ❑ M4 Sheldon's Plaid Pants 20.00 40.00
- ❑ M5 Howard's Purple V-Neck 15.00 30.00
- ❑ M6 Howard's Orange Shirt 15.00 30.00
- ❑ M7 Howard's Maroon Turtleneck 15.00 30.00
- ❑ M8 Howard's Green Pants 15.00 30.00
- ❑ M9 Leonard's Dress Shirt 15.00 30.00
- ❑ M10 Leonard's Red T-Shirt 15.00 30.00
- ❑ M11 Leonard's Green Hoodie 15.00 30.00
- ❑ M12 Raj's Purple Jacket 15.00 30.00
- ❑ M13 Raj's Yellow Shirt 15.00 30.00
- ❑ M14 Raj's Green Shirt 15.00 30.00
- ❑ M15 Penny's Hoodie 60.00 120.00
- ❑ M16 Penny's Sweatpants 60.00 120.00
- ❑ M17 Penny's Top 60.00 120.00
- ❑ M18 Sheldon's Pajamas SP 30.00 60.00
- ❑ NNO Five-Piece EXCH

2012 The Big Bang Theory Seasons One and Two Autographs

STATED ODDS 1:24
R=RARE, U=UNCOMMON

- ❑ A1 Johnny Galecki R 150.00 300.00
- ❑ A2 Jim Parsons R 300.00 500.00
- ❑ A3 Kaley Cuoco R 350.00 550.00
- ❑ A4 Simon Helberg R 125.00 225.00
- ❑ A5 Kunal Nayyar R 125.00 225.00
- ❑ A6 Kevin Sussman U 40.00 80.00
- ❑ A7 John Ross Bowie 12.00 30.00
- ❑ A8 Laurie Metcalf U 40.00 80.00
- ❑ A9 Brian George 10.00 25.00
- ❑ A10 Alice Amter 10.00 25.00
- ❑ A11 Courtney Henggeler 12.00 30.00

2012 The Big Bang Theory Seasons One and Two Behind the Scenes

COMPLETE SET (9) 25.00 50.00
OVERALL CHASE ODDS 1:6

- ❑ C1 Jim Parsons 4.00 10.00
- ❑ C2 Kunal Nayyar and Jim Parsons 4.00 10.00
- ❑ C3 Paintball 4.00 10.00
- ❑ C4 Kaley Cuoco and Jim Parsons 4.00 10.00
- ❑ C5 Kaley Cuoco 4.00 10.00
- ❑ C6 Filming 4.00 10.00
- ❑ C7 Johnny Galecki and Jim Parsons 4.00 10.00
- ❑ C8 Kaley Cuoco and Johnny Galecki 4.00 10.00
- ❑ C9 Johnny Galecki and Jim Parsons 4.00 10.00

2012 The Big Bang Theory Seasons One and Two Special Moments

COMPLETE SET (9) 10.00 25.00
OVERALL CHASE ODDS 1:6

- ❑ F1 Penny's Hug 2.00 5.00
- ❑ F2 Plea for Help 2.00 5.00
- ❑ F3 Borrowed Pillowcase 2.00 5.00
- ❑ F4 Too Much Freud 2.00 5.00
- ❑ F5 Queen Bee 2.00 5.00
- ❑ F6 An Exercise in Futility 2.00 5.00
- ❑ F7 Easier Than an Engine 2.00 5.00
- ❑ F8 I'm a Falcon 2.00 5.00
- ❑ F9 Scanners-esque 2.00 5.00

2012 The Big Bang Theory Seasons Three and Four

COMPLETE SET (68) 6.00 15.00

- ❑ 1 I Don't Know What Arctic .20 .50
- ❑ 2 Yeah I Just Stopped By .20 .50
- ❑ 3 You Fellas Are Planning .20 .50
- ❑ 4 Like the Proverbial Cheese .20 .50
- ❑ 5 Oh My God .20 .50
- ❑ 6 Howdy Ma'am .20 .50
- ❑ 7 I Sense I May Have Crossed .20 .50
- ❑ 8 The Science Chirps For Itself .20 .50
- ❑ 9 Oh I Really Don't Care Anymore .20 .50
- ❑ 10 Of Course I'm Right .20 .50
- ❑ 11 The Math Would Suggest .20 .50
- ❑ 12 Would You Like a Chocolate .20 .50
- ❑ 13 What's Going On .20 .50
- ❑ 14 Are We Gonna Talk .20 .50
- ❑ 15 I Couldn't Even Talk .20 .50
- ❑ 16 Alright Raj Looks Like .20 .50
- ❑ 17 The Year Was 1995 .20 .50
- ❑ 18 It's Like the Slogan Says .20 .50
- ❑ 19 Would You Like a Commemorative .20 .50
- ❑ 20 And She Wonders Why .20 .50
- ❑ 21 She Was My Second Cousin .20 .50
- ❑ 22 Cause of Accident .20 .50
- ❑ 23 It's a Warm Summer Evening .20 .50
- ❑ 24 Oh Yes the Waitress/Actress .20 .50
- ❑ 25 Howard, Artificial Women .20 .50
- ❑ 26 I am the Master .20 .50
- ❑ 27 Penny I Told You .20 .50
- ❑ 28 Let Me Get That Plate .20 .50
- ❑ 29 Before We Get to the Courthouse .20 .50
- ❑ 30 That's My Girl .20 .50
- ❑ 31 You Are My Boyfriend .20 .50
- ❑ 32 This Is Great .20 .50
- ❑ 33 Is Your Mother a Good .20 .50
- ❑ 34 I Don't Know About You .20 .50
- ❑ 35 Go Team Leonard .20 .50
- ❑ 36 So What You're Just Going .20 .50
- ❑ 37 So You Say You Can't .20 .50
- ❑ 38 As a Native Texan .20 .50
- ❑ 39 Why On Earth Would We .20 .50
- ❑ 40 Let Me Get My Cockamamie .20 .50
- ❑ 41 Just Like a Real Hand .20 .50
- ❑ 42 Hey Nice Knees .20 .50
- ❑ 43 He's a Lamb .20 .50
- ❑ 44 He Takes the Kitty to the Potty .20 .50
- ❑ 45 So You Decided to Get .20 .50
- ❑ 46 What Are You Doing In There .20 .50
- ❑ 47 Are You Still Depressed .20 .50
- ❑ 48 Now Get My Back Jack .20 .50
- ❑ 49 Excuse Me Madam .20 .50
- ❑ 50 It's Really Nice To See You .20 .50
- ❑ 51 Leonard, Call Me If You're Interested .20 .50
- ❑ 52 You Pop, Sparkle, and Buzz .20 .50
- ❑ 53 Penny, You Face Failure .20 .50
- ❑ 54 You're Peeing Aren't You .20 .50
- ❑ 55 We're Having a Conversation .20 .50
- ❑ 56 Galileo Did His Best Work .20 .50
- ❑ 57 Couldn't You Just Fool Around .20 .50
- ❑ 58 Where Would I Have Picked Up .20 .50
- ❑ 59 How Did You Get So Brave .20 .50
- ❑ 60 I've Said This Before .20 .50
- ❑ 61 Remember People .20 .50
- ❑ 62 Now When You Say Look After .20 .50
- ❑ 63 I Choose You .20 .50
- ❑ 64 Perhaps Your Talk .20 .50
- ❑ 65 Really Ten Miles .20 .50
- ❑ 66 Mommy Daddy You Remember .20 .50
- ❑ 67 Rajesh and I Have a Good Thing .20 .50
- ❑ NNO Checklist .20 .50

2012 The Big Bang Theory Seasons Three and Four Printing Plates Black

STATED PRINT RUN 1 SER. #'d SET
UNPRICED DUE TO SCARCITY

2012 The Big Bang Theory Seasons Three and Four Printing Plates Cyan

STATED PRINT RUN 1 SER. #'d SET
UNPRICED DUE TO SCARCITY

2012 The Big Bang Theory Seasons Three and Four Printing Plates Magenta

STATED PRINT RUN 1 SER. #'d SET
UNPRICED DUE TO SCARCITY

2012 The Big Bang Theory Seasons Three and Four Printing Plates Yellow

STATED PRINT RUN 1 SER. #'d SET
UNPRICED DUE TO SCARCITY

2012 The Big Bang Theory Seasons Three and Four Autograph Wardrobe Memorabilia

OVERALL AUTO ODDS 1:24

- ❑ A1 Johnny Galecki as Leonard 200.00 400.00
- ❑ A2 Jim Parsons as Sheldon 300.00 500.00
- ❑ A3 Kaley Cuoco as Penny 450.00 700.00
- ❑ A4 Simon Helberg as Howard 200.00 300.00
- ❑ A5 Kunal Nayyar as Raj 200.00 350.00
- ❑ A6 Mayim Bialik as Amy 300.00 500.00
- ❑ A7 Melissa Rauch as Bernadette 300.00 500.00

2012 The Big Bang Theory Seasons Three and Four Autographs

OVERALL AUTO ODDS 1:24

- ❑ A8 Aarti Mann as Priya 20.00 40.00
- ❑ A9 Kevin Sussman as Stuart 20.00 40.00
- ❑ A10 John Ross Bowie as Barry 8.00 20.00
- ❑ A11 Christine Baranski as Beverly Hofstadter 10.00 25.00
- ❑ A12 Laurie Metcalf as Mary Cooper 15.00 30.00
- ❑ A13 Alice Amter as Mrs. Koothrappali 8.00 20.00
- ❑ A14 Brian George as Dr. Koothrappali 8.00 20.00
- ❑ A15 Carol Ann Susi as Mrs. Wolowitz 10.00 25.00
- ❑ A16 Danica McKellar as Abby 30.00 60.00
- ❑ A17 Wil Wheaton 20.00 40.00
- ❑ A18 Rick Fox as Glenn 10.00 25.00
- ❑ A19 Levar Burton 20.00 50.00
- ❑ A20 Ian Scott Rudolph as Captain Sweatpants 8.00 20.00

2012 The Big Bang Theory Seasons Three and Four Dual Wardrobe Memorabilia

OVERALL WARDROBE ODDS 1:24

- ❑ DM1 Penny/Sheldon 50.00 100.00
- ❑ DM2 Amy/Sheldon 35.00 70.00
- ❑ DM3 Leonard/Sheldon 30.00 60.00
- ❑ DM4 Howard/Raj 30.00 60.00
- ❑ DM5 Penny/Leonard 50.00 100.00
- ❑ DM6 Howard/Bernadette 35.00 70.00
- ❑ DM7 Leonard/Raj 25.00 50.00

2012 The Big Bang Theory Seasons Three and Four Duos

COMPLETE SET (9) 10.00 25.00
STATED ODDS 1:12

- ❑ CPL1 Leonard/Penny 2.00 5.00
- ❑ CPL2 Howard/Bernadette 2.00 5.00
- ❑ CPL3 Sheldon/Penny 2.00 5.00
- ❑ CPL4 Sheldon/Mrs. Hofstadter 2.00 5.00
- ❑ CPL5 Leonard/Priya 2.00 5.00
- ❑ CPL6 Sheldon/Amy Farrah 2.00 5.00
- ❑ CPL7 Howard/Bernadette 2.00 5.00
- ❑ CPL8 Bernadette/Raj 2.00 5.00
- ❑ CPL9 Penny/Raj 2.00 5.00

2012 The Big Bang Theory Seasons Three and Four The Elevator

COMPLETE SET (9) 10.00 25.00
STATED ODDS 1:12

- ❑ E1 No, You Want the Crazy Guy 2.00 5.00
- ❑ E2 You May Want to Repaint 2.00 5.00
- ❑ E3 Initial Here 2.00 5.00
- ❑ E4 I Can't Speak for These Guys 2.00 5.00
- ❑ E5 Did It Occur to You 2.00 5.00
- ❑ E6 Oh, Yes 2.00 5.00
- ❑ E7 I Don't Have Play Dates 2.00 5.00
- ❑ E8 You Don't See You're Mistake 2.00 5.00
- ❑ E9 A Bad Thing 2.00 5.00

2012 The Big Bang Theory Seasons Three and Four Wardrobe Memorabilia

OVERALL WARDROBE ODDS 1:24

- ❑ M1 Sheldon's Purple Shirt 20.00 50.00
- ❑ M1.1 Shelbot's Purple Shirt 20.00 50.00
- ❑ M2 Leonard's Boxers 20.00 50.00
- ❑ M3 Penny's Blue Tank 35.00 70.00
- ❑ M4 Raj's Cream Shirt 15.00 40.00
- ❑ M5 Howard's Blue Shirt 15.00 40.00
- ❑ M6 Amy's Green Shirt 15.00 40.00
- ❑ M7 Bernadette's Floral Shirt 20.00 50.00
- ❑ M8 Sheldon's Green Shirt 20.00 50.00
- ❑ M9 Leonard's Blue Shirt 20.00 50.00
- ❑ M10 Penny's Yellow Tank 35.00 70.00
- ❑ M11 Howard's Green Shirt 15.00 40.00
- ❑ M12 Amy's Blue Plaid Shirt 15.00 40.00
- ❑ M13 Bernadette's Red Scarf 20.00 50.00
- ❑ M14 Sheldon's Lt. Blue Shirt 20.00 50.00
- ❑ M15 Leonard's Grey Sweatshirt 20.00 50.00
- ❑ M16 Penny's Floral Dress 35.00 70.00
- ❑ M17 Raj's Brown Shirt 15.00 40.00
- ❑ M18 Howard's Purple Shirt 15.00 40.00
- ❑ M19 Sheldon's Green Shirt 20.00 50.00
- ❑ M20 Leonard's Blue Shirt 20.00 50.00
- ❑ M21 Penny's Pink PJ Pants 35.00 70.00
- ❑ M22 Raj's Yellow Jacket 15.00 40.00
- ❑ M23 Sheldon's Purple Undershirt 20.00 50.00
- ❑ M24 Leonard's Red Shirt 20.00 50.00
- ❑ M25 Howard's Purple Shirt 15.00 40.00
- ❑ M26 Penny's Pink Tank 35.00 70.00
- ❑ M27 Sheldon's Red Shirt 20.00 50.00
- ❑ M28 Raj's Red Jacket 15.00 40.00
- ❑ M29 Howard's Yellow Shirt (Binder Exclusive) 25.00 50.00

2012 DC Comics Batman The Legend

COMPLETE SET (63) 6.00 15.00

- ❑ 1 Batman .20 .50
- ❑ 2 Bruce Wayne .20 .50
- ❑ 3 Robin .20 .50
- ❑ 4 Dick Grayson .20 .50
- ❑ 5 Jason Todd .20 .50
- ❑ 6 Tim Drake .20 .50
- ❑ 7 Alfred Pennyworth .20 .50
- ❑ 8 Commissioner James Gordon .20 .50
- ❑ 9 Batgirl .20 .50
- ❑ 10 Oracle .20 .50
- ❑ 11 Barbara Gordon .20 .50
- ❑ 12 The Joker .20 .50
- ❑ 13 The Penguin .20 .50
- ❑ 14 The Riddler .20 .50
- ❑ 15 Two-Face .20 .50
- ❑ 16 Harvey Dent .20 .50
- ❑ 17 Poison Ivy .20 .50
- ❑ 18 Catwoman .20 .50
- ❑ 19 Selina Kyle .20 .50
- ❑ 20 Batwoman .20 .50
- ❑ 21 Wayne Manor .20 .50
- ❑ 22 Bat-Mite .20 .50
- ❑ 23 Lucius Fox .20 .50
- ❑ 24 Nightwing .20 .50
- ❑ 25 DC Comics Red Hood .20 .50
- ❑ 26 The Court of Owls .20 .50
- ❑ 27 The Huntress .20 .50
- ❑ 28 Spoiler .20 .50
- ❑ 29 Ace, The Bat Hound .20 .50
- ❑ 30 The Scarecrow .20 .50
- ❑ 31 Mr. Freeze .20 .50
- ❑ 32 Ra's al Ghul .20 .50
- ❑ 33 Talia al Ghul .20 .50
- ❑ 34 Red Robin .20 .50
- ❑ 35 The Birds of Prey .20 .50
- ❑ 36 The Outsiders .20 .50
- ❑ 37 Kate Kane .20 .50
- ❑ 38 Batwing .20 .50
- ❑ 39 Bane .20 .50
- ❑ 40 Deadshot .20 .50
- ❑ 41 Calman .20 .50
- ❑ 42 Manhunter .20 .50
- ❑ 43 Anarky .20 .50
- ❑ 44 Azrael as Batman .20 .50
- ❑ 45 Talon .20 .50
- ❑ 46 Batman Beyond .20 .50
- ❑ 47 Black Mask .20 .50
- ❑ 48 Clayface .20 .50
- ❑ 49 Jokerz .20 .50
- ❑ 50 Vesper Fairchild .20 .50
- ❑ 51 Firefly .20 .50
- ❑ 52 Harley Quinn .20 .50
- ❑ 53 Kathy Kane .20 .50
- ❑ 54 Killer Croc .20 .50
- ❑ 55 Jervis Tetchc .20 .50
- ❑ 56 Man-Bat .20 .50
- ❑ 57 Batman Utility Belt .20 .50
- ❑ 58 Silver St. Cloud .20 .50
- ❑ 59 Leslie Thompkins, M.D. .20 .50
- ❑ 60 Ventriloquist and Scarface .20 .50
- ❑ 61 Batman of Earth Two .20 .50
- ❑ 62 Checklist .20 .50
- ❑ 63 Batman and Superman .20 .50
- ❑ P1 Batman/Joker PROMO .20 .50

2012 DC Comics Batman The Legend Bat-cave Puzzle

COMPLETE SET (9) 10.00 25.00
STATED ODDS

- ❑ TBC1 Batcave 2.00 5.00
- ❑ TBC2 Batcave 2.00 5.00
- ❑ TBC3 Batcave 2.00 5.00
- ❑ TBC4 Batcave 2.00 5.00
- ❑ TBC5 Batcave 2.00 5.00
- ❑ TBC6 Batcave 2.00 5.00
- ❑ TBC7 Batcave 2.00 5.00
- ❑ TBC8 Batcave 2.00 5.00
- ❑ TBC9 Batcave 2.00 5.00

2012 DC Comics Batman The Legend Batmobile

COMPLETE SET (9) 12.00 30.00
STATED ODDS

- ❑ BM1 Batmobile 2.00 5.00
- ❑ BM2 Batmobile 2.00 5.00
- ❑ BM3 Batmobile 2.00 5.00
- ❑ BM4 Batmobile 2.00 5.00
- ❑ BM5 Batmobile 2.00 5.00
- ❑ BM6 Batmobile 2.00 5.00
- ❑ BM7 Batmobile 2.00 5.00
- ❑ BM8 Batmobile 2.00 5.00
- ❑ BM9 Batmobile 2.00 5.00

2012 DC Comics Batman The Legend Circus of Villains

COMPLETE SET (8) 12.00 30.00
STATED ODDS

- ❑ CP1 The Joker 4.00 10.00
- ❑ CP2 Mr. Freeze 2.50 6.00
- ❑ CP3 The Penguin 2.50 6.00
- ❑ CP4 The Scarecrow 2.50 6.00
- ❑ CP5 Killer Croc 2.50 6.00
- ❑ CP6 Poison Ivy 2.50 6.00
- ❑ CP7 Two-Face 2.50 6.00
- ❑ CP8 Man-Bat 2.50 6.00

2012 DC Comics Batman The Legend Sketches

STATED ODDS 1:24

- ❑ 1 Adam DeKraker
- ❑ 2 Adriano Andy Carreon
- ❑ 3 Amber Shelton/40*
- ❑ 4 Amy Pronovost/50*
- ❑ 5 Andy Price
- ❑ 6 Anthony Hochrein
- ❑ 7 Anthony Wheeler
- ❑ 8 Ashleigh Popplewell
- ❑ 9 Aston Roy Cover
- ❑ 10 Autumn Rain Turkel
- ❑ 11 Benjamin Glendenning
- ❑ 12 Boo
- ❑ 13 Brendon and Brian Fraim
- ❑ 14 Brent Engstrom
- ❑ 15 Brian Kong
- ❑ 16 Bruce Gerlach
- ❑ 17 Bruno Bull de Oliveira
- ❑ 18 Buddy Prince
- ❑ 19 Bukshot
- ❑ 20 Cal Slayton/36*
- ❑ 21 Camila Fortuna
- ❑ 22 Carlos Sanchez
- ❑ 23 Chad Cicconi
- ❑ 24 Chad Hardin
- ❑ 25 Charles Hall
- ❑ 26 Charles Holbert
- ❑ 27 Chris Chuckry
- ❑ 28 Chris Foreman
- ❑ 29 Chris Glenn
- ❑ 30 Clayton McCormack
- ❑ 31 Cruddie Torian
- ❑ 32 Dan Bergren
- ❑ 33 Dan Borgonos
- ❑ 34 Dan Chaparro
- ❑ 35 Dan Schaefer
- ❑ 36 Dana Black
- ❑ 37 Daniel Gorman
- ❑ 38 Daniel HDR
- ❑ 39 Danielle Gransaull
- ❑ 40 Danny Devine
- ❑ 41 Dave Beaty
- ❑ 42 Dave Tata
- ❑ 43 David Baron
- ❑ 44 David Namisato
- ❑ 45 Dennis Crisostomo
- ❑ 46 Diana Greenhalgh/49*
- ❑ 47 Elliot Fernandez
- ❑ 48 Elvis Moura
- ❑ 49 Eric Van Elslande/80*
- ❑ 50 Erik Caines
- ❑ 51 Erik Maell
- ❑ 52 Frank A. Kadar/30*
- ❑ 53 Garry McKee
- ❑ 54 Gary Kezele
- ❑ 55 Gary Shipman
- ❑ 56 George Davis/50*
- ❑ 57 Gilbert Monsanto
- ❑ 58 Hanie Mohd
- ❑ 59 Hayden Davis
- ❑ 60 Irma Ahmed
- ❑ 61 Isaiah McAllister/50*
- ❑ 62 Jader Correa
- ❑ 63 Jason Keith Phillips
- ❑ 64 JC Fabul
- ❑ 65 Jed Thomas
- ❑ 66 Jeff Chandler
- ❑ 67 Jefferson Hojas
- ❑ 68 Jennifer Mercer
- ❑ 69 Jeremy Treece
- ❑ 70 Jerry Ma
- ❑ 71 Jezreel Rojales
- ❑ 72 Joe Hogan
- ❑ 73 Joe Pekar
- ❑ 74 John Haun/30*
- ❑ 75 John JAX Jackman
- ❑ 76 Jomar Bulda
- ❑ 77 Jonathan T. Racimo
- ❑ 78 Jonathan Wayshak
- ❑ 79 Josh Howard
- ❑ 80 Kat Laurange
- ❑ 81 Kate Glasheen
- ❑ 82 Kathryn Layno
- ❑ 83 Katie Cook
- ❑ 84 Ken Knudtsen
- ❑ 85 Kent Heidelman
- ❑ 86 Kevin Gentilcore/70*
- ❑ 87 Lance HaunRogue
- ❑ 88 Laura Inglis
- ❑ 89 Lawrence Snelly
- ❑ 90 Layron DeJarnette
- ❑ 91 Lee Ferguson
- ❑ 92 Luke Smarto
- ❑ 93 Marat Mychaels
- ❑ 94 Marcelo Ferreira
- ❑ 95 Marcus Smith
- ❑ 96 Mark Marvida
- ❑ 97 Mark Pennington
- ❑ 98 Matias Streb
- ❑ 99 Matt Hansen
- ❑ 100 Melike Acar
- ❑ 101 Michael Duron
- ❑ 102 Michael Kasinger
- ❑ 103 Michael Rooth
- ❑ 104 Mick and Matt Glebe/49*
- ❑ 105 Mike Legan
- ❑ 106 Mike Torrance

❑ 107 Nathan Watson
❑ 108 Neil Camera
❑ 109 Nestor Celario Jr.
❑ 110 Pablo Praino
❑ 111 Patricia Ross/51*
❑ 112 Patrick Finch
❑ 113 Patrick Gerrity
❑ 114 Patrick Larcada
❑ 115 Puis Calzada
❑ 116 Rain Lagunsad
❑ 117 Ramsey Raz Sibaja
❑ 118 Remi Doussel/30*
❑ 119 Remy Eisu Mokhtar/46*
❑ 120 Rhiannon Owens
❑ 121 Rich Woodall
❑ 122 Richard Cox/30*
❑ 123 Richard Dominguez
❑ 124 Richard Pace
❑ 125 Rodjer Goulart
❑ 126 Roger Andrews
❑ 127 Ryan Odagawa
❑ 128 Sara Richard
❑ 129 Sarah Wilkinson
❑ 130 Scott Gregory
❑ 131 Scott Houseman
❑ 132 Shane McCormack
❑ 133 Spencer Platt/50*
❑ 134 Stephanie Swanger
❑ 135 Ted Dastick Jr.
❑ 136 Ted Rechlin
❑ 137 Thomas Boatwright
❑ 138 Tim Levandoski
❑ 139 Tim Shay
❑ 140 Tom Nguyen
❑ 141 Tony Perna
❑ 142 Travis Walton
❑ 143 Vince Sunico
❑ 144 Vo
❑ 145 Wendy Chew
❑ 146 Will Nichols
❑ 147 William Donley III

2012 DC Comics The New 52

COMPLETE SET (61) 6.00 15.00
❑ 1 The New 52 .20 .50
❑ 2 Adam One .20 .50
❑ 3 Animal Man .20 .50
❑ 4 Aquaman .20 .50
❑ 5 Arsenal .20 .50
❑ 6 Batgirl .20 .50
❑ 7 Batman .20 .50
❑ 8 Batwoman .20 .50
❑ 9 Black Canary .20 .50
❑ 10 Blackhawks .20 .50
❑ 11 Blue Beetle .20 .50
❑ 12 Captain Atom .20 .50
❑ 13 Catwoman .20 .50
❑ 14 Cyborg .20 .50
❑ 15 Deadman .20 .50
❑ 16 Deadshot .20 .50
❑ 17 Deathstroke .20 .50
❑ 18 Dollmaker .20 .50
❑ 19 Fire .20 .50
❑ 20 Firestorm .20 .50
❑ 21 The Flash .20 .50
❑ 22 Frankenstein, Agent of S.H.A.D.E. .20 .50
❑ 23 Green Arrow .20 .50
❑ 24 Grifter .20 .50
❑ 25 Hal Jordan .20 .50
❑ 26 Harley Quinn .20 .50
❑ 27 Hawkman .20 .50
❑ 28 Huntress .20 .50
❑ 29 Ice .20 .50
❑ 30 The Joker .20 .50
❑ 31 Justice League Dark .20 .50
❑ 32 Legion Lost .20 .50
❑ 33 Legion of Super Heroes .20 .50
❑ 34 Martian Manhunter .20 .50
❑ 35 Massacre .20 .50
❑ 36 Mera .20 .50
❑ 37 Mirror .20 .50
❑ 38 Mister Terrific .20 .50
❑ 39 Nightwing .20 .50
❑ 40 OMAC .20 .50
❑ 41 Peraxxus .20 .50
❑ 42 DC Comics Red Hood .20 .50
❑ 43 Resurrection Man .20 .50
❑ 44 Robin .20 .50
❑ 45 Rocket Red .20 .50
❑ 46 Saiko .20 .50
❑ 47 Starfire .20 .50
❑ 48 Starling .20 .50
❑ 49 Stormwatch .20 .50
❑ 50 Suicide Squad .20 .50
❑ 51 Superboy .20 .50
❑ 52 Supergirl .20 .50
❑ 53 Superman .20 .50
❑ 54 Swamp Thing .20 .50
❑ 55 Talon .20 .50
❑ 56 Teen Titans .20 .50
❑ 57 The Guardians of the Universe .20 .50
❑ 58 Vixen .20 .50
❑ 59 Voodoo .20 .50
❑ 60 White Rabbit .20 .50
❑ 61 Wonder Woman .20 .50
❑ CL Checklist

2012 DC Comics The New 52 Foil Parallel

COMPLETE SET 50.00 100.00
*FOIL: 2.5X TO 6X BASIC CARDS
RANDOM INSERTS IN PACKS

2012 DC Comics The New 52 Binder Inserts

COMPLETE SET (9) 15.00 30.00
ONE SET PER BINDER
❑ B1 Wonder Woman 2.50 6.00
❑ B2 Supergirl 2.50 6.00
❑ B3 Green Lantern Corps 2.50 6.00
❑ B4 Green Arrow 2.50 6.00
❑ B5 Batman/Joker 2.50 6.00
❑ B6 Superman 2.50 6.00
❑ B7 Flash 2.50 6.00
❑ B8 Batman/Robin 2.50 6.00
❑ B9 Batman 2.50 6.00

2012 DC Comics The New 52 Lanterns

COMPLETE SET (9) 15.00 30.00
STATED ODDS 1:24
❑ LNTRN1 Hal Jordan 3.00 8.00
❑ LNTRN2 John Stewart 3.00 8.00
❑ LNTRN3 Kilowog 3.00 8.00
❑ LNTRN4 Star Sapphire 3.00 8.00
❑ LNTRN5 Black Hand 3.00 8.00
❑ LNTRN6 Saint Walker 3.00 8.00
❑ LNTRN7 Sinestro 3.00 8.00
❑ LNTRN8 Larfleeze 3.00 8.00
❑ LNTRN9 Atrocitus 3.00 8.00

2012 DC Comics The New 52 Oversized Art

ANNOUNCED PRINT RUN 1
UNPRICED DUE TO SCARCITY
EXCHANGE DEADLINE 9/1/2014

2012 DC Comics The New 52 Sketches

STATED ODDS 1:24
❑ 1 Achilleas Kokkinakis
❑ 2 Adam Cline/20*
❑ 3 Adam Talley
❑ 4 Alberto Foche
❑ 5 Amber Shelton/40*
❑ 6 Ana Sanchez
❑ 7 Andy Price/15*
❑ 8 Anthony Gay/30*
❑ 9 Anthony Wheeler/53*
❑ 10 Aston Roy Cover/100*
❑ 11 Axebone
❑ 12 Babisu Kourtis
❑ 13 Benjamin Glendenning/24*
❑ 14 Bianca Thompson
❑ 15 Blen Flores
❑ 16 Bill Thompson
❑ 17 Billy Martin
❑ 18 Bob Stevlic
❑ 19 Brandon Kenney
❑ 20 Brent Engstrom
❑ 21 Brian Kong
❑ 22 Bruce Gerlach
❑ 23 Bryan Turner
❑ 24 Bukshot!
❑ 25 Cal Slayton
❑ 26 Chad Cicconi
❑ 27 Chad Hardin
❑ 28 Chad Haverland/28*
❑ 29 Charles Hall
❑ 30 Chris Foreman
❑ 31 Chris Thorne/50*
❑ 32 Christian Thomas
❑ 33 Christopher Bradberry
❑ 34 Corey Brown
❑ 35 Cruddie Torian
❑ 36 Dan Borgonos/50*
❑ 37 Dan Schaefer
❑ 38 Dan Schoening
❑ 39 Dan Smith
❑ 40 Daniel Cooney
❑ 41 Daniel Gorman
❑ 42 Danielle Gransaull Soloud
❑ 43 Dave Beaty
❑ 44 Dave Strong
❑ 45 Dave Tata
❑ 46 David Baron
❑ 47 David Castro
❑ 48 David Rabbitte
❑ 49 David Ryan
❑ 50 Denae Frazier
❑ 51 Dennis Crisostomo
❑ 52 Dennis Culver
❑ 53 Dheeraj Verma
❑ 54 Dietrich Smith
❑ 55 Drew Moss
❑ 56 Eduardo Garcia
❑ 57 Eric Merced
❑ 58 Eric Ninaltowski/30*
❑ 59 Frank Kadar/20*
❑ 60 Gary Kezele/50*
❑ 61 Gene Gonzales
❑ 62 George Deep
❑ 63 Gilbert Monsanto
❑ 64 Glen Fernandez
❑ 65 Hanie Mohd
❑ 66 Henry Martinez
❑ 67 Ian Yoshio Roberts/50*
❑ 68 Iban Coello
❑ 69 Irma Ahmed
❑ 70 Isaiah McAllister/100*
❑ 71 Jack Redd
❑ 72 Jason Keith Phillips
❑ 73 Jason Sobol/30*
❑ 74 Javier Aranda
❑ 75 JC Fabul
❑ 76 Jeff Victor
❑ 77 Jefferson Hojas
❑ 78 Jennifer Mercer/10*
❑ 79 Jeremy Treece/20*
❑ 80 Jessica Hickman
❑ 81 Jezreel Rojales
❑ 82 Jim Hanna
❑ 83 John Jackman aka Jax
❑ 84 Jomar Bulda
❑ 85 Jonathan Gordon
❑ 86 Jonathan Racimo/120*
❑ 87 Jonathan Wayshak
❑ 88 Julius Abrera
❑ 89 Kat Laurange/25*
❑ 90 Kate Glasheen
❑ 91 Keith O'Malley
❑ 92 Kevin Gentilcore/90*
❑ 93 Lak Lim
❑ 94 Lawrence Reynolds
❑ 95 Lawrence Snelly
❑ 96 Layron DeJarnette
❑ 97 Lisa Redfern/30*
❑ 98 Lord Mesa
❑ 99 Luke Smarto
❑ 100 Lynne Anderson
❑ 101 Marat Mychaels
❑ 102 Marcelo Ferreira
❑ 103 Marcus Smith
❑ 104 Mark McKenna
❑ 105 Mark Pennington
❑ 106 Mat Nastos
❑ 107 Matthew Minor
❑ 108 Meghan Hetrick-Murante/12*
❑ 109 Melike Acar
❑ 110 Michael Duron
❑ 111 Michael Kasinger/50*
❑ 112 Michael Rooth
❑ 113 Mick and Matt Glebe
❑ 114 Mike Legan
❑ 115 Mike Torrance
❑ 116 Mike Vasquez
❑ 117 Pablo Diaz
❑ 118 Patrick Gerrity
❑ 119 Patrick Larcada
❑ 120 Penelope Rivera Gaylord
❑ 121 Rain Lagunsad
❑ 122 Ramsey Raz Sibaja/51*
❑ 123 Remi Doussel/20*
❑ 124 Remy Eisu Mokhtar
❑ 125 Rhiannon Owens
❑ 126 Rich Molinelli/100*
❑ 127 Rich Woodall
❑ 128 Ron Salas
❑ 129 Rusty Gilligan
❑ 130 Ryan Kinnaird
❑ 131 Ryan Odagawa
❑ 132 Sanna Umemoto
❑ 133 Scott Rorie
❑ 134 SpiderGuile
❑ 135 Stacey Kardash/40*
❑ 136 Ted Dastick Jr.
❑ 137 Thomas Boatwright
❑ 138 Tim Levandoski
❑ 139 Tim Shay
❑ 140 Tod Smith
❑ 141 Tom Hodges
❑ 142 Tom Nguyen
❑ 143 Tony Miello
❑ 144 Tony Perna/20*
❑ 145 Travis Walton
❑ 146 Victor Rodriguez
❑ 147 Vince Sunico
❑ 148 Virginia Kakava
❑ 149 Von Randal
❑ 150 William Bronson
❑ 151 William Withers
❑ 152 Wilson Ramos Jr.
❑ 153 Wu Wei

2012 DC Comics The New 52 Work in Progress

COMPLETE SET (9) 15.00 30.00
STATED ODDS 2:24
❑ WIP1 Catwoman 3.00 8.00
❑ WIP2 Batman 3.00 8.00
❑ WIP3 Superman 3.00 8.00
❑ WIP4 Cyborg 3.00 8.00
❑ WIP5 Batgirl 3.00 8.00
❑ WIP6 The Flash 3.00 8.00
❑ WIP7 Aquaman 3.00 8.00
❑ WIP8 Green Lantern 3.00 8.00
❑ WIP9 Wonder Woman 3.00 8.00

2012 Dexter Season Four

COMPLETE SET (72) 8.00 20.00
❑ 1 Dexter Morgan .20 .50
❑ 2 As a new and prolific serial killer .20 .50
❑ 3 Dexter is hungry .20 .50
❑ 4 Arthur Mitchell .20 .50
❑ 5 Arthur is a complicated man .20 .50
❑ 6 When he was 10 .20 .50
❑ 7 Vince Masuka .20 .50
❑ 8 Lt. Maria LaGuerta .20 .50
❑ 9 Sgt. Angel Batista .20 .50
❑ 10 Joey Quinn .20 .50
❑ 11 Special Agent Frank Lundy .20 .50
❑ 12 Debra Morgan .20 .50
❑ 13 Christine Hill .20 .50
❑ 14 Jonah Mitchell .20 .50
❑ 15 Sleep, Dexter .20 .50
❑ 16 Trinity Begins Again .20 .50
❑ 17 Lundy's Back .20 .50
❑ 18 Vacation Murder .20 .50
❑ 19 Found It .20 .50
❑ 20 Vandal .20 .50
❑ 21 Trinity Strikes Again .20 .50
❑ 22 Dex's New Woman .20 .50
❑ 23 So Close .20 .50
❑ 24 Victims: Deb and Lundy .20 .50
❑ 25 Lundy's Dead .20 .50
❑ 26 Rita's Mad .20 .50
❑ 27 Trinity Has Daddy Issues .20 .50
❑ 28 The Family Man .20 .50
❑ 29 Hammer .20 .50
❑ 30 Introducing .20 .50
❑ 31 Don't Touch My Sister .20 .50
❑ 32 Deer Killer .20 .50
❑ 33 Arthur's Coffin .20 .50
❑ 34 The Wrong Guy .20 .50
❑ 35 Dexter's Trip .20 .50
❑ 36 Arthur Reminisces .20 .50
❑ 37 Jumper .20 .50
❑ 38 Happy Thanksgiving .20 .50
❑ 39 Family Problems .20 .50
❑ 40 Hi, Dad .20 .50
❑ 41 Lost Boy .20 .50
❑ 42 I Know What You Did, Daddy .20 .50
❑ 43 Dexter, The Hero .20 .50
❑ 44 Christine Is Found Out .20 .50
❑ 45 Dexter Plants Evidence .20 .50
❑ 46 True Identity .20 .50
❑ 47 Let's Get Away Together .20 .50
❑ 48 Deb Knows .20 .50
❑ 49 Goodbye Trinity aka Arthur Mitchell .20 .50
❑ 50 Goodbye Rita aka Wife and Mother .20 .50
❑ 51 Lisa Bell/Tarla Grant .20 .50
❑ 52 Benito Gomez .20 .50
❑ 53 Zoey Kruger .20 .50
❑ 54 Jonathan Farrow .20 .50
❑ 55 Stan Beaudry .20 .50
❑ 56 Arthur Mitchell .20 .50
❑ 57 There's this cliché .20 .50
❑ 58 What is this .20 .50
❑ 59 Talk about your blood bath .20 .50
❑ 60 You've got a family to support .20 .50
❑ 61 I put her in a short skirt .20 .50
❑ 62 He's like me .20 .50
❑ 63 Every crime scene .20 .50
❑ 64 Please, we have three young children .20 .50
❑ 65 Two serial killers go for a ride .20 .50
❑ 66 Let's get a search team .20 .50
❑ 67 You can make anything sound perverted .20 .50
❑ 68 Love thy neighbor .20 .50
❑ 69 It doesn't matter what I do .20 .50
❑ 70 It's already over .20 .50
❑ 71 You think you're better than I am .20 .50
❑ 72 Checklist .20 .50

2012 Dexter Season Four Autographs

RANDOM INSERTS IN BOXES
❑ ACH Courtney Ford 15.00 40.00
who plays Christine Hill
❑ ADH Desmond Harrington 15.00 40.00
who plays Joey Quinn
❑ AJL John Lithgow 35.00 70.00
who plays Arthur Mitchell
❑ AMCH Michael C. Hall 40.00 80.00
who plays Dexter Morgan

2012 Dexter Season Four Costumes

TWO COSTUME OR PROP CARDS PER BOX
❑ CWS Four Walls One Heart shirt 6.00 15.00
❑ CABG Sgt. Angel Batista shirt 6.00 15.00
❑ CABR Sgt. Angel Batista shirt 6.00 15.00
❑ CAMJ Arthur Mitchell jacket 8.00 20.00
❑ CAMV Arthur Mitchell shirt 8.00 20.00
❑ CCHP Christine Hill purple dress 8.00 20.00
❑ CCHR Christine Hill red dress 8.00 20.00
❑ CDMC Dexter Morgan sleeve covers 8.00 20.00
❑ CJMB Johah Mitchell blue shirt 6.00 15.00
❑ CJMY Jonah Mitchell peach shirt 6.00 15.00
❑ CJQP Joey Quinn burgundy shirt 6.00 15.00
❑ CJQS Joey Quinn purple shirt 6.00 15.00
❑ CMLD Lt. Maria LaGuerta shirt 6.00 15.00
❑ CMLR Lt. Maria LaGuerta dress 6.00 15.00
❑ CSSP Scott Smith pajamas 6.00 15.00
❑ CVMC Vince Masuka white shirt 6.00 15.00
❑ CVMO Vince Masuka orange shirt 6.00 15.00

2012 Dexter Season Four Dexter's Justice

COMPLETE SET (9) 10.00 25.00
THREE CARDS PER BOX
❑ JM1 Prepping the Space 2.50 6.00
❑ JM2 The Stick 2.50 6.00
❑ JM3 Plastic Wrap 2.50 6.00
❑ JM4 Getting The Picture 2.50 6.00
❑ JM5 A Slice 2.50 6.00
❑ JM6 The Squeeze 2.50 6.00
❑ JM7 The Keeper 2.50 6.00
❑ JM8 A Neat Kill 2.50 6.00
❑ JM9 Clean Up 2.50 6.00

2012 Dexter Season Four Locations

COMPLETE SET (9) 10.00 25.00
THREE CARDS PER BOX
❑ L1 A Bloody Mess 2.50 6.00
❑ L2 Eyes 2.50 6.00
❑ L3 Jump, Mommy, Jump 2.50 6.00
❑ L4 C'mon, Hit Me 2.50 6.00
❑ L5 Hammer Time 2.50 6.00
❑ L6 Poor Little Arthur 2.50 6.00
❑ L7 Nostalgia 2.50 6.00
❑ L8 Set In Stone 2.50 6.00
❑ L9 All For Vera 2.50 6.00

2012 Dexter Season Four Promos

❑ CH Dexter hunched over 10.00 25.00
(issued at Chicago NS show)
❑ NY Dexter/Arthur 6.00 15.00
(issued at New York NS show)
❑ P1 Arthur Mitchell 2.00 5.00
❑ P2 Dexter Morgan 2.00 5.00
❑ P3 Dexter/Arthur 2.00 5.00
❑ PH Dexter with tools 6.00 15.00
(issued at Philly NS show)
❑ SD Dexter in a hoodie 3.00 8.00
(issued at SDCC)
❑ AP1 Dexter Morgan 5.00 12.00
(Album exclusive)
❑ AP2 Dexter Morgan 5.00 12.00
(Album exclusive)

2012 Dexter Season Four Props

TWO COSTUME OR PROP CARDS PER BOX
❑ PAB Miami Metro Archive Box 8.00 20.00
❑ PBP Blueprint 6.00 15.00
❑ PHR Hammer 20.00 40.00
❑ PKB Kidnapped Boy's Bag 6.00 15.00
❑ PKP Kill Room Plastic 8.00 20.00
❑ PLG Latex Glove 6.00 15.00
❑ PPC Postcard 12.00 30.00
❑ PWH 4 Walls 1 Heart Flyer 15.00 40.00

2012 Dexter Season Four Trinity's Kill

COMPLETE SET (9) 10.00 25.00
THREE CARDS PER BOX
❑ TM1 Dexter's Old Apartment 2.50 6.00
❑ TM2 Rita and Dexter's House 2.50 6.00
❑ TM3 Dexter's Crime Lab 2.50 6.00
❑ TM4 Miami Metro P D 2.50 6.00
❑ TM5 Slice Of Life 2.50 6.00
❑ TM6 The Mitchells' House 2.50 6.00
❑ TM7 The Blood-Spatter Room 2.50 6.00
❑ TM8 Dexter's New Shed 2.50 6.00
❑ TM9 Four Walls One Heart Build Site 2.50 6.00

2012 Dexter Season Four San Diego Comic Con Autographs

CARDS ISSUED IN 2012 SDCC MYSTERY PACKS
❑ 1 John Lithgow 40.00 80.00
who plays Arthur Mitchell
❑ 2 Michael C. Hall 40.00 80.00
who plays Dexter Morgan

2012 Dexter Season Four San Diego Comic Con Costumes

CARDS ISSUED IN 2012 SDCC MYSTERY PACKS
❑ CABB Sgt. Angel Batista shirt 6.00 15.00
❑ CAMS Arthur Mitchell shirt 8.00 20.00
❑ CCHT Christine Hill shirt 8.00 20.00
❑ CDMA Dexter Morgan apron 10.00 25.00

2012 Dexter Season Four San Diego Comic Con Props

CARDS ISSUED IN 2012 SDCC MYSTERY PACKS
❑ PBL Blood/35
❑ PSD Splatter Dummy/60 20.00 50.00
❑ PSH Silicone Hand/200 10.00 25.00
❑ PSH Silicone Head/299 10.00 25.00
❑ PVL Q-Tip/Latex Glove/255 12.00 30.00

2012 Essential Elvis

COMPLETE SET (35) 60.00 120.00
❑ 1 First Recording 2.50 6.00
❑ 2 First Hit Single 2.50 6.00
❑ 3 Louisiana Hayride 2.50 6.00
❑ 4 RCA Contract 2.50 6.00
❑ 5 First Gold Record 2.50 6.00
❑ 6 First Las Vegas Show 2.50 6.00
❑ 7 Hound Dog 2.50 6.00
❑ 8 Don't Be Cruel 2.50 6.00
❑ 9 The Ed Sullivan Show 2.50 6.00
❑ 10 Tupelo Homecoming 1956 2.50 6.00
❑ 11 First Movie (Love Me Tender) 2.50 6.00
❑ 12 Jailhouse Rock 2.50 6.00
❑ 13 King Creole 2.50 6.00
❑ 14 Military Dedication 2.50 6.00
❑ 15 Are You Lonesome Tonight 2.50 6.00
❑ 16 Memphis Charities 2.50 6.00
❑ 17 USS Arizona Benefit 2.50 6.00
❑ 18 Blue Hawaii 2.50 6.00
❑ 19 Viva Las Vegas 2.50 6.00
❑ 20 68 Special 2.50 6.00
❑ 21 International Hotel, Las Vegas 2.50 6.00
❑ 22 Final #1 Single 2.50 6.00
❑ 23 Record Attendance 2.50 6.00
❑ 24 That's the Way It Is 2.50 6.00
❑ 25 Distinguished Award 2.50 6.00
❑ 26 Lifetime Achievement Award 2.50 6.00
❑ 27 Historic MSG Shows 2.50 6.00
❑ 28 Golden Globe Winner (Documentary) 2.50 6.00
❑ 29 Aloha From Hawaii 2.50 6.00
❑ 30 Grammy Winner 2.50 6.00
❑ 31 Record New Year's Eve Show 2.50 6.00
❑ 32 Final Concert 2.50 6.00
❑ 33 Hall of Fame Induction 2.50 6.00
❑ 34 American Music Award of Merit 2.50 6.00
❑ 35 #1 in 17 Countries 2.50 6.00

2012 Essential Elvis Holofoil

STATED ODDS ONE PER BOX

2012 Essential Elvis Holofoil 1

STATED PRINT RUN 1 SER. #'d SET
UNPRICED DUE TO SCARCITY

2012 Essential Elvis Autographs Silver

OVERALL AUTO ODDS AT LEAST ONE PER BOX
RED INK VARIATIONS EXIST
❑ APAW Alfred Wertheimer 15.00 40.00
❑ APGK George Kalinsky 15.00 40.00
❑ ESBE Barbara Eden 20.00 50.00
❑ ESDJ DJ Fontana 12.00 30.00
❑ ESGK George Klein 12.00 30.00
❑ ESJA Julie Adams 12.00 30.00
❑ ESJB James Burton 12.00 30.00
❑ ESMM Marlyn Mason 12.00 30.00
❑ ESNS Nancy Sinatra 15.00 40.00
❑ ESPP Pat Priest 12.00 30.00
❑ ESYC Yvonne Craig 15.00 40.00
❑ ESMAM Mary Ann Mobley 15.00 40.00
❑ ESMTM Mary Tyler Moore 25.00 50.00

2012 Essential Elvis Autographs Gold

STATED PRINT RUN 100 SER. #'d SETS

2012 Essential Elvis Autographs Blue

STATED PRINT RUN 50 SER. #'d SETS

2012 Essential Elvis Autographs Red

STATED PRINT RUN 10 SER. #'d SETS
UNPRICED DUE TO SCARCITY

2012 Essential Elvis Cut Signatures

STATED PRINT RUN 1 SER. #'d SET
UNPRICED DUE TO SCARCITY
❑ 1 Elvis Presley
❑ 2 Elvis Presley
Vernon Presley
❑ 3 Elvis Presley MEM

2012 Essential Elvis Essential Materials Silver

*BLUE: .6X TO 1.5X SILVER
❑ EM1 Sun Records jacket 12.00 30.00
❑ EM2 Bathrobe 10.00 25.00
❑ EM3 Black shirt 10.00 25.00
White dickey
❑ EM5 Tweed jacket 10.00 25.00

2012 Essential Elvis Essential Materials Gold

STATED PRINT RUN 35-299
❑ EM4 Swim Trunks/149 15.00 40.00
❑ EM6 Kimono/199 15.00 40.00
❑ EMD1 Plaid PJs 20.00 50.00
Green warmup suit/149
❑ EMD2 Tweed jacket 20.00 50.00
Green warmup suit/199
❑ EMD3 Red smoking jacket 20.00 50.00
Tweed jacket/299
❑ EMQ1 Red smoking jacket 60.00 120.00
Plaid PJs/Tweed jacket/Green warmup suit/35
❑ EMT1 Red smoking jacket 30.00 60.00
Tweed jacket/Green warmup suit/99
❑ EMT2 Red smoking jacket 30.00 60.00
Plaid PJs/Tweed jacket/149

2012 Essential Elvis Essential Materials Blue

STATED PRINT RUN 10-25

2012 Essential Elvis Essential Materials Melting

STATED PRINT RUN 5 SER. #'d SETS
UNPRICED DUE TO SCARCITY

2012 Essential Elvis Essential Materials King Size Gold

STATED PRINT RUN 99-299
❑ KS1 Sun Records jacket/99 35.00 70.00
❑ KS2 Bathrobe/299 20.00 40.00
❑ KS3 Black shirt 35.00 70.00
White dickey/99

2012 Essential Elvis Essential Materials King Size Blue

STATED PRINT RUN 10-25

2012 Essential Elvis Essential Materials King Size Melting

STATED PRINT RUN 5 SER. #'d SETS
UNPRICED DUE TO SCARCITY

2012 Essential Elvis Joe Petruccio Sketches

STATED PRINT RUN 5-20
❑ 1 Blue Scarf/20
❑ 2 Eyes/5
❑ 3 Head Bowed/5
❑ 4 Silhouette/10
❑ 5 Singing (black background)/10

2012 Eureka Autograph Expansion

Chris Gauthier
Chris Gauthier
COMP.SET w/o INCENTIVES 60.00 120.00
ANNOUNCED PRINT RUN 250 SETS
❑ 1 Chris Gauthier 8.00 20.00
as Vincent
❑ 2 Colin Ferguson as Sheriff Carter/50* 200.00 300.00
issued as 5-set incentive)

❑ 3 Ed Quinn as Nathan Stark 10.00 25.00
❑ 4 Erica Cerra as Deputy Lupo 25.00 50.00
❑ 5 Joe Morton as Henry Deacon 8.00 20.00
❑ 6 Matt Frewer as Jim Taggart 10.00 25.00
❑ 7 Neil Grayston as Fargo/100* 60.00 120.00
(issued as 3-set incentive)

2012 Falling Skies Season One

COMPLETE SET (30) 20.00 50.00
❑ 1 Live and Learn 1.00 2.50
❑ 2 Live and Learn 1.00 2.50
❑ 3 Live and Learn 1.00 2.50
❑ 4 The Armory 1.00 2.50
❑ 5 The Armory 1.00 2.50
❑ 6 The Armory 1.00 2.50
❑ 7 Prisoner of war 1.00 2.50
❑ 8 Prisoner of war 1.00 2.50
❑ 9 Prisoner of war 1.00 2.50
❑ 10 Grace 1.00 2.50
❑ 11 Grace 1.00 2.50
❑ 12 Grace 1.00 2.50
❑ 13 Silent Kill 1.00 2.50
❑ 14 Silent Kill 1.00 2.50
❑ 15 Silent Kill 1.00 2.50
❑ 16 Sanctuary: Part 1 1.00 2.50
❑ 17 Sanctuary: Part 1 1.00 2.50
❑ 18 Sanctuary: Part 1 1.00 2.50
❑ 19 Sanctuary: Part 2 1.00 2.50
❑ 20 Sanctuary: Part 2 1.00 2.50
❑ 21 Sanctuary: Part 2 1.00 2.50
❑ 22 What Hides Beneath 1.00 2.50
❑ 23 What Hides Beneath 1.00 2.50
❑ 24 What Hides Beneath 1.00 2.50
❑ 25 Mutiny 1.00 2.50
❑ 26 Mutiny 1.00 2.50
❑ 27 Mutiny 1.00 2.50
❑ 28 Eight Hours 1.00 2.50
❑ 29 Eight Hours 1.00 2.50
❑ 30 Eight Hours 1.00 2.50

2012 Falling Skies Season One 2nd Mass

COMP. SET w/o SM10 (9) 25.00 50.00
STATED ODDS ONE PER PACK
STATED PRINT RUN 325 SER. #'d SETS
❑ SM1 Noah Wyle as Tom Mason 3.00 8.00
❑ SM2 Moon Bloodgood as Anne Glass 3.00 8.00
❑ SM3 Will Patton as Captain Weaver 3.00 8.00
❑ SM4 Drew Roy as Hal Mason 3.00 8.00
❑ SM5 Connor Jessup as Ben Mason 3.00 8.00
❑ SM6 Maxim Knight as Matt Mason 3.00 8.00
❑ SM7 Sarah Carter as Margaret 3.00 8.00
❑ SM8 Colin Cunningham as John Pope 3.00 8.00
❑ SM9 Peter Shinkoda as Dai 3.00 8.00
❑ SM10 Mpho Koaho as Anthony 12.00 30.00
(issued as a Rittenhouse Reward)

2012 Falling Skies Season One Autographs

STATED ODDS ONE PER PACK
❑ 1 Bruce Gray 8.00 20.00
as Uncle Scott
❑ 2 Colin Cunningham 20.00 50.00
as John Pope
❑ 3 Connor Jessup 15.00 40.00
as Ben Mason
❑ 4 Daniyah Ysrayl 6.00 15.00
as Rick
❑ 5 Drew Roy 15.00 40.00
as Hal Mason
❑ 6 Dylan Authors 8.00 20.00
as Jimmy Boland
❑ 7 Jessy Schram 25.00 50.00
as Karen
❑ 8 Maxim Knight 8.00 20.00
as Matt Mason
❑ 9 Melissa Kramer 8.00 20.00
as Sarah
❑ 10 Moon Bloodgood 60.00 120.00
❑ 11 Mpho Koaho 6.00 15.00
as Anthony
❑ 12 Noah Wyle 50.00 100.00
❑ 13 Peter Shinkoda 8.00 20.00
as Dai
❑ 14 Sarah Carter 30.00 60.00
as Margaret
❑ 15 Seychelle Gabriel 25.00 50.00
as Lourdes
❑ 16 Will Patton 20.00 50.00
as Captain Weaver

2012 Falling Skies Season One Costume Autographs

❑ 1 Connor Jessup 35.00 70.00
(issued as a 2-box incentive)
❑ 2 Moon Bloodgood 125.00 200.00
(issued as a 4-box incentive)

2012 Falling Skies Season One Costumes

STATED ODDS TWO PER PACK
STATED PRINT RUN 350 SER. #'d SETS
❑ CC1 Noah Wyle as 6.00 15.00
Tom Mason
❑ CC2 Noah Wyle as 6.00 15.00
Tom Mason
❑ CC3 Sarah Carter as 10.00 25.00
Maggie
❑ CC4 Moon Bloodgood as 8.00 20.00
Anne Glass
❑ CC5 Moon Bloodgood as 8.00 20.00
Anne Glass
❑ CC6 Will Patton as 6.00 15.00
Captain Weaver
❑ CC7 Drew Roy as 6.00 15.00
Hal Mason
❑ CC8 Dylan Authors as 6.00 15.00
Jimmy Boland
❑ CC9 Dylan Authors as 6.00 15.00
Jimmy Boland
❑ CC10 Dylan Authors as 6.00 15.00
Jimmy Boland
❑ CC11 Connor Jessup as 6.00 15.00
Ben Mason
❑ CC12 Connor Jessup as 6.00 15.00
Ben Mason
❑ CC13 Seychelle Gabriel as 8.00 20.00
Lourdes
❑ CC14 Seychelle Gabriel as 8.00 20.00
Lourdes
❑ CC15 Colin Cunningham as 6.00 15.00
Pope
❑ CC16 Colin Cunningham as 6.00 15.00
Pope
❑ CC17 Moon Bloodgood as 25.00 50.00
Anne Glass/200
❑ DC1 Drew Roy/Noah Wyle as 20.00 40.00
Hal Mason/Tom Mason/225/(issued as case topper)

2012 Falling Skies Season One Promos

❑ P1 Group of 6 1.50 4.00
(General Distribution)
❑ P2 Tom Mason 1.00 2.50
(San Diego Comic Con)

2012 Fringe Seasons One and Two

COMPLETE SET (72) 5.00 12.00
❑ 1 Unexplained Phenomenon .15 .40
❑ 2 Next of Kin .15 .40
❑ 3 Back in the Lab Again .15 .40
❑ 4 Infant Mortality .15 .40
❑ 5 Trapped in Amber .15 .40
❑ 6 The Beacon .15 .40
❑ 7 Grave Matters .15 .40
❑ 8 Bon Voyage, Beacon .15 .40
❑ 9 Power Hungry .15 .40
❑ 10 Mind-Melting .15 .40
❑ 11 Information Exchange .15 .40
❑ 12 Brief Interlude .15 .40
❑ 13 Heart Problems .15 .40
❑ 14 Back Again .15 .40
❑ 15 The Cage .15 .40
❑ 16 Walled In .15 .40
❑ 17 Uncommon .15 .40
❑ 18 Brainless .15 .40
❑ 19 Another One .15 .40
❑ 20 The Beast Within .15 .40
❑ 21 In Dreams .15 .40
❑ 22 Ability .15 .40
❑ 23 Empathy .15 .40
❑ 24 Spineless .15 .40
❑ 25 Food Poisoning .15 .40
❑ 26 Body Heat .15 .40
❑ 27 New Blood .15 .40
❑ 28 No Big Deal .15 .40
❑ 29 For Posterity .15 .40
❑ 30 Independent Research .15 .40
❑ 31 Baby Boy Hughes .15 .40
❑ 32 Tunnel Vision .15 .40
❑ 33 Elevated .15 .40
❑ 34 Bowling for Recovery .15 .40
❑ 35 Living Bombs .15 .40
❑ 36 Shrapnel .15 .40
❑ 37 Snack Break .15 .40
❑ 38 Nominal Aphasia .15 .40
❑ 39 Getting Ahead .15 .40
❑ 40 Misdirection .15 .40
❑ 41 Betrayal .15 .40
❑ 42 Workplace Violence .15 .40
❑ 43 Sleep Disorder .15 .40
❑ 44 Ashes, Ashes .15 .40
❑ 45 The Dark of Space .15 .40
❑ 46 August .15 .40
❑ 47 Making Sense of It All .15 .40
❑ 48 Snakehead .15 .40
❑ 49 Street Food .15 .40
❑ 50 Johari Window .15 .40
❑ 51 Red Mist .15 .40
❑ 52 Never Again .15 .40
❑ 53 Ubermenschen .15 .40
❑ 54 Race Against Time .15 .40
❑ 55 Fateful Moment .15 .40
❑ 56 Carcinogen .15 .40
❑ 57 Kindred Spirits .15 .40
❑ 58 The Body Electric .15 .40
❑ 59 White Tulip .15 .40
❑ 60 Misbegotten .15 .40
❑ 61 Newton .15 .40
❑ 62 Once Upon a Time .15 .40
❑ 63 Case Closed .15 .40
❑ 64 Noyo County .15 .40
❑ 65 Tracking Peter .15 .40
❑ 66 The Other Us .15 .40
❑ 67 Mr. Secretary .15 .40
❑ 68 Reunited .15 .40
❑ 69 Getting Him Back .15 .40
❑ 70 Assembled .15 .40
❑ 71 Peter .15 .40
❑ CL Checklist .15 .40
❑ P1 Olivia/Peter/Walter PROMO 2.50 6.00

2012 Fringe Seasons One and Two Authentic Wardrobe

STATED ODDS ONE PER BOX
❑ M1 Astrid's Burgundy Blouse 8.00 20.00
❑ M2 Brandon's Lab Coat 6.00 15.00
❑ M3 Broyles' Tie SP 30.00 60.00
❑ M4 Broyles' White Shirt 6.00 15.00
❑ M5 Broyles' Suit 6.00 15.00
❑ M6 Charlie's Blue Shirt 6.00 15.00
❑ M7 Charlie's Suit 6.00 15.00
❑ M8 Olivia's Striped Shirt 12.00 30.00
❑ M9 Olivia's Suit 10.00 25.00
❑ M10 Peter's Dark Gray Shirt 10.00 25.00
❑ M11 Peter's Gray Shirt 10.00 25.00
❑ M12 Rachel's Green Shirt 6.00 15.00
❑ M13 Rachel's Corduroy Pants 8.00 20.00
❑ M14 Walter's Gray Shirt 8.00 20.00
❑ M15 Walter's Green Shirt 8.00 20.00
❑ M16 Walter's Lab Coat 8.00 20.00
❑ M17 Officer's Jacket 10.00 25.00
(binder exclusive)

2012 Fringe Seasons One and Two Autographs

C = COMMON
U = UNCOMMON
R = RARE
STATED ODDS ONE PER BOX
❑ A1 Anna Torv R 250.00 450.00
❑ A2 Joshua Jackson R 200.00 350.00
❑ A3 Lance Reddick R 50.00 100.00
❑ A4 Blair Brown R 60.00 120.00
❑ A5 Jasika Nicole R 50.00 100.00
❑ A6 John Noble R 150.00 250.00
❑ A7 Seth Gabel R 50.00 100.00
❑ A8 Sebastian Roche U 6.00 15.00
❑ A9 Michael Cerveris U 15.00 40.00
❑ A10 Kevin Corrigan U 10.00 25.00
❑ A11 Ari Graynor C 10.00 25.00
❑ A12 Kirk Acevedo C 10.00 25.00
❑ A13 Chance Kelly C 6.00 15.00
❑ A14a Ryan McDonald C 6.00 15.00
❑ A14b Jeff Pinkner R 35.00 70.00
❑ A15 J.H. Wyman R 50.00 100.00
❑ A16 Meghan Markle U 12.00 30.00

2012 Fringe Seasons One and Two Our Universe

COMPLETE SET (9) 15.00 40.00
RANDOM INSERT IN PACKS
❑ F1 Olivia Dunham 4.00 10.00
❑ F2 Peter Bishop 3.00 8.00
❑ F3 Walter Bishop 3.00 8.00
❑ F4 Phillip Broyles 3.00 8.00
❑ F5 Charlie Francis 3.00 8.00
❑ F6 Astrid Farnsworth 3.00 8.00
❑ F7 Mitchell Loeb 3.00 8.00
❑ F8 Nina Sharp 3.00 8.00
❑ F9 The Observers 3.00 8.00

2012 Fringe Seasons One and Two Oversized Quad Wardrobe

❑ R1 Olivia/Walter
Astrid/Peter EXCH
❑ R2 Olivia/Walter
Astrid/Peter EXCH
❑ R3 Olivia/Walter
Astrid/Peter EXCH
❑ R4 Olivia/Walter
Astrid/Peter EXCH
❑ R5 Olivia/Walter
Astrid/Peter EXCH
❑ R6 Olivia/Walter
Astrid/Peter EXCH
❑ R7 Olivia/Walter
Astrid/Peter EXCH
❑ R8 Olivia/Walter
Astrid/Peter EXCH
❑ R9 Olivia/Walter
Astrid/Peter EXCH
❑ R10 Olivia/Walter
Astrid/Peter EXCH
❑ R11 Olivia/Walter
Astrid/Peter EXCH
❑ R12 Olivia/Walter
Astrid/Peter EXCH
❑ R13 Olivia/Walter
Astrid/Peter EXCH
❑ R14 Olivia/Walter
Astrid/Peter EXCH
❑ R15 Olivia/Walter
Astrid/Peter EXCH
❑ R16 Olivia/Walter
Astrid/Peter EXCH
❑ R17 Olivia/Walter
Astrid/Peter EXCH
❑ R18 Olivia/Walter
Astrid/Peter EXCH
❑ R19 Olivia/Walter
Astrid/Peter EXCH
❑ R20 Olivia/Walter
Astrid/Peter EXCH
❑ R21 Olivia/Walter
Astrid/Peter EXCH
❑ R22 Olivia/Walter
Astrid/Peter EXCH
❑ R23 Olivia/Walter
Astrid/Peter EXCH
❑ R24 Olivia/Walter
Astrid/Peter EXCH
❑ R25 Olivia/Walter
Astrid/Peter EXCH

2012 Fringe Seasons One and Two Universe B

COMPLETE SET (9) 15.00 40.00
RANDOM INSERT IN PACKS
❑ D1 Olivia Dunham 4.00 10.00
❑ D2 Peter Bishop 3.00 8.00
❑ D3 Walter Bishop 3.00 8.00
❑ D4 Phillip Broyles 3.00 8.00
❑ D5 Charlie Francis 3.00 8.00
❑ D6 Lincoln Lee 3.00 8.00
❑ D7 Fringe Division 3.00 8.00
❑ D8 ZFT 3.00 8.00
❑ D9 The Plot 3.00 8.00

2012 Game of Thrones Season One

COMPLETE SET (72) 5.00 12.00
T1/900 ISSUED AS CASE TOPPER
❑ 1 Winter is Coming .15 .40
❑ 2 Winter is Coming .15 .40
❑ 3 Winter is Coming .15 .40
❑ 4 The Kingsroad .15 .40
❑ 5 The Kingsroad .15 .40
❑ 6 The Kingsroad .15 .40
❑ 7 Lord Snow .15 .40
❑ 8 Lord Snow .15 .40
❑ 9 Lord Snow .15 .40
❑ 10 Cripples, Bastards and Broken Things .15 .40
❑ 11 Cripples, Bastards and Broken Things .15 .40
❑ 12 Cripples, Bastards and Broken Things .15 .40
❑ 13 The Wolf and the Lion .15 .40
❑ 14 The Wolf and the Lion .15 .40
❑ 15 The Wolf and the Lion .15 .40
❑ 16 A Golden Crown .15 .40
❑ 17 A Golden Crown .15 .40
❑ 18 A Golden Crown .15 .40
❑ 19 You Win or You Die .15 .40
❑ 20 You Win or You Die .15 .40
❑ 21 You Win or You Die .15 .40
❑ 22 The Pointy End .15 .40
❑ 23 The Pointy End .15 .40
❑ 24 The Pointy End .15 .40
❑ 25 Baelor .15 .40
❑ 26 Baelor .15 .40
❑ 27 Baelor .15 .40
❑ 28 Fire and Blood .15 .40
❑ 29 Fire and Blood .15 .40
❑ 30 Fire and Blood .15 .40
❑ 31 Maester Aemon .15 .40
❑ 32 Arya Stark .15 .40
❑ 33 Tyrion Lannister .15 .40
❑ 34 Petyr Littlefinger Baelish .15 .40
❑ 35 Prince Joffrey Baratheon .15 .40
❑ 36 Alliser Thorne .15 .40
❑ 37 Lancel Lannister .15 .40
❑ 38 Varys .15 .40
❑ 39 Sansa Stark .15 .40
❑ 40 Bronn .15 .40
❑ 41 Hodor .15 .40
❑ 42 Syrio Forel .15 .40
❑ 43 Robb Stark .15 .40
❑ 44 Samwell Tarly .15 .40
❑ 45 King Robert Baratheon .15 .40
❑ 46 Viserys Targaryen .15 .40
❑ 47 Ser Jaime Lannister .15 .40
❑ 48 Septa Mordane .15 .40
❑ 49 Ros .15 .40
❑ 50 Ser Jorah Mormont .15 .40
❑ 51 Jory Cassel .15 .40
❑ 52 Queen Cersei Lannister .15 .40
❑ 53 Rickon Stark .15 .40
❑ 54 Lord Commander Mormont .15 .40
❑ 55 Lord Eddard Ned Stark .15 .40
❑ 56 Lysa Arryn .15 .40
❑ 57 Gendry .15 .40
❑ 58 Lady Catelyn Stark .15 .40
❑ 59 Renly Baratheon .15 .40
❑ 60 Tywin Lannister .15 .40
❑ 61 Khal Drogo .15 .40
❑ 62 Grand Maester Pycelle .15 .40
❑ 63 Maester Luwin .15 .40
❑ 64 Jon Snow .15 .40
❑ 65 Rodrik Cassel .15 .40
❑ 66 Daenerys Targaryen .15 .40
❑ 67 Barristan Selmy .15 .40
❑ 68 Bran Stark .15 .40
❑ 69 Sandor Clegane The Hound .15 .40
❑ 70 Theon Greyjoy .15 .40
❑ 71 Magister Illyrio .15 .40
❑ 72 Checklist .15 .40
❑ T1 Title Sequence/900 10.00 25.00

2012 Game of Thrones Season One Foil Parallel

COMPLETE SET 25.00 60.00
STATED ODDS 1:3

2012 Game of Thrones Season One Autographs

L (LE) - LIMITED LOWER END: 300-400 COPIES
L (UE) - LIMITED UPPER END: 400-500 COPIES
OVERALL AUTO ODDS TWO PER BOX
❑ 1 Aidan Gillen 10.00 25.00
as Petyr Baelish Littlefinger L (UE)
❑ 2 Alfie Allen 10.00 25.00
as Theon Greyjoy L (UE)
❑ 3 Art Parkinson 15.00 40.00
as Rickon Stark L (LE)
❑ 4 Charles Dance 40.00 80.00
❑ 5 Conleth Hill 10.00 25.00
as Lord Varys L (UE)
❑ 6 Elyes Gabel 8.00 20.00
as Rakharo L (UE)
❑ 7 Emilia Clarke 150.00 250.00
❑ 8 Esme Bianco 15.00 40.00
as Ros L (UE)
❑ 9 Harry Lloyd 10.00 25.00
as Viserys Targaryen L (UE)
❑ 10 Ian McElhinney 8.00 20.00
as Barristan Selmy L (UE)
❑ 11 Isaac Hempstead-Wright 12.00 30.00
as Bran Stark L (UE)
❑ 12 Jack Gleeson 12.00 30.00
as Prince Joffrey Baratheon L (UE)
❑ 13 Jamie Sives 8.00 20.00
as Jory Cassel L (UE)
❑ 14 Jason Momoa 30.00 60.00
as Khal Drogo L (LE)
❑ 15 Jerome Flynn 10.00 25.00
as Bronn L (UE)
❑ 16 John Bradley 8.00 20.00
as Samwell Tarly L (UE)
❑ 17 Julian Glover 8.00 20.00
as Grand Maester Pycelle L (UE)
❑ 18 Kit Harington 50.00 100.00
❑ 19 Kristian Nairn 8.00 20.00
as Hodor L (UE)
❑ 20 Lena Headey 100.00 200.00
❑ 21 Maisie Williams 20.00 50.00
as Arya Stark L (UE)
❑ 22 Mark Addy 30.00 60.00
as King Robert Baratheon L (LE)
❑ 23 Michelle Fairley 40.00 80.00
❑ 24 Miltos Yerolemou 8.00 20.00
as Syrio Forel L (UE)
❑ 25 Nikolaj Coster-Waldau 40.00 80.00
❑ 26 Owen Teale 8.00 20.00
as Alliser Thorne L (UE)
❑ 27 Peter Dinklage 125.00 250.00
❑ 28 Richard Madden 75.00 150.00
❑ 29 Rory McCann 15.00 40.00
as Sandor Clegane The Hound L (UE)
❑ 30 Sean Bean 60.00 120.00

2012 Game of Thrones Season One Full Bleed Autographs

L (LE) - LIMITED LOWER END: 300-400 COPIES
L (UE) - LIMITED UPPER END: 400-500 COPIES
OVERALL AUTO ODDS TWO PER BOX
❑ 1 Aidan Gillen 10.00 25.00
as Petyr Baelish Littlefinger L (UE)
❑ 2 Alfie Allen 10.00 25.00
as Theon Greyjoy L (UE)
❑ 3 Art Parkinson 15.00 40.00
as Rickon Stark L (LE)
❑ 4 Conleth Hill 10.00 25.00
as Lord Varys L (UE)
❑ 5 Elyes Gabel 8.00 20.00
as Rakharo L (UE)
❑ 6 Esme Bianco 15.00 40.00
as Ros L (UE)
❑ 7 Harry Lloyd 10.00 25.00
as Viserys Targaryen L (UE)
❑ 8 Ian McElhinney 8.00 20.00
as Barristan Selmy L (UE)
❑ 9 Isaac Hempstead-Wright 12.00 30.00
as Bran Stark L (UE)
❑ 10 Jack Gleeson 12.00 30.00
as Prince Joffrey Baratheon L (UE)
❑ 11 Jamie Sives 8.00 20.00
as Jory Cassel L (UE)
❑ 12 Jason Momoa 30.00 60.00
as Khal Drogo L (LE)
❑ 13 Jerome Flynn 10.00 25.00
as Bronn L (UE)
❑ 14 John Bradley 8.00 20.00
as Samwell Tarly L (UE)
❑ 15 Julian Glover 8.00 20.00
as Grand Maester Pycelle L (UE)
❑ 16 Kristian Nairn 8.00 20.00
as Hodor L (UE)
❑ 17 Maisie Williams 20.00 50.00
as Arya Stark L (UE)
❑ 18 Mark Addy 30.00 60.00
as King Robert Baratheon L (LE)
❑ 19 Miltos Yerolemou 8.00 20.00
as Syrio Forel L (UE)
❑ 20 Owen Teale 8.00 20.00
as Alliser Thorne L (UE)
❑ 21 Rory McCann 15.00 40.00
as Sandor Clegane The Hound L (UE)

2012 Game of Thrones Season One Quotable Game of Thrones

COMPLETE SET (9) 8.00 20.00
STATED ODDS 1:12
❑ Q1 The Man Who Passes the Sentence 1.50 4.00
❑ Q2 Let Me Give You Some Advice 1.50 4.00
❑ Q3 Dothraki Have Two Things 1.50 4.00
❑ Q4 Everyone Who Isn't Us 1.50 4.00
❑ Q5 There Are No Men Like Me 1.50 4.00
❑ Q6 I Don't Believe That 1.50 4.00
❑ Q7 I'm Not a Cripple 1.50 4.00
❑ Q8 I Was Trained to Kill 1.50 4.00
❑ Q9 It's the Family Name That Lives 1.50 4.00
❑ Q10 What Do We Say to the God of Death 25.00 50.00

2012 Game of Thrones Season One Shadowbox

COMPLETE SET (6) 35.00 70.00
STATED ODDS 1:48
❑ 1 Cersei Lannister 8.00 20.00
❑ 2 Daenerys Targaryen 10.00 25.00
❑ 3 Eddard Stark 8.00 20.00
❑ 4 Jon Snow 8.00 20.00
❑ 5 Robb Stark 8.00 20.00
❑ 6 Tyrion Lannister 8.00 20.00

2012 Game of Thrones Season One The Houses

COMPLETE SET (9) 8.00 20.00
STATED ODDS 1:12
❑ H1 House Baratheon 1.50 4.00
❑ H2 House Stark 1.50 4.00
❑ H3 House Lannister 1.50 4.00
❑ H4 House Tully 1.50 4.00
❑ H5 House Targaryen 1.50 4.00
❑ H6 House Arryn 1.50 4.00
❑ H7 House Frey 1.50 4.00
❑ H8 House Tyrell 1.50 4.00
❑ H9 House Greyjoy 1.50 4.00

2012 Game of Thrones Season One You Win or You Die

COMPLETE SET (5) 10.00 25.00
STATED ODDS 1:24
❑ SP1 Eddard Stark 3.00 8.00
Winter Is Coming
❑ SP2 Cersei Lannister 3.00 8.00
Everyone But Us Is The Enemy
❑ SP3 Robert Baratheon 3.00 8.00
Killing Things Clears My Head
❑ SP4 Daenerys Targaryen 4.00 10.00
I Do Not Have A Gentle Heart
❑ SP5 Jon Snow 3.00 8.00
I Am The Watcher On The Wall

2012 Garbage Pail Kids

COMPLETE SET (110) 10.00 25.00
❑ 1a D. Jay .15 .40
❑ 1b Dee J. .15
❑ 2a Nate Inflate .15 .40
❑ 2b Balloony Bart .15 .40
❑ 3a Picky Nicky .15 .40
❑ 3b Pocketing Palmer .15 .40
❑ 4a Lifted Linda .15 .40
❑ 4b Smoothed Sally .15 .40
❑ 5a Steve Rotters .15 .40
❑ 5b Calvin America .15 .40
❑ 6a Lasso Luke .15 .40
❑ 6b Duke Ranch .15 .40
❑ 7a Ear Bud .15 .40
❑ 7b Waxy Wesley .15 .40
❑ 8a Bob Sled .15 .40
❑ 8b Crashed Craig .15 .40
❑ 9a Sushi Seth .15 .40
❑ 9b Chopped Chad .15 .40
❑ 10a Tooth Mary .15 .40
❑ 10b Fiona Fairy .15 .40
❑ 11a Sawing Sal .15 .40
❑ 11b Musical Mike .15 .40
❑ 12a Angry Al .15 .40
❑ 12b Birdbrain Bruce .15 .40
❑ 13a Chalk Linus .15 .40
❑ 13b Crime Scene Dean .15 .40
❑ 14a Laundro Matt .15 .40
❑ 14b Clean Gene .15 .40
❑ 15a Doughy Zoe .15 .40
❑ 15b Snotty Sally .15 .40
❑ 16a Jammin' Julie .15 .40
❑ 16b Jenny Jelly .15 .40
❑ 17a Rubber Roy .15 .40
❑ 17b Bouncing Bert .15 .40
❑ 18a Taffy Toby .15 .40
❑ 18b Pulled Pierre .15 .40
❑ 19a Sammy Stooge .15 .40
❑ 19b Triple Ted .15 .40
❑ 20a Relay Trey .15 .40
❑ 20b Racin' Ricky .15 .40
❑ 21a Hank Bank .15 .40
❑ 21b Piggy Peyton .15 .40
❑ 22a Screaming Stuart .15 .40
❑ 22b Terrified Terence .15 .40
❑ 23a Super Manny .15 .40
❑ 23b Airsick Vick .15 .40
❑ 24a Tricky Tracy .15 .40
❑ 24b Hallow Wendy .15 .40
❑ 25a Larry Lo Mein .15 .40
❑ 25b Takeout Tyler .15 .40
❑ 26a Academy Ward .15 .40
❑ 26b Grouchy Oscar .15 .40
❑ 27a Tina Trapeze .15 .40
❑ 27b Aerial Alice .15 .40
❑ 28a Jersey Jeff .15 .40
❑ 28b Situational Stan .15 .40
❑ 29a Brice Lice .15 .40
❑ 29b Infested Ian .15 .40
❑ 30a Complex Rex .15 .40
❑ 30b Water Lou .15 .40
❑ 31a Fillin' Phyllis .15 .40
❑ 31b Manicure Margaret .15 .40
❑ 32a Twisted Tom .15 .40
❑ 32b Salty Sean .15 .40
❑ 33a Ray Spray .15 .40
❑ 33b Brutal Barry .15 .40
❑ 34a 3-D Stevie .15 .40

34b Realistic Ralph .15 .40
35a Jack Snack .15 .40
35b Vending Vinnie .15 .40
36a Facial Harry .15 .40
36b Bearded Brent .15 .40
37a Vulgar Venus .15 .40
37b Stony Steph .15 .40
38a Thunder Todd .15 .40
38b Lightning Les .15 .40
39a Flatfoot Frank .15 .40
39b Doggy Dennis .15 .40
40a Pasty Pierce .15 .40
40b Rolled Up Ronald .15 .40
41a Jez Dispenser .15 .40
41b Candy Sandy .15 .40
42a Contact Carl .15 .40
42b Eyeball Paul .15 .40
43a Crystal Ball .15 .40
43b Fortune Terra .15 .40
44a Trashy Trixie .15 .40
44b Dustbin Daphne .15 .40
45a Messy Mario .15 .40
45b Lewd Luigi .15 .40
46a Proportional Pat .15 .40
46b Limber Leonardo .15 .40
47a Grillin' Greg .15 .40
47b Hotdog Harris .15 .40
48a Cannon Bill .15 .40
48b Explosive Earl .15 .40
49a Marshy Mel .15 .40
49b Gooey Hughie .15 .40
50a Pete Sheet .15 .40
50b Boo Bradley .15 .40
51a Tug Of Warren .15 .40
51b Stretched Saul .15 .40
52a Snowy Joey .15 .40
52b Blizzard Blake .15 .40
53a Clipper Claire .15 .40
53b Toenail Teresa .15 .40
54a Fried Frieda .15 .40
54b Fishy Florence .15 .40
55a Will Street .15 .40
55b Juan Percent .15 .40

2012 Garbage Pail Kids Green

COMPLETE SET 30.00 60.00
STATED ODDS 1:2

2012 Garbage Pail Kids Black

STATED ODDS 1:12 HOBBY

2012 Garbage Pail Kids Gold

STATED ODDS 1:124

2012 Garbage Pail Kids Adam Bomb Through History

COMPLETE SET (10) 4.00 10.00
STATED ODDS 1:2

1 The Big Bang .75 2.00
2 Extinction of the Dinosaurs .75 2.00
3 End of the Ice Age .75 2.00
4 Discovery of Fire .75 2.00
5 Fall of Troy .75 2.00
6 Destruction of Pompeii .75 2.00
7 Boston Tea Party .75 2.00
8 Hindenburg Disaster .75 2.00
9 Launch of Apollo 11 .75 2.00
10 Fall of the Berlin Wall .75 2.00

2012 Garbage Pail Kids Adam Bomb Through History Green

COMPLETE SET 8.00 20.00
*GREEN: .8X TO 2X BASIC CARDS
STATED ODDS 1:12

2012 Garbage Pail Kids Adam Bomb Through History Gold

*GOLD: 25X TO 50X BASIC CARDS
STATED ODDS 1:1,362

2012 Garbage Pail Kids Loco Motion

COMPLETE SET (10) 10.00 25.00
STATED ODDS 1:12

1 Stormy Heather 2.00 5.00
2 Adam Bomb 4.00 10.00
3 Clogged Duane 2.00 5.00
4 Bruised Lee 2.00 5.00
5 Meltin' Milton 2.00 5.00
6 Doughy Joey 2.00 5.00
7 See More Seymour 2.00 5.00
8 Homer Runt 2.00 5.00
9 Pumping Aaron 2.00 5.00
10 Scalped Ralph 2.00 5.00

2012 Garbage Pail Kids Mix 'n' Match

COMPLETE SET (10) 8.00 20.00
STATED ODDS 1:12

1 Adam Bomb 2.50 6.00
2 Mad Mike 1.50 4.00
3 Double Heather 1.50 4.00
4 Hot Scott 1.50 4.00
5 Wrinkled Rita 1.50 4.00
6 Tattoo Lou 1.50 4.00
7 Split Kit 1.50 4.00
8 Starin' Darren 1.50 4.00
9 Half-Nelson 1.50 4.00
10 See More Seymour 1.50 4.00

2012 Garbage Pail Kids Posters

COMPLETE SET (6) 10.00 20.00
ONE POSTER PER RACK PACK

1 D. Jay 2.00 5.00
2 Facial Harry 2.00 5.00
3 Messy Mario 2.00 5.00
4 Picky Nicky 2.00 5.00
5 Snowy Joey 2.00 5.00
6 Will Street 2.00 5.00

2012 Garbage Pail Kids Sketches

STATED ODDS 1:463

1 Brent Engstrom
2 Colin Walton
3 Fred Wheaton
4 James Warhola
5 Jeff Zapata
6 Joe Simko
7 Layron DeJarnette
8 Mark Pingitore
9 Neil Camera
10 Tom Bunk

2012 Garbage Pail Kids Magnets

COMPLETE SET (16) 10.00 20.00

1 Adam Bomb 1.25 3.00
2 Potty Scotty .75 2.00
3 Ghastly Ashley .75 2.00
4 Beasty Boyd .75 2.00
5 Stan Alive .75 2.00
6 Gary Goyle .75 2.00
7 Not Tobey .75 2.00
8 Tony Starch .75 2.00
9 Breezy Betty .75 2.00
10 Phan Tom .75 2.00
11 Sun Bernie .75 2.00
12 Dawn Pour .75 2.00
13 Topiary Terri .75 2.00
14 Noah Constrictor .75 2.00
15 IV Ivy .75 2.00
16 Curious Kate .75 2.00

2012 The Guild Seasons One Through Three

COMPLETE SET (63) 6.00 15.00

1 Awkward Break-up .15 .40
2 Doorstep'd .15 .40
3 Keyboard Chemistry .15 .40
4 OMG .15 .40
5 Photoshop'd .15 .40
6 Plus 5 Sexterity .15 .40
7 WTB Helm .15 .40
8 ... .15 .40
9 Cheese Gouging .15 .40
10 Secret Guild Meeting .15 .40
11 Maternal Instincts .15 .40
12 Mama Cougar .15 .40
13 Ethernoose .15 .40
14 Princess Codependent .15 .40
15 Headshot .15 .40
16 Boss Fight .15 .40
17 Tempta-T1-on .15 .40
18 That's a Lot of RAM .15 .40
19 DC .15 .40
20 The Orb of Nurr .15 .40
21 Squab .15 .40
22 Wade Wei .15 .40
23 Embrace the Tiger .15 .40
24 Teats for Tots .15 .40
25 Anything Phallic .15 .40
26 Not Your Average Zombie .15 .40
27 Remap'd .15 .40
28 Harlot .15 .40
29 Selfish Love .15 .40
30 Me-Weekend Bender .15 .40
31 Enhancements .15 .40
32 Jacked .15 .40
33 Vork-tanamo Bay .15 .40
34 It's Truth .15 .40
35 Two Choices .15 .40
36 Corrupting a Prince .15 .40
37 Survival of the Un-fittest .15 .40
38 The Way to Her Heart .15 .40
39 The Taking Kind .15 .40
40 The Challenge .15 .40
41 Fight Fight .15 .40
42 Revenge .15 .40
43 Corpse Run .15 .40
44 Feel the Excitement .15 .40
45 Axis of Anarchy .15 .40
46 Turncoat .15 .40
47 WTF .15 .40
48 Drive-Thru .15 .40
49 Hostile Raid Leader .15 .40
50 icanhazeurotrash .15 .40
51 Creepy Whisper .15 .40
52 Spork .15 .40
53 CASUALS .15 .40
54 Quatro Barras .15 .40
55 Negotiations .15 .40
56 Poo Face .15 .40
57 Down and Out .15 .40
58 Tiny Monster .15 .40
59 Bingo .15 .40
60 Eat That, Biceps .15 .40
61 2v1 .15 .40
62 Avatar Connection .15 .40
63 Uh-Oh .15 .40
P1 The Guild PROMO

2012 The Guild Seasons One Through Three Autographs

STATED ODDS 1:24

A1 Sandeep Parikh SP 30.00 60.00
A2 Felicia Day SP 150.00 250.00
A3 Jeff Lewis SP 30.00 60.00
A4 Amy Okuda SP 35.00 70.00
A5 Robin Thorsen SP 35.00 70.00
A6 Vincent Caso SP 40.00 80.00
A7 Sandeep Parikh 12.00 30.00
A8 Felicia Day 50.00 100.00
A9 Jeff Lewis 15.00 40.00
A10 Amy Okuda 15.00 40.00
A11 Robin Thorsen 10.00 25.00
A12 Vincent Caso 12.00 30.00
A13 Wil Wheaton 50.00 100.00
A14 Mike Rose 6.00 15.00
A15 Teal Sherer 6.00 15.00
A16 J. Teddy Garces 6.00 15.00
A17 Alexander Yi 8.00 20.00
A18 Michele Boyd 30.00 60.00
A19 Fernando Chien 8.00 20.00
A20 Brett Sheridan 6.00 15.00
A21 Viji Nathan 5.00 12.00
A22 Tara Caso 8.00 20.00
A24 Kim Evey 10.00 25.00
A25 Sean Becker 5.00 12.00

2012 The Guild Seasons One Through Three Characters

COMPLETE SET (6) 5.00 12.00
OVERALL CHASE ODDS 1:6

TG1 Felicia Day as Codex 2.00 5.00
TG2 Robin Thorsen as Clara 1.50 4.00
TG3 Sandeep Parikh as Zaboo 1.50 4.00
TG4 Amy Okuda as Tinkerballa 1.50 4.00
TG5 Jeff Lewis as Vork 1.50 4.00
TG6 Vincent Caso as Bladezz 1.50 4.00

2012 The Guild Seasons One Through Three Costumes

STATED ODDS 1:24

M1 Felicia Day 25.00 60.00
M2 Sandeep Parikh 8.00 20.00
M3 Jeff Lewis 8.00 20.00
M4 Amy Okuda 10.00 25.00
M5 Robin Thorsen 10.00 25.00
M6 Vincent Caso 8.00 20.00
M7 Vincent Caso 8.00 20.00

2012 The Guild Seasons One Through Three Vlog

COMPLETE SET (9) 5.00 12.00
OVERALL CHASE ODDS 1:6

1 Unintended Suicide 1.25 3.00
2 Not Ideal for Skulls 1.25 3.00
3 A Surge of Confidence 1.25 3.00
4 A Tiny Tiny Part 1.25 3.00
5 Questionable Sexuality 1.25 3.00
6 Infinite Wisdom 1.25 3.00
7 Always the Healer 1.25 3.00
8 A Unified Front 1.25 3.00
9 New Leadership 1.25 3.00

2012 James Bond 50th Anniversary

COMPLETE SET (198) 12.00 30.00
COMP.SER. 1 SET (99) 6.00 15.00
COMP.SER. 2 SET (99) 8.00 20.00
ODD #'d CARDS ISSUED IN SERIES 1
EVEN #'d CARDS ISSUED IN SERIES 2

1 Dr. No .15 .40
2 Dr. No .15 .40
3 Dr. No .15 .40
4 Dr. No .15 .40
5 Dr. No .15 .40
6 Dr. No .15 .40
7 Dr. No .15 .40
8 Dr. No .15 .40
9 Dr. No .15 .40
10 From Russia With Love .15 .40
11 From Russia With Love .15 .40
12 From Russia With Love .15 .40
13 From Russia With Love .15 .40
14 From Russia With Love .15 .40
15 From Russia With Love .15 .40
16 From Russia With Love .15 .40
17 From Russia With Love .15 .40
18 From Russia With Love .15 .40
19 Goldfinger .15 .40
20 Goldfinger .15 .40
21 Goldfinger .15 .40
22 Goldfinger .15 .40
23 Goldfinger .15 .40
24 Goldfinger .15 .40
25 Goldfinger .15 .40
26 Goldfinger .15 .40
27 Goldfinger .15 .40
28 Thunderball .15 .40
29 Thunderball .15 .40
30 Thunderball .15 .40
31 Thunderball .15 .40
32 Thunderball .15 .40
33 Thunderball .15 .40
34 Thunderball .15 .40
35 Thunderball .15 .40
36 Thunderball .15 .40
37 You Only Live Twice .15 .40
38 You Only Live Twice .15 .40
39 You Only Live Twice .15 .40
40 You Only Live Twice .15 .40
41 You Only Live Twice .15 .40
42 You Only Live Twice .15 .40
43 You Only Live Twice .15 .40
44 You Only Live Twice .15 .40
45 You Only Live Twice .15 .40
46 On Her Majesty's Secret Service .15 .40
47 On Her Majesty's Secret Service .15 .40
48 On Her Majesty's Secret Service .15 .40
49 On Her Majesty's Secret Service .15 .40
50 On Her Majesty's Secret Service .15 .40
51 On Her Majesty's Secret Service .15 .40
52 On Her Majesty's Secret Service .15 .40
53 On Her Majesty's Secret Service .15 .40
54 On Her Majesty's Secret Service .15 .40
55 Diamonds Are Forever .15 .40
56 Diamonds Are Forever .15 .40
57 Diamonds Are Forever .15 .40
58 Diamonds Are Forever .15 .40
59 Diamonds Are Forever .15 .40
60 Diamonds Are Forever .15 .40
61 Diamonds Are Forever .15 .40
62 Diamonds Are Forever .15 .40
63 Diamonds Are Forever .15 .40
64 Live And Let Die .15 .40
65 Live And Let Die .15 .40
66 Live And Let Die .15 .40
67 Live And Let Die .15 .40
68 Live And Let Die .15 .40
69 Live And Let Die .15 .40
70 Live And Let Die .15 .40
71 Live And Let Die .15 .40
72 Live And Let Die .15 .40
73 The Man With The Golden Gun .15 .40
74 The Man With The Golden Gun .15 .40
75 The Man With The Golden Gun .15 .40
76 The Man With The Golden Gun .15 .40
77 The Man With The Golden Gun .15 .40
78 The Man With The Golden Gun .15 .40
79 The Man With The Golden Gun .15 .40
80 The Man With The Golden Gun .15 .40
81 The Man With The Golden Gun .15 .40
82 The Spy Who Loved Me .15 .40
83 The Spy Who Loved Me .15 .40
84 The Spy Who Loved Me .15 .40
85 The Spy Who Loved Me .15 .40
86 The Spy Who Loved Me .15 .40
87 The Spy Who Loved Me .15 .40
88 The Spy Who Loved Me .15 .40
89 The Spy Who Loved Me .15 .40
90 The Spy Who Loved Me .15 .40
91 Moonraker .15 .40
92 Moonraker .15 .40
93 Moonraker .15 .40
94 Moonraker .15 .40
95 Moonraker .15 .40
96 Moonraker .15 .40
97 Moonraker .15 .40
98 Moonraker .15 .40
99 Moonraker .15 .40
100 For Your Eyes Only .15 .40
101 For Your Eyes Only .15 .40
102 For Your Eyes Only .15 .40
103 For Your Eyes Only .15 .40
104 For Your Eyes Only .15 .40
105 For Your Eyes Only .15 .40
106 For Your Eyes Only .15 .40
107 For Your Eyes Only .15 .40
108 For Your Eyes Only .15 .40
109 Octopussy .15 .40
110 Octopussy .15 .40
111 Octopussy .15 .40
112 Octopussy .15 .40
113 Octopussy .15 .40
114 Octopussy .15 .40
115 Octopussy .15 .40
116 Octopussy .15 .40
117 Octopussy .15 .40
118 Octopussy .15 .40
119 A View To A Kill .15 .40
120 A View To A Kill .15 .40
121 A View To A Kill .15 .40
122 A View To A Kill .15 .40
123 A View To A Kill .15 .40
124 A View To A Kill .15 .40
125 A View To A Kill .15 .40
126 A View To A Kill .15 .40
127 The Living Daylights .15 .40
128 The Living Daylights .15 .40
129 The Living Daylights .15 .40
130 The Living Daylights .15 .40
131 The Living Daylights .15 .40
132 The Living Daylights .15 .40
133 The Living Daylights .15 .40
134 The Living Daylights .15 .40
135 The Living Daylights .15 .40
136 Licence To Kill .15 .40
137 Licence To Kill .15 .40
138 Licence To Kill .15 .40
139 Licence To Kill .15 .40
140 Licence To Kill .15 .40
141 Licence To Kill .15 .40
142 Licence To Kill .15 .40
143 Licence To Kill .15 .40
144 Licence To Kill .15 .40
145 GoldenEye .15 .40
146 GoldenEye .15 .40
147 GoldenEye .15 .40
148 GoldenEye .15 .40
149 GoldenEye .15 .40
150 GoldenEye .15 .40
151 GoldenEye .15 .40
152 GoldenEye .15 .40
153 GoldenEye .15 .40
154 Tomorrow Never Dies .15 .40
155 Tomorrow Never Dies .15 .40
156 Tomorrow Never Dies .15 .40
157 Tomorrow Never Dies .15 .40
158 Tomorrow Never Dies .15 .40
159 Tomorrow Never Dies .15 .40
160 Tomorrow Never Dies .15 .40
161 Tomorrow Never Dies .15 .40
162 Tomorrow Never Dies .15 .40
163 The World Is Not Enough .15 .40
164 The World Is Not Enough .15 .40
165 The World Is Not Enough .15 .40
166 The World Is Not Enough .15 .40
167 The World Is Not Enough .15 .40
168 The World Is Not Enough .15 .40
169 The World Is Not Enough .15 .40
170 The World Is Not Enough .15 .40
171 The World Is Not Enough .15 .40
172 Die Another Day .15 .40
173 Die Another Day .15 .40
174 Die Another Day .15 .40
175 Die Another Day .15 .40
176 Die Another Day .15 .40
177 Die Another Day .15 .40
178 Die Another Day .15 .40
179 Die Another Day .15 .40
180 Die Another Day .15 .40
181 Casino Royale .15 .40
182 Casino Royale .15 .40
183 Casino Royale .15 .40
184 Casino Royale .15 .40
185 Casino Royale .15 .40
186 Casino Royale .15 .40
187 Casino Royale .15 .40
188 Casino Royale .15 .40
189 Casino Royale .15 .40
190 Quantum of Solace .15 .40
191 Quantum of Solace .15 .40
192 Quantum of Solace .15 .40
193 Quantum of Solace .15 .40
194 Quantum of Solace .15 .40
195 Quantum of Solace .15 .40
196 Quantum of Solace .15 .40
197 Quantum of Solace .15 .40
198 Quantum of Solace .15 .40
NNO SkyFall Movie Poster/700 10.00 25.00
(issued as Series 1 case topper)
CT1 James Bond (007 logo in background) 10.00 25.00
(issued as Series 2 case topper)
JBR27 Gustav Graves' Ice Palace Interior MEM/375 40.00 80.00
JBR28 Franz Sanchez's Airplane MEM/333 40.00 80.00
(issued as 3-case incentive)

2012 James Bond 50th Anniversary Parallel

COMPLETE SET (196) 50.00 100.00
COMP.SER. 1 SET (99) 25.00 60.00
COMP.SER. 2 SET (99) 25.00 60.00
STATED ODDS 1:3

2012 James Bond 50th Anniversary Autographs

OVERALL AUTO ODDS 3 PER BOX
L (LIMITED): 300-500 COPIES
VL (VERY LIMITED): 200-300 COPIES
EL (EXTREMELY LTD): UNDER 200 COPIES

A110 Daniel Craig EL 250.00 400.00
A138 Gemma Arterton EL 100.00 175.00
A145 Jill St. John L 15.00 40.00
A151 Eunice Gayson VL 20.00 50.00
A162 Anthony Zerbe L 10.00 25.00
A166 Luciana Paluzzi L 10.00 25.00
A167 Kim Norton 6.00 15.00
A168 Catherine Rabett L 8.00 20.00
A170 Nina Muschallik 6.00 15.00
A171 Francisca Tu 8.00 20.00
A172 Nina Young 6.00 15.00
A173 Michael Madsen L 12.00 30.00
A176 Lesley Langley L 6.00 15.00
A177 Joaquin Martinez L 8.00 20.00
A180 Toby Stephens L 6.00 15.00
A181 Simon Andreu L 6.00 15.00
A183 Cristina Contes L 8.00 20.00
A184 Sonny Caldinez 6.00 15.00
A186 Veruschka L 6.00 15.00
A189 Pierce Brosnan EL 250.00 350.00
A192 Carlos Leal L 6.00 15.00
A194 Joie Vejjajiva L 8.00 20.00
A195 David Yip L 6.00 15.00
A196 Mary Stavin VL 20.00 50.00
A198 Martine Beswicke EL 50.00 100.00
A199 Edward De Souza L 8.00 20.00
A200 Clifton James EL 75.00 150.00
A201 Christopher Muncke L 8.00 20.00
A202 Jeroen Krabbe L 8.00 20.00
A203 Sneh Gupta L 6.00 15.00
A204 Peter Fontaine L 6.00 15.00
A205 Al Matthews L 6.00 15.00
A207 Halle Berry EL 200.00 350.00
A208 Gotz Otto L 8.00 20.00
A209 Nadja Regin L 75.00 150.00
A210 Nadja Regin EL 75.00 150.00
A211 Simon Kunz L 6.00 15.00
A212 Irka Bochenko L 10.00 25.00
A213 Alizia Gur VL 30.00 60.00
A214 Pat Gill 6.00 15.00
A215 Tom So L 8.00 20.00
A216 Frank McRae L 6.00 15.00
A217 Beatrice Libert L 8.00 20.00
A218 Joe Flood L 6.00 15.00
A219 Jack Klaff L 6.00 15.00
A220 Gloria Hendry L 6.00 15.00
A221 Neville Jason L 6.00 15.00

2012 James Bond 50th Anniversary Bond...James Bond

COMPLETE SET (11) 8.00 20.00
STATED ODDS 1:12

B12 Roger Moore in For Your Eyes Only 2.00 5.00
B13 Roger Moore in Octopussy 2.00 5.00
B14 Roger Moore in A View To A Kill 2.00 5.00
B15 Timothy Dalton in The Living Daylights 2.00 5.00
B16 Timothy Dalton in License To Kill 2.00 5.00
B17 Pierce Brosnan in GoldenEye 2.00 5.00
B18 Pierce Brosnan in Tomorrow Never Dies 2.00 5.00
B19 Pierce Brosnan in The World Is Not Enough 2.00 5.00
B20 Pierce Brosnan in Die Another Day 2.00 5.00
B21 Daniel Craig in Casino Royale 2.00 5.00
B22 Daniel Craig in Quantum of Solace 2.00 5.00

2012 James Bond 50th Anniversary Dr. No Commemorative

COMPLETE SET (108) 12.00 30.00
STATED ODDS ONE PER SER. 1 PACK

1 Plot Synopsis for Dr. No .30 .75
2 Plot Synopsis for Dr. No .30 .75
3 Plot Synopsis for Dr. No .30 .75
4 Plot Synopsis for Dr. No .30 .75
5 Plot Synopsis for Dr. No .30 .75
6 Plot Synopsis for Dr. No .30 .75
7 Plot Synopsis for Dr. No .30 .75
8 Plot Synopsis for Dr. No .30 .75
9 Plot Synopsis for Dr. No .30 .75
10 Plot Synopsis for Dr. No .30 .75
11 Plot Synopsis for Dr. No .30 .75
12 Plot Synopsis for Dr. No .30 .75
13 Plot Synopsis for Dr. No .30 .75
14 Plot Synopsis for Dr. No .30 .75
15 Plot Synopsis for Dr. No .30 .75
16 Plot Synopsis for Dr. No .30 .75
17 Plot Synopsis for Dr. No .30 .75
18 Plot Synopsis for Dr. No .30 .75
19 Plot Synopsis for Dr. No .30 .75
20 Plot Synopsis for Dr. No .30 .75
21 Plot Synopsis for Dr. No .30 .75
22 Plot Synopsis for Dr. No .30 .75
23 Plot Synopsis for Dr. No .30 .75
24 Plot Synopsis for Dr. No .30 .75
25 Plot Synopsis for Dr. No .30 .75
26 Plot Synopsis for Dr. No .30 .75
27 Plot Synopsis for Dr. No .30 .75
28 Plot Synopsis for Dr. No .30 .75
29 Plot Synopsis for Dr. No .30 .75
30 Plot Synopsis for Dr. No .30 .75
31 Plot Synopsis for Dr. No .30 .75
32 Plot Synopsis for Dr. No .30 .75
33 Plot Synopsis for Dr. No .30 .75
34 Plot Synopsis for Dr. No .30 .75
35 Plot Synopsis for Dr. No .30 .75
36 Plot Synopsis for Dr. No .30 .75
37 Plot Synopsis for Dr. No .30 .75
38 Plot Synopsis for Dr. No .30 .75
39 Plot Synopsis for Dr. No .30 .75
40 Plot Synopsis for Dr. No .30 .75
41 Plot Synopsis for Dr. No .30 .75
42 Plot Synopsis for Dr. No .30 .75
43 Plot Synopsis for Dr. No .30 .75
44 Plot Synopsis for Dr. No .30 .75
45 Plot Synopsis for Dr. No .30 .75
46 Plot Synopsis for Dr. No .30 .75
47 Plot Synopsis for Dr. No .30 .75
48 Plot Synopsis for Dr. No .30 .75
49 Plot Synopsis for Dr. No .30 .75
50 Plot Synopsis for Dr. No .30 .75
51 Plot Synopsis for Dr. No .30 .75
52 Plot Synopsis for Dr. No .30 .75
53 Plot Synopsis for Dr. No .30 .75
54 Plot Synopsis for Dr. No .30 .75
55 Plot Synopsis for Dr. No .30 .75
56 Plot Synopsis for Dr. No .30 .75
57 Plot Synopsis for Dr. No .30 .75
58 Plot Synopsis for Dr. No .30 .75
59 Plot Synopsis for Dr. No .30 .75
60 Plot Synopsis for Dr. No .30 .75
61 Plot Synopsis for Dr. No .30 .75
62 Plot Synopsis for Dr. No .30 .75
63 Plot Synopsis for Dr. No .30 .75
64 Plot Synopsis for Dr. No .30 .75
65 Plot Synopsis for Dr. No .30 .75
66 Plot Synopsis for Dr. No .30 .75
67 Plot Synopsis for Dr. No .30 .75
68 Plot Synopsis for Dr. No .30 .75

❑ 69 Plot Synopsis for Dr. No .30 .75
❑ 70 Plot Synopsis for Dr. No .30 .75
❑ 71 Plot Synopsis for Dr. No .30 .75
❑ 72 Plot Synopsis for Dr. No .30 .75
❑ 73 Plot Synopsis for Dr. No .30 .75
❑ 74 Plot Synopsis for Dr. No .30 .75
❑ 75 Plot Synopsis for Dr. No .30 .75
❑ 76 Plot Synopsis for Dr. No .30 .75
❑ 77 Plot Synopsis for Dr. No .30 .75
❑ 78 Plot Synopsis for Dr. No .30 .75
❑ 79 Plot Synopsis for Dr. No .30 .75
❑ 80 Plot Synopsis for Dr. No .30 .75
❑ 81 Plot Synopsis for Dr. No .30 .75
❑ 82 Plot Synopsis for Dr. No .30 .75
❑ 83 Plot Synopsis for Dr. No .30 .75
❑ 84 Plot Synopsis for Dr. No .30 .75
❑ 85 Plot Synopsis for Dr. No .30 .75
❑ 86 Plot Synopsis for Dr. No .30 .75
❑ 87 Plot Synopsis for Dr. No .30 .75
❑ 88 Plot Synopsis for Dr. No .30 .75
❑ 89 Plot Synopsis for Dr. No .30 .75
❑ 90 Plot Synopsis for Dr. No .30 .75
❑ 91 Plot Synopsis for Dr. No .30 .75
❑ 92 Plot Synopsis for Dr. No .30 .75
❑ 93 Plot Synopsis for Dr. No .30 .75
❑ 94 Plot Synopsis for Dr. No .30 .75
❑ 95 Plot Synopsis for Dr. No .30 .75
❑ 96 Plot Synopsis for Dr. No .30 .75
❑ 97 Plot Synopsis for Dr. No .30 .75
❑ 98 Plot Synopsis for Dr. No .30 .75
❑ 99 Plot Synopsis for Dr. No .30 .75
❑ 100 Plot Synopsis for Dr. No .30 .75
❑ 101 Plot Synopsis for Dr. No .30 .75
❑ 102 Plot Synopsis for Dr. No .30 .75
❑ 103 Plot Synopsis for Dr. No .30 .75
❑ 104 Plot Synopsis for Dr. No .30 .75
❑ 105 Plot Synopsis for Dr. No .30 .75
❑ 106 Plot Synopsis for Dr. No .30 .75
❑ 107 Plot Synopsis for Dr. No .30 .75
❑ 108 Plot Synopsis for Dr. No .30 .75

2012 James Bond 50th Anniversary From Russia With Love Commemorative

COMPLETE SET (108) 15.00 40.00
STATED ODDS ONE PER SER. 2 PACK

❑ 1 From Russia With Love .30 .75
❑ 2 From Russia With Love .30 .75
❑ 3 From Russia With Love .30 .75
❑ 4 From Russia With Love .30 .75
❑ 5 From Russia With Love .30 .75
❑ 6 From Russia With Love .30 .75
❑ 7 From Russia With Love .30 .75
❑ 8 From Russia With Love .30 .75
❑ 9 From Russia With Love .30 .75
❑ 10 From Russia With Love .30 .75
❑ 11 From Russia With Love .30 .75
❑ 12 From Russia With Love .30 .75
❑ 13 From Russia With Love .30 .75
❑ 14 From Russia With Love .30 .75
❑ 15 From Russia With Love .30 .75
❑ 16 From Russia With Love .30 .75
❑ 17 From Russia With Love .30 .75
❑ 18 From Russia With Love .30 .75
❑ 19 From Russia With Love .30 .75
❑ 20 From Russia With Love .30 .75
❑ 21 From Russia With Love .30 .75
❑ 22 From Russia With Love .30 .75
❑ 23 From Russia With Love .30 .75
❑ 24 From Russia With Love .30 .75
❑ 25 From Russia With Love .30 .75
❑ 26 From Russia With Love .30 .75
❑ 27 From Russia With Love .30 .75
❑ 28 From Russia With Love .30 .75
❑ 29 From Russia With Love .30 .75
❑ 30 From Russia With Love .30 .75
❑ 31 From Russia With Love .30 .75
❑ 32 From Russia With Love .30 .75
❑ 33 From Russia With Love .30 .75
❑ 34 From Russia With Love .30 .75
❑ 35 From Russia With Love .30 .75
❑ 36 From Russia With Love .30 .75
❑ 37 From Russia With Love .30 .75
❑ 38 From Russia With Love .30 .75
❑ 39 From Russia With Love .30 .75
❑ 40 From Russia With Love .30 .75
❑ 41 From Russia With Love .30 .75
❑ 42 From Russia With Love .30 .75
❑ 43 From Russia With Love .30 .75
❑ 44 From Russia With Love .30 .75
❑ 45 From Russia With Love .30 .75
❑ 46 From Russia With Love .30 .75
❑ 47 From Russia With Love .30 .75
❑ 48 From Russia With Love .30 .75
❑ 49 From Russia With Love .30 .75
❑ 50 From Russia With Love .30 .75
❑ 51 From Russia With Love .30 .75
❑ 52 From Russia With Love .30 .75
❑ 53 From Russia With Love .30 .75
❑ 54 From Russia With Love .30 .75
❑ 55 From Russia With Love .30 .75
❑ 56 From Russia With Love .30 .75
❑ 57 From Russia With Love .30 .75
❑ 58 From Russia With Love .30 .75
❑ 59 From Russia With Love .30 .75
❑ 60 From Russia With Love .30 .75
❑ 61 From Russia With Love .30 .75
❑ 62 From Russia With Love .30 .75
❑ 63 From Russia With Love .30 .75
❑ 64 From Russia With Love .30 .75
❑ 65 From Russia With Love .30 .75
❑ 66 From Russia With Love .30 .75
❑ 67 From Russia With Love .30 .75
❑ 68 From Russia With Love .30 .75
❑ 69 From Russia With Love .30 .75
❑ 70 From Russia With Love .30 .75
❑ 71 From Russia With Love .30 .75
❑ 72 From Russia With Love .30 .75
❑ 73 From Russia With Love .30 .75
❑ 74 From Russia With Love .30 .75
❑ 75 From Russia With Love .30 .75
❑ 76 From Russia With Love .30 .75
❑ 77 From Russia With Love .30 .75
❑ 78 From Russia With Love .30 .75
❑ 79 From Russia With Love .30 .75
❑ 80 From Russia With Love .30 .75
❑ 81 From Russia With Love .30 .75
❑ 82 From Russia With Love .30 .75
❑ 83 From Russia With Love .30 .75
❑ 84 From Russia With Love .30 .75
❑ 85 From Russia With Love .30 .75
❑ 86 From Russia With Love .30 .75
❑ 87 From Russia With Love .30 .75
❑ 88 From Russia With Love .30 .75
❑ 89 From Russia With Love .30 .75
❑ 90 From Russia With Love .30 .75
❑ 91 From Russia With Love .30 .75
❑ 92 From Russia With Love .30 .75
❑ 93 From Russia With Love .30 .75
❑ 94 From Russia With Love .30 .75
❑ 95 From Russia With Love .30 .75
❑ 96 From Russia With Love .30 .75
❑ 97 From Russia With Love .30 .75
❑ 98 From Russia With Love .30 .75
❑ 99 From Russia With Love .30 .75
❑ 100 From Russia With Love .30 .75
❑ 101 From Russia With Love .30 .75
❑ 102 From Russia With Love .30 .75
❑ 103 From Russia With Love .30 .75
❑ 104 From Russia With Love .30 .75
❑ 105 From Russia With Love .30 .75
❑ 106 From Russia With Love .30 .75
❑ 107 From Russia With Love .30 .75
❑ 108 From Russia With Love .30 .75

2012 James Bond 50th Anniversary Full Bleed Autographs

OVERALL AUTO ODDS 3 PER BOX
L (LIMITED): 300-500 COPIES
VL (VERY LIMITED): 200-300 COPIES
EL (EXTREMELY LIMITED): LESS THAN 200 COPIES

❑ 1 Al Matthews L 6.00 15.00
❑ 2 Albert Moses L 6.00 15.00
❑ 3 Aleta Morrison L 6.00 15.00
❑ 4 Andreas Wisniewski L 6.00 15.00
❑ 5 Burt Kwouk VL 15.00 40.00
❑ 6 Carey Lowell EL 100.00 200.00
❑ 7 Catherina von Schell VL 30.00 60.00
❑ 8 Clifton James EL 75.00 150.00
❑ 9 Corinne Clery VL 35.00 70.00
❑ 10 Cristina Contes L 10.00 25.00
❑ 11 Daniel Benzali VL 25.00 50.00
❑ 12 David Meyer 5.00 12.00
❑ 13 David Yip L 6.00 15.00
❑ 14 Douglas Wilmer L 5.00 12.00
❑ 15 Earl Cameron L 5.00 12.00
❑ 16 Fernando Guillen Cuervo L 5.00 12.00
❑ 17 Fiona Fullerton VL 25.00 50.00
❑ 18 Frank McRae L 6.00 15.00
❑ 19 George Leech L 6.00 15.00
❑ 20 Honor Blackman 150.00 250.00
❑ 21 Jan Williams L 10.00 25.00
❑ 22 John Moreno L 6.00 15.00
❑ 23 Lois Chiles L 12.00 30.00
❑ 24 Mollie Peters L 12.00 30.00
❑ 25 Nadim Sawahla L 5.00 12.00
❑ 26 Nancy Sinatra L 15.00 40.00
❑ 27 Patrick Bauchau 5.00 12.00
❑ 28 Ricky Jay L 5.00 12.00
❑ 29 Simon Andreu L 5.00 12.00
❑ 30 Sneh Gupta L 6.00 15.00
❑ 31 Vernon Dobtcheff 5.00 12.00
❑ 32 Veruschka L 8.00 20.00
❑ 33 Vijay Amritraj 5.00 12.00
❑ 34 Anatole Taubman L 5.00 12.00
❑ 35 Anne Lonnberg L 6.00 15.00
❑ 36 Bogdan Kominowski L 5.00 12.00
❑ 37 Catherine Rabett L 6.00 15.00
❑ 38 Christopher Muncke L 5.00 12.00
❑ 39 Colin Salmon L 6.00 15.00
❑ 40 Edward De Souza L 6.00 15.00
❑ 41 George Leech L 5.00 12.00
❑ 42 Gotz Otto L 6.00 15.00
❑ 43 Honor Blackman EL 100.00 200.00
❑ 44 Jeroen Krabbe L 8.00 20.00
❑ 45 Joaquin Martinez L 5.00 12.00
❑ 46 John Rhys-Davies VL 50.00 100.00
❑ 47 John Wyman L 6.00 15.00
❑ 48 Joie Vejjajiva L 6.00 15.00
❑ 49 Lois Chiles L 15.00 40.00
❑ 50 Marilyn Galsworthy L 6.00 15.00
❑ 51 Michelle Yeoh L 35.00 70.00
❑ 52 Peter Fontaine L 5.00 12.00
❑ 53 Richard Kiel L 20.00 50.00
❑ 54 Roger Moore EL 100.00 200.00
❑ 55 Sean Bean L 20.00 40.00
❑ 56 Serena Gordon L 6.00 15.00
❑ 57 Steven Berkoff (hat) L 8.00 20.00
❑ 58 Tania Mallett L 12.00 30.00
❑ 59 Tony Meyer 5.00 12.00
❑ 60 Ulrich Thomsen L 6.00 15.00
❑ 61 Roger Moore/Richard Kiel 100.00 200.00
(issued as 6-case incentive)

2012 James Bond 50th Anniversary Gold Gallery

COMP.SET w/o SPs (36) 40.00 80.00
COMP.SER. 1 SET (18) 20.00 40.00
COMP.SER. 2 SET (18) 25.00 50.00
STATED ODDS 1:12

❑ GG1 Halle Berry as Jinx 2.00 5.00
in Die Another Day
❑ GG2 Sophie Marceau as Elektra King 2.00 5.00
in The World Is Not Enough
❑ GG3 Akiko Wakabayashi as Aki 2.00 5.00
in You Only Live Twice
❑ GG4 Cecilie Thomsen as Professor Inga Bergstrom 2.00
5.00
in Tomorrow Never Dies
❑ GG5 Carey Lowell as Pam Bouvier 2.00 5.00
in Licence To Kill
❑ GG6 Barbara Bach as Major Anya Amasova 2.00 5.00
in The Spy Who Loved Me
❑ GG7 Jane Seymour as Solitaire 2.00 5.00
in Live And Let Die
❑ GG8 Mie Hama as Kissy Suzuki 2.00 5.00
in You Only Live Twice
❑ GG9 Lois Maxwell as Miss Moneypenny 2.00 5.00
❑ GG10 Izabella Scorupco as Natalya Simonova 2.00 5.00
in GoldenEye
❑ GG11 Maud Adams as Octopussy 2.00 5.00
in Octopussy
❑ GG12 Gemma Arterton as Agent Fields 2.00 5.00
in Quantum of Solace
❑ GG13 Kristina Wayborn as Magda 2.00 5.00
in Octopussy
❑ GG14 Olga Kurylenko as Camille 2.00 5.00
in Quantum of Solace
❑ GG15 Helena Ronee as Israeli Girl 2.00 5.00
in On Her Majesty's Secret Service
❑ GG16 Talisa Soto as Lupe Lamora 2.00 5.00
in Licence To Kill
❑ GG17 Zena Marshall as Miss Taro 2.00 5.00
in Dr. No
❑ GG18 Eunice Gayson as Sylvia Trench 2.00 5.00
in Dr. No
❑ GG19 Ursula Andress as Honey Ryder 25.00 50.00
in Dr. No (issued as Rittenhouse Reward) SP
❑ GG20 Daniela Bianchi as Tatiana Romanova 2.00 5.00
in From Russia With Love
❑ GG21 Mollie Peters as Patricia Fearing 2.00 5.00
in Thunderball
❑ GG22 Luciana Paluzzi as Fiona Volpe 2.00 5.00
in Thunderball
❑ GG23 Jill St. John as Tiffany Case 2.00 5.00
in Diamonds Are Forever
❑ GG24 Gloria Hendry as Rosie Carver 2.00 5.00
in Live And Let Die
❑ GG25 Britt Ekland as Mary Goodnight 2.00 5.00
in The Man With The Golden Gun
❑ GG26 Caroline Munro as Naomi 2.00 5.00
in The Spy Who Loved Me
❑ GG27 Lois Chiles as Dr. Holly Goodhead 2.00 5.00
in Moonraker
❑ GG28 Carole Bouquet as Melina Havelock 2.00 5.00
in For Your Eyes Only
❑ GG29 Tanya Roberts as Stacey Sutton 2.00 5.00
in A View To A Kill
❑ GG30 Allison Doody as Jenny Flex 2.00 5.00
in A View To A Kill
❑ GG31 Grace Jones as May Day 2.00 5.00
in A View To A Kill
❑ GG32 Maryam d'Abo as Kara Milovy 2.00 5.00
in The Living Daylights
❑ GG33 Famke Janssen as Xenia Onatopp 2.00 5.00
in GoldenEye
❑ GG34 Teri Hatcher as Paris Carver 2.00 5.00
in Tomorrow Never Dies
❑ GG35 Michelle Yeoh as Wai Lin 2.00 5.00
in Tomorrow Never Dies
❑ GG36 Denise Richards as Dr. Christmas Jones2.00 5.00
in The World Is Not Enough
❑ GG37 Rosamund Pike as Miranda Frost 2.00 5.00
in Die Another Day
❑ GG38 Eva Green as Vesper Lynd 30.00 60.00
in Casino Royale/ (issued as Rittenhouse Reward) SP

2012 James Bond 50th Anniversary Gold Plaques

COMPLETE SET (22) 15.00 40.00
COMP.SER. 1 SET (11) 10.00 25.00
COMP.SER. 2 SET (11) 10.00 25.00
STATED ODDS 1:12

❑ P1 Dr. No 2.00 5.00
❑ P2 From Russia With Love 2.00 5.00
❑ P3 Goldfinger 2.00 5.00
❑ P4 Thunderball 2.00 5.00
❑ P5 You Only Live Twice 2.00 5.00
❑ P6 On Her Majesty's Secret Service 2.00 5.00
❑ P7 Diamonds Are Forever 2.00 5.00
❑ P8 Live And Let Die 2.00 5.00
❑ P9 The Man With The Golden Gun 2.00 5.00
❑ P10 The Spy Who Loved Me 2.00 5.00
❑ P11 Moonraker 2.00 5.00
❑ P12 For Your Eyes Only 2.00 5.00
❑ P13 Octopussy 2.00 5.00
❑ P14 A View To A Kill 2.00 5.00
❑ P15 The Living Daylights 2.00 5.00
❑ P16 Licence To Kill 2.00 5.00
❑ P17 GoldenEye 2.00 5.00
❑ P18 Tomorrow Never Dies 2.00 5.00
❑ P19 The World Is Not Enough 2.00 5.00
❑ P20 Die Another Day 2.00 5.00
❑ P21 Casino Royale 2.00 5.00
❑ P22 Quantum of Solace 2.00 5.00

2012 James Bond 50th Anniversary Promos

❑ P1 James Bond (Sean Connery)
Ser. 2 (General Distribution)
❑ P1 Honey Ryder 1.25 3.00
Ser. 1 (General Distribution)
❑ P2 James Bond (Timothy Dalton) 2.00 5.00
Ser. 2 (Non-Sport Update)
❑ P2 Tatiana Romanova 10.00 20.00
Ser. 1 (Non-Sport Update Magazine)
❑ P3 James Bond (Daniel Craig) 6.00 15.00
Ser. 1 (Album Exclusive)
❑ P3 Jinx 10.00 20.00
Ser. 2 (Album Exclusive)
❑ P4 J.W. Pepper 2.50 6.00
Ser. 2 (Fall 2012 Philly Non-Sport Show)
❑ P4 James Bond (Pierce Brosnan) 2.50 6.00
Ser. 1 (Spring 2012 Philly Non-Sport Show)
❑ UKP1 James Bond (Sean Connery) 6.00 15.00
Ser. 1 (UK Exclusive)

2012 James Bond 50th Anniversary Shadowbox

COMPLETE SET (6) 40.00 80.00
COMP.SER. 1 SET (3) 25.00 50.00
COMP.SER. 2 SET (3) 25.00 50.00
STATED ODDS 1:96

❑ S1 Sean Connery 10.00 25.00
❑ S2 George Lazenby 10.00 25.00
❑ S3 Roger Moore 10.00 25.00
❑ S4 Timothy Dalton 10.00 25.00
❑ S5 Pierce Brosnan 10.00 25.00
❑ S6 Daniel Craig 10.00 25.00

2012 James Bond 50th Anniversary SkyFall Posters

COMPLETE SET (4) 15.00 40.00
STATED ODDS 1:48

❑ SF1 James Bond 5.00 12.00
❑ SF2 Severine 5.00 12.00
❑ SF3 Silva 5.00 12.00
❑ SF4 Eve 5.00 12.00

2012 Leaf Poker Metal

❑ MBAE1 Antonio Esfandiari 3.00 8.00
❑ MBAO1 Annette Obrestad 5.00 12.00
❑ MBBE1 Bill Edler 3.00 8.00
❑ MBBG1 Brad Garrett SP 20.00 40.00
❑ MBCB1 Chad Brown 3.00 8.00
❑ MBCM1 Chris Moneymaker SP 6.00 15.00
❑ MBCM2 Cindy Margolis 8.00 20.00
❑ MBCV1 Cyndy Violette SP 5.00 12.00
❑ MBDB1 Doyle Brunson SP
❑ MBDC1 David Chiu SP 3.00 8.00
❑ MBDN1 Daniel Negreanu SP 10.00 25.00
❑ MBDP1 David Pham 3.00 8.00
❑ MBDW1 David Williams 3.00 8.00
❑ MBEB1 Eric Baldwin 3.00 8.00
❑ MBEL1 Erick Lindgren 3.00 8.00
❑ MBEN1 Evelyn Ng 5.00 12.00
❑ MBES1 Erica Schoenberg 5.00 12.00
❑ MBGR1 Greg Raymer
❑ MBGS1 Gavin Smith 3.00 8.00
❑ MBHB1 Humberto Brenes SP 3.00 8.00
❑ MBHC1 Hoyt Corkins SP 6.00 15.00
❑ MBHS1 Huck Seed SP
❑ MBIM1 Isabelle Mercier 8.00 20.00
❑ MBJA1 Jason Alexander SP 20.00 40.00
❑ MBJA2 Josh Arieh 3.00 8.00
❑ MBJB1 Jerry Buss 12.00 30.00
❑ MBJC1 Johnny Chan SP
❑ MBJC2 Jose Canseco SP 30.00 60.00
❑ MBJD1 Jonathan Duhamel 5.00 12.00
❑ MBJG1 Jamie Gold SP 3.00 8.00
❑ MBJH1 Jennifer Harman SP 6.00 15.00
❑ MBJH2 Joe Hachem SP 6.00 15.00
❑ MBJM1 Jason Mercier 5.00 12.00
❑ MBJRB Jean-Robert Bellande 3.00 8.00
❑ MBJS1 Joe Sebok 3.00 8.00
❑ MBLDP Lou Diamond Phillips SP 25.00 50.00
❑ MBLF1 Layne Flack SP 5.00 12.00
❑ MBLJ1 Lacey Jones 5.00 12.00
❑ MBMH1 Maria Ho 5.00 12.00
❑ MBMM1 Michael Mizrachi SP 5.00 12.00
❑ MBMM2 Mike Matusow SP 5.00 12.00
❑ MBMN1 Men Nguyen SP 3.00 8.00
❑ MBMT1 Marco Traniello 3.00 8.00
❑ MBNL1 Nam Le 3.00 8.00
❑ MBOH1 Orel Hershiser SP 20.00 40.00
❑ MBPA1 Patrik Antonius 3.00 8.00
❑ MBPF1 Prahlad Friedman 3.00 8.00
❑ MBPG1 Phil Gordon 3.00 8.00
❑ MBPH1 Phil Hellmuth SP 25.00 50.00
❑ MBPJ1 Peter Jetten 3.00 8.00
❑ MBPW1 Patrick Warburton SP 20.00 40.00
❑ MBPW1 Paul Wasicka 3.00 8.00
❑ MBSF1 Scott Fischman 3.00 8.00
❑ MBSM1 Scott Montgomery 3.00 8.00
❑ MBSN1 Scotty Nguyen SP 6.00 15.00
❑ MBTB1 Todd Brunson SP 5.00 12.00
❑ MBTD1 Tom Dwan 6.00 15.00
❑ MBTJC T.J. Cloutier SP 3.00 8.00
❑ MBTM1 Tiffany Michelle 6.00 15.00
❑ MBVR1 Vanessa Rousso 6.00 15.00

2012 Leaf Poker Metal Prismatic Silver

STATED PRINT RUN 25 SER. #'d SETS

2012 Leaf Poker Metal Prismatic Red

STATED PRINT RUN 5 SER. #'d SETS
UNPRICED DUE TO SCARCITY

2012 Leaf Poker Metal Prismatic Gold

STATED PRINT RUN 1 SER. #'d SET
UNPRICED DUE TO SCARCITY

2012 Leaf Poker Metal Printing Plates Black

STATED PRINT RUN 1 SER. #'d SET
UNPRICED DUE TO SCARCITY

2012 Leaf Poker Metal Printing Plates Cyan

STATED PRINT RUN 1 SER. #'d SET
UNPRICED DUE TO SCARCITY

2012 Leaf Poker Metal Printing Plates Magenta

STATED PRINT RUN 1 SER. #'d SET
UNPRICED DUE TO SCARCITY

2012 Leaf Poker Metal Printing Plates Yellow

STATED PRINT RUN 1 SER. #'d SET
UNPRICED DUE TO SCARCITY

2012 Leaf Poker Metal Bracelet Race Autographs

STATED PRINT RUN 2-11
UNPRICED DUE TO SCARCITY

❑ BRDC1 David Chiu/4
❑ BRJC1 Johnny Chan/10
❑ BRJH1 Jennifer Harman/2
❑ BRLF1 Layne Flack/6
❑ BRMN1 Men Nguyen/7
❑ BRPH1 Phil Hellmuth/11
❑ BRTJC T.J. Cloutier/6

2012 Leaf Poker Metal Bracelet Race Autographs Printing Plates Black

STATED PRINT RUN 1 SER. #'d SET
UNPRICED DUE TO SCARCITY

2012 Leaf Poker Metal Bracelet Race Autographs Printing Plates Cyan

STATED PRINT RUN 1 SER. #'d SET
UNPRICED DUE TO SCARCITY

2012 Leaf Poker Metal Bracelet Race Autographs Printing Plates Magenta

STATED PRINT RUN 1 SER. #'d SET
UNPRICED DUE TO SCARCITY

2012 Leaf Poker Metal Bracelet Race Autographs Printing Plates Yellow

STATED PRINT RUN 1 SER. #'d SET
UNPRICED DUE TO SCARCITY

2012 Leaf Poker Metal Faces of the Game Autographs

*PRIS.SILVER/25: .5X TO 1.2X BASIC CARDS

❑ FAMM1 Michael Mizrachi 8.00 20.00
❑ FAMM2 Mike Matusow 10.00 25.00
❑ FAPA1 Patrik Antonius 6.00 15.00
❑ FAPH1 Phil Hellmuth 12.00 30.00

2012 Leaf Poker Metal Faces of the Game Autographs Prismatic Silver

*PRIS.SILVER: .5X TO 1.2X BASIC CARDS
STATED PRINT RUN 25 SER. #'d SETS

2012 Leaf Poker Metal Hall of Fame Autographs

STATED PRINT RUN 10 SER. #'d SETS
UNPRICED DUE TO SCARCITY

❑ HOFJC Johnny Chan
❑ HOFDB1 Doyle Brunson
❑ HOFDN1 Daniel Negreanu
❑ HOFMN1 Men Nguyen
❑ HOFPH1 Phil Hellmuth
❑ HOFTJC T.J. Cloutier

2012 Leaf Poker Metal Hall of Fame Autographs Prismatic Red

STATED PRINT RUN 5 SER. #'d SETS
UNPRICED DUE TO SCARCITY

2012 Leaf Poker Metal Hall of Fame Autographs Prismatic Gold

STATED PRINT RUN 1 SER. #'d SET
UNPRICED DUE TO SCARCITY

2012 Leaf Poker Metal Hall of Fame Autographs Printing Plates Black

STATED PRINT RUN 1 SER. #'d SET
UNPRICED DUE TO SCARCITY

2012 Leaf Poker Metal Hall of Fame Autographs Printing Plates Cyan

STATED PRINT RUN 1 SER. #'d SET
UNPRICED DUE TO SCARCITY

2012 Leaf Poker Metal Hall of Fame Autographs Printing Plates Magenta

STATED PRINT RUN 1 SER. #'d SET
UNPRICED DUE TO SCARCITY

2012 Leaf Poker Metal Hall of Fame Autographs Printing Plates Yellow

STATED PRINT RUN 1 SER. #'d SET
UNPRICED DUE TO SCARCITY

2012 Leaf Poker Metal Legendary Ladies of Poker Autographs

❑ LLAO1 Annette Obrestad 6.00 15.00
❑ LLCM1 Cindy Margolis 6.00 15.00
❑ LLCV1 Cyndy Violette 5.00 12.00
❑ LLEN1 Evelyn Ng 6.00 15.00
❑ LLES1 Erica Schoenberg 5.00 12.00
❑ LLJH1 Jennifer Harman 6.00 15.00
❑ LLLJ1 Lacey Jones 5.00 12.00
❑ LLMH1 Maria Ho 5.00 12.00
❑ LLTM1 Tiffany Michelle 6.00 15.00
❑ LLVR1 Vanessa Rousso 6.00 15.00

2012 Leaf Poker Metal Legendary Ladies of Poker Autographs Prismatic Silver

*PRIS.SILVER: .6X TO 1.5X BASIC CARDS
STATED PRINT RUN 25 SER. #'d SETS

2012 Leaf Poker Metal Legendary Ladies of Poker Autographs Prismatic Red

STATED PRINT RUN 5 SER. #'d SETS
UNPRICED DUE TO SCARCITY

2012 Leaf Poker Metal Legendary Ladies of Poker Autographs Printing Plates Black

STATED PRINT RUN 1 SER. #'d SET
UNPRICED DUE TO SCARCITY

2012 Leaf Poker Metal Legendary Ladies of Poker Autographs Printing Plates Cyan

STATED PRINT RUN 1 SER. #'d SET
UNPRICED DUE TO SCARCITY

2012 Leaf Poker Metal Legendary Ladies of Poker Autographs Printing Plates Magenta

STATED PRINT RUN 1 SER. #'d SET
UNPRICED DUE TO SCARCITY

2012 Leaf Poker Metal Legendary Ladies of Poker Autographs Printing Plates Yellow

STATED PRINT RUN 1 SER. #'d SET
UNPRICED DUE TO SCARCITY

2012 Leaf Poker Metal National Pride Autographs

STATED PRINT RUN 25 SER. #'d SETS

❑ NPAO1 Annette Obrestad 15.00 30.00
❑ NPDN1 Daniel Negreanu 20.00 40.00
❑ NPEN1 Evelyn Ng 15.00 30.00
❑ NPES1 Erica Schoenberg 20.00 40.00
❑ NPGS1 Gavin Smith 10.00 20.00
❑ NPHS1 Huck Seed 15.00 30.00
❑ NPJC1 Jose Canseco 40.00 80.00
❑ NPJH1 Jennifer Harman 15.00 30.00
❑ NPJH2 Joe Hachem 10.00 20.00
❑ NPJRB Jean-Robert Bellande 10.00 20.00
❑ NPMT1 Marco Traniello 10.00 20.00
❑ NPOH1 Orel Hershiser 20.00 40.00
❑ NPPA1 Patrik Antonius 10.00 20.00
❑ NPPH1 Phil Hellmuth 25.00 50.00
❑ NPPJ1 Peter Jetten 10.00 20.00
❑ NPSN1 Scotty Nguyen 15.00 30.00

2012 Leaf Poker Metal National Pride Autographs Printing Plates Black

STATED PRINT RUN 1 SER. #'d SET
UNPRICED DUE TO SCARCITY

2012 Leaf Poker Metal National Pride Autographs Printing Plates Cyan

STATED PRINT RUN 1 SER. #'d SET
UNPRICED DUE TO SCARCITY

2012 Leaf Poker Metal National Pride Autographs Printing Plates Magenta

STATED PRINT RUN 1 SER. #'d SET
UNPRICED DUE TO SCARCITY

2012 Leaf Poker Metal National Pride Autographs Printing Plates Yellow

STATED PRINT RUN 1 SER. #'d SET
UNPRICED DUE TO SCARCITY

2012 Leaf Poker Metal World Series Cash Autographs

STATED PRINT RUN 11-79
NO PRICING ON CARDS #'d 20 OR LESS

❑ AE1 Antonio Esfandiari/13
❑ CB1 Chad Brown/30 8.00 20.00
❑ CV1 Cyndy Violette/29 8.00 20.00
❑ DC1 David Chiu/47 6.00 15.00
❑ DN1 Daniel Negreanu/48 15.00 40.00
❑ DW1 David Williams/19
❑ EL1 Erick Lindgren/25 10.00 25.00
❑ GR1 Greg Raymer/14
❑ GS1 Gavin Smith/18
❑ HB1 Humberto Brenes/58 8.00 20.00
❑ HC1 Hoyt Corkins/26 8.00 20.00
❑ HS1 Huck Seed/38 8.00 20.00
❑ JH1 Jennifer Harman/24 10.00 25.00
❑ JRB Jean-Robert Bellande/13
❑ LF1 Layne Flack/23 6.00 15.00
❑ MM1 Michael Mizrachi/23 10.00 25.00
❑ MM2 Mike Matusow/29 8.00 20.00
❑ MN1 Men Nguyen/70 6.00 15.00
❑ MT1 Marco Traniello/22 6.00 15.00
❑ NL1 Nam Le/16
❑ PH1 Phil Hellmuth/79 15.00 30.00

❑ SF1 Scott Fischman/11
❑ SN1 Scotty Nguyen/37 8.00 20.00
❑ TB1 Todd Brunson/28 8.00 20.00
❑ TC1 T.J. Cloutier/57 6.00 15.00
❑ VR1 Vanessa Rousso/13

2012 Leaf Poker Metal World Series Cash Autographs Printing Plates Black

STATED PRINT RUN 1 SER. #'d SET
UNPRICED DUE TO SCARCITY

2012 Leaf Poker Metal World Series Cash Autographs Printing Plates Cyan

STATED PRINT RUN 1 SER. #'d SET
UNPRICED DUE TO SCARCITY

2012 Leaf Poker Metal World Series Cash Autographs Printing Plates Magenta

STATED PRINT RUN 1 SER. #'d SET
UNPRICED DUE TO SCARCITY

2012 Leaf Poker Metal World Series Cash Autographs Printing Plates Yellow

STATED PRINT RUN 1 SER. #'d SET
UNPRICED DUE TO SCARCITY

2012 Mars Attacks Heritage

COMPLETE SET (55) 6.00 15.00

❑ 1 The Invasion Begins .40 1.00
❑ 2 Martians Approaching .20 .50
❑ 3 Attacking An Army Base .20 .50
❑ 4 Saucers Blast Our Jets .20 .50
❑ 5 Washington In Flames .20 .50
❑ 6 Burning Navy Ships .20 .50
❑ 7 Destroying The Bridge .20 .50
❑ 8 Terror In Times Square .20 .50
❑ 9 The Human Torch .20 .50
❑ 10 The Skyscraper Tumbles .20 .50
❑ 11 Destroy The City .20 .50
❑ 12 Death In The Cockpit .20 .50
❑ 13 Watching From Mars .20 .50
❑ 14 Charred By Martians .20 .50
❑ 15 Saucers Invade China .20 .50
❑ 16 Panic In Parliament .20 .50
❑ 17 Beast And The Beauty .20 .50
❑ 18 A Soldier Fights Back .20 .50
❑ 19 Burning Flesh .20 .50
❑ 20 Crushed To Death .20 .50
❑ 21 Prize Captive .20 .50
❑ 22 Burning Cattle .20 .50
❑ 23 The Frost Ray .20 .50
❑ 24 The Shrinking Ray .20 .50
❑ 25 Capturing A Martian .20 .50
❑ 26 The Tidal Wave .20 .50
❑ 27 The Giant Flies .20 .50
❑ 28 Helpless Victim .20 .50
❑ 29 Death In The Shelter .20 .50
❑ 30 Trapped!! .20 .50
❑ 31 The Monster Reaches In .20 .50
❑ 32 Robot Terror .20 .50
❑ 33 Removing The Victims .20 .50
❑ 34 Terror In The Railroad .20 .50
❑ 35 The Flame Throwers .20 .50
❑ 36 Destroying A Dog .20 .50
❑ 37 Creeping Menace .20 .50
❑ 38 Victims Of The Bug .20 .50
❑ 39 Army Of Giant Insects .20 .50
❑ 40 High Voltage Execution .20 .50
❑ 41 Horror In Paris .20 .50
❑ 42 Hairy Fiend .20 .50
❑ 43 Blasting The Bug .20 .50
❑ 44 Battle In The Air .20 .50
❑ 45 Fighting Giant Insects .20 .50
❑ 46 Blast Off For Mars .20 .50
❑ 47 Earth Bombs Mars .20 .50
❑ 48 Earthmen Land On Mars .20 .50
❑ 49 The Earthmen Charge .20 .50
❑ 50 Smashing The Enemy .20 .50
❑ 51 Crushing The Martians .20 .50
❑ 52 Giant Robot .20 .50
❑ 53 Martian City In Ruins .20 .50
❑ 54 Mars Explodes .20 .50
❑ 55 Checklist .30 .75

2012 Mars Attacks Heritage Green

COMPLETE SET 30.00 60.00
*GREEN: 1.5X TO 4X BASIC CARDS
STATED ODDS 1:3

2012 Mars Attacks Heritage Silver

*SILVER: 10X TO 25X BASIC CARDS
STATED ODDS 1:24

2012 Mars Attacks Heritage Gold

*GOLD/50: 50X TO 100X BASIC CARDS
STATED ODDS 1:101

2012 Mars Attacks Heritage 3D

COMPLETE SET (5) 8.00 20.00
STATED ODDS 1:8

❑ 1 The Invasion Begins 3.00 8.00
❑ 2 Martians Approaching 3.00 8.00
❑ 3 Beast And The Beauty 3.00 8.00
❑ 4 Robot Terror 3.00 8.00
❑ 5 Destroying A Dog 3.00 8.00

2012 Mars Attacks Heritage Deleted Scenes

COMPLETE SET (10) 5.00 12.00
STATED ODDS ONE PER PACK

❑ 1 Death By Impalement .75 2.00
❑ 2 Moscow Under Seige .75 2.00
❑ 3 The Chaos Spreads .75 2.00
❑ 4 Blood On City Streets .75 2.00
❑ 5 Robot Army Attacks .75 2.00
❑ 6 Battle In The Sky .75 2.00
❑ 7 Robots On The Run .75 2.00
❑ 8 On Enemy Turf .75 2.00
❑ 9 Flames Of Vengeance .75 2.00
❑ 10 A Martian's Last Stand .75 2.00

2012 Mars Attacks Heritage Len Brown Autographs

COMMON CARD 75.00 150.00
STATED ODDS 1:504 HOBBY

2012 Mars Attacks Heritage New Universe

COMPLETE SET (15) 5.00 12.00
STATED ODDS ONE PER PACK

❑ 1 Invasion Is Imminent .60 1.50
❑ 2 Early Encounters .60 1.50
❑ 3 Readying For War .60 1.50
❑ 4 The Novas Vira .60 1.50
❑ 5 Dead On Arrival .60 1.50
❑ 6 Sinking Ship .60 1.50
❑ 7 London Falling .60 1.50
❑ 8 The Best Defense .60 1.50
❑ 9 Sic 'Em .60 1.50
❑ 10 Changing Face Of Evil .60 1.50
❑ 11 Ordinary Heroes .60 1.50
❑ 12 Vigilance=Victory .60 1.50
❑ 13 Lord Of The Fleas .60 1.50
❑ 14 Patriot Act .60 1.50
❑ 15 Settling The Score .60 1.50

2012 Marvel Beginnings 2

COMPLETE SET (180) 15.00 40.00

❑ 181 Iron Man .15 .40
❑ 182 Nimrod .15 .40
❑ 183 Ultron .15 .40
❑ 184 Doop .15 .40
❑ 185 Siena Blaze .15 .40
❑ 186 Hulk .15 .40
❑ 187 Ahab .15 .40
❑ 188 Nova .15 .40
❑ 189 Demogoblin .15 .40
❑ 190 Squirrel Girl .15 .40
❑ 191 Xemnu .15 .40
❑ 192 Venom .15 .40
❑ 193 Cypher .15 .40
❑ 194 Wizard .15 .40
❑ 195 Zzzax .15 .40
❑ 196 Mandarin .15 .40
❑ 197 Ultimate Hawkeye .15 .40
❑ 198 Whirlwind .15 .40
❑ 199 Warpath .15 .40
❑ 200 Ultimate Captain America .15 .40
❑ 201 Baron Zemo .15 .40
❑ 202 Taskmaster .15 .40
❑ 203 Living Tribunal .15 .40
❑ 204 Garokk .15 .40
❑ 205 Isaiah Bradley .15 .40
❑ 206 Juggernaut .15 .40
❑ 207 Shanna The She-Devil .15 .40
❑ 208 General John Ryker .15 .40
❑ 209 Aunt May .15 .40
❑ 210 Silver Samurai .15 .40
❑ 211 Black Widow .15 .40
❑ 212 Flag Smasher .15 .40
❑ 213 Deathlok .15 .40
❑ 214 Jocasta .15 .40
❑ 215 Man-Beast .15 .40
❑ 216 Maria Hill .15 .40
❑ 217 Sersi .15 .40
❑ 218 Dracula .15 .40
❑ 219 Hepzibah .15 .40
❑ 220 Titania .15 .40
❑ 221 Spymaster .15 .40
❑ 222 Karma .15 .40
❑ 223 Phantom Rider .15 .40
❑ 224 Blizzard .15 .40
❑ 225 Puck .15 .40
❑ 226 Marrow .15 .40
❑ 227 Beast .15 .40
❑ 228 Mojo .15 .40
❑ 229 Black Tom .15 .40
❑ 230 Zombie .15 .40
❑ 231 Ghost Rider .15 .40
❑ 232 Unicorn .15 .40
❑ 233 Ultimate Hulk .15 .40
❑ 234 Magik .15 .40
❑ 235 Patriot .15 .40
❑ 236 Zaladane .15 .40
❑ 237 Doctor Faustus .15 .40
❑ 238 Chamber .15 .40
❑ 239 Hornet .15 .40
❑ 240 Spider-Ham .15 .40
❑ 241 Beta Ray Bill .15 .40
❑ 242 Tyrannus .15 .40
❑ 243 Gladiator .15 .40
❑ 244 Winter Soldier .15 .40
❑ 245 Foolkiller .15 .40
❑ 246 Lockjaw .15 .40
❑ 247 Lady Deathstrike .15 .40
❑ 248 Franklin Richards .15 .40
❑ 249 Wolverine .15 .40
❑ 250 Daken .15 .40
❑ 251 Wild Child .15 .40
❑ 252 X-23 .15 .40
❑ 253 Toad .15 .40
❑ 254 Moon Knight .15 .40
❑ 255 Genesis .15 .40
❑ 256 Rick Jones .15 .40
❑ 257 Black Panther .15 .40
❑ 258 Wasp .15 .40
❑ 259 Thing .15 .40
❑ 260 Sunfire .15 .40
❑ 261 Mach-V .15 .40
❑ 262 Jackal .15 .40
❑ 263 Zabu .15 .40
❑ 264 Hobgoblin .15 .40
❑ 265 Mad Thinker .15 .40
❑ 266 Byrrah .15 .40
❑ 267 Spider-Woman .15 .40
❑ 268 Vengeance .15 .40
❑ 269 Proteus .15 .40
❑ 270 Ghost .15 .40
❑ 271 Nitro .15 .40
❑ 272 Iron Fist .15 .40
❑ 273 Captain Britain .15 .40
❑ 274 Kraven .15 .40
❑ 275 Spider-Man .15 .40
❑ 276 Carrion .15 .40
❑ 277 Adam Warlock .15 .40
❑ 278 Red King .15 .40
❑ 279 Doctor Druid .15 .40
❑ 280 Sif .15 .40
❑ 281 Shang-Chi .15 .40
❑ 282 Count Nefaria .15 .40
❑ 283 Iron Patriot .15 .40
❑ 284 Mole Man .15 .40
❑ 285 Stranger .15 .40
❑ 286 Red Skull .15 .40
❑ 287 Ancient One .15 .40
❑ 288 Jester .15 .40
❑ 289 X-Cutioner .15 .40
❑ 290 Dr. MacTaggart .15 .40
❑ 291 Tinkerer .15 .40
❑ 292 Misty Knight .15 .40
❑ 293 Goliath .15 .40
❑ 294 Swordsman .15 .40
❑ 295 Snowbird .15 .40
❑ 296 Quasar .15 .40
❑ 297 Blade .15 .40
❑ 298 Punisher Noir .15 .40
❑ 299 Falcon .15 .40
❑ 300 Namor .15 .40
❑ 301 Azazel .15 .40
❑ 302 Morgan Le Fay .15 .40
❑ 303 Dark Beast .15 .40
❑ 304 Victoria Hand .15 .40
❑ 305 Professor X .15 .40
❑ 306 Callisto .15 .40
❑ 307 Sage .15 .40
❑ 308 Maestro .15 .40
❑ 309 Trauma .15 .40
❑ 310 She-Thing .15 .40
❑ 311 Psycho-Man .15 .40
❑ 312 Annihilus .15 .40
❑ 313 Thunderstrike .15 .40
❑ 314 X-Man .15 .40
❑ 315 Apocalypse .15 .40
❑ 316 Vindicator .15 .40
❑ 317 Ant-Man .15 .40
❑ 318 Satana .15 .40
❑ 319 Pixie .15 .40
❑ 320 Arana .15 .40
❑ 321 Prodigy .15 .40
❑ 322 Balder The Brave .15 .40
❑ 323 Captain Marvel .15 .40
❑ 324 Rage .15 .40
❑ 325 Angel .15 .40
❑ 326 M .15 .40
❑ 327 Living Monolith .15 .40
❑ 328 Bastion .15 .40
❑ 329 Heimdall .15 .40
❑ 330 Speed .15 .40
❑ 331 Corsair .15 .40
❑ 332 Green Goblin .15 .40
❑ 333 Hood .15 .40
❑ 334 Howard The Duck .15 .40
❑ 335 Gladiator .15 .40
❑ 336 Miss America .15 .40
❑ 337 Son of Satan .15 .40
❑ 338 Wendigo .15 .40
❑ 339 Pete Wisdom .15 .40
❑ 340 Captain Marvel .15 .40
❑ 341 Rhino .15 .40
❑ 342 Whiplash .15 .40
❑ 343 Mr. Fantastic .15 .40
❑ 344 Destroyer .15 .40
❑ 345 Abomination .15 .40
❑ 346 Scarlet Centurion .15 .40
❑ 347 Phalanx .15 .40
❑ 348 Marvel Girl .15 .40
❑ 349 Medusa .15 .40
❑ 350 Black Queen .15 .40
❑ 351 Boomerang .15 .40
❑ 352 Cable .15 .40
❑ 353 Moonstone .15 .40
❑ 354 Magnus .15 .40
❑ 355 Spymaster .15 .40
❑ 356 Mister Hyde .15 .40
❑ 357 Basilisk .15 .40
❑ 358 Nightcrawler .15 .40
❑ 359 Atlas .15 .40
❑ 360 Green Goblin .15 .40

2012 Marvel Beginnings 2 Printing Plates Black

STATED PRINT RUN 1 SER. #'d SET
UNPRICED DUE TO SCARCITY

2012 Marvel Beginnings 2 Printing Plates Cyan

STATED PRINT RUN 1 SER. #'d SET
UNPRICED DUE TO SCARCITY

2012 Marvel Beginnings 2 Printing Plates Magenta

STATED PRINT RUN 1 SER. #'d SET
UNPRICED DUE TO SCARCITY

2012 Marvel Beginnings 2 Printing Plates Yellow

STATED PRINT RUN 1 SER. #'d SET
UNPRICED DUE TO SCARCITY

2012 Marvel Beginnings 2 Avengers Die-Cut

COMPLETE SET (45) 20.00 40.00
STATED ODDS 1:2

❑ A1 Agent 13 .75 2.00
❑ A2 Ant-Man .75 2.00
❑ A3 Beast .75 2.00
❑ A4 Black Panther .75 2.00
❑ A5 Black Widow .75 2.00
❑ A6 Captain America .75 2.00
❑ A7 Captain America .75 2.00
❑ A8 Captain Britain .75 2.00
❑ A9 Captain Marvel .75 2.00
❑ A10 Doctor Strange .75 2.00
❑ A11 Echo .75 2.00
❑ A12 Falcon .75 2.00
❑ A13 Firestar .75 2.00
❑ A14 Giant-Man .75 2.00
❑ A15 Hawkeye .75 2.00
❑ A16 Hellcat .75 2.00
❑ A17 Hercules .75 2.00
❑ A18 Hulk .75 2.00
❑ A19 Iron Fist .75 2.00
❑ A20 Iron Man .75 2.00
❑ A21 Jewel .75 2.00
❑ A22 Justice .75 2.00
❑ A23 Luke Cage .75 2.00
❑ A24 Maria Hill .75 2.00
❑ A25 Mockingbird .75 2.00
❑ A26 Moon Knight .75 2.00
❑ A27 Ms. Marvel .75 2.00
❑ A28 Noh-Varr .75 2.00
❑ A29 Nova .75 2.00
❑ A30 Quicksilver .75 2.00
❑ A31 Red Hulk .75 2.00
❑ A32 Scarlet Witch .75 2.00
❑ A33 Sentry .75 2.00
❑ A34 She-Hulk .75 2.00
❑ A35 Spider-Man .75 2.00
❑ A36 Spider-Woman .75 2.00
❑ A37 Thing .75 2.00
❑ A38 Thor .75 2.00
❑ A39 Tigra .75 2.00
❑ A40 Valkyrie .75 2.00
❑ A41 Vision .75 2.00
❑ A42 War Machine .75 2.00
❑ A43 Wasp .75 2.00
❑ A44 Wolverine .75 2.00
❑ A45 Wonder Man .75 2.00

2012 Marvel Beginnings 2 Breakthrough Issues

COMPLETE SET (45) 10.00 25.00
STATED ODDS 1:1

❑ B46 The Amazing Spider-Man #121 .40 1.00
❑ B47 X-Men #1 .40 1.00
❑ B48 Ultimate Spider-Man #1 .40 1.00
❑ B49 Ultimate X-Men #1 .40 1.00
❑ B50 The Amazing Spider-Man #33 .40 1.00
❑ B51 Captain America #109 .40 1.00
❑ B52 The Avengers #1 .40 1.00
❑ B53 Fantastic Four #48 .40 1.00
❑ B54 The Amazing Spider-Man #14 .40 1.00
❑ B55 X-Men #4 .40 1.00
❑ B56 Fantastic Four #12 .40 1.00
❑ B57 Marvel Super Heroes Secert Wars #1 .40 1.00
❑ B58 The Incredible Hulk Vol.2 #340 .40 1.00
❑ B59 X-Men #58 .40 1.00
❑ B60 The Amazing Spider-Man #50 .40 1.00
❑ B61 Uncanny X-Men #94 .40 1.00
❑ B62 New Mutants #98 .40 1.00
❑ B63 Marvel Spotlight #5 .40 1.00
❑ B64 The Amazing Spider-Man #298 .40 1.00
❑ B65 Uncanny X-Men #303 .40 1.00
❑ B66 Uncanny X-Men #210 .40 1.00
❑ B67 X-Factor #1 .40 1.00
❑ B68 Uncanny X-Men #212 .40 1.00
❑ B69 Marvel Premier #15 .40 1.00
❑ B70 The Punisher War Journal #6 .40 1.00
❑ B71 The Amazing Spider-Man #31 .40 1.00
❑ B72 Captain America #117 .40 1.00
❑ B73 The Amazing Spider-Man #194 .40 1.00
❑ B74 X-Factor #24 .40 1.00
❑ B75 Uncanny X-Men #283 .40 1.00
❑ B76 Shadowland #1 .40 1.00
❑ B77 The Amazing Spider-Man #300 .40 1.00
❑ B78 Captain America #444 .40 1.00
❑ B79 Astonishing X-Men Vol.3 #7 .40 1.00
❑ B80 Captain America Vol 5 #25 .40 1.00
❑ B81 Captain America Vol.5 #18 .40 1.00
❑ B82 Thor Vol.3 #1 .40 1.00
❑ B83 X-Men First Class #1 .40 1.00
❑ B84 Punisher Vol.6 #1 .40 1.00
❑ B85 Secert Invasion: Dark Reign #1 .40 1.00
❑ B86 Spider-Man Noir #1 .40 1.00
❑ B87 Wolverine Noir #1 .40 1.00
❑ B88 Iron Man Vol.4 #1 .40 1.00
❑ B89 Daredevil Vol.2 #16 .40 1.00
❑ B90 Daredevil #131 .40 1.00

2012 Marvel Beginnings 2 Breakthrough Issues Printing Plates Black

STATED PRINT RUN 1 SER. #'d SET
UNPRICED DUE TO SCARCITY

2012 Marvel Beginnings 2 Breakthrough Issues Printing Plates Cyan

STATED PRINT RUN 1 SER. #'d SET
UNPRICED DUE TO SCARCITY

2012 Marvel Beginnings 2 Breakthrough Issues Printing Plates Magenta

STATED PRINT RUN 1 SER. #'d SET
UNPRICED DUE TO SCARCITY

2012 Marvel Beginnings 2 Breakthrough Issues Printing Plates Yellow

STATED PRINT RUN 1 SER. #'d SET
UNPRICED DUE TO SCARCITY

2012 Marvel Beginnings 2 Breakthrough Issues Autographs

OVERALL AUTO ODDS 1:48

❑ B46 Roy Thomas 20.00 50.00
❑ B47 Stan Lee 300.00 400.00
❑ B48A Brian Michael Bendis 15.00 40.00
❑ B48B Bill Jemas 15.00 40.00
❑ B50 Stan Lee 300.00 400.00
❑ B51 Stan Lee 300.00 400.00
❑ B52 Stan Lee
❑ B53 Stan Lee
❑ B54 Stan Lee 300.00 400.00
❑ B55 Stan Lee 300.00 400.00
❑ B56 Stan Lee
❑ B57A John Beatty 15.00 40.00
❑ B57B Mike Zeck 15.00 40.00
❑ B58 Tom DeFalco 30.00 60.00
❑ B59 Stan Lee
❑ B60 Stan Lee
❑ B61A Chris Claremont 15.00 40.00
❑ B61B Len Wein 15.00 40.00
❑ B62 Fabian Nicieza 15.00 40.00
❑ B63 Gary Friedrich 12.00 30.00
❑ B64A David Michelinie 15.00 40.00
❑ B64B Jim Salicrup 15.00 40.00
❑ B64C Janet Jay Jay Jackson 15.00 40.00
❑ B65 Tom DeFalco 30.00 60.00
❑ B66A Chris Claremont 15.00 40.00
❑ B66B Dan Green 15.00 40.00
❑ B66C Jim Shooter 30.00 60.00
❑ B67A Jim Shooter 30.00 60.00
❑ B67B Jackson Guice 15.00 40.00
❑ B68A Jim Shooter
❑ B68B Chris Claremont 15.00 40.00
❑ B69A Len Wein 15.00 40.00
❑ B69B Roy Thomas 15.00 40.00
❑ B70 Tom DeFalco 30.00 60.00
❑ B71 Stan Lee
❑ B72 Joe Sinnott 15.00 40.00
❑ B73 Marv Wolfman 15.00 40.00
❑ B74A Louise Simonson 12.00 30.00
❑ B74B Tom DeFalco 30.00 60.00
❑ B75 Whilce Portacio 15.00 40.00
❑ B76A Billy Tan 12.00 30.00
❑ B76B Christina Strain 12.00 30.00
❑ B77A Jim Salicrup 15.00 40.00
❑ B77B David Michelinie 15.00 40.00
❑ B78 Mark Waid 12.00 30.00
❑ B79A Laura Martin 15.00 40.00
❑ B79B Chris Eliopoulos 12.00 30.00
❑ B80A Frank D'Armata 15.00 40.00
❑ B80B Steve Epting 15.00 40.00
❑ B81A Steve Epting 15.00 40.00
❑ B81B Frank D'Armata 15.00 40.00
❑ B82A Laura Martin 15.00 40.00
❑ B82B Olivier Coipel 12.00 30.00
❑ B82C Mark Morales 15.00 40.00
❑ B83A Marko Djurdjevic 12.00 30.00
❑ B83B Val Staples 12.00 30.00
❑ B84 Tim Bradstreet 15.00 40.00
❑ B85 Alex Maleev 12.00 30.00
❑ B86 David Hine 12.00 30.00
❑ B87 Stuart Moore 12.00 30.00
❑ B88 Adi Granov 12.00 30.00
❑ B89A David Mack 12.00 30.00
❑ B89B Mark Morales 12.00 30.00
❑ B90 Marv Wolfman 15.00 40.00

2012 Marvel Beginnings 2 Breakthrough Issues Autographs Dual

OVERALL AUTO ODDS 1:48

❑ B48 Brian Michael Bendis 30.00 60.00
Bill Jemas
❑ B57 Tom DeFalco 35.00 70.00
John Beatty
❑ B64A Tom DeFalco 35.00 70.00
Jim Salicrup
❑ B64B David Michelinie 30.00 60.00
Janet Jay Jay Jackson
❑ B66 Chris Claremont 35.00 70.00
Jim Shooter
❑ B68 Jim Shooter 35.00 70.00
Chris Claremont
❑ B75 Tom DeFalco 35.00 70.00
Whilce Portacio
❑ B79 Chris Eliopoulos
Laura Martin
❑ B80 Frank D'Armata
Steve Epting
❑ B81 Steve Epting
Frank D'Armata
❑ B82 Laura Martin 30.00 60.00
Mark Morales
❑ B85 Brian Michael Bendis 30.00 60.00
Alex Maleev

2012 Marvel Beginnings 2 Comic Book Panels

STATED ODDS 1:288

❑ UM9 The Amazing Spider-Man #5 /77 40.00 80.00
❑ UM10 The Amazing Spider-Man #13 /80 40.00 80.00
❑ UM11 The Amazing Spider-Man #41
❑ UM15 Fantastic Four #12 /89 40.00 80.00
❑ UM16 Fantastic Four #18 /82 40.00 80.00
❑ UM17 Journey Into Mystery King Sized Annual #1
❑ UM18 Journey Into Mystery #85 /44 40.00 80.00
❑ UM19 Journey Into Mystery #104
❑ UM20 Giant Sized X-men #1 /124 40.00 80.00
❑ UM21 Marvel Premier #15 /50 40.00 80.00
❑ UM22 Marvel Spotlight #2

2012 Marvel Beginnings 2 Marvel Prime

COMPLETE SET (60) 35.00 70.00
STATED ODDS 1:2

❑ M1 Anti-Venom .75 2.00
❑ M2 Ares .75 2.00
❑ M3 Beta Ray Bill .75 2.00
❑ M4 Black Cat .75 2.00
❑ M5 Black Panther .75 2.00
❑ M6 Blade .75 2.00
❑ M7 Brother Voodoo .75 2.00
❑ M8 Captain America .75 2.00
❑ M9 Captain Marvel .75 2.00
❑ M10 Carnage .75 2.00
❑ M11 Cyclops .75 2.00
❑ M12 Daredevil .75 2.00
❑ M13 Deadpool .75 2.00
❑ M14 Deathlok .75 2.00
❑ M15 Doctor Doom .75 2.00
❑ M16 Daken .75 2.00
❑ M17 Fantomex .75 2.00
❑ M18 Gambit .75 2.00
❑ M19 Ghost Rider .75 2.00
❑ M20 Havok .75 2.00
❑ M21 Hawkeye .75 2.00
❑ M22 Howard The Duck .75 2.00
❑ M23 Hulk .75 2.00
❑ M24 Human Torch .75 2.00
❑ M25 Iceman .75 2.00
❑ M26 Iron Fist .75 2.00
❑ M27 Iron Man .75 2.00
❑ M28 Loki .75 2.00
❑ M29 Luke Cage .75 2.00
❑ M30 Magneto .75 2.00
❑ M31 Man-Thing .75 2.00
❑ M32 Misty Knight .75 2.00
❑ M33 Moon Knight .75 2.00
❑ M34 Multiple Man .75 2.00
❑ M35 Namor .75 2.00
❑ M36 Norman Osborn .75 2.00
❑ M37 Nova .75 2.00
❑ M38 Patriot .75 2.00
❑ M39 Psylocke .75 2.00
❑ M40 Punisher .75 2.00
❑ M41 Red Hulk .75 2.00
❑ M42 Red She-Hulk .75 2.00
❑ M43 Red Skull .75 2.00
❑ M44 Rescue .75 2.00
❑ M45 Rogue .75 2.00
❑ M46 Sentry .75 2.00
❑ M47 She-Hulk .75 2.00
❑ M48 Silver Surfer .75 2.00
❑ M49 Skaar .75 2.00
❑ M50 Spider-Man .75 2.00
❑ M51 Storm .75 2.00
❑ M52 Super Skrull .75 2.00
❑ M53 Taskmaster .75 2.00
❑ M54 Thing .75 2.00
❑ M55 Thor .75 2.00
❑ M56 Union Jack .75 2.00
❑ M57 Venom .75 2.00
❑ M58 Vulcan .75 2.00
❑ M59 Wolverine .75 2.00
❑ M60 X-23 .75 2.00

2012 Marvel Beginnings 2 Sketches

STATED ODDS 1:48

❑ 1 Adam Talley
❑ 2 Adriana Melo
❑ 3 Ashleigh Popplewell
❑ 4 Aston Roy Cover
❑ 5 Axebone
❑ 6 Bianca Thompson
❑ 7 Bill Pulkovski
❑ 8 Bob Stevlic
❑ 9 Boo
❑ 10 Bryan Tillman
❑ 11 Bryan Turner
❑ 12 Cal Slayton
❑ 13 Chadwick Haverland
❑ 14 Charles Holbert
❑ 15 Chris Foreman

- ❑ 16 Cruddie Torian
- ❑ 17 Dan Smith
- ❑ 18 Daniel Gorman
- ❑ 19 Daniel Vest
- ❑ 20 Danielle Gransaull
- ❑ 21 Danny Kuang
- ❑ 22 Daren Douglass
- ❑ 23 David Day
- ❑ 24 Dominike Stanton
- ❑ 25 Edward Cherniga
- ❑ 26 Elaine Perna
- ❑ 27 Effie Lebouleux
- ❑ 28 Elliot Fernandez
- ❑ 29 Elvin Hernandez
- ❑ 30 Erik Reeves
- ❑ 31 Eugene Commodore
- ❑ 32 Frankie Washington
- ❑ 33 Gavin Palmer
- ❑ 34 George Deep
- ❑ 35 Gilbert Monsanto
- ❑ 36 Guile Sharp
- ❑ 37 Ian Roberts
- ❑ 38 Isaiah Mcallister
- ❑ 39 j(ay)
- ❑ 40 James Riot Godfrey
- ❑ 41 James Slay
- ❑ 42 Jason Adams
- ❑ 43 Jason Durden
- ❑ 44 Jason Keith Phillips
- ❑ 45 Jason Metcalf
- ❑ 46 Jay Tracy
- ❑ 47 Jayson Kretzer
- ❑ 48 Jerry Gaylord
- ❑ 49 Jerry Ma
- ❑ 50 Jim Cheung
- ❑ 51 Joe Corroney
- ❑ 52 Joe Hogan
- ❑ 53 Joe Rubenstein
- ❑ 54 Joel Gomez
- ❑ 55 Jonathan Gordon
- ❑ 56 Jonathan Racimo
- ❑ 57 Jose Jaro
- ❑ 58 Kevin Sharpe
- ❑ 59 Kimberley Dunaway
- ❑ 60 Lak Lim
- ❑ 61 Layron DeJarnette
- ❑ 62 Livio Ramondelli
- ❑ 63 Marat Mychaels
- ❑ 64 Marat Rahmansky
- ❑ 65 Mark Henry
- ❑ 66 Mark Morales
- ❑ 67 Matt Slay
- ❑ 68 Matt Triano
- ❑ 69 Maurice Gilligan
- ❑ 70 Michael Duron
- ❑ 71 Michael Potter
- ❑ 72 Michael Watkins
- ❑ 73 Mick Glebe/Matt Glebe
- ❑ 74 Mike Mayhew
- ❑ 75 Pablo Diaz
- ❑ 76 Patti Ross
- ❑ 77 Penelope Gaylord
- ❑ 78 Randy Martinez
- ❑ 79 Remi Dousset
- ❑ 80 Remy Eisu Mokhtar
- ❑ 81 Rhiannon Owens
- ❑ 82 Robert Easby
- ❑ 83 Robert Thai
- ❑ 84 Rodney Ramos
- ❑ 85 Ryan Kincaid
- ❑ 86 Sara Richard
- ❑ 87 Scott Cohn
- ❑ 88 Soloud
- ❑ 89 Steve Scott
- ❑ 90 Tess Fowler
- ❑ 91 Tom Hodges
- ❑ 92 Tony Perna
- ❑ 93 Uko Smith
- ❑ 94 Vo Nguyen
- ❑ 95 Wendy Chew
- ❑ 96 Wes Huffer
- ❑ 97 Wesley Bernick
- ❑ 98 Wu Wei

2012 Marvel Beginnings 2 X-Men Hologram

STATED ODDS 1:72

- ❑ H43 Angel 25.00 50.00
- ❑ H44 Angel Salvadore 25.00 50.00
- ❑ H45 Armor 25.00 50.00
- ❑ H46 Aurora 25.00 50.00
- ❑ H47 Banshee 25.00 50.00
- ❑ H48 Beast 25.00 50.00
- ❑ H49 Bishop 25.00 50.00
- ❑ H50 Cable 25.00 50.00
- ❑ H51 Cannonball 25.00 50.00
- ❑ H52 Cloak 25.00 50.00
- ❑ H53 Colossus 25.00 50.00
- ❑ H54 Cyclops 25.00 50.00
- ❑ H55 Cypher 25.00 50.00
- ❑ H56 Dagger 25.00 50.00
- ❑ H57 Darwin 25.00 50.00
- ❑ H58 Dazzler 25.00 50.00
- ❑ H59 Domino 25.00 50.00
- ❑ H60 Emma Frost 25.00 50.00
- ❑ H61 Fantomex 25.00 50.00
- ❑ H62 Gambit 25.00 50.00
- ❑ H63 Havok 25.00 50.00
- ❑ H64 Hope 25.00 50.00
- ❑ H65 Iceman 25.00 50.00
- ❑ H66 Jean Grey 25.00 50.00
- ❑ H67 Jubilee 25.00 50.00
- ❑ H68 Kitty Pryde 25.00 50.00
- ❑ H69 Longshot 25.00 50.00
- ❑ H70 Magik 25.00 50.00
- ❑ H71 Marvel Girl 25.00 50.00
- ❑ H72 Mimic 25.00 50.00
- ❑ H73 Namor 25.00 50.00
- ❑ H74 Nightcrawler 25.00 50.00
- ❑ H75 Polaris 25.00 50.00
- ❑ H76 Professor X 25.00 50.00
- ❑ H77 Psylocke 30.00 60.00
- ❑ H78 Rogue 40.00 80.00
- ❑ H79 Storm 25.00 50.00
- ❑ H80 Thunderbird 25.00 50.00
- ❑ H81 Vulcan 25.00 50.00
- ❑ H82 Warpath 25.00 50.00
- ❑ H83 Wolverine 25.00 50.00
- ❑ H84 X-23 25.00 50.00

2012 Marvel Beginnings 3

COMPLETE SET (180) 15.00 30.00

- ❑ 361 Deadpool .15 .40
- ❑ 362 Power Princess .15 .40
- ❑ 363 Wingfoot .15 .40
- ❑ 364 Scarlet Witch .15 .40
- ❑ 365 Sasquatch .15 .40
- ❑ 366 Mesmero .15 .40
- ❑ 367 Justice .15 .40
- ❑ 368 Klaw .15 .40
- ❑ 369 Rocket Raccoon .15 .40
- ❑ 370 Ultimate Iron Man .15 .40
- ❑ 371 Half-Life .15 .40
- ❑ 372 Dum Dum Dugan .15 .40
- ❑ 373 Ultimate Thor .15 .40
- ❑ 374 Siryn .15 .40
- ❑ 375 Contemplator .15 .40
- ❑ 376 Man-Thing .15 .40
- ❑ 377 Nocturne .15 .40
- ❑ 378 Captain America .15 .40
- ❑ 379 Silvermane .15 .40
- ❑ 380 Cyclops .15 .40
- ❑ 381 Ant-Man .15 .40
- ❑ 382 Rusty .15 .40
- ❑ 383 Blue Blade .15 .40
- ❑ 384 Sentry .15 .40
- ❑ 385 Penance .15 .40
- ❑ 386 Yellowjacket .15 .40
- ❑ 387 Mystique .15 .40
- ❑ 388 Mysterio .15 .40
- ❑ 389 Firelord .15 .40
- ❑ 390 Puppet Master .15 .40
- ❑ 391 Spider-Man Noir .15 .40
- ❑ 392 Ultimate Spider-Man .15 .40
- ❑ 393 Grey Gargoyle .15 .40
- ❑ 394 Husk .15 .40
- ❑ 395 Doctor Octopus .15 .40
- ❑ 396 Odin .15 .40
- ❑ 397 Silver Surfer .15 .40
- ❑ 398 Kang The Conquerer .15 .40
- ❑ 399 Mister Sinister .15 .40
- ❑ 400 Aries .15 .40
- ❑ 401 Jack O'Lantern .15 .40
- ❑ 402 Star Brand .15 .40
- ❑ 403 Hydro-Man .15 .40
- ❑ 404 Pulsar .15 .40
- ❑ 405 Bruiser .15 .40
- ❑ 406 Songbird .15 .40
- ❑ 407 Echo .15 .40
- ❑ 408 Ronin .15 .40
- ❑ 409 Magneto .15 .40
- ❑ 410 Daredevil .15 .40
- ❑ 411 Mastermind .15 .40
- ❑ 412 Blazing Skull .15 .40
- ❑ 413 Viper .15 .40
- ❑ 414 Scorpion .15 .40
- ❑ 415 Bishop .15 .40
- ❑ 416 Ka-Zar .15 .40
- ❑ 417 Tombstone .15 .40
- ❑ 418 Owl .15 .40
- ❑ 419 Beetle .15 .40
- ❑ 420 Revanche .15 .40
- ❑ 421 Korath .15 .40
- ❑ 422 Guardsman .15 .40
- ❑ 423 Jubilee .15 .40
- ❑ 424 Human Torch .15 .40
- ❑ 425 Ricochet .15 .40
- ❑ 426 The Rawhide Kid .15 .40
- ❑ 427 US Agent .15 .40
- ❑ 428 Union Jack .15 .40
- ❑ 429 Glob .15 .40
- ❑ 430 Wolverine Noir .15 .40
- ❑ 431 Brother Voodoo .15 .40
- ❑ 432 Northstar .15 .40
- ❑ 433 Aurora .15 .40
- ❑ 434 Jean Grey .15 .40
- ❑ 435 Rose .15 .40
- ❑ 436 Big Wheel .15 .40
- ❑ 437 Sandman .15 .40
- ❑ 438 Nomad .15 .40
- ❑ 439 Jack of Hearts .15 .40
- ❑ 440 Red Ghost .15 .40
- ❑ 441 Armor .15 .40
- ❑ 442 Baron Zemo .15 .40
- ❑ 443 Batroc the Leaper .15 .40
- ❑ 444 Bob The Agent of Hydra .15 .40
- ❑ 445 MODOK .15 .40
- ❑ 446 Thunderbolt Ross .15 .40
- ❑ 447 Blob .15 .40
- ❑ 448 Punisher .15 .40
- ❑ 449 Bug .15 .40
- ❑ 450 Neutron .15 .40
- ❑ 451 Ezekiel .15 .40
- ❑ 452 Grim Reaper .15 .40
- ❑ 453 Anti-Venom .15 .40
- ❑ 454 Sauron .15 .40
- ❑ 455 Lizard .15 .40
- ❑ 456 Drax The Destroyer .15 .40
- ❑ 457 Black Knight .15 .40
- ❑ 458 Kaine .15 .40
- ❑ 459 Hawkeye .15 .40
- ❑ 460 3-D Man .15 .40
- ❑ 461 Darkhawk .15 .40
- ❑ 462 Talkback .15 .40
- ❑ 463 Stepford Cuckoos .15 .40
- ❑ 464 Cassandra Nova .15 .40
- ❑ 465 Ms. Marvel .15 .40
- ❑ 466 Luke Cage .15 .40
- ❑ 467 Starhawk .15 .40
- ❑ 468 Valkyrie .15 .40
- ❑ 469 Crossbones .15 .40
- ❑ 470 Dreadknight .15 .40
- ❑ 471 Titanium Man .15 .40
- ❑ 472 Psylocke .15 .40
- ❑ 473 Exodus .15 .40
- ❑ 474 Mockingbird .15 .40
- ❑ 475 Living Laser .15 .40
- ❑ 476 Armageddon .15 .40
- ❑ 477 Omega Red .15 .40
- ❑ 478 Rogue .15 .40
- ❑ 479 Enchantress .15 .40
- ❑ 480 Shadow King .15 .40
- ❑ 481 Dazzler .15 .40
- ❑ 482 Havok .15 .40
- ❑ 483 Groot .15 .40
- ❑ 484 Ares .15 .40
- ❑ 485 Jimmy Woo .15 .40
- ❑ 486 Holocaust .15 .40
- ❑ 487 Banshee .15 .40
- ❑ 488 Vanisher .15 .40
- ❑ 489 Forge .15 .40
- ❑ 490 Valerie Cooper .15 .40
- ❑ 491 Master Mold .15 .40
- ❑ 492 Sentinels .15 .40
- ❑ 493 Emma Frost .15 .40
- ❑ 494 Kitty Pryde .15 .40
- ❑ 495 Tusk .15 .40
- ❑ 496 Dead Girl .15 .40
- ❑ 497 Mary Jane Parker .15 .40
- ❑ 498 Bonebreaker .15 .40
- ❑ 499 Gateway .15 .40
- ❑ 500 Leech .15 .40
- ❑ 501 S'ym .15 .40
- ❑ 502 Caliban .15 .40
- ❑ 503 Ultimate Nick Fury .15 .40
- ❑ 504 Ulik .15 .40
- ❑ 505 Ezekiel Stane .15 .40
- ❑ 506 Super-Adaptoid .15 .40
- ❑ 507 Ultimo .15 .40
- ❑ 508 Fin Fang Foom .15 .40
- ❑ 509 Gamora .15 .40
- ❑ 510 Umar .15 .40
- ❑ 511 Dormammu .15 .40
- ❑ 512 Nightmare .15 .40
- ❑ 513 Wong .15 .40
- ❑ 514 Mephisto .15 .40
- ❑ 515 Warlock .15 .40
- ❑ 516 Magus .15 .40
- ❑ 517 Meggan .15 .40
- ❑ 518 Longshot .15 .40
- ❑ 519 Tyr .15 .40
- ❑ 520 Fandral .15 .40
- ❑ 521 Hogan .15 .40
- ❑ 522 Volstagg .15 .40
- ❑ 523 Thanos .15 .40
- ❑ 524 Scourge .15 .40
- ❑ 525 Dead Girl .15 .40
- ❑ 526 Betty Banner .15 .40
- ❑ 527 Sugar Man .15 .40
- ❑ 528 Norman Osborn .15 .40
- ❑ 529 Maker .15 .40
- ❑ 530 Maximus .15 .40
- ❑ 531 Terminus .15 .40
- ❑ 532 Skrulls .15 .40
- ❑ 533 Uatu the Watcher .15 .40
- ❑ 534 Kro .15 .40
- ❑ 535 Ultimate Spider-Man .15 .40
- ❑ 536 Vision .15 .40
- ❑ 537 Nebula .15 .40
- ❑ 538 Star-Lord .15 .40
- ❑ 539 Silver Sable .15 .40
- ❑ 540 Luke Cage Noir .15 .40

2012 Marvel Beginnings 3 Avengers Hologram

STATED ODDS 1:72

- ❑ HA1 Ant-Man 25.00 50.00
- ❑ HA2 Beast 25.00 50.00
- ❑ HA3 Black Panther 25.00 50.00
- ❑ HA4 Black Widow 25.00 50.00
- ❑ HA5 Captain America 25.00 50.00
- ❑ HA6 Captain Britain 25.00 50.00
- ❑ HA7 Captain Marvel 25.00 50.00
- ❑ HA8 Daredevil 25.00 50.00
- ❑ HA9 Doctor Strange 25.00 50.00
- ❑ HA10 Falcon 25.00 50.00
- ❑ HA11 Giant-Man 25.00 50.00
- ❑ HA12 Hawkeye 25.00 50.00
- ❑ HA13 Hellcat 25.00 50.00
- ❑ HA14 Hercules 25.00 50.00
- ❑ HA15 Hulk 25.00 50.00
- ❑ HA16 Iron Fist 25.00 50.00
- ❑ HA17 Iron Man 25.00 50.00
- ❑ HA18 Luke Cage 25.00 50.00
- ❑ HA19 Maria Hill 25.00 50.00
- ❑ HA20 Mockingbird 25.00 50.00
- ❑ HA21 Moon Knight 25.00 50.00
- ❑ HA22 Ms. Marvel 25.00 50.00
- ❑ HA23 Nova 25.00 50.00
- ❑ HA24 Quicksilver 25.00 50.00
- ❑ HA25 Red Hulk 25.00 50.00
- ❑ HA26 Scarlet Witch 25.00 50.00
- ❑ HA27 Sentry 25.00 50.00
- ❑ HA28 Shang-Chi 25.00 50.00
- ❑ HA29 She-Hulk 25.00 50.00
- ❑ HA30 Spider-Man 30.00 60.00
- ❑ HA31 Spider-Woman 25.00 50.00
- ❑ HA32 Squirrel Girl 25.00 50.00
- ❑ HA33 Storm 25.00 50.00
- ❑ HA34 Thing 25.00 50.00
- ❑ HA35 Thor 25.00 50.00
- ❑ HA36 Tigra 25.00 50.00
- ❑ HA37 US Agent 25.00 50.00
- ❑ HA38 Vision 25.00 50.00
- ❑ HA39 War Machine 25.00 50.00
- ❑ HA40 Wasp 25.00 50.00
- ❑ HA41 Wolverine 40.00 80.00
- ❑ HA42 Wonder Man 25.00 50.00

2012 Marvel Beginnings 3 Breakthrough Issues

COMPLETE SET (45) 10.00 25.00
STATED ODDS ONE PER PACK

- ❑ B91 Fantastic Four #1 .40 1.00
- ❑ B92 X-Men (vol. 1) #137 .40 1.00
- ❑ B93 X-Men (vol. 2) #1 .40 1.00
- ❑ B94 Daredevil #227 .40 1.00
- ❑ B95 Spider-Man (vol. 1) #1 .40 1.00
- ❑ B96 The Incredible Hulk (vol. 1) #181 .40 1.00
- ❑ B97 Future Foundation #1 .40 1.00
- ❑ B98 The Amazing Spider-Man (vol. 1) #1 .40 1.00
- ❑ B99 Daredevil (vol. 2) #1 .40 1.00
- ❑ B100 Tales of Suspense (vol. 1) #39 .40 1.00
- ❑ B101 Immortal Iron Fist #1 .40 1.00
- ❑ B102 The Amazing Spider-Man #3 .40 1.00
- ❑ B103 X-Men #2 .40 1.00
- ❑ B104 X-Men #3 .40 1.00
- ❑ B105 X-Men #12 .40 1.00
- ❑ B106 Ultimate Spider-Man (vol. 2) #1 .40 1.00
- ❑ B107 The Amazing Spider-Man (vol. 1) #129 .40 1.00
- ❑ B108 Fantastic Four #4 .40 1.00
- ❑ B109 X-Men #9 .40 1.00
- ❑ B110 Iron Fist #14 .40 1.00
- ❑ B111 The New Mutants #1 .40 1.00
- ❑ B112 Uncanny X-Men #129 .40 1.00
- ❑ B113 X-Men (vol. 2) #30 .40 1.00
- ❑ B114 Uncanny X-Men #172 .40 1.00
- ❑ B115 X-Factor (vol. 1) #6 .40 1.00
- ❑ B116 Uncanny X-Men #266 .40 1.00
- ❑ B117 Fantastic Four Annual #3 .40 1.00
- ❑ B118 The Avengers #57 .40 1.00
- ❑ B119 X-Men (vol. 2) #53 .40 1.00
- ❑ B120 Marvel Super Heroes: Secret Wars #8 .40 1.00
- ❑ B121 Captain Marvel (vol. 1) #34 .40 1.00
- ❑ B122 Iron Man (vol. 3) #1 .40 1.00
- ❑ B123 Fantastic Four (vol. 1) #232 .40 1.00
- ❑ B124 Astonishing X-Men (vol. 3) .40 1.00
- ❑ B125 Young Avengers #1 .40 1.00
- ❑ B126 Ultimate Spider-Man #160 .40 1.00
- ❑ B127 Captain America (vol. 4) #1 .40 1.00
- ❑ B128 The Hood #1 .40 1.00
- ❑ B129 Luke CageHero for Hire #1 .40 1.00
- ❑ B130 New Mutants #87 .40 1.00
- ❑ B131 Civil War #1 .40 1.00
- ❑ B132 Punisher Noir #1 .40 1.00
- ❑ B133 Iron Man Noir #1 .40 1.00
- ❑ B134 Marvel Comics #1 .40 1.00
- ❑ B135 Daredevil #168 .40 1.00

2012 Marvel Beginnings 3 Breakthrough Issues Autographs

OVERALL AUTO ODDS 1:48

- ❑ B91 Stan Lee 300.00 400.00
- ❑ B92 Glynis Oliver Marsh 15.00 40.00
- ❑ B94 Christie Scheele 8.00 20.00
- ❑ B95 Jim Salicrup 15.00 40.00
- ❑ B96A Len Wein
- ❑ B96B Glynis Oliver Marsh
- ❑ B97 Steve Epting 10.00 25.00
- ❑ B98 Stan Lee
- ❑ B99 Dan Kemp 8.00 20.00
- ❑ B100 Stan Lee 300.00 400.00
- ❑ B101 Matt Hollingsworth 10.00 25.00
- ❑ B102 Stan Lee
- ❑ B103 Stan Lee 300.00 400.00
- ❑ B104 Stan Lee 300.00 400.00
- ❑ B105 Stan Lee 300.00 400.00
- ❑ B106 Brian Michael Bendis
- ❑ B108 Stan Lee 300.00 400.00
- ❑ B109 Stan Lee
- ❑ B110 Dan Green 10.00 25.00
- ❑ B111A Chris Claremont 20.00 50.00
- ❑ B111B Mike Gustovich 8.00 20.00
- ❑ B112 Chris Claremont
- ❑ B113 Fabian Nicieza 12.00 30.00
- ❑ B115 Jackson Guice 10.00 25.00
- ❑ B116A Tom DeFalco
- ❑ B116B Mike Collins
- ❑ B117 Stan Lee 300.00 400.00
- ❑ B118 Stan Lee
- ❑ B119 Mark Waid 8.00 20.00
- ❑ B120A John Beatty 8.00 20.00
- ❑ B120B Mike Zeck 12.00 30.00
- ❑ B122 Sean Chen 15.00 40.00
- ❑ B123 Jim Salicrup 15.00 40.00
- ❑ B124 Laura Martin 10.00 25.00
- ❑ B125A Justin Ponsor 8.00 20.00
- ❑ B125B Jim Cheung 12.00 30.00
- ❑ B126A Andy Lanning 8.00 20.00
- ❑ B126B Brian Michael Bendis
- ❑ B126C Mark Bagley 10.00 25.00
- ❑ B127A John Ney Rieber 10.00 25.00
- ❑ B127B Stuart Moore 8.00 20.00
- ❑ B128 Kyle Hotz 8.00 20.00
- ❑ B129 Stan Lee
- ❑ B130 Louise Simonson 10.00 25.00
- ❑ B131A Steve McNiven 8.00 20.00
- ❑ B131B Dexter Vines 12.00 30.00
- ❑ B131C Chris Eliopoulos 8.00 20.00
- ❑ B132 Tim Bradstreet 12.00 30.00
- ❑ B133 Marta Martinez Garcia 8.00 20.00

2012 Marvel Beginnings 3 Breakthrough Issues Autographs Dual

OVERALL AUTO ODDS 1:48

- ❑ B92 Chris Claremont / Jim Salicrup
- ❑ B93 Tom DeFalco / Chris Claremont
- ❑ B95 Jim Salicrup / Tom DeFalco 35.00 70.00
- ❑ B96 Roy Thomas / Len Wein 60.00 120.00
- ❑ B107 Len Wein / Roy Thomas 60.00 120.00
- ❑ B111 Chris Claremont / Glynis Oliver Marsh
- ❑ B115A Jackson Guice / Joe Rubinstein 30.00 60.00
- ❑ B115B Jackson Guice / Louise Simonson
- ❑ B116 Joe Rubinstein / Mike Collins 35.00 70.00
- ❑ B119 Mark Waid / Richard Starkings 30.00 60.00
- ❑ B120 Mike Zeck / John Beatty 35.00 70.00
- ❑ B121 Len Wein / Roy Thomas 40.00 80.00
- ❑ B124 Laura Martin / Chris Eliopoulos 30.00 60.00
- ❑ B127 Richard Starkings / John Ney Rieber 30.00 60.00
- ❑ B130 Tom DeFalco / Louise Simonson 40.00 80.00

2012 Marvel Beginnings 3 Breakthrough Issues Autographs Triple

OVERALL ODDS 1:48

- ❑ B126 Justin Ponsor / Mark Bagley/ Andy Lanning

2012 Marvel Beginnings 3 Comic Book Panels

STATED ODDS 1:288

- ❑ UM11 The Amazing Spider-Man #7 /54 40.00 80.00
- ❑ UM17 Journey into Mystery #103 /41 40.00 80.00
- ❑ UM19 The Amazing Spider-Man #3 /56 40.00 80.00
- ❑ UM22 Journey into Mystery #112 /38 40.00 80.00
- ❑ UM24 Journey into Mystery #107 /49 40.00 80.00
- ❑ UM25 Daredevil (vol 1.) #7 /45 40.00 80.00
- ❑ UM26 Fantastic Four #52 /44 40.00 80.00
- ❑ UM27 Fantastic Four #5 /59 40.00 80.00
- ❑ UM28 Fantastic Four #4 /54 40.00 80.00
- ❑ UM29 The Amazing Spider-Man (vol. 1) #42 /4440.00 80.00
- ❑ UM30 Marvel Spotlight #32 /44 40.00 80.00

2012 Marvel Beginnings 3 Marvel Prime

COMPLETE SET (60) 35.00 70.00
STATED ODDS 1:2

- ❑ M1 A-Bomb .75 2.00
- ❑ M2 American Panther .75 2.00
- ❑ M3 Black Bolt .75 2.00
- ❑ M4 Black Panther .75 2.00
- ❑ M5 Black Widow .75 2.00
- ❑ M6 Cable .75 2.00
- ❑ M7 Captain America .75 2.00
- ❑ M8 Cyclops .75 2.00
- ❑ M9 Daredevil .75 2.00
- ❑ M10 Dark Phoenix .75 2.00
- ❑ M11 Deadpool .75 2.00
- ❑ M12 Death .75 2.00
- ❑ M13 Doctor Doom .75 2.00
- ❑ M14 Doctor Strange .75 2.00
- ❑ M15 Franklin Richards .75 2.00
- ❑ M16 Ghost Rider .75 2.00
- ❑ M17 Hawkeye .75 2.00
- ❑ M18 Hood .75 2.00
- ❑ M19 Hope .75 2.00
- ❑ M20 Hulk .75 2.00
- ❑ M21 Human Torch .75 2.00
- ❑ M22 Invisible Woman .75 2.00
- ❑ M23 Iron Lad .75 2.00
- ❑ M24 Iron Man .75 2.00
- ❑ M25 Iron Patriot .75 2.00
- ❑ M26 Lady Deadpool .75 2.00
- ❑ M27 Lockjaw .75 2.00
- ❑ M28 Medusa .75 2.00
- ❑ M29 Moon Knight .75 2.00
- ❑ M30 Ms. Marvel .75 2.00
- ❑ M31 Namorita .75 2.00
- ❑ M32 Nathaniel Richards .75 2.00
- ❑ M33 Night Thrasher .75 2.00
- ❑ M34 Nightcrawler .75 2.00
- ❑ M35 Patriot .75 2.00
- ❑ M36 Power-Man .75 2.00
- ❑ M37 Psylocke .75 2.00
- ❑ M38 Ragnarok .75 2.00
- ❑ M39 Scarlet Spider .75 2.00
- ❑ M40 Sentry .75 2.00
- ❑ M41 She-Hulk .75 2.00
- ❑ M42 Silver Samurai .75 2.00
- ❑ M43 Silver Surfer .75 2.00
- ❑ M44 Speedball .75 2.00
- ❑ M45 Spider-Man .75 2.00
- ❑ M46 Spider-Woman .75 2.00
- ❑ M47 Steve Rogers .75 2.00
- ❑ M48 Thing .75 2.00
- ❑ M49 Thor .75 2.00
- ❑ M50 Toxin .75 2.00
- ❑ M51 Ultimate Green Goblin .75 2.00
- ❑ M52 Ultimate Spider-Man .75 2.00
- ❑ M53 Ultron .75 2.00
- ❑ M54 War Machine .75 2.00
- ❑ M55 White Tiger .75 2.00
- ❑ M56 Winter Soldier .75 2.00
- ❑ M57 Wolverine .75 2.00
- ❑ M58 World War Hulk .75 2.00
- ❑ M59 X-23 .75 2.00
- ❑ M60 X-Man .75 2.00

2012 Marvel Beginnings 3 Villains Die-Cut

COMPLETE SET (45) 20.00 40.00
STATED ODDS 1:2

- ❑ V1 Abomination .75 2.00
- ❑ V2 Apocalypse .75 2.00
- ❑ V3 Baron Zemo .75 2.00
- ❑ V4 Black Cat .75 2.00
- ❑ V5 Bullseye .75 2.00
- ❑ V6 Carnage .75 2.00
- ❑ V7 Dark Phoenix .75 2.00
- ❑ V8 Doctor Doom .75 2.00
- ❑ V9 Doctor Octopus .75 2.00
- ❑ V10 Electro .75 2.00
- ❑ V11 Emma Frost .75 2.00
- ❑ V12 Galactus .75 2.00
- ❑ V13 Green Goblin .75 2.00
- ❑ V14 Hobgoblin .75 2.00
- ❑ V15 Hood .75 2.00
- ❑ V16 Jackal .75 2.00
- ❑ V17 Juggernaut .75 2.00
- ❑ V18 Kang The Conquerer .75 2.00
- ❑ V19 Kingpin .75 2.00
- ❑ V20 Kraven .75 2.00
- ❑ V21 Leader .75 2.00
- ❑ V22 Lizard .75 2.00
- ❑ V23 Loki .75 2.00
- ❑ V24 Magneto .75 2.00
- ❑ V25 Mandarin .75 2.00
- ❑ V26 Mephisto .75 2.00
- ❑ V27 Mister Sinister .75 2.00
- ❑ V28 MODOK .75 2.00
- ❑ V29 Mole Man .75 2.00
- ❑ V30 Mysterio .75 2.00
- ❑ V31 Mystique .75 2.00
- ❑ V32 Radioactive Man .75 2.00
- ❑ V33 Red Skull .75 2.00
- ❑ V34 Rhino .75 2.00
- ❑ V35 Sabretooth .75 2.00
- ❑ V36 Sandman .75 2.00
- ❑ V37 Satana .75 2.00
- ❑ V38 Scorpion .75 2.00
- ❑ V39 Sentinels .75 2.00
- ❑ V40 Shocker .75 2.00
- ❑ V41 Super Skrull .75 2.00
- ❑ V42 Thanos .75 2.00
- ❑ V43 Ulik .75 2.00
- ❑ V44 Ultron .75 2.00
- ❑ V45 Venom .75 2.00

2012 Marvel Bronze Age

COMPLETE SET (81) 6.00 15.00

- ❑ 1 Title Card .15 .40
- ❑ 2 X-Men #64 .15 .40
- ❑ 3 Fantastic Four #100 .15 .40
- ❑ 4 Amazing Adventures #1 .15 .40
- ❑ 5 Thor #180 .15 .40
- ❑ 6 Amazing Spider-Man #96 .15 .40
- ❑ 7 The Amazing Spider-Man #100 .15 .40
- ❑ 8 Marvel Spotlight #1 .15 .40
- ❑ 9 Marvel Feature #1 .15 .40
- ❑ 10 Marvel Premiere #1 .15 .40
- ❑ 11 Marvel Spotlight #2 .15 .40
- ❑ 12 Amazing Adventures #11 .15 .40
- ❑ 13 The Tomb of Dracula #1 .15 .40
- ❑ 14 Amazing Spider-Man #121 .15 .40
- ❑ 15 Avengers #100 .15 .40
- ❑ 16 Hero for Hire #1 .15 .40
- ❑ 17 Marvel Spotlight #5 .15 .40
- ❑ 18 The Cat #1 .15 .40
- ❑ 19 The Monster of Frankenstein .15 .40
- ❑ 20 The Defenders #4 .15 .40
- ❑ 21 Iron Man #55 .15 .40
- ❑ 22 The Tomb of Dracula #10 .15 .40
- ❑ 23 Supernatural Thrillers #5 .15 .40
- ❑ 24 Strange Tales #169 .15 .40
- ❑ 25 Vampire Tales #1 .15 .40

❑ 26 Special Marvel Edition #15 .15 .40
❑ 27 Captain America #170 .15 .40
❑ 28 The Amazing Spider-Man #129 .15 .40
❑ 29 Marvel Premiere #15 .15 .40
❑ 30 Giant-Size Creatures #1 .15 .40
❑ 31 Astonishing Tales #25 .15 .40
❑ 32 Giant Size Avengers #1 .15 .40
❑ 33 The Incredible Hulk #180 .15 .40
❑ 34 Giant Size X-Men #1 .15 .40
❑ 35 Legion of Monsters #1 .15 .40
❑ 36 Black Goliath #1 .15 .40
❑ 37 Star-Lord #1 .15 .40
❑ 38 The Champions #1 .15 .40
❑ 39 Deadly Hands of Kung Fu #19 .15 .40
❑ 40 Daredevil #131 .15 .40
❑ 41 Omega the Unknown #1 .15 .40
❑ 42 Nova #1 .15 .40
❑ 43 X-Men #101 .15 .40
❑ 44 Ms. Marvel #1 .15 .40
❑ 45 Black Panther #1 .15 .40
❑ 46 Rampaging Hulk #1 .15 .40
❑ 47 What If #1 .15 .40
❑ 48 Iron First #14 .15 .40
❑ 49 Spider-Woman #1 .15 .40
❑ 50 Devil Dinosaur #1 .15 .40
❑ 51 Uncanny X-Men #121 .15 .40
❑ 52 The Amazing Spider-Man #194 .15 .40
❑ 53 She-Hulk #1 .15 .40
❑ 54 Iron Man #128 .15 .40
❑ 55 Uncanny X-Men #130 .15 .40
❑ 56 Avengers #195 .15 .40
❑ 57 Uncanny X-Men #136 .15 .40
❑ 58 Moon Knight #1 .15 .40
❑ 59 Marvel Team-Up #100 .15 .40
❑ 60 Uncanny X-Men #141 .15 .40
❑ 61 Daredevil #168 .15 .40
❑ 62 Captain America 255 .15 .40
❑ 63 Avengers Annual #10 .15 .40
❑ 64 Marvel Fanfare #1 .15 .40
❑ 65 Daredevil #181 .15 .40
❑ 66 Bizarre Adventures #32 .15 .40
❑ 67 Wolverine #1 .15 .40
❑ 68 Vision and the Scarlet Witch #1 .15 .40
❑ 69 Marvel Graphic Novel #4 .15 .40
❑ 70 Uncanny X-Men #164 .15 .40
❑ 71 Hawkeye #1 .15 .40
❑ 72 Uncanny X-Men #173 .15 .40
❑ 73 Cloak and Dagger #1 .15 .40
❑ 74 Power Pack #1 .15 .40
❑ 75 West Coast Avengers #1 .15 .40
❑ 76 Marvel Super Heroes Secret Wars #7 .15 .40
❑ 77 Kitty Pryde and Wolverine #3 .15 .40
❑ 78 Marvel Team-Up #150 .15 .40
❑ 79 Web of Spider-Man #1 .15 .40
❑ 80 Longshot #1 .15 .40
❑ 81 Iron Man #200 .15 .40

2012 Marvel Bronze Age Parallel

COMPLETE SET 20.00 50.00
STATED ODDS 1:3

2012 Marvel Bronze Age Case Toppers

COMPLETE SET (2) 20.00 40.00
ONE PER CASE

❑ CT1 Marvel Comic Group 10.00 25.00
❑ CT2 Marvel Comic Group 10.00 25.00

2012 Marvel Bronze Age Classic Heroes

COMP.SET w/o SP (9) 8.00 20.00
STATED ODDS 1:12

❑ CH1 Captain America 1.50 4.00
❑ CH2 Thor 1.50 4.00
❑ CH3 Iron Man 1.50 4.00
❑ CH4 Hulk 1.50 4.00
❑ CH5 Spider-Man 1.50 4.00
❑ CH6 Thing 1.50 4.00
❑ CH7 Human Torch 1.50 4.00
❑ CH8 Mr. Fantastic 1.50 4.00
❑ CH9 Invisible Woman 1.50 4.00
❑ CH10 Silver Surfer 12.00 30.00
(issued as Rittenhouse Reward) SP

2012 Marvel Bronze Age Dual-Sided Posters

COMPLETE SET (18) 15.00 30.00
STATED ODDS 1:8

❑ PP1 Warriors of Kung-Fu/Hero for Hire 1.25 3.00
❑ PP2 Warriors of Kung-Fu/Hero for Hire 1.25 3.00
❑ PP3 Warriors of Kung-Fu/Hero for Hire 1.25 3.00
❑ PP4 Warriors of Kung-Fu/Hero for Hire 1.25 3.00
❑ PP5 Warriors of Kung-Fu/Hero for Hire 1.25 3.00
❑ PP6 Warriors of Kung-Fu/Hero for Hire 1.25 3.00
❑ PP7 Warriors of Kung-Fu/Hero for Hire 1.25 3.00
❑ PP8 Warriors of Kung-Fu/Hero for Hire 1.25 3.00
❑ PP9 Warriors of Kung-Fu/Hero for Hire 1.25 3.00
❑ PP10 Legion of Monsters/Sentinels of Space 1.25 3.00
❑ PP11 Legion of Monsters/Sentinels of Space 1.25 3.00
❑ PP12 Legion of Monsters/Sentinels of Space 1.25 3.00
❑ PP13 Legion of Monsters/Sentinels of Space 1.25 3.00
❑ PP14 Legion of Monsters/Sentinels of Space 1.25 3.00
❑ PP15 Legion of Monsters/Sentinels of Space 1.25 3.00
❑ PP16 Legion of Monsters/Sentinels of Space 1.25 3.00
❑ PP17 Legion of Monsters/Sentinels of Space 1.25 3.00
❑ PP18 Legion of Monsters/Sentinels of Space 1.25 3.00

2012 Marvel Bronze Age Embossed

COMPLETE SET (12) 15.00 40.00
STATED ODDS 1:24

❑ E1 Nova 2.50 6.00
❑ E2 Ms. Marvel 2.50 6.00
❑ E3 Moon Knight 2.50 6.00
❑ E4 Black Cat 2.50 6.00
❑ E5 Rogue 2.50 6.00
❑ E6 Iron First 2.50 6.00
❑ E7 Luke Cage 2.50 6.00
❑ E8 Elektra 2.50 6.00
❑ E9 Wolverine 2.50 6.00
❑ E10 Punisher 2.50 6.00
❑ E11 Tigra 2.50 6.00
❑ E12 Phoenix 2.50 6.00

2012 Marvel Bronze Age Promos

❑ P1 Wolverine/Hulk 1974 1.25 3.00
(General Distribution)
❑ P2 Spider-Man 1984 2.00 5.00
(Non-Sport Update)
❑ P3 Album Exclusive 10.00 20.00
❑ P4 X-Men 1976 1.00 2.50
(San Diego Comic Con)

2012 Marvel Bronze Age Sketches

ONE PER BOX

❑ 1 Adam Cleveland
❑ 2 Adam Cline
❑ 3 Al de Stefano
❑ 4 Albert Morales
❑ 5 Alberto Silva
❑ 6 Alcione da Silva
❑ 7 Alex Magno
❑ 8 Allen Geneta
❑ 9 Andre Toma
❑ 10 Andy Price
❑ 11 Anthony Tan
❑ 12 Apriyadi Kusbiantoro
❑ 13 Arie Monroe
❑ 14 Arley Tucker
❑ 15 Babisu Kourtis
❑ 16 Bienifer Flores
❑ 17 Bill Pulkovski
❑ 18 Bob Layton
❑ 19 Brian Shearer
❑ 20 Buddy Prince
❑ 21 Budi Setiawan
❑ 22 Butch Mapa
❑ 23 Caio Majado
❑ 24 Cal Slayton/90*
❑ 25 Cezar Razek
❑ 26 Charles Hall
❑ 27 Chris Bradberry
❑ 28 Chris Foreman
❑ 29 Chris Marrinan
❑ 30 Chris Moreno
❑ 31 Chuck George
❑ 32 Claire Pacheco
❑ 33 Dan Borgonos
❑ 34 Daniel HDR
❑ 35 Danielle Gransaull
❑ 36 Darren Chandler
❑ 37 Darryl Banks
❑ 38 Denver Brubaker
❑ 39 Eric McConnell/108*
❑ 40 Frank Kadar
❑ 41 Fred Hembeck
❑ 42 George Calloway
❑ 43 Greg Kirkpatrick
❑ 44 Hanie Mohd
❑ 45 Irma Ahmed
❑ 46 J. David Lee
❑ 47 Jack Redd
❑ 48 Jader Correa
❑ 49 Jake Sumbing
❑ 50 Jason Davies
❑ 51 Jason Potratz
❑ 52 Jason Sobol
❑ 53 Javier Gonzalez
❑ 54 Jay Fosgitt
❑ 55 Jayson Kretzer
❑ 56 JC Fabul
❑ 57 Jeanette Swift
❑ 58 Jeff Zapata
❑ 59 Jeremy Treece
❑ 60 Jim Kyle
❑ 61 Joe Pekar
❑ 62 Joe St. Pierre
❑ 63 John Czop
❑ 64 John Haun
❑ 65 John Jackman
❑ 66 Jomar Bulda
❑ 67 Jon Hughes
❑ 68 Joseph O'Brien
❑ 69 Juan Fontanez
❑ 70 Julius Dean Abrera
❑ 71 Justin Chung
❑ 72 Katie Cook
❑ 73 Kevin West
❑ 74 Kristin Allen
❑ 75 Lee Kohse
❑ 76 Leeahd Goldberg
❑ 77 Lui Antonio
❑ 78 Lynne Anderson
❑ 79 Marc Nguyen
❑ 80 Marcelo Ferreira
❑ 81 Mark Dos Santos
❑ 82 Mark Marvida
❑ 83 Mark Texeira
❑ 84 Mary Bellamy
❑ 85 Mary Jane Dizon Pajaron
❑ 86 Matias Streb
❑ 87 Matt Glebe
(issued as 9-case incentive)
❑ 88 Mauricio Dias
❑ 89 Mauro Fodra
❑ 90 Meghan Hetrick
❑ 91 Melike Acar
❑ 92 Michael Sta. Maria
❑ 93 Mick Glebe
(issued as 9-case incentive)
❑ 94 Mike Kaluta
❑ 95 Mike Rooth
❑ 96 Mitch Ballard
❑ 97 MJ San Juan
❑ 98 Nestor Celario
❑ 99 Newton Barbosa
❑ 100 Noah Salonga
❑ 101 Norman Jim Faustino
❑ 102 Noval Hernawan
❑ 103 Pablo Marcos
❑ 104 Patrick Larcada
❑ 105 Raimundo Nonato
❑ 106 Rainier Lagunsad
❑ 107 Randy Monces
❑ 108 Rhiannon Owens
❑ 109 Rich Hennemann
❑ 110 Rich Molinelli
❑ 111 Rich Woodall
❑ 112 Rodjer Goulart
❑ 113 Rodrigo Martins
❑ 114 Roy Cover
❑ 115 Saiful Remy Mokhtar
❑ 116 Sam Argo
❑ 117 Sara Richard
❑ 118 Scott Alan Gregory
❑ 119 Scott Rorie
❑ 120 Sean Moore
❑ 121 Stacey Kardash
❑ 122 Stefanie Battalene
❑ 123 Studio Mia
❑ 124 Thanh Bui
❑ 125 Tim Shay
❑ 126 Tone Rodriguez
❑ 127 Tony Perna
❑ 128 Tony Scott
❑ 129 Veronica O'Connell
❑ 130 Warren Martineck
❑ 131 Wendell Rubio Silva
❑ 132 Joe Rubinstein

2012 Marvel Greatest Heroes

COMPLETE SET (81) 6.00 15.00

❑ 1 Header Card .15 .40
❑ 2 Ant-Man .15 .40
❑ 3 Angel .15 .40
❑ 4 Beast .15 .40
❑ 5 Beta-Ray-Bill .15 .40
❑ 6 Black Bolt .15 .40
❑ 7 Black Knight .15 .40
❑ 8 Black Panther .15 .40
❑ 9 Black Widow .15 .40
❑ 10 Blade .15 .40
❑ 11 Blink .15 .40
❑ 12 Cable .15 .40
❑ 13 Captain America .15 .40
❑ 14 Captain Britain .15 .40
❑ 15 Captain Marvel .15 .40
❑ 16 Cloak .15 .40
❑ 17 Colossus .15 .40
❑ 18 Crystal .15 .40
❑ 19 Cyclops .15 .40
❑ 20 Dagger .15 .40
❑ 21 Daredevil .15 .40
❑ 22 Darkhawk .15 .40
❑ 23 Deadpool .15 .40
❑ 24 Deathlok .15 .40
❑ 25 Doctor Strange .15 .40
❑ 26 Doctor Voodoo .15 .40
❑ 27 Elektra .15 .40
❑ 28 Emma Frost .15 .40
❑ 29 Falcon .15 .40
❑ 30 Firestar .15 .40
❑ 31 Gambit .15 .40
❑ 32 Ghost Rider .15 .40
❑ 33 Gorilla Man .15 .40
❑ 34 Havok .15 .40
❑ 35 Hawkeye .15 .40
❑ 36 Hellcat .15 .40
❑ 37 Hercules .15 .40
❑ 38 Hulk .15 .40
❑ 39 Human Torch .15 .40
❑ 40 Invisible Woman .15 .40
❑ 41 Iron Fist .15 .40
❑ 42 Iron Man .15 .40
❑ 43 Jean Grey .15 .40
❑ 44 Jessica Jones .15 .40
❑ 45 Justice .15 .40
❑ 46 Ka-Zar .15 .40
❑ 47 Luke Cage .15 .40
❑ 48 Magik .15 .40
❑ 49 Man-Thing .15 .40
❑ 50 Mantis .15 .40
❑ 51 Medusa .15 .40
❑ 52 Misty Knight .15 .40
❑ 53 Mockingbird .15 .40
❑ 54 Moon Knight .15 .40
❑ 55 Mr. Fantastic .15 .40
❑ 56 Nightcrawler .15 .40
❑ 57 Nova .15 .40
❑ 58 Psylocke .15 .40
❑ 59 Quasar .15 .40
❑ 60 Red Hulk .15 .40
❑ 61 Rocket Raccoon .15 .40
❑ 62 Rogue .15 .40
❑ 63 Ronin .15 .40
❑ 64 Scarlet Witch .15 .40
❑ 65 Sentry .15 .40
❑ 66 She-Hulk .15 .40
❑ 67 Shroud .15 .40
❑ 68 Silver Surfer .15 .40
❑ 69 Spider-Girl .15 .40
❑ 70 Spider-Man .15 .40
❑ 71 Starhawk .15 .40
❑ 72 Storm .15 .40
❑ 73 Thing .15 .40
❑ 74 Thor .15 .40
❑ 75 Valkyrie .15 .40
❑ 76 Vision .15 .40
❑ 77 Warlock .15 .40
❑ 78 War-Machine .15 .40
❑ 79 Winter Soldier .15 .40
❑ 80 Wolverine .15 .40
❑ 81 X-23 .15 .40

2012 Marvel Greatest Heroes Silver Foil

COMPLETE SET (81) 25.00 50.00
STATED ODDS 1:3

2012 Marvel Greatest Heroes Avengers Case Toppers

COMPLETE SET (5) 40.00 80.00
STATED ODDS ONE PER CASE

❑ CT1 The Avengers 10.00 25.00
❑ CT2 The Avengers 10.00 25.00
❑ CT3 The Avengers 10.00 25.00
❑ CT4 The Avengers 10.00 25.00
❑ CT5 The Avengers 10.00 25.00

2012 Marvel Greatest Heroes I Am An Avenger

COMPLETE SET (19) 20.00 50.00
COMP.SET w/o SP 12.00 30.00
STATED ODDS 1:12

❑ IAM1 Finesse 2.00 5.00
❑ IAM2 Hazmat 2.00 5.00
❑ IAM3 Reptil 2.00 5.00
❑ IAM4 Striker 2.00 5.00
❑ IAM5 Veil 2.00 5.00
❑ IAM6 Captain America 2.00 5.00
❑ IAM7 Hawkeye 2.00 5.00
❑ IAM8 Spider-Woman 2.00 5.00
❑ IAM9 Thor 2.00 5.00
❑ IAM10 Beast 2.00 5.00
❑ IAM11 Valkyrie 2.00 5.00
❑ IAM12 Nova 2.00 5.00
❑ IAM13 War Machine 2.00 5.00
❑ IAM14 Steve Rogers 2.00 5.00
❑ IAM15 Jewel 2.00 5.00
❑ IAM16 Spider-Man 2.00 5.00
❑ IAM17 Thing 2.00 5.00
❑ IAM18 Wolverine 2.00 5.00
❑ IAM19 Luke Cage SP 12.00 30.00
(issued as Rittenhouse Reward)

2012 Marvel Greatest Heroes Icons Shadow-box

COMPLETE SET (6) 30.00 60.00
STATED ODDS 1:72

❑ S1 Captain America 6.00 15.00
❑ S2 Thor 6.00 15.00
❑ S3 Ms. Marvel 6.00 15.00
❑ S4 Iron Man 6.00 15.00
❑ S5 Ant Man 6.00 15.00
❑ S6 Hulk 6.00 15.00

2012 Marvel Greatest Heroes Promos

❑ P1 Spider-Man 1.00 2.50
Iron Man/ (General Distribution)
❑ P2 Steve Rogers 2.00 5.00
Captain America/ (Non-Sport Update Magazine)
❑ P3 Thor 8.00 20.00
Valkyrie/ (Binder Exclusive)
❑ P4 Black Widow 12.00 30.00
Black Panther (Shuri)/ (Chicago Non-Sports)

2012 Marvel Greatest Heroes Sketches

STATED ODDS ONE PER BOX

❑ 1 Adam Cleveland 15.00 40.00
❑ 2 Adriano Carreon 15.00 40.00
❑ 3 Albert Morales 20.00 50.00
❑ 4 Alberto Silva 25.00 60.00
❑ 5 Alcione da Silva 25.00 60.00
❑ 6 Alexandre Magno 15.00 40.00
❑ 7 Allen Geneta 15.00 40.00
❑ 8 Andre Toma 20.00 50.00
❑ 9 Andy Price
❑ 10 Anthony Tan 100.00 250.00
❑ 11 Anthony Wheeler 15.00 40.00
❑ 12 Apriyadi Kusbiantoro 20.00 50.00
❑ 13 Arie Monroe 20.00 50.00
❑ 14 Arley Tucker 20.00 50.00
❑ 15 Ashton Roy Cover 30.00 80.00
❑ 16 Axebone 125.00 250.00
❑ 17 Benjamin Glendenning 60.00 150.00
❑ 18 Bill Pulkovski 15.00 40.00
❑ 19 Bob Layton
❑ 20 Brian Shearer 15.00 40.00
❑ 21 Bryan Turner 25.00 60.00
❑ 22 Buddy Prince 20.00 50.00
❑ 23 Budi Setiawan 12.00 30.00
❑ 24 Butch Mapa 25.00 60.00
❑ 25 Caio Majado 12.00 30.00
❑ 26 Cal Slayton 20.00 50.00
❑ 27 Chachi Hernandez
❑ 28 Charles Hall 75.00 200.00
❑ 29 Chris Bradberry 150.00 250.00
❑ 30 Chris Foreman 20.00 50.00
❑ 31 Chris Gutierrez 25.00 60.00
❑ 32 Chris Marrinan 15.00 40.00
❑ 33 Chris Moreno 12.00 30.00
❑ 34 Chuck George 15.00 40.00
❑ 35 Claire Pacheco 40.00 100.00
❑ 36 Dan Borgonos 40.00 100.00
❑ 37 Daniel Gorman 25.00 60.00
❑ 38 Daniel HDR 20.00 50.00
❑ 39 Danielle Gransaull 25.00 60.00
❑ 40 Darren Chandler 15.00 40.00
❑ 41 Darryl Banks 25.00 60.00
❑ 42 Denae Frazier 50.00 100.00
❑ 43 Dennis Crisostomo 20.00 50.00
❑ 44 Denver Brubaker 15.00 40.00
❑ 45 Doug Cowan 15.00 40.00
❑ 46 Elvis Moura 12.00 30.00
❑ 47 Eman Casallos 100.00 200.00
❑ 48 Eric McConnell 30.00 80.00
❑ 49 Eugene Commodore 12.00 30.00
❑ 50 Felipe Massafera 30.00 80.00
❑ 51 Frank Kadar
❑ 52 George Calloway 75.00 150.00
❑ 53 George Davis 40.00 100.00
❑ 54 Greg Kirkpatrick 20.00 50.00
❑ 55 Hanie Mohd 20.00 50.00
❑ 56 Ian Yoshio Roberts 15.00 40.00
❑ 57 Irma Ahmed 20.00 50.00
❑ 58 Jack Redd 150.00 300.00
❑ 59 Jader Correa 40.00 100.00
❑ 60 Jake Minor 15.00 40.00
❑ 61 Jake Sumbing 20.00 50.00
❑ 62 Jason Davies 20.00 50.00
❑ 63 Jason Keith Phillips 25.00 60.00
❑ 64 Jayson Kretzer 20.00 50.00
❑ 65 Jason Sobol 15.00 40.00
❑ 66 Javier Gonzalez 15.00 40.00
❑ 67 Jay David Lee 15.00 40.00
❑ 68 Jay Fosgitt 20.00 50.00
❑ 69 JC Fabul 20.00 50.00
❑ 70 Jeanette Swift 15.00 40.00
❑ 71 Jeff Confer 50.00 120.00
❑ 72 Jerry Gaylord 20.00 50.00
❑ 73 Jim Kyle 50.00 120.00
❑ 74 Joe Pekar 30.00 80.00
❑ 75 Joe St.Pierre 60.00 150.00
❑ 76 John Czop 60.00 150.00
❑ 77 John Jackman 30.00 80.00
❑ 78 Jomar Bulda 20.00 50.00
❑ 79 Jon Hughes 25.00 60.00
❑ 80 Joseph O'Brien 20.00 50.00
❑ 81 Joshua Flower 60.00 150.00
❑ 82 Juan Fontanez Jr. 20.00 50.00
❑ 83 Justin Chung 25.00 60.00
❑ 84 Kat Laurange 30.00 80.00
❑ 85 Kathryn Layno 20.00 50.00
❑ 86 Katie Cook 125.00 250.00
❑ 87 Kevin West 100.00 200.00
❑ 88 Kristin Allen 25.00 60.00
❑ 89 Lak Lim 60.00 150.00
❑ 90 Larry Schlekewy
❑ 91 Lee Kohse 12.00 30.00
❑ 92 Lui Antonio 20.00 50.00
❑ 93 Luke Smarto 15.00 40.00
❑ 94 Lynne Anderson 40.00 100.00
❑ 95 Marcelo Ferreira 20.00 50.00
❑ 96 Mark Dos Santos 15.00 40.00
❑ 97 Mark Tannacore 20.00 50.00
❑ 98 Marlo Lodrigueza 40.00 100.00
❑ 99 Mary Bellamy 15.00 40.00
❑ 100 Matias Streb 50.00 120.00
❑ 101 Mauro Fodra 20.00 50.00
❑ 102 Melike Acar 700.00 1200.00
❑ 103 Michael Rooth 20.00 50.00
❑ 104 Michael Sta. Maria 40.00 100.00
❑ 105 MJ San Juan 20.00 50.00
❑ 106 Newton Barbosa 60.00 150.00
❑ 107 Nick Yakimovich 12.00 30.00
❑ 108 Noah Salonga 20.00 50.00
❑ 109 Noval Hernawan 20.00 50.00
❑ 110 Patrick Larcada 200.00 300.00
❑ 111 Rainier Lagunsad 20.00 50.00
❑ 112 Rhiannon Owens 60.00 150.00
❑ 113 Ricardo Teles 15.00 40.00
❑ 114 Rich Molinelli 15.00 40.00
❑ 115 Richard Cox 50.00 120.00
❑ 116 Rodjer Goulart 15.00 40.00
❑ 117 Rodrigo Martins 15.00 40.00
❑ 118 Ryan Kincaid 30.00 80.00
❑ 119 Saiful Remy Mokhtar 30.00 80.00
❑ 120 Sam Agro 20.00 50.00
❑ 121 Sanna Umemoto 50.00 120.00
❑ 122 Sarah Wilkinson 25.00 60.00
❑ 123 Fernando Scheidt 15.00 40.00
❑ 124 Scott Barnett
❑ 125 Scott Rorie 30.00 80.00
❑ 126 Sean Moore 12.00 30.00
❑ 127 Stacey Kardash 25.00 60.00
❑ 128 Stefanie Battalene 20.00 50.00
❑ 129 Steven Miller 20.00 50.00
❑ 130 Tess Fowler 25.00 60.00
❑ 131 Thanh Bui 15.00 40.00
❑ 132 Tim Shay
❑ 133 Tom Kelly 15.00 40.00
❑ 134 Tone Rodriguez 15.00 40.00
❑ 135 Tony Perna 250.00 450.00
❑ 136 Tony Scott 30.00 80.00
❑ 137 Vo Nguyen 25.00 60.00
❑ 138 Wendell Rubio Silva 12.00 30.00
❑ 139 Matt Glebe/ (issued as 6-case incentive)150.00 400.00
❑ 140 Mick Glebe/ (issued as 6-case incentive)150.00 400.00
❑ 141 Warren Martineck 250.00 400.00
(issued as 9-case incentive)

2012 Marvel Greatest Heroes Ultimate Heroes

COMPLETE SET (9) 15.00 40.00
STATED ODDS 1:36

❑ UH11 Captain America 3.00 8.00
❑ UH12 Hawkeye 3.00 8.00
❑ UH13 Iron Man 3.00 8.00
❑ UH14 Nick Fury 3.00 8.00
❑ UH15 Scalet Witch 3.00 8.00
❑ UH16 Spider-Man 3.00 8.00
❑ UH17 Thor 3.00 8.00
❑ UH18 Valkyrie 3.00 8.00
❑ UH19 Wasp 3.00 8.00

2012 Marvel Greatest Heroes Villains

COMPLETE SET (18) 10.00 25.00
STATED ODDS 1:6

❑ V1 Baron Zemo 1.25 3.00
❑ V2 Bullseye 1.25 3.00
❑ V3 Doctor Octopus 1.25 3.00
❑ V4 Dr. Doom 1.25 3.00
❑ V5 Green Goblin 1.25 3.00
❑ V6 Hood 1.25 3.00
❑ V7 Juggernaut 1.25 3.00
❑ V8 Kang 1.25 3.00
❑ V9 Loki 1.25 3.00
❑ V10 Magneto 1.25 3.00
❑ V11 Morgan Le Fay 1.25 3.00
❑ V12 Nightmare 1.25 3.00
❑ V13 Radioactive Man 1.25 3.00
❑ V14 Red Skull 1.25 3.00
❑ V15 Sphinx 1.25 3.00
❑ V16 Taskmaster 1.25 3.00
❑ V17 Thanos 1.25 3.00
❑ V18 Ultron 1.25 3.00

2012 Marvel Premier

STATED PRINT RUN 199 SER. #'d SETS

❑ 1 Mr. Fantastic 10.00 25.00
❑ 2 Invisible Woman 10.00 25.00
❑ 3 Thing 10.00 25.00
❑ 4 Human Torch 10.00 25.00
❑ 5 Spider-Man 10.00 25.00
❑ 6 Iron Man 10.00 25.00
❑ 7 Captain America 10.00 25.00
❑ 8 Thor 10.00 25.00
❑ 9 Hulk 10.00 25.00
❑ 10 Hawkeye 10.00 25.00
❑ 11 Wasp 10.00 25.00
❑ 12 Red Hulk 10.00 25.00
❑ 13 Iron Fist 10.00 25.00
❑ 14 Luke Cage 10.00 25.00
❑ 15 Doctor Strange 10.00 25.00
❑ 16 Black Panther 10.00 25.00
❑ 17 Spider-Woman 10.00 25.00
❑ 18 Ms. Marvel 10.00 25.00
❑ 19 Scarlet Witch 10.00 25.00
❑ 20 Wolverine 10.00 25.00
❑ 21 Emma Frost 10.00 25.00
❑ 22 Cyclops 10.00 25.00
❑ 23 Jean Grey 10.00 25.00
❑ 24 Gambit 10.00 25.00
❑ 25 Rogue 10.00 25.00
❑ 26 Iceman 10.00 25.00
❑ 27 Nightcrawler 10.00 25.00
❑ 28 Storm 10.00 25.00
❑ 29 X-23 10.00 25.00
❑ 30 Psylocke 10.00 25.00
❑ 31 Professor X 10.00 25.00
❑ 32 Silver Surfer 10.00 25.00
❑ 33 Daredevil 10.00 25.00
❑ 34 Deadpool 10.00 25.00
❑ 35 She-Hulk 10.00 25.00
❑ 36 Punisher 10.00 25.00
❑ 37 Ghost Rider 10.00 25.00
❑ 38 Elektra 10.00 25.00
❑ 39 Doctor Doom 10.00 25.00
❑ 40 Green Goblin 10.00 25.00
❑ 41 Venom 10.00 25.00
❑ 42 Red Skull 10.00 25.00
❑ 43 Loki 10.00 25.00
❑ 44 Magneto 10.00 25.00
❑ 45 Dark Phoenix 10.00 25.00
❑ 46 Sabretooth 10.00 25.00
❑ 47 Thanos 10.00 25.00
❑ 48 Mystique 10.00 25.00
❑ 49 Apocalypse 10.00 25.00
❑ 50 Galactus 10.00 25.00

2012 Marvel Premier Classic Corners

STATED ODDS 1:2.3
GROUP A ODDS 1:33.3
GROUP B ODDS 1:10.4
GROUP C ODDS 1:5.7
GROUP D ODDS 1:3.2

❑ CC1 X-Men #1 D 12.00 30.00
❑ CC2 The Avengers #1 D 12.00 30.00
❑ CC3 Fantastic Four #48 D 12.00 30.00
❑ CC4 Marvel Super Heroes Secert Wars #1 A200.00 300.00
❑ CC5 The Amazing Spider-Man #252 A 300.00 400.00
❑ CC6 Captain America #109 D 12.00 30.00

❑ CC7 Incredible Hulk (vol. 1) #102 D 12.00 30.00
❑ CC8 The Amazing Spider-Man #50 D 12.00 30.00
❑ CC9 Daredevil #1 D 15.00 40.00
❑ CC10 Deadly Hands of Kung Fu #1 C 12.00 30.00
❑ CC11 The Amazing Spider-Man #48 D 12.00 30.00
❑ CC12 Journey Into Mystery #91 D 12.00 30.00
❑ CC13 Sub-Mariner (vol. 1) #1 D 12.00 30.00
❑ CC14 Defenders (vol. 1) #1 C 15.00 40.00
❑ CC15 Tales to Astonish (vol. 1) #43 D 12.00 30.00
❑ CC16 Strange Tales (vol. 1) #108 D 12.00 30.00
❑ CC17 Silver Surfer #1 D 12.00 30.00
❑ CC18 Monsters on The Prowl #9 D 12.00 30.00
❑ CC19 Iron Man (vol. 1) #1 D 12.00 30.00
❑ CC20 Tomb of Dracula #10 C 12.00 30.00
❑ CC21 Amazing Adventures Inhumans and The Black Widow #1 D 12.00 30.00
❑ CC22 Amazing Adventures Black Bolt and The Inhumans #10 C 12.00 30.00
❑ CC23 Amazing Adventures The Beast #11 C 12.00 30.00
❑ CC24 Amazing Adventures The Beast #12 C 12.00 30.00
❑ CC25 The Amazing Spider-Man #279 A 300.00 500.00
❑ CC26 Western Gunfighters The Ghost Rider/Apache Kid #7 C 12.00 30.00
❑ CC27 The Amazing Spider-Man #250 B 20.00 40.00
❑ CC28 Marvel Presents Guardians of The Galaxy #3 B 20.00 40.00
❑ CC29 Amazing Spider-Man (vol. 2) #32 A 100.00 200.00
❑ CC30 The Amazing Spider-Man #200 B 20.00 40.00
❑ CC31 Amazing Spider-Man Annual (vol. 1) #7 D 12.00 30.00
❑ CC32 The Avengers #94 C 12.00 30.00
❑ CC33 Fear #1 D 12.00 30.00
❑ CC34 Adventure Into Fear With Man-Thing #10 C 12.00 30.00
❑ CC35 Wolverine Vol. 2 #1 C 15.00 40.00
❑ CC36 Beware #2 C 12.00 30.00
❑ CC37 Black Goliath #2 B 20.00 40.00
❑ CC38 Nova #1 B 30.00 60.00
❑ CC39 Nick Fury D 12.00 30.00
❑ CC40 Night Rider #1 B 20.00 40.00
❑ CC41 Luke Cage C 12.00 30.00
❑ CC42 Jungle Action (vol. 2) Featuring Black Panther C 12.00 30.00
❑ CC43 Howard The Duck #33 A 400.00 600.00
❑ CC44 Invaders (vol 1) #1 B 30.00 60.00
❑ CC45 The Human Torch (vol. 1) #1 C 12.00 30.00
❑ CC46 Marvel Two-in-One #22 B 20.00 40.00
❑ CC47 Marvel Tales #1 D 12.00 30.00
❑ CC48 Marvel Spotlight: Ghost Rider #5 C 12.00 30.00
❑ CC49 Marvel Spotlight: Warriors Three B 20.00 40.00
❑ CC50 Marvel Spotlight: Deathlok #33 B 20.00 40.00

2012 Marvel Premier Emotion Jason Adams Sketches

STATED PRINT RUN 50 SER. #'d SETS

❑ E1 Frustration - Thing 20.00 40.00
❑ E2 Responsibility - Spider-Man 35.00 70.00
❑ E3 Pride - Iron Man 20.00 40.00
❑ E4 Patriotism - Captain America 30.00 60.00
❑ E5 Honor - Thor 20.00 40.00
❑ E6 Anger - Hulk 20.00 40.00
❑ E7 Jealousy - Loki 20.00 40.00
❑ E8 Resentment - Magneto 20.00 40.00
❑ E9 Ferocity - Sabertooth 30.00 60.00
❑ E10 Mystic - Dr. Strange 20.00 40.00
❑ E11 Ambition - Dr. Doom 20.00 40.00
❑ E12 Torment - Wolverine 60.00 120.00
❑ E13 Control - Cyclops 20.00 40.00
❑ E14 Anxiety - Rogue 40.00 80.00
❑ E15 Joviality - Iceman 20.00 40.00
❑ E16 Turmoil - Psylocke 30.00 60.00
❑ E17 Horror - Venom 30.00 60.00
❑ E18 Insanity - Deadpool 20.00 40.00

2012 Marvel Premier Shadowbox

STATED ODDS 1:2.7
GROUP A ODDS 1:41.7
GROUP B ODDS 1:13
GROUP C ODDS 1:6.1
GROUP D ODDS 1:3.2

❑ S1 Spider-Man/Green Goblin D 12.00 30.00
❑ S2 Fantastic Four/Galactus D 12.00 30.00
❑ S3 Punisher/Spider-Man A 100.00 200.00
❑ S4 Captain America/Iron Man D 12.00 30.00
❑ S5 Wolverine/Magneto B 20.00 50.00
❑ S6 Bullseye/Daredevil D 12.00 30.00
❑ S7 Thor/Hulk D 12.00 30.00
❑ S8 Hulk/Red Hulk C 12.00 30.00
❑ S9 Dark Avengers/The Avengers A 300.00 450.00
❑ S10 The Avengers/Skrulls D 12.00 30.00
❑ S11 Ultimate Wolverine/Ultimate Hulk A 350.00 600.00
❑ S12 Spider-Man/Kraven D 12.00 30.00
❑ S13 Iron Patriot/Iron Man D 12.00 30.00
❑ S14 Venom/Spider-Man Carnage/Anti-Venom C 12.00 30.00
❑ S15 Red Skull/Captain America D 12.00 30.00
❑ S16 World War Hulk/Sentry C 12.00 30.00
❑ S17 Wolverine/Lady Deathstrike D 12.00 30.00
❑ S18 Silver Surfer/Thor D 12.00 30.00
❑ S19 Thor/Hercules C 12.00 30.00
❑ S20 X-Men/Sentinels D 15.00 40.00
❑ S21 Deadpool/Taskmaster D 15.00 40.00
❑ S22 Thing/Hulk D 12.00 30.00
❑ S23 Captain America/Baron Zemo C 12.00 30.00
❑ S24 Vulcan/Black Bolt C 12.00 30.00
❑ S25 Thor/Iron Man C 12.00 30.00
❑ S26 World War Hulk/Iron Man C 12.00 30.00
❑ S27 Thanos/Earth's Heroes C 15.00 40.00
❑ S28 Dark Avengers/X-Men C 12.00 30.00
❑ S29 Iron Fist/Hydra Foot Soliders B 15.00 40.00
❑ S30 Moon Knight/Bushman A 75.00 150.00
❑ S31 Thor/Frost Giants D 12.00 30.00
❑ S32 Thor/Loki D 12.00 30.00
❑ S33 Silver Surfer/Galactus D 12.00 30.00
❑ S34 Fantastic Four/Doctor Doom C 12.00 30.00
❑ S35 Brotherhood/X-Men B 15.00 40.00
❑ S36 Hulk/Namor B 15.00 40.00
❑ S37 Lizard/Spider-Man B 15.00 40.00
❑ S38 Iron Man/Mandarin B 15.00 40.00
❑ S39 Firelord/Spider-Man B 20.00 50.00
❑ S40 The Avengers/X-Men C 15.00 40.00
❑ S41 Sabretooth/Wolverine D 20.00 50.00
❑ S42 Professor X/Magneto B 20.00 50.00

2012 Music Music Music Single Memorabilia Silver

STATED PRINT RUN 15-80

❑ 1 Bing Crosby/90*
❑ 2 Britney Spears/90*
❑ 3 Bruce Springsteen/90*
❑ 4 Buddy Holly/90*
❑ 5 Carrie Underwood/90*
❑ 6 Courtney Love/90*
❑ 7 Dean Martin/80*
❑ 8 Diana Ross/80*
❑ 9 Elton John/80*
❑ 10 Elton John/15*
❑ 11 Elvis Presley/80*
❑ 12 Eric Clapton/80*
❑ 13 Frank Sinatra/80*
❑ 14 Gene Simmons/80*
❑ 15 James Brown/15*
❑ 16 Jimi Hendrix/15*
❑ 17 Keith Moon/80*
❑ 18 LeAnn Rimes/80*
❑ 19 Madonna/80*
❑ 20 MC Hammer/80*
❑ 21 Miranda Lambert/80*
❑ 22 Ray Charles/15*
❑ 23 Sammy Davis Jr./80*
❑ 24 Sammy Davis Jr./15*
❑ 25 Shania Twain/80*
❑ 26 Snoop Dogg/80*
❑ 27 Stevie Nicks/15*
❑ 28 Sting/80*
❑ 29 Usher/80*
❑ 30 Whitney Houston/80*

2012 Music Music Music Dual Memorabilia Silver

ANNOUNCED PRINT RUN 50

❑ 1 Bing Crosby Frank Sinatra
❑ 2 Britney Spears Madonna
❑ 3 Bruce Springsteen Elvis Presley
❑ 4 Bruce Springsteen Eric Clapton
❑ 5 Carrie Underwood LeAnn Rimes
❑ 6 Courtney Love Madonna
❑ 7 Dean Martin Sammy Davis Jr.
❑ 8 Diana Ross Whitney Houston
❑ 9 Dianna Ross Madonna
❑ 10 Elton John Elvis Presley
❑ 11 Elvis Presley Buddy Holly
❑ 12 Eric Clapton Keith Moon
❑ 13 Shania Twain Miranda Lambert
❑ 14 Snoop Dogg MC Hammer
❑ 15 Usher MC Hammer

2012 NCIS

COMPLETE SET (36) 35.00 70.00

❑ 1 Yankee White Left For Dead 1.25 3.00
❑ 2 Hung Out to Dry Eye Spy 1.25 3.00
❑ 3 Seadog My Other Left Foot 1.25 3.00
❑ 4 The Immortals One Shot, One Kill 1.25 3.00
❑ 5 The Curse The Good Samaritan 1.25 3.00
❑ 6 High Seas Enigma 1.25 3.00
❑ 7 Sub Rosa Bete Noire 1.25 3.00
❑ 8 Minimum Security The Truth Is Out There 1.25 3.00
❑ 9 Marine Down UnSEALed 1.25 3.00
❑ 10 Dead Man Talking The Bone Yard 1.25 3.00
❑ 11 Missing Terminal Leave 1.25 3.00
❑ 12 Split Decision Call of Silence 1.25 3.00
❑ 13 A Weak Link Heart Break 1.25 3.00
❑ 14 Reveille Forced Entry 1.25 3.00
❑ 15 See No Evil Chained 1.25 3.00
❑ 16 The Good Wives Club Black Water 1.25 3.00
❑ 17 Vanished Doppelgänger 1.25 3.00
❑ 18 Lt. Jane Doe The Meat Puzzle 1.25 3.00
❑ 19 Witness Twilight 1.25 3.00
❑ 20 Caught on Tape Kill Ari: Part 1 1.25 3.00
❑ 21 Pop Life Kill Ari: Part 2 1.25 3.00
❑ 22 An Eye for an Eye Mind Games 1.25 3.00
❑ 23 Bikini Wax Silver War 1.25 3.00
❑ 24 Conspiracy Theory Switch 1.25 3.00
❑ 25 Red Cell The Voyeur's Web 1.25 3.00
❑ 26 Hometown Hero Honor Code 1.25 3.00
❑ 27 SWAK Under Covers 1.25 3.00
❑ 28 Frame Up Bait 1.25 3.00
❑ 29 Probie Iced 1.25 3.00
❑ 30 Model Behavior Untouchable 1.25 3.00
❑ 31 Boxed In Bloodbath 1.25 3.00
❑ 32 Deception Jeopardy 1.25 3.00
❑ 33 Light Sleeper Hiatus: Part 1 1.25 3.00
❑ 34 Head Case Hiatus: Part 2 1.25 3.00
❑ 35 Family Secret Shalom 1.25 3.00
❑ 36 Ravenous Escaped 1.25 3.00

2012 NCIS Autograph Relics

❑ 1 Pauley Perrette 100.00 175.00
❑ 2 Rocky Carroll 75.00 125.00
(issued as 2-box incentive)

2012 NCIS Autographs

STATED ODDS ONE PER PACK

❑ 1 Alan Dale as Tom Morrow 8.00 20.00
❑ 2 Alicia Coppola as Faith Coleman 10.00 25.00
❑ 3 Bob Newhart as Doctor Walter Magnus 40.00 80.00
❑ 4 Brian Dietzen as Jimmy Palmer 20.00 40.00
❑ 5 Charles Durning as Ernie Yost 12.00 30.00
❑ 6 Cheryl Ladd as Mary Courtney 25.00 50.00
❑ 7 Diane Neal as Abigail Borin 12.00 30.00
❑ 8 Jessica Steen as Paula Cassidy 10.00 25.00
❑ 9 Lauren Holly as 50.00 100.00
❑ 10 Michael Nouri as Eli David 15.00 40.00
❑ 11 Pancho Demmings as Gerald Jackson 8.00 20.00
❑ 12 Pauley Perrette as 100.00 200.00
❑ 13 Rena Sofer as 15.00 40.00
❑ 14 Rocky Carroll as Leon Vance 20.00 50.00
❑ 15 Sandra Hess as Regine Smidt 12.00 30.00
❑ 16 Scottie Thompson as Jeanne Benoit 12.00 30.00
❑ 17 Sean Harmon as Young Leroy Jethro Gibbs 8.00 20.00
❑ 18 Stephanie Mello as Cynthia Sumner 10.00 25.00

2012 NCIS Character Quote Box Toppers

COMPLETE SET (2) 30.00 60.00
STATED ODDS ONE PER BOX
STATED PRINT RUN 225 SER. #'d SETS

❑ CT1 Leroy Jethro Gibbs 20.00 40.00
❑ CT2 Abby Sciuto 20.00 40.00

2012 NCIS Characters

COMPLETE SET (9) 20.00 40.00
STATED ODDS ONE PER PACK
STATED PRINT RUN 600 SER. #'d SETS

❑ C1 Mark Harmon as Special Agent Leroy Jethro Gibbs 3.00 8.00
❑ C2 Pauley Perrette as Abby Sciuto 3.00 8.00
❑ C3 Michael Weatherly as Special Agent Anthony Dinozzo 3.00 8.00
❑ C4 Sean Murray as Special Agent Timothy McGee 3.00 8.00
❑ C5 Cote de Pablo as Special Agent Ziva David 3.00 8.00
❑ C6 David McCallum as Dr. Donald Mallard 3.00 8.00
❑ C7 Sasha Alexander as Special Agent Caitlin Todd 3.00 8.00
❑ C8 Lauren Holly as Director Jenny Shepard 3.00 8.00
❑ C9 Rocky Carroll as Director Leon Vance 3.00 8.00

2012 NCIS Promos

❑ P1 6 cast shot (General Distribution) 1.25 3.00
❑ P2 7 cast shot (Non-Sport Update Magazine) 2.50 6.00
❑ P3 5 cast shot (Binder Exclusive) 12.00 30.00
❑ P4 5 cast shot (Philly NonSport Show) 2.00 5.00

2012 NCIS Relics

STATED ODDS TWO PER PACK
STATED PRINT RUN 500 SER. #'d SETS

❑ CC1 Abby Sciuto 8.00 20.00
❑ CC2 Dr. Donald Ducky Mallard 6.00 15.00
❑ CC3 Ziva David 10.00 25.00
❑ CC4 Leon Vance 6.00 15.00
❑ CC5 Timothy McGee 6.00 15.00
❑ CC6 Abby Sciuto 8.00 20.00
❑ CC7 Anthony Dinozzo/150 125.00 250.00
(issued as a Rittenhouse Reward)
❑ CC8 Jimmy Palmer 6.00 15.00
❑ CC9 Dr. Donald Ducky Mallard 6.00 15.00
❑ CC10 Anthony Dinozzo 8.00 20.00
❑ CC11 Leroy Jethro Gibbs 12.00 30.00
❑ CC12 Ziva David 10.00 25.00
❑ CC13 Timothy McGee 6.00 15.00
❑ CC14 Abby Sciuto 8.00 20.00
❑ CC15 Jimmy Palmer 6.00 15.00
❑ CC16 Ziva David 10.00 25.00
❑ CC17 Leroy Jethro Gibbs 12.00 30.00
❑ CC18 Leon Vance 6.00 15.00
❑ CC19 Dr. Donald Ducky Mallard 6.00 15.00
❑ CC20 Ziva David 10.00 25.00
❑ CC21 Anthony Dinozzo 8.00 20.00
❑ CC22 Abby Sciuto 12.00 30.00

2012 Platinum League Self Made

COMPLETE SET (87)
UNNUMBERED CARDS LISTED ALPHABETICALLY

2012 Pop Century

❑ BAAB1 Alex Borstein 6.00 15.00
❑ BAAB2 Amanda Beard 12.00 30.00
❑ BAAC1 Arianny Celeste 20.00 40.00
❑ BAAD1 Angie Dickinson 12.00 30.00
❑ BAAE1 Angie Everhart 8.00 20.00
❑ BAAF1 Amy Fisher 10.00 25.00
❑ BAAP1 Angelina Pivarnick 5.00 12.00
❑ BAAP2 Audrina Patridge 6.00 15.00
❑ BAAQ1 Aileen Quinn 8.00 20.00
❑ BAAR1 Austin Chumlee Russell 20.00 40.00
❑ BAASJ Antonio Sabato Jr. 5.00 12.00
❑ BAAW1 Adam West 25.00 50.00
❑ BABBS BooBoo Stewart 5.00 12.00
❑ BABD1 Bruce Dern 6.00 15.00
❑ BABDW Billy Dee Williams 25.00 50.00
❑ BABE1 Barbara Eden 25.00 50.00
❑ BABH1 Brooke Hogan 20.00 40.00
❑ BABJ1 Bruce Jenner 8.00 20.00
❑ BABK1 Bernie Kopell 6.00 15.00
❑ BABP1 Bristol Palin 12.00 30.00
❑ BABR1 Brande Roderick 8.00 20.00
❑ BABR2 Burt Reynolds 25.00 50.00
❑ BABS1 Britney Spears 200.00 300.00
❑ BABW1 Burt Ward 20.00 40.00
❑ BABZ1 Billy Zane 8.00 20.00
❑ BACA1 Christina Applegate 30.00 60.00
❑ BACE1 Carmen Electra 15.00 40.00
❑ BACH1 Corey Big Hoss Harrison 12.00 30.00
❑ BACL1 Carla Laemmle 10.00 25.00
❑ BACM1 Cindy Margolis 10.00 25.00
❑ BACP1 Cassandra Peterson 30.00 60.00
❑ BACS1 Charlie Sheen 40.00 80.00
❑ BACS2 Claire Sinclair 8.00 20.00
❑ BACT1 Cheryl Tiegs 35.00 70.00
❑ BADL1 David Lander 10.00 25.00
❑ BADMX DMX 12.00 30.00
❑ BADR1 Dennis Rodman 20.00 40.00
❑ BADS1 Dominique Swain 8.00 20.00
❑ BADT1 Donald J. Trump 25.00 50.00
❑ BADTJ Donald Trump Jr. 6.00 15.00
❑ BAEB1 Ernest Borgnine 20.00 40.00
❑ BAEE1 Erik Estrada 8.00 20.00
❑ BAEL1 Emmanuel Lewis 8.00 20.00
❑ BAEM1 Erin Moran 8.00 20.00
❑ BAEP1 Emily Procter 8.00 20.00
❑ BAFD1 Fred Dryer 6.00 15.00
❑ BAFW1 Fred Williamson 8.00 20.00
❑ BAGC1 Gina Carano 20.00 40.00
❑ BAGG1 Gilbert Gottfried 6.00 15.00
❑ BAGG2 Gina Gershon 25.00 50.00
❑ BAGLN Gena Lee Nolin 10.00 25.00
❑ BAGR1 Gretchen Rossi 6.00 15.00
❑ BAHA1 Harry Anderson 8.00 20.00
❑ BAHF1 Harrison Ford
❑ BAHF2 Heidi Fleiss 12.00 30.00
❑ BAHH1 Henry Hill 12.00 30.00
❑ BAHP1 Hayden Panettiere 60.00 120.00
❑ BAI1 Ichiro
❑ BAIS1 Ian Somerhalder 10.00 25.00
❑ BAIZ1 Ian Ziering 5.00 12.00
❑ BAJA1 Jason Alexander 25.00 50.00
❑ BAJA2 Julie Adams 12.00 30.00
❑ BAJC1 Joanna Cassidy 8.00 20.00
❑ BAJH1 Jessica Hall 8.00 20.00
❑ BAJJ1 Jenna Jameson 20.00 40.00
❑ BAJLO Jennifer Lopez 100.00 200.00
❑ BAJM1 Jackie Martling 5.00 12.00
❑ BAJN1 Jay North 12.00 30.00
❑ BAJP1 Jason Priestley 10.00 25.00
❑ BAJP2 Jeremy Piven 8.00 20.00
❑ BAJP3 Jon Provost 6.00 15.00
❑ BAJS1 Jordin Sparks 10.00 25.00
❑ BAJS2 Julian Sands 5.00 12.00
❑ BAKB1 Kate Beckinsale 175.00 300.00
❑ BAKB2 Kelly Bensimon 5.00 12.00
❑ BAKC1 Ken Climo 10.00 25.00
❑ BAKC2 Kristin Cavallari 10.00 25.00
❑ BAKDG Kara DioGuardi 5.00 12.00
❑ BAKS1 Kristy Swanson 12.00 30.00
❑ BALAW Lesley Ann Warren 10.00 25.00
❑ BALB1 Lo Bosworth 6.00 15.00
❑ BALF1 Lou Ferrigno 20.00 40.00
❑ BALH1 Larry Hagman 25.00 50.00
❑ BALL1 Lindsay Lohan 100.00 200.00
❑ BALL2 Lorenzo Lamas 5.00 12.00
❑ BALN1 Laraine Newman 5.00 12.00
❑ BAMCD Michael Clarke Duncan 25.00 50.00
❑ BAMF1 Morgan Fairchild 20.00 40.00
❑ BAML1 Martin Landau 20.00 40.00
❑ BAML2 Mike Lookinland 6.00 15.00
❑ BAMR1 Mickey Rourke 12.00 30.00
❑ BANH1 Natasha Henstridge 20.00 40.00
❑ BAPJS P.J. Soles 8.00 20.00
❑ BAPK1 Peter Kelamis 5.00 12.00
❑ BAPL1 Piper Laurie 8.00 20.00
❑ BAPP1 Pat Priest 10.00 25.00
❑ BAPP2 Priscilla Presley 30.00 60.00
❑ BAPS1 Patrick Stewart 30.00 60.00
❑ BAPS2 Pauly Shore 6.00 15.00
❑ BAPW1 Patrick Warburton 12.00 30.00
❑ BARD1 Richard Dreyfuss 30.00 60.00
❑ BARG1 Rupert Grint 30.00 60.00
❑ BARH1 Richard The Old Man Harrison 12.00 30.00
❑ BARH2 Rick Harrison 20.00 40.00
❑ BARK1 Rodney King 30.00 60.00
❑ BARS1 Ramona Singer 5.00 12.00
❑ BASE1 Shannon Elizabeth 25.00 50.00
❑ BASK1 Sally Kellerman 6.00 15.00
❑ BASP1 Sarah Palin 50.00 100.00
❑ BASU1 Sara Underwood 25.00 50.00
❑ BASW1 Steve Wilkos 6.00 15.00
❑ BATB1 Toni Basil 10.00 25.00
❑ BATF1 Tom Felton 30.00 60.00
❑ BATG1 Teresa Giudice 6.00 15.00
❑ BATG2 Tracey Gold 8.00 20.00
❑ BATL1 Tommy Lee 20.00 40.00
❑ BATL2 Traci Lords 30.00 60.00
❑ BATP1 The Professor
❑ BATW1 Torrie Wilson 12.00 30.00
❑ BAVN1 Vince Neil 10.00 25.00
❑ BAVT1 Verne Troyer 8.00 20.00
❑ BAVW1 Van Williams 12.00 30.00
❑ BAWAZ Winter Ave Zoli 6.00 15.00
❑ BAYB1 Yancy Butler 6.00 15.00

2012 Pop Century Silver

*SILVER/25: .5X TO 1.2X BASIC CARD
STATED PRINT RUN 3-25
NO PRICING ON CARDS #'d TO 10 OR LESS

2012 Pop Century Blue

STATED PRINT RUN 2-5
UNPRICED DUE TO SCARCITY

2012 Pop Century Gold

STATED PRINT RUN 1 SER. #'d SET
UNPRICED DUE TO SCARCITY

2012 Pop Century Award Winners Autographs

❑ AWAB2 Amanda Beard 20.00 40.00
❑ AWAD1 Angie Dickinson 20.00 40.00
❑ AWAQ1 Aileen Quinn 8.00 20.00
❑ AWBR1 Brande Roderick 8.00 20.00
❑ AWBR2 Burt Reynolds 20.00 40.00
❑ AWCS1 Charlie Sheen 50.00 100.00
❑ AWCS2 Claire Sinclair 8.00 20.00
❑ AWEB1 Ernest Borgnine 20.00 40.00
❑ AWIS1 Ian Somerhalder 10.00 25.00
❑ AWJC1 Joanna Cassidy 6.00 15.00
❑ AWJJ1 Jenna Jameson 25.00 50.00
❑ AWJLO Jennifer Lopez 150.00 250.00
❑ AWJP2 Jeremy Piven 6.00 15.00
❑ AWJP3 Jon Provost 6.00 15.00
❑ AWJS1 Jordin Sparks 8.00 20.00
❑ AWKC1 Ken Climo 10.00 25.00
❑ AWLAW Lesley Ann Warren 8.00 20.00
❑ AWLF1 Lou Ferrigno 12.00 30.00
❑ AWMCD Michael Clarke Duncan 20.00 40.00
❑ AWML1 Martin Landau 12.00 30.00
❑ AWNH1 Natasha Henstridge 20.00 40.00
❑ AWPL1 Piper Laurie 8.00 20.00
❑ AWRG1 Rupert Grint 30.00 60.00
❑ AWTF1 Tom Felton 30.00 60.00
❑ AWTL1 Tommy Lee 20.00 40.00
❑ AWYB1 Yancy Butler 8.00 20.00

2012 Pop Century Co-Stars Autographs

❑ AB1PW1 Alex Borstein Patrick Warburton 8.00 20.00
❑ AP2LB1 Audrina Patridge Lo Bosworth 10.00 25.00
❑ AR1CH1 Chumlee Russell Big Hoss Harrison 25.00 50.00
❑ AS1CA1 Antonio Sabato Jr. Christina Applegate 20.00 40.00
❑ AW1BW1 Adam West Burt Ward 60.00 120.00
❑ BD1EB1 Bruce Dern Ernest Borgnine 20.00 40.00
❑ BD1MR1 Bruce Dern Mickey Rourke 12.00 30.00
❑ BK1FW1 Bernie Kopell Fred Williamson 8.00 20.00
❑ BZ1NK1 Billy Zane Nastassja Kinski 12.00 30.00
❑ CE1CS1 Carmen Electra Charlie Sheen
❑ EL1VT1 Emmanuel Lewis Verne Troyer 15.00 40.00
❑ GG1LN1 Gilbert Gottfried Laraine Newman 8.00 20.00
❑ GG1PS2 Gilbert Gottfried Pauly Shore 8.00 20.00
❑ JA1GG1 Jason Alexander Gilbert Gottfried 15.00 40.00
❑ JA2TB1 Julie Adams Toni Basil 8.00 20.00
❑ JC1PJS Joanna Cassidy P.J. Soles 10.00 25.00
❑ JN1EL1 Jay North Emmanuel Lewis 10.00 25.00
❑ JN1JP3 Jay North Jon Provost 15.00 40.00
❑ JP1IZ1 Jason Priestley Ian Ziering 12.00 30.00
❑ JS2NK1 Julian Sands Nastassja Kinski 20.00 40.00
❑ KB2RS1 Kelly Bensimon Ramona Singer 8.00 20.00
❑ PA1CE1 Pamela Anderson Carmen Electra
❑ RH1RH2 Richard The Old Man Harrison Rick Harrison 30.00 60.00
❑ SK1FW1 Sally Kellerman Fred Williamson 10.00 25.00
❑ SK1VW1 Sally Kellerman Van Williams 15.00 40.00
❑ SP1BP1 Sarah Palin Bristol Palin
❑ VN1TL1 Vince Neil Tommy Lee 40.00 80.00
❑ PSC Richard Harrison Rick Harrison/Corey Harrison/Austin Russell 100.00 200.00
❑ SofM Charmain Carr Nicholas Hammond/Heather Menzies/Duane Chase/Angela Cartwright/Debbie Turner/Kym Karath 300.00 450.00

2012 Pop Century Dressing Room Autograph Memorabilia

RANDOM INSERT IN PACKS

❑ DRBS1 Britney Spears
❑ DRCS1 Charlie Sheen 75.00 150.00
❑ DRJP1 Jeremy Piven 25.00 50.00
❑ DRPA1 Pamela Anderson
❑ DRWS1 Richard Dreyfuss 25.00 50.00

2012 Pop Century Inscriptions Autographs Priscilla Presley

❑ IPP2a Priscilla Presley 75.00 150.00
❑ IPP2b Priscilla Presley/25 100.00 175.00
❑ IPP2c Priscilla Presley/5
❑ IPP2d Priscilla Presley/1

2012 Pop Century Keeping It Real Autographs

❑ KRAE1 Angie Everhart 10.00 25.00
❑ KRAF1 Amy Fisher 10.00 25.00
❑ KRAP1 Angelina Pivarnick 5.00 12.00
❑ KRAR1 Austin Chumlee Russell 20.00 40.00
❑ KRASJ Antonio Sabato Jr. 5.00 12.00
❑ KRBE1 Barbara Eden 25.00 50.00
❑ KRBH1 Brooke Hogan 20.00 40.00
❑ KRBP1 Bristol Palin 20.00 40.00
❑ KRBR1 Brande Roderick 8.00 20.00
❑ KRCE1 Carmen Electra 20.00 40.00
❑ KRCH1 Corey Big Hoss Harrison 12.00 30.00
❑ KRCM1 Cindy Margolis 8.00 20.00
❑ KRCP1 Cassandra Peterson 30.00 60.00
❑ KRDMX DMX 10.00 25.00
❑ KRDTJ Donald Trump Jr. 8.00 20.00
❑ KREE1 Erik Estrada 8.00 20.00
❑ KREL1 Emmanuel Lewis 8.00 20.00
❑ KREM1 Erin Moran
❑ KRGR1 Gretchen Rossi 6.00 15.00
❑ KRHF2 Heidi Fleiss 10.00 25.00
❑ KRJH1 Jessica Hall 6.00 15.00
❑ KRJLO Jennifer Lopez
❑ KRJS1 Jordin Sparks 10.00 25.00
❑ KRKB2 Kelly Bensimon 5.00 12.00
❑ KRKC2 Kristin Cavallari 10.00 25.00
❑ KRKS1 Kristy Swanson 10.00 25.00
❑ KRLB1 Lo Bosworth 5.00 12.00
❑ KRLF1 Lou Ferrigno 12.00 30.00
❑ KRLL2 Lorenzo Lamas 5.00 12.00
❑ KRMF1 Morgan Fairchild 12.00 30.00
❑ KRRH1 Richard The Old Man Harrison 12.00 30.00
❑ KRRH2 Rick Harrison 15.00 40.00
❑ KRRK1 Rodney King 25.00 50.00

❑ KRRS1 Ramona Singer 5.00 12.00
❑ KRSE1 Shannon Elizabeth 25.00 50.00
❑ KRSW1 Steve Wilkos 5.00 12.00
❑ KRTG1 Teresa Giudice 6.00 15.00
❑ KRTG2 Tracey Gold 8.00 20.00
❑ KRTW1 Torrie Wilson 12.00 30.00

2012 Pop Century Stunning Starlets Autographs

RANDOM INSERT IN PACKS
❑ SSAB2 Amanda Beard 15.00 40.00
❑ SSAC1 Arianny Celeste 20.00 40.00
❑ SSAD1 Angie Dickinson 20.00 40.00
❑ SSAE1 Angie Everhart 12.00 30.00
❑ SSBH1 Brooke Hogan 25.00 50.00
❑ SSBR1 Brande Roderick 10.00 25.00
❑ SSCM1 Cindy Margolis 10.00 25.00
❑ SSCS2 Claire Sinclair 10.00 25.00
❑ SSDS1 Dominique Swain 12.00 30.00
❑ SSEP1 Emily Procter 10.00 25.00
❑ SSGG2 Gina Gershon 25.00 50.00
❑ SSGR1 Gretchen Rossi 8.00 20.00
❑ SSJH1 Jessica Hall 8.00 20.00
❑ SSJJ1 Jenna Jameson 30.00 60.00
❑ SSJLO Jennifer Lopez 175.00 300.00
❑ SSKB2 Kelly Bensimon 8.00 20.00
❑ SSKC2 Kristin Cavallari 8.00 20.00
❑ SSKS1 Kristy Swanson 12.00 30.00
❑ SSLB1 Lo Bosworth 8.00 20.00
❑ SSMF1 Morgan Fairchild 15.00 40.00
❑ SSNH1 Natasha Henstridge 20.00 40.00
❑ SSNK1 Nastassja Kinski 30.00 60.00
❑ SSPL1 Piper Laurie 10.00 25.00
❑ SSPP2 Priscilla Presley 40.00 80.00
❑ SSSE1 Shannon Elizabeth 25.00 50.00
❑ SSSU1 Sara Underwood 25.00 50.00
❑ SSTL2 Traci Lords 30.00 60.00
❑ SSTW1 Torrie Wilson 12.00 30.00
❑ SSWAZ Winter Ave Zoli 8.00 20.00

2012 The Quotable Star Trek Voyager

COMPLETE SET (72) 5.00 12.00
❑ 1 The Caretaker .15 .40
❑ 2 The Caretaker .15 .40
❑ 3 The Caretaker .15
❑ 4 The Caretaker .15 .40
❑ 5 The Caretaker .15 .40
❑ 6 The Caretaker .15 .40
❑ 7 The Caretaker .15 .40
❑ 8 Time and Again .15 .40
❑ 9 The Cloud .15 .40
❑ 10 Parallax .15 .40
❑ 11 Twisted .15 .40
❑ 12 Phage .15 .40
❑ 13 The Cloud .15 .40
❑ 14 Emanations .15 .40
❑ 15 Prime Factors .15 .40
❑ 16 Faces .15 .40
❑ 17 Learning Curve .15 .40
❑ 18 The 37's .15 .40
❑ 19 Parallax .15 .40
❑ 20 Twisted .15 .40
❑ 21 Future's End, Part II .15 .40
❑ 22 Flesh and Blood .15 .40
❑ 23 Prototype .15 .40
❑ 24 Gravity .15 .40
❑ 25 Lifeline .15 .40
❑ 26 Message in a Bottle .15 .40
❑ 27 Displaced .15 .40
❑ 28 Tattoo .15 .40
❑ 29 Tattoo .15 .40
❑ 30 Cold Fire .15 .40
❑ 31 Alliances .15 .40
❑ 32 Death Wish .15 .40
❑ 33 Death Wish .15 .40
❑ 34 Death Wish .15 .40
❑ 35 Deadlock .15 .40
❑ 36 Innocence .15 .40
❑ 37 Flashback .15 .40
❑ 38 Basics, Part II .15 .40
❑ 39 Innocence .15 .40
❑ 40 Basics, Part II .15 .40
❑ 41 The Chute .15 .40
❑ 42 False Profits .15 .40
❑ 43 Future's End, Part I .15 .40
❑ 44 The Q and the Grey .15 .40
❑ 45 Darkling .15 .40
❑ 46 Before and After .15 .40
❑ 47 Displaced .15 .40
❑ 48 Displaced .15 .40
❑ 49 Worst Case Scenario .15 .40
❑ 50 Scorpion, Part I .15 .40
❑ 51 Scorpion, Part II .15 .40
❑ 52 The Gift .15 .40
❑ 53 The Gift .15 .40
❑ 54 The Gift .15 .40
❑ 55 Nemesis .15 .40
❑ 56 Revulsion .15 .40
❑ 57 The Raven .15 .40
❑ 58 Concerning Flight .15 .40
❑ 59 Year of Hell, Part II .15 .40
❑ 60 Random Thoughts .15 .40
❑ 61 Mortal Coil .15 .40
❑ 62 Hunters .15 .40
❑ 63 Prey .15 .40
❑ 64 Prey .15 .40
❑ 65 The Killing Game, Part II .15 .40
❑ 66 One .15 .40
❑ 67 Hope and Fear .15 .40
❑ 68 Drive .15 .40
❑ 69 Course: Oblivion .15 .40
❑ 70 Fair Heaven .15 .40
❑ 71 Ashes to Ashes .15 .40
❑ 72 Endgame .15 .40
❑ DF Delta Flyer PROP 100.00 175.00
(issued as a 3-case incentive)
❑ KM Kate Mulgrew 125.00 250.00
as Capt. Janeway AU MEM/(issued as a 6-case incentive)
❑ CC45 Captain Janeway MEM 25.00 50.00
(issued as case topper)

2012 The Quotable Star Trek Voyager Autographs

STATED ODDS 1:8
L (LIMITED): 300-500 COPIES
VL (VERY LIMITED): 200-300 COPIES
EL (EXTREMELY LIMITED): LESS THAN 200
❑ 1 Alicia Coppola 4.00 10.00
as Lt. Stadi L
❑ 2 Andy Dick 5.00 12.00
as EMH Mark II L
❑ 3 Andy Milder 4.00 10.00
as NAR
❑ 4 Anthony DeLongis 4.00 10.00
as First Maje Culluh L
❑ 5 Aron Eisenberg 4.00 10.00
as Kar L
❑ 6 Don Most 5.00 12.00
as Kadan L
❑ 7 Ed Begley, Jr. 12.00 30.00
as Henry Starling VL
❑ 8 Eric Pierpoint 8.00 20.00
as Kortar VL
❑ 9 Estelle Harris 20.00 40.00
as Old Woman EL
❑ 10 Ethan Phillips 25.00 50.00
as Neelix EL
❑ 11 Garrett Wang 25.00 50.00
as Harry Kim EL
❑ 12 Gregory Itzin 4.00 10.00
as Dr. Dysek
❑ 13 Harry Groener 6.00 15.00
as The Magistrate VL
❑ 14 J.G. Hertzler 4.00 10.00
as Hirogen Fighter L
❑ 15 Jeffrey Combs 5.00 12.00
as Penk L
❑ 16 Jennifer Lien 30.00 60.00
as Kes EL
❑ 17 Jeri Ryan 75.00 150.00
as Seven of Nine EL
❑ 18 John Aniston 4.00 10.00
as Quarren Ambassador L
❑ 19 John DeLancie 25.00 50.00
as Q EL
❑ 20 John Rhys-Davies 30.00 60.00
as Leonardo da Vinci EL
❑ 21 John Savage 5.00 12.00
as Captain Rudy Ransom L
❑ 22 Josh Clark 4.00 10.00
as Lt. Joe Carey
❑ 23 Karen Austin 8.00 20.00
as Miral VL
❑ 24 Kate Mulgrew 50.00 100.00
as Captain Janeway EL
❑ 25 Kathleen Garrett 4.00 10.00
as Tanis L
❑ 26 Kevin Tighe 6.00 15.00
as Henry Janeway
❑ 27 Kristanna Loken 35.00 70.00
as Malia EL
❑ 28 Leigh McCloskey 8.00 20.00
as Tieran VL
❑ 29 Leslie Jordan 4.00 10.00
as Kol
❑ 30 Manu Intiraymi 4.00 10.00
as Icheb L
❑ 31 Mark Harelik 4.00 10.00
as Kashyk L
❑ 32 Martha Hackett 8.00 20.00
as Seska VL
❑ 33 Martin Rayner 4.00 10.00
as Dr. Chaotica
❑ 34 Michael McKean 4.00 10.00
as The Clown L
❑ 35 Richard Herd 4.00 10.00
as Admiral Paris
❑ 36 Robert Beltran 35.00 70.00
as Chakotay EL
❑ 37 Robert Duncan McNeill 25.00 50.00
as Tom Paris EL
❑ 38 Robert Picardo 25.00 50.00
as The Doctor EL
❑ 39 Robin Sachs 4.00 10.00
as General Valen L
❑ 40 Roxann Dawson 35.00 70.00
as B'Elanna Torres EL
❑ 41 Scarlett Pomers 12.00 30.00
as Naomi Wildman VL
❑ 42 Sharon Lawrence 5.00 12.00
as Amelia Earhardt L
❑ 43 Susan Diol 4.00 10.00
as Danara Pel L
❑ 44 Susanna Thompson 20.00 40.00
as Borg Queen VL
❑ 45 Suzie Plakson 4.00 10.00
as Female Q L
❑ 46 Tim Russ 25.00 50.00
as Tuvok EL
❑ 47 Virgina Madsen 12.00 30.00
❑ 48 Zach Galligan 4.00 10.00
as Ensign David Gentry L

2012 The Quotable Star Trek Voyager Best of the Holodeck

COMPLETE SET (9) 5.00 12.00
STATED ODDS 1:12
❑ H1 Heroes and Demons 1.25 3.00
❑ H2 Warlord 1.25 3.00
❑ H3 Alter Ego 1.25 3.00
❑ H4 Concerning Flight 1.25 3.00
❑ H5 The Killing Game 1.25 3.00
❑ H6 Once Upon a Time 1.25 3.00
❑ H7 Bride of Chaotica 1.25 3.00
❑ H8 Fair Haven 1.25 3.00
❑ H9 Human Error 1.25 3.00

2012 The Quotable Star Trek Voyager Communicator Pins

STATED ODDS 1:96
STATED PRINT RUN 225 SER. #'d SETS
❑ 1 Captain Janeway 25.00 50.00
❑ 2 Chakotay 20.00 40.00
❑ 3 The Doctor 20.00 40.00
❑ 4 B'Elanna Torres 20.00 40.00
❑ 5 Tom Paris 20.00 40.00
❑ 6 Neelix 20.00 40.00
❑ 7 Seven of Nine 25.00 50.00
❑ 8 Tuvok 20.00 40.00
❑ 9 Harry Kim 20.00 40.00

2012 The Quotable Star Trek Voyager Starfleet's Finest

COMPLETE SET (10) 125.00 200.00
STATED ODDS 1:48
STATED PRINT RUN 399 SER. #'d SETS
❑ F1 Captain Janeway 10.00 25.00
❑ F2 Seven of Nine 12.00 30.00
❑ F3 Chakotay 10.00 25.00
❑ F4 Tom Paris 10.00 25.00
❑ F5 Harry Kim 10.00 25.00
❑ F6 B'Elanna Torres 10.00 25.00
❑ F7 Neelix 10.00 25.00
❑ F8 The Doctor 10.00 25.00
❑ F9 Tuvok 10.00 25.00
❑ F10 Kes 10.00 25.00

2012 The Quotable Star Trek Voyager U.S.S. Voyager

COMPLETE SET (9) 4.00 10.00
STATED ODDS 1:12
❑ V1 U.S.S. Voyager 1.00 2.50
❑ V2 U.S.S. Voyager 1.00 2.50
❑ V3 U.S.S. Voyager 1.00 2.50
❑ V4 U.S.S. Voyager 1.00 2.50
❑ V5 U.S.S. Voyager 1.00 2.50
❑ V6 U.S.S. Voyager 1.00 2.50
❑ V7 U.S.S. Voyager 1.00 2.50
❑ V8 U.S.S. Voyager 1.00 2.50
❑ V9 U.S.S. Voyager 1.00 2.50

2012 Smallville Seasons Seven Through Ten

COMPLETE SET (85) 8.00 20.00
❑ 1 Smallville The Final Seasons .15 .40
❑ 2 Clark Kent .15 .40
❑ 3 Lois Lane .15 .40
❑ 4 Chloe Sullivan .15 .40
❑ 5 Oliver Queen .15 .40
❑ 6 Tess Mercer .15 .40
❑ 7 Lex Luthor .15 .40
❑ 8 Jimmy Olsen .15 .40
❑ 9 Davis Bloom .15 .40
❑ 10 Zod .15 .40
❑ 11 Lana Lang .15 .40
❑ 12 Lionel Luthor .15 .40
❑ 13 Kara Zor-El Kent .15 .40
❑ 14 Jonathan Kent .15 .40
❑ 15 A Dark Challenge .15 .40
❑ 16 Ally or Enemy .15 .40
❑ 17 Bad and the Beautiful .15 .40
❑ 18 Mad Doctor of Smallville .15 .40
❑ 19 Warrior Angel .15 .40
❑ 20 Dreams of the Past .15 .40
❑ 21 A Powerful Paycheck .15 .40
❑ 22 Fortress Under Siege .15 .40
❑ 23 The Imperiled .15 .40
❑ 24 Lure of Dark Clark .15 .40
❑ 25 The Canary's Cry .15 .40
❑ 26 The Best of Lex .15 .40
❑ 27 The Powers of Pete Ross .15 .40
❑ 28 The Captive Clark .15 .40
❑ 29 Target: Lana Lang .15 .40
❑ 30 The Killing of Lionel .15 .40
❑ 31 The Reluctant Spy .15 .40
❑ 32 Another Path .15 .40
❑ 33 The Last Survivor .15 .40
❑ 34 The Truth Revealed .15 .40
❑ 35 In Search of Clark .15 .40
❑ 36 Explosive .15 .40
❑ 37 The Poisoning .15 .40
❑ 38 Their Love Revealed .15 .40
❑ 39 Killers at Large .15 .40
❑ 40 Mystery Solved .15 .40
❑ 41 The Bride of Zod .15 .40
❑ 42 The Infection .15 .40
❑ 43 The Wedding Crasher .15 .40
❑ 44 The Truth About Lana .15 .40
❑ 45 The Grudge .15 .40
❑ 46 Revelations .15 .40
❑ 47 Dangerous Crossings .15 .40
❑ 48 Metamorphosis .15 .40
❑ 49 Bloome's Legacy .15 .40
❑ 50 Unstable .15 .40
❑ 51 The Provokers .15 .40
❑ 52 Destiny of a Hero .15 .40
❑ 53 A New Beginning .15 .40
❑ 54 The Toyman Plays Again .15 .40
❑ 55 Speedy Betrayal .15 .40
❑ 56 Future Shock .15 .40
❑ 57 The Big Chill .15 .40
❑ 58 The Enchanted Comic .15 .40
❑ 59 What You Wish For .15 .40
❑ 60 Blood of a Hero .15 .40
❑ 61 Night of the Banshee .15 .40
❑ 62 A Most Dangerous Game .15 .40
❑ 63 The Return of Metallo .15 .40
❑ 64 After the Blur .15 .40
❑ 65 Threat of the Kandorians .15 .40
❑ 66 Battlefield Earth .15 .40
❑ 67 Chloe's Sacrifice .15 .40
❑ 68 Enter Cat Grant .15 .40
❑ 69 Going Public .15 .40
❑ 70 Reunion in Smallville .15 .40
❑ 71 A Goddess Reborn .15 .40
❑ 72 The Deadly Years .15 .40
❑ 73 The Orphanage .15 .40
❑ 74 Oliver's Ordeal .15 .40
❑ 75 Killer Clark .15 .40
❑ 76 Fall of a Hero .15 .40
❑ 77 Suspicion .15 .40
❑ 78 Threat of Desaad .15 .40
❑ 79 Name of the Game .15 .40
❑ 80 Return of a Killer .15 .40
❑ 81 Escape from the Phantom Zone .15 .40
❑ 82 Farewell to Smallville .15 .40
❑ 83 The Wedding .15 .40
❑ 84 Superman's Debut .15 .40
❑ 85 Checklist .15 .40

2012 Smallville Seasons Seven Through Ten Authentic Wardrobe

STATED ODDS THREE PER BOX
❑ M1 Clark Kent's Red Jacket 12.00 30.00
❑ M2 Clark Kent's Blue T-Shirt 12.00 30.00
❑ M3 Clark Kent's Dark Blue T-Shirt 12.00 30.00
❑ M4 Clark Kent's Black Blur Jacket 12.00 30.00
❑ M5 Clark Kent's Red Shield Jacket 15.00 40.00
❑ M6 Clark Kent's Red T-Shirt 10.00 25.00
❑ M7 Clark Kent's Blue Dress Shirt 10.00 25.00
❑ M8 Davis Bloome's Gray T-Shirt 8.00 20.00
❑ M9 Davis Bloome's Jacket 8.00 20.00
❑ M10 Davis Bloome's Blue Button-up Shirt 8.00 20.00
❑ M11 Jimmy Olsen's Blue Button-up Shirt 10.00 25.00
❑ M12 Lois Lane's Pink Wrap Top 15.00 40.00
❑ M13 Lois Lane's Purple Top 15.00 40.00
❑ M14 Chloe Sullivan's Green Dress 15.00 40.00
❑ M15 Chloe Sullivan's Plum Shirt 20.00 50.00
❑ M16 Kara Kent's Turquoise Crop Hoodie 30.00 60.00
❑ M17 Major Zod's Red Sweater 8.00 20.00
❑ M18 Major Zod's Military Jacket 8.00 20.00
❑ M19 Major Zod's Black Tank 8.00 20.00
❑ M20 Tess Mercer's Green Tank 25.00 50.00
❑ M21 Tess Mercer's Beige Tank 25.00 50.00
❑ M22 Tess Mercer's Green Military Pants 15.00 40.00
❑ M23 Tess Mercer's Red Blouse 15.00 40.00
❑ M24 Lionel Luthor's Black Dress Shirt 8.00 20.00
❑ M25 Lionel Luthor's Gray Dress Shirt 8.00 20.00
❑ M26 Linda Lake's Teal Dress 12.00 30.00
❑ M27 Dr. Curtis Knox's Leather Apron 10.00 25.00
❑ M28 Milton Fine's Black Shirt 8.00 20.00
❑ M29 Milton Fine's Green T-Shirt 8.00 20.00
❑ M30 Clark Kent's Black T-Shirt 10.00 25.00

2012 Smallville Seasons Seven Through Ten Autographs

STATED ODDS ONE PER BOX
❑ A1 Cassidy Freeman 35.00 70.00
as Tess Mercer
❑ A2 Justin Hartley 30.00 60.00
as Oliver Queen
❑ A3 Callum Blue 12.00 30.00
as Major Zod
❑ A4 John Glover 35.00 70.00
as Lionel Luthor
❑ A5 Sam Witwer 10.00 25.00
as Davis Bloome
❑ A6 Aaron Ashmore 40.00 80.00
as Jimmy Olsen
❑ A7 Eric Johnson 30.00 60.00
as Whitney Fordman
❑ A8 Laura Vandervoort 100.00 200.00
as Kara
❑ A9 Margot Kidder 45.00 90.00
as Dr. Bridgette Crosby
❑ A10 Dean Cain 15.00 40.00
as Dr. Curtis Cox
❑ A11 Tori Spelling 15.00 40.00
as Linda Lake
❑ A12 John Schneider 75.00 125.00
as Jonathan Kent
❑ A13 James Marsters 35.00 70.00
as Professor Milton Fine
❑ A14 Terence Stamp 40.00 80.00
as The Voice of Jor-El

2012 Smallville Seasons Seven Through Ten Behind the Scenes

COMPLETE SET (9) 8.00 20.00
RANDOM INSERT IN PACKS
❑ BTS1 Clark Kent vs. Green Arrow 1.50 4.00
❑ BTS2 Lex Luthor: Dead Man 1.50 4.00
❑ BTS3 New Direction 1.50 4.00
❑ BTS4 Heartthrob 1.50 4.00
❑ BTS5 Trouble in the Fortress of Solitude 1.50 4.00
❑ BTS6 Clark and Kara Kent 1.50 4.00
❑ BTS7 Lois Lane in Trouble 1.50 4.00
❑ BTS8 A Very Special Costume 1.50 4.00
❑ BTS9 Linda Lake's Take 1.50 4.00

2012 Smallville Seasons Seven Through Ten Clark and Lois

COMPLETE SET (9) 12.00 30.00
RANDOM INSERT IN PACKS
❑ LC1 A Distressing Damsel 2.00 5.00
❑ LC2 Daily Planet Drama 2.00 5.00
❑ LC3 Trouble in the Phantom Zone 2.00 5.00
❑ LC4 Clark Really Notices Lois 2.00 5.00
❑ LC5 Reporting Partners 2.00 5.00
❑ LC6 In Love 2.00 5.00
❑ LC7 Revelation 2.00 5.00
❑ LC8 Destiny 2.00 5.00
❑ LC9 Together Forever 2.00 5.00

2012 Smallville Seasons Seven Through Ten Oversized Dual Wardrobe

EXCH DEADLINE 3/20/2013
❑ R1 Clark Kent Red Jkt
Blue Shirt EXCH
❑ R2 Clark Kent Red Jkt
Blue Shirt EXCH
❑ R3 Clark Kent Red Jkt
Blue Shirt EXCH
❑ R4 Clark Kent Red Jkt
Blue Shirt EXCH
❑ R5 Clark Kent Red Jkt
Blue Shirt EXCH
❑ R6 Clark Kent Red Jkt
Blue Shirt EXCH
❑ R7 Clark Kent Red Jkt
Blue Shirt EXCH
❑ R8 Clark Kent Red Jkt
Blue Shirt EXCH
❑ R9 Clark Kent Red Jkt
Blue Shirt EXCH
❑ R10 Clark Kent Red Jkt
Blue Shirt EXCH
❑ R11 Clark Kent Red Jkt
Blue Shirt EXCH
❑ R12 Clark Kent Red Jkt
Blue Shirt EXCH
❑ R13 Clark Kent Red Jkt
Blue Shirt EXCH
❑ R14 Clark Kent Red Jkt
Blue Shirt EXCH
❑ R15 Clark Kent Red Jkt
Blue Shirt EXCH
❑ R16 Clark Kent Red Jkt
Blue Shirt EXCH
❑ R17 Clark Kent Red Jkt
Blue Shirt EXCH
❑ R18 Clark Kent Red Jkt
Blue Shirt EXCH
❑ R19 Clark Kent Red Jkt
Blue Shirt EXCH
❑ R20 Clark Kent Red Jkt
Blue Shirt EXCH
❑ R21 Clark Kent Red Jkt
Blue Shirt EXCH
❑ R22 Clark Kent Red Jkt
Blue Shirt EXCH
❑ R23 Clark Kent Red Jkt
Blue Shirt EXCH
❑ R24 Clark Kent Red Jkt
Blue Shirt EXCH
❑ R25 Clark Kent Red Jkt
Blue Shirt EXCH

2012 Smallville Seasons Seven Through Ten Promos

❑ P1 Clark Kent black jacket 2.00 5.00
(NSU Magazine)
❑ P2 Clark Kent red jacket 2.00 5.00
(C2E2)
❑ P3 Lois Lane/Clark Kent 1.50 4.00
(Non-Sport Philly)

2012 Spartacus Gods of the Arena

COMPLETE SET (18) 20.00 50.00
❑ G1 Past Transgressions 2.00 5.00
❑ G2 Past Transgressions 2.00 5.00
❑ G3 Past Transgressions 2.00 5.00
❑ G4 Missio 2.00 5.00
❑ G5 Missio 2.00 5.00
❑ G6 Missio 2.00 5.00
❑ G7 Paterfamilias 2.00 5.00
❑ G8 Paterfamilias 2.00 5.00
❑ G9 Paterfamilias 2.00 5.00
❑ G10 Beneath the Mask 2.00 5.00
❑ G11 Beneath the Mask 2.00 5.00
❑ G12 Beneath the Mask 2.00 5.00
❑ G13 Reckoning 2.00 5.00
❑ G14 Reckoning 2.00 5.00
❑ G15 Reckoning 2.00 5.00
❑ G16 The Bitter End 2.00 5.00
❑ G17 The Bitter End 2.00 5.00
❑ G18 The Bitter End 2.00 5.00
❑ CC1 Spartacus COSTUME 50.00 100.00
(issued as 2-box incentive)
❑ NNO Andy Whitfield Memorial Shadowbox 25.00 50.00
(issued as box topper)

2012 Spartacus Gods of the Arena Autographs

STATED ODDS TWO PER PACK
L (LIMITED): 300-500 COPIES
VL (VERY LIMITED): 200-300 COPIES
EL (EXTREMELY LIMITED): 200 OR LESS
❑ 1 Craig Walsh Wrightson as Solonius VL 20.00 40.00
❑ 2 David Austin as Medicus L 6.00 15.00
❑ 3 Dustin Clare as Gannicus VL 75.00 150.00
❑ 4 Gareth Williams as Vettius L 6.00 15.00
❑ 5 Jaime Murray as Gaia EL 75.00 150.00
❑ 6 Jason Hood as Cossutius L 6.00 15.00
❑ 7 Jeffrey Thomas as Titus L 6.00 15.00
❑ 8 Jessica Grace Smith as Diona L 10.00 25.00
❑ 9 John Bach as Magistrate Calavius L 6.00 15.00
❑ 10 John Hannah as Batiatus EL 60.00 120.00
❑ 11 Lliam Powell as Numerius L 6.00 15.00
❑ 12 Lucy Lawless as Lucretia EL 60.00 120.00
❑ 13 Manu Bennett as Crixis VL 20.00 50.00
❑ 14 Nick Tarabay as Ashur VL 15.00 30.00
❑ 15 Peter Feeney as Quintilius Varis L 6.00 15.00
❑ 16 Peter Mensah as Doctore 100.00 200.00
(issued as 4-box incentive)
❑ 17 Reuben de Jong as Theokoles L 8.00 20.00
❑ 18 Shane Rangi as Dagan L 6.00 15.00
❑ 19 Stephen Lovatt as Tullius L 6.00 15.00
❑ 20 Temuera Morrison as Doctore L 8.00 20.00

2012 Spartacus Gods of the Arena Battle for Freedom

COMPLETE SET (9) 15.00 30.00
STATED ODDS ONE PER PACK
❑ B1 Battle for Freedom 2.50 6.00
❑ B2 Battle for Freedom 2.50 6.00
❑ B3 Battle for Freedom 2.50 6.00
❑ B4 Battle for Freedom 2.50 6.00
❑ B5 Battle for Freedom 2.50 6.00
❑ B6 Battle for Freedom 2.50 6.00
❑ B7 Battle for Freedom 2.50 6.00
❑ B8 Battle for Freedom 2.50 6.00
❑ B9 Battle for Freedom 2.50 6.00

2012 Spartacus Gods of the Arena Die-Cut Gold Plaques

COMPLETE SET (12) 30.00 60.00
STATED ODDS ONE PER PACK
❑ GB1 Spartacus BAS 3.00 8.00
❑ GB2 Lucretia BAS 3.00 8.00
❑ GB3 Batiatus BAS 3.00 8.00
❑ GB4 Crixus BAS 3.00 8.00
❑ GB5 Doctore BAS 3.00 8.00
❑ GB6 Ilithya BAS 3.00 8.00
❑ GG1 Gannicus GOTA 3.00 8.00
❑ GG2 Gaia GOTA 3.00 8.00
❑ GG3 Solonius GOTA 3.00 8.00
❑ GG4 Ashur GOTA 3.00 8.00
❑ GG5 Tullius GOTA 3.00 8.00
❑ GG6 Melitta GOTA 3.00 8.00
❑ GG7 Barca GOTA SP 20.00 50.00
(issued as Rittenhouse Reward)

2012 Spartacus Gods of the Arena Gladiators In Action

COMPLETE SET (9) 15.00 30.00
STATED ODDS ONE PER PACK
❑ G1 Gladiators In Action 2.50 6.00
❑ G2 Gladiators In Action 2.50 6.00
❑ G3 Gladiators In Action 2.50 6.00
❑ G4 Gladiators In Action 2.50 6.00
❑ G5 Gladiators In Action 2.50 6.00
❑ G6 Gladiators In Action 2.50 6.00
❑ G7 Gladiators In Action 2.50 6.00
❑ G8 Gladiators In Action 2.50 6.00
❑ G9 Gladiators In Action 2.50 6.00

2012 Spartacus Gods of the Arena Promos

COMPLETE SET (2)
❑ P1 Spartacus
Gannicus/ (General Distribution)
❑ P2 Albums Exclusive

2012 Spartacus Gods of the Arena Vengeance

COMPLETE SET (9) 15.00 30.00
STATED ODDS ONE PER PACK
❑ V1 Vengeance 2.50 6.00
❑ V2 Vengeance 2.50 6.00
❑ V3 Vengeance 2.50 6.00
❑ V4 Vengeance 2.50 6.00
❑ V5 Vengeance 2.50 6.00
❑ V6 Vengeance 2.50 6.00
❑ V7 Vengeance 2.50 6.00
❑ V8 Vengeance 2.50 6.00
❑ V9 Vengeance 2.50 6.00

2012 Spartacus Gods of the Arena Women of Spartacus

COMPLETE SET (9) 20.00 40.00
COMPLETE SET 3.00 8.00
STATED ODDS ONE PER PACK
❑ WB1 Lucretia 3.00 8.00
❑ WB2 Ilithya 3.00 8.00

☐ WB3 Naevia 3.00 8.00
☐ WB4 Sura 3.00 8.00
☐ WB5 Mira 3.00 8.00
☐ WG1 Lucretia 3.00 8.00
☐ WG2 Gaia 3.00 8.00
☐ WG3 Naevia 3.00 8.00
☐ WG4 Melitta 3.00 8.00

2012 Sports Illustrated Swimsuit Decade of Supermodels

COMPLETE SET (70) 10.00 25.00
☐ 1 Ana Beatriz Barros .40 1.00
☐ 2 Angela Lindvall .40 1.00
☐ 3 Audrey Quock .40 1.00
☐ 4 Alicia Hall .40 1.00
☐ 5 Aline Nakashima .40 1.00
☐ 6 Amanda Beard .40 1.00
☐ 7 Ana Paula Araujo .40 1.00
☐ 8 Anne V .40 1.00
☐ 9 Ariel Meredith .40 1.00
☐ 10 Bridget Hall .40 1.00
☐ 11 Bar Refaeli .40 1.00
☐ 12 Beyonce 1.00 2.50
☐ 13 Brooklyn Decker .75 2.00
☐ 14 Carla Campbell .40 1.00
☐ 15 Carolyn Murphy .40 1.00
☐ 16 Chandra North .40 1.00
☐ 17 Cintia Dicker .40 1.00
☐ 18 Danica Patrick 6.00 15.00
☐ 19 Daniela Pestova .40 1.00
☐ 20 Daniella Sarahyba .40 1.00
☐ 21 Damaris Lewis .40 1.00
☐ 22 Sarah O'Hare .40 1.00
☐ 23 Elsa Benitez .40 1.00
☐ 24 Elle Macpherson .60 1.50
☐ 25 Esti Ginzburg .40 1.00
☐ 26 Fernanda Motta .40 1.00
☐ 27 Frankie Rayder .40 1.00
☐ 28 Fernanda Tavares .40 1.00
☐ 29 Heidi Klum .60 1.50
☐ 30 Hilary Rhoda .40 1.00
☐ 31 Isabeli Fontana .40 1.00
☐ 32 Irina Shayk .40 1.00
☐ 33 Jessica Van Deer Steen .40 1.00
☐ 34 Jessica White .40 1.00
☐ 35 Jarah Mariano .40 1.00
☐ 36 Jeisa Chiminazzo .40 1.00
☐ 37 Jessica Gomes .40 1.00
☐ 38 Jessica Hart .40 1.00
☐ 39 Julie Henderson .40 1.00
☐ 40 Kim Cloutier .40 1.00
☐ 41 Lucia Dvorska .40 1.00
☐ 42 Melissa Keller .40 1.00
☐ 43 Michelle Alves .40 1.00
☐ 44 May Anderson .40 1.00
☐ 45 Michelle Lombardo .40 1.00
☐ 46 Mallory Snyder .40 1.00
☐ 47 Maria Sharapova 2.00 5.00
☐ 48 Marisa Miller .60 1.50
☐ 49 Melissa Baker .40 1.00
☐ 50 Melissa Haro .40 1.00
☐ 51 Molly Sims .40 1.00
☐ 52 Noemie Lenoir .40 1.00
☐ 53 Oluchi Onweagba .40 1.00
☐ 54 Pania Rose .40 1.00
☐ 55 Petra Nemcova .40 1.00
☐ 56 Paulina Porizkova .40 1.00
☐ 57 Quiana Grant .40 1.00
☐ 58 Rachel Hunter .40 1.00
☐ 59 Racia Oliveria .40 1.00
☐ 60 Rebecca Romijn .40 1.00
☐ 61 Reka Ekergenyi .40 1.00
☐ 62 Stacey Williams .40 1.00
☐ 63 Shakara Ledard .40 1.00
☐ 64 Selita Ebanks .40 1.00
☐ 65 Tori Praver .40 1.00
☐ 66 Veronica Varekova .40 1.00
☐ 67 Yamila Diaz-Rahi .40 1.00
☐ 68 Yesica Toscanini .40 1.00
☐ 69 Yasmin Brunet .40 1.00
☐ 70 Checklist .40 1.00

2012 Sports Illustrated Swimsuit Decade of Supermodels Celebrities

COMPLETE SET (10) 12.00 30.00
STATED ODDS FOUR PER BOX
☐ C1 Amanda Beard 2.00 5.00
☐ C2 Beyonce 3.00 8.00
☐ C3 Brooklyn Decker 2.50 6.00
☐ C4 Danica Patrick 6.00 15.00
☐ C5 Daniela Hantuchova 2.00 5.00
☐ C6 Elle Macpherson 2.00 5.00
☐ C7 Maria Kirilenko 2.00 5.00
☐ C8 Maria Sharapova 4.00 10.00
☐ C9 Molly Sims 2.00 5.00
☐ C10 Tatiana Golovin 2.00 5.00

2012 Sports Illustrated Swimsuit Decade of Supermodels Danica Patrick Memorabilia

STATED ODDS ONE PER BOX
☐ DP1 Danica Patrick 25.00 60.00
☐ DP2 Danica Patrick 25.00 60.00
☐ DP3 Danica Patrick 25.00 60.00
☐ DP4 Danica Patrick 25.00 60.00
☐ DP5 Danica Patrick 25.00 60.00
☐ DP6 Danica Patrick 25.00 60.00
☐ DP7 Danica Patrick 25.00 60.00
☐ DP8 Danica Patrick 25.00 60.00
☐ DP9 Danica Patrick 25.00 60.00
☐ DP10 Danica Patrick 25.00 60.00

2012 Sports Illustrated Swimsuit Decade of Supermodels Decades Best

COMPLETE SET (10) 8.00 20.00
STATED ODDS FOUR PER BOX
☐ DB1 Bar Refaeli 2.50 6.00
☐ DB2 Brooklyn Decker 2.50 6.00
☐ DB3 Daniela Pestova 2.00 5.00
☐ DB4 Daniella Sarahyba 2.00 5.00
☐ DB5 Elle Macpherson 2.00 5.00
☐ DB6 Elsa Benitez 2.00 5.00
☐ DB7 Marisa Miller 2.50 6.00
☐ DB8 Molly Sims 2.00 5.00
☐ DB9 Petra Nemcova 2.00 5.00
☐ DB10 Veronica Varekova 2.00 5.00

2012 Sports Illustrated Swimsuit Decade of Supermodels Memorabilia

STATED ODDS TWO PER BOX
☐ AM Ariel Meredith 10.00 25.00
☐ AV Anne V 12.00 30.00
☐ BD Brooklyn Decker 25.00 50.00
☐ BR Bar Refaeli 15.00 40.00
☐ BR2 Bar Refaeli 15.00 40.00
☐ DP Daniela Pestova 12.00 30.00
☐ EB Elsa Benitez 10.00 25.00
☐ EM Elle Macpherson 15.00 40.00
☐ HK Heidi Klum 15.00 40.00
☐ JG Jessica Gomes 10.00 25.00
☐ JM Jarah Mariano 12.00 30.00
☐ KC Kim Cloutier 12.00 30.00
☐ MK Melissa Keller 10.00 25.00
☐ MK Maria Kirilenko 15.00 40.00
☐ ML Michelle Lombardo 10.00 25.00
☐ MM2 Marisa Miller 20.00 50.00
☐ MS Maria Sharapova 25.00 60.00
☐ PN Petra Nemcova 12.00 30.00
☐ TP Tori Praver 12.00 30.00
☐ YR Yamila Diaz-Rahi 10.00 25.00

2012 Sports Illustrated Swimsuit Decade of Supermodels Natural Colors

COMPLETE SET (10) 10.00 25.00
STATED ODDS FOUR PER BOX
☐ NC1 Bridget Hall 2.00 5.00
☐ NC2 Brooklyn Decker 2.50 6.00
☐ NC3 Jessica Gomes 2.00 5.00
☐ NC4 Irina Shayk 2.00 5.00
☐ NC5 Jessica White 2.00 5.00
☐ NC6 Tori Praver 2.00 5.00
☐ NC7 Melissa Keller 2.00 5.00
☐ NC8 Marisa Miller 2.50 6.00
☐ NC9 Noemie Lenoir 2.00 5.00
☐ NC10 Petra Nemcova 2.00 5.00

2012 Stargate SG-1 Expansion Autographs

ISSUED VIA RITTENHOUSE WEBSITE
☐ A70 Richard Dean Anderson/160* AU 150.00 200.00
☐ AC4 Christopher Judge/500* AU MEM 40.00 75.00
☐ AC5 Richard Dean Anderson/100* AU MEM200.00 250.00

2012 Tarzan 100th Anniversary

COMPLETE SET (55) 8.00 20.00
☐ 1 Tarzan .40 1.00
☐ 2 Tarzan .40 1.00
☐ 3 Tarzan .40 1.00
☐ 4 Tarzan .40 1.00
☐ 5 Tarzan .40 1.00
☐ 6 Tarzan .40 1.00
☐ 7 Tarzan .40 1.00
☐ 8 Tarzan .40 1.00
☐ 9 Tarzan .40 1.00
☐ 10 Tarzan .40 1.00
☐ 11 Tarzan .40 1.00
☐ 12 Tarzan .40 1.00
☐ 13 Tarzan .40 1.00
☐ 14 Tarzan .40 1.00
☐ 15 Tarzan .40 1.00
☐ 16 Tarzan .40 1.00
☐ 17 Tarzan .40 1.00
☐ 18 Tarzan .40 1.00
☐ 19 Tarzan .40 1.00
☐ 20 Tarzan .40 1.00
☐ 21 Tarzan .40 1.00
☐ 22 Tarzan .40 1.00
☐ 23 Tarzan .40 1.00
☐ 24 Tarzan .40 1.00
☐ 25 Tarzan .40 1.00
☐ 26 Tarzan .40 1.00
☐ 27 Tarzan .40 1.00
☐ 28 Tarzan .40 1.00
☐ 29 Tarzan .40 1.00
☐ 30 Tarzan .40 1.00
☐ 31 Tarzan .40 1.00
☐ 32 Tarzan .40 1.00
☐ 33 Tarzan .40 1.00
☐ 34 Tarzan .40 1.00
☐ 35 Tarzan .40 1.00
☐ 36 Tarzan .40 1.00
☐ 37 Tarzan .40 1.00
☐ 38 Tarzan .40 1.00
☐ 39 Tarzan .40 1.00
☐ 40 Tarzan .40 1.00
☐ 41 Tarzan .40 1.00
☐ 42 Tarzan .40 1.00
☐ 43 Tarzan .40 1.00
☐ 44 Tarzan .40 1.00
☐ 45 Tarzan .40 1.00
☐ 46 Tarzan .40 1.00
☐ 47 Tarzan .40 1.00
☐ 48 Tarzan .40 1.00
☐ 49 Tarzan .40 1.00
☐ 50 Tarzan .40 1.00
☐ 51 Tarzan .40 1.00
☐ 52 Tarzan .40 1.00
☐ 53 Tarzan .40 1.00
☐ 54 Tarzan .40 1.00
☐ 55 Tarzan .40 1.00

2012 Tarzan 100th Anniversary Autographs

ANNOUNCED PRINT RUN 1
UNPRICED DUE TO SCARCITY
☐ R1 Edgar Rice Burroughs EXCH
☐ R2 Edgar Rice Burroughs EXCH
☐ R3 Johnny Weissmuller EXCH

2012 Tarzan 100th Anniversary Book Covers

COMPLETE SET (9) 12.00 30.00
OVERALL CHASE ODDS 6:24
☐ B01 Tarzan of the Apes 2.50 6.00
☐ B02 The Return of Tarzan 2.50 6.00
☐ B03 Son of Tarzan 2.50 6.00
☐ B04 Tarzan and the Golden Lion 2.50 6.00
☐ B05 Tarzan, Lord of the Jungle 2.50 6.00
☐ B06 Tarzan at Earth's Core 2.50 6.00
☐ B07 Tarzan the Invincible 2.50 6.00
☐ B08 Tarzan the Magnificent 2.50 6.00
☐ B09 Tarzan and the Castaways 2.50 6.00

2012 Tarzan 100th Anniversary Characters

COMPLETE SET (9) 12.00 30.00
OVERALL CHASE ODDS 6:24
☐ FP01 Tarzan, Lord of the Jungle 2.50 6.00
☐ FP02 Jane Porter 2.50 6.00
☐ FP03 Jack Clayton 2.50 6.00
☐ FP04 Archimedes Q. Porter 2.50 6.00
☐ FP05 Paul d'Arnot 2.50 6.00
☐ FP06 La 2.50 6.00
☐ FP07 Muviro 2.50 6.00
☐ FP08 Nkima 2.50 6.00
☐ FP09 Jad-bal-ja 2.50 6.00

2012 Tarzan 100th Anniversary Movie Posters

COMPLETE SET (9) 12.00 30.00
OVERALL CHASE ODDS 6:24
☐ MOV01 Tarzan of the Apes 2.50 6.00
☐ MOV02 Tarzan and the Green Goddess 2.50 6.00
☐ MOV03 Tarzan's Secret Treasure 2.50 6.00
☐ MOV04 Tarzan's New York Adventure 2.50 6.00
☐ MOV05 Tarzan Triumphs 2.50 6.00
☐ MOV06 Tarzan and the Leopard Woman 2.50 6.00
☐ MOV07 Tarzan and the Mermaids 2.50 6.00
☐ MOV08 Tarzan the Magnificent 2.50 6.00
☐ MOV09 Tarzan and the Valley of Gold 2.50 6.00

2012 Tarzan 100th Anniversary Rhiannon Owens Oversized Art

ANNOUNCED PRINT RUN 1
UNPRICED DUE TO SCARCITY
☐ R6 Tarzan (Rhiannon Owens)
☐ R7 Tarzan (Rhiannon Owens)
☐ R8 Tarzan (Rhiannon Owens)
☐ R9 Tarzan (Rhiannon Owens)
☐ R10 Tarzan (Rhiannon Owens)
☐ R11 Tarzan (Rhiannon Owens)
☐ R12 Tarzan (Rhiannon Owens)
☐ R13 Tarzan (Rhiannon Owens)
☐ R14 Tarzan (Rhiannon Owens)
☐ R15 Tarzan (Rhiannon Owens)
☐ R16 Tarzan (Rhiannon Owens)
☐ R17 Tarzan (Rhiannon Owens)
☐ R18 Tarzan (Rhiannon Owens)
☐ R19 Tarzan (Rhiannon Owens)
☐ R20 Tarzan (Rhiannon Owens)
☐ R21 Tarzan (Rhiannon Owens)
☐ R22 Tarzan (Rhiannon Owens)
☐ R23 Tarzan (Rhiannon Owens)
☐ R24 Tarzan (Rhiannon Owens)
☐ R25 Tarzan (Rhiannon Owens)
☐ R26 Tarzan (Rhiannon Owens)
☐ R27 Tarzan (Rhiannon Owens)
☐ R28 Tarzan (Rhiannon Owens)
☐ R29 Tarzan (Rhiannon Owens)

2012 Tarzan 100th Anniversary Sketches

STATED ODDS 1:24
☐ 1 Achilleas Kokkinakis
☐ 2 Anthony Gay
☐ 3 Aston Roy Cover
☐ 4 Bien Flores
☐ 5 Bob Stevlic
☐ 6 Chad Cicconi
☐ 7 Chad Haverland
☐ 8 Babisu Kourtis
☐ 9 Chris Thorne
☐ 10 Corey Brown
☐ 11 Dan Borgonos
☐ 12 Dan Smith
☐ 13 Daniel Gorman
☐ 14 Danielle Soloud Gransaull
☐ 15 David Castro
☐ 16 David Hanson
☐ 17 David Ryan
☐ 18 Denise Parrish
☐ 19 Elliot Fernandez
☐ 20 Eric White
☐ 21 Gabby Untermayerova
☐ 22 Gary Kezele
☐ 23 George Deep
☐ 24 Henry Martinez
☐ 25 Ian Yoshio Roberts
☐ 26 Jason Roussel
☐ 27 JC Fabul
☐ 28 Jezreel Rojales
☐ 29 John Haun
☐ 30 Jomar Bulda
☐ 31 Julius Abrera
☐ 32 Matt Slay
☐ 33 Michael Rooth
☐ 34 Pablo Diaz
☐ 35 Rhiannon Owens
☐ 36 Rich Molinelli
☐ 37 Scott Rorie
☐ 38 Ted Dastick Jr.
☐ 39 Ted Rechlin
☐ 40 Thomas Boatwright
☐ 41 Tim Levandoski
☐ 42 Tim Shay
☐ 43 Victor Rodriguez
☐ 44 Vince Sunico
☐ 45 Wilson Ramos Jr.

2012 Tarzan 100th Anniversary Thomas Yeates Original Art

ANNOUNCED PRINT RUN 1
UNPRICED DUE TO SCARCITY
☐ R4 Thomas Yeates EXCH
☐ R5 Thomas Yeates EXCH

2012 True Blood Premiere

COMPLETE SET (98) 6.00 15.00
☐ 1 Strange Love .20 .50
☐ 2 Strange Love .20 .50
☐ 3 The First Taste .20 .50
☐ 4 The First Taste .20 .50
☐ 5 Mine .20 .50
☐ 6 Mine .20 .50
☐ 7 Escape From Dragon House .20 .50
☐ 8 Escape From Dragon House .20 .50
☐ 9 Sparks Fly Out .20 .50
☐ 10 Sparks Fly Out .20 .50
☐ 11 Cold Ground .20 .50
☐ 12 Cold Ground .20 .50
☐ 13 Burning House of Love .20 .50
☐ 14 Burning House of Love .20 .50
☐ 15 The Fourth Man in the Fire .20 .50
☐ 16 The Fourth Man in the Fire .20 .50
☐ 17 Plaisir d'amour .20 .50
☐ 18 Plaisir d'amour .20 .50
☐ 19 I Don't Wanna Know .20 .50
☐ 20 I Don't Wanna Know .20 .50
☐ 21 To Love is To Bury .20 .50
☐ 22 To Love is To Bury .20 .50
☐ 23 You'll Be the Death of Me .20 .50
☐ 24 You'll Be the Death of Me .20 .50
☐ 25 Nothing But the Blood .20 .50
☐ 26 Nothing But the Blood .20 .50
☐ 27 Keep This Party Going .20 .50
☐ 28 Keep This Party Going .20 .50
☐ 29 Scratches .20 .50
☐ 30 Scratches .20 .50
☐ 31 Shake and Fingerpop .20 .50
☐ 32 Shake and Fingerpop .20 .50
☐ 33 Never Let Me Go .20 .50
☐ 34 Never Let Me Go .20 .50
☐ 35 Hard-Hearted Hannah .20 .50
☐ 36 Hard-Hearted Hannah .20 .50
☐ 37 Release Me .20 .50
☐ 38 Release Me .20 .50
☐ 39 Timebomb .20 .50
☐ 40 Timebomb .20 .50
☐ 41 I Will Rise Up .20 .50
☐ 42 I Will Rise Up .20 .50
☐ 43 New World in My View .20 .50
☐ 44 New World in My View .20 .50
☐ 45 Frenzy .20 .50
☐ 46 Frenzy .20 .50
☐ 47 Beyond Here Lies Nothin' .20 .50
☐ 48 Beyond Here Lies Nothin' .20 .50
☐ 49 Bad Blood .20 .50
☐ 50 Bad Blood .20 .50
☐ 51 Beautifully Broken .20 .50
☐ 52 Beautifully Broken .20 .50
☐ 53 It Hurts Me, Too .20 .50
☐ 54 It Hurts Me, Too .20 .50
☐ 55 9 Crimes .20 .50
☐ 56 9 Crimes .20 .50
☐ 57 Trouble .20 .50
☐ 58 Trouble .20 .50
☐ 59 I Got a Right to Sing the Blues .20 .50
☐ 60 I Got a Right to Sing the Blues .20 .50
☐ 61 Hitting the Ground .20 .50
☐ 62 Hitting the Ground .20 .50
☐ 63 Night on the Sun .20 .50
☐ 64 Night on the Sun .20 .50
☐ 65 Everything is Broken .20 .50
☐ 66 Everything is Broken .20 .50
☐ 67 I Smell a Rat .20 .50
☐ 68 I Smell a Rat .20 .50
☐ 69 Fresh Blood .20 .50
☐ 70 Fresh Blood .20 .50
☐ 71 Evil is Going On .20 .50
☐ 72 Evil is Going On .20 .50
☐ 73 She's Not There .20 .50
☐ 74 She's Not There .20 .50
☐ 75 You Smell Like Dinner .20 .50
☐ 76 You Smell Like Dinner .20 .50
☐ 77 If You Love Me, Why am I Dyin'? .20 .50
☐ 78 If You Love Me, Why am I Dyin'? .20 .50
☐ 79 I'm Alive and On Fire .20 .50
☐ 80 I'm Alive and On Fire .20 .50
☐ 81 Me and the Devil .20 .50
☐ 82 Me and the Devil .20 .50
☐ 83 I Wish I Was the Moon .20 .50
☐ 84 I Wish I Was the Moon .20 .50
☐ 85 Cold Grey Light of Dawn .20 .50
☐ 86 Cold Grey Light of Dawn .20 .50
☐ 87 Spellbound .20 .50
☐ 88 Spellbound .20 .50
☐ 89 Let's Get out of Here .20 .50
☐ 90 Let's Get out of Here .20 .50
☐ 91 Burning Down the House .20 .50
☐ 92 Burning Down the House .20 .50
☐ 93 Soul of Fire .20 .50
☐ 94 Soul of Fire .20 .50
☐ 95 And When I Die .20 .50
☐ 96 And When I Die .20 .50
☐ 97 Checklist 1 .20 .50
☐ 98 Checklist 2 .20 .50
☐ CT Tru Blood Bottle DIECUT 10.00 25.00
(issued as case topper)

2012 True Blood Premiere Parallel

COMPLETE SET 30.00 60.00
*PARALLEL: 1.5X TO 4X BASIC CARDS
STATED ODDS 1:3

2012 True Blood Premiere Autographs

OVERALL AUTO ODDS 2 PER BOX
L (LIMITED): 300-500 COPIES
VL (VERY LIMITED): 200-300 COPIES
EL (EXTREMELY LIMITED): LESS THAN 200 COPIES
☐ 1 Adina Porter 6.00 15.00
as Lettie May Thornton L
☐ 2 Alexander Skarsgard 75.00 150.00
☐ 3 Allan Hyde 15.00 40.00
as Godric VL
☐ 4 Anna Camp 10.00 25.00
as Sarah Newlin L
☐ 5 Anna Paquin 100.00 200.00
☐ 6 Brit Morgan 10.00 25.00
as Debbie Pelt VL
☐ 7 Carrie Preston 12.00 30.00
as Arlene Fowler L
☐ 8 Courtney Ford 10.00 25.00
as Portia L
☐ 9 Dale Raoul 6.00 15.00
as Maxine Fortenberry L
☐ 10 Dan Buran 6.00 15.00
as Marcus Bozeman L
☐ 11 Deborah Ann Woll 40.00 80.00
☐ 12 Don Swayze 6.00 15.00
as Gus L
☐ 13 Grant Bowler 12.00 30.00
as Cooter VL
☐ 14 Jessica Tuck 10.00 25.00
as Nan Flanigan L
☐ 15 Jim Parrack 10.00 25.00
as Hoyt Fortenberry L
☐ 16 Kevin Alejandro 8.00 20.00
as Jesus Velasquez L
☐ 17 Kristin Bauer 40.00 80.00
☐ 18 Lauren Bowles 8.00 20.00
as Holly Cleary L
☐ 19 Lindsay Pulsipher 6.00 15.00
as Crystal Norris L
☐ 20 Lizzy Caplan 20.00 40.00
☐ 21 Mariana Klaveno 8.00 20.00
as Lorena L
☐ 22 Marshall Allman 8.00 20.00
as Tommy Mickens L
☐ 23 Melissa Rauch 10.00 25.00
as Summer
☐ 24 Michael Raymond James 8.00 20.00
as Rene Lenier L
☐ 25 Michelle Forbes 40.00 80.00
☐ 26 Nelsan Ellis 12.00 30.00
as Lafayette Reynolds L
☐ 27 Raoul Trujillo 6.00 15.00
as Longshadow L
☐ 28 Stephen Moyer 75.00 150.00
☐ 29 Todd Lowe 12.00 30.00
as Terry Bellefleur VL

2012 True Blood Premiere Black and White

COMPLETE SET (6) 10.00 25.00
STATED ODDS 1:18
☐ BW1 Sookie Stackhouse 4.00 10.00
☐ BW2 Bill Compton 4.00 10.00
☐ BW3 Eric Northman 3.00 8.00
☐ BW4 Sam Merlotte 3.00 8.00
☐ BW5 Tara Thornton 3.00 8.00
☐ BW6 Jason Stackhouse 3.00 8.00

2012 True Blood Premiere Characters

COMPLETE SET (9) 10.00 25.00
STATED ODDS 1:12
☐ D1 Sookie Stackhouse 2.50 6.00
☐ D2 Bill Compton 2.50 6.00
☐ D3 Sam Merlotte 2.00 5.00
☐ D4 Jason Stackhouse 2.00 5.00
☐ D5 Tara Thornton 2.00 5.00
☐ D6 Jessica Hamby 2.00 5.00
☐ D7 Lafayette Reynolds 2.00 5.00
☐ D8 Eric Northman 2.00 5.00
☐ D9 Pam De Beaufort 2.00 5.00

2012 True Blood Premiere Full Bleed Autographs

OVERALL AUTO ODDS 2 PER BOX
L (LIMITED): 300-500 COPIES
VL (VERY LIMITED): 200-300 COPIES
☐ 1 Adina Porter 6.00 15.00
as Lettie May Thornton L
☐ 2 Brit Morgan 10.00 25.00
as Debbie Pelt L
☐ 3 Courtney Ford 10.00 25.00
as Portia L
☐ 4 Dan Buran 6.00 15.00
as Marcus Bozeman L
☐ 5 Don Swayze 6.00 15.00
as Gus L
☐ 6 Lindsay Pulsipher 6.00 15.00
as Crystal Norris L
☐ 7 Lizzy Caplan 20.00 40.00
☐ 8 Mariana Klaveno 8.00 20.00
as Lorena L
☐ 9 Marshall Allman 8.00 20.00
as Tommy Mickens L
☐ 10 Michael Raymond James 8.00 20.00
as Rene Lenier L
☐ 11 Raoul Trujillo 6.00 15.00
as Longshadow L

2012 True Blood Premiere Quotable

COMP.SET w/o Q10 (9) 8.00 20.00
STATED ODDS 1:12
☐ Q1 Vampires Are Always In Some 2.00 5.00
☐ Q2 Jessica, I'm Going to Have 2.00 5.00
☐ Q3 The Only Vampire 2.00 5.00
☐ Q4 Your Hair is Like a Sunset 2.00 5.00
☐ Q5 You're So Warm 2.00 5.00
☐ Q6 I Find Myself Doubting 2.00 5.00
☐ Q7 Sookie, You Have No Future 2.00 5.00
☐ Q8 Is It My Fault 2.00 5.00
☐ Q9 Can I Ask You 2.00 5.00
☐ Q10 I'm Sorry You Fell In Love 10.00 25.00
(issued as a Rittenhouse Reward)

2012 True Blood Premiere Shadowbox

COMPLETE SET (4) 25.00 50.00
STATED ODDS 1:72
☐ 1 Bill Compton 6.00 15.00
☐ 2 Eric Northman 6.00 15.00
☐ 3 Sam Merlotte 6.00 15.00
☐ 4 Sookie Stackhouse 8.00 20.00

2012 Wacky Packages Series 9

COMPLETE SET (55) 6.00 15.00
☐ 1 Cornbutts .15 .40
☐ 2 Asparagus Jacks .15 .40
☐ 3 Juicy Newt .15 .40
☐ 4 Letgo .15 .40
☐ 5 Buzzard .15 .40
☐ 6 Oscar Tyer .15 .40
☐ 7 Velfeeta .15 .40
☐ 8 M&eMpty .15 .40
☐ 9 Combovers .15 .40
☐ 10 Strawberry Shortluse .15 .40
☐ 11 Sluggie .15 .40
☐ 12 Thums .15 .40
☐ 13 Blazin' Bran .15 .40
☐ 14 Fowlgers .15 .40
☐ 15 Hubble Bubble .15 .40
☐ 16 Sprout .15 .40
☐ 17 Dribbles 'n Spits .15 .40
☐ 18 Fig Leaf Nudetons .15 .40
☐ 19 Hells .15 .40
☐ 20 Weak Thins .15 .40
☐ 21 Motion Spray .15 .40
☐ 22 Windy's .15 .40
☐ 23 Klix .15 .40
☐ 24 Maxwell Louse .15 .40
☐ 25 Panters .15 .40
☐ 26 Lady Gag Me .15 .40
☐ 27 Miracle Glo .15 .40
☐ 28 Rhu-Barbie .15 .40
☐ 29 Alpha Bats .15 .40
☐ 30 Bulges .15 .40
☐ 31 Tridon't .15 .40
☐ 32 Brambles .15 .40
☐ 33 Speed Stink .15 .40
☐ 34 Yuck .15 .40
☐ 35 Lumpables .15 .40
☐ 36 Cheese Hips .15 .40
☐ 37 Juicy Dropped Pop .15 .40
☐ 38 Pimples .15 .40
☐ 39 Bull Parts .15 .40
☐ 40 Pureel .15 .40
☐ 41 E.Z. Pudge .15 .40
☐ 42 Stuckers .15 .40
☐ 43 Cheez Wuz .15 .40
☐ 44 Starburp .15 .40
☐ 45 Real Dull .15 .40
☐ 46 Slime Jim .15 .40
☐ 47 Dr. Shell's .15 .40
☐ 48 Hell-O .15 .40
☐ 49 Iworry .15 .40
☐ 50 Nutty Blubber .15 .40
☐ 51 Hun's .15 .40
☐ 52 Moose Attacks .15 .40
☐ 53 Hungry Hungry Hippies .15 .40
☐ 54 Fetchers .15 .40
☐ 55 Trux .15 .40

2012 Wacky Packages Series 9 Flash Foil
COMPLETE SET 200.00 300.00
*FLASH FOIL: 6X TO 15X BASIC CARDS
STATED ODDS 1:6

2012 Wacky Packages Series 9 Gold Flash Foil
COMMON CARD 100.00 175.00
STATED ODDS 1:308

2012 Wacky Packages Series 9 Awful Apps
COMPLETE SET (10) 4.00 10.00
STATED ODDS 1:3
❑ 1 Amazombie .60 1.50
❑ 2 Obey .60 1.50
❑ 3 TP Guide .60 1.50
❑ 4 ESP Scorecenter .60 1.50
❑ 5 Wickedpedia .60 1.50
❑ 6 Flushbook .60 1.50
❑ 7 Twitster .60 1.50
❑ 8 Doo Doo Jump .60 1.50
❑ 9 Words With Fiends .60 1.50
❑ 10 Angry Nerds .60 1.50

2012 Wacky Packages Series 9 Lame Games
COMPLETE SET (10) 4.00 10.00
STATED ODDS 1:3
❑ 1 Bubonic the Plaguehog .60 1.50
❑ 2 Super Mario Mothers .60 1.50
❑ 3 The Legend of Smelda .60 1.50
❑ 4 Litter Bug Planet .60 1.50
❑ 5 Ants Ants Revolution .60 1.50
❑ 6 Shock Band .60 1.50
❑ 7 Granny Theft Auto .60 1.50
❑ 8 Mass Defect .60 1.50
❑ 9 God of Warts .60 1.50
❑ 10 Hello .60 1.50

2012 Wacky Packages Series 9 Magnets
COMPLETE SET (10) 12.00 25.00
STATED ODDS 1:6
❑ 1 Campy Soup 2.00 5.00
❑ 2 Cracked Jerk 2.00 5.00
❑ 3 Moron Salt 2.00 5.00
❑ 4 Kook-Aid 2.00 5.00
❑ 5 Crakola 2.00 5.00
❑ 6 Gatoraid 2.00 5.00
❑ 7 Krazy 2.00 5.00
❑ 8 Play-Dumb 2.00 5.00
❑ 9 Hurtz 2.00 5.00
❑ 10 Life Servers 2.00 5.00

2012 Wacky Packages Series 9 Motion Luggage Tags
COMPLETE SET (9) 10.00 25.00
STATED ODDS 1:6
❑ 1 Kick Kat 2.00 5.00
❑ 2 Mrs. Blubberworth's 2.00 5.00
❑ 3 Sneez-It 2.00 5.00
❑ 4 Zilla Wafers 2.00 5.00
❑ 5 Raisin Brain 2.00 5.00
❑ 6 Crush 2.00 5.00
❑ 7 Froot Oops 2.00 5.00
❑ 8 Kreepy Kreme 2.00 5.00
❑ 9 Franken Bury 2.00 5.00

2012 Wacky Packages Series 9 Pink
COMPLETE SET 12.00 30.00
*PINK: 1X TO 2.5X BASIC CARDS
STATED ODDS ONE PER PACK

2012 The Walking Dead Season Two
COMPLETE SET (80) 12.00 30.00
❑ 1 The Walking Dead .30 .75
❑ 2 On the Road .30 .75
❑ 3 Memory Lane .30 .75
❑ 4 Traffic Jam .30 .75
❑ 5 Price of Supplies .30 .75
❑ 6 A Brief Reprieve .30 .75
❑ 7 Always Vigilant .30 .75
❑ 8 Gassing Up .30 .75
❑ 9 Just Like That .30 .75
❑ 10 Get Down .30 .75
❑ 11 On Their Own .30 .75
❑ 12 Quick Thinking .30 .75
❑ 13 Not Safe Yet .30 .75
❑ 14 Frightened and Alone .30 .75
❑ 15 A Tough Choice .30 .75
❑ 16 Gotta Know .30 .75
❑ 17 Guilt .30 .75
❑ 18 Searching for Sophia .30 .75
❑ 19 Opted Out .30 .75
❑ 20 Church Bells .30 .75
❑ 21 Faith .30 .75
❑ 22 Pure Joy .30 .75
❑ 23 Save My Son .30 .75
❑ 24 Solace from a Friend .30 .75
❑ 25 A Beautiful Place .30 .75
❑ 26 Saving Carl .30 .75
❑ 27 Overrun .30 .75
❑ 28 A Desperate Escape .30 .75
❑ 29 Erasing the Guilt .30 .75
❑ 30 White Lie .30 .75
❑ 31 Necessities .30 .75
❑ 32 Down a Well .30 .75
❑ 33 Cherokee Rose .30 .75
❑ 34 Up and Out .30 .75
❑ 35 Alone at Last .30 .75
❑ 36 Coming Clean .30 .75
❑ 37 A Gift from Dale .30 .75
❑ 38 A Clue .30 .75
❑ 39 Walker! .30 .75
❑ 40 A Safe Return .30 .75
❑ 41 He's Wearing Ears .30 .75
❑ 42 Roll in the Hay .30 .75
❑ 43 Target Practice .30 .75
❑ 44 Focus .30 .75
❑ 45 What Kind of a Future .30 .75
❑ 46 Andrea Steps Up .30 .75
❑ 47 Desperation .30 .75
❑ 48 This Is Home .30 .75
❑ 49 Seeing Red .30 .75
❑ 50 Fury .30 .75
❑ 51 The Search Ends .30 .75
❑ 52 A Mother's Cry .30 .75
❑ 53 Mourning .30 .75
❑ 54 We Bury the Ones We Love .30 .75
❑ 55 And Burn the Rest .30 .75
❑ 56 Quick Draw .30 .75
❑ 57 Saves on Ammo .30 .75
❑ 58 Drop Point .30 .75
❑ 59 Maggie's Schoolmate .30 .75
❑ 60 Masking His Scent .30 .75
❑ 61 A Second Chance .30 .75
❑ 62 Judge and Jury .30 .75
❑ 63 Terror in the Night .30 .75
❑ 64 Tragic End .30 .75
❑ 65 Honoring Dale .30 .75
❑ 66 Patrol .30 .75
❑ 67 Carl's Guilt .30 .75
❑ 68 Point of View .30 .75
❑ 69 Man-to-Man .30 .75
❑ 70 Tracking Down the Truth .30 .75
❑ 71 Showdown .30 .75
❑ 72 Back from the Dead .30 .75
❑ 73 First Kill .30 .75
❑ 74 Roaming Death .30 .75
❑ 75 Scattered .30 .75
❑ 76 Out of Gas .30 .75
❑ 77 A Need for Hope .30 .75
❑ 78 Infected .30 .75
❑ 79 Confessions .30 .75
❑ 80 Checklist .30 .75

2012 The Walking Dead Season Two Autographs
STATED ODDS 1:24 H, 1:2,000 R
❑ A1 Andrew Lincoln 125.00 200.00
as Rick Grimes
❑ A2 Jon Bernthal 35.00 70.00
as Shane Walsh
❑ A3 Jeffrey DeMunn 30.00 60.00
as Dale
❑ A4 Steven Yeun 30.00 60.00
as Glenn
❑ A5 Norman Reedus 100.00 200.00
as Daryl Dixon
❑ A6 Melissa Suzanne McBride 25.00 50.00
as Carol
❑ A7 Madison Lintz 50.00 100.00
as Sophia
❑ A8 Madison Lintz 50.00 100.00
as Walker Sophia
❑ A9 Lauren Cohan 40.00 80.00
as Maggie Greene
❑ A10 Scott Wilson 25.00 50.00
as Hershel Greene
❑ A11 IronE Singleton 25.00 50.00
as T-Dog
❑ A12 Greg Nicotero 25.00 50.00
Co-Executive Producer
❑ A13 Laurie Holden 50.00 100.00
as Andrea
❑ A14 Sarah Wayne Callies 40.00 80.00
as Lori Grimes

2012 The Walking Dead Season Two Character Bios
COMPLETE SET (9) 15.00 40.00
STATED ODDS 1:12
❑ CB1 Rick Grimes 4.00 10.00
❑ CB2 Lori Grimes 4.00 10.00
❑ CB3 Shane Walsh 3.00 8.00
❑ CB4 Carl Grimes 3.00 8.00
❑ CB5 Glenn 3.00 8.00
❑ CB6 Andrea 3.00 8.00
❑ CB7 Daryl Dixon 3.00 8.00
❑ CB8 Dale Horvath 3.00 8.00
❑ CB9 Carol 3.00 8.00

2012 The Walking Dead Season Two Dual Wardrobe Memorabilia
SINGLE/DUAL MEM ODDS 1:12 H, 1:2,000 R
❑ DM1 Rick Grimes green shirt 75.00 150.00
Sophia (walker) cargo pants
❑ DM2 Hershel Greene beige shirt 50.00 100.00
Maggie Greene green shirt
❑ DM3 Lori Grimes plaid shirt 50.00 100.00
Shane Walsh blue shirt

2012 The Walking Dead Season Two Puzzle
COMPLETE SET (9) 12.00 30.00
STATED ODDS 1:12
❑ 1 Top Left 2.50 6.00
❑ 2 Top Center 2.50 6.00
❑ 3 Top Right 2.50 6.00
❑ 4 Middle Left 2.50 6.00
❑ 5 Middle Center 2.50 6.00
❑ 6 Middle Right 2.50 6.00
❑ 7 Bottom Left 2.50 6.00
❑ 8 Bottom Center 2.50 6.00
❑ 9 Bottom Right 2.50 6.00

2012 The Walking Dead Season Two Shadowbox
COMPLETE SET (9) 40.00 80.00
STATED ODDS 1:24
❑ SB1 Safety 6.00 15.00
❑ SB2 Infected 6.00 15.00
❑ SB3 Brain Trauma 6.00 15.00
❑ SB4 Devoured 6.00 15.00
❑ SB5 Decay 6.00 15.00
❑ SB6 Relentless 6.00 15.00
❑ SB7 Roaming 6.00 15.00
❑ SB8 Fear the Living 6.00 15.00
❑ SB9 Impossible 6.00 15.00

2012 The Walking Dead Season Two Wardrobe Memorabilia
SINGLE/DUAL MEM ODDS 1:12 H, 1:2,000 R
❑ M1 Rick Grimes white t-shirt 40.00 80.00
❑ M2 T-Dog cargo pants 12.00 30.00
❑ M3 Shane Walsh blue jacket 25.00 60.00
❑ M4 Carl Grimes orange jacket 15.00 40.00
❑ M5 Andrea blue hoodie 25.00 50.00
❑ M6 Glenn brown shirt 15.00 40.00
❑ M7 Lori Grimes cream t-shirt 25.00 50.00
❑ M8 Dale Horvath white tank top 30.00 60.00
❑ M9 Sophia (human) blue shirt 25.00 50.00
❑ M10 Maggie Greene green tank 25.00 50.00
❑ M11 Shane Walsh blue shirt 15.00 40.00
❑ M12 Andrea striped top 30.00 60.00
❑ M13 Carol Peletier floral top 15.00 40.00
❑ M14 Hershel Greene beige shirt 15.00 40.00
❑ M15 Glenn blue shirt 15.00 40.00
❑ M16 Rick Grimes green shirt 40.00 80.00
❑ M17 Lori Grimes plaid shirt 30.00 60.00
❑ M18 Carl Grimes striped hoodie 15.00 40.00
❑ M19 Andrea cargo pants 15.00 40.00
❑ M20 Sophia (walker) cargo pants 30.00 60.00
❑ M21 Carol Peletier grey pants 15.00 40.00
❑ M22 Hershel Greene pinstripe shirt 15.00 40.00
❑ M23 Maggie Greene purple top 15.00 40.00
❑ M24 Dale Horvath Hawaiian shirt 15.00 40.00
❑ M25 T-Dog shirt 15.00 40.00
❑ M26 Andrea striped top 25.00 50.00
❑ M27 Daryl Dixon jeans 60.00 120.00
❑ M28 Walker Horde 8.00 20.00
❑ M29 Walker Horde 8.00 20.00
❑ M30 Walker Horde 8.00 20.00
❑ M31 Walker Horde 8.00 20.00
❑ M32 Walker Horde 8.00 20.00
❑ M33 Bus Walker blue uniform
(binder exclusive)

2012 Warehouse 13 Season Three
COMPLETE SET (26) 25.00 50.00
❑ 1 The New Guy 2.00 5.00
❑ 2 The New Guy 2.00 5.00
❑ 3 Trials 2.00 5.00
❑ 4 Trials 2.00 5.00
❑ 5 Love Sick 2.00 5.00
❑ 6 Love Sick 2.00 5.00
❑ 7 Queen For a Day 2.00 5.00
❑ 8 Queen For a Day 2.00 5.00
❑ 9 3.2.1 2.00 5.00
❑ 10 3.2.1 2.00 5.00
❑ 11 Don't Hate the Player 2.00 5.00
❑ 12 Don't Hate the Player 2.00 5.00
❑ 13 Past Imperfect 2.00 5.00
❑ 14 Past Imperfect 2.00 5.00
❑ 15 The 40th Floor 2.00 5.00
❑ 16 The 40th Floor 2.00 5.00
❑ 17 Shadows 2.00 5.00
❑ 18 Shadows 2.00 5.00
❑ 19 Insatiable 2.00 5.00
❑ 20 Insatiable 2.00 5.00
❑ 21 Emily Lake 2.00 5.00
❑ 22 Emily Lake 2.00 5.00
❑ 23 Stand 2.00 5.00
❑ 24 Stand 2.00 5.00
❑ 25 The Greatest Gift 2.00 5.00
❑ 26 The Greatest Gift 2.00 5.00

2012 Warehouse 13 Season Three Artifacts
COMPLETE SET (10) 20.00 50.00
COMP.SET w/o A38 (9) 15.00 40.00
STATED PRINT RUN 350 SER. #'d SETS
❑ A29 Mary Mallon's Butcher Knife 3.00 8.00
❑ A30 Joshua's Trumpet 3.00 8.00
❑ A31 Beatrix Potter Tea set 3.00 8.00
❑ A32 Collodi Bracelet 3.00 8.00
❑ A33 Mr. Mental's Mind Reading Fezzes 3.00 8.00
❑ A34 Marilyn Monroe's Hair Brush 3.00 8.00
❑ A35 Richard Nixon's Shoes 3.00 8.00
❑ A36 Pavlov's Bell 3.00 8.00
❑ A37 W.C. Fields' Juggling Balls 3.00 8.00
❑ A38 Van Doren Stern's Upholstery Brush 15.00 30.00
(issued as Rittenhouse Reward)

2012 Warehouse 13 Season Three Autograph Relics
❑ 1 Eddie McClintock 75.00 150.00
as Pete Lattimer/(issued as 4-box incentive)
❑ 2 Saul Rubinek 60.00 120.00
as Artie Nielsen/(issued as 2-box incentive)

2012 Warehouse 13 Season Three Autographs
L (LIMITED): 300-500 COPIES
VL (VERY LIMITED): 200-300 COPIES
EL (EXTREMELY LIMITED): LESS THAN 200 COPIES
❑ 1 Aaron Ashmore 15.00 40.00
as Steve Jinks VL
❑ 2 Allison Scagliotti 30.00 60.00
as Claudia Donovan VL
❑ 3 CCH Pounder 12.00 30.00
as Mrs. Irene Frederic VL
❑ 4 David Anders 8.00 20.00
as Jonah Raitt L
❑ 5 Eddie McClintock 20.00 50.00
as Pete Lattimer VL
❑ 6 Jeri Ryan 60.00 120.00
as Amanda Lattimer EL
❑ 7 Kate Mulgrew 60.00 120.00
as Jane Lattimer EL
❑ 8 Lindsay Wagner 60.00 120.00
as Dr. Vanessa Calder EL
❑ 9 Rene Auberjonois 12.00 30.00
as Hugo Miller VL
❑ 10 Sasha Roiz 8.00 20.00
as Marcus Diamond VL
❑ 11 Sasha Roiz 8.00 20.00
as Marcus Diamond VL
❑ 12 Saul Rubinek 15.00 40.00
as Artie Nielsen VL

2012 Warehouse 13 Season Three Promos
❑ P1 Artie/Myka/Pete 1.00 2.50
(General Distribution)
❑ P2 Four Ladies 6.00 15.00
(Box Topper)

2012 Warehouse 13 Season Three Relics
STATED ODDS TWO RELICS PER PACK
❑ 1 Amanda Lattimer 12.00 30.00
from Queen For a Day
❑ 2 Artie Nielsen jacket 6.00 15.00
from MacPherson
❑ 3 Artie Nielsen shirt 6.00 15.00
from MacPherson
❑ 4 Claudia Donovan 15.00 40.00
from Don't Hate the Player
❑ 5 Claudia Donovan 15.00 40.00
from Regrets
❑ 6 H.G. Wells jacket 10.00 25.00
from 3.2.1
❑ 7 H.G. Wells vest 10.00 25.00
from 3.2.1
❑ 8 H.G. Wells shirt 10.00 25.00
from Emily Lake
❑ 9 H.G. Wells sweater 10.00 25.00
from Emily Lake
❑ 10 Jane Lattimer 10.00 25.00
from Stand
❑ 11 Leena 6.00 15.00
from The New Guy
❑ 12 Marcus Diamond 6.00 15.00
from Emily Lake
❑ 13 Mrs. Irene Frederic 12.00 30.00
from The 40th Floor
❑ 14 Myka Bering 10.00 25.00
from 13.1
❑ 15 Myka Bering dress 10.00 25.00
from Duped
❑ 16 Myka Bering shirt 10.00 25.00
from Duped
❑ 17 Myka Bering 10.00 25.00
from Queen For a Day
❑ 18 Pete Lattimer hoodie 8.00 20.00
from 13.1
❑ 19 Pete Lattimer t-shirt 8.00 20.00
from 13.1
❑ 20 Pete Lattimer jacket 8.00 20.00
from Queen For a Day
❑ 21 Pete Lattimer shirt 8.00 20.00
from Queen For a Day
❑ 22 Steve Jinx 6.00 15.00
from The 40th Floor

2012 Yo Gabba Gabba
COMPLETE SET (90) 6.00 15.00
❑ 1 Muno .15 .40
❑ 2 Muno .15 .40
❑ 3 Muno .15 .40
❑ 4 Muno .15 .40
❑ 5 Muno .15 .40
❑ 6 Foofa .15 .40
❑ 7 Foofa .15 .40
❑ 8 Foofa .15 .40
❑ 9 Foofa .15 .40
❑ 10 Foofa .15 .40
❑ 11 Brobee .15 .40
❑ 12 Brobee .15 .40
❑ 13 Brobee .15 .40
❑ 14 Brobee .15 .40
❑ 15 Brobee .15 .40
❑ 16 Toodee .15 .40
❑ 17 Toodee .15 .40
❑ 18 Toodee .15 .40
❑ 19 Toodee .15 .40
❑ 20 Toodee .15 .40
❑ 21 Plex .15 .40
❑ 22 Plex .15 .40
❑ 23 Plex .15 .40
❑ 24 Plex .15 .40
❑ 25 Plex .15 .40
❑ 26 DJ Lance Rock .15 .40
❑ 27 DJ Lance Rock .15 .40
❑ 28 DJ Lance Rock .15 .40
❑ 29 DJ Lance Rock .15 .40
❑ 30 DJ Lance Rock .15 .40
❑ 31 Archibald .15 .40
❑ 32 Foofle .15 .40
❑ 33 Yo Dazzlers .15 .40
❑ 34 Barbara .15 .40
❑ 35 Sparkles .15 .40
❑ 36 Oskie Bugs .15 .40
❑ 37 Mr. Lizard .15 .40
❑ 38 Gooble .15 .40
❑ 39 Mrs. Fox .15 .40
❑ 40 Spooky Toast .15 .40
❑ 41 Muno's Family .15 .40
❑ 42 Play Pretend With Muno - Monkey .15 .40
❑ 43 Play Pretend With Muno - Dinosaur .15 .40
❑ 44 Play Pretend With Muno - Astronaut .15 .40
❑ 45 Play Pretend With Muno - Riding a Horse .15 .40
❑ 46 Play Pretend With Muno - Snake .15 .40
❑ 47 Play Pretend With Muno - Elephant .15 .40
❑ 48 Play Pretend With Muno - Christmas Tree .15 .40
❑ 49 Learn With Plex - Blowing Bubbles .15 .40
❑ 50 Learn With Plex - Making Lemonade .15 .40
❑ 51 Learn With Plex - Make Your Bed .15 .40
❑ 52 Learn With Plex - Put Your Toys Away .15 .40
❑ 53 Learn With Plex - Make a Snack .15 .40
❑ 54 Learn With Plex - Wash Your Hair .15 .40
❑ 55 Learn With Plex - Wash Your Hands .15 .40
❑ 56 Color With Brobee - Green .15 .40
❑ 57 Color With Brobee - Yellow .15 .40
❑ 58 Color With Brobee - Red .15 .40
❑ 59 Color With Brobee - Brown .15 .40
❑ 60 Color With Brobee - Purple .15 .40
❑ 61 Color With Brobee - Pink .15 .40
❑ 62 Color With Brobee - Blue .15 .40
❑ 63 Color With Brobee - Orange .15 .40
❑ 64 Sing-a-Long Songs - Yo Gabba Gabba .15 .40
❑ 65 Sing-a-Long Songs - Party in My Tummy .15 .40
❑ 66 Sing-a-Long Songs - Get the Sillies Out .15 .40
❑ 67 Sing-a-Long Songs - Hold Still .15 .40
❑ 68 Sing-a-Long Songs - I Love Bugs .15 .40
❑ 69 Sing-a-Long Songs - The Freeze Game .15 .40
❑ 70 Sing-a-Long Songs - Superhero .15 .40
❑ 71 Sing-a-Long Songs - The Name Game .15 .40
❑ 72 Sing-a-Long Songs - Pretend .15 .40
❑ 73 The Story Book Time .15 .40
❑ 74 The Story Book Time .15 .40
❑ 75 The Story Book Time .15 .40
❑ 76 The Story Book Time .15 .40
❑ 77 The Story Book Time .15 .40
❑ 78 The Story Book Time .15 .40
❑ 79 The Story Book Time .15 .40
❑ 80 The Story Book Time .15 .40
❑ 81 The Story Book Time .15 .40
❑ 82 The Story Book Time .15 .40
❑ 83 The Story Book Time .15 .40
❑ 84 The Story Book Time .15 .40
❑ 85 The Story Book Time .15 .40
❑ 86 The Story Book Time .15 .40
❑ 87 The Story Book Time .15 .40
❑ 88 The Story Book Time .15 .40
❑ 89 The Story Book Time .15 .40
❑ 90 The Story Book Time .15 .40
❑ NNO Yo Gabba Gabba PROMO 1.00 2.50

2012 Yo Gabba Gabba DJ Lance in Motion
COMPLETE SET (6) 10.00 25.00
STATED ODDS 1:24
❑ DL1 Let's Do It 3.00 8.00
❑ DL2 Are You Ready 3.00 8.00
❑ DL3 Let's Make a Funny Face 3.00 8.00
❑ DL4 Hey Everyone 3.00 8.00
❑ DL5 Now It's Time to Dance 3.00 8.00
❑ DL6 Let's Make a Funny Face 3.00 8.00

2012 Yo Gabba Gabba Mark's Magic Pictures
COMPLETE SET (6) 4.00 10.00
STATED ODDS 1:12
❑ MMP1 Elephant 1.50 4.00
❑ MMP2 TBD 1.50 4.00
❑ MMP3 Ant Farm 1.50 4.00
❑ MMP4 Potato Bug 1.50 4.00
❑ MMP5 TBD 1.50 4.00
❑ MMP6 Snowman 1.50 4.00

2012 Yo Gabba Gabba Pop-Ups
COMPLETE SET (6) 3.00 8.00
STATED ODDS 1:8
❑ PU1 Muno 1.00 2.50
❑ PU2 Foofa 1.00 2.50
❑ PU3 Brobee 1.00 2.50
❑ PU4 Toodee 1.00 2.50
❑ PU5 Plex 1.00 2.50
❑ PU6 DJ Lance 1.00 2.50

2012 Yo Gabba Gabba Stickers
*STICKER: 1X TO 2.5X BASIC CARDS
STATED ODDS ONE PER PACK

2013 Alphas Season One
COMPLETE SET (60) 5.00 12.00
❑ 1 Alphas .15 .40
❑ 2 An Unexpected Meeting .15 .40
❑ 3 Conundrum .15 .40
❑ 4 The Plot Thickens .15 .40
❑ 5 A Good Question .15 .40
❑ 6 An Unexpected Discovery .15 .40
❑ 7 A Good Analogy .15 .40
❑ 8 A World All His Own .15 .40
❑ 9 Hard at Work .15 .40
❑ 10 Waiting for the Next Move .15 .40
❑ 11 Red Flag .15 .40
❑ 12 Grocer Assassin? .15 .40
❑ 13 On Deaf Ears .15 .40
❑ 14 Caught in the Act .15 .40
❑ 15 Mindful Awakening .15 .40
❑ 16 Looking for Answers .15 .40
❑ 17 The Ghost .15 .40
❑ 18 Hard Questions and Difficult Answers .15 .40
❑ 19 A New Member .15 .40
❑ 20 Cold Charlie .15 .40
❑ 21 Unconvinced .15 .40
❑ 22 Finding a Ghost .15 .40
❑ 23 An Appeal for Redemption .15 .40
❑ 24 Something Isn't Right .15 .40
❑ 25 It's a Trap! .15 .40
❑ 26 The Second Gunman .15 .40
❑ 27 Friendly Fire .15 .40
❑ 28 A Desperate Move .15 .40
❑ 29 Unfolding Plans .15 .40
❑ 30 The Price of Blind Trust .15 .40
❑ 31 A Clever Ploy .15 .40
❑ 32 A Pyrrhic Victory .15 .40
❑ 33 A Friend Too Perfect .15 .40
❑ 34 An Uncertain Future .15 .40
❑ 35 A Lesson in Murphy's Law .15 .40
❑ 36 Trouble and Luck .15 .40
❑ 37 On the Threshold .15 .40
❑ 38 A Race against the Clock .15 .40
❑ 39 Fight and Flight .15 .40
❑ 40 A Friend in Need .15 .40
❑ 41 Failed Rescue .15 .40
❑ 42 Unfortunate Circumstances .15 .40
❑ 43 No Way Out .15 .40
❑ 44 Growing Suspicions .15 .40
❑ 45 Out of the Frying Pan .15 .40
❑ 46 Hiding Out .15 .40
❑ 47 A Respite and a Plan .15 .40
❑ 48 Hard Choices .15 .40
❑ 49 Running Out of Time .15 .40
❑ 50 Descending Forces .15 .40
❑ 51 A Traitor Revealed .15 .40
❑ 52 Betrayed .15 .40
❑ 53 Puppets and Strings .15 .40
❑ 54 A Final Moment Together .15 .40
❑ 55 The Puppet Master .15 .40
❑ 56 Sheep to the Slaughter .15 .40
❑ 57 Armed but Outclassed .15 .40
❑ 58 Making a Difference .15 .40
❑ 59 Beat Them at Their Own Game .15 .40
❑ 60 Checklist .15 .40

2013 Alphas Season One Autographs
STATED ODDS 1:24
❑ A1 Ryan Cartwright 10.00 25.00
as Gary Bell
❑ A2 Warren Christie 15.00 40.00
as Cameron Hicks
❑ A3 Azita Ghanizada 20.00 50.00
as Rachel Pirzad
❑ A4 Laura Mennell 15.00 40.00
as Nina Theroux
❑ A5 Malik Yoba 8.00 20.00
as Bill Harken
❑ A6 Mahershala Ali 8.00 20.00
as Agent Nathan Clay
❑ A7 Kathleen Gati 8.00 20.00
as Zahra Pirzad
❑ A8 Jane Moffat 8.00 20.00
as Sandra Bell
❑ A9 Liane Balaban 10.00 25.00
as Anna

2013 Alphas Season One Behind the Alphas
COMPLETE SET (9) 8.00 20.00
STATED ODDS 2:24
❑ CH1 Rachell 2.00 5.00
❑ CH2 Nina 2.00 5.00
❑ CH3 Bill 2.00 5.00
❑ CH4 Nina and Rachel 2.00 5.00
❑ CH5 Cameron 2.00 5.00
❑ CH6 Gary 2.00 5.00
❑ CH7 Dr. Rosen 2.00 5.00
❑ CH8 Dr. Rosen/Rachel/Bill/Nina 2.00 5.00
❑ CH9 The Alphas Team 2.00 5.00

2013 Alphas Season One Dual Wardrobe Memorabilia
STATED ODDS 1:96
❑ DM1 Cameron Hicks 8.00 20.00
Dr. Lee Rosen
❑ DM2 Rachel Pirzad 8.00 20.00
Gary Bell
❑ DM3 Bill Harken 8.00 20.00
Cameron Hicks

2013 Alphas Season One The Alphas Team
COMPLETE SET (7) 10.00 25.00
STATED ODDS 2:24
❑ CB1 Dr. Lee Rosen 2.50 6.00
❑ CB2 Cameron Hicks 2.50 6.00
❑ CB3 Nina Theroux 2.50 6.00
❑ CB4 Bill Harken 2.50 6.00
❑ CB5 Rachel Pirzad 2.50 6.00
❑ CB6 Gary Bell 2.50 6.00
❑ CB7 The Alphas Team 2.50 6.00

2013 Alphas Season One Wardrobe Memorabilia
STATED ODDS 1:24
❑ M1 Rachel Pirzad 8.00 20.00

❑ M2 Bill Harken (wearing jacket) 5.00 12.00
❑ M3 Bill Harken (wearing bloody shirt) 5.00 12.00
❑ M4 Cameron Hicks (wearing plaid flannel) 5.00 12.00
❑ M5 Cameron Hicks (wearing grey shirt) 5.00 12.00
❑ M6 Dr. Lee Rosen 5.00 12.00
❑ M7 Dr. Lee Rosen 5.00 12.00
❑ M8 Gary Bell (wearing dark jacket) 6.00 15.00
❑ M9 Gary Bell (wearing red shirt) 6.00 15.00
❑ M10 Nina Theroux 8.00 20.00
❑ M11 Rachel Pirzad (Binder Exclusive)

2013 American Horror Story Preview

COMPLETE SET (12)
❑ AP1 Murder House
❑ AP2 Back East
❑ AP3 A New Beginning
❑ AP4 Neighbors
❑ AP5 Talk Therapy
❑ AP6 Housekeeping
❑ AP7 A Bit of Naughty
❑ AP8 Bully
❑ AP9 On Edge
❑ AP10 Love and Bondage
❑ AP11 A Fiery Tale
❑ AP12 A Baby

2013 Castle Seasons One and Two

COMPLETE SET (72) 6.00 15.00
❑ 1 Castle .20 .50
❑ 2 The Golden Goose .20 .50
❑ 3 Flowers for Your Grave .20 .50
❑ 4 There's Always a Story .20 .50
❑ 5 It's in the Details .20 .50
❑ 6 Apples .20 .50
❑ 7 Inspiration .20 .50
❑ 8 Fluff Cycle .20 .50
❑ 9 The Horn and the Storm .20 .50
❑ 10 A Chill in Her Veins .20 .50
❑ 11 The White Whale .20 .50
❑ 12 Inner Beauty .20 .50
❑ 13 Saved by the Bell .20 .50
❑ 14 Daddy's Little Girl .20 .50
❑ 15 Up a Tree .20 .50
❑ 16 Castle's Bluff .20 .50
❑ 17 Back to Basics .20 .50
❑ 18 Airtight .20 .50
❑ 19 If Looks Could Kill .20 .50
❑ 20 The Grumpy Beaver .20 .50
❑ 21 To the Extraordinary KB .20 .50
❑ 22 Here Kitty Kitty .20 .50
❑ 23 If You're Listening .20 .50
❑ 24 All in the Family .20 .50
❑ 25 The Diabolical Cool Dad .20 .50
❑ 26 White Collar Pimp .20 .50
❑ 27 Too Many Wives .20 .50
❑ 28 All Grown Up .20 .50
❑ 29 The Ice Bullet Mystery .20 .50
❑ 30 The Benefits of Literature .20 .50
❑ 31 A Night for Martha .20 .50
❑ 32 Always a Bridesmaid .20 .50
❑ 33 The Shining Stars .20 .50
❑ 34 Crime and Punishment .20 .50
❑ 35 Fatherly Advice .20 .50
❑ 36 Rathborne .20 .50
❑ 37 Goldilocks Squatter .20 .50
❑ 38 Drago Double Date .20 .50
❑ 39 Third Strike .20 .50
❑ 40 Fallacious Arguments .20 .50
❑ 41 Slick Not Sticky .20 .50
❑ 42 Carry-On Baggage .20 .50
❑ 43 Tongue Tied .20 .50
❑ 44 The Love Shack .20 .50
❑ 45 Desperately Seeking Venom .20 .50
❑ 46 A Crime of Passion .20 .50
❑ 47 Federal Heat .20 .50
❑ 48 In the Light of Day .20 .50
❑ 49 Eagle Eye .20 .50
❑ 50 Smell the Coffee .20 .50
❑ 51 Death Awaits the Robber of Graves .20 .50
❑ 52 Castle and the Curse of Kan-Xul .20 .50
❑ 53 Want to Buy a Mummy .20 .50
❑ 54 She's Armed He's Dangerous .20 .50
❑ 55 Bobby Mann FTW .20 .50
❑ 56 A Steady Bag .20 .50
❑ 57 Mystery's in the Box .20 .50
❑ 58 The 54th .20 .50
❑ 59 Dirty Cop .20 .50
❑ 60 Misdirection .20 .50
❑ 61 Literally and Figuratively Cool .20 .50
❑ 62 Becks and Maddy .20 .50
❑ 63 Demming Schlemming .20 .50
❑ 64 A Tale of Two Leads .20 .50
❑ 65 Back to Square One .20 .50
❑ 66 Two Good Suspects .20 .50
❑ 67 Two-for-One .20 .50
❑ 68 Kissing Kate .20 .50
❑ 69 A Father's Trial .20 .50
❑ 70 A Game of Envy .20 .50
❑ 71 Ships in the Night .20 .50
❑ 72 Checklist .20 .50

2013 Castle Seasons One and Two Autographs

STATED ODDS 1:24
❑ A1 Nathan Fillion 60.00 120.00
❑ A2 Jon Huertas 20.00 40.00
❑ A3 Seamus Dever 20.00 40.00
❑ A4 Susan Sullivan 20.00 40.00
❑ A5 Tamala Jones 12.00 30.00
❑ A6 Ruben Santiago-Hudson 12.00 30.00
❑ A7 Dana Delany 50.00 100.00
❑ A8 Arye Gross 10.00 25.00
❑ A9 Scott Paulin 10.00 25.00
❑ A10 Michael Trucco 12.00 30.00
❑ A11 Juliana Dever 10.00 25.00
❑ A12 Monet Mazur 10.00 25.00
❑ AE1 Nathan Fillion MEM 125.00 250.00

2013 Castle Seasons One and Two Behind the Scenes

COMPLETE SET (9) 20.00 40.00
STATED ODDS 1:12
❑ BTS1 Behind the Scenes 3.00 8.00
❑ BTS2 Behind the Scenes 3.00 8.00
❑ BTS3 Behind the Scenes 3.00 8.00
❑ BTS4 Behind the Scenes 3.00 8.00
❑ BTS5 Behind the Scenes 3.00 8.00
❑ BTS6 Behind the Scenes 3.00 8.00
❑ BTS7 Behind the Scenes 3.00 8.00
❑ BTS8 Behind the Scenes 3.00 8.00
❑ BTS9 Behind the Scenes 3.00 8.00

2013 Castle Seasons One and Two Characters

COMPLETE SET (9) 20.00 40.00
STATED ODDS 1:12
❑ C1 Richard Castle 3.00 8.00
❑ C2 Kate Beckett 3.00 8.00
❑ C3 Javier Esposito 3.00 8.00
❑ C4 Kevin Ryan 3.00 8.00
❑ C5 Martha Rodgers 3.00 8.00
❑ C6 Alexis Castle 3.00 8.00
❑ C7 Lanie Parish 3.00 8.00
❑ C8 Captain Roy Montgomery 3.00 8.00
❑ C9 Cast of Castle 3.00 8.00

2013 Castle Seasons One and Two Dual Wardrobe Memorabilia

STATED ODDS 1:57
❑ DM1 Richard Castle Kate Beckett 30.00 60.00
❑ DM2 Richard Castle Alexis Castle 20.00 40.00
❑ DM3 Martha Rodgers Alexis Castle 20.00 40.00
❑ DM4 Javier Esposito Kevin Ryan 12.00 30.00
❑ DM5 Roy Montgomery Kate Beckett 20.00 40.00
❑ DM6 Richard Castle Martha Rodgers 20.00 40.00
❑ DM7 Kate Beckett Kevin Ryan 12.00 30.00
❑ DM8 Kate Beckett Javier Esposito 12.00 30.00
❑ DM9 Kate Beckett Lanie Parish 20.00 40.00
❑ DM10 Lanie Parish Javier Esposito 12.00 30.00
❑ DM11 Richard Castle Kate Beckett (Binder Exclusive) 20.00 40.00

2013 Castle Seasons One and Two Promos

❑ P1 Beckett/Castle San Diego Comic Con) 6.00 15.00
❑ P2 Beckett/Castle Non-Sport Update) 2.00 5.00
❑ P3 Cast (Licensing Show) 6.00 15.00

2013 Castle Seasons One and Two Scene of the Crime

COMPLETE SET (9) 15.00 30.00
STATED ODDS 1:12
❑ CS1 Flowers for Your Grave 2.50 6.00
❑ CS2 Hell Hath No Fury 2.50 6.00
❑ CS3 Nanny McDead 2.50 6.00
❑ CS4 A Chill Goes Through Her Veins 2.50 6.00
❑ CS5 The Double Down 2.50 6.00
❑ CS6 Inventing the Girl 2.50 6.00
❑ CS7 Famous Last Words 2.50 6.00
❑ CS8 The Fifth Bullet 2.50 6.00
❑ CS9 The Mistress Always Spanks Twice 2.50 6.00

2013 Castle Seasons One and Two Wardrobe Memorabilia

STATED ODDS 1:18
❑ M1 Javier Esposito Suit 10.00 25.00
❑ M2 Alexis Castle Coat 10.00 25.00
❑ M3 Kate Beckett Green Jacket 20.00 40.00
❑ M4 Richard Castle Suit 25.00 50.00
❑ M5 Lanie Parish Coat 10.00 25.00
❑ M6 Kevin Ryan Suit 10.00 25.00
❑ M7 Kate Beckett Dress 25.00 50.00
❑ M8 Richard Castle Burgundy Shirt 20.00 40.00
❑ M9 Martha Rodgers Dress 20.00 40.00
❑ M10 Kate Beckett Black Jacket 25.00 50.00
❑ M11 Alexis Castle Jacket 10.00 25.00
❑ M12 Javier Esposito Jeans 10.00 25.00
❑ M13 Kate Beckett Jeans 20.00 40.00
❑ M14 Lanie Parish Jeans 10.00 25.00
❑ M15 Richard Castle Lavender Shirt 20.00 40.00
❑ M16 Kevin Ryan Pants 10.00 25.00
❑ M17 Alexis Castle Shirt 10.00 25.00
❑ M18 Javier Esposito Pants 10.00 25.00
❑ M19 Roy Montgomery Shirt 10.00 25.00
❑ M20 Kate Beckett Shirt 25.00 50.00
❑ M21 Alexis Castle Pajamas 20.00 40.00
❑ M22 Richard Castle Pants 20.00 40.00
❑ M23 Kevin Ryan Gray Suit 10.00 25.00
❑ M24 Kate Beckett Brown Jacket 20.00 40.00
❑ M25 Lanie Parish Pants 10.00 25.00
❑ M26 Kevin Ryan Shirt 10.00 25.00
❑ M27 Richard Castle Pinstripe Shirt 20.00 40.00
❑ M28 Roy Montgomery Suit 10.00 25.00
❑ M29 Richard Castle Navy Suit 20.00 40.00
❑ M30 Martha Rodgers Shirt 10.00 25.00
❑ M31 Javier Esposito Shirt 10.00 25.00

2013 DC Comics Superman The Legend

COMPLETE SET (62) 6.00 15.00
❑ 1 Superman .15 .40
❑ 2 Supergirl .15 .40
❑ 3 Bizarro .15 .40
❑ 4 Brainiac .15 .40
❑ 5 Superman Beyond .15 .40
❑ 6 Cyborg Superman .15 .40
❑ 7 Darkseid .15 .40
❑ 8 Doomsday .15 .40
❑ 9 General Zod .15 .40
❑ 10 Encantadora .15 .40
❑ 11 Lex Luthor .15 .40
❑ 12 Eradicator .15 .40
❑ 13 Faora .15 .40
❑ 14 Fatal Five .15 .40
❑ 15 Lois Lane .15 .40
❑ 16 Fortress of Solitude .15 .40
❑ 17 Gangbuster .15 .40
❑ 18 Guardian .15 .40
❑ 19 Imperiex .15 .40
❑ 20 Toyman .15 .40
❑ 21 Krypto, The Superdog .15 .40
❑ 22 Lana Lang .15 .40
❑ 23 Lori Lemaris .15 .40
❑ 24 Perry White .15 .40
❑ 25 Metallo .15 .40
❑ 26 Mr. Mxyzptlk .15 .40
❑ 27 Jimmy Olsen .15 .40
❑ 28 Parasite .15 .40
❑ 29 Prankster .15 .40
❑ 30 Riot .15 .40
❑ 31 Outreach 1 Team .15 .40
❑ 32 Superboy .15 .40
❑ 33 Clark Kent .15 .40
❑ 34 Connor Kent .15 .40
❑ 35 Kara Kent .15 .40
❑ 36 Young Superman .15 .40
❑ 37 Jonathan Kent .15 .40
❑ 38 Martha Kent .15 .40
❑ 39 Pete Ross .15 .40
❑ 40 Chris Kent .15 .40
❑ 41 Cat Grant .15 .40
❑ 42 Captain Margaret Sawyer .15 .40
❑ 43 Inspector Henderson .15 .40
❑ 44 Morgan Edge .15 .40
❑ 45 Silver Banshee .15 .40
❑ 46 Lucy Lane .15 .40
❑ 47 General Sam Lane .15 .40
❑ 48 Lord Satanus .15 .40
❑ 49 Steel .15 .40
❑ 50 Jor-El and Lara .15 .40
❑ 51 Legion of Super-Heroes .15 .40
❑ 52 Phantom Zone .15 .40
❑ 53 Kryptonite .15 .40
❑ 54 Mon-El .15 .40
❑ 55 Kal-El .15 .40
❑ 56 Kingdom Come Superman .15 .40
❑ 57 Superman Red .15 .40
❑ 58 Superman Blue .15 .40
❑ 59 Bottle City of Kandor .15 .40
❑ 60 Black Banshee .15 .40
❑ 61 The Worldkillers .15 .40
❑ 62 Checklist .15 .40
❑ P1 Superman PROMO
❑ NNO Action Comics #844 Digital Comic Giveaway

2013 DC Comics Superman The Legend Alternate Worlds

COMPLETE SET (9) 8.00 20.00
OVERALL CHASE ODDS 4:24
❑ ARS1 President Superman 1.50 4.00
❑ ARS2 Superman from The Dark Knight Returns 1.50 4.00
❑ ARS3 Superman of Earth 2 1.50 4.00
❑ ARS4 Subject 1 1.50 4.00
❑ ARS5 Superman Beyond 1.50 4.00
❑ ARS6 Superman of Earth One 1.50 4.00
❑ ARS7 Red Son 1.50 4.00
❑ ARS8 Bizarro 1.50 4.00
❑ ARS9 Son of Darkseid 1.50 4.00

2013 DC Comics Superman The Legend Secret Origin

COMPLETE SET (6) 6.00 15.00
OVERALL CHASE ODDS 4:24
❑ SO1 Issue #1 1.50 4.00
❑ SO2 Issue #2 1.50 4.00
❑ SO3 Issue #3 1.50 4.00
❑ SO4 Issue #4 1.50 4.00
❑ SO5 Issue #5 1.50 4.00
❑ SO6 Issue #6 1.50 4.00

2013 DC Comics Superman The Legend Sketches

STATED ODDS 1:24
❑ 1 Aaron Felizmenio
❑ 2 Aaron Riley
❑ 3 Agnes Garbowska
❑ 4 Amy Clark Anderson
❑ 5 Ana Sanchez
❑ 6 Andrew Jones
❑ 7 Anthony Wheeler
❑ 8 Ashleigh Popplewell
❑ 9 Beck Seashols
❑ 10 Benjamin Glendenning
❑ 11 Bill McKay
❑ 12 Bill Pulkovski
❑ 13 Boo Dan Parsons
❑ 14 Brendon and Brian Fraim
❑ 15 Brent Engstrom
❑ 16 Brent Ragland
❑ 17 Brian Canio
❑ 18 Brian Kong
❑ 19 Bruce Gerlach
❑ 20 Buddy Prince
❑ 21 Bukshot!
❑ 22 Camila Fortuna
❑ 23 Cassandra James
❑ 24 Chris Chuckry
❑ 25 Chris Foreman
❑ 26 Chris Thorne
❑ 27 Clayton McCormack
❑ 28 Dan Borgonos
❑ 29 Dan Schaefer
❑ 30 Danielle Gransaull
❑ 31 Dave Beaty
❑ 32 Dave Lynch
❑ 33 Dave Sharpe
❑ 34 Dave Tata
❑ 35 David Baron
❑ 36 David Hunter
❑ 37 David Rabbitte
❑ 38 Elvis Moura
❑ 39 Eman Casallos
❑ 40 Erik Caines
❑ 41 Frank Kadar
❑ 42 Fritz Casas
❑ 43 Gary Shipman
❑ 44 George Davis
❑ 45 George Deep
❑ 46 Glen Fernandez
❑ 47 Hayden Davis
❑ 48 Irma Ahmed
❑ 49 Isaiah McAllister
❑ 50 Jader Correa
❑ 51 Jake Minor
❑ 52 Jamie Roberts
❑ 53 Jason Worthington
❑ 54 Javier Aranda
❑ 55 JC Fabul
❑ 56 Jed Thomas
❑ 57 Jeff Victor
❑ 58 Jennifer Mercer
❑ 59 Jeremy Treece
❑ 60 Jerry Ma
❑ 61 Jezreel Rojales
❑ 62 Joe Simko
❑ 63 John JAX Jackman
❑ 64 Jomar Bulda
❑ 65 Jon Hughes
❑ 66 Jonathan Racimo
❑ 67 Josh Howard
❑ 68 Kate Bradley
❑ 69 Kevin Gentilcore
❑ 70 Kris Cagle
❑ 71 Lark Sudol
❑ 72 Laura Inglis
❑ 73 Layron DeJarnette
❑ 74 Levi Espino
❑ 75 Luke Smarto
❑ 76 Marat Mychaels
❑ 77 Marcelo Ferreira
❑ 78 Mark Marvida
❑ 79 Mark Nasso
❑ 80 Matias Streb
❑ 81 Matthew Hansen
❑ 82 Matthew Minor
❑ 83 Mauricio Dias
❑ 84 Michael Duron
❑ 85 Michael Kasinger
❑ 86 Mike Vasquez
❑ 87 MJ San Juan
❑ 88 Nathan Watson
❑ 89 Neil Camera
❑ 90 Omar Bergonia
❑ 91 Rainier Lagunsad
❑ 92 Remy Mokhtar
❑ 93 Richard Brady
❑ 94 Richard Cox
❑ 95 Robert Hack
❑ 96 Rodjer Goulart
❑ 97 Ron McCain
❑ 98 Stacey Kardash
❑ 99 Stefanie Battalene
❑ 100 Stephanie Swanger
❑ 101 Thomas Boatwright
❑ 102 Thomas Tuomey
❑ 103 Tim Shay
❑ 104 Tom Nguyen
❑ 105 Tony Perna
❑ 106 Travis Walton
❑ 107 Vince Sunico
❑ 108 Vo
❑ 109 WAY$HAK
❑ 110 Will Nichols
❑ 111 William Bronson
❑ 112 William Donley III

2013 DC Comics Superman The Legend Women of Superman

COMPLETE SET (9) 8.00 20.00
OVERALL CHASE ODDS 4:24
❑ WOS1 Lara Lor-Van 1.50 4.00
❑ WOS2 Cat Grant 1.50 4.00
❑ WOS3 DC Comics Livewire 1.50 4.00
❑ WOS4 Supergirl 1.50 4.00
❑ WOS5 Lana Lang 1.50 4.00
❑ WOS6 DC Comics Maxima 1.50 4.00
❑ WOS7 Lois Lane 1.50 4.00
❑ WOS8 Silver Banshee 1.50 4.00
❑ WOS9 Ursa 1.50 4.00

2013 DC Comics Superman The Legend X-Ray Vision

COMPLETE SET (9) 8.00 20.00
OVERALL CHASE ODDS 4:24
❑ XR1 Nerd Club 1.50 4.00
❑ XR2 Muscle Building Club 1.50 4.00
❑ XR3 I Got This 1.50 4.00
❑ XR4 Retro 1.50 4.00
❑ XR5 Flying 1.50 4.00
❑ XR6 Punch 1.50 4.00
❑ XR7 Strength 1.50 4.00
❑ XR8 Landing 1.50 4.00
❑ XR9 The Legend 1.50 4.00

2013 Falling Skies Season Two

COMPLETE SET (30) 20.00 50.00
❑ 1 Worlds Apart 1.50 4.00
❑ 2 Worlds Apart 1.50 4.00
❑ 3 Worlds Apart 1.50 4.00
❑ 4 Shall We Gather at the River 1.50 4.00
❑ 5 Shall We Gather at the River 1.50 4.00
❑ 6 Shall We Gather at the River 1.50 4.00
❑ 7 Compass 1.50 4.00
❑ 8 Compass 1.50 4.00
❑ 9 Compass 1.50 4.00
❑ 10 Young Bloods 1.50 4.00
❑ 11 Young Bloods 1.50 4.00
❑ 12 Young Bloods 1.50 4.00
❑ 13 Love and Other Acts of Courage 1.50 4.00
❑ 14 Love and Other Acts of Courage 1.50 4.00
❑ 15 Love and Other Acts of Courage 1.50 4.00
❑ 16 Homecoming 1.50 4.00
❑ 17 Homecoming 1.50 4.00
❑ 18 Homecoming 1.50 4.00
❑ 19 Molon Labe 1.50 4.00
❑ 20 Molon Labe 1.50 4.00
❑ 21 Molon Labe 1.50 4.00
❑ 22 Death March 1.50 4.00
❑ 23 Death March 1.50 4.00
❑ 24 Death March 1.50 4.00
❑ 25 The Price of Greatness 1.50 4.00
❑ 26 The Price of Greatness 1.50 4.00
❑ 27 The Price of Greatness 1.50 4.00
❑ 28 A More Perfect Union 1.50 4.00
❑ 29 A More Perfect Union 1.50 4.00
❑ 30 A More Perfect Union 1.50 4.00
❑ BT1 Get Off My Planet (issued as box topper) 5.00 12.00

2013 Falling Skies Season Two Autograph Costumes

❑ NW Noah Wyle as Tom Mason (issued as 4-box incentive) 40.00 80.00
❑ WP Will Patton as Captain Weaver (issued as 2-box incentive) 30.00 60.00

2013 Falling Skies Season Two Autographs

ONE AUTO PER PACK
EL (EXTREMELY LIMITED): LESS THAN 200 COPIES
❑ 1 Billy Wickman as Boon EL 5.00 12.00
❑ 2 Brad Kelly as Lyle EL 8.00 20.00
❑ 3 Colin Cunningham as John Pope EL 15.00 40.00
❑ 4 Connor Jessup as Ben Mason EL 10.00 25.00
❑ 5 Daniyah Ysrayl as Rick EL 5.00 12.00
❑ 6 Drew Roy as Hal Mason EL 8.00 20.00
❑ 7 Dylan Authors as Jimmy Boland EL 5.00 12.00
❑ 8 Jessy Schram as Karen Nadler EL 12.00 30.00
❑ 9 Luciana Carro as Crazy Lee EL 10.00 25.00
❑ 10 Maxim Knight as Matt Mason EL 6.00 15.00
❑ 11 Melissa Kramer as Sarah EL 5.00 12.00
❑ 12 Moon Bloodgood as Anne Glass EL 40.00 80.00
❑ 13 Mpho Koaho as Anthony EL 5.00 12.00
❑ 14 Noah Wyle as Tom Mason EL 40.00 80.00
❑ 15 Peter Shinkoda as Dai EL 5.00 12.00
❑ 16 Sarah Carter as Maggie EL 15.00 40.00
❑ 17 Seychelle Gabriel as Lourdes EL 15.00 40.00
❑ 18 Terry O'Quinn as Arthur Manchester EL 20.00 50.00
❑ 19 Will Patton as Captain Weaver EL 20.00 50.00

2013 Falling Skies Season Two Costumes

TWO COSTUME CARDS PER PACK
STATED PRINT RUN 375 SER. #'d SETS
❑ CC18 Tom Mason shirt 5.00 12.00
❑ CC19 Anne Glass jacket 5.00 12.00
❑ CC20 Anne Glass shirt 5.00 12.00
❑ CC21 John Pope shirt 4.00 10.00
❑ CC22 John Pope shirt 4.00 10.00
❑ CC23 Hal Mason pants 4.00 10.00
❑ CC24 Ben Mason shirt 5.00 12.00
❑ CC25 Ben Mason shirt 5.00 12.00
❑ CC26 Maggie hoodie 6.00 15.00
❑ CC27 Maggie pants 6.00 15.00
❑ CC28 Lourdes shirt 4.00 10.00
❑ CC29 Captain Weaver shirt 4.00 10.00
❑ CC30 Captain Weaver pants 4.00 10.00
❑ CC31 Karen shirt 6.00 15.00
❑ CC32 Dai vest 4.00 10.00
❑ CC33 Porter jacket 4.00 10.00
❑ CC34 Jimmy Boland shirt 4.00 10.00
❑ CC35 Arthur Manchester shirt 4.00 10.00
❑ CC36 Arthur Manchester jacket 4.00 10.00

2013 Falling Skies Season Two International Pinups

COMPLETE SET (9) 15.00 40.00
STATED ODDS 1:2
❑ 1 Argentina 3.00 8.00
❑ 2 Mexico 3.00 8.00
❑ 3 German 3.00 8.00
❑ 4 Spain 3.00 8.00
❑ 5 Netherlands 3.00 8.00
❑ 6 Singapore 3.00 8.00
❑ 7 Australia 3.00 8.00
❑ 8 Japan 3.00 8.00
❑ 9 Sweden 3.00 8.00

2013 Falling Skies Season Two Promos

❑ P1 Cast (General Distribution) 1.25 3.00
❑ P2 Tom Mason (Binder Exclusive) 4.00 10.00
❑ P3 Four dudes (2013 San Diego Comic Con) 105.00 4.00

2013 Falling Skies Season Two Quotable

COMP.SET w/o RR (9) 15.00 40.00
STATED ODDS 1:2
❑ Q1 Tom Mason 3.00 8.00
❑ Q2 Anne Glass 3.00 8.00
❑ Q3 John Pope 3.00 8.00
❑ Q4 Dan Weaver 3.00 8.00
❑ Q5 Hal Mason 3.00 8.00
❑ Q6 Maggie 3.00 8.00
❑ Q7 Lourdes 3.00 8.00
❑ Q8 Ben Mason 3.00 8.00
❑ Q9 John Pope 3.00 8.00
❑ Q10 Captain Weaver (issued as Rittenhouse Reward) 25.00 60.00

2013 Fleer Retro Marvel

COMPLETE SET (60) 12.00 30.00
❑ 1 Black Bolt .60 1.50
❑ 2 Black Panther .60 1.50
❑ 3 Black Widow .60 1.50
❑ 4 Cable .60 1.50
❑ 5 Captain America .60 1.50
❑ 6 Captain Marvel .60 1.50
❑ 7 Colossus .60 1.50
❑ 8 Cyclops .60 1.50
❑ 9 Daredevil .60 1.50
❑ 10 Deadpool 1.25 3.00
❑ 11 Doctor Strange .60 1.50
❑ 12 Elektra .60 1.50
❑ 13 Emma Frost .60 1.50
❑ 14 Ghost Rider .60 1.50
❑ 15 Giant-Man .60 1.50
❑ 16 Hawkeye .60 1.50
❑ 17 Hulk .60 1.50
❑ 18 Human Torch .60 1.50
❑ 19 Iceman .60 1.50
❑ 20 Invisible Woman .60 1.50
❑ 21 Iron Fist .60 1.50
❑ 22 Iron Man .60 1.50
❑ 23 Luke Cage .60 1.50
❑ 24 Moon Knight .60 1.50
❑ 25 Mr. Fantastic .60 1.50
❑ 26 Namor .60 1.50
❑ 27 Nightcrawler .60 1.50
❑ 28 Northstar .60 1.50
❑ 29 Nova .60 1.50
❑ 30 Professor X .60 1.50
❑ 31 Psylocke .60 1.50
❑ 32 Punisher .60 1.50
❑ 33 Red Hulk .60 1.50
❑ 34 Red She-Hulk .60 1.50
❑ 35 Rocket Raccoon .60 1.50
❑ 36 Rogue .60 1.50
❑ 37 Scarlet Witch .60 1.50

38 She-Hulk .60 1.50
39 Silver Surfer .60 1.50
40 Spider-Man .75 2.00
41 Spider-Woman .60 1.50
42 Star-Lord .60 1.50
43 Storm .60 1.50
44 Thing .60 1.50
45 Thor .60 1.50
46 Ultimate Spider-Man .60 1.50
47 Venom .60 1.50
48 Wasp .60 1.50
49 Wolverine 1.00 2.50
50 X-23 .60 1.50
51 Daken .60 1.50
52 Doctor Doom .60 1.50
53 Galactus .60 1.50
54 Lizard .60 1.50
55 Loki .60 1.50
56 Magneto .60 1.50
57 Mojo .60 1.50
58 Mystique .60 1.50
59 Norman Osborn .60 1.50
60 Thanos .60 1.50

2013 Fleer Retro Marvel 1990 Impel Marvel Universe

COMPLETE SET (25) 40.00 80.00
STATED ODDS 1:6

1 Cable 2.00 5.00
2 Captain America 2.00 5.00
3 Captain Marvel 2.00 5.00
4 Colossus 2.00 5.00
5 Cyclops 2.00 5.00
6 Daredevil 2.00 5.00
7 Deadpool 4.00 10.00
8 Hawkeye 2.00 5.00
9 Hulk 2.00 5.00
10 Human Torch 2.00 5.00
11 Iceman 2.00 5.00
12 Invisible Woman 2.00 5.00
13 Iron Fist 2.00 5.00
14 Iron Man 2.00 5.00
15 Loki 2.00 5.00
16 Luke Cage 2.00 5.00
17 Wolverine 3.00 8.00
18 Mr. Fantastic 2.00 5.00
19 Nova 2.00 5.00
20 Spider-Man 3.00 8.00
21 Storm 2.00 5.00
22 Thing 2.00 5.00
23 Thor 2.00 5.00
24 Magneto 2.00 5.00
25 Red Skull 2.00 5.00

2013 Fleer Retro Marvel 1990 Impel Marvel Universe Autographs

STATED ODDS 1:576

1 Adi Granov Cable 10.00 25.00
2 Steve Epting Captain America 10.00 25.00
3 Ed McGuinness Captain Marvel 12.00 30.00
5 Adi Granov Cyclops 10.00 25.00
6 Mike Deodato Jr. Daredevil 12.00 30.00
7 Carlo Barberi Deadpool 20.00 50.00
8 Paul Renaud Hawkeye 10.00 25.00
9 Steve McNiven Hulk 12.00 30.00
11 Pablo Raimondi Iceman 12.00 30.00
12 Phil Noto Invisible Woman 10.00 25.00
13 Mike Deodato Jr. Iron Fist 12.00 30.00
14 Salvador Larroca Martinez Iron Man 15.00 40.00
16 Mike Deodato Jr. Luke Cage 12.00 30.00
17 Jim Cheung Wolverine 30.00 60.00
19 Clayton Henry Nova 12.00 30.00
20 Stefano Caselli Spider-Man 10.00 25.00

2013 Fleer Retro Marvel 1991 Impel Marvel Universe

COMPLETE SET (20) 40.00 80.00
STATED ODDS 1:7.5

1 Captain America 2.50 6.00
2 Captain Marvel 2.50 6.00
3 Colossus 2.50 6.00
4 Cyclops 2.50 6.00
5 Daredevil 2.50 6.00
6 Deadpool 5.00 12.00
7 Hulk 2.50 6.00
8 Human Torch 2.50 6.00
9 Iceman 2.50 6.00
10 Invisible Woman 2.50 6.00
11 Iron Man 2.50 6.00
12 Loki 2.50 6.00
13 Wolverine 4.00 10.00
14 Mr. Fantastic 2.50 6.00
15 Spider-Man 4.00 10.00
16 Storm 2.50 6.00
17 Thing 2.50 6.00
18 Thor 2.50 6.00
19 Magneto 2.50 6.00
20 Thanos 2.50 6.00

2013 Fleer Retro Marvel 1991 Impel Marvel Universe Autographs

STATED ODDS 1:720

2 Dexter Soy Captain Marvel 12.00 30.00
3 Adi Granov Colossus 10.00 25.00
4 Brandon Peterson Cyclops 10.00 25.00
5 Paolo Rivera Daredevil 12.00 30.00
6 Jason Pearson Deadpool
7 Carlo Pagulayan Hulk 12.00 30.00
10 Randy Green Invisible Woman 10.00 25.00
11 Scot Eaton Iron Man 10.00 25.00
12 Stephanie Hans Loki 10.00 25.00
14 Joe Jusko Mr. Fantastic 12.00 30.00
15 Brad Walker Spider-Man 15.00 40.00
16 Brandon Peterson Storm 10.00 25.00
17 Joe Jusko Thing 12.00 30.00
19 Paco Medina Magneto 15.00 40.00
20 Mark Bagley Thanos 10.00 25.00

2013 Fleer Retro Marvel 1992 Impel Marvel Universe

COMPLETE SET (15) 40.00 80.00
STATED ODDS 1:10

1 Captain America 2.50 6.00
2 Cyclops 2.50 6.00
3 Daredevil 2.50 6.00
4 Deadpool 5.00 12.00
5 Hulk 2.50 6.00
6 Human Torch 2.50 6.00
7 Iron Man 2.50 6.00
8 Loki 2.50 6.00
9 Mr. Fantastic 2.50 6.00
10 Spider-Man 4.00 10.00
11 Storm 2.50 6.00
12 Thor 2.50 6.00
13 Wolverine 4.00 10.00
14 Magneto 2.50 6.00
15 Thanos 2.50 6.00

2013 Fleer Retro Marvel 1992 Impel Marvel Universe Autographs

STATED ODDS 1:960

2 Giuseppe Camuncoli Cyclops 10.00 25.00
4 Patrick Zircher Deadpool 30.00 60.00
5 Michael Golden Hulk 10.00 25.00
6 Ryan Stegman Human Torch 12.00 30.00
8 Stephanie Hans Loki 10.00 25.00
9 Stefano Caselli Mr. Fantastic 12.00 30.00
10 Brad Walker Spider-Man 30.00 60.00
11 Arthur Adams Storm 15.00 40.00
13 Arthur Adams Wolverine 15.00 40.00
14 Mike Perkins Magneto 30.00 60.00
15 Mark Bagley Thanos 15.00 40.00

2013 Fleer Retro Marvel Autographs

STATED ODDS 1:10

1 Brandon Peterson Black Bolt 5.00 12.00
2 Adi Granov Black Panther 5.00 12.00
4 Dave Wilkins Cable 5.00 12.00
5 Steve Epting Captian America 5.00 12.00
6 Terry Dodson Captain Marvel 6.00 15.00
8 Jim Cheung Cyclops 5.00 12.00
9 Chris Samnee Daredevil 5.00 12.00
10 Paco Medina Deadpool 12.00 30.00
11 Leinil Francis Yu Doctor Strange 5.00 12.00
13 Giuseppe Camuncoli Emma Frost 5.00 12.00
14 Matthew Clark Ghost Rider 5.00 12.00
16 Mike Deodato Jr. Hawkeye 8.00 20.00
17 Olivier Coipel Hulk 6.00 15.00
19 Stuart Immonen Iceman 5.00 12.00
21 Mike Deodato Jr. Iron Fist 8.00 20.00
22 Salvador Larroca Martinez Iron Man 6.00 15.00
23 Mike Deodato Jr. Luke Cage 6.00 15.00
24 Alex Maleev Moon Knight 5.00 12.00
25 Steve Epting Mr. Fantastic 5.00 12.00
28 Dustin Weaver Northstar 5.00 12.00
29 Andy Lanning Nova 5.00 12.00
30 Giuseppe Camuncoli Professor X 6.00 15.00
31 Jorge Molina Psylocke 6.00 15.00
34 Carlo Pagulayan Red She-hulk 6.00 15.00
35 Salvador Larroca Martinez Rocket Raccon 6.00 15.00
36 Adi Granov Rogue 5.00 12.00
38 Ryan Stegman She-Hulk 5.00 12.00
39 Lee Weeks Silver Surfer 6.00 15.00
41 Alex Maleev Spider-Woman 5.00 12.00
42 Mark Bagley Star-Lord 5.00 12.00
43 David Lopez Storm 5.00 12.00
44 Ryan Stegman Thing 6.00 15.00
46 Jim Cheung Ultimate Spider-Man (miles) 6.00 15.00
47 Patrick Zircher Venom 6.00 15.00
48 Olivier Coipel Wasp 5.00 12.00
49 Clay Mann Wolverine 6.00 15.00
50 Stefano Caselli X-23 6.00 15.00
51 Giuseppe Camuncoli Daken 5.00 12.00
53 Barry Kitson Galactus
54 Chris Bachalo Lizard 5.00 12.00
55 Mike Mayhew Loki 5.00 12.00
56 Ale Garza Magneto 6.00 15.00
57 Adam Kubert Mojo 5.00 12.00
58 Adam Kubert Mystique 6.00 15.00
59 Mike Deodato Jr. Norman Osborn 6.00 15.00
60 Mark Bagley Thanos 6.00 15.00

2013 Fleer Retro Marvel Hardware

STATED ODDS 1:60

1 Punisher 8.00 20.00
2 Deadpool 12.00 30.00
3 Iron Man 8.00 20.00
4 Silver Samurai 8.00 20.00
5 Thor 8.00 20.00
6 Hawkeye 8.00 20.00
7 Ant-Man 8.00 20.00
8 Black Widow 8.00 20.00
9 Mandarin 8.00 20.00
10 H Ezekiel Stane 8.00 20.00

2013 Fleer Retro Marvel Holograms

COMPLETE SET (3) 50.00 100.00
STATED ODDS 1:80

H1 Fantastic Four vs Dr. Doom 15.00 40.00
H2 New Avengers vs Dark Avengers 15.00 40.00
H3 X-Men vs Brotherhood 15.00 40.00

2013 Fleer Retro Marvel Intimidation Nation

STATED ODDS 1:30

1 Wolverine 10.00 25.00
2 Deathlok 8.00 20.00
3 Hulk 8.00 20.00
4 Ghost Rider 8.00 20.00
5 Punisher 8.00 20.00
6 Silver Surfer 8.00 20.00
7 Black Panther 8.00 20.00
8 Red Hulk 8.00 20.00
9 Sabretooth 8.00 20.00
10 Deadpool 10.00 25.00
11 Galactus 8.00 20.00
12 Magneto 8.00 20.00
13 Red Skull 8.00 20.00
14 Green Goblin 8.00 20.00
15 Bullseye 8.00 20.00
16 Thanos 8.00 20.00
17 Venom 8.00 20.00
18 Carnage 8.00 20.00
19 Doctor Doom 8.00 20.00
20 Juggernaut 8.00 20.00

2013 Fleer Retro Marvel Jambalaya

STATED ODDS 1:200

1 Mr. Fantastic 75.00 150.00
2 Invisible Woman 100.00 200.00
3 Thing
4 Human Torch
5 Spider-Man 250.00 400.00
6 Iron Man 250.00 400.00
7 Captain 200.00 350.00
8 Thor 200.00 300.00
9 Hulk 100.00 200.00
10 Wolverine 350.00 550.00
11 Cyclops 100.00 200.00
12 Iceman 125.00 225.00
13 Storm 150.00 250.00
14 Silver Surfer 100.00 200.00
15 Daredevil 150.00 250.00
16 Deadpool 200.00 350.00
17 Punisher 200.00 300.00
18 Doctor Doom 100.00 200.00
19 Venom 125.00 225.00
20 Loki 150.00 250.00
21 Magneto 150.00 250.00

2013 Fleer Retro Marvel Metal

COMPLETE SET (42) 40.00 80.00
STATED ODDS 7:20

1 Mr. Fantastic 1.50 4.00
2 Invisible Woman 1.50 4.00
3 Thing 1.50 4.00
4 Human Torch 1.50 4.00
5 Spider-Man 3.00 8.00
6 Luke Cage 1.50 4.00
7 Domino 1.50 4.00
8 Iron Man 1.50 4.00
9 Captain America 1.50 4.00
10 Thor 1.50 4.00
11 Hulk 1.50 4.00
12 Iron Fist 1.50 4.00
13 Doctor Strange 1.50 4.00
14 Ms. Marvel 1.50 4.00
15 Scarlet Witch 1.50 4.00
16 Wolverine 3.00 8.00
17 Emma Frost 1.50 4.00
18 Cyclops 1.50 4.00
19 Jean Grey 1.50 4.00
20 Rogue 1.50 4.00
21 Iceman 1.50 4.00
22 Storm 1.50 4.00
23 Psylocke 1.50 4.00
24 Nova 1.50 4.00
25 Silver Surfer 1.50 4.00
26 Daredevil 1.50 4.00
27 Deadpool 5.00 12.00
28 She-Hulk 1.50 4.00
29 Punisher 2.50 6.00
30 Ghost Rider 1.50 4.00
31 Venom 1.50 4.00
32 Phoenix 1.50 4.00
33 Green Goblin 1.50 4.00
34 Red Skull 1.50 4.00
35 Loki 1.50 4.00
36 Magneto 1.50 4.00
37 Doctor Doom 1.50 4.00
38 Sabretooth 1.50 4.00
39 Thanos 1.50 4.00
40 Mystique 1.50 4.00
41 Apocalypse 1.50 4.00
42 Galactus 1.50 4.00

2013 Fleer Retro Marvel Metal Precious Metal Gems Blue

*BLUE/50: 6X TO 15X BASIC CARDS

2013 Fleer Retro Marvel Metal Precious Metal Gems Red

*RED/100: 4X TO 10X BASIC CARDS

2013 Fleer Retro Marvel Metal Precious Metal Gems Green

UNPRICED GREEN PRINT RUN 10 SER. #'d SETS

2013 Fleer Retro Marvel Power Blast

STATED ODDS 1:33

1 Black Panther 8.00 20.00
2 Black Widow 8.00 20.00
3 Cable 8.00 20.00
4 Captain America 8.00 20.00
5 Colossus 8.00 20.00
6 Cyclops 8.00 20.00
7 Daredevil 8.00 20.00
8 Deadpool 10.00 25.00
9 Ghost Rider 8.00 20.00
10 Hulk 8.00 20.00
11 Human Torch 8.00 20.00
12 Iron Man 8.00 20.00
13 Moon Knight 8.00 20.00
14 Namor 8.00 20.00
15 Nova 8.00 20.00
16 Punisher 8.00 20.00
17 Red Hulk 8.00 20.00
18 Spider-Man 10.00 25.00
19 Thing 8.00 20.00
20 War Machine 8.00 20.00
21 Wolverine 10.00 25.00

2013 Fleer Retro Marvel Quick Strike

STATED ODDS 1:40

1 Iron Fist 8.00 20.00
2 Spider-Man 10.00 25.00
3 Spider-Woman 8.00 20.00
4 Daredevil 8.00 20.00
5 Northstar 8.00 20.00
6 Silver Surfer 8.00 20.00
7 Nightcrawler 8.00 20.00
8 Gladiator 8.00 20.00
9 Black Panther 8.00 20.00
10 Beast 8.00 20.00
11 Captain America 8.00 20.00
12 Moon Knight 8.00 20.00
13 Longshot 8.00 20.00
14 Puck 8.00 20.00
15 Gamora 8.00 20.00
16 Ka-Zar 8.00 20.00
17 Tigra 8.00 20.00
18 Psylocke 8.00 20.00
19 Elektra 8.00 20.00
20 Iron Man 8.00 20.00
21 Quicksilver 8.00 20.00

2013 Fleer Retro Marvel Stickers

COMPLETE SET (25) 20.00 50.00
STATED ODDS 1:5

1 Mr. Fantastic 1.25 3.00
2 Invisible Woman 1.25 3.00
3 Thing 1.25 3.00
4 Human Torch 1.25 3.00
5 Spider-Man 2.00 5.00
6 Captain America 1.25 3.00
7 Hulk 1.25 3.00
8 Iron Man 1.25 3.00
9 Thor 1.25 3.00
10 Giant-Man 1.25 3.00
11 Wasp 1.25 3.00
12 Silver Surfer 1.25 3.00
13 Black Panther 1.25 3.00
14 Hawkeye 1.25 3.00
15 Daredevil 1.25 3.00
16 Doctor Strange 1.25 3.00
17 Namor 1.25 3.00
18 Iron Fist 1.25 3.00
19 Wolverine 2.00 5.00
20 Black Widow 1.25 3.00
21 Black Bolt 1.25 3.00
22 Magneto 1.25 3.00
23 Doctor Doom 1.25 3.00
24 Kang The Conquerer 1.25 3.00
25 Galactus 1.25 3.00

2013 Fleer Retro Marvel Ti-22

STATED ODDS 1:40

1 Captain America 10.00 25.00
2 Cyclops 10.00 25.00
3 Deadpool 15.00 40.00
4 Hulk 10.00 25.00
5 Human Torch 10.00 25.00
6 Iceman 10.00 25.00
7 Invisible Woman 10.00 25.00
8 Iron Fist 10.00 25.00
9 Iron Man 10.00 25.00
10 Mr. Fantastic 10.00 25.00
11 Ms. Marvel 10.00 25.00
12 Punisher 12.00 30.00
13 Silver Surfer 10.00 25.00
14 Spider-Man 12.00 30.00
15 Storm 10.00 25.00
16 Thing 10.00 25.00
17 Thor 10.00 25.00
18 War Machine 10.00 25.00
19 Wolverine 15.00 40.00
20 Doctor Doom 10.00 25.00
21 Magneto 10.00 25.00

2013 Fleer Retro Marvel Ultra Stars

STATED ODDS 1:40

1 Beta Ray Bill 8.00 20.00
2 Adam Warlock 8.00 20.00
3 Rocket Raccoon 8.00 20.00
4 Thanos 8.00 20.00
5 Thor 8.00 20.00
6 Mr. Fantastic 8.00 20.00
7 Thing 8.00 20.00
8 Invisible Woman 8.00 20.00
9 Human Torch 8.00 20.00
10 Nova 8.00 20.00
11 Star-Lord 8.00 20.00
12 Galactus 8.00 20.00
13 Odin 8.00 20.00
14 Black Bolt 8.00 20.00
15 Darkhawk 8.00 20.00

2013 Fleer Retro Marvel Ultra X-Men

COMPLETE SET (30) 35.00 70.00
STATED ODDS 1:4

1 Angel 1.50 4.00
2 Armor 1.50 4.00
3 Banshee 1.50 4.00
4 Beast 1.50 4.00
5 Bishop 1.50 4.00
6 Cable 1.50 4.00
7 Cannonball 1.50 4.00
8 Colossus 1.50 4.00
9 Cyclops 1.50 4.00
10 Domino 1.50 4.00
11 Emma Frost 1.50 4.00
12 Gambit 1.50 4.00
13 Havok 1.50 4.00
14 Hope 1.50 4.00
15 Iceman 1.50 4.00
16 Jean Grey 1.50 4.00
17 Jubilee 1.50 4.00
18 Kitty Pryde 1.50 4.00
19 Longshot 1.50 4.00
20 Magik 1.50 4.00
21 Marvel Girl 1.50 4.00
22 Namor 1.50 4.00
23 Nightcrawler 1.50 4.00
24 Professor X 1.50 4.00
25 Psylocke 1.50 4.00
26 Rogue 1.50 4.00
27 Storm 1.50 4.00
28 Warpath 1.50 4.00
29 Wolverine 3.00 8.00
30 X-23 1.50 4.00

2013 Fringe Seasons Three and Four

COMPLETE SET (73) 6.00 15.00

1 Our Olivia .20 .50
2 Their Olivia .20 .50
3 Deceived .20 .50
4 Deafening .20 .50
5 Mirage .20 .50
6 Dormancy .20 .50
7 War Wounds .20 .50
8 Activation .20 .50
9 Puzzle Pieces .20 .50
10 Gateway .20 .50
11 Discovered .20 .50
12 Equivalent Exchange .20 .50
13 World-Shattering .20 .50
14 Bobby .20 .50
15 Reciprocity .20 .50
16 Jellyfish .20 .50
17 Held Captive .20 .50
18 Pancakes .20 .50
19 Albatross .20 .50
20 Subject 13 .20 .50
21 Lost Boy .20 .50
22 Gravity .20 .50
23 Icarus .20 .50
24 Gene .20 .50
25 Lincoln .20 .50
26 Charged .20 .50
27 Abducted .20 .50
28 Accelerated .20 .50
29 Henry .20 .50
30 Tripping .20 .50
31 Breaking Character .20 .50
32 Gone .20 .50
33 Shifting Priorities .20 .50
34 Double Vision .20 .50
35 Run Down .20 .50
36 Hazardous .20 .50
37 Fun Guy .20 .50
38 Fractured .20 .50
39 Close Encounter .20 .50
40 Clues .20 .50
41 Emergence .20 .50
42 Novation .20 .50
43 Anomaly .20 .50
44 Unstuck .20 .50
45 Bachelor Pad .20 .50
46 Translucent .20 .50
47 Traitors .20 .50
48 Father and Son .20 .50
49 Enemy of My Enemy .20 .50
50 Irony .20 .50
51 Premonition .20 .50
52 Making Angels .20 .50
53 Respect .20 .50
54 Crazies .20 .50
55 Evacuation .20 .50
56 Subterfuge .20 .50
57 September Redux .20 .50
58 Anything for Love .20 .50
59 Familiar .20 .50
60 Hard to Face .20 .50
61 Grisly .20 .50
62 New Friends .20 .50
63 Consulting .20 .50
64 Duress .20 .50
65 Late Night .20 .50
66 New Old Nina .20 .50
67 Not Quite Right .20 .50
68 Henrietta .20 .50
69 Last Resort .20 .50
70 Job Well Done .20 .50
71 Godspeed .20 .50
72 Momentum .20 .50
73 Checklist .20 .50
NSP2 GTS Come and Play PROMO 10.00 25.00

2013 Fringe Seasons Three and Four Autographs

STATED ODDS 1:24

A1 Anna Torv 175.00 300.00
A3 John Noble 75.00 150.00
A4 Lance Reddick 50.00 100.00
A5 Blair Brown 50.00 100.00
A6 Jasika Nicole 50.00 100.00
A7 Seth Gabel 40.00 80.00
A8 Kirk Acevedo 8.00 20.00
A9 Leonard Nimoy 150.00 250.00

❑ A10 Ryan McDonald 8.00 20.00
❑ A11 Kevin Corrigan 8.00 20.00
❑ A12 Eugene Lipinski 8.00 20.00
❑ A13 Jarod Joseph 6.00 15.00
❑ A14 Michelle Krusiec 8.00 20.00
❑ A15 Philip Winchester 6.00 15.00
❑ A16 Paula Giroday 8.00 20.00
❑ A17 Neal Huff 6.00 15.00
❑ A18 Monte Markham 6.00 15.00
❑ A19 Lily Pilblad 12.00 30.00

2013 Fringe Seasons Three and Four Behind the Scenes

COMPLETE SET (9) 6.00 15.00
OVERALL CHASE ODDS 4:24

❑ D1 Season 3, Episode 12 1.25 3.00
❑ D2 Season 3, Episode 14 1.25 3.00
❑ D3 Season 3, Episode 3 1.25 3.00
❑ D4 Season 3, Episode 8 1.25 3.00
❑ D5 Season 3, Episode 10 1.25 3.00
❑ D6 Season 3, Episode 10 1.25 3.00
❑ D7 Season 3, Episode 11 1.25 3.00
❑ D8 Season 3, Episode 19 1.25 3.00
❑ D9 Season 3, Episode 17 1.25 3.00

2013 Fringe Seasons Three and Four The Other Side

COMPLETE SET (9) 8.00 20.00
OVERALL CHASE ODDS 4:24

❑ ALT1 Charlie's Problem 1.50 4.00
❑ ALT2 Intelligence 1.50 4.00
❑ ALT3 Crossing Over 1.50 4.00
❑ ALT4 Morning Pick-Me-Up 1.50 4.00
❑ ALT5 Amber Alert 1.50 4.00
❑ ALT6 Shape Shifting 1.50 4.00
❑ ALT7 Fringe Division 1.50 4.00
❑ ALT8 Agent Lee 1.50 4.00
❑ ALT9 Medical Science 1.50 4.00

2013 Fringe Seasons Three and Four Wardrobe Memorabilia

STATED ODDS 1:24

❑ M1 Peter Bishop 6.00 15.00
❑ M2 Olivia Dunham 10.00 25.00
❑ M3 Astrid Farnsworth 6.00 15.00
❑ M4 Phillip Broyles 10.00 25.00
❑ M5 Walter Bishop 8.00 20.00
❑ M6 Bolivia 10.00 25.00
❑ M7 Peter Bishop 6.00 15.00
❑ M8 Olivia Dunham 10.00 25.00
❑ M9 Astrid Farnsworth 6.00 15.00
❑ M10 Phillip Broyles 6.00 15.00
❑ M11 Walter Bishop 8.00 20.00
❑ M12 Bolivia 10.00 25.00
❑ M13 Peter Bishop 6.00 15.00
❑ M14 Olivia Dunham 10.00 25.00
❑ M15 Astrid Farnsworth 6.00 15.00
❑ M16 Peter Bishop 6.00 15.00
❑ M17 Phillip Broyles 6.00 15.00
❑ M18 Walter Bishop 8.00 20.00
❑ M19 Bolivia 10.00 25.00
❑ M20 Peter Bishop 6.00 15.00
❑ M21 Olivia Dunham 10.00 25.00
❑ M22 Astrid Farnsworth 6.00 15.00
❑ M23 Phillip Broyles 8.00 20.00
❑ M24 Bolivia 10.00 25.00
❑ M25 Peter Bishop 6.00 15.00
❑ M26 Walter Bishop 8.00 20.00
❑ M27 Olivia Dunham

2013 Game of Thrones Season Two

COMPLETE SET (88) 6.00 15.00

❑ 1 The North Remembers .15 .40
❑ 2 The North Remembers .15 .40
❑ 3 The North Remembers .15 .40
❑ 4 The Night Lands .15 .40
❑ 5 The Night Lands .15 .40
❑ 6 The Night Lands .15 .40
❑ 7 What Is Dead May Never Die .15 .40
❑ 8 What Is Dead May Never Die .15 .40
❑ 9 What Is Dead May Never Die .15 .40
❑ 10 Garden of Bones .15 .40
❑ 11 Garden of Bones .15 .40
❑ 12 Garden of Bones .15 .40
❑ 13 The Ghost of Harrenhal .15 .40
❑ 14 The Ghost of Harrenhal .15 .40
❑ 15 The Ghost of Harrenhal .15 .40
❑ 16 The Old Gods And The New .15 .40
❑ 17 The Old Gods And The New .15 .40
❑ 18 The Old Gods And The New .15 .40
❑ 19 A Man Without Honor .15 .40
❑ 20 A Man Without Honor .15 .40
❑ 21 A Man Without Honor .15 .40
❑ 22 The Prince of Winterfell .15 .40
❑ 23 The Prince of Winterfell .15 .40
❑ 24 The Prince of Winterfell .15 .40
❑ 25 Blackwater .15 .40
❑ 26 Blackwater .15 .40
❑ 27 Blackwater .15 .40
❑ 28 Valar Marghulis .15 .40
❑ 29 Valar Marghulis .15 .40
❑ 30 Valar Marghulis .15 .40
❑ 31 Sansa Stark .15 .40
❑ 32 Theon Greyjoy .15 .40
❑ 33 Petyr Littlefinger Baelish .15 .40
❑ 34 Tyrion Lannister .15 .40
❑ 35 Xaro Xoan Daxos .15 .40
❑ 36 Samwell Tarly .15 .40
❑ 37 King Joffrey Baratheon .15 .40
❑ 38 Gendry .15 .40
❑ 39 Irri .15 .40
❑ 40 Ygritte .15 .40
❑ 41 Arya Stark .15 .40
❑ 42 Bronn .15 .40
❑ 43 Tommen Baratheon .15 .40
❑ 44 Jaqen H'ghar .15 .40
❑ 45 Jon Snow .15 .40
❑ 46 Bran Stark .15 .40
❑ 47 Myrcella Baratheon .15 .40
❑ 48 Ser Loras Tyrell .15 .40
❑ 49 Brienne of Tarth .15 .40
❑ 50 Doreah .15 .40
❑ 51 Ser Davos Seaworth .15 .40
❑ 52 Pyat Pree .15 .40
❑ 53 Dagmer Cleftjaw .15 .40
❑ 54 Robb Stark .15 .40
❑ 55 Lady Talisa Maegyr .15 .40
❑ 56 Renly Baratheon .15 .40
❑ 57 Daenerys Targaryen .15 .40
❑ 58 Lord Commander Mormont .15 .40
❑ 59 Varys .15 .40
❑ 60 Lady Catelyn Stark .15 .40
❑ 61 Ser Jaime Lannister .15 .40
❑ 62 Yara Greyjoy .15 .40
❑ 63 Sandor Clegane The Hound .15 .40
❑ 64 Spice King .15 .40
❑ 65 Rakharo .15 .40
❑ 66 Grand Maester Pycelle .15 .40
❑ 67 Osha .15 .40
❑ 68 Stannis Baratheon .15 .40
❑ 69 Queen Cersei Lannister .15 .40
❑ 70 Qhorin Halfhand .15 .40
❑ 71 Hodor .15 .40
❑ 72 Janos Slynt .15 .40
❑ 73 Margaery Tyrell .15 .40
❑ 74 Balon Greyjoy .15 .40
❑ 75 Maester Luwin .15 .40
❑ 76 Grenn .15 .40
❑ 77 Matthos Seaworth .15 .40
❑ 78 Lancel Lannister .15 .40
❑ 79 Ser Rodrik Cassel .15 .40
❑ 80 Ser Jorah Mormont .15 .40
❑ 81 Yoren .15 .40
❑ 82 Lord Tywin Lannister .15 .40
❑ 83 Rickon Stark .15 .40
❑ 84 Shae .15 .40
❑ 85 Dragons .15 .40
❑ 86 Melisandre .15 .40
❑ 87 Checklist .15 .40
❑ 88 Checklist .15 .40

2013 Game of Thrones Season Two Foil

COMPLETE SET 30.00 60.00
STATED ODDS 1:3

2013 Game of Thrones Season Two Autographs

TWO AUTOGRAPHS PER BOX
L (LIMITED): 300-500 COPIES
VL (VERY LIMITED): 200-300

❑ 1 Aidan Gillen 12.00 30.00
as Petyr Baelish Littlefinger L
❑ 2 Aimee Richardson 10.00 25.00
as Myrcella Baratheon
❑ 3 Amrita Acharia 10.00 25.00
as Irri
❑ 4 Conan Stevens 12.00 30.00
as Gregor Clegane L
❑ 5 Conleth Hill 10.00 25.00
as Lord Varys L
❑ 6 D.B. Weiss (Executive Producer) 40.00 80.00
(issued as 3-case incentive)
❑ 7 David Benioff (Executive Producer) 40.00 80.00
(issued as 3-case incentive)
❑ 8 Dominic Carter 8.00 20.00
as Janos Slynt
❑ 9 Donald Sumpter 12.00 30.00
as Maester Luwin L
❑ 10 Emun Elliott 8.00 20.00
as Marillion
❑ 11 Eugene Simon 8.00 20.00
as Lancel Lannister
❑ 12 Finn Jones 8.00 20.00
as Loras Tyrell
❑ 13 Francis Magee 8.00 20.00
as Yoren
❑ 14 Gemma Whelan 10.00 25.00
as Yara Greyjoy
❑ 15 George RR Martin (Author) 100.00 200.00
(issued as 6-case incentive)
❑ 16 Gethin Anthony 10.00 25.00
as Renly Baratheon
❑ 17 Jack Gleeson 20.00 50.00
as King Joffrey Baratheon VL
❑ 18 John Bradley 8.00 20.00
as Samwell Tarly
❑ 19 Josef Altin 8.00 20.00
as Pypar
❑ 20 Kate Dickie 10.00 25.00
as Lysa Arryn
❑ 21 Kerr Logan 10.00 25.00
as Mathos Seaworth L
❑ 22 Laura Pradelska 12.00 30.00
as Quaithe L
❑ 23 Maisie Williams 30.00 60.00
as Arya Stark L
❑ 24 Natalie Dormer 20.00 50.00
as Margaery Tyrell
❑ 25 Natalia Tena 10.00 25.00
as Osha
❑ 26 Nicholas Blane 8.00 20.00
as Spice King
❑ 27 Ralph Ineson 8.00 20.00
as Dagmer Cleftjaw
❑ 28 Roger Allam 8.00 20.00
as Magister Illyrio
❑ 29 Rory McCann 12.00 30.00
as Sandor Clegane L
❑ 30 Roxanne McKee 12.00 30.00
as Doreah
❑ 31 Sibel Kekilli 20.00 50.00
as Shae L
❑ 32 Simon Armstrong 8.00 20.00
as Qhorin Halfhand
❑ 33 Stephen Dillane 40.00 80.00
as Stannis Baratheon VL
❑ 34 Susan Brown 8.00 20.00
as Septa Mordane

2013 Game of Thrones Season Two Battle of Blackwater Case Toppers

COMPLETE SET (2) 20.00 40.00
ONE PER CASE

❑ CT1 Battle of Blackwater 10.00 25.00
❑ CT2 Battle of Blackwater 10.00 25.00

2013 Game of Thrones Season Two Family Sigil

COMPLETE SET (6) 10.00 25.00
STATED ODDS 1:24

❑ S1 House Stark 3.00 8.00
❑ S2 House Baratheon 3.00 8.00
❑ S3 House Lannister 3.00 8.00
❑ S4 House Targaryen 3.00 8.00
❑ S5 House Greyjoy 3.00 8.00
❑ S6 House Tyrell 3.00 8.00

2013 Game of Thrones Season Two Full Bleed Autographs

TWO AUTOGRAPHS PER BOX
L (LIMITED): 300-500 COPIES
VL (VERY LIMITED): 200-300 COPIES

❑ 1 Charles Dance 30.00 60.00
as Tywin Lannister VL
❑ 2 Emilia Clarke 125.00 200.00
as Daenerys Targaryen VL
❑ 3 Gwendoline Christie 20.00 50.00
as Brienne of Tarth
❑ 4 Iain Glen 20.00 50.00
as Ser Jorah Mormont L
❑ 5 Ian Hanmore 8.00 20.00
as Pyat Pree
❑ 6 Kit Harington 40.00 80.00
as Jon Snow VL
❑ 7 Lena Headey 75.00 150.00
as Queen Cersei Lannister VL
❑ 8 Michelle Fairley 40.00 80.00
as Lady Catelyn Stark VL
❑ 9 Nikolaj Coster-Waldau 40.00 80.00
as Jaime Lannister VL
❑ 10 Nonso Anozie 8.00 20.00
as Xaro Xhoan Daxos
❑ 11 Peter Dinklage 75.00 150.00
as Tyrion Lannister VL
❑ 12 Richard Madden 40.00 80.00
as Robb Stark VL
❑ 13 Rose Leslie 20.00 50.00
as Ygritte
❑ 14 Sophie Turner 20.00 50.00
as Sansa Stark
❑ 15 Tom Wlaschiha 12.00 30.00
as Jaqen H'ghar

2013 Game of Thrones Season Two Gallery

COMPLETE SET (6) 20.00 50.00
STATED ODDS 1:48

❑ PL1 Tyrion Lannister 6.00 15.00
❑ PL2 Cersei Lannister 6.00 15.00
❑ PL3 Daenerys Targaryen 6.00 15.00
❑ PL4 Jaime Lannister 6.00 15.00
❑ PL5 Jon Snow 6.00 15.00
❑ PL6 Robb Stark 6.00 15.00

2013 Game of Thrones Season Two Promos

❑ P1 Daenerys Targaryen .75 2.00
(General Distribution)
❑ P2 King Joffrey Baratheon 2.50 6.00
(NSU Magazine)
❑ P3 Tyrion Lannister 10.00 25.00
(Binder Exclusive)
❑ P4 Robb Stark 6.00 15.00
(Spring 2013 Chicago Non-Sport Show)
❑ P5 Daenerys Targaryen 4.00 10.00
(Spring 2013 Philly Non-Sport Show)

2013 Game of Thrones Season Two Quotable Game of Thrones

COMP.SET w/o Q20 (9) 8.00 20.00
STATED ODDS 1:12

❑ Q11 You Love Your Children 1.50 4.00
❑ Q12 The King Can Do What He Likes 1.50 4.00
❑ Q13 I Will Hurt You 1.50 4.00
❑ Q14 How Can a Man be Brave 1.50 4.00
❑ Q15 I Saw You Kill a Man 1.50 4.00
❑ Q16 I've Not Much Liked My Head 1.50 4.00
❑ Q17 Do You Know How To Use That 1.50 4.00
❑ Q18 You're Quite Good At Being Hand 1.50 4.00
❑ Q19 We've Had Victorious Kings 1.50 4.00
❑ Q20 I'm Not Questioning Your Honor
(issued as Rittenhouse Reward)

2013 Game of Thrones Season Two Relics

STATED ODDS 1:48
PRINT RUN 300-625

❑ RB1 Robert Baratheon 10.00 25.00
(Baratheon House Banner)/300
❑ RB2 Joffrey Baratheon 10.00 25.00
(Baratheon House Banner)/300
❑ RB3 Queen Cersei (Baratheon House Banner)/300 10.00 25.00
❑ RB4 Myrcella Baratheon 10.00 25.00
(Baratheon House Banner)/300
❑ RB5 Tommen Baratheon 10.00 25.00
(Baratheon House Banner)/300
❑ RL1 Tywin Lannister 10.00 25.00
(Lannister House Banner)/325
❑ RL2 Tyrion Lannister 12.00 30.00
(Lannister House Banner)/325
❑ RL3 Cersei Lannister 12.00 30.00
(Lannister House Banner)/325
❑ RL4 Jaime Lannister 10.00 25.00
(Lannister House Banner)/325
❑ RL5 Lancel Lannister 10.00 25.00
(Lannister House Banner)/325
❑ RLG1 Lannister Guard Cape/575 8.00 20.00
❑ RLG2 Lannister Guard Cape/475 8.00 20.00
❑ RS1 Eddard Stark (Stark House Banner)/375 12.00 30.00
❑ RS2 Catelyn Stark (Stark House Banner)/375 10.00 25.00
❑ RS3 Robb Stark (Stark House Banner)/375 12.00 30.00
❑ RS4 Sansa Stark (Stark House Banner)/375 12.00 30.00
❑ RS5 Arya Stark (Stark House Banner)/375 12.00 30.00
❑ RS6 Bran Stark (Stark House Banner)/375 10.00 25.00
❑ RS7 Rickon Stark (Stark House Banner)/375 10.00 25.00
❑ RNW1 The Night's Watch Cloak/625 10.00 25.00

2013 Game of Thrones Season Two Sketches

❑ 1 David Desbois
❑ 2 David Desbois/Charles Hall
❑ 3 Sean Pence

2013 Game of Thrones Season Two Storyboard Art

COMPLETE SET (20) 12.00 30.00
STATED ODDS 1:12

❑ SB1 Winter is Coming 1.50 4.00
❑ SB2 The Kingsroad 1.50 4.00
❑ SB3 Lord Snow 1.50 4.00
❑ SB4 Cripples, Bastards, and Broken Things 1.50 4.00
❑ SB5 The Wolf and the Lion 1.50 4.00
❑ SB6 A Golden Crown 1.50 4.00
❑ SB7 You Win or You Die 1.50 4.00
❑ SB8 The Pointy End 1.50 4.00
❑ SB9 Baelor 1.50 4.00
❑ SB10 Fire and Blood 1.50 4.00
❑ SB11 The North Remembers 1.50 4.00
❑ SB12 The Night Lands 1.50 4.00
❑ SB13 What is Dead May Never Die 1.50 4.00
❑ SB14 Garden of Bones 1.50 4.00
❑ SB15 The Ghost of Harrenhal 1.50 4.00
❑ SB16 The Old Gods and the New 1.50 4.00
❑ SB17 A Man Withou Honor 1.50 4.00
❑ SB18 Blackwater 1.50 4.00
❑ SB19 Blackwater 1.50 4.00
❑ SB20 Winter is Coming 1.50 4.00

2013 Garbage Pail Kids Series Two

COMP.SET w/o SP's (146) 10.00 25.00

❑ 56a Mel Tin .20 .50
❑ 56b Marsh Marlow .20 .50
❑ 57a Chocolate Bonnie .20 .50
❑ 57b Esther Bunny .20 .50
❑ 58a Surf's Up Chuck .20 .50
❑ 58b Regurgi Tate .20 .50
❑ 59a Chalky Chester .20 .50
❑ 59b Cringing Carl .20 .50
❑ 60a i Padme .20 .50
❑ 60b Colleen Screen .20 .50
❑ 61a Capped Calvin .20 .50
❑ 61b Robed Rob .20 .50
❑ 62a Knot Ned .20 .50
❑ 62b Troy Scout .20 .50
❑ 63a Charnel Leon .20 .50
❑ 63b Blendin' Brendan .20 .50
❑ 64a Sleep Les .20 .50
❑ 64b Insomniac Zack .20 .50
❑ 65a Charlie Down .20 .50
❑ 65b Peanut Paul .20 .50
❑ 66a Brad Apple .20 .50
❑ 66b Apple A Ray .20 .50
❑ 67a Egg Sheldon .20 .50
❑ 67b Cracked Chris .20 .50
❑ 68a 8-Biff .20 .50
❑ 68b Pixelated Perry .20 .50
❑ 69a Sliding Sophie .20 .50
❑ 69b Separated Samantha .20 .50
❑ 70a Blown-Up Bruce .20 .50
❑ 70b Smashing Stan .20 .50
❑ 71a Frida Spirit .20 .50
❑ 71b Tie Dyna .20 .50
❑ 72a Fred Case .20 .50
❑ 72b Hidden Herman .20 .50
❑ 73a Roll-Up Ralph .20 .50
❑ 73b Frank Fruit .20 .50
❑ 74a Sketched Sal .20 .50
❑ 74b Etched Eric .20 .50
❑ 75a Goldie Locks .20 .50
❑ 75b Pauline Pudding .20 .50
❑ 76a Tongue Ty .20 .50
❑ 76b Licky Mickey .20 .50
❑ 77a Instant Wynn .20 .50
❑ 77b Lotto Otto .20 .50
❑ 78a Nicole Troll .20 .50
❑ 78b Orange Gina .20 .50
❑ 79a Misfired Merlin .20 .50
❑ 79b Spell Castor .20 .50
❑ 80a Piranha Finn .20 .50
❑ 80b Devoured Howard .20 .50
❑ 81a Allen Formation .20 .50
❑ 81b Jose Hoax .20 .50
❑ 82a Tad Tris .20 .50
❑ 82b Puzzled Parker .20 .50
❑ 83a Dominated David .20 .50
❑ 83b Little Lance .20 .50
❑ 84a Surprisin' Steph .20 .50
❑ 84b Toilet Trish .20 .50
❑ 85a Sheepish Seth .20 .50
❑ 85b Wade Wolf .20 .50
❑ 86a Blake Rake .20 .50
❑ 86b Hit Mitt .20 .50
❑ 87a Kool Aiden .20 .50
❑ 87b Pitcher Pierre .20 .50
❑ 88a Grating Gary .20 .50
❑ 88b Parma John .20 .50
❑ 89a Jake Mistake .20 .50
❑ 89b Dwight Out .20 .50
❑ 90a Mixed-Up Michelangelo .20 .50
❑ 90b Disordered Donatello .20 .50
❑ 91a Shane Shovel .20 .50
❑ 91b Sandy Andy .20 .50
❑ 92a Peter Pain .20 .50
❑ 92b Shad Ow .20 .50
❑ 93a Cheese Louise .20 .50
❑ 93b Lin Berger .20 .50
❑ 94a Straw Barry .20 .50
❑ 94b Deface Chase .20 .50
❑ 95a Drummed Dennis .20 .50
❑ 95b Bongo Bart .20 .50
❑ 96a Booger Barack .20 .50
❑ 96b Handy Hussein .20 .50
❑ 97a Luau Luann .20 .50
❑ 97b Peg Roast .20 .50
❑ 98a Firey Francis .20 .50
❑ 98b Reptilian Killian .20 .50
❑ 99a Dee Seeded .20 .50
❑ 99b Grace Vine .20 .50
❑ 100a Abduct Jed .20 .50
❑ 100b Take Ken .20 .50
❑ 101a Nasty Nick .20 .50
❑ 101b Garlic Rick .20 .50
❑ 101c Evil Eddie SP 125.00 250.00
❑ 102a Buggy Betty .20 .50
❑ 102b Squashed Sophia .20 .50
❑ 102c Green Jean SP 100.00 200.00
❑ 103a Gene E. .20 .50
❑ 103b Grant Wishes .20 .50
❑ 104a Drippy Dan .20 .50
❑ 104b Watery Wyatt .20 .50
❑ 104c Leaky Lou SP 100.00 200.00
❑ 105a Weird Wendy .20 .50
❑ 105b Wicked Wanda .20 .50
❑ 105c Haggy Maggie SP 100.00 200.00
❑ 106a Roller Debbie .20 .50
❑ 106b Kate Skate .20 .50
❑ 107a Oliver Twisted .20 .50
❑ 107b Brett Towel .20 .50
❑ 107c Dizzy Dave SP 100.00 200.00
❑ 108a Grim Jim .20 .50
❑ 108b Last Leg Lenny .20 .50
❑ 108c Beth Death SP 100.00 200.00
❑ 109a Charming Chessie .20 .50
❑ 109b Jeweled Julia .20 .50
❑ 110a Doug Plug .20 .50
❑ 110b Trey Spray .20 .50
❑ 110c Smelly Kelly SP 100.00 200.00
❑ 111a Fishy Phyllis .20 .50
❑ 111b Tuna Nettie .20 .50
❑ 111c Smelly Sally SP 100.00 200.00
❑ 112a Leafy Larry .20 .50
❑ 112b Waterin' Walter .20 .50
❑ 113a Guillo Tina .20 .50
❑ 113b Headless Harriet .20 .50
❑ 113c Cindy Lopper SP 100.00 200.00
❑ 114a Haunted Forrest .20 .50
❑ 114b Tim Ber .20 .50
❑ 114c Sappy Sarah SP 100.00 200.00
❑ 115a Duster Dorothy .20 .50
❑ 115b Taylor Twister .20 .50
❑ 116a Dead Ted .20 .50
❑ 116b Deliver Roy .20 .50
❑ 116c Jay Decay SP 100.00 200.00
❑ 117a Green Dean .20 .50
❑ 117b Vicious Venus .20 .50
❑ 117c Juicy Jessica SP 100.00 200.00
❑ 118a Matt Hatter .20 .50
❑ 118b Tea Time Terence .20 .50
❑ 119a Joel Hole .20 .50
❑ 119b Peyton Paddle .20 .50
❑ 119c Teed-Off Tom SP 100.00 200.00
❑ 120a Ali Gator .20 .50
❑ 120b Skinned Sam .20 .50
❑ 120c Marshy Marshall SP
❑ 121a Leo Tamer .20 .50
❑ 121b Cir Gus .20 .50
❑ 122a Cute Tippi .20 .50
❑ 122b Eerie Erin .20 .50
❑ 122c Waxy Wendy SP 100.00 200.00
❑ 123a Hector Collector .20 .50
❑ 123b Hoardin' Jordan .20 .50
❑ 123c G.P. Kay SP 125.00 250.00
❑ 124a Gargoyle Doyle .20 .50
❑ 124b Stone Sculpture .20 .50
❑ 125a Ill Jill .20 .50
❑ 125b Mothy Martha .20 .50
❑ 125c Retchin' Gretchen SP 125.00 250.00
❑ 126a Curt the Rope .20 .50
❑ 126b Halfed Harry .20 .50
❑ 127a Pat of Gold .20 .50
❑ 127b Lepre Shaun .20 .50
❑ 128a Adam Bomb .60 1.50
❑ 128b Protestin' Preston .20 .50
❑ 128c Blasted Billy SP 125.00 250.00

2013 Garbage Pail Kids Series Two Black

STATED ODDS 1:2

2013 Garbage Pail Kids Series Two Silver

STATED ODDS 1:12

2013 Garbage Pail Kids Series Two Gold

STATED ODDS 1:70

❑ 128a Adam Bomb 50.00 100.00

2013 Garbage Pail Kids Series Two Printing Plates Black

STATED PRINT RUN 1 SER. #'d SET
UNPRICED DUE TO SCARCITY

2013 Garbage Pail Kids Series Two Printing Plates Cyan

STATED PRINT RUN 1 SER. #'d SET
UNPRICED DUE TO SCARCITY

2013 Garbage Pail Kids Series Two Printing Plates Magenta

STATED PRINT RUN 1 SER. #'d SET
UNPRICED DUE TO SCARCITY

2013 Garbage Pail Kids Series Two Printing Plates Yellow

STATED PRINT RUN 1 SER. #'d SET
UNPRICED DUE TO SCARCITY

2013 Garbage Pail Kids Series Two 3D Motion

COMPLETE SET (10) 12.00 30.00
STATED ODDS 1:12

❑ 1 Weird Wendy 2.00 5.00
❑ 2 Hairy Carrie 2.00 5.00
❑ 3 Barren Aaron 2.00 5.00
❑ 4 Dyna Mike 2.00 5.00
❑ 5 Mel Tin 2.00 5.00
❑ 6 Surf's Up Chuck 2.00 5.00
❑ 7 Piranha Finn 2.00 5.00
❑ 8 Take Ken 2.00 5.00
❑ 9 Joel Hole 2.00 5.00
❑ 10 Faye Tall 2.00 5.00

2013 Garbage Pail Kids Series Two Bonus

STATED ODDS 1:24 HOBBY

❑ B7a Bridget Bride 8.00 20.00
❑ B7b Just Mary 8.00 20.00
❑ B8a Albert Alien 8.00 20.00
❑ B8b Spacey Scott 8.00 20.00
❑ B9a Son of Manny 8.00 20.00
❑ B9b Ripe Rene 8.00 20.00
❑ B10a Riveting Rosie 8.00 20.00
❑ B10b Propaganda Paula 8.00 20.00
❑ B11a Giant Gillian 4.00 10.00
❑ B11b Faye Tall 4.00 10.00
❑ B12a Crocked Davy 4.00 10.00
❑ B12b Bitten Brian 4.00 10.00
❑ B13a Ike Berg 6.00 15.00
❑ B13b Icy Ian 6.00 15.00
❑ B14a Taser Frasier 6.00 15.00
❑ B14b Shocked Sol 6.00 15.00
❑ B15a Dayna the Dead 6.00 15.00
❑ B15b Mia de los Muertos 6.00 15.00

2013 Garbage Pail Kids Series Two Foldees

COMPLETE SET (10) 5.00 12.00
STATED ODDS 1:4

❑ 1 Foldee 1 1.00 2.50
❑ 2 Foldee 2 1.00 2.50
❑ 3 Foldee 3 1.00 2.50
❑ 4 Foldee 4 1.00 2.50
❑ 5 Foldee 5 1.00 2.50
❑ 6 Foldee 6 1.00 2.50
❑ 7 Foldee 7 1.00 2.50
❑ 8 Foldee 8 1.00 2.50
❑ 9 Foldee 9 1.00 2.50
❑ 10 Foldee 10 1.00 2.50

2013 Garbage Pail Kids Series Two Glow in the Dark

COMPLETE SET (10) 8.00 20.00
STATED ODDS 1:6

❑ 1 Adam Bomb 2.00 5.00
❑ 2 Wacky Jackie 1.50 4.00
❑ 3 Slobby Robbie 1.50 4.00
❑ 4 Brainy Janie 1.50 4.00
❑ 5 New Wave Dave 1.50 4.00
❑ 6 Jolted Joel 1.50 4.00
❑ 7 Hot Scott 1.50 4.00
❑ 8 Roy Bot 1.50 4.00
❑ 9 Jules Drools 1.50 4.00
❑ 10 Invisible Manuel 1.50 4.00

2013 Garbage Pail Kids Series Two Sketches

STATED ODDS 1:96

❑ 1 Brent Engstrom

☐ 2 Colin Walton
☐ 3 Jeff Zapata
☐ 4 Joe Simko
☐ 5 Layron DeJarnette
☐ 6 Mark Pingatore
☐ 7 Neil Camera
☐ 8 Pat Barrett
☐ 9 Strephon Taylor
☐ 10 Tom Bunk

2013 Garbage Pail Kids Chrome Series One

COMP.SET w/o SPs (110) 15.00 40.00

☐ 1a Nasty Nick .60 1.50
☐ 1b Evil Eddie .60 1.50
☐ 2a Junkfood John .40 1.00
☐ 2b Ray Decay .40 1.00
☐ 3a Up Chuck .40 1.00
☐ 3b Heavin' Steven .40 1.00
☐ 4a Fryin' Brian .40 1.00
☐ 4b Electric Bill .40 1.00
☐ 5a Dead Ted .40 1.00
☐ 5b Jay Decay .40 1.00
☐ 6a Art Apart .40 1.00
☐ 6b Busted Bob .40 1.00
☐ 6c Pieced Reece SP 60.00 120.00
☐ 7a Stormy Heather .40 1.00
☐ 7b April Showers .40 1.00
☐ 8a Adam Bomb 1.00 2.50
☐ 8b Blasted Billy 1.00 2.50
☐ 9a Boozin' Bruce .40 1.00
☐ 9b Drunk Ken .40 1.00
☐ 10a Tee-Vee Stevie .40 1.00
☐ 10b Geeky Gary .40 1.00
☐ 11a Itchy Richie .40 1.00
☐ 11b Bugged Bert .40 1.00
☐ 12a Furry Fran .40 1.00
☐ 12b Hairy Mary .40 1.00
☐ 12c Wooly Whitney SP 60.00 120.00
☐ 13a Ashcan Andy .40 1.00
☐ 13b Spacey Stacy .40 1.00
☐ 14a Potty Scotty .40 1.00
☐ 14b Jason Basin .40 1.00
☐ 15a Ailin' Al .40 1.00
☐ 15b Mauled Paul .40 1.00
☐ 15c Injured Ira SP 60.00 120.00
☐ 16a Weird Wendy .40 1.00
☐ 16b Haggy Maggie .40 1.00
☐ 17a Wacky Jackie .40 1.00
☐ 17b Loony Lenny .40 1.00
☐ 18a Cranky Frankie .40 1.00
☐ 18b Bad Brad .40 1.00
☐ 19a Corroded Carl .40 1.00
☐ 19b Crater Chris .40 1.00
☐ 19c Kit Zit SP 60.00 120.00
☐ 20a Swell Mel .40 1.00
☐ 20b Dressy Jesse .40 1.00
☐ 21a Virus Iris .40 1.00
☐ 21b Sicky Vicky .40 1.00
☐ 21c Feverish Phyllis SP 60.00 120.00
☐ 22a Junky Jeff .40 1.00
☐ 22b Stinky Stan .40 1.00
☐ 22c Trashy Travis SP 60.00 120.00
☐ 23a Drippy Dan .40 1.00
☐ 23b Leaky Lou .40 1.00
☐ 24a Nervous Rex .40 1.00
☐ 24b Nerdy Norm .40 1.00
☐ 25a Creepy Carol .40 1.00
☐ 25b Scary Carrie .40 1.00
☐ 26a Slobby Robbie .40 1.00
☐ 26b Fat Matt .40 1.00
☐ 27a Brainy Janie .40 1.00
☐ 27b Jenny Genius .40 1.00
☐ 28a Oozy Suzy .40 1.00
☐ 28b Meltin' Melissa .40 1.00
☐ 28c Waxy Wynonna SP 60.00 120.00
☐ 29a Bony Joanie .40 1.00
☐ 29b Thin Lynn .40 1.00
☐ 30a New Wave Dave .40 1.00
☐ 30b Graffiti Petey .40 1.00
☐ 31a Run Down Rhoda .40 1.00
☐ 31b Flat Pat .40 1.00
☐ 32a Frigid Bridget .40 1.00
☐ 32b Chilly Millie .40 1.00
☐ 33a Mad Mike .40 1.00
☐ 33b Savage Stuart .40 1.00
☐ 33c Cruel Conan SP 60.00 120.00
☐ 34a Kim Kong .40 1.00
☐ 34b Anna Banana .40 1.00
☐ 35a Wrinkly Randy .40 1.00
☐ 35b Rockin' Robert .40 1.00
☐ 36a Wrappin' Ruth .40 1.00
☐ 36b Tommy Tomb .40 1.00
☐ 37a Guillo Tina .40 1.00
☐ 37b Cindy Lopper .40 1.00
☐ 38a Slimy Sam .40 1.00
☐ 38b Lizard Liz .40 1.00
☐ 39a Buggy Betty .40 1.00
☐ 39b Green Jean .40 1.00
☐ 40a Unstitched Mitch .40 1.00
☐ 40b Damaged Don .40 1.00
☐ 41a Mean Gene .40 1.00
☐ 41b Joltin' Joel .40 1.00
☐ 41c Armed Arnold SP 60.00 120.00
☐ L1a Pickled Pete .40 1.00
☐ L1b Formaldehyde Fred .40 1.00
☐ L2a Baby Abie .40 1.00
☐ L2b Missing Linc .40 1.00
☐ L3a Prickly Pete .40 1.00
☐ L3b Thorny Barb .40 1.00
☐ L4a Arach Ned .40 1.00
☐ L4b Web Jeb .40 1.00
☐ L5a Shadowy Sheila .40 1.00
☐ L5b Vaporized Val .40 1.00
☐ L6a Global Warren .40 1.00
☐ L6b Al Pocalypse .40 1.00
☐ L7a Stitched Stella .40 1.00
☐ L7b Patchwork Paula .40 1.00
☐ L8a Slammed Sloan .40 1.00
☐ L8b Keith Out .40 1.00
☐ L9a Raisin' Ella .40 1.00
☐ L9b Grape Vi .40 1.00
☐ L10a Finger-Paintin' Fifi .40 1.00
☐ L10b Libby Stick .40 1.00
☐ L11a Scrawled Saul .40 1.00
☐ L11b Bad Art .40 1.00
☐ L12a Noah Parking .40 1.00
☐ L12b Peter Meter .40 1.00
☐ L13a Dead Flora .40 1.00
☐ L13b Fetid Fern .40 1.00
☐ L14a Dunkin' Duncan .40 1.00
☐ L14b Will Hung .40 1.00

2013 Garbage Pail Kids Chrome Series One Refractors

STATED ODDS 1:3

☐ 1a Nasty Nick 4.00 10.00
☐ 1b Evil Eddie 4.00 10.00
☐ 8a Adam Bomb 8.00 20.00
☐ 8b Blasted Billy 8.00 20.00

2013 Garbage Pail Kids Chrome Series One Atomic Refractors

*ATOM.REF.: 4X TO 10X BASIC CARDS

2013 Garbage Pail Kids Chrome Series One Prism Refractors

ANNOUNCED PRINT RUN 199

☐ 1a Nasty Nick 20.00 50.00
☐ 1b Evil Eddie 20.00 50.00
☐ 8a Adam Bomb 40.00 80.00
☐ 8b Blasted Billy 40.00 80.00

2013 Garbage Pail Kids Chrome Series One Gold Refractors

ANNOUNCED PRINT RUN 50

2013 Garbage Pail Kids Chrome Series One John Pound Autographs

ANNOUNCED PRINT RUN 10

☐ 1a Nasty Nick 100.00 200.00
☐ 1b Evil Eddie 100.00 200.00
☐ 2a Junkfood John 60.00 120.00
☐ 2b Ray Decay 60.00 120.00
☐ 3a Up Chuck 60.00 120.00
☐ 3b Heavin' Steven 60.00 120.00
☐ 4a Fryin' Brian 60.00 120.00
☐ 4b Electric Bill 60.00 120.00
☐ 5a Dead Ted 60.00 120.00
☐ 5b Jay Decay 60.00 120.00
☐ 6a Art Apart 60.00 120.00
☐ 6b Busted Bob 60.00 120.00
☐ 7a Stormy Heather 60.00 120.00
☐ 7b April Showers 60.00 120.00
☐ 8a Adam Bomb 200.00 400.00
☐ 8b Blasted Billy 200.00 400.00
☐ 9a Boozin' Bruce 60.00 120.00
☐ 9b Drunk Ken 60.00 120.00
☐ 10a Tee-Vee Stevie 60.00 120.00
☐ 10b Geeky Gary 60.00 120.00
☐ 11a Itchy Richie 60.00 120.00
☐ 11b Bugged Bert 60.00 120.00
☐ 12a Furry Fran 60.00 120.00
☐ 12b Hairy Mary 60.00 120.00
☐ 13a Ashcan Andy 60.00 120.00
☐ 13b Spacey Stacy 60.00 120.00
☐ 14a Potty Scotty 60.00 120.00
☐ 14b Jason Basin 60.00 120.00
☐ 15a Ailin' Al 60.00 120.00
☐ 15b Mauled Paul 60.00 120.00
☐ 16a Weird Wendy 60.00 120.00
☐ 16b Haggy Maggie 60.00 120.00
☐ 17a Wacky Jackie 60.00 120.00
☐ 17b Loony Lenny 60.00 120.00
☐ 18a Cranky Frankie 60.00 120.00
☐ 18b Bad Brad 60.00 120.00
☐ 19a Corroded Carl 60.00 120.00
☐ 19b Crater Chris 60.00 120.00
☐ 20a Swell Mel 60.00 120.00
☐ 20b Dressy Jesse 60.00 120.00
☐ 21a Virus Iris 60.00 120.00
☐ 21b Sicky Vicky 60.00 120.00
☐ 22a Junky Jeff 60.00 120.00
☐ 22b Stinky Stan 60.00 120.00
☐ 23a Drippy Dan 60.00 120.00
☐ 23b Leaky Lou 60.00 120.00
☐ 24a Nervous Rex 60.00 120.00
☐ 24b Nerdy Norm 60.00 120.00
☐ 25a Creepy Carol 60.00 120.00
☐ 25b Scary Carrie 60.00 120.00
☐ 26a Slobby Robbie 60.00 120.00
☐ 26b Fat Matt 60.00 120.00
☐ 27a Brainy Janie 60.00 120.00
☐ 27b Jenny Genius 60.00 120.00
☐ 28a Oozy Suzy 60.00 120.00
☐ 28b Meltin' Melissa 60.00 120.00
☐ 29a Bony Joanie 60.00 120.00
☐ 29b Thin Lynn 60.00 120.00
☐ 30a New Wave Dave 60.00 120.00
☐ 30b Graffiti Petey 60.00 120.00
☐ 31a Run Down Rhoda 60.00 120.00
☐ 31b Flat Pat 60.00 120.00
☐ 32a Frigid Bridget 60.00 120.00
☐ 32b Chilly Millie 60.00 120.00
☐ 33a Mad Mike 60.00 120.00
☐ 33b Savage Stuart 60.00 120.00
☐ 34a Kim Kong 60.00 120.00
☐ 34b Anna Banana 60.00 120.00
☐ 35a Wrinkly Randy 60.00 120.00
☐ 35b Rockin' Robert 60.00 120.00
☐ 36a Wrappin' Ruth 60.00 120.00
☐ 36b Tommy Tomb 60.00 120.00
☐ 37a Guillo Tina 60.00 120.00
☐ 37b Cindy Lopper 60.00 120.00
☐ 38a Slimy Sam 60.00 120.00
☐ 38b Lizard Liz 60.00 120.00
☐ 39a Buggy Betty 60.00 120.00
☐ 39b Green Jean 60.00 120.00
☐ 40a Unstitched Mitch 60.00 120.00
☐ 40b Damaged Don 60.00 120.00
☐ 41a Mean Gene 60.00 120.00
☐ 41b Joltin' Joel 60.00 120.00
☐ L1a Pickled Pete 60.00 120.00
☐ L1b Formaldehyde Fred 60.00 120.00
☐ L2a Baby Abie 60.00 120.00
☐ L2b Missing Linc 60.00 120.00
☐ L3a Prickly Pete 60.00 120.00
☐ L3b Thorny Barb 60.00 120.00
☐ L4a Arach Ned 60.00 120.00
☐ L4b Web Jeb 60.00 120.00
☐ L5a Shadowy Sheila 60.00 120.00
☐ L5b Vaporized Val 60.00 120.00
☐ L6a Global Warren 60.00 120.00
☐ L6b Al Pocalypse 60.00 120.00
☐ L7a Stitched Stella 60.00 120.00
☐ L7b Patchwork Paula 60.00 120.00
☐ L8a Slammed Sloan 60.00 120.00
☐ L8b Keith Out 60.00 120.00
☐ L9a Raisin' Ella 60.00 120.00
☐ L9b Grape Vi 60.00 120.00
☐ L10a Finger-Paintin' Fifi 60.00 120.00
☐ L10b Libby Stick 60.00 120.00
☐ L11a Scrawled Saul 60.00 120.00
☐ L11b Bad Art 60.00 120.00
☐ L12a Noah Parking 60.00 120.00
☐ L12b Peter Meter 60.00 120.00
☐ L13a Dead Flora 60.00 120.00
☐ L13b Fetid Fern 60.00 120.00
☐ L14a Dunkin' Duncan 60.00 120.00
☐ L14b Will Hung 60.00 120.00

2013 Garbage Pail Kids Chrome Series One Pencil Art

COMPLETE SET (82) 60.00 120.00
STATED ODDS 1:6

☐ 1a Nasty Nick 2.50 6.00
☐ 1b Evil Eddie 2.50 6.00
☐ 2a Junkfood John 1.50 4.00
☐ 2b Ray Decay 1.50 4.00
☐ 3a Up Chuck 1.50 4.00
☐ 3b Heavin' Steven 1.50 4.00
☐ 4a Fryin' Brian 1.50 4.00
☐ 4b Electric Bill 1.50 4.00
☐ 5a Dead Ted 1.50 4.00
☐ 5b Jay Decay 1.50 4.00
☐ 6a Art Apart 1.50 4.00
☐ 6b Busted Bob 1.50 4.00
☐ 7a Stormy Heather 1.50 4.00
☐ 7b April Showers 1.50 4.00
☐ 8a Adam Bomb 4.00 10.00
☐ 8b Blasted Billy 4.00 10.00
☐ 9a Boozin' Bruce 1.50 4.00
☐ 9b Drunk Ken 1.50 4.00
☐ 10a Tee-Vee Stevie 1.50 4.00
☐ 10b Geeky Gary 1.50 4.00
☐ 11a Itchy Richie 1.50 4.00
☐ 11b Bugged Bert 1.50 4.00
☐ 12a Furry Fran 1.50 4.00
☐ 12b Hairy Mary 1.50 4.00
☐ 13a Ashcan Andy 1.50 4.00
☐ 13b Spacey Stacy 1.50 4.00
☐ 14a Potty Scotty 1.50 4.00
☐ 14b Jason Basin 1.50 4.00
☐ 15a Ailin' Al 1.50 4.00
☐ 15b Mauled Paul 1.50 4.00
☐ 16a Weird Wendy 1.50 4.00
☐ 16b Haggy Maggie 1.50 4.00
☐ 17a Wacky Jackie 1.50 4.00
☐ 17b Loony Lenny 1.50 4.00
☐ 18a Cranky Frankie 1.50 4.00
☐ 18b Bad Brad 1.50 4.00
☐ 19a Corroded Carl 1.50 4.00
☐ 19b Crater Chris 1.50 4.00
☐ 20a Swell Mel 1.50 4.00
☐ 20b Dressy Jesse 1.50 4.00
☐ 21a Virus Iris 1.50 4.00
☐ 21b Sicky Vicky 1.50 4.00
☐ 22a Junky Jeff 1.50 4.00
☐ 22b Stinky Stan 1.50 4.00
☐ 23a Drippy Dan 1.50 4.00
☐ 23b Leaky Lou 1.50 4.00
☐ 24a Nervous Rex 1.50 4.00
☐ 24b Nerdy Norm 1.50 4.00
☐ 25a Creepy Carol 1.50 4.00
☐ 25b Scary Carrie 1.50 4.00
☐ 26a Slobby Robbie 1.50 4.00
☐ 26b Fat Matt 1.50 4.00
☐ 27a Brainy Janie 1.50 4.00
☐ 27b Jenny Genius 1.50 4.00
☐ 28a Oozy Suzy 1.50 4.00
☐ 28b Meltin' Melissa 1.50 4.00
☐ 29a Bony Joanie 1.50 4.00
☐ 29b Thin Lynn 1.50 4.00
☐ 30a New Wave Dave 1.50 4.00
☐ 30b Graffiti Petey 1.50 4.00
☐ 31a Run Down Rhoda 1.50 4.00
☐ 31b Flat Pat 1.50 4.00
☐ 32a Frigid Bridget 1.50 4.00
☐ 32b Chilly Millie 1.50 4.00
☐ 33a Mad Mike 1.50 4.00
☐ 33b Savage Stuart 1.50 4.00
☐ 34a Kim Kong 1.50 4.00
☐ 34b Anna Banana 1.50 4.00
☐ 35a Wrinkly Randy 1.50 4.00
☐ 35b Rockin' Robert 1.50 4.00
☐ 36a Wrappin' Ruth 1.50 4.00
☐ 36b Tommy Tomb 1.50 4.00
☐ 37a Guillo Tina 1.50 4.00
☐ 37b Cindy Lopper 1.50 4.00
☐ 38a Slimy Sam 1.50 4.00
☐ 38b Lizard Liz 1.50 4.00
☐ 39a Buggy Betty 1.50 4.00
☐ 39b Green Jean 1.50 4.00
☐ 40a Unstitched Mitch 1.50 4.00
☐ 40b Damaged Don 1.50 4.00
☐ 41a Mean Gene 1.50 4.00
☐ 41b Joltin' Joel 1.50 4.00

2013 Horrors of War II

COMPLETE SET (40)
ANNOUNCED PRINT RUN 40

☐ 49 Battle of the Plains of Abraham
☐ 50 Battle of Lundy's Lane
☐ 51 Burning of Washington
☐ 52 Battle of Lake Champlain
☐ 53 Battle of Buena Vista
☐ 54 Charge of the Light Brigade
☐ 55 Battle of Fort Sumter
☐ 56 Second Battle of Bull Run
☐ 57 Pickett's Charge
☐ 58 Andersonville
☐ 59 Burning of Atlanta
☐ 60 Custer's Last Stand
☐ 61 Battle of Guantánamo Bay
☐ 62 Battle of San Juan Hill
☐ 63 First Battle of the Marne
☐ 64 First Battle of Ypres
☐ 65 Sinking of the Lusitania
☐ 66 Battle Of Verdun
☐ 67 Battle of the Somme
☐ 68 Passchendaele
☐ 69 Battle of Cambrai
☐ 70 The Spring Offensive
☐ 71 Armenian Holocaust
☐ 72 Guernica
☐ 73 Rape of Nanking
☐ 74 Desert Rats
☐ 75 Sinking of the Hood
☐ 76 Sinking of the Bismarck
☐ 77 Katyn Massacre
☐ 78 Doris Dorie Miller
☐ 79 Sinking of Hospital Ship Centaur
☐ 80 Malmedy Massacre
☐ 81 Code Talkers
☐ 82 Battle of Kapyong
☐ 83 John McCain, POW
☐ 84 Russian Invade Afghanistan
☐ 85 Norman Schwarzkopf
☐ 86 War in Afghanistan
☐ 87 Abu Ghraib
☐ 88 London Bombings

2013 Horrors of War II Cut Signatures

ANNOUNCED PRINT RUN 1
UNPRICED DUE TO SCARCITY

☐ 1 A.G. Dudgeon (WWII)
☐ 2 Aaron T. Bliss (Civil War)
☐ 3 Abie Abraham (WWII)
☐ 4 Abner Aust, Jr. (WWII)
☐ 5 Abraham Baum (WWII)
☐ 6 Adlai Stevenson, III (Korean War)
☐ 7 Adolf Galland (WWII)
☐ 8 Adolf Hitler (WWII)
☐ 9 Adolphus W. Greely (Civil War)
☐ 10 Aeneas Ranald Donald MacDonnell (WWII)
☐ 11 Aharon Remez (WWII)
☐ 12 Al Kilgore (WWII)
☐ 13 Alan Brooke, 1st Viscount Alanbrooke (WWI)
☐ 14 Alan Goodrich Kirk (WWII)
☐ 15 Albert C. Thompson (Civil War)
☐ 16 Albert C. Wedemeyer (WWII)
☐ 17 Albert Graf von der Goltz (WWI)
☐ 18 Albert Henze (WWII)
☐ 19 Albert K. Earnest (WWII)
☐ 20 Albert P. Clark (WWII)
☐ 21 Albert Parker Niblack (WWI)
☐ 22 Albert S. Barker (Civil War)
☐ 23 Albert Scott Crossfield (WWII)
☐ 24 Albert Wells (WWII)
☐ 25 Alden P. Rigby (WWII)
☐ 26 Alec Ingle (WWII)
☐ 27 Alex Vraciu (WWII)
☐ 28 Alexander A. Vandegrift (WWII)
☐ 29 Alexander Cambridge, 1st Earl of Athlone (WWI)
☐ 30 Alexander Kerensky (WWI)
☐ 31 Alexander M. Patch (WWII)
☐ 32 Alexander S. Wadsworth (War of 1812)
☐ 33 Alexandre de Beauharnais (French Revolutionary Wars)
☐ 34 Alf Larson (WWII)
☐ 35 Alfred Harmsworth, 1st Viscount Northcliffe (WWI)
☐ 36 Alfred James Peaches (WWII)
☐ 37 Alfred Keith Ogilvie (WWII)
☐ 38 Alfred M. Gray, Jr. (Korean War)
☐ 39 Alfred M. Gruenther (WWII)
☐ 40 Alfred M. Pride (WWII)
☐ 41 Alfred Philippi (WWI)
☐ 42 Alfred Regeniter (WWII)
☐ 43 Alfred V. Rascon (Vietnam)
☐ 44 Allan J. Kellogg, Jr. (Vietnam)
☐ 45 Allan Rawlinson (WWII)
☐ 46 Allen James Lynch (Vietnam)
☐ 47 Alois Schnaubelt (WWII)
☐ 48 Alonzo Nute (Civil War)
☐ 49 Alton W. Knappenberger (WWII)
☐ 50 Amos J. Cummings (Civil War)
☐ 51 Andrew E.K. Benham (Civil War)
☐ 52 Andrew J. Adams (WWII)
☐ 53 Andrew J. Goodpaster (WWII)
☐ 54 Anna Flynn Monkiewicz (WWII)
☐ 55 Anthony Wayne Vogdes (Spanish-American War)
☐ 56 Anton von Boksay (WWI)
☐ 57 Apollo Soucek (WWII)
☐ 58 Archibald Hope (WWII)
☐ 59 Archibald Wavell, 1st Earl Wavell (WWI)
☐ 60 Archibald Wavell, 1st Earl Wavell (WWII)
☐ 61 Archie Donahue (WWII)
☐ 62 Arleigh Burke (Cold War)
☐ 63 Arleigh Burke (Korean War)
☐ 64 Arleigh Burke (WWII)
☐ 65 Armando Diaz (WWI)
☐ 66 Armistead B. Chick Smith, Jr. (WWII)
☐ 67 Art Fiedler (WWII)
☐ 68 Arthur Babine (WWII)
☐ 69 Arthur D. Struble (WWII)
☐ 70 Arthur F. Jeffrey (WWII)
☐ 71 Arthur J. Jackson (Korean War)
☐ 72 Arthur J. Jackson (WWII)
☐ 73 Arthur John McChrystal (WWII)
☐ 74 Arthur Leenerman (WWII)
☐ 75 Arthur P. Fairfield (WWI)
☐ 76 Arthur Spurgin (WWII)
☐ 77 Arthur Tedder, 1st Baron Tedder (WWI)
☐ 78 Arthur W. Radford (WWI)
☐ 79 Arthur W. Radford (WWII)
☐ 80 Arthur W. Tedder (WWII)
☐ 81 Arval Roberson (WWII)
☐ 82 Aubrey Fitch (WWII)
☐ 83 Audie Murphy (WWII)
☐ 84 B.M. Bryan (WWII)
☐ 85 Barney Hajiro (WWII)
☐ 86 Barney M. Giles (WWI)
☐ 87 Barney M. Giles (WWII)
☐ 88 Barrie Davis (WWII)
☐ 89 Barry Goldwater (WWII)
☐ 90 Barton Kyle Yount (WWII)
☐ 91 Basil L. Plumley (Vietnam)
☐ 92 Beauford T. Anderson (WWII)
☐ 93 Ben Amsden (WWII)
☐ 94 Ben Kuroki (WWII)
☐ 95 Benito Mussolini (WWI)
☐ 96 Benito Mussolini (WWII)
☐ 97 Benjamin Foulois (Spanish-American War)
☐ 98 Benjamin Franklin Butler (Civil War)
☐ 99 Benjamin O. Davis, Jr. (WWII)
☐ 100 Bernard A. Schriever (WWII)
☐ 101 Bernard Duperier (WWII)
☐ 102 Bernard F. Fisher (Vietnam)
☐ 103 Bernard Moorcroft (WWII)
☐ 104 Bernard W. Rogers (Korean War)
☐ 105 Bernhard Henry Bieri (WWI)
☐ 106 Bernhard Henry Bieri (WWII)
☐ 107 Bernice Falk Haydu (WWII)
☐ 108 Bernt Balchen (WWII)
☐ 109 Bill Cullerton (WWII)
☐ 110 Bill Daniel (WWII)
☐ 111 Bill Overstreet (WWII)
☐ 112 Bill Shaeffer (WWII)
☐ 113 Bill Wratten (Gulf War)
☐ 114 Billy Bishop (WWI)
☐ 115 Billy G. Edens (WWII)
☐ 116 Bishop W. Perkins (Civil War)
☐ 117 Blanton Winship (Spanish-American War)
☐ 118 Bob Bunting (WWII)
☐ 119 Bob Dole (WWII)
☐ 120 Bob Feller (WWII)
☐ 121 Bob Kerrey (Vietnam)
☐ 122 Bob Kinzler (WWII)
☐ 123 Bob Pardo (Vietnam)
☐ 124 Bob Vickers (WWII)
☐ 125 Boleslaw Drobinski (WWII)
☐ 126 Bradford C. Freeman

(WWII)
❑ 127 Brian Thacker (Vietnam)
❑ 128 Brooke E. Allen (WWII)
❑ 129 Brooks Liles (WWII)
❑ 130 Bruce Bretherton (WWII)
❑ 131 Bruce C. Clarke (WWII)
❑ 132 Bruce K. Holloway (WWII)
❑ 133 Bruce Matheson (Vietnam)
❑ 134 Bruce Matheson (WWII)
❑ 135 Bruce McCandless (Cold War)
❑ 136 Bud Alley (Vietnam)
❑ 137 Buford Johnson (WWII)
❑ 138 C.E. Olsen (WWII)
❑ 139 C.J.S. Craig (Gulf War)
❑ 140 Caesar Augustus Rodney (War of 1812)
❑ 141 Carl Andrew Spaatz (Mexican Revolution)
❑ 142 Carl Andrew Spaatz (WWI)
❑ 143 Carl Andrew Spaatz (WWII)
❑ 144 Carl Bickel (WWII)
❑ 145 Carl H. Dodd (Korean War)
❑ 146 Carl Hayden (WWI)
❑ 147 Carl J. Luksic (WWII)
❑ 148 Carl S. Muscarello (WWII)
❑ 149 Carl-August von Schoenebeck (WWI)
❑ 150 Carroll W. McColpin (WWII)
❑ 151 Casimer Nastal (WWII)
❑ 152 Caspar Weinberger (WWII)
❑ 153 Cecil Calavan (WWII)
❑ 154 Chapman L. Anderson (Civil War)
❑ 155 Charity E. Adams (WWII)
❑ 156 Charles Maggie Magwood (WWII)
❑ 157 Charles Sandy McCorkle (WWII)
❑ 158 Charles A. Boutelle (Civil War)
❑ 159 Charles A. Lockwood (WWII)
❑ 160 Charles Alan Pownall (WWI)
❑ 161 Charles Aldrich (Civil War)
❑ 162 Charles Anderson Dana (Civil War)
❑ 163 Charles B. Stone, III (WWII)
❑ 164 Charles Bock, Jr. (Korean War)
❑ 165 Charles Bolte (WWII)
❑ 166 Charles Bond (WWII)
❑ 167 Charles C. Hagemeister (Vietnam)
❑ 168 Charles D. Mott (WWII)
❑ 169 Charles Dragich (WWII)
❑ 170 Charles E. Rosendahl (Mexican Revolution)
❑ 171 Charles E. Rosendahl (WWII)
❑ 172 Charles Edgar Clark (Spanish-American War)
❑ 173 Charles F. Bolden, Jr. (Vietnam)
❑ 174 Charles H. Chuck Older (Korean War)
❑ 175 Charles H. Chuck Older (WWII)
❑ 176 Charles H. Bonesteel, III (WWII)
❑ 177 Charles H. Coolidge (WWII)
❑ 178 Charles H. Haverland, Jr. (WWII)
❑ 179 Charles Henry Smith (Civil War)
❑ 180 Charles Horner (Vietnam)
❑ 181 Charles Hughes-Hallett (WWII)
❑ 182 Charles J. Ozuk (WWII)
❑ 183 Charles Johnston Badger (Spanish-American War)
❑ 184 Charles K. Duncan (WWII)
❑ 185 Charles Keighley-Peach (WWII)
❑ 186 Charles King (Spanish-American War)
❑ 187 Charles Kingsford Smith (WWI)
❑ 188 Charles L. Mullins, Jr. (WWII)
❑ 189 Charles Lane, Jr. (WWII)
❑ 190 Charles Lenfest (WWII)
❑ 191 Charles M. Kunz (WWII)
❑ 192 Charles M. Mallory (WWII)
❑ 193 Charles P. Murray, Jr. (WWII)
❑ 194 Charles Polack (WWI)
❑ 195 Charles Rene Magon de Medine (Napoleonic Wars)
❑ 196 Charles Stewart (Civil War)
❑ 197 Charles Sweeney (WWII)
❑ 198 Charles T. Menoher (WWI)
❑ 199 Charles W. Lindberg (WWII)
❑ 200 Charles W. Shea (WWII)
❑ 201 Chester W. Nimitz (WWI)
❑ 202 Chester W. Nimitz (WWII)
❑ 203 Christian Pineau (WWII)
❑ 204 Christopher Foxley-Norris (WWII)
❑ 205 Christopher P. Navarre (WWII)
❑ 206 Chuck Baisden (WWII)
❑ 207 Chuck DeBellevue (Vietnam)
❑ 208 Chuck Yeager (Vietnam)
❑ 209 Chuck Yeager (WWII)
❑ 210 Clancy Lyall (WWII)
❑ 211 Clarence A. Martin (WWII)
❑ 212 Clarence B. Craft (Korean War)
❑ 213 Clarence B. Craft (WWII)
❑ 214 Clarence Borley (WWII)
❑ 215 Clarence E. Bud Anderson (WWII)
❑ 216 Clarence Sasser (Vietnam)
❑ 217 Clark M. Clifford (Vietnam)
❑ 218 Clark Simmons (WWII)
❑ 219 Claude Dallemagne (American Revolution)
❑ 220 Clayton Campbell (WWII)
❑ 221 Clayton Kelly Gross (WWII)
❑ 222 Cleatus Lebow (WWII)
❑ 223 Clifford Quinn (WWII)
❑ 224 Clift Andrus (WWII)
❑ 225 Clive Caldwell (WWII)
❑ 226 Clovis E. Byers (WWII)
❑ 227 Clyde A. Curtin (Korean War)
❑ 228 Clyde East (Korean War)
❑ 229 Clyde East (WWII)
❑ 230 Colin Powell (Korean War)
❑ 231 Conolly Abel Smith (WWI)
❑ 232 Courtney Hodges (WWII)
❑ 233 Courtney Whitney (WWII)
❑ 234 Curt Souchay (WWII)
❑ 235 Curtis LeMay (Cold War)
❑ 236 Curtis LeMay (WWII)
❑ 237 Cyril Falls (WWI)
❑ 238 D.H. Clark (WWII)
❑ 239 Dabney N. Montgomery (WWII)
❑ 240 Dale F. Spencer (WWII)
❑ 241 Dale Karger (WWII)
❑ 242 Dame Ethel H. Becher (WWI)
❑ 243 Dan Carmichael (WWII)
❑ 244 Daniel E. Power (WWII)
❑ 245 Daniel Inouye (WWII)
❑ 246 Daniel Kerr (Civil War)
❑ 247 Daniel R. Rehm (WWII)
❑ 248 Daniel Sickles (Civil War)
❑ 249 Daniel Spry (WWII)
❑ 250 Darrell Shifty Powers (WWII)
❑ 251 Darwin S. Hall (Civil War)
❑ 252 Dave E. Severance (WWII)
❑ 253 David A. Clement (Vietnam)
❑ 254 David A. Harvey (Civil War)
❑ 255 David B. Henderson (Civil War)
❑ 256 David Cowan (WWI)
❑ 257 David Dixon Porter (Civil War)
❑ 258 David F. Thwaites (WWII)
❑ 259 David George Samuel Richardson Cox (WWII)
❑ 260 David H. McNerney (Vietnam)
❑ 261 David J. Thatcher (WWII)
❑ 262 David Lee Tex Hill (Korean War)
❑ 263 David Lee Tex Hill (WWII)
❑ 264 David Lloyd George (WWI)
❑ 265 David M. Davey Jones (WWII)
❑ 266 David McCampbell (WWII)
❑ 267 David Moriarty (WWII)
❑ 268 David Ogilvy, 11th Earl of Airlie (Second Boer War)
❑ 269 David Scott-Malden (WWII)
❑ 270 David Williams (WWII)
❑ 271 Dean Diz Laird (WWII)
❑ 272 Dean Davenport (WWII)
❑ 273 Dean E. Hess (WWII)
❑ 274 Delbert Kuehl (WWII)
❑ 275 deLesseps S. Morrison (WWII)
❑ 276 Denis Crowley-Milling (WWII)
❑ 277 Dennis L. Benchoff (Vietnam)
❑ 278 Dermot Boyle (WWII)
❑ 279 Desmond Doss (WWII)
❑ 280 Desmond Sheen (WWII)
❑ 281 Dewey F. Durnford (WWII)
❑ 282 Dick Stambook (WWII)
❑ 283 Dieter Dengler (Vietnam)
❑ 284 Don Blakeslee (WWII)
❑ 285 Don Cronin (WWII)
❑ 286 Don McGee (WWII)
❑ 287 Donald A. Williams (WWII)
❑ 288 Donald B. Beary (WWII)
❑ 289 Donald Beaty (WWII)
❑ 290 Donald Bryan (WWII)
❑ 291 Donald C. Henry (WWII)
❑ 292 Donald Dunstan (WWII)
❑ 293 Donald E. Ballard (Vietnam)
❑ 294 Donald E. Rudolph (WWII)
❑ 295 Donald H. Connolly (WWII)
❑ 296 Donald J. Strait (WWII)
❑ 297 Donald K. Ross (WWII)
❑ 298 Donald Kingaby (WWII)
❑ 299 Donald N. Yates (WWII)
❑ 300 Donald O. Aldridge (Vietnam)
❑ 301 Donald Paton (WWI)
❑ 302 Donald R. Burgett (WWII)
❑ 303 Donald Rudolph (Korean War)
❑ 304 Donald S. Lopez (WWII)
❑ 305 Donald Stratton (WWII)
❑ 306 Donald V. Bennett (WWII)
❑ 307 Donald Yandell (WWI)
❑ 308 Douglas Campbell (WWI)
❑ 309 Douglas Canning (WWII)
❑ 310 Douglas Haig, 1st Earl Haig (WWI)
❑ 311 Douglas MacArthur (Korean War)
❑ 312 Douglas MacArthur (WWI)
❑ 313 Douglas MacArthur (WWII)
❑ 314 Douglas Oxby (WWII)
❑ 315 Dr. Richard Hornberger (Korean War)
❑ 316 Drew Dix (Vietnam)
❑ 317 Duane E. Dewey (Korean War)
❑ 318 Duerr Schuh (WWII)
❑ 319 Dusan Simovitch (WWII)
❑ 320 E. A. Pollock (WWII)
❑ 321 E. Michael Burke (WWII)
❑ 322 E.J. Marquart (WWII)
❑ 323 E.J. Morris (WWII)
❑ 324 E.J. Timberlake (Korean War)
❑ 325 E.L. Mahar (WWII)
❑ 326 Earl McClung (WWII)
❑ 327 Earle E. Partridge (WWI)
❑ 328 Earle E. Partridge (WWII)
❑ 329 Earle G. Wheeler (WWII)
❑ 330 Ebenezer Webster (American Revolution)
❑ 331 Eckart Afheldt (WWII)
❑ 332 Ed Freeman (Vietnam)
❑ 333 Ed Harper (WWII)
❑ 334 Ed Johann (WWII)
❑ 335 Ed Koch (WWII)
❑ 336 Ed Mauser (WWII)
❑ 337 Ed Olander (WWII)
❑ 338 Ed Tipper (WWII)
❑ 339 Ed Wendorf (WWII)
❑ 340 Eddie Rickenbacker (WWI)
❑ 341 Edgar Harrell (WWII)
❑ 342 Edmund Allenby, 1st Viscount Allenby (WWI)
❑ 343 Edmund Hillary (WWII)
❑ 344 Edmund N. Morrill (Civil War)
❑ 345 Edmund P. Gaines (War of 1812)
❑ 346 Edward Bykowski (WWII)
❑ 347 Edward C. Kalbfus (Spanish-American War)
❑ 348 Edward C. Meyer (Vietnam)
❑ 349 Edward C. Waller (Korean War)
❑ 350 Edward Eberle (WWI)
❑ 351 Edward J. Saylor (WWII)
❑ 352 Edward L. Beach, Jr. (WWII)
❑ 353 Edward L. Stiles (WWII)
❑ 354 Edward M. Ned Almond (Korean War)
❑ 355 Edward M. Almond (WWI)
❑ 356 Edward P. Allen (Civil War)
❑ 357 Edward R. Hays (Civil War)
❑ 358 Edward R. Schowalter, Jr. (Korean War)
❑ 359 Edward Robinson (Vietnam)
❑ 360 Edward S. Bragg (Civil War)
❑ 361 Edward S. Popek (WWII)
❑ 362 Edward Tillman (WWII)
❑ 363 Edwards Pierrepont (Civil War)
❑ 364 Edwin Fobes (WWII)
❑ 365 Edwin S. Osborne (Civil War)
❑ 366 Edwin W. Rawlings (WWII)
❑ 367 Eedson L.M. Burns (WWII)
❑ 368 Eero Halonen (WWII)
❑ 369 Einar Harold Ingman, Jr. (Korean War)
❑ 370 Elaine Harmon (WWII)
❑ 371 Eldridge Williams (WWII)
❑ 372 Eleanor Maud Pat Cheramy (WWII)
❑ 373 Eli Wallach (WWII)
❑ 374 Elihu S. Williams (Civil War)
❑ 375 Elizabeth Strohfus (WWII)
❑ 376 Elliott Roosevelt (WWII)
❑ 377 Elmo Zumwalt, Jr. (WWII)
❑ 378 Elvin Lin Lindsay (WWII)
❑ 379 Elvin Homan (WWII)
❑ 380 Elwood R. Pete Quesada (WWII)
❑ 381 Emil R. Bedard (Vietnam)
❑ 382 Emmett O'Donnell (Korean War)
❑ 383 Emmett O'Donnell (WWII)
❑ 384 Ennis Whitehead (WWI)
❑ 385 Erastus J. Turner (Civil War)
❑ 386 Erhard Milch (WWII)
❑ 387 Eric Bols (WWII)
❑ 388 Erich Axthammer (WWII)
❑ 389 Erich Sommer (WWII)
❑ 390 Erik Shilling (WWII)
❑ 391 Ernest Borgnine (WWII)
❑ 392 Ernest D. Swinton (WWI)
❑ 393 Ernest E. West (Korean War)
❑ 394 Ernest Joseph King (Spanish-American War)
❑ 395 Ernest Joseph King (WWII)
❑ 396 Ernest Shipman (WWII)
❑ 397 Ernie Pyle (WWII)
❑ 398 Ernst Borngen (WWII)
❑ 399 Ernst Maisel (WWII)
❑ 400 Erroll Tremlett (WWII)
❑ 401 Erwin F. Hensch (WWII)
❑ 402 Erwin Prossl (WWII)
❑ 403 Erwin Rommel (WWI)
❑ 404 Erwin Rommel (WWII)
❑ 405 Eugene B. Fluckey (WWII)
❑ 406 Eugene H.C. Leutze (Civil War)
❑ 407 Eugene Ralph Hanks (WWII)
❑ 408 Everett Alvarez, Jr. (Vietnam)
❑ 409 Everett Miller (WWII)
❑ 410 Everett P. Pope (Korean War)
❑ 411 Everett P. Pope (WWII)
❑ 412 Ezer Weizman (WWII)
❑ 413 Ezra B. Taylor (Civil War)
❑ 414 F.H. Michaelis (WWII)
❑ 415 Fay R. Upthegrove (WWII)
❑ 416 Ferdinand Foch (WWI)
❑ 417 Ferdinand Maurice Felix West (WWI)
❑ 418 Fitz John Porter (Civil War)
❑ 419 Fitz John Porter (Mexican-American War)
❑ 420 Fitzhugh Lee (Civil War)
❑ 421 Floyd Gibbons (WWI)
❑ 422 Forde A. Todd (WWII)
❑ 423 Forrest Bradshaw (WWII)
❑ 424 Forrest L. Guth (WWII)
❑ 425 Forrest S. Petersen (WWII)
❑ 426 Francesco Cavalera (WWII)
❑ 427 Francis C. Denebrink (WWII)
❑ 428 Francis Gerard (WWII)
❑ 429 Francis M. Fleming (WWII)
❑ 430 Francis S. Currey (WWII)
❑ 431 Francis S. Gabreski (Korean War)
❑ 432 Francis S. Gabreski (WWII)
❑ 433 Francis W. Nye (WWII)
❑ 434 Francois Etienne de Kellermann (Napoleonic Wars)
❑ 435 Frank Pete Everest (WWII)
❑ 436 Frank A. Armstrong, Jr. (WWII)
❑ 437 Frank C. Mahin (WWI)
❑ 438 Frank C. Ransley (WWI)
❑ 439 Frank Carey (WWII)
❑ 440 Frank Friday Fletcher (WWI)
❑ 441 Frank H. Albright (WWI)
❑ 442 Frank Hurlbut (WWII)
❑ 443 Frank Losonsky (WWII)
❑ 444 Frank McCauley (WWII)
❑ 445 Frank O'Driscoll Hunter (WWI)
❑ 446 Frank S. Besson, Jr. (WWII)
❑ 447 Frank Soboleski (WWII)
❑ 448 Frank W. Klibbe (WWII)
❑ 449 Franklin A. Hart (WWII)
❑ 450 Franklin A. Nichols (WWII)
❑ 451 Franklin D. Miller (Vietnam)
❑ 452 Franklin Delano Roosevelt, Jr. (WWII)
❑ 453 Franklin Troup (WWII)

❑ 454 Frantisek Perina (WWII)
❑ 455 Franz Halder (WWII)
❑ 456 Fred J. Ascani (WWII)
❑ 457 Fred J. Christensen (WWII)
❑ 458 Fred Myers (WWI)
❑ 459 Fred Olivi (WWII)
❑ 460 Frederic T. Greenhalge (Civil War)
❑ 461 Frederick Taffy Higginson (WWII)
❑ 462 Frederick Bock (WWII)
❑ 463 Frederick C. Boots Blesse (Korean War)
❑ 464 Frederick C. Boots Blesse (Vietnam)
❑ 465 Frederick C. Sherman (WWI)
❑ 466 Frederick Dent Grant (Spanish-American War)
❑ 467 Frederick E. Bakutis (WWII)
❑ 468 Frederick E. Ferguson (Vietnam)
❑ 469 Frederick Funston (Spanish-American War)
❑ 470 Frederick L. Ashworth (WWII)
❑ 471 Frederick Lansing (Civil War)
❑ 472 Frederick Roberts, 1st Earl Roberts (Second Boer War)
❑ 473 Frederick Trafton, Jr. (WWII)
❑ 474 Friedrich Bottcher (WWII)
❑ 475 Friedrich Ruge (WWI)
❑ 476 Friedrich Ruge (WWII)
❑ 477 Friedrich von Bernhardi (Franco-Prussian War)
❑ 478 Friedrich von Bernhardi (WWI)
❑ 479 Fritz Henke (WWII)
❑ 480 Fritz Morzick (WWII)
❑ 481 Fritz Tegtmeier (WWII)
❑ 482 G. Hamilton-Gordon, 4th Earl Of Aberdeen (Crimean War)
❑ 483 G.E. Brookes (WWII)
❑ 484 Gail Halvorsen (WWII)
❑ 485 Gareth L. Nowell (WWII)
❑ 486 Garlen Eslick (WWII)
❑ 487 Gary B. Beikirch (Vietnam)
❑ 488 Gary G. Wetzel (Vietnam)
❑ 489 Gary L. Littrell (Vietnam)
❑ 490 Gene Derricotte (WWII)
❑ 491 Geoffrey Fisken (WWII)
❑ 492 George Bud Day (Korean War)
❑ 493 George Bud Day (Vietnam)
❑ 494 George Albert Whiting (WWII)
❑ 495 George B. Barth (WWII)
❑ 496 George Bennions (WWII)
❑ 497 George Boyd (WWII)
❑ 498 George C. Axtell (Korean War)
❑ 499 George C. Axtell (Vietnam)
❑ 500 George C. Axtell (WWII)
❑ 501 George C. Kenney (WWI)
❑ 502 George C. Lang (Vietnam)
❑ 503 George Carpenter (WWII)
❑ 504 George Chandler (WWII)
❑ 505 George Dewey (Spanish-American War)
❑ 506 George Doersch (WWII)
❑ 507 George E. Stratemeyer (WWI)
❑ 508 George Edward Whalen (Korean War)
❑ 509 George Edward Whalen (WWII)
❑ 510 George Elliott (Vietnam)
❑ 511 George F. Ceuleers (WWII)
❑ 512 George F. Hussey, Jr. (WWII)
❑ 513 George Fowler Hastings (Crimean War)
❑ 514 George G. Henson (WWII)
❑ 515 George G. Loving, Jr. (Korean War)
❑ 516 George Grunert (WWI)
❑ 517 George H. Brett (WWII)
❑ 518 George H. Gay, Jr. (WWII)
❑ 519 George H. O'Brien, Jr. (Korean War)
❑ 520 George Irving Back (WWII)
❑ 521 George J. Dufek (WWII)
❑ 522 George J. Richards (WWII)
❑ 523 George L. Jones (Korean War)
❑ 524 George L. Street, III (WWII)
❑ 525 George Loving, Jr. (WWII)
❑ 526 George M. Lamb (WWII)
❑ 527 George Marshall (Philippine-American War)
❑ 528 George Marshall (WWI)
❑ 529 George Marshall (WWII)
❑ 530 George Meyer (WWI)
❑ 531 George Robert Gleig (Napoleonic Wars)
❑ 532 George Robert Gleig (War of 1812)
❑ 533 George S. Patton, IV (Korean War)
❑ 534 George S. Patton, IV (Vietnam)
❑ 535 George Sakato (WWII)
❑ 536 Georges Carpentier (WWI)
❑ 537 Georg-Peter Eder (WWII)
❑ 538 Gerald Jerry O'Rourke (WWII)
❑ 539 Gerald A. Black (Vietnam)
❑ 540 Gerald Brown (WWII)
❑ 541 Gerald Ford (WWII)
❑ 542 Gerald L. Rounds (WWII)
❑ 543 Gerald Tyler (WWII)
❑ 544 Gerald W. Jerry Johnson (Vietnam)
❑ 545 Gerald W. Jerry Johnson (WWII)
❑ 546 Gerard E. Zinser (WWII)
❑ 547 Gerhard Matzky (WWII)
❑ 548 Gerhard Schoepfel (WWII)
❑ 549 Gerhard Sturt (WWII)
❑ 550 Gilbert L. Laws (Civil War)
❑ 551 Gino J. Merli (WWII)
❑ 552 Giuseppe Cimicchi (WWII)
❑ 553 Giuseppe Garibaldi (Franco-Prussian War)
❑ 554 Giuseppe Renzetti (WWII)
❑ 555 Glenn E. Duncan (WWII)
❑ 556 Glenn Frazier (WWII)
❑ 557 Glenn L. Bowers (WWII)
❑ 558 Gordon Ray Roberts (Vietnam)
❑ 559 Gordon Steege (WWII)
❑ 560 Gottfried Dulias (WWII)
❑ 561 Gottlieb von Haeseler (Franco-Prussian War)
❑ 562 Gough Whitlam (WWII)
❑ 563 Graham Seton Hutchison (WWI)
❑ 564 Guion Bluford (Vietnam)
❑ 565 Gunther Blumentritt (WWII)
❑ 566 Gunther Rall (WWII)
❑ 567 Gunther Rubell (WWII)
❑ 568 Gunther Schack (WWII)
❑ 569 Gus Hall (WWII)
❑ 570 Gustav Kastner-Kirdorf (WWI)
❑ 571 Guy Bordelon (Korean War)
❑ 572 Guy D. Simonds (WWII)
❑ 573 H. Clay Evans (Civil War)
❑ 574 H. Wickham Steed (WWI)
❑ 575 H.A. Young (WWII)
❑ 576 H.F.G. Letson (WWI)
❑ 577 Hajo Herrmann (WWII)
❑ 578 Hal Moore (Vietnam)
❑ 579 Hamilton Mac McWhorter, III (WWII)
❑ 580 Hamilton D. Coleman (Civil War)
❑ 581 Hamilton Fish, III (WWI)
❑ 582 Hank Dunn (Vietnam)
❑ 583 Hank Potter (WWII)
❑ 584 Hanns Heise (WWII)
❑ 585 Hanns Laengenfelder (WWII)
❑ 586 Hans Baur (WWII)
❑ 587 Hans Kreppel (WWII)
❑ 588 Hans Traupe (WWII)
❑ 589 Hans von Koester (Franco-Prussian War)
❑ 590 Hans-Joachim Jabs (WWII)
❑ 591 Harley L. Brown (WWII)
❑ 592 Harold A. Fritz (Vietnam)
❑ 593 Harold Alexander, Earl Alexander of Tunis (WWII)
❑ 594 Harold B. Sallada (WWII)
❑ 595 Harold Balfour (WWI)
❑ 596 Harold Bird-Wilson (WWII)
❑ 597 Harold Brown (Cold War)
❑ 598 Harold E. Comstock (WWII)
❑ 599 Harold E. Fischer (Korean War)
❑ 600 Harold E. Talbott (WWI)
❑ 601 Harold G. Bowen, Jr. (WWII)
❑ 602 Harold Johnson (WWII)
❑ 603 Harold Loch (WWII)
❑ 604 Harold Macmillan (WWI)
❑ 605 Harold R. Stark (WWII)
❑ 606 Harold Stassen (WWII)
❑ 607 Harold W. Blot (Vietnam)
❑ 608 Harrison Thyng (WWII)
❑ 609 Harry Butcher (WWII)
❑ 610 Harry C. Johnson (WWII)
❑ 611 Harry E. Yarnell (WWII)
❑ 612 Harry G. DeWolf (WWII)
❑ 613 Harry McCool (WWII)
❑ 614 Harry S. New (Spanish-American War)
❑ 615 Harry Secombe (WWII)
❑ 616 Harvey Alexander (WWII)
❑ 617 Harvey C. Barnum, Jr. (Vietnam)
❑ 618 Hasso von Manteuffel (WWII)
❑ 619 Hedworth Lambton (Second Boer War)
❑ 620 Heinrich Himmler (WWII)
❑ 621 Heinrich Nolte (WWII)
❑ 622 Heinz Gorlich (WWII)
❑ 623 Heinz Rothhardt (WWII)
❑ 624 Heinz-Oskar Laebe (WWII)
❑ 625 Helmuth Beukemann (WWII)
❑ 626 Henri Gouraud (WWI)
❑ 627 Henri Lafont (WWII)
❑ 628 Henry Bourgeois (WWII)
❑ 629 Henry Dundas, 1st Viscount Melville (French Revolutionary Wars)
❑ 630 Henry E. Erwin (WWII)
❑ 631 Henry Erben (Civil War)
❑ 632 Henry H. Hap Arnold (WWI)
❑ 633 Henry H. Hap Arnold (WWII)
❑ 634 Henry H. Carlton (Civil War)
❑ 635 Henry J. Spooner (Civil War)
❑ 636 Henry L. Morey (Civil War)
❑ 637 Henry Moore (WWII)
❑ 638 Henry R.B. Foote (WWII)
❑ 639 Henry S. Aurand (WWI)
❑ 640 Henry Schauer (WWII)
❑ 641 Henry Sewall (War of 1812)
❑ 642 Henry W. Slocum (Civil War)
❑ 643 Henry Zimmerman (WWII)
❑ 644 Herb Heilbrun (WWII)
❑ 645 Herb Holmes (Vietnam)
❑ 646 Herbert E. Regan (WWII)
❑ 647 Herbert H. Lehman (WWII)
❑ 648 Herbert Hallowes (WWII)
❑ 649 Herbert Plumer, 1st Viscount Plumer (WWI)
❑ 650 Herbert Weatherwax (WWII)
❑ 651 Herman Ernst (WWII)
❑ 652 Herman J. Rossi, Jr. (WWII)
❑ 653 Hermann Aldinger (WWII)
❑ 654 Hermann Goering (WWI)
❑ 655 Hermann Goering (WWII)
❑ 656 Hermann Greiner (WWII)
❑ 657 Hermann Hoth (WWII)
❑ 658 Hermann Niehoff (WWII)
❑ 659 Hermann Plocher (WWII)
❑ 660 Hermann Rauschenbusch (WWII)
❑ 661 Hermann-Heinrich Behrend (WWII)
❑ 662 Herschel Green (WWII)
❑ 663 Hershel W. Williams (WWII)
❑ 664 Hiram Cronk (War of 1812)
❑ 665 Hiroshi H. Miyamura (Korean War)
❑ 666 Holland M. Smith (WWI)
❑ 667 Homer E. Capehart (WWI)
❑ 668 Horace B. Moranville (WWII)
❑ 669 Horace E. Crouch (WWII)
❑ 670 Horst von Buttlar-Brandenfels (WWII)
❑ 671 Hosea Townsend (Civil War)
❑ 672 Howard J. Finn (WWII)
❑ 673 Howard P. Ady, Jr. (WWII)
❑ 674 Howard V. Lee (Vietnam)
❑ 675 Hoyt S. Vandenberg (WWII)
❑ 676 Hubert H. Humphrey (Vietnam)
❑ 677 Hugh Aloysius Drum (WWI)
❑ 678 Hugh Batten (WWII)
❑ 679 Hugh Dundas (WWII)
❑ 680 Hugh H. Gordon, Jr. (Spanish-American War)
❑ 681 Hugh J. Knerr (WWII)
❑ 682 Hugh L. Scott (WWI)
❑ 683 Hugh P. Harris (WWII)
❑ 684 Hugh Rodman (Spanish-American War)
❑ 685 Hugh Stockwell (WWII)
❑ 686 Hugo Osterhaus (WWI)
❑ 687 I.H. Cosby (WWII)
❑ 688 Ian Fraser (WWII)
❑ 689 Innes Westmacott (WWII)
❑ 690 Ira C. Eaker (WWII)
❑ 691 Isaac D. White (WWII)
❑ 692 Isaac S. Struble (Civil War)
❑ 693 Iva Toguri (WWII)
❑ 694 J. Edwin Reulet (WWII)
❑ 695 J. Hunter Reinburg (WWII)
❑ 696 J. Lawton Collins (Korean War)
❑ 697 J. Lawton Collins (WWI)
❑ 698 J. Lawton Collins (WWII)
❑ 699 J. Monroe Johnson (WWI)
❑ 700 J. Royden Stork (WWII)
❑ 701 J. Ted Crosby (WWII)
❑ 702 J.J. Broshek (WWII)
❑ 703 Jack A. Quinlan (WWII)
❑ 704 Jack Bryant (WWII)
❑ 705 Jack C. Montgomery (WWII)
❑ 706 Jack C. Price (WWII)
❑ 707 Jack Foley (WWII)
❑ 708 Jack H. Jacobs (Vietnam)
❑ 709 Jack Lenox, Jr. (WWII)
❑ 710 Jack Rose (WWII)
❑ 711 Jacklyn H. Lucas (WWII)
❑ 712 Jacob Beser (WWII)
❑ 713 Jacob DeShazer (WWII)
❑ 714 Jacques Francois Dugommier (French Revolutionary Wars)
❑ 715 Jacques Massu (WWII)
❑ 716 James A. Goodson (WWII)
❑ 717 James A. Sheppard (WWII)
❑ 718 James A. Van Fleet (Korean War)
❑ 719 James A. Van Fleet (WWI)
❑ 720 James A. Van Fleet (WWII)
❑ 721 James Allen Taylor (Vietnam)
❑ 722 James B. Morehead (WWII)
❑ 723 James B. Stockdale (Vietnam)
❑ 724 James B. Tapp (WWII)
❑ 725 James C. Adamson (Vietnam)
❑ 726 James C. Dozier (WWI)
❑ 727 James C. Fry (WWII)
❑ 728 James Callaghan (WWII)
❑ 729 James D. Ramage (Vietnam)
❑ 730 James D. Ramage (WWII)
❑ 731 James Doolittle (Cold War)
❑ 732 James Doolittle (WWII)
❑ 733 James E. Livingston (Vietnam)
❑ 734 James E. O'Donnell (WWII)
❑ 735 James E. Swett (WWII)
❑ 736 James F. Low (Korean War)
❑ 737 James G. Harbord (Mexican Revolution)
❑ 738 James G. Harbord (WWI)
❑ 739 James Gambier (Napoleonic Wars)
❑ 740 James H. Kasler (Korean War)
❑ 741 James H. Kasler (WWII)
❑ 742 James H. Shadden (Vietnam)
❑ 743 James Hodges (WWII)
❑ 744 James Jarvis (WWII)
❑ 745 James L. Brooks (WWII)
❑ 746 James L. Holloway, III (WWII)
❑ 747 James L. Holloway, Jr. (WWII)
❑ 748 James L. Pearce (WWII)
❑ 749 James Leathart (WWII)
❑ 750 James M. Burt (WWII)
❑ 751 James M. Gavin (WWII)
❑ 752 James M. Stagg (WWII)
❑ 753 James P. Fleming (Vietnam)
❑ 754 James P. Flick (Civil War)
❑ 755 James P. Kem (WWI)
❑ 756 James R. Hendrix (Korean War)
❑ 757 James R. Hendrix (WWII)
❑ 758 James R. Schlesinger (Cold War)
❑ 759 James Robinson Risner (Vietnam)
❑ 760 James Roy Starnes (WWII)
❑ 761 James Somerville (WWII)
❑ 762 James Storrar (WWII)
❑ 763 James Swope (WWII)
❑ 764 James T. Adams (WWI)
❑ 765 James W. Griffis (WWII)
❑ 766 James Warren (WWII)
❑ 767 Jan C. Smuts (WWI)
❑ 768 Jan van Arkel (WWII)
❑ 769 Jasper T. Acuff (WWII)
❑ 770 Jay R. Vargas (Vietnam)
❑ 771 Jay T. Robbins (WWII)
❑ 772 Jay Zeamer, Jr. (WWII)
❑ 773 Jean-Baptiste Meynier (Napoleonic Wars)
❑ 774 Jefferson Davis (Civil War)
❑ 775 Jefferson Dorroh (WWII)
❑ 776 Jefferson J. DeBlanc (WWII)
❑ 777 Jerauld Wright (WWII)
❑ 778 Jeremiah Denton (Vietnam)
❑ 779 Jerome L. Johnson (Vietnam)
❑ 780 Jerry O'Keefe (WWII)
❑ 781 Jesse G. Johnson

(WWII)
❑ 782 Jessica Lynch (War In Iraq)
❑ 783 Jim Billo (WWII)
❑ 784 Jim Hill (WWII)
❑ 785 Jim Whittaker (WWII)
❑ 786 Jimmie Doc Savage (WWII)
❑ 787 Jimmie Dean Coy (Gulf War)
❑ 788 Jimmy Carter (Cold War)
❑ 789 Joachim Melo (WWII)
❑ 790 Joe Forster (WWII)
❑ 791 Joe Foss (WWII)
❑ 792 Joe H. Kellwood (WWII)
❑ 793 Joe M. Jackson (Vietnam)
❑ 794 Joe Rosbert (WWII)
❑ 795 Johann Trummer (WWII)
❑ 796 Johannes Steinhoff (WWII)
❑ 797 Johannes Wiese (WWII)
❑ 798 John A. Shorty Powers (WWII)
❑ 799 John A. Blatnik (WWII)
❑ 800 John A. Buchanan (Civil War)
❑ 801 John A. Logan (Civil War)
❑ 802 John A. Roosevelt (WWII)
❑ 803 John A. Zink (WWII)
❑ 804 John Abizaid (War In Iraq)
❑ 805 John Alden Tilley (WWII)
❑ 806 John B. Montgomery (Cold War)
❑ 807 John Baca (Vietnam)
❑ 808 John Bartle (WWII)
❑ 809 John Bisley (WWII)
❑ 810 John Brooks Henderson (Civil War)
❑ 811 John C. Slessor (WWI)
❑ 812 John C. Tarsney (Civil War)
❑ 813 John Charles Gawen Roberts (Napoleonic Wars)
❑ 814 John Crittenden Watson (Civil War)
❑ 815 John Cruickshank (WWII)
❑ 816 John Cunningham (WWII)
❑ 817 John D. Bud Hawk (WWII)
❑ 818 John D. Bulkeley (Korean War)
❑ 819 John D. Bulkeley (WWII)
❑ 820 John D. Price (WWII)
❑ 821 John D. Stewart (Civil War)
❑ 822 John Dale Ryan (Vietnam)
❑ 823 John Dale Ryan (WWII)
❑ 824 John Duffy (Napoleonic Wars)
❑ 825 John E. Dahlquist (WWII)
❑ 826 John E. Pillsbury (Spanish-American War)
❑ 827 John E. Purdy (WWII)
❑ 828 John Ellacombe (WWII)
❑ 829 John F. Baker, Jr. (Vietnam)
❑ 830 John F. Bolt (WWII)
❑ 831 John F. Kinney (Korean War)
❑ 832 John F. Kinney (WWII)
❑ 833 John F. Lacey (Civil War)
❑ 834 John Gavin (Korean War)
❑ 835 John H. Ketcham (Civil War)
❑ 836 John H. Leahr (WWII)
❑ 837 John H. Towers (WWI)
❑ 838 John Heller (WWII)
❑ 839 John Herren (Vietnam)
❑ 840 John J. Pershing (Mexican Revolution)
❑ 841 John J. Pershing (Spanish-American War)
❑ 842 John J. Pershing (WWI)
❑ 843 John J. Tominac (WWII)
❑ 844 John K. Cannon (WWII)
❑ 845 John K. Norwell (WWII)
❑ 846 John K. Singlaub (WWII)
❑ 847 John Keith Wells (WWII)
❑ 848 John L. Jones (WWII)
❑ 849 John L. McCrea (WWI)
❑ 850 John Lapsley (WWII)
❑ 851 John Lind (Spanish-American War)
❑ 852 John M. Curran (Gulf War)
❑ 853 John M. Shalikashvili (Vietnam)
❑ 854 John M. Thompson (WWII)
❑ 855 John MacBride (Second Boer War)
❑ 856 John Major (Gulf War)
❑ 857 John McCain (Vietnam)
❑ 858 John McConnell (WWII)
❑ 859 John Morris Ellicott (Spanish-American War)
❑ 860 John Mulzac (WWII)
❑ 861 John Newman (WWII)
❑ 862 John Percival (War of 1812)
❑ 863 John Pope (Civil War)
❑ 864 John R. Allison (WWII)
❑ 865 John R. Allison (Korean War)
❑ 866 John R. Beardall (WWII)
❑ 867 John R. Crews (WWII)
❑ 868 John R. Strane (WWII)
❑ 869 John Raines (Civil War)
❑ 870 John Richard Rossi (WWII)
❑ 871 John S. Loisel (WWII)
❑ 872 John T. Sprague (Civil War)
❑ 873 John T. West (WWII)
❑ 874 John Urwin-Mann (WWII)
❑ 875 John V. McDuffie (Civil War)
❑ 876 John W. Rife (Civil War)
❑ 877 John W. Roper (WWI)
❑ 878 John W. Ruhsam (Korean War)
❑ 879 John W. Ruhsam (Vietnam)
❑ 880 John W. Ruhsam (WWII)
❑ 881 John W. Vessey, Jr. (Korean War)
❑ 882 John W. Vessey, Jr. (Vietnam)
❑ 883 John W. Vessey, Jr. (WWII)
❑ 884 John W. Vogt (WWII)
❑ 885 John Waddy (WWII)
❑ 886 John William Finn (WWII)
❑ 887 John Woodward Philip (Civil War)
❑ 888 John Woolston (WWII)
❑ 889 Johnnie Johnson (WWII)
❑ 890 Jon R. Cavaiani (Vietnam)
❑ 891 Jonathan H. Rowell (Civil War)
❑ 892 Jonathan M. Wainwright (WWI)
❑ 893 Jonathan M. Wainwright (WWII)
❑ 894 Jorma Karhunen (WWII)
❑ 895 Jose M. Lopez (WWII)
❑ 896 Josef Kammhuber (WWII)
❑ 897 Joseph Abbott (Civil War)
❑ 898 Joseph B. Cheadle (Civil War)
❑ 899 Joseph C. Rodriguez (Korean War)
❑ 900 Joseph Chamberlain (Second Boer War)
❑ 901 Joseph D. Taylor (Civil War)
❑ 902 Joseph Galloway (Vietnam)
❑ 903 Joseph Goebbels (WWII)
❑ 904 Joseph Griffin (WWII)
❑ 905 Joseph H. Moore (WWII)
❑ 906 Joseph H. Sweney (Civil War)
❑ 907 Joseph Habersham (American Revolution)
❑ 908 Joseph Hewitt (WWII)
❑ 909 Joseph Hooker (Civil War)
❑ 910 Joseph J. Doyle (WWII)
❑ 911 Joseph J. McCarthy (WWII)
❑ 912 Joseph Lagrange (French Revolutionary Wars)
❑ 913 Joseph M. Reeves (Spanish-American War)
❑ 914 Joseph M. Swing (WWII)
❑ 915 Joseph Malta (WWII)
❑ 916 Joseph O. Mauborgne (WWI)
❑ 917 Joseph Poshefko (WWII)
❑ 918 Joseph R. Reed (Civil War)
❑ 919 Joseph Strauss (WWI)
❑ 920 Joseph T. McNarney (WWI)
❑ 921 Joseph W. Kittinger, Jr (Korean War)
❑ 922 Joseph W. Kittinger, Jr (Vietnam)
❑ 923 Joseph Wheeler (Civil War)
❑ 924 Joseph Wheeler (Philippine-American War)
❑ 925 Joseph Wheeler (Spanish-American War)
❑ 926 Joseph Williams (American Revolution)
❑ 927 Josephus Daniels (WWI)
❑ 928 Judson C. Clements (Civil War)
❑ 929 Julian Byng, 1st Viscount Byng of Vimy (Second Boer War)
❑ 930 Julian Byng, 1st Viscount Byng of Vimy (WWI)
❑ 931 Julius C. Burrows (Civil War)
❑ 932 Julius Klein (WWII)
❑ 933 Karl Donitz (WWI)
❑ 934 Karl Eduard-Wilke (WWII)
❑ 935 Karl Heinz Lichte (WWII)
❑ 936 Karl Lang (WWI)
❑ 937 Karl Nagerl (WWII)
❑ 938 Karl-Adolf Hollidt (WWI)
❑ 939 Karl-Adolf Hollidt (WWII)
❑ 940 Karl-Adolf von Bodecker (WWII)
❑ 941 Karl-Ludwig Johanssen (WWII)
❑ 942 Kee J. Pon (WWII)
❑ 943 Ken Dahlberg (WWII)
❑ 944 Ken Jernstedt (WWII)
❑ 945 Kenneth A. Walsh (WWII)
❑ 946 Kenneth E. Stumpf (Vietnam)
❑ 947 Kenneth J. Houghton (Vietnam)
❑ 948 Kenneth L. Tallman (Vietnam)
❑ 949 Kenneth R. Bud Pool (WWII)
❑ 950 Kenneth S. Wherry (WWI)
❑ 951 Kermit A. Tyler (WWII)
❑ 952 Kohei Hanami/Arthur Evans (WWII)
❑ 953 Kuroki Tamemoto (Russo-Japanese War)
❑ 954 Larry Keighley (WWII)
❑ 955 Laurence Cardee Craigie (WWII)
❑ 956 Lauris Norstad (WWII)
❑ 957 Lawrence A. Clark (WWII)
❑ 958 Lawrence F. O'Neill (WWII)
❑ 959 Lawrence N. Guarino (Korean War)
❑ 960 Lawrence N. Guarino (Vietnam)
❑ 961 Lawrence N. Guarino (WWII)
❑ 962 Lawrence Powell (WWII)
❑ 963 Lee Baggett, Jr. (Cold War)
❑ 964 Leighton Willhite (WWII)
❑ 965 Leo Gray (WWII)
❑ 966 Leo H. Thebaud (WWII)
❑ 967 Leo K. Thorsness (Vietnam)
❑ 968 Leo W. Nadeau (WWII)
❑ 969 Leon Frankel (WWII)
❑ 970 Leonard B. Keller (Vietnam)
❑ 971 Leonard B. Smith (WWII)
❑ 972 Leonard Cheshire (WWII)
❑ 973 Leonard Rochford (WWI)
❑ 974 Leonard S. Reid (WWII)
❑ 975 Leonard Wood (Spanish-American War)
❑ 976 LeRoy Lutes (WWII)
❑ 977 Leroy Robinson (WWII)
❑ 978 Les Williams (WWII)
❑ 979 Leslie E. Brown (WWII)
❑ 980 Leslie Minchew (WWII)
❑ 981 Leslie Smith (WWII)
❑ 982 Levi Maish (Civil War)
❑ 983 Lew Wallace (Civil War)
❑ 984 Lewis E. Lyle (WWII)
❑ 985 Lewis L. Millett (Korean War)
❑ 986 Lindley Miller Garrison (WWI)
❑ 987 Lloyd Aspinwall (Civil War)
❑ 988 Lloyd L. Burke (Korean War)
❑ 989 Lloyd M. Bucher (WWII)
❑ 990 Lloyd McKeethen (WWII)
❑ 991 Lloyd P. Barto (WWII)
❑ 992 Lloyd W. Newton (Vietnam)
❑ 993 Loris Baldi (WWII)
❑ 994 Louis C. Menetrey (Vietnam)
❑ 995 Louis E. Atkinson (Civil War)
❑ 996 Louis E. Denfeld (WWI)
❑ 997 Louis E. Denfeld (WWII)
❑ 998 Louis H. Wilson, Jr. (WWII)
❑ 999 Louis Menard (WWII)
❑ 1000 Louis Mountbatten, Mountbatten of Burma (WWI)
❑ 1001 Louis Mountbatten, Mountbatten of Burma (WWII)
❑ 1002 Louis R. de Steiguer (Spanish-American War)
❑ 1003 Louis Schriber (WWII)
❑ 1004 Lucian Adams (WWII)
❑ 1005 Lucile Petry (WWII)
❑ 1006 Lucius D. Clay (WWII)
❑ 1007 Lucius D. Clay, Jr. (Vietnam)
❑ 1008 Ludwig Laubmeier (WWII)
❑ 1009 Luigi Gorrini (WWII)
❑ 1010 Lyell S. Pamperin (WWI)
❑ 1011 Lyle E. Umenhoffer (WWII)
❑ 1012 Lyman L. Lemnitzer (Cold War)
❑ 1013 Lyman L. Lemnitzer (Korean War)
❑ 1014 Lyman L. Lemnitzer (WWII)
❑ 1015 Lynde D. McCormick (WWI)
❑ 1016 Lyndon Marshall (WWII)
❑ 1017 Lynn Buck Compton (WWII)
❑ 1018 Lynn Jones (WWII)
❑ 1019 Lynn Zinck (Vietnam)
❑ 1020 M.L. Witherup (WWI)
❑ 1021 Manfred Beutner (WWII)
❑ 1022 Manfred Buttner (WWII)
❑ 1023 Marcel Albert (WWII)
❑ 1024 Marcus Robinson (WWII)
❑ 1025 Margaret Thatcher (Cold War)
❑ 1026 Mario Garcia Menocal (WWI)
❑ 1027 Marion E. Carl (WWII)
❑ 1028 Marion F. Kirby (WWII)
❑ 1029 Mark W. Clark (Korean War)
❑ 1030 Mark W. Clark (WWI)
❑ 1031 Mark W. Clark (WWII)
❑ 1032 Marquis Togo Heihachiro Saneyoshi (Russo-Japanese War)
❑ 1033 Marriott Brosius (Civil War)
❑ 1034 Marshall Beebe (WWII)
❑ 1035 Martin Bormann (WWII)
❑ 1036 Marvin Lubner (WWII)
❑ 1037 Masajiro Mike Kawato (WWII)
❑ 1038 Mason M. Patrick (WWI)
❑ 1039 Matthew B. Ridgway (Korean War)
❑ 1040 Matthew B. Ridgway (WWII)
❑ 1041 Maurice Britt (WWII)
❑ 1042 Maurice G. Long (WWII)
❑ 1043 Maurice Stephens (WWII)
❑ 1044 Max Miller (WWI)
❑ 1045 Max Zastrow (WWII)
❑ 1046 Maximo Gomez (Ten Years' War)
❑ 1047 Max-Josef Pemsel (WWII)
❑ 1048 Maxwell D. Taylor (Cold War)
❑ 1049 Maxwell D. Taylor (Korean War)
❑ 1050 Maxwell D. Taylor (WWII)
❑ 1051 Melvin E. Biddle (WWII)
❑ 1052 Melvin Laird (WWII)
❑ 1053 Melvin M. Boothman (Civil War)
❑ 1054 Merle Coons (WWII)
❑ 1055 Mervyn C. Shipard (WWII)
❑ 1056 Michael Carver, Baron Carver (WWII)
❑ 1057 Michael E. Thornton (Vietnam)
❑ 1058 Michael Gould (War on Terror)
❑ 1059 Michael J. Daly (WWII)
❑ 1060 Michael J. Novosel (Vietnam)
❑ 1061 Michael J. Novosel (WWII)
❑ 1062 Michael John Fitzmaurice (Vietnam)
❑ 1063 Michael Karatsonyi (WWII)
❑ 1064 Michael T. Russo (WWII)
❑ 1065 Michel Donnet (WWII)
❑ 1066 Mike Crosley (WWII)
❑ 1067 Miles Dempsey (WWII)
❑ 1068 Millard E. Tydings (WWI)
❑ 1069 Millie Davidson Dalrymple (WWII)
❑ 1070 Milton K. Young (WWII)
❑ 1071 Mitchell Paige (Korean War)
❑ 1072 Mitchell Paige (WWII)
❑ 1073 Montgomery M. Taylor (Spanish-American War)
❑ 1074 Morgan H. Vaux (WWII)
❑ 1075 Morris R. Jeppson (WWII)
❑ 1076 Morton Magoffin (WWII)
❑ 1077 Moses Hazen (American Revolution)
❑ 1078 Muir S. Fairchild (WWI)
❑ 1079 Myron H. McCord (Spanish-American War)
❑ 1080 N.P.W. Hancock (WWII)
❑ 1081 Nathan F. Twining (Mexican Revolution)
❑ 1082 Nathan F. Twining (WWII)
❑ 1083 Nathan Gordon (WWII)
❑ 1084 Neil H. McElroy (Cold War)
❑ 1085 Neil Ritchie (WWII)
❑ 1086 Nelson A. Miles (Civil War)
❑ 1087 Neville Duke (WWII)
❑ 1088 Neville McNamara (WWII)
❑ 1089 Nguyen Cao Ky (Vietnam)
❑ 1090 Nicholas Marshall Hephner (Civil War)
❑ 1091 Nicholas Oresko (WWII)
❑ 1092 Nick Bacon (Vietnam)
❑ 1093 Nicky Barr (WWII)
❑ 1094 Noel Gayler (WWII)
❑ 1095 Noel Harris (WWII)
❑ 1096 Norm Neitzke (WWII)
❑ 1097 Norman Williams (WWII)
❑ 1098 Odette Hallowes (WWII)
❑ 1099 Ola Lee Mize (Korean War)
❑ 1100 Ola Lee Mize (Vietnam)
❑ 1101 Olbert F. Lassiter (WWII)
❑ 1102 Oliver Goodall (WWII)
❑ 1103 Oliver North (Vietnam)
❑ 1104 Oliver Otis Howard (Civil War)
❑ 1105 Omar N. Bradley (Korean War)
❑ 1106 Omar N. Bradley (WWII)
❑ 1107 Ormsby B. Thomas (Civil War)
❑ 1108 Oscar S. Gifford (Civil War)

❑ 1109 Oscar W. Griswold (WWI)
❑ 1110 Oscar W. Griswold (WWII)
❑ 1111 Oscar Westover (WWII)
❑ 1112 Oskar Munzel (WWII)
❑ 1113 Oskar-Hubert Dennhardt (WWII)
❑ 1114 Otto Bertram (WWII)
❑ 1115 Otto Hitzfeld (WWII)
❑ 1116 Oveta Culp Hobby (WWII)
❑ 1117 P.G.T. Beauregard (Civil War)
❑ 1118 P.G.T. Beauregard (Mexican-American War)
❑ 1119 Paddy Barthropp (WWII)
❑ 1120 Pappy Boyington (WWII)
❑ 1121 Patrick Bellinger (WWII)
❑ 1122 Patrick Dunn (WWII)
❑ 1123 Patrick Henry Brady (Vietnam)
❑ 1124 Patrick J. Hurley (WWI)
❑ 1125 Patrick J. Hurley (WWII)
❑ 1126 Patrick Jameson (WWII)
❑ 1127 Patrick W. Brock (WWII)
❑ 1128 Paul Bucha (Vietnam)
❑ 1129 Paul C. Murphey, Jr. (WWII)
❑ 1130 Paul Conger (WWII)
❑ 1131 Paul Galanti (Vietnam)
❑ 1132 Paul Goodyear (WWII)
❑ 1133 Paul Hellyer (WWII)
❑ 1134 Paul J. Murphy (WWII)
❑ 1135 Paul J. Wiedorfer (WWII)
❑ 1136 Paul M. Herbert (WWI)
❑ 1137 Paul McGinnis (WWII)
❑ 1138 Paul Thayer (WWII)
❑ 1139 Paul W. Tibbets (WWII)
❑ 1140 Paul Webb (WWII)
❑ 1141 Paul-Georg Kleffel (WWII)
❑ 1142 Peppy Blount (WWII)
❑ 1143 Percy B. Laddle Lucas (WWII)
❑ 1144 Peter Buell Porter (War of 1812)
❑ 1145 Peter C. Lemon (Vietnam)
❑ 1146 Peter Goutiere (WWII)
❑ 1147 Peter J. Vander Linden (WWII)
❑ 1148 Peter M. Brothers (WWII)
❑ 1149 Peter Shaw (WWII)
❑ 1150 Peter Townsend (WWII)
❑ 1151 Peter V. Ayerst (WWII)
❑ 1152 Peter Williamson (WWII)
❑ 1153 Peter Wykeham (WWII)
❑ 1154 Peyton C. March (Spanish-American War)
❑ 1155 Peyton C. March (WWI)
❑ 1156 Phil Combies (WWII)
❑ 1157 Philip E. Colman (WWII)
❑ 1158 Philip H. Sheridan (Civil War)
❑ 1159 Philip Perugini (WWII)
❑ 1160 Philippe Guillaume de Deux-Ponts (American Revolution)
❑ 1161 Phillip M. Schaft (WWI)
❑ 1162 Pierre Cardon (WWI)
❑ 1163 Pierre M. Gallois (WWII)
❑ 1164 Pierre Soule (Civil War)
❑ 1165 Plutarco Elias Calles (Mexican Revolution)
❑ 1166 Price Daniel (WWII)
❑ 1167 Prince George, Duke of Cambridge (Crimean War)
❑ 1168 Quentin C. Aanenson (WWII)
❑ 1169 R. Bruce Porter (WWII)
❑ 1170 R.A. Beardsley (WWII)
❑ 1171 R.G. Guilbault (WWII)
❑ 1172 R.H. Bruce Lockhart (WWI)
❑ 1173 R.O. Davis (WWII)
❑ 1174 Ralph C. Jenkins (WWII)
❑ 1175 Ralph E. Foltz (WWII)
❑ 1176 Ralph Earle (Spanish-American War)
❑ 1177 Ralph Earle, Jr. (WWII)
❑ 1178 Ralph H. Wandrey (WWII)
❑ 1179 Ralph J. Doc Watson (WWII)
❑ 1180 Ralph O'Neill (WWI)
❑ 1181 Ralph Parr (Korean War)
❑ 1182 Randy Duke Cunningham (Vietnam)
❑ 1183 Ray Davis (Korean War)
❑ 1184 Ray Davis (Vietnam)
❑ 1185 Ray Davis (WWII)
❑ 1186 Ray Gallagher (WWII)
❑ 1187 Raymond G. Murphy (Korean War)
❑ 1188 Raymond M. Bank (WWII)
❑ 1189 Raymond Poincare (WWI)
❑ 1190 Red Adair (WWII)
❑ 1191 Reginald Llewellyn (WWII)
❑ 1192 Rex Bayly (WWII)
❑ 1193 Rex T. Barber (WWII)
❑ 1194 Richard A. Pittman (Vietnam)
❑ 1195 Richard B. Black (WWII)
❑ 1196 Richard C. Mangrum (WWII)
❑ 1197 Richard C. Suehr (WWII)
❑ 1198 Richard Cormier (WWII)
❑ 1199 Richard E. Bush (WWII)
❑ 1200 Richard E. Byrd (WWII)
❑ 1201 Richard E. Carey (Vietnam)
❑ 1202 Richard E. Cole (WWII)
❑ 1203 Richard E. Turner (WWII)
❑ 1204 Richard G. Stilwell (WWII)
❑ 1205 Richard H. Best (WWII)
❑ 1206 Richard H. Fleischer (WWII)
❑ 1207 Richard H. O'Kane (WWII)
❑ 1208 Richard Hobbs May (WWII)
❑ 1209 Richard K. Sorenson (WWII)
❑ 1210 Richard L. Bertelson (WWII)
❑ 1211 Richard M. Hoban (Korean War)
❑ 1212 Richard M. McCool, Jr. (Korean War)
❑ 1213 Richard M. McCool, Jr. (WWII)
❑ 1214 Richard Rutledge (WWII)
❑ 1215 Richard Schulze-Kossens (WWII)
❑ 1216 Richard Stephen Ritchie (Vietnam)
❑ 1217 Richard W. Anson (WWII)
❑ 1218 Richard W. Asbury (Korean War)
❑ 1219 Richard W. Asbury (WWII)
❑ 1220 Richard Wainwright (Civil War)
❑ 1221 Richard Wainwright (Spanish-American War)
❑ 1222 Richard West (WWI)
❑ 1223 Richard Williams (WWII)
❑ 1224 Richmond P. Hobson (Spanish-American War)
❑ 1225 Robert Bus Keeton (WWII)
❑ 1226 Robert Doc Carrara (Vietnam)
❑ 1227 Robert B. Carney (WWII)
❑ 1228 Robert B. McClure (WWI)
❑ 1229 Robert B. Nett (WWII)
❑ 1230 Robert Bunai (WWII)
❑ 1231 Robert C. Curtis (WWII)
❑ 1232 Robert C. Springer (Vietnam)
❑ 1233 Robert Coates (WWII)
❑ 1234 Robert Cowper (WWII)
❑ 1235 Robert D. Maxwell (WWII)
❑ 1236 Robert D. Wiegand (Vietnam)
❑ 1237 Robert E. Bush (WWII)
❑ 1238 Robert E. Galer (Korean War)
❑ 1239 Robert E. Galer (WWII)
❑ 1240 Robert E. Justice (WWII)
❑ 1241 Robert E. Simanek (Korean War)
❑ 1242 Robert Emmett O'Malley (Vietnam)
❑ 1243 Robert F. Foley (Vietnam)
❑ 1244 Robert F. Thomas (WWII)
❑ 1245 Robert G. Ingersoll (Civil War)
❑ 1246 Robert H. Barrow (WWII)
❑ 1247 Robert Hugo Dunlap (WWII)
❑ 1248 Robert J. Goebel (WWII)
❑ 1249 Robert J. Modrzejewski (Vietnam)
❑ 1250 Robert J. Natter (Vietnam)
❑ 1251 Robert J. Rankin (Korean War)
❑ 1252 Robert J. Rankin (WWII)
❑ 1253 Robert J. Shoens (WWII)
❑ 1254 Robert Kaestner (WWII)
❑ 1255 Robert L. Delashaw (Cold War)
❑ 1256 Robert L. Delashaw (WWII)
❑ 1257 Robert L. Eichelberger (WWII)
❑ 1258 Robert L. Hite (Korean War)
❑ 1259 Robert L. Hite (WWII)
❑ 1260 Robert L. Howard (Vietnam)
❑ 1261 Robert L. Liles (WWII)
❑ 1262 Robert L. Scott, Jr. (WWII)
❑ 1263 Robert L. Stewart (Vietnam)
❑ 1264 Robert Lee Bullard (Spanish-American War)
❑ 1265 Robert Lee Bullard (WWI)
❑ 1266 Robert M. DeHaven (WWII)
❑ 1267 Robert M. White (WWII)
❑ 1268 Robert Martin Patterson (Vietnam)
❑ 1269 Robert O. Carlson (WWII)
❑ 1270 Robert Ouellette (Vietnam)
❑ 1271 Robert P. Baldwin (Korean War)
❑ 1272 Robert P. Winks (WWII)
❑ 1273 Robert R. Ingram (Vietnam)
❑ 1274 Robert R. Watson (Korean War)
❑ 1275 Robert S. Beightler (WWI)
❑ 1276 Robert S. Beightler (WWII)
❑ 1277 Robert S. Johnson (WWII)
❑ 1278 Robert S. Scott (WWII)
❑ 1279 Robert S. Tuck (WWII)
❑ 1280 Robert Spurdle (WWII)
❑ 1281 Robert T. Smith (WWII)
❑ 1282 Robert W. Duncan (WWII)
❑ 1283 Robert W. McClurg (WWII)
❑ 1284 Robert Wade (WWII)
❑ 1285 Robert Wells Harper (WWII)
❑ 1286 Robin Olds (Vietnam)
❑ 1287 Robin Olds (WWII)
❑ 1288 Robley Dunglison Evans (Civil War)
❑ 1289 Robley Dunglison Evans (Spanish-American War)
❑ 1290 Rod Bain (WWII)
❑ 1291 Rod Steiger (WWII)
❑ 1292 Rod Strohl (WWII)
❑ 1293 Roderick A.B. Learoyd (WWII)
❑ 1294 Rodolfo P. Hernandez (Korean War)
❑ 1295 Roger Conant (WWII)
❑ 1296 Roger H.C. Donlon (Vietnam)
❑ 1297 Roger W. Mehle (WWII)
❑ 1298 Roland Beamont (WWII)
❑ 1299 Rolland L. Richardson (WWII)
❑ 1300 Ronald Ras Berry (WWII)
❑ 1301 Ronald E. Ray (Vietnam)
❑ 1302 Ronald E. Rosser (Korean War)
❑ 1303 Ronald Hamlyn (WWII)
❑ 1304 Roscoe C. Brown, Jr. (WWII)
❑ 1305 Rowland Bourke (WWI)
❑ 1306 Rowland Hill, 1st Viscount Hill (Napoleonic Wars)
❑ 1307 Roy Benavidez (Vietnam)
❑ 1308 Roy Hawthorne (WWII)
❑ 1309 Roy Redgrave (WWII)
❑ 1310 Roy Richardson (WWII)
❑ 1311 Roy W. Evans (WWII)
❑ 1312 Royal E. Ingersoll (WWI)
❑ 1313 Royce Priest (WWII)
❑ 1314 Rudolf Hess (WWII)
❑ 1315 Rufus E. Lester (Civil War)
❑ 1316 Russ Haworth (WWII)
❑ 1317 Russ McCarthy (Vietnam)
❑ 1318 Russell Bannock (WWII)
❑ 1319 Russell Dougherty (WWII)
❑ 1320 Russell E. Dunham (WWII)
❑ 1321 Russell L. Maxwell (WWII)
❑ 1322 Russell L. Reiserer (WWII)
❑ 1323 Russell S. Berkey (WWII)
❑ 1324 Sam L. Silber (WWI)
❑ 1325 Sammy L. Davis (Vietnam)
❑ 1326 Sammy Pierce (WWII)
❑ 1327 Samuel Brown (WWII)
❑ 1328 Samuel Dibble (Civil War)
❑ 1329 Samuel E. Anderson (WWII)
❑ 1330 Samuel Nicholl Benjamin (Civil War)
❑ 1331 Samuel Osgood (American Revolution)
❑ 1332 Samuel P. Snider (Civil War)
❑ 1333 Samuel R. Peters (Civil War)
❑ 1334 Samuel S. Yoder (Civil War)
❑ 1335 Sandy Johnstone (WWII)
❑ 1336 Sanford K. Moats (WWII)
❑ 1337 Sargent Shriver (WWII)
❑ 1338 Schumpert Jones (Vietnam)
❑ 1339 Sergai Karmarenko (WWII)
❑ 1340 Seymour Berry (WWII)
❑ 1341 Sheldon O. Hall (WWII)
❑ 1342 Shizuya Hayashi (WWII)
❑ 1343 Sidney C. Kirkman (WWII)
❑ 1344 Siegfried Westphal (WWII)
❑ 1345 Silvestre S. Herrera (WWII)
❑ 1346 Simon Bolivar Buckner (Civil War)
❑ 1347 Sir Alfred Milner, 1st Viscount Milner (WWI)
❑ 1348 Sir Allan Adair, 6th Baronet (WWII)
❑ 1349 Sir Anthony M. Synnot (WWII)
❑ 1350 Sir Archibald Montgomery-Massingberd (Second Boer War)
❑ 1351 Sir Arthur Coningham (WWII)
❑ 1352 Sir Arthur S. Wynne (Second Boer War)
❑ 1353 Sir Arthur T. Harris (WWI)
❑ 1354 Sir Augustus Phillimore (Carlist Wars)
❑ 1355 Sir Brian Burnett (WWII)
❑ 1356 Sir Brian G. Horrocks (WWI)
❑ 1357 Sir Brian G. Horrocks (WWII)
❑ 1358 Sir Charles J. Napier (Napoleonic Wars)
❑ 1359 Sir Charles Madden, 2nd Baronet (WWII)
❑ 1360 Sir Claude J.E. Auchinleck (WWII)
❑ 1361 Sir Clement Armitage (Second Boer War)
❑ 1362 Sir Cyprian Bridge (Crimean War)
❑ 1363 Sir Edward Heath (WWII)
❑ 1364 Sir Edward Hobart Seymour (Crimean War)
❑ 1365 Sir Edward Ian Jacob (WWII)
❑ 1366 Sir Evelyn Barker (WWII)
❑ 1367 Sir Evelyn Wood (Crimean War)
❑ 1368 Sir Frederick Rosier (WWII)
❑ 1369 Sir George S. White (Second Boer War)
❑ 1370 Sir Gordon MacMillan (WWII)
❑ 1371 Sir Guy Standing (WWI)
❑ 1372 Sir Harry Broadhurst (WWII)
❑ 1373 Sir Henry F. Ponsonby (Crimean War)
❑ 1374 Sir Henry Hardinge, 1st Viscount Hardinge (Napoleonic Wars)
❑ 1375 Sir James A. Rowland (WWII)
❑ 1376 Sir James Marshall-Cornwall (WWII)
❑ 1377 Sir John Baker-Carr (WWI)
❑ 1378 Sir John Macdonald (Napoleonic Wars)
❑ 1379 Sir John McCauley (WWII)
❑ 1380 Sir Osbert Sitwell (WWI)
❑ 1381 Sir Redvers H. Buller (Second Boer War)
❑ 1382 Sir Reginald Portal (WWII)
❑ 1383 Sir Richard O'Connor (WWII)
❑ 1384 Sir Ronald Forbes Adam (WWII)
❑ 1385 Sir Thomas A. Blamey (WWI)
❑ 1386 Sir Thomas A. Blamey (WWII)
❑ 1387 Sir Thomas Masterman Hardy (French Revolutionary Wars)
❑ 1388 Sir Varyl C. Begg (WWII)
❑ 1389 Sir W. R. Mansfield, 1st Baron Sandhurst (Crimean War)
❑ 1390 Slade Cutter (WWII)
❑ 1391 Smedley D. Butler (Spanish-American War)
❑ 1392 Spann Watson (WWII)
❑ 1393 Spencer Barker (WWII)
❑ 1394 Stan R. Sheridan (Vietnam)
❑ 1395 Stanley W. Swede Vejtasa (WWII)
❑ 1396 Stanley Walters (WWII)
❑ 1397 Stansfield Turner (Cold War)
❑ 1398 Stephen B. Elkins (Civil War)
❑ 1399 Stephen B. Packard (Civil War)
❑ 1400 Stephen J. Bonner, Jr. (WWII)
❑ 1401 Stephen J. Chamberlin (WWII)
❑ 1402 Stephen King-Hall (WWI)
❑ 1403 Stephen M. Young (WWI)
❑ 1404 Stephen Moylan (American Revolution)
❑ 1405 Stephen R. Gregg (WWII)
❑ 1406 Sterling Cale (WWII)
❑ 1407 Steve Pisanos (Vietnam)
❑ 1408 Steve Pisanos (WWII)
❑ 1409 Ted King (WWII)
❑ 1410 Teddy G. Allen (Vietnam)
❑ 1411 Terry de la Mesa Allen (WWI)
❑ 1412 Thad Allen (War on Terror)
❑ 1413 Thaddeus T. Coleman, Jr. (WWII)
❑ 1414 Theodor Busse (WWII)
❑ 1415 Theodore Dutch Van Kirk (WWII)
❑ 1416 Theodore F. Kane (Civil War)
❑ 1417 Theodore Hugh Winters (WWII)
❑ 1418 Thomas B. Fargo (War In Iraq)
❑ 1419 Thomas C. Catchings (Civil War)
❑ 1420 Thomas C. Hart (Spanish-American War)
❑ 1421 Thomas C. Hart (WWI)
❑ 1422 Thomas Cochrane, 10th Earl of Dundonald (Napoleonic Wars)
❑ 1423 Thomas D. White (WWII)
❑ 1424 Thomas E. Atkins (WWII)
❑ 1425 Thomas Ferebee (WWII)
❑ 1426 Thomas Fremantle (French Revolutionary Wars)
❑ 1427 Thomas G. Kelley (Vietnam)
❑ 1428 Thomas H. Moorer (WWII)
❑ 1429 Thomas H.B. Browne (Civil War)
❑ 1430 Thomas J. Classen (WWII)
❑ 1431 Thomas J. Henderson (Civil War)
❑ 1432 Thomas J. Hudner, Jr. (Korean War)
❑ 1433 Thomas James Kinsman (Vietnam)
❑ 1434 Thomas L. Hayes (WWII)
❑ 1435 Thomas M. Bayne (Civil War)
❑ 1436 Thomas M. Browne

(Civil War)
❑ 1437 Thomas Mayne Reid (Mexican-American War)
❑ 1438 Thomas Nelson Page (WWI)
❑ 1439 Thomas O. Selfridge (Civil War)
❑ 1440 Thomas Pike (WWII)
❑ 1441 Thomas S. Harris (WWII)
❑ 1442 Thomas W. Mellen (WWII)
❑ 1443 Timothy J. Keleher (WWII)
❑ 1444 Timothy Pickering (American Revolution)
❑ 1445 Tom Drake-Brockman (WWII)
❑ 1446 Tom Emrich (WWII)
❑ 1447 Tom Gleave (WWII)
❑ 1448 Tom Griffin (WWII)
❑ 1449 Tomas Vybiral (WWII)
❑ 1450 Tommy Franks (War In Iraq)
❑ 1451 Ture Mattila (WWII)
❑ 1452 Ulysses S. Grant (Civil War)
❑ 1453 Urban Drew (WWII)
❑ 1454 Utha Knox (WWII)
❑ 1455 Valston Eldridge Hancock (WWII)
❑ 1456 Van T. Barfoot (WWII)
❑ 1457 Vance C. McCormick (WWI)
❑ 1458 Varaztad Kazanjian (WWI)
❑ 1459 Vermont Garrison (WWII)
❑ 1460 Vernon E. Graham (WWII)
❑ 1461 Vernon J. Baker (WWII)
❑ 1462 Vernon McGarity (WWII)
❑ 1463 Victor Crutchley (WWII)
❑ 1464 Victor Goddard (WWII)
❑ 1465 Victor H. Brute Krulak (WWII)
❑ 1466 Victor McLaglen (WWI)
❑ 1467 Viscount Garnet J. Wolseley (Crimean War)
❑ 1468 Vivien Crea (War on Terror)
❑ 1469 W. Averell Harriman (WWII)
❑ 1470 W. Sefton Brancker (WWI)
❑ 1471 W.F. Tompkins (WWII)
❑ 1472 W.G.G. Duncan Smith (WWII)
❑ 1473 W.I. Burnham (WWI)
❑ 1474 Wade Hampton III (Civil War)
❑ 1475 Walker M. Bud Mahurin (Korean War)
❑ 1476 Walker M. Bud Mahurin (WWII)
❑ 1477 Wallace C. Strobel (WWII)
❑ 1478 Wallace R. Johnson (WWII)
❑ 1479 Wally Schirra (WWII)
❑ 1480 Walter A. Lundin (WWII)
❑ 1481 Walter Boomer (Gulf War)
❑ 1482 Walter D. Ehlers (WWII)
❑ 1483 Walter G. Benz (WWII)
❑ 1484 Walter Galligan (Vietnam)
❑ 1485 Walter Gericke (WWII)
❑ 1486 Walter Joseph Marm, Jr. (Vietnam)
❑ 1487 Walter Krupinski (WWII)
❑ 1488 Walter Matthau (WWII)
❑ 1489 Walter McCreary (WWII)
❑ 1490 Walter Mondale (Cold War)
❑ 1491 Walter T. Stewart (WWII)
❑ 1492 Walton H. Walker (Korean War)
❑ 1493 Walton H. Walker (WWI)
❑ 1494 Washington C. Whitthorne (Civil War)
❑ 1495 Wayne Blickenstaff (WWII)
❑ 1496 Wayne MacVeagh (Civil War)
❑ 1497 Wayne Morris (WWII)
❑ 1498 Webster Anderson (Vietnam)
❑ 1499 Werner Schroer (WWII)
❑ 1500 Werner Streib (WWII)
❑ 1501 Werner von Blomberg (WWI)
❑ 1502 Wesley L. Fox (Vietnam)
❑ 1503 Wilbur B. Webb (WWII)
❑ 1504 Wilburn K. Ross (WWII)
❑ 1505 Wiley D. Ganey (WWII)
❑ 1506 Wilfred Handel Miller (WWII)
❑ 1507 Wilhelm Hess (WWII)
❑ 1508 Wilhelm Miklas (WWII)
❑ 1509 Wilhelm Soth (WWII)
❑ 1510 Willard G. Wyman (Korean War)
❑ 1511 Willard G. Wyman (WWII)
❑ 1512 Willard W. Scott, Jr. (Vietnam)
❑ 1513 William A. Moffett (Spanish-American War)
❑ 1514 William B. Franke (Cold War)
❑ 1515 William B. Shubrick (War of 1812)
❑ 1516 William Badham (WWI)
❑ 1517 William Bower (WWII)
❑ 1518 William C. Cooper (Civil War)
❑ 1519 William C. Lovering (Civil War)
❑ 1520 William C. Westmoreland (Vietnam)
❑ 1521 William C. Westmoreland (WWII)
❑ 1522 William Claiborne Owens (Spanish-American War)
❑ 1523 William Driscoll (Vietnam)
❑ 1524 William E. Hall (WWII)
❑ 1525 William E. Haynes (Civil War)
❑ 1526 William E. Kepner (WWII)
❑ 1527 William E. Simonds (Civil War)
❑ 1528 William Elliott (Civil War)
❑ 1529 William F. Cassidy (Korean War)
❑ 1530 William F. Dean (Korean War)
❑ 1531 William F. Dean (WWII)
❑ 1532 William F. Halsey, Jr. (WWI)
❑ 1533 William F. Halsey, Jr. (WWII)
❑ 1534 William F. McCarthy (WWII)
❑ 1535 William Farrell (WWII)
❑ 1536 William Gibsone (WWI)
❑ 1537 William Glassford (WWI)
❑ 1538 William Grant Laidlaw (Civil War)
❑ 1539 William Grenville, 1st Baron Grenville (French Revolutionary Wars)
❑ 1540 William H. Hatch (Civil War)
❑ 1541 William H. Perry (Civil War)
❑ 1542 William H. Wescott (Korean War)
❑ 1543 William H.H. Cowles (Civil War)
❑ 1544 William Hayward (WWI)
❑ 1545 William Heler (WWII)
❑ 1546 William Hood Simpson (WWI)
❑ 1547 William Hood Simpson (WWII)
❑ 1548 William Irvine (American Revolution)
❑ 1549 William J. Crawford (WWII)
❑ 1550 William J. Knight (Vietnam)
❑ 1551 William J. Schildt (WWII)
❑ 1552 William K. Jones (WWII)
❑ 1553 William Kenny Giroux (WWII)
❑ 1554 William L. Birch (WWII)
❑ 1555 William L. Kenly (WWI)
❑ 1556 William L. Marcy (War of 1812)
❑ 1557 William L. Wilson (Civil War)
❑ 1558 William M. Meredith, Jr. (Korean War)
❑ 1559 William Mathis (WWII)
❑ 1560 William R. Anderson (WWII)
❑ 1561 William R. Beyer (WWII)
❑ 1562 William R. Charette (Korean War)
❑ 1563 William R. Lawley, Jr. (WWII)
❑ 1564 William Ralls Morrison (Civil War)
❑ 1565 William Reid (WWII)
❑ 1566 William Rufus Shafter (Civil War)
❑ 1567 William S. Clark (Civil War)
❑ 1568 William S. Cohen (War on Terror)
❑ 1569 William S. Cowles (Spanish-American War)
❑ 1570 William S. Rosecrans (Civil War)
❑ 1571 William S. Sims (WWI)
❑ 1572 William S. Smith (American Revolution)
❑ 1573 William Seawell (WWII)
❑ 1574 William Siborne (Napoleonic Wars)
❑ 1575 William Sinclair-Burgess (WWI)
❑ 1576 William Stratton (WWII)
❑ 1577 William Surcey (WWII)
❑ 1578 William T. Ellis (Civil War)
❑ 1579 William T. Sampson (Civil War)
❑ 1580 William T. Sampson (Spanish-American War)
❑ 1581 William Tecumseh Sherman (Civil War)
❑ 1582 William Vandever (Civil War)
❑ 1583 William W. Grout (Civil War)
❑ 1584 William W. Morrow (Civil War)
❑ 1585 William Wallace Atterbury (WWI)
❑ 1586 William Wells (Civil War)
❑ 1587 Wiltz Segura (WWII)
❑ 1588 Winfield Scott Hancock (Civil War)
❑ 1589 Winfield Scott Schley (Civil War)
❑ 1590 Winfield Scott Schley (Spanish-American War)
❑ 1591 Winton W. Bones Marshall (Korean War)
❑ 1592 Wolfgang Falck (WWII)
❑ 1593 Wolfgang Spate (WWII)
❑ 1594 Wolfram Eisenlohr (WWI)
❑ 1595 Wolfram Eisenlohr (WWII)
❑ 1596 Wolfram Freiherr von Richthofen (WWI)
❑ 1597 Woodrow W. Vaughan (WWII)
❑ 1598 Yenwith Whitney (WWII)
❑ 1599 Ynez Mendoza (WWII)
❑ 1600 Yves Ezanno (WWII)

2013 Horrors of War II Military Patches

ANNOUNCED PRINT RUN 1

❑ 1 100th Infantry Division
❑ 2 102nd Infantry Division
❑ 3 13th Air Force
❑ 4 14th Air Force
❑ 5 14th Army AAF Flying Tigers CBI Command
❑ 6 14th Army AAF Flying Tigers CBI Command Bullion
❑ 7 1st Air Force
❑ 8 1st Army
❑ 9 25th Infantry Division
❑ 10 26th Infantry Division
❑ 11 27th Infantry Division
❑ 12 28th Infantry Division
❑ 13 2nd Air Force
❑ 14 2nd Army
❑ 15 35th Infantry Division
❑ 16 37th Infantry Division
❑ 17 38th Infantry Division
❑ 18 39th Infantry Division
❑ 19 3rd Air Force
❑ 20 3rd Army
❑ 21 3rd Infantry Division
❑ 22 41st Infantry Division
❑ 23 44th Infantry Division
❑ 24 4th Infantry Division
❑ 25 4th Service Command
❑ 26 5th Air Force
❑ 27 5th Armored Division
❑ 28 5th Army
❑ 29 5th Service Command
❑ 30 65th Infantry Division
❑ 31 66th Infantry Division Second Design
❑ 32 69th Infantry Division
❑ 33 6th Air Force
❑ 34 6th Army Early Design
❑ 35 6th Army
❑ 36 6th Corps Area Service Command
❑ 37 70th Infantry Division
❑ 38 71st Infantry Division
❑ 39 75th Infantry Division
❑ 40 76th Infantry Division Official
❑ 41 78th Infantry Division
❑ 42 7th Army
❑ 43 VII Army Corps
❑ 44 7th Corps Area Service Command
❑ 45 7th Infantry Division
❑ 46 84th Infantry Division
❑ 47 86th Infantry Division
❑ 48 87th Infantry Division
❑ 49 88th Infantry Division
❑ 50 8th Air Force
❑ 51 8th Service Command
❑ 52 8th Army
❑ 53 95th Infantry Division
❑ 54 96th Infantry Division
❑ 55 97th Infantry Division
❑ 56 98th Infantry Division
❑ 57 9th Air Force
❑ 58 9th Infantry Division
❑ 59 9th Service Command
❑ 60 Alaska Defense Command
❑ 61 Army Air Corps Communications Specialist
❑ 62 Army Air Corps Engineering Specialist
❑ 63 Army Air Forces
❑ 64 Army Service Forces
❑ 65 European Theatre USA COM Z
❑ 66 German M-43 Cap Eagle
❑ 67 German Rank Patch
❑ 68 GHQ Reserve
❑ 69 Greenland Base Command
❑ 70 II Army Corps
❑ 71 III Army Corps OD Border
❑ 72 Naval Amphibious Forces
❑ 73 North African Theatre
❑ 74 Persian Gulf Command
❑ 75 Philippine Department
❑ 76 US Army 377th Support Brigade
❑ 77 United States Army Pacific
❑ 78 XXII Army Corps
❑ 79 US Army Air Corps Cadet
❑ 80 US Army Anti Aircraft Artillery Command
❑ 81 US Army Armored Headquarters Forces
❑ 82 US Army Corporal Insignia
❑ 83 US Army Labrador NE Canada Base Command
❑ 84 Supreme Headquarters Allied Expeditionary Force
❑ 85 V Army Corps
❑ 86 XII Army Corps
❑ 87 XIII Army Corps
❑ 88 XVI Army Corps

2013 Horrors of War II Military Relics

ANNOUNCED PRINT RUN 1-60

❑ 1 AAF Group 2nd Lieutenant Uniform/40
❑ 2 Army Dress Duty Visor/20
❑ 3 Army Field Jacket Rainbow Division/20
❑ 4 Army Garrison Cap/20
❑ 5 Army Tunic/60
❑ 6 Band of Brothers Jacket/40
❑ 7 British Paratrooper Shirt/10
❑ 8 British Side Cap/20
❑ 9 Colt 45 Ammo Clip Pouch/10
❑ 10 Colt Revolver Holster/5
❑ 11 Doughboy Tunic/40
❑ 12 Engineer's Mate Uniform/30
❑ 13 G2 AAF Bomber Flight Jacket/60
❑ 14 German Frock Coat/40
❑ 15 German Navy Shirt/40
❑ 16 Japanese Map Case/5
❑ 17 Japanese Navy Cap/20
❑ 18 Japanese Pith Helmet/20
❑ 19 Japanese Tropical Uniform/20
❑ 20 Leather Powder Flask/5
❑ 21 Luftwaffe Cap/20
❑ 22 M1 Airborne Camouflage Helmet Cover/20
❑ 23 Navy Donald Duck Cap/20
❑ 24 Nazi Chevrons/1
❑ 25 Nazi Uniform Coat/30
❑ 26 Russian Shoulder Board/3
❑ 27 Seawolf Flight Jacket/40
❑ 28 Staff Sergeant Ike Jacket/60
❑ 29 Union Wool Kepi/5
❑ 30 US Army 11th Armored Cavalry Regiment 85 Uniform/30
❑ 31 US Army Backpack/30
❑ 32 US Army Helmet/40
❑ 33 US Marines Trousers/30
❑ 34 US Marines Uniform/30
❑ 35 US Navy Flight Suit/60
❑ 36 US Navy Jumper/30
❑ 37 US Navy Officer's Uniform/20
❑ 38 US Navy Pacific Theatre Pith Helmet/10
❑ 39 US Navy Seabees Uniform/60

2013 Horrors of War II Original Art

ANNOUNCED PRINT RUN 10
UNPRICED DUE TO SCARCITY

❑ 1 Adolf Hitler
❑ 2 Archduke Franz Ferdinand
❑ 3 Benito Mussolini
❑ 4 Charles de Gaulle
❑ 5 Czar Nicholas II
❑ 6 Emperor Hirohito
❑ 7 General Douglas MacArthur
❑ 8 General Dwight D. Eisenhower
❑ 9 General Erwin Rommel
❑ 10 General Hideki Tojo
❑ 11 General Jimmy Doolittle
❑ 12 Heinrich Himmler
❑ 13 Joseph Stalin
❑ 14 Napoleon Bonaparte
❑ 15 Osama bin Laden
❑ 16 Winston Churchill

2013 Iron Man 3

COMPLETE SET (60)	6.00	15.00
❑ 1 A Proud Display of Iron Man	.20	.50
❑ 2 Tony Stark Continues to Push	.20	.50
❑ 3 The Stark Industries Research	.20	.50
❑ 4 Tony Stark Tries on a Component	.20	.50
❑ 5 The Mark XLII Armor	.20	.50
❑ 6 In Addition to His Regular Duties	.20	.50
❑ 7 Stark Industries CEO	.20	.50
❑ 8 Aldrich Killian of A.I.M.	.20	.50
❑ 9 Happy Hogan Introduces Himself	.20	.50
❑ 10 While Savin Waits for His Boss	.20	.50
❑ 11 A Suit of Armor Casually Reclining	.20	.50
❑ 12 Pepper Potts Has Become	.20	.50
❑ 13 Pepper Potts Descends	.20	.50
❑ 14 As Suspected, Tony Can Be	.20	.50
❑ 15 As Pepper Potts Exits	.20	.50
❑ 16 As Evidenced By the Armor	.20	.50
❑ 17 Eric Savin is Under	.20	.50
❑ 18 A Confrontation Heats Up	.20	.50
❑ 19 A Shadowy Figure	.20	.50
❑ 20 The Ominous Emblem	.20	.50
❑ 21 The President of the U.S.	.20	.50
❑ 22 Lt. Col. James Rhodes	.20	.50
❑ 23 Iron Patriot is Now Mission Ready	.20	.50
❑ 24 Both Tony Stark and Pepper	.20	.50
❑ 25 A Missile is Released	.20	.50
❑ 26 Missiles Crash Into Tony	.20	.50
❑ 27 With His Home Under Attack	.20	.50
❑ 28 As a Missile Destroys	.20	.50
❑ 29 Tony Achieves the Safety	.20	.50
❑ 30 Tony Stark is Buried	.20	.50
❑ 31 A Bruised Maya Hansen	.20	.50
❑ 32 A Rough Landing in the Woods	.20	.50
❑ 33 Tony Takes a Moment	.20	.50
❑ 34 Tony Strains Against the Dead	.20	.50
❑ 35 A Quick Phone Call	.20	.50
❑ 36 With an Important Phone Call	.20	.50
❑ 37 A Shed Full of Tools	.20	.50
❑ 38 Tony Takes a Seat	.20	.50
❑ 39 Tony's Shelter Has Become	.20	.50
❑ 40 The Resolute Harley Has Made	.20	.50
❑ 41 While Harley is Out Gathering	.20	.50
❑ 42 In the Aftermath of a Vicious	.20	.50
❑ 43 Mixed Among the Rubble	.20	.50
❑ 44 Pepper Examines a Helmet	.20	.50
❑ 45 Doing His Best to Blend In	.20	.50
❑ 46 While Expertly Disguised	.20	.50
❑ 47 Tony Can Rely Upon the Full	.20	.50
❑ 48 After Ditching His Country	.20	.50
❑ 49 Tony Takes in the Somber	.20	.50
❑ 50 Tony and His New Companion	.20	.50
❑ 51 As the Two Sit in the Soft	.20	.50
❑ 52 Although Harley is a Capable	.20	.50
❑ 53 This Small Town's Mysterious	.20	.50
❑ 54 Pepper Potts and Maya Hansen	.20	.50
❑ 55 The Two Brilliant Scientists	.20	.50
❑ 56 Tony Ducks Behind a Counter	.20	.50
❑ 57 Tony Watches the Glow	.20	.50
❑ 58 Fire and Ice Clash	.20	.50
❑ 59 Having Survived Another	.20	.50
❑ 60 Tony is Finally Reunited	.20	.50

2013 Iron Man 3 Foil

*FOIL: .8X TO 2X BASIC CARDS
STATED ODDS 1:1.2 H, 1:18 R

2013 Iron Man 3 Printing Plates Black

STATED PRINT RUN 1 SER. #'d SET
UNPRICED DUE TO SCARCITY

2013 Iron Man 3 Printing Plates Cyan

STATED PRINT RUN 1 SER. #'d SET
UNPRICED DUE TO SCARCITY

2013 Iron Man 3 Printing Plates Magenta

STATED PRINT RUN 1 SER. #'d SET
UNPRICED DUE TO SCARCITY

2013 Iron Man 3 Printing Plates Yellow

STATED PRINT RUN 1 SER. #'d SET
UNPRICED DUE TO SCARCITY

2013 Iron Man 3 Actor Autographs

STATED ODDS 1:144 H, 1:14,400 R

❑ FA Jon Favreau	30.00	60.00
❑ JF Jon Favreau	30.00	60.00
❑ RH Rebecca Hall	75.00	150.00
❑ SA William Sadler	40.00	80.00
❑ SB Shane Black	30.00	60.00
❑ WS William Sadler	40.00	80.00

2013 Iron Man 3 Comic Artist Autographs

STATED ODDS 1:144 H, 1:14,400 R

❑ IM3AG Adi Granov	15.00	40.00
❑ IM3BC Kurt Busiek		
❑ IM3BC Sean Chen		
❑ IM3DA David Michelinie	30.00	60.00
❑ IM3DM David Michelinie	30.00	60.00
❑ IM3HO Kevin Hopgood	15.00	40.00
❑ IM3KB Kurt Busiek		
❑ IM3LE Stan Lee	100.00	200.00
❑ IM3LK Len Kaminski	20.00	50.00
❑ IM3MD David Michelinie	30.00	60.00
❑ IM3MG Manuel Garcia	20.00	50.00
❑ IM3MI David Michelinie	30.00	60.00
❑ IM3ML Bob Layton		
❑ IM3ML David Michelinie	30.00	60.00
❑ IM3SC Sean Chen		
❑ IM3SG Scott Synder		
❑ IM3SG Manuel Garcia	20.00	50.00
❑ IM3SL Stan Lee	100.00	200.00

2013 Iron Man 3 Hall of Armor

COMPLETE SET (22)	175.00	300.00
STATED ODDS 1:36		
❑ HOA1 Mark I	8.00	20.00
❑ HOA2 Mark II	8.00	20.00
❑ HOA3 Mark III	8.00	20.00
❑ HOA4 Mark IV	8.00	20.00
❑ HOA5 Mark V	8.00	20.00
❑ HOA6 Mark VI	8.00	20.00
❑ HOA7 Mark VII	8.00	20.00
❑ HOA8 Mark XI	8.00	20.00
❑ HOA9 Mark XVI	8.00	20.00
❑ HOA10 Mark XVII	8.00	20.00
❑ HOA11 Mark XXV	8.00	20.00
❑ HOA12 Mark XXXIII	8.00	20.00
❑ HOA13 Mark XXXV	8.00	20.00
❑ HOA14 Mark XXXVII	8.00	20.00
❑ HOA15 Mark XXXVIII	8.00	20.00
❑ HOA16 Mark XXXIX	8.00	20.00
❑ HOA17 Mark XL	8.00	20.00
❑ HOA18 Mark XLI	8.00	20.00
❑ HOA19 Mark XLII	8.00	20.00
❑ HOA20 War Machine	8.00	20.00
❑ HOA21 War Machine	8.00	20.00
❑ HOA22 Iron Patriot	8.00	20.00

2013 Iron Man 3 Heroic Threads

OVERALL THREADS ODDS 1:12

❑ HT1 Tony Stark	8.00	20.00
❑ HT2 Tony Stark	8.00	20.00
❑ HT3 Savin	15.00	40.00
❑ HT4 Rhodey Rhodes	8.00	20.00
❑ HT5 Rhodey Rhodes	8.00	20.00
❑ HT6 Pepper Potts	40.00	80.00
❑ HT7 Maya Hansen	30.00	60.00
❑ HT8 Mandarin	6.00	15.00
❑ HT9 Killian	8.00	20.00
❑ HT10 Happy Hogan	8.00	20.00
❑ HT11 Harley	6.00	15.00
❑ HTP1 Tony Stark PATCH		

2013 Iron Man 3 Heroic Threads Autographs

❑ HTA2 Rebecca Hall	125.00	250.00
❑ HTA3 Jon Favreau	75.00	150.00

2013 Iron Man 3 Heroic Threads Dual

OVERALL THREADS ODDS 1:12

❑ HTD1 Savin Tony Stark	10.00	25.00
❑ HTD2 Rhodey Rhodes Tony Stark	12.00	30.00
❑ HTD3 Tony Stark Pepper Potts	15.00	40.00
❑ HTD4 Tony Stark Maya Hansen	12.00	30.00
❑ HTD5 Mandarin Tony Stark	10.00	25.00
❑ HTD6 Tony Stark Killian	12.00	30.00
❑ HTD7 Happy Hogan Tony Stark	10.00	25.00
❑ HTD8 Rhodey Rhodes Mandarin	10.00	25.00

MODERN ERA NON-SPORTS

❑ HTD9 Killian 12.00 30.00
Rhodey Rhodes
❑ HTD10 Pepper Potts 15.00 40.00
Maya Hansen
❑ HTD11 Killian 10.00 25.00
Maya Hansen
❑ HTD12 Killian 30.00 60.00
Mandarin
❑ HTD13 Savin 10.00 25.00
Killian
❑ HTD14 Killian 12.00 30.00
Pepper Potts
❑ HTD15 Happy Hogan 10.00 25.00
Savin
❑ HTD16 Happy Hogan 12.00 30.00
Pepper Potts

2013 Iron Man 3 Heroic Threads Quad

OVERALL THREADS ODDS 1:12
❑ HTQ1 Rhodey Rhodes 12.00 30.00
Tony Stark/ Killian/ Mandarin
❑ HTQ2 Savin 12.00 30.00
Killian/ Tony Stark/ Rhodey Rhodes
❑ HTQ3 Rhodey Rhodes 15.00 40.00
Tony Stark/ Pepper Potts/ Happy Hogan
❑ HTQ4 Killian 15.00 40.00
Maya Hansen/ Pepper Potts/ Tony Stark
❑ HTQ5 Tony Stark 15.00 40.00
Pepper Potts/ Rhodey Rhodes/ Killian

2013 Iron Man 3 Heroic Threads Triple

OVERALL THREADS ODDS 1:12
❑ HTT1 Tony Stark 12.00 30.00
Savin/ Mandarin
❑ HTT2 Savin 12.00 30.00
Tony Stark/ Killian
❑ HTT3 Rhodey Rhodes 12.00 30.00
Tony Stark/ Mandarin
❑ HTT4 Rhodey Rhodes 12.00 30.00
Tony Stark/ Mandarin
❑ HTT5 Rhodey Rhodes 12.00 30.00
Tony Stark/ Happy Hogan
❑ HTT6 Tony Stark 20.00 50.00
Pepper Potts/ Rhodey Rhodes
❑ HTT7 Tony Stark 20.00 50.00
Pepper Potts/ Happy Hogan
❑ HTT8 Maya Hansen 30.00 60.00
Tony Stark/ Pepper Potts
❑ HTT9 Maya Hansen 20.00 50.00
Tony Stark/ Killian
❑ HTT10 Mandarin 12.00 30.00
Tony Stark/ Killian
❑ HTT11 Maya Hansen 30.00 60.00
Pepper Potts/ Killian
❑ HTT12 Mandarin 12.00 30.00
Killian/ Savin
❑ HTT13 Happy Hogan 12.00 30.00
Killian/ Savin
❑ HTT14 Happy Hogan 15.00 40.00
Pepper Potts/ Rhodey Rhodes
❑ HTT15 Happy Hogan 15.00 40.00
Pepper Potts/ Killian

2013 Iron Man 3 Sketches

STATED ODDS 1:36 H, 1:14,400 R
❑ 1 Ajahy Cerezo
❑ 2 Albert Morales
❑ 3 Alex Magno
❑ 4 Anthony Tan
❑ 5 Arley Tucker
❑ 6 Ashleigh Popplewell
❑ 7 Austin Janowsky
❑ 8 Babisu Kourtis
❑ 9 Bienifer Flores
❑ 10 Bob Stevlic
❑ 11 Bridgit Scheide
❑ 12 Cal Slayton
❑ 13 Chadwick Haverland
❑ 14 Chris Bradberry
❑ 15 Cris Santos
❑ 16 Cruddie Torian
❑ 17 Darren Chandler
❑ 18 Dave Lynch
❑ 19 David Hindelang
❑ 20 Diana Greenhalgh
❑ 21 Dioscoro Dong Beniga Jr
❑ 22 Eduardo Garcia
❑ 23 Elvin Hernandez
❑ 24 Erik Reeves
❑ 25 Harold Edge
❑ 26 Ian Roberts
❑ 27 Ivan Rodriguez (Merc)
❑ 28 j(ay)
❑ 29 James Riot Godfrey
❑ 30 Jason Adams
❑ 31 Jason Keith Phillips
❑ 32 Jay David Lee
❑ 33 Jayson Kretzer
❑ 34 Jed Thomas
❑ 35 Jerry Ma
❑ 36 Jim Jimenez
❑ 37 Joe Hogan
❑ 38 Joel Gomez
❑ 39 Jomar Alejos Bulda
❑ 40 Jovenal Mendoza
❑ 41 Juan Francisco Calzada
❑ 42 Jun Lofamia
❑ 43 Juno Sanchez
❑ 44 Kevin Sharpe
❑ 45 Lawrence Reynolds
❑ 46 Layron DeJarnette
❑ 47 Lord Mesa
❑ 48 Mark Morales
❑ 49 Mark Peasley
❑ 50 Matt Slay
❑ 51 Mauro Fodra
❑ 52 Mel Joy San Juan
❑ 53 Melissa Uran
❑ 54 Michael Duron
❑ 55 Mike Vasquez
❑ 56 Natasa Kourtis
❑ 57 Nicole Virella
❑ 58 Rain Lagunsad
❑ 59 Rhiannon Owens
❑ 60 Robert Thai
❑ 61 Rodrigo Martins
❑ 62 Ryan Kincaid
❑ 63 Ryan Van Der Draaij
❑ 64 Tina Berardi
❑ 65 Val Mayerik
❑ 66 Walter Rice
❑ 67 Wendy Chew

2013 Marvel Greatest Battles

COMPLETE SET (90) 6.00 15.00
❑ 1 Iron Man vs. Mandarin .15 .40
❑ 2 Iron Man vs. Titanium Man .15 .40
❑ 3 Iron Man vs. Iron Monger .15 .40
❑ 4 Iron Man vs. Captain America .15 .40
❑ 5 Iron Man vs. Dr. Doom .15 .40
❑ 6 Iron Man vs. Ezekiel Stane .15 .40
❑ 7 Iron Man vs. Hulk .15 .40
❑ 8 Iron Man vs. Melter .15 .40
❑ 9 Iron Man vs. Controller .15 .40
❑ 10 Captain America vs. Task Master .15 .40
❑ 11 Captain America vs. Wolverine .15 .40
❑ 12 Captain America vs. Scourge .15 .40
❑ 13 Captain America vs. Baron Zemo .15 .40
❑ 14 Captain America vs. Red Skull .15 .40
❑ 15 Captain America vs. Punisher .15 .40
❑ 16 Captain America vs. Cyclops .15 .40
❑ 17 Captain America vs. Kang .15 .40
❑ 18 Captain America vs. Iron Man .15 .40
❑ 19 Hulk vs. Thing .15 .40
❑ 20 Hulk vs. Zeus .15 .40
❑ 21 Hulk vs. Hercules .15 .40
❑ 22 Hulk vs. Abomination .15 .40
❑ 23 Hulk vs. Red Hulk .15 .40
❑ 24 Hulk vs. Sentry .15 .40
❑ 25 Hulk vs. Red She-Hulk .15 .40
❑ 26 Hulk vs. Skaar .15 .40
❑ 27 Hulk vs. Punisher .15 .40
❑ 28 Thor vs. Loki .15 .40
❑ 29 Thor vs. Executioner .15 .40
❑ 30 Thor vs. Hercules .15 .40
❑ 31 Thor vs. Odin .15 .40
❑ 32 Thor vs. Beta-Ray-Bill .15 .40
❑ 33 Thor vs. Destroyer .15 .40
❑ 34 Thor vs. Wrecker .15 .40
❑ 35 Thor vs. Tanarus .15 .40
❑ 36 Thor vs. Blastaar .15 .40
❑ 37 Wolverine vs. Omega Red .15 .40
❑ 38 Wolverine vs. Mystique .15 .40
❑ 39 Wolverine vs. Sabretooth .15 .40
❑ 40 Wolverine vs. Magneto .15 .40
❑ 41 Wolverine vs. Deadpool .15 .40
❑ 42 Wolverine vs. Silver Samurai .15 .40
❑ 43 Wolverine vs. Cyclops .15 .40
❑ 44 Wolverine vs. Daken .15 .40
❑ 45 Wolverine vs. Gorgon .15 .40
❑ 46 Spider-Man vs. Doctor Octopus .15 .40
❑ 47 Spider-Man vs. Vulture .15 .40
❑ 48 Spider-Man vs. Sandman .15 .40
❑ 49 Spider-Man vs. Green Goblin .15 .40
❑ 50 Spider-Man vs. Rhino .15 .40
❑ 51 Spider-Man vs. Electro .15 .40
❑ 52 Spider-Man vs. Venom .15 .40
❑ 53 Spider-Man vs. Lizard .15 .40
❑ 54 Spider-Man vs. Scorpion .15 .40
❑ 55 Fantastic Four vs. Mole Man .15 .40
❑ 56 Fantastic Four vs. Klaw .15 .40
❑ 57 Fantastic Four vs. Super Skrull .15 .40
❑ 58 Fantastic Four vs. Galactus .15 .40
❑ 59 Fantastic Four vs. Annihilus .15 .40
❑ 60 Fantastic Four vs. Dr. Doom .15 .40
❑ 61 Fantastic Four vs. Psycho-Man .15 .40
❑ 62 Fantastic Four vs. Ramades .15 .40
❑ 63 Fantastic Four vs. Diablo .15 .40
❑ 64 Rogue vs. Ms. Marvel .15 .40
❑ 65 Rogue vs. She-Hulk .15 .40
❑ 66 Rogue vs. Iron Man .15 .40
❑ 67 Rogue vs. Ares .15 .40
❑ 68 Rogue vs. Danger .15 .40
❑ 69 Rogue vs. X-Men .15 .40
❑ 70 Rogue vs. Sunfire .15 .40
❑ 71 Rogue vs. Psylocke .15 .40
❑ 72 Rogue vs. Mystique .15 .40
❑ 73 Ms. Marvel vs. Rogue .15 .40
❑ 74 Ms. Marvel vs. Tigra .15 .40
❑ 75 Ms. Marvel vs. Moonstone .15 .40
❑ 76 Ms. Marvel vs. Brood .15 .40
❑ 77 Ms. Marvel vs. Warbird .15 .40
❑ 78 Ms. Marvel vs. Mystique .15 .40
❑ 79 Black Widow vs. Mockingbird .15 .40
❑ 80 Black Widow vs. Bullseye .15 .40
❑ 81 Black Widow vs. Magik .15 .40
❑ 82 Black Widow vs. Elektra .15 .40
❑ 83 Black Widow vs. Wolverine .15 .40
❑ 84 Black Widow vs. Daredevil .15 .40
❑ 85 Elektra vs. Echo .15 .40
❑ 86 Elektra vs. Hawkeye .15 .40
❑ 87 Elektra vs. Red Hulk .15 .40
❑ 88 Elektra vs. Hercules .15 .40
❑ 89 Elektra vs. Shroud .15 .40
❑ 90 Elektra vs. Daredevil .15 .40

2013 Marvel Greatest Battles Avengers vs X-Men

COMPLETE SET (18) 8.00 20.00
STATED ODDS 1:12
❑ VS1 Avengers vs X-Men 1.00 2.50
❑ VS2 Avengers vs X-Men 1.00 2.50
❑ VS3 Avengers vs X-Men 1.00 2.50
❑ VS4 Avengers vs X-Men 1.00 2.50
❑ VS5 Avengers vs X-Men 1.00 2.50
❑ VS6 Avengers vs X-Men 1.00 2.50
❑ VS7 Avengers vs X-Men 1.00 2.50
❑ VS8 Avengers vs X-Men 1.00 2.50
❑ VS9 Avengers vs X-Men 1.00 2.50
❑ VS10 Avengers vs X-Men 1.00 2.50
❑ VS11 Avengers vs X-Men 1.00 2.50
❑ VS12 Avengers vs X-Men 1.00 2.50
❑ VS13 Avengers vs X-Men 1.00 2.50
❑ VS14 Avengers vs X-Men 1.00 2.50
❑ VS15 Avengers vs X-Men 1.00 2.50
❑ VS16 Avengers vs X-Men 1.00 2.50
❑ VS17 Avengers vs X-Men 1.00 2.50
❑ VS18 Avengers vs X-Men 1.00 2.50

2013 Marvel Greatest Battles Battle Scars

COMPLETE SET (9) 6.00 15.00
STATED ODDS 1:12
❑ BS1 Spider-Man .75 2.00
❑ BS2 Iron Man .75 2.00
❑ BS3 Thor .75 2.00
❑ BS4 Captain America .75 2.00
❑ BS5 Hulk .75 2.00
❑ BS6 Wolverine .75 2.00
❑ BS7 Ms. Marvel .75 2.00
❑ BS8 Rogue .75 2.00
❑ BS9 Cyclops .75 2.00

2013 Marvel Greatest Battles Gold

STATED ODDS 1:24

2013 Marvel Greatest Battles Gold Covers

COMPLETE SET (9) 25.00 50.00
STATED ODDS 1:24
❑ GC1 Captain America 3.00 8.00
❑ GC2 Ghost Rider 3.00 8.00
❑ GC3 Hulk 3.00 8.00
❑ GC4 Iron Man 3.00 8.00
❑ GC5 Spider-Man 3.00 8.00
❑ GC6 Thor 3.00 8.00
❑ GC7 Wolverine 3.00 8.00
❑ GC8 Cyclops 3.00 8.00
❑ GC9 Storm 3.00 8.00
❑ GC10 Nova 20.00 50.00
(issued as Rittenhouse Reward)

2013 Marvel Greatest Battles Promos

❑ P1 Spider-Man 1.00 2.50
(General Distribution)
❑ P2 Wolverine 10.00 20.00
(Binder Exclusive)

2013 Marvel Greatest Battles Red

STATED ODDS 1:3

2013 Marvel Greatest Battles Secret Warriors Case Toppers

COMPLETE SET (2)
STATED ODDS ONE PER CASE
❑ CT1 Captain America and Nick Fury 10.00 25.00
❑ CT2 Captain America and Nick Fury 10.00 25.00

2013 Marvel Greatest Battles Sketches

ONE 2-CARD SKETCH PUZZLE PER BOX
L (LIMITED): 251+ SKETCHES
VL (VERY LIMITED): 151-250 SKETCHES
EL (EXTREMELY LTD): 51-150 SKETCHES
S (SCARCE): LESS THAN 50 SKETCHES
❑ 1 Adam Cleveland EL
❑ 2 Adam Cline S
❑ 3 Albert Morales S
❑ 4 Alberto Silva S
❑ 5 Alcione da Silva S
❑ 6 Alex Magno L
❑ 7 Alfredo Lopez Jr. S
❑ 8 Allen Geneta EL
❑ 9 Andre Toma S
❑ 10 Andy Price S
❑ 11 Anthony Tan S
❑ 12 Antonio Brandao S
❑ 13 Arley Tucker EL
❑ 14 Aston Roy Cover EL
❑ 15 Bien Flores S
❑ 16 Bill Mancuso S
❑ 17 Brent Ragland S
❑ 18 Bryan Tillman S
❑ 19 Buddy Prince EL
❑ 20 Cízar Razek EL
❑ 21 Charles Hall S
❑ 22 Chris Bradberry S
❑ 23 Chris Foreman EL
❑ 24 Chris Gutierrez S
❑ 25 Dan Borgonos S
❑ 26 Daniel HDR S
❑ 27 Darren Chandler S
❑ 28 Dave Beaty S
❑ 29 Dennis Crisostomo S
❑ 30 Denver Brubaker S
❑ 31 Edde Wagner EL
❑ 32 Edwin David S
❑ 33 Eli Rutten S
❑ 34 Gemma Magno EL
❑ 35 George Calloway S
❑ 36 George Davis S
❑ 37 Greg Kirkpatrick S
❑ 38 Ian Dorian S
❑ 39 Irma Ahmed S
❑ 40 J. David Lee L
❑ 41 Jader Correa S
❑ 42 Jake Minor S
❑ 43 Jake Sumbing VL
❑ 44 James Linares S
❑ 45 Jamie Snell S
❑ 46 Jason Sobol S
❑ 47 Jay Fosgitt EL
❑ 48 Jayson Kretzer S
❑ 49 JC Fabul VL
❑ 50 Jeanette Swift S
❑ 51 Jeff Confer S
❑ 52 Joe Pekar EL
❑ 53 John Czop S
❑ 54 John Haun S
❑ 55 Johndell Snead S
❑ 56 Jomar Bulda VL
❑ 57 Jon Hughes S
❑ 58 Jordan Butler EL
❑ 59 Jose Weingartner Jr. S
❑ 60 Joshua Flower S
❑ 61 Jovenal Mendoza S
❑ 62 Juan Fontanez S
❑ 63 Julia Pinto S
❑ 64 Julius Abrera S
❑ 65 Juno Sanchez EL
❑ 66 Kevin West S
❑ 67 Lee Bradley S
❑ 68 Leeahd Goldberg S
❑ 69 Lui Antonio S
❑ 70 Lynne Anderson S
❑ 71 Marcelo Ferreira S
❑ 72 Marco David Carrillo EL
❑ 73 Mark (Felix) Morales VL
❑ 74 Mark Marvida VL
❑ 75 Mark Tannacore S
❑ 76 Mary Jane Dizon Paragan S
❑ 77 Matias Streb S
❑ 78 Matt Glebe EL
❑ 79 Mauro Fodra VL
❑ 80 Meghan Hetrick
(issued as 6-case incentive)
❑ 81 Michael Duron S
❑ 82 Mick Glebe EL
❑ 83 Mike Thomas EL
❑ 84 Mitch Ballard EL
❑ 85 MJ San Juan EL
❑ 86 Nestor Celario Jr. S
❑ 87 Norman Jim Faustino EL
❑ 88 Noval Hernawan EL
❑ 89 Nur Hanie Mohd EL
❑ 90 Pablo Marcos EL
❑ 91 Puis Calzada S
❑ 92 Rainier Lagunsad S
❑ 93 Randy Monces EL
❑ 94 Rhiannon Owens S
❑ 95 Rich Molinelli S
❑ 96 Rodjer Goulart S
❑ 97 Rodrio Martins EL
❑ 98 Roger Medeiros S
❑ 99 Rogerio DeSouza S
❑ 100 Saiful Mokhtar EL
❑ 101 Sam Agro S
❑ 102 Scott Rorie S
❑ 103 Sean Moore S
❑ 104 Seth Ismart S
❑ 105 Stacey Kardash S
❑ 106 Stefanie Battalene S
❑ 107 Studio Mia VL
❑ 108 Thanh Bui S
❑ 109 Tim Levandoski S
❑ 110 Tony Santiago S
❑ 111 Tony Scott S
❑ 112 Vince Sunico S
❑ 113 Warren Martineck
(issued as 9-case incentive)
❑ 114 Wayne Beeman S
❑ 115 Wendell Rubio Silva S
❑ 116 William Allan Reyes EL
❑ 117 Yonami S

2013 Parks and Recreation

COMPLETE SET (90) 5.00 12.00
❑ 1 Pilot .15 .40
❑ 2 Canvassing .15 .40
❑ 3 The Reporter .15 .40
❑ 4 Boys' Club .15 .40
❑ 5 The Banquet .15 .40
❑ 6 Rock Show .15 .40
❑ 7 Pawnee Zoo .15 .40
❑ 8 The Stakeout .15 .40
❑ 9 Beauty Pageant .15 .40
❑ 10 The Practice Date .15 .40
❑ 11 Sister City .15 .40
❑ 12 KaBOOM .15 .40
❑ 13 Greg Pikitis .15 .40
❑ 14 Ron and Tammy .15 .40
❑ 15 The Camel .15 .40
❑ 16 Hunting Trip .15 .40
❑ 17 Tom's Divorce .15 .40
❑ 18 Christmas Scandal .15 .40
❑ 19 The Set-Up .15 .40
❑ 20 Leslie's House .15 .40
❑ 21 Sweetums .15 .40
❑ 22 Galentine's Day .15 .40
❑ 23 Woman of the Year .15 .40
❑ 24 The Possum .15 .40
❑ 25 Park Safety .15 .40
❑ 26 Summer Catalog .15 .40
❑ 27 94 Meetings .15 .40
❑ 28 Telethon .15 .40
❑ 29 The Master Plan .15 .40
❑ 30 Freddy Spaghetti .15 .40
❑ 31 Go Big or Go Home .15 .40
❑ 32 Flu Season .15 .40
❑ 33 Time Capsule .15 .40
❑ 34 Ron and Tammy: Part 2 .15 .40
❑ 35 Media Blitz .15 .40
❑ 36 Indianapolis .15 .40
❑ 37 Harvest Festival .15 .40
❑ 38 Camping .15 .40
❑ 39 Andy and April's Fancy Party .15 .40
❑ 40 Soulmates .15 .40
❑ 41 Jerry's Painting .15 .40
❑ 42 Eagleton .15 .40
❑ 43 The Fight .15 .40
❑ 44 Road Trip .15 .40
❑ 45 The Bubble .15 .40
❑ 46 Li'l Sebastian .15 .40
❑ 47 I'm Leslie Knope .15 .40
❑ 48 Ron and Tammys .15 .40
❑ 49 Born and Raised .15 .40
❑ 50 Pawnee Rangers .15 .40
❑ 51 Meet 'N' Greet .15 .40
❑ 52 End of the World .15 .40
❑ 53 The Treaty .15 .40
❑ 54 Smallest Park .15 .40
❑ 55 Trial of Leslie Knope .15 .40
❑ 56 Citizen Knope .15 .40
❑ 57 The Comeback Kid .15 .40
❑ 58 Campaign Ad .15 .40
❑ 59 Bowling for Votes .15 .40
❑ 60 Operation Ann .15 .40
❑ 61 Dave Returns .15 .40
❑ 62 Sweet Sixteen .15 .40
❑ 63 Campaign Shake-Up .15 .40
❑ 64 Lucky .15 .40
❑ 65 Live Ammo .15 .40
❑ 66 The Debate .15 .40
❑ 67 Bus Tour .15 .40
❑ 68 Win, Lose, or Draw .15 .40
❑ 69 Amy Poehler#1 as Leslie Knope .15 .40
❑ 70 Rashida Jones .15 .40
as Ann Perkins
❑ 71 Aziz Ansari .15 .40
as Tom Haverford
❑ 72 Nick Offerman .15 .40
as Ron Swanson
❑ 73 Aubrey Plaza .15 .40
as April Ludgate
❑ 74 Chris Pratt .15 .40
as Andy Dwyer
❑ 75 Jim O'Heir .15 .40
as Jerry Gergich
❑ 76 Retta .15 .40
as Donna Meagle
❑ 77 Adam Scott .15 .40
as Ben Wyatt
❑ 78 Rob Lowe .15 .40
as Chris Traeger
❑ 79 Jay Jackson .15 .40
as Perd Hapley
❑ 80 www.PawneeIndiana.com .15 .40
❑ 81 www.SnakeHoleLounge.com .15 .40
❑ 82 www.HoosierMate.com .15 .40
❑ 83 www.MissPawnee.com .15 .40
❑ 84 www.Entertainment720.com .15 .40
❑ 85 www.RentASwag.com .15 .40
❑ 86 www.Knope2012.com .15 .40
❑ 87 www.RonSwansonGrill.com .15 .40
❑ 88 www.DukeSilver.com .15 .40
❑ 89 www.ScarecrowBoat.com .15 .40
❑ 90 www.AwesomeSauceWedding.com .15 .40

2013 Parks and Recreation Foil

COMPLETE SET 8.00 20.00
STATED ODDS ONE PER PACK

2013 Parks and Recreation Autographs

STATED ODDS 1:12
❑ AP Aubrey Plaza 15.00 40.00
as April Ludgate
❑ AP1 Amy Poehler (gray jacket) 60.00 120.00
as Leslie Knope
❑ AP2 Amy Poehler (black jacket)
as Leslie Knope/ (issued as 4-case incentive)
❑ FA Fred Armisen 8.00 20.00
as Raul
❑ JJ Jay Jackson 5.00 12.00
as Perd Hapley
❑ JO Jim O'Heir 5.00 12.00
as Jerry Gergich
❑ MC Mo Collins 8.00 20.00
as Joan Callamezzo
❑ MM Megan Mullally 8.00 20.00
as Tammy Swanson
❑ NO Nick Offerman 15.00 40.00
as Ron Swanson
❑ PP Parker Posey 8.00 20.00
as Lindsay Carlisle Shay
❑ PR Paul Rudd 15.00 40.00
as Bobby Newport
❑ R Retta 5.00 12.00
as Donna Meagle
❑ RL Rob Lowe 30.00 60.00
as Chris Traeger

2013 Parks and Recreation Autographs Red Ink

PRINT RUN 26-173
❑ AA Aziz Ansari 15.00 40.00
as Tom Haverford/173*
❑ AP Aubrey Plaza 25.00 60.00
as April Ludgate/50*
❑ MM Megan Mullally 8.00 20.00
as Tammy Swanson/38*
❑ NO Nick Offerman 15.00 40.00
as Ron Swanson/55*
❑ PR Paul Rudd 20.00 50.00
as Bobby Newport/50*

2013 Parks and Recreation Autographs Gold Foil Red Ink

PRINT RUN 6-99
❑ AA Aziz Ansari 15.00 40.00
as Tom Haverford/99
❑ MC Mo Collins 8.00 20.00
as Joan Callamezzo/47*

2013 Parks and Recreation Autographs Red Foil

PRINT RUN 15-25

2013 Parks and Recreation Autographs Red Foil Red Ink

PRINT RUN 2-25

2013 Parks and Recreation Relics

STATED ODDS 1:24
❑ RAA Aziz Ansari suit jacket 6.00 15.00
as Tom Haverford
❑ RAS Adam Scott shirt 6.00 15.00
as Ben Wyatt
❑ RCP Chris Pratt shirt 6.00 15.00
as Andy Dwyer
❑ RNO Nick Offerman shirt 6.00 15.00
as Ron Swanson
❑ RRL Rob Lowe suit jacket 6.00 15.00
as Chris Traeger
❑ R1AP Amy Poehler dress 6.00 15.00
as Leslie Knope
❑ R2AP Amy Poehler suit jacket 6.00 15.00
as Leslie Knope
❑ R2RL Rob Lowe shirt 6.00 15.00
as Chris Traeger
❑ RAP2 Aubrey Plaza hoodie 8.00 20.00
as April Ludgate

2013 Parks and Recreation Relics Gold Foil

STATED PRINT RUN 99 SER. #'d SETS

2013 Parks and Recreation Relics Blue Foil

STATED PRINT RUN 25 SER. #'d SETS

2013 Parks and Recreation Relics Dual Gold Foil

PRINT RUN 50-99
❑ RDAA Aziz Ansari 8.00 20.00
Tom Haverford/99
❑ RDAP Amy Poehler 12.00 30.00
as Leslie Knope/99
❑ RDAS Adam Scott 8.00 20.00
as Ben Wyatt/50
❑ RDAP2 Aubrey Plaza 15.00 40.00
as April Ludgate/99

2013 Parks and Recreation Relics Dual Blue Foil

STATED PRINT RUN 25 SER. #'d SETS

2013 Parks and Recreation Relics Triple Gold Foil

PRINT RUN 50-99
❑ RTAP Amy Poehler
as Leslie Knope/99
❑ RTRL Rob Lowe
as Chris Traeger/50

2013 Parks and Recreation Relics Triple Blue Foil

STATED PRINT RUN 25 SER. #'d SETS

2013 Pop Century

❑ BAAD1 Andy Dick 3.00 8.00
❑ BAAD2 Angie Dickinson 12.00 30.00
❑ BAAGB Ashley Gold Broad 6.00 15.00
❑ BAAL1 Ali Landry 10.00 25.00
❑ BAAM1 Ali MacGraw 10.00 25.00
❑ BAAP1 Al Pacino
❑ BAAP3 Artimus Pyle 8.00 20.00
❑ BAAS1 Ashley Scott 6.00 15.00
❑ BABB1 Brooke Burns 8.00 20.00
❑ BABB2 Barry Bostwick 6.00 15.00
❑ BABG1 Bob Gibson 12.00 30.00
❑ BABH1 Bo Hopkins 3.00 8.00
❑ BABI1 Billy Idol 20.00 50.00
❑ BABJ1 Bruce Jenner 5.00 12.00
❑ BABM1 Bam Magera 6.00 15.00
❑ BABT1 Becca Tobin 5.00 12.00
❑ BABY1 Burt Young 8.00 20.00

❑ BAC1 Coolio 5.00 12.00
❑ BACB1 Candace Bailey 6.00 15.00
❑ BACF1 Carrie Fisher 50.00 100.00
❑ BACL1 Carl Lewis 10.00 25.00
❑ BACL2 Carla Laemmle 10.00 25.00
❑ BACP1 Carly Patterson 8.00 20.00
❑ BACP2 Chris Pontius 6.00 15.00
❑ BACRJ Cal Ripken Jr. 40.00 80.00
❑ BACS1 Connie Stevens 6.00 15.00
❑ BACW1 Cindy Williams 8.00 20.00
❑ BADB1 Drake Bell 4.00 10.00
❑ BADC1 Dean Cain 3.00 8.00
❑ BADD1 Donna Douglas 12.00 30.00
❑ BADG1 Debbie Gibson 15.00 40.00
❑ BADH1 Dave Hester 5.00 12.00
❑ BADR1 Debbie Reynolds 12.00 30.00
❑ BADR2 Dennis Rodman 8.00 20.00
❑ BADS1 Dee Snider 6.00 15.00
❑ BADS2 Dwight Schultz 10.00 25.00
❑ BAEA1 Ed Asner 6.00 15.00
❑ BAEA2 Erin Andrews 30.00 60.00
❑ BAEE1 Erika Eleniak 12.00 30.00
❑ BAEM1 Erin Murphy 6.00 15.00
❑ BAGC1 Gabrielle Carteris 4.00 10.00
❑ BAGL1 George Lazenby 15.00 40.00
❑ BAGM1 Garry Marshall 8.00 20.00
❑ BAHH1 Hulk Hogan 35.00 70.00
❑ BAHMC Holly Marie Combs 20.00 50.00
❑ BAHR1 Helen Reddy 6.00 15.00
❑ BAHS1 Hope Solo 20.00 50.00
❑ BAJC1 Joan Collins 12.00 30.00
❑ BAJE1 Jason Earles 3.00 8.00
❑ BAJG1 James Gandolfini 60.00 120.00
❑ BAJL1 Jennifer Lopez 60.00 120.00
❑ BAJL2 Jerry Lewis 30.00 60.00
❑ BAJL3 Jerry Lawler 10.00 25.00
❑ BAJL4 Judy Landers 8.00 20.00
❑ BAJM1 Jenny McCarthy 30.00 60.00
❑ BAJM2 Jeremy Miller 3.00 8.00
❑ BAKB1 Kate Beckinsale 150.00 250.00
❑ BAKS1 Katey Sagal 20.00 50.00
❑ BAKS2 Kevin Sorbo 6.00 15.00
❑ BAKV1 Kate Vernon 4.00 10.00
❑ BALA1 Loni Anderson 10.00 25.00
❑ BALB1 Linda Blair 10.00 25.00
❑ BALG1 Les Gold
❑ BALL1 Lindsay Lohan 75.00 150.00
❑ BALLJ Lolo Jones 15.00 40.00
❑ BALP1 Lori Petty 8.00 20.00
❑ BAMB1 Max Baer Jr. 10.00 25.00
❑ BAMBJ Mark Boone Jr. 8.00 20.00
❑ BAMDL Vini Mad Dog Lopez 8.00 20.00
❑ BAMF1 Morgan Fairchild 6.00 15.00
❑ BAML1 Mario Lopez 4.00 10.00
❑ BAMS1 Mark Spitz 6.00 15.00
❑ BANC1 Naked Cowboy 3.00 8.00
❑ BANK1 Nancy Kerrigan 8.00 20.00
❑ BANK2 Nastassja Kinski 12.00 30.00
❑ BAPD1 Patty Duke 8.00 20.00
❑ BAPG1 Pam Grier 6.00 15.00
❑ BAPR1 Pete Rose 8.00 20.00
❑ BAPT1 Peter Tork 10.00 25.00
❑ BAPW1 Patrick Warburton 8.00 20.00
❑ BARF1 Ric Flair 15.00 40.00
❑ BARH1 Richard Hatch 8.00 20.00
❑ BARL1 Robert Loggia 10.00 25.00
❑ BASF1 Samantha Fox 10.00 25.00
❑ BASG1 Seth Gold
❑ BASK1 Stacy Keach 8.00 20.00
❑ BASM1 Shannon Miller 8.00 20.00
❑ BASM2 Sofia Milos 6.00 15.00
❑ BASP1 Sarah Palin 40.00 80.00
❑ BASS1 Serinda Swan 8.00 20.00
❑ BAST1 Sam Trammell 6.00 15.00
❑ BATH1 Tippi Hedren 20.00 50.00
❑ BATH2 Tonya Harding 12.00 30.00
❑ BATN1 Ted Nugent 15.00 40.00
❑ BATO1 Tony Orlando 10.00 25.00
❑ BATW1 Tom Wopat 10.00 25.00
❑ BAVG1 Vida Guerra 12.00 30.00
❑ BAVM1 Virginia Madsen 12.00 30.00
❑ BAVP1 Vincent Pastore 5.00 12.00
❑ BAWM1 Wink Martindale 5.00 12.00
❑ BAYAT Y.A. Tittle 8.00 20.00

2013 Pop Century Silver

STATED PRINT RUN 25 SER. #'d SETS

2013 Pop Century And the Nomination Is Autographs

❑ ANAM1 Ali MacGraw 10.00 25.00
❑ ANAP1 Al Pacino 150.00 250.00
❑ ANBI1 Billy Idol 15.00 40.00
❑ ANDR1 Debbie Reynolds 12.00 30.00
❑ ANEA1 Ed Asner 6.00 15.00
❑ ANHR1 Helen Reddy 6.00 15.00
❑ ANJC1 Joan Collins 12.00 30.00
❑ ANJG1 James Gandolfini 60.00 120.00
❑ ANJL1 Jennifer Lopez 60.00 120.00
❑ ANKS1 Katey Sagal 15.00 40.00
❑ ANLB1 Linda Blair 10.00 25.00
❑ ANSK1 Stacy Keach 8.00 20.00
❑ ANSP1 Sarah Palin 40.00 80.00

2013 Pop Century Co-Stars Autographs

*SILVER/25: .5X TO 1.2X BASIC CARDS

❑ CS01 Ashley Gold Broad
Les Gold
❑ CS02 Ashley Gold Broad
Seth Gold
❑ CS03 Seth Gold 12.00 30.00
Les Gold
❑ CS04 Buster Douglas
Mike Tyson
❑ CS05 Bo Hopkins 6.00 15.00
Robert Loggia
❑ CS06 Connie Stevens 10.00 25.00
Ed Asner
❑ CS07 Cindy Williams 20.00 50.00
Penny Marshall
❑ CS08 Cindy Williams 8.00 20.00
David Lander
❑ CS09 David Lander 12.00 30.00
Penny Marshall
❑ CS10 Drake Bell 15.00 40.00
Jerry Lewis
❑ CS11 Dean Cain 6.00 15.00
Erika Eleniak
❑ CS12 Dean Cain 6.00 15.00
Barry Bostwick
❑ CS13 Donna Douglas 15.00 40.00
Max Baer Jr.
❑ CS14 Dicky Eklund 6.00 15.00
Micky Ward
❑ CS15 Dee Snider 12.00 30.00
Dennis Rodman
❑ CS16 Penny Marshall 15.00 40.00
Garry Marshall
❑ CS17 Holly Marie Combs 15.00 40.00
Angie Dickinson
❑ CS18 Katey Sagal 12.00 30.00
Mark Boone Junior
❑ CS19 Michael Oher 12.00 30.00
Quinton Aaron
❑ CS20 Tony Dow 15.00 40.00
Ken Osmond
❑ CS21 Catherine Bach 15.00 40.00
Tom Wopat
❑ CS22 James Gandolfini 60.00 120.00
Vincent Pastore
❑ CS23 Dominique Moceanu 15.00 40.00
Shannon Miller
❑ CS24 Mark Spitz 8.00 20.00
Janet Evans
❑ CS25 Ric Flair 15.00 40.00
Road Warrior Animal
❑ CS26 Nancy Kerrigan 15.00 40.00
Tonya Harding
❑ CS27 Danielle Harris 12.00 30.00
George Wilbur
❑ CS28 Nell Campbell 8.00 20.00
Patricia Quinn
❑ CS29 Ernest Thomas 8.00 20.00
Haywood Nelson
❑ CS30 Mark Lester 6.00 15.00
Shani Wallis
❑ CS007 Caroline Munro 50.00 100.00
Luciana Paluzzi/ Britt Ekland/ Lana Wood/ Maud Adams
❑ CSHPC Les Gold 15.00 40.00
Seth Gold/ Ashley Gold Broad
❑ CSWKRP Loni Anderson 20.00 50.00
Howard Hesseman/ Tim Reid

2013 Pop Century Co-Stars Autographs Silver

STATED PRINT RUN 20-25

2013 Pop Century Dressing Room Autograph Memorabilia

❑ DRJG1 James Gandolfini 75.00 150.00
❑ DRJG2 James Gandolfini 75.00 150.00
❑ DRJL1 Jennifer Lopez 100.00 175.00

2013 Pop Century Keeping It Real Autographs

*SILVER/25: .5X TO 1.2X BASIC CARDS

❑ KRAD1 Andy Dick 3.00 8.00
❑ KRBM1 Bam Magera 6.00 15.00
❑ KRC1 Coolio 4.00 10.00
❑ KRDH1 Dave Hester 3.00 8.00
❑ KRDR2 Dennis Rodman 6.00 15.00
❑ KRGC1 Gabrielle Carteris 4.00 10.00
❑ KRML1 Mario Lopez 4.00 10.00
❑ KRPR1 Pete Rose 8.00 20.00
❑ KRTN1 Ted Nugent 15.00 40.00
❑ KRVP1 Vincent Pastore 4.00 10.00

2013 Pop Century Keeping It Real Autographs Silver

STATED PRINT RUN 25 SER. #'d SETS

2013 Pop Century Keeping It Real Autographs Blue

STATED PRINT RUN 10 SER. #'d SETS
UNPRICED DUE TO SCARCITY

2013 Pop Century Perfectly Cast Autographs

*SILVER/25: .5X TO 1.2X BASIC CARDS

❑ PCALF Michu 6.00 15.00
❑ PCAP1 Al Pacino 200.00 300.00
❑ PCAP2 Al Pacino 200.00 300.00
❑ PCBE1 Barbara Eden 20.00 50.00
❑ PCDC1 Dean Cain 8.00 20.00
❑ PCGL1 George Lazenby 12.00 30.00
❑ PCJL1 Jennifer Lopez 60.00 120.00
❑ PCJL2 Jerry Lewis 35.00 70.00
❑ PCKS2 Kevin Sorbo 6.00 15.00
❑ PCLH1 Larry Hagman 20.00 50.00
❑ PCML1 Mario Lopez 6.00 15.00
❑ PCNC2 Nell Campbell 6.00 15.00
❑ PCPM1 Penny Marshall 12.00 30.00
❑ PCPQ1 Patricia Quinn 6.00 15.00
❑ PCST1 Sam Trammell 6.00 15.00

2013 Pop Century Perfectly Cast Autographs Silver

*SILVER/25: .5X TO 1.2X BASIC CARDS
PRINT RUN 5-25

2013 Pop Century Stunning Starlets Autographs

*SILVER/25: .5X TO 1.2X BASIC CARDS

❑ SSAL1 Ali Landry 12.00 30.00
❑ SSAS1 Ashley Scott 8.00 20.00
❑ SSBB1 Brook Burns 8.00 20.00
❑ SSBE1 Barbara Eden 15.00 40.00
❑ SSBT1 Becca Tobin 5.00 12.00
❑ SSJL4 Judy Landers 8.00 20.00
❑ SSJM1 Jenny McCarthy 15.00 40.00
❑ SSLB1 Linda Blair 12.00 30.00

2013 Pop Century Stunning Starlets Autographs Silver

STATED PRINT RUN 25 SER. #'d SETS

2013 Pop Century Stunning Starlets Autographs Blue

STATED PRINT RUN 10 SER. #'d SETS
UNPRICED DUE TO SCARCITY

2013 Pop Century Stunning Starlets Autographs Red

STATED PRINT RUN 5 SER. #'d SETS
UNPRICED DUE TO SCARCITY

2013 Spartacus Expansion

COMPLETE SET (22) 75.00 150.00
❑ C1 Spartacus 2.00 5.00
❑ C2 Crixus 2.00 5.00
❑ C3 Agron 2.00 5.00
❑ C4 Naevia 2.00 5.00
❑ C5 Nasir 2.00 5.00
❑ C6 Laeta 2.00 5.00
❑ C7 Crassus 2.00 5.00
❑ C8 Tiberius 2.00 5.00
❑ C9 Caesar 2.00 5.00
❑ C10 Kore 2.00 5.00
❑ E1 Enemies of Rome 2.00 5.00
❑ E2 Wolves at the Gate 2.00 5.00
❑ E3 Men of Honor 2.00 5.00
❑ E4 Decimation 2.00 5.00
❑ E5 Blood Brothers 2.00 5.00
❑ E6 Spoils of War 2.00 5.00
❑ E7 Mors Indecepta 2.00 5.00
❑ E8 Separate Paths 2.00 5.00
❑ E9 The Dead and the Dying 2.00 5.00
❑ E10 Victory 2.00 5.00
❑ LM Liam McIntyre 50.00 100.00
as Spartacus AUTO
❑ CAR Cynthia Addai-Robinson 30.00 60.00
as Naevia AUTO

2013 Spartacus Vengeance

COMPLETE SET (30) 30.00 60.00
❑ E1 Fugitivus 1.25 3.00
❑ E2 Fugitivus 1.25 3.00
❑ E3 Fugitivus 1.25 3.00
❑ E4 A Place in This World 1.25 3.00
❑ E5 A Place in This World 1.25 3.00
❑ E6 A Place in This World 1.25 3.00
❑ E7 The Greater Good 1.25 3.00
❑ E8 The Greater Good 1.25 3.00
❑ E9 The Greater Good 1.25 3.00
❑ E10 Empty Hands 1.25 3.00
❑ E11 Empty Hands 1.25 3.00
❑ E12 Empty Hands 1.25 3.00
❑ E13 Libertus 1.25 3.00
❑ E14 Libertus 1.25 3.00
❑ E15 Libertus 1.25 3.00
❑ E16 Chosen Path 1.25 3.00
❑ E17 Chosen Path 1.25 3.00
❑ E18 Chosen Path 1.25 3.00
❑ E19 Sacramentum 1.25 3.00
❑ E20 Sacramentum 1.25 3.00
❑ E21 Sacramentum 1.25 3.00
❑ E22 Balance 1.25 3.00
❑ E23 Balance 1.25 3.00
❑ E24 Balance 1.25 3.00
❑ E25 Monsters 1.25 3.00
❑ E26 Monsters 1.25 3.00
❑ E27 Monsters 1.25 3.00
❑ E28 Wrath of the Gods 1.25 3.00
❑ E29 Wrath of the Gods 1.25 3.00
❑ E30 Wrath of the Gods 1.25 3.00
❑ CT1 Spartacus Vengeance Poster 8.00 20.00
(issued as box topper)

2013 Spartacus Vengeance Autographs

TWO AUTOS PER PACK
L (LIMITED): 300-500 COPIES
VL (VERY LIMITED): 200-300 COPIES
EL (EXTREM. LTD): LESS THAN 200 COPIES

❑ 1 Brooke Williams 10.00 25.00
as Aurelia L
❑ 2 Conan Stevens 50.00 100.00
as Sedullus EL
❑ 3 Cynthia Addai-Robinson 50.00 100.00
as Naevia EL
❑ 4 Katrina Law 12.00 30.00
as Mira L
❑ 5 Katrina Law 12.00 30.00
as Mira L
❑ 6 Kevin J. Wilson 10.00 25.00
as Senator Albinius VL
❑ 7 Liam McIntyre 150.00 250.00
as Spartacus EL
❑ 8 Tom Hobbs 8.00 20.00
as Seppius L
❑ 9 Tom Hobbs 8.00 20.00
as Seppius L
❑ 10 Viva Bianca 25.00 50.00
as Ilithyia VL
❑ 11 Viva Bianca 25.00 50.00
as Ilithyia VL
❑ 12 Steven S. DeKnight 60.00 120.00
(issued as 4 box incentive)

2013 Spartacus Vengeance Blood and Sand Autographs

TWO AUTOS PER PACK
L (LIMITED): 300-500 COPIES
VL (VERY LIMITED): 200-300 COPIES
EL (EXTREM. LTD): LESS THAN 200 COPIES

❑ 1 Brooke Williams 10.00 25.00
as Aurelia L
❑ 2 Craig Parker 10.00 25.00
as Claudius Glaber
❑ 3 Craig Walsh Wrightson 10.00 25.00
as Solonius VL
❑ 4 Dan Feuerriegel 10.00 25.00
as Agron
❑ 5 Janine Burchett 8.00 20.00
as Domitia
❑ 6 Kevin J. Wilson 10.00 25.00
as Senator Albinius VL
❑ 7 Peter Mensah 50.00 100.00
as Doctore EL

2013 Spartacus Vengeance Die-Cut Gold Plaques

COMPLETE SET (8) 12.00 30.00
ONE PER PACK

❑ GV1 Spartacus 2.50 6.00
❑ GV2 Claudius Glaber 2.50 6.00
❑ GV3 Agron 2.50 6.00
❑ GV4 Seppia 2.50 6.00
❑ GV5 Seppius 2.50 6.00
❑ GV6 Naevia 2.50 6.00
❑ GV7 Senator Albinius 2.50 6.00
❑ GV8 Varinius 2.50 6.00

2013 Spartacus Vengeance Promos

❑ P1 Spartacus 1.25 3.00
(General Distribution)
❑ P2 Spartacus
(Binder Exclusive)

2013 Spartacus Vengeance Relics

ONE PER PACK

❑ 1 Claudius Glaber fabric 10.00 25.00
❑ 2 Claudius Glaber leather 10.00 25.00
❑ 3 Ilithyia 15.00 40.00
❑ 4 Lucretia 15.00 40.00
❑ 5 Seppia 12.00 30.00
❑ 6 Claudius Glaber's Undershirt HOR 10.00 25.00
❑ 7 Ilithyia's Dress HOR 15.00 40.00
❑ 8 Lucretia's Dress HOR 15.00 40.00
❑ 9 Seppia's Dress HOR 12.00 30.00
❑ 10 Doctore's Whip 10.00 25.00
❑ 11 Mira's Map 12.00 30.00
❑ 12 Glaber's Documents 10.00 25.00
❑ 13 Spartacus' Map 40.00 80.00
(issued as 2 box incentive)

2013 Star Trek Movies

COMPLETE SET (11) 350.00 500.00
❑ 1 Star Trek Into Darkness 3.00 8.00
❑ 2 Star Trek Into Darkness 3.00 8.00
❑ 3 Star Trek Into Darkness 3.00 8.00
❑ 4 Star Trek Into Darkness 3.00 8.00
❑ 5 Star Trek Into Darkness 3.00 8.00
❑ 6 Star Trek Into Darkness 3.00 8.00
❑ 7 Star Trek Into Darkness 3.00 8.00
❑ 8 Star Trek Into Darkness 3.00 8.00
❑ 9 Star Trek Into Darkness 3.00 8.00
❑ CP Chris Pine as Kirk AU MEM 200.00 350.00
❑ ZQ Zachary Quinto as Spock AU MEM 150.00 250.00

2013 Star Trek The Next Generation Heroes and Villains

COMPLETE SET (100) 6.00 15.00
❑ 1 Captain Jean-Luc Picard .15 .40
❑ 2 Commander William T. Riker .15 .40
❑ 3 Lt. Commander Data .15 .40
❑ 4 Lt. Commander Worf .15 .40
❑ 5 Lt. Commander Geordi La Forge .15 .40
❑ 6 Dr. Beverly Crusher .15 .40
❑ 7 Counselor Deanna Troi .15 .40
❑ 8 Wesley Crusher .15 .40
❑ 9 Guinan .15 .40
❑ 10 Katherine Pulaski .15 .40
❑ 11 Lt. Tasha Yar .15 .40
❑ 12 Doctor Selar .15 .40
❑ 13 Lt. Reginald Barclay .15 .40
❑ 14 Robin Lefler .15 .40
❑ 15 Leah Brahms .15 .40
❑ 16 K'Ehleyr .15 .40
❑ 17 Miles O'Brien .15 .40
❑ 18 Kieko Ishikawa .15 .40
❑ 19 Alexander Rozhenko .15 .40
❑ 20 Chief Engineer Argyle .15 .40
❑ 21 Nurse Alyssa Ogawa .15 .40
❑ 22 Kyle Riker .15 .40
❑ 23 Thomas Riker .15 .40
❑ 24 Ambassador Sarek .15 .40
❑ 25 Surna Kolrami .15 .40
❑ 26 Ro Laren .15 .40
❑ 27 Gowron .15 .40
❑ 28 Lwaxana Troi .15 .40
❑ 29 The Traveler .15 .40
❑ 30 Admiral Mark Jameson .15 .40
❑ 31 Kosinski .15 .40
❑ 32 Mediator Riva .15 .40
❑ 33 Thadiun Okona .15 .40
❑ 34 Salia, the Dauphin .15 .40
❑ 35 Ves Alkar .15 .40
❑ 36 Sarjenka .15 .40
❑ 37 Lt. Richard Castillo .15 .40
❑ 38 Captain Rachel Garrett .15 .40
❑ 39 Vash .15 .40
❑ 40 Tam Elbrun .15 .40
❑ 41 Dathon .15 .40
❑ 42 Ira Graves .15 .40
❑ 43 Ambassador Spock .15 .40
❑ 44 Admiral McCoy .15 .40
❑ 45 Montgomery Scott .15 .40
❑ 46 Dr. Noonian Soong .15 .40
❑ 47 Dr. Paul Stubbs .15 .40
❑ 48 Captain Jellico .15 .40
❑ 49 Commander Bruce Maddox .15 .40
❑ 50 Lal .15 .40
❑ 51 Nikolai Rozhenko .15 .40
❑ 52 Sito Jaxa .15 .40
❑ 53 Amanda Rogers .15 .40
❑ 54 Etana Jol .15 .40
❑ 55 Q .15 .40
❑ 56 Lore .15 .40
❑ 57 Duras .15 .40
❑ 58 Lursa .15 .40
❑ 59 B'Etor .15 .40
❑ 60 Ardra .15 .40
❑ 61 DaiMon Bok .15 .40
❑ 62 Kevin Uxbridge .15 .40
❑ 63 Locutus of Borg .15 .40
❑ 64 Sela .15 .40
❑ 65 Commander Tomalak .15 .40
❑ 66 Cyrus Redblock .15 .40
❑ 67 Captain Korris .15 .40
❑ 68 Armus .15 .40
❑ 69 Voval .15 .40
❑ 70 Romulan Admiral Alidar Jarok .15 .40
❑ 71 Kivas Fajo .15 .40
❑ 72 Commander Kieran McDuff .15 .40
❑ 73 Gul Madred .15 .40
❑ 74 Arctus Baran .15 .40
❑ 75 Hugh .15 .40
❑ 76 Roga Danar .15 .40
❑ 77 Crystalline Entity .15 .40
❑ 78 DaiMon Tog .15 .40
❑ 79 Crosis .15 .40
❑ 80 Toral .15 .40
❑ 81 Kahless .15 .40
❑ 82 Ronin .15 .40
❑ 83 Commander Dexter Remmick .15 .40
❑ 84 Captain Benjamin Maxwell .15 .40
❑ 85 Subcommander Selok .15 .40
❑ 86 Boothby .15 .40
❑ 87 Professor Moriarty .15 .40
❑ 88 Berlinghoff Rasmussen .15 .40
❑ 89 Admiral Alynna Nechayev .15 .40
❑ 90 Yuta .15 .40
❑ 91 Antedean Dignitary .15 .40
❑ 92 Dr. Timicin .15 .40
❑ 93 Pakled Captain .15 .40
❑ 94 Jev (Ullian) .15 .40
❑ 95 Tallera .15 .40
❑ 96 Senator Pardek .15 .40
❑ 97 The Bynars .15 .40
❑ 98 Devinoni Ral .15 .40
❑ 99 Radue (Aldean) .15 .40
❑ 100 The Galaxy Class U.S.S. Enterprise .15 .40

2013 Star Trek The Next Generation Heroes and Villains Retro Parallel

COMPLETE SET 15.00 40.00
STATED ODDS 1:3

2013 Star Trek The Next Generation Heroes and Villains Autographs

FOUR AUTOS PER BOX

❑ 1 Amick Byram 4.00 10.00
as Commander Ian Andrew Troi
❑ 2 Armin Shimerman 15.00 40.00
as Quark EL
❑ 3 Bebe Neuwirth 15.00 40.00
as Nurse Lanel VL
❑ 4 Brenda Strong 6.00 15.00
as Rashella
❑ 5 Brian Markinson 8.00 20.00
as Vorin VL
❑ 6 Brian Thompson 5.00 12.00
as Klag
❑ 7 Carolyn Seymour 6.00 15.00
as Commander Toreth L
❑ 8 Christopher McDonald 6.00 15.00
as Lt. Richard Castillo
❑ 9 Cristine Rose 10.00 25.00
as Gi'ral VL
❑ 10 Daniel Stewart 6.00 15.00
as Batai L
❑ 11 Eric Pierpoint 12.00 30.00
as Voval VL
❑ 12 Gates McFadden 40.00 80.00
as Dr. Beverly Crusher EL
❑ 13 Harry Groener 8.00 20.00
as Tam Elbrun VL
❑ 14 Howie Seago 5.00 12.00
as Riva L
❑ 15 James Horan 20.00 50.00
as Jo'Bril EL
❑ 16 James Horan 20.00 50.00
as Lt. Barnaby EL
❑ 17 James Sloyan 4.00 10.00
as K'Mtar L
❑ 18 Jerry Hardin 30.00 60.00
as Samuel Clemens EL
❑ 19 Jill Jacobson 4.00 10.00
as Vanessa
❑ 20 John DeMita 4.00 10.00
as Romulan L
❑ 21 Kathryn Leigh Scott 5.00 12.00
as Nuria L
❑ 22 Ken Olandt 4.00 10.00
as Jason Vigo L
❑ 23 Lee Arenberg 5.00 12.00
as Diamon Bok L
❑ 24 LeVar Burton 40.00 80.00
as Lt. Commander Geordi La Forge EL
❑ 25 Linda Thorson 12.00 30.00
as Gul Ocett VL
❑ 26 Margot Rose 10.00 25.00
as Eline VL
❑ 27 Marie Marshall 5.00 12.00
as Kelsey L
❑ 28 Mark Rolston 6.00 15.00
as Lt. Walter Pierce L
❑ 29 Maryann Plunkett 5.00 12.00
as Lt. Commander Susan Leijten L
❑ 30 Michael Bofshever 4.00 10.00
as Quantum Singularity Lifeform L
❑ 31 Michael Corbett 4.00 10.00
as Dr. Rabal L
❑ 32 Michael Dorn 40.00 80.00
as Lt. Worf EL
❑ 33 Michael Reilly Burke 4.00 10.00
as Goval L
❑ 34 Michelle Forbes 30.00 60.00
as Dara EL
❑ 35 Michelle Forbes 30.00 60.00
as Ensign Ro Laren EL
❑ 36 Michelle Scarabelli 4.00 10.00
as Lt. Jenna D'Sora
❑ 37 Mickey Cottrell 4.00 10.00
as Chancellor Alrik
❑ 38 Norman Lloyd 4.00 10.00
as Professor Galen
❑ 39 Olivia d'Abo 40.00 80.00
as Amanda Rogers EL
❑ 40 Patrick Massett 5.00 12.00
as Duras L
❑ 41 Patrick Stewart 75.00 150.00
as Captain Jean-Luc Picard EL
❑ 42 Paul Eiding 4.00 10.00
as Ambassador Loquel L
❑ 43 Paul Sorvino 8.00 20.00
as Nikolai Rozhenko L
❑ 44 Penny Johnson Jerald 12.00 30.00
as Dobara VL
❑ 45 Richard Gilbert-Hill 4.00 10.00
as Bosus
❑ 46 Richard Herd 6.00 15.00
as L'Kor L
❑ 47 Robert Duncan McNeill 15.00 40.00
as Cadet Nicholas Locarno EL
❑ 48 Robin Curtis 12.00 30.00
as Tallera EL
❑ 49 Robin Gammell 12.00 30.00
as Mauric EL
❑ 50 Ronny Cox 6.00 15.00
as Captain Edward Jellico
❑ 51 Scott MacDonald 15.00 40.00
as N'Vek EL
❑ 52 Shay Astar 5.00 12.00
as Isabella
❑ 53 Terry O'Quinn 20.00 50.00
as Admiral Erik Pressman EL
❑ 54 Tim DeZarn 10.00 25.00
as Satler VL
❑ 55 Tim O'Connor 4.00 10.00
as Ambassador Briam
❑ 56 Tim Russ 35.00 70.00
as Devor EL
❑ 57 Tom Jackson 4.00 10.00
as Lakanta

❑ 58 Tracey D'Arcy 4.00 10.00
as Young Woman
❑ 59 Tricia O'Neil 30.00 60.00
as Captain Rachel Garrett EL
❑ 60 Tricia O'Neil 30.00 60.00
as Kurak EL
❑ 61 Denise Crosby/Quotable TNG 40.00 80.00
(issued as 3-case incentive)
❑ 62 Brent Spiner MEM/275 125.00 200.00

2013 Star Trek The Next Generation Heroes and Villains Montage Case Toppers

COMPLETE SET (2) 15.00 30.00
ONE PER CASE
❑ CT1 Heroes Montage 8.00 20.00
❑ CT2 Villains Montage 8.00 20.00

2013 Star Trek The Next Generation Heroes and Villains Posters

COMPLETE SET (5) 10.00 25.00
STATED ODDS 1:48
❑ PC1 Engage/Picard 3.00 8.00
❑ PC2 Resolve/Geordi 3.00 8.00
❑ PC3 Honor/Worf 3.00 8.00
❑ PC4 Inquire/Data 3.00 8.00
❑ PC5 Boldly/Enterprise 3.00 8.00

2013 Star Trek The Next Generation Heroes and Villains Promos

❑ P1 Q/Picard .60 1.50
(General Distribution)
❑ P2 Data 2.50 6.00
(NSU Magazine)
❑ P3 Picard 8.00 20.00
(Binder Exclusive)
❑ P4 Data
(2013 San Diego Comic Con)

2013 Star Trek The Next Generation Heroes and Villains Relics

STATED ODDS 1:96
❑ C10 Dr. Noonien Soong Costume 15.00 40.00
❑ C11 Klingon Costume 15.00 40.00
❑ C12 Eli Hollander Wanted Posters 15.00 40.00
❑ C13 Q Costume 15.00 40.00
❑ C14 Chorgan Costume 15.00 40.00
❑ C15 Romulan Costume 15.00 40.00
❑ C16 Romulan Costume 15.00 40.00
❑ C17 Nausicaan Costume 15.00 40.00

2013 Star Trek The Next Generation Heroes and Villains Remastered

COMPLETE SET (18) 10.00 25.00
STATED ODDS 1:12
❑ R1 TNG Remastered 1.00 2.50
❑ R2 TNG Remastered 1.00 2.50
❑ R3 TNG Remastered 1.00 2.50
❑ R4 TNG Remastered 1.00 2.50
❑ R5 TNG Remastered 1.00 2.50
❑ R6 TNG Remastered 1.00 2.50
❑ R7 TNG Remastered 1.00 2.50
❑ R8 TNG Remastered 1.00 2.50
❑ R9 TNG Remastered 1.00 2.50
❑ R10 TNG Remastered 1.00 2.50
❑ R11 TNG Remastered 1.00 2.50
❑ R12 TNG Remastered 1.00 2.50
❑ R13 TNG Remastered 1.00 2.50
❑ R14 TNG Remastered 1.00 2.50
❑ R15 TNG Remastered 1.00 2.50
❑ R16 TNG Remastered 1.00 2.50
❑ R17 TNG Remastered 1.00 2.50
❑ R18 TNG Remastered 1.00 2.50

2013 Star Trek The Next Generation Heroes and Villains Romance

COMPLETE SET (18) 8.00 20.00
STATED ODDS 1:12
❑ L1 Data/Tasha Yar .75 2.00
❑ L2 Troi/Wyatt Miller .75 2.00
❑ L3 Riker/Beata .75 2.00
❑ L4 Picard/Jenice Manheim .75 2.00
❑ L5 Wesley/Salia .75 2.00
❑ L6 Worf/K'Ehleyr .75 2.00
❑ L7 Troi/Devanani Ral .75 2.00
❑ L8 Picard/Vash .75 2.00
❑ L9 Riker/Troi .75 2.00
❑ L10 Geordi/Kristy Henshaw .75 2.00
❑ L11 O'Brien/Keiko .75 2.00
❑ L12 Lwaxanna/Timicin .75 2.00
❑ L13 Wesley/Robin Lefler .75 2.00
❑ L14 Riker/Ro Laren .75 2.00
❑ L15 Picard/Kamala .75 2.00
❑ L16 Picard/Nella Daren .75 2.00
❑ L17 Tasha Yar/Lt. Castillo .75 2.00
❑ L18 Troi/Worf .75 2.00

2013 Star Trek The Next Generation Heroes and Villains Undercover Heroes

COMP.SET w/o SP (9) 8.00 20.00
STATED ODDS 1:24
❑ H1 Captain Picard 1.50 4.00
Romulan in Unification: Parts I and II
❑ H2 Counselor Troi 1.50 4.00
Romulan in Face of the Enemy
❑ H3 Commander Riker 1.50 4.00
Malcorian in First Contact
❑ H4 Dr. Crusher 1.50 4.00
Barkonian in Thine Own Self
❑ H5 Lt. Commander Data 1.50 4.00
Romulan in Unification: Parts I and II
❑ H6 Lt. Worf 1.50 4.00
Boraalan in Homeward
❑ H7 Commander Riker 1.50 4.00
Barkonian in Thine Own Self
❑ H8 Commander Riker 1.50 4.00
Bajoran in Preemptive Strike
❑ H9 Counselor Troi 1.50 4.00
Mintakan in Who Watches the Watchers
❑ H10 Commander Riker 20.00 40.00
Mintakan (issued as Rittenhouse Reward) SP

2013 Star Trek The Original Series Heroes and Villains

COMPLETE SET (100) 5.00 12.00
❑ 1 Captain Kirk .15 .40
❑ 2 Spock .15 .40
❑ 3 Dr. McCoy .15 .40
❑ 4 Scotty .15 .40
❑ 5 Lt. Uhura .15 .40
❑ 6 Lt. Sulu .15 .40
❑ 7 Ensign Chekov .15 .40
❑ 8 Nurse Christine Chapel .15 .40
❑ 9 Yeoman Janice Rand .15 .40
❑ 10 Captain Pike .15 .40
❑ 11 The Keeper .15 .40
❑ 12 Vina .15 .40
❑ 13 Lt. Cmdr. Gary Mitchell .15 .40
❑ 14 Dr. Elizabeth Dehner .15 .40
❑ 15 Balok's Puppet .15 .40
❑ 16 Evil Captain Kirk .15 .40
❑ 17 M-113 Salt Creature .15 .40
❑ 18 Robert Crater .15 .40
❑ 19 Charlie Evans .15 .40
❑ 20 Romulan Commander .15 .40
❑ 21 Ruk .15 .40
❑ 22 Roger Korby .15 .40
❑ 23 Tristan Adams .15 .40
❑ 24 Dr. Helen Noel .15 .40
❑ 25 Miri .15 .40
❑ 26 Jahn .15 .40
❑ 27 Anton Karidian .15 .40
❑ 28 Lenore Karidian .15 .40
❑ 29 Commissioner Ferris .15 .40
❑ 30 Finney .15 .40
❑ 31 Cogley .15 .40
❑ 32 Finnegan .15 .40
❑ 33 Trelane .15 .40
❑ 34 Gorn Captain .15 .40
❑ 35 Lazarus .15 .40
❑ 36 Marplon .15 .40
❑ 37 Landru .15 .40
❑ 38 Anan 7 .15 .40
❑ 39 Khan Noonian Singh .15 .40
❑ 40 Marla McGivers .15 .40
❑ 41 Kor .15 .40
❑ 42 Edith Keeler .15 .40
❑ 43 Sylvia .15 .40
❑ 44 Korob .15 .40
❑ 45 Zefram Cochrane .15 .40
❑ 46 Kras .15 .40
❑ 47 Apollo .15 .40
❑ 48 Lt. Palamas .15 .40
❑ 49 T'Pring .15 .40
❑ 50 T'Pau .15 .40
❑ 51 Commodore Matt Decker .15 .40
❑ 52 Hengist/Jack the Ripper .15 .40
❑ 53 Nomad .15 .40
❑ 54 Dr. Janet Wallace .15 .40
❑ 55 Arne Darvin .15 .40
❑ 56 Koloth .15 .40
❑ 57 Henoch .15 .40
❑ 58 Merik .15 .40
❑ 59 Claudius .15 .40
❑ 60 Thelev .15 .40
❑ 61 Nona .15 .40
❑ 62 Galt .15 .40
❑ 63 Shahna .15 .40
❑ 64 Ensign Garrovick .15 .40
❑ 65 Bella Oxmyx .15 .40
❑ 66 Jojo Krako .15 .40
❑ 67 Rojan .15 .40
❑ 68 Kelinda .15 .40
❑ 69 Dr. Ann Mulhall .15 .40
❑ 70 Stonn .15 .40
❑ 71 Melakon .15 .40
❑ 72 Dr. Richard Daystrom .15 .40
❑ 73 Captain Ronald Tracey .15 .40
❑ 74 Gary Seven .15 .40
❑ 75 Elaan .15 .40
❑ 76 Harry Mudd .15 .40
❑ 77 Romulan Commander .15 .40
❑ 78 Gorgan .15 .40
❑ 79 Kara .15 .40
❑ 80 Dr. Miranda Jones .15 .40
❑ 81 Gem .15 .40
❑ 82 Vians .15 .40
❑ 83 Kang .15 .40
❑ 84 Alexander .15 .40
❑ 85 Parmen .15 .40
❑ 86 Deela .15 .40
❑ 87 Rael .15 .40
❑ 88 Losira .15 .40
❑ 89 Bele .15 .40
❑ 90 Garth .15 .40
❑ 91 Marta .15 .40
❑ 92 Hodin .15 .40
❑ 93 Plasus .15 .40
❑ 94 Droxine .15 .40
❑ 95 Dr. Sevrin .15 .40
❑ 96 Abraham Lincoln .15 .40
❑ 97 Colonel Green .15 .40
❑ 98 Surak .15 .40
❑ 99 Kahless .15 .40
❑ 100 Dr. Janice Lester .15 .40

2013 Star Trek The Original Series Heroes and Villains Autographs

STATED ODDS ONE PER BOX
❑ A202 Maggie Thrett 10.00 25.00
as Ruth Bonaventure L
❑ A236 Victor Brandt 8.00 20.00
as Watson L
❑ A242 Arlene Martel 12.00 30.00
as T'Pring L
❑ A249 Steve Sandor 6.00 15.00
as Lars
❑ A250 Robert Phillips 6.00 15.00
as Space Officer
❑ A251 Carolyn Nelson 6.00 15.00
as Yeoman Atkins
❑ A253 Morgan Jones 6.00 15.00
as Colonel Nesvig
❑ A254 Dyanne Thorne 6.00 15.00
as First Girl
❑ A255 Garth Pillsbury 8.00 20.00
as Wilson L
❑ A257 Brioni Farrell 8.00 20.00
as Tula
❑ A258 Sean Morgan 8.00 20.00
as Phaser Specialist Brenner L
❑ A260 Michael Barrier 10.00 25.00
as Lt. DeSalle L
❑ A262 David L. Ross 10.00 25.00
as Lt. Galloway L
❑ A264 Diana Muldaur 50.00 100.00
as Ann Mulhall VL
❑ A268 Nichelle Nichols 75.00 150.00
as Uhura EL
❑ A269 William Shatner 200.00 350.00
as Captain Kirk EL
❑ LN Leonard Nimoy 200.00 300.00
(issued as 6-case incentive)
❑ NN Nichelle Nichols MEM 75.00 150.00
(issued as 3-case incentive)

2013 Star Trek The Original Series Heroes and Villains Dual Autographs

STATED ODDS ONE PER BOX
❑ DA5 Leslie Shatner 150.00 300.00
Lisabeth Shatner EL
❑ DA7 William Shatner 350.00 500.00
Joan Collins EL
❑ DA8 Grace Lee Whitney 15.00 40.00
Robert Walker, Jr. L
❑ DA14 Nichelle Nichols 60.00 120.00
Walter Koenig VL
❑ DA20 Venita Wolf 15.00 40.00
William Campbell L
❑ DA21 Anthony Call 10.00 25.00
Clint Howard
❑ DA22 Bruce Hyde 10.00 25.00
Stewart Moss
❑ DA24 Warren Stevens 12.00 30.00
Barbara Bouchet L
❑ DA25 Sherry Jackson 10.00 25.00
Harry Basch
❑ DA26 Charles Napier 30.00 60.00
Victor Brandt VL
❑ DA27 Victor Brandt 40.00 80.00
Deborah Downey VL
❑ DA28 Charles Napier 12.00 30.00
Deborah Downey L
❑ DA29 Susan Howard 15.00 40.00
Michael Ansara L
❑ DA30 Gary Combs 12.00 30.00
Bobby Clark L
❑ DA31 Michael Forest 12.00 30.00
Leslie Parrish L
❑ DA33 Diana Muldaur 50.00 100.00
David Frankham VL
❑ DA34 Joseph Ruskin 10.00 25.00
Steve Sandor

2013 Star Trek The Original Series Heroes and Villains Kirk's Battles

COMPLETE SET (9) 6.00 15.00
STATED ODDS 1:12
❑ GB1 Captain Kirk vs. Khan 1.25 3.00
in Space Seed
❑ GB2 Captain Kirk vs. Gary Mitchell 1.25 3.00
in Where No Man Has Gone Before
❑ GB3 Captain Kirk vs. Romulan Commander 1.25 3.00
in Balance of Terror
❑ GB4 Captain Kirk vs. The Gorn 1.25 3.00
in Arena
❑ GB5 Captain Kirk vs. Shahna 1.25 3.00
in The Gamesters of Triskelion
❑ GB6 Captain Kirk vs. Kang 1.25 3.00
in Day of the Dove
❑ GB7 Captain Kirk vs. Spock 1.25 3.00
in Amok Time
❑ GB8 Captain Kirk vs. Romulan Commander 1.25 3.00
in The Enterprise Incident
❑ GB9 Captain Kirk vs. Captain Kirk 1.25 3.00
in The Enemy Within

2013 Star Trek The Original Series Heroes and Villains Mirror Mirror

COMPLETE SET (9) 12.00 30.00
STATED ODDS 1:24
❑ MM1 Kirk/Mirror Kirk 2.50 6.00
❑ MM2 Spock/Mirror Spock 2.50 6.00
❑ MM3 McCoy/Mirror McCoy 2.50 6.00
❑ MM4 Scotty/Mirror Scotty 2.50 6.00
❑ MM5 Uhura/Mirror Uhura 2.50 6.00
❑ MM6 Sulu/Mirror Sulu 2.50 6.00
❑ MM7 Chekov/Mirror Chekov 2.50 6.00
❑ MM8 Marlena/Mirror Marlena 2.50 6.00
❑ MM9 U.S.S. Enterprise/I.S.S. Enterprise 2.50 6.00

2013 Star Trek The Original Series Heroes and Villains Montage Case Toppers

COMPLETE SET (2) 20.00 40.00
STATED ODDS ONE PER CASE
❑ CT1 Heroes Montage 10.00 25.00
❑ CT2 Villains Montage 10.00 25.00

2013 Star Trek The Original Series Heroes and Villains Promos

❑ P1 Khan/Kirk .75 2.00
(General Distribution)
❑ P2 Spock/Kor 2.00 5.00
(NSU Magazine)
❑ P3 Keeper/Pike 10.00 25.00
(Binder Exclusive)

2013 Star Trek The Original Series Heroes and Villains Retro Parallel

COMPLETE SET 20.00 50.00
STATED ODDS 1:3

2013 Star Trek The Original Series Heroes and Villains Shadowbox

COMPLETE SET (7) 25.00 50.00
STATED ODDS 1:41
❑ S1 Captain Kirk 6.00 15.00
❑ S2 Spock 6.00 15.00
❑ S3 Dr. McCoy 5.00 12.00
❑ S4 Scotty 5.00 12.00
❑ S5 Uhura 5.00 12.00
❑ S6 Sulu 5.00 12.00
❑ S7 Chekov 5.00 12.00

2013 Star Trek The Original Series Heroes and Villains Tribute

COMPLETE SET w/o SP (12) 5.00 12.00
STATED ODDS 1:6
❑ T38 Virgil Earp from Spectre of the Gun .75 2.00
❑ T39 Salish from The Paradise Syndrome .75 2.00
❑ T40 Gorgan from And the Children Shall Lead .75 2.00
❑ T41 Thann from The Empath .75 2.00
❑ T42 Deela from Wink of an Eye .75 2.00
❑ T43 Lt. D'Amato from That Which Survives .75 2.00
❑ T44 Garth from Whom Gods Destroy .75 2.00
❑ T45 Cory from Whom Gods Destroy .75 2.00
❑ T46 Plasus from The Cloud Minders .75 2.00
❑ T47 Flint from Requiem for Methuselah .75 2.00
❑ T48 Abraham Lincoln from The Savage Curtain .75 2.00
❑ T49 The Prosecutor from All Our Yesterdays .75 2.00
❑ T50 Harry Mudd from I, Mudd
(issued as Rittenhouse Reward) SP

2013 True Blood Archives

COMPLETE SET (72) 5.00 12.00
❑ 1 Sookie Stackhouse .15 .40
❑ 2 Bill Compton .15 .40
❑ 3 Eric Northman .15 .40
❑ 4 Sam Merlotte .15 .40
❑ 5 Jason Stackhouse .15 .40
❑ 6 Tara Thornton .15 .40
❑ 7 Andy Bellefleur .15 .40
❑ 8 Arlene Fowler .15 .40
❑ 9 Lafayette Reynolds .15 .40
❑ 10 Hoyt Fortenberry .15 .40
❑ 11 Terry Bellefleur .15 .40
❑ 12 Jessica Hamby .15 .40
❑ 13 Pam De Beaufort .15 .40
❑ 14 Sheriff Bud Dearborne .15 .40
❑ 15 Alcide Herveaux .15 .40
❑ 16 Holly Cleary .15 .40
❑ 17 Steve Newlin .15 .40
❑ 18 Jesus Velasquez .15 .40
❑ 19 Luna Garza .15 .40
❑ 20 Tommy Mickens .15 .40
❑ 21 Nan Flanagan .15 .40
❑ 22 Maxine Fortenberry .15 .40
❑ 23 Lettie Mae Thornton .15 .40
❑ 24 Russell Edgington .15 .40
❑ 25 Maryann Forrester .15 .40
❑ 26 Rene Lenier .15 .40
❑ 27 Crystal Norris .15 .40
❑ 28 Debbie Pelt .15 .40
❑ 29 Eggs Benedict Talley .15 .40
❑ 30 Lorena Krasiki .15 .40
❑ 31 Nora Gainsborough .15 .40
❑ 32 Marnie Stonebrook .15 .40
❑ 33 Salome Agrippa .15 .40
❑ 34 Patrick Devins .15 .40
❑ 35 Sarah Newlin .15 .40
❑ 36 Godric .15 .40
❑ 37 Adele Stackhouse .15 .40
❑ 38 Melinda Mickens .15 .40
❑ 39 Cooter .15 .40
❑ 40 Talbot .15 .40
❑ 41 Franklin Mott .15 .40
❑ 42 Martha Bozeman .15 .40
❑ 43 Marcus Bozeman .15 .40
❑ 44 Amy Burley .15 .40
❑ 45 Gus .15 .40
❑ 46 Rikki .15 .40
❑ 47 Portia Bellefleur .15 .40
❑ 48 Jackson Herveaux .15 .40
❑ 99 Turn! Turn! Turn! .15 .40
❑ 100 Turn! Turn! Turn! .15 .40
❑ 101 Authority Always Wins .15 .40
❑ 102 Authority Always Wins .15 .40
❑ 103 Whatever I Am, You Made Me .15 .40
❑ 104 Whatever I Am, You Made Me .15 .40
❑ 105 We'll Meet Again .15 .40
❑ 106 We'll Meet Again .15 .40
❑ 107 Let's Boot and Rally .15 .40
❑ 108 Let's Boot and Rally .15 .40
❑ 109 Hopeless .15 .40
❑ 110 Hopeless .15 .40
❑ 111 In The Beginning .15 .40
❑ 112 In The Beginning .15 .40
❑ 113 Somebody That I Used To Know .15 .40
❑ 114 Somebody That I Used To Know .15 .40
❑ 115 Everybody Wants To Rule The World .15 .40
❑ 116 Everybody Wants To Rule The World .15 .40
❑ 117 Gone, Gone, Gone .15 .40
❑ 118 Gone, Gone, Gone .15 .40
❑ 119 Sunset .15 .40
❑ 120 Sunset .15 .40
❑ 121 Save Yourself .15 .40
❑ 122 Save Yourself .15 .40
❑ CT1 Season Six Preview 8.00 20.00
(issued as case topper)

2013 True Blood Archives Foil

COMPLETE SET (72) 15.00 40.00
STATED ODDS 1:3

2013 True Blood Archives Autographs

STATED ODDS 1:12
L (LIMITED): 300-500 COPIES
VL (VERY LIMITED): 200-300 COPIES
EL (EXTREMELY LIMITED): LESS THAN 200 COPIES
❑ 1 Alexander Skarsgard 60.00 120.00
as Eric Northman EL
❑ 2 Allan Hyde 8.00 20.00
as Godric L
❑ 3 Anna Camp 15.00 40.00
as Sarah Newlin EL
❑ 4 Anna Paquin 75.00 150.00
as Sookie Stackhouse EL
❑ 5 Carrie Preston 8.00 20.00
as Arlene Fowler L
❑ 6 Chris Bauer 12.00 30.00
as Sheriff Andy Bellefleur EL
❑ 7 Dale Raoul 6.00 15.00
as Maxine Fortenberry L
❑ 8 Deborah Ann Woll 40.00 80.00
as Jessica Hamby (issued as 3-case incentive)
❑ 9 Denis O'Hare 12.00 30.00
as Russell Edgington VL
❑ 10 Grant Bowler 8.00 20.00
as Cooter VL
❑ 11 J. Smith-Cameron 6.00 15.00
as Melinda Mickens L
❑ 12 James Frain 12.00 30.00
as Franklin Mott EL
❑ 13 Janina Gavankar 30.00 60.00
as Luna Garza EL
❑ 14 Jessica Tuck 8.00 20.00
as Nan Flanigan L
❑ 15 Jim Parrack 6.00 15.00
as Hoyt Fortenberry L
❑ 16 Kelly Overton 30.00 60.00
as Rikki EL
❑ 17 Kevin Alejandro 8.00 20.00
as Jesus Velasquez L
❑ 18 Kristin Bauer 12.00 30.00
as Pam De Beaufort L
❑ 19 Lauren Bowles 8.00 20.00
as Holly Cleary L
❑ 20 Mehcad Brooks 10.00 25.00
as Eggs VL
❑ 21 Michelle Forbes 15.00 40.00
as Maryann Forrester EL
❑ 22 Nelson Ellis 8.00 20.00
as Lafayette Reynolds L
❑ 23 Rutina Wesley 30.00 60.00
as Tara Thornton EL
❑ 24 Ryan Kwanten 40.00 80.00
as Jason Stackhouse EL
❑ 25 Stephen Moyer 100.00 175.00
as Bill Compton (issued as 6-case incentive)
❑ 26 Todd Lowe 10.00 25.00
as Terry Bellefleur VL
❑ 27 Valentina Cervi 20.00 50.00
as Salome EL
❑ 28 William Sanderson 10.00 25.00
as Sheriff Bud Dearborne EL

2013 True Blood Archives Costumes

COSTUME/PROP ODDS 1:24
❑ C1 Sookie Stackhouse shirt 10.00 25.00
❑ C2 Jason Stackhouse shirt 10.00 25.00
❑ C3 Jessica Hamby shirt 12.00 30.00
❑ C4 Pam De Beaufort dress 10.00 25.00
❑ C5 Sookie Stackhouse dress 10.00 25.00
❑ C6 Lorena dress 8.00 20.00
❑ C7 Maryann Forrester dress 8.00 20.00
❑ C8 Sam Merlotte shirt 10.00 25.00
❑ C9 Russell Edgington jacket 10.00 25.00
❑ C10 Sookie Stackhouse shirt 15.00 40.00
❑ C11 Pam De Beaufort jacket 8.00 20.00
❑ C12 Sookie Stackhouse dress 10.00 25.00
❑ C13 Arlene Fowler shirt UER 8.00 20.00
(identified as Sookie on back)
❑ C14 Sookie Stackhouse dress 10.00 25.00
❑ C15 Eric Northman shirt 10.00 25.00

2013 True Blood Archives Gallery Characters

COMPLETE SET (11) 15.00 40.00
STATED ODDS 1:24
❑ PL01 Sookie Stackhouse 4.00 10.00
❑ PL02 Sam Merlotte 3.00 8.00
❑ PL03 Bill Compton 3.00 8.00
❑ PL04 Jason Stackhouse 3.00 8.00
❑ PL05 Pam De Beaufort 3.00 8.00
❑ PL06 Lafayette Reynolds 3.00 8.00
❑ PL07 Eric Northman 3.00 8.00
❑ PL08 Alcide Herveaux 3.00 8.00
❑ PL09 Jessica Hamby 3.00 8.00
❑ PL10 Tara Thornton 3.00 8.00
❑ PL11 Russell Edgington 3.00 8.00

2013 True Blood Archives Promos

❑ P1 Jessica Hamby 1.50 4.00
(General Distribution)
❑ P2 Sookie Stackhouse 2.50 6.00
(Non-Sport Update)
❑ P3 Bill Compton
(Binder Exclusive)
❑ P4 Tara Thornton 2.00 5.00
(2013 Spring Philly Non-Sport Show)
❑ P5 Pam De Beaufort 2.00 5.00
(2013 San Diego Comic Con)

2013 True Blood Archives Props

COSTUME/PROP ODDS 1:24
❑ R1 Merlotte's Match Packs 10.00 25.00
❑ R2 Tru Blood Bottle Labels 12.00 30.00
❑ R3 Merlotte's Menu - FRONT 10.00 25.00
❑ R4 Merlotte's Menu - INSIDE 10.00 25.00

2013 True Blood Archives Quotable

COMP.SET w/o RR (12) 8.00 20.00
STATED ODDS 1:12
❑ Q11 Color Me Impressed 1.25 3.00
❑ Q12 I'm a Gay Vampire American 1.25 3.00
❑ Q13 If You Can Use Your Magic Hands 1.25 3.00
❑ Q14 I've No Interest In Being 1.25 3.00
❑ Q15 Jesus, Stackhouse 1.25 3.00
❑ Q16 Turning Your Own Flesh and Blood 1.25 3.00
❑ Q17 It Is My Job to Protect 1.25 3.00
❑ Q18 I Ain't Been to Med School 1.25 3.00
❑ Q19 There Are Two Thing I Try 1.25 3.00
❑ Q20 If I Wanted to Look Like a Drag Queen 1.25 3.00
❑ Q21 I'm a *****, Not a Snitch 1.25 3.00
❑ Q22 I've Seen Enough Horror Movies 1.25 3.00
❑ Q23 I Made Her Vampire 15.00 40.00
(issued as Rittenhouse Reward)

2013 True Blood Archives Relationships

COMPLETE SET (18) 10.00 25.00
STATED ODDS 1:8
❑ R01 Sookie and Bill 1.00 2.50
❑ R02 Sookie and Eric 1.00 2.50
❑ R03 Sam and Tara 1.00 2.50
❑ R04 Jessica and Jason 1.00 2.50
❑ R05 Jessica and Hoyt 1.00 2.50
❑ R06 Arlene and Terry 1.00 2.50
❑ R07 Eric and Nora 1.00 2.50
❑ R08 Eric and Pam 1.00 2.50
❑ R09 Tara and Eggs 1.00 2.50
❑ R10 Sam and Luna 1.00 2.50
❑ R11 Russell and Talbot 1.00 2.50
❑ R12 Alcide and Debbie 1.00 2.50
❑ R13 Sookie and Alcide 1.00 2.50
❑ R14 Andy and Holly 1.00 2.50
❑ R15 Jason and Crystal 1.00 2.50
❑ R16 Jason and Amy 1.00 2.50
❑ R17 Lafayette and Jesus 1.00 2.50
❑ R18 Bill and Lorena 1.00 2.50

2013 The Vampire Diaries Season Two

COMPLETE SET (69) 8.00 20.00
❑ 1 Getting Ready to Leave .25 .60
❑ 2 Caught Red-Handed .25 .60
❑ 3 Hate…The Beginning of a Love Story .25 .60
❑ 4 Elena Cares for Stefan .25 .60
❑ 5 Tyler's Anger .25 .60
❑ 6 Friendly Competition .25 .60
❑ 7 You Suck .25 .60
❑ 8 Caroline Sees Matt .25 .60
❑ 9 What is Wrong With Me .25 .60
❑ 10 Searching for Answers .25 .60
❑ 11 Dig Deeper .25 .60
❑ 12 A Werewolf and a Full Moon .25 .60
❑ 13 Misdirection .25 .60
❑ 14 A New Enemy .25 .60

❑ 15 Doppelganger .25 .60
❑ 16 Bad Day Bad Century .25 .60
❑ 17 White Flag .25 .60
❑ 18 A Secret Revealed .25 .60
❑ 19 Hi Mom .25 .60
❑ 20 Plan To Kill .25 .60
❑ 21 A Budding Romance .25 .60
❑ 22 A Masked Threat .25 .60
❑ 23 Feel That .25 .60
❑ 24 My Witch is Better Than Yours .25 .60
❑ 25 Road Trip Bonding .25 .60
❑ 26 Elijah Meets Elena .25 .60
❑ 27 Elena's Rescue .25 .60
❑ 28 Elijah Staked .25 .60
❑ 29 Distraction .25 .60
❑ 30 Doppelganger Pursuit .25 .60
❑ 31 A New Spell .25 .60
❑ 32 Burning the Portrait .25 .60
❑ 33 Dr. Jonas Martin .25 .60
❑ 34 Bump in the Night .25 .60
❑ 35 Transformation .25 .60
❑ 36 New Info .25 .60
❑ 37 Elena's Failed Plan .25 .60
❑ 38 Exploring the Cellar .25 .60
❑ 39 You've Been Marked .25 .60
❑ 40 Aftermath .25 .60
❑ 41 Wolf Bite .25 .60
❑ 42 Hallucination .25 .60
❑ 43 Farewell .25 .60
❑ 44 Stefan Traps Tyler .25 .60
❑ 45 Alliance .25 .60
❑ 46 Rescuing Caroline .25 .60
❑ 47 Romantic Weekend .25 .60
❑ 48 Elijah Smith .25 .60
❑ 49 Stefan and Damon at Odds .25 .60
❑ 50 Daggering an Original .25 .60
❑ 51 Finding Elena .25 .60
❑ 52 Playing Elena .25 .60
❑ 53 Astral Projection .25 .60
❑ 54 A Couple's Fight .25 .60
❑ 55 A Declaration .25 .60
❑ 56 An Epic Moment .25 .60
❑ 57 Newfound Magic .25 .60
❑ 58 The 60s .25 .60
❑ 59 Picking an Outfit .25 .60
❑ 60 Flirting With Danger .25 .60
❑ 61 Learning the Truth .25 .60
❑ 62 Brothers at Odds .25 .60
❑ 63 An Alternate Plan .25 .60
❑ 64 Matt's Ruse .25 .60
❑ 65 Meeting Klaus .25 .60
❑ 66 A Final Confession .25 .60
❑ 67 The Sacrifice Ritual .25 .60
❑ 68 A Vampire a Werewolf and the Doppelganger .25 .60
❑ 69 Checklist .25 .60

2013 The Vampire Diaries Season Two Autograph Wardrobe Memorabilia

OVERALL AUTO ODDS ONE PER BOX

❑ A1 Nina Dobrev 250.00 450.00
❑ A2 Paul Wesley 100.00 200.00
❑ A3 Ian Somerhalder 150.00 250.00

2013 The Vampire Diaries Season Two Autographs

OVERALL AUTO ODDS ONE PER BOX

❑ A4 Steven R McQueen 30.00 60.00
❑ A5 Kat Graham 30.00 60.00
❑ A6 Candice Accola 60.00 120.00
❑ A7 Zach Roerig 25.00 50.00
❑ A8 Michael Trevino 20.00 40.00
❑ A9 Matt Davis 20.00 40.00
❑ A10 Joseph Morgan 60.00 120.00
❑ A11 Sara Canning 25.00 50.00
❑ A12 Daniel Gillies 20.00 40.00
❑ A13 Michaela McManus 15.00 30.00
❑ A14 Taylor Kinney 10.00 25.00
❑ A15 Lauren Cohan 20.00 40.00
❑ A16 Bryton James 8.00 20.00
❑ A17 Randy J. Goodwin 8.00 20.00
❑ A18 Trent Ford 8.00 20.00
❑ A19 Dawn Olivieri 8.00 20.00
❑ A20 Susan Walters 8.00 20.00
❑ A21 Marguerite MacIntyre 15.00 30.00

2013 The Vampire Diaries Season Two Behind the Scenes

COMPLETE SET (9) 10.00 25.00
STATED ODDS 2:24

❑ BTS1 Bad Moon Rising 2.00 5.00
❑ BTS2 Nina and Ian 2.00 5.00
❑ BTS3 Ian and Steven 2.00 5.00
❑ BTS4 Masquerade 2.00 5.00
❑ BTS5 The Trio 2.00 5.00
❑ BTS6 Katerina 2.00 5.00
❑ BTS7 The Descent 2.00 5.00
❑ BTS8 The Sun Also Rises 2.00 5.00
❑ BTS9 The Return 2.00 5.00

2013 The Vampire Diaries Season Two Dual Wardrobe Memorabilia

OVERALL WARDROBE ODDS ONE PER BOX

❑ DM1 Mason Lockwood 10.00 25.00
Sheriff Forbes
❑ DM2 Damon Salvatore 25.00 50.00
Stefan Salvatore
❑ DM3 Elena Gilbert 25.00 50.00
Stefan Salvatore
❑ DM4 Matt Donovan 20.00 40.00
Caroline Forbes
❑ DM5 Elena Gilbert 30.00 60.00
Damon Salvatore
❑ DM6 Jeremy Gilbert 20.00 40.00
Bonnie Bennett

2013 The Vampire Diaries Season Two Katerina Petrova

COMPLETE SET (7) 8.00 20.00
STATED ODDS 2:24

❑ KP1 Mystery Girl 2.00 5.00
❑ KP2 Waiting 2.00 5.00
❑ KP3 Call Me Klaus 2.00 5.00
❑ KP4 The Original Brothers and Katerina 2.00 5.00
❑ KP5 Entertaining Katerina 2.00 5.00
❑ KP6 True Love 2.00 5.00
❑ KP7 Return Home 2.00 5.00

2013 The Vampire Diaries Season Two Promos

❑ P1 Stefan/Elena/Damon 2.00 5.00
(Non-Sport Update)
❑ P2 Damon/Elena/Stefan 3.00 8.00
(Chicago Non-Sport)

2013 The Vampire Diaries Season Two Wardrobe Memorabilia

OVERALL WARDROBE ODDS ONE PER BOX

❑ M1 Tyler Lockwood 8.00 20.00
❑ M2 Caroline Forbes 15.00 40.00
❑ M3 Caroline Forbes 15.00 40.00
❑ M4 Mason Lockwood 6.00 15.00
❑ M5 Sheriff Forbes 6.00 15.00
❑ M6 Stefan Salvatore 12.00 30.00
❑ M7 Damon Salvatore 15.00 40.00
❑ M8 Stefan Salvatore 12.00 30.00
❑ M9 Elena Gilbert 25.00 50.00
❑ M10 Damon Salvatore 15.00 40.00
❑ M11 Katherine Pierce 25.00 50.00
❑ M12 Rose 12.00 30.00
❑ M13 Jules 10.00 25.00
❑ M14 Jenna Sommers 12.00 30.00
❑ M15 Jeremy Gilbert 10.00 25.00
❑ M16 Rose 12.00 30.00
❑ M17 Katherine Pierce 25.00 50.00
❑ M18 Luka 6.00 15.00
❑ M19 Tyler Lockwood 8.00 20.00
❑ M20 Elena Gilbert 25.00 50.00
❑ M21 Caroline Forbes 15.00 40.00
❑ M22 Jules 10.00 25.00
❑ M23 Bonnie Bennett 15.00 40.00
❑ M24 Luka 6.00 15.00
❑ M25 Elena Gilbert 25.00 50.00
❑ M26 Mason Lockwood 6.00 15.00
❑ M27 Matt Donovan 8.00 20.00
❑ M28 Sheriff Forbes 6.00 15.00
❑ M29 Elena Gilbert 25.00 50.00

2013 Wacky Packages Series 10

COMPLETE SET (55) 6.00 15.00

❑ 1 Mtn Doom .25 .60
❑ 2 Flustered Flakes .25 .60
❑ 3 Milk Deads .25 .60
❑ 4 Taco Belch .25 .60
❑ 5 Pooper Mario Doo-D Land .25 .60
❑ 6 Pillsburied .25 .60
❑ 7 Play-Gogh .25 .60
❑ 8 Lite Sabers .25 .60
❑ 9 Reeper's .25 .60
❑ 10 B.O. Shock Ew .25 .60
❑ 11 Dungeon Donuts .25 .60
❑ 12 Petsi .25 .60
❑ 13 Peter Pawn .25 .60
❑ 14 Tubby Grahams .25 .60
❑ 15 Zombie Fitness .25 .60
❑ 16 Might Be Dog .25 .60
❑ 17 Pull Pop .25 .60
❑ 18 Scream of Wheat .25 .60
❑ 19 Rold Cold .25 .60
❑ 20 Tomb Gator .25 .60
❑ 21 Helly Belly .25 .60
❑ 22 Hippy Meal .25 .60
❑ 23 Fiber Won .25 .60
❑ 24 Green Chant .25 .60
❑ 25 Chronic Degenerates .25 .60
❑ 26 Blow Hole Pop .25 .60
❑ 27 Wuss in Boots .25 .60
❑ 28 Jack Stinks .25 .60
❑ 29 Ultra Tite .25 .60
❑ 30 Deers of War .25 .60
❑ 31 Allmud Joy .25 .60
❑ 32 Battlesheep .25 .60
❑ 33 Fruit of the Loon .25 .60
❑ 34 Bogus Burgers .25 .60
❑ 35 The Legend of Zelduh .25 .60
❑ 36 Crawley Rancher .25 .60
❑ 37 Diarrhea of a Windy Kid .25 .60
❑ 38 Pop-Farts .25 .60
❑ 39 Klepto-Bismal .25 .60
❑ 40 Mortal Komrades .25 .60
❑ 41 Chia Pest .25 .60
❑ 42 Chux Mix .25 .60
❑ 43 Cementos .25 .60
❑ 44 Easy Muck .25 .60
❑ 45 Feet Fighter .25 .60
❑ 46 Tric Tac .25 .60
❑ 47 Benadrool .25 .60
❑ 48 Newts and Adders .25 .60
❑ 49 Ninjagoo .25 .60
❑ 50 Mimecraft .25 .60
❑ 51 Newtella .25 .60
❑ 52 Pampered .25 .60
❑ 53 Lucky Germs .25 .60
❑ 54 Monster Thigh .25 .60
❑ 55 Snakers .25 .60

2013 Wacky Packages Series 10 Black

BLACK ODDS ONE PER COLLECT. ED. PACK

2013 Wacky Packages Series 10 Blue

OVERALL BLUE ODDS ONE PER HOBBY PACK

2013 Wacky Packages Series 10 Cloth

ODDS 1:21 COLL. ED. PACK, 1:607 RETAIL

2013 Wacky Packages Series 10 Gold

STATED ODDS 1:355

2013 Wacky Packages Series 10 Ludlow Back Black

LUDLOW BLACK ODDS 1:14 COLLECT. ED. PACK

2013 Wacky Packages Series 10 Ludlow Back Red

LUDLOW RED ODDS 1:84 COLLECT. ED. PACK

2013 Wacky Packages Series 10 Red

RED ODDS ONE PER COLLECT. ED. PACK

2013 Wacky Packages Series 10 Silver

OVERALL SILVER ODDS 1:8

2013 Wacky Packages Series 10 Printing Plates Black

STATED PRINT RUN 1 SER. #'d SET
UNPRICED DUE TO SCARCITY

2013 Wacky Packages Series 10 Printing Plates Cyan

STATED PRINT RUN 1 SER. #'d SET
UNPRICED DUE TO SCARCITY

2013 Wacky Packages Series 10 Printing Plates Magenta

STATED PRINT RUN 1 SER. #'d SET
UNPRICED DUE TO SCARCITY

2013 Wacky Packages Series 10 Printing Plates Yellow

STATED PRINT RUN 1 SER. #'d SET
UNPRICED DUE TO SCARCITY

2013 Wacky Packages Series 10 Artist Autographs

STATED PRINT RUN 15 SER. #'d SETS

❑ 1 Smokin Joe McWilliams 30.00 60.00
❑ 2 Fred Wheaton 40.00 80.00
❑ 3 Junghwa Im 30.00 60.00
❑ 4 TBD
❑ 5 Brent Engstrom 50.00 100.00
❑ 6 Joe Simko 40.00 80.00
❑ 7 Junghwa Im 30.00 60.00
❑ 8 TBD
❑ 9 Neil Camera 35.00 70.00
❑ 10 Brent Engstrom 50.00 100.00
❑ 11 Smokin Joe McWilliams 30.00 60.00
❑ 12 TBD
❑ 13 TBD
❑ 14 Joe Simko 40.00 80.00
❑ 15 Brent Engstrom 50.00 100.00
❑ 16 Junghwa Im 30.00 60.00
❑ 17 Sam Gambino 30.00 60.00
❑ 18 Matthew Kirscht 20.00 40.00
❑ 19 Claude St. Aubin
❑ 20 Brent Engstrom 50.00 100.00
❑ 21 TBD
❑ 22 Smokin Joe McWilliams 30.00 60.00
❑ 23 Fred Wheaton 40.00 80.00
❑ 24 Pat Chaimuang
❑ 25 Brent Engstrom 50.00 100.00
❑ 26 Junghwa Im 30.00 60.00
❑ 27 Mark Pingitore
❑ 28 Sam Gambino 30.00 60.00
❑ 29 Smokin Joe McWilliams 30.00 60.00
❑ 30 TBD
❑ 31 Fred Wheaton 40.00 80.00
❑ 32 Joe Simko 40.00 80.00
❑ 33 TBD
❑ 34 Brent Engstrom 50.00 100.00
❑ 35 Brent Engstrom 50.00 100.00
❑ 36 Joe Simko 40.00 80.00
❑ 37 Neil Camera 35.00 70.00
❑ 38 Mark Pingitore
❑ 39 Junghwa Im 30.00 60.00
❑ 40 TBD
❑ 41 Sam Gambino 30.00 60.00
❑ 42 Junghwa Im 30.00 60.00
❑ 43 Neil Camera 35.00 70.00
❑ 44 Junghwa Im 30.00 60.00
❑ 45 Brent Engstrom 50.00 100.00
❑ 46 John Zeleznik
❑ 47 Junghwa Im 30.00 60.00
❑ 48 Brent Engstrom 50.00 100.00
❑ 49 John Zeleznik
❑ 50 Brent Engstrom 50.00 100.00
❑ 51 Junghwa Im 30.00 60.00
❑ 52 Brent Engstrom 50.00 100.00
❑ 53 Junghwa Im 30.00 60.00
❑ 54 Brent Engstrom 50.00 100.00
❑ 55 Smokin Joe McWilliams 30.00 60.00

2013 Wacky Packages Series 10 As Screamed on TV

COMPLETE SET (10) 6.00 15.00
*CLOTH: 1X TO 2.5X BASIC CARDS
STATED ODDS 1:2 HOBBY

❑ 1 Pillow Pest 1.00 2.50
❑ 2 Ya Mama Jeans 1.00 2.50
❑ 3 Lice-O-Matic 1.00 2.50
❑ 4 Oximoron Clean 1.00 2.50
❑ 5 Snake Weight 1.00 2.50
❑ 6 Edge of Glory 1.00 2.50
❑ 7 Pickpocket Fisherman 1.00 2.50
❑ 8 Magic Mullet 1.00 2.50
❑ 9 Pet Ridder 1.00 2.50
❑ 10 SlamPow 1.00 2.50

2013 Wacky Packages Series 10 As Screamed on TV Cloth

COMPLETE SET 6.00 15.00
OVERALL CLOTH ODDS 1:21 COLLECTOR EDITION PACK

2013 Wacky Packages Series 10 As Screamed on TV Printing Plates Black

STATED PRINT RUN 1 SER. #'d SET
UNPRICED DUE TO SCARCITY

2013 Wacky Packages Series 10 As Screamed on TV Printing Plates Cyan

STATED PRINT RUN 1 SER. #'d SET
UNPRICED DUE TO SCARCITY

2013 Wacky Packages Series 10 As Screamed on TV Printing Plates Magenta

STATED PRINT RUN 1 SER. #'d SET
UNPRICED DUE TO SCARCITY

2013 Wacky Packages Series 10 As Screamed on TV Printing Plates Yellow

STATED PRINT RUN 1 SER. #'d SET
UNPRICED DUE TO SCARCITY

2013 Wacky Packages Series 10 Awful Apps

COMPLETE SET (10) 5.00 12.00
*CLOTH: 1.2X TO 3X BASIC CARDS
STATED ODDS 1:2 HOBBY

❑ 1 Boogle .75 2.00
❑ 2 Ya-Who .75 2.00
❑ 3 Dump .75 2.00
❑ 4 Aimless .75 2.00
❑ 5 MySpaced .75 2.00
❑ 6 eAlimony .75 2.00
❑ 7 Instagrime .75 2.00
❑ 8 YouTube .75 2.00
❑ 9 Nyetflix .75 2.00
❑ 10 Cut the Cheese .75 2.00

2013 Wacky Packages Series 10 Awful Apps Cloth

COMPLETE SET
OVERALL CLOTH ODDS 1:21 COLLECTOR EDITION PACK

2013 Wacky Packages Series 10 Awful Apps Printing Plates Black

STATED PRINT RUN 1 SER. #'d SET
UNPRICED DUE TO SCARCITY

2013 Wacky Packages Series 10 Awful Apps Printing Plates Cyan

STATED PRINT RUN 1 SER. #'d SET
UNPRICED DUE TO SCARCITY

2013 Wacky Packages Series 10 Awful Apps Printing Plates Magenta

STATED PRINT RUN 1 SER. #'d SET
UNPRICED DUE TO SCARCITY

2013 Wacky Packages Series 10 Awful Apps Printing Plates Yellow

STATED PRINT RUN 1 SER. #'d SET
UNPRICED DUE TO SCARCITY

2013 Wacky Packages Series 10 Billboards

COMPLETE SET (6) 20.00 50.00
ONE PER COLLECTOR EDITION BOX

❑ 1 Crappy Barrel 5.00 12.00
❑ 2 Grab the Throne 5.00 12.00
❑ 3 Scare Bear Stare 5.00 12.00
❑ 4 Upchuck E. Cheese's 5.00 12.00
❑ 5 Windy's Burgers 5.00 12.00
❑ 6 Working Dead 5.00 12.00

2013 Wacky Packages Series 10 Bonus

COMPLETE SET (14)
B1-B6 ODDS
B7-B14 ODDS 1:14 COLLECTOR EDITION PACK

❑ B1 3 Racketeers
❑ B2 Special DK
❑ B3 Hi-Sea
❑ B4 Robo
❑ B5 Refuzit
❑ B6 Fancy Beast
❑ B7 Clubbed
❑ B8 Blue Bombit
❑ B9 Done
❑ B10 Taser's Choice
❑ B11 Ghoulette
❑ B12 5-Hour Anarchy
❑ B13 The Woman with the Draggin' Tattoo
❑ B14 Rice-A-Romney

2013 Wacky Packages Series 10 Cereal Box Bonus

COMPLETE SET (9)
STATED ODDS

❑ C1 Tix
❑ C2 Raisin Brain
❑ C3 Apple Jerks
❑ C4 Fruity Peppers
❑ C5 Honey Tomb
❑ C6 Grape News
❑ C7 Frite Loops
❑ C8 Frothing Flakes
❑ C9 Rice Kreepies

2013 Wacky Packages Series 10 Commercial Star Autographs

❑ 1 Jimmy Nelson 8.00 20.00
Nestle's Quik
❑ 2 John Gilchrist 12.00 30.00
Life Cereal
❑ 3 John Moschitta, Jr. 4.00 10.00
Micro Machines
❑ 4 Matt Frewer 10.00 25.00
Coca-Cola
❑ 5 Wendy Kaufman 6.00 15.00
Snapple

2013 Wacky Packages Series 10 Lost Wackys

STATED ODDS 1:84 COLLECTOR EDITION PACK

❑ L1 Growgerm 40.00 100.00
❑ L2 The Mumps 40.00 100.00
❑ L3 Shebad 40.00 100.00

2013 Wacky Packages Series 10 Magnets

COMPLETE SET (10) 30.00 70.00
STATED ODDS 1:12

❑ 1 Jolly Mean Giant 4.00 10.00
❑ 2 Cap'n Crud 4.00 10.00
❑ 3 Fool-Aid 4.00 10.00
❑ 4 Dirtycell 4.00 10.00
❑ 5 Kick Kat 4.00 10.00
❑ 6 Corn Butts 4.00 10.00
❑ 7 Asparagus Jacks 4.00 10.00
❑ 8 Slime Jim 4.00 10.00
❑ 9 Trux 4.00 10.00
❑ 10 Granny Theft Auto 4.00 10.00

2013 Wacky Packages Series 10 Tattoos

COMPLETE SET (10) 12.00 30.00
STATED ODDS 1:6

❑ 1 Burger Thing 2.00 5.00
❑ 2 My Spittle Pony 2.00 5.00
❑ 3 Jelly Bully 2.00 5.00
❑ 4 Ghoulfish 2.00 5.00
❑ 5 Crooker Jack 2.00 5.00
❑ 6 Chops Ahoy 2.00 5.00
❑ 7 Pooper Mario Doo-D Land 2.00 5.00
❑ 8 Battlesheep 2.00 5.00
❑ 9 Ninjagoo 2.00 5.00
❑ 10 Mimecraft 2.00 5.00

2013 The Walking Dead Comic Book 2 Something to Fear

COMPLETE SET (9)
STATED ODDS 2:24

❑ STF1 Part 1
❑ STF2 Part 2
❑ STF3 Part 3
❑ STF4 Part 4
❑ STF5 Part 5
❑ STF6 Part 6
❑ STF7 Negan Reprint Part 1
❑ STF8 Negan Reprint Part 2
❑ STF9 Negan Reprint Part 3

2013 Warehouse 13 Season Four

COMPLETE SET (20) 20.00 50.00

❑ 1 A New Hope 2.00 5.00
❑ 2 A New Hope 2.00 5.00
❑ 3 An Evil Within 2.00 5.00
❑ 4 An Evil Within 2.00 5.00
❑ 5 Personal Effects 2.00 5.00
❑ 6 Personal Effects 2.00 5.00
❑ 7 There's Always a Downside 2.00 5.00
❑ 8 There's Always a Downside 2.00 5.00
❑ 9 No Pain, No Gain 2.00 5.00
❑ 10 No Pain, No Gain 2.00 5.00
❑ 11 Fractures 2.00 5.00
❑ 12 Fractures 2.00 5.00
❑ 13 Endless Wonder 2.00 5.00
❑ 14 Endless Wonder 2.00 5.00
❑ 15 Second Chance 2.00 5.00
❑ 16 Second Chance 2.00 5.00
❑ 17 The Ones You Love 2.00 5.00
❑ 18 The Ones You Love 2.00 5.00
❑ 19 We All Fall Down 2.00 5.00
❑ 20 We All Fall Down 2.00 5.00
❑ BT1 Claudia/Pete/Myka/Artie 8.00 20.00
(issued as box topper)

2013 Warehouse 13 Season Four Autograph Relics

ONE AUTO OR AUTO RELIC PER PACK

❑ 1 Allison Scagliotti/150 50.00 100.00
as Claudia Donovan
❑ 2 Brent Spiner jacket/160 40.00 80.00
as Brother Adrian
❑ 3 CCH Pounder jacket/150 20.00 50.00
as Mrs. Irene Frederic from The 40th Floor
❑ 4 Genelle Williams blouse/150 20.00 50.00
as Leena from The New Guy
❑ 5 Jamie Murray/150 50.00 100.00
as H. G. Wells
❑ 6 Joanne Kelly jacket/160 40.00 80.00
as Myka Bering
❑ 7 Jeri Ryan dress/107 75.00 150.00
as Amanda from / (issued as 2-box incentive)
❑ 8 Eddie McClintock jacket
as Pete Lattimer from Pilot/ (issued as 4-box incentive)

2013 Warehouse 13 Season Four Autographs

ONE AUTO OR AUTO RELIC PER PACK

❑ 1 Allison Scagliotti 15.00 40.00
as Claudia Donovan
❑ 2 Ashley Williams 8.00 20.00
as Sally Stukowski
❑ 3 Brent Spiner 30.00 60.00
as Brother Adrian
❑ 4 CCH Pounder 8.00 20.00
as Mrs. Irene Frederic
❑ 5 Genelle Williams 10.00 25.00
as Leena
❑ 6 Jamie Murray 20.00 50.00
as H. G. Wells
❑ 7 Jeri Ryan 50.00 100.00
as Amanda
❑ 8 Joanne Kelly 15.00 40.00
as Myka Bering

2013 Warehouse 13 Season Four Grand Designs

COMPLETE SET (10) 20.00 50.00
OVERALL CHASE ODDS ONE PER PACK

❑ GD1 Grand Designs - Chapter 1 3.00 8.00
❑ GD2 Grand Designs - Chapter 2 3.00 8.00
❑ GD3 Grand Designs - Chapter 3 3.00 8.00
❑ GD4 Grand Designs - Chapter 4 3.00 8.00
❑ GD5 Grand Designs - Chapter 5 3.00 8.00
❑ GD6 Grand Designs - Chapter 6 3.00 8.00
❑ GD7 Grand Designs - Chapter 7 3.00 8.00
❑ GD8 Grand Designs - Chapter 8 3.00 8.00
❑ GD9 Grand Designs - Chapter 9 3.00 8.00
❑ GD10 Grand Designs - Chapter 10 3.00 8.00

2013 Warehouse 13 Season Four Of Monsters and Men

COMPLETE SET (10) 15.00 40.00
OVERALL CHASE ODDS ONE PER PACK

❑ MM1 The City of Ghouls - Chapter 1 2.50 6.00
❑ MM2 The City of Ghouls - Chapter 2 2.50 6.00
❑ MM3 The City of Ghouls - Chapter 3 2.50 6.00
❑ MM4 The City of Ghouls - Chapter 4 2.50 6.00
❑ MM5 The City of Ghouls - Chapter 5 2.50 6.00
❑ MM6 The City of Ghouls - Chapter 6 2.50 6.00
❑ MM7 The City of Ghouls - Chapter 7 2.50 6.00
❑ MM8 The City of Ghouls - Chapter 8 2.50 6.00
❑ MM9 The City of Ghouls - Chapter 9 2.50 6.00
❑ MM10 The City of Ghouls - Chapter 10 2.50 6.00

2013 Warehouse 13 Season Four Promos

❑ P1 Pete/Claudia/Steve .75 2.00
(General Distribution)
❑ P2 Artie/Claudia .60 1.50
(2013 Spring Philly Non-Sport)

2013 Warehouse 13 Season Four Relics

TWO RELICS PER PACK

❑ 1 Artie Nielsen red shirt/450 5.00 12.00
from A New Hope
❑ 2 Artie Nielsen tweed shirt/350 5.00 12.00
from Around the Bend
❑ 3 Brother Adrian jacket/150 15.00 40.00
from A New Hope
❑ 4 Claudia Donovan kimono/350 10.00 25.00
from No Pain No Gain
❑ 5 Claudia Donovan sweater/350 10.00 25.00
from Beyond Our Control
❑ 6 Dr. Vanessa Calder blouse/150 15.00 40.00
❑ 7 H.G. Wells shirt/150 30.00 60.00
❑ 8 Hugo Miller/350 DUAL 8.00 20.00
from 13.1
❑ 9 Kate Logan blouse/350 6.00 15.00
from Around the Bend
❑ 10 Kate Logan jacket/450 6.00 15.00
from Around the Bend
❑ 11 Leena blouse/450 6.00 15.00
from Resonance
❑ 12 Mrs. Irene Frederic/450 5.00 12.00
from Breakdown
❑ 13 Myka Bering jacket/350 8.00 20.00
from For the Team
❑ 14 Myka Bering shirt/450 8.00 20.00
from The New Guy
❑ 15 Pete Lattimer shirt/350 5.00 12.00
from Time Will Tell
❑ 16 Pete Lattimer skirt/450 5.00 12.00
from Don't Hate the Player
❑ 17 Sally Stukowski shirt/450 5.00 12.00
from The New Guy
❑ 18 Steve Jinks jacket/450 5.00 12.00
from We All Fall Down
❑ 19 Steve Jinks shirt/450 5.00 12.00
from Personal Effects
❑ 20 Pete Lattimer tie/150 25.00 50.00
from Age Before Beauty/ (issued as 2-box incentive)

STAR WARS

HOW TO USE

What's Listed
Products listed in the Price Guide typically: 1) are produced by licensed manufacturers, 2) are widely available and 3) have market activity on single items.

What the Columns Mean
The LO and HI columns reflect current retail selling ranges. The HI column on the right generally represents the full retail selling price. The LO column on the left generally represents the lowest price one would expect to find with extensive shopping.

Grading
All cards in the Price Guide are based on NrMint to Mint condition. Damaged cards are generally sold for 25 to 75 percent of Mint value. Toy prices are based on mint condition. Toys that are loose (out of package), are generally sold for 50 percent of the listed price.

Currency
This Price Guide is intended to reflect the entire North American market. All listed prices are in U.S. dollars.

Please Note: Beckett does not sell single cards or figures.

Beckett Star Wars price guide sponsored by wholesalegaming.com

1977-78 Star Wars 12-Backs
❑ 10 Ben Kenobi white hair 125.00 250.00
❑ 20 Ben Kenobi grey hair 125.00 250.00
❑ 30 C-3PO 75.00 150.00
❑ 40 Chewbacca 125.00 225.00
❑ 50 Darth Vader 150.00 300.00
❑ 51 Darth Vader/ telescoping lightsaber
❑ 60 Death Squad Commander 125.00 225.00
❑ 70 Han Solo large head 200.00 400.00
❑ 80 Han Solo small head 250.00 500.00
❑ 90 Jawa 150.00 300.00
❑ 91 Jawa plastic cape 1200.00 1600.00
❑ 100 Luke Skywalker/ blond hair 150.00 300.00
❑ 110 Luke Skywalker/ brown hair 200.00 400.00
❑ 120 Princess Leia 150.00 225.00
❑ 130 R2-D2 100.00 200.00
❑ 140 Stormtrooper 50.00 100.00
❑ 150 Tusken Raider 100.00 200.00

1977-78 Star Wars 20/21-Backs
❑ 10 Ben Kenobi grey hair 75.00 150.00
❑ 20 Ben Kenobi white hair 75.00 150.00
❑ 30 Boba Fett 250.00 500.00
❑ 40 C-3PO 50.00 100.00
❑ 50 Chewbacca 60.00 120.00
❑ 60 Darth Vader 100.00 200.00
❑ 70 Death Squad Commander 60.00 120.00
❑ 80 Death Star Droid 75.00 150.00
❑ 90 Greedo 60.00 120.00
❑ 100 Hammerhead 100.00 200.00
❑ 110 Han Solo/ large head 200.00 350.00
❑ 111 Han Solo/ small head 200.00 350.00
❑ 120 Jawa 75.00 150.00
❑ 130 Luke Skywalker/ blond hair 150.00 300.00
❑ 131 Luke Skywalker/ brown hair 200.00 400.00
❑ 140 Luke Skywalker X-wing 125.00 250.00
❑ 150 Princess Leia 125.00 225.00
❑ 160 Power Droid 50.00 100.00
❑ 170 R2-D2 50.00 100.00
❑ 180 R5-D4 75.00 150.00
❑ 190 Snaggletooth red 60.00 120.00
❑ 200 Stormtrooper 50.00 100.00
❑ 210 Tusken Raider 60.00 120.00
❑ 220 Walrusman 60.00 120.00

1977-78 Star Wars (loose)
❑ 10 Ben Kenobi grey hair 10.00 20.00
❑ 11 Ben Kenobi white hair 10.00 20.00
❑ 20 Boba Fett 25.00 50.00
❑ 30 C-3PO 10.00 20.00
❑ 40 Chewbacca 7.50 15.00
❑ 50 Darth Vader 10.00 20.00
❑ 60 Death Squad Commander 6.00 12.00
❑ 70 Death Star Droid 7.50 15.00
❑ 80 Greedo 7.50 15.00
❑ 90 Hammerhead 7.50 15.00
❑ 100 Han Solo large head 10.00 20.00
❑ 101 Han Solo small head 12.50 25.00
❑ 110 Jawa 7.50 15.00
❑ 120 Luke Skywalker blond hair 10.00 20.00
❑ 121 Luke Skywalker brown hair 12.50 25.00
❑ 130 Luke Skywalker X-wing 10.00 20.00
❑ 140 Power Droid 7.50 15.00
❑ 150 Princess Leia 7.50 15.00
❑ 160 R2-D2 7.50 15.00
❑ 170 R5-D4 7.50 15.00
❑ 180 Snaggletooth blue/ found in cantina playset7.50 15.00
❑ 181 Snaggletooth red 7.50 15.00
❑ 190 Stormtrooper 7.50 15.00
❑ 200 Tusken Raider 7.50 15.00
❑ 210 Walrusman 7.50 15.00

1978 Star Wars Accessories
❑ 10 Mini Collector's Case 50.00 100.00

1978 Star Wars Accessories (loose)
❑ 10 Mini Collector's Case 15.00 30.00

1978 Star Wars Playsets
❑ 10 Cantina Adventure Set/Greedo/Sanggletooth blue/Hammerhead/Walrusman 150.00 300.00
❑ 20 Death Star Space Station 250.00 500.00
❑ 30 Droid Factory 200.00 400.00
❑ 40 Land of the Jawas 60.00 120.00

1978 Star Wars Playsets (loose)
❑ 10 Cantina Adventure Set/Greedo/Sanggletooth blue/Hammerhead/Walrusman 50.00 100.00
❑ 20 Death Star Space Station 75.00 150.00
❑ 30 Droid Factory 30.00 60.00
❑ 40 Land of the Jawas 30.00 60.00

1978 Star Wars Vehicles
❑ 10 Imperial Troop Transporter 200.00 400.00
❑ 20 Land Speeder 125.00 250.00
❑ 30 Millenium Falcon 700.00 1200.00
❑ 40 Patrol Dewback 125.00 250.00
❑ 50 TIE Fighter 75.00 150.00
❑ 60 TIE Fighter Darth Vader 150.00 300.00
❑ 70 X-Wing Fighter 100.00 200.00

1978 Star Wars Vehicles (loose)
❑ 10 Imperial Troop Transporter 15.00 30.00
❑ 20 Land Speeder 15.00 30.00
❑ 30 Millenium Falcon 75.00 150.00
❑ 40 Patrol Dewback 25.00 50.00
❑ 50 TIE Fighter 25.00 50.00
❑ 60 TIE Fighter Darth Vader 30.00 60.00
❑ 70 X-Wing Fighter 30.00 60.00

1979-80 Star Wars 12-inch
❑ 10 Ben Kenobi 125.00 225.00
❑ 20 Boba Fett 250.00 500.00
❑ 30 C-3PO 125.00 250.00
❑ 40 Chewbacca 100.00 200.00
❑ 50 Darth Vader 150.00 300.00
❑ 60 Han Solo 125.00 250.00
❑ 70 IG-88 200.00 400.00
❑ 80 Jawa 100.00 200.00
❑ 90 Luke Skywalker 125.00 250.00
❑ 100 Princess Leia 125.00 250.00
❑ 110 R2-D2 100.00 200.00
❑ 120 Stormtrooper 200.00 350.00

1979-80 Star Wars 12-inch (loose)
❑ 10 Ben Kenobi 50.00 100.00
❑ 20 Boba Fett 60.00 120.00
❑ 30 C-3PO 20.00 40.00
❑ 40 Chewbacca 30.00 60.00
❑ 50 Darth Vader 50.00 100.00
❑ 60 Han Solo 60.00 120.00
❑ 70 IG-88 100.00 200.00
❑ 80 Jawa 25.00 50.00
❑ 90 Luke Skywalker 30.00 60.00
❑ 100 Princess Leia 30.00 60.00
❑ 110 R2-D2 25.00 50.00
❑ 120 Stormtrooper 25.00 50.00

1980 Star Wars Empire Strikes Back Micro Set
❑ 10 Bespin Control Room/Darth Vader/Darth Vader lightsaber/Luke Skywalker/L 30.00 60.00
❑ 20 Bespin Freeze Chamber/Boba Fett 75.00 150.00 Darth Vader/Han Solo in cuffs/Han Solo
❑ 30 Bespin Gantry/Darth Vader/Darth 40.00 80.00 Vader lightsaber/Luke Skywalker/Luke Sk
❑ 40 Bespin World/Boba Fett/Darth 100.00 200.00 Vader/Darth Vader lightsaber/Han Solo carb
❑ 50 Death Star Compactor/Ben 125.00 225.00 Kenobi/Darth Vader lightsaber/Han Solo stormtro
❑ 60 Death Star Escape/Chewbacca 40.00 80.00 Darth Vader/Luke Skywalker/Princess Leia/S
❑ 70 Death Star World/Ben Kenobi 125.00 225.00 Chewbacca/Darth Vader/Darth Vader lightsaber/Han Solo/Luke Skywalker/Luke Skywalker stormtrooper/Princess Leia/Princess Leia holding gun/Stormtrooper kneeling/Stormtrooper walking/Stormtrooper firing/Stormtrooper firing up/Stormtrooper injured
❑ 80 Hoth Generator Attack/AT-AT/AT-AT 30.00 60.00 Operator/Darth Vader unpainted/Rebel
❑ 90 Hoth Ion Cannon/Rebel on 50.00 100.00 Tauntaun/Rebel crouching/Rebel laying/Rebel wi
❑ 100 Hoth Turret Defense/Rebel on 40.00 80.00 Tauntaun blaster/Rebel crouching/Rebel layi
❑ 110 Hoth Wampa Cave/Chewbacca/Han 30.00 60.00 Solo/Luke Skywalker hanging/Probot/Wampa
❑ 120 Hoth World/Includes Hot Wampa 100.00 200.00 Cave/Hoth Ion Cannon/Hoth Generator Attack
❑ 130 Imperial TIE Fighter/TIE Fighter Pilot 50.00 100.00
❑ 140 Millenium Falcon/C-3PO/Chewbacca 150.00 300.00 with wrench/Lando Calrissian/Luke Skyw
❑ 150 Snowspeeder/X-Wing Pilot 75.00 150.00 sitting/X-Wing Pilot crouching
❑ 160 X-Wing/X-Wing Pilot 75.00 150.00

1980 Star Wars Empire Strikes Back Micro Set (loose)
❑ 10 Bespin Control Room 7.50 15.00
❑ 20 Bespin Freeze Chamber 12.50 25.00
❑ 30 Bespin Gantry 7.50 15.00
❑ 40 Bespin World 12.50 25.00
❑ 50 Death Star Compactor 12.50 25.00
❑ 60 Death Star Escape 7.50 15.00
❑ 70 Death Star World 12.50 25.00
❑ 80 Hoth Generator Attack 7.50 15.00
❑ 90 Hoth Ion Cannon 10.00 20.00
❑ 100 Hoth Turret Defense 6.00 12.00
❑ 110 Hoth Wampa Cave 7.50 15.00
❑ 120 Hoth World 12.50 25.00
❑ 130 Imperial Tie Fighter 6.00 12.00
❑ 140 Millenium Falcon 12.50 25.00
❑ 150 Snowspeeder 6.00 12.00
❑ 160 X-Wing 7.50 15.00
❑ 170 AT-AT 6.00 12.00
❑ 180 AT-AT Operator .75 2.00
❑ 190 Ben Kenobi 1.50 4.00
❑ 200 Boba Fett .75 2.00
❑ 210 C-3PO .75 2.00
❑ 220 Chewbacca .75 2.00
❑ 230 Chewbacca with wrench .75 2.00
❑ 240 Darth Vader 1.25 3.00
❑ 250 Darth Vader lightsaber 1.25 3.00
❑ 260 Darth Vader unpainted 1.25 3.00
❑ 270 Han Solo 1.25 3.00
❑ 280 Han Solo carbonite 1.25 3.00
❑ 290 Han Solo in cuffs 1.25 3.00
❑ 300 Han Solo stormtrooper 1.25 3.00
❑ 310 Lando Calrissian .75 2.00
❑ 320 Lobot .75 2.00
❑ 330 Luke Skywalker 1.25 3.00
❑ 340 Luke Skywalker hanging 1.25 3.00
❑ 350 Luke Skywalker lightsaber 1.25 3.00
❑ 360 Luke Skywalker stormtrooper 1.25 3.00
❑ 370 Princess Leia 1.25 3.00
❑ 380 Princess Leia holding gun 1.25 3.00
❑ 390 Probot .75 2.00
❑ 400 Rebel crouching .75 2.00
❑ 410 Rebel gun at side/ unpainted .75 2.00
❑ 420 Rebel gun on hip/ unpainted .75 2.00
❑ 430 Rebel gun on sholder/ unpainted .75 2.00
❑ 440 Rebel gun on shoulder .75 2.00
❑ 450 Rebel laying .75 2.00
❑ 460 Rebel laying unpainted .75 2.00
❑ 470 Rebel on Tauntaun .75 2.00
❑ 480 Rebel on Tauntaun blaster .75 2.00
❑ 490 Rebel with blaster at side .75 2.00
❑ 500 Rebel with blaster brown .75 2.00
❑ 510 Rebel with blaster white .75 2.00
❑ 520 Stormtrooper .75 2.00
❑ 530 Stormtrooper firing .75 2.00
❑ 540 Stormtrooper kneeling .75 2.00
❑ 550 Stormtrooper on gun .75 2.00
❑ 560 Stormtrooper walking .75 2.00
❑ 570 TIE Fighter Pilot .75 2.00
❑ 580 Turret Operator .75 2.00
❑ 590 Wampa 1.00 2.50
❑ 600 X-Wing Pilot .75 2.00
❑ 610 X-Wing Pilot crouching .75 2.00
❑ 620 X-Wing Pilot sitting .75 2.00

1980 Star Wars Empire Strikes Back Mini Rigs
❑ 10 CAP-2 10.00 20.00
❑ 20 INT-4 20.00 40.00
❑ 30 MLC-3 12.50 25.00
❑ 40 MTV-7 20.00 40.00
❑ 50 PDT-8 15.00 30.00
❑ 60 Tripod Laser Canon 20.00 40.00

1980 Star Wars Empire Strikes Back Mini Rigs (loose)
❑ 10 CAP-2 5.00 10.00
❑ 20 INT-4 7.50 15.00
❑ 30 MLC-3 5.00 10.00
❑ 40 MTV-7 6.00 12.00
❑ 50 PDT-8 7.50 15.00
❑ 60 Tripod Laser Canon 7.50 15.00

1980-82 Star Wars Empire Strikes Back
❑ 10 2-1B 30.00 60.00
❑ 20 4-LOM 75.00 150.00
❑ 30 AT-AT Commander 30.00 60.00
❑ 40 AT-AT Driver 40.00 80.00
❑ 50 Ben Kenobi grey hair 50.00 100.00
❑ 60 Ben Kenobi white hair 50.00 100.00
❑ 70 Bespin guard black 30.00 60.00
❑ 80 Bespin guard white 30.00 60.00
❑ 90 Boba Fett 150.00 300.00
❑ 100 Bossk 50.00 100.00
❑ 110 C-3PO 30.00 120.00
❑ 120 C-3PO removable limbs 30.00 120.00
❑ 130 Chewbacca 50.00 100.00
❑ 140 Cloud Car Pilot 80.00
❑ 150 Darth Vader 100.00 200.00
❑ 160 Death Squad Commander 150.00 300.00
❑ 170 Death Star Droid 50.00 100.00
❑ 180 Dengar 60.00 120.00
❑ 190 FX-7 50.00 100.00
❑ 200 Greedo 50.00 100.00
❑ 210 Hammerhead 50.00 100.00
❑ 220 Han Solo bespin 60.00 120.00
❑ 230 Han Solo hoth gear 50.00 100.00
❑ 240 Han Solo large head 60.00 120.00
❑ 250 Han Solo small head 60.00 120.00
❑ 260 IG-88 60.00 120.00
❑ 270 Imperial Commander 30.00 60.00
❑ 280 Imperial Stormtrooper 60.00 120.00
❑ 290 Jawa 40.00 80.00
❑ 300 Lando Calrissian 40.00 80.00
❑ 310 Lando Calrissian no teeth 40.00 80.00
❑ 360 Lobot 40.00 80.00
❑ 370 Luke Skywalker/ bespin fatigues 100.00 200.00 yellow hair tan legs
❑ 371 Luke Skywalker/ bespin fatigues/ yellow hair brown legs
❑ 380 Luke Skywalker/ bespin fatigues/ brown hair100.00 200.00
❑ 390 Luke Skywalker bespin/ white shirt blond hair100.00200.00
❑ 400 Luke Skywalker bespin 125.00 250.00 white shirt brown hair
❑ 410 Luke Skywalker hoth gear 50.00 100.00
❑ 420 Luke Skywalker X-wing 50.00 100.00
❑ 430 Power Droid 60.00 120.00
❑ 435 Princess Leia Organa/ bespin flesh neck60.00 120.00
❑ 436 Princess Leia Organa/ bespin turtle neck
❑ 437 Princess Leia Organa/ bespin gold neck/ sometimes looks green
❑ 438 Princess Leia Organa/ hoth gear 60.00 120.00
❑ 440 R2-D2 60.00 120.00
❑ 441 R2-D2 sensorscope 75.00 150.00
❑ 450 R5-D4
❑ 460 Rebel Commander 40.00 80.00
❑ 470 Rebel Soldier hoth gear 30.00 60.00
❑ 480 Snaggletooth red 40.00 80.00
❑ 490 Stormtrooper 50.00 100.00
❑ 500 TIE Fighter Pilot 50.00 100.00
❑ 510 Tusken Raider 50.00 100.00
❑ 520 Ugnaught 30.00 60.00
❑ 530 Walrusman 50.00 100.00
❑ 540 Wampa 50.00 100.00
❑ 550 Yoda brown snake 100.00 200.00
❑ 560 Yoda orange snake 75.00 150.00
❑ 570 Zuckuss 50.00 100.00

1980-82 Star Wars Empire Strikes Back Accessories
❑ 10 Darth Vader Case 200.00 350.00
❑ 20 Darth Vader Case/Boba Fett/IG88 200.00 400.00
❑ 30 Mini Collector's Case 125.00 225.00

1980-82 Star Wars Empire Strikes Back Accessories (loose)
❑ 10 Darth Vader Case 15.00 30.00
❑ 20 Mini Collector's Case 15.00 30.00

1980-82 Star Wars Empire Strikes Back (loose)
❑ 10 2-1B 6.00 12.00
❑ 20 4-LOM 12.50 25.00
❑ 30 AT-AT Commander 6.00 12.00
❑ 40 AT-AT Driver 7.50 15.00
❑ 50 Ben Kenobi grey hair 10.00 20.00
❑ 60 Ben Kenobi white hair 10.00 20.00
❑ 70 Bespin guard black 6.00 12.00
❑ 80 Bespin guard white 6.00 12.00
❑ 90 Boba Fett 25.00 50.00
❑ 100 Bossk 7.50 15.00
❑ 110 C-3PO 7.50 15.00
❑ 120 C-3PO removable limbs 7.50 15.00
❑ 130 Chewbacca 6.00 12.00
❑ 140 Cloud Car Pilot 6.00 12.00
❑ 150 Darth Vader 10.00 20.00
❑ 160 Death Squad Commander 10.00 20.00
❑ 170 Death Star Droid 6.00 12.00
❑ 180 Dengar 6.00 12.00
❑ 190 FX-7 6.00 12.00
❑ 200 Greedo 6.00 12.00
❑ 210 Hammerhead 6.00 12.00
❑ 220 Han Solo bespin 7.50 15.00
❑ 230 Han Solo hoth gear 6.00 12.00
❑ 240 Han Solo large head 6.00 12.00
❑ 250 Han Solo small head 6.00 12.00
❑ 260 IG-88 7.50 15.00
❑ 270 Imperial Commander 6.00 12.00
❑ 280 Imperial Stormtrooper 7.50 15.00
❑ 290 Jawa 6.00 12.00
❑ 300 Lando Calrissian 6.00 12.00
❑ 310 Lando Calrissian no teeth 6.00 12.00
❑ 360 Lobot 7.50 15.00
❑ 370 Luke Skywalker/ bespin fatigues 10.00 20.00 yellow hair tan legs
❑ 371 Luke Skywalker/ bespin fatigues/ yellow hair brown legs
❑ 380 Luke Skywalker/ bespin fatigues/ brown hair10.00 20.00
❑ 390 Luke Skywalker bespin/ white shirt blond hair12.50 20.00
❑ 400 Luke Skywalker bespin/ white shirt brown hair12.50 25.00
❑ 410 Luke Skywalker hoth gear 6.00 12.00
❑ 420 Luke Skywalker X-wing 6.00 12.00
❑ 430 Power Droid 7.50 15.00
❑ 435 Princess Leia Organa/ bespin flesh neck 7.50 15.00
❑ 436 Princess Leia Organa/ bespin turtle neck 7.50 15.00
❑ 437 Princess Leia Organa/ bespin gold neck/ sometimes looks green
❑ 438 Leia Organa hoth gear 7.50 15.00
❑ 440 R2-D2 7.50 15.00
❑ 441 R2-D2 sensorscope 7.50 15.00
❑ 450 R5-D4
❑ 460 Rebel Commander 6.00 12.00
❑ 470 Rebel Soldier hoth gear 6.00 12.00
❑ 480 Snaggletooth red 6.00 12.00
❑ 490 Stormtrooper 6.00 12.00
❑ 500 TIE Fighter Pilot 6.00 12.00
❑ 510 Tusken Raider 6.00 12.00
❑ 520 Ugnaught 12.00
❑ 530 Walrusman 6.00 12.00
❑ 540 Wampa 15.00 30.00
❑ 550 Yoda brown snake 7.50 15.00
❑ 560 Yoda orange snake 7.50 15.00
❑ 570 Zuckuss 6.00 12.00

1980-82 Star Wars Empire Strikes Back Playsets
❑ 10 Cloud City 200.00 400.00
❑ 20 Dagobah 125.00 250.00
❑ 30 Darth Vader/ Star Destroyer 125.00 250.00
❑ 40 Droid Factory 200.00 350.00
❑ 50 Hoth Ice Planet 75.00 150.00
❑ 60 Imperial Attack Base 125.00 225.00
❑ 70 Land of the Jawas 100.00 200.00
❑ 80 Rebel Command Center 100.00 200.00
❑ 90 Turret and Probot 40.00 80.00

1980-82 Star Wars Empire Strikes Back Playsets (loose)
❑ 10 Cloud City 30.00 60.00
❑ 20 Dagobah 25.00 50.00
❑ 30 Darth Vader/ Star Destroyer 25.00 50.00
❑ 40 Droid Factory 30.00 60.00
❑ 50 Hoth Ice Planet 20.00 40.00
❑ 60 Imperial Attack Base 30.00 60.00
❑ 70 Land of the Jawas 30.00 60.00
❑ 80 Rebel Command Center 30.00 60.00
❑ 90 Turret and Probot 12.50 25.00

1980-82 Star Wars Empire Strikes Back Vehicles
❑ 10 AT-AT 150.00 300.00
❑ 20 Imperial Cruiser 100.00 200.00
❑ 30 Imperial Transport 100.00 200.00
❑ 40 Millenium Falcon 150.00 300.00
❑ 50 Patrol Dewback 100.00 200.00
❑ 60 Rebel Transport 100.00 200.00
❑ 70 Scout Walker 75.00 150.00
❑ 80 Slave 1 100.00 200.00
❑ 90 Snowspeeder blue box 60.00 120.00
❑ 91 Snowspeeder pink box 75.00 150.00
❑ 100 Tauntaun 50.00 100.00
❑ 120 Tauntaun split belly 60.00 120.00
❑ 130 TIE Fighter 75.00 150.00
❑ 140 Twin Pod Cloud Car 40.00 80.00
❑ 150 X-Wing Fighter/ battle damage 100.00 200.00 red photo background box
❑ 160 X-Wing Fighter/ battle damage 100.00 200.00 landscape photo/ background box

1980-82 Star Wars Empire Strikes Back Vehicles (loose)
❑ 10 AT-AT 40.00 80.00
❑ 20 Imperial Cruiser 15.00 30.00

Powered By: www.WholesaleGaming.com

❑ 30 Imperial Transport 15.00 30.00
❑ 40 Millenium Falcon 50.00 100.00
❑ 50 Patrol Dewback 25.00 50.00
❑ 60 Rebel Transport 15.00 30.00
❑ 70 Scout Walker 15.00 30.00
❑ 80 Slave 1 20.00 40.00
❑ 90 Snowspeeder 15.00 30.00
❑ 100 Tauntaun 20.00 40.00
❑ 110 Tauntaun split belly 25.00 50.00
❑ 120 TIE Fighter 25.00 50.00
❑ 130 Twin Pod Cloud Car 20.00 40.00
❑ 140 X-Wing Fighter 30.00 60.00

1983 Star Wars Return of the Jedi

❑ 10 2-1B 40.00 80.00
❑ 20 4-LOM 40.00 80.00
❑ 30 8D8 25.00 50.00
❑ 40 Admiral Ackbar 25.00 50.00
❑ 50 AT-AT Commander 25.00 50.00
❑ 60 AT-AT Driver 40.00 80.00
❑ 70 AT-ST Driver 20.00 40.00
❑ 80 B-Wing Pilot 20.00 40.00
❑ 90 Ben Kenobi blue saber 30.00 60.00
❑ 100 Ben Kenobi grey hair 25.00 50.00
❑ 110 Ben Kenobi white hair 25.00 50.00
❑ 120 Bespin Guard black 30.00 60.00
❑ 130 Bespin Guard white 30.00 60.00
❑ 140 Bib Fortuna 25.00 50.00
❑ 150 Biker Scout/ long mask 40.00 80.00
❑ 151 Biker Scout/ short mask 75.00 150.00
❑ 160 Boba Fett/ photo card 150.00 300.00
❑ 161 Boba Fett/ space scene card 175.00 350.00
❑ 170 Bossk 40.00 80.00
❑ 180 C-3PO removable limbs 40.00 80.00
❑ 190 Chewbacca 40.00 80.00
❑ 200 Chief Chirpa 20.00 40.00
❑ 210 Cloud Car Pilot 30.00 60.00
❑ 220 Darth Vader 60.00 120.00
❑ 230 Death Squad Commander
❑ 240 Death Star Droid 30.00 60.00
❑ 250 Dengar 30.00 60.00
❑ 251 Dengar free/ nien nunb logo front 40.00 80.00
❑ 252 Dengar white face 50.00 100.00
❑ 260 Emperor 40.00 80.00
❑ 270 Emperors Royal Guard 40.00 80.00
❑ 280 FX-7 30.00 60.00
❑ 290 Gamorrean Guard 25.00 50.00
❑ 300 General Madine 20.00 40.00
❑ 310 Greedo 40.00 80.00
❑ 320 Hammerhead 25.00 50.00
❑ 330 Han Solo/ free emperor offer 100.00 200.00
❑ 340 Han Solo bespin 60.00 120.00
❑ 341 Han Solo bespin/ nien nunb logo front 60.00 120.00
❑ 360 Han Solo hoth gear 60.00 120.00
❑ 370 Han Solo trench coat 30.00 60.00
❑ 380 IG-88 30.00 60.00
❑ 390 Imperial Commander 40.00 80.00
❑ 400 Imperial Stormtrooper 40.00 80.00
❑ 405 Imperial TIE Fighter Pilot 50.00 100.00
❑ 410 Jawa 50.00 100.00
❑ 420 Klaatu 20.00 40.00
❑ 430 Klaatu skiff 20.00 40.00
❑ 431 Klaatu Skiff/ free coin sticker 20.00 40.00
❑ 440 Lando Calrissian 30.00 60.00
❑ 450 Lando Calrissian skiff 25.00 50.00
❑ 480 Lobot 30.00 60.00
❑ 490 Logray 20.00 40.00
❑ 500 Luke Skywalker
❑ 510 Luke Skywalker/ bespin fatigues 100.00 200.00
yellow hair tan legs
❑ 511 Luke Skywalker/ bespin fatigues 100.00 200.00
yellow hair brown legs
❑ 520 Luke Skywalker/ bespin fatigues/ brown hair150.00 300.00
❑ 530 Luke Skywalker bespin/ white shirt blond hair125.00225.00
❑ 540 Luke Skywalker bespin/ white shirt brown hair125.00250.00
❑ 550 Luke Skywalker/ gunner card 300.00 600.00
❑ 560 Luke Skywalker hoth gear 60.00 120.00
❑ 570 Luke Skywalker jedi/ blue lightsaber 75.00 150.00
❑ 580 Luke Skywalker jedi/ green lightsaber 75.00 150.00
❑ 590 Luke Skywalker X-wing 100.00 200.00
❑ 600 Lumat 40.00 80.00
❑ 610 Nien Nunb 25.00 50.00
❑ 620 Nikto 20.00 40.00
❑ 630 Paploo 40.00 80.00
❑ 640 Power Droid 50.00 100.00
❑ 650 Princess Leia Organa 400.00 800.00
❑ 655 Princess Leia Organa/ bespin flesh neck
❑ 656 Princess Leia Organa/ bespin turtle neck30.00 60.00
❑ 657 Princess Leia Organa/ bespin
gold neck/ sometimes looks green
❑ 660 Princess Leia Organa/ boussh 40.00 80.00
❑ 670 Princess Leia Organa/ hoth gear 125.00 225.00
❑ 680 Princess Leia Organa/ poncho 40.00 80.00
❑ 690 Prune Face 20.00 40.00
❑ 700 R2-D2 sensorscope 40.00 80.00
❑ 710 R5-D4 50.00 100.00
❑ 720 Rancor 40.00 80.00
❑ 730 Rancor Keeper 20.00 40.00
❑ 740 Rebel Commander 30.00 60.00
❑ 750 Rebel Commando 20.00 40.00
❑ 760 Rebel Soldier hoth gear 50.00 100.00
❑ 770 Ree-Yees 20.00 40.00
❑ 780 Sand People 40.00 80.00
❑ 790 Snaggletooth red 50.00 100.00
❑ 800 Squid Head 20.00 40.00
❑ 810 Stormtrooper 50.00 100.00
❑ 820 Sy Snootles/ and Rebo Band 40.00 80.00
Max Rebo/Droopy McCool
❑ 830 Teebo 20.00 40.00
❑ 840 TIE Fighter Pilot 40.00 80.00
❑ 850 Ugnaught 40.00 80.00
❑ 860 Walrusman 30.00 60.00
❑ 870 Weequay 20.00 40.00
❑ 880 Wicket 40.00 80.00
❑ 890 Yoda brown snake 60.00 120.00
❑ 900 Zuckuss 20.00 40.00

1983 Star Wars Return of the Jedi Accessories

❑ 10 C-3PO Case 30.00 60.00
❑ 20 Chewy Strap 25.00 50.00
❑ 30 Darth Vader Case 75.00 150.00
❑ 40 Jedi Vinyl Case 100.00 200.00
❑ 50 Laser Rifle Case 40.00 80.00

1983 Star Wars Return of the Jedi Accessories (loose)

❑ 10 C-3PO Case 15.00 30.00
❑ 20 Chewy Strap 15.00 30.00
❑ 30 Darth Vader Case 15.00 30.00
❑ 40 Jedi Vinyl Case 15.00 30.00
❑ 50 Laser Rifle Case 15.00 30.00

1983 Star Wars Return of the Jedi (loose)

❑ 10 2-1B 6.00 12.00
❑ 20 4-LOM 12.50 25.00
❑ 30 8D8 6.00 12.00
❑ 40 Admiral Ackbar 6.00 12.00
❑ 45 Amanaman 40.00 80.00
❑ 50 AT-AT Commander 6.00 12.00
❑ 60 AT-AT Driver 7.50 15.00
❑ 70 AT-ST Driver 6.00 12.00
❑ 80 B-Wing Pilot 5.00 10.00
❑ 85 Barada 10.00 20.00
❑ 90 Ben Kenobi blue saber 10.00 20.00
❑ 100 Ben Kenobi grey hair 10.00 20.00
❑ 110 Ben Kenobi white hair 10.00 20.00
❑ 120 Bespin Guard black 6.00 12.00
❑ 130 Bespin Guard white 6.00 12.00
❑ 140 Bib Fortuna 5.00 10.00
❑ 150 Biker Scout/ long mask 5.00 10.00
❑ 151 Biker Scout/ short mask 7.50 15.00
❑ 160 Boba Fett 25.00 50.00
❑ 170 Bossk 7.50 15.00
❑ 180 C-3PO removable limbs 7.50 15.00
❑ 190 Chewbacca 6.00 12.00
❑ 200 Chief Chirpa 5.00 10.00
❑ 210 Cloud Car Pilot 6.00 12.00
❑ 220 Darth Vader 10.00 20.00
❑ 230 Death Squad Commander 10.00 20.00
❑ 240 Death Star Droid 6.00 12.00
❑ 250 Dengar 6.00 12.00
❑ 251 Dengar white face 7.50 15.00
❑ 260 Emperor 7.50 15.00
❑ 270 Emperors Royal Guard 6.00 12.00
❑ 280 FX-7 6.00 12.00
❑ 290 Gamorrean Guard 5.00 10.00
❑ 300 General Madine 5.00 10.00
❑ 310 Greedo 6.00 12.00
❑ 320 Hammerhead 6.00 12.00
❑ 330 Han Solo 7.50 15.00
❑ 340 Han Solo bespin 6.00 12.00
❑ 345 Han Solo carbonite 40.00 80.00
❑ 350 Han Solo hoth gear 6.00 12.00
❑ 370 Han Solo trench coat 6.00 12.00
❑ 380 IG-88 7.50 15.00
❑ 390 Imperial Commander 6.00 12.00
❑ 395 Imperial Dignitary 20.00 40.00
❑ 397 Imperial Gunner 20.00 40.00
❑ 400 Imperial Stormtrooper 7.50 15.00
❑ 405 Imperial TIE Fighter Pilot 6.00 12.00
❑ 410 Jawa 6.00 12.00
❑ 420 Klaatu 5.00 10.00
❑ 430 Klaatu skiff 5.00 10.00
❑ 440 Lando Calrissian 6.00 12.00
❑ 450 Lando Calrissian skiff 6.00 12.00
❑ 480 Lobot 7.50 15.00
❑ 490 Logray 5.00 10.00
❑ 500 Luke Skywalker 10.00 20.00
❑ 510 Luke Skywalker/ bespin fatigues 10.00 20.00
yellow hair tan legs
❑ 511 Luke Skywalker/ bespin fatigues/ yellow hair brown legs
❑ 520 Luke Skywalker/ bespin fatigues/ brown hair10.00 20.00
❑ 530 Luke Skywalker bespin/ white shirt blond hair10.00 20.00
❑ 540 Luke Skywalker bespin/ white shirt brown hair12.50 25.00
❑ 560 Luke Skywalker hoth gear 6.00 12.00
❑ 570 Luke Skywalker jedi/ blue lightsaber 6.00 12.00
❑ 580 Luke Skywalker jedi/ green lightsaber 10.00 20.00
❑ 590 Luke Skywalker X-wing 50.00 100.00
❑ 600 Lumat 10.00 20.00
❑ 610 Nien Nunb 5.00 10.00
❑ 620 Nikto 5.00 10.00
❑ 630 Paploo 5.00 10.00
❑ 640 Power Droid 5.00 10.00
❑ 650 Princess Leia Organa 5.00 10.00
❑ 655 Princess Leia Organa/ bespin flesh neck 10.00 20.00
❑ 656 Princess Leia Organa/ bespin turtle neck 7.50 15.00
❑ 657 Princess Leia Organa/ bespin 7.50 15.00
gold neck/ sometimes looks green
❑ 660 Princess Leia Organa/ boussh
❑ 670 Princess Leia Organa/ hoth gear 7.50 15.00
❑ 680 Princess Leia Organa/ poncho 7.50 15.00
❑ 690 Prune Face 7.50 15.00
❑ 700 R2-D2 sensorscope 5.00 10.00
❑ 710 R5-D4 7.50 15.00
❑ 720 Rancor 7.50 15.00
❑ 730 Rancor Keeper 20.00 40.00
❑ 740 Rebel Commander 5.00 10.00
❑ 750 Rebel Commando 5.00 10.00
❑ 760 Rebel Soldier hoth gear 5.00 10.00
❑ 770 Ree-Yees 6.00 12.00
❑ 775 Romba 5.00 10.00
❑ 780 Sand People
❑ 790 Snaggletooth red 6.00 12.00
❑ 795 Snowtrooper 6.00 12.00
❑ 800 Squid Head 15.00 30.00
❑ 810 Stormtrooper 5.00 10.00
❑ 820 Sy Snootles 6.00 12.00
❑ 821 Droopy McCool 5.00 10.00
❑ 822 Max Rebo 5.00 10.00
❑ 830 Teebo 5.00 10.00
❑ 850 Ugnaught 5.00 10.00
❑ 858 Luke Skywalker/ stormtrooper 5.00 10.00
❑ 860 Walrusman 5.00 10.00
❑ 870 Weequay 6.00 12.00
❑ 880 Wicket 5.00 10.00
❑ 890 Yoda brown snake 7.50 15.00
❑ 900 Zuckuss 6.00 12.00

1983 Star Wars Return of the Jedi Playsets

❑ 10 Ewok Village 100.00 200.00
❑ 20 Jabba The Hutt(#Salacious Crumb 30.00 60.00
❑ 30 Jabba The Hutt Dungeon/Klaatu/Nikto/8D875.00 150.00
❑ 40 Jabba The Hutt Dungeon/EV-9D9/Amanaman/Barada 75.00 150.00

1983 Star Wars Return of the Jedi Playsets (loose)

❑ 10 Ewok Village 30.00 60.00
❑ 20 Jabba The Hutt 15.00 30.00
❑ 30 Jabba The Hutt Dungeon 20.00 40.00

1983 Star Wars Return of the Jedi Tri-Logo

❑ 10 2-1B 30.00 60.00
❑ 30 8D8 30.00 60.00
❑ 35 A-Wing Pilot 40.00 80.00
❑ 40 Admiral Ackbar 20.00 40.00
❑ 50 Amanaman 100.00 200.00
❑ 60 Anakin Skywalker 25.00 50.00
❑ 70 AT-AT Commander 20.00 40.00
❑ 80 AT-ST Driver 30.00 60.00
❑ 85 B-Wing Pilot 30.00 60.00
❑ 90 Barada 40.00 80.00
❑ 100 Ben Kenobi blue saber 60.00 120.00
❑ 120 Bespin Guard black/ tri-logo back only 150.00 300.00
❑ 130 Bespin Guard white/ tri-logo back only 250.00 500.00
❑ 140 Bib Fortuna 15.00 30.00
❑ 150 Biker Scout/ long mask 30.00 60.00
❑ 160 Boba Fett 350.00 700.00
❑ 170 Bossk 40.00 80.00
❑ 180 C-3PO removable limbs 40.00 80.00
❑ 190 Chewbacca 40.00 80.00
❑ 220 Darth Vader 75.00 150.00
❑ 240 Death Star Droid 40.00 80.00
❑ 250 Dengar 25.00 50.00
❑ 260 Emperor 30.00 60.00
❑ 270 Emperors Royal Guard 150.00 300.00
❑ 280 FX-7 30.00 60.00
❑ 290 Gamorrean Guard 30.00 60.00
❑ 300 General Madine 60.00 120.00
❑ 310 Greedo/ tri-logo back only 60.00 120.00
❑ 320 Hammerhead/ tri-logo back only 40.00 80.00
❑ 330 Han Solo 75.00 150.00
❑ 340 Han Solo carbonite 100.00 200.00
❑ 380 IG-88 100.00 200.00
❑ 390 Imperial Commander 50.00 100.00
❑ 400 Imperial Dignitary 50.00 100.00
❑ 410 Imperial Gunner 50.00 100.00
❑ 415 Jawa 500.00 1000.00
❑ 420 Klaatu 15.00 30.00
❑ 430 Klaatu skiff 25.00 50.00
❑ 440 Lando Calrissian 40.00 80.00
❑ 450 Lando Calrissian skiff 30.00 60.00
❑ 480 Lobot 30.00 60.00
❑ 520 Luke Skywalker/ bespin fatigues 200.00 400.00
❑ 550 Luke Skywalker/ gunner card 125.00 250.00
❑ 560 Luke Skywalker/ hoth gear 200.00 400.00
❑ 565 Luke Skywalker/ jedi 40.00 80.00
❑ 570 Luke Skywalker/ stormtrooper 150.00 300.00
❑ 580 Luke Skywalker/ poncho 30.00 60.00
❑ 590 Luke Skywalker X-wing 100.00 200.00
❑ 600 Lumat 30.00 60.00
❑ 610 Nien Nunb 50.00 100.00
❑ 620 Nikto 15.00 30.00
❑ 630 Paploo 15.00 30.00
❑ 650 Princess Leia Organa 60.00 120.00
❑ 655 Princess Leia Organa/ bespin turtle neck60.00 120.00
❑ 660 Princess Leia Organa/ boussh 75.00 150.00
❑ 680 Princess Leia Organa/ poncho 50.00 100.00
❑ 690 Prune Face 25.00 50.00
❑ 700 R2-D2 sensorscope/ blue background card20.00 40.00
❑ 701 R2-D2 sensorscope/ sparks card 75.00 120.00
❑ 710 R5-D4 30.00 60.00
❑ 720 Rancor 20.00 40.00
❑ 760 Rebel Soldier hoth gear 40.00 80.00
❑ 770 Ree-Yees 20.00 40.00
❑ 780 Romba 30.00 60.00
❑ 800 Squid Head 25.00 50.00
❑ 800 Snowtrooper 30.00 60.00
❑ 810 Stormtrooper 100.00 200.00
❑ 840 TIE Fighter Pilot 30.00 60.00
❑ 850 Ugnaught 30.00 60.00
❑ 860 Warok 50.00 100.00
❑ 880 Wicket 40.00 80.00
❑ 885 Yak Face 200.00 400.00
❑ 890 Yoda orange snake 500.00 900.00
❑ 890 Yoda brown snake 50.00 100.00

1983 Star Wars Return of the Jedi Vehicles

❑ 10 AT-AT 150.00 300.00
❑ 20 B-Wing Fighter 75.00 150.00
❑ 40 Ewok Assault Catapult 25.00 50.00
❑ 50 Ewok Battle Wagon
❑ 60 Ewok Glider 30.00 60.00
❑ 70 Imperial Shuttle 250.00 500.00
❑ 80 Millenium Falcon 125.00 250.00
❑ 90 Scout Walker 50.00 100.00
❑ 100 Speeder Bike 20.00 40.00
❑ 110 TIE Fighter/ battle damage 40.00 80.00
❑ 120 TIE Interceptor 60.00 120.00
❑ 130 X-Wing/ battle damage 75.00 150.00
❑ 140 Y-Wing 75.00 150.00

1983 Star Wars Return of the Jedi Vehicles (loose)

❑ 10 AT-AT 40.00 80.00
❑ 20 B-Wing Fighter 30.00 60.00
❑ 40 Ewok Assault Catapult 15.00 30.00
❑ 50 Ewok Battle Wagon
❑ 60 Ewok Glider 15.00 30.00
❑ 70 Imperial Shuttle 30.00 60.00
❑ 80 Millenium Falcon 50.00 100.00
❑ 90 Scout Walker 15.00 30.00
❑ 100 Speeder Bike 7.50 15.00
❑ 110 TIE Fighter/ battle damage 20.00 40.00
❑ 120 TIE Interceptor 20.00 40.00
❑ 130 X-Wing/ battle damage 30.00 60.00
❑ 140 Y-Wing 30.00 60.00

1985 Star Wars Droids Cartoon

❑ 10 A-Wing Pilot 75.00 150.00
❑ 20 Boba Fett 300.00 450.00
❑ 30 C-3PO 75.00 150.00
❑ 40 Jann Tosh 30.00 60.00
❑ 50 Jord Dusat 30.00 60.00
❑ 60 Kea Moll 30.00 60.00
❑ 70 Kez-Iban 30.00 60.00
❑ 80 R2-D2 75.00 150.00
❑ 90 Sise Fromm 125.00 250.00
❑ 100 Thall Joben 30.00 60.00
❑ 110 Tig Fromm 75.00 150.00
❑ 120 Uncle Gundy 30.00 60.00

1985 Star Wars Droids Cartoon Coins (loose)

❑ 10 A-Wing Pilot 4.00 10.00
❑ 20 Boba Fett 12.50 25.00
❑ 30 C-3PO 4.00 10.00
❑ 40 Jann Tosh 4.00 10.00
❑ 50 Jord Dusat 4.00 10.00
❑ 60 Kea Moll 4.00 10.00
❑ 70 Kez-Iban 4.00 10.00
❑ 80 R2-D2 5.00 12.00
❑ 90 Sise Fromm 5.00 12.00
❑ 100 Thall Joben 4.00 10.00
❑ 110 Tig Fromm 4.00 10.00
❑ 120 Uncle Gundy 4.00 10.00

1985 Star Wars Droids Cartoon (loose)

❑ 10 A-Wing Pilot 40.00 80.00
❑ 20 Boba Fett 125.00 225.00
❑ 30 C-3PO 40.00 80.00
❑ 40 Jann Tosh 15.00 30.00
❑ 50 Jord Dusat 15.00 30.00
❑ 60 Kea Moll 15.00 30.00
❑ 70 Kez-Iban 15.00 30.00
❑ 80 R2-D2 40.00 80.00
❑ 90 Sise Fromm 60.00 120.00
❑ 100 Thall Joben 15.00 30.00
❑ 110 Tig Fromm 40.00 80.00
❑ 120 Uncle Gundy 15.00 30.00

1985 Star Wars Droids Cartoon Vehicles

❑ 10 A-Wing Fighter 50.00 100.00
❑ 20 ATL Interceptor 50.00 100.00
❑ 30 Sidegunner 30.00 60.00

1985 Star Wars Droids Cartoon Vehicles (loose)

❑ 10 A-Wing Fighter 25.00 50.00
❑ 20 ATL Interceptor 25.00 50.00
❑ 30 Sidegunner 15.00 30.00

1985 Star Wars Ewoks Cartoons

❑ 10 Dulok Scout 25.00 50.00
❑ 20 Dulok Shaman 30.00 60.00
❑ 30 King Gorneesh 20.00 40.00
❑ 40 Lady Gorneesh 25.00 50.00
❑ 50 Logray 40.00 80.00
❑ 60 Wicket 50.00 100.00

1985 Star Wars Ewoks Cartoons Coins (loose)

❑ 10 Dulok Scout 4.00 10.00
❑ 20 Dulok Shaman 4.00 10.00
❑ 30 King Gorneesh 4.00 10.00
❑ 40 Lady Gorneesh 4.00 10.00
❑ 50 Logray 5.00 12.00
❑ 60 Wicket 5.00 12.00

1985 Star Wars Ewoks Cartoons (loose)

❑ 10 Dulok Scout 12.50 25.00
❑ 20 Dulok Shaman 15.00 30.00
❑ 30 King Gorneesh 10.00 20.00
❑ 40 Lady Gorneesh 12.50 25.00
❑ 50 Logray 20.00 40.00
❑ 60 Wicket 25.00 50.00

1985 Star Wars Power of the Force

❑ 5 2-1B
❑ 10 A-Wing Pilot 50.00 100.00
❑ 20 Amanaman 100.00 200.00
❑ 30 Anakin Skywalker
❑ 40 AT-AT Driver
❑ 50 AT-ST Driver 50.00 100.00
❑ 60 B-Wing Pilot 25.00 50.00
❑ 70 Barada 50.00 100.00
❑ 80 Ben Kenobi blue saber 60.00 120.00
❑ 90 Biker Scout 75.00 150.00
❑ 94 Boba Fett proof
❑ 95 Bossk proof
❑ 100 C-3PO removable limbs 50.00 100.00
❑ 110 Chewbacca 50.00 100.00
❑ 115 Cloud Car Pilot proof
❑ 120 Darth Vader 100.00 200.00
❑ 125 Dengar proof
❑ 130 Emperor 40.00 80.00
❑ 140 EV-9D9 60.00 120.00
❑ 145 FX-7 proof
❑ 150 Gamorrean Guard 200.00 400.00
❑ 155 Greedo proof
❑ 160 Han Solo carbonite 125.00 225.00
❑ 170 Han Solo trench coat 400.00 700.00
❑ 175 IG-88 proof
❑ 180 Imperial Dignitary 50.00 100.00
❑ 190 Imperial Gunner 50.00 100.00
❑ 200 Jawa 50.00 100.00
❑ 210 Lando Calrissian 60.00 120.00
❑ 211 Lando Calrissian skiff
❑ 215 Luke Skywalker bespin/ fatigues
❑ 216 Luke Skywalker bespin/ white shirt
❑ 220 Luke Skywalker hoth gear
❑ 230 Luke Skywalker jedi 75.00 150.00
❑ 240 Luke Skywalker poncho 60.00 120.00
❑ 250 Luke Skywalker/ stormtrooper 125.00 250.00
❑ 260 Luke Skywalker x-wing 60.00 120.00
❑ 270 Lumat 40.00 80.00
❑ 280 Nikto 1000.00 1500.00
❑ 290 Paploo 40.00 80.00
❑ 301 Princess Leia bespin proof
❑ 302 Princess Leia boushh proof
❑ 303 Princess Leia poncho 40.00 80.00
❑ 305 Prune Face poof
❑ 310 R2-D2 lightsaber 75.00 150.00
❑ 320 Romba 40.00 80.00
❑ 330 Stormtrooper 100.00 200.00
❑ 340 Teebo 60.00 120.00
❑ 350 TIE Fighter Pilot
❑ 355 Tusken Raider proof
❑ 360 Ugnaught
❑ 370 Warok 50.00 100.00
❑ 380 Wicket 40.00 80.00
❑ 390 Yak Face 1000.00 1400.00
❑ 400 Yoda brown snake 300.00 600.00
❑ 405 Zuckuss proof

1985 Star Wars Power of the Force Coins (loose)

❑ 10 A-Wing Pilot 6.00 12.00
❑ 20 Amanaman 6.00 12.00
❑ 30 Anakin Skywalker 20.00 40.00
❑ 40 AT-AT Driver
❑ 50 AT-ST Driver 5.00 10.00
❑ 60 B-Wing Pilot 5.00 10.00
❑ 70 Barada 7.50 15.00
❑ 80 Ben Kenobi blue saber 7.50 15.00
❑ 90 Biker Scout 7.50 15.00
❑ 100 C-3PO removable limbs 6.00 12.00
❑ 110 Chewbacca 7.50 15.00
❑ 120 Darth Vader 10.00 20.00
❑ 130 Emperor 7.50 15.00
❑ 140 EV-9D9 7.50 15.00
❑ 150 Gamorrean Guard 10.00 20.00
❑ 160 Han Solo carbonite 10.00 20.00
❑ 170 Han Solo trench coat 15.00 30.00
❑ 180 Imperial Dignitary 7.50 15.00
❑ 190 Imperial Gunner 5.00 10.00
❑ 200 Jawa 10.00 20.00
❑ 210 Lando Calrissian 6.00 12.00
❑ 220 Luke Skywalker hoth gear 10.00 20.00
❑ 230 Luke Skywalker jedi 10.00 20.00
❑ 240 Luke Skywalker poncho 10.00 20.00
❑ 250 Luke Skywalker trooper 15.00 30.00
❑ 260 Luke Skywalker X-wing 10.00 20.00
❑ 270 Lumat 5.00 10.00
❑ 280 Nikto
❑ 290 Paploo 5.00 10.00
❑ 300 Princess Leia poncho 7.50 15.00
❑ 310 R2-D2 lightsaber 7.50 15.00
❑ 320 Romba 5.00 10.00
❑ 330 Stormtrooper 10.00 20.00
❑ 340 Teebo 5.00 10.00
❑ 350 TIE Fighter Pilot
❑ 360 Ugnaught
❑ 370 Warok 6.00 12.00
❑ 380 Wicket 10.00 20.00
❑ 390 Yak Face 30.00 60.00
❑ 400 Yoda brown snake 20.00 40.00

1985 Star Wars Power of the Force (loose)

❑ 10 A-Wing Pilot 25.00 50.00
❑ 20 Amanaman 40.00 80.00
❑ 30 Anakin Skywalker 15.00 30.00
❑ 40 AT-AT Driver
❑ 50 AT-ST Driver 10.00 20.00
❑ 60 B-Wing Pilot 10.00 20.00
❑ 70 Barada 20.00 40.00
❑ 80 Ben Kenobi blue saber 20.00 40.00
❑ 90 Biker Scout 20.00 40.00
❑ 100 C-3PO removable limbs 10.00 20.00
❑ 110 Chewbacca 20.00 40.00
❑ 120 Darth Vader 20.00 40.00
❑ 130 Emperor 15.00 30.00
❑ 140 EV-9D9 25.00 50.00
❑ 150 Gamorrean Guard 50.00 100.00
❑ 160 Han Solo carbonite 30.00 60.00
❑ 170 Han Solo trench coat 125.00 225.00
❑ 180 Imperial Dignitary 30.00 60.00
❑ 190 Imperial Gunner 20.00 40.00
❑ 200 Jawa 20.00 40.00
❑ 210 Lando Calrissian 25.00 50.00
❑ 220 Luke Skywalker hoth gear 25.00 50.00
❑ 230 Luke Skywalker jedi 25.00 50.00
❑ 240 Luke Skywalker poncho 25.00 50.00
❑ 250 Luke Skywalker/ stormtrooper 40.00 80.00
❑ 260 Luke Skywalker x-wing 25.00 50.00
❑ 270 Lumat 15.00 30.00
❑ 280 Nikto
❑ 290 Paploo 12.50 25.00
❑ 300 Princess Leia poncho 20.00 40.00
❑ 310 R2-D2 lightsaber 40.00 80.00
❑ 320 Romba 15.00 30.00
❑ 330 Stormtrooper 30.00 60.00
❑ 340 Teebo 12.50 25.00
❑ 350 TIE Fighter Pilot
❑ 360 Ugnaught
❑ 370 Warok 20.00 40.00
❑ 380 Wicket 20.00 40.00
❑ 390 Yak Face 100.00 200.00
❑ 400 Yoda brown snake 75.00 150.00

1985 Star Wars Power of the Force Vehicles

❑ 10 Ewok Battle Wagon 125.00 250.00
❑ 20 Imperial Sniper Vehicle 75.00 150.00
❑ 30 Sand Skimmer 75.00 150.00
❑ 40 Security Scout 75.00 150.00
❑ 50 Tattoine Skiff 200.00 400.00

1985 Star Wars Power of the Force Vehicles (loose)

❑ 10 Ewok Battle Wagon 50.00 100.00
❑ 20 Imperial Sniper Vehicle 30.00 60.00
❑ 30 Sand Skimmer 30.00 60.00
❑ 40 Security Scout 30.00 60.00
❑ 50 Tattoine Skiff 100.00 200.00

1993 Star Wars Bend Ems

❑ 10 Admiral Ackbar 7.50 15.00
❑ 20 Ben Kenobi 10.00 20.00
❑ 30 Bib Fortuna 7.50 15.00
❑ 40 Boba Fett 15.00 30.00
❑ 50 C-3PO 10.00 20.00
❑ 60 Chewbacca 7.50 15.00
❑ 70 Darth Vader 12.50 25.00
❑ 80 Emperor 10.00 20.00
❑ 90 Emperor's Royal Guard 7.50 15.00
❑ 100 Gamorrean Guard 7.50 15.00
❑ 110 Han Solo 10.00 20.00
❑ 120 Lando Calrissian 7.50 15.00
❑ 130 Leia Organa 10.00 20.00
❑ 140 Luke Skywalker 10.00 20.00
❑ 150 Luke Skywalker X-wing 10.00 20.00
❑ 160 R2-D2 7.50 15.00
❑ 170 Stormtrooper 7.50 15.00
❑ 180 Tusken Raider 7.50 15.00
❑ 190 Wicket 7.50 15.00
❑ 200 Yoda 7.50 15.00
❑ 210 4-Piece A New Hope 20.00 40.00
Chewbacca/Luke Skywalker/R2-D2/Tusken Raider
❑ 220 4-Piece Empire Strikes 20.00 40.00
Back/Han Solo/Darth Vader/Yoda/Lando Calrissian
❑ 230 4-Piece Return of the 25.00 50.00
Jedi/Admiral Ackbar/Boba Fett/Wicket/Bib Fortuna
❑ 240 4-Piece Gift Se 1/[Ben 20.00 40.00
Kenobi/Leia Organa/Han Solo/C-3PO
❑ 250 4-Piece Gift Set 2/Storm 20.00 40.00
Trooper/Wicket/Yoda/Chewbacca
❑ 260 4-Piece Gift Set 3/Storm 20.00 40.00
Trooper/R2-D2/C-3PO/Darth Vader
❑ 270 4-Piece Gift Set 4/Emperor/C-3PO 20.00 40.00
Luke Skywalker/Darth Vader
❑ 280 6-Piece Gift Set 1/Darth Vader 25.00 50.00
Stormtrooper/Luke Skywalker/R2-D2/C-3PO
❑ 290 6-Piece Gift Set 2/Stormtrooper 25.00 50.00
Darth Vader/Emperor's Imperial Guard/Ad
❑ 300 8-Piece Gift Set/Darth 25.00 50.00
Vader/Luke Skywalker/C-3PO/Emperor/Stormtrooper
❑ 310 10-Piece Gift Set/R2-D2 30.00 60.00
Stormtrooper/Darth Vader/Admiral Ackbar/Chewba

1993 Star Wars Bend Ems (loose)

❑ 10 Admiral Ackbar 4.00 10.00
❑ 20 Ben Kenobi 5.00 12.00
❑ 30 Bib Fortuna 4.00 10.00
❑ 40 Boba Fett 8.00 20.00
❑ 50 C-3PO 5.00 12.00
❑ 60 Chewbacca 4.00 10.00
❑ 70 Darth Vader 6.00 15.00
❑ 80 Emperor 5.00 12.00
❑ 90 Emperor's Royal Guard 4.00 10.00
❑ 100 Gamorrean Guard 4.00 10.00
❑ 110 Han Solo 5.00 12.00
❑ 120 Lando Calrissian 4.00 10.00
❑ 130 Leia Organa 5.00 12.00
❑ 140 Luke Skywalker 5.00 12.00
❑ 150 Luke Skywalker X-wing 5.00 12.00
❑ 160 R2-D2 4.00 10.00
❑ 170 Stormtrooper 4.00 10.00
❑ 180 Tusken Raider 4.00 10.00
❑ 190 Wicket 4.00 10.00
❑ 200 Yoda 4.00 10.00

1995-96 Star Wars Power of the Force Red Accessories

❑ 10 C-3PO Carrying Case 30.00 60.00

1995-96 Star Wars Power of the Force Red Accessories (loose)

❑ 10 C-3PO Carrying Case 15.00 30.00

1995-96 Star Wars Power of the Force Red Cards

❑ 10 Ben Kenobi long saber/ 1/2 5.00 10.00
photo package back
❑ 11 Ben Kenobi long saber/ full 6.00 12.00
photo package back
❑ 20 Ben Kenobi short saber 5.00 10.00
❑ 21 Ben Kenobi short saber/ with 5.00 10.00
long saber package
❑ 22 Ben Kenobi short saber/ with hologram card7.50 15.00
❑ 23 Ben Kenobi short saber/ THX insert 7.50 15.00
❑ 30 Boba Fett full circle/ both hands 5.00 10.00
❑ 31 Boba Fett full circle/ one hand 100.00 200.00
❑ 32 Boba Fett half circle/ both hands 10.00 20.00
❑ 36 Boba Fett no emblem/ on chest 200.00 400.00
❑ 37 Boba Fett no skull/ on shoulder 300.00 600.00
❑ 80 C-3PO 5.00 10.00
❑ 81 C-3PO THX insert 7.50 15.00
❑ 90 Chewbacca 5.00 10.00
❑ 100 Darth Vader long saber 5.00 10.00

STAR WARS

❑ 110 Darth Vader short saber 5.00 10.00
❑ 111 Darth Vader short saber with long saber package 15.00 30.00
❑ 120 Death Star Gunner 6.00 12.00
❑ 130 Greedo/ small vest 5.00 10.00
❑ 150 Han Solo/ with gray holster 5.00 10.00
❑ 151 Han Solo/ with gray holster THX insert 7.50 15.00
❑ 160 Han Solo carbonite 5.00 10.00
❑ 170 Han Solo carbonite & freeze 5.00 10.00
❑ 180 Han Solo hoth closed hand 6.00 12.00
❑ 190 Han Solo hoth open hand 7.50 15.00
❑ 191 Jawas 7.50 15.00
❑ 210 Lando Calrissian 5.00 10.00
❑ 220 Momaw Nadon 6.00 12.00
❑ 230 Luke Skywalker/ long saber 6.00 12.00
❑ 231 Luke Skywalker/ long saber THX insert 7.50 15.00
❑ 240 Luke Skywalker/ short saber 6.00 12.00
❑ 250 Luke Skywalker dagobah/ long saber 5.00 10.00
❑ 260 Luke Skywalker dagobah/ short saber 5.00 10.00
❑ 261 Luke Skywalker dagobah/ short saber with/ long saber package
❑ 270 Luke Skywalker jedi/ black vest 6.00 12.00
❑ 280 Luke Skywalker jedi/ brown vest 12.50 25.00
❑ 290 Luke Skywalker stormtrooper 10.00 20.00
❑ 300 Luke Skywalker x-wing/ long saber 5.00 10.00
❑ 310 Luke Skywalker x-wing/ short saber 5.00 10.00
❑ 311 Luke Skywalker x-wing/ short saber with/ long saber package 7.50 15.00
❑ 320 Princess Leia Organa/ 2 band belt 5.00 10.00
❑ 330 Princess Leia Organa/ 3 band belt 5.00 10.00
❑ 340 R2-D2 5.00 10.00
❑ 341 R2-D2 THX insert 6.00 12.00
❑ 350 R5-D4 6.00 12.00
❑ 360 Sandtrooper 6.00 12.00
❑ 370 Stormtrooper/ image card 5.00 10.00
❑ 371 Stormtrooper/ hologram card 7.50 15.00
❑ 372 Stormtrooper/ TXH insert 7.50 15.00
❑ 380 TIE Fighter Pilot/ image card 5.00 10.00
❑ 381 TIE Fighter Pilot/ image card/ warning sticker 7.50 15.00
❑ 382 Tie Pilot/ hologram card 75.00 150.00
❑ 420 Tusken Raider/ closed hand 15.00 30.00
❑ 430 Tusken Raider/ open hand 5.00 10.00
❑ 440 Yoda/ image card 5.00 10.00
❑ 441 Yoda/ hologram card 10.00 20.00

1995-96 Star Wars Power of the Force Red Cards Deluxe

❑ 10 Crowd Control Stormtrooper with flight action thruster/ and capture claw 15.00 30.00
❑ 20 Han Solo with/ smuggler flight pack plus pivoting blaster/ cannons and 12.50 25.00
❑ 30 Luke Skywalker's/ desert sport skiff 12.50 25.00

1995-96 Star Wars Power of the Force Red Cards Deluxe (loose)

❑ 10 Crowd Control Stormtrooper with flight action thruster/ and capture claw 10.00 20.00
❑ 11 Han Solo with /smuggler flight pack plus pivoting blaster/ cannons and 7.50 15.00
❑ 12 Luke Skywalker's/ desert sport skiff 7.50 15.00

1995-96 Star Wars Power of the Force Red Classic Edition 4-Pack

❑ 10 Luke Skywalker/Han Solo/Darth Vader/Chewbacca 25.00 50.00

1995-96 Star Wars Power of the Force Red Die-Cast

❑ 10 6-Pack/Boba Fett/Han Solo Chewbacca/Darth Vader/Luke Skywalker/Stormt 20.00 40.00
❑ 20 4-Pack/C-3PO/Princess Leia/R2-D2/Obi-Wan Kenobi 15.00 30.00

1995-96 Star Wars Power of the Force Red Die-Cast (loose)

❑ 10 Boba Fett 4.00 10.00
❑ 11 Han Solo 3.00 8.00
❑ 12 Chewbacca 3.00 8.00
❑ 13 Darth Vader 4.00 10.00
❑ 14 Luke Skywalker 4.00 10.00
❑ 15 Stormtrooper 3.00 8.00
❑ 20 C-3PO 3.00 8.00
❑ 21 Princess Leia 4.00 10.00
❑ 22 R2-D2 3.00 8.00
❑ 23 Obi-Wan Kenobi 3.00 8.00

1995-96 Star Wars Power of the Force Red Playsets

❑ 10 Death Star Escape 7.50 15.00
❑ 20 Detention Block Rescue 7.50 15.00

1995-96 Star Wars Power of the Force Red Playsets (loose)

❑ 10 Death Star Escape 12.50 25.00
❑ 20 Detention Block Rescue 12.50 25.00

1995-96 Star Wars Power of the Force Red Vehicles

❑ 10 Immperial AT-ST 30.00 60.00
❑ 20 Landspeeder 20.00 40.00
❑ 30 Millennium Falcon 75.00 150.00
❑ 40 Rebel Snowspeeder 30.00 60.00
❑ 50 Slave I 40.00 80.00
❑ 60 Speeder Bike/Speeder Trooper 20.00 40.00
❑ 70 TIE Fighter 25.00 50.00

1995-96 Star Wars Power of the Force Red Vehicles (loose)

❑ 10 Immperial AT-ST 12.50 25.00
❑ 20 Landspeeder 10.00 20.00
❑ 30 Millennium Falcon 30.00 60.00
❑ 40 Rebel Snowspeeder 12.50 25.00
❑ 50 Slave I 20.00 40.00
❑ 60 Speeder Bike 10.00 20.00
❑ 70 TIE Fighter 15.00 30.00

1995-99 Star Wars Power of the Force Exclusives

❑ 10 Ben Kenobi's Spirit/ mail in offer 6.00 12.00
❑ 20 B'Omarr Monk/ mail in offer 7.50 15.00
❑ 30 Cantina Band Member/ mail in offer 5.00 10.00
❑ 40 Death Star Droid fan club/ mail in offer 15.00 30.00
❑ 50 Han Solo stormtrooper/ mail in offer 10.00 20.00
❑ 60 Kabe and Muftak/ mail in offer 15.00 30.00
❑ 70 Luke Skywalker/ Star Wars Trilogy Theater Edition/ promo figure 20.00 40.00
❑ 80 Mace Windue preview/ mail in offer 10.00 20.00
❑ 90 Oola and Salacious Crumb/ mail in offer 15.00 30.00
❑ 100 Pote Snitkin fan club/ mail in offer 7.50 15.00
❑ 110 Princess Leia hoth 12"/ fan club mail in 20.00 40.00

1995-99 Star Wars Power of the Force Exclusives (loose)

❑ 10 Ben Kenobi's Spirit/ mail in offer 2.50 6.00
❑ 20 B'Omarr Monk/ mail in offer 3.00 8.00
❑ 30 Cantina Band Member/ mail in offer 2.00 5.00
❑ 40 Death Star Droid fan club/ mail in offer 6.00 15.00
❑ 50 Han Solo stormtrooper/ mail in offer 4.00 10.00
❑ 60 Kabe and Muftak/ mail in offer 6.00 15.00
❑ 70 Luke Skywalker/ Star Wars Trilogy Theater Edition/ promo figure 7.50 20.00
❑ 80 Mace Windue preview/ mail in offer 4.00 10.00
❑ 90 Oola and Salacious Crumb/ mail in offer 6.00 15.00
❑ 100 Pote Snitkin fan club/ mail in offer 3.00 8.00
❑ 110 Princess Leia hoth 12"/ fan club mail in 7.50 20.00

1995-99 Star Wars Power of the Force (loose)

❑ 10 2-1B Medic Droid 2.00 5.00
❑ 20 4-LOM 2.00 5.00
❑ 30 8D8/ found in Green Freeze Frames Collection 2 2.00 5.00
❑ 40 Admiral Ackbar/ commlink wrist blaster 2.00 5.00
❑ 41 Admiral Ackbar/ wrist blaster 2.00 5.00
❑ 50 Admiral Moddi/ found in Green/ CommTech 2.50 6.00
❑ 60 Airspeeder Pilot/ found in Green Expanded Universe/ Vehicles 3.00 8.00
❑ 70 Anakin Skywalker/ found in Green Episode I Flashback 2.50 6.00
❑ 80 Anakin Skywalker/ jedi spirit/ found in Green/ Cinema Scenes 4.00 10.00
❑ 90 ASP-7 Droid 2.00 5.00
❑ 100 AT-AT Driver/ found in Green Freeze/ Frames Collection 1 4.00 10.00
❑ 110 AT-ST Driver 3.00 8.00
❑ 120 Aunt Beru/ found in Green Episode I Flashback 2.00 5.00
❑ 130 Bantha/ found in Green/ 2-Packs Real Feel 12.50 30.00
❑ 140 Barquin D'an/ found in Green/ Max Rebo Band Pairs 3.00 8.00
❑ 150 Ben (Obi-Wan) Kenobi/ cape with hood on/ found in Green/ Episode I Flash 2.00 5.00
❑ 160 Ben Kenobi long saber 2.50 6.00
❑ 170 Ben Kenobi short saber 2.50 6.00
❑ 180 Bib Fortuna 2.00 5.00
❑ 190 Biggs Darklighter/ found in Green Freeze/ Frames Collection 2 5.00 12.00
❑ 191 Biggs Darklighter/ no silver paint/ on chest/ found in Green Freeze/ Fr 25.00 50.00
❑ 200 Boba Fett full circle/ both hands 10.00 25.00
❑ 201 Boba Fett full circle/ one hand 60.00 120.00
❑ 210 Boba Fett no emblem/ on chest 125.00 250.00
❑ 220 Boba Fett no skull/ on shoulder 200.00 400.00
❑ 230 Bossk 2.00 5.00
❑ 240 C-3PO 2.50 6.00
❑ 250 C-3PO metalized body/ found in Green Freeze/ Frames Collection 1 2.50 6.00
❑ 260 C-3PO removable arm/ found in Green/ Episode I Flashback 2.00 5.00
❑ 270 C-3PO silver leg/ found in green Millennium Mint 2.00 5.00
❑ 280 Captain Piett/ rifle and pistol found in Green Freeze/ Frames Collectio 3.00 8.00
❑ 281 Captain Piett/ pistol and baton found in Green Freeze/ Frames Collectio 5.00 12.00
❑ 290 Chewbacca 2.50 6.00
❑ 300 Chewbacca boushh/ bounty hunter found in Green Freeze/ Frames Collectio 2.50 6.00
❑ 310 Chewbacca Hoth/ on card as Hoth Chewbacca/ found in Green/ Episode I F 2.50 6.00
❑ 320 Chewbacca/ mynock hunt/ found in Green/ Cinema Scenes 3.00 8.00
❑ 330 Clone Emperor Palpatine/ found in Green/ Expanded Universe 4.00 10.00
❑ 340 Cloud Car Pilot/ found in Green Expanded Universe/ Vehicles 3.00 8.00
❑ 350 Dark Trooper/ found in Green Expanded Universe 4.00 10.00
❑ 360 Darth Vader long saber 3.00 8.00
❑ 370 Darth Vader short saber 3.00 8.00
❑ 380 Darth Vader/ removable helmet found in Green Freeze/ Frames Collection 5.00 12.00
❑ 390 Death Star Droid/ found in Green Freeze/ Frames Collection 3 2.00 5.00
❑ 400 Death Star Gunner 2.50 6.00
❑ 410 Death Star Trooper/ found in Green Freeze/ Frames Collection 3 2.50 6.00
❑ 420 Dengar 2.00 5.00
❑ 430 Dewback/ found in Green 2-Packs 5.00 12.00
❑ 440 Doda Bodonawieedo/ found in Green Max Rebo Band Pairs 3.00 8.00
❑ 450 Dr. Evazan/ found in Green/ Cinema Scenes 2.00 5.00
❑ 460 Droopy McCool/ found in Green Max Rebo Band Pairs 4.00 10.00
❑ 470 Emperor Palpatine 2.00 5.00
❑ 480 Emperor Palpatine/ force lightning found in Green/ Episode I Flashback 2.50 6.00
❑ 490 Emperor's Royal Guard 2.00 5.00
❑ 500 Endor Rebel Soldier/ found in Green Freeze/ Frames Collection 1 2.00 5.00
❑ 510 EV-9D9 2.00 5.00
❑ 520 Gamorrean Guard 2.50 6.00
❑ 530 Garindan (Long Snoot) 2.00 5.00
❑ 540 Goink Droid/ foot holes found in Green/ CommTech with Jawa 2.00 5.00
❑ 541 Goink Droid/ one foot hole found in Green/ CommTech with Jawa 2.50 6.00
❑ 542 Goink Droid/ two foot holes found in Green/ CommTech with Jawa 2.50 6.00
❑ 550 Grand Admiral Thrawn/ found in Green/ Expanded Universe 3.00 8.00
❑ 560 Grand Moff Tarkin 2.50 6.00
❑ 570 Greeata/ found in Green/ Cinema Scenes 2.00 5.00
❑ 580 Greedo/ large vest/ found in Green CommTech 2.00 5.00
❑ 581 Greedo/ large vest/ yellow knee pins found in Green/ CommTech 4.00 10.00
❑ 590 Greedo/ small vest 2.00 5.00
❑ 600 Han Solo/ with brown holster found in Green/ CommTech 2.50 6.00
❑ 610 Han Solo/ with gray holster 2.00 5.00
❑ 620 Han Solo bespin 2.00 5.00
❑ 630 Han Solo carbonite 2.50 6.00
❑ 640 Han Solo carbonite & freeze 2.50 6.00
❑ 650 Han Solo endor/ blue pants 2.00 5.00
❑ 651 Han Solo endor/ brown pants 6.00 15.00
❑ 660 Han Solo hoth closed hand 2.50 6.00
❑ 670 Han Solo hoth open hand 2.50 6.00
❑ 680 Han Solo mynock hunt/ found in Green/ Cinema Scenes 3.00 8.00
❑ 690 Han Solo stormtrooper 4.00 10.00
❑ 700 Hoth Rebel 2.00 5.00
❑ 710 Hoth Rebel Soldier/ found in Green Freeze/ Frames Collection 1 2.00 5.00
❑ 720 Imperial Sentinel/ found in Green/ Expanded Universe 3.00 8.00
❑ 730 Interrogation Droid/ found in Green/ CommTech with Darth Vader 2.00 5.00
❑ 740 Ishi Tib gray pouch/ found in Green Freeze/ Frames Collection 3 2.50 6.00
❑ 741 Ishi Tib brown pouch/ found in Green Freeze/ Frames Collection 3 3.00 8.00
❑ 750 Jabba the Hut/ found in Green 2-Packs 5.00 12.00
❑ 760 Jawas 3.00 8.00
❑ 770 Joh Yowza/ found in Green Max Rebo Band Pairs 3.00 8.00
❑ 780 Kyle Katarn/ found in Green Expanded Universe 3.00 8.00
❑ 790 Labria/ found in Green/ Cinema Scenes 2.00 5.00
❑ 800 Lak Sivrak/ found in Green Freeze Frames Collection 2 2.00 5.00
❑ 810 Lando Calrissian 2.00 5.00
❑ 820 Lando Calrissian general/ found in Green Freeze/ Frames Collection 1 2.00 5.00
❑ 830 Lando Calrissian Skiff Guard 2.00 5.00
❑ 840 Lobot/ found in Green Freeze Frames Collection 1 2.00 5.00
❑ 850 Logray/ found in Green Freeze Frames Collection 1 2.50 6.00
❑ 860 Luke Skywalker/ long saber 2.50 6.00
❑ 870 Luke Skywalker/ short saber 2.50 6.00
❑ 880 Luke Skywalker bespin/ silver belt buckle/ found in Green Freeze/ Frames 2.00 5.00
❑ 881 Luke Skywalker bespin/ gold belt buckle/ found in Green Freeze/ Frames C 2.50 6.00
❑ 890 Luke Skywalker/ black robe with blue/black sleeves/ found in Green/ Ex 3.00 8.00
❑ 900 Luke Skywalker/ blast shield helmet found in Green Freeze/ Frames Colle 2.50 6.00
❑ 910 Luke Skywalker/ ceremonial 5.00 12.00
❑ 920 Luke Skywalker dagobah/ long saber 2.50 6.00
❑ 930 Luke Skywalker dagobah/ short saber 2.50 6.00
❑ 940 Luke Skywalker endor/ found in Green Vehicles/ with Speeder Bike/ and in 6.00 15.00
❑ 950 Luke Skywalker endor/ no glove found in Green Vehicles/ with Speeder Bi 10.00 25.00
❑ 960 Luke Skywalker hoth 4.00 10.00
❑ 970 Luke Skywalker hoth injured/ found in Green 2-Packs 6.00 15.00
❑ 980 Luke Skywalker jedi/ black vest 3.00 8.00
❑ 981 Luke Skywalker jedi/ brown vest 5.00 12.00
❑ 990 Luke Skywalker skyhopper/ found in Green/ CommTech 3.00 8.00
❑ 1000 Luke Skywalker stormtrooper 3.00 8.00
❑ 1010 Luke Skywalker tatooine/ with hat and goggles/ found in Green/ Episode I 2.50 6.00
❑ 1020 Luke Skywalker x-wing/ long saber 2.50 6.00
❑ 1030 Luke Skywalker x-wing/ short saber 2.50 6.00
❑ 1040 Lyn Me/ found in Green/ Cinema Scenes 2.00 5.00
❑ 1050 Malakili 2.00 5.00
❑ 1060 Mara Jade/ found in Green Expanded Universe 6.00 15.00
❑ 1070 Max Rebo/ found in Green 2-Packs 4.00 10.00
❑ 1080 Momaw Nadon 2.00 5.00
❑ 1090 Mon Mothma/ found in Green Freeze/ Frames Collection 1 2.00 5.00
❑ 1100 Nabrun Leids/ found in Green Cinema Scenes 2.00 5.00
❑ 1110 Nien Nunb 2.50 6.00
❑ 1120 Obi-Wan Kenobi/ found in Green Freeze/ Frames Collection 1 2.00 5.00
❑ 1130 Obi-Wan Kenobi/ jedi spirit found in Green/ Cinema Scenes 4.00 10.00
❑ 1140 Orrimaarko/ found in Green Freeze/ Frames Collection 3 2.00 5.00
❑ 1150 Ponda Baba black beard 5.00 12.00
❑ 1160 Ponda Baba gray beard 6.00 15.00
❑ 1170 Pote Snitkin/ found in Green Freeze Frames Collection 3 2.50 6.00
❑ 1180 Princess Leia Organa/ 2 band belt 2.00 5.00
❑ 1190 Princess Leia Organa/ 3 band belt 2.00 5.00
❑ 1200 Princess Leia Organa/ jabba's prisoner 3.00 8.00
❑ 1210 Princess Leia boushh 3.00 8.00
❑ 1220 Princess Leia/ ceremonial/ found in Green Princess/ Leia Collection 2-Pa 3.00 8.00
❑ 1230 Princess Leia/ ceremonial/ right arm bracelet/ found in Green/ Episode 2.50 6.00
❑ 1240 Princess Leia endor/ found in Green Vehicles/ with Speeder Bike/ and Mil 7.50 20.00
❑ 1250 Princess Leia/ ewok celebration found in Green Princess/ Leia Collectio 2.50 6.00
❑ 1260 Princess Leia hoth/ found in Green Freeze/ Frames Collection 3 2.00 5.00
❑ 1270 Princess Leia/ jabba's prisoner found in Green Freeze/ Frames Collectio 2.00 5.00
❑ 1280 Princess Leia/ mynock hunt/ found in Green/ Cinema Scenes 3.00 8.00
❑ 1290 Princess Leia/ red outfit/ found in Green Princess/ Leia Collection 2-Pa 2.50 6.00
❑ 1300 Princess Leia/ red/black robe/ red lightsaber/ found in Green/ Expanded 6.00 15.00
❑ 1310 Princess Leia/ white hooded gown found in Green/ CommTech 3.00 8.00
❑ 1320 R2-D2 2.00 5.00
❑ 1330 R2-D2 holo leia/ found in Green CommTech 2.50 6.00
❑ 1331 R2-D2 holo leia/ with foot peg/ found in Green/ CommTech 3.00 8.00
❑ 1340 R2-D2/ lightsaber left side/ found in Green/ Episode I Flashback 2.50 6.00
❑ 1341 R2-D2/ lightsaber right side/ found in Green/ Episode I Flashback 2.50 6.00
❑ 1350 R5-D4 2.00 5.00
❑ 1360 R5-D4 hooked button 2.50 6.00
❑ 1361 R5-D4 straight latch button 2.50 6.00
❑ 1370 Rancor/ found in Green/ 2-Packs Real Feel 20.00 40.00
❑ 1380 Rebel Fleet Trooper 2.50 6.00
❑ 1390 Rebel Speeder Bike/ Pilot found in Green/ Expanded Universe/ Vehicles 3.00 8.00
❑ 1400 Ree-Yees/ found in Green Freeze Frames Collection 3 3.00 8.00
❑ 1410 Ronto/ found in Green 2-Packs 4.00 10.00
❑ 1420 Rystall/ found in Green/ Cinema Scenes 2.00 5.00
❑ 1430 Saelt-Marae 2.00 5.00
❑ 1440 Sandtrooper 4.00 10.00
❑ 1450 Snowtrooper 4.00 10.00
❑ 1460 Spacetrooper/ found in Green Expanded Universe 6.00 15.00
❑ 1470 Speeder Trooper/ found in Red Vehicles/ with Speeder Bike 2.50 6.00
❑ 1480 Stormtrooper/ found in Green/ CommTech 2.50 6.00
❑ 1490 Sy Snootles/ found in Green/ Max Rebo Band Pairs 3.00 8.00
❑ 1500 Takeel/ found in Green/ Cinema Scenes 2.00 5.00
❑ 1510 Tauntaun/ found in Green 2-Packs 4.00 10.00
❑ 1520 TIE Fighter Pilot 2.00 5.00
❑ 1530 Tusken Raider/ closed hand 2.50 6.00
❑ 1540 Tusken Raider/ open hand 7.50 20.00
❑ 1550 Ugnaughts black/ found in Green Freeze/ Frames Collection 2 2.00 5.00
❑ 1560 Ugnaughts gray/ found in Green Freeze/ Frames Collection 2 2.00 5.00
❑ 1570 Uncle Owen Lars/ found in Green/ Cinema Scenes 4.00 10.00
❑ 1580 Wampa/ found in Green 2-Packs 7.50 20.00
❑ 1590 Wedge Antilles/ green stripes helmet/ found in Green/ Millennium Falcon 6.00 15.00
❑ 1591 Wedge Antilles/ red symbols helmet/ found in Green/ Millennium Falcon 10.00 25.00
❑ 1600 Weequay 4.00 10.00
❑ 1610 Wicket/ found in Green Princess Leia Collection 2-Packs/ and Green Free 3.00 8.00
❑ 1620 Wuher/ found in Green/ CommTech 3.00 8.00
❑ 1630 Yoda 3.00 8.00
❑ 1640 Yoda jedi spirit/ found in Green Cinema Scenes 4.00 10.00
❑ 1650 Yoda jedi trainer 2.50 6.00
❑ 1660 Yoda robe with/ maroon accents on neck and waist 4.00 10.00
❑ 1670 Zuckuss/ found in Green Freeze Frames Collection 3 2.50 6.00

1996 Star Wars Shadows Of The Empire

❑ 10 Boba Fett vs IG-88/ with comic book 12.50 25.00
❑ 20 Chewbacca/ bounty hunter disguise 7.50 15.00
❑ 30 Darth Vader vs Prince Xizor/ with comic book 12.50 25.00
❑ 40 Dash Rendar 6.00 12.00
❑ 50 Luke Skywalker/ imperial guard 10.00 20.00
❑ 60 Prince Xizor 6.00 12.00
❑ 70 Princess Leia/ boushh disguise 10.00 20.00

1996 Star Wars Shadows Of The Empire European

❑ 20 Chewbacca bounty/ hunter disguise 12.50 25.00
❑ 30 Dash Rendar 10.00 20.00
❑ 40 Luke Skywalker/ imperial guard 15.00 30.00
❑ 60 Princess Leia/ boushh disguise 10.00 20.00
❑ 80 Prince Xizor 15.00 30.00

1996 Star Wars Shadows Of The Empire (loose)

❑ 10 Boba Fett 6.00 12.00
❑ 20 Chewbacca bounty/ hunter disguise 5.00 10.00
❑ 30 Darth Vader 6.00 12.00
❑ 40 Dash Rendar 4.00 8.00
❑ 50 Endor Trooper/ found in Vehicles 4.00 8.00
❑ 60 IG-88 5.00 10.00
❑ 70 Luke Skywalker/ imperial guard 6.00 12.00
❑ 80 Prince Xizor 5.00 10.00
❑ 90 Princess Leia/ boushh disguise 7.50 15.00
❑ 100 Swoop Trooper/ found in Vehicles 4.00 8.00

1996 Star Wars Shadows Of The Empire Vehicles

❑ 10 Boba Fett's Slave I 40.00 80.00
❑ 20 Dash Rendar's Outrider 25.00 50.00
❑ 30 Swoop with Swoop Trooper 20.00 40.00
❑ 40 Speeder Bike/ with Endor Trooper 12.50 25.00

1996 Star Wars Shadows Of The Empire Vehicles (loose)

❑ 10 Boba Fett's Slave I 25.00 50.00
❑ 20 Dash Rendar's Outrider 12.50 25.00
❑ 30 Swoop 10.00 20.00
❑ 50 Speeder Bike 7.50 15.00

1996-97 Star Wars Power of the Force Green 2-Packs

❑ 10 Dewback/ and Sandtrooper 12.50 25.00
❑ 20 Jabba the Hut/ and Han Solo .00 12.50 25.00
❑ 21 Jabba the Hut/ and Han Solo .01 12.50 25.00
❑ 30 Luke Skywalker hoth/ and Tauntaun 12.50 25.00
❑ 40 Ronto and Jawa 10.00 20.00
❑ 50 Tauntaun and/ Han Solo hoth 12.50 25.00
❑ 60 Wampa and/ Luke Skywalker hoth injured 20.00 40.00

1996-97 Star Wars Power of the Force Green Accessories

❑ 10 Millennium Falcon/ carry case/Wedge Antilles/ green stripes helmet 20.00 40.00
❑ 20 Millennium Falcon/ carry case/Wedge Antilles/ red symbols helmet 30.00 60.00

1996-97 Star Wars Power of the Force Green Accessories (loose)

❑ 10 Millennium Falcon/ carry case 10.00 25.00

1996-97 Star Wars Power of the Force Green Cards Collection 1

❑ 10 Ben Kenobi 6.00 12.00
❑ 20 Bib Fortuna 7.50 15.00
❑ 30 Boba Fett full circle/ both hands 20.00 40.00
❑ 31 Boba Fett full circle/ one hand 125.00 250.00
❑ 40 C-3PO 7.50 15.00
❑ 50 Chewbacca/ hologram card 6.00 12.00
❑ 51 Chewbacca/ image card 5.00 10.00
❑ 60 Darth Vader 6.00 12.00
❑ 70 Death Star Gunner/ image card 6.00 12.00
❑ 71 Death Star Gunner/ hologram card 7.50 15.00
❑ 80 Emperor Palpatine/ hologram card 8.00
❑ 81 Emperor Palpatine/ image card 5.00 10.00
❑ 90 Greedo/ small vest/ hologram card 8.00
❑ 91 Greedo/ small vest/ image card 5.00 10.00
❑ 100 Han Solo/ with gray holster/ hologram card 5.00 10.00
❑ 101 Han Solo/ with gray holster/ image card 6.00 12.00
❑ 102 Han Solo/ with gray holster THX insert 7.50 15.00
❑ 110 Han Solo bespin/ hologram card 5.00 10.00
❑ 111 Han Solo bespin/ image card 6.00 12.00
❑ 120 Han Solo endor/ blue pants/ hologram card 5.00 10.00
❑ 121 Han Solo endor/ blue pants/ image card 6.00 12.00
❑ 122 Han Solo endor/ brown pants/ image card 12.50 25.00
❑ 130 Han Solo carbonite/ hologram card 5.00 10.00
❑ 131 Han Solo carbonite/ image card 6.00 12.00
❑ 140 Hoth Rebel/ hologram card 8.00
❑ 145 Lando Calrissian 15.00 30.00
❑ 150 Lando Calrissian Skiff Guard 5.00 10.00
❑ 160 Luke Skywalker ceremonial/ hologram card 10.00 20.00
❑ 161 Luke Skywalker ceremonial/ image card 12.50 25.00
❑ 170 Luke Skywalker hoth/ hologram card 5.00 10.00
❑ 171 Luke Skywalker hoth/ image card 6.00 12.00
❑ 180 Luke Skywalker jedi/ black vest hologram card 6.00 12.00
❑ 181 Luke Skywalker jedi/ black vest/ image card 7.50 15.00
❑ 190 Luke Skywalker stormtrooper/ hologram card 5.00 10.00
❑ 191 Luke Skywalker stormtrooper/ image card 6.00 12.00
❑ 200 Luke Skywalker x-wing/ hologram card 6.00 12.00
❑ 201 Luke Skywalker x-wing/ image card 7.50 15.00
❑ 210 Princess Leia Organa/ 2 bands on belt/ hologram card 5.00 10.00
❑ 211 Princess Leia Organa/ 2 bands on belt/ image card 6.00 12.00
❑ 212 Princess Leia Organa/ 3 bands on belt/ hologram card 5.00 10.00
❑ 213 Princess Leia Organa/ 3 bands on belt/ image card 6.00 12.00
❑ 220 Princess Leia boushh/ hologram card 6.00 12.00
❑ 221 Princess Leia boushh/ image card 7.50 15.00
❑ 230 Princess Leia Organa/ jabba's prisoner/ hologram card 6.00 12.00
❑ 231 Princess Leia Organa/ jabba's prisoner/ image card 7.50 15.00
❑ 235 R2-D2 6.00 12.00
❑ 240 Rebel Fleet Trooper 6.00 12.00
❑ 250 Sandtrooper/ hologram card 6.00 12.00
❑ 251 Sandtrooper/ image card 6.00 12.00
❑ 260 Yoda jedi trainer/ hologram card 6.00 12.00
❑ 261 Yoda jedi trainer/ image card 6.00 12.00

1996-97 Star Wars Power of the Force Green Cards Collection 2

❑ 10 2-1B Medic Droid/ image card 4.00 8.00
❑ 11 2-1B Medic Droid/ hologram card 5.00 10.00
❑ 20 4-LOM 6.00 12.00
❑ 30 Admiral Ackbar/ commlink wrist blaster 5.00 10.00
❑ 31 Admiral Ackbar/ wrist blaster 5.00 10.00
❑ 40 ASP-7 Droid/ hologram card 5.00 10.00
❑ 41 ASP-7 Droid/ image card 6.00 12.00
❑ 50 AT-ST Driver 6.00 12.00
❑ 60 Bib Fortuna 7.50 15.00
❑ 70 Bossk 5.00 10.00
❑ 80 Dengar 4.00 8.00
❑ 90 EV-9D9 5.00 10.00
❑ 100 Gamorrean Guard/ hologram card 6.00 12.00
❑ 101 Gamorrean Guard/ image card 7.50 15.00
❑ 110 Grand Moff Tarkin/ hologram card 6.00 12.00
❑ 120 Han Solo carbonite/ hologram card 6.00 12.00
❑ 130 Hoth Rebel/ hologram card 4.00 8.00
❑ 131 Hoth Rebel/ image card 5.00 10.00
❑ 140 Jawas/ hologram card 6.00 12.00
❑ 141 Jawas/ image card 7.50 15.00
❑ 150 Luke Skywalker ceremonial/ hologram card 10.00 20.00
❑ 151 Luke Skywalker ceremonial/ image card 12.50 25.00
❑ 160 Luke Skywalker hoth/ hologram card 5.00 10.00
❑ 161 Luke Skywalker hoth/ image card 6.00 12.00
❑ 170 Luke Skywalker jedi/ black vest hologram card 6.00 12.00
❑ 171 Luke Skywalker jedi/ black vest/ image card 7.50 15.00
❑ 180 Luke Skywalker stormtrooper/ hologram card 5.00 10.00
❑ 181 Luke Skywalker stormtrooper/ image card 6.00 12.00
❑ 190 Malakili/ hologram card 4.00 8.00
❑ 191 Malakili/ image card 5.00 10.00
❑ 200 Momaw Nadon/ hologram card 4.00 8.00
❑ 201 Momaw Nadon/ image card 5.00 10.00
❑ 210 Nien Nunb/ hologram card 6.00 12.00
❑ 211 Nien Nunb/ image card 7.50 15.00
❑ 215 Ponda Baba/ gray beard 12.50 25.00
❑ 216 Ponda Baba/ black beard 15.00 30.00
❑ 220 R5-D4 hooked button/ image card warning sticker 5.00 10.00
❑ 221 R5-D4 hooked button/ image card warning printed on card 6.00 12.00
❑ 222 R5-D4 hooked button hologram card warning sticker 5.00 10.00
❑ 223 R5-D4 hooked button/ hologram card warning printed on card 6.00 12.00
❑ 224 R5-D4 straight/ latch button/ no warning 7.50 15.00
❑ 225 R5-D4 straight/ latch button/ warning sticker 7.50 15.00
❑ 230 Rebel Fleet Trooper 6.00 12.00
❑ 240 Saelt-Marae/ hologram card 5.00 10.00
❑ 241 Saelt-Marae/ image card 6.00 12.00
❑ 250 Tusken Raider/ open hand/ hologram card 6.00 12.00
❑ 251 Tusken Raider/ open hand/ image card 6.00 12.00
❑ 252 Tusken Raider/ closed hand/ hologram card 20.00 40.00
❑ 253 Tusken Raider/ closed hand/ image card 20.00 40.00
❑ 260 Weequay/ hologram card 7.50 15.00
❑ 270 Yoda jedi trainer/ hologram card 7.50 15.00
❑ 271 Yoda jedi trainer/ image card 7.50 15.00

1996-97 Star Wars Power of the Force Green Cards Collection 3

❑ 10 AT-ST Driver 6.00 12.00
❑ 20 Boba Fett full circle/ both hands 12.50 25.00
❑ 21 Boba Fett full circle/ one hand
❑ 30 Darth Vader/ hologram card 6.00 12.00
❑ 31 Darth Vader/ image card 7.50 15.00
❑ 40 Death Star Gunner/ image card 6.00 12.00
❑ 41 Death Star Gunner/ hologram card 7.50 15.00
❑ 50 Emperor Palpatine/ hologram card 4.00 8.00
❑ 60 Emperor's Royal Guard/ image card 7.50 15.00
❑ 61 Emperor's Royal Guard/ hologram card 6.00 12.00
❑ 70 Garindan (Long Snoot)/ hologram card 5.00 10.00
❑ 71 Garindan (Long Snoot)/ image card 6.00 12.00
❑ 80 Grand Moff Tarkin/ image card 6.00 12.00
❑ 81 Grand Moff Tarkin/ hologram card 7.50 15.00
❑ 90 Ponda Baba gray beard/ hologram card 5.00 10.00
❑ 91 Ponda Baba gray beard/ image card 6.00 12.00
❑ 92 Ponda Baba black beard/ hologram card 6.00 12.00
❑ 93 Ponda Baba black beard/ image card 6.00 12.00
❑ 100 Sandtrooper 6.00 12.00
❑ 110 Snowtrooper/ hologram card 7.50 15.00
❑ 111 Snowtrooper/ image card 10.00 20.00
❑ 120 Weequay/ hologram card 6.00 12.00
❑ 121 Weequay/ image card 6.00 12.00

1996-97 Star Wars Power of the Force Green Cards Deluxe

❑ 10 Boba Fett/ wingblast rocket pack overhead cannon 7.50 15.00
❑ 20 Hoth Rebel Soldier/ anti vehicle laser cannon 7.50 15.00
❑ 30 Probe Droid/ proton torpedo and/ self destruct 7.50 15.00
❑ 40 Snowtrooper/ e-web heavy/ repeating blaster 7.50 15.00

1996-97 Star Wars Power of the Force Green Cards Deluxe (loose)

❑ 10 Boba Fett/ wingblast rocket pack overhead cannon 5.00 10.00
❑ 20 Hoth Rebel Soldier/ anti vehicle laser cannon 5.00 10.00
❑ 30 Probe Droid/ proton torpedo and/ self destruct 5.00 10.00
❑ 40 Snowtrooper/ e-web heavy/ repeating blaster 5.00 10.00

1996-97 Star Wars Power of the Force Green Cards Electronic Power FX

❑ 10 Darth Vader/ lightsaber with/ fighting action 7.50 15.00
❑ 20 Emperor Palpatine/ darkside energy bolts 7.50 15.00
❑ 30 Luke Skywalker/ lightsaber with/ dueling action 7.50 15.00
❑ 40 Obi-Wan Kenobi/ lightsaber with dueling action 6.00 12.00
❑ 50 R2-D2/ light up red eye/ remote control action 7.50 15.00

1996-97 Star Wars Power of the Force Green Cards Electronic Power FX (loose)

❑ 10 Darth Vader/ lightsaber with/ fighting action 4.00 10.00
❑ 20 Emperor Palpatine/ darkside energy bolts 4.00 10.00
❑ 30 Luke Skywalker/ lightsaber with/ dueling action 4.00 10.00
❑ 40 Obi-Wan Kenobi/ lightsaber with dueling action 4.00 10.00
❑ 50 R2-D2/ light up red eye/ remote control action 4.00 10.00

1996-97 Star Wars Power of the Force Green Cards Freeze Frames Collection 1

❑ 10 Bespin Han Solo .02 4.00 10.00
❑ 11 Bespin Han Solo .03 4.00 10.00
❑ 20 Bespin Luke Skywalker/ silver buckle .00 4.00 10.00
❑ 21 Bespin Luke Skywalker/ silver buckle .01 5.00 12.00
❑ 22 Bespin Luke Skywalker/ gold buckle .00 5.00 12.00
❑ 23 Bespin Luke Skywalker/ gold buckle .01 5.00 12.00
❑ 30 C-3PO metalized body 4.00 10.00
❑ 40 Chewbacca boushh/ bounty hunter 5.00 12.00
❑ 50 Endor Rebel Soldier .00 4.00 10.00
❑ 51 Endor Rebel Soldier .01 4.00 10.00
❑ 60 Lobot 4.00 10.00
❑ 70 Luke Skywalker/ blast shield helmet 4.00 10.00
❑ 80 Luke Skywalker ceremonial 4.00 10.00
❑ 90 Luke Skywalker/ stormtrooper .03 4.00 10.00
❑ 91 Luke Skywalker/ stormtrooper .04 4.00 10.00
❑ 100 Mon Mothma 4.00 10.00
❑ 110 Obi-Wan Kenobi .03 4.00 10.00
❑ 111 Obi-Wan Kenobi .04 4.00 10.00
❑ 120 Orrimaarko 4.00 10.00
❑ 130 Han Solo bespin 5.00 12.00

STAR WARS

- ☐ 140 Han Solo carbonite .04 5.00 12.00
- ☐ 141 Han Solo carbonite .05 4.00 10.00
- ☐ 150 Han Solo endor gear .01 4.00 10.00
- ☐ 151 Han Solo endor gear .02 4.00 10.00
- ☐ 160 Hoth Rebel Soldier .02 5.00 12.00
- ☐ 161 Hoth Rebel Soldier .03 5.00 12.00
- ☐ 170 Lando Calrissian general .00 4.00 10.00
- ☐ 171 Lando Calrissian general .01 4.00 10.00
- ☐ 180 Lando Calrissian skiff guard .01 4.00 10.00
- ☐ 181 Lando Calrissian skiff guard .02 4.00 10.00
- ☐ 190 Princess Leia Organa/ blaster 4.00 10.00
- ☐ 200 Princess Leia Organa/ ewok celebration .004.00 10.00
- ☐ 201 Princess Leia Organa/ ewok celebration .014.00 10.00
- ☐ 210 Princess Leia Organa/ jabbas prisoner .015.00 12.00
- ☐ 211 Princess Leia Organa/ jabbas prisoner .025.00 12.00
- ☐ 220 R2-D2 death star trash frame 7.50 15.00
- ☐ 221 R2-D2 imperial trash frame 20.00 40.00
- ☐ 230 Rebel Fleet Trooper .01 4.00 10.00
- ☐ 231 Rebel Fleet Trooper/ with sticker .01 4.00 10.00
- ☐ 232 Rebel Fleet Trooper .02 4.00 10.00

1996-97 Star Wars Power of the Force Green Cards Freeze Frames Collection 2

- ☐ 10 8D8 6.00 12.00
- ☐ 20 Admiral Ackbar/ commlink wrist blaster 6.00 12.00
- ☐ 30 Admiral Ackbar/ wrist blaster 6.00 12.00
- ☐ 40 Biggs Darklighter 10.00 20.00
- ☐ 41 Biggs Darklighter/ no silver paint/ on chest50.00 100.00
- ☐ 60 Ewoks Wicket & Logray 5.00 10.00
- ☐ 70 Gamorrean Guard 10.00 20.00
- ☐ 80 EV-9D9 6.00 12.00
- ☐ 80 Lak Sivrak 6.00 12.00
- ☐ 90 Malakili 5.00 10.00
- ☐ 100 Nien Nunb 5.00 10.00
- ☐ 110 Saelt-Marae 6.00 12.00
- ☐ 120 Ugnaughts 6.00 12.00

1996-97 Star Wars Power of the Force Green Cards Freeze Frames Collection 3

- ☐ 10 AT-AT Driver 20.00 40.00
- ☐ 20 AT-ST Driver 10.00 20.00
- ☐ 30 Boba Fett 25.00 50.00
- ☐ 31 Boba Fett 2 circle hands
- ☐ 40 Captain Piett/ rifle and pistol 7.50 15.00
- ☐ 50 Captain Piett/ pistol and baton 20.00 40.00
- ☐ 60 Darth Vader 7.50 15.00
- ☐ 61 Darth Vader/ removable helmet 15.00 30.00
- ☐ 70 Death Star Droid 6.00 12.00
- ☐ 80 Death Star Trooper 7.50 15.00
- ☐ 90 Emperor Palpatine 5.00 10.00
- ☐ 100 Emperor's Royal Guard 6.00 12.00
- ☐ 110 Garindan 7.50 15.00
- ☐ 120 Grand Moff Tarkin 7.50 15.00
- ☐ 130 Ishi Tib gray pouch 10.00 20.00
- ☐ 131 Ishi Tib brown pouch 12.50 25.00
- ☐ 140 Pote Snitkin 7.50 15.00
- ☐ 150 Princess Leia Organa/ hoth 5.00 10.00
- ☐ 160 Ree-Yees 10.00 20.00
- ☐ 170 Sandtrooper 25.00 50.00
- ☐ 180 Snowtrooper 7.50 15.00
- ☐ 190 Stormtrooper 6.00 12.00
- ☐ 200 TIE Fighter Pilot 12.50 25.00
- ☐ 210 Weequay 125.00 250.00
- ☐ 220 Zuckuss 10.00 20.00

1996-97 Star Wars Power of the Force Green Gunner Stations

- ☐ 10 Millennium Falcon/ with Han Solo 5.00 12.00
- ☐ 20 Millennium Falcon/ with Luke Skywalker 5.00 12.00
- ☐ 30 Tie Fighter with Darth Vader 5.00 12.00

1996-97 Star Wars Power of the Force Green Gunner Stations (loose)

- ☐ 10 Millennium Falcon/ with Han Solo 3.00 8.00
- ☐ 20 Millennium Falcon/ with Luke Skywalker 3.00 8.00
- ☐ 30 Tie Fighter with Darth Vader 3.00 8.00

1996-97 Star Wars Power of the Force Green Playsets

- ☐ 10 Endor Attack 25.00 50.00
- ☐ 20 Hoth Battle 25.00 50.00

1996-97 Star Wars Power of the Force Green Playsets (loose)

- ☐ 10 Endor Attack 12.50 25.00
- ☐ 20 Hoth Battle 12.50 25.00

1996-97 Star Wars Power of the Force Green Vehicles

- ☐ 10 A-Wing Fighter 20.00 40.00
- ☐ 20 Cruisemissile Trooper 15.00 30.00
- ☐ 30 Darth Vader's TIE Fighter 20.00 40.00
- ☐ 40 Dash Rendar's Outrider 20.00 40.00
- ☐ 50 Imperial AT-AT Walker 125.00 250.00
- ☐ 60 Luke's T-16 Skyhopper 20.00 40.00
- ☐ 70 Speeder Bike/Leia Organa .00 25.00 50.00
- ☐ 71 Speeder Bike/Leia Organa .01 25.00 50.00
- ☐ 80 Speeder Bike/Luke Skywalker 25.00 50.00
- ☐ 90 Speeder Bike/Luke Skywalker no glove 30.00 60.00
- ☐ 100 Slave I 40.00 80.00
- ☐ 110 X-Wing Fighter 50.00 100.00

1996-97 Star Wars Power of the Force Green Vehicles (loose)

- ☐ 10 A-Wing Fighter 10.00 20.00
- ☐ 20 Cruisemissile Trooper 7.50 15.00
- ☐ 30 Darth Vader's TIE Fighter 10.00 20.00
- ☐ 40 Dash Rendar's Outrider 10.00 20.00
- ☐ 50 Imperial AT-AT Walker 75.00 150.00
- ☐ 60 Luke's T-16 Skyhopper 10.00 20.00
- ☐ 70 Slave I 20.00 40.00
- ☐ 80 Speeder Bike 10.00 20.00
- ☐ 90 X-Wing Fighter 25.00 50.00

1996-98 Star Wars Power of the Force Collector Series 12-Inch

- ☐ 10 Admiral Ackbar 10.00 20.00
- ☐ 20 Boba Fett 30.00 60.00
- ☐ 30 C-3PO 20.00 40.00
- ☐ 40 Chewbacca 20.00 40.00
- ☐ 50 Darth Vader 20.00 40.00
- ☐ 60 Obi-Wan Kenobi/ light blue background 30.00 60.00
- ☐ 61 Obi-Wan Kenobi/ dark blue background 40.00 80.00
- ☐ 70 Han Solo/ light blue background 20.00 40.00
- ☐ 71 Han Solo/ dark blue background 30.00 60.00
- ☐ 80 Lando Calrissian 12.50 25.00
- ☐ 90 Luke Skywalker/ binoculars on belt 12.50 25.00
- ☐ 91 Luke Skywalker/ binoculars on board 12.50 25.00
- ☐ 100 Luke Skywalker bespin 10.00 20.00
- ☐ 110 Luke Skywalker x-wing 12.50 25.00
- ☐ 120 Princess Leia 125.00 250.00
- ☐ 130 Sandtrooper 25.00 50.00
- ☐ 140 Stormtrooper 20.00 40.00
- ☐ 150 TIE-Fighter Pilot 15.00 30.00
- ☐ 160 Tusken Raider blaster 10.00 20.00
- ☐ 170 Tusken Raider gaderffii 15.00 30.00

1996-98 Star Wars Power of the Force Collector Series 12-Inch Exclusives

- ☐ 10 AT-AT Driver/ Service Merchandise exclusive25.00 50.00
- ☐ 20 Grand Moff Tarkin/Imperial Gunner 25.00 50.00 FAO Schwartz exclusive
- ☐ 30 Han Solo & Luke Skywalker 40.00 80.00 stormtrooper gear/ Kay-Bee exclusive
- ☐ 40 Han Solo hoth & Tauntaun/ Toys R 30.00 60.00 Us exclusive
- ☐ 50 Hoth 4-Pack/Luke Skywalker hoth/ 25.00 50.00 Han Solo hoth/Snowtrooper/AT-AT Driver
- ☐ 60 Jedi Luke Skywalker/Bib Fortuna 25.00 50.00 white hands/ FAO Schwartz exclusive
- ☐ 70 Jedi Luke Skywalker/Bib Fortuna 25.00 50.00 blue hands/ FAO Schwartz exclusive
- ☐ 80 Luke Skywalker hoth vs Wampa/ Target exclusive 40.00 80.00

1996-98 Star Wars Power of the Force Collector Series 12-Inch Exclusives (loose)

- ☐ 10 AT-AT Driver/ Service Merchandise exclusive12.50 25.00
- ☐ 20 Grand Moff Tarkin/Imperial Gunner 12.50 25.00 FAO Schwartz exclusive
- ☐ 30 Han Solo & Luke Skywalker 20.00 40.00 stormtrooper gear/ Kay-Bee exclusive
- ☐ 40 Han Solo hoth & Tauntaun/ Toys R 15.00 30.00 Us exclusive
- ☐ 50 Hoth 4-Pack/Luke Skywalker 15.00 30.00 hoth/Han Solo hoth/Snowtrooper/AT-AT Driver
- ☐ 60 Jedi Luke Skywalker/Bib Fortuna white 12.50 25.00 hands/ FAO Schwartz exclusive
- ☐ 70 Jedi Luke Skywalker/Bib Fortuna 12.50 25.00 blue hands/ FAO Schwartz exclusive
- ☐ 80 Luke Skywalker hoth vs Wampa 25.00 50.00 Target exclusive

1996-98 Star Wars Power of the Force Collector Series 12-Inch (loose)

- ☐ 10 Admiral Ackbar 5.00 10.00
- ☐ 20 Boba Fett 12.50 25.00
- ☐ 30 C-3PO 10.00 20.00
- ☐ 40 Chewbacca 10.00 20.00
- ☐ 50 Darth Vader 12.50 25.00
- ☐ 60 Obi-Wan Kenobi 12.50 25.00
- ☐ 70 Han Solo 10.00 20.00
- ☐ 80 Lando Calrissian 6.00 12.00
- ☐ 90 Luke Skywalker 6.00 12.00
- ☐ 100 Luke Skywalker bespin 5.00 10.00
- ☐ 110 Luke Skywalker x-wing 6.00 12.00
- ☐ 120 Princess Leia 6.00 12.00
- ☐ 130 Sandtrooper 12.50 25.00
- ☐ 140 Stormtrooper 10.00 20.00
- ☐ 150 TIE-Fighter Pilot 7.50 15.00
- ☐ 160 Tusken Raider blaster 5.00 10.00
- ☐ 170 Tusken Raider gaderffii 7.50 15.00

1996-98 Star Wars Power of the Force Green 12-Inch

- ☐ 10 AT-AT Driver
- ☐ 20 Barquin D'an
- ☐ 30 Chewbacca
- ☐ 40 Chewbacca in chains
- ☐ 50 Darth Vader talking
- ☐ 60 Emperor Palpatine
- ☐ 70 Grand Moff Tarkin/ interrogation droid
- ☐ 80 Greedo
- ☐ 80 Obi-Wan Kenobi/ glowing lightsaber
- ☐ 90 Han Solo hoth/ firing rebel blaster
- ☐ 100 Han Solo with magnetic detonators
- ☐ 110 Jawa light up eyes
- ☐ 120 Luke Skywalker ceremonial/ with ceremonial medal
- ☐ 130 Luke Skywalker hoth/ firing rebel blaster
- ☐ 140 Luke Skywalker jedi/ glow in the dark lightsaber
- ☐ 150 Luke Skywalker stormtrooper/ with dianoga tenticle
- ☐ 160 Ponda Baba
- ☐ 170 Princess Leia jabba's prisoner
- ☐ 180 R2-D2 remote control
- ☐ 190 Sandtrooper imperial droid
- ☐ 200 Snowtrooper/ firing imperial blaster
- ☐ 210 Snowtrooper blue chestplate/ firing imperial blaster
- ☐ 220 Yoda fully poseable

1996-98 Star Wars Power of the Force Green 12-Inch Exclusives

- ☐ 10 Boba Fett talking/ Kay-Bee exclusive
- ☐ 20 C-3PO & R2-D2 electric/ Toys R Us exclusive
- ☐ 30 Cantina Band /Figrin D'an/ Wal-Mart exclusive
- ☐ 40 Cantina Band/Doikk N'ats/ Wal-Mart exclusive
- ☐ 50 Cantina Band/Ickabel/ Wal-Mart exclusive
- ☐ 60 Cantina Band/Nolan/ Wal-Mart exclusive
- ☐ 70 Cantina Band/Tech/ Wal-Mart exclusive
- ☐ 80 Cantina Band#Tedn/ Wal-Mart exclusive
- ☐ 90 Emperor Palpatine electric/Emperor's Royal Guard/ Target exclusive
- ☐ 100 Greedo/ JCPenney exclusive
- ☐ 110 Han Solo & Carbonite Block/ Target exclusive
- ☐ 120 Obi-Wan Kenobi vs Darth Vader/ electric JCPenney exclusive
- ☐ 130 Princess Leia Collection/Princess Leia jabba's prisoner/R2-D2 electric/
- ☐ 140 Princess Leia hoth/ firing rebel blaster/ Service Merchandise exclusive
- ☐ 150 R2-D2 fully posable with scope/ Wal-Mart exclusive
- ☐ 160 R5-D4 fully posable/ Wal-Mart exclusive
- ☐ 170 Rebel 3-Pack/Luke Skywalker tatooine/Princess Leia boushh/Han Solo bespi
- ☐ 180 Sandtrooper/ Diamond exclusive
- ☐ 190 Wicket fully posable/ Wal-Mart exclusive

1996-98 Star Wars Power of the Force Green 12-Inch Exclusives (loose)

- ☐ 10 Boba Fett talking/ Kay-Bee exclusive
- ☐ 20 C-3PO & R2-D2 electric/ Toys R Us exclusive
- ☐ 30 Cantina Band Figrin D'an/ Wal-Mart exclusive
- ☐ 40 Cantina Band/Doikk N'ats/ Wal-Mart exclusive
- ☐ 50 Cantina Band/Ickabel/ Wal-Mart exclusive
- ☐ 60 Cantina Band/Nolan/ Wal-Mart exclusive
- ☐ 70 Cantina Band/Tech/ Wal-Mart exclusive
- ☐ 80 Cantina Band#Tedn/ Wal-Mart exclusive
- ☐ 90 Emperor Palpatine electric/Emperor's Royal Guard/ Target exclusive
- ☐ 100 Greedo/ JCPenney exclusive
- ☐ 110 Han Solo & Carbonite Block/ Target exclusive
- ☐ 120 Obi-Wan Kenobi vs Darth Vader/ electric JCPenney exclusive
- ☐ 130 Princess Leia Collection/Princess Leia jabba's prisoner/R2-D2 electric/
- ☐ 140 Princess Leia hoth/ firing rebel blaster/ Service Merchandise exclusive
- ☐ 150 R2-D2 fully posable with scope/ Wal-Mart exclusive
- ☐ 160 R5-D4 fully posable/ Wal-Mart exclusive
- ☐ 170 Rebel 3-Pack/Luke Skywalker tatooine/Princess Leia boushh/Han Solo bespi
- ☐ 180 Sandtrooper/ Diamond exclusive
- ☐ 190 Wicket fully posable/ Wal-Mart exclusive

1996-98 Star Wars Power of the Force Green 12-Inch (loose)

- ☐ 10 AT-AT Driver
- ☐ 20 Barquin D'an
- ☐ 30 Chewbacca
- ☐ 40 Chewbacca in chains
- ☐ 50 Darth Vader talking
- ☐ 60 Emperor Palpatine
- ☐ 70 Grand Moff Tarkin/ interrogation droid
- ☐ 80 Greedo
- ☐ 90 Obi-Wan Kenobi/ glowing lightsaber
- ☐ 100 Han Solo hoth/ firing rebel blaster
- ☐ 110 Han Solo with magnetic detonators
- ☐ 120 Jawa light up eyes
- ☐ 130 Luke Skywalker ceremonial/ with ceremonial medal
- ☐ 140 Luke Skywalker hoth/ firing rebel blaster
- ☐ 150 Luke Skywalker jedi/ glow in the dark lightsaber
- ☐ 160 Luke Skywalker stormtrooper/ with dianoga tenticle
- ☐ 170 Ponda Baba
- ☐ 180 Princess Leia jabba's prisoner
- ☐ 190 R2-D2 remote control
- ☐ 200 Sandtrooper imperial droid
- ☐ 210 Snowtrooper/ firing imperial blaster
- ☐ 220 Snowtrooper blue chestplate/ firing imperial blaster
- ☐ 230 Yoda fully poseable

1997-98 Star Wars Power of the Force Green 2-Packs Real Feel

- ☐ 10 Bantha/ and Tusken Raider
- ☐ 20 Rancor/ and Luke Skywalker

1997-98 Star Wars Power of the Force Green Millennium Mint

- ☐ 10 Bespin Han Solo
- ☐ 11 Bespin Han Solo with/ new millennium/ minted coin text
- ☐ 20 C-3PO silver leg
- ☐ 30 Chewbacca
- ☐ 31 Chewbacca with/ new millennium/ minted coin text
- ☐ 40 Emperor Palpatine
- ☐ 50 Luke Skywalker/ endor .00
- ☐ 51 Luke Skywalker/ endor .01
- ☐ 60 Princess Leia/ endor .00
- ☐ 61 Princess Leia/ endor .01
- ☐ 70 Snowtrooper
- ☐ 71 Snowtrooper with/ new millennium/ minted coin text

1997-98 Star Wars Power of the Force Green Millennium Mint Coins (loose)

- ☐ 10 Bespin Han Solo
- ☐ 20 C-3PO
- ☐ 30 Chewbacca
- ☐ 40 Emperor Palpatine
- ☐ 50 Luke Skywalker
- ☐ 60 Princess Leia
- ☐ 70 Snowtrooper

1997-99 Star Wars Power of the Force Green Cinema Scenes

- ☐ 10 Cantina Aliens/Labria/Nabrun Leids/Takeel
- ☐ 20 Cantina Showdown/Dr. Evazan/Ponda Baba/Obi-Wan Kenobi
- ☐ 30 Death Star Escape/Han Solo stormtrooper/Luke Skywalker stormtrooper/Chew
- ☐ 40 Final Jedi Duel .00/Emperor Palpatine/Darth Vader/Luke Skywalker
- ☐ 41 Final Jedi Duel .01/Emperor Palpatine/Darth Vader/Luke Skywalker
- ☐ 50 Jabba the Hutt's Dancers/Rystall/Greeata/Lyn Me
- ☐ 60 Jedi Spirits/Anakin/Yoda/Obi-Wan
- ☐ 70 Mynock Hunt/Princess Leia/Han Solo/Chewbacca
- ☐ 80 Purchase of Droids/Uncle Owen Lars/C-3PO/Luke Skywalker bespin

1998 Star Wars Power of the Force Green Cards Princess Leia Collection

- ☐ 10 Princess Leia/ red outfit/Han Solo .00
- ☐ 11 Princess Leia/ red outfit/Han Solo .01
- ☐ 20 Princess Leia ceremonial/Luke Skywalker ceremonial .00
- ☐ 21 Princess Leia ceremonial/Luke Skywalker ceremonial .01
- ☐ 30 Princess Leia/R2-D2 .00
- ☐ 31 Princess Leia/R2-D2 .01
- ☐ 40 Princess Leia/ ewok celebration/Wicket .00
- ☐ 41 Princess Leia/ ewok celebration/Wicket .01

1998 Star Wars Power of the Force Green Complete Galaxy

- ☐ 10 Dagobah with Yoda
- ☐ 20 Death Star with Darth Vader
- ☐ 30 Endor with Ewok .00
- ☐ 31 Endor with Ewok .01
- ☐ 40 Tatooine with Luke Skywalker

1998 Star Wars Power of the Force Green Complete Galaxy (loose)

- ☐ 10 Dagobah with Yoda
- ☐ 20 Death Star with Darth Vader
- ☐ 30 Endor with Ewok
- ☐ 40 Tatooine with Luke Skywalker

1998 Star Wars Power of the Force Green Max Rebo Band Pairs Vendor Exclusive

- ☐ 10 Barquin D'an/Droopy McCool
- ☐ 20 Max Rebo/Doda Bodonawieedo
- ☐ 30 Joh Yowza/Sy Snootles

1998-99 Star Wars Power of the Force Green Cards CommTech

- ☐ 10 Admiral Motti
- ☐ 20 Darth Vader/with interrogation droid
- ☐ 30 Greedo/ large vest
- ☐ 31 Greedo/ large vest/ yellow knee pins V
- ☐ 40 Han Solo/ blaster holster
- ☐ 50 Jawa with goink droid/ with foot holes
- ☐ 51 Jawa with goink droid/ with one foot hole V
- ☐ 52 Jawa with goink droid/ no foot holes V
- ☐ 60 Luke Skywalker/ skyhopper
- ☐ 70 Princess Leia/ white hooded gown
- ☐ 80 R2-D2 with holographic/ Princess Leia
- ☐ 81 R2-D2 with foot peg and/ holographic Princess Leia V
- ☐ 90 Stormtrooper/ blaster rack
- ☐ 100 Wuher

1998-99 Star Wars Power of the Force Green Cards CommTech Chips (loose)

- ☐ 10 Admiral Motti
- ☐ 20 Darth Vader
- ☐ 30 Greedo
- ☐ 40 Han Solo
- ☐ 50 Jawa with Goink Droid
- ☐ 60 Luke Skywalker
- ☐ 70 Princess Leia
- ☐ 80 R2-D2
- ☐ 90 Stormtrooper
- ☐ 100 Wuher

1998-99 Star Wars Power of the Force Green Cards Episode I Flashback Photo

- ☐ 10 Anakin Skywalker
- ☐ 20 Aunt Beru
- ☐ 30 Ben (Obi-Wan) Kenobi/ cape with hood on
- ☐ 40 C-3PO removable arm
- ☐ 50 Darth Vader
- ☐ 60 Emperor Palpatine force lightning
- ☐ 70 Hoth Chewbacca
- ☐ 80 Luke Skywalker tatooine/ with hat and goggles
- ☐ 81 Luke Skywalker tatooine/ with had and goggles/ with Obi-Wan photo
- ☐ 90 Princess Leia/ ceremonial/-right arm bracelet
- ☐ 100 R2-D2 lightsaber left side
- ☐ 101 R2-D2 lightsaber right side
- ☐ 110 Yoda robe with/ maroon accents/ on neck and waist

1998-99 Star Wars Power of the Force Green Expanded Universe Collection 2

- ☐ 10 Clone Emperor Palpatine
- ☐ 20 Dark Trooper
- ☐ 30 Grand Admiral Thrawn
- ☐ 40 Imperial Sentinel
- ☐ 50 Kyle Katarn
- ☐ 60 Luke Skywalker/ black robe with/ blue/black sleeves
- ☐ 70 Mara Jade
- ☐ 80 Princess Leia/ red/black robe/ red lightsaber
- ☐ 90 Spacetrooper

1998-99 Star Wars Power of the Force Green Expanded Universe Vehicles

- ☐ 10 Airspeeder/Airspeeder Pilot
- ☐ 20 Cloud Car/Cloud Car Pilot
- ☐ 30 Speeder Bike/Rebel Speeder Bike Pilot

1998-99 Star Wars Power of the Force Green Expanded Universe Vehicles (loose)

- ☐ 10 Airspeeder
- ☐ 20 Cloud Car
- ☐ 30 Speeder Bike

1999 Star Wars Power of the Force Green 12-Inch Portrait Edition

- ☐ 10 Princess Leia ceremonial

1999 Star Wars Power of the Force Green 12-Inch Portrait Edition (loose)

- ☐ 10 Princess Leia ceremonial

1977 Star Wars

- COMPLETE SET (330) 125.00 250.00
- COMPLETE SERIES 1 (66) 25.00 50.00
- COMPLETE SERIES 2 (66) 25.00 50.00
- COMPLETE SERIES 3 (66) 25.00 50.00
- COMPLETE SERIES 4 (66) 25.00 50.00
- COMPLETE SERIES 5 (66) 25.00 50.00

- ☐ 1 Luke Skywalker .60 1.50
- ☐ 2 C-3PO and R2-D2 .60 1.50
- ☐ 3 The Little Droid R2-D2 .60 1.50
- ☐ 4 Space pirate Han Solo .60 1.50
- ☐ 5 Princess Leia Organa .60 1.50
- ☐ 6 Ben Kenobi .60 1.50
- ☐ 7 The villainous Darth Vader .60 1.50
- ☐ 8 Grand Moff Tarkin .60 1.50
- ☐ 9 Rebels defend their ship .60 1.50
- ☐ 10 Princess Leia captured! .60 1.50
- ☐ 11 Artoo is imprisoned by the Jawas .60 1.50
- ☐ 12 The droids are reunited! .60 1.50
- ☐ 13 A sale on droids! .60 1.50
- ☐ 14 Luke checks out his new droid .60 1.50
- ☐ 15 R2-D2 is left behind .60 1.50
- ☐ 16 Jawas of Tatooine .60 1.50
- ☐ 17 Lord Vader threatens Princess Leia .60 1.50
- ☐ 18 R2-D2 is missing! .60 1.50
- ☐ 19 Searching for the little droid .60 1.50
- ☐ 20 Hunted by the Sandpeople! .60 1.50
- ☐ 21 The Tusken Raiders .60 1.50
- ☐ 22 Rescued by Ben Kenobi .60 1.50
- ☐ 23 C-3PO is injured .60 1.50
- ☐ 24 Stormtroopers seek the droids .60 1.50
- ☐ 25 Luke rushed to save his loved ones .60 1.50
- ☐ 26 A horrified Luke sees family killed .60 1.50
- ☐ 27 Some repairs for C-3PO .60 1.50
- ☐ 28 Luke agrees to join Ben Kenobi .60 1.50
- ☐ 29 Stopped by Stormtroopers .60 1.50
- ☐ 30 Han in the Millennium falcom .60 1.50
- ☐ 31 Sighting the Death Star .60 1.50
- ☐ 32 Lord Vader's Guards .60 1.50
- ☐ 33 The droids in the control room .60 1.50
- ☐ 34 C-3PO diverts the guards .60 1.50
- ☐ 35 Luke and Han as stormtroopers .60 1.50
- ☐ 36 Blast of the laser rifle! .60 1.50
- ☐ 37 Cornered in the labyrinth .60 1.50
- ☐ 38 Luke and Han in the refuse room .60 1.50
- ☐ 39 Steel walls close in on out heroes! .60 1.50
- ☐ 40 Droids rescue their masters! .60 1.50
- ☐ 41 Facing the deadly chasm .60 1.50
- ☐ 42 Stromtroopers attack .60 1.50
- ☐ 43 Luke prepares to swing across the chasm .60 1.50
- ☐ 44 Han and Chewie shoot it out .60 1.50
- ☐ 45 The light sabre .60 1.50
- ☐ 46 A desperate moment for Ben .60 1.50
- ☐ 47 Luke prepares for the battle .60 1.50
- ☐ 48 R2-D2 is loaded aboard .60 1.50
- ☐ 49 The rebels monitor the raid .60 1.50
- ☐ 50 Rebel leaders wonder about their fate! .60 1.50
- ☐ 51 C-3PO and Princess Leia .60 1.50
- ☐ 52 Who will win the final Star War .60 1.50
- ☐ 53 Battle in outer space .60 1.50
- ☐ 54 The victors receive their reward .60 1.50
- ☐ 55 Han, Chewie, and Luke .60 1.50
- ☐ 56 A day of rejoicing .60 1.50
- ☐ 57 Mark Hamill as Luke Skywalker .60 1.50
- ☐ 58 Harrison Ford as Han Solo .60 1.50
- ☐ 59 Alec Guinness as Ben Kenobi .60 1.50
- ☐ 60 Peter Cushing as Grand Moff Tarkin .60 1.50
- ☐ 61 Mark Hamill in control room .60 1.50
- ☐ 62 Lord Vader's stormtroopers .60 1.50
- ☐ 63 May the Force be with you .60 1.50
- ☐ 64 Governor of Imperial Outlands .60 1.50
- ☐ 65 Carrie Fisher and Mark Hamill .60 1.50
- ☐ 66 Amazing Robot C-3PO .60 1.50
- ☐ 67 C-3PO and Luke .60 1.50
- ☐ 68 The Millennium Falcon .60 1.50
- ☐ 69 Threepio's desert Trek .60 1.50
- ☐ 70 Special mission for R2-D2 .60 1.50
- ☐ 71 The incredible C-3PO .60 1.50
- ☐ 72 Ben Kenobi rescues Luke .60 1.50
- ☐ 73 The droids wait for Luke .60 1.50
- ☐ 74 Luke Skywalker on Tatooine .60 1.50
- ☐ 75 Darth Vader strangles a rebel .60 1.50
- ☐ 76 R2-D2 on the rebel starship .60 1.50
- ☐ 77 Waiting in the control room .60 1.50
- ☐ 78 Droids to the rescue .60 1.50
- ☐ 79 Preparing to board Solo's spaceship .60 1.50
- ☐ 80 Where has R2-D2 gone? .60 1.50
- ☐ 81 Weapons of the Death Star .60 1.50
- ☐ 82 A daring rescue .60 1.50
- ☐ 83 Aboard the Millennium Falcon .60 1.50
- ☐ 84 Rebel pilot prepares for the raid .60 1.50
- ☐ 85 Luke on the sand planet .60 1.50
- ☐ 86 A mighty explosion .60 1.50
- ☐ 87 The droids try to rescue Luke .60 1.50
- ☐ 88 Stromtroopers guard Solo's ship .60 1.50
- ☐ 89 The imprisoned Princess Leia .60 1.50
- ☐ 90 Honoring the Victors .60 1.50
- ☐ 91 Solo and Chewie prepare to leave Luke .60 1.50
- ☐ 92 Advance of the Tusken Raider .60 1.50
- ☐ 93 Stormtroopers blast the rebels .60 1.50
- ☐ 94 Interrogated by Stormtroopers .60 1.50
- ☐ 95 Sighting R2-D2 .60 1.50
- ☐ 96 The droids on Tatooine .60 1.50
- ☐ 97 Meeting at the cantina .60 1.50
- ☐ 98 C-3PO .60 1.50
- ☐ 99 Ben with the light sabre .60 1.50
- ☐ 100 Our heroes at the spaceport .60 1.50
- ☐ 101 The Wookies Chewbacca .60 1.50
- ☐ 102 Rebels prepare for the big fight .60 1.50
- ☐ 103 Stormtroopers attack our heroes .60 1.50
- ☐ 104 Luke's uncle and aunt .60 1.50
- ☐ 105 Imperial soldiers burn through the starship .60 1.50
- ☐ 106 A message from Princess Leia .60 1.50
- ☐ 107 The Tusken Raider .60 1.50
- ☐ 108 Princess Leia observes the battle .60 1.50
- ☐ 109 Ben turns off the tractor beam .60 1.50
- ☐ 110 Threepio fools the guards .60 1.50
- ☐ 111 Chewie and Han Solo .60 1.50
- ☐ 112 Threatened by Sandpeople .60 1.50
- ☐ 113 Ben hides from Imperial stormtroopers .60 1.50
- ☐ 114 Planning to escape .60 1.50
- ☐ 115 Hiding in the Millennium Falcon .60 1.50
- ☐ 116 Honored for their heroism .60 1.50
- ☐ 117 Chewbacca posed as a prisoner .60 1.50
- ☐ 118 R2-D2 and C-3PO .60 1.50
- ☐ 119 Threepio, Ben and Luke .60 1.50
- ☐ 120 Luke destroys an Imperial ship .60 1.50
- ☐ 121 Han Solo and Chewbacca .60 1.50
- ☐ 122 The Millenium Falcon .60 1.50
- ☐ 123 Solo blasts a stormtrooper .60 1.50
- ☐ 124 Threepio searches for R2-D2 .60 1.50
- ☐ 125 Luke in disguise .60 1.50
- ☐ 126 A quizzical Threepio .60 1.50
- ☐ 127 The Rebel fleet .60 1.50
- ☐ 128 Roar of the Wookie .60 1.50
- ☐ 129 May the Force be with you .60 1.50
- ☐ 130 Pursued by the Jawas .60 1.50
- ☐ 131 Spectacular battle .60 1.50
- ☐ 132 Lord Vader and a soldier .60 1.50
- ☐ 133 Ben and Luke w .60 1.50 C-3PO
- ☐ 134 Luke dreams of being a star pilot .60 1.50
- ☐ 135 Cantina troubles .60 1.50
- ☐ 136 Danger from all sides .60 1.50
- ☐ 137 Luke attacked by a strange creature .60 1.50
- ☐ 138 On the track of the droids .60 1.50
- ☐ 139 Han Solo .60 1.50
- ☐ 140 R2-D2-where are you? .60 1.50
- ☐ 141 Some quick thinking by Luke .60 1.50
- ☐ 142 Darth Vader inspects the throttled ship .60 1.50
- ☐ 143 Droids on the sand planet .60 1.50
- ☐ 144 Harrison Ford as Han Solo .60 1.50
- ☐ 145 Escape from the Death Star .60 1.50
- ☐ 146 Luke Skywalkers aunt preparing dinner .60 1.50
- ☐ 147 Bargaining with the Jawas .60 1.50
- ☐ 148 The fearsome stormtroopers .60 1.50
- ☐ 149 The evil Grand Moff Tarkin .60 1.50
- ☐ 150 Shootout at the Chasm .60 1.50
- ☐ 151 Planning an escape .60 1.50
- ☐ 152 Spirited Princess Leia .60 1.50
- ☐ 153 The fantastic droid Threepio .60 1.50
- ☐ 154 Princess Leia comforts Luke .60 1.50
- ☐ 155 The Escape Pod is jettisoned .60 1.50
- ☐ 156 R2-D2 is lifted aboard .60 1.50
- ☐ 157 Learn about the Force, Luke .60 1.50
- ☐ 158 Rebel victory .60 1.50
- ☐ 159 Luke Skywalker's home .60 1.50
- ☐ 160 Destroying a world .60 1.50
- ☐ 161 Preparing for the raid .60 1.50
- ☐ 162 Han Solo cornered by Greedo .60 1.50
- ☐ 163 Caught in the tractor beam .60 1.50
- ☐ 164 Tusken Raiders capture Luke .60 1.50
- ☐ 165 Escaping from stormtroopers .60 1.50
- ☐ 166 A close call for Luke and Leia .60 1.50
- ☐ 167 Surrounded by Lord Vader's soldiers .60 1.50
- ☐ 168 Hunting the fugitives .60 1.50
- ☐ 169 Meeting at the Death Star .60 1.50
- ☐ 170 Luke and the Princess trapped .60 1.50
- ☐ 171 The walls are moving .60 1.50
- ☐ 172 Droids in the escape pod .60 1.50
- ☐ 173 The stormtroopers .60 1.50
- ☐ 174 Solo aims for trouble .60 1.50
- ☐ 175 A closer look at a Jawa .60 1.50
- ☐ 176 Luke Skywalkers dream .60 1.50
- ☐ 177 Solo swings into action .60 1.50
- ☐ 178 The Star Warriors .60 1.50
- ☐ 179 Stormtroopers search the spaceport .60 1.50
- ☐ 180 Princess Leia honors the victors .60 1.50
- ☐ 181 Peter Cushing as Grand Moff Tarkin .60 1.50
- ☐ 182 Deadly blasters .60 1.50
- ☐ 183 Dave Prowse as Darth Vader .60 1.50
- ☐ 184 Luke and his uncle .60 1.50
- ☐ 185 Luke on Tatooine .60 1.50
- ☐ 186 The Jawas .60 1.50
- ☐ 187 Threepio and friend .60 1.50
- ☐ 188 Starship under fire .60 1.50
- ☐ 189 Mark Hamill as Luke .60 1.50
- ☐ 190 Carrie Fisher as Princess Leia .60 1.50
- ☐ 191 Life on the desert world .60 1.50
- ☐ 192 Liberated Princess .60 1.50
- ☐ 193 Like's uncle buys Threepio .60 1.50
- ☐ 194 Stormtroopers attack .60 1.50
- ☐ 195 Alec Guinness as Ben Kenobi .60 1.50
- ☐ 196 Lord Darth Vader .60 1.50
- ☐ 197 Leia blasts a stormtrooper .60 1.50
- ☐ 198 Luke decides to leave Tatooine .60 1.50
- ☐ 199 The star warriors aim for action .60 1.50
- ☐ 200 C-3PO searches for his counterpart .60 1.50
- ☐ 201 Raid at Mos Eisley .60 1.50
- ☐ 202 Inquiring about Obi-Wan Kenobi .60 1.50
- ☐ 203 A band of Jawas .60 1.50
- ☐ 204 Stalking the corridors of the Death Star .60 1.50
- ☐ 205 Desperate moments for out heroes .60 1.50
- ☐ 206 Searching for the missing droid .60 1.50
- ☐ 207A C-3PO A.Daniels ERR Obscene 20.00 40.00
- ☐ 207B C-3PO A.Daniels COR Airbrushed .60 1.50
- ☐ 208 Luke Skywalker on the desert planet .60 1.50
- ☐ 209 The Rebel Troops .60 1.50
- ☐ 210 Princess Leia blasts the enemy .60 1.50
- ☐ 211 A proud moment for Han and Luke .60 1.50
- ☐ 212 A stormtrooper is blasted .60 1.50
- ☐ 213 Monitoring the battle .60 1.50
- ☐ 214 Luke and Leia .60 1.50
- ☐ 215 Han bows out of the battle .60 1.50

STAR WARS

☐ 216 Han and Leia quarrel .60 1.50
☐ 217 The Dark Lord of Sith .60 1.50
☐ 218 Luke Skywalker's home destroyed .60 1.50
☐ 219 The swing to freedom .60 1.50
☐ 220 Im going to regret this .60 1.50
☐ 221 Princess Leia .60 1.50
☐ 222 Evacuate? In our moment of triumph .60 1.50
☐ 223 Han Solo covers his friends .60 1.50
☐ 224 Luke's secret yen for action .60 1.50
☐ 225 Aunt Beru Lars .60 1.50
☐ 226 Portrait of a Princess .60 1.50
☐ 227 Instructing the Rebel pilots .60 1.50
☐ 228 R2-D2 is inspected by the Jawas .60 1.50
☐ 229 Grand Moff Tarkin .60 1.50
☐ 230 Guarding the Millennium Falcon .60 1.50
☐ 231 Discussing the Death Star's future .60 1.50
☐ 232 The Empire strikes back .60 1.50
☐ 233 Raiding the Rebel starship .60 1.50
☐ 234 Envisioning the Rebel's destruction .60 1.50
☐ 235 Luke Skywalker .60 1.50
☐ 236 Readying the Rebel Fleet .60 1.50
☐ 237 The deadly grip of Darth Vader .60 1.50
☐ 238 Uncle Owen Lars .60 1.50
☐ 239 The young star warrior .60 1.50
☐ 240 Artoo's desperate mission .60 1.50
☐ 241 The rebel fighter ships .60 1.50
☐ 242 Death Star shootout .60 1.50
☐ 243 Rebels in the trench .60 1.50
☐ 244 Waiting at Mos Eisley .60 1.50
☐ 245 Member of the evil Empire .60 1.50
☐ 246 Stormtrooper .60 1.50
☐ 247 Soldier of evil .60 1.50
☐ 248 Luke suspects the worst about his family .60 1.50
☐ 249 Ben Kenobi .60 1.50
☐ 250 Luke and Ben on Tatooine .60 1.50
☐ 251 An overjoyed Han Solo .60 1.50
☐ 252 The honored heroes .60 1.50
☐ 253 R2-D2 .60 1.50
☐ 254 Darth Vader .60 1.50
☐ 255 Luke poses with his weapon .60 1.50
☐ 256 The marvelous droid-C3PO .60 1.50
☐ 257 A pair of Jawas .60 1.50
☐ 258 Fighting impossible odds .60 1.50
☐ 259 Challenging the evil Empire .60 1.50
☐ 260 Han Solo .60 1.50
☐ 261 Fury of the Tusken Raider .60 1.50
☐ 262 Creature of Tatooine .60 1.50
☐ 263 The courage of Luke Skywalker .60 1.50
☐ 264 Star pilot Luke Skywalker .60 1.50
☐ 265 Anxious moments for the Rebels .60 1.50
☐ 266 Threepio and Leia monitor the battle .60 1.50
☐ 267 Non-nonsense privateer Han Solo .60 1.50
☐ 268 Ben prepares to turn off the tractor beam .60 1.50
☐ 269 Droids on the run .60 1.50
☐ 270 Luke Skywalker .60 1.50
☐ 271 Do you think they'll melt us down, Artoo? .60 1.50
☐ 272 Corridors of the Death Star .60 1.50
☐ 273 This is all your fault, Artoo! .60 1.50
☐ 274 Droids trick the Stormtrooper! .60 1.50
☐ 275 Guarding the Millenium Falcon .60 1.50
☐ 276 It's not wise to upset a Wookiee! .60 1.50
☐ 277 Bizarre inhabitants of the cantina! .60 1.50
☐ 278 A narrow escape! .60 1.50
☐ 279 Awaiting the Imperial attack .60 1.50
☐ 280 Remb.Luke,The Force will be w .60 1.50
you
☐ 281 A monstrous thirst! .60 1.50
☐ 282 Hurry up,we're gonna have company .60 1.50
☐ 283 The Cantina musicians .60 1.50
☐ 284 Distracted by Solo's assault .60 1.50
☐ 285 Spiffed up for the Awards Ceremony .60 1.50
☐ 286 Cantina denizens! .60 1.50
☐ 287 Han and Chewie ready for action! .60 1.50
☐ 288 Blasting the enemy! .60 1.50
☐ 289 The Rebel fighters take off! .60 1.50
☐ 290 Chewie aims for danger! .60 1.50
☐ 291 Lord Vader senses The Force .60 1.50
☐ 292 The Stormtroopers assemble .60 1.50
☐ 293 A friendly chat among alien friends! .60 1.50
☐ 294 Droids make their way to the Escape Pod .60 1.50
☐ 295 Han and the Rebel Pilots .60 1.50
☐ 296 Artoo-Detoo is abducted by Jawas! .60 1.50
☐ 297 Inside the Sandcrawler .60 1.50
☐ 298 Chewie gets riled! .60 1.50
☐ 299 Leia wishes Luke good luck! .60 1.50
☐ 300 A crucial moment for Luke Skywalker .60 1.50
☐ 301 Luke, the Star Warrior! .60 1.50
☐ 302 Threepio and Artoo .60 1.50
☐ 303 Various droids collected by the Jawas .60 1.50
☐ 304 The Jawas ready their new merchandise .60 1.50
☐ 305 Director George Lucas and Greedo .60 1.50
☐ 306 Technicians ready C-3PO for the cameras .60 1.50
☐ 307 A touch-up for Chewbacca .60 1.50
☐ 308 Directing the Cantina creatures .60 1.50
☐ 309 The birthday celebration for Sir Alec Guinness .60 1.50
☐ 310 Filming the Awards Ceremony .60 1.50
☐ 311 Model builders proudly display their work .60 1.50
☐ 312 Using the blue screen process for X-wings .60 1.50
☐ 313 The birth of a Droid .60 1.50
☐ 314 Shooting in Tunisia .60 1.50
☐ 315 Inside the Millenium Falcon .60 1.50
☐ 316 Photographing the miniature explosions .60 1.50
☐ 317 Filming explosions on the Death Star .60 1.50
☐ 318 Make-up for the Bantha .60 1.50
☐ 319 Dave Prowse and Alec Guinness rehearse .60 1.50
☐ 320 Flight of the Falcon .60 1.50
☐ 321 George Lucas directs counterpart Luke .60 1.50
☐ 322 Constructing the Star Destroyer .60 1.50
☐ 323 Aboard the Millenium Falcon .60 1.50
☐ 324 Chewbacca takes a breather .60 1.50
☐ 325 The princess .60 1.50
☐ 326 Animating the chessboard .60 1.50
☐ 327 Filming the sandcrawler .60 1.50
☐ 328 X-wings positioned for the cameras .60 1.50
☐ 329 Sir Alec Guinness .60 1.50
George Lucas
☐ 330 Filming Luke and Threepio .60 1.50

1977 Star Wars Stickers

Common Sticker (1-11)
Common Sticker (12-22)
Common Sticker (23-33)
Common Sticker (34-44)
Common Sticker (45-55)

☐ 1 Luke Skywalker
☐ 2 Princess Leia Organa
☐ 3 Han Solo
☐ 4 Chewbacca the Wookiee
☐ 5 See-Threepio
☐ 6 Artoo-Detoo
☐ 7 Lord Darth Vader
☐ 8 Grand Moff Tarkin
☐ 9 Ben (Obi-Wan) Kenobi
☐ 10 Tusken Raider
☐ 11 Battle in Outer Space
☐ 12 Han and Chewbacca
☐ 13 Alec Guinness as Ben
☐ 14 The Tusken Raider
☐ 15 See-Threepio
☐ 16 Chewbacca
☐ 17 Threatened by Sandpeople!
☐ 18 The Rebel Fleet
☐ 19 The Wookiee Chewbacca
☐ 20 R2-D2 and C-3PO
☐ 21 The Millennium Falcon Speeds
☐ 22 Spectacular Battle
☐ 23 Dave Prowse as Darth Vader
☐ 24 Droids on the Sand Planet
☐ 25 Escape Pod is Jettisoned
☐ 26 The Fantastic Droid See-Threepio
☐ 27 A Closer Look at a Jawa
☐ 28 Peter Cushing as Grand Moff Tarkin
☐ 29 Han Solo Hero Or Mercenary?
☐ 30 Stormtroopers
☐ 31 Princess Leia Comforts Luke
☐ 32 Preparing for the Raid
☐ 33 Solo Aims for Trouble
☐ 34 The Star Warriors Aim for Action!
☐ 35 Han Solo (Harrison Ford)
☐ 36 Star Pilot Luke Skywalker
☐ 37 The Marvelous Droid See-Threepio!
☐ 38 R2-D2 (Kenny Baker)
☐ 39 Creature of Tatooine
☐ 40 Darth Vader (David Prowse)
☐ 41 A Pair of Jawas
☐ 42 Luke Poses with His Weapon
☐ 43 Stormtrooper Tool of the Empire
☐ 44 Monitoring the Battle
☐ 45 A Crucial Moment for Luke Skywalker
☐ 46 Chewie Aims for Danger!
☐ 47 Droids on the Run
☐ 48 Inside the Sandcrawler
☐ 49 Luke, the Star Warrior!
☐ 50 George Lucas and Greedo
☐ 51 Technicians Ready C-3PO for the Cameras
☐ 52 The Jawas Ready their New Merchandise
☐ 53 Directing the Cantina Creatures
☐ 54 Leia Wishes Luke Good Luck!
☐ 55 A Touch-Up for Chewbacca

1977 Star Wars Wonder Bread

COMPLETE SET (16) 6.00 15.00
☐ 1 Luke Skywalker .50 1.25
☐ 2 Ben Kenobi .50 1.25
☐ 3 Princess L.Organa .50 1.25
☐ 4 Han Solo .50 1.25
☐ 5 Darth Vader .50 1.25
☐ 6 Grand Moff Tarkin .50 1.25
☐ 7 See-Threepio .50 1.25
☐ 8 Artoo-Detoo .50 1.25
☐ 9 Chewbacca .50 1.25
☐ 10 Jawas .50 1.25
☐ 11 Tusken Raiders .50 1.25
☐ 12 Stormtroopers .50 1.25
☐ 13 Millenium Falcon .50 1.25
☐ 14 Star Destroyer .50 1.25
☐ 15 X-Wing .50 1.25
☐ 16 Tie-Vader's Ship .50 1.25

1980 Star Wars Empire Strikes Back

COMPLETE SET (352) 60.00 120.00
☐ 1 Title Card Series I .15 .40
☐ 2 Luke Skywalker .15 .40
☐ 3 Princess Leia .15 .40
☐ 4 Han Solo .15 .40
☐ 5 Chewbacca .15 .40
☐ 6 See-Threepio .15 .40
☐ 7 Artoo-Detoo .15 .40
☐ 8 Lando Calrissian .15 .40
☐ 9 Yoda .15 .40
☐ 10 Darth Vader .15 .40
☐ 11 Boba Fett .15 .40
☐ 12 The Imperial Probot .15 .40
☐ 13 Planet of Ice .15 .40
☐ 14 Where's Luke? .15 .40
☐ 15 Droids on Patrol .15 .40
☐ 16 The Hidden Rebel Base .15 .40
☐ 17 New Rebel Strategy .15 .40
☐ 18 General Rieekan .15 .40
☐ 19 Leia's Plan .15 .40
☐ 20 Prey of the Wampa .15 .40
☐ 21 Examined: Luke's Tauntaun .15 .40
☐ 22 But Sir, I MMH .15 .40
☐ 23 In Search of Luke .15 .40
☐ 24 Frozen Death .15 .40
☐ 25 Skywalker's Rescue .15 .40
☐ 26 Luke's Fight for Life .15 .40
☐ 27 Rejuvenation Chamber .15 .40
☐ 28 Surgeon Droid .15 .40
☐ 29 Artoo's Icy Vigil .15 .40
☐ 30 Metal Monster .15 .40
☐ 31 Zeroing in on Chewie .15 .40
☐ 32 Han Aims for Action .15 .40
☐ 33 Destroying the Probot .15 .40
☐ 34 Death of Admiral Ozzel .15 .40
☐ 35 The Freedom Fighters .15 .40
☐ 36 Rebel Defenses .15 .40
☐ 37 Armed Against the Enemy .15 .40
☐ 38 Joined by Dack .15 .40
☐ 39 The Sound of Terror .15 .40
☐ 40 Suddenly Starfire .15 .40
☐ 41 Rattled by the Enemy .15 .40
☐ 42 Might of the Imperial Forces .15 .40
☐ 43 The Snow Walkers .15 .40
☐ 44 Luke Trapped .15 .40
☐ 45 Escape from Icy Peril .15 .40
☐ 46 Retreat! Retreat! .15 .40
☐ 47 Headquarters in Shambles .15 .40
☐ 48 Solo's Makeshift Escape .15 .40
☐ 49 Invaded .15 .40
☐ 50 Vader and the Snowtroopers .15 .40
☐ 51 Snowtroopers of the Empire .15 .40
☐ 52 Millennium Falcon: Getaway Ship! .15 .40
☐ 53 Emergency Blast Off .15 .40
☐ 54 Battle of the Star Destroyer .15 .40
☐ 55 Fix-It Man Han Solo .15 .40
☐ 56 A Sudden Change of Plan .15 .40
☐ 57 Misty World of Dagobah .15 .40
☐ 58 The Creature Called Yoda .15 .40
☐ 59 Welcome, Young Luke .15 .40
☐ 60 Journey Through the Swamp .15 .40
☐ 61 Yoda's House .15 .40
☐ 62 Artoo Peeking Through .15 .40
☐ 63 The Secret of Yoda .15 .40
☐ 64 The Princess Lends a Hand .15 .40
☐ 65 Repairing Hyperdrive .15 .40
☐ 66 Star Lovers .15 .40
☐ 67 Pardon Me, Sir But OHHH! .15 .40
☐ 68 Mysterious and Deadly Chamber .15 .40
☐ 69 Attacked by Batlike Creatures .15 .40
☐ 70 Use the Force, Luke .15 .40
☐ 71 Raising Luke's X-Wing .15 .40
☐ 72 A Need Beyond Reason .15 .40
☐ 73 A Gathering of Evils .15 .40
☐ 74 The Bounty Hunters .15 .40
☐ 75 IG-88 and Boba Fett .15 .40
☐ 76 Enter Lando Calrissian .15 .40
☐ 77 Warm Welcome for an Old Buddy .15 .40
☐ 78 Conniving Pals .15 .40
☐ 79 Greetings, Sweet Landy .15 .40
☐ 80 Calrissian's Main Man .15 .40
☐ 81 Pretty as a Princess .15 .40
☐ 82 A Swarm of Ugnaughts .15 .40
☐ 83 Threepio Blasted to Bits .15 .40
☐ 84 A Pile of See-Threepio .15 .40
☐ 85 Escorted by Lando .15 .40
☐ 86 Dinner Guests .15 .40
☐ 87 Host of Horror .15 .40
☐ 88 Deflecting Solo's Blasts .15 .40
☐ 89 Alas, Poor Threepio .15 .40
☐ 90 The Ordeal .15 .40
☐ 91 The Prize of Boba Fett .15 .40
☐ 92 His Day of Triumph .15 .40
☐ 93 The Carbon-Freezing Chamber .15 .40
☐ 94 End of the Star Warriors .15 .40
☐ 95 Pawn of the Evil One .15 .40
☐ 96 No This Can't Be Happening .15 .40
☐ 97 The Fate of Han Solo .15 .40
☐ 98 Boba's Special Delivery .15 .40
☐ 99 Observed By Luke .15 .40
☐ 100 Luke Arrives .15 .40
☐ 101 Ready for Action .15 .40
☐ 102 The Search for Vader .15 .40
☐ 103 Where Are You, Skywalker? .15 .40
☐ 104 Dark Lord of the Sith .15 .40
☐ 105 Weapon of Light .15 .40
☐ 106 The Confrontation .15 .40
☐ 107 Duel of the Lightsabres .15 .40
☐ 108 Escape from Their Captors .15 .40
☐ 109 Lando, Friend or Foe? .15 .40
☐ 110 Leia Takes Control .15 .40
☐ 111 Blasting the Stormtroopers .15 .40
☐ 112 Artoo to the Rescue .15 .40
☐ 113 Spectacular Battle .15 .40
☐ 114 Embrace the Dark Side .15 .40
☐ 115 Hate Me, Luke Destroy Me .15 .40
☐ 116 Luke's Last Stand .15 .40
☐ 117 Do You Have A Foot in My Size? .15 .40
☐ 118 Probot .15 .40
☐ 119 Falcon on Hoth .15 .40
☐ 120 Snowwalkers .15 .40
☐ 121 The Pursued .15 .40
☐ 122 Darth Vader .15 .40
☐ 123 Swamps of Dagobah .15 .40
☐ 124 Cloud City .15 .40
☐ 125 Lando's Greeting .15 .40
☐ 126 Threepio's Destruction .15 .40
☐ 127 Luke Battling Darth .15 .40
☐ 128 The Final Stand .15 .40
☐ 129 Rescue .15 .40
☐ 130 Ion Cannon .15 .40
☐ 131 Checklist 1-66 .15 .40
☐ 132 Checklist 67-132 .15 .40
☐ 133 Title Card Series II .15 .40
☐ 134 Millennium Falcon .15 .40
☐ 135 The Executor .15 .40
☐ 136 Imperial Star Destroyer .15 .40
☐ 137 Twin-Pod Cloud Car .15 .40
☐ 138 Slave! .15 .40
☐ 139 Rebel Armored Snowspeeder .15 .40
☐ 140 The Avenger .15 .40
☐ 141 The Fighter .15 .40
☐ 142 Rebel Transport .15 .40
☐ 143 TIE Bomber .15 .40
☐ 144 Preparing for Battle .15 .40
☐ 145 Seeking the Missing Luke .15 .40
☐ 146 The Searcher .15 .40
☐ 147 Star Pilot Luke Skywalker .15 .40
☐ 148 Luke's Patrol .15 .40
☐ 149 Shelter on Icy Hoth .15 .40
☐ 150 Imperial Spy .15 .40
☐ 151 Tracking the Probot .15 .40
☐ 152 Han Solo, Rescuer .15 .40
☐ 153 Medical Treatment .15 .40
☐ 154 Worried Droids on Hoth .15 .40
☐ 155 Imperial Assault .15 .40
☐ 156 Narrow Escape .15 .40
☐ 157 Fighting Against the Empire .15 .40
☐ 158 Roar of the Wookie .15 .40
☐ 159 Chewie's Task .15 .40
☐ 160 Moments Before the Escape .15 .40
☐ 161 Last Stages of the Battle .15 .40
☐ 162 Gallant Warrior .15 .40
☐ 163 Raise Those Ships .15 .40
☐ 164 The Awesome One .15 .40
☐ 165 Vader and his Snowtroopers .15 .40
☐ 166 Takeover of Rebel Base .15 .40
☐ 167 The Man Called Han Solo .15 .40
☐ 168 The Falcon in Repairs .15 .40
☐ 169 Skills of the Star Pilot .15 .40
☐ 170 Sir Wait for Me! .15 .40
☐ 171 Han's Desperate Plan .15 .40
☐ 172 An Overworked Wookiee .15 .40
☐ 173 Oh, Hello There, Chewbacca .15 .40
☐ 174 Artoo's Bumpy Landing .15 .40
☐ 175 Mysterious Planet .15 .40
☐ 176 Luke In Trouble? .15 .40
☐ 177 Working Against Time .15 .40
☐ 178 Han and the Princess .15 .40
☐ 179 Soldiers of the Empire .15 .40
☐ 180 The Wookiee at Work .15 .40
☐ 181 Vader and Bounty Hunter .15 .40
☐ 182 World of Darkness .15 .40
☐ 183 Taking No Chances .15 .40
☐ 184 Farewell to Yoda and Dagobah .15 .40
☐ 185 Racing to the Falcon .15 .40
☐ 186 The Ominous Vader .15 .40
☐ 187 The Dark Pursuer .15 .40
☐ 188 Young Senator From Alderaan .15 .40
☐ 189 Don't Fool with Han Solo .15 .40
☐ 190 Kindred Spirits .15 .40
☐ 191 Lobot's Task .15 .40
☐ 192 A Brave Princess .15 .40
☐ 193 Corridors of Bespin .15 .40
☐ 194 Lando's Aide Lobot .15 .40
☐ 195 Get Back Quick It's Vader .15 .40
☐ 196 Held by the Stormtroopers .15 .40
☐ 197 Han's Torment .15 .40
☐ 198 Lando's Game .15 .40
☐ 199 Deadly Device .15 .40
☐ 200 In Vader's Clutches .15 .40
☐ 201 A Tearful Farewell .15 .40
☐ 202 Han Faces His Fate .15 .40
☐ 203 Into the Carbon-Freezing Pit .15 .40
☐ 204 An Ugnaught .15 .40
☐ 205 Tears of a Princess .15 .40
☐ 206 Suspended in Carbon Freeze .15 .40
☐ 207 Gruesome Fate .15 .40
☐ 208 Evil Threatens .15 .40
☐ 209 This Deal is Getting Worse .15 .40
☐ 210 The Captor, Boba Fett .15 .40
☐ 211 Fear on Cloud City .15 .40
☐ 212 A Warrior Driven .15 .40
☐ 213 Courage of Skywalker .15 .40
☐ 214 The Pursuer .15 .40
☐ 215 Stalked By Vader .15 .40
☐ 216 A Droid Gone to Pieces .15 .40
☐ 217 Threepio's Free Ride .15 .40
☐ 218 Stormtrooper Takeover .15 .40
☐ 219 Princess Leia Under Guard .15 .40
☐ 220 Bounty Hunter Boba Fett .15 .40
☐ 221 Lando Covers Their Escape .15 .40
☐ 222 Tumbling to an Unknown Fate .15 .40
☐ 223 On the Verge of Defeat .15 .40
☐ 224 Gifted Performer .15 .40
☐ 225 Actress Carrie Fisher .15 .40
☐ 226 Harrison Ford .15 .40
☐ 227 Anthony Daniels as C-3PO .15 .40
☐ 228 Our Favorite Protocol Droid .15 .40
☐ 229 Kenny Baker as R2-D2 .15 .40
☐ 230 Mynocks Outside? Oh My! .15 .40
☐ 231 Actor Billy Dee Williams .15 .40
☐ 232 Galaxy's Most Loyal Droids .15 .40
☐ 233 Dashing Han Solo .15 .40
☐ 234 The Force and the Fury .15 .40
☐ 235 Yoda's Squabble with R2-D2 .15 .40
☐ 236 Blasted by Leia .15 .40
☐ 237 The Art of Levitation .15 .40
☐ 238 Snowswept Chewbacca .15 .40
☐ 239 Dreamworld or Trap? .15 .40
☐ 240 Swampland Peril .15 .40
☐ 241 Tried, Have You? .15 .40
☐ 242 Encounter on Dagobah .15 .40
☐ 243 Captain Solo Senses a Trap .15 .40
☐ 244 A Test for Luke .15 .40
☐ 245 R2-D2 on the Misty Bog .15 .40
☐ 246 Confronting the Dark Side .15 .40
☐ 247 Luke Battles Himself? .15 .40
☐ 248 Blooming Romance .15 .40
☐ 249 Chewie Retaliates .15 .40
☐ 250 Stormtrooper Battle .15 .40
☐ 251 Director Irvin Kershner .15 .40
☐ 252 Spiffing up a Wookiee .15 .40
☐ 253 Filming the Falcon .15 .40
☐ 254 Kershner Directs Mark Hamill .15 .40
☐ 255 Shooting the Exciting Climax .15 .40
☐ 256 Filming Vader in his Chamber .15 .40
☐ 257 Dagobah Comes to Life .15 .40
☐ 258 Building the Falcon .15 .40
☐ 259 Hoth Rebel Base Sequence .15 .40
☐ 260 Filming An Explosion .15 .40
☐ 261 Spectacular Swampland Set .15 .40
☐ 262 Acting Can be a Dirty Job! .15 .40
☐ 263 Checklist 133-198 .15 .40
☐ 264 Checklist 199-264 .15 .40
☐ 265 Title Card Series III .15 .40
☐ 266 Han Solo .15 .40
☐ 267 Princess Leia .15 .40
☐ 268 Luke Skywalker .15 .40
☐ 269 C-3PO .15 .40
☐ 270 R2-D2 .15 .40
☐ 271 Darth Vader .15 .40
☐ 272 Boba Fett .15 .40
☐ 273 Probot .15 .40
☐ 274 Dengar .15 .40
☐ 275 Bossk .15 .40
☐ 276 IG-88 .15 .40
☐ 277 FX-7 .15 .40
☐ 278 Chewbacca .15 .40
☐ 279 Lando Calrissian .15 .40
☐ 280 Stormtrooper .15 .40
☐ 281 Yoda .15 .40
☐ 282 Imperial Ships Approaching .15 .40
☐ 283 The Courageous Trench Fighters .15 .40
☐ 284 Too-Onebee .15 .40
☐ 285 Rebel Protocol Droids .15 .40
☐ 286 Within the Hidden Base .15 .40
☐ 287 Calrissian of Bespin .15 .40
☐ 288 Testing the Carbon-Freezing Process .15 .40
☐ 289 Flight of the X-Wing .15 .40
☐ 290 Dodging Deadly Laserblasts .15 .40
☐ 291 The Lovers Part .15 .40
☐ 292 Canyons of Death .15 .40
☐ 293 Magnificent Rebel Starship .15 .40
☐ 294 Old Friends Or Foes? .15 .40
☐ 295 Power of the Empire .15 .40
☐ 296 Threepio in a Jam .15 .40
☐ 297 Swamp Planet .15 .40
☐ 298 A Hasty Retreat .15 .40
☐ 299 Hostile World of Hoth .15 .40
☐ 300 Descent into Danger .15 .40
☐ 301 Luke Long Overdue .15 .40
☐ 302 Toward the Unknown .15 .40
☐ 303 In Search of Han .15 .40
☐ 304 Luke's Desperate Decision .15 .40
☐ 305 Emerging from the Pit .15 .40
☐ 306 Busy as a Wookiee .15 .40
☐ 307 Portrait of an Ugnaught .15 .40
☐ 308 The Wizard of Dagobah .15 .40
☐ 309 Emergency Repairs .15 .40
☐ 310 Han on the Icy Wasteland .15 .40
☐ 311 The Walkers Close In .15 .40
☐ 312 Toward Tomorrow .15 .40
☐ 313 In the Path of Danger .15 .40
☐ 314 The X-Wing Cockpit .15 .40
☐ 315 Hero of the Rebellion .15 .40
☐ 316 Vader's Private Chamber .15 .40
☐ 317 Aboard the Executor .15 .40
☐ 318 The Ominous One .15 .40
☐ 319 Lord Vader's Orders .15 .40
☐ 320 He's Still Alive .15 .40
☐ 321 Lando's Warm Reception .15 .40
☐ 322 The Landing .15 .40
☐ 323 Their Last Kiss? .15 .40
☐ 324 Bounty Hunter IG-88 .15 .40
☐ 325 The Icy Plains of Hoth .15 .40
☐ 326 Luke Astride his Tauntaun .15 .40
☐ 327 Rebel Snowspeeders Zero In .15 .40
☐ 328 Champions of Freedom .15 .40
☐ 329 Inside the Falcon .15 .40
☐ 330 The Training of a Jedi .15 .40
☐ 331 Yoda's Instruction .15 .40
☐ 332 The Warrior and the Jedi Master .15 .40
☐ 333 Imperial Snow Walker Attack .15 .40
☐ 334 The Asteroid Chase .15 .40
☐ 335 Approaching Planet Dagobah .15 .40
☐ 336 Power Generators .15 .40
☐ 337 Beauty of Bespin .15 .40
☐ 338 Dreamlike City .15 .40
☐ 339 Luke's Training .15 .40
☐ 340 Snow Walker Terror .15 .40
☐ 341 Tauntaun .15 .40
☐ 342 Cloud City Reactor Shaft .15 .40
☐ 343 Yoda's Home .15 .40
☐ 344 Escape from Bespin .15 .40
☐ 345 Deadly Stompers .15 .40
☐ 346 Snow Walker Model .15 .40
☐ 347 Of Helmets and Costumes .15 .40
☐ 348 Filming the Star Destroyer .15 .40
☐ 349 Millennium Falcon Miniature .15 .40
☐ 350 Launching An X-Wing .15 .40
☐ 351 Model Star Destroyer .15 .40
☐ 352 Checklist 265-352 .15 .40

1980 Star Wars Empire Strikes Back Stickers

COMPLETE SET (88) 10.00 25.00
☐ 1 F O .40 1.00
☐ 2 R I .40 1.00
☐ 3 A E .40 1.00
☐ 4 B X .40 1.00
☐ 5 U I .40 1.00
☐ 6 W U .40 1.00
☐ 7 M N .40 1.00
☐ 8 C D .40 1.00
☐ 9 O U .40 1.00
☐ 10 H E .40 1.00
☐ 11 E O .40 1.00
☐ 12 Y U .40 1.00
☐ 13 A K .40 1.00
☐ 14 A V .40 1.00
☐ 15 E S .40 1.00
☐ 16 Q L .40 1.00
☐ 17 A I .40 1.00
☐ 18 I O .40 1.00
☐ 19 Z T .40 1.00
☐ 20 G J .40 1.00
☐ 21 E I .40 1.00
☐ 22 A P .40 1.00
☐ 23 Luke, Darth, Luke, C-3PO .40 1.00
☐ 24 C-3PO .40 1.00
☐ 25 Luke & Yoda; Han & Tauntaun .40 1.00
☐ 26 Stormtrooper, Boba .40 1.00
☐ 27 Stormtrooper, Luke, Yoda .40 1.00
☐ 28 2-1B, Bossk, Lobot .40 1.00
☐ 29 Leia, Luke, Han, Chewie .40 1.00
☐ 30 Boba Fett .40 1.00
☐ 31 Stormtrooper, IG-88 .40 1.00
☐ 32 C-3PO, Lando, R2-D2 .40 1.00
☐ 33 Darth Vader .40 1.00
☐ 34 F O .40 1.00
☐ 35 R I .40 1.00
☐ 36 A E .40 1.00
☐ 37 B X .40 1.00
☐ 38 U I .40 1.00
☐ 39 W U .40 1.00
☐ 40 M N .40 1.00
☐ 41 C D .40 1.00
☐ 42 O U .40 1.00
☐ 43 H E .40 1.00
☐ 44 E O .40 1.00
☐ 45 Y U .40 1.00
☐ 46 A K .40 1.00
☐ 47 A V .40 1.00
☐ 48 E S .40 1.00
☐ 49 Q L .40 1.00
☐ 50 A I .40 1.00
☐ 51 I O .40 1.00
☐ 52 Z T .40 1.00
☐ 53 G J .40 1.00
☐ 54 E I .40 1.00
☐ 55 A P .40 1.00
☐ 56 Darth Vader .40 1.00
☐ 57 Boba Fett .40 1.00
☐ 58 Probot .40 1.00
☐ 59 Luke Skywalker .40 1.00
☐ 60 Princess Leia .40 1.00
☐ 61 Han Solo .40 1.00
☐ 62 Lando Calrissian .40 1.00
☐ 63 Chewbacca .40 1.00
☐ 64 R2-D2 .40 1.00
☐ 65 C-3PO .40 1.00
☐ 66 Yoda .40 1.00
☐ 67 F O .40 1.00
☐ 68 R I .40 1.00
☐ 69 A E .40 1.00
☐ 70 B X .40 1.00
☐ 71 U I .40 1.00
☐ 72 W U .40 1.00
☐ 73 M N .40 1.00
☐ 74 C D .40 1.00
☐ 75 O U .40 1.00
☐ 76 H E .40 1.00
☐ 77 E O .40 1.00
☐ 78 Y U .40 1.00
☐ 79 A K .40 1.00
☐ 80 A V .40 1.00
☐ 81 E S .40 1.00
☐ 82 Q L .40 1.00
☐ 83 A I .40 1.00
☐ 84 I O .40 1.00
☐ 85 Z T .40 1.00
☐ 86 G J .40 1.00
☐ 87 E I .40 1.00
☐ 88 A P .40 1.00

1983 Star Wars Return of the Jedi

COMPLETE SET (220) 15.00 40.00
☐ 1 Title Card .15 .40
☐ 2 Luke Skywalker .15 .40
☐ 3 Darth Vader .15 .40
☐ 4 Han Solo .15 .40
☐ 5 Princess Leia Organa .15 .40
☐ 6 Lando Calrissian .15 .40
☐ 7 Chewbacca .15 .40
☐ 8 C-3PO and R2-D2 .15 .40
☐ 9 The New Death Star .15 .40
☐ 10 The Inspection .15 .40
☐ 11 Toward the Desert Palace .15 .40
☐ 12 Bib Fortuna .15 .40
☐ 13 Court of Evil .15 .40
☐ 14 Jabba the Hutt .15 .40
☐ 15 Intergalactic Gangster .15 .40
☐ 16 Salacious Crumb .15 .40
☐ 17 A Message for Jabba the Hutt .15 .40
☐ 18 Dungeons of Jabba the Hutt .15 .40
☐ 19 Beedo and a Jawa .15 .40
☐ 20 Sy Snootles and the Rebo Band .15 .40
☐ 21 Droopy McCool .15 .40
☐ 22 Sy Snootles .15 .40
☐ 23 Watched by Boba Fett .15 .40
☐ 24 Boushh's Captive .15 .40
☐ 25 The Bounty Hunter Boushh .15 .40
☐ 26 The Villains Confer .15 .40
☐ 27 Hans Solo's Plight .15 .40
☐ 28 The Rescuer .15 .40
☐ 29 Decarbonized .15 .40
☐ 30 Princess Leia to the Rescue .15 .40
☐ 31 Heroes in Disguise .15 .40
☐ 32 The Princess Enslaved .15 .40
☐ 33 Luke Skywalker Arrives .15 .40
☐ 34 The Young Jedi .15 .40
☐ 35 The Court in Chaos .15 .40
☐ 36 The Rancor Pit .15 .40
☐ 37 Facing Jabba the Hutt .15 .40
☐ 38 The Sail Barge and The Desert Skiff .15 .40
☐ 39 Jabba The Hutt's New Dancing Girl .15 .40
☐ 40 On the Sail Barge .15 .40
☐ 41 A Monstrous Fate .15 .40
☐ 42 The Battle Begins .15 .40
☐ 43 Lando Calrissian's Fight for Life .15 .40
☐ 44 Fury of the Jedi .15 .40
☐ 45 Princess Leia Strikes Back .15 .40
☐ 46 The Demise of Jabba the Hutt .15 .40
☐ 47 Boba Fett's Last Stand .15 .40
☐ 48 The Rescue .15 .40
☐ 49 Gamorrean Guard .15 .40
☐ 50 The Deadly Cannon .15 .40

STAR WARS

❑ 51 The Raging Battle .15 .40
❑ 52 Princess Leia Swings Into Action .15 .40
❑ 53 Swing to Safety .15 .40
❑ 54 On the Death Star .15 .40
❑ 55 Guards of the Emperor .15 .40
❑ 56 The Deciders .15 .40
❑ 57 The Emperor .15 .40
❑ 58 Yoda, the Jedi Master .15 .40
❑ 59 A Word with Ben Kenobi .15 .40
❑ 60 The Allies Meet .15 .40
❑ 61 A New Challenge .15 .40
❑ 62 Pondering the Raid .15 .40
❑ 63 Mission: Destroy the Death Star .15 .40
❑ 64 Mon Mothma .15 .40
❑ 65 The Friends Depart .15 .40
❑ 66 Benevolent Creature .15 .40
❑ 67 The Plan Begins .15 .40
❑ 68 Forest of Endor .15 .40
❑ 69 Droids on the Move .15 .40
❑ 70 Blasting a Speeder Bike .15 .40
❑ 71 Approaching the Princess .15 .40
❑ 72 A New Found Friend .15 .40
❑ 73 Princess Leia's Smile .15 .40
❑ 74 Under Attack .15 .40
❑ 75 Imperial Scout Peril .15 .40
❑ 76 Entering the Throne Room .15 .40
❑ 77 The Skywalker Factor .15 .40
❑ 78 Captured by the Ewoks .15 .40
❑ 79 The Netted Droid .15 .40
❑ 80 All Hail See-Threepio .15 .40
❑ 81 Royal Treatment .15 .40
❑ 82 Sitting with Royalty .15 .40
❑ 83 Levitated by Luke .15 .40
❑ 84 The Ewok Leaders .15 .40
❑ 85 Logray and Chief Chirpa .15 .40
❑ 86 Help from Princess Leia .15 .40
❑ 87 Will Han Solo Be Dinner? .15 .40
❑ 88 The Baby Ewok .15 .40
❑ 89 The Forest Creatures .15 .40
❑ 90 The Droid and the Ewok .15 .40
❑ 91 R2-D2 Meets Wicket .15 .40
❑ 92 Unexpected Allies .15 .40
❑ 93 Serious Situation .15 .40
❑ 94 Luke Skywalker's Destiny .15 .40
❑ 95 Quiet, See-Threepio .15 .40
❑ 96 Imperial Biker Scout .15 .40
❑ 97 Biker Scout and the Battlefield .15 .40
❑ 98 Han Solo's Approach .15 .40
❑ 99 The Ultimate Mission .15 .40
❑ 100 Ready for Action .15 .40
❑ 101 Ambushed by the Empire .15 .40
❑ 102 Observed by the Ewoks .15 .40
❑ 103 The Courageous Ewoks .15 .40
❑ 104 Prisoners .15 .40
❑ 105 Revising Their Plan .15 .40
❑ 106 AT-ST .15 .40
❑ 107 The Forest Fighters .15 .40
❑ 108 Break for Freedom .15 .40
❑ 109 Artoo-Detoo .15 .40
❑ 110 Chewbacca Triumphant .15 .40
❑ 111 Ewoks to the Rescue .15 .40
❑ 112 Battle in the Forest .15 .40
❑ 113 Stormtrooper Attack .15 .40
❑ 114 The Victorious Rebels .15 .40
❑ 115 Time out for Love .15 .40
❑ 116 Facing the Emperor .15 .40
❑ 117 Master of Terror .15 .40
❑ 118 The Emperor's Offer .15 .40
❑ 119 Battle to the Jedi .15 .40
❑ 120 Lightsaber Battle .15 .40
❑ 121 Darth Vader is Down .15 .40
❑ 122 The Confrontation .15 .40
❑ 123 The Death Star Raid .15 .40
❑ 124 Military Leader Admiral Ackbar .15 .40
❑ 125 Within the Death Star .15 .40
❑ 126 Victory Celebration .15 .40
❑ 127 Congratulating Wedge .15 .40
❑ 128 The Triumphant Trio .15 .40
❑ 129 The Heroic Droids .15 .40
❑ 130 Toward Brighter Tomorrows .15 .40
❑ 131 Checklist 1-66 .15 .40
❑ 132 Checklist 67-132 .15 .40
❑ 133 Title Card Series II .15 .40
❑ 134 Path to Destiny .15 .40
❑ 135 Captured! .15 .40
❑ 136 The Courageous Jedi .15 .40
❑ 137 The Victors .15 .40
❑ 138 Wicket and Princess Leia .15 .40
❑ 139 The Emperor's Arrival .15 .40
❑ 140 Sail Barge Battle .15 .40
❑ 141 Luke Skywalker, The Jedi .15 .40
❑ 142 The Approach of Wicket .15 .40
❑ 143 A Close Call .15 .40
❑ 144 Above the Sarlacc Pit .15 .40
❑ 145 Adm. Ackbar's Defenders .15 .40
❑ 146 R2-D2 on Endor .15 .40
❑ 147 Boba Fett Attacks .15 .40
❑ 148 Deadly Plunge .15 .40
❑ 149 Lando Calrissian's Disguise .15 .40
❑ 150 Soldiers of the Empire .15 .40
❑ 151 A Curious Ewok .15 .40
❑ 152 A Pensive Luke Skywalker .15 .40
❑ 153 The Captive Princess .15 .40
❑ 154 Luke Skywalker Surrenders .15 .40
❑ 155 Thoughts of a Jedi .15 .40
❑ 156 The Jaws of Death .15 .40
❑ 157 Princess Leia has the Force .15 .40
❑ 158 Arrival of the Emperor .15 .40
❑ 159 Reunion on Endor .15 .40
❑ 160 Toward the Sarlacc Pit .15 .40
❑ 161 Sail Barge Creatures .15 .40
❑ 162 Friends of the Alliance .15 .40
❑ 163 The Dreaded Rancor .15 .40
❑ 164 Face of Terror .15 .40
❑ 165 Inside Jabba the Hutt's Palace .15 .40
❑ 166 The Ewok Village .15 .40
❑ 167 A Collection of Creatures .15 .40
❑ 168 Alert to Danger .15 .40
❑ 169 Walking the Plank .15 .40
❑ 170 A Gamorrean Guard Emerges .15 .40
❑ 171 The Imperial Fleet .15 .40
❑ 172 Jabba the Hutt on the Sail Barge .15 .40
❑ 173 Escorted to the Ewok Village .15 .40
❑ 174 A Monstrous Guest .15 .40
❑ 175 Village of the Ewoks .15 .40
❑ 176 Aboard the Sail Barge .15 .40
❑ 177 Confronting Their Destiny .15 .40
❑ 178 Where's Princess Leia? .15 .40
❑ 179 Horror From the Pit .15 .40
❑ 180 Give in to Your Hate .15 .40
❑ 181 Awaiting his Majesty .15 .40
❑ 182 A Mother Ewok and Child .15 .40
❑ 183 A Concerned Princess Leia .15 .40
❑ 184 Lead Singer Sy Snootles .15 .40
❑ 185 The Arrival of Boushh .15 .40
❑ 186 Master of His Court .15 .40
❑ 187 Star Lovers .15 .40
❑ 188 Luke Skywalker Now a Jedi .15 .40
❑ 189 Battle of the Bunker .15 .40
❑ 190 Portrait of Wicket .15 .40
❑ 191 Trapped by the Empire .15 .40
❑ 192 Their Secret Revealed .15 .40
❑ 193 Rethinking the Plan .15 .40
❑ 194 Snagged by the Ewoks .15 .40
❑ 195 Han Solo's in Trouble .15 .40
❑ 196 Is Han Solo Giving Up? .15 .40
❑ 197 The Royal Droid .15 .40
❑ 198 Princess Leia Intercedes .15 .40
❑ 199 Rescuing Han Solo .15 .40
❑ 200 Father Versus Son .15 .40
❑ 201 Luke Skywalker Jedi Warrior .15 .40
❑ 202 The Young Jedi Knight .15 .40
❑ 203 Han Solo is Alive! .15 .40
❑ 204 Lando Calrissian Undercover .15 .40
❑ 205 Horrendous Creature .15 .40
❑ 206 Corridors of the Imperial Destroyer .15 .40
❑ 207 Surrounded by Ewoks .15 .40
❑ 208 Gamorrean Guard Profile .15 .40
❑ 209 Hulking Gamorrean Guard .15 .40
❑ 210 Guests of Jabba the Hutt .15 .40
❑ 211 A Full Fledged Jedi .15 .40
❑ 212 Bizarre Alien Creatures .15 .40
❑ 213 Headquarters Frigate .15 .40
❑ 214 The Interceptor .15 .40
❑ 215 The Nearly Completed Death Star .15 .40
❑ 216 Rebel Cruiser .15 .40
❑ 217 The Interceptor .15 .40
❑ 218 The Emperor's Shuttle .15 .40
❑ 219 Portrait of Chewbacca .15 .40
❑ 220 Checklist 133-220 .15 .40

1983 Star Wars Return of the Jedi Stickers

COMPLETE SET (55) 10.00 25.00

❑ 1 Yoda .20 .50
❑ 2 Chief Chirpa .20 .50
❑ 3 Droopy McCool .20 .50
❑ 4 Jabba the Hut .20 .50
❑ 5 Ree-Yees .20 .50
❑ 6 Admiral Ackbar .20 .50
❑ 7 Boussh .20 .50
❑ 8 Han Solo .20 .50
❑ 9 Princess Leia .20 .50
❑ 10 Luke Skywalker .20 .50
❑ 11 Han Solo .20 .50
❑ 12 See-Threepio .20 .50
❑ 13 Chewbacca .20 .50
❑ 14 Sy Nootles .20 .50
❑ 15 Baby Ewok .20 .50
❑ 16 Nien Nunb .20 .50
❑ 17 Lando Calrissian .20 .50
❑ 18 R2-D2 .20 .50
❑ 19 Ben Kenobi .20 .50
❑ 20 Luke Skywalker .20 .50
❑ 21 Luke Skywalker .20 .50
❑ 22 Gamorrean Guard .20 .50
❑ 23 Salacious-Crumb .20 .50
❑ 24 Ewok .20 .50
❑ 25 Boba Fett .20 .50
❑ 26 The Ewok .20 .50
❑ 27 Jabba the Hutt .20 .50
❑ 28 Lando Calrissian in Skiff Disguise .20 .50
❑ 29 Max Rebo .20 .50
❑ 30 Princess Leia on Endor .20 .50
❑ 31 Princess Leia .20 .50
❑ 32 Han Solo .20 .50
❑ 33 Biker Scout .20 .50
❑ 34 Darth Vader .20 .50
❑ 35 Luke Skywalker .20 .50
❑ 36 Han Solo .20 .50
❑ 37 Princess Leia .20 .50
❑ 38 See-Threepio .20 .50
❑ 39 Artoo-Detoo .20 .50
❑ 40 Wicket .20 .50
❑ 41 Admiral Ackbar .20 .50
❑ 42 Chewbacca .20 .50
❑ 43 The Emperor .20 .50
❑ 44 Millennium Falcon .20 .50
❑ 45 Droids at the Door .20 .50
❑ 46 Hanging Han .20 .50
❑ 47 Desert Yacht .20 .50
❑ 48 Nien Numb and Lando .20 .50
❑ 49 Slave Girl Leia .20 .50
❑ 50 Heroes on Endor .20 .50
❑ 51 Threepio,Chewy .20 .50
❑ 52 Darth Vader .20 .50
❑ 53 R2 and Ewoks .20 .50
❑ 54 Pistol-Packin' Han .20 .50
❑ 55 Salacious Crumb .20 .50

1993-95 Star Wars Galaxy

COMPLETE SET (365) 15.00 40.00

❑ 1 Title Card .15 .40
❑ 2 George Lucas Art Montage .15 .40
❑ 3 Luke Skywalker .15 .40
❑ 4 Darth Vader .15 .40
❑ 5 Leia Organa .15 .40
❑ 6 Obi-Wan Ben Kenobi .15 .40
❑ 7 Han Solo .15 .40
❑ 8 Chewbacca .15 .40
❑ 9 Lando Calrissian .15 .40
❑ 10 Yoda .15 .40
❑ 11 C-3PO .15 .40
❑ 12 R2-D2 .15 .40
❑ 13 Boba Fett .15 .40
❑ 14 Emperor .15 .40
❑ 15 Ralph McQuarrie .15 .40
❑ 16 The Death Star Trench .15 .40
❑ 17 Ron Cobb .15 .40
❑ 18 Hammerhead .15 .40
❑ 19 Typical Wookiee Family .15 .40
❑ 20 Holiday Special .15 .40
❑ 21 Too-Onebee .15 .40
❑ 22 AT-AT .15 .40
❑ 23 Yoda .15 .40
❑ 24 A Space Slug .15 .40
❑ 25 IG-88 .15 .40
❑ 26 The Death Star .15 .40
❑ 27 Jabba The Hutt .15 .40
❑ 28 Costume Design .15 .40
❑ 29 Princess Leia .15 .40
❑ 30 Original Sketches .15 .40
❑ 31 Lando .15 .40
❑ 32 Yoda as Gremlin .15 .40
❑ 33 Bad Hair Day? .15 .40
❑ 34 The Rancor .15 .40
❑ 35 Jabba's Menagerie .15 .40
❑ 36 Gamorrean Guards .15 .40
❑ 37 Bib Fortuna .15 .40
❑ 38 Creature Collaboration .15 .40
❑ 39 Princess Leia's Hair .15 .40
❑ 40 Ewoks .15 .40
❑ 41 Leia as a Pin-Up .15 .40
❑ 42 Droid Torture Chamber .15 .40
❑ 43 The Max Rebo Band .15 .40
❑ 44 Luke's Confrontation .15 .40
❑ 45 The Speeder Bike Chase .15 .40
❑ 46 The Emperor Strikes Back .15 .40
❑ 47 Wedge Antilles .15 .40
❑ 48 Howard Chaykin .15 .40
❑ 49 John Berkey .15 .40
❑ 50 Berkey's Concept .15 .40
❑ 51 A Huge Space Battle .15 .40
❑ 52 Jim Campbell Poster .15 .40
❑ 53 Goozee .15 .40
(Siniger
❑ 54 Foreign Movie Posters .15 .40
❑ 55 White III .15 .40
(Struzan
❑ 56 Artists' Imaginations .15 .40
❑ 57 Druillet .15 .40
(McQuarrie
❑ 58 Italian Poster Art .15 .40
❑ 59 An Evil Darth Vader .15 .40
❑ 60 A Close Encounter .15 .40
❑ 61 If Droids Can Frolic .15 .40
❑ 62 Villains .15 .40
❑ 63 Dorman .15 .40
(Strain
❑ 64 Two Lukes .15 .40
❑ 65 International Art .15 .40
❑ 66 Sanjulian .15 .40
(Larry Noble
❑ 67 The Mountain .15 .40
❑ 68 The Noble TaunTaun .15 .40
❑ 69 A Pastiche .15 .40
❑ 70 The Rebels Transcend .15 .40
❑ 71 Borris Vallejo .15 .40
❑ 72 Male Bonding .15 .40
❑ 73 Revenge Poster .15 .40
(Sano
❑ 74 Heat Seems to Rise .15 .40
❑ 75 We're Moving .15 .40
❑ 76 Even Droids Celebrate .15 .40
❑ 77 Santa Threepio .15 .40
❑ 78 Strike Up the Droids .15 .40
❑ 79 Thomas Blackshear .15 .40
❑ 80 Jim Steranko .15 .40
❑ 81 Steranko's Empire .15 .40
❑ 82 Kyle Baker .15 .40
❑ 83 Bret Blevins .15 .40
❑ 84 Ted Boonthanakit .15 .40
❑ 85 June Brigman .15 .40
❑ 86 Paul Chadwick .15 .40
❑ 87 Howard Chaykin .15 .40
❑ 88 Mark Chiarello .15 .40
❑ 89 Geof Darrow .15 .40
❑ 90 Steve Ditko .15 .40
❑ 91 Dave Dorman .15 .40
❑ 92 George Evans .15 .40
❑ 93 Fastner & Larson .15 .40
❑ 94 Keith Giffen .15 .40
❑ 95 Paul Gulacy .15 .40
❑ 96 Bo Hampton .15 .40
❑ 97 Scott Hampton .15 .40
❑ 98 Michael Wm. Kaluta .15 .40
❑ 99 Gil Kane .15 .40
❑ 100 Gil Kane .15 .40
❑ 101 Cam Kennedy .15 .40
❑ 102 Dale Keown .15 .40
❑ 103 Karl Kesel .15 .40
❑ 104 Sam Keith .15 .40
❑ 105 Sam Keith .15 .40
❑ 106 David Lapham .15 .40
❑ 107 Mike Lemos .15 .40
❑ 108 Estoban Maroto .15 .40
❑ 109 Cynthia Martin .15 .40
❑ 110 Michael Mignola .15 .40
❑ 111 Moebius .15 .40
❑ 112 Jerome Moore .15 .40
❑ 113 Jon J. Muth .15 .40
❑ 114 Mark Nelson .15 .40
❑ 115 Earl Norem .15 .40
❑ 116 Allen Nunis .15 .40
❑ 117 Jason Palmer .15 .40
❑ 118 George Perez .15 .40
❑ 119 George Pratt .15 .40
❑ 120 Joe Quesada .15 .40
❑ 121 P. Craig Russell .15 .40
❑ 122 Mark Shultz .15 .40
❑ 123 Bill Seinkiewicz .15 .40
❑ 124 Walter Simonson .15 .40
❑ 125 Ken Steacy .15 .40
❑ 126 Brian Stelfreeze .15 .40
❑ 127 Brian Stelfreeze .15 .40
❑ 128 Dale Stevens .15 .40
❑ 129 William Stout .15 .40
❑ 130 Greg Theakston .15 .40
❑ 131 Angelo Torres .15 .40
❑ 132 Jim Valentino .15 .40
❑ 133 John Van Fleet .15 .40
❑ 134 Charles Vess .15 .40
❑ 135 Russell Walks .15 .40
❑ 136 Al Williamson .15 .40
❑ 137 Al Williamson .15 .40
❑ 138 Thomas Wm. Yeates II .15 .40
❑ 139 Bruce Zick .15 .40
❑ 140 Checklist .15 .40
❑ 141 Title Card .15 .40
❑ 142 Ralph McQuarrie .15 .40
❑ 143 A Giant Swamp Slug .15 .40
❑ 144 Imperial Walkers .15 .40
❑ 145 High Over Bespin .15 .40
❑ 146 The Entertainment .15 .40
❑ 147 The Imperial Palace .15 .40
❑ 148 Santa Yoda .15 .40
❑ 149 Marvel Comics .15 .40
❑ 150 Marvel's Series .15 .40
❑ 151 War in the Ice .15 .40
❑ 152 Luke Patrols .15 .40
❑ 153 Danger Uqnaughts .15 .40
❑ 154 The Duel Begins .15 .40
❑ 155 Blasting Their Way .15 .40
❑ 156 Marvel's Return .15 .40
❑ 157 Lumiya, a Half-Human .15 .40
❑ 158 Darth Vader's .15 .40
❑ 159 Ulic Qel-Droma .15 .40
❑ 160 Pirate Captain .15 .40
❑ 161 Dark Empire .15 .40
❑ 162 World Devastators .15 .40
❑ 163 Princess Leia .15 .40
❑ 164 Emperor Palpatine .15 .40
❑ 165 As Luke Fights .15 .40
❑ 166 Boris Vallejo .15 .40
❑ 167 Ken Barr .15 .40
❑ 168 Michael Whelan .15 .40
❑ 169 Melanie Taylor Kent .15 .40
❑ 170 George Gaadt .15 .40
❑ 171 Basil Gogos .15 .40
❑ 172 Scott Gustafson .15 .40
❑ 173 Sir Alec Guinness .15 .40
❑ 174 Tony Auth .15 .40
❑ 175 Todd Andrews .15 .40
❑ 176 Michael David Ward .15 .40
❑ 177 Morgan Weistling .15 .40
❑ 178 Joe Johnston .15 .40
❑ 179 Nilo Rodis-Jamero .15 .40
❑ 180 Ewok Break Time .15 .40
❑ 181 John Mollo .15 .40
❑ 182 Creatures Galore .15 .40
❑ 183 A Speeder Bike Pilot .15 .40
❑ 184 Assorted Aliens .15 .40
❑ 185 Although the Ewoks .15 .40
❑ 186 The Star Wars Holiday .15 .40
❑ 187 Imperial City On .15 .40
❑ 188 Kazuhiko Sano .15 .40
❑ 189 The Characters From .15 .40
❑ 190 A More Stylized .15 .40
❑ 191 The Star Wars Concert .15 .40
❑ 192 Luke Surveys All .15 .40
❑ 193 Vader is the Death Star .15 .40
❑ 194 Where's Luke? .15 .40
❑ 195 Telling a Story .15 .40
❑ 196 Merchandising .15 .40
❑ 197 A Tatooine Skiff .15 .40
❑ 198 The A-Wing Fighter .15 .40
❑ 199 Boba Fett .15 .40
❑ 200 Anakin Skywalker .15 .40
❑ 201 Pinball Wizards .15 .40
❑ 202 Star Wars Trilogy .15 .40
❑ 203 Gene Lemery .15 .40
❑ 204 Bill Schmidt .15 .40
❑ 205 Micael Allred .15 .40
❑ 206 Karl Altstaetter .15 .40
❑ 207 Thom Ang .15 .40
❑ 208 Sergio Aragones .15 .40
❑ 209 Marshall Arisman .15 .40
❑ 210 Dan Barry .15 .40
❑ 211 John Bolton .15 .40
❑ 212 Timothy Bradstreet .15 .40
❑ 213 Dan Brereton .15 .40
❑ 214 Ron Brown .15 .40
❑ 215 Frank Brunner .15 .40
❑ 216 Rich Buckler .15 .40
❑ 217 Greg Capullo .15 .40
❑ 218 Amanda Conner .15 .40
❑ 219 Ricardo Delgado .15 .40
❑ 220 Joe DeVito .15 .40
❑ 221 Colleen Doran .15 .40
❑ 222 Norm Dwyer .15 .40
❑ 223 Bob Fingerman .15 .40
❑ 224 Hugh Fleming .15 .40
❑ 225 Franchesco .15 .40
❑ 226 Drew Friedman .15 .40
❑ 227 Rick Geary .15 .40
❑ 228 Dave Gibbons .15 .40
❑ 229 Mike Grell .15 .40
❑ 230 Rebecca Guay .15 .40
❑ 231 Lurene Haines .15 .40
❑ 232 Matt Haley .15 .40
❑ 233 Cully Hamner .15 .40
❑ 234 Rich Hedden .15 .40
❑ 235 Dave Hoover .15 .40
❑ 236 Janine Johnston .15 .40
❑ 237 Jeffrey Jones .15 .40
❑ 238 Kelley Jones .15 .40
❑ 239 Miran Kim .15 .40
❑ 240 Jack Kirby .15 .40
❑ 241 Ray Lago .15 .40
❑ 242 Zohar Lazar .15 .40
❑ 243 Jae Lee .15 .40
❑ 244 Paul Lee .15 .40
❑ 245 John Paul Lona .15 .40
❑ 246 David Lowery .15 .40
❑ 247 Shawn C. Martinbrough .15 .40
❑ 248 Mike Mayhew .15 .40
❑ 249 Walter McDaniel .15 .40
❑ 250 Mike McMahon .15 .40
❑ 251 Linda Medley .15 .40
❑ 252 David O. Miller .15 .40
❑ 253 C. Scott Morse .15 .40
❑ 254 Nelson .15 .40
❑ 255 Hoang Nguyen .15 .40
❑ 256 Kevin O'Neill .15 .40
❑ 257 Mark Pacella .15 .40
❑ 258 Jimmy Palmiotti .15 .40
❑ 259 Jason Pearson .15 .40
❑ 260 Brandon Peterson .15 .40
❑ 261 Joe Phillips .15 .40
❑ 262 Whilce Portacio .15 .40
❑ 263 Ralph Reese .15 .40
❑ 264 Zina Saunders .15 .40
❑ 265 Chris Sprouse .15 .40
❑ 266 Jim Starlin .15 .40
❑ 267 Arthur Suydam .15 .40
❑ 268 Sylvain .15 .40
❑ 269 Tom Taggart .15 .40
❑ 270 Jill Thompson .15 .40
❑ 271 Tim Truman .15 .40
❑ 272 Keith Tucker .15 .40
❑ 273 Jeff Watts .15 .40
❑ 274 Mike Zeck .15 .40
❑ 275 Checklist .15 .40
❑ 276 Title Card .15 .40
❑ 277 The Glove of Darth Vader .15 .40
❑ 278 The Lost City of the Jedi .15 .40
❑ 279 Mission from Mount Yoda .15 .40
❑ 280 The Truce at Bakura .15 .40
❑ 281 The Courtship of Princess Leia .15 .40
❑ 282 The Crystal Star .15 .40
❑ 283 Ambush at Correllia .15 .40
❑ 284 Assault at Selonia .15 .40
❑ 285 Showdown at Centerpoint .15 .40
❑ 286 Children of the Jedi .15 .40
❑ 287 We Don't Do Weddings: The Band's Tale .15 .40
❑ 288 C-3PO Thinker .15 .40
❑ 289 C-3PO Birthday .15 .40
❑ 290 Luke and Starfighters .15 .40
❑ 291 C-3PO and R2-D2 .15 .40
❑ 292 Cantina Poster .15 .40
❑ 293 Bounty Hunters .15 .40
❑ 294 C-3PO Robot Book .15 .40
❑ 295 Luke With Gang .15 .40
❑ 296 Marvel Comic .15 .40
❑ 297 The Ewok Adventure .15 .40
❑ 298 Cindel and Ewok .15 .40
❑ 299 Wicket Finds a Way .15 .40
❑ 300 Lando Montage .15 .40
❑ 301 Boba Fett Cloud City .15 .40
❑ 302 C-3PO Director .15 .40
❑ 303 Mos Eisley Cantina .15 .40
❑ 304 Mos Eisley at Dark .15 .40
❑ 305 Christmas Card .15 .40
❑ 306 Magistrates of the Empire .15 .40
❑ 307 Grand Moff Tarkin .15 .40
❑ 308 Han and Chewie Fight Boba Fett .15 .40
❑ 309 The Tatooine Years .15 .40
❑ 310 The Four Jedi .15 .40
❑ 311 The Reluctant Jedi .15 .40
❑ 312 Nick Choles .15 .40
❑ 313 David Deitrick .15 .40
❑ 314 Gary Gianni .15 .40
❑ 315 Courtney Skinner .15 .40
❑ 316 Lou Harrison .15 .40
❑ 317 Les Dorscheid .15 .40
❑ 318 Brian Ashmore .15 .40
❑ 319 Hector Gomez .15 .40
❑ 320 Jae Lee .15 .40
❑ 321 Arthur Adams .15 .40
❑ 322 Dave Dorman .15 .40
❑ 323 Dave Dorman .15 .40
❑ 324 Hugh Fleming .15 .40
❑ 325 Hugh Fleming .15 .40
❑ 326 Kilian Plunkett .15 .40
❑ 327 June Brigman .15 .40
❑ 328 Dave Dorman .15 .40
❑ 329 Mark Harrison .15 .40
❑ 330 The Call to Adventure .15 .40
❑ 331 Supernatural Aid .15 .40
❑ 332 The Road of Trials .15 .40
❑ 333 The Ultimate Boon .15 .40
❑ 334 Joseph Campbell .15 .40
(George Lucas
❑ 335 The Force .15 .40
❑ 336 Leia .15 .40
❑ 337 Han Solo .15 .40
❑ 338 Skywalker .15 .40
(Vader
❑ 339 Kelly Freas .15 .40
❑ 340 Gene Colan .15 .40
❑ 341 Mitch O'Connell .15 .40
❑ 342 Mike Avon Deming .15 .40
❑ 343 Tim Eldred .15 .40
❑ 344 Cathleen Thole .15 .40
❑ 345 Don Punchatz .15 .40
❑ 346 John Pound .15 .40
❑ 347 Rick Buckler .15 .40
❑ 348 Scott Neely .15 .40
❑ 349 Joann Daley .15 .40
❑ 350 Jack Davis .15 .40
❑ 351 Mark McCreery .15 .40
❑ 352 Mike Smithson .15 .40
❑ 353 John Eaves .15 .40
❑ 354 Clark Schaffer .15 .40
❑ 355 Will Vinton Studios .15 .40
❑ 356 Gahan Wilson .15 .40
❑ 357 Steve Reiss .15 .40
❑ 358 Mark Harrison .15 .40
❑ 359 Cambell .15 .40
(Garner
❑ 360 Vince Locke .15 .40
❑ 361 John K. Snyder .15 .40
❑ 362 Therese Nielson .15 .40
❑ 363 Chris Moeller .15 .40
❑ 364 John Paul Leon .15 .40
❑ 365 Checklist .02 .10

1993-95 Star Wars Galaxy Millennium Falcon Foil

COMP.FACTORY SET (365) 50.00 100.00
*MIL.FALCON FOIL: .8X TO 2X BASE CARDS .30 .75
VADER HOLOGRAM ONE PER FACT.SET

❑ NNO Darth Vader HOLOGRAM 4.00 10.00

1993-95 Star Wars Galaxy 1st Day Production

COMPLETE SET (90) 40.00 100.00
*FIRST DAY: 1X TO 2.5X BASIC CARDS
STATED ODDS ONE PER SERIES 3 PACK

1993-95 Star Wars Galaxy Clearzone

COMPLETE SET (6) 15.00 40.00

❑ E1 Boba Fett 3.00 8.00
❑ E2 Bossk 3.00 8.00
❑ E3 4-LOM 3.00 8.00
❑ E4 IG-88 3.00 8.00
❑ E5 Zuckess 3.00 8.00
❑ E6 Dengar 3.00 8.00

1993-95 Star Wars Galaxy Etched Foil

COMPLETE SET (18) 60.00 120.00

❑ 1 Darth Vader 3.00 8.00
❑ 2 Han Solo 3.00 8.00
❑ 3 Luke Skywalker 3.00 8.00
❑ 4 Chewbacca 3.00 8.00
❑ 5 Obi-Wan Kenobi 3.00 8.00
Yoda
❑ 6 Princess Leia 3.00 8.00
❑ 7 Grand Moff Tarkin 3.00 8.00
❑ 8 Stormtrooper 3.00 8.00
❑ 9 Emperor 3.00 8.00
❑ 10 Boba Fett 3.00 8.00
❑ 11 Jabba the Hutt 3.00 8.00
❑ 12 Oola 3.00 8.00
❑ 13 Lando Calrissian 3.00 8.00
❑ 14 Millennium Falcon 3.00 8.00
❑ 15 Ewoks 3.00 8.00
❑ 16 Jawas 3.00 8.00
❑ 17 Tusken Raiders 3.00 8.00
❑ 18 Anakin 3.00 8.00
Yoda/Obi-Wan

1993-95 Star Wars Galaxy LucasArts

COMPLETE SET (12) 6.00 15.00

❑ L1 Dark Forces Display Art .60 1.50
❑ L2 Dark Forces Ad Art .60 1.50
❑ L3 Dark Trooper .60 1.50
❑ L4 Keith Carter .60 1.50
❑ L5 TIE Fighter .60 1.50
❑ L6 Defender of the Empire .60 1.50
❑ L7 Keith Carter .60 1.50
❑ L8 X-Wing .60 1.50
❑ L9 The Farlander Papers .60 1.50
❑ L10 Keith Carter .60 1.50
❑ L11 Rebel Assault .60 1.50
❑ L12 Keith Carter .60 1.50

1995 Star Wars Empire Strikes Back Widevision

COMPLETE SET (144) 6.00 15.00

❑ 1 Title Card .15 .40
❑ 2 Probe droid .15 .40
❑ 3 TaunTaun and rider .15 .40
❑ 4 Luke on TaunTaun .15 .40
❑ 5 Wampa .15 .40
❑ 6 C-3PO is quieted by Han .15 .40
❑ 7 Luke hanging in the cave .15 .40
❑ 8 Luke reaches out to ghost Obi .15 .40
❑ 9 Han waves to rescuers .15 .40
❑ 10 Luke in the bacta tank .15 .40
❑ 11 Luke gets a kiss .15 .40
❑ 12 Probe droid .15 .40
❑ 13 The Imperial fleet .15 .40
❑ 14 Vader's helmet .15 .40
❑ 15 The Imperial fleet .15 .40
❑ 16 Vader's meditation chamber .15 .40
❑ 17 Leia encourages the troops .15 .40
❑ 18 Hoth canon .15 .40
❑ 19 Rebel transport away .15 .40
❑ 20 Hoth troops .15 .40
❑ 21 Luke in Snowpeeder .15 .40
❑ 22 AT-ATs approach the base .15 .40
❑ 23 View of AT-AT from Snowpeeder .15 .40
❑ 24 AT-ATs on Hoth .15 .40
❑ 25 AT-AT driver .15 .40
❑ 26 Snowpeeders seen from AT-AT .15 .40
❑ 27 AT-AT seen from above .15 .40
❑ 28 Vader in hologram .15 .40
❑ 29 Winding up the legs of an AT-AT .15 .40
❑ 30 An AT-AT falls .15 .40
❑ 31 Snow trench .15 .40

STAR WARS

☐ 32 AT-ST .15 .40
☐ 33 Inside a Snowpeeder cockpit .15 .40
☐ 34 AT-ATs fire on fleeing rebels .15 .40
☐ 35 AT-AT in the snow .15 .40
☐ 36 An AT-AT explodes .15 .40
☐ 37 Fallen AT-AT .15 .40
☐ 38 ATATs attack .15 .40
☐ 39 View from an AT-AT cockpit .15 .40
☐ 40 Falcon leaving the main hangar at Hoth .15 .40
☐ 41 Star Destroyers' near miss .15 .40
☐ 42 The Falcon in an asteroid field .15 .40
☐ 43 Inside the Falcon's cockpit .15 .40
☐ 44 TIE fighters in pursuit .15 .40
☐ 45 Asteroids .15 .40
☐ 46 TIE fighters in asteroid field .15 .40
☐ 47 Into the asteroid field .15 .40
☐ 48 Falcon on an asteroid .15 .40
☐ 49 Falcon on an asteroid .15 .40
☐ 50 Asteroid cave .15 .40
☐ 51 Dagobah swamp .15 .40
☐ 52 Luke cleans up R2 .15 .40
☐ 53 Vader's skull .15 .40
☐ 54 Luke confronts Yoda .15 .40
☐ 55 Yoda .15 .40
☐ 56 C3PO interrupts Han and Leia's kiss .15 .40
☐ 57 Vader gives orders .15 .40
☐ 58 Emperor's image .15 .40
☐ 59 Emperor and Vader confer .15 .40
☐ 60 Yoda's house .15 .40
☐ 61 Yoda and Luke in Yoda's house .15 .40
☐ 62 TIE bombers .15 .40
☐ 63 Mynock on the Falcon's window .15 .40
☐ 64 The teeth of a cave .15 .40
☐ 65 Falcon and Space Slug .15 .40
☐ 66 Space Slug .15 .40
☐ 67 Yoda on looks back .15 .40
☐ 68 Yoda .15 .40
☐ 69 Duel in the tree cave .15 .40
☐ 70 The face of Luke's future .15 .40
☐ 71 Bossk .15 .40
☐ 72 Vader and Fett .15 .40
☐ 73 Avenger in asteroid field .15 .40
☐ 74 Falcon chased by Star Destroyer .15 .40
☐ 75 Falcon hit .15 .40
☐ 76 Falcon and Avenger in asteroid field .15 .40
☐ 77 Yoda on Luke's foot .15 .40
☐ 78 Yoda .15 .40
☐ 79 X-Wing rises above a bog .15 .40
☐ 80 Falcon on a Star Destroyer .15 .40
☐ 81 Boba Fett .15 .40
☐ 82 Luke does a hand stand .15 .40
☐ 83 The Falcon's cockpit .15 .40
☐ 84 Falcon and cloud cars .15 .40
☐ 85 Falcon .15 .40
☐ 86 The Falcon lands at Cloud City .15 .40
☐ 87 Lando walks out to meet Han .15 .40
☐ 88 Lando greets Han .15 .40
☐ 89 Lando kisses Leia's hand .15 .40
☐ 90 Falcon arrived at Cloud City .15 .40
☐ 91 Luke leaves Yoda in his X-Wing .15 .40
☐ 92 Ghost Obi and Yoda .15 .40
☐ 93 Exterior view Cloud City .15 .40
☐ 94 Darth blocks a blaster shot .15 .40
☐ 95 Darth and Boba .15 .40
☐ 96 Stormtroopers in cloud city .15 .40
☐ 97 Chewie reassembles C3PO .15 .40
☐ 98 Han is tortured .15 .40
☐ 99 Darth confers with Fett .15 .40
☐ 100 Lando .15 .40
☐ 101 X-Wing approaching Cloud City .15 .40
☐ 102 Gathering in the freezing chamber .15 .40
☐ 103 Leia and Han, a last look .15 .40
☐ 104 Leia and Han kiss .15 .40
☐ 105 Solo is prepared for freezing .15 .40
☐ 106 Frozen Han .15 .40
☐ 107 Luke enters the freezing chamber .15 .40
☐ 108 Vader in the freezing chamber .15 .40
☐ 109 Duel in the freezing chamber .15 .40
☐ 110 Chewie chokes Lando .15 .40
☐ 111 Captain Solo loaded onto Slave I .15 .40
☐ 112 Slave I leaves Cloud City .15 .40
☐ 113 Leia .15 .40
☐ 114 Vader leaps down .15 .40
☐ 115 Duel in the freezing chamber .15 .40
☐ 116 Luke seeks out Vader .15 .40
☐ 117 Luke flies out a window .15 .40
☐ 118 Luke hangs above the reactor shaft .15 .40
☐ 119 Chewie and C3PO in corridor .15 .40
☐ 120 Falcon on landing platform .15 .40
☐ 121 Falcon leaving Cloud City .15 .40
☐ 122 Cloud City Reactor Shaft .15 .40
☐ 123 Luke and Vader duel .15 .40
☐ 124 Luke and Vader duel .15 .40
☐ 125 Luke loses his hand .15 .40
☐ 126 Vader shakes his fist .15 .40
☐ 127 Luke - Nooo .15 .40
☐ 128 Vader extends a hand .15 .40
☐ 129 Reactor Shaft .15 .40
☐ 130 Luke beneath Cloud City .15 .40
☐ 131 Falcon and Cloud City .15 .40
☐ 132 Falcon beneath Cloud City .15 .40
☐ 133 Millennium Falcon and TIE fighters .15 .40
☐ 134 R2 and C-3PO .15 .40
☐ 135 Chewie repairs the Falcon .15 .40
☐ 136 Luke aboard the Falcon .15 .40
☐ 137 Millennium Falcon Cockpit .15 .40
☐ 138 Vader's Star Destroyer Bridge .15 .40
☐ 139 Luke's Mechanical Hand .15 .40
☐ 140 Luke and Leia .15 .40
☐ 141 Space - Millennium Falcon .15 .40
☐ 142 R2 and C3PO .15 .40
☐ 143 Luke, Leia and Droids .15 .40
☐ 144 Rebel Star Cruiser - Rebel Ships .15 .40

1995 Star Wars Empire Strikes Back Widevision Finest

COMPLETE SET (10) 40.00 100.00
STATED ODDS 1:12

☐ C1 Imperial Probe Droid 4.00 10.00
☐ C2 Luke Skywalker on tauntaun 4.00 10.00
☐ C3 Luke 4.00 10.00
AT-ATs
☐ C4 Fallen AT-AT 4.00 10.00
☐ C5 Yoda 4.00 10.00
Luke Skywalker
☐ C6 Millennium Falcon 4.00 10.00
Giant Worm
☐ C7 Cloud City 4.00 10.00
☐ C8 Luke Skywalker 4.00 10.00
Darth Vader
☐ C9 Luke Skywalker hanging around 4.00 10.00
☐ C10 Leia 4.00 10.00
Luke/MedDroid/C3PO

1995 Star Wars Empire Strikes Back Widevision Mini Posters

COMPLETE SET (6) 40.00 80.00
STATED ODDS ONE PER BOX

☐ 1 Advance Poster 6.00 15.00
☐ 2 Domestic Poster 6.00 15.00
☐ 3 Domestic Poster 6.00 15.00
☐ 4 Australian Poster 6.00 15.00
☐ 5 German Poster 6.00 15.00
☐ 6 Radio Show Poster 6.00 15.00

1995 Star Wars Widevision

COMPLETE SET (120) 15.00 40.00

☐ 1 Title Card .15 .50
☐ 2 Star Destroyer Belly .20 .50
☐ 3 The Tantive IV - Captured .20 .50
☐ 4 Droids in Hallway .20 .50
☐ 5 Rebels in Blockade Runner .20 .50
☐ 6 Battle in Hallway .20 .50
☐ 7 Leia and R2 .20 .50
☐ 8 Darth and Commander Antilles .20 .50
☐ 9 Leia .20 .50
☐ 10 Escape Pod View .20 .50
☐ 11 Alone in the Desert .20 .50
☐ 12 Shocked Droid .20 .50
☐ 13 Sandcrawler .20 .50
☐ 14 Reunited Droids .20 .50
☐ 15 Look Sir, Droids .20 .50
☐ 16 Owen, Luke and Jawa .20 .50
☐ 17 Luke Discovers Hologram .20 .50
☐ 18 Leia's Hologram .20 .50
☐ 19 Dinner Conversation .20 .50
☐ 20 Setting Suns .20 .50
☐ 21 Landspeeder .20 .50
☐ 22 Tusken Raiders .20 .50
☐ 23 Tuskens and Bantha .20 .50
☐ 24 Tusken Challenge .20 .50
☐ 25 Rescuing Luke .20 .50
☐ 26 Luke, Obi-Wan and C-3PO .20 .50
☐ 27 Luke with New Saber .20 .50
☐ 28 Discussing the Force .20 .50
☐ 29 Leia's Hologram .20 .50
☐ 30 Approaching the Death Star .20 .50
☐ 31 Imperial Conference .20 .50
☐ 32 Making a Point .20 .50
☐ 33 Choking on Vader's Response .20 .50
☐ 34 Lar's Homestead Destroyed .20 .50
☐ 35 Vader Interrogates Leia .20 .50
☐ 36 Ext. Tatooine - Wasteland .20 .50
☐ 37 Entering Mos Eisley .20 .50
☐ 38 Cantina Creatures .20 .50
☐ 39 Bartender Pointing .20 .50
☐ 40 Wolfman .20 .50
☐ 41 Mos Eisley Cantina .20 .50
☐ 42 Obi-Wan's Saber .20 .50
☐ 43 Han and Chewie .20 .50
☐ 44 Greedo and Han .20 .50
☐ 45 Look Greedo .20 .50
☐ 46 Mos Eisley Street .20 .50
☐ 47 At the Falcon .20 .50
☐ 48 The Falcon Takes Off .20 .50
☐ 49 Star Destroyers in Space .20 .50
☐ 50 Star Destroyer Chases Falcon .20 .50
☐ 51 Falcon Cockpit .20 .50
☐ 52 Tarkin and Leia .20 .50
☐ 53 Death Star Beam .20 .50
☐ 54 Taking Aim .20 .50
☐ 55 Alderaan .20 .50
☐ 56 Practicing with a Saber .20 .50
☐ 57 Playing Chess .20 .50
☐ 58 Remote Versus Luke .20 .50
☐ 59 Falcon .20 .50
☐ 60 In the Cockpit .20 .50
☐ 61 Approaching the Death Star .20 .50
☐ 62 Death Star Hangar Bay .20 .50
☐ 63 Hangar 2037 .20 .50
☐ 64 Darth in Hangar 2037 .20 .50
☐ 65 Out of Hiding - Falcon .20 .50
☐ 66 Stormtrooper Fires .20 .50
☐ 67 She's Rich .20 .50
☐ 68 Wookiee Prisoner .20 .50
☐ 69 Detention Area .20 .50
☐ 70 Into the Garbage Chute Flyboy .20 .50
☐ 71 Garbage Problems .20 .50
☐ 72 At the Tractor Beam .20 .50
☐ 73 Firing Across the Chasm .20 .50
☐ 74 Swinging .20 .50
☐ 75 Vader and Ben Duel .20 .50
☐ 76 Luke Fires .20 .50
☐ 77 Falcon Away .20 .50
☐ 78 Comforting Luke .20 .50
☐ 79 Han Mans the Guns .20 .50
☐ 80 Luke Mans the Guns .20 .50
☐ 81 Near Yavin .20 .50
☐ 82 Yavin's Moon .20 .50
☐ 83 Death Star Near Yavin .20 .50
☐ 84 Battle Plan .20 .50
☐ 85 Han and his Reward .20 .50
☐ 86 Hangar Deck .20 .50
☐ 87 Sentry .20 .50
☐ 88 X-Wing Formation .20 .50
☐ 89 X-Wings Approach Death Star .20 .50
☐ 90 Tower .20 .50
☐ 91 Watching the Battle .20 .50
☐ 92 TIEs .20 .50
☐ 93 TIE Chases X-Wing .20 .50
☐ 94 War Room .20 .50
☐ 95 TIE Cockpit View .20 .50
☐ 96 The Trench .20 .50
☐ 97 War Room Commanders .20 .50
☐ 98 Y-Wings .20 .50
☐ 99 X-Wings .20 .50
☐ 100 Exploded X-Wing .20 .50
☐ 101 Vader's TIE .20 .50
☐ 102 Vader in Cockpit .20 .50
☐ 103 Vader's View .20 .50
☐ 104 Death Star War Room .20 .50
☐ 105 Vader and Wingmen .20 .50
☐ 106 Falcon .20 .50
☐ 107 Leia Watches .20 .50
☐ 108 Luke Uses the Force .20 .50
☐ 109 Hitting the Target .20 .50
☐ 110 Exploding Death Star .20 .50
☐ 111 Han and Chewie .20 .50
☐ 112 Vader Unbalanced .20 .50
☐ 113 Back to Yavin .20 .50
☐ 114 Congratulations .20 .50
☐ 115 Entering Ceremony Hall .20 .50
☐ 116 Han Winks .20 .50
☐ 117 Heroes .20 .50
☐ 118 Assembled Heroes .20 .50
☐ 119 Art Card .20 .50
☐ 120 Art Card .20 .50

1995 Star Wars Widevision Finest

COMPLETE SET (10) 40.00 100.00

☐ C1 The Dune Sea 5.00 12.00
☐ C2 Luke Skywalker 5.00 12.00
☐ C3 Death Star 5.00 12.00
☐ C4 Princess Leia 5.00 12.00
Luke Skywalker
☐ C5 Lightsaber Battle 5.00 12.00
☐ C6 TIE Fighters 5.00 12.00
☐ C7 Y-Wing 5.00 12.00
☐ C8 Darth Vader 5.00 12.00
☐ C9 X-Wing 5.00 12.00
☐ C10 Procession 5.00 12.00

1996 Star Wars Finest

COMPLETE SET (90) 10.00 25.00

☐ 1 Header Card .20 .50
☐ 2 Luke Skywalker .20 .50
☐ 3 Princess Leia .20 .50
☐ 4 Mon Mothma .20 .50
☐ 5 Admiral Ackbar .20 .50
☐ 6 Gen. Jan Dodonna .20 .50
☐ 7 Han Solo .20 .50
☐ 8 Chewbacca .20 .50
☐ 9 Lando Calrissian .20 .50
☐ 10 Gen. Crix Madine .20 .50
☐ 11 Gen. Garm Bel Iblis .20 .50
☐ 12 Councilor Borsk Feylya .20 .50
☐ 13 Wedge Antilles .20 .50
☐ 14 Biggs Darklighter .20 .50
☐ 15 Nien Numb .20 .50
☐ 16 Winter .20 .50
☐ 17 Wicket Warrick .20 .50
☐ 18 Qwi Xux .20 .50
☐ 19 Emperor Palpatine .20 .50
☐ 20 Darth Vader .20 .50
☐ 21 Grand Moff Tarkin .20 .50
☐ 22 Jorus C'Baoth .20 .50
☐ 23 Grand Admiral Thrawn .20 .50
☐ 24 Cpt. Pellaeon .20 .50
☐ 25 Admiral Piett .20 .50
☐ 26 Admiral Daala .20 .50
☐ 27 General Veers .20 .50
☐ 28 Emperor's Royal Guard .20 .50
☐ 29 Death Star Gunners .20 .50
☐ 30 Stormtroopers .20 .50
☐ 31 TIE Fighter Pilots .20 .50
☐ 32 AT-AT Walker Pilots .20 .50
☐ 33 Biker Scouts .20 .50
☐ 34 Boba Fett .20 .50
☐ 35 Dengar .20 .50
☐ 36 Bossk .20 .50
☐ 37 Obi-Wan Kenobi .20 .50
☐ 38 Yoda .20 .50
☐ 39 Callista .20 .50
☐ 40 Jacen Solo .20 .50
☐ 41 Anakin Solo .20 .50
☐ 42 Jaina Solo .20 .50
☐ 43 Kyp Durron .20 .50
☐ 44 Kirana Ti .20 .50
☐ 45 Tionne .20 .50
☐ 46 Mara Jade .20 .50
☐ 47 Talon Karrde .20 .50
☐ 48 Salla Zend .20 .50
☐ 49 Zuckuss .20 .50
☐ 50 Lobot .20 .50
☐ 51 Gallandro .20 .50
☐ 52 Moruth Doole .20 .50
☐ 53 Garindan .20 .50
☐ 54 Lady Valarian .20 .50
☐ 55 Tusken Raiders .20 .50
☐ 56 Banthas .20 .50
☐ 57 Jawas .20 .50
☐ 58 Ugnaughts .20 .50
☐ 59 Noghri .20 .50
☐ 60 Ssi-Ruuk .20 .50
☐ 61 Wampa .20 .50
☐ 62 Tauntaun .20 .50
☐ 63 Sarlacc .20 .50
☐ 64 Greedo .20 .50
☐ 65 Cantina Band .20 .50
☐ 66 Labria .20 .50
☐ 67 Dr. Evazan .20 .50
☐ 68 Ponda Baba .20 .50
☐ 69 Feltipern Trevagg .20 .50
☐ 70 Kabe, Muftak .20 .50
☐ 71 Momaw Nadon .20 .50
☐ 72 Wuher Chalmun .20 .50
☐ 73 Jabba The Hutt .20 .50
☐ 74 Bib Fortuna .20 .50
☐ 75 Salacious Crumb .20 .50
☐ 76 Max Rebo Band .20 .50
☐ 77 Oola .20 .50
☐ 78 Rancor .20 .50
☐ 79 Gamorrean Guard .20 .50
☐ 80 Weequay .20 .50
☐ 81 Tessek .20 .50
☐ 82 C-3PO .20 .50
☐ 83 R2-D2 .20 .50
☐ 84 2-1B .20 .50
☐ 85 R5-D4 .20 .50
☐ 86 4-LOM .20 .50
☐ 87 Blue Max and Bollux .20 .50
☐ 88 EV-9D9 .20 .50
☐ 89 IG-88 .20 .50
☐ 90 Probot CL .20 .50

1996 Star Wars Finest Refractors

COMPLETE SET (90) 250.00 500.00
*REFRACTORS: 5X TO 12X BASE CARDS 2.50 6.00

1996 Star Wars Finest Embossed

COMPLETE SET (6) 10.00 25.00

☐ F1 Darth Vader 2.00 5.00
☐ F2 Luke Skywalker 2.00 5.00
☐ F3 Obi-Wan Kenobi 2.00 5.00
☐ F4 Jalina Solo 2.00 5.00
☐ F5 Princess Leia 2.00 5.00
☐ F6 Jacen Solo 2.00 5.00

1996 Star Wars Finest Matrix

COMPLETE SET (4) 6.00 15.00

☐ M1 Han Solo w 2.00 5.00
Chewbacca
☐ M2 R2-D2 and C-3PO 2.00 5.00
☐ M3 Emperor Palpatine 2.00 5.00
☐ M4 Boba Fett 2.00 5.00

1996 Star Wars Finest Promos

COMPLETE SET (3) 2.50 6.00

☐ SWF1 Boba Fett 1.00 2.50
☐ SWF2 Republic City 1.00 2.50
☐ SWF3 Jedi Council Chamber 1.00 2.50

1996 Star Wars Return of the Jedi Widevision

COMPLETE SET (144) 10.00 25.00

☐ 1 Title Card .20 .50
☐ 2 Star Destroyer, Death Star .20 .50
☐ 3 Shuttle .20 .50
☐ 4 Imperial Shuttle Cockpit .20 .50
☐ 5 The Docking Bay .20 .50
☐ 6 Main Docking Bay View .20 .50
☐ 7 Reviewing the Troops .20 .50
☐ 8 R2 and C-3PO .20 .50
☐ 9 C-3PO Meets a Door .20 .50
☐ 10 Bib Fortuna .20 .50
☐ 11 Jabba .20 .50
☐ 12 Luke's Holo Message .20 .50
☐ 13 Meet EV-9-D9 .20 .50
☐ 14 Droid Torture .20 .50
☐ 15 Max Rebo's Band .20 .50
☐ 16 Boushh .20 .50
☐ 17 Boba Fett .20 .50
☐ 18 Jabba's Palace .20 .50
☐ 19 Han Released .20 .50
☐ 20 A Kiss .20 .50
☐ 21 Jabba Looks Over Leia .20 .50
☐ 22 Bib and Luke .20 .50
☐ 23 Jabba's Throne .20 .50
☐ 24 Luke in Throne Room .20 .50
☐ 25 Leia and Lando .20 .50
☐ 26 Rancor .20 .50
☐ 27 Jabba and Fett .20 .50
☐ 28 In the Rancor's Grip .20 .50
☐ 29 Dead Rancor .20 .50
☐ 30 Luke and Han .20 .50
☐ 31 Skiff and Sailbarge .20 .50
☐ 32 On the Skiff .20 .50
☐ 33 Sarlacc .20 .50
☐ 34 Bib .20 .50
☐ 35 Walking the Plank .20 .50
☐ 36 Fighting Fett .20 .50
☐ 37 Firing on the Skiff .20 .50
☐ 38 Fett .20 .50
☐ 39 Fett Fires .20 .50
☐ 40 Han and Fett .20 .50
☐ 41 Leia Chokes Jabba .20 .50
☐ 42 Dangling to Reach Lando .20 .50
☐ 43 Sarlacc has a Meal .20 .50
☐ 44 Above the Pit .20 .50
☐ 45 Damaged C-3PO .20 .50
☐ 46 Salacious Crumb .20 .50
☐ 47 Leia Mans the Guns .20 .50
☐ 48 Luke and Leia Swing .20 .50
☐ 49 Droids in the Sand .20 .50
☐ 50 A Barge is Blown .20 .50
☐ 51 Shuttle of the Emperor .20 .50
☐ 52 The Emperor .20 .50
☐ 53 X-Wing on Dagobah .20 .50
☐ 54 Farewell to Yoda .20 .50
☐ 55 Ghost Ben and Luke .20 .50
☐ 56 The Rebel Fleet .20 .50
☐ 57 Mon Mothma Speaks .20 .50
☐ 58 Ackbar and Endor Map .20 .50
☐ 59 Ackbar and Mon Mothma .20 .50
☐ 60 Revealing the Target .20 .50
☐ 61 Death Star Core .20 .50
☐ 62 Lando .20 .50
☐ 63 Inside the Shuttle .20 .50
☐ 64 On Endor .20 .50
☐ 65 Bike Chase .20 .50
☐ 66 Luke and Leia Ride Bikes .20 .50
☐ 67 Scout Trooper .20 .50
☐ 68 Sparks Fly .20 .50
☐ 69 Leia Versus Trooper .20 .50
☐ 70 Luke Versus Trooper .20 .50
☐ 71 Darth in Emperor's Chamber .20 .50
☐ 72 Meet the Ewoks .20 .50
☐ 73 Ewok Village .20 .50
☐ 74 Baby Ewok .20 .50
☐ 75 Han for Dinner .20 .50
☐ 76 The Regal C-3PO .20 .50
☐ 77 Ewoks with Baby .20 .50
☐ 78 C-3PO Tells a Tale .20 .50
☐ 79 Luke and Leia .20 .50
☐ 80 The Shuttle Platform .20 .50
☐ 81 Vader and Shuttle .20 .50
☐ 82 AT-AT at Platform .20 .50
☐ 83 Luke Under Guard .20 .50
☐ 84 The Fleet Gathers .20 .50
☐ 85 Entering Hyperspace .20 .50
☐ 86 The Mon Calamari Bridge .20 .50
☐ 87 Ewok Bike Ride .20 .50
☐ 88 Luke, Vader and Emperor .20 .50
☐ 89 Falcon Cockpit .20 .50
☐ 90 Ackbar Surveys the Scene .20 .50
☐ 91 Approaching the Death Star .20 .50
☐ 92 Pulling Up .20 .50
☐ 93 X-Wings and Death Star .20 .50
☐ 94 The Battle .20 .50
☐ 95 Falcon Flees .20 .50
☐ 96 Endor Battle .20 .50
☐ 97 Glider .20 .50
☐ 98 Han Fires .20 .50
☐ 99 AT-ST .20 .50
☐ 100 TIEs Attack .20 .50
☐ 101 The Battle in Space .20 .50
☐ 102 Death Star Fires .20 .50
☐ 103 Ship Destroyed .20 .50
☐ 104 Another Explosion .20 .50
☐ 105 Falcon Moves in Close .20 .50
☐ 106 Duel Before the Emperor .20 .50
☐ 107 Wookiee on an AT-ST .20 .50
☐ 108 Crushing an AT-ST .20 .50
☐ 109 AT-ST Falls .20 .50
☐ 110 The Duel Continues .20 .50
☐ 111 A TIE is Destroyed .20 .50
☐ 112 Han - No Problem .20 .50
☐ 113 Setting a Timer .20 .50
☐ 114 Raised Saber .20 .50
☐ 115 Vader Loses a Hand .20 .50
☐ 116 Destroyed Bunker .20 .50
☐ 117 Emperor's Lightening .20 .50
☐ 118 Luke in Agony .20 .50
☐ 119 Lifted Emperor .20 .50
☐ 120 X-Ray Vader .20 .50
☐ 121 Central Core Shaft .20 .50
☐ 122 Luke and Vader .20 .50
☐ 123 The Falcon .20 .50
☐ 124 TIEs .20 .50
☐ 125 Flying in the Shaft .20 .50
☐ 126 Falcon .20 .50
☐ 127 Falcon Targets .20 .50
☐ 128 Star Destroyer Bridge Destroyed .20 .50
☐ 129 Ackbar .20 .50
☐ 130 Vader's Destroyer Nose Dives .20 .50
☐ 131 Vader Revealed .20 .50
☐ 132 X-Wing in the Shaft .20 .50
☐ 133 Explosions .20 .50
☐ 134 The Core Blows .20 .50
☐ 135 Falcon Flees the Destruction .20 .50
☐ 136 Exploding Free .20 .50
☐ 137 Last Look at Death Star .20 .50
☐ 138 Death Star Blows .20 .50
☐ 139 Explosion in the Sky .20 .50
☐ 140 Burning Vader's Body .20 .50
☐ 141 Ewok Celebration .20 .50
☐ 142 Luke and Leia Celebrate .20 .50
☐ 143 3 Ghost Jedi .20 .50
☐ 144 The Final Celebration .20 .50
☐ DIII Admiral Akbar

1996 Star Wars Return of the Jedi Widevision Finest

COMPLETE SET (10) 40.00 80.00
STATED ODDS 1:12

☐ C1 Darth Vader 4.00 10.00
☐ C2 R2-D2 4.00 10.00
C-3PO
☐ C3 Luke Skywalker 4.00 10.00
Han Solo
☐ C4 Rancor 4.00 10.00
Luke Skywalker
☐ C5 Floater 4.00 10.00
☐ C6 Speeder Bikes 4.00 10.00
☐ C7 X-Wings 4.00 10.00
☐ C8 Darth Vader 4.00 10.00
Luke Skywalker
☐ C9 Emperor 4.00 10.00
Luke Skywalker
☐ C10 Tower 4.00 10.00

1996 Star Wars Return of the Jedi Widevision Mini Posters

COMPLETE SET (6) 40.00 80.00
STATED ODDS ONE PER BOX

☐ 1 Advance Poster 6.00 15.00
☐ 2 Domestic Poster 6.00 15.00
☐ 3 Re-Release Poster 6.00 15.00
☐ 4 Japanese Poster 6.00 15.00
☐ 5 Japanese Poster 6.00 15.00
☐ 6 Polish Poster 6.00 15.00

1996 Star Wars Shadow of the Empire

COMPLETE SET (100) 15.00 40.00
73-78 STATED ODDS 1:9
79-82 STATED ODDS 1:18

☐ 1 Xizor is Lurking .15 .40
☐ 2 Leia's Recurring Nightmare .15 .40
☐ 3 Luke Feels the Dark Side .15 .40
☐ 4 Leia Defends Herself .15 .40
☐ 5 Reunion on Tatooine .15 .40
☐ 6 Xizor Greets Vader .15 .40
☐ 7 Xizor's Dirty Handiwork .15 .40
☐ 8 Ferreting Out a Traitor .15 .40
☐ 9 Beautiful . . . and Lethal .15 .40
☐ 10 Xizor Summons Jabba .15 .40
☐ 11 Leia Meets Dash Rendar .15 .40
☐ 12 Vader Stays Sharp .15 .40
☐ 13 Xizor Relishes the Good Life .15 .40
☐ 14 Fancy Flying .15 .40
☐ 15 Luke Scores a TIE .15 .40
☐ 16 Help Me, Obi-Wan .15 .40
☐ 17 Boba Fett Escapes From Gall .15 .40
☐ 18 Narrow Escape .15 .40
☐ 19 Dealing With Dash .15 .40
☐ 20 Vader Grows Wary of Xizor .15 .40
☐ 21 Xizor Wants it All .15 .40
☐ 22 The Emperor Insists .15 .40
☐ 23 It'th Greedo'th Uncle .15 .40
☐ 24 The Waiting Game .15 .40
☐ 25 Luke Hones His Lightsaber Skills .15 .40
☐ 26 Swoop Troop Attack .15 .40
☐ 27 Luke Axes a Swooper .15 .40
☐ 28 Good 'Ol Beggar's Canyon .15 .40
☐ 29 Vader Destroys the Rebel Base .15 .40
☐ 30 Guri Does Xizor's Dirty Work .15 .40
☐ 31 Luke and Dash's Bothan Mission .15 .40
☐ 32 Dash's Persuasive Charm .15 .40
☐ 33 Attack on the Suprosa .15 .40
☐ 34 Leia Meets Guri .15 .40
☐ 35 Luke and Melan are Ambushed .15 .40
☐ 36 Luke's Taken Prisoner .15 .40
☐ 37 Guri Turns the Tables .15 .40
☐ 38 Boarding Guri's Stinger .15 .40
☐ 39 Chewbacca in Disguise .15 .40
☐ 40 Leia and Chewie go Underground .15 .40
☐ 41 Leia Visits Spero's Plant Shop .15 .40
☐ 42 Vader Seethes Over Luke's Escape .15 .40
☐ 43 Leia Arrives at Xizor's Palace .15 .40
☐ 44 Leia Finally Meets Xizor .15 .40
☐ 45 Leia is Smitten .15 .40
☐ 46 Vader Senses His Son .15 .40
☐ 47 Leia Prepares for Xizor .15 .40
☐ 48 Hyperspace . . . at Last .15 .40
☐ 49 Xizor Prepares for Leia .15 .40
☐ 50 The Kiss .15 .40
☐ 51 Take That Xizor .15 .40
☐ 52 Xizor Sharpens his Claws .15 .40
☐ 53 Dash Does it Again .15 .40
☐ 54 Luke Becomes One With the Force .15 .40
☐ 55 Xizor's Troubled World .15 .40
☐ 56 Vader Uncovers Xizor's Secret Past .15 .40
☐ 57 Same Beast, Different Sewer .15 .40
☐ 58 Dash Fires the Guide .15 .40
☐ 59 Artoo and Threepio Helm the Falcon .15 .40
☐ 60 Luke Blocks Xizor's Fire .15 .40
☐ 61 Will Xizor Call Luke's Bluff? .15 .40
☐ 62 Five Minutes Until Impact .15 .40
☐ 63 Guri Goes Toe-to-Toe With Luke .15 .40
☐ 64 Xizor Narrowly Escapes .15 .40
☐ 65 Xizor's Castle Blows Up .15 .40
☐ 66 Battle Over Coruscant Part I .15 .40
☐ 67 Battle Over Coruscant Part II .15 .40
☐ 68 Battle Over Coruscant Part III .15 .40
☐ 69 Good Riddance, Xizor .15 .40
☐ 70 Watch Out, Dash .15 .40
☐ 71 Dash's Secret Getaway .15 .40
☐ 72 Luke Plans Han's Rescue .15 .40
☐ 73 Luke Skywalker 2.00 5.00
☐ 74 Leia and Chewbacca 2.00 5.00
☐ 75 Lando Calrissian 2.00 5.00
☐ 76 R2-D2 and C-3PO 2.00 5.00
☐ 77 Dash and Leebo 2.00 5.00
☐ 78 Xizor 2.00 5.00
☐ 79 Guri 3.00 8.00
☐ 80 Darth Vader 3.00 8.00
☐ 81 Jix and Big Gizz 3.00 8.00
☐ 82 Boba Fett 3.00 8.00
☐ 83 Millennium Falcon .15 .40
☐ 84 Outrider .15 .40
☐ 85 Virago .15 .40
☐ 86 Stinger .15 .40
☐ 87 Swoop .15 .40
☐ 88 Slave I .15 .40
☐ 89 Slave I in Battle .15 .40
☐ 90 Boba Fett .15 .40
☐ 91 Fett in Battle .15 .40
☐ 92 Fett and 4-Lom .15 .40
☐ 93 4-Lom .15 .40
☐ 94 Jabba's Palace .15 .40
☐ 95 AT-AT Under Attack .15 .40
☐ 96 Dash .15 .40
☐ 97 Dash on the Run .15 .40
☐ 98 Dash in Battle .15 .40
☐ 99 Ord Mantell Hovertram .15 .40
☐ 100 IG-88 .15 .40

1996 Star Wars 3Di

COMPLETE SET (63) 30.00 60.00
1M STATED ODDS 1:24

☐ 1 Opening Credits .60 1.50
☐ 2 Pursuit in Space .60 1.50
☐ 3 Droids in Crossfire .60 1.50
☐ 4 A Princess Strikes Back .60 1.50
☐ 5 Release of the Escape Pod .60 1.50
☐ 6 Toward Tatooine .60 1.50

STAR WARS

Card	Low	High
❑ 7 Jawas in Hiding	.60	1.50
❑ 8 Enter Luke Skywalker	.60	1.50
❑ 9 The Leia Hologram	.60	1.50
❑ 10 Spotting Sandpeople	.60	1.50
❑ 11 Attacked by Tuskan Raiders	.60	1.50
❑ 12 Rescued by Ben Kenobi	.60	1.50
❑ 13 A Message for Help	.60	1.50
❑ 14 Power of the Dark Side	.60	1.50
❑ 15 Fate of the Lars Homestead	.60	1.50
❑ 16 Cantina Denziens	.60	1.50
❑ 17 Meet Han and Chewie	.60	1.50
❑ 18 Alerting the Sandtrooper	.60	1.50
❑ 19 Perparing for Space Travel	.60	1.50
❑ 20 Escape from Tatooine	.60	1.50
❑ 21 Han Solo in Command	.60	1.50
❑ 22 Jumping into Hyperspace	.60	1.50
❑ 23 Target: Alderaan	.60	1.50
❑ 24 Laser of Destruction	.60	1.50
❑ 25 Leia's Ordeal	.60	1.50
❑ 26 Destruction of a Planet	.60	1.50
❑ 27 Lightsaber Pratice	.60	1.50
❑ 28 Approaching the Death Star	.60	1.50
❑ 29 Drawn into Danger	.60	1.50
❑ 30 Heroes in Hiding	.60	1.50
❑ 31 Accessing Imperial Data	.60	1.50
❑ 32 Luke's Rescue Plan	.60	1.50
❑ 33 A Captured Chewbacca	.60	1.50
❑ 34 Han Solo's Bluff	.60	1.50
❑ 35 Trapped in the Alcove	.60	1.50
❑ 36 Trash Compacter Peril	.60	1.50
❑ 37 The Power Generator Trench	.60	1.50
❑ 38 Shoot Out in the Shaft	.60	1.50
❑ 39 Swinging to Safety	.60	1.50
❑ 40 When Jedi Clash	.60	1.50
❑ 41 Run Luke, Run	.60	1.50
❑ 42 Escaping the Death Star	.60	1.50
❑ 43 I Can't Believe He 's Gone	.60	1.50
❑ 44 Skirmish in Space	.60	1.50
❑ 45 Got Him, I Got Him	.60	1.50
❑ 46 Destination: Yavin	.60	1.50
❑ 47 The Rebel Hideout	.60	1.50
❑ 48 Briefing the Rebels	.60	1.50
❑ 49 X-Wings Away	.60	1.50
❑ 50 Assault on the Death Star	.60	1.50
❑ 51 Monitoring the Battle	.60	1.50
❑ 52 Vader in the Trench	.60	1.50
❑ 53 Targets Coming Up	.60	1.50
❑ 54 Artoo Hanging On	.60	1.50
❑ 55 Blasted by Vader	.60	1.50
❑ 56 Luke Uses the Force	.60	1.50
❑ 57 Suprise Attack	.60	1.50
❑ 58 Vader's Final Stand	.60	1.50
❑ 59 Solo to the Resuce	.60	1.50
❑ 60 Death Star Departure	.60	1.50
❑ 61 The Victorious Rebels	.60	1.50
❑ 62 Honored for Their Bravery	.60	1.50
❑ 63 Heroes of the Rebellion	.60	1.50
❑ 1M Death Star Explosion	6.00	15.00

1997 Star Wars Stickers U.S.

COMPLETE SET (66)	7.50	20.00
❑ 1 Stormtroopers	.20	.50
❑ 2 1/2 - C-3PO	.20	.50
❑ 3 1/2 - R2	.20	.50
❑ 4 1/2 - Luke with Saber	.20	.50
❑ 5 1/2 - Obi-Wan Watching	.20	.50
❑ 6 Luke and Obi-Wan	.20	.50
❑ 7 Entering Mos Eisley	.20	.50
❑ 8 Leia and Darth	.20	.50
❑ 9 Firing in the Detention Block	.20	.50
❑ 10 Cantina Aliens	.20	.50
❑ 11 Blue Cantina Aliens	.20	.50
❑ 12 Chewie at the Bar	.20	.50
❑ 13 Falcon	.20	.50
❑ 14 Leia and Darth	.20	.50
❑ 15 Falcon Cockpit	.20	.50
❑ 16 Falcon Interior	.20	.50
❑ 17 Han, Chewie, Obi-Wan and Luke Meet	.20	.50
❑ 18 Obi-Wan Releasing Tractor Beam	.20	.50
❑ 19 Obi-Wan Releasing Tractor Beam	.20	.50
❑ 20 Obi-Wan	.20	.50
❑ 21 Darth and Obi-Wan Duel	.20	.50
❑ 22 Han and Chewie	.20	.50
❑ 23 Han	.20	.50
❑ 24 Leia Watches the Battle	.20	.50
❑ 25 C-3PO	.20	.50
❑ 26 Death Star Beam	.20	.50
❑ 27 Death Star Gunner	.20	.50
❑ 28 R2 and C-3PO	.20	.50
❑ 29 Awards Ceremony	.20	.50
❑ 30 Luke in Wampa Lair	.20	.50
❑ 31 Into the TaunTaun	.20	.50
❑ 32 Bacta	.20	.50
❑ 33 Battle on Hoth	.20	.50
❑ 34 Droids in Hoth Hallway	.20	.50
❑ 35 AT-ATs artwork	.20	.50
❑ 36 Darth	.20	.50
❑ 37 Falcon Cockpit	.20	.50
❑ 38 Falcon in Asteroid Field	.20	.50
❑ 39 1/2 - Chewie	.20	.50
❑ 40 1/2 - Chewie	.20	.50
❑ 41 X-Wing Approaches Dagobah	.20	.50
❑ 42 R2 as Voyeur	.20	.50
❑ 43 Luke in the Cave	.20	.50
❑ 44 Falcon at Cloud City	.20	.50
❑ 45 Leia, Han, Chewie and Lando	.20	.50
❑ 46 1/2 - Stormtroopers	.20	.50
❑ 47 1/2 - Stormtroopers with Lobot	.20	.50
❑ 48 Han Fires at Vader	.20	.50
❑ 49 1/2 - Vader	.20	.50
❑ 50 1/2 - Vader	.20	.50
❑ 51 Torturing Han	.20	.50
❑ 52 Vader talks to Fett	.20	.50
❑ 53 Leia Led Away	.20	.50
❑ 54 Luke and Vader Duel	.20	.50
❑ 55 Han in Carbonite	.20	.50
❑ 56 R2 and C-3PO	.20	.50
❑ 57 A Captured Chewie	.20	.50
❑ 58 Jabba, Leia and Bib	.20	.50
❑ 59 Desert Skiff	.20	.50
❑ 60 Luke Battles on Skiff	.20	.50
❑ 61 War Room	.20	.50
❑ 62 Shuttle Cockpit	.20	.50
❑ 63 Endor	.20	.50
❑ 64 Wicket and Leia	.20	.50
❑ 65 AT-ST fires on Bunker	.20	.50
❑ 66 Emperor	.20	.50

1997 Star Wars Trilogy Special Edition

COMPLETE SET (72)	6.00	15.00
13D ISSUED AS BOX TOPPER		
❑ 1 Escape Pod Away	.15	.40
❑ 2 Sandtroopers and Dewback	.15	.40
❑ 3 Dewback	.15	.40
❑ 4 Sandcrawler	.15	.40
❑ 5 Jawas at Lars Farm	.15	.40
❑ 6 Twin Suns	.15	.40
❑ 7 Landspeeder	.15	.40
❑ 8 Mos Eisley Overlook	.15	.40
❑ 9 Ranats Near Mos Eisley	.15	.40
❑ 10 Entering the City Streets	.15	.40
❑ 11 A View From Above	.15	.40
❑ 12 Rontos in the Distance	.15	.40
❑ 13 Droids at Work	.15	.40
❑ 14 Rearing Ronto	.15	.40
❑ 15 Falling Jawa	.15	.40
❑ 16 On Your Way	.15	.40
❑ 17 Jawa	.15	.40
❑ 18 Driving Past a Ronto	.15	.40
❑ 19 Outside the Cantina	.15	.40
❑ 20 Droids Outside the Cantina	.15	.40
❑ 21 Dismounting a Dewback	.15	.40
❑ 22 Cantina Aliens	.15	.40
❑ 23 Blowing Smoke	.15	.40
❑ 24 Patrolling Mos Eisley Streets	.15	.40
❑ 25 Patrolling With a Droid	.15	.40
❑ 26 The Young Jabba	.15	.40
❑ 27 Jabba Hands on Hips	.15	.40
❑ 28 Look Jabba	.15	.40
❑ 29 Han and Jabba	.15	.40
❑ 30 Stepped on Tail	.15	.40
❑ 31 Boba Fett	.15	.40
❑ 32 Falcon Surrounded	.15	.40
❑ 33 Falcon Takes Off	.15	.40
❑ 34 Leaving Mos Eisley	.15	.40
❑ 35 Death Star Near Alderaan	.15	.40
❑ 36 Nowhere to Go	.15	.40
❑ 37 Falcon Near Yavin	.15	.40
❑ 38 Massassi Temple	.15	.40
❑ 39 Yavin IV Forest	.15	.40
❑ 40 X-Wing Fleet	.15	.40
❑ 41 X-Wing	.15	.40
❑ 42 Fleet Approaches Death Star	.15	.40
❑ 43 Cockpit View	.15	.40
❑ 44 Death Star	.15	.40
❑ 45 Above the Death Star	.15	.40
❑ 46 Towers	.15	.40
❑ 47 Firing Towers	.15	.40
❑ 48 TIE Fires	.15	.40
❑ 49 TIE Chases X-Wing	.15	.40
❑ 50 Exploding TIE	.15	.40
❑ 51 Exploding X-Wing	.15	.40
❑ 52 Attack Formation	.15	.40
❑ 53 Surface Explosion	.15	.40
❑ 54 Firing in the Trench	.15	.40
❑ 55 Darth and Escorts	.15	.40
❑ 56 Explosion in the Trench	.15	.40
❑ 57 R2 Makes Repairs	.15	.40
❑ 58 The Exhaust Port	.15	.40
❑ 59 Leaving the Death Star Behind	.15	.40
❑ 60 Heroes Walk	.15	.40
❑ 61 Wampa Close-Up	.15	.40
❑ 62 Wampa Feasting	.15	.40
❑ 63 Wampa Approaches	.15	.40
❑ 64 Cloud City Sketch	.15	.40
❑ 65 Landing Platform Sketch	.15	.40
❑ 66 Bespin Sketch	.15	.40
❑ 67 New Dancers	.15	.40
❑ 68 New Band Members	.15	.40
❑ 69 Oola	.15	.40
❑ 70 Oola and Other Dancers	.15	.40
❑ 71 Band Sketch	.15	.40
❑ 72 Ewok Celebration Sketch	.15	.40
❑ 13D X-Wings Departing	6.00	15.00

1997 Star Wars Trilogy Special Edition Holograms

COMPLETE SET (2)	12.00	30.00
STATED ODDS 1:18		
❑ 1 X-Wing Fighter	6.00	15.00
❑ 2 Millennium Falcon	6.00	15.00

1997 Star Wars Trilogy Special Edition Laser

COMPLETE SET (6)	6.00	15.00
STATED ODDS 1:9		
❑ LC1 A New Customer	1.25	3.00
❑ LC2 It's Not My Fault	1.25	3.00
❑ LC3 The Tantive IV	1.25	3.00
❑ LC4 Chewbacca Led Away	1.25	3.00
❑ LC5 X-Wings Approach	1.25	3.00
❑ LC6 Imperial View	1.25	3.00

1997 Star Wars Trilogy The Complete Story

COMPLETE SET (72)	6.00	15.00
❑ 1 In the Belly of the Beast	.25	.60
❑ 2 Leia Feeds R2-D2	.25	.60
❑ 3 Demanding an Answer	.25	.60
❑ 4 A Desolate Desert	.25	.60
❑ 5 Look Sir, Droids	.25	.60
❑ 6 A Plea for Help	.25	.60
❑ 7 Alone in Thought	.25	.60
❑ 8 Sand People Strike	.25	.60
❑ 9 Kenobi Gets the Message	.25	.60
❑ 10 Into Mos Eisley	.25	.60
❑ 11 Greedo's Unlucky Day	.25	.60
❑ 12 A Deal is Struck	.25	.60
❑ 13 Moff Tarkin's Surprise	.25	.60
❑ 14 Let the Wookiee Win	.25	.60
❑ 15 Into the Enemy Lair	.25	.60
❑ 16 A Close and Smelly Call	.25	.60
❑ 17 Fight to the End	.25	.60
❑ 18 Han Hits His Mark	.25	.60
❑ 19 Preparing for Action	.25	.60
❑ 20 X-wings Attack	.25	.60
❑ 21 The Battle Unfolds	.25	.60
❑ 22 Into the Trench	.25	.60
❑ 23 The Dark Lord Attacks	.25	.60
❑ 24 Hitting their Target	.25	.60
❑ 25 Imperial Snoop	.25	.60
❑ 26 Abominable Wampa	.25	.60
❑ 27 Rejuvenating Bacta Bath	.25	.60
❑ 28 Vader's Meditation Ends	.25	.60
❑ 29 Lumbering Metal Monsters	.25	.60
❑ 30 Harpooning a Whale	.25	.60
❑ 31 Fire and Ice	.25	.60
❑ 32 Han Plays Chicken	.25	.60
❑ 33 Down in Desolate Dagobah	.25	.60
❑ 34 Luke Takes Aim	.25	.60
❑ 35 Vader and His Master	.25	.60
❑ 36 Shelter from a Storm	.25	.60
❑ 37 Smoking Them Out	.25	.60
❑ 38 Size Matters Not	.25	.60
❑ 39 Vader Hires Boba Fett	.25	.60
❑ 40 Chasing after Solo	.25	.60
❑ 41 Luke's Balancing Act	.25	.60
❑ 42 A Cloud City Welcome	.25	.60
❑ 43 Friend or Foe	.25	.60
❑ 44 A Surprise Dinner Guest	.25	.60
❑ 45 Loved Ones Part	.25	.60
❑ 46 Lightsaber Duel	.25	.60
❑ 47 A Terrible Blow	.25	.60
❑ 48 A Life Suspended	.25	.60
❑ 49 Under Construction	.25	.60
❑ 50 Vader Motivates the Troops	.25	.60
❑ 51 A Slimy Crime Kingpin	.25	.60
❑ 52 Han Comes to Life	.25	.60
❑ 53 A Jedi Tries to Reason	.25	.60
❑ 54 Sarlacc Sightseeing Tour	.25	.60
❑ 55 Fighting Fett	.25	.60
❑ 56 Luke and Leia Swing	.25	.60
❑ 57 The Emperor Arrives	.25	.60
❑ 58 Visit to an Old Friend	.25	.60
❑ 59 Rebel Fleet at the Ready	.25	.60
❑ 60 Into Enemy Territory	.25	.60
❑ 61 Chase Through the Forest	.25	.60
❑ 62 Threepio Tells Tales	.25	.60
❑ 63 Vader Comes for Luke	.25	.60
❑ 64 Leading the Attack	.25	.60
❑ 65 Running for Cover	.25	.60
❑ 66 Fully Operational	.25	.60
❑ 67 Crushing an Enemy	.25	.60
❑ 68 A Turn to the Dark Side	.25	.60
❑ 69 The Emperor's Lightning	.25	.60
❑ 70 The Emperor Goes Soaring	.25	.60
❑ 71 One Last Look	.25	.60
❑ 72 Together in the Force	.25	.60
❑ 0 Promo	1.00	2.00

1997 Star Wars Trilogy The Complete Story Laser

COMPLETE SET (6)	6.00	15.00
STATED ODDS 1:9		
❑ LC1 Luke Skywalker is entranced	1.25	3.00
❑ LC2 Han Solo and co-pilot Chewbacca	1.25	3.00
❑ LC3 Admiral Ozzel feels Darth Vader's	1.25	3.00
❑ LC4 A hologram of Emperor Palpatine	1.25	3.00
❑ LC5 A fate much worse	1.25	3.00
❑ LC6 Emperor Palpatine unleashes	1.25	3.00

1997 Star Wars Vehicles

COMPLETE SET (72)	5.00	12.00
❑ 1 Title Card	.15	.40
❑ 2 Millennium Falcon	.15	.40
❑ 3 A-Wing	.15	.40
❑ 4 B-Wing	.15	.40
❑ 5 Y-Wing	.15	.40
❑ 6 Z-95 Headhunter	.15	.40
❑ 7 X-Wing	.15	.40
❑ 8 V-Wing Air Speeder	.15	.40
❑ 9 E-Wing Fighter	.15	.40
❑ 10 Rebel Snowspeeder	.15	.40
❑ 11 Rebel Blockade Runner	.15	.40
❑ 12 Escape Pod	.15	.40
❑ 13 Rebel Cruiser	.15	.40
❑ 14 Rebel Transport	.15	.40
❑ 15 Mon Cal Cruiser	.15	.40
❑ 16 Nebulon Ranger	.15	.40
❑ 17 T-16 Skyhopper	.15	.40
❑ 18 Luke's Landspeeder	.15	.40
❑ 19 Jawa Sandcrawler	.15	.40
❑ 20 Sail Barge	.15	.40
❑ 21 Lady Luck	.15	.40
❑ 22 Twin-Pod Cloud Car	.15	.40
❑ 23 Slave I	.15	.40
❑ 24 IG-2000	.15	.40
❑ 25 Hound's Tooth	.15	.40
❑ 26 S-Swoop	.15	.40
❑ 27 Outrider	.15	.40
❑ 28 Virago	.15	.40
❑ 29 Stinger	.15	.40
❑ 30 AT-PT	.15	.40
❑ 31 AT-ST	.15	.40
❑ 32 AT-AT	.15	.40
❑ 33 Speeder Bike	.15	.40
❑ 34 Chariot Lav	.15	.40
❑ 35 TIE Fighter	.15	.40
❑ 36 TIE Bomber	.15	.40
❑ 37 TIE Interceptor	.15	.40
❑ 38 TIE Advanced	.15	.40
❑ 39 Lambda-Class Shuttle	.15	.40
❑ 40 I-7 Howltrunner	.15	.40
❑ 41 Interdictor Cruiser	.15	.40
❑ 42 Lancer Frigate	.15	.40
❑ 43 Imperial Star Destroyer	.15	.40
❑ 44 Victory Star Destroyer	.15	.40
❑ 45 Executor	.15	.40
❑ 46 Eclipse Star Destroyer	.15	.40
❑ 47 Sun Crusher	.15	.40
❑ 48 World Devastator	.15	.40
❑ 49 Death Star	.15	.40
❑ 50 Death Star II	.15	.40
❑ 51 Battle of Yavin - Strategy	.15	.40
❑ 52 Battle of Yavin - Warriors	.15	.40
❑ 53 Battle of Yavin - Hardware	.15	.40
❑ 54 Battle of Hoth - Strategy	.15	.40
❑ 55 Battle of Hot - Warriors	.15	.40
❑ 56 Battle of Hoth - Hardware	.15	.40
❑ 57 Battle of Endor - Strategy	.15	.40
❑ 58 Battle of Endor - Warriors	.15	.40
❑ 59 Battle of Endor - Hardware	.15	.40
❑ 60 Gun Port (Falcon subset)	.15	.40
❑ 61 Smuggler's Hold (Falcon subset)	.15	.40
❑ 62 Cockpit (Falcon subset)	.15	.40
❑ 63 Hyperdrive (Falcon subset)	.15	.40
❑ 64 Millennium Falcon (Han Solo)	.15	.40
❑ 65 X-Wing (Luke)	.15	.40
❑ 66 Executor (Darth Vader)	.15	.40
❑ 67 Mon Cal Cruiser (Ackbar)	.15	.40
❑ 68 Sail Barge (Jabba)	.15	.40
❑ 69 Slave 1 (Boba Fett)	.15	.40
❑ 70 Shuttle (Emperor Palpatine)	.15	.40
❑ 71 Jawa Sandcrawler (Jawas)	.15	.40
❑ 72 Checklist	.15	.40

1997 Star Wars Vehicles 3-D

STATED ODDS 1:36	Low	High
❑ 1 Princess Leia	8.00	20.00
❑ 2 Luke Skywalker	8.00	20.00
❑ 3 Princess Leia Luke Skywalker	15.00	40.00

1997 Star Wars Vehicles Cut Aways

COMPLETE SET (4)	7.50	20.00
STATED ODDS 1:18		
❑ C1 AT-ST	2.50	6.00
❑ C2 Slave I	2.50	6.00
❑ C3 X-Wing	2.50	6.00
❑ C4 Lambda Shuttle	2.50	6.00

1999 Star Wars Chrome Archives

COMPLETE SET (90)	10.00	25.00
❑ 1 Darth Vader strangles a Rebel	.20	.50
❑ 2 A message from Princess Leia	.20	.50
❑ 3 Princess Leia captured	.20	.50
❑ 4 The escape pod is jettisoned	.20	.50
❑ 5 The droids on Tatooine	.20	.50
❑ 6 Stormtroopers seek the droids	.20	.50
❑ 7 Luke checks out his new droid	.20	.50
❑ 8 The Tusken Raiders	.20	.50
❑ 9 Ben Kenobi rescues Luke	.20	.50
❑ 10 Interrogated by stormtroopers	.20	.50
❑ 11 Han Solo cornered by Greedo	.20	.50
❑ 12 Distracted by Solo's assault	.20	.50
❑ 13 The Millennium Falcon	.20	.50
❑ 14 Lord Vader threatens Princess Leia	.20	.50
❑ 15 Sighting the Death Star	.20	.50
❑ 16 Deadly Blasters	.20	.50
❑ 17 Planning an escape	.20	.50
❑ 18 Stormtroopers attack	.20	.50
❑ 19 Carrie Fisher and Mark Hamill	.20	.50
❑ 20 Han and Chewie	.20	.50
❑ 21 Ben with the lightsaber	.20	.50
❑ 22 The lightsaber	.20	.50
❑ 23 Han in the Millennium Falcon	.20	.50
❑ 24 Luke prepares for the battle	.20	.50
❑ 25 Who will win the final Star War	.20	.50
❑ 26 Preparing for the raid	.20	.50
❑ 27 The Empire strikes back	.20	.50
❑ 28 Battle in outer space	.20	.50
❑ 29 Spectacular battle	.20	.50
❑ 30 The honored heroes	.20	.50
❑ 31 Luke astride his Tauntaun	.20	.50
❑ 32 Rejuvenation Chamber	.20	.50
❑ 33 Imperial Spy	.20	.50
❑ 34 The Snow Walkers	.20	.50
❑ 35 Rebel Snowspeeders zero in	.20	.50
❑ 36 Vader and his Snowtroopers	.20	.50
❑ 37 Emergency blast off	.20	.50
❑ 38 Battle of the Star Destroyer	.20	.50
❑ 39 Canyons of Death	.20	.50
❑ 40 Misty World of Dagobah	.20	.50
❑ 41 Welcome, Young Luke	.20	.50
❑ 42 Journey through the swamp	.20	.50
❑ 43 Use the Force, Luke	.20	.50
❑ 44 Luke battles himself	.20	.50
❑ 45 The Bounty Hunters	.20	.50
❑ 46 Star Lovers	.20	.50
❑ 47 The Landing	.20	.50
❑ 48 Enter Lando Calrissian	.20	.50
❑ 49 Han's Torment	.20	.50
❑ 50 The prize of Boba Fett	.20	.50
❑ 51 His Day of Triumph	.20	.50
❑ 52 The Fate of Han Solo	.20	.50
❑ 53 Boba's Special Delivery	.20	.50
❑ 54 The Search for Vader	.20	.50
❑ 55 The Confrontation	.20	.50
❑ 56 The Force and the Fury	.20	.50
❑ 57 Embrace the Dark Side	.20	.50
❑ 58 Hate me, Luke! Destroy me!	.20	.50
❑ 59 Luke's Last Stand	.20	.50
❑ 60 Toward Tomorrow	.20	.50
❑ 61 The New Death Star	.20	.50
❑ 62 Intergalactic Gangster	.20	.50
❑ 63 Han Solo's Plight	.20	.50
❑ 64 The Princess Enslaved	.20	.50
❑ 65 The Young Jedi	.20	.50
❑ 66 The Dreaded Rancor	.20	.50
❑ 67 Toward the Sarlacc	.20	.50
❑ 68 Jabba the Hutt's new dancing girl	.20	.50
❑ 69 Boba Fett	.20	.50
❑ 70 The Raging Battle	.20	.50
❑ 71 Swing to Safety	.20	.50
❑ 72 The Deciders	.20	.50
❑ 73 Yoda, the Jedi Master	.20	.50
❑ 74 A word with Ben Kenobi	.20	.50
❑ 75 Droids on the move	.20	.50
❑ 76 Captured!	.20	.50
❑ 77 All Hail C-3PO	.20	.50
❑ 78 Unexpected Allies	.20	.50
❑ 79 Luke Skywalker's Destiny	.20	.50
❑ 80 Imperial Biker Scout	.20	.50
❑ 81 Ready for action	.20	.50
❑ 82 Artoo-Detoo	.20	.50
❑ 83 Chewbacca Triumphant	.20	.50
❑ 84 Facing the Emperor	.20	.50
❑ 85 The Emperor's offer	.20	.50
❑ 86 Darth Vader is down!	.20	.50
❑ 87 The Death Star raid	.20	.50
❑ 88 Admiral Ackbar	.20	.50
❑ 89 Within the Death Star	.20	.50
❑ 90 The Triumphant Trio	.20	.50
❑ P1 Hate me, Luke! Destroy me! PROMO	1.00	2.50
❑ P2 Welcome, young Luke PROMO	1.00	2.50

1999 Star Wars Chrome Archives Clearzone

COMPLETE SET (4)	7.50	20.00
❑ C1 Luke Skywalker	2.50	6.00
❑ C2 Darth Vader	2.50	6.00
❑ C3 Han Solo	2.50	6.00
❑ C4 Princess Leia	2.50	6.00

1999 Star Wars Chrome Archives Double Sided

COMPLETE SET (9)	40.00	100.00
❑ D1 Darth Vader	6.00	15.00
❑ D2 Luke Skywalker	6.00	15.00
❑ D3 Princess Leia	6.00	15.00
❑ D4 Han Solo	6.00	15.00
❑ D5 Chewbacca	6.00	15.00
❑ D6 Ben Kenobi	6.00	15.00
❑ D7 C-3PO	6.00	15.00
❑ D8 R2-D2	6.00	15.00
❑ D9 Tusken Raider	6.00	15.00

1999 Star Wars Episode One Widevision Series One

COMPLETE SET (80)	8.00	20.00
❑ 1 Title Card	.25	.60
❑ 2 Trade Federation Rendezvous	.25	.60
❑ 3 The Guardians of Peace	.25	.60
❑ 4 Begin Landing Your Troops	.25	.60
❑ 5 Protocol Droid Surprise	.25	.60
❑ 6 Over Naboo Swampland	.25	.60
❑ 7 An Awkward Introduction	.25	.60
❑ 8 New Friend of the Jedi	.25	.60
❑ 9 Destination: Otoh Gunga	.25	.60
❑ 10 In Big Dudu Dis Time	.25	.60
❑ 11 Jar Jar's Life-Debt	.25	.60
❑ 12 The Gungan Sub	.25	.60
❑ 13 What Lurks Behind	.25	.60
❑ 14 Tongue of Terror	.25	.60
❑ 15 Escaping the Opee Sea Killer	.25	.60
❑ 16 The Sando Aqua Monster	.25	.60
❑ 17 The Cold Claw Fish	.25	.60
❑ 18 The Queen's Palace in Theed	.25	.60
❑ 19 An Emergency Escape	.25	.60
❑ 20 Aboard the Transport Ship	.25	.60
❑ 21 The Dark Lord Called Maul	.25	.60
❑ 22 A Brave Little R2 Unit	.25	.60
❑ 23 Refueling and Repairing	.25	.60
❑ 24 Space Junk for Sale	.25	.60
❑ 25 Bargaining With Watto	.25	.60
❑ 26 A Message From Mos Espa	.25	.60
❑ 27 Obi-Wan on Board	.25	.60
❑ 28 A Tasty Treat for Jar Jar	.25	.60
❑ 29 Snagged by Sebulba	.25	.60
❑ 30 Anakin Confronts His Rival	.25	.60
❑ 31 Conscience of the Queen	.25	.60
❑ 32 Sio Bibble's Plea	.25	.60
❑ 33 Hit by a Sandstorm	.25	.60
❑ 34 Dinner in a Slave Hovel	.25	.60
❑ 35 Padme Doesn't Approve	.25	.60
❑ 36 Either Way, You Win	.25	.60
❑ 37 Young Hero ... Or Bug Squash?	.25	.60
❑ 38 Podrace Preparations	.25	.60
❑ 39 A Mouthful of Energy	.25	.60
❑ 40 Hard Working Astromech Droid	.25	.60
❑ 41 Darth Maul on Tatooine	.25	.60
❑ 42 Inside the Podrace Hangar	.25	.60
❑ 43 Skeptical Toydarian	.25	.60
❑ 44 A Day at the Podrace	.25	.60
❑ 45 Presiding Over the Podrace	.25	.60
❑ 46 They're Off	.25	.60
❑ 47 Intergalactic Spectators	.25	.60
❑ 48 He's on the Leader	.25	.60
❑ 49 Skywalker Rules	.25	.60
❑ 50 The Call to Destiny	.25	.60
❑ 51 Escape From Tatooine	.25	.60
❑ 52 On the Way to Coruscant	.25	.60
❑ 53 Palpatine's Political Ploy	.25	.60
❑ 54 Qui-Gon and the Jedi Council	.25	.60
❑ 55 The Galactic Senate	.25	.60
❑ 56 Twelve Concerned Jedi	.25	.60
❑ 57 Tested He Will Be	.25	.60
❑ 58 Facing Mace Windu	.25	.60
❑ 59 Judgement of the Jedi	.25	.60
❑ 60 Unspeakable Alliance	.25	.60
❑ 61 Binks Leads the Way	.25	.60
❑ 62 An Audience With Boss Nass	.25	.60
❑ 63 Her True Identity Revealed	.25	.60
❑ 64 The Mysterious Enemy	.25	.60
❑ 65 Trade Federation Tanks Close In	.25	.60
❑ 66 Orders From OOM-9	.25	.60
❑ 67 Battle Droid Formation	.25	.60
❑ 68 Preparing for the Assault	.25	.60
❑ 69 The Battle Droid Army	.25	.60
❑ 70 Qui-Gon's Fight for Life	.25	.60
❑ 71 Star Pilot Ric Olie	.25	.60
❑ 72 Attacking a Space Station	.25	.60
❑ 73 Unexpected Help From Anakin	.25	.60
❑ 74 Jedi vs. Sith	.25	.60
❑ 75 Young Skywalker's Gamble	.25	.60
❑ 76 Defeat of the Battle Droids	.25	.60
❑ 77 Their Evil Scheme Shattered	.25	.60
❑ 78 The Lightsaber Duel	.25	.60
❑ 79 A Jedi Falls	.25	.60
❑ 80 Checklist	.25	.60

1999 Star Wars Episode One Widevision Series One Chrome

COMPLETE SET (8)	30.00	60.00
STATED ODDS 1:12		
❑ C1 Palace of Queen Amidala	4.00	10.00
❑ C2 The Tatooine Adventure	4.00	10.00
❑ C3 Space Junk Dealer Watto	4.00	10.00
❑ C4 The Incomplete Threepio	4.00	10.00
❑ C5 Juggling Jar Jar Binks	4.00	10.00
❑ C6 Betting on Sebulba	4.00	10.00
❑ C7 A Gathering of Jedi	4.00	10.00
❑ C8 Forces of Justice Closing In	4.00	10.00

1999 Star Wars Episode One Widevision Series One Foil

COMPLETE SET (10)	30.00	60.00
❑ F1 Anakin Skywalker	3.00	8.00
❑ F2 Qui-Gon Jinn	3.00	8.00
❑ F3 Obi-Wan Kenobi	3.00	8.00
❑ F4 Queen Amidala	3.00	8.00
❑ F5 Jar Jar Binks	3.00	8.00
❑ F6 Watto	3.00	8.00
❑ F7 Darth Maul	3.00	8.00
❑ F8 Nute Gunray	3.00	8.00
❑ F9 Battle Droid	3.00	8.00
❑ F10 C-3P0 and R2-D2	3.00	8.00

1999 Star Wars Episode One Widevision Series One Expansion

COMPLETE SET (40)	30.00	60:00
STATED ODDS 1:2		
❑ X1 Pit Droids at Work	1.00	2.50
❑ X2 A Jarred Jar Jar	1.00	2.50
❑ X3 Droids in Watto's Junk Shop	1.00	2.50
❑ X4 Anakin's Podracer	1.00	2.50
❑ X5 Watching From on High	1.00	2.50
❑ X6 Monitoring the Podrace	1.00	2.50
❑ X7 A Final Word From Watto	1.00	2.50
❑ X8 Sebulba Gets Ready to Race	1.00	2.50
❑ X9 Flying Across the Desert	1.00	2.50
❑ X10 Winning the Podrace	1.00	2.50
❑ X11 With a Pal Like Jar Jar ...	1.00	2.50
❑ X12 Streets of Mos Espa	1.00	2.50
❑ X13 Knights of Light and Dark	1.00	2.50
❑ X14 Dark Lord of the Sith	1.00	2.50
❑ X15 The Jedi Council	1.00	2.50
❑ X16 Can This Boy Be a Jedi?	1.00	2.50
❑ X17 Questioning Anakin	1.00	2.50
❑ X18 Of Destiny and Great Danger	1.00	2.50
❑ X19 The Judgement of Mace Windu	1.00	2.50
❑ X20 Holo-View of Darth Sidious	1.00	2.50
❑ X21 Jar Jar of Otoh Gunga	1.00	2.50
❑ X22 A Toydarian Named Watto	1.00	2.50
❑ X23 Four-footed Transportation	1.00	2.50
❑ X24 Podrace Fever	1.00	2.50
❑ X25 Sebulba Coming up Fast	1.00	2.50
❑ X26 Anakin's Pals and Helpers	1.00	2.50
❑ X27 On-Screen Podrace Excitement	1.00	2.50
❑ X28 It's All up to Boss Nass	1.00	2.50
❑ X29 Citizens of the Sea	1.00	2.50
❑ X30 Battle Droid Flanking Viceroy	1.00	2.50
❑ X31 Awaiting the Jedi	1.00	2.50
❑ X32 Trade Federation Talks Upon the Hill	1.00	2.50
❑ X33 Armored Warships Advancing	1.00	2.50
❑ X34 OOM-9 Surveys the Battlefield	1.00	2.50
❑ X35 The Trade Federation's Finest	1.00	2.50
❑ X36 The Reconfigurators	1.00	2.50
❑ X37 Wardroids on the March	1.00	2.50
❑ X38 Naboo Fighter Surrounded	1.00	2.50
❑ X39 unknown	1.00	2.50
❑ X40 Day of the Battle Droid	1.00	2.50

1999 Star Wars Episode One Widevision Series One Stickers

COMPLETE SET (16)	8.00	20.00
❑ S1 Qui-Gon Jinn	.60	1.50
❑ S2 Obi-Wan Kenobi	.60	1.50
❑ S3 The Neimoidians	.60	1.50
❑ S4 Jar Jar Binks	.60	1.50
❑ S5 Darth Sidious	.60	1.50
❑ S6 Queen Amidala	.60	1.50
❑ S7 C-3PO	.60	1.50
❑ S8 Padme Naberrie	.60	1.50
❑ S9 Anakin Skywalker	.60	1.50
❑ S10 Watto	.60	1.50
❑ S11 Darth Maul	.60	1.50
❑ S12 Mace Windu	.60	1.50
❑ S13 Sebulba	.60	1.50
❑ S14 Battle Droids	.60	1.50
❑ S15 Boss Nass	.60	1.50
❑ S16 The Galactic Senate	.60	1.50

1999 Star Wars Episode One Widevision Series One Tin Inserts

COMPLETE SET (5)
STATED ODDS ONE PER RETAIL TIN

❑ 1 Anakin Skywalker

Card	Low	High
❑ 2 Darth Maul		
❑ 3 Obi-Wan Kenobi		
❑ 4 Queen Amidala		
❑ 5 Qui-Gon		

1999 Star Wars Episode One Widevision Series Two

Card	Low	High
COMPLETE SET (80)	8.00	20.00
❑ 1 Table of Contents	.25	.60
❑ 2 Qui-Gon Jinn	.25	.60
❑ 3 Obi-Wan Kenobi	.25	.60
❑ 4 Anakin Skywalker	.25	.60
❑ 5 Darth Maul	.25	.60
❑ 6 Captain Panaka and Queen Amidala	.25	.60
❑ 7 Jar Jar Binks	.25	.60
❑ 8 The Neimoidians	.25	.60
❑ 9 Boss Nass	.25	.60
❑ 10 R2-D2	.25	.60
❑ 11 C-3PO	.25	.60
❑ 12 Darth Sidious	.25	.60
❑ 13 The Jedi Council	.25	.60
❑ 14 Yoda	.25	.60
❑ 15 Sebulba	.25	.60
❑ 16 Watto	.25	.60
❑ 17 Jabba the Hutt	.25	.60
❑ 18 Captain Tarpals and the Gungan Warriors	.25	.60
❑ 19 Slave Community	.25	.60
❑ 20 Atop the Stone Head	.25	.60
❑ 21 Podracing Arena	.25	.60
❑ 22 Coruscant	.25	.60
❑ 23 Landing Ship Interior	.25	.60
❑ 24 Theed Power Generator	.25	.60
❑ 25 The Walking Droid Fighter	.25	.60
❑ 26 Jedi Reprisal	.25	.60
❑ 27 Blasted by the Force	.25	.60
❑ 28 Qui-gon Cuts Through	.25	.60
❑ 29 Destroyer Droids	.25	.60
❑ 30 STAP Warfare	.25	.60
❑ 31 Stampede	.25	.60
❑ 32 The Escape Party	.25	.60
❑ 33 Cutting down Battle Droids	.25	.60
❑ 34 Courageous Astromech Droid	.25	.60
❑ 35 Encountering Anakin	.25	.60
❑ 36 Watto's Gamble	.25	.60
❑ 37 Podracing Rivals	.25	.60
❑ 38 Teemto Gears Up	.25	.60
❑ 39 Podracers in Position	.25	.60
❑ 40 Quadinaros Makes Ready	.25	.60
❑ 41 Pit Droid Dispute	.25	.60
❑ 42 Arriving in the Arena	.25	.60
❑ 43 The Crowd Goes Wild	.25	.60
❑ 44 Anakin's Challenge	.25	.60
❑ 45 Through a Rocky Canyon	.25	.60
❑ 46 Sideline Friends	.25	.60
❑ 47 Beware of Tusken Raiders	.25	.60
❑ 48 Ratts Tyerell	.25	.60
❑ 49 Collision Up Ahead	.25	.60
❑ 50 Streaking across Tatooine	.25	.60
❑ 51 Sebulba's Foul Plan	.25	.60
❑ 52 High-Speed Climax	.25	.60
❑ 53 Fury of the Podrace	.25	.60
❑ 54 The Winning Podracer	.25	.60
❑ 55 The Mighty Gungan Army	.25	.60
❑ 56 Fantastic Weaponry	.25	.60
❑ 57 Blasting Through	.25	.60
❑ 58 Gungan Shields	.25	.60
❑ 59 Battlefield: Naboo	.25	.60
❑ 60 A Hapless Hero	.25	.60
❑ 61 Hostage to Their Will	.25	.60
❑ 62 Inside the Theed Central Hangar	.25	.60
❑ 63 Get to Your Ships	.25	.60
❑ 64 Naboo Starfighters Taking Off	.25	.60
❑ 65 The Queen's Volunteer Forces	.25	.60
❑ 66 Palace Attack	.25	.60
❑ 67 Releasing the Droid Starfighters	.25	.60
❑ 68 Blast of the Quadlaser Cannons	.25	.60
❑ 69 Celestial Combat	.25	.60
❑ 70 Droid Starfighter Assault	.25	.60
❑ 71 Droid Control Ship Crisis	.25	.60
❑ 72 Immobilizing the Enemy	.25	.60
❑ 73 The Menace of Maul	.25	.60
❑ 74 Fierce Combatants	.25	.60
❑ 75 His Moment of Truth	.25	.60
❑ 76 Battle to the Death	.25	.60
❑ 77 Dueling with Darth Maul	.25	.60
❑ 78 Hang On, Obi-Wan	.25	.60
❑ 79 A Time To Rejoice	.25	.60
❑ 80 Checklist	.25	.60

1999 Star Wars Episode One Widevision Series Two Chrome Hobby

Card	Low	High
COMPLETE SET (4)	12.00	25.00
STATED ODDS 1:18 HOBBY		
❑ HC1 Threat of the Destroyer Droids	4.00	10.00
❑ HC2 Departing an Underwater World	4.00	10.00
❑ HC3 An Appeal to Boss Nass	4.00	10.00
❑ HC4 Blasting the Gungans	4.00	10.00

1999 Star Wars Episode One Widevision Series Two Chrome Retail

Card	Low	High
COMPLETE SET (4)	20.00	40.00
STATED ODDS 1:18 RETAIL		
❑ C1 Sea Creature Peril	6.00	15.00
❑ C2 Escapees on Tatooine	6.00	15.00
❑ C3 Podrace Excitement	6.00	15.00
❑ C4 Control Ship Attack	6.00	15.00

1999 Star Wars Episode One Widevision Series Two Embossed Retail

Card	Low	High
COMPLETE SET (6)	20.00	40.00
STATED ODDS 1:12 RETAIL		
❑ E1 Commander Droid	4.00	10.00
❑ E2 Jar Jar Binks	4.00	10.00
❑ E3 Jabba the Hutt	4.00	10.00
❑ E4 Sebulba	4.00	10.00
❑ E5 Anakin Skywalker	4.00	10.00
❑ E6 Boss Nass	4.00	10.00

1999 Star Wars Episode One Widevision Series Two Jumbo Box Toppers

Card	Low	High
COMPLETE SET (3)	10.00	20.00
STATED ODDS ONE PER HOBBY BOX		
❑ 1 Darth Maul	4.00	10.00
❑ 2 Cutting Down the Battle Droids	4.00	10.00
❑ 3 Courageous Astromech Droid	4.00	10.00

2000 Star Wars Episode One 3-D

Card	Low	High
COMPLETE SET (46)	20.00	40.00
❑ 1 The Phantom Alliance	.50	1.25
❑ 2 To Trap a Jedi	.50	1.25
❑ 3 Besieged by Battle Droids	.50	1.25
❑ 4 Destroyer Droid Challenge	.50	1.25
❑ 5 Escaping the Neimoidians	.50	1.25
❑ 6 Planet Naboo Invaded	.50	1.25
❑ 7 Refuge in a Water World	.50	1.25
❑ 8 How Rude	.50	1.25
❑ 9 Facing Boss Nass	.50	1.25
❑ 10 Target: Planet Naboo	.50	1.25
❑ 11 Warcraft Closing In	.50	1.25
❑ 12 Rescuing Queen Amidala	.50	1.25
❑ 13 Valiant R2-D2	.50	1.25
❑ 14 The Sith Apprentice	.50	1.25
❑ 15 Encountering Anakin	.50	1.25
❑ 16 Day of the Podrace	.50	1.25
❑ 17 High-Speed Thrills	.50	1.25
❑ 18 Treacherous Dug	.50	1.25
❑ 19 The Fast and the Furious	.50	1.25
❑ 20 Racing Across Tatooine	.50	1.25
❑ 21 The Home Stretch	.50	1.25
❑ 22 Maul's Quarry	.50	1.25
❑ 23 Decision at Coruscant	.50	1.25
❑ 24 Facing the Jedi Council	.50	1.25
❑ 25 The Galactic Senate	.50	1.25
❑ 26 Amidala's Gamble	.50	1.25
❑ 27 A Phropecy Fulfilled	.50	1.25
❑ 28 Counterattack	.50	1.25
❑ 29 Face Off With Darth Maul	.50	1.25
❑ 30 Adversaries	.50	1.25
❑ 31 Regal Battlefield	.50	1.25
❑ 32 Reclaiming the Palace	.50	1.25
❑ 33 Gungans Go to War	.50	1.25
❑ 34 Trade Federation Offensive	.50	1.25
❑ 35 The Reluctant Hero	.50	1.25
❑ 36 Implacable Foes	.50	1.25
❑ 37 In the Generator Complex	.50	1.25
❑ 38 Fury of the Sith	.50	1.25
❑ 39 The Fate of Qui-Gon Jinn	.50	1.25
❑ 40 Starpilot Anakin	.50	1.25
❑ 41 Skywalker's First Battle	.50	1.25
❑ 42 The Enemy Within	.50	1.25
❑ 43 Vanquishing Darth Maul	.50	1.25
❑ 44 Naboo Liberated	.50	1.25
❑ 45 Yoda's Warning	.50	1.25
❑ 46 A Pause for Peace	.50	1.25
❑ P1 Qui-Gon Obi-Wan PROMO	3.00	8.00

2000 Star Wars Episode One 3-D Multi-Motion

Card	Low	High
COMPLETE SET (2)	10.00	25.00
❑ 1 Droideka	6.00	15.00
❑ 2 Lightsaber Duel	6.00	15.00

2001 Star Wars Evolution

Card	Low	High
COMPLETE SET (90)	5.00	12.00
❑ 1 4-Lom	.15	.40
❑ 2 Adi Gallia	.15	.40
❑ 3 Admiral Ackbar	.15	.40
❑ 4 Admiral Piett	.15	.40
❑ 5 Anakin Skywalker	.15	.40
❑ 6 Aurra Sing	.15	.40
❑ 7 Ben Quadrinaros	.15	.40
❑ 8 Beru Lars	.15	.40
❑ 9 Bib Fortuna	.15	.40
❑ 10 Biggs Darklighter	.15	.40
❑ 11 Boba Fett	.15	.40
❑ 12 Boss Nass	.15	.40
❑ 13 Bossk	.15	.40
❑ 14 C-3PO	.15	.40
❑ 15 Captain Needa	.15	.40
❑ 16 Captain Panaka	.15	.40
❑ 17 Captain Tarpals	.15	.40
❑ 18 Chancellor Valorum	.15	.40
❑ 19 Chewbacca	.15	.40
❑ 20 Darth Maul	.15	.40
❑ 21 Darth Vader	.15	.40
❑ 22 Dengar	.15	.40
❑ 23 Depa Billaba	.15	.40
❑ 24 Eeth Koth	.15	.40
❑ 25 Even Piell	.15	.40
❑ 26 Figrin D'an	.15	.40
❑ 27 Fode and Beed	.15	.40
❑ 28 General Carlist Rieekan	.15	.40
❑ 29 General Crix Madine	.15	.40
❑ 30 General Jan Dodonna	.15	.40
❑ 31 General Maximillian Veers	.15	.40
❑ 32 Grand Moff Tarkin	.15	.40
❑ 33 Greedo	.15	.40
❑ 34 Han Solo	.15	.40
❑ 35 IG-88	.15	.40
❑ 36 Jabba the Hutt	.15	.40
❑ 37 Jar Jar Binks	.15	.40
❑ 38 Jawa	.15	.40
❑ 39 Ki-Adi-Mundi	.15	.40
❑ 40 Klaatu	.15	.40
❑ 41 Lak Sivrak	.15	.40
❑ 42 Lando Calrissian	.15	.40
❑ 43 Lobot	.15	.40
❑ 44 Logray	.15	.40
❑ 45 Luke Skywalker	.15	.40
❑ 46 Mace Windu	.15	.40
❑ 47 Max Rebo	.15	.40
❑ 48 Moff Jerjerrod	.15	.40
❑ 49 Momaw Nadon	.15	.40
❑ 50 Mon Mothma	.15	.40
❑ 51 Muftak	.15	.40
❑ 52 Nien Nunb	.15	.40
❑ 53 Nute Gunray	.15	.40
❑ 54 Obi-Wan Kenobi	.15	.40
❑ 55 Oola	.15	.40
❑ 56 OOM-9	.15	.40
❑ 57 Oppo Rancisis	.15	.40
❑ 58 Owen Lars	.15	.40
❑ 59 Padme Amidala	.15	.40
❑ 60 Plo Koon	.15	.40
❑ 61 Ponda Baba	.15	.40
❑ 62 Princess Leia	.15	.40
❑ 63 Qui-Gon Jinn	.15	.40
❑ 64 R2-D2	.15	.40
❑ 65 R5-D4	.15	.40
❑ 66 Rancor	.15	.40
❑ 67 Ric Olie	.15	.40
❑ 68 Royal Guard	.15	.40
❑ 69 Rune Haako	.15	.40
❑ 70 Saesee Tiin	.15	.40
❑ 71 Salacious Crumb	.15	.40
❑ 72 Sebulba	.15	.40
❑ 73 Senator Palpatine	.15	.40
❑ 74 Shmi Skywalker	.15	.40
❑ 75 Sio Bibble	.15	.40
❑ 76 Stormtrooper	.15	.40
❑ 77 Sy Snootles	.15	.40
❑ 78 Tessek	.15	.40
❑ 79 Tusken Raider	.15	.40
❑ 80 Wald	.15	.40
❑ 81 Wampa	.15	.40
❑ 82 Watto	.15	.40
❑ 83 Wedge Antilles	.15	.40
❑ 84 Wicket	.15	.40
❑ 85 Wuher	.15	.40
❑ 86 Yaddle	.15	.40
❑ 87 Yarael Poof	.15	.40
❑ 88 Yoda	.15	.40
❑ 89 Zuckuss	.15	.40
❑ 90 Zutton	.15	.40
❑ C1 Anakin and Shmi CL	.15	.40
❑ C2 Luke and Darth Vader CL	.15	.40
❑ C3 Luke and Leia CL	.15	.40
❑ NNO Anakin PROMO		

2001 Star Wars Evolution Autographs

Card	Low	High
GROUP A/1000* STATED ODDS 1:37		
GROUP B/400* STATED ODDS 1:919		
GROUP C/300* STATED ODDS 1:2450		
GROUP D/100* STATED ODDS 1:3677		
❑ 1 Andrew Secombe/1000*	20.00	50.00
❑ 2 Anthony Daniels/100*	1000.00	1500.00
❑ 3 Billy Dee Williams/300*	200.00	400.00
❑ 4 Caroline Blakiston/1000*	15.00	40.00
❑ 5 Carrie Fisher/100*	1000.00	1500.00
❑ 6 Dalyn Chew/1000*	15.00	40.00
❑ 7 Dermot Crowley/1000*	15.00	40.00
❑ 8 Femi Taylor/1000*	15.00	40.00
❑ 9 Ian McDiarmid/400*	250.00	500.00
❑ 10 James Earl Jones/1000*	125.00	200.00
❑ 11 Jeremy Bulloch/1000*	50.00	100.00
❑ 12 Kenneth Colley/1000*	20.00	50.00
❑ 13 Kenny Baker/1000*	125.00	200.00
❑ 14 Lewis MacLeod/1000*	35.00	70.00
❑ 15 Mercedes Ngoh/1000*	20.00	50.00
❑ 16 Michael Culver/1000*	15.00	40.00
❑ 17 Michael Pennington/1000*	15.00	40.00
❑ 18 Michael Sheard/1000*	15.00	40.00
❑ 19 Michonne Bourriague/1000*	20.00	50.00
❑ 20 Mike Quinn/1000*	15.00	40.00
❑ 21 Paul Blake/1000*	15.00	40.00
❑ 22 Peter Mayhew/400*	100.00	200.00
❑ 23 Phil Brown/1000*	25.00	60.00
❑ 24 Tim Rose/1000*	15.00	40.00
❑ 25 Warwick Davis/1000*	20.00	50.00

2001 Star Wars Evolution Insert A

Card	Low	High
COMPLETE SET (12)	15.00	30.00
STATED ODDS 1:5		
❑ 1A Anakin Skywalker	1.50	4.00
❑ 2A Beru Lars	1.50	4.00
❑ 3A C-3PO	1.50	4.00
❑ 4A Han Solo	1.50	4.00
❑ 5A Lando Calrissian	1.50	4.00
❑ 6A Luke Skywalker	1.50	4.00
❑ 7A Obi-Wan Kenobi	1.50	4.00
❑ 8A Owen Lars	1.50	4.00
❑ 9A Padmé Amidala	1.50	4.00
❑ 10A Princess Leia	1.50	4.00
❑ 11A Qui-Gon Jinn	1.50	4.00
❑ 12A Yoda	1.50	4.00

2001 Star Wars Evolution Insert B

Card	Low	High
COMPLETE SET (8)	20.00	40.00
STATED ODDS 1:12		
❑ 1B Anakin Skywalker	2.50	6.00
❑ 2B C-3PO	2.50	6.00
❑ 3B Han Solo	2.50	6.00
❑ 4B Lando Calrissian	2.50	6.00
❑ 5B Luke Skywalker	2.50	6.00
❑ 6B Obi-Wan Kenobi	2.50	6.00
❑ 7B Padmé Amidala	2.50	6.00
❑ 8B Princess Leia	2.50	6.00

2002 Star Wars Attack of the Clones

Card	Low	High
COMPLETE SET (100)	5.00	12.00
❑ 1 Title Card	.15	.40
❑ 2 Anakin Skywalker	.15	.40
❑ 3 Padme Amidala	.15	.40
❑ 4 Obi-Wan Kenobi	.15	.40
❑ 5 Yoda	.15	.40
❑ 6 Mace Windu	.15	.40
❑ 7 Count Dooku	.15	.40
❑ 8 Chancellor Palpatine	.15	.40
❑ 9 Zam Wesell	.15	.40
❑ 10 Jango Fett	.15	.40
❑ 11 Boba Fett	.15	.40
❑ 12 Cliegg Lars	.15	.40
❑ 13 Owen Lars	.15	.40
❑ 14 Beru Whitesun	.15	.40
❑ 15 C-3PO and R2-D2	.15	.40
❑ 16 Jar Jar Binks	.15	.40
❑ 17 Nute Gunray	.15	.40
❑ 18 Lama Su	.15	.40
❑ 19 Ki-Adi-Mundi	.15	.40
❑ 20 Clone Trooper	.15	.40
❑ 21 Super Battle Droid	.15	.40
❑ 22 Landing at Coruscant	.15	.40
❑ 23 A Decoy's Sacrifice	.15	.40
❑ 24 The Republic in Turmoil	.15	.40
❑ 25 Senator Amidala Lives	.15	.40
❑ 26 The Padme Delegation	.15	.40
❑ 27 Old Friends Reunited	.15	.40
❑ 28 Under Jedi Protection	.15	.40
❑ 29 Guarding Against Evil	.15	.40
❑ 30 A Deadly Delivery	.15	.40
❑ 31 Attack of the Kouhuns	.15	.40
❑ 32 Off on a Probe Droid	.15	.40
❑ 33 Obi-Wan Drops In	.15	.40
❑ 34 Downward Trajectory	.15	.40
❑ 35 Into the Industrial Sector	.15	.40
❑ 36 That was too close	.15	.40
❑ 37 Anakin's Short Cut	.15	.40
❑ 38 Assault on a Speeder	.15	.40
❑ 39 Nightclub Brawl	.15	.40
❑ 40 Darted and Deceived	.15	.40
❑ 41 On Her Way to Safety	.15	.40
❑ 42 A Lead From Dexter	.15	.40
❑ 43 The Jedi Archives	.15	.40
❑ 44 Help From Jocasta Nu	.15	.40
❑ 45 Not Exactly Home Cooking	.15	.40
❑ 46 Yoda's Youthful Proteges	.15	.40
❑ 47 Young Heroes in Disguise	.15	.40
❑ 48 Elsewhere in the Galaxy	.15	.40
❑ 49 Tipoca City, Planet Kamino	.15	.40
❑ 50 An Audience With Lama Su	.15	.40
❑ 51 The Majesty of Naboo	.15	.40
❑ 52 A Talk and a Tour	.15	.40
❑ 53 Inside the Clone Center	.15	.40
❑ 54 Bring on the Clones	.15	.40
❑ 55 Meant for Each Other	.15	.40
❑ 56 Meeting Jango and Boba	.15	.40
❑ 57 Fun in the Naboo Manor	.15	.40
❑ 58 Anakin's Dinner Theater	.15	.40
❑ 59 Destiny's Players	.15	.40
❑ 60 Reporting to Mace and Yoda	.15	.40
❑ 61 At the Landing Platform	.15	.40
❑ 62 Rocket-Powered Warrior	.15	.40
❑ 63 Attack from on High	.15	.40
❑ 64 Snared and Dragged	.15	.40
❑ 65 Fly D624But You Can't Hide	.15	.40
❑ 66 Return to Tatooine	.15	.40
❑ 67 Watto's Revelation	.15	.40
❑ 68 The Space Chase Begins	.15	.40
❑ 69 A Sea of Asteroids	.15	.40
❑ 70 Rocked by Laser Blasts	.15	.40
❑ 71 Obi-Wan's Deception	.15	.40
❑ 72 The Lars Family	.15	.40
❑ 73 In Search of his Mother	.15	.40
❑ 74 Penetrating the Tusken Camp	.15	.40
❑ 75 Menace of the Dark Side	.15	.40
❑ 76 Obi-Wan's Holo-Message	.15	.40
❑ 77 The Jedi's Last Words	.15	.40
❑ 78 Padme's Rescue Plan	.15	.40
❑ 79 The Capture of Kenobi	.15	.40
❑ 80 Threat of the Geonosians	.15	.40
❑ 81 Surviving the Droid Factory	.15	.40
❑ 82 Jar Jar in the Senate	.15	.40
❑ 83 Death in the Arena	.15	.40
❑ 84 To Live and Die as a Jedi	.15	.40
❑ 85 The Deadly Power of Dooku	.15	.40
❑ 86 Fury of a Jedi Knight	.15	.40
❑ 87 Clash of the Lightsabers	.15	.40
❑ 88 Challenge of Count Dooku	.15	.40
❑ 89 A Fantastic Duel	.15	.40
❑ 90 Anakin Loses an Arm	.15	.40
❑ 91 Creating High-Tech Transports	.15	.40
❑ 92 Aliens on the Set	.15	.40
❑ 93 The Many Faces of Anthony Daniels	.15	.40
❑ 94 Young Lovers Get the Brush	.15	.40
❑ 95 Mace Sets the Pace	.15	.40
❑ 96 Bringing the Speeder to Life	.15	.40
❑ 97 Readying Nute for the Cameras	.15	.40
❑ 98 From Dracula to Dooku	.15	.40
❑ 99 Jedi Tall and Jedi Small	.15	.40
❑ 100 Checklist	.02	.10
❑ P1 Sage Continues PROMO	1.00	2.50
❑ P2 Sage Continues PROMO	1.00	2.50
❑ P3 Sage Continues PROMO	1.00	2.50

2002 Star Wars Attack of the Clones Foil

Card	Low	High
COMPLETE SET (10)	6.00	15.00
❑ 1 Jango Fett	.75	2.00
❑ 2 Padme Amidala	.75	2.00
❑ 3 Anakin Skywalker	.75	2.00
❑ 4 Count Dooku	.75	2.00
❑ 5 Mace Windu	.75	2.00
❑ 6 Obi-Wan Kenobi	.75	2.00
❑ 7 Obi-Wan Kenobi	.75	2.00
❑ 8 Anakin Skywalker	.75	2.00
❑ 9 Count Dooku	.75	2.00
❑ 10 Jango Fett	.75	2.00

2002 Star Wars Attack of the Clones Panoramic Fold-Outs

Card	Low	High
COMPLETE SET (5)	12.00	30.00
STATED ODDS 1:12		
❑ 1 Lightsaber Battle	3.00	8.00
❑ 2 Imperial Troops	3.00	8.00
❑ 3 Good Guys	3.00	8.00
❑ 4 Bad Guys	3.00	8.00
❑ 5 Space Battle	3.00	8.00

2002 Star Wars Attack of the Clones Prisms

Card	Low	High
COMPLETE SET (8)	7.50	20.00
❑ 1 Anakin Skywalker	1.25	3.00
❑ 2 Count Dooku	1.25	3.00
❑ 3 Jango Fett	1.25	3.00
❑ 4 Zam Wesell	1.25	3.00
❑ 5 Padme Amidala	1.25	3.00
❑ 6 Obi-Wan Kenobi	1.25	3.00
❑ 7 Mace Windu	1.25	3.00
❑ 8 C-3PO and R2-D2	1.25	3.00

2002 Star Wars Attack of the Clones Widevision

Card	Low	High
COMPLETE SET (80)	5.00	12.00
❑ 1 Senator Amidala's Starship	.15	.40
❑ 2 Amidala and Her Jedi Allies	.15	.40
❑ 3 The Senator's Anxious Protector	.15	.40
❑ 4 A Deadly Scheme	.15	.40
❑ 5 The Jedi Pursuers above Coruscant	.15	.40
❑ 6 Danger Dead Ahead	.15	.40
❑ 7 Spectacular Speeder Chase	.15	.40
❑ 8 Running for Her Life	.15	.40
❑ 9 Saying No to Death Sticks	.15	.40
❑ 10 The Mysterious Assassin	.15	.40
❑ 11 The Jedi Council's Plan	.15	.40
❑ 12 A Chat with Dexter Jettster	.15	.40
❑ 13 Yoda's Students Light the Way	.15	.40
❑ 14 The Secrets of the Planet Kamino	.15	.40
❑ 15 Kamino's Amazing Clone Factory	.15	.40
❑ 16 On the Way to Jango Fett	.15	.40
❑ 17 Star-Crossed Young Lovers	.15	.40
❑ 18 Skywalker's Destiny Beckons	.15	.40
❑ 19 Obi-Wan vs. Jango Fett	.15	.40
❑ 20 The Kamino Landing Pad Battle	.15	.40
❑ 21 Return to Mos Espa	.15	.40
❑ 22 Jango and Boba on the Run	.15	.40
❑ 23 Dodging a Galactic Blast	.15	.40
❑ 24 Obi-Wan's Daring Maneuver	.15	.40
❑ 25 Anakin's Quest	.15	.40
❑ 26 The Tusken Raider Camp	.15	.40
❑ 27 Possessed by the Dark Side	.15	.40
❑ 28 A Final Farewell... And Promise	.15	.40
❑ 29 Obi-Wan's Desperate Message	.15	.40
❑ 30 To Rescue a Jedi	.15	.40
❑ 31 Enter... The Droid Factory	.15	.40
❑ 32 A Jedi Takes Control	.15	.40
❑ 33 Conveyor Belt Peril		.40
❑ 34 An Attacker... Stomped	.15	.40
❑ 35 A Titan Rides the Belt	.15	.40
❑ 36 Challenge of the Geonosians	.15	.40
❑ 37 Airborne Rescuer R2-D2	.15	.40
❑ 38 The Vat of Death	.15	.40
❑ 39 A Disassembled Droid	.15	.40
❑ 40 Have Lightsaber, Will Throttle	.15	.40
❑ 41 Surrender... To Fight Another Day	.15	.40
❑ 42 Dooku's Moment of Triumph	.15	.40
❑ 43 Outworlders at the Stake	.15	.40
❑ 44 Roar of the Savage Reek	.15	.40
❑ 45 Insect-Like Behemoth	.15	.40
❑ 46 Padmé on Top of Things	.15	.40
❑ 47 Clash of the Arena Beasts	.15	.40
❑ 48 Droids on All Sides	.15	.40
❑ 49 Fett's Blast of Death	.15	.40
❑ 50 Jedi Warriors in Action	.15	.40
❑ 51 The Politician and the Padawan	.15	.40
❑ 52 Where Are We? A Battle? Oh No!	.15	.40
❑ 53 Attack of the Super Battle Droids	.15	.40
❑ 54 Against Overwhelming Numbers	.15	.40
❑ 55 Help from On High	.15	.40
❑ 56 Salvation from the Skies	.15	.40
❑ 57 Yoda and His Clone Troopers	.15	.40
❑ 58 Clones Attack Dooku's Forces	.15	.40
❑ 59 March to Enemy Headquarters	.15	.40
❑ 60 No Chance against the Enemy	.15	.40
❑ 61 Fantastic Droid Warfare	.15	.40
❑ 62 Against the Big Guns	.15	.40
❑ 63 Juggernaut of Justice	.15	.40
❑ 64 Geonosian Fortress under Siege	.15	.40
❑ 65 Dooku's Makeshift Escape	.15	.40
❑ 66 On the Trail of Count Dooku	.15	.40
❑ 67 An Impulsive Anakin... Overwhelmed	.15	.40
❑ 68 The Power of a Jedi Knight	.15	.40
❑ 69 Lightsaber Slugfest	.15	.40
❑ 70 Master Yoda Uses the Force	.15	.40
❑ 71 Against the Evil Might of Dooku	.15	.40
❑ 72 A Contest of Skill and Power	.15	.40
❑ 73 Duel of the Jedi Masters	.15	.40
❑ 74 The Last Jedi Standing	.15	.40
❑ 75 Dooku's Escape from Geonosis	.15	.40
❑ 76 Parners in Galactic Tyranny	.15	.40
❑ 77 A New Order for the Universe	.15	.40
❑ 78 Beginning of the Great Clone War	.15	.40
❑ 79 The Wedding of Anakin and Padme	.15	.40
❑ 80 Checklist	.15	.40

2002 Star Wars Attack of the Clones Widevision Autographs

Card	Low	High
COMPLETE SET (24)	600.00	1200.00
STATED ODDS 1:24		
❑ 1 Ahmed Best Jar Jar Binks	15.00	40.00
❑ 2 Alethea McGrath Jocasta Nu	15.00	40.00
❑ 3 Amy Allen Aayla Secura	30.00	60.00
❑ 4 Andrew Secombe the voice of Watto	15.00	40.00
❑ 5 Ayesha Dharker Queen Jamillia	15.00	40.00
❑ 6 Bodie Taylor Clone Trooper	15.00	40.00
❑ 7 Bonnie Piesse Beru Whitesun	40.00	80.00
❑ 8 Daniel Logan Boba Fett	75.00	125.00
❑ 9 David Bowers Mas Amedda	15.00	40.00
❑ 10 Frank Oz Yoda	250.00	400.00
❑ 11 Jay Laga'aia Captain Typho	15.00	40.00
❑ 12 Jesse Jensen Saesee Tiin	15.00	40.00
❑ 13 Joel Edgerton Owen Lars	20.00	50.00
❑ 14 Kenny Baker R2-D2	20.00	50.00
❑ 15 Leeanna Walsman Zam Wesell	15.00	40.00
❑ 16 Mary Oyaya Luminara Unduli	15.00	40.00
❑ 17 Matt Doran Elan Sleazebaggano	15.00	40.00
❑ 18 Matt Sloan Plo Koon	15.00	40.00
❑ 19 Nalini Krishan Barriss Offee	15.00	40.00
❑ 20 Rena Owen Taun We	15.00	40.00
❑ 21 Ronald Falk Dexter Jettster	15.00	40.00
❑ 22 Silas Carson Ki-Adi-Mundi	25.00	50.00
❑ 23 Silas Carson Nute Gunray	25.00	50.00
❑ 24 Zachariah Jensen Kit Fisto	15.00	40.00

2002 Star Wars Attack of the Clones Widevision Promos

Card	Low	High
COMPLETE SET (1)	.60	1.50
❑ P1 Spider Droid	.60	1.50

2004 Star Wars Clone Wars Cartoon

Card	Low	High
COMPLETE SET (90)	5.00	12.00
❑ 1 Anakin Skywalker	.15	.40
❑ 2 Obi-Wan Kenobi	.15	.40
❑ 3 Mace Windu	.15	.40
❑ 4 Yoda	.15	.40
❑ 5 Kit Fisto	.15	.40
❑ 6 Arc Troopers	.15	.40
❑ 7 Durge	.15	.40
❑ 8 Asajj Ventress	.15	.40
❑ 9 Count Dooku	.15	.40
❑ 10 A Galaxy in Conflict	.15	.40
❑ 11 The Power of Windu	.15	.40
❑ 12 Troops of the Republic	.15	.40
❑ 13 Master and Padawan	.15	.40
❑ 14 A Most Gifted Student	.15	.40
❑ 15 The Chancellor's Decision	.15	.40
❑ 16 Onward to his Destiny	.15	.40
❑ 17 Of Skills and Maturity	.15	.40
❑ 18 Squadrons Launched	.15	.40
❑ 19 Arc Troopers Deploy	.15	.40
❑ 20 Against a Droid Army	.15	.40
❑ 21 Arc Troopers Assault	.15	.40
❑ 22 Soldiers Under Siege	.15	.40
❑ 23 Attacking an AAT	.15	.40
❑ 24 Target Sighted	.15	.40
❑ 25 Troopers Take Over	.15	.40
❑ 26 Unfriendly Persuasion	.15	.40
❑ 27 The Mercenary Army	.15	.40
❑ 28 Taking on the Republic	.15	.40
❑ 29 A Sniper Strikes Back	.15	.40
❑ 30 Assault Vehicles Destroyed	.15	.40
❑ 31 Durge Triumphant	.15	.40
❑ 32 Crisis on Mon Calamari	.15	.40
❑ 33 Jedi of the Sea	.15	.40
❑ 34 Slashed by Kit Fisto	.15	.40
❑ 35 Using the Force	.15	.40
❑ 36 Twin Terrors	.15	.40
❑ 37 Fisto's Final Strike	.15	.40
❑ 38 Arena of Death	.15	.40
❑ 39 Count Dooku Welcomed	.15	.40
❑ 40 The New Combatant	.15	.40
❑ 41 Malice Against Metal	.15	.40
❑ 42 Monstrous Rampage	.15	.40
❑ 43 Battling Asajj Ventress	.15	.40
❑ 44 I Am Sith	.15	.40
❑ 45 Apprentice or Adversary	.15	.40
❑ 46 The Power of Dooku	.15	.40
❑ 47 The Trials of Asajj	.15	.40
❑ 48 War of the Sith	.15	.40
❑ 49 Asajj vs. Dooku	.15	.40
❑ 50 Ventress Vanquished	.15	.40
❑ 51 Master of Evil	.15	.40
❑ 52 Kenobi's Battle Plan	.15	.40
❑ 53 Skewering a Droid	.15	.40
❑ 54 Obi-Wan's Charge	.15	.40
❑ 55 The Fatal Thrust?	.15	.40
❑ 56 Flame and the Fury	.15	.40
❑ 57 A Clash of Titans	.15	.40
❑ 58 We are in Position	.15	.40
❑ 59 Arc Forces Close In	.15	.40
❑ 60 A Droid Dispatched	.15	.40
❑ 61 The Face of Defeat	.15	.40
❑ 62 The Return of Durge	.15	.40
❑ 63 Durge the Unstoppable	.15	.40
❑ 64 Obi-Wan Engulfed	.15	.40
❑ 65 Victory at Last	.15	.40
❑ 66 Battle in Outer Space	.15	.40
❑ 67 Anakin's Bold Move	.15	.40
❑ 68 Space Raiders	.15	.40
❑ 69 All Ships Fire	.15	.40
❑ 70 Annihilating the Enemy	.15	.40
❑ 71 Collision Course	.15	.40

❑ 72 General Grievous .15 .40
❑ 73 Episode II Clone Trooper .15 .40
❑ 74 The Defense of Kamino .15 .40
❑ 75 Durge's Debut .15 .40
❑ 76 Deadly Dud .15 .40
❑ 77 Attack of the Dark Jedi .15 .40
❑ 78 The Battle of Jabim .15 .40
❑ 79 Anakin Unleashed .15 .40
❑ 80 Padawans Fight Alone .15 .40
❑ 81 Troops of the Republic .15 .40
❑ 82 Old Enemies, New Dangers .15 .40
❑ 83 Dark Side Rising .15 .40
❑ 84 Dark Jedi Triumphant .15 .40
❑ 85 Power of the Dark Side .15 .40
❑ 86 The Phantom Menace .15 .40
❑ 87 In War and Peace .15 .40
❑ 88 An Epic Struggle .15 .40
❑ 89 Jedi Knights Forever .15 .40
❑ 90 Checklist .15 .40

2004 Star Wars Clone Wars Cartoon Autographs

❑ NNO Jack Thomson 15.00 30.00
❑ NNO Anthony Phelan 15.00 30.00

2004 Star Wars Clone Wars Cartoon Battle Motion

COMPLETE SET (10) 15.00 40.00
❑ B1 Anakin Skywalker 2.00 5.00
❑ B2 Mace Windu 2.00 5.00
❑ B3 Obi-Wan Kenobi 2.00 5.00
❑ B4 Asajj Ventress 2.00 5.00
❑ B5 Clone Troopers 2.00 5.00
❑ B6 Yoda 2.00 5.00
❑ B7 Durge 2.00 5.00
❑ B8 Count Dooku 2.00 5.00
❑ B9 Amidala 2.00 5.00
❑ B10 Arc Troopers 2.00 5.00

2004 Star Wars Clone Wars Cartoon Sketches

❑ 1 Joe Corroney
❑ 2 Dave Dorman
❑ 3 Davide Fabbri
❑ 4 Tomas Giorello
❑ 5 Rafael Kayanan
❑ 6 John McCrea
❑ 7 Pop Mhan
❑ 8 Rodolfo Migliari
❑ 9 Kilian Plunkett
❑ 10 Paul Ruddish
❑ 11 Genndy Tartakovsky
❑ 12 Robert Teranishi
❑ 13 Doug Wheatley

2004 Star Wars Clone Wars Cartoon Stickers

COMPLETE SET (10) 3.00 8.00
❑ 1 Anakin Skywalker .40 1.00
❑ 2 Obi-Wan Kenobi .40 1.00
❑ 3 Arc Trooper .40 1.00
❑ 4 Yoda .40 1.00
❑ 5 Mace Windu .40 1.00
❑ 6 Durge .40 1.00
❑ 7 Count Dooku .40 1.00
❑ 8 Asajj Ventress .40 1.00
❑ 9 C-3PO .40 1.00
❑ 10 R2-D2 .40 1.00

2004 Star Wars Heritage

COMPLETE SET (120) 8.00 20.00
❑ 1 The Blockade Runner Attacked .15 .40
❑ 2 Darth Vader's Fury .15 .40
❑ 3 No Escape For The Princess .15 .40
❑ 4 Sandcrawler Droid .15 .40
❑ 5 Discovering The Holo-Message .15 .40
❑ 6 Will Leia Betray The Rebellion? .15 .40
❑ 7 The Mos Eisley Cantina .15 .40
❑ 8 Don't Mess With Ben Kenobi .15 .40
❑ 9 Greedo's Prisoner .15 .40
❑ 10 A Visit From Jabba .15 .40
❑ 11 Facing Grand Moff Tarkin .15 .40
❑ 12 He Made A Fair Move .15 .40
❑ 13 Striking Back At The Empire .15 .40
❑ 14 It Came From The Garbage Chute .15 .40
❑ 15 Your Powers Are Weak, Old Man .15 .40
❑ 16 Ben Kenobi's Sacrifice .15 .40
❑ 17 Old Friends Reunited .15 .40
❑ 18 Star Pilot Luke Skywalker .15 .40
❑ 19 Death Star Under Attack .15 .40
❑ 20 The Battle Station Obliterated .15 .40
❑ 21 There's More To Him Than Money .15 .40
❑ 22 Honored For Their Heroism .15 .40
❑ 23 Fury Of The Wampa .15 .40
❑ 24 That's Two You Owe Me .15 .40
❑ 25 Probot Attack On Hoth .15 .40
❑ 26 Aboard The Executor .15 .40
❑ 27 You Have Failed Me .15 .40
❑ 28 At-Ats On The March .15 .40
❑ 29 Speeders Against The Enemy .15 .40
❑ 30 Firepower Of The At-At .15 .40
❑ 31 Luke Nearly Stomped .15 .40
❑ 32 Never Tell Me The Odds .15 .40
❑ 33 A Jedi Master On Dagobah .15 .40
❑ 34 The Princess And The Pirate .15 .40
❑ 35 Darth Vader's Scheme .15 .40
❑ 36 Beheading A Tyrant .15 .40
❑ 37 Darth Vader And Boba Fett .15 .40
❑ 38 The Carbon Frozen Captain .15 .40
❑ 39 The Great Confrontation .15 .40
❑ 40 Jedi Against Sith .15 .40
❑ 41 Truth And Consequences .15 .40
❑ 42 Luke's Temptation .15 .40
❑ 43 A New Hand For Luke .15 .40
❑ 44 We'll Get Him Back .15 .40
❑ 45 Luke Bargains For Solo .15 .40
❑ 46 Entertaining Jabba's Denizens .15 .40
❑ 47 The Unfreezing Of Han .15 .40
❑ 48 Enslaved By Jabba The Hutt .15 .40
❑ 49 Challenge Of The Rancor .15 .40
❑ 50 Luke's Counterattack .15 .40
❑ 51 Facing Off Against Fett .15 .40
❑ 52 Prey Of The Sarlacc .15 .40
❑ 53 A Walk On The Dark Side .15 .40
❑ 54 The Passing Of Yoda .15 .40
❑ 55 Ben's Revelations .15 .40
❑ 56 United Against The Empire .15 .40
❑ 57 Two On A Speeder Bike .15 .40
❑ 58 Perilous Bike Chase .15 .40
❑ 59 Against The New Death Star .15 .40
❑ 60 Skirmish At The Bunker .15 .40
❑ 61 Father Versus Son .15 .40
❑ 62 Will The Dark Side Prevail? .15 .40
❑ 63 The Last Of Anakin .15 .40
❑ 64 His Soul Redeemed .15 .40
❑ 65 A Family Made Whole .15 .40
❑ 66 Blessings From Beyond .15 .40
❑ 67 Trapped By The Trade Federation .15 .40
❑ 68 Don't Let Them Escape .15 .40
❑ 69 An Undersea Kingdom .15 .40
❑ 70 Boss Nass Of The Gungans .15 .40
❑ 71 Help From Astromech Droids .15 .40
❑ 72 Bargaining With Watto .15 .40
❑ 73 Sebulba's Boast .15 .40
❑ 74 C-3PO, Meet R2-D2 .15 .40
❑ 75 Day Of The Podrace .15 .40
❑ 76 Watching From The Stands .15 .40
❑ 77 High-Speed Daredevils .15 .40
❑ 78 A Farewell To Mom .15 .40
❑ 79 Attacked By Darth Maul .15 .40
❑ 80 Onward Against The Invaders .15 .40
❑ 81 An Army Of Battle Droids .15 .40
❑ 82 Penetrating The Palace .15 .40
❑ 83 Amidala's Bold Assault .15 .40
❑ 84 Qui-Gon Jinn Vs. Darth Maul .15 .40
❑ 85 Obi-Wan's Greatest Challenge .15 .40
❑ 86 Anakin Joins The Battle .15 .40
❑ 87 Galactic Combat .15 .40
❑ 88 Yoda's Misgivings .15 .40
❑ 89 A Noble Sacrifice .15 .40
❑ 90 The Eager Apprentice .15 .40
❑ 91 Death Of A Bounty Hunter .15 .40
❑ 92 Help From Dexter Jettster .15 .40
❑ 93 Troubled Young Lovers .15 .40
❑ 94 Kamino's Master Cloners .15 .40
❑ 95 Battle With Jango Fett .15 .40
❑ 96 The Fate Of Shmi Skywalker .15 .40
❑ 97 Held Captive By The Count .15 .40
❑ 98 Droid Factory Peril .15 .40
❑ 99 Spearing An Acklay .15 .40
❑ 100 Use The Force, Anakin .15 .40
❑ 101 Jedi Knights Surrounded .15 .40
❑ 102 Outnumbered By Battle Droids .15 .40
❑ 103 The Republic Strikes Back .15 .40
❑ 104 Battlefield: Geonosis .15 .40
❑ 105 Anakin Takes On Dooku .15 .40
❑ 106 Power Of The Dark Lord .15 .40
❑ 107 Fighting An Old Friend .15 .40
❑ 108 Saving His Jedi Allies .15 .40
❑ 109 Begun, The Clone War Has .15 .40
❑ 110 Sharing A Dark Destiny .15 .40
❑ 111 Galactic Conflict .15 .40
❑ 112 Ace Star Pilot Skywalker .15 .40
❑ 113 A Dark Awakening .15 .40
❑ 114 Palpatine's Protege? .15 .40
❑ 115 Anakin And The Jedi Council .15 .40
❑ 116 Mace Windu's Concerns .15 .40
❑ 117 Yoda's Discovery .15 .40
❑ 118 Fear For The Future .15 .40
❑ 119 A Jedi Knight Emergency .15 .40
❑ 120 The Star Wars Saga CL .15 .40

2004 Star Wars Heritage Alphabet Stickers

COMPLETE SET (30) 12.00 30.00
STATED ODDS 1:3 RETAIL
❑ 1 A K .50 1.25
❑ 2 B X .50 1.25
❑ 3 E I .50 1.25
❑ 4 N T .50 1.25
❑ 5 F O .50 1.25
❑ 6 Y U .50 1.25
❑ 7 S A .50 1.25
❑ 8 M E .50 1.25
❑ 9 C D .50 1.25
❑ 10 R H .50 1.25
❑ 11 A V .50 1.25
❑ 12 B P .50 1.25
❑ 13 H E .50 1.25
❑ 14 I R .50 1.25
❑ 15 O U .50 1.25
❑ 16 F S .50 1.25
❑ 17 E T .50 1.25
❑ 18 N C .50 1.25
❑ 19 M G .50 1.25
❑ 20 D A .50 1.25
❑ 21 A P .50 1.25
❑ 22 B C .50 1.25
❑ 23 E S .50 1.25
❑ 24 O I .50 1.25
❑ 25 U W .50 1.25
❑ 26 Z T .50 1.25
❑ 27 M N .50 1.25
❑ 28 D R .50 1.25
❑ 29 G J .50 1.25
❑ 30 Q L .50 1.25

2004 Star Wars Heritage Autographs

STATED ODDS 1:578
❑ NNO Mark Hamill 500.00 800.00
❑ NNO James Earl Jones 75.00 150.00
❑ NNO Carrie Fisher 200.00 400.00

2004 Star Wars Heritage Etched Wave One

COMPLETE SET (6) 6.00 15.00
STATED ODDS 1:9
❑ 1 Obi-Wan and Qui-Gon 1.25 3.00
❑ 2 Anakin Skywalker 1.25 3.00
❑ 3 Mace Windu and Yoda 1.25 3.00
❑ 4 Darth Maul, Palpatine, Count Dooku 1.25 3.00
❑ 5 Amidala and Clone Troopers 1.25 3.00
❑ 6 Bounty Hunters 1.25 3.00

2004 Star Wars Heritage Etched Wave Two

COMPLETE SET (6) 6.00 15.00
STATED ODDS 1:9
❑ 1 Palpatine, Organa, and Binks 1.25 3.00
❑ 2 C-3PO, R2-D2, and creature 1.25 3.00
❑ 3 Young Anakin, Watto, and Anakin's Mother 1.25 3.00
❑ 4 Jedi in battle 1.25 3.00
❑ 5 Female Jedi in battle 1.25 3.00
❑ 6 General Grievous 1.25 3.00

2005 Star Wars Revenge of the Sith

COMPLETE SET (90) 5.00 12.00
❑ 1 Anakin Skywalker .15 .40
❑ 2 Darth Vader .15 .40
❑ 3 Padme Amidala .15 .40
❑ 4 Obi-Wan Kenobi .15 .40
❑ 5 Yoda .15 .40
❑ 6 Mace Windu .15 .40
❑ 7 Chancellor Palpatine .15 .40
❑ 8 Darth Sidious .15 .40
❑ 9 Count Dooku .15 .40
❑ 10 General Grievous .15 .40
❑ 11 Chewbacca .15 .40
❑ 12 Tarfful .15 .40
❑ 13 Bail Organa .15 .40
❑ 14 C-3PO and R2-D2 .15 .40
❑ 15 Nute Gunray .15 .40
❑ 16 Jedi .15 .40
❑ 17 Sith .15 .40
❑ 18 Separatists .15 .40
❑ 19 Senators .15 .40
❑ 20 Clone Troopers .15 .40
❑ 21 Separatist Droids .15 .40
❑ 22 Jedi Knights To The Rescue .15 .40
❑ 23 Anakin's Daring Raid .15 .40
❑ 24 Battling The Buzz Droids .15 .40
❑ 25 Facing An Old Enemy .15 .40
❑ 26 Clashing With The Count .15 .40
❑ 27 The Fury Of Dooku .15 .40
❑ 28 Count Dooku's Execution .15 .40
❑ 29 R2 Does His Part .15 .40
❑ 30 What About Plan B .15 .40
❑ 31 Enter...General Grievous .15 .40
❑ 32 Beheading A Droid .15 .40
❑ 33 Dueling With General Grievous .15 .40
❑ 34 To Fight Another Day .15 .40
❑ 35 Another Happy Landing .15 .40
❑ 36 Dream Or Premonition .15 .40
❑ 37 Star-Crossed Lovers .15 .40
❑ 38 Seeking Yoda's Advice .15 .40
❑ 39 Heir To The Future .15 .40
❑ 40 Conferring With The Council .15 .40
❑ 41 The Secret Of Eternal Life .15 .40
❑ 42 Obi-Wan's Plan Of Attack .15 .40
❑ 43 Utapau On Alert .15 .40
❑ 44 The Rampaging Wheel .15 .40
❑ 45 Formidable Foes .15 .40
❑ 46 Vanquishing Grievous .15 .40
❑ 47 Arresting The Chancellor .15 .40
❑ 48 A Sith Lord Revealed .15 .40
❑ 49 Mace vs. Palpatine .15 .40
❑ 50 The Jedi Betrayed .15 .40
❑ 51 Unstoppable Clones .15 .40
❑ 52 Planet Of The Wookiees .15 .40
❑ 53 A Farewell To Friends .15 .40
❑ 54 The Terrible Truth .15 .40
❑ 55 The Sith Apprentice .15 .40
❑ 56 An Alliance Severed .15 .40
❑ 57 Slaughter Of The Separatists .15 .40
❑ 58 His Mad Reign Begins .15 .40
❑ 59 Yoda's Fight For Life .15 .40
❑ 60 The Path I Cannot Follow .15 .40
❑ 61 War of the Jedi .15 .40
❑ 62 Brother Against Brother .15 .40
❑ 63 Struggle In The Senate .15 .40
❑ 64 The Force Unleashed .15 .40
❑ 65 Consumed By The Dark Site .15 .40
❑ 66 Anakin's Fiery Fate .15 .40
❑ 67 Escaping From Palpatine .15 .40
❑ 68 The Birth Of Luke And Leia .15 .40
❑ 69 More Machine Than Man .15 .40
❑ 70 An Alliance Of Evil .15 .40
❑ 71 Dark Days Brighter Tomorrows .15 .40
❑ 72 Saving Luke Skywalker .15 .40
❑ 73 Coruscant .15 .40
❑ 74 Utapau .15 .40
❑ 75 Kashyyyk .15 .40
❑ 76 Mustafar .15 .40
❑ 77 Buzz Droids .15 .40
❑ 78 Lightsabers .15 .40
❑ 79 Jedi Starfighters .15 .40
❑ 80 ARC170 Starfighters .15 .40
❑ 81 Droid Tri Fighters .15 .40
❑ 82 Galactic Rescue .15 .40
❑ 83 Wookiee World .15 .40
❑ 84 A Deadly Duel .15 .40
❑ 85 Showdown On Mustafar .15 .40
❑ 86 In Exile On Dagobah .15 .40
❑ 87 From Jedi To Sith .15 .40
❑ 88 Old Friends Revisited .15 .40
❑ 89 A Trilogy Fulfilled .15 .40
❑ 90 Checklist .02 .10
❑ P1 The Circle is Complete PROMO 1.00 2.50
❑ P2 The Circle is Complete PROMO 1.00 2.50
❑ P3 The Circle is Complete PROMO 15.00 40.00
Star Wars Shop
❑ P4 The Circle is Complete PROMO 1.00 2.50
❑ P5 The Circle is Complete PROMO 1.00 2.50

2005 Star Wars Revenge of the Sith Blister Bonus

COMPLETE SET (3) 6.00 15.00
STATED ODDS ONE PER BLISTER PACK
❑ B1 General Grievous 2.50 6.00
❑ B2 Yoda 2.50 6.00
❑ B3 Clone Trooper 2.50 6.00

2005 Star Wars Revenge of the Sith Embossed Foil

COMPLETE SET (10) 20.00 50.00
STATED ODDS 1:6 RETAIL
❑ 1 Darth Vader 2.50 6.00
❑ 2 Darth Vader 2.50 6.00
❑ 3 Darth Vader 2.50 6.00
❑ 4 Darth Vader 2.50 6.00
❑ 5 Darth Vader 2.50 6.00
❑ 6 Darth Vader 2.50 6.00
❑ 7 Darth Vader 2.50 6.00
❑ 8 Darth Vader 2.50 6.00
❑ 9 Darth Vader 2.50 6.00
❑ 10 Darth Vader 2.50 6.00

2005 Star Wars Revenge of the Sith Etched Foil Puzzle

COMPLETE SET (6) 12.00 30.00
STATED ODDS 1:6
❑ 1 Bail 2.50 6.00
Leia/Beru/Luke/Owen
❑ 2 Darth Vader 2.50 6.00
❑ 3 Poggle 2.50 6.00
Nute Gunray/San Hill
❑ 4 Chewbacca 2.50 6.00
Tarfful
❑ 5 Saesee Tinn 2.50 6.00
Plo Koon/Quinlan Vos
❑ 6 Luminara Unduli 2.50 6.00
Adi Gallia/Barriss Offee

2005 Star Wars Revenge of the Sith Holograms

COMPLETE SET (3) 5.00 12.00
STATED ODDS 1:14 RETAIL
❑ 1 Yoda 2.00 5.00
❑ 2 Clone Trooper 2.00 5.00
❑ 3 Darth Vader 2.00 5.00

2005 Star Wars Revenge of the Sith Lenticular Morph Hobby

COMPLETE SET (2) 5.00 12.00
STATED ODDS 1:24 HOBBY
❑ 1 Padawan 3.00 8.00
Vader
❑ 2 Vader 3.00 8.00

2005 Star Wars Revenge of the Sith Lenticular Morph Retail

COMPLETE SET (2) 5.00 12.00
STATED ODDS 1:24 RETAIL
❑ 1 Anakin 3.00 8.00
Vader
❑ 2 Anakin 3.00 8.00
Vader

2005 Star Wars Revenge of the Sith Sketches

COMPLETE SET (41)
STATED ODDS 1:36
GROUP A ODDS 1:777
GROUP B ODDS 1:357
GROUP C ODDS 1:493
GROUP D ODDS 1:663
GROUP E ODDS 1:194
GROUP F ODDS 1:1,131
GROUP G ODDS 1:134
GROUP H ODDS 1:333
GROUP I ODDS 1:221
❑ NNO Chris Eliopoulos A
❑ NNO Juan Carlos Ramos A
❑ NNO Kieron Dwyer B
❑ NNO David Rabbitte B
❑ NNO Joseph Booth C
❑ NNO Brian Rood C
❑ NNO Matt Busch E
❑ NNO Robert Teranishi E
❑ NNO Davide Fabbri G
❑ NNO Thomas Hodges H
❑ NNO Jeff Chandler A
❑ NNO Monte Moore A
❑ NNO Cynthia Cummens B
❑ NNO Brandon McKinney B
❑ NNO Russ Walks B
❑ NNO Matt Haley C
❑ NNO William O'Neill D
❑ NNO Dan Norton E
❑ NNO James Hodgkins F
❑ NNO John McCrea G
❑ NNO Justin Chung A
❑ NNO Kilian Plunkett A
❑ NNO Dave Dorman B
❑ NNO Amy Pronovost B
❑ NNO Brent Woodside B
❑ NNO Mike Lilly C
❑ NNO Ryan Benjamin E
❑ NNO Dan Parsons E
❑ NNO Christian Dalla Vecchia G
❑ NNO Howard Shum G
❑ NNO Jeff Carlisle A
❑ NNO Dave Fox A
❑ NNO Cat Staggs A
❑ NNO Scott Erwert B
❑ NNO Chris Trevas B
❑ NNO Joe Corroney C
❑ NNO Otis Frampton D
❑ NNO Paul Gutierrez E
❑ NNO Sarah Wilkinson E
❑ NNO Grant Gould G
❑ NNO Randy Martinez I

2005 Star Wars Revenge of the Sith Stickers

COMPLETE SET (10) 2.50 6.00
STATED ODDS 1:3 RETAIL
❑ 1 Helmet .40 1.00
❑ 2 General Grievous .40 1.00
❑ 3 Darth Vader .40 1.00
Chewbacca/Anakin Skywalker/Yoda
❑ 4 Jedi .40 1.00
❑ 5 Sith .40 1.00
❑ 6 Darth Vader .40 1.00
❑ 7 Yoda .40 1.00
❑ 8 Darth Vader .40 1.00
❑ 9 Sith .40 1.00
❑ 10 Darth Vader Helmet .40 1.00

2005 Star Wars Revenge of the Sith Tattoos

COMPLETE SET (10) 4.00 10.00
STATED ODDS 1:3 RETAIL
❑ 1 Flaming Vader 1.00 2.50
❑ 2 Clone Trooper 1.00 2.50
❑ 3 Vader 1.00 2.50
❑ 4 Vader Shield 1.00 2.50
❑ 5 Yoda 1.00 2.50
❑ 6 Sith 1.00 2.50
❑ 7 Jedi 1.00 2.50
❑ 8 Grievous 1.00 2.50
❑ 9 Vader Gear 1.00 2.50
❑ 10 Sith Lord 1.00 2.50

2005 Star Wars Revenge of the Sith Tin Gold

COMPLETE SET (6) 5.00 12.00
STATED ODDS ONE PER TIN
❑ A Darth Vader 1.00 2.50
❑ B Lightsaber duel 1.00 2.50
❑ C Darth Vader 1.00 2.50
❑ D Darth Vader 1.00 2.50
❑ E Darth Vader 1.00 2.50
❑ F Darth Vader 1.00 2.50
Darth Sidious

2005 Star Wars Revenge of the Sith Tin Story

COMPLETE SET (6) 5.00 12.00
STATED ODDS ONE PER TIN
❑ 1 Rescuing Palpatine 1.00 2.50
❑ 2 What Price Love 1.00 2.50
❑ 3 Battling General Grievous 1.00 2.50
❑ 4 Destroy All Jedi 1.00 2.50
❑ 5 At War With Darth Sidious 1.00 2.50
❑ 6 Clash of the Jedi 1.00 2.50

2005 Star Wars Revenge of the Sith Widevision

COMPLETE SET (80) 5.00 12.00
❑ 1 The Rescue Mission .15 .40
❑ 2 Conflict in Space .15 .40
❑ 3 The Jedi's Daring Raid .15 .40
❑ 4 Buzz Droid .15 .40
❑ 5 Aboard the Enemy Ship .15 .40
❑ 6 The General's Command .15 .40
❑ 7 Artoo Strikes Back .15 .40
❑ 8 Count Dooku's Challenge .15 .40
❑ 9 Against a Sith Lord .15 .40
❑ 10 Duel to the Death .15 .40
❑ 11 A Dangerous Drop .15 .40
❑ 12 Shorter than Expected .15 .40
❑ 13 At War with the General .15 .40
❑ 14 Droids against Them .15 .40
❑ 15 A Wicked Escape Move .15 .40
❑ 16 Spaceship in Distress .15 .40
❑ 17 Desperate Plunge .15 .40
❑ 18 Emergency Landing .15 .40
❑ 19 Conferring with Sidious .15 .40
❑ 20 Anakin's Great Fear .15 .40
❑ 21 Seeking Answers .15 .40
❑ 22 Reporting to the Council .15 .40
❑ 23 Jedi Concerns .15 .40
❑ 24 Secrets of Eternal Life .15 .40
❑ 25 Showdown on Kashyyyk .15 .40
❑ 26 Wookiees Rally for War .15 .40
❑ 27 Repelling a Sea Attack .15 .40
❑ 28 Fire Power of the Enemy .15 .40
❑ 29 Fury Unleashed .15 .40
❑ 30 Astride Boga .15 .40
❑ 31 An Assemblage of Evil .15 .40
❑ 32 The General's Surprise .15 .40
❑ 33 Lightsaber Challenge .15 .40
❑ 34 Grievous on the Move .15 .40
❑ 35 The Great Chase .15 .40
❑ 36 Ally or Sith Lord? .15 .40
❑ 37 High Speed Pursuit .15 .40
❑ 38 A Mortal Weakness .15 .40
❑ 39 Blasted by Obi-Wan .15 .40
❑ 40 Grievous Annihilated .15 .40
❑ 41 A Fateful Decision .15 .40
❑ 42 The Chancellor Exposed .15 .40
❑ 43 Desperate Battle .15 .40
❑ 44 Mace Windu Betrayed .15 .40
❑ 45 Evil Triumphant .15 .40
❑ 46 Darth Vader .15 .40
❑ 47 Chancellor's Orders .15 .40
❑ 48 Slaughter of the Jedi .15 .40
❑ 49 Invading the Jedi Temple .15 .40
❑ 50 A Padawan Retaliates .15 .40
❑ 51 Yoda Senses a Trap .15 .40
❑ 52 Vader's Grim Task .15 .40
❑ 53 Dawning of a Dark Era .15 .40
❑ 54 Journey to Mustafar .15 .40
❑ 55 Let Her Go Anakin .15 .40
❑ 56 Friend against Friend .15 .40
❑ 57 A Minor Distraction .15 .40
❑ 58 Unlimited Power .15 .40
❑ 59 When Jedi Collide .15 .40
❑ 60 Duel of the Titans .15 .40
❑ 61 Yoda's Greatest Battle .15 .40
❑ 62 Trashing the Senate .15 .40
❑ 63 To Fight Another Day .15 .40
❑ 64 Turning on His Master .15 .40
❑ 65 A Friendship in Flames .15 .40
❑ 66 I Have the High Ground .15 .40
❑ 67 Fall of a Jedi .15 .40
❑ 68 Anakin's Tragic Fate .15 .40
❑ 69 A Matter of Death and Life .15 .40
❑ 70 He's Still Alive .15 .40
❑ 71 Rebuilding Darth Vader .15 .40
❑ 72 A Twice-Blessed Event .15 .40
❑ 73 A Mechanical Prison .15 .40
❑ 74 Man in the Iron Mask .15 .40
❑ 75 Cold Steel, Broken Heart .15 .40
❑ 76 An Evil Alliance .15 .40
❑ 77 The Passing of Padme .15 .40
❑ 78 Tomorrow's Heroes .15 .40
❑ 79 A New Hope .15 .40
❑ 80 Checklist .02 .10

2005 Star Wars Revenge of the Sith Widevision Autographs

STATED ODDS 1:48 HOBBY
❑ NNO Amy Allen 20.00 50.00
❑ NNO Samuel L. Jackson 600.00 1000.00
❑ NNO Peter Mayhew 50.00 100.00
❑ NNO Matthew Wood 50.00 100.00
❑ NNO Michael Kingma 20.00 50.00

2005 Star Wars Revenge of the Sith Widevision Chrome Hobby

COMPLETE SET (10) 12.50 30.00
STATED ODDS 1:6 HOBBY
❑ H1 Pursuit in Outer Space 1.50 4.00
❑ H2 The Doomed Cruiser 1.50 4.00
❑ H3 A Night at the Opera 1.50 4.00
❑ H4 The Wookiee Planet 1.50 4.00
❑ H5 The Galactic Senate 1.50 4.00
❑ H6 The Traitorous Troopers 1.50 4.00
❑ H7 Betting on Boga 1.50 4.00
❑ H8 Visions of Mustafar 1.50 4.00
❑ H9 Palpatine's Secret Chamber 1.50 4.00
❑ H10 Technological Terrors 1.50 4.00

2005 Star Wars Revenge of the Sith Widevision Chrome Retail

COMPLETE SET (10) 15.00 40.00
STATED ODDS 1:60 RETAIL
❑ R1 A Galactic Rescue Mission 2.00 5.00
❑ R2 Forces of the Republic 2.00 5.00
❑ R3 The Splendors of Coruscant 2.00 5.00
❑ R4 Showdown on Kashyyyk 2.00 5.00
❑ R5 Against Formidable Foes 2.00 5.00
❑ R6 High-Speed Pursuit 2.00 5.00
❑ R7 Possessed by the Dark Side 2.00 5.00
❑ R8 Luke and Leia's Birthplace 2.00 5.00
❑ R9 Darth Vader Reborn 2.00 5.00
❑ R10 A Home for Princess Leia 2.00 5.00

2005 Star Wars Revenge of the Sith Widevision Flix Pix

COMPLETE SET (10) 15.00 40.00
STATED ODDS 1:6
❑ 1 Anakin Skywalker 2.00 5.00
❑ 2 Obi-Wan Kenobi 2.00 5.00
❑ 3 Darth Vader 2.00 5.00
❑ 4 Darth Sidious 2.00 5.00
❑ 5 Yoda 2.00 5.00
❑ 6 Mace Windu 2.00 5.00
❑ 7 General Grievous 2.00 5.00
❑ 8 Count Dooku 2.00 5.00
❑ 9 Aayla Secura 2.00 5.00
❑ 10 Kai-Adi Mundi 2.00 5.00

2006 Star Wars Evolution Update

COMPLETE SET (90) 5.00 12.00
1D ISSUED AS DAMAGED AUTO REPLACEMENT
❑ 1 Aayla Secura .15 .40
❑ 2 Agen Kolar .15 .40
❑ 3 Anakin Skywalker .15 .40
❑ 4 Bail Organa .15 .40
❑ 5 Barriss Offee .15 .40
❑ 6 Battle Droid .15 .40
❑ 7 Beru Whitesun .15 .40
❑ 8 Boba Fett .15 .40
❑ 9 C-3PO .15 .40
❑ 10 Captain Antilles .15 .40
❑ 11 Captain Typho .15 .40
❑ 12 Chancellor Palpatine .15 .40
❑ 13 Chewbacca .15 .40
❑ 14 Chi Eekway .15 .40
❑ 15 Cliegg Lars .15 .40
❑ 16 Clone Trooper .15 .40
❑ 17 Count Dooku .15 .40
❑ 18 Darth Maul .15 .40
❑ 19 Darth Sidious .15 .40
❑ 20 Darth Vader .15 .40
❑ 21 Dexter Jettster .15 .40
❑ 22 Droideka .15 .40
❑ 23 Elan Sleazebagano .15 .40
❑ 24 Fang Zar .15 .40
❑ 25 General Grievous .15 .40
❑ 26 Giddean Danu .15 .40
❑ 27 Governor Tarkin .15 .40
❑ 28 Han Solo .15 .40
❑ 29 Jango Fett .15 .40
❑ 30 Jar Jar .15 .40
❑ 31 Jocasta Nu .15 .40
❑ 32 Ki Adi Mundi .15 .40
❑ 33 Kit Fisto .15 .40
❑ 34 Lama Su .15 .40
❑ 35 Lando Calrissian .15 .40
❑ 36 Luke Skywalker .15 .40
❑ 37 Luminara Unduli .15 .40
❑ 38 Mace Windu .15 .40

❑ 39 MagnaGuards .15 .40
❑ 40 Mas Amedda .15 .40
❑ 41 Meena Tills .15 .40
❑ 42 Mon Mothma .15 .40
❑ 43 Nute Gunray .15 .40
❑ 44 Obi-Wan Kenobi .15 .40
❑ 45 Orn Free Taa .15 .40
❑ 46 Owen Lars .15 .40
❑ 47 Padme .15 .40
❑ 48 Passel Argente .15 .40
❑ 49 Plo Koon .15 .40
❑ 50 Poggle the Lesser .15 .40
❑ 51 Po Nudo .15 .40
❑ 52 Princess Leia .15 .40
❑ 53 Queen Apailana .15 .40
❑ 54 Queen Jamillia .15 .40
❑ 55 Qui-Gon Jinn .15 .40
❑ 56 Rune Kaako .15 .40
❑ 57 R2-D2 .15 .40
❑ 58 Saesee Tiin .15 .40
❑ 59 San Hill .15 .40
❑ 60 Shaak Ti .15 .40
❑ 61 Shu Mai .15 .40
❑ 62 Sly Moore .15 .40
❑ 63 Stass Allie .15 .40
❑ 64 Stormtrooper .15 .40
❑ 65 Super Battle Droid .15 .40
❑ 66 Tarfful .15 .40
❑ 67 Taun We .15 .40
❑ 68 Terr Taneel .15 .40
❑ 69 Tion Medon .15 .40
❑ 70 Tusken Raider .15 .40
❑ 71 Wat Tambor .15 .40
❑ 72 Watto .15 .40
❑ 73 Yoda .15 .40
❑ 74 Zam Wesell .15 .40
❑ 75 Zett Jukassa .15 .40
❑ 76 Acklay .15 .40
❑ 77 Airwha .15 .40
❑ 78 Bantha .15 .40
❑ 79 Boga .15 .40
❑ 80 Dewback .15 .40
❑ 81 Kaadu .15 .40
❑ 82 Nexu .15 .40
❑ 83 Opee Sea Killer .15 .40
❑ 84 Reek .15 .40
❑ 85 Sarlacc .15 .40
❑ 86 Space Slug .15 .40
❑ 87 Tauntaun .15 .40
❑ 88 Death Star .15 .40
❑ 89 Millennium Falcon .15 .40
❑ 90 Slave I .15 .40
❑ 1D Luke Skywalker SP 2.00 5.00
❑ P1 Obi-Wan Kenobi PROMO 1.00 2.50
❑ P2 Darth Vader PROMO 1.00 2.50

2006 Star Wars Evolution Update Autographs

STATED ODDS 1:24 HOBBY
GROUP A ODDS 1:2,005
GROUP B ODDS 1:231
GROUP C ODDS 1:81
GROUP D ODDS 1:259
GROUP E ODDS 1:48

❑ NNO James Earl Jones A 200.00 400.00
❑ NNO Bob Keen B 25.00 50.00
❑ NNO Michonne Bourriague C 10.00 25.00
❑ NNO Richard LeParmentier C 10.00 25.00
❑ NNO Zach Jensen E 10.00 25.00
❑ NNO George Lucas
❑ NNO John Coppinger B 25.00 50.00
❑ NNO Wayne Pygram B 50.00 100.00
❑ NNO Sandi Finlay C 10.00 25.00
❑ NNO Garrick Hagon E 10.00 25.00
❑ NNO Peter Cushing
❑ NNO Hayden Christensen A 600.00 1000.00
❑ NNO Mike Edmonds B 25.00 50.00
❑ NNO Mike Quinn B 25.00 50.00
❑ NNO Michael Kingma C 10.00 25.00
❑ NNO Jesse Jensen E 10.00 25.00
❑ NNO Alec Guinness
❑ NNO David Barclay B 25.00 50.00
❑ NNO Toby Philpott B 25.00 50.00
❑ NNO Maria de Aragon C 10.00 25.00
❑ NNO Nalini Krishan D 10.00 25.00
❑ NNO Matt Sloan E 10.00 25.00

2006 Star Wars Evolution Update Galaxy Crystals

COMPLETE SET (10) 12.50 30.00
STATED ODDS 1:4 RETAIL

❑ G1 Luke 1.50 4.00
Anakin
❑ G2 Leia 1.50 4.00
Padme
❑ G3 Obi-Wan 1.50 4.00
Qui-Gon
❑ G4 Darth Vader 1.50 4.00
Darth Sidious
❑ G5 Han Solo 1.50 4.00
Chewbacca
❑ G6 Yoda 1.50 4.00
Mace Windu
❑ G7 Boba Fett 1.50 4.00
Jango Fett
❑ G8 Darth Maul 1.50 4.00
Count Dooku
❑ G9 C-3PO 1.50 4.00
R2-D2
❑ G10 Stormtrooper 1.50 4.00
Clone

2006 Star Wars Evolution Update Etched Foil Puzzle

COMPLETE SET (6) 6.00 15.00
STATED ODDS 1:6

❑ 1 Anakin Skywalker 1.25 3.00
❑ 2 Obi-Wan Kenobi 1.25 3.00
❑ 3 Padme Amidala 1.25 3.00
❑ 4 Wraith-bot 1.25 3.00
❑ 5 Chancellor Palpatine 1.25 3.00
❑ 6 Clone Trooper 1.25 3.00

2006 Star Wars Evolution Update Insert A

COMPLETE SET (20) 20.00 40.00
STATED ODDS 1:6

❑ 1A Anakin Skywalker 1.50 4.00
❑ 2A Bail Organa 1.50 4.00
❑ 3A Boba Fett 1.50 4.00
❑ 4A Chancellor Palpatine 1.50 4.00
❑ 5A Clone Trooper 1.50 4.00
❑ 6A Darth Sidious 1.50 4.00
❑ 7A Darth Vader 1.50 4.00
❑ 8A General Grievous 1.50 4.00
❑ 9A Governor Tarkin 1.50 4.00
❑ 10A Han Solo 1.50 4.00
❑ 11A Jango Fett 1.50 4.00
❑ 12A Lando Calrissian 1.50 4.00
❑ 13A Luke Skywalker 1.50 4.00
❑ 14A Obi-Wan Kenobi 1.50 4.00
❑ 15A Padmé Amidala 1.50 4.00
❑ 16A Princess Leia 1.50 4.00
❑ 17A Stormtrooper 1.50 4.00
❑ 18A Tusken Raider 1.50 4.00
❑ 19A Death Star 1.50 4.00
❑ 20A Slave I 1.50 4.00

2006 Star Wars Evolution Update Insert B

COMPLETE SET (15) 20.00 40.00
STATED ODDS 1:12

❑ 1B Anakin Skywalker 2.00 5.00
❑ 2B Bail Organa 2.00 5.00
❑ 3B Chancellor Palpatine 2.00 5.00
❑ 4B Clone Trooper 2.00 5.00
❑ 5B Darth Sidious 2.00 5.00
❑ 6B Han Solo 2.00 5.00
❑ 7B Jango Fett 2.00 5.00
❑ 8B Lando Calrissian 2.00 5.00
❑ 9B Luke Skywalker 2.00 5.00
❑ 10B Obi-Wan Kenobi 2.00 5.00
❑ 11B Padmé Amidala 2.00 5.00
❑ 12B Princess Leia 2.00 5.00
❑ 13B Stormtrooper 2.00 5.00
❑ 14B Tusken Raider 2.00 5.00
❑ 15B Death Star 2.00 5.00

2006 Star Wars Evolution Update Luke and Leia

COMPLETE SET (2)
STATED ODDS 1:1975 HOBBY
STATED PRINT RUN 100 SER. #'d SETS

❑ 1C Luke Skywalker
❑ 2C Princess Leia

2007 Star Wars 30th Anniversary

COMPLETE SET (120) 5.00 12.00

❑ 1 The 30th Anniversary .15 .40
❑ 2 The George Lucas Legacy .15 .40
❑ 3 Characters '77 .15 .40
❑ 4 Characters '77 .15 .40
❑ 5 Characters '77 .15 .40
❑ 6 Characters '77 .15 .40
❑ 7 Characters '77 .15 .40
❑ 8 Characters '77 .15 .40
❑ 9 Characters '77 .15 .40
❑ 10 Episode IV .15 .40
❑ 11 Episode IV .15 .40
❑ 12 Episode IV .15 .40
❑ 13 Episode IV .15 .40
❑ 14 Episode IV .15 .40
❑ 15 Episode IV .15 .40
❑ 16 Episode IV .15 .40
❑ 17 Episode IV .15 .40
❑ 18 Episode IV .15 .40
❑ 19 Episode V .15 .40
❑ 20 Episode V .15 .40
❑ 21 Episode V .15 .40
❑ 22 Episode V .15 .40
❑ 23 Episode V .15 .40
❑ 24 Episode V .15 .40
❑ 25 Episode V .15 .40
❑ 26 Episode V .15 .40
❑ 27 Episode V .15 .40
❑ 28 Episode VI .15 .40
❑ 29 Episode VI .15 .40
❑ 30 Episode VI .15 .40
❑ 31 Episode VI .15 .40
❑ 32 Episode VI .15 .40
❑ 33 Episode VI .15 .40
❑ 34 Episode VI .15 .40
❑ 35 Episode VI .15 .40
❑ 36 Episode VI .15 .40
❑ 37 Episode IV SE .15 .40
❑ 38 Episode IV SE .15 .40
❑ 39 Episode IV SE .15 .40
❑ 40 Episode V SE .15 .40
❑ 41 Episode V SE .15 .40
❑ 42 Episode V SE .15 .40
❑ 43 Episode VI SE .15 .40
❑ 44 Episode VI SE .15 .40
❑ 45 Episode VI SE .15 .40
❑ 46 Episode I .15 .40
❑ 47 Episode I .15 .40
❑ 48 Episode I .15 .40
❑ 49 Episode I .15 .40
❑ 50 Episode I .15 .40
❑ 51 Episode I .15 .40
❑ 52 Episode I .15 .40
❑ 53 Episode I .15 .40
❑ 54 Episode I .15 .40
❑ 55 Episode II .15 .40
❑ 56 Episode II .15 .40
❑ 57 Episode II .15 .40
❑ 58 Episode II .15 .40
❑ 59 Episode II .15 .40
❑ 60 Episode II .15 .40
❑ 61 Episode II .15 .40
❑ 62 Episode II .15 .40
❑ 63 Episode II .15 .40
❑ 64 Episode III .15 .40
❑ 65 Episode III .15 .40
❑ 66 Episode III .15 .40
❑ 67 Episode III .15 .40
❑ 68 Episode III .15 .40
❑ 69 Episode III .15 .40
❑ 70 Episode III .15 .40
❑ 71 Episode III .15 .40
❑ 72 Episode III .15 .40
❑ 73 Episode IV .15 .40
❑ 74 Episode IV .15 .40
❑ 75 Episode V .15 .40
❑ 76 Episode V .15 .40
❑ 77 Episode VI .15 .40
❑ 78 Episode VI .15 .40
❑ 79 Episode I .15 .40
❑ 80 Episode II .15 .40
❑ 81 Episode III .15 .40
❑ 82 Episode IV .15 .40
❑ 83 Episode IV .15 .40
❑ 84 Episode V .15 .40
❑ 85 Episode V .15 .40
❑ 86 Episode VI .15 .40
❑ 87 Episode VI .15 .40
❑ 88 Episode I .15 .40
❑ 89 Episode II .15 .40
❑ 90 Episode III .15 .40
❑ 91 Holiday Special .15 .40
❑ 92 Holiday Special .15 .40
❑ 93 Holiday Special .15 .40
❑ 94 Caravan of Courage .15 .40
❑ 95 Caravan of Courage .15 .40
❑ 96 Caravan of Courage .15 .40
❑ 97 Battle for Endor .15 .40
❑ 98 Battle for Endor .15 .40
❑ 99 Battle for Endor .15 .40
❑ 100 Holiday Special .15 .40
❑ 101 Holiday Special .15 .40
❑ 102 Ewoks .15 .40
❑ 103 Droids .15 .40
❑ 104 Clone Wars I .15 .40
❑ 105 Clone Wars I .15 .40
❑ 106 Clone Wars II .15 .40
❑ 107 Clone Wars II .15 .40
❑ 108 Clone Wars II .15 .40
❑ 109 Episode IV .15 .40
❑ 110 Episode IV .15 .40
❑ 111 Episode IV .15 .40
❑ 112 Episode V .15 .40
❑ 113 Episode VI .15 .40
❑ 114 Episode VI .15 .40
❑ 115 Fan Films .15 .40
❑ 116 Fan Films .15 .40
❑ 117 Fan Films .15 .40
❑ 118 Sneak Preview .15 .40
❑ 119 Sneak Preview .15 .40
❑ 120 Checklist .02 .10

2007 Star Wars 30th Anniversary Blue

*BLUE: 4X TO 10X BASIC CARDS
STATED ODDS 1:12

❑ 1 The 30th Anniversary 1.50 4.00
❑ 2 The George Lucas Legacy 1.50 4.00
❑ 3 Characters '77 1.50 4.00
❑ 4 Characters '77 1.50 4.00
❑ 5 Characters '77 1.50 4.00
❑ 6 Characters '77 1.50 4.00
❑ 7 Characters '77 1.50 4.00
❑ 8 Characters '77 1.50 4.00
❑ 9 Characters '77 1.50 4.00
❑ 10 Episode IV 1.50 4.00
❑ 11 Episode IV 1.50 4.00
❑ 12 Episode IV 1.50 4.00
❑ 13 Episode IV 1.50 4.00
❑ 14 Episode IV 1.50 4.00
❑ 15 Episode IV 1.50 4.00
❑ 16 Episode IV 1.50 4.00
❑ 17 Episode IV 1.50 4.00
❑ 18 Episode IV 1.50 4.00
❑ 19 Episode V 1.50 4.00
❑ 20 Episode V 1.50 4.00
❑ 21 Episode V 1.50 4.00
❑ 22 Episode V 1.50 4.00
❑ 23 Episode V 1.50 4.00
❑ 24 Episode V 1.50 4.00
❑ 25 Episode V 1.50 4.00
❑ 26 Episode V 1.50 4.00
❑ 27 Episode V 1.50 4.00
❑ 28 Episode VI 1.50 4.00
❑ 29 Episode VI 1.50 4.00
❑ 30 Episode VI 1.50 4.00
❑ 31 Episode VI 1.50 4.00
❑ 32 Episode VI 1.50 4.00
❑ 33 Episode VI 1.50 4.00
❑ 34 Episode VI 1.50 4.00
❑ 35 Episode VI 1.50 4.00
❑ 36 Episode VI 1.50 4.00
❑ 37 Episode IV SE 1.50 4.00
❑ 38 Episode IV SE 1.50 4.00
❑ 39 Episode IV SE 1.50 4.00
❑ 40 Episode V SE 1.50 4.00
❑ 41 Episode V SE 1.50 4.00
❑ 42 Episode V SE 1.50 4.00
❑ 43 Episode VI SE 1.50 4.00
❑ 44 Episode VI SE 1.50 4.00
❑ 45 Episode VI SE 1.50 4.00
❑ 46 Episode I 1.50 4.00
❑ 47 Episode I 1.50 4.00
❑ 48 Episode I 1.50 4.00
❑ 49 Episode I 1.50 4.00
❑ 50 Episode I 1.50 4.00
❑ 51 Episode I 1.50 4.00
❑ 52 Episode I 1.50 4.00
❑ 53 Episode I 1.50 4.00
❑ 54 Episode I 1.50 4.00
❑ 55 Episode II 1.50 4.00
❑ 56 Episode II 1.50 4.00
❑ 57 Episode II 1.50 4.00
❑ 58 Episode II 1.50 4.00
❑ 59 Episode II 1.50 4.00
❑ 60 Episode II 1.50 4.00
❑ 61 Episode II 1.50 4.00
❑ 62 Episode II 1.50 4.00
❑ 63 Episode II 1.50 4.00
❑ 64 Episode III 1.50 4.00
❑ 65 Episode III 1.50 4.00
❑ 66 Episode III 1.50 4.00
❑ 67 Episode III 1.50 4.00
❑ 68 Episode III 1.50 4.00
❑ 69 Episode III 1.50 4.00
❑ 70 Episode III 1.50 4.00
❑ 71 Episode III 1.50 4.00
❑ 72 Episode III 1.50 4.00
❑ 73 Episode IV 1.50 4.00
❑ 74 Episode IV 1.50 4.00
❑ 75 Episode V 1.50 4.00
❑ 76 Episode V 1.50 4.00
❑ 77 Episode VI 1.50 4.00
❑ 78 Episode VI 1.50 4.00
❑ 79 Episode I 1.50 4.00
❑ 80 Episode II 1.50 4.00
❑ 81 Episode III 1.50 4.00
❑ 82 Episode IV 1.50 4.00
❑ 83 Episode IV 1.50 4.00
❑ 84 Episode V 1.50 4.00
❑ 85 Episode V 1.50 4.00
❑ 86 Episode VI 1.50 4.00
❑ 87 Episode VI 1.50 4.00
❑ 88 Episode I 1.50 4.00
❑ 89 Episode II 1.50 4.00
❑ 90 Episode III 1.50 4.00
❑ 91 Holiday Special 1.50 4.00
❑ 92 Holiday Special 1.50 4.00
❑ 93 Holiday Special 1.50 4.00
❑ 94 Caravan of Courage 1.50 4.00
❑ 95 Caravan of Courage 1.50 4.00
❑ 96 Caravan of Courage 1.50 4.00
❑ 97 Battle for Endor 1.50 4.00
❑ 98 Battle for Endor 1.50 4.00
❑ 99 Battle for Endor 1.50 4.00
❑ 100 Holiday Special 1.50 4.00
❑ 101 Holiday Special 1.50 4.00
❑ 102 Ewoks 1.50 4.00
❑ 103 Droids 1.50 4.00
❑ 104 Clone Wars I 1.50 4.00
❑ 105 Clone Wars I 1.50 4.00
❑ 106 Clone Wars II 1.50 4.00
❑ 107 Clone Wars II 1.50 4.00
❑ 108 Clone Wars II 1.50 4.00
❑ 109 Episode IV 1.50 4.00
❑ 110 Episode IV 1.50 4.00
❑ 111 Episode IV 1.50 4.00
❑ 112 Episode V 1.50 4.00
❑ 113 Episode VI 1.50 4.00
❑ 114 Episode VI 1.50 4.00
❑ 115 Fan Films 1.50 4.00
❑ 116 Fan Films 1.50 4.00
❑ 117 Fan Films 1.50 4.00
❑ 118 Sneak Preview 1.50 4.00
❑ 119 Sneak Preview 1.50 4.00
❑ 120 Checklist 1.50 4.00

2007 Star Wars 30th Anniversary Red

*RED: 8X TO 20X BASIC CARDS
STATED ODDS 1:24

❑ 1 The 30th Anniversary 3.00 8.00
❑ 2 The George Lucas Legacy 3.00 8.00
❑ 3 Characters '77 3.00 8.00
❑ 4 Characters '77 3.00 8.00
❑ 5 Characters '77 3.00 8.00
❑ 6 Characters '77 3.00 8.00
❑ 7 Characters '77 3.00 8.00
❑ 8 Characters '77 3.00 8.00
❑ 9 Characters '77 3.00 8.00
❑ 10 Episode IV 3.00 8.00
❑ 11 Episode IV 3.00 8.00
❑ 12 Episode IV 3.00 8.00
❑ 13 Episode IV 3.00 8.00
❑ 14 Episode IV 3.00 8.00
❑ 15 Episode IV 3.00 8.00
❑ 16 Episode IV 3.00 8.00
❑ 17 Episode IV 3.00 8.00
❑ 18 Episode IV 3.00 8.00
❑ 19 Episode V 3.00 8.00
❑ 20 Episode V 3.00 8.00
❑ 21 Episode V 3.00 8.00
❑ 22 Episode V 3.00 8.00
❑ 23 Episode V 3.00 8.00
❑ 24 Episode V 3.00 8.00
❑ 25 Episode V 3.00 8.00
❑ 26 Episode V 3.00 8.00
❑ 27 Episode V 3.00 8.00
❑ 28 Episode VI 3.00 8.00
❑ 29 Episode VI 3.00 8.00
❑ 30 Episode VI 3.00 8.00
❑ 31 Episode VI 3.00 8.00
❑ 32 Episode VI 3.00 8.00
❑ 33 Episode VI 3.00 8.00
❑ 34 Episode VI 3.00 8.00
❑ 35 Episode VI 3.00 8.00
❑ 36 Episode VI 3.00 8.00
❑ 37 Episode IV SE 3.00 8.00
❑ 38 Episode IV SE 3.00 8.00
❑ 39 Episode IV SE 3.00 8.00
❑ 40 Episode V SE 3.00 8.00
❑ 41 Episode V SE 3.00 8.00
❑ 42 Episode V SE 3.00 8.00
❑ 43 Episode VI SE 3.00 8.00
❑ 44 Episode VI SE 3.00 8.00
❑ 45 Episode VI SE 3.00 8.00
❑ 46 Episode I 3.00 8.00
❑ 47 Episode I 3.00 8.00
❑ 48 Episode I 3.00 8.00
❑ 49 Episode I 3.00 8.00
❑ 50 Episode I 3.00 8.00
❑ 51 Episode I 3.00 8.00
❑ 52 Episode I 3.00 8.00
❑ 53 Episode I 3.00 8.00
❑ 54 Episode I 3.00 8.00
❑ 55 Episode II 3.00 8.00
❑ 56 Episode II 3.00 8.00
❑ 57 Episode II 3.00 8.00
❑ 58 Episode II 3.00 8.00
❑ 59 Episode II 3.00 8.00
❑ 60 Episode II 3.00 8.00
❑ 61 Episode II 3.00 8.00
❑ 62 Episode II 3.00 8.00
❑ 63 Episode II 3.00 8.00
❑ 64 Episode III 3.00 8.00
❑ 65 Episode III 3.00 8.00
❑ 66 Episode III 3.00 8.00
❑ 67 Episode III 3.00 8.00
❑ 68 Episode III 3.00 8.00
❑ 69 Episode III 3.00 8.00
❑ 70 Episode III 3.00 8.00
❑ 71 Episode III 3.00 8.00
❑ 72 Episode III 3.00 8.00
❑ 73 Episode IV 3.00 8.00
❑ 74 Episode IV 3.00 8.00
❑ 75 Episode V 3.00 8.00
❑ 76 Episode V 3.00 8.00
❑ 77 Episode VI 3.00 8.00
❑ 78 Episode VI 3.00 8.00
❑ 79 Episode I 3.00 8.00
❑ 80 Episode II 3.00 8.00
❑ 81 Episode III 3.00 8.00
❑ 82 Episode IV 3.00 8.00
❑ 83 Episode IV 3.00 8.00
❑ 84 Episode V 3.00 8.00
❑ 85 Episode V 3.00 8.00
❑ 86 Episode VI 3.00 8.00
❑ 87 Episode VI 3.00 8.00
❑ 88 Episode I 3.00 8.00
❑ 89 Episode II 3.00 8.00
❑ 90 Episode III 3.00 8.00
❑ 91 Holiday Special 3.00 8.00
❑ 92 Holiday Special 3.00 8.00
❑ 93 Holiday Special 3.00 8.00
❑ 94 Caravan of Courage 3.00 8.00
❑ 95 Caravan of Courage 3.00 8.00
❑ 96 Caravan of Courage 3.00 8.00
❑ 97 Battle for Endor 3.00 8.00
❑ 98 Battle for Endor 3.00 8.00
❑ 99 Battle for Endor 3.00 8.00
❑ 100 Holiday Special 3.00 8.00
❑ 101 Holiday Special 3.00 8.00
❑ 102 Ewoks 3.00 8.00
❑ 103 Droids 3.00 8.00
❑ 104 Clone Wars I 3.00 8.00
❑ 105 Clone Wars I 3.00 8.00
❑ 106 Clone Wars II 3.00 8.00
❑ 107 Clone Wars II 3.00 8.00
❑ 108 Clone Wars II 3.00 8.00
❑ 109 Episode IV 3.00 8.00
❑ 110 Episode IV 3.00 8.00
❑ 111 Episode IV 3.00 8.00
❑ 112 Episode V 3.00 8.00
❑ 113 Episode VI 3.00 8.00
❑ 114 Episode VI 3.00 8.00
❑ 115 Fan Films 3.00 8.00
❑ 116 Fan Films 3.00 8.00
❑ 117 Fan Films 3.00 8.00
❑ 118 Sneak Preview 3.00 8.00
❑ 119 Sneak Preview 3.00 8.00
❑ 120 Checklist 3.00 8.00

2007 Star Wars 30th Anniversary Gold

STATED ODDS 1:287
STATED PRINT RUN 30 SER.#'d SETS

❑ 1 The 30th Anniversary 75.00 150.00
❑ 2 The George Lucas Legacy 75.00 150.00
❑ 3 Characters '77 75.00 150.00
❑ 4 Characters '77 75.00 150.00
❑ 5 Characters '77 75.00 150.00
❑ 6 Characters '77 75.00 150.00
❑ 7 Characters '77 75.00 150.00
❑ 8 Characters '77 75.00 150.00
❑ 9 Characters '77 75.00 150.00
❑ 10 Episode IV 75.00 150.00
❑ 11 Episode IV 75.00 150.00
❑ 12 Episode IV 75.00 150.00
❑ 13 Episode IV 75.00 150.00
❑ 14 Episode IV 75.00 150.00
❑ 15 Episode IV 75.00 150.00
❑ 16 Episode IV 75.00 150.00
❑ 17 Episode IV 75.00 150.00
❑ 18 Episode IV 75.00 150.00
❑ 19 Episode V 75.00 150.00
❑ 20 Episode V 75.00 150.00
❑ 21 Episode V 75.00 150.00
❑ 22 Episode V 75.00 150.00
❑ 23 Episode V 75.00 150.00
❑ 24 Episode V 75.00 150.00
❑ 25 Episode V 75.00 150.00
❑ 26 Episode V 75.00 150.00
❑ 27 Episode V 75.00 150.00
❑ 28 Episode VI 75.00 150.00
❑ 29 Episode VI 75.00 150.00
❑ 30 Episode VI 75.00 150.00
❑ 31 Episode VI 75.00 150.00
❑ 32 Episode VI 75.00 150.00
❑ 33 Episode VI 75.00 150.00
❑ 34 Episode VI 75.00 150.00
❑ 35 Episode VI 75.00 150.00
❑ 36 Episode VI 75.00 150.00
❑ 37 Episode IV SE 75.00 150.00
❑ 38 Episode IV SE 75.00 150.00
❑ 39 Episode IV SE 75.00 150.00
❑ 40 Episode V SE 75.00 150.00
❑ 41 Episode V SE 75.00 150.00
❑ 42 Episode V SE 75.00 150.00
❑ 43 Episode VI SE 75.00 150.00
❑ 44 Episode VI SE 75.00 150.00
❑ 45 Episode VI SE 75.00 150.00
❑ 46 Episode I 75.00 150.00
❑ 47 Episode I 75.00 150.00
❑ 48 Episode I 75.00 150.00
❑ 49 Episode I 75.00 150.00
❑ 50 Episode I 75.00 150.00
❑ 51 Episode I 75.00 150.00
❑ 52 Episode I 75.00 150.00
❑ 53 Episode I 75.00 150.00
❑ 54 Episode I 75.00 150.00
❑ 55 Episode II 75.00 150.00
❑ 56 Episode II 75.00 150.00
❑ 57 Episode II 75.00 150.00
❑ 58 Episode II 75.00 150.00
❑ 59 Episode II 75.00 150.00
❑ 60 Episode II 75.00 150.00
❑ 61 Episode II 75.00 150.00
❑ 62 Episode II 75.00 150.00
❑ 63 Episode II 75.00 150.00
❑ 64 Episode III 75.00 150.00
❑ 65 Episode III 75.00 150.00
❑ 66 Episode III 75.00 150.00
❑ 67 Episode III 75.00 150.00
❑ 68 Episode III 75.00 150.00
❑ 69 Episode III 75.00 150.00
❑ 70 Episode III 75.00 150.00
❑ 71 Episode III 75.00 150.00
❑ 72 Episode III 75.00 150.00
❑ 73 Episode IV 75.00 150.00
❑ 74 Episode IV 75.00 150.00
❑ 75 Episode V 75.00 150.00
❑ 76 Episode V 75.00 150.00
❑ 77 Episode VI 75.00 150.00
❑ 78 Episode VI 75.00 150.00
❑ 79 Episode I 75.00 150.00
❑ 80 Episode II 75.00 150.00
❑ 81 Episode III 75.00 150.00
❑ 82 Episode IV 75.00 150.00
❑ 83 Episode IV 75.00 150.00
❑ 84 Episode V 75.00 150.00
❑ 85 Episode V 75.00 150.00
❑ 86 Episode VI 75.00 150.00
❑ 87 Episode VI 75.00 150.00
❑ 88 Episode I 75.00 150.00
❑ 89 Episode II 75.00 150.00
❑ 90 Episode III 75.00 150.00
❑ 91 Holiday Special 75.00 150.00
❑ 92 Holiday Special 75.00 150.00
❑ 93 Holiday Special 75.00 150.00
❑ 94 Caravan of Courage 75.00 150.00
❑ 95 Caravan of Courage 75.00 150.00
❑ 96 Caravan of Courage 75.00 150.00
❑ 97 Battle for Endor 75.00 150.00
❑ 98 Battle for Endor 75.00 150.00
❑ 99 Battle for Endor 75.00 150.00
❑ 100 Holiday Special 75.00 150.00
❑ 101 Holiday Special 75.00 150.00
❑ 102 Ewoks 75.00 150.00
❑ 103 Droids 75.00 150.00
❑ 104 Clone Wars I 75.00 150.00
❑ 105 Clone Wars I 75.00 150.00
❑ 106 Clone Wars II 75.00 150.00
❑ 107 Clone Wars II 75.00 150.00
❑ 108 Clone Wars II 75.00 150.00
❑ 109 Episode IV 75.00 150.00
❑ 110 Episode IV 75.00 150.00
❑ 111 Episode IV 75.00 150.00
❑ 112 Episode V 75.00 150.00
❑ 113 Episode VI 75.00 150.00
❑ 114 Episode VI 75.00 150.00
❑ 115 Fan Films 75.00 150.00
❑ 116 Fan Films 75.00 150.00
❑ 117 Fan Films 75.00 150.00
❑ 118 Sneak Preview 75.00 150.00
❑ 119 Sneak Preview 75.00 150.00
❑ 120 Checklist 75.00 150.00

2007 Star Wars 30th Anniversary Animation Cels

COMPLETE SET (9) 6.00 15.00
STATED ODDS 1:6 RETAIL

❑ 1 Star Wars Holiday Special 1.50 4.00
❑ 2 Star Wars Holiday Special 1.50 4.00
❑ 3 Droids 1.50 4.00
❑ 4 Adventures 1.50 4.00
❑ 5 Cartoon Network's Clone Wars 1.50 4.00
❑ 6 Cartoon Network's Clone Wars 1.50 4.00
❑ 7 Cartoon Network's Clone Wars 1.50 4.00
❑ 8 Cartoon Network's Clone Wars 1.50 4.00
❑ 9 Cartoon Network's Clone Wars 1.50 4.00

2007 Star Wars 30th Anniversary Autographs

STATED ODDS 1:43 HOBBY

❑ NNO Harrison Ford
❑ NNO David Prowse 300.00 600.00
❑ NNO John Dykstra 25.00 50.00
❑ NNO Lorne Peterson 15.00 30.00
❑ NNO Joe Viskocil 20.00 40.00
❑ NNO Paul Blake 10.00 20.00
❑ NNO Richard LeParmentier 10.00 20.00
❑ NNO Carrie Fisher
❑ NNO George Roubichek 15.00 30.00
❑ NNO Gary Kurtz 10.00 20.00
❑ NNO Norman Reynolds 25.00 50.00
❑ NNO Rusty Goffe 25.00 50.00
❑ NNO Garrick Hagon 10.00 20.00
❑ NNO Anthony Daniels 700.00 1200.00

STAR WARS

❑ NNO Colin Higgins 10.00 20.00
❑ NNO Richard Edlund 20.00 40.00
❑ NNO Ken Ralston 20.00 40.00
❑ NNO John Williams 150.00 300.00
❑ NNO Maria deAragon 20.00 40.00
❑ NNO Peter Mayhew 150.00 300.00
❑ NNO Jon Berg 10.00 20.00
❑ NNO John Mollo 10.00 20.00
❑ NNO Phil Tippet 25.00 50.00
❑ NNO Kenny Baker 25.00 50.00
❑ NNO Christine Hewett 15.00 30.00

2007 Star Wars 30th Anniversary Blister Bonus

COMPLETE SET (3) 2.50 6.00
STATED ODDS ONE PER BLISTER PACK

❑ 1 Luke Skywalker 1.25 3.00
❑ 2 Princess Leia 1.25 3.00
❑ 3 Han Solo 1.25 3.00

2007 Star Wars 30th Anniversary Magnets

COMPLETE SET (9) 12.00 30.00
STATED ODDS 1:8 RETAIL

❑ NNO Luke Skywalker 1.50 4.00
❑ NNO Han Solo 1.50 4.00
❑ NNO Death Star Battle 1.50 4.00
❑ NNO Princess Leia 1.50 4.00
❑ NNO Tusken Raider 1.50 4.00
❑ NNO Jawas 1.50 4.00
❑ NNO Stormtroopers 1.50 4.00
❑ NNO Darth Vader 1.50 4.00
Gov. Tarkin
❑ NNO Droids 1.50 4.00

2007 Star Wars 30th Anniversary Original Series Box Toppers

COMPLETE SET (330)
STATED ODDS ONE PER BOX

❑ 1 Luke Skywalker
❑ 2 C-3PO and R2-D2
❑ 3 The Little Droid R2-D2
❑ 4 Space pirate Han Solo
❑ 5 Princess Leia Organa
❑ 6 Ben Kenobi
❑ 7 The villainous Darth Vader
❑ 8 Grand Moff Tarkin
❑ 9 Rebels defend their ship
❑ 10 Princess Leia captured!
❑ 11 Artoo is imprisoned by the Jawas
❑ 12 The droids are reunited!
❑ 13 A sale on droids!
❑ 14 Luke checks out his new droid
❑ 15 R2-D2 is left behind
❑ 16 Jawas of Tatooine
❑ 17 Lord Vader threatens Princess Leia
❑ 18 R2-D2 is missing!
❑ 19 Searching for the little droid
❑ 20 Hunted by the Sandpeople!
❑ 21 The Tusken Raiders
❑ 22 Rescued by Ben Kenobi
❑ 23 C-3PO is injured
❑ 24 Stormtroopers seek the droids
❑ 25 Luke rushed to save his loved ones
❑ 26 A horrified Luke sees family killed
❑ 27 Some repairs for C-3PO
❑ 28 Luke agrees to join Ben Kenobi
❑ 29 Stopped by Stormtroopers
❑ 30 Han in the Millennium falcom
❑ 31 Sighting the Death Star
❑ 32 Lord Vader's Guards
❑ 33 The droids in the control room
❑ 34 C-3PO diverts the guards
❑ 35 Luke and Han as stormtroopers
❑ 36 Blast of the laser rifle!
❑ 37 Cornered in the labyrinth
❑ 38 Luke and Han in the refuse room
❑ 39 Steel walls close in on out heroes!
❑ 40 Droids rescue their masters!
❑ 41 Facing the deadly chasm
❑ 42 Stromtroopers attack
❑ 43 Luke prepares to swing across the chasm
❑ 44 Han and Chewie shoot it out
❑ 45 The light sabre
❑ 46 A desperate moment for Ben
❑ 47 Luke prepares for the battle
❑ 48 R2-D2 is loaded aboard
❑ 49 The rebels monitor the raid
❑ 50 Rebel leaders wonder about their fate!
❑ 51 C-3PO and Princess Leia
❑ 52 Who will win the final Star War
❑ 53 Battle in outer space
❑ 54 The victors receive their reward
❑ 55 Han, Chewie, and Luke
❑ 56 A day of rejoicing
❑ 57 Mark Hamill as Luke Skywalker
❑ 58 Harrison Ford as Han Solo
❑ 59 Alec Guinness as Ben Kenobi
❑ 60 Peter Cushing as Grand Moff Tarkin
❑ 61 Mark Hamill in control room
❑ 62 Lord Vader's stormtroopers
❑ 63 May the Force be with you
❑ 64 Governor of Imperial Outlands
❑ 65 Carrie Fisher and Mark Hamill
❑ 66 Amazing Robot C-3PO
❑ 67 C-3PO and Luke
❑ 68 The Millennium Falcon
❑ 69 Threeplo's desert Trek
❑ 70 Special mission for R2-D2
❑ 71 The incredible C-3PO
❑ 72 Ben Kenobi rescues Luke
❑ 73 The droids wait for Luke
❑ 74 Luke Skywalker on Tatooine
❑ 75 Darth Vader strangles a rebel
❑ 76 R2-D2 on the rebel starship
❑ 77 Waiting in the control room
❑ 78 Droids to the rescue
❑ 79 Preparing to board Solo's spaceship
❑ 80 Where has R2-D2 gone?
❑ 81 Weapons of the Death Star
❑ 82 A daring rescue
❑ 83 Aboard the Millennium Falcon
❑ 84 Rebel pilot prepares for the raid
❑ 85 Luke on the sand planet
❑ 86 A mighty explosion
❑ 87 The droids try to rescue Luke
❑ 88 Stromtroopers guard Solo's ship
❑ 89 The imprisoned Princess Leia
❑ 90 Honoring the Victors
❑ 91 Solo and Chewie prepare to leave Luke
❑ 92 Advance of the Tusken Raider
❑ 93 Stormtroopers blast the rebels
❑ 94 Interrogated by Stormtroopers
❑ 95 Sighting R2-D2
❑ 96 The droids on Tatooine
❑ 97 Meeting at the cantina
❑ 98 C-3PO
❑ 99 Ben with the light sabre
❑ 100 Our heroes at the spaceport
❑ 101 The Wookies Chewbacca
❑ 102 Rebels prepare for the big fight
❑ 103 Stormtroopers attack our heroes
❑ 104 Luke's uncle and aunt
❑ 105 Imperial soldiers burn through the starship
❑ 106 A message from Princess Leia
❑ 107 The Tusken Raider
❑ 108 Princess Leia observes the battle
❑ 109 Ben turns off the tractor beam
❑ 110 Threepio fools the guards
❑ 111 Chewie and Han Solo
❑ 112 Threatened by Sandpeople
❑ 113 Ben hides from Imperial stormtroopers
❑ 114 Planning to escape
❑ 115 Hiding in the Millennium Falcon
❑ 116 Honored for their heroism
❑ 117 Chewbacca posed as a prisoner
❑ 118 R2-D2 and C-3PO
❑ 119 Threepio, Ben and Luke
❑ 120 Luke destroys an Imperial ship
❑ 121 Han Solo and Chewbacca
❑ 122 The Millenium Falcon
❑ 123 Solo blasts a stormtrooper
❑ 124 Threepio searches for R2-D2
❑ 125 Luke in disguise
❑ 126 A quizzical Threepio
❑ 127 The Rebel fleet
❑ 128 Roar of the Wookie
❑ 129 May the Force be with you
❑ 130 Pursued by the Jawas
❑ 131 Spectacular battle
❑ 132 Lord Vader and a soldier
❑ 133 Ben and Luke w
C-3PO
❑ 134 Luke dreams of being a star pilot
❑ 135 Cantina troubles
❑ 136 Danger from all sides
❑ 137 Luke attacked by a strange creature
❑ 138 On the track of the droids
❑ 139 Han Solo
❑ 140 R2-D2-where are you?
❑ 141 Some quick thinking by Luke
❑ 142 Darth Vader inspects the throttled ship
❑ 143 Droids on the sand planet
❑ 144 Harrison Ford as Han Solo
❑ 145 Escape from the Death Star
❑ 146 Luke Skywalkers aunt preparing dinner
❑ 147 Bargaining with the Jawas
❑ 148 The fearsome stormtroopers
❑ 149 The evil Grand Moff Tarkin
❑ 150 Shootout at the Chasm
❑ 151 Planning an escape
❑ 152 Spirited Princess Leia
❑ 153 The fantastic droid Threepio
❑ 154 Princess Leia comforts Luke
❑ 155 The Escape Pod is jettisoned
❑ 156 R2-D2 is lifted aboard
❑ 157 Learn about the Force, Luke
❑ 158 Rebel victory
❑ 159 Luke Skywalker's home
❑ 160 Destroying a world
❑ 161 Preparing for the raid
❑ 162 Han Solo cornered by Greedo
❑ 163 Caught in the tractor beam
❑ 164 Tusken Raiders capture Luke
❑ 165 Escaping from stormtroopers
❑ 166 A close call for Luke and Leia
❑ 167 Surrounded by Lord Vader's soldiers
❑ 168 Hunting the fugitives
❑ 169 Meeting at the Death Star
❑ 170 Luke and the Princess trapped
❑ 171 The walls are moving
❑ 172 Droids in the escape pod
❑ 173 The stormtroopers
❑ 174 Solo aims for trouble
❑ 175 A closer look at a Jawa
❑ 176 Luke Skywalkers dream
❑ 177 Solo swings into action
❑ 178 The Star Warriors
❑ 179 Stormtroopers search the spaceport
❑ 180 Princess Leia honors the victors
❑ 181 Peter Cushing as Grand Moff Tarkin
❑ 182 Deadly blasters
❑ 183 Dave Prowse as Darth Vader
❑ 184 Luke and his uncle
❑ 185 Luke on Tatooine
❑ 186 The Jawas
❑ 187 Threepio and friend
❑ 188 Starship under fire
❑ 189 Mark Hamill as Luke
❑ 190 Carrie Fisher as Princess Leia
❑ 191 Life on the desert world
❑ 192 Liberated Princess
❑ 193 Luke's uncle buys Threepio
❑ 194 Stormtroopers attack
❑ 195 Alec Guinness as Ben Kenobi
❑ 196 Lord Darth Vader
❑ 197 Leia blasts a stormtrooper
❑ 198 Luke decides to leave Tatooine
❑ 199 The star warriors aim for action
❑ 200 C-3PO searches for his counterpart
❑ 201 Raid at Mos Eisley
❑ 202 Inquiring about Obi-Wan Kenobi
❑ 203 A band of Jawas
❑ 204 Stalking the corridors of the Death Star
❑ 205 Desperate moments for our heroes
❑ 206 Searching for the missing droid
❑ 207 C-3PO Anthony Daniels
❑ 208 Luke Skywalker on the desert planet
❑ 209 The Rebel Troops
❑ 210 Princess Leia blasts the enemy
❑ 211 A proud moment for Han and Luke
❑ 212 A stormtrooper is blasted
❑ 213 Monitoring the battle
❑ 214 Luke and Leia
❑ 215 Han bows out of the battle
❑ 216 Han and Leia quarrel
❑ 217 The Dark Lord of Sith
❑ 218 Luke Skywalker's home destroyed
❑ 219 The swing to freedom
❑ 220 Im going to regret this
❑ 221 Princess Leia
❑ 222 Evacuate? In our moment of triumph
❑ 223 Han Solo covers his friends
❑ 224 Luke's secret yen for action
❑ 225 Aunt Beru Lars
❑ 226 Portrait of a Princess
❑ 227 Instructing the Rebel pilots
❑ 228 R2-D2 is inspected by the Jawas
❑ 229 Grand Moff Tarkin
❑ 230 Guarding the Millennium Falcon
❑ 231 Discussing the Death Star's future
❑ 232 The Empire strikes back
❑ 233 Raiding the Rebel starship
❑ 234 Envisioning the Rebel's destruction
❑ 235 Luke Skywalker
❑ 236 Readying the Rebel Fleet
❑ 237 The deadly grip of Darth Vader
❑ 238 Uncle Owen Lars
❑ 239 The young star warrior
❑ 240 Artoo's desperate mission
❑ 241 The rebel fighter ships
❑ 242 Death Star shootout
❑ 243 Rebels in the trench
❑ 244 Waiting at Mos Eisley
❑ 245 Member of the evil Empire
❑ 246 Stormtrooper
❑ 247 Soldier of evil
❑ 248 Luke suspects the worst about his family
❑ 249 Ben Kenobi
❑ 250 Luke and Ben on Tatooine
❑ 251 An overjoyed Han Solo
❑ 252 The honored heroes
❑ 253 R2-D2
❑ 254 Darth Vader
❑ 255 Luke poses with his weapon
❑ 256 The marvelous droid-C3PO
❑ 257 A pair of Jawas
❑ 258 Fighting impossible droids
❑ 259 Challenging the evil Empire
❑ 260 Han Solo
❑ 261 Fury of the Tusken Raider
❑ 262 Creature of Tatooine
❑ 263 The courage of Luke Skywalker
❑ 264 Star pilot Luke Skywalker
❑ 265 Anxious moments for the Rebels
❑ 266 Threepio and Leia monitor the battle
❑ 267 Non-nonsense privateer Han Solo
❑ 268 Ben prepares to turn off the tractor beam
❑ 269 Droids on the run
❑ 270 Luke Skywalker
❑ 271 Do you think they'll melt us down, Artoo?
❑ 272 Corridors of the Death Star
❑ 273 This is all your fault, Artoo!
❑ 274 Droids trick the Stormtrooper!
❑ 275 Guarding the Millenium Falcon
❑ 276 It's not wise to upset a Wookiee!
❑ 277 Bizarre inhabitants of the cantina!
❑ 278 A narrow escape!
❑ 279 Awaiting the Imperial attack
❑ 280 Remb.Luke,The Force will be w
you
❑ 281 A monstrous thirst!
❑ 282 Hurry up,we're gonna have company
❑ 283 The Cantina musicians
❑ 284 Distracted by Solo's assault
❑ 285 Spiffed up for the Awards Ceremony
❑ 286 Cantina denizens!
❑ 287 Han and Chewie ready for action!
❑ 288 Blasting the enemy!
❑ 289 The Rebel fighters take off!
❑ 290 Chewie aims for danger!
❑ 291 Lord Vader senses The Force
❑ 292 The Stormtroopers assemble
❑ 293 A friendly chat among alien friends!
❑ 294 Droids make their way to the Escape Pod
❑ 295 Han and the Rebel Pilots
❑ 296 Artoo-Detoo is abducted by Jawas!
❑ 297 Inside the Sandcrawler
❑ 298 Chewie gets riled!
❑ 299 Leia wishes Luke good luck!
❑ 300 A crucial moment for Luke Skywalker
❑ 301 Luke, the Star Warrior!
❑ 302 Threepio and Artoo
❑ 303 Various droids collected by the Jawas
❑ 304 The Jawas ready their new merchandise
❑ 305 Director George Lucas and Greedo
❑ 306 Technicians ready C-3PO for the cameras
❑ 307 A touch-up for Chewbacca
❑ 308 Directing the Cantina creatures
❑ 309 The birthday celebration for Sir Alec Guinness
❑ 310 Filming the Awards Ceremony
❑ 311 Model builders proudly display their work
❑ 312 Using the blue screen process for X-wings
❑ 313 The birth of a Droid
❑ 314 Shooting in Tunisia
❑ 315 Inside the Millenium Falcon
❑ 316 Photographing the miniature explosions
❑ 317 Filming explosions on the Death Star
❑ 318 Make-up for the Bantha
❑ 319 Dave Prowse and Alec Guinness rehearse
❑ 320 Flight of the Falcon
❑ 321 George Lucas directs counterpart Luke
❑ 322 Constructing the Star Destroyer
❑ 323 Aboard the Millenium Falcon
❑ 324 Chewbacca takes a breather
❑ 325 The princess
❑ 326 Animating the chessboard
❑ 327 Filming the sandcrawler
❑ 328 X-wings positioned for the cameras
❑ 329 Sir Alec Guinness
George Lucas
❑ 330 Filming Luke and Threepio

2007 Star Wars 30th Anniversary Promos

COMPLETE SET (3) 2.00 5.00

❑ P1 Enter Darth Vader 1.00 2.50
❑ P2 May the Force Be With You 1.00 2.50
❑ P3 The Power of the Dark Side 1.00 2.50

2007 Star Wars 30th Anniversary Sketches

STATED ODDS 1:50 HOBBY

❑ NNO Dave Dorman
❑ NNO Tom Hodges
❑ NNO Sean Pence
❑ NNO Katie Cook
❑ NNO Jessica Hickman
❑ NNO Cat Staggs
❑ NNO Christian Dalla Vecch
❑ NNO Robert Teranishi
❑ NNO Matt Busch
❑ NNO Craig Rousseau
❑ NNO Len Bellinger
❑ NNO Alexander Buechel
❑ NNO Ingrid Hardy
❑ NNO Kevin Graham
❑ NNO Allison Sohn
❑ NNO Ryan Waterhouse
❑ NNO Russell Walks
❑ NNO Joe Corroney
❑ NNO Adam Hughes
❑ NNO Leah Mangue
❑ NNO Mark Brooks
❑ NNO Gabe Hernandez
❑ NNO Brian Rood
❑ NNO Jeff Chandler
❑ NNO David Rabbitte
❑ NNO Amy Pronovost
❑ NNO Stephane Roux
❑ NNO Brian Denham
❑ NNO Rafael Kayanan
❑ NNO Doug Cowan
❑ NNO Jan Duursema
❑ NNO Cynthis Cummens
❑ NNO Juan Carlos Ramos
❑ NNO Otis Frampton
❑ NNO Josh Howard
❑ NNO Joseph Booth
❑ NNO Josh Fargher
❑ NNO Phil Noto
❑ NNO Justin Chung
❑ NNO Chris Eliopoulous
❑ NNO Brian Ashmore
❑ NNO John Watkins-Chow
❑ NNO Paul Gutierrez
❑ NNO Brandon McKinney
❑ NNO Sarah Wilkinson
❑ NNO Grant Gould
❑ NNO Davidé Fabbri

2007 Star Wars 30th Anniversary Triptych Puzzle

COMPLETE SET (27) 12.00 25.00
STATED ODDS 1:3

❑ 1 Bravery 1 .75 2.00
❑ 2 Bravery 2 .75 2.00
❑ 3 Bravery 3 .75 2.00
❑ 4 Escaping Fate 1 .75 2.00
❑ 5 Escaping Fate 2 .75 2.00
❑ 6 Escaping Fate 3 .75 2.00
❑ 7 Hidden in Plain Sight 1 .75 2.00
❑ 8 Hidden in Plain Sight 2 .75 2.00
❑ 9 Hidden in Plain Sight 3 .75 2.00
❑ 10 Imprisonment 1 .75 2.00
❑ 11 Imprisonment 2 .75 2.00
❑ 12 Imprisonment 3 .75 2.00
❑ 13 Insurmountable Odds 1 .75 2.00
❑ 14 Insurmountable Odds 2 .75 2.00
❑ 15 Insurmountable Odds 3 .75 2.00
❑ 16 Master and Apprentice 1 .75 2.00
❑ 17 Master and Apprentice 2 .75 2.00
❑ 18 Master and Apprentice 3 .75 2.00
❑ 19 The Power of the Force 1 .75 2.00
❑ 20 The Power of the Force 2 .75 2.00
❑ 21 The Power of the Force 3 .75 2.00
❑ 22 The Underworld 1 .75 2.00
❑ 23 The Underworld 2 .75 2.00
❑ 24 The Underworld 3 .75 2.00
❑ 25 Tyranny 1 .75 2.00
❑ 26 Tyranny 2 .75 2.00
❑ 27 Tyranny 3 .75 2.00

2008 Star Wars Clone Wars

COMPLETE SET (90) 5.00 12.00

❑ 1 The Clone Wars: An Animated Adventure .15 .40
❑ 2 Anakin Skywalker .15 .40
❑ 3 Ahsoka Tano .15 .40
❑ 4 Obi-Wan Kenobi .15 .40
❑ 5 Padmé Amidala .15 .40
❑ 6 Captain Rex .15 .40
❑ 7 Yoda .15 .40
❑ 8 Chancellor Palpatine .15 .40
❑ 9 Commander Cody .15 .40
❑ 10 Asajj Ventress .15 .40
❑ 11 Count Dooku .15 .40
❑ 12 General Loathsom .15 .40
❑ 13 Jabba the Hutt .15 .40
❑ 14 Ziro the Hutt .15 .40
❑ 15 Rotta the Huttlet .15 .40
❑ 16 R2-D2 .15 .40
❑ 17 C-3PO .15 .40
❑ 18 4A-7 .15 .40
❑ 19 A Galaxy Divided .15 .40
❑ 20 Clash on Christophsis .15 .40
❑ 21 Attack of the Clones .15 .40
❑ 22 Patterns of Force .15 .40
❑ 23 Octuptarra Peril .15 .40
❑ 24 Loathsom's New Ploy .15 .40
❑ 25 The New Padawan .15 .40
❑ 26 Battle of Crystal City .15 .40
❑ 27 Jedi in the Fray .15 .40
❑ 28 Destroying a Droid .15 .40
❑ 29 A Bold Deception .15 .40
❑ 30 Crossing the Lines .15 .40
❑ 31 Against a Destroyer Droid .15 .40
❑ 32 Smashing the Enemy .15 .40
❑ 33 The Surrender of Obi-Wan .15 .40
❑ 34 Space Armada .15 .40
❑ 35 Ready or Reckless .15 .40
❑ 36 Droid Trouble .15 .40
❑ 37 Triumph of the Jedi .15 .40
❑ 38 The Shield Is Down .15 .40
❑ 39 Heroes Assembled .15 .40
❑ 40 Galactic Struggle .15 .40
❑ 41 An Unlikely Alliance .15 .40
❑ 42 The Rescue Mission .15 .40
❑ 43 Droid Blasters .15 .40
❑ 44 Tank Girl .15 .40
❑ 45 Unstoppable Advance .15 .40
❑ 46 Inside Teth Castle .15 .40
❑ 47 Dooku's Deception .15 .40
❑ 48 Rescued or Kidnapped .15 .40
❑ 49 Heroes Under Fire .15 .40
❑ 50 Restraining Rex .15 .40
❑ 51 An Escape Route Blasted .15 .40
❑ 52 Vulture Droid Attack .15 .40
❑ 53 Little Girl, Big Challenge .15 .40
❑ 54 Starfighters .15 .40
❑ 55 Attack from Space .15 .40
❑ 56 In Vulture's Shadow .15 .40
❑ 57 Towering Terror .15 .40
❑ 58 A Message from Ventress .15 .40
❑ 59 Rex on the Rampage .15 .40
❑ 60 Terrors of Teth .15 .40
❑ 61 A Leap for Life .15 .40
❑ 62 Ventress Cuts Through .15 .40
❑ 63 Ahsoka's Greatest Challenge .15 .40
❑ 64 The Winged Rescuer .15 .40
❑ 65 Why You Tin-Plated Traitor .15 .40
❑ 66 Fury of the Republic .15 .40
❑ 67 Attack and Retreat .15 .40
❑ 68 Kenobi vs. Ventress .15 .40
❑ 69 Dark Forces of Dooku .15 .40
❑ 70 Hold On, Ahsoka! .15 .40
❑ 71 Unlikely Shipmates .15 .40
❑ 72 Concern on Coruscant .15 .40
❑ 73 Padmé's Plan .15 .40
❑ 74 Memories of Tatooine .15 .40
❑ 75 Ziro's Vile Scheme .15 .40
❑ 76 Jailed but Not for Long .15 .40
❑ 77 Power of the Dark Count .15 .40
❑ 78 Force against Force .15 .40
❑ 79 Clash of the Titans .15 .40
❑ 80 No Rest for Ahsoka .15 .40
❑ 81 A Padawan Imperiled .15 .40
❑ 82 Ahsoka Rules .15 .40
❑ 83 Ziro Surrounded .15 .40
❑ 84 Anakin to the Rescue .15 .40
❑ 85 Desperately Seeking Ahsoka .15 .40
❑ 86 Return of the Huttlet .15 .40
❑ 87 His Nasty Plot Revealed .15 .40
❑ 88 Hope and Fear .15 .40
❑ 89 Clone War Victory .15 .40
❑ 90 Checklist .15 .40

2008 Star Wars Clone Wars Gold

COMPLETE SET (90)
*GOLD: 8X TO 20X BASIC CARD
STATED ODDS 1:24 HOBBY
STATED PRINT RUN 205 SER. #'d SETS

2008 Star Wars Clone Wars Animation Cels

COMPLETE SET (10) 7.50 15.00
STATED ODDS 1:6

❑ 1 Taking Aim 1.25 3.00
❑ 2 Battle on Christophsis 1.25 3.00
❑ 3 The New Master and Apprentice 1.25 3.00
❑ 4 The March of Asaji Ventress 1.25 3.00
❑ 5 Testing Anakin's Skill 1.25 3.00
❑ 6 Heroes for the Republic 1.25 3.00
❑ 7 Saber Slashing the Droideka 1.25 3.00
❑ 8 Master and Apprentice Reunited 1.25 3.00
❑ 9 Preparing for Galactic Civil War 1.25 3.00
❑ 10 Meeting with the Masters 1.25 3.00

2008 Star Wars Clone Wars Coins Purple

COMPLETE SET (12)

❑ 1 Anakin
❑ 2 Ahsoka
❑ 3 Obi-Wan
❑ 4 Asajj
❑ 5 Yoda
❑ 6 Padme
❑ 7 C-3PO
R2-D2
❑ 8 Palpatine
❑ 9 Rex
❑ 10 Dooku
❑ 11 Cody
❑ 12 Jabba

2008 Star Wars Clone Wars Foil

COMPLETE SET (10) 12.00 25.00
STATED ODDS 1:3 RETAIL

❑ 1 Anakin 2.00 5.00
❑ 2 Obi-Wan 2.00 5.00
❑ 3 Ahsoka 2.00 5.00
❑ 4 C-3PO 2.00 5.00
❑ 5 Clone Trooper 2.00 5.00
❑ 6 R2-D2 2.00 5.00
❑ 7 Rex 2.00 5.00
❑ 8 Yoda 2.00 5.00
❑ 9 Jedi 2.00 5.00
❑ 10 Ventress 2.00 5.00

2008 Star Wars Clone Wars Motion

COMPLETE SET (5) 4.00 8.00
STATED ODDS 1:8 RETAIL

❑ 1 R2-D2 1.25 3.00
Ahsoka
❑ 2 Anakin 1.25 3.00
Ahsoka
❑ 3 Anakin 1.25 3.00
❑ 4 Hyperspace 1.25 3.00
❑ 5 Asajj 1.25 3.00
Obi-Wan

2008 Star Wars Clone Wars Sketches

STATED ODDS 1:24 HOBBY

❑ 1 Amy Pronovost
❑ 2 Anthony Ermio
❑ 3 Ben Curtis Jones
❑ 4 Bosco Ng
❑ 5 Brent Engstrom
❑ 6 Brian Ashmore
❑ 7 Brian Denham
❑ 8 Brian Kalin O'Connell
❑ 9 Brian Kong
❑ 10 Brian Miller
❑ 11 Bryan Morton
❑ 12 Cat Staggs
❑ 13 Chelsea Brown
❑ 14 Chris Henderson
❑ 15 Chris Trevas
❑ 16 Christian Dalla Vecchia
❑ 17 Clay McCormack
❑ 18 Cynthia Cummens
❑ 19 Dan Parsons
❑ 20 Daniel Cooney
❑ 21 Danny Keller
❑ 22 Dave Filoni
❑ 23 Dave Fox
❑ 24 David Le Merrer
❑ 25 David Rabbitte
❑ 26 Davide Fabbri
❑ 27 Dennis Budd
❑ 28 Don Pedicini Jr.
❑ 29 Doug Cowan
❑ 30 Dwayne Clare
❑ 31 Edward Pun
❑ 32 Erik Maell
❑ 33 Francis Hsu
❑ 34 Gabe Hernandez
❑ 35 Giancarlo Volpe
❑ 36 Grant Gould
❑ 37 Hamilton Cline
❑ 38 Howard Shum
❑ 39 Ingrid Hardy
❑ 40 Irma Ahmed (Aimo)
❑ 41 Jackson Sze
❑ 42 Jake Minor
❑ 43 Jake Myler
❑ 44 James Bukauskas (Bukshot)
❑ 45 James Hodgkins
❑ 46 Jamie Snell
❑ 47 Jan Duursema
❑ 48 Jason Hughes
❑ 49 Jason Potratz
❑ 50 Jason Potratz
Jack Hai
❑ 51 Jason Sobol
❑ 52 Jeff Carlisle
❑ 53 Jeff Chandler
❑ 54 Jessica Hickman
❑ 55 Jim Kyle
❑ 56 Joanne Ellen Mutch
❑ 57 Joe Corroney
❑ 58 Joel Carroll
❑ 59 John McCrea
❑ 60 John Watkins-Chow
❑ 61 Jon Morris
❑ 62 Josh Fargher
❑ 63 Josh Howard
❑ 64 Juan Carlos Ramos
❑ 65 Justin Chung
❑ 66 Karen Krajenbrink
❑ 67 Kate Bradley
❑ 68 Kate Glasheen
❑ 69 Katie Cook-Wilcox
❑ 70 Keith Phillips
❑ 71 Kelsey Mann
❑ 72 Kevin Doyle
❑ 73 Kevin Graham
❑ 74 Kilian Plunkett
❑ 75 Kyle Babbitt
❑ 76 Lance Sawyer
❑ 77 Le Tang
❑ 78 Leah Mangue
❑ 79 Lee Kohse
❑ 80 Len Bellinger
❑ 81 Lord Mesa

❑ 82 Mark McHaley
❑ 83 Mark Walters
❑ 84 Matt Gaser
❑ 85 Matt Olsen
❑ 86 Matthew Goodmanson
❑ 87 Michael Duron
❑ 88 Nicole Falk
❑ 89 Noah Albrecht
❑ 90 Pat Presley
❑ 91 Patrick Hamill
❑ 92 Paul Alan Ballard
❑ 93 Paul Gutierrez
❑ 94 Randy Bantog
❑ 95 Rich Molinelli
❑ 96 Rich Woodall
❑ 97 Rob Teranishi
❑ 98 Russel G. Chong
❑ 99 Sergio Paez
❑ 100 Shelli Paroline
❑ 101 Spencer Brinkerhoff
❑ 102 Stephanie Yue
❑ 103 Steven Oatney
❑ 104 Steward Lee
❑ 105 Thang Le
❑ 106 Tod Smith
❑ 107 Tom Hodges
❑ 108 Wayne Lo
❑ 109 William O'Neill
❑ 110 Zack Giallongo

2009 Star Wars Clone Wars Widevision

COMPLETE SET (80) 5.00 12.00

❑ 1 The Clone Wars: Season One .15 .40
❑ 2 Summit on Rugosa .15 .40
❑ 3 Yoda's Strategy .15 .40
❑ 4 Introspection in the Cave .15 .40
❑ 5 Yoda's Victory .15 .40
❑ 6 A New Galactic Threat .15 .40
❑ 7 Hunting Survivors .15 .40
❑ 8 Out of the Storm .15 .40
❑ 9 Weapon of Malevolence .15 .40
❑ 10 Target: Malevolence .15 .40
❑ 11 Attacking Malevolence .15 .40
❑ 12 Pawn of Malevolence .15 .40
❑ 13 Jedi Conference .15 .40
❑ 14 Fate of Malevolence .15 .40
❑ 15 Rescue on Malevolence .15 .40
❑ 16 Day of the Rookies .15 .40
❑ 17 Tension on Rishi's Moon .15 .40
❑ 18 Destroy the Outpost .15 .40
❑ 19 The Republic Swoops in .15 .40
❑ 20 Skywalker's Trap .15 .40
❑ 21 Rescuing Artoo .15 .40
❑ 22 Anakin's Master Evasion .15 .40
❑ 23 Target: Skytop Station .15 .40
❑ 24 Jedi Free Fall .15 .40
❑ 25 Grievous' Cantankerous Ally .15 .40
❑ 26 Ahsoka's Deadly Duel .15 .40
❑ 27 Padmé's New Peril .15 .40
❑ 28 Battle Droids Attack .15 .40
❑ 29 Binks to the Rescue .15 .40
❑ 30 A Liability Named Nute .15 .40
❑ 31 Gunray Prison Break .15 .40
❑ 32 Enemies on All Sides .15 .40
❑ 33 Jedi Showdown .15 .40
❑ 34 An Unexpected Discovery .15 .40
❑ 35 The Testing of Grievous .15 .40
❑ 36 The Rules of War .15 .40
❑ 37 In Search of Dooku .15 .40
❑ 38 Peril of the Pirates .15 .40
❑ 39 A Visit to Dooku .15 .40
❑ 40 Betrayl is Imminant .15 .40
❑ 41 An Awkward Truce .15 .40
❑ 42 Weequay Pirates .15 .40
❑ 43 An Unexpected Strategy .15 .40
❑ 44 The Rescue of Secura .15 .40
❑ 45 Crack-Up on Maridun .15 .40
❑ 46 Is it Right to Fight .15 .40
❑ 47 In the Care of Wag Too .15 .40
❑ 48 In Defense of the Lurmen .15 .40
❑ 49 Wave of Death .15 .40
❑ 50 Whose Pantora is it .15 .40
❑ 51 Enter the Talz .15 .40
❑ 52 An Avoidable Conflict .15 .40
❑ 53 The Challenge of Peace .15 .40
❑ 54 An Enemy Among Us .15 .40
❑ 55 The Informer .15 .40
❑ 56 Asajj's Breakout Escape .15 .40
❑ 57 The Hidden Enemy .15 .40
❑ 58 Shaak Herding .15 .40
❑ 59 A very Quick Capture .15 .40
❑ 60 Derailing a Mad Doctor .15 .40
❑ 61 Dr. Vindi Fires Away .15 .40
❑ 62 Clones in the Bomb Room .15 .40
❑ 63 Seeking the Reeksa Root .15 .40
❑ 64 Jaybo Bids Farewell .15 .40
❑ 65 Ahsoka's Big Mistake .15 .40
❑ 66 Anakin's Stern Guidance .15 .40
❑ 67 Ahsoka Strikes Back .15 .40
❑ 68 Ryloth Imprisoned .15 .40
❑ 69 The Living Shield .15 .40
❑ 70 Gutkurr Attack .15 .40
❑ 71 Victory for Ghost Company .15 .40
❑ 72 An Unexpected Ally .15 .40
❑ 73 Cham's Great Fear .15 .40
❑ 74 The Bridge to Lessu .15 .40
❑ 75 Holding Tambor at Bay .15 .40
❑ 76 Attack on the Senate .15 .40
❑ 77 Trapped by a Bounty Hunter .15 .40
❑ 78 Attack on Anakin .15 .40
❑ 79 Hostage Crisis .15 .40
❑ 80 Checklist .15 .40

2009 Star Wars Clone Wars Widevision Silver

COMPLETE SET (80) 150.00 300.00
*SILVER: 5X TO 12X BASIC CARDS
STATED ODDS 1:17
STATED PRINT RUN 500 SER. #'d SETS

2009 Star Wars Clone Wars Widevision Gold

STATED ODDS 1:8222
UNPRICED GOLD PRINT RUN 1

2009 Star Wars Clone Wars Widevision Animation Cels

COMPLETE SET (10) 6.00 15.00
STATED ODDS 1:4

❑ 1 Threepio and Jar Jar .75 2.00
❑ 2 Yoda .75 2.00
❑ 3 Kit and Nahdar .75 2.00
❑ 4 Battle Droids .75 2.00
❑ 5 Padme with Gun .75 2.00
❑ 6 Ahsoka .75 2.00
❑ 7 Clone Snowtroopers .75 2.00
❑ 8 Talz Warriors .75 2.00
❑ 9 Anakin and Obi-Wan .75 2.00
❑ 10 Anakin and Padmé kiss .75 2.00

2009 Star Wars Clone Wars Widevision Animator Sketches

STATED ODDS 1:223

❑ LE Thang Le
❑ LO Wayne Lo
❑ NG Bosco Ng
❑ TA Don Ta
❑ MIN Ken Min
❑ SZE Jackson Sze
❑ VOY Chris Voy
❑ BANT Randy Bantog
❑ BROC Tim Brock
❑ CHON Russell Chong
❑ ERMI Anthony Ermio
❑ FILO Dave Filoni
❑ LEME Davide Le Merrer
❑ MARS Darren Marshall
❑ OCON Brian Kalin O'Connell
❑ PAEZ Sergio Paez
❑ PLUN Kilian Plunkett
❑ PRES Pat Presley
❑ SLEE Stew Lee
❑ STEP Jacob Stephens
❑ TANG Le Tang
❑ VLEE Vince Lee
❑ VOLP Giancarlo Volpe

2009 Star Wars Clone Wars Widevision Artist Sketches

STATED ODDS 1:27

❑ DAY David Day
❑ YUE Stephanie Yue
❑ AHME Irma Ahmed
❑ ALCO Soni Alcorn-Hender
❑ ASHM Brian Ashmore
❑ BABB Kyle Babbitt
❑ BERG Dan Bergren
❑ BMIL Brian Miller
❑ BRIN Spencer Brinkerhoff III
❑ BUDD Dennis Budd
❑ BUEC Alex Buechel
❑ BUKA James Bukauskas
❑ CHAN Bernard Chang
❑ CHEN Chris Henderson
❑ CHER Matte Chero
❑ CHUN Justin Chung
❑ CLIN Hamilton Cline
❑ COOK Katie Cook
❑ CORR Joe Corroney
❑ DABO Jerome Dabos
❑ DAST Ted Dastick Jr.
❑ DAVI Hayden Davis
❑ DENH Brian Denham
❑ DORA Colleen Doran
❑ DOYL Kevin Doyle
❑ DURO Michael Duron (Locoduck)
❑ ECKL Darla Ecklund
❑ EDLU Nina Edlund
❑ EDWA Carolyn Edwards
❑ ENGS Brent Engstrom
❑ FALK Nicole Falk
❑ FARB Gabe Farber
❑ FARG Josh Fargher
❑ GARB Agnieszka Garbowska
❑ GERL Bruce Gerlach
❑ GIAL Zack Giallongo
❑ GLAS Kate Glasheen
❑ GOUL Grant Gould
❑ GRAH Kevin Graham
❑ HARD Ingrid Hardy
❑ HICK Jess Hickman
❑ HODG Tom Hodges
❑ HUGH Jason Hughes
❑ JMIN Jake Minor
❑ JONE Ben Curtis Jones
❑ JSNE Jamie Snell
❑ KELL Danny Kelly
❑ KOHS Lee Kohse
❑ KRAJ Karen Krajenbrink
❑ KYLE Jim Kyle
❑ LAMB Braden Lamb
❑ LIEL Kevin Liell
❑ LMAR Laura Martin
❑ LSNE Lawrence Snelly
❑ MAEL Erik Maell
❑ MANG Leah Mangue
❑ MCHA Mark McHaley
❑ MESA Lord Mesa
❑ MMIN Matt Minor
❑ MOLI Rich Molinelli
❑ MOOR Monte Moore
❑ MORR Jon Morris
❑ MORT Bryan Morton
❑ NARC Cynthia (Cummens) Narcisi
❑ NWOO Nolan Woodward
❑ OATN Steve Oatney
❑ OWEN Rhiannon Owens
❑ PARO Shelli Paroline
❑ PEDI Don Pedicini Jr.
❑ PENC Sean Pence
❑ PHIL Jason Keith Phillips
❑ PROC Tim Proctor
❑ PRON Amy Pronovost
❑ PULK Bill Pulkovski
❑ RABB David Rabbitte
❑ RADI Darin Radimaker
❑ RAMO Juan Carlos Ramos
❑ RHEN Robert Hendrickson
❑ RIVE Adrien Rivera
❑ RMAR Randy Martinez
❑ ROOD Brian Rood
❑ ROUS Craig Rousseau
❑ ROUX Stephane Roux
❑ RWOO Rich Woodall
❑ SAWY Lance Sawyer
❑ SEGU Neil Segura
❑ SHUM Howard Shum
❑ SIMM Scott D. M. Simmons
❑ SMIL Steven Miller
❑ SOBO Jason Sobol
❑ SORI Carlo Sinfuego Soriano
❑ SOUK John Soukup
❑ STAG Cat Staggs
❑ TATA Dave Pops Tata
❑ TERA Rob Teranishi
❑ TREE Jeremy Treece
❑ TSAI Francis Tsai
❑ TSMI Tod Allen Smith
❑ USMI Uko Smith
❑ VASQ Denise Vasquez
❑ VILL Frank Villarreal
❑ WALE John P. Wales
❑ WALK Russ Walks
❑ WILK Sarah Wilkinson
❑ GREEN David Green

2009 Star Wars Clone Wars Widevision Autographs

STATED ODDS 1:67

❑ AD Anthony Daniels
❑ CT Catherine Taber 12.00 30.00
❑ IA Ian Abercrombie 12.00 30.00
❑ ML Matt Lanter 8.00 20.00
❑ NF Nika Futterman 12.00 30.00
❑ TK Tom Kane 12.00 30.00
❑ DBB Dee Bradley Baker 12.00 30.00
❑ JAT James Arnold Taylor 8.00 20.00
❑ MW1 Matthew Wood 10.00 25.00
as Battle Droids
❑ MW2 Matthew Wood 10.00 25.00
as General Grievous

2009 Star Wars Clone Wars Widevision Foil Characters

COMPLETE SET (20) 15.00 40.00
STATED ODDS 1:3

❑ 1 Anakin Skywalker 1.00 2.50
❑ 2 Ahsoka Tano 1.00 2.50
❑ 3 Obi-Wan Kenobi 1.00 2.50
❑ 4 Plo Koon 1.00 2.50
❑ 5 Yoda 1.00 2.50
❑ 6 General Grievous 1.00 2.50
❑ 7 Count Dooku 1.00 2.50
❑ 8 Mace Windu 1.00 2.50
❑ 9 Padme Amidala 1.00 2.50
❑ 10 Asajj Ventress 1.00 2.50
❑ 11 C-3PO 1.00 2.50
❑ 12 R2-D2 1.00 2.50
❑ 13 Captain Rex 1.00 2.50
❑ 14 Commander Cody 1.00 2.50
❑ 15 Commander Gree 1.00 2.50
❑ 16 Commander Bly 1.00 2.50
❑ 17 Luminara Unduli 1.00 2.50
❑ 18 Kit Fisto 1.00 2.50
❑ 19 Aayla Secura 1.00 2.50
❑ 20 Palpatine 1.00 2.50
Darth Sidious

2009 Star Wars Clone Wars Widevision Motion

COMPLETE SET (5) 6.00 15.00
STATED ODDS 1:8

❑ 1 Anakin's Jedi Starfighter 1.50 4.00
❑ 2 Obi-Wan's Jedi Starfighter 1.50 4.00
❑ 3 Y-Wing Fighter 1.50 4.00
❑ 4 Ahsoka's Jedi Starfighter 1.50 4.00
❑ 5 General Grievous' Starship 1.50 4.00

2009 Star Wars Clone Wars Widevision Season Two Previews

COMPLETE SET (8) 3.00 8.00
STATED ODDS 1:2

❑ PV1 Anakin, Ahsoka and Clones .50 1.25
❑ PV2 Obi-Wan and Friend .50 1.25
❑ PV3 Mandalorian .50 1.25
❑ PV4 Clones in Battle .50 1.25
❑ PV5 Ahsoka and Changling Clawdite .50 1.25
❑ PV6 Obi-Wan and Rodian .50 1.25
❑ PV7 Obi-Wan and Mace .50 1.25
❑ PV8 Padmé and friend .50 1.25

2009 Star Wars Galaxy Series 4

COMPLETE SET (120) 5.00 12.00

❑ 1 Return to the Galaxy .15 .40
❑ 2 Luke Skywalker .15 .40
❑ 3 Leia Organa .15 .40
❑ 4 Darth Vader .15 .40
❑ 5 Obi-Wan Kenobi .15 .40
❑ 6 Han Solo .15 .40
❑ 7 Chewbacca .15 .40
❑ 8 Lando Calrissian .15 .40
❑ 9 Grand Moff Tarkin .15 .40
❑ 10 Yoda .15 .40
❑ 11 Darth Sidious Palpatine .15 .40
❑ 12 Young Obi-Wan .15 .40
❑ 13 Qui-Gon Jinn .15 .40
❑ 14 Anakin Skywalker .15 .40
❑ 15 Padme Amidala .15 .40
❑ 16 Jango Fett .15 .40
❑ 17 Mace Windu .15 .40
❑ 18 Count Dooku .15 .40
❑ 19 Adventure on Ilum .15 .40
❑ 20 Duel Against Lumiya .15 .40
❑ 21 Night of the Red Ghost .15 .40
❑ 22 The Empire on Hoth .15 .40
❑ 23 Heroes on the Move .15 .40
❑ 24 Obi-Wan, the Warrior .15 .40
❑ 25 Making a Cargo Dump .15 .40
❑ 26 Becoming Boushh .15 .40
❑ 27 Bounty Hunters Assembled .15 .40
❑ 28 Yoda on Dagobah .15 .40
❑ 29 A Padawan's Challenge .15 .40
❑ 30 Preparing the New Slave Girl .15 .40
❑ 31 Darth Vader vs. Ben Kenobi .15 .40
❑ 32 Chewbacca Menaced by Darth Maul .15 .40
❑ 33 Stormtrooper in the Field .15 .40
❑ 34 Yoda in Action .15 .40
❑ 35 Teaching the Younglings .15 .40
❑ 36 Doomed Romance .15 .40
❑ 37 Garage: Padme and Anakin .15 .40
❑ 38 Garage: Luke and Leia .15 .40
❑ 39 Call to Vengeance .15 .40
❑ 40 Conflict on Utapau .15 .40
❑ 41 Abducting a Princess .15 .40
❑ 42 An Unlikely Duo .15 .40
❑ 43 Cantina Scene .15 .40
❑ 44 Rancor and Rancor Keeper .15 .40
❑ 45 Once Allies .15 .40
❑ 46 A Well-Earned Prize .15 .40
❑ 47 Two of a Kind .15 .40
❑ 48 The Last Sunrise .15 .40
❑ 49 Episode I - The Call to Adventure .15 .40
❑ 50 Episode II - The Road of Trials .15 .40
❑ 51 Episode III - The Abyss .15 .40
❑ 52 Episode IV - Illumination .15 .40
❑ 53 Episode V - The Ultimate Prize .15 .40
❑ 54 Episode VI - The Return .15 .40
❑ 55 Episode IV Poster .15 .40
❑ 56 Episode V Poster .15 .40
❑ 57 Episode VI Poster .15 .40
❑ 58 A New Epic Begins .15 .40
❑ 59 Bring in the Clones .15 .40
❑ 60 Dark Clumination .15 .40
❑ 61 A Classic Clash .15 .40
❑ 62 Illustrating the Order .15 .40
❑ 63 Shattering Journey .15 .40
❑ 64 A Master's Master .15 .40
❑ 65 Her Name Is Mara Jade .15 .40
❑ 66 Old Friends, New Art .15 .40
❑ 67 Early Adventuring .15 .40
❑ 68 Inside the Insider .15 .40
❑ 69 Warriors of the Force .15 .40
❑ 70 The Fury of Mace Windu .15 .40
❑ 71 The Essential Leia .15 .40
❑ 72 A More-than-Worthy Foe .15 .40
❑ 73 Like Father, Like Son .15 .40
❑ 74 Sins of the Father .15 .40
❑ 75 The Dark Side .15 .40
❑ 76 General Grievous .15 .40
❑ 77 Men of Good Will .15 .40
❑ 78 From Hero to Villain .15 .40
❑ 79 Two Forces of Good .15 .40
❑ 80 The Fury of Maul .15 .40
❑ 81 The Fett Legacy .15 .40
❑ 82 Senator and the Separatist .15 .40
❑ 83 Another Battlefield .15 .40
❑ 84 In the Trenches .15 .40
❑ 85 Weapons of Warfare .15 .40
❑ 86 Old Republic, New Twists .15 .40
❑ 87 A Stark Challenge .15 .40
❑ 88 Target Black Sun .15 .40
❑ 89 Adapting Episode One .15 .40
❑ 90 The Fury of Aurra Sing .15 .40
❑ 91 Adapting Episode Two .15 .40
❑ 92 Naboo under Siege .15 .40
❑ 93 Jedi vs. Bounty Hunters .15 .40
❑ 94 Operation Purge .15 .40
❑ 95 Vader the Enforcer .15 .40
❑ 96 Classic Adventures .15 .40
❑ 97 At War with Boba Fett .15 .40
❑ 98 Palpatine's Galaxy .15 .40
❑ 99 In the Clutches of Amanin .15 .40
❑ 100 From Pilot to General .15 .40
❑ 101 Boba Fett Unleashed .15 .40
❑ 102 Romance in Deep Space .15 .40
❑ 103 The Rogue Squadron .15 .40
❑ 104 The Threat of Thrawn .15 .40
❑ 105 The Empire Rises Again .15 .40
❑ 106 Rebel Heroes Under Attack .15 .40
❑ 107 Tales of Chewbacca .15 .40
❑ 108 A Jedi No Longer .15 .40
❑ 109 Conflict in All Eras .15 .40
❑ 110 The Struggle Rages On .15 .40
❑ 111 Astonishing Power .15 .40
❑ 112 Kashyyyk Under Siege .15 .40
❑ 113 The Force Repulse .15 .40
❑ 114 Of Rancors and Banthas .15 .40
❑ 115 Aboard the Death Star .15 .40
❑ 116 Unleashing the Force .15 .40
❑ 117 Survival of Kazdan Paratus .15 .40
❑ 118 Leave No Witnesses .15 .40
❑ 119 Ultimate Power .15 .40
❑ 120 Checklist .15 .40

2009 Star Wars Galaxy Series 4 Printing Plates Black

STATED PRINT RUN 1 SER. #'d SET
UNPRICED DUE TO SCARCITY

2009 Star Wars Galaxy Series 4 Printing Plates Cyan

STATED PRINT RUN 1 SER. #'d SET
UNPRICED DUE TO SCARCITY

2009 Star Wars Galaxy Series 4 Printing Plates Magenta

COMPLETE SET (
UNPRICED DUE TO SCARCITY

2009 Star Wars Galaxy Series 4 Printing Plates Yellow

STATED PRINT RUN 1 SER. #'d SET
UNPRICED DUE TO SCARCITY

2009 Star Wars Galaxy Series 4 Autographs

STATED ODDS 1:95 HOBBY

❑ 205 Michael Allred
❑ 206 Karl Alstaetter
❑ 207 Thom Ang
❑ 209 Marshall Arisman
❑ 211 John Bolton
❑ 213 Daniel Brereton
❑ 214 Ron Brown
❑ 216 Rich Buckler
❑ 218 Amanda Conner
❑ 220 Joe DeVito
❑ 221 Colleen Doran
❑ 222 Norm Dwyer
❑ 223 Bob Fingerman
❑ 224 Hugh Fleming
❑ 226 Drew Friedman
❑ 227 Rick Geary
❑ 228 Dave Gibbons
❑ 231 Lurene Haines
❑ 232 Matt Haley
❑ 237 Jeffrey Jones
❑ 239 Miran Kim
❑ 241 Ray Lago
❑ 242 Zohar Lazar
❑ 244 Paul Lee
❑ 248 Mike Mayhew
❑ 251 Linda Medley
❑ 252 David O. Miller
❑ 253 C. Scott Morse
❑ 254 Nelson De Castro
❑ 255 Hoang Nguyen
❑ 257 Mark Pacella
❑ 258 Jimmy Palmiotti
❑ 261 Joe Phillips
❑ 262 Whilce Portacio
❑ 263 Ralph Reese
❑ 264 Zina Saunders
❑ 265 Chris Sprouse
❑ 266 Jim Starlin
❑ 267 Arthur Suydam
❑ 268 Sylvain Despretz
❑ 269 Tom Taggart
❑ 271 Tim Truman
❑ 274 Mike Zeck

2009 Star Wars Galaxy Series 4 Die-Cut Sketches

STATED ODDS 1:191 HOBBY

❑ 1 Amy Vutiya
❑ 2 Andy Heng
❑ 3 Art Denka
❑ 4 Artbot 138
❑ 5 Ayleen Gaspar
❑ 6 Brian Kong
❑ 7 Brian Slivka
❑ 8 Bryce Ward
❑ 9 Chanmen
❑ 10 Daniel Cantrell
❑ 11 Datadub
❑ 12 Fetts
❑ 13 Gargamel Katope
❑ 14 George Gaspar
❑ 15 Ghanmenu
❑ 16 Gio Chiappetta
❑ 17 Goccodo
❑ 18 Hans Yim
❑ 19 iguodo
❑ 20 Jaguar Nono
❑ 21 Jason Atomic
❑ 22 Jeff McMillan
❑ 23 Jeremy Madl
❑ 24 Jesse Moore
❑ 25 JK5
❑ 26 Justin Rudy
❑ 27 Kemilyn
❑ 28 Kerry Lee
❑ 29 L'amour Supreme
❑ 30 Luc Hudson
❑ 31 Mad Barbarian
❑ 32 Matt Doughty
❑ 33 MCA
❑ 34 McEavill
❑ 35 Michael Leavitt
❑ 36 Mishka NYC
❑ 37 Neil Winn
❑ 38 Natalie To
❑ 39 Nick the Ring
❑ 40 Nix Toxic
❑ 41 Patrick Francisco
❑ 42 Phetus
❑ 43 Rob Ames
❑ 44 Russell Walks
❑ 45 RYCA
❑ 46 Sara! Antoinette Martin
❑ 47 Simeon Lipman
❑ 48 Sket One
❑ 49 Suckadelic
❑ 50 Tulip
❑ 51 Urban Medium

2009 Star Wars Galaxy Series 4 Etched Foil

COMPLETE SET (6) 6.00 12.00
STATED ODDS 1:6

❑ 1 Anakin 1.50 4.00
Padme
❑ 2 Darth Sidious 1.50 4.00
❑ 3 Luke 1.50 4.00
Han
❑ 4 Anakin Skywalker 1.50 4.00
❑ 5 C-3PO 1.50 4.00
R2-D2
❑ 6 Leia 1.50 4.00
Vader

2009 Star Wars Galaxy Series 4 Galaxy Evolutions

COMPLETE SET (6)
STATED ODDS 1:24 RETAIL

❑ 1 Darth Vader
❑ 2 Anakin
❑ 3 Anakin
❑ 4 Anakin
❑ 5 Anakin
❑ 6 Anakin

2009 Star Wars Galaxy Series 4 Lost Galaxy

COMPLETE SET (5) 12.00 25.00
STATED ODDS 1:24
YODA'S WORLD/999 STATED ODDS 1:277
JOHN RHEAUME AUTO STATED ODDS 1:2,789

❑ 1 Under the Helmets 3.00 8.00
❑ 2 Myth Behind the Man 3.00 8.00
❑ 3 Younglings at Play 3.00 8.00
❑ 4 A Child of Destiny 3.00 8.00
❑ 5 The Jedi Slayer 3.00 8.00
❑ NNO Yoda's World/999 15.00 30.00
❑ NNOAU Yoda's World/ (signed by artist John Rheaume)

2009 Star Wars Galaxy Series 4 Promos

❑ P1A Ventress 1.50 4.00
Dooku/ (general distribution)
❑ P1B Starcruiser crash/ (Fan Club exclusive) 6.00 15.00
❑ P2 Vader .50 1.00
Padme/ (NSU exclusive)
❑ P3 Group shot/ (Wizard World 2008 exclusive)2.00 5.00

2009 Star Wars Galaxy Series 4 Silver Foil

COMPLETE SET (15) 5.00 12.00
STATED ODDS 1:3

❑ 1 Luke Skywalker .60 1.50
❑ 2 Princess Leia .60 1.50
❑ 3 Han Solo .60 1.50
❑ 4 Darth Vader .60 1.50
❑ 5 Obi-Wan Kenobi .60 1.50
❑ 6 Chewbacca .60 1.50
❑ 7 Boba Fett .60 1.50
❑ 8 Anakin Skywalker .60 1.50
❑ 9 Padme Amidala .60 1.50
❑ 10 Obi-Wan Kenobi .60 1.50
❑ 11 Qui-Gon Jinn .60 1.50
❑ 12 Yoda .60 1.50
❑ 13 Darth Maul .60 1.50
❑ 14 Darth Sidious .60 1.50
❑ 15 Boba Fett .60 1.50

2009 Star Wars Galaxy Series 4 Bronze Foil

COMPLETE SET (15) 25.00 60.00
*BRONZE: 2X TO 5X BASIC CARDS 3.00 8.00
STATED ODDS 1:24

2009 Star Wars Galaxy Series 4 Gold Foil

COMPLETE SET (15) 60.00 120.00
STATED ODDS 1:47
STATED PRINT RUN 500 SER. #'d SETS

2009 Star Wars Galaxy Series 4 Silver Foil Refractor

STATED PRINT RUN 1 SER. #'d SET
UNPRICED DUE TO SCARCITY

2009 Star Wars Galaxy Series 4 Sketches

STATED ODDS 1:24 HOBBY

❑ 1 Allison Sohn
❑ 2 Amy Pronovost
❑ 3 Art Grafunkel
❑ 4 Brent Engstrom
❑ 5 Brent Schoonover
❑ 6 Brian Kong
❑ 7 Brian Miller
❑ 8 Brian Rood
❑ 9 Bruce Gerlach
❑ 10 Bryan Morton
❑ 11 Carolyn Edwards
❑ 12 Cat Staggs
❑ 13 Chris Henderson
❑ 14 Cynthia Cummens
❑ 15 Dan Cooney
❑ 16 Daniel Bergren
❑ 17 David Rabbitte
❑ 18 Denise Vasquez
❑ 19 Dennis Budd
❑ 20 Don Pedicini Jr.
❑ 21 Doug Cowan
❑ 22 Edward Pun
❑ 23 Erik Maell
❑ 24 Gabe Hernandez
❑ 25 Grant Gould
❑ 26 Howard Shum
❑ 27 Ingrid Hardy
❑ 28 Irma Aimo Ahmed
❑ 29 Jake Minor
❑ 30 Jamie Snell
❑ 31 Jason Davies

☐ 32 Jason Hughes
☐ 33 Jason Keith Phillips
☐ 34 Jason Sobol
☐ 35 Javier Guzman
☐ 36 Jeff Carlisle
☐ 37 Jerry Vanderstelt
☐ 38 Jessica Hickman
☐ 39 Jim Kyle
☐ 40 Joanne Ellen Mutch
☐ 41 Joe Corroney
☐ 42 Joel Carroll
☐ 43 John McCrea
☐ 44 John Soukup
☐ 45 John Watkins-Chow
☐ 46 Jon Morris
☐ 47 Jon Ocampo
☐ 48 Joseph Booth
☐ 49 Josh Fargher
☐ 50 Josh Howard
☐ 51 Justin Chung
☐ 52 Justin Jusscope Orr
☐ 53 Karen Krajenbrink
☐ 54 Kate Glasheen
☐ 55 Kate Red Bradley
☐ 56 Katie Cook
☐ 57 Katie McDee
☐ 58 Ken Branch
☐ 59 Kevin Caron
☐ 60 Kevin Doyle
☐ 61 Kevin Graham
☐ 62 Kyle Babbitt
☐ 63 Lance Sawyer
☐ 64 Leah Mangue
☐ 65 Lee Kohse
☐ 66 Len Bellinger
☐ 67 Lord Mesa
☐ 68 Mark McHaley
☐ 69 Mark Walters
☐ 70 Matt Minor
☐ 71 Micheal Locoduck Duron
☐ 72 Monte Moore
☐ 73 Nate Lovett
☐ 74 Nathan E. Hamill
☐ 75 Nicole Falk
☐ 76 Nik Neocleous
☐ 77 Nina Edlund
☐ 78 Noah Albrecht
☐ 79 Otto Dieffenbach
☐ 80 Patrick Hamill
☐ 81 Patrick Richardson
☐ 82 Paul Allan Ballard
☐ 83 Paul Gutierrez
☐ 84 Pete Pachoumis
☐ 85 Randy Martinez
☐ 86 Randy Siplon
☐ 87 Rich Molinelli
☐ 88 Rich Woodall
☐ 89 Russell Walks
☐ 90 Sarah Wilkinson
☐ 91 Scott Zirkel
☐ 92 Sean Pence
☐ 93 Spencer Brinkerhoff
☐ 94 Stephanie Yue
☐ 95 Ted Dastick Jr.
☐ 96 Tod Allen Smith
☐ 97 Tom Hodges
☐ 98 Zack Giallongo

2009 Star Wars Galaxy Series 4 Sketches Retail Red

STATED ODDS 1:48 RETAIL

☐ 1 Brent Engstrom
☐ 2 Brent Schoonover
☐ 3 Brian Kong
☐ 4 Brian Miller
☐ 5 Brian Rood
☐ 6 Bryan Morton
☐ 7 Cat Staggs
☐ 8 Chris Henderson
☐ 9 Dan Cooney
☐ 10 David Rabbitte
☐ 11 Don Pedicini Jr.
☐ 12 Gabe Hernandez
☐ 13 Grant Gould
☐ 14 Howard Shum
☐ 15 Ingrid Hardy
☐ 16 Jamie Snell
☐ 17 Jason Davies
☐ 18 Jason Keith Phillips
☐ 19 Jason Sobol
☐ 20 Javier Guzman
☐ 21 Jessica Hickman
☐ 22 Jim Kyle
☐ 23 John McCrea
☐ 24 Jon Morris
☐ 25 Karen Krajenbrink
☐ 26 Kate Glasheen
☐ 27 Katie McDee
☐ 28 Kevin Doyle
☐ 29 Kevin Graham
☐ 30 Leah Mangue
☐ 31 Lee Kohse
☐ 32 Matt Minor
☐ 33 Nicole Falk
☐ 34 Paul Allan Ballard
☐ 35 Paul Gutierrez
☐ 36 Randy Martinez
☐ 37 Rich Molinelli
☐ 38 Rich Woodall
☐ 39 Russell Walks
☐ 40 Sarah Wilkinson
☐ 41 Sean Pence
☐ 42 Ted Dastick Jr.
☐ 43 Tom Hodges

2010 Star Wars Clone Wars Rise of the Bounty Hunters

COMPLETE SET (90) 4.00 10.00

☐ 1 The Clone Wars: Season 2 .10 .30
☐ 2 Plo Koon in Space .10 .30
☐ 3 Bane's Bold Move .10 .30
☐ 4 Stealing Their Secrets .10 .30
☐ 5 Cato Apprehended .10 .30
☐ 6 The Torture of Bolla .10 .30
☐ 7 Courageous Assault .10 .30
☐ 8 The Power of Rex .10 .30
☐ 9 The Stolen Holocron .10 .30
☐ 10 Battle Scars .10 .30
☐ 11 Abduction of the Innocent .10 .30
☐ 12 The Young Adept .10 .30
☐ 13 Springing the Trap! .10 .30
☐ 14 Padme's Plan .10 .30
☐ 15 Lover of Enemy .10 .30
☐ 16 An Old Enemy .10 .30
☐ 17 In the Arms of Clovis .10 .30
☐ 18 Poggle the Lesser .10 .30
☐ 19 Return to Geonosis .10 .30
☐ 20 An Improvised Attack .10 .30
☐ 21 Dealing in Fire .10 .30
☐ 22 Surveying the Battle .10 .30
☐ 23 The Master's Assault .10 .30
☐ 24 A Fateful Decision .10 .30
☐ 25 Master and Apprentice .10 .30
☐ 26 A Grim Report .10 .30
☐ 27 A Monstrous Surprise .10 .30
☐ 28 The Worm Turns .10 .30
☐ 29 Poggle's Prisoner .10 .30
☐ 30 Brain Invaders .10 .30
☐ 31 Night of the Undead .10 .30
☐ 32 The Mind Benders .10 .30
☐ 33 Barriss' Transformation .10 .30
☐ 34 Grievous' Attack .10 .30
☐ 35 To Rescue a Jedi .10 .30
☐ 36 Surrounded .10 .30
☐ 37 Another Grievous Battle .10 .30
☐ 38 Grievous' Cruelty .10 .30
☐ 39 A Warm Welcome .10 .30
☐ 40 Jedi Assault .10 .30
☐ 41 A Clone in Defense .10 .30
☐ 42 Starting the Search .10 .30
☐ 43 A Desperate Padawan .10 .30
☐ 44 To Catch a Thief .10 .30
☐ 45 A Thief's Cowardice .10 .30
☐ 46 The Mandalore Plot .10 .30
☐ 47 A Deceptive Duchess .10 .30
☐ 48 Conspiracy on Concordia .10 .30
☐ 49 Behold: The Darksaber .10 .30
☐ 50 A Fruitless Search .10 .30
☐ 51 Of Passion and Peril .10 .30
☐ 52 A Traitor Among Them .10 .30
☐ 53 A Safe Arrival .10 .30
☐ 54 Duchess of Mandalore .10 .30
☐ 55 The Duchess Framed .10 .30
☐ 56 Satine's Desparation .10 .30
☐ 57 Jedi vs. Mandalorian .10 .30
☐ 58 Padme's Plea .10 .30
☐ 59 Padme's Investigation .10 .30
☐ 60 The Invisible Enemy .10 .30
☐ 61 Funeral for a Friend .10 .30
☐ 62 Admiral Trench .10 .30
☐ 63 New Weapon, Old Foe .10 .30
☐ 64 The Fall of Trench .10 .30
☐ 65 The Invincible's End .10 .30
☐ 66 The World of Felucia .10 .30
☐ 67 Unexpected Protectors .10 .30
☐ 68 Pirate Attack .10 .30
☐ 69 Freeing the Farm .10 .30
☐ 70 The Dug Dilemma .10 .30
☐ 71 After the Bomb .10 .30
☐ 72 Monster from the Past .10 .30
☐ 73 Battling the Beast .10 .30
☐ 74 The Great Escape .10 .30
☐ 75 The Behemoth Walks .10 .30
☐ 76 Creature of Destruction .10 .30
☐ 77 The Professor Flees .10 .30
☐ 78 Here's Lucky .10 .30
☐ 79 The Mysterious Newbie .10 .30
☐ 80 Fett's Daring Assault .10 .30
☐ 81 A Dark Fate .10 .30
☐ 82 Gandark Patrol .10 .30
☐ 83 Boxed-In by Boba .10 .30
☐ 84 Friends or Foes .10 .30
☐ 85 A Jedi Rescue .10 .30
☐ 86 Boba's Challenge .10 .30
☐ 87 Slave 1 .10 .30
☐ 88 An Unusual Success .10 .30
☐ 89 Aurra Sing Caught .10 .30
☐ 90 Checklist .10 .30

2010 Star Wars Clone Wars Rise of the Bounty Hunters Silver

COMPLETE SET (90)
STATED PRINT RUN 100 SER. #'d SETS

2010 Star Wars Clone Wars Rise of the Bounty Hunters Gold

STATED PRINT RUN 1 SER. #'d SET
UNPRICED DUE TO SCARCITY

2010 Star Wars Clone Wars Rise of the Bounty Hunters Animator Sketches

STATED ODDS 1:335

☐ 1 Brian Kalin O'Connell 40.00 80.00
☐ 2 Chris Glenn 60.00 120.00
☐ 3 Juan Hernandez 30.00 60.00
☐ 4 Ken Min 60.00 120.00
☐ 5 Polina Hristova 20.00 40.00
☐ 6 Will Nichols 20.00 40.00

2010 Star Wars Clone Wars Rise of the Bounty Hunters Cels Red

COMPLETE SET (5) 8.00 20.00
STATED ODDS

☐ 1 Obi-Wan and Cad Bane 3.00 8.00
☐ 2 Ahsoka and Anakin 3.00 8.00
☐ 3 A Great Deception 3.00 8.00
☐ 4 Death Watch 3.00 8.00
☐ 5 Aurra Sing 3.00 8.00

2010 Star Wars Clone Wars Rise of the Bounty Hunters Cels Yellow

COMPLETE SET (5)
STATED ODDS

☐ 1 Satine and Obi-Wan
☐ 2 Ahsoka Tano
☐ 3 Commander Cody
☐ 4 Kit and Anakin
☐ 5 Eeth Koth

2010 Star Wars Clone Wars Rise of the Bounty Hunters Foil

COMPLETE SET (20) 8.00 20.00
STATED ODDS 1:3

☐ 1 Anakin Skywalker .60 1.50
☐ 2 Ahsoka Tano .60 1.50
☐ 3 Obi-Wan Kenobi .60 1.50
☐ 4 Plo Koon .60 1.50
☐ 5 Yoda .60 1.50
☐ 6 General Grievous .60 1.50
☐ 7 Ki-Adi-Mundi .60 1.50
☐ 8 Mace Windu .60 1.50
☐ 9 Padme Amidala .60 1.50
☐ 10 Cad Bane .60 1.50
☐ 11 Aurra Sing .60 1.50
☐ 12 Bossk .60 1.50
☐ 13 Captain Rex .60 1.50
☐ 14 Commander Cody .60 1.50
☐ 15 Boba Fett .60 1.50
☐ 16 Pre Vizsla .60 1.50
☐ 17 Luminara Unduli .60 1.50
☐ 18 C-3PO and R2-D2 .60 1.50
☐ 19 Bariss Offee .60 1.50
☐ 20 Satine Kryze .60 1.50

2010 Star Wars Clone Wars Rise of the Bounty Hunters Motion

COMPLETE SET (5) 6.00 15.00
STATED ODDS 1:6

☐ 1 Pre Vizsla 1.50 4.00
☐ 2 Pre Vizsla 2 1.50 4.00
☐ 3 Obi-Wan Kenobi 1.50 4.00
☐ 4 Anakin and Hondo 1.50 4.00
☐ 5 Ahsoka and Barriss 1.50 4.00

2010 Star Wars Clone Wars Rise of the Bounty Hunters Sketches

STATED ODDS 1:24 HOBBY, 1:48 RETAIL

☐ 1 Adrien Rivera
☐ 2 Alex Buechel
☐ 3 Amy Pronovost
☐ 4 Beck Kramer
☐ 5 Bill Pulkovski
☐ 6 Bob Stevlic
☐ 7 Braden Lamb
☐ 8 Brent Engstrom
☐ 9 Brian Miller
☐ 10 Brian Rood
☐ 11 Bruce Gerlach
☐ 12 Cal Slayton
☐ 13 Cat Staggs
☐ 14 Dan Bergren
☐ 15 Dan Masso
☐ 16 David Day
☐ 17 David Rabbitte
☐ 18 Denise Vasquez
☐ 19 Don Pedicini Jr
☐ 20 Doug Cowan
☐ 21 Gabe Farber
☐ 22 Gary Kezele
☐ 23 Geoff Munn
☐ 24 George Davis
☐ 25 Grant Gould
☐ 26 Hayden Davis
☐ 27 Howard Shum
☐ 28 Ingrid Hardy
☐ 29 Irma Ahmed
☐ 30 Jamie Snell
☐ 31 Jason Hughes
☐ 32 Jason Keith Philips
☐ 33 Jason Sobol
☐ 34 Jeff Confer
☐ 35 Jeremy Treece
☐ 36 Jerry Gaylord
☐ 37 Jessica Hickman
☐ 38 Jim Kyle
☐ 39 John Beatty
☐ 40 John P. Wales
☐ 41 John Soukup
☐ 42 Jon Morris
☐ 43 Juan Carlos Ramos
☐ 44 Katie Cook
☐ 45 Kevin Doyle
☐ 46 Kevin Graham
☐ 47 Kevin Liell
☐ 48 Lance Sawyer
☐ 49 Lawrence Snelly
☐ 50 Lee Kohse
☐ 51 M. Jason Reed
☐ 52 Mark Slater
☐ 53 Martheus Wade
☐ 54 Matt Minor
☐ 55 Michael Duron
☐ 56 Nolan Woodward
☐ 57 Otis Frampton
☐ 58 Patrick Richardson
☐ 59 Randy Martinez
☐ 60 Rhiannon Owens
☐ 61 Rich Molinelli
☐ 62 Robert Teranishi
☐ 63 Ryan Hungerford
☐ 64 Sarah Wilkinson
☐ 65 Scott Zambelli
☐ 66 Shea Standefer
☐ 67 Shelli Paroline
☐ 68 Spencer Brinkerhoff
☐ 69 Stephanie Yue
☐ 70 Steve Oatney
☐ 71 Tim Proctor
☐ 72 Tod Allen Smith
☐ 73 Tom Hodges
☐ 74 Zack Giallongo

2010 Star Wars The Empire Strikes Back 3D

COMPLETE SET (48) 10.00 25.00

☐ 1 Peril of the Probot .40 1.00
☐ 2 Wampa of the Prowl .40 1.00
☐ 3 Will Han go Solo? .40 1.00
☐ 4 Wrong Answer Princess .40 1.00
☐ 5 Is Luke Lost Forever .40 1.00
☐ 6 The Force is With Him .40 1.00
☐ 7 A Friend in Need .40 1.00
☐ 8 Back from the Brink .40 1.00
☐ 9 Finding Rebels .40 1.00
☐ 10 Preparing for Battle .40 1.00
☐ 11 Luke Speeds into Danger .40 1.00
☐ 12 March of the Walkers .40 1.00
☐ 13 Target:Power Generators .40 1.00
☐ 14 Han's Escape Plan .40 1.00
☐ 15 Vader Invades! .40 1.00
☐ 16 Persuing the Falcon .40 1.00
☐ 17 Asteroids Dead Ahead .40 1.00
☐ 18 The Artful Dodgers .40 1.00
☐ 19 Mysteries of Dagobah .40 1.00
☐ 20 Hunters and the Hunted .40 1.00
☐ 21 Judge Him Not by His Size .40 1.00
☐ 22 An Inconvienent Update .40 1.00
☐ 23 Escaping the Space Slug .40 1.00
☐ 24 Face Behind the Mask .40 1.00
☐ 25 Vader's Bounty Trackers .40 1.00
☐ 26 There is no try .40 1.00
☐ 27 Master of the Force .40 1.00
☐ 28 Scanned by Boba Fett .40 1.00
☐ 29 Having His Ups and Downs .40 1.00
☐ 30 Arrival on Bespin .40 1.00
☐ 31 Magnificent Cloud City .40 1.00
☐ 32 An Unexpected Welcome .40 1.00
☐ 33 Lando's Betrayal .40 1.00
☐ 34 Solo's Ordeal .40 1.00
☐ 35 The Carbon Freeze Chamber .40 1.00
☐ 36 She Loves Him and He Knows It .40 1.00
☐ 37 Barely Alive .40 1.00
☐ 38 To Save His Friends .40 1.00
☐ 39 Opposers Face to Face .40 1.00
☐ 40 Dual at Bespin .40 1.00
☐ 41 Turning the Tables .40 1.00
☐ 42 In Persuit of Vader .40 1.00
☐ 43 The Cloud City Imperiled .40 1.00
☐ 44 Tempted by the Dark Lord .40 1.00
☐ 45 Ben! Why Didn't You Tell Me .40 1.00
☐ 46 Plans for His Son .40 1.00
☐ 47 Stop Wasting Time, Artoo .40 1.00
☐ 48 Toward Tatooine .40 1.00
☐ P1 Luke Skywalker PROMO 8.00 20.00

2010 Star Wars The Empire Strikes Back 3D Autographs

STATED ODDS 1:1,055

☐ 1 Irvin Kershner 250.00 400.00
☐ 2 Ralph McQuarrie 500.00 800.00
☐ 3 Peter Mayhew 200.00 350.00
☐ 4 David Prowse 500.00 800.00
☐ 5 Kenny Baker 200.00 350.00
☐ 6 Carrie Fisher 500.00 800.00
☐ 7 Jeremy Bulloch 150.00 300.00
☐ 8 Mark Hamill 400.00 600.00

2010 Star Wars The Empire Strikes Back 3D Sketches

STATED ODDS 1:24 H, 1:72 R

☐ 1 Irma Ahmed 20.00 50.00
☐ 2 Soni Alcorn-Hender 150.00 250.00
☐ 3 Alex Alderete
☐ 4 Brian Ashmore
☐ 5 John Beatty 15.00 40.00
☐ 6 Dan Bergren 20.00 50.00
☐ 7 Dennis Budd 10.00 25.00
☐ 8 Alex Buechel 25.00 60.00
☐ 9 Jeff Confer
☐ 10 Katie Cook 300.00 500.00
☐ 11 Joe Corroney 200.00 350.00
☐ 12 Cynthia Cummens Narcisi 15.00 40.00
☐ 13 Dan Curto 25.00 60.00
☐ 14 Scott Daly 20.00 50.00
☐ 15 Ted Dastick 25.00 60.00
☐ 16 Jason Davies
☐ 17 Hayden Davis 30.00 80.00
☐ 18 David Day 25.00 60.00
☐ 19 Mark Dos Santos 40.00 100.00
☐ 20 Michael Duron 25.00 60.00
☐ 21 Jan Duursema 20.00 50.00
☐ 22 Carolyn Edwards 40.00 100.00
☐ 23 Chris Eliopoulos 50.00 120.00
☐ 24 Brent Engstrom 40.00 100.00
☐ 25 Gabe Farber 40.00 100.00
☐ 26 Bruce Gerlach 12.00 30.00
☐ 27 Zack Giallongo 10.00 25.00
☐ 28 Kevin Graham 30.00 80.00
☐ 29 Ingrid Hardy 30.00 80.00
☐ 30 John Haun 100.00 200.00
☐ 31 Chris Henderson 40.00 100.00
☐ 32 Robert Hendrickson 40.00 100.00
☐ 33 Jessica Hickman
☐ 34 Tom Hodges
☐ 35 Chris Houghton 20.00 50.00
☐ 36 Jason Hughes 10.00 25.00
☐ 37 Ryan Hungerford 25.00 60.00
☐ 38 Ben Curtis Jones
☐ 39 Brandon Kenney 30.00 80.00
☐ 40 Lee Kohse 30.00 80.00
☐ 41 Karen Krajenbrink
☐ 42 Beck Kramer 30.00 80.00
☐ 43 Jim Kyle
☐ 44 Braden Lamb 12.00 30.00
☐ 45 Kevin Liell 30.00 80.00
☐ 46 Erik Maell 50.00 120.00
☐ 47 Leah Mangue
☐ 48 Randy Martinez 25.00 60.00
☐ 49 Dan Masso
☐ 50 Clay McCormack 25.00 60.00
☐ 51 John McCrea 20.00 50.00
☐ 52 Katie McDee 15.00 40.00
☐ 53 Jen Mercer
☐ 54 Lord Mesa 30.00 80.00
☐ 55 Steven Miller 25.00 60.00
☐ 56 Jake Minor 20.00 50.00
☐ 57 Matt Minor 15.00 40.00
☐ 58 Rich Molinelli
☐ 59 Monte Moore 15.00 40.00
☐ 60 Jon Morris 20.00 50.00
☐ 61 Bryan Morton 50.00 120.00
☐ 62 Steve Oatney 15.00 40.00
☐ 63 Matt Olson
☐ 64 Rhiannon Owens 30.00 80.00
☐ 65 Shelli Paroline 10.00 25.00
☐ 66 Sean Pence
☐ 67 Lauren Perry 25.00 60.00
☐ 68 Jason Keith Phillips 25.00 60.00
☐ 69 Tim Proctor
☐ 70 Bill Pulkovski
☐ 71 Mark Raats 40.00 100.00
☐ 72 David Rabbitte
☐ 73 Darrin Radimaker 10.00 25.00
☐ 74 Juan Carlos Ramos 12.00 30.00
☐ 75 Adrian Rivera 20.00 50.00
☐ 76 Brian Rood 15.00 40.00
☐ 77 Scott Rorie
☐ 78 Lance Sawyer 12.00 30.00
☐ 79 Howard Shum 10.00 25.00
☐ 80 Cassandra Siemon 20.00 50.00
☐ 81 Scott DM Simmons
☐ 82 Cal Slayton 30.00 80.00
☐ 83 Tod Allen Smith 25.00 60.00
☐ 84 Jamie Snell 25.00 60.00
☐ 85 Lawrence Snelly 10.00 25.00
☐ 86 Jason Sobol 15.00 40.00
☐ 87 John Soukup 40.00 100.00
☐ 88 Cat Staggs
☐ 89 Shea Standefer
☐ 90 Steve Stanley 60.00 150.00
☐ 91 Tomoko Taniguchi 30.00 80.00
☐ 92 Robert Teranishi 20.00 50.00
☐ 93 Jeremy Treece 20.00 50.00
☐ 94 Chris Uminga 50.00 120.00
☐ 95 Jerry Vanderstelt
☐ 96 Denise Vasquez
☐ 97 Martheus Wade
☐ 98 Sarah Wilkinson 30.00 80.00
☐ 99 Rich Woodall
☐ 100 Nolan Woodard 40.00 100.00
☐ 101 Lin Workman 125.00 250.00
☐ 102 Stephanie Yue 20.00 50.00
☐ 103 Scott Zirkel 30.00 80.00
☐ 104 James Bukauskas
☐ 105 Kevin Doyle
☐ 106 Mark McHaley
☐ 107 Geoff Munn
☐ 108 John P. Wales
☐ 109 Spencer Brinkerhoff III

2010 Star Wars Galaxy Series 5

COMPLETE SET (120) 8.00 20.00

☐ 1 Star Wars Galaxy 5 .15 .40
☐ 2 The New Queen's Fitting .15 .40
☐ 3 Ewok Kong .15 .40
☐ 4 You will become a Jedi .15 .40
☐ 5 We'll take him together .15 .40
☐ 6 Battle for the Republic .15 .40
☐ 7 I have the high ground .15 .40
☐ 8 You can't win Darth .15 .40
☐ 9 One with the Force .15 .40
☐ 10 Princess Leia Organa .15 .40
☐ 11 Mara Jade .15 .40
☐ 12 Assaj Ventress .15 .40
☐ 13 Padme Amidala .15 .40
☐ 14 Dani .15 .40
☐ 15 Aayla Secura .15 .40
☐ 16 Female X-wing pilot .15 .40
☐ 17 Ahsoka Tano .15 .40
☐ 18 Republic: Unite .15 .40
☐ 19 Rebellion: Celebrate .15 .40
☐ 20 New Republic: Together .15 .40
☐ 21 Enlist Today .15 .40
☐ 22 Loose Lips .15 .40
☐ 23 Rebuild The Death Star .15 .40
☐ 24 Regrets .15 .40
☐ 25 Palpatine plays Possem .15 .40
☐ 26 Infiltrator .15 .40
☐ 27 Vader's Brutal Interrogation .15 .40
☐ 28 Assaj and Anakin .15 .40
☐ 29 Tension in the Force .15 .40
☐ 30 Han's Dective Skills .15 .40
☐ 31 Luke's Ground Assault .15 .40
☐ 32 Surveyed by the Dark Lord .15 .40
☐ 33 Wampa Breakfast .15 .40
☐ 34 Fridgid Disappearance .15 .40
☐ 35 The Battle of Hoth .15 .40
☐ 36 Sandtrooper Patrol .15 .40
☐ 37 Loser Buys .15 .40
☐ 38 Wuher's Domain .15 .40
☐ 39 Deal Gone Bad .15 .40
☐ 40 Mos Eisley Cantina .15 .40
☐ 41 Undercover Jedi .15 .40
☐ 42 Blasting Falcon .15 .40
☐ 43 Dealt in Han's Favor .15 .40
☐ 44 The Great Escape .15 .40
☐ 45 Dagobah Landing .15 .40
☐ 46 Trial by Empire .15 .40
☐ 47 Lightsaber Construction .15 .40
☐ 48 Tatooine Training .15 .40
☐ 49 Endor Chase .15 .40
☐ 50 Troopers .15 .40
☐ 51 Star Wars:1917 .15 .40
☐ 52 Star Wars: 1927 .15 .40
☐ 53 Star Wars: 1937 .15 .40
☐ 54 Star Wars: 1947 .15 .40
☐ 55 In Evil's Service .15 .40
☐ 56 Recruiting Poster .15 .40
☐ 57 Leia vs. The Empire .15 .40
☐ 58 Best of Both Worlds .15 .40
☐ 59 Born to Be Bad .15 .40
☐ 60 Fated to Suffer .15 .40
☐ 61 Heart of the Saga .15 .40
☐ 62 The Original Epic .15 .40
☐ 63 Rebel Hero #1 .15 .40
☐ 64 Wrath of Vader .15 .40
☐ 65 The Slave Princess .15 .40
☐ 66 The New Hopers .15 .40
☐ 67 Bounty Hunters .15 .40
☐ 68 Powers of the Force .15 .40
☐ 69 Han and Chewie .15 .40
☐ 70 Luke Skywalker .15 .40
☐ 71 The Evil Empire .15 .40
☐ 72 Obi-Wan Kenobi .15 .40
☐ 73 Leia and Han .15 .40
☐ 74 Anakin Skywalker .15 .40
☐ 75 Senior Jedi .15 .40
☐ 76 Galactic Underworld .15 .40
☐ 77 Clone Troopers .15 .40
☐ 78 Freedom Fighters .15 .40
☐ 79 Vive Le Jedi .15 .40
☐ 80 Comic Art of France .15 .40
☐ 81 The Incredible Drew Struzan .15 .40
☐ 82 In Persuit of Fett .15 .40
☐ 83 Red Squadron .15 .40
☐ 84 Luke's Vision .15 .40
☐ 85 Advarsaries .15 .40
☐ 86 On Tatooine .15 .40
☐ 87 Death and Life .15 .40
☐ 88 Hero to the Max .15 .40
☐ 89 Armored and Dangerous .15 .40
☐ 90 Anakin's Galaxy .15 .40
☐ 91 Leia Means Business .15 .40
☐ 92 The Jedi Beam On .15 .40
☐ 93 A Universe Expanding .15 .40
☐ 94 Mandalorian Lore .15 .40
☐ 95 Unseen McQuarrie .15 .40
☐ 96 Unseen McQuarrie .15 .40
☐ 97 Star Wars Visions 2010 .15 .40
☐ 98 Star Wars Visions 2010 .15 .40
☐ 99 Star Wars Visions 2010 .15 .40
☐ 100 The Gang's All Here .15 .40
☐ 101 A Man Called Solo .15 .40
☐ 102 The Completed Circle .15 .40
☐ 103 The Heroes of Hoth .15 .40
☐ 104 Here Comes Trouble .15 .40
☐ 105 Frozen, Encased and Alive .15 .40
☐ 106 Jabba's World .15 .40
☐ 107 Leia As We Love Her .15 .40
☐ 108 A Fateful Gamble .15 .40
☐ 109 The Invisible Threat .15 .40
☐ 110 Into the Temple .15 .40
☐ 111 Armed and Dangerous .15 .40
☐ 112 Sith Infiltration .15 .40
☐ 113 Brutal Galactic Conflict .15 .40
☐ 114 Sith Acolyte .15 .40
☐ 115 Jedi Killer .15 .40
☐ 116 In Defense of the Temple .15 .40
☐ 117 Clash of the Foils .15 .40
☐ 118 Eye to Eye .15 .40
☐ 119 Jedi Temple Attacked .15 .40
☐ 120 Checklist .15 .40

2010 Star Wars Galaxy Series 5 Printing Plates Black

OVERALL PRINTING PLATE ODDS 1:571
UNPRICED PRINT PLATE PRINT RUN 1

2010 Star Wars Galaxy Series 5 Printing Plates Cyan

OVERALL PRINTING PLATE ODDS 1:571
UNPRICED PRINT PLATE PRINT RUN 1

2010 Star Wars Galaxy Series 5 Printing Plates Magenta

OVERALL PRINTING PLATE ODDS 1:571
UNPRICED PRINT PLATE PRINT RUN 1

2010 Star Wars Galaxy Series 5 Printing Plates Yellow

OVERALL PRINTING PLATE ODDS 1:571
UNPRICED PRINT PLATE PRINT RUN 1

2010 Star Wars Galaxy Series 5 Artist Sketches

STATED ODDS 1:24 HOBBY, 1:72 RETAIL

☐ AHME Irma Ahmed 25.00 60.00
☐ ALCO Soni Alcorn-Hender 125.00 250.00
☐ BABB Kyle Babbitt
☐ BALL Paul Allan Ballard 100.00 200.00
☐ BEAT John Beatty 25.00 60.00
☐ BELL Len Bellinger 150.00 300.00
☐ BERG Dan Bergren 20.00 50.00
☐ BMIL Brian Miller 40.00 100.00
☐ BRAD Kate Bradley 50.00 120.00

❑ BRIN Spencer Brinkerhoff III 15.00 40.00
❑ BUDD Dennis Budd 10.00 25.00
❑ BUEC Alex Buechel 20.00 50.00
❑ BUKA James Bukaskas 8.00 20.00
❑ BUSC Matt Busch 15.00 40.00
❑ CHEN Chris Henderson 60.00 150.00
❑ CHER Matte Chero 20.00 50.00
❑ CHUN Justin Chung
❑ COOK Katie Cook 200.00 400.00
❑ CORR Joe Corroney 150.00 300.00
❑ DAST Ted Dastick Jr.
❑ DAY David Day 20.00 50.00
❑ DIFF Otto Diffenbach 10.00 25.00
❑ DOYL Kevin Doyle 25.00 60.00
❑ DURO Michael Duron 40.00 100.00
❑ ECKL Darla Ecklund 8.00 20.00
❑ EDLU Nina Edlund 125.00 250.00
❑ ENGS Brent Engstrom 15.00 40.00
❑ FALK Nicole Falk
❑ FARB Gabe Farber 40.00 100.00
❑ FOSG Jay Fosgitt 20.00 50.00
❑ FOUS Dustin Foust 25.00 60.00
❑ GERL Bruce Gerlach 20.00 50.00
❑ GIAL Zack Giallongo 8.00 20.00
❑ GLAS Kate Glasheen 25.00 60.00
❑ GOUL Grant Gould 15.00 40.00
❑ GRAF Art Grafunkel 25.00 60.00
❑ GRAH Kevin Graham 25.00 60.00
❑ HARD Ingrid Hardy 50.00 120.00
❑ HAUN John Haun 40.00 100.00
❑ HDAV Hayden Davis 40.00 100.00
❑ HICK Jessica Hickman 10.00 25.00
❑ HODG Tom Hodges
❑ HUNG Ryan Hungerford 25.00 60.00
❑ JDAV Jason Davies 30.00 80.00
❑ JMIN Jake Minor 30.00 80.00
❑ JONE Ben Curtis Jones 25.00 60.00
❑ JSNE Jamie Snell 25.00 60.00
❑ KENN Brandon Kenney 50.00 120.00
❑ KOHS Lee Kohse 40.00 100.00
❑ KONG Brian Kong 30.00 80.00
❑ KRAJ Karen Krajenbrink 20.00 50.00
❑ KYLE Jim Kyle 20.00 50.00
❑ LAMB Braden D. Lamb 15.00 40.00
❑ LIEL Kevin Liell 20.00 50.00
❑ LSNE Lawrence Snelly 15.00 40.00
❑ MAEL Erik Maell 40.00 100.00
❑ MANG Leah Mangue 25.00 60.00
❑ MART Randy Martinez 20.00 50.00
❑ MASS Dan Masso 40.00 100.00
❑ MCHA Mark McHaley
❑ MERC Jennifer Mercer 25.00 60.00
❑ MESA Lord Mesa 15.00 40.00
❑ MMIN Matt Minor 20.00 50.00
❑ MOLI Rich Molinelli 10.00 25.00
❑ MOOR Monte Moore 25.00 60.00
❑ MORR Jon Morris 15.00 40.00
❑ MORT Bryan Morton 20.00 50.00
❑ NARC Cynthia Narcisi
❑ NWOO Nolan Woodward
❑ OATN Steve Oatney 20.00 50.00
❑ OWEN Rhiannon Owens 40.00 100.00
❑ PARO Shelli Paroline 15.00 40.00
❑ PENC Sean Pence
❑ PHIL Jason Keith Phillips 15.00 40.00
❑ PROC Tim Proctor 50.00 120.00
❑ PRON Amy Pronovost 20.00 50.00
❑ PULK Bill Pulkovski 40.00 100.00
❑ RABB David Rabbitte 25.00 60.00
❑ RADI Darrin Radimaker 25.00 60.00
❑ RAMO Wilson Ramos Jr. 25.00 60.00
❑ RHEN Robert Hendrickson 60.00 150.00
❑ RIVE Adrien Rivera 15.00 40.00
❑ ROOD Brian Rood 20.00 50.00
❑ RORI Scott Rorie 60.00 150.00
❑ ROUS Craig Rousseau 15.00 40.00
❑ RWOO Rich Woodall 20.00 50.00
❑ SAWY Lance Sawyer 30.00 80.00
❑ SCHO Patrick Schoenmaker 100.00 200.00
❑ SHST Shea Standefer
❑ SHUM Howard Shum 8.00 20.00
❑ SIMM Scott DM Simmons 25.00 60.00
❑ SIPL Randy Siplon 60.00 120.00
❑ SMIL Steven Miller 100.00 200.00
❑ SMIT Tod Allen Smith 25.00 60.00
❑ SOBO Jason Sobol 30.00 80.00
❑ SOUK John Soukup 60.00 150.00
❑ STAG Cat Staggs 60.00 150.00
❑ STST Steve Stanley 40.00 100.00
❑ TATA Dave Tata 10.00 25.00
❑ TERA Robert Teranishi 10.00 25.00
❑ TREE Jeremy Treece 20.00 50.00
❑ UMIN Chris Uminga 40.00 100.00
❑ VAND Jerry Vanderstelt 60.00 150.00
❑ VASQ Denise Vasquez 15.00 40.00
❑ VILL Frank Villareal 10.00 25.00
❑ WADE Martheus Wade
❑ WALE John P. Wales 8.00 20.00
❑ WALK Russ Walks
❑ WALT Mark Walters 10.00 25.00
❑ WATK John Watkins-Chow 50.00 120.00
❑ WILK Sarah Wilkinson 40.00 100.00
❑ YUE Stephanie Yue 15.00 40.00
❑ ZULL Chrissie Zullo 40.00 100.00

2010 Star Wars Galaxy Series 5 Autographs

STATED ODDS 1:274 HOBBY

❑ DP David Prowse 40.00 80.00
❑ JB Jeremy Bulloch 50.00 100.00
❑ JJ James Earl Jones 75.00 150.00
❑ KB Kenny Baker 35.00 70.00
❑ MH Mark Hamill 300.00 450.00
❑ PM Peter Mayhew 35.00 70.00

2010 Star Wars Galaxy Series 5 Die-Cut Sketches

STATED ODDS 1:192 HOBBY

❑ ADAM Jason Adams
❑ APPR Appro Nation 200.00 300.00
❑ ATOM Jason Atomic 75.00 150.00
❑ AUSG Anthony Ausgang
❑ AUXP Auxpeer
❑ BANG Burt Banger 30.00 80.00
❑ BELL Len Bellinger 150.00 300.00
❑ DANG Dangeruss 50.00 120.00
❑ DAVI Collin David 40.00 100.00
❑ DEAL Jared Deal 40.00 100.00
❑ DEVI Devil Robots
❑ DUTC Angie Dutchess 75.00 150.00
❑ FLYN Brian Flynn 40.00 100.00
❑ GOTH Gothic Hangman 40.00 100.00
❑ HARI Hariken
❑ HERN Jesse Hernandez
❑ ILAN Ilanena 40.00 100.00
❑ KANO Kano 40.00 100.00
❑ KING King
❑ KOLE Adriean Koleric
❑ KOSB Kosbe 40.00 100.00
❑ LEAV Michael Leavitt 100.00 200.00
❑ LEDE Rolo Ledesma 50.00 120.00
❑ MCMU Bill McMullen 50.00 120.00
❑ MONS Buff Monster 30.00 80.00
❑ MRDE Mr. Den 25.00 60.00
❑ MURA Mio Murakami 50.00 120.00
❑ NAMI Hiroshi Namiki
❑ PLAS Plasticgod 100.00 200.00
❑ ROID Billy Roids 40.00 100.00
❑ SKUL Skull Toys 60.00 150.00
❑ SUCK Suckadelic 50.00 120.00
❑ TOUM Touma 60.00 150.00
❑ TULI Tulip 60.00 150.00
❑ UAMO Uamou
❑ WALK Russell Walks
❑ WALT Colin Walton 20.00 50.00
❑ KELLY Mike Kelly 30.00 80.00

2010 Star Wars Galaxy Series 5 Etched Foil

COMPLETE SET (6) 4.00 10.00
STATED ODDS 1:6 H/R

❑ 1 Luke 1.25 3.00
Han Solo
❑ 2 Darth Vader 1.25 3.00
Imperial Fleet
❑ 3 Yoda 1.25 3.00
Obi-Wan/R2-D2
❑ 4 Leia 1.25 3.00
Lando/Chewbacca/C-3PO
❑ 5 Luke 1.25 3.00
Darth Vader
❑ 6 Boba Fett 1.25 3.00
Bounty Hunters

2010 Star Wars Galaxy Series 5 Lost Galaxy

COMPLETE SET (5) 10.00 25.00
STATED ODDS 1:24 HOBBY

❑ 1 The Skywalker Flame 3.00 8.00
❑ 2 Coronation of Evil 3.00 8.00
❑ 3 The Rancor Keeper 3.00 8.00
❑ 4 Thrawn Tactics 3.00 8.00
❑ 5 Behind Death Star Doors 3.00 8.00

2010 Star Wars Galaxy Series 5 Manga Sketches

STATED ODDS 1:274 HOBBY

❑ AXER Axer 20.00 50.00
❑ DURA Vanessa Duran 30.00 80.00
❑ GORD Dax Gordine 25.00 60.00
❑ RAMO Wilson Ramos Jr. 25.00 60.00
❑ ROSE Jennyson Allan Borlongan Rosero (2NGAW)200.00300.00
❑ SMIT Tim Smith 25.00 60.00
❑ TANI Tomoko Taniguchi 150.00 300.00
❑ VEDD Eric Vedder 40.00 100.00

2010 Star Wars Galaxy Series 5 Silver Foil

COMPLETE SET (15) 6.00 15.00
STATED ODDS 1:3 H/R

❑ 1 Anakin Skywalker .60 1.50
❑ 2 Boba Fett .60 1.50
❑ 3 Chewbacca .60 1.50
❑ 4 Count Dooku .60 1.50
❑ 5 Darth Maul .60 1.50
❑ 6 Han Solo .60 1.50
❑ 7 Lando Calrissian .60 1.50
❑ 8 Luke Skywalker .60 1.50
❑ 9 Obi-Wan Kenobi .60 1.50
❑ 10 Padme Amidala .60 1.50
❑ 11 Emperor Palpatine .60 1.50
❑ 12 Princess Leia Organa .60 1.50
❑ 13 Qui-Gon Jinn .60 1.50
❑ 14 Darth Vader .60 1.50
❑ 15 Yoda .60 1.50

2010 Star Wars Galaxy Series 5 Bronze Foil

COMPLETE SET (15) 20.00 50.00
STATED ODDS 1:24 H/R

2010 Star Wars Galaxy Series 5 Gold Foil

COMPLETE SET (15) 100.00 200.00
STATED PRINT RUN 770 SER. #'d SETS
STATED ODDS 1:39 H/R

2010 Star Wars Galaxy Series 5 Silver Foil Refractor

STATED ODDS 1:17,488 HOBBY
UNPRICED REFRACTOR PRINT RUN 1

2011 Star Wars Galaxy Series 6

COMPLETE SET (120) 8.00 20.00

❑ 1 Star Wars Galaxy .15 .40
❑ 2 The Death of Kai Justiss .15 .40
❑ 3 A Sad Farewell .15 .40
❑ 4 The Fallen Gungan .15 .40
❑ 5 The Myrkr Forest .15 .40
❑ 6 Reflections on Endor .15 .40
❑ 7 The Dangers of Felucia .15 .40
❑ 8 The Solitary Wicket .15 .40
❑ 9 Jedi-to-Jedi Chat .15 .40
❑ 10 The Terror of Talon .15 .40
❑ 11 Spectral Witness .15 .40
❑ 12 Gamorrean Guard .15 .40
❑ 13 The Nightsister .15 .40
❑ 14 The Charge of Thrawn .15 .40
❑ 15 Offbeat Buddies .15 .40
❑ 16 In Fun and War .15 .40
❑ 17 A Job Well Done .15 .40
❑ 18 Watto the Betrayer .15 .40
❑ 19 The Darkest Lord .15 .40
❑ 20 We Come Bearing Gifts .15 .40
❑ 21 An Alternative to Hoth .15 .40
❑ 22 The Boarding Party .15 .40
❑ 23 Master and Commander .15 .40
❑ 24 Curiosity Zaps Threepio .15 .40
❑ 25 Fall of the Jedi .15 .40
❑ 26 The End of Darth Plagueis .15 .40
❑ 27 Princess of Destruction .15 .40
❑ 28 Keeping it All in the Family .15 .40
❑ 29 What a Woman .15 .40
❑ 30 Boba's Prize .15 .40
❑ 31 Darth Vader .15 .40
❑ 32 Clash of the Bounty Hunters .15 .40
❑ 33 Ahsoka Kicks Metal Butt .15 .40
❑ 34 Preparation of the Droids .15 .40
❑ 35 Journey to the Needles .15 .40
❑ 36 Secura's Grace .15 .40
❑ 37 Mostly Unsung Hero .15 .40
❑ 38 Inside a Complex Hero .15 .40
❑ 39 Rancor Ranks Best of Beasts .15 .40
❑ 40 Helmets .15 .40
❑ 41 Vigilant Watch .15 .40
❑ 42 The Memory Remains .15 .40
❑ 43 Landspeeder .15 .40
❑ 44 TIE Fighter .15 .40
❑ 45 X-Wing .15 .40
❑ 46 Daring Escape .15 .40
❑ 47 Logray's Hunt .15 .40
❑ 48 Peace and Love, Man .15 .40
❑ 49 Seeing Without Eyes .15 .40
❑ 50 Fate of a Slave Dancer .15 .40
❑ 51 The Birth of Evil .15 .40
❑ 52 Tool Time .15 .40
❑ 53 Jungle Fury .15 .40
❑ 54 The Good, the Bad, and the Imperial .15 .40
❑ 55 Who's Running This Show .15 .40
❑ 56 Cellblock Blasters .15 .40
❑ 57 Hope Springs Eternal .15 .40
❑ 58 Revenge and Retribution .15 .40
❑ 59 Destroy the Death .15 .40
❑ 60 The Hard Sell .15 .40
❑ 61 Brotherhood of the Blade .15 .40
❑ 62 In the Beginning .15 .40
❑ 63 A Long Time Ago .15 .40
❑ 64 In a Galaxy Far, Far Away .15 .40
❑ 65 No Shields, No Guts .15 .40
❑ 66 The Dagobah Scene .15 .40
❑ 67 Scrap Yard Power Droid .15 .40
❑ 68 Face of a Raider .15 .40
❑ 69 Salacious Attacks .15 .40
❑ 70 On Dewback Patrol .15 .40
❑ 71 Soul of the Galaxy .15 .40
❑ 72 Encounter on Dagobah .15 .40
❑ 73 Bounty Acquired .15 .40
❑ 74 Master vs. Pupil .15 .40
❑ 75 In-Your-Face Wookiee .15 .40
❑ 76 Red Squadron Assembled .15 .40
❑ 77 Secret Lord of Dagobah .15 .40
❑ 78 Unhappy New Arrival .15 .40
❑ 79 Sandtrooper Plus .15 .40
❑ 80 Hidden Horrors of Hoth .15 .40
❑ 81 Reunion on Endor .15 .40
❑ 82 Dual Saber Showdown .15 .40
❑ 83 The Secret Apprentice .15 .40
❑ 84 Confronting Yoda .15 .40
❑ 85 Gripped by Force Lightning .15 .40
❑ 86 Unleashing the Force .15 .40
❑ 87 Starkiller's Challenge .15 .40
❑ 88 Rescue at Bespin .15 .40
❑ 89 Face of a Jedi Master .15 .40
❑ 90 Anakin's Universe .15 .40
❑ 91 Daring Aerial Raid .15 .40
❑ 92 The Darkest Shadows .15 .40
❑ 93 The Weak-Minded .15 .40
❑ 94 Lightsaber Wielders .15 .40
❑ 95 A Wookiee's World .15 .40
❑ 96 At War with the Empire .15 .40
❑ 97 Hardware in Space .15 .40
❑ 98 Let the Games Begin .15 .40
❑ 99 To Rescue a Princess .15 .40
❑ 100 Sith Vixen .15 .40
❑ 101 Rampage of the Walkers .15 .40
❑ 102 Ackbar's Plan of Attack .15 .40
❑ 103 Two For the High Road .15 .40
❑ 104 Can Solo be Saved .15 .40
❑ 105 Can Vader be Stopped .15 .40
❑ 106 Will Fett be Thwarted .15 .40
❑ 107 A Jedi in Jabba's Court .15 .40
❑ 108 The Reluctant Farmboy .15 .40
❑ 109 The Challenge of Darth Maul .15 .40
❑ 110 Podrace Pandemonium .15 .40
❑ 111 To Serve and Protect .15 .40
❑ 112 Orders to Exterminate .15 .40
❑ 113 Boba and Bossk .15 .40
❑ 114 Aquatic Jedi .15 .40
❑ 115 The Darkest Apprentice .15 .40
❑ 116 Jettster at Work .15 .40
❑ 117 The Beckoning .15 .40
❑ 118 Face Behind the Mask .15 .40
❑ 119 King of the Monsters .15 .40
❑ 120 Checklist .15 .40

2011 Star Wars Galaxy Series 6 Printing Plates Black

STATED PRINT RUN 1 SER. #'d SET
UNPRICED DUE TO SCARCITY

2011 Star Wars Galaxy Series 6 Printing Plates Cyan

STATED PRINT RUN 1 SER. #'d SET
UNPRICED DUE TO SCARCITY

2011 Star Wars Galaxy Series 6 Printing Plates Magenta

STATED PRINT RUN 1 SER. #'d SET
UNPRICED DUE TO SCARCITY

2011 Star Wars Galaxy Series 6 Printing Plates Yellow

STATED PRINT RUN 1 SER. #'d SET
UNPRICED DUE TO SCARCITY

2011 Star Wars Galaxy Series 6 Animation Cel

COMPLETE SET (9) 20.00 40.00
STATED ODDS 1:4 RETAIL

❑ 1 Luke Skywalker 3.00 8.00
❑ 2 Obi-Wan 3.00 8.00
Luke
❑ 3 Darth Vader 3.00 8.00
Princess Leia
❑ 4 Stormtroopers 3.00 8.00
C-3PO
❑ 5 Stormtroopers 3.00 8.00
C-3PO
❑ 6 C-3PO 3.00 8.00
❑ 7 Darth Vader 3.00 8.00
❑ 8 R2-D2 3.00 8.00
C-3PO
❑ 9 Jawas 3.00 8.00
R2-D2

2011 Star Wars Galaxy Series 6 Etched Foil

COMPLETE SET (6) 5.00 12.00
STATED ODDS 1:6

❑ 1 Durge 1.25 3.00
Aurra Sing
❑ 2 Boba Fett 1.25 3.00
❑ 3 Zam Wessel 1.25 3.00
Jango Fett
❑ 4 Greedo/4-LOM 1.25 3.00
Bossk
❑ 5 Boushh 1.25 3.00
Zuckuss
❑ 6 Dengar 1.25 3.00
IG-88

2011 Star Wars Galaxy Series 6 Foil Silver

COMPLETE SET (10) 6.00 15.00
STATED ODDS 1:3

❑ 1 Luke Skywalker 1.00 2.50
❑ 2 Obi-Wan Kenobi 1.00 2.50
❑ 3 Darth Maul 1.00 2.50
❑ 4 Greedo 1.00 2.50
❑ 5 Han Solo 1.00 2.50
❑ 6 Boba Fett 1.00 2.50
❑ 7 Lando Calrissian 1.00 2.50
❑ 8 Princess Leia Organa 1.00 2.50
❑ 9 Boba Fett 1.00 2.50
❑ 10 Darth Vader 1.00 2.50

2011 Star Wars Galaxy Series 6 Foil Bronze

COMPLETE SET (10) 25.00 50.00
STATED ODDS 1:24

2011 Star Wars Galaxy Series 6 Foil Gold

COMPLETE SET (10) 100.00 150.00
STATED ODDS 1:49
STATED PRINT RUN 600 SER. #'d SETS

2011 Star Wars Galaxy Series 6 Foil Refractor

STATED PRINT RUN 1 SER. #'d SET
UNPRICED DUE TO SCARCITY

2011 Star Wars Galaxy Series 6 Sketchagraphs

STATED ODDS 1:135 HOBBY

❑ 1 Amy Allen
Adam Hughes
❑ 2 Amy Allen
Alex Buechel
❑ 3 Amy Allen
Allison Sohn
❑ 4 Amy Allen
Brian Rood
❑ 5 Amy Allen
Cat Staggs
❑ 6 Amy Allen
Doug Cowan
❑ 7 Amy Allen
Grant Gould
❑ 8 Amy Allen
Jamie Snell
❑ 9 Amy Allen
Jim Kyle
❑ 10 Amy Allen
John Haun
❑ 11 Amy Allen
Kevin Doyle
❑ 12 Amy Allen
Kevin Graham
❑ 13 Amy Allen
Lin Workman
❑ 14 Amy Allen
Kyle Babbitt
❑ 15 Amy Allen
Otis Frampton
❑ 16 Amy Allen
Randy Martinez
❑ 17 Amy Allen
Rich Molinelli
❑ 18 Amy Allen
Sarah Wilkinson
❑ 19 Amy Allen
Sean Pence
❑ 20 Amy Allen
Steve Stanley
❑ 21 Amy Allen
Tim Proctor
❑ 22 Amy Allen
Tom Hodges
❑ 23 Carrie Fisher
Adam Hughes
❑ 24 Carrie Fisher
Alex Buechel
❑ 25 Carrie Fisher
Allison Sohn
❑ 26 Carrie Fisher
Brian Rood
❑ 27 Carrie Fisher
Cat Staggs
❑ 28 Carrie Fisher
Doug Cowan
❑ 29 Carrie Fisher
Grant Gould
❑ 30 Carrie Fisher
Jamie Snell
❑ 31 Carrie Fisher
Jim Kyle
❑ 32 Carrie Fisher
John Haun
❑ 33 Carrie Fisher
Kevin Doyle
❑ 34 Carrie Fisher
Kevin Graham
❑ 35 Carrie Fisher
Lin Workman
❑ 36 Carrie Fisher
Kyle Babbitt
❑ 37 Carrie Fisher
Otis Frampton
❑ 38 Carrie Fisher
Randy Martinez
❑ 39 Carrie Fisher
Rich Molinelli
❑ 40 Carrie Fisher
Sarah Wilkinson
❑ 41 Carrie Fisher
Sean Pence
❑ 42 Carrie Fisher
Steve Stanley
❑ 43 Carrie Fisher
Tim Proctor
❑ 44 Carrie Fisher
Tom Hodges
❑ 45 Jake Lloyd
Adam Hughes
❑ 46 Jake Lloyd
Alex Buechel
❑ 47 Jake Lloyd
Allison Sohn
❑ 48 Jake Lloyd
Brian Rood
❑ 49 Jake Lloyd
Cat Staggs
❑ 50 Jake Lloyd
Doug Cowan
❑ 51 Jake Lloyd
Grant Gould
❑ 52 Jake Lloyd
Jamie Snell
❑ 53 Jake Lloyd
Jim Kyle
❑ 54 Jake Lloyd
John Haun
❑ 55 Jake Lloyd
Kevin Doyle
❑ 56 Jake Lloyd
Kevin Graham
❑ 57 Jake Lloyd
Lin Workman
❑ 58 Jake Lloyd
Kyle Babbitt
❑ 59 Jake Lloyd
Otis Frampton
❑ 60 Jake Lloyd
Randy Martinez
❑ 61 Jake Lloyd
Rich Molinelli
❑ 62 Jake Lloyd
Sarah Wilkinson
❑ 63 Jake Lloyd
Sean Pence
❑ 64 Jake Lloyd
Steve Stanley
❑ 65 Jake Lloyd
Tim Proctor
❑ 66 Jake Lloyd
Tom Hodges
❑ 67 John Morton
Adam Hughes
❑ 68 John Morton
Alex Buechel
❑ 69 John Morton
Allison Sohn
❑ 70 John Morton
Brian Rood
❑ 71 John Morton
Cat Staggs
❑ 72 John Morton
Doug Cowan
❑ 73 John Morton
Grant Gould
❑ 74 John Morton
Jamie Snell
❑ 75 John Morton
Jim Kyle
❑ 76 John Morton
John Haun
❑ 77 John Morton
Kevin Doyle
❑ 78 John Morton
Kevin Graham
❑ 79 John Morton
Lin Workman
❑ 80 John Morton
Kyle Babbitt
❑ 81 John Morton
Otis Frampton
❑ 82 John Morton
Randy Martinez
❑ 83 John Morton
Rich Molinelli
❑ 84 John Morton
Sarah Wilkinson
❑ 85 John Morton
Sean Pence
❑ 86 John Morton
Steve Stanley
❑ 87 John Morton
Tim Proctor
❑ 88 John Morton
Tom Hodges
❑ 89 Jon Berg
Adam Hughes
❑ 90 Jon Berg
Alex Buechel
❑ 91 Jon Berg
Allison Sohn
❑ 92 Jon Berg
Brian Rood
❑ 93 Jon Berg
Cat Staggs
❑ 94 Jon Berg
Doug Cowan
❑ 95 Jon Berg
Grant Gould
❑ 96 Jon Berg
Jamie Snell
❑ 97 Jon Berg
Jim Kyle
❑ 98 Jon Berg
John Haun
❑ 99 Jon Berg
Kevin Doyle
❑ 100 Jon Berg
Kevin Graham
❑ 101 Jon Berg
Lin Workman
❑ 102 Jon Berg
Kyle Babbitt
❑ 103 Jon Berg
Otis Frampton
❑ 104 Jon Berg
Randy Martinez
❑ 105 Jon Berg
Rich Molinelli
❑ 106 Jon Berg
Sarah Wilkinson
❑ 107 Jon Berg
Sean Pence
❑ 108 Jon Berg
Steve Stanley
❑ 109 Jon Berg
Tim Proctor
❑ 110 Jon Berg
Tom Hodges
❑ 111 Mark Hamill
Adam Hughes
❑ 112 Mark Hamill
Alex Buechel
❑ 113 Mark Hamill
Allison Sohn
❑ 114 Mark Hamill
Brian Rood
❑ 115 Mark Hamill
Cat Staggs
❑ 116 Mark Hamill
Doug Cowan
❑ 117 Mark Hamill
Grant Gould
❑ 118 Mark Hamill
Jamie Snell
❑ 119 Mark Hamill
Jim Kyle
❑ 120 Mark Hamill
John Haun
❑ 121 Mark Hamill
Kevin Doyle
❑ 122 Mark Hamill
Kevin Graham
❑ 123 Mark Hamill
Lin Workman
❑ 124 Mark Hamill
Kyle Babbitt
❑ 125 Mark Hamill
Otis Frampton
❑ 126 Mark Hamill
Randy Martinez
❑ 127 Mark Hamill
Rich Molinelli
❑ 128 Mark Hamill
Sarah Wilkinson
❑ 129 Mark Hamill
Sean Pence
❑ 130 Mark Hamill
Steve Stanley
❑ 131 Mark Hamill
Tim Proctor

❑ 132 Mark Hamill
Tom Hodges
❑ 133 Mike Quinn
Adam Hughes
❑ 134 Mike Quinn
Alex Buechel
❑ 135 Mike Quinn
Allison Sohn
❑ 136 Mike Quinn
Brian Rood
❑ 137 Mike Quinn
Cat Staggs
❑ 138 Mike Quinn
Doug Cowan
❑ 139 Mike Quinn
Grant Gould
❑ 140 Mike Quinn
Jamie Snell
❑ 141 Mike Quinn
Jim Kyle
❑ 142 Mike Quinn
John Haun
❑ 143 Mike Quinn
Kevin Doyle
❑ 144 Mike Quinn
Kevin Graham
❑ 145 Mike Quinn
Lin Workman
❑ 146 Mike Quinn
Kyle Babbitt
❑ 147 Mike Quinn
Otis Frampton
❑ 148 Mike Quinn
Randy Martinez
❑ 149 Mike Quinn
Rich Molinelli
❑ 150 Mike Quinn
Sarah Wilkinson
❑ 151 Mike Quinn
Sean Pence
❑ 152 Mike Quinn
Steve Stanley
❑ 153 Mike Quinn
Tim Proctor
❑ 154 Mike Quinn
Tom Hodges
❑ 155 Orli Shoshan
Adam Hughes
❑ 156 Orli Shoshan
Alex Buechel
❑ 157 Orli Shoshan
Allison Sohn
❑ 158 Orli Shoshan
Brian Rood
❑ 159 Orli Shoshan
Cat Staggs
❑ 160 Orli Shoshan
Doug Cowan
❑ 161 Orli Shoshan
Grant Gould
❑ 162 Orli Shoshan
Jamie Snell
❑ 163 Orli Shoshan
Jim Kyle
❑ 164 Orli Shoshan
John Haun
❑ 165 Orli Shoshan
Kevin Doyle
❑ 166 Orli Shoshan
Kevin Graham
❑ 167 Orli Shoshan
Lin Workman
❑ 168 Orli Shoshan
Kyle Babbitt
❑ 169 Orli Shoshan
Otis Frampton
❑ 170 Orli Shoshan
Randy Martinez
❑ 171 Orli Shoshan
Rich Molinelli
❑ 172 Orli Shoshan
Sarah Wilkinson
❑ 173 Orli Shoshan
Sean Pence
❑ 174 Orli Shoshan
Steve Stanley
❑ 175 Orli Shoshan
Tim Proctor
❑ 176 Orli Shoshan
Tom Hodges
❑ 177 Ray Park
Adam Hughes
❑ 178 Ray Park
Alex Buechel
❑ 179 Ray Park
Allison Sohn
❑ 180 Ray Park
Brian Rood
❑ 181 Ray Park
Cat Staggs
❑ 182 Ray Park
Doug Cowan
❑ 183 Ray Park
Grant Gould
❑ 184 Ray Park
Jamie Snell
❑ 185 Ray Park
Jim Kyle
❑ 186 Ray Park
John Haun
❑ 187 Ray Park
Kevin Doyle
❑ 188 Ray Park
Kevin Graham
❑ 189 Ray Park
Lin Workman
❑ 190 Ray Park
Kyle Babbitt
❑ 191 Ray Park
Otis Frampton
❑ 192 Ray Park
Randy Martinez
❑ 193 Ray Park
Rich Molinelli
❑ 194 Ray Park
Sarah Wilkinson
❑ 195 Ray Park
Sean Pence
❑ 196 Ray Park
Steve Stanley
❑ 197 Ray Park
Tim Proctor
❑ 198 Ray Park
Tom Hodges

2011 Star Wars Galaxy Series 6 Sketches

OVERALL SKETCH ODDS 1:24 HOBBY, 1:65 RETAIL

❑ 1 Katie Cook
❑ 2 Beck Seashols
❑ 3 Art O'Callaghan
❑ 4 Cat Staggs
❑ 5 Kevin Liell
❑ 6 Len Bellinger
❑ 7 Ryan Hungerford
❑ 8 Otis Frampton
❑ 9 Jamie Snell
❑ 10 Scott Zambelli
❑ 11 Gabe Farber
❑ 12 Steve Stanley
❑ 13 Matt Busch
❑ 14 Scott Rorie
❑ 15 Robert Hendrickson
❑ 16 Chris Henderson
❑ 17 Lin Workman
❑ 18 Tom Hodges
❑ 19 Jason Williams
❑ 20 Charles Hall
❑ 21 Jason Sobol
❑ 22 Soni Alcorn-Hender
❑ 23 Jason Keith Phillips
❑ 24 Denae Frazier
❑ 25 Shea Standefer
❑ 26 Alex Buechel
❑ 27 Sanna U
❑ 28 Sarah Wilkinson
❑ 29 M. Jason Reed
❑ 30 Rhiannon Owens
❑ 31 Michael Locoduck Duron
❑ 32 Kate Bradley
❑ 33 Don Pedicini Jr.
❑ 34 Lawrence Reynolds
❑ 35 Bob Stevlic
❑ 36 Gary Kezele
❑ 37 Amy Pronovost
❑ 38 Lord Mesa
❑ 39 Matthew Minor
❑ 40 Lee Kohse
❑ 41 David Day
❑ 42 D Douglas
❑ 43 Linzy Zorn
❑ 44 Rachel Kaiser
❑ 45 Vanessa Banky Farano
❑ 46 Manny Mederos
❑ 47 Jim Kyle
❑ 48 Eli Rutten
❑ 49 Kevin Doyle
❑ 50 Ted Dastick Jr.
❑ 51 Adrian Rivera
❑ 52 Agnes Garbowska
❑ 53 Brent Engstrom
❑ 54 Tomoko Taniguchi
❑ 55 Leah Mangue
❑ 56 David Green
❑ 57 David Rabbitte
❑ 58 Erik Maell
❑ 59 Hayden Davis
❑ 60 Jason Adams
❑ 61 Tim Proctor
❑ 62 Tod Smith
❑ 63 Stephanie Swanger
❑ 64 Monte Moore
❑ 65 Irma Ahmed
❑ 66 Kevin Graham
❑ 67 Joe Hogan
❑ 68 Jay Shimko
❑ 69 Steve Oatney
❑ 70 Shelli Paroline
❑ 71 Robert Teranishi
❑ 72 Brian Kong
❑ 73 Steve Miller
❑ 74 Jonathan D. Gordon
❑ 75 Dennis Budd
❑ 76 Bruce Gerlach
❑ 77 Nina Edlund
❑ 78 Nolan Woodard
❑ 79 Ingrid Hardy
❑ 80 Cynthia Narcisi
❑ 81 Randy Martinez
❑ 82 Rich Woodall
❑ 83 Tim Smith
❑ 84 Bryan Morton
❑ 85 Juan Carlos Ramos
❑ 86 Doug Cowan
❑ 87 Wilson Ramos Jr.
❑ 88 Dennis Hart
❑ 89 Geoff Munn
❑ 90 Mick and Matt Glebe
❑ 91 Braden D. Lamb
❑ 92 Sean Pence
❑ 93 Jessica Hickman
❑ 94 Martheus Wade
❑ 95 Bill Pulkovski
❑ 96 Dan Bergren
❑ 97 Jerry The Franchize Gaylord
❑ 98 John Haun
❑ 99 Russell Walks
❑ 100 Zack Giallongo
❑ 101 Jason Durden
❑ 102 Joe Corroney
❑ 103 Kyle Babbitt

2011 Star Wars Galaxy Series 6 Sketches Die-Cut

OVERALL SKETCH ODDS 1:24 HOBBY, 1:65 RETAIL

❑ 1 Abe Lincoln Jr.
❑ 2 Arbito
❑ 3 Aya Kakeda
❑ 4 Billy Roids
❑ 5 Brian Mead
❑ 6 Burt Banger
❑ 7 Chris Ryniak
❑ 8 Dan Bina
❑ 9 Dan Goodsell
❑ 10 Dave Savage
❑ 11 Doktor A
❑ 12 Free Humanity
❑ 13 Gothic Hangman
❑ 14 JRYU
❑ 15 Jason Atomic
❑ 16 Jermaine Rogers
❑ 17 John Spanky Stokes
❑ 18 Jon-Paul Kaiser
❑ 19 Jordana Lake
❑ 20 Julie West
❑ 21 Larz
❑ 22 Len Bellinger
❑ 23 Lorne Colon
❑ 24 Lou Pimentel
❑ 25 Luke Gibbons-Reich
❑ 26 Martin Hsu
❑ 27 Martina Secondo Russo
Frank Russo
❑ 28 Marty Hansen THEGODBEAST
❑ 29 Mike Egan
❑ 30 Mike Mendez NEMO
❑ 31 Mio Murakami
❑ 32 Nathan Hamill
❑ 33 olive47
❑ 34 Omen
❑ 35 Ritzy Periwinkle
❑ 36 Sarah Jo Marks
❑ 37 Scott Tolleson
❑ 38 Sergey Safonov
❑ 39 SHAWNIMALS
❑ 40 Stella Bouzakis
❑ 41 Steve Talkowski
❑ 42 Steven Daily
❑ 43 The Suckford
❑ 44 Tyson Bodnarchuk
❑ 45 VISE ONE
❑ 46 Wade Lageose

2011 Star Wars Galaxy Series 6 Sketches Retail Red

OVERALL RETAIL SKETCH ODDS 1:65

❑ 1 Alex Buechel
❑ 2 Bill Pulkovski
❑ 3 Chris Henderson
❑ 4 David Day
❑ 5 David Rabbitte
❑ 6 Erik Maell
❑ 7 Howard Shum
❑ 8 Jerry The Franchize Gaylord
❑ 9 John P. Wales
❑ 10 Justin Chung
❑ 11 Mark Slater
❑ 12 Michael Locoduck Duron
❑ 13 Mick and Matt Glebe
❑ 14 Rhiannon Owens
❑ 15 Scott Zambelli
❑ 16 Shea Standefer
❑ 17 Shelli Paroline
❑ 18 Stephanie Swanger
❑ 19 Wilson Ramos Jr.
❑ 20 Zack Giallongo
❑ 21 Stephanie Yue
❑ 22 Lee Bradley
❑ 23 Don Pedicini Jr.
❑ 24 Ted Dastick Jr.
❑ 25 Tim Proctor
❑ 26 Tim Smith 3
❑ 27 Tod Smith
❑ 28 Beck Seashols
❑ 29 Juan Carlos Ramos

2012 Star Wars Galactic Files

COMPLETE SET (350) 25.00 50.00

❑ 1 Star Wars Galactic Files .15 .40
❑ 2 Qui-Gon Jinn .15 .40
❑ 3 Obi-Wan Kenobi .15 .40
❑ 4 Padme Naberrie .15 .40
❑ 5 Anakin Skywalker .15 .40
❑ 6 Darth Maul .15 .40
❑ 7 Senator Palpatine .15 .40
❑ 8 Darth Sidious .15 .40
❑ 9 Rune Haako .15 .40
❑ 10 Nute Gunray .15 .40
❑ 11 Sebulba .15 .40
❑ 12 Queen Amidala .15 .40
❑ 13 Jar Jar Binks .15 .40
❑ 14 Sabe .15 .40
❑ 15 Chancellor Valorum .15 .40
❑ 16 Shmi Skywalker .15 .40
❑ 17 C-3PO .15 .40
❑ 18 R2-D2 .15 .40
❑ 19 Captain Panaka .15 .40
❑ 20 Watto .15 .40
❑ 21 Yoda .15 .40
❑ 22 Mace Windu .15 .40
❑ 23 Boss Nass .15 .40
❑ 24 Captain Tarpals .15 .40
❑ 25 Lott Dod .15 .40
❑ 26 Adi Gallia .15 .40
❑ 27 Saesee Tiin .15 .40
❑ 28 Even Piell .15 .40
❑ 29 Yarael Poof .15 .40
❑ 30 Mas Amedda .15 .40
❑ 31 Ric Olie .15 .40
❑ 32 Aurra Sing .15 .40
❑ 33 Obi-Wan Kenobi .15 .40
❑ 34 Anakin Skywalker .15 .40
❑ 35 Padme Amidala .15 .40
❑ 36 Count Dooku .15 .40
❑ 37 Yoda .15 .40
❑ 38 Mace Windu .15 .40
❑ 39 Supreme Chancellor Palpatine .15 .40
❑ 40 Jango Fett .15 .40
❑ 41 Boba Fett .15 .40
❑ 42 Zam Wesell .15 .40
❑ 43 Bail Organa .15 .40
❑ 44 Cliegg Lars .15 .40
❑ 45 Owen Lars .15 .40
❑ 46 Beru Whitesun .15 .40
❑ 47 Jar Jar Binks .15 .40
❑ 48 Dorme .15 .40
❑ 49 Corde .15 .40
❑ 50 Dexter Jettster .15 .40
❑ 51 Captain Typho .15 .40
❑ 52 C-3PO .15 .40
❑ 53 R2-D2 .15 .40
❑ 54 Taun We .15 .40
❑ 55 Lama Su .15 .40
❑ 56 Jocasta Nu .15 .40
❑ 57 Poggle the Lesser .15 .40
❑ 58 Kit Fisto .15 .40
❑ 59 Luminara Unduli .15 .40
❑ 60 Barriss Offee .15 .40
❑ 61 Sly Moore .15 .40
❑ 62 Wat Tambor .15 .40
❑ 63 San Hill .15 .40
❑ 64 Shu Mai .15 .40
❑ 65 Shaak Ti .15 .40
❑ 66 Anakin Skywalker .15 .40
❑ 67 Obi-Wan Kenobi .15 .40
❑ 68 Padme Amidala .15 .40
❑ 69 Supreme Chancellor Palpatine .15 .40
❑ 70 Mace Windu .15 .40
❑ 71 Yoda .15 .40
❑ 72 C-3PO .15 .40
❑ 73 R2-D2 .15 .40
❑ 74 General Grievous .15 .40
❑ 75 Darth Sidious .15 .40
❑ 76 Darth Vader (Jedi Purge) SP 12.00 30.00
❑ 76 Darth Vader (Sith Apprentice) .15 .40
❑ 77 Chewbacca .15 .40
❑ 78 Kit Fisto .15 .40
❑ 79 Ki-Adi-Mundi .15 .40
❑ 80 Agen Kolar .15 .40
❑ 81 Aayla Secura .15 .40
❑ 82 Plo Koon .15 .40
❑ 83 Stass Allie .15 .40
❑ 84 Commander Cody .15 .40
❑ 85 Rune Haako .15 .40
❑ 86 Nute Gunray .15 .40
❑ 87 Passel Argente .15 .40
❑ 88 Po Nudo .15 .40
❑ 89 Tion Medon .15 .40
❑ 90 Tarfful .15 .40
❑ 91 Mon Mothma .15 .40
❑ 92 Count Dooku .15 .40
❑ 93 C-3PO .15 .40
❑ 94 R2-D2 .15 .40
❑ 95 Princess Leia Organa .15 .40
❑ 96 Luke Skywalker (Farmboy) .15 .40
❑ 96 Luke Skywalker (Stormtrooper) SP 12.00 30.00
❑ 97 Han Solo .15 .40
❑ 98 Ben (Obi-Wan) Kenobi .15 .40
❑ 99 Darth Vader .15 .40
❑ 100 Grand Moff Tarkin .15 .40
❑ 101 Chewbacca .15 .40
❑ 102 Uncle Owen .15 .40
❑ 103 Aunt Beru .15 .40
❑ 104 Greedo .15 .40
❑ 105 Garindan .15 .40
❑ 106 Momaw Nadon .15 .40
❑ 107 Ponda Baba .15 .40
❑ 108 Dr. Cornelius Evazan .15 .40
❑ 109 Figran D'an .15 .40
❑ 110 BoShek .15 .40
❑ 111 Wuher .15 .40
❑ 112 Admiral Motti .15 .40
❑ 113 Chief Bast .15 .40
❑ 114 General Tagge .15 .40
❑ 115 Captain Antilles .15 .40
❑ 116 R5-D4 .15 .40
❑ 117 Jan Dodonna .15 .40
❑ 118 Wedge Antilles .15 .40
❑ 119 Biggs Darklighter .15 .40
❑ 120 Jek Porkins .15 .40
❑ 121 Garvin Dreis .15 .40
❑ 122 John D. Branon .15 .40
❑ 123 Luke Skywalker .15 .40
❑ 124 Han Solo .15 .40
❑ 125 Princess Leia Organa (Despair on Hoth) SP 12.00 30.00
❑ 125 Princess Leia Organa (Rebel Leader) .15 .40
❑ 126 Chewbacca .15 .40
❑ 127 C-3PO .15 .40
❑ 128 R2-D2 .15 .40
❑ 129 Lando Calrissian .15 .40
❑ 130 Darth Vader .15 .40
❑ 131 Boba Fett .15 .40
❑ 132 Lobot .15 .40
❑ 133 Yoda .15 .40
❑ 134 Emperor Palpatine .15 .40
❑ 135 Bossk .15 .40
❑ 136 4-LOM .15 .40
❑ 137 Dengar .15 .40
❑ 138 Zuckuss .15 .40
❑ 139 IG-88 .15 .40
❑ 140 General Veers .15 .40
❑ 141 Admiral Piett .15 .40
❑ 142 Captain Needa .15 .40
❑ 143 Admiral Ozzel .15 .40
❑ 144 General Rieekan .15 .40
❑ 145 Wedge Antilles .15 .40
❑ 146 Dak Ralter .15 .40
❑ 147 Zev Senesca .15 .40
❑ 148 Hobbie Klivian .15 .40
❑ 149 Ben (Obi-Wan) Kenobi .15 .40
❑ 150 2-1B .15 .40
❑ 151 FX-7 .15 .40
❑ 152 Toryn Farr .15 .40
❑ 153 Luke Skywalker .15 .40
❑ 154 Princess Leia Organa .15 .40
❑ 155 Han Solo .15 .40
❑ 156 Lando Calrissian .15 .40
❑ 157 Chewbacca .15 .40
❑ 158 C-3PO .15 .40
❑ 159 R2-D2 .15 .40
❑ 160 Darth Vader .15 .40
❑ 161 Emperor Palpatine .15 .40
❑ 162 Boba Fett .15 .40
❑ 163 Jabba the Hutt .15 .40
❑ 164 Bib Fortuna .15 .40
❑ 165 Moff Jerjerrod .15 .40
❑ 166 General Madine .15 .40
❑ 167 Admiral Ackbar .15 .40
❑ 168 Nien Numb .15 .40
❑ 169 Wicket W. Warrick .15 .40
❑ 170 Chief Chirpa .15 .40
❑ 171 Logray .15 .40
❑ 172 Teebo .15 .40
❑ 173 Yoda .15 .40
❑ 174 Mon Mothma .15 .40
❑ 175 Wedge Antilles .15 .40
❑ 176 Boushh .15 .40
❑ 177 Oola .15 .40
❑ 178 Ten Numb .15 .40
❑ 179 Arvel Crynyd .15 .40
❑ 180 Max Rebo .15 .40
❑ 181 Salacious B. Crumb .15 .40
❑ 182 Sy Snootles .15 .40
❑ 183 Droopy McCool .15 .40
❑ 184 Kyle Katarn .15 .40
❑ 185 Galen Marek .15 .40
❑ 186 Darth Malak .15 .40
❑ 187 Darth Revan .15 .40
❑ 188 Bastila Shan .15 .40
❑ 189 Darth Nihilus .15 .40
❑ 190 General Rahm Kota .15 .40
❑ 191 HK-47 .15 .40
❑ 192 Dash Rendar .15 .40
❑ 193 Prince Xizor .15 .40
❑ 194 Darth Malgus .15 .40
❑ 195 Maris Brood .15 .40
❑ 196 Darth Sion .15 .40
❑ 197 Proxy .15 .40
❑ 198 Jerec .15 .40
❑ 199 Darth Traya .15 .40
❑ 200 Captain Pellaeon .15 .40
❑ 201 Talon Karrde .15 .40
❑ 202 Joruus C'baoth .15 .40
❑ 203 Mara Jade .15 .40
❑ 204 Grand Admiral Thrawn .15 .40
❑ 205 Winter .15 .40
❑ 206 Darth Bane .15 .40
❑ 207 Natasi Daala .15 .40
❑ 208 Kyp Durron .15 .40
❑ 209 Exar Kun .15 .40
❑ 210 Darth Plagueis .15 .40
❑ 211 Anakin Solo .15 .40
❑ 212 Jacen Solo .15 .40
❑ 213 Jaina Solo .15 .40
❑ 214 Ben Skywalker .15 .40
❑ 215 Cade Skywalker .15 .40
❑ 216 Kir Kanos .15 .40
❑ 217 Lumiya .15 .40
❑ 218 Dark Luke Skywalker .15 .40
❑ 219 Clone Emperor .15 .40
❑ 220 Darth Talon .15 .40
❑ 221 Jaster Mereel .15 .40
❑ 222 Carnie .15 .40
❑ 223 Fixer .15 .40
❑ 224 Quinlan Vos .15 .40
❑ 225 Grand Moff Trachta .15 .40
❑ 226 Darth Krayt .15 .40
❑ 227 Darth Nihl .15 .40
❑ 228 Dellan Blue .15 .40
❑ 229 Durge .15 .40
❑ 230 Asajj Ventress .15 .40
❑ 231 Ahsoka Tano .15 .40
❑ 232 Hondo Ohnaka .15 .40
❑ 233 Captain Rex .15 .40
❑ 234 Cad Bane .15 .40
❑ 235 Pre Vizsla .15 .40
❑ 236 Savage Opress .15 .40
❑ 237 Wulff Yularen .15 .40
❑ 238 Nahdar Vebb .15 .40
❑ 239 Satine Kryze .15 .40
❑ 240 Mortis Son .15 .40
❑ 241 Republic Cruiser .15 .40
❑ 242 Naboo Royal Starship .15 .40
❑ 243 Anakin's Podracer .15 .40
❑ 244 Sebulba's Podracer .15 .40
❑ 245 Naboo Starfighter .15 .40
❑ 246 Sith Infiltrator .15 .40
❑ 247 Vulture Droid .15 .40
❑ 248 Trade Federation Battleship .15 .40
❑ 249 Naboo Cruiser .15 .40
❑ 250 Anakin's Speeder .15 .40
❑ 251 Zam's Speeder .15 .40
❑ 252 Obi-Wan's Starfighter (Delta 7) .15 .40
❑ 253 Slave 1 (Jango Fett) .15 .40
❑ 254 Republic Gunship .15 .40
❑ 255 Solar Sailer .15 .40
❑ 256 Hailfire Droid .15 .40
❑ 257 Anakin's Starfighter .15 .40
❑ 258 Obi-Wan's Starfighter (ETA-2) .15 .40
❑ 259 Separatist Cruiser .15 .40
❑ 260 AT-TE .15 .40
❑ 261 Droid Tri-Fighter .15 .40
❑ 262 ARC-170 Starfighter .15 .40
❑ 263 AT-RT .15 .40
❑ 264 AT-AP .15 .40
❑ 265 Padme's Starship .15 .40
❑ 266 Republic Attack Cruiser .15 .40
❑ 267 Tantive IV .15 .40
❑ 268 Star Destroyer .15 .40
❑ 269 Luke's Landspeeder .15 .40
❑ 270 Sandcrawler .15 .40
❑ 271 Millennium Falcon .15 .40
❑ 272 X-Wing Fighter .15 .40
❑ 273 Y-Wing Fighter .15 .40
❑ 274 TIE Fighter .15 .40
❑ 275 Darth Vader's TIE Fighter .15 .40
❑ 276 Death Star .15 .40
❑ 277 Snowspeeder .15 .40
❑ 278 AT-AT .15 .40
❑ 279 Super Star Destroyer Executor .15 .40
❑ 280 Luke's X-Wing Fighter .15 .40
❑ 281 Slave 1 (Boba Fett) .15 .40
❑ 282 TIE Bomber .15 .40
❑ 283 Twin-Pod Cloud Car .15 .40
❑ 284 Rebel Transport .15 .40
❑ 285 Medical Frigate .15 .40
❑ 286 Jabba's Sail Barge .15 .40
❑ 287 Desert Skiff .15 .40
❑ 288 Imperial Shuttle .15 .40
❑ 289 Death Star II .15 .40
❑ 290 A-Wing Fighter .15 .40
❑ 291 B-Wing Fighter .15 .40
❑ 292 AT-ST .15 .40
❑ 293 Speeder Bike .15 .40
❑ 294 TIE Interceptor .15 .40
❑ 295 Mon Calamari Cruiser .15 .40
❑ 296 Eopie .15 .40
❑ 297 Kaadu .15 .40
❑ 298 Fambaa .15 .40
❑ 299 Opee Sea Killer .15 .40
❑ 300 Acklay .15 .40
❑ 301 Reek .15 .40
❑ 302 Nexu .15 .40
❑ 303 Massiff .15 .40
❑ 304 Varactyl .15 .40
❑ 305 Tusken Raiders .15 .40
❑ 306 Jawas .15 .40
❑ 307 Dewback .15 .40
❑ 308 Bantha .15 .40
❑ 309 Dianoga .15 .40
❑ 310 Wampa .15 .40
❑ 311 Tauntaun .15 .40
❑ 312 Mynock .15 .40
❑ 313 Space Slug .15 .40
❑ 314 Rancor .15 .40
❑ 315 Sarlacc .15 .40
❑ 316 Battle Droid .15 .40
❑ 317 Droideka .15 .40
❑ 318 Gungan .15 .40
❑ 319 Naboo Palace Guard .15 .40
❑ 320 Naboo Pilot .15 .40
❑ 321 Naboo Security .15 .40
❑ 322 Clone Trooper .15 .40
❑ 323 Geonosian Soldier Drone .15 .40
❑ 324 Super Battle Droid .15 .40
❑ 325 Clone Trooper .15 .40
❑ 326 Magnaguard .15 .40
❑ 327 Clone Pilot .15 .40
❑ 328 Shock Trooper .15 .40
❑ 329 AT-RT Driver .15 .40
❑ 330 Wookiee Army .15 .40
❑ 331 Stormtrooper .15 .40
❑ 332 Rebel Fleet Trooper .15 .40
❑ 333 Sandtrooper .15 .40
❑ 334 Death Star Gunner .15 .40
❑ 335 Death Star Trooper .15 .40
❑ 336 Rebel Honor Guard .15 .40
❑ 337 TIE Fighter Pilot .15 .40
❑ 338 Snowtrooper .15 .40
❑ 339 Rebel Soldier (Hoth) .15 .40
❑ 340 Rebel Officer (Hoth) .15 .40
❑ 341 AT-AT Driver .15 .40
❑ 342 Imperial Officer .15 .40
❑ 343 Ugnaught .15 .40
❑ 344 Gamorrean Guard .15 .40
❑ 345 Scout Trooper .15 .40
❑ 346 Royal Guard .15 .40
❑ 347 Endor Rebel Trooper .15 .40
❑ 348 AT-ST Driver .15 .40
❑ 349 Skiff Guards .15 .40
❑ 350 Ewok .15 .40

2012 Star Wars Galactic Files Blue Foil

STATED PRINT RUN 350 SER. #'d SETS

2012 Star Wars Galactic Files Red Foil

STATED PRINT RUN 35 SER. #'d SETS

2012 Star Wars Galactic Files Gold Foil

STATED PRINT RUN 1 SER. #'d SET
UNPRICED DUE TO SCARCITY

2012 Star Wars Galactic Files Autographs

STATED ODDS ONE AUTO OR PATCH PER HOBBY BOX

❑ 1 Amy Allen 15.00 40.00
as Aayla Secura
❑ 2 Anthony Forrest 12.00 30.00
as Fixer
❑ 3 Bonnie Piese 12.00 30.00
as Beru Whitesun

STAR WARS

❑ 4 Carrie Fisher 300.00 500.00
❑ 5 Daniel Logan 15.00 40.00
as Boba Fett
❑ 6 Felix Silla 15.00 40.00
as Widdle Warrick
❑ 7 Harrison Ford 2500.00 4000.00
as Han Solo
❑ 8 Irvin Kershner 750.00 1250.00
❑ 9 Jake Lloyd 15.00 40.00
as Anakin Skywalker
❑ 10 James Earl Jones 200.00 400.00
as Darth Vader
❑ 11 Jeremy Bulloch 30.00 60.00
as Boba Fett
❑ 12 Mark Hamill 300.00 500.00
❑ 13 Matthew Wood 25.00 50.00
as General Grievous
❑ 14 Michonne Bourrigue 12.00 30.00
as Aurra Sing
❑ 15 Peter Mayhew 25.00 50.00
❑ 16 Ray Park 25.00 50.00
❑ 17 Richard LeParmentier 12.00 30.00
as Admiral Motti

2012 Star Wars Galactic Files Classic Lines

COMPLETE SET (10) 3.00 8.00
STATED ODDS 1:4

❑ CL1 Help Me Obi-Wan Kenobi .75 2.00
❑ CL2 I Find Your Lack of Faith Disturbing .75 2.00
❑ CL3 Do, or Do Not. There Is No Try .75 2.00
❑ CL4 I Know .75 2.00
❑ CL5 There is a Great Disturbance .75 2.00
❑ CL6 I Call This Aggressive Negotiations .75 2.00
❑ CL7 This Is Where the Fun Begins .75 2.00
❑ CL8 Uggh. So Uncivilized .75 2.00
❑ CL9 I Am a Jedi, Like My Father .75 2.00
❑ CL10 This Deal Is Getting Worse .75 2.00

2012 Star Wars Galactic Files Duels of Fate

COMPLETE SET (10) 4.00 10.00
STATED ODDS 1:6

❑ DF1 Obi-Wan/Qui-Gon vs. Darth Maul 1.00 2.50
❑ DF2 Count Dooku vs. Anakin/Obi-Wan 1.00 2.50
❑ DF3 Yoda vs. Count Dooku 1.00 2.50
❑ DF4 Anakin/Obi-Wan vs. Count Dooku 1.00 2.50
❑ DF5 Mace Windu vs. Darth Sidious 1.00 2.50
❑ DF6 Darth Sidious vs. Yoda 1.00 2.50
❑ DF7 Obi-Wan vs. Darth Vader 1.00 2.50
❑ DF8 Darth Vader vs. Obi-Wan 1.00 2.50
❑ DF9 Darth Vader vs. Luke Skywalker 1.00 2.50
❑ DF10 Luke Skywalker vs. Darth Vader 1.00 2.50

2012 Star Wars Galactic Files Galactic Moments

COMPLETE SET (20) 20.00 40.00
STATED ODDS 1:6

❑ GM1 Han vs. Greedo 1.50 4.00
❑ GM2 Princess and the Plans 1.50 4.00
❑ GM3 Introducing Yoda 1.50 4.00
❑ GM4 Defense of the Death Star 1.50 4.00
❑ GM5 Destruction of Alderaan 1.50 4.00
❑ GM6 Dagobah Training 1.50 4.00
❑ GM7 Luke's Lack of Vision 1.50 4.00
❑ GM8 Duel to the Truth 1.50 4.00
❑ GM9 Entertaining the Emperor 1.50 4.00
❑ GM10 Assembling the Bounty Hunters 1.50 4.00
❑ GM11 I Know 1.50 4.00
❑ GM12 A Pensive Prisoner 1.50 4.00
❑ GM13 The Luring of Skywalker 1.50 4.00
❑ GM14 Chewbacca Imprisoned 1.50 4.00
❑ GM15 Tracking the Invasion 1.50 4.00
❑ GM16 You Must Learn the Ways 1.50 4.00
❑ GM17 The Rancor Outage 1.50 4.00
❑ GM18 A Well Earned Victory 1.50 4.00
❑ GM19 Luke Sells His Landspeeder 1.50 4.00
❑ GM20 You Were In the Rebellion 1.50 4.00

2012 Star Wars Galactic Files Heroes on Both Sides

COMPLETE SET (10) 4.00 10.00
STATED ODDS 1:6

❑ HB1 Battle of Naboo 1.00 2.50
❑ HB2 Standoff on Kamino 1.00 2.50
❑ HB3 Battle of Geonosis 1.00 2.50
❑ HB4 Battle of Coruscant 1.00 2.50
❑ HB5 Battle of Kashyyyk 1.00 2.50
❑ HB6 Invasion of Utapau 1.00 2.50
❑ HB7 Capturing the Tantive IV 1.00 2.50
❑ HB8 Battle of Yavin 1.00 2.50
❑ HB9 Battle of Hoth 1.00 2.50
❑ HB10 Battle of Endor 1.00 2.50

2012 Star Wars Galactic Files I Have a Bad Feeling About This

COMPLETE SET (8) 3.00 8.00
STATED ODDS 1:4

❑ BF1 Qui-Gon/Obi-Wan .75 2.00
❑ BF2 Anakin Skywalker .75 2.00
❑ BF3 Obi-Wan Kenobi .75 2.00
❑ BF4 Chewie/Luke/Obi-Wan/Han .75 2.00
❑ BF5 Leia/Han/Luke .75 2.00
❑ BF6 Leia/Han .75 2.00
❑ BF7 C-3PO/R2-D2 .75 2.00
❑ BF8 Han/Luke/Chewie .75 2.00

2012 Star Wars Galactic Files Patches

STATED ODDS ONE AUTO OR PATCH PER HOBBY BOX

❑ PR1 X-Wing Fighter Pilots: Red Leader 50.00 100.00
❑ PR2 X-Wing Fighter Pilots: Red Two 50.00 100.00
❑ PR3 X-Wing Fighter Pilots: Red Three 50.00 100.00
❑ PR4 X-Wing Fighter Pilots: Red Four 50.00 100.00
❑ PR5 X-Wing Fighter Pilots: Red Five 100.00 200.00
❑ PR6 X-Wing Fighter Pilots: Red Six 50.00 100.00
❑ PR7 Naboo Starfighter Pilots: Bravo Leader 8.00 20.00
❑ PR8 Naboo Starfighter Pilots: Bravo Four 8.00 20.00
❑ PR9 Naboo Starfighter Pilots: Bravo Five 8.00 20.00
❑ PR10 AT-AT Walker Crew: Blizzard One 8.00 20.00
❑ PR11 AT-AT Walker Crew: Blizzard One 8.00 20.00
❑ PR12 Jedi Starfighter Pilots 12.00 30.00
Obi-Wan Kenobi
❑ PR13 Jedi Starfighter Pilots 15.00 40.00
❑ PR14 Jedi Starfighter Pilots 12.00 30.00
❑ PR15 A-Wing Fighter Pilots 8.00 20.00
❑ PR16 ARC-170 Clone Fighters 8.00 20.00
❑ PR17 Snowspeeder Pilots: Rogue Leader 60.00 120.00
❑ PR18 Snowspeeder Pilots: Rogue Two 40.00 80.00
❑ PR19 Snowspeeder Pilots: Rogue Three 40.00 80.00
❑ PR20 Snowspeeder Pilots: Rogue Four 30.00 60.00
❑ PR21 Snowspeeder Pilots: Rogue Leader (Gunner)30.00 60.00
❑ PR22 TIE Fighter Squadron 8.00 20.00
❑ PR23 Death Star Command 15.00 40.00
❑ PR24 Death Star Command 15.00 40.00
Darth Vader
❑ PR25 Millennium Falcon Pilots 35.00 70.00
Han Solo
❑ PR26 Millennium Falcon Pilots 15.00 40.00
Chewbacca
❑ PR27 Millennium Falcon Pilots: Gold Leader25.00 50.00
❑ PR28 Millennium Falcon Pilots: Gold Leader15.00 40.00
❑ PR29 B-Wing Pilot: Endor Veterans 8.00 20.00
❑ PR30 Endor Scout Trooper Patrol 8.00 20.00

2012 Star Wars Galactic Files Sketches

STATED ODDS 1:24 H, 1:96 R

❑ 1 Adam Talley
❑ 2 Alex Buechel
❑ 3 Amy Pronovost
❑ 4 Angelina Benedetti
❑ 5 Ashleigh Popplewell
❑ 6 Bill Pulkovski
❑ 7 Bob Stevlic
❑ 8 Brent Engstrom
❑ 9 Brian DeGuire
❑ 10 Chris Raimo
❑ 11 Clay Rodery
❑ 12 Dan Bergren
❑ 13 Darla Ecklund
❑ 14 Dave Strong
❑ 15 David Green
❑ 16 David Rabbitte
❑ 17 Denae Frazier
❑ 18 Denise Vasquez
❑ 19 Diego Jourdan
❑ 20 Eli Rutten
❑ 21 Gary Kezele
❑ 22 Howard Shum
❑ 23 Ian Roberts
❑ 24 Ingrid Hardy
❑ 25 Irma Ahmed
❑ 26 Jamie Snell
❑ 27 Jason Durden
❑ 28 Jason Goad
❑ 29 Jason Sobol
❑ 30 Jay Shimko
❑ 31 Jennifer Mercer
❑ 32 Jeremy Scott
❑ 33 Joe Hogan
❑ 34 John Ottinger
❑ 35 Justin Chung
❑ 36 Kate Glasheen
❑ 37 Katie Cook
❑ 38 Kevin Bloomfield
❑ 39 Kevin Reinke
❑ 40 Kimberly Dunaway
❑ 41 Lak Lim
❑ 42 Lance Sawyer
❑ 43 Lark Sudol
❑ 44 Leah Mangue
❑ 45 Lee Kohse
❑ 46 Lee Lightfoot
❑ 47 Lin Workman
❑ 48 Lord Mesa
❑ 49 M. Jason Reed
❑ 50 Mario Rojas
❑ 51 Matte Chero
❑ 52 Mike Hampton
❑ 53 Mike Vasquez
❑ 54 Mikey Babinski
❑ 55 Nina Edlund
❑ 56 Pablo Diaz
❑ 57 Puis Calzada
❑ 58 Rachel Kaiser
❑ 59 Randy Martinez
❑ 60 Rhiannon Owens
❑ 61 Rich Molinelli
❑ 62 Robert Teranishi
❑ 63 Russ Maheras
❑ 64 Scott Rorie
❑ 65 Scott Zambelli
❑ 66 Stephanie Swanger
❑ 67 Ted Dastick
❑ 68 Tim Proctor
❑ 69 Trev Murphy
❑ 70 Tyler Scarlet
❑ 71 Val Hochberg
❑ 72 Van Davis
❑ 73 Vanessa Banky Farano
❑ 74 Wilson Ramos Jr.
❑ 75 Adrien Rivera
❑ 76 Tony Miello

2012 Star Wars Galaxy Series 7

COMPLETE SET (110) 8.00 20.00

❑ 1 The Wrath of Maul .15 .40
❑ 2 Educating Luke .15 .40
❑ 3 Best Friends Forever .15 .40
❑ 4 A Different Side of Leia .15 .40
❑ 5 His Worst Fears Realized .15 .40
❑ 6 A Jedi on Tatooine .15 .40
❑ 7 Fett's Grand Destiny .15 .40
❑ 8 The Finest of Naboo .15 .40
❑ 9 Talon's Dark Reach .15 .40
❑ 10 The Rogue Years .15 .40
❑ 11 Birth of a Hero .15 .40
❑ 12 Life with Leia .15 .40
❑ 13 The Pity of Darth Vader .15 .40
❑ 14 A Daring Deception .15 .40
❑ 15 Fighting for Naboo .15 .40
❑ 16 Spying on Stormtroopers .15 .40
❑ 17 Facing a Frozen Fate .15 .40
❑ 18 A Menace Named Maul .15 .40
❑ 19 A Dark Victory .15 .40
❑ 20 Discovering Darth Maul .15 .40
❑ 21 Vader's Optimism .15 .40
❑ 22 The Eve of Infiltration .15 .40
❑ 23 The Hopeful Princess .15 .40
❑ 24 Not Part of the Bargain .15 .40
❑ 25 A Dark Side Destiny .15 .40
❑ 26 Desert Nomads .15 .40
❑ 27 Vader's Revenge .15 .40
❑ 28 Podrace Spectator .15 .40
❑ 29 Ahsoka Grows Up .15 .40
❑ 30 In Search of Han .15 .40
❑ 31 The Spiritual Jedi .15 .40
❑ 32 The Warrior Kenobi .15 .40
❑ 33 In the Court of the Evil Hutt .15 .40
❑ 34 The Millennium Falcon's Great Escape .15 .40
❑ 35 Boba Fett's Grand Return .15 .40
❑ 36 Luke's Dark Journey .15 .40
❑ 37 A Hutt Called Jabba .15 .40
❑ 38 Dueling with Dooku .15 .40
❑ 39 Unclear Omnisignal Unicode .15 .40
❑ 40 When Ewoks Attack .15 .40
❑ 41 Pursued by Rancors .15 .40
❑ 42 A Pensive Princess .15 .40
❑ 43 Leia's Vigil .15 .40
❑ 44 The Kessel Run .15 .40
❑ 45 The Odd Couple .15 .40
❑ 46 Mourning for Padme .15 .40
❑ 47 Mighty Mace Windu .15 .40
❑ 48 Beyond the Cave .15 .40
❑ 49 Portrait in Black .15 .40
❑ 50 A Friend in Need .15 .40
❑ 51 Rites of Passage .15 .40
❑ 52 Jedi a la Kurosawa .15 .40
❑ 53 Dashing Derring-Do .15 .40
❑ 54 The Karloff Connection .15 .40
❑ 55 Boba Fett's Prize .15 .40
❑ 56 See Action Now .15 .40
❑ 57 The Clash of Lightsabers .15 .40
❑ 58 The Hunter and His Prey .15 .40
❑ 59 Legacy of the Empire .15 .40
❑ 60 In the Clutches of Darth Vader .15 .40
❑ 61 30 Years .15 .40
❑ 62 Searching for Solo .15 .40
❑ 63 The Bounty of Bossk .15 .40
❑ 64 A Long Time Ago .15 .40
❑ 65 The Battle Continues .15 .40
❑ 66 The Empire Falls .15 .40
❑ 67 A Brand New Hope .15 .40
❑ 68 The Empire Strikes Again .15 .40
❑ 69 Return to the Saga .15 .40
❑ 70 Han Shot First .15 .40
❑ 71 A Wretched Hive .15 .40
❑ 72 The Truth Unfurled .15 .40
❑ 73 Knight of Passage .15 .40
❑ 74 Unite .15 .40
❑ 75 Victory is Imminant .15 .40
❑ 76 Geonosis Reflections .15 .40
❑ 77 Qui-Gon .15 .40
❑ 78 Resurrection .15 .40
❑ 79 Use the Force, Luke .15 .40
❑ 80 Wookie Rage .15 .40
❑ 81 Cruise the Galaxy .15 .40
❑ 82 Luke and the Force .15 .40
❑ 83 Vader Triumphant .15 .40
❑ 84 Han's Narrow Escape .15 .40
❑ 85 The Lando Factor .15 .40
❑ 86 Ready for Adventure .15 .40
❑ 87 A Truly Classic Cover .15 .40
❑ 88 A Mystery Named Maul .15 .40
❑ 89 The Nefarious Opposition .15 .40
❑ 90 Alliance of Evil .15 .40
❑ 91 Against the Dark Side .15 .40
❑ 92 A Portrais of Leia .15 .40
❑ 93 A Collection of Fiends .15 .40
❑ 94 A Jedi's Destiny .15 .40
❑ 95 Trouble on Tatooine .15 .40
❑ 96 Splintered Together .15 .40
❑ 97 Star Lovers .15 .40
❑ 98 The Fate of Palpatine .15 .40
❑ 99 Revenge of the Tribute .15 .40
❑ 100 A Brand New Master .15 .40
❑ 101 Luke's Loss of Innocence .15 .40
❑ 102 Against Dooku's Might .15 .40
❑ 103 The Bounty Hunter's Prize .15 .40
❑ 104 A Dark Challenge .15 .40
❑ 105 The Crimson Crusader .15 .40
❑ 106 For Blood and Money .15 .40
❑ 107 Pods Away! .15 .40
❑ 108 Checking Out Threepio .15 .40
❑ 109 Showdown With Grievous .15 .40
❑ 110 Checklist .15 .40

2012 Star Wars Galaxy Series 7 Printing Plates Black

STATED PRINT RUN 1 SER. #'d SET
UNPRICED DUE TO SCARCITY

2012 Star Wars Galaxy Series 7 Printing Plates Cyan

STATED PRINT RUN 1 SER. #'d SET
UNPRICED DUE TO SCARCITY

2012 Star Wars Galaxy Series 7 Printing Plates Magenta

STATED PRINT RUN 1 SER. #'d SET
UNPRICED DUE TO SCARCITY

2012 Star Wars Galaxy Series 7 Printing Plates Yellow

STATED PRINT RUN 1 SER. #'d SET
UNPRICED DUE TO SCARCITY

2012 Star Wars Galaxy Series 7 Cels

COMPLETE SET (9) 35.00 70.00
STATED ODDS

❑ 1 Asajj Vendress 4.00 10.00
❑ 2 Battle of Hoth 4.00 10.00
❑ 3 Boba Fett 4.00 10.00
❑ 4 Darth Maul 4.00 10.00
❑ 5 Darth Vader 4.00 10.00
❑ 6 C-3PO 4.00 10.00
R2-D2
❑ 7 Sandtrooper 4.00 10.00
❑ 8 Scout Trooper 4.00 10.00
❑ 9 Yoda 4.00 10.00

2012 Star Wars Galaxy Series 7 Etched Foil

COMPLETE SET (6) 5.00 12.00
STATED ODDS 1:6

❑ 1 Asajj Ventress 1.50 4.00
❑ 2 Emperor Palpatine 1.50 4.00
❑ 3 Darth Revan 1.50 4.00
Nihilus/Malgus
❑ 4 Darth Maul 1.50 4.00
Count Dooku
❑ 5 Darth Vader 1.50 4.00
❑ 6 Darth Talon 1.50 4.00

2012 Star Wars Galaxy Series 7 Etched Foil Original Art

COMPLETE SET
ANNOUNCED PRINT RUN 1
UNPRICED DUE TO SCARCITY

❑ 1 Asajj Ventress
❑ 2 Emperor Palpatine
❑ 3 Darth Revan
Nihilus/Malgus
❑ 4 Darth Maul
Count Dooku
❑ 5 Darth Vader
❑ 6 Darth Talon

2012 Star Wars Galaxy Series 7 Foil Silver

COMPLETE SET (15) 6.00 15.00
STATED ODDS 1:3

❑ 1 Anakin Skywalker .75 2.00
❑ 2 Cad Bane .75 2.00
❑ 3 Obi-Wan Kenobi .75 2.00
❑ 4 Bossk .75 2.00
❑ 5 Chewbacca .75 2.00
❑ 6 Boba Fett .75 2.00
❑ 7 Slave Leia .75 2.00
❑ 8 Princess Leia .75 2.00
❑ 9 Luke Skywalker .75 2.00
❑ 10 Darth Maul .75 2.00
❑ 11 Senator Palpatine .75 2.00
❑ 12 Han Solo .75 2.00
❑ 13 Grand Moff Tarkin .75 2.00
❑ 14 Darth Vader .75 2.00
❑ 15 Yoda .75 2.00

2012 Star Wars Galaxy Series 7 Foil Bronze

COMPLETE SET (15) 25.00 60.00
*BRONZE: 1.5X TO 4X SILVER
STATED ODDS 1:24

2012 Star Wars Galaxy Series 7 Foil Gold

COMPLETE SET (15) 75.00 125.00
*GOLD: 3X TO 8X SILVER
STATED ODDS 1:48

2012 Star Wars Galaxy Series 7 Foil Refractor

STATED ODDS 16,096
STATED PRINT RUN 1 SER. #'d SET
UNPRICED DUE TO SCARCITY

2012 Star Wars Galaxy Series 7 Sketchagraphs

STATED ODDS 1:230

❑ 1 Alan Flying
Allison Sohn
❑ 2 Alan Flying
Brian Rood
❑ 3 Alan Flying
Bruce Gerlach
❑ 4 Alan Flying
Dan Bergren
❑ 5 Alan Flying
David Day
❑ 6 Alan Flying
Gabe Farber
❑ 7 Alan Flying
Gary Kezele
❑ 8 Alan Flying
Hayden Davis
❑ 9 Alan Flying
Jake Minor
❑ 10 Alan Flying
Jamie Snell
❑ 11 Alan Flying
Jim Kyle
❑ 12 Alan Flying
John Haun
❑ 13 Alan Flying
Kevin Doyle
❑ 14 Alan Flying
Kevin Graham
❑ 15 Alan Flying
Kyle Babbitt
❑ 16 Alan Flying
Leah Mangue
❑ 17 Alan Flying
Matthew Minor
❑ 18 Alan Flying
Rich Molinelli
❑ 19 Alan Flying
Robert Hendrickson
❑ 20 Alan Flying
Robert Teranishi
❑ 21 Alan Flying
Sarah Wilkinson
❑ 22 Alan Flying
Sean Pence
❑ 23 Alan Flying
Steve Oatney
❑ 24 Alan Flying
Tim Proctor
❑ 25 Alan Flying
Tom Hodges
❑ 26 Ashley Eckstein
Allison Sohn
❑ 27 Ashley Eckstein
Brian Rood
❑ 28 Ashley Eckstein
Bruce Gerlach
❑ 29 Ashley Eckstein
Dan Bergren
❑ 30 Ashley Eckstein
David Day
❑ 31 Ashley Eckstein
Gabe Farber
❑ 32 Ashley Eckstein
Gary Kezele
❑ 33 Ashley Eckstein
Hayden Davis
❑ 34 Ashley Eckstein
Jake Minor
❑ 35 Ashley Eckstein
Jamie Snell
❑ 36 Ashley Eckstein
Jim Kyle
❑ 37 Ashley Eckstein
John Haun
❑ 38 Ashley Eckstein
Kevin Doyle
❑ 39 Ashley Eckstein
Kevin Graham
❑ 40 Ashley Eckstein
Kyle Babbitt
❑ 41 Ashley Eckstein
Leah Mangue
❑ 42 Ashley Eckstein
Matthew Minor
❑ 43 Ashley Eckstein
Rich Molinelli
❑ 44 Ashley Eckstein
Robert Hendrickson
❑ 45 Ashley Eckstein
Robert Teranishi
❑ 46 Ashley Eckstein
Sarah Wilkinson
❑ 47 Ashley Eckstein
Sean Pence
❑ 48 Ashley Eckstein
Steve Oatney
❑ 49 Ashley Eckstein
Tim Proctor
❑ 50 Ashley Eckstein
Tom Hodges
❑ 51 Ben Burtt
Allison Sohn
❑ 52 Ben Burtt
Brian Rood
❑ 53 Ben Burtt
Bruce Gerlach
❑ 54 Ben Burtt
Dan Bergren
❑ 55 Ben Burtt
David Day
❑ 56 Ben Burtt
Gabe Farber
❑ 57 Ben Burtt
Gary Kezele
❑ 58 Ben Burtt
Hayden Davis
❑ 59 Ben Burtt
Jake Minor
❑ 60 Ben Burtt
Jamie Snell
❑ 61 Ben Burtt
Jim Kyle
❑ 62 Ben Burtt
John Haun
❑ 63 Ben Burtt
Kevin Doyle
❑ 64 Ben Burtt
Kevin Graham
❑ 65 Ben Burtt
Kyle Babbitt
❑ 66 Ben Burtt
Leah Mangue
❑ 67 Ben Burtt
Matthew Minor
❑ 68 Ben Burtt
Rich Molinelli
❑ 69 Ben Burtt
Robert Hendrickson
❑ 70 Ben Burtt
Robert Teranishi
❑ 71 Ben Burtt
Sarah Wilkinson
❑ 72 Ben Burtt
Sean Pence
❑ 73 Ben Burtt
Steve Oatney
❑ 74 Ben Burtt
Tim Proctor
❑ 75 Ben Burtt
Tom Hodges
❑ 76 Carrie Fisher
Allison Sohn
❑ 77 Carrie Fisher
Brian Rood
❑ 78 Carrie Fisher
Bruce Gerlach
❑ 79 Carrie Fisher
Dan Bergren
❑ 80 Carrie Fisher
David Day
❑ 81 Carrie Fisher
Gabe Farber
❑ 82 Carrie Fisher
Gary Kezele
❑ 83 Carrie Fisher
Hayden Davis
❑ 84 Carrie Fisher
Jake Minor
❑ 85 Carrie Fisher
Jamie Snell
❑ 86 Carrie Fisher
Jim Kyle
❑ 87 Carrie Fisher
John Haun
❑ 88 Carrie Fisher
Kevin Doyle
❑ 89 Carrie Fisher
Kevin Graham
❑ 90 Carrie Fisher
Kyle Babbitt
❑ 91 Carrie Fisher
Leah Mangue
❑ 92 Carrie Fisher
Matthew Minor
❑ 93 Carrie Fisher
Rich Molinelli
❑ 94 Carrie Fisher
Robert Hendrickson
❑ 95 Carrie Fisher
Robert Teranishi
❑ 96 Carrie Fisher
Sarah Wilkinson
❑ 97 Carrie Fisher
Sean Pence
❑ 98 Carrie Fisher
Steve Oatney
❑ 99 Carrie Fisher
Tim Proctor
❑ 100 Carrie Fisher
Tom Hodges
❑ 101 Catherine Taber
Allison Sohn
❑ 102 Catherine Taber
Brian Rood
❑ 103 Catherine Taber
Bruce Gerlach
❑ 104 Catherine Taber
Dan Bergren
❑ 105 Catherine Taber
David Day
❑ 106 Catherine Taber
Gabe Farber
❑ 107 Catherine Taber
Gary Kezele
❑ 108 Catherine Taber
Hayden Davis
❑ 109 Catherine Taber
Jake Minor
❑ 110 Catherine Taber
Jamie Snell
❑ 111 Catherine Taber
Jim Kyle
❑ 112 Catherine Taber
John Haun
❑ 113 Catherine Taber
Kevin Doyle
❑ 114 Catherine Taber
Kevin Graham
❑ 115 Catherine Taber
Kyle Babbitt
❑ 116 Catherine Taber
Leah Mangue
❑ 117 Catherine Taber
Matthew Minor
❑ 118 Catherine Taber
Rich Molinelli
❑ 119 Catherine Taber
Robert Hendrickson
❑ 120 Catherine Taber
Robert Teranishi
❑ 121 Catherine Taber
Sarah Wilkinson
❑ 122 Catherine Taber
Sean Pence
❑ 123 Catherine Taber
Steve Oatney
❑ 124 Catherine Taber
Tim Proctor
❑ 125 Catherine Taber
Tom Hodges
❑ 126 Dickey Beer
Allison Sohn
❑ 127 Dickey Beer
Brian Rood
❑ 128 Dickey Beer
Bruce Gerlach
❑ 129 Dickey Beer
Dan Bergren
❑ 130 Dickey Beer
David Day
❑ 131 Dickey Beer
Gabe Farber
❑ 132 Dickey Beer
Gary Kezele
❑ 133 Dickey Beer

Hayden Davis
❑ 134 Dickey Beer
Jake Minor
❑ 135 Dickey Beer
Jamie Snell
❑ 136 Dickey Beer
Jim Kyle
❑ 137 Dickey Beer
John Haun
❑ 138 Dickey Beer
Kevin Doyle
❑ 139 Dickey Beer
Kevin Graham
❑ 140 Dickey Beer
Kyle Babbitt
❑ 141 Dickey Beer
Leah Mangue
❑ 142 Dickey Beer
Matthew Minor
❑ 143 Dickey Beer
Rich Molinelli
❑ 144 Dickey Beer
Robert Hendrickson
❑ 145 Dickey Beer
Robert Teranishi
❑ 146 Dickey Beer
Sarah Wilkinson
❑ 147 Dickey Beer
Sean Pence
❑ 148 Dickey Beer
Steve Oatney
❑ 149 Dickey Beer
Tim Proctor
❑ 150 Dickey Beer
Tom Hodges
❑ 151 James Arnold Taylor
Allison Sohn
❑ 152 James Arnold Taylor
Brian Rood
❑ 153 James Arnold Taylor
Bruce Gerlach
❑ 154 James Arnold Taylor
Dan Bergren
❑ 155 James Arnold Taylor
David Day
❑ 156 James Arnold Taylor
Gabe Farber
❑ 157 James Arnold Taylor
Gary Kezele
❑ 158 James Arnold Taylor
Hayden Davis
❑ 159 James Arnold Taylor
Jake Minor
❑ 160 James Arnold Taylor
Jamie Snell
❑ 161 James Arnold Taylor
Jim Kyle
❑ 162 James Arnold Taylor
John Haun
❑ 163 James Arnold Taylor
Kevin Doyle
❑ 164 James Arnold Taylor
Kevin Graham
❑ 165 James Arnold Taylor
Kyle Babbitt
❑ 166 James Arnold Taylor
Leah Mangue
❑ 167 James Arnold Taylor
Matthew Minor
❑ 168 James Arnold Taylor
Rich Molinelli
❑ 169 James Arnold Taylor
Robert Hendrickson
❑ 170 James Arnold Taylor
Robert Teranishi
❑ 171 James Arnold Taylor
Sarah Wilkinson
❑ 172 James Arnold Taylor
Sean Pence
❑ 173 James Arnold Taylor
Steve Oatney
❑ 174 James Arnold Taylor
Tim Proctor
❑ 175 James Arnold Taylor
Tom Hodges
❑ 176 Mark Hamill
Allison Sohn
❑ 177 Mark Hamill
Brian Rood
❑ 178 Mark Hamill
Bruce Gerlach
❑ 179 Mark Hamill
Dan Bergren
❑ 180 Mark Hamill
David Day
❑ 181 Mark Hamill
Gabe Farber
❑ 182 Mark Hamill
Gary Kezele
❑ 183 Mark Hamill
Hayden Davis
❑ 184 Mark Hamill
Jake Minor
❑ 185 Mark Hamill
Jamie Snell
❑ 186 Mark Hamill
Jim Kyle
❑ 187 Mark Hamill
John Haun
❑ 188 Mark Hamill
Kevin Doyle
❑ 189 Mark Hamill
Kevin Graham
❑ 190 Mark Hamill
Kyle Babbitt
❑ 191 Mark Hamill
Leah Mangue
❑ 192 Mark Hamill
Matthew Minor
❑ 193 Mark Hamill
Rich Molinelli
❑ 194 Mark Hamill
Robert Hendrickson
❑ 195 Mark Hamill
Robert Teranishi
❑ 196 Mark Hamill
Sarah Wilkinson
❑ 197 Mark Hamill
Sean Pence
❑ 198 Mark Hamill
Steve Oatney
❑ 199 Mark Hamill
Tim Proctor
❑ 200 Mark Hamill
Tom Hodges
❑ 201 Matt Wood
Allison Sohn
❑ 202 Matt Wood
Brian Rood
❑ 203 Matt Wood
Bruce Gerlach
❑ 204 Matt Wood
Dan Bergren
❑ 205 Matt Wood
David Day
❑ 206 Matt Wood
Gabe Farber
❑ 207 Matt Wood
Gary Kezele
❑ 208 Matt Wood
Hayden Davis
❑ 209 Matt Wood
Jake Minor
❑ 210 Matt Wood
Jamie Snell
❑ 211 Matt Wood
Jim Kyle
❑ 212 Matt Wood
John Haun
❑ 213 Matt Wood
Kevin Doyle
❑ 214 Matt Wood
Kevin Graham
❑ 215 Matt Wood
Kyle Babbitt
❑ 216 Matt Wood
Leah Mangue
❑ 217 Matt Wood
Matthew Minor
❑ 218 Matt Wood
Rich Molinelli
❑ 219 Matt Wood
Robert Hendrickson
❑ 220 Matt Wood
Robert Teranishi
❑ 221 Matt Wood
Sarah Wilkinson
❑ 222 Matt Wood
Sean Pence
❑ 223 Matt Wood
Steve Oatney
❑ 224 Matt Wood
Tim Proctor
❑ 225 Matt Wood
Tom Hodges
❑ 226 Peter Mayhew
Allison Sohn
❑ 227 Peter Mayhew
Brian Rood
❑ 228 Peter Mayhew
Bruce Gerlach
❑ 229 Peter Mayhew
Dan Bergren
❑ 230 Peter Mayhew
David Day
❑ 231 Peter Mayhew
Gabe Farber
❑ 232 Peter Mayhew
Gary Kezele
❑ 233 Peter Mayhew
Hayden Davis
❑ 234 Peter Mayhew
Jake Minor
❑ 235 Peter Mayhew
Jamie Snell
❑ 236 Peter Mayhew
Jim Kyle
❑ 237 Peter Mayhew
John Haun
❑ 238 Peter Mayhew
Kevin Doyle
❑ 239 Peter Mayhew
Kevin Graham
❑ 240 Peter Mayhew
Kyle Babbitt
❑ 241 Peter Mayhew
Leah Mangue
❑ 242 Peter Mayhew
Matthew Minor
❑ 243 Peter Mayhew
Rich Molinelli
❑ 244 Peter Mayhew
Robert Hendrickson
❑ 245 Peter Mayhew
Robert Teranishi
❑ 246 Peter Mayhew
Sarah Wilkinson
❑ 247 Peter Mayhew
Sean Pence
❑ 248 Peter Mayhew
Steve Oatney
❑ 249 Peter Mayhew
Tim Proctor
❑ 250 Peter Mayhew
Tom Hodges
❑ 251 Timothy Zahn
Allison Sohn
❑ 252 Timothy Zahn
Brian Rood
❑ 253 Timothy Zahn
Bruce Gerlach
❑ 254 Timothy Zahn
Dan Bergren
❑ 255 Timothy Zahn
David Day
❑ 256 Timothy Zahn
Gabe Farber
❑ 257 Timothy Zahn
Gary Kezele
❑ 258 Timothy Zahn
Hayden Davis
❑ 259 Timothy Zahn
Jake Minor
❑ 260 Timothy Zahn
Jamie Snell
❑ 261 Timothy Zahn
Jim Kyle
❑ 262 Timothy Zahn
John Haun
❑ 263 Timothy Zahn
Kevin Doyle
❑ 264 Timothy Zahn
Kevin Graham
❑ 265 Timothy Zahn
Kyle Babbitt
❑ 266 Timothy Zahn
Leah Mangue
❑ 267 Timothy Zahn
Matthew Minor
❑ 268 Timothy Zahn
Rich Molinelli
❑ 269 Timothy Zahn
Robert Hendrickson
❑ 270 Timothy Zahn
Robert Teranishi
❑ 271 Timothy Zahn
Sarah Wilkinson
❑ 272 Timothy Zahn
Sean Pence
❑ 273 Timothy Zahn
Steve Oatney
❑ 274 Timothy Zahn
Tim Proctor
❑ 275 Timothy Zahn
Tom Hodges
❑ 276 Tom Kane
Allison Sohn
❑ 277 Tom Kane
Brian Rood
❑ 278 Tom Kane
Bruce Gerlach
❑ 279 Tom Kane
Dan Bergren
❑ 280 Tom Kane
David Day
❑ 281 Tom Kane
Gabe Farber
❑ 282 Tom Kane
Gary Kezele
❑ 283 Tom Kane
Hayden Davis
❑ 284 Tom Kane
Jake Minor
❑ 285 Tom Kane
Jamie Snell
❑ 286 Tom Kane
Jim Kyle
❑ 287 Tom Kane
John Haun
❑ 288 Tom Kane
Kevin Doyle
❑ 289 Tom Kane
Kevin Graham
❑ 290 Tom Kane
Kyle Babbitt
❑ 291 Tom Kane
Leah Mangue
❑ 292 Tom Kane
Matthew Minor
❑ 293 Tom Kane
Rich Molinelli
❑ 294 Tom Kane
Robert Hendrickson
❑ 295 Tom Kane
Robert Teranishi
❑ 296 Tom Kane
Sarah Wilkinson
❑ 297 Tom Kane
Sean Pence
❑ 298 Tom Kane
Steve Oatney
❑ 299 Tom Kane
Tim Proctor
❑ 300 Tom Kane
Tom Hodges

2012 Star Wars Galaxy Series 7 Sketches

STATED ODDS 1:24 H, 1:116 R

❑ 1 Adrian Rivera	8.00	20.00
❑ 2 Agnes Garbowska	30.00	80.00
❑ 3 Alex Buechel	25.00	60.00
❑ 4 Amy Beth Christenson	20.00	50.00
❑ 5 Ashleigh Popplewell	40.00	100.00
❑ 6 Beck Seashols	20.00	50.00
❑ 7 Ben Dale	12.00	30.00
❑ 8 Bill Pulkovski	15.00	40.00
❑ 9 Bob Stevlic	40.00	100.00
❑ 10 Brandon Kenney	150.00	300.00
❑ 11 Brent Engstrom	50.00	125.00
❑ 12 Brian DeGuire	15.00	40.00
❑ 13 Brian Miller	30.00	80.00
❑ 14 Brian Rood	25.00	60.00
❑ 15 Bruce Gerlach	15.00	40.00
❑ 16 Cal Slayton	15.00	40.00
❑ 17 Charles Hall	200.00	400.00
❑ 18 Chris Henderson	25.00	60.00
❑ 19 Colin Walton	8.00	20.00
❑ 20 Cory Hamscher	15.00	40.00
❑ 21 Cynthia Narcisi	30.00	80.00
❑ 22 D'Douglas	15.00	40.00
❑ 23 Dan Bergren	60.00	150.00
❑ 24 Dan Curto	25.00	60.00
❑ 25 Darla Ecklund		
❑ 26 David Day	40.00	100.00
❑ 27 David Rabbitte	40.00	100.00
❑ 28 Denae Frazier	50.00	125.00
❑ 29 Denis Medri	20.00	50.00
❑ 30 Dennis Budd	10.00	25.00
❑ 31 Don Pedicini Jr.	15.00	40.00
❑ 32 Eli Rutten	100.00	250.00
❑ 33 Erik Maell	40.00	100.00
❑ 34 Gabe Farber	40.00	100.00
❑ 35 Gary Kezele	100.00	250.00
❑ 36 Hayden Davis	30.00	80.00
❑ 37 Ingrid Hardy	25.00	60.00
❑ 38 Irma Ahmed	50.00	125.00
❑ 39 Jamie Snell	30.00	80.00
❑ 40 Jason Atomic	30.00	80.00
❑ 41 Jason Davies	40.00	100.00
❑ 42 Jason Durden	20.00	50.00
❑ 43 Jason Hughes	15.00	40.00
❑ 44 Jason Sobol	30.00	80.00
❑ 45 Jason Keith Phillips	40.00	100.00
❑ 46 Jay Shimko	30.00	80.00
❑ 47 Jerry Ma	15.00	40.00
❑ 48 Jim Kyle	12.00	30.00
❑ 49 Joe Corroney	100.00	250.00
❑ 50 Joe Hogan	40.00	100.00
❑ 51 John Beatty	15.00	40.00
❑ 52 John Soukup	40.00	100.00
❑ 53 John P Wales	8.00	20.00
❑ 54 Jonathan D. Gordon		
❑ 55 Kate Glasheen	15.00	40.00
❑ 56 Katie Cook	300.00	600.00
❑ 57 Keven Reinke	75.00	175.00
❑ 58 Kevin Doyle	15.00	40.00
❑ 59 Kevin Graham	30.00	80.00
❑ 60 Kevin Liell	30.00	80.00
❑ 61 Killian Plunkett	150.00	300.00
❑ 62 Kyle Babbitt	10.00	25.00
❑ 63 Lak Lim	60.00	150.00
❑ 64 Lance Sawyer	8.00	20.00
❑ 65 Lawrence Reynolds	100.00	250.00
❑ 66 Lee Bradley	15.00	40.00
❑ 67 Lee Kohse	50.00	125.00
❑ 68 Lin Workman	40.00	100.00
❑ 69 Lord Mesa	30.00	80.00
❑ 70 Mark McHaley	60.00	150.00
❑ 71 Mark Slater	8.00	20.00
❑ 72 Mike Duron	60.00	150.00
❑ 73 Nathan Hamill		
❑ 74 Nathen Reinke	100.00	200.00
❑ 75 Nicole Falk	25.00	60.00
❑ 76 Nigel Sade		
❑ 77 Nina Edlund		
❑ 78 Pat Presley	30.00	80.00
❑ 79 Patrick Richardson	60.00	150.00
❑ 80 Patrick Schoenmaker	60.00	150.00
❑ 81 Randy Martinez	100.00	250.00
❑ 82 Randy Siplon	40.00	100.00
❑ 83 Rhiannon Owens	15.00	40.00
❑ 84 Rich Molinelli	25.00	60.00
❑ 85 Rob Liefeld		
❑ 86 Robert Hendrickson	40.00	100.00
❑ 87 Russell Walks		
❑ 88 Scott Rorie	40.00	100.00
❑ 89 Scott Zambelli	25.00	60.00
❑ 90 Shea Standefer	25.00	60.00
❑ 91 Shelli Paroline	8.00	20.00
❑ 92 Sian Mandrake	8.00	20.00
❑ 93 Steph Swanger	30.00	80.00
❑ 94 Ted Dastick Jr.	60.00	150.00
❑ 95 Tim Proctor	60.00	150.00
❑ 96 Tod Allen Smith	15.00	40.00
❑ 97 Tom Hodges	100.00	250.00
❑ 98 Trev Murphy	150.00	350.00
❑ 99 Vanessa Banky Farano	40.00	100.00
❑ 100 Veronica O'Connell	150.00	350.00
❑ 101 Zack Giallongo	8.00	20.00
❑ 102 Brian Kong	50.00	125.00
❑ 103 Cat Staggs	100.00	200.00
❑ 104 Chris Glenn	20.00	50.00
❑ 105 Cole Higgins	10.00	25.00
❑ 106 David Green	15.00	40.00
❑ 107 Eric Komalieh	30.00	80.00
❑ 108 Jenn DePaola	40.00	100.00
❑ 109 Jessica Hickman	8.00	20.00
❑ 110 Linzy Zorn	25.00	60.00
❑ 111 Marat Mychaels	15.00	40.00
❑ 112 Matt Busch	30.00	80.00
❑ 113 Mikey Babinski	100.00	200.00
❑ 114 Nicole Goff		
❑ 115 Sarah Wilkinson	25.00	60.00
❑ 116 Sean Pence	600.00	1000.00
❑ 117 Vince Lee	10.00	25.00
❑ 118 Will Nichols	30.00	80.00
❑ 119 Lizzie Carr	20.00	50.00

2012 Star Wars Galaxy Series 7 Sketches Retail Red

STATED ODDS 1:116 RETAIL

❑ 1 Adrian Rivera	6.00	15.00
❑ 2 Agnes Garbowska	60.00	120.00
❑ 3 Beck Seashols	30.00	60.00
❑ 4 Bruce Gerlach	15.00	40.00
❑ 5 David Rabbitte	20.00	50.00
❑ 6 Denae Frazier		
❑ 7 Denis Medri		
❑ 8 Erik Maell	40.00	80.00
❑ 9 Howard Shum	8.00	20.00
❑ 10 Jason Davies		
❑ 11 Jason Durden	15.00	40.00
❑ 12 Jay Shimko	25.00	60.00
❑ 13 Jessica Hickman	6.00	15.00
❑ 14 Joe Hogan	25.00	60.00
❑ 15 John P Wales	8.00	20.00
❑ 16 Jonathan D. Gordon		
❑ 17 Kate Glasheen	20.00	50.00
❑ 18 Kevin Doyle		
❑ 19 Lee Bradley	8.00	20.00
❑ 20 Lee Kohse	60.00	120.00
❑ 21 Lord Mesa		
❑ 22 Mark Slater	6.00	15.00
❑ 23 Rich Molinelli	25.00	60.00
❑ 24 Scott Zambelli	30.00	60.00
❑ 25 Shelli Paroline	12.00	30.00
❑ 26 Sian Mandrake	6.00	15.00
❑ 27 Steph Swanger	25.00	60.00
❑ 28 Tod Allen Smith		
❑ 29 Trev Murphy	125.00	250.00
❑ 30 Veronica O'Connell	125.00	250.00
❑ 31 Wilson Ramos Jr.	25.00	60.00

2013 Star Wars Galactic Files 2

COMP.SET w/o SPs (350)	12.00	30.00
❑ 351 Teemto Pagalies	.15	.40
❑ 352 Ratts Tyerell	.15	.40
❑ 353 Gasgano	.15	.40
❑ 354 Ben Quadinaros	.15	.40
❑ 355 Mars Guo	.15	.40
❑ 356 Ody Mandrell	.15	.40
❑ 357 Elan Sleazebaggano	.15	.40
❑ 358 Luke Skywalker	.15	.40
❑ 359 Bom Vimdin	.15	.40
❑ 360 Pons Limbic	.15	.40
❑ 361 Djas Puhr	.15	.40
❑ 362 Baniss Keeg	.15	.40
❑ 363 Ellorrs Madak	.15	.40
❑ 364 Muftak	.15	.40
❑ 365 Kabe	.15	.40
❑ 366 Princess Leia Organa	.15	.40
❑ 367 Han Solo	.15	.40
❑ 368 Wooof	.15	.40
❑ 369 Amanaman	.15	.40
❑ 370 Barada	.15	.40
❑ 371 Malakili	.15	.40
❑ 372 EV-9D9	.15	.40
❑ 373 Ephant Mon	.15	.40
❑ 374 Tessek	.15	.40
❑ 375 Qui-Gon Jinn	.15	.40
❑ 376 Obi-Wan Kenobi	.15	.40
❑ 377 Padmé Naberrie	.15	.40
❑ 378 Anakin Skywalker	.15	.40
❑ 379 Darth Maul	.15	.40
❑ 380 Chancellor Palpatine	.15	.40
❑ 381 Darth Sidious	.15	.40
❑ 382 Rune Haako	.15	.40
❑ 383 Nute Gunray	.15	.40
❑ 384 Sio Bibble	.15	.40
❑ 385 Queen Amidala	.15	.40
❑ 386 Jar Jar Binks	.15	.40
❑ 387 Saché	.15	.40
❑ 388 Yané	.15	.40
❑ 389 Rabé	.15	.40
❑ 390 C-3PO	.15	.40
❑ 391 R2-D2	.15	.40
❑ 392 Fode and Beed	.15	.40
❑ 393 Yaddle	.15	.40
❑ 394 Depa Billaba	.15	.40
❑ 395 Oppo Rancisis	.15	.40
❑ 396 Eeth Koth	.15	.40
❑ 397 Rum Sleg	.15	.40
❑ 398 Kitster	.15	.40
❑ 399 Wald	.15	.40
❑ 400 Obi-Wan Kenobi	.15	.40
❑ 401 Anakin Skywalker	.15	.40
❑ 402 Padmé Amidala	.15	.40
❑ 403 Darth Tyranus	.15	.40
❑ 404 Yoda	.15	.40
❑ 405 Mace Windu	.15	.40
❑ 406 Supreme Chancellor Palpatine	.15	.40
❑ 407 Jango Fett	.15	.40
❑ 408 Boba Fett	.15	.40
❑ 409 Queen Jamillia	.15	.40
❑ 410 Sarrissa Jeng	.15	.40
❑ 411 Watto	.15	.40
❑ 412 Toonbuck Toora	.15	.40
❑ 413 Pablo-Jill	.15	.40
❑ 414 Hermione Bagwa	.15	.40
❑ 415 Lexi Dio	.15	.40
❑ 416 Danni Faytonni	.15	.40
❑ 417 Gilramos Libkath	.15	.40
❑ 417 Ayy Vida	.15	.40
❑ 418 C-3PO	.15	.40
❑ 419 R2-D2	.15	.40
❑ 420 Coleman Trebor	.15	.40
❑ 421 Achk Med-Beq	.15	.40
❑ 422 Bultar Swan	.15	.40
❑ 423 Fi-Ek Sirch	.15	.40
❑ 424 Aayla Secura	.15	.40
❑ 425 Saesee Tiin	.15	.40
❑ 426 Plo Koon	.15	.40
❑ 427 Ki-Adi-Mundi	.15	.40
❑ 428 Sun Fac	.15	.40
❑ 429 J.K. Burtola	.15	.40
❑ 430 Ashla	.15	.40
❑ 431 Que-Mars Redath-Gom	.15	.40
❑ 432 Anakin Skywalker	.15	.40
❑ 433 Obi-Wan Kenobi	.15	.40
❑ 434 Padme Amidala	.15	.40
❑ 435 Supreme Chancellor Palpatine	.15	.40
❑ 436 Mace Windu	.15	.40
❑ 437 Yoda	.15	.40
❑ 438 C-3PO	.15	.40
❑ 439 R2-D2	.15	.40
❑ 440 General Grievous	.15	.40
❑ 441 Darth Sidious	.15	.40
❑ 442 Darth Vader	.15	.40
❑ 443 Chewbacca	.15	.40
❑ 444 Obi-Wan Kenobi	.15	.40
❑ 445 Captain Colton	.15	.40
❑ 446 Zett Jukassa	.15	.40
❑ 447 Captain Antilles	.15	.40
❑ 448 Ask Aak	.15	.40
❑ 449 Queen Apailana	.15	.40
❑ 450 Breha Organa	.15	.40
❑ 451 Merumeru	.15	.40
❑ 452 Odd Ball	.15	.40
❑ 453 Commander Gree	.15	.40
❑ 454 Commander Bacara	.15	.40
❑ 455 Commander Bly	.15	.40
❑ 456 Commander Neyo	.15	.40
❑ 457 Luke Skywalker	.15	.40
❑ 458 Leia Organa	.15	.40
❑ 459 C-3PO	.15	.40
❑ 460 R2-D2	.15	.40
❑ 461 Princess Leia Organa	.15	.40
❑ 462 Luke Skywalker	.15	.40
❑ 463a Han Solo Falcon Pilot	.15	.40
❑ 463b Han Solo Stormtrooper SP	4.00	10.00
❑ 464 Ben (Obi-Wan) Kenobi	.15	.40
❑ 465 Darth Vader	.15	.40
❑ 466 Grand Moff Tarkin	.15	.40
❑ 467 Chewbacca	.15	.40
❑ 468 Daine Jir	.15	.40
❑ 469 Hem Dazon	.15	.40
❑ 470 Nabrun Leids	.15	.40
❑ 471 Wioslea	.15	.40
❑ 472 Lak Sivrak	.15	.40
❑ 473 Wulff Yularen	.15	.40
❑ 474 Boba Fett	.15	.40
❑ 475 Commander Willard	.15	.40
❑ 476 Dutch Vander	.15	.40
❑ 477 Tiree	.15	.40
❑ 478 Davish Pops Krail	.15	.40
❑ 479 Theron Nett	.15	.40
❑ 480 Han Solo	.15	.40
❑ 481a Luke Skywalker Hoth	.15	.40
❑ 481b Luke Skywalker Bacta Tank SP	4.00	10.00
❑ 482 Han Solo	.15	.40
❑ 483 Princess Leia Organa	.15	.40
❑ 484 Chewbacca	.15	.40
❑ 485 C-3PO	.15	.40
❑ 486 R2-D2	.15	.40
❑ 487 Lando Calrissian	.15	.40
❑ 488 Darth Vader	.15	.40
❑ 489 Boba Fett	.15	.40
❑ 490 Yoda	.15	.40
❑ 491 Willrow Hood	.15	.40
❑ 492 M'Kae	.15	.40
❑ 493 General McQuarrie	.15	.40
❑ 494 Bren Derlin	.15	.40
❑ 495 Edian	.15	.40
❑ 496 K-3PO	.15	.40
❑ 497 Tamizander Rey	.15	.40
❑ 498 Kesin Ommis	.15	.40
❑ 499 Commander Nemet	.15	.40
❑ 500 Captain Lennox	.15	.40
❑ 501 Captain Bewil	.15	.40
❑ 502 Tigran Jamiro	.15	.40
❑ 503 Jeroen Webb	.15	.40
❑ 504 Cal Alder	.15	.40
❑ 505 Cabbel	.15	.40
❑ 506 Lieutenant Sheckil	.15	.40
❑ 507 Luke Skywalker	.15	.40
❑ 508 Han Solo	.15	.40
❑ 509 Luke Skywalker	.15	.40
❑ 510a Princess Leia Rebel General	.15	.40
❑ 510b Princess Leia Slave Girl SP	4.00	10.00
❑ 511 Han Solo	.15	.40
❑ 512 Lando Calrissian	.15	.40
❑ 513 Chewbacca	.15	.40
❑ 514 C-3PO	.15	.40
❑ 515 R2-D2	.15	.40
❑ 516 Darth Vader	.15	.40
❑ 517 Emperor Palpatine	.15	.40
❑ 518 Boba Fett	.15	.40
❑ 519 Jabba the Hutt	.15	.40
❑ 520 Anakin Skywalker	.15	.40
❑ 521 Paploo	.15	.40
❑ 522 Romba	.15	.40
❑ 523 Lumat	.15	.40
❑ 524 Widdle Warrick	.15	.40
❑ 525 Leektar	.15	.40
❑ 526 Kren Blista-Vanee	.15	.40
❑ 527 Sim Aloo	.15	.40
❑ 528 Colonel Cracken	.15	.40
❑ 529 Major Panno	.15	.40
❑ 530 Orrimaarko	.15	.40
❑ 531 Giran	.15	.40
❑ 532 Saelt-Marae	.15	.40
❑ 533 Princess Leia Organa	.15	.40
❑ 534 Luke Skywalker	.15	.40
❑ 535 Han Solo	.15	.40
❑ 536 Bria Tharen	.15	.40
❑ 537 Kiro	.15	.40
❑ 538 Dani	.15	.40
❑ 539 Guri	.15	.40
❑ 540 Allana Solo	.15	.40
❑ 541 Juno Eclipse	.15	.40

STAR WARS

❑ 542 Borsk Fey'lya .15 .40
❑ 543 Garm Bel Iblis .15 .40
❑ 544 Darth Caedus .15 .40
❑ 545 Kazdan Paratus .15 .40
❑ 546 Corran Horn .15 .40
❑ 547 Padme Amidala .15 .40
❑ 548 Shae Vizla .15 .40
❑ 549 Jodo Kast .15 .40
❑ 550 Shira Brie .15 .40
❑ 551 Nom Anor .15 .40
❑ 552 Jaxxon .15 .40
❑ 553 Vestara Khai .15 .40
❑ 554 Darth Zannah .15 .40
❑ 555 Noa Briqualon .15 .40
❑ 556 Cindel Towani .15 .40
❑ 557 Teek .15 .40
❑ 558 Mace Towani .15 .40
❑ 559 Voolvif Monn .15 .40
❑ 560 Fenn Shysa .15 .40
❑ 561 Admiral Isard .15 .40
❑ 562 Canderous Ordo .15 .40
❑ 563 Baron Soontir Fel .15 .40
❑ 564 Jahan Cross .15 .40
❑ 565 K'Kruhk .15 .40
❑ 566 Deena Shan .15 .40
❑ 567 Kerra Holt .15 .40
❑ 568 Luke Skywalker .15 .40
❑ 569 Obi-Wan Kenobi .15 .40
❑ 570 Mortis Father .15 .40
❑ 571 Steela Gerrera .15 .40
❑ 572 Saw Gerrera .15 .40
❑ 573 Katooni .15 .40
❑ 574 Byph .15 .40
❑ 575 Petro .15 .40
❑ 576 Zatt .15 .40
❑ 577 Gungi .15 .40
❑ 578 Ganodi .15 .40
❑ 579 Darth Maul .15 .40
❑ 580 Bo-Katan .15 .40
❑ 581 Embo .15 .40
❑ 582 Letta Turmond .15 .40
❑ 583 Lux Bonteri .15 .40
❑ 584 Satine Kryze .15 .40
❑ 585 Latts Razzi .15 .40
❑ 586 Mother Talzin .15 .40
❑ 587 Asajj Ventress .15 .40
❑ 588 Rako Hardeen .15 .40
❑ 589 Mortis Daughter .15 .40
❑ 590 Qui-Gon Jinn's Lightsaber .15 .40
❑ 591 Obi-Wan Kenobi's Lightsaber .15 .40
❑ 592 ELG-3A Blaster Pistol .15 .40
❑ 593 CR-2 Blaster Pistol .15 .40
❑ 594 S-5 Blaster Rifle .15 .40
❑ 595 Darth Maul's Lightsaber .15 .40
❑ 596 Booma .15 .40
❑ 597 E-5 Blaster Rifle .15 .40
❑ 598 Gungan Personal Energy Shield .15 .40
❑ 599 DC-15 Blaster Rifle .15 .40
❑ 600 DC-15a Blaster .15 .40
❑ 601 Kamino saberdart .15 .40
❑ 602 WESTAR-34 blaster pistol .15 .40
❑ 603 ZX miniature flame projector .15 .40
❑ 604 Yoda's Lightsaber .15 .40
❑ 605 Mace Windu's Lightsaber .15 .40
❑ 606 Anakin Skywalker's First Lightsaber .15 .40
❑ 607 Anakin Skywalker's Second Lightsaber .15 .40
❑ 608 Count Dooku's Lightsaber .15 .40
❑ 609 Electrostaff .15 .40
❑ 610 Force Pike .15 .40
❑ 611 Senate Guard Ceremonial Blaster Rifle .15 .40
❑ 612 Gaderffii Stick .15 .40
❑ 613 RT-97C Heavy Blaster Rifle .15 .40
❑ 614 Han Solo's Modified DL-44 .15 .40
❑ 615 DLT-19 Heavy Blaster Rifle .15 .40
❑ 616 DH-17 Blaster Pistol .15 .40
❑ 617 Obi-Wan Kenobi's Third Lightsaber .15 .40
❑ 618 Tusken Cycler .15 .40
❑ 619 T-21 light repeating blaster .15 .40
❑ 620 E-11 Blaster Rifle .15 .40
❑ 621 Jawa Ionization Blaster .15 .40
❑ 622 SE-14C blaster pistol .15 .40
❑ 623 Darth Vader's Lightsaber .15 .40
❑ 624 Defender Sporting Blaster Pistol .15 .40
❑ 625 A280 blaster rifle .15 .40
❑ 626 IG-88's Pulse Cannon .15 .40
❑ 627 EE-3 Carbine Rifle .15 .40
❑ 628 Mark II Blaster Cannon .15 .40
❑ 629 Scout Blaster .15 .40
❑ 630 DL-44 Blaster Pistol .15 .40
❑ 631 Chewbacca's Bowcaster .15 .40
❑ 632 DL-18 blaster pistol .15 .40
❑ 633 Defender Sporting Blaster (Variant) .15 .40
❑ 634 BD-1 Cutter vibro-ax .15 .40
❑ 635 Luke Skywalker's Lightsaber .15 .40
❑ 636 Class-A thermal detonator .15 .40
❑ 637 DL-21 blaster pistol .15 .40
❑ 638 Theed Palace .15 .40
❑ 639 Mos Espa .15 .40
❑ 640 Galactic Senate Building .15 .40
❑ 641 Jedi Temple .15 .40
❑ 642 Theed Hangar Bay .15 .40
❑ 643 Padmé's Apartment .15 .40
❑ 644 Outlander Club .15 .40
❑ 645 Tipoca City .15 .40
❑ 646 Geonosis Arena .15 .40
❑ 647 Pau City .15 .40
❑ 648 Galaxies Opera House .15 .40
❑ 649 Senate Office Building .15 .40
❑ 650 Klegger Corp Mining Facility .15 .40
❑ 651 Polis Massan Medical Facility .15 .40
❑ 652 Ben Kenobi's Hut .15 .40
❑ 653 Lars Homestead .15 .40
❑ 654 Chalmun's Cantina .15 .40
❑ 655 Docking Bay 94 .15 .40
❑ 656 Garbage Compactor 3263827 .15 .40
❑ 657 Docking Control Room 327 .15 .40
❑ 658 Docking Bay 327 .15 .40
❑ 659 Massassi Temple .15 .40
❑ 660 Echo Base .15 .40
❑ 661 Wampa Cave .15 .40
❑ 662 Yoda's Hut .15 .40
❑ 663 Vader's Meditation Chamber .15 .40
❑ 664 East Platform .15 .40
❑ 665 Carbon-Freezing Chamber .15 .40
❑ 666 Jabba's Palace .15 .40
❑ 667 Great Pit of Carkoon .15 .40
❑ 668 Rebel Briefing Room .15 .40
❑ 669 Emperor's Throne Room .15 .40
❑ 670 Endor Shield Generator Bunker .15 .40
❑ 671 Ewok Village .15 .40
❑ 672 Naboo .15 .40
❑ 673 Tatooine .15 .40
❑ 674 Coruscant .15 .40
❑ 675 Kamino .15 .40
❑ 676 Geonosis .15 .40
❑ 677 Utapau .15 .40
❑ 678 Mustafar .15 .40
❑ 679 Kashyyyk .15 .40
❑ 680 Felucia .15 .40
❑ 681 Mygeeto .15 .40
❑ 682 Alderaan .15 .40
❑ 683 Yavin 4 .15 .40
❑ 684 Hoth .15 .40
❑ 685 Dagobah .15 .40
❑ 686 Bespin .15 .40
❑ 687 Endor .15 .40
❑ 688 Dantooine .15 .40
❑ 689 Corellia .15 .40
❑ 690 Ralltiir .15 .40
❑ 691 Cato Neimoidia .15 .40
❑ 692 Ord Mantell .15 .40
❑ 693 Mandalore .15 .40
❑ 694 Anoat .15 .40
❑ 695 Sullust .15 .40
❑ 696 Taanab .15 .40
❑ 697 Mon Calamari .15 .40
❑ 698 Ansion .15 .40
❑ 699 Nar Shaddaa .15 .40

2013 Star Wars Galactic Files 2 Blue Foil

*BLUE/350: 2X TO 5X BASIC CARDS

2013 Star Wars Galactic Files 2 Autographs

STATED ODDS 1:55

❑ 1 John Ratzenberger 20.00 50.00
❑ 2 Ashley Eckstein 15.00 40.00
❑ 3 Peter Mayhew 20.00 50.00
❑ 4 Jett Lucas 12.00 30.00
❑ 5 Tom Kane 15.00 40.00
❑ 6 Tim Rose 12.00 30.00
❑ 7 Alan Harris 15.00 40.00
❑ 8 Ralph Brown 12.00 30.00
❑ 9 Daniel Logan 12.00 30.00
❑ 10 Carrie Fisher 250.00 400.00
❑ 11 James Earl Jones 200.00 350.00
❑ 12 Mark Hamill 350.00 500.00
❑ 13 Billy Dee Williams 75.00 150.00
❑ 14 Kenneth Colley 12.00 30.00
❑ 15 Chris Parsons 12.00 30.00
❑ 16 Jeremy Bulloch 20.00 50.00
❑ 17 Ian McDiarmid 350.00 500.00

2013 Star Wars Galactic Files 2 Autographs Dual

ANNOUNCED COMBINED PRINT RUN 200

❑ 1 Ashley Eckstein 100.00 200.00
Tom Kane
❑ 2 Jeremy Bulloch 150.00 250.00
Alan Harris
❑ 3 James Earl Jones
Ian McDiarmid
❑ 4 Carrie Fisher
Mark Hamill
❑ 5 Harrison Ford
Peter Mayhew

2013 Star Wars Galactic Files 2 Classic Lines

COMPLETE SET (10) 3.00 8.00
STATED ODDS 1:4

❑ CL1 Princess Leia Organa .60 1.50
❑ CL2 Luke Skywalker .60 1.50
❑ CL3 Han Solo .60 1.50
❑ CL4 Darth Vader .60 1.50
❑ CL5 Obi-Wan Kenobi .60 1.50
❑ CL6 Padme Amidala .60 1.50
❑ CL7 C-3PO .60 1.50
❑ CL8 Anakin Skywalker .60 1.50
❑ CL9 Boba Fett .60 1.50
❑ CL10 Admiral Ackbar .60 1.50

2013 Star Wars Galactic Files 2 Galactic Moments

COMPLETE SET (20) 30.00 60.00
STATED ODDS 1:12

❑ GM1 Stormtroopers 2.00 5.00
❑ GM2 Stuck on the Sandcrawler 2.00 5.00
❑ GM3 Scum and Villainy 2.00 5.00
❑ GM4 Droids in the Desert 2.00 5.00
❑ GM5 Two New Friends 2.00 5.00
❑ GM6 Kenobi alone 2.00 5.00
❑ GM7 The Dark Side on Bespin 2.00 5.00
❑ GM8 A Dinner Surprise 2.00 5.00
❑ GM9 The Burden of Darth Vader 2.00 5.00
❑ GM10 Clash in the Gantry 2.00 5.00
❑ GM11 Looking for Luke 2.00 5.00
❑ GM12 The Rescue of Chewbacca 2.00 5.00
❑ GM13 Leia's Great Escape 2.00 5.00
❑ GM14 Vader's Peace 2.00 5.00
❑ GM15 Commanding Dengar 2.00 5.00
❑ GM16 Luke Laying low 2.00 5.00
❑ GM17 Jabba's New Prize 2.00 5.00
❑ GM18 Jabba's Grand Company 2.00 5.00
❑ GM19 The Emperor's Last Show 2.00 5.00
❑ GM20 In Service of the Emperor 2.00 5.00

2013 Star Wars Galactic Files 2 Honor the Fallen

COMPLETE SET (10) 4.00 10.00
STATED ODDS 1:6

❑ HF1 Battle of Naboo .75 2.00
❑ HF2 Battle of Geonosis .75 2.00
❑ HF3 Battle of Coruscant .75 2.00
❑ HF4 Order 66 .75 2.00
❑ HF5 Operation Nightfall .75 2.00
❑ HF6 Mission to Mustafar .75 2.00
❑ HF7 Battle of Yavin .75 2.00
❑ HF8 Battle of Hoth .75 2.00
❑ HF9 Battle of the Great Pit of Carkoon .75 2.00
❑ HF10 Battle of Endor .75 2.00

2013 Star Wars Galactic Files 2 Medallions

STATED ODDS 1:55

❑ MD1 Luke Skywalker 20.00 50.00
❑ MD2 Biggs Darklighter 10.00 25.00
❑ MD3 Han Solo 20.00 50.00
❑ MD4 Chewbacca 15.00 40.00
❑ MD5 Lando Calrissian 12.00 30.00
❑ MD6 Han Solo 100.00 175.00
❑ MD7 Boba Fett 35.00 70.00
❑ MD8 Jango Fett 10.00 25.00
❑ MD9 Princess Leia Organa 20.00 50.00
❑ MD10 Bail Organa 10.00 25.00
❑ MD11 AT-AT Driver 10.00 25.00
❑ MD12 General Veers 35.00 70.00
❑ MD13 Jawa 20.00 50.00
❑ MD14 C-3PO 35.00 70.00
❑ MD15 R2-D2 20.00 50.00
❑ MD16 R5-D4 12.00 30.00
❑ MD17 Darth Maul 10.00 25.00
❑ MD18 Darth Sidious 12.00 30.00
❑ MD19 Luke Skywalker 30.00 60.00
❑ MD20 Obi-Wan Kenobi 12.00 30.00
❑ MD21 C-3PO & R2-D2 40.00 80.00
❑ MD22 TIE Fighter Pilot 10.00 25.00
❑ MD23 Darth Vader 15.00 40.00
❑ MD24 Stormtrooper 12.00 30.00
❑ MD25 Obi-Wan Kenobi 12.00 30.00
❑ MD26 Plo Koon 12.00 30.00
❑ MD27 Captain Panaka 12.00 30.00
❑ MD28 Qui-Gon Jinn 12.00 30.00
❑ MD29 Obi-Wan Kenobi 15.00 40.00
❑ MD30 Queen Amidala 40.00 80.00

2013 Star Wars Galactic Files 2 Ripples in the Galaxy

COMPLETE SET (10) 4.00 10.00
STATED ODDS 1:6

❑ RG1 Death of Qui-Gon Jinn .75 2.00
❑ RG2 The Tusken Raider Camp .75 2.00
❑ RG3 Anakin Skywalker Falls to the Dark Side .75 2.00
❑ RG4 Order 66 .75 2.00
❑ RG5 Destruction of Alderaan .75 2.00
❑ RG6 The Training of Luke Skywalker .75 2.00
❑ RG7 The Torture of Han Solo .75 2.00
❑ RG8 Death of Yoda .75 2.00
❑ RG9 Death of Emperor Palpatine .75 2.00
❑ RG10 Redemption of Anakin Skywalker .75 2.00

2013 Star Wars Galactic Files 2 The Weak Minded

COMPLETE SET (7) 2.50 6.00
STATED ODDS 1:3

❑ WM1 Ben (Obi-Wan) Kenobi .60 1.50
to Sandtrooper
❑ WM2 Obi-Wan Kenobi .60 1.50
to Elan Sleazebaggano
❑ WM3 Ben (Obi-Wan) Kenobi .60 1.50
to Stormtroopers
❑ WM4 Luke Skywalker .60 1.50
to Bib Fortuna
❑ WM5 Qui-Gon Jinn .60 1.50
to Boss Nass
❑ WM6 Luke Skywalker .60 1.50
to Jabba the Hutt
❑ WM7 Qui-Gon Jinn to Watto .60 1.50

2013 Star Wars Jedi Legacy

COMPLETE SET (90) 6.00 15.00

❑ 1A Clandestine Birth .20 .50
Anakin Skywalker
❑ 1L Clandestine Birth .20 .50
Luke Skywalker
❑ 2A Fatherless as a Child .20 .50
Anakin Skywalker
❑ 2L Fatherless as a Child .20 .50
Luke Skywalker
❑ 3A Tatooine .20 .50
Anakin Skywalker
❑ 3L Tatooine .20 .50
Luke Skywalker
❑ 4A Isolation in Youth .20 .50
Anakin Skywalker
❑ 4L Isolation in Youth .20 .50
Luke Skywalker
❑ 5A Befriending a Droid .20 .50
Anakin Skywalker
❑ 5L Befriending a Droid .20 .50
Luke Skywalker
❑ 6A Death of a Guardian .20 .50
Anakin Skywalker
❑ 6L Death of a Guardian .20 .50
Luke Skywalker
❑ 7A Technical Ability .20 .50
Anakin Skywalker
❑ 7L Technical Ability .20 .50
Luke Skywalker
❑ 8A Daredevil Abilities .20 .50
Anakin Skywalker
❑ 8L Daredevil Abilities .20 .50
Luke Skywalker
❑ 9A Fantastic Adventure .20 .50
Anakin Skywalker
❑ 9L Fantastic Adventure .20 .50
Luke Skywalker
❑ 10A Introduction of Royalty .20 .50
Anakin Skywalker
❑ 10L Introduction of Royalty .20 .50
Luke Skywalker
❑ 11A A Royal Rescue .20 .50
Anakin Skywalker
❑ 11L A Royal Rescue .20 .50
Luke Skywalker
❑ 12A Death of a Mentor .20 .50
Anakin Skywalker
❑ 12L Death of a Mentor .20 .50
Luke Skywalker
❑ 13A Late Jedi Training .20 .50
Anakin Skywalker
❑ 13L Late Jedi Training .20 .50
Luke Skywalker
❑ 14A Act of Extreme Bravery .20 .50
Anakin Skywalker
❑ 14L Act of Extreme Bravery .20 .50
Luke Skywalker
❑ 15A Celebration of Heroism .20 .50
Anakin Skywalker
❑ 15L Celebration of Heroism .20 .50
Luke Skywalker
❑ 16A Pilot Squad Leader .20 .50
Anakin Skywalker
❑ 16L Pilot Squad Leader .20 .50
Luke Skywalker
❑ 17A Clever Thinking in the Heart of Battle .20 .50
Anakin Skywalker
❑ 17L Clever Thinking in the Heart of Battle .20 .50
Luke Skywalker
❑ 18A Too Old to Train .20 .50
Anakin Skywalker
❑ 18L Too Old to Train .20 .50
Luke Skywalker
❑ 19A Truncated Trial .20 .50
Anakin Skywalker
❑ 19L Truncated Trial .20 .50
Luke Skywalker
❑ 20A Fear of Potential .20 .50
Anakin Skywalker
❑ 20L Fear of Potential .20 .50
Luke Skywalker
❑ 21A Temptation of the Dark Side .20 .50
Anakin Skywalker
❑ 21L Temptation of the Dark Side .20 .50
Luke Skywalker
❑ 22A A Dark Premonition .20 .50
Anakin Skywalker
❑ 22L A Dark Premonition .20 .50
Luke Skywalker
❑ 23A A Life-Changing Disregard of Advisement .20 .50
Anakin Skywalker
❑ 23L A Life-Changing Disregard of Advisement .20 .50
Luke Skywalker
❑ 24A To the Distress of Dear Friends .20 .50
Anakin Skywalker
❑ 24L To the Distress of Dear Friends .20 .50
Luke Skywalker
❑ 25A Trial By Fett .20 .50
Anakin Skywalker
❑ 25L Trial By Fett .20 .50
Luke Skywalker
❑ 26A Springing the Trap .20 .50
Anakin Skywalker
❑ 26L Springing the Trap .20 .50
Luke Skywalker
❑ 27A In the Lair of Scum and Villainy .20 .50
Anakin Skywalker
❑ 27L In the Lair of Scum and Villainy .20 .50
Luke Skywalker
❑ 28A Challenge of a Fallen Jedi .20 .50
Anakin Skywalker
❑ 28L Challenge of a Fallen Jedi .20 .50
Luke Skywalker
❑ 29A Loss to Powerful Dark Opponent .20 .50
Anakin Skywalker
❑ 29L Loss to Powerful Dark Opponent .20 .50
Luke Skywalker
❑ 30A Dismemberment .20 .50
Anakin Skywalker
❑ 30L Dismemberment .20 .50
Luke Skywalker
❑ 31A Mechanical Limb .20 .50
Anakin Skywalker
❑ 31L Mechanical Limb .20 .50
Luke Skywalker
❑ 32A A Daring Rescue .20 .50
Anakin Skywalker
❑ 32L A Daring Rescue .20 .50
Luke Skywalker
❑ 33A A Difficult Truth .20 .50
Anakin Skywalker
❑ 33L A Difficult Truth .20 .50
Luke Skywalker
❑ 34A The Jabba Factor .20 .50
Anakin Skywalker
❑ 34L The Jabba Factor .20 .50
Luke Skywalker
❑ 35A Wrath of a Great Beast .20 .50
Anakin Skywalker
❑ 35L Wrath of a Great Beast .20 .50
Luke Skywalker
❑ 36A Proposition of Palpatine .20 .50
Anakin Skywalker
❑ 36L Proposition of Palpatine .20 .50
Luke Skywalker
❑ 37A A Civil Confrontation .20 .50
Anakin Skywalker
❑ 37L A Civil Confrontation .20 .50
Luke Skywalker
❑ 38A Fear For a Loved One .20 .50
Anakin Skywalker
❑ 38L Fear For a Loved One .20 .50
Luke Skywalker
❑ 39A The Moment of Truth .20 .50
Anakin Skywalker
❑ 39L The Moment of Truth .20 .50
Luke Skywalker
❑ 40A A Galaxy at War .20 .50
Anakin Skywalker
❑ 40L A Galaxy at War .20 .50
Luke Skywalker
❑ 41A Battle Through Blood .20 .50
Anakin Skywalker
❑ 41L Battle Through Blood .20 .50
Luke Skywalker
❑ 42A Dark Urging of the Emperor .20 .50
Anakin Skywalker
❑ 42L Dark Urging of the Emperor .20 .50
Luke Skywalker
❑ 43A Moment of Clarity .20 .50
Anakin Skywalker
❑ 43L Moment of Clarity .20 .50
Luke Skywalker
❑ 44A Together We Conquer .20 .50
Anakin Skywalker
❑ 44L Together We Conquer .20 .50
Luke Skywalker
❑ 45A Balance is Achieved .20 .50
Anakin Skywalker
❑ 45L Balance is Achieved .20 .50
Luke Skywalker

2013 Star Wars Jedi Legacy Blue

COMPLETE SET 25.00 50.00
STATED ODDS ONE PER PACK

2013 Star Wars Jedi Legacy Magenta

COMPLETE SET
STATED ODDS 1:6

2013 Star Wars Jedi Legacy Green

COMPLETE SET
STATED ODDS 1:24

2013 Star Wars Jedi Legacy Gold

ANNCD PRINT RUN 10

2013 Star Wars Jedi Legacy Printing Plates Black

STATED PRINT RUN 1 SER. #'d SET
UNPRICED DUE TO SCARCITY

2013 Star Wars Jedi Legacy Printing Plates Cyan

STATED PRINT RUN 1 SER. #'d SET
UNPRICED DUE TO SCARCITY

2013 Star Wars Jedi Legacy Printing Plates Magenta

STATED PRINT RUN 1 SER. #'d SET
UNPRICED DUE TO SCARCITY

2013 Star Wars Jedi Legacy Printing Plates Yellow

STATED PRINT RUN 1 SER. #'d SET
UNPRICED DUE TO SCARCITY

2013 Star Wars Jedi Legacy Autographs

STATED ODDS 1:72

❑ 1 Alan Harris 20.00 50.00
❑ 2 Amy Allen 10.00 25.00
❑ 3 Anthony Daniels 250.00 400.00
❑ 4 Anthony Forrest 10.00 25.00
❑ 5 Billy Dee Williams 125.00 250.00
❑ 6 Bonnie Piesse 10.00 25.00
❑ 7 Carrie Fisher 300.00 500.00
❑ 8 Garrick Hagon 10.00 25.00
❑ 9 Harrison Ford 1750.00 2500.00
❑ 10 Ian McDiarmid 300.00 500.00
❑ 11 James Earl Jones 200.00 350.00
❑ 12 Jeremy Bulloch 30.00 60.00
❑ 13 John Morton 15.00 40.00
❑ 14 Kenneth Colley 15.00 40.00
❑ 15 Kenny Baker 30.00 60.00
❑ 16 Mark Hamill 400.00 600.00
❑ 17 Tim Rose 15.00 40.00

2013 Star Wars Jedi Legacy Chewbacca Fur Relics

STATED ODDS 1:720

❑ CR1 Chewbacca 75.00 150.00
❑ CR2 Chewbacca 75.00 150.00
❑ CR3 Chewbacca 75.00 150.00
❑ CR4 Chewbacca 75.00 150.00

2013 Star Wars Jedi Legacy Connections

COMPLETE SET (15) 5.00 12.00
STATED ODDS 1:2

❑ C1 Obi-Wan Kenobi .60 1.50
❑ C2 Yoda .60 1.50
❑ C3 Owen Lars .60 1.50
❑ C4 R2-D2 .60 1.50
❑ C5 C-3PO .60 1.50
❑ C6 Emperor Palpatine .60 1.50
❑ C7 Princess Leia Organa .60 1.50
❑ C8 Boba Fett .60 1.50
❑ C9 Padme Amidala .60 1.50
❑ C10 The Force .60 1.50
❑ C11 Anakin's Lightsaber .60 1.50
❑ C12 Death Star .60 1.50
❑ C13 Tatooine .60 1.50
❑ C14 Tusken Raiders .60 1.50
❑ C15 Jabba The Hutt .60 1.50

2013 Star Wars Jedi Legacy Ewok Fur Relics

STATED ODDS 1:120

❑ ER1 Wicket W. Warrick 35.00 70.00
❑ ER2 Teebo 20.00 50.00
❑ ER3 Logray 20.00 50.00
❑ ER4 Widdle Warrick 50.00 100.00
❑ ER5 Ewok 20.00 50.00
❑ ER6 Ewok 20.00 50.00
❑ ER7 Ewok 20.00 50.00
❑ ER8 Ewok 20.00 50.00

2013 Star Wars Jedi Legacy Film Cels

STATED ODDS ONE PER BOX

❑ FR1 Luke Skywalker 12.00 30.00
❑ FR2 Luke Skywalker 12.00 30.00
❑ FR3 Darth Vader/Obi Wan Kenobi 12.00 30.00
❑ FR4 Darth Vader 12.00 30.00
❑ FR5 X-Wing Fighter 12.00 30.00
❑ FR6 Darth Vader 20.00 50.00
❑ FR7 Princess Leia/Luke Skywalker 12.00 30.00
❑ FR8 Luke Skywalker/Biggs Darklighter 12.00 30.00
❑ FR9 Admiral Motti/Darth Vader 12.00 30.00
❑ FR10 Luke Skywalker 12.00 30.00
❑ FR11 Luke Skywalker 12.00 30.00
❑ FR12 Emperor Palpatine 12.00 30.00
❑ FR13 Luke Skywalker/Yoda 12.00 30.00
❑ FR14 Luke Skywalker/Yoda 12.00 30.00
❑ FR15 Luke Skywalker 12.00 30.00
❑ FR16 Darth Vader 12.00 30.00
❑ FR17 Princess Leia/Luke Skywalker 12.00 30.00
❑ FR18 Han Solo/Darth Vader 12.00 30.00
❑ FR19 Darth Vader 12.00 30.00
❑ FR20 Darth Vader 12.00 30.00
❑ FR21 Darth Vader 12.00 30.00
❑ FR22 Luke Skywalker 12.00 30.00
❑ FR23 Yoda/Luke Skywalker 12.00 30.00
❑ FR24 Luke Skywalker 12.00 30.00
❑ FR25 Darth Vader 12.00 30.00
❑ FR26 Luke Skywalker 12.00 30.00
❑ FR27 Darth Vader 12.00 30.00
❑ FR28 Anakin Skywalker 12.00 30.00
❑ FR29 Luke Skywalker 12.00 30.00
❑ FR30 Luke Skywalker 12.00 30.00

2013 Star Wars Jedi Legacy Film Cels Dual

STATED ODDS 1:144

❑ DFR1 Darth Vader/Luke Skywalker 30.00 60.00
❑ DFR2 Luke Skywalker/Darth Vader 20.00 50.00
❑ DFR3 Luke Skywalker 20.00 50.00
❑ DFR4 Darth Vader/Luke Skywalker 20.00 50.00
❑ DFR5 Darth Vader/Luke Skywalker 20.00 50.00
❑ DFR6 Darth Vader/Luke Skywalker 20.00 50.00

2013 Star Wars Jedi Legacy Film Cels Triple

STATED ODDS 1:144

❑ TFR1 Luke Skywalker/Yoda 30.00 60.00
❑ TFR2 Princess Leia/Luke Skywalker 30.00 60.00
❑ TFR3 Luke Skywalker 30.00 60.00
❑ TFR4 Luke Skywalker 30.00 60.00
❑ TFR5 Luke Skywalker 30.00 60.00
❑ TFR6 Darth Vader 30.00 60.00
❑ TFR7 Darth Vader 30.00 60.00
❑ TFR8 Darth Vader 30.00 60.00
❑ TFR9 Darth Vader 30.00 60.00
❑ TFR10 Darth Vader 30.00 60.00

2013 Star Wars Jedi Legacy Influencers

COMPLETE SET (18) 5.00 12.00
STATED ODDS 1:2

❑ I1 Qui-Gon Jinn .50 1.25
❑ I2 Shmi Skywalker .50 1.25
❑ I3 Mace Windu .50 1.25
❑ I4 Ahsoka Tano .50 1.25
❑ I5 Watto .50 1.25
❑ I6 Jar Jar Binks .50 1.25
❑ I7 Grand Moff Tarkin .50 1.25
❑ I8 Luke Skywalker .50 1.25
❑ I9 Count Dooku .50 1.25
❑ I10 Biggs Darklighter .50 1.25
❑ I11 Han Solo .50 1.25
❑ I12 Wedge Antilles .50 1.25
❑ I13 Beru Lars .50 1.25
❑ I14 Lando Calrissian .50 1.25
❑ I15 Chewbacca .50 1.25
❑ I16 Tosche Station .50 1.25
❑ I17 Anakin Skywalker .50 1.25
❑ I18 Dagobah .50 1.25

2013 Star Wars Jedi Legacy Jabba's Sail Barge Relics

STATED ODDS 1:336

❑ JR1 Luke Skywalker 100.00 175.00
❑ JR2 Leia Organa 100.00 175.00
❑ JR3 Boba Fett 75.00 150.00
❑ JR4 Nysad (Nikto Gunner) 50.00 100.00
❑ JR5 R2-D2 50.00 100.00

2013 Star Wars Jedi Legacy The Circle is Now Complete

COMPLETE SET (12) 35.00 70.00
STATED ODDS 1:12

❑ CC1 Luke Skywalker 4.00 10.00
❑ CC2 Luke Skywalker 4.00 10.00
❑ CC3 Luke Skywalker 4.00 10.00
❑ CC4 Luke Skywalker 4.00 10.00
❑ CC5 Luke Skywalker 4.00 10.00
❑ CC6 Luke Skywalker 4.00 10.00
❑ CC7 Darth Vader 4.00 10.00
❑ CC8 Darth Vader 4.00 10.00
❑ CC9 Darth Vader 4.00 10.00
❑ CC10 Darth Vader 4.00 10.00
❑ CC11 Darth Vader 4.00 10.00
❑ CC12 Darth Vader 4.00 10.00
❑ LS Luke Skywalker
(Round Promo)

STAR WARS